Holt McDougal Geometry Features Quicklist

	SEE PAGE(S)
PROVEN INSTRUCTIONAL DESIGN	
• Consistent lesson format of **Example, Solution, Check It Out** provides a logical instructional approach.	216–218
• Step-by-step examples and color-coded explanations help students become independent learners.	224–226
• Know-it Notes indicate key concepts for students to remember and correspond to entries in the students' **Know-it Notebook**.	224
• Exercises matched to examples mean no homework surprises!	256
COMPREHENSIVE DIFFERENTIATED INSTRUCTION	
• Reaching All Learners includes strategies for adapting the material for all types of learners.	TE 224
• English Language Learners identifies strategies particularly effective with this group of students.	TE 253
• Geometry Labs allow students to explore math concepts through manipulatives.	240–241
• Technology Labs assist students in the use of graphing calculators, spreadsheets, and dynamic geometry software.	250–252
• Reteach, Practice, Challenge, Reading Strategies, and Problem Solving reduced images make selecting worksheets quick and easy.	TE 228–229
• Teaching Tips provide suggestions for addressing various learning styles.	TE 235
• Additional Examples offer more classroom review for struggling students.	TE 232
• Assignment Guide recommends homework assignments based on student ability.	TE 234
• Power Presentations are editable PowerPoint® presentations for every lesson as well as extra examples and quizzes.	TE 237
BUILT-IN ASSESSMENT AND INTERVENTION	
• Are You Ready? at the beginning of each chapter assesses students' prerequisite skills.	213
• Ready to Go On? diagnoses students' skill development within the chapter.	239
• Check It Out and Try This questions enable students to check their understanding after every example and activity.	225, 240
• Questioning Strategies aid on-the-spot intervention with questions crafted to assess student comprehension.	TE 243
• Common Error Alert helps teachers anticipate potential pitfalls for students.	TE 229
• Alternative Assessment provides options to monitor student progress.	TE 249
• Chapter Test assesses students' mastery of concepts and skills.	288

	SEE PAGE(S)
READING AND WRITING MATH FOR COMPREHENSION	
• Reading and Writing Math helps students develop strong communication skills as they master math concepts.	215
• Reading Connection recommends math-themed literature that ties into chapter content.	TE 215
• Reading Math and Writing Math hints appear throughout each chapter to help students use the language of math.	81, 273
• Write About It exercises require students to explain a math concept or procedure.	220
• Journal suggestions encourage students to write about math.	TE 237
• Think and Discuss questions in every lesson extend and enrich student knowledge.	255
• Graphic Organizers in every lesson help students organize and remember key information.	269
• Glossary contains definitions and illustrations of key mathematical terms in English and Spanish.	G1–G46
ENGAGING CONNECTIONS AND APPLICATIONS	
• Links spark student interest by giving them the opportunity to apply math skills to other disciplines and the real world.	220, 248, 271
• Connecting Geometry to Algebra provides review and application of previously learned geometry concepts.	226, 266
• Career Path relates math concepts to the real world.	237
• Real-World Connection uses real-world scenarios to develop higher-order thinking.	294–295
INTEGRATED TEST PREP	
• Countdown to Testing prepares students for state tests with daily practice questions.	T4–T27
• Test Prep exercises provide daily practice in standardized test format.	230
• Test Prep Doctor addresses specific test-taking strategies related to the lesson.	TE 259
• Multi-Step Test Prep uses real-world scenarios to develop higher order thinking skills.	229, 238
• Test Tackler targets specific test-taking strategies to help students become savvy test-takers.	290–291
• College Entrance Exam Practice provides practice for college entrance exams such as the SAT and ACT.	289
• Standardized Test Prep provides cumulative assessment in standardized test format.	292–293
STUDENT SUPPORT	
• Study Guide: Preview prepares students for concepts in the chapter and connects the concepts to the real world.	214
• Student to Student shares advice from other students on how to approach the math in the lesson.	233
• Homework Help Online provides stepped-out solutions and additional practice for students as they work independently.	256
• Study Guide: Review highlights lesson vocabulary and key skills and offers additional examples and practice exercises.	284–287

TEACHER'S EDITION

Geometry

Edward B. Burger
David J. Chard
Paul A. Kennedy
Steven J. Leinwand
Freddie L. Renfro
Tom W. Roby
Dale G. Seymour
Bert K. Waits

HOLT McDOUGAL

 HOUGHTON MIFFLIN HARCOURT

Geometry Contents in Brief

Printed in the U.S.A.

ISBN-13 978-0-030-99578-1

ISBN-10 0-030-99578-7

3 4 5 6 7 8 9 10 0868 18 17 16 15 14 13 12 11 4500282876

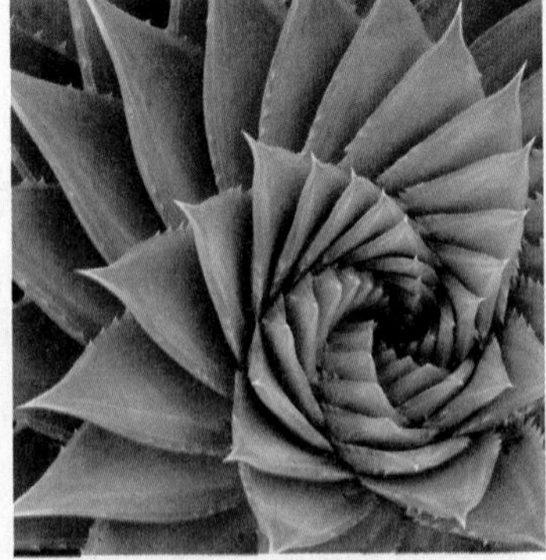

Cover photo: © Micha Pawlitzki/Corbis

Geometry Teacher's Edition

Contents in Brief

Contributing Authors

Linda Antinone
Fort Worth, TX
Ms. Antinone teaches mathematics at R. L. Paschal High School in Fort Worth, Texas. She has received the Presidential Award for Excellence in Teaching Mathematics and the National Radio Shack Teacher award. She has coauthored several books for Texas Instruments on the use of technology in mathematics.

Carmen Whitman
Pflugerville, TX
Ms. Whitman travels nationally helping districts improve mathematics education. She has been a program coordinator on the mathematics team at the Charles A. Dana Center, and has served as a secondary math specialist for the Austin Independent School District.

Reviewers

Robert Brouhle
Mathematics Department Chair, retired
Marina High School
Huntington Beach, CA

Carey Carter
Mathematics Teacher
Everman Joe C. Bean High School
Everman, TX

Greg Davis
Department Chair, retired
Lodi High School
Lodi, WI

Roger Fuller
Mathematics Department Chair
Grand Prairie High School
Grand Prairie, TX

Anthony Gugliotta
Supervisor of Math & Science
Rumson-Fair Haven Regional HS
Rumson, NJ

Marieta W. Harris
Mathematics Specialist
Memphis, TN

Debbie Hecky
Geometry Teacher
Scott High School
Covington, KY

Cynthia Hodges
Department Chair
Shoemaker High School
Killeen, TX

Kathleen Kelly
Mathematics Department Chair, retired
Lawrence High School
Fairfield, ME

Mike Kingery
Mathematics Teacher
Mayfield High School
Las Cruces, NM

Joy Lindsay
Mathematics Instructor
Bonita High School
LaVerne, CA

Kim Loggins
Geometry Teacher
Los Alamitos High School
Los Alamitos, CA

Elaine Pappas
Mathematics Department Chair
Cedar Shoals High School
Athens, GA

Terri Salas
Mathematics Consultant
Corpus Christi, TX

Jane Schneider
Mathematics Department Chair
Parkway West High School
Ballwin, MO

Jamae Sellari
Mathematics Instructor
Forest Hill High School
Jackson, MS

Caren Sorrells
Mathematics Coordinator
Birdville ISD
Haltom City, TX

E. Robin Staudenmeier
Middle/High School Math Coordinator
Olympia Community USD 16
Stanford, IL

Maureen "Marnie" Stockman
Geometry Specialist and Consultant
Cordova, MD

Anna Valdez
Geometry Teacher
Nikki Rowe High School
McAllen, TX

Lauralea Wright
Mathematics Teacher
Mauldin High School
Mauldin, SC

Denise Young
Mathematics Teacher
Blue Valley West High School
Overland Park, KS

Contributing Writer

Karen Droga Campe
Instructor
Yale University
New Haven, CT

Field Test Participants

Jill Morris
Navasota High School
Navasota, TX

Ruth Stutzman
Jefferson Forest High School
Forest, VA

Carey Carter
Alvarado High School
Alvarado, TX

Preparing for Standardized Tests

Holt McDougal Geometry provides many opportunities for you to prepare for standardized tests.

Test Prep Exercises

Use the Test Prep Exercises for daily practice of standardized test questions in various formats.

Multiple Choice—choose your answer.

Gridded Response—write your answer in a grid and fill in the corresponding bubbles.

Short Response—write open-ended responses that are scored with a 2-point rubric.

Extended Response—write open-ended responses that are scored with a 4-point rubric.

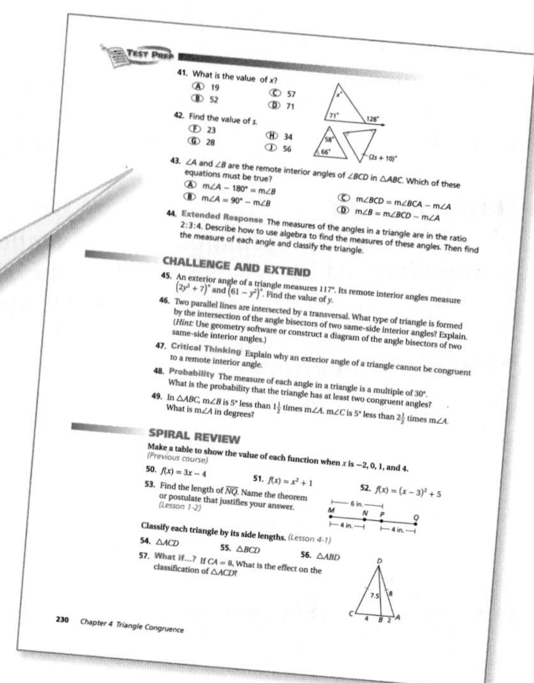

TEST PREP

41. What is the value of x?
Ⓐ 19 Ⓑ 52 Ⓒ 57 Ⓓ 71

42. Find the value of s.
Ⓕ 23 Ⓖ 28 Ⓗ 34 Ⓙ 56

43. ∠A and ∠B are the remote interior angles of ∠BCD in △ABC. Which of these equations must be true?
Ⓐ m∠A − 180° = m∠B
Ⓑ m∠A = 90° − m∠B
Ⓒ m∠BCD = m∠BCA − m∠A
Ⓓ m∠B = m∠BCD − m∠A

44. Extended Response The measures of the angles in a triangle are in the ratio 2:3:4. Describe how to use algebra to find the measures of these angles. Then find the measure of each angle and classify the triangle.

CHALLENGE AND EXTEND

45. An exterior angle of a triangle measures 117°. Its remote interior angles measure $(2y^2 + 7)°$ and $(61 - y^2)°$. Find the value of y.

46. Two parallel lines are intersected by a transversal. What type of triangle is formed by the intersection of the angle bisectors of two same-side interior angles? Explain. (Hint: Use geometry software or construct a diagram of the angle bisectors of two same-side interior angles.)

47. Critical Thinking Explain why an exterior angle of a triangle cannot be congruent to a remote interior angle.

48. Probability The measure of each angle in a triangle is a multiple of 30°. What is the probability that the triangle has at least two congruent angles?

49. In △ABC, m∠B is 5° less than $1\frac{1}{2}$ times m∠A. m∠C is 5° less than $2\frac{1}{2}$ times m∠A. What is m∠A in degrees?

SPIRAL REVIEW

Make a table to show the value of each function when x is −2, 0, 1, and 4. (Previous course)

50. $f(x) = 3x - 4$ 51. $f(x) = x^2 + 1$ 52. $f(x) = (x - 3)^2 + 5$

53. Find the length of $\overline{NQ}$. Name the theorem or postulate that justifies your answer. (Lesson 1-2)

Classify each triangle by its side lengths. (Lesson 4-1)

54. △ACD 55. △BCD 56. △ABD

57. What if...? If CA = 8, what is the effect on the classification of △ACD?

230 Chapter 4 Triangle Congruence

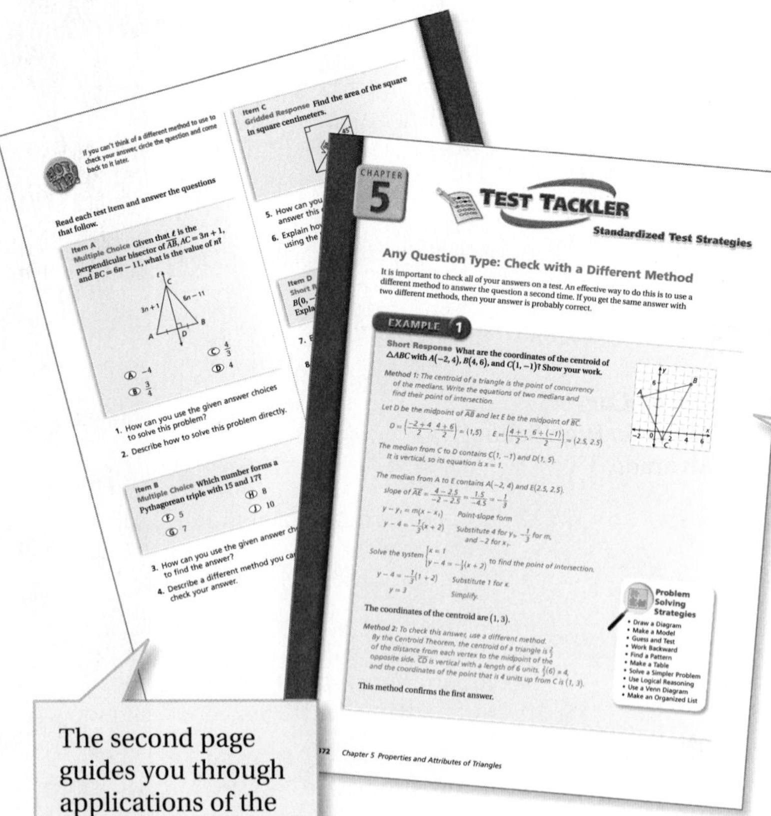

CHAPTER 5 TEST TACKLER

Standardized Test Strategies

Any Question Type: Check with a Different Method

It is important to check all of your answers on a test. An effective way to do this is to use a different method to answer the question a second time. If you get the same answer with two different methods, then your answer is probably correct.

EXAMPLE 1

Short Response What are the coordinates of the centroid of △ABC with A(−2, 4), B(4, 6), and C(1, −1)? Show your work.

The coordinates of the centroid are (1, 3).

This method confirms the first answer.

372 Chapter 5 Properties and Attributes of Triangles

Test Tackler

Use the Test Tackler to become familiar with and practice test-taking strategies.

The first page of this feature explains and shows an example of a test-taking strategy.

The second page guides you through applications of the test-taking strategy.

Standardized Test Prep

Use the Standardized Test Prep to apply test-taking strategies.

The Hot Tip provides test-taking tips to help you succeed on your tests.

These pages include practice with multiple choice, gridded response, short response, and extended response test items.

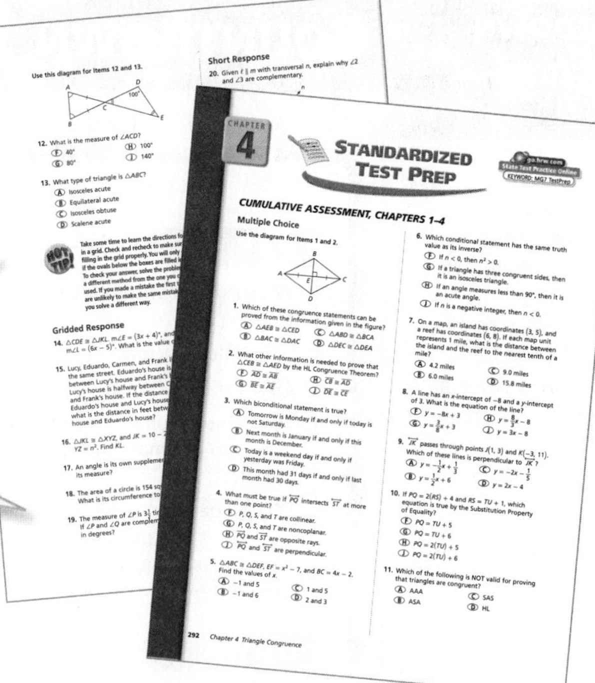

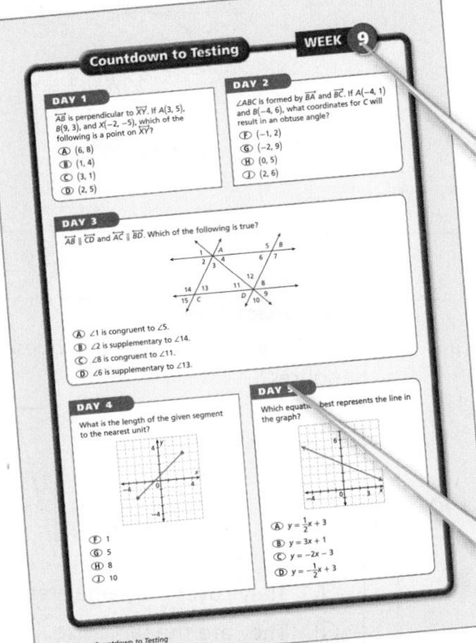

Countdown to Testing

Use the Countdown to Testing to practice for your state test every day.

There are 24 pages of practice for your state test. Each page is designed to be used in a week so that all practice will be completed before your state test is given.

Each week's page has five practice test items, one for each day of the week.

Test-Taking Tips

- Get plenty of sleep the night before the test. A rested mind thinks more clearly and you won't feel like falling asleep while taking the test.
- Draw a figure when one is not provided with the problem. If a figure is given, write any details from the problem on the figure.
- Read each problem carefully. As you finish each problem, read it again to make sure your answer is reasonable.
- Review the formula sheet that will be supplied with the test. Make sure you know when to use each formula.
- First answer problems that you know how to solve. If you do not know how to solve a problem, skip it and come back to it when you have finished the others.
- Use other test-taking strategies that can be found throughout this book, such as working backward and eliminating answer choices.

Countdown to Testing

Each problem on the *Countdown to Testing* is correlated to the 12th grade NAEP Assessment Standards. These correlations are shown at the bottom of each page.

Week 1

Day 1

Which statement about a number line is true?

- Ⓐ Values increase toward the right.
- Ⓑ Values increase toward the left.
- Ⓒ Whole numbers are toward the right and decimal numbers are toward the left.
- Ⓓ Negative numbers are toward the right and positive numbers are toward the left.

Day 2

If $a = b$ and $b = c$, which statement must be true?

- Ⓕ $a > c$
- Ⓖ $-a - c = 0$
- Ⓗ $a + c = 0$
- Ⓙ $a = c$

Day 3

If the width of each square in the grid is 1 centimeter, what is the diameter of the circle?

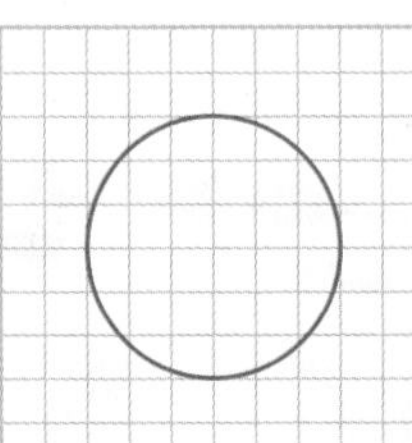

- Ⓐ 1 centimeter
- Ⓑ 3 centimeters
- Ⓒ 6 centimeters
- Ⓓ 12 centimeters

Day 4

Which shape is NOT included in the figure?

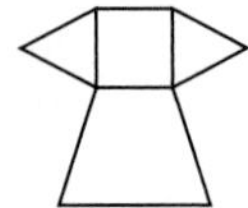

- Ⓕ Circle
- Ⓖ Square
- Ⓗ Triangle
- Ⓙ Trapezoid

Day 5

Which statement best describes these two figures?

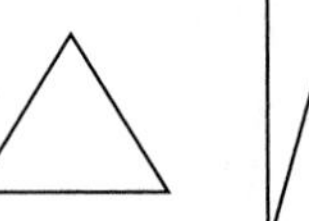

- Ⓐ They cover the same area.
- Ⓑ They are the same size.
- Ⓒ They have the same number of sides.
- Ⓓ The distance around each figure is the same.

Week 1	NAEP Standards Grade 12
1	Number Properties and Operations – Number sense: 12.1.1.d
2	Algebra – Algebraic representations: 12.5.2.e
3	Measurement – Measuring physical attributes: 12.2.1.h
4	Geometry – Dimension and shape: 12.3.1.c
5	Geometry – Relationships between geometric figures: 12.3.3.b

Countdown to Testing WEEK 2

DAY 1

What is the length of $\overline{FD}$?

Ⓐ 0
Ⓑ 3
Ⓒ 6
Ⓓ 9

DAY 2

$\angle ABC$ is an obtuse angle. Which of these could be the measure of $\angle ABC$?

Ⓕ 0°
Ⓖ 53°
Ⓗ 90°
Ⓙ 108°

DAY 3

Which point is described by the coordinates $(-2, 3)$?

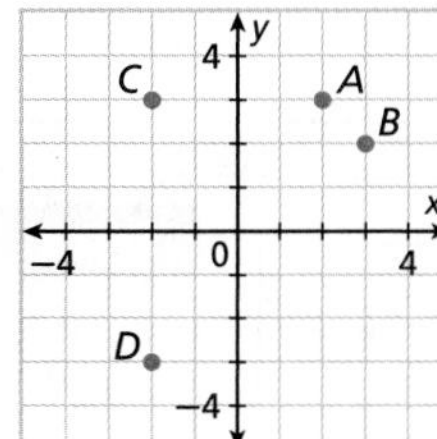

Ⓐ *A*
Ⓑ *B*
Ⓒ *C*
Ⓓ *D*

DAY 4

An architect is sketching a blueprint of a patio for a new home. On the blueprint, *C* is the midpoint of $\overline{AD}$, which represents one side of the patio. Point *B* is the midpoint of $\overline{AC}$. If $BC = 8$ feet, what is the length of $\overline{AD}$?

Ⓕ 8 feet
Ⓖ 16 feet
Ⓗ 24 feet
Ⓙ 32 feet

DAY 5

$\overrightarrow{OB}$ bisects $\angle AOC$, and $m\angle AOC = 60°$. What is $m\angle BOE$?

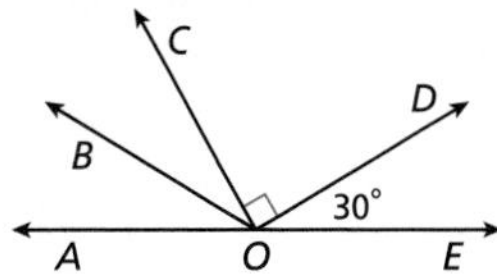

Ⓐ 30°
Ⓑ 60°
Ⓒ 120°
Ⓓ 150°

Week 2	NAEP Standards Grade 12
1	Measurement – Measuring physical attributes: 12.2.1.e
2	Measurement – Measuring physical attributes: 12.2.1.f
3	Algebra – Algebraic representations: 12.5.2.c
4	Measurement – Measuring physical attributes: 12.2.1.e
5	Measurement – Measuring physical attributes: 12.2.1.f

Countdown to Testing WEEK 3

DAY 1

The figure below shows the first three elements in a pattern. The area of the white region in the first element is 8 cm^2, and the area of the white region in the second element is 16 cm^2. What will the area of the white region be when an element contains six circles?

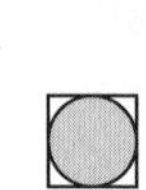
$A_w = 8$ cm^2

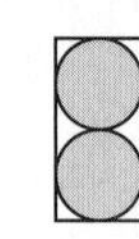
$A_w = 16$ cm^2

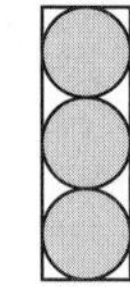
$A_w = 24$ cm^2

Ⓐ 36 square centimeters
Ⓑ 48 square centimeters
Ⓒ 144 square centimeters
Ⓓ 168 square centimeters

DAY 2

Which of these is a unit that can describe the perimeter of a figure?

Ⓕ Meters
Ⓖ Square centimeters
Ⓗ Cubic inches
Ⓙ Seconds

DAY 3

Point X is the midpoint of $\overline{HI}$. What is the coordinate of the point X?

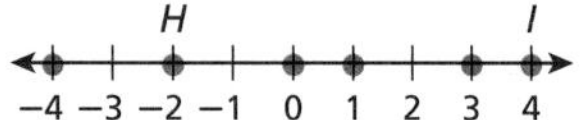

Ⓐ −4
Ⓑ 0
Ⓒ 1
Ⓓ 3

DAY 4

Which expression best represents the perimeter of the figure below?

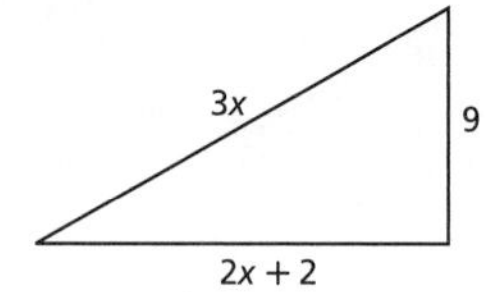

Ⓕ $27x$
Ⓖ $5x + 11$
Ⓗ $9x + 9$
Ⓙ $11x + 5$

DAY 5

A line segment is drawn between the points $(5, 8)$ and $(-1, 6)$. What are the coordinates of the midpoint of the segment?

Ⓐ $(3, 1)$
Ⓑ $(4, 14)$
Ⓒ $(2, 7)$
Ⓓ $\left(-\frac{1}{2}, 3\right)$

Week 3	NAEP Standards Grade 12
1	Algebra – Patterns, relations, and functions: 12.5.1.a
2	Measurement – Systems of measurement: 12.2.2.a
3	Measurement – Measuring physical attributes: 12.2.1.e
4	Algebra – Variables, expressions, and operations: 12.5.3.b
5	Measurement – Measuring physical attributes: 12.2.1.e

Countdown to Testing WEEK 4

DAY 1

Which equation below represents the second step of the solution process?

Step 1: $6x - 12 = 3(5 - x)$

Step 2: ?

Step 3: $9x - 12 = 15$

Step 4: $9x = 27$

Step 5: $x = 3$

(A) $6x - 12 = 15 - x$

(B) $6x - 12 = 15 - 3x$

(C) $6x - 12 = 5 - 3x$

(D) $6x = 3(5 - x) - 12$

DAY 2

Which conjecture best describes a rule for the pattern below?

(F) Rotate counterclockwise 90°

(G) Rotate clockwise 90°

(H) Rotate counterclockwise 180°

(J) Rotate clockwise 180°

DAY 3

Given: A triangle is a right triangle.

Conclusion: Two of the sides are congruent.

This conclusion—

(A) is true because right triangles have exactly one angle that measures 90°.

(B) is true because all right triangles have two congruent angles.

(C) is false because, for example, the sides of a 30°-60°-90° right triangle have different lengths.

(D) is false because a right triangle cannot have two congruent angles.

DAY 4

Which of the following best describes the value of $4n + 1$ when n is an integer?

(F) The value is always negative.

(G) The value is always positive.

(H) The value is always even.

(J) The value is always odd.

DAY 5

$\overrightarrow{MN}$ bisects $\angle LMO$. Which statement must be true?

(A) $m\angle LMN = m\angle OMN$

(B) $m\angle LMO = m\angle OMN$

(C) $m\angle LMN = m\angle OML$

(D) $m\angle LMO = m\angle ONM$

Week 4	NAEP Standards Grade 12
1	Number Properties and Operations – Properties of number and operations: 12.1.5.e
2	Geometry – Transformation of shapes and preservation of properties: 12.3.2.d
3	Geometry – Mathematical reasoning: 12.3.5.a
4	Number Properties and Operations – Properties of number and operations: 12.1.5.f
5	Measurement – Measuring physical attributes: 12.2.1.f

Countdown to Testing WEEK 5

DAY 1

Which statement is the converse of the conditional statement "If m$\angle A = 48°$, then $\angle A$ is acute?"

(A) If $\angle A$ is not acute, then m$\angle A \neq 48°$.

(B) If $\angle A$ is acute, then m$\angle A = 48°$.

(C) If m$\angle A \neq 48°$, then $\angle A$ is not acute.

(D) If $\angle A$ is not acute, then it must be obtuse.

DAY 2

Which of the following statements is true, based on the figure?

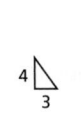

(F) $\angle 2$ and $\angle 4$ are not adjacent but form a linear pair.

(G) $\angle 2$ and $\angle 4$ are adjacent angles that form a linear pair.

(H) $\angle 1$ and $\angle 3$ are adjacent angles and form a linear pair.

(J) $\angle 1$ and $\angle 3$ are not adjacent angles but form a linear pair.

DAY 3

Let a represent "Three points are not collinear," and let b represent "The three points lie in exactly one plane." Which symbolic sentence represents the statement "If three points lie in exactly one plane, then the three points are not collinear"?

(A) $a \rightarrow b$

(B) $b \rightarrow a$

(C) $\sim a \rightarrow \sim b$

(D) $\sim b \rightarrow \sim a$

DAY 4

The figure below shows a pattern of right triangles and their areas, A. Based on the pattern, what will be the area of a right triangle with a height of 64 units?

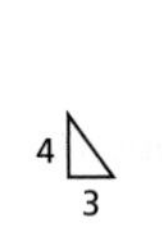

$A = 6$ square units

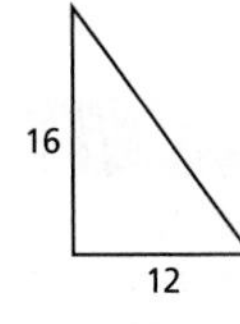

$A = 24$ square units

16, 12

$A = 96$ square units

(F) 4 square units

(G) 100 square units

(H) 364 square units

(J) 1536 square units

DAY 5

How many pairs of vertical angles are in the diagram?

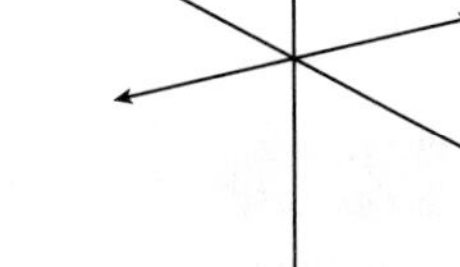

(A) 2

(B) 3

(C) 6

(D) 12

Week 5	NAEP Standards Grade 12
1	Geometry – Mathematical reasoning: 12.3.5.a
2	Geometry – Relationships between geometric figures: 12.3.3.g
3	Geometry – Mathematical reasoning: 12.3.5.a
4	Geometry – Transformation of shapes and preservation of properties: 12.3.2.e
5	Geometry – Position and direction: 12.3.4.b

Countdown to Testing WEEK 6

DAY 1

A transversal crosses two parallel lines. If two angles are on opposite sides of the transversal and inside the two parallel lines, then they are alternate interior angles. If two angles are alternate interior angles, then they are congruent. ∠1 and ∠2 are alternate interior angles.

Which conclusion can be drawn from the given information?

Ⓐ ∠1 and ∠2 are parallel.
Ⓑ ∠1 and ∠2 are suppplementary
Ⓒ ∠1 and ∠2 are complementary.
Ⓓ ∠1 and ∠2 are congruent.

DAY 2

Two angles are labeled in the figure below. Which of the following statements best describes this angle pair?

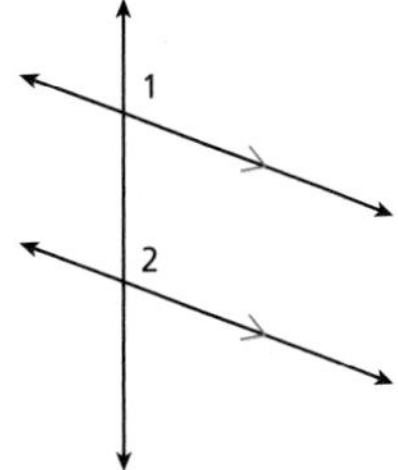

Ⓕ They are complementary angles.
Ⓖ They are congruent angles.
Ⓗ They are supplementary angles.
Ⓙ They are parallel angles.

DAY 3

If line *a* is parallel to line *b*, and m∠8 = 62°, what is m∠1?

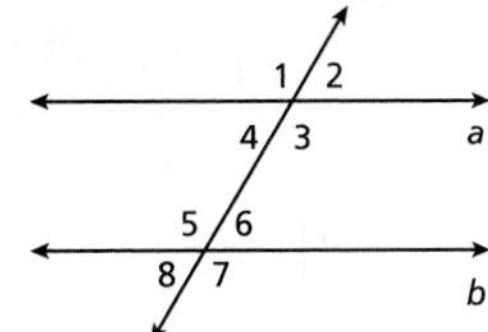

Ⓐ 28°
Ⓑ 62°
Ⓒ 118°
Ⓓ 180°

DAY 4

The area of a circle is about 7 cm^2. By how many times will the area increase if the radius of the circle is tripled?

Ⓕ 1.5
Ⓖ 3
Ⓗ 6
Ⓙ 9

DAY 5

B is in the interior of ∠*AOC*. Which of the following statements must be true?

Ⓐ m∠*AOB* + m∠*BOC* = m∠*AOC*
Ⓑ m∠*AOB* = m∠*BOC*
Ⓒ m∠*AOB* + m∠*AOC* = m∠*BOC*
Ⓓ m∠*BOC* + m∠*AOC* = m∠*AOB*

Week 6	NAEP Standards Grade 12
1	Geometry – Relationships between geometric figures: 12.3.3.g
2	Geometry – Relationships between geometric figures: 12.3.3.g
3	Geometry – Relationships between geometric figures: 12.3.3.g
4	Measurement – Measuring physical attributes: 12.2.1.h
5	Measurement – Measuring physical attributes: 12.2.1.f

Countdown to Testing — WEEK 7

DAY 1

Four rays are drawn from the origin through each of the following points: $S(-2, 5)$, $T(0, 4)$, $U(-1, -3)$, and $V(2, 6)$. Which point is on the ray that forms an acute angle with the ray in the figure?

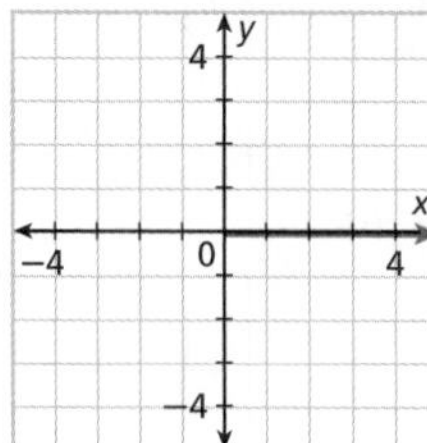

Ⓐ S
Ⓑ T
Ⓒ U
Ⓓ V

DAY 2

What must be true if two nonvertical lines are perpendicular?

Ⓕ Their slopes add to 0.
Ⓖ The product of their slopes is −1.
Ⓗ Their slopes are equal.
Ⓙ Their y-intercepts are equal.

DAY 3

Which line is parallel to $y = 2x + 3$?

Ⓐ $y = 2x - 8$
Ⓑ $y = 3x + 2$
Ⓒ $2y = -4x + 6$
Ⓓ $y = -2x + 3$

DAY 4

Which expression best represents the perimeter of the rectangle?

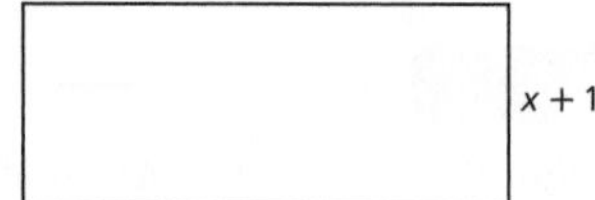

Ⓕ $4x + 1$
Ⓖ $6x + 4$
Ⓗ $8x + 2$
Ⓙ $3x^2 + 3x$

DAY 5

Two parallel lines are cut by a transversal. The measures of two corresponding angles are $(x + 20)°$ and $(3x - 10)°$. What is the value of x?

Ⓐ 7
Ⓑ 15
Ⓒ 35
Ⓓ 42

Week 7	NAEP Standards Grade 12
1	Measurement – Measuring physical attributes: 12.2.1.e
2	Geometry – Relationships between geometric figures: 12.3.3.g
3	Geometry – Relationships between geometric figures: 12.3.3.g
4	Algebra – Variables, expressions, and operations: 12.5.3.b
5	Geometry – Relationships between geometric figures: 12.3.3.g

Countdown to Testing WEEK 8

DAY 1

What is the slope of the given line segment?

Ⓐ −2
Ⓑ $-\frac{1}{2}$
Ⓒ 1
Ⓓ 2

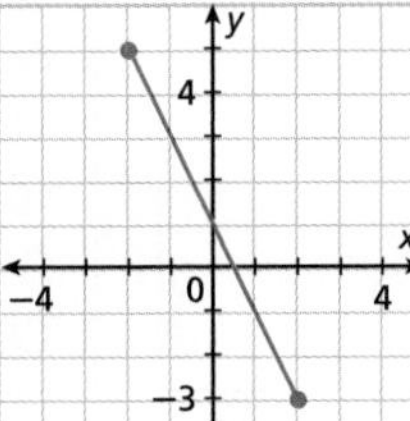

DAY 2

Which two lines are perpendicular?

Ⓕ $y = -5x + 2$ and $2y - 10x = 4$
Ⓖ $y = \frac{1}{4}x + 1$ and $y = 4x + 2$
Ⓗ $y = 3x + 1$ and $y - 4x = 6$
Ⓙ $y = \frac{1}{2}x + 2$ and $y + 2x = -4$

DAY 3

Which of the following is the best classification for the given triangle?

Ⓐ Equilateral
Ⓑ Isosceles
Ⓒ Scalene
Ⓓ Right

DAY 4

$\triangle SQT$ is an equilateral triangle. $\overline{QR}$ bisects $\angle SQT$. What are the measures of the angles of $\triangle SQR$?

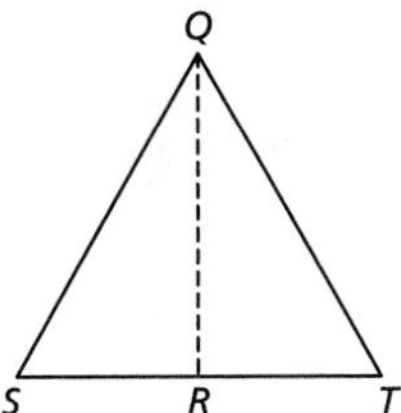

Ⓕ 30°-30°-30°
Ⓖ 30°-60°-90°
Ⓗ 30°-60°-60°
Ⓙ 60°-60°-60°

DAY 5

What is the area of a circle with a radius of $2y$?

Ⓐ $2\pi y$
Ⓑ $4\pi y$
Ⓒ $4\pi y^2$
Ⓓ $8\pi y^2$

Week 8	NAEP Standards Grade 12
1	Measurement – Measuring physical attributes: 12.2.1.e
2	Geometry – Relationships between geometric figures: 12.3.3.g
3	Geometry – Dimension and shape: 12.3.1.c
4	Measurement – Measuring physical attributes: 12.2.1.f
5	Measurement – Measuring physical attributes: 12.2.1.h

Countdown to Testing WEEK 9

DAY 1

$\overleftrightarrow{AB}$ is perpendicular to $\overleftrightarrow{XY}$. If $A(3, 5)$, $B(9, 3)$, and $X(-2, -5)$, which of the following is a point on $\overleftrightarrow{XY}$?

- Ⓐ (6, 8)
- Ⓑ (1, 4)
- Ⓒ (3, 1)
- Ⓓ (2, 5)

DAY 2

$\angle ABC$ is formed by $\overrightarrow{BA}$ and $\overrightarrow{BC}$. If $A(-4, 1)$ and $B(-4, 6)$, what coordinates for C will result in an obtuse angle?

- Ⓕ (−1, 2)
- Ⓖ (−2, 9)
- Ⓗ (0, 5)
- Ⓙ (2, 6)

DAY 3

$\overleftrightarrow{AB} \parallel \overleftrightarrow{CD}$ and $\overleftrightarrow{AC} \parallel \overleftrightarrow{BD}$. Which of the following is true?

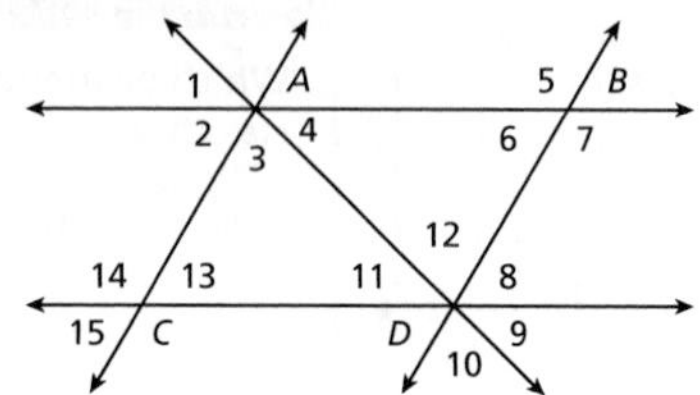

- Ⓐ $\angle 1$ is congruent to $\angle 5$.
- Ⓑ $\angle 2$ is supplementary to $\angle 14$.
- Ⓒ $\angle 8$ is congruent to $\angle 11$.
- Ⓓ $\angle 6$ is supplementary to $\angle 13$.

DAY 4

What is the length of the given segment to the nearest unit?

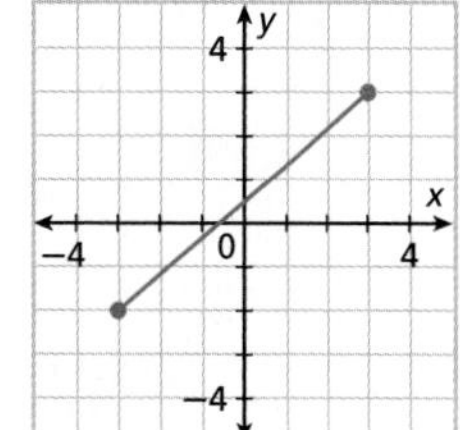

- Ⓕ 1
- Ⓖ 5
- Ⓗ 8
- Ⓙ 10

DAY 5

Which equation best represents the line in the graph?

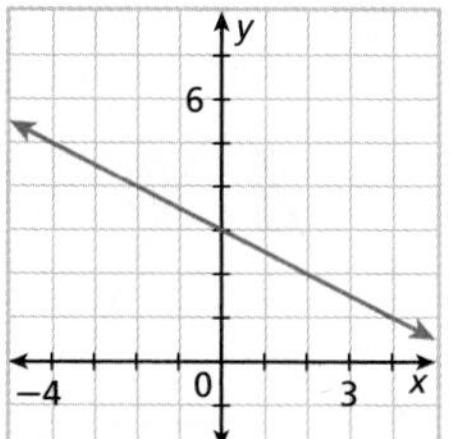

- Ⓐ $y = \frac{1}{2}x + 3$
- Ⓑ $y = 3x + 1$
- Ⓒ $y = -2x - 3$
- Ⓓ $y = -\frac{1}{2}x + 3$

Week 9	NAEP Standards Grade 12
1	Measurement – Measuring physical attributes: 12.2.1.e
2	Measurement – Measuring physical attributes: 12.2.1.e
3	Geometry – Relationships between geometric figures: 12.3.3.g
4	Measurement – Measuring physical attributes: 12.2.1.e
5	Algebra – Algebraic representations: 12.5.2.a

Countdown to Testing WEEK 10

DAY 1

Which set of angle measures can be used to conclude that lines x and y are parallel?

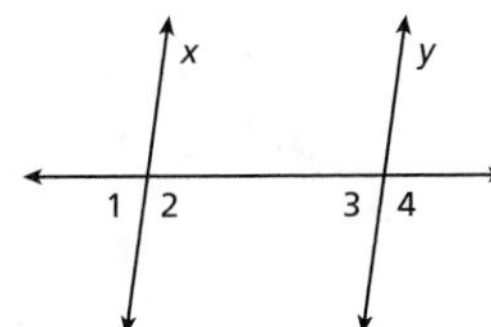

(A) $m\angle 1 = 87°$ and $m\angle 3 = 93°$
(B) $m\angle 1 = 82°$ and $m\angle 4 = 98°$
(C) $m\angle 1 = 80°$ and $m\angle 2 = 100°$
(D) $m\angle 3 = 88°$ and $m\angle 4 = 92°$

DAY 2

Which postulate or theorem can be used to prove that these triangles are congruent?

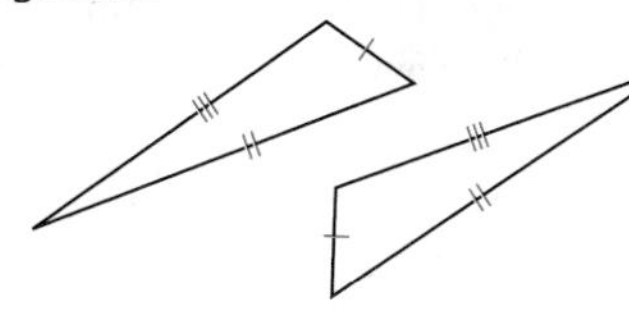

(F) SAS
(G) ASA
(H) AAS
(J) SSS

DAY 3

Which of the following conjectures is false?

(A) The product of an even number and an odd number is even.
(B) The difference of two negative numbers is a positive number.
(C) If x is negative, then $-x$ is positive.
(D) If x is even, then $x + 1$ is odd.

DAY 4

How many line segments can be determined by four points, no three of which are collinear?

(F) 4
(G) 6
(H) 8
(J) 10

DAY 5

The centroid of a triangle divides each median of the triangle into two segments. What of the following is the ratio of the length of the longer segment to the length of the shorter segment?

(A) 1:1
(B) 1:3
(C) 2:3
(D) 2:1

Week 10	NAEP Standards Grade 12
1	Geometry – Relationships between geometric figures: 12.3.3.g
2	Geometry – Transformation of shapes and preservation of properties: 12.3.2.e
3	Geometry – Mathematical reasoning: 12.3.5.a
4	Algebra – Patterns, relations, and functions: 12.5.1.a
5	Geometry – Relationships between geometric figures: 12.3.3.f

Countdown to Testing WEEK 11

DAY 1

What conclusion can you draw from the figure?

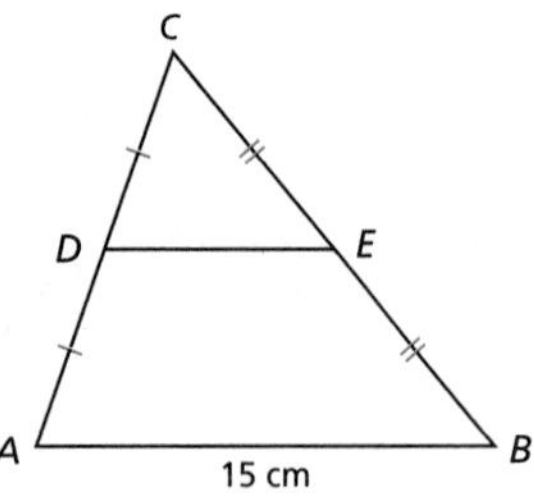

Ⓐ $\triangle ABC$ is isosceles.

Ⓑ The perimeter of $\triangle ABC$ is 45 centimeters.

Ⓒ $DE = 10$ centimeters

Ⓓ $DE = \frac{1}{2} AB$

DAY 2

Jan drew the figure below and claims that line ℓ is parallel to line m. Which of the following proves her statement true?

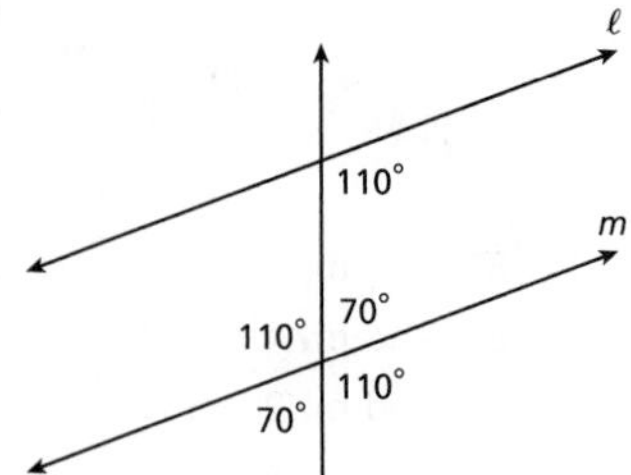

Ⓕ Angles on opposite sides of the transversal are equal.

Ⓖ Corresponding angles on the same side of the transversal are congruent.

Ⓗ More than two angles in the diagram have the same value.

Ⓙ Two straight lines pass through the same transversal.

DAY 3

Which of the following can you use to prove that two angles are complementary?

Ⓐ The sum of their measures is 90°.

Ⓑ The sum of their measures is 180°.

Ⓒ The angles have the same measure.

Ⓓ The measure of one angle is twice the other measure.

DAY 4

If $X(5, 5)$ and $Y(0, 0)$, what are the coordinates of Z so that $m\angle XYZ = 90°$?

Ⓕ $(5, -5)$

Ⓖ $(-5, -5)$

Ⓗ $(5, 0)$

Ⓙ $(0, 5)$

DAY 5

$\overrightarrow{OZ}$ is a bisector of $\angle XOY$. Which of the following statements is NOT true?

Ⓐ $2m\angle ZOY = m\angle XOY$

Ⓑ $2m\angle XOZ = m\angle XOY$

Ⓒ $m\angle ZOY = m\angle XOY$

Ⓓ $m\angle XOZ = \frac{1}{2}m\angle XOY$

Week 11	NAEP Standards Grade 12
1	Geometry – Relationships between geometric figures: 12.3.3.b
2	Geometry – Relationships between geometric figures: 12.3.3.g
3	Geometry – Mathematical reasoning: 12.3.5.a
4	Measurement – Measuring physical attributes: 12.2.1.e
5	Measurement – Measuring physical attributes: 12.2.1.f

Countdown to Testing WEEK 12

DAY 1

Which of the following correctly completes the congruence statement?

$\overline{AB} \cong$ ___?___

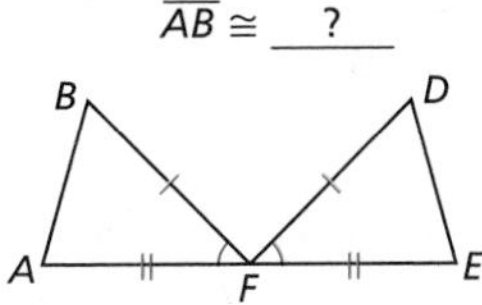

Ⓐ $\overline{FD}$

Ⓑ $\overline{AF}$

Ⓒ $\overline{EF}$

Ⓓ $\overline{ED}$

DAY 2

Based on the figure, which inequality is correct?

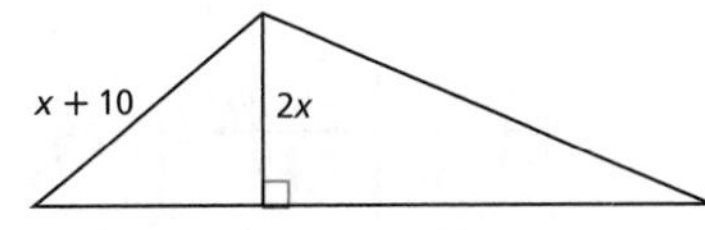

Ⓕ $2x > x + 10$

Ⓖ $2x < 10$

Ⓗ $x < 10$

Ⓙ $x > 8$

DAY 3

Roberta is attaching wooden trim around a stained glass window. The window is made up of eight congruent isosceles triangles.

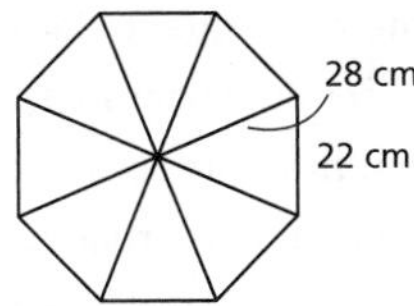

What length of trim does Roberta need in order to surround the entire window?

Ⓐ 22 centimeters

Ⓑ 78 centimeters

Ⓒ 176 centimeters

Ⓓ 624 centimeters

DAY 4

How many different segments can be created from eight colinear points?

Ⓕ 8

Ⓖ 13

Ⓗ 28

Ⓙ 36

DAY 5

Which of these conditional statements is true?

Ⓐ If two angles are vertical angles, then they are congruent.

Ⓑ If two angles are congruent, then they are right angles.

Ⓒ If four points are given, then they lie in exactly one plane.

Ⓓ If one angle of a triangle measures 60°, then the triangle is a right triangle.

Week 12	NAEP Standards Grade 12
1	Geometry – Transformation of shapes and preservation of properties: 12.3.2.e
2	Geometry – Relationships between geometric figures: 12.3.3.b
3	Measurement – Measuring physical attributes: 12.2.1.h
4	Algebra – Patterns, relations, and functions: 12.5.1.a
5	Geometry – Mathematical reasoning: 12.3.5.a

Countdown to Testing WEEK 13

DAY 1

What are the coordinates of point *P*?

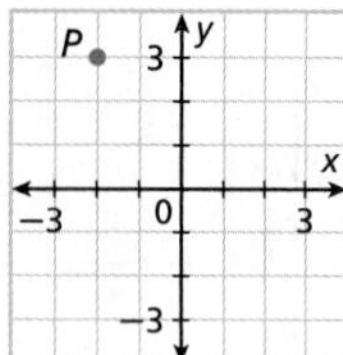

(A) (3, −2)
(B) (−2, 3)
(C) (3, 2)
(D) (2, −3)

DAY 2

Which postulate or theorem can be used to verify the congruence of these two triangles?

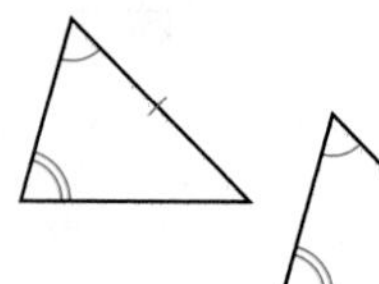

(F) SSS
(G) HL
(H) AAS
(J) SAS

DAY 3

Which conjecture is true?

(A) If a figure is a rectangle, its perimeter is equal to its area.
(B) If a figure is a triangle, all three sides are congruent.
(C) If a figure is a quadrilateral, then it has four sides.
(D) If a figure is a circle, its area is always greater than its circumference.

DAY 4

The layout of a swimming pool is plotted on the coordinate grid below. If each unit on the grid represents 2 meters, what is the length of the pool?

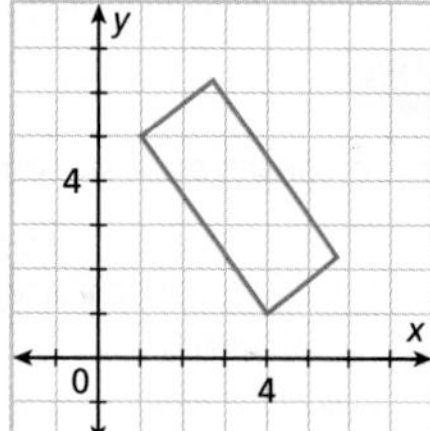

(F) 5 meters
(G) 8 meters
(H) 10 meters
(J) 25 meters

DAY 5

$\triangle LMN$ is shown on the grid. What is the slope of $\overline{MN}$?

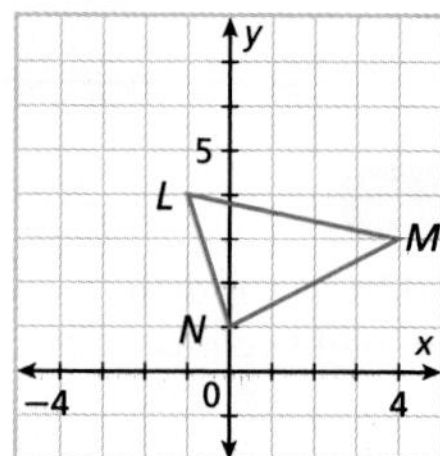

(A) $-\frac{1}{2}$
(B) −4
(C) $\frac{1}{2}$
(D) 2

Week 13	NAEP Standards Grade 12
1	Algebra – Algebraic representations: 12.5.2.c
2	Geometry – Transformation of shapes and preservation of properties: 12.3.2.e
3	Geometry – Mathematical reasoning: 12.3.5.a
4	Measurement – Measuring physical attributes: 12.2.1.e
5	Measurement – Measuring physical attributes: 12.2.1.e

Countdown to Testing WEEK 14

DAY 1

A ceramic tile is in the shape of a 30°-60°-90° triangle. The side across from the 30° angle is 6.25 centimeters long. How long is the hypotenuse of the tile?

Ⓐ 3.125 centimeters

Ⓑ $6.25\sqrt{3}$ centimeters

Ⓒ 12.5 centimeters

Ⓓ 15 centimeters

DAY 2

What is the slope of this line?

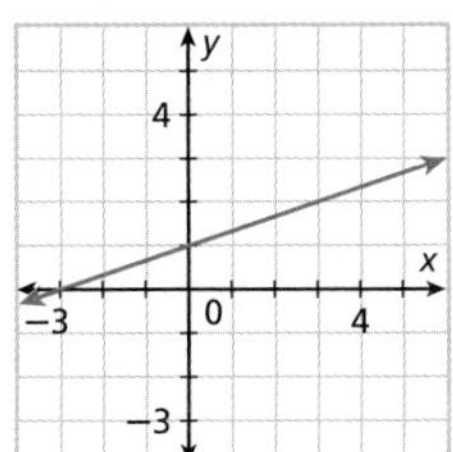

Ⓕ 1

Ⓖ $\frac{1}{3}$

Ⓗ 3

Ⓙ $-\frac{1}{3}$

DAY 3

Which equation should Aretha use to find the distance *c* between two points across a river?

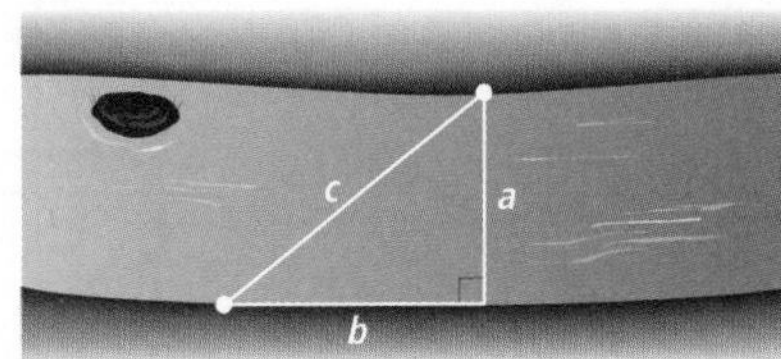

Ⓐ $c = a^2 + b^2$

Ⓑ $c = a + b$

Ⓒ $c^2 = \sqrt{a + b}$

Ⓓ $c = \sqrt{a^2 + b^2}$

DAY 4

The sums of the angle measures of three polygons are given. Based on the pattern, what will be the sum of the measures of a hexagon?

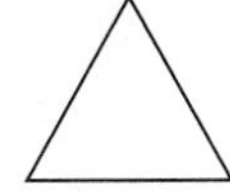 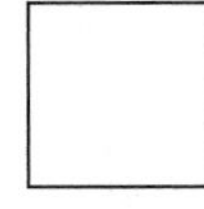 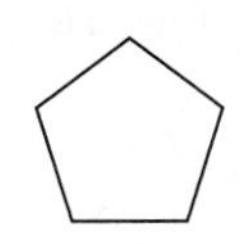

180° 360° 540°

Ⓕ 240°

Ⓖ 420°

Ⓗ 600°

Ⓙ 720°

DAY 5

Which line in the graph is described by the equation $y = x + 2$?

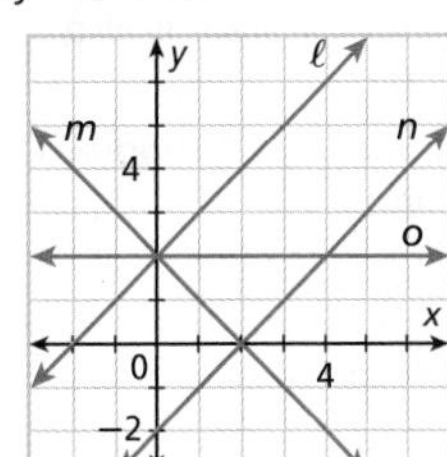

Ⓐ ℓ

Ⓑ m

Ⓒ n

Ⓓ o

Week 14	NAEP Standards Grade 12
1	Geometry – Relationships between geometric figures: 12.3.3.d
2	Measurement – Measuring physical attributes: 12.2.1.e
3	Geometry – Relationships between geometric figures: 12.3.3.d
4	Algebra – Patterns, relations, and functions: 12.5.1.a
5	Algebra – Algebraic representations: 12.5.2.a

Countdown to Testing WEEK 15

DAY 1

Three coordinates of ▱*ABCD* are *A*(4, 5), *C*(7, 3), and *D*(1, 3). Which coordinates could represent point *B*?

Ⓐ (1, 5)
Ⓑ (3, 7)
Ⓒ (5, 1)
Ⓓ (10, 5)

DAY 2

Which two lines are parallel?

Ⓕ $y = 6x + 8$ and $y + \frac{1}{6}x = 3$
Ⓖ $y = \frac{1}{3}x - 1$ and $y = 3x + 1$
Ⓗ $y - 2x = 2$ and $y = 2 - 2x$
Ⓙ $y = \frac{1}{4}x$ and $y - \frac{1}{4}x = 1$

DAY 3

What is the midpoint of $\overline{QR}$?

Ⓐ (1, −2)
Ⓑ (−2, 1)
Ⓒ (1, 2)
Ⓓ (−1, −2)

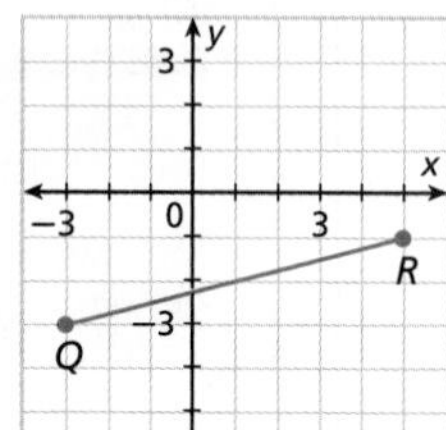

DAY 4

Which of these statements is true?

Ⓕ All quadrilaterals are parallelograms.
Ⓖ Every rectangle is a parallelogram.
Ⓗ Every parallelogram is also a rectangle.
Ⓙ The diagonals of a rhombus are congruent.

DAY 5

Which expression describes the total number of diagonals in a polygon with *n* sides?

No. of sides	3	4	5	6	7
No. of diagonals	0	2	5	9	14

Ⓐ $\frac{n(n-3)}{2}$
Ⓑ $2n$
Ⓒ $\frac{3n}{2}$
Ⓓ $\frac{2n+6}{3}$

Week 15	NAEP Standards Grade 12
1	Geometry – Dimension and shape: 12.3.1.c
2	Geometry – Relationships between geometric figures: 12.3.3.g
3	Measurement – Measuring physical attributes: 12.2.1.e
4	Geometry – Mathematical reasoning: 12.3.5.a
5	Algebra – Patterns, relations, and functions: 12.5.1.b

Countdown to Testing WEEK 16

DAY 1

The coordinates of the vertices of $\triangle ABC$ are (1, 1), (6, 1) and (1, 8). Which of the following could be the coordinates of the vertices of a triangle congruent to $\triangle ABC$?

Ⓐ (−8, −2), (−3, −2), (−3, −9)
Ⓑ (4, 1), (6, 2), (8, 10)
Ⓒ (−2, 5), (−2, −9), (−8, 3)
Ⓓ (0, 0), (−1, 8), (5, 2)

DAY 2

Natalia is using indirect measurement to find the distance across a pond. Which Pythagorean triple is represented by the triangle?

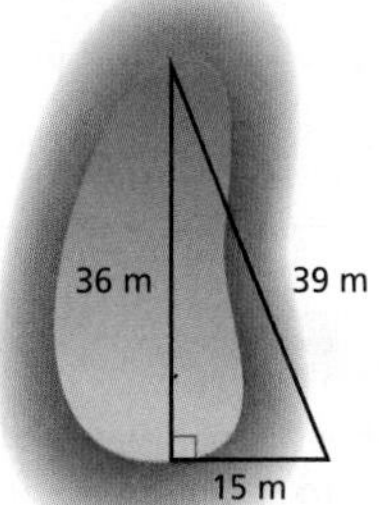

Ⓕ 3-4-5
Ⓖ 5-12-13
Ⓗ 8-15-17
Ⓙ 7-24-25

DAY 3

Which of the following sets of measurements could represent the side lengths of a right triangle?

Ⓐ 3, 5, 9
Ⓑ 4.5, 12, 8.5
Ⓒ 6, 7, 10
Ⓓ 2.5, 6, 6.5

DAY 4

What is the area of the composite figure?

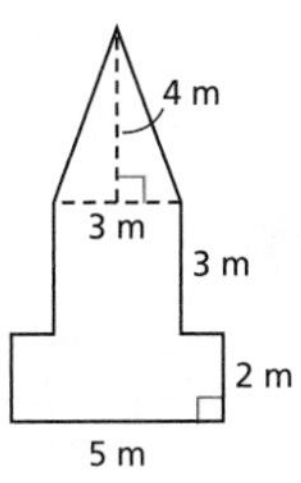

Ⓕ 8 square meters
Ⓖ 21 square meters
Ⓗ 25 square meters
Ⓙ 45 square meters

DAY 5

What is the measure of $\angle 3$ in the regular hexagon?

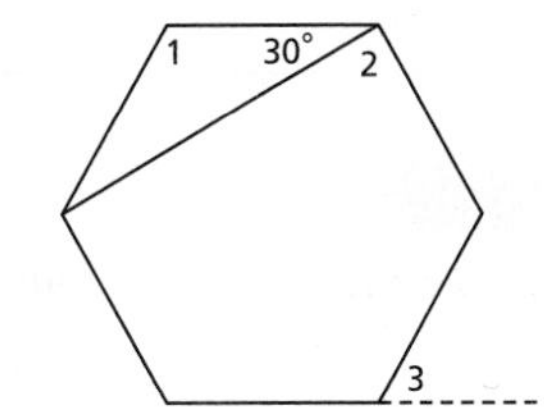

Ⓐ 30°
Ⓑ 60°
Ⓒ 90°
Ⓓ 120°

Week 16	NAEP Standards Grade 12
1	Geometry – Transformation of shapes and preservation of properties: 12.3.2.c
2	Measurement – Measuring physical attributes: 12.2.1.k
3	Geometry – Relationships between geometric figures: 12.3.3.d
4	Measurement – Measuring physical attributes: 12.2.1.h
5	Measurement – Measuring physical attributes: 12.2.1.f

Countdown to Testing WEEK 17

DAY 1

Which two lines are perpendicular?

(A) $y = x + 6$ and $y = x - 6$

(B) $y + \frac{2}{3}x = 1$ and $y = \frac{3}{2}x - 4$

(C) $y = \frac{1}{2}x - 2$ and $y = -\frac{1}{2}x + 3$

(D) $y - 2x = 5$ and $y = 2x + 2$

DAY 2

What is the perimeter of the composite figure to the nearest centimeter?

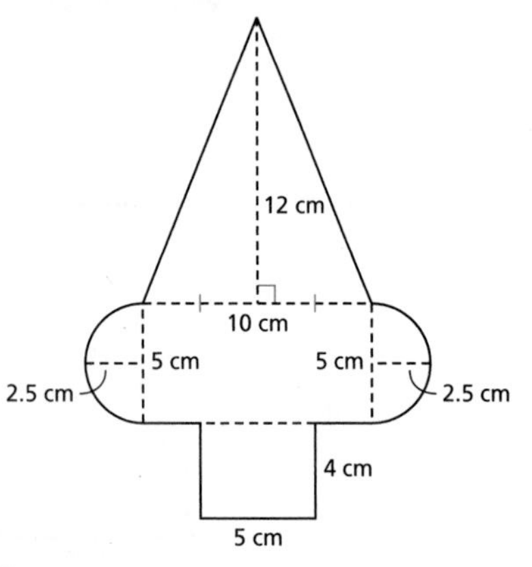

(F) 44 centimeters

(G) 52 centimeters

(H) 60 centimeters

(J) 83 centimeters

DAY 3

What is the measure of ∠1 in the triangle below?

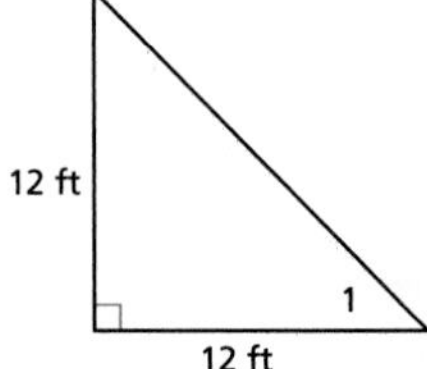

(A) 30°

(B) 45°

(C) 60°

(D) 90°

DAY 4

What is the sixth item in the pattern below?

64, 32, 16, 8, …

(F) 0

(G) $\frac{1}{2}$

(H) 2

(J) 4

DAY 5

The vertices of polygon *ABCD* are *A*(1, 5), *B*(8, 5), *C*(8, 3), and *D*(1, 3). Which of the following statements about this polygon is true?

(A) It is a square.

(B) Its width is 2 units.

(C) Its perimeter is 6 units.

(D) Its area is 9 square units.

Week 17	NAEP Standards Grade 12
1	Geometry – Relationships between geometric figures: 12.3.3.g
2	Measurement – Measuring physical attributes: 12.2.1.h
3	Measurement – Measuring physical attributes: 12.2.1.f
4	Number Properties and Operations – Properties of number and operations: 12.1.5.a
5	Measurement – Measuring physical attributes: 12.2.1.e

Countdown to Testing WEEK 18

DAY 1

Based on the pattern of similar triangles below, what is the value of x?

Ⓐ 2
Ⓑ 4
Ⓒ $4\sqrt{3}$
Ⓓ 8

DAY 2

Which ratio is equivalent to $\sin B$?

Ⓕ $\frac{2\sqrt{3}}{3}$
Ⓖ $\sqrt{3}$
Ⓗ $\frac{\sqrt{3}}{2}$
Ⓙ $\frac{1}{2}$

DAY 3

What is the value of x to the nearest tenth of a millimeter?

Ⓐ 52.0 millimeters
Ⓑ 61.6 millimeters
Ⓒ 78.8 millimeters
Ⓓ 140.4 millimeters

DAY 4

What is the value of x in the regular pentagon below?

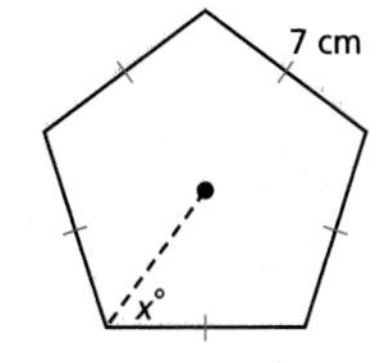

Ⓕ 54°
Ⓖ 90°
Ⓗ 108°
Ⓙ 180°

DAY 5

Which conjecture about polygons is NOT true?

Ⓐ The area of a parallelogram is the product of its base and height.
Ⓑ A rhombus has four right angles.
Ⓒ A square has four congruent sides.
Ⓓ A trapezoid has exactly one pair of parallel sides.

Week 18	NAEP Standards Grade 12
1	Geometry – Transformation of shapes and preservation of properties: 12.3.2.e
2	Measurement – Measuring physical attributes: 12.2.1.m
3	Measurement – Measuring physical attributes: 12.2.1.m
4	Measurement – Measuring physical attributes: 12.2.1.f
5	Geometry – Mathematical reasoning: 12.3.5.a

Countdown to Testing WEEK 19

DAY 1

Which two line segments are congruent?

Ⓐ $\overline{AB}$ and $\overline{DF}$
Ⓑ $\overline{CE}$ and $\overline{GH}$
Ⓒ $\overline{GH}$ and $\overline{AB}$
Ⓓ $\overline{CD}$ and $\overline{DE}$

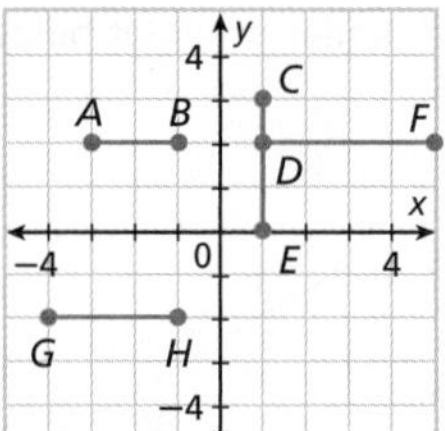

DAY 2

Based on the table, which algebraic expression best represents the number of triangles formed by drawing all of the diagonals from one vertex in a polygon with *n* sides?

No. of sides	3	4	5	8
No. of triangles formed	1	2	3	6

Ⓕ n
Ⓖ $2n - 1$
Ⓗ $n - 2$
Ⓙ $\frac{n+2}{2}$

DAY 3

At a certain time of the day, a 24-foot tree casts an 18-foot shadow. How long is the shadow cast by a 4-foot mailbox at the same time of day?

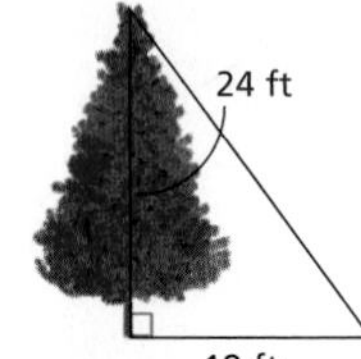

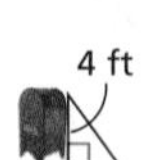

Ⓐ 1.3 feet
Ⓑ 3 feet
Ⓒ 4.5 feet
Ⓓ 5 feet

DAY 4

A school increases the width of its rectangular playground from 25 meters to 40 meters and the length from 45 meters to 60 meters. By how much does the perimeter of the playground increase?

Ⓕ 30 meters
Ⓖ 60 meters
Ⓗ 200 meters
Ⓙ 225 meters

DAY 5

What is *x*?

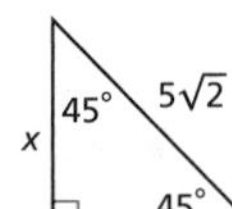

Ⓐ 2
Ⓑ 5
Ⓒ 10
Ⓓ 30

Week 19	NAEP Standards Grade 12
1	Measurement – Measuring physical attributes: 12.2.1.e
2	Algebra – Patterns, relations, and functions: 12.5.1.b
3	Measurement – Measuring physical attributes: 12.2.1.k
4	Measurement – Measuring physical attributes: 12.2.1.h
5	Geometry – Relationships between geometric figures: 12.3.3.d

Countdown to Testing WEEK 20

DAY 1

The figure shows the measure of each interior angle for several regular polygons.

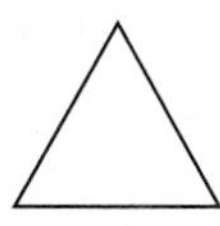
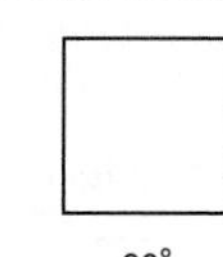
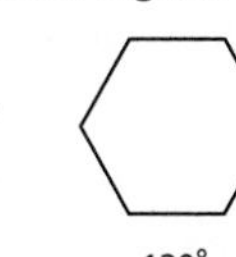

60° 90° 108° 120°

Which algebraic expression best represents the measure of an interior angle of a regular polygon with n sides?

(A) $\frac{(n-2)180}{n}$ (C) $(n-2)180$

(B) $\frac{360n}{n+2}$ (D) $\frac{180n}{2}$

DAY 2

Which coordinates represent a vertex of the hexagon?

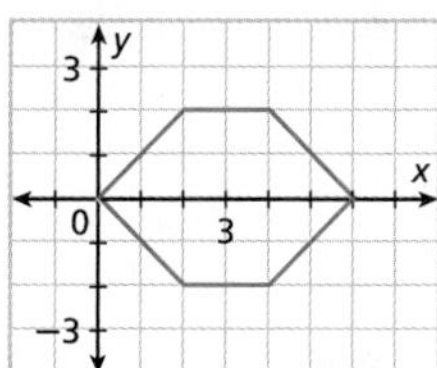

(F) (0, 2)

(G) (4, −2)

(H) (3, 2)

(J) (−2, 2)

DAY 3

The two triangles in the figure are similar. What is the length of $\overline{MN}$?

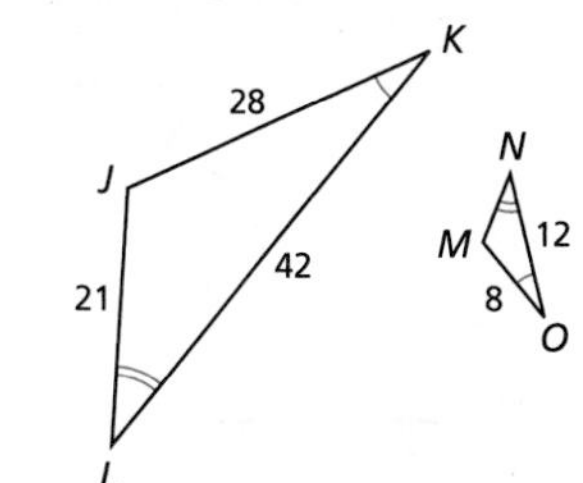

(A) 3.5 (C) 7

(B) 6 (D) 17.5

DAY 4

Two regular pentagons have perimeters of 30 and 75 respectively. What scale factor relates the smaller figure to the larger one?

(F) 1:2.5

(G) 1:6

(H) 1:15

(J) 1:21

DAY 5

Alissa is painting a diagonal line across a square tile. What is the length of the line?

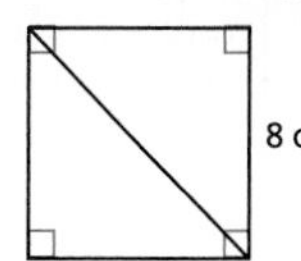

(A) $2\sqrt{8}$ centimeters

(B) 6 centimeters

(C) 8 centimeters

(D) $8\sqrt{2}$ centimeters

Week 20	NAEP Standards Grade 12
1	Algebra – Patterns, relations, and functions: 12.5.1.b
2	Algebra – Algebraic representations: 12.5.2.c
3	Measurement – Systems of measurement: 12.2.2.g
4	Geometry – Transformation of shapes and preservation of properties: 12.3.2.e
5	Geometry – Relationships between geometric figures: 12.3.3.d

Countdown to Testing WEEK 21

DAY 1

The table lists the measure of an exterior angle for the given regular polygon. Which expression best represents the measure of an exterior angle of a regular polygon with n sides?

Figure	Quadrilateral	Pentagon	Decagon
Exterior angle	90°	72°	36°

Ⓐ $\frac{360}{n-2}$

Ⓑ $\frac{360+n}{2+n}$

Ⓒ $360n$

Ⓓ $\frac{360}{n}$

DAY 2

Carrie is building a skateboard ramp with the dimensions below. What is the approximate measure of x?

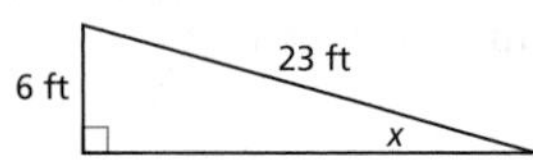

Ⓕ 4°

Ⓖ 8°

Ⓗ 12°

Ⓙ 15°

DAY 3

What is the value of z?

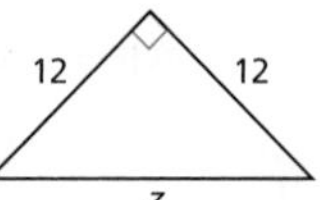

Ⓐ 12

Ⓑ $12\sqrt{2}$

Ⓒ $12\sqrt{3}$

Ⓓ 17

DAY 4

Which equation best describes the line containing the hypotenuse of this triangle?

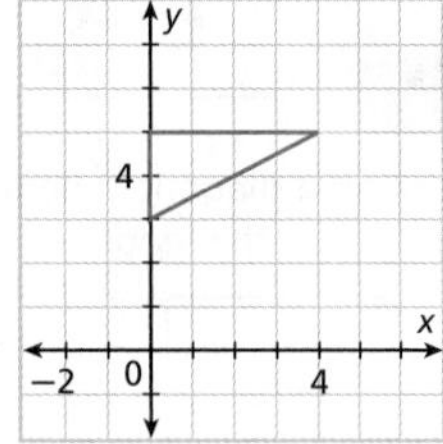

Ⓕ $y = \frac{1}{2}x + 3$

Ⓖ $y = 5$

Ⓗ $y = x + 3$

Ⓙ $y = -\frac{1}{2}x - 3$

DAY 5

The center of circle C is the midpoint of $\overline{AB}$. What are the coordinates of the midpoint?

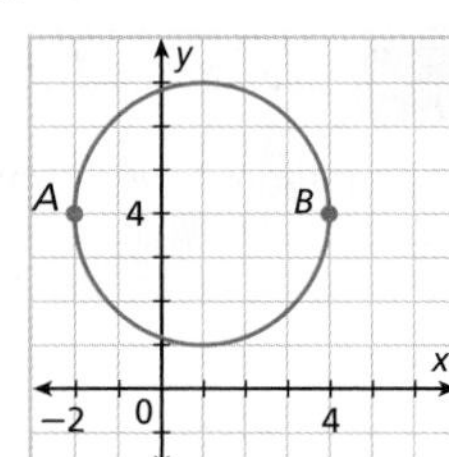

Ⓐ (0, 4)

Ⓑ (1, 4)

Ⓒ (2, 4)

Ⓓ (3, 3)

Week 21	NAEP Standards Grade 12
1	Algebra – Patterns, relations, and functions: 12.5.1.b
2	Measurement – Measuring physical attributes: 12.2.1.m
3	Geometry – Relationships between geometric figures: 12.3.3.d
4	Algebra – Algebraic representations: 12.5.2.a
5	Measurement – Measuring physical attributes: 12.2.1.e

Countdown to Testing WEEK 22

DAY 1

If this pattern is continued, how many shaded triangles will there be in the fourth element of the pattern?

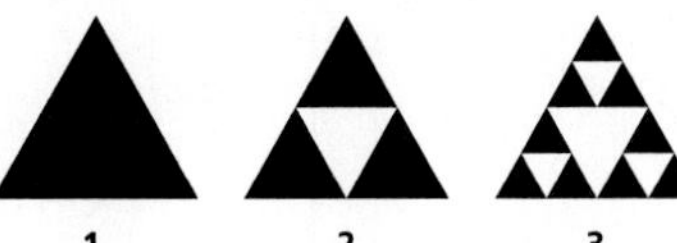

Ⓐ 9
Ⓑ 13
Ⓒ 27
Ⓓ 40

DAY 2

What is the slope of the line?

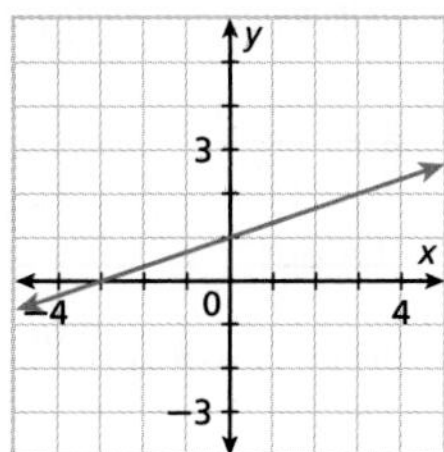

Ⓕ $-\frac{1}{2}$
Ⓖ $\frac{1}{3}$
Ⓗ $\frac{1}{2}$
Ⓙ 3

DAY 3

A delivery truck travels 13.5 mi east and then 18 mi north. How far is the truck from its starting point?

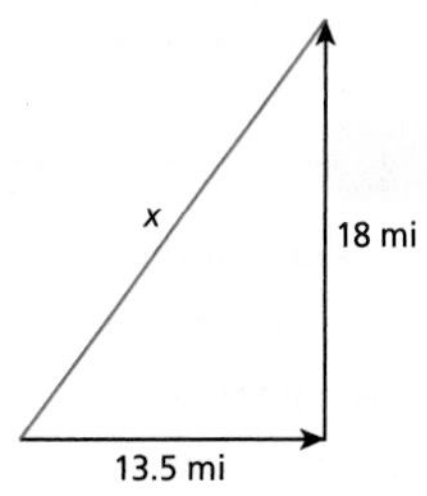

Ⓐ 4.5 miles
Ⓑ 20.25 miles
Ⓒ 22.5 miles
Ⓓ 31.5 miles

DAY 4

What are the side lengths of the triangle?

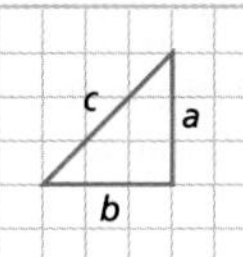

Ⓕ 3, 4, and 5
Ⓖ 2, 3, and 5
Ⓗ 3, 3, and 3
Ⓙ 3, 3, and $3\sqrt{2}$

DAY 5

An 18-foot ladder reaches the top of a building when placed at an angle of 45° with the horizontal. What is the approximate height of the building?

Ⓐ 9.0 feet
Ⓑ 12.7 feet
Ⓒ 14.4 feet
Ⓓ 30.9 feet

Week 22	NAEP Standards Grade 12
1	Algebra – Patterns, relations, and functions: 12.5.1.a
2	Algebra – Algebraic representations: 12.5.2.a
3	Geometry – Position and direction: 12.3.4.e
4	Geometry – Relationships between geometric figures: 12.3.3.d
5	Geometry – Relationships between geometric figures: 12.3.3.d

Countdown to Testing WEEK 23

DAY 1

$\triangle RST$ is a 30°-60°-90° triangle. What is the y-coordinate of R if $a = -5$ and $c = -2$?

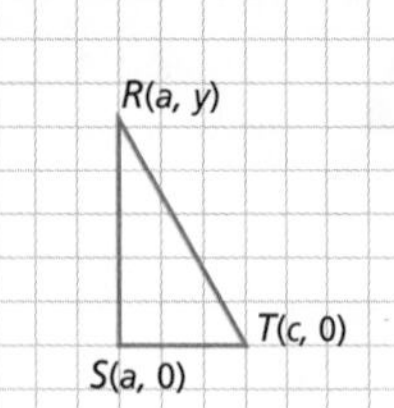

Ⓐ 3
Ⓑ $3\sqrt{2}$
Ⓒ $3\sqrt{3}$
Ⓓ 6

DAY 2

What is x if y is 12.8 and z is 16 in the right triangle below?

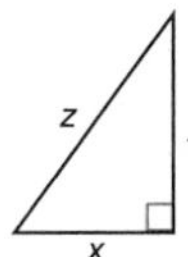

Ⓕ 3.2
Ⓖ 4.0
Ⓗ 9.6
Ⓙ 12.8

DAY 3

How does the slope of the hypotenuse of $\triangle ABC$ compare with that of $\triangle DBC$?

Ⓐ They have the same value.
Ⓑ They have opposite signs.
Ⓒ They have the same sign.
Ⓓ They are reciprocals.

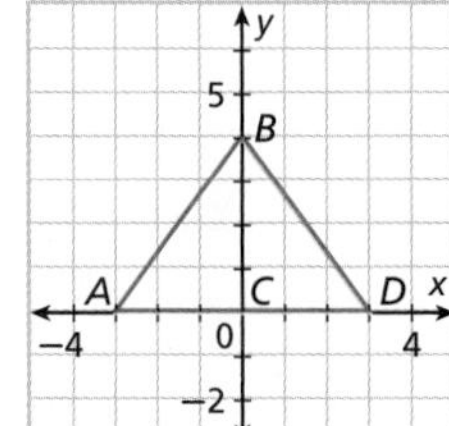

DAY 4

How many sides does a regular polygon have if each interior angle measures 120°?

Ⓕ 3
Ⓖ 4
Ⓗ 6
Ⓙ 8

DAY 5

An electrician is standing at the top of a tower. He sees a truck at an angle of depression of 3°. If the tower is 300 feet tall, about how far away is the truck?

Ⓐ 16 feet
Ⓑ 300 feet
Ⓒ 1052 feet
Ⓓ 5724 feet

Week 23	NAEP Standards Grade 12
1	Geometry – Relationships between geometric figures: 12.3.3.d
2	Geometry – Relationships between geometric figures: 12.3.3.d
3	Measurement – Measuring physical attributes: 12.2.1.e
4	Measurement – Measuring physical attributes: 12.2.1.f
5	Measurement – Measuring physical attributes: 12.2.1.k

Countdown to Testing WEEK 24

DAY 1

Quadrilaterals *ABCD* and *WXYZ* are similar. What is *XY*?

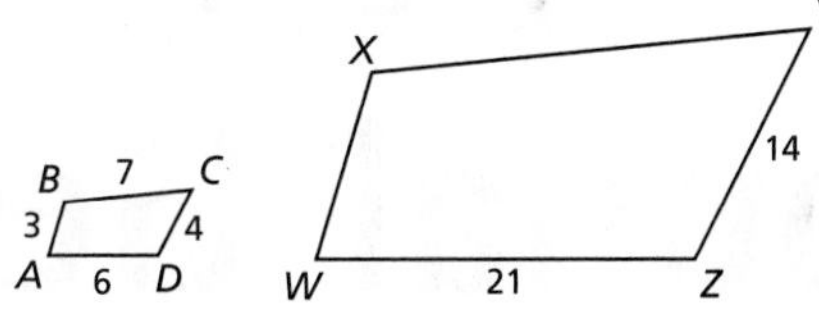

Ⓐ 3.5
Ⓑ 21
Ⓒ 24.5
Ⓓ 35

DAY 2

What is the second term in a proportion in which the first, third, and fourth terms are 3, 9, and 12, respectively?

Ⓕ 3
Ⓖ 4
Ⓗ 6
Ⓙ 8

DAY 3

The endpoints of a segment are $Q(-2, 6)$ and $R(5, -4)$. What is the length of the segment to the nearest tenth?

Ⓐ 3.6 units
Ⓑ 4.1 units
Ⓒ 8.5 units
Ⓓ 12.2 units

DAY 4

Which Pythagorean triple would be most helpful in finding the value of *a*?

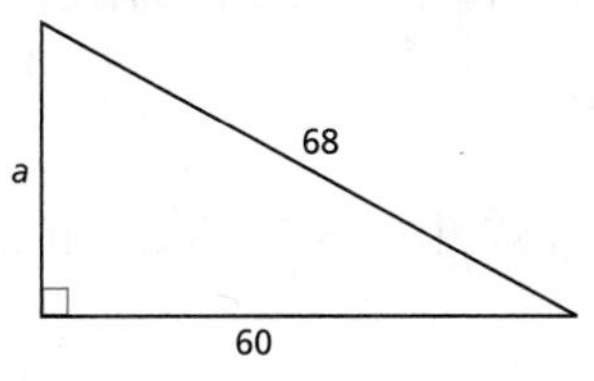

Ⓕ 3-4-5
Ⓖ 5-12-14
Ⓗ 8-15-17
Ⓙ 7-24-25

DAY 5

What is the perimeter of the square?

Ⓐ 6
Ⓑ 12
Ⓒ 24
Ⓓ 36

Week 24	NAEP Standards Grade 12
1	Measurement – Systems of measurement: 12.2.2.g
2	Number Properties and Operations – Ratios and Proportional Reasoning: 12.1.4.b
3	Measurement – Measuring physical attributes: 12.2.1.e
4	Measurement – Systems of measurement: 12.2.2.g
5	Measurement – Measuring physical attributes: 12.2.1.h

You can count on **Holt McDougal Geometry** for...

1 Built-in Assessment and Intervention.
Prescribe the resources your students need when they need them in order to lead your students to success.

2 Comprehensive Differentiated Instruction.
Ensure all students have the opportunity to succeed with strategies designed to reach students of all learning styles and skill levels.

3 Success on High-Stakes Tests.
Prepare students for success on test day with standards-based test preparation that's embedded into daily lessons.

4 Integrated Technology That Enhances Learning.
Motivate your students to excel and manage your classroom with maximum effectiveness using Holt McDougal technology.

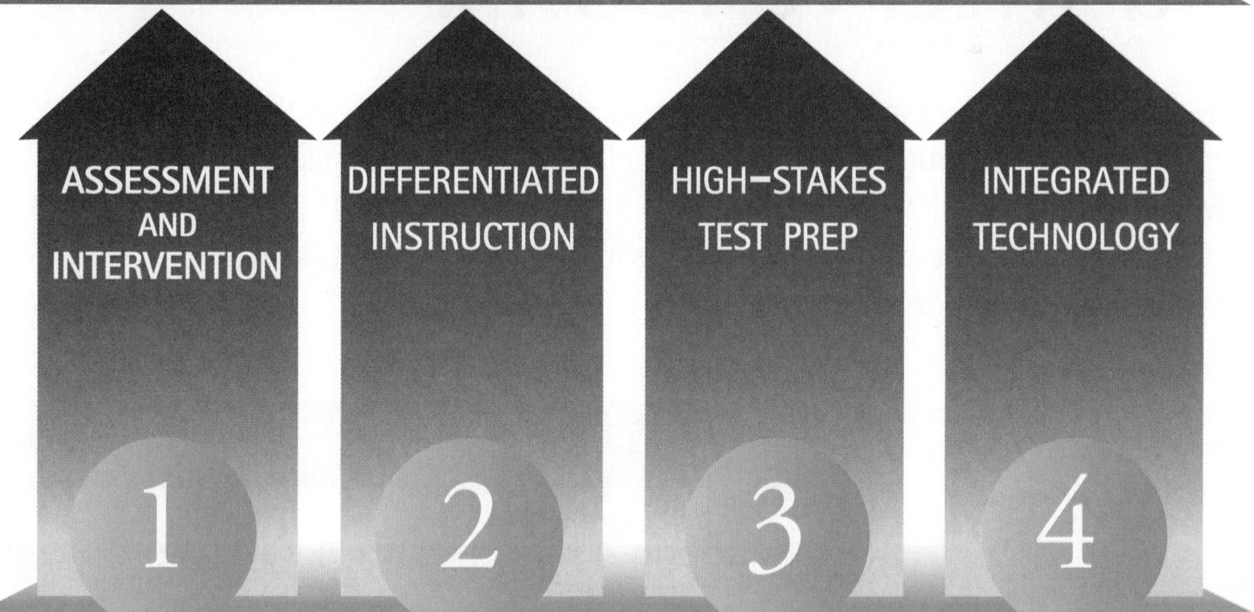

Built for Student Success… from the Ground Up

Every student is unique with individual strengths and weaknesses. Starting with **Holt McDougal Mathematics** for middle school through **Holt McDougal Algebra 1, Geometry,** and **Algebra 2,** this series provides the instruction and resources you need to reach and teach every one of your students. Weather it's an alternative approach to a lesson, a modification for a visual learner, or extra practice with basic skills, **Holt McDougal** has what you need to help all of your students succeed.

> *"Deep and abstract ideas are challenging to all, but the challenge should be a pleasurable one that students want to conquer."*
>
> **– Dr. Edward B. Burger, Holt author**

Program Highlights

Built-in Assessment and Intervention...

You need to know how well your students understand the lesson BEFORE they take the test. With **Holt McDougal Geometry**, informal and formal assessment options are given at every stage within the chapter. Response to Intervention (RtI) resources allow you to reteach or review material without simply sending students back to previous lessons in the book.

Assess Prior Knowledge

to make sure all students start the chapter on solid footing

- **Intervene** with alternate teaching strategies and basic skills review in *Are You Ready? Intervention and Enrichment*

Formative Assessment

to diagnose skill development within the chapter

- **Intervene** with *Ready to Go On?, Lesson Tutorial Videos, Homework Help Online,* and more

Summative Assessment

to allow students to demonstrate their mastery of the concepts

- **Intervene** with *Reteach* and *Lesson Tutorial Videos*

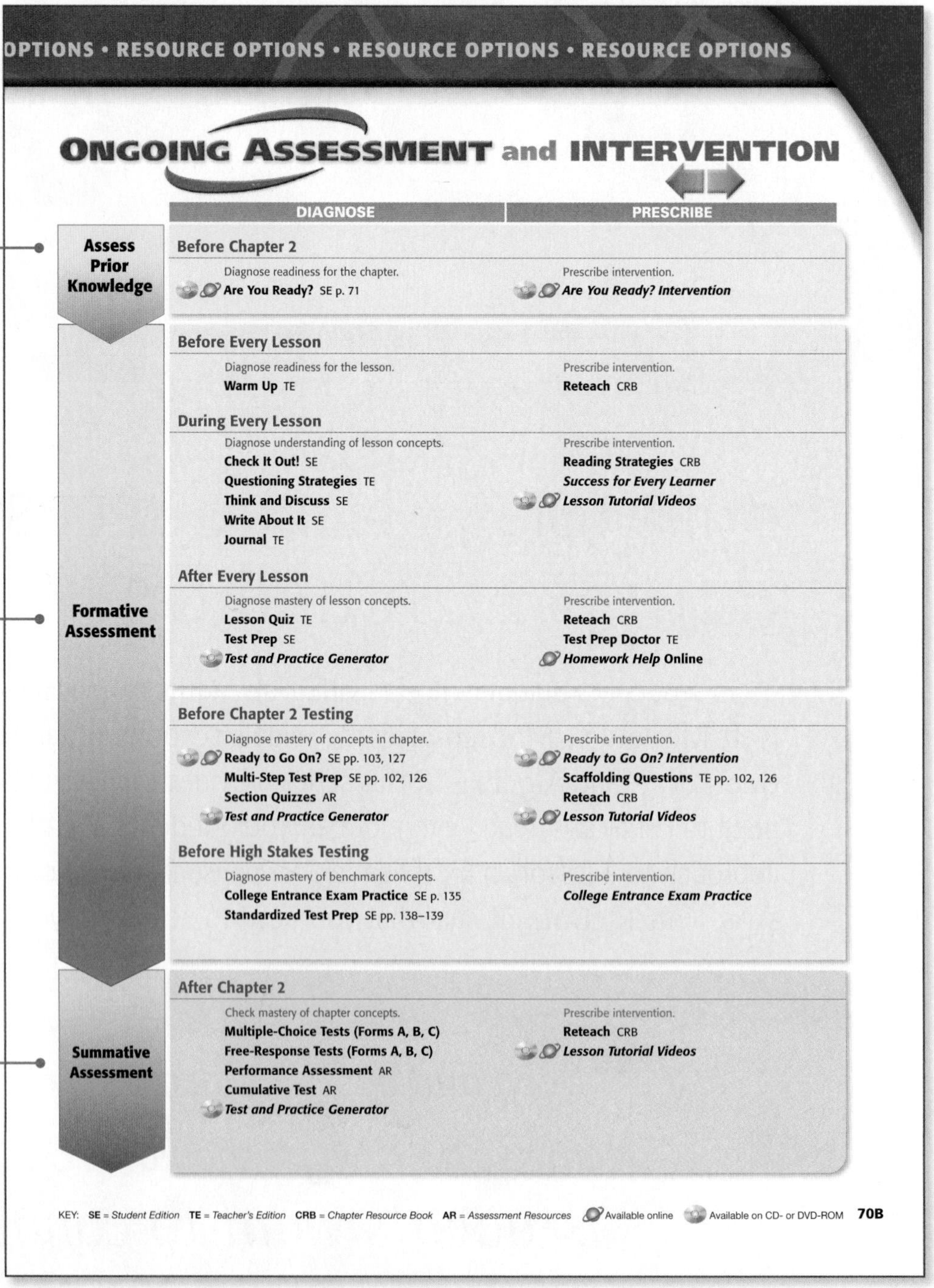

OPTIONS • RESOURCE OPTIONS • RESOURCE OPTIONS • RESOURCE OPTIONS

ONGOING ASSESSMENT and INTERVENTION

	DIAGNOSE	PRESCRIBE
Assess Prior Knowledge	**Before Chapter 2** Diagnose readiness for the chapter. ***Are You Ready?*** SE p. 71	Prescribe intervention. ***Are You Ready? Intervention***
Formative Assessment	**Before Every Lesson** Diagnose readiness for the lesson. **Warm Up** TE	Prescribe intervention. **Reteach** CRB
	During Every Lesson Diagnose understanding of lesson concepts. **Check It Out!** SE **Questioning Strategies** TE **Think and Discuss** SE **Write About It** SE **Journal** TE	Prescribe intervention. **Reading Strategies** CRB ***Success for Every Learner*** ***Lesson Tutorial Videos***
	After Every Lesson Diagnose mastery of lesson concepts. **Lesson Quiz** TE **Test Prep** SE ***Test and Practice Generator***	Prescribe intervention. **Reteach** CRB **Test Prep Doctor** TE **Homework Help Online**
	Before Chapter 2 Testing Diagnose mastery of concepts in chapter. **Ready to Go On?** SE pp. 103, 127 **Multi-Step Test Prep** SE pp. 102, 126 **Section Quizzes** AR ***Test and Practice Generator***	Prescribe intervention. ***Ready to Go On? Intervention*** **Scaffolding Questions** TE pp. 102, 126 **Reteach** CRB ***Lesson Tutorial Videos***
	Before High Stakes Testing Diagnose mastery of benchmark concepts. **College Entrance Exam Practice** SE p. 135 **Standardized Test Prep** SE pp. 138–139	Prescribe intervention. ***College Entrance Exam Practice***
Summative Assessment	**After Chapter 2** Check mastery of chapter concepts. **Multiple-Choice Tests (Forms A, B, C)** **Free-Response Tests (Forms A, B, C)** **Performance Assessment** AR **Cumulative Test** AR ***Test and Practice Generator***	Prescribe intervention. **Reteach** CRB ***Lesson Tutorial Videos***

KEY: **SE** = *Student Edition* **TE** = *Teacher's Edition* **CRB** = *Chapter Resource Book* **AR** = *Assessment Resources* Available online Available on CD- or DVD-ROM **70B**

...using Data-Driven Instruction

When students are struggling, they don't want to keep re-reading the same lesson in the hope that eventually it will make sense. They need to try a new approach to the lesson. This is the core of the assessment and intervention system in **Holt McDougal Geometry**.

Are You Ready? Intervention and Enrichment

RtI Tier 2

Diagnose mastery of *prerequisite skills* and prescribe intervention

- Strengthens weaknesses with direct instruction, conceptual models, and scaffolded practice
- Enriches every chapter with critical thinking activities
- Available in print, on CD-ROM, and online

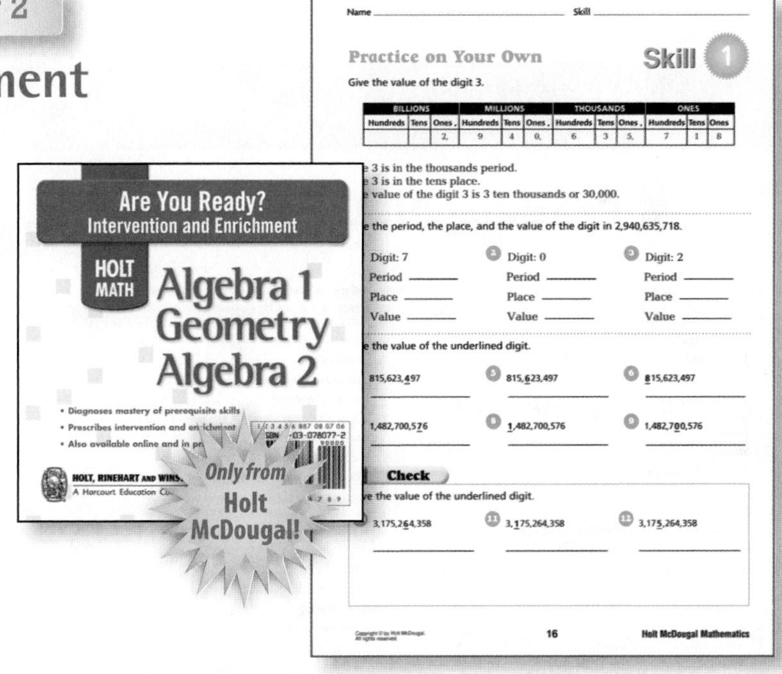

Name Date Class

SECTION 4A **Ready to Go On? Skills Intervention**
4-1 Classifying Triangles

Find these vocabulary words in Lesson 4-1 and the Multilingual Glossary.

Vocabulary: acute triangle, equiangular triangle, right triangle, obtuse triangle, equilateral triangle, isosceles triangle, scalene triangle

Classifying Triangles by Angle Measures

A. △PQS
A right angle has a measure of ______.
Since ∠QPS is a ______ angle, △PQS is a ______ triangle.

B. △PRQ
First, find m∠QRP. Since ∠QRP and ∠SRP form a ______ pair, the ...
______. To find m∠QRP, subtract 54° from ______.
m∠QRP = ______ − 54° = ______
What kind of angle is ∠QRP? ______. So, △PRQ is an ______ tria...

C. △PRS
First, find m∠RPS.
Since ∠RPS and ∠RPQ form a ______ angle, the angles are ______
To find m∠RPS, subtract 23° from ______.
m∠RPS = ______ − 23° = ______
What kind of angle is ∠RPS? ______.
What kind of angles are ∠SRP and ∠PSR? ______
So, △PRS is an ______ triangle.

Classifying Triangles by Side Lengths

A. △JKL
How many sides are congruent in △JKL? ______
What kind of triangle is △JKL? ______

B. ∠KML
Find KL. ______ How many sides are congruent, or have the same measure, in △KML? ______ So, what kind of triangle is △KML? ______

41 Holt Geometry

Ready to Go On?
Intervention and Enrichment
HOLT
Geometry
• Diagnoses mastery of newly taught skills
• Prescribes intervention and enrichment
• Also available online and in print
Only from Holt McDougal!

Ready to Go On? Intervention and Enrichment

RtI Tier 2

Diagnose mastery of *newly taught skills* and prescribe intervention

- Addresses deficiencies with alternative instruction and practice
- Checks progress with post-tests
- Available in print, on CD-ROM, and online

> "*Closing the gap* in academic achievement occurs when the teacher responds to the learner's needs with flexible strategies and ongoing assessment."
>
> **– Freddie L. Renfro, Holt McDougal author**

Differentiated Instruction... 2

Holt McDougal Geometry provides you with a multitude of instructional resources for Universal Access. The program also provides data resources for early intervention and monitoring as prescribed in Response to Intervention (RtI).

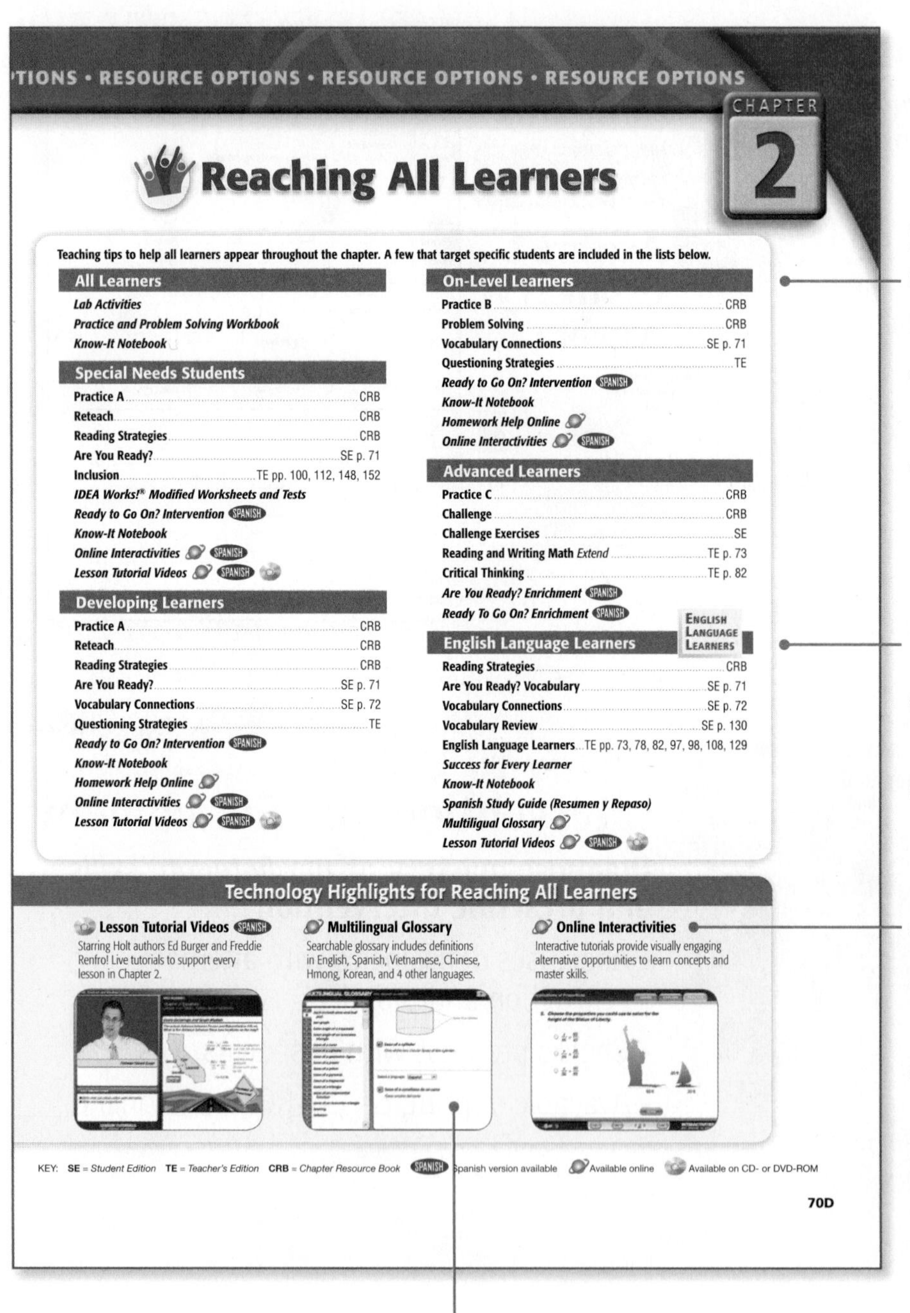

TIONS • RESOURCE OPTIONS • RESOURCE OPTIONS • RESOURCE OPTIONS

CHAPTER 2

Reaching All Learners

Teaching tips to help all learners appear throughout the chapter. A few that target specific students are included in the lists below.

All Learners

- *Lab Activities*
- *Practice and Problem Solving Workbook*
- *Know-It Notebook*

Special Needs Students

Practice A	CRB
Reteach	CRB
Reading Strategies	CRB
Are You Ready?	SE p. 71
Inclusion	TE pp. 100, 112, 148, 152
IDEA Works!® Modified Worksheets and Tests	
Ready to Go On? Intervention SPANISH	
Know-It Notebook	
Online Interactivities SPANISH	
Lesson Tutorial Videos SPANISH	

Developing Learners

Practice A	CRB
Reteach	CRB
Reading Strategies	CRB
Are You Ready?	SE p. 71
Vocabulary Connections	SE p. 72
Questioning Strategies	TE
Ready to Go On? Intervention SPANISH	
Know-It Notebook	
Homework Help Online	
Online Interactivities SPANISH	
Lesson Tutorial Videos SPANISH	

On-Level Learners

Practice B	CRB
Problem Solving	CRB
Vocabulary Connections	SE p. 71
Questioning Strategies	TE
Ready to Go On? Intervention SPANISH	
Know-It Notebook	
Homework Help Online	
Online Interactivities SPANISH	

Advanced Learners

Practice C	CRB
Challenge	CRB
Challenge Exercises	SE
Reading and Writing Math *Extend*	TE p. 73
Critical Thinking	TE p. 82
Are You Ready? Enrichment SPANISH	
Ready To Go On? Enrichment SPANISH	

English Language Learners ENGLISH LANGUAGE LEARNERS

Reading Strategies	CRB
Are You Ready? Vocabulary	SE p. 71
Vocabulary Connections	SE p. 72
Vocabulary Review	SE p. 130
English Language Learners	TE pp. 73, 78, 82, 97, 98, 108, 129
Success for Every Learner	
Know-It Notebook	
Spanish Study Guide (Resumen y Repaso)	
Multilingual Glossary	
Lesson Tutorial Videos SPANISH	

Technology Highlights for Reaching All Learners

Lesson Tutorial Videos SPANISH
Starring Holt authors Ed Burger and Freddie Renfro! Live tutorials to support every lesson in Chapter 2.

Multilingual Glossary
Searchable glossary includes definitions in English, Spanish, Vietnamese, Chinese, Hmong, Korean, and 4 other languages.

Online Interactivities
Interactive tutorials provide visually engaging alternative opportunities to learn concepts and master skills.

KEY: **SE** = *Student Edition* **TE** = *Teacher's Edition* **CRB** = *Chapter Resource Book* SPANISH Spanish version available · Available online · Available on CD- or DVD-ROM

70D

Special Needs, Developing, On-Level, and Advanced Learners

- Identifies features within the Teacher's Edition that target various skill levels
- Lists resources appropriate for different skill levels including 7 levels of lesson worksheets

English Language Learners

- Provides extensive support for English language learners
- Identifies appropriate reading strategies and vocabulary development

Online Interactivities

- Contains interactive tutorials with audio
- Features interactive exploration and practice items

Multilingual Glossary

- Includes an illustrated glossary in 13 languages
- Features English and Spanish audio

Program Highlights

...to Reach All Learners

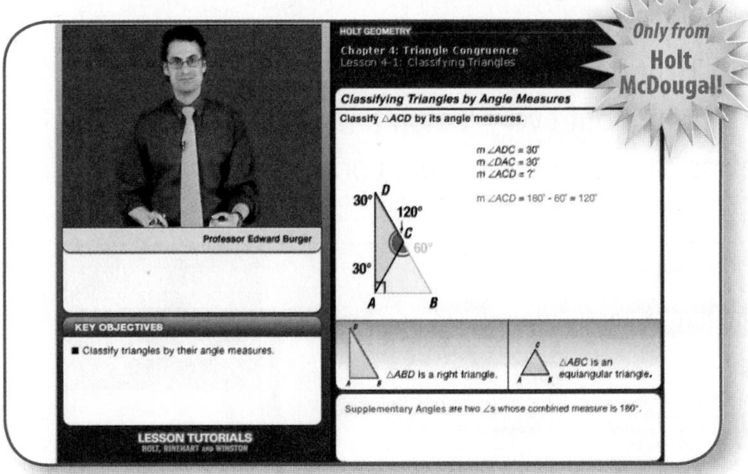

Lesson Tutorial Videos DVD-ROM

RtI Tiers 1,2

Illustrate every example using 348 videos

- Reaches visual and auditory learners
- Provides an at-home tutor for students who need to see the explanation again
- Includes Spanish subtitles
- Also available online

Only from Holt McDougal!

Name ______________ Date ________ Class ________

Problem Solving

Angles Formed by Parallel Lines and Transversals

Find each value. Name the postulate or theorem that you used to find the values.

1. In the diagram, roads a and b are parallel.

   Solution:

   The two given angles are **alternate exterior** angles.

   By the Alternate Exterior Angles Theorem, the angles are congruent,

   so their measures are ____________.

   Solve for x: $(x + 40)^\circ = (2x - 22)^\circ$
   $40^\circ = (x - 22)^\circ$
   $62^\circ = x$

   Evaluate the expression for $\angle PQR$:
   $(2x - 22)^\circ$

IDEA Works!® Modified Worksheets and Tests

RtI Tier 2

Offers adapted formats for students with special needs

- Provides modified practice and problem solving for every lesson
- Features modified tests and quizzes and vocabulary flash cards for every chapter
- Provides customization options through editable worksheets and tests

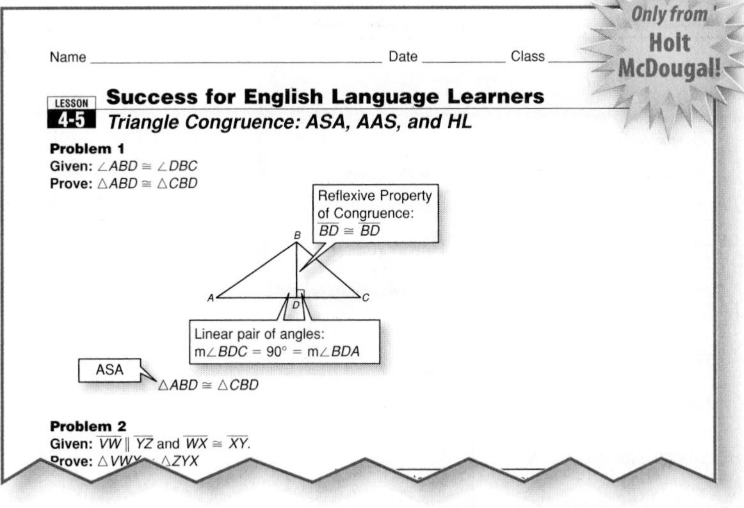

Only from Holt McDougal!

Name ______________ Date ________ Class ________

LESSON 4-5 **Success for English Language Learners**

Triangle Congruence: ASA, AAS, and HL

Problem 1
Given: $\angle ABD \cong \angle DBC$
Prove: $\triangle ABD \cong \triangle CBD$

Problem 2
Given: $\overline{VW} \parallel \overline{YZ}$ and $\overline{WX} \cong \overline{XY}$.
Prove: $\triangle VWX \cong \triangle ZYX$

Success for Every Learner

RtI Tier 2

Ideal for developing, visual, and English Language Learners

- Explains lesson concepts with fewer words and more visuals
- Suggests alternate teaching strategies for English Language Learners

"Key to effective instructional design is differentiated levels of support or scaffolding to support student learning when and where they need it." — Dr. David J. Chard, Holt author

Program Highlights

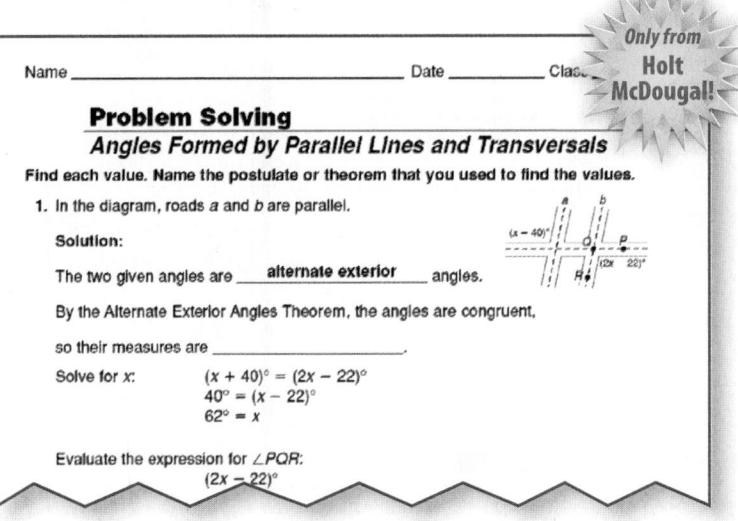

Standards Mastery...

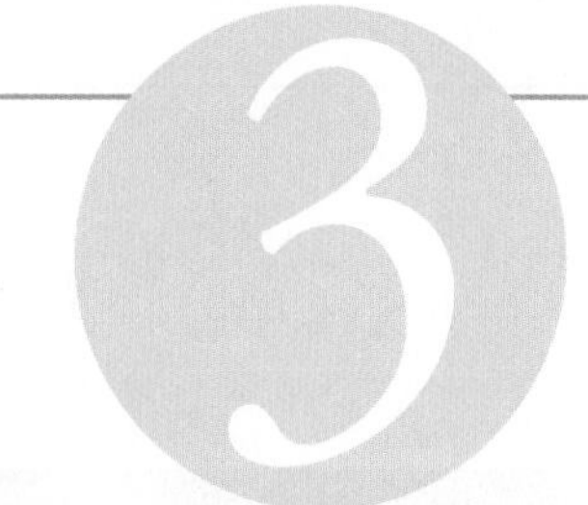

Integrated test prep means no surprises on test day. **Holt McDougal Geometry** includes lesson and cumulative review in standardized test format throughout every lesson and chapter to develop student confidence in test-taking skills without taking time away from core content.

Countdown to Testing

- Provides 120 days of test prep items to be used as daily warm-up exercises
- Items are located in the front of the Student Edition for easy access
- Teacher's Edition provides a correlation of the items to the NAEP standards

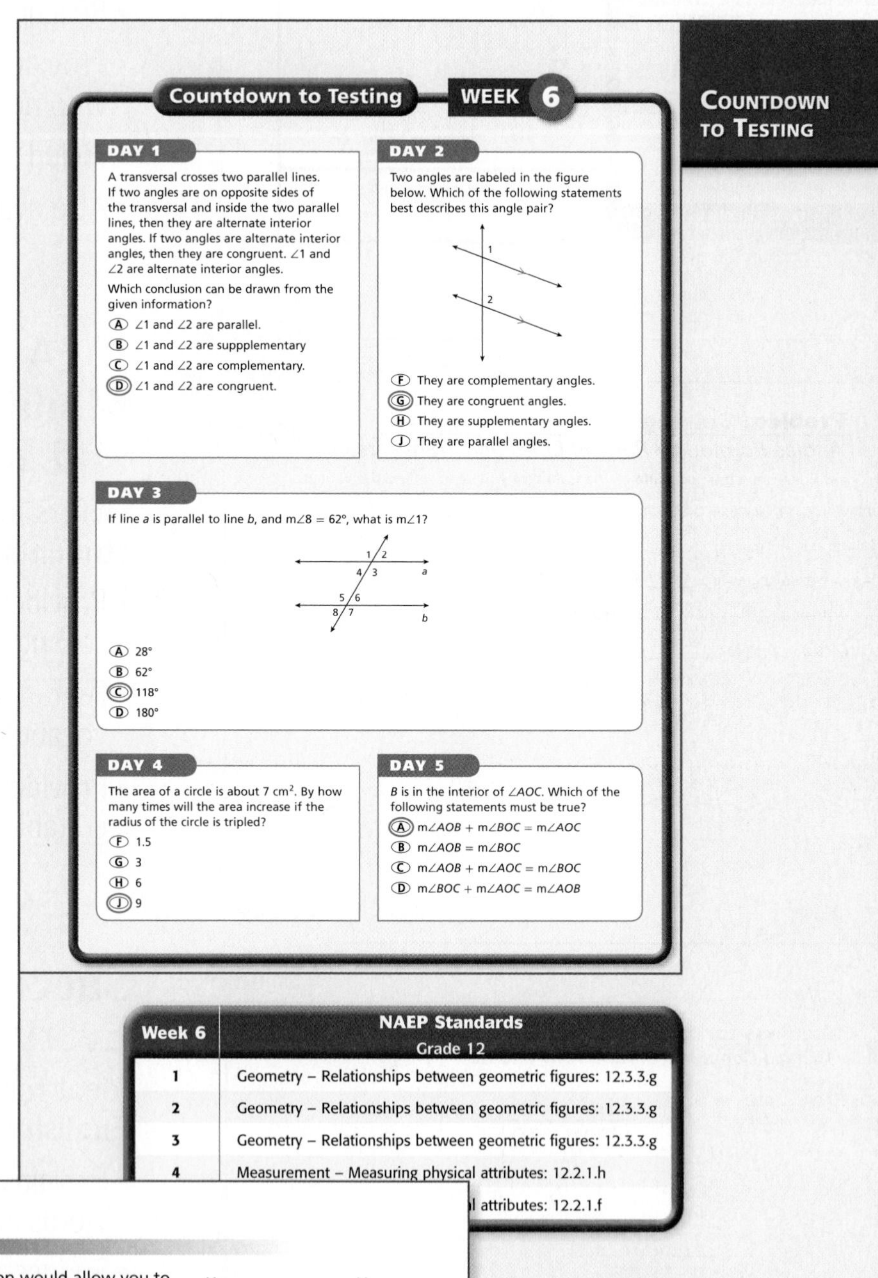

COUNTDOWN TO TESTING

Countdown to Testing WEEK 6

DAY 1

A transversal crosses two parallel lines. If two angles are on opposite sides of the transversal and inside the two parallel lines, then they are alternate interior angles. If two angles are alternate interior angles, then they are congruent. $\angle 1$ and $\angle 2$ are alternate interior angles.

Which conclusion can be drawn from the given information?

(A) $\angle 1$ and $\angle 2$ are parallel.
(B) $\angle 1$ and $\angle 2$ are suppplementary
(C) $\angle 1$ and $\angle 2$ are complementary.
(D) $\angle 1$ and $\angle 2$ are congruent.

DAY 2

Two angles are labeled in the figure below. Which of the following statements best describes this angle pair?

(F) They are complementary angles.
(G) They are congruent angles.
(H) They are supplementary angles.
(J) They are parallel angles.

DAY 3

If line *a* is parallel to line *b*, and $m\angle 8 = 62°$, what is $m\angle 1$?

(A) 28°
(B) 62°
(C) 118°
(D) 180°

DAY 4

The area of a circle is about 7 cm². By how many times will the area increase if the radius of the circle is tripled?

(F) 1.5
(G) 3
(H) 6
(J) 9

DAY 5

B is in the interior of $\angle AOC$. Which of the following statements must be true?

(A) $m\angle AOB + m\angle BOC = m\angle AOC$
(B) $m\angle AOB = m\angle BOC$
(C) $m\angle AOB + m\angle AOC = m\angle BOC$
(D) $m\angle BOC + m\angle AOC = m\angle AOB$

Week 6	NAEP Standards Grade 12
1	Geometry – Relationships between geometric figures: 12.3.3.g
2	Geometry – Relationships between geometric figures: 12.3.3.g
3	Geometry – Relationships between geometric figures: 12.3.3.g
4	Measurement – Measuring physical attributes: 12.2.1.h
	l attributes: 12.2.1.f

Test Prep

- Provides daily practice of new and previously taught skills
- Uses various standardized test formats

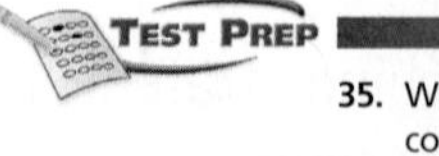

35. What additional information would allow you to conclude that *WXYZ* is a parallelogram?

(A) $\overline{XY} \cong \overline{ZW}$ (C) $\overline{WY} \cong \overline{WZ}$
(B) $\overline{WX} \cong \overline{YZ}$ (D) $\angle XWY \cong \angle ZYW$

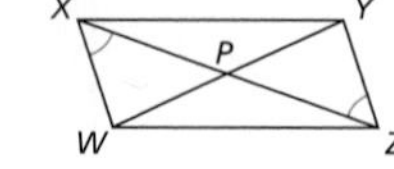

36. Which could be the coordinates of the fourth vertex of ▱*ABCD* with *A*(−1, −1), *B*(1, 3), and *C*(6, 1)?

(F) *D*(8, 5) (G) *D*(4, −3) (H) *D*(13, 3) (J) *D*(3, 7)

37. Short Response The vertices of quadrilateral *RSTV* are *R*(−5, 0), *S*(−1, 3), *T*(5, 1), and *V*(2, −2). Is *RSTV* a parallelogram? Justify your answer. no

Program Highlights

...and Test Preparation

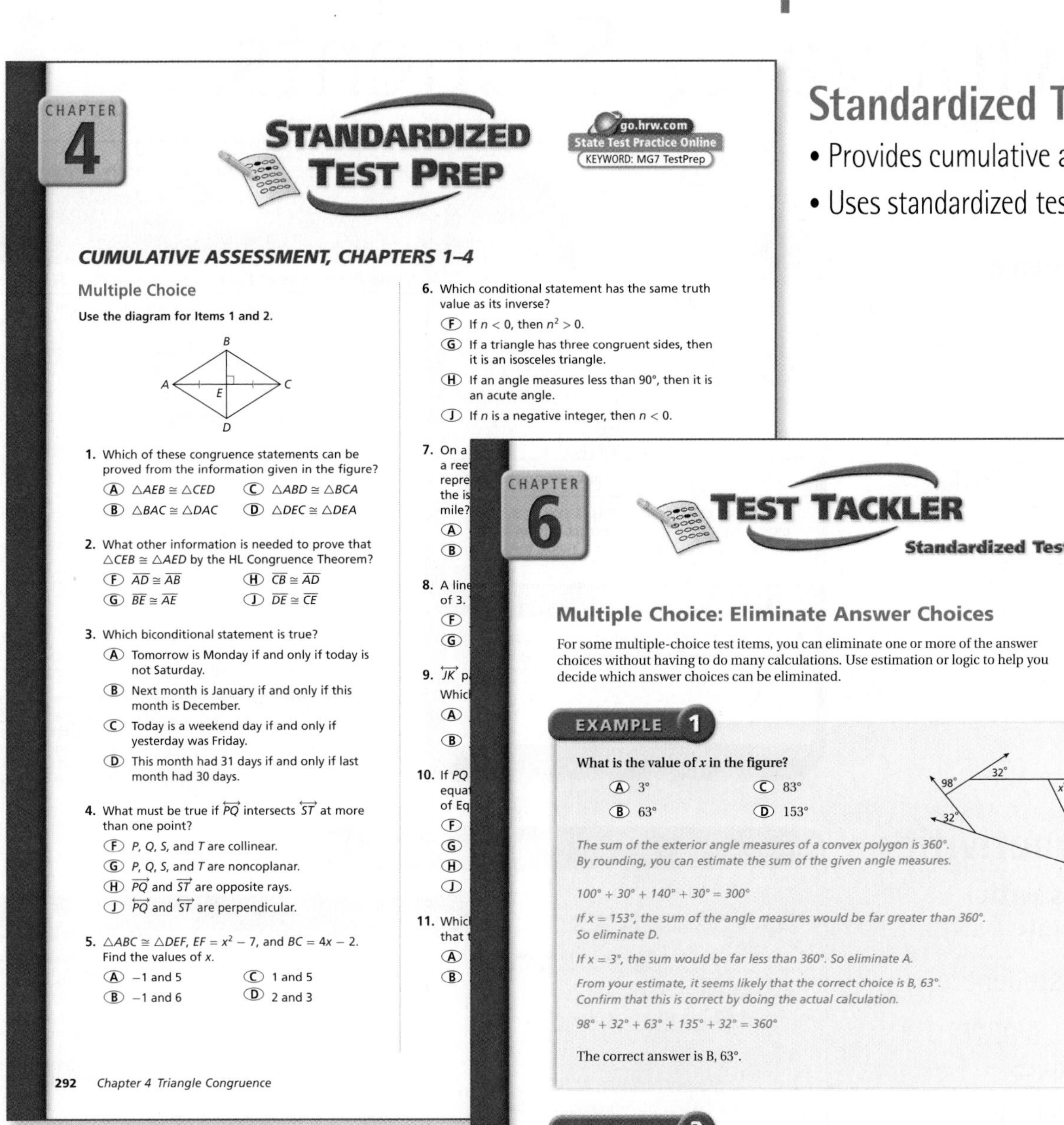
CHAPTER 4

STANDARDIZED TEST PREP

go.hrw.com
State Test Practice Online
KEYWORD: MG7 TestPrep

CUMULATIVE ASSESSMENT, CHAPTERS 1–4

Multiple Choice

Use the diagram for Items 1 and 2.

1. Which of these congruence statements can be proved from the information given in the figure?
   Ⓐ $\triangle AEB \cong \triangle CED$ Ⓒ $\triangle ABD \cong \triangle BCA$
   Ⓑ $\triangle BAC \cong \triangle DAC$ Ⓓ $\triangle DEC \cong \triangle DEA$
2. What other information is needed to prove that $\triangle CEB \cong \triangle AED$ by the HL Congruence Theorem?
   Ⓕ $\overline{AD} \cong \overline{AB}$ Ⓗ $\overline{CB} \cong \overline{AD}$
   Ⓖ $\overline{BE} \cong \overline{AE}$ Ⓙ $\overline{DE} \cong \overline{CE}$
3. Which biconditional statement is true?
   Ⓐ Tomorrow is Monday if and only if today is not Saturday.
   Ⓑ Next month is January if and only if this month is December.
   Ⓒ Today is a weekend day if and only if yesterday was Friday.
   Ⓓ This month had 31 days if and only if last month had 30 days.
4. What must be true if $\overleftrightarrow{PQ}$ intersects $\overleftrightarrow{ST}$ at more than one point?
   Ⓕ P, Q, S, and T are collinear.
   Ⓖ P, Q, S, and T are noncoplanar.
   Ⓗ $\overrightarrow{PQ}$ and $\overrightarrow{ST}$ are opposite rays.
   Ⓙ $\overleftrightarrow{PQ}$ and $\overleftrightarrow{ST}$ are perpendicular.
5. $\triangle ABC \cong \triangle DEF$, $EF = x^2 - 7$, and $BC = 4x - 2$. Find the values of x.
   Ⓐ −1 and 5 Ⓒ 1 and 5
   Ⓑ −1 and 6 Ⓓ 2 and 3
6. Which conditional statement has the same truth value as its inverse?
   Ⓕ If $n < 0$, then $n^2 > 0$.
   Ⓖ If a triangle has three congruent sides, then it is an isosceles triangle.
   Ⓗ If an angle measures less than 90°, then it is an acute angle.
   Ⓙ If n is a negative integer, then $n < 0$.
7. On a ... a ree... repre... the is... mile?
8. A line ... of 3.
9. $\overleftrightarrow{JK}$ p... Which
10. If PQ ... equa... of Eq...
11. Which ... that

292 Chapter 4 Triangle Congruence

CHAPTER 6

TEST TACKLER

Standardized Test Strategies

Multiple Choice: Eliminate Answer Choices

For some multiple-choice test items, you can eliminate one or more of the answer choices without having to do many calculations. Use estimation or logic to help you decide which answer choices can be eliminated.

EXAMPLE 1

What is the value of x in the figure?

Ⓐ 3° Ⓒ 83°
Ⓑ 63° Ⓓ 153°

The sum of the exterior angle measures of a convex polygon is 360°. By rounding, you can estimate the sum of the given angle measures.

100° + 30° + 140° + 30° = 300°

If x = 153°, the sum of the angle measures would be far greater than 360°. So eliminate D.

If x = 3°, the sum would be far less than 360°. So eliminate A.

From your estimate, it seems likely that the correct choice is B, 63°. Confirm that this is correct by doing the actual calculation.

98° + 32° + 63° + 135° + 32° = 360°

The correct answer is B, 63°.

EXAMPLE 2

What is m∠B in the isosceles trapezoid?

Ⓕ 216° Ⓗ 72°
Ⓖ 108° Ⓙ 58°

Base angles of an isosceles trapezoid are congruent. Since ∠D and ∠B are not a pair of base angles, their measures are not equal. Eliminate G, 108°.

∠D and ∠C are base angles, so m∠C = 108°. ∠B and ∠C are same-side interior angles formed by parallel lines. So they are supplementary angles. Therefore the measure of angle B cannot be greater than 180°. You can eliminate F.

m∠B = 180° − 108° = 72°

The correct answer is H, 72°.

444 Chapter 6 Polygons and Quadrilaterals

Standardized Test Prep

- Provides cumulative assessment
- Uses standardized test formats

Test Tackler

- Targets specific test-taking strategies to help students become savvy test-takers

"Assessment should enhance mathematics learning. What we assess and how we assess it communicates what we value."

— Steven J. Leinwand, Holt McDougal author

Integrated Technology that Motivates Students...

4

Program Highlights

Lesson Tutorial Videos DVD-ROM

Illustrates every example using 348 videos

- Provides personal take-home tutor
- Keeps students learning when a substitute teacher is necessary
- Helps absent students learn concepts
- Also available online

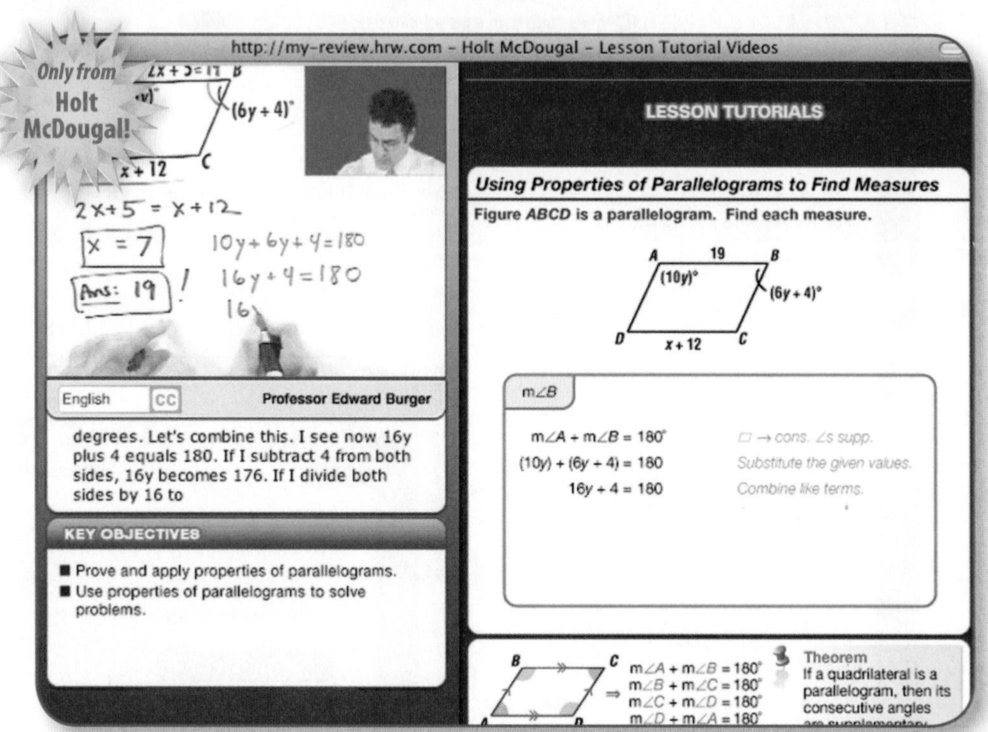

Online Interactivities

Engages students with interactive tutorials

- Visually engages students
- Provides at-home support with online examples
- Spanish audio available
- Found online

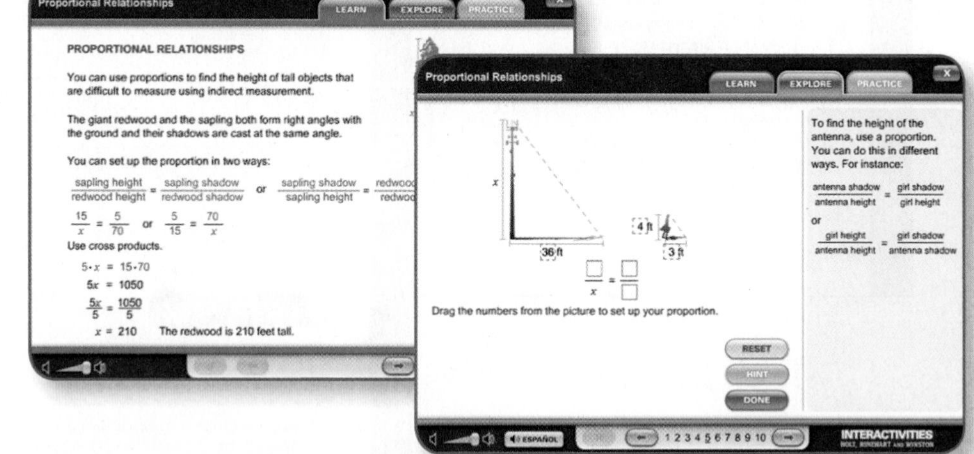

Homework Help Online

Provides interactive homework help

- Includes access to *Lesson Tutorial Videos* and *Online Interactivities*
- Provides interactive practice similar to lesson exercises
- Contains stepped-out solutions and hints for selected lesson exercises

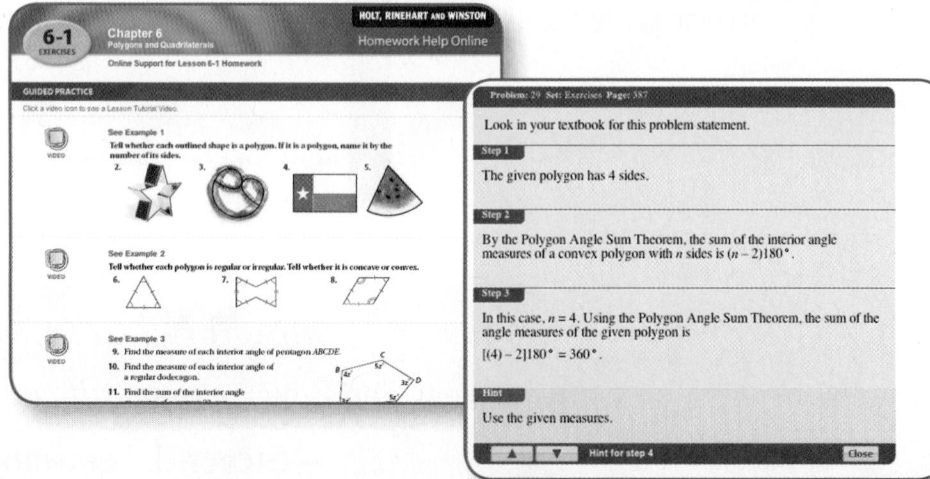

HOLT, RINEHART AND WINSTON
6-1
Chapter 6
Homework Help Online
GUIDED PRACTICE
Look in your textbook for this problem statement.
Step 1
The given polygon has 4 sides.
Step 2
By the Polygon Angle Sum Theorem, the sum of the interior angle measures of a convex polygon with n sides is (n − 2)180°.
Step 3
In this case, n = 4. Using the Polygon Angle Sum Theorem, the sum of the angle measures of the given polygon is
[(4) − 2]180° = 360°.
Hint
Use the given measures.
Hint for step 4
Close

...Enhances Instruction...

Interactive Answers and Solutions CD-ROM

Create customized answer keys that contain only what you need

- Project the answers to only the exercises you assigned
- Make customized answer transparencies
- Display the complete solution for any exercise at the click of a mouse!

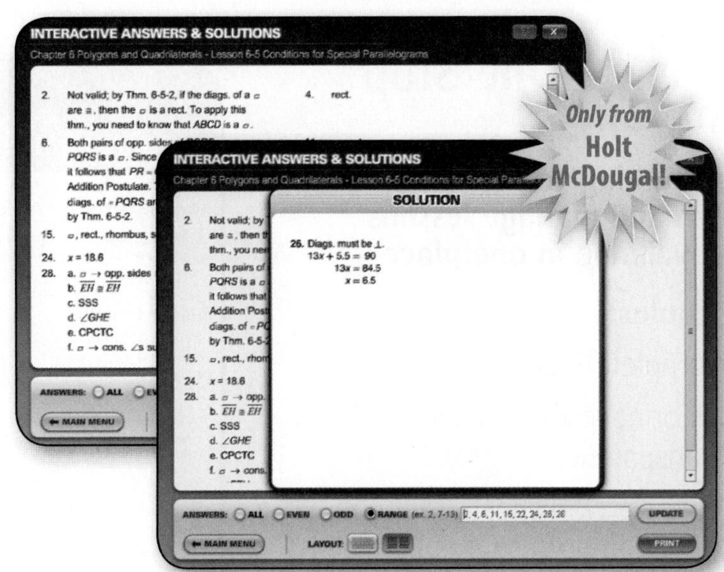

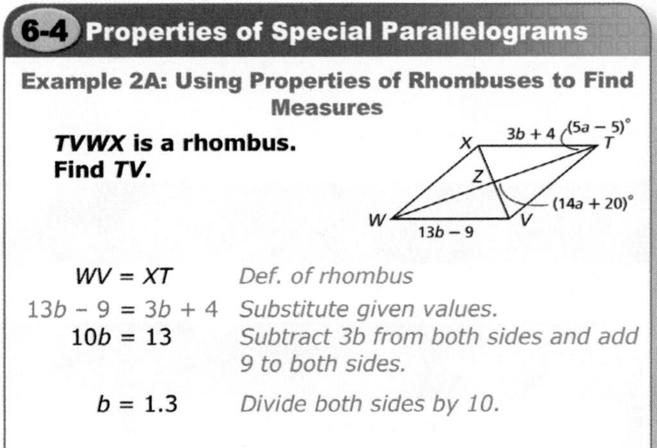

Power Presentations CD-ROM

Enlivens instruction through Power Point® presentations

- Includes Warm-Ups, Lesson Quizzes, and complete stepped-out lesson presentations
- Customizable to match your teaching style
- Found with the Teacher One-Stop™

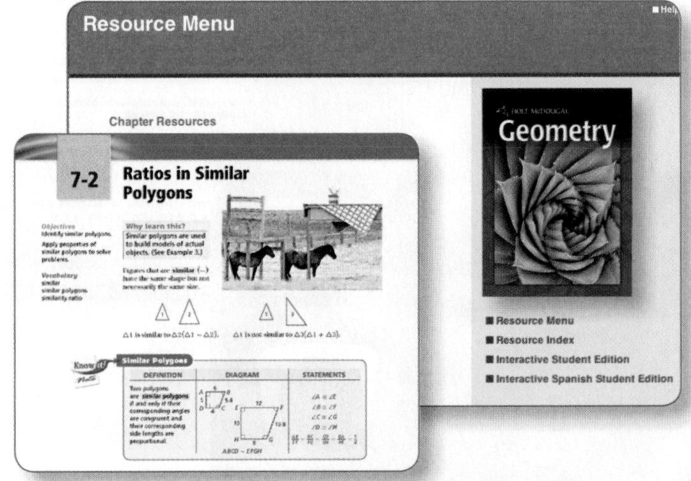

Student One Stop™ CD-ROM

Provides resources for students who may not have Internet access

- Contains entire Student Edition and all workbooks
- Includes both *Are You Ready? Intervention and Enrichment*, and *Ready to Go On? Intervention and Enrichment*

> "*Technology, when used appropriately, can improve students' mathematical understanding and problem-solving skills.*"
>
> **– Dr. Bert K. Waits, Holt author**

Program Highlights

...Simplifies Planning and...

Teacher One Stop™ DVD-ROM

Everything you need to plan and manage lessons is available in one place

Includes:

- Complete Teacher's Edition
- All print resources and transparencies
- Editable worksheets found in the Chapter Resource Books
- Customizable lesson plans
- Calendar Planner
- PuzzleView
- MindPoint® Quiz Show
- Resources for TI Technology
- ExamView® Assessment Suite
- Editable Power Point® Presentations

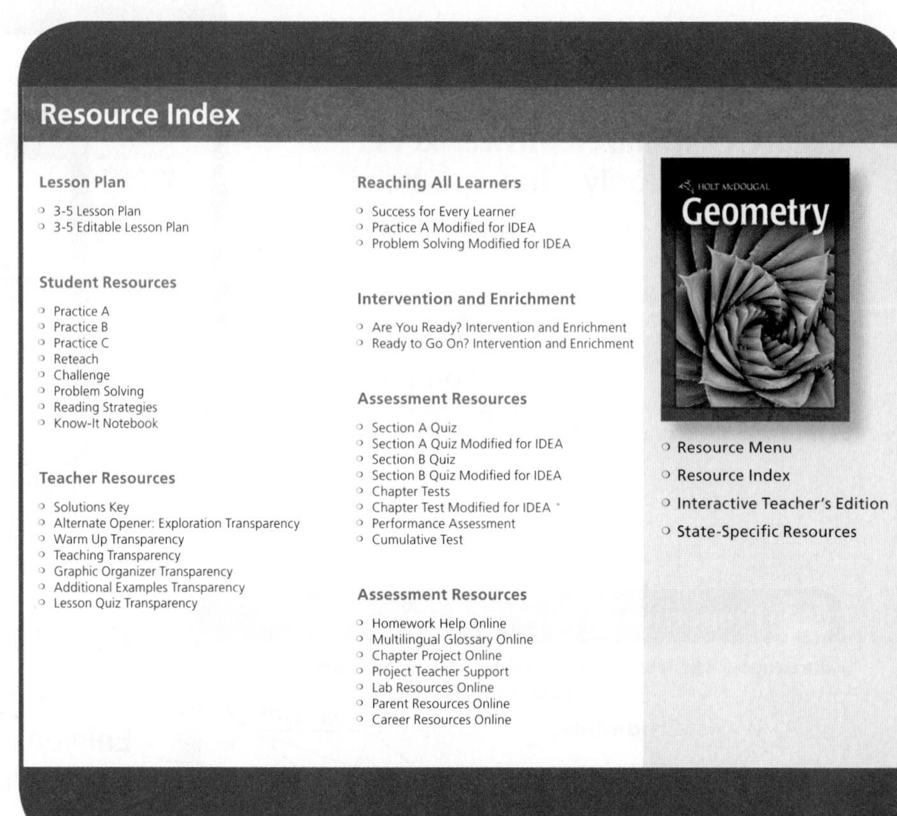

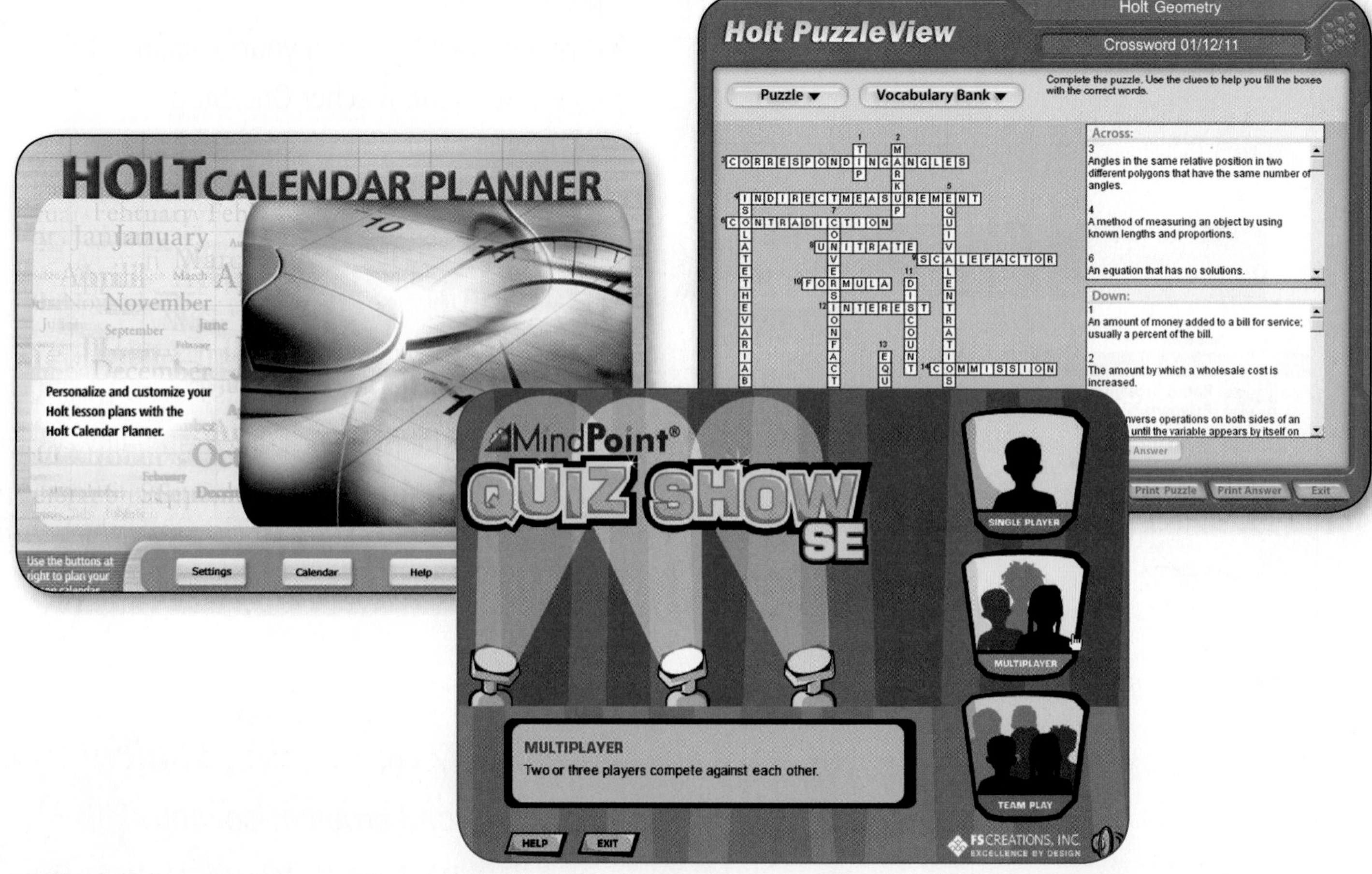

...Makes Online Resources Accessible

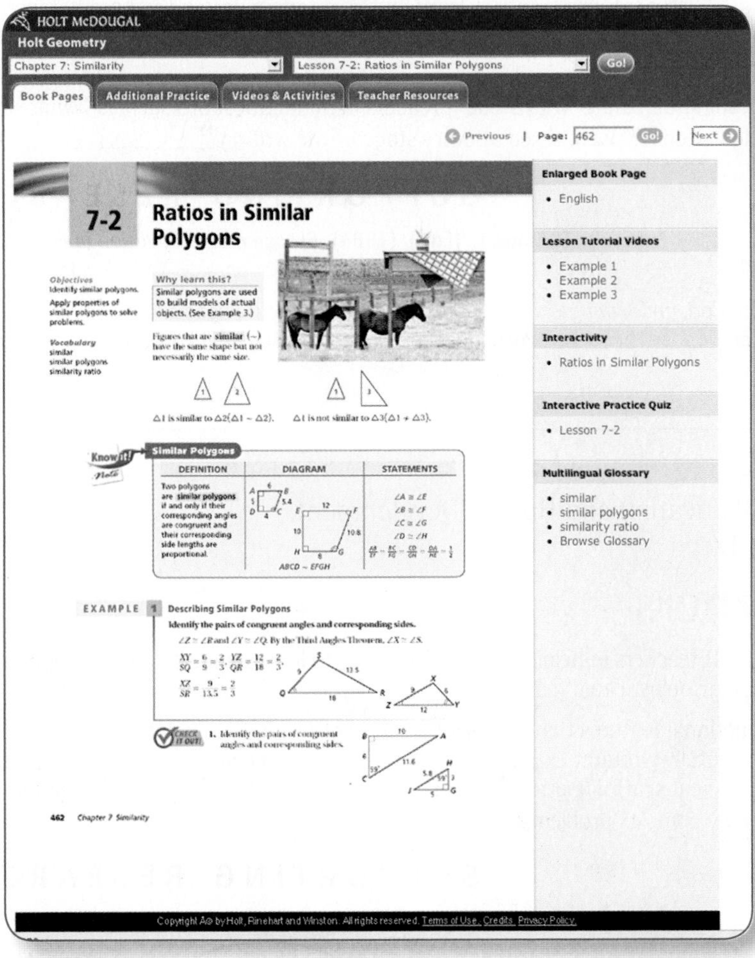

Online Edition

Go home empty-handed and work online

For teacher:

- Editable lesson plans and worksheets
- Lesson transparencies
- PowerPoint® presentations
- Leveled practice worksheets for every lesson
- *IDEA Works!* modified worksheets, quizzes, and tests for special needs students
- *Are You Ready?* and *Ready to Go On? Intervention and Enrichment*
- *Success for Every Learner* teaching strategies and worksheets

For students:

- Entire Student Edition
- Lesson Tutorial Videos
- Online Interactivities
- Homework Help Online
- Extra practice
- Interactive quizzes and tests
- All workbooks
- Graphing calculator
- Virtual manipulatives
- Parent resources

and much more...

Online Assessment

Automatically scores online assessments and prescribes and assigns intervention

- Analyze mastery by topic or standard
- Generate a variety of reports
- Seamlessly integrate content with the **ExamView® Assessment Suite**

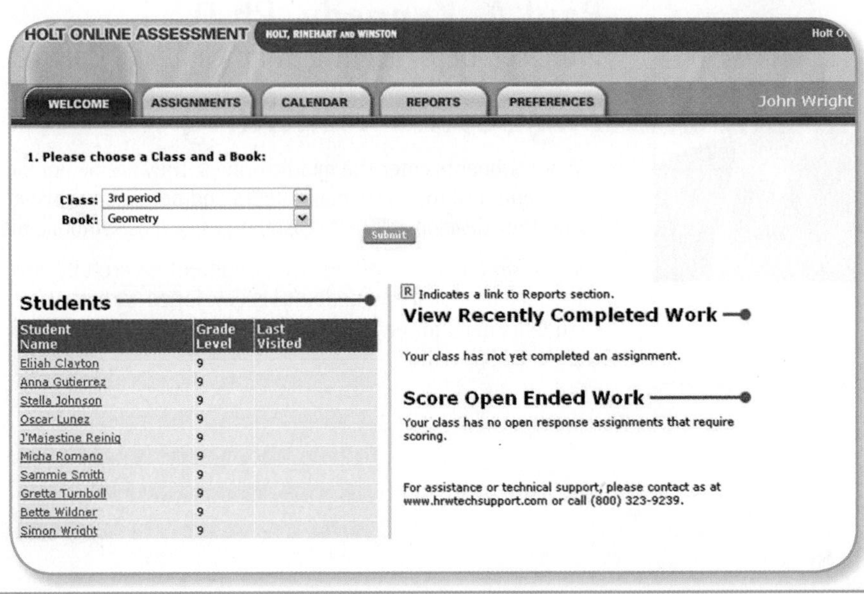

Edward B. Burger, Ph.D.

Professor of Mathematics and Chair | Williams College, MA

Student Engagement

"Learning should be fun. Deep and abstract ideas are challenging to all, but the challenge should be a pleasurable one that students want to conquer. Thus we offer levity throughout the *Holt McDougal* series— jokes for the teachers to share with their students and entertaining antics on the accompanying videos, mixing mathematical insights with laughs. There is no better student than the student who wants to learn. In this program we worked hard to make learning fun so students enjoy the journey and, as a result, attain a deeper understanding of the mathematics they explore.

The mathematics is developed in a meaningful manner with student readers in mind. Questions such as "What would resonate with real middle school students today?" were asked at every stage of the writing."

SUPPORTING RESEARCH

Ames, R., & Ames, C. (Eds.). (1984). *Research on motivation in education: Vol. 1. Student motivation.* New York: Academic Press.

Brewster, Cori, and Jennifer Fager. (2000). Increasing Student Engagement and Motivation: From Time-on-Task to Homework. **Portland, Ore.: Northwest Regional Educational Laboratory.**

David J. Chard, Ph.D.

Leon Simmons Dean, School of Education and Human Development, Southern Methodist University, TX

Reaching All Learners

"*Holt McDougal Math* is designed to assist teachers in helping all their students to learn conceptual knowledge, skills, and strategies essential to understanding sophisticated mathematics.

This program was designed with instructional features that represent a coherent pedagogical approach to mathematics instruction. Each lesson begins with carefully wrought examples of all of the skills, concepts, and strategies addressed. Key to any instructional program is sufficient scaffolding to support student learning. This ensures that all students are able to understand and solve increasingly complex problems."

SUPPORTING RESEARCH

Bransford, J. D., Brown, A. L., & Cocking, R. R. (Eds.). (2000). *How people learn: Brain, mind, experience, and school.* Washington, DC: National Research Council.

Gersten, R., Chard, D. J., Baker, S., et al. (2005). A meta-analysis of research on mathematics instruction for students with learning disabilities. **Signal Hill, CA: Instructional Research Group.**

Paul A. Kennedy, Ph.D.

Professor, Department of Mathematics | Colorado State University, CO

Algebraic Thinking

"When students enter the middle grades, they are beginning the preparation for the transition to more advanced mathematical topics such as algebra and geometry while enhancing their basic arithmetic knowledge. It is crucial that they develop abstract reasoning as well as symbolic manipulation skills.

In the *Holt McDougal Math* series, content is carefully developed using methods aligned with standard best practices. The idea of "doing and undoing" is developed early in the program and carried thought the series. Additionally students need to see the relationships between the math they are learning and real-world scenarios."

SUPPORTING RESEARCH

Vygotsky, L.S. (1978). *Mind and society: The development of higher mental processes.* Cambridge, MA: Harvard University Press.

Driscoll, Mark J. (1997). *Fostering algebraic thinking.* **Portsmouth, NH.; Heinemann.**

Steven J. Leinwand
Principal Research Annalyst, American Institutes for Research | Washington, DC

Assessing Student Understanding

"As the mathematics curriculum has broadened to encompass communicating and conceptualizing, problem solving and reasoning, so too must our traditional view of assessment broaden. To reflect today's curriculum and more accurately determine students' progress, assessment should be an integral part of the teaching and learning process. Questioning strategies, such as those found in the *Holt McDougal Math* series, can be integral to daily assessment, along with lesson quizzes.

Additionally, assessment should provide opportunities for students to evaluate, reflect upon, and improve their work. The Are You Ready? feature allows students to determine if they have the skills to complete the chapter successfully. And more importantly Ready to Go On? provided understanding the material and to work several times in a chapter to improve their work before the Chapter Test (rather then after)."

SUPPORTING RESEARCH

NCTM Assessment Standards Working Groups (1995). *Assessment Standards for School Mathematics. National Council of Teachers of Mathematics. Reston, VA.*

National Research Council (1989). *Everybody Counts. Washington, DC; National Academy Press.*

Freddie L. Renfro
Former Director of Mathematics Instruction K–12 | Texas City Independent School District, TX

Differentiated Instruction

"Imagine a classroom where diversity in learning is the norm, and the teacher responds to the learners' needs with flexible strategies, open dialogue, and ongoing assessment.

Every child is unique. Finding ways to tailor instruction to meet individual student needs in the classroom can be a manageable task with the right support. In the *Holt McDougal Math* series, we promote differentiated instruction by including activities that address a variety of learning styles: discovery learning, the use of concrete examples, and student interaction, to name a few.

The Teacher's Edition offers suggestions for differentiated assessment as well so that students have the opportunity to demonstrate their understanding in a manner that reflects their learning style."

SUPPORTING RESEARCH

Tomlinson, C. (1999). *The differentiated classroom: Responding to the needs of all learners.* Alexandria, VA: Association for Supervision and Curriculum Development.

Willis, S. and Mann, Larry. (2000). *Differentiating instruction.* Alexandria, VA: Association for Supervision and Curriculum Development.

Tom Roby, Ph. D.
Associate Professor and Director of Quantitative Learning Center | University of Connecticut, CT

Intervention

"The middle grades mark a key transition for students, from basic arithmetical knowledge to the more abstract topics of algebra and geometry. Students need to understand the fundamental properties of numbers, not just the procedures of arithmetic, in order to become comfortable when numbers are replaced by variables. This transition from the concrete to the abstract can be facilitated by using manipulatives and pictures, as is done systematically in the *Holt McDougal Math* series.

The program is carefully designed so that topics fit together natura lly. Just addressing each topic is not enough, since students can easily find themselves memorizing many specific individual procedures without ever seeing the bigger picture. Ensuring that the mathematics are not only accurate, but also coherent within the grade and well articulated from one grade to the next, is key to helping students succeed at this level and in those to come."

SUPPORTING RESEARCH

All National Research Council. (2001). *Adding it up: Helping Children learn mathematics.* J. Kilpatriack, J.. Swafford, and B. Findell (Eds.) Mathematics Learning Study Committee, Center for Education, Division of Behavioral and Social Sciences and Education: Washington, CD: National Academy Press. **Wu, H. H. (2001)** *How to prepare students for algebra.* American Educator 25 (2): 10–17.

Program Highlights

Dale G. Seymour
Author, Speaker, Publisher, and Former Mathematics Teacher | Founder, Creative Publications
Founder of Creative Publications Palo Alto, California

Geometry Instructional Design

"Connections in mathematics are key to understanding and appreciating the beauty of mathematics. These connections need to be demonstrated so that students can view mathematics as an integrated whole.

In the *Holt McDougal Algebra 1/Geometry/Algebra 2* series we use graphical illustrations to help students envision complex mathematical concepts. Many students can comprehend a difficult concept more quickly if they see it as a whole rather than attempt to understand it as an abstraction. Visualizations in the textbook as well as in the series' accompanying posters enable students to make connections among interrelated ideas."

SUPPORTING RESEARCH

Fuys, D., Geddes, D., & Tischler, R. (1988). The van Hiele model of thinking in geometry among adolescents. *Journal for Research in Mathematics Education.*

Gagatsis, A. & Patronis, T. (1990, February). Using geometrical models in a process of reflective thinking in learning and teaching mathematics. *Educational Studies in Mathematics, 21, 1, 29-54.*

Bert K. Waits, Ph.D.
Professor Emeritus of Mathematics | The Ohio State University, OH

Technology to Enhance Learning

"Research has demonstrated that technology, when used appropriately, can improve students' mathematical understanding and problem-solving skills. Similarly, technological tools can help teachers challenge students to use and understand mathematics in real-world scenarios.

The *Holt McDougal Math* series presents a balanced approach to learning. We stress that students must utilize all available tools, including mental and paper-and- pencil skills and technology, in the mathematics-learning process. This series uses technology not as an end in itself, but rather as a means for understanding and application. Current research supports this use of computer software including spreadsheets, dynamic geometry software, and graphing calculators."

SUPPORTING RESEARCH

Graham, A.T., & J.O.J. Thomas. (2000). Building a versatile understanding of algebraic variables with a graphic calculator. *Educational Studies in Mathematics*, 41 (3), 265-282.

Hallar, Jeannie C., & Karen Norwood. (1999). The effects of a graphing-approach intermediate algebra curriculum on students' understanding of function. *Journal for Research in Mathematics Education*, 30 (2), 220-226.

Holt McDougal Geometry Program Components

Student Edition

Student One Stop™ CD-ROM

Premier Online Edition

Teacher's Edition

Assessment and Intervention

Are You Ready? Intervention and Enrichment

Assessment Resources

Ready to Go On? Intervention and Enrichment

Differentiated Instruction

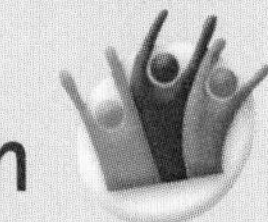

Alternate Openers: Explorations Transparencies

Chapter Resources

IDEA Works!® Modified Worksheets and Tests

Lab Activities

Lesson Tutorial Videos DVD-ROM and Online

Manipulatives Kits

Multilingual Glossary

Premier Online Edition

Student One Stop™ CD-ROM

Success for Every Learner

Workbooks

Know-It Notebook™
and Teacher's Guide

Practice and Problem Solving Workbook
and Teacher's Guide

Spanish Resources

Spanish Summary of Geometry Student Edition

Integrated Technology

Are You Ready? Intervention and Enrichment
CD-ROM and Online

Homework Help Online

Interactive Answers and Solutions CD-ROM

Interactivities Online

Lesson Tutorial Videos DVD-ROM and Online

Premier Online Edition

Ready to Go On? Intervention and Enrichment
CD-ROM and Online

Student One Stop™ CD-ROM

Teacher One Stop™ DVD-ROM

Additional Teaching Resources

Lesson Plans

Solutions Key

Teacher's Manipulatives Kit

HOLT McDOUGAL
a division of Houghton Mifflin Harcourt

To preview all Holt McDougal Geomerty products, go to hmhschool.com/virtualsampling/

Foundations for Geometry

Tools for Success

CHAPTER 2

Geometric Reasoning

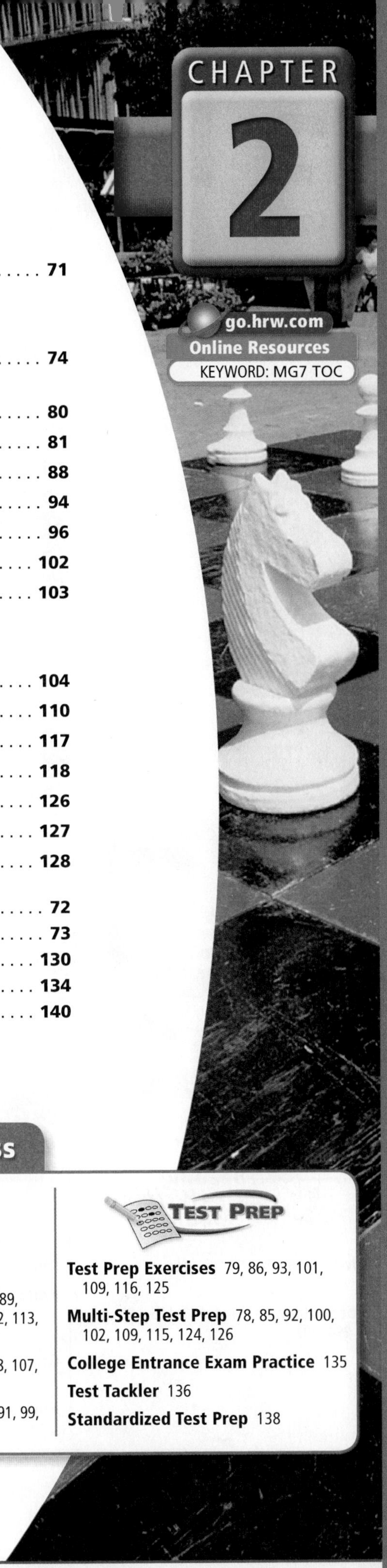

go.hrw.com
Online Resources
KEYWORD: MG7 TOC

Tools for Success

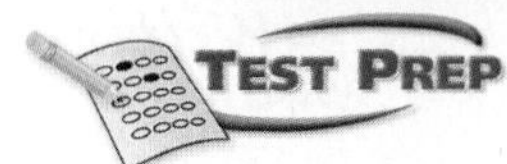

CHAPTER 3

Parallel and Perpendicular Lines

go.hrw.com
Online Resources
KEYWORD: MG7 TOC

Tools for Success

CHAPTER 4

Triangle Congruence

go.hrw.com
Online Resources
KEYWORD: MG7 TOC

Tools for Success

Properties and Attributes of Triangles

Tools for Success

Polygons and Quadrilaterals

CHAPTER 6

go.hrw.com
Online Resources
KEYWORD: MG7 TOC

Tools for Success

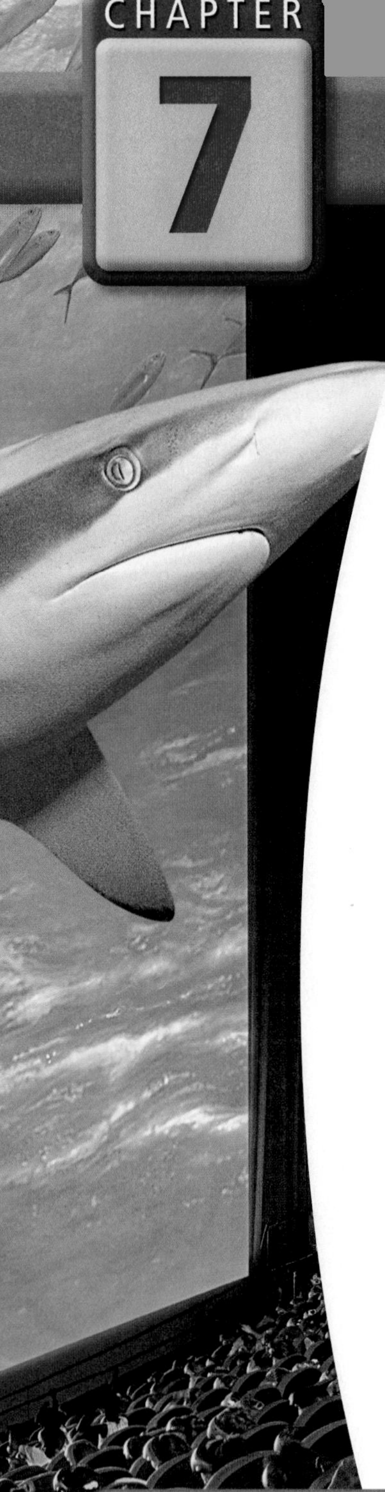

CHAPTER 7

Similarity

Tools for Success

Right Triangles and Trigonometry

go.hrw.com
Online Resources
KEYWORD: MG7 TOC

Tools for Success

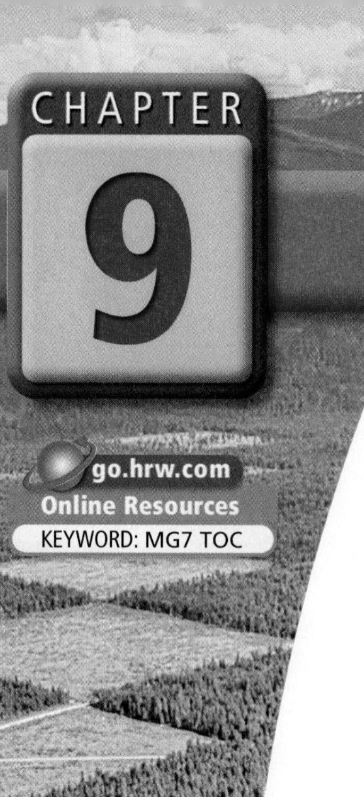

go.hrw.com
Online Resources
KEYWORD: MG7 TOC

Extending Perimeter, Circumference, and Area

Tools for Success

CHAPTER 10

Spatial Reasoning

go.hrw.com
Online Resources
KEYWORD: MG7 TOC

Tools for Success

Circles

Tools for Success

CHAPTER 12

Extending Transformational Geometry

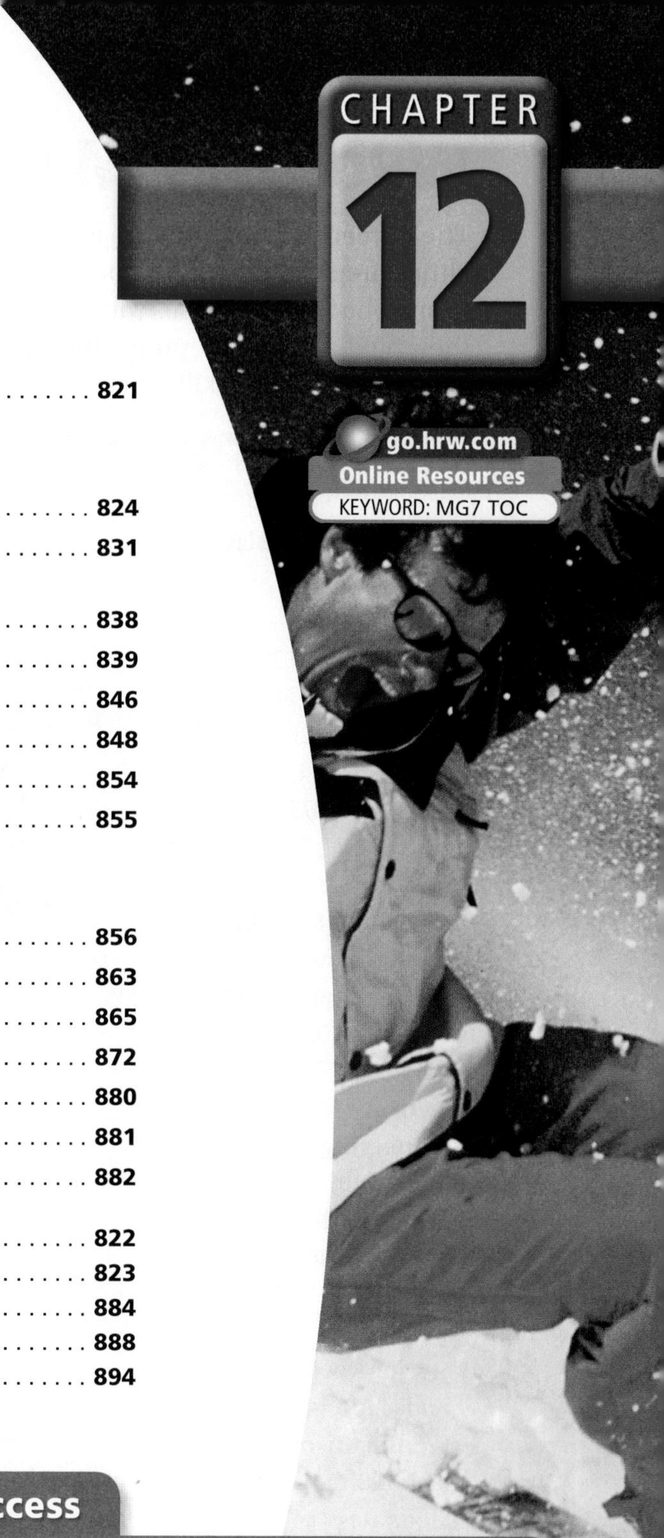

go.hrw.com
Online Resources
KEYWORD: MG7 TOC

Tools for Success

WHO USES MATHEMATICS?

The Career Path features are a set of interviews with young adults who are either preparing for or just beginning in different career fields. These people share what math courses they studied in high school, how math is used in their field, and what options the future holds. Also, many exercises throughout the book highlight skills used in various career fields.

Career Path

go.hrw.com
Career Resources Online
KEYWORD: MG7 Career

Career Applications

ELECTRICIAN *p. 320*

Electricians install and maintain the systems that provide many of the modern-day comforts we rely on, such as climate control, lighting, and technology. Look on page 320 to find out how Alex Peralta got started on this career path.

TECHNICAL WRITER *p. 612*

Have you ever wondered who writes manuals for operating televisions or stereos? A technical writer not only writes manuals for operating electronics, but also documents maintenance procedures for airplanes. Look at the Career Path on page 612 to find out how to become a technical writer.

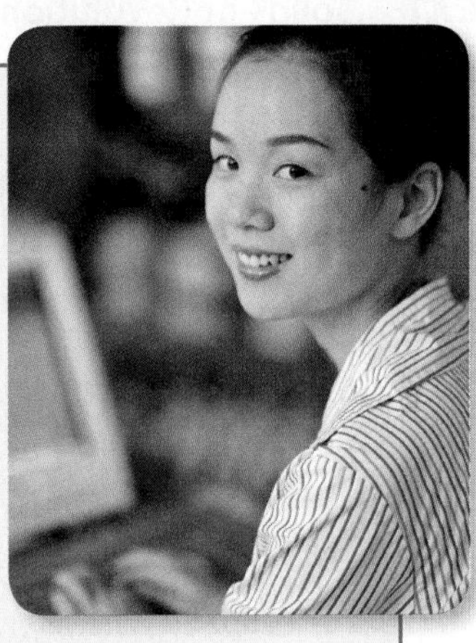

FURNITURE MAKER *p. 805*

A furniture maker must take precise measurements and be aware of spatial relationships in order to build a quality finished product. The Career Path on page 805 describes the kind of experience needed to be successful as a furniture maker.

Why Learn Mathematics?

Links to interesting topics may accompany real-world applications in the examples or exercises. These links help you see how math is used in the real world. For a complete list of all applications in ***Holt McDougal Geometry,*** see the Index.

40. If two angles are adjacent, then they share a vertex.

41. If you use sunscreen, then you will not get sunburned.
Possible answer: You did not go out in the sun.

LINK

Geology

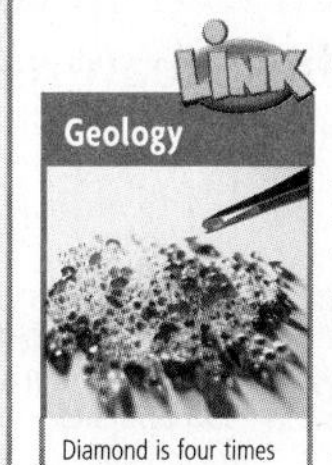

Diamond is four times as hard as the next mineral on Mohs' scale, corundum (ruby and sapphire).

Geology Mohs' scale is used to identify minerals. A mineral with a higher number is harder than a mineral with a lower number.

Use the table and the statements below for Exercises 42–47. Write each conditional and find its truth value.

p: calcite — q: not apatite

r: a hardness of 3 — s: a hardness less than 5

42. $p \rightarrow r$ **43.** $s \rightarrow q$ **44.** $q \rightarrow s$

45. $q \rightarrow p$ **46.** $r \rightarrow q$ **47.** $p \rightarrow s$

48. Critical Thinking Consider the conditional "If two angles are congruent, then they have the same measure." Write the converse, inverse, and contrapositive and find the truth value of each. Use the related conditionals to draw a Venn diagram that represents the relationship

Mohs'
Hardness
1
2
3
4
5
6
7
8
9
10

Real-World LINKS

LINK

Animation

Each frame of a computer-animated feature represents $\frac{1}{24}$ of a second of film.

Source: www.pixar.com

LINK

Monument

The height of the Statue of Liberty from the foundation of the pedestal to the torch is 305 ft. Her index finger measures 8 ft, and the fingernail is 13 in. by 10 in.

Source: libertystatepark.org

LINK

Space Shuttle

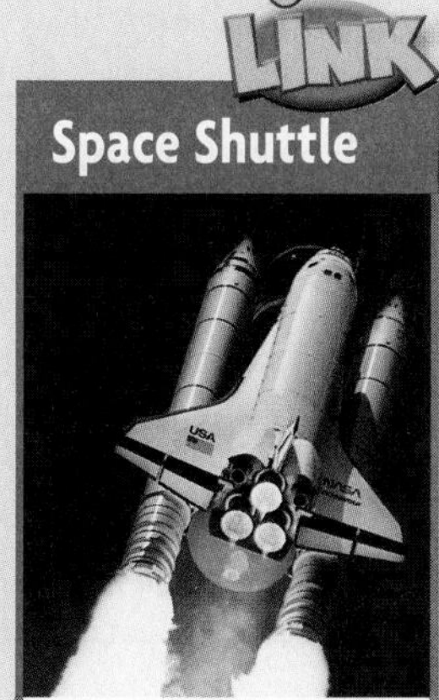

During its launch, a space shuttle accelerates to more than 27,359 km/h in just over 8 minutes. So the shuttle travels 3219 km/h faster each minute.

How to Study Geometry

This book has many features designed to help you learn and study effectively. Becoming familiar with these features will prepare you for greater success on your exams.

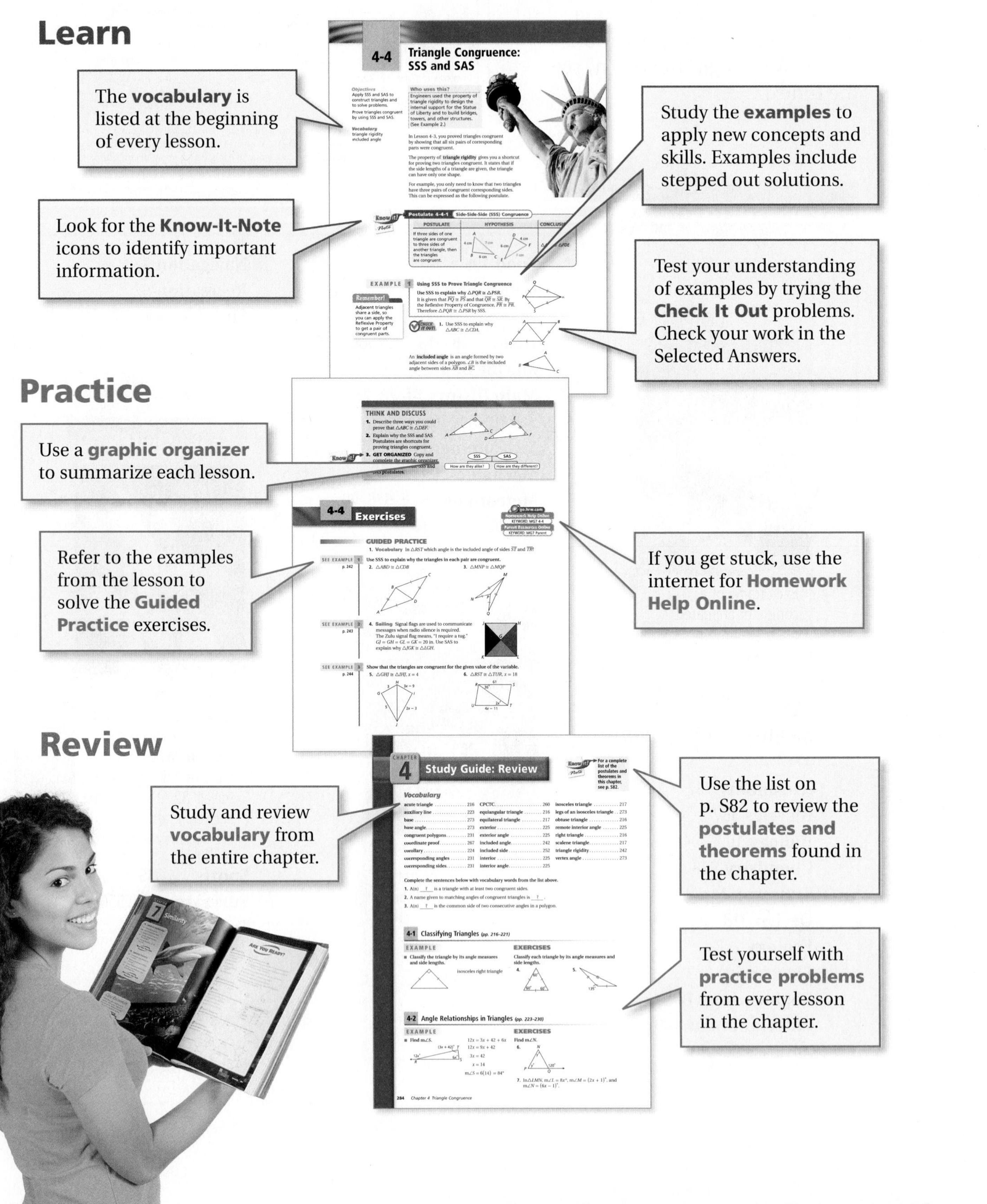

Learn
The **vocabulary** is listed at the beginning of every lesson.
Look for the **Know-It-Note** icons to identify important information.
Study the **examples** to apply new concepts and skills. Examples include stepped out solutions.
Test your understanding of examples by trying the **Check It Out** problems. Check your work in the Selected Answers.
4-4 Triangle Congruence: SSS and SAS
Practice
Use a **graphic organizer** to summarize each lesson.
Refer to the examples from the lesson to solve the **Guided Practice** exercises.
If you get stuck, use the internet for **Homework Help Online**.
4-4 Exercises
Review
Study and review **vocabulary** from the entire chapter.
Use the list on p. S82 to review the **postulates and theorems** found in the chapter.
Test yourself with **practice problems** from every lesson in the chapter.
Study Guide: Review

Tools of Geometry

In geometry, it is important to use tools correctly in order to measure accurately and produce accurate figures. One important tool is your pencil. Always use a sharp pencil with a good eraser.

Ruler

The ruler shown has a mark every $\frac{1}{8}$ inch, so the accuracy is to the nearest $\frac{1}{8}$ inch.

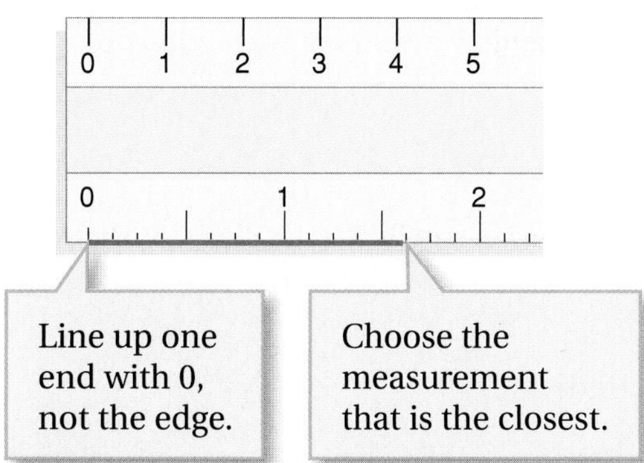

Protractor

To use a protractor to measure an angle, you may need to extend the sides of the angle.

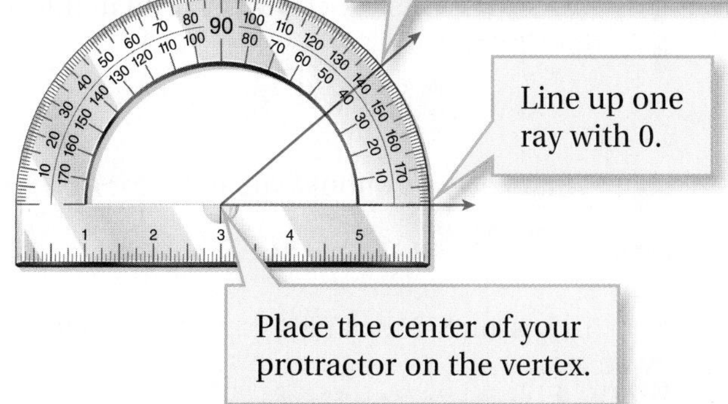

Compass

A compass is used to draw arcs and circles. If you have trouble keeping the point in place, try keeping the compass still and turning the paper.

Straightedge

A straightedge is used to draw a line through two points. If you use a ruler as a straightedge, do not use the marks on the ruler.

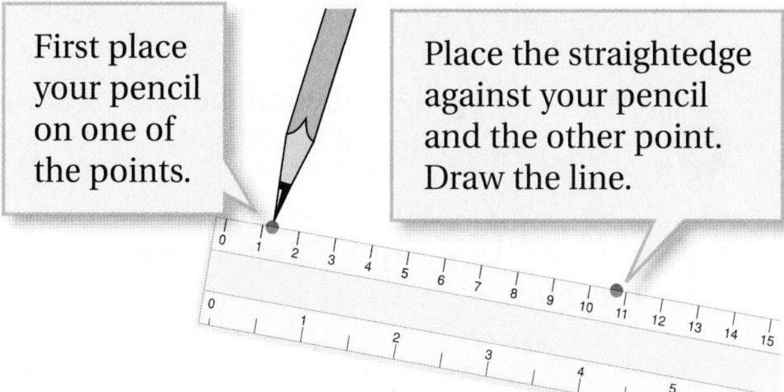

First place your pencil on one of the points.
Place the straightedge against your pencil and the other point. Draw the line.

Geometry Software

Geometry software can be used to create figures and explore their properties.

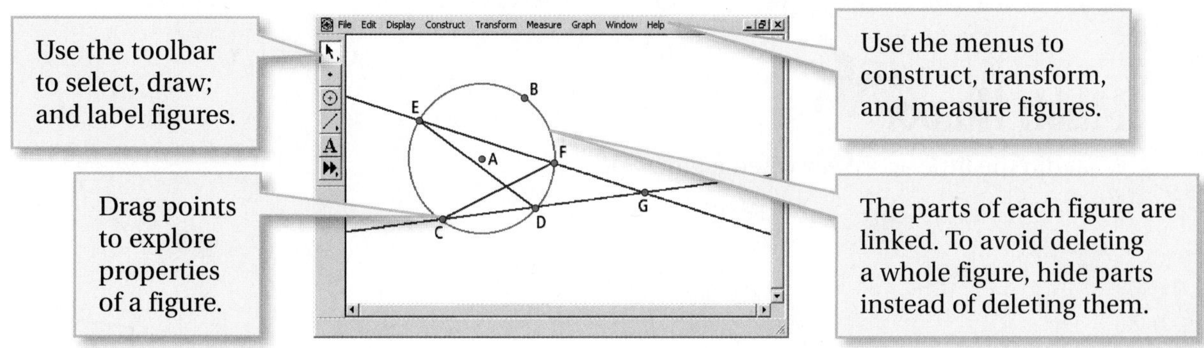

Scavenger Hunt

Use this scavenger hunt to discover a few of the many tools in ***Holt McDougal Geometry*** that you can use to become an independent learner. On a separate sheet of paper, write the answers to each question below. Within each answer, one letter will be in a yellow box. After you have answered every question, identify the letters that would be in yellow boxes and rearrange them to reveal the answer to the question at the bottom of the page.

1. What is the first **Vocabulary** term in the Study Guide: Preview for Chapter 1?
   ANGLE

2. What keyword should you enter for **Homework Help** for Lesson 3-3?
   MG7 3-3

3. In Lesson 8-2, what is **Example 4** teaching you to find?
   LENGTHS

4. What theorem are you asked about in the **Know-It Note** on page 352?
   PYTHAGOREAN

5. What mathematician is featured in the **Math History** link on page 318?
   GIOVANNI CEVA

6. Whose job is described in the **Career Path** on page 612?
   TECHNICAL WRITER

7. In the **Study Guide: Review** for Lesson 11-1, what do the lines intersect?
   CIRCLE

8. What advice does Chapter 1's **Test Tackler** give about how to answer a multiple choice test item you don't know how to solve?
   WORK BACKWARD

Math Humor

What did the little acorn say when it grew up?

GEOMETRY

Focus on Problem Solving

The Problem Solving Plan

Mathematical problems are a part of daily life. You need to use a good problem-solving plan to be a good problem solver. The plan used in this textbook is outlined below.

UNDERSTAND the Problem

First make sure you understand the problem you are asked to solve.

- **What are you asked to find?** Restate the question in your own words.
- **What information is given?** Identify the key facts given in the problem.
- **What information do you need?** Determine what information you need to solve the problem.
- **Do you have all the information needed?** Determine if you need more information.
- **Do you have too much information?** Determine if there is unnecessary information and eliminate it from your list of important facts.

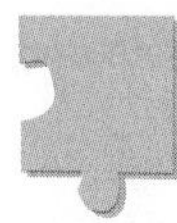

Make a PLAN

Plan how to use the information you are given.

- **Have you solved similar problems?** Think about similar problems you have solved successfully.
- **What problem solving strategy or strategies could you use to solve this problem?** Choose an appropriate problem solving strategy and decide how you will use it.

SOLVE

Use your plan to solve the problem. Show the steps in the solution, and write a final statement that gives the solution to the problem.

LOOK BACK

Check your answer against the original problem.

- **Have you answered the question?** Make sure you have answered the original question.
- **Is the answer reasonable?** The answer must make sense in relation to the question.
- **Are your calculations correct?** Check to make sure your calculations are accurate.
- **Can you use another strategy or solve the problem in another way?** Using another strategy is a good way to check your answer.
- **Did you learn anyting that could help you solve similar problems in the future?** Try to remember the types of problems you have solved and the strategies you applied.

Foundations for Geometry

Section 1A	Section 1B
Euclidean and Construction Tools	**Coordinate and Transformation Tools**
1-1 Understanding Points, Lines, and Planes	**1-5 Using Formulas in Geometry**
1-2 Technology Lab Explore Properties Associated with Points	**Connecting Geometry to Algebra** Unit Conversions
1-2 Measuring and Constructing Segments	**1-6 Midpoint and Distance in the Coordinate Plane**
1-3 Measuring and Constructing Angles	**1-7 Transformations in the Coordinate Plane**
1-4 Pairs of Angles	**1-7 Technology Lab** Explore Transformations

Pacing Guide for 45-Minute Classes

Teacher One Stop™
Calendar Planner®

Chapter 1 — **Countdown Weeks 1, 2**

DAY 1	DAY 2	DAY 3	DAY 4	DAY 5
1-1 Lesson	1-2 Technology Lab	1-2 Lesson	1-3 Lesson	1-4 Lesson
DAY 6	**DAY 7**	**DAY 8**	**DAY 9**	**DAY 10**
Multi-Step Test Prep Ready to Go On?	1-5 Lesson	Connecting Geometry to Algebra 1-6 Lesson	1-7 Lesson	1-7 Technology Lab
DAY 11	**DAY 12**	**DAY 13**		
Multi-Step Test Prep Ready to Go On?	Chapter 1 Review	Chapter 1 Test		

Pacing Guide for 90-Minute Classes

Teacher One Stop™
Calendar Planner®

Chapter 1

DAY 1	DAY 2	DAY 3	DAY 4	DAY 5
1-1 Lesson 1-2 Technology Lab	1-2 Lesson 1-3 Lesson	1-4 Lesson Multi-Step Test Prep Ready to Go On?	1-5 Lesson Connecting Geometry to Algebra 1-6 Lesson	1-7 Lesson 1-7 Technology Lab
DAY 6	**DAY 7**			
Multi-Step Test Prep Ready to Go On? Chapter 1 Review	Chapter 1 Test 2-1 Lesson			

ONGOING ASSESSMENT and INTERVENTION

Assess Prior Knowledge

Before Chapter 1

DIAGNOSE	PRESCRIBE
Diagnose readiness for the chapter.	Prescribe intervention.
 **Are You Ready?** SE p. 3	 ***Are You Ready? Intervention***

Formative Assessment

Before Every Lesson

DIAGNOSE	PRESCRIBE
Diagnose readiness for the lesson.	Prescribe intervention.
Warm Up TE	**Reteach** CRB

During Every Lesson

DIAGNOSE	PRESCRIBE
Diagnose understanding of lesson concepts.	Prescribe intervention.
Check It Out! SE	**Reading Strategies** CRB
Questioning Strategies TE	***Success for Every Learner***
Think and Discuss SE	***Lesson Tutorial Videos***
Write About It SE	
Journal TE	

After Every Lesson

DIAGNOSE	PRESCRIBE
Diagnose mastery of lesson concepts.	Prescribe intervention.
Lesson Quiz TE	**Reteach** CRB
Test Prep SE	**Test Prep Doctor** TE
Test and Practice Generator	***Homework Help*** **Online**

Before Chapter 1 Testing

DIAGNOSE	PRESCRIBE
Diagnose mastery of concepts in chapter.	Prescribe intervention.
Ready to Go On? SE pp. 35, 59	***Ready to Go On? Intervention***
Multi-Step Test Prep SE pp. 34, 58	**Scaffolding Questions** TE pp. 34, 58
Section Quizzes AR	**Reteach** CRB
Test and Practice Generator	***Lesson Tutorial Videos***

Before High Stakes Testing

DIAGNOSE	PRESCRIBE
Diagnose mastery of benchmark concepts.	Prescribe intervention.
College Entrance Exam Practice SE p. 65	***College Entrance Exam Practice***
Standardized Test Prep SE pp. 68–69	

Summative Assessment

After Chapter 1

DIAGNOSE	PRESCRIBE
Check mastery of chapter concepts.	Prescribe intervention.
Multiple-Choice Tests (Forms A, B, C)	**Reteach** CRB
Free-Response Tests (Forms A, B, C)	***Lesson Tutorial Videos***
Performance Assessment AR	
Cumulative Test AR	
Test and Practice Generator	

KEY: **SE** = *Student Edition* **TE** = *Teacher's Edition* **CRB** = *Chapter Resource Book* **AR** = *Assessment Resources* Available online Available on CD- or DVD-ROM

CHAPTER 1

Lesson Resources

Before the Lesson

Prepare ***Teacher One Stop*** 
- Editable lesson plans
- Calendar Planner
- Easy access to all chapter resources

Lesson Transparencies 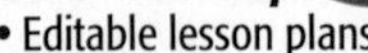
- Teacher Tools

Teach the Lesson

Introduce ***Alternate Openers: Explorations***

Lesson Transparencies
- Warm Up
- Problem of the Day

Teach ***Lesson Transparencies*** 
- Teaching Transparencies

Know-It Notebook™
- Vocabulary
- Key Concepts

Power Presentations

Lesson Tutorial Videos  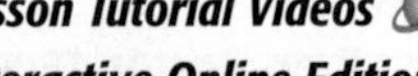 

Interactive Online Edition
- Lesson Activities
- Lesson Tutorial Videos

Lab Activities

Lab Resources Online

Online Interactivities  

TechKeys 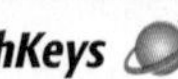

Practice the Lesson

Practice ***Chapter Resources***
- Practice A, B, C

Practice and Problem Solving Workbook

IDEA Works!® Modified Worksheets and Tests

ExamView Test and Practice Generator

Homework Help Online

Online Interactivities

Interactive Online Edition
- Homework Help

Apply ***Chapter Resources***
- Problem Solving

Practice and Problem Solving Workbook

Interactive Online Edition 
- Chapter Project

Project Teacher Support

After the Lesson

Reteach ***Chapter Resources***
- Reteach
- Reading Strategies ELL

Success for Every Learner

Review ***Interactive Answers and Solutions***

Solutions Key

Know-It Notebook™
- Big Ideas
- Chapter Review

Extend ***Chapter Resources***
- Challenge

Technology Highlights for the Teacher

 Power Presentations

Dynamic presentations to engage students. Complete PowerPoint® presentations for every lesson in Chapter 1.

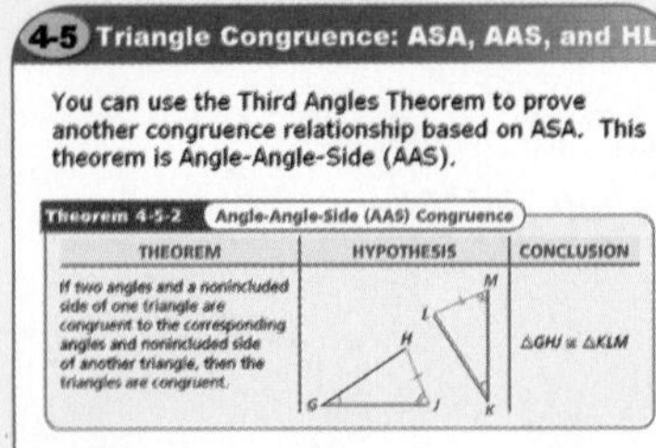

Teacher One Stop SPANISH

Easy access to Chapter 1 resources and assessments. Includes lesson planning, test generation, and puzzle creation software.

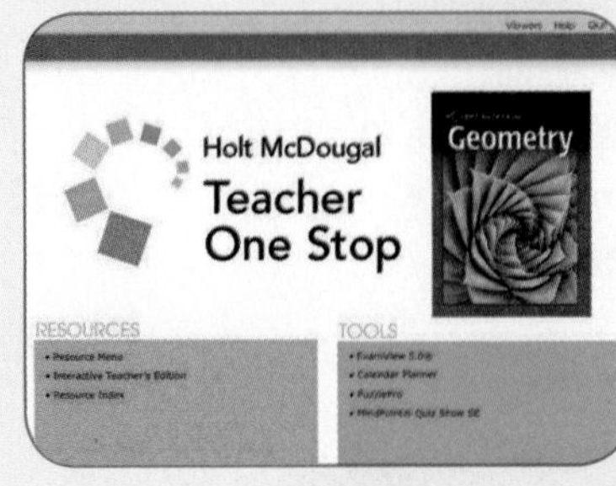

 Premier Online Edition 

Chapter 1 includes Tutorial Videos, Lesson Activities, Lesson Quizzes, Homework Help, and Chapter Project.

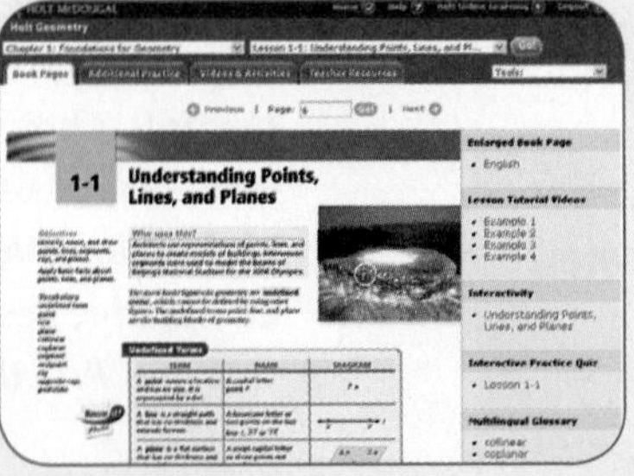

 KEY: **SE** = *Student Edition* **TE** = *Teacher's Edition*  English Language Learners  Spanish version available 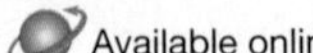 Available online  Available on CD- or DVD-ROM

CHAPTER 1

Reaching All Learners

Teaching tips to help all learners appear throughout the chapter. A few that target specific students are included in the lists below.

All Learners

Lab Activities
Practice and Problem Solving Workbook
Know-It Notebook

Special Needs Students

Practice A .... CRB
Reteach .... CRB
Reading Strategies .... CRB
Are You Ready? .... SE p. 3
Inclusion .... TE pp. 18, 25, 30, 36, 42, 45, 51
IDEA Works!® Modified Worksheets and Tests
Ready to Go On? Intervention SPANISH
Know-It Notebook
Online Interactivities SPANISH
Lesson Tutorial Videos 

Developing Learners

Practice A .... CRB
Reteach .... CRB
Reading Strategies .... CRB
Are You Ready? .... SE p. 3
Vocabulary Connections .... SE p. 4
Questioning Strategies .... TE
Ready to Go On? Intervention SPANISH
Know-It Notebook
Homework Help Online
Online Interactivities SPANISH
Lesson Tutorial Videos 

On-Level Learners

Practice B .... CRB
Problem Solving .... CRB
Vocabulary Connections .... SE p. 4
Questioning Strategies .... TE
Ready to Go On? Intervention SPANISH
Know-It Notebook
Homework Help Online
Online Interactivities SPANISH

Advanced Learners

Practice C .... CRB
Challenge .... CRB
Challenge Exercises .... SE
Reading and Writing Math *Extend* .... TE p. 5
Critical Thinking .... TE p. 14
Are You Ready? Enrichment SPANISH
Ready To Go On? Enrichment SPANISH

English Language Learners

ENGLISH LANGUAGE LEARNERS

Reading Strategies .... CRB
Are You Ready? Vocabulary .... SE p. 3
Vocabulary Connections .... SE p. 4
Vocabulary Review .... SE p. 60
English Language Learners .... TE pp. 5, 7, 22, 23, 39
Success for Every Learner
Know-It Notebook
Spanish Study Guide (Resumen y Repaso)
Multilingual Glossary
Lesson Tutorial Videos  

Technology Highlights for Reaching All Learners

Lesson Tutorial Videos SPANISH

Starring Holt authors Ed Burger and Freddie Renfro! Live tutorials to support every lesson in Chapter 1.

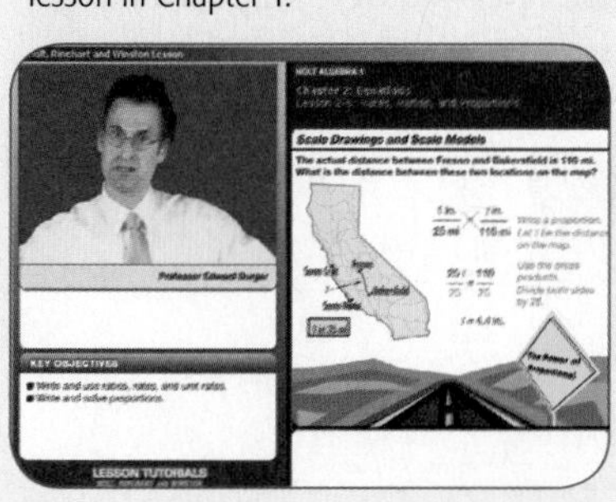

Multilingual Glossary

Searchable glossary includes definitions in English, Spanish, Vietnamese, Chinese, Hmong, Korean, and 4 other languages.

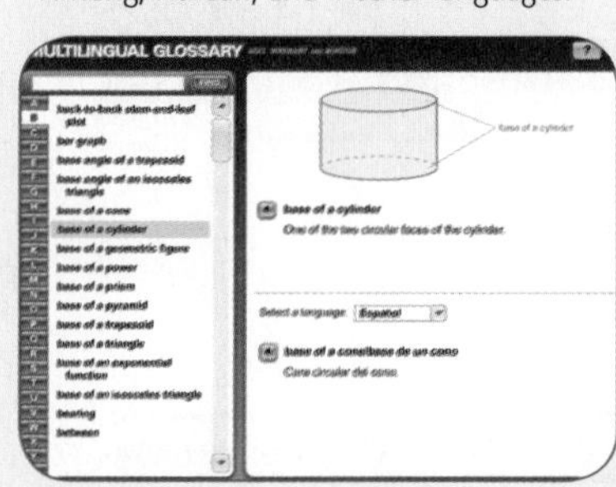

Online Interactivities

Interactive tutorials provide visually engaging alternative opportunities to learn concepts and master skills.

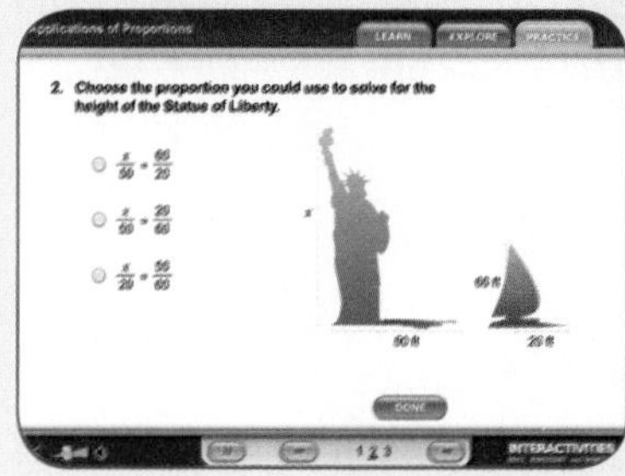

KEY: **SE** = *Student Edition* **TE** = *Teacher's Edition* **CRB** = *Chapter Resource Book* SPANISH Spanish version available  Available online Available on CD- or DVD-ROM

Ongoing Assessment

Assessing Prior Knowledge

Determine whether students have the prerequisite concepts and skills for success in Chapter 1.

Are You Ready? SPANISH .... SE p. 3
Warm Up .... TE

Test Preparation

Provide review and practice for Chapter 1 and standardized tests.

Multi-Step Test Prep .... SE pp. 34, 58
Study Guide: Review .... SE pp. 60–61
Test Tackler .... SE pp. 66–67
Standardized Test Prep .... SE pp. 68–69
College Entrance Exam Practice .... SE p. 65
Countdown to Testing .... SE pp. C4-C27
IDEA Works!® Modified Worksheets and Tests

Alternative Assessment

Assess students' understanding of Chapter 1 concepts and combined problem-solving skills.

Chapter 1 Project .... SE p. 2
Alternative Assessment .... TE
Performance Assessment .... AR
Portfolio Assessment .... AR

Lesson Assessment

Provide formative assessment for each lesson of Chapter 1.

Questioning Strategies .... TE
Think and Discuss .... SE
Check It Out! Exercises .... SE
Write About It .... SE
Journal .... TE
Lesson Quiz .... TE
Alternative Assessment .... TE
IDEA Works!® Modified Worksheets and Tests

Weekly Assessment

Provide formative assessment for each section of Chapter 1.

Multi-Step Test Prep .... SE pp. 34, 58
Ready to Go On? SPANISH .... SE pp. 35, 59
Section Quizzes .... AR
Test and Practice Generator .... *Teacher One Stop*

Chapter Assessment

Provide summative assessment of Chapter 1 mastery.

Chapter 1 Test .... SE p. 64
Chapter Test (Levels A, B, C) .... AR
• Multiple Choice • Free Response
Cumulative Test .... AR
Test and Practice Generator .... *Teacher One Stop*
IDEA Works!® Modified Worksheets and Tests

Technology Highlights for Assessment

Are You Ready? SPANISH

Automatically assess readiness and prescribe intervention for Chapter 1 prerequisite skills.

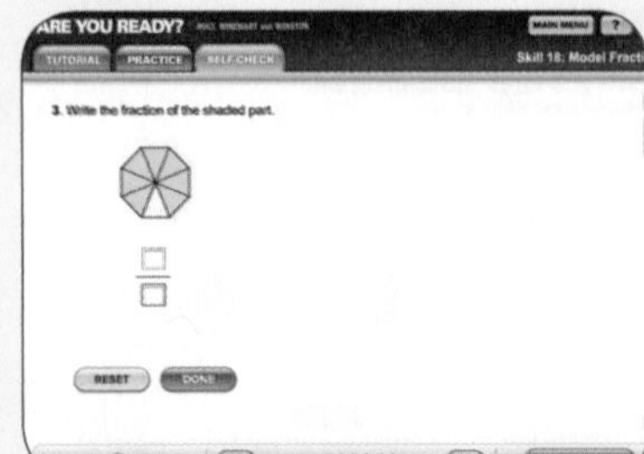

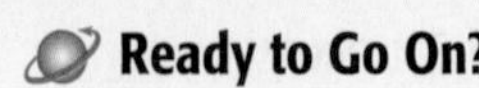

Ready to Go On?

Automatically assess understanding of and prescribe intervention for Sections 1A and 1B.

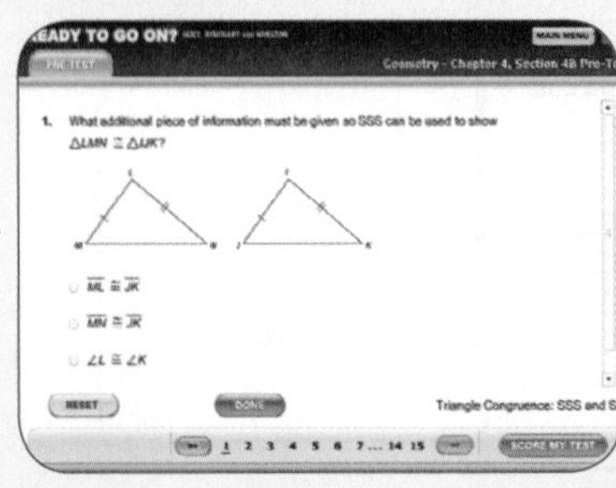

Test and Practice Generator

Use Chapter 1 problem banks to create assessments and worksheets to print out or deliver online. Includes dynamic problems.

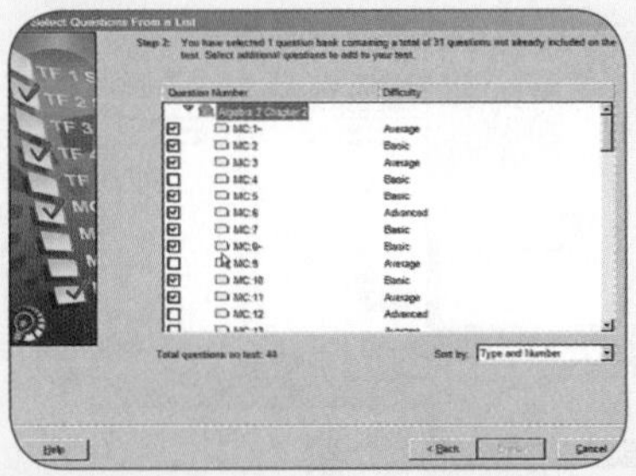

KEY: **SE** = *Student Edition* **TE** = *Teacher's Edition* **AR** = *Assessment Resources*  Spanish version available 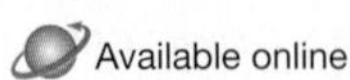 Available online Available on CD- or DVD-ROM

CHAPTER 1

Formal Assessment

Three levels (A, B, C) of multiple-choice and free-response chapter tests, along with a performance assessment, are available in the *Assessment Resources.*

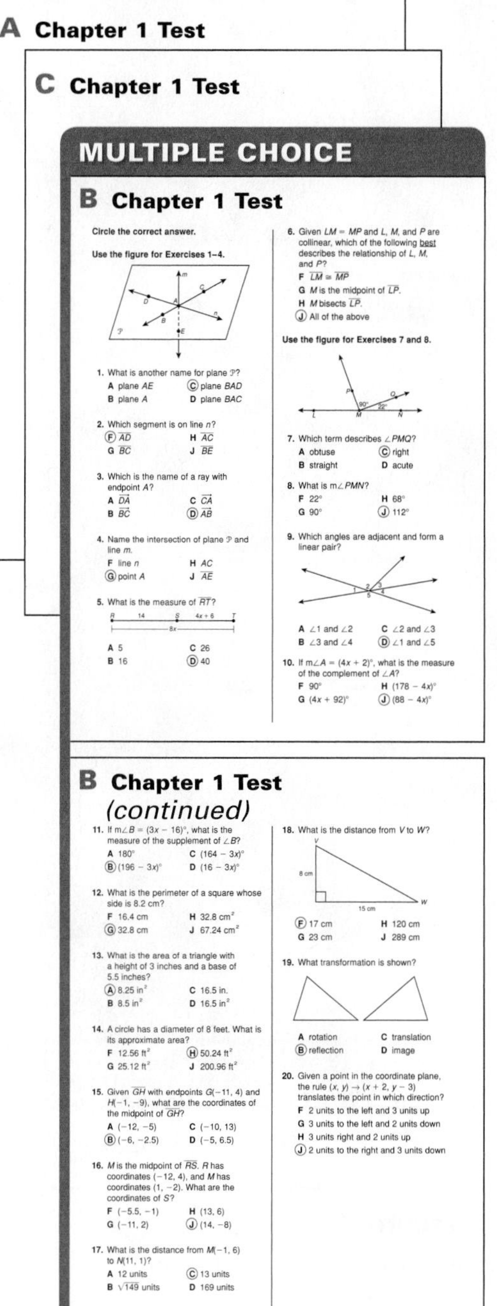

A Chapter 1 Test

C Chapter 1 Test

MULTIPLE CHOICE

B Chapter 1 Test

Circle the correct answer.

Use the figure for Exercises 1–4.

1. What is another name for plane $\mathcal{P}$?
A plane AE C plane BAD
B plane A D plane BAC

2. Which segment is on line n?
F $\overline{AD}$ H $\overline{AC}$
G $\overline{BC}$ J $\overline{BE}$

3. Which is the name of a ray with endpoint A?
A $\overrightarrow{DA}$ C $\overrightarrow{CA}$
B $\overrightarrow{BC}$ D $\overrightarrow{AB}$

4. Name the intersection of plane $\mathcal{P}$ and line m.
F line n H AC
G point A J $\overline{AE}$

5. What is the measure of $\overline{RT}$?
A 5 C 26
B 16 D 40

6. Given $LM = MP$ and L, M, and P are collinear, which of the following best describes the relationship of L, M, and P?
F $\overline{LM} \cong \overline{MP}$
G M is the midpoint of $\overline{LP}$.
H M bisects $\overline{LP}$.
J All of the above

Use the figure for Exercises 7 and 8.

7. Which term describes $\angle PMQ$?
A obtuse C right
B straight D acute

8. What is $m\angle PMN$?
F 22° H 68°
G 90° J 112°

9. Which angles are adjacent and form a linear pair?
A $\angle 1$ and $\angle 2$ C $\angle 2$ and $\angle 3$
B $\angle 3$ and $\angle 4$ D $\angle 1$ and $\angle 5$

10. If $m\angle A = (4x + 2)°$, what is the measure of the complement of $\angle A$?
F 90° H $(178 - 4x)°$
G $(4x + 92)°$ J $(88 - 4x)°$

B Chapter 1 Test (continued)

11. If $m\angle B = (3x - 16)°$, what is the measure of the supplement of $\angle B$?
A 180° C $(164 - 3x)°$
B $(196 - 3x)°$ D $(16 - 3x)°$

12. What is the perimeter of a square whose side is 8.2 cm?
F 16.4 cm H 32.8 cm^2
G 32.8 cm J 67.24 cm^2

13. What is the area of a triangle with a height of 3 inches and a base of 5.5 inches?
A 8.25 in^2 C 16.5 in.
B 8.5 in^2 D 16.5 in^2

14. A circle has a diameter of 8 feet. What is its approximate area?
F 12.56 ft^2 H 50.24 ft^2
G 25.12 ft^2 J 200.96 ft^2

15. Given $\overline{GH}$ with endpoints $G(-11, 4)$ and $H(-1, -9)$, what are the coordinates of the midpoint of $\overline{GH}$?
A $(-12, -5)$ C $(-10, 13)$
B $(-6, -2.5)$ D $(-5, 6.5)$

16. M is the midpoint of $\overline{RS}$. R has coordinates $(-12, 4)$, and M has coordinates $(1, -2)$. What are the coordinates of S?
F $(-5.5, -1)$ H $(13, 6)$
G $(-11, 2)$ J $(14, -8)$

17. What is the distance from $M(-1, 6)$ to $N(11, 1)$?
A 12 units C 13 units
B $\sqrt{149}$ units D 169 units

18. What is the distance from V to W?
F 17 cm H 120 cm
G 23 cm J 289 cm

19. What transformation is shown?
A rotation C translation
B reflection D image

20. Given a point in the coordinate plane, the rule $(x, y) \rightarrow (x + 2, y - 3)$ translates the point in which direction?
F 2 units to the left and 3 units up
G 3 units to the left and 2 units down
H 3 units right and 2 units up
J 2 units to the right and 3 units down

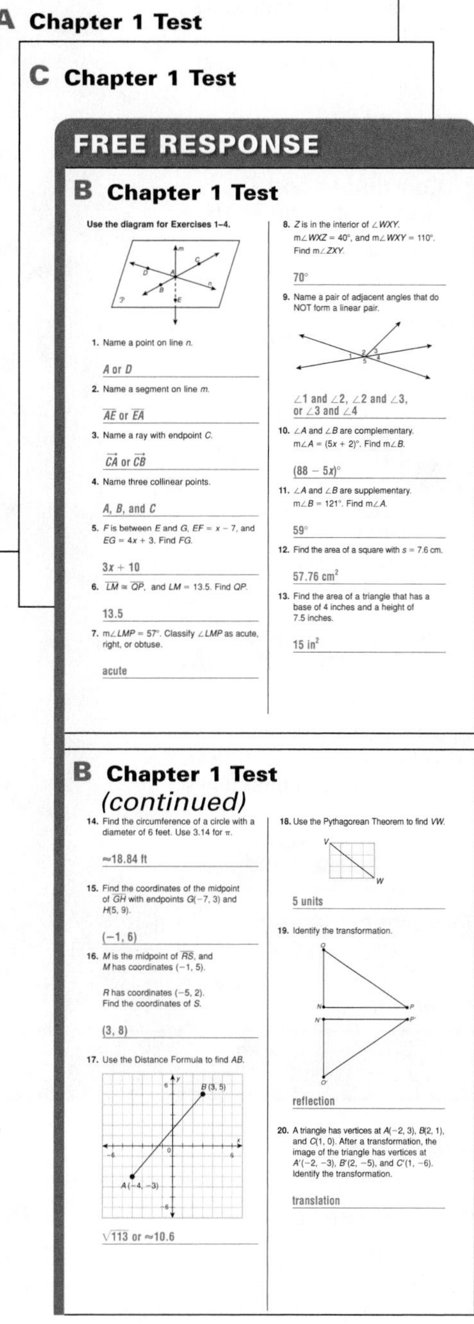

A Chapter 1 Test

C Chapter 1 Test

FREE RESPONSE

B Chapter 1 Test

Use the diagram for Exercises 1–4.

1. Name a point on line n.
A or D

2. Name a segment on line m.
$\overline{AE}$ or $\overline{EA}$

3. Name a ray with endpoint C.
$\overrightarrow{CA}$ or $\overrightarrow{CB}$

4. Name three collinear points.
A, B, and C

5. F is between E and G, $EF = x - 7$, and $EG = 4x + 3$. Find FG.
$3x + 10$

6. $\overline{LM} \cong \overline{QP}$, and $LM = 13.5$. Find QP.
13.5

7. $m\angle LMP = 57°$. Classify $\angle LMP$ as acute, right, or obtuse.
acute

8. Z is in the interior of $\angle WXY$. $m\angle WXZ = 40°$, and $m\angle WXY = 110°$. Find $m\angle ZXY$.
70°

9. Name a pair of adjacent angles that do NOT form a linear pair.
$\angle 1$ and $\angle 2$, $\angle 2$ and $\angle 3$, or $\angle 3$ and $\angle 4$

10. $\angle A$ and $\angle B$ are complementary. $m\angle A = (5x + 2)°$. Find $m\angle B$.
$(88 - 5x)°$

11. $\angle A$ and $\angle B$ are supplementary. $m\angle B = 121°$. Find $m\angle A$.
59°

12. Find the area of a square with $s = 7.6$ cm.
57.76 cm^2

13. Find the area of a triangle that has a base of 4 inches and a height of 7.5 inches.
15 in^2

B Chapter 1 Test (continued)

14. Find the circumference of a circle with a diameter of 6 feet. Use 3.14 for π.
≈18.84 ft

15. Find the coordinates of the midpoint of $\overline{GH}$ with endpoints $G(-7, 3)$ and $H(5, 9)$.
$(-1, 6)$

16. M is the midpoint of $\overline{RS}$, and M has coordinates $(-1, 5)$.
R has coordinates $(-5, 2)$. Find the coordinates of S.
$(3, 8)$

17. Use the Distance Formula to find AB.
$\sqrt{113}$ or ≈10.6

18. Use the Pythagorean Theorem to find VW.
5 units

19. Identify the transformation.
reflection

20. A triangle has vertices at $A(-2, 3)$, $B(2, 1)$, and $C(1, 0)$. After a transformation, the image of the triangle has vertices at $A'(-2, -3)$, $B'(2, -5)$, and $C'(1, -6)$. Identify the transformation.
translation

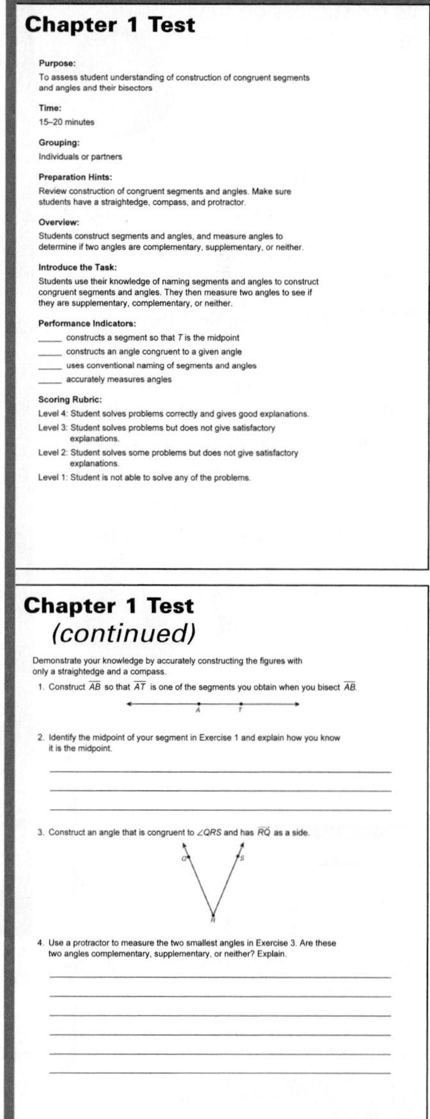

PERFORMANCE ASSESSMENT

Chapter 1 Test

Purpose:
To assess student understanding of construction of congruent segments and angles and their bisectors

Time:
15–20 minutes

Grouping:
Individuals or partners

Preparation Hints:
Review construction of congruent segments and angles. Make sure students have a straightedge, compass, and protractor.

Overview:
Students construct segments and angles, and measure angles to determine if two angles are complementary, supplementary, or neither.

Introduce the Task:
Students use their knowledge of naming segments and angles to construct congruent segments and angles. They then measure two angles to see if they are supplementary, complementary, or neither.

Performance Indicators:
_____ constructs a segment so that T is the midpoint
_____ constructs an angle congruent to a given angle
_____ uses conventional naming of segments and angles
_____ accurately measures angles

Scoring Rubric:
Level 4: Student solves problems correctly and gives good explanations.
Level 3: Student solves problems but does not give satisfactory explanations.
Level 2: Student solves some problems but does not give satisfactory explanations.
Level 1: Student is not able to solve any of the problems.

Chapter 1 Test (continued)

Demonstrate your knowledge by accurately constructing the figures with only a straightedge and a compass.

1. Construct $\overline{AB}$ so that $\overline{AT}$ is one of the segments you obtain when you bisect $\overline{AB}$.

2. Identify the midpoint of your segment in Exercise 1 and explain how you know it is the midpoint.

3. Construct an angle that is congruent to $\angle QRS$ and has $\overrightarrow{RQ}$ as a side.

4. Use a protractor to measure the two smallest angles in Exercise 3. Are these two angles complementary, supplementary, or neither? Explain.

Teacher One Stop™

Test & Practice Generator

Create and customize Chapter 1 Tests. Instantly generate multiple test versions, answer keys, and practice versions of test items.

Modified chapter tests that address special learning needs are available in *IDEA Works!® Modified Worksheets and Tests.*

CHAPTER 1

SECTION 1A
Euclidean and Construction Tools

MULTI-STEP TEST PREP

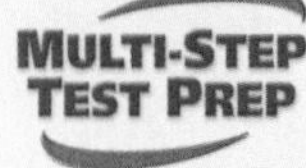

On page 34, students analyze a diagram of an archaeological dig by applying definitions, using the distance formula, and classifying angles.

Exercises designed to prepare students for success on the Multi-Step Test Prep can be found on pages 10, 18, 26, and 32.

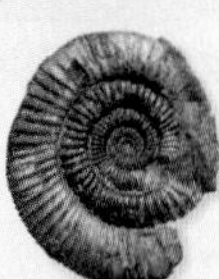

SECTION 1B
Coordinate and Transformation Tools

MULTI-STEP TEST PREP

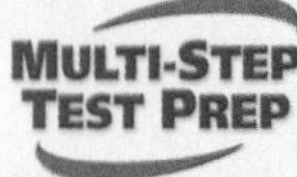

On page 58, students find the area and perimeter of a patio to determine the total cost of the paving stones used. They use distance, midpoint, and transformations to create the construction plans for the patio.

Exercises designed to prepare students for success on the Multi-Step Test Prep can be found on pages 39, 48, and 54.

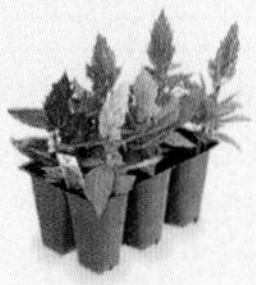

Interactivities Online ▶

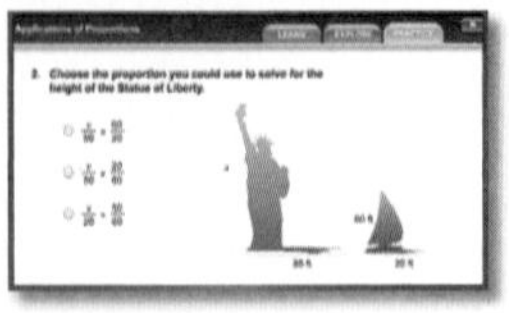

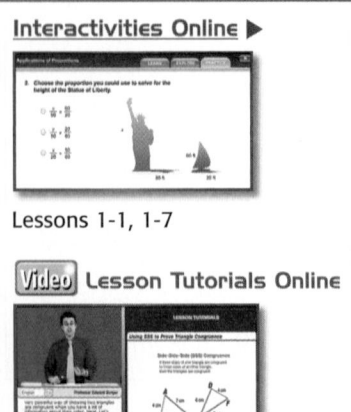

Lessons 1-1, 1-7

Video Lesson Tutorials Online

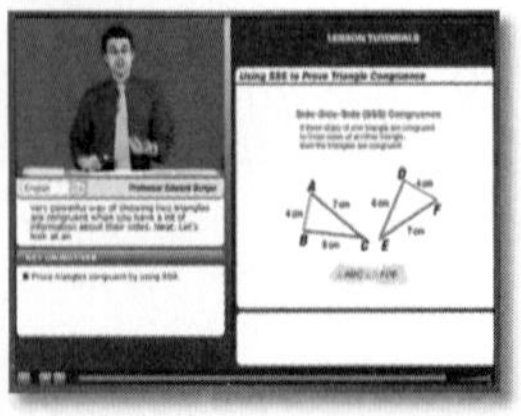

Lesson Tutorial Videos are available for EVERY example.

CHAPTER 1

Foundations for Geometry

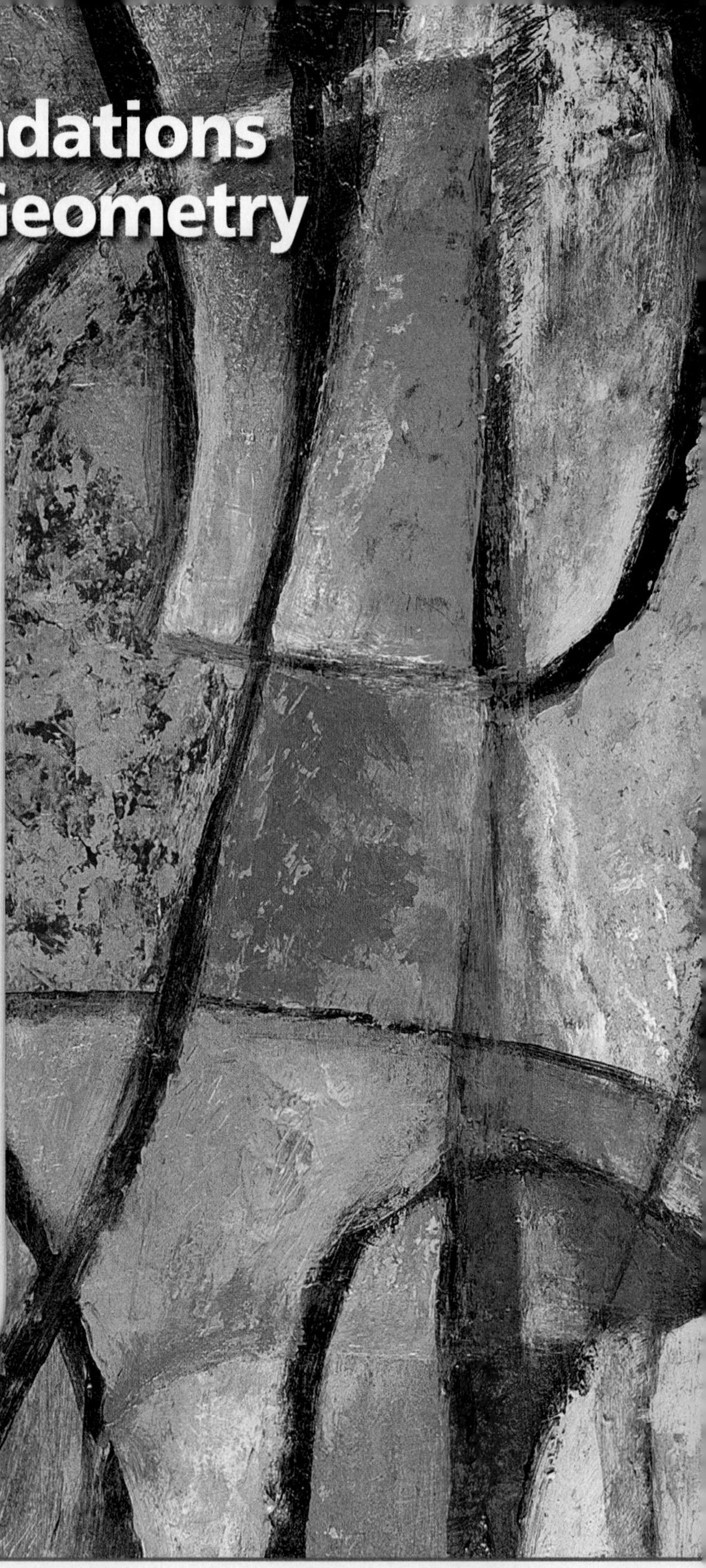

Chapter Focus

- Use the correct terminology for basic geometric figures.
- Apply basic formulas in and out of the coordinate plane.

Picture This!

Many geometric concepts and shapes may be used in creating works of art. Unique designs can be made using only points, lines, planes, or circles.

go.hrw.com
Chapter Project Online
KEYWORD: MG7 ChProj

Picture This

About the Project

Students begin by using geoboards to explore designs based on line segments. Then they use a compass and paper folding to make star designs. Finally, students use everything they've learned to produce an original piece of string art.

Project Resources

All project resources for teachers and students are provided online.

Materials:

- Activity 1: geoboard, colored rubber bands or colored string
- Activity 2: compass, straightedge
- Activity 3: straightedge
- Activity 4: wooden board, small nails, hammer, colored string or thread

go.hrw.com
Project Teacher Support
KEYWORD: MG7 ProjectTS

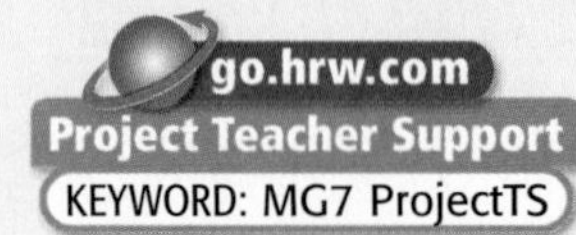

ARE YOU READY?

Vocabulary

Match each term on the left with a definition on the right.

1. coordinate C
2. metric system of measurement E
3. expression A
4. order of operations D

A. a mathematical phrase that contains operations, numbers, and/or variables
B. the measurement system often used in the United States
C. one of the numbers of an ordered pair that locates a point on a coordinate graph
D. a list of rules for evaluating expressions
E. a decimal system of weights and measures that is used universally in science and commonly throughout the world

Measure with Customary and Metric Units

For each object tell which is the better measurement.

5. length of an unsharpened pencil $7\frac{1}{2}$ in. or $9\frac{3}{4}$ in. $7\frac{1}{2}$ in.
6. the diameter of a quarter 1 m or $2\frac{1}{2}$ cm $2\frac{1}{2}$ cm
7. length of a soccer field 100 yd or 40 yd **100 yd**
8. height of a classroom 5 ft or 10 ft **10 ft**
9. height of a student's desk 30 in. or 4 ft **30 in.**
10. length of a dollar bill 15.6 cm or 35.5 cm **15.6 cm**

Combine Like Terms

Simplify each expression.

11. $-y + 3y - 6y + 12y$ $8y$
12. $63 + 2x - 7 - 4x$ $-2x + 56$
13. $-5 - 9 - 7x + 6x$ $-x - 14$
14. $24 - 3y + y + 7$ $-2y + 31$

Evaluate Expressions

Evaluate each expression for the given value of the variable.

15. $x + 3x + 7x$ for $x = -5$ -55
16. $5p + 10$ for $p = 78$ 400
17. $2a - 8a$ for $a = 12$ -72
18. $3n - 3$ for $n = 16$ 45

Ordered Pairs

Write the ordered pair for each point.

19. A (0, 7)
20. B (−5, 4)
21. C (6, 3)
22. D (−8, −2)
23. E (3, −5)
24. F (6, −4)

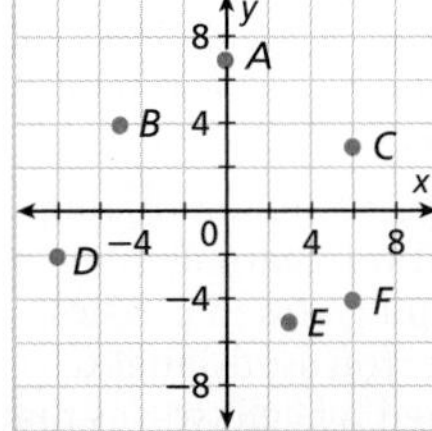

CHAPTER 1

ARE YOU READY?

Organizer

Objective: Assess students' understanding of prerequisite skills.

Prerequisite Skills

Measure with Customary and Metric Units
Combine Like Terms
Evaluate Expressions
Ordered Pairs

Assessing Prior Knowledge

INTERVENTION

Diagnose and Prescribe

Use this page to determine whether intervention is necessary or whether enrichment is appropriate.

Resources

Are You Ready? Intervention and Enrichment **Worksheets**

***Are You Ready?* CD-ROM**

***Are You Ready?* Online**

my.hrw.com

ARE YOU READY?

Diagnose and Prescribe

NO INTERVENE

Prerequisite Skill	*Are You Ready? Intervention,* Chapter 1 Worksheets	CD-ROM	Online
Measure with Customary and Metric Units	Skill 20	Activity 20	Diagnose and Prescribe Online
Combine Like Terms	Skill 57	Activity 57	
Evaluate Expressions	Skill 60	Activity 60	
Ordered Pairs	Skill 79	Activity 79	

YES ENRICH

Are You Ready? Enrichment, Chapter 1
Worksheets
CD-ROM
Online

CHAPTER 1 Study Guide: Preview

Organizer

Objective: Help students organize the new concepts they will learn in Chapter 1.

Online Edition
Multilingual Glossary

Resources

Teacher One Stop™
PuzzleView

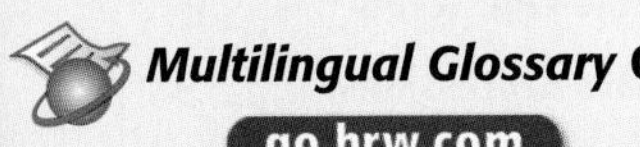

***Multilingual Glossary* Online**
go.hrw.com
KEYWORD: MG7 Glossary

Answers to *Vocabulary Connections*

1. An undefined term is a term that is not defined with a word or phrase.
2. A coordinate plane is a flat surface that has numbers on it to describe locations.
3. Possible answer: tip of a sharpened pencil
4. *Transformation* means "to change or move a shape."

CHAPTER 1 Study Guide: Preview

Where You've Been

Previously, you
- used the order of operations.
- used variables and expressions to represent situations.
- located points in the coordinate plane.
- solved equations.

In This Chapter

You will study
- applying basic facts about points, lines, planes, segments, and angles.
- measuring and constructing segments and angles.
- using formulas to find distance and the coordinates of a midpoint.
- identifying reflections, rotations, and translations.

Where You're Going

You can use the skills learned in this chapter
- to find distances between cities.
- to determine how much material is needed to make a rectangular or triangular object.
- in classes such as Biology, when you learn about gene mapping and in physics, when you study angles formed by light waves that bounce off objects.

Key Vocabulary/Vocabulario

angle	ángulo
area	área
coordinate plane	plano cartesiano
line	línea
perimeter	perímetro
plane	plano
point	punto
transformation	transformación
undefined term	término indefinido

Vocabulary Connections

To become familiar with some of the vocabulary terms in the chapter, consider the following. You may refer to the chapter, the glossary, or a dictionary if you like.

1. A *definition* is a statement that gives the meaning of a word or phrase. What do you think the phrase **undefined term** means?
2. *Coordinates* are numbers used to describe a location. A *plane* is a flat surface. How can you use these meanings to understand the term **coordinate plane**?
3. A **point** is often represented by a dot. What real-world items could represent points?
4. *Trans-* is a prefix that means "across," as in movement. A *form* is a shape. How can you use these meanings to understand the term **transformation**?

Reading Strategy: Use Your Book for Success

Understanding how your textbook is organized will help you locate and use helpful information.

As you read through an example problem, pay attention to the notes in the **margin.** These notes highlight key information about the concept and will help you to avoid common mistakes.

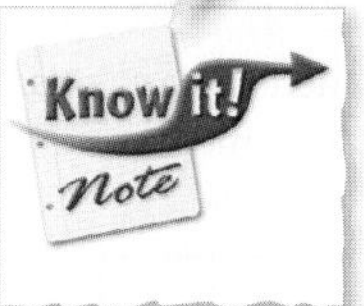

Writing Math — Writing a similarity statement is like writing a congruent statement—be sur

Helpful Hint — When writing an indirect proof, look for a contradiction of one of the followi

Caution! — Consider all cases when you assume the opposite. If the conclusion is $QR >$

The **Glossary** is found in the back of your textbook. Use it when you need a definition of an unfamiliar word or phrase.

The **Index** is located at the end of your textbook. If you need to locate the page where a particular concept is explained, use the **Index** to find the corresponding page number.

The **Problem-Solving Handbook** is found in the back of your textbook. These pages review strategies that can help you solve real-world problems.

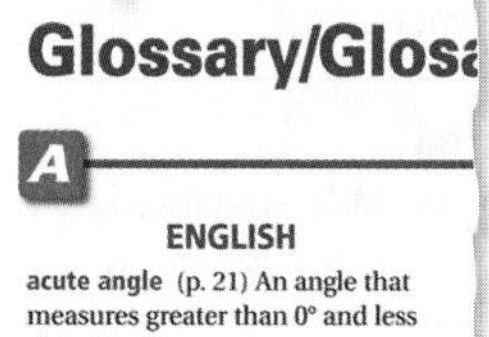

Glossary/Glos
A
ENGLISH
acute angle (p. 21) An angle that measures greater than 0° and less than 90°.

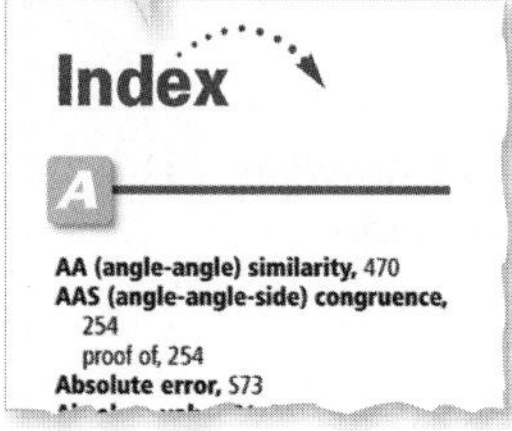

Index
A
AA (angle-angle) similarity, 470
AAS (angle-angle-side) congruence, 254
proof of, 254
Absolute error, 573

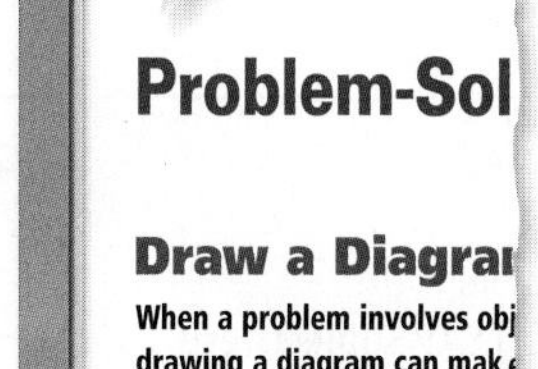

Use your textbook for the following problems.

1. Use the index to find the page where *right angle* is defined.
2. What formula does the Know-It Note on the first page of Lesson 1-6 refer to?
3. Use the glossary to find the definition of *congruent segments.*

Reading and Writing Math

Organizer

Objective: Help students apply strategies to understand and retain key concepts.

ENGLISH LANGUAGE LEARNERS

Reading Strategy: Use Your Book for Success

Discuss The index, glossary, margin notes, and Problem-Solving Handbook can provide students with a great deal of useful information as they use this textbook.

Extend Ask students to find a term they do not know and look it up in the glossary. Then ask them to enter the definition in their journal. Challenge the students to use information in the book that was not mentioned. For example, look at the table of contents, highlighted words, words in italics, or words in boldface.

Answers to *Try This*

1. p. 21
2. Mdpt. Formula
3. segs. that have the same length

Reading Connection

Flatland
by Edwin A. Abbott

First published in 1880, this classic work of mathematical fiction satirizes the human habit of assuming that what we see is all there is. After living for years as a square in Flatland, the protagonist visits one-dimensional Lineland and three-dimensional Spaceland. There his eyes are opened, and he grasps the idea not only of a third dimension but of a fourth dimension as well.

Activity *Flatland* describes a cube as a three-dimensional square. Have students report on the *tesseract,* a four-dimensional cube. Have them explain how a tesseract's properties are related to those of a cube.

SECTION

1A Euclidean and Construction Tools

One-Minute Section Planner

Lesson	Lab Resources	Materials
Lesson 1-1 Understanding Points, Lines, and Planes • Identify, name, and draw points, lines, segments, rays, and planes. • Apply basic facts about points, lines, and planes. ☑ SAT-10 ☑ NAEP ☑ ACT ☑ SAT ☑ SAT Subject Tests		**Required** straightedge (MK) **Optional** raw spaghetti, index cards, straw, clay, gumdrops, toothpicks
1-2 Technology Lab Explore Properties Associated with Points • Use geometry software to measure distances and explore properties of points on segments. ☑ SAT-10 ☑ NAEP ☑ ACT ☐ SAT ☐ SAT Subject Tests	***Technology Lab Activities*** 1-2 Lab Recording Sheet	**Required** geometry software **Optional** ruler (MK)
Lesson 1-2 Measuring and Constructing Segments • Use length and midpoint of a segment. • Construct midpoints and congruent segments. ☑ SAT-10 ☑ NAEP ☑ ACT ☑ SAT ☐ SAT Subject Tests	***Geometry Lab Activities*** 1-2 Geometry Lab	**Required** compass (MK), straightedge **Optional** road map, masking tape, butcher paper, small plastic disks, meter stick
Lesson 1-3 Measuring and Constructing Angles • Name and classify angles. • Measure and construct angles and angle bisectors. ☐ SAT-10 ☑ NAEP ☑ ACT ☑ SAT ☐ SAT Subject Tests	***Geometry Lab Activities*** 1-3 Geometry Lab	**Required** compass (MK), straightedge, protractor (MK), geometry software **Optional** yarn, index cards, pictures of angles, origami paper, sticky notes, acetate or tracing paper, clock (MK), Mira
Lesson 1-4 Pairs of Angles • Identify adjacent, vertical, complementary, and supplementary angles. • Find measures of pairs of angles. ☐ SAT-10 ☑ NAEP ☑ ACT ☑ SAT ☐ SAT Subject Tests		**Required** protractor (MK)

MK = *Manipulatives Kit*

Math Background

known work in which a logical, deductive system of reasoning is used as a means of unifying all mathematical knowledge.

The essential doctrine of *Elements* is that when a certain set of fundamental ideas or understandings are assumed to be true, all other mathematical results can be logically derived and proved from these foundations. To that end, the first of the thirteen books in Euclid's *Elements* presents five postulates (also known as axioms).

1. Between any two points a straight line may be drawn.
2. A line segment can be extended forever in a straight line.
3. Given a line segment, a circle may be drawn having one endpoint as the center and the segment as a radius.
4. All right angles are congruent.
5. If a straight line falling on two straight lines makes the interior angles on the same side less than two right angles, then the straight lines, if extended indefinitely, meet on the side on which the angles lie.

The fifth postulate, which is known as the Parallel Postulate, has an important history and will be discussed further in the Math Background notes for Section 3A.

This book begins with a somewhat different set of postulates, but its purpose is the same as that of *Elements:* to build a logically coherent system of facts by using deductive reasoning. Some facts that are theorems (i.e., that can be proved by using postulates and previously established theorems) are presented here as postulates. This presentation is used because a completely rigorous development of Euclidean

ot particularly illuminating. developing the most lts.

ONS

1-2, 1-3

Constructions with compass and straightedge date to antiquity. In fact, Euclid's first three postulates describe how these tools may be used. The straightedge is used to draw a line through two points or to extend an existing line segment. In contrast to a ruler, the unmarked straightedge is never used for measuring distance. Although a compass is often thought of as a tool for making circles, its primary use in constructions is marking equal distances.

Using these two seemingly primitive tools and working within the limits described above, one can construct virtually all of the fundamental figures of Euclidean geometry, including equilateral triangles, squares, and regular pentagons. All compass-and-straightedge constructions depend on a handful of basic constructions that are introduced in Chapter 1: copying a segment, copying an angle, bisecting a segment, and bisecting an angle.

ANGLES

Lesson 1-3

An angle is defined as the figure that is formed by two rays with a common endpoint. Note that in some textbooks an angle is defined as the figure formed by two *noncollinear* rays with a common endpoint. This restriction eliminates straight angles and thus removes some of the ambiguity that can arise when straight angles are considered. (For example, either side of a straight angle could be considered the interior or exterior of the angle.) On the other hand, angles with measures greater than or equal to 180° are essential in trigonometry and other areas of higher mathematics. For this reason, straight angles are discussed in this course. Students should be aware, however, that when working with proofs, the term *angle* generally refers to angles formed by noncollinear rays unless otherwise stated.

1-1 Organizer

Pacing: Traditional 1 day
Block $\frac{1}{2}$ day

Objectives: Identify, name, and draw points, lines, segments, rays, and planes.

Apply basic facts about points, lines, and planes.

Online Edition
Tutorial Videos, Interactivity

Countdown Week 1

Power Presentations with PowerPoint®

Warm Up

Graph each inequality.

1. $x \geq 3$

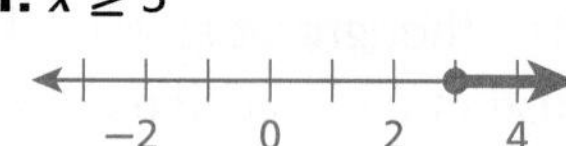

2. $2 \leq x \leq 6$

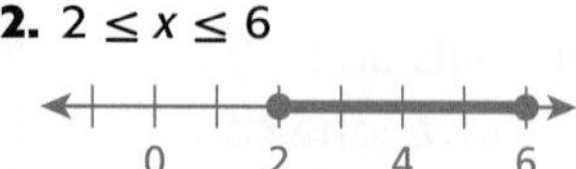

3. $x < 1$ or $x > 0$

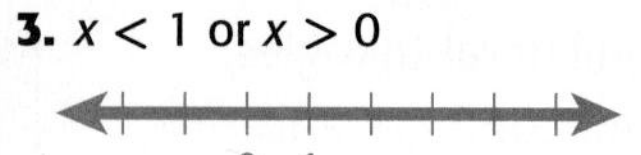

Also available on transparency

Math Humor

Q: What did the little acorn say when it grew up?

A: "Geometry"

1-1 Understanding Points, Lines, and Planes

Objectives
Identify, name, and draw points, lines, segments, rays, and planes.

Apply basic facts about points, lines, and planes.

Vocabulary
undefined term
point
line
plane
collinear
coplanar
segment
endpoint
ray
opposite rays
postulate

Who uses this?

Architects use representations of points, lines, and planes to create models of buildings. Interwoven segments were used to model the beams of Beijing's National Stadium for the 2008 Olympics.

The most basic figures in geometry are **undefined terms**, which cannot be defined by using other figures. The undefined terms *point, line,* and *plane* are the building blocks of geometry.

Know it! Note

Undefined Terms

TERM	NAME	DIAGRAM
A **point** names a location and has no size. It is represented by a dot.	A capital letter point *P*	*P* •
A **line** is a straight path that has no thickness and extends forever.	A lowercase letter or two points on the line line ℓ, $\overleftrightarrow{XY}$ or $\overleftrightarrow{YX}$	*X* *Y* ℓ
A **plane** is a flat surface that has no thickness and extends forever.	A script capital letter or three points not on a line plane $\mathcal{R}$ or plane *ABC*	*A* • *C* • $\mathcal{R}$ *B* •

Points that lie on the same line are **collinear**. *K, L,* and *M* are collinear. *K, L,* and *N* are *noncollinear.* Points that lie in the same plane are **coplanar**. Otherwise they are *noncoplanar.*

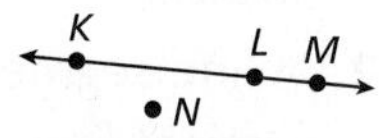

EXAMPLE 1 Naming Points, Lines, and Planes

Helpful Hint

A plane may be named by any three noncollinear points on that plane. Plane *ABC* may also be named *BCA, CAB, CBA, ACB,* or *BAC.*

Refer to the design in the roof of Beijing's National Stadium.

A **Name four coplanar points.**
K, L, M, and *N* all lie in plane $\mathcal{R}$.

B **Name three lines.**
$\overleftrightarrow{AB}$, $\overleftrightarrow{BC}$, and $\overleftrightarrow{CA}$.

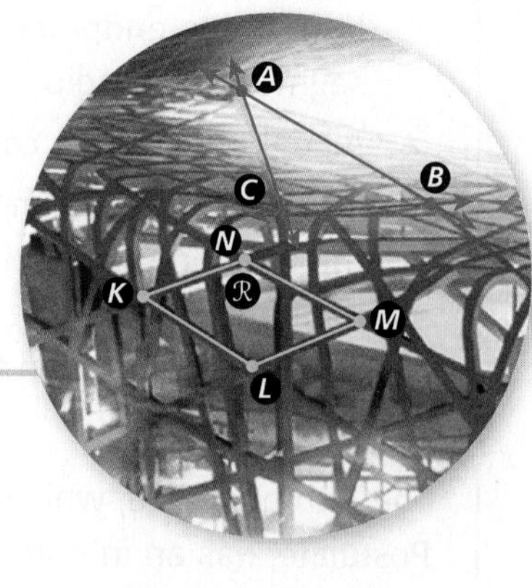

1. Use the diagram to name two planes.
Possible answer: plane $\mathcal{R}$ and plane *ABC*

State Resources

1 Introduce

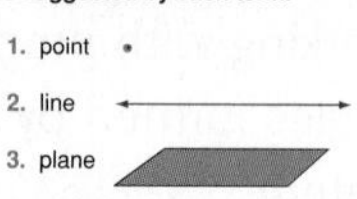

EXPLORATION

1-1 Understanding Points, Lines, and Planes

The following are some of the terms used as the basic building blocks of geometry. Describe a real-world object that is suggested by each term.

1. point •
2. line
3. plane
4. Tell whether each of the following is most like a point, a line, or a plane.
   a. a desktop
   b. a speck of dust
   c. a jet contrail

THINK AND DISCUSS

5. **Explain** what is represented by the arrowhead at each end of the line in Problem 2.
6. **Discuss** whether the surface of Earth can be an example of a plane.

Motivate

Point out different objects in the classroom that are representations of points, segments, and planes, such as the tips of pushpins on the bulletin board, rulers, and desktops. Discuss with students what these items have in common.

Ask students to give examples of other objects that have these same characteristics and can be found in the world around them, such as the locations of cities on a map, the lines on a football field, and the bases on a baseball field.

Explorations and answers are provided in *Alternate Openers: Explorations Transparencies.*

Segments and Rays

DEFINITION	NAME	DIAGRAM
A **segment**, or line segment, is the part of a line consisting	The two endpoints	

Draw and label each of the following.

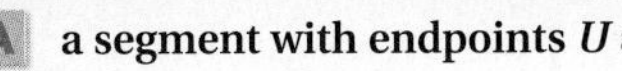

A a segment with endpoints *U* and *V*

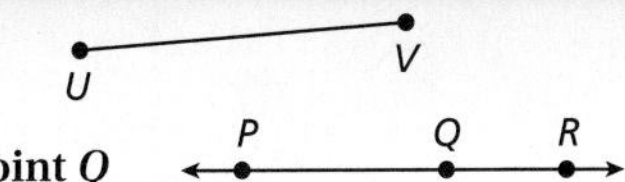

B opposite rays with a common endpoint *Q*

2. Draw and label a ray with endpoint *M* that contains *N*.

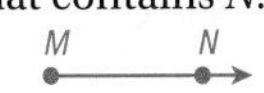

A **postulate**, or *axiom*, is a statement that is accepted as true without proof. Postulates about points, lines, and planes help describe geometric properties.

Postulates Points, Lines, and Planes

1-1-1 Through any two points there is exactly one line.

1-1-2 Through any three noncollinear points there is exactly one plane containing them.

1-1-3 If two points lie in a plane, then the line containing those points lies in the plane.

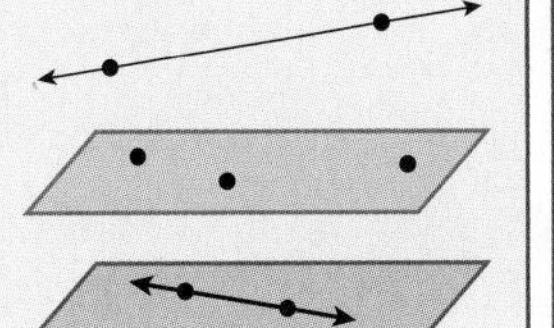

EXAMPLE 3 Identifying Points and Lines in a Plane

Name a line that passes through two points.

There is exactly one line *n* passing through *G* and *H*.

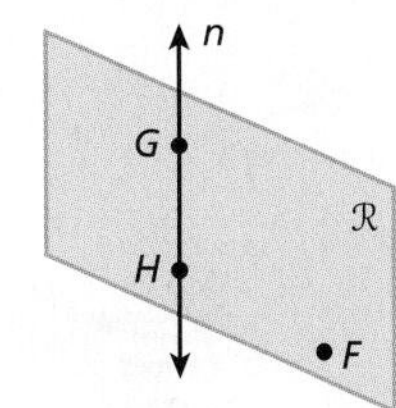

3. Name a plane that contains three noncollinear points. **Possible answer: plane *GHF***

Power Presentations with PowerPoint®

Additional Examples

Example 1

A. segment with endpoints *M* and *N*

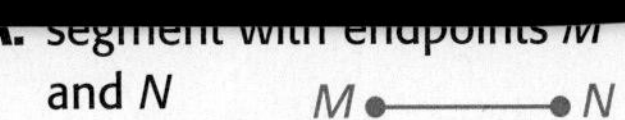

B. opposite rays with common endpoint *T*

Example 3

Name a line that passes through two points. $\overleftrightarrow{XY}$

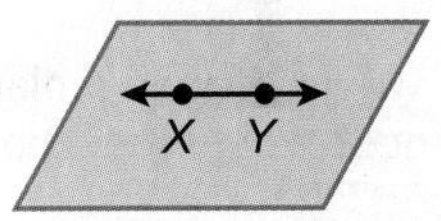

Teaching Tip **Reading Math** The phrase "exactly one" means that one exists and it is unique.

ENGLISH LANGUAGE LEARNERS

INTERVENTION 

Questioning Strategies

EXAMPLE 1

- What are the different ways you can name the planes represented in the stadium roof?
- How else could you name the lines?

EXAMPLE 2

- What figure is formed by two opposite rays? Is there a way to name the opposite rays? Give an example.

EXAMPLE 3

- Are there other ways to name the line determined by the points in the diagram? Explain.

2 Teach

Guided Instruction

Show students how to draw a plane. Discuss all the different ways of labeling a line, segment, ray, and plane. Explain that $\overrightarrow{CD}$ and $\overrightarrow{DC}$ are not the same ray.

Visual Point out to students that the diagrams of planes, lines, and rays extend forever, but we cannot draw them that way.

Reaching All Learners

Through Modeling

Have students work in small groups to use physical models, such as raw spaghetti and index cards, to illustrate Postulates 1-1-3, 1-1-4, and 1-1-5. Use contrasting colors of paper to emphasize the different planes in Postulate 1-1-5.

Power Presentations with PowerPoint®

Additional Examples

Example 4

A. Sketch two lines intersecting in exactly one point.

B. Sketch a figure that shows a line that lies in a plane.

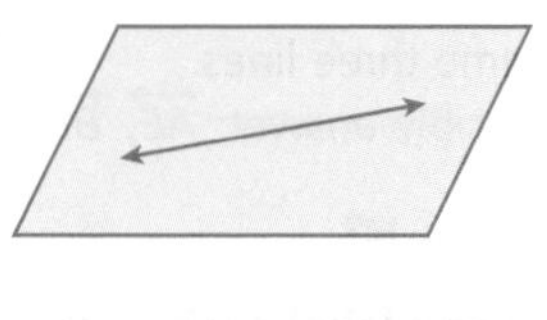

INTERVENTION

Questioning Strategies

EXAMPLE 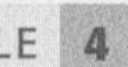

- Must any two planes intersect? Why or why not? Name planes in the classroom that support your answer.
- What would happen if planes were extended? Would they then all intersect?
- If a line lies in a plane, how many points of intersection do the line and the plane have?

Recall that a system of equations is a set of two or more equations containing two or more of the same variables. The coordinates of the solution of the system satisfy all equations in the system. These coordinates also locate the point where all the graphs of the equations in the system *intersect*.

An *intersection* is the set of all points that two or more figures have in common. The next two postulates describe intersections involving lines and planes.

Know it! Note

Postulates **Intersection of Lines and Planes**

1-1-4 If two lines intersect, then they intersect in exactly one point.

1-1-5 If two planes intersect, then they intersect in exactly one line.

Use a dashed line to show the hidden parts of any figure that you are drawing. A dashed line will indicate the part of the figure that is not seen.

EXAMPLE 4 Representing Intersections

Sketch a figure that shows each of the following.

A **A line intersects a plane, but does not lie in the plane.**

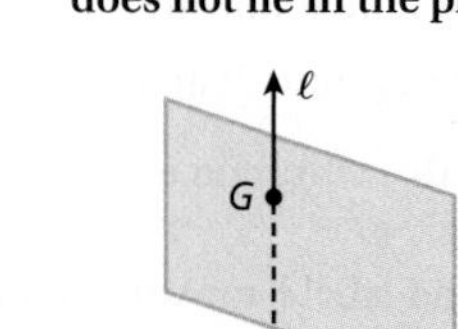

B **Two planes intersect in one line.**

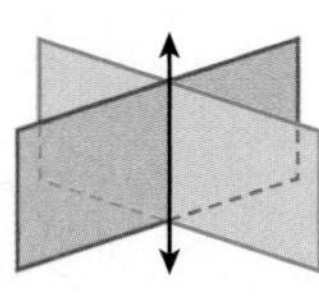

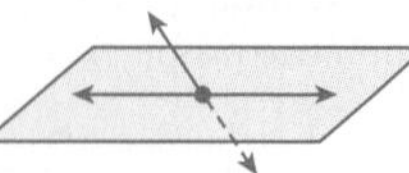

4. Sketch a figure that shows two lines intersect in one point in a plane, but only one of the lines lies in the plane.

THINK AND DISCUSS

1. Explain why any two points are collinear.

2. Which postulate explains the fact that two straight roads cannot cross each other more than once?

3. Explain why points and lines may be coplanar even when the plane containing them is not drawn.

4. Name all the possible lines, segments, and rays for the points *A* and *B*. Then give the maximum number of planes that can be determined by these points.

5. GET ORGANIZED Copy and complete the graphic organizer below. In each box, name, describe, and illustrate one of the undefined terms.

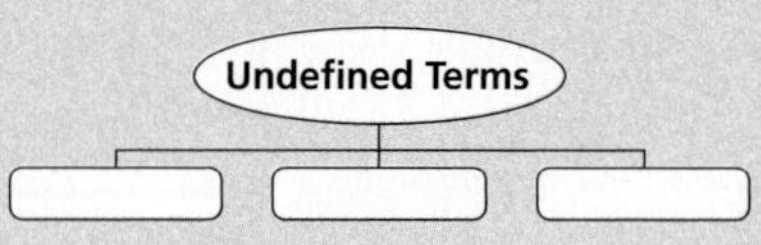

Undefined Terms

3 Close

Summarize

Ask students to name the different terms introduced in this lesson and write the notation for each. Give students the postulates with some missing words and ask them to fill in the blanks. Ask students to explain the meaning of the word *postulate*. to assume or claim as true

ONGOING ASSESSMENT and INTERVENTION 

Diagnose ***Before*** **the Lesson**
1-1 Warm Up, TE p. 6

Monitor ***During*** **the Lesson**
Check It Out! Exercises, SE pp. 6–8
Questioning Strategies, TE pp. 7–8

Assess ***After*** **the Lesson**
1-1 Lesson Quiz, TE p. 11
Alternative Assessment, TE p. 11

Answers to *Think and Discuss*

Possible answers:

1. By Post. 1-1-1, through any 2 pts. there is a line. Therefore any 2 pts. are collinear.
2. Post. 1-1-4
3. Any 3 noncollinear pts. determine a plane.
4. $\overleftrightarrow{AB}$, $\overline{AB}$, $\overrightarrow{AB}$, $\overrightarrow{BA}$; 0 planes
5. See p. A2.

go.hrw.com Homework Help Online

1-1 Exercises

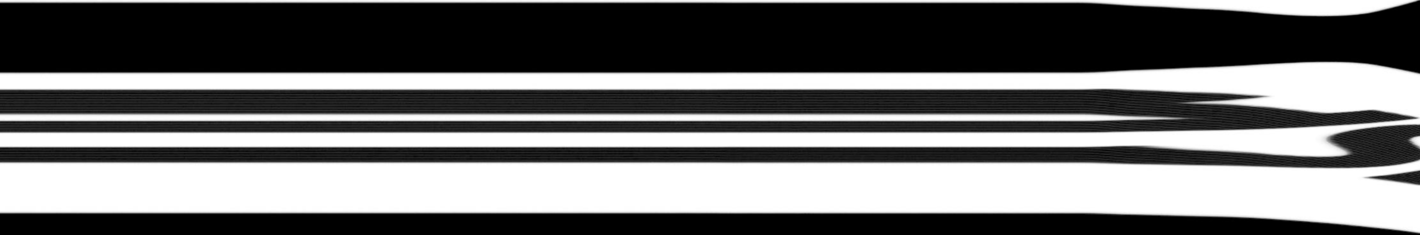

p. 7

9. a line that contains A and C $\overleftrightarrow{AB}$

10. a plane that contains A, D, and C Possible answer: plane ABD

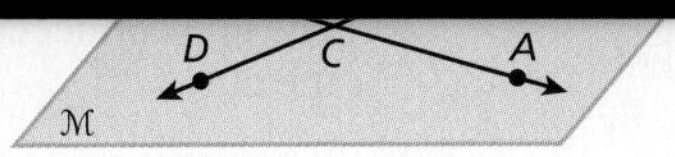

SEE EXAMPLE 4 p. 8

Sketch a figure that shows each of the following.

11. three coplanar lines that intersect in a common point

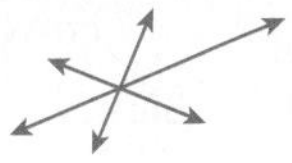

12. two lines that do not intersect

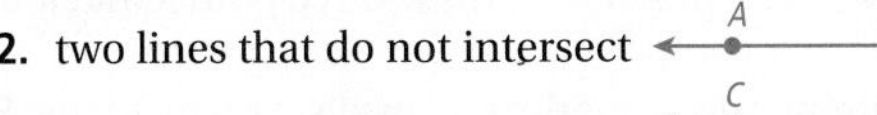

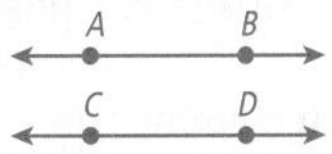

Teaching Tip **Communicating Math** In **Exercises 3–6,** students sometimes forget to place a symbol above the letters that are used to name lines, segments, and rays. Remind students that two letters without a symbol represent a distance.

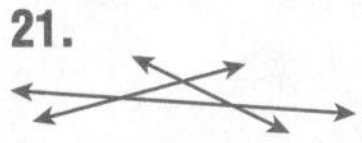

Homework Quick Check

Quickly check key concepts.
Exercises: 14–20 even, 24, 26, 28, 32

PRACTICE AND PROBLEM SOLVING

Independent Practice	
For Exercises	See Example
13–15	1
16–17	2
18–19	3
20–21	4

Extra Practice
Skills Practice p. S4
Application Practice p. S28

Use the figure to name each of the following.

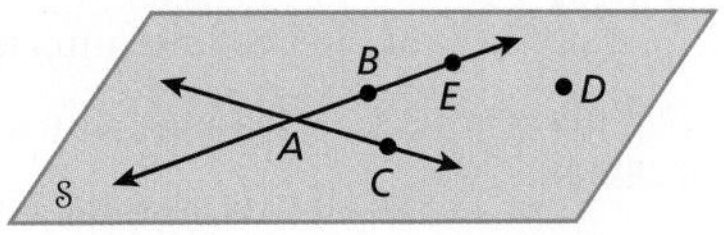

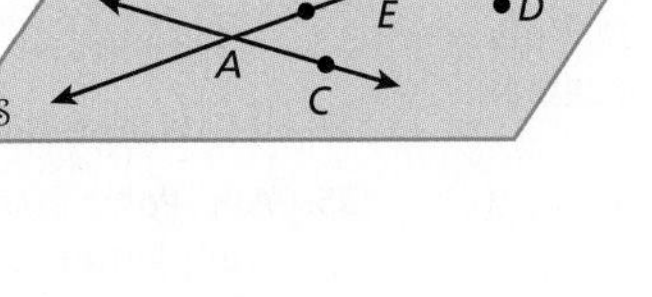

13. three collinear points B, E, A

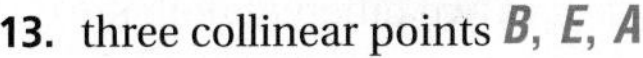

14. four coplanar points Possible answer: B, C, D, E

15. a plane containing E Possible answer: plane ABC

Draw and label each of the following.

16. a line containing X and Y

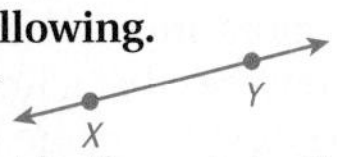

17. a pair of opposite rays that both contain R

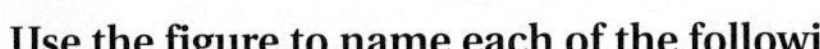

Use the figure to name each of the following.

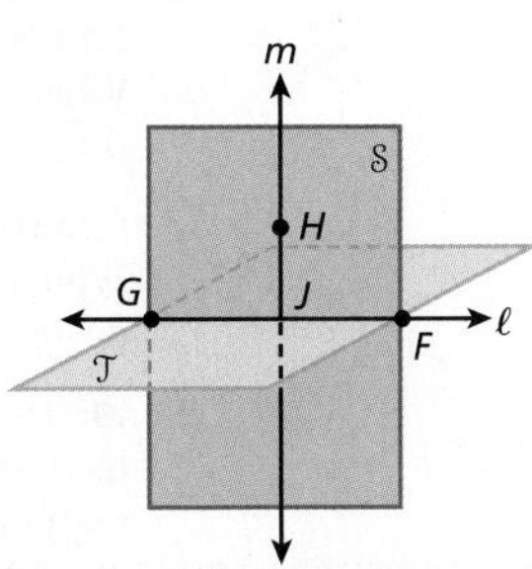

18. two points and a line that lie in plane $\mathcal{T}$ Possible answer: G, J, and ℓ

19. two planes that contain ℓ Possible answer: planes $\mathcal{T}$ and $\mathcal{S}$

Sketch a figure that shows each of the following.

20. a line that intersects two nonintersecting planes

21. three coplanar lines that intersect in three different points

20.

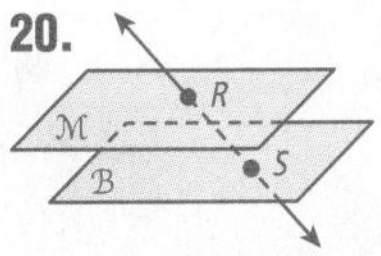

21.

State Resources

MULTI-STEP TEST PREP **Exercise 22** involves identifying geometric shapes at an archaeological site. This exercise prepares students for the Multi-Step Test Prep on page 34.

Teaching Tip **Visual** For **Exercise 36,** have students make an organized list of all the combinations of three points that could be chosen and then select those that are collinear.

Answers

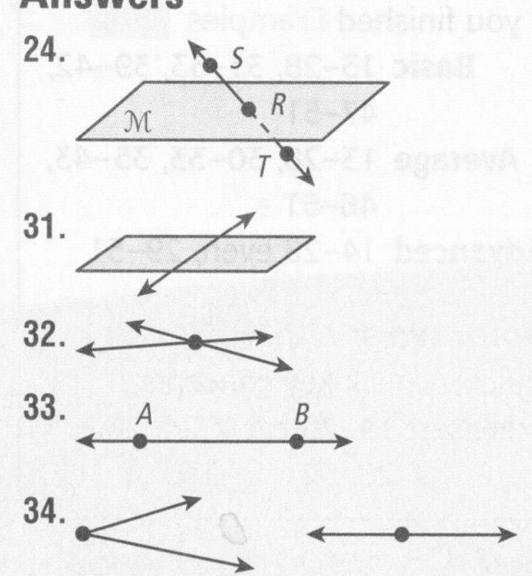

38. Lines may not intersect: 0 pts. of intersection.

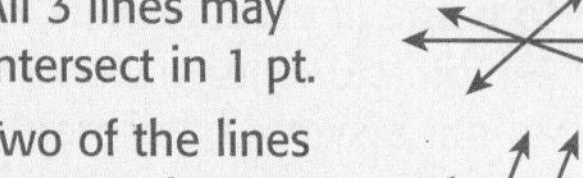

All 3 lines may intersect in 1 pt.

Two of the lines may not intersect, but they might each intersect a third line.

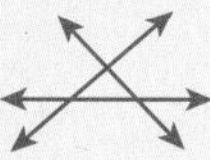

Each line may intersect each of the other lines.

MULTI-STEP TEST PREP

22. This problem will prepare you for the Multi-Step Test Prep on page 34. Name an object at the archaeological site shown that is represented by each of the following.
   a. a point
   b. a segment
   c. a plane

22. Possible answers:
a. tip of a stake
b. string
c. grid formed by string

28. If 2 pts. lie in a plane, then the line containing those pts. lies in the plane.

30. It is not possible. By Post. 1-1-2, any 3 noncollinear pts. are contained in a unique plane. If the 3 pts. are collinear, they are contained in infinitely many planes. In either case, the 3 pts. will be coplanar.

35. Post. 1-1-3

Draw each of the following.

23. plane $\mathcal{H}$ containing two lines that intersect at M
24. $\overleftrightarrow{ST}$ intersecting plane $\mathcal{M}$ at R

Use the figure to name each of the following.

25. the intersection of $\overleftrightarrow{TV}$ and $\overleftrightarrow{US}$ U
26. the intersection of $\overleftrightarrow{US}$ and plane $\mathcal{R}$ U
27. the intersection of $\overline{TU}$ and $\overline{UV}$ U

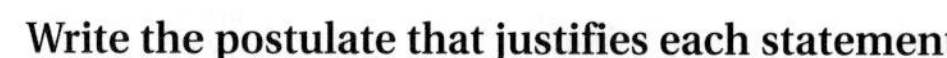

Write the postulate that justifies each statement.

28. The line connecting two dots on a sheet of paper lies on the same sheet of paper as the dots.
29. If two ants are walking in straight lines but in different directions, their paths cannot cross more than once. If 2 lines intersect, then they intersect in exactly 1 pt.
30. **Critical Thinking** Is it possible to draw three points that are noncoplanar? Explain.

S A N

Tell whether each statement is sometimes, always, or never true. Support your answer with a sketch.

31. If two planes intersect, they intersect in a straight line. A
32. If two lines intersect, they intersect at two different points. N
33. $\overleftrightarrow{AB}$ is another name for $\overleftrightarrow{BA}$. A
34. If two rays share a common endpoint, then they form a line. S
35. **Art** Pointillism is a technique in which tiny dots of complementary colors are combined to form a picture. Which postulate ensures that a line connecting two of these points also lies in the plane containing the points?
36. **Probability** Three of the labeled points are chosen at random. What is the probability that they are collinear? $\frac{1}{4}$

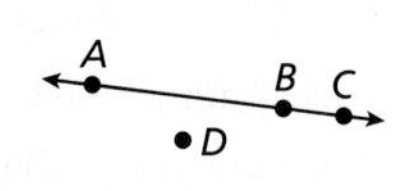

37. Campers often use a cooking stove with three legs. Which postulate explains why they might prefer this design to a stove that has four legs? Post. 1-1-2

38. **Write About It** Explain why three coplanar lines may have zero, one, two, or three points of intersection. Support your answer with a sketch.

1-1 PRACTICE A

1-1 PRACTICE C

1-1 PRACTICE B

Use the figure for Exercises 1–7.

1. Name a plane. Possible answer: plane BCD
2. Name a segment. $\overline{BD}$, $\overline{BC}$, $\overline{BE}$, or $\overline{CE}$
3. Name a line. Possible answer: $\overleftrightarrow{EC}$
4. Name three collinear points. points B, C, and E
5. Name three noncollinear points. Possible answer: points B, C, and D
6. Name the intersection of a line and a segment not on the line. point B
7. Name a pair of opposite rays. $\overrightarrow{BC}$ and $\overrightarrow{BE}$

Use the figure for Exercises 8–11.

8. Name the points that determine plane $\mathcal{R}$. points X, Y, and Z
9. Name the point at which line m intersects plane $\mathcal{R}$. point Z
10. Name two lines in plane $\mathcal{R}$ that intersect line m. $\overleftrightarrow{XZ}$ and $\overleftrightarrow{YZ}$
11. Name a line in plane $\mathcal{R}$ that does not intersect line m. $\overleftrightarrow{XY}$

Draw your answers in the space provided.

Michelle Kwan won a bronze medal in figure skating at the 2002 Salt Lake City Winter Olympic Games.

12. Michelle skates straight ahead from point L and stops at point M. Draw her path.
13. Michelle skates straight ahead from point L and continues through point M. Name a figure that represents her path. Draw her path. ray
14. Michelle and her friend Alexei start back to back at point L and skate in opposite directions. Michelle skates through point M, and Alexei skates through point K. Draw their paths.

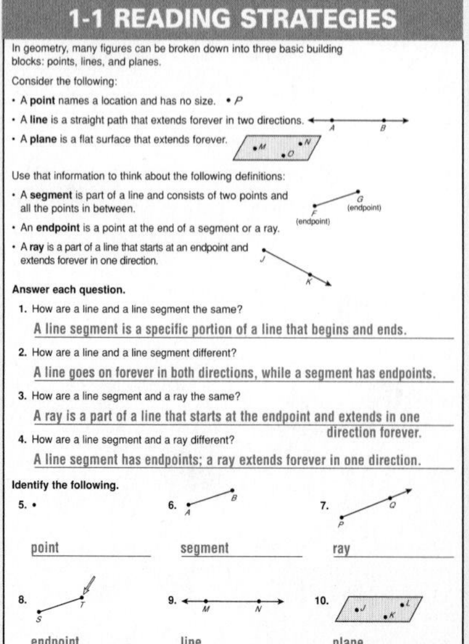

1-1 READING STRATEGIES

In geometry, many figures can be broken down into three basic building blocks: points, lines, and planes.

Consider the following:

- A **point** names a location and has no size. • P
- A **line** is a straight path that extends forever in two directions.
- A **plane** is a flat surface that extends forever.

Use that information to think about the following definitions:

- A **segment** is part of a line and consists of two points and all the points in between.
- An **endpoint** is a point at the end of a segment or a ray.
- A **ray** is a part of a line that starts at an endpoint and extends forever in one direction.

Answer each question.

1. How are a line and a line segment the same?
   A line segment is a specific portion of a line that begins and ends.
2. How are a line and a line segment different?
   A line goes on forever in both directions, while a segment has endpoints.
3. How are a line segment and a ray the same?
   A ray is a part of a line that starts at the endpoint and extends in one direction forever.
4. How are a line segment and a ray different?
   A line segment has endpoints; a ray extends forever in one direction.

Identify the following.

5. point
6. segment
7. ray
8. endpoint
9. line
10. plane

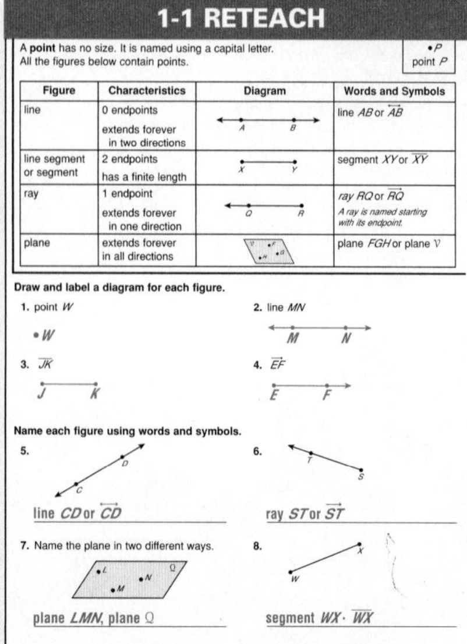

1-1 RETEACH

A **point** has no size. It is named using a capital letter. All the figures below contain points. • P point P

Figure	Characteristics	Diagram	Words and Symbols
line	0 endpoints; extends forever in two directions		line AB or $\overleftrightarrow{AB}$
line segment or segment	2 endpoints; has a finite length		segment XY or $\overline{XY}$
ray	1 endpoint; extends forever in one direction		ray RQ or $\overrightarrow{RQ}$; *A ray is named starting with its endpoint.*
plane	extends forever in all directions		plane FGH or plane $\mathcal{V}$

Draw and label a diagram for each figure.

1. point W
2. line MN
3. $\overline{JK}$
4. $\overrightarrow{EF}$

Name each figure using words and symbols.

5. line CD or $\overleftrightarrow{CD}$
6. ray ST or $\overrightarrow{ST}$
7. Name the plane in two different ways. plane LMN, plane $\mathcal{Q}$
8. segment $WX \cdot \overline{WX}$

TEST PREP

39. Which of the following is a set of noncollinear points?

(A) P, R, T (C) P, Q, R

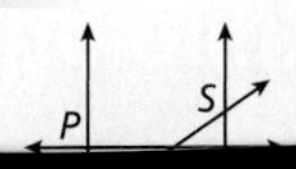

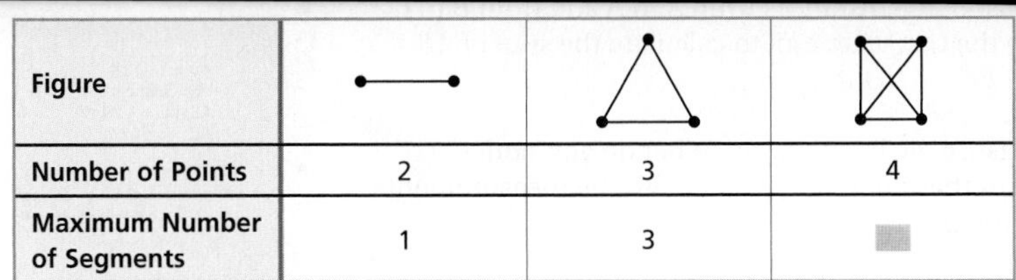

Figure	●—●	triangle	square with diagonals
Number of Points	2	3	4
Maximum Number of Segments	1	3	■

43. What is the maximum number of segments determined by 4 points? **6**

44. **Multi-Step** Extend the table. What is the maximum number of segments determined by 10 points? **45**

$\frac{n(n-1)}{2}$ 45. Write a formula for the maximum number of segments determined by n points.

46. **Critical Thinking** Explain how rescue teams could use two of the postulates from this lesson to locate a distress signal.

SPIRAL REVIEW

47. The combined age of a mother and her twin daughters is 58 years. The mother was 25 years old when the twins were born. Write and solve an equation to find the age of each of the three people. *(Previous course)* **Mother is 36; twins are 11.**

Determine whether each set of ordered pairs is a function. *(Previous course)*

48. $\{(0, 1), (1, -1), (5, -1), (-1, 2)\}$ **yes**

49. $\{(3, 8), (10, 6), (9, 8), (10, -6)\}$ **no**

Find the mean, median, and mode for each set of data. *(Previous course)*

50. 0, 6, 1, 3, 5, 2, 7, 10
mean: 4.25; median: 4; mode: none

51. 0.47, 0.44, 0.4, 0.46, 0.44
mean: 0.442; median: 0.44; mode: 0.44

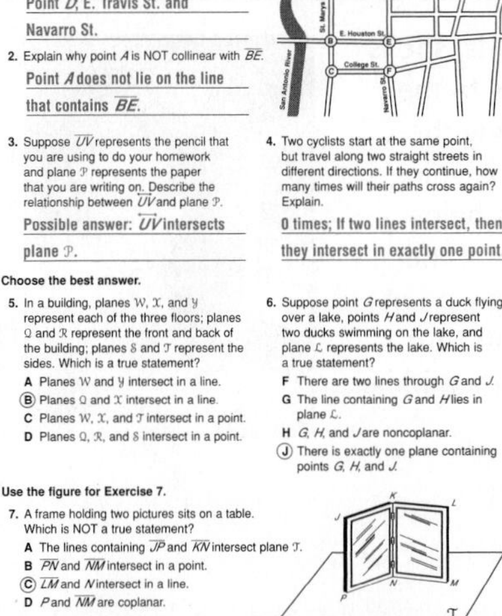

1-1 PROBLEM SOLVING

Use the map of part of San Antonio for Exercises 1 and 2.

1. Name a point that appears to be collinear with $\overline{EF}$. Which streets intersect at this point?
Point D, E. Travis St. and Navarro St.

2. Explain why point A is NOT collinear with $\overline{BE}$.
Point A does not lie on the line that contains $\overline{BE}$.

3. Suppose $\overline{UV}$ represents the pencil that you are using to do your homework and plane $\mathcal{P}$ represents the paper that you are writing on. Describe the relationship between $\overleftrightarrow{UV}$ and plane $\mathcal{P}$.
Possible answer: $\overleftrightarrow{UV}$ intersects plane $\mathcal{P}$.

4. Two cyclists start at the same point, but travel along two straight streets in different directions. If they continue, how many times will their paths cross again? Explain.
0 times; If two lines intersect, then they intersect in exactly one point.

Choose the best answer.

5. In a building, planes $\mathcal{W}$, $\mathcal{X}$, and $\mathcal{Y}$ represent each of the three floors; planes $\mathcal{Q}$ and $\mathcal{R}$ represent the front and back of the building; planes $\mathcal{S}$ and $\mathcal{T}$ represent the sides. Which is a true statement?
A Planes $\mathcal{W}$ and $\mathcal{Y}$ intersect in a line.
(B) Planes $\mathcal{Q}$ and $\mathcal{X}$ intersect in a line.
C Planes $\mathcal{W}$, $\mathcal{X}$, and $\mathcal{T}$ intersect in a point.
D Planes $\mathcal{Q}$, $\mathcal{R}$, and $\mathcal{S}$ intersect in a point.

6. Suppose point G represents a duck flying over a lake, points H and J represent two ducks swimming on the lake, and plane $\mathcal{L}$ represents the lake. Which is a true statement?
F There are two lines through G and J.
G The line containing G and H lies in plane $\mathcal{L}$.
H G, H, and J are noncoplanar.
(J) There is exactly one plane containing points G, H, and J.

Use the figure for Exercise 7.

7. A frame holding two pictures sits on a table. Which is NOT a true statement?
A The lines containing $\overline{JP}$ and $\overline{KN}$ intersect plane $\mathcal{T}$.
B $\overline{PN}$ and $\overline{NM}$ intersect in a point.
(C) $\overline{LM}$ and N intersect in a line.
D P and $\overline{NM}$ are coplanar.

Answers

46. Rescue teams can use the principles of Post. 1-1-1 and Post. 1-1-4. A distress signal is received by 2 rescue teams. By Post. 1-1-1, 2 pts. determine a line. So 2 lines are created by the 3 pts., the locations of the rescue teams and the distress signal. By Post. 1-1-4, the intersection of the 2 lines will be the location of the distress signal.

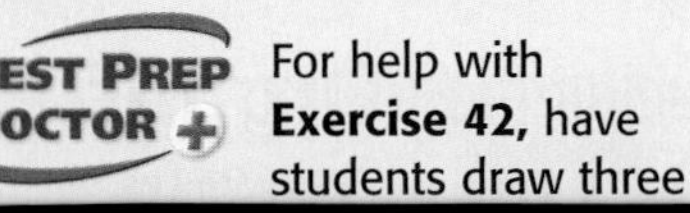

TEST PREP DOCTOR

For help with **Exercise 42,** have students draw three

ALTERNATIVE ASSESSMENT

Have students make physical models using straw and clay, or gumdrops and marshmallows with toothpicks, to illustrate the postulates in this lesson. Have them explain their models.

Power Presentations with PowerPoint®

1-1 Lesson Quiz

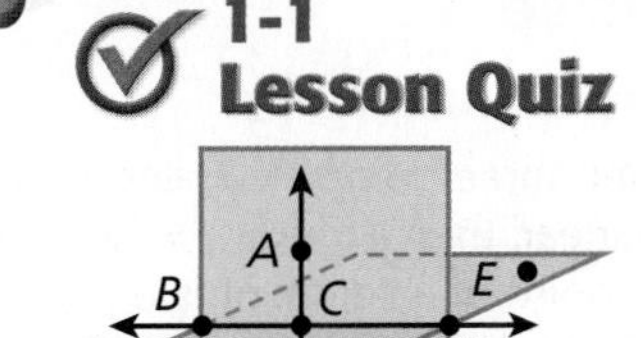

Name each of the following.

1. two opposite rays $\overrightarrow{CB}$ and $\overrightarrow{CD}$
2. a point on $\overrightarrow{BC}$
Possible answer: D
3. the intersection of plane $\mathcal{N}$ and plane $\mathcal{T}$
Possible answer: $\overleftrightarrow{BD}$
4. a plane containing E, D, and B
plane $\mathcal{T}$

Draw each of the following.

5. a line intersecting a plane at one point

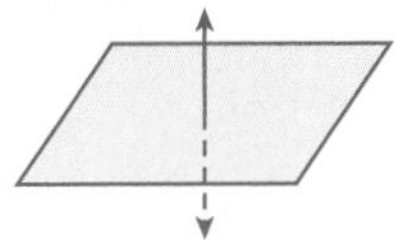
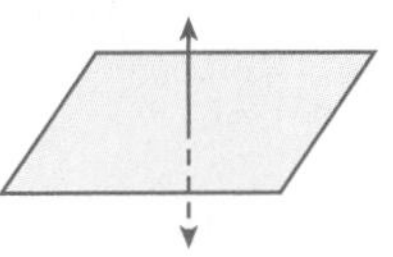

6. a ray with endpoint P that passes through Q

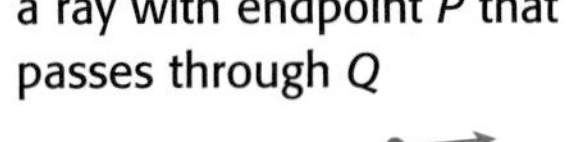

Also available on transparency

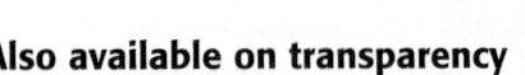

Technology Lab Organizer

Use with Lesson 1-2

Pacing:

Traditional $\frac{1}{2}$ day

Block $\frac{1}{4}$ day

Objective: Use geometry software to measure distances and explore properties of points on segments.

Materials: geometry software

Online Edition
TechKeys

Countdown Week 1

Resources

Technology Lab Activities
1-2 Lab Recording Sheet

Teach

Discuss

Emphasize that there are infinitely many points on a line segment between its endpoints, but only one of these points is the midpoint.

Close

Key Concept

When three points *A*, *B*, and *C* are collinear, then $AB + BC = AC$. The midpoint of a segment is equidistant from each endpoint.

Assessment

Journal Have students summarize how they determine, given three collinear points, if the point between the endpoints is the midpoint. Then have them support their answer with a sketch.

State Resources

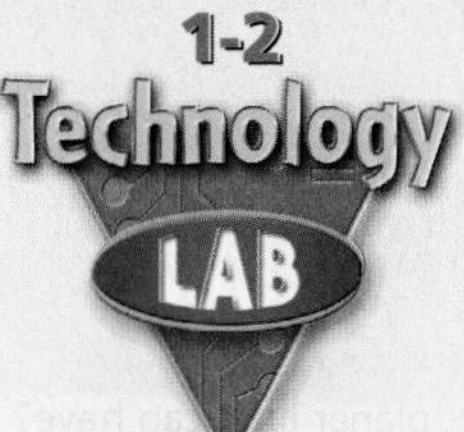

Use with Lesson 1-2

Explore Properties Associated with Points

The two endpoints of a segment determine its length. Other points on the segment are *between* the endpoints. Only one of these points is the *midpoint* of the segment. In this lab, you will use geometry software to measure lengths of segments and explore properties of points on segments.

go.hrw.com
Lab Resources Online
KEYWORD: MG7 Lab1

Activity

1. Construct a segment and label its endpoints *A* and *C*.
2. Create point *B* on $\overline{AC}$.
3. Measure the distances from *A* to *B* and from *B* to *C*. Use the Calculate tool to calculate the sum of *AB* and *BC*.

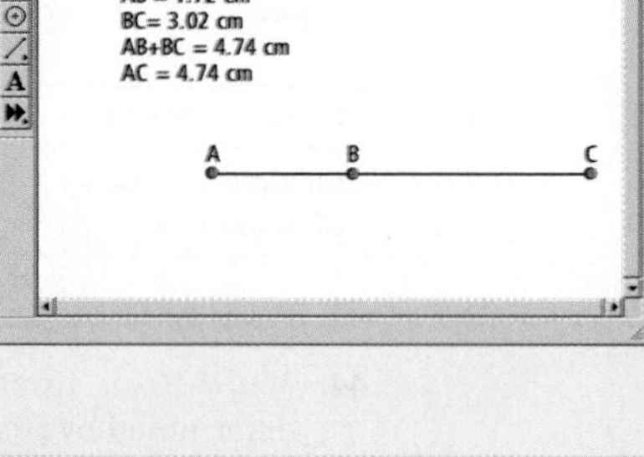

4. Measure the length of $\overline{AC}$. What do you notice about this length compared with the measurements found in Step 3?
5. Drag point *B* along $\overline{AC}$. Drag one of the endpoints of $\overline{AC}$. What relationships do you think are true about the three measurements?
6. Construct the midpoint of $\overline{AC}$ and label it *M*.
7. Measure $\overline{AM}$ and $\overline{MC}$. What relationships do you think are true about the lengths of $\overline{AC}$, $\overline{AM}$, and $\overline{MC}$? Use the Calculate tool to confirm your findings.
8. How many midpoints of $\overline{AC}$ exist?

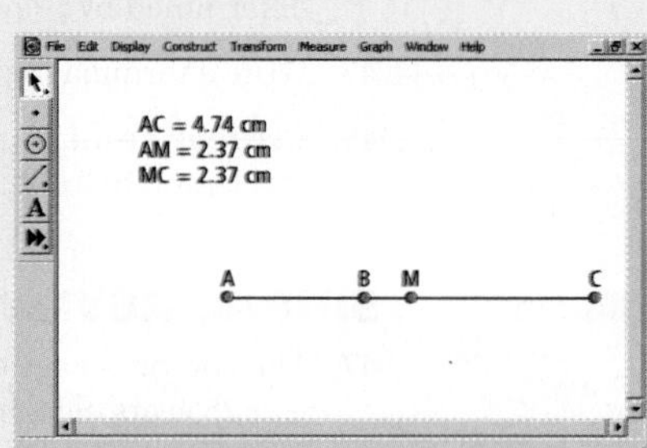

Try This

1. Repeat the activity with a new segment. Drag each of the points in your figure (the endpoints, the point on the segment, and the midpoint). Write down any relationships you observe about the measurements. **Check students' work.**
2. Create a point *D* not on $\overline{AC}$. Measure $\overline{AD}$, $\overline{DC}$, and $\overline{AC}$. Does $AD + DC = AC$? What do you think has to be true about *D* for the relationship to always be true? **No; *D* must be between *A* and *C*.**

Teacher to Teacher

To introduce the concept of midpoint, I like to tell the following riddle to the class.

Q: A hunter walks into the woods and keeps walking in the same direction. At what point does the hunter begin to leave the woods?

A: The midpoint.

Then I can explain to students that once the hunter is halfway through the woods, she is as close to the end as to the beginning. After passing the midpoint, the hunter is going out instead of in. This helps students remember that the midpoint is not just any point between the endpoints, but exactly one point in the middle.

Teresa Salas
Corpus Christi, TX

1-2 Measuring and Constructing Segments

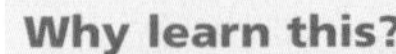

Objectives

Use length and midpoint of a segment.

Construct midpoints and congruent segments.

Vocabulary

coordinate
distance
length
congruent segments
construction
between
midpoint
bisect
segment bisector

Why learn this?

You can measure a segment to c... distance between two loc... race are used to show... stations on the cours...

A ruler can be used to meas... two points. A point correspon... only one number on the ruler. T... is called a **coordinate** . The followin... postulate summarizes this concept.

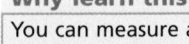

Postulate 1-2-1 Ruler Postulate

The points on a line can be put into a one-to-one correspondence with the real numbers.

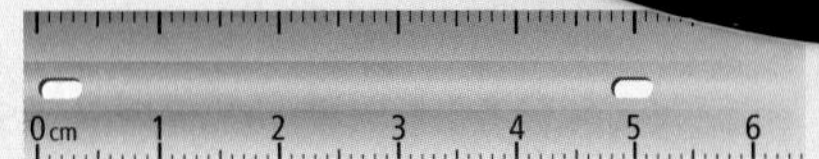

The **distance** between any two points is the absolute value of the difference of the coordinates. If the coordinates of points A and B are a and b, then the distance between A and B is $|a - b|$ or $|b - a|$. The distance between A and B is also called the **length** of $\overline{AB}$, or AB.

$$AB = |a - b| = |b - a|$$

EXAMPLE 1 Finding the Length of a Segment

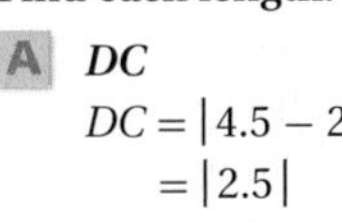

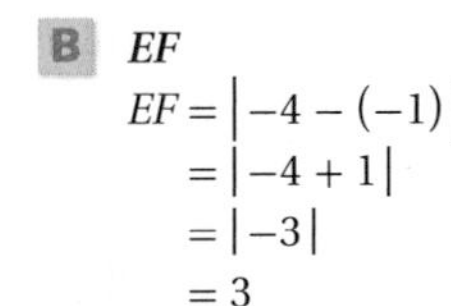

Find each length.

A DC

$DC = |4.5 - 2|$
$= |2.5|$
$= 2.5$

B EF

$EF = |-4 - (-1)|$
$= |-4 + 1|$
$= |-3|$
$= 3$

CHECK IT OUT! Find each length.

1a. XY $3\frac{1}{2}$

1b. XZ $4\frac{1}{2}$

Caution!

PQ represents a number, while $\overline{PQ}$ represents a geometric figure. Be sure to use equality for numbers ($PQ = RS$) and congruence for figures ($\overline{PQ} \cong \overline{RS}$).

Congruent segments are segments that have the same length. In the diagram, $PQ = RS$, so you can write $\overline{PQ} \cong \overline{RS}$. This is read as "segment PQ is congruent to segment RS." *Tick marks* are used in a figure to show congruent segments.

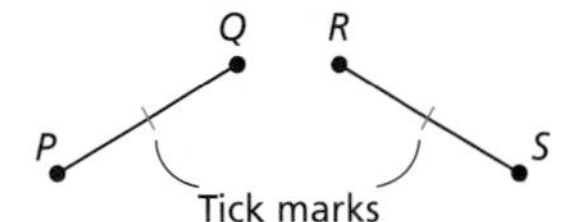

1-2 Organizer

Pacing: Traditional $\frac{1}{2}$ day

Power Presentations with PowerPoint®

Warm Up

Simplify.

1. $7 - (-3)$ 10
2. $-1 - (-13)$ 12
3. $|-7 - 1|$ 8

Solve each equation.

4. $2x + 3 = 9x - 11$ 2
5. $3x = 4x - 5$ 5
6. How many real numbers are there between $\frac{1}{2}$ and $\frac{3}{4}$? infinitely many

Also available on transparency

Math Humor

Carpenter 1: Why did you leave your tape measure in the truck?

Carpenter 2: Because we're entering a construction zone.

1 Introduce

EXPLORATION

1-2 Measuring and Constructing Segments

Use geometry software or a ruler for the following Exploration.

1. Draw $\overline{AC}$. Then place B on the segment between A and C.
2. Measure $\overline{AB}$, $\overline{BC}$, and $\overline{AC}$ in inches. Then measure each segment in centimeters and millimeters. Record the lengths in a table like the one shown.

Unit	Length of $\overline{AB}$	Length of $\overline{BC}$	Length of $\overline{AC}$
Inch			
Centimeter			
Millimeter			

THINK AND DISCUSS

3. **Describe** the relationship among the lengths of $\overline{AB}$, $\overline{BC}$, and $\overline{AC}$. Is this relationship the same no matter what measurement unit you use?
4. **Discuss** what would happen if you located D between A and B. What would be the relationship among the lengths of $\overline{AD}$, $\overline{DB}$, $\overline{BC}$, and $\overline{AC}$?

Motivate

Show students a road map. Ask them to locate a place that is midway between two other places. Ask questions about distance between locations on a straight road. "Suppose you are driving to a relative's house. The only place to stop for food is 75 miles from home, and it is $\frac{1}{3}$ of the total trip. How far from the food stop does your relative live?" 150 mi

Explorations and answers are provided in *Alternate Openers: Explorations Transparencies.*

State Resources

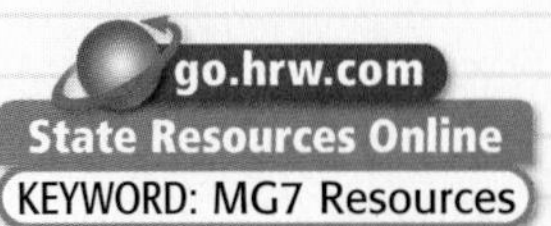

Power Presentations with PowerPoint®

Additional Examples

Example 1

Find each length.

A. BC 2 **B.** AC 5

INTERVENTION

Questioning Strategies

EXAMPLE 1

- To find the length of a segment, why do you subtract the coordinates instead of adding them?
- What equation can you create using BC, AC, and AB?

Construction

Discuss techniques to make an accurate construction, including using a sharp pencil, lining up the compass tip and the pencil tip, and being sure the compass stays the same size.

Teaching Tip **Communicating Math** Have students look up the word *between* in the dictionary and compare that definition with the mathematical definition. Emphasize that the mathematical definition of *between* includes collinearity.

ENGLISH LANGUAGE LEARNERS

Teaching Tip **Critical Thinking** Point out that just as there are infinitely many real numbers between any two real numbers, there are infinitely many points between any two points on a line.

You can make a sketch or measure and draw a segment. These may not be exact. A **construction** is a way of creating a figure that is more precise. One way to make a geometric construction is to use a compass and straightedge.

Construction Congruent Segment

Construct a segment congruent to $\overline{AB}$.

1

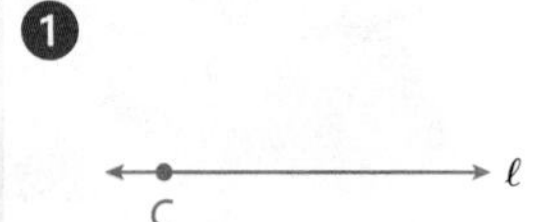

Draw ℓ. Choose a point on ℓ and label it C.

2

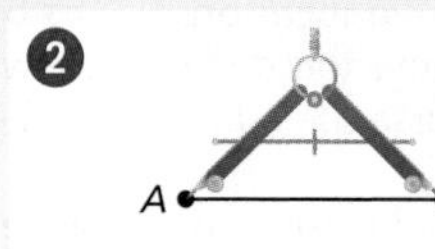

Open the compass to distance AB.

3

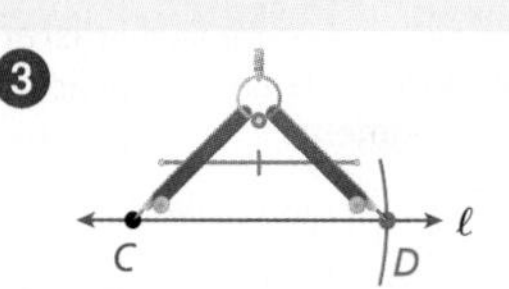

Place the point of the compass at C and make an arc through ℓ. Find the point where the arc and ℓ intersect and label it D.

$\overline{CD} \cong \overline{AB}$

EXAMPLE 2 Copying a Segment

Sketch, draw, and construct a segment congruent to $\overline{MN}$.

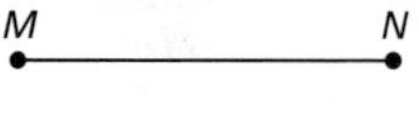

Step 1 Estimate and sketch.
Estimate the length of $\overline{MN}$ and sketch $\overline{PQ}$ approximately the same length.

Step 2 Measure and draw.
Use a ruler to measure $\overline{MN}$. MN appears to be 3.1 cm. Use a ruler and draw $\overline{XY}$ to have length 3.1 cm.

Step 3 Construct and compare.
Use a compass and straightedge to construct $\overline{ST}$ congruent to $\overline{MN}$.

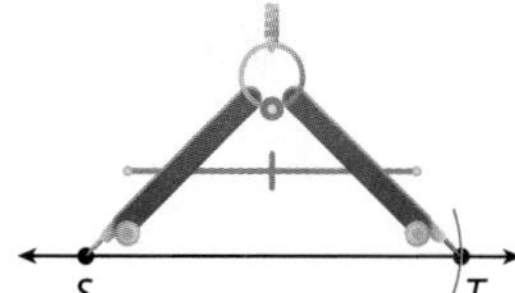

A ruler shows that $\overline{PQ}$ and $\overline{XY}$ are approximately the same length as $\overline{MN}$, but $\overline{ST}$ is precisely the same length.

2. Sketch, draw, and construct a segment congruent to $\overline{JK}$.

Check students' work.

In order for you to say that a point B is **between** two points A and C, all three of the points must lie on the same line, and $AB + BC = AC$.

Postulate 1-2-2 Segment Addition Postulate

If B is between A and C, then $AB + BC = AC$.

A B C

2 Teach

Guided Instruction

Discuss how to read PQ, $\overleftrightarrow{PQ}$, and $\overline{PQ}$. Ask students to explain the Ruler Postulate in their own words. Stress that $CD = DC$, and that distances can never be negative. Have students dramatize Postulate 1-2-2. Locate three students as A, B, and C on a line in the classroom. Then ask one of the students to move off the line to illustrate when one point is not *between* the other two. Find distances between points by counting floor tiles or paces, or by using a meterstick.

Reaching All Learners

Through Concrete Manipulatives

Have students use masking tape or draw a long number line, either on their notebook paper or on a long piece of butcher paper taped to the floor. Give them small plastic disks to put on their number lines to represent points. They can then use these to count the spaces between the points.

EXAMPLE 3 Using the Segment Addition Postulate

x^2y Algebra

A **B is between A and C, $AC = 14$, and $BC = 11.4$. Find AB.**

$AC = AB + BC$	*Seg. Add. Post.*
$14 = AB + 11.4$	*Substitute 14 for AC and 11.4 for BC.*
$-11.4 \quad -11.4$	*Subtract 11.4 from both sides.*
$2.6 = AB$	*Simplify.*

B **S is between R and T. Find RT.**

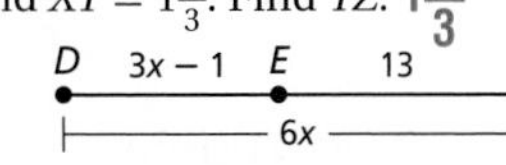

$RT = RS + ST$	*Seg. Add. Post.*
$4x = (2x + 7) + 28$	*Substitute the given values.*
$4x = 2x + 35$	*Simplify.*
$-2x \quad -2x$	*Subtract 2x from both sides.*
$2x = 35$	*Simplify.*
$\frac{2x}{2} = \frac{35}{2}$	*Divide both sides by 2.*
$x = \frac{35}{2}$, or 17.5	*Simplify.*
$RT = 4x$	
$= 4(17.5) = 70$	*Substitute 17.5 for x.*

CHECK IT OUT!

3a. Y is between X and Z, $XZ = 3$, and $XY = 1\frac{1}{3}$. Find YZ. $1\frac{2}{3}$

3b. E is between D and F. Find DF. **24**

The **midpoint** M of $\overline{AB}$ is the point that **bisects**, or divides, the segment into two congruent segments. If M is the midpoint of $\overline{AB}$, then $AM = MB$. So if $AB = 6$, then $AM = 3$ and $MB = 3$.

EXAMPLE 4 *Recreation Application*

x^2y Algebra

The map shows the route for a race. You are 365 m from drink station R and 2 km from drink station S. The first-aid station is located at the midpoint of the two drink stations. How far are you from the first-aid station?

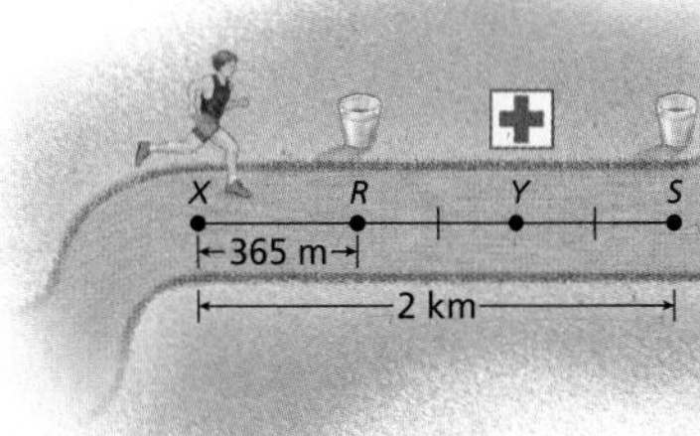

Let your current location be X and the location of the first-aid station be Y.

$XR + RS = XS$	*Seg. Add. Post.*
$365 + RS = 2000$	*Substitute 365 for XR and 2000 for XS.*
$-365 \quad -365$	*Subtract 365 from both sides.*
$RS = 1635$	*Simplify.*
$RY = 817.5$	*Y is the mdpt. of $\overline{RS}$, so $RY = \frac{1}{2}RS$.*
$XY = XR + RY$	
$= 365 + 817.5 = 1182.5$ m	*Substitute 365 for XR and 817.5 for RY.*

You are 1182.5 m from the first-aid station.

CHECK IT OUT!

4. What is the distance to a drink station located at the midpoint between your current location and the first-aid station? **591.25 m**

Teaching Tip **Communicating Math** Help students understand that when numbers represent measurements of physical quantities, they must be accompanied by a unit. For example, in Example 4, if you only wrote 1182.5 as the answer, you would not know if the answer is 1182.5 km or 1182.5 m. You must use a unit to best communicate your answer.

When solving equations as in **Examples 3** and **4,** students sometimes forget to do the inverse operation. Review inverse operations if necessary.

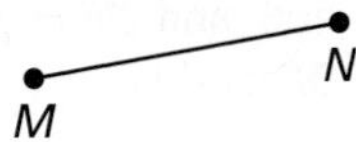

Additional Examples

Example 2

Sketch, draw, and construct a segment congruent to $\overline{MN}$.

Check students' drawings and constructions. The segment should be approximately $1\frac{1}{4}$ in.

Example 3

A. G is between F and H, $FG = 6$, and $FH = 11$. Find GH. 5

B. M is between N and O. Find NO. 27

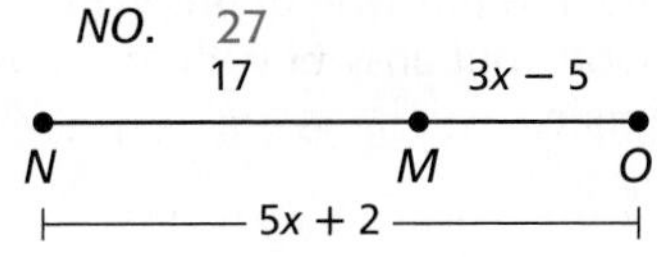

Example 4

The map shows the route for a race. You are at X, 6000 ft from the first checkpoint C. The second checkpoint D is located at the midpoint between C and the end of the race Y. The total race is 3 miles. How far apart are the 2 checkpoints? 4920 feet

5280

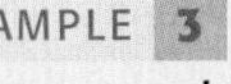

INTERVENTION

Questioning Strategies

EXAMPLE 2

- How are drawing and constructing different? How are they alike? Which is more accurate?

EXAMPLE 3

- Do you need to know that one of the points is between the other two? Why or why not?

EXAMPLE 4

- If you are given the midpoint and one endpoint of a segment, what three distances do you know?

Construction

Give each student a ruler. These can be found in the Manipulatives Kit **(MK)**. Use paper other than patty paper and have students bend the line over the ruler. Then fold the paper along the line. Fold the paper end to end to locate the midpoint.

Power Presentations with PowerPoint®

Additional Examples

Example 5

D is the midpoint of *EF*, $ED = 4x + 6$, and $DF = 7x - 9$. Find *ED*, *DF*, and *EF*. 26; 26; 52

INTERVENTION

Questioning Strategies

EXAMPLE 5

- Is it possible for *x* to be a negative number in this type of problem? Support your answer with an example.

A **segment bisector** is any ray, segment, or line that intersects a segment at its midpoint. It divides the segment into two equal parts at its midpoint.

Construction Segment Bisector

1

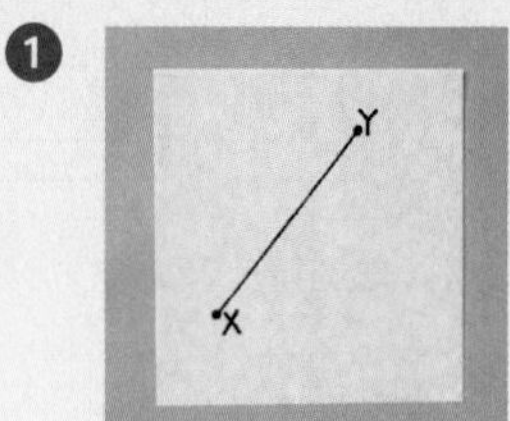

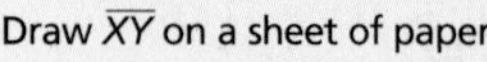

Draw $\overline{XY}$ on a sheet of paper.

2

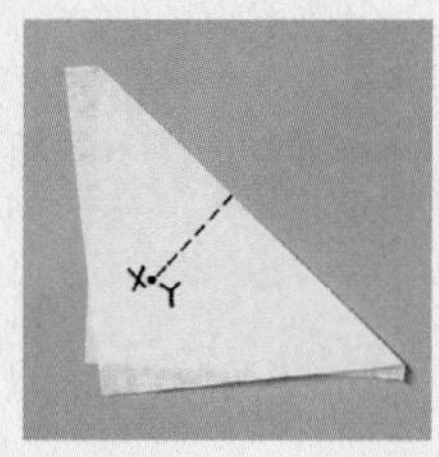

Fold the paper so that *Y* is on top of *X*.

3

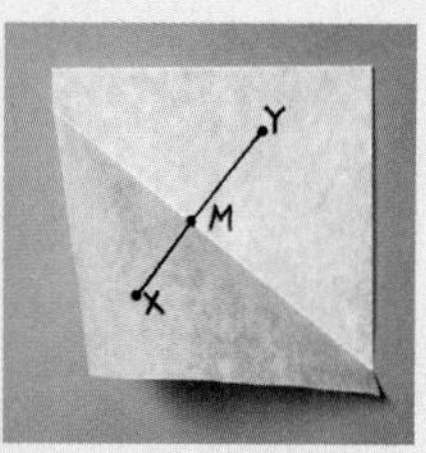

Unfold the paper. The line represented by the crease bisects $\overline{XY}$. Label the midpoint *M*.

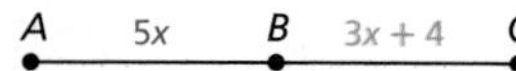

$XM = MY$

EXAMPLE 5 Using Midpoints to Find Lengths

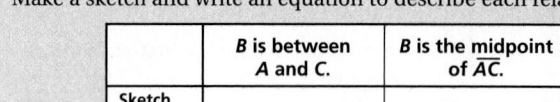

Algebra

B is the midpoint of $\overline{AC}$, $AB = 5x$, and $BC = 3x + 4$. Find AB, BC, and AC.

Step 1 Solve for *x*.

$AB = BC$	*B is the mdpt. of $\overline{AC}$.*
$5x = 3x + 4$	*Substitute 5x for AB and 3x + 4 for BC.*
$-3x \quad -3x$	*Subtract 3x from both sides.*
$2x = 4$	*Simplify.*
$\frac{2x}{2} = \frac{4}{2}$	*Divide both sides by 2.*
$x = 2$	*Simplify.*

Step 2 Find *AB*, *BC*, and *AC*.

$AB = 5x = 5(2) = 10$ $\quad BC = 3x + 4 = 3(2) + 4 = 10$ $\quad AC = AB + BC = 10 + 10 = 20$

CHECK IT OUT!

5. *S* is the midpoint of *RT*, $RS = -2x$, and $ST = -3x - 2$. Find *RS*, *ST*, and *RT*. $RS = 4$; $ST = 4$; $RT = 8$

THINK AND DISCUSS

1. Suppose *R* is the midpoint of $\overline{ST}$. Explain how *SR* and *ST* are related.

Know it! Note

2. GET ORGANIZED Copy and complete the graphic organizer. Make a sketch and write an equation to describe each relationship.

	B is between *A* and *C*.	*B* is the midpoint of $\overline{AC}$.
Sketch		
Equation		

3 Close

Summarize

Review the Segment Addition Postulate, emphasizing that betweenness involves collinearity. Remind students that a segment has exactly one midpoint. Review the steps used to construct a segment congruent to a given segment.

ONGOING ASSESSMENT and INTERVENTION

Diagnose **Before** the Lesson
1-2 Warm Up, TE p. 13

Monitor **During** the Lesson
Check It Out! Exercises, SE pp. 13–16
Questioning Strategies, TE pp. 14–16

Assess **After** the Lesson
1-2 Lesson Quiz, TE p. 19
Alternative Assessment, TE p. 19

Answers to *Think and Discuss*

1. Since *R* is the mdpt. of $\overline{ST}$, you know $SR = RT$. Also, $ST = SR + RT$. By subst., $ST = SR + SR = 2SR$. So *ST* is twice *SR*.
2. See p. A2.

1-2 Exercises

go.hrw.com
Homework Help Online
KEYWORD: MG7 1-2
Parent Resources Online
KEYWORD: MG7 Parent

GUIDED PRACTICE

Vocabulary Apply the vocabulary from this lesson to answer each question.

1. Line ℓ bisects $\overline{XY}$ at M and divides $\overline{XY}$ into two equal parts. Name a pair of congruent segments. $\overline{XM}$ and $\overline{MY}$

2. __?__ is the amount of space between two points on a line. It is always expressed as a nonnegative number. (*distance* or *midpoint*) distance

SEE EXAMPLE 1 p. 13

Find each length.

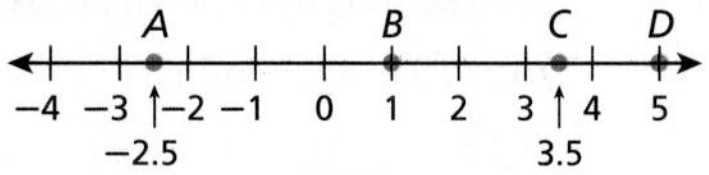

3. AB 3.5
4. BC 2.5

SEE EXAMPLE 2 p. 14

5. Sketch, draw, and construct a segment congruent to $\overline{RS}$. Check students' work.

SEE EXAMPLE 3 p. 15

6. B is between A and C, $AC = 15.8$, and $AB = 9.9$. Find BC. 5.9

7. Find MP. 29

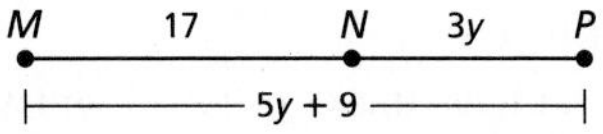

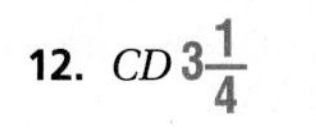

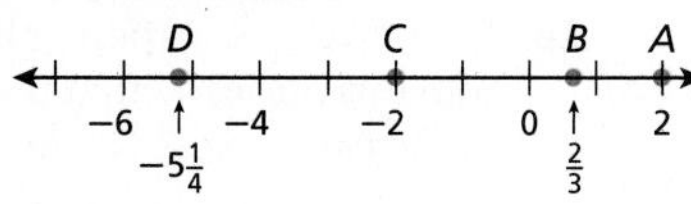

SEE EXAMPLE 4 p. 15

8. **Travel** If a picnic area is located at the midpoint between Sacramento and Oakland, find the distance to the picnic area from the road sign. 66.5 mi

Roseville	5
Sacramento	23
Oakland	110

SEE EXAMPLE 5 p. 16

9. **Multi-Step** K is the midpoint of $\overline{JL}$, $JL = 4x - 2$, and $JK = 7$. Find x, KL, and JL. $x = 4$; $KL = 7$; $JL = 14$

10. E bisects $\overline{DF}$, $DE = 2y$, and $EF = 8y - 3$. Find DE, EF, and DF. $DE = EF = 1$; $DF = 2$

PRACTICE AND PROBLEM SOLVING

Independent Practice

For Exercises	See Example
11–12	1
13	2
14–15	3
16	4
17–18	5

Extra Practice
Skills Practice p. S4
Application Practice p. S28

Find each length.

11. DB $5\frac{11}{12}$
12. CD $3\frac{1}{4}$

13. Sketch, draw, and construct a segment twice the length of $\overline{AB}$. Check students' work.

14. D is between C and E, $CE = 17.1$, and $DE = 8$. Find CD. 9.1

15. Find MN. 5

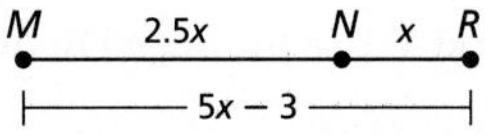

16. **Sports** During a football game, a quarterback standing at the 9-yard line passes the ball to a receiver at the 24-yard line. The receiver then runs with the ball halfway to the 50-yard line. How many total yards (passing plus running) did the team gain on the play? 28 yd

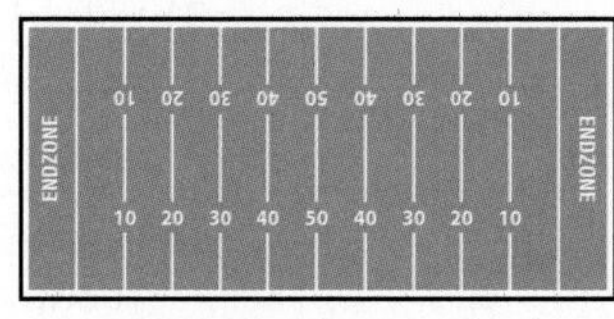

17. **Multi-Step** E is the midpoint of $\overline{DF}$, $DE = 2x + 4$, and $EF = 3x - 1$. Find DE, EF, and DF. $DE = EF = 14$; $DF = 28$

18. Q bisects $\overline{PR}$, $PQ = 3y$, and $PR = 42$. Find y and QR. $y = 7$; $QR = 21$

1-2 Exercises

Assignment Guide

Assign *Guided Practice* exercises as necessary.

If you finished Examples 1–3
Basic 11–15, 20, 24, 26
Average 11–15, 20, 24, 26, 28–30, 35, 36, 43
Advanced 11–15, 20, 24, 26, 28–30, 35, 36, 42–45

If you finished Examples 1–5
Basic 11–20, 22, 27, 28, 31, 34, 35, 37–40, 46–53
Average 11–28, 30–32, 34–41, 43–53
Advanced 12–14, 16–20, 22–30 even, 31, 32, 34–53

Homework Quick Check
Quickly check key concepts.
Exercises: 12–14, 16, 18, 20, 22, 31

Teaching Tip
Algebra For **Exercise 17,** remind students that they have to substitute the value of x into the expressions $2x + 4$ and $3x - 1$ to find DE, EF, and DF.

State Resources

go.hrw.com
State Resources Online
KEYWORD: MG7 Resources

Exercise 19 involves finding distances between points. This exercise prepares students for the Multi-Step Test Prep on page 34.

Kinesthetic To demonstrate the difference between equal length and congruence in **Exercise 24,** have students place one hand over the other to show how they match for congruence. Then, for equality, have them show 5 fingers on each hand for 5 = 5.

Inclusion If students are using a ruler for a straightedge in **Exercise 35,** be sure that they are not using the marks on the ruler to measure distances, and that they show construction arcs.

Multiple Representations For **Exercise 40,** encourage students to draw and label a diagram with all the given information before attempting to solve the problem.

19. This problem will prepare you for the Multi-Step Test Prep on page 34. Archaeologists at Valley Forge were eager to find what remained of the winter camp that soldiers led by George Washington called home for several months. The diagram represents one of the restored log cabins.

a. How is C related to $\overline{AE}$? **C is the mdpt. of $\overline{AE}$.**

b. If $AC = 7$ ft, $EF = 2(AC) + 2$, and $AB = 2(EF) - 16$, what are AB and EF? **16**

Use the diagram for Exercises 20–23.

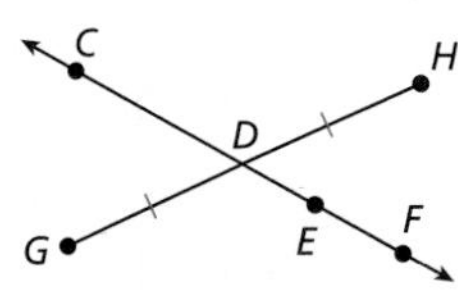

20. $GD = 4\frac{2}{3}$. Find GH. **$9\frac{1}{3}$**

21. $\overline{CD} \cong \overline{DF}$, E bisects $\overline{DF}$, and $CD = 14.2$. Find EF. **7.1**

22. $GH = 4x - 1$, and $DH = 8$. Find x. **4.25**

23. $\overline{GH}$ bisects $\overline{CF}$, $CF = 2y - 2$, and $CD = 3y - 11$. Find CD. **4**

Tell whether each statement is sometimes, always, or never true. Support each of your answers with a sketch.

24. Two segments that have the same length must be congruent. **A;**

25. If M is between A and B, then M bisects $\overline{AB}$. **S;** A M B A M B

26. If Y is between X and Z, then X, Y, and Z are collinear. **A** X Y Z

27. $\overline{AM} \cong \overline{MB}$ is incorrect. The statement should be written as $AM \cong MB$, not as 2 distances that are $\cong$.

27. **///ERROR ANALYSIS///** Below are two statements about the midpoint of $\overline{AB}$. Which is incorrect? Explain the error.

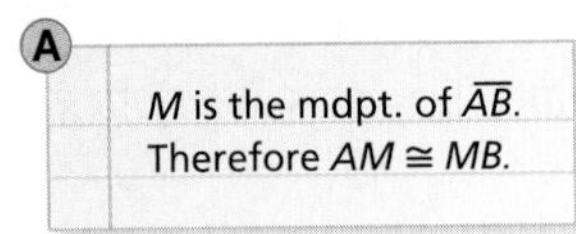
A

M is the mdpt. of $\overline{AB}$.
Therefore $AM \cong MB$.

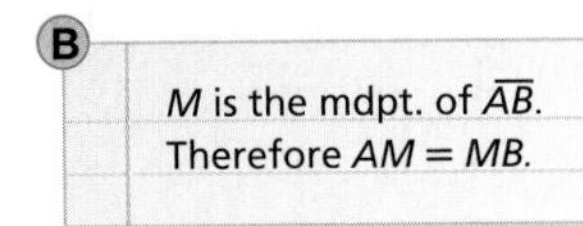
B

M is the mdpt. of $\overline{AB}$.
Therefore $AM = MB$.

28. **Carpentry** A carpenter has a wooden dowel that is 72 cm long. She wants to cut it into two pieces so that one piece is 5 times as long as the other. What are the lengths of the two pieces? **60 cm; 12 cm**

29. The coordinate of M is 2.5, and $MN = 4$. What are the possible coordinates for N? **6.5; −1.5**

30. D E F **Possible answer: $\overline{DE} + \overline{EF} = \overline{DF}$**

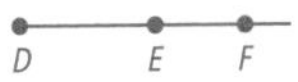

30. Draw three collinear points where E is between D and F. Then write an equation using these points and the Segment Addition Postulate.

Suppose S is between R and T. Use the Segment Addition Postulate to solve for each variable.

31. $RS = 7y - 4$
$ST = y + 5$
$RT = 28$ **3.375**

32. $RS = 3x + 1$
$ST = \frac{1}{2}x + 3$
$RT = 18$ **4**

33. $RS = 2z + 6$
$ST = 4z - 3$
$RT = 5z + 12$ **9**

34. **Write About It** In the diagram, B is not between A and C. Explain. **B is not between A and C, because A, B, and C are not collinear.**

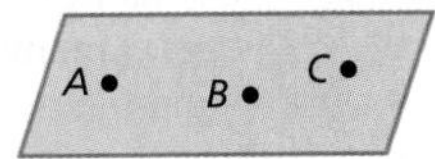

35. **Construction** Use a compass and straightedge to construct a segment whose length is $AB + CD$. **Check students' constructions.**

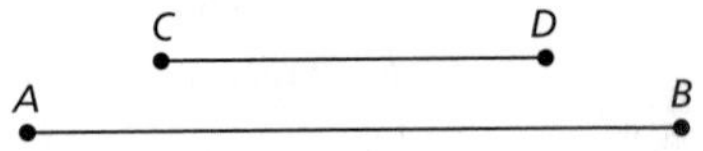

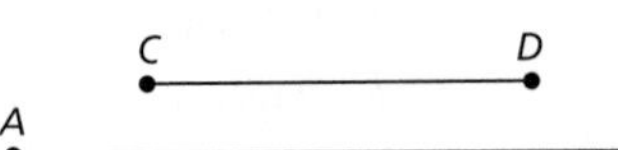

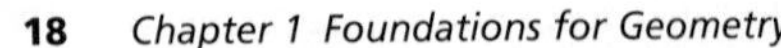

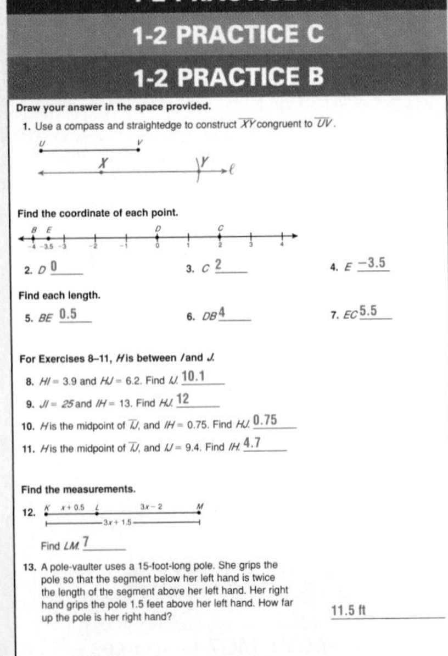

1-2 PRACTICE A

1-2 PRACTICE C

1-2 PRACTICE B

Draw your answer in the space provided.

1. Use a compass and straightedge to construct $\overline{XY}$ congruent to $\overline{UV}$.

Find the coordinate of each point.

2. D **0** 3. C **2** 4. E **−3.5**

Find each length.

5. BE **0.5** 6. DB **4** 7. EC **5.5**

For Exercises 8–11, H is between I and J.

8. $HI = 3.9$ and $HJ = 6.2$. Find IJ. **10.1**

9. $JI = 25$ and $IH = 13$. Find HJ. **12**

10. H is the midpoint of $\overline{IJ}$, and $IH = 0.75$. Find HJ. **0.75**

11. H is the midpoint of $\overline{IJ}$, and $IJ = 9.4$. Find IH. **4.7**

Find the measurements.

12. K $x + 0.5$ L $3x - 2$ M; $3x + 1.5$

Find LM. **7**

13. A pole-vaulter uses a 15-foot-long pole. She grips the pole so that the segment below her left hand is twice the length of the segment above her left hand. Her right hand grips the pole 1.5 feet above her left hand. How far up the pole is her right hand? **11.5 ft**

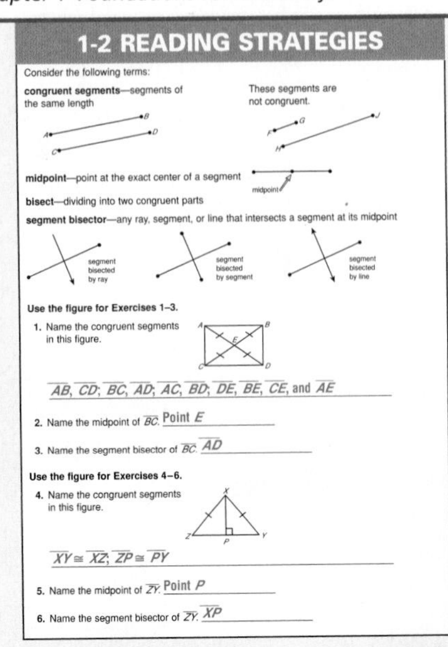

1-2 READING STRATEGIES

Consider the following terms:

congruent segments—segments of the same length

These segments are not congruent.

midpoint—point at the exact center of a segment

bisect—dividing into two congruent parts

segment bisector—any ray, segment, or line that intersects a segment at its midpoint

segment bisected by ray / segment bisected by segment / segment bisected by line

Use the figure for Exercises 1–3.

1. Name the congruent segments in this figure.
$\overline{AB}$, $\overline{CD}$; $\overline{BC}$, $\overline{AD}$; $\overline{AC}$, $\overline{BD}$; $\overline{DE}$, $\overline{BE}$, $\overline{CE}$, and $\overline{AE}$

2. Name the midpoint of $\overline{BC}$. **Point E**

3. Name the segment bisector of $\overline{BC}$. **$\overline{AD}$**

Use the figure for Exercises 4–6.

4. Name the congruent segments in this figure.
$\overline{XY} \cong \overline{XZ}$; $\overline{ZP} \cong \overline{PY}$

5. Name the midpoint of $\overline{ZY}$. **Point P**

6. Name the segment bisector of $\overline{ZY}$. **$\overline{XP}$**

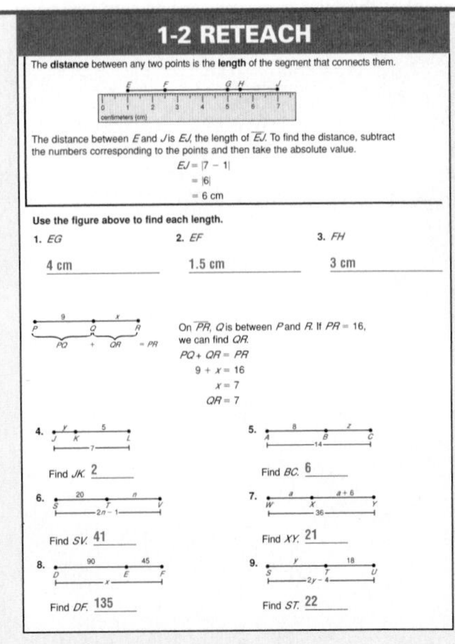

1-2 RETEACH

The **distance** between any two points is the **length** of the segment that connects them.

The distance between E and J is EJ, the length of $\overline{EJ}$. To find the distance, subtract the numbers corresponding to the points and then take the absolute value.

$EJ = |7 - 1|$
$= |6|$
$= 6$ cm

Use the figure above to find each length.

1. EG **4 cm** 2. EF **1.5 cm** 3. FH **3 cm**

On $\overline{PR}$, Q is between P and R. If $PR = 16$, we can find QR.

$PQ + QR = PR$
$9 + x = 16$
$x = 7$
$QR = 7$

4. Find JK. **2** 5. Find BC. **6**

6. Find SV. **41** 7. Find XY. **21**

8. Find DF. **135** 9. Find ST. **22**

TEST PREP

36. Q is between P and R. S is between Q and R, and R is between Q and T. $PT = 34$, $QR = 8$, and $PQ = SQ = SR$. What is the length of $\overline{RT}$?
 (A) 9 (B) 10 (C) 18 **(D) 22**

37. C is the midpoint of $\overline{AD}$. B is the midpoint of $\overline{AC}$. $BC = 12$. What is the length of $\overline{AD}$?
 (F) 12 (G) 24 (H) 36 **(J) 48**

38. Which expression correctly states that $\overline{XY}$ is congruent to $\overline{VW}$?
 (A) $XY \cong VW$ **(B) $\overline{XY} \cong \overline{VW}$** (C) $\overline{XY} = \overline{VW}$ (D) $XY = VW$

39. A, B, C, D, and E are collinear points. $AE = 34$, $BD = 16$, and $AB = BC = CD$. What is the length of $\overline{CE}$?
 (F) 10 (G) 16 **(H) 18** (J) 24

CHALLENGE AND EXTEND

40. HJ is twice JK. J is between H and K. If $HJ = 4x$ and $HK = 78$, find JK. **26**

41. A, D, N, and X are collinear points. D is between N and A. $NA + AX = NX$. Draw a diagram that represents this information. X A D N

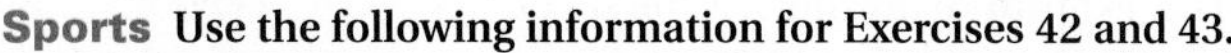

LINK Sports

Joanna Hayes, of the United States, clears a hurdle on her way to winning the gold medal in the women's 100 m hurdles during the 2004 Olympic Games.

Sports Use the following information for Exercises 42 and 43.

The table shows regulation distances between hurdles in women's and men's races. In both the women's and men's events, the race consists of a straight track with 10 equally spaced hurdles.

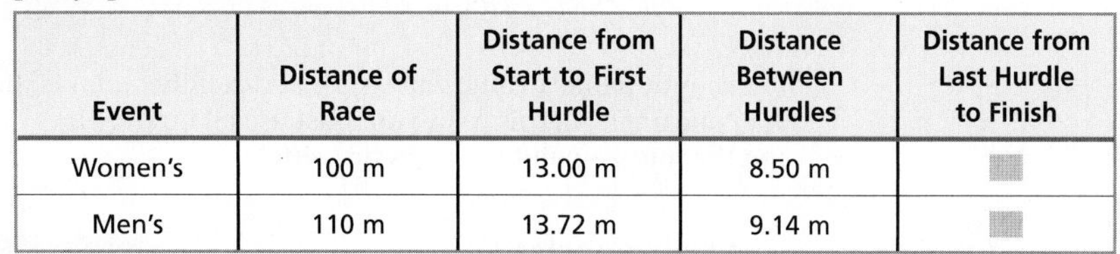

Event	Distance of Race	Distance from Start to First Hurdle	Distance Between Hurdles	Distance from Last Hurdle to Finish
Women's	100 m	13.00 m	8.50 m	
Men's	110 m	13.72 m	9.14 m	

42. Find the distance from the last hurdle to the finish line for the women's race. **10.5 m**

43. Find the distance from the last hurdle to the finish line for the men's race. **14.02 m**

44. **Critical Thinking** Given that J, K, and L are collinear and that K is between J and L, is it possible that $JK = JL$? If so, draw an example. If not, explain. **JK cannot be equal to JL because $JK + KL = JL$ and $KL \neq 0$.**

SPIRAL REVIEW

Evaluate each expression. *(Previous course)*

45. $|20 - 8|$ **12**
46. $|-9 + 23|$ **14**
47. $-|4 - 27|$ **−23**

Simplify each expression. *(Previous course)*

48. $8a - 3(4 + a) - 10$ **$5a - 22$**
49. $x + 2(5 - 2x) - (4 + 5x)$ **$-8x + 6$**

Use the figure to name each of the following. *(Lesson 1-1)*

50. two lines that contain B **$\overleftrightarrow{AB}$, $\overleftrightarrow{CB}$**
51. two segments containing D **$\overline{AD}$, $\overline{BD}$**
52. three collinear points **A, B, D**
53. a ray with endpoint C **$\overrightarrow{CB}$**

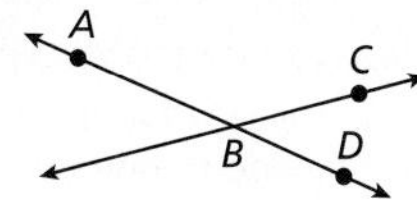

COMMON ERROR ALERT

In **Exercise 36,** students might interpret the word *between* to mean at the *midpoint*. Remind them that *between* does not imply midway, and suggest that they draw a diagram to help them sort out the information.

Journal

Have students define the midpoint of a segment in their own words and illustrate what it means for one point to be between two other points.

ALTERNATIVE ASSESSMENT

Have students create and solve a real-world problem involving algebraic expressions that illustrate distance and midpoint. Ask them to include a diagram and explain their problem.

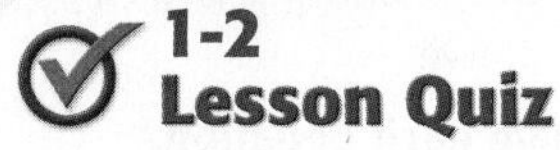

1-2 Lesson Quiz

1. M is between N and O, $MO = 15$, and $MN = 7.6$. Find NO. 22.6

2. S is the midpoint of $\overline{TV}$, $TS = 4x - 7$, and $SV = 5x - 15$. Find TS, SV, and TV. 25, 25, 50

3. Sketch, draw, and construct a segment congruent to $\overline{CD}$.

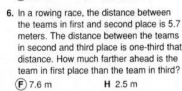

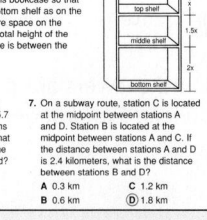

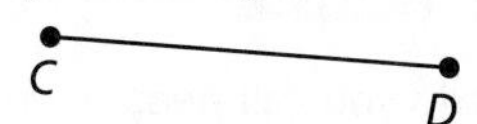

Check students' constructions.

4. $\overline{LH}$ bisects $\overline{GK}$ at M. $GM = 2x + 6$, and $GK = 24$. Find x. 3

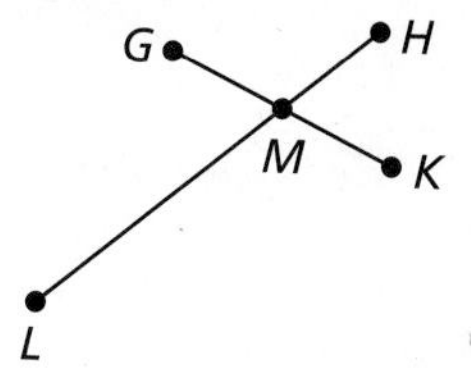

5. Tell whether the statement below is sometimes, always, or never true. Support your answer with a sketch.
If M is the midpoint of $\overline{KL}$, then M, K, and L are collinear.
A

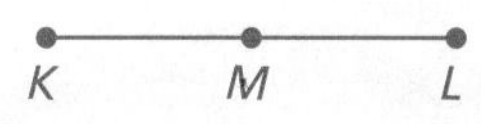

Also available on transparency

1-2 PROBLEM SOLVING

For Exercises 1 and 2, use the figure. It shows the top view of a stage that has three trap doors.

stage; x, 8 ft, x, 8 ft, x; trap door; A; B; $26\frac{1}{2}$ ft

1. The total length of the stage is 76 feet. If the trap doors are centered across the stage, what is the distance from the left side of the stage to the first trap door?
 $24\frac{3}{4}$ ft

2. An actor starts at point A, walks across the stage, and then stops at point B before disappearing through the trap door. How far did he walk across the stage?
 23 ft

3. Anna is 26 feet high on a rock-climbing wall. She descends to the 15-foot mark, rests, and then climbs down until she reaches her friend, who is 8 feet from the ground. How many feet has Anna descended?
 18 ft

4. Jamilla has a piece of ribbon that is 48.5 centimeters long. For her scrapbook, she cuts it into two pieces so that one piece is 4 times as long as the other. What are the lengths of the pieces?
 9.7 cm and 38.8 cm

Choose the best answer.

5. Jordan wants to adjust the shelves in his bookcase so that there is twice as much space on the bottom shelf as on the top shelf, and one and a half times more space on the middle shelf as on the top shelf. If the total height of the bookcase is 0.9 meter, how much space is between the top and middle shelves?
 A 0.2 m C 0.4 m
 (B) 0.3 m D 0.5 m

top shelf; middle shelf; bottom shelf; x; 1.5x; 2x

6. In a rowing race, the distance between the teams in first and second place is 5.7 meters. The distance between the teams in second and third place is one-third that distance. How much farther ahead is the team in first place than the team in third?
 (F) 7.6 m H 2.5 m
 G 5.7 m J 1.9 m

7. On a subway route, station C is located at the midpoint between stations A and D. Station B is located at the midpoint between stations A and C. If the distance between stations A and D is 2.4 kilometers, what is the distance between stations B and D?
 A 0.3 km C 1.2 km
 B 0.6 km **(D) 1.8 km**

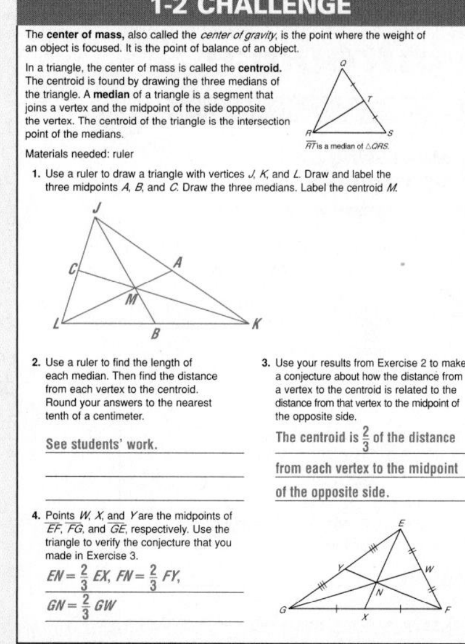

1-2 CHALLENGE

The **center of mass,** also called the *center of gravity*, is the point where the weight of an object is focused. It is the point of balance of an object.

In a triangle, the center of mass is called the **centroid.** The centroid is found by drawing the three medians of the triangle. A **median** of a triangle is a segment that joins a vertex and the midpoint of the side opposite the vertex. The centroid of the triangle is the intersection point of the medians.

$\overline{RT}$ is a median of $\triangle QRS$.

Materials needed: ruler

1. Use a ruler to draw a triangle with vertices J, K, and L. Draw and label the three midpoints A, B, and C. Draw the three medians. Label the centroid M.

2. Use a ruler to find the length of each median. Then find the distance from each vertex to the centroid. Round your answers to the nearest tenth of a centimeter.
 See students' work.

3. Use your results from Exercise 2 to make a conjecture about how the distance from a vertex to the centroid is related to the distance from that vertex to the midpoint of the opposite side.
 The centroid is $\frac{2}{3}$ of the distance from each vertex to the midpoint of the opposite side.

4. Points W, X, and Y are the midpoints of $\overline{EF}$, $\overline{FG}$, and $\overline{GE}$, respectively. Use the triangle to verify the conjecture that you made in Exercise 3.
 $EN = \frac{2}{3}EX$, $FN = \frac{2}{3}FY$, $GN = \frac{2}{3}GW$

1-3 Organizer

Pacing: Traditional 1 day
Block $\frac{1}{2}$ day

Objectives: Name and classify angles.

Measure and construct angles and angle bisectors.

Geometry Lab
In Geometry Lab Activities

Online Edition
Tutorial Videos, TechKeys

Countdown Week 1

Power Presentations with PowerPoint®

Warm Up

1. Draw $\overrightarrow{AB}$ and $\overrightarrow{AC}$, where A, B, and C are noncollinear. Check students' drawings
2. Draw opposite rays $\overrightarrow{DE}$ and $\overrightarrow{DF}$. Check students' drawings

Solve each equation.

3. $2x + 3 + x - 4 + 3x - 5 = 180$ 31
4. $5x + 2 = 8x - 10$ 4

Also available on transparency

Math Humor

Q: What do you call people who are in favor of tractors?

A: Protractors!

State Resources

1-3 Measuring and Constructing Angles

Objectives
Name and classify angles.
Measure and construct angles and angle bisectors.

Vocabulary
angle
vertex
interior of an angle
exterior of an angle
measure
degree
acute angle
right angle
obtuse angle
straight angle
congruent angles
angle bisector

Who uses this?
Surveyors use angles to help them measure and map the earth's surface. (See Exercise 27.)

A transit is a tool for measuring angles. It consists of a telescope that swivels horizontally and vertically. Using a transit, a surveyor can measure the *angle* formed by his or her location and two distant points.

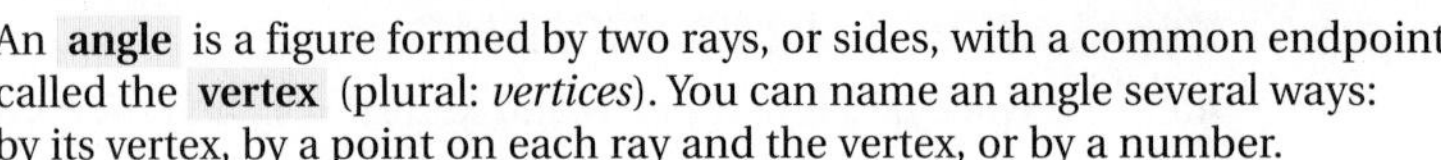

An **angle** is a figure formed by two rays, or sides, with a common endpoint called the **vertex** (plural: *vertices*). You can name an angle several ways: by its vertex, by a point on each ray and the vertex, or by a number.

The set of all points between the sides of the angle is the **interior of an angle**. The **exterior of an angle** is the set of all points outside the angle.

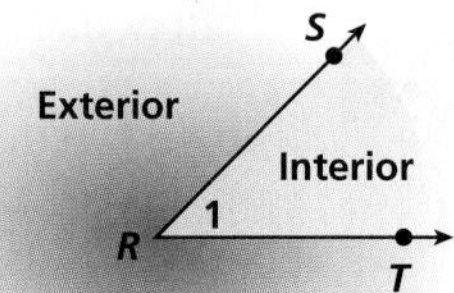

Angle Name

$\angle R$, $\angle SRT$, $\angle TRS$, or $\angle 1$

You cannot name an angle just by its vertex if the point is the vertex of more than one angle. In this case, you must use all three points to name the angle, and the middle point is always the vertex.

EXAMPLE 1 **Naming Angles**

A surveyor recorded the angles formed by a transit (point *T*) and three distant points, *Q*, *R*, and *S*. Name three of the angles.

$\angle QTR$, $\angle QTS$, and $\angle RTS$

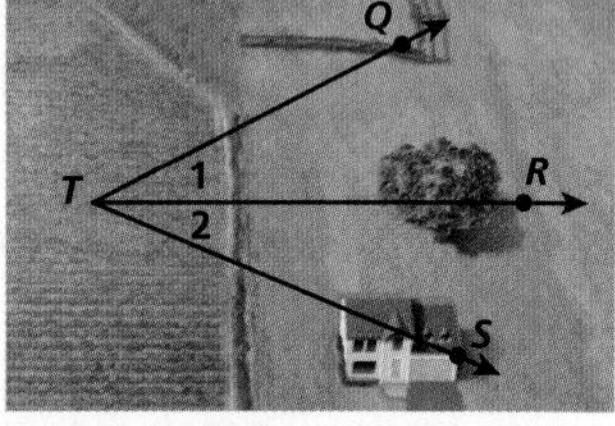

CHECK IT OUT! 1. Write the different ways you can name the angles in the diagram. $\angle RTQ$, $\angle STR$, $\angle 1$, $\angle 2$

The **measure** of an angle is usually given in degrees. Since there are 360° in a circle, one **degree** is $\frac{1}{360}$ of a circle. When you use a protractor to measure angles, you are applying the following postulate.

Postulate 1-3-1 **Protractor Postulate**

Given $\overleftrightarrow{AB}$ and a point O on $\overleftrightarrow{AB}$, all rays that can be drawn from O can be put into a one-to-one correspondence with the real numbers from 0 to 180.

1 Introduce

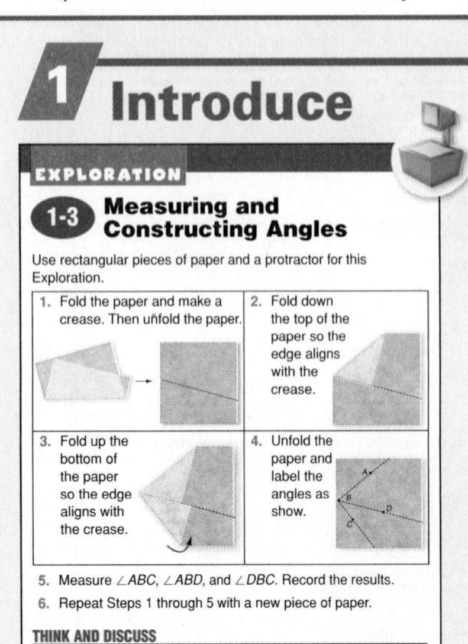
EXPLORATION

1-3 Measuring and Constructing Angles

Use rectangular pieces of paper and a protractor for this Exploration.

1. Fold the paper and make a crease. Then unfold the paper.
2. Fold down the top of the paper so the edge aligns with the crease.
3. Fold up the bottom of the paper so the edge aligns with the crease.
4. Unfold the paper and label the angles as show.
5. Measure $\angle ABC$, $\angle ABD$, and $\angle DBC$. Record the results.
6. Repeat Steps 1 through 5 with a new piece of paper.

THINK AND DISCUSS

7. **Describe** what you notice about the measure of $\angle ABC$.
8. **Discuss** the relationship among the measures of $\angle ABC$.

Motivate

Point out examples of different types of angles in the classroom, such as the corner of a piece of paper for a right angle, and open scissors to show an acute angle or an obtuse angle. Have students get in groups of three and use a long strand of yarn and three index cards, each labeled with a different letter, to model for the class the different angles that can be formed.

Explorations and answers are provided in *Alternate Openers: Explorations Transparencies.*

Student to Student

Using a Protractor

José Muñoz
Lincoln High School

Most protractors have two sets of numbers around the edge. When I measure an angle and need to know which number to use, I first ask myself whether the angle is acute, right, or obtuse. For example, ∠RST looks like it is obtuse, so I know its measure must be 110°, not 70°.

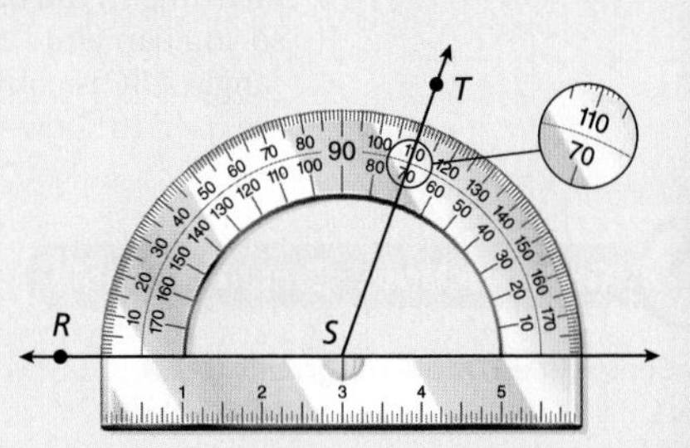

You can use the Protractor Postulate to help you classify angles by their measure. The measure of an angle is the absolute value of the difference of the real numbers that the rays correspond with on a protractor. If $\overrightarrow{OC}$ corresponds with c and $\overrightarrow{OD}$ corresponds with d, $m\angle DOC = |d - c|$ or $|c - d|$.

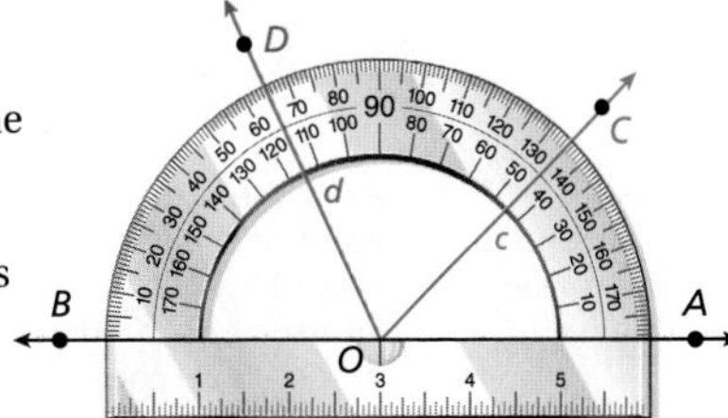

Types of Angles

Acute Angle	Right Angle	Obtuse Angle	Straight Angle
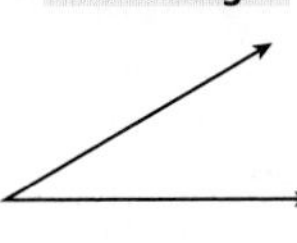	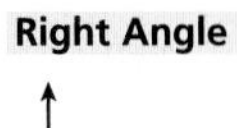	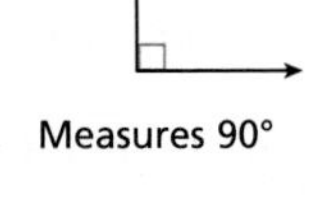	
Measures greater than 0° and less than 90°	Measures 90°	Measures greater than 90° and less than 180°	Formed by two opposite rays and meaures 180°

EXAMPLE 2 **Measuring and Classifying Angles**

Find the measure of each angle. Then classify each as acute, right, or obtuse.

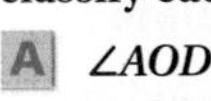

A ∠AOD

$m\angle AOD = 165°$

∠AOD is obtuse.

B ∠COD

$m\angle COD = |165 - 75| = 90°$

∠COD is a right angle.

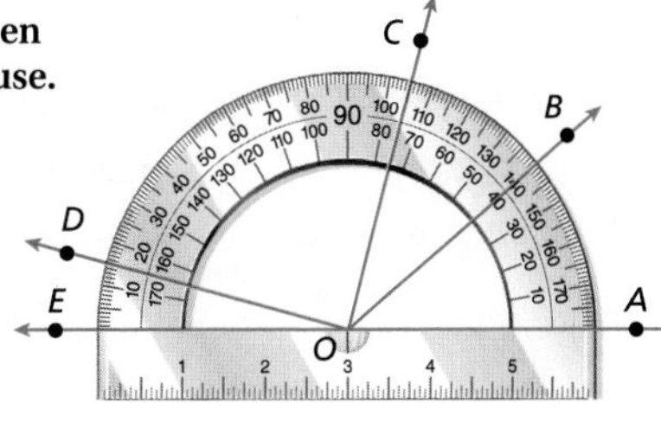

CHECK IT OUT! **Use the diagram to find the measure of each angle. Then classify each as acute, right, or obtuse.**

2a. ∠BOA **40°; acute**
2b. ∠DOB **125°; obtuse**
2c. ∠EOC **105°; obtuse**

COMMON ERROR ALERT

Remind students to place the center mark of the protractor (MK) on the vertex and to align one side of the angle with the 0° mark. Some protractors have their zero line on the bottom edge, while others have it higher.

Power Presentations with PowerPoint®

Additional Examples

Example 1

A surveyor recorded the angles formed by a transit (point *A*) and three distant points, *B*, *C*, and *D*. Name three of the angles.

Possible answer: ∠BAC, ∠CAD, ∠BAD

Example 2

Find the measure of each angle. Then classify each as acute, right, or obtuse.

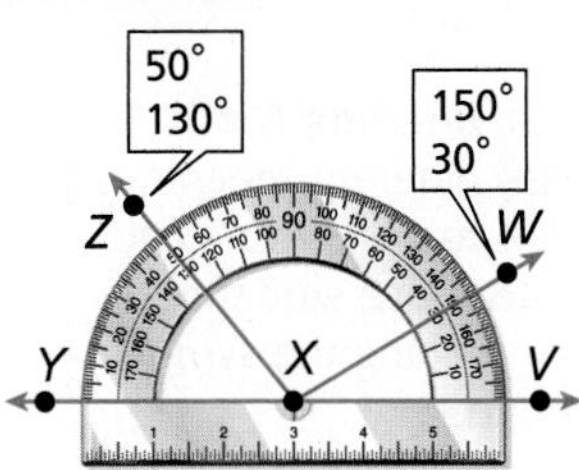

A. ∠WXV 30°; acute

B. ∠ZXW 100°; obtuse

2 Teach

Guided Instruction

Discuss how to name angles. The vertex is always the middle letter, or is used as the single letter name. Show students how to use a protractor to measure angles and how to write their measure. Explain that the *measure* of ∠A is written as m∠A. Describe each step of the constructions. Emphasize that congruent angles have equal measures and that an angle bisector divides an angle into two congruent angles.

Reaching All Learners

Through Visual Cues

Use pictures from magazines of angles of different sizes. Ask students to identify the type of angle and estimate the measure. Then have students measure the angles with a protractor. If protractors are not available, they can use index cards or origami paper. The edge is already a 90° angle, and anything greater would be an obtuse angle. A half-fold forms a 45° angle, a tri-fold approximately 30°, and so on. The pictures can be posted by classification and used for reference.

INTERVENTION

Questioning Strategies

EXAMPLE 1

- Does the order of the letters matter when you name an angle? Explain.

EXAMPLE 2

- Does the order in which the real numbers are subtracted matter? Explain.
- Do the lengths of the sides of an angle affect its measure?

Visual Remind students to show all arcs in their construction. In **Step 4,** they should use the same compass span *BC* when drawing the arcs. Have students practice constructing both acute and obtuse angles.

Power Presentations with PowerPoint®

Additional Examples

Example 3

$m\angle DEG = 115°$, and $m\angle DEF = 48°$. Find $m\angle FEG$. 67°

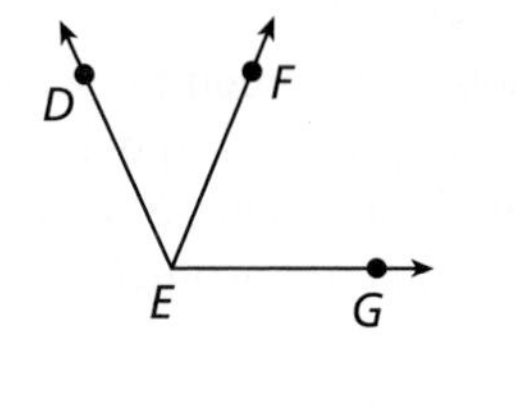

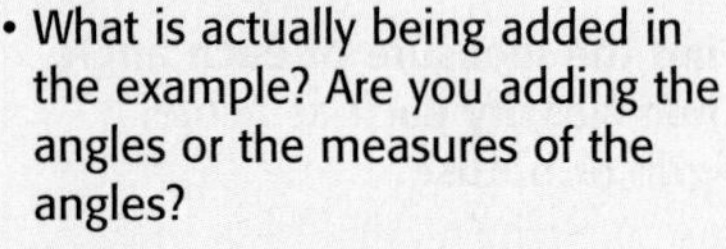

INTERVENTION

Questioning Strategies

EXAMPLE 3

- What is actually being added in the example? Are you adding the angles or the measures of the angles?

Reading Math Review the different meanings of $m\angle A = m\angle B$ and $\angle A \cong \angle B$. Have students practice reading the symbols aloud.

ENGLISH LANGUAGE LEARNERS

Congruent angles are angles that have the same measure. In the diagram, $m\angle ABC = m\angle DEF$, so you can write $\angle ABC \cong \angle DEF$. This is read as "angle *ABC* is congruent to angle *DEF*." *Arc marks* are used to show that the two angles are congruent.

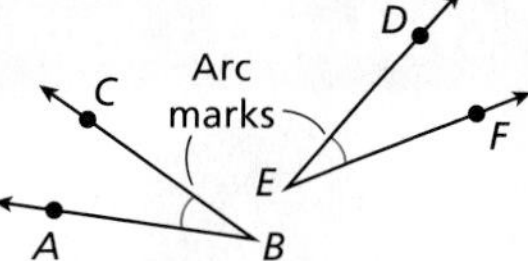

Construction Congruent Angle

Construct an angle congruent to $\angle A$.

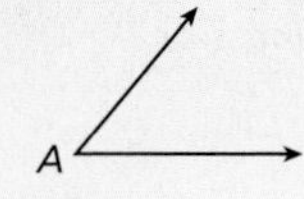

1. 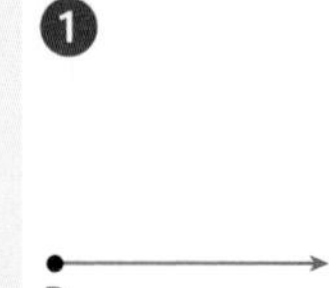

Use a straightedge to draw a ray with endpoint *D*.

2. 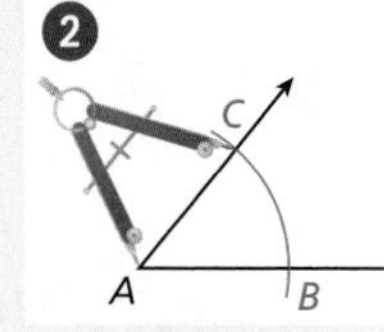

Place the compass point at *A* and draw an arc that intersects both sides of $\angle A$. Label the intersection points *B* and *C*.

3. 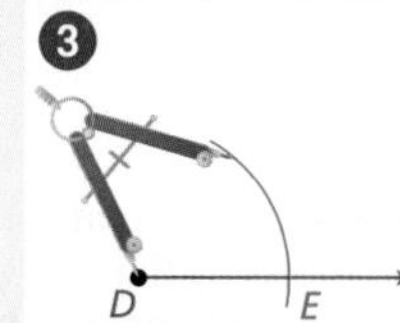

Using the same compass setting, place the compass point at *D* and draw an arc that intersects the ray. Label the intersection *E*.

4. 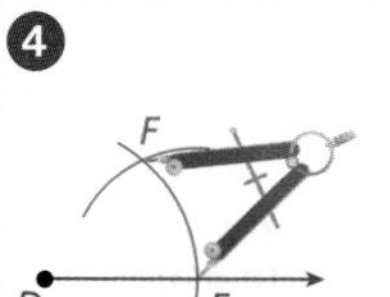

Place the compass point at *B* and open it to the distance *BC*. Place the point of the compass at *E* and draw an arc. Label its intersection with the first arc *F*.

5. 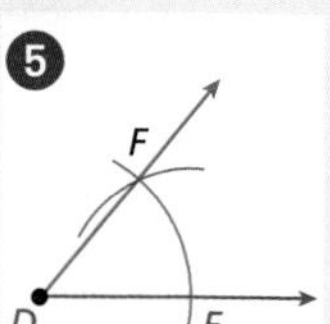

Use a straightedge to draw $\overrightarrow{DF}$.

$\angle D \cong \angle A$

The Angle Addition Postulate is very similar to the Segment Addition Postulate that you learned in the previous lesson.

Postulate 1-3-2 Angle Addition Postulate

If *S* is in the interior of $\angle PQR$, then $m\angle PQS + m\angle SQR = m\angle PQR$.

($\angle$ Add. Post.)

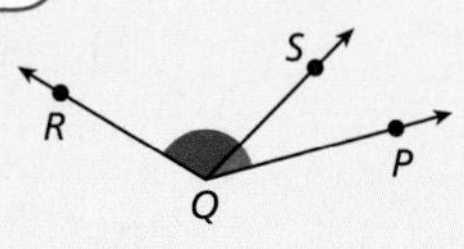

EXAMPLE 3 Using the Angle Addition Postulate

Algebra

$m\angle ABD = 37°$ and $m\angle ABC = 84°$. Find $m\angle DBC$.

$m\angle ABC = m\angle ABD + m\angle DBC$	*$\angle$ Add. Post.*
$84° = 37° + m\angle DBC$	*Substitute the given values.*
$-37 \quad -37$	*Subtract 37 from both sides.*
$47° = m\angle DBC$	*Simplify.*

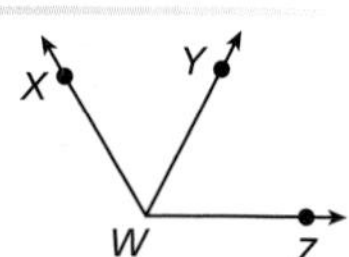

3. $m\angle XWZ = 121°$ and $m\angle XWY = 59°$. Find $m\angle YWZ$. **62°**

An **angle bisector** is a ray that divides an angle into two congruent angles. $\overrightarrow{JK}$ bisects $\angle LJM$; thus $\angle LJK \cong \angle KJM$.

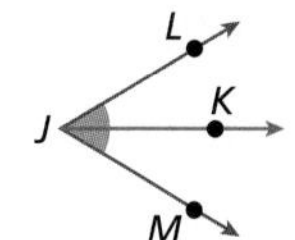

Construction Angle Bisector

Construct the bisector of ∠A.

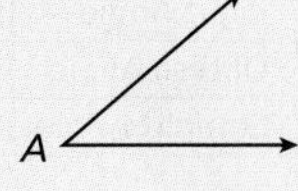

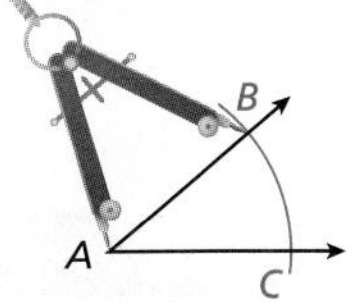

Place the point of the compass at *A* and draw an arc. Label its points of intersection with ∠*A* as *B* and *C*.

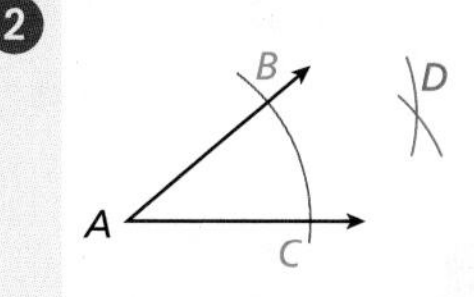

Without changing the compass setting, draw intersecting arcs from *B* and *C*. Label the intersection of the arcs as *D*.

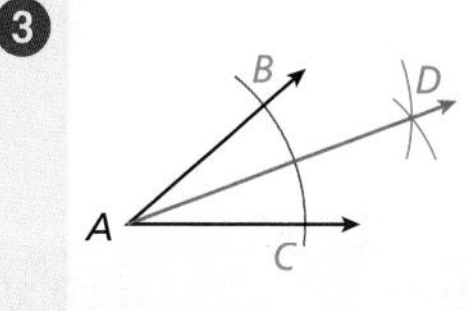

Use a straightedge to draw $\overrightarrow{AD}$. $\overrightarrow{AD}$ bisects ∠*A*.

EXAMPLE 4 **Finding the Measure of an Angle**

Algebra

$\overrightarrow{BD}$ bisects $\angle ABC$, $m\angle ABD = (6x + 3)°$, and $m\angle DBC = (8x - 7)°$. Find $m\angle ABD$.

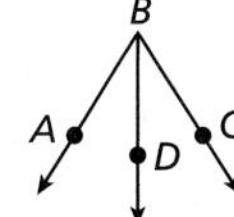

Step 1 Find x.

$m\angle ABD = m\angle DBC$	*Def. of ∠ bisector*
$(6x + 3)° = (8x - 7)°$	*Substitute the given values.*
$+7 \qquad +7$	*Add 7 to both sides.*
$6x + 10 = 8x$	*Simplify.*
$-6x \qquad -6x$	*Subtract 6x from both sides.*
$10 = 2x$	*Simplify.*
$\frac{10}{2} = \frac{2x}{2}$	*Divide both sides by 2.*
$5 = x$	*Simplify.*

Step 2 Find $m\angle ABD$.

$m\angle ABD = 6x + 3$	
$= 6(5) + 3$	*Substitute 5 for x.*
$= 33°$	*Simplify.*

Find the measure of each angle.

4a. $\overrightarrow{QS}$ bisects $\angle PQR$, $m\angle PQS = (5y - 1)°$, and $m\angle PQR = (8y + 12)°$. Find $m\angle PQS$. **34°**

4b. $\overrightarrow{JK}$ bisects $\angle LJM$, $m\angle LJK = (-10x + 3)°$, and $m\angle KJM = (-x + 21)°$. Find $m\angle LJM$. **46°**

COMMON ERROR ALERT

In the constructions, if students' compass settings are not tightly fixed, the compass setting may change without students being aware. Stress to students that they must check compass tightness and keep the same fixed compass setting for accuracy.

Reading Math Explain the *bi* is a prefix meaning "two" and *sect* means "to cut," as into sections.

ENGLISH LANGUAGE LEARNERS

Power Presentations with PowerPoint®

Additional Examples

Example 4

$\overrightarrow{KM}$ bisects $\angle JKL$, $m\angle JKM = (4x + 6)°$, and $m\angle MKL = (7x - 12)°$. Find $m\angle JKM$. 30°

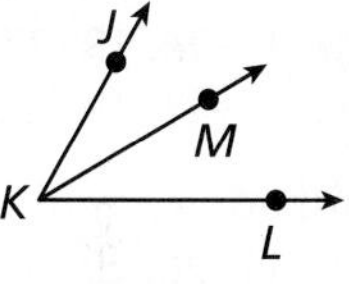

INTERVENTION

Questioning Strategies

EXAMPLE 4

- When do you set the angle measures equal to solve for the variable?
- How can you solve for the variable if you are given the measures of the bisected angle and one of the congruent angles?

3 Close

Summarize

Review with students the parts of an angle, the names of the types of angles, and how to measure angles. Review the Angle Addition Postulate and how it relates to the bisector of an angle.

ONGOING ASSESSMENT and INTERVENTION

***Diagnose Before* the Lesson**
1-3 Warm Up, TE p. 20

***Monitor During* the Lesson**
Check It Out! Exercises, SE pp. 20–23
Questioning Strategies, TE pp. 21–23

***Assess After* the Lesson**
1-3 Lesson Quiz, TE p. 27
Alternative Assessment, TE p. 27

Answers to *Think and Discuss*

1. Two ∠s with the same measure are ≅. All rt. ∠s measure 90°, so any 2 rt. ∠s are ≅.
2. $m\angle ABD = m\angle DBC = \frac{1}{2}m\angle ABC$
3. See p. A2.

THINK AND DISCUSS

1. Explain why any two right angles are congruent.
2. $\overrightarrow{BD}$ bisects ∠ABC. How are m∠ABC, m∠ABD, and m∠DBC related?
3. **GET ORGANIZED** Copy and complete the graphic organizer. In the cells sketch, measure, and name an example of each angle type.

	Diagram	Measure	Name
Acute Angle			
Right Angle			
Obtuse Angle			
Straight Angle			

1-3 Exercises

1-3 Exercises

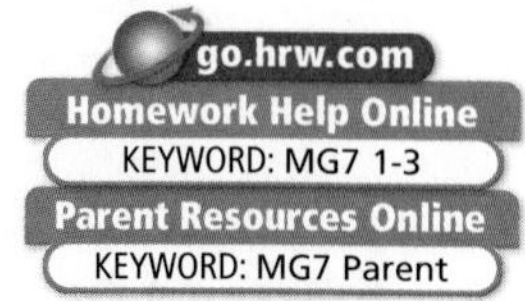

Assignment Guide

Assign *Guided Practice* exercises as necessary.

If you finished Examples **1–2**
Basic 11–14, 19–26, 33–35
Average 11–14, 19–27, 32–36
Advanced 11–14, 19–27, 32–36

If you finished Examples **1–4**
Basic 11–26, 29–31, 33–35, 38, 41–45, 51–58
Average 11–37, 39–46, 48–58
Advanced 11, 12–22 even, 23, 26–58

Homework Quick Check
Quickly check key concepts.
Exercises: 11, 12, 16, 18, 20, 26, 30

State Resources

go.hrw.com
State Resources Online
KEYWORD: MG7 Resources

GUIDED PRACTICE

Vocabulary **Apply the vocabulary from this lesson to answer each question.**

1. ∠A is an acute angle. ∠O is an obtuse angle. ∠R is a right angle. Put ∠A, ∠O, and ∠R in order from least to greatest by measure. **∠A, ∠R, ∠O**
2. Which point is the vertex of ∠BCD? Which rays form the sides of ∠BCD? **C; $\overrightarrow{CB}$, $\overrightarrow{CD}$**

SEE EXAMPLE 1 p. 20

3. **Music** Musicians use a metronome to keep time as they play. The metronome's needle swings back and forth in a fixed amount of time. Name all of the angles in the diagram.

3. ∠AOB, ∠BOA, or ∠1; ∠BOC, ∠COB, or ∠2; ∠AOC or ∠COA

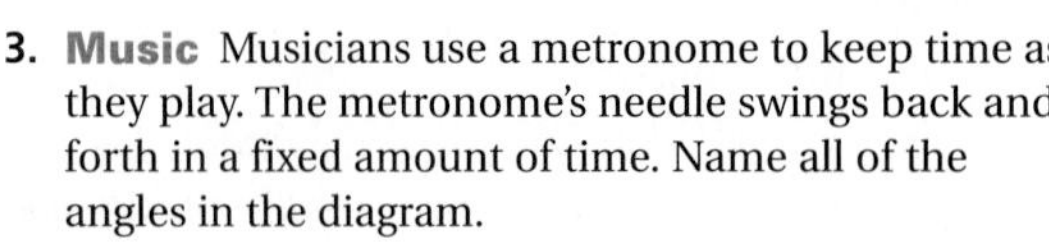

SEE EXAMPLE 2 p. 21

Use the protractor to find the measure of each angle. Then classify each as acute, right, or obtuse.

4. ∠VXW **15°; acute**
5. ∠TXW **105°; obtuse**
6. ∠RXU **110°; obtuse**

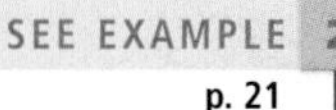

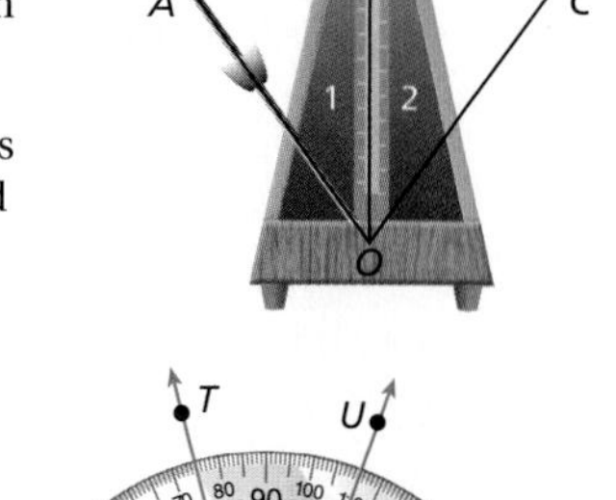

SEE EXAMPLE 3 p. 22

L is in the interior of ∠JKM. Find each of the following.

7. m∠JKM if m∠JKL = 42° and m∠LKM = 28° **70°**
8. m∠LKM if m∠JKL = 56.4° and m∠JKM = 82.5° **26.1°**

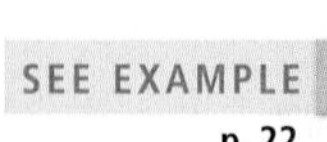

SEE EXAMPLE 4 p. 23

Multi-Step $\overrightarrow{BD}$ **bisects ∠ABC. Find each of the following.**

9. m∠ABD if m∠ABD = $(6x + 4)°$ and m∠DBC = $(8x - 4)°$ **28°**
10. m∠ABC if m∠ABD = $(5y - 3)°$ and m∠DBC = $(3y + 15)°$ **84°**

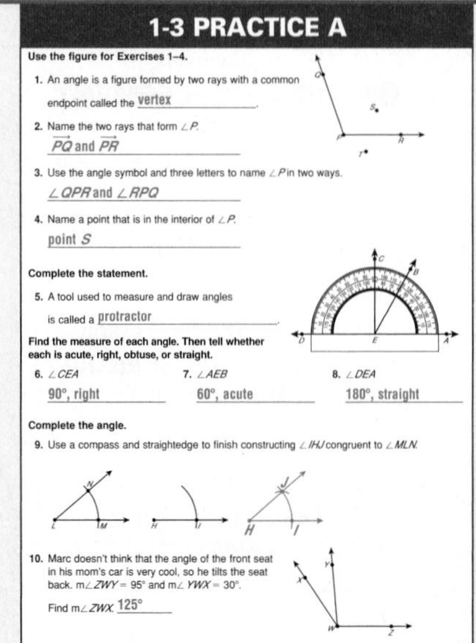

1-3 PRACTICE A

Use the figure for Exercises 1–4.

1. An angle is a figure formed by two rays with a common endpoint called the vertex.
2. Name the two rays that form ∠P. $\overrightarrow{PQ}$ and $\overrightarrow{PR}$
3. Use the angle symbol and three letters to name ∠P in two ways. ∠QPR and ∠RPQ
4. Name a point that is in the interior of ∠P. point S

Complete the statement.

5. A tool used to measure and draw angles is called a protractor

Find the measure of each angle. Then tell whether each is acute, right, obtuse, or straight.

6. ∠CEA 90°, right
7. ∠AEB 60°, acute
8. ∠DEA 180°, straight

Complete the angle.

9. Use a compass and straightedge to finish constructing ∠HIJ congruent to ∠MLN.

10. Marc doesn't think that the angle of the front seat in his mom's car is very cool, so he tilts the seat back. m∠ZWY = 95° and m∠YWX = 30°. Find m∠ZWX. 125°

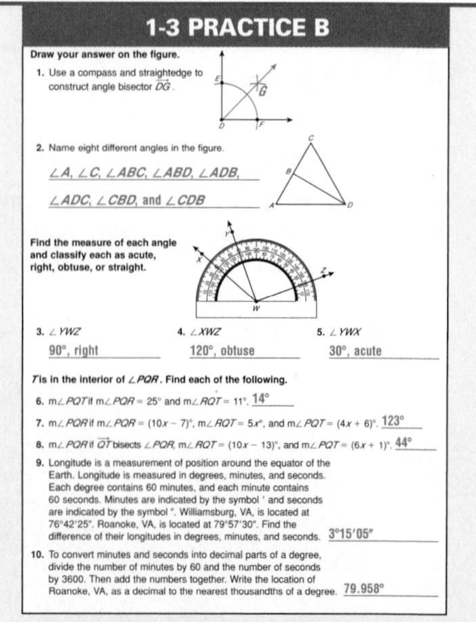

1-3 PRACTICE B

Draw your answer on the figure.

1. Use a compass and straightedge to construct angle bisector $\overrightarrow{DG}$.
2. Name eight different angles in the figure. ∠A, ∠C, ∠ABC, ∠ABD, ∠ADB, ∠ADC, ∠CBD, and ∠CDB

Find the measure of each angle and classify each as acute, right, obtuse, or straight.

3. ∠YWZ 90°, right
4. ∠XWZ 120°, obtuse
5. ∠YWX 30°, acute

T is in the interior of ∠PQR. Find each of the following.

6. m∠PQT if m∠PQR = 25° and m∠RQT = 11°. 14°
7. m∠PQR if m∠PQR = (10x − 7)°, m∠RQT = 5x°, and m∠PQT = (4x + 6)°. 123°
8. m∠PQR if $\overrightarrow{QT}$ bisects ∠PQR, m∠RQT = (10x − 13)°, and m∠PQT = (6x + 1)°. 44°
9. Longitude is a measurement of position around the equator of the Earth. Longitude is measured in degrees, minutes, and seconds. Each degree contains 60 minutes, and each minute contains 60 seconds. Minutes are indicated by the symbol ′ and seconds are indicated by the symbol ″. Williamsburg, VA, is located at 76°42′25″. Roanoke, VA, is located at 79°57′30″. Find the difference of their longitudes in degrees, minutes, and seconds. 3°15′05″
10. To convert minutes and seconds into decimal parts of a degree, divide the number of minutes by 60 and the number of seconds by 3600. Then add the numbers together. Write the location of Roanoke, VA, as a decimal to the nearest thousandths of a degree. 79.958°

PRACTICE AND PROBLEM SOLVING

Independent Practice	
For Exercises	See Example
11	1
12–14	2
15–16	3
17–18	4

Extra Practice
Skills Practice p. S4
Application Practice p. S28

11. **Physics** Pendulum clocks have been used since 1656 to keep time. The pendulum swings back and forth once or twice per second. Name all of the angles in the diagram.
∠1 or ∠JMK; ∠2 or ∠LMK; ∠M or ∠JML

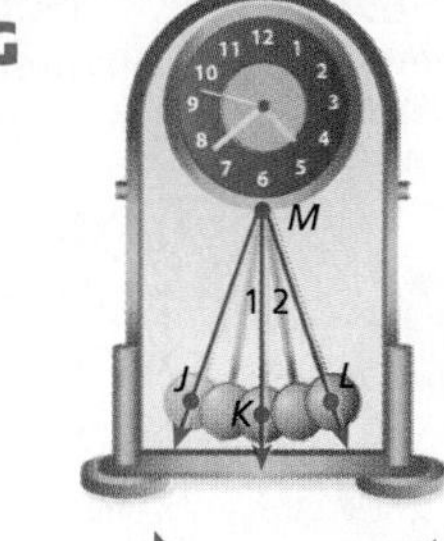

Use the protractor to find the measure of each angle. Then classify each as acute, right, or obtuse.

12. ∠*CGE* **90°; rt.**
13. ∠*BGD* **93°; obtuse**
14. ∠*AGB* **20°; acute**

T is in the interior of ∠RSU. Find each of the following.

15. m∠RSU if m∠RST = 38° and m∠TSU = 28.6° **66.6°**
16. m∠RST if m∠TSU = 46.7° and m∠RSU = 83.5° **36.8°**

Multi-Step $\overrightarrow{SP}$ **bisects ∠RST. Find each of the following.**

17. m∠RST if m∠RSP = $(3x - 2)°$ and m∠PST = $(9x - 26)°$ **20°**
18. m∠RSP if m∠RST = $\frac{5}{2}y°$ and m∠PST = $(y + 5)°$ **25°**

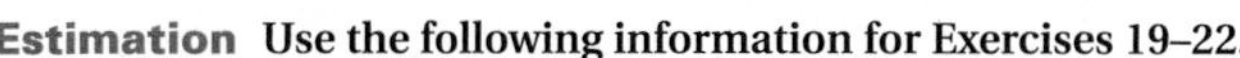

Estimation Use the following information for Exercises 19–22.

Assume the corner of a sheet of paper is a right angle. Use the corner to estimate the measure and classify each angle in the diagram.

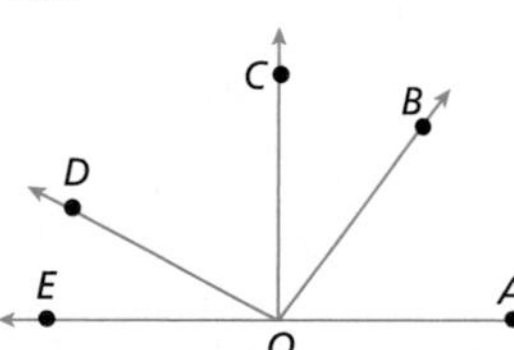

19. ∠*BOA* **acute**
20. ∠*COA* **rt.**

21. ∠*EOD* **acute**
22. ∠*EOB* **obtuse**

Use a protractor to draw an angle with each of the following measures.

23–26. Check students' drawings.

23. 33°
24. 142°
25. 90°
26. 168°

27. **Surveying** A surveyor at point S discovers that the angle between peaks A and B is 3 times as large as the angle between peaks B and C. The surveyor knows that ∠ASC is a right angle. Find m∠ASB and m∠BSC.
67.5°; 22.5°

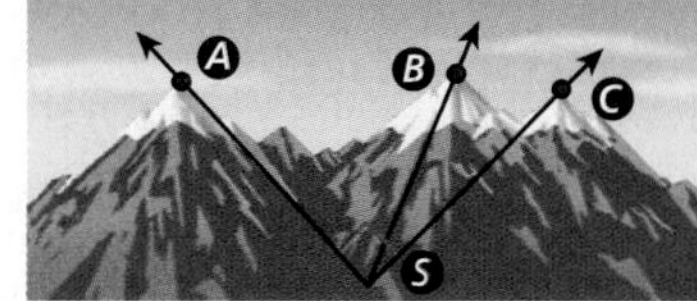

28. **Math History** As far back as the 5th century B.C., mathematicians have been fascinated by the problem of trisecting an angle. It is possible to construct an angle with $\frac{1}{4}$ the measure of a given angle. Explain how to do this.

Find the value of x.

29. m∠AOC = $7x - 2$, m∠DOC = $2x + 8$, m∠EOD = 27 **$16\frac{1}{3}$**
30. m∠AOB = $4x - 2$, m∠BOC = $5x + 10$, m∠COD = $3x - 8$ **10**
31. m∠AOB = $6x + 5$, m∠BOC = $4x - 2$, m∠AOC = $8x + 21$ **9**
32. **Multi-Step** Q is in the interior of right ∠PRS. If m∠PRQ is 4 times as large as m∠QRS, what is m∠PRQ? **72°**

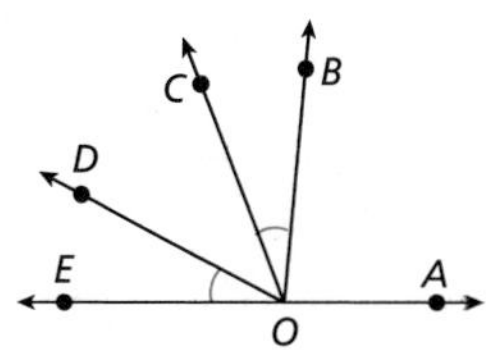

COMMON ERROR ALERT

In **Exercise 32,** students may multiply the wrong angle by 4. They can avoid making this error by making a drawing of ∠*PRS* and *Q*.

Teaching Tip **Visual** For **Exercises 4–6** and **12–14,** show students how to extend the rays using index cards or sticky notes.

Teaching Tip **Inclusion** For **Exercises 12–14,** use acetate or tracing paper to draw individual angles, and then measure with a protractor on the acetate sheet. Color overlays also help students see the angles more clearly.

Teaching Tip **Algebra** For **Exercise 18,** have students multiply both sides of the equation by 2 to turn the fraction into a whole number.

Answers

28. First construct the bisector of the given ∠. Then choose one of the smaller ∠s that was constructed and construct its bisector. The resulting ∠s will have $\frac{1}{4}$ the measure of the original ∠.

1-3 PRACTICE C

Use the figure for Exercises 1–3.

1. Name the obtuse angle. **∠BAE**
2. Name two acute angles. **∠BAC and ∠DAE**
3. Name two right angles. **∠BAD and ∠CAE**

Keisha has a straightedge and a compass, but no protractor.

4. What kind of angle can Keisha draw exactly with only a straightedge?
straight angle
5. Describe how Keisha can draw an exact 45° angle using only a straightedge and a compass.
First, Keisha can draw a straight angle (180°). She can then bisect the straight angle to make two right angles (90°). Keisha can then bisect the right angles to make a 45° angle.

Draw your answer in the space provided.

6. Construct a 135° angle using only a straightedge and a compass. **135°**
7. An acute angle measures $(6x - 45)°$. Write an inequality to describe the range of all possible values of x. **$7.5 < x < 22.5$**

Use the chart to complete the exercise.

Dive	Difficulty
Back $3\frac{1}{2}$ somersault	3.6
Forward $3\frac{1}{2}$ somersault 1 twist	3.6
Reverse $1\frac{1}{2}$ somersault $4\frac{1}{2}$ twists	3.7
Back $2\frac{1}{2}$ somersault $2\frac{1}{2}$ twists	3.8

8. In diving, a somersault is a full forward rotation and a twist is a full turn. The chart names some of the most difficult platform dives according to the International Swimming Federation. Name the dive in which the diver moves through a total of exactly 1800°.
back $2\frac{1}{2}$ somersault $2\frac{1}{2}$ twists
9. $\overrightarrow{HJ}$ bisects ∠IHL, $\overrightarrow{HK}$ bisects ∠JHL, and m∠IHK = 51°. Find m∠IHL. **68°**
10. m∠XWY is twice m∠XWZ. Tell if $\overrightarrow{WZ}$ must be the angle bisector of ∠XWY.
No, $\overrightarrow{WZ}$ does not have to be the angle bisector of ∠XWY.

Exercise 33 involves using algebra to find the measures of congruent angles formed by an angle bisector. This exercise prepares students for the Multi-Step Test Prep on page 34.

Kinesthetic For **Exercise 40,** have students investigate how to find the bisector of the angle using patty paper or a Mira. Draw an angle on a piece of patty paper, and then fold the paper so that the two sides of the angle overlap. The crease created defines a bisector of the angle. To use a Mira, place the Mira on the vertex of the angle so that one side is reflected onto the other side. Then draw the Mira line.

TEST PREP DOCTOR In **Exercise 44,** if students chose **C,** they divided 90° by 2 and then added 30 instead of dividing the original angle by 2.

Answers

34. $m\angle AOB = 90°$, rt.; $m\angle BOC = 126°$, obtuse; $m\angle COD = 36°$, acute; $m\angle DOA = 108°$, obtuse

MULTI-STEP TEST PREP

33. This problem will prepare you for the Multi-Step Test Prep on page 34. An archaeologist standing at O looks for clues on where to dig for artifacts.
    a. What value of x will make the angle between the pottery and the arrowhead measure 57°? **9**
    b. What value of x makes $\angle LOJ \cong \angle JOK$? **12**
    c. What values of x make $\angle LOK$ an acute angle? **$0 < x < 15.6$**

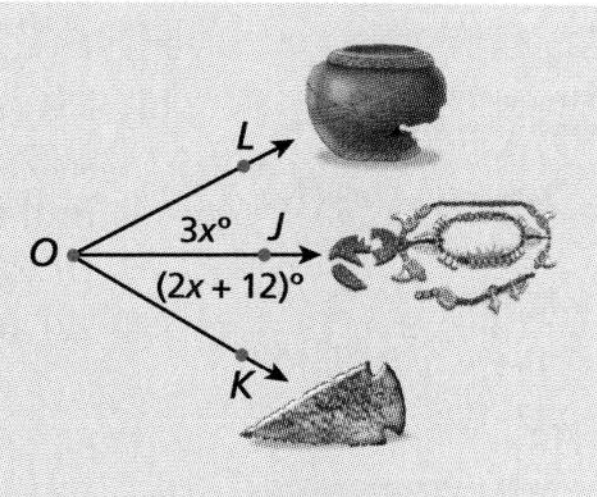

Data Analysis Use the circle graph for Exercises 34–36.

34. Find $m\angle AOB$, $m\angle BOC$, $m\angle COD$, and $m\angle DOA$. Classify each angle as acute, right, or obtuse.

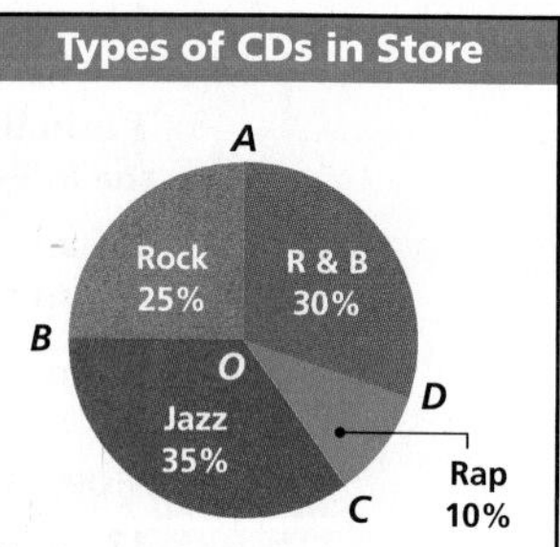

35. **What if...?** Next year, the music store will use some of the shelves currently holding jazz music to double the space for rap. What will $m\angle COD$ and $m\angle BOC$ be next year?

35. $m\angle COD = 72°$; $m\angle BOC = 90°$

36. Suppose a fifth type of music, salsa, is added. If the space is divided equally among the five types, what will be the angle measure for each type of music in the circle graph? **72°**

37. **Critical Thinking** Can an obtuse angle be congruent to an acute angle? Why or why not?

37. No; an obtuse ∠ measures greater than 90°, so it cannot be ≅ to an acute ∠ (less than 90°).

38. The measure of an obtuse angle is $(5x + 45)°$. What is the largest value for x? **27**

39. **Write About It** $\overrightarrow{FH}$ bisects $\angle EFG$. Use the Angle Addition Postulate to explain why $m\angle EFH = \frac{1}{2}m\angle EFG$.

39. $m\angle EFG = m\angle EFH + m\angle HFG = 2m\angle EFH$, so $m\angle EFH = \frac{1}{2}m\angle EFG$

40. **Multi-Step** Use a protractor to draw a 70° angle. Then use a compass and straightedge to bisect the angle. What do you think will be the measure of each angle formed? Use a protractor to support your answer. **Check students' constructions. Each ∠ should be 35°.**

TEST PREP

41. $m\angle UOW = 50°$, and $\overrightarrow{OV}$ bisects $\angle UOW$. What is $m\angle VOY$?
    (A) 25° (B) 65° (C) 130° **(D) 155°**

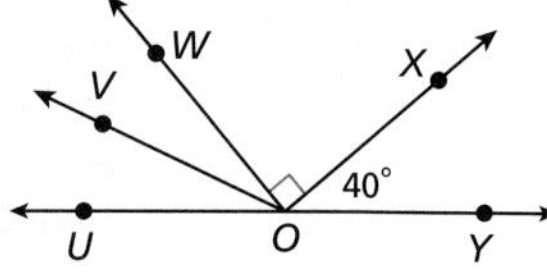

42. What is $m\angle UOX$?
    (F) 50° (G) 115° **(H) 140°** (J) 165°

43. $\overrightarrow{BD}$ bisects $\angle ABC$, $m\angle ABC = (4x + 5)°$, and $m\angle ABD = (3x - 1)°$. What is the value of x?
    (A) 2.2 (B) 3 **(C) 3.5** (D) 7

44. If an angle is bisected and then 30° is added to the measure of the bisected angle, the result is the measure of a right angle. What is the measure of the original angle?
    (F) 30° (G) 60° (H) 75° **(J) 120°**

45. **Short Response** If an obtuse angle is bisected, are the resulting angles acute or obtuse? Explain. **The ∠s are acute. An obtuse ∠ measures between 90° and 180°. Since $\frac{1}{2}$ of 180 is 90, the resulting ∠s must measure less than 90°.**

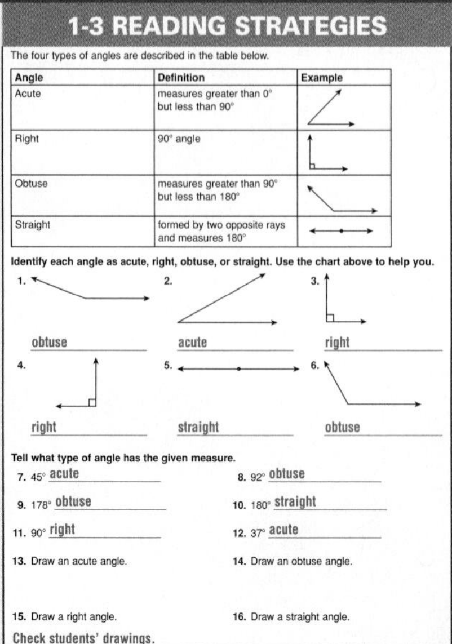

1-3 READING STRATEGIES

The four types of angles are described in the table below.

Angle	Definition	Example
Acute	measures greater than 0° but less than 90°	
Right	90° angle	
Obtuse	measures greater than 90° but less than 180°	
Straight	formed by two opposite rays and measures 180°	

Identify each angle as acute, right, obtuse, or straight. Use the chart above to help you.

1. obtuse 2. acute 3. right
4. right 5. straight 6. obtuse

Tell what type of angle has the given measure.

7. 45° acute
8. 92° obtuse
9. 178° obtuse
10. 180° straight
11. 90° right
12. 37° acute
13. Draw an acute angle.
14. Draw an obtuse angle.
15. Draw a right angle.
16. Draw a straight angle.

Check students' drawings.

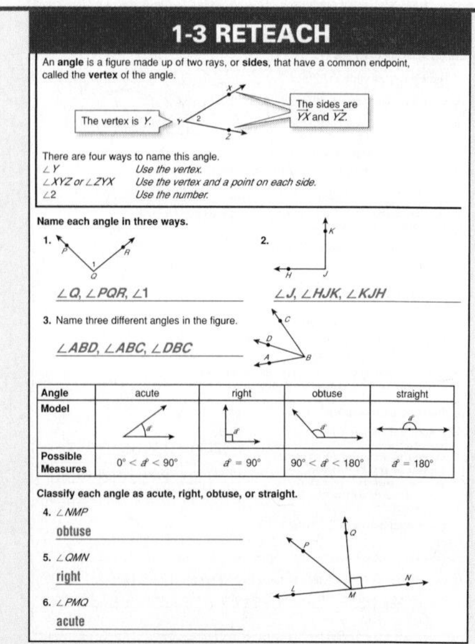

1-3 RETEACH

An **angle** is a figure made up of two rays, or **sides**, that have a common endpoint, called the **vertex** of the angle.

The vertex is Y. The sides are $\overrightarrow{YX}$ and $\overrightarrow{YZ}$.

There are four ways to name this angle.
∠Y — Use the vertex.
∠XYZ or ∠ZYX — Use the vertex and a point on each side.
∠2 — Use the number.

Name each angle in three ways.

1. ∠Q, ∠PQR, ∠1
2. ∠J, ∠HJK, ∠KJH
3. Name three different angles in the figure. ∠ABD, ∠ABC, ∠DBC

Angle	acute	right	obtuse	straight
Model				
Possible Measures	0° < a° < 90°	a° = 90°	90° < a° < 180°	a° = 180°

Classify each angle as acute, right, obtuse, or straight.

4. ∠NMP obtuse
5. ∠QMN right
6. ∠PMQ acute

CHALLENGE AND EXTEND

46. Find the measure of the angle formed by the hands of a clock when it is 7:00. **150°**

47. $\overrightarrow{QS}$ bisects $\angle PQR$, $m\angle PQR = (x^2)°$, and $m\angle PQS = (2x + 6)°$. Find all the possible measures for $\angle PQR$. **36° or 4°**

48. For more precise measurements, a degree can be divided into 60 minutes, and each minute can be divided into 60 seconds. An angle measure of 42 degrees, 30 minutes, and 10 seconds is written as 42°30′10″. Subtract this angle measure from the measure 81°24′15″. **38°54′5″**

49. If 1 degree equals 60 minutes and 1 minute equals 60 seconds, how many seconds are in 2.25 degrees? **8100**

50. $\angle ABC \cong \angle DBC$. $m\angle ABC = \left(\frac{3x}{2} + 4\right)°$ and $m\angle DBC = \left(2x - 27\frac{1}{4}\right)°$. Is $\angle ABD$ a straight angle? Explain. **No; $x = 62.5$, and substituting this value into the expressions for the ∠ measures gives a sum of 195.5.**

SPIRAL REVIEW

51. What number is 64% of 35? **22.4**

52. What percent of 280 is 33.6? *(Previous course)* **12%**

Sketch a figure that shows each of the following. *(Lesson 1-1)*

53. a line that contains $\overline{AB}$ and $\overrightarrow{CB}$ (A, B, C on a line)

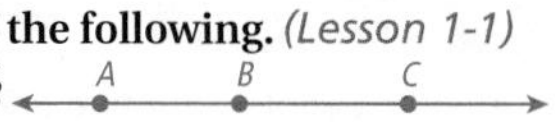

54. two different lines that intersect $\overline{MN}$

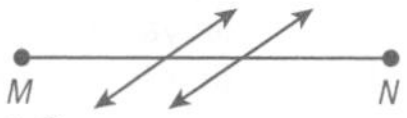

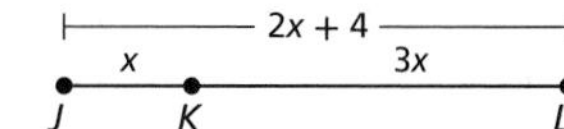

55. a plane and a ray that intersect only at Q

55.

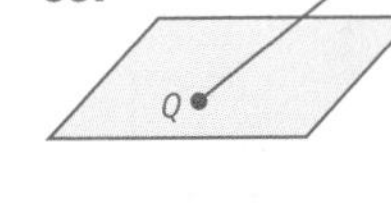

Find the length of each segment. *(Lesson 1-2)*

56. $\overline{JK}$ **2**   57. $\overline{KL}$ **6**   58. $\overline{JL}$ **8**

Using Technology   Segment and Angle Bisectors

1. Construct the bisector of $\overline{MN}$.

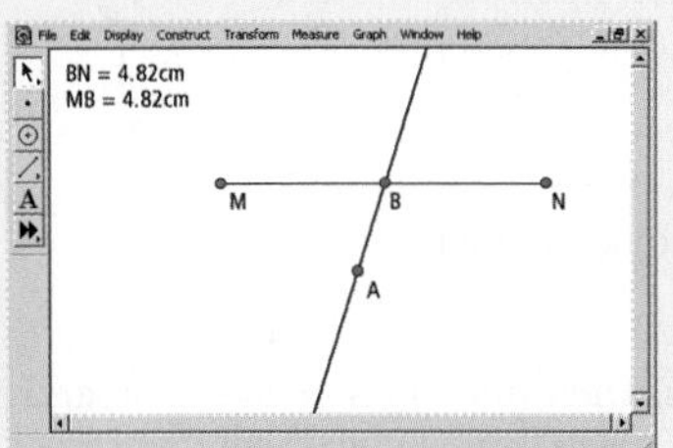

a. Draw $\overline{MN}$ and construct the midpoint B.
b. Construct a point A not on the segment.
c. Construct bisector $\overleftrightarrow{AB}$ and measure $\overline{MB}$ and $\overline{NB}$.
d. Drag M and N and observe MB and NB.

2. Construct the bisector of $\angle BAC$.

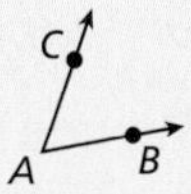

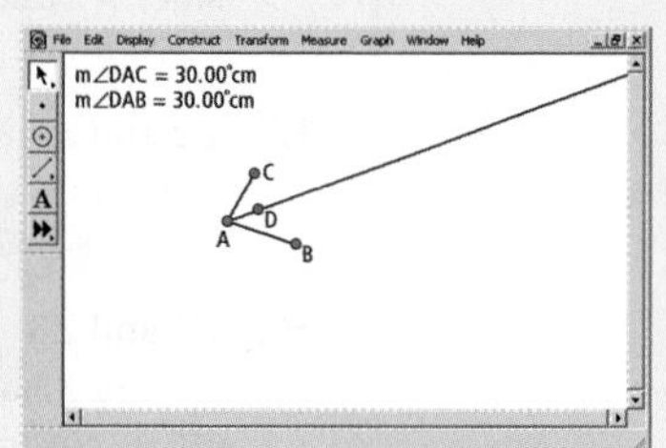

a. Draw $\angle BAC$.
b. Construct the angle bisector $\overrightarrow{AD}$ and measure $\angle DAC$ and $\angle DAB$.
c. Drag the angle and observe $m\angle DAB$ and $m\angle DAC$.

1-3 PROBLEM SOLVING

Projection drawings are often used to represent three-dimensional molecules. The projection drawing of a methane molecule is shown below, along with the angles that are formed in the drawing.

Methane Molecule

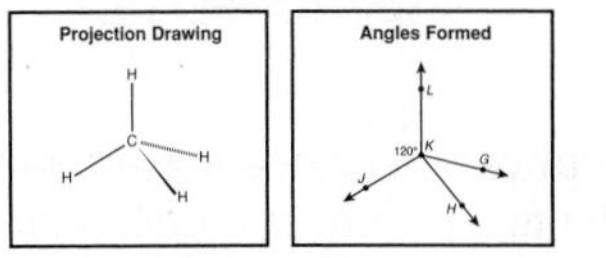

Projection Drawing | Angles Formed (120°, K, L, G, H, J)

1. Name five different angles that are formed in the drawing.
   Possible answer: ∠LKG, ∠GKH, ∠HKJ, ∠JKL, ∠LKH
2. If m∠LKH = m∠JKL + 20° and m∠HKG = 37°, what is m∠GKL? 103°
3. Find m∠JKH. 100°

The diagram shows the proper way to sit at a computer to avoid straining your back or eyes. Use the figure for Exercises 4 and 5.

4. The *total viewing angle* is ∠DAB. If m∠DAC = $\frac{1}{2}$(m∠ACB), what is the measure of the total viewing angle?
   65°
5. The *optimum viewing angle* is 38° below the horizontal. If $\overrightarrow{AV}$ is drawn to form this angle with $\overrightarrow{AB}$, what is the measure of ∠DAV?
   27°

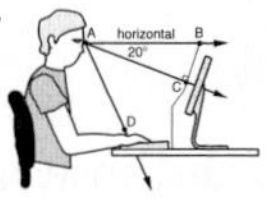

Choose the best answer.

6. $\overrightarrow{QR}$ is in the interior of obtuse ∠PQS, and ∠PQR is a right angle. Classify ∠SQR.
   (A) acute   B right   C obtuse   D straight
7. $\overrightarrow{VX}$ bisect ∠WVY, m∠WVX = (6x)°, and m∠WVY = (16x − 42)°. What is the value of x?
   F $\frac{21}{11}$ G $\frac{42}{13}$ H 4.2   (J) 10.5

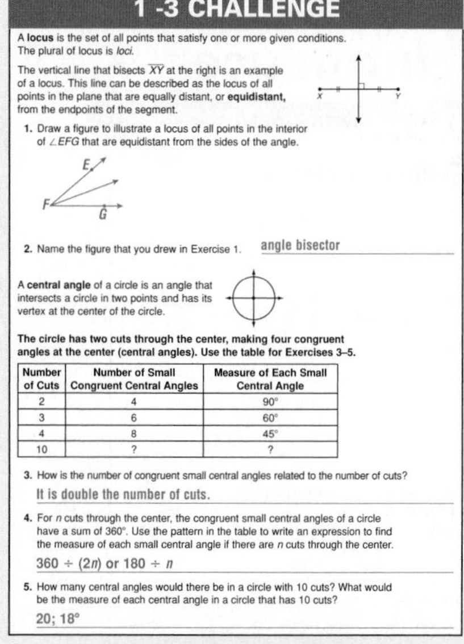

1 -3 CHALLENGE

A **locus** is the set of all points that satisfy one or more given conditions. The plural of locus is *loci*.

The vertical line that bisects $\overline{XY}$ at the right is an example of a locus. This line can be described as the locus of all points in the plane that are equally distant, or **equidistant,** from the endpoints of the segment.

1. Draw a figure to illustrate a locus of all points in the interior of ∠EFG that are equidistant from the sides of the angle.
2. Name the figure that you drew in Exercise 1. angle bisector

A **central angle** of a circle is an angle that intersects a circle in two points and has its vertex at the center of the circle.

The circle has two cuts through the center, making four congruent angles at the center (central angles). Use the table for Exercises 3–5.

Number of Cuts	Number of Small Congruent Central Angles	Measure of Each Small Central Angle
2	4	90°
3	6	60°
4	8	45°
10	?	?

3. How is the number of congruent small central angles related to the number of cuts?
   It is double the number of cuts.
4. For n cuts through the center, the congruent small central angles of a circle have a sum of 360°. Use the pattern in the table to write an expression to find the measure of each small central angle if there are n cuts through the center.
   360 ÷ (2n) or 180 ÷ n
5. How many central angles would there be in a circle with 10 cuts? What would be the measure of each central angle in a circle that has 10 cuts?
   20; 18°

COMMON ERROR ALERT

For **Exercise 47,** students may not try the negative value for *x*. Remind students to check both values of *x* by substituting them back into the expression.

Visual For **Exercise 46,** use a representation of a clock, such as a paper plate with arrows attached with a brad to represent the hands. Given a measurement, students can show the possible time on the clock. Given a time, students can form and then classify the angle.

Journal

Have students name and give the definition of at least 5 other words that use *bi* to mean "two."

ALTERNATIVE ASSESSMENT

Have students create a diagram containing each type of angle introduced in this lesson. They should identify the angles in their diagram, measure each with their protractor, choose one to copy, and bisect another.

Power Presentations with PowerPoint®

Classify each angle as acute, right, or obtuse.

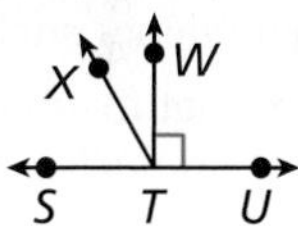

1. ∠XTS acute
2. ∠WTU right
3. K is in the interior of ∠LMN, m∠LMK = 52°, and m∠KMN = 12°. Find m∠LMN. 64°
4. $\overrightarrow{BD}$ bisects ∠ABC, m∠ABD = $\left(\frac{1}{2}y + 10\right)°$, and m∠DBC = (y + 4)°. Find m∠ABC. 32°
5. Use a protractor to draw an angle with a measure of 165°. Check students' work.
6. m∠WYZ = (2x − 5)° and m∠XYW = (3x + 10)°. Find the value of x. 35

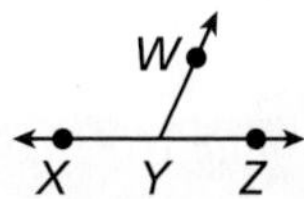

Also available on transparency

1-4 Organizer

Pacing: Traditional 1 day
Block $\frac{1}{2}$ day

Objectives: Identify adjacent, vertical, complementary, and supplementary angles.

Find measures of pairs of angles.

Online Edition
Tutorial Videos

Countdown Week 1

Power Presentations with PowerPoint®

Warm Up

Simplify each expression.

1. $90 - (x + 20)$ $70 - x$
2. $180 - (3x - 10)$ $190 - 3x$

Write an algebraic expression for each of the following.

3. 4 more than twice a number $2n + 4$
4. 6 less than half a number $\frac{1}{2}n - 6$

Also available on transparency

Math Humor

Teacher: Today we are going to learn about complementary angles.

Student: Does that mean the angles are nice to each other?

1-4 Pairs of Angles

Objectives
Identify adjacent, vertical, complementary, and supplementary angles.

Find measures of pairs of angles.

Vocabulary
adjacent angles
linear pair
complementary angles
supplementary angles
vertical angles

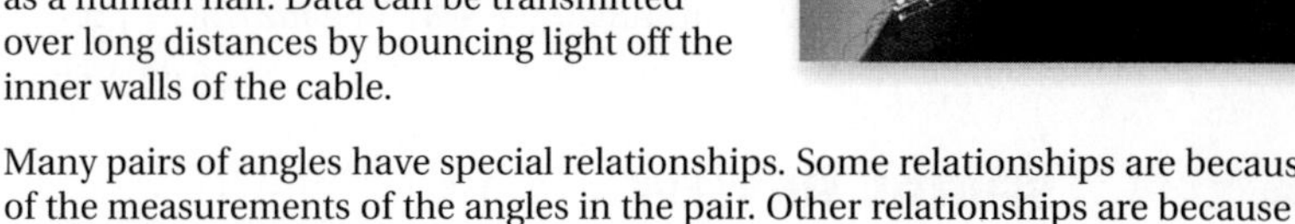

Who uses this?
Scientists use properties of angle pairs to design fiber-optic cables. (See Example 4.)

A fiber-optic cable is a strand of glass as thin as a human hair. Data can be transmitted over long distances by bouncing light off the inner walls of the cable.

Many pairs of angles have special relationships. Some relationships are because of the measurements of the angles in the pair. Other relationships are because of the positions of the angles in the pair.

Know it! Note

Pairs of Angles

Adjacent angles are two angles in the same plane with a common vertex and a common side, but no common interior points. ∠1 and ∠2 are adjacent angles.

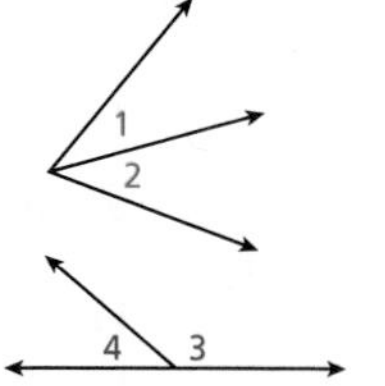

A **linear pair** of angles is a pair of adjacent angles whose noncommon sides are opposite rays. ∠3 and ∠4 form a linear pair.

EXAMPLE 1 **Identifying Angle Pairs**

Tell whether the angles are only adjacent, adjacent and form a linear pair, or not adjacent.

A ∠1 and ∠2

∠1 and ∠2 have a common vertex, *B*, a common side, $\overrightarrow{BC}$, and no common interior points. Therefore ∠1 and ∠2 are only adjacent angles.

B ∠2 and ∠4

∠2 and ∠4 share $\overline{BC}$ but do not have a common vertex, so ∠2 and ∠4 are not adjacent angles.

C ∠1 and ∠3

∠1 and ∠3 are adjacent angles. Their noncommon sides, $\overrightarrow{BC}$ and $\overrightarrow{BA}$, are opposite rays, so ∠1 and ∠3 also form a linear pair.

Tell whether the angles are only adjacent, adjacent and form a linear pair, or not adjacent.

1a. ∠5 and ∠6 adj.; lin. pair
1b. ∠7 and ∠*SPU* not adj.
1c. ∠7 and ∠8 not adj.

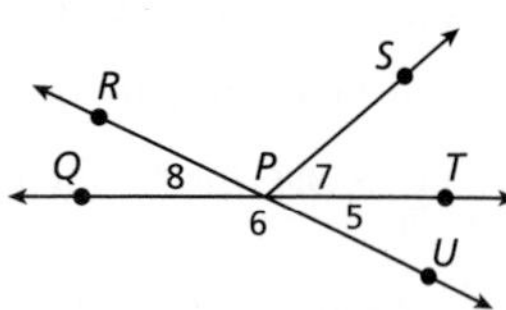

State Resources

go.hrw.com
State Resources Online
KEYWORD: MG7 Resources

1 Introduce

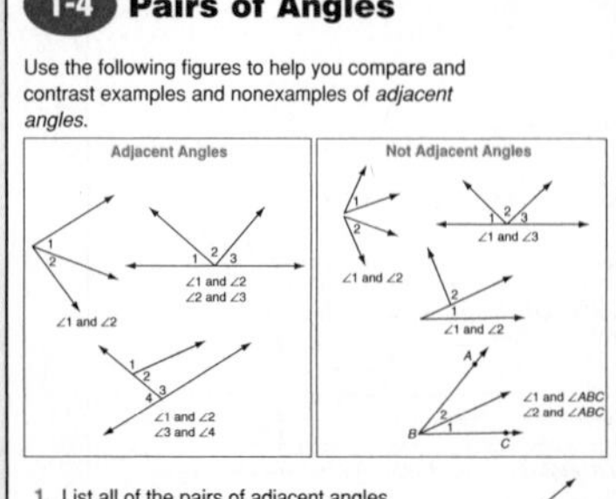

EXPLORATION
1-4 Pairs of Angles
Use the following figures to help you compare and contrast examples and nonexamples of adjacent angles.
Adjacent Angles
Not Adjacent Angles
1. List all of the pairs of adjacent angles in the figure.
2. Complete this definition: Adjacent angles are two angles in the same plane with a common ? and a common ? , but with no common interior points.

Motivate

Angles are used in physics, engineering, art and design. Show students a picture of a quilt pattern with angle pairs in it. Discuss the relationships between different pairs of angles. Ask students what they think the angle measures must be so the pieces will fit together.

Explorations and answers are provided in *Alternate Openers: Explorations Transparencies.*

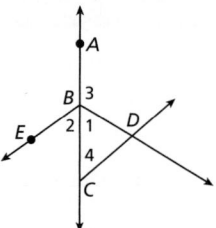

Complementary and Supplementary Angles

Complementary angles are two angles whose measures have a sum of 90°. $\angle A$ and $\angle B$ are complementary.

Supplementary angles are two angles whose measures have a sum of 180°. $\angle A$ and $\angle C$ are supplementary.

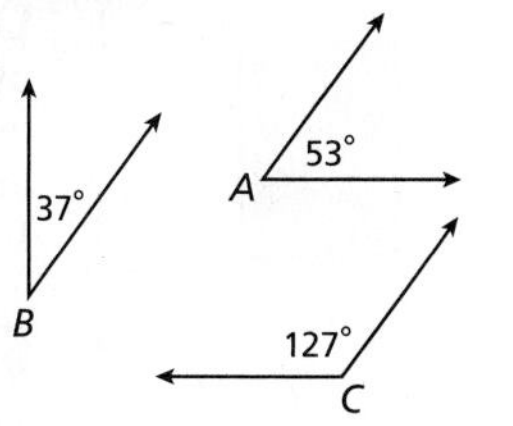

You can find the complement of an angle that measures $x°$ by subtracting its measure from 90°, or $(90 - x)°$. You can find the supplement of an angle that measures $x°$ by subtracting its measure from 180°, or $(180 - x)°$.

EXAMPLE 2 Finding the Measures of Complements and Supplements

Find the measure of each of the following.

A complement of $\angle M$

$(90 - x)°$

$90° - 26.8° = 63.2°$

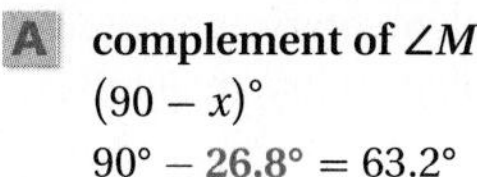

B supplement of $\angle N$

$(180 - x)°$

$180° - (2y + 20)° = 180° - 2y - 20$

$= (160 - 2y)°$

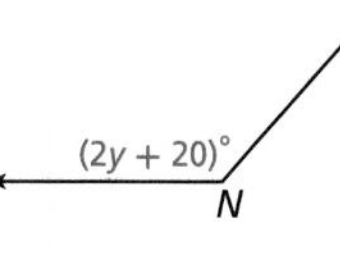

Find the measure of each of the following.

2a. complement of $\angle E$ **$(102 - 7x)°$**

2b. supplement of $\angle F$ **$63\frac{1}{2}°$**

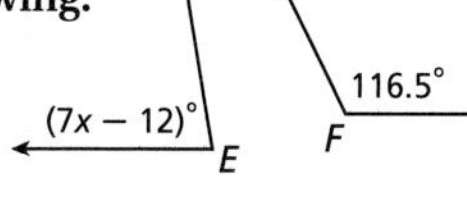

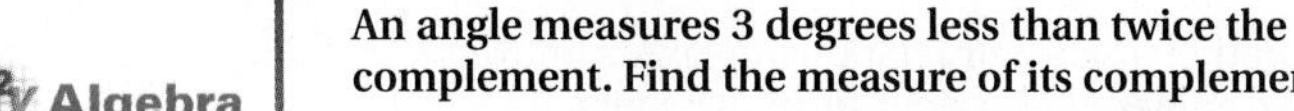

EXAMPLE 3 Using Complements and Supplements to Solve Problems

2 Algebra

An angle measures 3 degrees less than twice the measure of its complement. Find the measure of its complement.

Step 1 Let $m\angle A = x°$. Then $\angle B$, its complement, measures $(90 - x)°$.

Step 2 Write and solve an equation.

$m\angle A = 2m\angle B - 3$

$x = 2(90 - x) - 3$	*Substitute x for m∠A and 90 − x for m∠B.*
$x = 180 - 2x - 3$	*Distrib. Prop.*
$x = 177 - 2x$	*Combine like terms.*
$+2x \quad +2x$	*Add 2x to both sides.*
$3x = 177$	*Simplify.*
$\frac{3x}{3} = \frac{177}{3}$	*Divide both sides by 3.*
$x = 59$	*Simplify.*

The measure of the complement, $\angle B$, is $(90 - 59)° = 31°$.

3. An angle's measure is 12° more than $\frac{1}{2}$ the measure of its supplement. Find the measure of the angle. **68°**

COMMON ERROR ALERT

In **Example 2,** students may not apply the Distributive Property correctly. Stress that in the expression $180 - (2y + 20)$, both $2y$ and 20 must be multiplied by -1 to get $160 - 2y$.

Power Presentations with PowerPoint®

Additional Examples

Example 1

Tell whether the angles are only adjacent, adjacent and form a linear pair, or not adjacent.

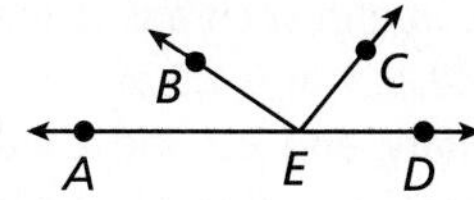

A. $\angle AEB$ and $\angle BED$ lin. pair and adjacent

B. $\angle AEB$ and $\angle BEC$ only adj.

C. $\angle DEC$ and $\angle AEB$ not adj.

Example 2

Find the measure of each of the following.

A. complement of $\angle F$ 31°

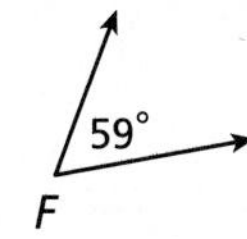

B. supplement of $\angle G$ $(170 - 7x)°$

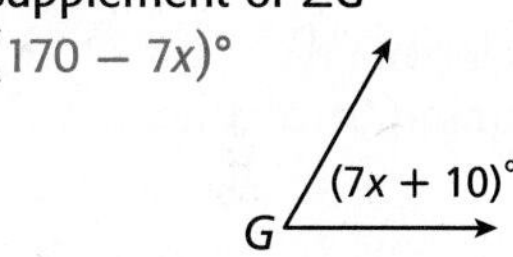

Example 3

An angle is 10° more than 3 times the measure of its complement. Find the measure of the complement. 20°

2 Teach

Guided Instruction

Discuss vertical, complementary, supplementary, and adjacent angles and linear pairs. Have students use mental math to find complements and supplements of angles before using variables or expressions.

Cognitive Strategies One way to help students remember that complementary angles add to 90° and that supplementary angles add to 180° is that 90 comes before 180 and *C* comes before *S* in the alphabet.

Reaching All Learners

Through Cooperative Learning

Each student should create a simple puzzle by dividing a square into six regions using segments. Students should measure all of the angles formed and write several hints for the puzzle solver. For example, a hint might be that one corner of the square is made up of a 15° angle and a 75° angle. Students should then exchange puzzles with a partner and try to reassemble the original square.

INTERVENTION

Questioning Strategies

EXAMPLE 1

- What type of angle is formed by a pair of adjacent angles that form a linear pair?

EXAMPLES 2–3

- Do two angles have to be adjacent to be complementary or supplementary?

Teaching Tip **Visual** The following is another way for students to remember which sum is 90 and which is 180: "Complementary" and "corner" both start with the letter "c," and corners are often right angles. "Supplementary" and "straight" both start with the letter "s," and a straight line is a 180° angle.

Power Presentations with PowerPoint®

Additional Examples

Example 4

Light passing through a fiber-optic cable reflects off the walls of the cable in such a way that ∠1 ≅ ∠2, ∠1 and ∠3 are complementary, and ∠2 and ∠4 are complementary. If m∠1 = 47°, find m∠2, m∠3, and m∠4. 47°; 43°; 43°

Example 5

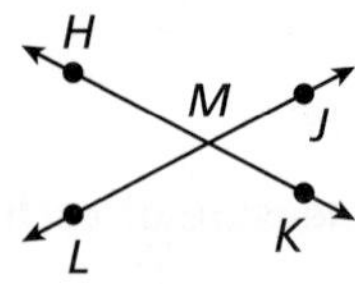

Name the pairs of vertical angles. *∠HML and ∠JMK; ∠HMJ and ∠LMK*

INTERVENTION

Questioning Strategies

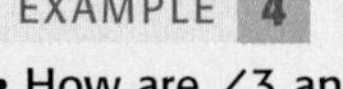

EXAMPLE 4

- How are ∠3 and ∠4 related? Explain.

EXAMPLE 5

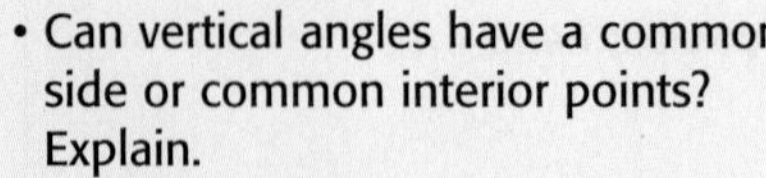

- Can vertical angles have a common side or common interior points? Explain.

Teaching Tip **Inclusion** Remind students that the shape of the letter *x* suggests the idea of vertical angles.

EXAMPLE 4 *Problem-Solving Application*

Light passing through a fiber optic cable reflects off the walls in such a way that ∠1 ≅ ∠2. ∠1 and ∠3 are complementary, and ∠2 and ∠4 are complementary.
If m∠1 = 38°, find m∠2, m∠3, and m∠4.

1 Understand the Problem

The **answers** are the measures of ∠2, ∠3, and ∠4.
List the important information:

- ∠1 ≅ ∠2
- ∠1 and ∠3 are complementary, and ∠2 and ∠4 are complementary.
- m∠1 = 38°

2 Make a Plan

If ∠1 ≅ ∠2, then m∠1 = m∠2.
If ∠3 and ∠1 are complementary, then m∠3 = (90 − 38)°.
If ∠4 and ∠2 are complementary, then m∠4 = (90 − 38)°.

3 Solve

By the Transitive Property of Equality, if m∠1 = 38° and m∠1 = m∠2, then m∠2 = 38°. Since ∠3 and ∠1 are complementary, m∠3 = 52°. Similarly, since ∠2 and ∠4 are complementary, m∠4 = 52°.

4 Look Back

The answer makes sense because 38° + 52° = 90°, so ∠1 and ∠3 are complementary, and ∠2 and ∠4 are complementary. Thus m∠2 = 38°, m∠3 = 52°, and m∠4 = 52°.

CHECK IT OUT! **4. What if...?** Suppose m∠3 = 27.6°. Find m∠1, m∠2, and m∠4.
m∠1 = m∠2 = 62.4°; m∠4° = 27.6°

Another angle pair relationship exists between two angles whose sides form two pairs of opposite rays. **Vertical angles** are two nonadjacent angles formed by two intersecting lines. ∠1 and ∠3 are vertical angles, as are ∠2 and ∠4.

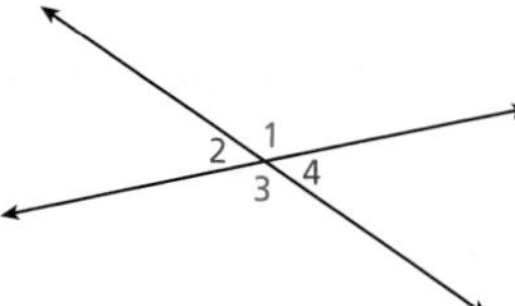

EXAMPLE 5 Identifying Vertical Angles

Name one pair of vertical angles. Do they appear to have the same measure? Check by measuring with a protractor.

∠EDF and *∠GDH* are vertical angles and appear to have the same measure.

Check m∠*EDF* ≈ m∠*GDH* ≈ *135°.*

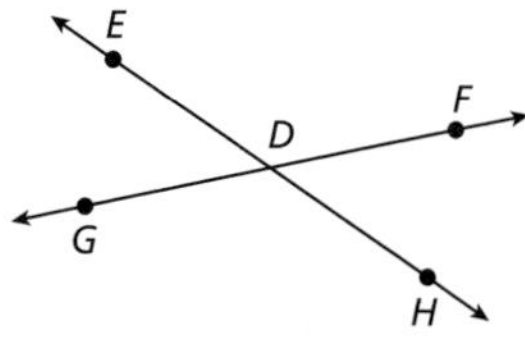

Possible answer: ∠EDG and ∠FDH; m∠EDG ≈ m∠FDH ≈ 45°

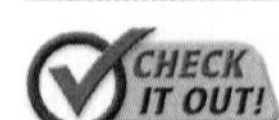

CHECK IT OUT! **5.** Name another pair of vertical angles. Do they appear to have the same measure? Check by measuring with a protractor.

3 Close

Summarize

Review the different angle pairs and illustrations in the lesson. Remind students that a linear pair is a pair of adjacent and supplementary angles, but not all complementary and supplementary angles are adjacent. Then have students identify what kind of angle is a complement of an acute angle, a supplement of an obtuse angle, and the supplement of a right angle. acute, acute, right

ONGOING ASSESSMENT and INTERVENTION

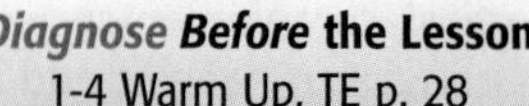

***Diagnose Before* the Lesson**
1-4 Warm Up, TE p. 28

***Monitor During* the Lesson**
Check It Out! Exercises, SE pp. 28–30
Questioning Strategies, TE pp. 29–30

***Assess After* the Lesson**
1-4 Lesson Quiz, TE p. 33
Alternative Assessment, TE p. 33

THINK AND DISCUSS

1. Explain why any two right angles are supplementary.
2. Is it possible for a pair of vertical angles to also be adjacent? Explain.
3. **GET ORGANIZED** Copy and complete the graphic organizer below. In each box, draw a diagram and write a definition of the given angle pair.

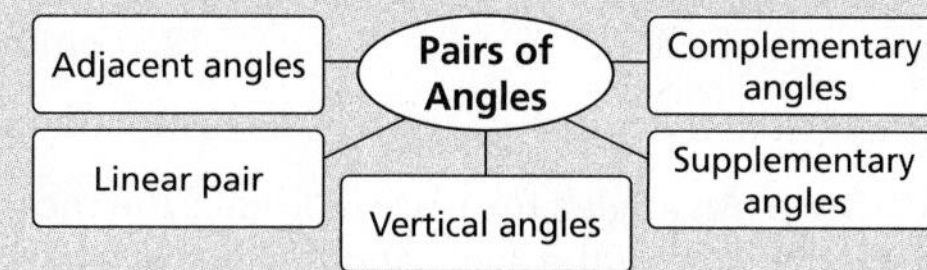

1-4 Exercises

go.hrw.com
Homework Help Online
KEYWORD: MG7 1-4
Parent Resources Online
KEYWORD: MG7 Parent

GUIDED PRACTICE

Vocabulary Apply the vocabulary from this lesson to answer each question.

1. An angle measures $x°$. What is the measure of its *complement*? What is the measure of its *supplement*? $(90 - x)°$; $(180 - x)°$
2. $\angle ABC$ and $\angle CBD$ are *adjacent angles*. Which side do the angles have in common? $\overrightarrow{BC}$

SEE EXAMPLE 1 p. 28

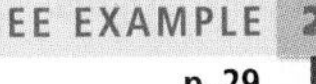

Tell whether the angles are only adjacent, adjacent and form a linear pair, or not adjacent.

3. $\angle 1$ and $\angle 2$ adj.;
4. $\angle 1$ and $\angle 3$ not adj.
5. $\angle 2$ and $\angle 4$ lin. pair not adj.
6. $\angle 2$ and $\angle 3$ only adj.

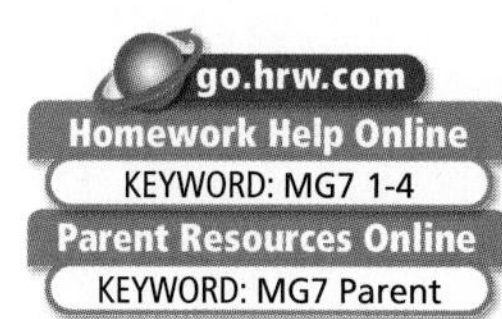

SEE EXAMPLE 2 p. 29

Find the measure of each of the following.

7. supplement of $\angle A$ 98.8°
8. complement of $\angle A$ 8.8°
9. supplement of $\angle B$ $(185 - 6x)°$
10. complement of $\angle B$ $(95 - 6x)°$

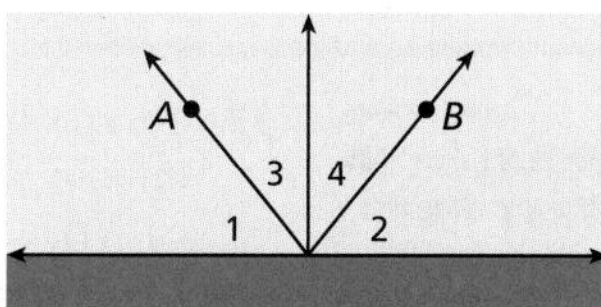

SEE EXAMPLE 3 p. 29

11. **Multi-Step** An angle's measure is 6 degrees more than 3 times the measure of its complement. Find the measure of the angle. 69°

SEE EXAMPLE 4 p. 30

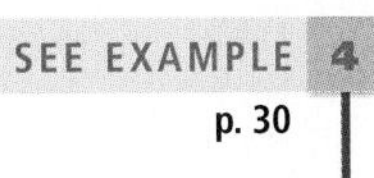

12. **Landscaping** A sprinkler swings back and forth between A and B in such a way that $\angle 1 \cong \angle 2$. $\angle 1$ and $\angle 3$ are complementary, and $\angle 2$ and $\angle 4$ are complementary. If $m\angle 1 = 47.5°$, find $m\angle 2$, $m\angle 3$, and $m\angle 4$. $m\angle 2 = 47.5°$; $m\angle 3 = m\angle 4 = 42.5°$

SEE EXAMPLE 5 p. 30

13. Name each pair of vertical angles. $\angle ABE$, $\angle CBD$; $\angle ABC$, $\angle EBD$

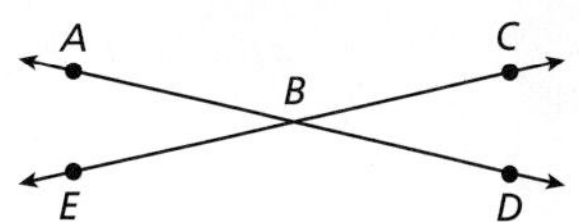

Answers to *Think and Discuss*

1. All rt. ∠s measure 90°, so the sum of the measures of any 2 rt. ∠s is 180°. Therefore any 2 rt. ∠s are supp.
2. Vert. ∠s cannot be adj. ∠s because the def. of vert. ∠s states that they are nonadj. ∠s formed by intersecting lines.
3. See p. A2.

1-4 Exercises

Assignment Guide

Assign *Guided Practice* exercises as necessary.

If you finished Examples **1–3**
Basic 14–22, 25, 27–30, 34
Average 14–22, 25, 27–35
Advanced 14–22, 25, 27–35, 37

If you finished Examples **1–5**
Basic 14–22, 24–30, 33, 34, 37–43, 47–55
Average 14–44, 47–55
Advanced 14–55

Homework Quick Check
Quickly check key concepts.
Exercises: 14, 18, 22, 24, 28, 30, 34

State Resources

MULTI-STEP TEST PREP Exercise 33 involves using algebra to find measures of complementary angles, congruent angles, and linear pairs. This exercise prepares students for the Multi-Step Test Prep on page 34.

Answers

33a.

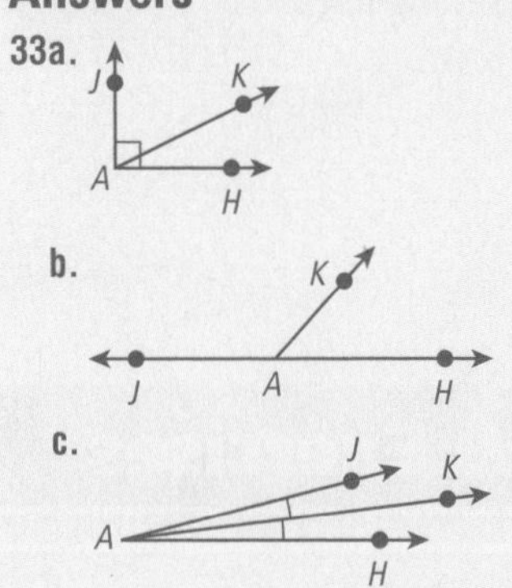

PRACTICE AND PROBLEM SOLVING

Independent Practice	
For Exercises	See Example
14–17	1
18–21	2
22	3
23	4
24	5

Extra Practice
Skills Practice p. S4
Application Practice p. S28

Tell whether the angles are only adjacent, adjacent and form a linear pair, or not adjacent.

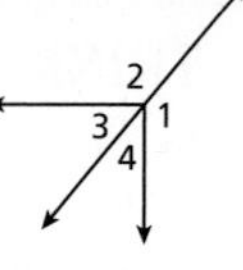

14. ∠1 and ∠4 adj.; lin. pair
15. ∠2 and ∠3 adj.; lin. pair
16. ∠3 and ∠4 only adj.
17. ∠3 and ∠1 not adj.

Given $m\angle A = 56.4°$ and $m\angle B = (2x - 4)°$, find the measure of each of the following.

18. supplement of ∠A 123.6°
19. complement of ∠A 33.6°
20. supplement of ∠B $(184 - 2x)°$
21. complement of ∠B $(94 - 2x)°$
22. **Multi-Step** An angle's measure is 3 times the measure of its complement. Find the measure of the angle and the measure of its complement. 67.5°; 22.5°
23. **Art** In the stained glass pattern, $\angle 1 \cong \angle 2$. ∠1 and ∠3 are complementary, and ∠2 and ∠4 are complementary. If $m\angle 1 = 22.3°$, find m∠2, m∠3, and m∠4.
 $m\angle 2 = 22.3°$; $m\angle 3 = m\angle 4 = 67.7°$

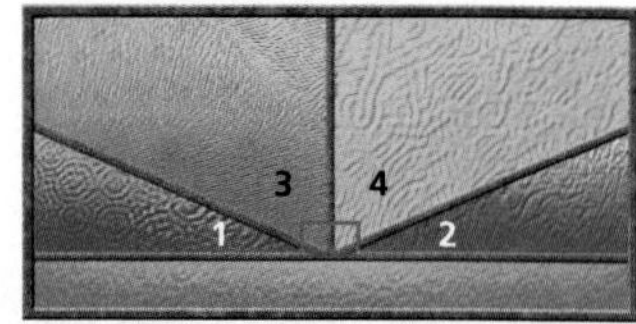

24. Name the pairs of vertical angles.
 ∠PTU, ∠VTR; ∠UTQ, ∠STV; ∠QTR, ∠PTS; ∠PTQ, ∠STR; ∠UTR, ∠PTV; ∠QTV, ∠UTS
25. **Probability** The angle measures 30°, 60°, 120°, and 150° are written on slips of paper. You choose two slips of paper at random. What is the probability that the angle measures are supplementary? $\frac{1}{3}$

Multi-Step **∠ABD and ∠BDE are supplementary. Find the measures of both angles.**

26. $m\angle ABD = 5x°$, $m\angle BDE = (17x - 18)°$ 45°; 135°
27. $m\angle ABD = (3x + 12)°$, $m\angle BDE = (7x - 32)°$ 72°; 108°
28. $m\angle ABD = (12x - 12)°$, $m\angle BDE = (3x + 48)°$ 103.2°; 76.8°

Multi-Step **∠ABD and ∠BDC are complementary. Find the measures of both angles.**

29. $m\angle ABD = (5y + 1)°$, $m\angle BDC = (3y - 7)°$ 61°; 29°
30. $m\angle ABD = (4y + 5)°$, $m\angle BDC = (4y + 8)°$ 43.5°; 46.5°
31. $m\angle ABD = (y - 30)°$, $m\angle BDC = 2y°$ 10°; 80°
32. **Critical Thinking** Explain why an angle that is supplementary to an acute angle must be an obtuse angle.

32. The measure of an acute ∠ is less than 90°. Therefore the measure of its supp. must be between 90° and 180°, which means the supp. is an obtuse ∠.

MULTI-STEP TEST PREP

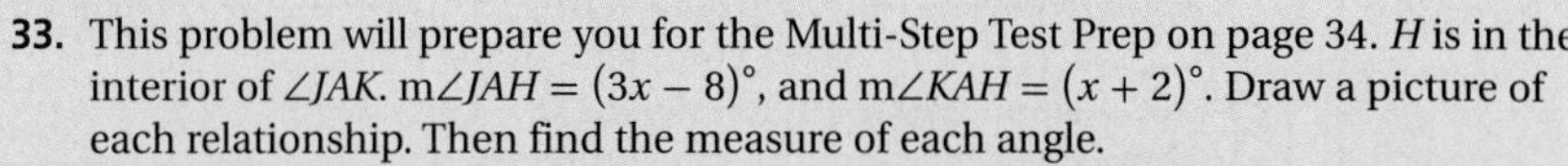

33. This problem will prepare you for the Multi-Step Test Prep on page 34. *H* is in the interior of ∠JAK. $m\angle JAH = (3x - 8)°$, and $m\angle KAH = (x + 2)°$. Draw a picture of each relationship. Then find the measure of each angle.

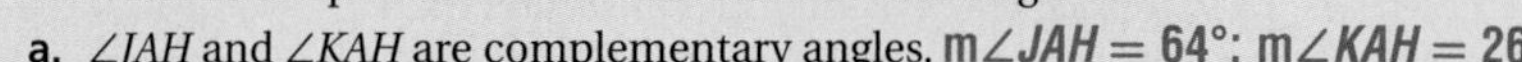

 a. ∠JAH and ∠KAH are complementary angles. $m\angle JAH = 64°$; $m\angle KAH = 26°$

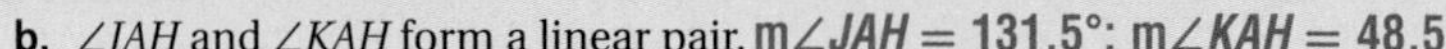

 b. ∠JAH and ∠KAH form a linear pair. $m\angle JAH = 131.5°$; $m\angle KAH = 48.5°$
 c. ∠JAH and ∠KAH are congruent angles. $m\angle JAH = m\angle KAH = 7°$

1-4 PRACTICE A
1-4 PRACTICE C
1-4 PRACTICE B

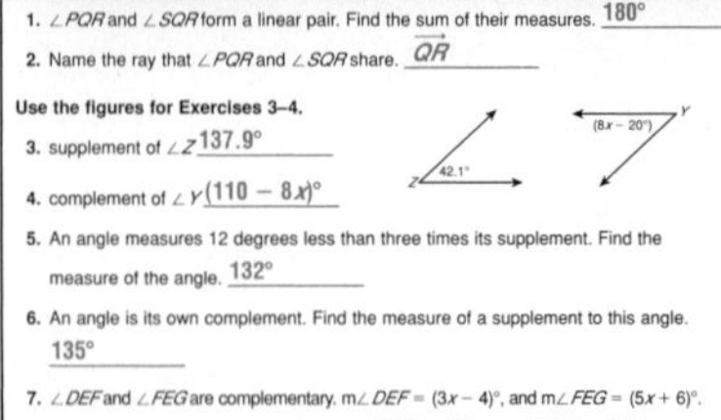

1. ∠PQR and ∠SQR form a linear pair. Find the sum of their measures. 180°
2. Name the ray that ∠PQR and ∠SQR share. $\overrightarrow{QR}$

Use the figures for Exercises 3–4.

3. supplement of ∠Z 137.9°
4. complement of ∠Y $(110 - 8x)°$
5. An angle measures 12 degrees less than three times its supplement. Find the measure of the angle. 132°
6. An angle is its own complement. Find the measure of a supplement to this angle. 135°
7. ∠DEF and ∠FEG are complementary. $m\angle DEF = (3x - 4)°$, and $m\angle FEG = (5x + 6)°$. Find the measures of both angles. $m\angle DEF = 29°$; $m\angle FEG = 61°$
8. ∠DEF and ∠FEG are supplementary. $m\angle DEF = (9x + 1)°$, and $m\angle FEG = (8x + 9)°$. Find the measures of both angles. $m\angle DEF = 91°$; $m\angle FEG = 89°$

Use the figure for Exercises 9–10.
In 2004, several nickels were minted to commemorate the Louisiana Purchase and Lewis and Clark's expedition into the American West. One nickel shows a pipe and a hatchet crossed to symbolize peace between the American government and Native American tribes.

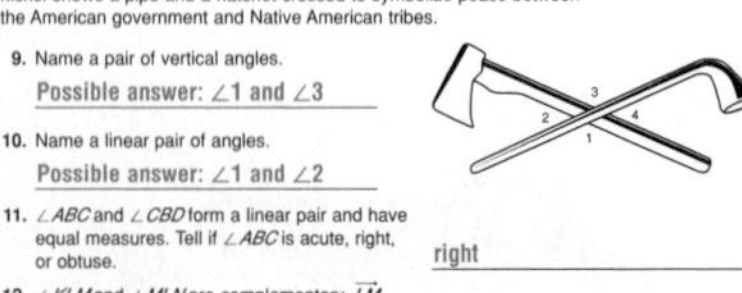

9. Name a pair of vertical angles. Possible answer: ∠1 and ∠3
10. Name a linear pair of angles. Possible answer: ∠1 and ∠2
11. ∠ABC and ∠CBD form a linear pair and have equal measures. Tell if ∠ABC is acute, right, or obtuse. right
12. ∠KLM and ∠MLN are complementary. $\overrightarrow{LM}$ bisects ∠KLN. Find the measures of ∠KLM and ∠MLN. 45°; 45°

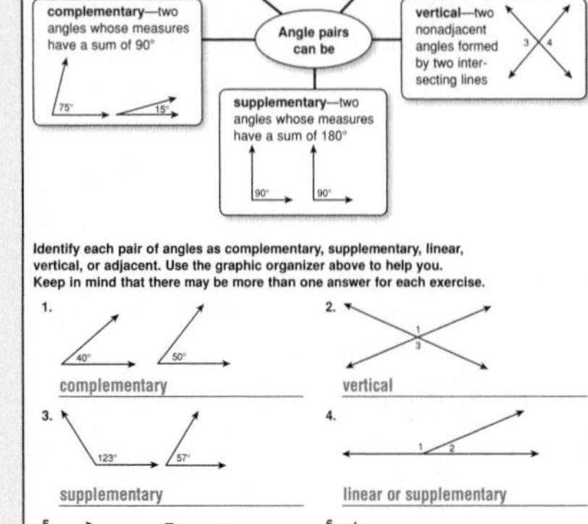

1-4 READING STRATEGIES

The graphic organizer below outlines the different possibilities for a pair of angles.

Angle pairs can be
- **adjacent**—two angles in the same plane with a common vertex and a common side but no common interior points
- **linear**—adjacent angles whose noncommon sides are opposite rays
- **complementary**—two angles whose measures have a sum of 90°
- **vertical**—two nonadjacent angles formed by two intersecting lines
- **supplementary**—two angles whose measures have a sum of 180°

Identify each pair of angles as complementary, supplementary, linear, vertical, or adjacent. Use the graphic organizer above to help you. Keep in mind that there may be more than one answer for each exercise.

1. complementary
2. vertical
3. supplementary
4. linear or supplementary
5. adjacent
6. complementary

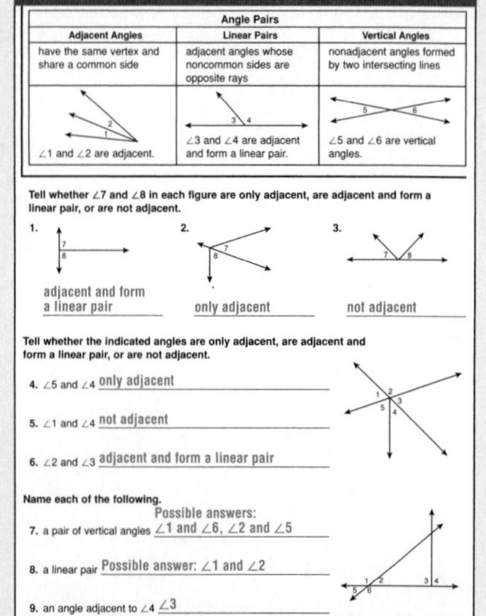

1-4 RETEACH

Angle Pairs		
Adjacent Angles	Linear Pairs	Vertical Angles
have the same vertex and share a common side	adjacent angles whose noncommon sides are opposite rays	nonadjacent angles formed by two intersecting lines
∠1 and ∠2 are adjacent.	∠3 and ∠4 are adjacent and form a linear pair.	∠5 and ∠6 are vertical angles.

Tell whether ∠7 and ∠8 in each figure are only adjacent, are adjacent and form a linear pair, or are not adjacent.

1. adjacent and form a linear pair
2. only adjacent
3. not adjacent

Tell whether the indicated angles are only adjacent, are adjacent and form a linear pair, or are not adjacent.

4. ∠5 and ∠4 only adjacent
5. ∠1 and ∠4 not adjacent
6. ∠2 and ∠3 adjacent and form a linear pair

Name each of the following.

7. a pair of vertical angles Possible answers: ∠1 and ∠6, ∠2 and ∠5
8. a linear pair Possible answer: ∠1 and ∠2
9. an angle adjacent to ∠4 ∠3

Determine whether each statement is true or false. If false, explain why.

34. F; the supp. must be greater than the comp.

34. If an angle is acute, then its complement must be greater than its supplement.

35. A pair of vertical angles may also form a linear pair. F; vert. ∡ cannot be adj. ∡, so they cannot form a lin. pair.

36. If two angles are supplementary and congruent, the measure of each angle is 90°. T

37. If a ray divides an angle into two complementary angles, then the original angle is a right angle. T

38. Write About It Describe a situation in which two angles are both congruent and complementary. Explain. The 2 ∡ must both measure 45°. 45° + 45° = 90°, so the ∡ are comp. and ≅.

39. What is the value of x in the diagram?

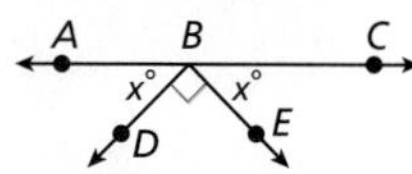

Ⓐ 15 Ⓑ 30 ⓒ 45 Ⓓ 90

40. The ratio of the measures of two complementary angles is 1:2. What is the measure of the larger angle? (*Hint:* Let x and $2x$ represent the angle measures.)

Ⓕ 30° Ⓖ 45° ⓗ 60° Ⓙ 120°

41. m∠A = 3y, and m∠B = 2m∠A. Which value of y makes ∠A supplementary to ∠B?

Ⓐ 10 Ⓑ 18 ⓒ 20 Ⓓ 36

42. The measures of two supplementary angles are in the ratio 7:5. Which value is the measure of the smaller angle? (*Hint:* Let $7x$ and $5x$ represent the angle measures.)

Ⓕ 37.5 Ⓖ 52.5 ⓗ 75 Ⓙ 105

CHALLENGE AND EXTEND

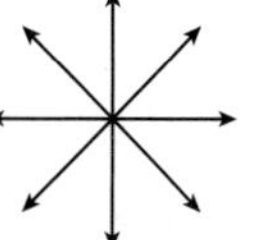

43. How many pairs of vertical angles are in the diagram? 12

44. The supplement of an angle is 4 more than twice its complement. Find the measure of the angle. 4°

45. An angle's measure is twice the measure of its complement. The larger angle is how many degrees greater than the smaller angle? 30°

46. The supplement of an angle is 36° less than twice the supplement of the complement of the angle. Find the measure of the supplement. 168°

SPIRAL REVIEW

Solve each equation. Check your answer. *(Previous course)*

47. $4x + 10 = 42$ 8

48. $5m - 9 = m + 4$ 3.25

49. $2(y + 3) = 12$ 3

50. $-(d + 4) = 18$ −22

***Y* is between *X* and *Z*, *XY* = 3*x* + 1, *YZ* = 2*x* − 2, and *XZ* = 84. Find each of the following.** *(Lesson 1-2)*

51. x 17

52. XY 52

53. YZ 32

$\overrightarrow{XY}$ bisects ∠WYZ. Given m∠WYX = 26°, find each of the following. *(Lesson 1-3)*

54. m∠XYZ 26°

55. m∠WYZ 52°

If students chose **F** for **Exercise 40,** they did not substitute the value for x in the expression $2x$ and find the larger angle. If they chose **D** for **Exercise 41,** they wrote the equation $3y + 2y = 180$ instead of multiplying $3y$ by 2.

Journal

Have students draw and then define vertical angles in their own words. Ask them to give examples of vertical angles used in real-world structures.

ALTERNATIVE ASSESSMENT

Have students name and draw the various pairs of angles introduced in this lesson. Ask them to write and solve a word problem using complementary or supplementary angles on index cards, and then rotate for other students to solve.

Power Presentations with PowerPoint®

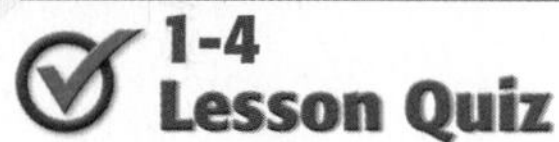

m∠A = 64.1°, and m∠B = (4x − 30)°. Find the measure of each of the following.

1. supplement of ∠A 115.9°
2. complement of ∠B (120 − 4x)°
3. Determine whether this statement is true or false. If false, explain why. If two angles are complementary and congruent, then the measure of each is 90°. False; each is 45°.

m∠XYZ = 2x° and m∠PQR = (8x − 20)°.

4. If ∠XYZ and ∠PQR are supplementary, find the measure of each angle. 40°; 140°
5. If ∠XYZ and ∠PQR are complementary, find the measure of each angle. 22°; 68°

Also available on transparency

1-4 PROBLEM SOLVING

Use the drawing of part of the Eiffel Tower for Exercises 1–5.

1. Name a pair of angles that appear to be complementary.
   Possible answer: ∠ALB and ∠BLC
2. Name a pair of supplementary angles.
   Possible answer: ∠AML and ∠YML
3. If m∠CSW = 45°, what is m∠JST? How do you know?
   45°; They are vertical angles.
4. If m∠FKB = 135°, what is m∠BKL? How do you know?
   45°; The angles are supplementary.
5. Name three angles whose measures sum to 180°.
   Possible answer: ∠ABM, ∠MBK, and ∠KBC

Choose the best answer.

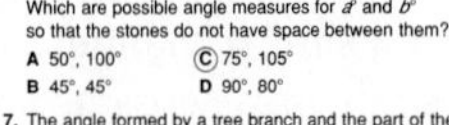

6. A landscaper uses paving stones for a walkway. Which are possible angle measures for $a°$ and $b°$ so that the stones do not have space between them?
   A 50°, 100° ⓒ 75°, 105°
   B 45°, 45° D 90°, 80°
7. The angle formed by a tree branch and the part of the trunk above it is 68°. What is the measure of the angle that is formed by the branch and the part of the trunk below it?
   F 22° H 158°
   ⓖ 112° J 180°
8. ∠R and ∠S are complementary. If m∠R = (7 + 3x)° and m∠S = (2x + 13)°, which is a true statement?
   ⓐ ∠R is acute. C ∠R and ∠S are right angles.
   B ∠R is obtuse. D m∠S > m∠R

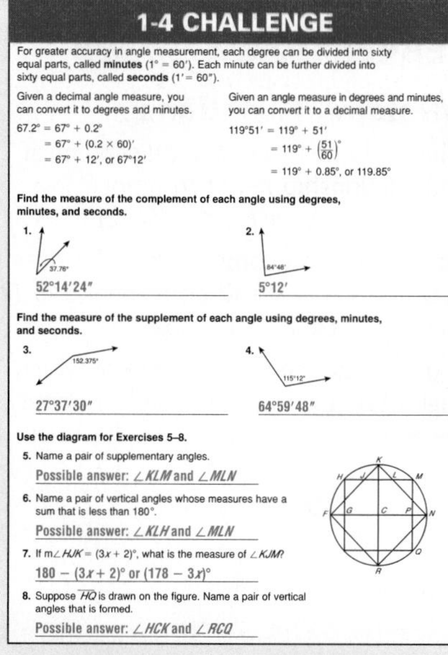

1-4 CHALLENGE

For greater accuracy in angle measurement, each degree can be divided into sixty equal parts, called **minutes** (1° = 60′). Each minute can be further divided into sixty equal parts, called **seconds** (1′ = 60″).

Given a decimal angle measure, you can convert it to degrees and minutes.

67.2° = 67° + 0.2°
= 67° + (0.2 × 60)′
= 67° + 12′, or 67°12′

Given an angle measure in degrees and minutes, you can convert it to a decimal measure.

119°51′ = 119° + 51′
= $119° + \left(\frac{51}{60}\right)°$
= 119° + 0.85°, or 119.85°

Find the measure of the complement of each angle using degrees, minutes, and seconds.

1. 37.76° — 52°14′24″
2. 84°48′ — 5°12′

Find the measure of the supplement of each angle using degrees, minutes, and seconds.

3. 152.375° — 27°37′30″
4. 115°12′ — 64°59′48″

Use the diagram for Exercises 5–8.

5. Name a pair of supplementary angles.
   Possible answer: ∠KLM and ∠MLN
6. Name a pair of vertical angles whose measures have a sum that is less than 180°.
   Possible answer: ∠KLH and ∠MLN
7. If m∠HJK = (3x + 2)°, what is the measure of ∠KJM?
   180 − (3x + 2)° or (178 − 3x)°
8. Suppose $\overline{HQ}$ is drawn on the figure. Name a pair of vertical angles that is formed.
   Possible answer: ∠HCK and ∠RCQ

Organizer

Objective: Assess students' ability to apply concepts and skills in Lessons 1-1 through 1-4 in a real-world format.

Online Edition

Resources

Geometry Assessments
www.mathtekstoolkit.org

Problem	Text Reference
1	Lesson 1-1
2	Lesson 1-2
3	Lesson 1-3
4	Lesson 1-4

State Resources

CHAPTER 1

MULTI-STEP TEST PREP

SECTION 1A

Euclidean and Construction Tools

Can You Dig It? A group of college and high school students participated in an archaeological dig. The team discovered four fossils. To organize their search, Sierra used a protractor and ruler to make a diagram of where different members of the group found fossils. She drew the locations based on the location of the campsite. The campsite is located at X on $\overleftrightarrow{XB}$. The four fossils were found at R, T, W, and M.

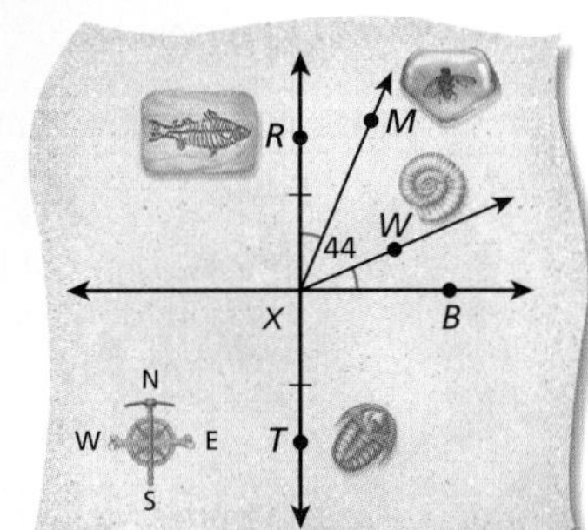

1. Are the locations of the campsite at X and the fossils at R and T collinear or noncollinear? **1. collinear**
2. How is X related to $\overline{RT}$? If $RX = 10x - 6$ and $XT = 3x + 8$, what is the distance between the locations of the fossils at R and T? **2. mdpt.; 28 ft**
3. $\angle RXB$ and $\angle BXT$ are right angles. Find the measure of each angle formed by the locations of the fossils and the campsite. Then classify each angle by its measure.
4. Identify the special angle pairs shown in the diagram of the archaeological dig.

3. $m\angle RXM = 23°$; acute; $m\angle RXW = 67°$; acute; $m\angle WXB = 23°$; acute; $m\angle MXW = 44°$; acute; $m\angle RXT = 180°$; straight; $m\angle MXT = 157°$; obtuse; $m\angle WXT = 113°$; obtuse

4. adj.; adj. and a lin. pair; supp.; comp.; vert.

INTERVENTION

Scaffolding Questions

1. What term describes the placement of and relationship between points? Possible answer: X, R, and T are collinear.
2. How would you compare the distances between X and R and between X and T? The distances are the same.
3. You can assume the measure of which angle? What is the term used to classify the angle? $\angle RXT = 180°$; it is a straight $\angle$.
4. How are the angle pairs $\angle RXM$ and $\angle MXB$, and $\angle RXM$ and $\angle MXT$ alike? How are they different? Both $\angle$ pairs are adj. angles. $\angle RXM$ and $\angle MXB$ are comp. $\angle RXM$ and $\angle MXT$ are supp. and a lin. pair.

Extension

What occupations can you name that use angles and directions in a similar manner? Possible answer: Draftspersons use compasses for greater accuracy in their drawings.

Quiz for Lessons 1-1 Through 1-4

1-1 Understanding Points, Lines, and Planes

Draw and label each of the following.

1. a segment with endpoints X and Y
2. a ray with endpoint M that passes through P
3. three coplanar lines intersecting at a point
4. two points and a line that lie in a plane

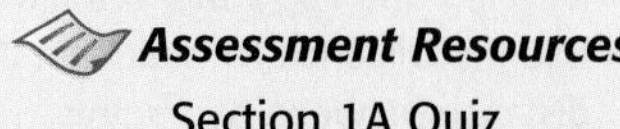

Use the figure to name each of the following.

5. three coplanar points **5. Possible answer: T, V, W**
6. two lines **$\overleftrightarrow{XZ}$ and $\overleftrightarrow{WY}$**
7. a plane containing T, V, and X **plane TVX**
8. a line containing V and Z **ℓ**

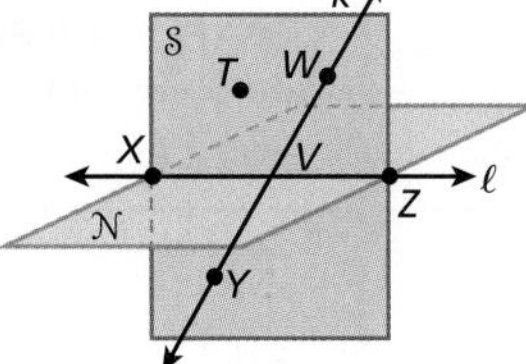

1-2 Measuring and Constructing Segments

Find the length of each segment.

9. $\overline{SV}$ **6.5**
10. $\overline{TR}$ **6**
11. $\overline{ST}$ **3.5**

12. The diagram represents a straight highway with three towns, Henri, Joaquin, and Kenard. Find the distance from Henri H to Joaquin J. **30**

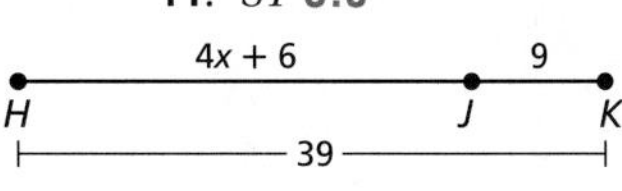

13. Sketch, draw, and construct a segment congruent to $\overline{CD}$. **Check students' work.**
14. Q is the midpoint of $\overline{PR}$, $PQ = 2z$, and $PR = 8z - 12$. Find z, PQ, and PR. **3; 6; 12**

1-3 Measuring and Constructing Angles

15. Name all the angles in the diagram.
∠LMN, ∠NML, or ∠1; ∠NMP, ∠PMN, or ∠2; ∠LMP, ∠PML

Classify each angle by its measure.

16. $m\angle PVQ = 21°$ **acute**
17. $m\angle RVT = 96°$ **obtuse**
18. $m\angle PVS = 143°$ **obtuse**
19. $\overrightarrow{RS}$ bisects $\angle QRT$, $m\angle QRS = (3x + 8)°$, and $m\angle SRT = (9x - 4)°$. Find $m\angle SRT$. **14°**
20. Use a protractor and straightedge to draw a 130° angle. Then bisect the angle. **Check students' work.**

1-4 Pairs of Angles

Tell whether the angles are only adjacent, adjacent and form a linear pair, or not adjacent.

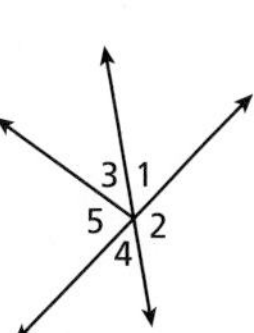

21. ∠1 and ∠2 **adj.; lin. pair**
22. ∠4 and ∠5 **only adj.**
23. ∠3 and ∠4 **not adj.**

If $m\angle T = (5x - 10)°$, find the measure of each of the following.

24. supplement of ∠T **$(190 - 5x)°$**
25. complement of ∠T **$(100 - 5x)°$**

READY TO GO ON? SECTION 1A

Organizer

Objective: Assess students' mastery of concepts and skills in Lessons 1-1 through 1-4.

Resources

Section 1A Quiz

Teacher One Stop™

Test & Practice Generator

INTERVENTION

Resources

Ready to Go On? Intervention and Enrichment **Worksheets**

Ready to Go On? **CD-ROM**

Ready to Go On? **Online**

my.hrw.com

READY TO GO ON? Diagnose and Prescribe

NO — INTERVENE

Ready to Go On? Intervention	Worksheets	CD-ROM	Online
	Ready to Go On? Intervention, Section 1A		
Lesson 1-1	1-1 Intervention	Activity 1-1	Diagnose and Prescribe Online
Lesson 1-2	1-2 Intervention	Activity 1-2	
Lesson 1-3	1-3 Intervention	Activity 1-3	
Lesson 1-4	1-4 Intervention	Activity 1-4	

YES — ENRICH

Ready to Go On? Enrichment, Section 1A

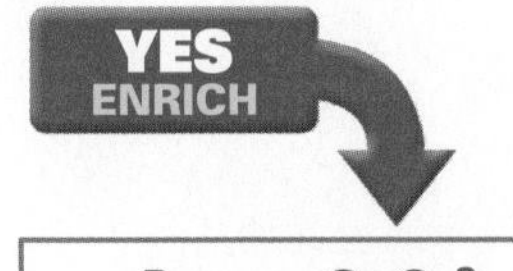

Worksheets
CD-ROM
Online

SECTION **1B**

Coordinate and Transformation Tools

One-Minute Section Planner

Lesson	Lab Resources	Materials
Lesson 1-5 Using Formulas in Geometry • Apply formulas for perimeter, area, and circumference. ☑ SAT-10 ☑ NAEP ☑ ACT ☑ SAT ☑ SAT Subject Tests	***Geometry Lab Activities*** 1-5 Geometry Labs	**Optional** quilt patterns
Lesson 1-6 Midpoint and Distance in the Coordinate Plane • Develop and apply the formula for midpoint. • Use the Distance Formula and the Pythagorean Theorem to find the distance between two points. ☑ SAT-10 ☑ NAEP ☑ ACT ☑ SAT ☐ SAT Subject Tests		**Optional** coordinate grid with points representing a house and a school, graph paper
Lesson 1-7 Transformations in the Coordinate Plane • Identify reflections, rotations, and translations. • Graph transformations in the coordinate plane. ☐ SAT-10 ☑ NAEP ☑ ACT ☐ SAT ☑ SAT Subject Tests		**Required** graph paper, straightedge **Optional** mirror (MK); examples of tessellations, translations, rotations, and reflections; coordinate grid and cut-out triangle, geometry software
1-7 Technology Lab Explore Transformations • Use geometry software to perform transformations and explore their properties. ☐ SAT-10 ☑ NAEP ☑ ACT ☐ SAT ☐ SAT Subject Tests	***Technology Lab Activities*** 1-7 Lab Recording Sheet	**Required** geometry software

MK = *Manipulatives Kit*

COORDINATE GEOMETRY

Lesson 1-6

Coordinate geometry, also known as analytic geometry, is the branch of mathematics that merges geometry and algebra. The French mathematician René Descartes is credited with introducing the key principles of coordinate geometry in his 1637 work, *Discourse on Method.* In honor of Descartes, coordinate geometry is also called "Cartesian geometry."

The coordinate plane is the tool that links algebra and geometry. For example, through the use of the coordinate plane, a straight line is not only "a straight path that has no thickness and extends forever" but also the graph of a linear equation. These two definitions have far-reaching ramifications. In synthetic geometry (the deductive approach studied by Euclid and others), two lines are perpendicular if and only if they intersect to form right angles. A coordinate-geometry perspective provides a powerful test of perpendicularity: two lines are perpendicular if and only if the product of their slopes is -1.

The familiar Cartesian coordinate system uniquely names a point in the plane using two numbers, called the coordinates of the point. The coordinates are defined with respect to two perpendicular axes that intersect at a point called the origin.

It is worth noting that the standard Cartesian coordinate system is just one of many possible coordinate systems. Polar coordinates provide another familiar example of a coordinate system. In addition, it is sometimes useful to name points using an oblique coordinate system in which the axes are not perpendicular to each other. In the oblique system shown here, the axes intersect at an angle of $\alpha°$. (When $\alpha = 90$, the system is an ordinary Cartesian system.) The point P has coordinates (5, 3).

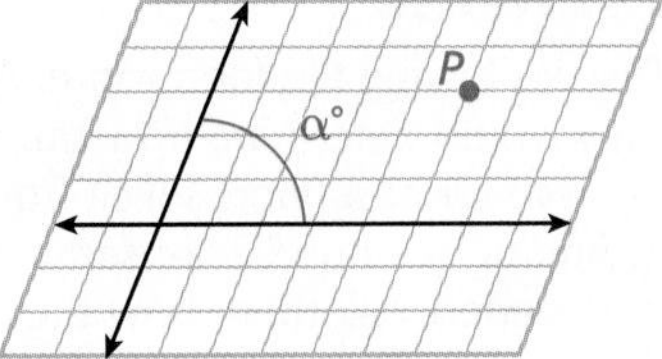

DISTANCE

Lesson 1-6

Although the idea of the distance between two points is intuitively familiar, it is instructive to look at the concept of distance from a purely mathematical point of view. Mathematicians define a distance function (called a *metric*) as a function that assigns a real number to any two points A and B in a plane such that:

- $d(A, B) = d(B, A)$;
- $d(A, B) \geq 0$, with $d(A, B) = 0$ if and only if $A = B$;
- $d(A, B) \leq d(A, C) + d(C, B)$ for any point C.

Our standard notion of the distance between two points, based on the Distance Formula, satisfies all three of the above properties. The last property, known as the Triangle Inequality, will be discussed further in Chapter 5.

TRANSFORMATIONS

Lesson 1-7

A transformation is a function that changes the position, size, or shape of a figure. In this course, the emphasis is on transformations that are most closely linked to congruence and similarity: reflections, translations, rotations, and dilations. However, it is important to understand that there exist many other transformations.

Perhaps the simplest transformation is the transformation that maps every point to itself. This is known as the identity transformation. Another simple transformation is the one that maps every point to the origin. As a more complex example, a *shear* is a transformation in which the points on a given line ℓ remain fixed while all other points are shifted parallel to ℓ by a distance proportional to their distance from ℓ. A shear has the effect of mapping a rectangle to a parallelogram, as shown below.

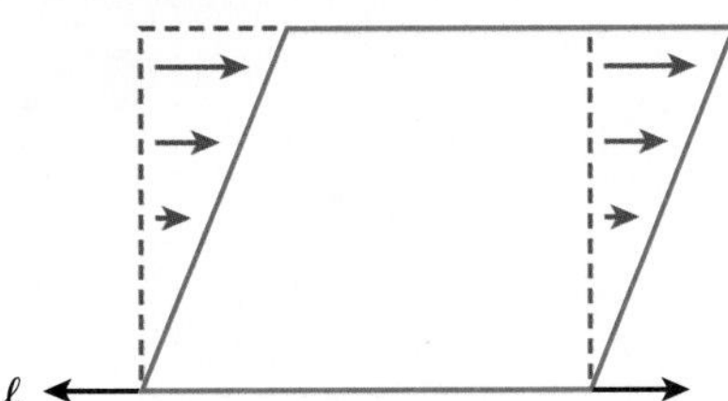

1-5 Organizer

Pacing: Traditional 1 day
Block $\frac{1}{2}$ day

Objectives: Apply formulas for perimeter, area, and circumference.

Geometry Lab
In *Geometry Lab Activities*

Online Edition
Tutorial Videos

Countdown Week 2

Power Presentations with PowerPoint®

Warm Up

Evaluate. Round to the nearest hundredth.

1. 12^2 144 **2.** 7.6^2 57.76

3. $\sqrt{64}$ 8 **4.** $\sqrt{54}$ 7.35

5. $3^2(\pi)$ 28.27 **6.** $(3\pi)^2$ 88.83

Also available on transparency

Math Humor

Q: What is the hidden math term?

A: Square root

Inclusion Perimeter is a measure of the distance around a figure, and a distance (or length) is a one-dimensional measurement. Area can be thought of as a measure of how many 1 x 1 squares can fit inside a figure. Squares are two-dimensional figures, so area is a two-dimensional measurement.

State Resources

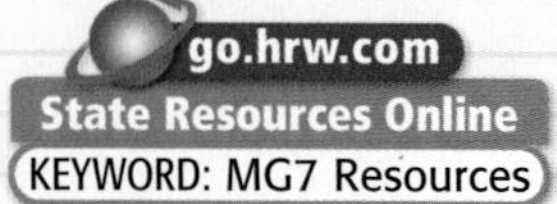

1-5 Using Formulas in Geometry

Objective
Apply formulas for perimeter, area, and circumference.

Vocabulary
perimeter
area
base
height
diameter
radius
circumference
pi

Why learn this?
Puzzles use geometric-shaped pieces. Formulas help determine the amount of materials needed. (See Exercise 6.)

The **perimeter** P of a plane figure is the sum of the side lengths of the figure. The **area** A of a plane figure is the number of nonoverlapping square units of a given size that exactly cover the figure.

area = 2 units × 5 units
= 10 square units

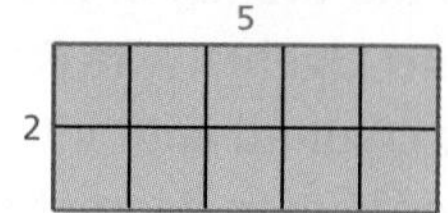

Know it! Note — **Perimeter and Area**

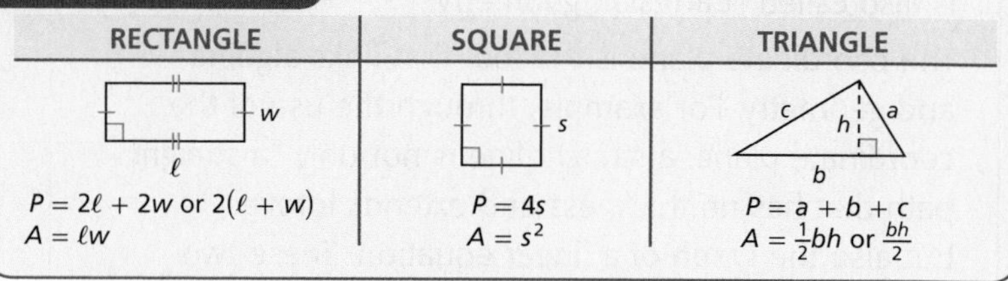

RECTANGLE	SQUARE	TRIANGLE
$P = 2\ell + 2w$ or $2(\ell + w)$ $A = \ell w$	$P = 4s$ $A = s^2$	$P = a + b + c$ $A = \frac{1}{2}bh$ or $\frac{bh}{2}$

The **base** b can be any side of a triangle. The **height** h is a segment from a vertex that forms a right angle with a line containing the base. The height may be a side of the triangle or in the interior or the exterior of the triangle.

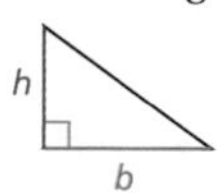
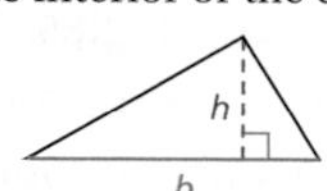
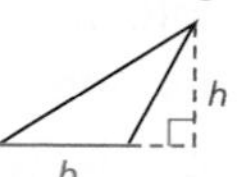

Remember!
Perimeter is expressed in linear units, such as inches (in.) or meters (m). Area is expressed in square units, such as square centimeters (cm²).

EXAMPLE 1 Finding Perimeter and Area

Find the perimeter and area of each figure.

A rectangle in which $\ell = 17$ cm and $w = 5$ cm

$P = 2\ell + 2w$
$= 2(17) + 2(5)$
$= 34 + 10 = 44$ cm
$A = \ell w$
$= (17)(5) = 85 \text{ cm}^2$

B triangle in which $a = 8$, $b = (x + 1)$, $c = 4x$, and $h = 6$

$P = a + b + c$
$= 8 + (x + 1) + 4x$
$= 5x + 9$
$A = \frac{1}{2}bh$
$= \frac{1}{2}(x + 1)(6) = 3x + 3$

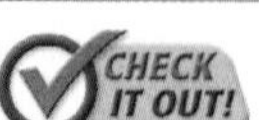

1. Find the perimeter and area of a square with $s = 3.5$ in.
$P = 14$ in.; $A = 12.25 \text{ in}^2$

1 Introduce

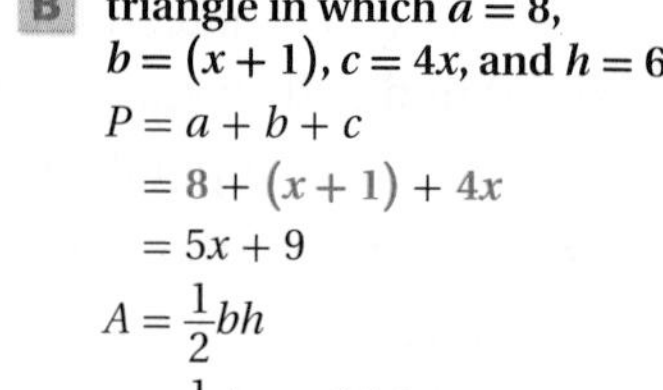

EXPLORATION
1-5 Using Formulas in Geometry

Recall that the area of a rectangle is the product of its length and width. You can use this fact to develop the formula for the area of a triangle.

1. Use a straightedge to draw a triangle. Then cut out the triangle.
2. Trace around the triangle to make a copy of it. Then cut out this second triangle.
3. Arrange the two triangles as shown.
4. Cut off one end of the figure and move it to the other side to make a rectangle.
5. Suppose the original triangle has base b and height h. What are the length and width of the rectangle in terms of b and h?

THINK AND DISCUSS

6. Show how you can write the area of the rectangle in terms of b and h.

Motivate

Discuss buying tile for a room. Ask students how they would determine how much tile they would need to cover a floor. Solicit from them the idea of finding the number of same-sized squares that are needed. Ask them how they could determine the length of baseboard needed to trim the room.

Explorations and answers are provided in *Alternate Openers: Explorations Transparencies.*

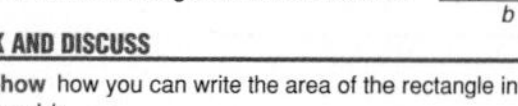

EXAMPLE 2 Crafts Application

The Texas Treasures quilt block includes 24 purple triangles. The base and height of each triangle are about 3 in. Find the approximate amount of fabric used to make the 24 triangles.

The area of one triangle is

$A = \frac{1}{2}bh = \frac{1}{2}(3)(3) = 4\frac{1}{2}\text{ in}^2.$

The total area of the 24 triangles is

$24\left(4\frac{1}{2}\right) = 108\text{ in}^2.$

2. Find the amount of fabric used to make the four rectangles. Each rectangle has a length of $6\frac{1}{2}$ in. and a width of $2\frac{1}{2}$ in. **65 in^2**

In a circle a **diameter** is a segment that passes through the center of the circle and whose endpoints are on the circle. A **radius** of a circle is a segment whose endpoints are the center of the circle and a point on the circle. The **circumference** of a circle is the distance around the circle.

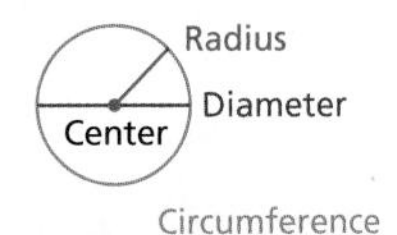

Circumference and Area of a Circle

The circumference C of a circle is given by the formula $C = \pi d$ or $C = 2\pi r$.

The area A of a circle is given by the formula $A = \pi r^2$.

The ratio of a circle's circumference to its diameter is the same for all circles. This ratio is represented by the Greek letter **π (pi)**. The value of π is irrational. Pi is often approximated as 3.14 or $\frac{22}{7}$.

EXAMPLE 3 Finding the Circumference and Area of a Circle

Find the circumference and area of the circle.

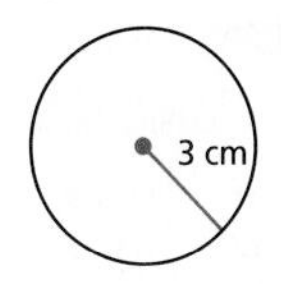

$C = 2\pi r$
$= 2\pi(3) = 6\pi$
$\approx 18.8\text{ cm}$

$A = \pi r^2$
$= \pi(3)^2 = 9\pi$
$\approx 28.3\text{ cm}^2$

3. Find the circumference and area of a circle with radius 14 m. **$C \approx 88.0$ m; $A \approx 615.8$ m^2**

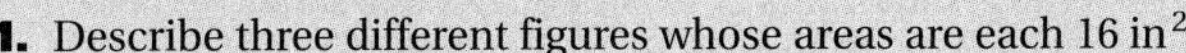

THINK AND DISCUSS

1. Describe three different figures whose areas are each 16 in^2.

2. **GET ORGANIZED** Copy and complete the graphic organizer. In each shape, write the formula for its area and perimeter.

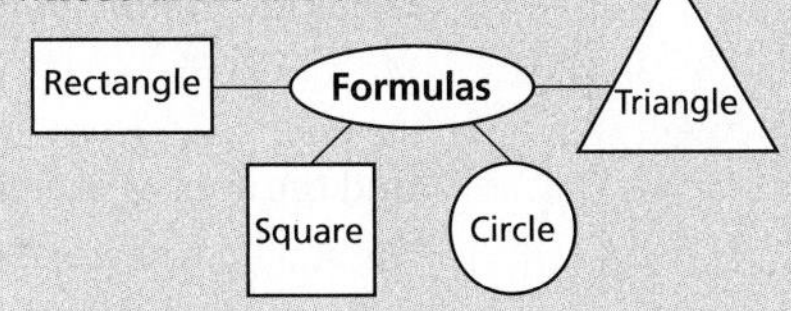

Power Presentations with PowerPoint®

Additional Examples

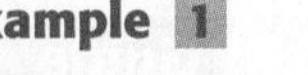

Example 1

Find the perimeter and area of each figure.

A.

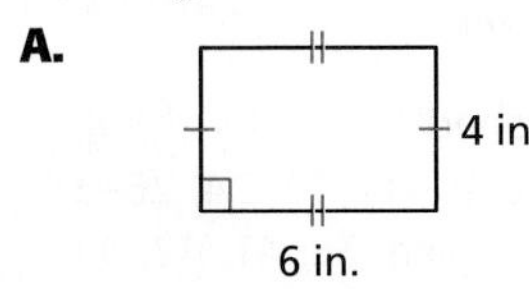

20 in.; 24 in^2

B.

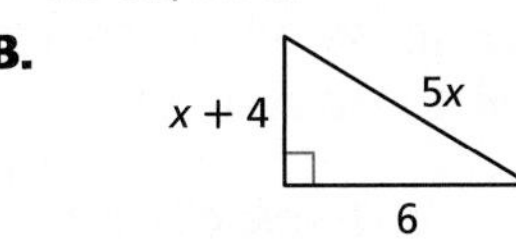

$6x + 10$; $3x + 12$

Example 2

The Queens Quilt block includes 12 blue triangles. The base and height of each triangle are about 4 in. Find the approximate amount of fabric used to make the 12 triangles. 96 in^2

Example 3

Find the circumference and area of a circle with radius 8 cm. Use the π key on your calculator. Then round the answer to the nearest tenth. 50.3 cm; 201.1 cm^2

INTERVENTION

Questioning Strategies

EXAMPLES 1–2

- How does knowing the formula for the area of a rectangle help you find the area of a triangle?

EXAMPLE 3

- Compare the results when you multiply 6 by π and multiply 6 by 3.14.

2 Teach

Guided Instruction

Review the meanings of *perimeter, area,* and *circumference*, and the parts of a circle. Show examples of triangles having interior and exterior heights. Give examples of finding the area and circumference of a circle, leaving answers in terms of π, and rounding. Remind students that the diameter d is twice the radius r or $d = 2r$.

3 Close

Summarize

Review the formulas for finding the area and perimeter (circumference) of a rectangle, triangle, and circle.

Answers to *Think and Discuss*

1. Possible answer: A rect. with length 8 in. and width 2 in.; a square with sides 4 in. long; a △ with base 4 in. and height 8 in.
2. See p. A2.

ONGOING ASSESSMENT and INTERVENTION

***Diagnose Before* the Lesson**
1-5 Warm Up, TE p. 36

***Monitor During* the Lesson**
Check It Out! Exercises, SE pp. 36–37
Questioning Strategies, TE p. 37

***Assess After* the Lesson**
1-5 Lesson Quiz, TE p. 41
Alternative Assessment, TE p. 41

1-5 Exercises

Assignment Guide

Assign *Guided Practice* exercises as necessary.

If you finished Examples  1–3

Basic 10–17, 19–24, 26–34 even, 38, 41, 42, 44, 46–50, 56–62

Average 10–30, 32–52, 56–62

Advanced 10–30 even, 31–62

Homework Quick Check

Quickly check key concepts.

Exercises: 10, 14, 24, 34, 36, 38, 42

Teaching Tip

Math Background

Exercise 13 involves quilt patterns. Plan ahead and ask students whether their families have quilts they may bring in as examples of different geometric patterns.

State Resources

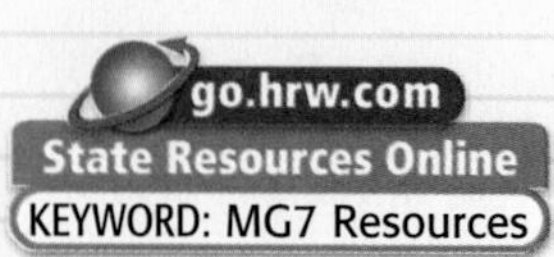

1-5 Exercises

go.hrw.com
Homework Help Online
KEYWORD: MG7 1-5
Parent Resources Online
KEYWORD: MG7 Parent

GUIDED PRACTICE

1. Both terms refer to the dist. around a figure.

Vocabulary **Apply the vocabulary from this lesson to answer each question.**

1. Explain how the concepts of *perimeter* and *circumference* are related.
2. For a rectangle, length and width are sometimes used in place of __?__. (*base and height* or *radius and diameter*) **base and height**

SEE EXAMPLE 1 p. 36

Find the perimeter and area of each figure.

3. 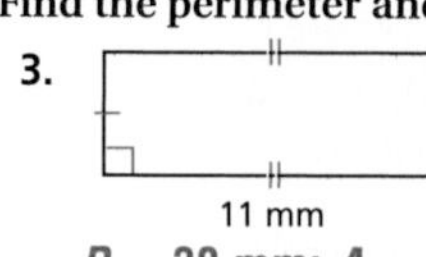

$P = 30$ mm; $A = 44$ mm^2

4. 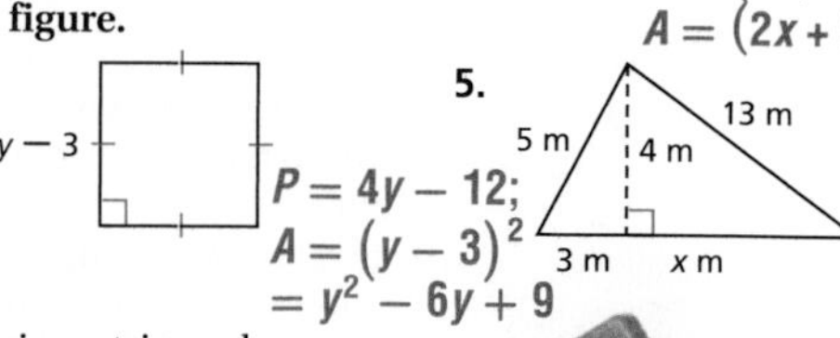

$P = 4y - 12$; $A = (y-3)^2 = y^2 - 6y + 9$

5. $P = (x + 21)$ m; $A = (2x + 6)$ m^2

SEE EXAMPLE 2 p. 37

6. **Manufacturing** A puzzle contains a triangular piece with a base of 3 in. and a height of 4 in. A manufacturer wants to make 80 puzzles. Find the amount of wood used if each puzzle contains 20 triangular pieces. **9600 in^2**

SEE EXAMPLE 3 p. 37

Find the circumference and area of each circle. Use the π key on your calculator. Round to the nearest tenth.

7. 

$C \approx 13.2$ m; $A \approx 13.9$ m^2

8. 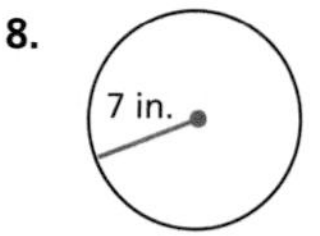

$C \approx 44.0$ in.; $A \approx 153.9$ in^2

9. 16 cm
$C \approx 50.3$ cm; $A \approx 201.1$ cm^2

PRACTICE AND PROBLEM SOLVING

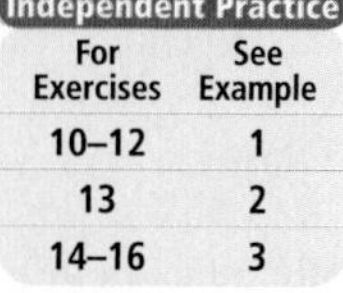

Independent Practice

For Exercises	See Example
10–12	1
13	2
14–16	3

Extra Practice
Skills Practice p. S5
Application Practice p. S28

Find the perimeter and area of each figure.

10. 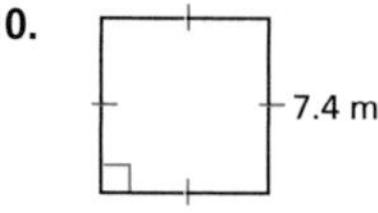

$P = 29.6$ m; $A = 54.76$ m^2

11. 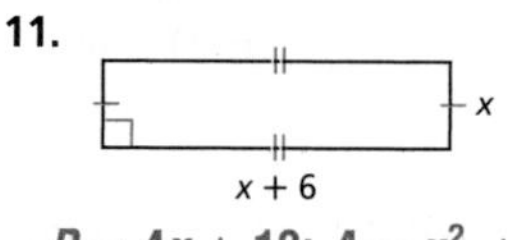

$P = 4x + 12$; $A = x^2 + 6x$

12. 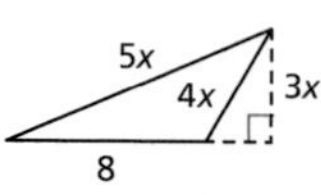

$P = 9x + 8$; $A = 12x$

13. **Crafts** The quilt pattern includes 32 small triangles. Each has a base of 3 in. and a height of 1.5 in. Find the amount of fabric used to make the 32 triangles. **72 in^2**

Find the circumference and area of each circle with the given radius or diameter. Use the π key on your calculator. Round to the nearest tenth.

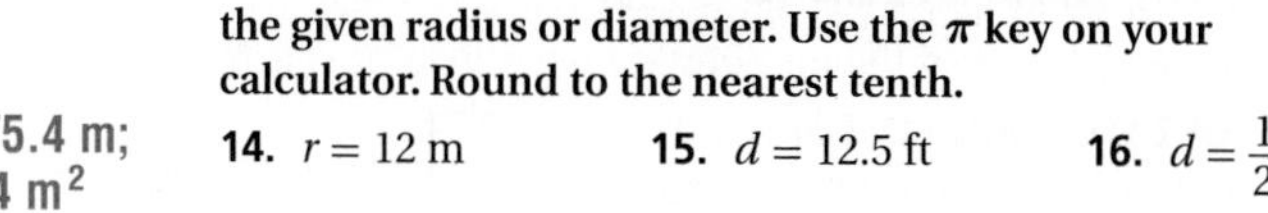

14. $r = 12$ m
15. $d = 12.5$ ft
16. $d = \frac{1}{2}$ mi

14. $C \approx 75.4$ m; $A \approx 452.4$ m^2
15. $C \approx 39.3$ ft; $A \approx 122.7$ ft^2
16. $C \approx 1.6$ mi; $A \approx 0.2$ mi^2

Find the area of each of the following.

17. square whose sides are 9.1 yd in length **82.81 yd^2**
18. square whose sides are $(x + 1)$ in length $x^2 + 2x + 1$
19. triangle whose base is $5\frac{1}{2}$ in. and whose height is $2\frac{1}{4}$ in. **6.1875 in^2**

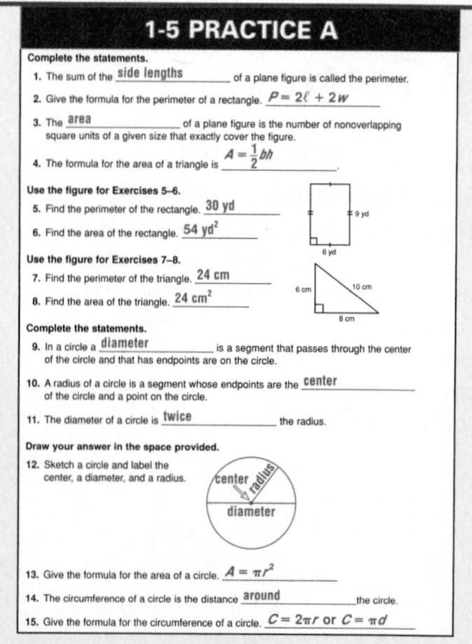

1-5 PRACTICE A

Complete the statements.

1. The sum of the __side lengths__ of a plane figure is called the perimeter.
2. Give the formula for the perimeter of a rectangle. __$P = 2\ell + 2w$__
3. The __area__ of a plane figure is the number of nonoverlapping square units of a given size that exactly cover the figure.
4. The formula for the area of a triangle is __$A = \frac{1}{2}bh$__.

Use the figure for Exercises 5–6.

5. Find the perimeter of the rectangle. __30 yd__
6. Find the area of the rectangle. __54 yd^2__

9 yd
6 yd

Use the figure for Exercises 7–8.

7. Find the perimeter of the triangle. __24 cm__
8. Find the area of the triangle. __24 cm^2__

6 cm
10 cm
8 cm

Complete the statements.

9. In a circle a __diameter__ is a segment that passes through the center of the circle and that has endpoints are on the circle.
10. A radius of a circle is a segment whose endpoints are the __center__ of the circle and a point on the circle.
11. The diameter of a circle is __twice__ the radius.

Draw your answer in the space provided.

12. Sketch a circle and label the center, a diameter, and a radius.

center
radius
diameter

13. Give the formula for the area of a circle. __$A = \pi r^2$__
14. The circumference of a circle is the distance __around__ the circle.
15. Give the formula for the circumference of a circle. __$C = 2\pi r$ or $C = \pi d$__

Given the area of each of the following figures, find each unknown measure.

20. The area of a triangle is 6.75 m^2. If the base of the triangle is 3 m, what is the height of the triangle? **4.5 m**

21. A rectangle has an area of 347.13 cm^2. If the length is 20.3 cm, what is the width of the rectangle? **17.1 cm**

22. The area of a circle is 64π. Find the radius of the circle. $r = 8$

23. **/// ERROR ANALYSIS ///** Below are two statements about the area of the circle. Which is incorrect? Explain the error.

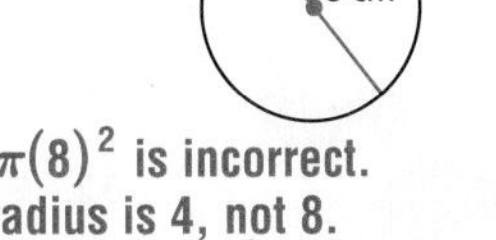

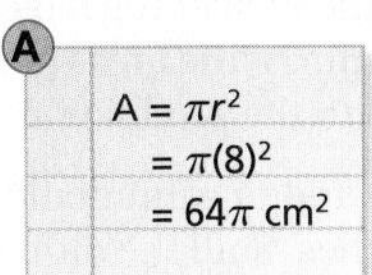

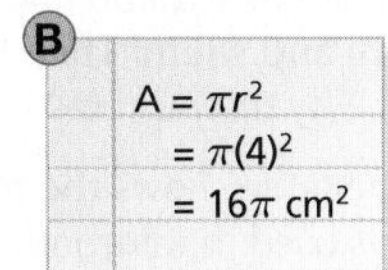

$A = \pi(8)^2$ is incorrect. The radius is 4, not 8. $A = \pi r^2 = \pi(4)^2 = 16\pi\text{ cm}^2$

Find the area of each circle. Leave answers in terms of π.

24. circle with a diameter of 28 m $196\pi\text{ m}^2$

25. circle with a radius of $3y$ $9y^2\pi$

26. **Geography** The radius r of the earth at the equator is approximately 3964 mi. Find the distance around the earth at the equator. Use the π key on your calculator and round to the nearest mile. **24,907 mi**

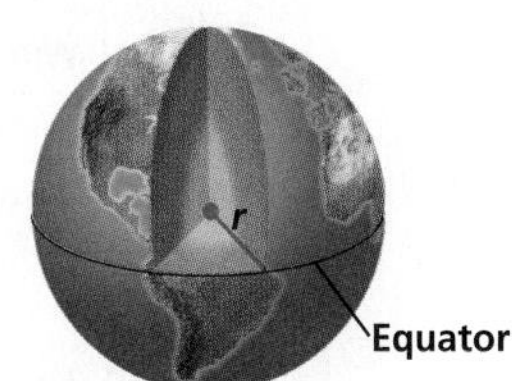

27. **Critical Thinking** Explain how the formulas for the perimeter and area of a square may be derived from the corresponding formulas for a rectangle.

28. Find the perimeter and area of a rectangle whose length is $(x + 1)$ and whose width is $(x - 3)$. Express your answer in terms of x.

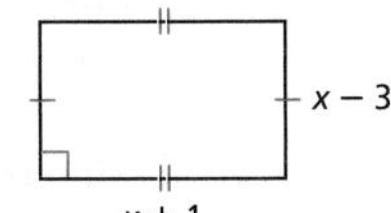

29. **Multi-Step** If the height h of a triangle is 3 inches less than the length of the base b, and the area A of the triangle is 19 times the length of the base, find b and h. $b = 41$ in.; $h = 38$ in.

27. For a square, the length and width are both s, so $P = 2\ell + 2w = 2s + 2s = 4s$ and $A = \ell w = s(s) = s^2$

28. $P = 4x - 4$; $A = (x + 1)(x - 3) = x^2 - 2x - 3$

MULTI-STEP TEST PREP

30. This problem will prepare you for the Multi-Step Test Prep on page 58.

A landscaper is to install edging around a garden. The edging costs \$1.39 for each 24-inch-long strip. The landscaper estimates it will take 4 hours to install the edging.

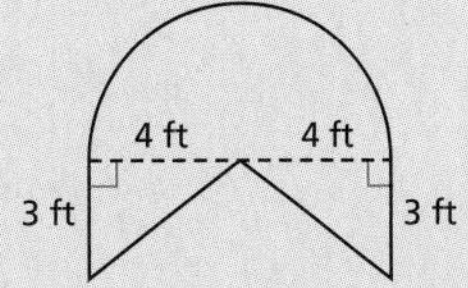

a. If the total cost is \$120.30, what is the cost of the material purchased? **\$20.85**

b. What is the charge for labor? **\$99.45**

c. What is the area of the semicircle to the nearest tenth? 25.1 ft^2

d. What is the area of each triangle? 6 ft^2

e. What is the total area of the garden to the nearest foot? 37 ft^2

**COMMON ERROR /// ALERT **

In **Exercises 24** and **25,** students may confuse πr^2 in the area formula and $2\pi r$ in the circumference formula. Remind them that area is measured in square units, so they should use the formula in which r is squared.

Reading Math In **Exercises 24** and **25,** remind students that the direction to leave answers in terms of π means that π is part of the answer. **ENGLISH LANGUAGE LEARNERS**

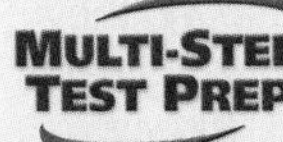

Exercise 30 involves perimeters of triangles and the circumference of a semicircle. This exercise prepares students for the Multi-Step Test Prep on page 58.

1-5 PRACTICE B

Use the figures for Exercises 1–3.

1. Find the perimeter of triangle *A*. **12 ft**
2. Find the area of triangle *A*. 6 ft^2
3. Triangle *A* is identical to triangle *B*. Find the height h of triangle *B*. **2.4 ft or $2\frac{2}{5}$ ft**

A: 3 ft, 4 ft, 5 ft
B: h, 5 ft

Find the perimeter and area of each shape.

4. square with a side 2.4 m in length
$P = 9.6$ m; $A = 5.76\text{ m}^2$
5. rectangle with length $(x + 3)$ and width 7
$P = 2x + 20$; $A = 7x + 21$
6. Although a circle does not have sides, it does have a perimeter. What is the term for the perimeter of a circle? **circumference**

Find the circumference and area of each circle.

7. 14 mi. Use $\frac{22}{7}$ for π.
$C \approx 44$ mi
$A \approx 154\text{ mi}^2$
8. 1.5 cm. Use 3.14 for π.
$C \approx 9.42$ cm
$A \approx 7.065\text{ cm}^2$
9. $x + 1$. Leave π as π.
$C \approx 2\pi(x + 1)$
$A \approx \pi(x^2 + 2x + 1)$
10. The area of a square is $\frac{1}{4}\text{ in}^2$. Find the perimeter. **2 in.**
11. The area of a triangle is 152 m^2, and the height is 16 m. Find the base. **19 m**
12. The circumference of a circle is 25π mm. Find the radius. **12.5 mm**

Use the figure for Exercises 13–14.

Lucas has a 39-foot-long rope. He uses all the rope to outline this T-shape in his backyard. All the angles in the figure are right angles.

9 ft, 3 ft, 3 ft, 3.5 ft, 3.5 ft, x, x

13. Find x. **7.5 ft**
14. Find the area enclosed by the rope. 42 ft^2

1-5 PRACTICE C

1. Find the length of the sides of a square whose area and perimeter are the same nonzero number. **4**
2. Find the length of the radius of a circle whose area and circumference are the same nonzero number. **2**
3. Explain why the area and the perimeter (or the circumference) of a figure can never be equal; they can only have equal numbers.
Area is measured in square units; perimeter is measured in linear units.

Find the measurements.

4. Faye has 44 feet of fencing to enclose a rectangular garden. She wants to enclose as much area as possible. Use trial-and-error to find the maximum area Faye can enclose with all 44 feet of fence. Name the length and width that give the maximum area.
$A = 121\text{ ft}^2$; $\ell = 11$ ft; $w = 11$ ft
5. Explain what the answer to Exercise 4 implies about the relationship of perimeter to area for rectangles.
For a given perimeter, a rectangle with sides of equal length (a square) encloses the maximum area.
6. Faye decides to use her 44 feet of fencing to enclose a circular garden. Find the area of the garden. (Use $\frac{22}{7}$ for π.) **about 154 ft^2**
7. Find the difference between the area Faye can enclose by a circle and the maximum area she can enclose by a rectangle. **about 33 ft^2**
8. Explain what the answer to Exercise 7 implies about the relationship of perimeter to area for rectangles and circles.
If a rectangle and a circle have the same perimeter, then the circle has the greater area.
9. A rectangular box of tissues is 9.5 inches long, 4.5 inches wide, and 4 inches high. Find the area of the surface of the box. 197.5 in^2
10. A right triagnle has two legs with lengths a and b and a hypotenuse with length c. In this triangle, the area and perimeter are the same nonzero number. Find the length a if $b = 6$. (Hint: Use the Pythagorean Theorem, $a^2 + b^2 = c^2$.) $a = 8$

Diversity **Exercise 32** gives dimensions of international soccer fields. The size of the playing field in Paralympics soccer, for athletes with cerebral palsy, is 75 m long and 55 m wide.

Number Sense For **Exercises 41–43,** explain to students that leaving the answer in terms of π gives an exact answer. Point out that the decimal answer of the diameter found by using the π key on a calculator is an approximation.

If students chose **D** for **Exercise 47,** they divided by 2 instead of taking the square root. If they chose **F** for **Exercise 48,** they found the length instead of the width. If they chose **G** for **Exercise 50,** they did not divide by 2 in the equation representing the area.

Answers

31a. This must be equal to $(a + b)(c + d)$ because the sum of the areas of the 4 small rects. equals the area of the large rect.

b. This must be equal to the product $(a + 1)(c + 1)$ because the sum of the areas of the 4 small rects. equals the area of the large rect.

c. This must be equal to the product $(a + 1)^2$ because the sum of the areas of the 4 small rects. equals the area of the large rect.

31. Algebra The large rectangle has length $a + b$ and width $c + d$. Therefore, its area is $(a + b)(c + d)$.

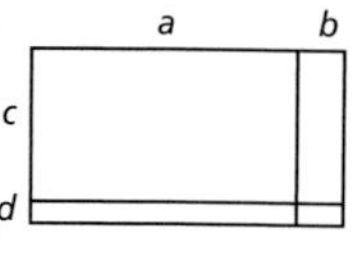

a. Find the area of each of the four small rectangles in the figure. Then find the sum of these areas. Explain why this sum must be equal to the product $(a + b)(c + d)$. $ac + ad + bc + bd$

b. Suppose $b = d = 1$. Write the area of the large rectangle as a product of its length and width. Then find the sum of the areas of the four small rectangles. Explain why this sum must be equal to the product $(a + 1)(c + 1)$.

c. Suppose $b = d = 1$ and $a = c$. Write the area of the large rectangle as a product of its length and width. Then find the sum of the areas of the four small rectangles. Explain why this sum must be equal to the product $(a + 1)^2$.

b. $(a + 1)(c + 1)$; $ac + a + c + 1$

c. $(a + 1)^2$; $a^2 + 2a + 1$

32. Sports The table shows the minimum and maximum dimensions for rectangular soccer fields used in international matches. Find the difference in area of the largest possible field and the smallest possible field. 1850 m^2

	Minimum	Maximum
Length	100 m	110 m
Width	64 m	75 m

Find the value of each missing measure of a triangle.

33. $b = 2$ ft; $h =$ ▒ ft; $A = 28 \text{ ft}^2$ **28 ft**

34. $b =$ ▒ ft; $h = 22.6$ yd; $A = 282.5 \text{ yd}^2$ **25 yd**

Find the area of each rectangle with the given base and height.

35. 9.8 ft; 2.7 ft 26.46 ft^2

36. 4 mi 960 ft; 440 ft $9{,}715{,}200 \text{ ft}^2$, or $0.\overline{348} \text{ mi}^2$

37. 3 yd 12 ft; 11 ft $25\frac{2}{3} \text{ yd}^2$ or 231 ft^2

Find the perimeter of each rectangle with the given base and height.

38. 21.4 in.; 7.8 in. **58.4 in.**

39. 4 ft 6 in.; 6 in. **10 ft**

40. 2 yd 8 ft; 6 ft **13 yd 1 ft**

Find the diameter of the circle with the given measurement. Leave answers in terms of π.

41. $C = 14$ $\frac{14}{\pi}$

42. $A = 100\pi$ **20**

43. $C = 50\pi$ **50**

44. A skate park consists of a two adjacent rectangular regions as shown. Find the perimeter and area of the park. $P = 52$ yd; $A = 137 \text{ yd}^2$

17 yd
9 yd
4 yd
4 yd

45. Critical Thinking Explain how you would measure a triangular piece of paper if you wanted to find its area.

45. Measure any side as the base. Then measure the height of the △ at a rt. ∠ to the base.

46. Write About It A student wrote in her journal, "To find the perimeter of a rectangle, add the length and width together and then double this value." Does her method work? Explain. The method works because adding the length and width together and doubling the result is $2(\ell + w)$, which is equivalent to $2\ell + 2w$.

47. Manda made a circular tabletop that has an area of 452 in^2. Which is closest to the radius of the tabletop?

Ⓐ 9 in. Ⓑ 12 in. Ⓒ 24 in. Ⓓ 72 in.

48. A piece of wire 48 m long is bent into the shape of a rectangle whose length is twice its width. Find the length of the rectangle.

Ⓕ 8 m Ⓖ 16 m Ⓗ 24 m Ⓙ 32 m

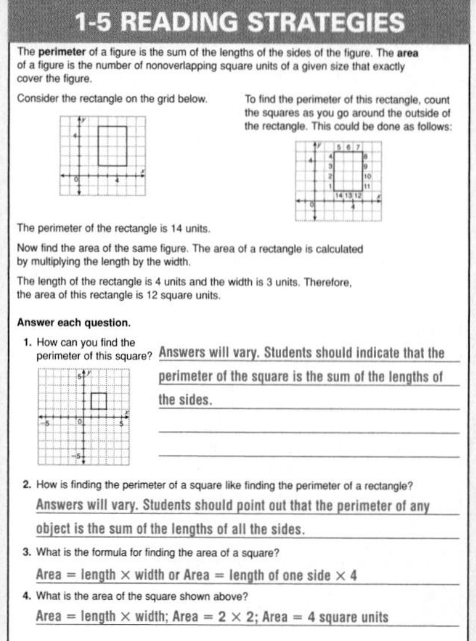

1-5 READING STRATEGIES

The **perimeter** of a figure is the sum of the lengths of the sides of the figure. The **area** of a figure is the number of nonoverlapping square units of a given size that exactly cover the figure.

Consider the rectangle on the grid below.

To find the perimeter of this rectangle, count the squares as you go around the outside of the rectangle. This could be done as follows:

The perimeter of the rectangle is 14 units.

Now find the area of the same figure. The area of a rectangle is calculated by multiplying the length by the width.

The length of the rectangle is 4 units and the width is 3 units. Therefore, the area of this rectangle is 12 square units.

Answer each question.

1. How can you find the perimeter of this square? Answers will vary. Students should indicate that the perimeter of the square is the sum of the lengths of the sides.

2. How is finding the perimeter of a square like finding the perimeter of a rectangle? Answers will vary. Students should point out that the perimeter of any object is the sum of the lengths of all the sides.

3. What is the formula for finding the area of a square? Area = length × width or Area = length of one side × 4

4. What is the area of the square shown above? Area = length × width; Area = 2 × 2; Area = 4 square units

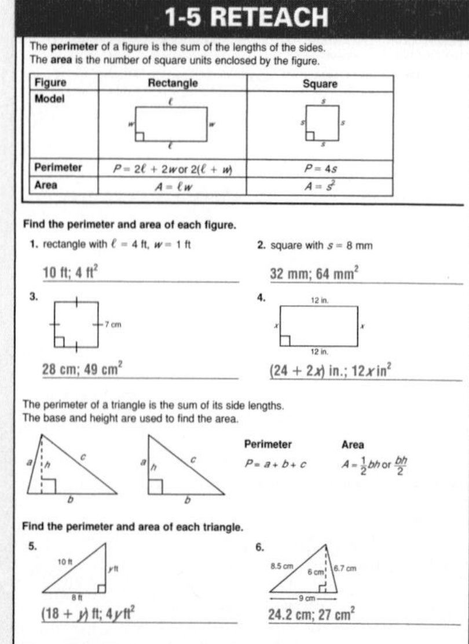

1-5 RETEACH

The **perimeter** of a figure is the sum of the lengths of the sides.
The **area** is the number of square units enclosed by the figure.

Figure	Rectangle	Square
Model		
Perimeter	$P = 2\ell + 2w$ or $2(\ell + w)$	$P = 4s$
Area	$A = \ell w$	$A = s^2$

Find the perimeter and area of each figure.

1. rectangle with $\ell = 4$ ft, $w = 1$ ft — 10 ft; 4 ft^2

2. square with $s = 8$ mm — 32 mm; 64 mm^2

3. 7 cm — 28 cm; 49 cm^2

4. 12 in.; x — $(24 + 2x)$ in.; $12x \text{ in}^2$

The perimeter of a triangle is the sum of its side lengths.
The base and height are used to find the area.

Perimeter: $P = a + b + c$

Area: $A = \frac{1}{2}bh$ or $\frac{bh}{2}$

Find the perimeter and area of each triangle.

5. 10 ft; y ft; 8 ft — $(18 + y)$ ft; $4y \text{ ft}^2$

6. 8.5 cm; 6 cm; 6.7 cm; 9 cm — 24.2 cm; 27 cm^2

49. Which equation best represents the area A of the triangle?

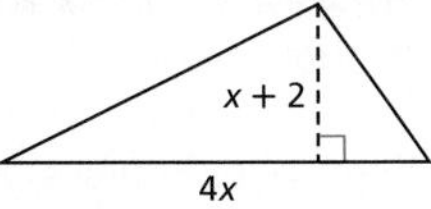

(A) $A = 2x^2 + 4x$
(B) $A = 4x(x + 2)$
(C) $A = 2x^2 + 2$
(D) $A = 4x^2 + 8$

50. Ryan has a 30 ft piece of string. He wants to use the string to lay out the boundary of a new flower bed in his garden. Which of these shapes would use all the string?

(F) A circle with a radius of about 37.2 in.
(G) A rectangle with a length of 6 ft and a width of 5 ft
(H) A triangle with each side 9 ft long
(J) A square with each side 90 in. long

CHALLENGE AND EXTEND

51. A circle with a 6 in. diameter is stamped out of a rectangular piece of metal as shown. Find the area of the remaining piece of metal. Use the π key on your calculator and round to the nearest tenth. **83.7 in^2**

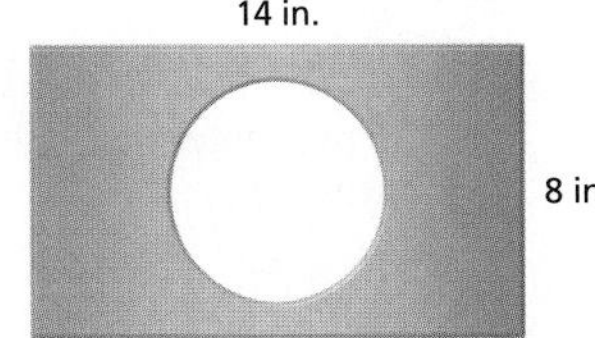

52. a. Solve $P = 2\ell + 2w$ for w. **$w = \frac{P - 2\ell}{2}$**

b. Use your result from part **a** to find the width of a rectangle that has a perimeter of 9 ft and a length of 3 ft. **1.5 ft**

53. Find all possible areas of a rectangle whose sides are natural numbers and whose perimeter is 12. **5; 8; 9**

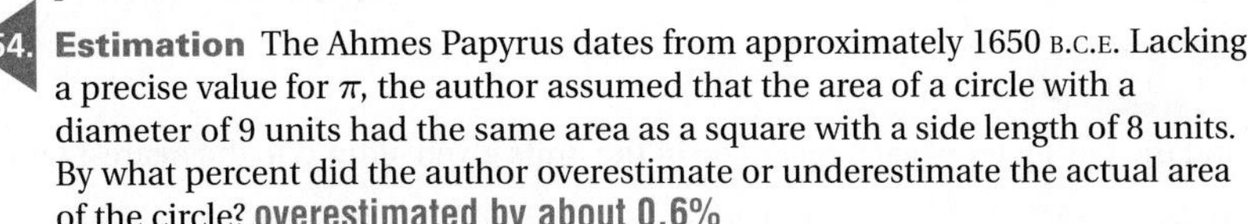

54. **Estimation** The Ahmes Papyrus dates from approximately 1650 B.C.E. Lacking a precise value for π, the author assumed that the area of a circle with a diameter of 9 units had the same area as a square with a side length of 8 units. By what percent did the author overestimate or underestimate the actual area of the circle? **overestimated by about 0.6%**

55. **Multi-Step** The width of a painting is $\frac{4}{5}$ the measure of the length of the painting. If the area is 320 in^2, what are the length and width of the painting? **width = 16 in.; length = 20 in.**

LINK — Math History

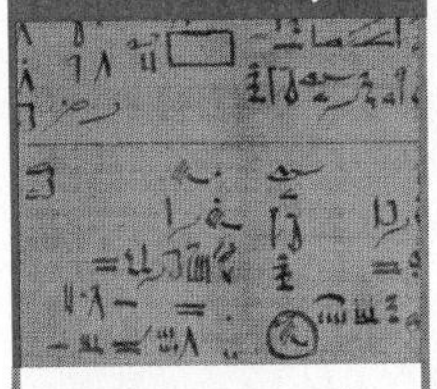

The Ahmes Papyrus is an ancient Egyptian source of information about mathematics. A page of the Ahmes Papyrus is about 1 foot wide and 18 feet long.

Source: scholars.nus.edu.sg

SPIRAL REVIEW

Determine the domain and range of each function. *(Previous course)*

56. $\{(2, 4), (-5, 8), (-3, 4)\}$ **D: {2, −5, −3}; R: {4, 8}**

57. $\{(4, -2), (-2, 8), (16, 0)\}$ **D: {4, −2, 16}; R: {−2, 8, 0}**

Name the geometric figure that each item suggests. *(Lesson 1-1)*

58. the wall of a classroom **plane**

59. the place where two walls meet **line or segment**

60. Marion has a piece of fabric that is 10 yd long. She wants to cut it into 2 pieces so that one piece is 4 times as long as the other. Find the lengths of the two pieces. *(Lesson 1-2)* **8 yd; 2 yd**

61. Suppose that A, B, and C are collinear points. B is the midpoint of $\overline{AC}$. The coordinate of A is -8, and the coordinate of B is -2.5. What is the coordinate of C? *(Lesson 1-2)* **3**

62. An angle's measure is 9 degrees more than 2 times the measure of its supplement. Find the measure of the angle. *(Lesson 1-4)* **123°**

COMMON ERROR ALERT

In **Exercise 51,** some students may attempt to subtract the area of the rectangle from the area of the circle. Explain that they must subtract the smaller area from the larger area, or the result will be a negative number.

Teaching Tip **Algebra** For **Exercise 54,** you might need to review that you find the percent of change by dividing the difference by the original.

Journal

Have students draw a rectangle, a triangle, and a circle on a grid and explain how they would find the area and perimeter (or circumference) of each figure, using their own dimensions.

ALTERNATIVE ASSESSMENT

Give students the area, perimeter, and circumference of three figures. Then ask students to find the dimensions and draw the figures that match the corresponding values.

Power Presentations with PowerPoint®

1-5 Lesson Quiz

Find the area and perimeter of each figure.

1.

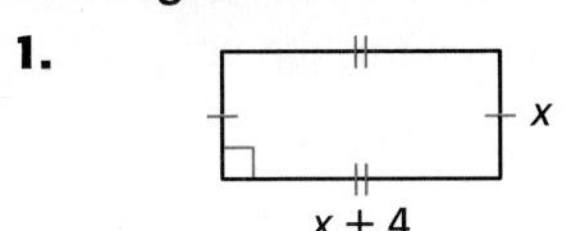

$x^2 + 4x$; $4x + 8$

2.

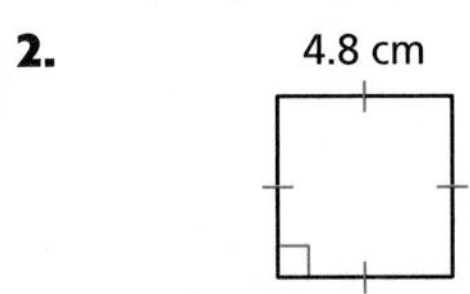

23.04 cm^2; 19.2 cm

3. (triangle with sides $3x$, $x + 6$, height $2x$, base 10)

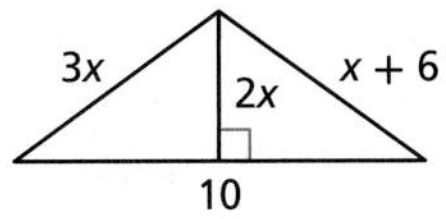

$10x$; $4x + 16$

Find the circumference and area of each circle. Leave answers in terms of π.

4. radius 2 cm 4π cm; $4\pi^2$ cm

5. diameter 12 ft 12π ft; $36\pi^2$ ft

6. The area of a rectangle is 74.82 in^2, and the length is 12.9 in. Find the width. 5.8 in.

Also available on transparency

1-5 PROBLEM SOLVING

Use the table for Exercises 1–6.

Figure	Perimeter or Circumference	Area
rectangle	$P = 2\ell + 2w$ or $2(\ell + w)$	$A = \ell w$
triangle	$P = a + b + c$	$A = \frac{1}{2}bh$
circle	$C = 2\pi r$	$A = \pi r^2$

Use the diagram of a hockey field for Exercises 1–4.

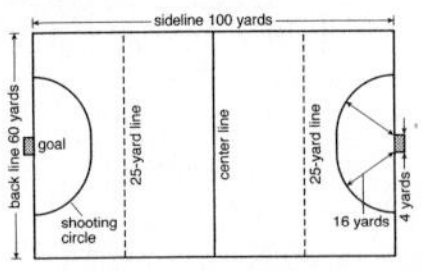

(sideline 100 yards; back line 60 yards; goal; 25-yard line; center line; 25-yard line; shooting circle; 16 yards; 4 yards)

1. What is the perimeter of the field? 320 yd
2. What is the area of the field? 6000 yd^2
3. What is the area of each of the shooting circles? Use 3.14 for π. about 401.92 yd^2
4. What is the area of the field between the two 25-yard lines? 3000 yd^2

Choose the best answer.

5. A rectangular counter 3 feet wide and 5 feet long has a circle cut out of it in order to have a sink installed. The circle has a diameter of 18 inches. What is the approximate area of the remaining countertop surface? Use 3.14 for π.
(A) 13.2 ft^2 C 18.9 ft^2
B 15.0 ft^2 D 29.5 ft^2

6. The base of a triangular garden measures 5.5 feet. Its height is 3 feet. If 4 pounds of mulch are needed to cover a square foot, how many pounds of mulch will be needed to cover the garden?
F 8.25 lb (G) 33 lb
H 16.5 lb J 66 lb

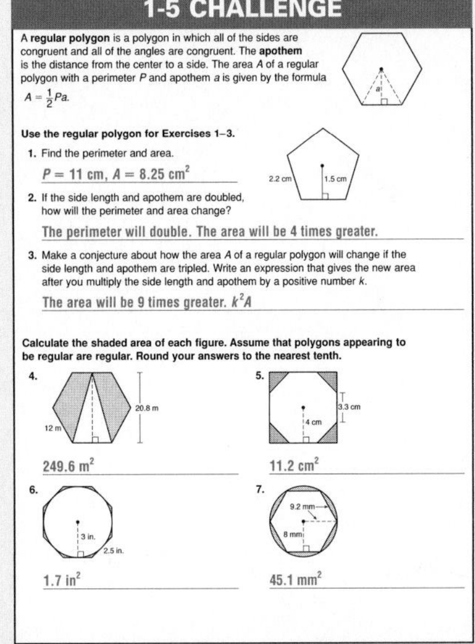

1-5 CHALLENGE

A **regular polygon** is a polygon in which all of the sides are congruent and all of the angles are congruent. The **apothem** is the distance from the center to a side. The area A of a regular polygon with a perimeter P and apothem a is given by the formula $A = \frac{1}{2}Pa$.

Use the regular polygon for Exercises 1–3.

1. Find the perimeter and area. $P = 11$ cm, $A = 8.25$ cm^2
2. If the side length and apothem are doubled, how will the perimeter and area change? The perimeter will double. The area will be 4 times greater.
3. Make a conjecture about how the area A of a regular polygon will change if the side length and apothem are tripled. Write an expression that gives the new area after you multiply the side length and apothem by a positive number k. The area will be 9 times greater. k^2A

Calculate the shaded area of each figure. Assume that polygons appearing to be regular are regular. Round your answers to the nearest tenth.

4. 249.6 m^2
5. 11.2 cm^2
6. 1.7 in^2
7. 45.1 mm^2

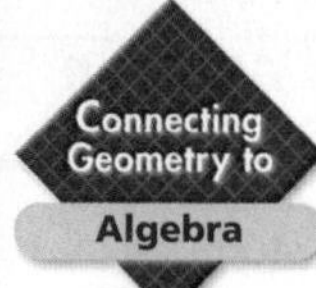

Organizer

Pacing:
Traditional $\frac{1}{2}$ day
Block $\frac{1}{4}$ day

Objective: Use conversion factors to convert measurements.

 **Online Edition**

 **Countdown Week 2**

Teach

Remember

Students review how to convert measurements to different units using conversion factors.

Critical Thinking Students may want to convert the dimensions of the shapes before calculating perimeter and area. Explain that converting first and using the rounded results can change the final answer. Have students work Exercise 1 both ways to demonstrate.

Close

Assess

Have students find the answers to Exercises 5 and 10 on p. 38 in feet.

5b. Square the numerator and denominator of the conversion factor.

State Resources

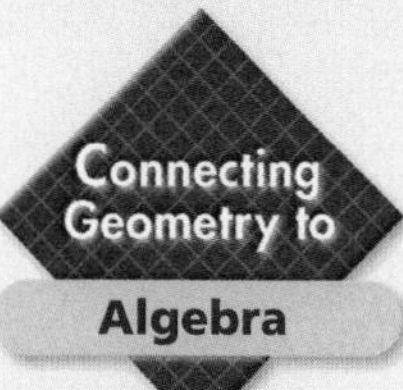

Unit Conversions

In previous courses, you learned to convert a measurement from one unit to another by multiplying it by a *conversion factor.* A conversion factor is a ratio of two equal quantities in different units of measurement.

Example

Find the perimeter, in centimeters, of the rectangle. (*Hint:* 1 in. = 2.54 cm.)

Find the perimeter in inches first.

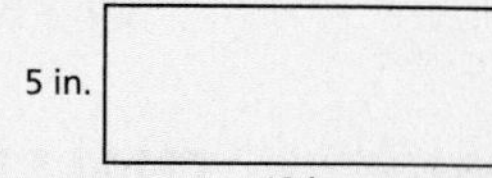

$p = 2\ell + 2w$

$p = 2(13) + 2(5)$ *Substitute 13 for ℓ and 5 for w.*

$s = 26 + 10 = 36$ *Simplify.*

The perimeter of the rectangle is 36 in. Multiply by a conversion factor to change the unit to centimeters.

$36 \text{ in} \times \frac{2.54 \text{ cm}}{1 \text{ in.}}$ *Write the conversion factor*

$= 36 \not{\text{in}} \times \frac{2.54 \text{ cm}}{1 \not{\text{in.}}}$ *Cancel out the like units and simplify.*

$= 36 \times 2.54 \text{ cm} = 91.44 \text{ cm}$

The perimeter of the rectangle is 91.44 cm.

Try This

Find the perimeter of each rectangle in the units given. Round to the nearest tenth.

1. feet **42.7 ft**
(*Hint:* 1 ft = 0.3048 m)

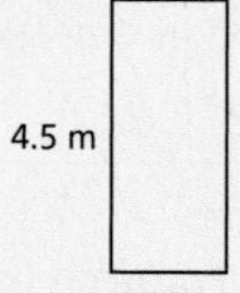

2. kilometers **7.7 km**
(*Hint:* 1 mi ≈ 1.609 km)

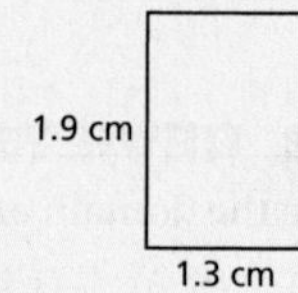

3. millimeters **64 mm**

1.9 cm
1.3 cm

4. The radius of a circle is 3.5 in. Find the circumference of the circle in centimeters. Use 3.14 for π, and round your answer to the nearest tenth. **55.8 cm**
5. The side length of a square is 7 in.
   a. What is the area of the square in square inches? **49 in.^{2}**
   b. How could you change the conversion factor from the example to convert square inches to square centimeters? **See margin.**
   c. Find the area of the square in square centimeters. Round to the nearest tenth. **316.1 cm^2**

1-6 Midpoint and Distance in the Coordinate Plane

Objectives
Develop and apply the formula for midpoint.

Use the Distance Formula and the Pythagorean Theorem to find the distance between two points.

Vocabulary
coordinate plane
leg
hypotenuse

Why learn this?
You can use a coordinate plane to help you calculate distances. (See Example 5.)

Major League baseball fields are laid out according to strict guidelines. Once you know the dimensions of a field, you can use a coordinate plane to find the distance between two of the bases.

A **coordinate plane** is a plane that is divided into four regions by a horizontal line (x-axis) and a vertical line (y-axis). The location, or coordinates, of a point are given by an ordered pair (x, y).

You can find the midpoint of a segment by using the coordinates of its endpoints. Calculate the average of the x-coordinates and the average of the y-coordinates of the endpoints.

Midpoint Formula

The midpoint M of $\overline{AB}$ with endpoints $A(x_1, y_1)$ and $B(x_2, y_2)$ is found by

$$M\left(\frac{x_1 + x_2}{2}, \frac{y_1 + y_2}{2}\right).$$

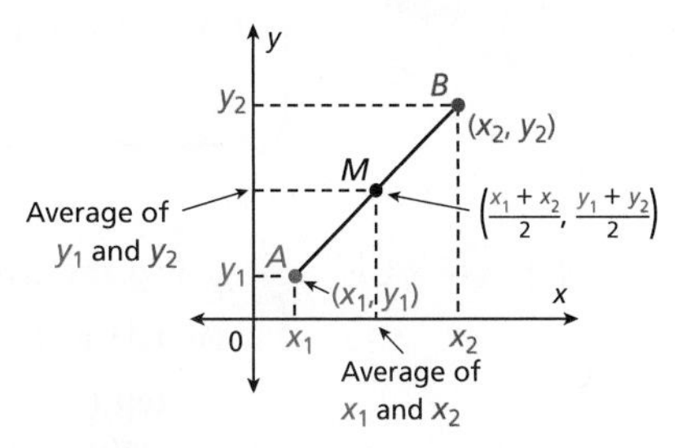

EXAMPLE 1 Finding the Coordinates of a Midpoint

Helpful Hint
To make it easier to picture the problem, plot the segment's endpoints on a coordinate plane.

Find the coordinates of the midpoint of $\overline{CD}$ with endpoints $C(-2, -1)$ and $D(4, 2)$.

$$M\left(\frac{x_1 + x_2}{2}, \frac{y_1 + y_2}{2}\right)$$

$$\frac{-2 + 4}{2}, \frac{-1 + 2}{2} = \left(\frac{2}{2}, \frac{1}{2}\right)$$

$$= \left(1, \frac{1}{2}\right)$$

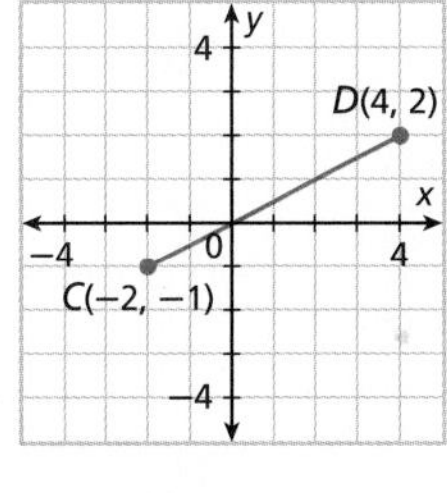

1. Find the coordinates of the midpoint of $\overline{EF}$ with endpoints $E(-2, 3)$ and $F(5, -3)$. $\left(\frac{3}{2}, 0\right)$

1-6 Organizer

Pacing: Traditional $\frac{1}{2}$ day
Block $\frac{1}{4}$ day

Objectives: Develop and apply the formula for midpoint.

Use the Distance Formula and the Pythagorean Theorem to find the distance between two points.

Online Edition
Tutorial Videos

Countdown Week 2

Power Presentations with PowerPoint®

Warm Up

1. Graph $A(-2, 3)$ and $B(1, 0)$.

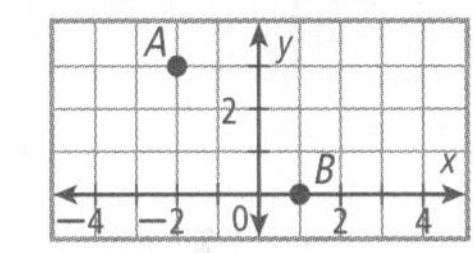

2. Find CD. 8

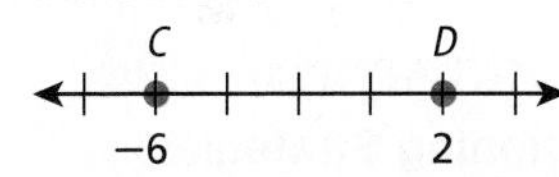

3. Find the coordinate of the midpoint of $\overline{CD}$. −2

4. Simplify. $\sqrt{(3-(-1))^2}$ 4

Also available on transparency

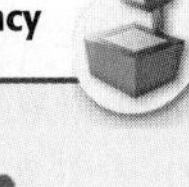

Math Humor

Q: What keeps a square from moving?

A: Square roots.

1 Introduce

EXPLORATION

1-6 Midpoint and Distance in the Coordinate Plane

The coordinate plane shows graphs of four line segments that are each named $\overline{AB}$. Copy each segment onto a sheet of graph paper.

1. Fold each segment so that A matches up with B. Use the fold to find the midpoint of the segment. In a table, record the coordinates of each segment's endpoints and midpoint.

Segment	Coordinates of A	Coordinates of B	Coordinates of Midpoint
1			
2			
3			
4			

2. For segments 1 and 2, how are the x-coordinates of each segment's midpoint related to the x-coordinates of its endpoints?
3. For segments 3 and 4, how are the y-coordinates of each segment's midpoint related to the y-coordinates of its endpoints?

THINK AND DISCUSS

Motivate

Give students a coordinate graph on which a house and a school have been graphed. Ask them to estimate the distance between the school and the house and to estimate the point that is halfway between these two locations.

Explorations and answers are provided in *Alternate Openers: Explorations Transparencies.*

State Resources

go.hrw.com
State Resources Online
KEYWORD: MG7 Resources

Power Presentations with PowerPoint®

Additional Examples

Example 1

Find the coordinates of the midpoint of $\overline{PQ}$ with endpoints $P(-8, 3)$ and $Q(-2, 7)$. $(-5, 5)$

Example 2

M is the midpoint of $\overline{XY}$. X has coordinates $(2, 7)$, and M has coordinates $(6, 1)$. Find the coordinates of Y. $(10, -5)$

Example 3

Find FG and JK. Then determine whether $\overline{FG} \cong \overline{JK}$. $5; 3\sqrt{2}$; no

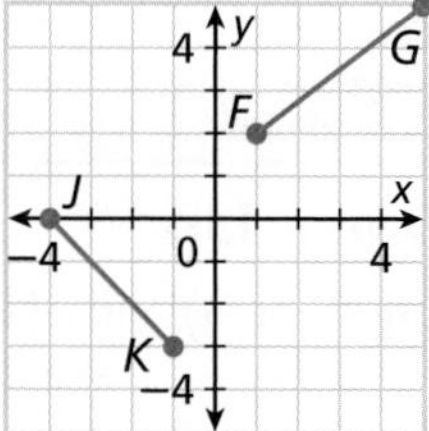

INTERVENTION

Questioning Strategies

EXAMPLE 1

- Does it matter which point is represented by (x_1, y_1)? Explain.

EXAMPLE 2

- Given the midpoint and one endpoint of a segment, how is the Midpoint Formula used to find the missing endpoint?

EXAMPLE 3

- How do you substitute the coordinates of two points into the Distance Formula?

EXAMPLE 2 Finding the Coordinates of an Endpoint

x^2y Algebra

M is the midpoint of $\overline{AB}$. A has coordinates $(2, 2)$, and M has coordinates $(4, -3)$. Find the coordinates of B.

Step 1 Let the coordinates of B equal (x, y).

Step 2 Use the Midpoint Formula: $(4, -3) = \left(\frac{2+x}{2}, \frac{2+y}{2}\right)$.

Step 3 Find the x-coordinate. Find the y-coordinate.

x-coordinate		y-coordinate
$4 = \frac{2+x}{2}$	*Set the coordinates equal.*	$-3 = \frac{2+y}{2}$
$2(4) = 2\left(\frac{2+x}{2}\right)$	*Multiply both sides by 2.*	$2(-3) = 2\left(\frac{2+y}{2}\right)$
$8 = 2 + x$	*Simplify.*	$-6 = 2 + y$
$-2 \quad -2$	*Subtract 2 from both sides.*	$-2 \quad -2$
$6 = x$	*Simplify.*	$-8 = y$

The coordinates of B are $(6, -8)$.

2. S is the midpoint of $\overline{RT}$. R has coordinates $(-6, -1)$, and S has coordinates $(-1, 1)$. Find the coordinates of T. **(4, 3)**

The Ruler Postulate can be used to find the distance between two points on a number line. The Distance Formula is used to calculate the distance between two points in a coordinate plane.

Know it! Note

Distance Formula

In a coordinate plane, the distance d between two points (x_1, y_1) and (x_2, y_2) is

$$d = \sqrt{(x_2 - x_1)^2 + (y_2 - y_1)^2}.$$

EXAMPLE 3 Using the Distance Formula

Find AB and CD. Then determine if $\overline{AB} \cong \overline{CD}$.

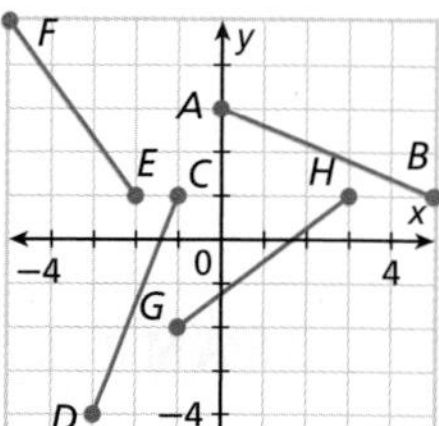

Step 1 Find the coordinates of each point.
$A(0, 3)$, $B(5, 1)$, $C(-1, 1)$, and $D(-3, -4)$

Step 2 Use the Distance Formula.

$$d = \sqrt{(x_2 - x_1)^2 + (y_2 - y_1)^2}$$

$$AB = \sqrt{(5-0)^2 + (1-3)^2} = \sqrt{5^2 + (-2)^2} = \sqrt{25 + 4} = \sqrt{29}$$

$$CD = \sqrt{[-3-(-1)]^2 + (-4-1)^2} = \sqrt{(-2)^2 + (-5)^2} = \sqrt{4 + 25} = \sqrt{29}$$

Since $AB = CD$, $\overline{AB} \cong \overline{CD}$.

3. Find EF and GH. Then determine if $\overline{EF} \cong \overline{GH}$.
$EF = 5$; $GH = 5$; $\overline{EF} \cong \overline{GH}$

2 Teach

Guided Instruction

Before teaching the Midpoint Formula, remind students how to find the average of two numbers. Connect average, a measure of central tendency, to the idea of midpoint. Review how to subtract positive and negative numbers to avoid subtracting errors in the Distance Formula. When finding midpoints and distances on a coordinate plane, relate your instruction to finding distances and midpoints on a number line.

Reaching All Learners

Through Cognitive Strategies

Have students use mental math to estimate the midpoint or distance. Then have them use a calculator to support their answer.

You can also use the Pythagorean Theorem to find the distance between two points in a coordinate plane. You will learn more about the Pythagorean Theorem in Chapter 5.

In a right triangle, the two sides that form the right angle are the **legs**. The side across from the right angle that stretches from one leg to the other is the **hypotenuse**. In the diagram, a and b are the lengths of the shorter sides, or legs, of the right triangle. The longest side is called the hypotenuse and has length c.

Theorem 1-6-1 Pythagorean Theorem

In a right triangle, the sum of the squares of the lengths of the *legs* is equal to the square of the length of the *hypotenuse*.

$$a^2 + b^2 = c^2$$

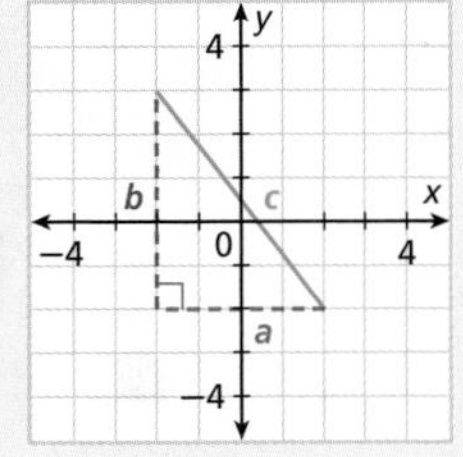

EXAMPLE 4 Finding Distances in the Coordinate Plane

Use the Distance Formula and the Pythagorean Theorem to find the distance, to the nearest tenth, from A to B.

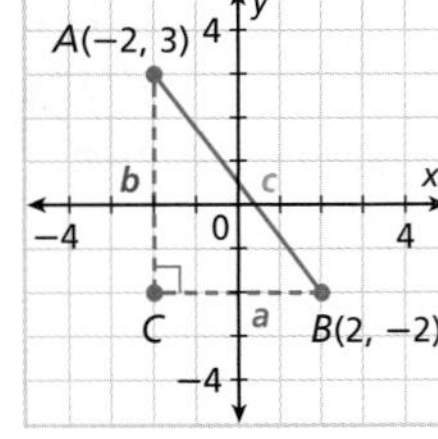

Method 1

Use the Distance Formula. Substitute the values for the coordinates of A and B into the Distance Formula.

$$AB = \sqrt{(x_2 - x_1)^2 + (y_2 - y_1)^2}$$
$$= \sqrt{[2 - (-2)]^2 + (-2 - 3)^2}$$
$$= \sqrt{4^2 + (-5)^2}$$
$$= \sqrt{16 + 25}$$
$$= \sqrt{41}$$
$$\approx 6.4$$

Method 2

Use the Pythagorean Theorem. Count the units for sides a and b.

$a = 4$ and $b = 5$.

$$c^2 = a^2 + b^2$$
$$= 4^2 + 5^2$$
$$= 16 + 25$$
$$= 41$$
$$c = \sqrt{41}$$
$$c \approx 6.4$$

Use the Distance Formula and the Pythagorean Theorem to find the distance, to the nearest tenth, from R to S.

4a. $R(3, 2)$ and $S(-3, -1)$ **6.7**

4b. $R(-4, 5)$ and $S(2, -1)$ **8.5**

Students may incorrectly label the sides of a triangle when using $a^2 + b^2 = c^2$. Remind them that sides a and b are interchangeable, and represent the two shorter sides that form the right angle. The side opposite the right angle is called the hypotenuse and is labeled as c.

Power Presentations with PowerPoint®

Additional Examples

Example 4

Use the Distance Formula and the Pythagorean Theorem to find the distance, to the nearest tenth, from $D(3, 4)$ to $E(-2, -5)$. 10.3

INTERVENTION

Questioning Strategies

EXAMPLE 4

- Do you think it is easier to use the Pythagorean Theorem or the Distance Formula to find the distance between two points? Explain.

Algebra Review with students that $\sqrt{3^2 + 4^2} \neq 3 + 4$. They must first square each number and then take the square root of the sum. The answer is 5, not 7.

Inclusion Have students label the coordinates of any two points they are given as (x_1, y_1) and (x_2, y_2) before substituting the numbers into the Midpoint Formula or Distance Formula.

Power Presentations with PowerPoint®

Additional Examples

Example 5

A player throws the ball from first base to a point located between third base and home plate and 10 feet from third base. What is the distance of the throw, to the nearest tenth? 120.4 ft

INTERVENTION

Questioning Strategies

EXAMPLE 5

- How do you find the coordinates of the endpoints used in the Distance Formula?
- Is the pitcher's mound the midpoint between home plate and second base? Explain.

EXAMPLE 5 Sports Application

The four bases on a baseball field form a square with 90 ft sides. When a player throws the ball from home plate to second base, what is the distance of the throw, to the nearest tenth?

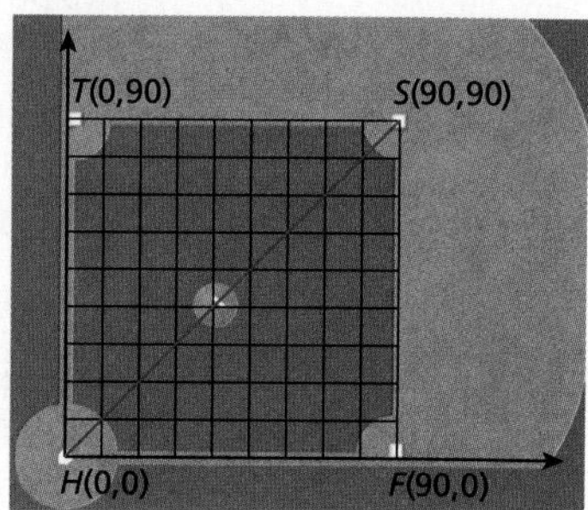

Set up the field on a coordinate plane so that home plate H is at the origin, first base F has coordinates (90, 0), second base S has coordinates (90, 90), and third base T has coordinates (0, 90).

The distance HS from home plate to second base is the length of the hypotenuse of a right triangle.

$$HS = \sqrt{(x_2 - x_1)^2 + (y_2 - y_1)^2}$$
$$= \sqrt{(90 - 0)^2 + (90 - 0)^2}$$
$$= \sqrt{90^2 + 90^2}$$
$$= \sqrt{8100 + 8100}$$
$$= \sqrt{16{,}200}$$
$$\approx 127.3 \text{ ft}$$

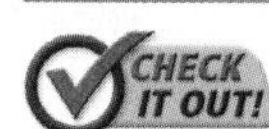

5. The center of the pitching mound has coordinates (42.8, 42.8). When a pitcher throws the ball from the center of the mound to home plate, what is the distance of the throw, to the nearest tenth? **60.5 ft**

THINK AND DISCUSS

1. Can you exchange the coordinates (x_1, y_1) and (x_2, y_2) in the Midpoint Formula and still find the correct midpoint? Explain.
2. A right triangle has sides lengths of r, s, and t. Given that $s^2 + t^2 = r^2$, which variables represent the lengths of the legs and which variable represents the length of the hypotenuse?
3. Do you always get the same result using the Distance Formula to find distance as you do when using the Pythagorean Theorem? Explain your answer.
4. Why do you think that most cities are laid out in a rectangular grid instead of a triangular or circular grid?

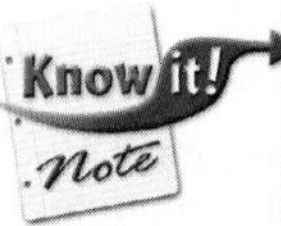

5. **GET ORGANIZED** Copy and complete the graphic organizer below. In each box, write a formula. Then make a sketch that will illustrate the formula.

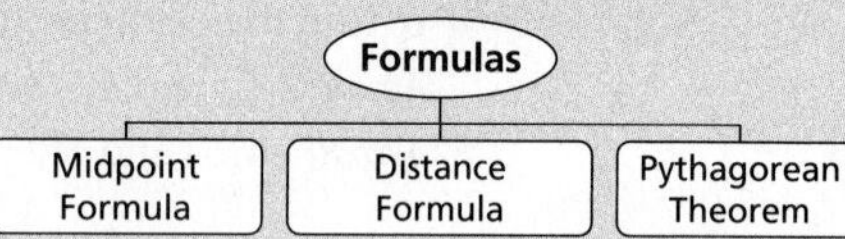

3 Close

Summarize

Review with students how to use the Midpoint Formula and Distance Formula to find the midpoint of a segment and the distance between two points, given their coordinates.

ONGOING ASSESSMENT and INTERVENTION

Diagnose **Before the Lesson**
1-6 Warm Up, TE p. 43

Monitor **During the Lesson**
Check It Out! Exercises, SE pp. 43–46
Questioning Strategies, TE pp. 44–46

Assess **After the Lesson**
1-6 Lesson Quiz, TE p. 49
Alternative Assessment, TE p. 49

Answers to *Think and Discuss*

1. yes; $\frac{x_1 + x_2}{2} = \frac{x_2 + x_1}{2}$ and $\frac{y_1 + y_2}{2} = \frac{y_2 + y_1}{2}$
2. s and t represent the lengths of the legs. r represents the length of the hyp.
3. Yes; you can use either method to find the dist. between 2 pts.
4. Possible answer: to make locating addresses easier
5. See p. A2.

1-6 Exercises

go.hrw.com
Homework Help Online
KEYWORD: MG7 1-6
Parent Resources Online
KEYWORD: MG7 Parent

GUIDED PRACTICE

1. **Vocabulary** The __?__ is the side of a right triangle that is directly across from the right angle. (*hypotenuse* or *leg*) **hypotenuse**

SEE EXAMPLE 1 p. 43

Find the coordinates of the midpoint of each segment.

2. $\overline{AB}$ with endpoints $A(4, -6)$ and $B(-4, 2)$ **$(0, -2)$**
3. $\overline{CD}$ with endpoints $C(0, -8)$ and $D(3, 0)$ **$\left(1\frac{1}{2}, -4\right)$**

SEE EXAMPLE 2 p. 44

4. M is the midpoint of $\overline{LN}$. L has coordinates $(-3, -1)$, and M has coordinates $(0, 1)$. Find the coordinates of N. **$(3, 3)$**
5. B is the midpoint of $\overline{AC}$. A has coordinates $(-3, 4)$, and B has coordinates $\left(-1\frac{1}{2}, 1\right)$. Find the coordinates of C. **$(0, -2)$**

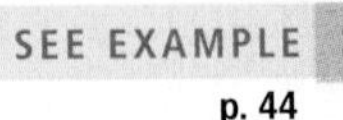
SEE EXAMPLE 3 p. 44

Multi-Step Find the length of the given segments and determine if they are congruent.

6. $\overline{JK}$ and $\overline{FG}$ **$\sqrt{29}$; $\sqrt{29}$; yes**
7. $\overline{JK}$ and $\overline{RS}$ **$\sqrt{29}$; $3\sqrt{5}$; no**

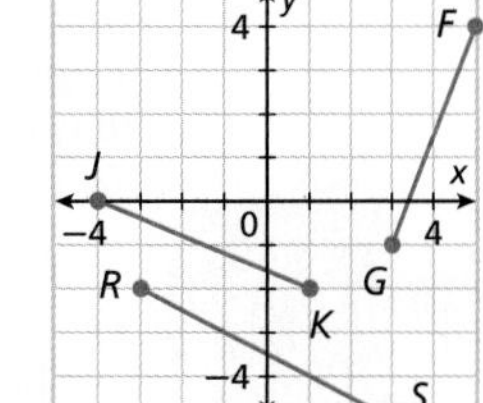

SEE EXAMPLE 4 p. 45

Use the Distance Formula and the Pythagorean Theorem to find the distance, to the nearest tenth, between each pair of points.

8. $A(1, -2)$ and $B(-4, -4)$ **5.4**
9. $X(-2, 7)$ and $Y(-2, -8)$ **15.0**
10. $V(2, -1)$ and $W(-4, 8)$ **10.8**

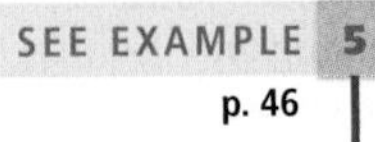
SEE EXAMPLE 5 p. 46

11. **Architecture** The plan for a rectangular living room shows electrical wiring will be run in a straight line from the entrance E to a light L at the opposite corner of the room. What is the length of the wire to the nearest tenth? **27.2 ft**

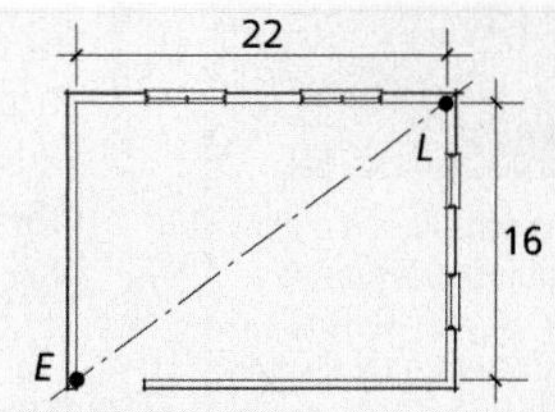

PRACTICE AND PROBLEM SOLVING

For Exercises	See Example
12–13	1
14–15	2
16–17	3
18–20	4
21	5

Independent Practice

Extra Practice
Skills Practice p. S5
Application Practice p. S28

Find the coordinates of the midpoint of each segment.

12. $\overline{XY}$ with endpoints $X(-3, -7)$ and $Y(-1, 1)$ **$(-2, -3)$**
13. $\overline{MN}$ with endpoints $M(12, -7)$ and $N(-5, -2)$ **$\left(3\frac{1}{2}, -4\frac{1}{2}\right)$**
14. M is the midpoint of $\overline{QR}$. Q has coordinates $(-3, 5)$, and M has coordinates $(7, -9)$. Find the coordinates of R. **$(17, -23)$**
15. D is the midpoint of $\overline{CE}$. E has coordinates $(-3, -2)$, and D has coordinates $\left(2\frac{1}{2}, 1\right)$. Find the coordinates of C. **$(8, 4)$**

Multi-Step Find the length of the given segments and determine if they are congruent.

16. $\overline{DE}$ and $\overline{FG}$ **$2\sqrt{5}$; $2\sqrt{5}$; yes**
17. $\overline{DE}$ and $\overline{RS}$ **$2\sqrt{5}$; $\sqrt{29}$; no**

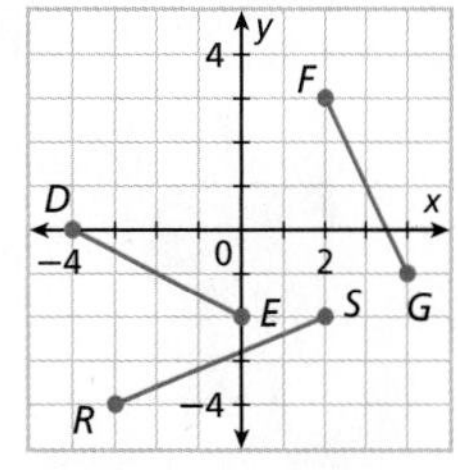

1-6 Exercises

Assignment Guide

Assign *Guided Practice* exercises as necessary.

If you finished Examples **1–3**
Basic 12–17, 22, 26, 27, 33
Average 12–17, 22, 24–27, 33, 38
Advanced 12–17, 22, 24–27, 33, 36, 38

If you finished Examples **1–5**
Basic 12–23, 26–28, 30, 32–37, 42–50
Average 12–39, 42–50
Advanced 12–50

Homework Quick Check
Quickly check key concepts.
Exercises: 12, 14, 16, 18, 21, 26, 30

State Resources

MULTI-STEP TEST PREP Exercise 33 involves finding the distance between points on a coordinate plane. This exercise prepares students for the Multi-Step Test Prep on page 58.

Answers

32. When 2 pts. lie on a horiz. or vert. line, they share a common x-coordinate or y-coordinate. To find the dist. between the pts., find the difference of the other coordinates.

Use the Distance Formula and the Pythagorean Theorem to find the distance, to the nearest tenth, between each pair of points.

10.4 **18.** $U(0, 1)$ and $V(-3, -9)$ 8.9 **19.** $M(10, -1)$ and $N(2, -5)$ 15.5 **20.** $P(-10, 1)$ and $Q(5, 5)$

18 in. **21. Consumer Application** Televisions and computer screens are usually advertised based on the length of their diagonals. If the height of a computer screen is 11 in. and the width is 14 in., what is the length of the diagonal? Round to the nearest inch.

$\overline{CD}, \overline{EF}, \overline{AB}$ **22. Multi-Step** Use the Distance Formula to order $\overline{AB}$, $\overline{CD}$, and $\overline{EF}$ from shortest to longest.

4.47 **23.** Use the Pythagorean Theorem to find the distance from A to E. Round to the nearest hundredth.

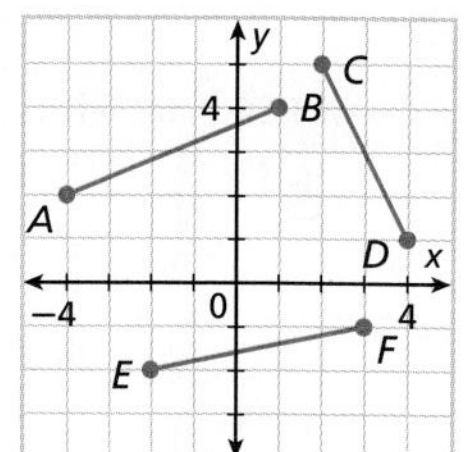

$\left(-2a, \frac{3}{2}a\right)$ **24.** X has coordinates $(a, 3a)$, and Y has coordinates $(-5a, 0)$. Find the coordinates of the midpoint of (XY).

Divide each coord. by 2. **25.** Describe a shortcut for finding the midpoint of a segment when one of its endpoints has coordinates (a, b) and the other endpoint is the origin.

On the map, each square of the grid represents 1 square mile. Find each distance to the nearest tenth of a mile.

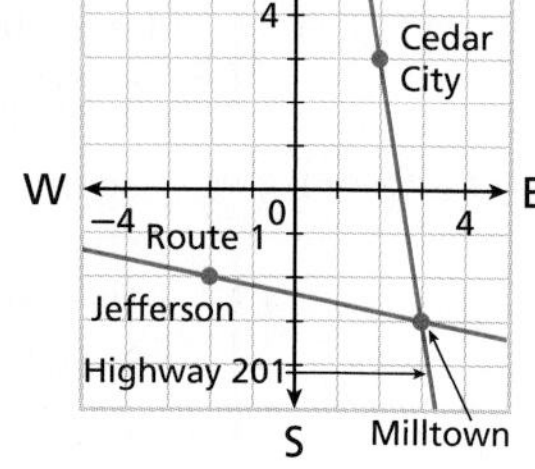

26. Find the distance along Highway 201 from Cedar City to Milltown. 6.1 mi

27. A car breaks down on Route 1, at the midpoint between Jefferson and Milltown. A tow truck is sent out from Jefferson. How far does the truck travel to reach the car? 2.5 mi

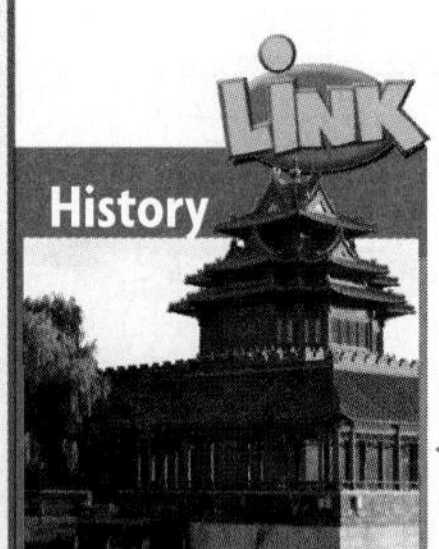

The construction of the Forbidden City lasted for 14 years. It began in 1406 with an estimated workforce of 200,000 men.
Source: www.wikipedia.com

28. History The Forbidden City in Beijing, China, is the world's largest palace complex. Surrounded by a wall and a moat, the rectangular complex is 960 m long and 750 m wide. Find the distance, to the nearest meter, from one corner of the complex to the opposite corner. 1218 m

29. Critical Thinking Give an example of a line segment with midpoint $(0, 0)$.
Possible answer: seg. with endpts. $(1, 2)$ and $(-1, -2)$

The coordinates of the vertices of $\triangle ABC$ are $A(1, 4)$, $B(-2, -1)$, and $C(-3, -2)$.

30. Find the perimeter of $\triangle ABC$ to the nearest tenth. 14.5

31. The height h to side $\overline{BC}$ is $\sqrt{2}$, and b is the length of $\overline{BC}$. What is the area of $\triangle ABC$? 1

32. Write About It Explain why the Distance Formula is not needed to find the distance between two points that lie on a horizontal or a vertical line.

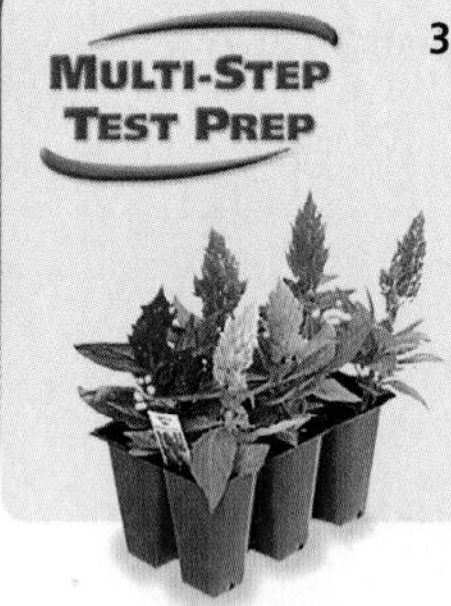

33. This problem will prepare you for the Multi-Step Test Prep on page 58. Tania uses a coordinate plane to map out plans for landscaping a rectangular patio area. On the plan, one square represents 2 feet. She plans to plant a tree at the midpoint of $\overline{AC}$. How far from each corner of the patio does she plant the tree? Round to the nearest tenth. Let M be the mdpt. of $\overline{AC}$; $AM = MC = 5.0$ ft; $MB = MD \approx 6.4$ ft.

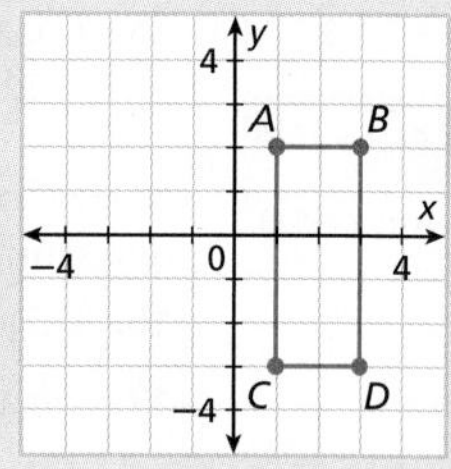

1-6 PRACTICE A
1-6 PRACTICE C
1-6 PRACTICE B

Find the coordinates of the midpoint of each segment.

1. $\overline{TU}$ with endpoints $T(5, -1)$ and $U(1, -5)$ — $(3, -3)$
2. $\overline{VW}$ with endpoints $V(-2, -6)$ and $W(x + 2, y + 3)$ — $\left(\frac{x}{2}, \frac{y-3}{2}\right)$
3. Y is the midpoint of $\overline{XZ}$. X has coordinates (2, 4), and Y has coordinates (–1, 1). Find the coordinates of Z. — $(-4, -2)$

Use the figure for Exercises 4–7.

4. Find AB. $\sqrt{26}$
5. Find BC. $\sqrt{26}$
6. Find CA. $4\sqrt{2}$
7. Name a pair of congruent segments. $\overline{AB}$ and $\overline{BC}$

Find the distances.

8. Use the Distance Formula to find the distance, to the nearest tenth, between $K(-7, -4)$ and $L(-2, 0)$. — 6.4
9. Use the Pythagorean Theorem to find the distance, to the nearest tenth, between $F(9, 5)$ and $G(-2, 2)$. — 11.4

Use the figure for Exercises 10–11.

Snooker is a kind of pool or billiards played on a 6-foot-by-12-foot table. The side pockets are halfway down the rails (long sides).

10. Find the distance, to the nearest tenth of a foot, diagonally across the table from corner pocket to corner pocket. — 13.4 ft
11. Find the distance, to the nearest tenth of an inch, diagonally across the table from corner pocket to side pocket. — 101.8 in.

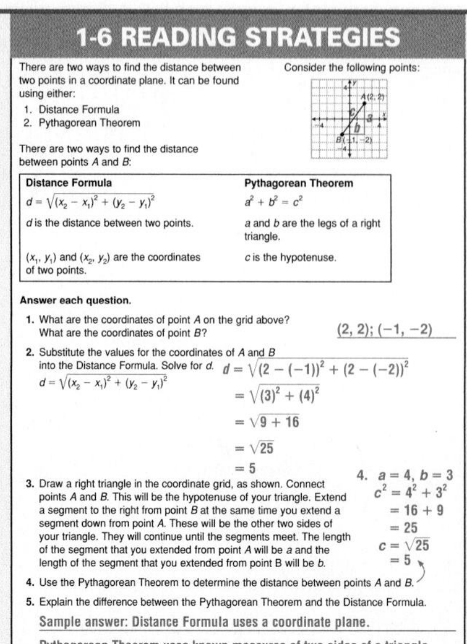

1-6 READING STRATEGIES

There are two ways to find the distance between two points in a coordinate plane. It can be found using either:

1. Distance Formula
2. Pythagorean Theorem

Consider the following points: $A(2, 2)$, $B(-1, -2)$

There are two ways to find the distance between points A and B:

Distance Formula	Pythagorean Theorem
$d = \sqrt{(x_2 - x_1)^2 + (y_2 - y_1)^2}$	$a^2 + b^2 = c^2$
d is the distance between two points.	a and b are the legs of a right triangle.
(x_1, y_1) and (x_2, y_2) are the coordinates of two points.	c is the hypotenuse.

Answer each question.

1. What are the coordinates of point A on the grid above? What are the coordinates of point B? — (2, 2); (−1, −2)
2. Substitute the values for the coordinates of A and B into the Distance Formula. Solve for d. $d = \sqrt{(x_2 - x_1)^2 + (y_2 - y_1)^2}$
$$d = \sqrt{(2-(-1))^2 + (2-(-2))^2} = \sqrt{(3)^2 + (4)^2} = \sqrt{9 + 16} = \sqrt{25} = 5$$
3. Draw a right triangle in the coordinate grid, as shown. Connect points A and B. This will be the hypotenuse of your triangle. Extend a segment to the right from point B at the same time you extend a segment down from point A. These will be the other two sides of your triangle. They will continue until the segments meet. The length of the segment that you extended from point A will be a and the length of the segment that you extended from point B will be b.
4. Use the Pythagorean Theorem to determine the distance between points A and B.
4. $a = 4, b = 3$; $c^2 = 4^2 + 3^2 = 16 + 9 = 25$; $c = \sqrt{25} = 5$
5. Explain the difference between the Pythagorean Theorem and the Distance Formula.
Sample answer: Distance Formula uses a coordinate plane.
Pythagorean Theorem uses known measures of two sides of a triangle.

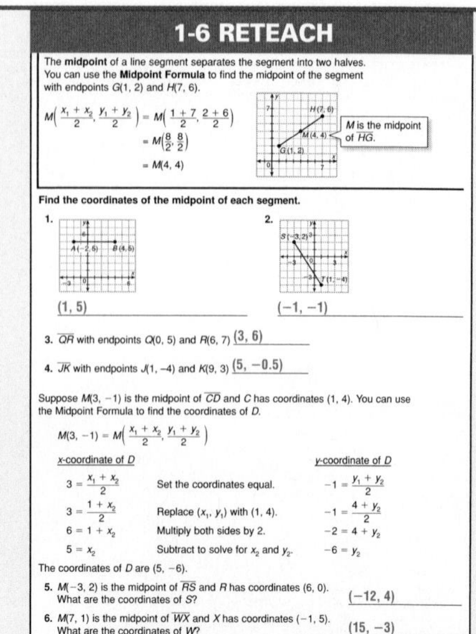

1-6 RETEACH

The **midpoint** of a line segment separates the segment into two halves. You can use the **Midpoint Formula** to find the midpoint of the segment with endpoints $G(1, 2)$ and $H(7, 6)$.

$$M\left(\frac{x_1 + x_2}{2}, \frac{y_1 + y_2}{2}\right) = M\left(\frac{1+7}{2}, \frac{2+6}{2}\right) = M\left(\frac{8}{2}, \frac{8}{2}\right) = M(4, 4)$$

M is the midpoint of $\overline{HG}$.

Find the coordinates of the midpoint of each segment.

1. $A(-2, 5)$, $B(4, 5)$ — (1, 5)
2. $S(-3, 2)$, $T(1, -4)$ — (−1, −1)
3. $\overline{QR}$ with endpoints $Q(0, 5)$ and $R(6, 7)$ — (3, 6)
4. $\overline{JK}$ with endpoints $J(1, -4)$ and $K(9, 3)$ — (5, −0.5)

Suppose $M(3, -1)$ is the midpoint of $\overline{CD}$ and C has coordinates (1, 4). You can use the Midpoint Formula to find the coordinates of D.

$$M(3, -1) = M\left(\frac{x_1 + x_2}{2}, \frac{y_1 + y_2}{2}\right)$$

x-coordinate of D		y-coordinate of D
$3 = \frac{x_1 + x_2}{2}$	Set the coordinates equal.	$-1 = \frac{y_1 + y_2}{2}$
$3 = \frac{1 + x_2}{2}$	Replace (x_1, y_1) with (1, 4).	$-1 = \frac{4 + y_2}{2}$
$6 = 1 + x_2$	Multiply both sides by 2.	$-2 = 4 + y_2$
$5 = x_2$	Subtract to solve for x_2 and y_2.	$-6 = y_2$

The coordinates of D are (5, −6).

5. $M(-3, 2)$ is the midpoint of $\overline{RS}$ and R has coordinates (6, 0). What are the coordinates of S? — (−12, 4)
6. $M(7, 1)$ is the midpoint of $\overline{WX}$ and X has coordinates (−1, 5). What are the coordinates of W? — (15, −3)

TEST PREP

34. Which segment has a length closest to 4 units?

Ⓐ $\overline{EF}$ Ⓒ $\overline{JK}$

Ⓑ $\overline{GH}$ Ⓓ $\overline{LM}$

35. Find the distance, to the nearest tenth, between the midpoints of $\overline{LM}$ and $\overline{JK}$.

Ⓕ 1.8 Ⓗ 4.0

Ⓖ 3.6 Ⓙ 5.3

36. What are the coordinates of the midpoint of a line segment that connects the points $(7, -3)$ and $(-5, 6)$?

Ⓐ $\left(6, -4\frac{1}{2}\right)$ Ⓒ $\left(2, \frac{1}{2}\right)$

Ⓑ $(2, 3)$ **Ⓓ $\left(1, 1\frac{1}{2}\right)$**

37. A coordinate plane is placed over the map of a town. A library is located at $(-5, 1)$, and a museum is located at $(3, 5)$. What is the distance, to the nearest tenth, from the library to the museum?

Ⓕ 4.5 Ⓖ 5.7 Ⓗ 6.3 **Ⓙ 8.9**

CHALLENGE AND EXTEND

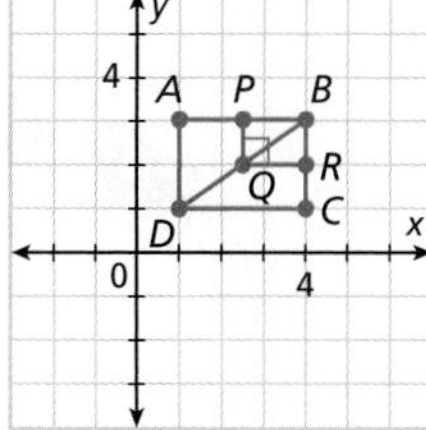

38. Use the diagram to find the following.
   a. P is the midpoint of $\overline{AB}$, and R is the midpoint of $\overline{BC}$. Find the coordinates of Q. **$Q(2.5, 2)$**
   b. Find the area of rectangle $PBRQ$. **1.5**
   c. Find DB. Round to the nearest tenth. **$\sqrt{13} \approx 3.6$**

39. The coordinates of X are $(a - 5, -2a)$. The coordinates of Y are $(a + 1, 2a)$. If the distance between X and Y is 10, find the value of a. **± 2**

40. Find two points on the y-axis that are a distance of 5 units from $(4, 2)$. **$(0, 5)$; $(0, -1)$**

41. Given $\angle ACB$ is a right angle of $\triangle ABC$, $AC = x$, and $BC = y$, find AB in terms of x and y. **$AB = \sqrt{x^2 + y^2}$**

SPIRAL REVIEW

Determine if the ordered pair $(-1, 4)$ satisfies each function. *(Previous course)*

42. $y = 3x - 1$ **no**
43. $f(x) = 5 - x^2$ **yes**
44. $g(x) = x^2 - x + 2$ **yes**

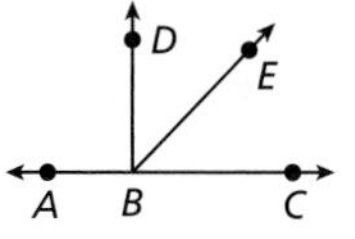

$\overrightarrow{BD}$ bisects straight angle ABC, and $\overrightarrow{BE}$ bisects $\angle CBD$. Find the measure of each angle and classify it as acute, right, or obtuse. *(Lesson 1-3)*

45. $\angle ABD$ **90°; rt.**
46. $\angle CBE$ **45°; acute**
47. $\angle ABE$ **135°; obtuse**

Find the area of each of the following. *(Lesson 1-5)*

48. square whose perimeter is 20 in. **25 in^2**
49. triangle whose height is 2 ft and whose base is twice its height **4 ft^2**
50. rectangle whose length is x and whose width is $(4x + 5)$ **$4x^2 + 5x$**

1-6 PROBLEM SOLVING

For Exercises 1 and 2, use the diagram of a tennis court.

1. A singles tennis court is a rectangle 27 feet wide and 78 feet long. Suppose a player at corner A hits the ball to her opponent in the diagonally opposite corner B. Approximately how far does the ball travel, to the nearest tenth of a foot? **82.5 ft**
2. A doubles tennis court is a rectangle 36 feet wide and 78 feet long. If two players are standing in diagonally opposite corners, about how far apart are they, to the nearest tenth of a foot? **85.9 ft**

A map of an amusement park is shown on a coordinate plane, where each square of the grid represents 1 square meter. The water ride is at (−17, 12), the roller coaster is at (26, −8), and the Ferris wheel is at (2, 20). Find each distance to the nearest tenth of a meter.

3. What is the distance between the water ride and the roller coaster? **47.4 m**
4. A caricature artist is at the midpoint between the roller coaster and the Ferris wheel. What is the distance from the artist to the Ferris wheel? **18.4 m**

Use the map of the Sacramento Zoo on a coordinate plane for Exercises 5–7. Choose the best answer.

5. To the nearest tenth of a unit, how far is it from the tigers to the hyenas?
   A 5.1 units C 9.9 units
   B 7.1 units D 50.0 units
6. Between which of these exhibits is the distance the least?
   F tigers and primates
   G hyenas and gibbons
   H otters and gibbons
   J tigers and otters
7. Suppose you walk straight from the jaguars to the tigers and then to the otters. What is the total distance to the nearest tenth of a unit?
   A 11.4 units **C 13.9 units**
   B 13.0 units D 14.2 units

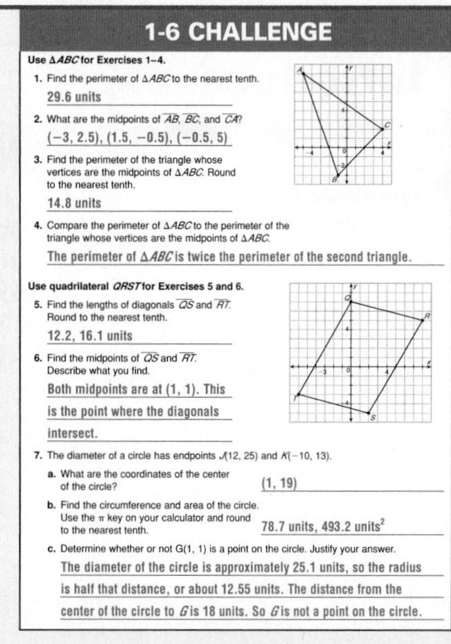

1-6 CHALLENGE

Use $\triangle ABC$ for Exercises 1–4.

1. Find the perimeter of $\triangle ABC$ to the nearest tenth. **29.6 units**
2. What are the midpoints of $\overline{AB}$, $\overline{BC}$, and $\overline{CA}$? **(−3, 2.5), (1.5, −0.5), (−0.5, 5)**
3. Find the perimeter of the triangle whose vertices are the midpoints of $\triangle ABC$. Round to the nearest tenth. **14.8 units**
4. Compare the perimeter of $\triangle ABC$ to the perimeter of the triangle whose vertices are the midpoints of $\triangle ABC$. **The perimeter of $\triangle ABC$ is twice the perimeter of the second triangle.**

Use quadrilateral $QRST$ for Exercises 5 and 6.

5. Find the lengths of diagonals $\overline{QS}$ and $\overline{RT}$. Round to the nearest tenth. **12.2, 16.1 units**
6. Find the midpoints of $\overline{QS}$ and $\overline{RT}$. Describe what you find. **Both midpoints are at (1, 1). This is the point where the diagonals intersect.**
7. The diameter of a circle has endpoints $J(12, 25)$ and $K(-10, 13)$.
   a. What are the coordinates of the center of the circle? **(1, 19)**
   b. Find the circumference and area of the circle. Use the π key on your calculator and round to the nearest tenth. **78.7 units, 493.2 units^2**
   c. Determine whether or not $G(1, 1)$ is a point on the circle. Justify your answer. **The diameter of the circle is approximately 25.1 units, so the radius is half that distance, or about 12.55 units. The distance from the center of the circle to G is 18 units. So G is not a point on the circle.**

COMMON ERROR ALERT

In **Exercise 39,** students may think that 2 is the only value of a. Remind them that coordinates can be negative, and thus −2 is also a value of a.

TEST PREP DOCTOR If students have difficulty with **Exercise 34,** have them mark off a segment on a piece of paper that is four units long and compare it to the four segments that are shown on the graph.

Journal

Have students compare the distance and midpoint formulas. Ask them to draw an example on a grid.

ALTERNATIVE ASSESSMENT

Have students draw and measure the sides of a right triangle on a coordinate plane. They should label the vertices and find the locations of the midpoints of each side. Then they should find the distances between the vertices.

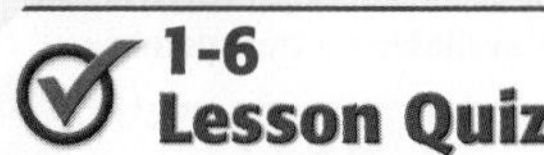

Power Presentations with PowerPoint®

1-6 Lesson Quiz

1. Find the coordinates of the midpoint of $\overline{MN}$ with endpoints $M(-2, 6)$ and $N(8, 0)$. $(3, 3)$
2. K is the midpoint of $\overline{HL}$. H has coordinates $(1, -7)$, and K has coordinates $(9, 3)$. Find the coordinates of L. $(17, 13)$
3. Find the distance, to the nearest tenth, between $S(6, 5)$ and $T(-3, -4)$. 12.7
4. The coordinates of the vertices of $\triangle ABC$ are $A(2, 5)$, $B(6, -1)$, and $C(-4, -2)$. Find the perimeter of $\triangle ABC$, to the nearest tenth. 26.5
5. Find the lengths of $\overline{AB}$ and $\overline{CD}$ and determine whether they are congruent. $\sqrt{10}$; $\sqrt{10}$; yes

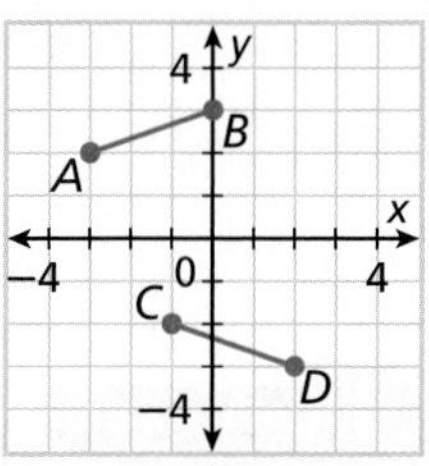

Also available on transparency

1-7 Organizer

Pacing: Traditional 1 day
Block $\frac{1}{2}$ day

Objectives: Identify reflections, rotations, and translations.

Graph transformations in the coordinate plane.

Online Edition
Tutorial Videos, Interactivity

Countdown Week 2

Power Presentations with PowerPoint®

Warm Up

1. Draw a line that divides a right angle in half.

2. Draw three different squares with (3, 2) as one vertex.
Check students' drawings.

3. Find the values of x and y if $(3, -2) = (x + 1, y - 3)$
$x = 2; y = 1$

Also available on transparency

Math Humor

Spanish teacher: Why didn't you translate the verb?

Student: I did. I moved it 3 inches right and 2 inches down.

1-7 Transformations in the Coordinate Plane

Objectives
Identify reflections, rotations, and translations.

Graph transformations in the coordinate plane.

Vocabulary
transformation
preimage
image
reflection
rotation
translation

Who uses this?
Artists use transformations to create decorative patterns. (See Example 4.)

The Alhambra, a 13th-century palace in Granada, Spain, is famous for the geometric patterns that cover its walls and floors. To create a variety of designs, the builders based the patterns on several different *transformations.*

A **transformation** is a change in the position, size, or shape of a figure. The original figure is called the **preimage**. The resulting figure is called the **image**. A transformation *maps* the preimage to the image. Arrow notation (→) is used to describe a transformation, and primes (′) are used to label the image.

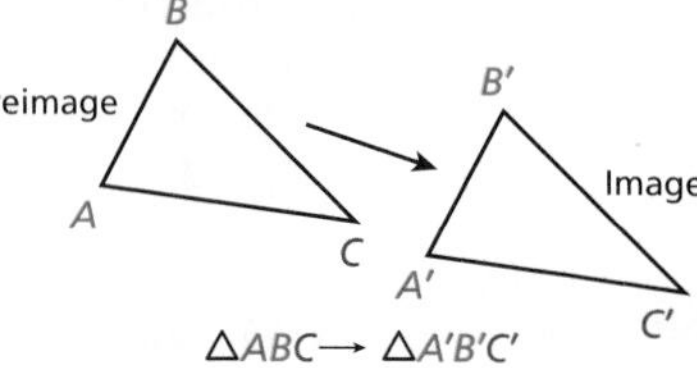

Know it! Note

Transformations

REFLECTION	ROTATION	TRANSLATION
B, B′, A, C, C′, A′	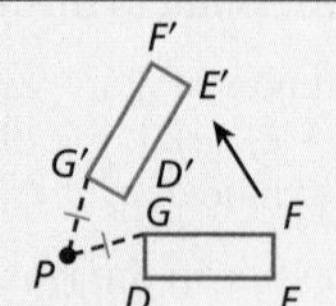	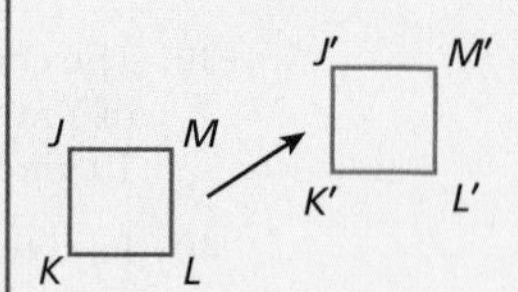
A **reflection** (or *flip*) is a transformation across a line, called the line of reflection. Each point and its image are the same distance from the line of reflection.	A **rotation** (or *turn*) is a transformation about a point P, called the center of rotation. Each point and its image are the same distance from P.	A **translation** (or *slide*) is a transformation in which all the points of a figure move the same distance in the same direction.

EXAMPLE 1 Identifying Transformations

Identify the transformation. Then use arrow notation to describe the transformation.

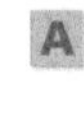

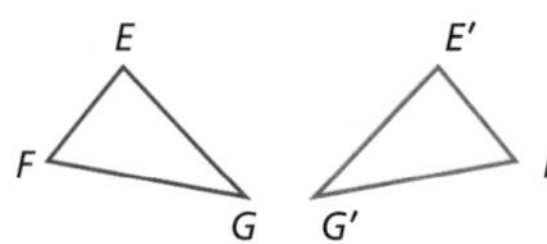

The transformation cannot be a translation because each point and its image are not in the same position.

The transformation is a reflection. $\triangle EFG \rightarrow \triangle E'F'G'$

State Resources

go.hrw.com
State Resources Online
KEYWORD: MG7 Resources

1 Introduce

EXPLORATION

1-7 Transformations in the Coordinate Plane

Use geometry software to reflect a triangle across a line segment.

1. Draw $\overline{AB}$. (This will be the *line of reflection.*)
2. Draw $\triangle RST$ on one side of $\overline{AB}$.
3. Select $\overline{AB}$ and choose Mark Mirror from the Transform menu. Then select $\triangle RST$ and choose Reflect from the Transform menu. Label the new triangle as $\triangle R'S'T'$.
4. Construct $\overline{TT'}$. Then select $\overline{TT'}$ and $\overline{AB}$ and use the Construct menu to construct their intersection X. Measure $\overline{TX}$, $\overline{T'X}$, and $\angle TXB$.
5. Drag T. What do you notice about the measurements as you do so?

Motivate

Show students examples of tessellations, translations, rotations, and reflections in the real world, from magazines or advertisements. Ask students to demonstrate transformations by standing and sliding two steps right and then rotating 90° clockwise.

Explorations and answers are provided in *Alternate Openers: Explorations Transparencies.*

Identify the transformation. Then use arrow notation to describe the transformation.

B 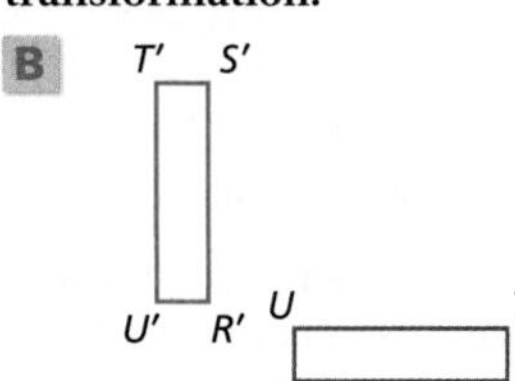

The transformation cannot be a reflection because each point and its image are not the same distance from a line of reflection.

The transformation is a 90° rotation. $RSTU \rightarrow R'S'T'U'$

Identify each transformation. Then use arrow notation to describe the transformation.

1a. 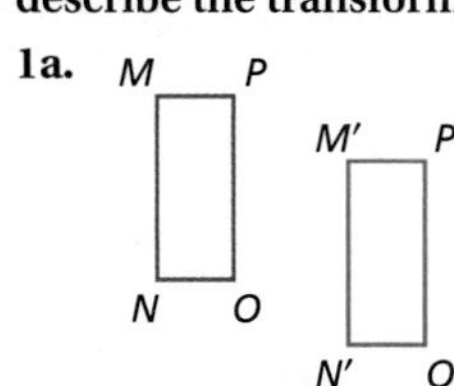

translation; $MNOP \rightarrow M'N'O'P'$

1b. 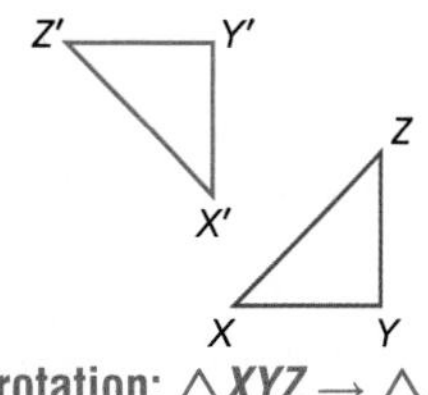

rotation; $\triangle XYZ \rightarrow \triangle X'Y'Z'$

EXAMPLE **2** **Drawing and Identifying Transformations**

A figure has vertices at $A(-1, 4)$, $B(-1, 1)$, and $C(3, 1)$. After a transformation, the image of the figure has vertices at $A'(-1, -4)$, $B'(-1, -1)$, and $C'(3, -1)$. Draw the preimage and image. Then identify the transformation.

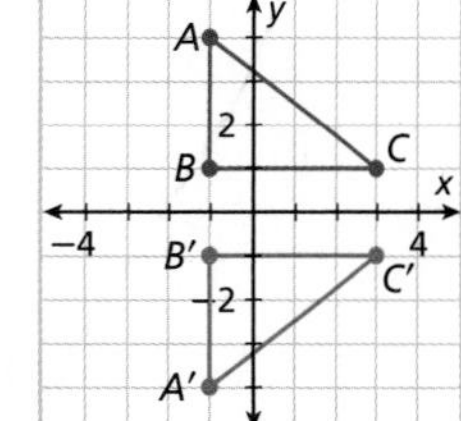

Plot the points. Then use a straightedge to connect the vertices.

The transformation is a reflection across the x-axis because each point and its image are the same distance from the x-axis.

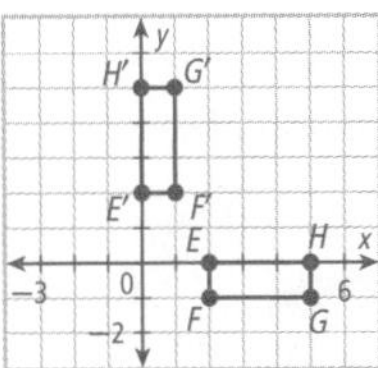

2. A figure has vertices at $E(2, 0)$, $F(2, -1)$, $G(5, -1)$, and $H(5, 0)$. After a transformation, the image of the figure has vertices at $E'(0, 2)$, $F'(1, 2)$, $G'(1, 5)$, and $H'(0, 5)$. Draw the preimage and image. Then identify the transformation. rotation; 90°

To find coordinates for the image of a figure in a translation, add a to the x-coordinates of the preimage and add b to the y-coordinates of the preimage. Translations can also be described by a rule such as $(x, y) \rightarrow (x + a, y + b)$.

EXAMPLE **3** **Translations in the Coordinate Plane**

Find the coordinates for the image of $\triangle ABC$ after the translation $(x, y) \rightarrow (x + 3, y - 4)$. Draw the image.

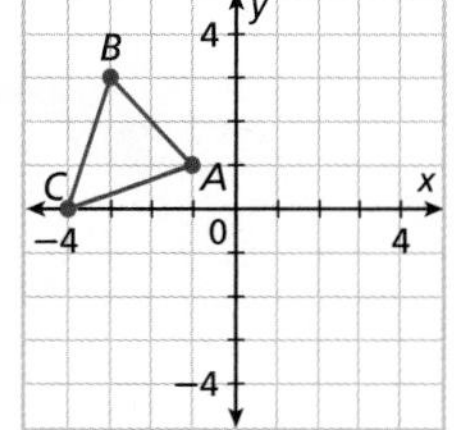

Step 1 Find the coordinates of $\triangle ABC$.

The vertices of $\triangle ABC$ are $A(-1, 1)$, $B(-3, 3)$, and $C(-4, 0)$.

Power Presentations with PowerPoint®

Additional Examples

Example 1

Identify the transformation. Then use arrow notation to describe the transformation.

A. 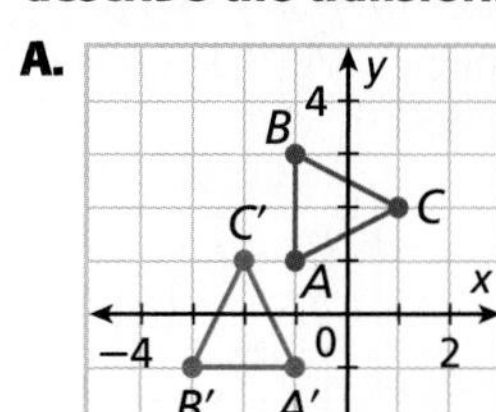

90° rotation, $\triangle ABC \rightarrow \triangle A'B'C'$

B. 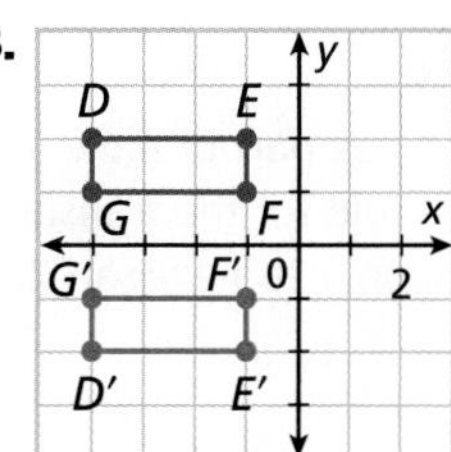

reflection, $DEFG \rightarrow D'E'F'G'$

Example 2

A figure has vertices at $A(1, -1)$, $B(2, 3)$, and $C(4, -2)$. After a transformation, the image of the figure has vertices at $A'(-1, -1)$, $B'(-2, 3)$, and $C'(-4, -2)$. Draw the preimage and image. Then identify the transformation.

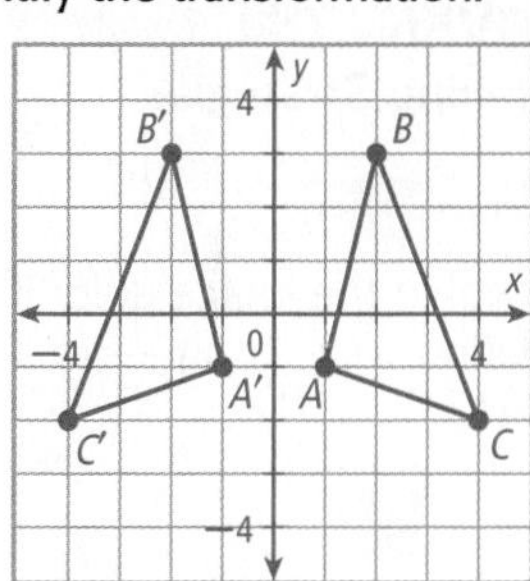

reflection across the y-axis

2 Teach

Guided Instruction

Explain the concepts of reflection, rotation, and translation; the terms *preimage* and *image*; and prime notation before using examples on a coordinate plane.

Inclusion Have students look in a mirror (MK). They are the *preimage before* they see themselves in the mirror. The image is their reflection in the mirror.

Reaching All Learners

Through Concrete Manipulatives

Give students a coordinate grid and a cut-out triangle. Have them slide the figure to a new location, rotate it about the origin, and reflect it over a specified line to find the image. Show students why a reflection is not equivalent to a 180° rotation. Use notebook paper with a large *F* marked on one side to show that the image in a rotation is upside down.

INTERVENTION

Questioning Strategies

EXAMPLE 1

- How would each image in **Example 1A** and **Example 1B** differ if the transformation were a translation?

EXAMPLE 2

- How did you decide what type of transformation this was?

Power Presentations with PowerPoint®

Additional Examples

Example 3

Find the coordinates for the image of $\triangle ABC$ after the translation $(x, y) \rightarrow (x + 2, y - 1)$. Draw the image. $A'(-2, 1)$, $B'(-1, 3)$, $C'(1, 0)$

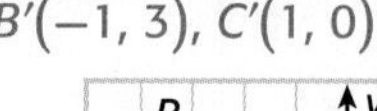

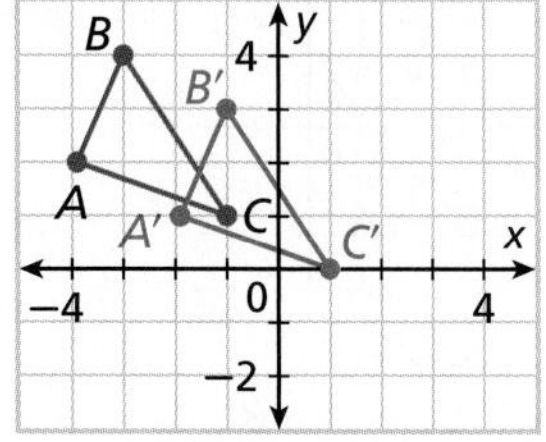

Example 4

The figure shows part of a tile floor. Write a rule for the translation of hexagon 1 to hexagon 2.

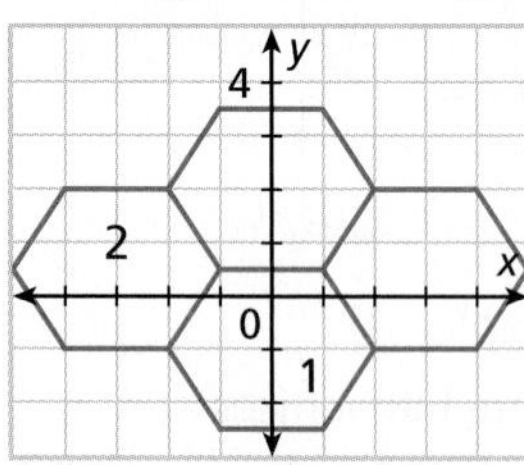

$(x, y) \rightarrow (x - 3, y + 1.5)$

INTERVENTION
Questioning Strategies

EXAMPLE 3

- How would the image differ if the translation were $(x, y) \rightarrow (x - 2, y + 1)$?

EXAMPLE 4

- To write a rule for the translation, does it matter which point on the figure you choose? Why or why not?

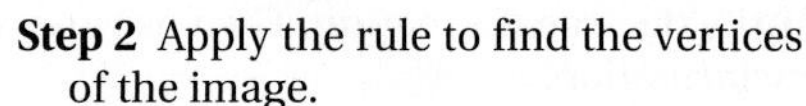

Step 2 Apply the rule to find the vertices of the image.

$A'(-1 + 3, 1 - 4) = A'(2, -3)$
$B'(-3 + 3, 3 - 4) = B'(0, -1)$
$C'(-4 + 3, 0 - 4) = C'(-1, -4)$

Step 3 Plot the points. Then finish drawing the image by using a straightedge to connect the vertices.

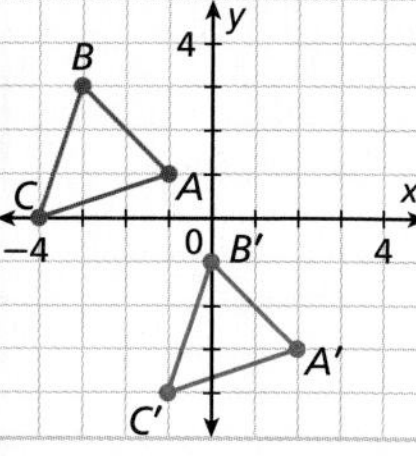

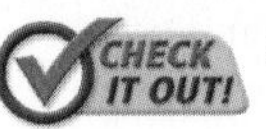

3. Find the coordinates for the image of $JKLM$ after the translation $(x, y) \rightarrow (x - 2, y + 4)$. Draw the image. $J'(-1, 5)$; $K'(1, 5)$; $L'(1, 0)$; $M'(-1, 0)$

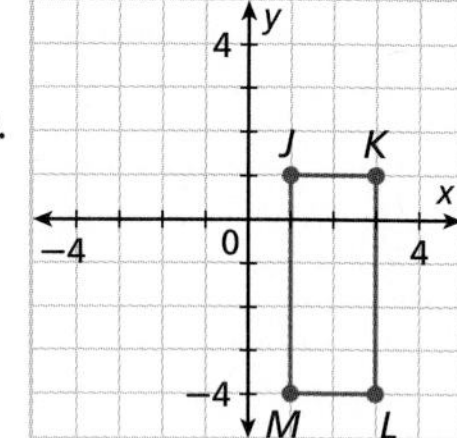

EXAMPLE 4 Art History Application

The pattern shown is similar to a pattern on a wall of the Alhambra. Write a rule for the translation of square 1 to square 2.

Step 1 Choose 2 points

Choose a point A on the preimage and a corresponding point A' on the image. A has coordinates $(3, 1)$, and A' has coordinates $(1, 3)$.

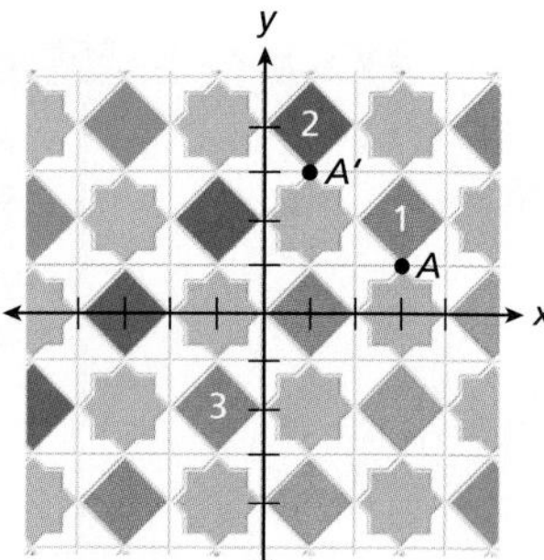

Step 2 Translate

To translate A to A', 2 units are subtracted from the x-coordinate and 2 units are added to the y-coordinate. Therefore, the translation rule is $(x, y) \rightarrow (x - 2, y + 2)$.

4. Use the diagram to write a rule for the translation of square 1 to square 3. $(x, y) \rightarrow (x - 4, y - 4)$

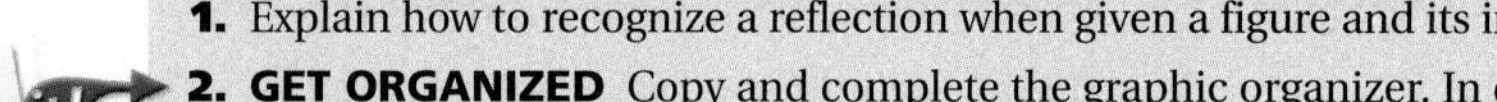

THINK AND DISCUSS

1. Explain how to recognize a reflection when given a figure and its image.

2. GET ORGANIZED Copy and complete the graphic organizer. In each box, sketch an example of each transformation.

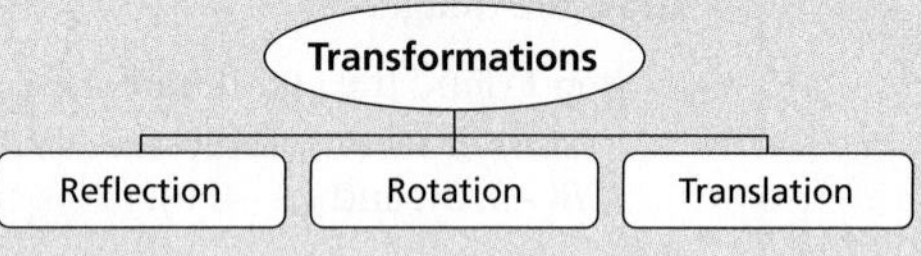

3 Close

Summarize

Review the three types of transformations and give an example of each.

ONGOING ASSESSMENT and INTERVENTION

***Diagnose Before* the Lesson**
1-7 Warm Up, TE p. 50

***Monitor During* the Lesson**
Check It Out! Exercises, SE pp. 51–52
Questioning Strategies, TE pp. 51–52

***Assess After* the Lesson**
1-7 Lesson Quiz, TE p. 55
Alternative Assessment, TE p. 55

Answers to *Think and Discuss*

Possible answers:

1. The preimage and image will be mirror images of each other.
2. See p. A2.

1-7 Exercises

go.hrw.com
Homework Help Online
KEYWORD: MG7 1-7
Parent Resources Online
KEYWORD: MG7 Parent

GUIDED PRACTICE

Vocabulary **Apply the vocabulary from this lesson to answer each question.**

1. Given the transformation $\triangle XYZ \rightarrow \triangle X'Y'Z'$, name the preimage and image of the transformation. **Preimage is $\triangle XYZ$; image is $\triangle X'Y'Z'$.**

2. The types of transformations of geometric figures in the coordinate plane can be described as a slide, a flip, or a turn. What are the other names used to identify these transformations? **translation; reflection; rotation**

SEE EXAMPLE 1 p. 50

Identify each transformation. Then use arrow notation to describe the transformation.

3.

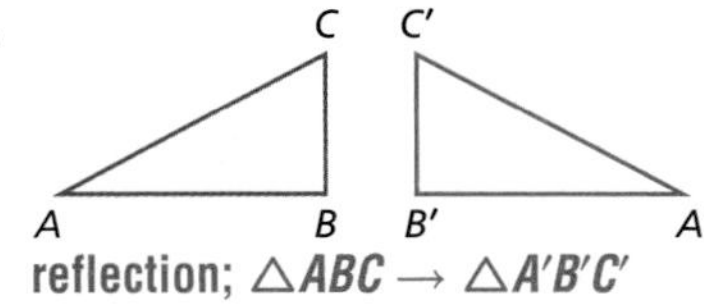

reflection; $\triangle ABC \rightarrow \triangle A'B'C'$

4.

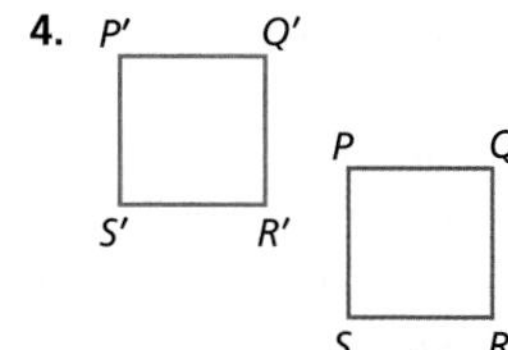

translation; $PQRS \rightarrow P'Q'R'S'$

SEE EXAMPLE 2 p. 51

5. A figure has vertices at $A(-3, 2)$, $B(-1, -1)$, and $C(-4, -2)$. After a transformation, the image of the figure has vertices at $A'(3, 2)$, $B'(1, -1)$, and $C'(4, -2)$. Draw the preimage and image. Then identify the transformation. **reflection across the y-axis**

SEE EXAMPLE 3 p. 51

6. $D'(-1, 1)$; $E'(-2, -1)$; $F'(1, -2)$

6. **Multi-Step** The coordinates of the vertices of $\triangle DEF$ are $D(2, 3)$, $E(1, 1)$, and $F(4, 0)$. Find the coordinates for the image of $\triangle DEF$ after the translation $(x, y) \rightarrow (x - 3, y - 2)$. Draw the preimage and image.

SEE EXAMPLE 4 p. 52

7. **Animation** In an animated film, a simple scene can be created by translating a figure against a still background. Write a rule for the translation that maps the rocket from position 1 to position 2.
$(x, y) \rightarrow (x + 4, y + 4)$

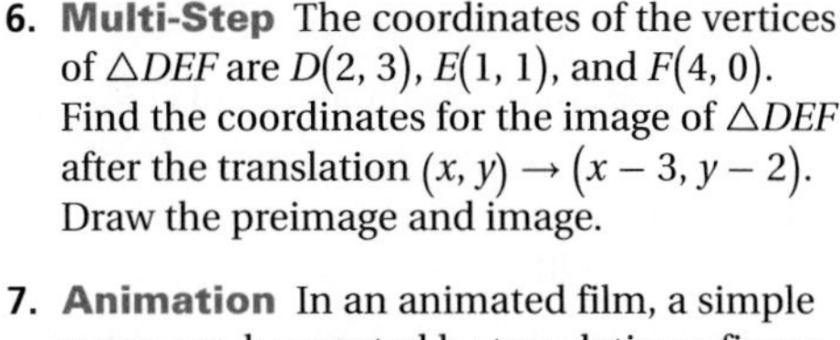

PRACTICE AND PROBLEM SOLVING

Independent Practice	
For Exercises	See Example
8–9	1
10	2
11	3
12	4

Extra Practice
Skills Practice p. S5
Application Practice p. S28

Identify each transformation. Then use arrow notation to describe the transformation.

8.

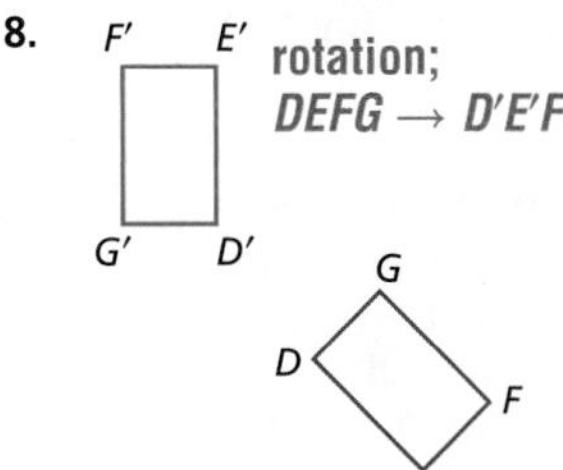

rotation; $DEFG \rightarrow D'E'F'G'$

9.

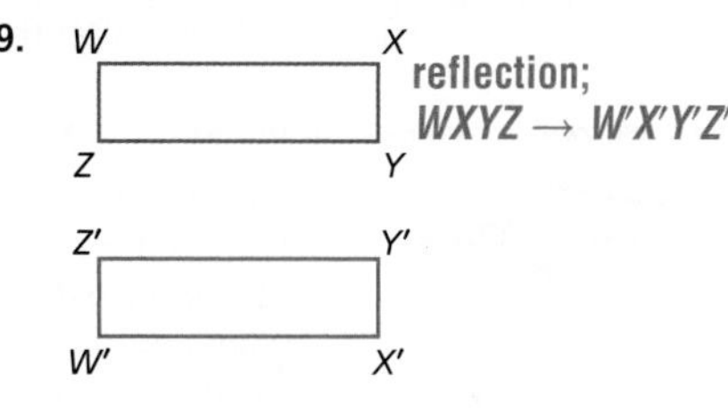

reflection; $WXYZ \rightarrow W'X'Y'Z'$

10. A figure has vertices at $J(-2, 3)$, $K(0, 3)$, $L(0, 1)$, and $M(-2, 1)$. After a transformation, the image of the figure has vertices at $J'(2, 1)$, $K'(4, 1)$, $L'(4, -1)$, and $M'(2, -1)$. Draw the preimage and image. Then identify the transformation. **translation**

Answers

10.

M, J, K, L, J′, K′, M′, L′; axes x, y; 4, −4, 0, −2

1-7 Exercises

Assignment Guide

Assign *Guided Practice* exercises as necessary.

If you finished Examples **1–2**
Basic 8–10, 13–15, 17–22
Average 8–10, 13–15, 17–22
Advanced 8–10, 13–15, 17–22, 34

If you finished Examples **1–4**
Basic 8–18, 26–32, 38–47
Average 8–33, 38-47
Advanced 8–47

Homework Quick Check

Quickly check key concepts.
Exercises: 8, 10–12, 14, 18, 26, 28

Answers

5.

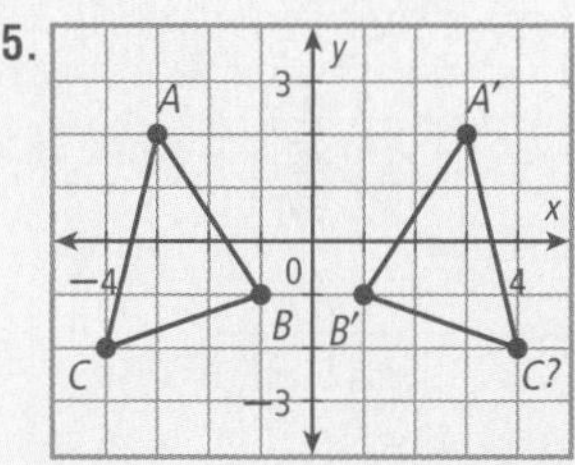

6.

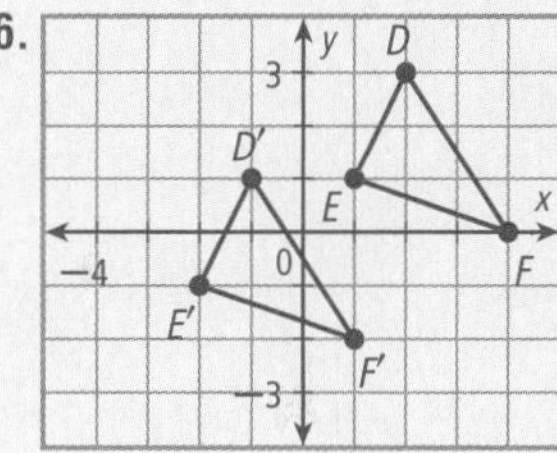

State Resources

go.hrw.com
State Resources Online
KEYWORD: MG7 Resources

Communicating Math In **Exercises 16** and **17,** stress to students that when reflecting across the x-axis, the x-coordinate stays the same, and, when reflecting across the y-axis, the y-coordinate stays the same.

Exercise 28 involves applying a combination of transformations to obtain a given image. This exercise prepares students for the Multi-Step Test Prep on page 58.

Answers

11.

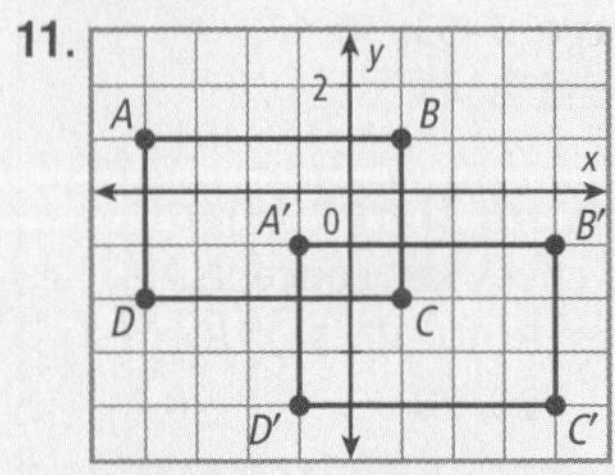

16.

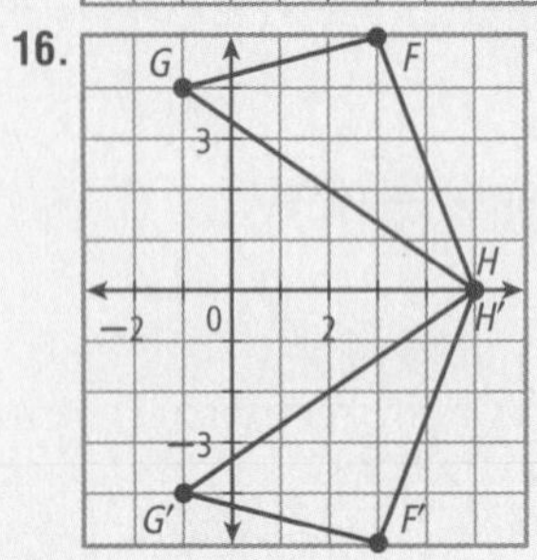

24–27. See p. A11.

---

11. $A'(-1, -1)$, $B'(4, -1)$, $C'(4, -4)$, $D'(-1, -4)$

11. Multi-Step The coordinates of the vertices of rectangle $ABCD$ are $A(-4, 1)$, $B(1, 1)$, $C(1, -2)$, and $D(-4, -2)$. Find the coordinates for the image of rectangle $ABCD$ after the translation $(x, y) \rightarrow (x + 3, y - 2)$. Draw the preimage and the image.

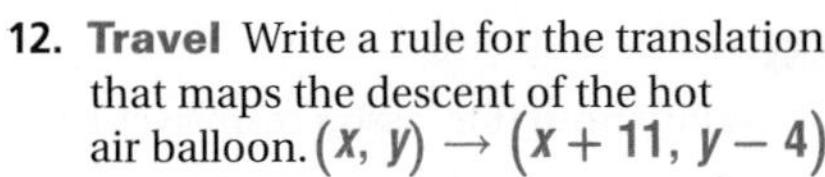

12. Travel Write a rule for the translation that maps the descent of the hot air balloon. $(x, y) \rightarrow (x + 11, y - 4)$

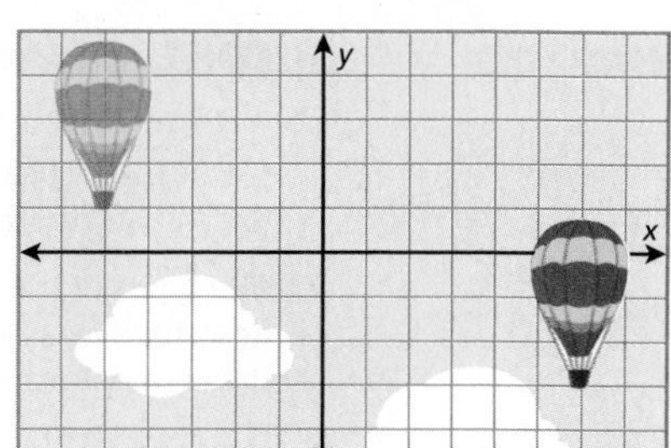

Which transformation is suggested by each of the following?

13. mountain range and its image on a lake **reflection**
14. straight line path of a band marching down a street **translation**
15. wings of a butterfly **reflection**

Given points $F(3, 5)$, $G(-1, 4)$, and $H(5, 0)$, draw $\triangle FGH$ and its reflection across each of the following lines.

16. the x-axis
17. the y-axis

17. (answer graph)

18. Find the vertices of one of the triangles on the graph. Then use arrow notation to write a rule for translating the other three triangles.

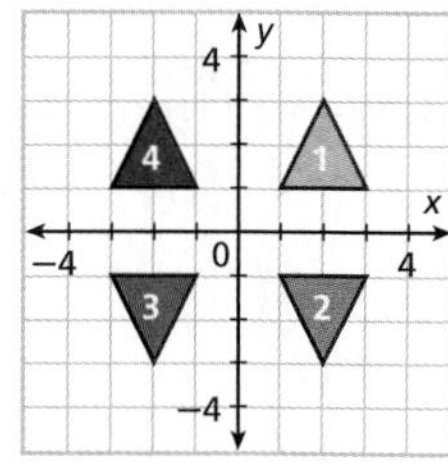

18. $\triangle 1$ to $\triangle 2$: $(x, y) \rightarrow (x, -y)$; $\triangle 2$ to $\triangle 3$: $(x, y) \rightarrow (-x, y)$; $\triangle 3$ to $\triangle 4$: $(x, y) \rightarrow (x, -y)$

A transformation maps A onto B and C onto D.

19. Name the image of A. **B**
20. Name the preimage of B. **A**
21. Name the image of C. **D**
22. Name the preimage of D. **C**
23. Find the coordinates for the image of $\triangle RST$ with vertices $R(1, -4)$, $S(-1, -1)$, and $T(-5, 1)$ after the translation $(x, y) \rightarrow (x - 2, y - 8)$. **$R'(-1, -12)$; $S'(-3, -9)$; $T'(-7, -7)$**
24. **Critical Thinking** Consider the translations $(x, y) \rightarrow (x + 5, y + 3)$ and $(x, y) \rightarrow (x + 10, y + 5)$. Compare the two translations.

Graph each figure and its image after the given translation.

25. $\overline{MN}$ with endpoints $M(2, 8)$ and $N(-3, 4)$ after the translation $(x, y) \rightarrow (x + 2, y - 5)$
26. $\overline{KL}$ with endpoints $K(-1, 1)$ and $L(3, -4)$ after the translation $(x, y) \rightarrow (x - 4, y + 3)$
27. **Write About It** Given a triangle in the coordinate plane, explain how to draw its image after the translation $(x, y) \rightarrow (x + 1, y + 1)$.

MULTI-STEP TEST PREP

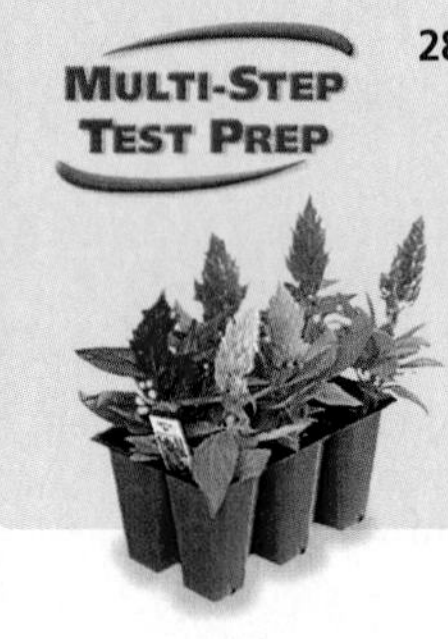

28. This problem will prepare you for the Multi-Step Test Prep on page 58. Greg wants to rearrange the triangular pattern of colored stones on his patio. What combination of transformations could he use to transform $\triangle CAE$ to the image on the coordinate plane?
Possible answer: 2 reflections (across the y-axis and across $\overleftrightarrow{EC}$)

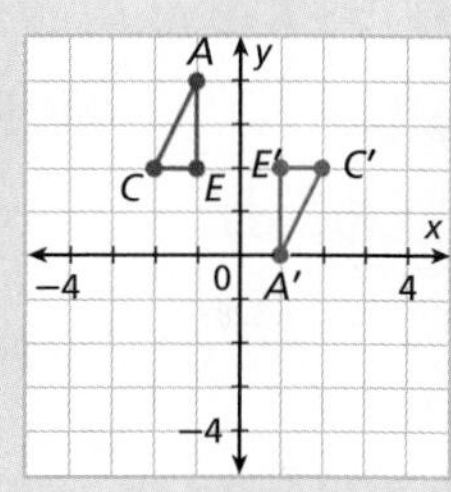

1-7 PRACTICE A

1-7 PRACTICE C

1-7 PRACTICE B

Use the figure for Exercises 1–3.

The figure in the plane at right shows the preimage in the transformation $ABCD \rightarrow A'B'C'D'$. Match the number of the image (below) with the name of the correct transformation.

1. rotation 2
2. translation 1
3. reflection 3
4. A figure has vertices at $D(-2, 1)$, $E(-3, 3)$, and $F(0, 3)$. After a transformation, the image of the figure has vertices at $D'(-1, -2)$, $E'(-3, -3)$, and $F'(-3, 0)$. Draw the preimage and the image. Then identify the transformation. rotation
5. A figure has vertices at $G(0, 0)$, $H(-1, -2)$, $I(-1.5, 0)$, and $J(-2.5, 2)$. Find the coordinates for the image of $GHIJ$ after the translation $(x, y) \rightarrow (x - 2.5, y + 4)$. $G'(-2.5, 4)$, $H'(-3.5, 2)$, $I'(-4, 4)$, $J'(-5, 6)$

Use the figure for Exercise 6.

6. A parking garage attendant will make the most money when the maximum number of cars fits in the parking garage. To fit one more car in, the attendant moves a car from position 1 to position 2. Write a rule for this translation. $(x, y) \rightarrow (x - 7, y + 5)$
7. A figure has vertices at $X(-1, 1)$, $Y(-2, 3)$, and $Z(0, 4)$. Draw the image of XYZ after the translation $(x, y) \rightarrow (x - 2, y)$ and a 180° rotation around x.

1-7 READING STRATEGIES

Figures in a coordinate plane can be moved within the coordinate plane. These movements are called **transformations.** There are three types of transformations, described in the table below.

Transformation	Definition	Example
Reflection	A transformation across a line. Each point and its image are the same distance from the line of reflection.	
Rotation	A transformation around a point. Each point and its image are the same distance from the central point.	
Translation	All the points of a figure move the same distance in the same direction.	

Use the information in the chart to answer the questions below.

1. What type of transformation moves figure A to figure B? Possible answer: translation
2. What type of transformation moves point C to point D? Possible answer: rotation
3. What type of transformation moves figure F to figure G? reflection

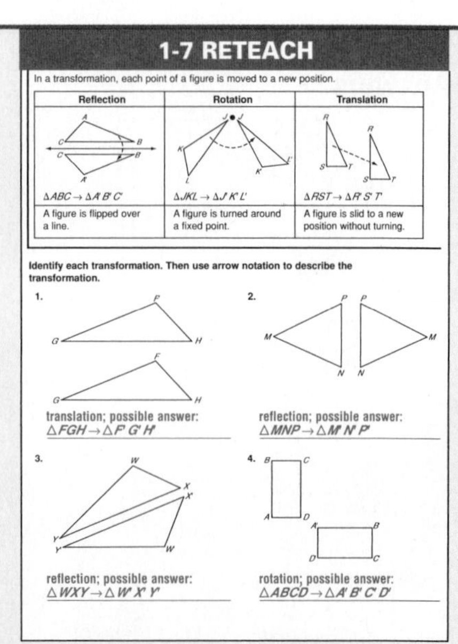

1-7 RETEACH

In a transformation, each point of a figure is moved to a new position.

Reflection	Rotation	Translation
$\triangle ABC \rightarrow \triangle A'B'C'$	$\triangle JKL \rightarrow \triangle J'K'L'$	$\triangle RST \rightarrow \triangle R'S'T'$
A figure is flipped over a line.	A figure is turned around a fixed point.	A figure is slid to a new position without turning.

Identify each transformation. Then use arrow notation to describe the transformation.

1. translation; possible answer: $\triangle FGH \rightarrow \triangle F'G'H'$
2. reflection; possible answer: $\triangle MNP \rightarrow \triangle M'N'P'$
3. reflection; possible answer: $\triangle WXY \rightarrow \triangle W'X'Y'$
4. rotation; possible answer: $\triangle ABCD \rightarrow \triangle A'B'C'D'$

TEST PREP

29. Which type of transformation maps $\triangle XYZ$ to $\triangle X'Y'Z'$?

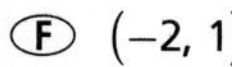

(A) Reflection (circled) (C) Translation
(B) Rotation (D) Not here

30. $\triangle DEF$ has vertices at $D(-4, 2)$, $E(-3, -3)$, and $F(1, 4)$. Which of these points is a vertex of the image of $\triangle DEF$ after the translation $(x, y) \rightarrow (x - 2, y + 1)$?

(F) $(-2, 1)$ (H) $(-5, -2)$ (circled)
(G) $(3, 3)$ (J) $(-6, -1)$

31. Consider the translation $(1, 4) \rightarrow (-2, 3)$. What number was added to the x-coordinate?

(A) -3 (circled) (B) -1 (C) 1 (D) 7

32. Consider the translation $(-5, -7) \rightarrow (-2, -1)$. What number was added to the y-coordinate?

(F) -3 (G) 3 (H) 6 (circled) (J) 8

CHALLENGE AND EXTEND

33. $\triangle RST$ with vertices $R(-2, -2)$, $S(-3, 1)$, and $T(1, 1)$ is translated by $(x, y) \rightarrow (x - 1, y + 3)$. Then the image, $\triangle R'S'T'$, is translated by $(x, y) \rightarrow (x + 4, y - 1)$, resulting in $\triangle R''S''T''$.

a. Find the coordinates for the vertices of $\triangle R''S''T''$. $R''(1, 0)$; $S''(0, 3)$; $T''(4, 3)$

b. Write a rule for a single translation that maps $\triangle RST$ to $\triangle R''S''T''$. $(x, y) \rightarrow (x + 3, y + 2)$

34. Find the angle through which the minute hand of a clock rotates over a period of 12 minutes. 72°

35. A triangle has vertices $A(1, 0)$, $B(5, 0)$, and $C(2, 3)$. The triangle is rotated 90° counterclockwise about the origin. Draw and label the image of the triangle.

35. (answer graph with A', B', C')

Determine the coordinates for the reflection image of any point $A(x, y)$ across the given line.

36. x-axis $(x, -y)$

37. y-axis $(-x, y)$

SPIRAL REVIEW

Use factoring to find the zeros of each function. *(Previous course)*

38. $y = x^2 + 12x + 35$ $-5, -7$

39. $y = x^2 + 3x - 18$ $-6, 3$

40. $y = x^2 - 18x + 81$ 9

41. $y = x^2 - 3x + 2$ $1, 2$

Given $m\angle A = 76.1°$, find the measure of each of the following. *(Lesson 1-4)*

42. supplement of $\angle A$ 103.9°

43. complement of $\angle A$ 13.9°

Use the Distance Formula and the Pythagorean Theorem to find the distance, to the nearest tenth, between each pair of points. *(Lesson 1-6)*

44. $(2, 3)$ and $(4, 6)$ 3.6

45. $(-1, 4)$ and $(0, 8)$ 4.1

46. $(-3, 7)$ and $(-6, -2)$ 9.5

47. $(5, 1)$ and $(-1, 3)$ 6.3

1-7 PROBLEM SOLVING

Use the diagram of the starting positions of five basketball players for Exercises 1 and 2.

1. After the first step of a play, player 3 is at $(-1.5, 0)$ and player 4 is at $(1, 0.5)$. Write a rule to describe the translations of players 3 and 4 from their starting positions to their new positions.

player 3: $(x, y) \rightarrow (x + 4.5, y - 1)$;
player 4: $(x, y) \rightarrow (x - 4, y + 1)$

2. For the second step of the play, player 3 is to move to a position described by the rule $(x, y) \rightarrow (x - 4, y - 2)$ and player 4 is to move to a position described by the rule $(x, y) \rightarrow (x + 3, y - 2)$. What are the positions of these two players after this step of the play?

player 3: $(-5.5, -2)$; player 4: $(4, -1.5)$

Use the diagram for Exercises 3–5.

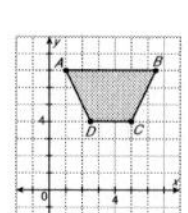

3. Find the coordinates of the image of $ABCD$ after it is moved 6 units left and 2 units up.

$(-5, 9)$, $\left(\frac{1}{2}, 9\right)$, $(-1, 6)$, $\left(-3\frac{1}{2}, 6\right)$

4. The original image is moved so that its new coordinates are $A'(-1, 7)$, $B'(-6\frac{1}{2}, 7)$, $C'(-5, 4)$, and $D'(-2\frac{1}{2}, 4)$. Identify the transformation.

reflection across the y-axis

5. The original image is translated so that the coordinates of B are $(11\frac{1}{2}, 17)$. What are the coordinates of the other three vertices of the image after this translation?

$A'(6, 17)$, $C'(10, 14)$, $D'\left(7\frac{1}{2}, 14\right)$

6. Triangle HJK has vertices $H(0, -9)$, $J(-1, -5)$, and $K(7, 8)$. What are the coordinates of the vertices after the translation $(x, y) \rightarrow (x - 1, y - 3)$?

A $H'(-1, 12)$, $J'(-2, 8)$, $K'(6, -5)$
(C) $H'(-1, -12)$, $J'(-2, -8)$, $K'(6, 5)$
B $H'(1, -12)$, $J'(2, -8)$, $K'(-6, 5)$
D $H'(1, 12)$, $J'(2, 8)$, $K'(-6, -5)$

7. A segment has endpoints at $S(2, 3)$ and $T(-2, 8)$. After a transformation, the image has endpoints at $S'(2, 3)$ and $T'(6, 8)$. Which best describes the transformation?

F reflection across the y-axis
H rotation about the origin
G translation $(x, y) \rightarrow (x + 8, y)$
(J) rotation about the point $(2, 3)$

1-7 CHALLENGE

In Exercises 1 and 2, each image was the result of more than one transformation of the preimage. Show the steps that you can use to get from the preimage to the image. Graph the intermediate image and describe each step.

1. Possible answer: first, a reflection across the y-axis. Then, a translation 3 units right and 5 units down.

2. Possible answer: first, a reflection across the line $y = 3$. Then, a translation 8 units left and 4 units down.

Trapezoid $W''X''Y''Z''$ resulted after two transformations.

3. Make a conjecture about the coordinates of the vertices of trapezoid $WXYZ$. Explain.

$W'(-7, -5)$, $X'(-3, -5)$, $Y'(-4, -2)$, $Z'(-6, -2)$; preimage reflected across x-axis; image translated by $(x, y) \rightarrow (x + 8, y + 3)$.

4. Is this the only possible solution for the coordinates of $WXYZ$? Explain.

No, coordinates could be $W'(1, 8)$, $X'(5, 8)$, $Y'(4, 5)$, $Z'(2, 5)$.

TEST PREP DOCTOR If students chose **D** for **Exercise 31,** remind them to find the x-coordinate instead of the y-coordinate. If they chose **G** in **Exercise 32,** they found the x-coordinate instead.

Journal

Have students explain and give an example on a coordinate plane of a reflection, a translation, and a rotation. Have them write a rule for their translation.

ALTERNATIVE ASSESSMENT

Have students create a figure and its image under a reflection, a rotation, and a translation. Then write rules for each and compare the results.

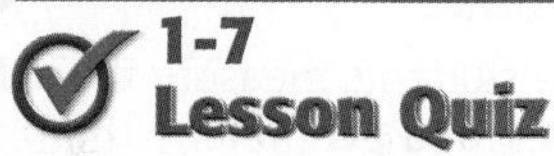

Power Presentations with PowerPoint®

1-7 Lesson Quiz

1. A figure has vertices at $X(-1, 1)$, $Y(1, 4)$, and $Z(2, 2)$. After a transformation, the image of the figure has vertices at $X'(-3, 2)$, $Y'(-1, 5)$, and $Z'(0, 3)$. Draw the preimage and the image. Identify the transformation. translation

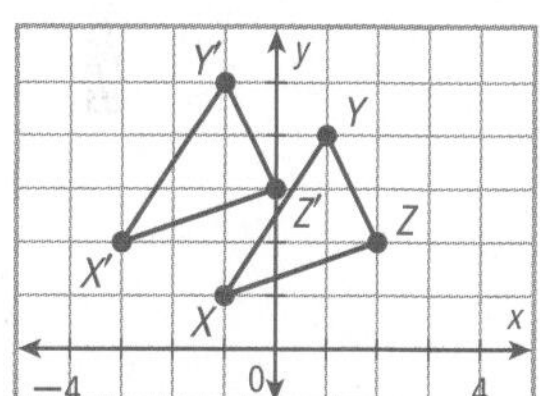

2. What transformation is suggested by the wings of an airplane? reflection

3. Given points $P(-2, -1)$ and $Q(-1, 3)$, draw $\overline{PQ}$ and its reflection across the y-axis.

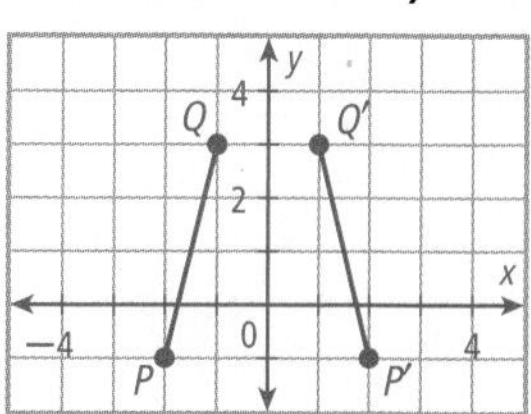

4. Find the coordinates of the image of $F(2, 7)$ after the translation $(x, y) \rightarrow (x + 5, y - 6)$. $(7, 1)$

Also available on transparency

Organizer

Use with Lesson 1-7

Pacing:

Traditional 1 day

Block $\frac{1}{2}$ day

Objective: Use geometry software to perform transformations and explore their properties.

Materials: geometry software

Online Edition

TechKeys

Countdown Week 2

Resources

Technology Lab Activities

1-7 Lab Recording Sheet

Teach

Discuss

Have students measure the sides, angles, and perimeter of both the preimage and the image of $\triangle ABC$. Discuss whether any of these measures change after a translation or a rotation. no Discuss the arrow and prime notation to make sure students understand the difference in naming the preimage and image. Ask students whether the area of the image is affected by either a translation or a rotation. no

State Resources

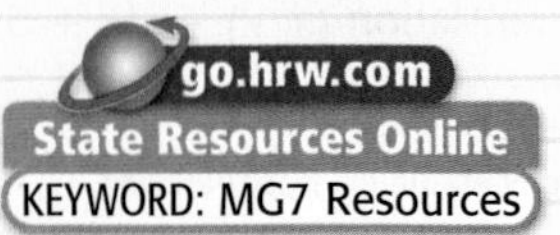

1-7 Technology LAB

Explore Transformations

Use with Lesson 1-7

A transformation is a movement of a figure from its original position (preimage) to a new position (image). In this lab, you will use geometry software to perform transformations and explore their properties.

Activity 1

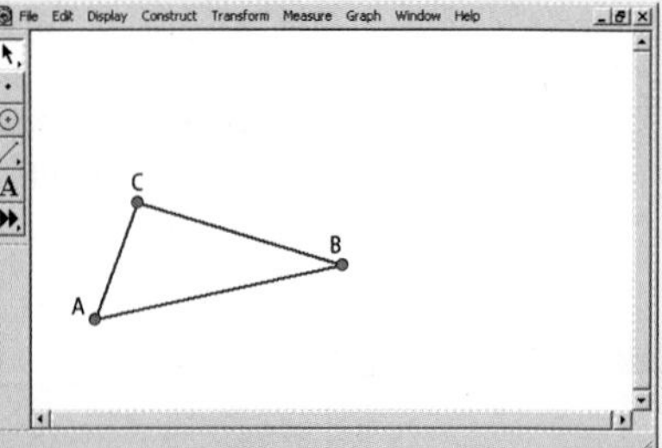

1. Construct a triangle using the segment tool. Use the text tool to label the vertices *A*, *B*, and *C*.
2. Select points *A* and *B* in that order. Choose Mark Vector from the Transform menu.

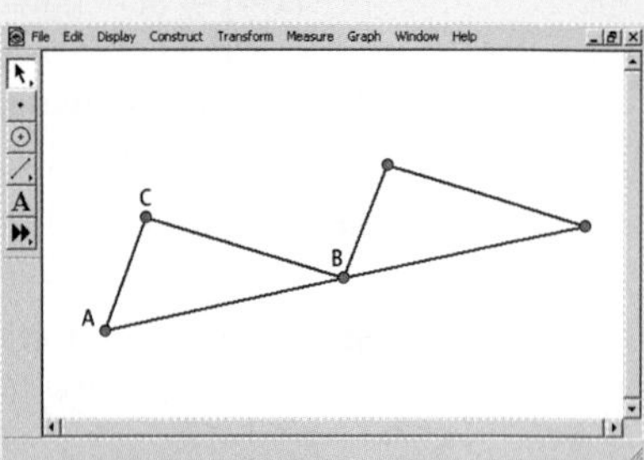

3. Select $\triangle ABC$ by clicking on all three segments of the triangle.
4. Choose Translate from the Transform menu, using *Marked* as the translation vector. What do you notice about the relationship between your preimage and its image?
   They appear to be $\cong$.
5. What happens when you drag a vertex or a side of $\triangle ABC$?
   The $\triangle s$ move together and stay the same size and shape.

Try This

1. The image of the $\triangle$ moves in the same direction as the endpt.

2. The $\triangle s$ move together and remain a fixed dist. apart.

For Problems 1 and 2 choose New Sketch from the File menu.

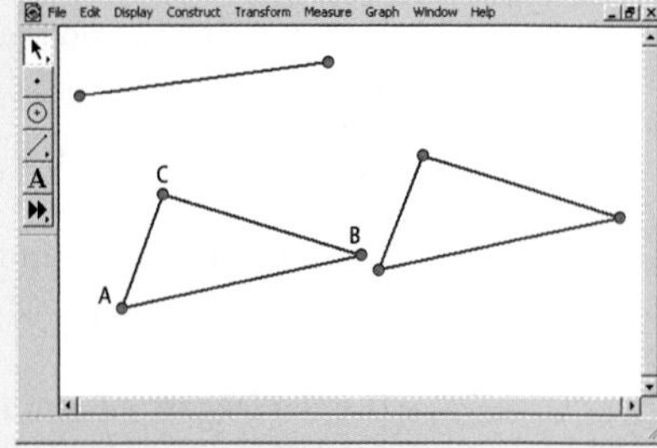

1. Construct a triangle and a segment outside the triangle. Mark this segment as a translation vector as you did in Step 2 of Activity 1. Use Step 4 of Activity 1 to translate the triangle. What happens when you drag an endpoint of the new segment?
2. Instead of translating by a marked vector, use *Rectangular* as the translation vector and translate by a horizontal distance of 1 cm and a vertical distance of 2 cm. Compare this method with the marked vector method. What happens when you drag a side or vertex of the triangle?
3. Select the angles and sides of the preimage and image triangles. Use the tools in the Measure menu to measure length, angle measure, perimeter, and area. What do you think is true about these two figures? **Each measurement is the same for the preimage and image $\triangle s$. The $\triangle s$ appear to be $\cong$.**

Activity 2

1. Construct a triangle. Label the vertices *G*, *H*, and *I*.

2. Select point *H* and choose Mark Center from the Transform menu.

3. Select ∠*GHI* by selecting points *G*, *H*, and *I* in that order. Choose Mark Angle from the Transform menu.

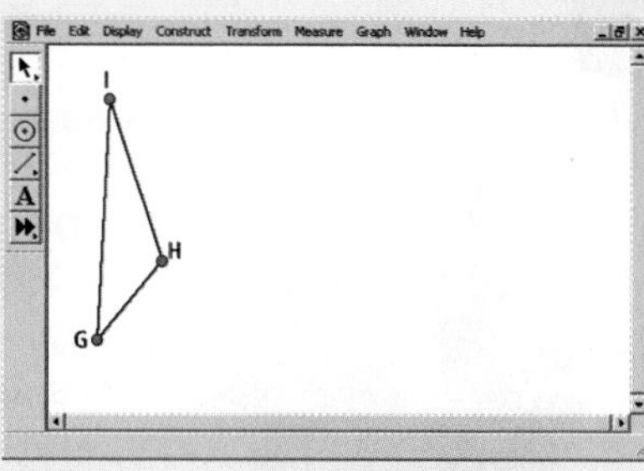

4. Select the entire triangle △*GHI* by dragging a selection box around the figure.

5. Choose Rotate from the Transform menu, using *Marked Angle* as the angle of rotation.

6. What happens when you drag a vertex or a side of △*GHI*? **The △ and its image rotate by the same ∠ measure and remain the same size and shape.**

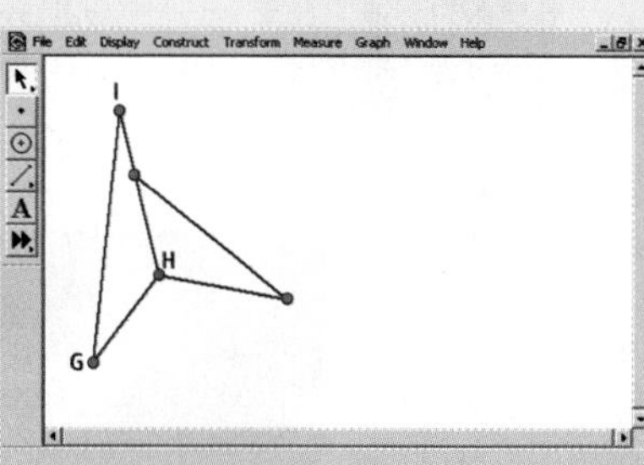

Try This

For Problems 4–6 choose New Sketch from the File menu.

4. Instead of selecting an angle of the triangle as the rotation angle, draw a new angle outside of the triangle. Mark this angle. Mark ∠*GHI* as Center and rotate the triangle. What happens when you drag one of the points that form the rotation angle? **The image rotates by the same ∠ measure as the marked ∠.**

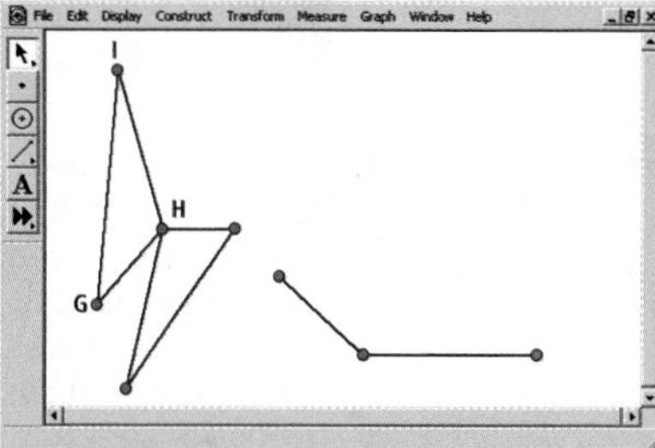

The △ rotates by the same ∠ measure. When *P* is inside, the image overlaps the △. When *P* coincides with a vertex, the image also coincides with the vertex.

5. Construct △*QRS*, a new rotation angle, and a point *P* not on the triangle. Mark *P* as the center and mark the angle. Rotate the triangle. What happens when you drag *P* outside, inside, or on the preimage triangle?

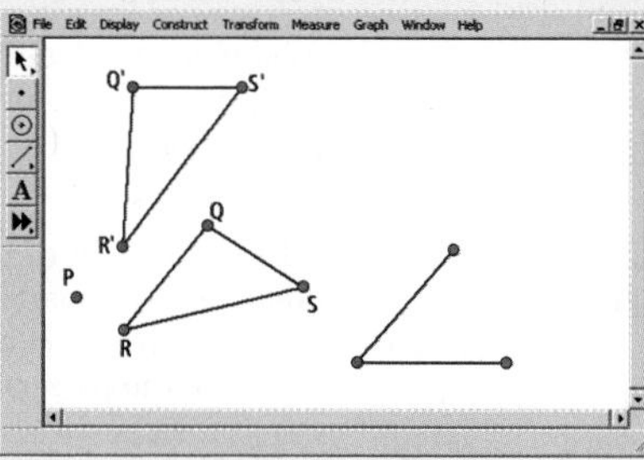

6. Instead of rotating by a marked angle, use *Fixed Angle* as the rotation method and rotate by a fixed angle measure of 30°. Compare this method with the marked angle method.

7. Using the fixed angle method of rotation, can you find an angle measure that will result in an image figure that exactly covers the preimage figure? **360°**

6. The △ rotated by an ∠ of 30°, not by the measure of the marked ∠.

Close

Key Concept

When you translate or rotate a figure, the lengths of sides, angle measures, perimeter, and area do not change. The image is congruent to the preimage.

Assessment

Journal Have students explain how the preimage and image of a figure compare under a translation and a rotation. Have them discuss which properties are preserved.

Organizer

Objective: Assess students' ability to apply concepts and skills in Lessons 1-5 through 1-7 in a real-world format.

Online Edition

Resources

Geometry Assessments
www.mathtekstoolkit.org

Problem	Text Reference
1	Lesson 1-5
2	Lesson 1-6
3	Lesson 1-7

State Resources

Coordinate and Transformation Tools

Pave the Way Julia wants to use L-shaped paving stones to pave a patio. Two stones will cover a 12 in. by 18 in. rectangle.

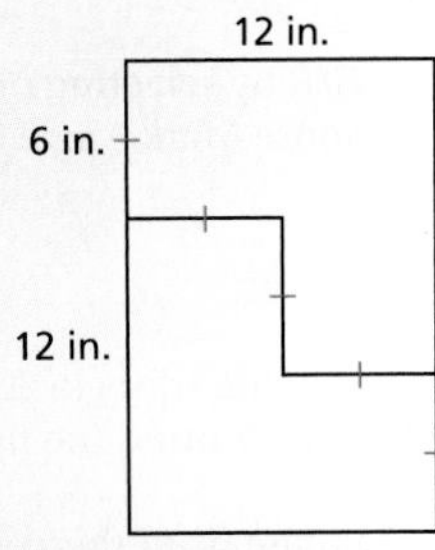

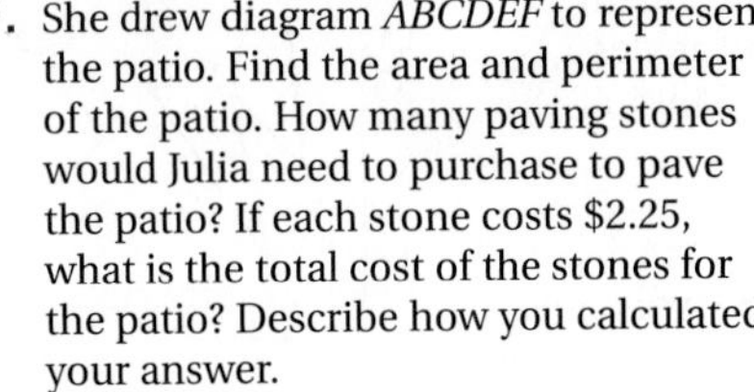

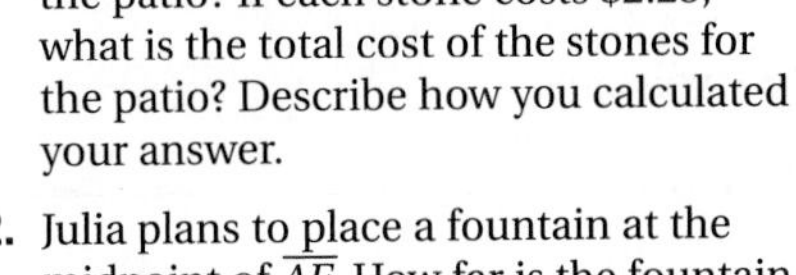

1. $A = 36 + 72 = 108 \text{ ft}^2$; $P = 48$ ft; She would need 144 stones. Total cost is \$324.00. Explanation: 2 stones make a 12 in. by 18 in. rect. $12(18) = 216$ in. $= 1.5 \text{ ft}^2$. $\frac{108}{1.5} = 72$. Since 2 stones make up each of the rects., $72(2) = 144$ stones, and $144(2.25) = 324$.

2. from $B \approx 8.5$ ft; from $C = 6.0$ ft; from $E \approx 13.4$ ft; from $F = 6.0$ ft

3. She used a reflection across $\overline{AB}$. Check students' drawings; possible answers: reflection across $\overline{AF}$; rotation about B; translation from D to F; rotation about E; translation from F to E.

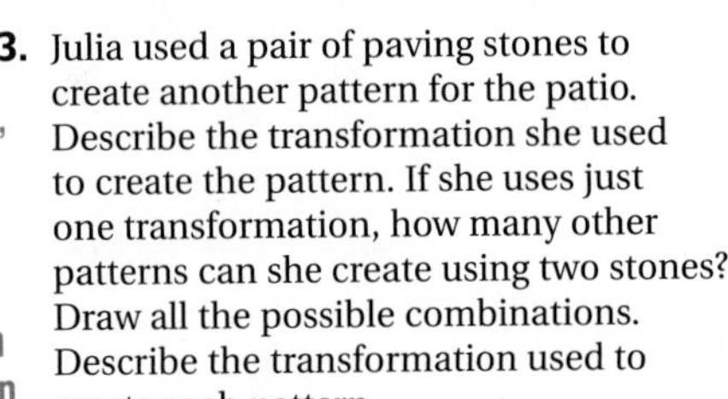

1. She drew diagram *ABCDEF* to represent the patio. Find the area and perimeter of the patio. How many paving stones would Julia need to purchase to pave the patio? If each stone costs \$2.25, what is the total cost of the stones for the patio? Describe how you calculated your answer.
2. Julia plans to place a fountain at the midpoint of $\overline{AF}$. How far is the fountain from *B*, *C*, *E*, and *F*? Round to the nearest tenth.
3. Julia used a pair of paving stones to create another pattern for the patio. Describe the transformation she used to create the pattern. If she uses just one transformation, how many other patterns can she create using two stones? Draw all the possible combinations. Describe the transformation used to create each pattern.

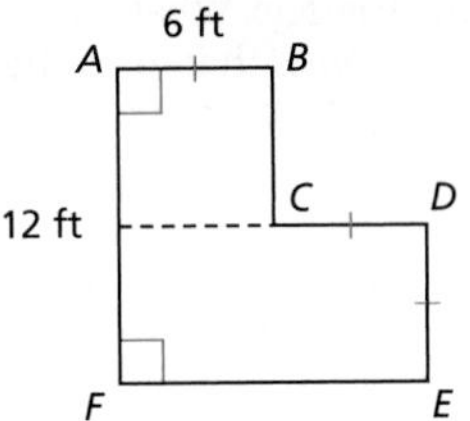

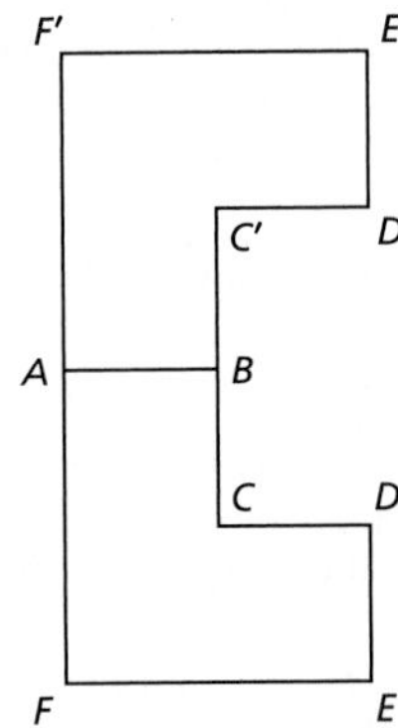

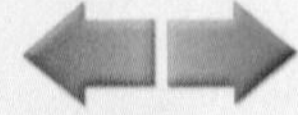

INTERVENTION

Scaffolding Questions

1. What is the significance of the way the sides of the stones are marked? How can you find the area of this figure? The marks on the sides of the figure mean that these sides are the same length. Right angle marks tell you that $\angle A$ and $\angle F$ measure 90°. You will use the formulas for the area of a rectangle and the area of a square to find the areas of the two parts of the figure. Then add the two areas together.
2. What formulas will you use to find the location of the fountain? First you will find the midpoint of a segment. Then use the Distance Formula to find the distance between the fountain and each point.
3. How can you decide which transformation to use? What is meant by creating different patterns? You can use a reflection, a rotation, or a translation. You just need to be sure that the sides of the figures will touch when you repeat your pattern. Different patterns can be created using the two tiles and one transformation.

Extension

Have students choose a pattern and reproduce it on graph paper. They could also create the tile patterns using geometry software.

Quiz for Lessons 1-5 Through 1-7

1-5 Using Formulas in Geometry

Find the perimeter and area of each figure.

1. 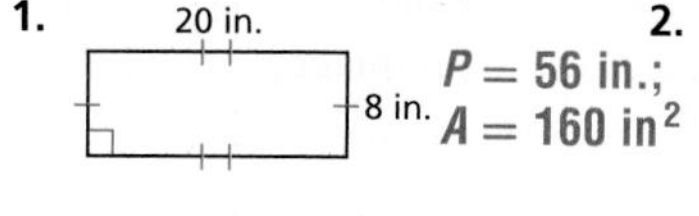

$P = 56$ in.; $A = 160$ in^2

2. 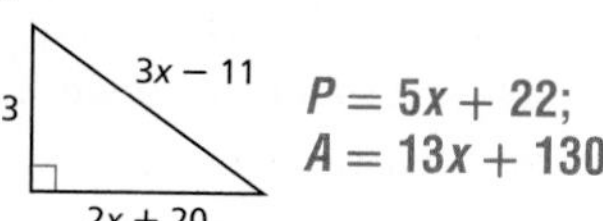

$P = 5x + 22$; $A = 13x + 130$

3. 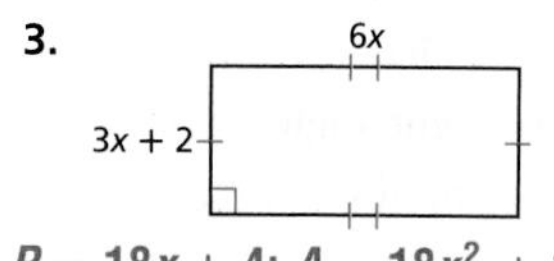

$P = 18x + 4$; $A = 18x^2 + 12x$

4. 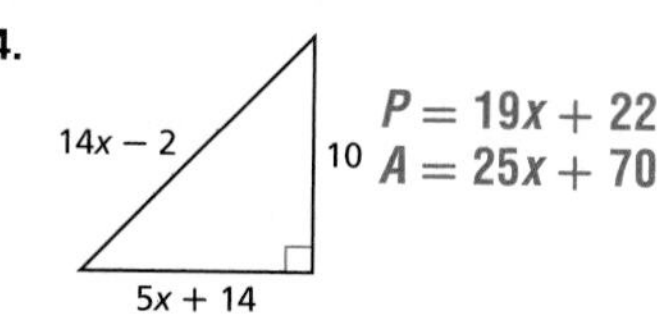

$P = 19x + 22$; $A = 25x + 70$

5. Find the circumference and area of a circle with a radius of 6 m. Use the π key on your calculator and round to the nearest tenth. $C \approx 37.7$ m; $A \approx 113.1$ m^2

1-6 Midpoint and Distance in the Coordinate Plane

6. Find the coordinates for the midpoint of $\overline{XY}$ with endpoints $X(-4, 6)$ and $Y(3, 8)$. $(-0.5, 7)$
7. J is the midpoint of $\overline{HK}$, H has coordinates $(6, -2)$, and J has coordinates $(9, 3)$. Find the coordinates of K. $(12, 8)$
8. Using the Distance Formula, find QR and ST to the nearest tenth. Then determine if $\overline{QR} \cong \overline{ST}$. $QR \approx 7.3$; $ST \approx 7.3$; $\overline{QR} \cong \overline{ST}$
9. Using the Distance Formula and the Pythagorean Theorem, find the distance, to the nearest tenth, from $F(4, 3)$ to $G(-3, -2)$. 8.6

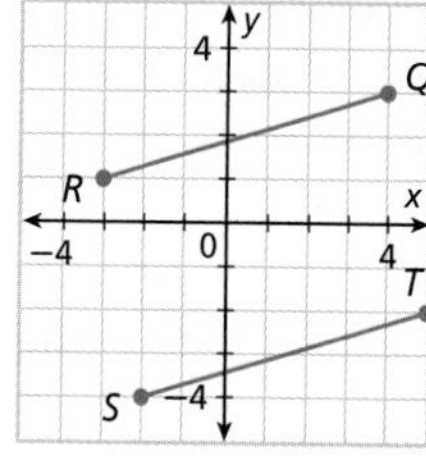

1-7 Transformations in the Coordinate Plane

Identify the transformation. Then use arrow notation to describe the transformation.

10. 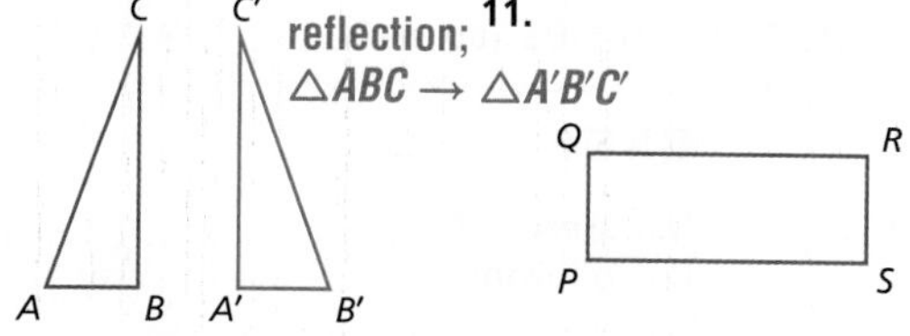

reflection; $\triangle ABC \rightarrow \triangle A'B'C'$

11.
translation; $PQRS \rightarrow P'Q'R'S'$

12. A graphic designer used the translation $(x, y) \rightarrow (x - 3, y + 2)$ to transform square $HJKL$. Find the coordinates and graph the image of square $HJKL$.
13. A figure has vertices at $X(1, 1)$, $Y(3, 1)$, and $Z(3, 4)$. After a transformation, the image of the figure has vertices at $X'(-1, -1)$, $Y'(-3, -1)$, and $Z'(-3, -4)$. Graph the preimage and image. Then identify the transformation.

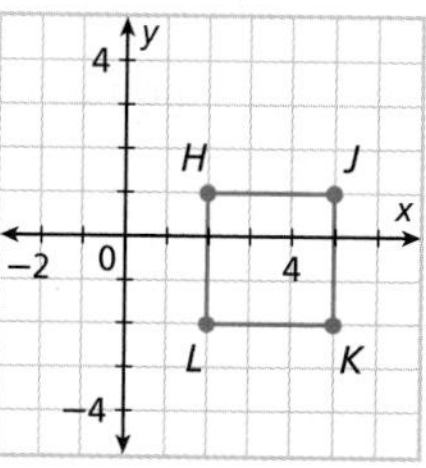

12. $H'(-1, 3)$; $J'(2, 3)$; $K'(2, 0)$; $L'(-1, 0)$

Ready To Go On? Section 1B

Organizer

Objective: Assess students' mastery of concepts and skills in Lessons 1-5 through 1-7.

Resources

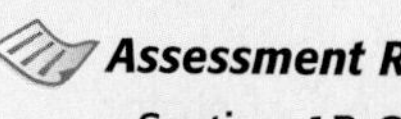

Assessment Resources
Section 1B Quiz

Teacher One Stop™
Test & Practice Generator

INTERVENTION

Resources

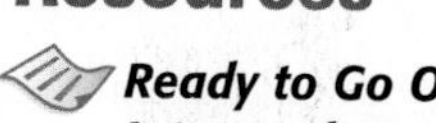

***Ready to Go On? Intervention and Enrichment* Worksheets**

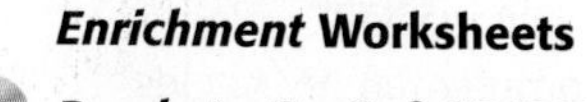

***Ready to Go On?* CD-ROM**

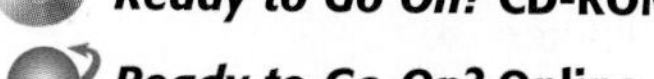

***Ready to Go On?* Online**

my.hrw.com

Answers

12–13. See p. A11.

Ready To Go On? Diagnose and Prescribe

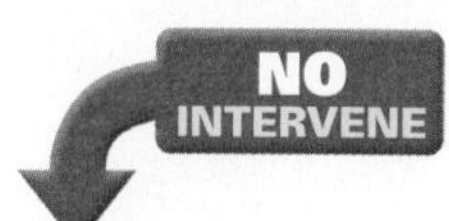

NO INTERVENE

Ready to Go On? Intervention	Ready to Go On? Intervention, Section 1B: Worksheets	CD-ROM	Online
Lesson 1-5	1-5 Intervention	Activity 1-5	Diagnose and Prescribe Online
Lesson 1-6	1-6 Intervention	Activity 1-6	
Lesson 1-7	1-7 Intervention	Activity 1-7	

YES ENRICH

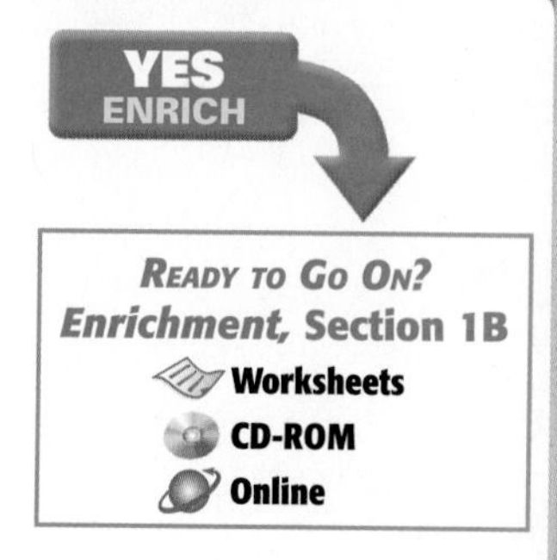

Ready to Go On? Enrichment, Section 1B
Worksheets
CD-ROM
Online

CHAPTER 1

Study Guide: Review

Organizer

Objective: Help students organize and review key concepts and skills presented in Chapter 1.

Resources

Teacher One Stop™
PuzzleView
Test & Practice Generator

Lesson Tutorial Videos
CD-ROM

Answers

1. angle bisector
2. complementary angles
3. hypotenuse
4. *A, F, E, G* or *C, G, D, B*
5. Possible answer: $\overleftrightarrow{GC}$
6. Possible answer: plane *AEG*

CHAPTER 1

Study Guide: Review

For a complete list of the postulates and theorems in this chapter, see p. PS12.

Vocabulary

Complete the sentences below with vocabulary words from the list above.

1. A(n) ___?___ divides an angle into two congruent angles.
2. ___?___ are two angles whose measures have a sum of 90°.
3. The length of the longest side of a right triangle is called the ___?___ .

1-1 Understanding Points, Lines, and Planes *(pp. 6–11)*

EXAMPLES

- **Name the common endpoint of $\overrightarrow{SR}$ and $\overrightarrow{ST}$.**

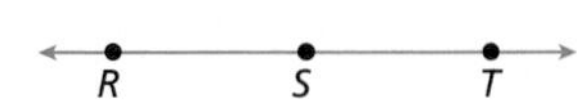

$\overrightarrow{SR}$ and $\overrightarrow{ST}$ are opposite rays with common endpoint *S*.

EXERCISES

Name each of the following.

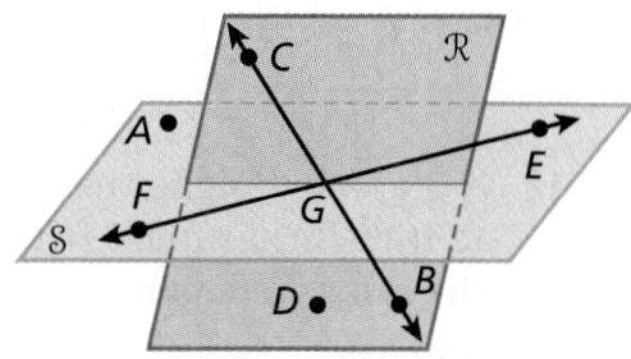

4. four coplanar points
5. line containing *B* and *C*
6. plane that contains *A*, *G*, and *E*

- **Draw and label three coplanar lines intersecting in one point.**

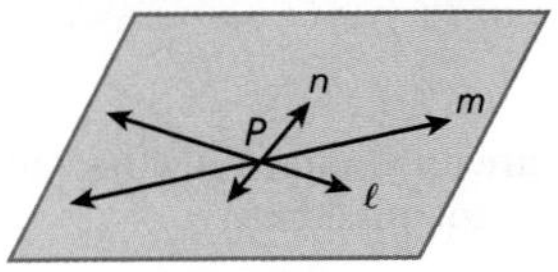

Draw and label each of the following.

7. line containing P and Q
8. pair of opposite rays both containing C
9. $\overleftrightarrow{CD}$ intersecting plane $\mathcal{P}$ at B

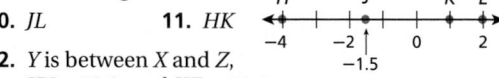

1-2 Measuring and Constructing Segments *(pp. 13–19)*

EXAMPLES

- **Find the length of $\overline{XY}$.**

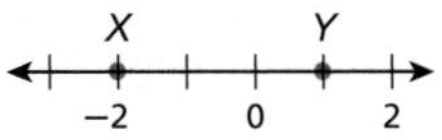

$XY = |-2 - 1|$
$= |-3| = 3$

- **S is between R and T. Find RT.**

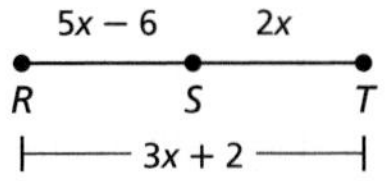

$RT = RS + ST$
$3x + 2 = 5x - 6 + 2x$
$3x + 2 = 7x - 6$
$x = 2$
$RT = 3(2) + 2 = 8$

EXERCISES

Find each length.

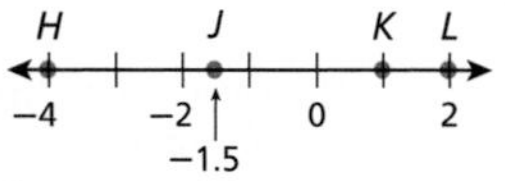

10. JL
11. HK
12. Y is between X and Z, $XY = 13.8$, and $XZ = 21.4$. Find YZ.
13. Q is between P and R. Find PR.

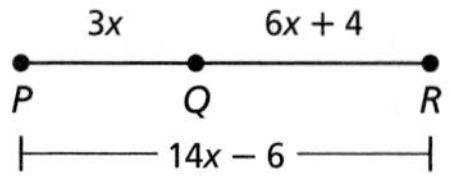

14. U is the midpoint of $\overline{TV}$, $TU = 3x + 4$, and $UV = 5x - 2$. Find TU, UV, and TV.
15. E is the midpoint of $\overline{DF}$, $DE = 9x$, and $EF = 4x + 10$. Find DE, EF, and DF.

1-3 Measuring and Constructing Angles *(pp. 20–27)*

EXAMPLES

- **Classify each angle as acute, right, or obtuse.**

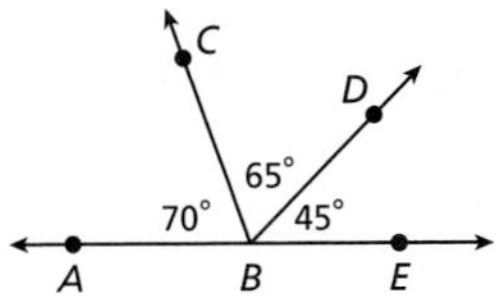

$\angle ABC$ acute;
$\angle CBD$ acute;
$\angle ABD$ obtuse;
$\angle DBE$ acute;
$\angle CBE$ obtuse

- **$\overrightarrow{KM}$ bisects $\angle JKL$, $m\angle JKM = (3x + 4)°$, and $m\angle MKL = (6x - 5)°$. Find $m\angle JKL$.**

$3x + 4 = 6x - 5$	*Def. of ∠ bisector*
$3x + 9 = 6x$	*Add 5 to both sides.*
$9 = 3x$	*Subtract 3x from both sides.*
$x = 3$	*Divide both sides by 3.*

$m\angle JKL = 3x + 4 + 6x - 5$
$= 9x - 1$
$= 9(3) - 1 = 26°$

EXERCISES

16. Classify each angle as acute, right, or obtuse.

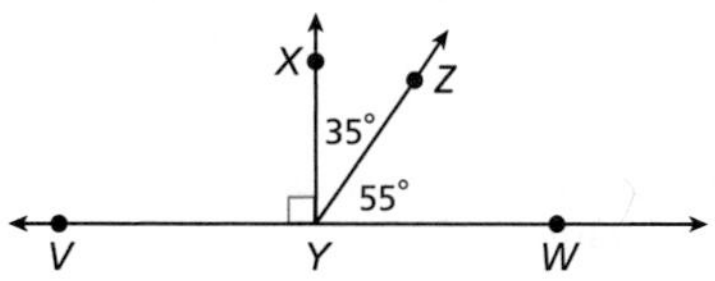

17. $m\angle HJL = 116°$. Find $m\angle HJK$.
18. $\overrightarrow{NP}$ bisects $\angle MNQ$, $m\angle MNP = (6x - 12)°$, and $m\angle PNQ = (4x + 8)°$. Find $m\angle MNQ$.

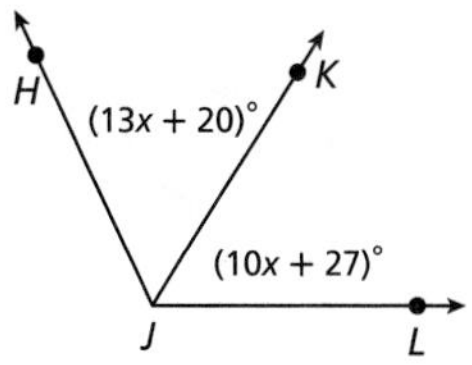

Answers

7. 

8. 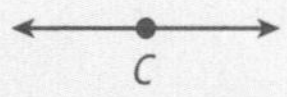

9. 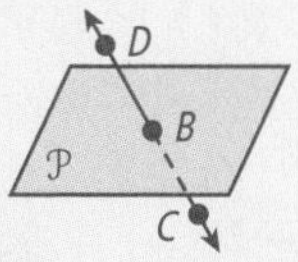

10. 3.5
11. 5
12. 7.6
13. 22
14. 13; 13; 26
15. 18; 18; 36
16. $\angle VYX$: rt; $\angle VYZ$: obtuse; $\angle XYZ$: acute; $\angle XYW$: rt.; $\angle ZYW$: acute; $\angle VYW$: straight
17. 59°
18. 96°

Answers

19. only adj.
20. adj. and a lin. pair
21. not adj.
22. 15.4°; 105.4°
23. $(94 - 2x)°$; $(184 - 2x)°$
24. 73°
25. $14x - 2$; $12x^2 - 3x$
26. $4x + 16$; $x^2 + 8x + 16$
27. $x + 15$; $4x - 20$
28. $10x + 54$; $100x + 140$
29. $A \approx 1385.4$ m^2; $C \approx 131.9$ m
30. $A \approx 153.9$ ft^2; $C \approx 44.0$ ft
31. 12 m

1-4 Pairs of Angles *(pp. 28–33)*

EXAMPLES

- **Tell whether the angles are only adjacent, adjacent and form a linear pair, or not adjacent.**

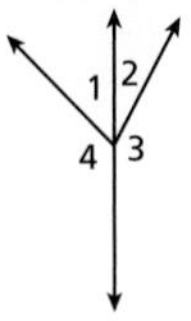

$\angle 1$ and $\angle 2$ are only adjacent.

$\angle 2$ and $\angle 4$ are not adjacent.

$\angle 2$ and $\angle 3$ are adjacent and form a linear pair.

$\angle 1$ and $\angle 4$ are adjacent and form a linear pair.

- **Find the measure of the complement and supplement of each angle.**

$90 - 67.3 = 22.7°$

$180 - 67.3 = 112.7°$

$90 - (3x - 8) = (98 - 3x)°$

$180 - (3x - 8) = (188 - 3x)°$

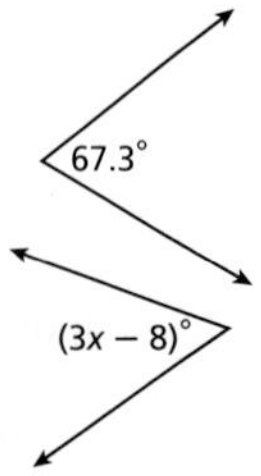

EXERCISES

Tell whether the angles are only adjacent, adjacent and form a linear pair, or not adjacent.

19. $\angle 1$ and $\angle 2$
20. $\angle 3$ and $\angle 4$
21. $\angle 2$ and $\angle 5$

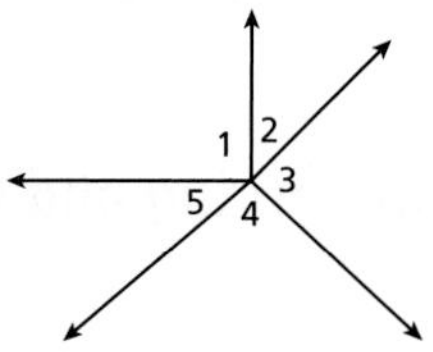

Find the measure of the complement and supplement of each angle.

22.

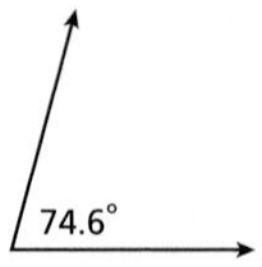

23.

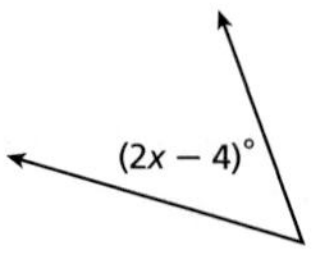

24. An angle measures 5 degrees more than 4 times its complement. Find the measure of the angle.

1-5 Using Formulas in Geometry *(pp. 36–41)*

EXAMPLES

- **Find the perimeter and area of the triangle.**

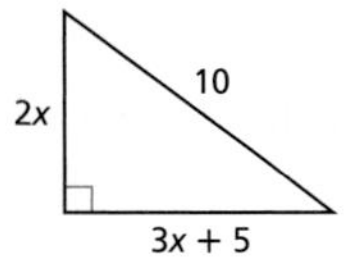

$P = 2x + 3x + 5 + 10$
$= 5x + 15$

$A = \frac{1}{2}(3x + 5)(2x)$
$= 3x^2 + 5x$

- **Find the circumference and area of the circle to the nearest tenth.**

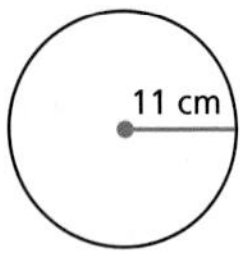

$C = 2\pi r$
$= 2\pi(11)$
$= 22\pi$
≈ 69.1 cm

$A = \pi r^2$
$= \pi(11)^2$
$= 121\pi$
≈ 380.1 cm^2

EXERCISES

Find the perimeter and area of each figure.

25.

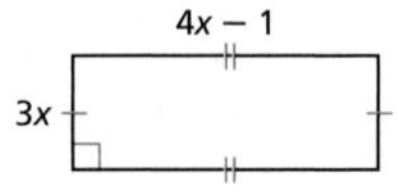

26.

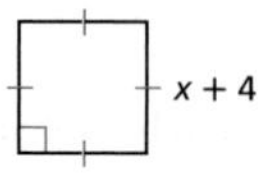

27.

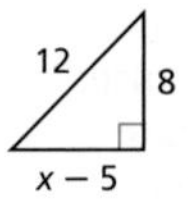

28.

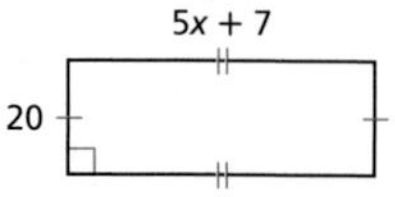

Find the circumference and area of each circle to the nearest tenth.

29.

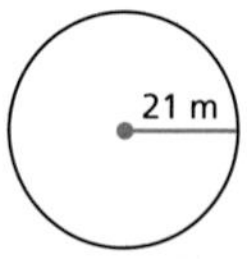

30.

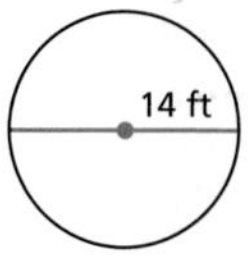

31. The area of a triangle is 102 m^2. The base of the triangle is 17 m. What is the height of the triangle?

1-6 Midpoint and Distance in the Coordinate Plane *(pp. 43–49)*

EXAMPLES

- **X is the midpoint of $\overline{CD}$. C has coordinates $(-4, 1)$, and X has coordinates $(3, -2)$. Find the coordinates of D.**

$(3, -2) = \left(\frac{-4 + x}{2}, \frac{1 + y}{2}\right)$

$3 = \frac{-4 + x}{2}$ $\quad$ $-2 = \frac{1 + y}{2}$

$6 = -4 + x$ $\quad$ $-4 = 1 + y$

$10 = x$ $\quad$ $-5 = y$

The coordinates of D are $(10, -5)$.

- **Use the Distance Formula and the Pythagorean Theorem to find the distance, to the nearest tenth, from $(1, 6)$ to $(4, 2)$.**

$d = \sqrt{(4 - 1)^2 + (2 - 6)^2}$ $\quad$ $c^2 = a^2 + b^2$

$= \sqrt{3^2 + (-4)^2}$ $\quad$ $= 3^2 + 4^2$

$= \sqrt{9 + 16}$ $\quad$ $= 9 + 16 = 25$

$= \sqrt{25}$ $\quad$ $c = \sqrt{25}$

$= 5.0$ $\quad$ $= 5.0$

EXERCISES

Y is the midpoint of $\overline{AB}$. Find the missing coordinates of each point.

32. $A(3, 2)$; $B(-1, 4)$; $Y(■, ■)$

33. $A(5, 0)$; $B(■, ■)$; $Y(-2, 3)$

34. $A(■, ■)$; $B(-4, 4)$; $Y(-2, 3)$

Use the Distance Formula and the Pythagorean Theorem to find the distance, to the nearest tenth, between each pair of points.

35. $X(-2, 4)$ and $Y(6, 1)$

36. $H(0, 3)$ and $K(-2, -4)$

37. $L(-4, 2)$ and $M(3, -2)$

1-7 Transformations in the Coordinate Plane *(pp. 50–55)*

EXAMPLES

- **Identify the transformation. Then use arrow notation to describe the transformation.**

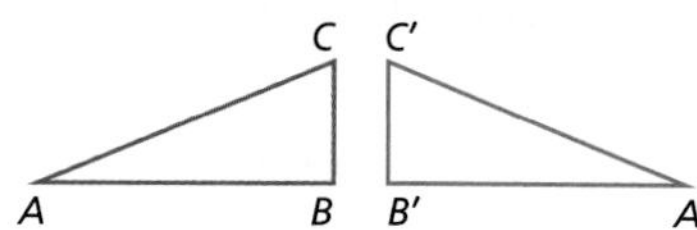

The transformation is a reflection.
$\triangle ABC \rightarrow \triangle A'B'C'$

- **The coordinates of the vertices of rectangle $HJKL$ are $H(2, -1)$, $J(5, -1)$, $K(5, -3)$, and $L(2, -3)$. Find the coordinates of the image of rectangle $HJKL$ after the translation $(x, y) \rightarrow (x - 4, y + 1)$.**

$H' = (2 - 4, -1 + 1) = H'(-2, 0)$

$J' = (5 - 4, -1 + 1) = J'(1, 0)$

$K' = (5 - 4, -3 + 1) = K'(1, -2)$

$L' = (2 - 4, -3 + 1) = L'(-2, -2)$

EXERCISES

Identify each transformation. Then use arrow notation to describe the transformation.

38.

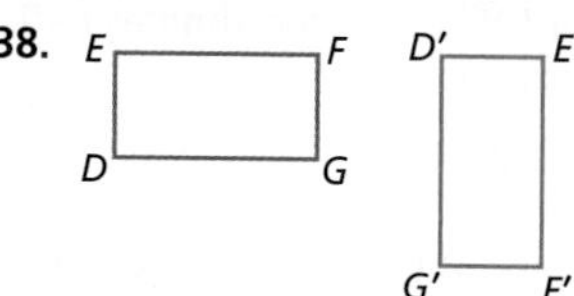

39.

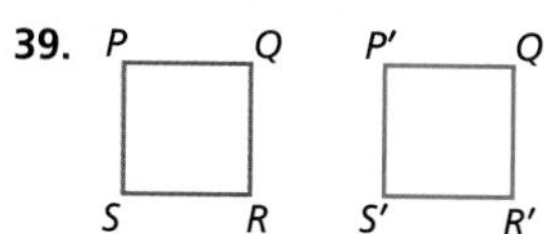

40. The coordinates for the vertices of $\triangle XYZ$ are $X(-5, -4)$, $Y(-3, -1)$, and $Z(-2, -2)$. Find the coordinates for the image of $\triangle XYZ$ after the translation $(x, y) \rightarrow (x + 4, y + 5)$.

Answers

32. $Y(1, 3)$
33. $B(-9, 6)$
34. $A(0, 2)$
35. 8.5
36. 7.3
37. 8.1
38. 90° rotation; $DEFG \rightarrow D'E'F'G'$
39. translation; $PQRS \rightarrow P'Q'R'S'$
40. $X'(-1, 1)$; $Y'(1, 4)$; $Z'(2, 3)$

Organizer

Objective: Assess students' mastery of concepts and skills in Chapter 1.

 **Online Edition**

Resources

 ***Assessment Resources***

Chapter 1 Tests
- Free Response (Levels A, B, C)
- Multiple Choice (Levels A, B, C)
- Performance Assessment

Teacher One Stop™
Test & Practice Generator

State Resources

1. Draw and label plane $\mathcal{N}$ containing two lines that intersect at B.

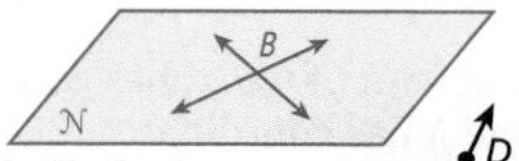

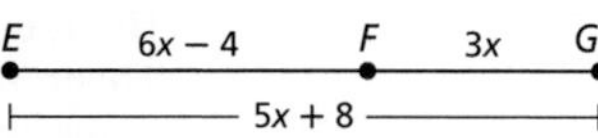

Use the figure to name each of the following.

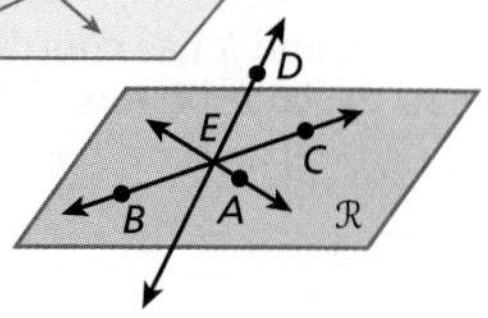

2. four noncoplanar points **2. Possible answer: D, E, C, A**
3. line containing B and E **3. Possible Answer: $\overleftrightarrow{BE}$**
4. The coordinate of A is -3, and the coordinate of B is 0.5. Find AB. **3.5**
5. E, F, and G represent mile markers along a straight highway. Find EF. **14**
   (Figure: E — $6x - 4$ — F — $3x$ — G; $EG = 5x + 8$)
6. J is the midpoint of $\overline{HK}$. Find HJ, JK, and HK. **9; 9; 18**
   (Figure: H — $3x + 5$ — J — $9x - 3$ — K)

Classify each angle by its measure.

7. $m\angle LMP = 70°$ **acute**
8. $m\angle QMN = 90°$ **rt.**
9. $m\angle PMN = 125°$ **obtuse**
10. $\overrightarrow{TV}$ bisects $\angle RTS$. If the $m\angle RTV = (16x - 6)°$ and $m\angle VTS = (13x + 9)°$, what is the $m\angle RTV$? **74°**
11. An angle's measure is 5 degrees less than 3 times the measure of its supplement. Find the measure of the angle and its supplement. **133.75°; 46.25°**

Tell whether the angles are only adjacent, adjacent and form a linear pair, or not adjacent.

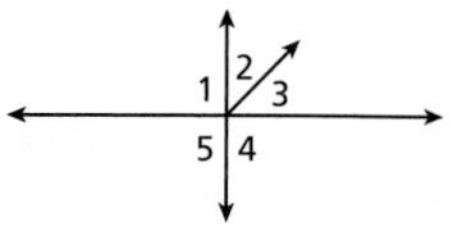

12. $\angle 2$ and $\angle 3$ **only adj.**
13. $\angle 4$ and $\angle 5$ **adj. and a lin. pair**
14. $\angle 1$ and $\angle 4$ **not adj.**
15. Find the perimeter and area of a rectangle with $b = 8$ ft and $h = 4$ ft. **$P = 24$ ft; $A = 32$ ft^2**

Find the circumference and area of each circle to the nearest tenth.

16. $r = 15$ m **16. 94.2 m; 706.9 m^2**
17. $d = 25$ ft **17. 78.5 ft; 490.9 ft^2**
18. $d = 2.8$ cm **8.8 cm; 6.2 cm^2**
19. Find the midpoint of the segment with endpoints $(-4, 6)$ and $(3, 2)$. **$(-0.5, 4)$**
20. M is the midpoint of $\overline{LN}$. M has coordinates $(-5, 1)$, and L has coordinates $(2, 4)$. Find the coordinates of N. **$(-12, -2)$**
21. Given $A(-5, 1)$, $B(-1, 3)$, $C(1, 4)$, and $D(4, 1)$, is $\overline{AB} \cong \overline{CD}$? Explain. **no; $AB \approx 4.5$; $CD \approx 4.2$**

Identify each transformation. Then use arrow notation to describe the transformation.

22. 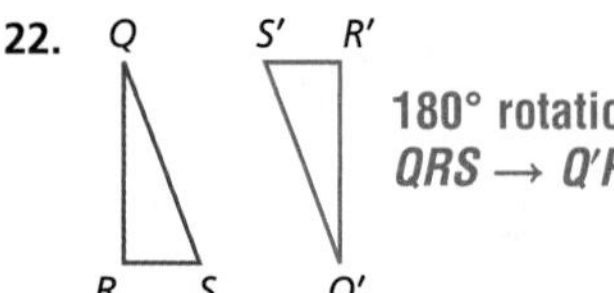

180° rotation; $QRS \rightarrow Q'R'S'$

23. 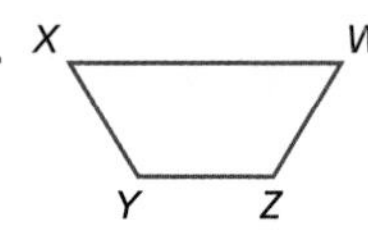

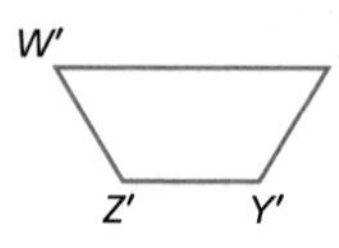

reflection; $WXYZ \rightarrow W'X'Y'Z'$

24. A designer used the translation $(x, y) \rightarrow (x + 3, y - 3)$ to transform a triangular-shaped pin ABC. Find the coordinates and draw the image of $\triangle ABC$.
$A'(-2, -2)$; $B'(1, 1)$; $C'(2, -2)$

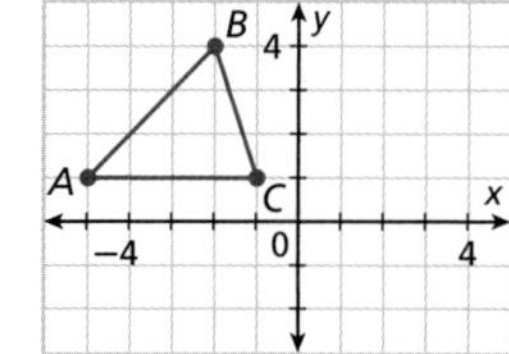

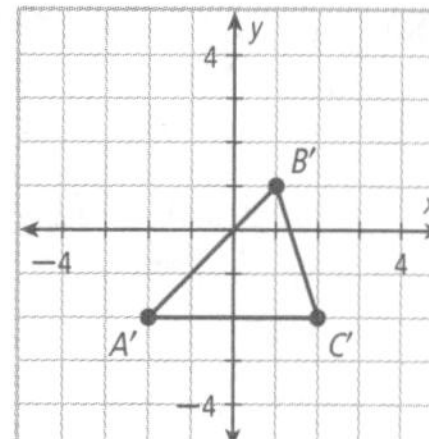

COLLEGE ENTRANCE EXAM PRACTICE

FOCUS ON SAT

The SAT* has three sections: Mathematics, Critical Reading, and Writing. Your SAT scores show how you compare with other students. It can be used by colleges to determine admission and to award merit-based financial aid.

On SAT multiple-choice questions, you receive one point for each correct answer, but you lose a fraction of a point for each incorrect response. Guess only when you can eliminate at least one of the answer choices.

You may want to time yourself as you take this practice test. It should take you about 6 minutes to complete.

1. Points D, E, F, and G are on a line, in that order. If $DE = 2$, $FG = 5$, and $DF = 6$, what is the value of $EG(DG)$?

(A) 13

(B) 18

(C) 19

(D) 42

(E) 99

2. $\overrightarrow{QS}$ bisects $\angle PQR$, $m\angle PQR = (4x + 2)°$, and $m\angle SQR = (3x - 6)°$. What is the value of x?

(A) 1

(B) 4

(C) 7

(D) 10

(E) 19

3. A rectangular garden is enclosed by a brick border. The total length of bricks used to enclose the garden is 42 meters. If the length of the garden is twice the width, what is the area of the garden?

(A) 7 meters

(B) 14 meters

(C) 42 meters

(D) 42 square meters

(E) 98 square meters

4. What is the area of the square?

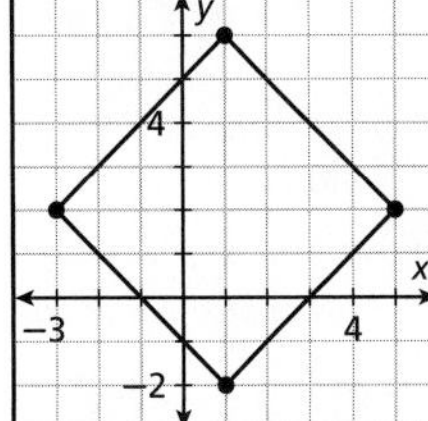

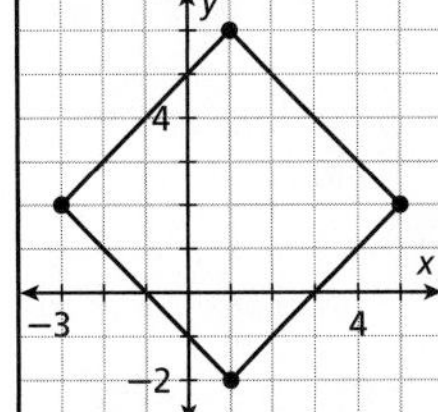

(A) 16

(B) 25

(C) 32

(D) 36

(E) 41

5. If $\angle BFD$ and $\angle AFC$ are right angles and $m\angle CFD = 72°$, what is the value of x?

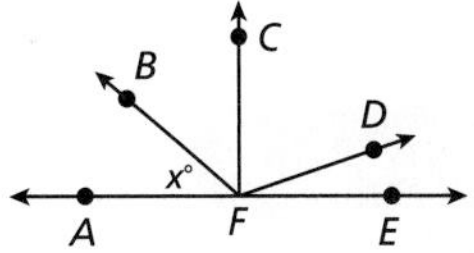

Note: Figure not drawn to scale.

(A) 18

(B) 36

(C) 72

(D) 90

(E) 108

*SAT is a registered trademark of the College Board, which was not involved in the production of, and does not endorse, this product.

Organizer

Objective: Provide practice for college entrance exams such as the SAT.

Resources

Questions on the SAT represent the following math strands:

Number and Operation, 20–25%

Algebra and Functions, 35–40%

Geometry and Measurement, 25–30%

Data Analysis, Statistics, and Probability, 10–15%

Items on this page focus on:

- Number and Operation
- Algebra and Functions
- Geometry and Measurement

Text References:

Item	1	2	3	4	5
Lesson	1-2	1-3	1-5	1-6	1-3

TEST PREP DOCTOR

1. Students may choose **B** because they have found the incorrect value of *EF*, possibly by subtracting 2 from 5. Remind students to sketch a figure of the situation.

2. Students may choose **A** because they did not do the opposite operation. Also remind students of the definition of *bisect* and the relationship of bisected angles.

3. Students may choose **C** or **D** because they calculated the perimeter of the garden. Remind students to read each test item carefully to determine what question is being asked.

4. Students may choose **A** or **D** because they incorrectly calculated the length of a side of the square. Remind students of the Distance Formula.

5. Students may choose **E** because they assumed the angles were complementary. Remind students that they cannot assume information that is not given in the test item.

Organizer

Objective: Provide opportunities to learn and practice common test-taking strategies.

This Test Tackler focuses on how to work backward to obtain an answer to a multiple-choice test item. When faced with a test item they do not know how to solve, students should be encouraged not to skip the item, but to use the answer choices provided in order to make an educated guess. By substituting each answer choice into the test question, students can determine whether the choice makes the test question correct and/or reasonable.

Standardized Test Strategies

Multiple Choice: Work Backward

When you do not know how to solve a multiple-choice test item, use the answer choices and work the question backward. Plug in the answer choices to see which choice makes the question true.

EXAMPLE 1

T is the midpoint of $\overline{RC}$, $RT = 12x - 8$, and $TC = 28$. What is the value of x?

Ⓐ -4 Ⓒ 3

Ⓑ 2 Ⓓ 28

12x − 8, 28; R, T, C

Since T is the midpoint of $\overline{RC}$, then $RT = RC$, or $12x - 8 = 28$. Find what value of x makes the left side of the equation equal 28.

Try choice A: If $x = -4$, then $12x - 8 = 12(-4) - 8 = -56$. This choice is not correct because length is always a positive number.

Try choice B: If $x = 2$, then $12x - 8 = 12(2) - 8 = 16$. Since $16 \neq 28$, choice B is not the answer.

Try choice C: If $x = 3$, then $12x - 8 = 12(3) - 8 = 28$.

Since $28 = 28$, the correct answer is C, 3.

EXAMPLE 2

Joel used 6400 feet of fencing to make a rectangular horse pen. The width of the pen is 4 times as long as the length. What is the length of the horse pen?

Ⓕ 25 feet Ⓗ 640 feet

Ⓖ 480 feet Ⓙ 1600 feet

ℓ, 4ℓ

Use the formula $P = 2\ell + 2w$. $P = 6400$ and $w = 4\ell$. You can work backward to determine which answer choice is the most reasonable.

Try choice J: Use mental math. If $\ell = 1600$, then $4\ell = 6400$. This choice is not reasonable because the perimeter of the pen would then be far greater than 6400 feet.

Try choice F: Use mental math. If $\ell = 25$, then $4\ell = 100$. This choice is incorrect because the perimeter of the pen is 6400 ft, which is far greater than $2(25) + 2(100)$.

Try choice H: If $\ell = 640$, then $4\ell = 2560$. When you substitute these values into the perimeter formula, it makes a true statement.

The correct answer is H, 640 ft.

Read each test item and answer the questions that follow.

Item A
The measure of an angle is 3 times as great as that of its complement. Which value is the measure of the smaller angle?

Ⓐ 22.5° Ⓒ 63.5°
Ⓑ 27.5° Ⓓ 67.5°

1. Are there any definitions that you can use to solve this problem? If so, what are they?
2. Describe how to work backward to find the correct answer.

Item B
In a town's annual relay marathon race, the second runner of each team starts at mile marker 4 and runs to the halfway point of the 26-mile marathon. At that point the second runner passes the relay baton to the third runner of the team. How many total miles does the second runner of each team run?

Ⓕ 4 miles Ⓗ 9 miles
Ⓖ 6.5 miles Ⓙ 13 miles

3. Which answer choice should you plug in first? Why?
4. Describe, by working backward, how you know that choices F and G are not correct.

Item C
Consider the translation $(-2, 8) \rightarrow (8, -4)$. What number was added to the x-coordinate?

Ⓐ −12 Ⓒ 4
Ⓑ −6 Ⓓ 10

5. Which answer choice should you plug in first? Why?
6. Explain how to work the test question backward to determine the correct answer.

When you work a test question backward start with choice C. The choices are usually listed in order from least to greatest. If choice C is incorrect because it is too low, you do not need to plug in the smaller numbers.

Item D
$\triangle QRS$ has vertices at $Q(3, 5)$, $R(3, 9)$, and $S(7, 5)$. Which of these points is a vertex of the image of $\triangle QRS$ after the translation $(x, y) \rightarrow (x - 7, y - 6)$?

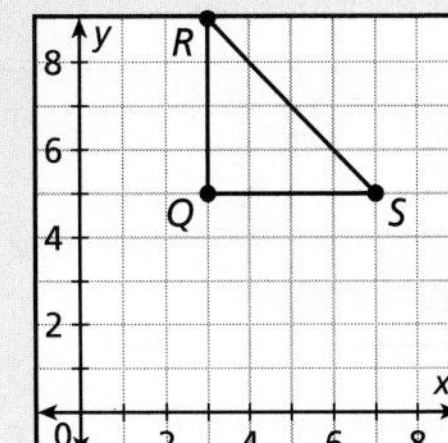

Ⓕ $(-4, 3)$ Ⓗ $(4, 1)$
Ⓖ $(0, 0)$ Ⓙ $(4, -3)$

7. Explain how to use mental math to find an answer that is NOT reasonable.
8. Describe, by working backward, how you can determine the correct answer.

Item E
$\overrightarrow{TS}$ bisects $\angle PTR$. If $m\angle PTS = (9x + 2)°$ and $m\angle STR = (x + 18)°$, what is the value of x?

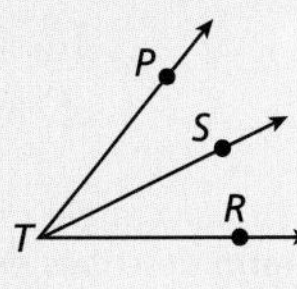

Ⓐ −10 Ⓒ 2
Ⓑ 0 Ⓓ 20

9. Explain how to use mental math to find an answer that is NOT reasonable.
10. Describe how to use the answer choices to work backward to find which answer is reasonable.

Answers

Possible answers:

1. yes; the def. of comp. ∠s and the comp. of an ∠
2. Multiply the ∠ measure given in choice **A** by 3 to get the greater ∠ measure. Then determine whether the sum of the larger ∠ measure and the ∠ measure given in choice **A** equals 90°. Repeat this process with choices **B** and **C**, or until the correct answer is found.
3. Plug in **H** first. If **H** is too high, the answer is **F** or **G**. If **H** is too low, the answer is **J**.
4. One-half of 26 equals 13, and 13 minus 4 does not equal 4, so choice **F** is incorrect; and 13 minus 6.5 does not equal 4, so choice **G** is incorrect.
5. Plug in **C** first. If **C** is too high, the answer is **A** or **B**. If **C** is too low, the answer is **D**.
6. Subtract the value given in each answer choice from 8, the x-coordinate of the translated pt., and see if you get −2, the x-coordinate of the original pt.
7. If you add −7 to the x-coordinate and −6 to the y-coordinate of any of the original pts., you do not get (0, 0). **G** is not a reasonable choice.
8. Add 7 to the x-value of the pt. in choice **F**, and add 6 to the y-value of the pt. in choice **F**. Look to see if this new pt. matches any of the original vertices of the △. If not, repeat this process until the correct answer is found.

State Resources

Answers to Test Items

A. A
B. H
C. D
D. F
E. C

Answers

Possible answers:

9. If you substitute −10 into $(9x + 2)$, the result is neg. Since an ∠ measure cannot be a neg. value, choice **A** is not reasonable.
10. Substitute the value of x given in choice **B** into both ∠ measures, and simplify. If the resulting values are equivalent, then that value of x is the correct answer. Repeat this process with choices **C** and **D**, or until the correct answer is found.

go.hrw.com
State Resources Online
KEYWORD: MG7 Resources

Organizer

Objective: Provide review and practice for Chapter 1 and standardized tests.

Resources

Assessment Resources

Chapter 1 Cumulative Test

go.hrw.com
KEYWORD: MG7 Resources

State Resources

CUMULATIVE ASSESSMENT, CHAPTER 1

Multiple Choice

Use the diagram for Items 1–3.

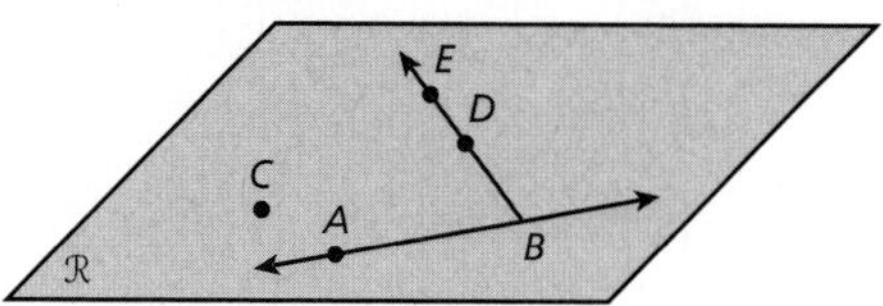

1. Which points are collinear?
   (A) *A*, *B*, and *C*
   (B) *B*, *C*, and *D*
   (C) *A*, *B*, and *E*
   (D) *B*, *D*, and *E*

2. What is another name for plane *R*?
   (F) Plane $\mathcal{C}$
   (G) Plane *AB*
   (H) Plane *ACE*
   (J) Plane *BDE*

3. Use your protractor to find the approximate measure of $\angle ABD$.
   (A) 123°
   (B) 117°
   (C) 77°
   (D) 63°

4. *S* is between *R* and *T*. The distance between *R* and *T* is 4 times the distance between *S* and *T*. If $RS = 18$, what is *RT*?
   (F) 24
   (G) 22.5
   (H) 14.4
   (J) 6

5. A ray bisects a straight angle into two congruent angles. Which term describes each of the congruent angles that are formed?
   (A) Acute
   (B) Obtuse
   (C) Right
   (D) Straight

6. Which expression states that $\overline{AB}$ is congruent to $\overline{CD}$?
   (F) $AB \cong CD$
   (G) $AB = CD$
   (H) $\overline{AB} = \overline{CD}$
   (J) $\overline{AB} \cong \overline{CD}$

7. The measure of an angle is 35°. What is the measure of its complement?
   (A) 35°
   (B) 45°
   (C) 55°
   (D) 145°

Use the diagram for Items 8–10.

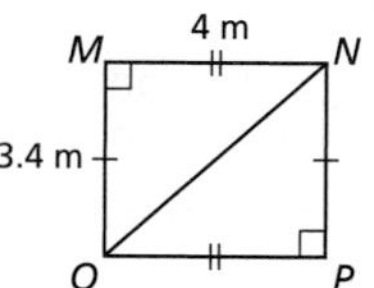

8. Which of these angles is adjacent to $\angle MQN$?
   (F) $\angle QMN$
   (G) $\angle NPQ$
   (H) $\angle QNP$
   (J) $\angle PQN$

9. What is the area of $\triangle NQP$?
   (A) 3.7 square meters
   (B) 6.8 square meters
   (C) 7.4 square meters
   (D) 13.6 square meters

10. Which of the following pairs of angles are complementary?
    (F) $\angle MNQ$ and $\angle QNP$
    (G) $\angle NQP$ and $\angle QPN$
    (H) $\angle MNP$ and $\angle QNP$
    (J) $\angle QMN$ and $\angle NPQ$

11. *K* is the midpoint of $\overline{JL}$. *J* has coordinates $(2, -1)$, and *K* has coordinates $(-4, 3)$. What are the coordinates of *L*?
    (A) $(3, -2)$
    (B) $(1, -1)$
    (C) $(-1, 1)$
    (D) $(-10, 7)$

12. A circle with a diameter of 10 inches has a circumference equal to the perimeter of a square. To the nearest tenth, what is the length of each side of the square?
    (F) 2.5 inches
    (G) 3.9 inches
    (H) 5.6 inches
    (J) 7.9 inches

13. The map coordinates of a campground are $(1, 4)$, and the coordinates of a fishing pier are $(4, 7)$. Each unit on the map represents 1 kilometer. If Alejandro walks in a straight line from the campground to the pier, how many kilometers, to the nearest tenth, will he walk?
    (A) 3.5 kilometers
    (B) 4.2 kilometers
    (C) 6.0 kilometers
    (D) 12.1 kilometers

Answers

1. D
2. H
3. D
4. F
5. C
6. J
7. C
8. J
9. B
10. F
11. D
12. J
13. B
14. H
15. A
16. H
17. C
18. 144
19. 1.75
20. 17
21. 90
22. 72

For many types of geometry problems, it may be helpful to draw a diagram and label it with the information given in the problem. This method is a good way of organizing the information and helping you decide how to solve the problem.

14. $m\angle R$ is 57°. What is the measure of its supplement?

(F) 33° (H) 123°
(G) 43° (J) 133°

15. What rule would you use to translate a triangle 4 units to the right?

(A) $(x, y) \rightarrow (x + 4, y)$
(B) $(x, y) \rightarrow (x - 4, y)$
(C) $(x, y) \rightarrow (x, y + 4)$
(D) $(x, y) \rightarrow (x, y - 4)$

16. If $\overrightarrow{WZ}$ bisects $\angle XWY$, which of the following statements is true?

(F) $m\angle XWZ > m\angle YWZ$
(G) $m\angle XWZ < m\angle YWZ$
(H) $m\angle XWZ = m\angle YWZ$
(J) $m\angle XWZ \cong m\angle YWZ$

17. The x- and y-axes separate the coordinate plane into four regions, called quadrants. If (c, d) is a point that is not on the axes, such that $c < 0$ and $d < 0$, which quadrant would contain point (c, d)?

(A) I (C) III
(B) II (D) IV

Gridded Response

18. The measure of $\angle 1$ is 4 times the measure of its supplement. What is the measure, in degrees, of $\angle 1$?

19. The exits for Market St. and Finch St. are 3.5 miles apart on a straight highway. The exit for King St. is at the midpoint between these two exits. How many miles apart are the King St. and Finch St. exits?

20. R has coordinates $(-4, 9)$. S has coordinates $(4, -6)$. What is RS?

21. If $\angle A$ is a supplement of $\angle B$ and is a right angle, then what is $m\angle B$ in degrees?

22. $\angle C$ and $\angle D$ are complementary. $m\angle C$ is 4 times $m\angle D$. What is $m\angle C$?

Short Response

23. $\triangle ABC$ has vertices $A(-2, 0)$, $B(0, 0)$, and $C(0, 3)$. The image of $\triangle ABC$ has vertices $A'(1, -4)$, $B'(3, -4)$, and $C'(3, -1)$.

a. Draw $\triangle ABC$ and its image $\triangle A'B'C'$ on a coordinate plane.

b. Write a rule for the transformation of $\triangle ABC$ using arrow notation.

24. You are given the measure of $\angle 4$. You also know the following angles are supplementary: $\angle 1$ and $\angle 2$, $\angle 2$ and $\angle 3$, and $\angle 1$ and $\angle 4$.

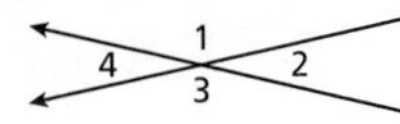

Explain how you can determine the measures of $\angle 1$, $\angle 2$, and $\angle 3$.

25. Marian is making a circular tablecloth from a rectangular piece of fabric that measures 6 yards by 4 yards. What is the area of the largest circular piece that can be cut from the fabric? Leave your answer in terms of π. Show your work or explain in words how you found your answer.

Extended Response

26. Demara is creating a design using a computer illustration program. She begins by drawing the rectangle shown on the coordinate grid.

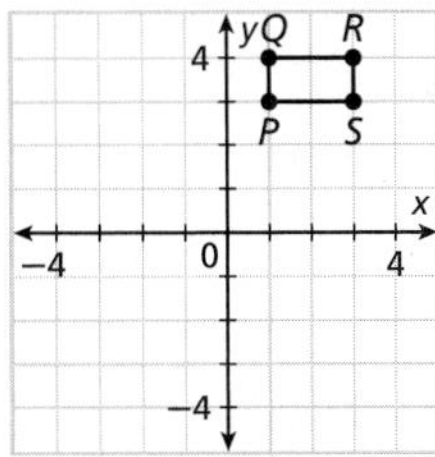

a. Demara translates rectangle $PQRS$ using the rule $(x, y) \rightarrow (x - 4, y - 6)$. On a copy of the coordinate grid, draw this translation and label each vertex.

b. Describe one way that Demara could have moved rectangle $PQRS$ to the same position in part **a** using a reflection and then a translation.

c. On the same coordinate grid, Demara reflects rectangle $PQRS$ across the x-axis. She draws a figure with vertices at $(1, -3)$, $(3, -3)$, $(3, -5)$, and $(1, -5)$. Did Demara reflect rectangle $PQRS$ correctly? Explain your answer.

Short-Response Rubric

Items 23–25

2 Points = The student's answer is an accurate and complete execution of the task or tasks.

1 Point = The student's answer contains attributes of an appropriate response but is flawed.

0 Points = The student's answer contains no attributes of an appropriate response.

Extended-Response Rubric

Item 26

4 Points = The student correctly performs the translation on a coordinate grid. Explanations are complete, and work demonstrates a thorough understanding of transformations.

3 Points = The student's translation and explanations are correct but may contain minor flaws. Work demonstrates an understanding of major concepts related to transformation.

2 Points = The student answers correctly, but only part of the problem is answered or explanations are incomplete. Work demonstrates a limited understanding of transformations.

1 Point = The student answers incorrectly but makes a reasonable attempt to show work or offer an explanation.

0 Points = The student does not answer correctly and does not attempt all parts of the problem.

Answers

23a.

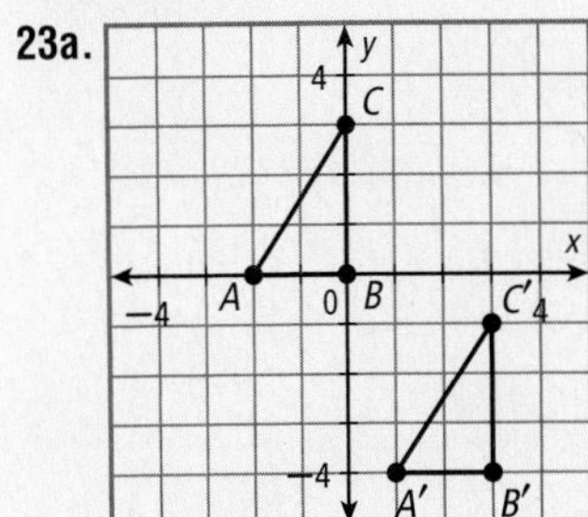

23b. $(x, y) \rightarrow (x + 3, y - 4)$

24. Possible answer: $\angle 1$ is supp. to $\angle 4$, so $m\angle 1 = 180° - m\angle 4$. You continue to subtract from 180° to find the measure of each $\angle$.

25. 4π yd^2; possible answer: The largest circular piece can have a diam. no larger than the width of the fabric. The width of the fabric is 4 yd. If the diam. of the circular piece is 4 yd, then its radius is 2 yd and its area is $\pi(2^2) = 4\pi$ yd^2.

26a.

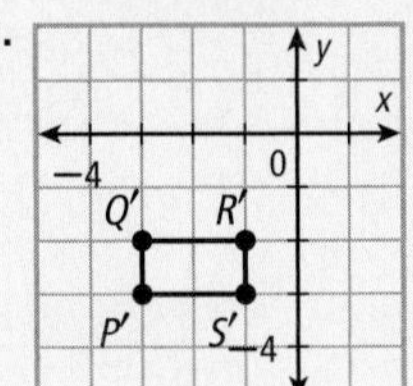

26b. Possible answer: She could have reflected rect. $PQRS$ across the y-axis and then translated it 6 units down.

26c. No; possible answer: a figure and its reflected image should be the same size and shape. Rect. $PQRS$ has a length of 2 units and a width of 1 unit. The image Demara drew is a square with a side length of 2 units. Because the 2 figures have different shapes, Demara did not perform the reflection correctly.

Geometric Reasoning

Section 2A

Inductive and Deductive Reasoning

2-1 Using Inductive Reasoning to Make Conjectures
Connecting Geometry to Number Theory Venn Diagrams
2-2 Conditional Statements
2-3 Using Deductive Reasoning to Verify Conjectures
2-3 Geometry Lab Solve Logic Puzzles
2-4 Biconditional Statements and Definitions

Section 2B

Mathematical Proof

2-5 Algebraic Proof
2-6 Geometric Proof
2-6 Geometry Lab Design Plans for Proofs
2-7 Flowchart and Paragraph Proofs
EXTENSION Introduction to Symbolic Logic

Pacing Guide for 45-Minute Classes

Teacher One Stop™
Calendar Planner®

Chapter 2

Countdown Weeks 3, 4

DAY 1	DAY 2	DAY 3	DAY 4	DAY 5
2-1 Lesson Connecting Geometry to Number Theory	2-2 Lesson	2-3 Lesson	2-3 Geometry Lab	2-4 Lesson
DAY 6	**DAY 7**	**DAY 8**	**DAY 9**	**DAY 10**
Multi-Step Test Prep Ready to Go On?	2-5 Lesson	2-6 Lesson	2-6 Lesson	2-6 Geometry Lab
DAY 11	**DAY 12**	**DAY 13**	**DAY 14**	**DAY 15**
2-7 Lesson	Multi-Step Test Prep Ready to Go On?	Extension	Chapter 2 Review	Chapter 2 Test

Pacing Guide for 90-Minute Classes

Teacher One Stop™
Calendar Planner®

Chapter 2

DAY 1	DAY 2	DAY 3	DAY 4	DAY 5
Chapter 1 Test 2-1 Lesson Connecting Geometry to Number Theory	2-2 Lesson 2-3 Lesson	2-3 Geometry Lab 2-4 Lesson	Multi-Step Test Prep Ready to Go On? 2-5 Lesson	2-6 Lesson
DAY 6	**DAY 7**	**DAY 8**		
2-6 Geometry Lab 2-7 Lesson	Multi-Step Test Prep Ready to Go On? Extension	Chapter 2 Review Chapter 2 Test		

ONGOING ASSESSMENT and INTERVENTION

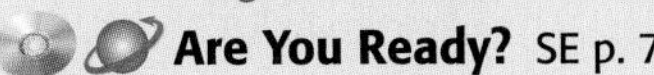

	DIAGNOSE	PRESCRIBE
Assess Prior Knowledge	**Before Chapter 2**	
	Diagnose readiness for the chapter.	Prescribe intervention.
	Are You Ready? SE p. 71	***Are You Ready? Intervention***
Formative Assessment	**Before Every Lesson**	
	Diagnose readiness for the lesson.	Prescribe intervention.
	Warm Up TE	**Reteach** CRB
	During Every Lesson	
	Diagnose understanding of lesson concepts.	Prescribe intervention.
	Check It Out! SE	**Reading Strategies** CRB
	Questioning Strategies TE	***Success for Every Learner***
	Think and Discuss SE	***Lesson Tutorial Videos***
	Write About It SE	
	Journal TE	
	After Every Lesson	
	Diagnose mastery of lesson concepts.	Prescribe intervention.
	Lesson Quiz TE	**Reteach** CRB
	Test Prep SE	**Test Prep Doctor** TE
	Test and Practice Generator	***Homework Help* Online**
	Before Chapter 2 Testing	
	Diagnose mastery of concepts in chapter.	Prescribe intervention.
	Ready to Go On? SE pp. 103, 127	***Ready to Go On? Intervention***
	Multi-Step Test Prep SE pp. 102, 126	**Scaffolding Questions** TE pp. 102, 126
	Section Quizzes AR	**Reteach** CRB
	Test and Practice Generator	***Lesson Tutorial Videos***
	Before High Stakes Testing	
	Diagnose mastery of benchmark concepts.	Prescribe intervention.
	College Entrance Exam Practice SE p. 135	***College Entrance Exam Practice***
	Standardized Test Prep SE pp. 138–139	
Summative Assessment	**After Chapter 2**	
	Check mastery of chapter concepts.	Prescribe intervention.
	Multiple-Choice Tests (Forms A, B, C)	**Reteach** CRB
	Free-Response Tests (Forms A, B, C)	***Lesson Tutorial Videos***
	Performance Assessment AR	
	Cumulative Test AR	
	Test and Practice Generator	

KEY: **SE** = *Student Edition* **TE** = *Teacher's Edition* **CRB** = *Chapter Resource Book* **AR** = *Assessment Resources* Available online Available on CD- or DVD-ROM

CHAPTER 2

Lesson Resources

Before the Lesson

Prepare ***Teacher One Stop***  
- Editable lesson plans
- Calendar Planner
- Easy access to all chapter resources

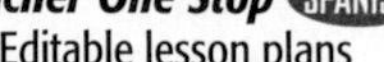

Lesson Transparencies
- Teacher Tools

Teach the Lesson

Introduce ***Alternate Openers: Explorations***

Lesson Transparencies 
- Warm Up
- Problem of the Day

Teach ***Lesson Transparencies***
- Teaching Transparencies

Know-It Notebook™
- Vocabulary
- Key Concepts

Power Presentations 

Lesson Tutorial Videos 

Interactive Online Edition 
- Lesson Activities
- Lesson Tutorial Videos

Lab Activities

Lab Resources Online 

Online Interactivities 

TechKeys 

Practice the Lesson

Practice ***Chapter Resources***
- Practice A, B, C

Practice and Problem Solving Workbook

IDEA Works!® Modified Worksheets and Tests

ExamView Test and Practice Generator

Homework Help Online

Online Interactivities

Interactive Online Edition
- Homework Help

Apply ***Chapter Resources***
- Problem Solving

Practice and Problem Solving Workbook

Interactive Online Edition
- Chapter Project

Project Teacher Support

After the Lesson

Reteach ***Chapter Resources***
- Reteach
- Reading Strategies ELL

Success for Every Learner

Review ***Interactive Answers and Solutions***

Solutions Key

Know-It Notebook™
- Big Ideas
- Chapter Review

Extend ***Chapter Resources***
- Challenge

Technology Highlights for the Teacher

 **Power Presentations**

Dynamic presentations to engage students. Complete PowerPoint® presentations for every lesson in Chapter 2.

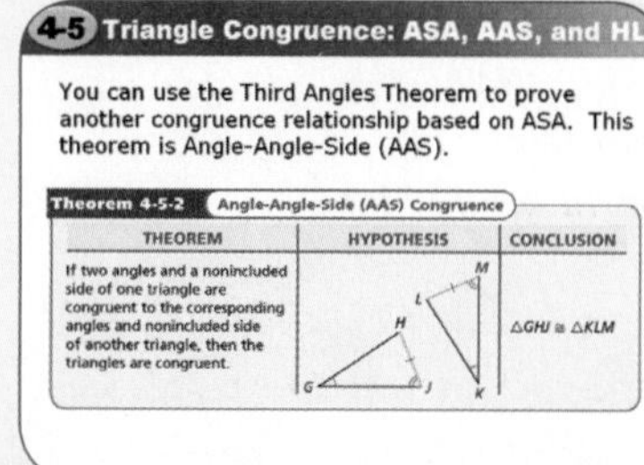

 **Teacher One Stop** SPANISH

Easy access to Chapter 2 resources and assessments. Includes lesson planning, test generation, and puzzle creation software.

 **Premier Online Edition** SPANISH

Chapter 2 includes Tutorial Videos, Lesson Activities, Lesson Quizzes, Homework Help, and Chapter Project.

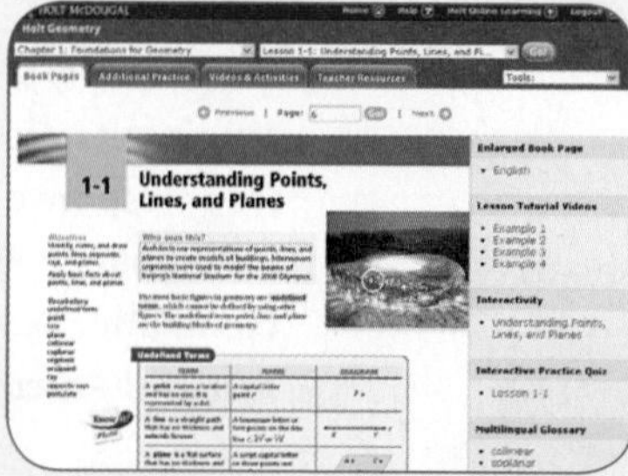

KEY: **SE** = *Student Edition* **TE** = *Teacher's Edition*  ELL English Language Learners   SPANISH Spanish version available 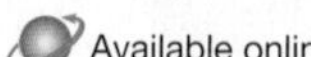 Available online  Available on CD- or DVD-ROM

Reaching All Learners

Teaching tips to help all learners appear throughout the chapter. A few that target specific students are included in the lists below.

All Learners

Lab Activities
Practice and Problem Solving Workbook
Know-It Notebook

Special Needs Students

Practice A .... CRB
Reteach .... CRB
Reading Strategies .... CRB
Are You Ready? .... SE p. 71
Inclusion .... TE pp. 100, 112, 148, 152
IDEA Works!® Modified Worksheets and Tests
Ready to Go On? Intervention SPANISH
Know-It Notebook
Online Interactivities  SPANISH
Lesson Tutorial Videos SPANISH

Developing Learners

Practice A .... CRB
Reteach .... CRB
Reading Strategies .... CRB
Are You Ready? .... SE p. 71
Vocabulary Connections .... SE p. 72
Questioning Strategies .... TE
Ready to Go On? Intervention SPANISH
Know-It Notebook
Homework Help Online

Online Interactivities  SPANISH

Lesson Tutorial Videos SPANISH

On-Level Learners

Practice B .... CRB
Problem Solving .... CRB
Vocabulary Connections .... SE p. 71
Questioning Strategies .... TE
Ready to Go On? Intervention SPANISH
Know-It Notebook
Homework Help Online  
Online Interactivities SPANISH

Advanced Learners

Practice C .... CRB
Challenge .... CRB
Challenge Exercises .... SE
Reading and Writing Math *Extend* .... TE p. 73
Critical Thinking .... TE p. 82
Are You Ready? Enrichment SPANISH
Ready To Go On? Enrichment SPANISH

English Language Learners

ENGLISH LANGUAGE LEARNERS

Reading Strategies .... CRB
Are You Ready? Vocabulary .... SE p. 71
Vocabulary Connections .... SE p. 72
Vocabulary Review .... SE p. 130
English Language Learners ... TE pp. 73, 78, 82, 97, 98, 108, 129
Success for Every Learner
Know-It Notebook
Spanish Study Guide (Resumen y Repaso)
Multilingual Glossary
Lesson Tutorial Videos  

Technology Highlights for Reaching All Learners

Lesson Tutorial Videos SPANISH

Starring Holt authors Ed Burger and Freddie Renfro! Live tutorials to support every lesson in Chapter 2.

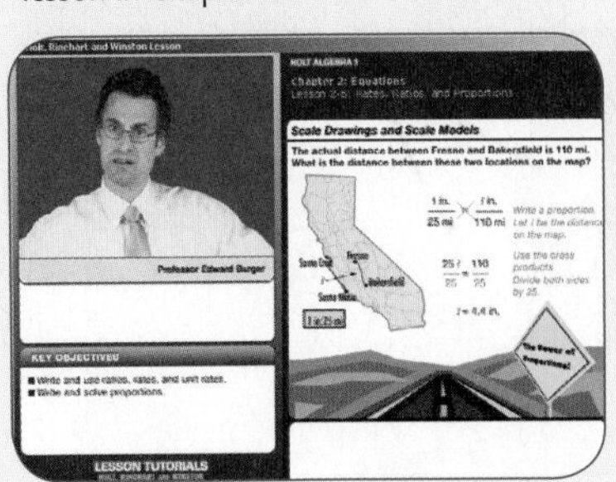

Multilingual Glossary

Searchable glossary includes definitions in English, Spanish, Vietnamese, Chinese, Hmong, Korean, and 4 other languages.

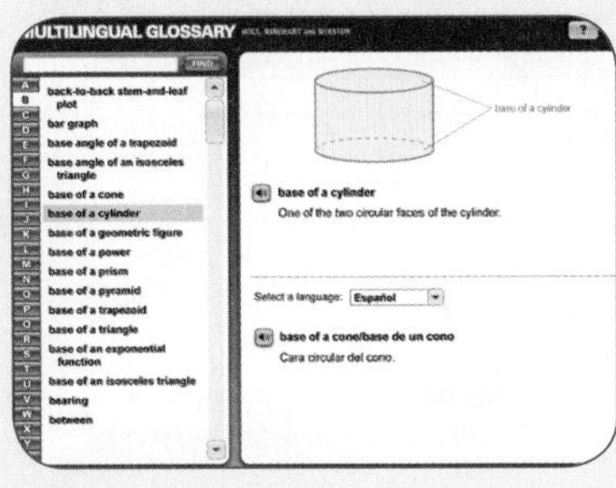

Online Interactivities

Interactive tutorials provide visually engaging alternative opportunities to learn concepts and master skills.

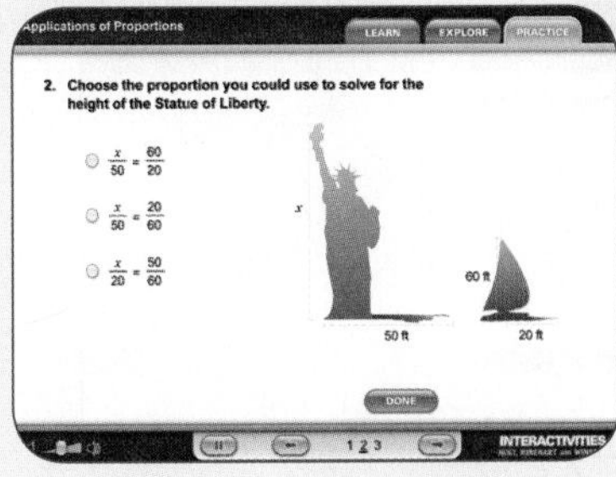

KEY: **SE** = *Student Edition* **TE** = *Teacher's Edition* **CRB** = *Chapter Resource Book* SPANISH Spanish version available · Available online · Available on CD- or DVD-ROM

CHAPTER 2

Ongoing Assessment

Assessing Prior Knowledge

Determine whether students have the prerequisite concepts and skills for success in Chapter 2.

Are You Ready? SPANISH .... SE p. 71
Warm Up .... TE

Test Preparation

Provide review and practice for Chapter 2 and standardized tests.

Multi-Step Test Prep .... SE pp. 102, 106
Study Guide: Review .... SE pp. 130–133
Test Tackler .... SE pp. 136–137
Standardized Test Prep .... SE pp. 138–139
College Entrance Exam Practice .... SE p. 135
Countdown to Testing .... SE pp. C4-C27
IDEA Works!® Modified Worksheets and Tests

Alternative Assessment

Assess students' understanding of Chapter 2 concepts and combined problem-solving skills.

Chapter 2 Project .... SE p. 70
Alternative Assessment .... TE
Performance Assessment .... AR
Portfolio Assessment .... AR

Lesson Assessment

Provide formative assessment for each lesson of Chapter 2.

Questioning Strategies .... TE
Think and Discuss .... SE
Check It Out! Exercises .... SE
Write About It .... SE
Journal .... TE
Lesson Quiz .... TE
Alternative Assessment .... TE
IDEA Works!® Modified Worksheets and Tests

Weekly Assessment

Provide formative assessment for each section of Chapter 2.

Multi-Step Test Prep .... SE pp. 102, 106
Ready to Go On? SPANISH .... SE pp. 103, 127
Section Quizzes .... AR
Test and Practice Generator .... *Teacher One Stop*

Chapter Assessment

Provide summative assessment of Chapter 2 mastery.

Chapter 2 Test .... SE p. 134
Chapter Test (Levels A, B, C) .... AR
• Multiple Choice • Free Response
Cumulative Test .... AR
Test and Practice Generator .... *Teacher One Stop*
IDEA Works!® Modified Worksheets and Tests

Technology Highlights for Assessment

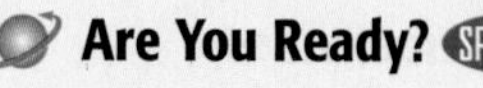

Are You Ready? SPANISH

Automatically assess readiness and prescribe intervention for Chapter 2 prerequisite skills.

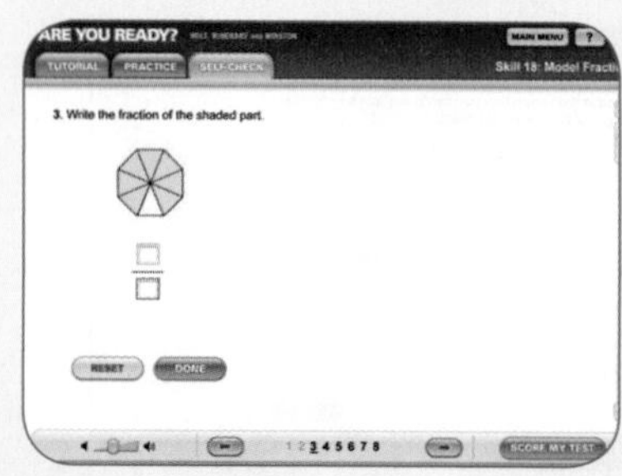

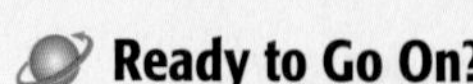

Ready to Go On?

Automatically assess understanding of and prescribe intervention for Sections 2A and 2B.

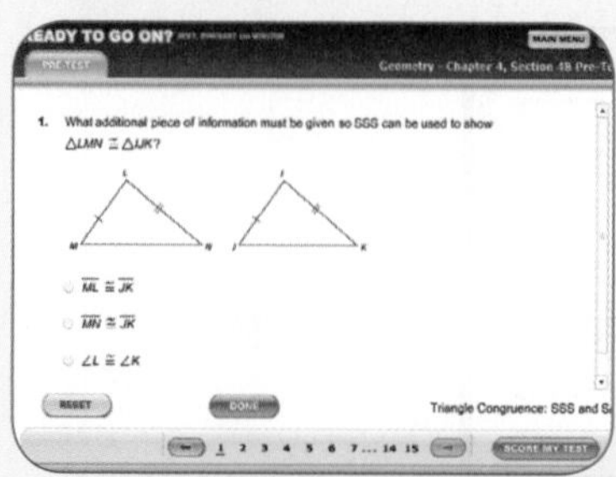

Test and Practice Generator

Use Chapter 2 problem banks to create assessments and worksheets to print out or deliver online. Includes dynamic problems.

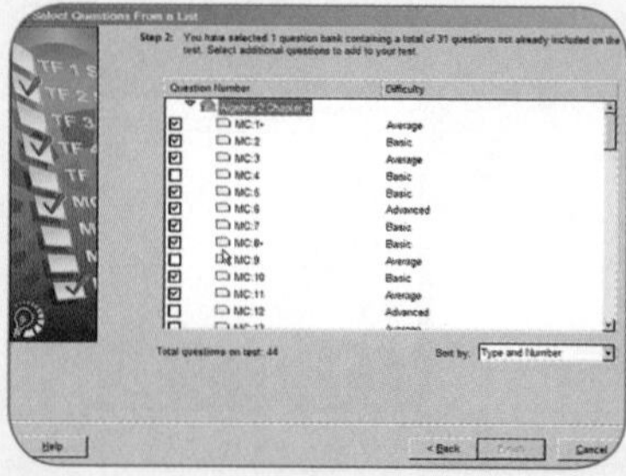

KEY: **SE** = *Student Edition* **TE** = *Teacher's Edition* **AR** = *Assessment Resources* SPANISH Spanish version available 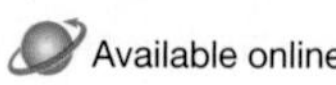 Available online  Available on CD- or DVD-ROM

Formal Assessment

Three levels (A, B, C) of multiple-choice and free-response chapter tests, along with a performance assessment, are available in the *Assessment Resources.*

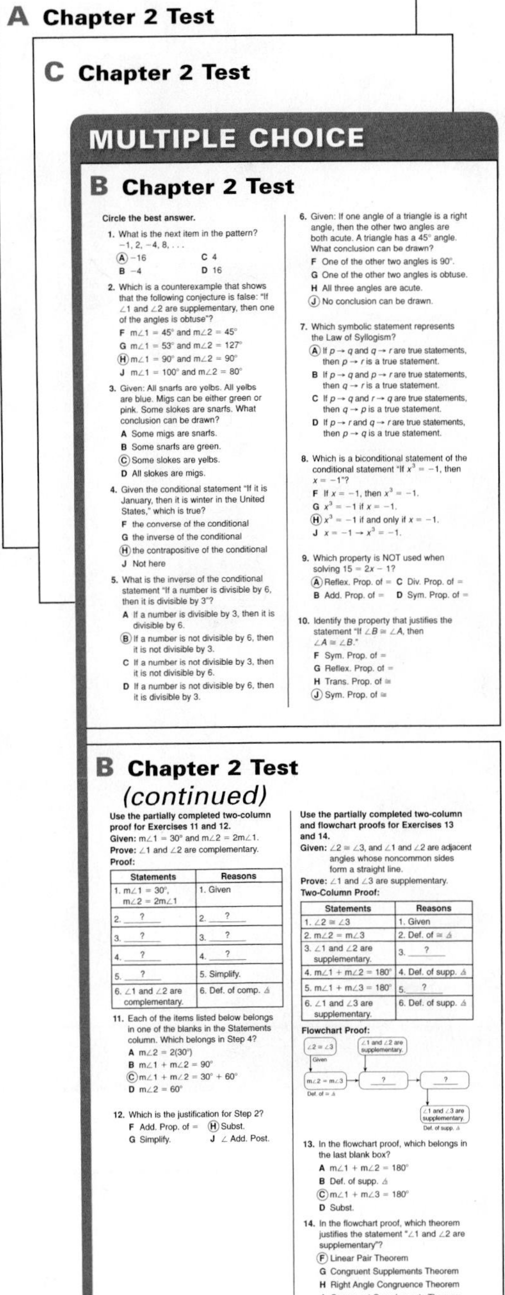

A Chapter 2 Test

C Chapter 2 Test

MULTIPLE CHOICE

B Chapter 2 Test

Circle the best answer.

1. What is the next item in the pattern?
   $-1, 2, -4, 8, \ldots$
   (A) -16 C 4
   B -4 D 16
2. Which is a counterexample that shows that the following conjecture is false: "If ∠1 and ∠2 are supplementary, then one of the angles is obtuse"?
   F m∠1 = 45° and m∠2 = 45°
   G m∠1 = 53° and m∠2 = 127°
   (H) m∠1 = 90° and m∠2 = 90°
   J m∠1 = 100° and m∠2 = 80°
3. Given: All snarfs are yelbs. All yelbs are blue. Migs can be either green or pink. Some slokes are snarfs. What conclusion can be drawn?
   A Some migs are snarfs.
   B Some snarfs are green.
   (C) Some slokes are yelbs.
   D All slokes are migs.
4. Given the conditional statement "If it is January, then it is winter in the United States," which is true?
   F the converse of the conditional
   G the inverse of the conditional
   (H) the contrapositive of the conditional
   J Not here
5. What is the inverse of the conditional statement "If a number is divisible by 6, then it is divisible by 3"?
   A If a number is divisible by 3, then it is divisible by 6.
   (B) If a number is not divisible by 6, then it is not divisible by 3.
   C If a number is not divisible by 3, then it is not divisible by 6.
   D If a number is not divisible by 6, then it is divisible by 3.
6. Given: If one angle of a triangle is a right angle, then the other two angles are both acute. A triangle has a 45° angle. What conclusion can be drawn?
   F One of the other two angles is 90°.
   G One of the other two angles is obtuse.
   H All three angles are acute.
   (J) No conclusion can be drawn.
7. Which symbolic statement represents the Law of Syllogism?
   (A) If $p \rightarrow q$ and $q \rightarrow r$ are true statements, then $p \rightarrow r$ is a true statement.
   B If $p \rightarrow q$ and $p \rightarrow r$ are true statements, then $q \rightarrow r$ is a true statement.
   C If $p \rightarrow q$ and $r \rightarrow q$ are true statements, then $q \rightarrow p$ is a true statement.
   D If $p \rightarrow r$ and $q \rightarrow r$ are true statements, then $p \rightarrow q$ is a true statement.
8. Which is a biconditional statement of the conditional statement "If $x^3 = -1$, then $x = -1$"?
   F If $x = -1$, then $x^3 = -1$.
   G $x^3 = -1$ if $x = -1$.
   (H) $x^3 = -1$ if and only if $x = -1$.
   J $x = -1 \rightarrow x^3 = -1$.
9. Which property is NOT used when solving $15 = 2x - 1$?
   (A) Reflex. Prop. of = C Div. Prop. of =
   B Add. Prop. of = D Sym. Prop. of =
10. Identify the property that justifies the statement "If ∠B ≅ ∠A, then ∠A ≅ ∠B."
   F Sym. Prop. of =
   G Reflex. Prop. of =
   H Trans. Prop. of ≅
   (J) Sym. Prop. of ≅

B Chapter 2 Test (continued)

Use the partially completed two-column proof for Exercises 11 and 12.

Given: m∠1 = 30° and m∠2 = 2m∠1.
Prove: ∠1 and ∠2 are complementary.
Proof:

Statements	Reasons
1. m∠1 = 30°, m∠2 = 2m∠1	1. Given
2. ?	2. ?
3. ?	3. ?
4. ?	4. ?
5. ?	5. Simplify.
6. ∠1 and ∠2 are complementary.	6. Def. of comp. ∡

11. Each of the items listed below belongs in one of the blanks in the Statements column. Which belongs in Step 4?
   A m∠2 = 2(30°)
   B m∠1 + m∠2 = 90°
   (C) m∠1 + m∠2 = 30° + 60°
   D m∠2 = 60°
12. Which is the justification for Step 2?
   F Add. Prop. of = (H) Subst.
   G Simplify. J ∠ Add. Post.

Use the partially completed two-column and flowchart proofs for Exercises 13 and 14.

Given: ∠2 ≅ ∠3, and ∠1 and ∠2 are adjacent angles whose noncommon sides form a straight line.
Prove: ∠1 and ∠3 are supplementary.
Two-Column Proof:

Statements	Reasons
1. ∠2 ≅ ∠3	1. Given
2. m∠2 = m∠3	2. Def. of ≅ ∡
3. ∠1 and ∠2 are supplementary.	3. ?
4. m∠1 + m∠2 = 180°	4. Def. of supp. ∡
5. m∠1 + m∠3 = 180°	5. ?
6. ∠1 and ∠3 are supplementary.	6. Def. of supp. ∡

Flowchart Proof:

13. In the flowchart proof, which belongs in the last blank box?
   A m∠1 + m∠2 = 180°
   B Def. of supp. ∡
   (C) m∠1 + m∠3 = 180°
   D Subst.
14. In the flowchart proof, which theorem justifies the statement "∠1 and ∠2 are supplementary"?
   (F) Linear Pair Theorem
   G Congruent Supplements Theorem
   H Right Angle Congruence Theorem
   J Congruent Complements Theorem

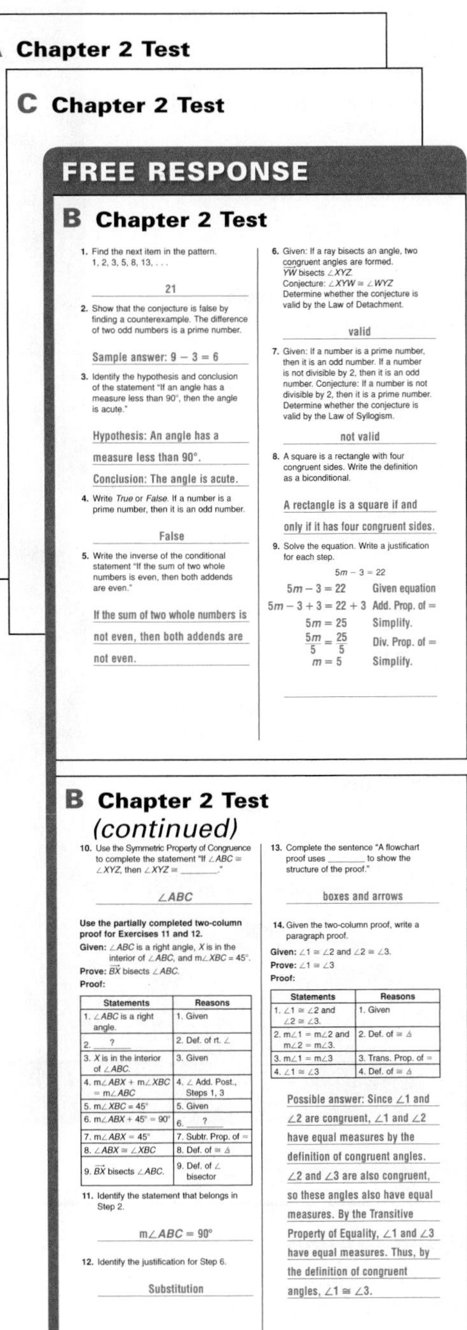

A Chapter 2 Test

C Chapter 2 Test

FREE RESPONSE

B Chapter 2 Test

1. Find the next item in the pattern.
   1, 2, 3, 5, 8, 13, . . .
   21
2. Show that the conjecture is false by finding a counterexample. The difference of two odd numbers is a prime number.
   Sample answer: $9 - 3 = 6$
3. Identify the hypothesis and conclusion of the statement "If an angle has a measure less than 90°, then the angle is acute."
   Hypothesis: An angle has a measure less than 90°.
   Conclusion: The angle is acute.
4. Write *True* or *False*. If a number is a prime number, then it is an odd number.
   False
5. Write the inverse of the conditional statement "If the sum of two whole numbers is even, then both addends are even."
   If the sum of two whole numbers is not even, then both addends are not even.
6. Given: If a ray bisects an angle, two congruent angles are formed. $\overrightarrow{YW}$ bisects ∠XYZ.
   Conjecture: ∠XYW ≅ ∠WYZ
   Determine whether the conjecture is valid by the Law of Detachment.
   valid
7. Given: If a number is a prime number, then it is an odd number. If a number is not divisible by 2, then it is an odd number. Conjecture: If a number is not divisible by 2, then it is a prime number. Determine whether the conjecture is valid by the Law of Syllogism.
   not valid
8. A square is a rectangle with four congruent sides. Write the definition as a biconditional.
   A rectangle is a square if and only if it has four congruent sides.
9. Solve the equation. Write a justification for each step.
   $5m - 3 = 22$

$5m - 3 = 22$	Given equation
$5m - 3 + 3 = 22 + 3$	Add. Prop. of =
$5m = 25$	Simplify.
$\frac{5m}{5} = \frac{25}{5}$	Div. Prop. of =
$m = 5$	Simplify.

B Chapter 2 Test (continued)

10. Use the Symmetric Property of Congruence to complete the statement "If ∠ABC ≅ ∠XYZ, then ∠XYZ ≅ ______."
   ∠ABC

Use the partially completed two-column proof for Exercises 11 and 12.

Given: ∠ABC is a right angle, X is in the interior of ∠ABC, and m∠XBC = 45°.
Prove: $\overrightarrow{BX}$ bisects ∠ABC.
Proof:

Statements	Reasons
1. ∠ABC is a right angle.	1. Given
2. ?	2. Def. of rt. ∠
3. X is in the interior of ∠ABC.	3. Given
4. m∠ABX + m∠XBC = m∠ABC	4. ∠ Add. Post., Steps 1, 3
5. m∠XBC = 45°	5. Given
6. m∠ABX + 45° = 90°	6. ?
7. m∠ABX = 45°	7. Subtr. Prop. of =
8. ∠ABX ≅ ∠XBC	8. Def. of ≅ ∡
9. $\overrightarrow{BX}$ bisects ∠ABC.	9. Def. of ∠ bisector

11. Identify the statement that belongs in Step 2.
   m∠ABC = 90°
12. Identify the justification for Step 6.
   Substitution
13. Complete the sentence "A flowchart proof uses ______ to show the structure of the proof."
   boxes and arrows
14. Given the two-column proof, write a paragraph proof.

Given: ∠1 ≅ ∠2 and ∠2 ≅ ∠3.
Prove: ∠1 ≅ ∠3
Proof:

Statements	Reasons
1. ∠1 ≅ ∠2 and ∠2 ≅ ∠3.	1. Given
2. m∠1 = m∠2 and m∠2 = m∠3.	2. Def. of ≅ ∡
3. m∠1 = m∠3	3. Trans. Prop. of =
4. ∠1 ≅ ∠3	4. Def. of ≅ ∡

Possible answer: Since ∠1 and ∠2 are congruent, ∠1 and ∠2 have equal measures by the definition of congruent angles. ∠2 and ∠3 are also congruent, so these angles also have equal measures. By the Transitive Property of Equality, ∠1 and ∠3 have equal measures. Thus, by the definition of congruent angles, ∠1 ≅ ∠3.

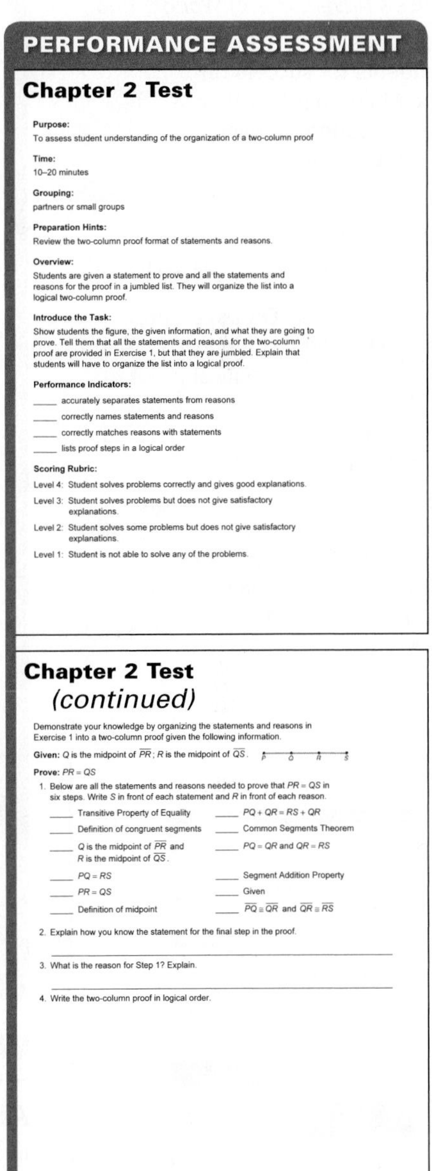

PERFORMANCE ASSESSMENT

Chapter 2 Test

Purpose:
To assess student understanding of the organization of a two-column proof

Time:
10–20 minutes

Grouping:
partners or small groups

Preparation Hints:
Review the two-column proof format of statements and reasons.

Overview:
Students are given a statement to prove and all the statements and reasons for the proof in a jumbled list. They will organize the list into a logical two-column proof.

Introduce the Task:
Show students the figure, the given information, and what they are going to prove. Tell them that all the statements and reasons for the two-column proof are provided in Exercise 1, but that they are jumbled. Explain that students will have to organize the list into a logical proof.

Performance Indicators:

_____ accurately separates statements from reasons
_____ correctly names statements and reasons
_____ correctly matches reasons with statements
_____ lists proof steps in a logical order

Scoring Rubric:

Level 4: Student solves problems correctly and gives good explanations.
Level 3: Student solves problems but does not give satisfactory explanations.
Level 2: Student solves some problems but does not give satisfactory explanations.
Level 1: Student is not able to solve any of the problems.

Chapter 2 Test (continued)

Demonstrate your knowledge by organizing the statements and reasons in Exercise 1 into a two-column proof given the following information.

Given: Q is the midpoint of $\overline{PR}$; R is the midpoint of $\overline{QS}$.

Prove: PR = QS

1. Below are all the statements and reasons needed to prove that PR = QS in six steps. Write S in front of each statement and R in front of each reason.
   _____ Transitive Property of Equality
   _____ PQ + QR = RS + QR
   _____ Definition of congruent segments
   _____ Common Segments Theorem
   _____ Q is the midpoint of $\overline{PR}$ and R is the midpoint of $\overline{QS}$.
   _____ PQ = QR and QR = RS
   _____ PQ = RS
   _____ Segment Addition Property
   _____ PR = QS
   _____ Given
   _____ Definition of midpoint
   _____ $\overline{PQ} \cong \overline{QR}$ and $\overline{QR} \cong \overline{RS}$
2. Explain how you know the statement for the final step in the proof.
3. What is the reason for Step 1? Explain.
4. Write the two-column proof in logical order.

Modified chapter tests that address special learning needs are available in *IDEA Works!*® *Modified Worksheets and Tests.*

Teacher One Stop™

Test & Practice Generator

Create and customize Chapter 2 Tests. Instantly generate multiple test versions, answer keys, and practice versions of test items.

CHAPTER 2

SECTION 2A
Inductive and Deductive Reasoning

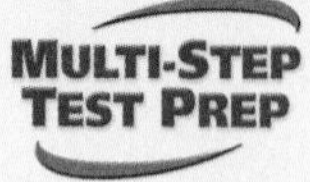

MULTI-STEP TEST PREP On page 102, students use inductive and deductive reasoning to decipher the wordplay in Lewis Carroll's *Alice's Adventures in Wonderland.*

Exercises designed to prepare students for success on the Multi-Step Test Prep can be found on pages 78, 85, 92, and 100.

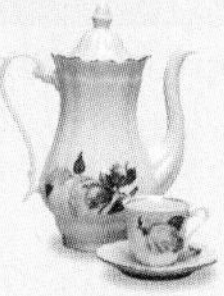

SECTION 2B
Mathematical Proof

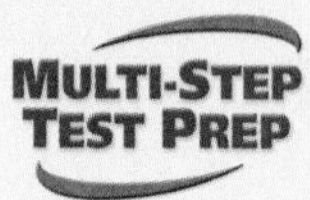

MULTI-STEP TEST PREP On page 126, students use mathematical proof to investigate the geometric properties of intersecting highways.

Exercises designed to prepare students for success on the Multi-Step Test Prep can be found on pages 109, 115, and 124.

Interactivities Online ▶

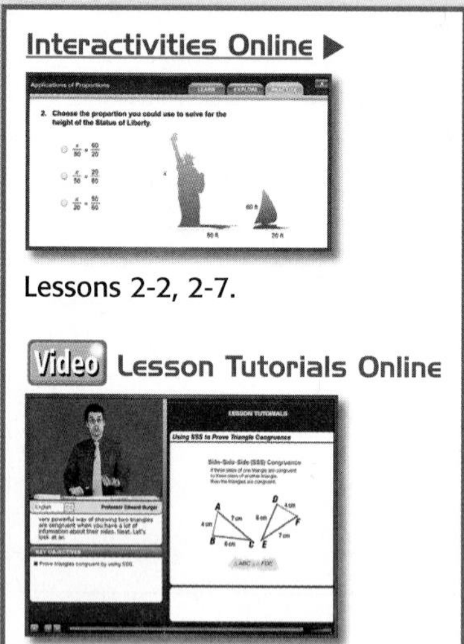

Lessons 2-2, 2-7.

Video Lesson Tutorials Online

Lesson Tutorial Videos are available for EVERY example.

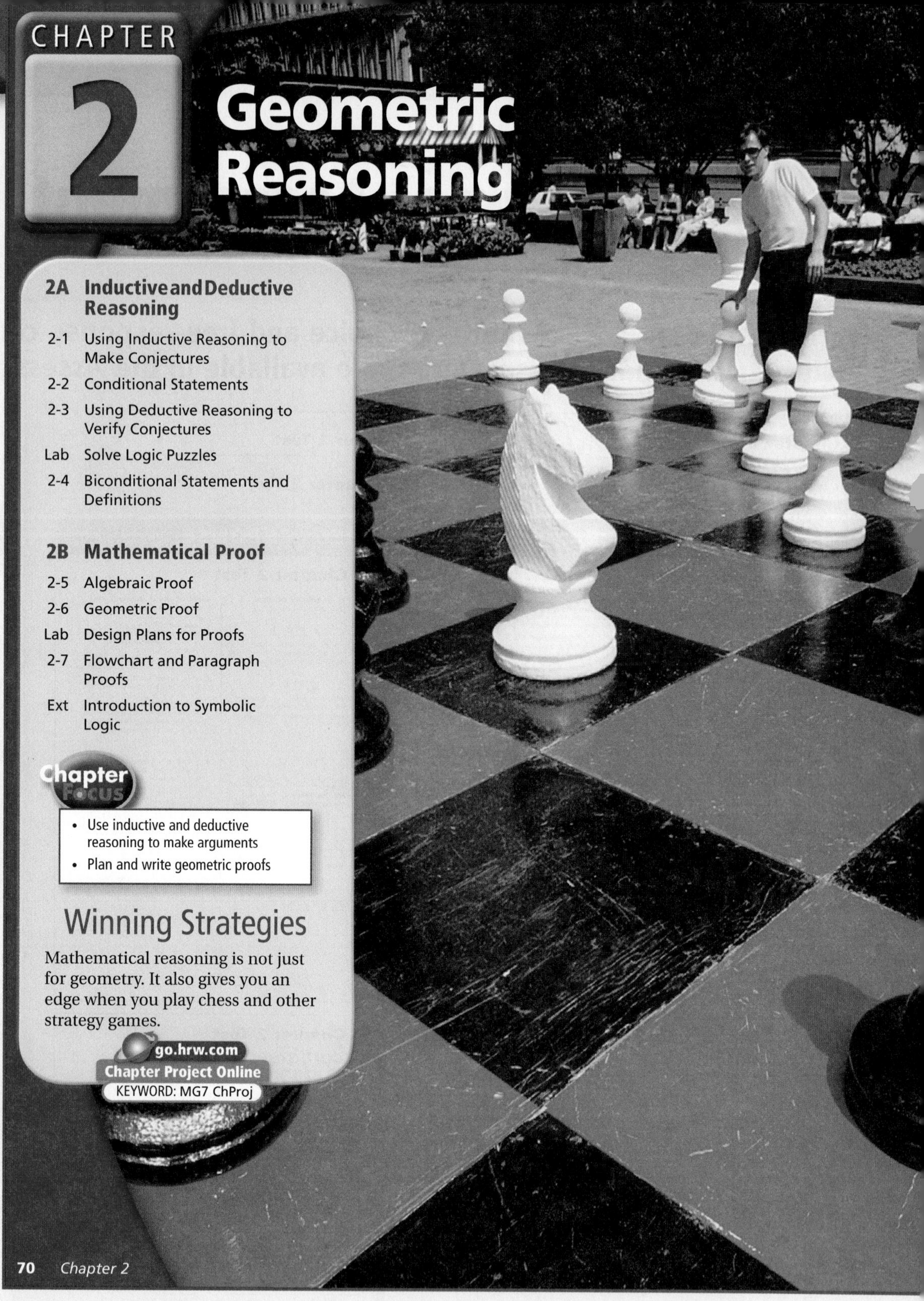

CHAPTER 2 Geometric Reasoning

Chapter Focus
- Use inductive and deductive reasoning to make arguments
- Plan and write geometric proofs

Winning Strategies

Mathematical reasoning is not just for geometry. It also gives you an edge when you play chess and other strategy games.

go.hrw.com
Chapter Project Online
KEYWORD: MG7 ChProj

Winning Strategies

About the Project

In the Chapter Project, students use logical reasoning to develop strategies for a paper-and-pencil game and to solve a mathematical puzzle.

Project Resources

All project resources for teachers and students are provided online.

go.hrw.com
Project Teacher Support
KEYWORD: MG7 ProjectTS

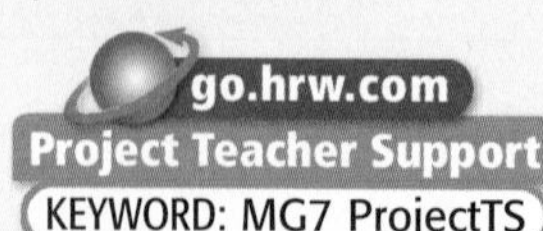

ARE YOU READY?

Vocabulary

Match each term on the left with a definition on the right.

1. angle B
2. line A
3. midpoint F
4. plane C
5. segment D

A. a straight path that has no thickness and extends forever
B. a figure formed by two rays with a common endpoint
C. a flat surface that has no thickness and extends forever
D. a part of a line between two points
E. names a location and has no size
F. a point that divides a segment into two congruent segments

Angle Relationships

Select the best description for each labeled angle pair.

6. linear pair or vertical angles **lin. pair**
7. 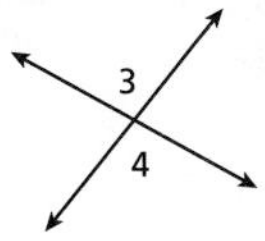 adjacent angles or vertical angles **vert. ∠s**
8. 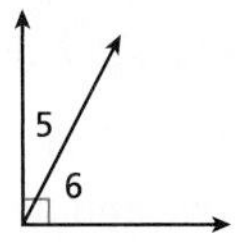 supplementary angles or complementary angles **comp. ∠s**

Classify Real Numbers

Tell if each number is a natural number, a whole number, an integer, or a rational number. Give all the names that apply.

9. 6 natural, whole, integer, rational
10. −0.8 rational
11. −3 integer, rational
12. 5.2 rational
13. $\frac{3}{8}$ rational
14. 0 whole, integer, rational

Points, Lines, and Planes

Name each of the following. 15–19. Possible answers:

15. a point B
16. a line $\overleftrightarrow{BD}$
17. a ray $\overrightarrow{CA}$
18. a segment $\overline{CD}$
19. a plane plane $\mathcal{F}$

Solve One-Step Equations

Solve.

20. $8 + x = 5$ −3
21. $6y = -12$ −2
22. $9 = 6s$ 1.5
23. $p - 7 = 9$ 16
24. $\frac{z}{5} = 5$ 25
25. $8.4 = -1.2r$ −7

ARE YOU READY?

Organizer

Objective: Assess students' understanding of prerequisite skills.

Prerequisite Skills

Angle Relationships
Classify Real Numbers
Points, Lines, and Planes
Solve One-Step Equations

Assessing Prior Knowledge

INTERVENTION

Diagnose and Prescribe

Use this page to determine whether intervention is necessary or whether enrichment is appropriate.

Resources

***Are You Ready? Intervention and Enrichment* Worksheets**

***Are You Ready?* CD-ROM**

***Are You Ready?* Online**

my.hrw.com

ARE YOU READY?

Diagnose and Prescribe

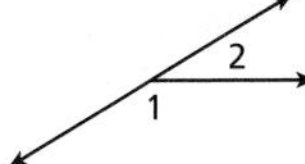

Prerequisite Skill	*Are You Ready? Intervention*, Chapter 2 — Worksheets	CD-ROM	Online
Angle Relationships	Skill 25	Activity 25	Diagnose and Prescribe Online
Classify Real Numbers	Skill 17	Activity 17	
Points, Lines, and Planes	Skill 22	Activity 22	
Solve One-Step Equations	Skill 68	Activity 68	

***Are You Ready? Enrichment*, Chapter 2**

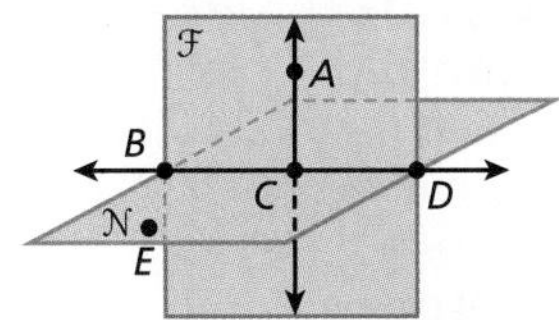

Worksheets

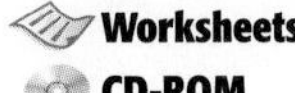
CD-ROM

Online

Organizer

Objective: Help students organize the new concepts they will learn in Chapter 2.

Online Edition
Multilingual Glossary

Resources

Teacher One Stop™
PuzzleView

***Multilingual Glossary* Online**
go.hrw.com
KEYWORD: MG7 Glossary

Answers to *Vocabulary Connections*

1. Possible answer: a number that is not positive, such as −3
2. Possible answer: a general conclusion
3. Possible answer: You start with general principles to get to a specific conclusion.
4. Possible answer: *Polygon* might mean "a figure with many ∠s."

Study Guide: Preview

Where You've Been

Previously, you

- studied relationships among points, lines, and planes.
- identified congruent segments and angles.
- examined angle relationships.
- used geometric formulas for perimeter and area.

In This Chapter

You will study

- inductive and deductive reasoning.
- using conditional statements and biconditional statements.
- justifying solutions to algebraic equations.
- writing two-column, flowchart, and paragraph proofs.

Where You're Going

You can use the skills learned in this chapter

- when you write proofs in geometry, algebra, and advanced math courses.
- when you use logical reasoning to draw conclusions in science and social studies courses.
- when you assess the validity of arguments in politics and advertising.

Key Vocabulary/Vocabulario

conjecture	conjetura
counterexample	contraejemplo
deductive reasoning	razonamiento deductivo
inductive reasoning	razonamiento inductivo
polygon	polígono
proof	demostración
quadrilateral	cuadrilátero
theorem	teorema
triangle	triángulo

Vocabulary Connections

To become familiar with some of the vocabulary terms in the chapter, consider the following. You may refer to the chapter, the glossary, or a dictionary if you like.

1. The word **counterexample** is made up of two words: *counter* and *example*. In this case, *counter* is related to the Spanish word *contra*, meaning "against." What is a counterexample to the statement "All numbers are positive"?
2. The root of the word **inductive** is *ducere*, which means "to lead." When you are inducted into a club, you are "led into" membership. When you use inductive reasoning in math, you start with specific examples. What do you think inductive reasoning leads you to?
3. The word **deductive** comes from *de*, which means "down from," and *ducere*, the same root as *inductive*. What do you think the phrase "lead down from" would mean when applied to reasoning in math?
4. In Greek, the word *poly* means "many," and the word *gon* means "angle." How can you use these meanings to understand the term **polygon**?

Reading Strategy: Read and Interpret a Diagram

A diagram is an informational tool. To correctly read a diagram, you must know what you can and cannot assume based on what you see in it.

What You CAN Assume	What You CANNOT Assume
✔ Collinear points	✘ Measures of segments
✔ Betweenness of points	✘ Measures of angles
✔ Coplanar points	✘ Congruent segments
✔ Straight angles and lines	✘ Congruent angles
✔ Adjacent angles	✘ Right angles
✔ Linear pairs of angles	
✔ Vertical angles	

If a diagram includes labeled information, such as an angle measure or a right angle mark, treat this information as given.

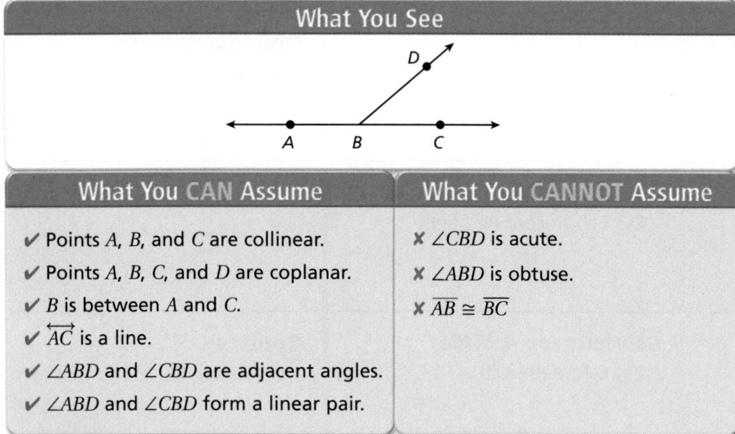

What You CAN Assume	What You CANNOT Assume
✔ Points A, B, and C are collinear.	✘ $\angle CBD$ is acute.
✔ Points A, B, C, and D are coplanar.	✘ $\angle ABD$ is obtuse.
✔ B is between A and C.	✘ $\overline{AB} \cong \overline{BC}$
✔ $\overleftrightarrow{AC}$ is a line.	
✔ $\angle ABD$ and $\angle CBD$ are adjacent angles.	
✔ $\angle ABD$ and $\angle CBD$ form a linear pair.	

Try This

List what you can and cannot assume from each diagram.

1.

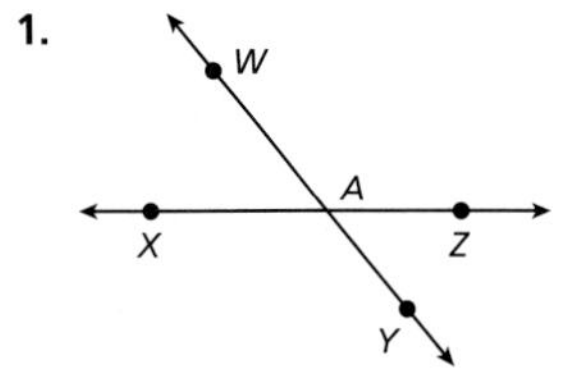

2.

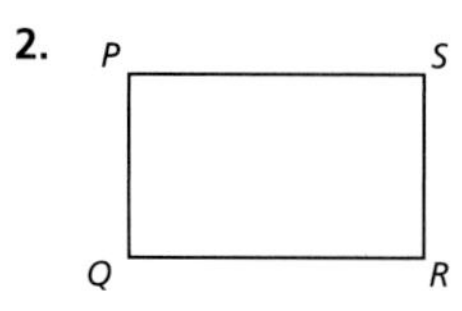

Reading and Writing Math CHAPTER 2

Organizer

Objective: Help students apply strategies to understand and retain key concepts.

Resources

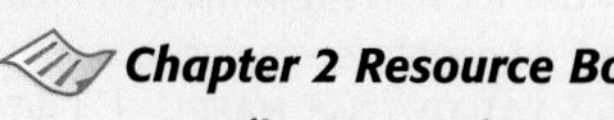

Reading Strategies

ENGLISH LANGUAGE LEARNERS

Reading Strategy: Read and Interpret a Diagram

Discuss Emphasize to students that knowing what they can and cannot assume from a diagram will be essential to their success in writing proofs and in solving problems throughout the course.

Extend As students work through Chapter 2, have them discuss what can be assumed from the diagrams. Ask them to list this information in their journals and to refer to the list when writing proofs.

Answers to *Try This*

1, 2. See p. A11.

Reading Connection

Euclid's Window
by Leonard Mlodinow

The author's thesis is that the great revolutions in mathematics from Pythagoras to Stephen Hawking could not have occurred without Euclid and his invention and formalization of the system of geometric proof. Part I of this book details the historical events leading to Euclid's development of the method of deductive reasoning through the application of axioms and theorems.

Activity Have students research Euclid's five "common notions" (e.g., #2: "If equals are added to equals, then the wholes are equals") and restate and name each notion using modern terminology (#2 is the Addition Property of Equality).

SECTION **2A**

Inductive and Deductive Reasoning

One-Minute Section Planner

Lesson	Lab Resources	Materials
Lesson 2-1 Using Inductive Reasoning to Make Conjectures • Use inductive reasoning to identify patterns and make conjectures. • Find counterexamples to disprove conjectures. ☑ SAT-10 ☑ NAEP ☐ ACT ☑ SAT ☐ SAT Subject Tests		**Optional** toothpicks, science textbook, magazine
Lesson 2-2 Conditional Statements • Identify, write, and analyze the truth value of conditional statements. • Write the inverse, converse, and contrapositive of a conditional statement. ☐ SAT-10 ☑ NAEP ☐ ACT ☐ SAT ☐ SAT Subject Tests	***Geometry Lab Activities*** 2-2 Geometry Lab	**Optional** magazine or newspaper advertisements
Lesson 2-3 Using Deductive Reasoning to Verify Conjectures • Apply the Law of Detachment and the Law of Syllogism in logical reasoning. ☑ SAT-10 ☑ NAEP ☐ ACT ☑ SAT ☐ SAT Subject Tests		**Optional** globe
2-3 Geometry Lab Solve Logic Puzzles • Use tables to solve logic puzzles. • Use networks to solve logic puzzles. ☐ SAT-10 ☐ NAEP ☐ ACT ☐ SAT ☐ SAT Subject Tests	***Geometry Lab Activities*** 2-3 Lab Recording Sheet	
Lesson 2-4 Biconditional Statements and Definitions • Write and analyze biconditional statements. ☐ SAT-10 ☑ NAEP ☐ ACT ☐ SAT ☐ SAT Subject Tests	***Geometry Lab Activities*** 2-4 Geometry Lab	**Optional** dictionary, reversible vest or jacket

MK = *Manipulatives Kit*

Math Background

Professional Learning

INDUCTIVE REASONING

Lesson 2-1

Inductive reasoning is the process of concluding that a general rule or principle is true because specific cases of the rule are true. For example, suppose that you observe 50 bees and notice that all of them have two pairs of wings. When you then conclude that *all* bees have two pairs of wings, you are using inductive reasoning.

Students should understand the role of inductive reasoning in mathematics and they should use inductive reasoning often to develop geometric intuition. They should know that mathematical principles are frequently discovered via inductive reasoning. For example, drawing a wide variety of triangles and constructing the medians to each side will show that the medians are concurrent in every triangle. This naturally leads to the conjecture that the medians of any triangle are concurrent.

However, it is equally essential for students to recognize that inductive reasoning never constitutes a proof of a conjecture. In the example above, no matter how many triangles are checked, it is logically possible (until shown otherwise through deductive reasoning) that there is one elusive triangle for which the conjecture does not hold.

DEDUCTIVE REASONING

Lesson 2-3

Deductive reasoning is the process of using logic to draw conclusions from established facts. A *deduction* is a sequence of statements in which each statement can be logically derived from the preceding one. The question of how to logically support the first statement, which has no predecessor, illustrates the necessity of postulates (statements accepted as true without proof).

A deductive argument, then, begins with a set of statements, or *premises*, known or assumed to be true. Given the premises, it may be possible to draw a conclusion by using logical reasoning:

Premises: Insects are animals.
Bees are insects.

Conclusion: Bees are animals.

An argument is defined to be *logically sound* when all of the premises are true and when the line of reasoning is valid, as in the preceding example. Some additional examples make it clear why both truth *and* validity are required elements of a sound argument.

In the following situation, the premises are true but the reasoning is invalid:

Premises: Insects are animals.
Reptiles are animals.

Conclusion: Reptiles are insects.

The next example illustrates a situation in which the reasoning is valid but one of the premises is false:

Premises: Insects are reptiles.
Bees are insects.

Conclusion: Bees are reptiles.

Thus, for a logical argument to be considered a correct mathematical proof, it must be a sound argument; that is, it must be based on *both* true premises *and* on valid reasoning.

BICONDITIONAL STATEMENTS

Lesson 2-4

The biconditional statement "p if and only if q" connects the statements p and q by asserting that either both statements are true or both statements are false. Biconditional statements are sometimes written in the form "p is necessary and sufficient for q."

Students generally need to see many examples to appreciate the logical subtleties of *if* versus *if and only if*. It may be helpful to begin with nonmathematical examples. Consider the following.

- Paul will go to the movies tomorrow if it rains.
- Paul will go to the movies tomorrow if and only if it rains.

Based on the first statement, you can say that if it rains tomorrow, Paul will go the movies. However, the statement gives no information about Paul's plans if it is sunny—he may go to the movies anyway. The second statement says that Paul will go to the movies if it rains and that this is the *only* situation in which he will go to the movies.

2-1 Organizer

Pacing: Traditional $\frac{1}{2}$ day
Block $\frac{1}{4}$ day

Objectives: Use inductive reasoning to identify patterns and make conjectures.

Find counterexamples to disprove conjectures.

Online Edition
Tutorial Videos

Countdown Week 3

Power Presentations with PowerPoint®

Warm Up

Complete each sentence.

1. __?__ points are points that lie on the same line. Collinear
2. __?__ points are points that lie in the same plane. Coplanar
3. The sum of the measures of two __?__ angles is 90°. complementary

Also available on transparency

Math Fact !!!

Some patterns have more than one correct rule. For example, the pattern 1, 2, 4, ... can be extended with 8 (by multiplying each term by 2) or 7 (by adding consecutive numbers to each term).

State Resources

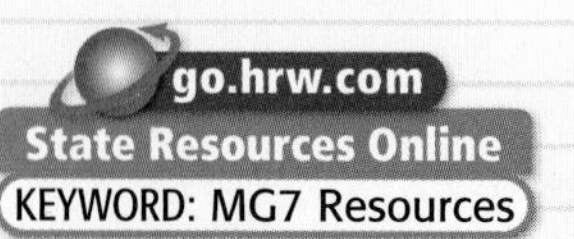

State Resources Online
KEYWORD: MG7 Resources

2-1 Using Inductive Reasoning to Make Conjectures

Objectives
Use inductive reasoning to identify patterns and make conjectures.

Find counterexamples to disprove conjectures.

Vocabulary
inductive reasoning
conjecture
counterexample

Who uses this?
Biologists use inductive reasoning to develop theories about migration patterns.

Biologists studying the migration patterns of California gray whales developed two theories about the whales' route across Monterey Bay. The whales either swam directly across the bay or followed the shoreline.

EXAMPLE 1 Identifying a Pattern

Find the next item in each pattern.

A **Monday, Wednesday, Friday, ...**
Alternating days of the week make up the pattern.
The next day is Sunday.

B **3, 6, 9, 12, 15, ...**
Multiples of 3 make up the pattern. The next multiple is 18.

C ←, ↖, ↑, ...
In this pattern, the figure rotates 45° clockwise each time.
The next figure is ↗.

1. Find the next item in the pattern 0.4, 0.04, 0.004, ... **0.0004**

When several examples form a pattern and you assume the pattern will continue, you are applying *inductive reasoning*. **Inductive reasoning** is the process of reasoning that a rule or statement is true because specific cases are true. You may use inductive reasoning to draw a conclusion from a pattern. A statement you believe to be true based on inductive reasoning is called a **conjecture**.

EXAMPLE 2 Making a Conjecture

Complete each conjecture.

A **The product of an even number and an odd number is __?__.**
List some examples and look for a pattern.
$(2)(3) = 6 \quad (2)(5) = 10 \quad (4)(3) = 12 \quad (4)(5) = 20$
The product of an even number and an odd number is even.

1 Introduce

EXPLORATION

2-1 Using Inductive Reasoning to Make Conjectures

The figure shows a pattern of squares made from toothpicks. Use the figure to complete the following.

1 × 1 2 × 2 3 × 3 4 × 4

1. Count the number of toothpicks that are needed to make the 1 × 1 square, the 2 × 2 square, the 3 × 3 square, and the 4 × 4 square.
2. Record your results in the table.

Size of Square	1 × 1	2 × 2	3 × 3	4 × 4	5 × 5	...	$n \times n$
Toothpicks							

3. Look for a pattern. Predict the number of toothpicks that are needed to make a 5 × 5 square. Record this value in the table.

Motivate

Ask students to describe a science experiment in which they collected data and formed a hypothesis based on their data. Explain that this kind of reasoning, in which generalizations are based on examples, is called *inductive reasoning*.

Explorations and answers are provided in *Alternate Openers: Explorations Transparencies.*

Complete each conjecture.

B **The number of segments formed by n collinear points is ___?___.**

Draw a segment. Mark points on the segment, and count the number of individual segments formed. Be sure to include overlapping segments.

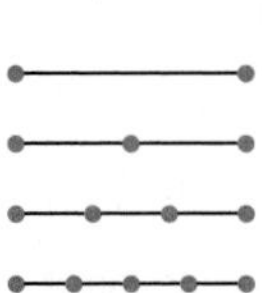

Points	Segments
2	1
3	$2 + 1 = 3$
4	$3 + 2 + 1 = 6$
5	$4 + 3 + 2 + 1 = 10$

The number of segments formed by n collinear points is the sum of the whole numbers less than n.

2. Complete the conjecture: The product of two odd numbers is ___?___. odd

EXAMPLE 3 ***Biology Application***

To learn about the migration behavior of California gray whales, biologists observed whales along two routes. For seven days they counted the numbers of whales seen along each route. Make a conjecture based on the data.

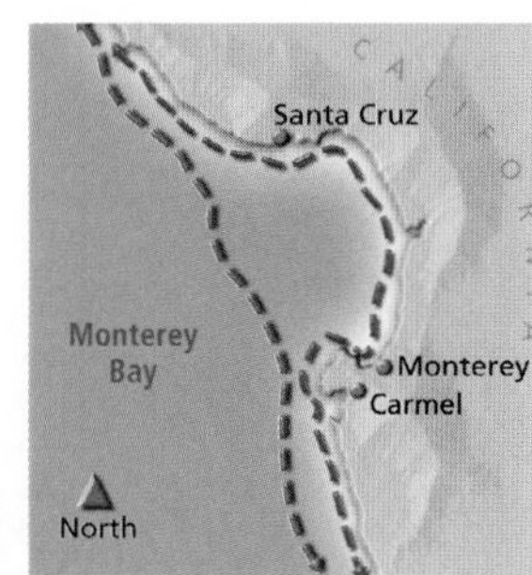

Numbers of Whales Each Day							
Direct Route	1	3	0	2	1	1	0
Shore Route	7	9	5	8	8	6	7

More whales were seen along the shore route each day. The data supports the conjecture that most California gray whales migrate along the shoreline.

3. Make a conjecture about the lengths of male and female whales based on the data.

Female whales are longer than male whales.

Average Whale Lengths						
Length of Female (ft)	49	51	50	48	51	47
Length of Male (ft)	47	45	44	46	48	48

To show that a conjecture is always true, you must prove it. To show that a conjecture is false, you have to find only one example in which the conjecture is not true. This case is called a **counterexample**. A counterexample can be a drawing, a statement, or a number.

Inductive Reasoning
1. Look for a pattern
2. Make a conjecture.
3. Prove the conjecture or find a counterexample.

COMMON ERROR ALERT

When testing conjectures about numbers, students may fail to find a counterexample because they try only the same type of number. Remind students to try various types of numbers, such as whole numbers and fractions, positive numbers, negative numbers, and zero.

Power Presentations with PowerPoint®

Additional Examples

Example 1

Find the next item in each pattern.

A. January, March, May, ... July

B. 7, 14, 21, 28, ... 35

C.  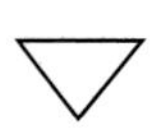 

Example 2

Complete each conjecture.

A. The sum of two positive numbers is ___?___. positive

B. The number of lines formed by 4 points, no three of which are collinear, is ___?___. 6

Example 3

The cloud of water leaving a whale's blowhole when it exhales is called its *blow*. A biologist observed blue-whale blows of 25 ft, 29 ft, 27 ft, and 24 ft. Another biologist recorded humpback-whale blows of 8 ft, 7 ft, 8 ft, and 9 ft. Make a conjecture based on the data. The height of a blue whale's blow is greater than a humpback whale's.

2 Teach

Guided Instruction

Many of the examples and exercises in this lesson use the vocabulary learned in Chapter 1. Review terms such as *collinear* and *coplanar,* the different types of angles, linear pairs of angles, and *complementary* and *supplementary* angles.

Teaching Tip **Science** You may want to use a science textbook so you can review the steps of the scientific method. Relate the lesson to students' experiences doing experiments in their science classes.

Reaching All Learners

Through Cooperative Learning

Have students work in small groups. The first student writes a number or draws a shape. The next student writes or draws a second item, beginning a pattern. Have them continue until each student has contributed to the pattern. Then ask the first student to describe a rule for the pattern. Have the groups repeat this activity until each student has gone first.

INTERVENTION

Questioning Strategies

EXAMPLE 1

- Do you have to find a general rule to find the next item in a pattern?

EXAMPLE 2

- How many examples do you need to look at to complete a conjecture? Explain.

EXAMPLE 3

- How do you read the data to find what conjecture is supported?

Power Presentations with PowerPoint®

Additional Examples

Example 4

Show that each conjecture is false by finding a counterexample. Possible answers:

A. For every integer n, n^3 is positive. $n = -3$

B. Two complementary angles are not congruent. 45° and 45°

C. Based on the data in **Example 4C,** the monthly high temperature in Abilene is never below 90°F for two months in a row. Jan–Feb

INTERVENTION

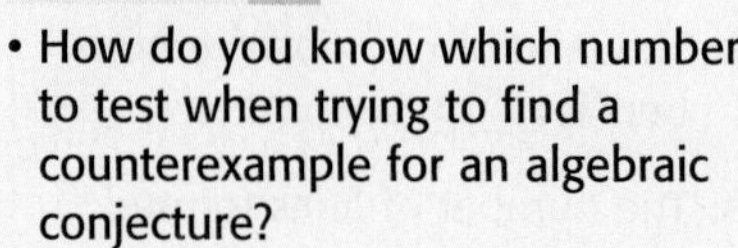

Questioning Strategies

EXAMPLE 4

- How do you know which numbers to test when trying to find a counterexample for an algebraic conjecture?

EXAMPLE 4 **Finding a Counterexample**

Show that each conjecture is false by finding a counterexample.

A For all positive numbers n, $\frac{1}{n} \leq n$.

Pick positive values for n and substitute them into the equation to see if the conjecture holds.

Let $n = 1$. Since $\frac{1}{n} = 1$ and $1 \leq 1$, the conjecture holds.

Let $n = 2$. Since $\frac{1}{n} = \frac{1}{2}$ and $\frac{1}{2} \leq 2$, the conjecture holds.

Let $n = \frac{1}{2}$. Since $\frac{1}{n} = \frac{1}{\frac{1}{2}} = 2$ and $2 \not\leq \frac{1}{2}$, the conjecture is false.

$n = \frac{1}{2}$ is a counterexample.

B For any three points in a plane, there are three different lines that contain two of the points.

Draw three collinear points.

If the three points are collinear, the conjecture is false.

C The temperature in Abilene, Texas, never exceeds 100°F during the spring months (March, April, and May).

Monthly High Temperatures (°F) in Abilene, Texas

Jan	Feb	Mar	Apr	May	Jun	Jul	Aug	Sep	Oct	Nov	Dec
88	89	97	99	107	109	110	107	106	103	92	89

The temperature in May was 107°F, so the conjecture is false.

Show that each conjecture is false by finding a counterexample.

4a. For any real number x, $x^2 \geq x$. Possible answer: $x = \frac{1}{2}$

4b. Supplementary angles are adjacent.

4c. The radius of every planet in the solar system is less than 50,000 km. Jupiter or Saturn

4b. Possible answer:

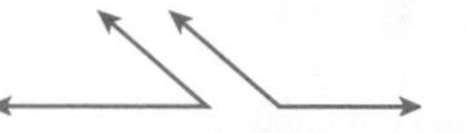

Planets' Diameters (km)

Mercury	Venus	Earth	Mars	Jupiter	Saturn	Uranus	Neptune
4880	12,100	12,800	6790	143,000	121,000	51,100	49,500

THINK AND DISCUSS

1. Can you prove a conjecture by giving one example in which the conjecture is true? Explain your reasoning.

2. GET ORGANIZED Copy and complete the graphic organizer. In each box, describe the steps of the inductive reasoning process.

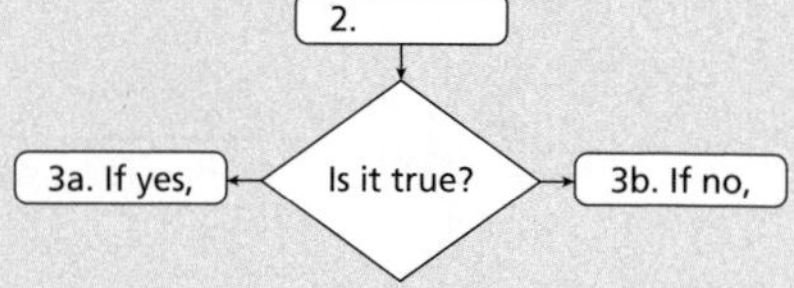

3 Close

Summarize

Review with students the three steps of the inductive reasoning process:

- Look for a pattern.
- Make a conjecture.
- Prove the conjecture or find a counterexample.

Explain to students that they will learn to prove a conjecture later in the chapter.

ONGOING ASSESSMENT and INTERVENTION

Diagnose **Before** the Lesson
2-1 Warm Up, TE p. 74

Monitor **During** the Lesson
Check It Out! Exercises, SE pp. 74–76
Questioning Strategies, TE pp. 75–76

Assess **After** the Lesson
2-1 Lesson Quiz, TE p. 79
Alternative Assessment, TE p. 79

Answers to *Think and Discuss*

1. No; possible answer: a conjecture cannot be proven true just by giving examples, no matter how many.
2. See p. A2.

2-1 Exercises

go.hrw.com
Homework Help Online
KEYWORD: MG7 2-1
Parent Resources Online
KEYWORD: MG7 Parent

GUIDED PRACTICE

1. **Vocabulary** Explain why a *conjecture* may be true or false.

SEE EXAMPLE 1 p. 74

Find the next item in each pattern.

2. March, May, July, ... September
3. $\frac{1}{3}, \frac{2}{4}, \frac{3}{5}, \ldots$ $\frac{4}{6}$
4. ...

SEE EXAMPLE 2 p. 74

Complete each conjecture.

5. The product of two even numbers is _?_. even
6. A rule in terms of n for the sum of the first n odd positive integers is _?_. n^2

SEE EXAMPLE 3 p. 75

7. **Biology** A laboratory culture contains 150 bacteria. After twenty minutes, the culture contains 300 bacteria. After one hour, the culture contains 1200 bacteria. Make a conjecture about the rate at which the bacteria increases. The number of bacteria doubles every 20 minutes.

SEE EXAMPLE 4 p. 76

Show that each conjecture is false by finding a counterexample.

8. Kennedy is the youngest U.S. president to be inaugurated. Roosevelt was inaugurated at age 42.
9. Three points on a plane always form a triangle.
10. For any real number x, if $x^2 \geq 1$, then $x \geq 1$. Possible answer: $x = -3$

President	Age at Inauguration
Washington	57
T. Roosevelt	42
Truman	60
Kennedy	43
Clinton	46

9. The 3 pts. are collinear.

PRACTICE AND PROBLEM SOLVING

Independent Practice	
For Exercises	See Example
11–13	1
14–15	2
16	3
17–19	4

Extra Practice
Skills Practice p. S6
Application Practice p. S29

Find the next item in each pattern.

11. 8 A.M., 11 A.M., 2 P.M., ... 5 P.M.
12. 75, 64, 53, ... 42
13. △, □, ⬠, ...

Complete each conjecture.

14. A rule in terms of n for the sum of the first n even positive integers is _?_. $n(n + 1)$
15. The number of nonoverlapping segments formed by n collinear points is _?_. $n - 1$
16. **Industrial Arts** About 5% of the students at Lincoln High School usually participate in the robotics competition. There are 526 students in the school this year. Make a conjecture about the number of students who will participate in the robotics competition this year. About 26 students will participate.

Show that each conjecture is false by finding a counterexample.

17. If $1 - y > 0$, then $0 < y < 1$. Possible answer: $y = -1$
18. For any real number x, $x^3 \geq x^2$. Possible answer: $x = -1$
19. Every pair of supplementary angles includes one obtuse angle. $m\angle 1 = m\angle 2 = 90°$

Make a conjecture about each pattern. Write the next two items.

20. 2, 4, 16, ...
21. $\frac{1}{2}, \frac{1}{4}, \frac{1}{8}, \ldots$
22. −3, 6, −9, 12, ...
23. Draw a square of dots. Make a conjecture about the number of dots needed to increase the size of the square from $n \times n$ to $(n + 1) \times (n + 1)$. $2n + 1$

20. Each term is the square of the previous term; 256, 65,536.
21. Possible answer: each term is the previous term multiplied by $\frac{1}{2}$; $\frac{1}{16}, \frac{1}{32}$.
22. The terms are multiples of 3 with alternating signs; −15, 18.

2-1 Exercises

Assignment Guide

Assign *Guided Practice* exercises as necessary.

If you finished Examples 1–2
Basic 11–15, 20–22, 31–33
Average 11–15, 20–22, 28–33, 41
Advanced 11–15, 20–23, 28–33, 41–43

If you finished Examples 1–4
Basic 11–27, 31–33, 36–39, 44–53
Average 11–22, 24–29, 31, 32, 34–40, 44–53
Advanced 12, 14, 16, 18, 20–53

Homework Quick Check
Quickly check key concepts.
Exercises: 12, 14, 16, 18, 24, 26, 32

Teaching Tip **Communicating Math** For **Exercises 11–13,** have students describe each pattern in words.

Answers

1. Possible answer: A conjecture is based on observation and is not true until proven true in every case.

State Resources

go.hrw.com
State Resources Online
KEYWORD: MG7 Resources

Teaching Tip

Reading Math In **Exercise 34,** some students may have trouble understanding the information given in the text and the table. Explain the concept of "turnaround date" and how this relates to the numbers in the table.

ENGLISH LANGUAGE LEARNERS

MULTI-STEP TEST PREP **Exercise 36** involves interpreting text from *Alice's Adventures in Wonderland* and translating these words into a mathematical pattern. This exercise prepares students for the Multi-Step Test Prep on page 102.

Answers

26. Possible answer:

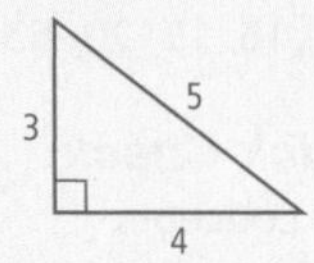

3
5
4

29. $\frac{1}{11} = 0.\overline{09}$, $\frac{2}{11} = 0.\overline{18}$, $\frac{3}{11} = 0.\overline{27}$, ...; the fraction pattern is multiples of $\frac{1}{11}$, and the decimal pattern is repeating multiples of 0.09.

30. $6 = 3 + 3$; $8 = 5 + 3$; $10 = 5 + 5$; $12 = 7 + 5$; $14 = 7 + 7$

31. 34, 55, 89; each term is the sum of the 2 previous terms.

32. The middle number is the mean of the other 2 numbers.

35. Possible answer: Even numbers are divisible by 2, but odd numbers are not. So the conjecture, while true for even numbers, does not necessarily hold true for all numbers.

Determine if each conjecture is true. If not, write or draw a counterexample.

24. Points X, Y, and Z are coplanar. **T**

25. If n is an integer, then $-n$ is positive. **F; possible answer: $n = 2$**

26. In a triangle with one right angle, two of the sides are congruent. **F**

27. If $\overrightarrow{BD}$ bisects $\angle ABC$, then $m\angle ABD = m\angle CBD$. **T**

28. **Estimation** The Westside High School band is selling coupon books to raise money for a trip. The table shows the amount of money raised for the first four days of the sale. If the pattern continues, estimate the amount of money raised during the sixth day. **about $400**

Day	Money Raised ($)
1	146.25
2	195.75
3	246.25
4	295.50

29. Write each fraction in the pattern $\frac{1}{11}, \frac{2}{11}, \frac{3}{11}, \ldots$ as a repeating decimal. Then write a description of the fraction pattern and the resulting decimal pattern.

LINK Math History

Goldbach first stated his conjecture in a letter to Leonhard Euler in 1742. Euler, a Swiss mathematician who published over 800 papers, replied, "I consider [the conjecture] a theorem which is quite true, although I cannot demonstrate it."

30. **Math History** Remember that a prime number is a whole number greater than 1 that has exactly two factors, itself and 1. Goldbach's conjecture states that every even number greater than 2 can be written as the sum of two primes. For example, $4 = 2 + 2$. Write the next five even numbers as the sum of two primes.

31. The pattern 1, 1, 2, 3, 5, 8, 13, 21, ... is known as the *Fibonacci sequence.* Find the next three terms in the sequence and write a conjecture for the pattern.

32. Look at a monthly calendar and pick any three squares in a row—across, down, or diagonal. Make a conjecture about the number in the middle.

12	13	14
19	20	21
26	27	28

33. Make a conjecture about the value of $2n - 1$ when n is an integer. **odd**

34. **Critical Thinking** The turnaround date for migrating gray whales occurs when the number of northbound whales exceeds the number of southbound whales. Make a conjecture about the turnaround date, based on the table below. What factors might affect the validity of your conjecture in the future?

Migration Direction of Gray Whales

	Feb. 16	Feb. 17	Feb. 18	Feb. 19	Feb. 20	Feb. 21	Feb. 22
Southbound	0	2	3	0	1	1	0
Northbound	0	0	2	5	3	2	1

34. **Feb. 19; possible answer: the weather or the whales' health**

35. **Write About It** Explain why a true conjecture about even numbers does not necessarily hold for all numbers. Give an example to support your answer.

MULTI-STEP TEST PREP

36. This problem will prepare you for the Multi-Step Test Prep on page 102.
   a. For how many hours did the Mock Turtle do lessons on the third day? **8**
   b. On what day did the Mock Turtle do 1 hour of lessons? **tenth**

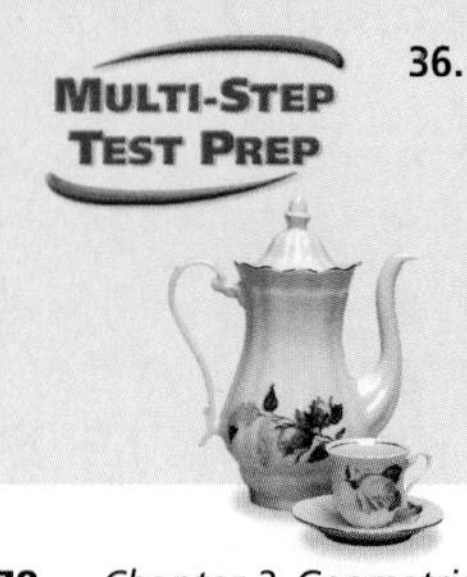

"And how many hours a day did you do lessons?" said Alice, in a hurry to change the subject.

"Ten hours the first day," said the Mock Turtle: "nine the next, and so on."

The Granger Collection, New York

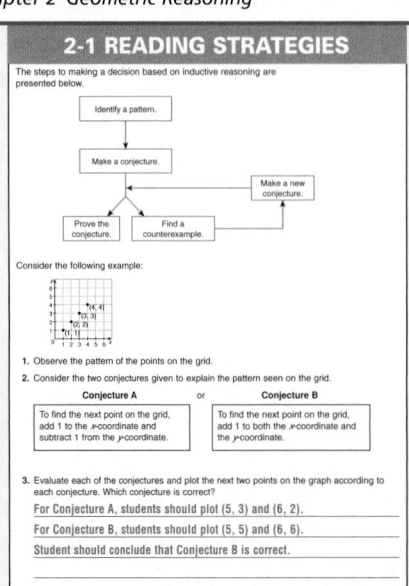

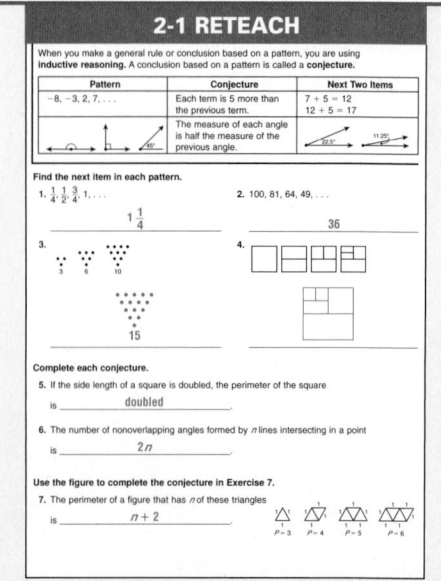

2-1 PRACTICE A
2-1 PRACTICE C
2-1 PRACTICE B

Find the next item in each pattern.

1. 100, 81, 64, 49, . . . **36**

2. 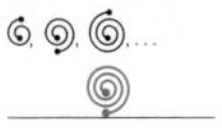

3. Alabama, Alaska, Arizona, . . . **Arkansas**

4. west, south, east, . . . **north**

Complete each conjecture.

5. The square of any negative number is **positive**.

6. The number of segments determined by n points is $\frac{n(n-1)}{2}$.

Show that each conjecture is false by finding a counterexample.

7. For any integer n, $n^3 > 0$.
Possible answers: zero, any negative number

8. Each angle in a right triangle has a different measure.

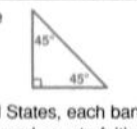

45°
45°

9. For many years in the United States, each bank printed its own currency. The variety of different bills led to widespread counterfeiting. By the time of the Civil War, a significant fraction of the currency in circulation was counterfeit. If one Civil War soldier had 48 bills, 16 of which were counterfeit, and another soldier had 39 bills, 13 of which were counterfeit, make a conjecture about what fraction of bills were counterfeit at the time of the Civil War.
One-third of the bills were counterfeit.

Make a conjecture about each pattern. Write the next two items.

10. 1, 2, 2, 4, 8, 32, . . .
Each item, starting with the third, is the product of the two preceding items; 256, 8192.

11. 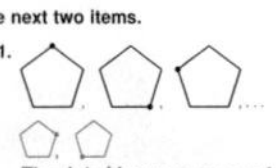
The dot skips over one vertex in a clockwise direction.

2-1 READING STRATEGIES

The steps to making a decision based on inductive reasoning are presented below.

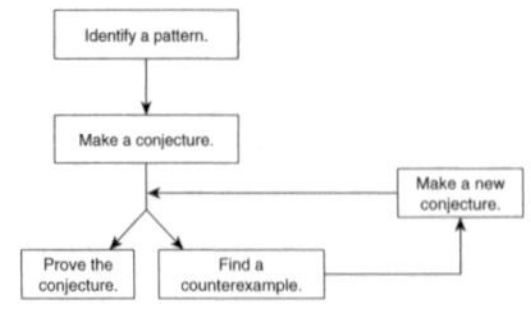

Identify a pattern.
Make a conjecture.
Make a new conjecture.
Prove the conjecture.
Find a counterexample.

Consider the following example:

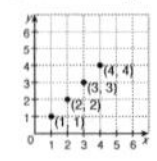

(4, 4)
(3, 3)
(2, 2)
(1, 1)

1. Observe the pattern of the points on the grid.
2. Consider the two conjectures given to explain the pattern seen on the grid.

Conjecture A	or	Conjecture B
To find the next point on the grid, add 1 to the x-coordinate and subtract 1 from the y-coordinate.		To find the next point on the grid, add 1 to both the x-coordinate and the y-coordinate.

3. Evaluate each of the conjectures and plot the next two points on the graph according to each conjecture. Which conjecture is correct?
For Conjecture A, students should plot (5, 3) and (6, 2).
For Conjecture B, students should plot (5, 5) and (6, 6).
Student should conclude that Conjecture B is correct.

2-1 RETEACH

When you make a general rule or conclusion based on a pattern, you are using **inductive reasoning.** A conclusion based on a pattern is called a **conjecture.**

Pattern	Conjecture	Next Two Items
−8, −3, 2, 7, . . .	Each term is 5 more than the previous term.	7 + 5 = 12 12 + 5 = 17
(angles: 180°, 90°, 45°)	The measure of each angle is half the measure of the previous angle.	(angles: 22.5°, 11.25°)

Find the next item in each pattern.

1. $\frac{1}{4}, \frac{1}{2}, \frac{3}{4}, 1, \ldots$ $1\frac{1}{4}$

2. 100, 81, 64, 49, . . . **36**

3. 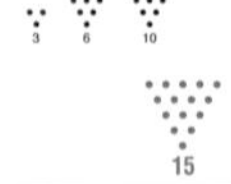

3
6
10
15

4. 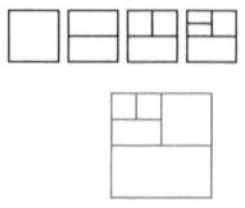

Complete each conjecture.

5. If the side length of a square is doubled, the perimeter of the square is **doubled**.

6. The number of nonoverlapping angles formed by n lines intersecting in a point is $2n$.

Use the figure to complete the conjecture in Exercise 7.

7. The perimeter of a figure that has n of these triangles is $n + 2$.

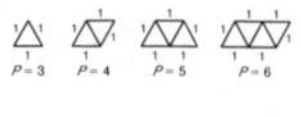

P = 3
P = 4
P = 5
P = 6

TEST PREP

37. Which of the following conjectures is false?
   - (A) If x is odd, then $x + 1$ is even.
   - (B) The sum of two odd numbers is even.
   - **(C)** The difference of two even numbers is positive.
   - (D) If x is positive, then $-x$ is negative.

38. A student conjectures that if x is a prime number, then $x + 1$ is not prime. Which of the following is a counterexample?

   (F) $x = 11$ (G) $x = 6$ (H) $x = 3$ **(J)** $x = 2$

39. The class of 2004 holds a reunion each year. In 2005, 87.5% of the 120 graduates attended. In 2006, 90 students went, and in 2007, 75 students went. About how many students do you predict will go to the reunion in 2010?

   (A) 12 (B) 15 (C) 24 **(D)** 30

CHALLENGE AND EXTEND

40. **Multi-Step** Make a table of values for the rule $x^2 + x + 11$ when x is an integer from 1 to 8. Make a conjecture about the type of number generated by the rule. Continue your table. What value of x generates a counterexample?

41. **Political Science** Presidential elections are held every four years. U.S. senators are elected to 6-year terms, but only $\frac{1}{3}$ of the Senate is up for election every two years. If $\frac{1}{3}$ of the Senate is elected during a presidential election year, how many years must pass before these same senate seats are up for election during another presidential election year? **12 years**

42. **Physical Fitness** Rob is training for the President's Challenge physical fitness program. During his first week of training, Rob does 15 sit-ups each day. He will add 20 sit-ups to his daily routine each week. His goal is to reach 150 sit-ups per day.
   a. Make a table of the number of sit-ups Rob does each week from week 1 through week 10.
   b. During which week will Rob reach his goal?
   c. Write a conjecture for the number of sit-ups Rob does during week n.

43. **Construction** Draw $\overline{AB}$. Then construct point C so that it is not on $\overline{AB}$ and is the same distance from A and B. Construct $\overline{AC}$ and $\overline{BC}$. Compare $m\angle CAB$ and $m\angle CBA$ and compare AC and CB. Make a conjecture.

SPIRAL REVIEW

Determine if the given point is a solution to $y = 3x - 5$. *(Previous course)*

44. $(1, 8)$ **no** 45. $(-2, -11)$ **yes** 46. $(3, 4)$ **yes** 47. $(-3.5, 0.5)$ **no**

Find the perimeter or circumference of each of the following. Leave answers in terms of x. *(Lesson 1-5)*

48. a square whose area is x^2 **$4x$**
49. a rectangle with dimensions x and $4x - 3$ **$10x - 6$**
50. a triangle with side lengths of $x + 2$ **$3x + 6$**
51. a circle whose area is $9\pi x^2$ **$6\pi x$**

A triangle has vertices $(-1, -1)$, $(0, 1)$, and $(4, 0)$. Find the coordinates for the vertices of the image of the triangle after each transformation. *(Lesson 1-7)*

52. $(x, y) \rightarrow (x, y + 2)$
53. $(x, y) \rightarrow (x + 4, y - 1)$

52. $(-1, 1)$, $(0, 3)$, and $(4, 2)$
53. $(3, -2)$, $(4, 0)$, and $(8, -1)$

COMMON ERROR ALERT

If students do not recognize the pattern in **Exercise 31,** give them the hint that for each term they should look at the two previous terms.

TEST PREP DOCTOR In **Exercise 38,** point out to students that the hypothesis "if x is a prime number" eliminates choice **G.** They can use the given values of x in choices **F, H,** and **J** to determine whether $x + 1$ is prime.

Answers

40, 42–43. See p. A11.

Journal

Have students write a conjecture about numbers and then use examples to determine whether it is true.

ALTERNATIVE ASSESSMENT

Have students find a pattern in a magazine and describe it in words. Have students make up one conjecture about numbers that is true and one that is false, giving a counterexample to disprove it.

Power Presentations with PowerPoint®

2-1 Lesson Quiz

Find the next item in each pattern.

1. 0.7, 0.07, 0.007, ... 0.0007
2. 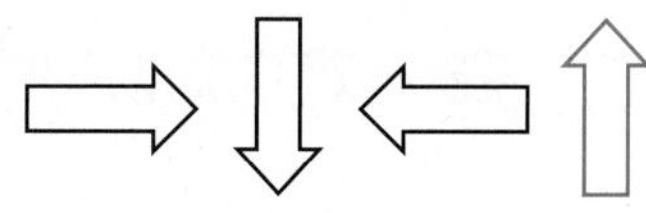

Determine if each conjecture is true. If false, give a counterexample.

3. The quotient of two negative numbers is a positive number. T
4. Every prime number is odd. F; 2
5. Two supplementary angles are not congruent. F; 90° and 90°
6. The square of an odd integer is odd. T

Also available on transparency

2-1 PROBLEM SOLVING

The table shows the lengths of five green iguanas after birth and then after 1 year.

Iguana	Length after Hatching (in.)	Length after 1 Year (in.)
1	10	36
2	9	34
3	11	35
4	12	35
5	10	37

1. Estimate the length of a green iguana after 1 year if it was 8 inches long when it hatched.
   Possible answer: 33 in.
2. Make a conjecture about the average growth of a green iguana during the first year.
   Possible answer: The average growth of a green iguana during the first year is about 2 ft.

The times for the first eight matches of the Santa Barbara Open women's volleyball tournament are shown. Show that each conjecture is false by finding a counterexample.

Match	1	2	3	4	5	6	7	8
Time	0:31	0:56	0:51	0:18	0:50	0:34	1:03	0:36

3. Every one of the first eight matches lasted less than 1 hour.
   Match 7 lasted 1 hour 3 minutes.
4. These matches were all longer than a half hour.
   Match 4 was 18 minutes long.

Choose the best answer.

Sample	Number of Cells		
	Interphase	Prophase	Metaphase
1	86	22	5
2	70	28	3
3	76	32	3
4	91	25	5
5	65	16	4
6	89	34	6

5. The table shows the number of cells present during three phases of mitosis. If a sample contained 80 cells during interphase, which is the best prediction for the number of cells present during prophase?
   A 18 cells **(B)** 24 cells C 40 cells D 80 cells
6. About 75% of the students at Jackson High School volunteer to clean up a half-mile stretch of road every year. If there are 408 students in the school this year, about how many are expected to volunteer for the clean-up?
   F 102 students G 204 students **(H)** 306 students J 333 students
7. Mara earned \$25, \$25, \$20, and \$28 in the last 4 weeks for walking her neighbor's dogs. If her earnings continue in this way, which is the best estimate for her average weekly earnings for next month?
   A \$20.50 B \$23.33 **(C)** \$24.50 D \$25.00

2-1 CHALLENGE

The pattern shown is known as *Pascal's Triangle*.

row 1	1
row 2	1 1
row 3	1 2 1
row 4	1 3 3 1
row 5	1 4 6 4 1
row 6	1 5 10 10 5 1

1. If the pattern is extended, find the terms in row 7.
   1, 6, 15, 20, 15, 6, 1
2. Make a conjecture for the pattern.
   Each row has 1 as the first and last number. Each of the other numbers is found by adding the two numbers that appear just above it.
3. Make a conjecture about the sum of the terms in each row.
   The sum of each row of terms after the first is twice the sum of the terms in the previous row.

Refer to the pattern of figures for Exercises 4 and 5.

Figure 1 Figure 2 Figure 3

4. If the pattern continues, how many black triangles will there be in Figure 4? in Figure 5? 27; 81
5. Write an algebraic expression for the number of black triangles in figure n. 3^{n-1}

Find a counterexample for each statement.

6. For every integer x, $x^2 + 2x - 1$ is divisible by 2. Possible answer: $x = 2$
7. For every integer n, $n^2 + n$ is prime. Possible answer: $n = -2$
8. Make a table of values for the expression $4^a - 1$, where a is a positive integer. Make a conjecture about the type of number that is generated by the rule.

a	$4^a - 1$
1	3
2	15
3	63
4	255
5	1023

Possible answer: All values of $4^a - 1$ are divisible by 3.

Organizer

Pacing:
Traditional $\frac{1}{2}$ day
Block $\frac{1}{4}$ day

Objective: Apply reasoning skills to drawing Venn diagrams of number sets.

Online Edition

Teach

Remember

Students review sets of numbers.

Teaching Tip **Communicating Math** Show students diagrams of two concentric circles, two overlapping circles, and two circles that do not intersect. Have students describe sets of everyday things, such as animals, for each Venn diagram.

Close

Assess

Have students draw a Venn diagram that shows the relationship between integers and rational numbers.

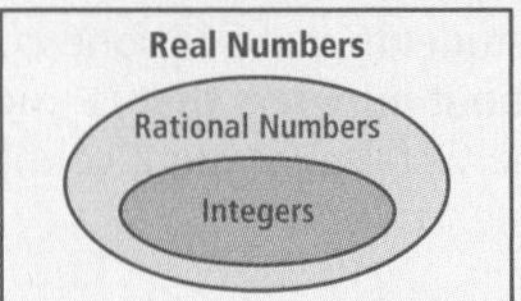

State Resources

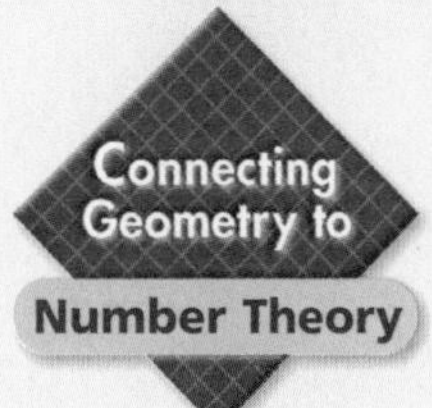

Venn Diagrams

Recall that in a Venn diagram, ovals are used to represent each set. The ovals can overlap if the sets share common elements.

The real number system contains an infinite number of subsets. The following chart shows some of them. Other examples of subsets are even numbers, multiples of 3, and numbers less than 6.

Set	Description	Examples
Natural numbers	The counting numbers	1, 2, 3, 4, 5, …
Whole numbers	The set of natural numbers and 0	0, 1, 2, 3, 4, …
Integers	The set of whole numbers and their opposites	…, −2, −1, 0, 1, 2, …
Rational numbers	The set of numbers that can be written as a ratio of integers	$-\frac{3}{4}$, 5, −2, 0.5, 0
Irrational numbers	The set of numbers that cannot be written as a ratio of integers	$\pi, \sqrt{10}, 8 + \sqrt{2}$

Example

Draw a Venn diagram to show the relationship between the set of even numbers and the set of natural numbers.

The set of even numbers includes all numbers that are divisible by 2. This includes natural numbers such as 2, 4, and 6. But even numbers such as –4 and –10 are not natural numbers.

So the set of even numbers includes some, but not all, elements in the set of natural numbers. Similarly, the set of natural numbers includes some, but not all, even numbers.

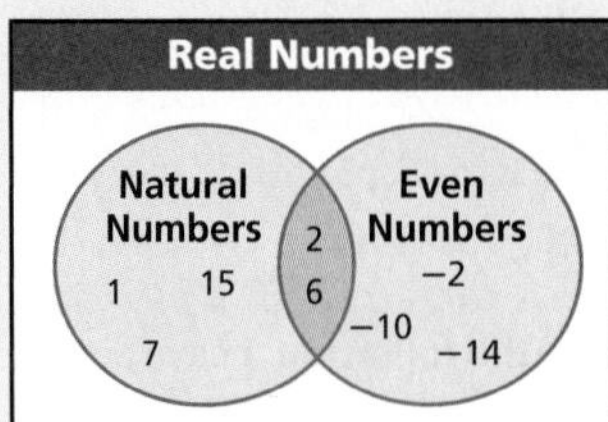

Draw a rectangle to represent all real numbers.

Draw overlapping ovals to represent the sets of even and natural numbers. You may write individual elements in each region.

Try This

Draw a Venn diagram to show the relationship between the given sets.

1. natural numbers, whole numbers
2. odd numbers, whole numbers
3. irrational numbers, integers

Answers to *Try This*

1.

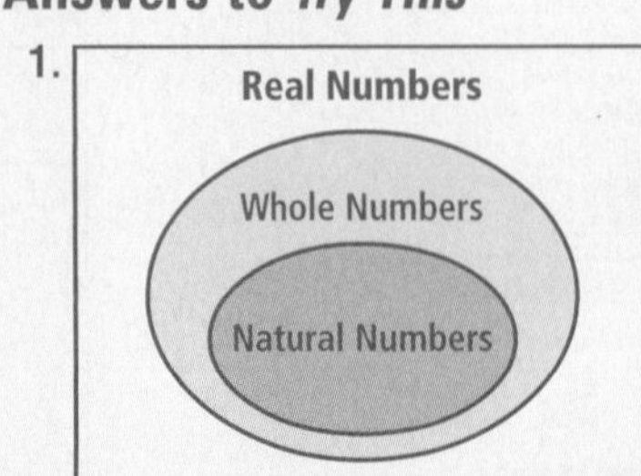

2.

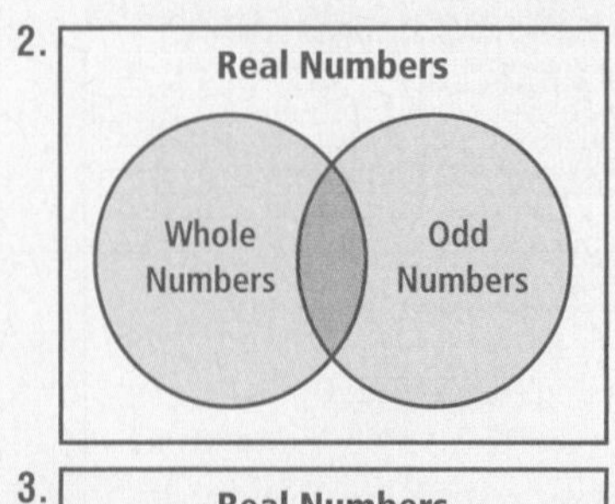

3.

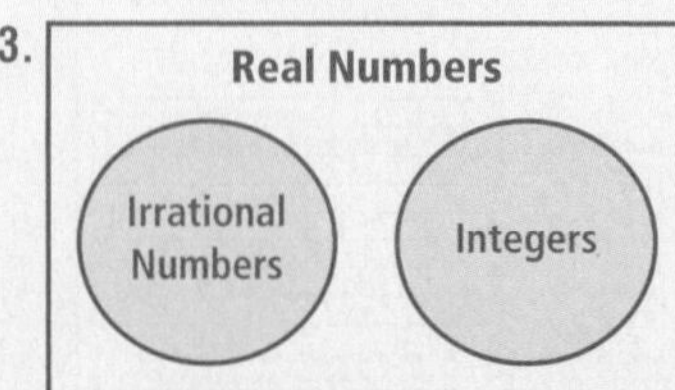

2-2 Conditional Statements

Objectives
Identify, write, and analyze the truth value of conditional statements.

Write the inverse, converse, and contrapositive of a conditional statement.

Vocabulary
conditional statement
hypothesis
conclusion
truth value
negation
converse
inverse
contrapositive
logically equivalent statements

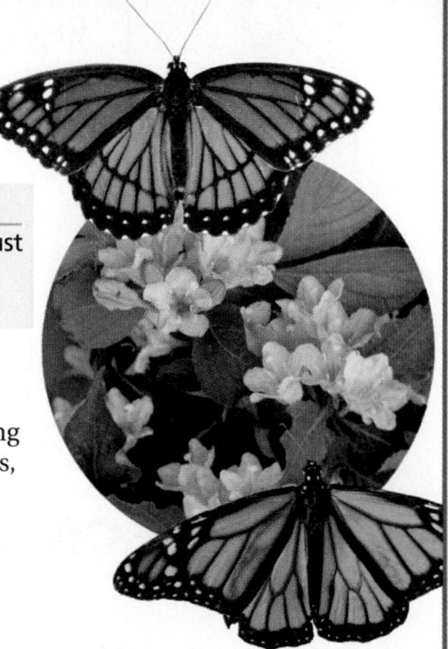

Why learn this?
To identify a species of butterfly, you must know what characteristics one butterfly species has that another does not.

It is thought that the viceroy butterfly mimics the bad-tasting monarch butterfly to avoid being eaten by birds. By comparing the appearance of the two butterfly species, you can make the following conjecture:

If a butterfly has a curved black line on its hind wing, then it is a viceroy.

Know it! Note

Conditional Statements

DEFINITION	SYMBOLS	VENN DIAGRAM
A **conditional statement** is a statement that can be written in the form "if p, then q."		
The **hypothesis** is the part p of a conditional statement following the word *if*.	$p \to q$	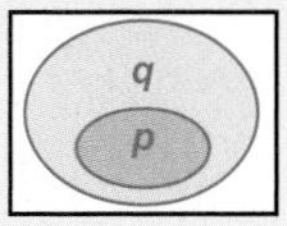 (Venn diagram: circle p inside circle q)
The **conclusion** is the part q of a conditional statement following the word *then*.		

By phrasing a conjecture as an if-then statement, you can quickly identify its hypothesis and conclusion.

Writing Math
"If p, then q" can also be written as "if p, q," "q, if p," "p implies q," and "p only if q."

EXAMPLE 1 Identifying the Parts of a Conditional Statement

Identify the hypothesis and conclusion of each conditional.

A **If a butterfly has a curved black line on its hind wing, then it is a viceroy.**
Hypothesis: A butterfly has a curved black line on its hind wing.
Conclusion: The butterfly is a Viceroy.

B **A number is an integer if it is a natural number.**
Hypothesis: A number is a natural number.
Conclusion: The number is an integer.

1. Identify the hypothesis and conclusion of the statement "A number is divisible by 3 if it is divisible by 6."

Many sentences without the words *if* and *then* can be written as conditionals. To do so, identify the sentence's hypothesis and conclusion by figuring out which part of the statement depends on the other.

2-2 Organizer

Pacing: Traditional 1 day
Block $\frac{1}{2}$ day

Objectives: Identify, write, and analyze the truth value of conditional statements.

Write the inverse, converse, and contrapositive of a conditional statement.

Geometry Lab
In *Geometry Lab Activities*

Online Edition
Tutorial Videos, Interactivity

Countdown Week 3

Power Presentations with PowerPoint®

Warm Up

Determine if each statement is true or false.

1. The measure of an obtuse angle is less than 90°. F
2. All perfect-square numbers are positive. T
3. Every prime number is odd. F
4. Any three points are coplanar. T

Also available on transparency

Math Humor

Teacher: Which month has 28 days?
Student: All of them!

1 Introduce

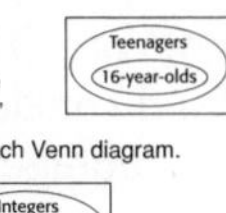

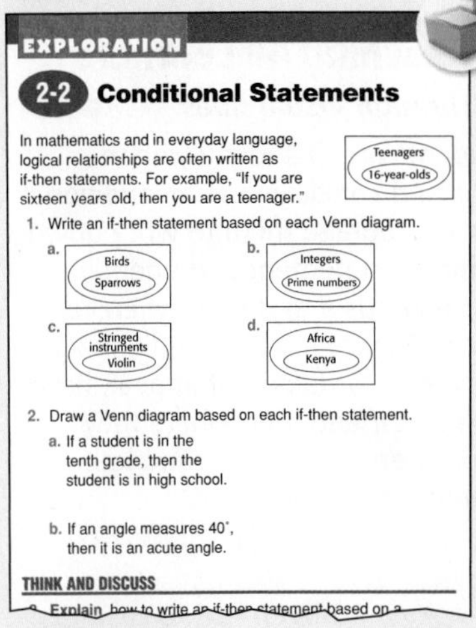

EXPLORATION

2-2 Conditional Statements

In mathematics and in everyday language, logical relationships are often written as if-then statements. For example, "If you are sixteen years old, then you are a teenager."

(Venn diagram: Teenagers, 16-year-olds)

1. Write an if-then statement based on each Venn diagram.
   a. Birds / Sparrows
   b. Integers / Prime numbers
   c. Stringed instruments / Violin
   d. Africa / Kenya
2. Draw a Venn diagram based on each if-then statement.
   a. If a student is in the tenth grade, then the student is in high school.
   b. If an angle measures 40°, then it is an acute angle.

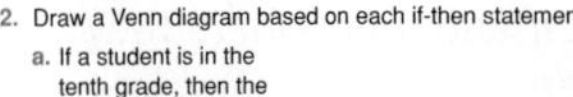

THINK AND DISCUSS

Motivate

Have students bring in advertisements that promise certain results if you buy a particular product. Ask students to restate the advertising claims in the form "If..., then...." Explain to students that statements of this form are called *conditional statements.*

Explorations and answers are provided in *Alternate Openers: Explorations Transparencies.*

State Resources

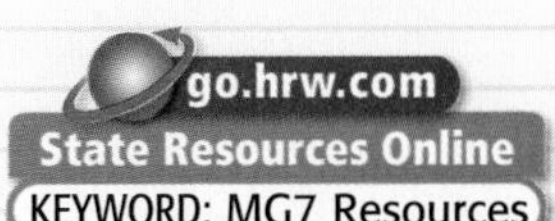

Power Presentations with PowerPoint®

Additional Examples

Example 1

Identify the hypothesis and conclusion of each conditional.

A. If today is Thanksgiving Day, then today is Thursday.

B. A number is a rational number if it is an integer.

Example 2

Write a conditional statement from each of the following.

A. An obtuse triangle has exactly one obtuse angle. If a triangle is obtuse, then it has exactly one obtuse angle.

B.

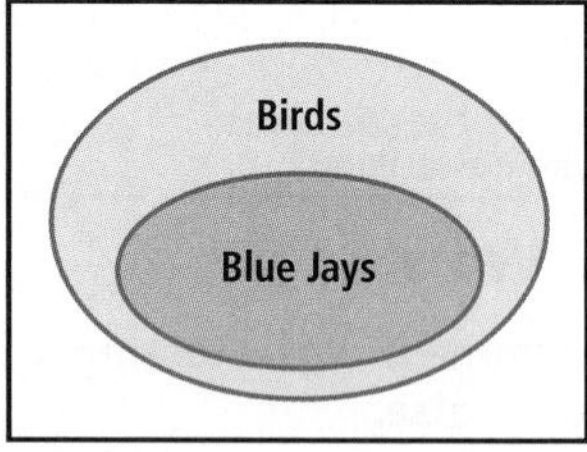

If an animal is a blue jay, then it is a bird.

INTERVENTION

Questioning Strategies

EXAMPLE 1

- When the word *then* does not appear in a conditional statement, how can you tell which part is the conclusion?

EXAMPLE 2

- If the information is given in a Venn diagram, how can you identify the hypothesis and conclusion?

Multiple Representations Have students draw Venn diagrams to represent the written conditional statements in **Examples 1** and **2**.

Critical Thinking Explain to students how to find the negation of statements containing the words *all, some,* or *none.*

EXAMPLE 2 Writing a Conditional Statement

Write a conditional statement from each of the following.

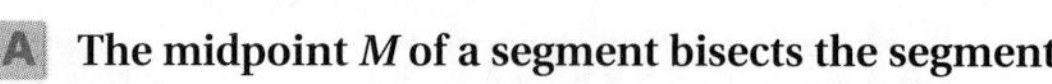

A **The midpoint M of a segment bisects the segment.**

The midpoint M of a segment bisects the segment. *Identify the hypothesis and conclusion.*

Conditional: If M is the midpoint of a segment, then M bisects the segment.

B

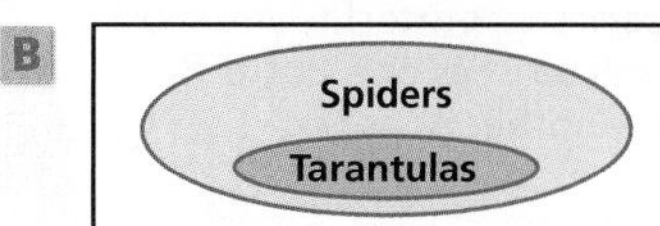

The inner oval represents the hypothesis, and the outer oval represents the conclusion.

Conditional: If an animal is a tarantula, then it is a spider.

2. Write a conditional statement from the sentence "Two angles that are complementary are acute."
If 2 ∠s are comp., then they are acute.

A conditional statement has a **truth value** of either true (T) or false (F). It is false only when the hypothesis is true and the conclusion is false. Consider the conditional "If I get paid, I will take you to the movie." If I don't get paid, I haven't broken my promise. So the statement is still true.

To show that a conditional statement is false, you need to find only one counterexample where the hypothesis is true and the conclusion is false.

EXAMPLE 3 Analyzing the Truth Value of a Conditional Statement

Determine if each conditional is true. If false, give a counterexample.

A **If today is Sunday, then tomorrow is Monday.**

When the hypothesis is true, the conclusion is also true because Monday follows Sunday. So the conditional is true.

B **If an angle is obtuse, then it has a measure of 100°.**

You can draw an obtuse angle whose measure is not 100°. In this case, the hypothesis is true, but the conclusion is false. Since you can find a counterexample, the conditional is false.

C **If an odd number is divisible by 2, then 8 is a perfect square.**

An odd number is never divisible by 2, so the hypothesis is false. The number 8 is not a perfect square, so the conclusion is false. However, the conditional is true because the hypothesis is false.

Remember!

If the hypothesis is false, the conditional statement is true, regardless of the truth value of the conclusion.

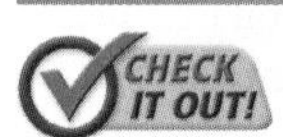

3. Determine if the conditional "If a number is odd, then it is divisible by 3" is true. If false, give a counterexample.
F; possible answer: 7

The **negation** of statement p is "not p," written as $\sim p$. The negation of the statement "M is the midpoint of $\overline{AB}$" is "M is *not* the midpoint of $\overline{AB}$." The negation of a true statement is false, and the negation of a false statement is true. Negations are used to write related conditional statements.

2 Teach

Guided Instruction

Be sure students are able to identify conditional statements in various forms before analyzing their truth values. Explain that to find a counterexample for a conditional, you must find a case in which the hypothesis is true and the conclusion is false. Finally, show students how each related conditional is formed.

ENGLISH LANGUAGE LEARNERS

Reaching All Learners

Through Visual Cues

When students are first identifying the hypothesis and conclusion in a conditional statement, encourage them to write down the conditional statement and underline or circle the words *if* and *then* wherever they appear. As you discuss conditionals in which these words do not appear, have students insert *if* and *then* where they belong and then rewrite the complete statement in if-then form.

Related Conditionals

DEFINITION	SYMBOLS
A conditional is a statement that can be written in the form "If p, then q."	$p \to q$
The **converse** is the statement formed by exchanging the hypothesis and conclusion.	$q \to p$
The **inverse** is the statement formed by negating the hypothesis and the conclusion.	$\sim p \to \sim q$
The **contrapositive** is the statement formed by both exchanging and negating the hypothesis and conclusion.	$\sim q \to \sim p$

EXAMPLE 4 Biology Application

Moth

Butterfly

Write the converse, inverse, and contrapositive of the conditional statement. Use the photos to find the truth value of each.

If an insect is a butterfly, then it has four wings.

If an insect is a butterfly, then it has four wings.

Converse: If an insect has four wings, then it is a butterfly.

A moth also is an insect with four wings. So the converse is false.

Inverse: If an insect is not a butterfly, then it does not have four wings.

A moth is not a butterfly, but it has four wings. So the inverse is false.

Contrapositive: If an insect does not have four wings, then it is not a butterfly.

Butterflies must have four wings. So the contrapositive is true.

4. Converse: If an animal has 4 paws, then it is a cat; F. Inverse: If an animal is not a cat, then it does not have 4 paws; F. Contrapositive: If an animal does not have 4 paws, then it is not a cat; T.

4. Write the converse, inverse, and contrapositive of the conditional statement "If an animal is a cat, then it has four paws." Find the truth value of each.

The logical equivalence of a conditional and its contrapositive is known as the Law of Contrapositive.

In the example above, the conditional statement and its contrapositive are both true, and the converse and inverse are both false. Related conditional statements that have the same truth value are called **logically equivalent statements**. A conditional and its contrapositive are logically equivalent, and so are the converse and inverse.

Statement	Example	Truth Value
Conditional	If $m\angle A = 95°$, then $\angle A$ is obtuse.	T
Converse	If $\angle A$ is obtuse, then $m\angle A = 95°$.	F
Inverse	If $m\angle A \neq 95°$, then $\angle A$ is not obtuse.	F
Contrapositive	If $\angle A$ is not obtuse, then $m\angle A \neq 95°$.	T

However, the converse of a true conditional is not necessarily false. All four related conditionals can be true, or all four can be false, depending on the statement.

Many students think that a conditional with a false hypothesis is false. To help students remember when a conditional is false, describe a conditional as a promise, as explained on page 82.

Power Presentations with PowerPoint®

Additional Examples

Example 3

Determine if each conditional is true. If false, give a counterexample.

A. If this month is August, then next month is September. T

B. If two angles are acute, then they are congruent. F; possible answer: 80° and 30°

C. If an even number greater than 2 is prime, then $5 + 4 = 8$. T

Example 4

Write the converse, inverse, and contrapositive of the conditional statement. Use the Science Fact to find the truth value of each.

If an animal is an adult insect, then it has six legs.

Science Fact

Adult insects have six legs.
No other animals have six legs.

Conv.: If an animal has six legs, then it is an adult insect; T. Inv.: If an animal is not an adult insect, then it does not have 6 legs; T. Contra.: If an animal does not have six legs, then it is not an adult insect; T.

3 Close

Summarize

Ask students to describe the relationship between a conditional statement and its converse, inverse, and contrapositive. Conv.: Exchange the hypothesis and conclusion. Inv.: Negate the hypothesis and conclusion. Contra.: Exchange and negate the hypothesis and conclusion. Ask "Which pairs of related conditional statements are always logically equivalent?" cond. and contra.; conv. and inv.

ONGOING ASSESSMENT and INTERVENTION

Diagnose ***Before*** **the Lesson**
2-2 Warm Up, TE p. 81

Monitor ***During*** **the Lesson**
Check It Out! Exercises, SE pp. 81–83
Questioning Strategies, TE pp. 82–83

Assess ***After*** **the Lesson**
2-2 Lesson Quiz, TE p. 87
Alternative Assessment, TE p. 87

INTERVENTION
Questioning Strategies

EXAMPLE 3

- What steps should you take to determine the truth value of a conditional statement?

EXAMPLE 4

- How can you remember the characteristics of the converse, inverse, and contrapositive of a conditional?

Answers to *Think and Discuss*

1. T; F
2. T
3. Yes; possible answer: "If $x = 3$, then $2x = 6$" is true, and so is the conv. "If $2x = 6$, then $x = 3$."
4. See p. A2.

THINK AND DISCUSS

1. If a conditional statement is false, what are the truth values of its hypothesis and conclusion?
2. What is the truth value of a conditional whose hypothesis is false?
3. Can a conditional statement and its converse be logically equivalent? Support your answer with an example.

4. **GET ORGANIZED** Copy and complete the graphic organizer. In each box, write the definition and give an example.

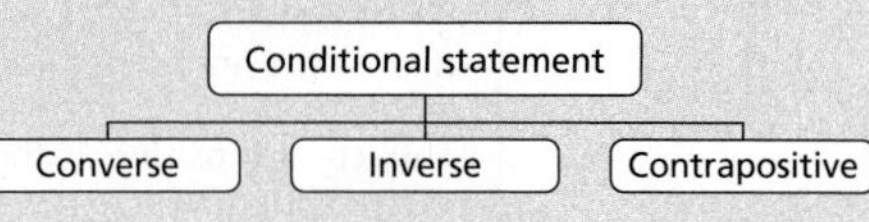

2-2 Exercises

2-2 Exercises

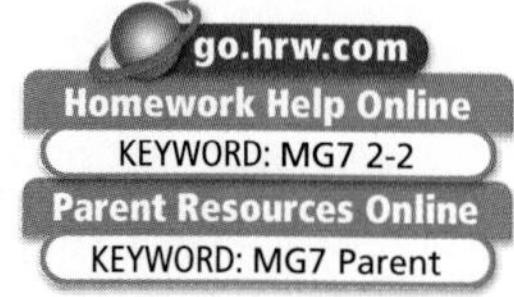

Assignment Guide

Assign *Guided Practice* exercises as necessary.

If you finished Examples **1–2**
Basic 13–18, 30–33
Average 13–18, 30–36, 54
Advanced 13–18, 30–36, 54–55

If you finished Examples **1–4**
Basic 13–23, 30–37, 42–47, 49–53, 58–66
Average 13–29, 36–55, 58–66
Advanced 13–29, 36–66

Homework Quick Check
Quickly check key concepts.
Exercises: 14, 18, 20, 22, 36, 40

GUIDED PRACTICE

Vocabulary **Apply the vocabulary from this lesson to answer each question.**

1. The __?__ of a *conditional statement* is formed by exchanging the hypothesis and conclusion. (*converse, inverse,* or *contrapositive*) **converse**
2. A *conditional* and its *contrapositive* are __?__ because they have the same truth value. (*logically equivalent* or *converses*) **logically equivalent**

SEE EXAMPLE 1 p. 81

Identify the hypothesis and conclusion of each conditional.

3. If a person is at least 16 years old, then the person can drive a car.
4. A figure is a parallelogram if it is a rectangle.
5. The statement $a - b < a$ implies that b is a positive number.

SEE EXAMPLE 2 p. 82

Write a conditional statement from each of the following.

6. Eighteen-year-olds are eligible to vote.
7. $\left(\frac{a}{b}\right)^2 < \frac{a}{b}$ when $0 < a < b$.
   If $0 < a < b$, then $\left(\frac{a}{b}\right)^2 < \frac{a}{b}$.
8. 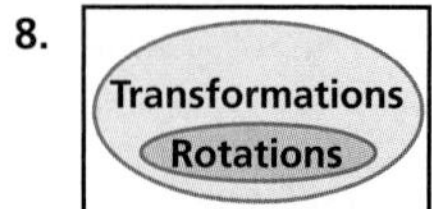

   If something is a rotation, then it is a transformation.

SEE EXAMPLE 3 p. 82

Determine if each conditional is true. If false, give a counterexample.

9. If three points form the vertices of a triangle, then they lie in the same plane. T
10. If $x > y$, then $|x| > |y|$. F; possible answer: $x = 2$ and $y = -4$
11. If the season is spring, then the month is March. F; possible answer: April

SEE EXAMPLE 4 p. 83

12. **Travel** Write the converse, inverse, and contrapositive of the following conditional statement. Find the truth value of each.

    If Brielle drives at exactly 30 mi/h, then she travels 10 mi in 20 min.

Answers

6. If a person is 18 years old, then that person is eligible to vote.
12. Converse: If Brielle travels 10 mi in 20 min, then she drives at exactly 30 mi/h; F. Inverse: If Brielle does not drive at exactly 30 mi/h, then she does not travel 10 mi in 20 min; F. Contrapositive: If Brielle does not travel 10 mi in 20 min, then she does not drive at exactly 30 mi/h; T.

State Resources

go.hrw.com
State Resources Online
KEYWORD: MG7 Resources

PRACTICE AND PROBLEM SOLVING

Independent Practice	
For Exercises	See Example
13–15	1
16–18	2
19–21	3
22–23	4

Extra Practice

Skills Practice p. S6

Application Practice p. S29

Identify the hypothesis and conclusion of each conditional.

13. If an animal is a tabby, then it is a cat.
14. Four angles are formed if two lines intersect.
15. If 8 ounces of cereal cost \$2.99, then 16 ounces of cereal cost \$5.98.

Write a conditional statement from each sentence.

16. You should monitor the heart rate of a patient who is ill. If a patient is ill, then you should monitor the patient's heart rate.
17. After three strikes, the batter is out. If the batter makes 3 strikes, then the batter is out.
18. Congruent segments have equal measures. If segs. are ≅, then they have equal measures.

Determine if each conditional is true. If false, give a counterexample.

19. If you subtract −2 from −6, then the result is −4. T
20. If two planes intersect, then they intersect in exactly one point. F; by Postulate 1-1-5, 2 planes intersect in exactly 1 line.
21. If a cat is a bird, then today is Friday. T

Write the converse, inverse, and contrapositive of each conditional statement. Find the truth value of each.

22. **Probability** If the probability of an event is 0.1, then the event is unlikely to occur.
23. **Meteorology** If freezing rain is falling, then the air temperature is 32°F or less. (*Hint:* The freezing point of water is 32°F.)

Find the truth value of each statement.

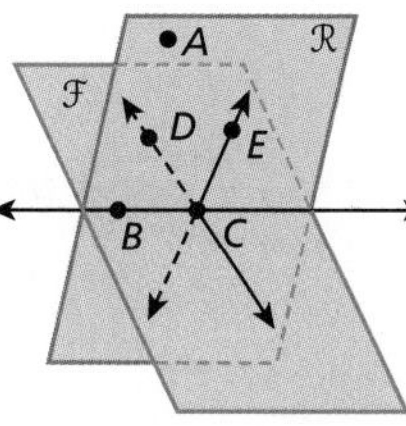

24. *E* lies in plane ℛ. T
25. $\overleftrightarrow{CD}$ lies in plane ℱ. T
26. *C*, *E*, and *D* are coplanar. T
27. Plane ℱ contains $\overrightarrow{ED}$. F
28. *B* and *E* are collinear. T
29. $\overleftrightarrow{BC}$ contains ℱ and ℛ. F

Draw a Venn diagram.

30. All integers are rational numbers.
31. All natural numbers are real.
32. All rectangles are quadrilaterals.
33. Plane is an undefined term.

Write a conditional statement from each Venn diagram.

34. 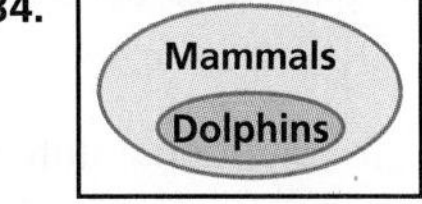

35. 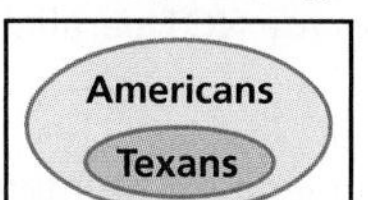

36. 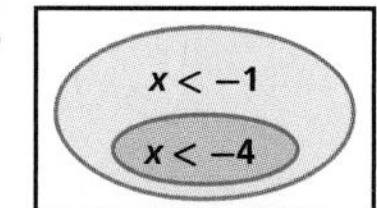

34. If an animal is a dolphin, then it is a mammal.

35. If a person is a Texan, then the person is an American.

36. If $x < -4$, then $x < -1$.

MULTI-STEP TEST PREP

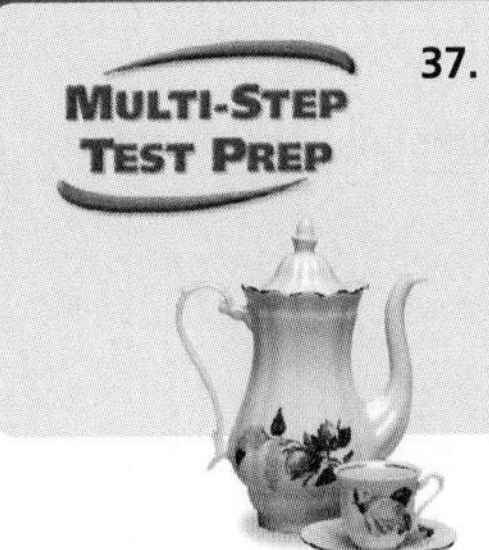

37. This problem will prepare you for the Multi-Step Test Prep on page 102.
    a. Identify the hypothesis and conclusion in the Duchess's statement.
    b. Rewrite the Duchess's claim as a conditional statement.

"Tut, tut, child!" said the Duchess. "Everything's got a moral, if only you can find it." And she squeezed herself up closer to Alice's side as she spoke.

Teaching Tip

Algebra If students have difficulty with **Exercise 10,** review the definition of absolute value. If students try only positive numbers for *x* and *y*, they may come to the incorrect conclusion that the conditional is true. Remind them to consider all combinations of positive and negative numbers that can be substituted for the variables.

MULTI-STEP TEST PREP **Exercise 37** involves identifying the hypothesis and conclusion in an implied conditional statement. This exercise prepares students for the Multi-Step Test Prep on page 102.

Answers

22. Converse: If an event is unlikely to occur, then the probability of the event is 0.1; F. Inverse: If the probability of an event is not 0.1, then the event is likely to occur; F. Contrapositive: If an event is likely to occur, then the probability of the event is not 0.1; T.
23. Converse: If the air temperature is 32°F or less, then freezing rain is falling; F.
    Inverse: If freezing rain is not falling, then the air temperature is greater than 32°F; F.
    Contrapositive: If the air temperature is greater than 32°F, then freezing rain is not falling; T.

30. 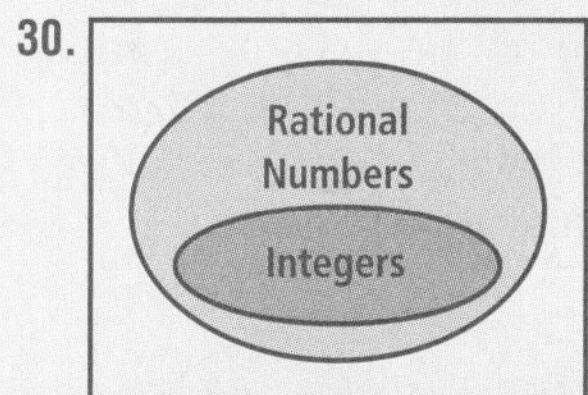

Answers

31. 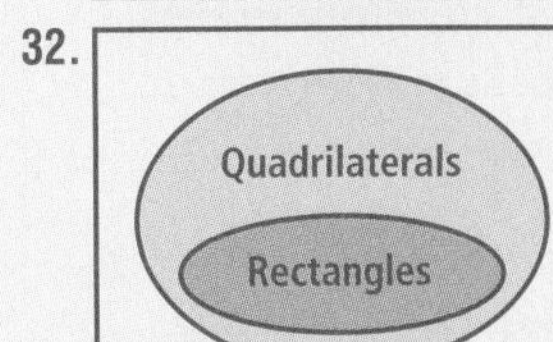

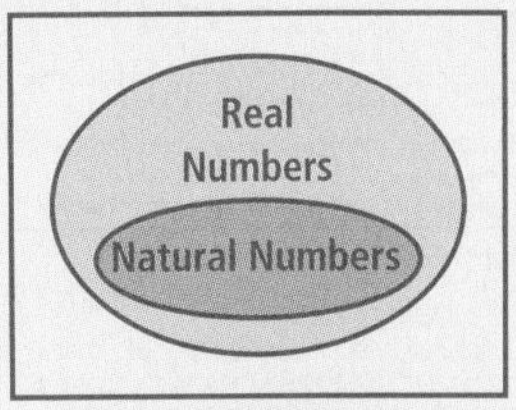

32.

33. 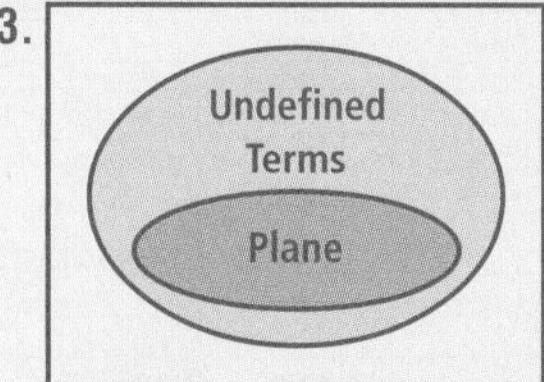

37a. H: Only you can find it. C: Everything's got a moral.
b. If only you can find it, then everything's got a moral.

2-2 PRACTICE A

2-2 PRACTICE C

2-2 PRACTICE B

Identify the hypothesis and conclusion of each conditional.

1. If you can see the stars, then it is night.
   Hypothesis: You can see the stars.
   Conclusion: It is night.
2. A pencil writes well if it is sharp.
   Hypothesis: A pencil is sharp.
   Conclusion: The pencil writes well.

Write a conditional statement from each of the following.

3. Three noncollinear points determine a plane.
   If three points are noncollinear, then they determine a plane.
4. 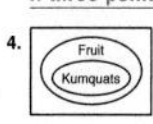 If a food is a kumquat, then it is a fruit.

Determine if each conditional is true. If false, give a counterexample.

5. If two points are noncollinear, then a right triangle contains one obtuse angle.
   true
6. If a liquid is water, then it is composed of hydrogen and oxygen.
   true
7. If a living thing is green, then it is a plant.
   false; possible answer: a frog
8. "If *G* is at 4, then *GH* is 3." Write the converse, inverse, and contrapositive of this statement. Find the truth value of each. 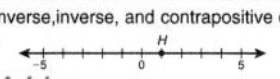
   Converse: If *GH* is 3, then *G* is at 4; false
   Inverse: If *G* is not at 4, then *GH* is not 3; false
   Contrapositive: If *GH* is not 3, then *G* is not at 4; true

This chart shows a small part of the *Mammalia* class of animals, the mammals. Write a conditional to describe the relationship between each given pair.

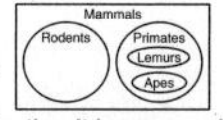

9. primates and mammals If an animal is a primate, then it is a mammal.
10. lemurs and rodents Possible answer: If an animal is a lemur, then it is not a rodent.
11. rodents and apes Possible answer: If an animal is a rodent, then it is not an ape.
12. apes and mammals If an animal is an ape, then it is a mammal.

TEST PREP DOCTOR If students answer **Exercise 53** incorrectly, have them write the hypothesis and conclusion of each statement separately and then switch them to form the converse. If the students are unsure of the truth value of any of the statements, review the necessary concepts with them.

Answers

39. Possible answer:

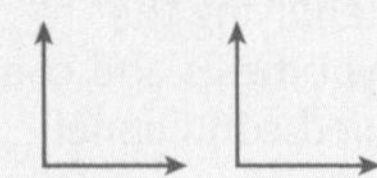

40. Possible answer:

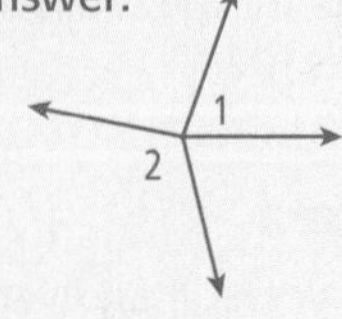

42. If a mineral is calcite, then it has a hardness of 3; T.
43. If a mineral has a hardness less than 5, then it is not apatite; T.
44. If a mineral is not apatite, then it has a hardness less than 5; F.
45. If a mineral is not apatite, then it is calcite; F.
46. If a mineral has a hardness of 3, then it is not apatite; T.
47. If a mineral is calcite, then it has a hardness less than 5; T.
48. Converse: If 2 ∡ have the same measure, then they are ≅; T. Inverse: If 2 ∡ are not ≅, then they do not have the same measure; T. Contrapositive: If 2 ∡ do not have the same measure, then they are not ≅; T.

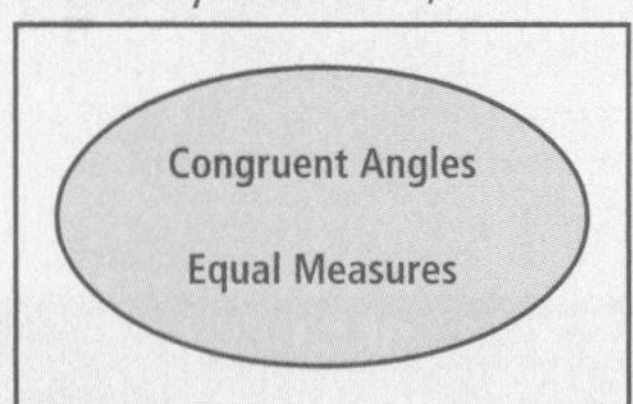

49. Possible answer: A conditional statement is false when its hypothesis is true and its conclusion is false. A conditional statement with a false hypothesis is true because nothing has been guaranteed by the hypothesis.

56a. Possible answer: Figure A is not a rect., so it belongs outside the larger oval in the Venn diagram. It cannot be inside the smaller oval, so it cannot be a square.

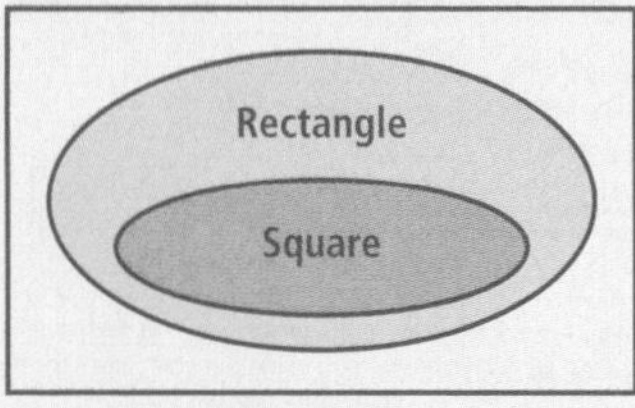

Find a counterexample to show that the converse of each conditional is false.

38. If $x = -5$, then $x^2 = 25$. $x = 5$
39. If two angles are vertical angles, then they are congruent.
40. If two angles are adjacent, then they share a vertex.
41. If you use sunscreen, then you will not get sunburned.

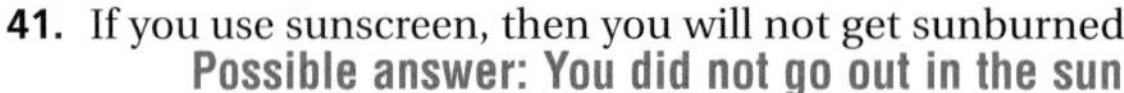
Possible answer: You did not go out in the sun.

LINK Geology

Diamond is four times as hard as the next mineral on Mohs' scale, corundum (ruby and sapphire).

Geology Mohs' scale is used to identify minerals. A mineral with a higher number is harder than a mineral with a lower number.

Mohs' Scale	
Hardness	**Mineral**
1	Talc
2	Gypsum
3	Calcite
4	Fluorite
5	Apatite
6	Orthoclase
7	Quartz
8	Topaz
9	Corundum
10	Diamond

Use the table and the statements below for Exercises 42–47. Write each conditional and find its truth value.

p: calcite q: not apatite
r: a hardness of 3 s: a hardness less than 5

42. $p \to r$ 43. $s \to q$ 44. $q \to s$
45. $q \to p$ 46. $r \to q$ 47. $p \to s$

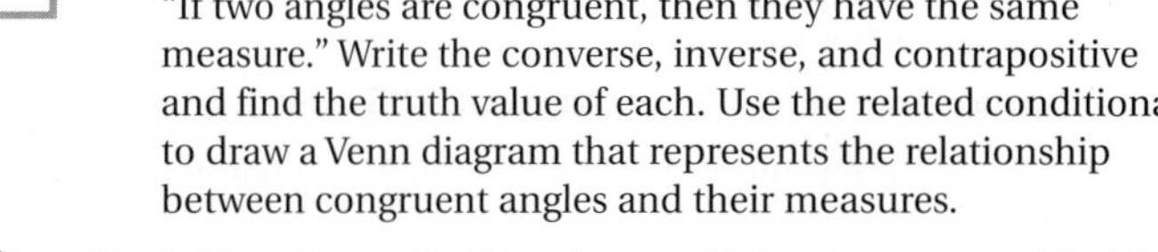

48. **Critical Thinking** Consider the conditional "If two angles are congruent, then they have the same measure." Write the converse, inverse, and contrapositive and find the truth value of each. Use the related conditionals to draw a Venn diagram that represents the relationship between congruent angles and their measures.

49. **Write About It** When is a conditional statement false? Explain why a true conditional statement can have a hypothesis that is false.

TEST PREP

50. What is the inverse of "If it is Saturday, then it is the weekend"?
 (A) If it is the weekend, then it is Saturday.
 (B) If it is not Saturday, then it is the weekend.
 (C) If it is not Saturday, then it is not the weekend.
 (D) If it is not the weekend, then it is not Saturday.

51. Let a represent "Two lines are parallel to the same line," and let b represent "The two lines are parallel." Which symbolic statement represents the conditional "If two lines are NOT parallel, then they are parallel to the same line"?
 (F) $a \to b$ (G) $b \to a$ (H) $\sim b \to a$ (J) $b \to \sim a$

52. Which statement is a counterexample for the conditional statement "If $f(x) = \sqrt{25 - x^2}$, then $f(x)$ is positive"?
 (A) $x = 0$ (B) $x = 3$ (C) $x = 4$ (D) $x = 5$

53. Which statement has the same truth value as its converse?
 (F) If a triangle has a right angle, its side lengths are 3 centimeters, 4 centimeters, and 5 centimeters.
 (G) If an angle measures 104°, then the angle is obtuse.
 (H) If a number is an integer, then it is a natural number.
 (J) If an angle measures 90°, then it is an acute angle.

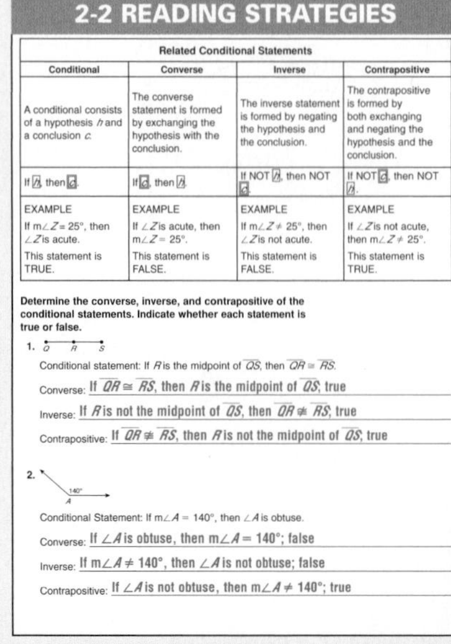

2-2 READING STRATEGIES

Related Conditional Statements			
Conditional	**Converse**	**Inverse**	**Contrapositive**
A conditional consists of a hypothesis h and a conclusion c.	The converse statement is formed by exchanging the hypothesis with the conclusion.	The inverse statement is formed by negating the hypothesis and the conclusion.	The contrapositive is formed by both exchanging and negating the hypothesis and the conclusion.
If h, then c.	If c, then h.	If NOT h, then NOT c.	If NOT c, then NOT h.
EXAMPLE If m∠Z = 25°, then ∠Z is acute. This statement is TRUE.	EXAMPLE If ∠Z is acute, then m∠Z = 25°. This statement is FALSE.	EXAMPLE If m∠Z ≠ 25°, then ∠Z is not acute. This statement is FALSE.	EXAMPLE If ∠Z is not acute, then m∠Z ≠ 25°. This statement is TRUE.

Determine the converse, inverse, and contrapositive of the conditional statements. Indicate whether each statement is true or false.

1. Q R S

Conditional statement: If R is the midpoint of $\overline{QS}$, then $\overline{QR} \cong \overline{RS}$.

Converse: If $\overline{QR} \cong \overline{RS}$, then R is the midpoint of $\overline{QS}$; true

Inverse: If R is not the midpoint of $\overline{QS}$, then $\overline{QR} \ncong \overline{RS}$; true

Contrapositive: If $\overline{QR} \ncong \overline{RS}$, then R is not the midpoint of $\overline{QS}$; true

2. 140° A

Conditional Statement: If m∠A = 140°, then ∠A is obtuse.

Converse: If ∠A is obtuse, then m∠A = 140°; false

Inverse: If m∠A ≠ 140°, then ∠A is not obtuse; false

Contrapositive: If ∠A is not obtuse, then m∠A ≠ 140°; true

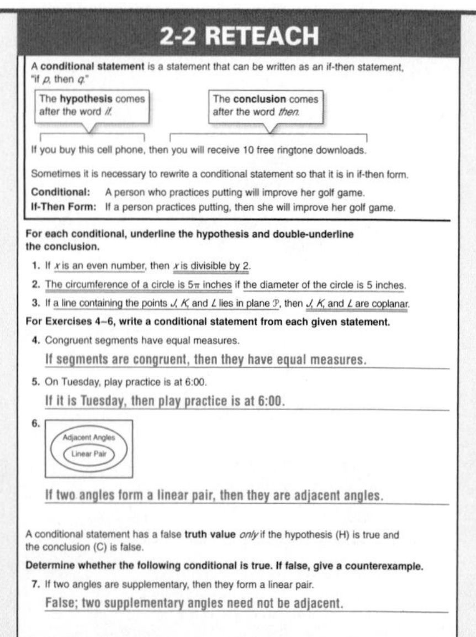

2-2 RETEACH

A **conditional statement** is a statement that can be written as an if-then statement, "if p, then q."

The **hypothesis** comes after the word *if*. The **conclusion** comes after the word *then*.

If you buy this cell phone, then you will receive 10 free ringtone downloads.

Sometimes it is necessary to rewrite a conditional statement so that it is in if-then form.

Conditional: A person who practices putting will improve her golf game.
If-Then Form: If a person practices putting, then she will improve her golf game.

For each conditional, underline the hypothesis and double-underline the conclusion.

1. If x is an even number, then x is divisible by 2.
2. The circumference of a circle is 5π inches if the diameter of the circle is 5 inches.
3. If a line containing the points J, K, and L lies in plane $\mathcal{P}$, then J, K, and L are coplanar.

For Exercises 4–6, write a conditional statement from each given statement.

4. Congruent segments have equal measures.
 If segments are congruent, then they have equal measures.
5. On Tuesday, play practice is at 6:00.
 If it is Tuesday, then play practice is at 6:00.
6. Adjacent Angles / Linear Pair
 If two angles form a linear pair, then they are adjacent angles.

A conditional statement has a false **truth value** *only* if the hypothesis (H) is true and the conclusion (C) is false.

Determine whether the following conditional is true. If false, give a counterexample.

7. If two angles are supplementary, then they form a linear pair.
 False; two supplementary angles need not be adjacent.

CHALLENGE AND EXTEND

For each Venn diagram, write two statements beginning with *Some*, *All*, or *No*.

54. No lines are pts. No pts. are lines.

55. Some students are adults. Some adults are students.

56b. If a figure is not a rect., then it is not a square. By the contrapositive, since figure A is not a rect., it is not a square.

54.

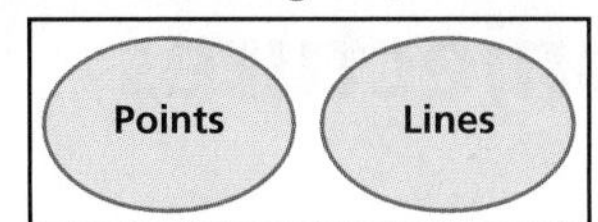

55.

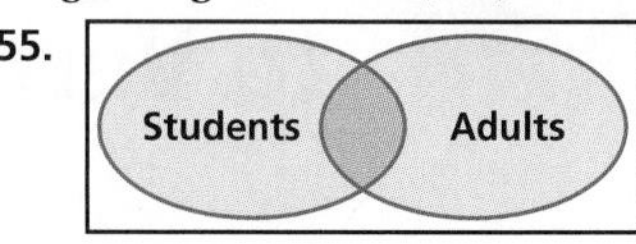

56. Given: If a figure is a square, then it is a rectangle. Figure A is not a rectangle. Conclusion: Figure A is not a square.

 a. Draw a Venn diagram to represent the given conditional statement. Use the Venn diagram to explain why the conclusion is valid.

 b. Write the contrapositive of the given conditional. How can you use the contrapositive to justify the conclusion?

57. Multi-Step How many true conditionals can you write using the statements below?

p: n is an integer. q: n is a whole number. r: n is a natural number.

3

SPIRAL REVIEW

Write a rule to describe each relationship. *(Previous course)*

58. $y = x + 3$

59. $y = 2x + 1$

60. $y = \frac{5}{2}x - 4$

58.

x	−8	4	7	9
y	−5	7	10	12

59.

x	−3	−1	0	4
y	−5	−1	1	9

60.

x	−2	0	4	6
y	−9	−4	6	11

Determine whether each statement is true or false. If false, explain why. *(Lesson 1-4)*

61. If two angles are complementary and congruent, then the measure of each is 45°. T

62. A pair of acute angles can be supplementary. F

63. A linear pair of angles is also a pair of supplementary angles. T

Find the next item in each pattern. *(Lesson 2-1)*

64. 1, 13, 131, 1313, ... 13,131

65. $2, \frac{2}{3}, \frac{2}{9}, \frac{2}{27}, \ldots$ $\frac{2}{81}$

66. $x, 2x^2, 3x^3, 4x^4, \ldots$ $5x^5$

Career Path

Stephanie Poulin
Desktop Publisher
Daily Reporter

Q: What high school math classes did you take?

A: I took three years of math: Pre-Algebra, Algebra, and Geometry.

Q: What training do you need to be a desktop publisher?

A: Most of my training was done on the job. The computer science and typing classes I took in high school have been helpful.

Q: How do you use math?

A: Part of my job is to make sure all the text, charts, and photographs are formatted to fit the layout of each page. I have to manipulate things by comparing ratios, calculating areas, and using estimation.

Q: What future plans do you have?

A: My goal is to start my own business as a freelance graphic artist.

2-2 PROBLEM SOLVING

1. Write the converse, inverse, and contrapositive of the conditional statement. Find the truth value of each.

If it is April, then there are 30 days in the month.

Conv.: If there are 30 days in the month, then it is April; false. Inv.: If it is not April, then there are not 30 days in the month; false. Contra.: If there are not 30 days in the month, then it is not April; true.

2. Write a conditional statement from the diagram. Then write the converse, inverse, and contrapositive. Find the truth value of each.

Yard
Enclosed by a fence
Has swimming pool

Cond.: If a yard has a swimming pool, then the yard is enclosed by a fence. Conv.: If a yard is enclosed by a fence, then it has a swimming pool; false. Inv.: If a yard does not have a swimming pool, then it is not enclosed by a fence; false. Contra.: If a yard is not enclosed by a fence, then it does not have a swimming pool; true.

Use the table and the statements listed. Write each conditional and find its truth value.

U.S. Flag	
Year	Number of Stars
1777	13
1818	20
1848	30
1959	50

p: 1777 q: 30 stars r: after 1818 s: less than 50 stars

3. $p \rightarrow q$ If the year is 1777, then the U.S. flag has 30 stars; false.

4. $r \rightarrow s$ If it is after 1818, then the U.S. flag has less than 50 stars; false.

5. $q \rightarrow s$ If the U.S. flag has 30 stars, then it is after 1818; true.

Choose the best answer.

6. What is the converse of "If you saw the movie, then you know how it ends"?
 (A) If you know how the movie ends, then you saw the movie.
 B If you did not see the movie, then you do not know how it ends.
 C If you do not know how the movie ends, then you did not see the movie.
 D If you do not know how the movie ends, then you saw the movie.

7. What is the inverse of "If you received a text message, then you have a cell phone"?
 F If you have a cell phone, then you received a text message.
 G If you do not have a cell phone, then you did not receive a text message.
 (H) If you did not receive a text message, then you do not have a cell phone.
 J If you received a text message, then you do not have a cell phone.

Answers

62. Possible answer: Acute ∠s measure less than 90°, so the sum of the measures of 2 acute ∠s must be less than 180°. Therefore, 2 acute ∠s cannot be supp.

In **Exercises 38–41,** some students may try to find a counterexample for the given statement rather than its converse. Remind them to switch the hypothesis and conclusion to form the converse before finding the truth value.

Visual Encourage students to draw graphs for **Exercises 58–60.**

Journal

Have students make up a true conditional statement for which the converse, inverse, and contrapositive are all true.

ALTERNATIVE ASSESSMENT

Ask students to write one conditional that is true and one that is false, using any subject that interests them. Then ask them to write the converse, inverse, and contrapositive of each of their original statements and determine the truth values of each.

Power Presentations with PowerPoint®

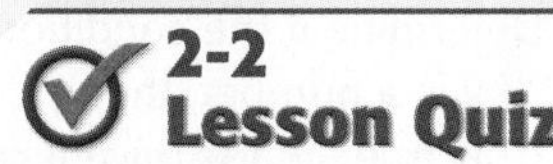

Identify the hypothesis and conclusion of each conditional.

1. A triangle with one right angle is a right triangle. H: A triangle has one right angle. C: The triangle is a right triangle.

2. All even numbers are divisible by 2. H: A number is even. C: The number is divisible by 2.

3. Determine if the statement "If $n^2 = 144$, then $n = 12$" is true. If false, give a counterexample. F; $n = -12$

4. Write the converse, inverse, and contrapositive of the conditional statement "If Maria's birthday is February 29, then she was born in a leap year." Find the truth value of each. Conv.: If Maria was born in a leap year, then her birthday is February 29; F. Inv.: If Maria's birthday is not February 29, then she was not born in a leap year; F. Contra.: If Maria was not born in a leap year, then her birthday is not February 29; T.

Also available on transparency

2-3 Organizer

Pacing: Traditional 1 day
Block $\frac{1}{2}$ day

Objective: Apply the Law of Detachment and the Law of Syllogism in logical reasoning.

Online Edition
Tutorial Videos

Countdown Week 3

Power Presentations with PowerPoint®

Warm Up

Identify the hypothesis and conclusion of each conditional.

1. A mapping that is a reflection is a type of transformation. H: A mapping is a reflection. C: The mapping is a transformation.
2. The quotient of two negative numbers is positive. H: Two numbers are negative. C: The quotient is positive.
3. Determine if the conditional "If x is a number, then $|x| > 0$" is true. If false, give a counterexample. F; $x = 0$

Also available on transparency

Math Humor

Q: How is a geometry classroom like the United Nations?

A: They both have lots of rulers.

State Resources

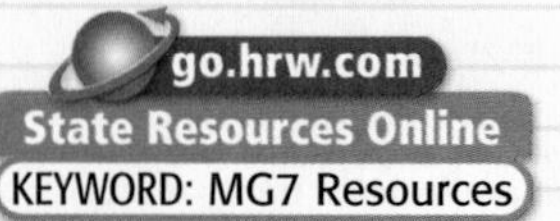

go.hrw.com
State Resources Online
KEYWORD: MG7 Resources

2-3 Using Deductive Reasoning to Verify Conjectures

Objective
Apply the Law of Detachment and the Law of Syllogism in logical reasoning.

Vocabulary
deductive reasoning

Why learn this?
You can use inductive and deductive reasoning to decide whether a common myth is accurate.

You learned in Lesson 2-1 that one counterexample is enough to disprove a conjecture. But to prove that a conjecture is true, you must use *deductive reasoning.* **Deductive reasoning** is the process of using logic to draw conclusions from given facts, definitions, and properties.

EXAMPLE 1 ***Media Application***

Urban legends and modern myths spread quickly through the media. Many Web sites and television shows are dedicated to confirming or disproving such myths. Is each conclusion a result of inductive or deductive reasoning?

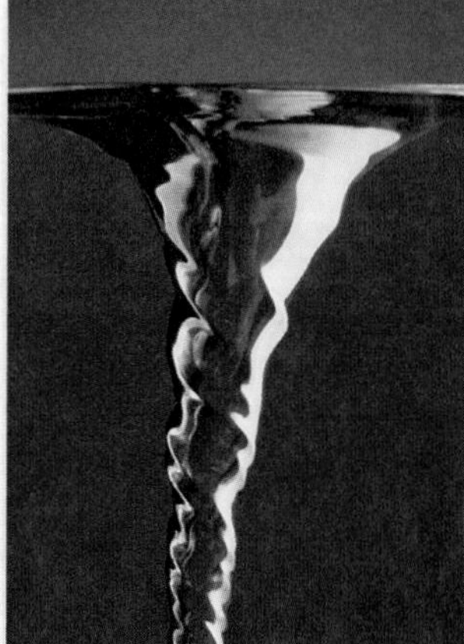

A **There is a myth that toilets and sinks drain in opposite directions in the Southern and Northern Hemispheres. However, if you were to observe sinks draining in the two hemispheres, you would see that this myth is false.**

Since the conclusion is based on a pattern of observation, it is a result of inductive reasoning.

B **There is a myth that you should not touch a baby bird that has fallen from its nest because the mother bird will disown the baby if she detects human scent. However, biologists have shown that birds cannot detect human scent. Therefore, the myth cannot be true.**

The conclusion is based on logical reasoning from scientific research. It is a result of deductive reasoning.

CHECK IT OUT! 1. There is a myth that an eelskin wallet will demagnetize credit cards because the skin of the electric eels used to make the wallet holds an electric charge. However, eelskin products are not made from electric eels. Therefore, the myth cannot be true. Is this conclusion a result of inductive or deductive reasoning? **deductive reasoning**

In deductive reasoning, if the given facts are true and you apply the correct logic, then the conclusion must be true. The Law of Detachment is one valid form of deductive reasoning.

1 Introduce

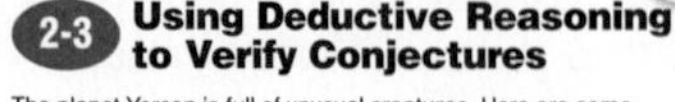

EXPLORATION

2-3 Using Deductive Reasoning to Verify Conjectures

The planet Yercon is full of unusual creatures. Here are some facts about the creatures.

If you are a zintoid, then you are a quorg.
If you are a meerk, then you are a ving.
If you are a quorg, then you are a wiklop.

1. Dorla is a meerk. What else must be true about Dorla?
2. Zim is a quorg. What else must be true about Zim?
3. In general, suppose you know that $p \rightarrow q$ is a true statement and that p is true. What can you conclude?
4. Use the facts about the creatures to write a new conditional statement about zintoids: If you are a zintoid, then __?__.
5. In general, suppose you know that $p \rightarrow q$ and $q \rightarrow r$ are true statements. What can you conclude?

THINK AND DISCUSS

Motivate

Discuss with students the meaning of *myth* (a story of unknown authorship, usually serving to explain some phenomenon of nature, the origin of man, or cultural customs and institutions). Have students recall a myth or legend that they have read or heard. Ask students if the myth is true, and have them explain how they know whether it is true.

Explorations and answers are provided in *Alternate Openers: Explorations Transparencies.*

Law of Detachment

If $p \rightarrow q$ is a true statement and p is true, then q is true.

EXAMPLE 2 Verifying Conjectures by Using the Law of Detachment

Determine if each conjecture is valid by the Law of Detachment.

A **Given: If two segments are congruent, then they have the same length. $\overline{AB} \cong \overline{XY}$.**

Conjecture: $AB = XY$

Identify the hypothesis and conclusion in the given conditional.

If two segments are congruent, then they have the same length.

The given statement $\overline{AB} \cong \overline{XY}$ matches the hypothesis of a true conditional. By the Law of Detachment $AB = XY$. The conjecture is valid.

B **Given: If you are tardy 3 times, you must go to detention. Shea is in detention.**

Conjecture: Shea was tardy at least 3 times.

Identify the hypothesis and conclusion in the given conditional.

If you are tardy 3 times, you must go to detention.

The given statement "Shea is in detention" matches the conclusion of a true conditional. But this does not mean the hypothesis is true. Shea could be in detention for another reason. The conjecture is not valid.

2. Determine if the conjecture is valid by the Law of Detachment. Given: If a student passes his classes, the student is eligible to play sports. Ramon passed his classes. Conjecture: Ramon is eligible to play sports. valid

Another valid form of deductive reasoning is the Law of Syllogism. It allows you to draw conclusions from two conditional statements when the conclusion of one is the hypothesis of the other.

Law of Syllogism

If $p \rightarrow q$ and $q \rightarrow r$ are true statements, then $p \rightarrow r$ is a true statement.

EXAMPLE 3 Verifying Conjectures by Using the Law of Syllogism

Determine if each conjecture is valid by the Law of Syllogism.

A **Given: If $m\angle A < 90°$, then $\angle A$ is acute. If $\angle A$ is acute, then it is not a right angle.**

Conjecture: If $m\angle A < 90°$, then it is not a right angle.

Let p, q, and r represent the following.

p: The measure of an angle is less than 90°.

q: The angle is acute.

r: The angle is not a right angle.

You are given that $p \rightarrow q$ and $q \rightarrow r$. Since q is the conclusion of the first conditional and the hypothesis of the second conditional, you can conclude that $p \rightarrow r$. The conjecture is valid by the Law of Syllogism.

Power Presentations with PowerPoint®

Additional Examples

Example 1

Is each conclusion a result of inductive or deductive reasoning?

A. There is a myth that you can balance an egg on its end only on the spring equinox. A person was able to balance an egg on July 8, September 21, and December 19. Therefore, this myth is false. inductive reasoning

B. There is a myth that the Great Wall of China is the only man-made object visible from the Moon. The Great Wall is barely visible in photographs taken from 180 miles above Earth. The Moon is about 237,000 miles from Earth. Therefore, the myth cannot be true. deductive reasoning

Example 2

Determine if each conjecture is valid by the Law of Detachment.

A. Given: If the side lengths of a triangle are 5 cm, 12 cm, and 13 cm, then the area of the triangle is 30 cm^2. The area of $\triangle PQR$ is 30 cm^2.

Conjecture: The side lengths of $\triangle PQR$ are 5 cm, 12 cm, and 13 cm. not valid

B. Given: In the World Series, if a team wins four games, then the team wins the series. The Red Sox won four games in the 2004 World Series.

Conjecture: The Red Sox won the 2004 World Series. valid

2 Teach

Guided Instruction

Review the concept of inductive reasoning, and discuss the differences between inductive and deductive reasoning. Have students give examples of each. Then introduce the Law of Detachment and the Law of Syllogism.

Algebra Show students how the Law of Syllogism is similar to the Transitive Property of Equality used in algebra. Both involve the same term in the middle.

Reaching All Learners

Through Auditory Cues

For each example, read each conditional statement aloud for students. Suggest that they listen for the key words *if* and *then*. Students can then recite back the conditionals in the order needed to apply the Law of Detachment or the Law of Syllogism. Remind students not to worry about the truth value of individual conditionals, but rather to make sure the law is applied correctly.

INTERVENTION 

Questioning Strategies

EXAMPLE 1

- How can you tell the difference between inductive and deductive reasoning?

EXAMPLES 2–3

- How can you recognize when to apply the Law of Detachment versus when to apply the Law of Syllogism?

Power Presentations with PowerPoint®

Additional Examples

Example 3

Determine if each conjecture is valid by the Law of Syllogism.

A. Given: If a figure is a kite, then it is a quadrilateral. If a figure is a quadrilateral, then it is a polygon.

Conjecture: If a figure is a kite, then it is a polygon. valid

B. Given: If a number is divisible by 2, then it is even. If a number is even, then it is an integer.

Conjecture: If a number is an integer, then it is divisible by 2. not valid

Example 4

Draw a conclusion from the given information.

A. Given: If $2y = 4$, then $z = -1$. If $x + 3 = 12$, then $2y = 4$. $x + 3 = 12$ $z = -1$

B. If the sum of the measures of two angles is 180°, then the angles are supplementary. If two angles are supplementary, they are not angles of a triangle. $m\angle A = 135°$, and $m\angle B = 45°$. $\angle A$ and $\angle B$ are not angles of a triangle.

INTERVENTION

Questioning Strategies

EXAMPLE 4

- When applying the Law of Syllogism, does the order of the conditional statements matter? Explain.

Caution!

It is possible to arrive at a true conclusion by applying invalid logical reasoning, as in Example 3B.

Determine if each conjecture is valid by the Law of Syllogism.

B **Given: If a number is divisible by 4, then it is divisible by 2. If a number is even, then it is divisible by 2.**

Conjecture: If a number is divisible by 4, then it is even.

Let x, y, and z represent the following.

x: A number is divisible by 4.

y: A number is divisible by 2.

z: A number is even.

You are given that $x \rightarrow y$ and $z \rightarrow y$. The Law of Syllogism cannot be used to draw a conclusion since y is the conclusion of both conditionals. Even though the conjecture $x \rightarrow z$ is true, the logic used to draw the conclusion is not valid.

3. Determine if the conjecture is valid by the Law of Syllogism.
Given: If an animal is a mammal, then it has hair.
If an animal is a dog, then it is a mammal.
Conjecture: If an animal is a dog, then it has hair. **valid**

EXAMPLE  4 Applying the Laws of Deductive Reasoning

Draw a conclusion from the given information.

A **Given: If a team wins 10 games, then they play in the finals. If a team plays in the finals, then they travel to Boston. The Ravens won 10 games.**

Conclusion: The Ravens will travel to Boston.

B **Given: If two angles form a linear pair, then they are adjacent. If two angles are adjacent, then they share a side. $\angle 1$ and $\angle 2$ form a linear pair.**

Conclusion: $\angle 1$ and $\angle 2$ share a side.

4. Draw a conclusion from the given information.
Given: If a polygon is a triangle, then it has three sides.
If a polygon has three sides, then it is not a quadrilateral. Polygon P is a triangle.
Polygon P is not a quad.

THINK AND DISCUSS

1. Could "A square has exactly two sides" be the conclusion of a valid argument? If so, what do you know about the truth value of the given information?
2. Explain why writing conditional statements as symbols might help you evaluate the validity of an argument.

3. **GET ORGANIZED** Copy and complete the graphic organizer. Write each law in your own words and give an example of each.

Deductive Reasoning

Law of Detachment | Law of Syllogism

3 Close

Summarize

Remind students of the difference between inductive reasoning (based on patterns) and deductive reasoning (based on logic). Review the Law of Detachment and the Law of Syllogism given on page 89.

ONGOING ASSESSMENT and INTERVENTION

Diagnose ***Before*** **the Lesson**
2-3 Warm Up, TE p. 88

Monitor ***During*** **the Lesson**
Check It Out! Exercises, SE pp. 88–90
Questioning Strategies, TE pp. 89–90

Assess ***After*** **the Lesson**
2-3 Lesson Quiz, TE p. 93
Alternative Assessment, TE p. 93

Answers to *Think and Discuss*

1. Yes; the given information is false.
2. Possible answer: Using symbols instead of words forces you to look at the validity of the argument itself, without being distracted by the truth value of the individual statements.
3. See p. A2.

2-3 Exercises

go.hrw.com
Homework Help Online
KEYWORD: MG7 2-3
Parent Resources Online
KEYWORD: MG7 Parent

GUIDED PRACTICE

1. **Vocabulary** Explain how *deductive reasoning* differs from inductive reasoning.

SEE EXAMPLE 1 p. 88

Does each conclusion use inductive or deductive reasoning?

2. At Bell High School, students must take Biology before they take Chemistry. Sam is in Chemistry, so Marcia concludes that he has taken Biology. **deductive reasoning**
3. A detective learns that his main suspect was out of town the day of the crime. He concludes that the suspect is innocent. **deductive reasoning**

SEE EXAMPLE 2 p. 89

Determine if each conjecture is valid by the Law of Detachment.

4. Given: If you want to go on a field trip, you must have a signed permission slip. Zola has a signed permission slip.
   Conjecture: Zola wants to go on a field trip. **invalid**
5. Given: If the side lengths of a rectangle are 3 ft and 4 ft, then its area is 12 ft^2. A rectangle has side lengths of 3 ft and 4 ft.
   Conjecture: The area of the rectangle is 12 ft^2. **valid**

SEE EXAMPLE 3 p. 89

Determine if each conjecture is valid by the Law of Syllogism.

6. Given: If you fly from Texas to California, you travel from the central to the Pacific time zone. If you travel from the central to the Pacific time zone, then you gain two hours.
   Conjecture: If you fly from Texas to California, you gain two hours. **valid**
7. Given: If a figure is a square, then the figure is a rectangle. If a figure is a square, then it is a parallelogram.
   Conjecture: If a figure is a parallelogram, then it is a rectangle. **invalid**

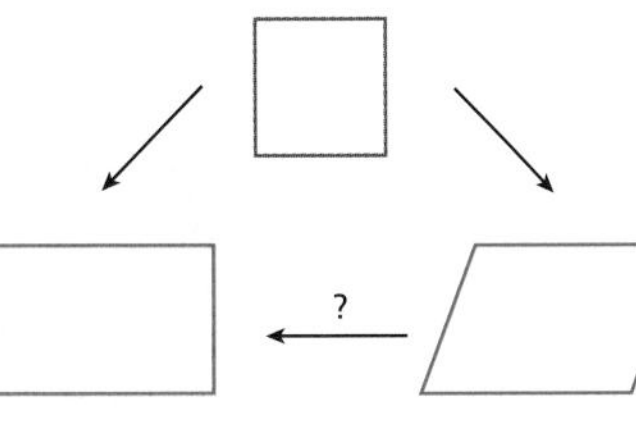

SEE EXAMPLE 4 p. 90

8. Draw a conclusion from the given information.
   Given: If you leave your car lights on overnight, then your car battery will drain. If your battery is drained, your car might not start. Alex left his car lights on last night. **Alex's car might not start.**

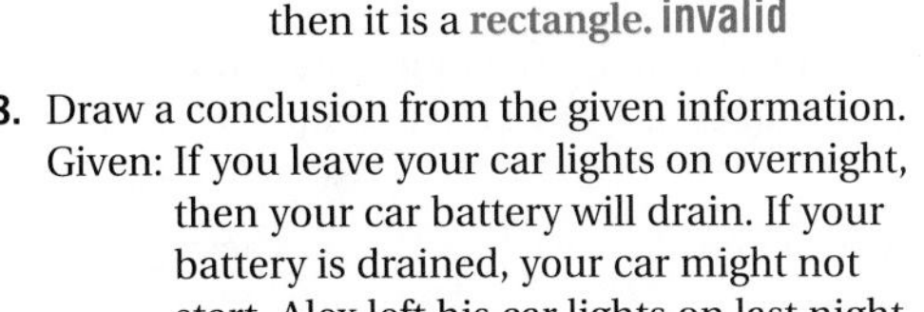
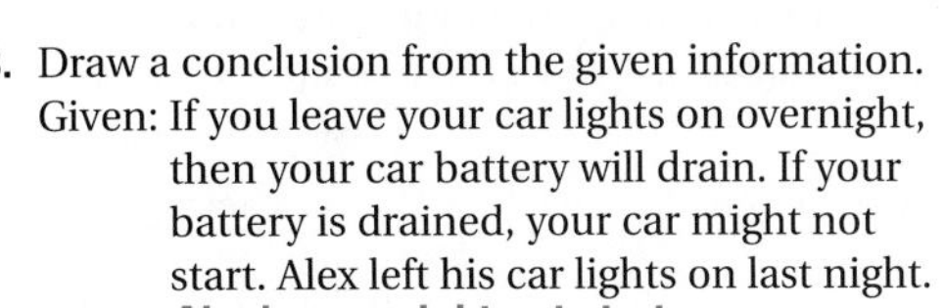

PRACTICE AND PROBLEM SOLVING

Independent Practice	
For Exercises	See Example
9–10	1
11	2
12	3
13	4

Extra Practice
Skills Practice p. S6
Application Practice p. S29

Does each conclusion use inductive or deductive reasoning?

9. The sum of the angle measures of a triangle is 180°. Two angles of a triangle measure 40° and 60°, so Kandy concludes that the third angle measures 80°. **deductive reasoning**
10. All of the students in Henry's Geometry class are juniors. Alexander takes Geometry, but has another teacher. Henry concludes that Alexander is also a junior. **inductive reasoning**
11. Determine if the conjecture is valid by the Law of Detachment.
    Given: If one integer is odd and another integer is even, their product is even. The product of two integers is 24.
    Conjecture: One of the two integers is odd. **invalid**

2-3 Exercises

Assignment Guide

Assign *Guided Practice* exercises as necessary.

If you finished Examples 1–2
Basic 9–11
Average 9–11, 14
Advanced 9–11, 14

If you finished Examples 1–4
Basic 9–13, 15–18, 20, 22–25, 29–37
Average 9–14, 16, 18–25, 28–37
Advanced 9–14, 16, 18, 19, 21–37

Homework Quick Check
Quickly check key concepts.
Exercises: 10–13, 16, 18

Teaching Tip
Diversity Some students may not be familiar with time zones. For **Exercise 6,** you may want to use a globe to show how Earth is divided into 24 time zones. Explain that as you travel west, you gain one hour for each time zone you pass through. This accounts for Earth's rotation.

Answers

1. Possible answer: Inductive reasoning is based on a pattern of specific cases. Deductive reasoning is based on logical reasoning.

State Resources

go.hrw.com
State Resources Online
KEYWORD: MG7 Resources

Exercise 22 involves rewriting a given statement as a conditional and using logic to determine whether a conclusion is valid. This exercise prepares students for the Multi-Step Test Prep on page 102.

Answers

21. Possible answers: If Mary goes to the store, then I will go with her. Mary goes to the store. The conclusion "I will go with her" is valid by the Law of Detachment. If Jon goes to the movies, then he will eat popcorn. If Jon eats popcorn, then he needs a drink. The conclusion "If Jon goes to the movies, then he needs a drink" is valid by the Law of Syllogism.

22a. If a creature is a serpent, then it eats eggs.

b. No; possible answer: the Pigeon did not correctly apply the Law of Detachment; "Alice eats eggs" matches the conclusion of the conditional, not the hypothesis.

27a. If you live in San Diego, then you live in the United States.

b. If you do not live in California, then you do not live in San Diego. If you do not live in the United States, then you do not live in California.

c. If you do not live in the United States, then you do not live in San Diego.

d. They are contrapositives of each other.

12. **Science** Determine if the conjecture is valid by the Law of Syllogism.
Given: If an element is an alkali metal, then it reacts with water. If an element is in the first column of the periodic table, then it is an alkali metal.
Conjecture: If an element is in the first column of the periodic table, then it reacts with water. **valid**

13. Draw a conclusion from the given information.
Given: If Dakota watches the news, she is informed about current events.
If Dakota knows about current events, she gets better grades in Social Studies.
Dakota watches the news. **Dakota gets better grades in Social Studies.**

14. **Technology** Joseph downloads a file in 18 minutes with a dial-up modem. How long would it take to download the file with a Cheetah-Net cable modem? **0.24 min or 14.4 s**

CHEETAH-NET CABLE
75 Times As Fast As Dial-Up

LINK

Recreation

When the Gemini roller coaster opened in Cedar Point in 1978, it was the fastest roller coaster in the world. It no longer holds this title, but it is still a popular attraction.

Recreation **Use the true statements below for Exercises 15–18. Determine whether each conclusion is valid.**

I. The Gemini is at Cedar Point amusement park in Sandusky, OH.
II. Carter and Mary go to Cedar Point.
III. The Gemini roller coaster reaches speeds of 60 mi/h.
IV. When Carter goes to an amusement park, he rides all the roller coasters.

15. Carter went to Sandusky, OH. **valid**
16. Mary rode the Gemini. **invalid**
17. Carter rode a roller coaster that travels 60 mi/h. **valid**
18. Mary rode a roller coaster that travels 60 mi/h. **invalid**
19. **Critical Thinking** Is the argument below a valid application of the Law of Syllogism? Is the conclusion true? Explain your answers.
If $3 - x < 5$, then $x < -2$. If $x < -2$, then $-5x > 10$. Thus, if $3 - x < 5$, then $-5x > 10$.
yes; no; because the first conditional is false

20. **ERROR ANALYSIS** Below are two conclusions. Which is incorrect? Explain the error.
If two angles are complementary, their measures add to 90°. If an angle measures 90°, then it is a right angle. $\angle A$ and $\angle B$ are complementary.

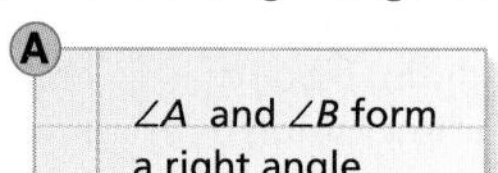

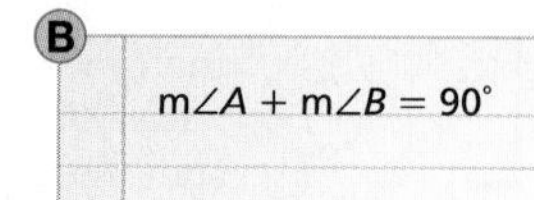

20. A; comp. ∠s are not necessarily adj., so they may not form a rt. ∠.

21. **Write About It** Write one example of a real-life logical argument that uses the Law of Detachment and one that uses the Law of Syllogism. Explain why the conclusions are valid.

22. This problem will prepare you for the Multi-Step Test Prep on page 102.
When Alice meets the Pigeon in Wonderland, the Pigeon thinks she is a serpent. The Pigeon reasons that serpents eat eggs, and Alice confirms that she has eaten eggs.
a. Write "Serpents eat eggs" as a conditional statement.
b. Is the Pigeon's conclusion that Alice is a serpent valid? Explain your reasoning.

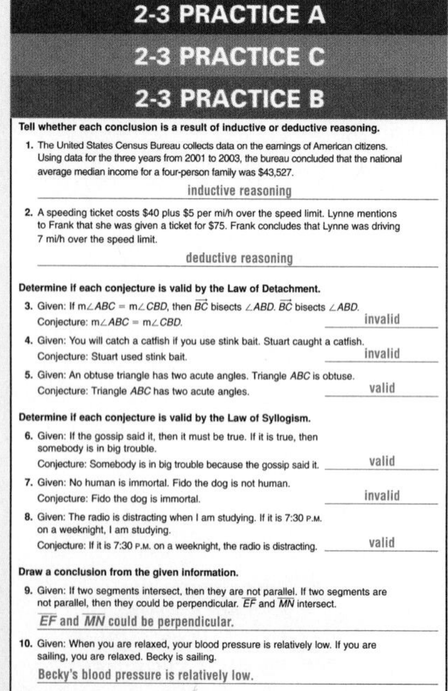

2-3 PRACTICE A
2-3 PRACTICE C
2-3 PRACTICE B

Tell whether each conclusion is a result of inductive or deductive reasoning.

1. The United States Census Bureau collects data on the earnings of American citizens. Using data for the three years from 2001 to 2003, the bureau concluded that the national average median income for a four-person family was $43,527.
inductive reasoning
2. A speeding ticket costs $40 plus $5 per mi/h over the speed limit. Lynne mentions to Frank that she was given a ticket for $75. Frank concludes that Lynne was driving 7 mi/h over the speed limit.
deductive reasoning

Determine if each conjecture is valid by the Law of Detachment.

3. Given: If $m\angle ABC = m\angle CBD$, then $\overrightarrow{BC}$ bisects $\angle ABD$. $\overrightarrow{BC}$ bisects $\angle ABD$.
Conjecture: $m\angle ABC = m\angle CBD$. **invalid**
4. Given: You will catch a catfish if you use stink bait. Stuart caught a catfish.
Conjecture: Stuart used stink bait. **invalid**
5. Given: An obtuse triangle has two acute angles. Triangle *ABC* is obtuse.
Conjecture: Triangle *ABC* has two acute angles. **valid**

Determine if each conjecture is valid by the Law of Syllogism.

6. Given: If the gossip said it, then it must be true. If it is true, then somebody is in big trouble.
Conjecture: Somebody is in big trouble because the gossip said it. **valid**
7. Given: No human is immortal. Fido the dog is not human.
Conjecture: Fido the dog is immortal. **invalid**
8. Given: The radio is distracting when I am studying. If it is 7:30 P.M. on a weeknight, I am studying.
Conjecture: If it is 7:30 P.M. on a weeknight, the radio is distracting. **valid**

Draw a conclusion from the given information.

9. Given: If two segments intersect, then they are not parallel. If two segments are not parallel, then they could be perpendicular. $\overline{EF}$ and $\overline{MN}$ intersect.
$\overline{EF}$ and $\overline{MN}$ could be perpendicular.
10. Given: When you are relaxed, your blood pressure is relatively low. If you are sailing, you are relaxed. Becky is sailing.
Becky's blood pressure is relatively low.

2-3 READING STRATEGIES

Conjectures can be verified by using deductive reasoning.

Types of Deductive Reasoning
- Law of Detachment: If $p \rightarrow q$ is a true statement and p is true, then q is true.
  Given: If I get over 90%, I will receive an A. I got 96%. Conjecture: I have an A.
- Law of Syllogism: If $p \rightarrow q$ and $q \rightarrow r$ are true statements, then $p \rightarrow r$ is a true statement.
  Given: If I oversleep, I will miss the bus. If I miss the bus, I will have to walk to school. Conjecture: If I oversleep, I will have to walk to school.

Apply the Laws of Deductive Reasoning.

1. If two angles are congruent, then they have the same measure. $\angle BAC \cong \angle CAD$.
Conjecture: **$m\angle BAC = m\angle CAD$**
Hypothesis: **Two angles are congruent.**
The conjecture is (valid/invalid) **valid** using the Law of **Detachment**.

2. (132°, S)
You are given the following statements about $\angle S$:
If $90° < m\angle S < 180°$, then $\angle S$ is obtuse. If $\angle S$ is obtuse, then it is not a right angle.
Conjecture: **If $90° < m\angle S < 180°$, then it is not a right angle.**
If $p \rightarrow q$ and $q \rightarrow r$, determine p, q, and r.
p: **The measure of $\angle S$ is greater than 90° and less than 180°.**
q: **The angle is obtuse.**
r: **The angle is not a right angle.**
The conjecture is (valid/invalid) **valid** based on the Law of **Syllogism**.

2-3 RETEACH

With inductive reasoning, you use examples to make a conjecture. With **deductive reasoning,** you use facts, definitions, and properties to draw conclusions and prove that conjectures are true.

Given: If two points lie in a plane, then the line containing those points also lies in the plane. *A* and *B* lie in plane $\mathcal{N}$.
Conjecture: $\overleftrightarrow{AB}$ lies in plane $\mathcal{N}$.

One valid form of deductive reasoning that lets you draw conclusions from true facts is called the **Law of Detachment.**

Given	If you have $2, then you can buy a snack. You have $2.	If you have $2, then you can buy a snack. You can buy a snack.
Conjecture	You can buy a snack.	You have $2.
Valid Conjecture?	Yes; the conditional is true and the hypothesis is true.	No; the hypothesis may or may not be true. For example, if you borrowed money, you could also buy a snack.

Tell whether each conclusion uses inductive or deductive reasoning.

1. A sign in the cafeteria says that a car wash is being held on the last Saturday of May. Tomorrow is the last Saturday of May, so Justin concludes that the car wash is tomorrow. **deductive**
2. So far, at the beginning of every Latin class, the teacher has had students review vocabulary. Latin class is about to start, and Jamilla assumes that they will first review vocabulary. **inductive**
3. Opposite rays are two rays that have a common endpoint and form a line. $\overrightarrow{YX}$ and $\overrightarrow{YZ}$ are opposite rays. **deductive**

Determine whether each conjecture is valid by the Law of Detachment.

4. Given: If you ride the Titan roller coaster in Arlington, Texas, then you will drop 255 feet.
Michael rode the Titan roller coaster.
Conjecture: Michael dropped 255 feet. **valid**
5. Given: A segment that is a diameter of a circle has endpoints on the circle.
$\overline{GH}$ has endpoints on a circle.
Conjecture: $\overline{GH}$ is a diameter. **invalid**

TEST PREP

23. The Supershots scored over 75 points in each of ten straight games. The newspaper predicts that they will score more than 75 points tonight. Which form of reasoning is this conclusion based on?
   - (A) Deductive reasoning, because the conclusion is based on logic
   - (B) Deductive reasoning, because the conclusion is based on a pattern
   - (C) Inductive reasoning, because the conclusion is based on logic
   - **(D)** Inductive reasoning, because the conclusion is based on a pattern

24. $\overrightarrow{HF}$ bisects $\angle EHG$. Which conclusion is NOT valid?
   - (F) E, F, and G are coplanar.
   - **(H)** $\overline{EF} \cong \overline{FG}$
   - (G) $\angle EHF \cong \angle FHG$
   - (J) $m\angle EHF = m\angle FHG$

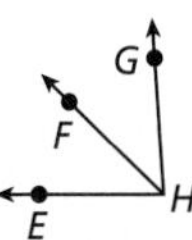

25. **Gridded Response** If Whitney plays a low G on her piano, the frequency of the note is 24.50 hertz. The frequency of a note doubles with each octave. What is the frequency in hertz of a G note that is 3 octaves above low G? **196**

CHALLENGE AND EXTEND

26. **Political Science** To be eligible to hold the office of the president of the United States, a person must be at least 35 years old, be a natural-born U.S. citizen, and have been a U.S. resident for at least 14 years. Given this information, what conclusion, if any, can be drawn from the statements below? Explain your reasoning.

   Andre is not eligible to be the president of the United States.
   Andre has lived in the United States for 16 years.

26. Either Andre is less than 35 years old, or he is not a natural-born citizen. Possible answer: Since there are 3 criteria to be eligible and he meets 1, he must not meet 1 of the remaining 2.

27. **Multi-Step** Consider the two conditional statements below.
   If you live in San Diego, then you live in California.
   If you live in California, then you live in the United States.
   a. Draw a conclusion from the given conditional statements.
   b. Write the contrapositive of each conditional statement.
   c. Draw a conclusion from the two contrapositives.
   d. How does the conclusion in part **a** relate to the conclusion in part **c**?

28. If Cassie goes to the skate park, Hanna and Amy will go. If Hanna or Amy goes to the skate park, then Marc will go. If Marc goes to the skate park, then Dallas will go. If only two of the five people went to the skate park, who were they? **Marc and Dallas**

SPIRAL REVIEW

Simplify each expression. *(Previous course)*

29. $2(x + 5)$ **$2x + 10$**
30. $(4y + 6) - (3y - 5)$ **$y + 11$**
31. $(3c + 4c) + 2(-7c + 7)$ **$-7c + 14$**

Find the coordinates of the midpoint of the segment connecting each pair of points. *(Lesson 1-6)*

32. $(1, 2)$ and $(4, 5)$ **$(2.5, 3.5)$**
33. $(-3, 6)$ and $(0, 1)$ **$(-1.5, 3.5)$**
34. $(-2.5, 9)$ and $(2.5, -3)$ **$(0, 3)$**

Identify the hypothesis and conclusion of each conditional statement. *(Lesson 2-2)*

35. If the fire alarm rings, then everyone should exit the building.
36. If two different lines intersect, then they intersect at exactly one point.
37. The statement $\overline{AB} \cong \overline{CD}$ implies that $AB = CD$.

TEST PREP DOCTOR For **Exercise 23,** remind students that they can use the definitions of *inductive reasoning* and *deductive reasoning* to eliminate choices **B** and **C.** Ask students whether the conclusion is based on a pattern or on logic, which should lead them to the correct choice, **D.**

Journal

Have students rewrite the Law of Detachment and the Law of Syllogism in words without using symbols.

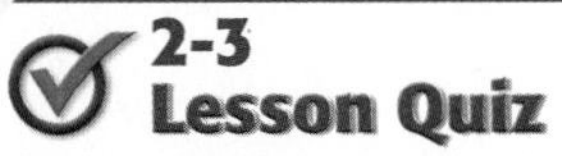

ALTERNATIVE ASSESSMENT

Have students write a valid and an invalid application of the Law of Detachment and the Law of Syllogism. Have students exchange papers with a partner and then explain why each conclusion is or is not valid.

Power Presentations with PowerPoint®

2-3 Lesson Quiz

1. Is the conclusion a result of inductive or deductive reasoning?

   At Reagan High School, students must pass Geometry before they take Algebra 2. Emily is in Algebra 2, so she must have passed Geometry. **deductive reasoning**

Determine if each conjecture is valid.

2. Given: If n is a natural number, then n is an integer. If n is an integer, then n is a rational number. 0.875 is a rational number.

   Conjecture: 0.875 is a natural number. **not valid**

3. Given: If an American citizen is at least 18 years old, then he or she is eligible to vote. Anna is a 20-year-old American citizen.

   Conjecture: Anna is eligible to vote. **valid**

Also available on transparency

2-3 PROBLEM SOLVING

Use the information in the table and the given statement to draw a valid conclusion for each. If a valid conclusion cannot be made, explain why not.

Volcanic Eruptions
I. A category 2 eruption produces a plume of ash 1–5 kilometers high.
II. An explosive volcano produces a volume of ash between 1 million and 10 million cubic meters.
III. If a volume of ash 10,000–1,000,000 cubic meters is produced, the eruption is classified as a category 1 eruption.
IV. If the eruption is severe, then it produces a plume of ash between 3 and 5 kilometers high.

1. **Given:** When Mt. Kilauea in Hawaii erupted, it produced a volume of ash between 10,000 and 1 million cubic meters.
   Conclusion: Mt. Kilauea's eruption in Hawaii was a category 1 eruption.
2. **Given:** The eruption of a volcano in Unzen, Japan, was not explosive.
   No valid conclusion can be made. Possible answer: The negation of the hypothesis does not produce a valid conclusion given a true conditional.
3. **Given:** The eruption of a volcano in Stromboli, Italy, was a category 2 eruption.
   Conclusion: The eruption of the volcano in Stromboli, Italy, produced a plume of ash 1–5 kilometers high.

Choose the best answer.

4. A sports store has running shoes 25% off original prices. Andrea sees a pair of running shoes that she likes for $65.00. Which is a valid conclusion?
   - A The sale price of the shoes is $40.00.
   - **(B)** The sale price of the shoes is $48.75.
   - C Andrea will buy the shoes.
   - D Andrea will not buy the shoes.
5. If Zack makes $1\frac{1}{2}$ quarts of lemonade, then he uses 6 lemons. If Zack makes $1\frac{1}{2}$ quarts of lemonade, then he makes 4 servings. Zack uses 5 lemons. Which is a valid conclusion?
   - F Zack makes 3 servings.
   - H Zack makes 1 quart.
   - G Zack makes 2 servings.
   - **(J)** Zack does not make $1\frac{1}{2}$ quarts.

2-3 CHALLENGE

Jake, Anna, and Ling are each originally from different states: California, Texas, and New Jersey. One of the students is on Student Council, one is on the swim team, and one is in the math club. The following statements are true.

a. Ling is not involved with student government this year, and she has never been to Texas.
b. Anna rides the bus with the person from New Jersey.
c. Jake is not from California.
d. Jake likes to go to his friend's swim meets.
e. The person from California is Ling's neighbor. It is the person she goes to for math questions.
f. The person on Student Council was born in the same month as Anna.

Use the information to answer each question.

1. Use statement b to formulate a conditional statement that is helpful in solving this puzzle.
   Possible answer: If Anna rides the bus with the person from New Jersey, then Anna is not from New Jersey. So Anna must be from California or Texas.
2. Determine whether or not each conjecture is valid. Explain.
   a. If a person is not involved with student government, then he or she is not on Student Council. Ling is not involved with student government. So Ling is not on Student Council.
      Yes; the conditional is true and the hypothesis is true.
   b. If a person is not from the West Coast, then he or she is not from California. Jake is not from California. Therefore, Jake is not from the West Coast.
      No; a true conditional and a true conclusion do not necessarily make the hypothesis true. Jake could be from a different West Coast state.
3. Use one of the statements listed above to write a conditional statement and make a valid conjecture. Describe how it is helpful in solving the puzzle.
   Possible answer: If Jake likes to go to his friend's swim meets, then he is not on the swim team. Conjecture: Jake is not on the swim team. So Jake is on Student Council or in the math club.
4. Apply what you know about deductive reasoning to tell where Jake, Anna, and Ling are from and in which activity they are involved.
   Jake is from Texas and is on Student Council. Anna is from California and is in the math club. Ling is from New Jersey and is on the swim team.

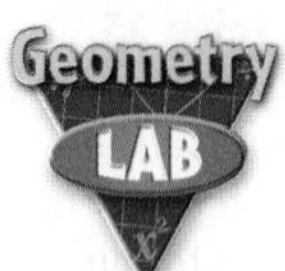

Organizer

Use with Lesson 2-3

Pacing:
Traditional 1 day
Block $\frac{1}{2}$ day

Objectives: Use tables to solve logic puzzles.

Use networks to solve logic puzzles.

Online Edition

Countdown Week 3

Resources

Geometry Lab Activities
2-3 Lab Recording Sheet

Teach

Discuss

Emphasize that the key to solving logic puzzles is to systematically work through the given information one piece at a time. As you read each clue, draw any conclusions you can and mark the diagram carefully before moving on to the next clue. In **Activity 2,** suggest that students redraw the network on their own paper.

State Resources

go.hrw.com
State Resources Online
KEYWORD: MG7 Resources

2-3 Geometry LAB

Solve Logic Puzzles

Use with Lesson 2-3

In Lesson 2-3, you used deductive reasoning to analyze the truth values of conditional statements. Now you will learn some methods for diagramming conditional statements to help you solve logic puzzles.

Activity 1

Bonnie, Cally, Daphne, and Fiona own a bird, cat, dog, and fish. No girl has a type of pet that begins with the same letter as her name. Bonnie is allergic to animal fur. Daphne feeds Fiona's bird when Fiona is away. Make a table to determine who owns which animal.

1. Since no girl has a type of pet that starts with the same letter as her name, place an X in each box along the diagonal of the table.

	Bird	Cat	Dog	Fish
Bonnie	×			
Cally		×		
Daphne			×	
Fiona				×

2. Bonnie cannot have a cat or dog because of her allergy. So she must own the fish, and no other girl can have the fish.

	Bird	Cat	Dog	Fish
Bonnie	×	×	×	✓
Cally		×		×
Daphne			×	×
Fiona				×

3. Fiona owns the bird, so place a check in Fiona's row, in the bird column. Place an X in the remaining boxes in the same column and row.

	Bird	Cat	Dog	Fish
Bonnie	×	×	×	✓
Cally	×	×		×
Daphne	×		×	×
Fiona	✓	×	×	×

4. Therefore, Daphne owns the cat, and Cally owns the dog.

	Bird	Cat	Dog	Fish
Bonnie	×	×	×	✓
Cally	×	×	✓	×
Daphne	×	✓	×	×
Fiona	✓	×	×	×

Try This

1. Because no one else can own the bird and Fiona owns only 1 pet.

1. After figuring out that Fiona owns the bird in Step 3, why can you place an X in every other box in that row and column?
2. Ally, Emily, Misha, and Tracy go to a dance with Danny, Frank, Jude, and Kian. Ally and Frank are siblings. Jude and Kian are roommates. Misha does not know Kian. Emily goes with Kian's roommate. Tracy goes with Ally's brother. Who went to the dance with whom?

	Danny	Frank	Jude	Kian
Ally	×	×	×	✓
Emily	×	×	✓	×
Misha	✓	×	×	×
Tracy	×	✓	×	×

Activity 2

A farmer has a goat, a wolf, and a cabbage. He wants to transport all three from one side of a river to the other. He has a boat, but it has only enough room for the farmer and one thing. The wolf will eat the goat if they are left alone together, and the goat will eat the cabbage if they are left alone. How can the farmer get everything to the other side of the river?

You can use a *network* to solve this kind of puzzle. A **network** is a diagram of *vertices* and *edges*, also known as a graph. An **edge** is a curve or a segment that joins two *vertices* of the graph. A **vertex** is a point on the graph.

1. Let *F* represent the farmer, *W* represent the wolf, *G* represent the goat, and *C* represent the cabbage. Use an ordered pair to represent what is on each side of the river. The first ordered pair is (*FWGC*, —), and the desired result is (—, *FWGC*).

2. Draw a vertex and label it with the first ordered pair. Then draw an edge and vertex for each possible trip the farmer could make across the river. If at any point a path results in an unworkable combination of things, no more edges can be drawn from that vertex.

3. From each workable vertex, continue to draw edges and vertices that represent the next trip across the river. When you get to a vertex for (—, *FWGC*), the network is complete.

4. Use the network to write out the solution in words.

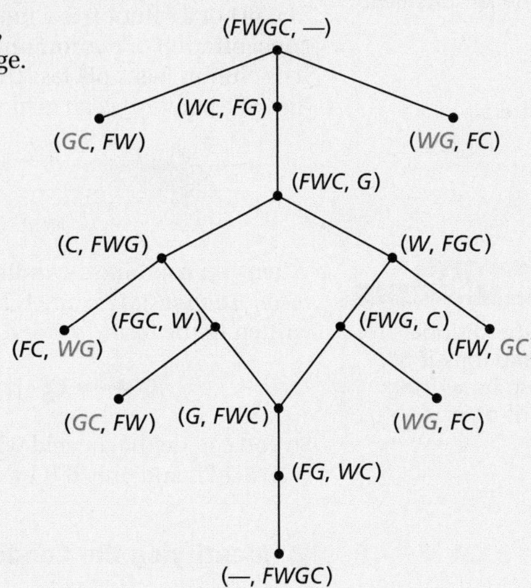

Try This

3. What combinations are unworkable? Why? **WG and GC; because the wolf will eat the goat and the goat will eat the cabbage**
4. How many solutions are there to the farmer's transport problem? How many steps does each solution take? **2; 7**
5. What is the advantage of drawing a complete solution network rather than working out one solution with a diagram?
6. Madeline has two measuring cups—a 1-cup measuring cup and a $\frac{3}{4}$-cup measuring cup. Neither cup has any markings on it. How can Madeline get exactly $\frac{1}{2}$ cup of flour in the larger measuring cup? Complete the network below to solve the problem.

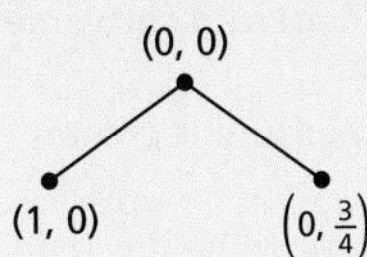

Close

Key Concept

Many logic puzzles can be solved by the process of elimination if you work with the given clues in a careful and systematic way. Diagrams can be used to organize each piece of the puzzle and to help visualize the final outcome.

Assessment

Journal Have students explain how they reached their conclusions in one of the *Try This* puzzles.

Answers

5. Possible answer: You can see all solutions instead of just 1 possible solution.

6.

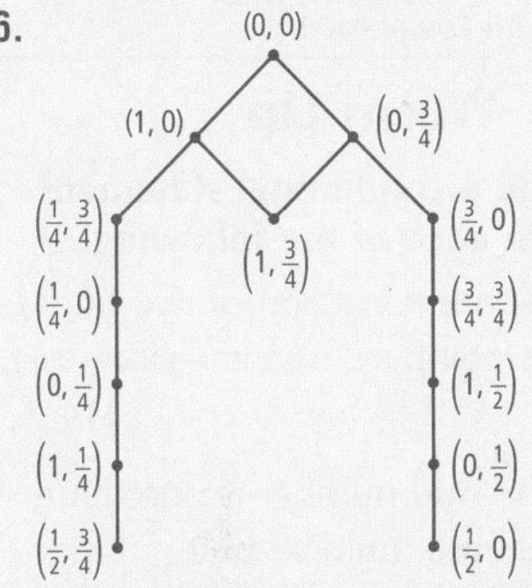

Possible answer: Fill the 1 c cup. Pour the contents into the $\frac{3}{4}$ c cup. Empty the $\frac{3}{4}$ c cup so you have $\frac{1}{4}$ c in the larger cup. Transfer this to the $\frac{3}{4}$ c cup, and fill the 1 c cup. Use the contents of the 1c cup to fill the $\frac{3}{4}$ c cup, leaving $\frac{1}{2}$ c in the 1 c cup.

Teacher to Teacher

Some students really enjoy logic puzzles. I like to challenge these students with more complicated puzzles that don't have the grid already provided. Creating the grid makes students organize the information in the puzzle before trying to solve it.

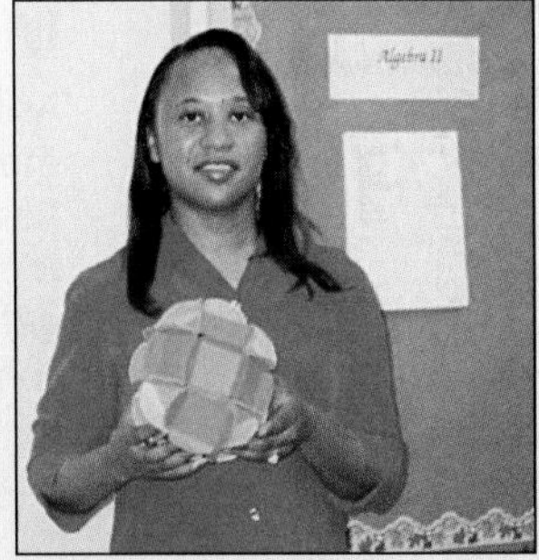

Many grocery stores and bookstores sell magazines with logic puzzles. Internet sites are another good resource for logic puzzles.

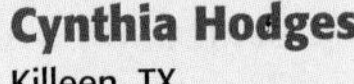

Cynthia Hodges
Killeen, TX

2-4 Organizer

Pacing: Traditional 1 day
Block $\frac{1}{2}$ day

Objective: Write and analyze biconditional statements.

Geometry Lab
In *Geometry Lab Activities*

Online Edition
Tutorial Videos

Countdown Week 3

Warm Up

Write a conditional statement from each of the following.

1. The intersection of two lines is a point. If two lines intersect, then they intersect in a point.
2. An odd number is one more than a multiple of 2. If a number is odd, then it is one more than a multiple of 2.
3. Write the converse of the conditional "If Pedro lives in Chicago, then he lives in Illinois." Find its truth value. If Pedro lives in Illinois, then he lives in Chicago; F.

Also available on transparency

Math Humor

Q: Why was the math book sad?
A: It had too many problems.

2-4 Biconditional Statements and Definitions

Objective
Write and analyze biconditional statements.

Vocabulary
biconditional statement
definition
polygon
triangle
quadrilateral

Who uses this?
A gardener can plan the color of the hydrangeas she plants by checking the pH of the soil.

The pH of a solution is a measure of the concentration of hydronium ions in the solution. If a solution has a pH less than 7, it is an acid. Also, if a solution is an acid, it has a pH less than 7.

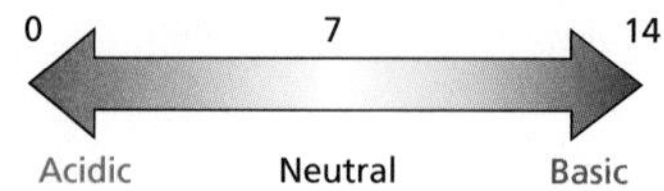

Writing Math
The biconditional "p if and only if q" can also be written as "p iff q" or $p \leftrightarrow q$.

When you combine a conditional statement and its converse, you create a *biconditional statement.* A **biconditional statement** is a statement that can be written in the form "p if and only if q." This means "if p, then q" and "if q, then p."

$$p \leftrightarrow q \text{ means } p \rightarrow q \text{ and } q \rightarrow p$$

So you can define an acid with the following biconditional statement: A solution is an acid if and only if it has a pH less than 7.

EXAMPLE 1 Identifying the Conditionals within a Biconditional Statement

Write the conditional statement and converse within each biconditional.

A **Two angles are congruent if and only if their measures are equal.**

Let p and q represent the following.

p: Two angles are congruent.
q: Two angle measures are equal.

The two parts of the biconditional $p \leftrightarrow q$ are $p \rightarrow q$ and $q \rightarrow p$.
Conditional: If **two angles are congruent,** then their measures are equal.
Converse: If two angle measures are equal, then **the angles are congruent.**

B **A solution is a base $\leftrightarrow$ it has a pH greater than 7.**

Let x and y represent the following.

x: A solution is a base.
y: A solution has a pH greater than 7.

The two parts of the biconditional $x \leftrightarrow y$ are $x \rightarrow y$ and $y \rightarrow x$.
Conditional: If **a solution is a base,** then it has a pH greater than 7.
Converse: If a solution has a pH greater than 7, then **it is a base.**

CHECK IT OUT! **Write the conditional statement and converse within each biconditional.**

1a. An angle is acute iff its measure is greater than 0° and less than 90°.

1b. Cho is a member if and only if he has paid the \$5 dues.

1a. Conditional: If an ∠ is acute, then its measure is greater than 0° and less than 90°. Converse: If an ∠'s measure is greater than 0° and less than 90°, then the ∠ is acute.

1b. Conditional: If Cho is a member, then he has paid the \$5 dues. Converse: If Cho has paid the \$5 dues, then he is a member.

State Resources

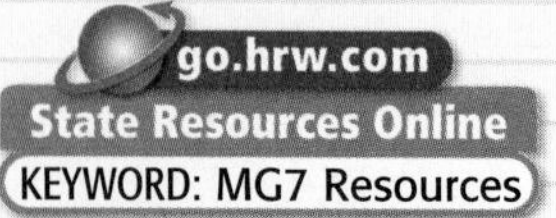

1 Introduce

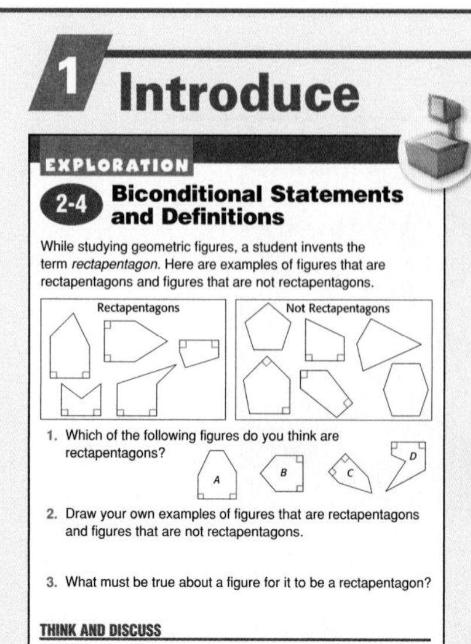

Motivate

Ask students to give a definition for a common classroom object, such as a piece of chalk. Possible answer: something you write with Use the students' answers to demonstrate why a definition must be precise. For example, a pen is something you write with, but it is not chalk. Have the students refine their definition until it is sufficiently precise.

Explorations and answers are provided in *Alternate Openers: Explorations Transparencies.*

EXAMPLE 2 **Writing a Biconditional Statement**

For each conditional, write the converse and a biconditional statement.

A **If $2x + 5 = 11$, then $x = 3$.**

Converse: If $x = 3$, then $2x + 5 = 11$.
Biconditional: $2x + 5 = 11$ if and only if $x = 3$.

B **If a point is a midpoint, then it divides the segment into two congruent segments.**

Converse: If a point divides a segment into two congruent segments, then the point is a midpoint.
Biconditional: A point is a midpoint if and only if it divides the segment into two congruent segments.

2a. Converse: If it is Independence Day, then the date is July 4th. Biconditional: It is July 4th if and only if it is Independence Day.

2b. Converse: If pts. are collinear, then they lie on the same line. Biconditional: Pts. lie on the same line if and only if they are collinear.

For each conditional, write the converse and a biconditional statement.

2a. If the date is July 4th, then it is Independence Day.

2b. If points lie on the same line, then they are collinear.

For a biconditional statement to be true, both the conditional statement and its converse must be true. If either the conditional or the converse is false, then the biconditional statement is false.

EXAMPLE 3 **Analyzing the Truth Value of a Biconditional Statement**

Determine if each biconditional is true. If false, give a counterexample.

A **A square has a side length of 5 if and only if it has an area of 25.**

Conditional: If a square has a side length of 5, then it has an area of 25. *The conditional is true.*
Converse: If a square has an area of 25, then it has a side length of 5. *The converse is true.*
Since the conditional and its converse are true, the biconditional is true.

B **The number n is a positive integer ↔ $2n$ is a natural number.**

Conditional: If n is a positive integer, then $2n$ is a natural number. *The conditional is true.*
Converse: If $2n$ is a natural number, then n is a positive integer. *The converse is false.*
If $2n = 1$, then $n = \frac{1}{2}$, which is not an integer. Because the converse is false, the biconditional is false.

Determine if each biconditional is true. If false, give a counterexample.

3a. An angle is a right angle iff its measure is 90°. T

3b. $y = -5 \leftrightarrow y^2 = 25$ F; $y = 5$

In geometry, biconditional statements are used to write *definitions*. A **definition** is a statement that describes a mathematical object and can be written as a true biconditional. Most definitions in the glossary are not written as biconditional statements, but they can be. The "if and only if" is implied.

Power Presentations with PowerPoint®

Additional Examples

Example 1

Write the conditional statement and converse within each biconditional.

A. An angle is obtuse if and only if its measure is greater than 90° and less than 180°.
Cond.: If an ∠ is obtuse, then its measure is greater than 90° and less than 180°. Conv.: If the measure of an ∠ is greater than 90° and less than 180°, then the ∠ is obtuse.

B. A solution is neutral ↔ its pH is 7.
Cond.: If a solution is neutral, then its pH is 7. Conv.: If the pH of a solution is 7, then it is neutral.

Example 2

For each conditional, write the converse and a biconditional statement.

A. If $5x - 8 = 37$, then $x = 9$.
Conv.: If $x = 9$, then $5x - 8 = 37$. Bicond.: $5x - 8 = 37$ if and only if $x = 9$.

B. If two angles have the same measure, then they are congruent. Conv.: If 2 ∠s are ≅, then they have the same measure. Bicond.: 2 ∠s have the same measure if and only if they are ≅.

INTERVENTION

Questioning Strategies

EXAMPLE 1

- What would be the effect if you reversed the order of the two statements that make up a biconditional? Explain.

EXAMPLE 2

- How do you form the converse of a conditional if the words *if* and *then* do not appear in the given statement?

2 Teach

ENGLISH LANGUAGE LEARNERS

Guided Instruction

Be sure that students understand the relationship between a conditional and its converse—that they are not necessarily logically equivalent—before introducing biconditional statements. Emphasize that biconditionals are used for definitions because they are conditionals in which the converse is also true. You may want to model something reversible for students, such as a reversible vest or jacket.

Reaching All Learners

Through Cooperative Learning

After you have discussed the concept of precise definitions on page 98, have each student write five definitions in biconditional form using the vocabulary terms from Chapters 1 and 2. Then have the students exchange papers and rewrite each definition in everyday language.

Reading Math Explain to students that *bi-* means "two." So the word *biconditional* means "two conditions." ENGLISH LANGUAGE LEARNERS

Power Presentations with PowerPoint®

Additional Examples

Example 3

Determine if each biconditional is true. If false, give a counterexample.

A. A rectangle has side lengths of 12 cm and 25 cm if and only if its area is 300 cm^2.
F; possible answer: a rectangle with side lengths of 30 cm and 10 cm

B. A natural number n is odd $\leftrightarrow$ n^2 is odd. T

Example 4

Write each definition as a biconditional.

A. A pentagon is a five-sided polygon. A figure is a pentagon if and only if it is a 5-sided polygon.

B. A right angle measures 90°. An ∠ is a rt. ∠ if and only if it measures 90°.

INTERVENTION
Questioning Strategies

EXAMPLE 3

- How do you find a counterexample for a biconditional?

EXAMPLE 4

- Can any definition be written as a biconditional? Explain.

In the glossary, a **polygon** is defined as a closed plane figure formed by three or more line segments. Each segment intersects exactly two other segments only at their endpoints, and no two segments with a common endpoint are collinear.

A **triangle** is defined as a three-sided polygon, and a **quadrilateral** is a four-sided polygon.

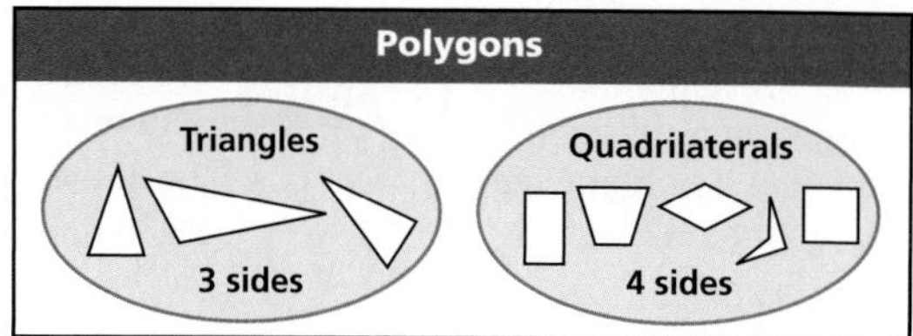

A good, precise definition can be used forward and backward. For example, if a figure is a quadrilateral, then it is a four-sided polygon. If a figure is a four-sided polygon, then it is a quadrilateral. To make sure a definition is precise, it helps to write it as a biconditional statement.

Helpful Hint

Think of definitions as being reversible. Postulates, however, are not necessarily true when reversed.

EXAMPLE 4 Writing Definitions as Biconditional Statements

Write each definition as a biconditional.

A **A triangle is a three-sided polygon.**
A figure is a triangle if and only if it is a three-sided polygon.

B **A segment bisector is a ray, segment, or line that divides a segment into two congruent segments.**
A ray, segment, or line is a segment bisector if and only if it divides a segment into two congruent segments.

CHECK IT OUT! **Write each definition as a biconditional.**

4a. A quadrilateral is a four-sided polygon.
4b. The measure of a straight angle is 180°.

4a. A figure is a quad. if and only if it is a 4-sided polygon.

4b. An ∠ is a straight ∠ if and only if its measure is 180°.

THINK AND DISCUSS

1. How do you determine if a biconditional statement is true or false?
2. Compare a triangle and a quadrilateral.
3. **GET ORGANIZED** Copy and complete the graphic organizer. Use the definition of a polygon to write a conditional, converse, and biconditional in the appropriate boxes.

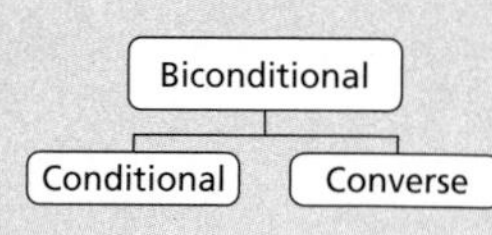

3 Close

Summarize

Ask students the following questions.

- "Why is it necessary to be able to write a definition as a biconditional statement?" Possible answer: so the definition is precise and reversible
- "When is a biconditional statement true?" when the cond. statement and conv. it contains are both true

ONGOING ASSESSMENT and INTERVENTION

Diagnose **Before the Lesson**
2-4 Warm Up, TE p. 96

Monitor **During the Lesson**
Check It Out! Exercises, SE pp. 96–98
Questioning Strategies, TE pp. 97–98

Assess **After the Lesson**
2-4 Lesson Quiz, TE p. 101
Alternative Assessment, TE p. 101

Answers to *Think and Discuss*

1. Possible answer: Find the truth value of the conditional and the converse it contains. If both are true, then the biconditional is true.
2. A △ has 3 sides and 3 vertices. A quad. has 4 sides and 4 vertices.
3. See p. A3.

2-4 Exercises

go.hrw.com
Homework Help Online
KEYWORD: MG7 2-4
Parent Resources Online
KEYWORD: MG7 Parent

GUIDED PRACTICE

1. **Vocabulary** How is a *biconditional statement* different from a conditional statement?

SEE EXAMPLE 1 p. 96

Write the conditional statement and converse within each biconditional.

2. Perry can paint the entire living room if and only if he has enough paint.
3. Your medicine will be ready by 5 P.M. if and only if you drop your prescription off by 8 A.M.

SEE EXAMPLE 2 p. 97

For each conditional, write the converse and a biconditional statement.

4. If a student is a sophomore, then the student is in the tenth grade.
5. If two segments have the same length, then they are congruent.

SEE EXAMPLE 3 p. 97

Multi-Step Determine if each biconditional is true. If false, give a counterexample.

6. $xy = 0 \leftrightarrow x = 0$ or $y = 0$. T
7. A figure is a quadrilateral if and only if it is a polygon. F; a △ is a polygon but not a quad.

SEE EXAMPLE 4 p. 98

Write each definition as a biconditional.

8. Parallel lines are two coplanar lines that never intersect.
9. A hummingbird is a tiny, brightly colored bird with narrow wings, a slender bill, and a long tongue.

PRACTICE AND PROBLEM SOLVING

Independent Practice

For Exercises	See Example
10–12	1
13–15	2
16–17	3
18–19	4

Extra Practice
Skills Practice p. S6
Application Practice p. S29

Write the conditional statement and converse within each biconditional.

10. Three points are coplanar if and only if they lie in the same plane.
11. A parallelogram is a rectangle if and only if it has four right angles.
12. A lunar eclipse occurs if and only if Earth is between the Sun and the Moon.

For each conditional, write the converse and a biconditional statement.

13. If today is Saturday or Sunday, then it is the weekend.
14. If Greg has the fastest time, then he wins the race.
15. If a triangle contains a right angle, then it is a right triangle.

Multi-Step Determine if each biconditional is true. If false, give a counterexample.

16. Felipe is a swimmer if and only if he is an athlete.
17. The number $2n$ is even if and only if n is an integer. T

16. F; possible answer: Felipe could be a runner.

Write each definition as a biconditional.

18. A circle is the set of all points in a plane that are a fixed distance from a given point.
19. A catcher is a baseball player who is positioned behind home plate and who catches throws from the pitcher.

2-4 Exercises

Assignment Guide

Assign *Guided Practice* exercises as necessary.

If you finished Examples 1–2
Basic 10–15
Average 10–15
Advanced 10–15

If you finished Examples 1–4
Basic 10–21, 24, 28, 30–34, 37–41, 46–54
Average 10–32, 35–41, 43–44, 46–54
Advanced 10–29, 30–34 even, 35–54

Homework Quick Check
Quickly check key concepts.
Exercises: 10, 14, 16, 18, 24, 30

Answers

1. Possible answer: A biconditional contains the conditional and its converse. A conditional is not reversible, but a biconditional is.
2. Conditional: If Perry can paint the entire living room, then he has enough paint. Converse: If Perry has enough paint, then he can paint the entire living room.
3. Conditional: If your medicine will be ready by 5 P.M., then you dropped your prescription off by 8 A.M. Converse: If you drop your prescription off by 8 A.M., then your medicine will be ready by 5 P.M.

State Resources

go.hrw.com
State Resources Online
KEYWORD: MG7 Resources

Answers

4. Converse: If a student is in the tenth grade, then the student is a sophomore. Biconditional: A student is a sophomore if and only if the student is in the tenth grade.
5. Converse: If 2 segs. are ≅, then they have the same length. Biconditional: 2 segs. have the same length if and only if they are ≅.
8. 2 lines are ∥ if and only if they are coplanar and never intersect.
9. An animal is a hummingbird if and only if it is a tiny, brightly colored bird with narrow wings, a slender bill, and a long tongue.
10. Conditional: If 3 pts. are coplanar, then they lie in the same plane. Converse: If 3 pts. lie in the same plane, then they are coplanar.
11. Conditional: If a ▱ is a rect., then it has 4 rt. ∡. Converse: If a ▱ has 4 rt. ∡, then it is a rect.
12. Conditional: If a lunar eclipse occurs, then Earth is between the Sun and the Moon. Converse: If Earth is between the Sun and the Moon, then a lunar eclipse occurs.
13. Converse: If it is the weekend, then today is Saturday or Sunday. Biconditional: Today is Saturday or Sunday if and only if it is the weekend.

14–15, 18–19. See p. A11.

Inclusion If students have difficulty with **Exercises 21** and **22,** suggest that they solve the equation in the hypothesis and in the conclusion and see if the solutions are the same.

MULTI-STEP TEST PREP **Exercise 37** involves writing statements as conditionals and then determining the truth value of the resulting biconditional. This exercise prepares students for the Multi-Step Test Prep on page 102.

Answers

24. An equil. △ is a △ with 3 ≅ sides.
25. A square is a quad. with 4 ≅ sides and 4 rt. ∠s.
26. A cell is a white blood cell if and only if it defends the body against invading organisms by engulfing them or releasing antibodies.
27. Possible answer: A bicycle also moves along the ground but is not an automobile.
28. Possible answer: A computer is a machine that performs computations but is not a calculator.
29. Possible answer: The definition does not say that the rays have a common endpoint.

35–37. See p. A11.

Algebra **Determine if a true biconditional can be written from each conditional statement. If not, give a counterexample.**

20. If $a = b$, then $|a| = |b|$. **no; possible answer: $a = 3$, $b = -3$**
21. If $3x - 2 = 13$, then $\frac{4}{5}x + 8 = 12$. **yes**
22. If $y^2 = 64$, then $3y = 24$. **no; possible answer: $y = -8$**
23. If $x > 0$, then $x^2 > 0$. **no; possible answer: $x = -2$**

Use the diagrams to write a definition for each figure.

24. 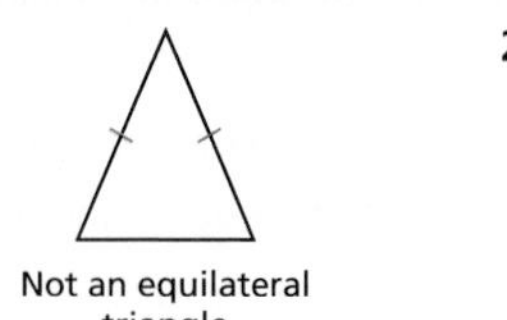

25. 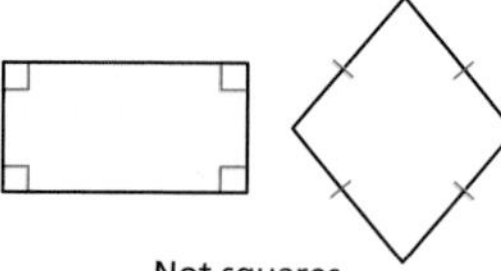

LINK Biology

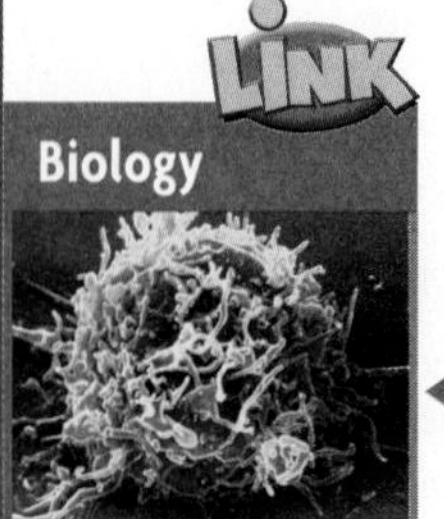

White blood cells live less than a few weeks. A drop of blood can contain anywhere from 7000 to 25,000 white blood cells.

26. **Biology** White blood cells are cells that defend the body against invading organisms by engulfing them or by releasing chemicals called *antibodies*. Write the definition of a white blood cell as a biconditional statement.

Explain why the given statement is not a definition.

27. An automobile is a vehicle that moves along the ground.
28. A calculator is a machine that performs computations with numbers.
29. An angle is a geometric object formed by two rays.

Chemistry **Use the table for Exercises 30–32. Determine if a true biconditional statement can be written from each conditional.**

pH	Examples
0	Battery Acid
4	Acid rain, tomato juice
6	Saliva
8	Sea water
13	Bleach, oven cleaner
14	Drain cleaner

30. If a solution has a pH of 4, then it is tomato juice. **no**
31. If a solution is bleach, then its pH is 13. **no**
32. If a solution has a pH greater than 7, then it is not battery acid. **no**

Complete each statement to form a true biconditional.

33. The circumference of a circle is 10π if and only if its radius is __?__ . **5**
34. Four points in a plane form a __?__ if and only if no three of them are collinear. **quad.**
35. **Critical Thinking** Write the definition of a biconditional statement as a biconditional statement. Use the conditional and converse within the statement to explain why your biconditional is true.

36. **Write About It** Use the definition of an angle bisector to explain what is meant by the statement "A good definition is reversible."

MULTI-STEP TEST PREP

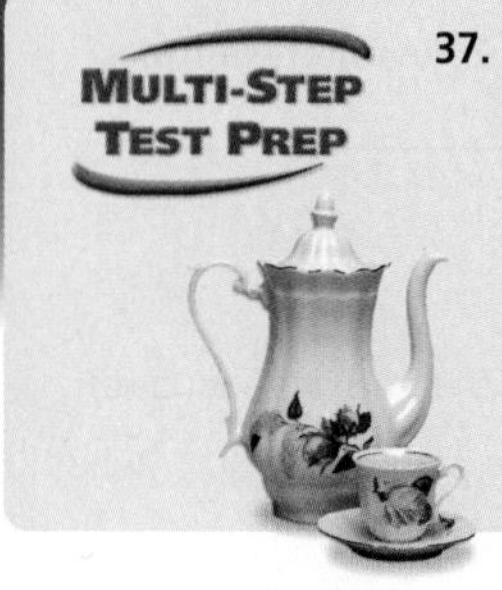

37. This problem will prepare you for the Multi-Step Test Prep on page 102.
    a. Write "I say what I mean" and "I mean what I say" as conditionals.
    b. Explain why the biconditional statement implied by Alice is false.

"Then you should say what you mean," the March Hare went on.

"I do," Alice hastily replied; "at least—at least I mean what I say—that's the same thing, you know."

The Granger Collection, New York

2-4 PRACTICE A
2-4 PRACTICE C
2-4 PRACTICE B

Write the conditional statement and converse within each biconditional.

1. The tea kettle is whistling if and only if the water is boiling.
   Conditional: If the tea kettle is whistling, then the water is boiling.
   Converse: If the water is boiling, then the tea kettle is whistling.
2. A biconditional is true if and only if the conditional and converse are both true.
   Conditional: If a biconditional is true, then the conditional and converse are both tru
   Converse: If the conditional and converse are both true, then the biconditional is tru

For each conditional, write the converse and a biconditional statement.

3. Conditional: If n is an odd number, then $n - 1$ is divisible by 2.
   Converse: If $n - 1$ is divisible by 2, then n is an odd number.
   Biconditional: n is an odd number if and only if $n - 1$ is divisible by 2.
4. Conditional: An angle is obtuse when it measures between 90° and 180°.
   Converse: If an angle measures between 90° and 180°, then the angle is obtuse.
   Biconditional: An angle is obtuse if and only if it measures between 90° and 180°.

Determine whether a true biconditional can be written from each conditional statement. If not, give a counterexample.

5. If the lamp is unplugged, then the bulb does not shine.
   No; possible answer: The switch could be off.
6. The date can be the 29th if and only if it is not February.
   No; possible answer: Leap years have a Feb. 29th.

Write each definition as a biconditional.

7. A cube is a three-dimensional solid with six square faces.
   A figure is a cube if and only if it is a three-dimensional solid with six square faces.
8. Tanya claims that the definition of *doofus* is "her younger brother."
   A person is a doofus if and only if the person is Tanya's younger brother.

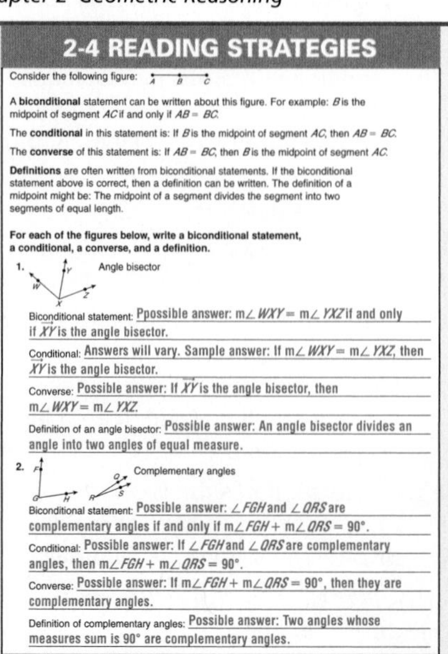

2-4 READING STRATEGIES

Consider the following figure: A B C

A **biconditional** statement can be written about this figure. For example: B is the midpoint of segment AC if and only if $AB = BC$.

The **conditional** in this statement is: If B is the midpoint of segment AC, then $AB = BC$.

The **converse** of this statement is: If $AB = BC$, then B is the midpoint of segment AC.

Definitions are often written from biconditional statements. If the biconditional statement above is correct, then a definition can be written. The definition of a midpoint might be: The midpoint of a segment divides the segment into two segments of equal length.

For each of the figures below, write a biconditional statement, a conditional, a converse, and a definition.

1. Angle bisector
   Biconditional statement: Ppossible answer: $m\angle WXY = m\angle YXZ$ if and only if $\overrightarrow{XY}$ is the angle bisector.
   Conditional: Answers will vary. Sample answer: If $m\angle WXY = m\angle YXZ$, then $\overrightarrow{XY}$ is the angle bisector.
   Converse: Possible answer: If $\overrightarrow{XY}$ is the angle bisector, then $m\angle WXY = m\angle YXZ$.
   Definition of an angle bisector: Possible answer: An angle bisector divides an angle into two angles of equal measure.
2. Complementary angles
   Biconditional statement: Possible answer: $\angle FGH$ and $\angle QRS$ are complementary angles if and only if $m\angle FGH + m\angle QRS = 90°$.
   Conditional: Possible answer: If $\angle FGH$ and $\angle QRS$ are complementary angles, then $m\angle FGH + m\angle QRS = 90°$.
   Converse: Possible answer: If $m\angle FGH + m\angle QRS = 90°$, then they are complementary angles.
   Definition of complementary angles: Possible answer: Two angles whose measures sum is 90° are complementary angles.

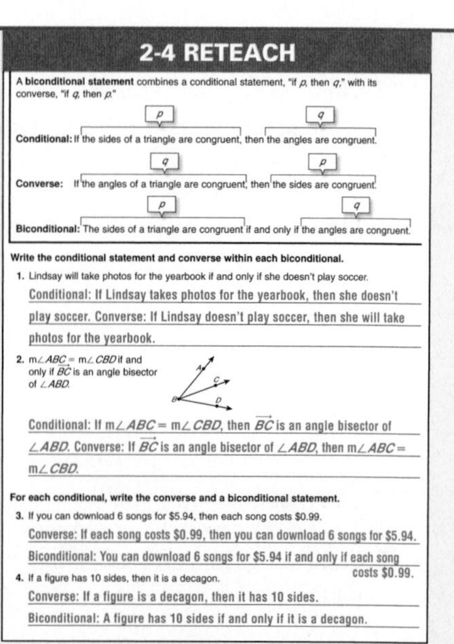

2-4 RETEACH

A **biconditional statement** combines a conditional statement, "if p, then q," with its converse, "if q, then p."

Conditional: If [the sides of a triangle are congruent]$_p$, then [the angles are congruent]$_q$.

Converse: If [the angles of a triangle are congruent]$_q$, then [the sides are congruent]$_p$.

Biconditional: [The sides of a triangle are congruent]$_p$ if and only if [the angles are congruent]$_q$.

Write the conditional statement and converse within each biconditional.

1. Lindsay will take photos for the yearbook if and only if she doesn't play soccer.
   Conditional: If Lindsay takes photos for the yearbook, then she doesn't play soccer. Converse: If Lindsay doesn't play soccer, then she will take photos for the yearbook.
2. $m\angle ABC = m\angle CBD$ if and only if $\overrightarrow{BC}$ is an angle bisector of $\angle ABD$.
   Conditional: If $m\angle ABC = m\angle CBD$, then $\overrightarrow{BC}$ is an angle bisector of $\angle ABD$. Converse: If $\overrightarrow{BC}$ is an angle bisector of $\angle ABD$, then $m\angle ABC = m\angle CBD$.

For each conditional, write the converse and a biconditional statement.

3. If you can download 6 songs for \$5.94, then each song costs \$0.99.
   Converse: If each song costs \$0.99, then you can download 6 songs for \$5.94.
   Biconditional: You can download 6 songs for \$5.94 if and only if each song costs \$0.99.
4. If a figure has 10 sides, then it is a decagon.
   Converse: If a figure is a decagon, then it has 10 sides.
   Biconditional: A figure has 10 sides if and only if it is a decagon.

38. Which is a counterexample for the biconditional "An angle measures 80° if and only if the angle is acute"?
   (A) $m\angle S = 60°$ (B) $m\angle S = 115°$ (C) $m\angle S = 90°$ (D) $m\angle S = 360°$

39. Which biconditional is equivalent to the spelling phrase "*I* before *E* except after *C*"?
   (F) The letter *I* comes before *E* if and only if *I* follows *C*.
   (G) The letter *E* comes before *I* if and only if *E* follows *C*.
   (H) The letter *E* comes before *I* if and only if *E* comes before *C*.
   (J) The letter *I* comes before *E* if and only if *I* comes before *C*.

40. Which conditional statement can be used to write a true biconditional?
   (A) If a number is divisible by 4, then it is even.
   (B) If a ratio compares two quantities measured in different units, the ratio is a rate.
   (C) If two angles are supplementary, then they are adjacent.
   (D) If an angle is right, then it is not acute.

41. **Short Response** Write the two conditional statements that make up the biconditional "You will get a traffic ticket if and only if you are speeding." Is the biconditional true or false? Explain your answer.

CHALLENGE AND EXTEND

42. **Critical Thinking** Describe what the Venn diagram of a true biconditional statement looks like. How does this support the idea that a definition can be written as a true biconditional?

43. Consider the conditional "If an angle measures 105°, then the angle is obtuse."
   a. Write the inverse of the conditional statement.
   b. Write the converse of the inverse.
   c. How is the converse of the inverse related to the original conditional?
   d. What is the truth value of the biconditional statement formed by the inverse of the original conditional and the converse of the inverse? Explain.

43a. If an ∠ does not measure 105°, then the ∠ is not obtuse.
b. If an ∠ is not obtuse, then it does not measure 105°.
c. It is the contrapositive of the original.
d. F; the inverse is false, and its converse is true.

44. Suppose *A*, *B*, *C*, and *D* are coplanar, and *A*, *B*, and *C* are not collinear. What is the truth value of the biconditional formed from the true conditional "If $m\angle ABD + m\angle DBC = m\angle ABC$, then *D* is in the interior of $\angle ABC$"? Explain.

45. Find a counterexample for "*n* is divisible by 4 if and only if n^2 is even." **Possible answer: $n = 2$**

SPIRAL REVIEW

Describe how the graph of each function differs from the graph of the parent function $y = x^2$. *(Previous course)*

46. $y = \frac{1}{2}x^2 + 5$ 47. $y = -2x^2 - 1$ 48. $y = (x - 2)(x + 2)$ **The graph is shifted 4 units down.**

46. The graph is shifted 5 units up and is wider than the graph of the parent function.

A transformation maps *S* onto *T* and *X* onto *Y*. Name each of the following. *(Lesson 1-7)*

49. the image of *S* **T** 50. the image of *X* **Y** 51. the preimage of *T* **S**

Determine if each conjecture is true. If not, give a counterexample. *(Lesson 2-1)*

52. If $n \geq 0$, then $\frac{n}{2} > 0$. 53. If *x* is prime, then $x + 2$ is also prime.

54. The vertices of the image of a figure under the translation $(x, y) \rightarrow (x + 0, y + 0)$ have the same coordinates as the preimage. **T**

52. F; possible answer: $n = 0$
53. F; possible answer: $x = 2$

2-4 PROBLEM SOLVING

Use the table for Exercises 1–4. Determine if a true biconditional statement can be written from each conditional. If so, then write a biconditional. If not, then explain why not.

Mountain Bike Races	Characteristics
Cross-country	A massed-start race. Riders must carry their own tools to make repairs.
Downhill	Riders start at intervals. The rider with the lowest time wins.
Freeride	Courses contain cliffs, drops, and ramps. Scoring depends on the style and the time.
Marathon	A massed-start race that covers more than 250 kilometers.

1. If a mountain bike race is mass-started, then it is a cross-country race.
   No; marathon races are also mass-started, so the conditional is false.
2. If a mountain bike race is downhill, then time is a factor in who wins.
   No; time is also a factor in freeride races, so the converse is false.
3. If a mountain bike race covers more than 250 kilometers, then it is a marathon race.
   Yes; a mountain bike race covers 250 kilometers if and only if it is a marathon race.
4. If a race course contains cliffs, drops, and ramps, then it is not a marathon race.
   No; a downhill race does not contain cliffs, drops, and ramps, so the converse is false.

Choose the best answer.

5. The cat is the only species that can hold its tail vertically while it walks.
   A The converse of this statement is false.
   B The biconditional of this statement is false.
   (C) The biconditional of this statement is true.
   D This statement cannot be written as a biconditional.
6. Which conditional statement can be used to write a true biconditional?
   F If you travel 2 miles in 4 minutes, then distance is a function of time.
   (G) If the distance depends on the time, then distance is a function of time.
   H If *y* increases as *x* increases, then *y* is a function of *x*.
   J If *y* is not a function of *x*, then *y* does not increase as *x* increases.

2-4 CHALLENGE

A **truth table** is used to represent all of the possible outcomes of compound statements, where *p* is the hypothesis and *q* is the conclusion.

1. Complete the truth table below.

Hypothesis	Conclusion	Conditional	Converse	Biconditional
p	q	$p \rightarrow q$	$q \rightarrow p$	$p \leftrightarrow q$
T	T	T	T	T
T	F	F	T	F
F	T	T	F	F
F	F	T	T	T

2. Under what circumstances is a biconditional statement true?
   when *p* and *q* are both true or when *p* and *q* are both false
3. Compare and contrast the truth values of conditional and biconditional statements.
   The truth values are the same except when the hypothesis is false and the conclusion is true. In this case, the conditional is true and the biconditional is false.
4. Two statements are **logically equivalent** if they have the same truth table values. Suppose "Contrapositive" were added to the truth table. Which of the statements is logically equivalent to the contrapositive of $p \rightarrow q$?
   $p \rightarrow q$; both are true except for the case when *p* is true and *q* is false.
5. Give an example in which a conditional statement is true, but its biconditional is false. Then explain why the biconditional is false.
   Possible answer: If an angle measures 105°, then it is obtuse. Biconditional: An angle measures 105° if and only if it is obtuse. The biconditional is false because the converse is false.

Rewrite each definition in biconditional form.

6. The midpoint of $\overline{AB}$ is the point *M* such that *M* is on $\overline{AB}$ and $AM = MB$.
   M is the midpoint of $\overline{AB}$ if and only if *M* is on $\overline{AB}$ and $AM = MB$.
7. A bisector of a segment is a line, ray, or segment that intersects the segment at its midpoint.
   A figure is a bisector of a segment if and only if it is a line, ray, or segment that intersects the segment at its midpoint.
8. A chord of a circle is a segment that has its endpoints on the circle.
   A segment is a chord of a circle if and only if the endpoints of the segment

COMMON ERROR ALERT

For **Exercise 20,** students may have forgotten the concept of absolute value. Encourage them to try different combinations of positive and negative numbers. They should discover that if *a* and *b* are opposites, then the converse is false. So a true biconditional cannot be written.

TEST PREP DOCTOR If students answer **Exercise 38** incorrectly, ask them to write out the conditional and its converse as two separate statements and determine whether each is true or false. In this problem, the conditional is true, but its converse is false. The counterexample must be an acute angle, so the answer is **A.**

Answers

41–42, 44, 47. See p. A11.

Journal

Ask students to use an example to explain a biconditional statement and to describe how it is related to the two conditionals it contains.

ALTERNATIVE ASSESSMENT

Have students look up two everyday words, such as shirt, book, tricycle, or house, in the dictionary. Have them use the dictionary definition to write a biconditional statement for each term. Then have them explain whether the dictionary definition qualifies as a "good" definition.

Power Presentations with PowerPoint®

2-4 Lesson Quiz

1. For the conditional "If an angle is right, then its measure is 90°," write the converse and a biconditional statement. Conv.: If an ∠ measures 90°, then the ∠ is rt. Bicond.: An ∠ is rt. iff its measure is 90°.
2. Determine if the biconditional "Two angles are complementary if and only if they are both acute" is true. If false, give a counterexample. F; possible answer: 30° and 40°
3. Write the definition "An acute triangle is a triangle with three acute angles" as a biconditional. A △ is acute iff it has 3 acute ∠s.

Also available on transparency

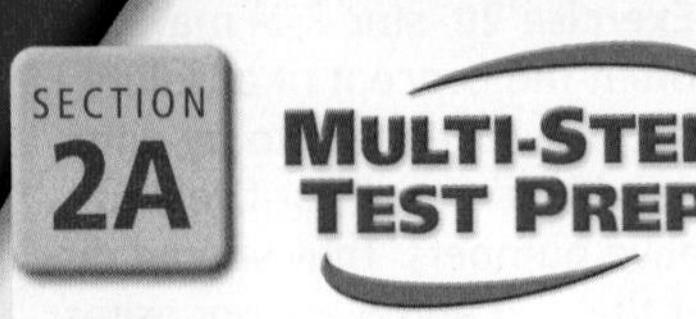

Organizer

Objective: Assess students' ability to apply concepts and skills in Lessons 2-1 through 2-4 in a real-world format.

 **Online Edition**

Resources

 ***Geometry Assessments***
www.mathtekstoolkit.org

Problem	Text Reference
1	Lesson 2-1
2	Lesson 2-2
3	Lesson 2-3
4	Lesson 2-4

Answers

3. No; no hypothesis is known to be true, so the Law of Detachment cannot be applied. No conclusion matches another hypothesis, so the Law of Syllogism cannot be applied.
4. I breathe if and only if I sleep. This biconditional is made of 2 conditionals: If I breathe, then I sleep, and if I sleep, then I breathe. The second is true, but the first is not. So the biconditional is false.

State Resources

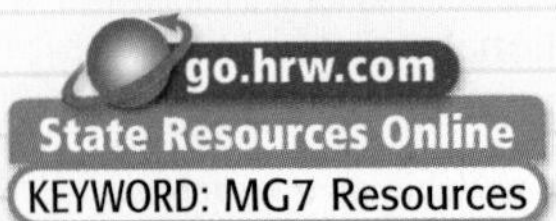

CHAPTER 2

MULTI-STEP TEST PREP

SECTION 2A

Inductive and Deductive Reasoning

Rhyme or Reason
Alice's Adventures in Wonderland originated as a story told by Charles Lutwidge Dodgson (Lewis Carroll) to three young traveling companions. The story is famous for its wordplay and logical absurdities.

1. When Alice first meets the Cheshire Cat, she asks what sort of people live in Wonderland. The Cat explains that everyone in Wonderland is mad. What conjecture might the Cat make since Alice, too, is in Wonderland? **Alice is mad.**

2. **"I don't much care where—" said Alice.**
"Then it doesn't matter which way you go," said the Cat.
"—so long as I get *somewhere*," Alice added as an explanation.
"Oh, you're sure to do that," said the Cat, "if you only walk long enough."

Write the conditional statement implied by the Cat's response to Alice. **If you only walk long enough, then you're sure to get somewhere.**

3. **"Well, then," the Cat went on, "you see a dog growls when it's angry, and wags its tail when it's pleased. Now I growl when I'm pleased, and wag my tail when I'm angry. Therefore I'm mad."**

Is the Cat's conclusion valid by the Law of Detachment or the Law of Syllogism? Explain your reasoning.

4. **"You might just as well say," added the Dormouse, who seemed to be talking in his sleep, "that 'I breathe when I sleep' is the same thing as 'I sleep when I breathe'!"**

Write a biconditional statement from the Dormouse's example. Explain why the biconditional statement is false.

Black and White Detail. The Pierpont Morgan Library Art Resource, NY

INTERVENTION

Scaffolding Questions

1. What pattern has the Cat noticed about the people in Wonderland? They are all mad.
2. What is the hypothesis of the Cat's statement? You walk long enough. What is the conclusion? You'll get somewhere.
3. What conditionals can be formed from the Cat's statements? If a dog is angry, then it growls. If a dog is pleased, then it wags its tail. If the Cat is pleased, then it growls. If the Cat is angry, then it wags its tail.
4. What conditional can you write based on the Dormouse's words? If I sleep, then I breathe. What is the converse? If I breathe, then I sleep.

Extension

The Footman tells Alice, "There might be some sense in your knocking, if we had the door between us." Assume that there is no sense in Alice's knocking. What can you conclude about a door between them? Explain. There is no door between them, by the Law of Contrapositive.

CHAPTER 2

SECTION 2A

Quiz for Lessons 2-1 Through 2-4

2-1 Using Inductive Reasoning to Make Conjectures

Find the next item in each pattern.

1. 1, 10, 18, 25, ... 31
2. July, May, March, ... January
3. $\frac{1}{8}, -\frac{1}{4}, \frac{1}{2}, \ldots$ −1
4. |, ┼, ╫, ... ╫╫
5. A biologist recorded the following data about the weight of male lions in a wildlife park in Africa. Use the table to make a conjecture about the average weight of a male lion.

ID Number	Weight (lb)
A1902SM	387.2
A1904SM	420.5
A1920SM	440.6
A1956SM	398.7
A1974SM	415.0

6. Complete the conjecture "The sum of two negative numbers is __?__." negative
7. Show that the conjecture "If an even number is divided by 2, then the result is an even number" is false by finding a counterexample. Possible answer: 6

2-2 Conditional Statements

8. Identify the hypothesis and conclusion of the conditional statement "An angle is obtuse if its measure is 107°."

Write a conditional statement from each of the following.

9. A whole number is an integer. If a number is a whole number, then it is an integer.
10. 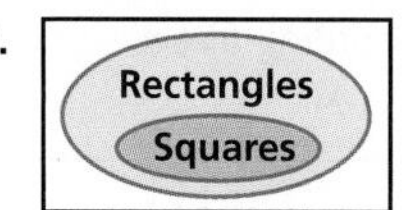

10. If a figure is a square, then it is a rect.
11. The diagonals of a square are congruent. If a figure is a square, then its diags. are ≅.

Determine if each conditional is true. If false, give a counterexample.

12. If an angle is acute, then it has a measure of 30°. F; possible answer: an ∠ that measures 60°
13. If $9x - 11 = 2x + 3$, then $x = 2$. T
14. Write the converse, inverse, and contrapositive of the statement "If a number is even, then it is divisible by 4." Find the truth value of each.

2-3 Using Deductive Reasoning to Verify Conjectures

15. Determine if the following conjecture is valid by the Law of Detachment.
Given: If Sue finishes her science project, she can go to the movie. Sue goes to the movie. not valid
Conjecture: Sue finished her science project.
16. Use the Law of Syllogism to draw a conclusion from the given information.
Given: If one angle of a triangle is 90°, then the triangle is a right triangle. If a triangle is a right triangle, then its acute angle measures are complementary.
If 1 ∠ of a △ is 90°, then its acute ∠ measures are comp.

2-4 Biconditional Statements and Definitions

17. For the conditional "If two angles are supplementary, the sum of their measures is 180°," write the converse and a biconditional statement.
18. Determine if the biconditional "$\sqrt{x} = 4$ if and only if $x = 16$" is true. If false, give a counterexample. T

READY TO GO ON? SECTION 2A

Organizer

Objective: Assess students' mastery of concepts and skills in Lessons 2-1 through 2-4.

Resources

Assessment Resources
Section 2A Quiz

Teacher One Stop™
Test & Practice Generator

INTERVENTION

Resources

***Ready to Go On? Intervention and Enrichment* Worksheets**

***Ready to Go On?* CD-ROM**

***Ready to Go On?* Online**

my.hrw.com

Answers

5, 14, 17. See p. A12.

READY TO GO ON?
Diagnose and Prescribe

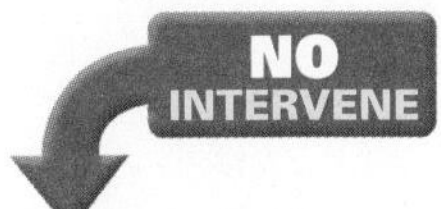

Ready to Go On? Intervention	*Ready to Go On? Intervention*, Section 2A		
	Worksheets	CD-ROM	Online
Lesson 2-1	2-1 Intervention	Activity 2-1	Diagnose and Prescribe Online
Lesson 2-2	2-2 Intervention	Activity 2-2	
Lesson 2-3	2-3 Intervention	Activity 2-3	
Lesson 2-4	2-4 Intervention	Activity 2-4	

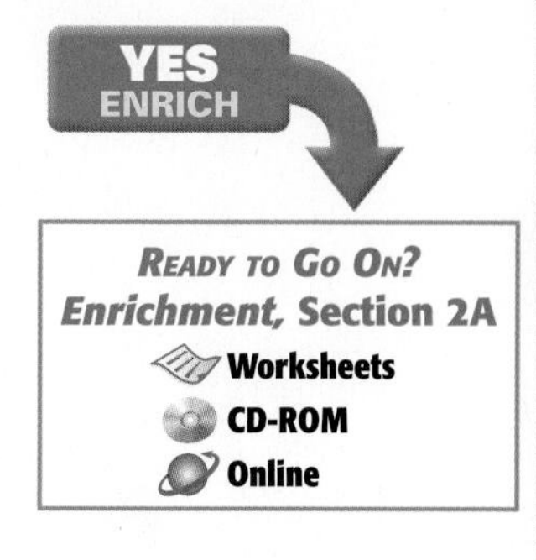

***Ready to Go On? Enrichment*, Section 2A**
Worksheets
CD-ROM
Online

SECTION 2B

Equations and Formulas

One-Minute Section Planner

Lesson	Lab Resources	Materials
Lesson 2-5 Algebraic Proof • Review properties of equality and use them to write algebraic proofs. • Identify properties of equality and congruence. ☐ SAT-10 ☑ NAEP ☑ ACT ☐ SAT ☑ SAT Subject Tests		**Optional** mirror
Lesson 2-6 Geometric Proof • Write two-column proofs. • Prove geometric theorems by using deductive reasoning. ☑ SAT-10 ☑ NAEP ☑ ACT ☐ SAT ☐ SAT Subject Tests		**Optional** geometry software, strips of paper
2-6 Geometry Lab Design Plans for Proofs • Learn strategies for planning the logical steps of a proof. ☐ SAT-10 ☐ NAEP ☐ ACT ☐ SAT ☐ SAT Subject Tests	***Geometry Lab Activities*** 2-6 Lab Recording Sheet	
Lesson 2-7 Flowchart and Paragraph Proofs • Write flowchart and paragraph proofs. • Prove geometric theorems by using deductive reasoning. ☑ SAT-10 ☑ NAEP ☐ ACT ☐ SAT ☐ SAT Subject Tests	***Technology Lab Activities*** 2-7 Technology Lab	**Optional** patty paper, colored pencils
Extension Introduction to Symbolic Logic • Analyze the truth value of conjunctions and disjunctions. • Construct truth tables to determine the truth value of logical statements. ☐ SAT-10 ☑ NAEP ☐ ACT ☐ SAT ☐ SAT Subject Tests		**Optional** index cards

MK = *Manipulatives Kit*

Math Background

Professional Learning

ALGEBRAIC PROOF

Lesson 2-5

Traditionally, students did not encounter formal proofs until they studied Euclidean geometry. However, students who have solved equations in an algebra course and have justified the steps in those solutions have already had experience in creating and presenting a mathematical proof.

As described in the Math Background notes for Section 2A, a proof is nothing more than a sound argument—an argument based on true premises and valid reasoning. When describing the solution of an equation as an algebraic proof, the premises for the proof are the given equation, the properties of equality, and the properties of real numbers. These premises may be used as justifications for each step in the solution of an equation, as shown below.

$2(3x + 1) = 32$	*Given equation*
$6x + 2 = 32$	*Distributive Property*
$6x = 30$	*Subtraction Property of Equality*
$x = 5$	*Division Property of Equality*

In writing algebraic proofs, students must understand that the justification for each step is not simply a description of the operation ("Subtract 2 from both sides.") but rather a general mathematical principle (Subtraction Property of Equality). This process is analogous to the process that students will use when they write geometric proofs.

GEOMETRIC PROOF

Lesson 2-6

Starting with the initial postulates and definitions presented in Chapter 1, geometric proofs provide the logical structure that supports an increasingly complex and powerful set of theorems. In a geometric proof, the premises are definitions, postulates, properties, and previously proven theorems.

By necessity, the early theorems in this course may seem trivial to students, and writing proofs for such apparently obvious statements can seem strange. However, students should recognize that these theorems are needed for later work. Also, the early theorems provide an opportunity for students to become familiar with the key elements of a proof.

In any case, it is worth noting that the theorems that come a bit later in the logical sequence (Chapters 3, 4, and beyond) are often more easily appreciated by students because the need to justify the theorems seems clearer.

PROOF FORMATS

Lessons 2-6, 2-7

This course introduces students to two-column proofs, flowchart proofs, and paragraph proofs. However, the main purpose of any proof, regardless of its format, is to present a logically sound argument. To that end, it is essential to point out to students that finding a proof and communicating a proof are two entirely different things.

Students who see completed proofs should understand that these are models for how to present a finished logical argument; they are *not* models of the step-by-step thought process for finding a proof. The process of finding a proof is rarely a linear one. Instead, it is more often a matter of sorting through the pieces of a puzzle, looking for logical connections, stumbling into blind alleys, and returning to the starting point (sometimes more than once). Once this hit-and-miss process has been completed, the proof can be organized and communicated in any format.

It is interesting to note that the first two-column proofs began appearing in textbooks around 1900. Since then, such proofs have often occupied a central role in geometry courses, and their prominence has led to misconceptions about their role, even among educators. According to a study that appeared in the *Journal for Research in Mathematics Education*, many pre-service teachers believe that an argument must be in two-column format in order to constitute a mathematical proof. Although the two-column format is practical because it reminds students that every statement must be supported with a reason, students should be reminded that the heart of any proof is the validity of the argument, not the format.

2-5 Organizer

Pacing: Traditional 1 day
Block $\frac{1}{2}$ day

Objectives: Review properties of equality and use them to write algebraic proofs.

Identify properties of equality and congruence.

Online Edition
Tutorial Videos

Countdown Week 4

Power Presentations with PowerPoint®

Warm Up

Solve each equation.

1. $3x + 5 = 17 \quad x = 4$

2. $r - 3.5 = 8.7 \quad r = 12.2$

3. $4t - 7 = 8t + 3 \quad t = -\frac{5}{2}$

4. $\frac{n+8}{5} = -6 \quad n = -38$

5. $2(y - 5) - 20 = 0 \quad y = 15$

Also available on transparency

Customer: How much are two eggs?

Waitress: $1.75.

Customer: How much is one egg?

Waitress: $1.50.

Customer: Then I'll have the other one.

2-5 Algebraic Proof

Objectives
Review properties of equality and use them to write algebraic proofs.

Identify properties of equality and congruence.

Vocabulary
proof

Who uses this?
Game designers and animators solve equations to simulate motion. (See Example 2.)

A **proof** is an argument that uses logic, definitions, properties, and previously proven statements to show that a conclusion is true.

If you've ever solved an equation in Algebra, then you've already done a proof! An algebraic proof uses algebraic properties such as the properties of equality and the Distributive Property.

Remember!
The Distributive Property states that $a(b + c) = ab + ac$.

Properties of Equality

Addition Property of Equality	If $a = b$, then $a + c = b + c$.
Subtraction Property of Equality	If $a = b$, then $a - c = b - c$.
Multiplication Property of Equality	If $a = b$, then $ac = bc$.
Division Property of Equality	If $a = b$ and $c \neq 0$, then $\frac{a}{c} = \frac{b}{c}$.
Reflexive Property of Equality	$a = a$
Symmetric Property of Equality	If $a = b$, then $b = a$.
Transitive Property of Equality	If $a = b$ and $b = c$, then $a = c$.
Substitution Property of Equality	If $a = b$, then b can be substituted for a in any expression.

As you learned in Lesson 2-3, if you start with a true statement and each logical step is valid, then your conclusion is valid.

An important part of writing a proof is giving justifications to show that every step is valid. For each justification, you can use a definition, postulate, property, or a piece of information that is given.

EXAMPLE 1 **Solving an Equation in Algebra**

Solve the equation $-5 = 3n + 1$. Write a justification for each step.

$-5 = 3n + 1$	Given equation
$\underline{-1 \qquad -1}$	Subtraction Property of Equality
$-6 = 3n$	Simplify.
$\frac{-6}{3} = \frac{3n}{3}$	Division Property of Equality
$-2 = n$	Simplify.
$n = -2$	Symmetric Property of Equality

1. Solve the equation $\frac{1}{2}t = -7$. Write a justification for each step.

$\frac{1}{2}t = -7$ (Given); $2\left(\frac{1}{2}t\right) = 2(-7)$ (Mult. Prop. of =); $t = -14$ (Simplify.)

State Resources

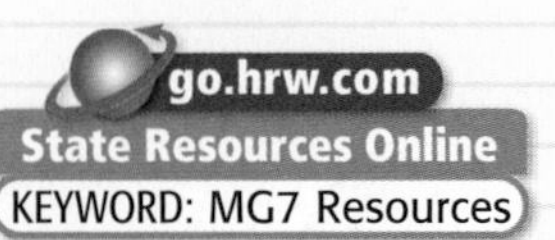

go.hrw.com
State Resources Online
KEYWORD: MG7 Resources

1 Introduce

EXPLORATION

2-5 Algebraic Proof

The solution to an algebraic equation is a type of proof. The steps must appear in the correct order, and you must be able to justify each step.

1. Write a step-by-step solution of the linear equation by placing the given equations in the correct order.

$3x - 12 + 5 = 17$
$3x = 24$
$3x - 7 = 17$
$3(x - 4) + 5 = 17$
$x = 8$

2. What property do you use to go from step a to step b?
3. What do you do to the equation to go from step c to step d?
4. What do you do to the equation to go from step d to step e?

Motivate

Ask students to raise their hands if they have ever written a proof. Then ask students to raise their hands if they have ever solved an algebraic equation. Explain to students that if they have solved an equation, then they have already written a type of proof.

Explorations and answers are provided in *Alternate Openers: Explorations Transparencies.*

COMMON ERROR ALERT

Some students incorrectly use the equal sign versus the congruence symbol. Remind them that numbers are equal and figures are congruent. Stress that $\overline{AB}$ and $\angle PQR$ are *figures,* so they cannot be equal, and AB and $m\angle PQR$ are *measures,* and thus are numbers.

Power Presentations with PowerPoint®

Additional Examples

Example 1

Solve the equation $4m - 8 = -12$. Write a justification for each step.

$4m - 8 = -12$ (Given); $4m = -4$ (Add. Prop. of =); $m = -1$ (Div. Prop. of =)

Example 2

What is the temperature in degrees Fahrenheit F when it is 15°C? Solve the equation $F = \frac{9}{5}C + 32$ for F and justify each step.

$F = \frac{9}{5}C + 32$ (Given);
$F = \frac{9}{5}(15) + 32$ (Subst.);
$F = 27 + 32$ (Simplify.); $F = 59$ (Simplify.)

EXAMPLE 2 Problem-Solving Application

To simulate the motion of an object in a computer game, the designer uses the formula $sr = 3.6p$ to find the number of pixels the object must travel during each second of animation. In the formula, s is the desired speed of the object in kilometers per hour, r is the scale of pixels per meter, and p is the number of pixels traveled per second.

The graphics in a game are based on a scale of 6 pixels per meter. The designer wants to simulate a vehicle moving at 75 km/h. How many pixels must the vehicle travel each second? Solve the equation for p and justify each step.

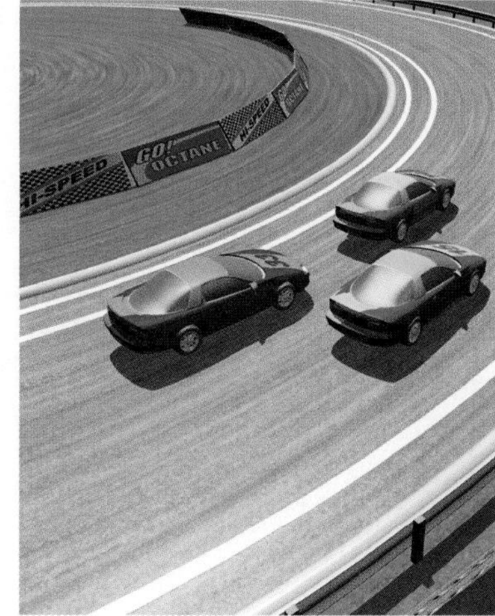

1 Understand the Problem

The **answer** will be the number of pixels traveled per second.

List the important information:

- $sr = 3.6p$
- $s = 75$ km/h
- p: pixels traveled per second
- $r = 6$ pixels per meter

2 Make a Plan

Substitute the given information into the formula and solve.

3 Solve

$sr = 3.6p$	Given equation
$(75)(6) = 3.6p$	Substitution Property of Equality
$450 = 3.6p$	Simplify.
$\frac{450}{3.6} = \frac{3.6p}{3.6}$	Division Property of Equality
$125 = p$	Simplify.
$p = 125$ pixels	Symmetric Property of Equality

4 Look Back

Check your answer by substituting it back into the original formula.

$sr = 3.6p$
$(75)(6) = 3.6(125)$
$450 = 450$ ✓

2. $C = \frac{5}{9}(F - 32)$ (Given);
$C = \frac{5}{9}(86 - 32)$ (Subst.);
$C \frac{5}{9}(54)$ (Simplify.);
$C = 30$ (Simplify.)

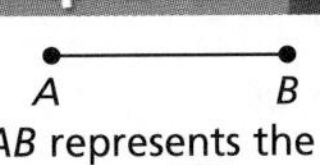

Helpful Hint

AB represents the length of $\overline{AB}$, so you can think of AB as a variable representing a number.

CHECK IT OUT! **2.** What is the temperature in degrees Celsius C when it is 86°F? Solve the equation $C = \frac{5}{9}(F - 32)$ for C and justify each step.

Like algebra, geometry also uses numbers, variables, and operations. For example, segment lengths and angle measures are numbers. So you can use these same properties of equality to write algebraic proofs in geometry.

INTERVENTION

Questioning Strategies

EXAMPLE 1

- When an equation contains multiple operations, how do you know which step to do first?

EXAMPLE 2

- When you are working with a formula that contains several variables, how can you make sure you are substituting the correct numbers for the variables?

2 Teach

Guided Instruction

Review how to solve linear equations by using inverse operations to isolate the variable. Explain that each step is valid because it uses a property of equality. Then show students how to identify the properties of congruence, and explain that any of these properties can be used as a justification in a geometric proof.

Teaching Tip **Visual** Go through the examples on the board to show how the justifications validate each step.

Reaching All Learners

Through Kinesthetic Experience

Have students act out the properties of congruence. For the Reflexive Property, have students look in a mirror. For the Symmetric Property, have two students stand next to each other and then change places. For the Transitive Property, have one student give a second student a sheet of paper, and have the second student give the paper to a third. The result is the same as if the first student had given the paper directly to the third.

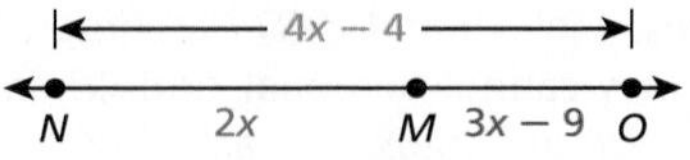

Additional Examples

Example 3

Write a justification for each step.

$NO = NM + MO$ Seg. Add. Post.

$4x - 4 = 2x + (3x - 9)$ Subst. Prop. of =

$4x - 4 = 5x - 9$ Simplify.

$-4 = x - 9$ Subtr. Prop. of =

$5 = x$ Add. Prop. of =

Example 4

Identify the property that justifies each statement.

A. $\angle QRS \cong \angle QRS$ Reflex. Prop. of ≅

B. $m\angle 1 = m\angle 2$, so $m\angle 2 = m\angle 1$. Sym. Prop. of =

C. $\overline{AB} \cong \overline{CD}$ and $\overline{CD} \cong \overline{EF}$, so $\overline{AB} \cong \overline{EF}$. Trans. Prop. of ≅

D. $32° = 32°$ Reflex. Prop. of =

INTERVENTION 

Questioning Strategies

EXAMPLE 3

- What properties are you using when you simplify in this equation?

EXAMPLE 4

- How can you remember the difference between the Reflexive, Symmetric, and Transitive Properties?

Auditory Say the words *reflexive, symmetric,* and *transitive* aloud, and ask students what the words bring to mind. For example, *reflexive* might remind students of a reflection in a mirror. You see the same thing on both sides of a mirror, so $a = a$.

EXAMPLE 3 Solving an Equation in Geometry

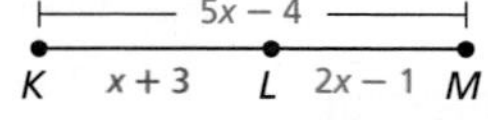

Write a justification for each step.

$KM = KL + LM$	Segment Addition Postulate
$5x - 4 = (x + 3) + (2x - 1)$	Substitution Property of Equality
$5x - 4 = 3x + 2$	Simplify.
$2x - 4 = 2$	Subtraction Property of Equality
$2x = 6$	Addition Property of Equality
$x = 3$	Division Property of Equality

3. Write a justification for each step.

$m\angle ABC = m\angle ABD + m\angle DBC$

$8x° = (3x + 5)° + (6x - 16)°$

$8x = 9x - 11$

$-x = -11$

$x = 11$

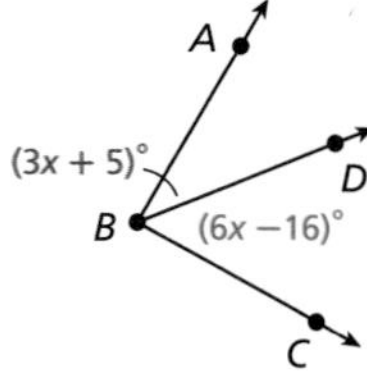

3. ∠ Add. Post.
Subst.
Simplify.
Subtr. Prop. of =
Mult. Prop. of =

You learned in Chapter 1 that segments with equal lengths are congruent and that angles with equal measures are congruent. So the Reflexive, Symmetric, and Transitive Properties of Equality have corresponding properties of congruence.

Know it! Note

SYMBOLS	EXAMPLE
Reflexive Property of Congruence figure A ≅ figure A (Reflex. Prop. of ≅)	$\overline{EF} \cong \overline{EF}$
Symmetric Property of Congruence If figure A ≅ figure B, then figure B ≅ figure A. (Sym. Prop. of ≅)	If $\angle 1 \cong \angle 2$, then $\angle 2 \cong \angle 1$.
Transitive Property of Congruence If figure A ≅ figure B and figure B ≅ figure C, then figure A ≅ figure C. (Trans. Prop. of ≅)	If $\overline{PQ} \cong \overline{RS}$ and $\overline{RS} \cong \overline{TU}$, then $\overline{PQ} \cong \overline{TU}$.

EXAMPLE 4 Identifying Properties of Equality and Congruence

Remember! Numbers are equal (=) and figures are congruent (≅).

Identify the property that justifies each statement.

A	$m\angle 1 = m\angle 1$	Reflex. Prop. of =
B	$\overline{XY} \cong \overline{VW}$, so $\overline{VW} \cong \overline{XY}$.	Sym. Prop. of ≅
C	$\angle ABC \cong \angle ABC$	Reflex. Prop. of ≅
D	$\angle 1 \cong \angle 2$, and $\angle 2 \cong \angle 3$. So $\angle 1 \cong \angle 3$.	Trans. Prop. of ≅

Identify the property that justifies each statement.

4a. $DE = GH$, so $GH = DE$. **4b.** $94° = 94°$

4c. $0 = a$, and $a = x$. So $0 = x$. **4d.** $\angle A \cong \angle Y$, so $\angle Y \cong \angle A$.

4a. Sym. Prop. of =
4b. Reflex. Prop. of =
4c. Trans. Prop. of =
4d. Sym. Prop. of ≅

3 Close

Summarize

Review the eight properties of equality on page 104. Ask students which properties of equality have corresponding properties of congruence. reflexive, symmetric, and transitive Also remind students when to use an equal sign and when to use a congruence symbol.

ONGOING ASSESSMENT

and INTERVENTION 

Diagnose ***Before*** **the Lesson**
2-5 Warm Up, TE p. 104

Monitor ***During*** **the Lesson**
Check It Out! Exercises, SE pp. 104–106
Questioning Strategies, TE pp. 105–106

Assess ***After*** **the Lesson**
2-5 Lesson Quiz, TE p. 109
Alternative Assessment, TE p. 109

THINK AND DISCUSS

1. Tell what property you would use to solve the equation $\frac{k}{6} = 3.5$.
2. Explain when to use a congruence symbol instead of an equal sign.

3. **GET ORGANIZED** Copy and complete the graphic organizer. In each box, write an example of the property, using the correct symbol.

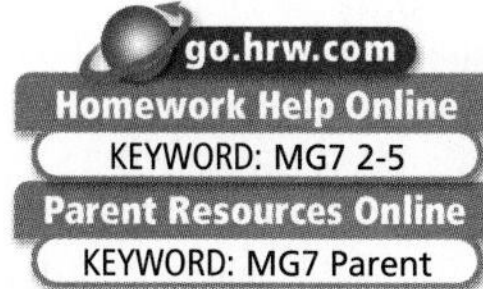

Property	Equality	Congruence
Reflexive		
Symmetric		
Transitive		

Answers to *Think and Discuss*

1. Mult. Prop. of =
2. Use a ≅ symbol for geometric figures. Use an = sign for numbers.
3. See p. A3.

2-5 Exercises

go.hrw.com
Homework Help Online
KEYWORD: MG7 2-5
Parent Resources Online
KEYWORD: MG7 Parent

GUIDED PRACTICE

1. **Vocabulary** Write the definition of *proof* in your own words.

SEE EXAMPLE 1 p. 104

Multi-Step **Solve each equation. Write a justification for each step.**

2. $y + 1 = 5$
3. $t - 3.2 = -8.3$
4. $2p - 30 = -4p + 6$
5. $\frac{x+3}{-2} = 8$
6. $\frac{1}{2}n = \frac{3}{4}$
7. $0 = 2(r - 3) + 4$

SEE EXAMPLE 2 p. 105

8. **Nutrition** Amy's favorite breakfast cereal has 102 Calories per serving. The equation $C = 9f + 90$ relates the grams of fat f in one serving to the Calories C in one serving. How many grams of fat are in one serving of the cereal? Solve the equation for f and justify each step.

9. **Movie Rentals** The equation $C = \$5.75 + \$0.89m$ relates the number of movie rentals m to the monthly cost C of a movie club membership. How many movies did Elias rent this month if his membership cost \$11.98? Solve the equation for m and justify each step.

SEE EXAMPLE 3 p. 106

Write a justification for each step.

10. 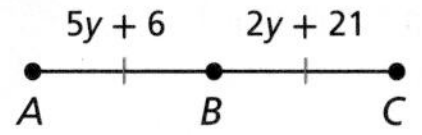 (Segment A, B, C with $AB = 5y + 6$, $BC = 2y + 21$)

Statement	Justification
$AB = BC$	Def. of ≅ segs.
$5y + 6 = 2y + 21$	Subst.
$3y + 6 = 21$	Subtr. Prop. of =
$3y = 15$	Subtr. Prop. of =
$y = 5$	Div. Prop. of =

11. 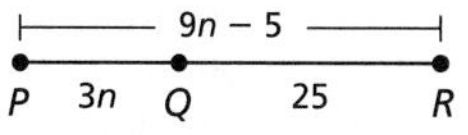 (Segment P, Q, R with $PQ = 3n$, $QR = 25$, $PR = 9n - 5$)

Statement	Justification
$PQ + QR = PR$	Seg. Add. Post.
$3n + 25 = 9n - 5$	Subst.
$25 = 6n - 5$	Subtr. Prop. of =
$30 = 6n$	Add. Prop. of =
$5 = n$	Div. Prop. of =

SEE EXAMPLE 4 p. 106

Identify the property that justifies each statement.

12. $\overline{AB} \cong \overline{AB}$
13. $m\angle 1 = m\angle 2$, and $m\angle 2 = m\angle 4$. So $m\angle 1 = m\angle 4$.
14. $x = y$, so $y = x$.
15. $\overline{ST} \cong \overline{YZ}$, and $\overline{YZ} \cong \overline{PR}$. So $\overline{ST} \cong \overline{PR}$.

2-5 Exercises

Assignment Guide

Assign *Guided Practice* exercises as necessary.

If you finished Examples **1–2**
Basic 16–22, 33
Average 16–22, 33–35
Advanced 16–22, 29, 34, 35

If you finished Examples **1–4**
Basic 16–28, 30–33, 37–42, 46–50
Average 16–28, 30–34, 36–43, 45–50
Advanced 16–29, 33–50

Homework Quick Check
Quickly check key concepts.
Exercises: 20, 22, 24, 28, 34

Answers

1. Possible answer: A proof is an argument that uses logic, definitions, and previously proven statements to show that another statement is always true.

State Resources

Answers

2. $y + 1 = 5$ (Given); $y = 4$ (Subtr. Prop. of =)
3. $t - 3.2 = -8.3$ (Given); $t = -5.1$ (Add. Prop. of =)
4. $2p - 30 = -4p + 6$ (Given); $6p - 30 = 6$ (Add. Prop. of =); $6p = 36$ (Add. Prop. of =); $p = 6$ (Div. Prop. of =)
5. $\frac{x+3}{-2} = 8$ (Given); $x + 3 = -16$ (Mult. Prop. of =); $x = -19$ (Subtr. Prop. of =)
6. $\frac{1}{2}n = \frac{3}{4}$ (Given); $n = \frac{3}{2}$ (Mult. Prop. of =)
7. $0 = 2(r - 3) + 4$ (Given); $0 = 2r - 6 + 4$ (Distrib. Prop.); $0 = 2r - 2$ (Simplify.); $2 = 2r$ (Add. Prop. of =); $1 = r$ (Div. Prop. of =)
8. $C = 9f + 90$ (Given); $102 = 9f + 90$ (Subst.); $12 = 9f$ (Subtr. Prop. of =); $\frac{4}{3} = f$ (Div. Prop. of =)
9. $C = \$5.75 + \$0.89m$ (Given); $\$11.98 = \$5.75 + \$0.89m$ (Subst.); $\$6.23 = \$0.89m$ (Subtr. Prop. of =); $m = 7$ (Div. Prop. of =)
12. Reflex. Prop. of ≅
13. Trans. Prop. of =
14. Sym. Prop. of =
15. Trans. Prop. of ≅

Teaching Tip **Reading Math** In **Exercises 33–35,** students might have more difficulty writing an equation for the problem than actually solving the equation. Walk students through the problem, translating each phrase into a mathematical expression one phrase at a time.

ENGLISH LANGUAGE LEARNERS

Answers

16. $5x - 3 = 4(x + 2)$ (Given); $5x - 3 = 4x + 8$ (Distrib. Prop.); $x - 3 = 8$ (Subtr. Prop. of =); $x = 11$ (Add. Prop. of =)

17. $1.6 = 3.2n$ (Given); $0.5 = n$ (Div. Prop. of =)

18. $\frac{z}{3} - 2 = -10$ (Given); $\frac{z}{3} = -8$ (Add. Prop. of =); $z = -24$ (Mult. Prop. of =)

19. $-(h + 3) = 72$ (Given); $-h - 3 = 72$ (Distrib. Prop.); $-h = 75$ (Add. Prop. of =); $h = -75$ (Mult. Prop. of =)

20. $9y + 17 = -19$ (Given); $9y = -36$ (Subtr. Prop. of =); $y = -4$ (Div. Prop. of =)

21. $\frac{1}{2}(p - 16) = 13$ (Given);
$\frac{1}{2}p - 8 = 13$ (Distrib. Prop.);
$\frac{1}{2}p = 21$ (Add. Prop. of =);
$p = 42$ (Mult. Prop. of =)

22. $T = 0.03c + 0.05b$ (Given); $147 = 0.03c + 0.05(150)$ (Subst.); $147 = 0.03c + 7.5$ (Simplify.); $139.5 = 0.03c$ (Subtr. Prop. of =); $4650 = c$ (Div. Prop. of =)

29, 33–35a, 36. See p. A12.

2-5 PRACTICE A
2-5 PRACTICE C
2-5 PRACTICE B

Solve each equation. Show all your steps and write a justification for each step.

1. $\frac{1}{5}(a + 10) = -3$
   $5\left[\frac{1}{5}(a + 10)\right] = 5(-3)$ (Mult. Prop. of =)
   $a + 10 = -15$ (Simplify.)
   $a + 10 - 10 = -15 - 10$ (Subtr. Prop. of =)
   $a = -25$ (Simplify.)

2. $t + 6.5 = 3t - 1.3$
   $t + 6.5 - t = 3t - 1.3 - t$ (Subtr. Prop. of =)
   $6.5 = 2t - 1.3$ (Simplify.)
   $6.5 + 1.3 = 2t - 1.3 + 1.3$ (Add. Prop. of =)
   $7.8 = 2t$ (Simplify.)
   $\frac{7.8}{2} = \frac{2t}{2}$ (Div. Prop. of =)
   $3.9 = t$ (Simplify.)
   $t = 3.9$ (Symmetric Prop. of =)

3. The formula for the perimeter P of a rectangle with length ℓ and width w is $P = 2(\ell + w)$. Find the length of the rectangle shown here if the perimeter is $9\frac{1}{2}$ feet. Solve the equation for ℓ and justify each step. Possible answer:
   $P = 2(\ell + w)$ (Given)
   $9\frac{1}{2} = 2(\ell + 1\frac{1}{4})$ (Subst. Prop. of =)
   $9\frac{1}{2} = 2\ell + 2\frac{1}{2}$ (Distrib. Prop.)
   $9\frac{1}{2} - 2\frac{1}{2} = 2\ell + 2\frac{1}{2} - 2\frac{1}{2}$ (Subtr. Prop. of =)
   $7 = 2\ell$ (Simplify.)
   $\frac{7}{2} = \frac{2\ell}{2}$ (Div. Prop. of =)
   $3\frac{1}{2} = \ell$ (Simplify.)
   $\ell = 3\frac{1}{2}$ (Symmetric Prop. of =)

Write a justification for each step.

4. H, I, J; $7x - 3$; $2x + 6$; $3x - 3$
   $HJ = HI + IJ$ — Seg. Add. Post.
   $7x - 3 = (2x + 6) + (3x - 3)$ — Subst. Prop. of =
   $7x - 3 = 5x + 3$ — Simplify.
   $7x = 5x + 6$ — Add. Prop. of =
   $2x = 6$ — Subtr. Prop. of =
   $x = 3$ — Div. Prop. of =

Identify the property that justifies each statement.

5. $m = n$, so $n = m$. — Symmetric Prop. of =
6. $\angle ABC \cong \angle ABC$ — Reflexive Prop. of ≅
7. $\overline{KL} \cong \overline{LK}$ — Reflexive Prop. of ≅
8. $p = q$ and $q = -1$, so $p = -1$. — Transitive Prop. of = or Subst.

PRACTICE AND PROBLEM SOLVING

Independent Practice	
For Exercises	See Example
16–21	1
22	2
23–24	3
25–28	4

Extra Practice
Skills Practice p. S7
Application Practice p. S29

Multi-Step Solve each equation. Write a justification for each step.

16. $5x - 3 = 4(x + 2)$ **17.** $1.6 = 3.2n$ **18.** $\frac{z}{3} - 2 = -10$

19. $-(h + 3) = 72$ **20.** $9y + 17 = -19$ **21.** $\frac{1}{2}(p - 16) = 13$

22. Ecology The equation $T = 0.03c + 0.05b$ relates the numbers of cans c and bottles b collected in a recycling rally to the total dollars T raised. How many cans were collected if $147 was raised and 150 bottles were collected? Solve the equation for c and justify each step.

Write a justification for each step.

23. $m\angle XYZ = m\angle 2 + m\angle 3$
$4n - 6 = 58 + (2n - 12)$
$4n - 6 = 2n + 46$
$2n - 6 = 46$
$2n = 52$
$n = 26$

23. ∠ Add. Post.
Subst.
Simplify.
Subtr. Prop. of =
Add. Prop. of =
Div. Prop. of =

24. $m\angle WYV = m\angle 1 + m\angle 2$
$5n = 3(n - 2) + 58$
$5n = 3n - 6 + 58$
$5n = 3n + 52$
$2n = 52$
$n = 26$

24. ∠ Add. Post.
Subst.
Distrib. Prop.
Simplify.
Subtr. Prop. of =
Div. Prop. of =

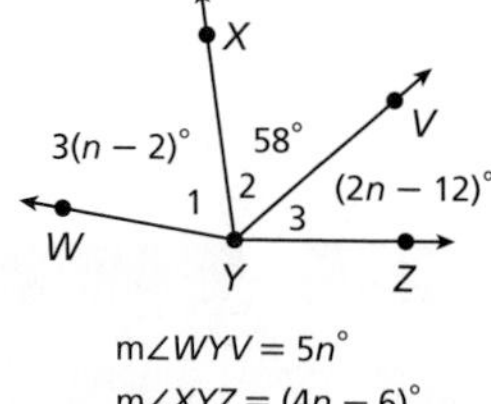

Identify the property that justifies each statement.

25. $\overline{KL} \cong \overline{PR}$, so $\overline{PR} \cong \overline{KL}$. Sym. Prop. of ≅
26. $412 = 412$ Reflex. Prop. of =

27. If $a = b$ and $b = 0$, then $a = 0$. Trans. Prop. of =
28. figure $A \cong$ figure A Reflex. Prop. of ≅

29. Estimation Round the numbers in the equation $2(3.1x - 0.87) = 94.36$ to the nearest whole number and estimate the solution. Then solve the equation, justifying each step. Compare your estimate to the exact solution.

Use the indicated property to complete each statement.

30. Reflexive Property of Equality: $3x - 1 = \underline{\ ?\ }$ $3x - 1$

31. Transitive Property of Congruence: If $\angle A \cong \angle X$ and $\angle X \cong \angle T$, then $\underline{\ ?\ }$. $\angle A \cong \angle T$

32. Symmetric Property of Congruence: If $\overline{BC} \cong \overline{NP}$, then $\underline{\ ?\ }$. $\overline{NP} \cong \overline{BC}$

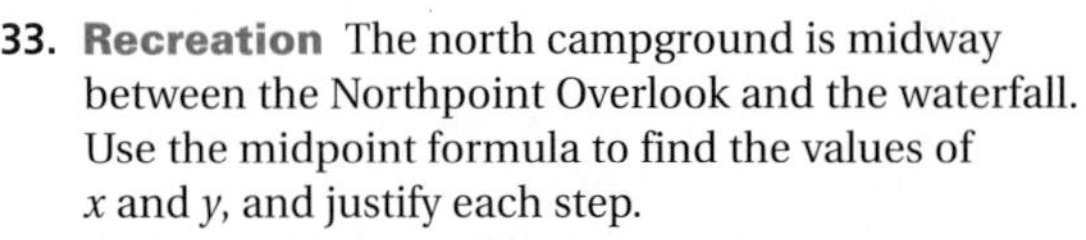

33. Recreation The north campground is midway between the Northpoint Overlook and the waterfall. Use the midpoint formula to find the values of x and y, and justify each step.

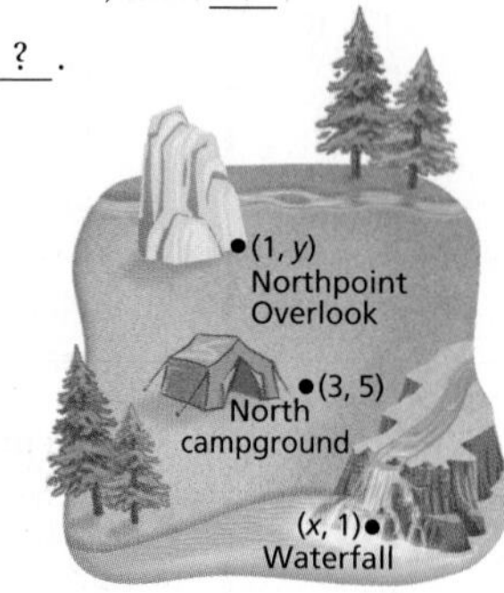

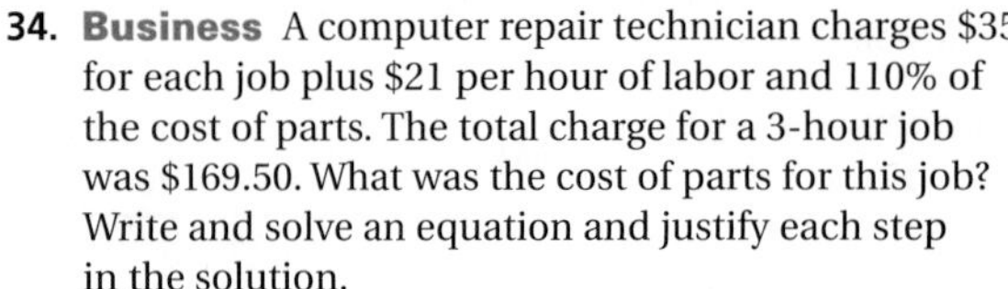

34. Business A computer repair technician charges $35 for each job plus $21 per hour of labor and 110% of the cost of parts. The total charge for a 3-hour job was $169.50. What was the cost of parts for this job? Write and solve an equation and justify each step in the solution.

35. Finance Morgan spent a total of $1,733.65 on her car last year. She spent $92.50 on registration, $79.96 on maintenance, and $983 on insurance. She spent the remaining money on gas. She drove a total of 10,820 miles.

a. How much on average did the gas cost per mile? Write and solve an equation and justify each step in the solution.

b. What if...? Suppose Morgan's car averages 32 miles per gallon of gas. How much on average did Morgan pay for a gallon of gas? $1.71

36. Critical Thinking Use the definition of segment congruence and the properties of equality to show that all three properties of congruence are true for segments.

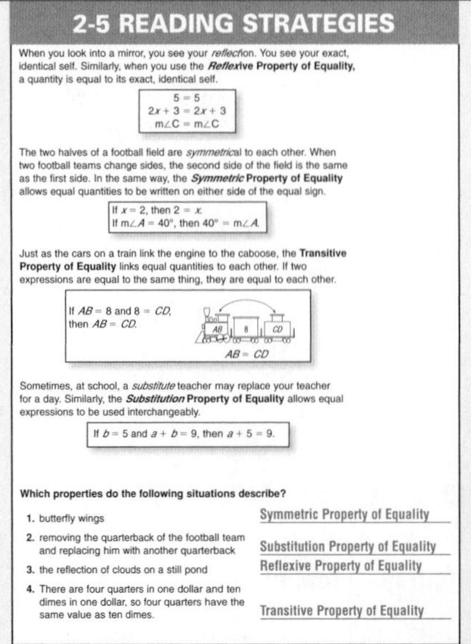

2-5 READING STRATEGIES

When you look into a mirror, you see your *reflection*. You see your exact, identical self. Similarly, when you use the ***Reflexive* Property of Equality,** a quantity is equal to its exact, identical self.

$5 = 5$
$2x + 3 = 2x + 3$
$m\angle C = m\angle C$

The two halves of a football field are *symmetrical* to each other. When two football teams change sides, the second side of the field is the same as the first side. In the same way, the ***Symmetric* Property of Equality** allows equal quantities to be written on either side of the equal sign.

If $x = 2$, then $2 = x$.
If $m\angle A = 40°$, then $40° = m\angle A$.

Just as the cars on a train link the engine to the caboose, the **Transitive Property of Equality** links equal quantities to each other. If two expressions are equal to the same thing, they are equal to each other.

If $AB = 8$ and $8 = CD$, then $AB = CD$.

AB 8 CD
$AB = CD$

Sometimes, at school, a *substitute* teacher may replace your teacher for a day. Similarly, the ***Substitution* Property of Equality** allows equal expressions to be used interchangeably.

If $b = 5$ and $a + b = 9$, then $a + 5 = 9$.

Which properties do the following situations describe?

1. butterfly wings — Symmetric Property of Equality
2. removing the quarterback of the football team and replacing him with another quarterback — Substitution Property of Equality
3. the reflection of clouds on a still pond — Reflexive Property of Equality
4. There are four quarters in one dollar and ten dimes in one dollar, so four quarters have the same value as ten dimes. — Transitive Property of Equality

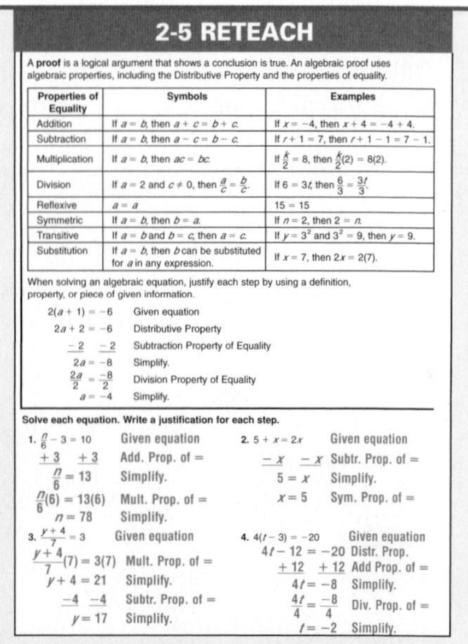

2-5 RETEACH

A **proof** is a logical argument that shows a conclusion is true. An algebraic proof uses algebraic properties, including the Distributive Property and the properties of equality.

Properties of Equality	Symbols	Examples
Addition	If $a = b$, then $a + c = b + c$.	If $x = -4$, then $x + 4 = -4 + 4$.
Subtraction	If $a = b$, then $a - c = b - c$.	If $r + 1 = 7$, then $r + 1 - 1 = 7 - 1$.
Multiplication	If $a = b$, then $ac = bc$.	If $\frac{k}{2} = 8$, then $\frac{k}{2}(2) = 8(2)$.
Division	If $a = 2$ and $c \neq 0$, then $\frac{a}{c} = \frac{b}{c}$.	If $6 = 3t$, then $\frac{6}{3} = \frac{3t}{3}$.
Reflexive	$a = a$	$15 = 15$
Symmetric	If $a = b$, then $b = a$.	If $n = 2$, then $2 = n$.
Transitive	If $a = b$ and $b = c$, then $a = c$.	If $y = 3^2$ and $3^2 = 9$, then $y = 9$.
Substitution	If $a = b$, then b can be substituted for a in any expression.	If $x = 7$, then $2x = 2(7)$.

When solving an algebraic equation, justify each step by using a definition, property, or piece of given information.

$2(a + 1) = -6$ Given equation
$2a + 2 = -6$ Distributive Property
$\underline{-2}\ \ \underline{-2}$ Subtraction Property of Equality
$2a = -8$ Simplify.
$\frac{2a}{2} = \frac{-8}{2}$ Division Property of Equality
$a = -4$ Simplify.

Solve each equation. Write a justification for each step.

1. $\frac{n}{6} - 3 = 10$ Given equation
   $\underline{+3}\ \ \underline{+3}$ Add. Prop. of =
   $\frac{n}{6} = 13$ Simplify.
   $\frac{n}{6}(6) = 13(6)$ Mult. Prop. of =
   $n = 78$ Simplify.

2. $5 + x = 2x$ Given equation
   $\underline{-x}\ \ \underline{-x}$ Subtr. Prop. of =
   $5 = x$ Simplify.
   $x = 5$ Sym. Prop. of =

3. $\frac{y+4}{7} = 3$ Given equation
   $\frac{y+4}{7}(7) = 3(7)$ Mult. Prop. of =
   $y + 4 = 21$ Simplify.
   $\underline{-4}\ \ \underline{-4}$ Subtr. Prop. of =
   $y = 17$ Simplify.

4. $4(t - 3) = -20$ Given equation
   $4t - 12 = -20$ Distr. Prop.
   $\underline{+12}\ \ \underline{+12}$ Add Prop. of =
   $4t = -8$ Simplify.
   $\frac{4t}{4} = \frac{-8}{4}$ Div. Prop. of =
   $t = -2$ Simplify.

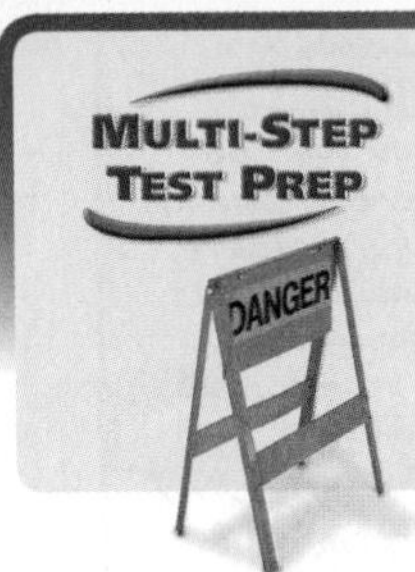

37. This problem will prepare you for the Multi-Step Test Prep on page 126.
Recall from Algebra 1 that the Multiplication and Division Properties of Inequality tell you to reverse the inequality sign when multiplying or dividing by a negative number.

a. Solve the inequality $x + 15 \le 63$ and write a justification for each step.

b. Solve the inequality $-2x > 36$ and write a justification for each step.

38. Write About It Compare the conclusion of a deductive proof and a conjecture based on inductive reasoning.

39. Which could NOT be used to justify the statement $\overline{AB} \cong \overline{CD}$?

Ⓐ Definition of congruence
Ⓑ Reflexive Property of Congruence (circled)
Ⓒ Symmetric Property of Congruence
Ⓓ Transitive Property of Congruence

40. A club membership costs $35 plus $3 each time t the member uses the pool. Which equation represents the total cost C of the membership?

Ⓕ $35 = C + 3t$ Ⓖ $C + 35 = 3t$ Ⓗ $C = 35 + 3t$ (circled) Ⓙ $C = 35t + 3$

41. Which statement is true by the Reflexive Property of Equality?

Ⓐ $x = 35$ Ⓑ $\overline{CD} = \overline{CD}$ Ⓒ $\overline{RT} \cong \overline{TR}$ Ⓓ $CD = CD$ (circled)

42. Gridded Response In the triangle, $m\angle 1 + m\angle 2 + m\angle 3 = 180°$. If $m\angle 3 = 2m\angle 1$ and $m\angle 1 = m\angle 2$, find $m\angle 3$ in degrees. **90**

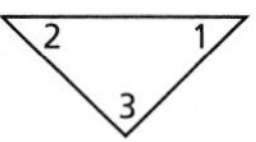

CHALLENGE AND EXTEND

43. In the gate, $PA = QB$, $QB = RA$, and $PA = 18$ in. Find PR, and justify each step.

44. Critical Thinking Explain why there is no Addition Property of Congruence.

44. Possible answer: You cannot add geometric figures.

45. Algebra Justify each step in the solution of the inequality $7 - 3x > 19$.

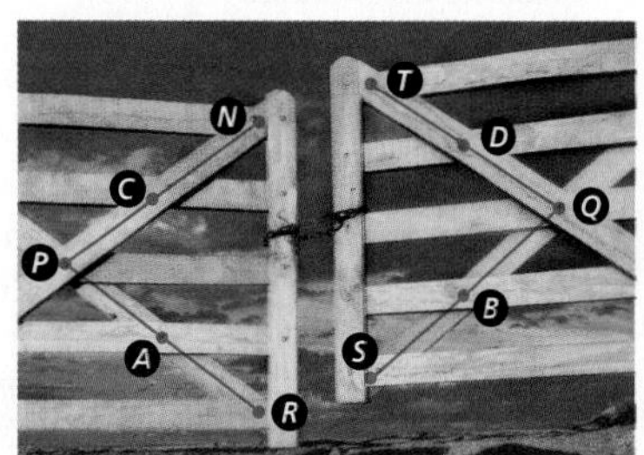

SPIRAL REVIEW

46. The members of a high school band have saved $600 for a trip. They deposit the money in a savings account. What additional information is needed to find the amount of interest the account earns during a 3-month period? *(Previous course)*
the interest rate the account earns

Use a compass and straightedge to construct each of the following. *(Lesson 1-2)*

47. $\overline{JK}$ congruent to $\overline{MN}$

M •———————• N

48. a segment bisector of $\overline{JK}$
47–48. Check students' constructions.

Identify whether each conclusion uses inductive or deductive reasoning. *(Lesson 2-3)*

49. A triangle is obtuse if one of its angles is obtuse. Jacob draws a triangle with two acute angles and one obtuse angle. He concludes that the triangle is obtuse.
49. deductive reasoning

50. Tonya studied 3 hours for each of her last two geometry tests. She got an A on both tests. She concludes that she will get an A on the next test if she studies for 3 hours.
50. inductive reasoning

Exercise 37 involves solving linear inequalities. This exercise prepares students for the Multi-Step Test Prep on page 126.

Students who answer **Exercise 40** incorrectly may have difficulty writing an algebraic equation. Remind students who chose **F** or **G** that the total cost is the sum of the fixed and variable costs. If students chose **J**, ask them which part of the cost varies based on the number of times the member uses the pool.

Answers

37–38, 43, 45. See p. A12.

Journal

Have students use an example to compare the process of solving an algebraic equation with the process of writing an algebraic proof.

ALTERNATIVE ASSESSMENT

Have students write and solve equations to show each property of equality in the lesson. Then have students write a statement that illustrates each property of congruence.

2-5 Lesson Quiz

Solve each equation. Write a justification for each step.

1. $\frac{z-5}{6} = -2$ $\frac{z-5}{6} = -2$ (Given); $z - 5 = -12$ (Mult. Prop. of =); $z = -7$ (Add. Prop. of =)

2. $6r - 3 = -2(r + 1)$
$6r - 3 = -2(r + 1)$ (Given); $6r - 3 = -2r - 2$ (Distrib. Prop.); $8r - 3 = -2$ (Add. Prop. of =); $8r = 1$ (Add. Prop. of =); $r = \frac{1}{8}$ (Div. Prop. of =)

Identify the property that justifies each statement.

3. $x = y$ and $y = z$, so $x = z$. Trans. Prop. of =

4. $\angle DEF \cong \angle DEF$ Reflex. Prop. of ≅

5. $\overline{AB} \cong \overline{CD}$, so $\overline{CD} \cong \overline{AB}$. Sym. Prop. of ≅

Also available on transparency

2-5 PROBLEM SOLVING

1. Because of a recent computer glitch, an airline mistakenly sold tickets for round-trip flights at a discounted price. The equation $n(p + t) = 3298.75$ relates the number of discounted tickets sold n, the price of each ticket p, and the tax per ticket t. What was the discounted price of each ticket if 1015 tickets were sold and the tax per ticket was $1.39? Solve the equation for p. Justify each step.

$n(p + t) = 3298.75$	Given equation
$1015(p + 1.39) = 3298.75$	Subst. Prop. of =
$p + 1.39 = 3.25$	Div. Prop. of =
$p = \$1.86$	Subtr. Prop. of =

2. The equation $C = 7.25s + 15.95a$ describes the total cost of admission C to the aquarium. How many student tickets were sold if the total cost for the entire class and 6 adults was $298.70? Solve the equation for s. Justify each step.

s = number of student tickets
a = number of adult tickets
C = total cost of admission

$C = 7.25s + 15.95a$	Given equation
$298.70 = 7.25s + 15.95(6)$	Subst. Prop. of =
$298.70 = 7.25s + 95.7$	Simplify.
$203 = 7.25s$	Subtr. Prop. of =
$28 = s$	Div. Prop. of =
$s = 28$ students	Sym. Prop. of =

Refer to the figure. Choose the best answer.

3. Which could be used to find the value of x?
A Segment Addition Postulate
Ⓑ Angle Addition Postulate (circled)
C Transitive Property of Congruence
D Definition of supplementary angles

4. What is $m\angle SQR$?
Ⓕ 28° (circled) H 61°
G 29° J 62°

R, S, $(x - 1)°$, $(2x + 4)°$, P, Q

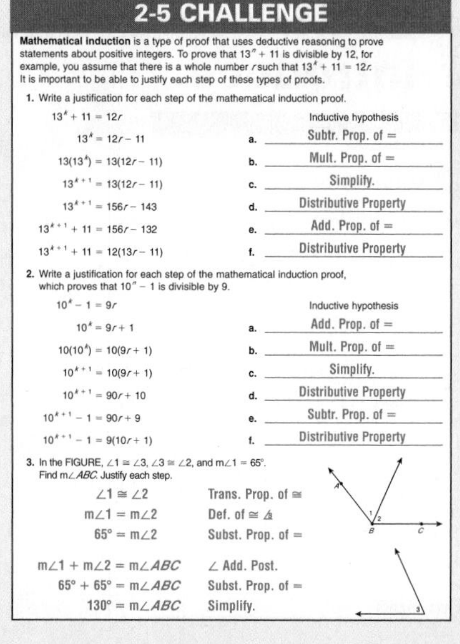
2-5 CHALLENGE

Mathematical induction is a type of proof that uses deductive reasoning to prove statements about positive integers. To prove that $13^n + 11$ is divisible by 12, for example, you assume that there is a whole number r such that $13^k + 11 = 12r$. It is important to be able to justify each step of these types of proofs.

1. Write a justification for each step of the mathematical induction proof.

$13^k + 11 = 12r$		Inductive hypothesis
$13^k = 12r - 11$	a.	Subtr. Prop. of =
$13(13^k) = 13(12r - 11)$	b.	Mult. Prop. of =
$13^{k+1} = 13(12r - 11)$	c.	Simplify.
$13^{k+1} = 156r - 143$	d.	Distributive Property
$13^{k+1} + 11 = 156r - 132$	e.	Add. Prop. of =
$13^{k+1} + 11 = 12(13r - 11)$	f.	Distributive Property

2. Write a justification for each step of the mathematical induction proof, which proves that $10^n - 1$ is divisible by 9.

$10^k - 1 = 9r$		Inductive hypothesis
$10^k = 9r + 1$	a.	Add. Prop. of =
$10(10^k) = 10(9r + 1)$	b.	Mult. Prop. of =
$10^{k+1} = 10(9r + 1)$	c.	Simplify.
$10^{k+1} = 90r + 10$	d.	Distributive Property
$10^{k+1} - 1 = 90r + 9$	e.	Subtr. Prop. of =
$10^{k+1} - 1 = 9(10r + 1)$	f.	Distributive Property

3. In the FIGURE, $\angle 1 \cong \angle 3$, $\angle 3 \cong \angle 2$, and $m\angle 1 = 65°$. Find $m\angle ABC$. Justify each step.

$\angle 1 \cong \angle 2$	Trans. Prop. of ≅
$m\angle 1 = m\angle 2$	Def. of ≅ ∠s
$65° = m\angle 2$	Subst. Prop. of =
$m\angle 1 + m\angle 2 = m\angle ABC$	∠ Add. Post.
$65° + 65° = m\angle ABC$	Subst. Prop. of =
$130° = m\angle ABC$	Simplify.

2-6 Organizer

Pacing: Traditional 2 days
Block 1 day

Objectives: Write two-column proofs.

Prove geometric theorems by using deductive reasoning.

Online Edition
Tutorial Videos

Countdown Week 4

Power Presentations with PowerPoint®

Warm Up

Determine whether each statement is true or false. If false, give a counterexample.

1. If two angles are complementary, then they are not congruent. F; 45° and 45°
2. If two angles are congruent to the same angle, then they are congruent to each other. T
3. Supplementary angles are congruent. F; 60° and 120°

Also available on transparency

Math Humor

Q: What do you have to know to get top grades in geometry?

A: All the angles!

2-6 Geometric Proof

SO WHAT ABOUT RAISING MY ALLOWANCE, DAD?

WELL, SINCE YOU DON'T DO YOUR CHORES, MY COST-BENEFIT ANALYSIS WOULD INDICATE THAT YOUR ALLOWANCE HAS COSTS BUT NO BENEFITS. THEREFORE, YOUR BUDGET INCREASE IS DENIED.

I LIKED YOU BETTER BEFORE THE MANAGEMENT CLASS.

Objectives
Write two-column proofs.

Prove geometric theorems by using deductive reasoning.

Vocabulary
theorem
two-column proof

Who uses this?
To persuade your parents to increase your allowance, your argument must be presented logically and precisely.

When writing a geometric proof, you use deductive reasoning to create a chain of logical steps that move from the hypothesis to the conclusion of the conjecture you are proving. By proving that the conclusion is true, you have proven that the original conjecture is true.

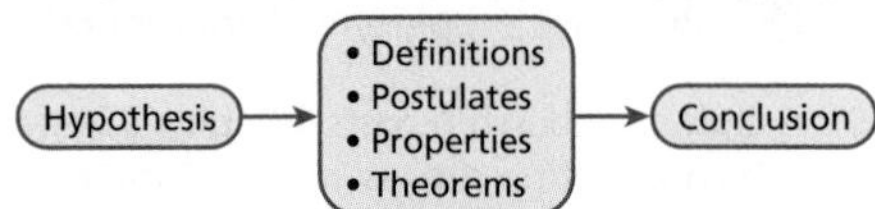

When writing a proof, it is important to justify each logical step with a reason. You can use symbols and abbreviations, but they must be clear enough so that anyone who reads your proof will understand them.

Helpful Hint
When a justification is based on more than the previous step, you can note this after the reason, as in Example 1 Step 5.

EXAMPLE 1 Writing Justifications

Write a justification for each step, given that ∠A and ∠B are complementary and ∠A ≅ ∠C.

1. ∠A and ∠B are complementary.	Given information
2. $m\angle A + m\angle B = 90°$	Def. of comp. ∠s
3. ∠A ≅ ∠C	Given information
4. $m\angle A = m\angle C$	Def. of ≅ ∠s
5. $m\angle C + m\angle B = 90°$	Subst. Prop. of = *Steps 2, 4*
6. ∠C and ∠B are complementary.	Def. of comp. ∠s

1. Write a justification for each step, given that B is the midpoint of $\overline{AC}$ and $\overline{AB} \cong \overline{EF}$.
   1. B is the midpoint of $\overline{AC}$.
   2. $\overline{AB} \cong \overline{BC}$
   3. $\overline{AB} \cong \overline{EF}$
   4. $\overline{BC} \cong \overline{EF}$

1. Given
2. Def. of mdpt.
3. Given
4. Trans. Prop. of ≅

A **theorem** is any statement that you can prove. Once you have proven a theorem, you can use it as a reason in later proofs.

Know it! Note

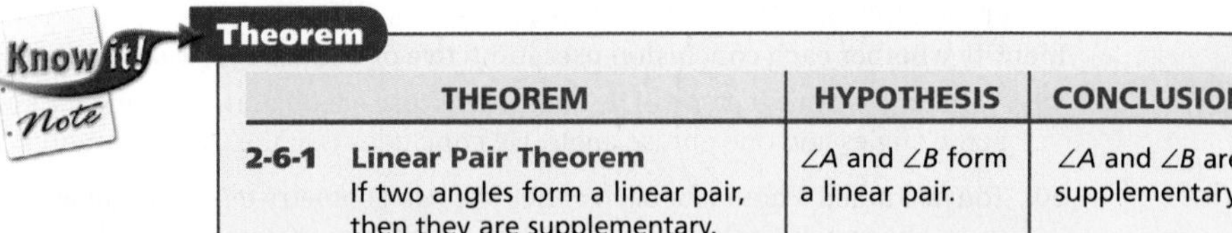

Theorem

	THEOREM	HYPOTHESIS	CONCLUSION
2-6-1	**Linear Pair Theorem** If two angles form a linear pair, then they are supplementary.	∠A and ∠B form a linear pair.	∠A and ∠B are supplementary.

State Resources

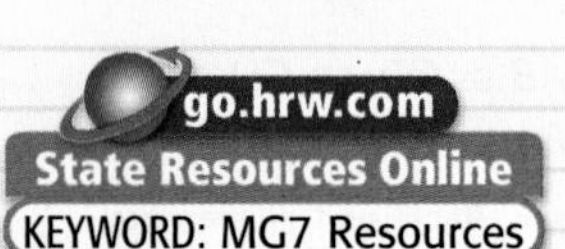

go.hrw.com
State Resources Online
KEYWORD: MG7 Resources

1 Introduce

EXPLORATION
2-6 Geometric Proof
Use geometry software to construct angles that form a linear pair.
1. Draw a segment $\overline{AB}$.
2. Construct a point C between A and B.
3. Draw a segment $\overline{CD}$ such that point D is not on $\overline{AB}$.
4. Measure ∠ACD and ∠BCD. Calculate the sum of m∠ACD and m∠BCD.
5. Drag point C. What do you notice?
6. Drag point D. What do you notice?
THINK AND DISCUSS

Motivate

Discuss with students the scenario in the opening cartoon. Ask "If the student's argument for a raise in allowance is not precise, what might the parent's reaction be?" Possible answer: The parent might not agree to raise the student's allowance. Have students describe the argument they would use. Explain that this lesson focuses on how to write precise, logical arguments in geometry.

Explorations and answers are provided in *Alternate Openers: Explorations Transparencies.*

Theorem

THEOREM	HYPOTHESIS	CONCLUSION
2-6-2 Congruent Supplements Theorem If two angles are supplementary to the same angle (or to two congruent angles), then the two angles are congruent.	$\angle 1$ and $\angle 2$ are supplementary. $\angle 2$ and $\angle 3$ are supplementary.	$\angle 1 \cong \angle 3$

A geometric proof begins with *Given* and *Prove* statements, which restate the hypothesis and conclusion of the conjecture. In a **two-column proof**, you list the steps of the proof in the left column. You write the matching reason for each step in the right column.

EXAMPLE 2 Completing a Two-Column Proof

Fill in the blanks to complete a two-column proof of the Linear Pair Theorem.
Given: $\angle 1$ and $\angle 2$ form a linear pair.
Prove: $\angle 1$ and $\angle 2$ are supplementary.
Proof:

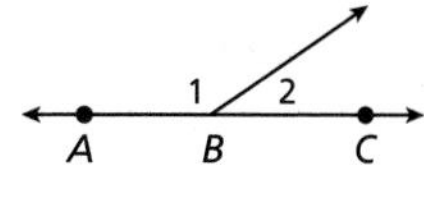

Statements	Reasons
1. $\angle 1$ and $\angle 2$ form a linear pair.	1. Given
2. $\overrightarrow{BA}$ and $\overrightarrow{BC}$ form a line.	2. Def. of lin. pair
3. $m\angle ABC = 180°$	3. Def. of straight $\angle$
4. a. ___?___	4. $\angle$ Add. Post.
5. b. ___?___	5. Subst. *Steps 3, 4*
6. $\angle 1$ and $\angle 2$ are supplementary.	6. c. ___?___

Writing Math

Since there is no other substitution property, the Substitution Property of Equality is often written as "Substitution" or "Subst."

Use the existing statements and reasons in the proof to fill in the blanks.

a. $m\angle 1 + m\angle 2 = m\angle ABC$ — *The $\angle$ Add. Post. is given as the reason.*
b. $m\angle 1 + m\angle 2 = 180°$ — *Substitute 180° for $m\angle ABC$.*
c. Def. of supp. $\angle$s — *The measures of supp. $\angle$s add to 180° by def.*

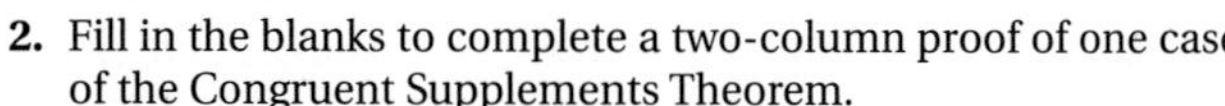

2. Fill in the blanks to complete a two-column proof of one case of the Congruent Supplements Theorem.
Given: $\angle 1$ and $\angle 2$ are supplementary, and $\angle 2$ and $\angle 3$ are supplementary.
Prove: $\angle 1 \cong \angle 3$
Proof:

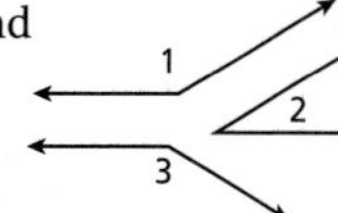

Statements	Reasons
1. a. ___?___	1. Given
2. $m\angle 1 + m\angle 2 = 180°$ $m\angle 2 + m\angle 3 = 180°$	2. Def. of supp. $\angle$s
3. b. ___?___	3. Subst.
4. $m\angle 2 = m\angle 2$	4. Reflex. Prop. of =
5. $m\angle 1 = m\angle 3$	5. c. ___?___
6. d. ___?___	6. Def. of $\cong$ $\angle$s

2a. $\angle 1$ and $\angle 2$ are supp., and $\angle 2$ and $\angle 3$ are supp.
2b. $m\angle 1 + m\angle 2 = m\angle 2 + m\angle 3$
2c. Subtr. Prop. of =
2d. $\angle 1 \cong \angle 3$

COMMON ERROR ALERT

When writing a proof, some students may incorrectly assume things from the figure. If students make this mistake, refer them back to page 73.

Power Presentations with PowerPoint®

Additional Examples

Example 1

Write a justification for each step, given that $\angle A$ and $\angle B$ are supplementary and $m\angle A = 45°$.

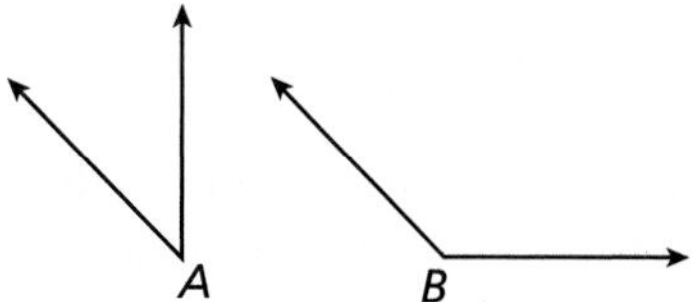

1. $\angle A$ and $\angle B$ are supplementary. $m\angle A = 45°$ Given
2. $m\angle A + \angle B = 180°$ Def. of supp. $\angle$s
3. $45° + m\angle B = 180°$ Subst.
4. $m\angle B = 135°$ Subtr. Prop. of =

Example 2

Fill in the blanks to complete the two-column proof.
Given: $\overline{XY}$
Prove: $\overline{XY} \cong \overline{XY}$

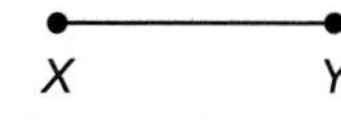

1. ___?___ (Given) $\overline{XY}$
2. $XY = XY$ (___?___) Reflex. Prop. of =
3. ___?___ (Def. of $\cong$ segs.) $\overline{XY} \cong \overline{XY}$

2 Teach

Guided Instruction

Explain to students that in a proof, every statement must be justified by a reason. Use the graphic on page 110 to emphasize that the reasons will be definitions, postulates, properties, and theorems, as well as information in the Given statement.

Auditory When reviewing the examples, say each step of the proof aloud and have students speak each justification.

Reaching All Learners

Through Critical Thinking

Have students write the statements and reasons for the proofs presented in the examples on individual strips of paper. Have students exchange complete sets and rearrange them into a two-column proof.

INTERVENTION
Questioning Strategies

EXAMPLE 1

- Is it possible that two different reasons could be used to justify a step in a proof? Why or why not?

EXAMPLE 2

- When filling in missing information in a proof, should you work down the columns or across the rows?

Power Presentations with PowerPoint®

Additional Examples

Example 3

Use the given plan to write a two-column proof.

Given: ∠1 and ∠2 are supp. ∠1 ≅ ∠3

Prove: ∠3 and ∠2 are supp.

Plan: Use the definitions of supplementary and congruent angles and substitution to show that m∠3 + m∠2 = 180°. By the definition of supplementary angles, ∠3 and ∠2 are supplementary.

Answer Note: Two-column proofs in the answers are given in the format *Statement* (*Reason*).

1. ∠1 and ∠2 are supp. ∠1 ≅ ∠3 (Given)
2. m∠1 + m∠2 = 180° (Def. of supp. ∡)
3. m∠1 = m∠3 (Def. of ≅ ∡)
4. m∠3 + m∠2 = 180° (Subst.)
5. ∠3 and ∠2 are supp. (Def. of supp. ∡)

INTERVENTION

Questioning Strategies

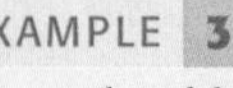
EXAMPLE 3

- How should you mark a figure when starting a proof?
- How does a plan help in writing a two-column proof?

Kinesthetic Some students may have difficulty deciding which statement a reason goes with. Have students point at the conclusion of the reason. The conclusion must match the statement that it is aligned with.

Inclusion When students are using a definition as a justification, suggest that they write the definition as a conditional statement in the order needed to apply it.

Before you start writing a proof, you should plan out your logic. Sometimes you will be given a plan for a more challenging proof. This plan will detail the major steps of the proof for you.

Theorems

THEOREM		HYPOTHESIS	CONCLUSION
2-6-3	**Right Angle Congruence Theorem** All right angles are congruent.	∠A and ∠B are right angles.	∠A ≅ ∠B
2-6-4	**Congruent Complements Theorem** If two angles are complementary to the same angle (or to two congruent angles), then the two angles are congruent.	∠1 and ∠2 are complementary. ∠2 and ∠3 are complementary.	∠1 ≅ ∠3

Helpful Hint

If a diagram for a proof is not provided, draw your own and mark the given information on it. But do not mark the information in the Prove statement on it.

EXAMPLE 3 Writing a Two-Column Proof from a Plan

Use the given plan to write a two-column proof of the Right Angle Congruence Theorem.
Given: ∠1 and ∠2 are right angles.
Prove: ∠1 ≅ ∠2

Plan: Use the definition of a right angle to write the measure of each angle. Then use the Transitive Property and the definition of congruent angles.

Proof:

Statements	Reasons
1. ∠1 and ∠2 are right angles.	1. Given
2. m∠1 = 90°, m∠2 = 90°	2. Def. of rt. ∠
3. m∠1 = m∠2	3. Trans. Prop. of =
4. ∠1 ≅ ∠2	4. Def. of ≅ ∡

3. Use the given plan to write a two-column proof of one case of the Congruent Complements Theorem.
Given: ∠1 and ∠2 are complementary, and ∠2 and ∠3 are complementary.
Prove: ∠1 ≅ ∠3
Plan: The measures of complementary angles add to 90° by definition. Use substitution to show that the sums of both pairs are equal. Use the Subtraction Property and the definition of congruent angles to conclude that ∠1 ≅ ∠3.

1. ∠1 and ∠2 are comp. ∠2 and ∠3 are comp. (Given)
2. m∠1 + m∠2 = 90°, m∠2 + m∠3 = 90° (Def. of comp. ∡)
3. m∠1 + m∠2 = m∠2 + m∠3 (Subst.)
4. m∠2 = m∠2 (Reflex. Prop. of =)
5. m∠1 = m∠3 (Subtr. Prop. of =)
6. ∠1 ≅ ∠3 (Def. of ≅ ∡)

The Proof Process
1. Write the conjecture to be proven.
2. Draw a diagram to represent the hypothesis of the conjecture.
3. State the given information and mark it on the diagram.
4. State the conclusion of the conjecture in terms of the diagram.
5. Plan your argument and prove the conjecture.

3 Close

Summarize

Review with students the steps of the proof process in the summary box on page 112. Ask students to list the four parts of a two-column proof. Given statement, Prove statement, statements, and reasons

Also review the four theorems presented in the lesson:

- Linear Pair Theorem
- Congruent Supplements Theorem
- Right Angle Congruence Theorem
- Congruent Complements Theorem

ONGOING ASSESSMENT and INTERVENTION

Diagnose ***Before*** **the Lesson**
2-6 Warm Up, TE p. 110

Monitor ***During*** **the Lesson**
Check It Out! Exercises, SE pp. 110–112
Questioning Strategies, TE pp. 111–112

Assess ***After*** **the Lesson**
2-6 Lesson Quiz, TE p. 116
Alternative Assessment, TE p. 116

THINK AND DISCUSS

1. Which step in a proof should match the Prove statement?
2. Why is it important to include every logical step in a proof?
3. List four things you can use to justify a step in a proof.

4. **GET ORGANIZED** Copy and complete the graphic organizer. In each box, describe the steps of the proof process.

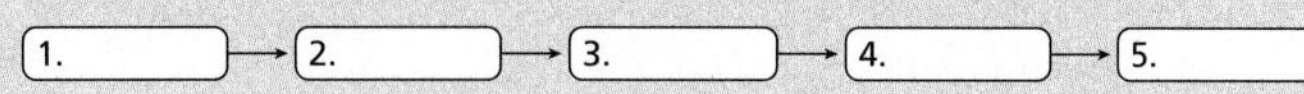

Answers to *Think and Discuss*

1. the last step
2. Possible answer: so another person can follow your proof and you can verify that your logical reasoning is correct.
3. postulate; theorem; definition; property
4. See p. A3.

2-6 Exercises

go.hrw.com
Homework Help Online
KEYWORD: MG7 2-6
Parent Resources Online
KEYWORD: MG7 Parent

GUIDED PRACTICE

Vocabulary **Apply the vocabulary from this lesson to answer each question.**

1. In a *two-column proof,* you list the ___?___ in the left column and the ___?___ in the right column. (*statements* or *reasons*) **statements; reasons**

2. A ___?___ is a statement you can prove. (*postulate* or *theorem*) **theorem**

SEE EXAMPLE 1 p. 110

3. Write a justification for each step, given that $m\angle A = 60°$ and $m\angle B = 2m\angle A$.
   1. $m\angle A = 60°$, $m\angle B = 2m\angle A$ **Given**
   2. $m\angle B = 2(60°)$ **Subst.**
   3. $m\angle B = 120°$ **Simplify.**
   4. $m\angle A + m\angle B = 60° + 120°$ **Add. Prop. of =**
   5. $m\angle A + m\angle B = 180°$ **Simplify.**
   6. $\angle A$ and $\angle B$ are supplementary. **Def. of supp. ∠s**

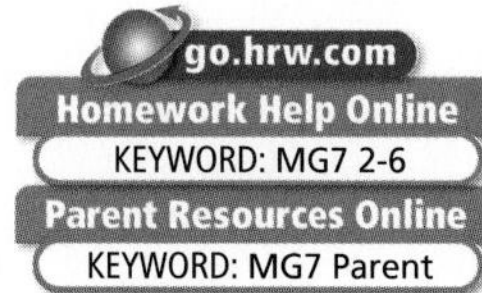

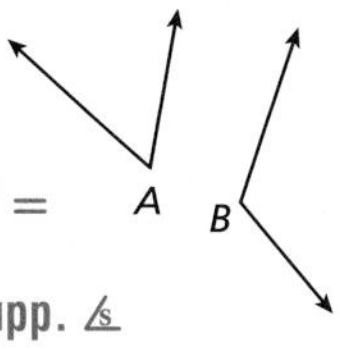

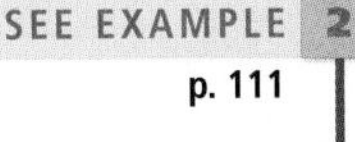

p. 111

4. Fill in the blanks to complete the two-column proof.
   Given: $\angle 2 \cong \angle 3$
   Prove: $\angle 1$ and $\angle 3$ are supplementary.
   Proof:

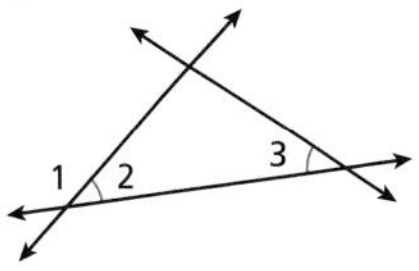

Statements	Reasons
1. $\angle 2 \cong \angle 3$	1. Given
2. $m\angle 2 = m\angle 3$	2. a. ___?___
3. b. ___?___	3. Lin. Pair Thm.
4. $m\angle 1 + m\angle 2 = 180°$	4. Def. of supp. ∠s
5. $m\angle 1 + m\angle 3 = 180°$	5. c. ___?___ *Steps 2, 4*
6. d. ___?___	6. Def. of supp. ∠s

a. Def. of ≅ ∠s
b. ∠1 and ∠2 are supp.
c. Subst.
d. ∠1 and ∠3 are supp.

SEE EXAMPLE 3 p. 112

5. Use the given plan to write a two-column proof.
   Given: X is the midpoint of $\overline{AY}$, and Y is the midpoint of $\overline{XB}$.
   Prove: $\overline{AX} \cong \overline{YB}$
   Plan: By the definition of midpoint, $\overline{AX} \cong \overline{XY}$, and $\overline{XY} \cong \overline{YB}$. Use the Transitive Property to conclude that $\overline{AX} \cong \overline{YB}$.

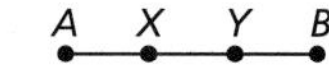

2-6 Exercises

Assign *Guided Practice* exercises as necessary.

If you finished Examples **1–2**
Basic 6–8, 12
Average 6–8, 11, 12, 14
Advanced 6–8, 11, 12–22 even

If you finished Examples **1–3**
Basic 6–12, 16–20, 22–27, 31–36
Average 6–16, 18–22 even, 23–27, 31–36
Advanced 6–16, 18, 21–36

Homework Quick Check
Quickly check key concepts.
Exercises: 6, 8, 10, 16, 20

Answers

5. 1. X is the mdpt. of $\overline{AY}$. Y is the mdpt. of $\overline{XB}$. (Given)
   2. $\overline{AX} \cong \overline{XY}$, $\overline{XY} \cong \overline{YB}$ (Def. of mdpt.)
   3. $\overline{AX} \cong \overline{YB}$ (Trans. Prop. of ≅)

State Resources

Answers

9. 1. $\overline{BE} \cong \overline{CE}, \overline{DE} \cong \overline{AE}$ (Given)
   2. $BE = CE, DE = AE$ (Def. of ≅ segs.)
   3. $AE + BE = AB, CE + DE = CD$ (Seg. Add. Post.)
   4. $DE + CE = AB$ (Subst.)
   5. $AB = CD$ (Subst.)
   6. $\overline{AB} \cong \overline{CD}$ (Def. of ≅ segs.)

7a. $m\angle 1 + m\angle 2 = 180°$, $m\angle 3 + m\angle 4 = 180°$

PRACTICE AND PROBLEM SOLVING

Independent Practice	
For Exercises	See Example
6	1
7–8	2
9–10	3

Extra Practice
Skills Practice p. S7
Application Practice p. S29

6. Write a justification for each step, given that $\overrightarrow{BX}$ bisects $\angle ABC$ and $m\angle XBC = 45°$.
   1. $\overrightarrow{BX}$ bisects $\angle ABC$.
   2. $\angle ABX \cong \angle XBC$
   3. $m\angle ABX = m\angle XBC$
   4. $m\angle XBC = 45°$
   5. $m\angle ABX = 45°$
   6. $m\angle ABX + m\angle XBC = m\angle ABC$
   7. $45° + 45° = m\angle ABC$
   8. $90° = m\angle ABC$
   9. $\angle ABC$ is a right angle.

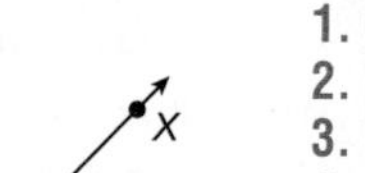

1. Given
2. Def. of ∠ bisector
3. Def. of ≅ ∡
4. Given
5. Subst.
6. ∠ Add. Post.
7. Subst.
8. Simplify.
9. Def. of rt. ∠

Fill in the blanks to complete each two-column proof.

7. **Given:** ∠1 and∠2 are supplementary, and ∠3 and ∠4 are supplementary. ∠2 ≅ ∠3
   Prove: ∠1 ≅ ∠4
   Proof:

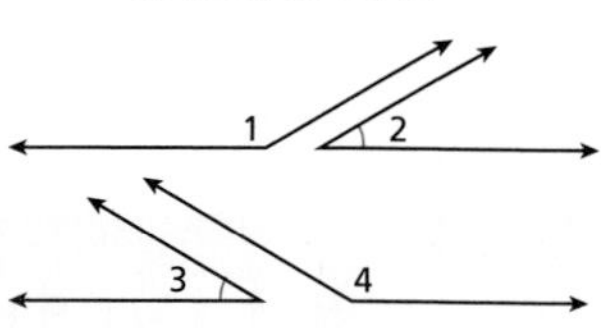

Statements	Reasons
1. ∠1 and ∠2 are supplementary. ∠3 and ∠4 are supplementary.	1. Given
2. a. ___?___	2. Def. of supp. ∡
3. $m\angle 1 + m\angle 2 = m\angle 3 + m\angle 4$	3. b. ___?___ Subst.
4. ∠2 ≅ ∠3	4. Given
5. $m\angle 2 = m\angle 3$	5. Def. of ≅ ∡
6. c. ___?___ $m\angle 1 = m\angle 4$	6. Subtr. Prop. of = *Steps 3, 5*
7. ∠1 ≅ ∠4	7. d. ___?___ Def. of ≅ ∡

8. **Given:** ∠BAC is a right angle. ∠2 ≅ ∠3
   Prove: ∠1 and ∠3 are complementary.
   Proof:

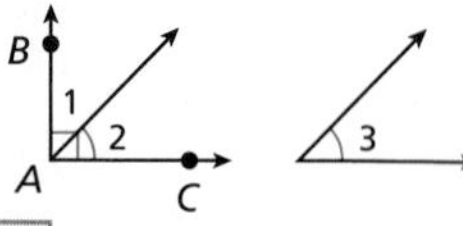

Statements	Reasons
1. ∠BAC is a right angle.	1. Given
2. $m\angle BAC = 90°$	2. a. ___?___
3. b. ___?___	3. ∠ Add. Post.
4. $m\angle 1 + m\angle 2 = 90°$	4. Subst. *Steps 2, 3*
5. ∠2 ≅ ∠3	5. Given
6. c. ___?___	6. Def. of ≅ ∡
7. $m\angle 1 + m\angle 3 = 90°$	7. d. ___?___ *Steps 4, 6*
8. e. ___?___	8. Def. of comp. ∡

a. Def. of rt. ∠
b. $m\angle 1 + m\angle 2 = m\angle BAC$
c. $m\angle 2 = m\angle 3$
d. Subst.
e. ∠1 and ∠3 are comp.

Use the given plan to write a two-column proof.

9. **Given:** $\overline{BE} \cong \overline{CE}, \overline{DE} \cong \overline{AE}$
   Prove: $\overline{AB} \cong \overline{CD}$
   Plan: Use the definition of congruent segments to write the given information in terms of lengths. Then use the Segment Addition Postulate to show that $AB = CD$ and thus $\overline{AB} \cong \overline{CD}$.

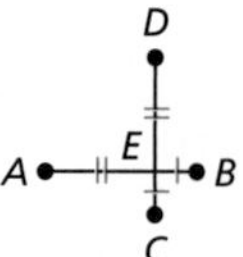

2-6 PRACTICE A
2-6 PRACTICE C
2-6 PRACTICE B

Write a justification for each step.

Given: $AB = EF$, B is the midpoint of $\overline{AC}$, and E is the midpoint of $\overline{DF}$.

1. B is the midpoint of $\overline{AC}$, and E is the midpoint of $\overline{DF}$. — Given
2. $\overline{AB} \cong \overline{BC}$, and $\overline{DE} \cong \overline{EF}$. — Def. of mdpt.
3. $AB = BC$, and $DE = EF$. — Def. of ≅ segments
4. $AB + BC = AC$, and $DE + EF = DF$. — Seg. Add. Post.
5. $2AB = AC$, and $2EF = DF$. — Subst.
6. $AB = EF$ — Given
7. $2AB = 2EF$ — Mult. Prop. of =
8. $AC = DF$ — Subst. Prop. of =
9. $\overline{AC} \cong \overline{DF}$ — Def. of ≅ segments

Fill in the blanks to complete the two-column proof.

10. **Given:** ∠HKJ is a straight angle. $\overrightarrow{KI}$ bisects ∠HKJ.
    Prove: ∠IKJ is a right angle.
    Proof:

Statements	Reasons
1. a. ∠HKJ is a straight angle.	1. Given
2. $m\angle HKJ = 180°$	2. b. Def. of straight ∠
3. c. $\overrightarrow{KI}$ bisects ∠HKJ	3. Given
4. ∠IKJ ≅ ∠IKH	4. Def. of ∠ bisector
5. $m\angle IKJ = m\angle IKH$	5. Def. of ≅ ∡
6. d. $m\angle IKJ + m\angle IKH = m\angle HKJ$	6. ∠ Add. Post.
7. $2m\angle IKJ = 180°$	7. e. Subst. (Steps 2, 5, 6)
8. $m\angle IKJ = 90°$	8. Div. Prop. of =
9. ∠IKJ is a right angle.	9. f. Def. of right ∠

2-6 READING STRATEGIES

The following five steps are used to give geometric proofs:

The Proof Process
1. Write the conjecture to be proven.
2. Draw a diagram if one is not provided.
3. State the given information and mark it on the diagram.
4. State the conclusion of the conjecture in terms of the diagram.
5. Plan your argument and prove your conjecture.

Mark the diagram and answer the questions about the following proof.

Given: $\overrightarrow{FD}$ bisects ∠EFC. $\overrightarrow{FC}$ bisects ∠DFB.
Prove: ∠EFD ≅ ∠CFB
Proof:

1. $\overrightarrow{FD}$ bisects ∠EFC, $\overrightarrow{FC}$ bisects ∠DFB.	1. Given
2. ∠EFD ≅ ∠DFC, ∠DFC ≅ ∠CFB	2. Definition of ∠ bisector
3. $m\angle EFD = m\angle DFC$, $m\angle DFC = m\angle CFB$	3. Definition of ≅ ∡
4. $m\angle EFD = m\angle CFB$	4. Transitive Property of Equality
5. ∠EFD ≅ ∠CFB	5. Definition of ≅ ∡

1. What was the given information?
   $\overrightarrow{FD}$ bisects ∠EFC, $\overrightarrow{FC}$ bisects ∠DFB
2. What should be marked in the diagram?
   All three angles should be marked congruent to each other.
3. What was the conjecture to be proved?
   ∠EFD ≅ ∠CFB
4. What titles should be put above the two columns?
   Statements and *Reasons*
5. What property of equality was used to prove the angles congruent?
   Transitive Property of Equality

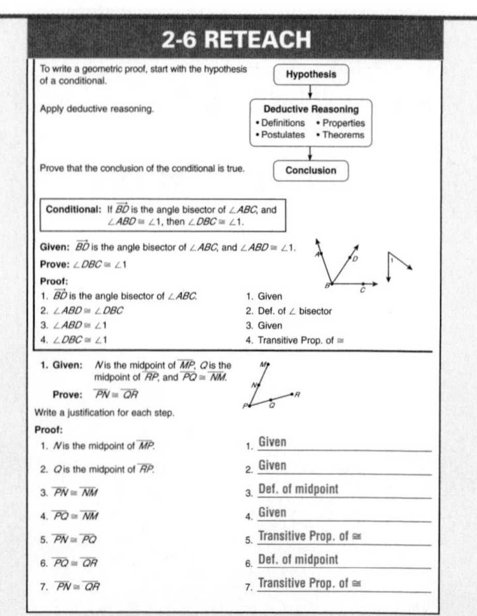

2-6 RETEACH

To write a geometric proof, start with the hypothesis of a conditional. — **Hypothesis**

Apply deductive reasoning. — **Deductive Reasoning** • Definitions • Properties • Postulates • Theorems

Prove that the conclusion of the conditional is true. — **Conclusion**

Conditional: If $\overrightarrow{BD}$ is the angle bisector of ∠ABC, and ∠ABD ≅ ∠1, then ∠DBC ≅ ∠1.

Given: $\overrightarrow{BD}$ is the angle bisector of ∠ABC, and ∠ABD ≅ ∠1.
Prove: ∠DBC ≅ ∠1
Proof:

1. $\overrightarrow{BD}$ is the angle bisector of ∠ABC. — 1. Given
2. ∠ABD ≅ ∠DBC — 2. Def. of ∠ bisector
3. ∠ABD ≅ ∠1 — 3. Given
4. ∠DBC ≅ ∠1 — 4. Transitive Prop. of ≅

1. **Given:** N is the midpoint of $\overline{MP}$, Q is the midpoint of $\overline{RP}$, and $\overline{PQ} \cong \overline{NM}$.
   Prove: $\overline{PN} \cong \overline{QR}$

Write a justification for each step.

Proof:

1. N is the midpoint of $\overline{MP}$. — 1. Given
2. Q is the midpoint of $\overline{RP}$. — 2. Given
3. $\overline{PN} \cong \overline{NM}$ — 3. Def. of midpoint
4. $\overline{PQ} \cong \overline{NM}$ — 4. Given
5. $\overline{PN} \cong \overline{PQ}$ — 5. Transitive Prop. of ≅
6. $\overline{PQ} \cong \overline{QR}$ — 6. Def. of midpoint
7. $\overline{PN} \cong \overline{QR}$ — 7. Transitive Prop. of ≅

Use the given plan to write a two-column proof.

10. **Given:** $\angle 1$ and $\angle 3$ are complementary, and $\angle 2$ and $\angle 4$ are complementary. $\angle 3 \cong \angle 4$

Prove: $\angle 1 \cong \angle 2$

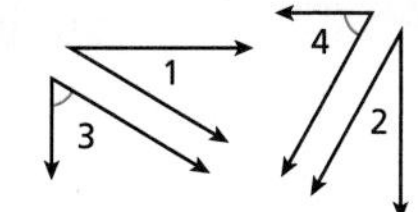

Plan: Since $\angle 1$ and $\angle 3$ are complementary and $\angle 2$ and $\angle 4$ are complementary, both pairs of angle measures add to 90°. Use substitution to show that the sums of both pairs are equal. Since $\angle 3 \cong \angle 4$, their measures are equal. Use the Subtraction Property of Equality and the definition of congruent angles to conclude that $\angle 1 \cong \angle 2$.

LINK

Engineering

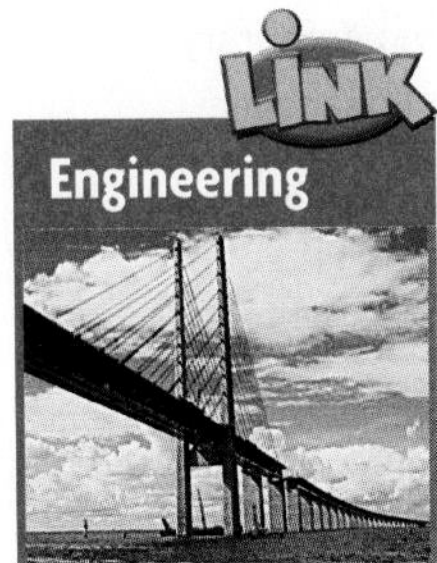

The Oresund Bridge, at 7845 meters long, is the world's longest single bridge. It carries both rail and car traffic between Denmark and Sweden.

Find each angle measure.

11. $m\angle 1$ 132°

12. $m\angle 2$ 27°

13. $m\angle 3$ 59°

14. **Engineering** The Oresund Bridge, which connects the countries of Denmark and Sweden, was completed in 1999. If $\angle 1 \cong \angle 2$, which theorem can you use to conclude that $\angle 3 \cong \angle 4$? $\cong$ Supps. Thm.

15. **Critical Thinking** Explain why there are two cases to consider when proving the Congruent Supplements Theorem and the Congruent Complements Theorem.

Tell whether each statement is sometimes, always, or never true.

16. An angle and its complement are congruent. S

17. A pair of right angles forms a linear pair. S

18. An angle and its complement form a right angle. S

19. A linear pair of angles is complementary. N

Algebra **Find the value of each variable.**

20. 15

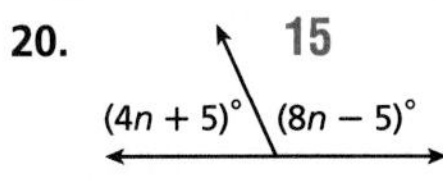

21. 16

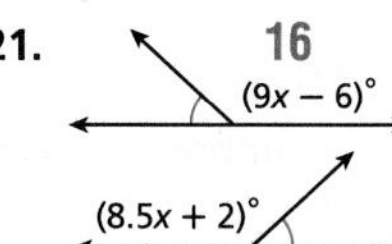

22. 12

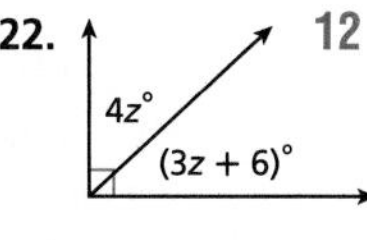

23. **Write About It** How are a theorem and a postulate alike? How are they different?

MULTI-STEP TEST PREP

24. This problem will prepare you for the Multi-Step Test Prep on page 126.

Sometimes you may be asked to write a proof without a specific statement of the Given and Prove information being provided for you. For each of the following situations, use the triangle to write a Given and Prove statement.

a. The segment connecting the midpoints of two sides of a triangle is half as long as the third side.

b. The acute angles of a right triangle are complementary.

c. In a right triangle, the sum of the squares of the legs is equal to the square of the hypotenuse.

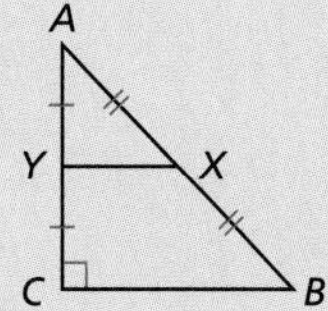

Teaching Tip **Communicating Math** Remind students that arc marks are used to indicate congruent angles in **Exercises 13** and **21.**

MULTI-STEP TEST PREP **Exercise 24** involves writing the Given and Prove statements for a proof when they are not explicitly stated. This exercise prepares students for the Multi-Step Test Prep on page 126.

Answers

10. 1. $\angle 1$ and $\angle 3$ are comp. $\angle 2$ and $\angle 4$ are comp. (Given)
    2. $m\angle 1 + m\angle 3 = 90°$, $m\angle 2 + m\angle 4 = 90°$ (Def. of comp. ∡)
    3. $m\angle 1 + m\angle 3 = m\angle 2 + m\angle 4$ (Subst.)
    4. $\angle 3 \cong \angle 4$ (Given)
    5. $m\angle 3 = m\angle 4$ (Def. of $\cong$ ∡)
    6. $m\angle 1 = m\angle 2$ (Subtr. Prop. of =)
    7. $\angle 1 \cong \angle 2$ (Def. of $\cong$ ∡)

15. Possible answer: because the ∡ can be supp. or comp. to the same $\angle$ or to 2 $\cong$ ∡

23. Possible answer: A thm. and a post. are both true statements of geometric facts. They are different because a post. is assumed to be true, while a thm. must be proven to be true.

24a. **Given:** Y is the mdpt. of $\overline{AC}$. X is the mdpt. of $\overline{AB}$.
Prove: $XY = \frac{1}{2}BC$

b. **Given:** $\angle C$ is a rt. $\angle$.
Prove: $\angle A$ and $\angle B$ are comp.

c. **Given:** $\angle C$ is a rt. $\angle$.
Prove: $(AB)^2 = (AC)^2 + (BC)^2$

2-6 PROBLEM SOLVING

1. Refer to the diagram of the stained-glass window and use the given plan to write a two-column proof.

Given: $\angle 1$ and $\angle 3$ are supplementary.
$\angle 2$ and $\angle 4$ are supplementary.
$\angle 3 \cong \angle 4$

Prove: $\angle 1 \cong \angle 2$

Plan: Use the definition of supplementary angles to write the given information in terms of angle measures. Then use the Substitution Property of Equality and the Subtraction Property of Equality to conclude that $\angle 1 \cong \angle 2$.

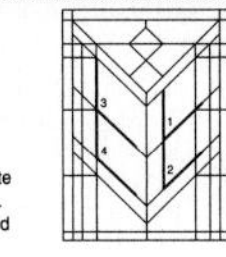

Statements	Reasons
1. $\angle 1$ and $\angle 3$ are supplementary. $\angle 2$ and $\angle 4$ are supplementary.	1. Given
2. $m\angle 1 + m\angle 3 = 180°$ $m\angle 2 + m\angle 4 = 180°$	2. Def. of supp. ∡
3. $m\angle 1 + m\angle 3 = m\angle 2 + m\angle 4$	3. Subst. Prop. of $\cong$
4. $\angle 3 \cong \angle 4$	4. Given
5. $m\angle 3 = m\angle 4$	5. Def. of $\cong$ ∡
6. $m\angle 1 + m\angle 4 = m\angle 2 + m\angle 4$	6. Subst. Prop. of =
7. $m\angle 4 = m\angle 4$	7. Reflex. Prop. of =
8. $m\angle 1 = m\angle 2$	8. Subtr. Prop. of =
9. $\angle 1 \cong \angle 2$	9. Def. of $\cong$ ∡

The position of a sprinter at the starting blocks is shown in the diagram. Which statement can be proved using the given information? Choose the best answer.

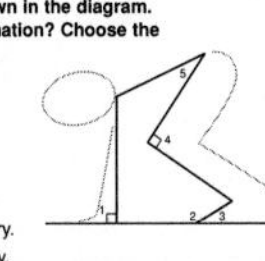

2. **Given:** $\angle 1$ and $\angle 4$ are right angles.
   A $\angle 3 \cong \angle 5$ C $m\angle 1 + m\angle 4 = 90°$
   (B) $\angle 1 \cong \angle 4$ D $m\angle 3 + m\angle 5 = 180°$

3. **Given:** $\angle 2$ and $\angle 3$ are supplementary.
   $\angle 2$ and $\angle 5$ are supplementary.
   (F) $\angle 3 \cong \angle 5$ H $\angle 3$ and $\angle 5$ are complementary.
   G $\angle 2 \cong \angle 5$ J $\angle 1$ and $\angle 2$ are supplementary.

2-6 CHALLENGE

In a proof, you can often determine the **Given** information from the figure.

Write the information that is given in each figure. Then make a conjecture about what you could prove using the given information.

1. Given: $\angle 1 \cong \angle 4$ and $\angle ABC$ is a right $\angle$. Possible answer: Prove $\angle 2 \cong \angle 3$.

2. Given: $EF \cong EJ$ and $FG \cong JH$. Possible answer: Prove $\overline{EH} \cong \overline{EG}$.

3. Write a two-column proof.

Given: $\angle KLM$ and $\angle NML$ are right angles.
$\angle 2 \cong \angle 3$

Prove: $\angle 1 \cong \angle 4$

Possible answer:

Statements	Reasons
1. $\angle KLM$ and $\angle NML$ are right angles.	1. Given
2. $\angle KLM \cong \angle NML$	2. Rt. $\angle \cong$ Thm.
3. $m\angle KLM = m\angle NML$	3. Def. of $\cong$ ∡
4. $m\angle KLM = m\angle 1 + m\angle 2$, $m\angle NML = m\angle 3 + m\angle 4$	4. $\angle$ Add. Post.
5. $m\angle 1 + m\angle 2 = m\angle 3 + m\angle 4$	5. Subst. Prop. of =
6. $\angle 2 \cong \angle 3$	6. Given
7. $m\angle 2 = m\angle 3$	7. Def. of $\cong$ ∡
8. $m\angle 1 + m\angle 2 = m\angle 2 + m\angle 4$	8. Subst. Prop. of =
9. $m\angle 2 = m\angle 2$	9. Reflex. Prop. of =
10. $m\angle 1 = m\angle 4$	10. Subtr. Prop. of =
11. $\angle 1 \cong \angle 4$	11. Def. of $\cong$ ∡

TEST PREP

25. Which theorem justifies the conclusion that $\angle 1 \cong \angle 4$?

   (A) Linear Pair Theorem
   (B) Congruent Supplements Theorem
   (C) Congruent Complements Theorem
   (D) Right Angle Congruence Theorem

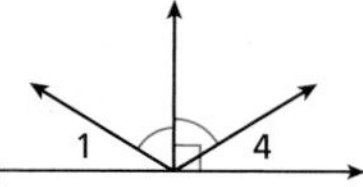

26. What can be concluded from the statement $m\angle 1 + m\angle 2 = 180°$?

   (F) $\angle 1$ and $\angle 2$ are congruent.
   (G) $\angle 1$ and $\angle 2$ are supplementary.
   (H) $\angle 1$ and $\angle 2$ are complementary.
   (J) $\angle 1$ and $\angle 2$ form a linear pair.

27. Given: Two angles are complementary. The measure of one angle is 10° less than the measure of the other angle. Conclusion: The measures of the angles are 85° and 95°. Which statement is true?

   (A) The conclusion is correct because 85° is 10° less than 95°.
   (B) The conclusion is verified by the first statement given.
   (C) The conclusion is invalid because the angles are not congruent.
   (D) The conclusion is contradicted by the first statement given.

CHALLENGE AND EXTEND

28. Write a two-column proof.
   Given: $m\angle LAN = 30°$, $m\angle 1 = 15°$
   Prove: $\overrightarrow{AM}$ bisects $\angle LAN$.

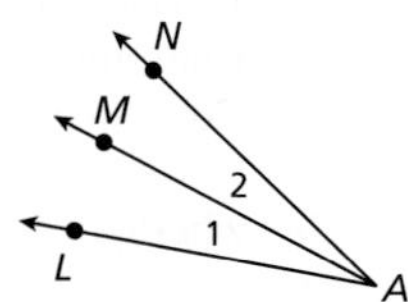

Multi-Step Find the value of the variable and the measure of each angle.

29.

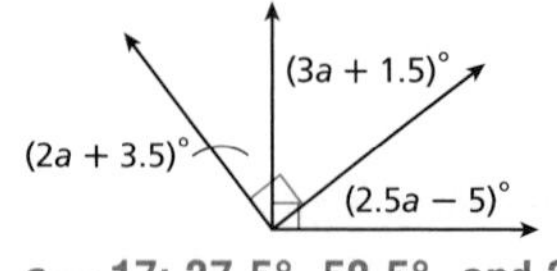

$a = 17$; 37.5°, 52.5°, and 37.5°

30. $(4x^2 - 6)°$ $(-2x^2 + 19x)°$

$x = 6$; 138° and 42°

SPIRAL REVIEW

The table shows the number of tires replaced by a repair company during one week, classified by the mileage on the tires when they were replaced. Use the table for Exercises 31 and 32. *(Previous course)*

Mileage on Replaced Tires	
Mileage	**Tires**
40,000–49,999	60
50,000–59,999	82
60,000–69,999	54
70,000–79,999	40
80,000–89,999	14

31. What percent of the tires had mileage between 40,000 and 49,999 when replaced? 24%

32. If the company replaces twice as many tires next week, about how many tires would you expect to have lasted between 80,000 and 89,999 miles? 28 tires

Sketch a figure that shows each of the following. *(Lesson 1-1)* **33–34. Possible answers:**

33. Through any two collinear points, there is more than one plane containing them.

34. A pair of opposite rays forms a line.

Identify the property that justifies each statement. *(Lesson 2-5)*

35. $\overline{JK} \cong \overline{KL}$, so $\overline{KL} \cong \overline{JK}$. Sym. Prop. of ≅

36. If $m = n$ and $n = p$, then $m = p$. Trans. Prop. of =

Answers

28. 1. $m\angle LAN = 30°$ (Given)
2. $m\angle 1 + m\angle 2 = m\angle LAN$ (∠ Add. Post.)
3. $m\angle 1 + m\angle 2 = 30°$ (Subst.)
4. $m\angle 1 = 15°$ (Given)
5. $15° + m\angle 2 = 30°$ (Subst.)
6. $m\angle 2 = 15°$ (Subtr. Prop. of =)
7. $m\angle 1 = m\angle 2$ (Trans. Prop. of =)
8. $\angle 1 \cong \angle 2$ (Def. of ≅ ∠s)
9. $\overrightarrow{AM}$ bisects $\angle LAN$. (Def. of ∠ bisector)

TEST PREP DOCTOR For **Exercise 26,** students who chose **H** are confusing *complementary* with *supplementary*. For students who chose **J,** sketch two angles that are supplementary but not adjacent.

Journal

Have students describe what to do if they get stuck while writing a proof. Then you can have students share their ideas with the class.

ALTERNATIVE ASSESSMENT

Have students draw a diagram with angle pairs and write a true statement about their figures. Then have students exchange papers, and ask them to write a two-column proof of the other student's statement.

Power Presentations with PowerPoint®

2-6 Lesson Quiz

1. Write a justification for each step, given that $m\angle ABC = 90°$ and $m\angle 1 = 4m\angle 2$.

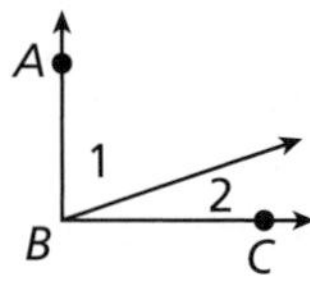

   1. $m\angle ABC = 90°$, $m\angle 1 = 4m\angle 2$ Given
   2. $m\angle 1 + m\angle 2 = m\angle ABC$ ∠ Add. Post.
   3. $4m\angle 2 + m\angle 2 = 90°$ Subst.
   4. $5m\angle 2 = 90°$ Simplify.
   5. $m\angle 2 = 18°$ Div. Prop. of =

2. Use the given plan to write a two-column proof.

Given: $\angle 1$, $\angle 2$, $\angle 3$, and $\angle 4$
Prove: $m\angle 1 + m\angle 2 = m\angle 1 + m\angle 4$

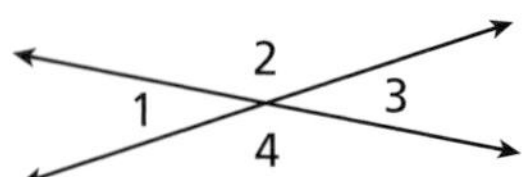

Plan: Use the Linear Pair Theorem to show that the angle pairs are supplementary. Then use the definition of supplementary and substitution.

1. $\angle 1$ and $\angle 2$ are supp. $\angle 1$ and $\angle 4$ are supp. (Lin. Pair Thm.)
2. $m\angle 1 + m\angle 2 = 180°$, $m\angle 1 + m\angle 4 = 180°$ (Def. of supp. ∠s)
3. $m\angle 1 + m\angle 2 = m\angle 1 + m\angle 4$ (Subst.)

Also available on transparency

2-6

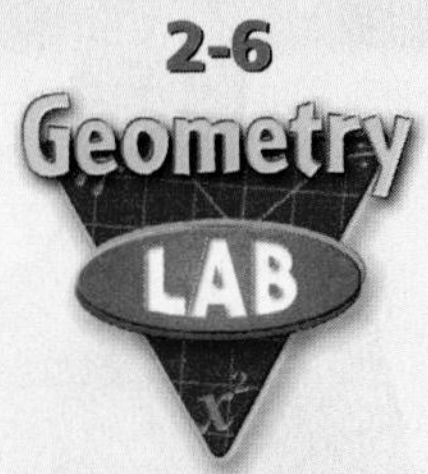

Design Plans for Proofs

Use with Lesson 2-6

Sometimes the most challenging part of writing a proof is planning the logical steps that will take you from the Given statement to the Prove statement. Like working a jigsaw puzzle, you can start with any piece. Write down everything you know from the Given statement. If you don't see the connection right away, start with the Prove statement and work backward. Then connect the pieces into a logical order.

Prove the Common Angles Theorem.
Given: $\angle AXB \cong \angle CXD$
Prove: $\angle AXC \cong \angle BXD$

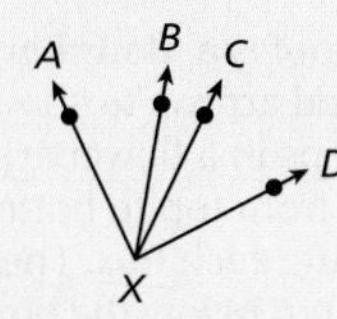

1. Start by considering the difference in the Given and Prove statements. How does $\angle AXB$ compare to $\angle AXC$? How does $\angle CXD$ compare to $\angle BXD$?
   In both cases, $\angle BXC$ is combined with the first angle to get the second angle.
2. The situation involves combining adjacent angle measures, so list any definitions, properties, postulates, and theorems that might be helpful.
   Definition of congruent angles, Angle Addition Postulate, properties of equality, and Reflexive, Symmetric, and Transitive Properties of Congruence
3. Start with what you are given and what you are trying to prove and then work toward the middle.

$\angle AXB \cong \angle CXD$	*The first reason will be "Given."*
$m\angle AXB = m\angle CXD$	*Def. of $\cong$ ∠s*
???	???
$m\angle AXC = m\angle BXD$	???
$\angle AXC \cong \angle BXD$	*The last statement will be the Prove statement.*

4. Based on Step 1, $\angle BXC$ is the missing piece in the middle of the logical flow. So write down what you know about $\angle BXC$.

$\angle BXC \cong \angle BXC$	*Reflex. Prop. of $\cong$*
$m\angle BXC = m\angle BXC$	*Reflex. Prop. of =*

5. Now you can see that the Angle Addition Postulate needs to be used to complete the proof.

$m\angle AXB + m\angle BXC = m\angle AXC$	*∠ Add. Post.*
$m\angle BXC + m\angle CXD = m\angle BXD$	*∠ Add. Post.*

6. Use the pieces to write a complete two-column proof of the Common Angles Theorem.

1. Describe how a plan for a proof differs from the actual proof.
2. Write a plan and a two-column proof.
   Given: $\overrightarrow{BD}$ bisects $\angle ABC$.
   Prove: $2m\angle 1 = m\angle ABC$

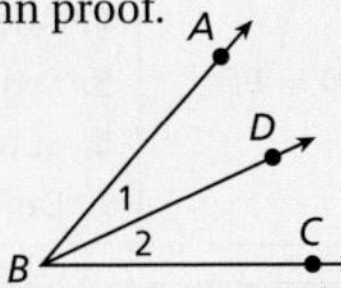

3. Write a plan and a two-column proof.
   Given: $\angle LXN$ is a right angle.
   Prove: $\angle 1$ and $\angle 2$ are complementary.

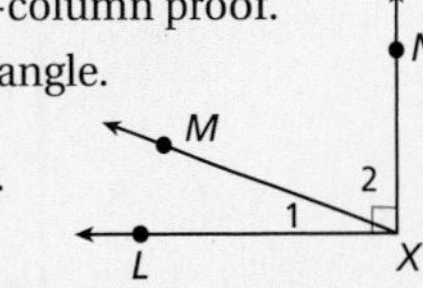

Answers to *Activity*

6. 1. $\angle AXB \cong \angle CXD$ (Given)
   2. $m\angle AXB = m\angle CXD$ (Def. of $\cong$ ∠s)
   3. $m\angle BXC = m\angle BXC$ (Reflex. Prop. of =)
   4. $m\angle AXB + m\angle BXC = m\angle CXD + m\angle BXC$ (Add. Prop. of =)
   5. $m\angle AXB + m\angle BXC = m\angle AXC$, $m\angle BXC + m\angle CXD = m\angle BXD$ (∠ Add. Post.)
   6. $m\angle AXC = m\angle BXD$ (Subst.)
   7. $\angle AXC \cong \angle BXD$ (Def. of $\cong$ ∠s)

Answers to *Try This*

1. Possible answer: A plan for a proof is less formal than a proof. A formal proof presents every logical step in detail, but a plan describes only the key logical steps.

2–3. See p. A12.

Organizer

Use with Lesson 2-6

Pacing:
Traditional 1 day
Block $\frac{1}{2}$ day

Objective: Learn strategies for planning the logical steps of a proof.

Online Edition

Countdown Week 4

Resources

Geometry Lab Activities
2-6 Lab Recording Sheet

Teach

Discuss

Emphasize that writing a proof requires an organized approach similar to solving logic puzzles. Instruct students to think about what they are trying to prove before they begin writing. Does it make sense? Why? Brainstorming like this can give students an idea of how to start the proof.

Close

Key Concept

As with problem solving, there are many strategies for writing a proof. Writing a plan first helps you organize your thoughts.

Assessment

Journal Have students describe in their own words what they have learned about planning a geometric proof.

State Resources

2-7 Organizer

Pacing: Traditional 1 day
Block $\frac{1}{2}$ day

Objectives: Write flowchart and paragraph proofs.

Prove geometric theorems by using deductive reasoning.

Technology Lab
In *Technology Lab Activities*

Online Edition
Tutorial Videos, Interactivity

Countdown Week 4

Power Presentations with PowerPoint®

Warm Up

Complete each sentence.

1. If the measures of two angles are ___?___, then the angles are congruent. equal
2. If two angles form a ___?___, then they are supplementary. linear pair
3. If two angles are complementary to the same angle, then the two angles are ___?___. congruent

Also available on transparency

Math Humor

Q: What do you call two fishermen standing up?

A: Vertical anglers.

2-7 Flowchart and Paragraph Proofs

Objectives
Write flowchart and paragraph proofs.
Prove geometric theorems by using deductive reasoning.

Vocabulary
flowchart proof
paragraph proof

Why learn this?
Flowcharts make it easy to see how the steps of a process are linked together.

A second style of proof is a **flowchart proof**, which uses boxes and arrows to show the structure of the proof. The steps in a flowchart proof move from left to right or from top to bottom, shown by the arrows connecting each box. The justification for each step is written below the box.

Know it! Note

Theorem 2-7-1 Common Segments Theorem

THEOREM	HYPOTHESIS	CONCLUSION
Given collinear points A, B, C, and D arranged as shown, if $\overline{AB} \cong \overline{CD}$, then $\overline{AC} \cong \overline{BD}$. (A B C D)	$\overline{AB} \cong \overline{CD}$	$\overline{AC} \cong \overline{BD}$

EXAMPLE 1 Reading a Flowchart Proof

Use the given flowchart proof to write a two-column proof of the Common Segments Theorem.

Given: $\overline{AB} \cong \overline{CD}$

Prove: $\overline{AC} \cong \overline{BD}$

Flowchart proof:

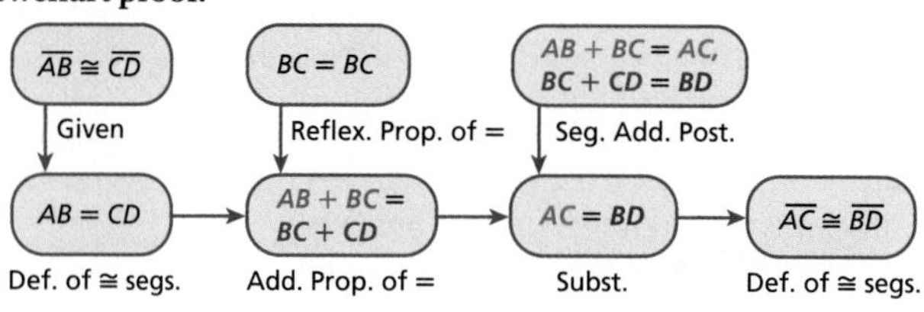

Two-column proof:

Statements	Reasons
1. $\overline{AB} \cong \overline{CD}$	1. Given
2. $AB = CD$	2. Def. of ≅ segs.
3. $BC = BC$	3. Reflex. Prop. of =
4. $AB + BC = BC + CD$	4. Add. Prop. of =
5. $AB + BC = AC$, $BC + CD = BD$	5. Seg. Add. Post.
6. $AC = BD$	6. Subst.
7. $\overline{AC} \cong \overline{BD}$	7. Def. of ≅ segs.

State Resources

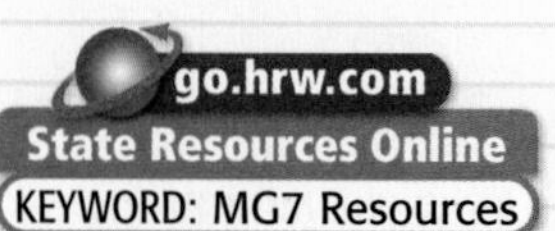

1 Introduce

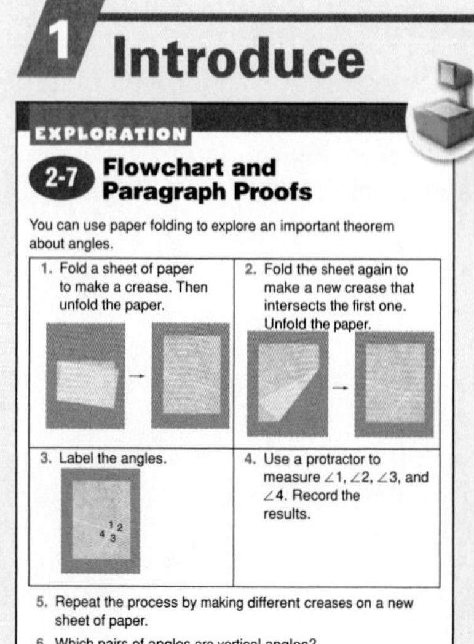

EXPLORATION
2-7 Flowchart and Paragraph Proofs
You can use paper folding to explore an important theorem about angles.
1. Fold a sheet of paper to make a crease. Then unfold the paper.
2. Fold the sheet again to make a new crease that intersects the first one. Unfold the paper.
3. Label the angles.
4. Use a protractor to measure ∠1, ∠2, ∠3, and ∠4. Record the results.
5. Repeat the process by making different creases on a new sheet of paper.
6. Which pairs of angles are vertical angles?

Motivate

Ask students to name different styles of poetry they may have seen in their language arts classes. Possible answers: sonnet, limerick, ballad, haiku, free verse Discuss the idea that just as thoughts and feelings can be expressed in different forms of poetry, a logical argument can be presented in different styles of proof. Writers may have a favorite poetry style, and students may have a favorite proof style.

Explorations and answers are provided in *Alternate Openers: Explorations Transparencies.*

1. Use the given flowchart proof to write a two-column proof.

Given: $RS = UV$, $ST = TU$

Prove: $\overline{RT} \cong \overline{TV}$

R S T U V

Flowchart proof:

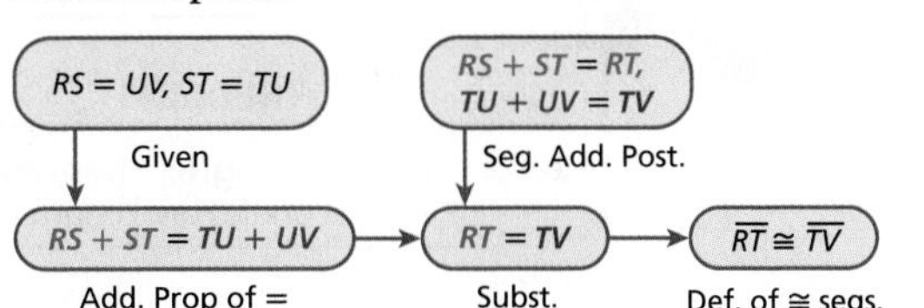

1. $RS = UV$, $ST = TU$ (Given)
2. $RS + ST = TU + UV$ (Add. Prop. of =)
3. $RS + ST = RT$, $TU + UV = TV$ (Seg. Add. Post.)
4. $RT = TV$ (Subst.)
5. $\overline{RT} \cong \overline{TV}$ (Def. of ≅ segs.)

EXAMPLE 2 Writing a Flowchart Proof

Use the given two-column proof to write a flowchart proof of the Converse of the Common Segments Theorem.

Given: $\overline{AC} \cong \overline{BD}$

Prove: $\overline{AB} \cong \overline{CD}$

A B C D

Two-column proof:

Statements	Reasons
1. $\overline{AC} \cong \overline{BD}$	1. Given
2. $AC = BD$	2. Def. of ≅ segs.
3. $AB + BC = AC$, $BC + CD = BD$	3. Seg. Add. Post.
4. $AB + BC = BC + CD$	4. Subst. *Steps 2, 3*
5. $BC = BC$	5. Reflex. Prop. of =
6. $AB = CD$	6. Subtr. Prop. of =
7. $\overline{AB} \cong \overline{CD}$	7. Def. of ≅ segs.

Flowchart proof:

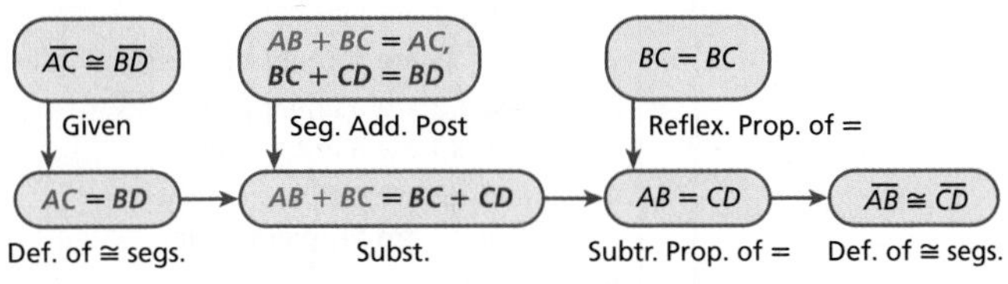

Helpful Hint

Like the converse of a conditional statement, the converse of a theorem is found by switching the hypothesis and conclusion.

2. Use the given two-column proof to write a flowchart proof.

Given: $\angle 2 \cong \angle 4$

Prove: $m\angle 1 = m\angle 3$

1 2 3 4

Two-column proof:

Statements	Reasons
1. $\angle 2 \cong \angle 4$	1. Given
2. $\angle 1$ and $\angle 2$ are supplementary. $\angle 3$ and $\angle 4$ are supplementary.	2. Lin. Pair Thm.
3. $\angle 1 \cong \angle 3$	3. ≅ Supps. Thm.
4. $m\angle 1 = m\angle 3$	4. Def. of ≅ ∡

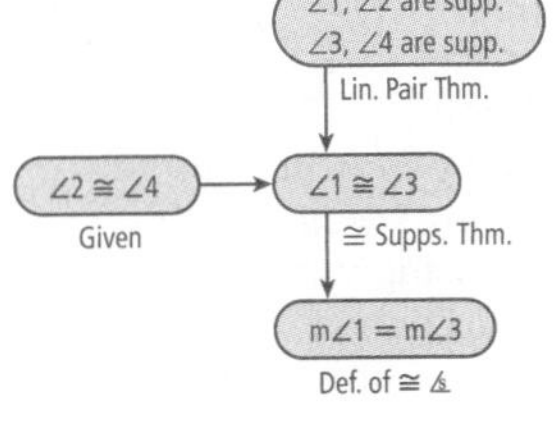

Power Presentations with PowerPoint®

Additional Examples

Example 1

Use the given flowchart proof to write a two-column proof.

Given: $\angle 2$ and $\angle 3$ are comp. $\angle 1 \cong \angle 3$

Prove: $\angle 2$ and $\angle 1$ are comp.

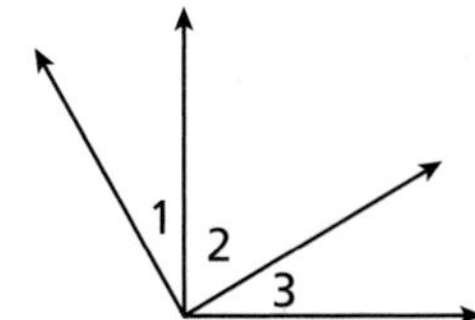

Flowchart proof:

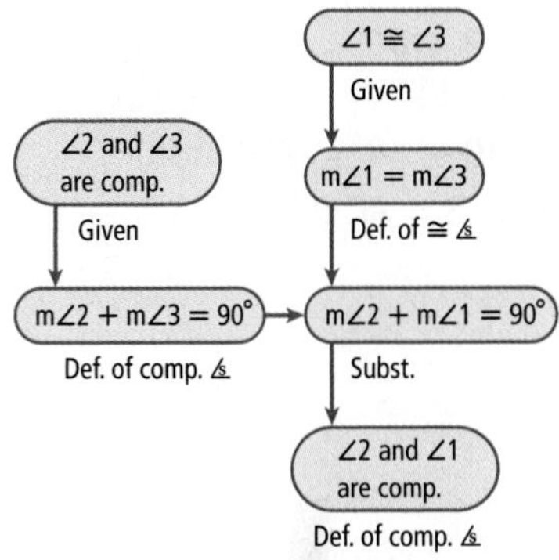

1. $\angle 2$ and $\angle 3$ are comp. $\angle 1 \cong \angle 3$ (Given)
2. $m\angle 2 + m\angle 3 = 90°$ (Def. of comp. ∡)
3. $m\angle 1 = m\angle 3$ (Def. of ≅ ∡)
4. $m\angle 2 + m\angle 1 = 90°$ (Subst.)
5. $\angle 2$ and $\angle 1$ are comp. (Def. of comp. ∡)

Example 2

See TE margin on p. 120.

INTERVENTION

Questioning Strategies

EXAMPLE 1

- When you change a proof from flowchart style to two-column style, how do you decide what order to list the steps in?

2 Teach

Guided Instruction

Remind students of the structure of a two-column proof. Explain that flowchart and paragraph proofs are two more styles of proofs. Point out that some boxes in a flowchart proof may have more than one arrow pointing to or away from them.

Teaching Tip **Multiple Representations** Writing proofs in different styles lets students see different representations of the same logical argument. Some students may find it easier to follow the logic in a flowchart proof.

Reaching All Learners

Through Visual Cues

Emphasize the importance of focusing on the diagram and the Given statement before beginning to write a proof. For every proof, students should first copy the diagram from the textbook onto their paper. They should ask themselves what the diagram tells them. Then they should mark the diagram with any additional information from the Given statement, such as congruent segments, congruent angles, or right angles.

A **paragraph proof** is a style of proof that presents the steps of the proof and their matching reasons as sentences in a paragraph. Although this style of proof is less formal than a two-column proof, you still must include every step.

Theorems

	THEOREM	HYPOTHESIS	CONCLUSION
2-7-2	**Vertical Angles Theorem** Vertical angles are congruent.	$\angle A$ and $\angle B$ are vertical angles.	$\angle A \cong \angle B$
2-7-3	If two congruent angles are supplementary, then each angle is a right angle. ($\cong$ ∡ supp. → rt. ∡)	$\angle 1 \cong \angle 2$; $\angle 1$ and $\angle 2$ are supplementary.	$\angle 1$ and $\angle 2$ are right angles.

EXAMPLE 3 Reading a Paragraph Proof

Use the given paragraph proof to write a two-column proof of the Vertical Angles Theorem.

Given: $\angle 1$ **and** $\angle 3$ **are vertical angles.**
Prove: $\angle 1 \cong \angle 3$

Paragraph proof: $\angle 1$ and $\angle 3$ are vertical angles, so they are formed by intersecting lines. Therefore $\angle 1$ and $\angle 2$ are a linear pair, and $\angle 2$ and $\angle 3$ are a linear pair. By the Linear Pair Theorem, $\angle 1$ and $\angle 2$ are supplementary, and $\angle 2$ and $\angle 3$ are supplementary. So by the Congruent Supplements Theorem, $\angle 1 \cong \angle 3$.

Two-column proof:

Statements	Reasons
1. $\angle 1$ and $\angle 3$ are vertical angles.	1. Given
2. $\angle 1$ and $\angle 3$ are formed by intersecting lines.	2. Def. of vert. ∡
3. $\angle 1$ and $\angle 2$ are a linear pair. $\angle 2$ and $\angle 3$ are a linear pair.	3. Def. of lin. pair
4. $\angle 1$ and $\angle 2$ are supplementary. $\angle 2$ and $\angle 3$ are supplementary.	4. Lin. Pair Thm.
5. $\angle 1 \cong \angle 3$	5. $\cong$ Supps. Thm.

3. Use the given paragraph proof to write a two-column proof.

Given: $\angle WXY$ is a right angle. $\angle 1 \cong \angle 3$
Prove: $\angle 1$ and $\angle 2$ are complementary.

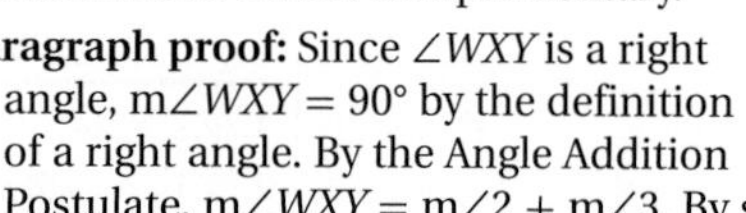
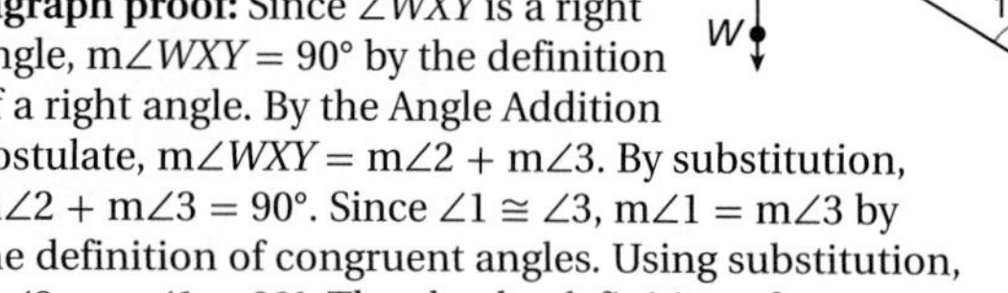

Paragraph proof: Since $\angle WXY$ is a right angle, $m\angle WXY = 90°$ by the definition of a right angle. By the Angle Addition Postulate, $m\angle WXY = m\angle 2 + m\angle 3$. By substitution, $m\angle 2 + m\angle 3 = 90°$. Since $\angle 1 \cong \angle 3$, $m\angle 1 = m\angle 3$ by the definition of congruent angles. Using substitution, $m\angle 2 + m\angle 1 = 90°$. Thus by the definition of complementary angles, $\angle 1$ and $\angle 2$ are complementary.

1. $\angle WXY$ is a rt. $\angle$. (Given)
2. $m\angle WXY = 90°$ (Def. of rt. $\angle$)
3. $m\angle 2 + m\angle 3 = m\angle WXY$ ($\angle$ Add. Post.)
4. $m\angle 2 + m\angle 3 = 90°$ (Subst.)
5. $\angle 1 \cong \angle 3$ (Given)
6. $m\angle 1 = m\angle 3$ (Def. of $\cong$ ∡)
7. $m\angle 2 + m\angle 1 = 90°$ (Subst.)
8. $\angle 1$ and $\angle 2$ are comp. (Def. of comp. ∡)

Power Presentations with PowerPoint®

Additional Examples

Example 2

Use the given two-column proof to write a flowchart proof.

Given: B is the midpoint of $\overline{AC}$.
Prove: $2AB = AC$

A ———•——— C (B)

Two-Column proof:

1. B is the midpoint of $\overline{AC}$. (Given)
2. $\overline{AB} \cong \overline{BC}$ (Def. of mdpt.)
3. $AB = BC$ (Def. of $\cong$ segs.)
4. $AB + BC = AC$ (Seg. Add. Post.)
5. $AB + AB = AC$ (Subst.)
6. $2AB = AC$ (Simplify.)

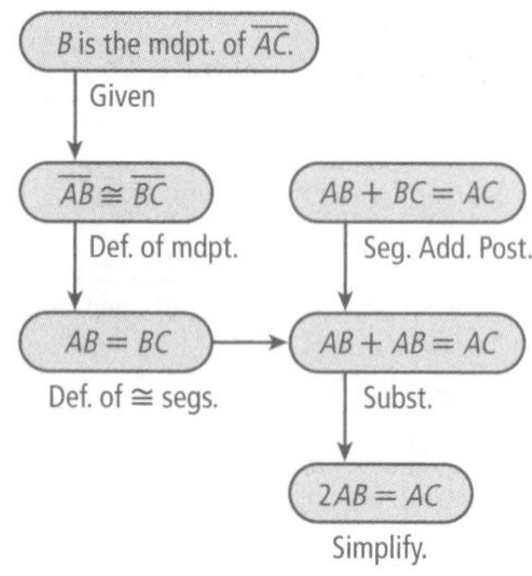

Example 3

Use the given paragraph proof to write a two-column proof.

Given: $m\angle 1 + m\angle 2 = m\angle 4$
Prove: $m\angle 3 + m\angle 1 + m\angle 2 = 180°$

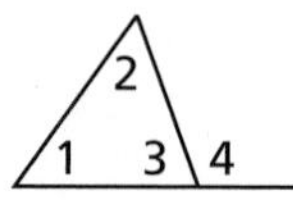

Paragraph proof: It is given that $m\angle 1 + m\angle 2 = m\angle 4$. $\angle 3$ and $\angle 4$ are supplementary by the Lin. Pair Thm. So $m\angle 3 + m\angle 4 = 180°$ by def. By Subst., $m\angle 3 + m\angle 1 + m\angle 2 = 180°$.

1. $m\angle 1 + m\angle 2 = m\angle 4$ (Given)
2. $\angle 3$ and $\angle 4$ are supp. (Lin. Pair Thm.)
3. $m\angle 3 + m\angle 4 = 180°$ (Def. of supp. ∡)
4. $m\angle 3 + m\angle 1 + m\angle 2 = 180°$ (Subst.)

INTERVENTION
Questioning Strategies

EXAMPLE 2

- Why might a flowchart proof you write look different from another person's flowchart proof of the same thing?

EXAMPLE 3

- In a paragraph proof, what distinguishes between the statements and the reasons?

Student to Student

Writing a Proof

Claire Jeffords
Riverbend High School

When I have to write a proof and I don't see how to start, I look at what I'm supposed to be proving and see if it makes sense. If it does, I ask myself why. Sometimes this helps me to see what the reasons in the proof might be. If all else fails, I just start writing down everything I know based on the diagram and the given statement. By brainstorming like this, I can usually figure out the steps of the proof. You can even write each thing on a separate piece of paper and arrange the pieces of paper like a flowchart.

EXAMPLE  4 Writing a Paragraph Proof

Use the given two-column proof to write a paragraph proof of Theorem 2-7-3.

Given: $\angle 1$ and $\angle 2$ are supplementary. $\angle 1 \cong \angle 2$
Prove: $\angle 1$ and $\angle 2$ are right angles.

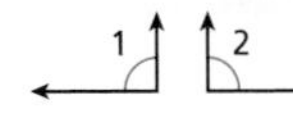

Two-column proof:

Statements	Reasons
1. $\angle 1$ and $\angle 2$ are supplementary. $\angle 1 \cong \angle 2$	1. Given
2. $m\angle 1 + m\angle 2 = 180°$	2. Def. of supp. $\angle$s
3. $m\angle 1 = m\angle 2$	3. Def. of $\cong$ $\angle$s *Step 1*
4. $m\angle 1 + m\angle 1 = 180°$	4. Subst. *Steps 2, 3*
5. $2m\angle 1 = 180°$	5. Simplification
6. $m\angle 1 = 90°$	6. Div. Prop. of =
7. $m\angle 2 = 90°$	7. Trans. Prop. of = *Steps 3, 6*
8. $\angle 1$ and $\angle 2$ are right angles.	8. Def. of rt. $\angle$

Paragraph proof: $\angle 1$ and $\angle 2$ are supplementary, so $m\angle 1 + m\angle 2 = 180°$ by the definition of supplementary angles. They are also congruent, so their measures are equal by the definition of congruent angles. By substitution, $m\angle 1 + m\angle 1 = 180°$, so $m\angle 1 = 90°$ by the Division Property of Equality. Because $m\angle 1 = m\angle 2$, $m\angle 2 = 90°$ by the Transitive Property of Equality. So both are right angles by the definition of a right angle.

4. Use the given two-column proof to write a paragraph proof.

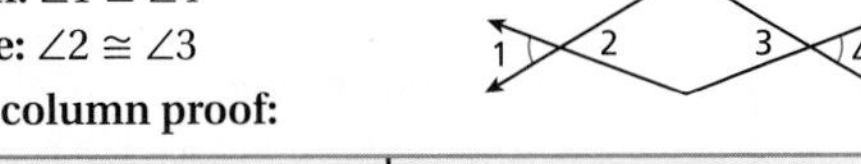

Given: $\angle 1 \cong \angle 4$
Prove: $\angle 2 \cong \angle 3$

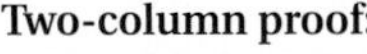

Two-column proof:

Statements	Reasons
1. $\angle 1 \cong \angle 4$	1. Given
2. $\angle 1 \cong \angle 2$, $\angle 3 \cong \angle 4$	2. Vert. $\angle$s Thm.
3. $\angle 2 \cong \angle 4$	3. Trans. Prop. of $\cong$ *Steps 1, 2*
4. $\angle 2 \cong \angle 3$	4. Trans. Prop. of $\cong$ *Steps 2, 3*

It is given that $\angle 1 \cong \angle 4$. By the Vert. $\angle$s Thm., $\angle 1 \cong \angle 2$ and $\angle 3 \cong \angle 4$. By the Trans. Prop. of $\cong$, $\angle 2 \cong \angle 4$. Similarly, $\angle 2 \cong \angle 3$.

COMMON ERROR ALERT

In paragraph proofs, you may find that some students leave out one or more reasons or perhaps an entire step. Have students number each step and its reason in the paragraph proof to match the numbering of the corresponding two-column proof.

Power Presentations with PowerPoint®

Additional Examples

Example 4

Use the given two-column proof to write a paragraph proof.

Given: $\angle 1$ and $\angle 2$ are comp.
Prove: $\angle 3$ and $\angle 4$ are comp.

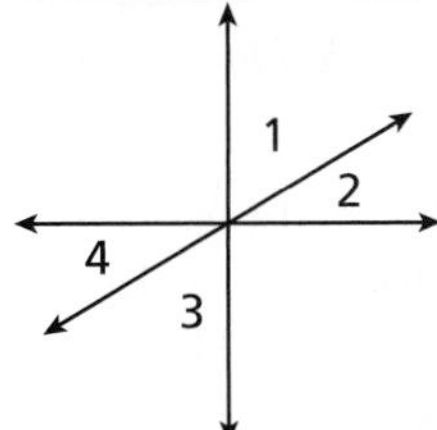

Two-Column proof:

1. $\angle 1$ and $\angle 2$ are comp. (Given)
2. $m\angle 1 + m\angle 2 = 90°$ (Def. of comp. $\angle$s)
3. $\angle 1 \cong \angle 3$, $\angle 2 \cong \angle 4$ (Vert. $\angle$s Thm.)
4. $m\angle 1 = m\angle 3$, $m\angle 2 = m\angle 4$ (Def. of $\cong$ $\angle$s)
5. $m\angle 3 + m\angle 4 = 90°$ (Subst.)
6. $m\angle 3$ and $m\angle 4$ are comp. (Def. of comp. $\angle$s)

$\angle 1$ and $\angle 2$ are comp., so $m\angle 1 + m\angle 2 = 90°$ by the def. of comp. $\angle$s. $\angle 1 \cong \angle 3$ and $\angle 2 \cong \angle 4$ by the Vert. $\angle$s Thm. So $m\angle 1 = m\angle 3$ and $m\angle 2 = m\angle 4$ by the def. of $\cong$ $\angle$s. By Subst., $m\angle 3 + m\angle 4 = 90°$, so $\angle 3$ and $\angle 4$ are comp. by the def. of comp. $\angle$s.

3 Close

Summarize

Review the three proof styles that have been introduced. Lead a brief discussion on how to write a proof in one format and how to rewrite it in a different format.

Also review the three theorems presented in the lesson:

- Common Segments Theorem
- Vertical Angles Theorem
- If two congruent angles are supplementary, then each is a right angle.

ONGOING ASSESSMENT and INTERVENTION

***Diagnose Before* the Lesson**
2-7 Warm Up, TE p. 118

***Monitor During* the Lesson**
Check It Out! Exercises, SE pp. 119–121
Questioning Strategies, TE pp. 119–121

***Assess After* the Lesson**
2-7 Lesson Quiz, TE p. 125
Alternative Assessment, TE p. 125

INTERVENTION

Questioning Strategies

EXAMPLE 4

- When you write a paragraph proof, how can you be sure that you haven't left out any of the reasons?

Answers to *Think and Discuss*

1. Possible answer: There may be more than one thm. that you can apply to a proof, and the steps in a proof may sometimes be written in a different order.
2. Answers will vary.
3. See p. A3.

THINK AND DISCUSS

1. Explain why there might be more than one correct way to write a proof.
2. Describe the steps you take when writing a proof.

3. **GET ORGANIZED** Copy and complete the graphic organizer. In each box, describe the proof style in your own words.

Proof Styles: Two-column | Flowchart | Paragraph

2-7 Exercises

Assignment Guide

Assign *Guided Practice* exercises as necessary.

If you finished Examples **1–2**
- **Basic** 7, 8, 12–16
- **Average** 7, 8, 11, 12–16 even
- **Advanced** 7, 8, 11–16

If you finished Examples **1–4**
- **Basic** 7–18, 20–23, 28–36
- **Average** 7–10, 12–16 even, 17–23, 26–36
- **Advanced** 7–10, 12–16 even, 18–36

Homework Quick Check
Quickly check key concepts.
Exercises: 7–10, 12, 16

State Resources

2-7 Exercises

GUIDED PRACTICE

Vocabulary **Apply the vocabulary from this lesson to answer each question.**

1. In a __?__ proof, the logical order is represented by arrows that connect each step. (*flowchart* or *paragraph*) **flowchart**

2. The steps and reasons of a __?__ proof are written out in sentences. (*flowchart* or *paragraph*) **paragraph**

SEE EXAMPLE 1 p. 118

3. Use the given flowchart proof to write a two-column proof.
Given: $\angle 1 \cong \angle 2$
Prove: $\angle 1$ and $\angle 2$ are right angles.
Flowchart proof:

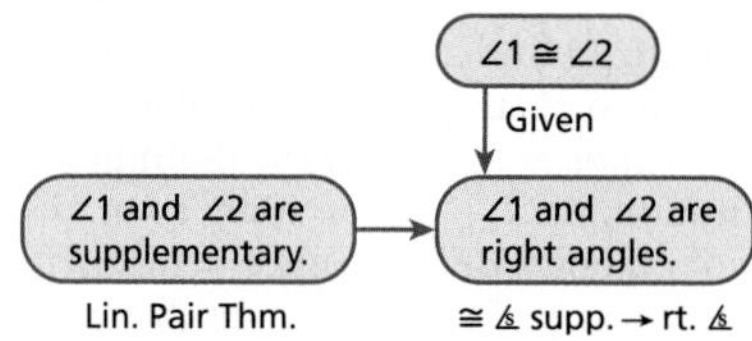

1. $\angle 1 \cong \angle 2$ (Given)
2. $\angle 1$ and $\angle 2$ are supp. (Lin. Pair Thm.)
3. $\angle 1$ and $\angle 2$ are rt. ∡. (≅ ∡ supp. → rt. ∡)

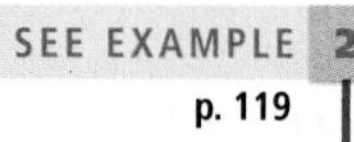
SEE EXAMPLE 2 p. 119

4. Use the given two-column proof to write a flowchart proof.
Given: $\angle 2$ and $\angle 4$ are supplementary.
Prove: $m\angle 2 = m\angle 3$
Two-column proof:

Statements	Reasons
1. $\angle 2$ and $\angle 4$ are supplementary.	1. Given
2. $\angle 3$ and $\angle 4$ are supplementary.	2. Lin. Pair Thm.
3. $\angle 2 \cong \angle 3$	3. ≅ Supps. Thm. *Steps 1, 2*
4. $m\angle 2 = m\angle 3$	4. Def. of ≅ ∡

Answers

4.

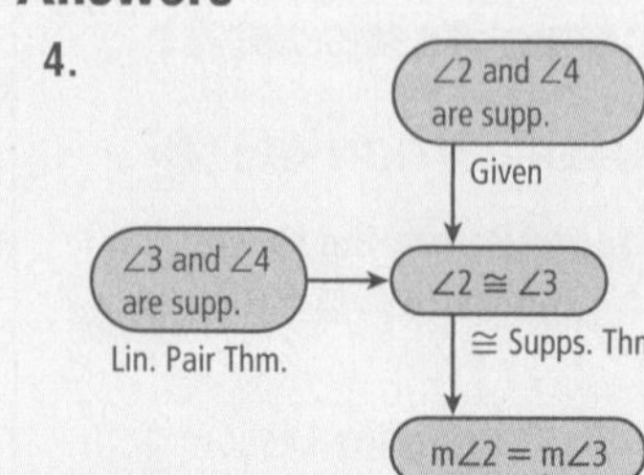

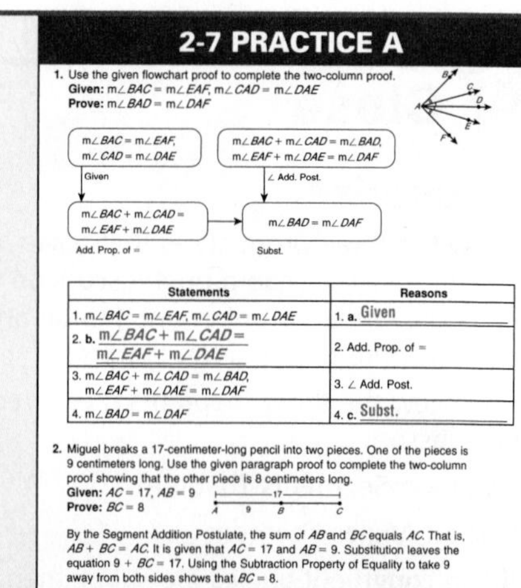

2-7 PRACTICE A

1. Use the given flowchart proof to complete the two-column proof.
Given: $m\angle BAC = m\angle EAF$, $m\angle CAD = m\angle DAE$
Prove: $m\angle BAD = m\angle DAF$

$m\angle BAC = m\angle EAF$, $m\angle CAD = m\angle DAE$ (Given) → $m\angle BAC + m\angle CAD = m\angle EAF + m\angle DAE$ (Add. Prop. of =)
$m\angle BAC + m\angle CAD = m\angle BAD$, $m\angle EAF + m\angle DAE = m\angle DAF$ (∠ Add. Post.) → $m\angle BAD = m\angle DAF$ (Subst.)

Statements	Reasons
1. $m\angle BAC = m\angle EAF$, $m\angle CAD = m\angle DAE$	1. a. Given
2. b. $m\angle BAC + m\angle CAD = m\angle EAF + m\angle DAE$	2. Add. Prop. of =
3. $m\angle BAC + m\angle CAD = m\angle BAD$, $m\angle EAF + m\angle DAE = m\angle DAF$	3. ∠ Add. Post.
4. $m\angle BAD = m\angle DAF$	4. c. Subst.

2. Miguel breaks a 17-centimeter-long pencil into two pieces. One of the pieces is 9 centimeters long. Use the given paragraph proof to complete the two-column proof showing that the other piece is 8 centimeters long.
Given: $AC = 17$, $AB = 9$
Prove: $BC = 8$

By the Segment Addition Postulate, the sum of AB and BC equals AC. That is, $AB + BC = AC$. It is given that $AC = 17$ and $AB = 9$. Substitution leaves the equation $9 + BC = 17$. Using the Subtraction Property of Equality to take 9 away from both sides shows that $BC = 8$.

Statements	Reasons
1. $AB + BC = AC$	1. a. Seg. Add. Post.
2. $AC = 17$, $AB = 9$	2. Given
3. b. $9 + BC = 17$	3. Subst.
4. c. $BC = 8$	4. Subtr. Prop. of =

SEE EXAMPLE 3 p. 120

5. Use the given paragraph proof to write a two-column proof.

Given: $\angle 2 \cong \angle 4$

Prove: $\angle 1 \cong \angle 3$

1. $\angle 2 \cong \angle 4$ (Given)
2. $\angle 1 \cong \angle 2$, $\angle 3 \cong \angle 4$ (Vert. ∠s Thm.)
3. $\angle 1 \cong \angle 4$ (Trans. Prop. of ≅)
4. $\angle 1 \cong \angle 3$ (Trans. Prop. of ≅)

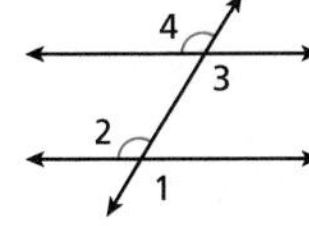

Paragraph proof: By the Vertical Angles Theorem, $\angle 1 \cong \angle 2$, and $\angle 3 \cong \angle 4$. It is given that $\angle 2 \cong \angle 4$. By the Transitive Property of Congruence, $\angle 1 \cong \angle 4$, and thus $\angle 1 \cong \angle 3$.

SEE EXAMPLE 4 p. 121

6. Use the given two-column proof to write a paragraph proof.

Given: $\overrightarrow{BD}$ bisects $\angle ABC$.

Prove: $\overrightarrow{BG}$ bisects $\angle FBH$.

Two-column proof:

Statements	Reasons
1. $\overrightarrow{BD}$ bisects $\angle ABC$.	1. Given
2. $\angle 1 \cong \angle 2$	2. Def. of ∠ bisector
3. $\angle 1 \cong \angle 4$, $\angle 2 \cong \angle 3$	3. Vert. ∠s Thm.
4. $\angle 4 \cong \angle 2$	4. Trans. Prop. of ≅ *Steps 2, 3*
5. $\angle 4 \cong \angle 3$	5. Trans. Prop. of ≅ *Steps 3, 4*
6. $\overrightarrow{BG}$ bisects $\angle FBH$.	6. Def. of ∠ bisector

PRACTICE AND PROBLEM SOLVING

Independent Practice

For Exercises	See Example
7	1
8	2
9	3
10	4

Extra Practice

Skills Practice p. S7
Application Practice p. S29

7. Use the given flowchart proof to write a two-column proof.

Given: B is the midpoint of $\overline{AC}$.
$AD = EC$

Prove: $DB = BE$

Flowchart proof:

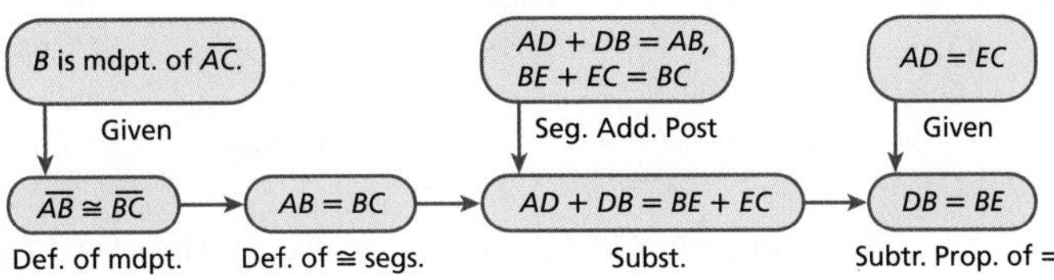

8. Use the given two-column proof to write a flowchart proof.

Given: $\angle 3$ is a right angle.

Prove: $\angle 4$ is a right angle.

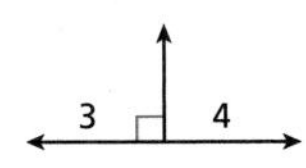

Two-column proof:

Statements	Reasons
1. $\angle 3$ is a right angle.	1. Given
2. $m\angle 3 = 90°$	2. Def. of rt. ∠
3. $\angle 3$ and $\angle 4$ are supplementary.	3. Lin. Pair Thm.
4. $m\angle 3 + m\angle 4 = 180°$	4. Def. of supp. ∠s
5. $90° + m\angle 4 = 180°$	5. Subst. *Steps 2, 4*
6. $m\angle 4 = 90°$	6. Subtr. Prop. of =
7. $\angle 4$ is a right angle.	7. Def. of rt. ∠

Teaching Tip

Reading Math Some students may have difficulty following the logic in a paragraph proof since the steps are not always clearly separated. In **Exercise 5,** have students rewrite the paragraph proof on their own paper and then underline each statement in a different color of pencil. Have them circle the corresponding reason in the same color. This is very helpful with long paragraph proofs, such as in **Exercise 9.**

Answers

6. It is given that $\overrightarrow{BD}$ bisects $\angle ABC$, so $\angle 1 \cong \angle 2$ by the def. of ∠ bisector. By the Vert. ∠s Thm., $\angle 1 \cong \angle 4$ and $\angle 2 \cong \angle 3$. By the Trans. Prop. of ≅, $\angle 4 \cong \angle 2$, and thus $\angle 4 \cong \angle 3$. Therefore $\overrightarrow{BG}$ bisects $\angle FBH$ by the def. of ∠ bisector.
7. 1. B is the mdpt. of $\overline{AC}$. (Given)
   2. $\overline{AB} \cong \overline{BC}$ (Def. of mdpt.)
   3. $AB = BC$ (Def. of ≅ segs.)
   4. $AD + DB = AB$, $BE + EC = BC$ (Seg. Add. Post.)
   5. $AD + DB = BE + EC$ (Subst.)
   6. $AD = EC$ (Given)
   7. $DB = BE$ (Subtr. Prop. of =)
8.

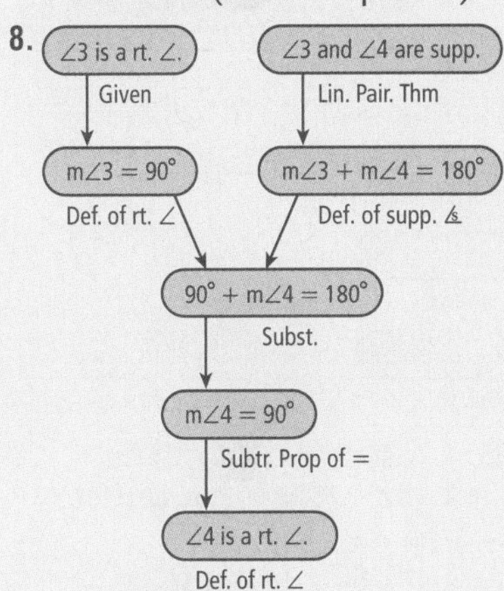

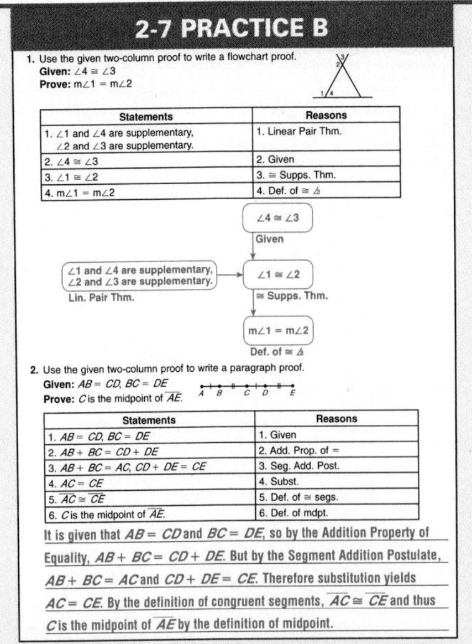

2-7 PRACTICE B

1. Use the given two-column proof to write a flowchart proof.

Given: $\angle 4 \cong \angle 3$

Prove: $m\angle 1 = m\angle 2$

Statements	Reasons
1. $\angle 1$ and $\angle 4$ are supplementary, $\angle 2$ and $\angle 3$ are supplementary.	1. Linear Pair Thm.
2. $\angle 4 \cong \angle 3$	2. Given
3. $\angle 1 \cong \angle 2$	3. ≅ Supps. Thm.
4. $m\angle 1 = m\angle 2$	4. Def. of ≅ ∠s

∠4 ≅ ∠3 — Given
∠1 and ∠4 are supplementary, ∠2 and ∠3 are supplementary. — Lin. Pair Thm.
∠1 ≅ ∠2 — ≅ Supps. Thm.
m∠1 = m∠2 — Def. of ≅ ∠s

2. Use the given two-column proof to write a paragraph proof.

Given: $AB = CD$, $BC = DE$

Prove: C is the midpoint of $\overline{AE}$.

Statements	Reasons
1. $AB = CD$, $BC = DE$	1. Given
2. $AB + BC = CD + DE$	2. Add. Prop. of =
3. $AB + BC = AC$, $CD + DE = CE$	3. Seg. Add. Post.
4. $AC = CE$	4. Subst.
5. $\overline{AC} \cong \overline{CE}$	5. Def. of ≅ segs.
6. C is the midpoint of $\overline{AE}$.	6. Def. of mdpt.

It is given that $AB = CD$ and $BC = DE$, so by the Addition Property of Equality, $AB + BC = CD + DE$. But by the Segment Addition Postulate, $AB + BC = AC$ and $CD + DE = CE$. Therefore substitution yields $AC = CE$. By the definition of congruent segments, $\overline{AC} \cong \overline{CE}$ and thus C is the midpoint of $\overline{AE}$ by the definition of midpoint.

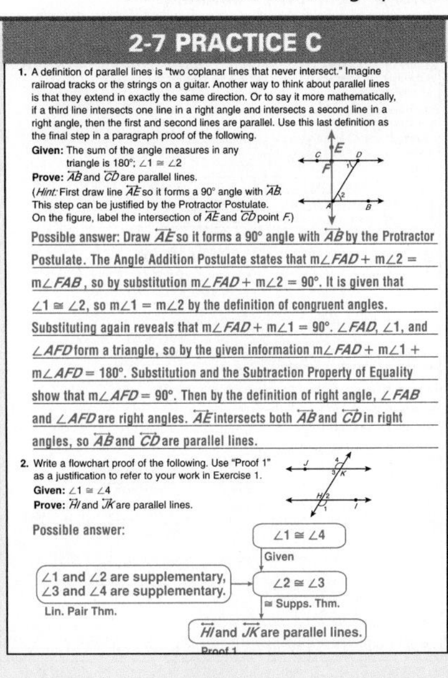

2-7 PRACTICE C

1. A definition of parallel lines is "two coplanar lines that never intersect." Imagine railroad tracks or the strings on a guitar. Another way to think about parallel lines is that they extend in exactly the same direction. Or to say it more mathematically, if a third line intersects one line in a right angle and intersects a second line in a right angle, then the first and second lines are parallel. Use this last definition as the final step in a paragraph proof of the following.

Given: The sum of the angle measures in any triangle is 180°; $\angle 1 \cong \angle 2$

Prove: $\overleftrightarrow{AB}$ and $\overleftrightarrow{CD}$ are parallel lines.

(*Hint:* First draw line $\overleftrightarrow{AE}$ so it forms a 90° angle with $\overleftrightarrow{AB}$. This step can be justified by the Protractor Postulate. On the figure, label the intersection of $\overleftrightarrow{AE}$ and $\overleftrightarrow{CD}$ point F.)

Possible answer: Draw $\overleftrightarrow{AE}$ so it forms a 90° angle with $\overleftrightarrow{AB}$ by the Protractor Postulate. The Angle Addition Postulate states that $m\angle FAD + m\angle 2 = m\angle FAB$, so by substitution $m\angle FAD + m\angle 2 = 90°$. It is given that $\angle 1 \cong \angle 2$, so $m\angle 1 = m\angle 2$ by the definition of congruent angles. Substituting again reveals that $m\angle FAD + m\angle 1 = 90°$. $\angle FAD$, $\angle 1$, and $\angle AFD$ form a triangle, so by the given information $m\angle FAD + m\angle 1 + m\angle AFD = 180°$. Substitution and the Subtraction Property of Equality show that $m\angle AFD = 90°$. Then by the definition of right angle, $\angle FAB$ and $\angle AFD$ are right angles. $\overleftrightarrow{AE}$ intersects both $\overleftrightarrow{AB}$ and $\overleftrightarrow{CD}$ in right angles, so $\overleftrightarrow{AB}$ and $\overleftrightarrow{CD}$ are parallel lines.

2. Write a flowchart proof of the following. Use "Proof 1" as a justification to refer to your work in Exercise 1.

Given: $\angle 1 \cong \angle 4$

Prove: $\overleftrightarrow{HI}$ and $\overleftrightarrow{JK}$ are parallel lines.

Possible answer:

∠1 ≅ ∠4 — Given
∠1 and ∠2 are supplementary, ∠3 and ∠4 are supplementary. — Lin. Pair Thm.
∠2 ≅ ∠3 — ≅ Supps. Thm.
$\overleftrightarrow{HI}$ and $\overleftrightarrow{JK}$ are parallel lines. — Proof 1

Exercise 18 involves arranging the pieces of a logical argument into a flowchart proof. This exercise prepares students for the Multi-Step Test Prep on page 126.

Answers

18.

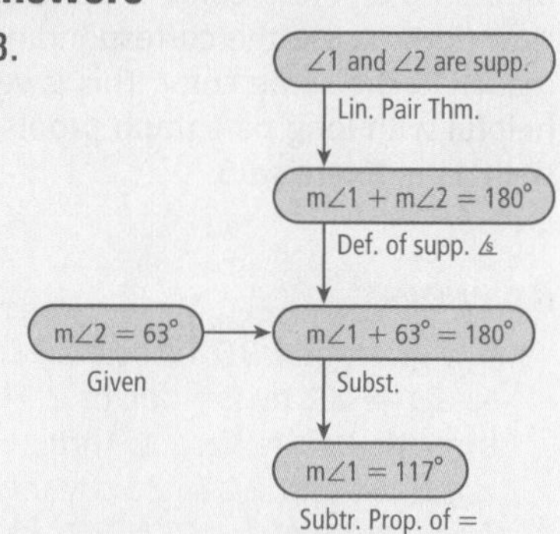

19. Possible answer: Both $\angle$s adj. to the given rt. $\angle$ must be rt. $\angle$s because they form lin. pairs with the given $\angle$. The fourth $\angle$ is a vert. $\angle$ of the given $\angle$, so it, too, is a rt. $\angle$. Since all 4 $\angle$s are rt. $\angle$s, they are all $\cong$ by the Rt. $\angle \cong$ Thm.

24.

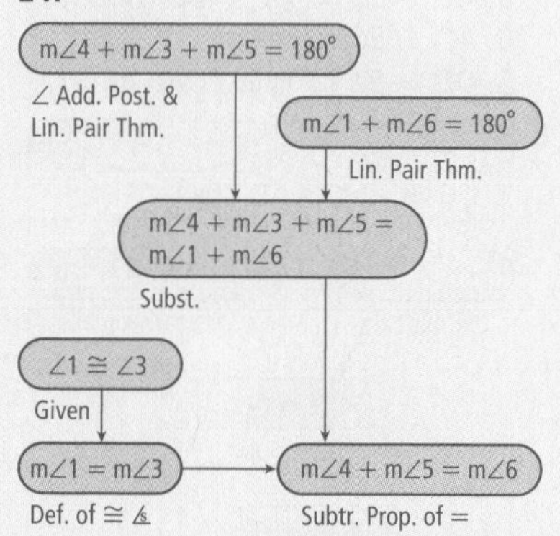

25. 1. $\angle AOC \cong \angle BOD$ (Given)
    2. $m\angle AOC = m\angle BOD$ (Def. of $\cong$ $\angle$s)
    3. $m\angle AOB + m\angle BOC = m\angle AOC$, $m\angle BOC + m\angle COD = m\angle BOD$ ($\angle$ Add. Post.)
    4. $m\angle AOB + m\angle BOC = m\angle BOC + m\angle COD$ (Subst.)
    5. $m\angle BOC = m\angle BOC$ (Reflex. Prop. of =)
    6. $m\angle AOB = m\angle COD$ (Subtr. Prop. of =)
    7. $\angle AOB \cong \angle COD$ (Def. of $\cong$ $\angle$s)

26. It is given that $\angle 2$ and $\angle 5$ are rt. $\angle$s. So by the Rt. $\angle \cong$ Thm., $\angle 2 \cong \angle 5$. By the def. of $\cong$ $\angle$s, $m\angle 2 = m\angle 5$. It is also given that $m\angle 1 + m\angle 2 + m\angle 3 = m\angle 4 + m\angle 5 + m\angle 6$. By the Subtr. Prop. of =, $m\angle 1 + m\angle 3 = m\angle 4 + m\angle 6$. $\angle 3 \cong \angle 6$ by the Vert. $\angle$s Thm., so $m\angle 3 = m\angle 6$ by the def. of $\cong$ $\angle$s. By the Subtr. Prop. of =, $m\angle 1 = m\angle 4$. So by the def. of $\cong$ $\angle$s, $\angle 1 \cong \angle 4$.

1. $\angle 1 \cong \angle 4$ (Given)
2. $\angle 1 \cong \angle 2$ (Vert. $\angle$s Thm.)
3. $\angle 4 \cong \angle 2$ (Trans. Prop. of $\cong$)
4. $m\angle 4 = m\angle 2$ (Def. of $\cong$ $\angle$s)
5. $\angle 3$ and $\angle 4$ are supp. (Lin. Pair Thm.)
6. $m\angle 3 + m\angle 4 = 180°$ (Def. of supp. $\angle$s)
7. $m\angle 3 + m\angle 2 = 180°$ (Subst.)
8. $\angle 2$ and $\angle 3$ are supp. (Def. of supp. $\angle$s)

9. Use the given paragraph proof to write a two-column proof.

Given: $\angle 1 \cong \angle 4$

Prove: $\angle 2$ and $\angle 3$ are supplementary.

Paragraph proof:

$\angle 4$ and $\angle 3$ form a linear pair, so they are supplementary by the Linear Pair Theorem. Therefore, $m\angle 4 + m\angle 3 = 180°$. Also, $\angle 1$ and $\angle 2$ are vertical angles, so $\angle 1 \cong \angle 2$ by the Vertical Angles Theorem. It is given that $\angle 1 \cong \angle 4$. So by the Transitive Property of Congruence, $\angle 4 \cong \angle 2$, and by the definition of congruent angles, $m\angle 4 = m\angle 2$. By substitution, $m\angle 2 + m\angle 3 = 180°$, so $\angle 2$ and $\angle 3$ are supplementary by the definition of supplementary angles.

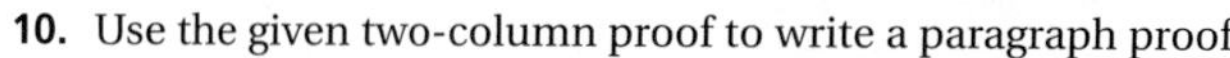

10. Use the given two-column proof to write a paragraph proof.

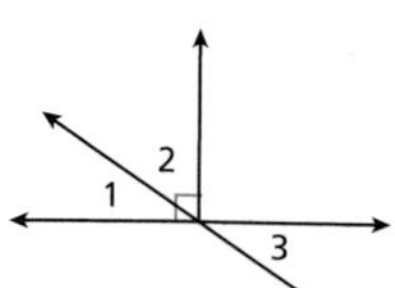

Given: $\angle 1$ and $\angle 2$ are complementary.

Prove: $\angle 2$ and $\angle 3$ are complementary.

Two-column proof:

Statements	Reasons
1. $\angle 1$ and $\angle 2$ are complementary.	1. Given
2. $m\angle 1 + m\angle 2 = 90°$	2. Def. of comp. $\angle$s
3. $\angle 1 \cong \angle 3$	3. Vert. $\angle$s Thm.
4. $m\angle 1 = m\angle 3$	4. Def. of $\cong$ $\angle$s
5. $m\angle 3 + m\angle 2 = 90°$	5. Subst. *Steps 2, 4*
6. $\angle 2$ and $\angle 3$ are complementary.	6. Def. of comp. $\angle$s

Since $\angle 1$ and $\angle 2$ are comp., $m\angle 1 + m\angle 2 = 90°$. $\angle 1 \cong \angle 3$ by the Vert. $\angle$s Thm. Thus $m\angle 1 = m\angle 3$. By subst., $m\angle 2 + m\angle 3 = 90°$, so $\angle 2$ and $\angle 3$ are comp.

Find each measure and name the theorem that justifies your answer.

11. AB **12.** $m\angle 2$ **13.** $m\angle 3$

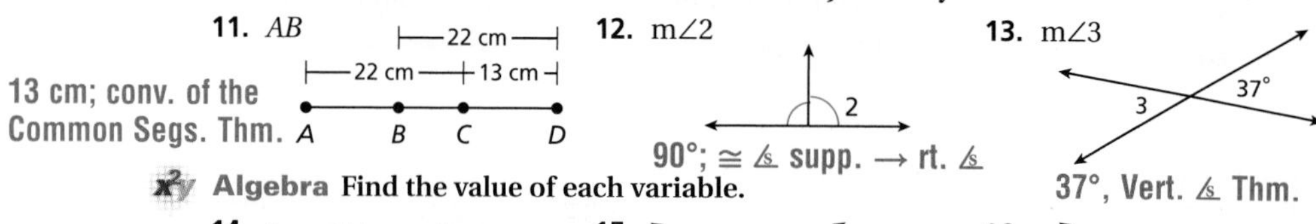

11. 13 cm; conv. of the Common Segs. Thm.

12. 90°; $\cong$ $\angle$s supp. → rt. $\angle$s

13. 37°, Vert. $\angle$s Thm.

Algebra Find the value of each variable.

14. **15.** **16.**

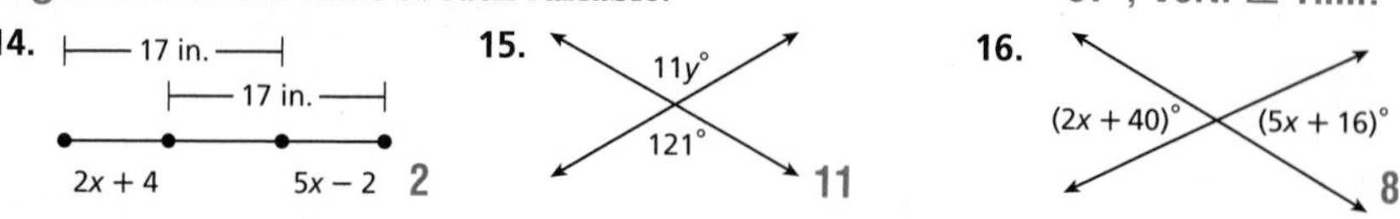

14. 2 15. 11 16. 8

17. **ERROR ANALYSIS** Below are two drawings for the given proof. Which is incorrect? Explain the error.

Given: $\overline{AB} \cong \overline{BC}$

Prove: $\angle A \cong \angle C$

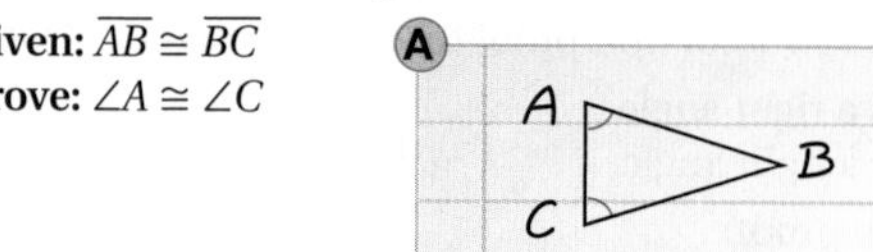

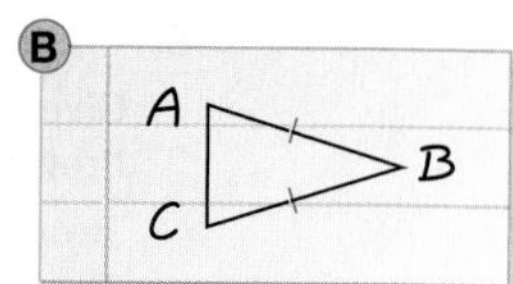

17. A; the diagram is marked with the Prove information instead of the Given information.

MULTI-STEP TEST PREP

18. This problem will prepare you for the Multi-Step Test Prep on page 126. Rearrange the pieces to create a flowchart proof.

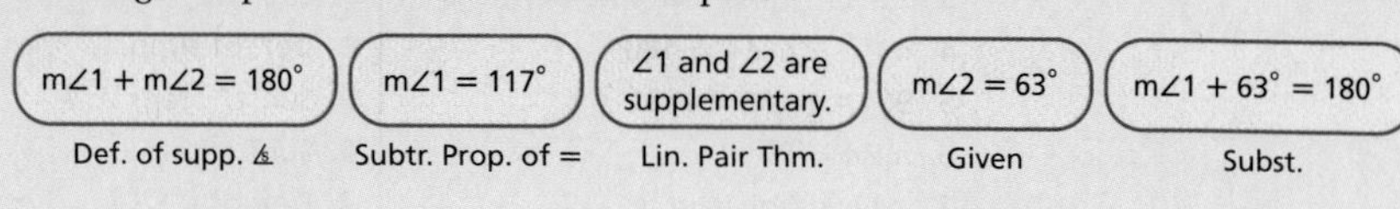

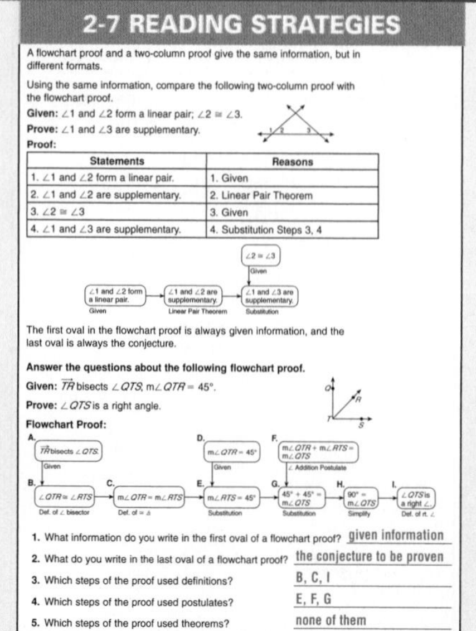

2-7 READING STRATEGIES

A flowchart proof and a two-column proof give the same information, but in different formats.

Using the same information, compare the following two-column proof with the flowchart proof.

Given: $\angle 1$ and $\angle 2$ form a linear pair; $\angle 2 \cong \angle 3$.

Prove: $\angle 1$ and $\angle 3$ are supplementary.

Proof:

Statements	Reasons
1. $\angle 1$ and $\angle 2$ form a linear pair.	1. Given
2. $\angle 1$ and $\angle 2$ are supplementary.	2. Linear Pair Theorem
3. $\angle 2 \cong \angle 3$	3. Given
4. $\angle 1$ and $\angle 3$ are supplementary.	4. Substitution Steps 3, 4

∠2 ≅ ∠3 (Given); ∠1 and ∠2 form a linear pair. (Given) → ∠1 and ∠2 are supplementary. (Linear Pair Theorem) → ∠1 and ∠3 are supplementary. (Substitution)

The first oval in the flowchart proof is always given information, and the last oval is always the conjecture.

Answer the questions about the following flowchart proof.

Given: $\overrightarrow{TR}$ bisects $\angle QTS$, $m\angle QTR = 45°$.

Prove: $\angle QTS$ is a right angle.

Flowchart Proof:

A. $\overrightarrow{TR}$ bisects $\angle QTS$. (Given)
B. $\angle QTR \cong \angle RTS$ (Def. of $\angle$ bisector)
C. $m\angle QTR = m\angle RTS$ (Def. of $\cong$ $\angle$s)
D. $m\angle QTR = 45°$ (Given)
E. $m\angle RTS = 45°$ (Substitution)
F. $m\angle QTR + m\angle RTS = m\angle QTS$ ($\angle$ Addition Postulate)
G. $45° + 45° = m\angle QTS$ (Substitution)
H. $90° = m\angle QTS$ (Simplify)
I. $\angle QTS$ is a right $\angle$. (Def. of rt. $\angle$)

1. What information do you write in the first oval of a flowchart proof? given information
2. What do you write in the last oval of a flowchart proof? the conjecture to be proven
3. Which steps of the proof used definitions? B, C, I
4. Which steps of the proof used postulates? E, F, G
5. Which steps of the proof used theorems? none of them

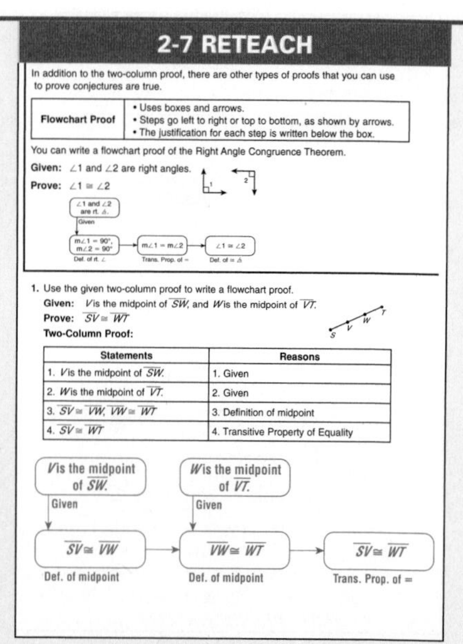

2-7 RETEACH

In addition to the two-column proof, there are other types of proofs that you can use to prove conjectures are true.

Flowchart Proof	• Uses boxes and arrows. • Steps go left to right or top to bottom, as shown by arrows. • The justification for each step is written below the box.

You can write a flowchart proof of the Right Angle Congruence Theorem.

Given: $\angle 1$ and $\angle 2$ are right angles.

Prove: $\angle 1 \cong \angle 2$

∠1 and ∠2 are rt. ∠s. (Given) → m∠1 = 90°, m∠2 = 90° (Def. of rt. ∠) → m∠1 = m∠2 (Trans. Prop. of =) → ∠1 ≅ ∠2 (Def. of ≅ ∠s)

1. Use the given two-column proof to write a flowchart proof.

Given: V is the midpoint of $\overline{SW}$, and W is the midpoint of $\overline{VT}$.

Prove: $\overline{SV} \cong \overline{WT}$

Two-Column Proof:

Statements	Reasons
1. V is the midpoint of $\overline{SW}$.	1. Given
2. W is the midpoint of $\overline{VT}$.	2. Given
3. $\overline{SV} \cong \overline{VW}$, $\overline{VW} \cong \overline{WT}$	3. Definition of midpoint
4. $\overline{SV} \cong \overline{WT}$	4. Transitive Property of Equality

V is the midpoint of $\overline{SW}$. (Given) → $\overline{SV} \cong \overline{VW}$ (Def. of midpoint); W is the midpoint of $\overline{VT}$. (Given) → $\overline{VW} \cong \overline{WT}$ (Def. of midpoint) → $\overline{SV} \cong \overline{WT}$ (Trans. Prop. of =)

19. **Critical Thinking** Two lines intersect, and one of the angles formed is a right angle. Explain why all four angles are congruent.

20. **Write About It** Which style of proof do you find easiest to write? to read?
Answers will vary.

21. Which pair of angles in the diagram must be congruent?

Ⓐ ∠1 and ∠5 **Ⓒ ∠5 and ∠8** (circled)
Ⓑ ∠3 and ∠4 Ⓓ None of the above

22. What is the measure of ∠2?

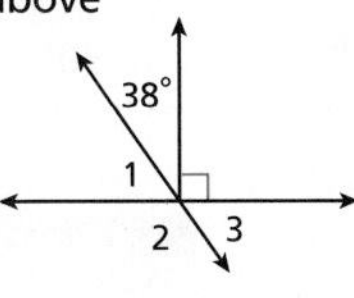

Ⓕ 38° **Ⓗ 128°** (circled)
Ⓖ 52° Ⓙ 142°

23. Which statement is NOT true if ∠2 and ∠6 are supplementary?

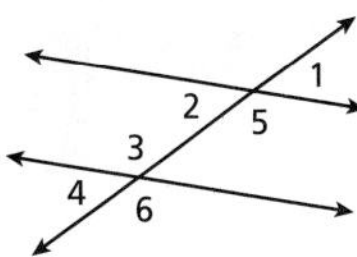

Ⓐ m∠2 + m∠6 = 180°
Ⓑ ∠2 and ∠3 are supplementary.
Ⓒ ∠1 and ∠6 are supplementary.
Ⓓ m∠1 + m∠4 = 180° (circled)

CHALLENGE AND EXTEND

24. **Textiles** Use the woven pattern to write a flowchart proof.
Given: ∠1 ≅ ∠3
Prove: m∠4 + m∠5 = m∠6

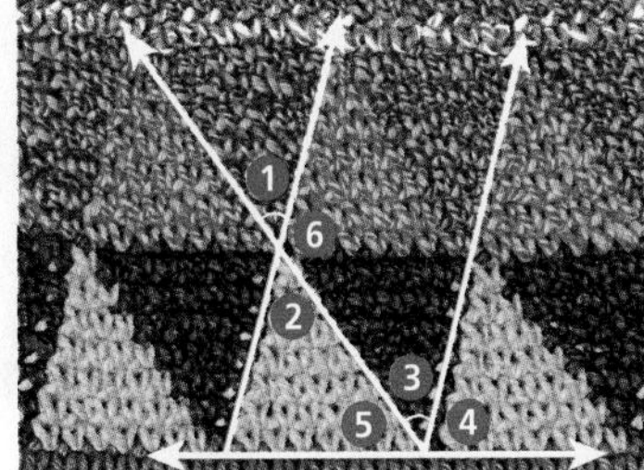

25. Write a two-column proof.
Given: ∠AOC ≅ ∠BOD
Prove: ∠AOB ≅ ∠COD

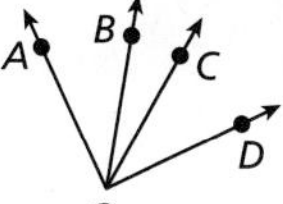

26. Write a paragraph proof.
Given: ∠2 and ∠5 are right angles.
m∠1 + m∠2 + m∠3 = m∠4 + m∠5 + m∠6
Prove: ∠1 ≅ ∠4

27. **Multi-Step** Find the value of each variable and the measures of all four angles.
$x = 31$ and $y = 11.5$; 86°, 94°, 86°, and 94°

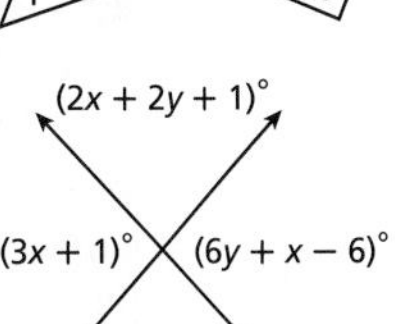

SPIRAL REVIEW

Solve each system of equations. Check your solution. *(Previous course)*

28. $\begin{cases} y = 2x + 14 \\ y = -6x + 18 \end{cases}$ $\left(\frac{1}{2}, 15\right)$

29. $\begin{cases} 7x - y = -33 \\ 3x + y = -7 \end{cases}$ $(-4, 5)$

30. $\begin{cases} 2x + y = 8 \\ -x + 3y = 10 \end{cases}$ $(2, 4)$

Use a protractor to draw an angle with each of the following measures. *(Lesson 1-3)*

31. 125° 32. 38° 33. 94° 34. 175°
31–34. Check students' drawings.

For each conditional, write the converse and a biconditional statement. *(Lesson 2-4)*

35. If a positive integer has more than two factors, then it is a composite number.

36. If a quadrilateral is a trapezoid, then it has exactly one pair of parallel sides.

35. Converse: If a positive integer is a composite number, then it has more than 2 factors. Biconditional: A positive integer has more than 2 factors if and only if it is a composite number.

36. Converse: If a quad. has exactly 1 pair of ∥ sides, then it is a trap. Biconditional: A quad. is a trap. if and only if it has exactly 1 pair of ∥ sides.

TEST PREP DOCTOR For **Exercise 21,** students who chose **A** or **B** made false assumptions from the diagram. Remind students who chose **D** about the Vertical Angles Theorem and ask them to identify pairs of vertical angles in the diagram.

Journal

Have students write about what advice they would give to a fellow student who is just starting to learn to write proofs.

ALTERNATIVE ASSESSMENT

Ask students to draw a figure similar to those used in the proofs in this lesson. Have students write a hypothesis and conclusion that apply to this figure. Then ask students to write a proof of their conjecture using one of the three styles they have learned.

Power Presentations with PowerPoint®

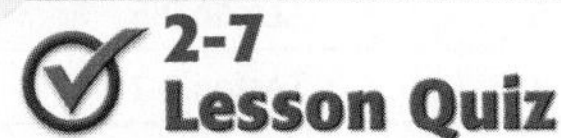

Use the two-column proof below to write the following.

1. a flowchart proof

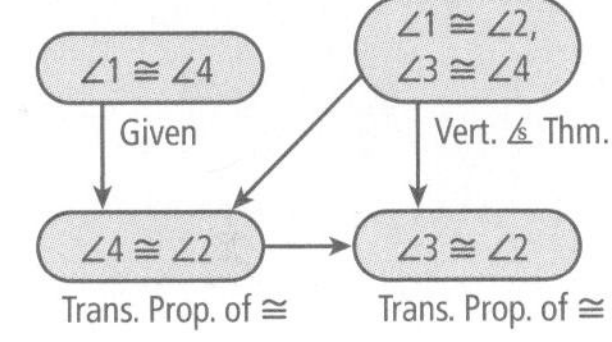

2. a paragraph proof
It is given that ∠1 ≅ ∠4. By the Vertical Angles Theorem, ∠1 ≅ ∠2 and ∠3 ≅ ∠4. By the Transitive Property of Congruence, ∠4 ≅ ∠2 and ∠3 ≅ ∠2.

Given: ∠1 ≅ ∠4
Prove: ∠3 ≅ ∠2

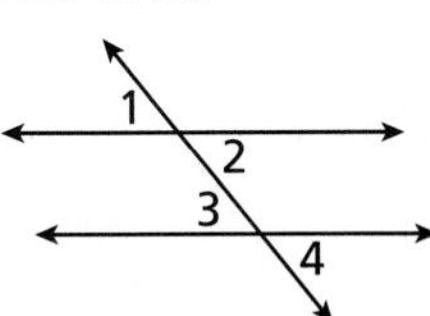

Two-Column proof

1. ∠1 ≅ ∠4 (Given)
2. ∠1 ≅ ∠2, ∠3 ≅ ∠4 (Vert. ∡ Thm.)
3. ∠4 ≅ ∠2 (Trans. Prop. of ≅)
4. ∠3 ≅ ∠2 (Trans. Prop. of ≅)

Also available on transparency

2-7 PROBLEM SOLVING

The diagram shows the second-floor glass railing at a mall.

1. Use the given two-column proof to write a flowchart proof.
Given: ∠2 and ∠3 are supplementary.
Prove: ∠1 and ∠3 are supplementary.
Two-Column Proof:

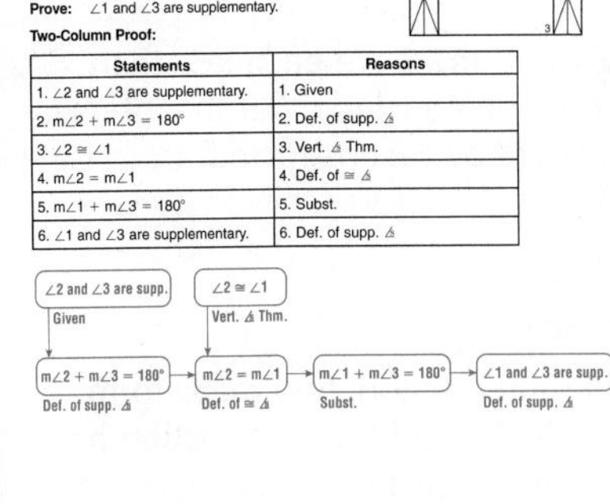

Statements	Reasons
1. ∠2 and ∠3 are supplementary.	1. Given
2. m∠2 + m∠3 = 180°	2. Def. of supp. ∡
3. ∠2 ≅ ∠1	3. Vert. ∡ Thm.
4. m∠2 = m∠1	4. Def. of ≅ ∡
5. m∠1 + m∠3 = 180°	5. Subst.
6. ∠1 and ∠3 are supplementary.	6. Def. of supp. ∡

Choose the best answer.

2. Which would NOT be included in a paragraph proof of the two-column proof above?
Ⓐ Since ∠2 and ∠3 are supplementary, m∠2 = m∠3. (circled)
B ∠2 ≅ ∠1 by the Vertical Angles Theorem.
C Using substitution, m∠1 + m∠3 = 180°.
D m∠2 = m∠1 by the definition of congruent angles.

2-7 CHALLENGE

A **flowchart proof** is a visual representation of the deductive reasoning process. To write a flowchart proof, it may be helpful to first write a two-column proof.

1. Write a flowchart proof.
Given: $\overline{EF} \cong \overline{BC}$, B is the midpoint of $\overline{AC}$.
Prove: $\overline{EF} \cong \overline{AB}$

Possible answer:
- B is the midpoint of $\overline{AC}$. (Given) → $\overline{AB} \cong \overline{BC}$ (Def. of midpoint) → $AB = BC$ (Def. of ≅ seg.)
- $\overline{EF} \cong \overline{AB}$ (Given) → $EF = BC$ (Def. of ≅ seg.)
- $EF = BC$ → $AB = BC$ → $EF = AB$ (Subst.) → $\overline{EF} \cong \overline{AB}$ (Def. of ≅ seg.)

2. Write a flowchart proof.
Given: ∠STV ≅ ∠TVU, ∠STU ≅ ∠UVS
Prove: ∠SVT ≅ ∠UTV

Possible answer:
- ∠STV ≅ ∠TVU, ∠STU ≅ ∠SVU (Given) → m∠STV = m∠TVU, m∠STU = m∠SVU (Def. of ≅ ∡)
- m∠SVT + m∠TVU = m∠SVU (∠ Add. Post.); m∠STV + m∠UTV = m∠STU (∠ Add. Post.) → m∠SVT + m∠TVU = m∠STV + m∠UTV (Subst.)
- → m∠SVT + m∠STV = m∠STV + m∠UTV (Subst.)
- m∠STV = m∠STV (Reflex. Prop. of =) → m∠SVT = m∠UTV (Subtr. Prop. of =) → ∠SVT ≅ ∠UTV (Def. of ≅ ∡)

Organizer

Objective: Assess students' ability to apply concepts and skills in Lessons 2-5 through 2-7 in a real-world format.

Resources

Geometry Assessments
www.mathtekstoolkit.org

Problem	Text Reference
1	Previous course
2	Previous course Lesson 2-5
3	Lesson 2-6
4	Lesson 2-7

Answers

3–4. See p. A12.

State Resources

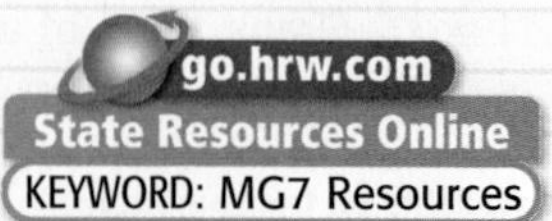

SECTION 2B

Mathematical Proof

Intersection Inspection According to the U.S. Department of Transportation, it is ideal for two intersecting streets to form four 90° angles. If this is not possible, roadways should meet at an angle of 75° or greater for maximum safety and visibility.

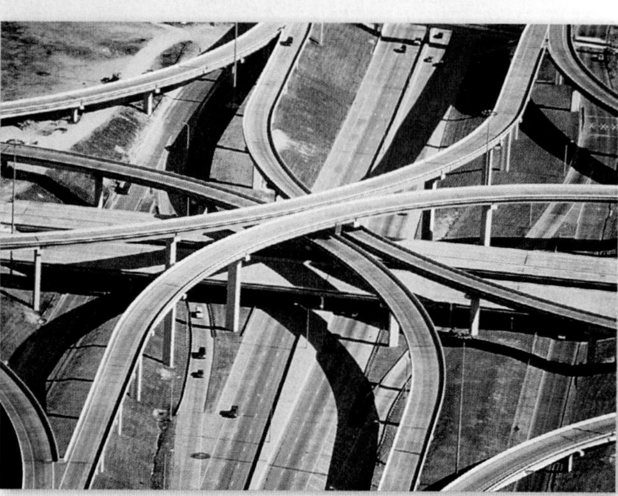

1. Write a compound inequality to represent the range of measures an angle in an intersection should have. $75° \leq x \leq 90°$
2. Suppose that an angle in an intersection meets the guidelines specified by the U.S. Department of Transportation. Find the range of measures for the adjacent angle in the intersection. $90° \leq y \leq 105°$

The intersection of West Elm Street and Lamar Boulevard has a history of car accidents. The Southland neighborhood association is circulating a petition to have the city reconstruct the intersection. A surveyor measured the intersection, and one of the angles measures 145°.

3. Given that $m\angle 2 = 145°$, write a two-column proof to show that $m\angle 1$ and $m\angle 3$ are less than 75°.
4. Write a paragraph proof to justify the argument that the intersection of West Elm Street and Lamar Boulevard should be reconstructed.

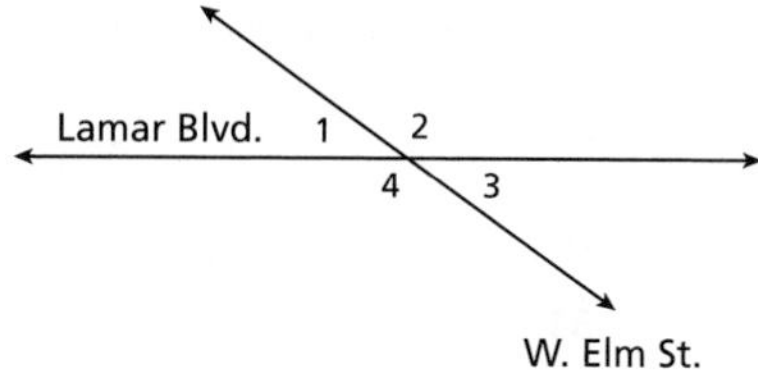

INTERVENTION

Scaffolding Questions

1. Which word or words in the problem indicate an inequality? greater
2. When four angles are formed by intersecting lines, what is the relationship between the measures of an angle and an adjacent angle? They are supp. Which theorem or postulate justifies this? Lin. Pair Thm.
3. What is the relationship between ∠2 and ∠1? They are supp. What is the relationship between ∠1 and ∠3? They are ≅.
4. If $m\angle 1$ and $m\angle 3$ are each less than 75°, why can you conclude that the intersection should be reconstructed? because the DOT guidelines specify that these angles should each measure at least 75°

Extension

At another intersection, two roads form a 106° angle. Should this intersection be reconstructed? Explain. Yes, because the adjacent angle measures 74°, which does not meet the DOT guidelines.

CHAPTER 2

SECTION 2B

Quiz for Lessons 2-5 Through 2-7

2-5 Algebraic Proof

Solve each equation. Write a justification for each step.

1. $m - 8 = 13$
2. $4y - 1 = 27$
3. $-\frac{x}{3} = 2$

1. $m - 8 = 13$ (Given); $m = 21$ (Add. Prop. of $=$)

2. $4y - 1 = 27$ (Given); $4y = 28$ (Add. Prop. of $=$); $y = 7$ (Div. Prop. of $=$)

3. $-\frac{x}{3} = 2$ (Given); $-x = 6$ (Mult. Prop. of $=$); $x = -6$ (Div. Prop. of $=$)

Identify the property that justifies each statement.

4. $m\angle XYZ = m\angle PQR$, so $m\angle PQR = m\angle XYZ$. **Sym. Prop. of $=$**
5. $\overline{AB} \cong \overline{AB}$ **Reflex. Prop. of $\cong$**
6. $\angle 4 \cong \angle A$, and $\angle A \cong \angle 1$. So $\angle 4 \cong \angle 1$. **Trans. Prop. of $\cong$**
7. $k = 7$, and $m = 7$. So $k = m$. **Trans. Prop. of $=$**

2-6 Geometric Proof

8. Fill in the blanks to complete the two-column proof.
   Given: $m\angle 1 + m\angle 3 = 180°$
   Prove: $\angle 1 \cong \angle 4$
   Proof:

Statements	Reasons
1. $m\angle 1 + m\angle 3 = 180°$	1. a. ___?___
2. b. ___?___	2. Def. of supp. ∡
3. $\angle 3$ and $\angle 4$ are supplementary.	3. Lin. Pair Thm.
4. $\angle 3 \cong \angle 3$	4. c. ___?___
5. d. ___?___	5. $\cong$ Supps. Thm.

a. Given
b. $\angle 1$ and $\angle 3$ are supp.
c. Reflex. Prop. of $\cong$
d. $\angle 1 \cong \angle 4$

9. Use the given plan to write a two-column proof of the Symmetric Property of Congruence.
   Given: $\overline{AB} \cong \overline{EF}$
   Prove: $\overline{EF} \cong \overline{AB}$
   Plan: Use the definition of congruent segments to write $\overline{AB} \cong \overline{EF}$ as a statement of equality. Then use the Symmetric Property of Equality to show that $EF = AB$. So $\overline{EF} \cong \overline{AB}$ by the definition of congruent segments.

2-7 Flowchart and Paragraph Proofs

Use the given two-column proof to write the following.
Given: $\angle 1 \cong \angle 3$
Prove: $\angle 2 \cong \angle 4$
Proof:

Statements	Reasons
1. $\angle 1 \cong \angle 3$	1. Given
2. $\angle 1 \cong \angle 2$, $\angle 3 \cong \angle 4$	2. Vert. ∡ Thm.
3. $\angle 2 \cong \angle 3$	3. Trans. Prop. of $\cong$
4. $\angle 2 \cong \angle 4$	4. Trans. Prop. of $\cong$

10. a flowchart proof
11. a paragraph proof

11. It is given that $\angle 1 \cong \angle 3$. By the Vert. ∡ Thm., $\angle 1 \cong \angle 2$ and $\angle 3 \cong \angle 4$. By the Trans. Prop. of $\cong$, $\angle 2 \cong \angle 3$. Thus, $\angle 2 \cong \angle 4$.

READY TO GO ON? SECTION 2B

Organizer

Objective: Assess students' mastery of concepts and skills in Lessons 2-5 through 2-7.

Resources

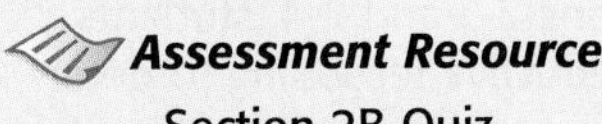

Section 2B Quiz

Teacher One Stop™
Test & Practice Generator

INTERVENTION

Resources

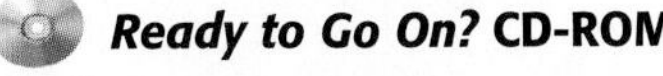

Ready to Go On? **Intervention and Enrichment Worksheets**

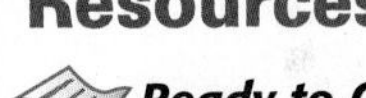

Ready to Go On? **CD-ROM**

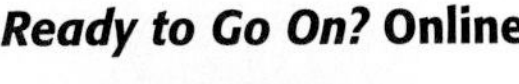

Ready to Go On? **Online**

my.hrw.com

Answers

9–10. See p. A12.

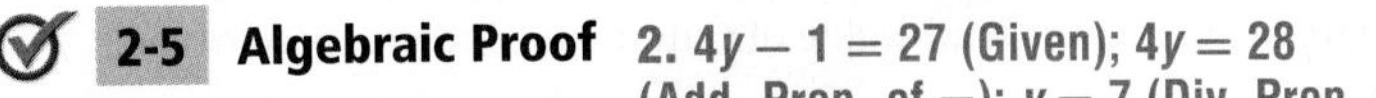

READY TO GO ON? Diagnose and Prescribe

NO INTERVENE

Ready to Go On? Intervention	Worksheets	CD-ROM	Online
	Ready to Go On? Intervention, Section 2B		
Lesson 2-5	2-5 Intervention	Activity 2-5	Diagnose and Prescribe Online
Lesson 2-6	2-6 Intervention	Activity 2-6	
Lesson 2-7	2-7 Intervention	Activity 2-7	

YES ENRICH

Ready to Go On? Enrichment, Section 2B
Worksheets
CD-ROM
Online

CHAPTER 2

Organizer

Pacing: Traditional 1 day

Block $\frac{1}{2}$ day

Objectives: Analyze the truth value of conjunctions and disjunctions.

Construct truth tables to determine the truth value of logical statements.

Using the Extension

In Lessons 2-3 and 2-4, students used deductive reasoning to determine the truth value of written statements. In this extension, students learn to write truth tables to evaluate symbolic statements in an organized way. This is a brief introduction to symbolic logic, which is studied in depth in higher-level mathematics and philosophy courses.

State Resources

EXTENSION

Introduction to Symbolic Logic

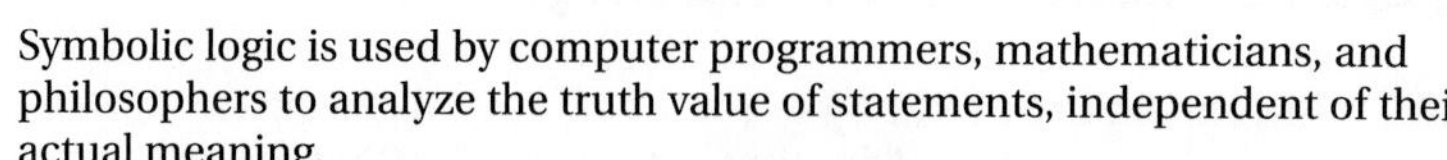

Objectives

Analyze the truth value of conjunctions and disjunctions.

Construct truth tables to determine the truth value of logical statements.

Vocabulary

compound statement

conjunction

disjunction

truth table

Symbolic logic is used by computer programmers, mathematicians, and philosophers to analyze the truth value of statements, independent of their actual meaning.

A **compound statement** is created by combining two or more statements. Suppose p and q each represent a statement. Two compound statements can be formed by combining p and q: a *conjunction* and a *disjunction*.

Know it! Note

Compound Statements

TERM	WORDS	SYMBOLS	EXAMPLE
Conjunction	A compound statement that uses the word *and*	p AND q $p \wedge q$	Pat is a band member AND Pat plays tennis.
Disjunction	A compound statement that uses the word *or*	p OR q $p \vee q$	Pat is a band member OR Pat plays tennis.

A conjunction is true only when all of its parts are true. A disjunction is true if any one of its parts is true.

EXAMPLE 1 Analyzing Truth Values of Conjunctions and Disjunctions

Use p, q, and r to find the truth value of each compound statement.

p: Washington, D.C., is the capital of the United States.

q: The day after Monday is Tuesday.

r: California is the largest state in the United States.

A $q \vee r$

Since q is true, the disjunction is true.

B $r \wedge p$

Since r is false, the conjunction is false.

CHECK IT OUT! **Use the information given above to find the truth value of each compound statement.**

1a. $r \vee p$ T

1b. $p \wedge q$ T

A table that lists all possible combinations of truth values for a statement is called a **truth table**. A truth table shows you the truth value of a compound statement, based on the possible truth values of its parts.

Caution!

Make sure you include all possible combinations of truth values for each piece of the compound statement.

p	q	$p \to q$	$p \wedge q$	$p \vee q$
T	T	T	T	T
T	F	F	F	T
F	T	T	F	T
F	F	T	F	F

1 Introduce

Motivate

In Lesson 2-3, students learned how to determine whether a logical argument is valid based on the Law of Detachment or the Law of Syllogism. By representing statements with symbols, you can evaluate the validity of an argument without being distracted by the words themselves. A truth table provides a systematic way to consider the different combinations of true and false statements that make up a logical argument.

2 Teach

Guided Instruction

Review how symbols were used to represent statements in Lessons 2-2, 2-3, and 2-4. Remind students that a conditional statement is false *only* when the hypothesis is true and the conclusion is false.

Teaching Tip **Visual** Have students write basic truth tables for $p \to q$, $p \vee q$, $p \wedge q$, and $\sim p$ on index cards as a reference for more complicated truth tables.

EXAMPLE 2 Constructing Truth Tables for Compound Statements

Construct a truth table for the compound statement $\sim u \wedge (v \vee w)$.

Since u, v, and w can each be either true or false, the truth table will have $(2)(2)(2) = 8$ rows.

Remember!

The negation (~) of a statement has the opposite truth value.

u	v	w	~u	v ∨ w	~u ∧ (v ∨ w)
T	T	T	F	T	F
T	T	F	F	T	F
T	F	T	F	T	F
T	F	F	F	F	F
F	T	T	T	T	T
F	T	F	T	T	T
F	F	T	T	T	T
F	F	F	T	F	F

CHECK IT OUT! 2. Construct a truth table for the compound statement $\sim u \wedge \sim v$.

u	v	~u	~v	~u ∧ ~v
T	T	F	F	F
T	F	F	T	F
F	T	T	F	F
F	F	T	T	T

EXTENSION Exercises

Use p, q, and r to find the truth value of each compound statement.

p: The day after Friday is Sunday.

q: $\frac{1}{2} = 0.5$

r: If $-4x - 2 = 10$, then $x = 3$.

1. $r \wedge q$ F
2. $r \vee p$ F
3. $p \vee r$ F
4. $q \wedge \sim q$ F
5. $\sim q \vee q$ T
6. $q \vee r$ T

Construct a truth table for each compound statement.

7. $s \wedge \sim t$
8. $\sim u \vee t$
9. $\sim u \vee (s \wedge t)$

Use a truth table to show that the two statements are logically equivalent.

10. $p \rightarrow q$; $\sim q \rightarrow \sim p$
11. $q \rightarrow p$; $\sim p \rightarrow \sim q$
12. A biconditional statement can be written as $(p \rightarrow q) \wedge (q \rightarrow p)$. Construct a truth table for this compound statement.
13. DeMorgan's Laws state that $\sim(p \wedge q) = \sim p \vee \sim q$ and that $\sim(p \vee q) = \sim p \wedge \sim q$.
    a. Use truth tables to show that both statements are true.
    b. If you think of disjunction and conjunction as inverse operations, DeMorgan's Laws are similar to which algebraic property? Distrib. Prop.
14. The Law of Disjunctive Inference states that if $p \vee q$ is true and p is false, then q must be true.
    a. Construct a truth table for $p \vee q$.
    b. Use the truth table to explain why the Law of Disjunctive Inference is true.

COMMON ERROR ALERT

Some students assume that a conjunction is true only if one, but not both, statements are true. Explain the difference between the *inclusive* OR used in mathematics, which means "one or the other or both," and the *exclusive* OR used in English, which means "one or the other, but *not* both."

ENGLISH LANGUAGE LEARNERS

Power Presentations with PowerPoint®

Additional Examples

Example 1

Use p, q, and r to find the truth value of each compound statement.

p: The month after April is May.

q: The next prime number after 13 is 17.

r: Half of 19 is 9.

A. $p \vee q$ T

B. $q \wedge r$ F

Example 2

Construct a truth table for the compound statement $\sim p \vee \sim q$.

p	q	~p	~q	~p ∨ ~q
T	T	F	F	F
T	F	F	T	T
F	T	T	F	T
F	F	T	T	T

Also available on transparency

INTERVENTION 

Questioning Strategies

EXAMPLE 1

- How can you remember which symbol means "and" and which symbol means "or"?

EXAMPLE 2

- When you construct a truth table, how do you decide what to put at the top of each column?
- If you constructed a truth table for a valid form of argument, such as the Law of Detachment or the Law of Syllogism, what would you expect to find in the last column?

3 Close

Summarize

Remind students that the variables in a truth table represent a statement that can be either true or false. Have students complete the truth table below.

p	q	~p	~p ∧ q
T	T	F	F
T	F	F	F
F	T	T	T
F	F	T	F

Answers

7–13a. See p. A12.

14a.

p	q	p ∨ q
T	T	T
T	F	T
F	T	T
F	F	F

b. $p \vee q$ is true in the first, second, and third lines. p is false in the third and fourth lines. So the third line contains the premises of the Law of Disjunctive Inference, and in this case, q is true.

Organizer

Objective: Help students organize and review key concepts and skills presented in Chapter 2.

Online Edition
Multilingual Glossary

Countdown Week 4

Resources

Teacher One Stop™
PuzzleView
Test & Practice Generator

***Multilingual Glossary* Online**
go.hrw.com
KEYWORD: MG7 Glossary

Lesson Tutorial Videos
CD-ROM

Answers

1. theorem
2. deductive reasoning
3. counterexample
4. conjecture
5. The rightmost △ is duplicated, rotated 180°, and shifted to the right. The next 2 items are 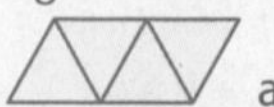 and 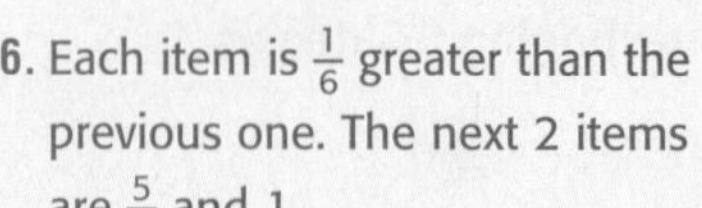.
6. Each item is $\frac{1}{6}$ greater than the previous one. The next 2 items are $\frac{5}{6}$ and 1.
7. The white section is halved. If the white section is a rect. but not a square, it is halved horiz. and the upper portion is colored yellow. If the white section is a square, it is halved vert. and the left portion is colored yellow. The next 2 items are 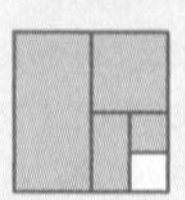 and 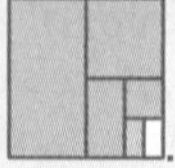.
8. odd
9. positive
10. F; 0
11. T
12. T
13. F; during a leap year, there are 29 days in February.
14. Check students' constructions. Possible answer: The 3 ∠ bisectors of a △ intersect in the int. of the △.

CHAPTER 2 Study Guide: Review

For a complete list of the postulates and theorems in this chapter, see p. PS12.

Vocabulary

- **biconditional statement** 96
- **conclusion** 81
- **conditional statement** 81
- **conjecture** 74
- **contrapositive** 83
- **converse** 83
- **counterexample** 75
- **deductive reasoning** 88
- **definition** 97
- **flowchart proof** 118
- **hypothesis** 81
- **inductive reasoning** 74
- **inverse** 83
- **logically equivalent statements** 83
- **negation** 82
- **paragraph proof** 120
- **polygon** 98
- **proof** 104
- **quadrilateral** 98
- **theorem** 110
- **triangle** 98
- **truth value** 82
- **two-column proof** 111

Complete the sentences below with vocabulary words from the list above.

1. A statement you can prove and then use as a reason in later proofs is a(n) __?__ .
2. __?__ is the process of using logic to draw conclusions from given facts, definitions, and properties.
3. A(n) __?__ is a case in which a conjecture is not true.
4. A statement you believe to be true based on inductive reasoning is called a(n) __?__ .

2-1 Using Inductive Reasoning to Make Conjectures *(pp. 74–79)*

EXAMPLES

■ **Find the next item in the pattern below.**

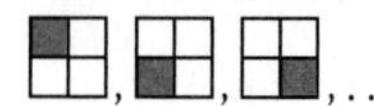

The red square moves in the counterclockwise direction. The next figure is [figure].

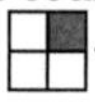

■ **Complete the conjecture "The sum of two odd numbers is __?__ ."**

List some examples and look for a pattern.

$1 + 1 = 2 \quad 3 + 5 = 8 \quad 7 + 11 = 18$

The sum of two odd numbers is even.

■ **Show that the conjecture "For all non-zero integers, $-x < x$" is false by finding a counterexample.**

Pick positive and negative values for x and substitute to see if the conjecture holds.

Let $n = 3$. Since $-3 < 3$, the conjecture holds.

Let $n = -5$. Since $-(-5)$ is 5 and $5 \nless -5$, the conjecture is false.

$n = -5$ is a counterexample.

EXERCISES

Make a conjecture about each pattern. Write the next two items.

5.  [figure: triangles pattern], ...

6. $\frac{1}{6}, \frac{1}{3}, \frac{1}{2}, \frac{2}{3}, \ldots$

7.  [figure: rectangles pattern], ...

Complete each conjecture.

8. The sum of an even number and an odd number is __?__ .
9. The square of a natural number is __?__ .

Determine if each conjecture is true. If not, write or draw a counterexample.

10. All whole numbers are natural numbers.
11. If C is the midpoint of $\overline{AB}$, then $\overline{AC} \cong \overline{BC}$.
12. If $2x + 3 = 15$, then $x = 6$.
13. There are 28 days in February.
14. Draw a triangle. Construct the bisectors of each angle of the triangle. Make a conjecture about where the three angle bisectors intersect.

2-2 Conditional Statements *(pp. 81–87)*

EXAMPLES

- **Write a conditional statement from the sentence "A rectangle has congruent diagonals."**

  If a figure is a rectangle, then it has congruent diagonals.

- **Write the inverse, converse, and contrapositive of the conditional statement "If $m\angle 1 = 35°$, then $\angle 1$ is acute." Find the truth value of each.**

  Converse: If $\angle 1$ is acute, then $m\angle 1 = 35°$. Not all acute angles measure 35°, so this is false.

  Inverse: If $m\angle 1 \neq 35°$, then $\angle 1$ is not acute. You can draw an acute angle that does not measure 35°, so this is false.

  Contrapositive: If $\angle 1$ is not acute, then $m\angle 1 \neq 35°$. An angle that measures 35° must be acute. So this statement is true.

EXERCISES

Write a conditional statement from each Venn diagram.

15. 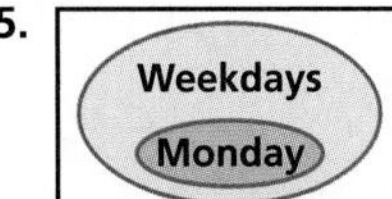

16. 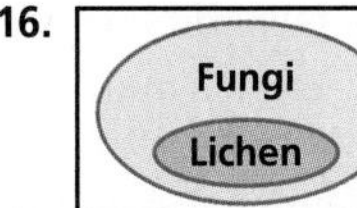

Determine if each conditional is true. If false, give a counterexample.

17. If two angles are adjacent, then they have a common ray.
18. If you multiply two irrational numbers, the product is irrational.

Write the converse, inverse, and contrapositive of each conditional statement. Find the truth value of each.

19. If $\angle X$ is a right angle, then $m\angle X = 90°$.
20. If x is a whole number, then $x = 2$.

2-3 Using Deductive Reasoning to Verify Conjectures *(pp. 88–93)*

EXAMPLES

- **Determine if the conjecture is valid by the Law of Detachment or the Law of Syllogism.**

  Given: If $5c = 8y$, then $2w = -15$. If $5c = 8y$, then $x = 17$.

  Conjecture: If $2w = -15$, then $x = 17$.

  Let p be $5c = 8y$, q be $2w = -15$, and r be $x = 17$.

  Using symbols, the given information is written as $p \rightarrow q$ and $p \rightarrow r$. Neither the Law of Detachment nor the Law of Syllogism can be applied. The conjecture is not valid.

- **Draw a conclusion from the given information.**

  Given: If two points are distinct, then there is one line through them. *A* and *B* are distinct points.

  Let p be the hypothesis: two points are distinct.

  Let q be the conclusion: there is one line through the points.

  The statement "A and B are distinct points" matches the hypothesis, so you can conclude that there is one line through A and B.

EXERCISES

Use the true statements below to determine whether each conclusion is true or false.

Sue is a member of the swim team. When the team practices, Sue swims. The team begins practice when the pool opens. The pool opens at 8 A.M. on weekdays and at 12 noon on Saturday.

21. The swim team practices on weekdays only.
22. Sue swims on Saturdays.
23. Swim team practice starts at the same time every day.

Use the following information for Exercises 24–26.

The expression $2.15 + 0.07x$ gives the cost of a long-distance phone call, where x is the number of minutes after the first minute.

If possible, draw a conclusion from the given information. If not possible, explain why.

24. The cost of Sara's long-distance call is \$2.57.
25. Paulo makes a long-distance call that lasts ten minutes.
26. Asa's long-distance phone bill for the month is \$19.05.

Answers

15. If it is Monday, then it is a weekday.
16. If something is a lichen, then it is a fungus.
17. T
18. F; possible answer: $\sqrt{2}$ and $\sqrt{2}$
19. Conv.: If $m\angle X = 90°$, then $\angle X$ is a rt. $\angle$; T. Inv.: If $\angle X$ is not a rt. $\angle$, then $m\angle X \neq 90°$; T. Contra.: If $m\angle X \neq 90°$, then $\angle X$ is not a rt. $\angle$; T.
20. Conv.: If $x = 2$, then x is a whole number; T. Inv.: If x is not a whole number, then $x \neq 2$; T. Contra.: If $x \neq 2$, then x is not a whole number; F.
21. F
22. T
23. F
24. Sara's call lasted 7 min.
25. The cost of Paulo's long-distance call is \$2.78.
26. No conclusion; the number and length of calls are unknown.

Answers

27. yes
28. no; possible answer: $x = 2$
29. no; possible answer: a seg. with endpoints $(3, 7)$ and $(-5, -1)$
30. yes
31. comp.
32. positive
33. greater than 50 mi/h
34. $4s$
35. $\frac{m}{-5} + 3 = -4.5$ (Given); $\frac{m}{-5} = -7.5$ (Subtr. Prop. of =); $m = 37.5$ (Mult. Prop. of =)
36. $-47 = 3x - 59$ (Given); $12 = 3x$ (Add. Prop. of =); $4 = x$ (Div. Prop. of =)
37. Reflex. Prop. of =
38. Sym. Prop. of $\cong$
39. Trans. Prop. of =
40. figure *ABCD*
41. $m\angle 5 = m\angle 2$
42. $\overline{CD} \cong \overline{EF}$
43. $I = Prt$ (Given); $4200 = P(0.06)(4)$ (Subst.); $4200 = P(0.24)$ (Simplify.); $17{,}500 = P$ (Div. Prop. of =)

2-4 Biconditional Statements and Definitions *(pp. 96–101)*

EXAMPLES

- **For the conditional "If a number is divisible by 10, then it ends in 0", write the converse and a biconditional statement.**

  Converse: If a number ends in 0, then it is divisible by 10.

  Biconditional: A number is divisible by 10 if and only if it ends in 0.

- **Determine if the biconditional "The sides of a triangle measure 3, 7, and 15 if and only if the perimeter is 25" is true. If false, give a counterexample.**

  Conditional: If the sides of a triangle measure 3, 7, and 15, then the perimeter is 25. True.

  Converse: If the perimeter of a triangle is 25, then its sides measure 3, 7, and 15. False; a triangle with side lengths of 6, 10, and 9 also has a perimeter of 25.

  Therefore the biconditional is false.

EXERCISES

Determine if a true biconditional can be written from each conditional statement. If not, give a counterexample.

27. If $3 - \frac{2x}{5} = 2$, then $x = \frac{5}{2}$.
28. If $x < 0$, then the value of x^4 is positive.
29. If a segment has endpoints at $(1, 5)$ and $(-3, 1)$, then its midpoint is $(-1, 3)$.
30. If the measure of one angle of a triangle is 90°, then the triangle is a right triangle.

Complete each statement to form a true biconditional.

31. Two angles are __?__ if and only if the sum of their measures is 90°.
32. $x^3 > 0$ if and only if x is __?__.
33. Trey can travel 100 miles in less than 2 hours if and only if his average speed is __?__.
34. The area of a square is equal to s^2 if and only if the perimeter of the square is __?__.

2-5 Algebraic Proof *(pp. 104–109)*

EXAMPLES

- **Solve the equation $5x - 3 = -18$. Write a justification for each step.**

$5x - 3 = -18$	Given
$+3 \quad +3$	Add. Prop. of =
$5x = -15$	Simplify.
$\frac{5x}{5} = \frac{-15}{5}$	Div. Prop. of =
$x = -3$	Simplify.

- **Write a justification for each step.**

$RS = ST$	Given
$5x - 18 = 4x$	Subst. Prop. of =
$x - 18 = 0$	Subtr. Prop. of =
$x = 18$	Add. Prop. of =

R
5x − 18
S
4x
T

Identify the property that justifies each statement.

- $\angle X \cong \angle 2$, so $\angle 2 \cong \angle X$.

  Symmetric Property of Congruence

- If $m\angle 2 = 180°$ and $m\angle 3 = 180°$, then $m\angle 2 = m\angle 3$.

  Transitive Property of Equality

EXERCISES

Solve each equation. Write a justification for each step.

35. $\frac{m}{-5} + 3 = -4.5$
36. $-47 = 3x - 59$

Identify the property that justifies each statement.

37. $a + b = a + b$
38. If $\angle RST \cong \angle ABC$, then $\angle ABC \cong \angle RST$.
39. $2x = 9$, and $y = 9$. So $2x = y$.

Use the indicated property to complete each statement.

40. Reflex. Prop. of $\cong$: figure $ABCD \cong$ __?__
41. Sym. Prop. of =: If $m\angle 2 = m\angle 5$, then __?__.
42. Trans. Prop. of $\cong$: If $\overline{AB} \cong \overline{CD}$ and $\overline{AB} \cong \overline{EF}$, then __?__.
43. Kim borrowed money at an annual simple interest rate of 6% to buy a car. How much did she borrow if she paid $4200 in interest over the life of the 4-year loan? Solve the equation $I = Prt$ for P and justify each step.

2-6 Geometric Proof *(pp. 110–116)*

EXAMPLES

- **Write a justification for each step, given that $m\angle 2 = 2m\angle 1$.**

1. $\angle 1$ and $\angle 2$ supp.	Lin. Pair Thm.
2. $m\angle 1 + m\angle 2 = 180°$	Def. of supp. ∡
3. $m\angle 2 = 2m\angle 1$	Given
4. $m\angle 1 + 2m\angle 1 = 180°$	Subst. *Steps 2, 3*
5. $3m\angle 1 = 180°$	Simplify
6. $m\angle 1 = 60°$	Div. Prop. of =

- **Use the given plan to write a two-column proof.**

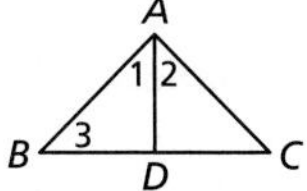

Given: $\overline{AD}$ bisects $\angle BAC$.
$\angle 1 \cong \angle 3$

Prove: $\angle 2 \cong \angle 3$

Plan: Use the definition of angle bisector to show that $\angle 1 \cong \angle 2$. Use the Transitive Property to conclude that $\angle 2 \cong \angle 3$.

Two-column proof:

Statements	Reasons
1. $\overline{AD}$ bisects $\angle BAC$.	1. Given
2. $\angle 1 \cong \angle 2$	2. Def. of ∠ bisector
3. $\angle 1 \cong \angle 3$	3. Given
4. $\angle 2 \cong \angle 3$	4. Trans. Prop. of ≅

EXERCISES

44. Write a justification for each step, given that $\angle 1$ and $\angle 2$ are complementary, and $\angle 1 \cong \angle 3$.

1. $\angle 1$ and $\angle 2$ comp.
2. $m\angle 1 + m\angle 2 = 90°$
3. $\angle 1 \cong \angle 3$
4. $m\angle 1 = m\angle 3$
5. $m\angle 3 + m\angle 2 = 90°$
6. $\angle 3$ and $\angle 2$ comp.

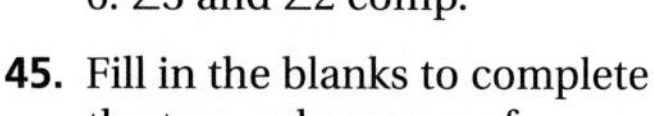

45. Fill in the blanks to complete the two-column proof.

Given: $\overline{TU} \cong \overline{UV}$

Prove: $SU + TU = SV$

Two-column proof:

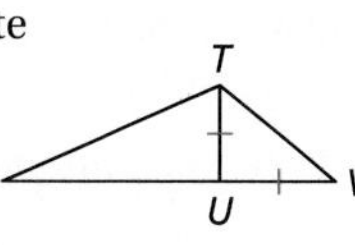

Statements	Reasons
1. $\overline{TU} \cong \overline{UV}$	1. a. ___?___
2. b. ___?___	2. Def. of ≅ segs.
3. c. ___?___	3. Seg. Add. Post.
4. $SU + TU = SV$	4. d. ___?___

Find the value of each variable.

46.

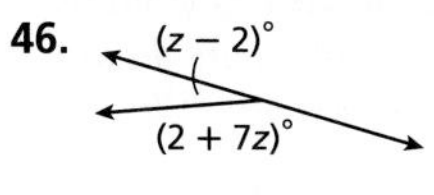

47.

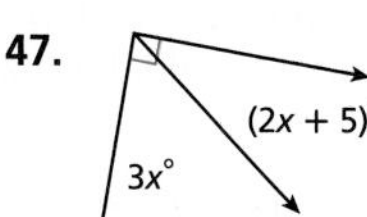

2-7 Flowchart and Paragraph Proofs *(pp. 118–125)*

EXAMPLES

Use the two-column proof in the example for Lesson 2-6 above to write each of the following.

- a flowchart proof

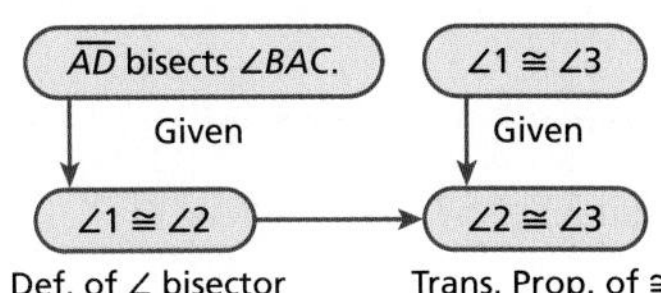

- a paragraph proof

Since $\overline{AD}$ bisects $\angle BAC$, $\angle 1 \cong \angle 2$ by the definition of angle bisector. It is given that $\angle 1 \cong \angle 3$. Therefore, $\angle 2 \cong \angle 3$ by the Transitive Property of Congruence.

EXERCISES

Use the given plan to write each of the following.

Given: $\angle ADE$ and $\angle DAE$ are complementary.
$\angle ADE$ and $\angle BAC$ are complementary.

Prove: $\angle DAC \cong \angle BAE$

Plan: Use the Congruent Complements Theorem to show that $\angle DAE \cong \angle BAC$. Since $\angle CAE \cong \angle CAE$, $\angle DAC \cong \angle BAE$ by the Common Angles Theorem.

48. a flowchart proof **49.** a paragraph proof

Find the value of each variable and name the theorem that justifies your answer.

50.

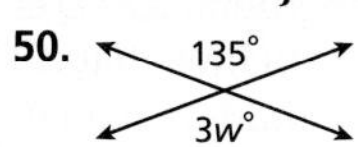

51.

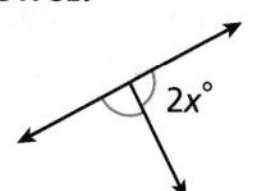

Answers

44. 1. Given
2. Def. of comp. ∡
3. Given
4. Def. of ≅ ∡
5. Subst.
6. Def. of comp. ∡

45a. Given
b. $TU = UV$
c. $SU + UV = SV$
d. Subst.

46. $z = 22.5$

47. $x = 17$

48.

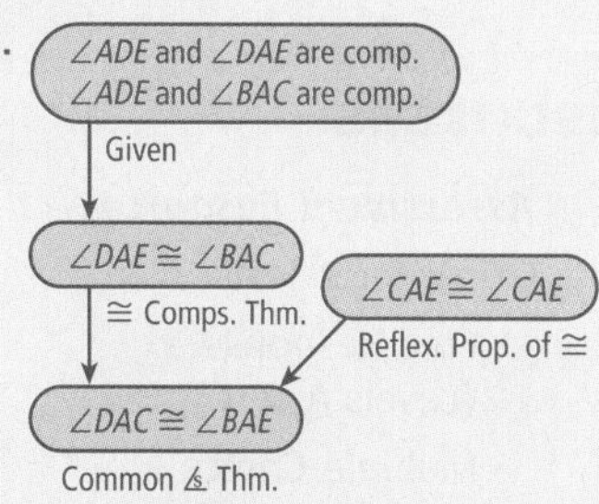

∠ADE and ∠DAE are comp.
∠ADE and ∠BAC are comp.
Given
∠DAE ≅ ∠BAC
≅ Comps. Thm.
∠CAE ≅ ∠CAE
Reflex. Prop. of ≅
∠DAC ≅ ∠BAE
Common ∡ Thm.

49. It is given that $\angle ADE$ and $\angle DAE$ are comp. and $\angle ADE$ and $\angle BAC$ are comp. By the ≅ Comps. Thm., $\angle DAE \cong \angle BAC$. By the Reflex. Prop. of ≅, $\angle CAE \cong \angle CAE$. By the Common ∡ Thm., $\angle DAC \cong \angle BAE$.

50. $w = 45$; Vert. ∡ Thm.

51. $x = 45$; ≅ ∡ supp. → rt. ∡

Organizer

Objective: Assess students' mastery of concepts and skills in Chapter 2.

Online Edition

Resources

Assessment Resources

Chapter 2 Tests

- Free Response (Levels A, B, C)
- Multiple Choice (Levels A, B, C)
- Performance Assessment

Teacher One Stop™

Test & Practice Generator

State Resources

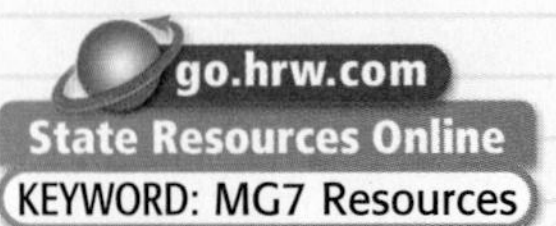

Find the next item in each pattern.

1. ...
2. 405, 135, 45, 15, ... **5**
3. Complete the conjecture "The sum of two even numbers is __?__." **even**
4. Show that the conjecture "All complementary angles are adjacent" is false by finding a counterexample.
5. Identify the hypothesis and conclusion of the conditional statement "The show is cancelled if it rains."
6. Write a conditional statement from the sentence "Parallel lines do not intersect." **If 2 lines are ||, then they do not intersect.**

Determine if each conditional is true. If false, give a counterexample.

7. If two lines intersect, then they form four right angles. **F**
8. If a number is divisible by 10, then it is divisible by 5. **T**

Use the conditional "If you live in the United States, then you live in Kentucky" for Items 9–11. Write the indicated type of statement and determine its truth value.

9. converse
10. inverse
11. contrapositive
12. Determine if the following conjecture is valid by the Law of Detachment.
Given: If it is colder than 50°F, Tom wears a sweater. It is 46°F today.
Conjecture: Tom is wearing a sweater. **valid**
13. Use the Law of Syllogism to draw a conclusion from the given information.
Given: If a figure is a square, then it is a quadrilateral. If a figure is a quadrilateral, then it is a polygon. Figure $ABCD$ is a square. **Figure *ABCD* is a polygon.**
14. Write the conditional statement and converse within the biconditional "Chad will work on Saturday if and only if he gets paid overtime."
15. Determine if the biconditional "B is the midpoint of $\overline{AC}$ iff $AB = BC$" is true. If false, give a counterexample. **F; *B* is not between *A* and *C*.**

Solve each equation. Write a justification for each step.

16. $8 - 5s = 1$
17. $0.4t + 3 = 1.6$
18. $38 = -3w + 2$

Identify the property that justifies each statement.

19. If $2x = y$ and $y = 7$, then $2x = 7$. **Trans. Prop. of =**
20. $m\angle DEF = m\angle DEF$ **Reflex. Prop. of =**
21. $\angle X \cong \angle P$, and $\angle P \cong \angle D$. So $\angle X \cong \angle D$. **Trans. Prop. of ≅**
22. If $\overline{ST} \cong \overline{XY}$, then $\overline{XY} \cong \overline{ST}$. **Sym. Prop. of ≅**

Use the given plan to write a proof in each format.

Given: $\angle AFB \cong \angle EFD$
Prove: $\overrightarrow{FB}$ bisects $\angle AFC$.
Plan: Since vertical angles are congruent, $\angle EFD \cong \angle BFC$. Use the Transitive Property to conclude that $\angle AFB \cong \angle BFC$. Thus $\overrightarrow{FB}$ bisects $\angle AFC$ by the definition of angle bisector.

23. two-column proof
24. paragraph proof
25. flowchart proof

Answers

4. Possible answer: $\angle 1$ and $\angle 2$ are comp., but not adj.

7. Possible answer:

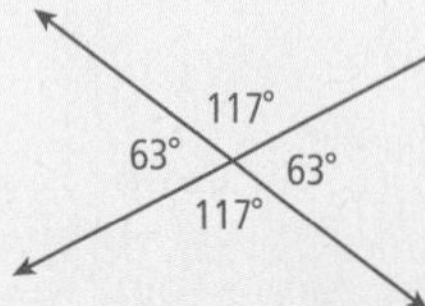

9. If you live in Kentucky, then you live in the United States; T.
10. If you do not live in the United States, then you do not live in Kentucky; T.
11. If you do not live in Kentucky, then you do not live in the United States; F.
14. Conditional: If Chad works on Saturday, then he gets paid overtime. Converse: If Chad gets paid overtime, then he will work on Saturday.
16. $8 - 5s = 1$ (Given); $-5s = -7$ (Subtr. Prop. of =); $s = 1.4$ (Div. Prop. of =)
17. $0.4t + 3 = 1.6$ (Given); $0.4t = -1.4$ (Subtr. Prop. of =); $t = -3.5$ (Div. Prop. of =)
18. $38 = -3w + 2$ (Given); $36 = -3w$ (Subtr. Prop. of =); $-12 = w$ (Div. Prop. of =)

23–25. See p. A13.

COLLEGE ENTRANCE EXAM PRACTICE

FOCUS ON SAT MATHEMATICS SUBJECT TESTS

Some colleges require that you take the SAT Subject Tests. There are two math subject tests—Level 1 and Level 2. Take the Mathematics Subject Test Level 1 when you have completed three years of college-prep mathematics courses.

HOT TIP! On SAT Mathematics Subject Test questions, you receive one point for each correct answer, but you lose a fraction of a point for each incorrect response. Guess only when you can eliminate at least one of the answer choices.

You may want to time yourself as you take this practice test. It should take you about 6 minutes to complete.

1. In the figure below, m∠1 = m∠2. What is the value of *y*?

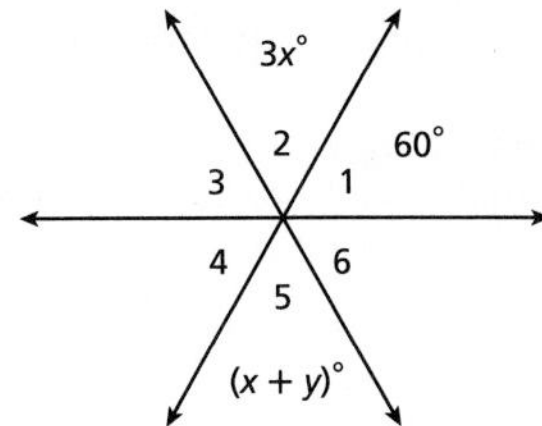

Note: Figure not drawn to scale.

(A) 10
(B) 30
(C) 40
(D) 50
(E) 60

2. The statement "I will cancel my appointment if and only if I have a conflict" is true. Which of the following can be concluded?

I. If I have a conflict, then I will cancel my appointment.

II. If I do not cancel my appointment, then I do not have a conflict.

III. If I cancel my appointment, then I have a conflict.

(A) I only
(B) II only
(C) III only
(D) I and III
(E) I, II, and III

3. What is the contrapositive of the statement "If it is raining, then the football team will win"?

(A) If it is not raining, then the football team will not win.

(B) If it is raining, then the football team will not win.

(C) If the football team wins, then it is raining.

(D) If the football team does not win, then it is not raining.

(E) If it is not raining, then the football team will win.

4. Given the points $D(1, 5)$ and $E(-2, 3)$, which conclusion is NOT valid?

(A) The midpoint of $\overline{DE}$ is $\left(-\frac{1}{2}, 4\right)$.

(B) *D* and *E* are collinear.

(C) The distance between *D* and *E* is $\sqrt{5}$.

(D) $\overline{DE} \cong \overline{ED}$

(E) *D* and *E* are distinct points.

5. For all integers *x*, what conclusion can be drawn about the value of the expression $\frac{x^2}{2}$?

(A) The value is negative.

(B) The value is not negative.

(C) The value is even.

(D) The value is odd.

(E) The value is not a whole number.

Organizer

Objective: Provide practice for college entrance exams such as the SAT Mathematics Subject Test Level 1.

Online Edition

Resources

College Entrance Exam Practice

Questions on the SAT Mathematics Subject Test Level 1 represent the following math content areas:

Number and Operations, 10-14%

Algebra and Functions, 38-42%

Geometry and Measurment, 38-42%

- **Plane Euclidean,** 18-22%
- **Coordinate,** 8-12%
- **Three-dimensional,** 4-6%
- **Trigonometry,** 6-8%

Data Analysis, Statistics, and Probability, 6-10%

Items on this page focus on:

- Algebra
- Plane Euclidean Geometry
- Coordinate Geometry
- Miscellaneous

Text References:

Item	1	2	3	4	5
Lesson	2-7	2-4	2-2	2-5	2-1

TEST PREP DOCTOR

1. Students may not know how to approach this problem. Suggest that they use the fact that m∠1 = m∠2 to solve for *x*, and then use the Vertical Angles Theorem to solve for *y*.

2. Students may choose **D** if they do not recognize that II is the contrapositive of the conditional within the given biconditional. Remind students that a conditional and its contrapositive are logically equivalent, and that a biconditional is true only when the conditional and its converse are true.

3. Students who chose **A** chose the inverse of the statement, and students who chose **C** chose the converse of the statement. Remind students that the contrapositive of a statement is found by exchanging and negating the hypothesis and conclusion.

4. Students who chose **B** may not remember that any two points are collinear. Students who chose **E** may not know what the term *distinct* means. Encourage students to check each answer choice before choosing their final answer.

5. Remind students to substitute multiple values for the variable before making a conjecture. Students who chose **C**, **D**, or **E** may have selected only one value for *x*. Remind students that the square of any number is not negative, so the correct answer is **B**.

Organizer

Objective: Provide opportunities to learn and practice common test-taking strategies.

This Test Tackler focuses on how to correctly fill in a grid when answering gridded-response items. Often students solve the test item correctly, but get the problem wrong because they fill in the answer improperly. This strategy reviews the rules for filling in an answer and helps students identify common mistakes in gridded answers.

Remind students that it is okay for the first answer box at the top of the grid to be blank, as long as there are no blanks between numbers. Compare the gridded answers in the examples to demonstrate.

Standardized Test Strategies

Gridded Response: Record Your Answer

When responding to a gridded-response test item, you must fill out the grid on your answer sheet correctly, or the item will be marked as incorrect.

EXAMPLE 1

Gridded Response: Solve the equation $25 - 2(3x - 4) = 13$.

1	0	/	3	

The value of x is $\frac{20}{6}$, $\frac{10}{3}$, $3\frac{1}{3}$, or $3.\overline{3}$.

- Mixed numbers and repeating decimals cannot be gridded, so you must grid the answer as $\frac{20}{6}$ or $\frac{10}{3}$.
- Using a pencil, write your answer in the answer boxes at the top of the grid.
- Put only one digit or symbol in each box. On some grids, the fraction bar and decimal point have a designated column.
- Do not leave a blank box in the middle of an answer.
- For each digit or symbol, shade the bubble that is in the same column as the digit or symbol in the answer box.

EXAMPLE 2

Gridded Response: The perimeter of a rectangle is 90 in. The width of the rectangle is 18 in. Find the length of the rectangle in feet.

	2	.	2	5

The length of the rectangle is 27 inches, but the problem asks for the measurement in feet.

27 inches = 2.25 or $\frac{9}{4}$ feet

- Using a pencil, write your answer in the answer boxes at the top of the grid.
- Put only one digit or symbol in each box. On some grids, the fraction bar and the decimal point have a designated column.
- Do not leave a blank box in the middle of an answer.
- For each digit or symbol, shade the bubble that is in the same column as the digit or symbol in the answer box.

You cannot grid a negative number in a gridded-response item because the grid does not include the negative sign (−). So if you get a negative answer to a test item, rework the problem. You probably made a math error.

Read each statement and answer the questions that follow.

Sample A

The correct answer to a test item is $\frac{1}{6}$. A student gridded this answer as shown.

1. What error did the student make when filling out the grid?
2. Another student got an answer of $-\frac{1}{6}$. Explain why the student knew this answer was wrong.

Sample B

The perimeter of a triangle is $2\frac{3}{4}$ feet. A student gridded this answer as shown.

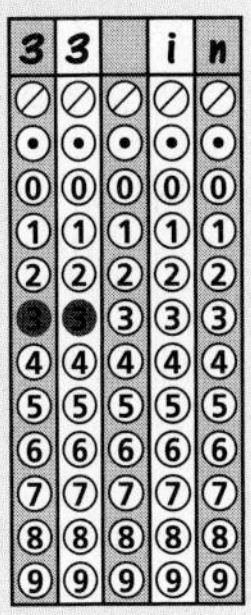

3. What error did the student make when filling out the grid?
4. Explain two ways to correctly grid the answer.

Sample C

The length of a segment is $7\frac{2}{5}$ units. A student gridded this answer as shown.

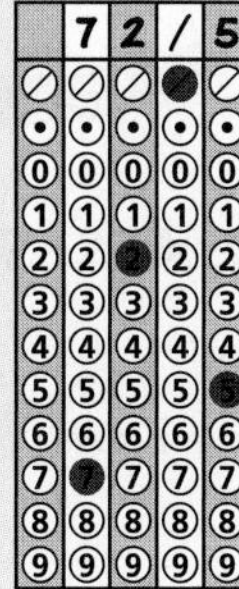

5. What answer does the grid show?
6. Explain why you cannot grid a mixed number.
7. Write the answer $7\frac{2}{5}$ in two forms that could be entered in the grid correctly.

Sample D

The measure of an angle is 48.9°. A student gridded this answer as shown.

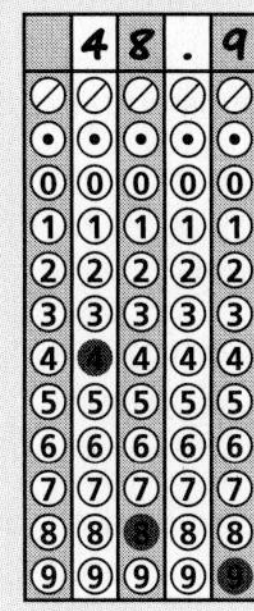

8. What error did the student make when filling out the grid?
9. Explain how to correctly grid the answer.
10. Another student plans to grid this answer as an improper fraction. Can this fraction be gridded? Explain.

Answers

Possible answers:

1. The student left a space between / and 6.
2. You cannot grid a negative number, so the correct answer cannot possibly be negative.
3. You cannot grid units of measurement, so you must grid the answer in the units asked for in the problem.
4. You can grid the answer as an improper fraction, $\frac{11}{4}$, or as a decimal, 2.75.
5. The grid shows $\frac{72}{5}$, which is 14.4.
6. Since spaces cannot be included in the grid, a mixed number would appear to be an improper fraction.
7. You can grid the answer as an improper fraction, $\frac{37}{5}$, or as a decimal, 7.4.
8. The student forgot to fill in the bubble for the decimal.
9. Fill in the bubble for the decimal in the fourth column of the grid.
10. No; there are not enough columns in the grid to fit the equivalent improper fraction, which is $\frac{489}{10}$.

State Resources

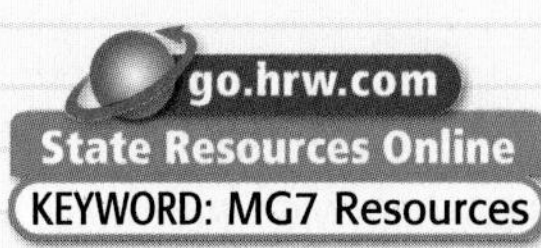

Organizer

Objective: Provide review and practice for Chapters 1–2 and standardized tests.

 Online Edition

Resources

Chapter 2 Cumulative Test

go.hrw.com
KEYWORD: MG7 Resources

State Resources

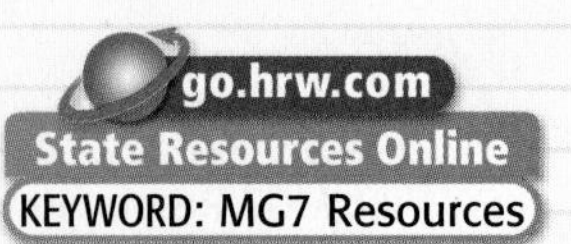

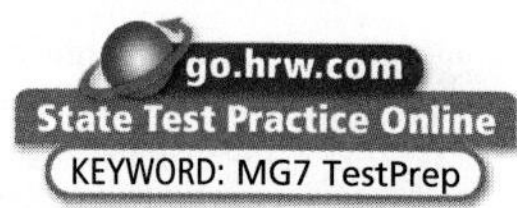

CUMULATIVE ASSESSMENT, CHAPTERS 1–2

Multiple Choice

Use the figure below for Items 1 and 2. In the figure, $\overrightarrow{DB}$ bisects ∠ADC.

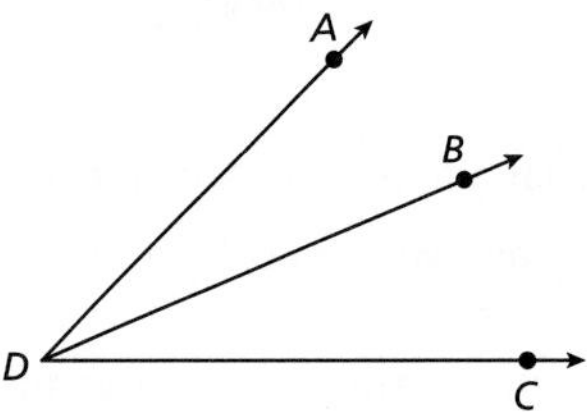

1. Which best describes the intersection of ∠*ADB* and ∠*BDC*?
   - (A) Exactly one ray
   - (B) Exactly one point
   - (C) Exactly one angle
   - (D) Exactly one segment

2. Which expression is equal to the measure of ∠*ADC*?
   - (F) 2(m∠*ADB*)
   - (G) 90° − m∠*BDC*
   - (H) 180° − 2(m∠*ADC*)
   - (J) m∠*BDC* − m∠*ADB*

3. What is the inverse of the statement, "If a polygon has 8 sides, then it is an octagon"?
   - (A) If a polygon is an octagon, then it has 8 sides.
   - (B) If a polygon is not an octagon, then it does not have 8 sides.
   - (C) If an octagon has 8 sides, then it is a polygon.
   - (D) If a polygon does not have 8 sides, then it is not an octagon.

4. Lily conjectures that if a number is divisible by 15, then it is also divisible by 9. Which of the following is a counterexample?
   - (F) 45
   - (G) 50
   - (H) 60
   - (J) 72

5. A diagonal of a polygon connects nonconsecutive vertices. The table shows the number of diagonals in a polygon with *n* sides.

Number of Sides	Number of Diagonals
4	2
5	5
6	9
7	14

If the pattern continues, how many diagonals does a polygon with 8 sides have?
   - (A) 17
   - (B) 19
   - (C) 20
   - (D) 21

6. Which type of transformation maps figure *LMNP* onto figure *L′M′N′P′*?

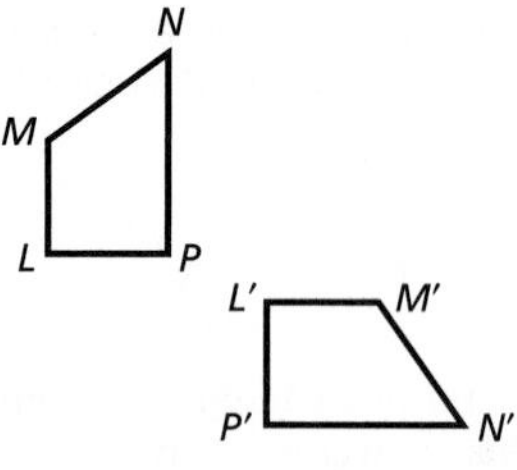

   - (F) Reflection
   - (G) Rotation
   - (H) Translation
   - (J) None of these

7. Miyoko went jogging on July 25, July 28, July 31, and August 3. If this pattern continues, when will Miyoko go jogging next?
   - (A) August 5
   - (B) August 6
   - (C) August 7
   - (D) August 8

8. Congruent segments have equal measures. A segment bisector divides a segment into two congruent segments. $\overleftrightarrow{XY}$ intersects $\overline{DE}$ at *X* and bisects $\overline{DE}$. Which conjecture is valid?
   - (F) m∠*YXD* = m∠*YXE*
   - (G) *Y* is between *D* and *E*.
   - (H) *DX* = *XE*
   - (J) *DE* = *YE*

Answers

1. A
2. F
3. D
4. H
5. C
6. G
7. B
8. H
9. C
10. J
11. B
12. H
13. 10
14. 105
15. 0.16
16. 2(*AB*) + 16 = 24 (Given); 2(*AB*) = 8 (Subtr. Prop. of =); *AB* = 4 (Div. Prop. of =)

9. Which statement is true by the Symmetric Property of Congruence?

Ⓐ $\overline{ST} \cong \overline{ST}$

Ⓑ $15 + MN = MN + 15$

Ⓒ If $\angle P \cong \angle Q$, then $\angle Q \cong \angle P$.

Ⓓ If $\angle D \cong \angle E$ and $\angle E \cong \angle F$, then $\angle D \cong \angle F$.

To find a counterexample for a biconditional statement, write the conditional statement and converse it contains. Then try to find a counterexample for one of these statements.

10. Which is a counterexample for the following biconditional statement?

A pair of angles is supplementary if and only if the angles form a linear pair.

Ⓕ The measures of supplementary angles add to 180°.

Ⓖ A linear pair of angles is supplementary.

Ⓗ Complementary angles do not form a linear pair.

Ⓙ Two supplementary angles are not adjacent.

11. K is between J and L. The distance between J and K is 3.5 times the distance between K and L. If $JK = 14$, what is JL?

Ⓐ 10.5 Ⓒ 24.5

Ⓑ 18 Ⓓ 49

12. What is the length of the segment connecting the points $(-7, -5)$ and $(5, -2)$?

Ⓕ $\sqrt{13}$ Ⓗ $3\sqrt{17}$

Ⓖ $\sqrt{53}$ Ⓙ $\sqrt{193}$

Gridded Response

13. A segment has an endpoint at $(5, -2)$. The midpoint of the segment is $(2, 2)$. What is the length of the segment?

14. $\angle P$ measures 30° more than the measure of its supplement. What is the measure of $\angle P$ in degrees?

15. The perimeter of a square field is 1.6 kilometers. What is the area of the field in square kilometers?

Short Response

16. Solve the equation $2(AB) + 16 = 24$ to find the length of segment AB. Write a justification for each step.

17. Use the given two-column proof to write a flowchart proof.

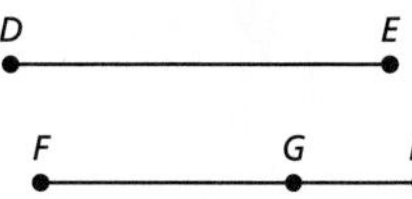

Given: $\overline{DE} \cong \overline{FH}$
Prove: $DE = FG + GH$

Two-column proof:

Statements	Reasons
1. $\overline{DE} \cong \overline{FH}$	**1.** Given
2. $DE = FH$	**2.** Def. of ≅ segs.
3. $FG + GH = FH$	**3.** Seg. Add. Post.
4. $DE = FG + GH$	**4.** Subst.

18. Consider the following conditional statement.

If two angles are complementary, then the angles are acute.

a. Determine if the conditional is true or false. If false, give a counterexample.

b. Write the converse of the conditional statement.

c. Determine whether the converse is true or false. If false, give a counterexample.

Extended Response

19. The figure below shows the intersection of two lines.

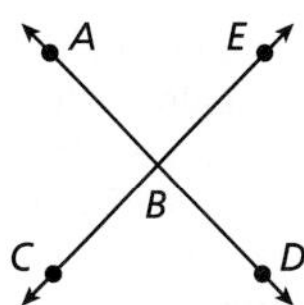

a. Name the linear pairs of angles in the figure. What conclusion can you make about each pair? Explain your reasoning.

b. Name the pairs of vertical angles in the figure. What conclusion can you make about each pair? Explain your reasoning.

c. Suppose $m\angle EBD = 90°$. What are the measures of the other angles in the figure? Write a two-column proof to support your answer.

Short-Response Rubric

Items 16–18

2 Points = The student's answer is an accurate and complete execution of the task or tasks.

1 Point = The student's answer contains attributes of an appropriate response but is flawed.

0 Points = The student's answer contains no attributes of an appropriate response.

Extended-Response Rubric

Item 19

4 Points = The student correctly identifies the linear pairs of angles and the pairs of vertical angles, describing the correct relationship between each type of pair. All steps of the proof in part **c** are shown.

3 Points = The student correctly identifies some of the angle pairs in parts **a** and **b** but does not justify their relationships. The proof in part **c** is correct but contains minor flaws.

2 Points = The student answers parts **a** and **b** correctly but without justification. The student answers part **c** but does not write a proof to justify the conclusion.

1 Point = The student attempts to answer all parts of the problem, but does not do so correctly. The student attempts to justify the answers.

0 Points = The student does not answer correctly and does not attempt all parts of the problem.

17. $\overline{DE} \cong \overline{FH}$ (Given) → $DE = FH$ (Def. of ≅ segs.); $FG + GH = FH$ (Seg. Add. Post.); $DE = FH$ and $FG + GH = FH$ → $DE = FG + GH$ (Subst.)

18a. True

18b. If 2 ∡ are acute, then they are comp.

18c. F; possible answer: if $m\angle 1 = 60°$ and $m\angle 2 = 80°$, then the ∡ are acute, but they are not comp.

19a. $\angle ABC$ and $\angle CBD$, $\angle CBD$ and $\angle DBE$, $\angle DBE$ and $\angle EBA$, and $\angle EBA$ and $\angle ABC$; each pair of ∡ is supp. by the Lin. Pair Thm.

b. $\angle ABC$ and $\angle DBE$, $\angle EBA$ and $\angle CBD$; each pair of vert. ∡ is ≅ by the Vert. ∡ Thm.

19c. If $m\angle EBD = 90°$, then $m\angle EBA = m\angle ABC = m\angle CBD = 90°$.
Two-column proof:

1. $m\angle EBD = 90°$ (Given)
2. $m\angle EBD$ and $\angle CBD$ are supp. (Lin. Pair Thm.)
3. $m\angle EBD + m\angle CBD = 180°$ (Def. of supp. ∡)
4. $90° + m\angle CBD = 180°$ (Subst.)
5. $m\angle CBD = 90°$ (Subtr. Prop. of =)
6. $\angle CBD \cong \angle EBA$, $\angle EBD \cong \angle ABC$ (Vert. ∡ Thm.)
7. $m\angle CBD = m\angle EBA$, $m\angle EBD = m\angle ABC$ (Def. of ≅ ∡)
8. $m\angle EBA = 90°$, $m\angle ABC = 90°$ (Trans. Prop. of =)

Real-World CONNECTIONS

Organizer

Objective: Choose appropriate problem-solving strategies and use them with skills from Chapters 1 and 2 to solve real-world problems.

The Myrtle Beach Marathon

Reading Strategies

Encourage students to write down the important information as they read **Problem 1.** Then have students explain what they must do in order to solve the problem. Also ask them what units they will use in their answers. Find a speed in mi/h and a time in hours.

Using Data Ask students to explain in their own words the connection between distance, rate, and time. Distance equals rate multiplied by time. Also ask students what is meant by average speed. The average speed is the total distance for a trip divided by the total time for the trip.

State Resources

The Myrtle Beach Marathon

Every year in early February, runners take to the streets of Myrtle Beach to participate in a 26-mile marathon. It's an ideal time and place for long-distance running, with temperatures that average 60°F and a flat course that features breathtaking ocean views.

Choose one or more strategies to solve each problem.

1. During the marathon, a runner maintains a steady pace and completes the first 2.6 miles in 20 minutes. After 1 hour 20 minutes, she has completed 10.4 miles. Make a conjecture about the runner's average speed in miles per hour. How long do you expect it to take her to complete the marathon? **7.8 mi/h; $3\frac{1}{3}$ h**
2. Along the course, medical stations are available every 2 miles. Portable toilets are available every 3 miles and at the end of the course. At how many points are there both a medical station and portable toilets? **5**

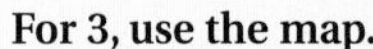

For 3, use the map.

3. The course includes a straight section along Ocean Blvd. Along this section, runners pass a viewing stand and the race headquarters. The distance from the beginning of the straight section at 29th Ave. N. to the headquarters is 3.25 times the distance from 29th Ave. N. to the viewing stand. What is the distance from the viewing stand to the headquarters? **1.8 mi**

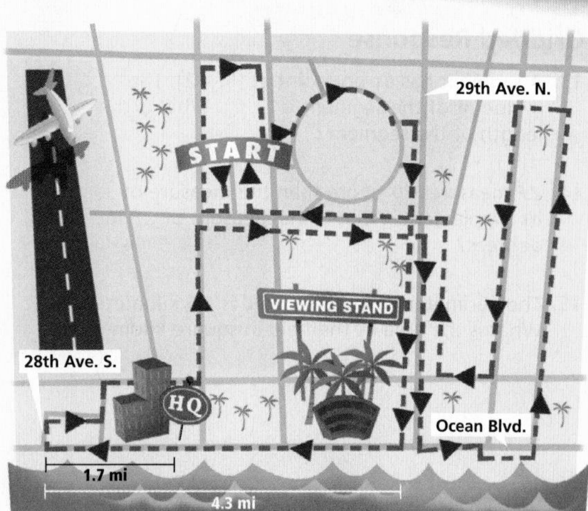

Problem-Solving Focus

For **Problem 2,** focus on the second step of the problem-solving process:
(2) Make a Plan. Ask students what strategy or strategies they can use to solve the problem. Possible answer: Use the strategies Make an Organized List and Find a Pattern. The medical stations and portable toilets both occur at multiples of 6 miles and at the end of the course, for a total of 5 locations.

 South Carolina's Waterfalls

The northwest corner of South Carolina is crisscrossed by hiking trails that lead to dozens of waterfalls, ranging from shallow cascades to the spectacular, 420-foot Raven Cliff Falls.

1. Mill Creek Falls or Yellow Branch Falls

Choose one or more strategies to solve each problem.

1. A hiker made a round-trip hike of at least 3 miles and saw a waterfall that is less than 100 feet tall. Which waterfalls might the hiker have visited?

2. A travel brochure includes the following statements about South Carolina's waterfalls. Determine if each statement is true or false. If false, explain why.
   a. If your round-trip hike is greater than 4 miles, you will be rewarded with an incredible view of a waterfall that is more than 400 feet tall.
   b. If you haven't been to Lower Whitewater Falls, then you haven't seen a waterfall at least 200 feet tall.
   c. If you don't want to hike 3 or more miles but want to see a 70-foot waterfall, then you should visit King Creek Falls. T

3. Lower Brasstown Falls is a 120-foot waterfall consisting of three separate falls. The upper falls are 15 feet taller than the middle falls. The middle falls and lower falls are the same height. What is the height of each falls?
   35 ft, 35 ft, 50 ft

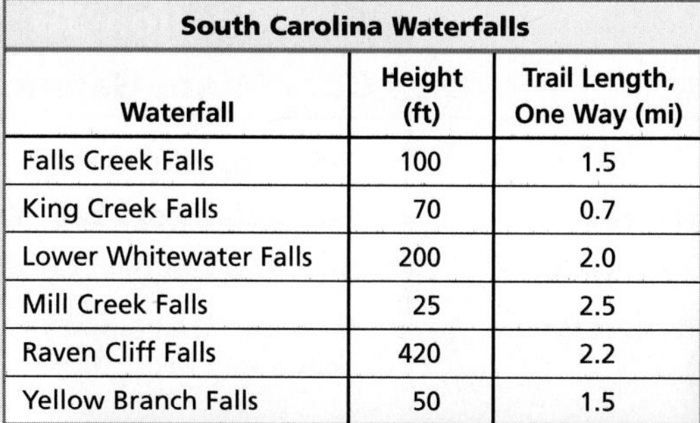

South Carolina Waterfalls

Waterfall	Height (ft)	Trail Length, One Way (mi)
Falls Creek Falls	100	1.5
King Creek Falls	70	0.7
Lower Whitewater Falls	200	2.0
Mill Creek Falls	25	2.5
Raven Cliff Falls	420	2.2
Yellow Branch Falls	50	1.5

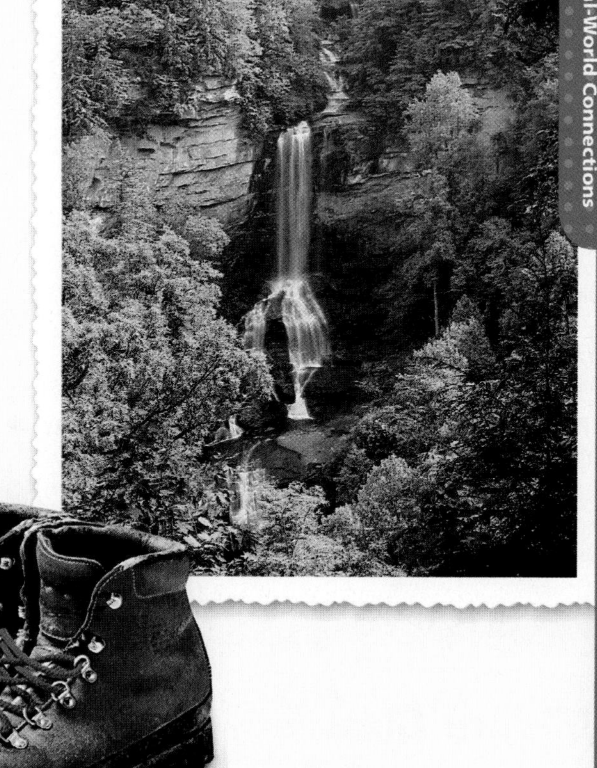

Answers

2a. F; a round-trip hike to Mill Creek Falls is greater than 4 mi, but the falls are less than 400 ft tall.

b. F; if you hike to Raven Cliff, then you have seen a waterfall that is at least 200 ft tall.

South Carolina's Waterfalls

Reading Strategies

ENGLISH LANGUAGE LEARNERS

Make sure that students understand what is meant by a one-way hike and a round-trip hike. If students are unfamiliar with the terms *one-way* and *round-trip,* draw and label a simple sketch that illustrates these terms.

Using Data Have students review the data in the table before they begin solving the problems. Ask if there is any connection between the height of a waterfall and the length of the trail to the waterfall. No. Also ask how students can find the round-trip hiking distances from the given information. Double the distances in the table. Students may wish to copy the table and add a fourth column showing the round-trip distances.

Problem-Solving Focus

Ask students to explain what strategy they would use to solve **Problem 1.** Possible answer: Use a Venn diagram. One region contains names of waterfalls with round-trip hikes of at least 3 mi, and the other region contains names of waterfalls less than 100 ft tall. The intersection of the regions is the solution.

Discuss additional reasoning questions similar to the ones posed in **Problems 1** and **2.** For example, encourage students to use the data in the table to develop their own true or false conditional statements. Then have students share the statements with classmates, challenging them to determine the truth value of each.

Parallel and Perpendicular Lines

Section 3A

Lines with Transversals

- **3-1 Lines and Angles**
- **Connecting Geometry to Algebra** Systems of Equations
- **3-2 Technology Lab** Explore Parallel Lines and Transversals
- **3-2 Angles Formed by Parallel Lines and Transversals**
- **3-3 Proving Lines Parallel**
- **3-3 Geometry Lab** Construct Parallel Lines
- **3-4 Perpendicular Lines**
- **3-4 Geometry Lab** Construct Perpendicular Lines

Section 3B

Coordinate Geometry

- **3-5 Slopes of Lines**
- **3-6 Technology Lab** Explore Parallel and Perpendicular Lines
- **3-6 Lines in the Coordinate Plane**
- **Connecting Geometry to Data Analysis** Scatter Plots and Lines of Best Fit

Pacing Guide for 45-Minute Classes

Teacher One Stop™
Calendar Planner®

Chapter 3

Countdown Weeks 5, 6

DAY 1	DAY 2	DAY 3	DAY 4	DAY 5
3-1 Lesson	Connecting Geometry to Algebra 3-2 Technology Lab	3-2 Lesson	3-3 Lesson	3-3 Geometry Lab 3-4 Lesson
DAY 6	**DAY 7**	**DAY 8**	**DAY 9**	**DAY 10**
3-4 Lesson 3-4 Geometry Lab	Multi-Step Test Prep Ready to Go On?	3-5 Lesson	3-6 Technology Lab 3-6 Lesson	3-6 Lesson Connecting Geometry to Data Analysis
DAY 11	**DAY 12**	**DAY 13**		
Multi-Step Test Prep Ready to Go On?	Chapter 3 Review	Chapter 3 Test		

Pacing Guide for 90-Minute Classes

Teacher One Stop™
Calendar Planner®

Chapter 3

DAY 1	DAY 2	DAY 3	DAY 4	DAY 5
3-1 Lesson Connecting Geometry to Algebra 3-2 Technology Lab	3-2 Lesson 3-3 Lesson	3-3 Geometry Lab 3-4 Lesson 3-4 Geometry Lab	Multi-Step Test Prep Ready to Go On? 3-5 Lesson	3-6 Technology Lab 3-6 Lesson Connecting Geometry to Data Analysis
DAY 6	**DAY 7**			
Multi-Step Test Prep Ready to Go On? Chapter 3 Review	Chapter 3 Test 4-1 Lesson 4-2 Geometry Lab			

ONGOING ASSESSMENT and INTERVENTION

	DIAGNOSE	PRESCRIBE
Assess Prior Knowledge	**Before Chapter 3**	
	Diagnose readiness for the chapter.	Prescribe intervention.
	Are You Ready? SE p. 143	***Are You Ready? Intervention***
Formative Assessment	**Before Every Lesson**	
	Diagnose readiness for the lesson.	Prescribe intervention.
	Warm Up TE	**Reteach** CRB
	During Every Lesson	
	Diagnose understanding of lesson concepts.	Prescribe intervention.
	Check It Out! SE	**Reading Strategies** CRB
	Questioning Strategies TE	***Success for Every Learner***
	Think and Discuss SE	***Lesson Tutorial Videos***
	Write About It SE	
	Journal TE	
	After Every Lesson	
	Diagnose mastery of lesson concepts.	Prescribe intervention.
	Lesson Quiz TE	**Reteach** CRB
	Test Prep SE	**Test Prep Doctor** TE
	Test and Practice Generator	***Homework Help*** **Online**
	Before Chapter 3 Testing	
	Diagnose mastery of concepts in chapter.	Prescribe intervention.
	Ready to Go On? SE pp. 181, 201	***Ready to Go On? Intervention***
	Multi-Step Test Prep SE pp. 180, 200	**Scaffolding Questions** TE pp. 180, 200
	Section Quizzes AR	**Reteach** CRB
	Test and Practice Generator	***Lesson Tutorial Videos***
	Before High Stakes Testing	
	Diagnose mastery of benchmark concepts.	Prescribe intervention.
	College Entrance Exam Practice SE p. 207	***College Entrance Exam Practice***
	Standardized Test Prep SE pp. 210–211	
Summative Assessment	**After Chapter 3**	
	Check mastery of chapter concepts.	Prescribe intervention.
	Multiple-Choice Tests (Forms A, B, C)	**Reteach** CRB
	Free-Response Tests (Forms A, B, C)	***Lesson Tutorial Videos***
	Performance Assessment AR	
	Cumulative Test AR	
	Test and Practice Generator	

KEY: **SE** = *Student Edition* **TE** = *Teacher's Edition* **CRB** = *Chapter Resource Book* **AR** = *Assessment Resources* 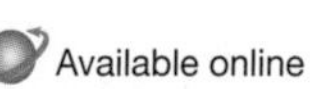 Available online Available on CD- or DVD-ROM

CHAPTER 3

Lesson Resources

Before the Lesson

Prepare ***Teacher One Stop*** 
- Editable lesson plans 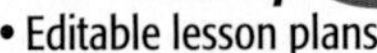
- Calendar Planner
- Easy access to all chapter resources

Lesson Transparencies
- Teacher Tools

Teach the Lesson

Introduce ***Alternate Openers: Explorations***

Lesson Transparencies
- Warm Up
- Problem of the Day

Teach ***Lesson Transparencies***
- Teaching Transparencies

Know-It Notebook™
- Vocabulary
- Key Concepts

Power Presentations

Lesson Tutorial Videos 

Interactive Online Edition 
- Lesson Activities 
- Lesson Tutorial Videos 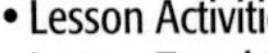

Lab Activities 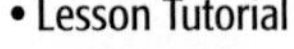

Lab Resources Online 

Online Interactivities  

TechKeys 

Practice the Lesson

Practice ***Chapter Resources***
- Practice A, B, C

Practice and Problem Solving Workbook

IDEA Works!® Modified Worksheets and Tests

ExamView Test and Practice Generator

Homework Help Online

Online Interactivities

Interactive Online Edition
- Homework Help

Apply ***Chapter Resources***
- Problem Solving

Practice and Problem Solving Workbook

Interactive Online Edition
- Chapter Project

Project Teacher Support

After the Lesson

Reteach ***Chapter Resources***
- Reteach
- Reading Strategies ELL

Success for Every Learner 

Review ***Interactive Answers and Solutions***

Solutions Key

Know-It Notebook™
- Big Ideas
- Chapter Review

Extend ***Chapter Resources***
- Challenge

Technology Highlights for the Teacher

 **Power Presentations**

Dynamic presentations to engage students. Complete PowerPoint® presentations for every lesson in Chapter 3.

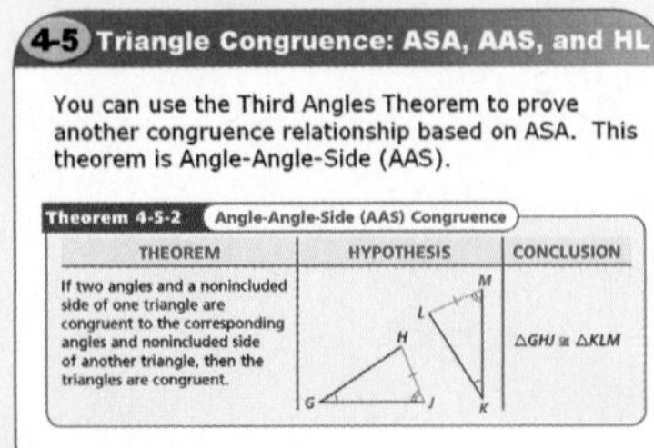

 **Teacher One Stop** SPANISH

Easy access to Chapter 3 resources and assessments. Includes lesson planning, test generation, and puzzle creation software.

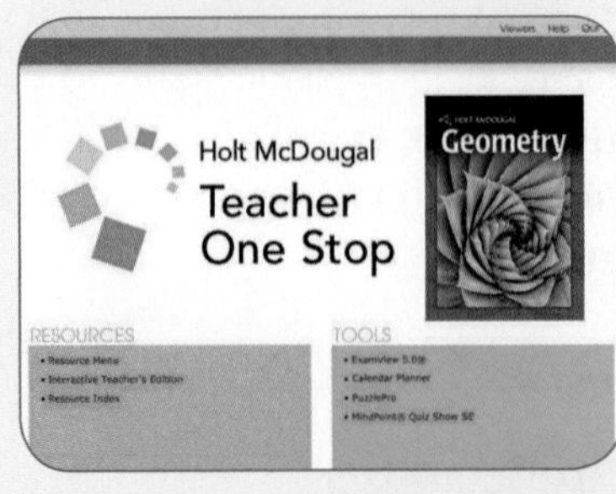

 **Premier Online Edition** SPANISH

Chapter 3 includes Tutorial Videos, Lesson Activities, Lesson Quizzes, Homework Help, and Chapter Project.

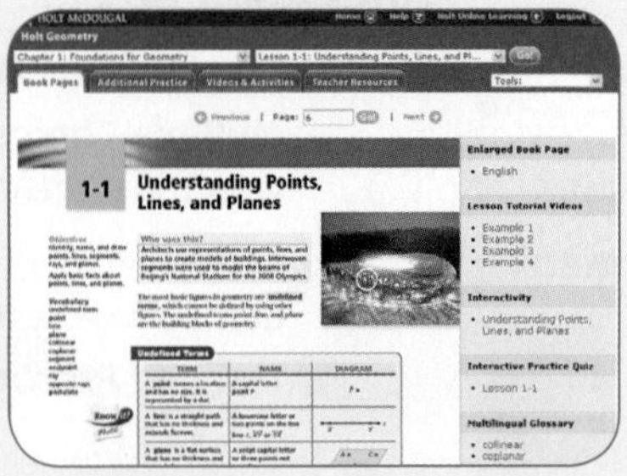

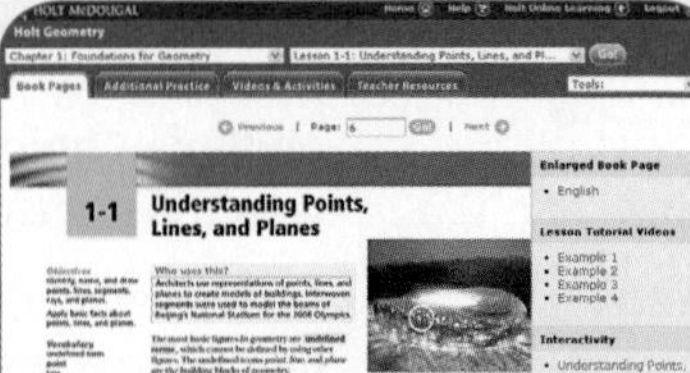

KEY: **SE** = *Student Edition* **TE** = *Teacher's Edition*  English Language Learners  Spanish version available 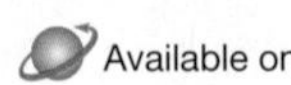 Available online  Available on CD- or DVD-ROM

Reaching All Learners

Teaching tips to help all learners appear throughout the chapter. A few that target specific students are included in the lists below.

All Learners

Lab Activities
Practice and Problem Solving Workbook
Know-It Notebook

Special Needs Students

Practice A .... CRB
Reteach .... CRB
Reading Strategies .... CRB
Are You Ready? .... SE p. 143
Inclusion .... TE pp. 176, 184, 186, 195
IDEA Works!® Modified Worksheets and Tests
Ready to Go On? Intervention SPANISH
Know-It Notebook
Online Interactivities 
Lesson Tutorial Videos 

Developing Learners

Practice A .... CRB
Reteach .... CRB
Reading Strategies .... CRB
Are You Ready? .... SE p. 143
Vocabulary Connections .... SE p. 144
Questioning Strategies .... TE
Ready to Go On? Intervention SPANISH
Know-It Notebook
Homework Help Online
Online Interactivities 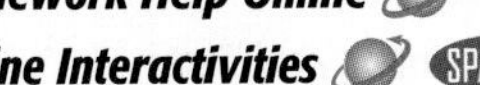
Lesson Tutorial Videos  

On-Level Learners

Practice B .... CRB
Problem Solving .... CRB
Vocabulary Connections .... SE p. 144
Questioning Strategies .... TE
Ready to Go On? Intervention SPANISH
Know-It Notebook
Homework Help Online
Online Interactivities 

Advanced Learners

Practice C .... CRB
Challenge .... CRB
Challenge Exercises .... SE
Reading and Writing Math *Extend* .... TE p. 145
Critical Thinking .... TE p. 175
Are You Ready? Enrichment SPANISH
Ready To Go On? Enrichment 

English Language Learners

ENGLISH LANGUAGE LEARNERS

Reading Strategies .... CRB
Are You Ready? Vocabulary .... SE p. 143
Vocabulary Connections .... SE p. 144
Vocabulary Review .... SE p. 202
English Language Learners .... TE pp. 141, 145, 147, 165, 191
Success for Every Learner
Know-It Notebook
Spanish Study Guide (Resumen y Repaso)
Multilingual Glossary
Lesson Tutorial Videos  

Technology Highlights for Reaching All Learners

 Lesson Tutorial Videos 

Starring Holt authors Ed Burger and Freddie Renfro! Live tutorials to support every lesson in Chapter 3.

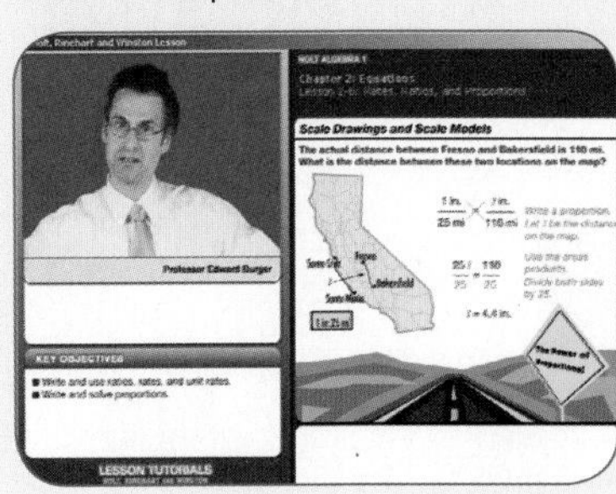

Multilingual Glossary

Searchable glossary includes definitions in English, Spanish, Vietnamese, Chinese, Hmong, Korean, and 4 other languages.

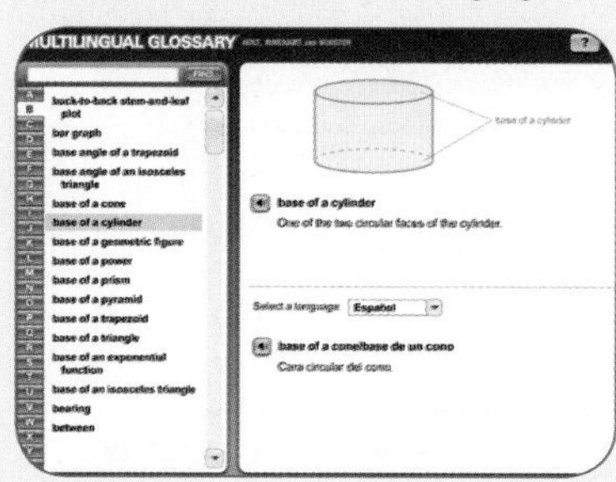

Online Interactivities

Interactive tutorials provide visually engaging alternative opportunities to learn concepts and master skills.

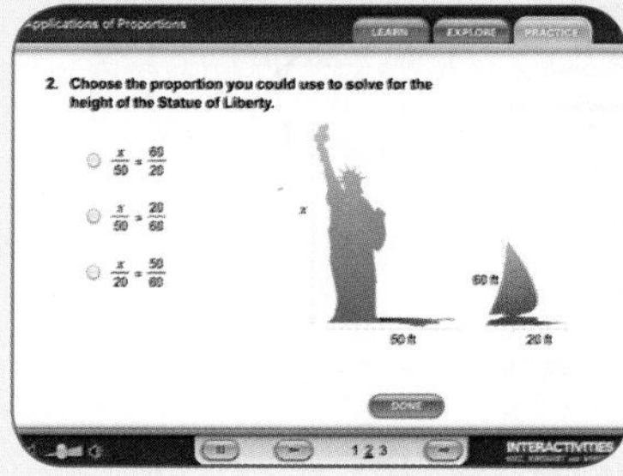

KEY: **SE** = *Student Edition* **TE** = *Teacher's Edition* **CRB** = *Chapter Resource Book*  Spanish version available  Available online Available on CD- or DVD-ROM

Ongoing Assessment

Assessing Prior Knowledge

Determine whether students have the prerequisite concepts and skills for success in Chapter 3.

Are You Ready? SPANISH .... SE p. 143
Warm Up .... TE

Test Preparation

Provide review and practice for Chapter 3 and standardized tests.

Multi-Step Test Prep .... SE pp. 180, 200
Study Guide: Review .... SE pp. 202–205
Test Tackler .... SE pp. 208–209
Standardized Test Prep .... SE pp. 210–211
College Entrance Exam Practice .... SE p. 207
Countdown to Testing .... SE pp. C4-C27
IDEA Works!® Modified Worksheets and Tests

Alternative Assessment

Assess students' understanding of Chapter 3 concepts and combined problem-solving skills.

Chapter 3 Project .... SE p. 142
Alternative Assessment .... TE
Performance Assessment .... AR
Portfolio Assessment .... AR

Lesson Assessment

Provide formative assessment for each lesson of Chapter 3.

Questioning Strategies .... TE
Think and Discuss .... SE
Check It Out! Exercises .... SE
Write About It .... SE
Journal .... TE
Lesson Quiz .... TE
Alternative Assessment .... TE
IDEA Works!® Modified Worksheets and Tests

Weekly Assessment

Provide formative assessment for each section of Chapter 3.

Multi-Step Test Prep .... SE pp. 180, 200
Ready to Go On? SPANISH .... SE pp. 181, 201
Section Quizzes .... AR
Test and Practice Generator .... *Teacher One Stop*

Chapter Assessment

Provide summative assessment of Chapter 3 mastery.

Chapter 3 Test .... SE p. 206
Chapter Test (Levels A, B, C) .... AR
• Multiple Choice • Free Response
Cumulative Test .... AR
Test and Practice Generator .... *Teacher One Stop*
IDEA Works!® Modified Worksheets and Tests

Technology Highlights for Assessment

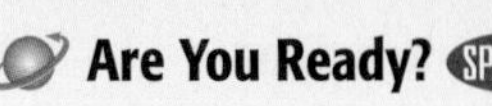

Are You Ready? SPANISH

Automatically assess readiness and prescribe intervention for Chapter 3 prerequisite skills.

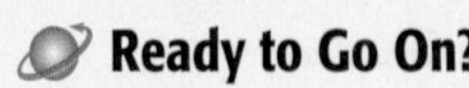

Ready to Go On?

Automatically assess understanding of and prescribe intervention for Sections 3A and 3B.

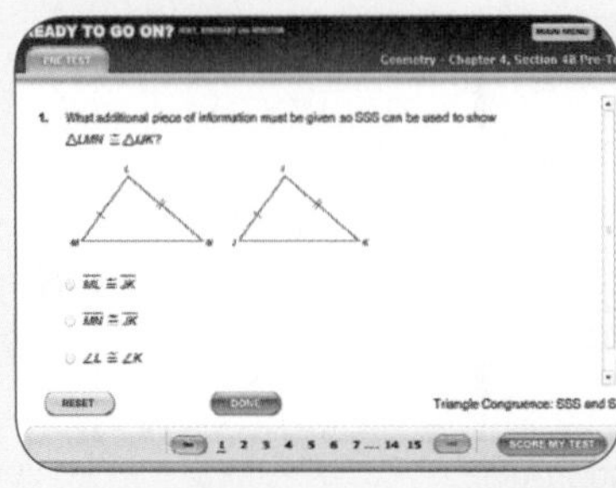

Test and Practice Generator

Use Chapter 3 problem banks to create assessments and worksheets to print out or deliver online. Includes dynamic problems.

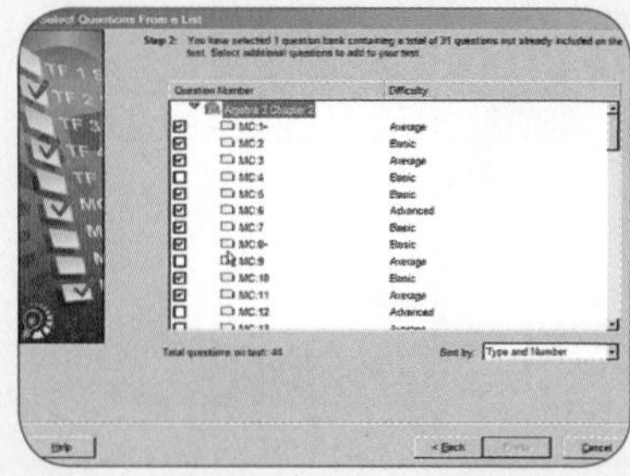

KEY: **SE** = *Student Edition* **TE** = *Teacher's Edition* **AR** = *Assessment Resources* SPANISH Spanish version available  Available online Available on CD- or DVD-ROM

CHAPTER 3

Formal Assessment

Three levels (A, B, C) of multiple-choice and free-response chapter tests, along with a performance assessment, are available in the *Assessment Resources.*

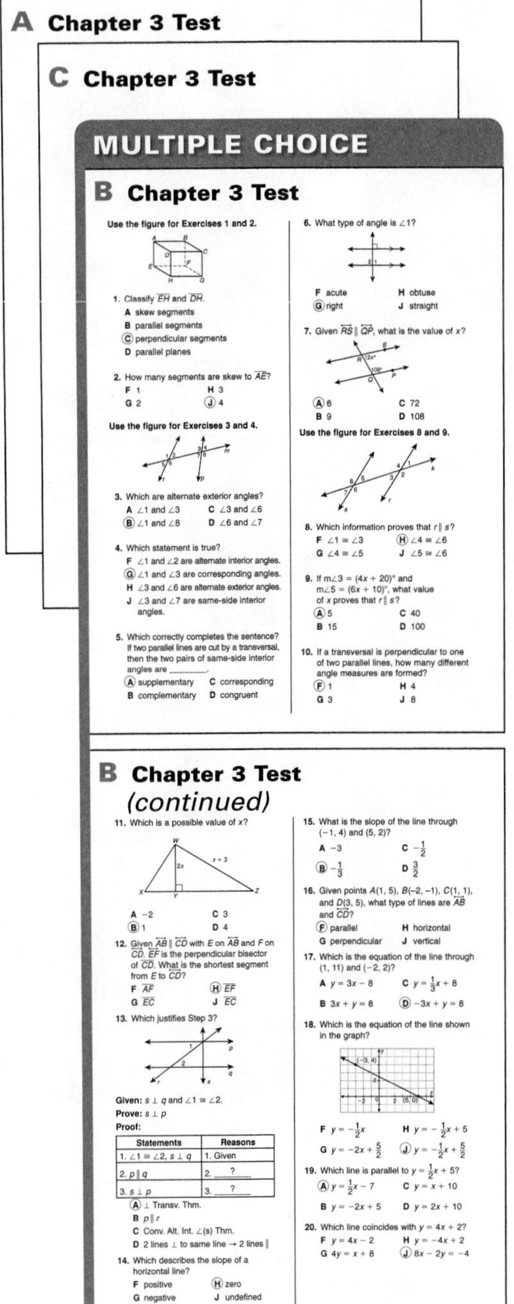

A Chapter 3 Test

C Chapter 3 Test

MULTIPLE CHOICE

B Chapter 3 Test

Use the figure for Exercises 1 and 2.

1. Classify $\overline{EH}$ and $\overline{DH}$.
   A skew segments
   B parallel segments
   Ⓒ perpendicular segments
   D parallel planes

2. How many segments are skew to $\overline{AE}$?
   F 1 H 3
   G 2 Ⓙ 4

Use the figure for Exercises 3 and 4.

3. Which are alternate exterior angles?
   A ∠1 and ∠3 C ∠3 and ∠6
   Ⓑ ∠1 and ∠8 D ∠6 and ∠7

4. Which statement is true?
   F ∠1 and ∠2 are alternate interior angles.
   Ⓖ ∠1 and ∠3 are corresponding angles.
   H ∠3 and ∠6 are alternate exterior angles.
   J ∠3 and ∠7 are same-side interior angles.

5. Which correctly completes the sentence? If two parallel lines are cut by a transversal, then the two pairs of same-side interior angles are ________.
   Ⓐ supplementary C corresponding
   B complementary D congruent

6. What type of angle is ∠1?
   F acute H obtuse
   Ⓖ right J straight

7. Given $\overleftrightarrow{RS} \parallel \overleftrightarrow{QP}$, what is the value of x?
   Ⓐ 6 C 72
   B 9 D 108

Use the figure for Exercises 8 and 9.

8. Which information proves that $r \parallel s$?
   F ∠1 ≅ ∠3 Ⓗ ∠4 ≅ ∠6
   G ∠4 ≅ ∠5 J ∠5 ≅ ∠6

9. If m∠3 = $(4x + 20)°$ and m∠5 = $(6x + 10)°$, what value of x proves that $r \parallel s$?
   Ⓐ 5 C 40
   B 15 D 100

10. If a transversal is perpendicular to one of two parallel lines, how many different angle measures are formed?
    Ⓕ 1 H 4
    G 3 J 8

B Chapter 3 Test *(continued)*

11. Which is a possible value of x?
    A −2 C 3
    Ⓑ 1 D 4

12. Given $\overleftrightarrow{AB} \parallel \overleftrightarrow{CD}$ with E on $\overleftrightarrow{AB}$ and F on $\overleftrightarrow{CD}$. $\overleftrightarrow{EF}$ is the perpendicular bisector of $\overline{CD}$. What is the shortest segment from E to $\overleftrightarrow{CD}$?
    F $\overline{AF}$ Ⓗ $\overline{EF}$
    G $\overline{EC}$ J $\overline{EC}$

13. Which justifies Step 3?
    Given: $s \perp q$ and ∠1 ≅ ∠2.
    Prove: $s \perp p$
    Proof:

Statements	Reasons
1. ∠1 ≅ ∠2, $s \perp q$	1. Given
2. $p \parallel q$	2. ___?___
3. $s \perp p$	3. ___?___

   Ⓐ ⊥ Transv. Thm.
   B $p \parallel r$
   C Conv. Alt. Int. ∠(s) Thm.
   D 2 lines ⊥ to same line → 2 lines ∥

14. Which describes the slope of a horizontal line?
    F positive Ⓗ zero
    G negative J undefined

15. What is the slope of the line through (−1, 4) and (5, 2)?
    A −3 C $-\frac{1}{2}$
    Ⓑ $-\frac{1}{3}$ D $\frac{3}{2}$

16. Given points $A(1, 5)$, $B(-2, -1)$, $C(1, 1)$, and $D(3, 5)$, what type of lines are $\overleftrightarrow{AB}$ and $\overleftrightarrow{CD}$?
    Ⓕ parallel H horizontal
    G perpendicular J vertical

17. Which is the equation of the line through (1, 11) and (−2, 2)?
    A $y = 3x - 8$ C $y = \frac{1}{3}x + 8$
    B $3x + y = 8$ Ⓓ $-3x + y = 8$

18. Which is the equation of the line shown in the graph?
    F $y = -\frac{1}{2}x$ H $y = -\frac{1}{2}x + 5$
    G $y = -2x + \frac{5}{2}$ Ⓙ $y = -\frac{1}{2}x + \frac{5}{2}$

19. Which line is parallel to $y = \frac{1}{2}x + 5$?
    Ⓐ $y = \frac{1}{2}x - 7$ C $y = x + 10$
    B $y = -2x + 5$ D $y = 2x + 10$

20. Which line coincides with $y = 4x + 2$?
    F $y = 4x - 2$ H $y = -4x + 2$
    G $4y = x + 8$ Ⓙ $8x - 2y = -4$

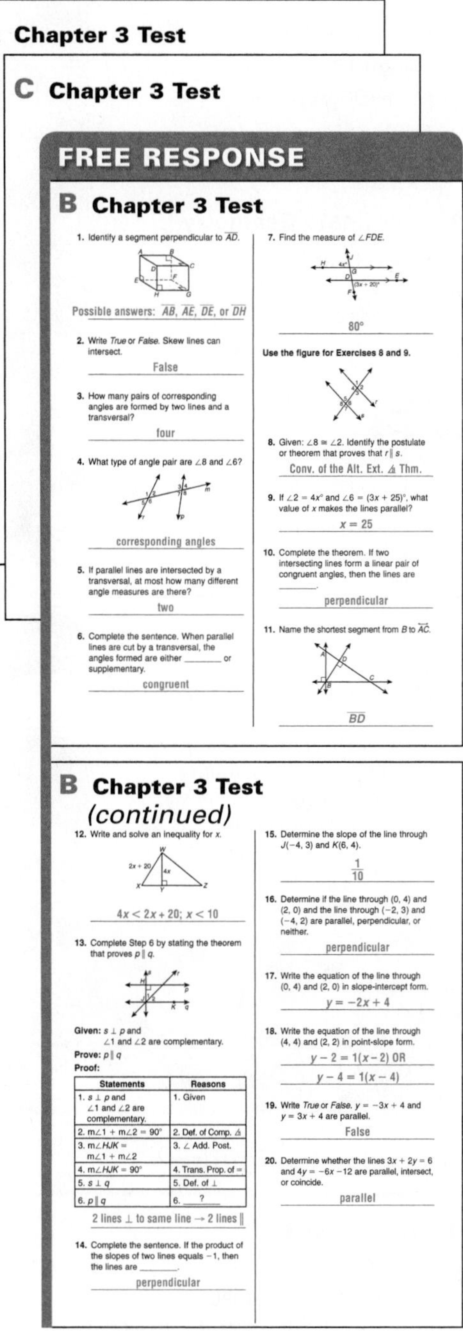

A Chapter 3 Test

C Chapter 3 Test

FREE RESPONSE

B Chapter 3 Test

1. Identify a segment perpendicular to $\overline{AD}$.
   Possible answers: $\overline{AB}$, $\overline{AE}$, $\overline{DE}$, or $\overline{DH}$

2. Write *True* or *False*. Skew lines can intersect.
   False

3. How many pairs of corresponding angles are formed by two lines and a transversal?
   four

4. What type of angle pair are ∠8 and ∠6?
   corresponding angles

5. If parallel lines are intersected by a transversal, at most how many different angle measures are there?
   two

6. Complete the sentence. When parallel lines are cut by a transversal, the angles formed are either ________ or supplementary.
   congruent

7. Find the measure of ∠FDE.
   80°

Use the figure for Exercises 8 and 9.

8. Given: ∠8 ≅ ∠2. Identify the postulate or theorem that proves that $r \parallel s$.
   Conv. of the Alt. Ext. ∠s Thm.

9. If ∠2 = $4x°$ and ∠6 = $(3x + 25)°$, what value of x makes the lines parallel?
   $x = 25$

10. Complete the theorem. If two intersecting lines form a linear pair of congruent angles, then the lines are ________.
    perpendicular

11. Name the shortest segment from B to $\overleftrightarrow{AC}$.
    $\overline{BD}$

B Chapter 3 Test *(continued)*

12. Write and solve an inequality for x.
    $4x < 2x + 20$; $x < 10$

13. Complete Step 6 by stating the theorem that proves $p \parallel q$.
    Given: $s \perp p$ and ∠1 and ∠2 are complementary.
    Prove: $p \parallel q$
    Proof:

Statements	Reasons
1. $s \perp p$ and ∠1 and ∠2 are complementary.	1. Given
2. m∠1 + m∠2 = 90°	2. Def. of Comp. ∠s
3. m∠HJK = m∠1 + m∠2	3. ∠ Add. Post.
4. m∠HJK = 90°	4. Trans. Prop. of =
5. $s \perp q$	5. Def. of ⊥
6. $p \parallel q$	6. ___?___

   2 lines ⊥ to same line → 2 lines ∥

14. Complete the sentence. If the product of the slopes of two lines equals −1, then the lines are ________.
    perpendicular

15. Determine the slope of the line through $J(-4, 3)$ and $K(6, 4)$.
    $\frac{1}{10}$

16. Determine if the line through (0, 4) and (2, 0) and the line through (−2, 3) and (−4, 2) are parallel, perpendicular, or neither.
    perpendicular

17. Write the equation of the line through (0, 4) and (2, 0) in slope-intercept form.
    $y = -2x + 4$

18. Write the equation of the line through (4, 4) and (2, 2) in point-slope form.
    $y - 2 = 1(x - 2)$ OR $y - 4 = 1(x - 4)$

19. Write *True* or *False*. $y = -3x + 4$ and $y = 3x + 4$ are parallel.
    False

20. Determine whether the lines $3x + 2y = 6$ and $4y = -6x - 12$ are parallel, intersect, or coincide.
    parallel

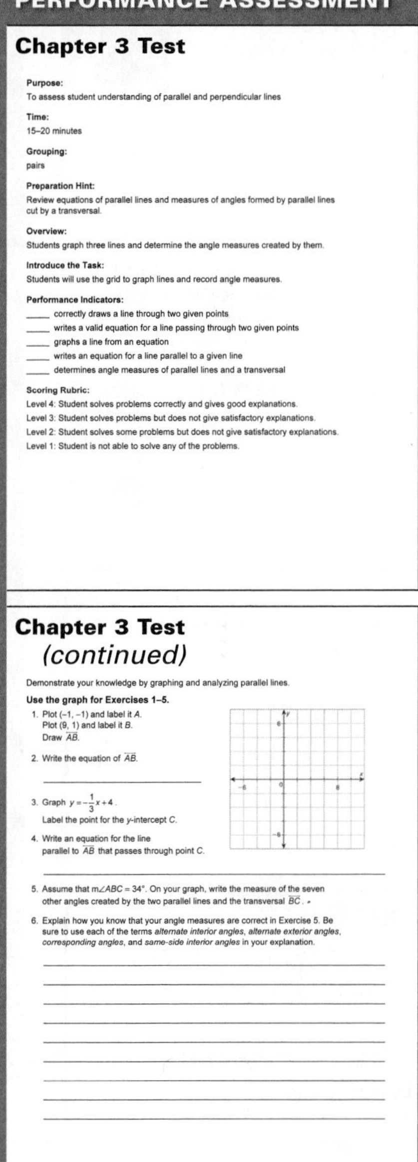

PERFORMANCE ASSESSMENT

Chapter 3 Test

Purpose:
To assess student understanding of parallel and perpendicular lines

Time:
15–20 minutes

Grouping:
pairs

Preparation Hint:
Review equations of parallel lines and measures of angles formed by parallel lines cut by a transversal.

Overview:
Students graph three lines and determine the angle measures created by them.

Introduce the Task:
Students will use the grid to graph lines and record angle measures.

Performance Indicators:
_____ correctly draws a line through two given points
_____ writes a valid equation for a line passing through two given points
_____ graphs a line from an equation
_____ writes an equation for a line parallel to a given line
_____ determines angle measures of parallel lines and a transversal

Scoring Rubric:
Level 4: Student solves problems correctly and gives good explanations.
Level 3: Student solves problems but does not give satisfactory explanations.
Level 2: Student solves some problems but does not give satisfactory explanations.
Level 1: Student is not able to solve any of the problems.

Chapter 3 Test *(continued)*

Demonstrate your knowledge by graphing and analyzing parallel lines.

Use the graph for Exercises 1–5.

1. Plot (−1, −1) and label it A. Plot (9, 1) and label it B. Draw $\overleftrightarrow{AB}$.
2. Write the equation of $\overleftrightarrow{AB}$.
3. Graph $y = -\frac{1}{3}x + 4$. Label the point for the y-intercept C.
4. Write an equation for the line parallel to $\overleftrightarrow{AB}$ that passes through point C.
5. Assume that m∠ABC = 34°. On your graph, write the measure of the seven other angles created by the two parallel lines and the transversal $\overleftrightarrow{BC}$.
6. Explain how you know that your angle measures are correct in Exercise 5. Be sure to use each of the terms *alternate interior angles*, *alternate exterior angles*, *corresponding angles*, and *same-side interior angles* in your explanation.

Teacher One Stop™
Test & Practice Generator

Create and customize Chapter 3 Tests. Instantly generate multiple test versions, answer keys, and practice versions of test items.

Modified chapter tests that address special learning needs are available in *IDEA Works!®* *Modified Worksheets and Tests.*

CHAPTER 3

SECTION 3A
Lines with Transversals

On page 180, students use properties of parallel and perpendicular lines to model a real-world attraction known as a mystery spot.

Exercises designed to prepare students for success on the Multi-Step Test Prep can be found on pages 150, 160, 168, and 176.

SECTION 3B
Coordinate Geometry

On page 200, students write equations and graph lines to model a real-world traffic situation.

Exercises designed to prepare students for success on the Multi-Step Test Prep can be found on pages 186 and 196.

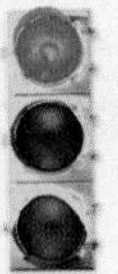

Interactivities Online ▶

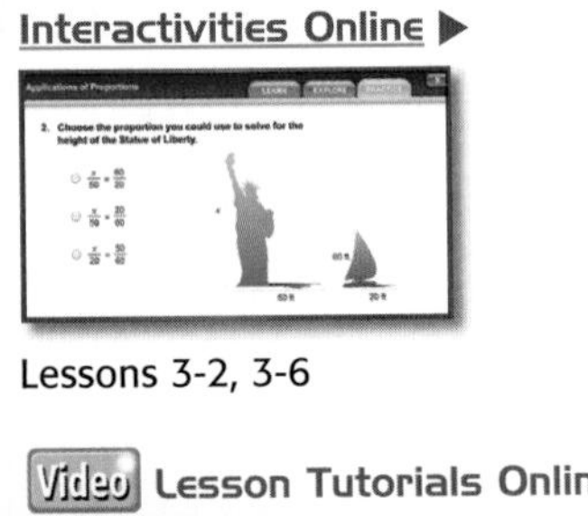

Lessons 3-2, 3-6

Video Lesson Tutorials Online

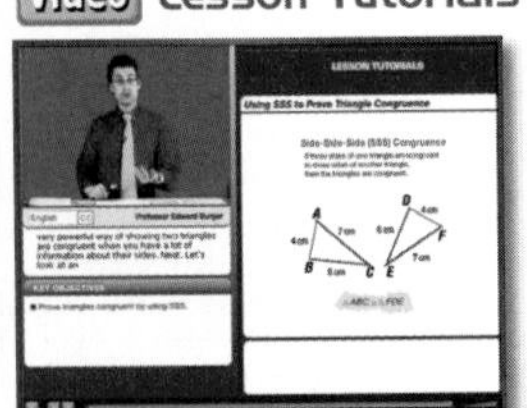

Lesson Tutorial Videos are available for EVERY example.

CHAPTER 3

Parallel and Perpendicular Lines

Chapter Focus

- Use and prove properties of parallel lines and the angles formed by parallel lines and transversals.
- Represent lines in the coordinate plane.

Seeing is Disbelieving!

Many optical illusions are based on parallel and perpendicular lines. You can use these types of lines to create your own optical illusions.

Seeing is Disbelieving

About the Project

In this Chapter Project, students study the mathematics behind optical illusions. They begin by using parallel lines and transversals to draw an "impossible figure." Then they use theorems from the chapter to analyze an optical illusion and create one of their own.

Project Resources

All project resources for teachers and students are provided online.

ARE YOU READY?

Vocabulary

Match each term on the left with a definition on the right.

1. acute angle F
2. congruent angles D
3. obtuse angle B
4. collinear E
5. congruent segments A

A. segments that have the same length
B. an angle that measures greater than 90° and less than 180°
C. points that lie in the same plane
D. angles that have the same measure
E. points that lie on the same line
F. an angle that measures greater than 0° and less than 90°

Conditional Statements

Identify the hypothesis and conclusion of each conditional.

6. If E is on $\overleftrightarrow{AC}$, then E lies in plane $\mathcal{P}$.
7. If A is not in plane $\mathcal{Q}$, then A is not on $\overleftrightarrow{BD}$.
8. If plane $\mathcal{P}$ and plane $\mathcal{Q}$ intersect, then they intersect in a line.

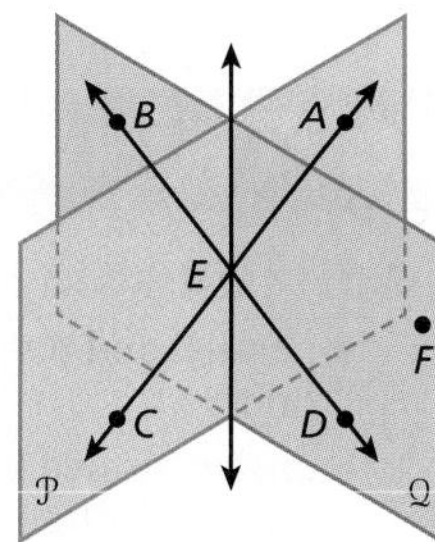

Name and Classify Angles

Name and classify each angle. Possible answers:

9. 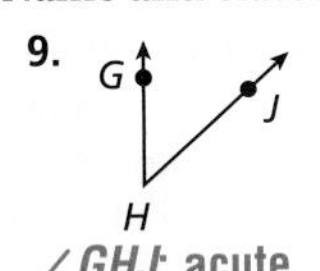

∠GHJ; acute

10. 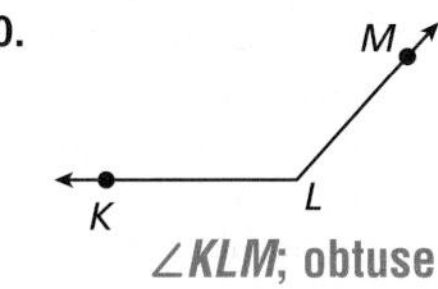

∠KLM; obtuse

11. 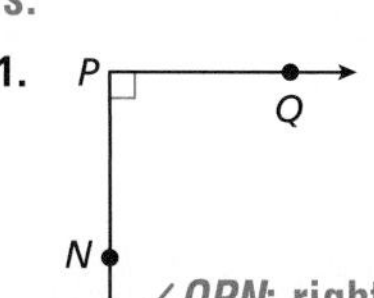

∠QPN; right

12. 

∠RST; straight

Angle Relationships

Give an example of each angle pair. Possible answers:

13. vertical angles ∠AGB and ∠EGD
14. adjacent angles ∠AGB and ∠BGC
15. complementary angles ∠BGC and ∠CGD
16. supplementary angles ∠AGC and ∠CGD

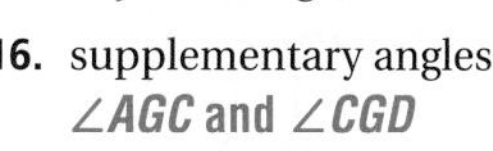

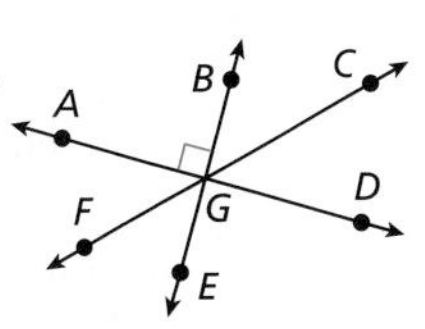

Evaluate Expressions

Evaluate each expression for the given value of the variable.

17. $4x + 9$ for $x = 31$ 133
18. $6x - 16$ for $x = 43$ 242
19. $97 - 3x$ for $x = 20$ 37
20. $5x + 3x + 12$ for $x = 17$ 148

Solve Multi-Step Equations

Solve each equation for x.

21. $4x + 8 = 24$ $x = 4$
22. $2 = 2x - 8$ $x = 5$
23. $4x + 3x + 6 = 90$ $x = 12$
24. $21x + 13 + 14x - 8 = 180$ $x = 5$

CHAPTER 3

ARE YOU READY?

Organizer

Objective: Assess students' understanding of prerequisite skills.

Prerequisite Skills

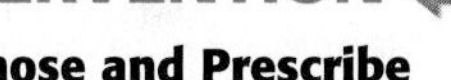

Conditional Statements
Name and Classify Angles
Angle Relationships
Evaluate Expressions
Solve Multi-Step Equations

Assessing Prior Knowledge

INTERVENTION

Diagnose and Prescribe

Use this page to determine whether intervention is necessary or whether enrichment is appropriate.

Resources

 ***Are You Ready? Intervention and Enrichment*** **Worksheets**

 ***Are You Ready?*** **CD-ROM**

 ***Are You Ready?*** **Online**

my.hrw.com

ARE YOU READY?

Diagnose and Prescribe

NO INTERVENE

Prerequisite Skill	*Are You Ready? Intervention,* Chapter 3 — Worksheets	CD-ROM	Online
Conditional Statements	Skill 88	Activity 88	Diagnose and Prescribe Online
Name and Classify Angles	Skill 23	Activity 23	
Angle Relationships	Skill 25	Activity 25	
Evaluate Expressions	Skill 60	Activity 60	
Solve Multi-Step Equations	Skill 69	Activity 69	

YES ENRICH

Are You Ready? Enrichment, Chapter 3

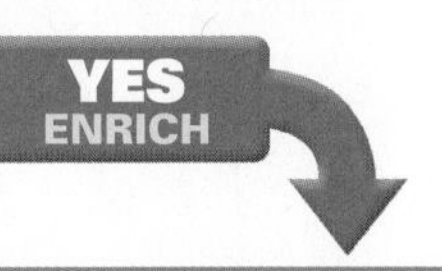

Worksheets
CD-ROM
Online

CHAPTER 3

Study Guide: Preview

Organizer

Objective: Help students organize the new concepts they will learn in Chapter 3.

Online Edition
Multilingual Glossary

Resources

Teacher One Stop™
PuzzleView

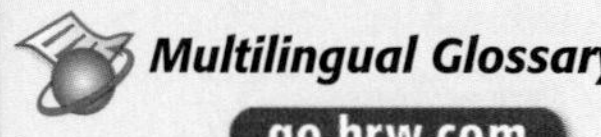
Multilingual Glossary **Online**

go.hrw.com
KEYWORD: MG7 Glossary

Answers to *Vocabulary Connections*

1. crosses the two lines
2. the steepness of the line in a plane
3. matching; ∡ that are in matching positions
4. inside; the area between the lines; between the two lines, on opposite sides of the third line

CHAPTER 3

Study Guide: Preview

Where You've Been

Previously, you

- identified and named points, lines, and planes.
- named and classified angles.
- found measures of angle pairs.
- developed and applied the formula for midpoint.

In This Chapter

You will study

- parallel and perpendicular lines.
- angles formed by parallel lines and a transversal.
- lines in a coordinate plane.

Where You're Going

You can use the skills learned in this chapter

- in Calculus, to find slopes of lines tangent to curves.
- in other classes, such as Physics and Economics, to analyze rates of change.
- in fields such as architecture and construction, to ensure that opposite walls of a building are parallel and adjacent walls are perpendicular.

Key Vocabulary/Vocabulario

alternate exterior angles	ángulos alternos externos
alternate interior angles	ángulos alternos internos
corresponding angles	ángulos correspondientes
parallel lines	líneas paralelas
perpendicular bisector	mediatriz
perpendicular lines	líneas perpendiculares
same-side interior angles	ángulos internos del mismo lado
slope	pendiente
transversal	transversal

Vocabulary Connections

To become familiar with some of the vocabulary terms in the chapter, answer the following questions. You may refer to the chapter, the glossary, or a dictionary if you like.

1. The root *trans-* means "across." What do you think a **transversal** of two lines does?
2. The *slope* of a mountain trail describes the steepness of the climb. What might the **slope** of a line describe?
3. What does the word *corresponding* mean? What do you think the term **corresponding angles** means?
4. What does the word *interior* mean? What might the phrase "interior of a pair of lines" describe? The word *alternate* means "to change from one to another." If two lines are crossed by a third line, where do you think a pair of **alternate interior angles** might be?

Study Strategy: Take Effective Notes

Taking effective notes is an important study strategy. The Cornell system of note taking is a good way to organize and review main ideas. In the Cornell system, the paper is divided into three main sections. The note-taking column is where you take notes during lecture. The cue column is where you write questions and key phrases as you review your notes. The summary area is where you write a brief summary of the lecture.

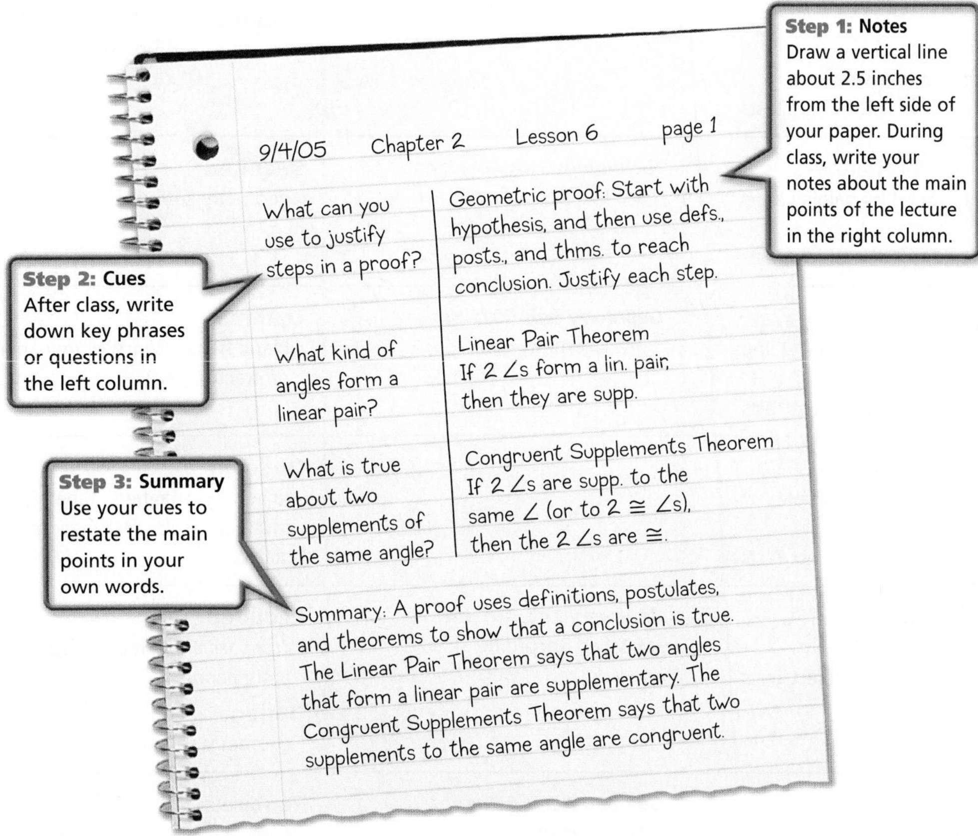

Step 1: Notes
Draw a vertical line about 2.5 inches from the left side of your paper. During class, write your notes about the main points of the lecture in the right column.
9/4/05 Chapter 2 Lesson 6 page 1
What can you use to justify steps in a proof?
Geometric proof: Start with hypothesis, and then use defs., posts., and thms. to reach conclusion. Justify each step.
Step 2: Cues
After class, write down key phrases or questions in the left column.
What kind of angles form a linear pair?
Linear Pair Theorem
If 2 ∠s form a lin. pair, then they are supp.
Step 3: Summary
Use your cues to restate the main points in your own words.
What is true about two supplements of the same angle?
Congruent Supplements Theorem
If 2 ∠s are supp. to the same ∠ (or to 2 ≅ ∠s), then the 2 ∠s are ≅.
Summary: A proof uses definitions, postulates, and theorems to show that a conclusion is true. The Linear Pair Theorem says that two angles that form a linear pair are supplementary. The Congruent Supplements Theorem says that two supplements to the same angle are congruent.

Try This

1. Research and write a paragraph describing the Cornell system of note taking. Describe how you can benefit from using this type of system.
2. In your next class, use the Cornell system of note taking. Compare these notes to your notes from a previous lecture.

Reading and Writing Math CHAPTER 3

Organizer

Objective: Apply study strategies to understand and retain key concepts.

Online Edition

Resources

Chapter 3 Resource Book

Reading Strategies

Study Strategy: Take Effective Notes

ENGLISH LANGUAGE LEARNERS

Discuss The physical act of writing helps students reinforce the concepts that they hear and see.

Extend Too often students do not refer to their notes because the notes are disorganized and difficult to follow. Encourage students to use a notetaking system and to review their notes regularly.

Throughout Chapter 3, ask students to share questions and summaries. Any student having difficulty understanding a topic may benefit from hearing other explanations.

Answers to *Try This*

1–2. Check students' work.

Reading Connection

The Fifth Postulate
by Jason Socrates Bardi

Two thousand years after Euclid, mathematicians still had not proven Euclid's fifth postulate, which assumes the existence of parallel lines. The reasons behind the failure became clear only in the nineteenth century, when non-Euclidean geometries were developed. Bardi tells the story of this evolving idea in vivid prose.

Activity The Fifth Postulate is often stated as follows: "Exactly one line can be drawn through any point not on a given line parallel to the given line in a plane." In fact, Euclid put it quite differently. Have students find Euclid's version and compare it with the version above.

SECTION

3A Lines with Transversals

One-Minute Section Planner

Lesson	Lab Resources	Materials
Lesson 3-1 Lines and Angles • Identify parallel, perpendicular, and skew lines. • Identify the angles formed by two lines and a transversal. ☐ SAT-10 ☑ NAEP ☑ ACT ☑ SAT ☑ SAT Subject Tests		**Optional** straws or toothpicks, paper
3-2 Technology Lab Explore Parallel Lines and Transversals • Use geometry software to explore angles formed by parallel lines and transversals. ☐ SAT-10 ☑ NAEP ☑ ACT ☑ SAT ☑ SAT Subject Tests	***Technology Lab Activities*** 3-2 Lab Recording Sheet	**Required** geometry software
Lesson 3-2 Angles Formed by Parallel Lines and Transversals • Prove and use theorems about the angles formed by parallel lines and a transversal. ☐ SAT-10 ☑ NAEP ☑ ACT ☑ SAT ☑ SAT Subject Tests	***Geometry Lab Activities*** 3-2 Geometry Lab	**Optional** blank transparency, patty paper, protractor (MK)
Lesson 3-3 Proving Lines Parallel • Use the angles formed by a transversal to prove two lines are parallel. ☐ SAT-10 ☑ NAEP ☑ ACT ☑ SAT ☑ SAT Subject Tests		**Optional** uncooked spaghetti, tape, protractor, ruler (MK), geometry software
3-3 Geometry Lab Construct Parallel Lines • Use various methods to construct parallel lines. ☐ SAT-10 ☐ NAEP ☑ ACT ☑ SAT ☑ SAT Subject Tests	***Geometry Lab Activities*** 3-3 Lab Recording Sheet	**Required** compass and straightedge (MK), patty paper **Optional** geometry software
Lesson 3-4 Perpendicular Lines • Prove and apply theorems about perpendicular lines. ☐ SAT-10 ☑ NAEP ☑ ACT ☑ SAT ☐ SAT Subject Tests	***Geometry Lab Activities*** 3-4 Geometry Lab	**Required** compass and straightedge (MK) **Optional** patty paper
3-4 Geometry Lab Construct Perpendicular Lines • Construct a line perpendicular to a given line through a given point. ☐ SAT-10 ☐ NAEP ☑ ACT ☑ SAT ☑ SAT Subject Tests	***Geometry Lab Activities*** 3-4 Lab Recording Sheet	**Required** compass and straightedge (MK)

MK = *Manipulatives Kit*

Math Background

Professional Learning

THE PARALLEL POSTULATE

Lesson 3-3

As discussed in the Math Background notes for Chapter 1, the Parallel Postulate was the fifth postulate proposed in Euclid's *Elements.* Euclid worded the postulate as follows.

If a straight line falling on two straight lines makes the interior angles on the same side less than two right angles, then the straight lines, if extended indefinitely, meet on the side on which the angles lie.

Today, the postulate is usually presented in a logically equivalent form that is sometimes known as Playfair's Axiom:

Through a point P not on line ℓ, there is exactly one line parallel to ℓ.

The Parallel Postulate has played an important role in the history of mathematics, initially because many mathematicians believed it was actually a theorem that could be proved from Euclid's first four postulates. It was only in the nineteenth century that Eugenio Beltrami proved that the Parallel Postulate could not be proven from Euclid's four other axioms.

It was also in the nineteenth century that mathematicians began to recognize that logically consistent mathematical systems can be developed without assuming the Parallel Postulate. These systems, called non-Euclidean geometries, have their own theorems, which may or may not match those of Euclidean geometry.

When presenting the Parallel Postulate (as Playfair's Axiom) to students, it is worth focusing on the postulate's language. In particular, the postulate asserts that through a point P not on a line ℓ, there is *exactly one* line parallel to ℓ. In other words, a parallel line exists, *and it is unique.* Thus, non-Euclidean geometries are based on one of two assumptions: that there is no line through P parallel to ℓ (which gives rise to elliptic geometry) or that there are multiple lines through P parallel to ℓ (which gives rise to hyperbolic geometry).

PERPENDICULARITY

Lesson 3-4

Thus far, the concept of distance has been defined only for two points. However, it is possible to extend the notion of distance to other situations. For example, the distance from a point P to a line ℓ is defined as the length of the perpendicular segment from P to ℓ. As shown in the figure, this perpendicular segment is the shortest segment from the point to the line.

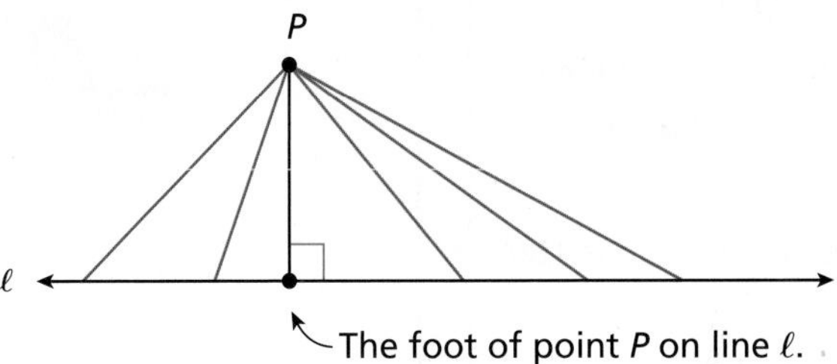

The point at which the perpendicular segment through P intersects line ℓ is sometimes called the *foot* of the point on the line.

CONSTRUCTIONS

Lessons 3-3, 3-4

The Parallel Postulate guarantees that through a point P not on a line ℓ, there is a line through P parallel to ℓ. However, the postulate gives no indication of how to construct this line. Instead, the construction is based on the logically equivalent postulate that states that if two coplanar lines are cut by a transversal such that two corresponding angles are congruent, then the two lines are parallel. Hence, the construction of the required line amounts to constructing a congruent copy of an angle.

The construction of the perpendicular segment from a point to a line is similar to the construction of the perpendicular bisector of a segment. Both of these constructions can be shown to be valid using triangle congruence theorems and the fact that corresponding parts of congruent triangles are congruent (CPCTC). Students will be asked to write proofs justifying these constructions in Chapter 4 (see pages 282–283).

3-1 Organizer

Pacing: Traditional 1 day
Block $\frac{1}{2}$ day

Objectives: Identify parallel, perpendicular, and skew lines.

Identify the angles formed by two lines and a transversal.

Online Edition
Tutorial Videos

Countdown Week 5

Power Presentations with PowerPoint®

Warm Up

Identify each of the following.

1. points that lie in the same plane coplanar points
2. two angles whose sum is 180° supplementary angles
3. the intersection of two distinct intersecting lines point
4. a pair of adjacent angles whose noncommon sides are opposite rays linear pair

Math Humor

Line ℓ: Look out! You almost intersected me!

Line m: Well, *skew's* me!

3-1 Lines and Angles

Objectives
Identify parallel, perpendicular, and skew lines.

Identify the angles formed by two lines and a transversal.

Vocabulary
parallel lines
perpendicular lines
skew lines
parallel planes
transversal
corresponding angles
alternate interior angles
alternate exterior angles
same-side interior angles

Who uses this?
Card architects use playing cards to build structures that contain parallel and perpendicular planes.

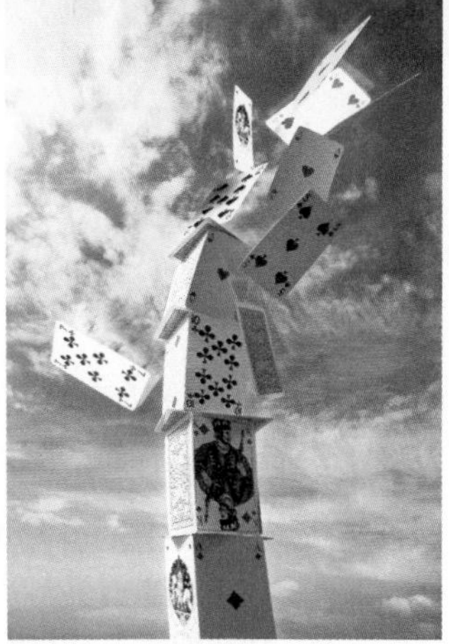

In 1992, Bryan Berg broke the Guinness World Record for card structures by building a tower 14 feet 6 inches tall. Since then, he has built structures more than 25 feet tall.

Know it! Note

Parallel, Perpendicular, and Skew Lines

Parallel lines (∥) are coplanar and do not intersect. In the figure, $\overleftrightarrow{AB} \parallel \overleftrightarrow{EF}$, and $\overleftrightarrow{EG} \parallel \overleftrightarrow{FH}$.

Perpendicular lines (⊥) intersect at 90° angles. In the figure, $\overleftrightarrow{AB} \perp \overleftrightarrow{AE}$, and $\overleftrightarrow{EG} \perp \overleftrightarrow{GH}$.

Skew lines are not coplanar. Skew lines are not parallel and do not intersect. In the figure, $\overleftrightarrow{AB}$ and $\overleftrightarrow{EG}$ are skew.

Parallel planes are planes that do not intersect. In the figure, plane $ABE \parallel$ plane CDG.

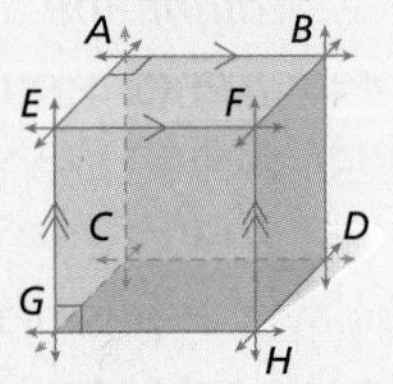

Arrows are used to show that $\overleftrightarrow{AB} \parallel \overleftrightarrow{EF}$ and $\overleftrightarrow{EG} \parallel \overleftrightarrow{FH}$.

EXAMPLE 1 **Identifying Types of Lines and Planes**

Helpful Hint
Segments or rays are parallel, perpendicular, or skew if the lines that contain them are parallel, perpendicular, or skew.

Identify each of the following.

A a pair of parallel segments
$\overline{KN} \parallel \overline{PS}$

B a pair of skew segments
$\overline{LM}$ and $\overline{RS}$ are skew.

C a pair of perpendicular segments
$\overline{MR} \perp \overline{RS}$

D a pair of parallel planes
plane $KPS \parallel$ plane LQR

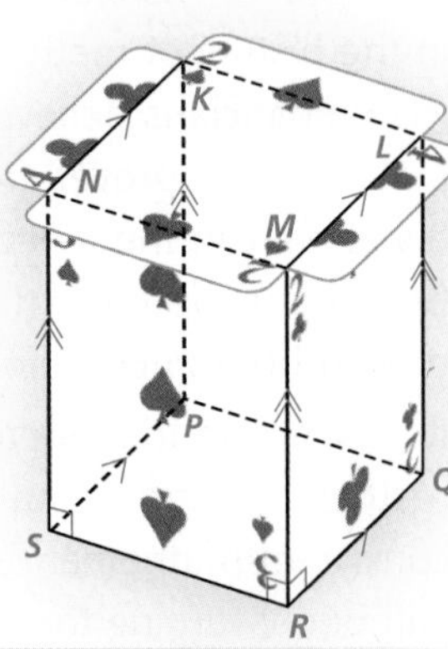

CHECK IT OUT! Identify each of the following.

1a. a pair of parallel segments
1b. a pair of skew segments
1c. a pair of perpendicular segments
1d. a pair of parallel planes

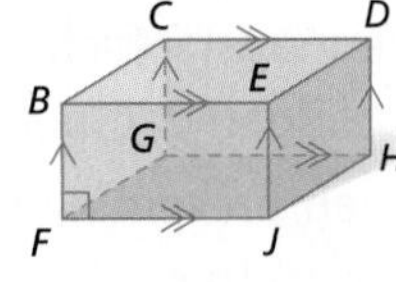

Possible answers:
1a. $\overline{BF} \parallel \overline{EJ}$
1b. $\overline{BF}$ and $\overline{DE}$ are skew.
1c. $\overline{BF} \perp \overline{FJ}$
1d. plane $FJH \parallel$ plane BCD

146 *Chapter 3 Parallel and Perpendicular Lines*

State Resources

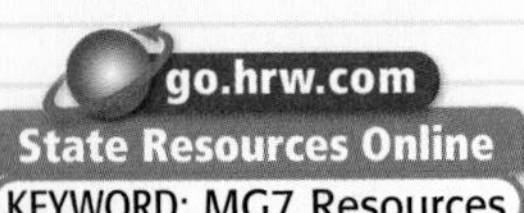

go.hrw.com
State Resources Online
KEYWORD: MG7 Resources

1 Introduce

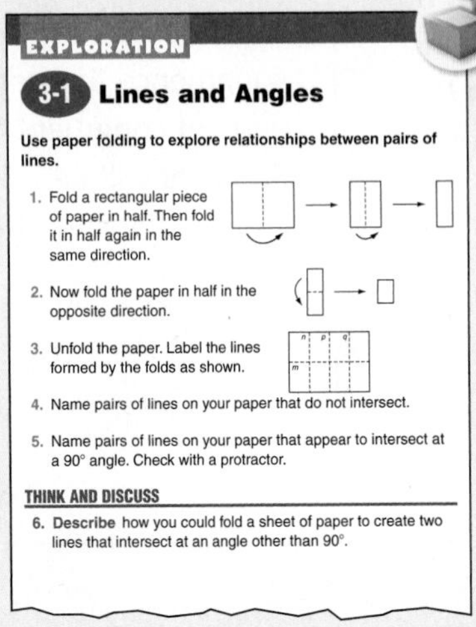

EXPLORATION

3-1 Lines and Angles

Use paper folding to explore relationships between pairs of lines.

1. Fold a rectangular piece of paper in half. Then fold it in half again in the same direction.
2. Now fold the paper in half in the opposite direction.
3. Unfold the paper. Label the lines formed by the folds as shown.
4. Name pairs of lines on your paper that do not intersect.
5. Name pairs of lines on your paper that appear to intersect at a 90° angle. Check with a protractor.

THINK AND DISCUSS

6. Describe how you could fold a sheet of paper to create two lines that intersect at an angle other than 90°.

Motivate

Have students describe in their own words the relationship between the lines represented by the two vertical sides of a door. Be sure students recognize that the lines are always the same distance apart. Then ask students to describe the relationship between the lines represented by the top and one of the vertical sides of the door. Lead them to conclude that these lines form a right angle.

Explorations and answers are provided in *Alternate Openers: Explorations Transparencies.*

Angle Pairs Formed by a Transversal

TERM	EXAMPLE
A **transversal** is a line that intersects two coplanar lines at two different points. The transversal *t* and the other two lines *r* and *s* form eight angles.	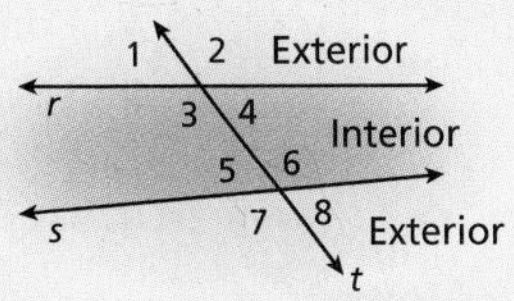 (diagram: lines *r*, *s*, transversal *t*; angles 1–8; Exterior, Interior, Exterior)
Corresponding angles lie on the same side of the transversal *t*, on the same sides of lines *r* and *s*.	∠1 and ∠5
Alternate interior angles are nonadjacent angles that lie on opposite sides of the transversal *t*, between lines *r* and *s*.	∠3 and ∠6
Alternate exterior angles lie on opposite sides of the transversal *t*, outside lines *r* and *s*.	∠1 and ∠8
Same-side interior angles or *consecutive interior angles* lie on the same side of the transversal *t*, between lines *r* and *s*.	∠3 and ∠5

EXAMPLE 2 Classifying Pairs of Angles

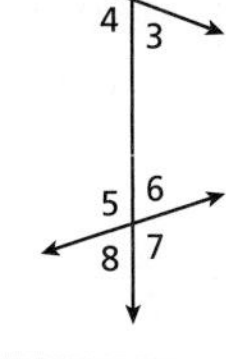

Give an example of each angle pair.

A corresponding angles
∠4 and ∠8

B alternate interior angles
∠4 and ∠6

C alternate exterior angles
∠2 and ∠8

D same-side interior angles
∠4 and ∠5

Give an example of each angle pair.

2a. corresponding angles
2b. alternate interior angles
2c. alternate exterior angles
2d. same-side interior angles

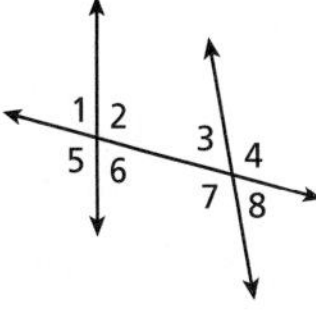

Possible answers:
2a. ∠1 and ∠3
2b. ∠2 and ∠7
2c. ∠1 and ∠8
2d. ∠2 and ∠3

EXAMPLE 3 Identifying Angle Pairs and Transversals

Identify the transversal and classify each angle pair.

A ∠1 and ∠5
transversal: *n*; alternate interior angles

B ∠3 and ∠6
transversal: *m*; corresponding angles

C ∠1 and ∠4
transversal: *ℓ*; alternate exterior angles

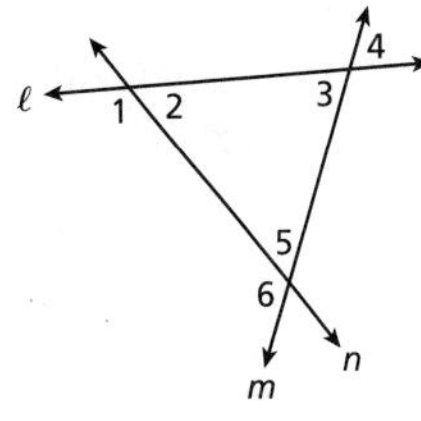

Helpful Hint

To determine which line is the transversal for a given angle pair, locate the line that connects the vertices.

3. Identify the transversal and classify the angle pair ∠2 and ∠5 in the diagram above. transv.: *n*; same-side int. ∠s

Power Presentations with PowerPoint®

Additional Examples

Example 1

Use the diagram in Example 1. Identify each of the following.

A. a pair of parallel segments
$\overline{LM} \parallel \overline{QR}$

B. a pair of skew segments
$\overline{KN}$ and $\overline{PQ}$

C. a pair of perpendicular segments $\overline{NS} \perp \overline{SP}$

D. a pair of parallel planes
plane *NMR* ∥ plane *KLQ*

Example 2

Use the diagram in Example 2. Give an example of each angle pair.

A. corresponding angles
∠1 and ∠5

B. alternate interior angles
∠3 and ∠5

C. alternate exterior angles
∠1 and ∠7

D. same-side interior angles
∠3 and ∠6

Example 3

Use the diagram in Example 3. Identify the transversal and classify each angle pair.

A. ∠1 and ∠3 line *ℓ*; corr. ∠s

B. ∠2 and ∠6 line *n*; alt. int. ∠s

C. ∠4 and ∠6 line *m*; alt. ext. ∠s

Also available on transparency

INTERVENTION
Questioning Strategies

EXAMPLES 1–3

- Can you identify more possible answers?

2 Teach

Guided Instruction

Review the definition of a linear pair of angles. Also discuss the meanings of the words *alternate, interior,* and *exterior*. Be sure that students can identify a transversal before introducing the pairs of angles in the lesson.

Reading Math Corresponding angles are in corresponding, or matching, positions on the same side of the transversal.

ENGLISH LANGUAGE LEARNERS

3 Close

Summarize

Have students name the different pairs of angles formed when two lines are cut by a transversal. Alt. int. angles, alt. ext. angles, corr. angles, and same-side int. angles

Have students explain the difference between parallel lines and skew lines. Parallel lines are coplanar; skew lines are not.

ONGOING ASSESSMENT and INTERVENTION

***Diagnose Before* the Lesson**
3-1 Warm Up, TE p. 146

***Monitor During* the Lesson**
Check It Out! Exercises, SE pp. 146–147
Questioning Strategies, TE p. 147

***Assess After* the Lesson**
3-1 Lesson Quiz, TE p. 151
Alternative Assessment, TE p. 151

Answers to *Think and Discuss*

1. Intersecting lines can intersect at any ∠. ⊥ lines intersect at 90° ∠s.
2. The ∠s are outside lines m and n, on opposite sides of line p.
3. See p. A3.

THINK AND DISCUSS

1. Compare perpendicular and intersecting lines.
2. Describe the positions of two alternate exterior angles formed by lines m and n with transversal p.

3. **GET ORGANIZED** Copy the diagram and graphic organizer. In each box, list all the angle pairs of each type in the diagram.

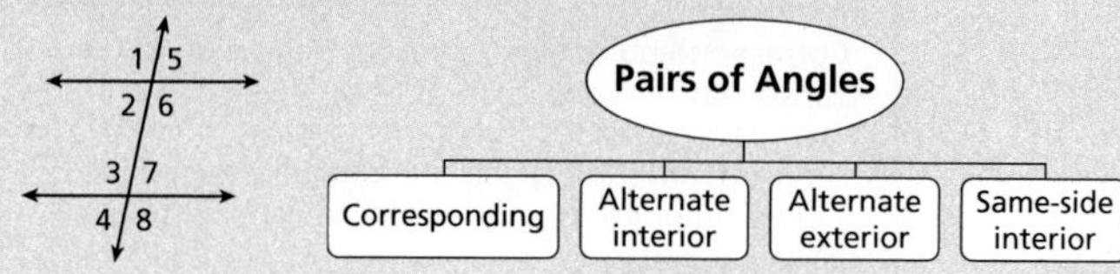

3-1 Exercises

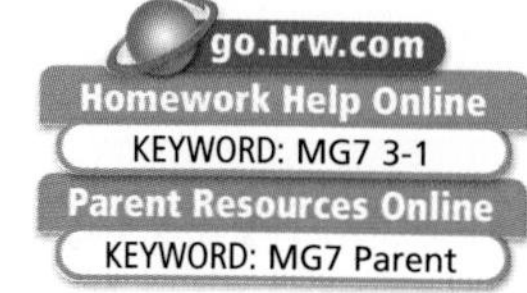

Assignment Guide

Assign *Guided Practice* exercises as necessary.

If you finished Examples **1–3**

Basic 14–29, 33, 35–37, 43–48, 55–62
Average 14–24 even, 26–52, 55–62
Advanced 14–24 even, 26–34, 41–62

Homework Quick Check
Quickly check key concepts.
Exercises: 14, 18, 22, 28, 40

Inclusion To determine which line is the transversal in **Exercises 10–13,** locate the line that connects the vertices of the angles.

GUIDED PRACTICE

1. **Vocabulary** __?__ are located on opposite sides of a transversal, between the two lines that intersect the transversal. (*corresponding angles, alternate interior angles, alternate exterior angles,* or *same-side interior angles*) alternate interior angles

SEE EXAMPLE 1 p. 146

Identify each of the following. Possible answers:

2. one pair of perpendicular segments $\overline{EH} \perp \overline{DH}$
3. one pair of skew segments $\overline{AB}$ and $\overline{DH}$ are skew.
4. one pair of parallel segments $\overline{AB} \parallel \overline{CD}$
5. one pair of parallel planes plane ABC ∥ plane EFG

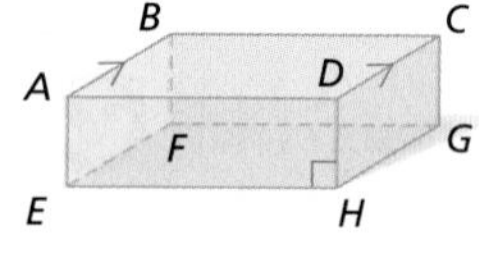

SEE EXAMPLE 2 p. 147

Give an example of each angle pair. Possible answers:

6. alternate interior angles ∠2 and ∠4
7. alternate exterior angles ∠6 and ∠8
8. corresponding angles ∠6 and ∠3
9. same-side interior angles ∠2 and ∠3

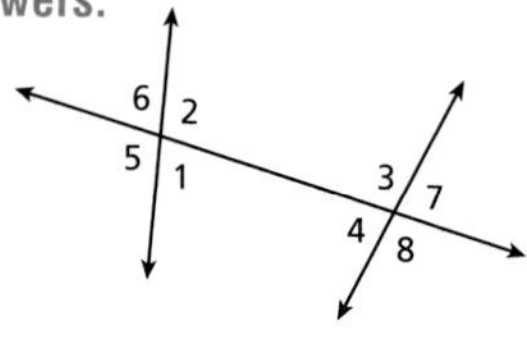

SEE EXAMPLE 3 p. 147

Identify the transversal and classify each angle pair.

10. ∠1 and ∠2 transv.: n; corr. ∠s
11. ∠2 and ∠3 transv.: m; alt. ext. ∠s
12. ∠2 and ∠4 transv.: n; alt. int. ∠s
13. ∠4 and ∠5 transv.: p; same-side int. ∠s

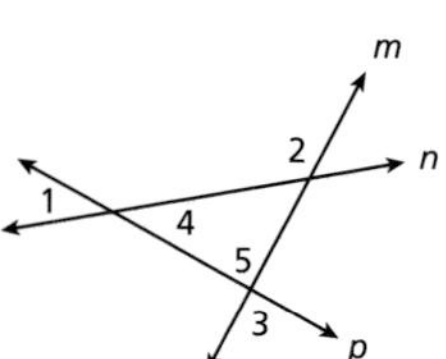

State Resources

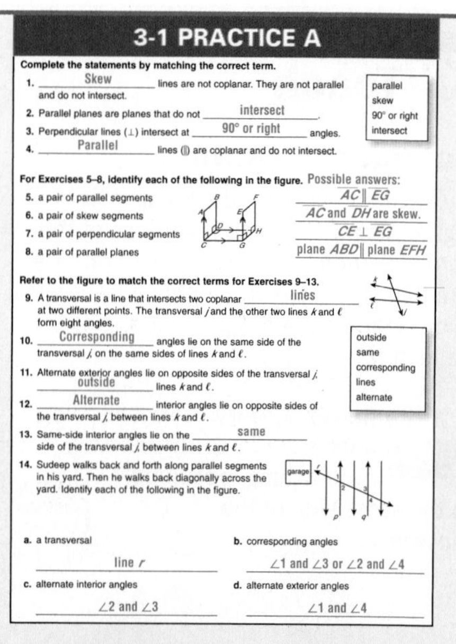

3-1 PRACTICE A

Complete the statements by matching the correct term.

1. Skew lines are not coplanar. They are not parallel and do not intersect.
2. Parallel planes are planes that do not intersect.
3. Perpendicular lines (⊥) intersect at 90° or right angles.
4. Parallel lines (∥) are coplanar and do not intersect.

parallel / skew / 90° or right / intersect

For Exercises 5–8, identify each of the following in the figure. Possible answers:

5. a pair of parallel segments $\overline{AC} \parallel \overline{EG}$
6. a pair of skew segments $\overline{AC}$ and $\overline{DH}$ are skew.
7. a pair of perpendicular segments $\overline{CE} \perp \overline{EG}$
8. a pair of parallel planes plane ABD ∥ plane EFH

Refer to the figure to match the correct terms for Exercises 9–13.

9. A transversal is a line that intersects two coplanar lines at two different points. The transversal j and the other two lines k and ℓ form eight angles.
10. Corresponding angles lie on the same side of the transversal j, on the same sides of lines k and ℓ.
11. Alternate exterior angles lie on opposite sides of the transversal j, outside lines k and ℓ.
12. Alternate interior angles lie on opposite sides of the transversal j, between lines k and ℓ.
13. Same-side interior angles lie on the same side of the transversal j, between lines k and ℓ.

outside / same / corresponding / lines / alternate

14. Sudeep walks back and forth along parallel segments in his yard. Then he walks back diagonally across the yard. Identify each of the following in the figure.

a. a transversal line r
b. corresponding angles ∠1 and ∠3 or ∠2 and ∠4
c. alternate interior angles ∠2 and ∠3
d. alternate exterior angles ∠1 and ∠4

PRACTICE AND PROBLEM SOLVING

Independent Practice	
For Exercises	See Example
14–17	1
18–21	2
22–25	3

Extra Practice
Skills Practice p. S8
Application Practice p. S30

Identify each of the following. Possible answers:

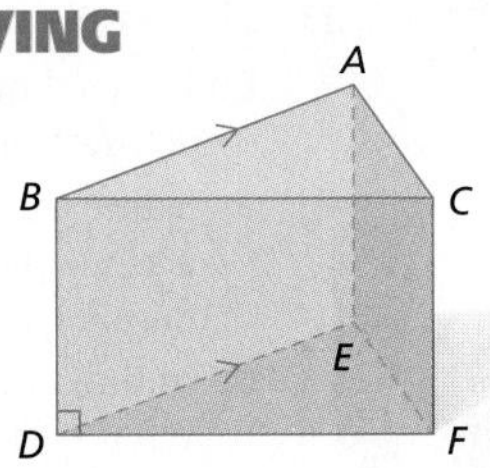

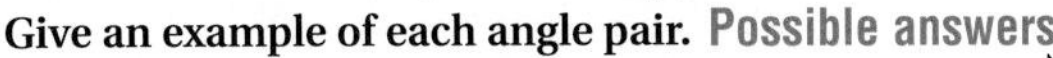

14. one pair of parallel segments $\overline{AB} \parallel \overline{DE}$

15. one pair of skew segments $\overline{AB}$ and $\overline{CF}$ are skew.

16. one pair of perpendicular segments $\overline{BD} \perp \overline{DF}$

17. one pair of parallel planes plane $ABC \parallel$ plane DEF

Give an example of each angle pair. Possible answers:

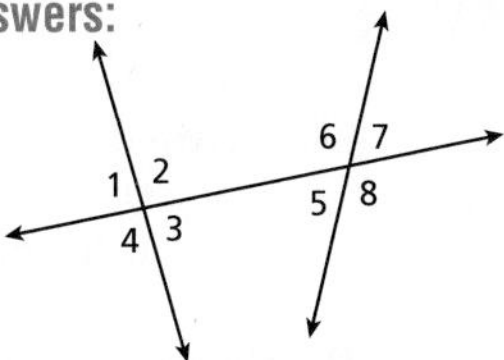

18. same-side interior angles $\angle 2$ and $\angle 6$

19. alternate exterior angles $\angle 1$ and $\angle 8$

20. corresponding angles $\angle 1$ and $\angle 6$

21. alternate interior angles $\angle 2$ and $\angle 5$

Identify the transversal and classify each angle pair.

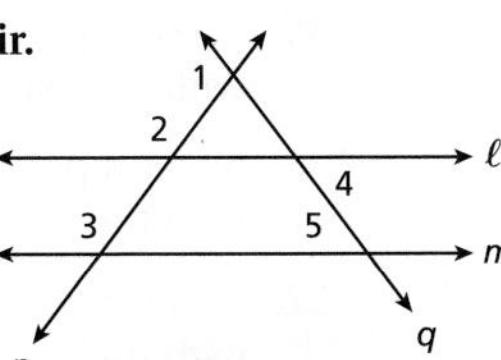

22. $\angle 2$ and $\angle 3$ transv.: p; corr. ∠s

23. $\angle 4$ and $\angle 5$ transv.: q; alt. int. ∠s

24. $\angle 2$ and $\angle 4$ transv.: ℓ; alt. ext. ∠s

25. $\angle 1$ and $\angle 2$ transv.: p; same-side int. ∠s

26. **Sports** A football player runs across the 30-yard line at an angle. He continues in a straight line and crosses the goal line at the same angle. Describe two parallel lines and a transversal in the diagram. The 30-yard line and goal line are ∥, and the path of the runner is the transv.

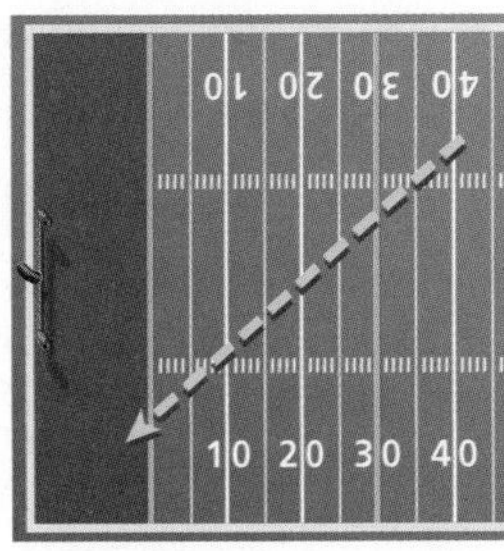

Name the type of angle pair shown in each letter. Possible answers:

27. F corr. ∠s

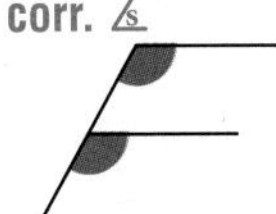

28. Z alt. int. ∠s

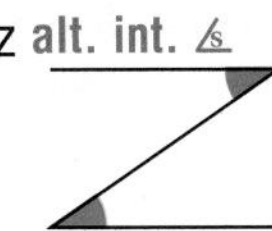

29. C same-side int. ∠s

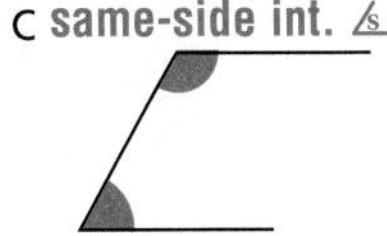

LINK

Entertainment

In an Ames room, two people of the same height that are standing in different parts of the room appear to be different sizes.

Entertainment Use the following information for Exercises 30–32.

In an Ames room, the floor is tilted and the back wall is closer to the front wall on one side.

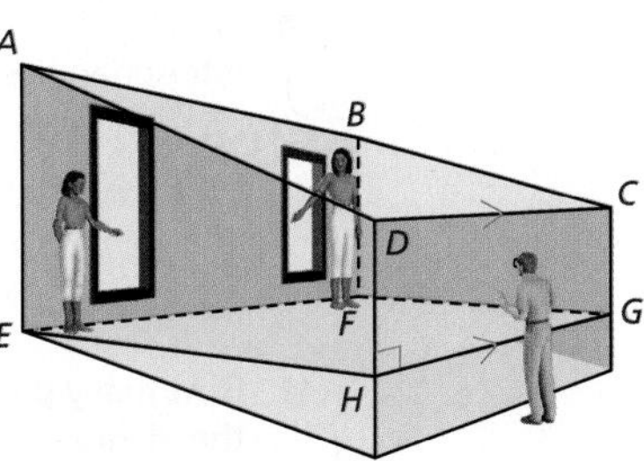

30. Name a pair of parallel segments in the diagram. $\overline{CD} \parallel \overline{GH}$

31. Name a pair of skew segments in the diagram. Possible answer: $\overline{CD}$ and $\overline{FG}$

32. Name a pair of perpendicular segments in the diagram. $\overline{DH} \perp \overline{GH}$

COMMON ERROR ALERT

In **Exercises 38–40,** some students may have difficulty choosing the correct transversal because three intersecting lines can be visually distracting. Suggest that these students redraw or trace the diagram for each exercise, labeling only the necessary angles.

Teaching Tip **Kinesthetic** Students who have trouble visualizing skew lines in **Exercise 15** may benefit from building models of skew lines and parallel lines out of straws or toothpicks.

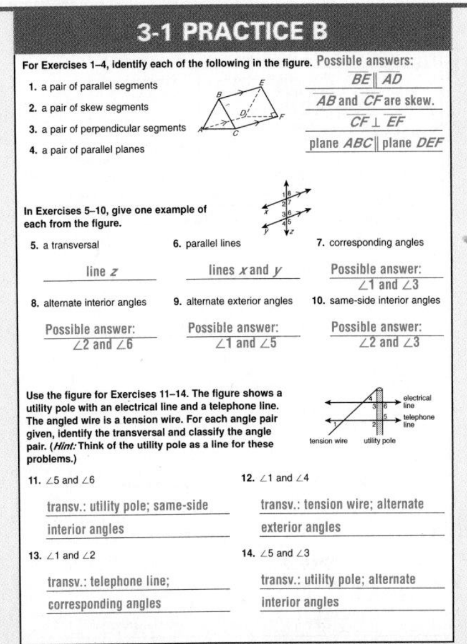

3-1 PRACTICE B

For Exercises 1–4, identify each of the following in the figure. Possible answers:

1. a pair of parallel segments $\overline{BE} \parallel \overline{AD}$
2. a pair of skew segments $\overline{AB}$ and $\overline{CF}$ are skew.
3. a pair of perpendicular segments $\overline{CF} \perp \overline{EF}$
4. a pair of parallel planes plane $ABC \parallel$ plane DEF

In Exercises 5–10, give one example of each from the figure.

5. a transversal line z
6. parallel lines lines x and y
7. corresponding angles Possible answer: $\angle 1$ and $\angle 3$
8. alternate interior angles Possible answer: $\angle 2$ and $\angle 6$
9. alternate exterior angles Possible answer: $\angle 1$ and $\angle 5$
10. same-side interior angles Possible answer: $\angle 2$ and $\angle 3$

Use the figure for Exercises 11–14. The figure shows a utility pole with an electrical line and a telephone line. The angled wire is a tension wire. For each angle pair given, identify the transversal and classify the angle pair. (*Hint:* Think of the utility pole as a line for these problems.)

electrical line
telephone line
tension wire
utility pole

11. $\angle 5$ and $\angle 6$ transv.: utility pole; same-side interior angles
12. $\angle 1$ and $\angle 4$ transv.: tension wire; alternate exterior angles
13. $\angle 1$ and $\angle 2$ transv.: telephone line; corresponding angles
14. $\angle 5$ and $\angle 3$ transv.: utility pole; alternate interior angles

3-1 PRACTICE C

For Exercises 1–4, sketch an example and state the apparent relationship between lines j and ℓ.

1. Line j is parallel to line k and line ℓ is parallel to line k. Lines ℓ and j are coplanar.
   Possible answer: 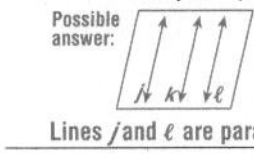
   Lines j and ℓ are parallel.
2. Line k is perpendicular to lines j and ℓ. Lines ℓ and j are not coplanar. 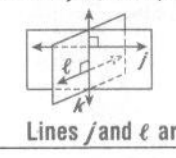
   Lines j and ℓ are skew.
3. Line k is parallel to line j. Line ℓ is perpendicular to line k. Lines ℓ and j are coplanar. 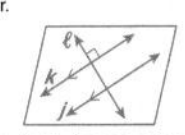
   Lines j and ℓ are perpendicular.
4. Line j is parallel to line k and line ℓ is parallel to line k. Lines ℓ, k, and j are not coplanar. 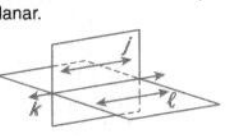
   Lines j and ℓ are parallel.

Luke and JoAnne make up a game. For a game board, they draw two lines crossed by a transversal and then they take turns placing and in the angles. Corresponding angles score 10, alternate interior angles score 20, alternate exterior angles score 30, and same-side interior angles score 40. Tally the score for and on each game board below.

5. = 10; = 10
6. = 40; = 80

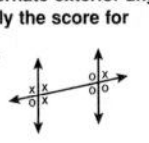

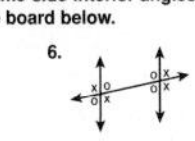

Draw a filled-in game board that satisfies each condition.

7. Neither player scores any points. 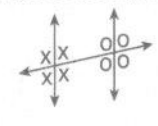
8. X scores the maximum possible amount.

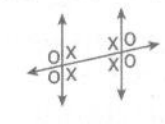

MULTI-STEP TEST PREP **Exercise 33** involves identifying parallel and nonparallel planes. This exercise prepares students for the Multi-Step Test Prep on page 180.

TEST PREP DOCTOR If students have difficulty with **Exercise 44,** review the meanings of *alternate* and *interior*. Ask students to identify which two angles are on opposite sides of the transversal and between the other two lines.

In **Exercise 46,** remind students who did not choose **C** that since all of the lines in the diagram lie in the same plane, none of them can be skew.

Answers

33a. plane *MNR* || plane *KLP*; plane *LMQ* || plane *KNP*; plane *PQR* || plane *KLM*

b. same-side int. ∠s

34. parallel or skew;

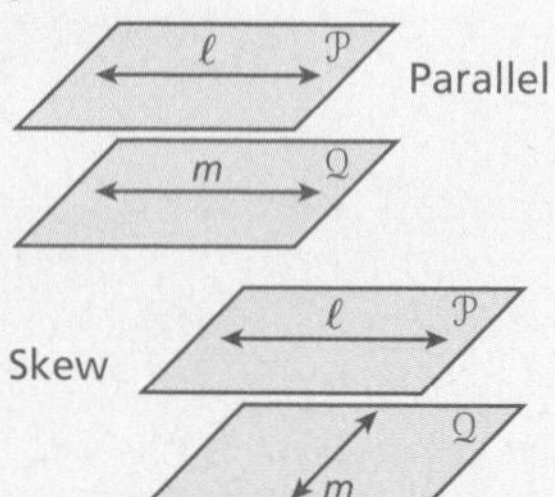

43. Possible answer: In a room, the intersection of the front wall and ceiling forms part of one line, and the intersection of the right wall and the floor forms part of another line. The two lines are skew.

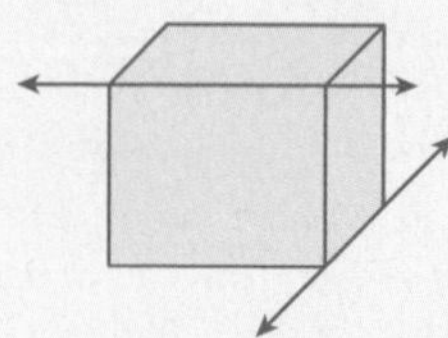

MULTI-STEP TEST PREP

33. This problem will prepare you for the Multi-Step Test Prep on p 180.
Buildings that are tilted like the one shown are sometimes called mystery spots.
  a. Name a plane parallel to plane *KLP*, a plane parallel to plane *KNP*, and a plane parallel to *KLM*.
  b. In the diagram, $\overline{QR}$ is a transversal to $\overline{PQ}$ and $\overline{RS}$. What type of angle pair is ∠*PQR* and ∠*QRS*?

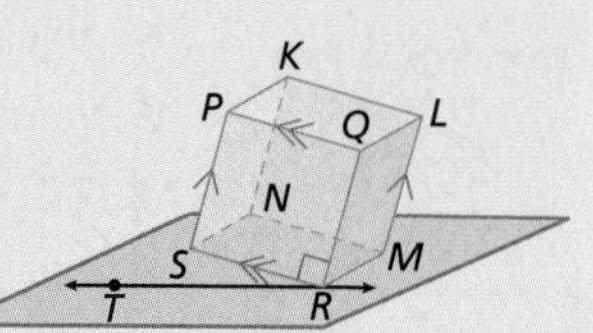

34. **Critical Thinking** Line ℓ is contained in plane *P* and line *m* is contained in plane *Q*. If *P* and *Q* are parallel, what are the possible classifications of ℓ and *m*? Include diagrams to support your answer.

Use the diagram for Exercises 35–40. Possible answers:

35. Name a pair of alternate interior angles with transversal *n*. ∠5 and ∠8
36. Name a pair of same-side interior angles with transversal ℓ. ∠2 and ∠7
37. Name a pair of corresponding angles with transversal *m*. ∠1 and ∠5
38. Identify the transversal and classify the angle pair for ∠3 and ∠7. transv.: ℓ; corr. ∠s

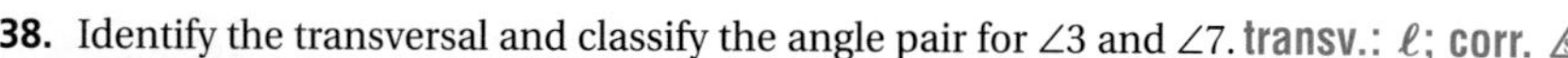

39. Identify the transversal and classify the angle pair for ∠5 and ∠8. transv.: *m*; alt. int. ∠s
40. Identify the transversal and classify the angle pair for ∠1 and ∠6. transv.: *m*; alt. ext. ∠s
41. **Aviation** Describe the type of lines formed by two planes when flight 1449 is flying from San Francisco to Atlanta at 32,000 feet and flight 2390 is flying from Dallas to Chicago at 28,000 feet. The lines are skew.

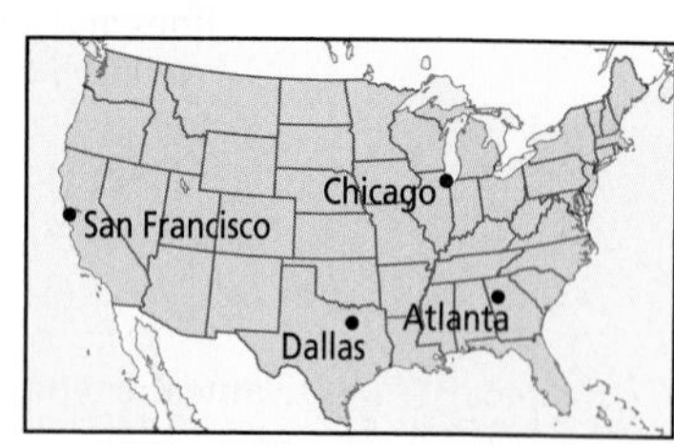

42. **Multi-Step** Draw line *p*, then draw two lines *m* and *n* that are both perpendicular to *p*. Make a conjecture about the relationship between lines *m* and *n*. *m* || *n*

43. **Write About It** Discuss a real-world example of skew lines. Include a sketch.

TEST PREP

44. Which pair of angles in the diagram are alternate interior angles?
  (A) ∠1 and ∠5
  (B) ∠2 and ∠6
  (C) ∠7 and ∠5
  (D) ∠2 and ∠3

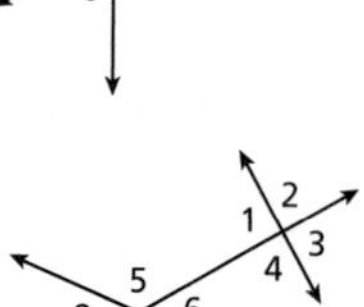

45. How many pairs of corresponding angles are in the diagram?
  (F) 2
  (G) 4
  (H) 8
  (J) 16

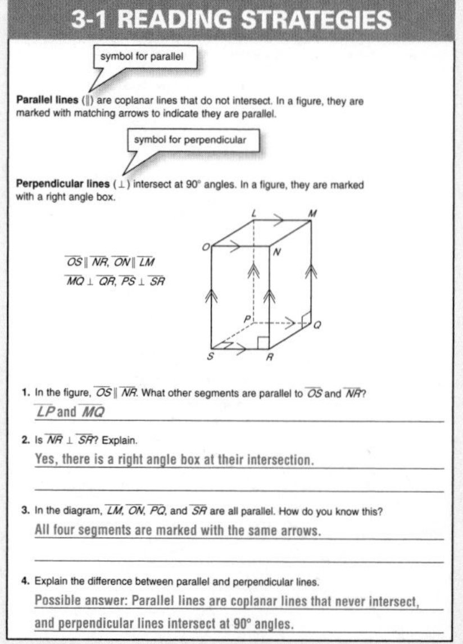

3-1 READING STRATEGIES

symbol for parallel

Parallel lines (||) are coplanar lines that do not intersect. In a figure, they are marked with matching arrows to indicate they are parallel.

symbol for perpendicular

Perpendicular lines (⊥) intersect at 90° angles. In a figure, they are marked with a right angle box.

$\overline{OS} \parallel \overline{NR}$, $\overline{ON} \parallel \overline{LM}$
$\overline{MQ} \perp \overline{QR}$, $\overline{PS} \perp \overline{SR}$

1. In the figure, $\overline{OS} \parallel \overline{NR}$. What other segments are parallel to $\overline{OS}$ and $\overline{NR}$?
$\overline{LP}$ and $\overline{MQ}$
2. Is $\overline{NR} \perp \overline{SR}$? Explain.
Yes, there is a right angle box at their intersection.
3. In the diagram, $\overline{LM}$, $\overline{ON}$, $\overline{PQ}$, and $\overline{SR}$ are all parallel. How do you know this?
All four segments are marked with the same arrows.
4. Explain the difference between parallel and perpendicular lines.
Possible answer: Parallel lines are coplanar lines that never intersect, and perpendicular lines intersect at 90° angles.

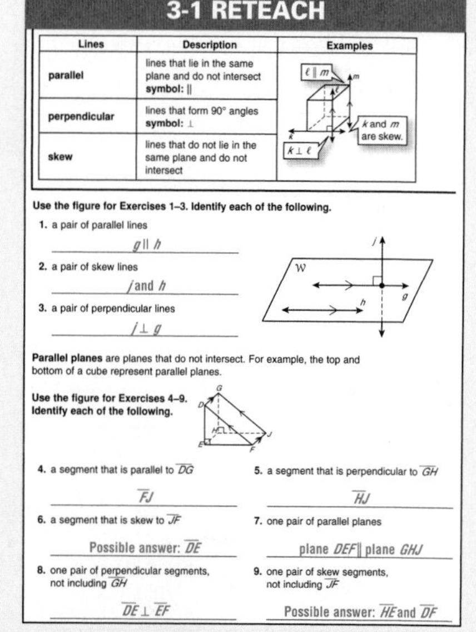

3-1 RETEACH

Lines	Description	Examples
parallel	lines that lie in the same plane and do not intersect **symbol:** ||	ℓ || m
perpendicular	lines that form 90° angles **symbol:** ⊥	k ⊥ ℓ
skew	lines that do not lie in the same plane and do not intersect	k and m are skew.

Use the figure for Exercises 1–3. Identify each of the following.

1. a pair of parallel lines
g || *h*
2. a pair of skew lines
j and *h*
3. a pair of perpendicular lines
j ⊥ *g*

Parallel planes are planes that do not intersect. For example, the top and bottom of a cube represent parallel planes.

Use the figure for Exercises 4–9. Identify each of the following.

4. a segment that is parallel to $\overline{DG}$
$\overline{FJ}$
5. a segment that is perpendicular to $\overline{GH}$
$\overline{HJ}$
6. a segment that is skew to $\overline{JF}$
Possible answer: $\overline{DE}$
7. one pair of parallel planes
plane *DEF* || plane *GHJ*
8. one pair of perpendicular segments, not including $\overline{GH}$
$\overline{DE} \perp \overline{EF}$
9. one pair of skew segments, not including $\overline{JF}$
Possible answer: $\overline{HE}$ and $\overline{DF}$

46. Which type of lines are NOT represented in the diagram?

Ⓐ Parallel lines
(C) Skew lines (circled)
Ⓑ Intersecting lines
Ⓓ Perpendicular lines

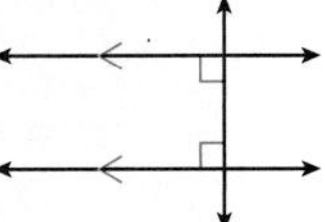

47. For two lines and a transversal, ∠1 and ∠8 are alternate exterior angles, and ∠1 and ∠5 are corresponding angles. Classify the angle pair ∠5 and ∠8.

(F) Vertical angles (circled)
Ⓖ Alternate interior angles
Ⓗ Adjacent angles
Ⓙ Same-side interior angles

48. Which angles in the diagram are NOT corresponding angles?

Ⓐ ∠1 and ∠5
Ⓒ ∠4 and ∠8
Ⓑ ∠2 and ∠6
(D) ∠2 and ∠7 (circled)

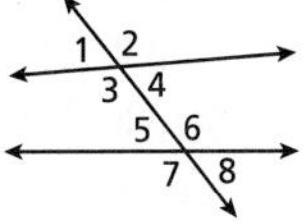

CHALLENGE AND EXTEND

Name all the angle pairs of each type in the diagram. Identify the transversal for each pair.

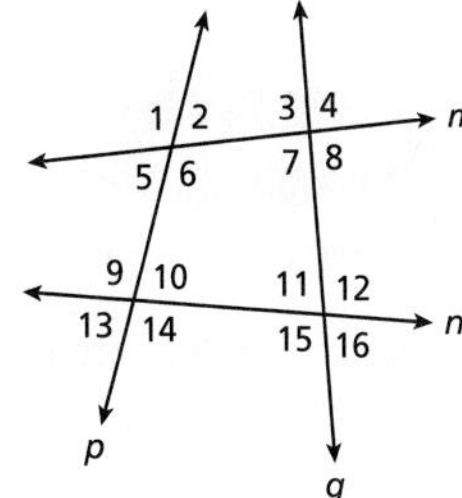

49. corresponding
50. alternate interior
51. alternate exterior
52. same-side interior
53. **Multi-Step** Draw two lines and a transversal such that ∠1 and ∠3 are corresponding angles, ∠1 and ∠2 are alternate interior angles, and ∠3 and ∠4 are alternate exterior angles. What type of angle pair is ∠2 and ∠4? corr. ∠s
54. If the figure shown is folded to form a cube, which faces of the cube will be parallel? the red and orange faces, the blue and purple faces, and the yellow and green faces

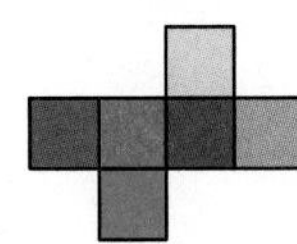

SPIRAL REVIEW

Evaluate each function for $x = -1, 0, 1, 2,$ and 3. *(Previous course)*

55. $y = 4x^2 - 7$
−3; −7; −3; 9; 29
56. $y = -2x^2 + 5$
3; 5; 3; −3; −13
57. $y = (x + 3)(x - 3)$
−8; −9; −8;−5; 0

Find the circumference and area of each circle. Use the π key on your calculator and round to the nearest tenth. *(Lesson 1-5)*

58. 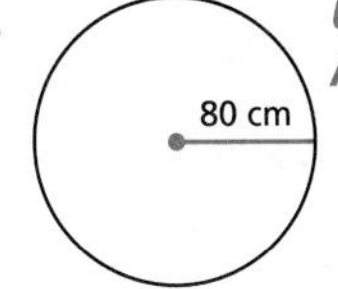

$C = 502.7$ cm; $A = 20{,}106.2\ \text{cm}^2$

59. 3.8 m
$C = 11.9$ m; $A = 11.3\ \text{m}^2$

Write a justification for each statement, given that ∠1 and ∠3 are right angles. *(Lesson 2-6)*

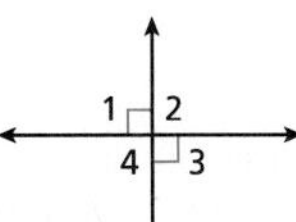

60. ∠1 ≅ ∠3 Rt. ∠ ≅ Thm. or Vert. ∠s Thm.
61. m∠1 + m∠2 = 180° Lin. Pair Thm.
62. ∠2 ≅ ∠4 Vert. ∠s Thm.

COMMON ERROR ALERT

In **Exercise 47,** students who try to visualize the angles may be less likely to choose the correct answer. Encourage students to first draw a sketch showing the given relationships among ∠1, ∠5, and ∠8.

Answers

49–53. See p. A13.

Journal

Have students draw a cube with each vertex labeled. Ask them to list a pair of perpendicular segments, a pair of parallel segments, and a pair of skew segments.

ALTERNATIVE ASSESSMENT

Have students sketch two parallel planes. Include an example of parallel lines, perpendicular lines, and skew lines in the sketch. Then have them sketch two lines cut by a transversal. Ask them to identify all pairs of alternate interior angles, alternate exterior angles, same-side interior angles, and corresponding angles.

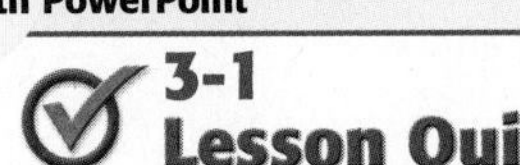

3-1 Lesson Quiz

Identify each of the following.

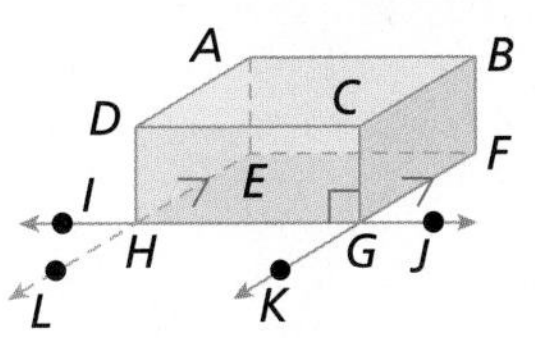

1. one pair of parallel segments $\overline{EH} \parallel \overline{FG}$
2. one pair of skew segments $\overline{BF}$ and $\overline{EH}$
3. one pair of perpendicular segments $\overline{CG} \perp \overline{GH}$
4. one pair of parallel planes *ABC* and *EFG*
5. one pair of alternate interior angles ∠*EHG* and ∠*HGK*
6. one pair of corresponding angles ∠*EHG* and ∠*FGJ*
7. one pair of alternate exterior angles ∠*IHE* and ∠*JGK*
8. one pair of same-side interior angles ∠*EHG* and ∠*HGF*

Also available on transparency

3-1 PROBLEM SOLVING

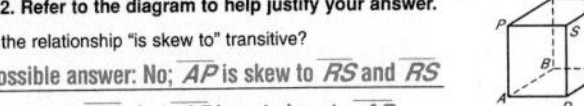

Use the diagram of the rectangular box for Exercises 1 and 2. Refer to the diagram to help justify your answer.

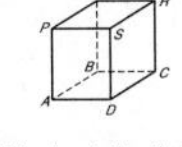

1. Is the relationship "is skew to" transitive?
Possible answer: No; $\overline{AP}$ is skew to $\overline{RS}$ and $\overline{RS}$ is skew to $\overline{AD}$, but $\overline{AP}$ is not skew to $\overline{AD}$.
2. If a segment is skew to one of two parallel segments, must it be skew to the other?
Possible answer: No; $\overline{PQ}$ is skew to $\overline{AD}$ but not to $\overline{PS}$.

Use the flag of Puerto Rico for Exercises 3 and 4.

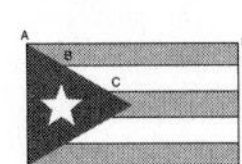

3. If ∠*DFC* and ∠*ACF* are same-side interior angles, identify the transversal.
$\overline{CF}$
4. Name a pair of alternate interior angles if the transversal is $\overline{BE}$.
Possible answer: ∠*DEB* and ∠*CBE*

Choose the best answer.

5. Describe the type of lines suggested by the two skis of a person water skiing.
A intersecting lines
(B) parallel lines (circled)
C perpendicular lines
D skew lines
6. Describe the type of lines suggested by the paths of two people at a fair when one person is riding the aerial ride from one end of the fair to the other, and the other person is walking in a different direction on the ground.
F intersecting
H perpendicular
G parallel
(J) skew (circled)
7. In the quilt pattern, which is a true statement about the angles formed by the transversal $\overline{HK}$ and $\overline{HM}$ and $\overline{JL}$?
(A) ∠*LSK* and ∠*PHQ* are corresponding angles. (circled)
B ∠*JSQ* and ∠*JQH* are corresponding angles.
C ∠*LSK* and ∠*QSJ* are same-side interior angles.
D ∠*PHQ* and ∠*RLS* are same-side interior angles.

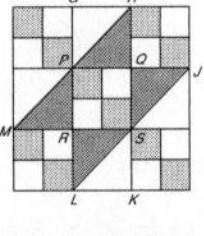

3-1 CHALLENGE

In Euclidean geometry, a line is a straight path that extends forever in two directions in a plane. In *spherical geometry,* a line is a **great circle.** This is a circle that divides a sphere into equal halves.

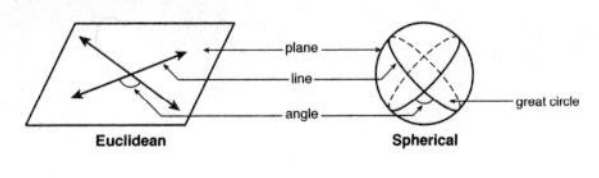

Answer *yes* or *no* for Exercises 1 and 2.

1. Does a line have endpoints in Euclidean geometry? in spherical geometry?
no; no
2. Does a line have a measurable length in Euclidean geometry? in spherical geometry?
no; yes

Use the figures at right for Exercises 3 and 4.

In each figure, *P*, *Q*, and *R* are collinear points and *R* is between points *P* and *Q*.

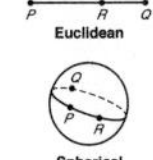

3. In the Euclidean figure, what conclusion is drawn from the Segment Addition Postulate?
$PR + RQ = PQ$
4. Can you draw the same conclusion about the spherical figure? Explain.
The distance $PR + RQ$, the length of the path from *P* to *Q* traveling in a *counterclockwise* direction, is much longer than the length of the path traveling from *P* to *Q* in a *clockwise* direction. So, $PR + RQ \neq PQ$.

Each statement below is true in Euclidean geometry. Explain why it is false in spherical geometry.

5. If two lines intersect, then their intersection is exactly one point.
Any two lines will intersect at exactly two points.
6. One and only one line contains two given points.
If the two points are at opposite "poles," then infinitely many lines will pass through them.

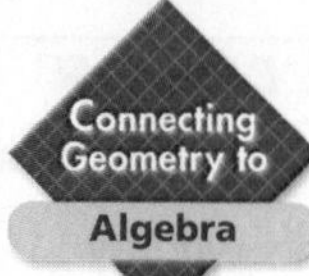

Organizer

Pacing:
Traditional $\frac{1}{2}$ day
Block $\frac{1}{4}$ day

Objective: Find angle measures by solving systems of equations.

Teach

Remember

Review with students the properties of vertical angles and linear pairs and how to solve systems of equations.

Inclusion Some students may prefer solving systems of equations by other methods, such as graphing or substitution.

Close

Assess

Have students draw two intersecting lines and measure the angles formed. Have them choose values of x and y, and then write linear expressions in terms of x and y for two of the angle measures to form a system of equations. Have them show how to solve the system to find x and y.

Systems of Equations

Sometimes angle measures are given as algebraic expressions. When you know the relationship between two angles, you can write and solve a system of equations to find angle measures.

Solving Systems of Equations by Using Elimination

Step 1 Write the system so that like terms are under one another.
Step 2 Eliminate one of the variables.
Step 3 Substitute that value into one of the original equations and solve.
Step 4 Write the answers as an ordered pair, (x, y).
Step 5 Check your solution.

Example 1

Solve for x and y.

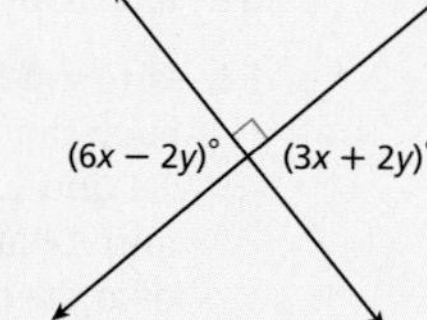

Since the lines are perpendicular, all of the angles are right angles. To write two equations, you can set each expression equal to 90°.

$$(3x + 2y)^\circ = 90^\circ,\ (6x - 2y)^\circ = 90^\circ$$

Step 1	$3x + 2y = 90$ $\underline{6x - 2y = 90}$	*Write the system so that like terms are under one another.*
Step 2	$9x + 0 = 180$	*Add like terms on each side of the equations. The y-term has been eliminated.*
	$x = 20$	*Divide both sides by 9 to solve for x.*
Step 3	$3x + 2y = 90$	*Write one of the original equations.*
	$3(20) + 2y = 90$	*Substitute 20 for x.*
	$60 + 2y = 90$	*Simplify.*
	$2y = 30$	*Subtract 60 from both sides.*
	$y = 15$	*Divide by 2 on both sides.*
Step 4	$(20, 15)$	*Write the solution as an ordered pair.*
Step 5	Check the solution by substituting 20 for x and 15 for y in the original equations.	

$3x + 2y$	$= 90$
$3(20) + 2(15)$	90
$60 + 30$	90
90	90 ✓

$6x - 2y$	$= 90$
$6(20) - 2(15)$	90
$120 - 30$	90
90	90 ✓

In some cases, before you can do Step 1 you will need to multiply one or both of the equations by a number so that you can eliminate a variable.

Example 2

Solve for x and y.

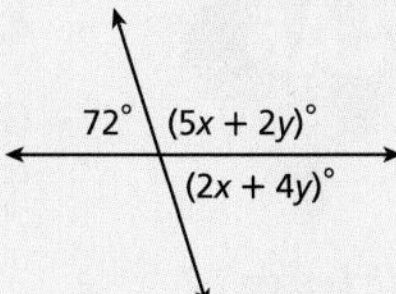

$(2x + 4y)^\circ = 72^\circ$ *Vertical Angles Theorem*

$(5x + 2y)^\circ = 108^\circ$ *Linear Pair Theorem*

The equations cannot be added or subtracted to eliminate a variable. Multiply the second equation by -2 to get opposite y-coefficients.

$5x + 2y = 108 \rightarrow -2(5x + 2y) = -2(108) \rightarrow -10x - 4y = -216$

Step 1 $2x + 4y = 72$; $-10x - 4y = -216$ *Write the system so that like terms are under one another.*

Step 2 $-8x = -144$ *Add like terms on both sides of the equations. The y-term has been eliminated.*

$x = 18$ *Divide both sides by −8 to solve for x.*

Step 3 $2x + 4y = 72$ *Write one of the original equations.*

$2(18) + 4y = 72$ *Substitute 18 for x.*

$36 + 4y = 72$ *Simplify.*

$4y = 36$ *Subtract 36 from both sides.*

$y = 9$ *Divide by 4 on both sides.*

Step 4 $(18, 9)$ *Write the solution as an ordered pair.*

Step 5 Check the solution by substituting 18 for x and 9 for y in the original equations.

$2x + 4y$	$= 72$
$2(18) + 4(9)$	72
$36 + 36$	72
72	72 ✓

$5x + 2y$	$= 108$
$5(18) + 2(9)$	108
$90 + 18$	108
108	108 ✓

Try This

Solve for x and y.

1. $x = 5;\ y = 10$

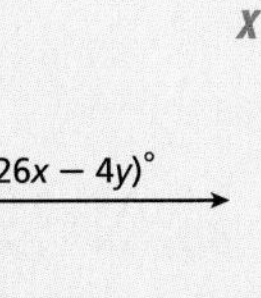

2. $x = 6;\ y = 9$

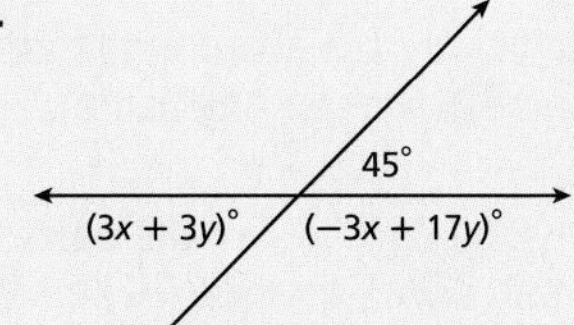

3. $x = 4;\ y = 12$

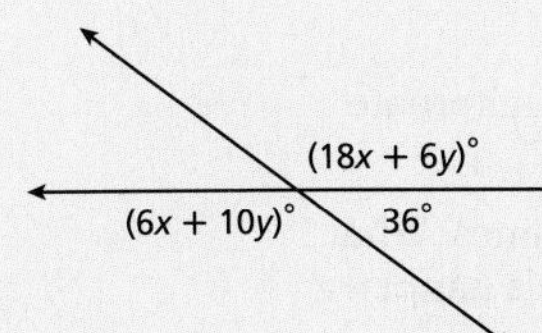

4. $x = 2;\ y = 13$

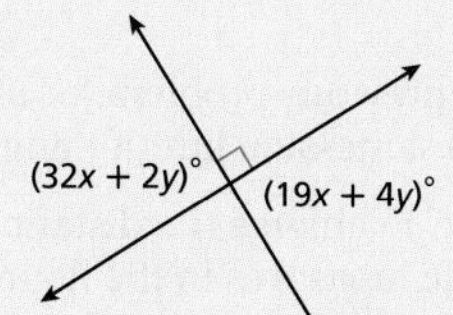

Connecting Geometry to Algebra 153

Organizer

Use with Lesson 3-2

Pacing:
Traditional $\frac{1}{2}$ day
Block $\frac{1}{4}$ day

Objective: Use geometry software to explore angles formed by parallel lines and transversals.

Materials: geometry software

Online Edition
TechKeys

Countdown Week 5

Resources

Technology Lab Activities
3-2 Lab Recording Sheet

Teach

Discuss

Ask students what they think is true of any pair of angles they created. They are either supp. or ≅.

Close

Key Concept

For two parallel lines cut by a transversal, the corr., alt. int., and alt. ext. ∠s are ≅, and the same-side int. ∠s are supp.

Assessment

Journal Have students draw two nonparallel lines and a transversal, measure the angles formed, and make a conjecture.

State Resources

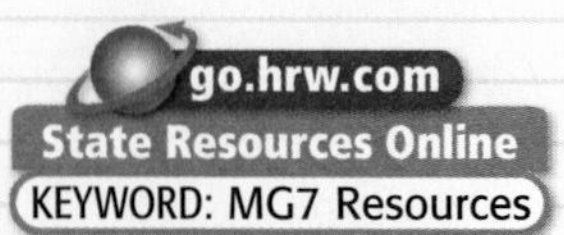

Explore Parallel Lines and Transversals

Use with Lesson 3-2

Geometry software can help you explore angles that are formed when a transversal intersects a pair of parallel lines.

Activity

1. Construct a line and label two points on the line *A* and *B*.

2. Create point *C* not on $\overleftrightarrow{AB}$. Construct a line parallel to $\overleftrightarrow{AB}$ through point *C*. Create another point on this line and label it *D*.

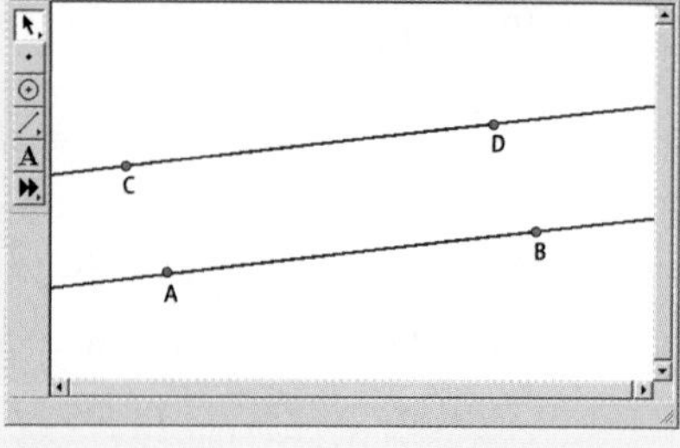

3. Create two points outside the two parallel lines and label them *E* and *F*. Construct transversal $\overleftrightarrow{EF}$. Label the points of intersection *G* and *H*.

4. Measure the angles formed by the parallel lines and the transversal. Write the angle measures in a chart like the one below. Drag point *E* or *F* and chart with the new angle measures. What relationships do you notice about the angle measures? What conjectures can you make?

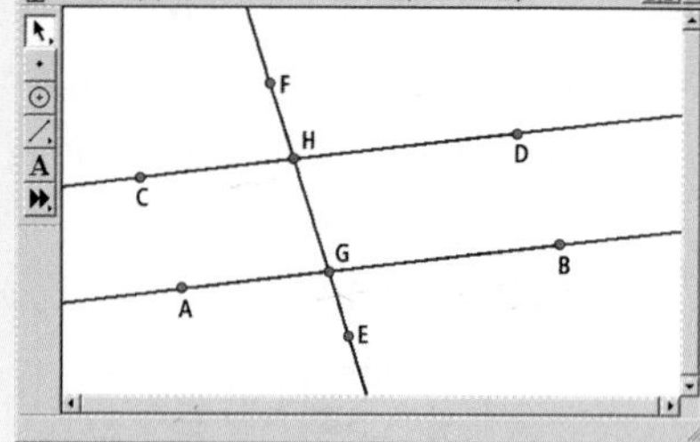

Angle	∠AGE	∠BGE	∠AGH	∠BGH	∠CHG	∠DHG	∠CHF	∠DHF
Measure	100°	80°	80°	100°	100°	80°	80°	100°
Measure	72°	108°	108°	72°	72°	108°	108°	72°

4. Possible measures are given in the table. Possible answer: All acute ∠s are ≅. All obtuse ∠s are ≅. Any acute ∠ is supp. to any obtuse ∠.

Try This

1. The corr. ∠s are the pairs *∠AGE* and *∠CHG*, *∠BGE* and *∠DHG*, *∠AGH* and *∠CHF*, and *∠BGH* and *∠DHF*. The ∠s in each pair have = measures.

1. Identify the pairs of corresponding angles in the diagram. What conjecture can you make about their angle measures? Drag a point in the figure to confirm your conjecture.
2. Repeat steps in the previous problem for alternate interior angles, alternate exterior angles, and same-side interior angles.
3. Try dragging point *C* to change the distance between the parallel lines. What happens to the angle measures in the figure? Why do you think this happens?

Answers to *Try This*

2. The alt. int. ∠s are the pairs ∠CHG and ∠BGH, and ∠AGH and ∠DHG.
The ∠s in each pair have = measures.
The alt. ext. ∠s are the pairs ∠AGE and ∠DHF, and ∠BGE and ∠CHF.
The ∠s in each pair have = measures.
The same-side int. ∠s are the pairs ∠CHG and ∠AGH, and ∠BGH and ∠DHG.
The angles in each pair have measures that add up to 180°.

3. Possible answer: If the || lines are dragged farther apart or closer together, there is no change in the ∠ measures. Since the lines remain ||, the amount of "tilt" of the line remains the same, so the ∠ measures remain the same.

3-2 Angles Formed by Parallel Lines and Transversals

Objective
Prove and use theorems about the angles formed by parallel lines and a transversal.

Who uses this?
Piano makers use parallel strings for the higher notes. The longer strings used to produce the lower notes can be viewed as transversals. (See Example 3.)

When parallel lines are cut by a transversal, the angle pairs formed are either congruent or supplementary.

Know it! Note

Postulate 3-2-1 Corresponding Angles Postulate

POSTULATE	HYPOTHESIS	CONCLUSION
If two parallel lines are cut by a transversal, then the pairs of corresponding angles are congruent.	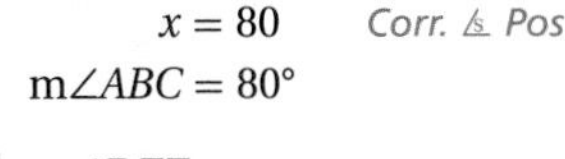	$\angle 1 \cong \angle 3$ $\angle 2 \cong \angle 4$ $\angle 5 \cong \angle 7$ $\angle 6 \cong \angle 8$

EXAMPLE 1 Using the Corresponding Angles Postulate

Find each angle measure.

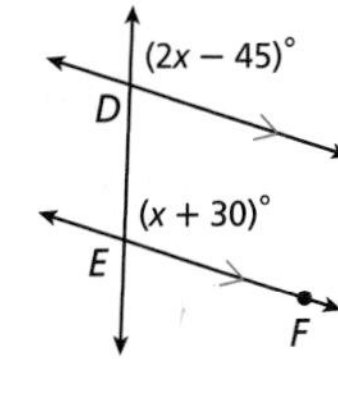

A $m\angle ABC$

$x = 80$ *Corr. ∡ Post.*

$m\angle ABC = 80°$

Algebra

B $m\angle DEF$

$(2x - 45)° = (x + 30)°$ *Corr. ∡ Post.*

$x - 45 = 30$ *Subtract x from both sides.*

$x = 75$ *Add 45 to both sides.*

$m\angle DEF = x + 30$

$= 75 + 30$ *Substitute 75 for x.*

$= 105°$

CHECK IT OUT! 1. Find $m\angle QRS$.
$m\angle QRS = 62°$

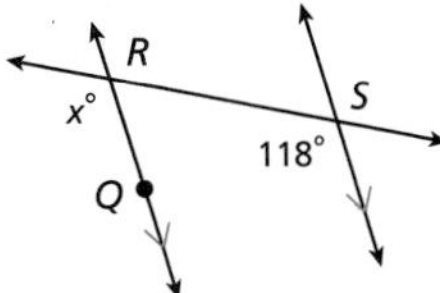

Remember that postulates are statements that are accepted without proof. Since the Corresponding Angles Postulate is given as a postulate, it can be used to prove the next three theorems.

3-2 Organizer

Pacing: Traditional 1 day
Block $\frac{1}{2}$ day

Objective: Prove and use theorems about the angles formed by parallel lines and a transversal.

Geometry Lab
In *Geometry Lab Activities*

Online Edition
Tutorial Videos, Interactivity

Countdown Week 5

Power Presentations with PowerPoint®

Warm Up

Identify each angle pair.

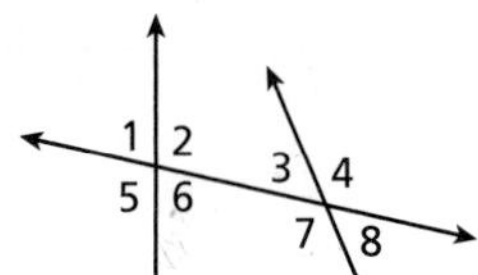

1. $\angle 1$ and $\angle 3$ corr. ∡
2. $\angle 3$ and $\angle 6$ alt. int. ∡
3. $\angle 4$ and $\angle 5$ alt. ext. ∡
4. $\angle 6$ and $\angle 7$ same-side int. ∡

Also available on transparency

Math Humor

Home owner: How do I know these two doors are the same size?

Carpenter: They're alternate exterior doors.

1 Introduce

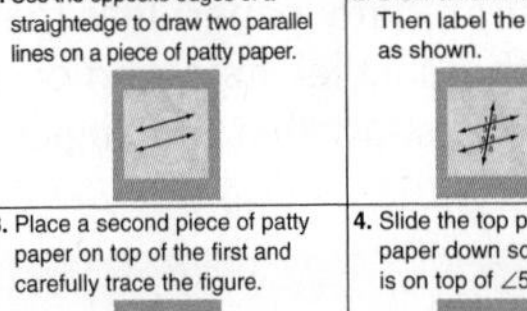

EXPLORATION

3-2 Angles Formed by Parallel Lines and Transversals

Use two pieces of patty paper to explore the angles formed by two parallel lines and a transversal.

1. Use the opposite edges of a straightedge to draw two parallel lines on a piece of patty paper.
2. Draw a transversal. Then label the angles as shown.
3. Place a second piece of patty paper on top of the first and carefully trace the figure.
4. Slide the top piece of paper down so that ∠1 is on top of ∠5.
5. How are the following pairs of angles related? ∠1 and ∠5 ∠1 and ∠8 ∠3 and ∠6 ∠3 and ∠5

THINK AND DISCUSS

6. Describe the pairs of congruent angles that are formed when parallel lines are cut by a transversal.

Motivate

Have students look through magazines to find pictures with parallel lines and transversals, such as bridges, fences, furniture, etc. Use markers or colored tape to mark the lines, and then identify angles that appear to be congruent and angles that appear to be supplementary.

Explorations and answers are provided in *Alternate Openers: Explorations Transparencies.*

State Resources

go.hrw.com
State Resources Online
KEYWORD: MG7 Resources

Power Presentations with PowerPoint®

Additional Examples

Example 1

Find each angle measure.

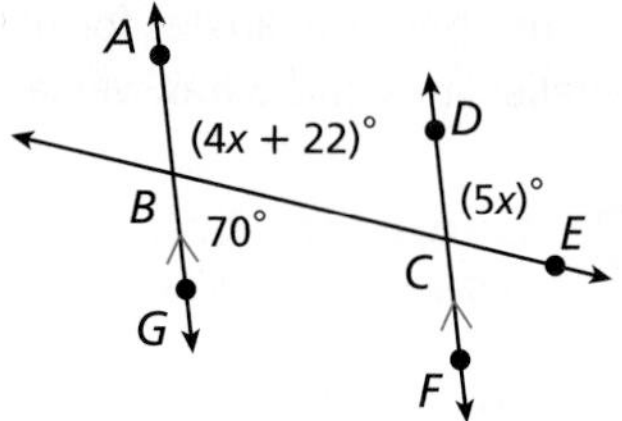

A. m∠*ECF* 70°

B. m∠*DCE* 110°

Example 2

Find each angle measure.

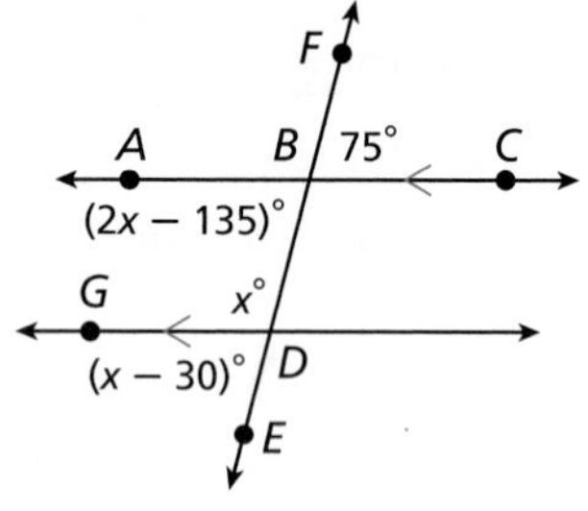

A. m∠*EDG* 75°

B. m∠*BDG* 105°

INTERVENTION

Questioning Strategies

EXAMPLES 1–2

- What theorem or postulate was used to find the answer in each part of the example? How was it used?
- What equation was used to find the answer?
- Is the answer always *x*? Why or why not?

Visual Have students use lined paper to draw two parallel lines and a transversal that is not perpendicular to the lines. Instruct students to shade the acute angles one color and the obtuse angles another color. Let students use a protractor (MK) to see that all the angles shaded the same color are congruent and that pairs of angles shaded different colors are supplementary. Protractors can be found in the Manipulatives Kit (MK).

Theorems Parallel Lines and Angle Pairs

	THEOREM	HYPOTHESIS	CONCLUSION
3-2-2	**Alternate Interior Angles Theorem** If two parallel lines are cut by a transversal, then the pairs of alternate interior angles are congruent.		∠1 ≅ ∠3 ∠2 ≅ ∠4
3-2-3	**Alternate Exterior Angles Theorem** If two parallel lines are cut by a transversal, then the two pairs of alternate exterior angles are congruent.		∠5 ≅ ∠7 ∠6 ≅ ∠8
3-2-4	**Same-Side Interior Angles Theorem** If two parallel lines are cut by a transversal, then the two pairs of same-side interior angles are supplementary.		m∠1 + m∠4 = 180° m∠2 + m∠3 = 180°

You will prove Theorems 3-2-3 and 3-2-4 in Exercises 25 and 26.

Helpful Hint

If a transversal is perpendicular to two parallel lines, all eight angles are congruent.

PROOF **Alternate Interior Angles Theorem**

Given: $\ell \parallel m$

Prove: ∠2 ≅ ∠3

Proof:

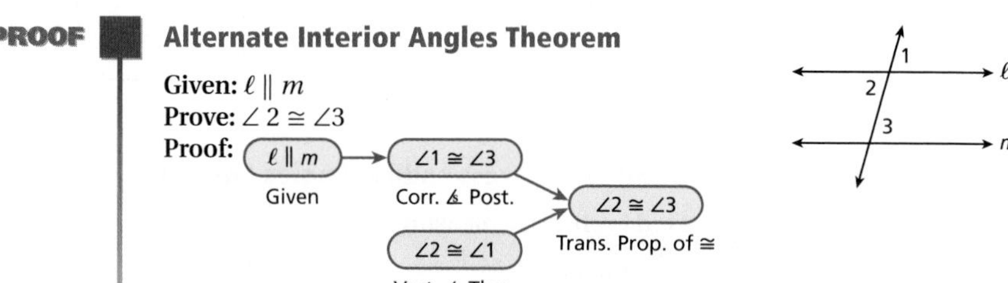

EXAMPLE 2 **Finding Angle Measures**

Find each angle measure.

A m∠*EDF*

$x = 125$

m∠*EDF* = 125° *Alt. Ext. ∠s Thm.*

Algebra

B m∠*TUS*

$13x° + 23x° = 180°$	*Same-Side Int. ∠s Thm.*
$36x = 180$	*Combine like terms.*
$x = 5$	*Divide both sides by 36.*
m∠*TUS* = 23(5) = 115°	*Substitute 5 for x.*

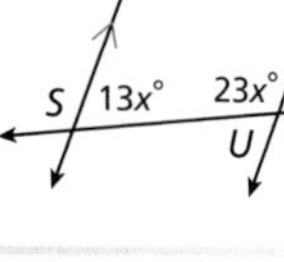

2. Find m∠*ABD*.

m∠*ABD* = 60°

2 Teach

Guided Instruction

Review pairs of angles that are formed when two lines are cut by a transversal. Discuss the angle measures when the two lines are parallel. Remind students that arrows on a figure indicate parallel lines.

Multiple Representations Draw parallel lines and a transversal on a transparency. Trace an acute angle and an obtuse angle onto another transparency, and move them over each angle to show congruence.

Reaching All Learners

Through Kinesthetic Experience

Have students draw a pair of parallel lines and a transversal on patty paper. Tear the paper between the parallel lines, and overlay the two parts to show that the angles are congruent.

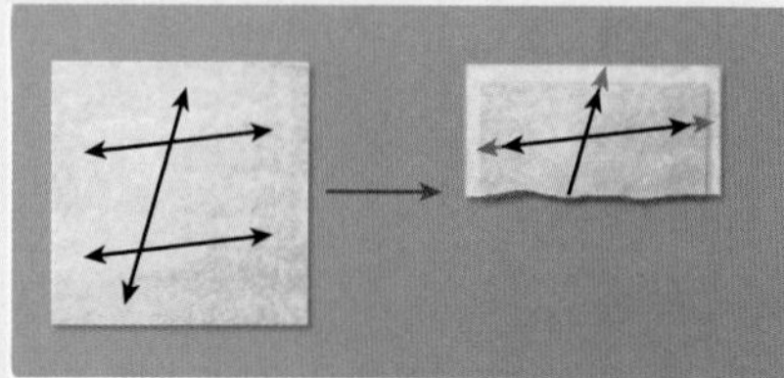

Student to Student

Parallel Lines and Transversals

Nancy Martin
East Branch
High School

When I solve problems with parallel lines and transversals, I remind myself that every pair of angles is either congruent or supplementary.

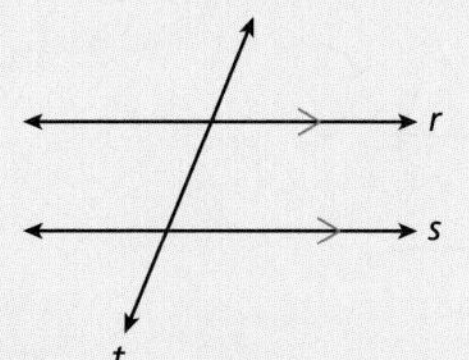

If r ∥ s, all the acute angles are congruent and all the obtuse angles are congruent. The acute angles are supplementary to the obtuse angles.

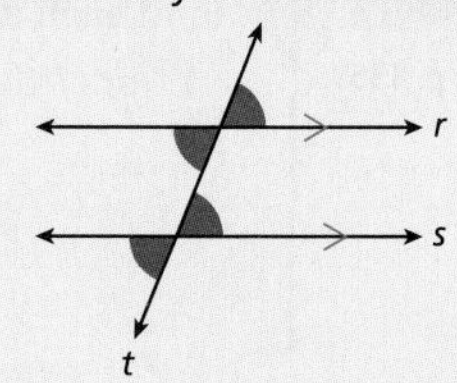

COMMON ERROR ALERT

Students may incorrectly apply the postulates and theorems presented in this lesson when lines cut by a transversal are not parallel. Remind them that the postulates and theorems are only true for parallel lines.

Teaching Tip **Auditory** As you work through the examples, call on students to read aloud the statement of each postulate or theorem when it is used as a justification in a solution.

EXAMPLE 3 Music Application

 Algebra

The treble strings of a grand piano are parallel. Viewed from above, the bass strings form transversals to the treble strings. Find x and y in the diagram.

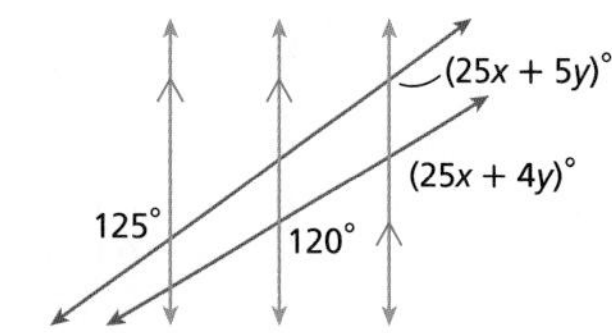

By the Alternate Exterior Angles Theorem, $(25x + 5y)^\circ = 125^\circ$.

By the Corresponding Angles Postulate, $(25x + 4y)^\circ = 120^\circ$.

$25x + 5y = 125$

$-(25x + 4y = 120)$ *Subtract the second equation from the first equation.*

$y = 5$

$25x + 5(5) = 125$ *Substitute 5 for y in 25x + 5y = 125. Simplify and solve for x.*

$x = 4, y = 5$

3. Find the measures of the acute angles in the diagram.
55° and 60°

Power Presentations with PowerPoint®

Additional Examples

Example 3

Find x and y in the diagram.

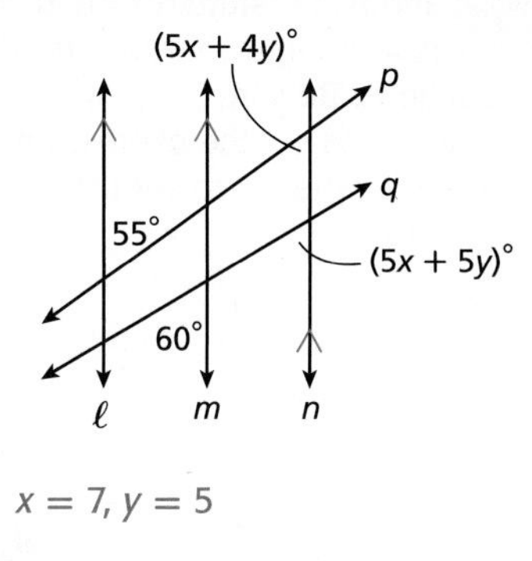

$x = 7, y = 5$

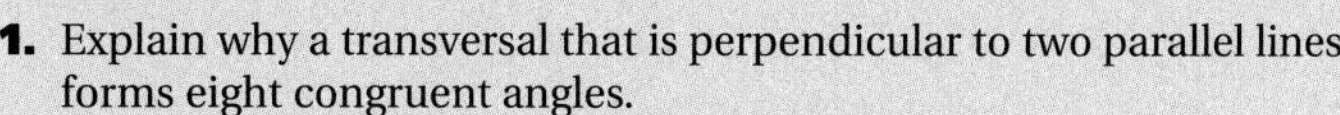

THINK AND DISCUSS

1. Explain why a transversal that is perpendicular to two parallel lines forms eight congruent angles.

2. **GET ORGANIZED** Copy the diagram and graphic organizer. Complete the graphic organizer by explaining why each of the three theorems is true.

INTERVENTION 

Questioning Strategies

EXAMPLE 3

- Which transversals intersect parallel lines?
- Which transversals intersect nonparallel lines?

3 Close

Summarize

Have students look at the diagram for the Corresponding Angles Postulate on p. 155. Have them identify the following:

Parallel lines *p* and *q*
Transversal *t*
Congruent angles:
Corresponding $\angle 1 \cong \angle 3$; $\angle 2 \cong \angle 4$; $\angle 5 \cong \angle 7$; $\angle 6 \cong \angle 8$
Alternate interior $\angle 2 \cong \angle 7$; $\angle 3 \cong \angle 6$
Alternate exterior $\angle 1 \cong \angle 8$; $\angle 4 \cong \angle 5$
Supplementary angles:
Same-side interior $\angle 2$ and $\angle 3$; $\angle 6$ and $\angle 7$

ONGOING ASSESSMENT and INTERVENTION 

Diagnose ***Before*** **the Lesson**
3-2 Warm Up, TE p. 155

Monitor ***During*** **the Lesson**
Check It Out! Exercises, SE pp. 155–157
Questioning Strategies, TE pp. 156–157

Assess ***After*** **the Lesson**
3-2 Lesson Quiz, TE p. 161
Alternative Assessment, TE p. 161

Answers to *Think and Discuss*

1. If the transv. is ⊥, all the ∠s formed are rt. ∠s, and all rt. ∠s are ≅.
2. See p. A3.

3-2 Exercises

Assignment Guide

Assign *Guided Practice* exercises as necessary.

If you finished Examples **1–3**

Basic 6–25, 29, 31, 33–36, 41–47

Average 6–12, 14–18 even, 20–38, 41–47

Advanced 6–12, 14–18 even, 20–30, 32–47

Homework Quick Check

Quickly check key concepts.

Exercises: 6, 8, 12, 20, 25

Teaching Tip

Algebra For **Exercises 7** and **9–11,** students need to write and solve multi-step equations. Be sure students know whether to set the expressions equal to each other or to set their sum equal to 180°.

State Resources

3-2 Exercises

go.hrw.com
Homework Help Online
KEYWORD: MG7 3-2
Parent Resources Online
KEYWORD: MG7 Parent

GUIDED PRACTICE

SEE EXAMPLE 1 p. 155

Find each angle measure.

1. m∠*JKL*

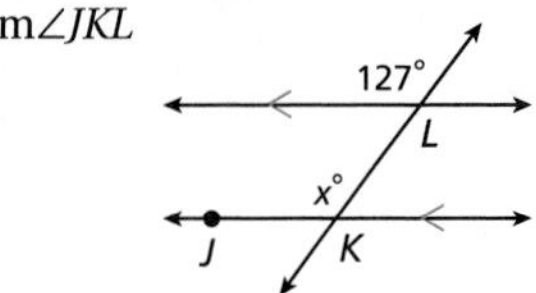

m∠*JKL* = 127°

2. m∠*BEF*

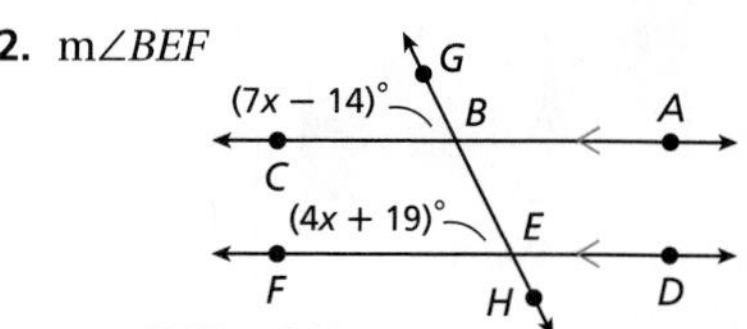

m∠*BEF* = 63°

SEE EXAMPLE 2 p. 156

3. m∠1

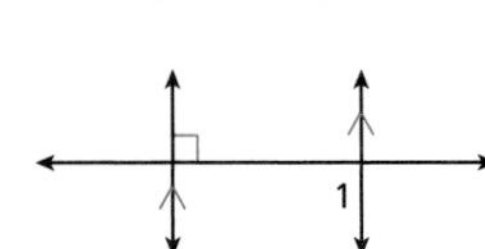

m∠1 = 90°

4. m∠*CBY*

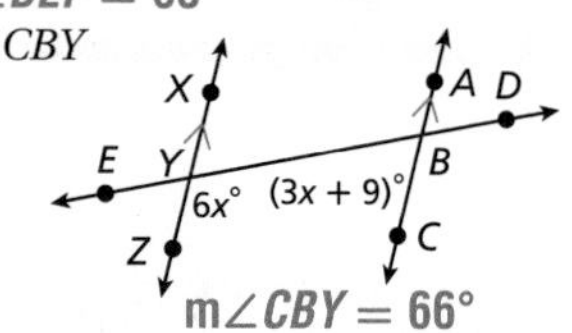

m∠*CBY* = 66°

SEE EXAMPLE 3 p. 157

5. Safety The railing of a wheelchair ramp is parallel to the ramp. Find *x* and *y* in the diagram.

x = 8; *y* = 9

PRACTICE AND PROBLEM SOLVING

Independent Practice

For Exercises	See Example
6–7	1
8–11	2
12	3

Extra Practice

Skills Practice p. S8

Application Practice p. S30

Find each angle measure.

6. m∠*KLM*

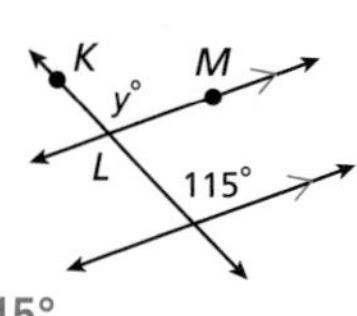

m∠*KLM* = 115°

7. m∠*VYX*

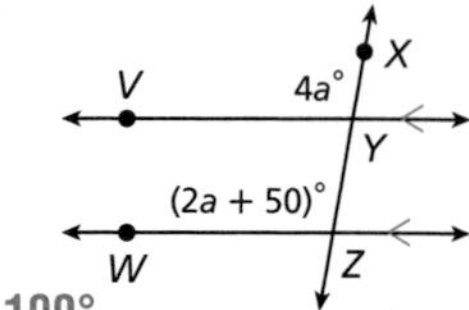

m∠*VYX* = 100°

8. m∠*ABC*

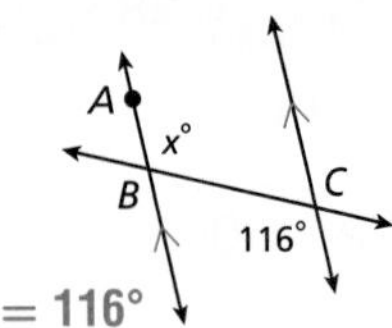

m∠*ABC* = 116°

9. m∠*EFG*

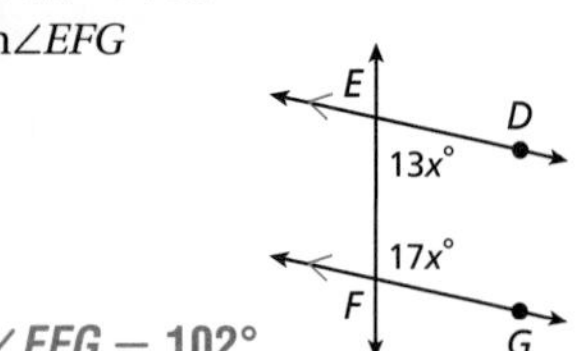

m∠*EFG* = 102°

10. m∠*PQR*

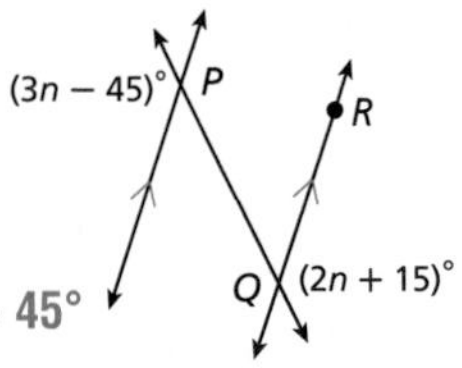

(3*n* − 45)° *P* *R* *Q* (2*n* + 15)°

m∠*PQR* = 45°

11. m∠*STU*

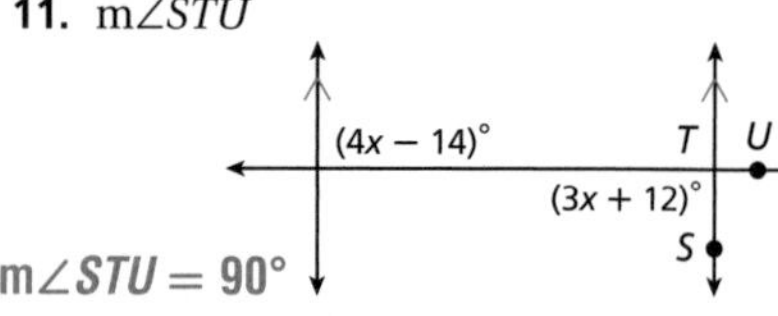

m∠*STU* = 90°

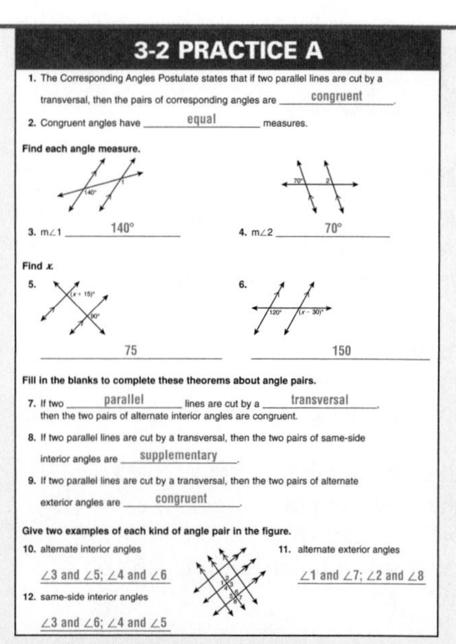

3-2 PRACTICE A

1. The Corresponding Angles Postulate states that if two parallel lines are cut by a transversal, then the pairs of corresponding angles are ___congruent___.
2. Congruent angles have ___equal___ measures.

Find each angle measure.

3. m∠1 ___140°___
4. m∠2 ___70°___

Find *x*.

5. ___75___
6. ___150___

Fill in the blanks to complete these theorems about angle pairs.

7. If two ___parallel___ lines are cut by a ___transversal___, then the two pairs of alternate interior angles are congruent.
8. If two parallel lines are cut by a transversal, then the two pairs of same-side interior angles are ___supplementary___.
9. If two parallel lines are cut by a transversal, then the two pairs of alternate exterior angles are ___congruent___.

Give two examples of each kind of angle pair in the figure.

10. alternate interior angles ___∠3 and ∠5; ∠4 and ∠6___
11. alternate exterior angles ___∠1 and ∠7; ∠2 and ∠8___
12. same-side interior angles ___∠3 and ∠6; ∠4 and ∠5___

13. 120°; Corr. ∠s Post.

14. 60°; Lin. Pair Thm.

15. 60°; Same-Side Int. ∠s Thm.

16. 120°; Alt. Int. ∠s Thm.

17. 60°; Lin. Pair Thm.

18. 60°; Lin. Pair Thm.

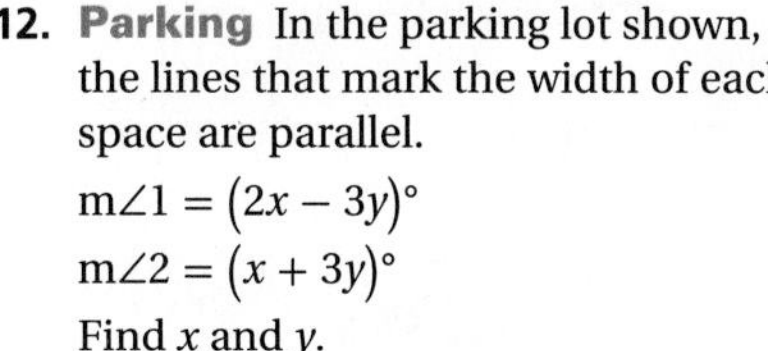

12. Parking In the parking lot shown, the lines that mark the width of each space are parallel.

$m\angle 1 = (2x - 3y)^\circ$

$m\angle 2 = (x + 3y)^\circ$

Find x and y.

$x = 60$, $y = 20$

Find each angle measure. Justify each answer with a postulate or theorem.

13. $m\angle 1$ **14.** $m\angle 2$ **15.** $m\angle 3$

16. $m\angle 4$ **17.** $m\angle 5$ **18.** $m\angle 6$

19. $m\angle 7$ **120°; Vert. ∠s Thm.**

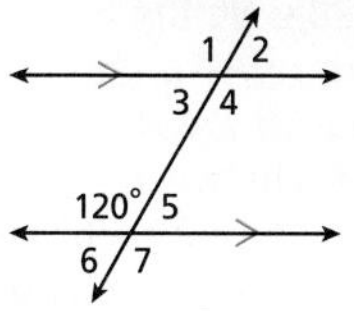

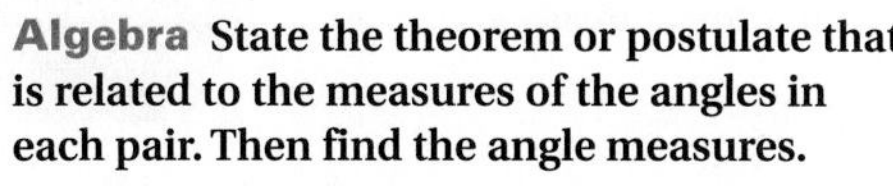

Algebra **State the theorem or postulate that is related to the measures of the angles in each pair. Then find the angle measures.**

20. $m\angle 1 = (7x + 15)^\circ$, $m\angle 2 = (10x - 9)^\circ$

21. $m\angle 3 = (23x + 11)^\circ$, $m\angle 4 = (14x + 21)^\circ$

22. $m\angle 4 = (37x - 15)^\circ$, $m\angle 5 = (44x - 29)^\circ$

23. $m\angle 1 = (6x + 24)^\circ$, $m\angle 4 = (17x - 9)^\circ$

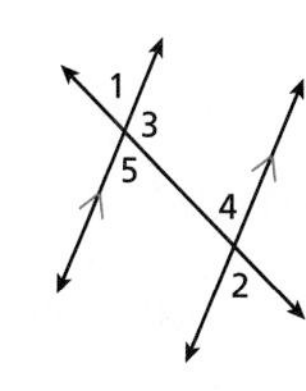

20. $x = 8$; Alt. Ext. ∠s Thm.; $m\angle 1 = m\angle 2 = 71°$

21. $x = 4$; Same-Side Int. ∠s Thm.; $m\angle 3 = 103°$; $m\angle 4 = 77°$

LINK

Architecture

The Luxor hotel is 600 feet wide, 600 feet long, and 350 feet high. The atrium in the hotel measures 29 million cubic feet.

24. Architecture The Luxor Hotel in Las Vegas, Nevada, is a 30-story pyramid. The hotel uses an elevator called an inclinator to take people up the side of the pyramid. The inclinator travels at a 39° angle. Which theorem or postulate best illustrates the angles formed by the path of the inclinator and each parallel floor? (*Hint:* Draw a picture.) **Corr. ∠s Post.**

25. Complete the two-column proof of the Alternate Exterior Angles Theorem.

Given: $\ell \parallel m$

Prove: $\angle 1 \cong \angle 2$

Proof:

Statements	Reasons
1. $\ell \parallel m$	1. Given
2. a. ___?___	2. Vert. ∠s Thm.
3. $\angle 3 \cong \angle 2$	3. b. ___?___
4. c. ___?___	4. d. ___?___

a. $\angle 1 \cong \angle 3$
b. Corr. ∠s Post.
c. $\angle 1 \cong \angle 2$
d. Trans. Prop. of ≅

26. Write a paragraph proof of the Same-Side Interior Angles Theorem.

Given: $r \parallel s$

Prove: $m\angle 1 + m\angle 2 = 180°$

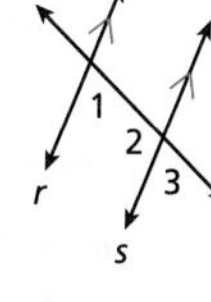

Draw the given situation or tell why it is impossible.

27. Two parallel lines are intersected by a transversal so that the corresponding angles are supplementary.

28. Two parallel lines are intersected by a transversal so that the same-side interior angles are complementary.

28. The situation is impossible because when ∥ lines are intersected by a transv., same-side int. ∠s are supp.

COMMON ERROR ALERT

In **Exercise 12,** students may not remember how to begin solving a system of equations with two variables. Review how to solve systems by adding each side of the equations together, or by solving for one variable in one equation and substituting the expression into the other equation.

Diversity The architecture in **Example 24** can provide an opportunity to discuss pyramids built by people of many different cultures.

Answers

22. $x = 2$; Alt. Int. ∠s Thm.; $m\angle 4 = m\angle 5 = 59°$

23. $x = 3$; Corr. ∠s Post.; $m\angle 1 = m\angle 4 = 42°$

26. It is given that $r \parallel s$. By the Corr. ∠s Post., $\angle 1 \cong \angle 3$; so $m\angle 1 = m\angle 3$ by def. of ≅ ∠s. By the Lin. Pair Thm., $m\angle 3 + m\angle 2 = 180°$. By subst. $m\angle 1 + m\angle 2 = 180°$.

27.

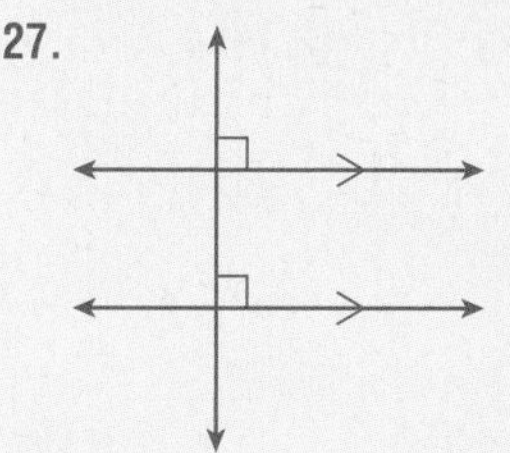

3-2 PRACTICE B

Find each angle measure.

1. $m\angle 1$ 47°
2. $m\angle 2$ 119°
3. $m\angle ABC$ 97°
4. $m\angle DEF$ 62°

Complete the two-column proof to show that same-side exterior angles are supplementary.

5. **Given:** $p \parallel q$

Prove: $m\angle 1 + m\angle 3 = 180°$

Proof:

Statements	Reasons
1. $p \parallel q$	1. Given
2. a. $m\angle 2 + m\angle 3 = 180°$	2. Lin. Pair Thm.
3. $\angle 1 \cong \angle 2$	3. b. Corr. ∠s Post.
4. c. $m\angle 1 = m\angle 2$	4. Def. of ≅ ∠s
5. d. $m\angle 1 + m\angle 3 = 180°$	5. e. Subst.

6. Ocean waves move in parallel lines toward the shore. The figure shows Sandy Beaches windsurfing across several waves. For this exercise, think of Sandy's wake as a line. $m\angle 1 = (2x + 2y)^\circ$ and $m\angle 2 = (2x + y)^\circ$. Find x and y.

$x =$ 15

$y =$ 40

3-2 PRACTICE C

1. A *parallelogram* is a quadrilateral formed by two pairs of parallel lines. Use what you know about parallel lines and angle measures to find the sum of the measures of the four angles inside the parallelogram. Explain your answer.

Possible answer: $m\angle 1 + m\angle 2 = 180°$ and $m\angle 3 + m\angle 4 = 180°$ by the Same-Side Int. ∠s Thm. Thus, the total of the angle measures is 360°.

2. A *trapezoid* is a quadrilateral formed by one pair of parallel lines. Use what you know about parallel lines and angle measures to find the sum of the measures of the four angles inside the trapezoid. 360°

3. A *trapezium* is a quadrilateral formed by four lines, no two of which are parallel. Find the sum of the measures of the four angles inside the trapezium. Write a two-column proof to justify your answer. (*Hint:* Draw $\overline{BE}$ parallel to $\overleftrightarrow{AD}$ and having E on $\overleftrightarrow{CD}$. Write *Construction* to justify this step.)

Given: The sum of the measures of the angles in a triangle is 180°.

Prove: $m\angle 1 + m\angle 2 + m\angle 3 + m\angle 4 =$ 360°; possible answer:

Statements	Reasons
1. Draw $\overline{BE}$ parallel to $\overleftrightarrow{AD}$.	1. Construction
2. $m\angle 1 + m\angle ABE = 180°$, $m\angle 4 + m\angle DEB = 180°$	2. Same-Side Int. ∠s Thm.
3. $m\angle 1 + m\angle 4 + m\angle ABE + m\angle DEB = 360°$	3. Add. Prop. of =
4. $m\angle 3 + m\angle CEB + m\angle CBE = 180°$	4. Given
5. $m\angle DEB + m\angle CEB = 180°$	5. Lin. Pair Thm.
6. $m\angle 3 + m\angle CEB + m\angle CBE = m\angle DEB + m\angle CEB$	6. Subst. (Steps 4, 5)
7. $m\angle 3 + m\angle CBE = m\angle DEB$	7. Subtr. Prop. of =
8. $m\angle 1 + m\angle 3 + m\angle 4 + m\angle ABE + m\angle CBE = 360°$	8. Subst. (Steps 3, 7)
9. $m\angle 2 = m\angle ABE + m\angle CBE$	9. Angle Add. Post.
10. $m\angle 1 + m\angle 2 + m\angle 3 + m\angle 4 = 360°$	10. Subst. (Steps 8, 9)

Exercise 29 involves using the Same-Side Interior Angles Theorem. This exercise prepares students for the Multi-Step Test Prep on page 180.

Visual Students may find it easier to visualize the angle relationships in **Exercise 29** by redrawing the sketch so that sides $\overleftrightarrow{PS}$ and $\overleftrightarrow{QR}$ are horizontal.

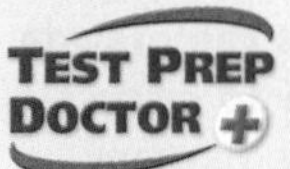

If students chose **A** in **Exercise 34,** ask them what relationship x has to $m\angle RVT$.

Answers

33.

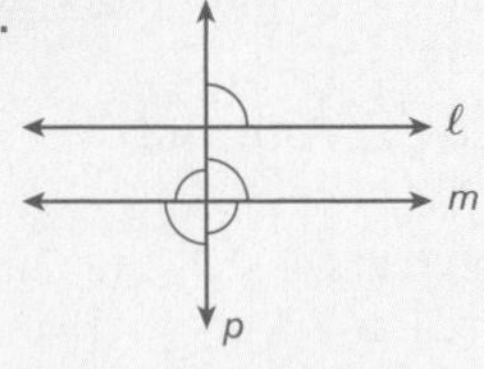

If all ∡ formed by m and p are ≅, then $m \perp p$. If the ∠ formed by ℓ and p is ≅ to the ∡ formed by m and p, it must be a rt. ∠, so $\ell \perp p$.

MULTI-STEP TEST PREP

29. This problem will prepare you for the Multi-Step Test Prep on page 180.

In the diagram, which represents the side view of a mystery spot, $m\angle SRT = 25°$. $\overleftrightarrow{RT}$ is a transversal to $\overleftrightarrow{PS}$ and $\overleftrightarrow{QR}$.

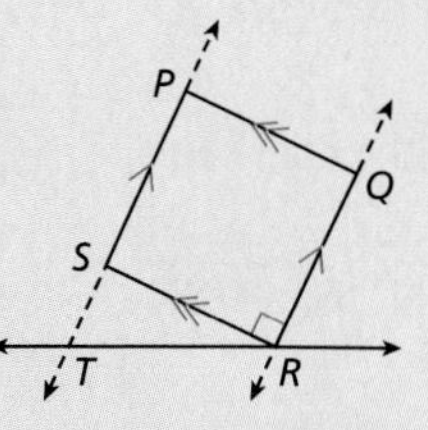

a. What type of angle pair is $\angle QRT$ and $\angle STR$? **same-side int. ∡**

b. Find $m\angle STR$. Use a theorem or postulate to justify your answer.

29b. By the Same-Side Int. ∡ Thm., $m\angle QRT + m\angle STR = 180°$. $m\angle QRT = 25° + 90° = 115°$, so $m\angle STR = 65°$.

30. **Land Development** A piece of property lies between two parallel streets as shown. $m\angle 1 = (2x + 6)°$, and $m\angle 2 = (3x + 9)°$. What is the relationship between the angles? What are their measures?

30. The ∡ are same-side int. ∡; $m\angle 1 = 72°$; and $m\angle 2 = 108°$.

31. **ERROR ANALYSIS** In the figure, $m\angle ABC = (15x + 5)°$, and $m\angle BCD = (10x + 25)°$. Which value of $m\angle BCD$ is incorrect? Explain.

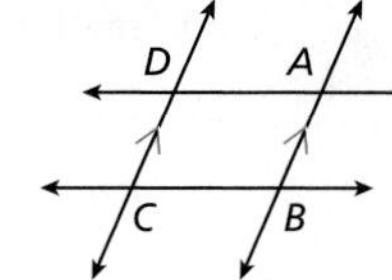

31. A is incorrect because the ∡ are supp, not ≅.

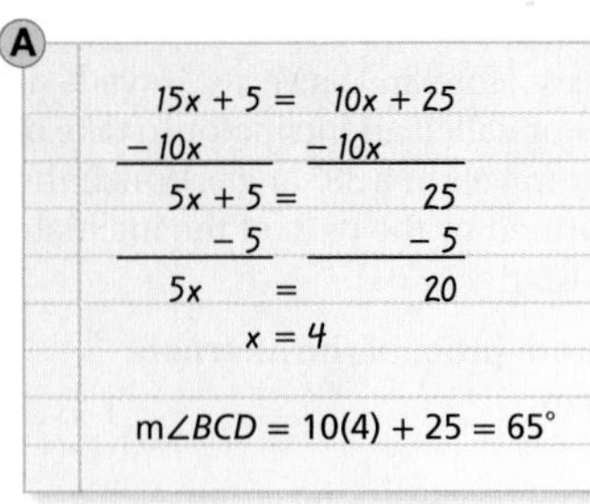

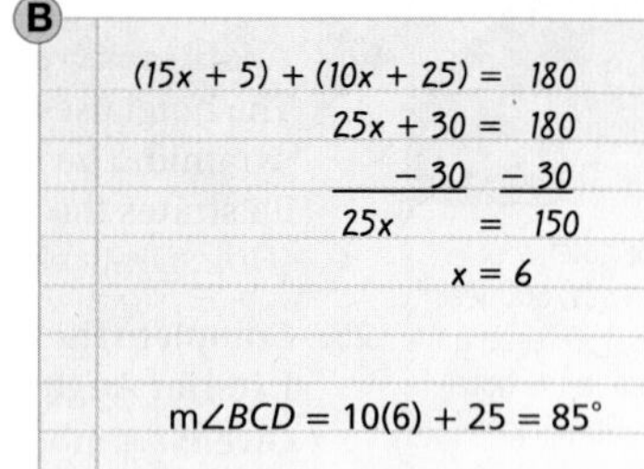

32. **Critical Thinking** In the diagram, $\ell \parallel m$. Explain why $\frac{x}{y} = 1$.

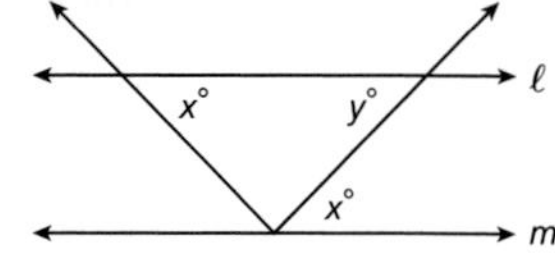

32. By the Alt. Int. ∡ Thm., $x° = y°$, so $\frac{x}{y} = 1$.

33. **Write About It** Suppose that lines ℓ and m are intersected by transversal p. One of the angles formed by ℓ and p is congruent to every angle formed by m and p. Draw a diagram showing lines ℓ, m, and p, mark any congruent angles that are formed, and explain what you know is true.

34. $m\angle RST = (x + 50)°$, and $m\angle STU = (3x + 20)°$. Find $m\angle RVT$.

Ⓐ 15°
Ⓑ 27.5°
Ⓒ 65°
Ⓓ 77.5°

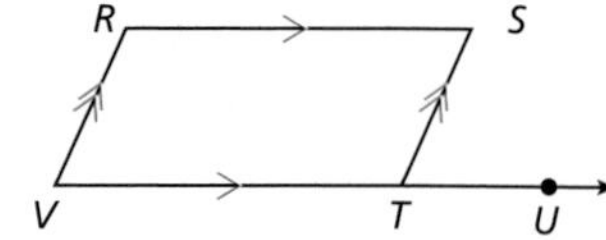

3-2 READING STRATEGIES

The angles in this figure can be compared using the following rules:

Corresponding Angles Postulate	If two parallel lines are cut by a transversal, then the pairs of corresponding angles are **congruent.**	Name the pairs of angles *congruent* by the Corresponding Angles Postulate. 1. ∠1 ≅ ∠5 2. ∠2 ≅ ∠6 3. ∠3 ≅ ∠7 4. ∠4 ≅ ∠8
Alternate Interior Angles Theorem	If two parallel lines are cut by a transversal, then the two pairs of alternate interior angles are **congruent.**	Name the pairs of angles *congruent* by the Alternate Interior Angles Theorem. 5. ∠2 ≅ ∠8 6. ∠3 ≅ ∠5
Alternate Exterior Angles Theorem	If two parallel lines are cut by a transversal, then the two pairs of alternate exterior angles are **congruent.**	Name the pairs of angles *congruent* by the Alternate Exterior Angles Theorem. 7. ∠1 ≅ ∠7 8. ∠4 ≅ ∠6
Same-Side Interior Angles Theorem	If two parallel lines are cut by a transversal, then the two pairs of same-side interior angles are **supplementary.**	Name the pairs of angles *supplementary* by the Same-Side Interior Angles Theorem. 9. m∠2 + m∠5 = 180° 10. m∠3 + m∠8 = 180°

11. If m∠2 = 47°, then what is m∠6? How do you know?
m∠6 = 47° by the Corresponding Angles Postulate

12. Based on the value for ∠6 from Exercise 11, what is ∠3? How do you know?
m∠3 = 133° by the Same-Side Interior Angles Theorem

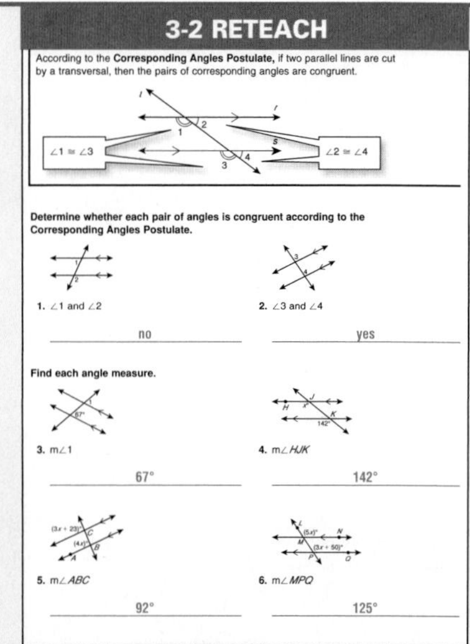
3-2 RETEACH

According to the **Corresponding Angles Postulate,** if two parallel lines are cut by a transversal, then the pairs of corresponding angles are congruent.

∠1 ≅ ∠3 ∠2 ≅ ∠4

Determine whether each pair of angles is congruent according to the Corresponding Angles Postulate.

1. ∠1 and ∠2 — no
2. ∠3 and ∠4 — yes

Find each angle measure.

3. m∠1 — 67°
4. m∠HJK — 142°
5. m∠ABC — 92°
6. m∠MPQ — 125°

35. For two parallel lines and a transversal, $m\angle 1 = 83°$. For which pair of angle measures is the sum the least?

Ⓕ $\angle 1$ and a corresponding angle

Ⓖ $\angle 1$ and a same-side interior angle

Ⓗ $\angle 1$ and its supplement

Ⓙ (circled) $\angle 1$ and its complement

36. **Short Response** Given $a \parallel b$ with transversal t, explain why $\angle 1$ and $\angle 3$ are supplementary.

36. By the Lin. Pair Thm., $m\angle 1 + m\angle 2 = 180°$. By the Alt. Int. ∠Thm., $\angle 2 \cong \angle 3$, so $m\angle 2 = m\angle 3$. By subst., $m\angle 1 + m\angle 3 = 180°$, so $\angle 1$ and $\angle 3$ are supp.

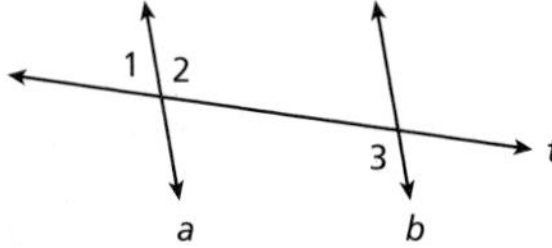

CHALLENGE AND EXTEND

Multi-Step **Find $m\angle 1$ in each diagram. (*Hint:* Draw a line parallel to the given parallel lines.)**

37. $m\angle 1 = 75°$

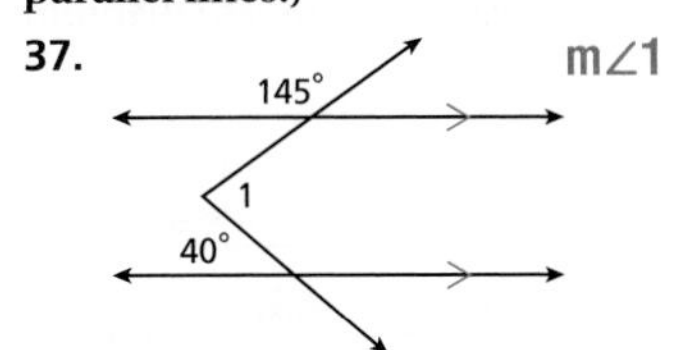

38. $m\angle 1 = 155°$

39. Find x and y in the diagram. Justify your answer.

39. By the Same-Side Int. ⦣ Thm., $10x + 5y + 80 = 180$ and $15x + 4y + 72 = 180$. So $x = 4$ and $y = 12$.

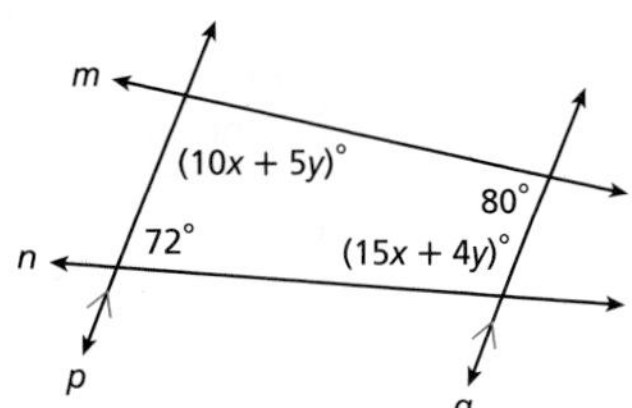

40. Two lines are parallel. The measures of two corresponding angles are $a°$ and $2b°$, and the measures of two same-side interior angles are $a°$ and $b°$. Find the value of a. $a = 120$

SPIRAL REVIEW

If the first quantity increases, tell whether the second quantity is likely to increase, decrease, or stay the same. *(Previous course)*

41. time in years and average cost of a new car **increase**

42. age of a student and length of time needed to read 500 words **decrease**

Use the Law of Syllogism to draw a conclusion from the given information. *(Lesson 2-3)*

43. If two angles form a linear pair, then they are supplementary. If two angles are supplementary, then their measures add to 180°. $\angle 1$ and $\angle 2$ form a linear pair. $m\angle 1 + m\angle 2 = 180°$

44. If a figure is a square, then it is a rectangle. If a figure is a rectangle, then its sides are perpendicular. Figure *ABCD* is a square. **The sides of *ABCD* are ⊥.**

Give an example of each angle pair. *(Lesson 3-1)* **Possible answers:**

45. alternate interior angles $\angle 3$ and $\angle 6$

46. alternate exterior angles $\angle 1$ and $\angle 8$

47. same-side interior angles $\angle 3$ and $\angle 5$

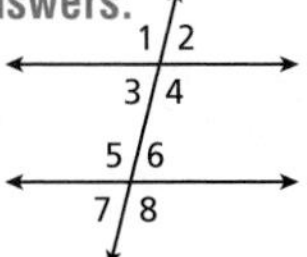

COMMON ERROR ALERT

In **Exercise 40,** students may not be sure how to label the angles in their diagrams correctly. Explain that there is more than one possible placement for the corresponding angle that measures $a°$. Tell them that if they label two different angles with a, they must make sure that those two angles are, in fact, congruent.

Journal

Have students list examples in the real world where they have seen parallel lines cut by a transversal.

ALTERNATIVE ASSESSMENT

Have students sketch and label two parallel lines cut by a transversal. Have them use a protractor to measure the angles. Then they should use the sketch to explain the relationships among all the angles.

Power Presentations with PowerPoint®

3-2 Lesson Quiz

State the theorem or postulate that is related to the measures of the angles in each pair. Then find the unknown angle measures.

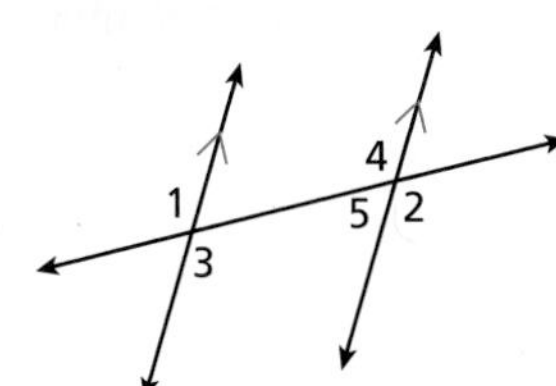

1. $m\angle 1 = 120°$, $m\angle 2 = (60x)°$ Alt. Ext. ⦣ Thm.; $m\angle 2 = 120°$

2. $m\angle 2 = (75x - 30)°$, $m\angle 3 = (30x + 60)°$ Corr. ⦣ Post.; $m\angle 2 = 120°$, $m\angle 3 = 120°$

3. $m\angle 3 = (50x + 20)°$, $m\angle 4 = (100x - 80)°$ Alt. Int. ⦣ Thm.; $m\angle 3 = 120°$, $m\angle 4 = 120°$

4. $m\angle 3 = (45x + 30)°$, $m\angle 5 = (25x + 10)°$ Same-Side Int. ⦣ Thm.; $m\angle 3 = 120°$, $m\angle 5 = 60°$

Also available on transparency

3-2 PROBLEM SOLVING

Find each value. Name the postulate or theorem that you used to find the values.

1. In the diagram of movie theater seats, the incline of the floor, f, is parallel to the seats, s.

If $m\angle 1 = 68°$, what is x?

17; Alt. Int. ⦣ Thm.

2. In the diagram, roads a and b are parallel.

What is the measure of $\angle PQR$?

102°; Alt. Ext. ⦣ Thm.

3. In the diagram of the gate, the horizontal bars are parallel and the vertical bars are parallel. Find x and y.

$x = 10$; $y = 3$; $(12x + 2y)° = 126°$ by the Corr. ⦣ Post. and $(3x + 2y)° = 36°$ by the Alt. Int. ⦣ Thm.

Use the diagram of a staircase railing for Exercises 4 and 5. $\overline{AG} \parallel \overline{CJ}$ and $\overline{AD} \parallel \overline{FJ}$. Choose the best answer.

4. Which is a true statement about the measure of $\angle DCJ$?

A It equals 30°, by the Alternate Interior Angles Theorem.

B It equals 30°, by the Corresponding Angles Postulate.

C It equals 50°, by the Alternate Interior Angles Theorem.

Ⓓ It equals 50°, by the Corresponding Angles Postulate.

5. Which is a true statement about the value of n?

F It equals 25°, by the Alternate Interior Angles Theorem.

G It equals 25°, by the Same-Side Interior Angles Theorem.

Ⓗ It equals 35°, by the Alternate Interior Angles Theorem.

J It equals 35°, by the Same-Side Interior Angles Theorem.

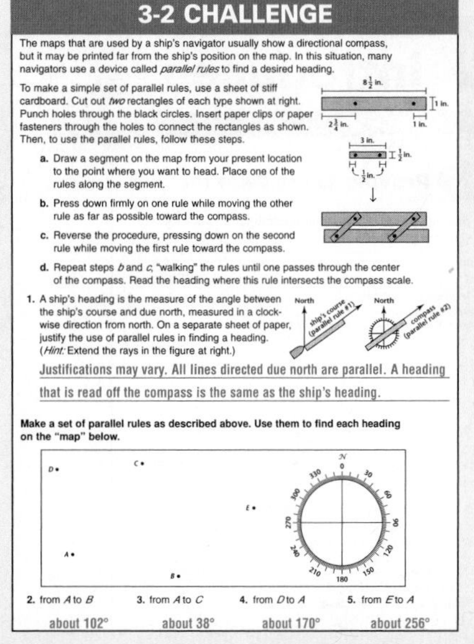

3-2 CHALLENGE

The maps that are used by a ship's navigator usually show a directional compass, but it may be printed far from the ship's position on the map. In this situation, many navigators use a device called *parallel rules* to find a desired heading.

To make a simple set of parallel rules, use a sheet of stiff cardboard. Cut out *two* rectangles of each type shown at right. Punch holes through the black circles. Insert paper clips or paper fasteners through the holes to connect the rectangles as shown. Then, to use the parallel rules, follow these steps.

a. Draw a segment on the map from your present location to the point where you want to head. Place one of the rules along the segment.

b. Press down firmly on one rule while moving the other rule as far as possible toward the compass.

c. Reverse the procedure, pressing down on the second rule while moving the first rule toward the compass.

d. Repeat steps b and c, "walking" the rules until one passes through the center of the compass. Read the heading where this rule intersects the compass scale.

1. A ship's heading is the measure of the angle between the ship's course and due north, measured in a clockwise direction from north. On a separate sheet of paper, justify the use of parallel rules in finding a heading. (*Hint:* Extend the rays in the figure at right.)

Justifications may vary. All lines directed due north are parallel. A heading that is read off the compass is the same as the ship's heading.

Make a set of parallel rules as described above. Use them to find each heading on the "map" below.

2. from A to B about 102°

3. from A to C about 38°

4. from D to A about 170°

5. from E to A about 256°

3-3 Organizer

Pacing: Traditional 1 day
Block $\frac{1}{2}$ day

Objective: Use the angles formed by a transversal to prove two lines are parallel.

Online Edition
Tutorial Videos

Countdown Week 5

Power Presentations with PowerPoint®

Warm Up

State the converse of each statement.

1. If $a = b$, then $a + c = b + c$. If $a + c = b + c$, then $a = b$.
2. If $m\angle A + m\angle B = 90°$, then $\angle A$ and $\angle B$ are complementary. If $\angle A$ and $\angle B$ are complementary, then $m\angle A + m\angle B = 90°$.
3. If $AB + BC = AC$, then A, B, and C are collinear. If A, B, and C are collinear, then $AB + BC = AC$.

Also available on transparency

Math Humor

Q: Why didn't the two parallel lines recognize each other?

A: Because they had never met.

3-3 Proving Lines Parallel

Objective
Use the angles formed by a transversal to prove two lines are parallel.

Who uses this?
Rowers have to keep the oars on each side parallel in order to travel in a straight line. (See Example 4.)

Recall that the converse of a theorem is found by exchanging the hypothesis and conclusion. The converse of a theorem is not automatically true. If it is true, it must be stated as a postulate or proved as a separate theorem.

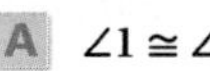

Postulate 3-3-1 Converse of the Corresponding Angles Postulate

POSTULATE	HYPOTHESIS	CONCLUSION
If two coplanar lines are cut by a transversal so that a pair of corresponding angles are congruent, then the two lines are parallel.	$\angle 1 \cong \angle 2$ 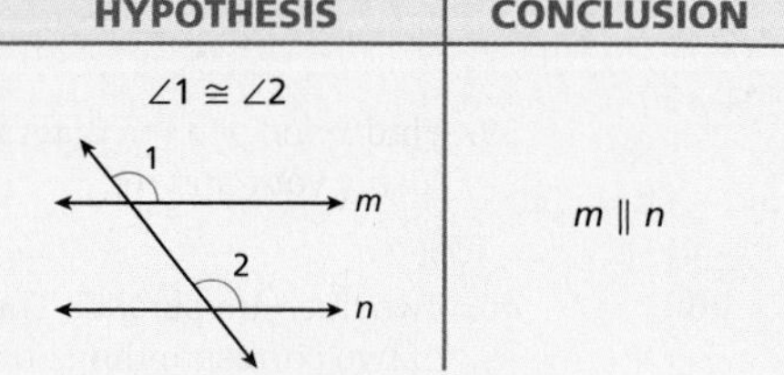	$m \parallel n$

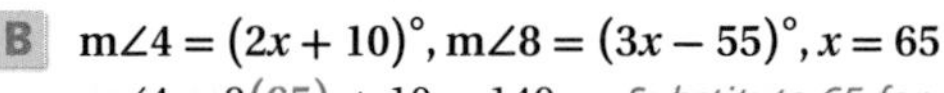

EXAMPLE 1 Using the Converse of the Corresponding Angles Postulate

Use the Converse of the Corresponding Angles Postulate and the given information to show that $\ell \parallel m$.

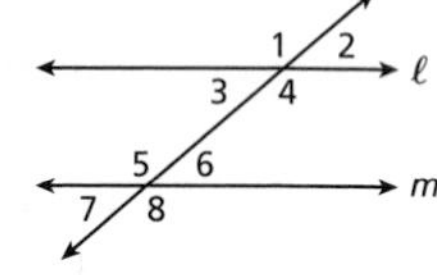

A $\angle 1 \cong \angle 5$

$\angle 1 \cong \angle 5$ — *$\angle 1$ and $\angle 5$ are corresponding angles.*
$\ell \parallel m$ — *Conv. of Corr. $\angle$s Post.*

B $m\angle 4 = (2x + 10)°, m\angle 8 = (3x - 55)°, x = 65$

$m\angle 4 = 2(65) + 10 = 140$ — *Substitute 65 for x.*
$m\angle 8 = 3(65) - 55 = 140$ — *Substitute 65 for x.*
$m\angle 4 = m\angle 8$ — *Trans. Prop. of Equality*
$\angle 4 \cong \angle 8$ — *Def. of $\cong$ $\angle$s*
$\ell \parallel m$ — *Conv. of Corr. $\angle$s Post.*

CHECK IT OUT! Use the Converse of the Corresponding Angles Postulate and the given information to show that $\ell \parallel m$.

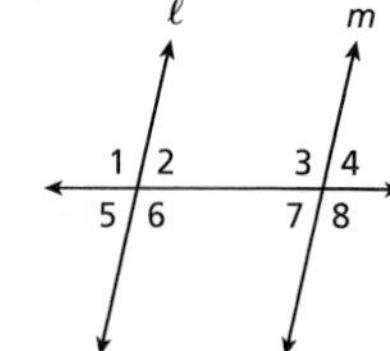

1a. $m\angle 1 = m\angle 3$
1b. $m\angle 7 = (4x + 25)°$, $m\angle 5 = (5x + 12)°$, $x = 13$

1a. $\angle 1 \cong \angle 3$, so $\ell \parallel m$ by the Conv. of the Corr. $\angle$s Post.

1b. $m\angle 7 = 77°$ and $m\angle 5 = 77°$, so $\angle 7 \cong \angle 5$. $\ell \parallel m$ by the Conv. of the Corr. $\angle$s Post.

State Resources

go.hrw.com
State Resources Online
KEYWORD: MG7 Resources

1 Introduce

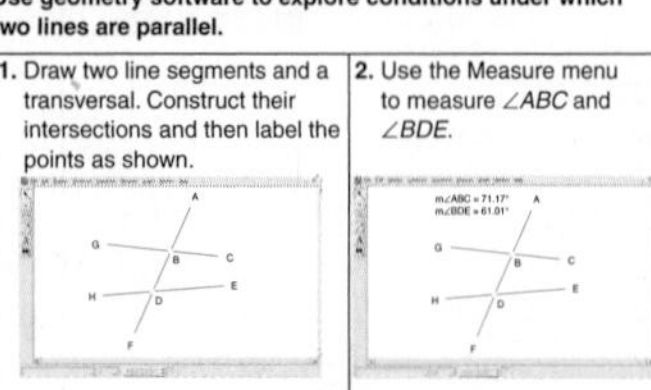

EXPLORATION

3-3 Proving Lines Parallel

Use geometry software to explore conditions under which two lines are parallel.

1. Draw two line segments and a transversal. Construct their intersections and then label the points as shown.
2. Use the Measure menu to measure $\angle ABC$ and $\angle BDE$.
3. Drag one or more points so that $m\angle ABC = m\angle BDE$. What appears to be true about $\overline{GC}$ and $\overline{HE}$?
4. Drag the segments into new positions and then measure $\angle ABC$ and $\angle HDF$. Drag points so that $m\angle ABC = m\angle HDF$. What appears to be true about $\overline{GC}$ and $\overline{HE}$?
5. Drag the segments into new positions and then measure $\angle GBD$ and $\angle BDE$. Drag points so that $m\angle GBD = m\angle BDE$. What appears to be true about $\overline{GC}$ and $\overline{HE}$?

Motivate

Review the concept of converses with students. Have a volunteer state a conditional statement that is not about geometry. Then have another volunteer state its converse. Repeat this activity a few times. Then state the Corresponding Angles Postulate and ask students to state its converse.

Explorations and answers are provided in *Alternate Openers: Explorations Transparencies.*

Postulate 3-3-2 **Parallel Postulate**

Through a point P not on line ℓ, there is exactly one line parallel to ℓ.

The Converse of the Corresponding Angles Postulate is used to construct parallel lines. The Parallel Postulate guarantees that for any line ℓ, you can always construct a parallel line through a point that is not on ℓ.

Construction Parallel Lines

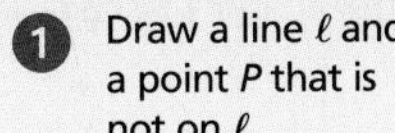

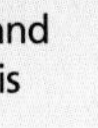

1. Draw a line ℓ and a point P that is not on ℓ.

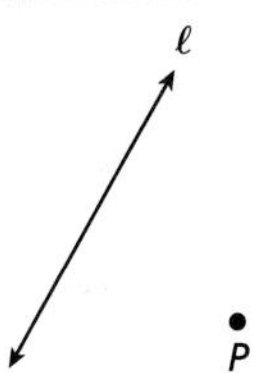

2. Draw a line m through P that intersects ℓ. Label the angle 1.

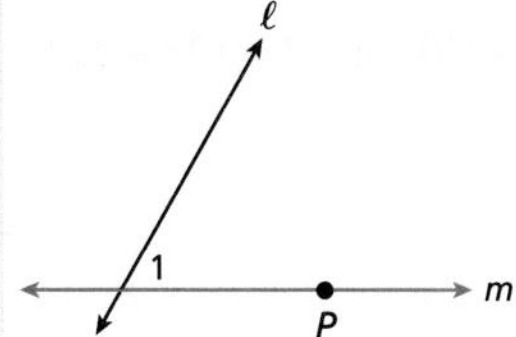

3. Construct an angle congruent to $\angle 1$ at P. By the converse of the Corresponding Angles Postulate, $\ell \parallel n$.

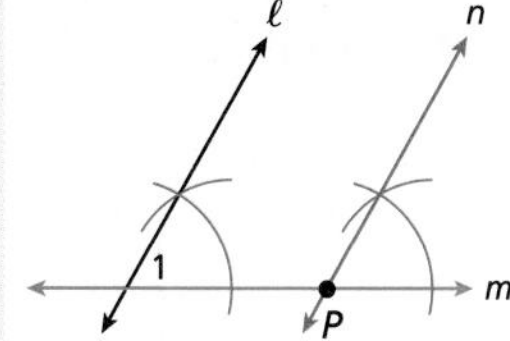

Theorems **Proving Lines Parallel**

	THEOREM	HYPOTHESIS	CONCLUSION
3-3-3	**Converse of the Alternate Interior Angles Theorem** If two coplanar lines are cut by a transversal so that a pair of alternate interior angles are congruent, then the two lines are parallel.	$\angle 1 \cong \angle 2$	$m \parallel n$
3-3-4	**Converse of the Alternate Exterior Angles Theorem** If two coplanar lines are cut by a transversal so that a pair of alternate exterior angles are congruent, then the two lines are parallel.	$\angle 3 \cong \angle 4$	$m \parallel n$
3-3-5	**Converse of the Same-Side Interior Angles Theorem** If two coplanar lines are cut by a transversal so that a pair of same-side interior angles are supplementary, then the two lines are parallel.	$m\angle 5 + m\angle 6 = 180°$	$m \parallel n$

You will prove Theorems 3-3-3 and 3-3-5 in Exercises 38–39.

Teach

Guided Instruction

As you present the postulates and theorems in this lesson, have students compare them with their related postulates and theorems in the previous lesson.

In Lesson 3-2, parallel lines and a transversal were used to prove that angles were congruent. In this lesson, congruent angles will be used to prove that lines are parallel.

Reaching All Learners

Through Concrete Manipulatives

Have students tape two pieces of uncooked spaghetti together to form four angles, and measure one angle. Have them place another piece of spaghetti so that the corresponding angle is congruent to the measured angle. Repeat with different angle pairs.

COMMON ERROR ALERT

As you work through the examples, watch for students who use a postulate or theorem for justification when its converse should be used. To help them choose the correct conditional, point out that any given information corresponds to the hypothesis in a conditional statement.

Power Presentations with PowerPoint®

Additional Examples

Example 1

Use the Converse of the Corresponding Angles Postulate and the given information to show that $\ell \parallel m$.

A. $\angle 4 \cong \angle 8$

$\angle 4$ and $\angle 8$ are corr. ∠s., so $\ell \parallel m$ by the Conv. of Corr. ∠s Post.

B. $m\angle 3 = (4x - 80)°$, $m\angle 7 = (3x - 50)°$, $x = 30$

$m\angle 3 = 4(30) - 80 = 40$

$m\angle 7 = 3(30) - 50 = 40$

$m\angle 3 = m\angle 7$, so $\angle 3 \cong \angle 7$.

$\ell \parallel m$ by the Conv. of Corr. ∠s Post.

INTERVENTION

Questioning Strategies

EXAMPLE 1

- What other pairs of angles can you use with the Converse of the Corresponding Angles Postulate to prove the lines parallel?

Construction

Ask students why the lines constructed must be parallel. We constructed congruent corresponding angles.

Math Background The Parallel Postulate is needed to prove many important theorems in Euclidean geometry. It is not true in spherical geometry, which will be studied in Chapter 10.

PROOF

Converse of the Alternate Exterior Angles Theorem

Given: $\angle 1 \cong \angle 2$
Prove: $\ell \parallel m$

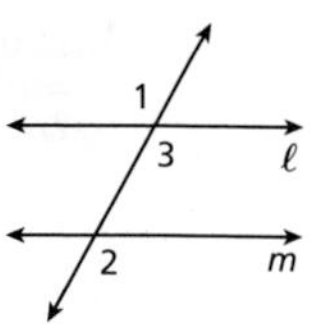

Proof: It is given that $\angle 1 \cong \angle 2$. Vertical angles are congruent, so $\angle 1 \cong \angle 3$. By the Transitive Property of Congruence, $\angle 2 \cong \angle 3$. So $\ell \parallel m$ by the Converse of the Corresponding Angles Postulate.

EXAMPLE 2 Determining Whether Lines are Parallel

Use the given information and the theorems you have learned to show that $r \parallel s$.

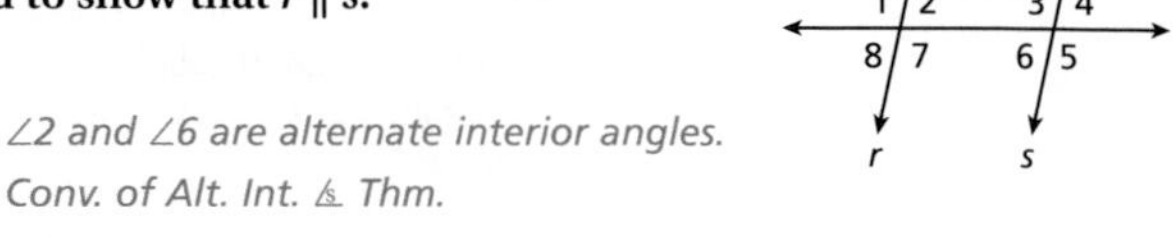

A $\angle 2 \cong \angle 6$

$\angle 2 \cong \angle 6$ — *$\angle 2$ and $\angle 6$ are alternate interior angles.*
$r \parallel s$ — *Conv. of Alt. Int. ∠s Thm.*

Algebra

B $m\angle 6 = (6x + 18)°$, $m\angle 7 = (9x + 12)°$, $x = 10$

$m\angle 6 = 6x + 18$
$= 6(10) + 18 = 78°$ — *Substitute 10 for x.*
$m\angle 7 = 9x + 12$
$= 9(10) + 12 = 102°$ — *Substitute 10 for x.*
$m\angle 6 + m\angle 7 = 78° + 102°$
$= 180°$ — *$\angle 6$ and $\angle 7$ are same-side interior angles.*
$r \parallel s$ — *Conv. of Same-Side Int. ∠s Thm.*

CHECK IT OUT! Refer to the diagram above. Use the given information and the theorems you have learned to show that $r \parallel s$.

2a. $m\angle 4 = m\angle 8$ **2b.** $m\angle 3 = 2x°$, $m\angle 7 = (x + 50)°$, $x = 50$

EXAMPLE 3 Proving Lines Parallel

Given: $\ell \parallel m$, $\angle 1 \cong \angle 3$
Prove: $r \parallel p$

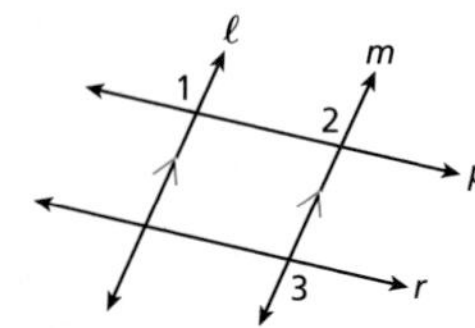

Proof:

Statements	Reasons
1. $\ell \parallel m$	1. Given
2. $\angle 1 \cong \angle 2$	2. Corr. ∠s Post.
3. $\angle 1 \cong \angle 3$	3. Given
4. $\angle 2 \cong \angle 3$	4. Trans. Prop. of ≅
5. $r \parallel p$	5. Conv. of Alt. Ext. ∠s Thm.

CHECK IT OUT! **3.** **Given:** $\angle 1 \cong \angle 4$, $\angle 3$ and $\angle 4$ are supplementary.
Prove: $\ell \parallel m$

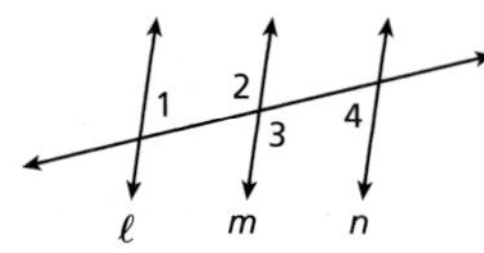

2a. $\angle 4 \cong \angle 8$, so $r \parallel s$ by the Conv. of the Alt. Ext. ∠s Thm.

2b. $m\angle 3 = 100°$ and $m\angle 7 = 100°$, so $\angle 3 \cong \angle 7$. $r \parallel s$ by the Conv. of the Alt. Int. ∠s Thm.

1. $\angle 1 \cong \angle 4$ (Given)
2. $m\angle 1 = m\angle 4$ (Def. ≅ ∠s)
3. $\angle 3$ and $\angle 4$ are supp. (Given)
4. $m\angle 3 + m\angle 4 = 180°$ (Def. supp. ∠s)
5. $m\angle 3 + m\angle 1 = 180°$ (Subst.)
6. $m\angle 2 = m\angle 3$ (Vert. ∠s Thm.)
7. $m\angle 2 + m\angle 1 = 180°$ (Subst.)
8. $\ell \parallel m$ (Conv. of Same-Side Int. ∠s Thm.)

Power Presentations with PowerPoint®

Additional Examples

Example 2

Use the diagram in Example 2, the given information, and the theorems you have learned to show that $r \parallel s$.

A. $\angle 4 \cong \angle 8$

$\angle 4$ and $\angle 8$ are alt. ext. ∠s, so $r \parallel s$ by the Conv. of Alt. Ext. ∠s Thm.

B. $m\angle 2 = (10x + 8)°$, $m\angle 3 = (25x - 3)°$, $x = 5$

$m\angle 2 = 58°$; $m\angle 3 = 122°$; $m\angle 2 + m\angle 3 = 58° + 122° = 180°$; $\angle 2$ and $\angle 3$ are supp. same-side int. ∠s, so $r \parallel s$ by the Conv. of Same-Side Int. ∠s Thm.

Example 3

Use the diagram in Example 3.

Given: $p \parallel r$, $\angle 1 \cong \angle 3$
Prove: $\ell \parallel m$

1. $p \parallel r$ (Given)
2. $\angle 3 \cong \angle 2$ (Alt. Ext. ∠s Thm.)
3. $\angle 1 \cong \angle 3$ (Given)
4. $\angle 1 \cong \angle 2$ (Trans. Prop. of ≅)
5. $\ell \parallel m$ (Conv. of Corr. ∠s Post.)

INTERVENTION

Questioning Strategies

EXAMPLE 2

- What are some angle pairs that must be congruent for the lines to be parallel?
- What are some angle pairs that must be supplementary for the lines to be parallel?

EXAMPLE 3

- Classify the special angle pairs in the diagram. What is the transversal for each pair?

EXAMPLE 4 **Sports Application**

During a race, all members of a rowing team should keep the oars parallel on each side. If $m\angle 1 = (3x + 13)°$, $m\angle 2 = (5x - 5)°$, and $x = 9$, show that the oars are parallel.

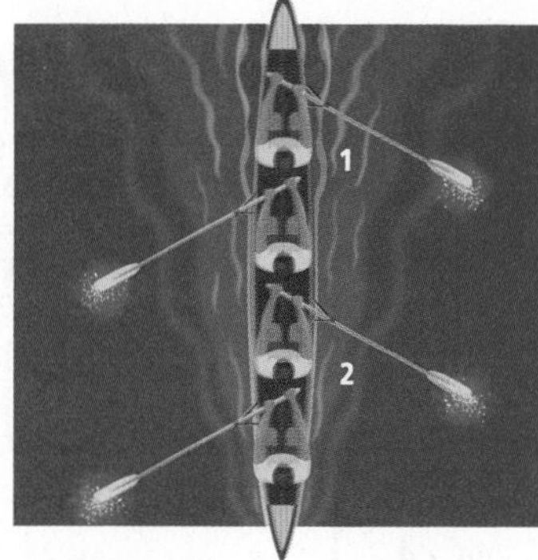

A line through the center of the boat forms a transversal to the two oars on each side of the boat.

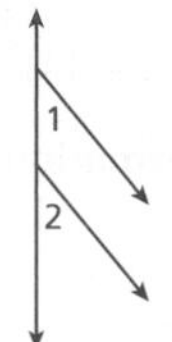

$\angle 1$ and $\angle 2$ are corresponding angles. If $\angle 1 \cong \angle 2$, then the oars are parallel.

Substitute 9 for x in each expression:

$m\angle 1 = 3x + 13$

$= 3(9) + 13 = 40°$ *Substitute 9 for x in each expression.*

$m\angle 2 = 5x - 5$

$= 5(9) - 5 = 40°$ *$m\angle 1 = m\angle 2$, so $\angle 1 \cong \angle 2$.*

The corresponding angles are congruent, so the oars are parallel by the Converse of the Corresponding Angles Postulate.

4. **What if...?** Suppose the corresponding angles on the opposite side of the boat measure $(4y - 2)°$ and $(3y + 6)°$, where $y = 8$. Show that the oars are parallel.

$4y - 2 = 4(8) - 2 = 30°$ $3y + 6 = 3(8) + 6 = 30°$

The ∠s are ≅, so the oars are ∥ by the Conv. of the Corr. ∠s Post.

THINK AND DISCUSS

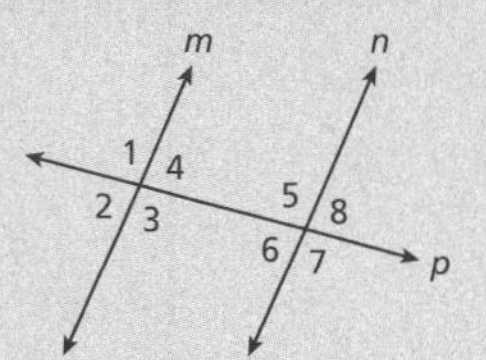

1. Explain three ways of proving that two lines are parallel.
2. If you know $m\angle 1$, how could you use the measures of $\angle 5$, $\angle 6$, $\angle 7$, or $\angle 8$ to prove $m \parallel n$?

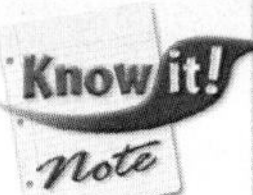

3. **GET ORGANIZED** Copy and complete the graphic organizer. Use it to compare the Corresponding Angles Postulate with the Converse of the Corresponding Angles Postulate.

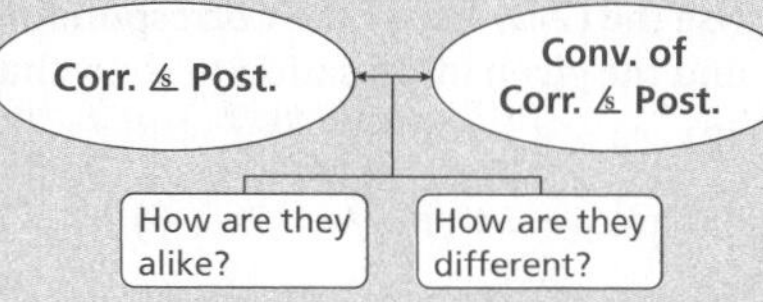

Power Presentations with PowerPoint®

Additional Examples

Example 4

A carpenter is creating a woodwork pattern and wants two long pieces to be parallel. $m\angle 1 = (8x + 20)°$ and $m\angle 2 = (2x + 10)°$. If $x = 15$, show that pieces A and B are parallel.

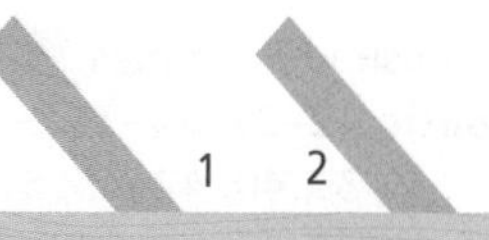

The horizontal piece forms a transversal to pieces A and B. Substituting 15 for x, $m\angle 1 = 140°$ and $m\angle 2 = 40°$. Since $\angle 1$ and $\angle 2$ are same-side interior angles, pieces A and B are parallel by the Conv. of Same-Side Int. ∠s Thm.

INTERVENTION

Questioning Strategies

EXAMPLE 4

- What other pair of angles could you use to determine if the oars or wood pieces are parallel?

Reading Math Point out to students that the word *converse* comes from the Latin *conversus*, which means "to turn around".

ENGLISH LANGUAGE LEARNERS

3 Close

Summarize

Review the four angle relationships that would prove that two lines are parallel.

- a pair of corresponding angles that are congruent
- a pair of alternate interior angles that are congruent
- a pair of alternate exterior angles that are congruent
- a pair of same-side interior angles that are supplementary

ONGOING ASSESSMENT and INTERVENTION

***Diagnose Before* the Lesson**
3-3 Warm Up, TE p. 162

***Monitor During* the Lesson**
Check It Out! Exercises, SE pp. 162–165
Questioning Strategies, TE pp. 163–165

***Assess After* the Lesson**
3-3 Lesson Quiz, TE p. 169
Alternative Assessment, TE p. 169

Answers to *Think and Discuss*

1. Prove 2 corr. ∠s are ≅, prove 2 same-side int. ∠s are supp., or prove 2 alt. int. ∠s are ≅.
2. If $m\angle 5 = m\angle 1$, then $m \parallel n$ by the Conv. of the Corr. ∠s Post. If $m\angle 7 = m\angle 1$, then $m \parallel n$ by the Conv. of the Alt. Ext. ∠s Thm. $\angle 6$ and $\angle 8$ each form a lin. pair with $\angle 5$, so you could use the Lin. Pair Thm. and the Conv. of the Corr. ∠s Post.
3. See p. A3.

Assignment Guide

Assign *Guided Practice* exercises as necessary.

If you finished Examples **1–2**
Basic 12–20, 24–34 even
Average 12–20, 24–34
Advanced 12–20, 24–35

If you finished Examples **1–4**
Basic 12–21, 24–36 even, 37, 40, 42–45, 57–65
Average 12–22 even, 25–53, 57–65
Advanced 12–36 even, 37–65

Homework Quick Check
Quickly check key concepts.
Exercises: 12, 16, 21, 22, 28, 34

Answers

2. $m\angle 1 = 128°$, and $m\angle 8 = 128°$, so $\angle 1 \cong \angle 8$. $p \parallel q$ by the Conv. of the Corr. $\angle$s Post.
3. $m\angle 4 = 47°$, and $m\angle 5 = 47°$, so $\angle 4 \cong \angle 5$. $p \parallel q$ by the Conv. of the Corr. $\angle$s Post.
7. $m\angle 4 = 61°$, and $m\angle 8 = 61°$, so $\angle 4 \cong \angle 8$. $r \parallel s$ by the Conv. of the Alt. Int. $\angle$s Thm.
8. $m\angle 8 = 139°$, and $m\angle 7 = 41°$. $139° + 41° = 180°$, so $\angle 8$ and $\angle 7$ are supp. $r \parallel s$ by the Conv. of the Same-Side Int. $\angle$s Thm.
13. $m\angle 4 = 54°$, and $m\angle 8 = 54°$, so $\angle 4 \cong \angle 8$. $\ell \parallel m$ by the Conv. of the Corr. $\angle$s Post.
14. $m\angle 2 = 124°$, and $m\angle 6 = 124°$, so $\angle 2 \cong \angle 6$. $\ell \parallel m$ by the Conv. of the Corr. $\angle$s Post.

State Resources

3-3 Exercises

go.hrw.com
Homework Help Online
KEYWORD: MG7 3-3
Parent Resources Online
KEYWORD: MG7 Parent

GUIDED PRACTICE

SEE EXAMPLE 1 p. 162

Use the Converse of the Corresponding Angles Postulate and the given information to show that $p \parallel q$.

1. $\angle 4 \cong \angle 5$ — $\angle 4 \cong \angle 5$, so $p \parallel q$ by the Conv. of the Corr. $\angle$s Post.
2. $m\angle 1 = (4x + 16)°$, $m\angle 8 = (5x - 12)°$, $x = 28$
3. $m\angle 4 = (6x - 19)°$, $m\angle 5 = (3x + 14)°$, $x = 11$

SEE EXAMPLE 2 p. 164

Use the theorems and given information to show that $r \parallel s$.

4. $\angle 1 \cong \angle 5$ — 4. $\angle 1 \cong \angle 5$, so $r \parallel s$ by the Conv. of the Alt. Ext. $\angle$s Thm.
5. $m\angle 3 + m\angle 4 = 180°$ — 5. $\angle 3$ and $\angle 4$ are supp., so $r \parallel s$ by the Conv. of the Same-Side Int. $\angle$s Thm.
6. $\angle 3 \cong \angle 7$ — 6. $\angle 3 \cong \angle 7$, so $r \parallel s$ by the Conv. of the Alt. Int. $\angle$s Thm.
7. $m\angle 4 = (13x - 4)°$, $m\angle 8 = (9x + 16)°$, $x = 5$
8. $m\angle 8 = (17x + 37)°$, $m\angle 7 = (9x - 13)°$, $x = 6$
9. $m\angle 2 = (25x + 7)°$, $m\angle 6 = (24x + 12)°$, $x = 5$ — 9. $m\angle 2 = 132°$, and $m\angle 6 = 132°$, so $\angle 2 \cong \angle 6$. $r \parallel s$ by the Conv. of the Alt. Ext. $\angle$s Thm.

SEE EXAMPLE 3 p. 164

10. Complete the following two-column proof.

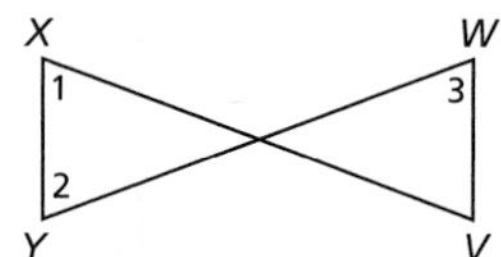

Given: $\angle 1 \cong \angle 2$, $\angle 3 \cong \angle 1$
Prove: $XY \parallel WV$
Proof:

Statements	Reasons
1. $\angle 1 \cong \angle 2$, $\angle 3 \cong \angle 1$	1. Given
2. $\angle 2 \cong \angle 3$	2. a. ___?___ Trans. Prop. of $\cong$
3. b. ___?___ $\overline{XY} \parallel \overline{WV}$	3. c. ___?___ Conv. of the Alt. Int. $\angle$s Thm.

SEE EXAMPLE 4 p. 165

11. **Architecture** In the fire escape, $m\angle 1 = (17x + 9)°$, $m\angle 2 = (14x + 18)°$, and $x = 3$. Show that the two landings are parallel.
$m\angle 1 = 60°$, and $m\angle 2 = 60°$, so $\angle 1 \cong \angle 2$. By the Conv. of the Alt. Int. $\angle$s Thm., the landings are $\parallel$.

PRACTICE AND PROBLEM SOLVING

Use the Converse of the Corresponding Angles Postulate and the given information to show that $\ell \parallel m$.

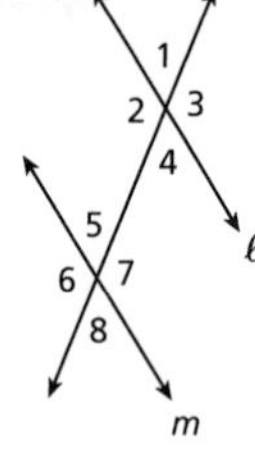

12. $\angle 3 \cong \angle 7$ — $\angle 3 \cong \angle 7$, so $\ell \parallel m$ by the Conv. of the Corr. $\angle$s Post.
13. $m\angle 4 = 54°$, $m\angle 8 = (7x + 5)°$, $x = 7$
14. $m\angle 2 = (8x + 4)°$, $m\angle 6 = (11x - 41)°$, $x = 15$
15. $m\angle 1 = (3x + 19)°$, $m\angle 5 = (4x + 7)°$, $x = 12$ — 15. $m\angle 1 = 55°$, and $m\angle 5 = 55°$, so $\angle 1 \cong \angle 5$. $\ell \parallel m$ by the Conv. of the Corr. $\angle$s Post.

3-3 PRACTICE A

1. The Converse of the Corresponding Angles Postulate states that if two coplanar lines are cut by a transversal so that a pair of corresponding angles is congruent, then the two lines are ___parallel___.

Use the figure for Exercises 2 and 3. Given the information in each exercise, state the reason why lines *b* and *c* are parallel.

2. $\angle 4 \cong \angle 8$
Conv. of Corr. $\angle$s Post.

3. $m\angle 3 = 68°$, $m\angle 7 = (5x + 3)°$, $x = 13$
$m\angle 7 = 68°$, $\angle 3 \cong \angle 7$, Conv. of Corr. $\angle$s Post.

Fill in the blanks to complete these theorems about parallel lines.

4. If two coplanar lines are cut by a ___transversal___ so that a pair of alternate interior angles are ___congruent___, then the two lines are parallel.
5. If two coplanar lines are cut by a transversal so that a pair of same-side interior angles are ___supplementary___, then the two lines are parallel.
6. If two coplanar lines are cut by a transversal so that a pair of alternate exterior angles are congruent, then the two lines are ___parallel___.
7. Shu believes that a theorem is missing from the lesson. His conjecture is that if two coplanar lines are cut by a transversal so that a pair of same-side exterior angles are supplementary, then the two lines are parallel. Complete the two-column proof with the statements and reasons provided.

Given: $\angle 1$ and $\angle 3$ are supplementary.
Prove: $m \parallel n$
Proof:

$m \parallel n$,
$\angle 2$ and $\angle 3$ are supplementary.
Given
$\cong$ Supps. Thm.

Statements	Reasons
1. $\angle 1$ and $\angle 3$ are supplementary.	1. a. ___Given___
2. b. ___$\angle 2$ and $\angle 3$ are supplementary.___	2. Linear Pair Thm.
3. $\angle 1 \cong \angle 2$	3. c. ___$\cong$ Supps. Thm.___
4. d. ___$m \parallel n$___	4. Conv. of Corr. $\angle$s Post.

3-3 PRACTICE B

Use the figure for Exercises 1–8. Tell whether lines *m* and *n* must be parallel from the given information. If they are, state your reasoning. (*Hint:* The angle measures may change for each exercise, and the figure is for reference only.)

1. $\angle 7 \cong \angle 3$
$m \parallel n$, Conv. of Alt. Int. $\angle$s Thm.
2. $m\angle 3 = (15x + 22)°$, $m\angle 1 = (19x - 10)°$, $x = 8$
$m \parallel n$, Conv. of Corr. $\angle$s Post.
3. $\angle 7 \cong \angle 6$
m and *n* do not have to be parallel.
4. $m\angle 2 = (5x + 3)°$, $m\angle 3 = (8x - 5)°$, $x = 14$
$m \parallel n$, Conv. of Same-Side Int. $\angle$s Thm.
5. $m\angle 8 = (6x - 1)°$, $m\angle 4 = (5x + 3)°$, $x = 9$
m and *n* are not parallel.
6. $\angle 5 \cong \angle 7$
$m \parallel n$, Conv. of Corr. $\angle$s Post.
7. $\angle 1 \cong \angle 5$
$m \parallel n$, Conv. of Alt. Ext. $\angle$s Thm.
8. $m\angle 6 = (x + 10)°$, $m\angle 2 = (x + 15)°$
m and *n* are not parallel.
9. Look at some of the printed letters in a textbook. The small horizontal and vertical segments attached to the ends of the letters are called *serifs*. Most of the letters in a textbook are in a serif typeface. The letters on this page do not have serifs, so these letters are in a sans-serif typeface. (*Sans* means "without" in French.) The figure shows a capital letter *A* with serifs. Use the given information to write a paragraph proof that the serif, segment $\overline{HI}$, is parallel to segment $\overline{JK}$.

Given: $\angle 1$ and $\angle 3$ are supplementary.
Prove: $\overline{HI} \parallel \overline{JK}$

Possible answer: The given information states that $\angle 1$ and $\angle 3$ are supplementary. $\angle 1$ and $\angle 2$ are also supplementary by the Linear Pair Theorem. Therefore $\angle 3$ and $\angle 2$ must be congruent by the Congruent Supplements Theorem. Since $\angle 3$ and $\angle 2$ are congruent, $\overline{HI}$ and $\overline{JK}$ are parallel by the Converse of the Corresponding Angles Postulate.

Independent Practice

For Exercises	See Example
12–15	1
16–21	2
22	3
23	4

Extra Practice
Skills Practice p. S8
Application Practice p. S30

Use the theorems and given information to show that $n \parallel p$.

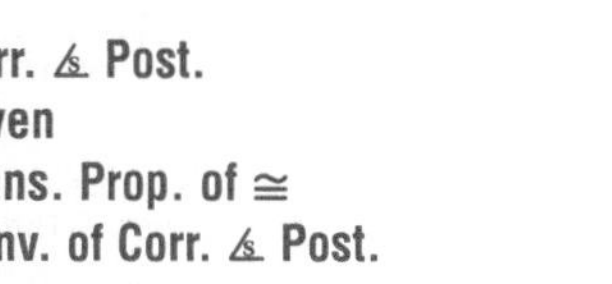

16. $\angle 3 \cong \angle 6$
17. $\angle 2 \cong \angle 7$
18. $m\angle 4 + m\angle 6 = 180°$
19. $m\angle 1 = (8x - 7)°$, $m\angle 8 = (6x + 21)°$, $x = 14$
20. $m\angle 4 = (4x + 3)°$, $m\angle 5 = (5x - 22)°$, $x = 25$
21. $m\angle 3 = (2x + 15)°$, $m\angle 5 = (3x + 15)°$, $x = 30$
22. Complete the following two-column proof.
    Given: $\overline{AB} \parallel \overline{CD}$, $\angle 1 \cong \angle 2$, $\angle 3 \cong \angle 4$
    Prove: $\overline{BC} \parallel \overline{DE}$
    Proof:

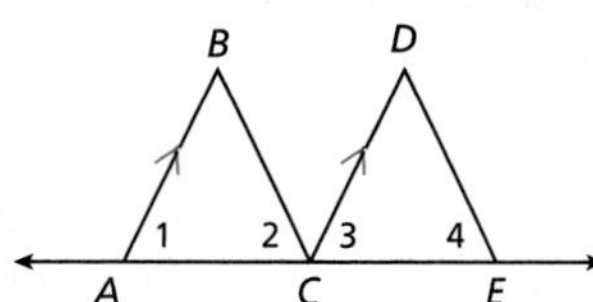

Statements	Reasons
1. $\overline{AB} \parallel \overline{CD}$	1. Given
2. $\angle 1 \cong \angle 3$	2. a. ___?___ Corr. ∠s Post.
3. $\angle 1 \cong \angle 2$, $\angle 3 \cong \angle 4$	3. b. ___?___ Given
4. $\angle 2 \cong \angle 4$	4. c. ___?___ Trans. Prop. of ≅
5. d. ___?___ $\overline{BC} \parallel \overline{DE}$	5. e. ___?___ Conv. of Corr. ∠s Post.

23. **Art** Edmund Dulac used perspective when drawing the floor titles in this illustration for *The Wind's Tale* by Hans Christian Andersen. Show that $DJ \parallel EK$ if $m\angle 1 = (3x + 2)°$, $m\angle 2 = (5x - 10)°$, and $x = 6$.

23. If $x = 6$, then $m\angle 1 = 20°$ and $m\angle 2 = 20°$. So $\overline{DJ} \parallel \overline{EK}$ by the Conv. of the Corr. ∠s Post.

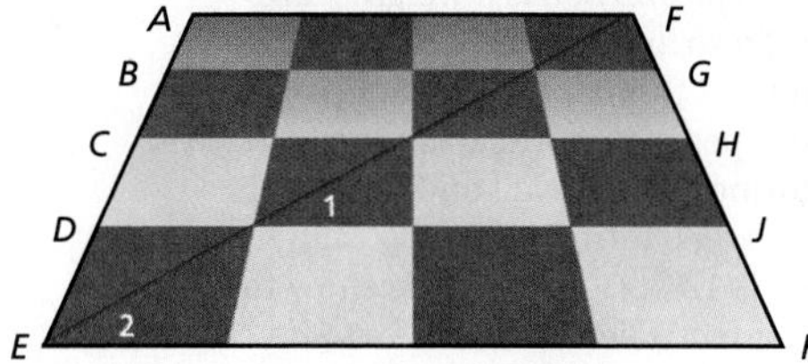

Name the postulate or theorem that proves that $\ell \parallel m$.

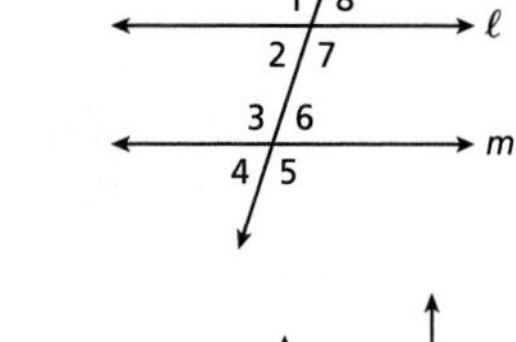

24. $\angle 8 \cong \angle 6$
25. $\angle 8 \cong \angle 4$
26. $\angle 2 \cong \angle 6$
27. $\angle 7 \cong \angle 5$
28. $\angle 3 \cong \angle 7$
29. $m\angle 2 + m\angle 3 = 180°$

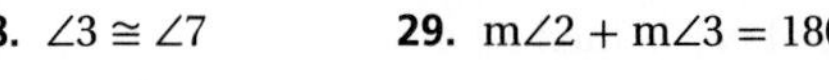

24. Conv. of the Corr. ∠s Post.
25. Conv. of the Alt. Ext. ∠s Thm.
26. Conv. of the Alt. Int. ∠s Thm.
27. Conv. of the Corr. ∠s Post.
28. Conv. of the Alt. Int. ∠s Thm.
29. Conv. of the Same-Side Int. ∠s Thm.

For the given information, tell which pair of lines must be parallel. Name the postulate or theorem that supports your answer.

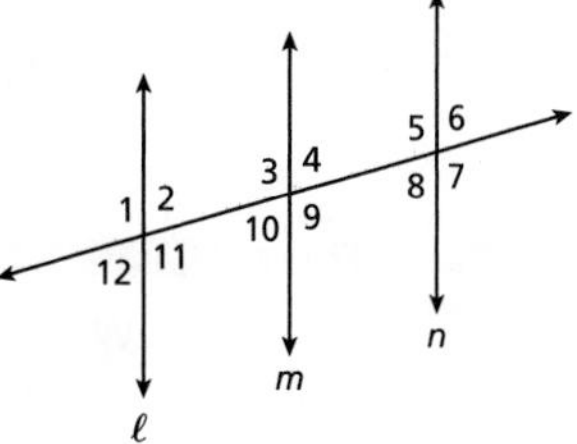

30. $m\angle 2 = m\angle 10$
31. $m\angle 8 + m\angle 9 = 180°$
32. $\angle 1 \cong \angle 7$
33. $m\angle 10 = m\angle 6$
34. $\angle 11 \cong \angle 5$
35. $m\angle 2 + m\angle 5 = 180°$
36. **Multi-Step** Two lines are intersected by a transversal so that $\angle 1$ and $\angle 2$ are corresponding angles, $\angle 1$ and $\angle 3$ are alternate exterior angles, and $\angle 3$ and $\angle 4$ are corresponding angles. If $\angle 2 \cong \angle 4$, what theorem or postulate can be used to prove the lines parallel? Conv. of Alt. Int. ∠s Thm.

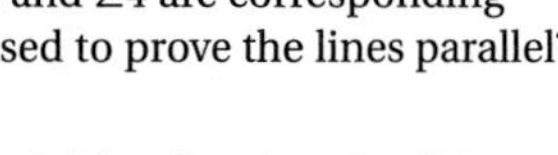

COMMON ERROR ALERT

Students who justified **Step 2** in **Exercise 22,** with the incorrect theorem may benefit from drawing just $\overleftrightarrow{AB}$, $\overleftrightarrow{CD}$, $\overleftrightarrow{AE}$, $\angle 1$, and $\angle 3$. This may make it easier to see the relationship between the angles and the lines.

Teaching Tip

Algebra In **Step 4** of **Exercise 22,** help students understand the double application of the Transitive Property of Congruence. Ask them what conclusion they can draw if $a = b$, $b = c$, and $c = d$, using the Transitive Property of Equality. $a = d$

Answers

16. $\angle 3 \cong \angle 6$, so $n \parallel p$ by the Conv. of the Alt. Int. ∠s Thm.
17. $\angle 2 \cong \angle 7$, so $n \parallel p$ by the Conv. of the Alt. Ext. ∠s Thm.
18. $\angle 4$ and $\angle 6$ are supp., so $n \parallel p$ by the Conv. of the Same-Side Int. ∠s Thm.
19. $m\angle 1 = 105°$, and $m\angle 8 = 105°$, so $\angle 1 \cong \angle 8$. $n \parallel p$ by the Conv. of the Alt. Ext. ∠s Thm.
20. $m\angle 4 = 103°$, and $m\angle 5 = 103°$, so $\angle 4 \cong \angle 5$. $n \parallel p$ by the Conv. of the Alt. Int. ∠s Thm.
21. $m\angle 3 = 75°$, and $m\angle 5 = 105°$. $75° + 105° = 180°$, so $\angle 3$ and $\angle 5$ are supp. $n \parallel p$ by the Conv. of the Same-Side Int. ∠s Thm.
30. $\ell \parallel m$; Conv. of the Alt. Int. ∠s Thm.
31. $m \parallel n$; Conv. of the Same-Side Int. ∠s Thm.
32. $\ell \parallel n$; Conv. of the Alt. Ext. ∠s Thm.
33. $m \parallel n$; Conv. of the Alt. Ext. ∠s Thm.
34. $\ell \parallel n$; Conv. of the Alt. Int. ∠s Thm.
35. $\ell \parallel n$; Conv. of the Same-Side Int. ∠s Thm.

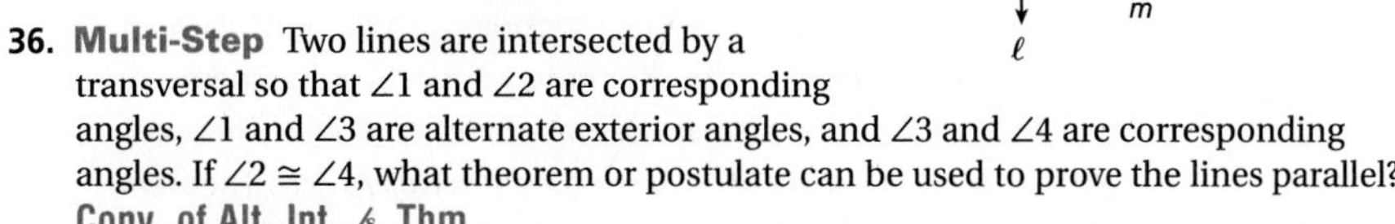

3-3 PRACTICE C

1. $p \parallel q$, $m\angle 1 = (6x + y - 4)°$, $m\angle 2 = (x - 9y + 1)°$, $m\angle 3 = (11x + 2)°$. Find x, y, and the measures of $\angle 1$, $\angle 2$, and $\angle 3$.
   $x = 11$; $y = -5$; $m\angle 1 = 57°$; $m\angle 2 = 57°$; $m\angle 3 = 123°$
2. Use the figure and the given information to write a paragraph proof that the sum of the measures of the three angles in a triangle is 180°. (*Hint:* Begin by constructing $\overleftrightarrow{FG}$ through point C and parallel to $\overline{AB}$.)
   Given: ABC is a triangle.
   Prove: $m\angle 1 + m\angle 2 + m\angle 3 = 180°$
   Possible answer: Construct $\overleftrightarrow{FG}$ through point C and parallel to $\overline{AB}$. $\angle 3$ and $\angle 4$ are a linear pair, so $m\angle 3 + m\angle 4 = 180°$ by the Linear Pair Theorem. But the Angle Addition Postulate shows that $m\angle 4 = m\angle ACF + m\angle FCD$, so by substitution $m\angle 3 + m\angle ACF + m\angle FCD = 180°$. $m\angle 1 = m\angle ACF$ by the Alternate Interior Angles Theorem and $m\angle 2 = m\angle FCD$ by the Corresponding Angles Postulate. Therefore $m\angle 1 + m\angle 2 + m\angle 3 = 180°$ by substitution.
3. In an *isosceles triangle*, at least two of the angles are congruent. To construct isosceles triangle DEH, begin by drawing $\overrightarrow{DE}$ and $\overrightarrow{DF}$. If you copy $\angle FDE$ and let the angle open in the same direction, the ray would be parallel to $\overrightarrow{DF}$. Instead, copy $\angle FDE$ and draw $\overrightarrow{EG}$ so that the ray intersects $\overrightarrow{DF}$. Label the intersection point H. Use your compass to measure $\overline{DH}$ and $\overline{EH}$. What is remarkable about the measures of these segments?
   The measures of the segments are equal.
4. Construct another isosceles triangle with angles and side lengths different from the triangle you drew in Exercise 3. Again measure the lengths of the sides opposite the congruent angles. Write a conjecture about the measures of the side lengths in isosceles triangles.
   Possible answer: If a triangle is isosceles, then the sides opposite the congruent angles are congruent.
   Possible answer:

Exercise 37 involves using the Converse of the Same-Side Interior Angles Theorem to prove that lines are parallel. This exercise prepares students for the Multi-Step Test Prep on page 180.

In **Exercise 43,** to help students choose the best answer, ask them to choose the answer that will allow them to directly prove $\ell \parallel m$.

Answers

37a. $\angle URT$; $m\angle URT = m\angle URS + m\angle SRT$ by the $\angle$ Add. Post. It is given that $m\angle SRT = 25°$ and $m\angle URS = 90°$, so $m\angle URT = 25° + 90° = 115°$.

b. It is given that $m\angle SUR = 65°$. From part **a,** $m\angle URT = 115°$. $65° + 115° = 180°$, so $\overleftrightarrow{SU} \parallel \overleftrightarrow{RT}$ by the Conv. of the Same-Side Int. ∡ Thm.

39. It is given that ∠1 and ∠2 are supp., so $m\angle 1 + m\angle 2 = 180°$. By the Lin. Pair Thm., $m\angle 2 + m\angle 3 = 180°$. By the Trans. Prop. of =, $m\angle 1 + m\angle 2 = m\angle 2 + m\angle 3$. By the Subtr. Prop. of =, $m\angle 1 = m\angle 3$. By the Conv. of the Corr. ∡ Post., $\ell \parallel m$.

40. The ∠ formed by the wall and the roof and the ∠ formed by the plumb line and the roof are corr. ∡. If they have the same measure, then they are ≅, so the wall is ∥ to the plumb line, by the Conv. of the Corr. ∡ Post. Since the plumb line is perfectly vertical, the wall must also be perfectly vertical.

41. The Reflex. Prop. is not true for ∥ lines, because a line is not ∥ to itself. The Sym. Prop. is true, because if $\ell \parallel m$, then ℓ and m are coplanar and do not intersect. So $m \parallel \ell$. The Trans. Prop. is not true for ∥ lines, because if $\ell \parallel m$ and $m \parallel n$, then ℓ and n could be the same line. So they would not be ∥.

42. Yes; by the Vert. ∡ Thm.; the ∠ that forms a same-side int. ∠ with the 55° ∠ measures 125°. $125° + 55° = 180°$, so the same-side int. ∡ are supp. By the Conv. of the Same-Side Int. ∡ Thm., $a \parallel b$.

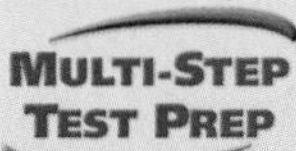

37. This problem will prepare you for the Multi-Step Test Prep on page 180.

In the diagram, which represents the side view of a mystery spot, $m\angle SRT = 25°$, and $m\angle SUR = 65°$.

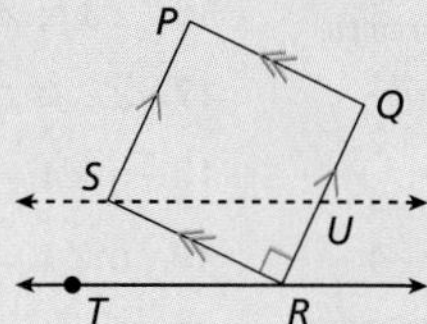

a. Name a same-side interior angle of $\angle SUR$ for lines $\overleftrightarrow{SU}$ and $\overleftrightarrow{RT}$ with transversal $\overline{RU}$. What is its measure? Explain your reasoning.

b. Prove that $\overleftrightarrow{SU}$ and $\overleftrightarrow{RT}$ are parallel.

38. Complete the flowchart proof of the Converse of the Alternate Interior Angles Theorem.

Given: $\angle 2 \cong \angle 3$
Prove: $\ell \parallel m$
Proof:

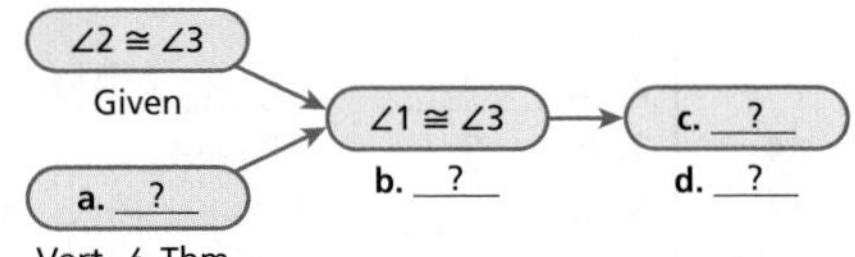

a. $\angle 1 \cong \angle 2$
b. Trans. Prop. of ≅
c. $\ell \parallel m$
d. Conv. of Corr. ∡ Post.

39. Use the diagram to write a paragraph proof of the Converse of the Same-Side Interior Angles Theorem.

Given: ∠1 and ∠2 are supplementary.
Prove: $\ell \parallel m$

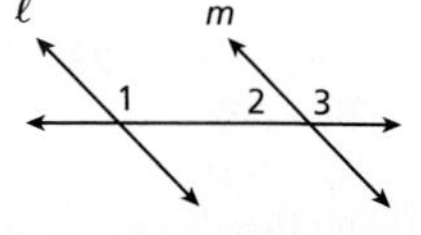

40. Carpentry A *plumb bob* is a weight hung at the end of a string, called a *plumb line*. The weight pulls the string down so that the plumb line is perfectly vertical. Suppose that the angle formed by the wall and the roof is 123° and the angle formed by the plumb line and the roof is 123°. How does this show that the wall is perfectly vertical?

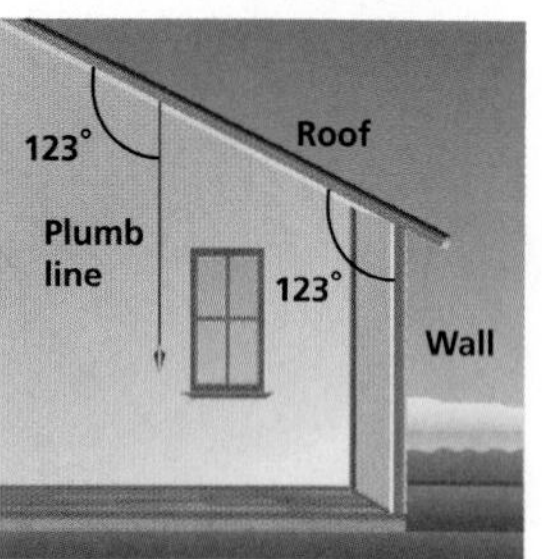

41. Critical Thinking Are the Reflexive, Symmetric, and Transitive Properties true for parallel lines? Explain why or why not.

Reflexive: $\ell \parallel \ell$
Symmetric: If $\ell \parallel m$, then $m \parallel \ell$.
Transitive: If $\ell \parallel m$ and $m \parallel n$, then $\ell \parallel n$.

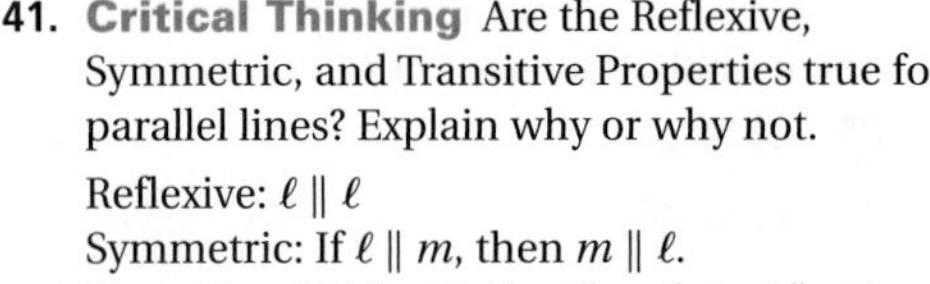

42. Write About It Does the information given in the diagram allow you to conclude that $a \parallel b$? Explain.

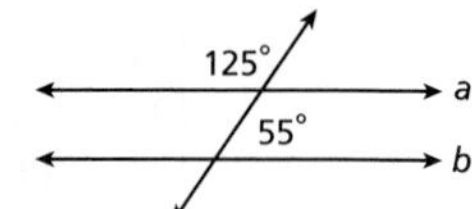

43. Which postulate or theorem can be used to prove $\ell \parallel m$?

(A) Converse of the Corresponding Angles Postulate
(B) Converse of the Alternate Interior Angles Theorem
(C) Converse of the Alternate Exterior Angles Theorem
(D) Converse of the Same-Side Interior Angles Theorem

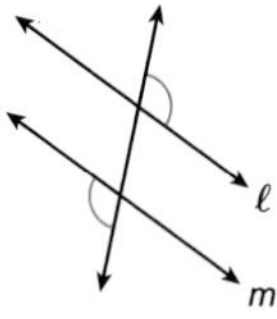

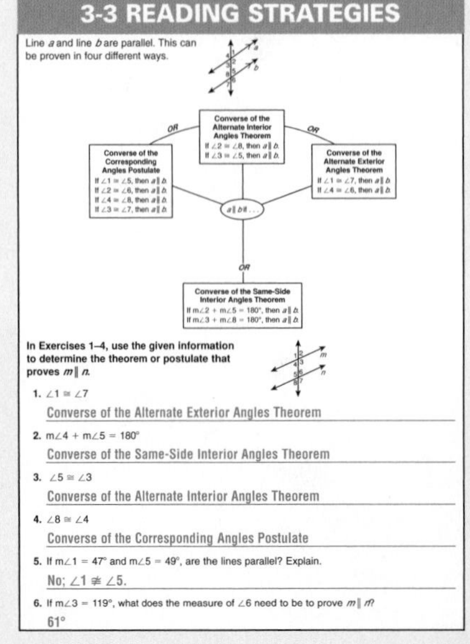

3-3 READING STRATEGIES

Line a and line b are parallel. This can be proven in four different ways.

Converse of the Corresponding Angles Postulate
If ∠1 ≅ ∠5, then $a \parallel b$.
If ∠2 ≅ ∠6, then $a \parallel b$.
If ∠4 ≅ ∠8, then $a \parallel b$.
If ∠3 ≅ ∠7, then $a \parallel b$.

OR

Converse of the Alternate Interior Angles Theorem
If ∠2 ≅ ∠8, then $a \parallel b$.
If ∠3 ≅ ∠5, then $a \parallel b$.

OR

Converse of the Alternate Exterior Angles Theorem
If ∠1 ≅ ∠7, then $a \parallel b$.
If ∠4 ≅ ∠6, then $a \parallel b$.

$a \parallel b$ if . . .

OR

Converse of the Same-Side Interior Angles Theorem
If $m\angle 2 + m\angle 5 = 180°$, then $a \parallel b$.
If $m\angle 3 + m\angle 8 = 180°$, then $a \parallel b$.

In Exercises 1–4, use the given information to determine the theorem or postulate that proves $m \parallel n$.

1. ∠1 ≅ ∠7
Converse of the Alternate Exterior Angles Theorem

2. $m\angle 4 + m\angle 5 = 180°$
Converse of the Same-Side Interior Angles Theorem

3. ∠5 ≅ ∠3
Converse of the Alternate Interior Angles Theorem

4. ∠8 ≅ ∠4
Converse of the Corresponding Angles Postulate

5. If $m\angle 1 = 47°$ and $m\angle 5 = 49°$, are the lines parallel? Explain.
No; ∠1 ≇ ∠5.

6. If $m\angle 3 = 119°$, what does the measure of ∠6 need to be to prove $m \parallel n$?
61°

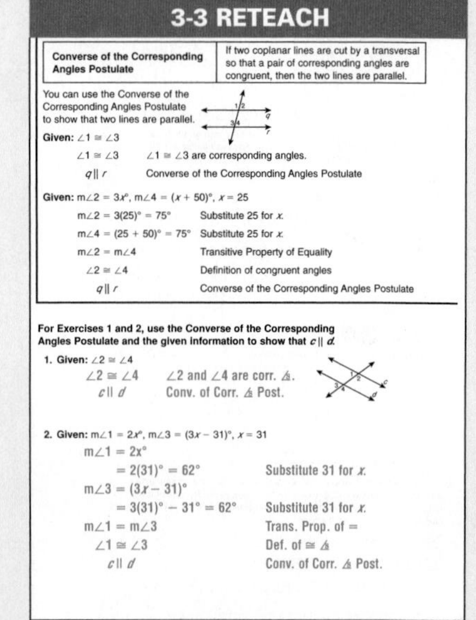

3-3 RETEACH

Converse of the Corresponding Angles Postulate	If two coplanar lines are cut by a transversal so that a pair of corresponding angles are congruent, then the two lines are parallel.

You can use the Converse of the Corresponding Angles Postulate to show that two lines are parallel.

Given: ∠1 ≅ ∠3

∠1 ≅ ∠3 — ∠1 ≅ ∠3 are corresponding angles.
$q \parallel r$ — Converse of the Corresponding Angles Postulate

Given: $m\angle 2 = 3x°$, $m\angle 4 = (x + 50)°$, $x = 25$

$m\angle 2 = 3(25)° = 75°$ — Substitute 25 for x.
$m\angle 4 = (25 + 50)° = 75°$ — Substitute 25 for x.
$m\angle 2 = m\angle 4$ — Transitive Property of Equality
∠2 ≅ ∠4 — Definition of congruent angles
$q \parallel r$ — Converse of the Corresponding Angles Postulate

For Exercises 1 and 2, use the Converse of the Corresponding Angles Postulate and the given information to show that $c \parallel d$.

1. **Given:** ∠2 ≅ ∠4
∠2 ≅ ∠4 — ∠2 and ∠4 are corr. ∡.
$c \parallel d$ — Conv. of Corr. ∡ Post.

2. **Given:** $m\angle 1 = 2x°$, $m\angle 3 = (3x - 31)°$, $x = 31$
$m\angle 1 = 2x°$
$= 2(31)° = 62°$ — Substitute 31 for x.
$m\angle 3 = (3x - 31)°$
$= 3(31)° - 31° = 62°$ — Substitute 31 for x.
$m\angle 1 = m\angle 3$ — Trans. Prop. of =
∠1 ≅ ∠3 — Def. of ≅ ∡
$c \parallel d$ — Conv. of Corr. ∡ Post.

44. Two coplanar lines are cut by a transversal. Which condition does NOT guarantee that the two lines are parallel?

Ⓐ A pair of alternate interior angles are congruent.
Ⓑ A pair of same-side interior angles are supplementary.
Ⓒ A pair of corresponding angles are congruent.
Ⓓ A pair of alternate exterior angles are complementary.

45. **Gridded Response** Find the value of x so that $\ell \parallel m$. **15**

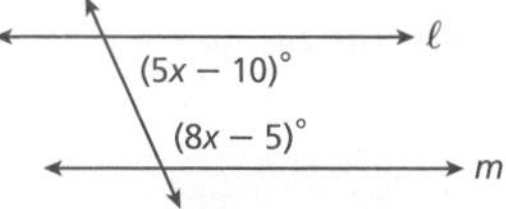

CHALLENGE AND EXTEND

Determine which lines, if any, can be proven parallel using the given information. Justify your answers.

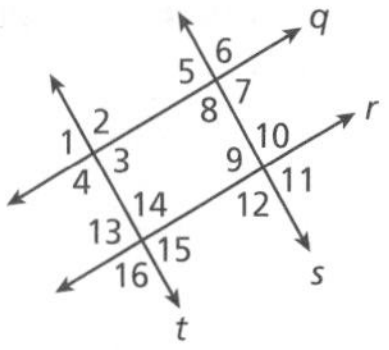

46. $\angle 1 \cong \angle 15$ 47. $\angle 8 \cong \angle 14$

48. $\angle 3 \cong \angle 7$ 49. $\angle 8 \cong \angle 10$

50. $\angle 6 \cong \angle 8$ 51. $\angle 13 \cong \angle 11$

52. $m\angle 12 + m\angle 15 = 180°$ 53. $m\angle 5 + m\angle 8 = 180°$

54. Write a paragraph proof that $\overline{AE} \parallel \overline{BD}$.

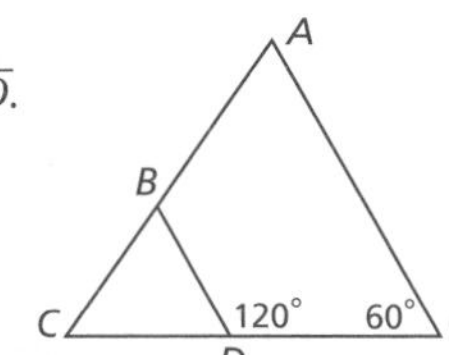

53. No lines can be proven ∥.

54. It is given that $m\angle E = 60°$ and $m\angle BDE = 120°$, so $m\angle E + m\angle BDE = 180°$. $\angle E$ and $\angle BDE$ are supp., so $\overline{AE} \parallel \overline{BD}$ by the Conv. of the Same-Side Int. ∠s Thm.

46. $q \parallel r$ by the Conv. of the Alt. Ext. ∠s Thm.

47. No lines can be proven ∥.

48. $s \parallel t$ by the Conv. of the Corr. ∠s Post.

49. $q \parallel r$ by the Conv. of the Alt. Int. ∠s Thm.

50. No lines can be proven ∥.

51. $s \parallel t$ by the Conv. of the Alt. Ext. ∠s Thm.

52. $s \parallel t$ by the Conv. of the Same-Side Int. ∠s Thm.

Use the diagram for Exercises 55 and 56.

55. **Given:** $m\angle 2 + m\angle 3 = 180°$
Prove: $\ell \parallel m$

56. **Given:** $m\angle 2 + m\angle 5 = 180°$
Prove: $\ell \parallel n$

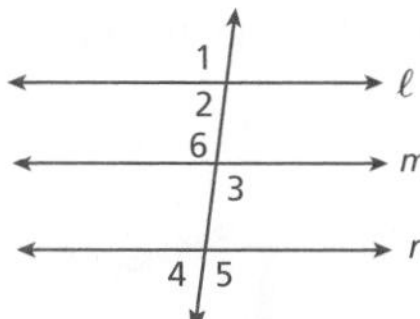

SPIRAL REVIEW

Solve each equation for the indicated variable. *(Previous course)*

57. $a - b = -c$, for a **$a = b - c$**

58. $y = \frac{1}{2}x - 10$, for x **$x = 2y + 20$**

59. $4y + 6x = 12$, for y **$y = -\frac{3}{2}x + 3$**

Write the converse, inverse, and contrapositive of each conditional statement. Find the truth value of each. *(Lesson 2-2)*

60. If an animal is a bat, then it has wings.

61. If a polygon is a triangle, then it has exactly three sides.

62. If the digit in the ones place of a whole number is 2, then the number is even.

Identify each of the following. *(Lesson 3-1)*

63. one pair of parallel segments **$\overline{AD} \parallel \overline{BC}$**

64. one pair of skew segments

65. one pair of perpendicular segments **$\overline{AB} \perp \overline{AD}$**

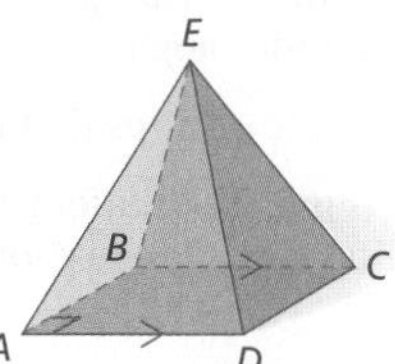

64. Possible answer: $\overline{AB}$ and $\overline{DE}$ are skew.

COMMON ERROR ALERT

In **Exercises 46–53,** remind students that they should not assume that lines in the diagram are parallel only because they appear to be parallel. They should justify each answer with a postulate or theorem learned in this lesson.

Answers

55–56, 60–62. See p. A13.

Journal

Have students explain how to construct parallel lines using one of the postulates or theorems in the lesson.

ALTERNATIVE ASSESSMENT

Have students draw two lines by holding a ruler (MK) in place and drawing a line on each side. Then have students draw a transversal and use angle measures to confirm that the lines are parallel.

Power Presentations with PowerPoint®

3-3 Lesson Quiz

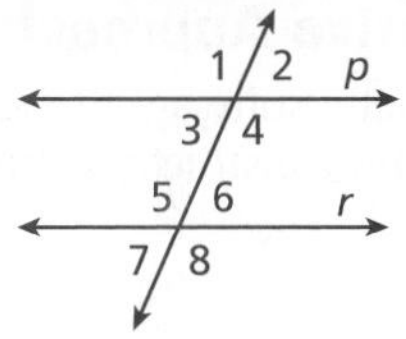

Name the postulate or theorem that proves $p \parallel r$.

1. $\angle 4 \cong \angle 5$
Conv. of Alt. Int. ∠s Thm.

2. $\angle 2 \cong \angle 7$
Conv. of Alt. Ext. ∠s Thm.

3. $\angle 3 \cong \angle 7$
Conv. of Corr. ∠s Post.

4. $\angle 3$ and $\angle 5$ are supplementary. Conv. of Same-Side Int. ∠s Thm.

Use the theorems and given information to prove $p \parallel r$.

5. $m\angle 2 = (5x + 20)°$, $m\angle 7 = (7x + 8)°$, and $x = 6$
$m\angle 2 = 5(6) + 20 = 50°$
$m\angle 7 = 7(6) + 8 = 50°$
$m\angle 2 = m\angle 7$, so $\angle 2 \cong \angle 7$.
$p \parallel r$ by the Conv. of Alt. Ext. ∠s Thm.

Also available on transparency

3-3 PROBLEM SOLVING

1. A bedroom has sloping ceilings as shown. Marcel is hanging a shelf below a rafter. If $m\angle 1 = (8x - 1)°$, $m\angle 2 = (6x + 7)°$, and $x = 4$, show that the shelf is parallel to the rafter above it.

$m\angle 1 = (8x - 1) = 8(4) - 1 = 31°$ Replace x with 4.
$m\angle 2 = (6x + 7) = 6(4) + 7 = 31°$ Replace x with 4.
∠1 and ∠2 are corr. ∠s and they are congruent, so the shelf is parallel to the rafter by the Conv. of Corr. ∠s Post.

2. In the sign, $m\angle 3 = (3y + 7)°$, $m\angle 4 = (5y + 5)°$, and $y = 21$. Show that the sign posts are parallel.

$m\angle 3 = (3y + 7) = 3(21) + 7 = 70°$ Replace y with 21.
$m\angle 4 = (5y + 5) = 5(21) + 5 = 110°$ Replace y with 21.
$m\angle 3 + m\angle 4 = 70° + 110° = 180°$
∠3 and ∠4 are supp. ∠s, so the sign posts are parallel by the Conv. of Same-Side Int. ∠s Thm.

Choose the best answer.

3. In the bench, $m\angle EFG = (4n + 16)°$, $m\angle FJL = (3n + 40)°$, $m\angle GKL = (3n + 22)°$, and $n = 24$. Which is a true statement?
Ⓐ $\overline{FG} \parallel \overline{HK}$ by the Converse of the Corr. ∠s Post.
B $\overline{FG} \parallel \overline{HK}$ by the Converse of the Alt. Int. ∠s Thm.
C $\overline{EJ} \parallel \overline{GK}$ by the Converse of the Corr. ∠s Post.
D $\overline{EJ} \parallel \overline{GK}$ by the Converse of the Alt. Int. ∠s Thm.

4. In the windsurfing sail, $m\angle 5 = (7c + 1)°$, $m\angle 6 = (9c - 1)°$, $m\angle 7 = (17c)°$, and $c = 6$. Which is a true statement?
F $\overline{RV}$ is parallel to $\overline{SW}$.
G $\overline{SW}$ is parallel to $\overline{TX}$.
H $\overline{RT}$ is parallel to $\overline{VX}$.
Ⓙ Cannot conclude that two segments are parallel

The figure shows Natalia's initials, which are monogrammed on her duffel bag. Use the figure for Exercises 5 and 6.

5. If $m\angle 1 = (4x - 24)°$, $m\angle 2 = (2x + 8)°$, and $x = 16$, show that the sides of the letter N are parallel.
$m\angle 1 = 40°$ and $m\angle 2 = 40°$, so the sides are ∥ by the Conv. of the Alt. Int. ∠s Thm.

6. If $m\angle 3 = (7x + 13)°$, $m\angle 4 = (5x + 35)°$, and $x = 11$, show that the sides of the letter H are parallel.
$m\angle 3 = 90°$ and $m\angle 4 = 90°$, so the sides are ∥ by the Conv. of the Same-Side Int. ∠s Thm.

3-3 CHALLENGE

In the figure at right, what value of the variable b guarantees that lines ℓ and m are parallel? Notice that the angles with measures $(9b - 8)°$ and $(7b + 10)°$ are a pair of alternate exterior angles. If these measures are equal, it follows that $\ell \parallel m$. So you can write and solve an equation that reflects this fact.

$$9b - 8 = 7b + 10$$
$$9b - 8 + 8 = 7b + 10 + 8$$
$$9b = 7b + 18$$
$$9b - 7b = 7b + 18 - 7b$$
$$2b = 18$$
$$b = 9$$

When $b = 9$, $(9b - 8)° = 73°$ and $(7b + 10)° = 73°$, giving $\ell \parallel m$.

Find the value of a that guarantees $r \parallel s$.

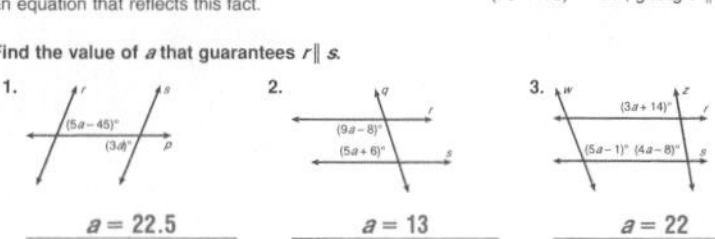

1. **$a = 22.5$** 2. **$a = 13$** 3. **$a = 22$**

4. Refer to the figure at right. Explain why it is not possible to find a value of n that guarantees $j \parallel k$.
Explanations may vary.

5. a. Refer to the figure at right. Explain why $u \parallel v$ for any reasonable values of c and d.
Explanations may vary.
b. Give the range of reasonable values for c and d.
$0 < c < 20$; $0 < d < 100$

6. The diagram at right is a plan for drawing a stylized version of the letter A. A person using this plan may choose any reasonable values for p and q. Enlarge the plan on a separate sheet of paper.
a. Using variable expressions, label the measures of all the acute and obtuse angles. Assume that all segments that appear parallel are, indeed, parallel. (*Hint:* It will help to extend the segments and to draw at least one additional line.)
$m\angle 1 = m\angle 2 = m\angle 6 = (180 - p)°$
$m\angle 3 = m\angle 4 = m\angle 5 = (180 - q)°$
$m\angle 7 = p°$; $m\angle 8 = q°$
$m\angle 9 = (180 - p - q)$
b. What is a range of reasonable values for p and q?
$0 < q < 90$; $p < q$

Organizer

Use with Lesson 3-3

Pacing:
Traditional $\frac{1}{2}$ day
Block $\frac{1}{4}$ day

Objective: Use various methods to construct parallel lines.

Materials: compass, protractor, straightedge, and patty paper

Online Edition

Countdown Week 5

Resources

Geometry Lab Activities
3-3 Lab Recording Sheet

Teach

Discuss

One method of constructing parallel lines was shown in Lesson 3-3. Two more methods are shown in this lab. The first method uses a property of a *rhombus,* which will be discussed in Chapter 6. The second method uses a theorem from Lesson 3-4.

For the first construction, check for compasses (MK) that will not keep their settings. Remind students to sharpen their pencils.

Alternative Approach

Use geometry software to perform either of the constructions from this lab.

State Resources

3-3

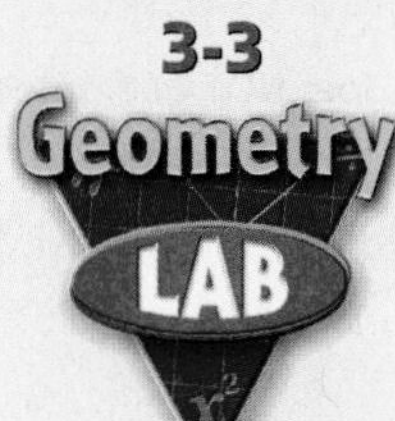

Construct Parallel Lines

Use with Lesson 3-3

In Lesson 3-3, you learned one method of constructing parallel lines using a compass and straightedge. Another method, called the rhombus method, uses a property of a figure called a *rhombus,* which you will study in Chapter 6. The rhombus method is shown below.

Activity 1

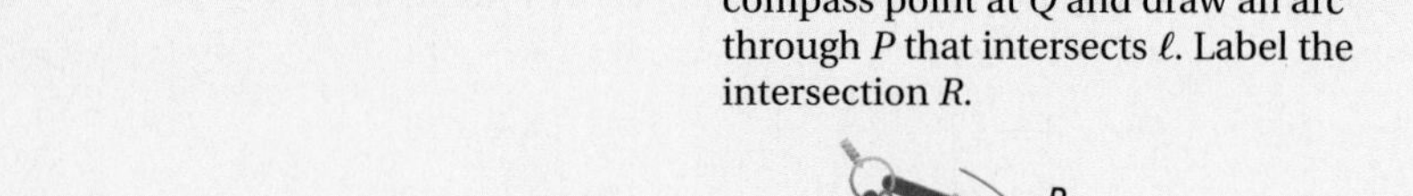

1. Draw a line ℓ and a point P not on the line.

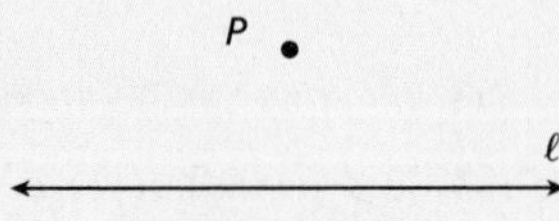

2. Choose a point Q on the line. Place your compass point at Q and draw an arc through P that intersects ℓ. Label the intersection R.

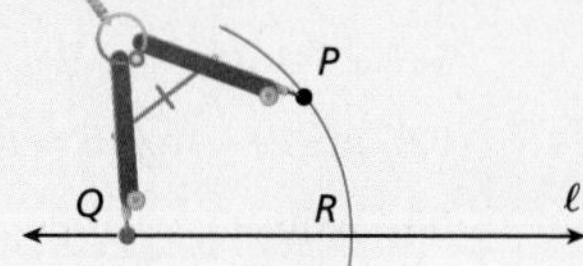

3. Using the same compass setting as the first arc, draw two more arcs: one from P, the other from R. Label the intersection of the two arcs S.

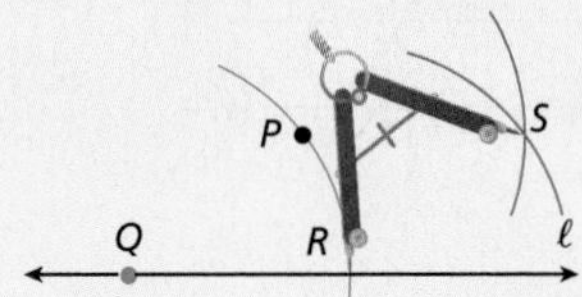

4. Draw $\overleftrightarrow{PS} \parallel \ell$.

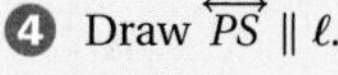

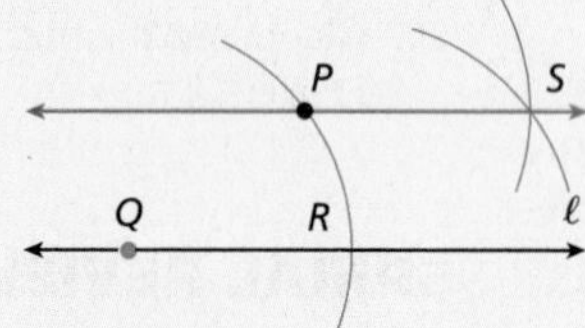

Try This

1. Repeat Activity 1 using a different point not on the line. Are your results the same? **Yes; the lines are still ||.**
2. Using the lines you constructed in Problem 1, draw transversal $\overleftrightarrow{PQ}$. Verify that the lines are parallel by using a protractor to measure alternate interior angles. **Check students' work.**
3. What postulate ensures that this construction is always possible? **|| Post.**
4. A *rhombus* is a quadrilateral with four congruent sides. Explain why this method is called the rhombus method. **If you draw quadrilateral *PQRS* in the diagram, then it is a rhombus, because the same compass setting was used to construct all 4 side lengths.**

Activity 2

1. Draw a line ℓ and point P on a piece of patty paper.

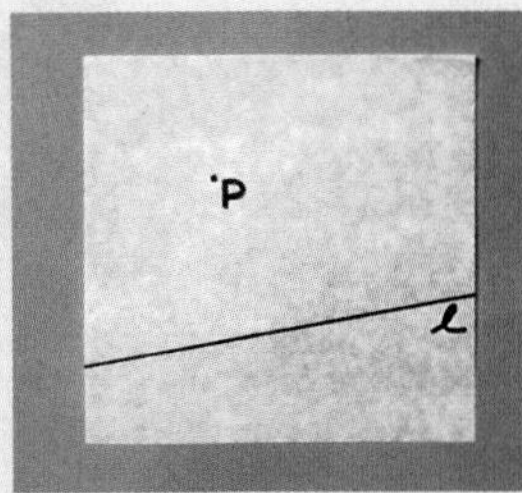

2. Fold the paper through P so that both sides of line ℓ match up

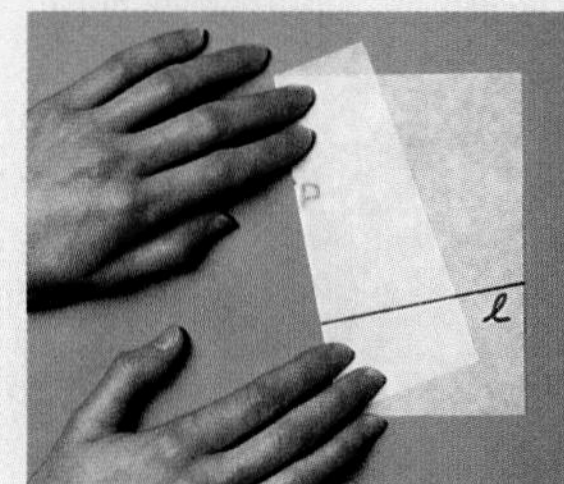

3. Crease the paper to form line m. P should be on line m.

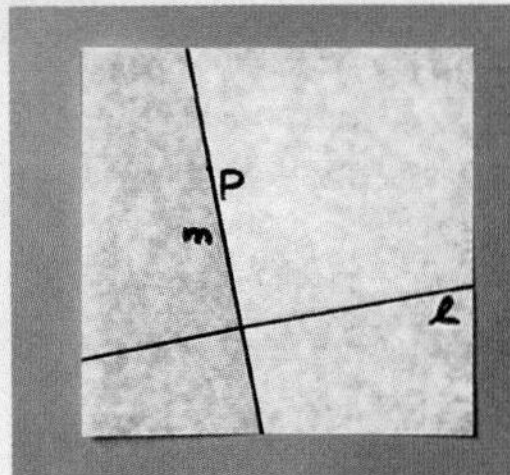

4. Fold the paper again through P so that both sides of line m match up.

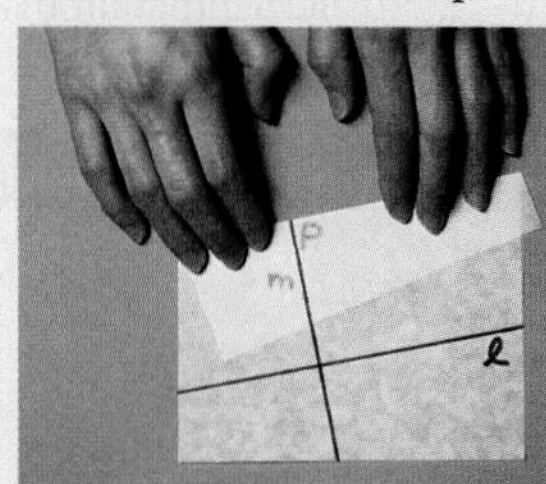

5. Crease the paper to form line n. Line n is parallel to line ℓ through P.

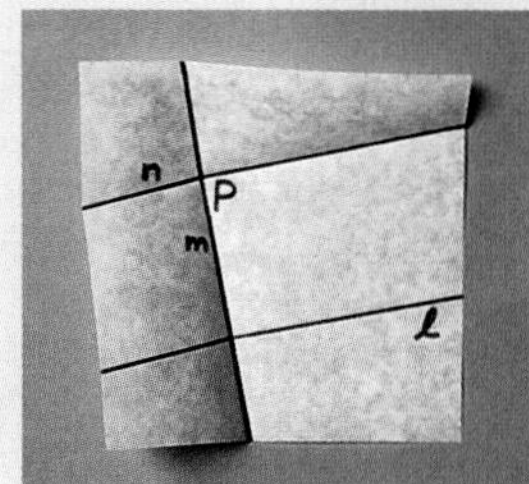

Try This

5. Repeat Activity 2 using a point in a different place not on the line. Are your results the same? **Yes; the lines are still ||.**
6. Use a protractor to measure corresponding angles. How can you tell that the lines are parallel? **The corr. ∠s measure 90°. By the Conv. of the Corr. ∠s Post., the lines must be ||.**
7. Draw a triangle and construct a line parallel to one side through the vertex that is not on that side. **Check students' work.**
8. Line m is perpendicular to both ℓ and n. Use this statement to complete the following conjecture: If two lines in a plane are perpendicular to the same line, then ___?___. **the lines are ||**

Close

Key Concepts

You can use properties of a figure called a *rhombus* to construct parallel lines.

You can also use this fact, which is stated as a theorem in Lesson 3-4: If two coplanar lines are perpendicular to a third line, then those two lines are parallel to each other.

Assessment

Journal Have students use the postulate and theorems from Lesson 3-3 to explain why the lines in each construction are parallel.

Teacher to Teacher

I like to give students the opportunity to try these constructions using geometry software. Although constructing parallel lines is much easier with geometry software, the following instructions allow students to duplicate the rhombus method.

Draw a line $\overleftrightarrow{AB}$ and a point P. Draw a circle centered at A that passes through P. This circle intersects line $\overleftrightarrow{AB}$ in two places. Label point C, the intersection closer to point P. Draw a circle centered at P that passes through A. Then draw another circle centered at C that passes through A. These circles intersect at point A and another point. Label the other point Q. Draw line $\overleftrightarrow{PQ}$. Then $\overleftrightarrow{AB} \parallel \overleftrightarrow{PQ}$.

Anthony Gugliotta
Rumson, NJ

3-4 Organizer

Pacing: Traditional 1 day
Block $\frac{1}{2}$ day

Objective: Prove and apply theorems about perpendicular lines.

Geometry Lab
In *Geometry Lab Activities*

Online Edition
Tutorial Videos

Countdown Week 6

Power Presentations with PowerPoint®

Warm Up

Solve each inequality.

1. $x - 5 < 8$ $\quad x < 13$

2. $3x + 1 > x$ $\quad x > -\frac{1}{2}$

Solve each equation.

3. $5y = 90$ $\quad y = 18$

4. $5x + 15 = 90$ $\quad x = 15$

Solve the system of equations.

5. $\begin{cases} 6y = 90 \\ 8y - 3x = 90 \end{cases}$

$x = 10, y = 15$

Also available on transparency

Math Humor

Q: Why is the angle formed by two perpendicular lines never wrong?

A: Because it's always *right*!

State Resources

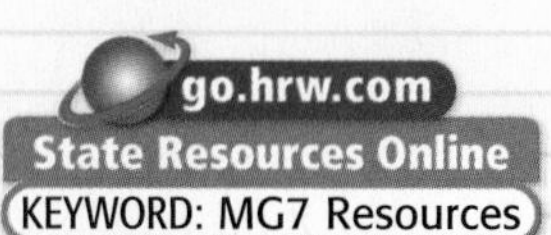

3-4 Perpendicular Lines

Objective
Prove and apply theorems about perpendicular lines.

Vocabulary
perpendicular bisector
distance from a point to a line

Why learn this?
Rip currents are strong currents that flow away from the shoreline and are perpendicular to it. A swimmer who gets caught in a rip current can get swept far out to sea. (See Example 3.)

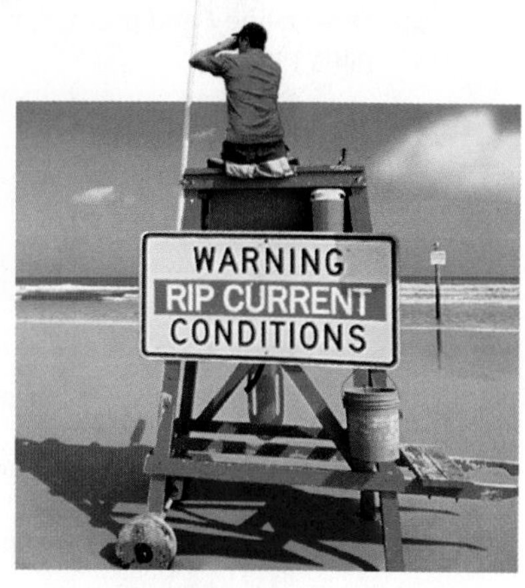

The **perpendicular bisector** of a segment is a line perpendicular to a segment at the segment's midpoint. A construction of a perpendicular bisector is shown below.

Construction Perpendicular Bisector of a Segment

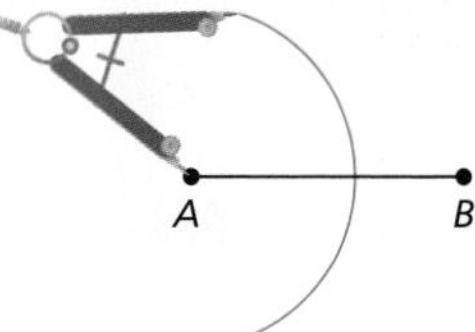

1. Draw $\overline{AB}$. Open the compass wider than half of AB and draw an arc centered at A.

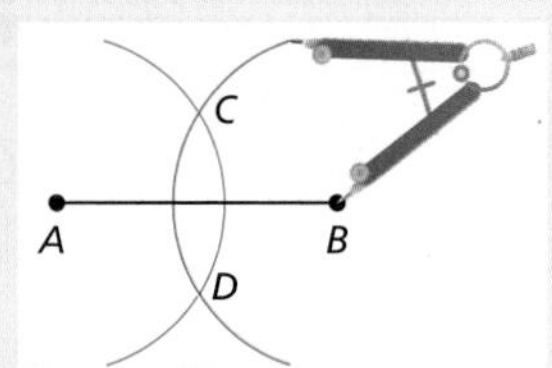

2. Using the same compass setting, draw an arc centered at B that intersects the first arc at C and D.

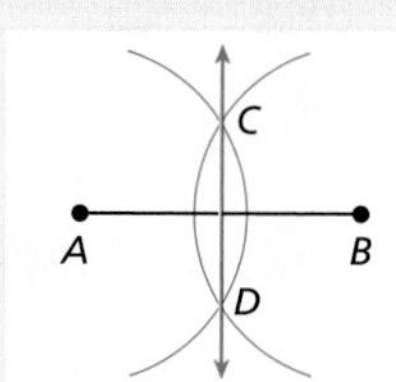

3. Draw $\overleftrightarrow{CD}$. $\overleftrightarrow{CD}$ is the perpendicular bisector of $\overline{AB}$.

The shortest segment from a point to a line is perpendicular to the line. This fact is used to define the **distance from a point to a line** as the length of the perpendicular segment from the point to the line.

EXAMPLE 1 Distance From a Point to a Line

A **Name the shortest segment from P to $\overleftrightarrow{AC}$.**

The shortest distance from a point to a line is the length of the perpendicular segment, so $\overline{PB}$ is the shortest segment from P to $\overleftrightarrow{AC}$.

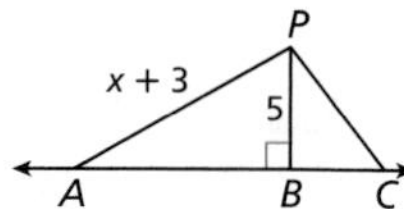

B **Write and solve an inequality for x.**

$PA > PB$ — *$\overline{PB}$ is the shortest segment.*

$x + 3 > 5$ — *Substitute $x + 3$ for PA and 5 for PB.*

$\underline{-3 \quad -3}$ — *Subtract 3 from both sides of the inequality.*

$x > 2$

CHECK IT OUT!

1a. Name the shortest segment from A to $\overleftrightarrow{BC}$.

1b. Write and solve an inequality for x.

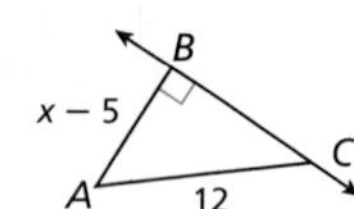

1a. $\overline{AB}$

1b. $x - 5 < 12$; $x < 17$

1 Introduce

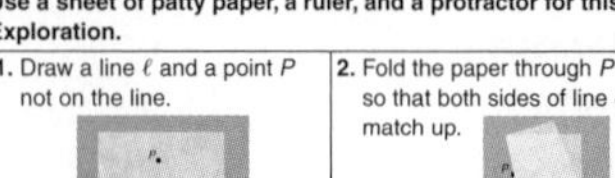

EXPLORATION

3-4 Perpendicular Lines

Use a sheet of patty paper, a ruler, and a protractor for this Exploration.

1. Draw a line ℓ and a point P not on the line.	2. Fold the paper through P so that both sides of line ℓ match up.
3. Unfold the paper. Label the intersection of the fold and line ℓ as point X.	4. Make three more folds that pass through P and that intersect line ℓ. Label them as shown.

5. Use a protractor to measure ∠PXC. What is special about the line through point X?
6. Use a ruler to measure $\overline{PX}$, $\overline{PA}$, $\overline{PB}$, and $\overline{PC}$. Which segment is shortest?

THINK AND DISCUSS

7. **Describe** the shortest segment from a point to a line.

Motivate

Show students a sketch or picture of a rectangular picture frame. Explain that in order to make the glass fit correctly in the frame, the framer must make sure that both sides are perpendicular to the top and the bottom of the frame. Ask students to name other objects in which sides must be perpendicular.

Explorations and answers are provided in *Alternate Openers: Explorations Transparencies.*

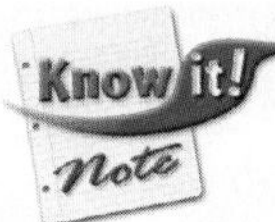

Theorems

	THEOREM	HYPOTHESIS	CONCLUSION
3-4-1	If two intersecting lines form a linear pair of congruent angles, then the lines are perpendicular. (2 intersecting lines form lin. pair of ≅ ∡ → lines ⊥.)	ℓ, m	$\ell \perp m$
3-4-2	**Perpendicular Transversal Theorem** In a plane, if a transversal is perpendicular to one of two parallel lines, then it is perpendicular to the other line.	n, p, q	$q \perp p$
3-4-3	If two coplanar lines are perpendicular to the same line, then the two lines are parallel to each other. (2 lines ⊥ to same line → 2 lines ∥.)	r, s, t	$r \parallel s$

You will prove Theorems 3-4-1 and 3-4-3 in Exercises 37 and 38.

PROOF **Perpendicular Transversal Theorem**

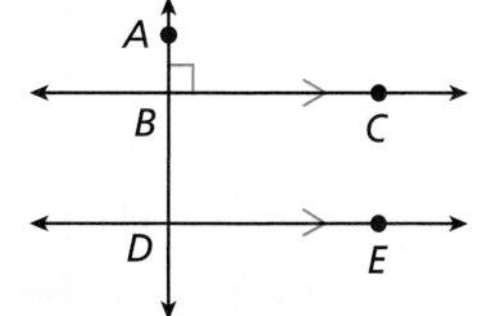

Given: $\overleftrightarrow{BC} \parallel \overleftrightarrow{DE}$, $\overleftrightarrow{AB} \perp \overleftrightarrow{BC}$

Prove: $\overleftrightarrow{AB} \perp \overleftrightarrow{DE}$

Proof:

It is given that $\overleftrightarrow{BC} \parallel \overleftrightarrow{DE}$, so $\angle ABC \cong \angle BDE$ by the Corresponding Angles Postulate. It is also given that $\overleftrightarrow{AB} \perp \overleftrightarrow{BC}$, so $m\angle ABC = 90°$. By the definition of congruent angles, $m\angle ABC = m\angle BDE$, so $m\angle BDE = 90°$ by the Transitive Property of Equality. By the definition of perpendicular lines, $\overleftrightarrow{AB} \perp \overleftrightarrow{DE}$.

EXAMPLE 2 Proving Properties of Lines

Write a two-column proof.

Given: $\overleftrightarrow{AD} \parallel \overleftrightarrow{BC}$, $\overleftrightarrow{AD} \perp \overleftrightarrow{AB}$, $\overleftrightarrow{BC} \perp \overleftrightarrow{DC}$

Prove: $\overleftrightarrow{AB} \parallel \overleftrightarrow{DC}$

Proof:

Statements	Reasons
1. $\overleftrightarrow{AD} \parallel \overleftrightarrow{BC}$, $\overleftrightarrow{BC} \perp \overleftrightarrow{DC}$	1. Given
2. $\overleftrightarrow{AD} \perp \overleftrightarrow{DC}$	2. ⊥ Transv. Thm.
3. $\overleftrightarrow{AD} \perp \overleftrightarrow{AB}$	3. Given
4. $\overleftrightarrow{AB} \parallel \overleftrightarrow{DC}$	4. 2 lines ⊥ to same line → 2 lines ∥.

1. $\angle EHF \cong \angle HFG$ (Given)
2. $\overleftrightarrow{EH} \parallel \overleftrightarrow{FG}$ (Conv. of Alt. Int. ∡ Thm.)
3. $\overleftrightarrow{FG} \perp \overleftrightarrow{GH}$ (Given)
4. $\overleftrightarrow{EH} \perp \overleftrightarrow{GH}$ (⊥ Transv. Thm.)

2. Write a two-column proof.
Given: $\angle EHF \cong \angle HFG$, $\overleftrightarrow{FG} \perp \overleftrightarrow{GH}$
Prove: $\overleftrightarrow{EH} \perp \overleftrightarrow{GH}$

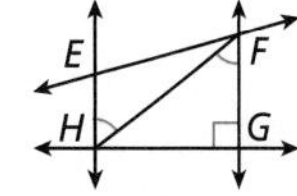

2 Teach

Guided Instruction

Make sure students understand that a perpendicular bisector of a segment must be perpendicular to the segment *and* that it must bisect the segment. Compare and contrast the theorems in the lesson.

Reading Math Discuss how the definition of the distance from a point to a line may differ from students' idea of the distance from their school to the street where they live.

Reaching All Learners

Through Modeling

Students who have difficulty with compass and straightedge constructions may want to use patty paper or a Mira to construct the perpendicular bisector of a segment.

Auditory Ask for several volunteers to demonstrate the construction of a perpendicular bisector of a segment. As they construct the bisector, ask them to explain what they are doing in each step.

COMMON ERROR ALERT

Students may want to state all the given information in a proof in the first statement of the proof. Call their attention to how the given information, as presented in **Example 2,** clearly shows the logical progression of thought.

Power Presentations with PowerPoint®

Additional Examples

Example 1

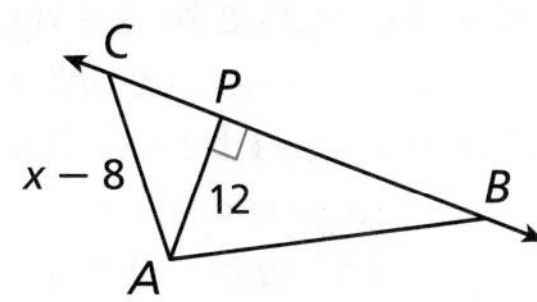

A. Name the shortest segment from point A to $\overleftrightarrow{BC}$. $\overline{AP}$

B. Write and solve an inequality for x. $AC > AP$; $x - 8 > 12$; $x > 20$

Example 2

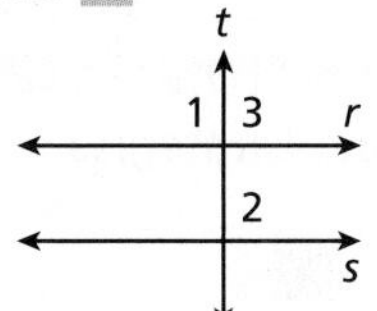

Write a two-column proof.
Given: $r \parallel s$, $\angle 1 \cong \angle 2$
Prove: $r \perp t$

1. $r \parallel s$, $\angle 1 \cong \angle 2$ (Given)
2. $\angle 2 \cong \angle 3$ (Corr. ∡ Post.)
3. $\angle 1 \cong \angle 3$ (Trans. Prop. of ≅)
4. $r \perp t$ (2 intersecting lines form lin. pair of ≅ ∡ → lines ⊥)

INTERVENTION

Questioning Strategies

EXAMPLE 1

- How does the solution in **Example 1B** confirm your choice for the shortest segment?

EXAMPLE 2

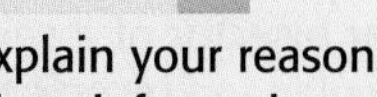

- Explain your reasoning from the given information to the conclusion.

Power Presentations with PowerPoint®

Additional Examples

Example 3

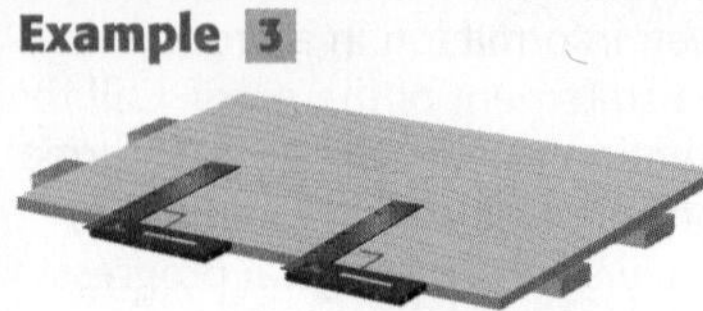

A *carpenter's square* forms a right angle. A carpenter places the square so that one side is parallel to an edge of a board, and then draws a line along the other side of the square. Then he slides the square to the right and draws a second line. Why must the two lines be parallel?

Both lines are perpendicular to the edge of the board. If two coplanar lines are perpendicular to the same line, then the two lines are parallel to each other, so the lines must be parallel to each other.

INTERVENTION 

Questioning Strategies

EXAMPLE 3

- What is the given information?
- What do you need to show?
- Which theorem will you use?

EXAMPLE 3 Oceanography Application

Rip currents may be caused by a sandbar parallel to the shoreline. Waves cause a buildup of water between the sandbar and the shoreline. When this water breaks through the sandbar, it flows out in a direction perpendicular to the sandbar. Why must the rip current be perpendicular to the shoreline?

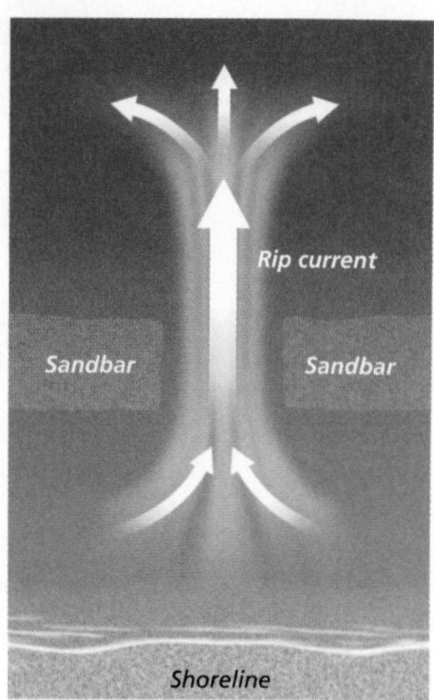

The rip current forms a transversal to the shoreline and the sandbar.

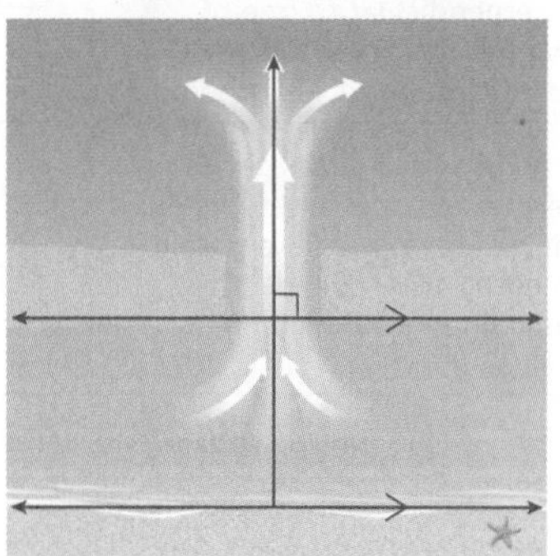

The shoreline and the sandbar are parallel, and the rip current is perpendicular to the sandbar. So by the Perpendicular Transversal Theorem, the rip current is perpendicular to the shoreline.

3. A swimmer who gets caught in a rip current should swim in a direction perpendicular to the current. Why should the path of the swimmer be parallel to the shoreline?
The shoreline and the path of the swimmer should both be ⊥ to the current, so they should be || to each other.

THINK AND DISCUSS

1. Describe what happens if two intersecting lines form a linear pair of congruent angles.
2. Explain why a transversal that is perpendicular to two parallel lines forms eight congruent angles.

3. **GET ORGANIZED** Copy and complete the graphic organizer. Use the diagram and the theorems from this lesson to complete the table.

Diagram	If you are given . . .	Then you can conclude . . .
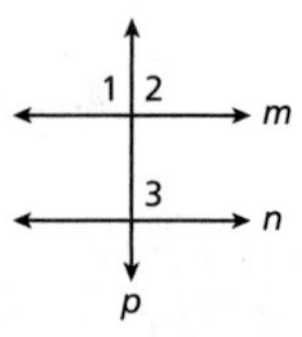 (diagram: lines m, n, p; angles 1, 2, 3)	$m\angle 1 = m\angle 2$	$m \perp p$
	$m\angle 2 = 90°$ $m\angle 3 = 90°$	$m \parallel n$
	$m\angle 2 = 90°$ $m \parallel n$	$n \perp p$

3 Close

Summarize

Review the main points of the lesson:

- A perpendicular bisector of a segment is both perpendicular and bisects the segment.
- The distance from a point not on a line to the line is the perpendicular distance.

Review the three theorems with the given diagrams on page 173.

ONGOING ASSESSMENT and INTERVENTION 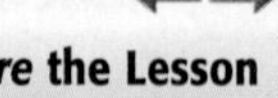

Diagnose **Before the Lesson**
3-4 Warm Up, TE p. 172

Monitor **During the Lesson**
Check It Out! Exercises, SE pp. 172–174
Questioning Strategies, TE pp. 173–174

Assess **After the Lesson**
3-4 Lesson Quiz, TE p. 178
Alternative Assessment, TE p. 178

Answers to *Think and Discuss*

1. If two intersecting lines form a lin. pair of ≅ ∠s, then the ∠s in the lin. pair have the same measure. By the Lin. Pair Thm., they are also supp., so their measures add to 180°. This means the measure of each ∠ must be 90°, so the lines must be ⊥.
2. If a transv. is ⊥ to the || lines, all pairs of corr. ∠s must be rt. ∠s. Since all rt. ∠s are ≅, the transv. and the || lines form 8 ≅ ∠s.

3-4 Exercises

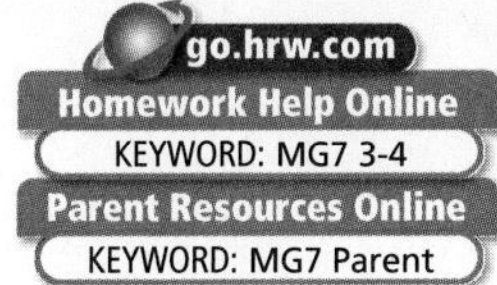

GUIDED PRACTICE

1. **Vocabulary** $\overleftrightarrow{CD}$ is the *perpendicular bisector* of $\overline{AB}$. $\overleftrightarrow{CD}$ intersects $\overline{AB}$ at C. What can you say about $\overline{AB}$ and $\overleftrightarrow{CD}$? What can you say about $\overline{AC}$ and $\overline{BC}$? **$\overline{AB}$ and $\overleftrightarrow{CD}$ are $\perp$. $\overline{AC}$ and $\overline{BC}$ are $\cong$.**

SEE EXAMPLE 1 p. 172

2. Name the shortest segment from point E to $\overleftrightarrow{AD}$. **$\overline{EB}$**
3. Write and solve an inequality for x. **$x + 12 > 7$; $x > -5$**

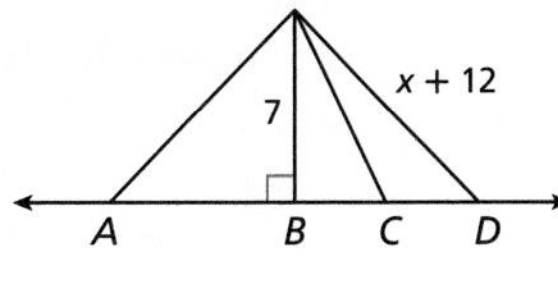

SEE EXAMPLE 2 p. 173

4. Complete the two-column proof.
Given: $\angle ABC \cong \angle CBE$, $\overleftrightarrow{DE} \perp \overleftrightarrow{AF}$
Prove: $\overleftrightarrow{CB} \parallel \overleftrightarrow{DE}$
Proof:

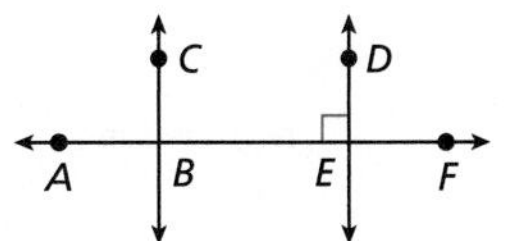

Statements	Reasons
1. $\angle ABC \cong \angle CBE$	1. Given
2. $\overleftrightarrow{CB} \perp \overleftrightarrow{AF}$	2. a. ___?___
3. b. ___?___ $\overleftrightarrow{DE} \perp \overleftrightarrow{AF}$	3. Given
4. $\overleftrightarrow{CB} \parallel \overleftrightarrow{DE}$	4. c. ___?___

a. 2 intersecting lines form lin. pair of $\cong$ ∠s → lines $\perp$.
c. 2 lines $\perp$ to same line → 2 lines $\parallel$.

SEE EXAMPLE 3 p. 174

5. **Sports** The center line in a tennis court is perpendicular to both service lines. Explain why the service lines must be parallel to each other.
The service lines are coplanar lines that are $\perp$ to the same line (the center line), so they must be $\parallel$ to each other.

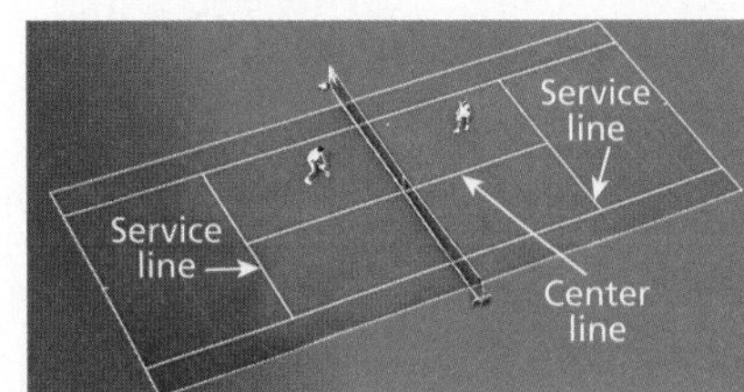

PRACTICE AND PROBLEM SOLVING

Independent Practice	
For Exercises	See Example
6–7	1
8	2
9	3

Extra Practice
Skills Practice p. S9
Application Practice p. S30

6. Name the shortest segment from point W to $\overline{XZ}$. **$\overline{WY}$**
7. Write and solve an inequality for x. **$x + 8 < 19$; $x < 11$**

8. Complete the two-column proof below.
Given: $\overleftrightarrow{AB} \perp \overleftrightarrow{BC}$, $m\angle 1 + m\angle 2 = 180°$
Prove: $\overleftrightarrow{BC} \perp \overleftrightarrow{CD}$
Proof:

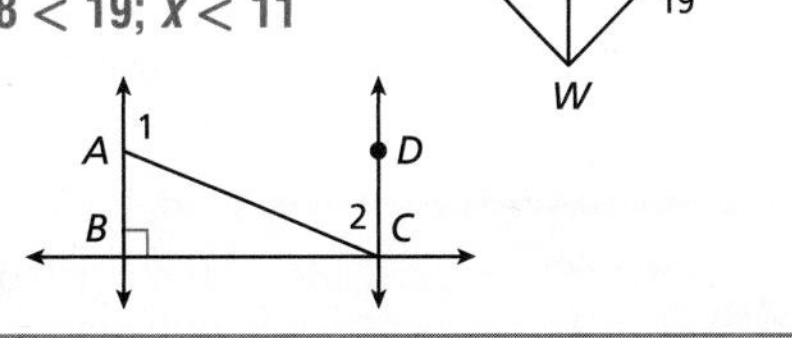

Statements	Reasons
1. $\overleftrightarrow{AB} \perp \overleftrightarrow{BC}$	1. Given
2. $m\angle 1 + m\angle 2 = 180°$	2. a. ___?___ **Given**
3. $\angle 1$ and $\angle 2$ are supplementary.	3. Def. of supplementary
4. b. ___?___ **$\overleftrightarrow{AB} \parallel \overleftrightarrow{CD}$**	4. Converse of the Same-Side Interior Angles Theorem
5. $\overleftrightarrow{BC} \perp \overleftrightarrow{CD}$	5. c. ___?___ **$\perp$ Transv. Thm.**

3-4 Exercises

Assignment Guide

Assign *Guided Practice* exercises as necessary.

If you finished Examples **1–3**
Basic 6–9, 10–20 even, 23–24, 27–28, 31–35, 39–45
Average 6–26, 28–36, 39–45
Advanced 6–23, 25–45

Homework Quick Check
Quickly check key concepts.
Exercises: 6, 8, 9, 10, 12

Teaching Tip **Visual** For **Exercise 1,** students may find it helpful to draw a diagram.

Teaching Tip **Critical Thinking** Ask students why the Perpendicular Transversal Theorem cannot be the reason for **Step 4** in **Exercise 4.** In the theorem, parallel lines are part of the hypothesis and perpendicular lines are part of the conclusion.

State Resources

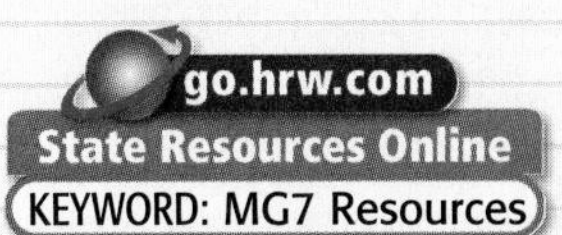

Teaching Tip **Inclusion** To make **Exercise 15** easier to visualize, once the parallel lines have been identified, suggest that students redraw the diagram without the perpendicular transversal and then rotate it so the parallel lines are horizontal.

Exercise 23 involves using the Perpendicular Transversal Theorem. This exercise prepares students for the Multi-Step Test Prep on page 180.

Answers

22. The Reflex. Prop. is not true for $\perp$ lines because a line is not $\perp$ to itself. The Sym. Prop. is true, because if $\ell \perp m$, then ℓ and m intersect to form a 90° angle. So $m \perp \ell$. The Trans. Prop. is not true, because if $\ell \perp m$ and $m \perp n$, then $\ell \parallel n$.

23a. It is given that $\overline{QR} \perp \overline{PQ}$ and $\overline{PQ} \parallel \overline{RS}$, so $\overline{QR} \perp \overline{RS}$ by the $\perp$ Transv. Thm. It is given that $\overline{PS} \parallel \overline{QR}$. Since $\overline{QR} \perp \overline{RS}$, $\overline{PS} \perp \overline{RS}$ by the $\perp$ Transv. Thm.

b. It is given that $\overline{PS} \parallel \overline{QR}$ and $\overline{QR} \perp \overline{PQ}$. So $\overline{PQ} \perp \overline{PS}$ by the $\perp$ Transv. Thm.

9. **Music** The *frets* on a guitar are all perpendicular to one of the strings. Explain why the frets must be parallel to each other.
The frets are lines that are $\perp$ to the same line (the string), so the frets must be $\parallel$ to each other.

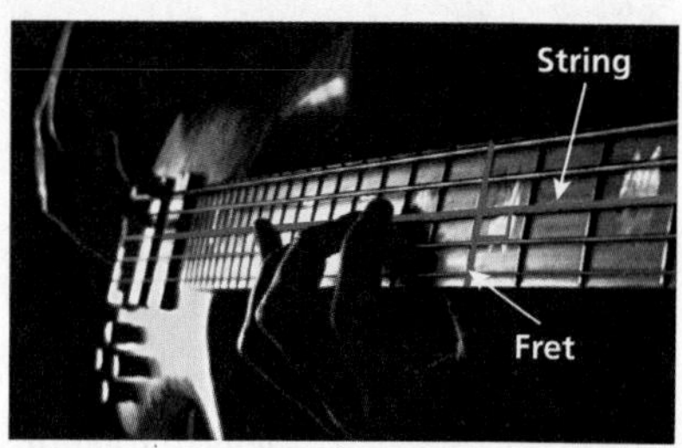

For each diagram, write and solve an inequality for x.

10. 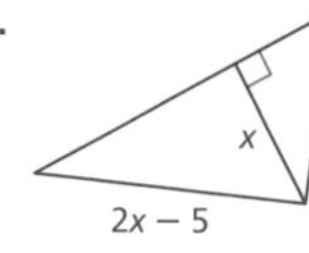

$2x - 5 > x$; $x > 5$

11. 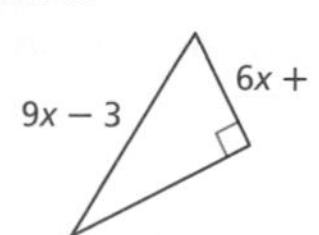

$9x - 3 > 6x + 5$; $x > \frac{8}{3}$

Multi-Step Solve to find x and y in each diagram.

12. $2x°$, $(3y - 2x)°$ **$x = 45$; $y = 60$**

13. 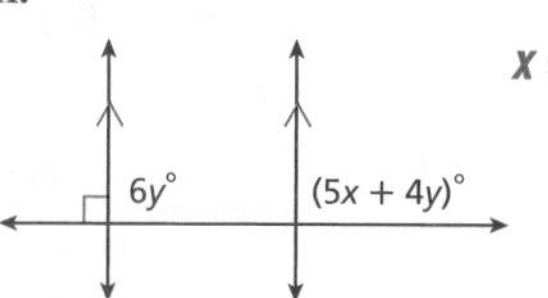

$x = 6$, $y = 15$

14. $(2x + y)°$, $(10x - 4y)°$ **$x = 25$, $y = 40$**

15. 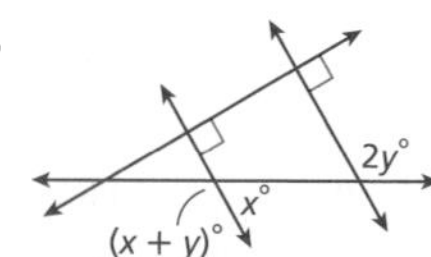
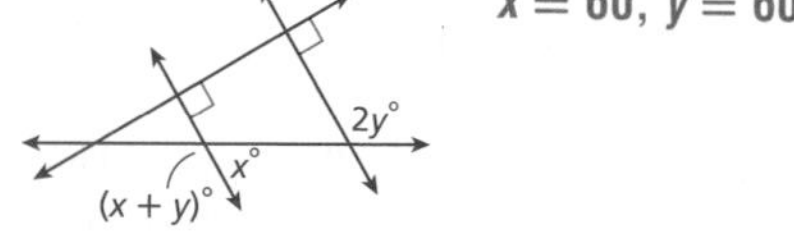

$x = 60$, $y = 60$

Determine if there is enough information given in the diagram to prove each statement.

16. $\angle 1 \cong \angle 2$ **yes**
17. $\angle 1 \cong \angle 3$ **no**
18. $\angle 2 \cong \angle 3$ **no**
19. $\angle 2 \cong \angle 4$ **no**
20. $\angle 3 \cong \angle 4$ **yes**
21. $\angle 3 \cong \angle 5$ **yes**

22. **Critical Thinking** Are the Reflexive, Symmetric, and Transitive Properties true for perpendicular lines? Explain why or why not.
Reflexive: $\ell \perp \ell$
Symmetric: If $\ell \perp m$, then $m \perp \ell$.
Transitive: If $\ell \perp m$ and $m \perp n$, then $\ell \perp n$.

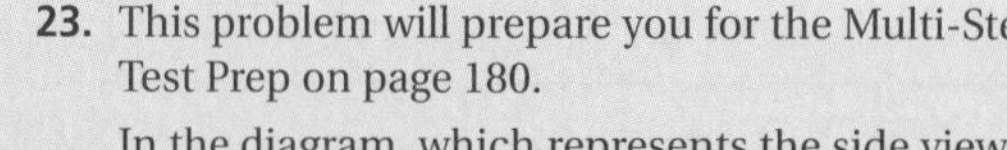

MULTI-STEP TEST PREP

23. This problem will prepare you for the Multi-Step Test Prep on page 180.
In the diagram, which represents the side view of a mystery spot, $\overline{QR} \perp \overline{PQ}$, $\overline{PQ} \parallel \overline{RS}$, and $\overline{PS} \parallel \overline{QR}$.
a. Prove $\overline{QR} \perp \overline{RS}$ and $\overline{PS} \perp \overline{RS}$.
b. Prove $\overline{PQ} \perp \overline{PS}$.

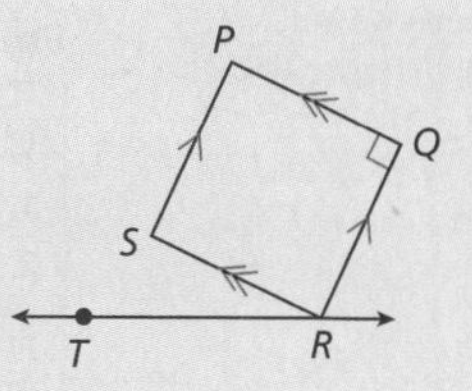

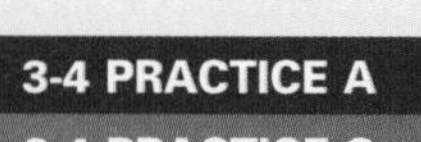

3-4 PRACTICE B

For Exercises 1–4, name the shortest segment from the point to the line and write an inequality for x. (*Hint:* One answer is a double inequality.)

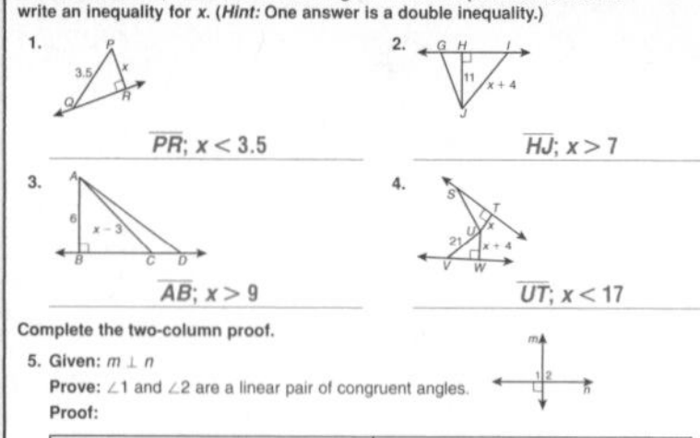

1. **$\overline{PR}$; $x < 3.5$**
2. **$\overline{HJ}$; $x > 7$**
3. **$\overline{AB}$; $x > 9$**
4. **$\overline{UT}$; $x < 17$**

Complete the two-column proof.

5. **Given:** $m \perp n$
Prove: $\angle 1$ and $\angle 2$ are a linear pair of congruent angles.
Proof:

Statements	Reasons
1. a. **$m \perp n$**	1. Given
2. b. **$m\angle 1 = 90°$, $m\angle 2 = 90°$**	2. Def. of $\perp$
3. $\angle 1 \cong \angle 2$	3. c. **Def. of $\cong$ ∠s**
4. $m\angle 1 + m\angle 2 = 180°$	4. Add. Prop. of =
5. d. **$\angle 1$ and $\angle 2$ are a linear pair.**	5. Def. of linear pair

6. The Four Corners National Monument is at the intersection of the borders of Arizona, Colorado, New Mexico, and Utah. It is called the four corners because the intersecting borders are perpendicular. If you were to lie down on the intersection, you could be in four states at the same time—the only place in the United States where this is possible. The figure shows the Colorado-Utah border extending north in a straight line until it intersects the Wyoming border at a right angle. Explain why the Colorado-Wyoming border must be parallel to the Colorado–New Mexico border. **Possible answer:**
All the borders are straight lines, and the Colorado–Utah border is a transversal to the Colorado–Wyoming and the Colorado–New Mexico borders. Because the transversal is perpendicular to both borders, the borders must be parallel.

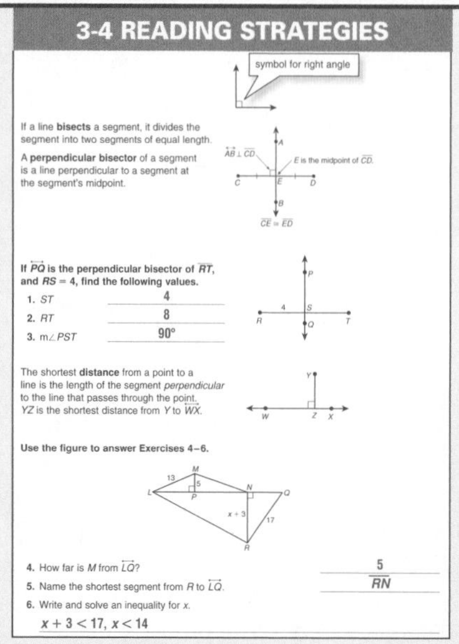

3-4 READING STRATEGIES

If a line **bisects** a segment, it divides the segment into two segments of equal length.

A **perpendicular bisector** of a segment is a line perpendicular to a segment at the segment's midpoint.

If $\overleftrightarrow{PQ}$ is the perpendicular bisector of $\overline{RT}$, and $RS = 4$, find the following values.

1. ST **4**
2. RT **8**
3. $m\angle PST$ **90°**

The shortest **distance** from a point to a line is the length of the segment *perpendicular* to the line that passes through the point. YZ is the shortest distance from Y to $\overleftrightarrow{WX}$.

Use the figure to answer Exercises 4–6.

4. How far is M from $\overleftrightarrow{LQ}$? **5**
5. Name the shortest segment from R to $\overleftrightarrow{LQ}$. **$\overline{RN}$**
6. Write and solve an inequality for x.
$x + 3 < 17$, $x < 14$

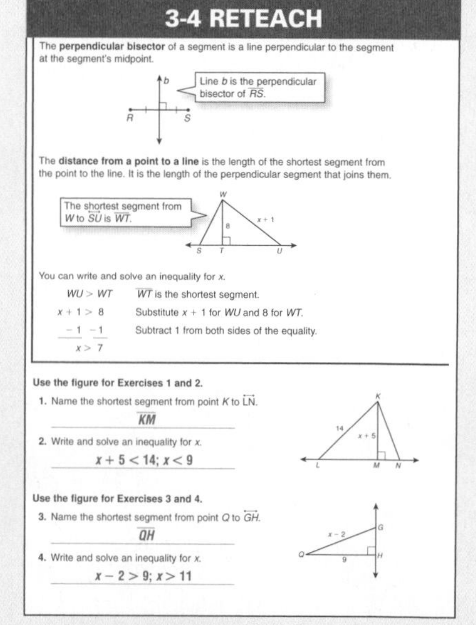

3-4 RETEACH

The **perpendicular bisector** of a segment is a line perpendicular to the segment at the segment's midpoint.

The **distance from a point to a line** is the length of the shortest segment from the point to the line. It is the length of the perpendicular segment that joins them.

The shortest segment from W to $\overleftrightarrow{SU}$ is $\overline{WT}$.

You can write and solve an inequality for x.

$WU > WT$	$\overline{WT}$ is the shortest segment.
$x + 1 > 8$	Substitute $x + 1$ for WU and 8 for WT.
$-1 \quad -1$	Subtract 1 from both sides of the equality.
$x > 7$	

Use the figure for Exercises 1 and 2.

1. Name the shortest segment from point K to $\overleftrightarrow{LN}$.
$\overline{KM}$
2. Write and solve an inequality for x.
$x + 5 < 14$; $x < 9$

Use the figure for Exercises 3 and 4.

3. Name the shortest segment from point Q to $\overleftrightarrow{GH}$.
$\overline{QH}$
4. Write and solve an inequality for x.
$x - 2 > 9$; $x > 11$

24. **Geography** Felton Avenue, Arlee Avenue, and Viehl Avenue are all parallel. Broadway Street is perpendicular to Felton Avenue. Use the satellite photo and the given information to determine the values of x and y. $x = 6$; $y = 6$

25. **Estimation** Copy the diagram onto a grid with 1 cm by 1 cm squares. Estimate the distance from point P to line ℓ. Possible answer: 1.6 cm

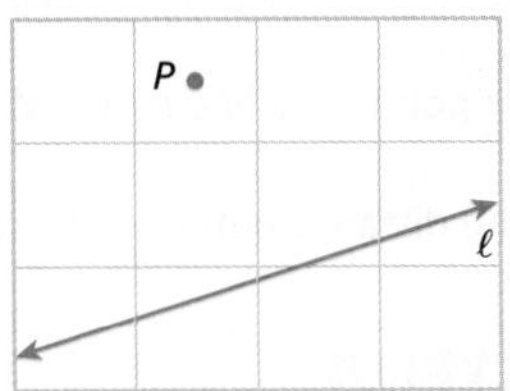

26. **Critical Thinking** Draw a figure to show that Theorem 3-4-3 is not true if the lines are not in the same plane.

27. Draw a figure in which $\overline{AB}$ is a perpendicular bisector of $\overline{XY}$ but $\overline{XY}$ is not a perpendicular bisector of $\overline{AB}$.

28. **Write About It** A ladder is formed by rungs that are perpendicular to the sides of the ladder. Explain why the rungs of the ladder are parallel.

Construction **Construct a segment congruent to each given segment and then construct its perpendicular bisector.**

29. 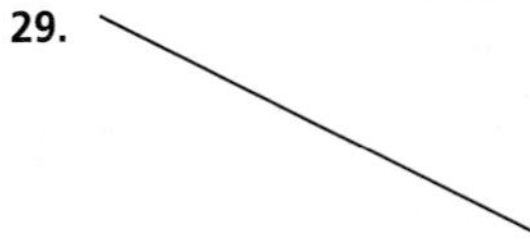

Check students' work.

30. 

Check students' work.

TEST PREP

31. Which inequality is correct for the given diagram?

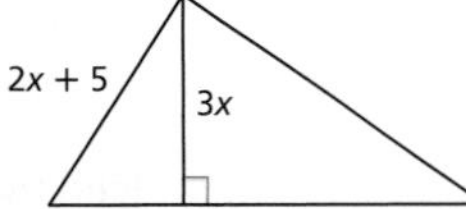

(A) $2x + 5 < 3x$
(C) $2x + 5 > 3x$ (circled)
(B) $x > 1$
(D) $x > 5$

32. In the diagram, $\ell \perp m$. Find x and y.

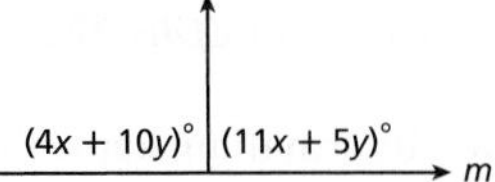

(F) $x = 5, y = 7$ (circled)
(G) $x = 7, y = 5$
(H) $x = 90, y = 90$
(J) $x = 10, y = 5$

33. If $\ell \perp m$, which statement is NOT correct?

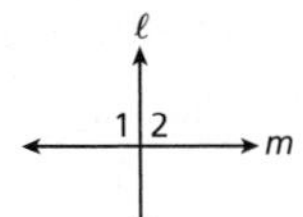

(A) $m\angle 2 = 90°$
(B) $m\angle 1 + m\angle 2 = 180°$
(C) $\angle 1 \cong \angle 2$
(D) $\angle 1 \perp \angle 2$ (circled)

Construction

In **Exercises 29** and **30,** you may want to ask students how they can check their constructions by using paper folding.

TEST PREP DOCTOR Students who chose D in **Exercise 31** may need to review the Multiplication Property of Inequality. Remind students that for all real numbers a and b, if $a > b$, then $-a < -b$.

Encourage students to substitute their values for x and y in the variable expressions in **Exercise 32** before choosing their answer.

Answers

26. Possible answer: The two edges of the cube that are skew are ⊥ to a third edge, but they are not ∥.

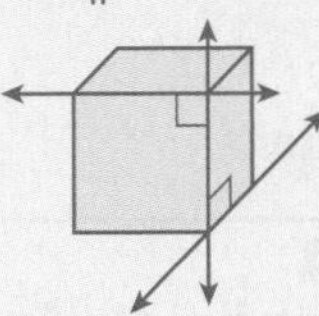

27. Possible answer:

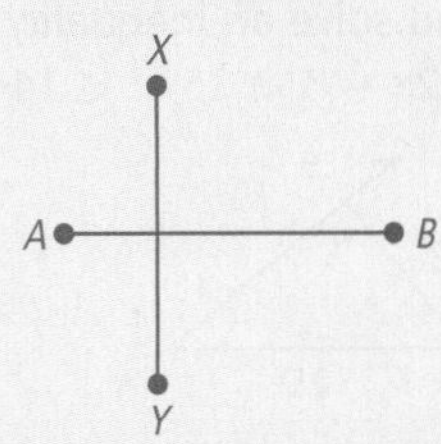

28. The rungs of the ladder are lines that are all ⊥ to the same line, a side of the ladder, so the rungs must be ∥.

3-4 PROBLEM SOLVING

A wall rack for holding CDs is shown. Use the figure for Exercises 1 and 2.

1. Explain why $\overline{HK}$ must be perpendicular to $\overline{KL}$.
$\overline{HK}$ is a transversal to $\overline{GH}$ and $\overline{KL}$. $\overline{GH}$ and $\overline{KL}$ are parallel, and $\overline{HK} \perp \overline{GH}$. So by the Perpendicular Transversal Theorem, $\overline{HK} \perp \overline{KL}$.

2. If $\overline{JM} \perp \overline{HK}$, explain why $\overline{JM} \parallel \overline{GH}$.
$\overline{JM} \perp \overline{HK}$ and $\overline{GH} \perp \overline{HK}$. If two coplanar lines are perpendicular to the same line, then the two lines are parallel to each other. Since $\overline{JM}$ and $\overline{GH}$ are both perpendicular to $\overline{HK}$, it follows that $\overline{JM} \parallel \overline{GH}$.

3. The valve pistons on a trumpet are all perpendicular to the lead pipe. Explain why the valve pistons must be parallel to each other.
lead pipe
valve piston
The valve pistons are lines that are ⊥ to the same line (the lead pipe), so the valve pistons must be ∥ to each other.

Use the diagram of a bocce court for Exercises 4 and 5. Choose the best answer.

A B C D E F
pitch line
volo lines
pitch line
1 2
G H J K L M

4. If $m\angle 1 = m\angle 2$, what can you conclude?
(A) $\overline{BH} \perp \overline{GJ}$ (circled)
C $\overline{BH} \parallel \overline{CJ}$
B $\overline{AC} \perp \overline{BH}$
D $\overline{AC} \parallel \overline{GJ}$

5. The pitch lines are parallel, and the first pitch line is perpendicular to the long sides of the court. Which is a correct conclusion?
F $BH = CJ$
(H) $\overline{EL} \perp \overline{AF}$ (circled)
G $\overline{BH} \parallel \overline{CJ}$
J $\overline{DK} \perp \overline{AF}$

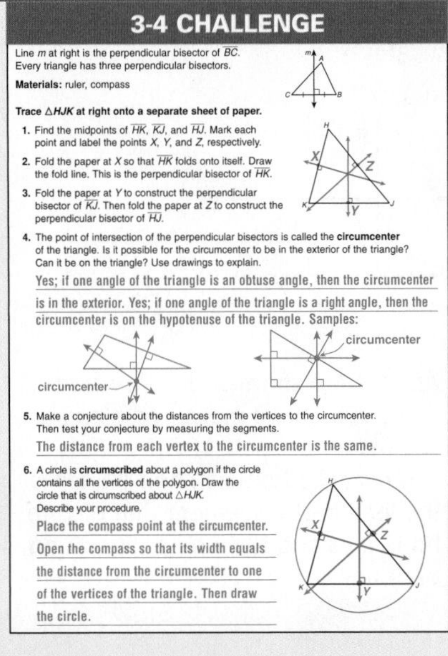

3-4 CHALLENGE

Line m at right is the perpendicular bisector of $\overline{BC}$. Every triangle has three perpendicular bisectors.

Materials: ruler, compass

Trace △HJK at right onto a separate sheet of paper.

1. Find the midpoints of $\overline{HK}$, $\overline{KJ}$, and $\overline{HJ}$. Mark each point and label the points X, Y, and Z, respectively.
2. Fold the paper at X so that $\overline{HK}$ folds onto itself. Draw the fold line. This is the perpendicular bisector of $\overline{HK}$.
3. Fold the paper at Y to construct the perpendicular bisector of $\overline{KJ}$. Then fold the paper at Z to construct the perpendicular bisector of $\overline{HJ}$.
4. The point of intersection of the perpendicular bisectors is called the **circumcenter** of the triangle. Is it possible for the circumcenter to be in the exterior of the triangle? Can it be on the triangle? Use drawings to explain.
Yes; if one angle of the triangle is an obtuse angle, then the circumcenter is in the exterior. Yes; if one angle of the triangle is a right angle, then the circumcenter is on the hypotenuse of the triangle. Samples:
circumcenter
circumcenter
5. Make a conjecture about the distances from the vertices to the circumcenter. Then test your conjecture by measuring the segments.
The distance from each vertex to the circumcenter is the same.
6. A circle is **circumscribed** about a polygon if the circle contains all the vertices of the polygon. Draw the circle that is circumscribed about △HJK. Describe your procedure.
Place the compass point at the circumcenter. Open the compass so that its width equals the distance from the circumcenter to one of the vertices of the triangle. Then draw the circle.

Journal

Ask students to explain how to make the steps of a staircase parallel. Have them include a sketch in their explanation.

ALTERNATIVE ASSESSMENT

Have students write the hypothesis and conclusion of the three theorems on page 173. Then ask them to draw a sketch and restate the hypotheses and conclusions in terms of their sketches.

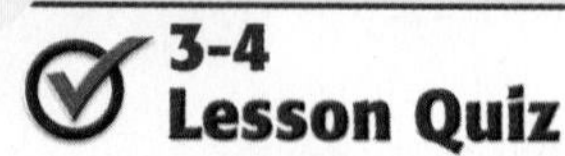

Power Presentations with PowerPoint®

3-4 Lesson Quiz

1. Write and solve an inequality for x. $2x - 3 < 25; x < 14$

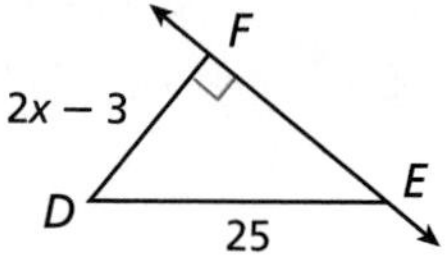

2. Solve to find x and y in the diagram.

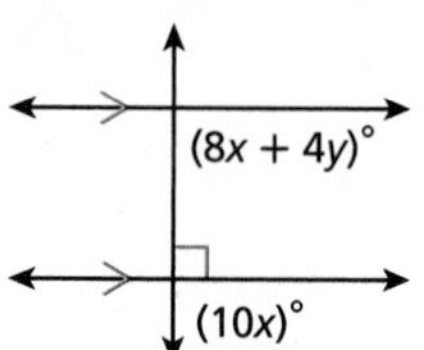

$x = 9, y = 4.5$

3. Complete the two-column proof below.

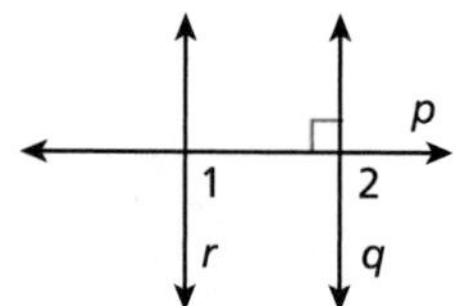

Given: $\angle 1 \cong \angle 2, p \perp q$
Prove: $p \perp r$
Proof:
1. $\angle 1 \cong \angle 2$ (Given)
2. $q \parallel r$ (__?__) Conv. of Corr. ∠s Post.
3. $p \perp q$ (__?__) Given
4. $p \perp r$ (__?__) ⊥ Transv. Thm.

Also available on transparency

34. In a plane, both lines m and n are perpendicular to both lines p and q. Which conclusion CANNOT be made?
    (A) $p \parallel q$
    (B) $m \parallel n$
    (C) $p \perp q$ (circled)
    (D) All angles formed by lines m, n, p, and q are congruent.

35. **Extended Response** Lines m and n are parallel. Line p intersects line m at A and line n at B, and is perpendicular to line m.
    a. What is the relationship between line n and line p? Draw a diagram to support your answer.
    b. What is the distance from point A to line n? What is the distance from point B to line m? Explain.
    c. How would you define the distance between two parallel lines in a plane?

CHALLENGE AND EXTEND

36. **Multi-Step** Find $m\angle 1$ in the diagram. (*Hint:* Draw a line parallel to the given parallel lines.) $m\angle 1 = 135°$

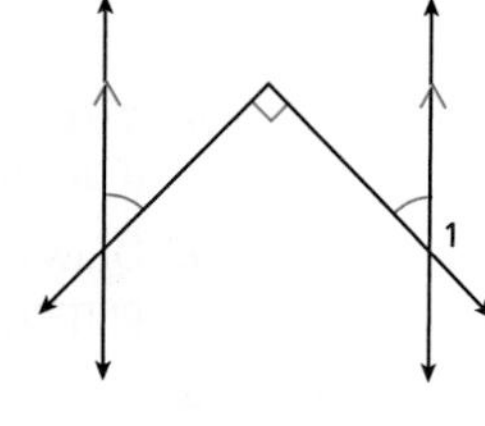

37. Prove Theorem 3-4-1: If two intersecting lines form a linear pair of congruent angles, then the two lines are perpendicular.

37. Label the ≅ ∠s ∠1 and ∠2. By def. of ≅ ∠s, $m\angle 1 = m\angle 2$. By the Lin. Pair Thm., $m\angle 1 + m\angle 2 = 180°$. By subst., $m\angle 1 + m\angle 1 = 180°$, so $2(m\angle 1) = 180°$. By Div. Prop. of =, $m\angle 1 = 90°$, so the lines are ⊥ by the def. of ⊥ lines.

38. Prove Theorem 3-4-3: If two coplanar lines are perpendicular to the same line, then the two lines are parallel to each other.
    Label a pair of corr. rt. ∠s ∠1 and ∠2. By the Rt. ∠ ≅ Thm., $\angle 1 \cong \angle 2$. So $r \parallel s$ by the Conv. of the Corr. ∠s Post.

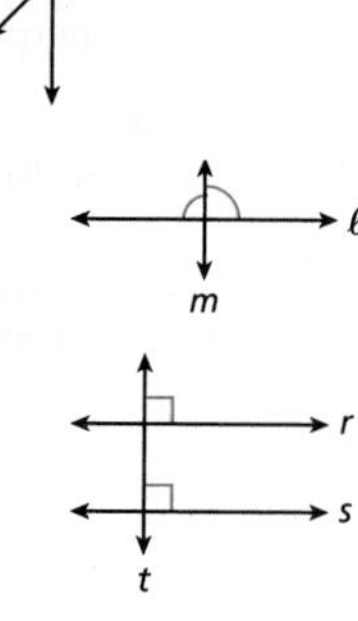

SPIRAL REVIEW

39. A soccer league has 6 teams. During one season, each team plays each of the other teams 2 times. What is the total number of games played in the league during one season? *(Previous course)* 30 games

Find the measure of each angle. *(Lesson 1-4)*

40. the supplement of $\angle DJE$ 152°
41. the complement of $\angle FJG$ 25°
42. the supplement of $\angle GJH$ 155°

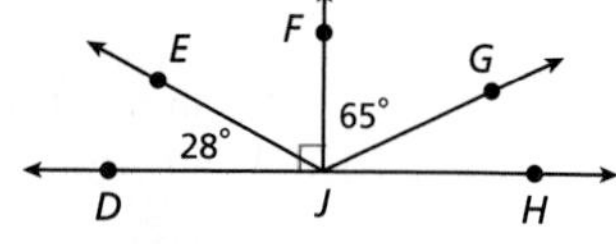

For the given information, name the postulate or theorem that proves $\ell \parallel m$. *(Lesson 3-3)*

43. $\angle 2 \cong \angle 7$ Conv. of Alt. Ext. ∠s Thm.
44. $\angle 3 \cong \angle 6$ Conv. of Alt. Int. ∠s Thm.
45. $m\angle 4 + m\angle 6 = 180°$ Conv. of Same-Side Int. ∠s Thm.

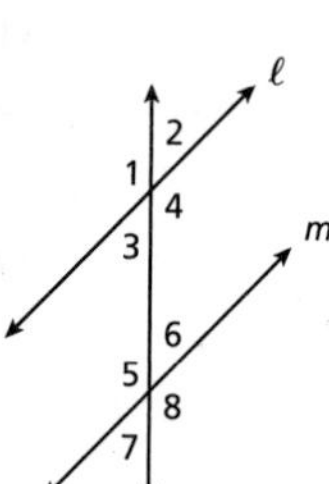

Answers

35a. $n \perp p$

b. AB; AB; the shortest distance from a point to a line is measured along a ⊥ segment.

c. The distance between two ∥ lines is the length of a segment that is ⊥ to both lines and has one endpoint on each line.

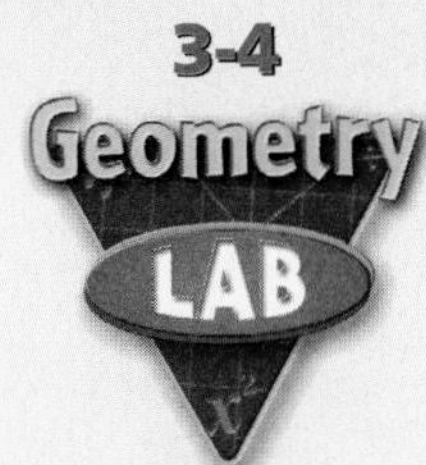

Construct Perpendicular Lines

Use with Lesson 3-4

In Lesson 3-4, you learned to construct the perpendicular bisector of a segment. This is the basis of the construction of a line perpendicular to a given line through a given point. The steps in the construction are the same whether the point is on or off the line.

Activity

Copy the given line ℓ and point P.

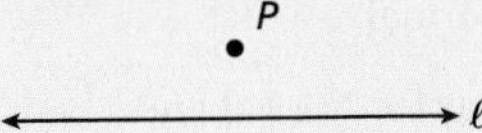

1. Place the compass point on P and draw an arc that intersects ℓ at two points. Label the points A and B.

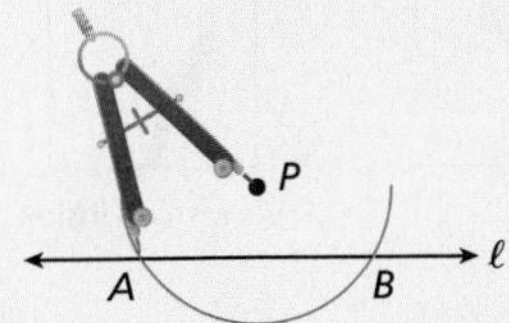

2. Construct the perpendicular bisector of $\overline{AB}$.

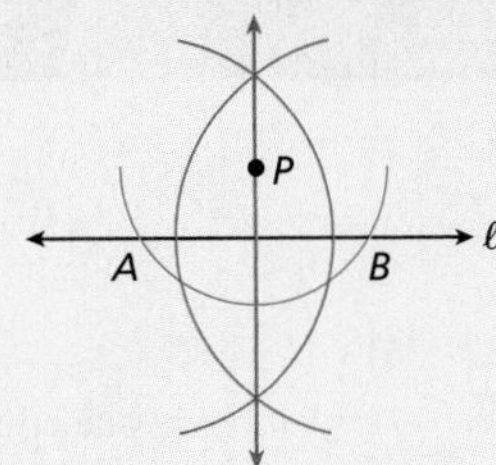

Try This

Copy each diagram and construct a line perpendicular to line ℓ through point P. Use a protractor to verify that the lines are perpendicular.

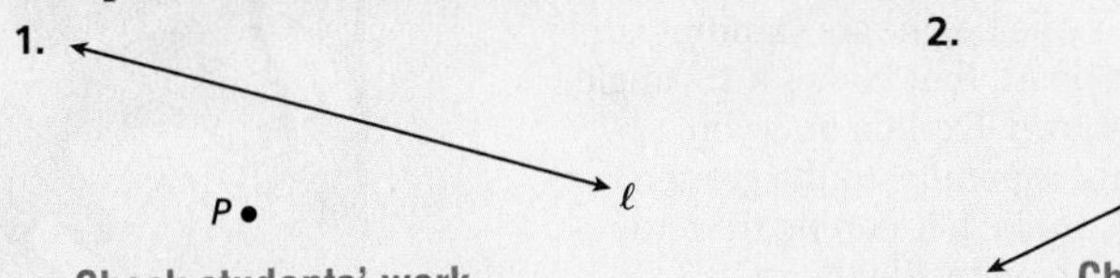

1. Check students' work.

2. Check students' work.

3. Follow the steps below to construct two parallel lines. Explain why $\ell \parallel n$.

Step 1 Given a line ℓ, draw a point P not on ℓ.

Step 2 Construct line m perpendicular to ℓ through P.

Step 3 Construct line n perpendicular to m through P.

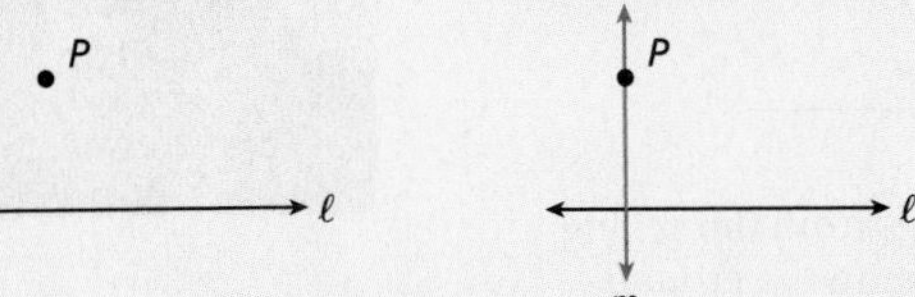

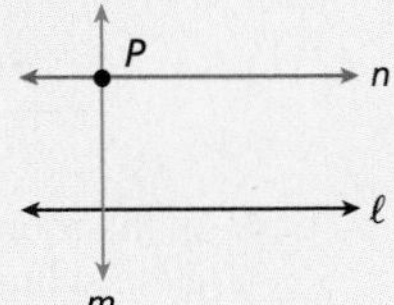

Check students' work. The lines are $\parallel$ because two lines that are $\perp$ to the same line are $\parallel$ to each other.

Organizer

Use with Lesson 3-4

Pacing:

Traditional $\frac{1}{2}$ day
Block $\frac{1}{4}$ day

Objective: Construct a line perpendicular to a given line through a given point.

Materials: compass and protractor

Online Edition

Countdown Week 5

Resources

Geometry Lab Activities

3-4 Lab Recording Sheet

Teach

Discuss

Relate the construction on page 172 of the perpendicular bisector of a segment to this construction.

Close

Key Concept

You can use the construction of the perpendicular bisector of a segment to construct a line perpendicular to a given line through a given point.

Assessment

Journal Have students draw a line m and a point Q not on m. Ask them to explain how to construct $\overleftrightarrow{QR} \perp m$.

State Resources

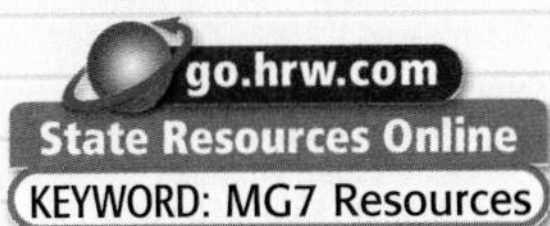

Organizer

Objective: Assess students' ability to apply concepts and skills in Lessons 3-1 through 3-4 in a real-world format.

Online Edition

Resources

 ***Geometry Assessments***

www.mathtekstoolkit.org

Problem	Text Reference
1	Lesson 3-1
2	Lesson 3-2
3	Lesson 3-3
4	Lesson 3-4

Answers

1–4. See p. A13.

CHAPTER 3

MULTI-STEP TEST PREP

SECTION 3A

Parallel and Perpendicular Lines and Transversals

On the Spot Inside a mystery spot building, objects can appear to roll uphill, and people can look as if they are standing at impossible angles. This is because there is no view of the outside, so the room appears to be normal.

Suppose that the ground is perfectly level and the floor of the building forms a 25° angle with the ground. The floor and ceiling are parallel, and the walls are perpendicular to the floor.

View from outside

View from inside

1. A table is placed in the room. The legs of the table are perpendicular to the floor, and the top is perpendicular to the legs. Draw a diagram and describe the relationship of the tabletop to the floor, walls, and ceiling of the room.
2. Find the angle of the table top relative to the ground. Suppose a ball is placed on the table. Describe what would happen and how it would appear to a person in the room.
3. Two people of the same height are standing on opposite ends of a board that makes a 25° angle with the floor, as shown. Explain how you know that the board is parallel to the ground. What would appear to be happening from the point of view of a person inside the room?

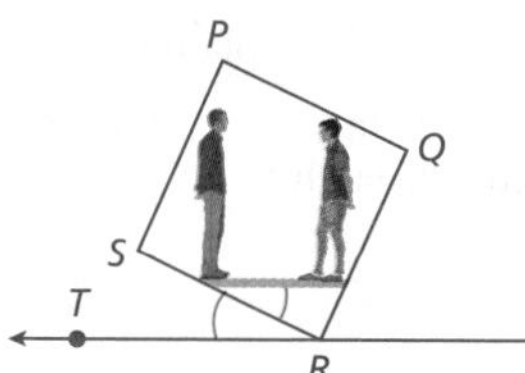

4. In the room, a lamp hangs from the ceiling along a line perpendicular to the ground. Find the angle the line makes with the walls. Describe how it would appear to a person standing in the room.

INTERVENTION 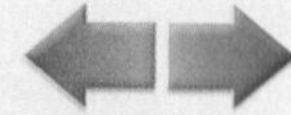

Scaffolding Questions

1. If you extended the tabletop, at what angle would it intersect the walls? 90°
2. If you extended the tabletop, would it intersect the ground? Yes Which pair of congruent corresponding angles would be formed? the angle formed by the floor and the ground and the angle formed by the tabletop and the ground
3. What is m$\angle SRT$? 25° What type of angle pair are $\angle SRT$ and the angle formed by the board and the floor? alternate interior angles
4. What angle do the walls make with the ground? 65° How can you use this angle to find the angle the line makes with the walls? The angles are complementary.

Extension

A ball appears to roll up a ramp on the floor of the room. What can you say about the angle that the ramp makes with the floor? The angle is less than 25°.

SECTION 3A

Quiz for Lessons 3-1 Through 3-4

3-1 Lines and Angles

Identify each of the following. $\overline{AE} \perp \overline{AB}$

1. a pair of perpendicular segments
2. a pair of skew segments
3. a pair of parallel segments $\overline{AE} \parallel \overline{FB}$
4. a pair of parallel planes
plane $AEF \parallel$ plane DHG

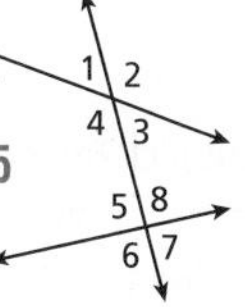

2. Possible answer: $\overline{AB}$ and $\overline{FG}$ are skew.

Give an example of each angle pair. 5–8. Possible answers:

5. alternate interior angles $\angle 3$ and $\angle 5$
6. alternate exterior angles $\angle 1$ and $\angle 7$
7. corresponding angles $\angle 2$ and $\angle 8$
8. same-side interior angles $\angle 4$ and $\angle 5$

3-2 Angles Formed by Parallel Lines and Transversals

Find each angle measure.

9. 135°

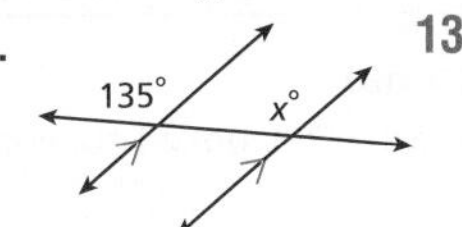

10. 23°

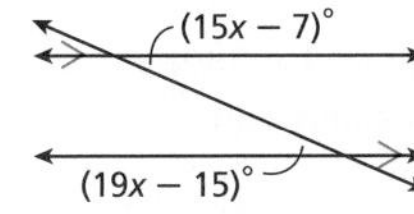

11. 122°

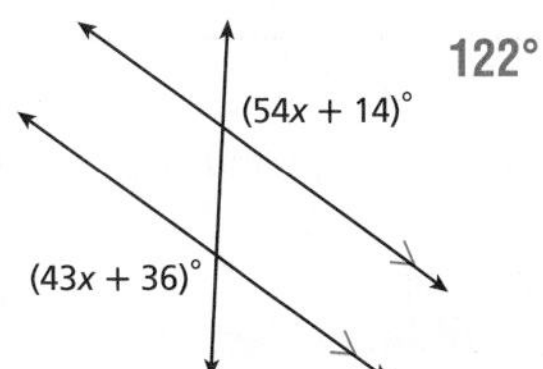

3-3 Proving Lines Parallel

Use the given information and the theorems and postulates you have learned to show that $a \parallel b$.

12. $m\angle 8 = (13x + 20)^\circ$, $m\angle 6 = (7x + 38)^\circ$, $x = 3$
13. $\angle 1 \cong \angle 5$
14. $m\angle 8 + m\angle 7 = 180^\circ$
15. $m\angle 8 = m\angle 4$
16. The tower shown is supported by guy wires such that $m\angle 1 = (3x + 12)^\circ$, $m\angle 2 = (4x - 2)^\circ$, and $x = 14$. Show that the guy wires are parallel.

16. $m\angle 1 = 3(14) + 12 = 54^\circ$, and $m\angle 2 = 4(14) - 2 = 54^\circ$, so $\angle 1 \cong \angle 2$. The guy wires are $\parallel$ by the Conv. of the Corr. ∠s Post.

3-4 Perpendicular Lines

17. Write a two-column proof.
Given: $\angle 1 \cong \angle 2$, $\ell \perp n$
Prove: $\ell \perp p$

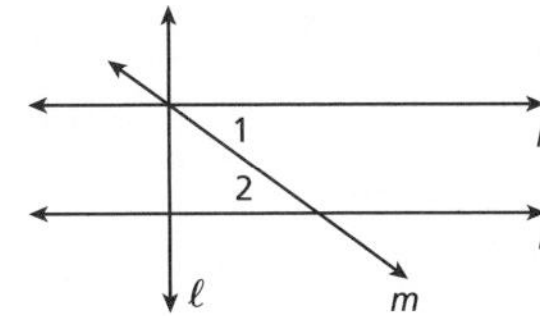

1. $\angle 1 \cong \angle 2$, $\ell \perp n$ (Given)
2. $p \parallel n$ (Conv. of Alt. Int. ∠s Thm.)
3. $\ell \perp p$ (⊥Transv. Thm.)

READY TO GO ON?

Organizer

Objective: Assess students' mastery of concepts and skills in Lessons 3-1 through 3-4.

Resources

 ***Assessment Resources***
Section 3A Quiz

Teacher One Stop™
Test & Practice Generator

INTERVENTION

Resources

 ***Ready to Go On? Intervention and Enrichment Worksheets***

 ***Ready to Go On?* CD-ROM**

 ***Ready to Go On?* Online**

my.hrw.com

Answers

12–15. See p. A13.

READY TO GO ON? Diagnose and Prescribe

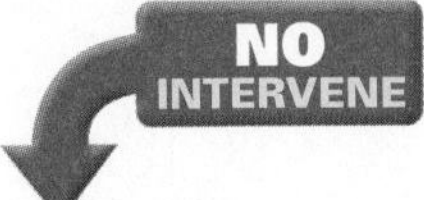

NO INTERVENE

Ready to Go On? Intervention	READY TO GO ON? Intervention, Section 3A		
	Worksheets	CD-ROM	Online
Lesson 3-1	3-1 Intervention	Activity 3-1	Diagnose and Prescribe Online
Lesson 3-2	3-2 Intervention	Activity 3-2	
Lesson 3-3	3-3 Intervention	Activity 3-3	
Lesson 3-4	3-4 Intervention	Activity 3-4	

YES ENRICH

***READY TO GO ON? Enrichment,* Section 3A**
Worksheets
CD-ROM
Online

SECTION 3B

Coordinate Geometry

One-Minute Section Planner

Lesson	Lab Resources	Materials
Lesson 3-5 Slopes of Lines • Find the slope of a line. • Use slopes to identify parallel and perpendicular lines. ☐ SAT-10 ☑ NAEP ☑ ACT ☑ SAT ☑ SAT Subject Tests	***Geometry Lab Activities*** 3-5 Geometry Lab	**Optional** compass and straightedge
3-6 Technology Lab Explore Parallel and Perpendicular Lines • Use a graphing calculator to graph parallel and perpendicular lines. ☐ SAT-10 ☑ NAEP ☑ ACT ☑ SAT ☑ SAT Subject Tests	***Technology Lab Activities*** 3-6 Lab Recording Sheet	**Required** graphing calculator
Lesson 3-6 Lines in the Coordinate Plane • Graph lines, and write their equations in slope-intercept and point-slope form. • Classify lines as parallel, intersecting, or coinciding. ☐ SAT-10 ☑ NAEP ☑ ACT ☑ SAT ☑ SAT Subject Tests	***Technology Lab Activities*** 3-6 Technology Lab	**Optional** straws or uncooked spaghetti

MK = *Manipulatives Kit*

Math Background

Professional Learning

PERPENDICULAR LINES

Lesson 3-5

One of the central theorems of this chapter states that two nonvertical lines in a coordinate plane are perpendicular if and only if the product of their slopes is -1. Students learn and use this theorem in Algebra 1, often with the caveat that they will not be able to prove it until they study geometry. The proof of the theorem is outlined below. Note that the proof requires some ideas that are not introduced until Chapter 7.

The first part of the proof is to show that if two nonvertical lines are perpendicular, then the product of their slopes is -1. Assume that nonvertical lines k and ℓ are perpendicular and intersect at P; also assume that line ℓ has positive slope m. Then it is possible to construct a right triangle PQR with its hypotenuse along line ℓ and with legs of length m and 1 as shown.

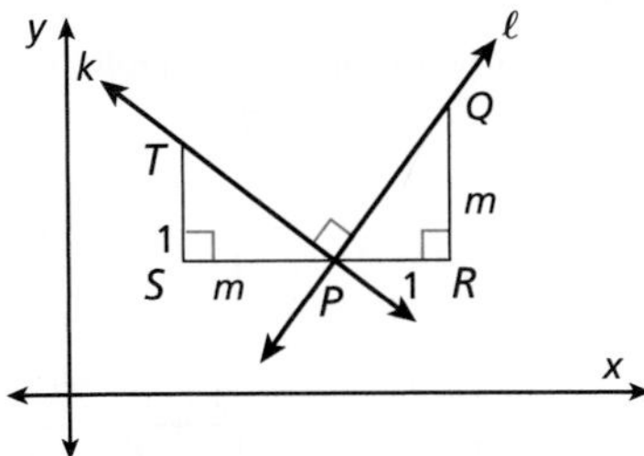

Extend $\overline{PR}$ through P and mark off a length of m along the line (at point S). Construct a perpendicular segment from S to k to form right triangle TPS. Now $\angle PQR \cong \angle TPS$ since both angles are complementary to $\angle QPR$. Thus, $\triangle PQR \cong \triangle TPS$ by ASA Congruence, and $\overline{TS} \cong \overline{PR}$, so $TS = 1$. The slope of line k is $-\frac{1}{m}$, and $-\frac{1}{m} \cdot m = -1$.

The second part of the proof is to show that if the product of the slopes of two lines is -1, then the lines are perpendicular. To begin, construct $\triangle PQR$ and $\triangle TPS$ as above, with $\overline{QR} \cong \overline{SP}$.

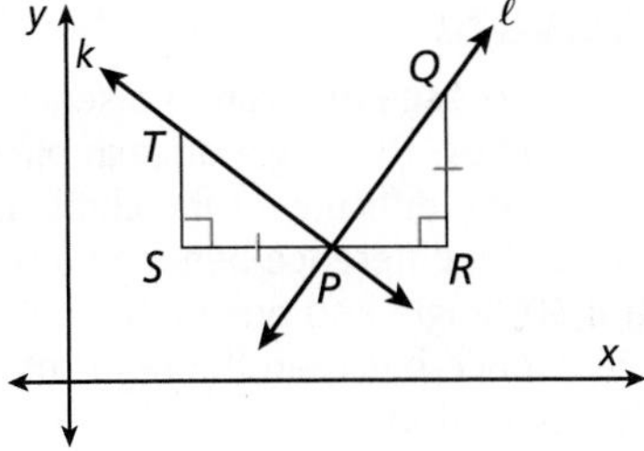

Based on these triangles, the slope of line ℓ is $\frac{QR}{PR}$ and the slope of line k is $-\frac{ST}{SP}$. Since the product of the slopes is -1, they must be opposite reciprocals of each other.

Therefore, $\frac{QR}{PR} = \frac{SP}{ST}$ and $\frac{QR}{SP} = \frac{PR}{ST}$. By SAS Similarity, $\triangle PQR \sim \triangle TPS$, and so $\angle PQR \cong \angle TPS$. Because they are the acute angles of a right triangle, $\angle PQR$ and $\angle QPR$ are complementary. Therefore, $\angle TPS$ and $\angle QPR$ are also complementary, and so $\angle TPQ$ is a right angle.

LINEAR EQUATIONS

Lesson 3-6

This course allows students to prove another important fact from Algebra 1: the graph of a linear function is a straight line. The proof, outlined below, again requires ideas from Chapter 7.

Any linear function may be written in the form $y = mx + b$. Assume $m \neq 0$ and let P, Q, and R be three points whose coordinates satisfy the equation. The goal is to show that the points are collinear by showing that $m\angle PQR = 180°$.

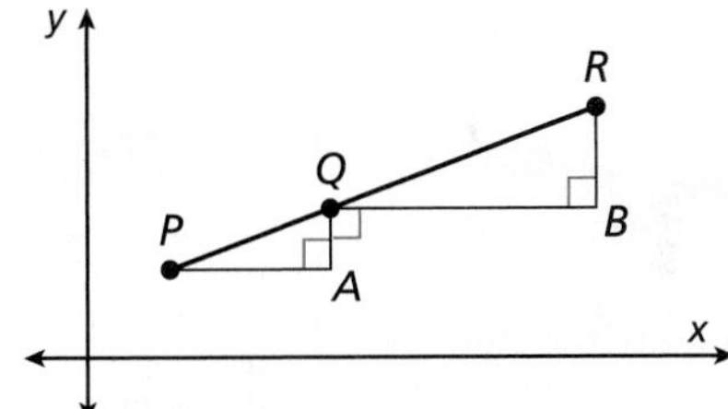

Construct right triangles PAQ and QBR as shown and assign general coordinates to the points. For example, assign P the coordinates (x_P, y_P) or $(x_P, mx_P + b)$. Using these coordinates, it is straightforward to show that $\frac{QA}{PA} = m$ and $\frac{RB}{QB} = m$. Thus, $\frac{QA}{PA} = \frac{RB}{QB}$ and $\frac{QA}{RB} = \frac{PA}{QB}$, so $\triangle PQA \sim \triangle QRB$ by SAS Similarity. This means $\angle QPA \cong \angle RQB$, so $\angle PQA$ and $\angle RQB$ are complementary, and $m\angle PQR = 180°$.

3-5 Organizer

Pacing: Traditional 1 day
Block $\frac{1}{2}$ day

Objectives: Find the slope of a line.

Use slopes to identify parallel and perpendicular lines.

Geometry Lab
In *Geometry Lab Activities*

Online Edition
Tutorial Videos

Countdown Week 6

Power Presentations with PowerPoint®

Warm Up

Find the value of *m*.

1. $m = \frac{7-5}{8-3}$ $\frac{2}{5}$

2. $m = \frac{(-3)-6}{5-(-1)}$ $-\frac{3}{2}$

3. $m = \frac{4-(-4)}{2-2}$ undefined

4. $m = \frac{-3+3}{1-6}$ 0

Also available on transparency

Math Humor

Q: How do the geometry teacher and track coach wake up their son?

A: It's time to rise and run!

3-5 Slopes of Lines

Objectives
Find the slope of a line.

Use slopes to identify parallel and perpendicular lines.

Vocabulary
rise
run
slope

Why learn this?
You can use the graph of a line to describe your rate of change, or speed, when traveling. (See Example 2.)

The *slope* of a line in a coordinate plane is a number that describes the steepness of the line. Any two points on a line can be used to determine the slope.

Know it! Note — **Slope of a Line**

DEFINITION	EXAMPLE
The **rise** is the difference in the *y*-values of two points on a line.	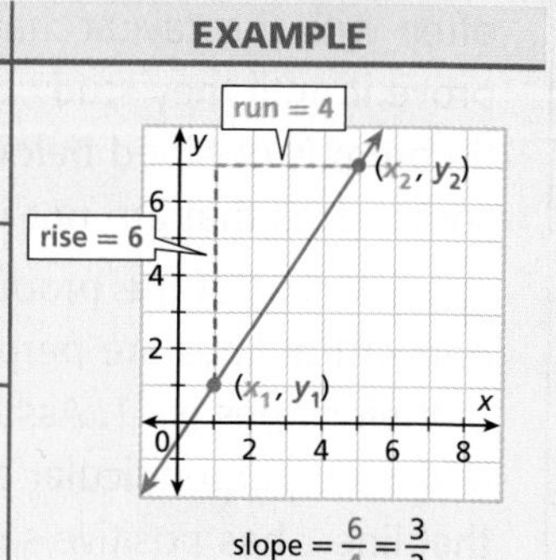
The **run** is the difference in the *x*-values of two points on a line.	
The **slope** of a line is the ratio of rise to run. If (x_1, y_1) and (x_2, y_2) are any two points on a line, the slope of the line is $m = \frac{y_2 - y_1}{x_2 - x_1}$.	slope $= \frac{6}{4} = \frac{3}{2}$

EXAMPLE 1 Finding the Slope of a Line

Algebra

Use the slope formula to determine the slope of each line.

A $\overleftrightarrow{AB}$

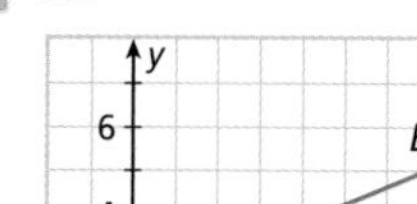
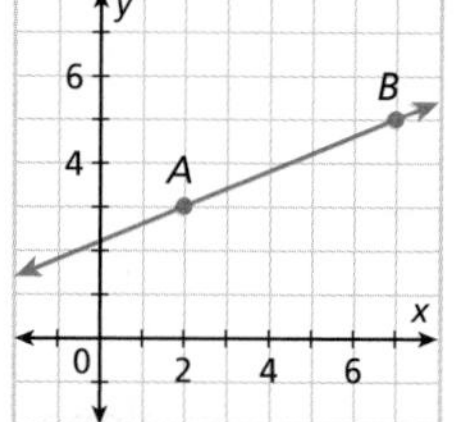

Substitute $(2, 3)$ for (x_1, y_1) and $(7, 5)$ for (x_2, y_2) in the slope formula and then simplify.

$$m = \frac{y_2 - y_1}{x_2 - x_1} = \frac{5-3}{7-2} = \frac{2}{5}$$

B $\overleftrightarrow{CD}$

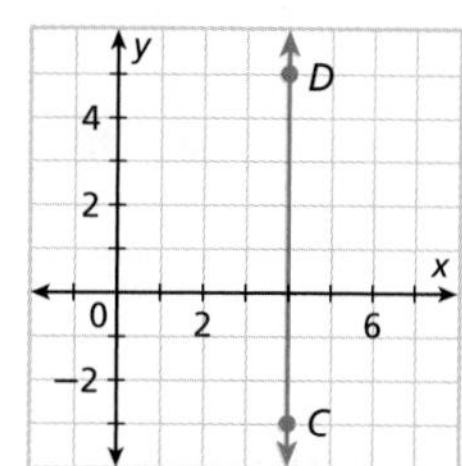

Substitute $(4, -3)$ for (x_1, y_1) and $(4, 5)$ for (x_2, y_2) in the slope formula and then simplify.

$$m = \frac{y_2 - y_1}{x_2 - x_1} = \frac{5-(-3)}{4-4} = \frac{8}{0}$$

The slope is undefined.

Remember!
A fraction with zero in the denominator is undefined because it is impossible to divide by zero.

State Resources

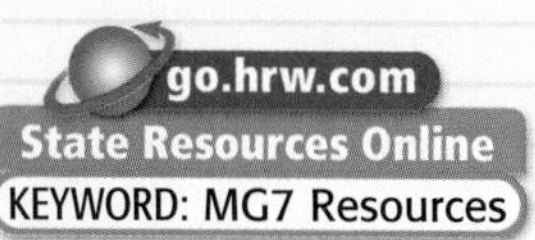
go.hrw.com
State Resources Online
KEYWORD: MG7 Resources

1 Introduce

EXPLORATION

3-5 Slopes of Lines

Recall that the slope of a line that passes through the points (x_1, y_1) and (x_2, y_2) is given by slope $= \frac{\text{rise}}{\text{run}} = \frac{y_2 - y_1}{x_2 - x_1}$.

1. Copy line ℓ and point *P*. Use a compass and straightedge to construct a line *m* that passes through *P* and is parallel to line ℓ.
2. Find the slope of line ℓ and line *m*. How are the slopes related?
3. Construct another pair of parallel lines to see if the same result holds.
4. Use a compass and straightedge to construct a line *n* that passes through *P* and is perpendicular to line ℓ.
5. Find the slope of line ℓ and line *n*. How are the slopes related?
6. Construct another pair of perpendicular lines to see if the same result holds.

THINK AND DISCUSS

7. **Discuss** whether your conclusions about lines ℓ and *m* hold for horizontal and vertical lines.
8. **Explain** how you would find the slope of a line that is perpendicular to the line through $(-3, 1)$ and $(3, 3)$.

Motivate

Ice climbers ascend a cliff in a series of stages called *pitches*. The angle of each pitch can contribute to the difficulty of the climb. Discuss with students the difference between a section of cliff with a 30° angle and one with a 15° angle. Show the difference between the ratios of rise to run of each cliff section.

Explorations and answers are provided in *Alternate Openers: Explorations Transparencies.*

Use the slope formula to determine the slope of each line.

C  $\overleftrightarrow{EF}$

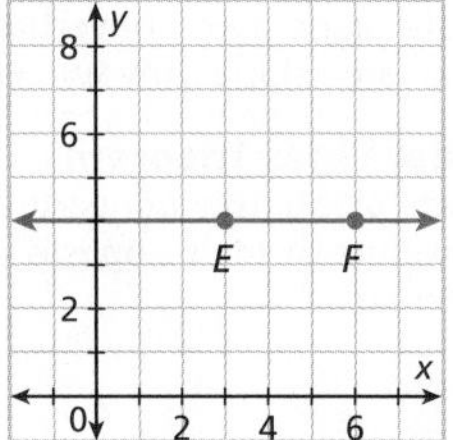

Substitute $(3, 4)$ for (x_1, y_1) and $(6, 4)$ for (x_2, y_2) in the slope formula and then simplify.

$$m = \frac{y_2 - y_1}{x_2 - x_1} = \frac{4 - 4}{6 - 3} = \frac{0}{3} = 0$$

D 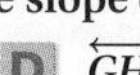 $\overleftrightarrow{GH}$

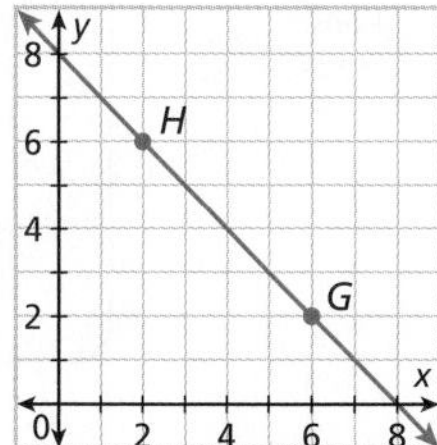

Substitute $(6, 2)$ for (x_1, y_1) and $(2, 6)$ for (x_2, y_2) in the slope formula and then simplify.

$$m = \frac{y_2 - y_1}{x_2 - x_1} = \frac{6 - 2}{2 - 6} = \frac{4}{-4} = -1$$

1. Use the slope formula to determine the slope of $\overleftrightarrow{JK}$ through $J(3, 1)$ and $K(2, -1)$. $m = 2$

Summary: Slope of a Line

Positive Slope	Negative Slope	Zero Slope	Undefined Slope

One interpretation of slope is a *rate of change.* If y represents miles traveled and x represents time in hours, the slope gives the rate of change in miles per hour.

EXAMPLE 2 *Transportation Application*

Tony is driving from Dallas, Texas, to Atlanta, Georgia. At 3:00 P.M., he is 180 miles from Dallas. At 5:30 P.M., he is 330 miles from Dallas. Graph the line that represents Tony's distance from Dallas at a given time. Find and interpret the slope of the line.

Distance from Dallas

Use the points $(3, 180)$ and $(5.5, 330)$ to graph the line and find the slope.

$$m = \frac{330 - 180}{5.5 - 3} = \frac{150}{2.5} = 60$$

The slope is 60, which means he is traveling at an average speed of 60 miles per hour.

2. **What if...?** Use the graph above to estimate how far Tony will have traveled by 6:30 P.M. if his average speed stays the same. **390 mi**

2 Teach

Guided Instruction

When calculating the slope of a line through two points, encourage students to graph the line to see the relationship between the value of the slope and the graph. Graph pairs of lines with the same slope and pairs of lines whose slopes are opposite reciprocals, and ask the students to make a conjecture about the lines. Then discuss the two theorems that relate the slopes of parallel and perpendicular lines.

Reaching All Learners

Through Kinesthetic Experience

To help students remember the order for writing the slope ratio tell them that, if you are sitting at your desk, you have to get up before you can go somewhere. In other words, you have to *rise* before you can *run*. Students should place the rise in the numerator before placing the run in the denominator.

Power Presentations with PowerPoint®

Additional Examples

Example 1

Use the slope formula to determine the slope of each line.

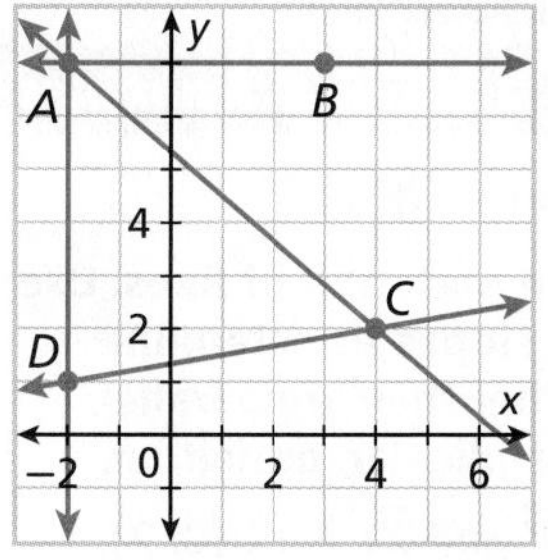

A. $\overleftrightarrow{AB}$ 0 **B.** $\overleftrightarrow{AC}$ $-\frac{5}{6}$

C. $\overleftrightarrow{AD}$ undefined **D.** $\overleftrightarrow{CD}$ $\frac{1}{6}$

Example 2

Justin is driving from home to his college dormitory. At 4:00 P.M., he is 260 miles from home. At 7:00 P.M., he is 455 miles from home. Graph the line that represents Justin's distance from home at a given time. Find and interpret the slope of the line.

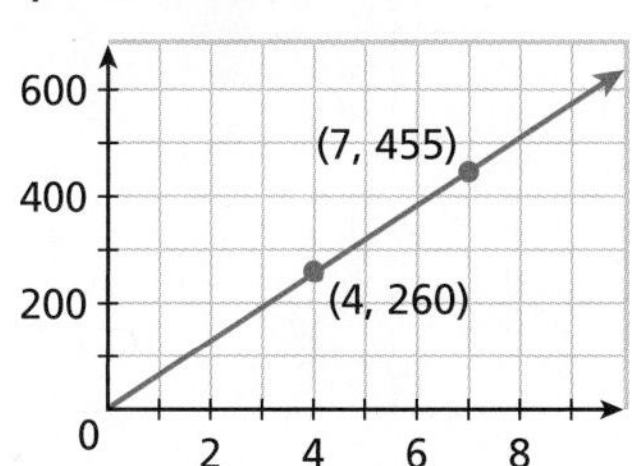

65; Justin is traveling at an average speed of 65 mi/h.

INTERVENTION

Questioning Strategies

EXAMPLE 1

- How much horizontal distance does the line gain for every y units it rises?

EXAMPLE 2

- Explain how to interpret the slope of a line.

Inclusion For **Example 3,** remind students that lines that appear parallel or perpendicular on the graph may not be. They must use slopes to prove the relationship algebraically.

Power Presentations with PowerPoint®

Additional Examples

Example 3

Graph each pair of lines. Use their slopes to determine whether they are parallel, perpendicular, or neither.

A. $\overleftrightarrow{UV}$ and $\overleftrightarrow{XY}$ for $U(0, 2)$, $V(-1, -1)$, $X(3, 1)$, and $Y(-3, 3)$

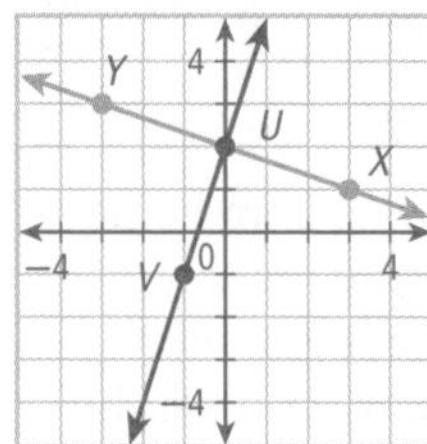

$3, -\frac{1}{3}$; perpendicular

B. $\overleftrightarrow{GH}$ and $\overleftrightarrow{IJ}$ for $G(-3, -2)$, $H(1, 2)$, $I(-2, 4)$, and $J(2, -4)$

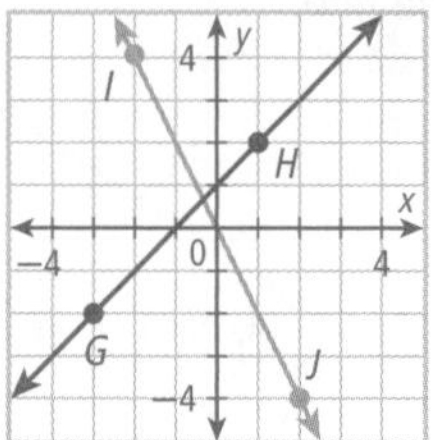

1, −2; neither

B. $\overleftrightarrow{CD}$ and $\overleftrightarrow{EF}$ for $C(-1, -3)$, $D(1, 1)$, $E(-1, 1)$, and $F(0, 3)$

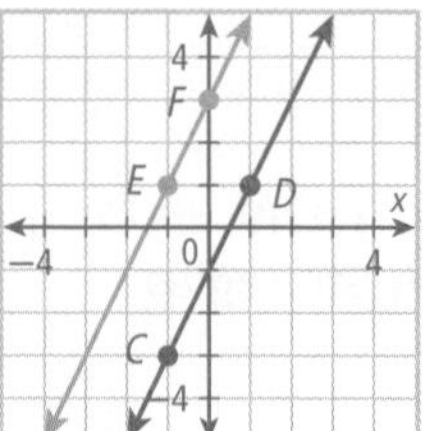

2, 2; parallel

Know it! Note

Slopes of Parallel and Perpendicular Lines

3-5-1 Parallel Lines Theorem
In a coordinate plane, two nonvertical lines are parallel if and only if they have the same slope. Any two vertical lines are parallel.

3-5-2 Perpendicular Lines Theorem
In a coordinate plane, two nonvertical lines are perpendicular if and only if the product of their slopes is −1. Vertical and horizontal lines are perpendicular.

If a line has a slope of $\frac{a}{b}$, then the slope of a perpendicular line is $-\frac{b}{a}$. The ratios $\frac{a}{b}$ and $-\frac{b}{a}$ are called *opposite reciprocals.*

EXAMPLE 3 **Determining Whether Lines Are Parallel, Perpendicular, or Neither**

x^2y **Algebra**

Graph each pair of lines. Use slopes to determine whether the lines are parallel, perpendicular, or neither.

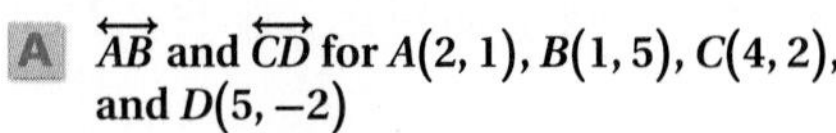

A $\overleftrightarrow{AB}$ **and** $\overleftrightarrow{CD}$ **for** $A(2, 1)$, $B(1, 5)$, $C(4, 2)$, **and** $D(5, -2)$

slope of $\overleftrightarrow{AB} = \frac{5-1}{1-2} = \frac{4}{-1} = -4$

slope of $\overleftrightarrow{CD} = \frac{-2-2}{5-4} = \frac{-4}{1} = -4$

The lines have the same slope, so they are parallel.

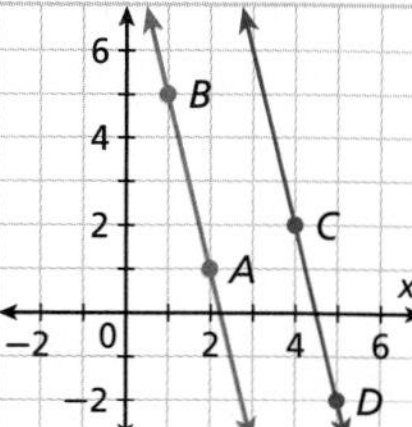

B $\overleftrightarrow{ST}$ **and** $\overleftrightarrow{UV}$ **for** $S(-2, 2)$, $T(5, -1)$, $U(3, 4)$, **and** $V(-1, -4)$

slope of $\overleftrightarrow{ST} = \frac{-1-2}{5-(-2)} = \frac{-3}{7} = -\frac{3}{7}$

slope of $\overleftrightarrow{UV} = \frac{-4-4}{-1-3} = \frac{-8}{-4} = 2$

The slopes are not the same, so the lines are not parallel. The product of the slopes is not −1, so the lines are not perpendicular.

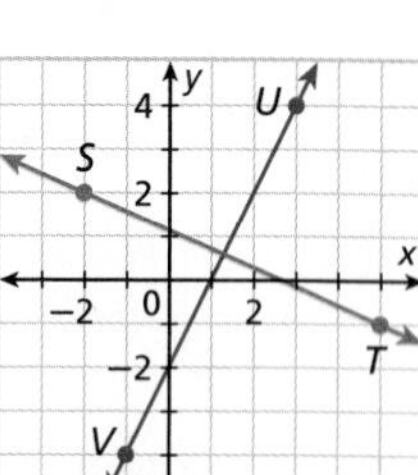

Caution!

Four given points do not always determine two lines. Graph the lines to make sure the points are not collinear.

C $\overleftrightarrow{FG}$ **and** $\overleftrightarrow{HJ}$ **for** $F(1, 1)$, $G(2, 2)$, $H(2, 1)$, **and** $J(1, 2)$

slope of $\overleftrightarrow{FG} = \frac{2-1}{2-1} = \frac{1}{1} = 1$

slope of $\overleftrightarrow{HJ} = \frac{2-1}{1-2} = \frac{1}{-1} = -1$

The product of the slopes is $1(-1) = -1$, so the lines are perpendicular.

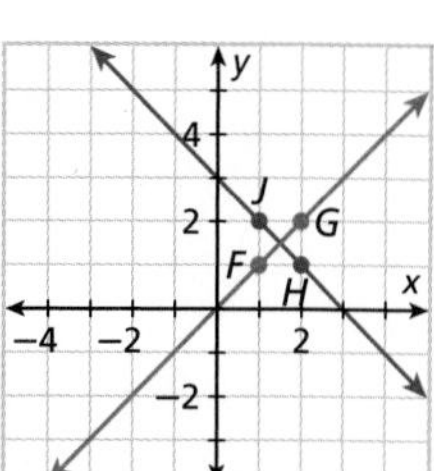

CHECK IT OUT! **Graph each pair of lines. Use slopes to determine whether the lines are parallel, perpendicular, or neither.**

⊥ **3a.** $\overleftrightarrow{WX}$ and $\overleftrightarrow{YZ}$ for $W(3, 1)$, $X(3, -2)$, $Y(-2, 3)$, and $Z(4, 3)$

neither **3b.** $\overleftrightarrow{KL}$ and $\overleftrightarrow{MN}$ for $K(-4, 4)$, $L(-2, -3)$, $M(3, 1)$, and $N(-5, -1)$

∥ **3c.** $\overleftrightarrow{BC}$ and $\overleftrightarrow{DE}$ for $B(1, 1)$, $C(3, 5)$, $D(-2, -6)$, and $E(3, 4)$

INTERVENTION

Questioning Strategies

EXAMPLE 3

- Which numbers should be subtracted in the numerator? in the denominator?
- How can you tell by their slopes whether two lines are parallel or perpendicular?

3 Close

Summarize

Remind students that the slope of a line is the ratio of the *rise* to the *run,* and describes the steepness of a line. The slope of the line can be used to classify parallel and perpendicular lines using the Parallel Lines Theorem and the Perpendicular Lines Theorem.

ONGOING ASSESSMENT

and INTERVENTION

Diagnose ***Before*** **the Lesson**
3-5 Warm Up, TE p. 182

Monitor ***During*** **the Lesson**
Check It Out! Exercises, SE pp. 183–184
Questioning Strategies, TE pp. 183–184

Assess ***After*** **the Lesson**
3-5 Lesson Quiz, TE p. 187
Alternative Assessment, TE p. 187

THINK AND DISCUSS

1. Explain how to find the slope of a line when given two points.
2. Compare the slopes of horizontal and vertical lines.

3. **GET ORGANIZED** Copy and complete the graphic organizer.

Pairs of Lines		
Type	Slopes	Example
Parallel		
Perpendicular		

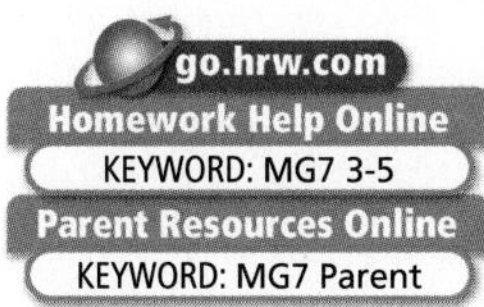

3-5 Exercises

go.hrw.com
Homework Help Online
KEYWORD: MG7 3-5
Parent Resources Online
KEYWORD: MG7 Parent

GUIDED PRACTICE

1. **Vocabulary** The *slope* of a line is the ratio of its __?__ to its __?__. (*rise* or *run*) **rise; run**

SEE EXAMPLE 1 p. 182

Use the slope formula to determine the slope of each line.

2. $\overleftrightarrow{MN}$ $m = \frac{6}{7}$

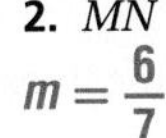

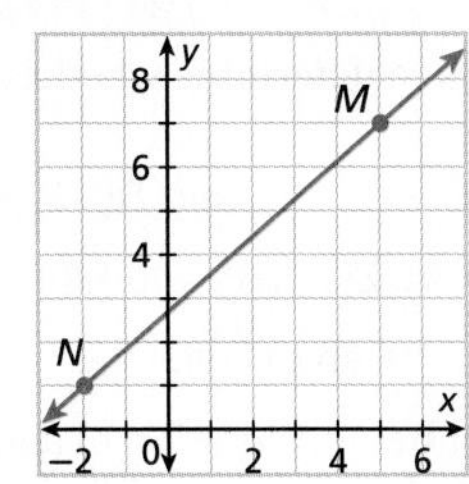

3. $\overleftrightarrow{CD}$ $m = -\frac{5}{9}$

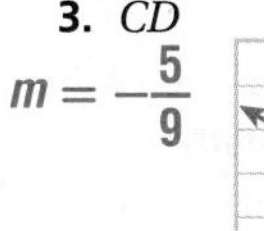

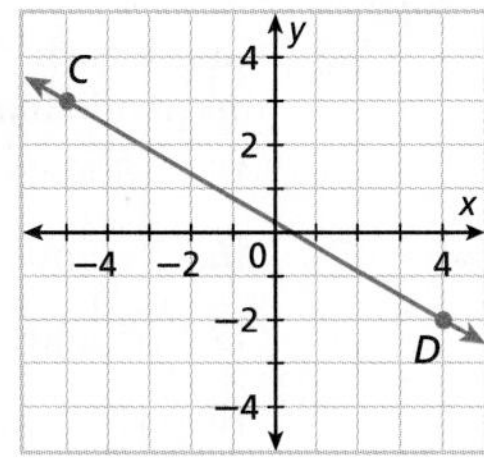

4. $\overleftrightarrow{AB}$ $m = 0$

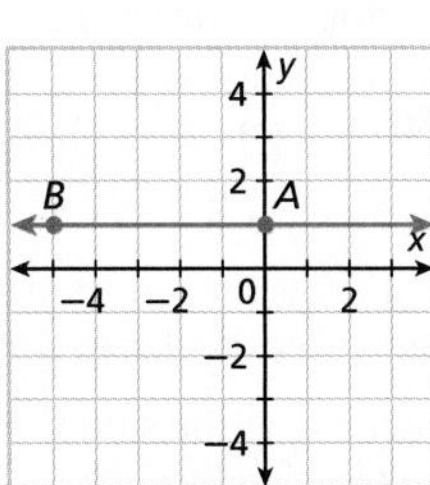

5. $\overleftrightarrow{ST}$ $m = \frac{5}{2}$

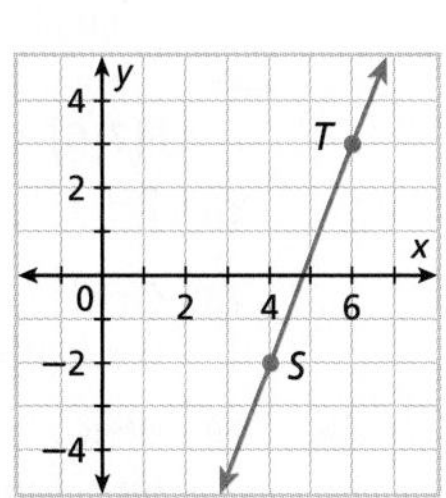

SEE EXAMPLE 2 p. 183

6. **Biology** A migrating bird flying at a constant speed travels 80 miles by 8:00 A.M. and 200 miles by 11:00 A.M. Graph the line that represents the bird's distance traveled. Find and interpret the slope of the line. **$m = 40$, which means that the bird is flying at an average speed of 40 mi/h.**

SEE EXAMPLE 3 p. 184

Graph each pair of lines. Use slopes to determine whether the lines are parallel, perpendicular, or neither.

7. $\overleftrightarrow{HJ}$ and $\overleftrightarrow{KM}$ for $H(3, 2)$, $J(4, 1)$, $K(-2, -4)$, and $M(-1, -5)$ $\parallel$
8. $\overleftrightarrow{LM}$ and $\overleftrightarrow{NP}$ for $L(-2, 2)$, $M(2, 5)$, $N(0, 2)$, and $P(3, -2)$ $\perp$
9. $\overleftrightarrow{QR}$ and $\overleftrightarrow{ST}$ for $Q(6, 1)$, $R(-2, 4)$, $S(5, 3)$, and $T(-3, -1)$ **neither**

Answers to *Think and Discuss*

1. Subtract the first *y*-value from the second *y*-value and the first *x*-value from the second *x*-value. Divide the difference of the *y*-values by the difference of the *x*-values.
2. Any 2 points on a horiz. line have the same *y*-value, so the numerator of the slope is 0. Thus the slope of a horiz. line is 0. Any 2 points on a vert. line have the same *x*-value, so the denominator of the slope is 0. Thus the slope of a vert. line is undefined.
3. See p. A3.

3-5 Exercises

Assignment Guide

Assign *Guided Practice* exercises as necessary.

If you finished Examples 1–3

Basic 10–14, 16–22 even, 24–28, 34–40
Average 10–14, 16–22 even, 23–30, 34–40
Advanced 10–14 even, 15–40

Homework Quick Check
Quickly check key concepts.
Exercises: 12, 14, 16, 18, 20

Teaching Tip **Science Link** The migration of birds is discussed in **Exercise 6.** You may want to mention that many birds have three basic flying speeds: cruising, migration, and emergency.

State Resources

go.hrw.com
State Resources Online
KEYWORD: MG7 Resources

Answers

7.

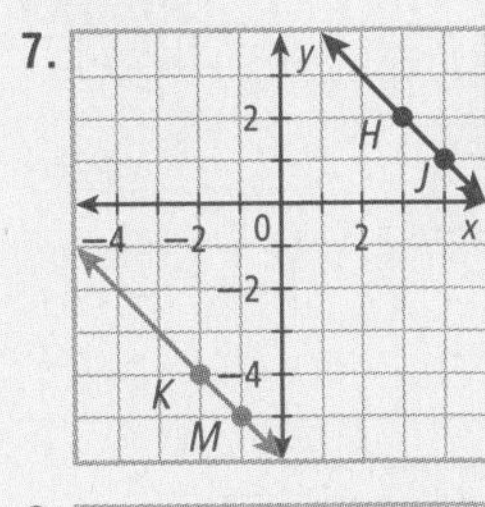

8.

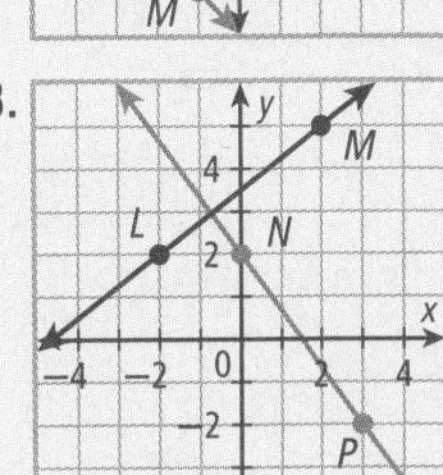

9.

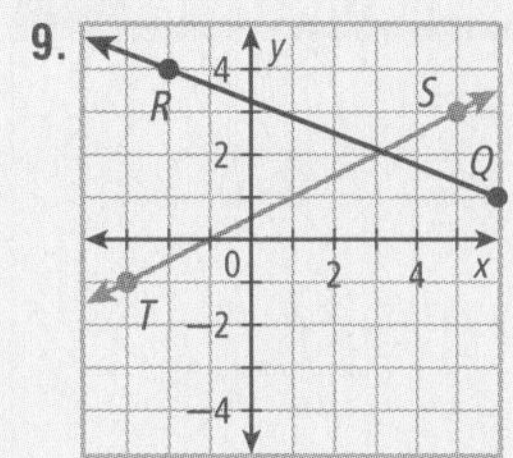

Inclusion In **Exercise 14,** students may make an error in the sign of the slope or place the run over the rise. Tell students to graph the line and estimate the slope by looking at whether it goes up or down and how steep it is.

Exercise 25 involves finding a car's rate of speed. This exercise prepares students for the Multi-Step Test Prep on page 200.

Answers

15–17. For graphs, see p. A14.

18. $m = \frac{1150}{2400} \approx 0.5$; the average change in elevation of the river is about 0.5 m per kilometer of length.

24. The lines have the same slope. They are either ||, or they are the same line.

PRACTICE AND PROBLEM SOLVING

Independent Practice	
For Exercises	See Example
10–13	1
14	2
15–17	3

Extra Practice
Skills Practice p. S9
Application Practice p. S30

Use the slope formula to determine the slope of each line.

10. $\overleftrightarrow{AB}$ *m* is undefined.

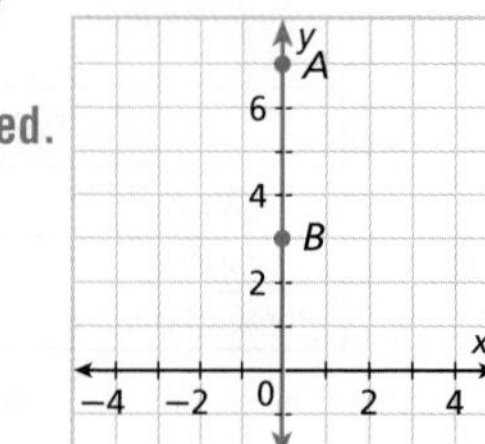

11. $\overleftrightarrow{CD}$ $m = 0$

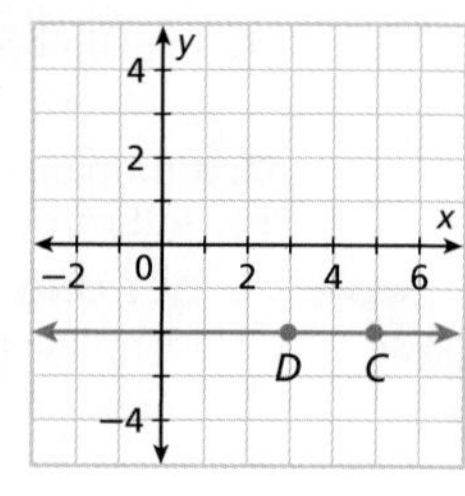

12. $\overleftrightarrow{EF}$ $m = -1$

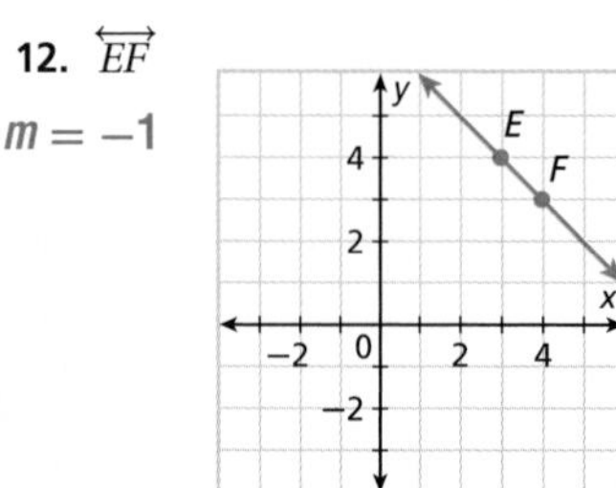

13. $\overleftrightarrow{GH}$ $m = -\frac{7}{3}$

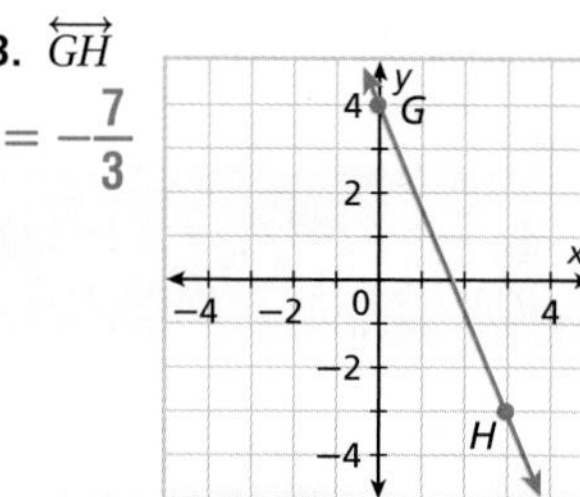

14. **Aviation** A pilot traveling at a constant speed flies 100 miles by 2:30 P.M. and 475 miles by 5:00 P.M. Graph the line that represents the pilot's distance flown. Find and interpret the slope of the line.

14. $m = 150$, which means that the plane is flying at an average speed of 150 mi/h.

Graph each pair of lines. Use slopes to determine whether the lines are parallel, perpendicular, or neither.

15. $\overleftrightarrow{AB}$ and $\overleftrightarrow{CD}$ for $A(2, -1)$, $B(7, 2)$, $C(2, -3)$, and $D(-3, -6)$ $\parallel$

16. $\overleftrightarrow{XY}$ and $\overleftrightarrow{ZW}$ for $X(-2, 5)$, $Y(6, -2)$, $Z(-3, 6)$, and $W(4, 0)$ neither

17. $\overleftrightarrow{JK}$ and $\overleftrightarrow{JL}$ for $J(-4, -2)$, $K(4, -2)$, and $L(-4, 6)$ $\perp$

18. **Geography** A point on a river has an elevation of about 1150 meters above sea level. The length of the river from that point to where it enters the sea is about 2400 km. Find and interpret the slope of the river.

For $F(7, 6)$, $G(-3, 5)$, $H(-2, -3)$, $J(4, -2)$, and $K(6, 1)$, find each slope.

19. $\overleftrightarrow{FG}$ $m = \frac{1}{10}$ 20. $\overleftrightarrow{GJ}$ $m = -1$ 21. $\overleftrightarrow{HK}$ $m = \frac{1}{2}$ 22. $\overleftrightarrow{GK}$ $m = -\frac{4}{9}$

23. **Critical Thinking** The slope of $\overleftrightarrow{AB}$ is greater than 0 and less than 1. Write an inequality for the slope of a line perpendicular to $\overleftrightarrow{AB}$. $m < -1$

24. **Write About It** Two cars are driving at the same speed. What is true about the lines that represent the distance traveled by each car at a given time?

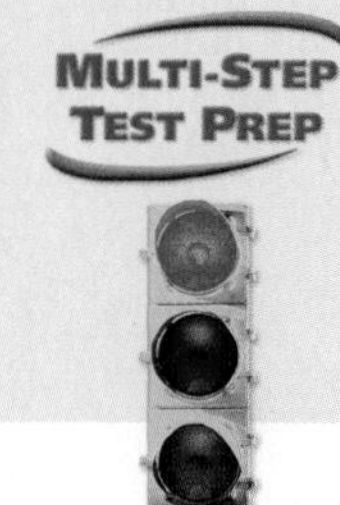

25. This problem will prepare you for the Multi-Step Test Prep on page 200.

A traffic engineer calculates the speed of vehicles as they pass a traffic light. While the light is green, a taxi passes at a constant speed. After 2 s the taxi is 132 ft past the light. After 5 s it is 330 ft past the light.

a. Find the speed of the taxi in feet per second. 66 ft/s

b. Use the fact that 22 ft/s = 15 mi/h to find the taxi's speed in miles per hour. 45 mi/h

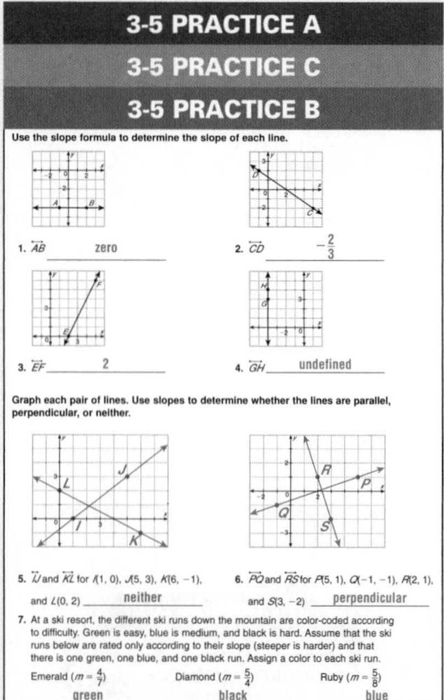

3-5 PRACTICE A

3-5 PRACTICE C

3-5 PRACTICE B

Use the slope formula to determine the slope of each line.

1. $\overleftrightarrow{AB}$ zero 2. $\overleftrightarrow{CD}$ $-\frac{2}{3}$

3. $\overleftrightarrow{EF}$ 2 4. $\overleftrightarrow{GH}$ undefined

Graph each pair of lines. Use slopes to determine whether the lines are parallel, perpendicular, or neither.

5. $\overleftrightarrow{IJ}$ and $\overleftrightarrow{KL}$ for $I(1, 0)$, $J(5, 3)$, $K(6, -1)$, and $L(0, 2)$ neither

6. $\overleftrightarrow{PQ}$ and $\overleftrightarrow{RS}$ for $P(5, 1)$, $Q(-1, -1)$, $R(2, 1)$, and $S(3, -2)$ perpendicular

7. At a ski resort, the different ski runs down the mountain are color-coded according to difficulty. Green is easy, blue is medium, and black is hard. Assume that the ski runs below are rated only according to their slope (steeper is harder) and that there is one green, one blue, and one black run. Assign a color to each ski run.

Emerald ($m = \frac{4}{7}$) green Diamond ($m = \frac{5}{4}$) black Ruby ($m = \frac{5}{8}$) blue

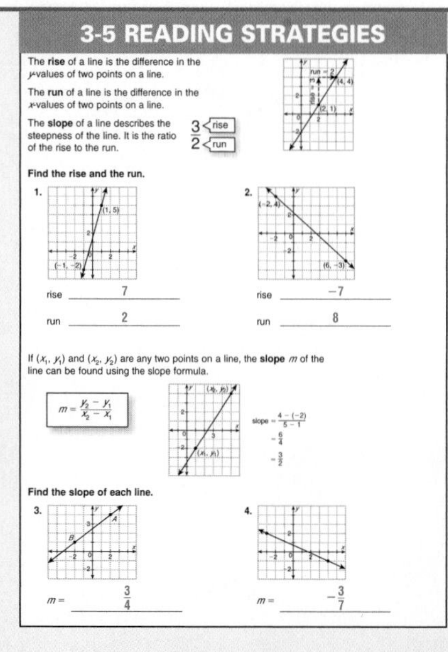

3-5 READING STRATEGIES

The **rise** of a line is the difference in the *y*-values of two points on a line.

The **run** of a line is the difference in the *x*-values of two points on a line.

The **slope** of a line describes the steepness of the line. It is the ratio of the rise to the run. $\frac{3}{2}$ rise / run

Find the rise and the run.

1. rise 7 run 2

2. rise −7 run 8

If (x_1, y_1) and (x_2, y_2) are any two points on a line, the **slope** *m* of the line can be found using the slope formula.

$m = \frac{y_2 - y_1}{x_2 - x_1}$

Find the slope of each line.

3. $m =$ $\frac{3}{4}$

4. $m =$ $-\frac{3}{7}$

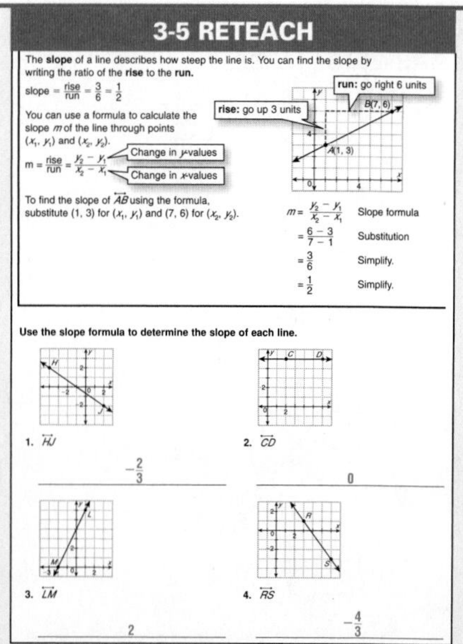

3-5 RETEACH

The **slope** of a line describes how steep the line is. You can find the slope by writing the ratio of the **rise** to the **run**.

slope $= \frac{\text{rise}}{\text{run}} = \frac{3}{6} = \frac{1}{2}$

You can use a formula to calculate the slope *m* of the line through points (x_1, y_1) and (x_2, y_2).

$m = \frac{\text{rise}}{\text{run}} = \frac{y_2 - y_1}{x_2 - x_1}$ Change in *y*-values / Change in *x*-values

To find the slope of $\overleftrightarrow{AB}$ using the formula, substitute (1, 3) for (x_1, y_1) and (7, 6) for (x_2, y_2).

$m = \frac{y_2 - y_1}{x_2 - x_1}$ Slope formula

$= \frac{6 - 3}{7 - 1}$ Substitution

$= \frac{3}{6}$ Simplify.

$= \frac{1}{2}$ Simplify.

Use the slope formula to determine the slope of each line.

1. $\overleftrightarrow{HJ}$ $-\frac{2}{3}$ 2. $\overleftrightarrow{CD}$ 0

3. $\overleftrightarrow{LM}$ 2 4. $\overleftrightarrow{RS}$ $-\frac{4}{3}$

TEST PREP

26. $\overleftrightarrow{AB} \perp \overleftrightarrow{CD}$ for $A(1, 3)$, $B(4, -2)$, $C(6, 1)$, and $D(x, y)$. Which are possible values of x and y?
    - (A) $x = 1, y = -2$ (circled)
    - (B) $x = 3, y = 6$
    - (C) $x = 3, y = -4$
    - (D) $x = -2, y = -4$

27. Classify $\overleftrightarrow{MN}$ and $\overleftrightarrow{PQ}$ for $M(-3, 1)$, $N(1, 3)$, $P(8, 4)$, and $Q(2, 1)$.
    - (F) Parallel (circled)
    - (G) Perpendicular
    - (H) Vertical
    - (J) Skew

28. In the formula $d = rt$, d represents distance, and r represents the rate of change, or slope. Which ray on the graph represents a slope of 45 miles per hour?
    - (A) A
    - (B) B
    - (C) C (circled)
    - (D) D

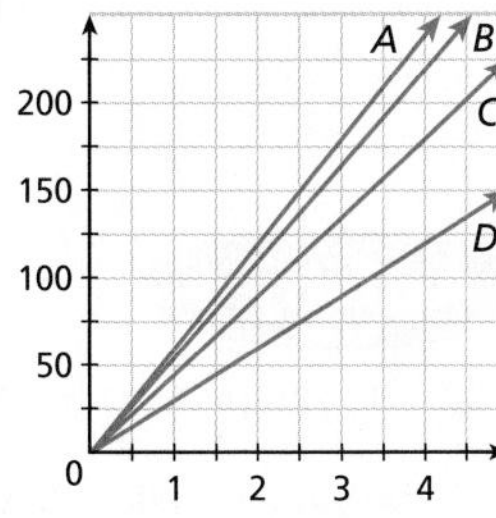

CHALLENGE AND EXTEND

Use the given information to classify $\overleftrightarrow{JK}$ for $J(a, b)$ and $K(c, d)$.

29. $a = c$ $\overleftrightarrow{JK}$ is a vert. line.

30. $b = d$ $\overleftrightarrow{JK}$ is a horiz. line.

31. The vertices of square $ABCD$ are $A(0, -2)$, $B(6, 4)$, $C(0, 10)$, $D(-6, 4)$.
    - a. Show that the opposite sides are parallel.
    - b. Show that the consecutive sides are perpendicular.
    - c. Show that all sides are congruent.

32. $\overleftrightarrow{ST} \parallel \overleftrightarrow{VW}$ for $S(-3, 5)$, $T(1, -1)$, $V(x, -3)$, and $W(1, y)$. Find a set of possible values for x and y. Possible answer: $x = 3$, $y = 0$

33. $\overleftrightarrow{MN} \perp \overleftrightarrow{PQ}$ for $M(2, 1)$, $N(-3, 0)$, $P(x, 4)$, and $Q(3, y)$. Find a set of possible values for x and y. Possible answer: $x = 1$, $y = -6$

SPIRAL REVIEW

Find the x- and y-intercepts of the line that contains each pair of points. *(Previous course)*

34. $(-5, 0)$ and $(0, -5)$ x-int.: -5; y-int.: -5

35. $(0, 1)$ and $(2, -7)$ x-int.: 0.25; y-int.: 1

36. $(1, -3)$ and $(3, 3)$ x-int.: 2; y-int.: -6

Use the given paragraph proof to write a two-column proof. *(Lesson 2-7)*

37. **Given:** $\angle 1$ is supplementary to $\angle 3$.
    Prove: $\angle 2 \cong \angle 3$
    Proof: It is given that $\angle 1$ is supplementary to $\angle 3$. $\angle 1$ and $\angle 2$ are a linear pair by the definition of a linear pair. By the Linear Pair Theorem, $\angle 1$ and $\angle 2$ are supplementary. Thus $\angle 2 \cong \angle 3$ by the Congruent Supplements Theorem.

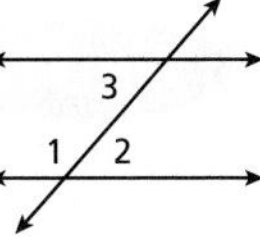

37.
1. $\angle 1$ is supp. to $\angle 3$. (Given)
2. $\angle 1$ and $\angle 2$ are supp. (Lin. Pair Thm.)
3. $\angle 2 \cong \angle 3$ ($\cong$ Supps. Thm.)

Given that $m\angle 2 = 75°$, tell whether each statement is true or false. Justify your answer with a postulate or theorem. *(Lesson 3-2)*

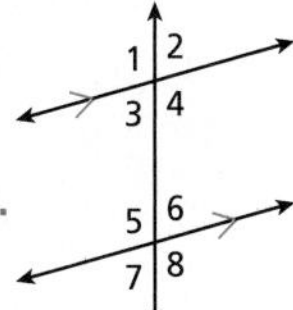

38. $\angle 1 \cong \angle 8$ T; Alt. Ext. ∠s Thm.

39. $\angle 2 \cong \angle 6$ T; Corr. ∠s Post.

40. $\angle 3 \cong \angle 5$ F; Same-Side Int. ∠s Thm.

TEST PREP DOCTOR In **Exercise 26,** you may have to remind students that they are looking for the opposite reciprocal, not just the reciprocal, of the slope of $\overleftrightarrow{AB}$.

In **Exercise 28,** suggest to students that they choose points whose coordinates are easily determined from the graph.

Answers

31. See p. A14.

Journal

Have students explain two ways to determine the slope of a line. Ask them to draw graphs of pairs of parallel lines and perpendicular lines and to explain how their slopes are related.

ALTERNATIVE ASSESSMENT

Have students draw three graphs on three coordinate planes: one of parallel lines, one of perpendicular lines, and one of lines that are neither parallel nor perpendicular. Have them use slopes to support their drawings.

Power Presentations with PowerPoint®

3-5 Lesson Quiz

1. Use the slope formula to determine the slope of the line that passes through $M(3, 7)$ and $N(-3, 1)$. $m = 1$

Graph each pair of lines. Use slopes to determine whether they are parallel, perpendicular, or neither.

2. $\overleftrightarrow{AB}$ and $\overleftrightarrow{XY}$ for $A(-2, 5)$, $B(-3, 1)$, $X(0, -2)$, and $Y(1, 2)$ 4, 4; parallel

3. $\overleftrightarrow{MN}$ and $\overleftrightarrow{ST}$ for $M(0, -2)$, $N(4, -4)$, $S(4, 1)$, and $T(1, -5)$ 2, $-\frac{1}{2}$; perpendicular

2–3.

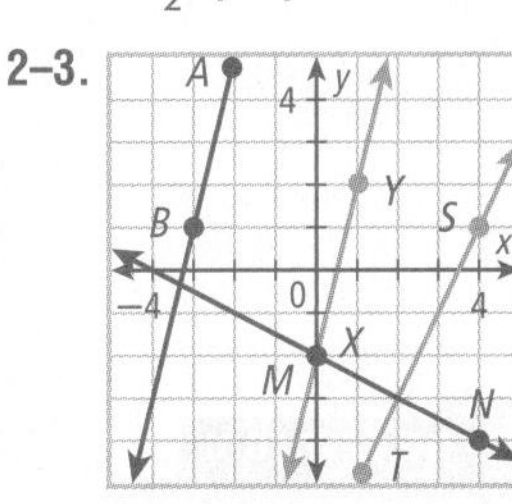

Also available on transparency

3-5 PROBLEM SOLVING

Graph the line that represents each situation. Then find and interpret the slope of the line.

1. Mara is jogging at a constant speed. She jogs 2 miles in 14 minutes. After 35 minutes, she has jogged 5 miles. Graph the line that represents Mara's distance traveled.

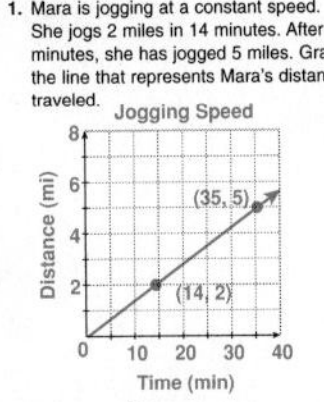

The slope is $\frac{1}{7}$, which means that Mara is jogging at an average speed of $\frac{1}{7}$ mi/min.

2. A turtle swimming at a constant speed travels 12 miles by 3:00 P.M. and 28 miles by 7:00 P.M. Graph the line that represents the turtle's distance traveled.

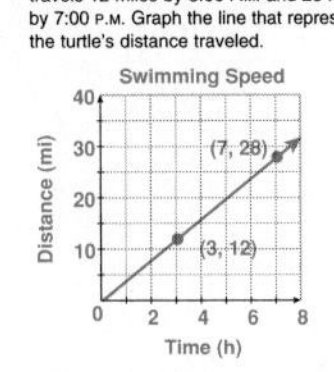

The slope is 4, which means that the turtle is swimming at an average speed of 4 mi/h.

Choose the best answer.

3. A hang glider who started at 7:55 A.M. has traveled at a constant speed as shown in the table.

Time	Distance Traveled
8:00 A.M.	2 mi
8:30 A.M.	14 mi

If the line that represents the hang glider's distance traveled is graphed, which is a true interpretation of the slope?
- (A) The hang glider is traveling at an average speed of 24 miles per hour. (circled)
- B The hang glider is traveling at an average speed of 16 miles per hour.
- C The hang glider is traveling at an average speed of 12 miles per minute.
- D The hang glider is traveling at an average speed of 7 miles per minute.

4. The line represents the distance traveled by an in-line skater traveling at a constant speed. What is the rate of change represented in the graph?

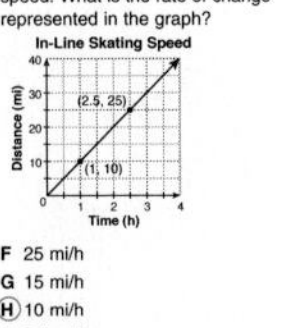

- F 25 mi/h
- G 15 mi/h
- (H) 10 mi/h (circled)
- J 0.1 mi/h

3-5 CHALLENGE

Quadrilateral	Properties	Models
parallelogram	Both pairs of opposite sides are parallel.	N P R Q
trapezoid	Exactly one pair of opposite sides is parallel.	C D G F

Determine whether each quadrilateral with the given vertices is a parallelogram, a trapezoid, or neither. Explain your reasoning.

1. $A(-9, -1)$, $B(-5, 2)$, $C(6, 2)$, $D(-10, -10)$
   Trapezoid; $\overline{AB}$ and $\overline{CD}$ both have a slope of $\frac{3}{4}$. The slope of $\overline{AD}$ is 9 and the slope of $\overline{BC}$ is 0. So exactly one pair of opposite sides is parallel.

2. $R(-14, 8)$, $S(11, -7)$, $T(2, 11)$, $V(0, 7)$
   Neither; the slope of $\overline{RS}$ is $-\frac{3}{5}$, the slope of $\overline{ST}$ is -2, the slope of $\overline{TV}$ is 2, and the slope of $\overline{VR}$ is $-\frac{1}{14}$. So neither pair of sides is parallel.

3. $J(4, 4)$, $K(2, 1)$, $L(-3, 2)$, $M(-1, 5)$
   Parallelogram; $\overline{JK}$ and $\overline{LM}$ both have a slope of $\frac{3}{2}$. $\overline{KL}$ and $\overline{MJ}$ both have a slope of $-\frac{1}{5}$. Opposite sides have the same slope, so they are parallel.

4. If a quadrilateral is a parallelogram and the diagonals are perpendicular, then the figure is a rhombus. Determine whether quadrilateral $WXYZ$ is a rhombus. Explain.
   No; the slopes of $\overline{WX}$ and $\overline{ZY}$ are $\frac{1}{5}$ and the slopes of $\overline{XY}$ and $\overline{WZ}$ are $-\frac{4}{3}$. So the figure is a parallelogram. The slopes of $\overline{WY}$ and $\overline{XZ}$ are $\frac{5}{2}$ and $-\frac{3}{8}$, respectively. Since they are not opposite reciprocals, the diagonals are not perpendicular.

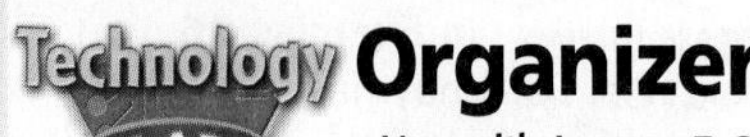

Organizer

Use with Lesson 3-6

Pacing:

Traditional $\frac{1}{2}$ day

Block $\frac{1}{4}$ day

Objective: Use a graphing calculator to graph parallel and perpendicular lines.

Materials: graphing calculator

Online Edition

Graphing Calculator, TechKeys

Countdown Week 6

Resources

Technology Lab Activities

3-6 Lab Recording Sheet

Teach

Discuss

Have students use the table feature to make a table of values for $y = 3x - 4$ and $y = 3x + 1$. Use the table to find two points on each line, and calculate the slopes to verify that the lines are parallel. Then make a table of values for $y = 3x - 4$ and $y = -\frac{1}{3}x$, find two points, and calculate the slopes to verify that the lines are perpendicular.

State Resources

go.hrw.com

State Resources Online

KEYWORD: MG7 Resources

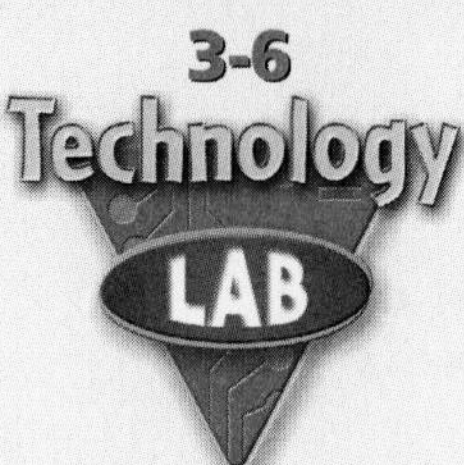

3-6 Technology LAB

Use with Lesson 3-6

Explore Parallel and Perpendicular Lines

A graphing calculator can help you explore graphs of parallel and perpendicular lines. To graph a line on a calculator, you can enter the equation of the line in *slope-intercept form*. The slope-intercept form of the equation of a line is $y = mx + b$, where m is the slope and b is the y-intercept. For example, the line $y = 2x + 3$ has a slope of 2 and crosses the y-axis at (0, 3).

go.hrw.com

Lab Resources Online

KEYWORD: MG7 Lab3

Activity 1

1. On a graphing calculator, graph the lines $y = 3x - 4$, $y = -3x - 4$, and $y = 3x + 1$. Which lines appear to be parallel? What do you notice about the slopes of the parallel lines?
   $y = 3x - 4$ and $y = 3x + 1$ appear to be ||. The slopes of the lines are the same.

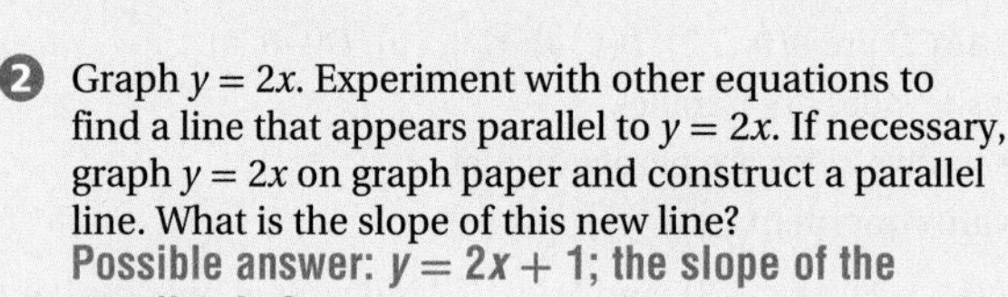

2. Graph $y = 2x$. Experiment with other equations to find a line that appears parallel to $y = 2x$. If necessary, graph $y = 2x$ on graph paper and construct a parallel line. What is the slope of this new line?
   Possible answer: $y = 2x + 1$; the slope of the new line is 2.

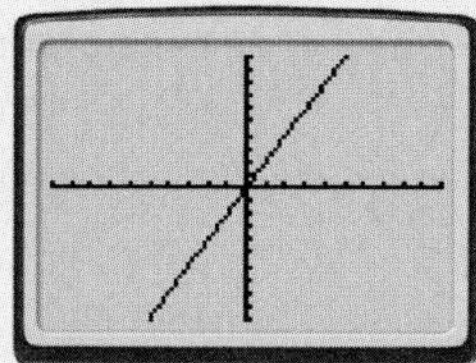

3. Graph $y = -\frac{1}{2}x + 3$. Try to graph a line that appears parallel to $y = -\frac{1}{2}x + 3$. What is the slope of this new line?
   Possible answer: $y = -\frac{1}{2}x + 1$; the slope of the new line is $-\frac{1}{2}$.

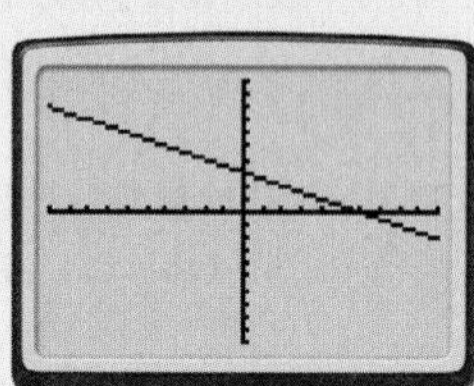

Try This

2. Possible answer: Yes; the lines are still || if the window setting is changed; both lines appear steeper.

1. Create two new equations of lines that you think will be parallel. Graph these to confirm your conjecture. **Possible answer: $y = x$ and $y = x + 1$**
2. Graph two lines that you think are parallel. Change the window settings on the calculator. Do the lines still appear parallel? Describe your results.
3. Try changing the y-intercepts of one of the parallel lines. Does this change whether the lines appear to be parallel? **Changing the y-intercept of the lines does not change whether they are ||.**

On a graphing calculator, perpendicular lines may not appear to be perpendicular on the screen. This is because the unit distances on the x-axis and y-axis can have different lengths. To make sure that the lines appear perpendicular on the screen, use a *square window*, which shows the x-axis and y-axis as having equal unit distances.

One way to get a square window is to use the **Zoom** feature. On the **Zoom** menu, the **ZDecimal** and **ZSquare** commands change the window to a square window. The **ZStandard** command does not produce a square window.

Activity 2

1. Graph the lines $y = x$ and $y = -x$ in a square window. Do the lines appear to be perpendicular? **yes**

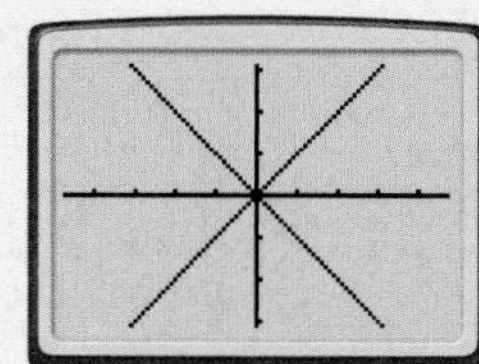

2. Graph $y = 3x - 2$ in a square window. Experiment with other equations to find a line that appears perpendicular to $y = 3x - 2$. If necessary, graph $y = 3x - 2$ on graph paper and construct a perpendicular line. What is the slope of this new line?
Possible answer: $y = -\frac{1}{3}x + 1$; the slope of the new line is $-\frac{1}{3}$.

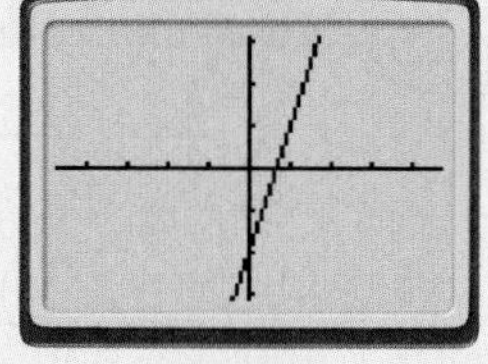

3. Graph $y = \frac{2}{3}x$ in a square window. Try to graph a line that appears perpendicular to $y = \frac{2}{3}x$. What is the slope of this new line?
Possible answer: $y = -\frac{3}{2}x$; the slope of the new line is $-\frac{3}{2}$.

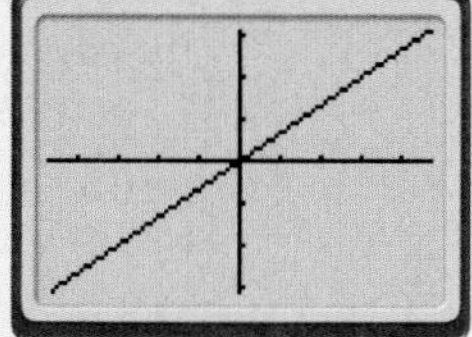

Try This

The students' equations should have slopes that are opp. reciprocals of each other. The product of the 2 slopes should be –1.

4. Create two new equations of lines that you think will be perpendicular. Graph these in a square window to confirm your conjecture.
5. Graph two lines that you think are perpendicular. Change the window settings on the calculator. Do the lines still appear perpendicular? Describe your results.
Possible answers: No; the lines still intersect, but the ∠ does not look like a rt. ∠.
6. Try changing the y-intercepts of one of the perpendicular lines. Does this change whether the lines appear to be perpendicular?
Changing the y-intercept of the lines does not change whether they are ⊥.

Close

Key Concepts

Parallel lines have the same slope and different y-intercepts.

The slopes of two perpendicular lines are opposite reciprocals of each other.

Assessment

Journal Have students explain how they can tell from the equations of two lines if the lines are parallel or perpendicular.

3-6 Organizer

Pacing: Traditional 1 day
Block $\frac{1}{2}$ day

Objectives: Graph lines and write their equations in slope-intercept and point-slope form.

Classify lines as parallel, intersecting, or coinciding.

Technology Lab
In *Technology Lab Activities*

Online Edition
Tutorial Videos, Interactivity

Countdown Week 6

Power Presentations with PowerPoint®

Warm Up

Substitute the given values of *m, x,* and *y* into the equation $y = mx + b$ and solve for *b*.

1. $m = 2, x = 3,$ and $y = 0$
   $b = -6$
2. $m = -1, x = 5,$ and $y = -4$
   $b = 1$

Solve each equation for *y*.

3. $y - 6x = 9$ $\quad y = 6x + 9$
4. $4x - 2y = 8$ $\quad y = 2x - 4$

Also available on transparency

Math Humor

Q: What do two lines with the same slope do when it rains?

A: Coincide.

State Resources

go.hrw.com
State Resources Online
KEYWORD: MG7 Resources

3-6 Lines in the Coordinate Plane

Objectives
Graph lines and write their equations in slope-intercept and point-slope form.

Classify lines as parallel, intersecting, or coinciding.

Vocabulary
point-slope form
slope-intercept form

Why learn this?
The cost of some health club plans includes a one-time enrollment fee and a monthly fee. You can use the equations of lines to determine which plan is best for you. (See Example 4.)

"A one-year membership is \$10,000, but to encourage you to work out, we give you back \$25 every time you use the facility."

The equation of a line can be written in many different forms. The *point-slope* and *slope-intercept* forms of a line are equivalent. Because the slope of a vertical line is undefined, these forms cannot be used to write the equation of a vertical line.

Know it! Note

Forms of the Equation of a Line

FORM	EXAMPLE
The **point-slope form** of a line is $y - y_1 = m(x - x_1)$, where m is the slope and (x_1, y_1) is a given point on the line.	$y - 3 = 2(x - 4)$ $m = 2, (x_1, y_1) = (4, 3)$
The **slope-intercept form** of a line is $y = mx + b$, where m is the slope and b is the y-intercept.	$y = 3x + 6$ $m = 3, b = 6$
The equation of a vertical line is $x = a$, where a is the x-intercept.	$x = 5$
The equation of a horizontal line is $y = b$, where b is the y-intercept.	$y = 2$

You will use a proof to derive the slope-intercept form of a line in Exercise 54.

PROOF **Point-Slope Form of a Line**

Given: The slope of a line through points (x_1, y_1) and (x_2, y_2) is $m = \frac{y_2 - y_1}{x_2 - x_1}$.
Prove: The equation of the line through (x_1, y_1) with slope m is $y - y_1 = m(x - x_1)$.
Proof:
Let (x, y) be any point on the line.

$m = \frac{y_2 - y_1}{x_2 - x_1}$	*Slope formula*
$m = \frac{y - y_1}{x - x_1}$	*Substitute (x, y) for (x_2, y_2).*
$(x - x_1)m = (x - x_1)\frac{y - y_1}{x - x_1}$	*Multiply both sides by $(x - x_1)$.*
$m(x - x_1) = (y - y_1)$	*Simplify.*
$y - y_1 = m(x - x_1)$	*Sym. Prop. of =*

1 Introduce

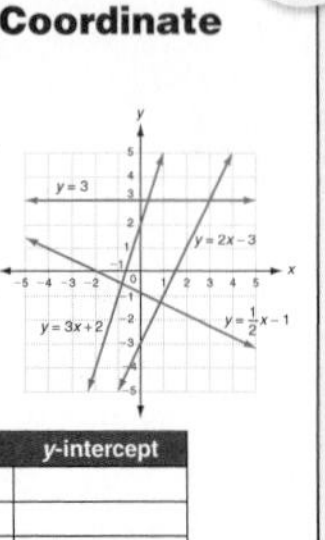

EXPLORATION

3-6 Lines in the Coordinate Plane

Use the given lines to explore equations, slopes, and y-intercepts.

1. Find the slope of each line. Record the slopes in the table.
2. Find the y-intercept of each line. Record the y-intercepts in the table.

Equation	Slope	y-intercept
$y = 3x + 2$		
$y = 2x - 3$		
$y = -\frac{1}{2}x - 1$		
$y = 3$		

3. What do you notice? How are the slopes and y-intercepts related to the equations?

THINK AND DISCUSS

4. Explain how you can identify the y-intercept of the line $y = -7x + 4$ without graphing it.

Motivate

Show students the instructions for baking a cake from a packaged cake mix. Point out that the baking times are different at higher altitudes because the air pressure is less at higher elevations than at sea level. Tell students that the graph of a linear equation can be used to determine how long a cake should be baked at a particular altitude.

Explorations and answers are provided in *Alternate Openers: Explorations Transparencies.*

EXAMPLE 1 **Writing Equations of Lines**

Algebra

Write the equation of each line in the given form.

A the line with slope 3 through $(2, 1)$ in point-slope form

$y - y_1 = m(x - x_1)$ *Point-slope form*

$y - 1 = 3(x - 2)$ *Substitute 3 for m, 2 for x_1, and 1 for y_1.*

B the line through $(0, 4)$ and $(-1, 2)$ in slope-intercept form

$m = \frac{2 - 4}{-1 - 0} = \frac{-2}{-1} = 2$ *Find the slope.*

$y = mx + b$ *Slope-intercept form*

$4 = 2(0) + b$ *Substitute 2 for m, 0 for x, and 4 for y to find b.*

$4 = b$ *Simplify.*

$y = 2x + 4$ *Write in slope-intercept form using m = 2 and b = 4.*

Remember!

A line with y-intercept b contains the point $(0, b)$.
A line with x-intercept a contains the point $(a, 0)$.

C the line with x-intercept 2 and y-intercept 3 in point-slope form

$m = \frac{3 - 0}{0 - 2} = -\frac{3}{2}$ *Use the points (2, 0) and (0, 3) to find the slope.*

$y - y_1 = m(x - x_1)$ *Point-slope form*

$y - 0 = -\frac{3}{2}(x - 2)$ *Substitute $-\frac{3}{2}$ for m, 2 for x_1, and 0 for y_1.*

$y = -\frac{3}{2}(x - 2)$ *Simplify.*

CHECK IT OUT! Write the equation of each line in the given form.

1a. the line with slope 0 through (4, 6) in slope-intercept form $y = 6$

1b. the line through (−3, 2) and (1, 2) in point-slope form $y - 2 = 0$

EXAMPLE 2 **Graphing Lines**

Algebra

Graph each line.

A $y = \frac{3}{2}x + 3$

The equation is given in slope-intercept form, with a slope of $\frac{3}{2}$ and a y-intercept of 3.

Plot the point $(0, 3)$ and then rise 3 and run 2 to find another point.

Draw the line containing the two points.

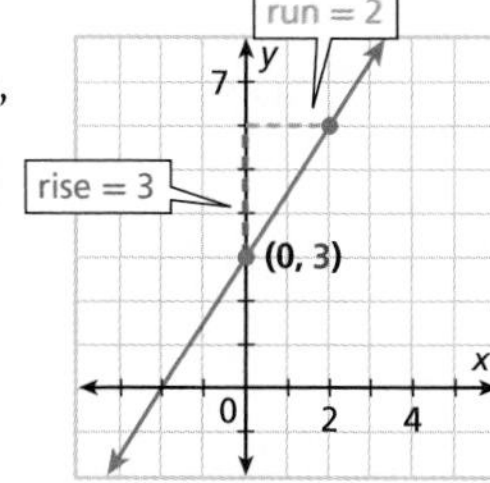

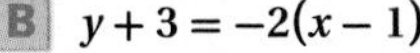

B $y + 3 = -2(x - 1)$

The equation is given in point-slope form, with a slope of $-2 = \frac{-2}{1}$ through the point $(1, -3)$.

Plot the point $(1, -3)$ and then rise −2 and run 1 to find another point.

Draw the line containing the two points.

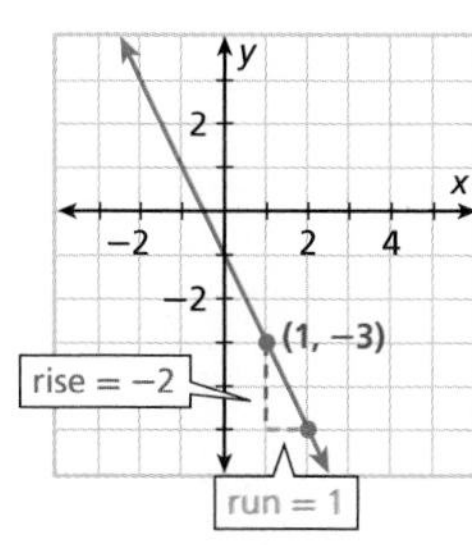

Students sometimes make errors substituting a negative coordinate into the point-slope form of an equation. Remind students that subtracting y is equivalent to adding the opposite of y.

Power Presentations with PowerPoint®

Additional Examples

Example 1

Write the equation of each line in the given form.

A. the line with slope 6 through $(3, -4)$ in point-slope form $y + 4 = 6(x - 3)$

B. the line through $(-1, 0)$ and $(1, 2)$ in slope-intercept form $y = x + 1$

C. the line with x-intercept 3 and y-intercept −5 in point-slope form $y = \frac{5}{3}(x - 3)$

Example 2

Graph each line.

A. $y = \frac{1}{2}x + 1$

B. $y - 3 = -2(x + 4)$

C. $y = -3$

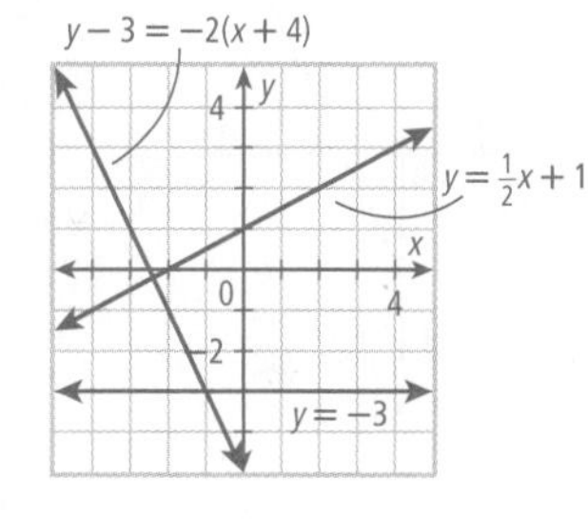

2 Teach

Guided Instruction

Before writing equations of lines, discuss the meaning of the points (x_1, y_1) and (x_2, y_2). As you work through the lesson, relate the equations of parallel, intersecting, and coinciding lines to their graphs.

Reaching All Learners

Through Curriculum Integration

Give groups of students a thermometer showing Fahrenheit and Celsius temperatures. Ask them to write two ordered pairs (°F, °C) that relate the boiling and freezing temperatures in Fahrenheit to the corresponding temperatures in Celsius. Then have them write the slope-intercept form of the equation of the line through the two points.

INTERVENTION

Questioning Strategies

EXAMPLE 1

- In **Example 1B,** how do you find the y-intercept b after you find the slope?
- How do you use the intercepts to find the slope in **Example 1C**?

EXAMPLE 2

- Describe how you graph each line.

Power Presentations with PowerPoint®

Additional Examples

Example 3

Determine whether the lines are parallel, intersect, or coincide.

A. $y = 3x + 7$, $y = -3x - 4$
intersect

B. $y = -\frac{1}{3}x + 5$, $6y = -2x + 12$
parallel

C. $2y - 4x = 16$,
$y - 10 = 2(x - 1)$ coincide

INTERVENTION
Questioning Strategies

EXAMPLE 3

- How can you tell that two lines are parallel?
- How is it helpful to solve equations for y?
- How can lines that have different equations be coinciding lines?

Answers to Check It Out!

2a.

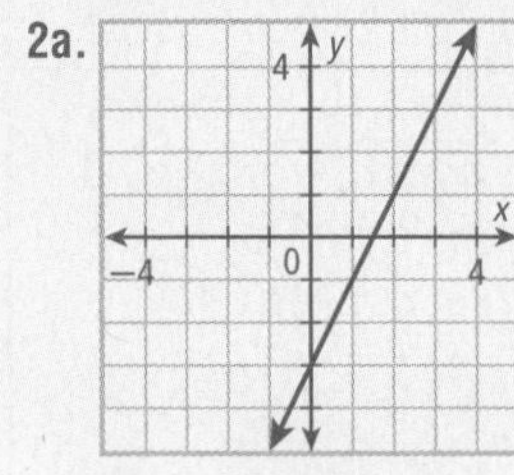

b.

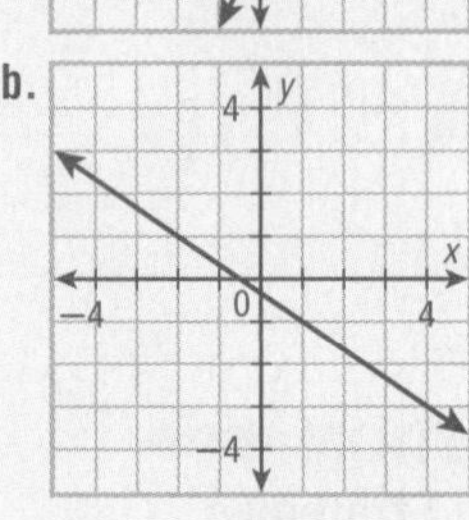

c.

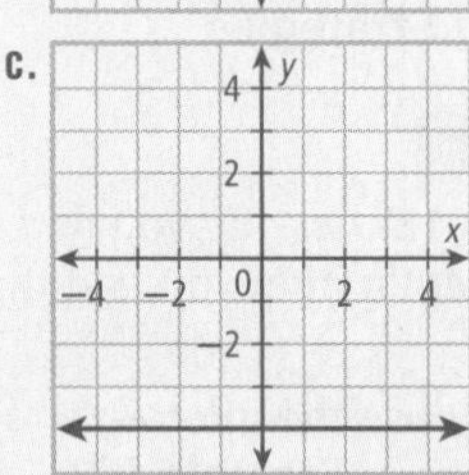

Graph the line.

C $x = 3$
The equation is given in the form for a vertical line with an x-intercept of 3.
The equation tells you that the x-coordinate of every point on the line is 3. Draw the vertical line through $(3, 0)$.

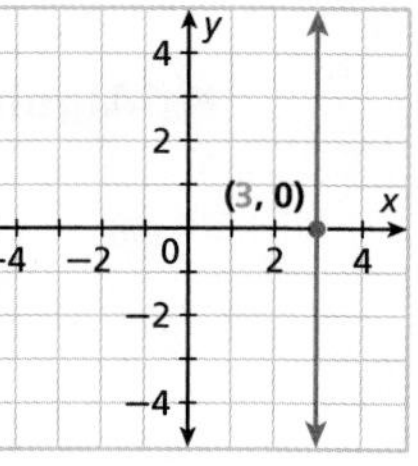

Graph each line.
2a. $y = 2x - 3$ **2b.** $y - 1 = -\frac{2}{3}(x + 2)$ **2c.** $y = -4$

A system of two linear equations in two variables represents two lines. The lines can be parallel, intersecting, or coinciding. Lines that coincide are the same line, but the equations may be written in different forms.

Know it! Note

Pairs of Lines

Parallel Lines	Intersecting Lines	Coinciding Lines
$y = 5x + 8$ $y = 5x - 4$	$y = 2x - 5$ $y = 4x + 3$	$y = 2x - 4$ $y = 2x - 4$
Same slope different y-intercept	Different slopes	Same slope same y-intercept

EXAMPLE 3 Classifying Pairs of Lines

Determine whether the lines are parallel, intersect, or coincide.

A $y = 2x + 3$, $y = 2x - 1$
Both lines have a slope of 2, and the y-intercepts are different. So the lines are parallel.

B $y = 3x - 5$, $6x - 2y = 10$
Solve the second equation for y to find the slope-intercept form.
$6x - 2y = 10$
$-2y = -6x + 10$
$y = 3x - 5$
Both lines have a slope of 3 and a y-intercept of -5, so they coincide.

C $3x + 2y = 7$, $3y = 4x + 7$
Solve both equations for y to find the slope-intercept form.

$3x + 2y = 7$
$2y = -3x + 7$
$y = -\frac{3}{2}x + \frac{7}{2}$ *The slope is $-\frac{3}{2}$.*

$3y = 4x + 7$
$y = \frac{4}{3}x + \frac{7}{3}$ *The slope is $\frac{4}{3}$.*

The lines have different slopes, so they intersect.

3. Determine whether the lines $3x + 5y = 2$ and $3x + 6 = -5y$ are parallel, intersect, or coincide. parallel

Teaching Tip

Math Background An equation of the form $Ax + By = C$ can be written in slope-intercept form as $y = \frac{-A}{B}x + \frac{C}{B}$. So a quick way to check whether lines have the same slope is to find $\frac{-A}{B}$ for both lines. If the slopes are the same, then find $\frac{C}{B}$ to see if the lines coincide.

EXAMPLE 4 Problem-Solving Application

Audrey is trying to decide between two health club plans. After how many months would both plans' total costs be the same?

	Plan A	Plan B
Enrollment Fee	\$140	\$60
Monthly Fee	\$35	\$55

1 Understand the Problem

The **answer** is the number of months after which the costs of the two plans would be the same. Plan A costs \$140 for enrollment and \$35 per month. Plan B costs \$60 for enrollment and \$55 per month.

2 Make a Plan

Write an equation for each plan, and then graph the equations. The solution is the intersection of the two lines. Find the intersection by solving the system of equations.

3 Solve

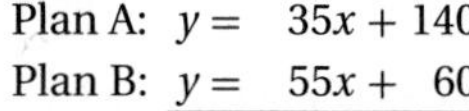

Plan A: $y = 35x + 140$
Plan B: $y = 55x + 60$
$0 = -20x + 80$ *Subtract the second equation from the first.*

$x = 4$ *Solve for x.*
$y = 35(4) + 140 = 280$ *Substitute 4 for x in the first equation.*

The lines cross at $(4, 280)$.
Both plans cost \$280 after 4 months.

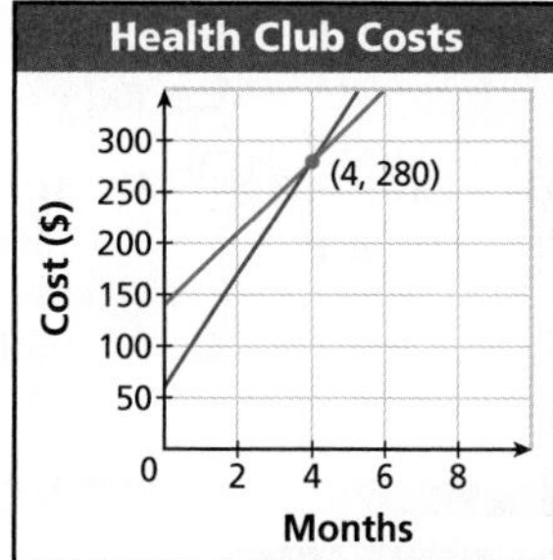

4 Look Back

Check your answer for each plan in the original problem. For 4 months, plan A costs \$140 plus $\$35(4) = \$140 + \$140 = \$280$. Plan B costs $\$60 + \$55(4) = \$60 + \$220 = \$280$, so the plans cost the same.

CHECK IT OUT! Use the information above to answer the following.

4. **What if...?** Suppose the rate for Plan B was also \$35 per month. What would be true about the lines that represent the cost of each plan? **The lines would be ∥.**

THINK AND DISCUSS

1. Explain how to use the slopes and y-intercepts to determine if two lines are parallel.
2. Describe the relationship between the slopes of perpendicular lines.
3. **GET ORGANIZED** Copy and complete the graphic organizer.

Know it! Note

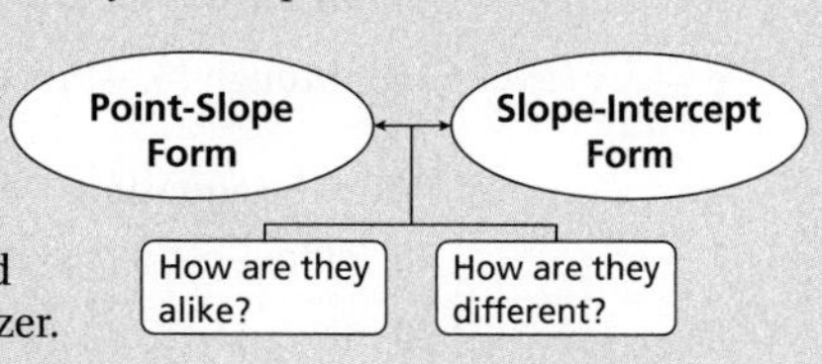

COMMON ERROR ALERT

In **Example 4,** students may forget to subtract 60 from 140, resulting in $y = -20x + 200$. Suggest that they align the equations vertically and change the sign of each term in the bottom equation, or suggest that students solve $35x + 140 = 55x + 60$ instead.

Power Presentations with PowerPoint®

Additional Examples

Example 4

Erica is trying to decide between two car rental plans. For how many miles will the plans cost the same?

	Plan A	Plan B
Initial Fee	\$100.00	\$85.00
Mileage Fee	\$0.35/mi	\$0.50

Both plans cost \$135 for 100 miles.

INTERVENTION

Questioning Strategies

EXAMPLE 4

- Which fee in each plan is related to the slope of the line? Which fee in each plan is related to the y-intercept of the line?

3 Close

Summarize

Review the point-slope and slope-intercept forms of the equations of a line and how to use each form to graph a line. Graph a line and show students how to write both the point-slope and slope-intercept forms of the equation. Compare and contrast pairs of lines that are parallel, perpendicular, or coinciding.

ONGOING ASSESSMENT and INTERVENTION

Diagnose ***Before*** **the Lesson**
3-6 Warm Up, TE p. 190

Monitor ***During*** **the Lesson**
Check It Out! Exercises, SE pp. 191–193
Questioning Strategies, TE pp. 191–193

Assess ***After*** **the Lesson**
3-6 Lesson Quiz, TE p. 197
Alternative Assessment, TE p. 197

Answers to *Think and Discuss*

1. If the slopes are the same and the y-intercepts are different, then the lines are ∥.
2. If the slopes of 2 ⊥ lines are multiplied, the product is −1. Each slope is the opp. reciprocal of the other slope.
3. See p. A3.

Assignment Guide

Assign *Guided Practice* exercises as necessary.

If you finished Examples **1–2**
- **Basic** 13–18, 24–30
- **Average** 13–18, 24–31
- **Advanced** 13–18, 24–31, 46

If you finished Examples **1–4**
- **Basic** 12–23, 24–44 even, 45–46, 53, 57–61, 67–73
- **Average** 14–22 even, 23–31, 32–52 even, 53, 54, 56–64, 67–73
- **Advanced** 12–23, 24–44 even, 47–52 even, 53–73

Homework Quick Check
Quickly check key concepts.
Exercises: 14, 16, 22, 23, 28, 36

Teaching Tip

Kinesthetic Let students use straws or uncooked spaghetti and graph paper to model a line that passes through the points in **Exercise 2.** Have them use the models to find the slope of the line and then write the equation of the line in slope-intercept form.

Answers

1, 5–7, 12, 16–18. See p. A14.

24–31. For graphs, see p. A14.

State Resources

3-6 Exercises

go.hrw.com
Homework Help Online
KEYWORD: MG7 3-6
Parent Resources Online
KEYWORD: MG7 Parent

GUIDED PRACTICE

1. **Vocabulary** How can you recognize the *slope-intercept form* of an equation?

SEE EXAMPLE 1 p. 191

Write the equation of each line in the given form.

2. the line through $(4, 7)$ and $(-2, 1)$ in slope-intercept form $y = x + 3$
3. the line through $(-4, 2)$ with slope $\frac{3}{4}$ in point-slope form. $y - 2 = \frac{3}{4}(x + 4)$
4. the line with x-intercept 4 and y-intercept -2 in slope-intercept form $y = \frac{1}{2}x - 2$

SEE EXAMPLE 2 p. 191

Graph each line.

5. $y = -3x + 4$ 6. $y + 4 = \frac{2}{3}(x - 6)$ 7. $x = 5$

SEE EXAMPLE 3 p. 192

Determine whether the lines are parallel, intersect, or coincide.

8. $y = -3x + 4$, $y = -3x + 1$ $\parallel$
9. $6x - 12y = -24$, $3y = 2x + 18$ **intersect**
10. $y = \frac{1}{3}x + \frac{2}{3}$, $3y = x + 2$ **coincide**
11. $4x + 2y = 10$, $y = -2x + 15$ $\parallel$

SEE EXAMPLE 4 p. 193

12. **Transportation** A speeding ticket in Conroe costs \$115 for the first 10 mi/h over the speed limit and \$1 for each additional mi/h. In Lakeville, a ticket costs \$50 for the first 10 mi/h over the speed limit and \$10 for each additional mi/h. If the speed limit is 55 mi/h, at what speed will the tickets cost approximately the same?

PRACTICE AND PROBLEM SOLVING

Homework Help

For Exercises	See Example
13–15	1
16–18	2
19–22	3
23	4

Extra Practice
Skills Practice p. S9
Application Practice p. S30

Write the equation of each line in the given form.

13. the line through $(0, -2)$ and $(4, 6)$ in point-slope form $y + 2 = 2x$
14. the line through $(5, 2)$ and $(-2, 2)$ in slope-intercept form $y = 2$
15. the line through $(6, -4)$ with slope $\frac{2}{3}$ in point-slope form $y + 4 = \frac{2}{3}(x - 6)$

Graph each line.

16. $y - 7 = x + 4$ 17. $y = \frac{1}{2}x - 2$ 18. $y = 2$

Determine whether the lines are parallel, intersect, or coincide.

19. $y = x - 7$, $y = -x + 3$ **intersect**
20. $y = \frac{5}{2}x + 4$, $2y = 5x - 4$ $\parallel$
21. $x + 2y = 6$, $y = -\frac{1}{2}x + 3$ **coincide**
22. $7x + 2y = 10$, $3y = 4x - 5$ **intersect**
23. **Business** Chris is comparing two sales positions that he has been offered. The first pays a weekly salary of \$375 plus a 20% commission. The second pays a weekly salary of \$325 plus a 25% commission. How much must he make in sales per week for the two jobs to pay the same? **\$1000 per week**

Write the equation of each line in slope-intercept form. Then graph the line.

24. through $(-6, 2)$ and $(3, 6)$ $y = \frac{4}{9}x + \frac{14}{3}$
25. horizontal line through $(2, 3)$ $y = 3$
26. through $(5, -2)$ with slope $\frac{2}{3}$ $y = \frac{2}{3}x - \frac{16}{3}$
27. x-intercept 4, y-intercept -3 $y = \frac{3}{4}x - 3$

Write the equation of each line in point-slope form. Then graph the line.

28. slope $-\frac{1}{2}$, y-intercept 2 $y - 2 = -\frac{1}{2}x$
29. slope $\frac{3}{4}$, x-intercept -2 $y = \frac{3}{4}(x + 2)$
30. through $(5, -1)$ with slope -1 $y + 1 = -(x - 5)$
31. through $(4, 6)$ and $(-2, -5)$

31. $y - 6 = \frac{11}{6}(x - 4)$

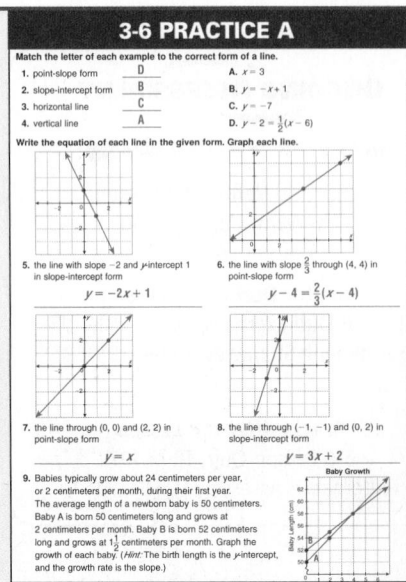

3-6 PRACTICE A

Match the letter of each example to the correct form of a line.

1. point-slope form D
2. slope-intercept form B
3. horizontal line C
4. vertical line A

A. $x = 3$
B. $y = -x + 1$
C. $y = -7$
D. $y - 2 = \frac{1}{2}(x - 6)$

Write the equation of each line in the given form. Graph each line.

5. the line with slope -2 and y-intercept 1 in slope-intercept form $y = -2x + 1$
6. the line with slope $\frac{2}{3}$ through $(4, 4)$ in point-slope form $y - 4 = \frac{2}{3}(x - 4)$
7. the line through $(0, 0)$ and $(2, 2)$ in point-slope form $y = x$
8. the line through $(-1, -1)$ and $(0, 2)$ in slope-intercept form $y = 3x + 2$
9. Babies typically grow about 24 centimeters per year, or 2 centimeters per month, during their first year. The average length of a newborn baby is 50 centimeters. Baby A is born 50 centimeters long and grows at 2 centimeters per month. Baby B is born 52 centimeters long and grows at $1\frac{1}{2}$ centimeters per month. Graph the growth of each baby. (*Hint:* The birth length is the y-intercept, and the growth rate is the slope.)

Baby Growth

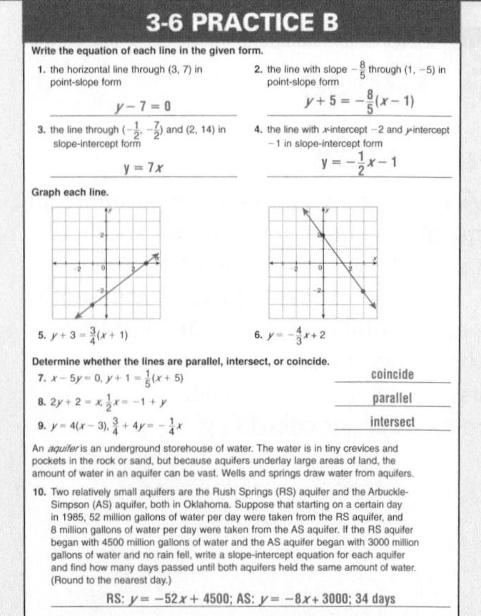

3-6 PRACTICE B

Write the equation of each line in the given form.

1. the horizontal line through $(3, 7)$ in point-slope form $y - 7 = 0$
2. the line with slope $-\frac{8}{5}$ through $(1, -5)$ in point-slope form $y + 5 = -\frac{8}{5}(x - 1)$
3. the line through $(-\frac{1}{2}, -\frac{7}{2})$ and $(2, 14)$ in slope-intercept form $y = 7x$
4. the line with x-intercept -2 and y-intercept -1 in slope-intercept form $y = -\frac{1}{2}x - 1$

Graph each line.

5. $y + 3 = \frac{3}{4}(x + 1)$
6. $y = -\frac{4}{3}x + 2$

Determine whether the lines are parallel, intersect, or coincide.

7. $x - 5y = 0$, $y + 1 = \frac{1}{5}(x + 5)$ coincide
8. $2y + 2 = x$, $\frac{1}{2}x = -1 + y$ parallel
9. $y = 4(x - 3)$, $\frac{3}{4} + 4y = -\frac{1}{4}x$ intersect

An *aquifer* is an underground storehouse of water. The water is in tiny crevices and pockets in the rock or sand, but because aquifers underlay large areas of land, the amount of water in an aquifer can be vast. Wells and springs draw water from aquifers.

10. Two relatively small aquifers are the Rush Springs (RS) aquifer and the Arbuckle-Simpson (AS) aquifer, both in Oklahoma. Suppose that starting on a certain day in 1985, 52 million gallons of water per day were taken from the RS aquifer, and 8 million gallons of water per day were taken from the AS aquifer. If the RS aquifer began with 4500 million gallons of water and the AS aquifer began with 3000 million gallons of water and no rain fell, write a slope-intercept equation for each aquifer and find how many days passed until both aquifers held the same amount of water. (Round to the nearest day.)

RS: $y = -52x + 4500$; AS: $y = -8x + 3000$; 34 days

32. **ERROR ANALYSIS** Write the equation of the line with slope −2 through the point $(-4, 3)$ in slope-intercept form. Which equation is incorrect? Explain.

A
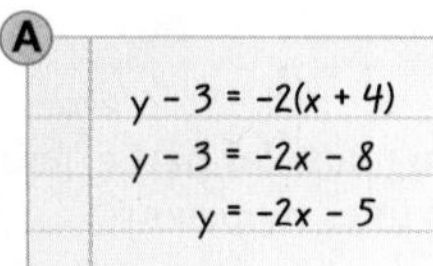

B
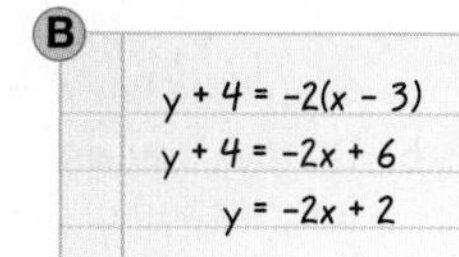

B is incorrect. In B, the x- and y-values of the pt. used to find the pt.-slope form are interchanged.

Determine whether the lines are perpendicular.

33. $y = 3x - 5,\ y = -3x + 1$ **no**

34. $y = -x + 1,\ y = x + 2$ **yes**

35. $y = -\frac{2}{3}x + 5,\ y = \frac{3}{2}x - 8$, **yes**

36. $y = -2x + 4,\ y = -\frac{1}{2}x - 2$ **no**

Multi-Step **Given the equation of the line and point P not on the line, find the equation of a line parallel to the given line and a line perpendicular to the given line through the given point.**

37. $y = 3x + 7,\ P(2, 3)$

38. $y = -2x - 5,\ P(-1, 4)$

39. $4x + 3y = 8,\ P(4, -2)$

40. $2x - 5y = 7,\ P(-2, 4)$

Multi-Step **Use slope to determine if each triangle is a right triangle. If so, which angle is the right angle?**

41. $A(-5, 3), B(0, -2), C(5, 3)$ **yes; $\angle B$**

42. $D(1, 0), E(2, 7), F(5, 1)$ **no**

43. $G(3, 4), H(-3, 4), J(1, -2)$ **no**

44. $K(-2, 4), L(2, 1), M(1, 8)$ **yes; $\angle K$**

LINK

Food

In 2004, the world's largest pizza was baked in Italy. The diameter of the pizza was 5.19 m (about 17 ft) and it weighed 124 kg (about 273 lb).

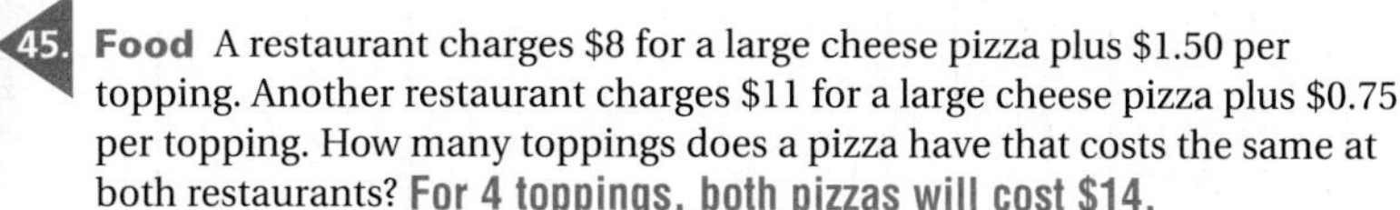

45. **Food** A restaurant charges \$8 for a large cheese pizza plus \$1.50 per topping. Another restaurant charges \$11 for a large cheese pizza plus \$0.75 per topping. How many toppings does a pizza have that costs the same at both restaurants? **For 4 toppings, both pizzas will cost \$14.**

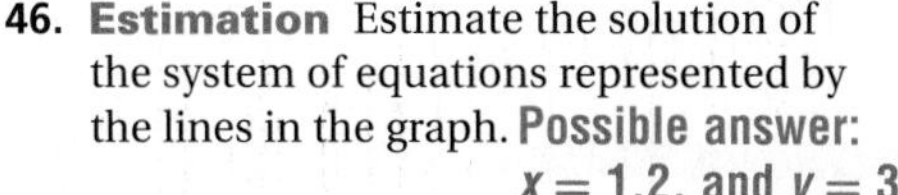

46. **Estimation** Estimate the solution of the system of equations represented by the lines in the graph. **Possible answer: $x = 1.2$, and $y = 3.7$**

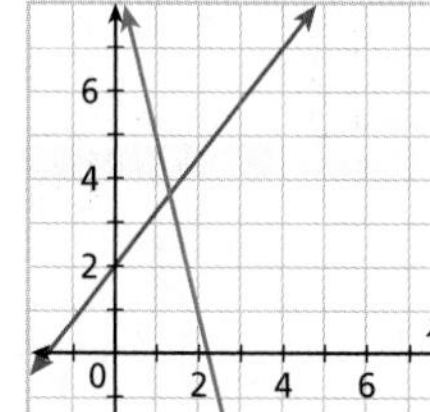

Write the equation of the perpendicular bisector of the segment with the given endpoints.

47. $(2, 5)$ and $(4, 9)$ $y = -\frac{1}{2}x + \frac{17}{2}$

48. $(1, 1)$ and $(3, 1)$ $x = 2$

49. $(1, 3)$ and $(-1, 4)$ $y = 2x + \frac{7}{2}$

50. $(-3, 2)$ and $(-3, -10)$ $y = -4$

51. Line ℓ has equation $y = -\frac{1}{2}x + 4$, and point P has coordinates $(3, 5)$. $y = 2x - 1$
    a. Find the equation of line m that passes through P and is perpendicular to ℓ.
    b. Find the coordinates of the intersection of ℓ and m. $(2, 3)$
    c. What is the distance from P to ℓ? $\sqrt{5}$ **units**

52. Line p has equation $y = x + 3$, and line q has equation $y = x - 1$. **Possible answers:**
    a. Find the equation of a line r that is perpendicular to p and q. $y = -x + 1$
    b. Find the coordinates of the intersection of p and r and the coordinates of the intersection of q and r. $(-1, 2)$; $(1, 0)$
    c. Find the distance between lines p and q. $2\sqrt{2}$ **units**

Teaching Tip

Inclusion For **Exercises 41–44,** suggest that students first graph each triangle. Ask them if any angle looks like a right angle. Then have them verify their answer by finding the rise and run of the segments that form the angle.

Answers

37. ∥ line: $y = 3x - 3$;
    ⊥ line: $y = -\frac{1}{3}x + \frac{11}{3}$

38. ∥ line: $y = -2x + 2$;
    ⊥ line: $y = \frac{1}{2}x + \frac{9}{2}$

39. ∥ line: $y = -\frac{4}{3}x + \frac{10}{3}$;
    ⊥ line: $y = \frac{3}{4}x - 5$

40. ∥ line: $y = \frac{2}{5}x + \frac{24}{5}$;
    ⊥ line: $y = -\frac{5}{2}x - 1$

3-6 PRACTICE C

1. Line p is the graph of $y = 2.6x + 3.4$. Line q is parallel to line p. $\overline{AB}$, $\overline{CD}$, and $\overline{EF}$ each have endpoints on p and q, one endpoint on each line. $\overleftrightarrow{AB}$ is the graph of $y = -\frac{5}{13}x + \frac{6}{7}$. $\overleftrightarrow{CD}$ is the graph of $y = \frac{4}{17}x - \frac{1}{3}$. $\overleftrightarrow{EF}$ is the graph of $y = -0.7x + 1.1$. Name the shortest segment. Explain your answer.
   $\overline{AB}$ is the shortest segment because the shortest distance between parallel lines is a segment perpendicular to both lines. Lines p and q both have a slope of $2.6 = \frac{13}{5}$. A segment perpendicular to these lines must have a slope of $-\frac{5}{13}$. $\overline{AB}$ is the only segment listed that has this slope.

2. A graphic designer draws line m determined by the equation $y = -2x + 4$. She needs to create parallel lines on either side of line m that are exactly 5 units away. Use the slope formula, the distance formula, and your knowledge of parallel and perpendicular lines to find equations for the parallel lines. (*Hint:* Although you can get the correct equations by starting from any point on m, using the y-intercept is easiest. Begin by using the slope formula to relate x and y on the line perpendicular to line m through the y-intercept. Then substitute into the distance formula.)
   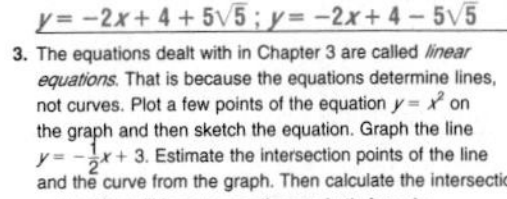
   $y = -2x + 4 + 5\sqrt{5}$; $y = -2x + 4 - 5\sqrt{5}$

3. The equations dealt with in Chapter 3 are called *linear equations*. That is because the equations determine lines, not curves. Plot a few points of the equation $y = x^2$ on the graph and then sketch the equation. Graph the line $y = -\frac{1}{2}x + 3$. Estimate the intersection points of the line and the curve from the graph. Then calculate the intersection points. You will have to use the quadratic formula.
   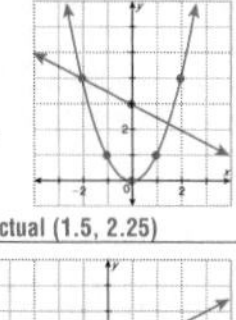
   Possible answers: $(-2, 4)$, $(1.5, 2.25)$; $(-2, 4)$, Actual $(1.5, 2.25)$

4. Plot a few points of the equation $y = \sqrt{16 - x^2}$ on the graph and then sketch the equation. Graph the line $y = \frac{1}{2}x + 3$. Estimate the intersection points of the line and the curve from the graph. Then calculate the intersection points.
   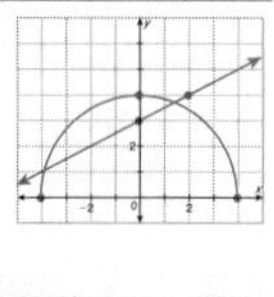
   Possible answers: $(-3.9, 1.1)$, $(1.5, 3.75)$;
   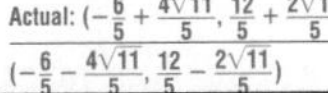
   Actual: $\left(-\frac{6}{5} + \frac{4\sqrt{11}}{5}, \frac{12}{5} + \frac{2\sqrt{11}}{5}\right)$, $\left(-\frac{6}{5} - \frac{4\sqrt{11}}{5}, \frac{12}{5} - \frac{2\sqrt{11}}{5}\right)$

Exercise 53 involves graphing two lines and interpreting their intersection. This exercise prepares students for the Multi-Step Test Prep on page 200.

For Exercise 58, encourage students to write the equations in slope-intercept form and eliminate any graphs that have the wrong *y*-intercepts. This will immediately eliminate choices **B** and **C.**

Data Collection For help with Exercise 55, see *Technology Lab Activities*.

Answers

53a–b.

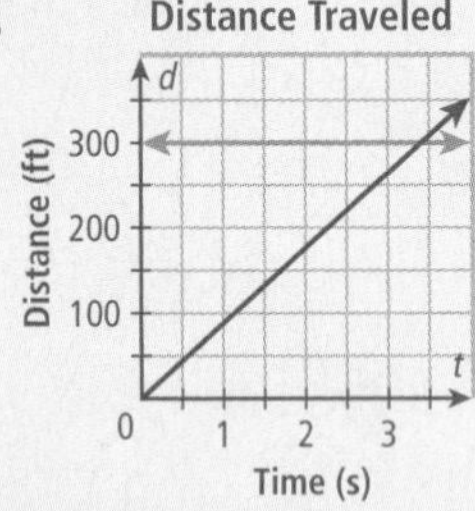

b. the time when the car has traveled 300 ft

c. Possible answer: 3.5 s

54. It is given that the eqn. of the line through (x_1, y_1) with slope m is $y - y_1 = m(x - x_1)$. Let $(0, b)$ be a pt. on the line. Then 0 is a possible value for x_1, and b is a possible value for y_1. Substitute these values into the eqn. $y - y_1 = m(x - x_1)$ to get $y - b = m(x - 0)$. Simplify to get $y - b = mx$. By the Add. Prop. of =, $y = mx + b$. Thus the eqn. of the line through $(0, b)$ with slope m is $y = mx + b$.

56. The slope of the line is $m = \frac{2-6}{2+4} = -\frac{2}{3}$. The pt-slope form of the line is $y - 6 = -\frac{2}{3}(x + 4)$. To see if the line crosses the *x*-axis at $(5, 0)$, substitute 5 for *x* and 0 for *y*:

$0 - 6 = -\frac{2}{3}(5 + 4)$

$-6 = -\frac{2}{3}(9)$

$-6 = -6$

These values make the equation true, so $(5, 0)$ is on the line.

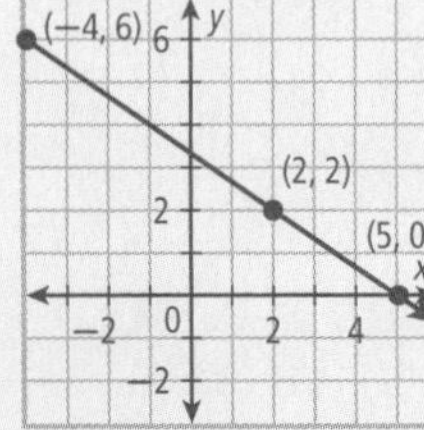

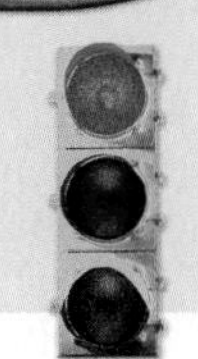

53. This problem will prepare you for the Multi-Step Test Prep on page 200.
For a car moving at 60 mi/h, the equation $d = 88t$ gives the distance in feet d that the car travels in t seconds.
    a. Graph the line $d = 88t$.
    b. On the same graph you made for part **a**, graph the line $d = 300$. What does the intersection of the two lines represent?
    c. Use the graph to estimate the number of seconds it takes the car to travel 300 ft.

54. Prove the slope-intercept form of a line, given the point-slope form.
Given: The equation of the line through (x_1, y_1) with slope m is $y - y_1 = m(x - x_1)$.
Prove: The equation of the line through $(0, b)$ with slope m is $y = mx + b$.
Plan: Substitute $(0, b)$ for (x_1, y_1) in the equation $y - y_1 = m(x - x_1)$ and simplify.

55. **Data Collection** Use a graphing calculator and a motion detector to do the following: Walk in front of the motion detector at a constant speed, and write the equation of the resulting graph. **Check students' work.**

56. **Critical Thinking** A line contains the points $(-4, 6)$ and $(2, 2)$. Write a convincing argument that the line crosses the *x*-axis at $(5, 0)$. Include a graph to verify your argument.

57. **Write About It** Determine whether the lines are parallel. Use slope to explain your answer.
The top line passes through $(-4, 0)$ and $(0, 3)$, so its slope is $m = \frac{3-0}{0+4} = \frac{3}{4}$. The bottom line passes through $(0, -2)$ and $(3, 0)$, so its slope is $m = \frac{-0-(-2)}{3-0} = \frac{2}{3}$. The lines do not have the same slope, so they are not ∥.

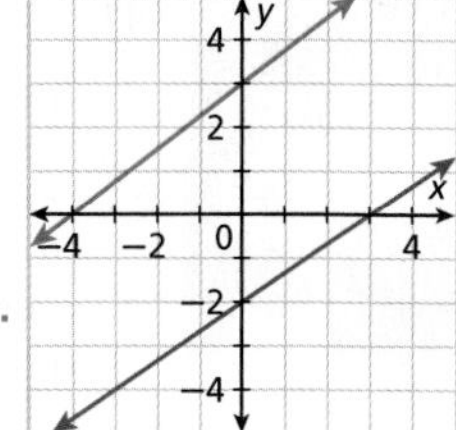

58. Which graph best represents a solution to this system of equations?

$$\begin{cases} -3x + y = 7 \\ 2x + y = -3 \end{cases}$$

Ⓐ

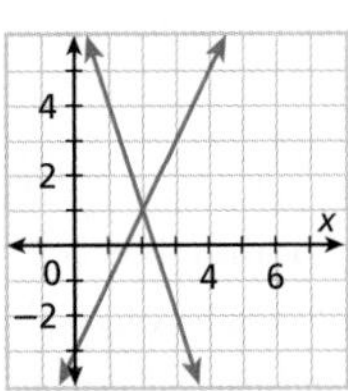

Ⓑ

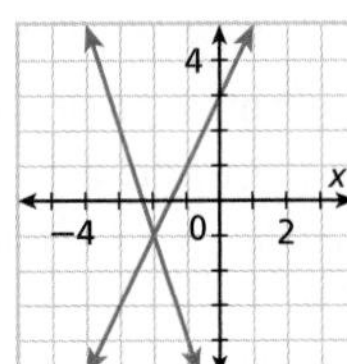

Ⓒ

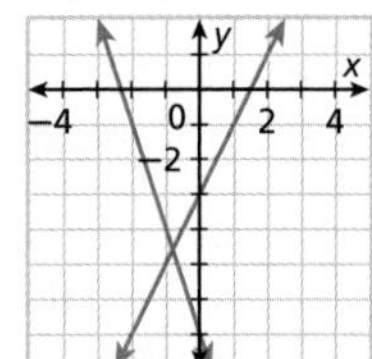

Ⓓ (circled)

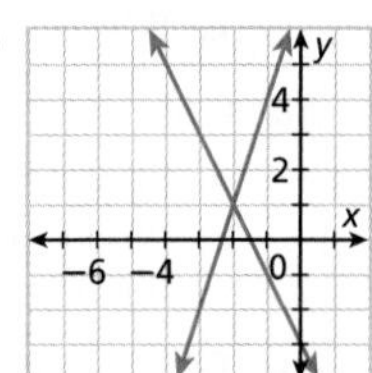

3-6 READING STRATEGIES

Equation of a line → Point-slope form: $y - y_1 = m(x - x_1)$; m is the slope. (x_1, y_1) is a given point.
Equation of a line → Slope-intercept form: $y = mx + b$; m is the slope. b is the y-intercept.

1. Why do you think $y - y_1 = m(x - x_1)$ is called point-slope form?
Looking at the equation, you can see the slope and a point on the line.

2. Why do you think $y = mx + b$ is called the slope-intercept form of the line?
Looking at the equation, m is the slope and b is the y-intercept.

3. How is the point-slope form of an equation like the slope-intercept form of the equation?
They are both equations of the line, and they both plug in the slope and a point on the line.

4. If you know two points on a line, which form of the equation is easier to write?
point-slope form

Write the equations of the following lines.

5. Use the point-slope form.
$y + 2 = \frac{4}{5}(x + 2)$ or $y - 2 = \frac{4}{5}(x - 3)$

6. Use the slope-intercept form.
$y = 3x - 2$

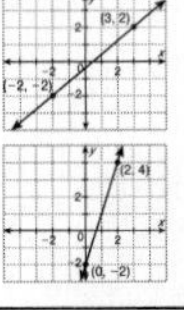

3-6 RETEACH

Slope-Intercept Form	Point-Slope Form
$y = mx + b$ (slope: m; y-intercept: b) $y = 4x + 7$	$y - y_1 = m(x - x_1)$ (slope: m) $y - 2 = \frac{1}{3}(x + 5)$ point on the line: $(x_1, y_1) = (-5, 2)$

Write the equation of the line through (0, 1) and (2, 7) in slope-intercept form.

Step 1: Find the slope.

$m = \frac{y_2 - y_1}{x_2 - x_1}$ Formula for slope

$= \frac{7-1}{2-0} = \frac{6}{2} = 3$

Step 2: Find the y-intercept.

$y = mx + b$ Slope-intercept form

$1 = 3(0) + b$ Substitute 3 for m, 0 for x, and 1 for y.

$1 = b$ Simplify.

Step 3: Write the equation.

$y = mx + b$ Slope-intercept form

$y = 3x + 1$ Substitute 3 for m and 1 for b.

Write the equation of each line in the given form.

1. the line through (4, 2) and (8, 5) in slope-intercept form
$y = \frac{3}{4}x - 1$

2. the line through (4, 6) with slope $\frac{1}{2}$ in point-slope form
$y - 6 = \frac{1}{2}(x - 4)$

3. the line through (−5, 1) with slope 2 in point-slope form
$y - 1 = 2(x + 5)$

4. the line with x-intercept −5 and y-intercept 3 in slope-intercept form
$y = \frac{3}{5}x + 3$

5. the line through (8, 0) with slope $-\frac{3}{4}$ in slope-intercept form
$y = -\frac{3}{4}x + 6$

6. the line through (1, 7) and (−6, 7) in point-slope form
$y - 7 = 0$

59. Which line is parallel to the line with the equation $y = -2x + 5$?

Ⓕ $\overleftrightarrow{AB}$ through $A(2, 3)$ and $B(1, 1)$ Ⓗ $4x + 2y = 10$

Ⓖ $y = -\frac{1}{2}x - 3$ Ⓙ (circled) $x + \frac{1}{2}y = 1$

60. Which equation best describes the graph shown?

Ⓐ $y = -\frac{3}{2}x + 3$ Ⓒ $y = -\frac{2}{3}x + 2$

Ⓑ $y = 3x - \frac{2}{3}$ Ⓓ (circled) $y = -\frac{2}{3}x + 3$

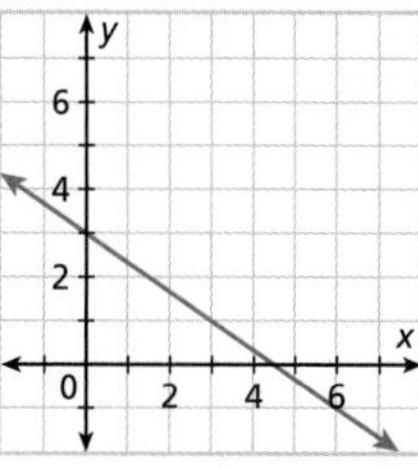

61. Which line includes the points $(-4, 2)$ and $(6, -3)$?

Ⓕ $y = 2x - 4$ Ⓗ $y = -\frac{1}{2}x - 4$

Ⓖ $y = 2x$ Ⓙ (circled) $y = -\frac{1}{2}x$

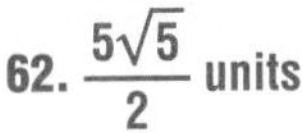

CHALLENGE AND EXTEND

62. $\frac{5\sqrt{5}}{2}$ units

62. A right triangle is formed by the x-axis, the y-axis, and the line $y = -2x + 5$. Find the length of the hypotenuse.

63. If the length of the hypotenuse of a right triangle is 17 units and the legs lie along the x-axis and y-axis, find a possible equation that describes the line that contains the hypotenuse. Possible answer: $y = -\frac{8}{15}x + 8$

64. Possible answer: $x = 0$, $y = 0$, $y = -\frac{5}{12}x + 5$

64. Find the equations of three lines that form a triangle with a hypotenuse of 13 units.

65. **Multi-Step** Are the points $(-2, -4)$, $(5, -2)$ and $(2, -3)$ collinear? Explain the method you used to determine your answer. no

66. For the line $y = x + 1$ and the point $P(3, 2)$, let d represent the distance from P to a point (x, y) on the line.

a. Write an expression for d^2 in terms of x and y. Substitute the expression $x + 1$ for y and simplify. $d^2 = 2x^2 - 8x + 10$

b. How could you use this expression to find the shortest distance from P to the line? Compare your result to the distance along a perpendicular line.

SPIRAL REVIEW

67. The cost of renting DVDs from an online company is \$5.00 per month plus \$2.50 for each DVD rented. Write an equation for the total cost c of renting d DVDs from the company in one month. Graph the equation. How many DVDs did Sean rent from the company if his total bill for one month was \$20.00? *(Previous course)*

Use the coordinate plane for Exercises 68–70. Find the coordinates of the midpoint of each segment. *(Lesson 1-6)*

70. $\left(-\frac{3}{2}, -1\right)$

68. $\overline{AB}$ $\left(-\frac{1}{2}, 2\right)$ 69. $\overline{BC}$ $(1, 0)$ 70. $\overline{AC}$

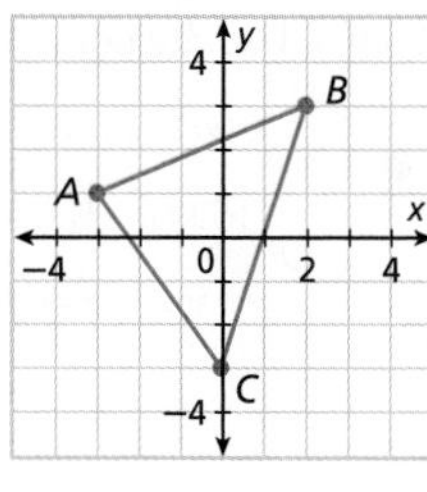

Use the slope formula to find the slope of each segment. *(Lesson 3-5)*

73. $m = -\frac{4}{3}$

71. $\overline{AB}$ $m = \frac{2}{5}$ 72. $\overline{BC}$ $m = 3$ 73. $\overline{AC}$

COMMON ERROR ALERT

For **Exercise 57,** students may base their answers on the appearance of the lines. Remind them to calculate the slopes.

Answers

65. Possible answer: I found the equation of the line through the first 2 pts., which is $y = \frac{2}{7}x - \frac{24}{7}$. Then I substituted the x- and y-values for the third pt. to see if it lies on the line. The values did not make the equation true, so the pts. are not collinear.

Journal

Have students explain how to use two points or one point and the slope to write the equation of a line. Have them include examples.

ALTERNATIVE ASSESSMENT

Ask students to draw a pair of parallel lines, a pair of intersecting lines, and a pair of coinciding lines, and then write a system of equations for each pair.

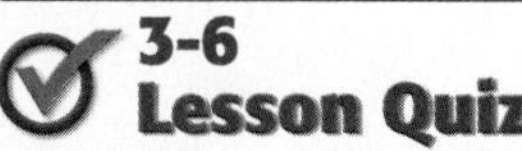

3-6 Lesson Quiz

Write the equation of each line in the given form. Then graph each line.

1. the line through $(-1, 3)$ and $(3, -5)$ in slope-intercept form $y = -2x + 1$

2. the line through $(5, -1)$ with slope $\frac{2}{5}$ in point-slope form $y + 1 = \frac{2}{5}(x - 5)$

1–2.

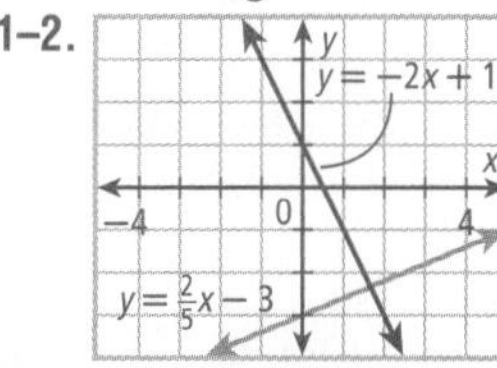

Determine whether the lines are parallel, intersect, or coincide.

3. $y - 3 = -\frac{1}{2}x$, $y - 5 = 2(x + 3)$ intersect

4. $2y = 4x + 12$, $4x - 2y = 8$ parallel

Also available on transparency

3-6 PROBLEM SOLVING

Use the following information for Exercises 1 and 2. Josh can order 1 color ink cartridge and 2 black ink cartridges for his printer for \$78. He can also order 1 color ink cartridge and 1 black ink cartridge for \$53.

1. Let x equal the cost of a color ink cartridge and y equal the cost of a black ink cartridge. Write a system of equations to represent this situation.

$x + 2y = 78$, $x + y = 53$

2. What is the cost of each cartridge?

color: \$28, black: \$25

3. Ms. Williams is planning to buy T-shirts for the cheerleading camp that she is running. After buying how many T-shirts would both companies' total costs be the same? Use a graph to find your solution.

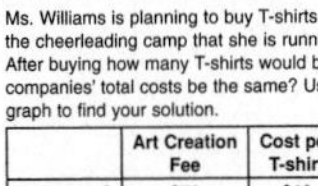

	Art Creation Fee	Cost per T-shirt
Company A	\$70	\$10
Company B	\$50	\$12

Both companies total costs would be the same for 10 T-shirts.

T-shirt Costs
Total Cost (\$): 250, 200, 150, 100, 50
Number of T-shirts: 0, 4, 8, 12, 16, 20
(10, 170)

Choose the best answer.

4. Two floats begin a parade at different times, but travel at the same speeds. Which is a true statement about the lines that represent the distance traveled by each float at a given time?
A The lines intersect.
Ⓑ The lines are parallel.
C The lines are the same.
D The lines have a negative slope.

5. A piano teacher charges \$20 for each half hour lesson, plus an initial fee of \$50. Another teacher charges \$40 per hour, plus a fee of \$50. Which is a true statement about the lines that represent the total cost by each piano teacher?
F The lines intersect.
G The lines are parallel.
Ⓗ The lines are the same.
J The lines have a negative slope.

6. Serina is trying to decide between two similar packages for starting her own Web site. Which is a true statement?
A Both packages cost \$235.50 for 5 months.
Ⓑ Both packages cost \$295 for 10 months.
C Both packages cost \$355 for 15 months.
D The packages will never have the same cost.

	Design and Setup	Monthly Fee to Host
Package A	\$150.00	\$14.50
Package B	\$175.00	\$12.00

Answers

66b. See p. A15.

67. $c = 2.5d + 5$

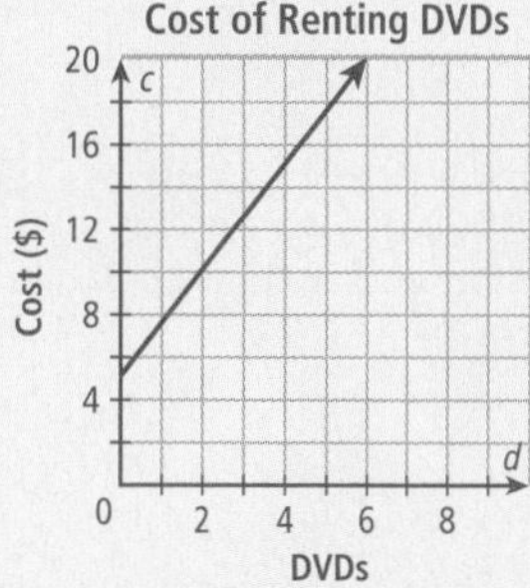

If his bill was \$20.00, Sean rented 6 DVDs.

Organizer

Pacing:
Traditional $\frac{1}{2}$ day
Block $\frac{1}{4}$ day

Objective: Apply linear equation skills learned in Lesson 3-6 to graphing and writing equations for lines associated with data sets.

Teach

Remember

Students review scatter plots and lines of best fit.

Teaching Tip

Technology A graphing calculator uses *linear regression* to find the equation of the line of best fit, which will be studied in statistics.

Close

Assess

Have students use data such as shoe size versus length of bare foot or arm span versus height to create a scatter plot, and then estimate the equation of the line of best fit.

State Resources

Scatter Plots and Lines of Best Fit

Recall that a line has an infinite number of points on it. You can compute the slope of a line if you can identify two distinct points on the line.

Example 1

The table shows several possible measures of an angle and its supplement. Graph the points in the table. Then draw the line that best represents the data and write the equation of the line.

x	$y = 180 - x$
30	150
60	120
90	90
120	60
150	30

Step 1
Use the table to write ordered pairs $(x, 180 - x)$ and then plot the points.

(30, 150), (60, 120), (90, 90), (120, 60), (150, 30)

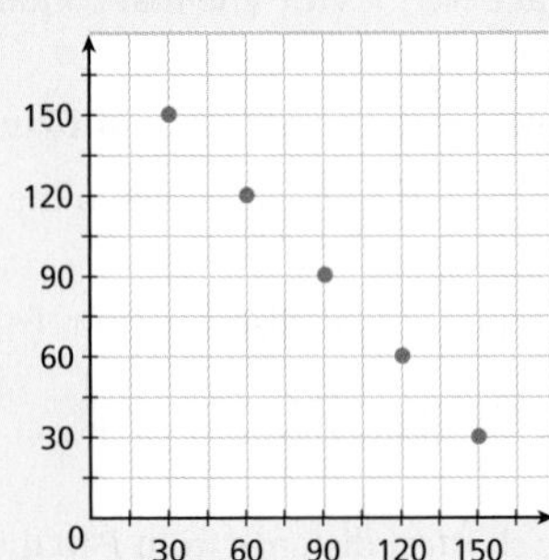

Step 2
Draw a line that passes through all the points.

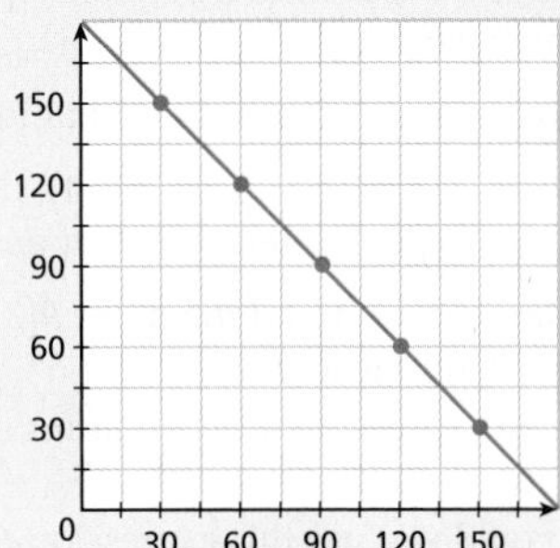

Step 3 Choose two points from the line, such as (30, 150) and (120, 60). Use them to find the slope.

$$m = \frac{y_2 - y_1}{x_2 - x_1}$$ *Slope formula*

$$= \frac{60 - 150}{120 - 30}$$ *Substitute (30, 150) for (x_1, y_1) and (120, 60) for (x_2, y_2).*

$$= \frac{-90}{90} = -1$$ *Simplify.*

Step 4 Use the point-slope form to find the equation of the line and then simplify.

$$y - y_1 = m(x - x_1)$$ *Point-slope form*

$$y - 150 = -1(x - 30)$$ *Substitute (30, 150) for (x_1, y_1) and -1 for m.*

$$y = -x + 180$$ *Simplify.*

If you can draw a line through all the points in a set of data, the relationship is linear. If the points are close to a line, you can approximate the relationship with a *line of best fit*.

Example 2

A physical therapist evaluates a client's progress by measuring the angle of motion of an injured joint. The table shows the angle of motion of a client's wrist over six weeks. Estimate the equation of the line of best fit.

Week	Angle Measure
1	30
2	36
3	46
4	48
5	54
6	62

Step 1
Use the table to write ordered pairs and then plot the points.

(1, 30), (2, 36), (3, 46), (4, 48), (5, 54), (6, 62)

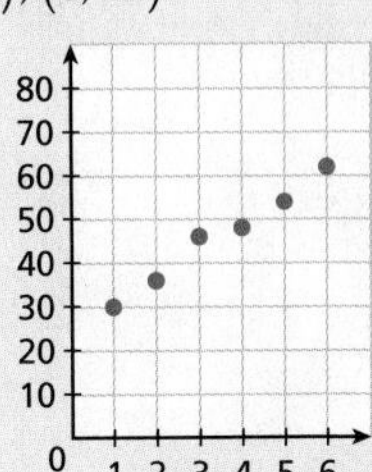

Step 2
Use a ruler to estimate a line of best fit. Try to get the edge of the ruler closest to all the points on the line.

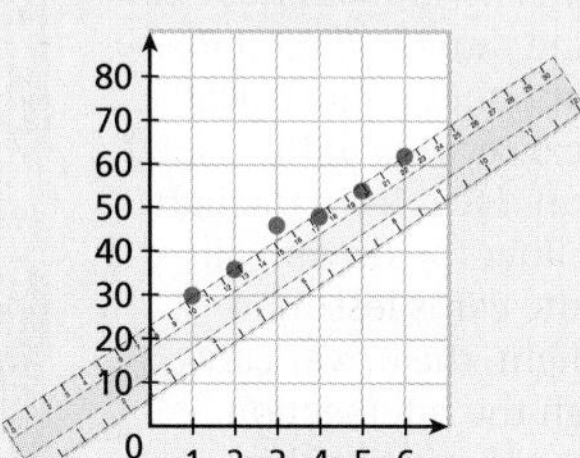

Step 3 A line passing through (2, 36) and (6, 62) seems to be closest to all the points. Draw this line. Use the points (2, 36) and (6, 62) to find the slope of the line.

$m = \frac{y_2 - y_1}{x_2 - x_1} = \frac{62 - 36}{6 - 2} = 6.5$ *Substitute (2, 36) for (x_1, y_1) and (6, 62) for (x_2, y_2).*

Step 4 Use the point-slope form to find the equation of the line and then simplify.

$y - y_1 = m(x - x_1)$ *Point-slope form*

$y - 36 = 6.5(x - 2)$ *Substitute (2, 36) for (x_1, y_1) and 6.5 for m.*

$y = 6.5x + 23$ *Simplify.*

Try This

Estimate the equation of the line of best fit for each relationship. **1–2. Possible answers:**

1. $y = -\frac{4}{3}x + \frac{34}{3}$

2. the relationship between an angle and its complement **$y = 90 - x$**

3. Data Collection Use a graphing calculator and a motion detector to do the following: Set the equipment so that the graph shows distance on the *y*-axis and time on the *x*-axis. Walk in front of the motion dector while varying your speed slightly and use the resulting graph. **Check students' work.**

Data Collection For help with Try This 3, see *Technology Lab Activities.*

Organizer

Objective: Assess students' ability to apply concepts and skills in Lessons 3-5 through 3-6 in a real-world format.

 **Online Edition**

Resources

 ***Geometry Assessments***
www.mathtekstoolkit.org

Problem	Text Reference
1	Lesson 3-5
2	Lesson 3-6

Answers

2. $d = \frac{22}{15}(45)t$
$d = 66t$

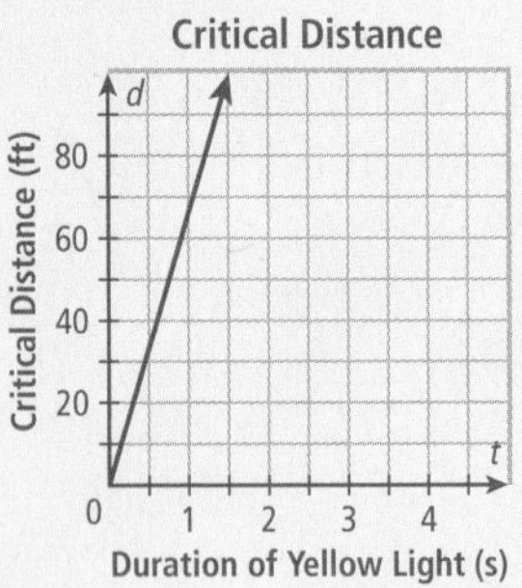

State Resources

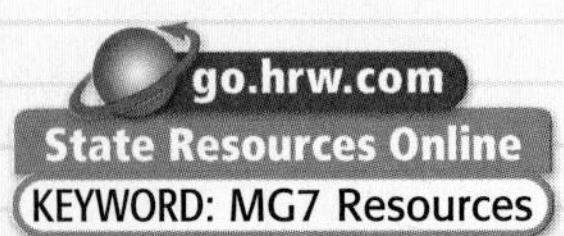

Coordinate Geometry

Red Light, Green Light When a driver approaches an intersection and sees a yellow traffic light, she must decide if she can make it through the intersection before the light turns red. Traffic engineers use graphs and equations to study this situation.

1. Traffic engineers can set the duration of the yellow lights on Lincoln Road for any length of time t up to 10 seconds. For each value of t, there is a critical distance d. If a car moving at the speed limit is more than d feet from the light when it turns yellow, the driver will have to stop. If the car is less than d feet from the light, the driver can continue through the intersection. The graph shows the relationship between t and d. Find the speed limit on Lincoln Road in miles per hour. (*Hint:* 22 ft/s = 15 mi/h) **30 mi/h**

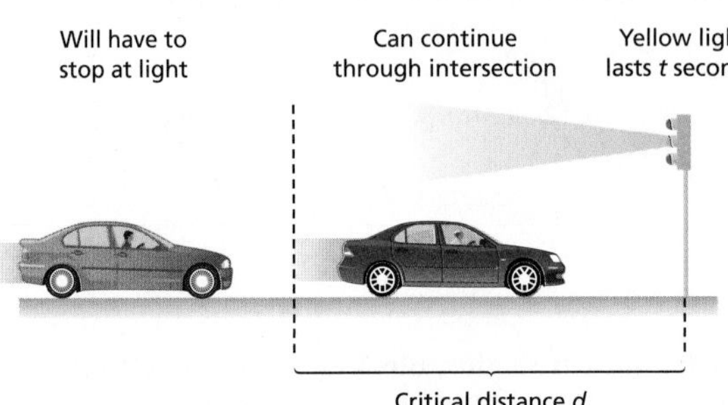

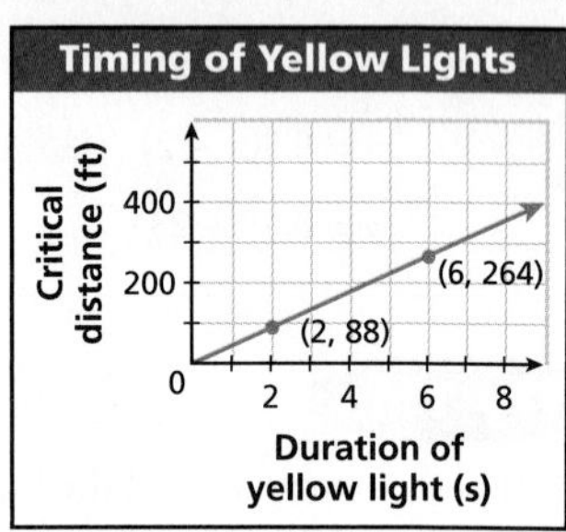

2. Traffic engineers use the equation $d = \frac{22}{15}st$ to determine the critical distance for various durations of a yellow light. In the equation, s is the speed limit. The speed limit on Porter Street is 45 mi/h. Write the equation of the critical distance for a yellow light on Porter Street and then graph the line. Does this line intersect the line for Lincoln Road? If so, where? Is the line for Porter Street steeper or flatter than the line for Lincoln Road? Explain how you know.

Yes, the lines intersect at (0, 0). The line for Porter Street is steeper because the slope of the line is greater.

INTERVENTION

Scaffolding Questions

1. In the graph, what does the slope of the line represent? the rate (i.e., the speed limit) What information do you need in order to calculate the slope of the line? coordinates of 2 points on the line If you know a speed in feet per second, how can you convert it to miles per hour? Multiply by $\frac{15}{22}$.

2. How can you simplify the equation when $s = 45$? $d = 66t$ What is the slope of the line? 66 How does this slope compare to the slope of the line in **Problem 1**? The slope is greater than in **Problem 1**.

Extension

Suppose the duration of a yellow light is 6 sec. How much greater is the critical distance for a car moving at 45 mi/h compared to that of a car moving at 30 mi/h? 132 ft

READY TO GO ON?

CHAPTER 3
SECTION 3B

Quiz for Lesson 3-5 Through 3-6

3-5 Slopes of Lines

Use the slope formula to determine the slope of each line.

1. $\overleftrightarrow{AC}$ $m = -1$
2. $\overleftrightarrow{CD}$ $m = -\frac{1}{9}$
3. $\overleftrightarrow{AB}$ $m = -\frac{2}{3}$
4. $\overleftrightarrow{BD}$ $m = \frac{3}{7}$

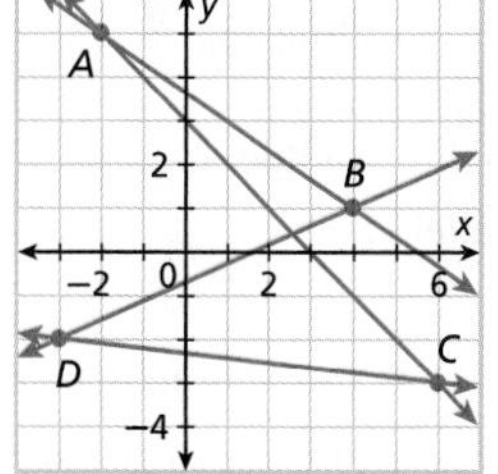

Find the slope of the line through the given points.

5. $M(2, 3)$ and $N(0, 7)$ $m = -2$
6. $F(-1, 4)$ and $G(5, -1)$ $m = -\frac{5}{6}$
7. $P(4, 0)$ and $Q(1, -3)$ $m = 1$
8. $K(4, 2)$ and $L(-3, 2)$ $m = 0$
9. Sonia is walking 2.5 miles home from school. She leaves at 4:00 P.M., and gets home at 4:45 P.M. Graph the line that represents Sonia's distance from school at a given time. Find and interpret the slope of the line.

9. Possible answer: $m = \frac{10}{3} \approx 3.3$; Sonia's average speed was about 3.3 mi/h.

Graph each pair of lines and use their slopes to determine if they are parallel, perpendicular, or neither.

10. $\overleftrightarrow{EF}$ and $\overleftrightarrow{GH}$ for $E(-2, 3)$, $F(6, 1)$, $G(6, 4)$, and $H(2, 5)$ $\parallel$
11. $\overleftrightarrow{JK}$ and $\overleftrightarrow{LM}$ for $J(4, 3)$, $K(5, -1)$, $L(-2, 4)$, and $M(3, -5)$ neither
12. $\overleftrightarrow{NP}$ and $\overleftrightarrow{QR}$ for $N(5, -3)$, $P(0, 4)$, $Q(-3, -2)$, and $R(4, 3)$ $\perp$
13. $\overleftrightarrow{ST}$ and $\overleftrightarrow{VW}$ for $S(0, 3)$, $T(0, 7)$, $V(2, 3)$, and $W(5, 3)$ $\perp$

3-6 Lines in the Coordinate Plane

Write the equation of each line in the given form.

14. the line through $(3, 8)$ and $(-3, 4)$ in slope-intercept form $y = \frac{2}{3}x + 6$
15. the line through $(-5, 4)$ with slope $\frac{2}{3}$ in point-slope form $y - 4 = \frac{2}{3}(x + 5)$
16. the line with y-intercept 2 through the point $(4, 1)$ in slope-intercept form $y = -\frac{1}{4}x + 2$

Graph each line.

17. $y = -2x + 5$
18. $y + 3 = \frac{1}{4}(x - 4)$
19. $x = 3$

Write the equation of each line.

20. 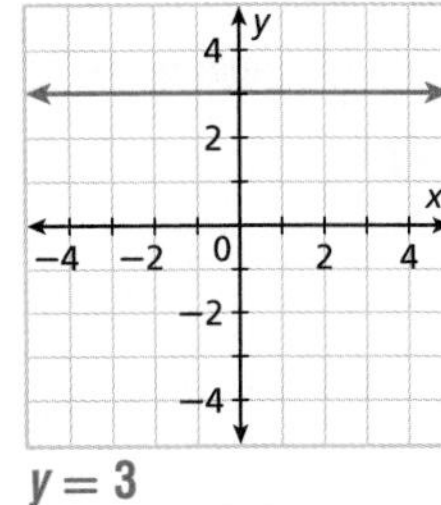
$y = 3$

21. 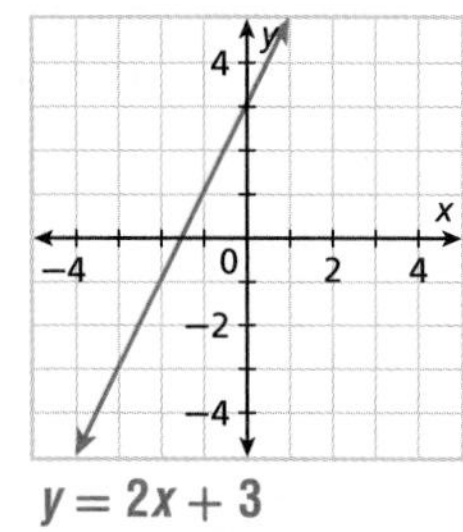
$y = 2x + 3$

22. 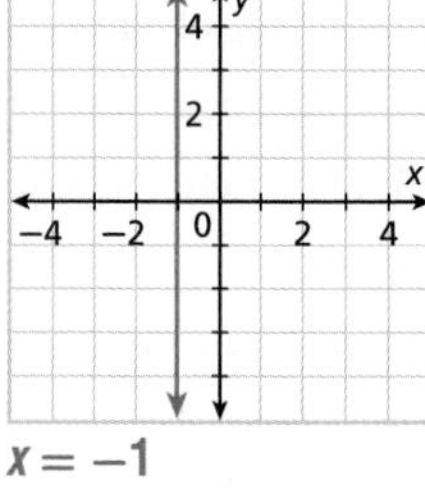
$x = -1$

Determine whether the lines are parallel, intersect, or coincide.

23. $y = -2x + 5$, $y = -2x - 5$ $\parallel$
24. $3x + 2y = 8$, $y = -\frac{3}{2}x + 4$ coincide
25. $y = 4x - 5$, $3x + 4y = 7$ intersect

READY TO GO ON? SECTION 3B

Organizer

Objective: Assess students' mastery of concepts and skills in Lessons 3-5 through 3-6.

Resources

Assessment Resources
Section 3B Quiz

Teacher One Stop™
Test & Practice Generator

INTERVENTION

Resources

Ready to Go On? Intervention and Enrichment Worksheets

***Ready to Go On?* CD-ROM**

***Ready to Go On?* Online**

my.hrw.com

Answers

10–13, 17–19. See p. A15.

READY TO GO ON? Diagnose and Prescribe

NO INTERVENE

Ready to Go On? Intervention	Ready to Go On? Intervention, Section 3B: Worksheets	CD-ROM	Online
Lesson 3-5	3-5 Intervention	Activity 3-5	Diagnose and Prescribe Online
Lesson 3-6	3-6 Intervention	Activity 3-6	

YES ENRICH

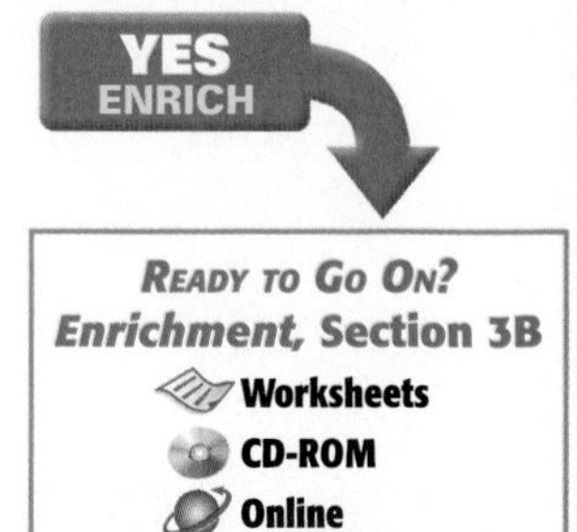
Ready to Go On? Enrichment, Section 3B
Worksheets
CD-ROM
Online

CHAPTER 3 Study Guide: Review

Organizer

Objective: Help students organize and review key concepts and skills presented in Chapter 3.

 Online Edition

Resources

Teacher One Stop™
Test & Practice Generator

 ***Multilingual Glossary*** **Online**
go.hrw.com
KEYWORD: MG7 Glossary

 ***Lesson Tutorial Videos*** **CD-ROM**

Answers

1. alternate interior angles
2. skew lines
3. transversal
4. point-slope form
5. rise; run
6. possible answer: $\overline{DE}$ and $\overline{BC}$ are skew.
7. $\overline{AB} \parallel \overline{DE}$
8. $\overline{AD} \perp \overline{DE}$
9. plane $ABC \parallel$ plane DEF

CHAPTER 3

Study Guide: Review

For a complete list of the postulates and theorems in this chapter, see p. PS12.

Vocabulary

Complete the sentences below with vocabulary words from the list above.

1. Angles on opposite sides of a transversal and between the lines it intersects are __?__ .
2. Lines that are in different planes are __?__ .
3. A(n) __?__ is a line that intersects two coplanar lines at two points.
4. The __?__ is used to write the equation of a line with a given slope that passes through a given point.
5. The slope of a line is the ratio of the __?__ to the __?__ .

3-1 Lines and Angles *(pp. 146–151)*

EXAMPLES

Identify each of the following.

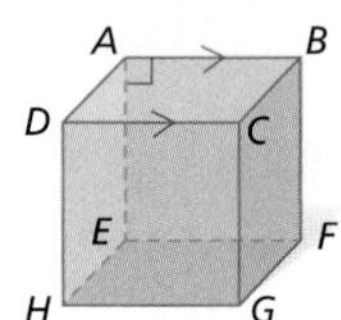

- a pair of parallel segments
  $\overline{AB} \parallel \overline{CD}$
- a pair of parallel planes
  plane $ABC \parallel$ plane EFG
- a pair of perpendicular segments
  $\overline{AB} \perp \overline{AE}$
- a pair of skew segments
  $\overline{AB}$ and $\overline{FG}$ are skew.

EXERCISES

Identify each of the following.

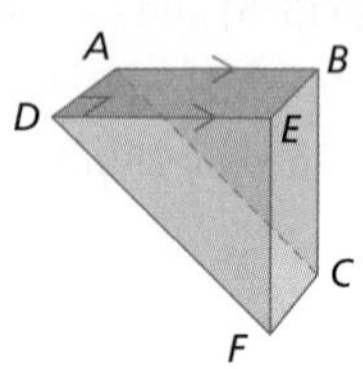

6. a pair of skew segments
7. a pair of parallel segments
8. a pair of perpendicular segments
9. a pair of parallel planes

Identify the transversal and classify each angle pair.

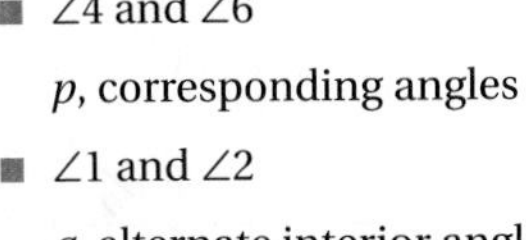
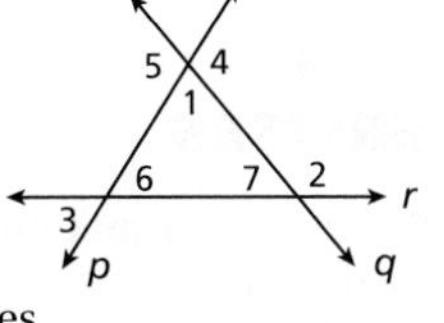

- $\angle 4$ and $\angle 6$

  p, corresponding angles
- $\angle 1$ and $\angle 2$

  q, alternate interior angles
- $\angle 3$ and $\angle 4$

  p, alternate exterior angles
- $\angle 6$ and $\angle 7$

  r, same-side interior angles

Identify the transversal and classify each angle pair.

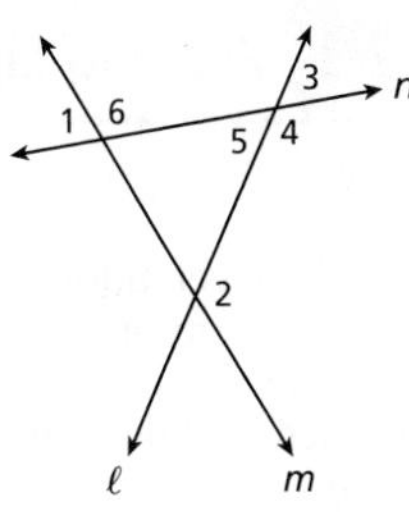

10. $\angle 5$ and $\angle 2$

11. $\angle 6$ and $\angle 3$

12. $\angle 2$ and $\angle 4$

13. $\angle 1$ and $\angle 2$

3-2 Angles Formed by Parallel Lines and Transversals *(pp. 155–161)*

EXAMPLES

Find each angle measure.

- $m\angle TUV$

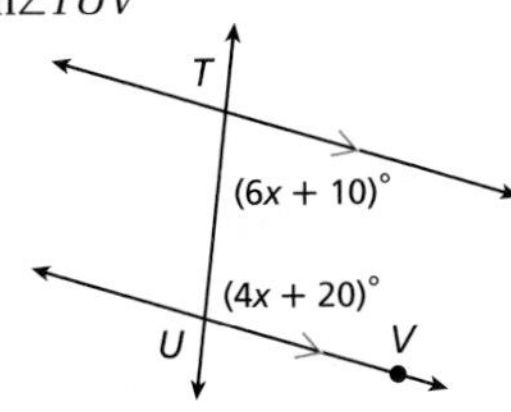

By the Same-Side Interior Angles Theorem, $(6x + 10) + (4x + 20) = 180$.

$x = 15$ *Solve for x.*

Substitute the value for *x* into the expression for $m\angle TUV$.
$m\angle TUV = 4(15) + 20 = 80°$

- $m\angle ABC$

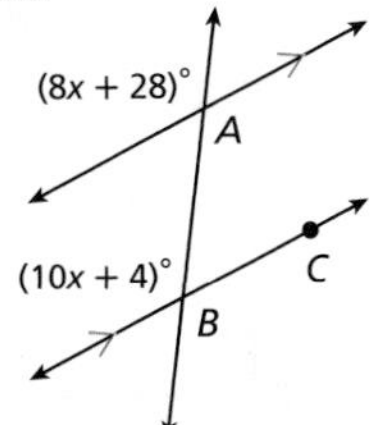

By the Corresponding Angles Postulate, $8x + 28 = 10x + 4$.

$x = 12$ *Solve for x.*

Substitute the value for *x* into the expression for one of the obtuse angles.
$10(12) + 4 = 124°$

$\angle ABC$ is supplementary to the 124° angle, so $m\angle ABC = 180 - 124 = 56°$.

EXERCISES

Find each angle measure.

14. $m\angle WYZ$

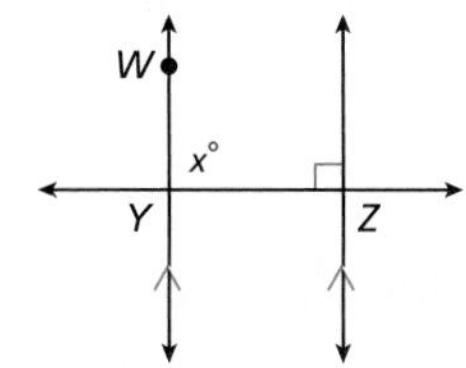

15. $m\angle KLM$

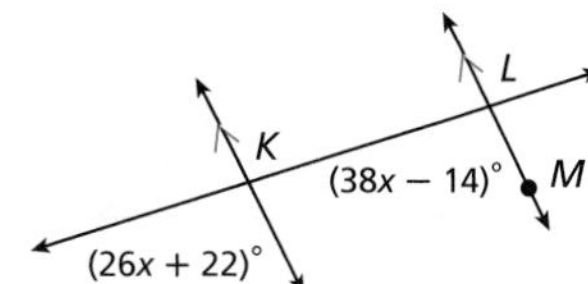

16. $m\angle DEF$

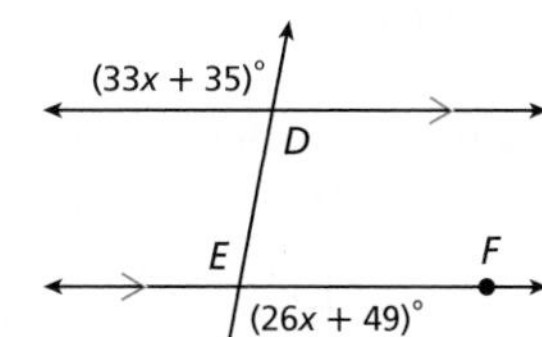

17. $m\angle QRS$

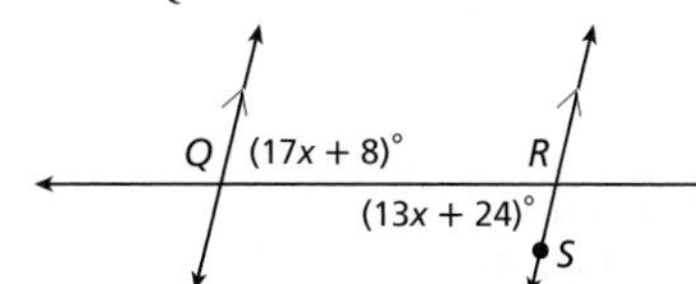

Answers

10. ℓ; alt. int. ∡s
11. *n*; corr. ∡s
12. ℓ; same-side int. ∡s
13. *m*; alt. ext. ∡s
14. $m\angle WYZ = 90°$
15. $m\angle KLM = 100°$
16. $m\angle DEF = 79°$
17. $m\angle QRS = 76°$

Answers

18. $\angle 4 \cong \angle 6$, so $c \parallel d$ by the Conv. of the Alt. Int. ⦞ Thm.
19. $m\angle 1 = 107°$; and $m\angle 5 = 107°$, so $\angle 1 \cong \angle 5$. $c \parallel d$ by the Conv. of the Corr. ⦞ Post.
20. $m\angle 6 = 66°$, $m\angle 3 = 114°$, and $66° + 114° = 180°$, so $\angle 6$ and $\angle 3$ are supp. $c \parallel d$ by the Conv. of the Same-Side Int. ⦞ Thm.
21. $m\angle 1 = 99°$, and $m\angle 7 = 99°$, so $\angle 1 \cong \angle 7$. $c \parallel d$ by the Conv. of the Alt. Ext. ⦞ Thm.
22. $\overline{KM}$
23. $x - 5 < 8$; $x < 13$
24. 1. $\overline{AD} \parallel \overline{BC}$, $\overline{AD} \perp \overline{AB}$, $\overline{DC} \perp \overline{BC}$ (Given);
    2. $\overline{AB} \perp \overline{BC}$ ($\perp$ Transv. Thm.);
    3. $\overline{AB} \parallel \overline{CD}$ (2 lines $\perp$ to same line $\rightarrow$ 2 lines $\parallel$)

3-3 Proving Lines Parallel *(pp. 162–169)*

EXAMPLES

Use the given information and theorems and postulates you have learned to show that $p \parallel q$.

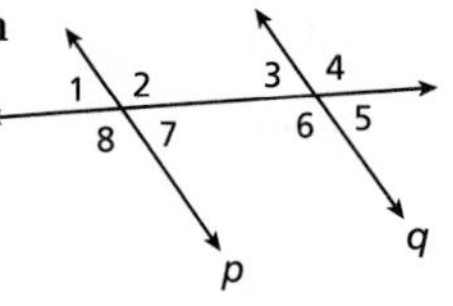

- $m\angle 2 + m\angle 3 = 180°$

  $\angle 2$ and $\angle 3$ are supplementary, so $p \parallel q$ by the Converse of the Same-Side Interior Angles Theorem.

- $\angle 8 \cong \angle 6$

  $\angle 8 \cong \angle 6$, so $p \parallel q$ by the Converse of the Corresponding Angles Postulate.

- $m\angle 1 = (7x - 3)°$, $m\angle 5 = 5x + 15$, $x = 9$

  $m\angle 1 = 60°$, and $m\angle 5 = 60°$. So $\angle 1 \cong \angle 5$. $p \parallel q$ by the Converse of the Alternate Exterior Angles Theorem.

EXERCISES

Use the given information and theorems and postulates you have learned to show that $c \parallel d$.

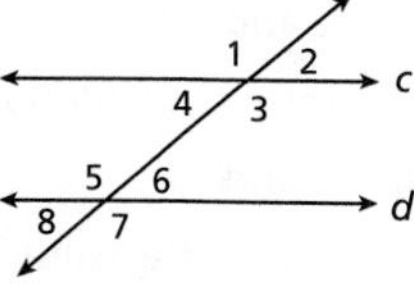

18. $m\angle 4 = 58°$, $m\angle 6 = 58°$
19. $m\angle 1 = (23x + 38)°$, $m\angle 5 = (17x + 56)°$, $x = 3$
20. $m\angle 6 = (12x + 6)°$, $m\angle 3 = (21x + 9)°$, $x = 5$
21. $m\angle 1 = 99°$, $m\angle 7 = (13x + 8)°$, $x = 7$

3-4 Perpendicular Lines *(pp. 172–178)*

EXAMPLES

- **Name the shortest segment from point X to $\overline{WY}$.**

  $\overline{XZ}$

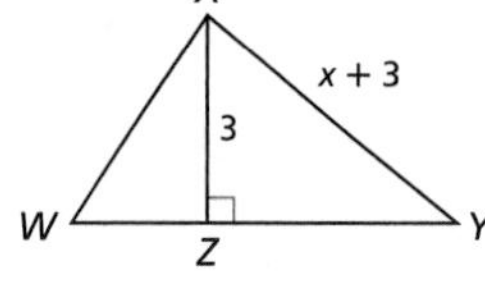

- **Write and solve an inequality for x.**

  $x + 3 > 3$

  $x > 0$ *Subtract 3 from both sides.*

- **Given:** $m \perp p$, $\angle 1$ and $\angle 2$ are complementary.
  Prove: $p \parallel q$

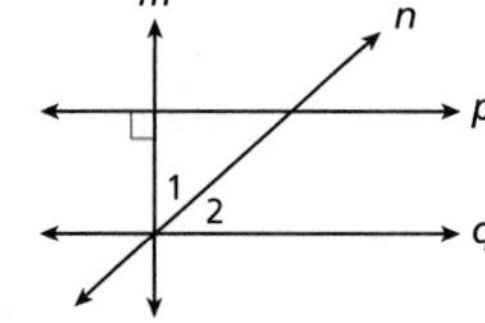

Proof:
It is given that $m \perp p$. $\angle 1$ and $\angle 2$ are complementary, so $m\angle 1 + m\angle 2 = 90°$. Thus $m \perp q$. Two lines perpendicular to the same line are parallel, so $p \parallel q$.

EXERCISES

22. Name the shortest segment from point K to $\overline{LN}$.
23. Write and solve an inequality for x.

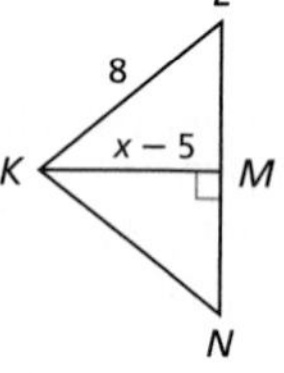

24. **Given:** $\overline{AD} \parallel \overline{BC}$, $\overline{AD} \perp \overline{AB}$, $\overline{DC} \perp \overline{BC}$

    Prove: $\overline{AB} \parallel \overline{CD}$

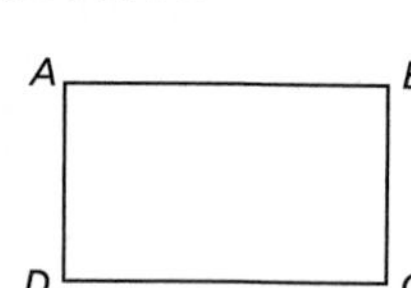

3-5 Slopes of Lines *(pp. 182–187)*

EXAMPLES

- **Use the slope formula to determine the slope of the line.**

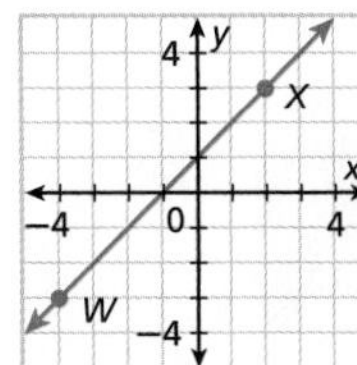

slope of $\overleftrightarrow{WX} = \frac{y_2 - y_1}{x_2 - x_1} = \frac{3 - (-3)}{2 - (-4)} = \frac{6}{6} = 1$

- **Use slopes to determine whether $\overleftrightarrow{AB}$ and $\overleftrightarrow{CD}$ are parallel, perpendicular, or neither for $A(-1, 5)$, $B(-3, 4)$, $C(3, -1)$, and $D(4, -3)$.**

slope of $\overleftrightarrow{AB} = \frac{4 - 5}{-3 - (-1)} = \frac{1}{2}$

slope of $\overleftrightarrow{CD} = \frac{-3 - (-1)}{4 - 3} = \frac{-2}{1} = -2$

The slopes are opposite reciprocals, so the lines are perpendicular.

EXERCISES

Use the slope formula to determine the slope of each line.

25.

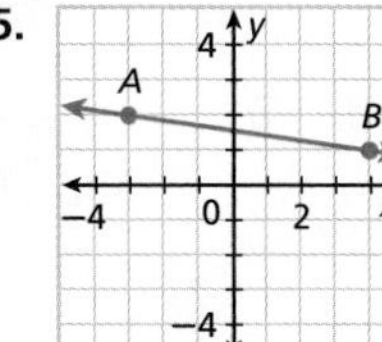

26.

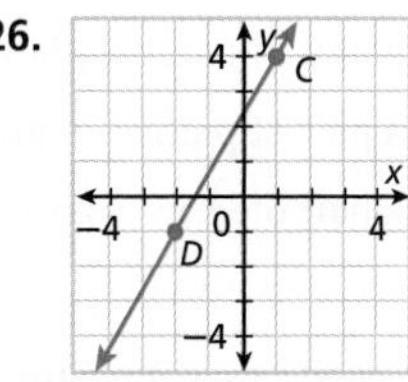

Use slopes to determine if the lines are parallel, perpendicular, or neither.

27. $\overleftrightarrow{EF}$ and $\overleftrightarrow{GH}$ for $E(8, 2)$, $F(-3, 4)$, $G(6, 1)$, and $H(-4, 3)$

28. $\overleftrightarrow{JK}$ and $\overleftrightarrow{LM}$ for $J(4, 3)$, $K(-4, -2)$, $L(5, 6)$, and $M(-3, 1)$

29. $\overleftrightarrow{ST}$ and $\overleftrightarrow{UV}$ for $S(-4, 5)$, $T(2, 3)$, $U(3, 1)$, and $V(4, 4)$

3-6 Lines in the Coordinate Plane *(pp. 190–197)*

EXAMPLES

- **Write the equation of the line through $(5, -2)$ with slope $\frac{3}{5}$ in slope-intercept form.**

$y - (-2) = \frac{3}{5}(x - 5)$ *Point-slope form*

$y + 2 = \frac{3}{5}x - 3$ *Simplify.*

$y = \frac{3}{5}x - 5$ *Solve for y.*

- **Determine whether the lines $y = 4x + 6$ and $8x - 2y = 4$ are parallel, intersect, or coincide.**

Solve the second equation for y to find the slope-intercept form.

$8x - 2y = 4$

$y = 4x - 2$

Both the lines have a slope of 4 and have different y-intercepts, so they are parallel.

EXERCISES

Write the equation of each line in the given form.

30. the line through $(6, 1)$ and $(-3, 5)$ in slope-intercept form

31. the line through $(-3, -4)$ with slope $\frac{2}{3}$ in slope-intercept form

32. the line with x-intercept 1 and y-intercept -2 in point-slope form

Determine whether the lines are parallel, intersect, or coincide.

33. $-3x + 2y = 5$, $6x - 4y = 8$

34. $y = 4x - 3$, $5x + 2y = 1$

35. $y = 2x + 1$, $2x - y = -1$

Answers

25. $m = -\frac{1}{7}$
26. $m = \frac{5}{3}$
27. neither
28. $\parallel$
29. $\perp$
30. $y = -\frac{4}{9}x + \frac{11}{3}$
31. $y = \frac{2}{3}x - 2$
32. $y - 0 = 2(x - 1)$
33. $\parallel$
34. intersect
35. coincide

Organizer

Objective: Assess students' mastery of concepts and skills in Chapter 3.

Online Edition

Resources

Assessment Resources

Chapter 3 Tests
- Free Response (Levels A, B, C)
- Multiple Choice (Levels A, B, C)
- Performance Assessment

Teacher One Stop™
Test & Practice Generator

State Resources

Identify each of the following.

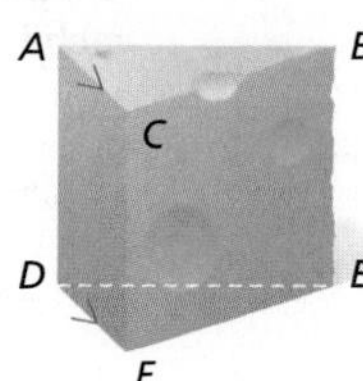

1. a pair of parallel planes
2. a pair of parallel segments $\overline{AC} \parallel \overline{DF}$
3. a pair of skew segments

Find each angle measure.

4. 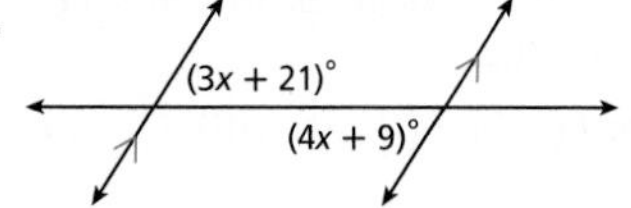

5. 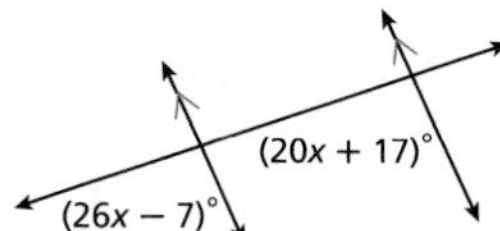

6. 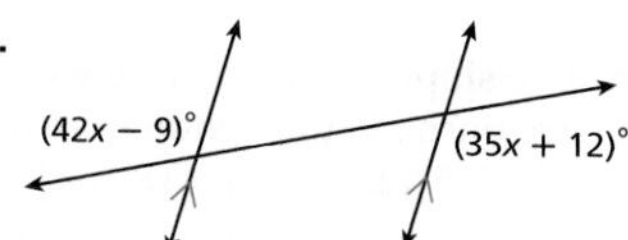

Use the given information and the theorems and postulates you have learned to show $f \parallel g$.

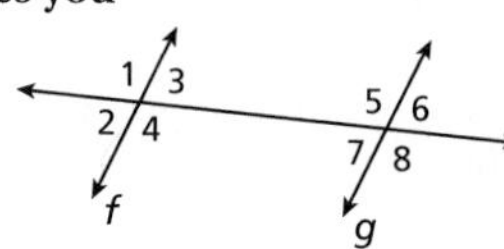

7. $m\angle 4 = (16x + 20)°$, $m\angle 5 = (12x + 32)°$, $x = 3$
8. $m\angle 3 = (18x + 6)°$, $m\angle 5 = (21x + 18)°$, $x = 4$

Write a two-column proof.

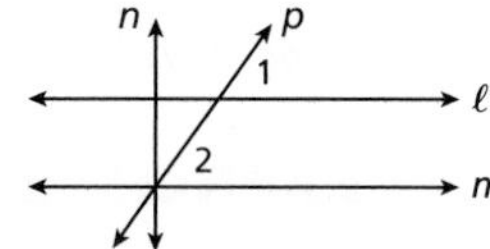

9. Given: $\angle 1 \cong \angle 2$, $n \perp \ell$

   Prove: $n \perp m$

Use the slope formula to determine the slope of each line.

10. 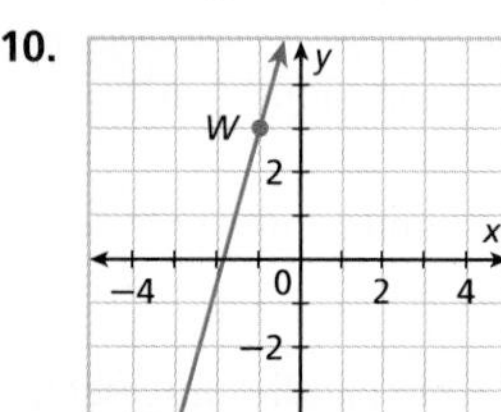 $m = \frac{7}{2}$

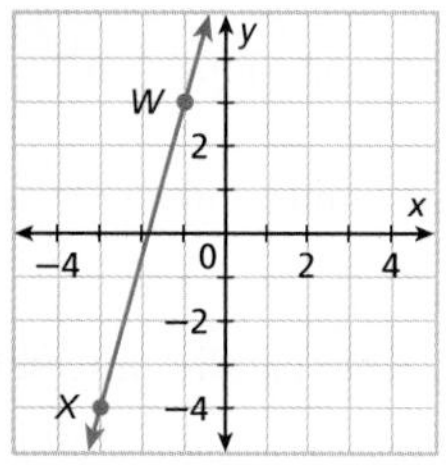

11. 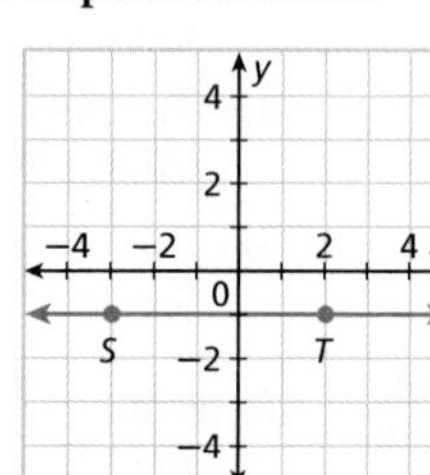 $m = 0$

12. 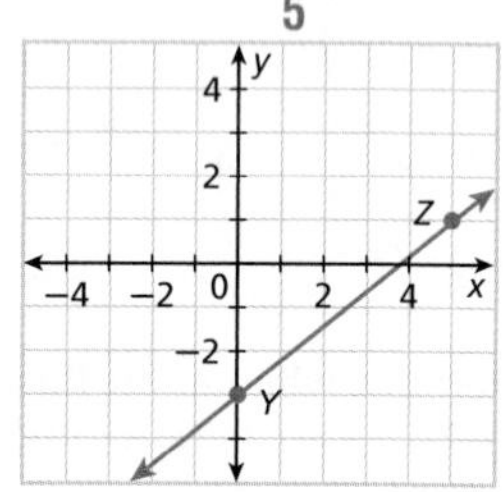 $m = \frac{4}{5}$

13. Greg is on a 32-mile bicycle trail from Elroy, Wisconsin, to Sparta, Wisconsin. He leaves Elroy at 9:30 A.M. and arrives in Sparta at 2:00 P.M. Graph the line that represents Greg's distance from Elroy at a given time. Find and interpret the slope of the line. $m = \frac{32}{4.5} \approx 7.1$; **Greg's average speed was about 7.1 mi/h.**

14. Graph $\overleftrightarrow{QR}$ and $\overleftrightarrow{ST}$ for $Q(3, 3)$, $R(6, -5)$, $S(-4, 6)$, and $T(-1, -2)$. Use slopes to determine whether the lines are parallel, perpendicular, or neither.

15. Write the equation of the line through $(-2, -5)$ with slope $-\frac{3}{4}$ in point-slope form. $y + 5 = -\frac{3}{4}(x + 2)$

16. Determine whether the lines $6x + y = 3$ and $2x + 3y = 1$ are parallel, intersect, or coincide. **intersect**

Answers

1. plane $ABC \parallel$ plane DEF
3. Possible answer: $\overline{AB}$ and $\overline{CF}$ are skew.
4. Both labeled angles measure 57°.
5. Both labeled angles measure 97°.
6. Both labeled angles measure 117°.
7. $m\angle 4 = 68°$, and $m\angle 5 = 68°$, so $\angle 4 \cong \angle 5$. $f \parallel g$ by the Conv. of Alt. Int. ∠s Thm.
8. $m\angle 3 = 78°$, and $m\angle 5 = 102°$, so $m\angle 3 + m\angle 5 = 180°$. $f \parallel g$ by the Conv. of Same-Side Int. ∠s Thm.
9. 1. $\angle 1 \cong \angle 2$, $n \perp \ell$ (Given)
   2. $\ell \parallel m$ (Conv. of Corr. ∠s Post.)
   3. $n \perp m$ (⊥ Transv. Thm.)

14. 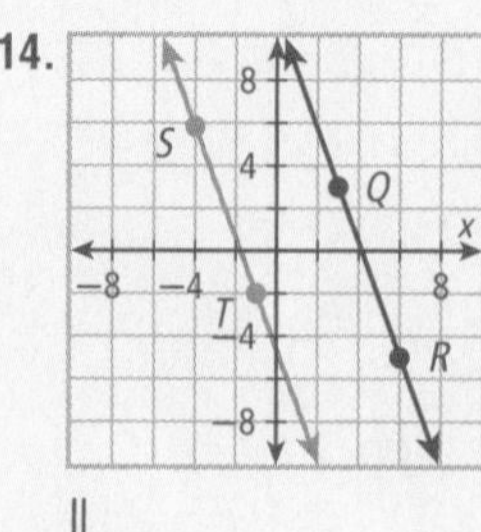

$\parallel$

COLLEGE ENTRANCE EXAM PRACTICE

CHAPTER 3

FOCUS ON ACT

When you take the ACT Mathematics Test, you receive a separate subscore for each of the following areas:
- Pre-Algebra/Elementary Algebra,
- Intermediate Algebra/Coordinate Geometry, and
- Plane Geometry/Trigonometry.

Find out what percent of questions are from each area and concentrate on content that represents the greatest percent of questions.

You may want to time yourself as you take this practice test. It should take you about 5 minutes to complete.

1. Which of the following is an equation of the line that passes through the point $(2, -3)$ and is parallel to the line $4x - 5y = 1$?
   (A) $-4x + 5y = -23$
   (B) $-5x - 4y = 2$
   (C) $-2x - 5y = 11$
   (D) $-4x - 5y = 7$
   (E) $-5x + 4y = -22$

2. In the figure below, line t crosses parallel lines ℓ and m. Which of the following statements are true?

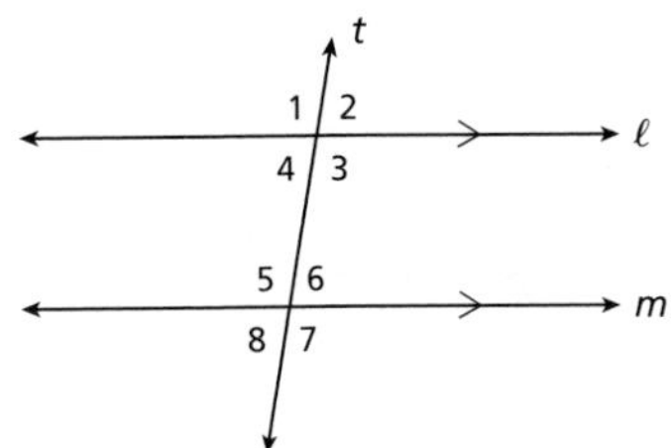

   I. $\angle 1$ and $\angle 6$ are alternate interior angles.
   II. $\angle 2 \cong \angle 4$
   III. $\angle 2 \cong \angle 8$
   (F) I only
   (G) II only
   (H) III only
   (J) I and II only
   (K) II and III only

3. In the standard (x, y) coordinate plane, the line that passes through $(1, -7)$ and $(-8, 5)$ is perpendicular to the line that passes through $(3, 6)$ and $(-1, b)$. What is the value of b?
   (A) 2
   (B) 3
   (C) 7
   (D) 9
   (E) 10

4. Lines m and n are cut by a transversal so that $\angle 2$ and $\angle 5$ are corresponding angles. If $m\angle 2 = (x + 18)°$ and $m\angle 5 = (2x - 28)°$, which value of x makes lines m and n parallel?
   (F) $3\frac{1}{3}$
   (G) $33\frac{1}{3}$
   (H) 46
   (J) $63\frac{1}{3}$
   (K) 72

5. What is the distance between point $G(4, 2)$ and the line through the points $E(1, -2)$ and $F(7, -2)$?
   (A) 3
   (B) 4
   (C) 5
   (D) 6
   (E) 7

COLLEGE ENTRANCE EXAM PRACTICE — CHAPTER 3

Organizer

Objective: Provide practice for college entrance exams such as the ACT.

Resources

College Entrance Exam Practice

Questions on the ACT represent the following content areas:
Pre-Algebra, 23%
Elementary Algebra, 17%
Intermediate Algebra, 15%
Coordinate Geometry, 15%
Plane Geometry, 23%
Trigonometry, 7%

Items on this page focus on:
- Parallel Lines and Transversals
- Lines in the Coordinate Plane

Text References:

Item	1	2	3	4	5
Lesson	3-5, 3-6	3-2	3-6	3-3	3-4

TEST PREP DOCTOR

1. Students who chose **B** found the equation of the line perpendicular to the given line and through the given point. Remind students that parallel lines have the same slope.
2. Students who chose **G** may not recognize that $\angle 2$ and $\angle 8$ are alternate exterior angles and are therefore congruent. Students who chose **F** or **J** may not understand the definition of alternate interior angles.
3. Students who chose **A** or **E** found the equation of a line parallel to the line through the points $(1, -7)$ and $(-8, 5)$, rather than a perpendicular line. Students who chose **D** found a line such that the product of the slopes is 1 rather than -1.
4. Students who chose **B** found the value of x that makes the angles formed by lines m and n complementary. Students who chose **D** found the value of x that makes the angles formed by lines m and n supplementary. Remind students of the definition of corresponding angles.
5. Students may not know how to approach this problem. Suggest that they draw a diagram, and remind students that the distance between a point and a line is measured along a line perpendicular to the line.

Organizer

Objective: Provide students with opportunities to learn and practice common test-taking strategies.

This Test Tackler explains how short response test items are scored and demonstrates how to write a response to receive full credit. Students need to be aware that points are awarded based on the completeness and correctness of each answer. It may help for students to understand that scoring guides are designed so that different graders will assign the same score for a given response.

Standardized Test Strategies

Short Response: Write Short Responses

Short response test items are designed to test mathematical understanding. In your response, you have to show your work and possibly describe your reasoning to show that you understand the concept. Scores are based on a 2-point scoring rubric.

Some short response questions require you to draw and label a diagram. Make sure you draw the figure as described in the problem statement and provide all markings and labeling as needed.

EXAMPLE 1

Short Response Draw and label $\angle ABC$ and $\angle CBD$, a pair of adjacent, supplementary angles. Then draw a line perpendicular to line AD though point B and name two right angles.

Scoring Rubric

2 points: The student shows an understanding of adjacent and supplementary angles and perpendicular lines. The diagram is correct, and all labels and markings are included. The student correctly names two right angles.

1 point: The student correctly sketches the diagram, but labels it incorrectly, does not name two right angles, or incorrectly names two right angles. OR the student makes minor flaws in the diagram but correctly names two right angles.

0 points: The diagram is completely incorrect, or the student gives no response.

Here are examples of how different responses were scored using the scoring rubric shown.

2-point response:

$\angle ABG$ and $\angle GBD$ are right angles.

Notice that the diagram is correct and all labels and markings are included. Student correctly identified two right angles.

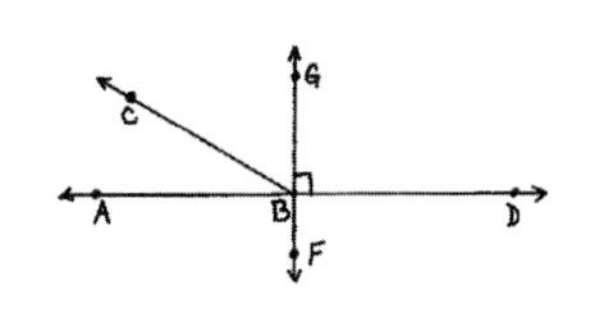

1-point response:

$\angle GCD$ is a right angle.

Notice that the diagram is almost correct, but points B and C are mislabeled. Also, the student only identified one right angle, not two.

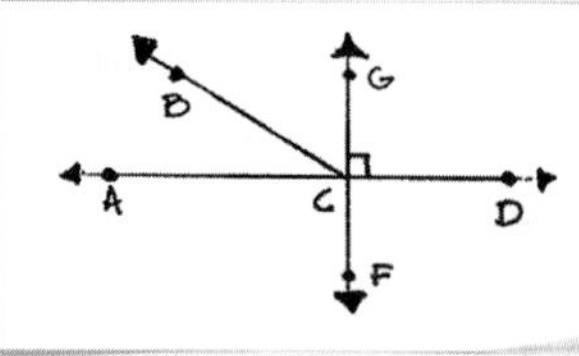

0-point response:

Notice that the student did not complete the required diagram, and it appears to be completely incorrect.

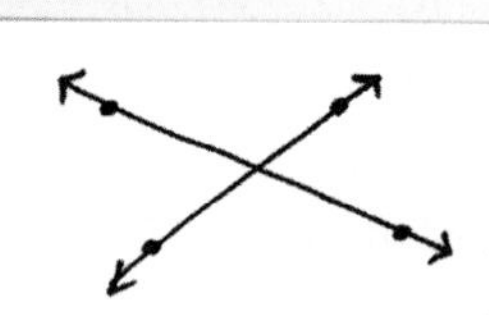

Read each test item, and use the scoring rubric to answer each question.

Scoring Rubric

2 points: The student demonstrates an understanding of the concept, correctly answers the question, and provides a complete explanation.

1 point: The student correctly answers the question but does not show all work or does not provide an explanation.

1 point: The student makes minor errors resulting in an incorrect solution but shows an understanding of the concept.

0 points: The student gives a response showing no work or explanation, or the student gives no response.

Item A

Short Response Find $m\angle JKM$. Identify any postulates used to determine the answer.

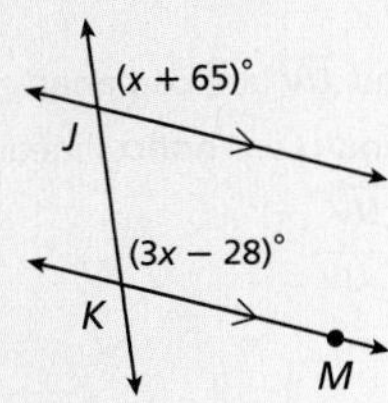

1. What should be included in a student's response in order to receive 2 points?
2. A student wrote this response:

The angles look like they have the same measure, so:

$(x+65)° = (3x-28)°$

$-2x = -93$

$x = 46.5$

$(3x-28) = 3(46.5) - 28 = 111.5$

$m\angle JKM = 111.5°$

What score should this response receive? What needs to be added to the response, if anything, in order to receive 2 points?

To receive full credit, make sure your explanations or descriptions are complete sentences.

Item B

Short Response Write a paragraph proof.

Given: $YT \parallel ZW$; $XZ \perp ZW$

Prove: $XY \perp YT$

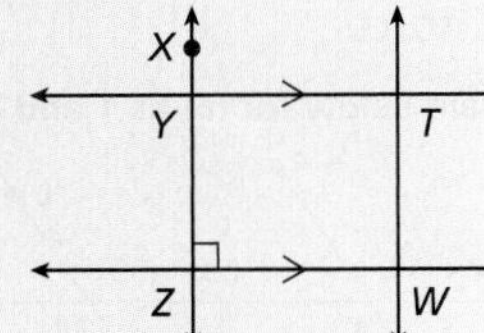

So far, Issac has these thoughts written down on his paper.

I know $\overleftrightarrow{YT} \parallel \overleftrightarrow{ZW}$, and it looks like $\overleftrightarrow{YZ} \parallel \overleftrightarrow{TW}$. $\angle YZW$ and $\angle XYT$ are corr. ∠s, so they must be ≅.

I also know $\overleftrightarrow{XZ} \perp \overleftrightarrow{ZW}$, so the ∠s formed by these lines are rt. ∠s. It also looks like $\overleftrightarrow{TW} \perp \overleftrightarrow{ZW}$, which means more rt. ∠s.

I think I need to show $\angle YZW \cong \angle XYT$ so that I can say they both measure 90°. Then by def. of ⊥ lines, $\overleftrightarrow{XY} \perp \overleftrightarrow{YT}$.

3. What information is NOT necessary for Isaac to include in his proof?
4. Rewrite Issac's paragraph so that it would receive 2 points.

Answers

1. The response should include a correct answer with the equation used to find the measure. The steps of solving the equation should be shown and each step should be justified. Also, any postulates or theorems used should be identified.
2. 1 point; the answer is correct, but the explanation needs to identify the Corr. ∠s Post. to justify that the ∠s are ≅.
3. It looks like $\overleftrightarrow{YZ} \parallel \overleftrightarrow{TW}$, and it looks like $\overleftrightarrow{TW} \perp \overleftrightarrow{ZW}$.
4. It is given that $\overleftrightarrow{YT} \parallel \overleftrightarrow{ZW}$. By the Corr. ∠s Post., $\angle XZW \cong \angle XYT$. It is also given that $\overleftrightarrow{XZ} \perp \overleftrightarrow{ZW}$, so $m\angle XZW = 90°$. By def. of ≅ ∠s, $m\angle XYT = 90°$. So by def. of ⊥ lines, $\overleftrightarrow{XY} \perp \overleftrightarrow{YT}$.

State Resources

go.hrw.com
State Resources Online
KEYWORD: MG7 Resources

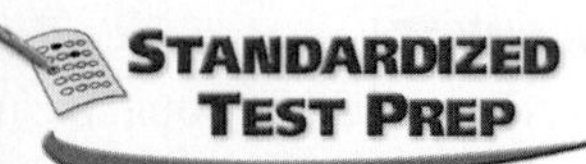

Organizer

Objective: Provide review and practice for Chapters 1–3 and standardized tests.

Online Edition

Resources

Assessment Resources

Chapter 3 Cumulative Test

go.hrw.com
KEYWORD: MG7 Resources

State Resources

CUMULATIVE ASSESSMENT, CHAPTERS 1–3

Multiple Choice

Use the diagram below for Items 1 and 2.

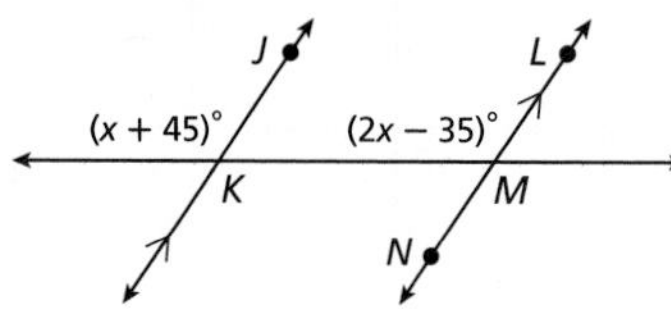

1. What type of angle pair are $\angle JKM$ and $\angle KMN$?

Ⓐ Corresponding angles
Ⓑ Alternate exterior angles
Ⓒ Same-side interior angles
Ⓓ Alternate interior angles

2. What is $m\angle KML$?

Ⓕ 57° Ⓗ 102°
Ⓖ 80° Ⓙ 125°

3. What is a possible value of x in the diagram?

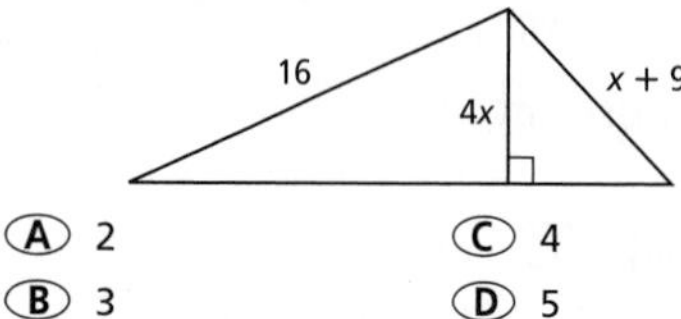

Ⓐ 2 Ⓒ 4
Ⓑ 3 Ⓓ 5

4. A graphic artist used a computer illustration program to draw a line connecting points with coordinates $(3, -1)$ and $(4, 6)$. She needs to draw a second line parallel to the first line. What slope should the second line have?

Ⓕ $\frac{1}{7}$ Ⓗ 5
Ⓖ $\frac{1}{5}$ Ⓙ 7

5. Which term describes a pair of vertical angles that are also supplementary?

Ⓐ Acute Ⓒ Right
Ⓑ Obtuse Ⓓ Straight

6. What is the equation of the line that passes through the points $(-1, 8)$ and $(4, -2)$?

Ⓕ $y = -2x + 6$ Ⓗ $y = \frac{1}{2}x - 4$
Ⓖ $y = -\frac{1}{2}x$ Ⓙ $y = 2x + 10$

7. Given the points $R(-5, 3)$, $S(-5, 4)$, $T(-3, 4)$, and $U(-3, 1)$, which line is perpendicular to $\overleftrightarrow{TU}$?

Ⓐ $\overleftrightarrow{RS}$ Ⓒ $\overleftrightarrow{ST}$
Ⓑ $\overleftrightarrow{RT}$ Ⓓ $\overleftrightarrow{SU}$

8. Which of following is true if $\overleftrightarrow{XY}$ and $\overleftrightarrow{UV}$ are skew?

Ⓕ $\overleftrightarrow{XY}$ and $\overleftrightarrow{UV}$ are coplanar.
Ⓖ X, Y, and U are noncollinear.
Ⓗ $\overleftrightarrow{XY} \parallel \overleftrightarrow{UV}$
Ⓙ $\overleftrightarrow{XY} \perp \overleftrightarrow{UV}$

Make sure that you answer the question that is asked. Some problems require more than one step. You must perform *all* of the steps to get the correct answer.

9. Point C is the midpoint of $\overline{AB}$ for $A(1, -2)$ and $B(7, 2)$. What is the length of $\overline{AC}$? Round to the nearest tenth.

Ⓐ 3.0 Ⓒ 5.0
Ⓑ 3.6 Ⓓ 7.2

Use the diagram below for Items 10 and 11.

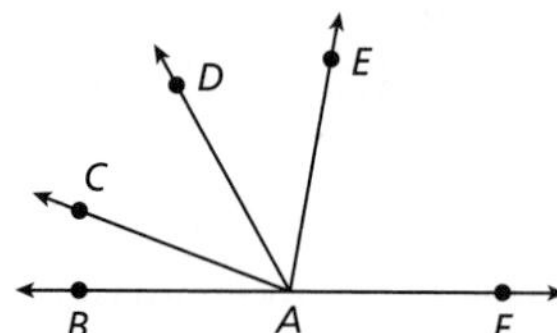

10. $\overrightarrow{AD}$ bisects $\angle CAE$, and $\overrightarrow{AE}$ bisects $\angle CAF$. If $m\angle DAF = 120°$, what is $m\angle DAE$?

Ⓕ 40° Ⓖ 60° Ⓗ 80° Ⓙ 100°

11. What is the intersection of $\overrightarrow{AF}$ and $\overrightarrow{AD}$?

Ⓐ A Ⓑ F Ⓒ $\overline{FD}$ Ⓓ $\angle DAF$

Answers

1. D
2. J
3. A
4. J
5. C
6. F
7. C
8. G
9. B
10. F
11. A
12. H
13. B
14. J
15. 37.5
16. 0.75
17. 24
18. 11
19. 30
20. 91

12. Which statement is true by the Transitive Property of Equality?

Ⓕ If $x + 3 = y$, then $y = x + 3$.

Ⓖ If $k = 6$, then $2k = 12$.

Ⓗ If $a = b$ and $b = 8$, then $a = 8$.

Ⓙ If $m = n$, then $m + 7 = n + 7$.

13. Which condition guarantees that $r \parallel s$?

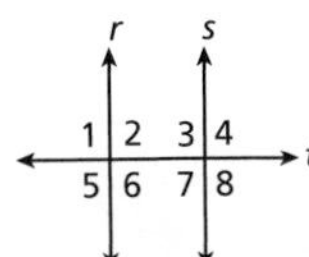

Ⓐ $\angle 1 \cong \angle 2$

Ⓑ $\angle 2 \cong \angle 7$

Ⓒ $\angle 2 \cong \angle 3$

Ⓓ $\angle 1 \cong \angle 4$

14. What is the converse of the following statement?

If $x = 2$, then $x + 3 = 5$.

Ⓕ If $x \neq 2$, then $x + 3 = 5$.

Ⓖ If $x = 2$, then $x + 3 \neq 5$.

Ⓗ If $x + 3 \neq 5$, then $x \neq 2$.

Ⓙ If $x + 3 = 5$, then $x = 2$.

Gridded Response

15. Two lines a and b are cut by a transversal so that $\angle 1$ and $\angle 2$ are same-side interior angles. If $m\angle 1 = (2x + 30)°$ and $m\angle 2 = (4x - 75)°$, what value of x proves that $a \parallel b$?

16. What is the slope of the line that passes through (3, 7) and (−5, 1)?

17. $\angle 1$ and $\angle 2$ form a linear pair. $m\angle 1 = (4x + 18)°$ and $m\angle 2 = (3x - 6)°$. What is the value of x?

18. Points A, B, and C are collinear, and B is between A and C. $AB = 16$ and $AC = 27$. What is the distance BC?

19. Ms. Nelson wants to put a chain-link fence around 3 sides of a square-shaped lawn. Chain-link fencing is sold in sections that are each 6 feet wide. If Ms. Nelson's lawn has an area of 3600 square feet, how many sections of fencing will she need?

20. What is the next number in this pattern?

67, 76, 83, 88,...

Short Response

21. Given $\ell \parallel m$ with transversal t, explain why $\angle 1$ and $\angle 8$ are supplementary.

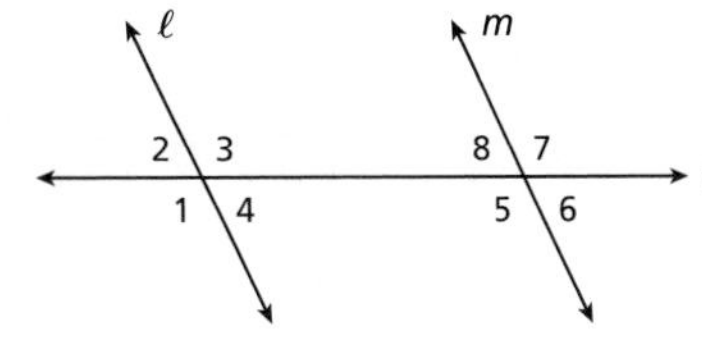

22. Read the following conditional statement.

If two angles are vertical angles, then they are congruent.

a. Write the converse of this conditional statement.

b. Give a counterexample to show that the converse is false.

23. Assume that the following statements are true when the bases are loaded in a baseball game.

If a batter hits the ball over the fence, then the batter hits a home run.
A batter hits a home run if and only if the result is four runs scored.

a. If a batter hits the ball over the fence when the bases are loaded, can you conclude that four runs were scored? Explain your answer.

b. If a batter hits a home run when the bases are loaded, can you conclude that the batter hit the ball over the fence? Explain your answer.

Extended Response

24. A car passes through a tollbooth at 8:00 A.M. and begins traveling east at an average speed of 45 miles per hour. A second car passes through the same tollbooth an hour later and begins traveling east at an average speed of 60 miles per hour.

a. Write an equation for each car that relates the number of hours x since 8:00 A.M. to the distance in miles y the car has traveled. Explain what the slope of each equation represents.

b. Graph the system of equations on the coordinate plane.

c. If neither car stops, at what time will the second car catch up to the first car? Explain how you determined your answer.

Short-Response Rubric

Items 21–23

2 Points = The student's answer is an accurate and complete execution of the task or tasks.

1 Point = The student's answer contains attributes of an appropriate response but is flawed.

0 Points = The student's answer contains no attributes of an appropriate response.

Extended-Response Rubric

Item 24

4 Points = The student's equations are written, graphed, and analyzed correctly. Work demonstrates a thorough understanding of concepts related to equations of lines and lines in the coordinate plane.

3 Points = The student's equations, graph, and answers are correct but may contain minor flaws. Work demonstrates an understanding of major concepts.

2 Points = The student answers correctly, but explanations are missing or incomplete, or the student only answers part of the problem. Work demonstrates a limited understanding of concepts.

1 Point = The student answers incorrectly but makes a reasonable attempt to show work and write and graph the equations.

0 Points = The student does not answer correctly and does not attempt all parts of the problem.

Answers

21. Possible answer: $\angle 1 \cong \angle 5$ by the Corr. ∡ Post. $\angle 5$ is supp. to $\angle 8$ by the Lin. Pair Thm. Therefore, $\angle 1$ is supp to $\angle 8$ by the ≅ Supp. Thm.

22a. If 2 ∡ are ≅, then they are vert. ∡.

b. Possible answer: $\angle A \cong \angle B$, but $\angle A$ and $\angle B$ are not vert. ∡ because they are not formed by 2 intersecting lines.

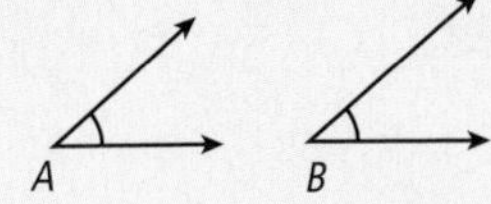

23a. Yes; possible answer: based on the given statements, if a batter hits the ball over the fence, then the batter hits a home run. If a batter hits a home run, then the batter hits in 4 runs. Therefore, by the Law of Syllogism, if a batter hits the ball over the fence, then the batter hits in 4 runs.

b. No; possible answer: the converse of the statement, "If a batter hits the ball over the fence, then the batter hits a home run," is not necessarily true.

24a. First car: $y = 45x$; second car: $y = 60x - 60$; the slope of each equation represents the car's average speed.

b.

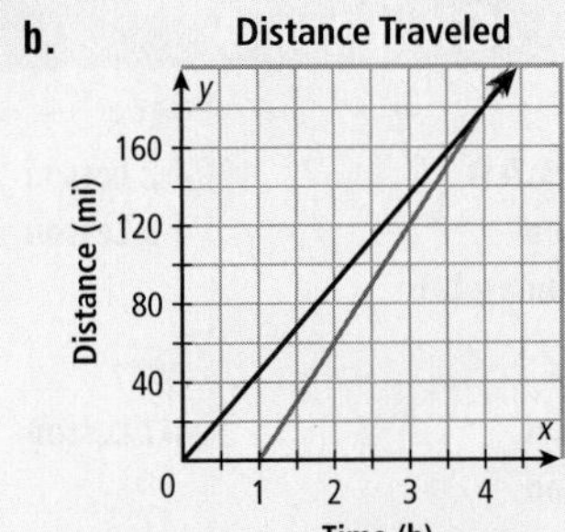

24c. Noon; possible answer: the point where the lines cross represents the time when the second car catches up to the first car. The lines cross at (4, 180). The second car catches up to the first car 4 hours after 8:00 A.M., when both cars have traveled 180 mi.

Triangle Congruence

Pacing Guide for 45-Minute Classes

Teacher One Stop™
Calendar Planner®

Chapter 4

Countdown Weeks 7, 8, 9

DAY 1	DAY 2	DAY 3	DAY 4	DAY 5
4-1 Lesson 4-2 Geometry Lab	4-2 Lesson	4-3 Lesson	Multi-Step Test Prep Ready to Go On?	4-4 Geometry Lab
DAY 6	**DAY 7**	**DAY 8**	**DAY 9**	**DAY 10**
4-4 Lesson	4-4 Lesson	4-5 Technology Lab	4-5 Lesson	4-5 Lesson
DAY 11	**DAY 12**	**DAY 13**	**DAY 14**	**DAY 15**
4-6 Lesson Connecting Geometry to Algebra	4-7 Lesson	4-7 Lesson	4-8 Lesson	Extension
DAY 16	**DAY 17**	**DAY 18**		
Multi-Step Test Prep Ready to Go On?	Chapter 4 Review	Chapter 4 Test		

Pacing Guide for 90-Minute Classes

Teacher One Stop™
Calendar Planner®

Chapter 4

DAY 1	DAY 2	DAY 3	DAY 4	DAY 5
Chapter 3 Test 4-1 Lesson 4-2 Geometry Lab	4-2 Lesson 4-3 Lesson	Multi-Step Test Prep Ready to Go On? 4-4 Geometry Lab	4-4 Lesson	4-5 Technology Lab 4-5 Lesson
DAY 6	**DAY 7**	**DAY 8**	**DAY 9**	**DAY 10**
4-5 Lesson 4-6 Lesson Connecting Geometry to Algebra	4-7 Lesson	4-8 Lesson Extension	Multi-Step Test Prep Ready to Go On? Chapter 4 Review	Chapter 4 Test 5-1 Lesson

ONGOING ASSESSMENT and INTERVENTION

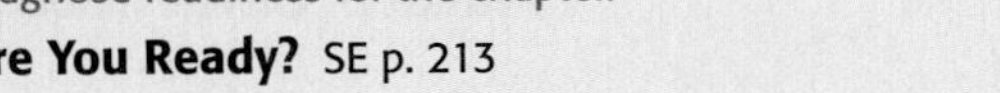

	DIAGNOSE	PRESCRIBE
Assess Prior Knowledge	**Before Chapter 4**	
	Diagnose readiness for the chapter.	Prescribe intervention.
	Are You Ready? SE p. 213	***Are You Ready? Intervention***
Formative Assessment	**Before Every Lesson**	
	Diagnose readiness for the lesson.	Prescribe intervention.
	Warm Up TE	**Reteach** CRB
	During Every Lesson	
	Diagnose understanding of lesson concepts.	Prescribe intervention.
	Check It Out! SE	**Reading Strategies** CRB
	Questioning Strategies TE	***Success for Every Learner***
	Think and Discuss SE	***Lesson Tutorial Videos***
	Write About It SE	
	Journal TE	
	After Every Lesson	
	Diagnose mastery of lesson concepts.	Prescribe intervention.
	Lesson Quiz TE	**Reteach** CRB
	Test Prep SE	**Test Prep Doctor** TE
	Test and Practice Generator	***Homework Help* Online**
	Before Chapter 4 Testing	
	Diagnose mastery of concepts in chapter.	Prescribe intervention.
	Ready to Go On? SE pp. 239, 281	***Ready to Go On? Intervention***
	Multi-Step Test Prep SE pp. 238, 280	**Scaffolding Questions** TE pp. 238, 280
	Section Quizzes AR	**Reteach** CRB
	Test and Practice Generator	***Lesson Tutorial Videos***
	Before High Stakes Testing	
	Diagnose mastery of benchmark concepts.	Prescribe intervention.
	College Entrance Exam Practice SE p. 289	***College Entrance Exam Practice***
	Standardized Test Prep SE pp. 292–293	
Summative Assessment	**After Chapter 4**	
	Check mastery of chapter concepts.	Prescribe intervention.
	Multiple-Choice Tests (Forms A, B, C)	**Reteach** CRB
	Free-Response Tests (Forms A, B, C)	***Lesson Tutorial Videos***
	Performance Assessment AR	
	Cumulative Test AR	
	Test and Practice Generator	

KEY: **SE** = *Student Edition* **TE** = *Teacher's Edition* **CRB** = *Chapter Resource Book* **AR** = *Assessment Resources* Available online Available on CD- or DVD-ROM

CHAPTER 4

Lesson Resources

Before the Lesson

Prepare ***Teacher One Stop*** SPANISH 
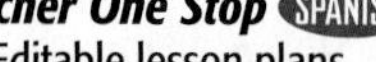
- Editable lesson plans
- Calendar Planner
- Easy access to all chapter resources

Lesson Transparencies
- Teacher Tools

Teach the Lesson

Introduce ***Alternate Openers: Explorations***
Lesson Transparencies 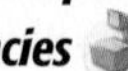
- Warm Up
- Problem of the Day

Teach ***Lesson Transparencies***
- Teaching Transparencies

Know-It Notebook™
- Vocabulary
- Key Concepts

Power Presentations 
Lesson Tutorial Videos  SPANISH

Interactive Online Edition  
- Lesson Activities
- Lesson Tutorial Videos

Lab Activities
Lab Resources Online 
Online Interactivities   SPANISH
TechKeys  

Practice the Lesson

Practice ***Chapter Resources***
- Practice A, B, C

Practice and Problem Solving Workbook
IDEA Works!® Modified Worksheets and Tests
ExamView Test and Practice Generator
Homework Help Online
Online Interactivities   SPANISH
Interactive Online Edition 
- Homework Help

Apply ***Chapter Resources***
- Problem Solving

Practice and Problem Solving Workbook
Interactive Online Edition
- Chapter Project

Project Teacher Support

After the Lesson

Reteach ***Chapter Resources***
- Reteach
- Reading Strategies  ELL

Success for Every Learner

Review ***Interactive Answers and Solutions*** 
Solutions Key
Know-It Notebook™
- Big Ideas
- Chapter Review

Extend ***Chapter Resources***
- Challenge

Technology Highlights for the Teacher

 **Power Presentations**

Dynamic presentations to engage students. Complete PowerPoint® presentations for every lesson in Chapter 4.

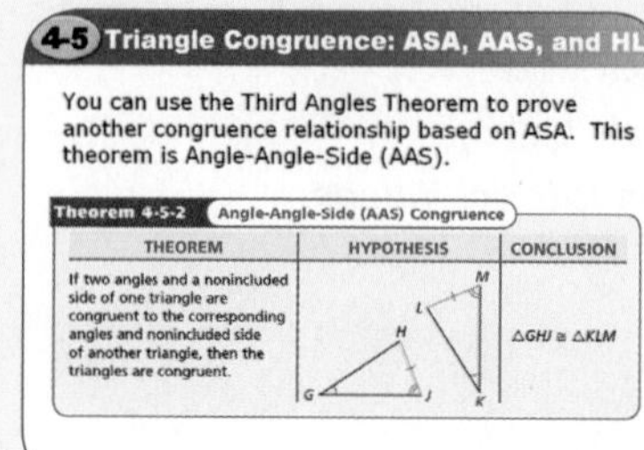

 **Teacher One Stop** SPANISH

Easy access to Chapter 4 resources and assessments. Includes lesson planning, test generation, and puzzle creation software.

 **Premier Online Edition** SPANISH

Chapter 4 includes Tutorial Videos, Lesson Activities, Lesson Quizzes, Homework Help, and Chapter Project.

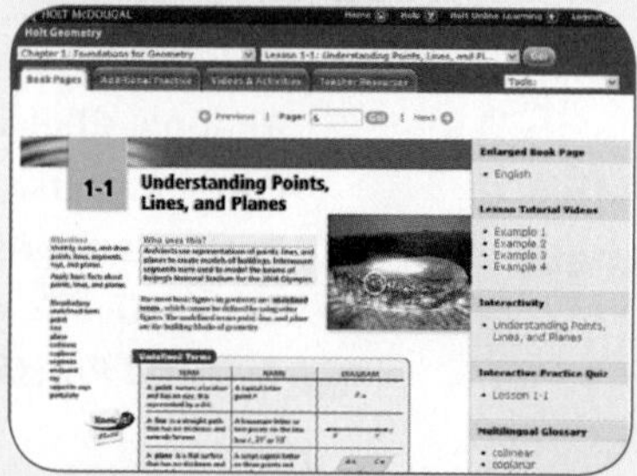

KEY: **SE** = *Student Edition* **TE** = *Teacher's Edition*  English Language Learners  Spanish version available  Available online  Available on CD- or DVD-ROM

CHAPTER 4

Reaching All Learners

Teaching tips to help all learners appear throughout the chapter. A few that target specific students are included in the lists below.

All Learners

Lab Activities
Practice and Problem Solving Workbook
Know-It Notebook

Special Needs Students

Practice A .... CRB
Reteach .... CRB
Reading Strategies .... CRB
Are You Ready? .... SE p. 213
Inclusion .... TE pp. 217, 235, 253, 255, 269, 282
IDEA Works!® Modified Worksheets and Tests
Ready to Go On? Intervention SPANISH
Know-It Notebook

Online Interactivities SPANISH

Lesson Tutorial Videos SPANISH

Developing Learners

Practice A .... CRB
Reteach .... CRB
Reading Strategies .... CRB
Are You Ready? .... SE p. 213
Vocabulary Connections .... SE p. 214
Questioning Strategies .... TE
Ready to Go On? Intervention SPANISH
Know-It Notebook
Homework Help Online
Online Interactivities SPANISH

Lesson Tutorial Videos SPANISH

On-Level Learners

Practice B .... CRB
Problem Solving .... CRB
Vocabulary Connections .... SE p. 214
Questioning Strategies .... TE
Ready to Go On? Intervention SPANISH
Know-It Notebook
Homework Help Online
Online Interactivities SPANISH

Advanced Learners

Practice C .... CRB
Challenge .... CRB
Challenge Exercises .... SE
Reading and Writing Math *Extend* .... TE p. 215
Critical Thinking .... TE pp. 245, 262, 266
Are You Ready? Enrichment SPANISH
Ready To Go On? Enrichment SPANISH

English Language Learners

ENGLISH LANGUAGE LEARNERS

Reading Strategies .... CRB
Are You Ready? Vocabulary .... SE p. 213
Vocabulary Connections .... SE p. 214
Vocabulary Review .... SE p. 284
English Language Learners TE pp. 215, 225, 232, 253, 294, 295
Success for Every Learner
Know-It Notebook
Spanish Study Guide (Resumen y Repaso)
Multilingual Glossary

Lesson Tutorial Videos SPANISH

Technology Highlights for Reaching All Learners

Lesson Tutorial Videos SPANISH

Starring Holt authors Ed Burger and Freddie Renfro! Live tutorials to support every lesson in Chapter 4.

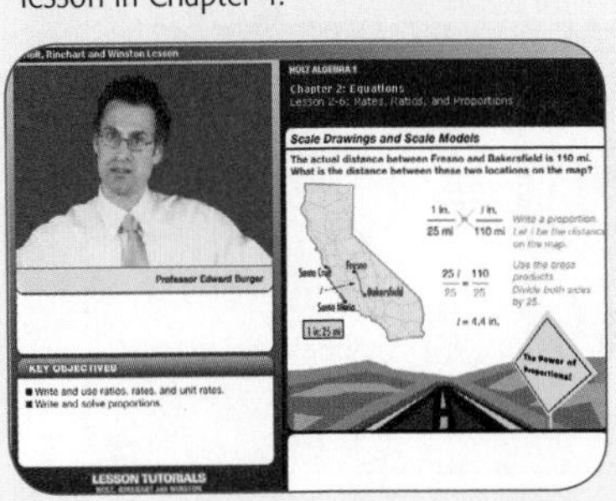

Multilingual Glossary

Searchable glossary includes definitions in English, Spanish, Vietnamese, Chinese, Hmong, Korean, and 4 other languages.

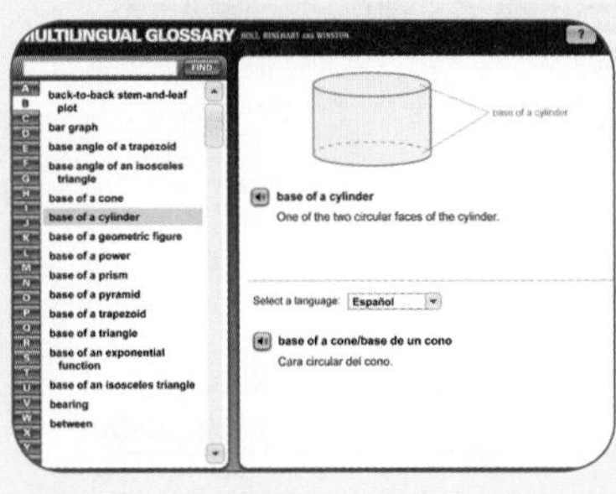

Online Interactivities

Interactive tutorials provide visually engaging alternative opportunities to learn concepts and master skills.

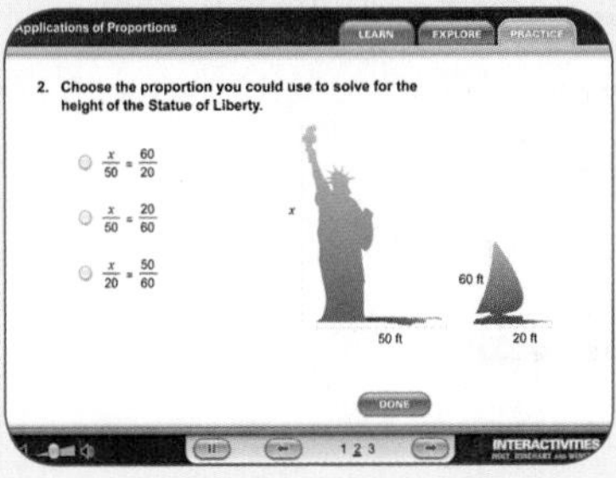

KEY: **SE** = *Student Edition* **TE** = *Teacher's Edition* **CRB** = *Chapter Resource Book* SPANISH Spanish version available; Available online; Available on CD- or DVD-ROM

Ongoing Assessment

Assessing Prior Knowledge

Determine whether students have the prerequisite concepts and skills for success in Chapter 4.

Are You Ready? SPANISH .... SE p. 213
Warm Up .... TE

Test Preparation

Provide review and practice for Chapter 4 and standardized tests.

Multi-Step Test Prep .... SE pp. 238, 280
Study Guide: Review .... SE pp. 284–287
Test Tackler .... SE pp. 290–291
Standardized Test Prep .... SE pp. 292–293
College Entrance Exam Practice .... SE p. 289
Countdown to Testing .... SE pp. C4-C27
IDEA Works!® Modified Worksheets and Tests

Alternative Assessment

Assess students' understanding of Chapter 4 concepts and combined problem-solving skills.

Chapter 4 Project .... SE p. 212
Alternative Assessment .... TE
Performance Assessment .... AR
Portfolio Assessment .... AR

Lesson Assessment

Provide formative assessment for each lesson of Chapter 4.

Questioning Strategies .... TE
Think and Discuss .... SE
Check It Out! Exercises .... SE
Write About It .... SE
Journal .... TE
Lesson Quiz .... TE
Alternative Assessment .... TE
IDEA Works!® Modified Worksheets and Tests

Weekly Assessment

Provide formative assessment for each section of Chapter 4.

Multi-Step Test Prep .... SE pp. 238, 280
Ready to Go On? SPANISH .... SE pp. 239, 281
Section Quizzes .... AR
Test and Practice Generator .... *Teacher One Stop*

Chapter Assessment

Provide summative assessment of Chapter 4 mastery.

Chapter 4 Test .... SE p. 288
Chapter Test (Levels A, B, C) .... AR
- Multiple Choice
- Free Response

Cumulative Test .... AR
Test and Practice Generator .... *Teacher One Stop*
IDEA Works!® Modified Worksheets and Tests

Technology Highlights for Assessment

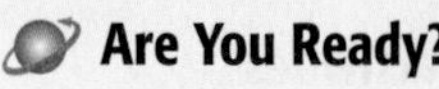

Are You Ready? SPANISH

Automatically assess readiness and prescribe intervention for Chapter 4 prerequisite skills.

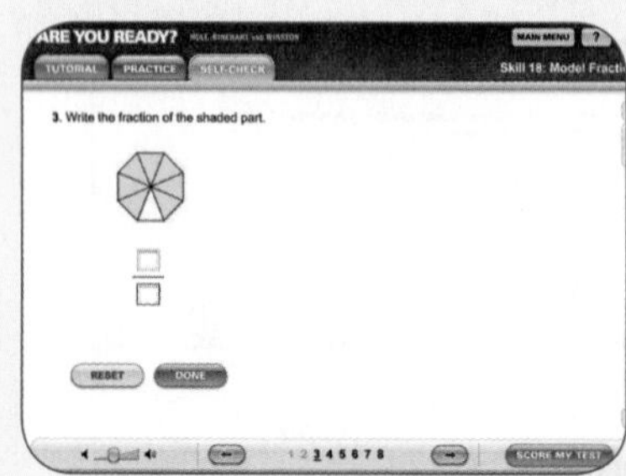

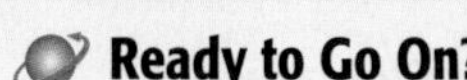

Ready to Go On?

Automatically assess understanding of and prescribe intervention for Sections 4A and 4B.

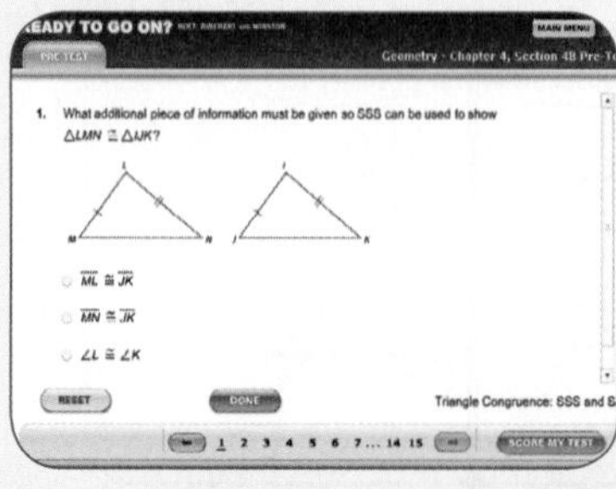

Test and Practice Generator

Use Chapter 4 problem banks to create assessments and worksheets to print out or deliver online. Includes dynamic problems.

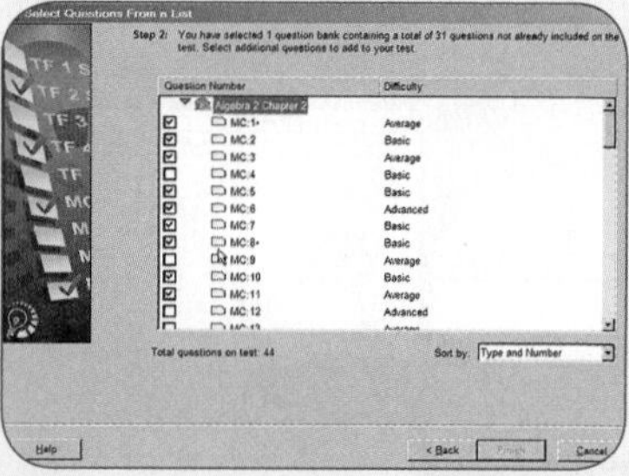

KEY: **SE** = *Student Edition* **TE** = *Teacher's Edition* **AR** = *Assessment Resources* SPANISH Spanish version available; Available online; Available on CD- or DVD-ROM

Formal Assessment

Three levels (A, B, C) of multiple-choice and free-response chapter tests, along with a performance assessment, are available in the *Assessment Resources.*

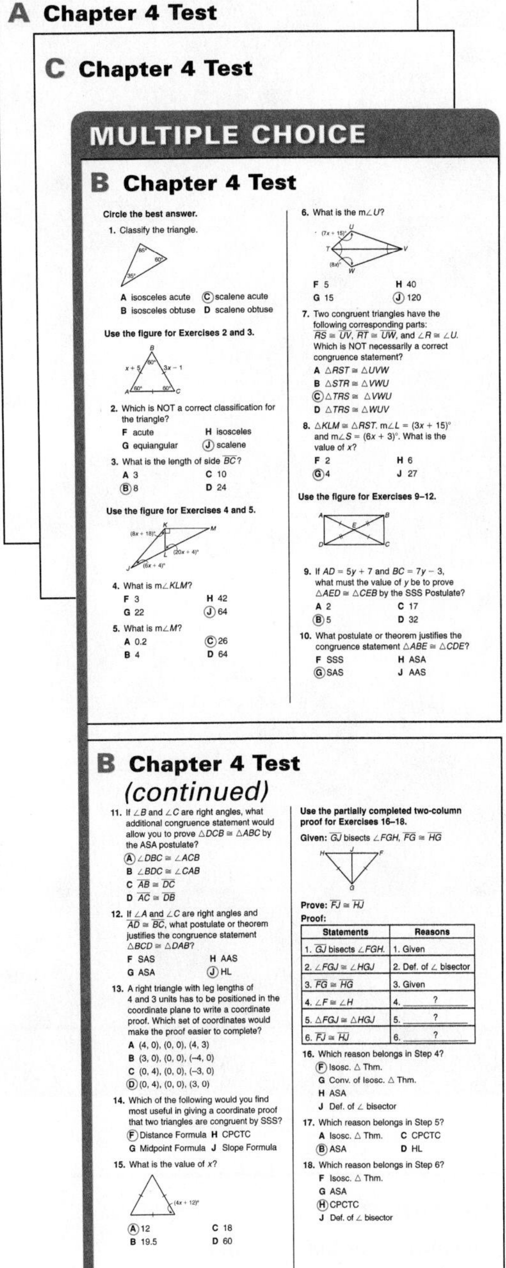

A Chapter 4 Test

C Chapter 4 Test

MULTIPLE CHOICE

B Chapter 4 Test

Circle the best answer.

1. Classify the triangle.
   A isosceles acute (C) scalene acute
   B isosceles obtuse D scalene obtuse

Use the figure for Exercises 2 and 3.

2. Which is NOT a correct classification for the triangle?
   F acute H isosceles
   G equiangular (J) scalene
3. What is the length of side $\overline{BC}$?
   A 3 C 10
   (B) 8 D 24

Use the figure for Exercises 4 and 5.

4. What is $m\angle KLM$?
   F 3 H 42
   G 22 (J) 64
5. What is $m\angle M$?
   A 0.2 (C) 26
   B 4 D 64
6. What is the $m\angle U$?
   F 5 H 40
   G 15 (J) 120
7. Two congruent triangles have the following corresponding parts: $\overline{RS} \cong \overline{UV}$, $\overline{RT} \cong \overline{UW}$, and $\angle R \cong \angle U$. Which is NOT necessarily a correct congruence statement?
   A $\triangle RST \cong \triangle UVW$
   B $\triangle STR \cong \triangle VWU$
   (C) $\triangle TRS \cong \triangle VWU$
   D $\triangle TRS \cong \triangle WUV$
8. $\triangle KLM \cong \triangle RST$. $m\angle L = (3x + 15)°$ and $m\angle S = (6x + 3)°$. What is the value of x?
   F 2 H 6
   (G) 4 J 27

Use the figure for Exercises 9–12.

9. If $AD = 5y + 7$ and $BC = 7y - 3$, what must the value of y be to prove $\triangle AED \cong \triangle CEB$ by the SSS Postulate?
   A 2 C 17
   (B) 5 D 32
10. What postulate or theorem justifies the congruence statement $\triangle ABE \cong \triangle CDE$?
    F SSS H ASA
    (G) SAS J AAS

B Chapter 4 Test (continued)

11. If $\angle B$ and $\angle C$ are right angles, what additional congruence statement would allow you to prove $\triangle DCB \cong \triangle ABC$ by the ASA postulate?
    (A) $\angle DBC \cong \angle ACB$
    B $\angle BDC \cong \angle CAB$
    C $\overline{AB} \cong \overline{DC}$
    D $\overline{AC} \cong \overline{DB}$
12. If $\angle A$ and $\angle C$ are right angles and $\overline{AD} \cong \overline{BC}$, what postulate or theorem justifies the congruence statement $\triangle BCD \cong \triangle DAB$?
    F SAS H AAS
    G ASA (J) HL
13. A right triangle with leg lengths of 4 and 3 units has to be positioned in the coordinate plane to write a coordinate proof. Which set of coordinates would make the proof easier to complete?
    A (4, 0), (0, 0), (4, 3)
    B (3, 0), (0, 0), (−4, 0)
    C (0, 4), (0, 0), (−3, 0)
    (D) (0, 4), (0, 0), (3, 0)
14. Which of the following would you find most useful in giving a coordinate proof that two triangles are congruent by SSS?
    (F) Distance Formula H CPCTC
    G Midpoint Formula J Slope Formula
15. What is the value of x?
    (A) 12 C 18
    B 19.5 D 60

Use the partially completed two-column proof for Exercises 16–18.

Given: $\overline{GJ}$ bisects $\angle FGH$, $\overline{FG} \cong \overline{HG}$

Prove: $\overline{FJ} \cong \overline{HJ}$

Proof:

Statements	Reasons
1. $\overline{GJ}$ bisects $\angle FGH$.	1. Given
2. $\angle FGJ \cong \angle HGJ$	2. Def. of $\angle$ bisector
3. $\overline{FG} \cong \overline{HG}$	3. Given
4. $\angle F \cong \angle H$	4. ?
5. $\triangle FGJ \cong \triangle HGJ$	5. ?
6. $\overline{FJ} \cong \overline{HJ}$	6. ?

16. Which reason belongs in Step 4?
    (F) Isosc. △ Thm.
    G Conv. of Isosc. △ Thm.
    H ASA
    J Def. of ∠ bisector
17. Which reason belongs in Step 5?
    A Isosc. △ Thm. C CPCTC
    (B) ASA D HL
18. Which reason belongs in Step 6?
    F Isosc. △ Thm.
    G ASA
    (H) CPCTC
    J Def. of ∠ bisector

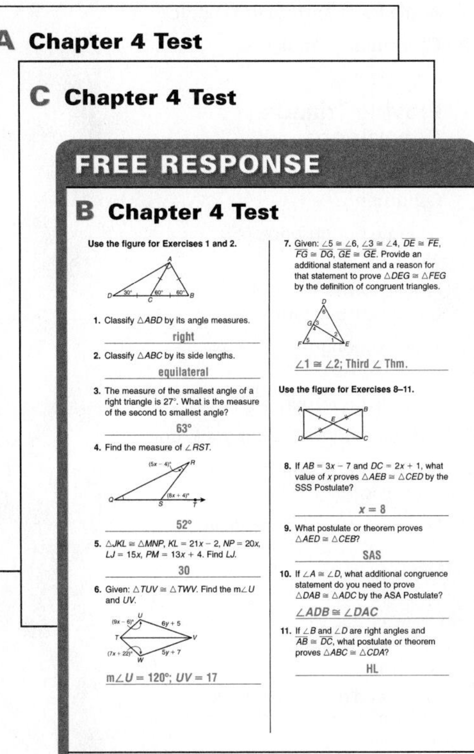

A Chapter 4 Test

C Chapter 4 Test

FREE RESPONSE

B Chapter 4 Test

Use the figure for Exercises 1 and 2.

1. Classify $\triangle ABD$ by its angle measures. right
2. Classify $\triangle ABC$ by its side lengths. equilateral
3. The measure of the smallest angle of a right triangle is 27°. What is the measure of the second to smallest angle? 63°
4. Find the measure of $\angle RST$. 52°
5. $\triangle JKL \cong \triangle MNP$, $KL = 21x - 2$, $NP = 20x$, $LJ = 15x$, $PM = 13x + 4$. Find LJ. 30
6. Given: $\triangle TUV \cong \triangle TWV$. Find the $m\angle U$ and UV. $m\angle U = 120°$; $UV = 17$
7. Given: $\angle 5 \cong \angle 6$, $\angle 3 \cong \angle 4$, $\overline{DE} \cong \overline{FE}$, $\overline{FG} \cong \overline{DG}$, $\overline{GE} \cong \overline{GE}$. Provide an additional statement and a reason for that statement to prove $\triangle DEG \cong \triangle FEG$ by the definition of congruent triangles. $\angle 1 \cong \angle 2$; Third ∠ Thm.

Use the figure for Exercises 8–11.

8. If $AB = 3x - 7$ and $DC = 2x + 1$, what value of x proves $\triangle AEB \cong \triangle CED$ by the SSS Postulate? $x = 8$
9. What postulate or theorem proves $\triangle AED \cong \triangle CEB$? SAS
10. If $\angle A \cong \angle D$, what additional congruence statement do you need to prove $\triangle DAB \cong \triangle ADC$ by the ASA Postulate? $\angle ADB \cong \angle DAC$
11. If $\angle B$ and $\angle D$ are right angles and $\overline{AB} \cong \overline{DC}$, what postulate or theorem proves $\triangle ABC \cong \triangle CDA$? HL

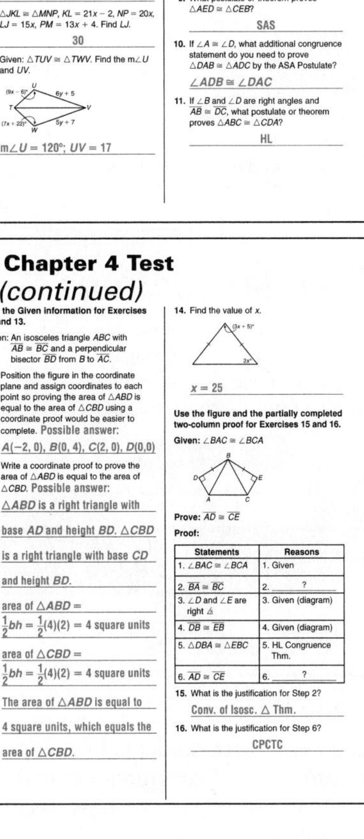

B Chapter 4 Test (continued)

Use the Given information for Exercises 12 and 13.

Given: An isosceles triangle ABC with $\overline{AB} \cong \overline{BC}$ and a perpendicular bisector $\overline{BD}$ from B to $\overline{AC}$.

12. Position the figure in the coordinate plane and assign coordinates to each point so proving the area of $\triangle ABD$ is equal to the area of $\triangle CBD$ using a coordinate proof would be easier to complete. Possible answer: $A(-2, 0)$, $B(0, 4)$, $C(2, 0)$, $D(0,0)$
13. Write a coordinate proof to prove the area of $\triangle ABD$ is equal to the area of $\triangle CBD$. Possible answer: $\triangle ABD$ is a right triangle with base AD and height BD. $\triangle CBD$ is a right triangle with base CD and height BD. area of $\triangle ABD = \frac{1}{2}bh = \frac{1}{2}(4)(2) = 4$ square units; area of $\triangle CBD = \frac{1}{2}bh = \frac{1}{2}(4)(2) = 4$ square units. The area of $\triangle ABD$ is equal to 4 square units, which equals the area of $\triangle CBD$.
14. Find the value of x. $x = 25$

Use the figure and the partially completed two-column proof for Exercises 15 and 16.

Given: $\angle BAC \cong \angle BCA$

Prove: $\overline{AD} \cong \overline{CE}$

Proof:

Statements	Reasons
1. $\angle BAC \cong \angle BCA$	1. Given
2. $\overline{BA} \cong \overline{BC}$	2. ?
3. $\angle D$ and $\angle E$ are right ∠s	3. Given (diagram)
4. $\overline{DB} \cong \overline{EB}$	4. Given (diagram)
5. $\triangle DBA \cong \triangle EBC$	5. HL Congruence Thm.
6. $\overline{AD} \cong \overline{CE}$	6. ?

15. What is the justification for Step 2? Conv. of Isosc. △ Thm.
16. What is the justification for Step 6? CPCTC

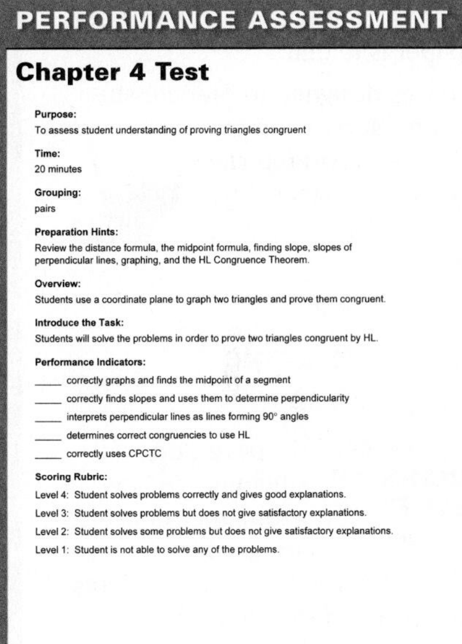

PERFORMANCE ASSESSMENT

Chapter 4 Test

Purpose:
To assess student understanding of proving triangles congruent

Time:
20 minutes

Grouping:
pairs

Preparation Hints:
Review the distance formula, the midpoint formula, finding slope, slopes of perpendicular lines, graphing, and the HL Congruence Theorem.

Overview:
Students use a coordinate plane to graph two triangles and prove them congruent.

Introduce the Task:
Students will solve the problems in order to prove two triangles congruent by HL.

Performance Indicators:
_____ correctly graphs and finds the midpoint of a segment
_____ correctly finds slopes and uses them to determine perpendicularity
_____ interprets perpendicular lines as lines forming 90° angles
_____ determines correct congruencies to use HL
_____ correctly uses CPCTC

Scoring Rubric:
Level 4: Student solves problems correctly and gives good explanations.
Level 3: Student solves problems but does not give satisfactory explanations.
Level 2: Student solves some problems but does not give satisfactory explanations.
Level 1: Student is not able to solve any of the problems.

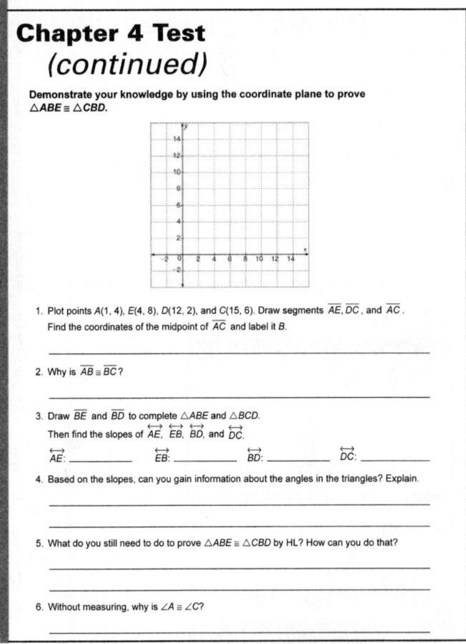

Chapter 4 Test (continued)

Demonstrate your knowledge by using the coordinate plane to prove $\triangle ABE \cong \triangle CBD$.

1. Plot points $A(1, 4)$, $E(4, 8)$, $D(12, 2)$, and $C(15, 6)$. Draw segments $\overline{AE}$, $\overline{DC}$, and $\overline{AC}$. Find the coordinates of the midpoint of $\overline{AC}$ and label it B.
2. Why is $\overline{AB} \cong \overline{BC}$?
3. Draw $\overline{BE}$ and $\overline{BD}$ to complete $\triangle ABE$ and $\triangle BCD$. Then find the slopes of $\overleftrightarrow{AE}$, $\overleftrightarrow{EB}$, $\overleftrightarrow{BD}$, and $\overleftrightarrow{DC}$.
   $\overleftrightarrow{AE}$: _____ $\overleftrightarrow{EB}$: _____ $\overleftrightarrow{BD}$: _____ $\overleftrightarrow{DC}$: _____
4. Based on the slopes, can you gain information about the angles in the triangles? Explain.
5. What do you still need to do to prove $\triangle ABE \cong \triangle CBD$ by HL? How can you do that?
6. Without measuring, why is $\angle A \cong \angle C$?

Teacher One Stop™

Test & Practice Generator

Create and customize Chapter 4 Tests. Instantly generate multiple test versions, answer keys, and practice versions of test items.

Modified chapter tests that address special learning needs are available in *IDEA Works!® Modified Worksheets and Tests.*

CHAPTER 4

SECTION 4A

Triangles and Congruence

On page 238, students use the ancient art of paper folding to make an origami swan. They answer questions about the sides, angles, and triangles created when a square piece of paper is folded.

Exercises designed to prepare students for success on the Multi-Step Test Prep can be found on pages 220, 229, and 236.

SECTION 4B

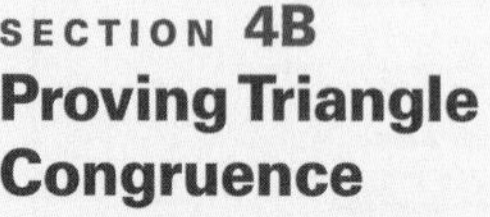

Proving Triangle Congruence

On page 280, students see how geometric concepts are used to design and construct a doghouse. Students prove several facts about the triangles used in the design, including that they are congruent.

Exercises designed to prepare students for success on the Multi-Step Test Prep can be found on pages 247, 258, 264, 271, and 278.

Interactivities Online ▶

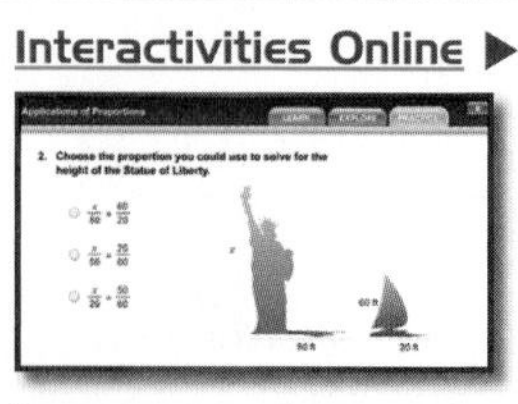

Lessons 4-3, 4-8.

Video Lesson Tutorials Online

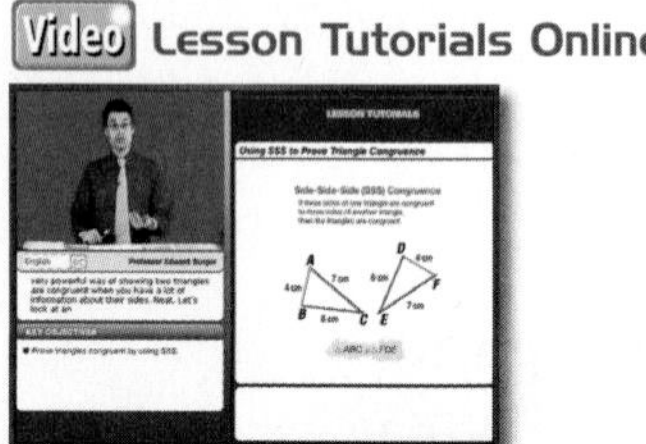

Lesson Tutorial Videos are available for EVERY example.

CHAPTER 4

Triangle Congruence

Chapter Focus

- Prove and use the Triangle Sum Theorem
- Understand congruence and prove and apply congruence relationships for triangles

Flexible Creations

When you turn a kaleidoscope, the shapes flip to form a variety of designs. You can create flexagons that also flip to form patterns.

go.hrw.com
Chapter Project Online
KEYWORD: MG7 ChProj

Flexible Creations

About the Project

In the Chapter Project, students fold strips of paper to form rows of congruent equilateral triangles. Then they use these strips to create their own polygonal flexagons.

Project Resources

All project resources for teachers and students are provided online.

Materials:

- paper, scissors, glue, ruler and protractor or straightedge and compass
- geometry software

ARE YOU READY?

Vocabulary

Match each term on the left with a definition on the right.

1. acute angle F
2. congruent segments D
3. obtuse angle B
4. postulate A
5. triangle E

A. a statement that is accepted as true without proof
B. an angle that measures greater than 90° and less than 180°
C. a statement that you can prove
D. segments that have the same length
E. a three-sided polygon
F. an angle that measures greater than 0° and less than 90°

Measure Angles

Use a protractor to measure each angle.

6. 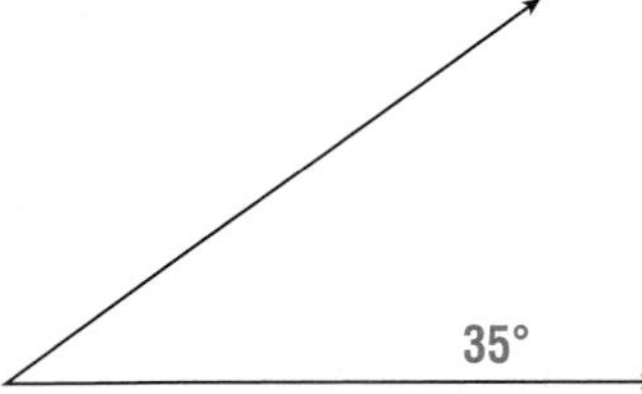 35°

7.  90°

Use a protractor to draw an angle with each of the following measures.

8. 20°
9. 63°
10. 105°
11. 158°

For exercises 8–11 check students' drawings.

Solve Equations with Fractions

Solve.

12. $\frac{9}{2}x + 7 = 25$ 4
13. $3x - \frac{2}{3} = \frac{4}{3}$ $\frac{2}{3}$
14. $x - \frac{1}{5} = \frac{12}{5}$ $2\frac{3}{5}$
15. $2y = 5y - \frac{21}{2}$ $3\frac{1}{2}$

Connect Words and Algebra

Write an equation for each statement.

16. Tanya's age t is three times Martin's age m. $t = 3m$
17. Twice the length of a segment x is 9 ft. $2x = 9$
18. The sum of 53° and twice an angle measure y is 90°. $53 + 2y = 90$
19. The price of a radio r is $25 less than the price of a CD player p. $r = p - 25$
20. Half the amount of liquid j in a jar is 5 oz more than the amount of liquid b in a bowl. $\frac{1}{2}j = b + 5$

CHAPTER 4

ARE YOU READY?

Organizer

Objective: Assess students' understanding of prerequisite skills.

Prerequisite Skills

Measure Angles
Solve Equations with Fractions
Connect Words and Algebra

Assessing Prior Knowledge

INTERVENTION

Diagnose and Prescribe

Use this page to determine whether intervention is necessary or whether enrichment is appropriate.

Resources

 ***Are You Ready? Intervention and Enrichment*** **Worksheets**

 ***Are You Ready?*** **CD-ROM**

 ***Are You Ready?*** **Online**

my.hrw.com

ARE YOU READY?

Diagnose and Prescribe

NO INTERVENE

Prerequisite Skill	*Are You Ready? Intervention*, Chapter 4 — Worksheets	CD-ROM	Online
Measure Angles	Skill 24	Activity 24	Diagnose and Prescribe Online
Solve Equations with Fractions	Skill 71	Activity 71	
Connect Words and Algebra	Skill 58	Activity 58	

YES ENRICH

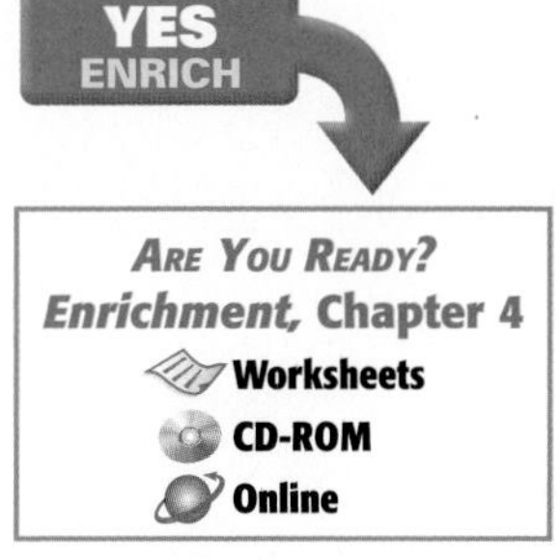

***Are You Ready? Enrichment*, Chapter 4**
Worksheets
CD-ROM
Online

Study Guide: Preview

Organizer

Objective: Help students organize the new concepts they will learn in Chapter 4.

Online Edition
Multilingual Glossary

Resources

Teacher One Stop™
PuzzleView

***Multilingual Glossary* Online**
go.hrw.com
KEYWORD: MG7 Glossary

Answers to *Vocabulary Connections*

1. 
Possible answer: Yes, I think the △ is acute.
2. Possible answer: *Exterior* means "outside." An ext. ∠ of a △ is located outside the △.
3. Possible answer: An obtuse △ is a △ that contains an obtuse ∠.
4. Possible answer:

CHAPTER 4

Study Guide: Preview

Where You've Been

Previously, you
- measured and classified angles.
- wrote definitions for triangles and other polygons.
- used deductive reasoning.
- planned and wrote proofs.

In This Chapter

You will study
- classifying triangles.
- proving triangles congruent.
- using corresponding parts of congruent triangles in proofs.
- positioning figures in the coordinate plane for use in proofs.
- proving theorems about isosceles and equilateral triangles.

Where You're Going

You can use the skills learned in this chapter
- in Algebra 2 and Precalculus.
- in other classes, such as in Physics when you solve for various measures of a triangle and in Geography when you identify a location using coordinates.
- outside of school to make greeting cards or to design jewelry or whenever you create sets of objects that have the same size and shape.

Key Vocabulary/Vocabulario

acute triangle	triángulo acutángulo
congruent polygons	polígonos congruentes
corollary	corolario
equilateral triangle	triángulo equilátero
exterior angle	ángulo externo
interior angle	ángulo interno
isosceles triangle	triángulo isósceles
obtuse triangle	triángulo obtusángulo
right triangle	triángulo rectángulo
scalene triangle	triángulo escaleno

Vocabulary Connections

To become familiar with some of the vocabulary terms in the chapter, consider the following. You may refer to the chapter, the glossary, or a dictionary if you like.

1. The Latin word *acutus* means "pointed" or "sharp." Draw a triangle that looks pointed or sharp. Do you think this is an **acute triangle**?
2. Consider the everyday meaning of the word *exterior*. Where do you think an **exterior angle** of a triangle is located?
3. You already know the definition of an obtuse angle. Use this meaning to make a conjecture about an **obtuse triangle**.
4. *Scalene* comes from a Greek word that means "uneven." If the sides of a **scalene triangle** are uneven, draw an example of such a triangle.

Reading Strategy: Read Geometry Symbols

In Geometry we often use symbols to communicate information.
When studying each lesson, read both the symbols and the words slowly and carefully. Reading aloud can sometimes help you translate symbols into words.

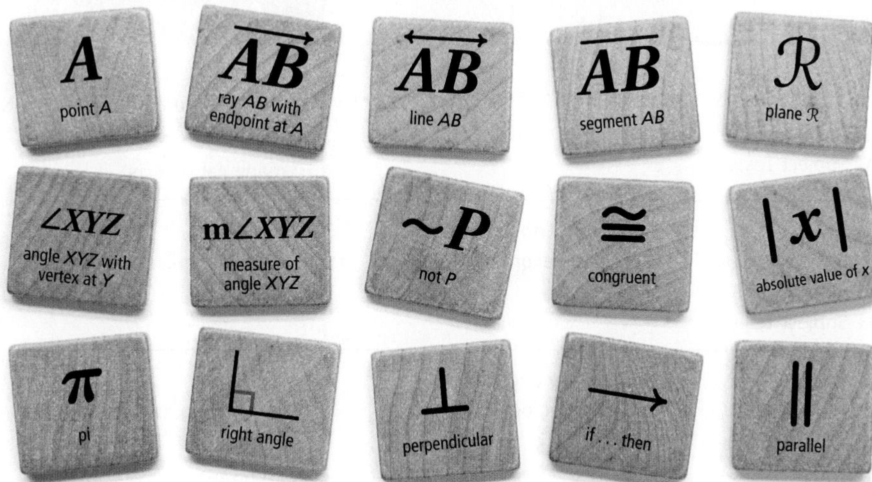

Throughout this course, you will use these symbols and combinations of these symbols to represent various geometric statements.

Symbol Combinations	Translated into Words
$\overleftrightarrow{ST} \parallel \overleftrightarrow{UV}$	Line *ST* is parallel to line *UV*.
$\overline{BC} \perp \overline{GH}$	Segment *BC* is perpendicular to segment *GH*.
$p \rightarrow q$	If *p*, then *q*.
$m\angle QRS = 45°$	The measure of angle *QRS* is 45 degrees.
$\angle CDE \cong \angle LMN$	Angle *CDE* is congruent to angle *LMN*.

Try This

Rewrite each statement using symbols.

1. the absolute value of 2 times pi
2. The measure of angle 2 is 125 degrees.
3. Segment *XY* is perpendicular to line *BC*.
4. If not *p*, then not *q*.

Translate the symbols into words.

5. $m\angle FGH = m\angle VWX$
6. $\overleftrightarrow{ZA} \parallel \overleftrightarrow{TU}$
7. $\sim p \rightarrow q$
8. $\overrightarrow{ST}$ bisects $\angle TSU$.

Reading and Writing Math

Organizer

Objective: Help students apply the strategies to understand and retain key concepts.

Online Edition

Resources

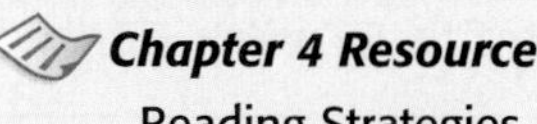

Chapter 4 Resource Book

Reading Strategies

ENGLISH LANGUAGE LEARNERS

Reading Strategy: Read Geometry Symbols

Discuss Students benefit from reading geometric symbols and their meanings aloud.

Extend Throughout Chapter 4, have students present proofs and read the geometric symbols in them. Discuss how the proofs would differ if the symbols were changed or left out.

Answers to *Try This*

1. $|2\pi|$
2. $m\angle 2 = 125°$
3. $\overline{XY} \perp \overleftrightarrow{BC}$
4. $\sim p \rightarrow \sim q$
5. The measure of angle *FGH* equals the measure of angle *VWX*.
6. Line *ZA* is parallel to line *TU*.
7. If not *p*, then *q*.
8. Ray *ST* bisects angle *TSU*.

Reading Connection

Compass Constructions
by Christopher M. Freeman

The author presents scores of constructions, including triangles of all types, quadrilaterals, and the Golden Ratio. Each construction is precisely described and illustrated.

Activity Have students construct two overlapping circles with the same radius. Have them connect the centers of the two circles with a line segment, and then connect the endpoints of the segment to one of the two intersections of the circles. Ask students to explain why the resulting triangle must be equilateral. All three sides are radii of congruent circles.

SECTION 4A

Triangles and Congruence

One-Minute Section Planner

Lesson	Lab Resources	Materials
Lesson 4-1 Classifying Triangles • Classify triangles by their angle measures and side lengths. • Use triangle classification to find angle measures and side lengths. ☑ SAT-10 ☑ NAEP ☑ ACT ☑ SAT ☑ SAT Subject Tests		**Required** straightedge and compass (MK) **Optional** triangular objects
4-2 Geometry Lab Develop the Triangle Sum Theorem • Use patty paper to discover the relationship between the measures of the interior angles of a triangle. ☐ SAT-10 ☑ NAEP ☑ ACT ☐ SAT ☐ SAT Subject Tests	***Geometry Lab Activities*** 4-2 Lab Recording Sheet	**Required** patty or similar paper
Lesson 4-2 Angle Relationships in Triangles • Find the measures of interior and exterior angles of triangles. • Apply theorems about the interior and exterior angles of triangles. ☑ SAT-10 ☑ NAEP ☑ ACT ☑ SAT ☑ SAT Subject Tests	***Technology Lab Activities*** 4-2 Technology Lab	**Optional** geometry software
Lesson 4-3 Congruent Triangles • Use properties of congruent triangles. • Prove triangles congruent by using the definition of congruence. ☐ SAT-10 ☑ NAEP ☑ ACT ☑ SAT ☑ SAT Subject Tests		**Optional** patterns with congruent triangles, color pencils, ruler (MK), tracing paper

MK = *Manipulatives Kit*

Math Background

Professional Learning

TRIANGLE GEOMETRY

Lessons 4-1 to 4-3

In 1816, the French mathematician August Leopold Crelle stated, "It is indeed wonderful that so simple a figure as the triangle is so inexhaustible in properties." The study of these seemingly inexhaustible properties begins in Chapter 4 with a system for classifying triangles and a proof of the Triangle Sum Theorem. Building logically on these foundations, it is possible to develop and prove theorems that are increasingly elegant and unexpected. For example, in Lesson 5-3, students encounter the rather surprising fact that the three altitudes of any triangle are concurrent.

As students study Chapter 4 and the following chapters, it is helpful to highlight this "family tree" of triangle geometry. As described below, the Parallel Postulate leads to the Triangle Sum Theorem. This theorem in turn leads to a handful of useful corollaries (results whose proofs follow immediately from another theorem). Continuing in this way, one can trace the "logical ancestry" of the concurrency theorems and triangle inequalities of Chapter 5. Drawing attention to this logical thread that connects the milestones of triangle geometry helps students understand that the triangle theorems are not simply isolated facts to be memorized, but part of an interconnected scaffolding that gives mathematics a coherent structure.

THE TRIANGLE SUM THEOREM

Lesson 4-2

The Triangle Sum Theorem states that the sum of the angle measures of a triangle is 180°. For many students, this is the first true geometry theorem that they see, perhaps as early as the intermediate grades or middle school. Students should recognize, however, that it is only now that they can prove this central fact.

It is also important to note that the proof of the Triangle Sum Theorem depends very directly on the Parallel Postulate. In fact, the first step of the proof requires drawing a line ℓ that is parallel to one side of the triangle such that ℓ passes through the vertex not on that side of the triangle.

Furthermore, the Triangle Sum Theorem can be shown to be logically equivalent to the Parallel Postulate. That is, either of the two statements may be taken as a postulate. Then, given this postulate plus the other axioms of Euclidean geometry, the other statement can be proved. As discussed in the Math Background notes for Section 3A, non-Euclidean geometries assume that the Parallel Postulate does not hold. Therefore, in any non-Euclidean geometry, the sum of the angles of a triangle is not 180°.

The Triangle Sum Theorem shows that the standard triangle classifications by angle measures make sense. For example, an obtuse triangle is defined to be a triangle with one obtuse angle. The Triangle Sum Theorem shows that it is impossible for a triangle to have more than one obtuse angle.

TRIANGLE CONGRUENCE

Lesson 4-3

Two geometric figures are congruent if they are the same size and shape; in other words, if one of the figures can be moved so that it fits perfectly on top of the other figure. This is the intuitive idea behind the more rigorous mathematical definition of congruence: two figures are congruent if one can be transformed into the other by an isometry (that is, by a combination of translations, reflections, and rotations).

For polygons, the definition of congruence can be stated in terms of corresponding sides and angles. In particular, two triangles are congruent if and only if the sides and angles can be matched up so that the corresponding sides are congruent and the corresponding angles are congruent. This definition of triangle congruence means that six correspondences must be checked in order to conclude that two triangles are congruent (three pairs of corresponding sides and three pairs of corresponding angles). The congruence theorems in Section 4B provide shortcuts for proving triangles congruent.

4-1 Organizer

Pacing: Traditional $\frac{1}{2}$ day
Block $\frac{1}{4}$ day

Objectives: Classify triangles by their angle measures and side lengths.

Use triangle classification to find angle measures and side lengths.

Online Edition
Tutorial Videos

Countdown Week 7

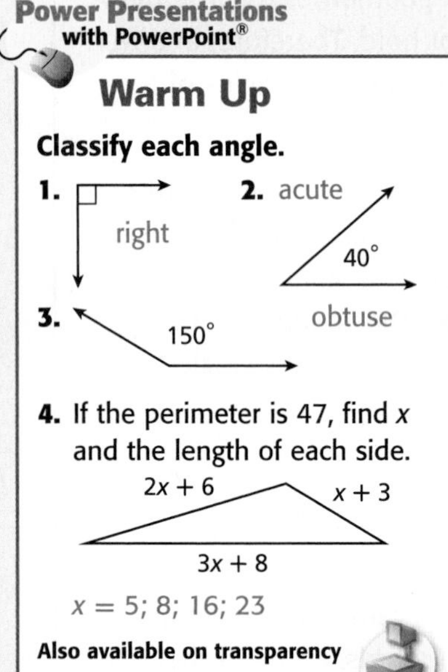

Power Presentations with PowerPoint®

Warm Up

Classify each angle.

1. right

2. acute 40°

3. 150° obtuse

4. If the perimeter is 47, find x and the length of each side.

$2x + 6$, $x + 3$, $3x + 8$

$x = 5$; 8; 16; 23

Also available on transparency

Q: What do you call a tall kettle on the stove?

A: Hypotenuse!

4-1 Classifying Triangles

Objectives

Classify triangles by their angle measures and side lengths.

Use triangle classification to find angle measures and side lengths.

Vocabulary

acute triangle
equiangular triangle
right triangle
obtuse triangle
equilateral triangle
isosceles triangle
scalene triangle

Who uses this?

Manufacturers use properties of triangles to calculate the amount of material needed to make triangular objects. (See Example 4.)

A triangle is a steel percussion instrument in the shape of an *equilateral triangle.* Different-sized triangles produce different musical notes when struck with a metal rod.

Recall that a *triangle* ($\triangle$) is a polygon with three sides. Triangles can be classified in two ways: by their angle measures or by their side lengths.

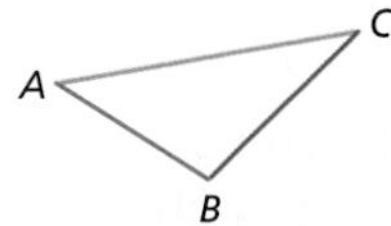

$\overline{AB}$, $\overline{BC}$, and $\overline{AC}$ are the *sides* of $\triangle ABC$. A, B, and C are the triangle's *vertices*.

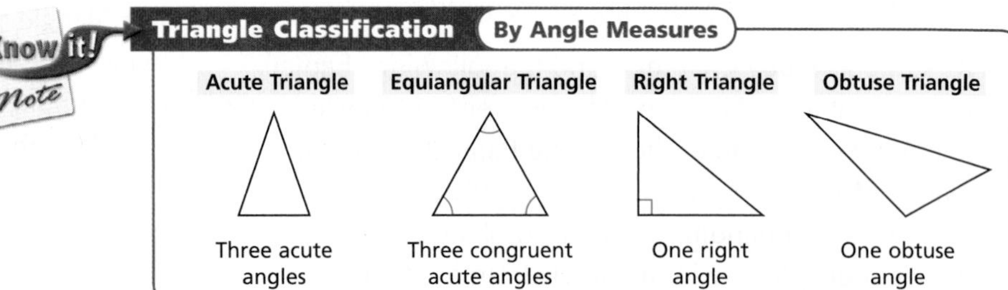

Triangle Classification **By Angle Measures**

Acute Triangle	Equiangular Triangle	Right Triangle	Obtuse Triangle
Three acute angles	Three congruent acute angles	One right angle	One obtuse angle

EXAMPLE 1 Classifying Triangles by Angle Measures

Classify each triangle by its angle measures.

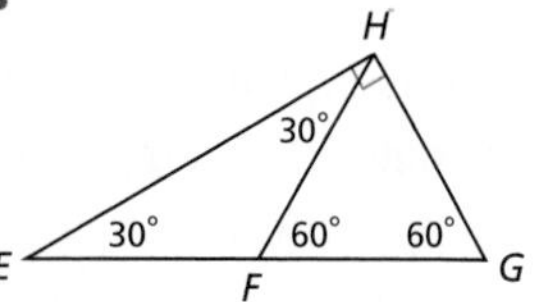

A $\triangle EHG$

$\angle EHG$ is a right angle. So $\triangle EHG$ is a right triangle.

B $\triangle EFH$

$\angle EFH$ and $\angle HFG$ form a linear pair, so they are supplementary. Therefore $m\angle EFH + m\angle HFG = 180°$. By substitution, $m\angle EFH + 60° = 180°$. So $m\angle EFH = 120°$. $\triangle EFH$ is an obtuse triangle by definition.

1. Use the diagram to classify $\triangle FHG$ by its angle measures. **equiangular**

State Resources

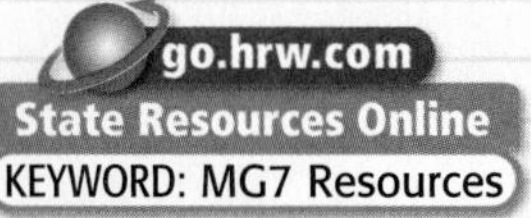

1 Introduce

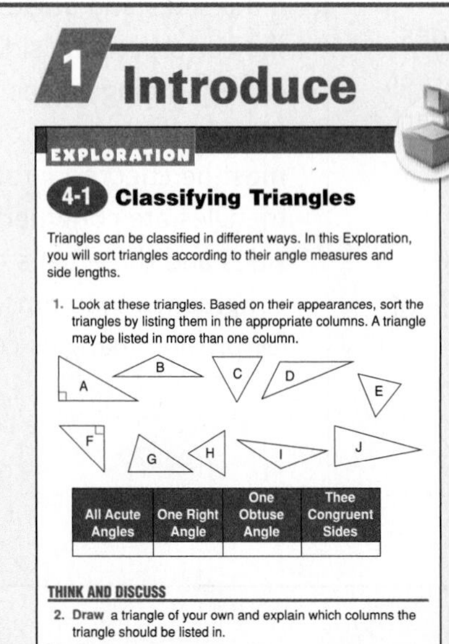

EXPLORATION

4-1 Classifying Triangles

Triangles can be classified in different ways. In this Exploration, you will sort triangles according to their angle measures and side lengths.

1. Look at these triangles. Based on their appearances, sort the triangles by listing them in the appropriate columns. A triangle may be listed in more than one column.

All Acute Angles	One Right Angle	One Obtuse Angle	Thee Congruent Sides

THINK AND DISCUSS

2. Draw a triangle of your own and explain which columns the triangle should be listed in.

Motivate

Ask students to identify different types of triangles found in the classroom and/or in the real world, such as musical triangles, art sponges, or roof tops. Give them models of different types of triangles and have them measure the sides and angles. Explain that they will learn how to classify these triangles according to their side lengths and their angle measures. Triangle models can be found in the Manipulatives Kit (MK).

Explorations and answers are provided in *Alternate Openers: Explorations Transparencies.*

Triangle Classification | **By Side Lengths**

Equilateral Triangle	Isosceles Triangle	Scalene Triangle
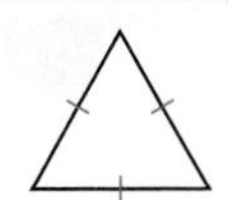	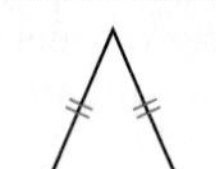	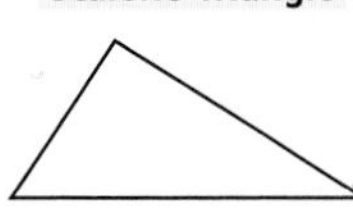
Three congruent sides	At least two congruent sides	No congruent sides

EXAMPLE 2 Classifying Triangles by Side Lengths

Remember!

When you look at a figure, you cannot assume segments are congruent based on their appearance. They must be marked as congruent.

Classify each triangle by its side lengths.

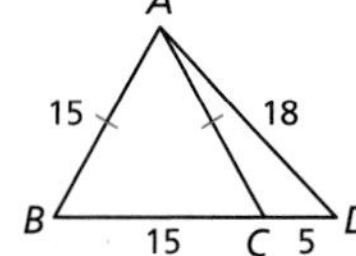

A $\triangle ABC$

From the figure, $\overline{AB} \cong \overline{AC}$. So $AC = 15$, and $\triangle ABC$ is equilateral.

B $\triangle ABD$

By the Segment Addition Postulate, $BD = BC + CD = 15 + 5 = 20$. Since no sides are congruent, $\triangle ABD$ is scalene.

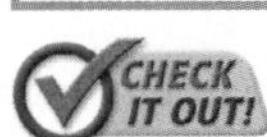

2. Use the diagram to classify $\triangle ACD$ by its side lengths. scalene

EXAMPLE 3 Using Triangle Classification

Find the side lengths of the triangle.

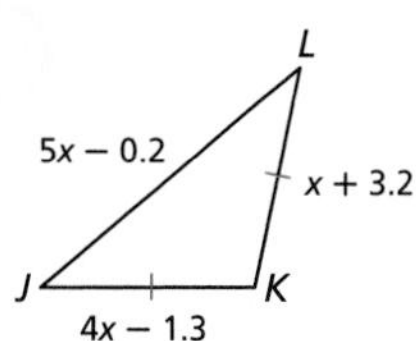

Step 1 Find the value of x.

$\overline{JK} \cong \overline{KL}$	*Given*
$JK = KL$	*Def. of ≅ segs.*
$(4x - 1.3) = (x + 3.2)$	*Substitute (4x − 13) for JK and (x + 3.2) for KL.*
$3x = 4.5$	*Add 1.3 and subtract x from both sides.*
$x = 1.5$	*Divide both sides by 3.*

Step 2 Substitute 1.5 into the expressions to find the side lengths.

$JK = 4x - 1.3$
$= 4(1.5) - 1.3 = 4.7$
$KL = x + 3.2$
$= (1.5) + 3.2 = 4.7$
$JL = 5x - 0.2$
$= 5(1.5) - 0.2 = 7.3$

3. Find the side lengths of equilateral $\triangle FGH$. 17; 17; 17

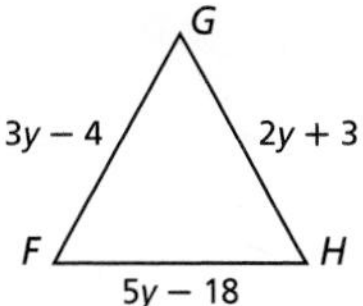

2 Teach

Guided Instruction

Explain how to classify a triangle by its angles as acute, equiangular, right, or obtuse. Show that triangles can also be classified by their side lengths as equilateral, isosceles, or scalene. Then explain that some classifications can occur together. For example, a triangle can be right and isosceles.

Inclusion Remind students that $\triangle ABC$ is a triangle and $\angle ABC$ is one angle of the triangle.

Reaching All Learners

Through Auditory Cues

Have students work with a partner. Ask one student to describe a triangle classified by its angles and the other student to draw a diagram of what it would look like. Then have them reverse roles and have one student describe a triangle classified by its sides and the partner draw a diagram of what it would look like.

COMMON ERROR ALERT

Students sometimes think that a triangle is acute if it has one acute angle. Remind them that for a triangle to be acute, all three of its angles must be acute.

Power Presentations with PowerPoint®

Additional Examples

Example 1

Classify each triangle by its angle measures.

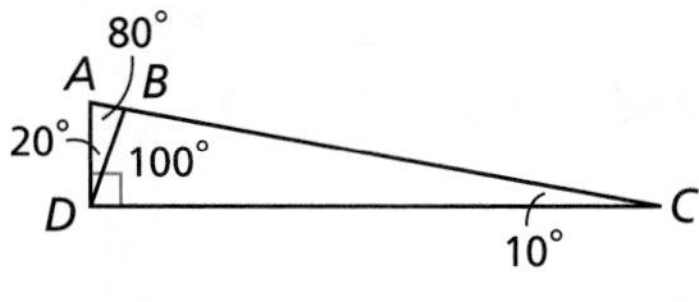

A. $\triangle BDC$ obtuse

B. $\triangle ABD$ acute

Example 2

Classify each triangle by its side lengths.

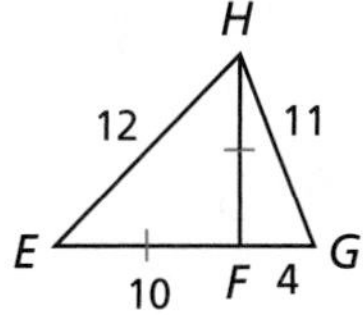

A. $\triangle EHF$ isosceles

B. $\triangle EHG$ scalene

Example 3

Find the side lengths of the triangle. 23.3; 23.3; 44.5

4x − 10.7 K 2x + 6.3
J L
5x + 2

INTERVENTION

Questioning Strategies

EXAMPLE 1

- How do you find the measure of the other angles in the triangles?

EXAMPLES 2–3

- What segment length can you change so that there is an equilateral triangle?

Algebra In **Example 3,** stress that students substitute1.5 for x as a way to find and verify the answer to the problem.

Power Presentations with PowerPoint®

Additional Examples

Example 4

A steel mill produces roof supports by welding pieces of steel beams into equilateral triangles. Each side of the triangle is 18 feet long. How many triangles can be formed from 420 feet of steel beam? 7

INTERVENTION

Questioning Strategies

EXAMPLE 4

- Why do you round the answer down instead of rounding the answer up?

EXAMPLE 4 *Music Application*

A manufacturer produces musical triangles by bending pieces of steel into the shape of an equilateral triangle. The triangles are available in side lengths of 4 inches, 7 inches, and 10 inches. How many 4-inch triangles can the manufacturer produce from a 100 inch piece of steel?

The amount of steel needed to make one triangle is equal to the perimeter P of the equilateral triangle.

$P = 3(4)$
$= 12$ in.

To find the number of triangles that can be made from 100 inches. of steel, divide 100 by the amount of steel needed for one triangle.

$100 \div 12 = 8\frac{1}{3}$ triangles

There is not enough steel to complete a ninth triangle. So the manufacturer can make 8 triangles from a 100 in. piece of steel.

CHECK IT OUT! **Each measure is the side length of an equilateral triangle. Determine how many triangles can be formed from a 100 in. piece of steel.**

4a. 7 in. 4 **4b.** 10 in. 3

THINK AND DISCUSS

1. For $\triangle DEF$, name the three pairs of consecutive sides and the vertex formed by each.
2. Sketch an example of an obtuse isosceles triangle, or explain why it is not possible to do so.
3. Is every acute triangle equiangular? Explain and support your answer with a sketch.
4. Use the Pythagorean Theorem to explain why you cannot draw an equilateral right triangle.
5. **GET ORGANIZED** Copy and complete the graphic organizer. In each box, describe each type of triangle.

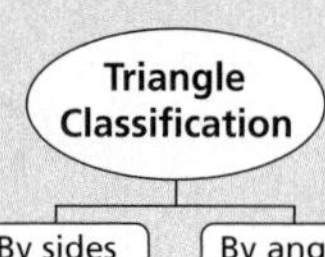

3 Close

Summarize

Review triangle classifications by angle measures and side lengths. Draw an example of each. Emphasize what sides or angles need to be congruent to classify each triangle.

ONGOING ASSESSMENT and INTERVENTION

Diagnose ***Before*** **the Lesson**
4-1 Warm Up, TE p. 216

Monitor ***During*** **the Lesson**
Check It Out! Exercises, SE pp. 216–218
Questioning Strategies, TE pp. 217–218

Assess ***After*** **the Lesson**
4-1 Lesson Quiz, TE p. 221
Alternative Assessment, TE p. 221

Answers to *Think and Discuss*

1. $\overline{DE}, \overline{EF}, E$; $\overline{EF}, \overline{FD}, F$; $\overline{FD}, \overline{DE}, D$
2. Possible answer:

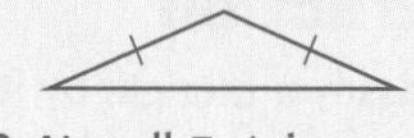

3. No; all 3 ∠s in an acute △ must be acute, but they do not have to have the same measure; possible answer:

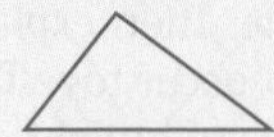

4. In an equil. rt. △, all 3 sides have the same length. By the Pyth. Thm., the 3 sides lengths are related by the formula $c^2 = a^2 + b^2$, making the hyp. c greater than either a or b. So the 3 sides cannot have the same length.
5. See p. A3.

4-1 Exercises

go.hrw.com
Homework Help Online
KEYWORD: MG7 4-1
Parent Resources Online
KEYWORD: MG7 Parent

GUIDED PRACTICE

Vocabulary **Apply the vocabulary from this lesson to answer each question.**

1. In $\triangle JKL$, JK, KL, and JL are *equal.* How does this help you classify $\triangle JKL$ by its side lengths? **An equilateral △ has 3 ≅ sides.**

2. $\triangle XYZ$ is an *obtuse* triangle. What can you say about the types of angles in $\triangle XYZ$? **One of the ∠s is obtuse, and the other 2 ∠s are acute.**

SEE EXAMPLE 1 p. 216

Classify each triangle by its angle measures.

3. $\triangle DBC$ **rt.**
4. $\triangle ABD$ **rt.**
5. $\triangle ADC$ **obtuse**

D, 31°, 70°, A, 59°, B, 20°, C

SEE EXAMPLE 2 p. 217

Classify each triangle by its side lengths.

6. $\triangle EGH$ **isosc.**
7. $\triangle EFH$ **scalene**
8. $\triangle HFG$ **scalene**

H, 7.4, 8, E, 3, F, G

SEE EXAMPLE 3 p. 217

Multi-Step **Find the side lengths of each triangle.**

9. 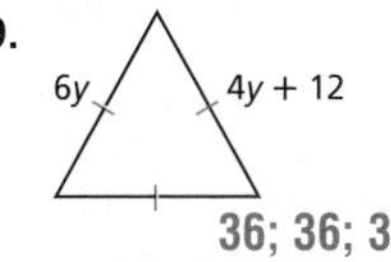

36; 36; 36

10. $4x + 0.5$, $x + 2.4$, $2x + 1.7$ **3.1; 3.1; 3.3**

SEE EXAMPLE 4 p. 218

11. **Crafts** A jeweler creates triangular earrings by bending pieces of silver wire. Each earring is an isosceles triangle with the dimensions shown. How many earrings can be made from a piece of wire that is 50 cm long? **6**

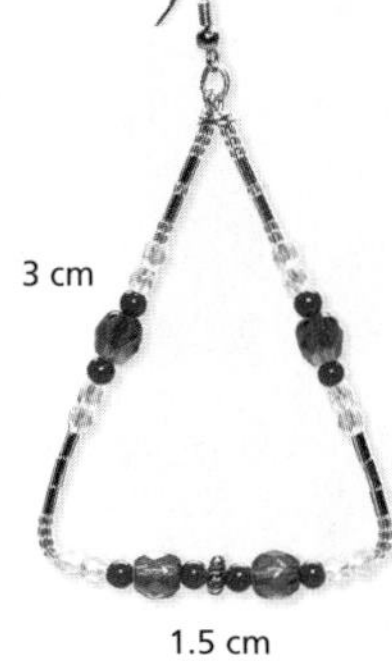

PRACTICE AND PROBLEM SOLVING

Independent Practice

For Exercises	See Example
12–14	1
15–17	2
18–20	3
21–22	4

Extra Practice
Skills Practice p. S10
Application Practice p. S31

Classify each triangle by its angle measures.

12. $\triangle BEA$ **rt.**
13. $\triangle DBC$ **obtuse**
14. $\triangle ABC$ **equiangular**

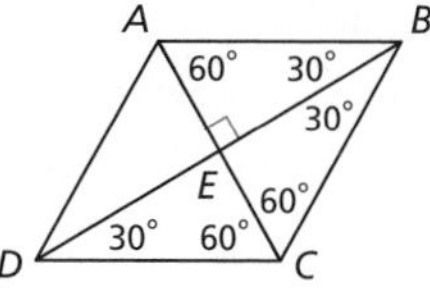

Classify each triangle by its side lengths.

15. $\triangle PST$ **equil.**
16. $\triangle RSP$ **isosc.**
17. $\triangle RPT$ **scalene**

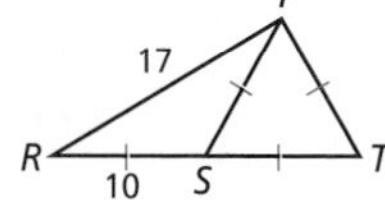

Multi-Step **Find the side lengths of each triangle.**

18. $z + 5$, $4z - 4$, $3z - 1$ **8; 8; 8**

19. $2x + 6.8$, $8x + 1.4$ **8.6; 8.6**

20. Draw a triangle large enough to measure. Label the vertices X, Y, and Z.
    a. Name the three sides and three angles of the triangle.
    b. Use a ruler and protractor to classify the triangle by its side lengths and angle measures.

20. Check students' drawings.
a. $\overline{XY}$, $\overline{YZ}$, $\overline{XZ}$, $\angle X$, $\angle Y$, $\angle Z$
b. Possible answer: scalene obtuse

4-1 Exercises

Assignment Guide

Assign *Guided Practice* exercises as necessary.

If you finished Examples **1–2**
Basic 12–17, 20, 23–31, 35–37
Average 12–17, 20, 23–31, 35–37, 39
Advanced 12–17, 20, 23–31, 35–37, 39, 46

If you finished Examples **1–4**
Basic 12–29, 35, 36, 39–44, 49–58
Average 12–23, 24–32 even, 33, 34, 38–44, 48–58
Advanced 12–22, 24–30 even, 32–34, 38–58

Homework Quick Check
Quickly check key concepts.
Exercises: 12, 16, 18, 22, 24, 28

Teaching Tip

Visual For **Exercises 15–17,** introduce the orientation of isosceles $\triangle RSP$. Point out that the triangle is not "upside down" but that the orientation is just different.

For **Exercise 20,** have students use a different color for each side of the triangle so they can refer to the angles by the colors that form them.

State Resources

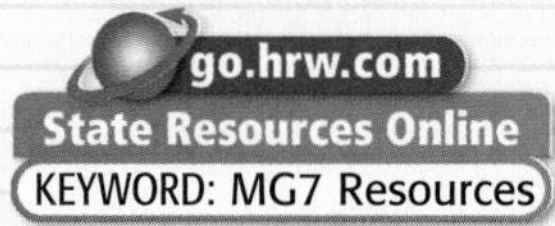

Construction

For help with **Exercise 39,** have students first construct $\overline{AB}$. Then have them set their compasses to the width AB. Draw an arc centered at A and then another arc centered at B. Label the intersection C and draw $\triangle ABC$.

MULTI-STEP TEST PREP **Exercise 40** involves using the Pythagorean Theorem to find the length of the hypotenuse of a right triangle. This exercise prepares students for the Multi-Step Test Prep on page 238.

Answers

23. 25.

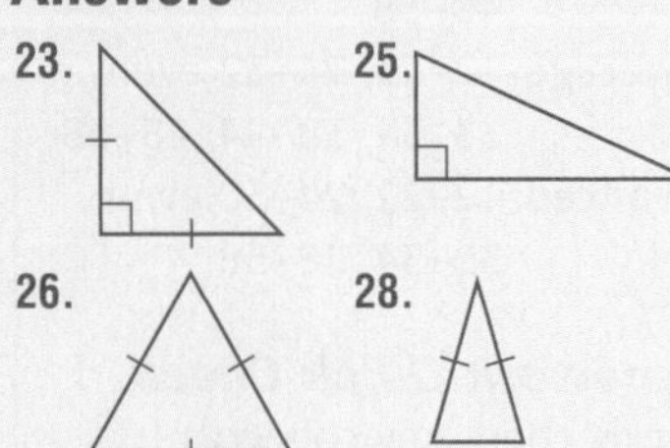

26. 28.

34. No; yes; not every isosc. △ is equil. because only 2 of the 3 sides must be ≅. Every equil. △ is isosc. because an equil. △ has 3 ≅ sides, and the def. of an isosc. △ requires that at least 2 sides be ≅.

35. 36.

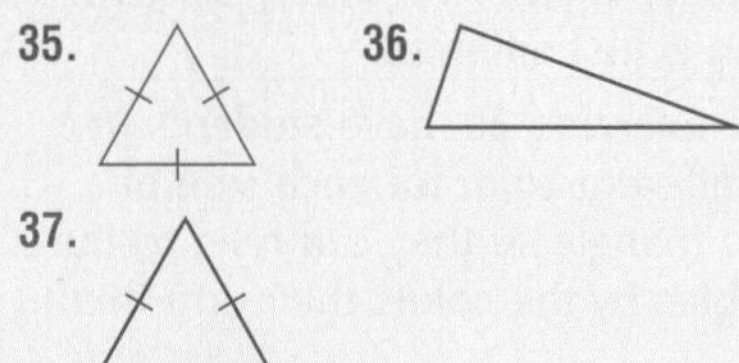

37.

38. $s = \frac{P}{3}$. The perimeter of an equil. △ is 3 times the length of any 1 side, or $P = 3s$. Solve this formula for s by dividing both sides by 3.

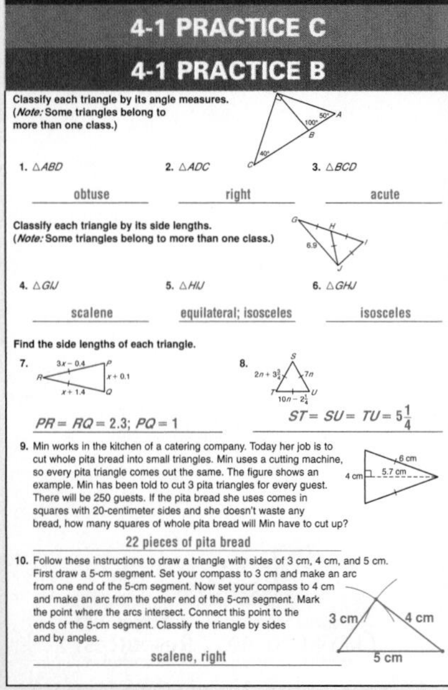

4-1 PRACTICE A

4-1 PRACTICE C

4-1 PRACTICE B

Classify each triangle by its angle measures. (*Note:* Some triangles belong to more than one class.)

1. $\triangle ABD$ obtuse
2. $\triangle ADC$ right
3. $\triangle BCD$ acute

Classify each triangle by its side lengths. (*Note:* Some triangles belong to more than one class.)

4. $\triangle GIJ$ scalene
5. $\triangle HIJ$ equilateral; isosceles
6. $\triangle GHJ$ isosceles

Find the side lengths of each triangle.

7. $PR = RQ = 2.3$; $PQ = 1$
8. $ST = SU = TU = 5\frac{1}{4}$

9. Min works in the kitchen of a catering company. Today her job is to cut whole pita bread into small triangles. Min uses a cutting machine, so every pita triangle comes out the same. The figure shows an example. Min has been told to cut 3 pita triangles for every guest. There will be 250 guests. If the pita bread she uses comes in squares with 20-centimeter sides and she doesn't waste any bread, how many squares of whole pita bread will Min have to cut up?
22 pieces of pita bread

10. Follow these instructions to draw a triangle with sides of 3 cm, 4 cm, and 5 cm. First draw a 5-cm segment. Set your compass to 3 cm and make an arc from one end of the 5-cm segment. Now set your compass to 4 cm and make an arc from the other end of the 5-cm segment. Mark the point where the arcs intersect. Connect this point to the ends of the 5-cm segment. Classify the triangle by sides and by angles.
scalene, right

24. Not possible; an equiangular. △ must contain only acute ∠s.

27. Not possible; an equiangular △ must also be equil.

Carpentry Use the following information for Exercises 21 and 22.
A manufacturer makes trusses, or triangular supports, for the roofs of houses. Each truss is the shape of an isosceles triangle in which $\overline{PQ} \cong \overline{PR}$. The length of the base $\overline{QR}$ is $\frac{4}{3}$ the length of each of the congruent sides.

21. The perimeter of each truss is 60 ft. Find each side length. **18 ft; 18 ft; 24 ft**

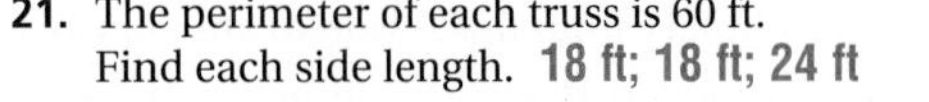

22. How many trusses can the manufacturer make from 150 feet of lumber? **2**

Draw an example of each type of triangle or explain why it is not possible.

23. isosceles right
24. equiangular obtuse
25. scalene right
26. equilateral acute
27. scalene equiangular
28. isosceles acute

29. An equilateral triangle has a perimeter of 105 in. What is the length of each side of the triangle? **35 in.**

Classify each triangle by its angles and sides.

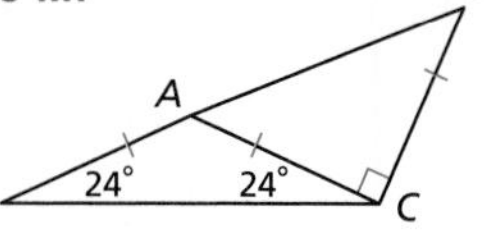

30. $\triangle ABC$ **isosc. obtuse**
31. $\triangle ACD$ **isosc. rt.**

32. An isosceles triangle has a perimeter of 34 cm. The congruent sides measure $(4x - 1)$ cm. The length of the third side is x cm. What is the value of x? **4**

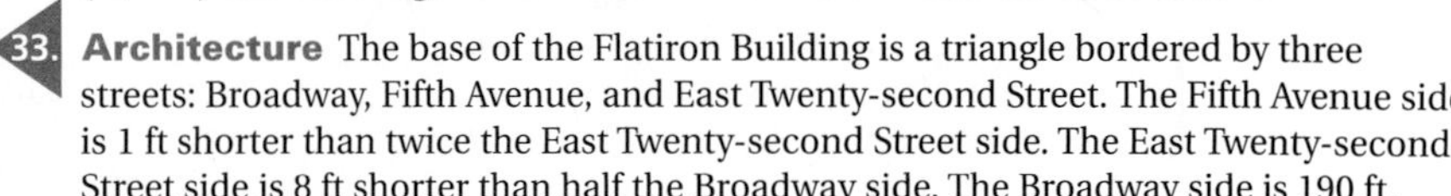

LINK Architecture

Daniel Burnham designed and built the 22-story Flatiron Building in New York City in 1902.

Source: www.greatbuildings.com

33. **Architecture** The base of the Flatiron Building is a triangle bordered by three streets: Broadway, Fifth Avenue, and East Twenty-second Street. The Fifth Avenue side is 1 ft shorter than twice the East Twenty-second Street side. The East Twenty-second Street side is 8 ft shorter than half the Broadway side. The Broadway side is 190 ft.
a. Find the two unknown side lengths. **173 ft; 87 ft**
b. Classify the triangle by its side lengths. **scalene**

34. **Critical Thinking** Is every isosceles triangle equilateral? Is every equilateral triangle isosceles? Explain.

Tell whether each statement is sometimes, always, or never true. Support your answer with a sketch.

35. An acute triangle is a scalene triangle. **S**
36. A scalene triangle is an obtuse triangle. **S**
37. An equiangular triangle is an isosceles triangle. **A**

38. **Write About It** Write a formula for the side length s of an equilateral triangle, given the perimeter P. Explain how you derived the formula.

39. **Construction** Use the method for constructing congruent segments to construct an equilateral triangle. **Check students' constructions.**

MULTI-STEP TEST PREP

40. This problem will prepare you for the Multi-Step Test Prep on page 238.
Marc folded a rectangular sheet of paper, $ABCD$, in half along $\overline{EF}$. He folded the resulting square diagonally and then unfolded the paper to create the creases shown.
a. Use the Pythagorean Theorem to find DE and CE. **$5\sqrt{2}$**
b. What is the m∠DEC? **90°**
c. Classify $\triangle DEC$ by its side lengths and by its angle measures. **isosc. △; rt. △**

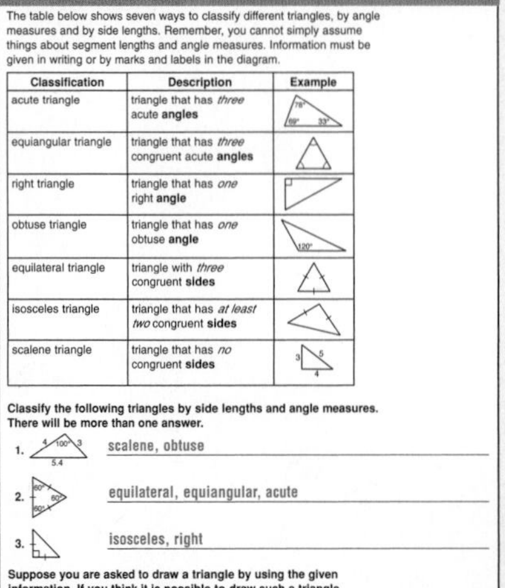

4-1 READING STRATEGIES

The table below shows seven ways to classify different triangles, by angle measures and by side lengths. Remember, you cannot simply assume things about segment lengths and angle measures. Information must be given in writing or by marks and labels in the diagram.

Classification	Description	Example
acute triangle	triangle that has *three* acute **angles**	
equiangular triangle	triangle that has *three* congruent acute **angles**	
right triangle	triangle that has *one* right **angle**	
obtuse triangle	triangle that has *one* obtuse **angle**	
equilateral triangle	triangle with *three* congruent **sides**	
isosceles triangle	triangle that has *at least two* congruent **sides**	
scalene triangle	triangle that has *no* congruent **sides**	

Classify the following triangles by side lengths and angle measures. There will be more than one answer.

1. scalene, obtuse
2. equilateral, equiangular, acute
3. isosceles, right

Suppose you are asked to draw a triangle by using the given information. If you think it is possible to draw such a triangle, classify the triangle. Otherwise write *no such triangle*.

4. $\triangle ABC$ with $AB = 3$, $BC = 3$, and $CA = 5$ — isosceles triangle
5. $\triangle XOZ$ with m∠X = 92°, m∠O = 92°, and m∠Z = 27° — no such triangle
6. $\triangle MNK$ with m∠M = 90°, m∠N = 60°, and m∠K = 30° — right triangle

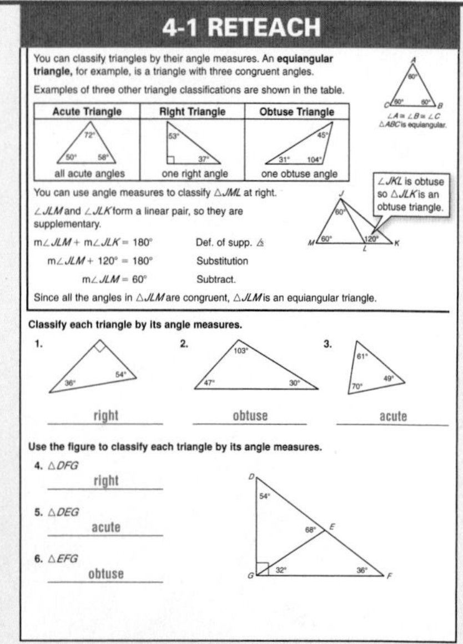

4-1 RETEACH

You can classify triangles by their angle measures. An **equiangular triangle,** for example, is a triangle with three congruent angles.

∠A ≅ ∠B ≅ ∠C
△ABC is equiangular.

Examples of three other triangle classifications are shown in the table.

Acute Triangle	Right Triangle	Obtuse Triangle
all acute angles	one right angle	one obtuse angle

You can use angle measures to classify $\triangle JML$ at right.

∠JLM and ∠JLK form a linear pair, so they are supplementary.

m∠JLM + m∠JLK = 180° Def. of supp. ∠s
m∠JLM + 120° = 180° Substitution
m∠JLM = 60° Subtract.

∠JKL is obtuse so $\triangle JLK$ is an obtuse triangle.

Since all the angles in $\triangle JLM$ are congruent, $\triangle JLM$ is an equiangular triangle.

Classify each triangle by its angle measures.

1. right
2. obtuse
3. acute

Use the figure to classify each triangle by its angle measures.

4. $\triangle DFG$ right
5. $\triangle DEG$ acute
6. $\triangle EFG$ obtuse

41. What is the side length of an equilateral triangle with a perimeter of $36\frac{2}{3}$ inches?

Ⓐ $36\frac{2}{3}$ inches Ⓒ $12\frac{1}{3}$ inches
Ⓑ $18\frac{1}{3}$ inches Ⓓ $12\frac{2}{9}$ inches

42. The vertices of $\triangle RST$ are $R(3, 2)$, $S(-2, 3)$, and $T(-2, 1)$. Which of these best describes $\triangle RST$?

Ⓕ Isosceles Ⓖ Scalene Ⓗ Equilateral Ⓙ Right

43. Which of the following is NOT a correct classification of $\triangle LMN$?

Ⓐ Acute Ⓒ Isosceles
Ⓑ Equiangular Ⓓ Right

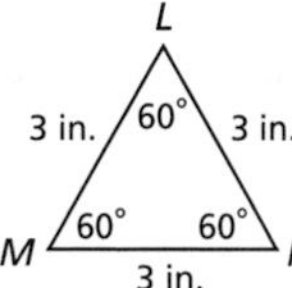

44. **Gridded Response** $\triangle ABC$ is isosceles, and $\overline{AB} \cong \overline{AC}$. $AB = \left(\frac{1}{2}x + \frac{1}{4}\right)$, and $BC = \left(\frac{5}{2} - x\right)$. What is the perimeter of $\triangle ABC$? **3**

CHALLENGE AND EXTEND

45. It is an isosc. △ since 2 sides of the △ have length *a*. It is also a rt. △ since 2 sides of the △ lie on the coord. axes and form a rt. ∠.

45. A triangle has vertices with coordinates $(0, 0)$, $(a, 0)$, and $(0, a)$, where $a \neq 0$. Classify the triangle in two different ways. Explain your answer.

46. Write a two-column proof.
Given: $\triangle ABC$ is equiangular.
$EF \parallel AC$
Prove: $\triangle EFB$ is equiangular.

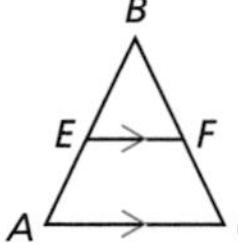

47. Two sides of an equilateral triangle measure $(y + 10)$ units and $(y^2 - 2)$ units. If the perimeter of the triangle is 21 units, what is the value of y? **−3**

48. **Multi-Step** The average length of the sides of $\triangle PQR$ is 24. How much longer then the average is the longest side? **8**

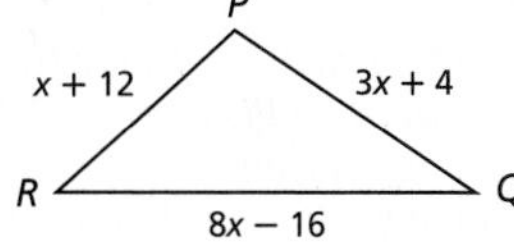

SPIRAL REVIEW

Name the parent function of each function. *(Previous course)*

49. $y = 5x^2 + 4$ **$y = x^2$** 50. $2y = 3x + 4$ **$y = x$** 51. $y = 2(x - 8)^2 + 6$ **$y = x^2$**

Determine if each biconditional is true. If false, give a counterexample. *(Lesson 2-4)*

52. Two lines are parallel if and only if they do not intersect.
F; skew lines do not intersect and are not parallel.

53. A triangle is equiangular if and only if it has three congruent angles. **T**

54. A number is a multiple of 20 if and only if the number ends in a 0.
F; possible answer: 30 has a 0 in the ones place, but 30 is not a multiple of 20.

Determine whether each line is parallel to, is perpendicular to, or coincides with $y = 4x$. *(Lesson 3-6)*

55. $y = 4x + 2$ **∥** 56. $4y = -x + 8$ **⊥**

57. $\frac{1}{2}y = 2x$ **coincides** 58. $-2y = \frac{1}{2}x$ **⊥**

COMMON ERROR ALERT

In **Exercise 45,** students may assume that a must be positive. Explain that the variable a can represent any real number.

TEST PREP DOCTOR If students chose **C** for **Exercise 41,** they may be having difficulty dividing $\frac{2}{3}$ by 3. In **Exercise 44,** students may forget that there are two congruent sides in an isosceles triangle. Remind them to add $\frac{1}{2}x + \frac{1}{4}$ twice. Make sure that they realize the variables will add to 0.

Journal

Have students describe at least three real-world examples of isosceles and equilateral triangles and include a sketch or magazine picture of each.

Have students sketch and identify an example of each type of triangle in this lesson. Then ask them to verify their answers by measuring with a ruler and a protractor (MK).

4-1 PROBLEM SOLVING

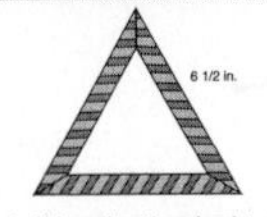

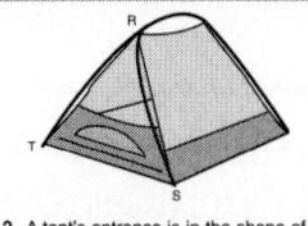

1. Aisha makes triangular picture frames by gluing three pieces of wood together in the shape of an equilateral triangle and covering the wood with ribbon. Each side of a frame is $6\frac{1}{2}$ inches long. How many frames can she cover with 2 yards of ribbon?
3 frames

2. A tent's entrance is in the shape of an isosceles triangle in which $\overline{RT} \cong \overline{RS}$. The length of $\overline{TS}$ is 1.2 times the length of a side. The perimeter of the entrance is 14 feet. Find each side length.
$4\frac{3}{8}$ ft; $4\frac{3}{8}$ ft; $5\frac{1}{4}$ ft

Use the figure and the following information for Exercises 3 and 4.

The distance "as the crow flies" between Santa Fe and Phoenix is 609 kilometers. This is 245 kilometers less than twice the distance between Santa Fe and El Paso. Phoenix is 48 kilometers closer to El Paso than it is to Santa Fe.

Santa Fe, New Mexico
Phoenix, Arizona
El Paso, Texas

3. What is the distance between each pair of cities?
Santa Fe and El Paso, 427 km; El Paso and Phoenix, 561 km; Phoenix and Santa Fe, 609 km

4. Classify the triangle that connects the cities by its side lengths. **scalene**

Choose the best answer.

A *gable,* as shown in the diagram, is the triangular portion of a wall between a sloping roof.

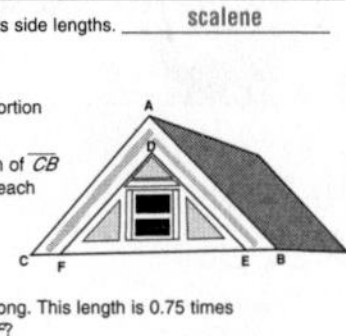

5. Triangle *ABC* is an isosceles triangle. The length of $\overline{CB}$ is 12 feet 4 inches and the congruent sides are each $\frac{3}{4}$ this length. What is the perimeter of $\triangle ABC$?
A 31 ft 4 in. C 21 ft 7 in.
Ⓑ 30 ft 10 in. D 18 ft 6 in.

6. In $\triangle DEF$, $\overline{DE}$ and $\overline{DF}$ are each 6 feet 3 inches long. This length is 0.75 times the length of $\overline{FE}$. What is the perimeter of $\triangle DEF$?
F 12 ft 4 in. H 17 ft 2 in.
G 14 ft 7 in. Ⓙ 20 ft 10 in.

Answers

46. 1. $\triangle ABC$ is equiangular. (Given)
2. $\angle A \cong \angle B \cong \angle C$ (Def. of equiangular △)
3. $\overline{EF} \parallel \overline{AC}$ (Given)
4. $\angle BEF \cong \angle A$, $\angle BFE \cong \angle C$, (Corr. ∠s Post.)
5. $\angle BEF \cong \angle B$, $\angle BFE \cong \angle B$, (Trans. Prop. of ≅)
6. $\angle BEF \cong \angle BFE$ (∠s ≅ to the same ∠ are ≅.)
7. $\triangle EFB$ is equiangular. (Def. of equiangular △)

4-1 Lesson Quiz

Classify each triangle by its angles and sides.

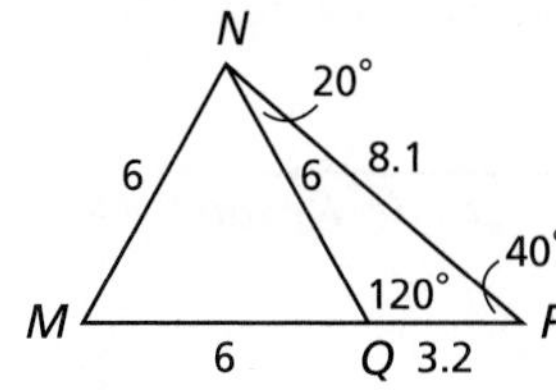

1. $\triangle MNQ$ acute; equilateral
2. $\triangle NQP$ obtuse; scalene
3. $\triangle MNP$ acute; scalene
4. Find the side lengths of the triangle. 29; 29; 23

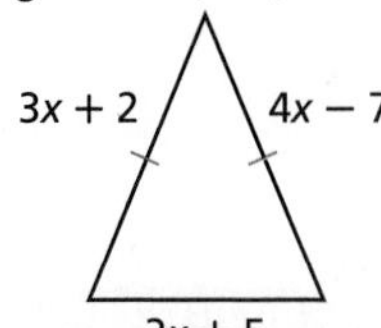

Also available on transparency

Organizer

Use with Lesson 4-2

Pacing:

Traditional $\frac{1}{2}$ day

Block $\frac{1}{4}$ day

Objective: Use patty paper to discover the relationship between the measures of the interior angles of a triangle.

Materials: patty paper

Online Edition

Countdown Week 7

Resources

Geometry Lab Activities

4-2 Lab Recording Sheet

Teach

Discuss

Discuss the algebraic language used to describe the relationship between the angles of a triangle.

Alternative Approach

Have students use geometry software to draw a triangle, measure the interior angles, and drag the vertices. Lead them to the conjecture that the angle sum is always 180°.

Close

Key Concept

The sum of the measures of the angles of any triangle is 180°.

Assessment

Journal Have students draw different-shaped triangles, measure the angles, and find the sum. Then compare their results.

State Resources

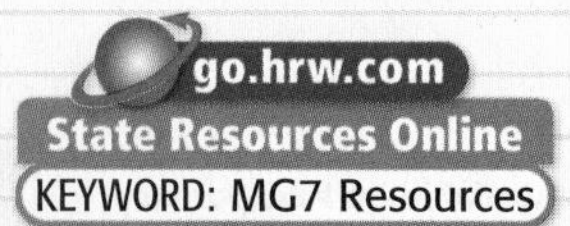

go.hrw.com
State Resources Online
KEYWORD: MG7 Resources

4-2 Geometry LAB

Develop the Triangle Sum Theorem

Use with Lesson 4-2

In this lab, you will use patty paper to discover a relationship between the measures of the interior angles of a triangle.

Activity

1. Draw and label $\triangle ABC$ on a sheet of notebook paper.

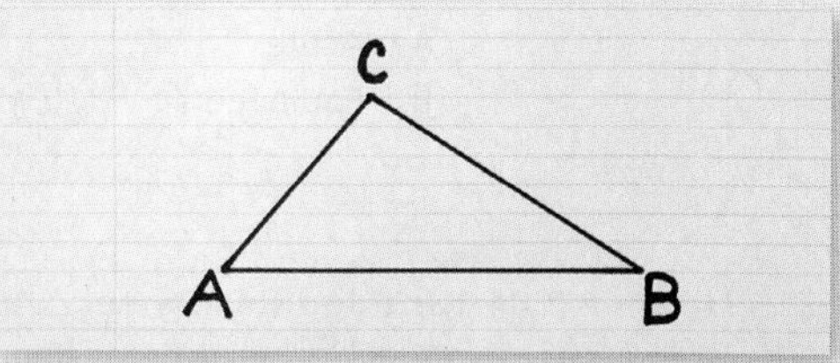

2. On patty paper draw a line ℓ and label a point P on the line.

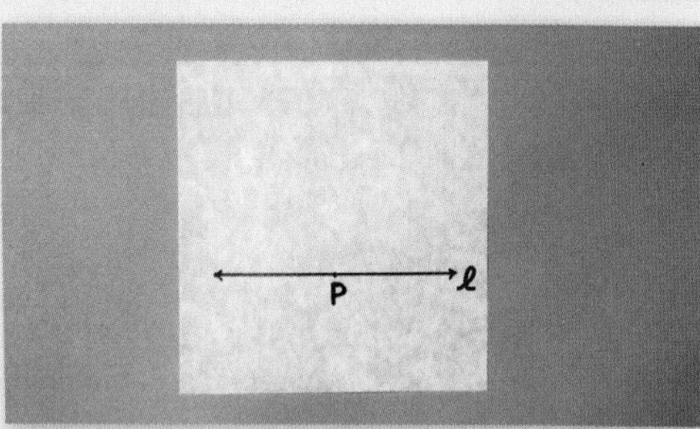

3. Place the patty paper on top of the triangle you drew. Align the papers so that $\overline{AB}$ is on line ℓ and P and B coincide. Trace $\angle B$. Rotate the triangle and trace $\angle C$ adjacent to $\angle B$. Rotate the triangle again and trace $\angle A$ adjacent to $\angle C$. The diagram shows your final step.

Try This

1. What do you notice about the three angles of the triangle that you traced? **When placed together the 3 ∡ form a line.**
2. Repeat the activity two more times using two different triangles. Do you get the same results each time? **yes**
3. Write an equation describing the relationship among the measures of the angles of $\triangle ABC$. $m\angle A + m\angle B + m\angle C = 180°$
4. Use inductive reasoning to write a conjecture about the sum of the measures of the angles of a triangle. **The sum of the measures of the ∡ of a △ is 180°.**

Teacher to Teacher

A pencil can be used to "swing" through the angles of a triangle. At the final move the pencil point will face the opposite direction–a rotation of 180°.

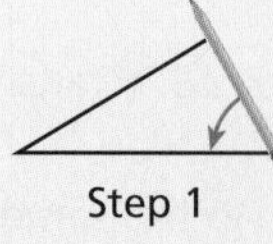

Step 1

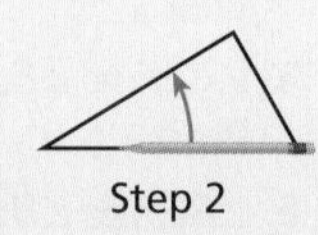

Step 2

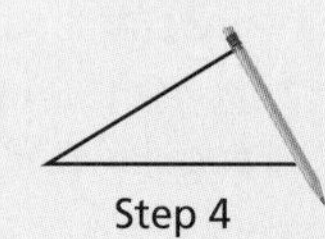

Step 3

Step 4

Kathleen Kelly
Fairfield, ME

4-2 Angle Relationships in Triangles

Objectives
Find the measures of interior and exterior angles of triangles.

Apply theorems about the interior and exterior angles of triangles.

Vocabulary
auxiliary line
corollary
interior
exterior
interior angle
exterior angle
remote interior angle

Who uses this?
Surveyors use triangles to make measurements and create boundaries. (See Example 1.)

This engraving shows the county surveyor and commissioners laying out the town of Baltimore in 1730.

Triangulation is a method used in surveying. Land is divided into adjacent triangles. By measuring the sides and angles of one triangle and applying properties of triangles, surveyors can gather information about adjacent triangles.

Know it! Note

Theorem 4-2-1 Triangle Sum Theorem

The sum of the angle measures of a triangle is 180°.

$m\angle A + m\angle B + m\angle C = 180°$

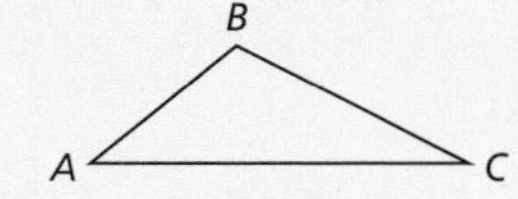

The proof of the Triangle Sum Theorem uses an *auxiliary line*. An **auxiliary line** is a line that is added to a figure to aid in a proof.

PROOF **Triangle Sum Theorem**

Given: $\triangle ABC$
Prove: $m\angle 1 + m\angle 2 + m\angle 3 = 180°$

Proof:

Draw $\ell \parallel \overline{AC}$ through B. — Parallel Post.

$\angle 1 \cong \angle 4$ — Alt. Int. ∠s Thm.

$\angle 3 \cong \angle 5$ — Alt. Int. ∠s Thm.

$m\angle 1 = m\angle 4$ — Def. of ≅ ∠s

$m\angle 3 = m\angle 5$ — Def. of ≅ ∠s

$m\angle 4 + m\angle 2 + m\angle 5 = 180°$ — ∠ Add. Post. & def. of straight ∠

$m\angle 1 + m\angle 2 + m\angle 3 = 180°$ — Subst.

4-2 Organizer

Pacing: Traditional 1 day
Block $\frac{1}{2}$ day

Objectives: Find the measures of interior and exterior angles of triangles.

Apply theorems about the interior and exterior angles of triangles.

Technology Lab
In *Technology Lab Activities*

Online Edition
Tutorial Videos

Countdown Week 7

Power Presentations with PowerPoint®

Warm Up

1. Find the measure of exterior $\angle DBA$ of $\triangle BCD$, if $m\angle DBC = 30°$, $m\angle C = 70°$, and $m\angle D = 80°$. 150°
2. What is the complement of an angle with measure 17°? 73°
3. How many lines can be drawn through N parallel to $\overline{MP}$? Why? 1; Parallel Post.

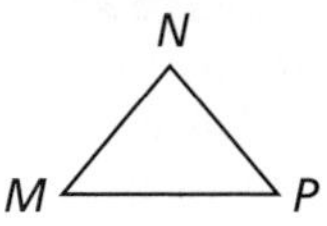

Also available on transparency

Math Humor

Q: How many feet are in a yard?

A: It depends on how many people are in the yard!

1 Introduce

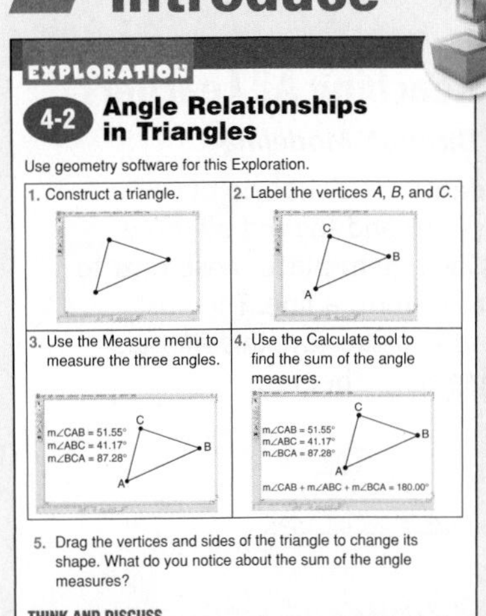
EXPLORATION

4-2 Angle Relationships in Triangles

Use geometry software for this Exploration.

1. Construct a triangle.
2. Label the vertices A, B, and C.
3. Use the Measure menu to measure the three angles.
4. Use the Calculate tool to find the sum of the angle measures.
5. Drag the vertices and sides of the triangle to change its shape. What do you notice about the sum of the angle measures?

THINK AND DISCUSS

Motivate

Have students trace a circular object to create a protractor-like shape. Then have them label their drawings with estimated angle measures every ten degrees. Have students use the protractor they created to measure and find the sum of the interior angles of a triangle. Finally have them draw an exterior angle of a triangle and measure it. Students should check their estimates with an actual protractor.

Explorations and answers are provided in *Alternate Openers: Explorations Transparencies.*

State Resources Online
KEYWORD: MG7 Resources

Power Presentations with PowerPoint®

Additional Examples

Example 1

After an accident, the positions of cars are measured by law enforcement to investigate the collision. Use the diagram drawn from the information collected to find the indicated angle measures.

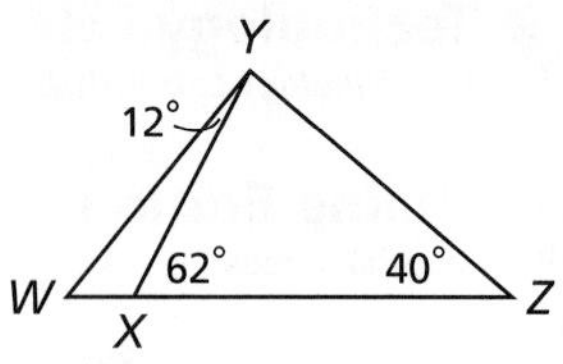

A. m∠XYZ 78°

B. m∠YWZ 50°

INTERVENTION

Questioning Strategies

EXAMPLE 1

- What properties do you need to know about triangles when using the triangulation method to calculate the measures of angles?

Language Arts The word *auxiliary* means "giving assistance." Emphasize that an *auxiliary line* drawn from a vertex of a triangle to the opposite side may *assist* with a proof.

EXAMPLE 1 Surveying Application

The map of France commonly used in the 1600s was significantly revised as a result of a triangulation land survey. The diagram shows part of the survey map. Use the diagram to find the indicated angle measures.

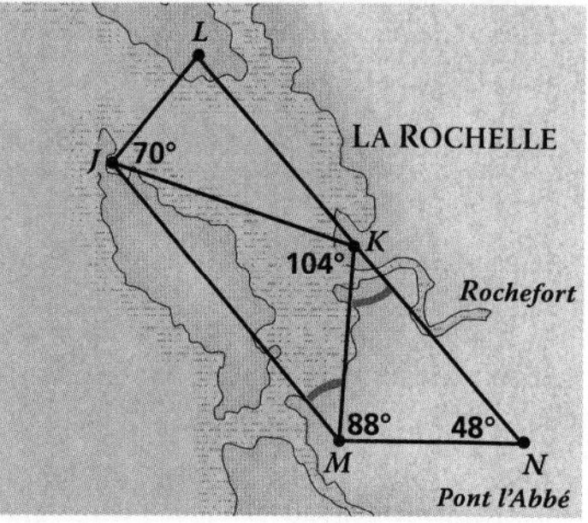

Algebra

A $m\angle NKM$

$m\angle KMN + m\angle MNK + m\angle NKM = 180°$	*△ Sum Thm.*
$88 + 48 + m\angle NKM = 180$	*Substitute 88 for m∠KMN and 48 for m∠MNK.*
$136 + m\angle NKM = 180$	*Simplify.*
$m\angle NKM = 44°$	*Subtract 136 from both sides.*

B $m\angle JLK$

Step 1 Find $m\angle JKL$.

$m\angle NKM + m\angle MKJ + m\angle JKL = 180°$	*Lin. Pair Thm. & ∠ Add. Post.*
$44 + 104 + m\angle JKL = 180$	*Substitute 44 for m∠NKM and 104 for m∠MKJ.*
$148 + m\angle JKL = 180$	*Simplify.*
$m\angle JKL = 32°$	*Subtract 148 from both sides.*

Step 2 Use substitution and then solve for $m\angle JLK$.

$m\angle JLK + m\angle JKL + m\angle KJL = 180°$	*△ Sum Thm.*
$m\angle JLK + 32 + 70 = 180$	*Substitute 32 for m∠JKL and 70 for m∠KJL.*
$m\angle JLK + 102 = 180$	*Simplify.*
$m\angle JLK = 78°$	*Subtract 102 from both sides.*

CHECK IT OUT! **1.** Use the diagram to find $m\angle MJK$. 32°

A **corollary** is a theorem whose proof follows directly from another theorem. Here are two corollaries to the Triangle Sum Theorem.

Know it! Note

Corollaries

COROLLARY		HYPOTHESIS	CONCLUSION
4-2-2	The acute angles of a right triangle are complementary.		∠D and ∠E are complementary. $m\angle D + m\angle E = 90°$
4-2-3	The measure of each angle of an equiangular triangle is 60°.		$m\angle A = m\angle B = m\angle C = 60°$

You will prove Corollaries 4-2-2 and 4-2-3 in Exercises 24 and 25.

2 Teach

Guided Instruction

Review the method of constructing a parallel line before proving the Triangle Sum Theorem. Explain why an auxiliary line was added to the figure in the proof. Compare the two corollaries to the Triangle Sum Theorem. Review the meanings of interior, exterior, and remote before introducing the Exterior Angle Theorem. Show how the Third Angles Theorem is related to the Triangle Sum Theorem.

Reaching All Learners

Through Modeling

Have students cut a triangle out of a sheet of paper and tear off all three corners. Have them place these next to each other to form a line. Then ask students to explain how this models the Triangle Sum Theorem.

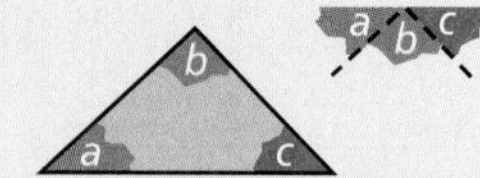

EXAMPLE 2 Finding Angle Measures in Right Triangles

One of the acute angles in a right triangle measures 22.9°. What is the measure of the other acute angle?

Let the acute angles be $\angle M$ and $\angle N$, with $m\angle M = 22.9°$.

$m\angle M + m\angle N = 90$ *Acute ∠s of rt. △ are comp.*

$22.9 + m\angle N = 90$ *Substitute 22.9 for m∠M.*

$m\angle N = 67.1°$ *Subtract 22.9 from both sides.*

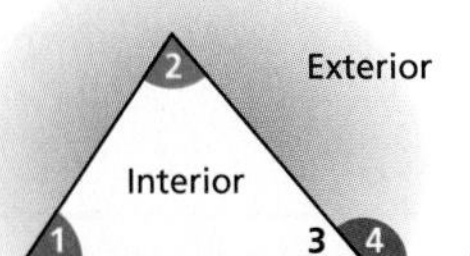

The measure of one of the acute angles in a right triangle is given. What is the measure of the other acute angle?

2a. 63.7° 26.3° **2b.** $x°$ $(90 - x)°$ **2c.** $48\frac{2}{5}°$ $41\frac{3}{5}°$

The **interior** is the set of all points inside the figure. The **exterior** is the set of all points outside the figure. An **interior angle** is formed by two sides of a triangle. An **exterior angle** is formed by one side of the triangle and the extension of an adjacent side. Each exterior angle has two *remote interior angles.* A **remote interior angle** is an interior angle that is not adjacent to the exterior angle.

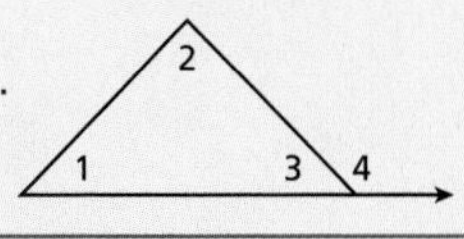

$\angle 4$ is an exterior angle. Its remote interior angles are $\angle 1$ and $\angle 2$.

Know it! Note

Theorem 4-2-4 **Exterior Angle Theorem**

The measure of an exterior angle of a triangle is equal to the sum of the measures of its remote interior angles.

$m\angle 4 = m\angle 1 + m\angle 2$

You will prove Theorem 4-2-4 in Exercise 28.

EXAMPLE 3 Applying the Exterior Angle Theorem

Find $m\angle J$.

(6x − 1)°, H, 126°, F, G, J, (5x + 17)°

$m\angle J + m\angle H = m\angle FGH$ *Ext. ∠ Thm.*

$5x + 17 + 6x - 1 = 126$ *Substitute 5x + 17 for m∠J, 6x − 1 for m∠H, and 126 for m∠FGH.*

$11x + 16 = 126$ *Simplify.*

$11x = 110$ *Subtract 16 from both sides.*

$x = 10$ *Divide both sides by 11.*

$m\angle J = 5x + 17 = 5(10) + 17 = 67°$

CHECK IT OUT!

3. Find $m\angle ACD$. 141°

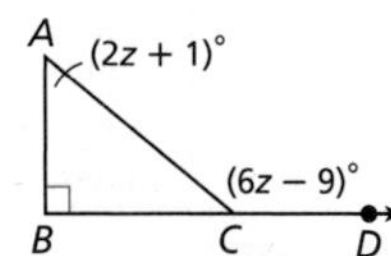

COMMON ERROR ALERT

For **Check It Out Problem 2b,** students may write $(x - 90)°$. Show them that if the given angle has a measure of 10° for example, the remaining acute angle would have measure $(90 - 10)°$, not $(10 - 90)°$.

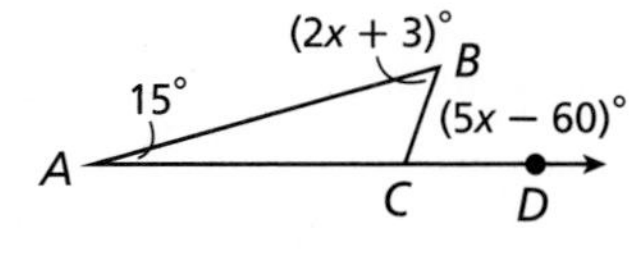

Additional Examples

Example 2

One of the acute angles in a right triangle measures $2x°$. What is the measure of the other acute angle? $(90 - 2x)°$

Example 3

Find $m\angle B$. 55°

(2x + 3)°, B, 15°, (5x − 60)°, A, C, D

INTERVENTION

Questioning Strategies

EXAMPLE 2

- What corollary to the Triangle Sum Theorem is used to find the acute angles of a right triangle? Does this apply to every right triangle?

EXAMPLE 3

- What is the relationship between the angle formed by extending one of the sides of a triangle and each interior angle?

Teaching Tip

Reading Math Remind students of the meanings of *interior, exterior,* and *remote.* An *interior* angle is *inside* the figure, an *exterior* angle is *outside* the figure, and a *remote interior angle* is *interior and away* from the exterior angle. Relate the idea of a remote interior angle to a television remote control that sends a signal across the room and away from you.

ENGLISH LANGUAGE LEARNERS

Power Presentations with PowerPoint®

Additional Examples

Example 4

Find m∠K and m∠J. 80°, 80°

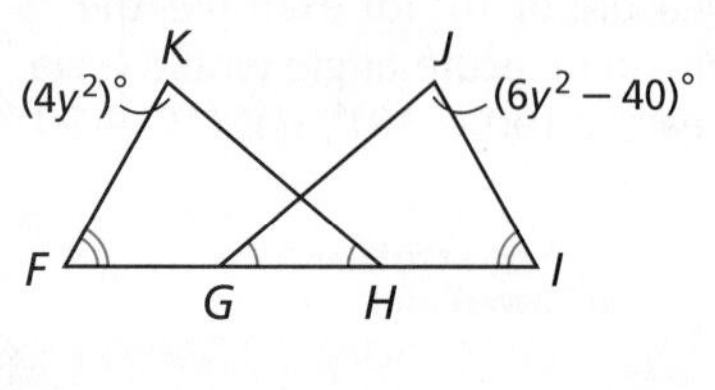

INTERVENTION

Questioning Strategies

EXAMPLE 4

- Why is it not necessary to solve for *y* to find the missing measures of the angles?

Know it! Note

Theorem 4-2-5 Third Angles Theorem

THEOREM	HYPOTHESIS	CONCLUSION
If two angles of one triangle are congruent to two angles of another triangle, then the third pair of angles are congruent.	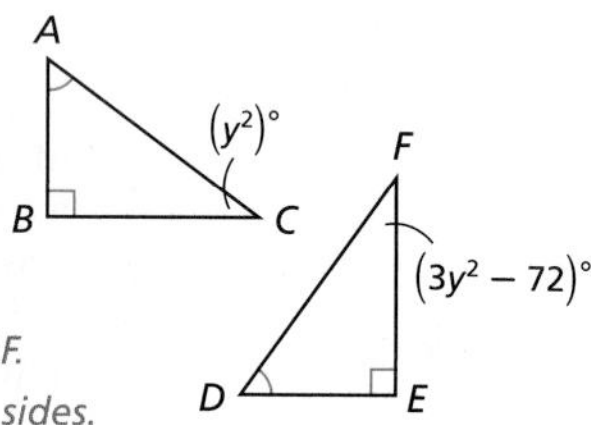	$\angle N \cong \angle T$

You will prove Theorem 4-2-5 in Exercise 27.

EXAMPLE 4 **Applying the Third Angles Theorem**

Algebra

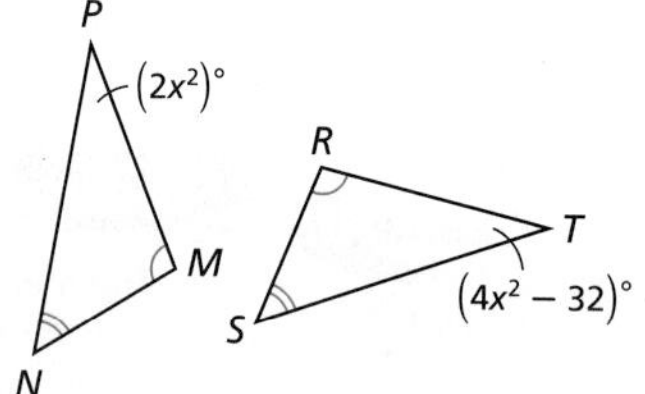

Find m∠C and m∠F.

$\angle C \cong \angle F$	*Third ∆ Thm.*
$m\angle C = m\angle F$	*Def. of ≅ ∆.*
$y^2 = 3y^2 - 72$	*Substitute y^2 for m∠C and $3y^2 - 72$ for m∠F.*
$-2y^2 = -72$	*Subtract $3y^2$ from both sides.*
$y^2 = 36$	*Divide both sides by −2.*

So m∠C = 36°.

Since m∠F = m∠C, m∠F = 36°.

Helpful Hint

You can use substitution to verify that m∠F = 36°. m∠F = (3·36 − 72) = 36°.

CHECK IT OUT! **4.** Find m∠P and m∠T. 32°; 32°

P, $(2x^2)°$, M, N, R, T, S, $(4x^2 - 32)°$

THINK AND DISCUSS

1. Use the Triangle Sum Theorem to explain why the supplement of one of the angles of a triangle equals in measure the sum of the other two angles of the triangle. Support your answer with a sketch.

2. Sketch a triangle and draw all of its exterior angles. How many exterior angles are there at each vertex of the triangle? How many total exterior angles does the triangle have?

Know it! Note

3. GET ORGANIZED Copy and complete the graphic organizer. In each box, write each theorem in words and then draw a diagram to represent it.

Theorem	Words	Diagram
Triangle Sum Theorem		
Exterior Angle Theorem		
Third Angles Theorem		

3 Close

Summarize

Review the Triangle Sum Theorem, the Exterior Angle Theorem, and the Third Angles Theorem. Have several large triangles as models for each theorem. Highlight the specific math concept on each triangle with different colors. Students should then elaborate and discuss each theorem.

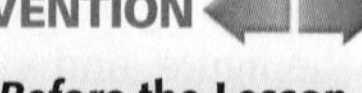

ONGOING ASSESSMENT and INTERVENTION

Diagnose **Before** the Lesson
4-2 Warm Up, TE p. 223

Monitor **During** the Lesson
Check It Out! Exercises, SE pp. 224–226
Questioning Strategies, TE pp. 224–226

Assess **After** the Lesson
4-2 Lesson Quiz, TE p. 230
Alternative Assessment, TE p. 230

Answers to *Think and Discuss*

1. Since ∠3 and ∠4 are supp. ∆, m∠3 + m∠4 = 180° by def. ∠1 + ∠2 + ∠3 = 180° by the △ Sum Thm. By the Trans. Prop. of =, m∠3 + m∠4 = m∠1 + m∠2 + m∠3. Subtract m∠3 from both sides. Then m∠4 = m∠1 + m∠2.

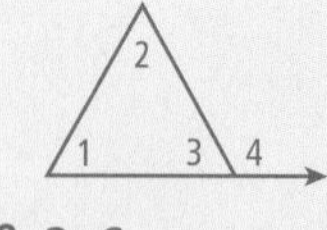

2. 2; 6

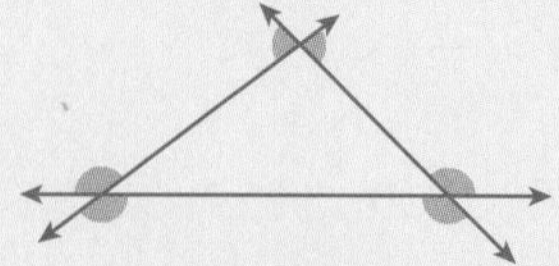

3. See p. A4.

4-2 Exercises

go.hrw.com
Homework Help Online
KEYWORD: MG7 4-2
Parent Resources Online
KEYWORD: MG7 Parent

GUIDED PRACTICE

Vocabulary **Apply the vocabulary from this lesson to answer each question.**

1. To remember the meaning of *remote interior angle*, think of a television remote control. What is another way to remember the term *remote*? **Possible answer: Think "out of the way"**
2. An *exterior angle* is drawn at vertex E of $\triangle DEF$. What are its *remote interior angles*? **$\angle D$; $\angle F$**
3. What do you call segments, rays, or lines that are added to a given diagram? **auxiliary lines**

SEE EXAMPLE 1 p. 224

Astronomy **Use the following information for Exercises 4 and 5.**

An *asterism* is a group of stars that is easier to recognize than a constellation. One popular asterism is the Summer Triangle, which is composed of the stars Deneb, Altair, and Vega.

4. What is the value of y? **17**
5. What is the measure of each angle in the Summer Triangle? **36°; 80°; 64°**

SEE EXAMPLE 2 p. 225

The measure of one of the acute angles in a right triangle is given. What is the measure of the other acute angle?

6. 20.8° **69.2°**
7. $y°$ **$(90 - y)°$**
8. $24\frac{2}{3}°$ **$65\frac{1}{3}°$**

SEE EXAMPLE 3 p. 225

Find each angle measure.

9. $m\angle M$ **28°**

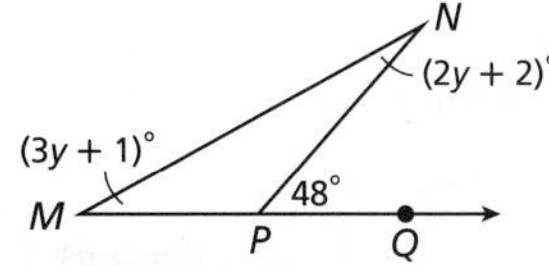

10. $m\angle L$ **41°**

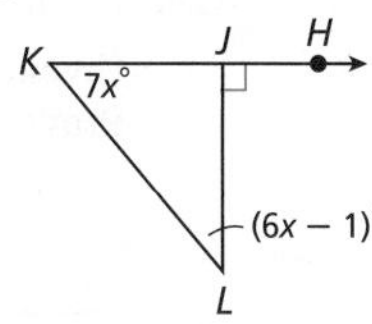

11. In $\triangle ABC$, $m\angle A = 65°$, and the measure of an exterior angle at C is 117°. Find $m\angle B$ and the $m\angle BCA$. **52°; 63°**

SEE EXAMPLE 4 p. 226

12. $m\angle C$ and $m\angle F$ **100°; 100°**

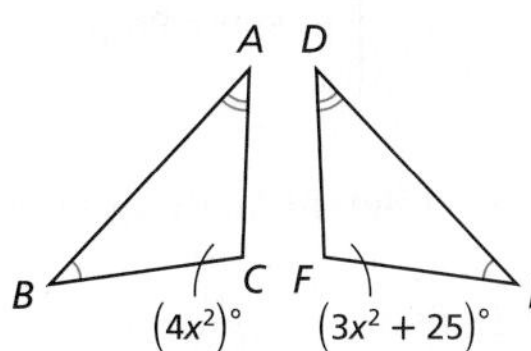

13. $m\angle S$ and $m\angle U$ **89°; 89°**

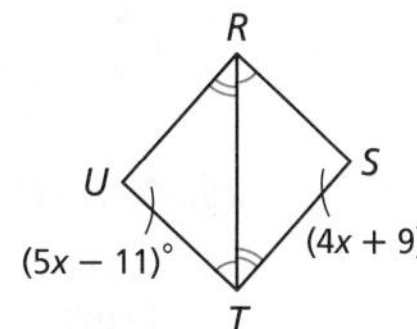

14. For $\triangle ABC$ and $\triangle XYZ$, $m\angle A = m\angle X$ and $m\angle B = m\angle Y$. Find the measures of $\angle C$ and $\angle Z$ if $m\angle C = 4x + 7$ and $m\angle Z = 3(x + 5)$. **39°**

4-2 Exercises

Assignment Guide

Assign *Guided Practice* exercises as necessary.

If you finished Examples **1–2**
- **Basic** 15–18, 23, 24, 29–31, 35
- **Average** 15–18, 23–26, 29–31, 35
- **Advanced** 15–18, 23–26, 29–31, 35, 46, 48, 49

If you finished Examples **1–4**
- **Basic** 15–24, 29–32, 35, 40–44, 50–57
- **Average** 15–24, 29–35, 38–44, 49–57
- **Advanced** 15–29, 33–57

Homework Quick Check
Quickly check key concepts.
Exercises: 15, 16, 20, 22, 24, 29

Algebra In **Exercises 21** and **22,** remind students that they do not have to find the value of y or x, only y^2 and x^2.

Answers

25. Possible answer:
    1. $\triangle ABC$ is equiangular. (Given)
    2. $m\angle A = m\angle B = m\angle C$ (Def. of equiangular)
    3. $m\angle A + m\angle B + m\angle C = 180°$ ($\triangle$ Sum Thm.)
    4. $m\angle A + m\angle A + m\angle A = 180°$ $m\angle B + m\angle B + m\angle B = 180°$ $m\angle C + m\angle C + m\angle C = 180°$ (Subst. Prop.)
    5. $3m\angle A = 180°$, $3m\angle B = 180°$, $3m\angle C = 180°$ (Simplify)
    6. $m\angle A = 60°$, $m\angle B = 60°$, $m\angle C = 60°$ (Div. Prop. of =)

27. 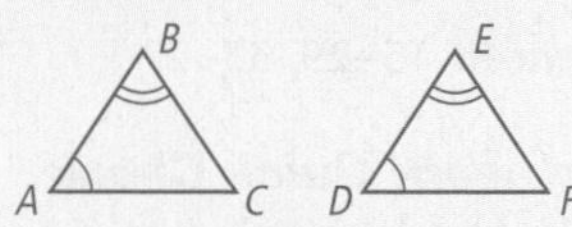

    1. $\triangle ABC$, $\triangle DEF$, $\angle A \cong \angle D$, $\angle B \cong \angle E$ (Given)
    2. $m\angle A + m\angle B + m\angle C = 180°$ ($\triangle$ Sum Thm.)
    3. $m\angle C = 180° - m\angle A - m\angle B$ (Subtr. Prop. of =)
    4. $m\angle D + m\angle E + m\angle F = 180°$ ($\triangle$ Sum Thm.)
    5. $m\angle F = 180° - m\angle D - m\angle E$ (Subtr. Prop. of =)
    6. $m\angle A = m\angle D$, $m\angle B = m\angle E$, (Def. of $\cong$ ∡)
    7. $m\angle F = 180° - m\angle A - m\angle B$ (Subst.)
    8. $m\angle F = m\angle C$ (Trans. Prop. of =)
    9. $\angle F \cong \angle C$ (Def. of $\cong$ ∡)

PRACTICE AND PROBLEM SOLVING

Independent Practice

For Exercises	See Example
15	1
16–18	2
19–20	3
21–22	4

Extra Practice

Skills Practice p. S10
Application Practice p. S31

15. **Navigation** A sailor on ship A measures the angle between ship B and the pier and finds that it is 39°. A sailor on ship B measures the angle between ship A and the pier and finds that it is 57°. What is the measure of the angle between ships A and B? **84°**

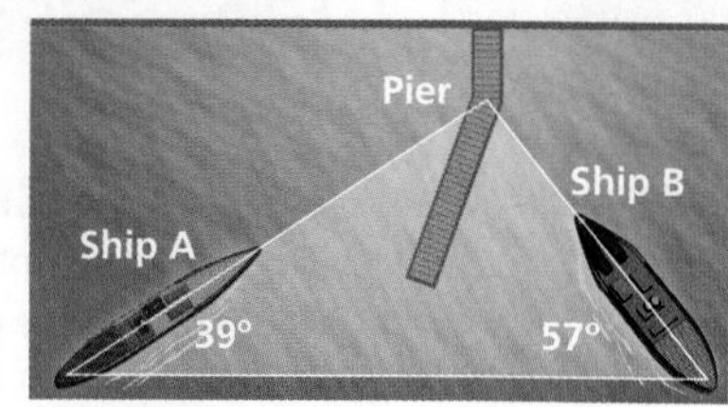

The measure of one of the acute angles in a right triangle is given. What is the measure of the other acute angle?

16. $76\frac{1}{4}°$ **$13\frac{3}{4}°$**　　17. $2x°$ **$(90 - 2x)°$**　　18. 56.8° **33.2°**

Find each angle measure.

19. $m\angle XYZ$ **162°**

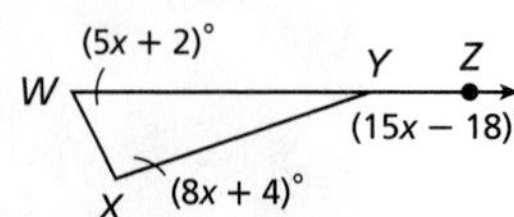

20. $m\angle C$ **61°**

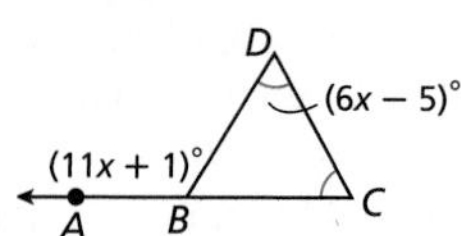

21. $m\angle N$ and $m\angle P$ **48°; 48°**

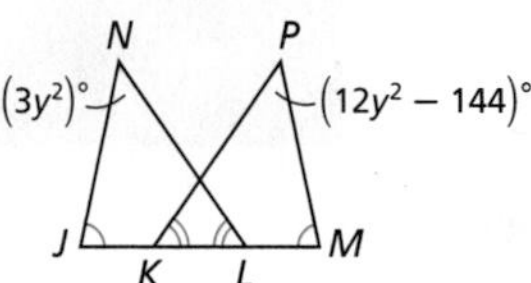

22. $m\angle Q$ and $m\angle S$ **128°; 128°**

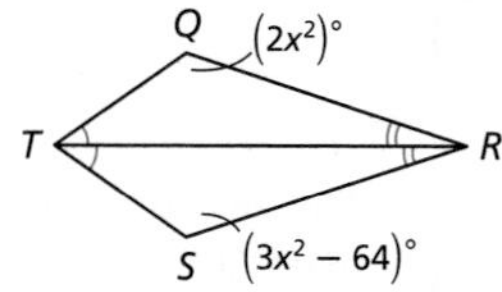

23. **Multi-Step** The measures of the angles of a triangle are in the ratio 1:4:7. What are the measures of the angles? (*Hint:* Let x, $4x$, and $7x$ represent the angle measures.) **15°; 60°; 105°**

24. Complete the proof of Corollary 4-2-2.
    Given: $\triangle DEF$ with right $\angle F$
    Prove: $\angle D$ and $\angle E$ are complementary.
    Proof:

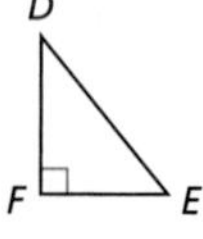

Statements	Reasons
1. $\triangle DEF$ with rt. $\angle F$	1. a. __?__
2. b. __?__	2. Def. of rt. $\angle$
3. $m\angle D + m\angle E + m\angle F = 180°$	3. c. __?__
4. $m\angle D + m\angle E + 90° = 180°$	4. d. __?__
5. e. __?__	5. Subtr. Prop.
6. $\angle D$ and $\angle E$ are comp.	6. f. __?__

a. Given
b. $m\angle F = 90°$
c. $\triangle$ Sum Thm.
d. Subst.
e. $m\angle D + m\angle E = 90°$
f. Def. of comp. ∡

25. Prove Corollary 4-2-3 using two different methods of proof.
    Given: $\triangle ABC$ is equiangular.
    Prove: $m\angle A = m\angle B = m\angle C = 60°$

26. **Multi-Step** The measure of one acute angle in a right triangle is $1\frac{1}{4}$ times the measure of the other acute angle. What is the measure of the larger acute angle? **50°**

27. Write a two-column proof of the Third Angles Theorem.

4-2 PRACTICE A

4-2 PRACTICE C

4-2 PRACTICE B

1. An area in central North Carolina is known as the Research Triangle because of the relatively large number of high-tech companies and research universities located there. Duke University, the University of North Carolina at Chapel Hill, and North Carolina State University are all within this area. The Research Triangle is roughly bounded by the cities of Chapel Hill, Durham, and Raleigh. From Chapel Hill, the angle between Durham and Raleigh measures 54.8°. From Raleigh, the angle between Chapel Hill and Durham measures 24.1°. Find the angle between Chapel Hill and Raleigh from Durham. **101.1°**
2. The acute angles of right triangle ABC are congruent. Find their measures. **45°**

The measure of one of the acute angles in a right triangle is given. Find the measure of the other acute angle.

3. 44.9° **45.1°**　　4. $(90 - z)°$ **$z°$**　　5. 0.3° **89.7°**

Find each angle measure.

6. $m\angle B$ **60°**　　7. $m\angle PRS$ **47°**
8. In $\triangle LMN$, the measure of an exterior angle at N measures 99°. $m\angle L = \frac{1}{3}x°$ and $m\angle M = \frac{2}{3}x°$. Find $m\angle L$, $m\angle M$, and $m\angle LNM$. **33°; 66°; 81°**
9. $m\angle E$ and $m\angle G$ **44°; 44°**　　10. $m\angle T$ and $m\angle V$ **108°; 108°**

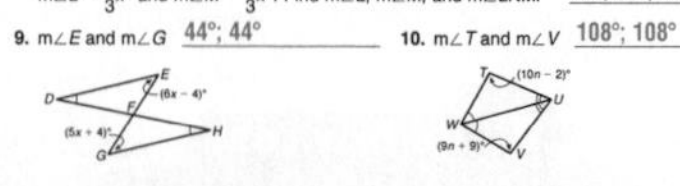

11. In $\triangle ABC$ and $\triangle DEF$, $m\angle A = m\angle D$ and $m\angle B = m\angle E$. Find $m\angle F$ if an exterior angle at A measures 107°, $m\angle B = (5x + 2)°$, and $m\angle C = (5x + 5)°$. **55°**
12. The angle measures of a triangle are in the ratio 3:4:3. Find the angle measures of the triangle. **54°; 72°; 54°**

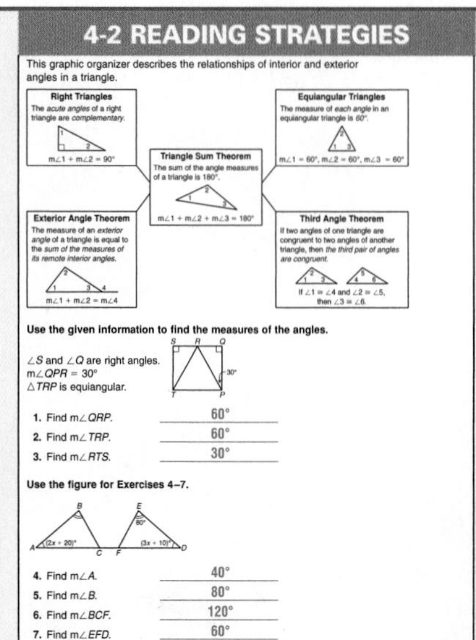

4-2 READING STRATEGIES

This graphic organizer describes the relationships of interior and exterior angles in a triangle.

Right Triangles
The *acute angles* of a right triangle are *complementary*.
$m\angle 1 + m\angle 2 = 90°$

Equiangular Triangles
The measure of *each angle* in an equiangular triangle is *60°*.
$m\angle 1 = 60°$, $m\angle 2 = 60°$, $m\angle 3 = 60°$

Triangle Sum Theorem
The sum of the angle measures of a triangle is 180°.
$m\angle 1 + m\angle 2 + m\angle 3 = 180°$

Exterior Angle Theorem
The measure of an *exterior angle* of a triangle is equal to the *sum of the measures of its remote interior angles.*
$m\angle 1 + m\angle 2 = m\angle 4$

Third Angle Theorem
If two angles of one triangle are congruent to two angles of another triangle, then *the third pair of angles are congruent.*
If $\angle 1 \cong \angle 4$ and $\angle 2 \cong \angle 5$, then $\angle 3 \cong \angle 6$.

Use the given information to find the measures of the angles.

$\angle S$ and $\angle Q$ are right angles.
$m\angle QPR = 30°$
$\triangle TRP$ is equiangular.

1. Find $m\angle QRP$. **60°**
2. Find $m\angle TRP$. **60°**
3. Find $m\angle RTS$. **30°**

Use the figure for Exercises 4–7.

4. Find $m\angle A$. **40°**
5. Find $m\angle B$. **80°**
6. Find $m\angle BCF$. **120°**
7. Find $m\angle EFD$. **60°**

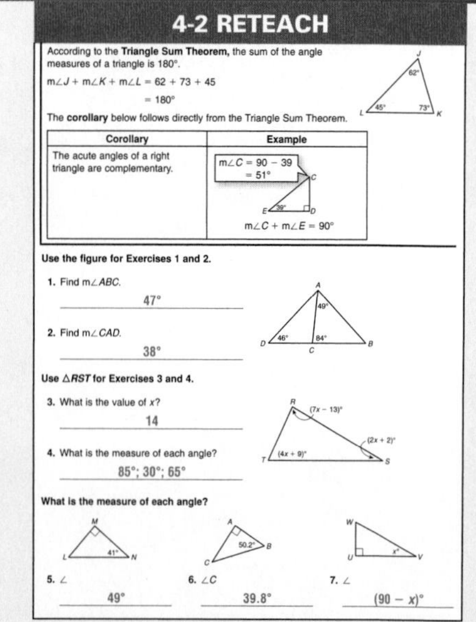

4-2 RETEACH

According to the **Triangle Sum Theorem,** the sum of the angle measures of a triangle is 180°.

$m\angle J + m\angle K + m\angle L = 62 + 73 + 45$
$= 180°$

The **corollary** below follows directly from the Triangle Sum Theorem.

Corollary	Example
The acute angles of a right triangle are complementary.	$m\angle C = 90 - 39 = 51°$; $m\angle C + m\angle E = 90°$

Use the figure for Exercises 1 and 2.

1. Find $m\angle ABC$. **47°**
2. Find $m\angle CAD$. **38°**

Use $\triangle RST$ for Exercises 3 and 4.

3. What is the value of x? **14**
4. What is the measure of each angle? **85°; 30°; 65°**

What is the measure of each angle?

5. $\angle$ **49°**　　6. $\angle C$ **39.8°**　　7. $\angle$ **$(90 - x)°$**

28. Prove the Exterior Angle Theorem.
Given: $\triangle ABC$ with exterior angle $\angle ACD$
Prove: $m\angle ACD = m\angle A + m\angle B$
(*Hint:* $\angle BCA$ and $\angle DCA$ form a linear pair.)

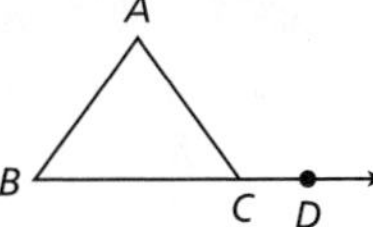

Find each angle measure.

29. $\angle UXW$ **36°**
30. $\angle UWY$ **48°**
31. $\angle WZX$ **48°**
32. $\angle XYZ$ **42°**

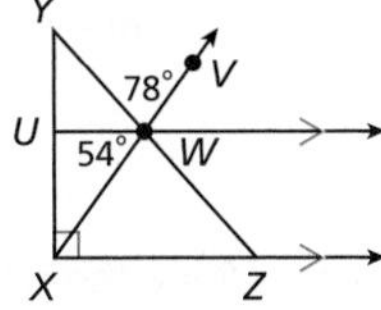

33. **Critical Thinking** What is the measure of any exterior angle of an equiangular triangle? What is the sum of the exterior angle measures? **120°; 360°**

34. Find $m\angle SRQ$, given that $\angle P \cong \angle U$, $\angle Q \cong \angle T$, and $m\angle RST = 37.5°$. **37.5°**

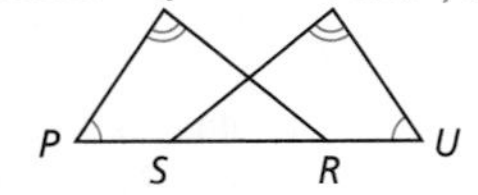

35. **Multi-Step** In a right triangle, one acute angle measure is 4 times the other acute angle measure. What is the measure of the smaller angle? **18°**

36. **Aviation** To study the forces of lift and drag, the Wright brothers built a glider, attached two ropes to it, and flew it like a kite. They modeled the two wind forces as the legs of a right triangle.

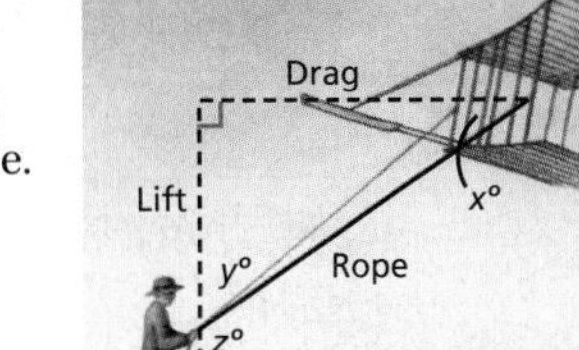

a. What part of a right triangle is formed by each rope?
b. Use the Triangle Sum Theorem to write an equation relating the angle measures in the right triangle.
c. Simplify the equation from part **b**. What is the relationship between x and y?
d. Use the Exterior Angle Theorem to write an expression for z in terms of x.
e. If $x = 37°$, use your results from parts **c** and **d** to find y and z.

36a. hyp.
b. $x° + y° + 90° = 180°$
c. $x° + y° = 90°$; x and y are comp. ∠s
d. $z° = x° + 90°$
e. 53°; 127°

37. **Estimation** Draw a triangle and two exterior angles at each vertex. Estimate the measure of each angle. How are the exterior angles at each vertex related? Explain.

38. **Given:** $\overline{AB} \perp \overline{BD}$, $\overline{BD} \perp \overline{DC}$, $\angle A \cong \angle C$
Prove: $\overline{AD} \parallel \overline{CB}$

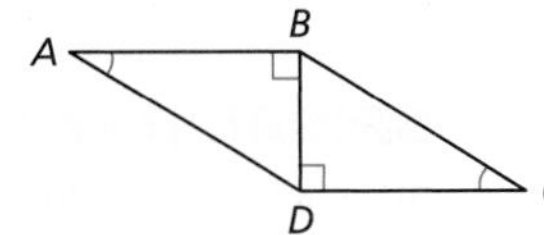

39. **Write About It** A triangle has angle measures of 115°, 40°, and 25°. Explain how to find the measures of the triangle's exterior angles. Support your answer with a sketch.

39. Check students' drawings. The measures of the ext. ∠s will be the sum of the pairs of remote int. ∠s: 155°, 65°, and 140°.

MULTI-STEP TEST PREP

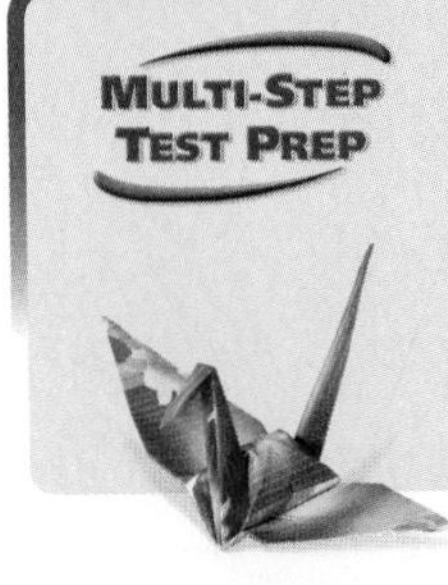

40. This problem will prepare you for the Multi-Step Test Prep on page 238.
One of the steps in making an origami crane involves folding a square sheet of paper into the shape shown.

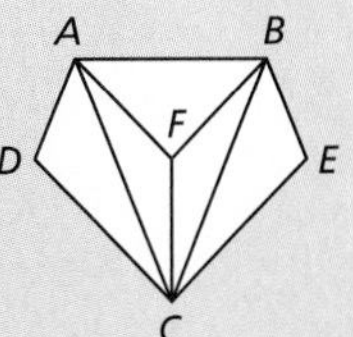

a. $\angle DCE$ is a right angle. $\overline{FC}$ bisects $\angle DCE$, and $\overline{BC}$ bisects $\angle FCE$. Find $m\angle FCB$. **22.5°**
b. Use the Triangle Sum Theorem to find $m\angle CBE$. **67.5°**

COMMON ERROR ALERT

In **Exercise 26,** students may not remember how to solve $x + 1\frac{1}{4}x = 90$. Remind them that x means $1x$, so $1x + 1\frac{1}{4}x$ is $2\frac{1}{4}x$. Then be sure they divide 90 by $2\frac{1}{4}$ or multiply 90 by $\frac{4}{9}$, not $\frac{9}{4}$, to find x.

MULTI-STEP TEST PREP **Exercise 40** involves folding a sheet of paper into a given shape. This exercise prepares students for the Multi-Step Test Prep on page 238.

Answers

28. 1. $\triangle ABC$ with ext. $\angle ACD$ (Given)
2. $m\angle A + m\angle B + m\angle ACB = 180°$ (△ Sum Thm.)
3. $m\angle ACB + m\angle ACD = 180°$ (Lin. Pair Thm.)
4. $m\angle ACD = 180° - m\angle ACB$ (Subtr. Prop. of =)
5. $m\angle ACD = (m\angle A + m\angle B + m\angle ACB) - m\angle ACB$ (Subst.)
6. $m\angle ACD = m\angle A + m\angle B$ (Simplify)

37.

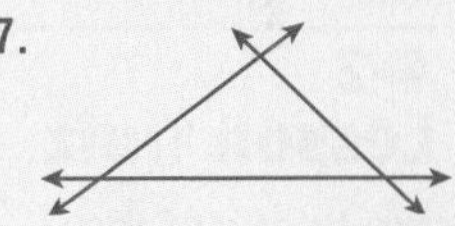

The ext. ∠s at the same vertex of a △ are vert. ∠s. Since vert. ∠s are ≅, the 2 ext. ∠s have the same measure.

38. 1. $\overline{AB} \perp \overline{BD}$, $\overline{BD} \perp \overline{DC}$, $\angle A \cong \angle C$ (Given)
2. $\angle ABD$ and $\angle CDB$ are rt. ∠s. (Def. of ⊥ lines)
3. $m\angle ABD = m\angle CDB$ (Def. of rt. ∠s)
4. $\angle ABD \cong \angle CDB$ (Rt. ∠ ≅ Thm.)
5. $\angle ADB \cong \angle CBD$ (Third ∠s Thm.)
6. $\overline{AD} \parallel \overline{CB}$ (Conv. of Alt. Int. ∠s Thm.)

4-2 PROBLEM SOLVING

1. The locations of three food stands on a fair's midway are shown. What is the measure of the angle labeled $x°$?
121°

2. A large triangular piece of plywood is to be painted to look like a mountain for the spring musical. The angles at the base of the plywood measure 76° and 45°. What is the measure of the top angle that represents the mountain peak?
59°

Use the figure of the banner for Exercises 3 and 4.

3. What is the value of n?
$n = 12$

4. What is the measure of each angle in the banner?
76°, 76°, 28°

Use the figure of the athlete pole vaulting for Exercises 5 and 6.

5. What is $x°$, the measure of the angle that the pole makes when it first touches the ground?
32°

6. At takeoff, $a° = 23°$. What is $c°$, the measure of the angle the pole makes with the athlete's body?
113°

The figure shows a path through a garden. Choose the best answer.

7. What is the measure of $\angle QLP$?
A 20° C 110°
(B) 70° D 125°

8. What is the measure of $\angle LPM$?
F 85° (H) 95°
G 90° J 125°

9. What is the measure of $\angle PMN$?
A 98° C 60°
(B) 68° D 55°

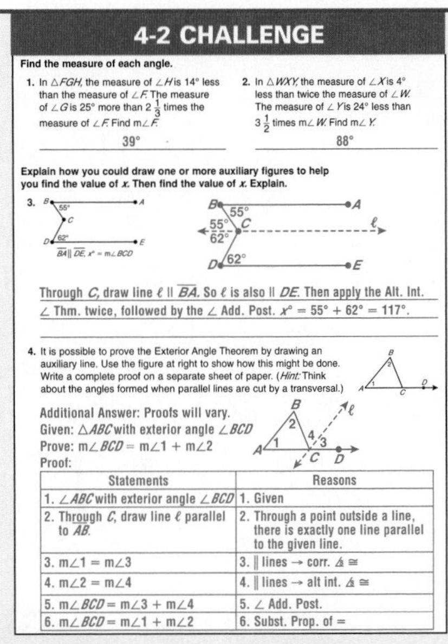

4-2 CHALLENGE

Find the measure of each angle.

1. In $\triangle FGH$, the measure of $\angle H$ is 14° less than the measure of $\angle F$. The measure of $\angle G$ is 25° more than $2\frac{1}{3}$ times the measure of $\angle F$. Find $m\angle F$.
39°

2. In $\triangle WXY$, the measure of $\angle X$ is 4° less than twice the measure of $\angle W$. The measure of $\angle Y$ is 24° less than $3\frac{1}{2}$ times $m\angle W$. Find $m\angle Y$.
88°

Explain how you could draw one or more auxiliary figures to help you find the value of x. Then find the value of x. Explain.

3. $\overline{BA} \parallel \overline{DE}$, $x° = m\angle BCD$

Through C, draw line $\ell \parallel \overline{BA}$. So ℓ is also $\parallel DE$. Then apply the Alt. Int. ∠ Thm. twice, followed by the ∠ Add. Post. $x° = 55° + 62° = 117°$.

4. It is possible to prove the Exterior Angle Theorem by drawing an auxiliary line. Use the figure at right to show how this might be done. Write a complete proof on a separate sheet of paper. (*Hint:* Think about the angles formed when parallel lines are cut by a transversal.)

Additional Answer: Proofs will vary.
Given: $\triangle ABC$ with exterior angle $\angle BCD$
Prove: $m\angle BCD = m\angle 1 + m\angle 2$
Proof:

Statements	Reasons
1. $\angle ABC$ with exterior angle $\angle BCD$	1. Given
2. Through C, draw line ℓ parallel to $\overline{AB}$.	2. Through a point outside a line, there is exactly one line parallel to the given line.
3. $m\angle 1 = m\angle 3$	3. ∥ lines → corr. ∠s ≅
4. $m\angle 2 = m\angle 4$	4. ∥ lines → alt int. ∠s ≅
5. $m\angle BCD = m\angle 3 + m\angle 4$	5. ∠ Add. Post.
6. $m\angle BCD = m\angle 1 + m\angle 2$	6. Subst. Prop. of =

TEST PREP DOCTOR  If students have difficulty with **Exercise 43,** have them draw and label $\triangle ABC$ with $\overline{AC}$ extended to D and then use reasonable angle measures to estimate the answer.

Journal

Have students describe how they remember which angles are remote interior angles and which ones are exterior angles.

ALTERNATIVE ASSESSMENT

Have small groups of students compare answers to statements that are always, sometimes, or never true. For example, the supplement of one of the angles of a triangle is equal to the sum of the other two angles of the triangle. Then have the students write a statement to justify their answers. Encourage students to draw diagrams to support their answers.

Power Presentations with PowerPoint®

4-2 Lesson Quiz

1. The measure of one of the acute angles in a right triangle is $56\frac{2}{3}°$. What is the measure of the other acute angle? $33\frac{1}{3}°$
2. Find m∠ABD. 124°

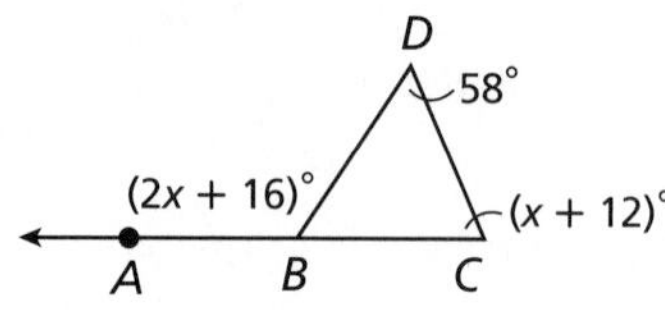

3. Find m∠N and m∠P. 75°, 75°

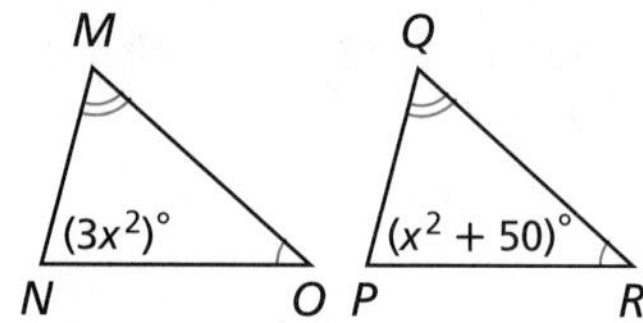

4. The diagram is a map showing John's house, Kay's house, and the grocery store. What is the angle the two houses make with the store? 30°

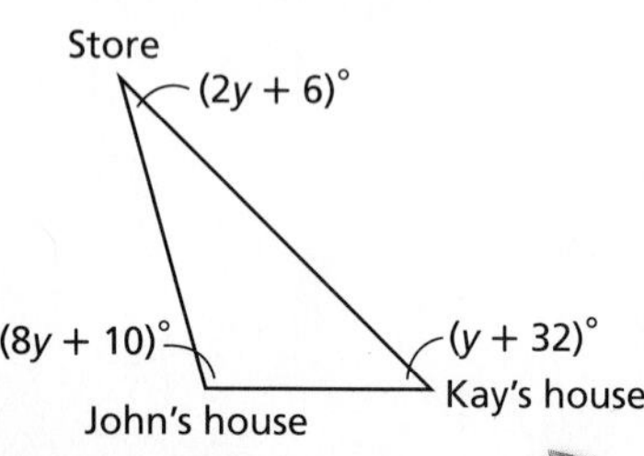

Also available on transparency

TEST PREP

41. What is the value of x?
   (A) 19 (B) 52 **(C) 57** (D) 71

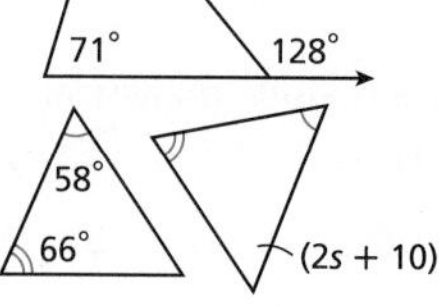

42. Find the value of s.
   (F) 23 (G) 28 (H) 34 (J) 56

43. ∠A and ∠B are the remote interior angles of ∠BCD in △ABC. Which of these equations must be true?
   (A) m∠A − 180° = m∠B
   (B) m∠A = 90° − m∠B
   (C) m∠BCD = m∠BCA − m∠A
   (D) m∠B = m∠BCD − m∠A

44. **Extended Response** The measures of the angles in a triangle are in the ratio 2:3:4. Describe how to use algebra to find the measures of these angles. Then find the measure of each angle and classify the triangle.

CHALLENGE AND EXTEND

45. An exterior angle of a triangle measures 117°. Its remote interior angles measure $(2y^2 + 7)°$ and $(61 - y^2)°$. Find the value of y. **7 or −7**
46. Two parallel lines are intersected by a transversal. What type of triangle is formed by the intersection of the angle bisectors of two same-side interior angles? Explain. (*Hint:* Use geometry software or construct a diagram of the angle bisectors of two same-side interior angles.)

46. A rt. △ is formed. The 2 same-side int. ∠s are supp., so the 2 ∠s formed by their bisectors must be comp. That means the remaining ∠ of the △ must measure 90°.

47. **Critical Thinking** Explain why an exterior angle of a triangle cannot be congruent to a remote interior angle.
48. **Probability** The measure of each angle in a triangle is a multiple of 30°. What is the probability that the triangle has at least two congruent angles? $\frac{2}{3}$
49. In △ABC, m∠B is 5° less than $1\frac{1}{2}$ times m∠A. m∠C is 5° less than $2\frac{1}{2}$ times m∠A. What is m∠A in degrees? **38°**

SPIRAL REVIEW

Make a table to show the value of each function when x is −2, 0, 1, and 4. *(Previous course)*

50. $f(x) = 3x - 4$
51. $f(x) = x^2 + 1$
52. $f(x) = (x - 3)^2 + 5$
53. Find the length of $\overline{NQ}$. Name the theorem or postulate that justifies your answer. *(Lesson 1-2)* **6 in.; Seg. Add. Post.**

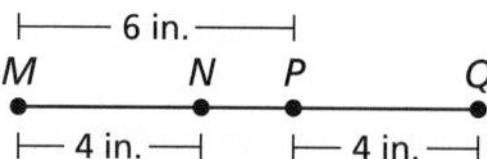

Classify each triangle by its side lengths. *(Lesson 4-1)*

54. △ACD **isosc.**
55. △BCD **scalene**
56. △ABD **scalene**
57. **What if...?** If CA = 8, What is the effect on the classification of △ACD? **△ACD is equil.**

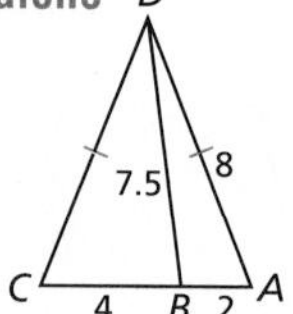

Answers

44. Let 2x, 3x, and 4x represent the ∠ measures. The sum of the ∠ measures of a △ is 180°, so 2x + 3x + 4x = 180°. Solving the eqn. for the value of x, yields x = 20. Find each measure by substituting 20 for x in each expression. 2x = 2(20) = 40; 3x = 3(20) = 60; 4x = 4(20) = 80. Since all of the ∠s measure less than 90°, they are acute ∠s by def. Thus the △ is acute.
47. Since an ext. ∠ is = to a sum of 2 remote int. ∠s, it must be greater than either ∠. Therefore it cannot be ≅ to a remote int. ∠.

50–52. See p. A15.

4-3 Congruent Triangles

Objectives
Use properties of congruent triangles.

Prove triangles congruent by using the definition of congruence.

Vocabulary
corresponding angles
corresponding sides
congruent polygons

Who uses this?
Machinists used triangles to construct a model of the International Space Station's support structure.

Geometric figures are congruent if they are the same size and shape. **Corresponding angles** and **corresponding sides** are in the same position in polygons with an equal number of sides. Two polygons are **congruent polygons** if and only if their corresponding angles and sides are congruent. Thus triangles that are the same size and shape are congruent.

Know it! Note — **Properties of Congruent Polygons**

DIAGRAM	CORRESPONDING ANGLES	CORRESPONDING SIDES
$\triangle ABC \cong \triangle DEF$	$\angle A \cong \angle D$ $\angle B \cong \angle E$ $\angle C \cong \angle F$	$\overline{AB} \cong \overline{DE}$ $\overline{BC} \cong \overline{EF}$ $\overline{AC} \cong \overline{DF}$
polygon $PQRS \cong$ polygon $WXYZ$	$\angle P \cong \angle W$ $\angle Q \cong \angle X$ $\angle R \cong \angle Y$ $\angle S \cong \angle Z$	$\overline{PQ} \cong \overline{WX}$ $\overline{QR} \cong \overline{XY}$ $\overline{RS} \cong \overline{YZ}$ $\overline{PS} \cong \overline{WZ}$

Helpful Hint

Two vertices that are the endpoints of a side are called consecutive vertices. For example, *P* and *Q* are consecutive vertices.

To name a polygon, write the vertices in consecutive order. For example, you can name polygon *PQRS* as *QRSP* or *SRQP*, but **not** as *PRQS*. In a congruence statement, the order of the vertices indicates the corresponding parts.

EXAMPLE 1 Naming Congruent Corresponding Parts

$\triangle RST$ and $\triangle XYZ$ represent the triangles of the space station's support structure. If $\triangle RST \cong \triangle XYZ$, identify all pairs of congruent corresponding parts.

Angles: $\angle R \cong \angle X$, $\angle S \cong \angle Y$, $\angle T \cong \angle Z$

Sides: $\overline{RS} \cong \overline{XY}$, $\overline{ST} \cong \overline{YZ}$, $\overline{RT} \cong \overline{XZ}$

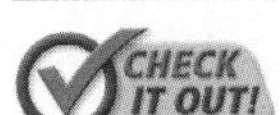

CHECK IT OUT! 1. If polygon $LMNP \cong$ polygon $EFGH$, identify all pairs of corresponding congruent parts.

$\angle L \cong \angle E$, $\angle M \cong \angle F$, $\angle N \cong \angle G$, $\angle P \cong \angle H$, $\overline{LM} \cong \overline{EF}$, $\overline{MN} \cong \overline{FG}$, $\overline{NP} \cong \overline{GH}$, $\overline{LP} \cong \overline{EH}$

4-3 Organizer

Pacing: Traditional 1 day
Block $\frac{1}{2}$ day

Objectives: Use properties of congruent triangles.

Prove triangles congruent by using the definition of congruence.

Online Edition
Tutorial Videos, Interactivity

Countdown Week 7

Power Presentations with PowerPoint®

Warm Up

1. Name all sides and angles of $\triangle FGH$. $\overline{FG}$, $\overline{GH}$, $\overline{FH}$, $\angle F$, $\angle G$, $\angle H$
2. What is true about $\angle K$ and $\angle L$? Why? $\cong$; Third ∡ Thm.

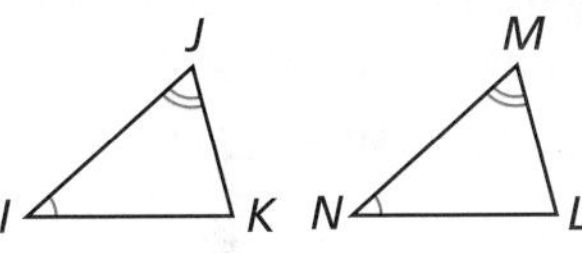

3. What does it mean for two segments to be congruent? They have the same length.

Also available on transparency

Math Humor

Q: What quantity is represented by three congruent dirty trees?

A: 99. dirty tree + dirty tree + dirty tree

1 Introduce

EXPLORATION

4-3 Congruent Triangles

In this Exploration you will investigate triangles that have the same size and shape.

1. Draw a large scalene $\triangle ABC$.
2. Use a ruler to find the midpoint of each side. Connect the midpoints to form $\triangle DEF$.

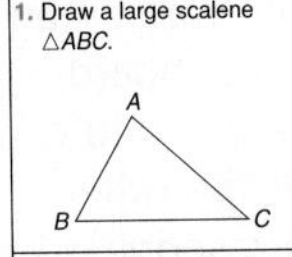

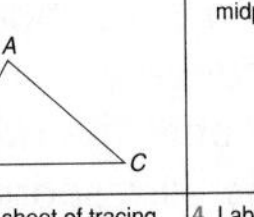

3. Place a sheet of tracing paper over your drawing and copy $\triangle DEF$.
4. Label the interior of each angle of $\triangle DEF$ with the letter of its vertex. Cut out $\triangle DEF$.
5. Place the cutout triangle on top of the figure in Step 2. Find all the triangles that are the same size and shape as $\triangle DEF$. List these triangles.
6. Choose one of the triangles that has the same size and shape as $\triangle DEF$. When the cutout triangle is placed on top of this triangle, which pairs of angles match up? Which pairs of sides match up?

THINK AND DISCUSS

Motivate

Show students a quilt or other pattern and ask them to identify all the triangles that look identical in size and shape. Explain that they will learn the properties used to prove certain triangles are identical, or congruent. Encourage students to think of examples where congruent triangles may be used or seen in the real world, such as in furniture, buildings, art, and floor tiles.

Explorations and answers are provided in *Alternate Openers: Explorations Transparencies.*

State Resources

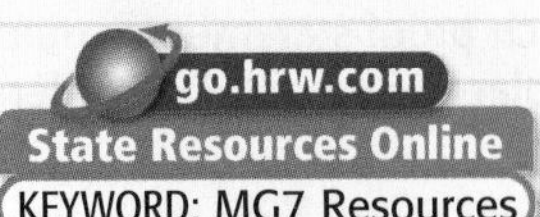

Power Presentations with PowerPoint®

Additional Examples

Example 1

Given: $\triangle PQR \cong \triangle STW$. Identify all pairs of congruent corresponding parts. $\angle P \cong \angle S$, $\angle Q \cong \angle T$, $\angle R \cong \angle W$, $\overline{PQ} \cong \overline{ST}$, $\overline{PR} \cong \overline{SW}$, $\overline{QR} \cong \overline{TW}$

Example 2

Given: $\triangle ABC \cong \triangle DBC$

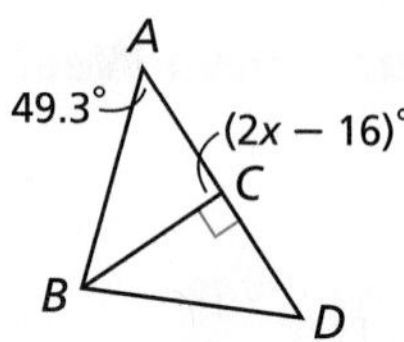

A. Find the value of x. 53

B. Find $m\angle DBC$. 40.7°

Example 3

Given: $\angle YWX$ and $\angle YWZ$ are right angles. $\overline{YW}$ bisects $\angle XYZ$. W is the midpoint of $\overline{XZ}$. $\overline{XY} \cong \overline{YZ}$.

Prove: $\triangle XYW \cong \triangle ZYW$

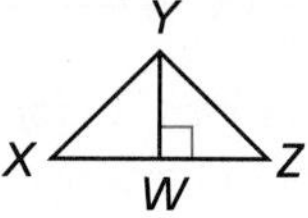

1. $\angle YWX$ and $\angle YWZ$ are rt. ∡. (Given)
2. $\angle YWX \cong \angle YWZ$ (Rt. $\angle \cong$ Thm.)
3. $\overline{YW}$ bisects $\angle XYZ$. (Given)
4. $\angle XYW \cong \angle ZYW$ (Def. of $\angle$ bisector)
5. W is mdpt. of $\overline{XZ}$. (Given)
6. $\overline{XW} \cong \overline{ZW}$ (Def. of mdpt.)
7. $\overline{YW} \cong \overline{YW}$ (Reflex. Prop. of $\cong$)
8. $\angle X \cong \angle Z$ (Third ∡ Thm.)
9. $\overline{XY} \cong \overline{YZ}$ (Given)
10. $\triangle XYW \cong \triangle ZYW$ (Def. of $\cong$ ▵)

INTERVENTION 

Questioning Strategies

EXAMPLE 1

- How does a triangle congruence statement indicate corresponding parts?

EXAMPLE 2

- What properties do you use to find the measure of the angle?

EXAMPLE 3

- Which proof statements could not be placed in a different order?

EXAMPLE 2 **Using Corresponding Parts of Congruent Triangles**

x^2_y **Algebra**

Given: $\triangle EFH \cong \triangle GFH$

F, 21.6°, E, (6x – 12)° H, G

A **Find the value of x.**

$\angle FHE$ and $\angle FHG$ are rt. ∡.	*Def. of ⊥ lines*
$\angle FHE \cong \angle FHG$	*Rt. $\angle \cong$ Thm.*
$m\angle FHE = m\angle FHG$	*Def. of $\cong$ ∡*
$(6x - 12)^\circ = 90^\circ$	*Substitute values for $m\angle FHE$ and $m\angle FHG$.*
$6x = 102$	*Add 12 to both sides.*
$x = 17$	*Divide both sides by 6.*

Helpful Hint

When you write a statement such as $\triangle ABC \cong \triangle DEF$, you are also stating which parts are congruent.

B **Find $m\angle GFH$.**

$m\angle EFH + m\angle FHE + m\angle E = 180^\circ$	*△ Sum Thm.*
$m\angle EFH + 90 + 21.6 = 180$	*Substitute values for $m\angle FHE$ and $m\angle E$.*
$m\angle EFH + 111.6 = 180$	*Simplify.*
$m\angle EFH = 68.4$	*Subtract 111.6 from both sides.*
$\angle GFH \cong \angle EFH$	*Corr. ∡ of $\cong$ ▵ are $\cong$.*
$m\angle GFH = m\angle EFH$	*Def. of $\cong$ ∡*
$m\angle GFH = 68.4^\circ$	*Trans. Prop. of =*

Given: $\triangle ABC \cong \triangle DEF$

2a. Find the value of x.

2b. Find $m\angle F$.

2a. 4

2b. 37°

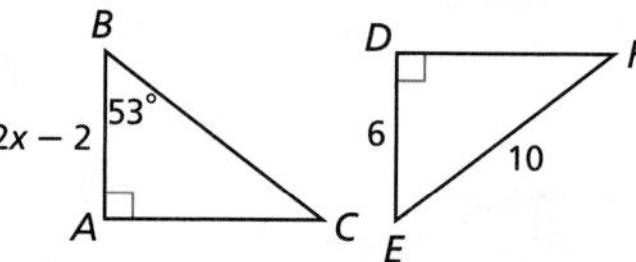

EXAMPLE 3 **Proving Triangles Congruent**

Given: $\angle P$ and $\angle M$ are right angles.
R is the midpoint of $\overline{PM}$.
$\overline{PQ} \cong \overline{MN}$, $\overline{QR} \cong \overline{NR}$

Prove: $\triangle PQR \cong \triangle MNR$

Proof:

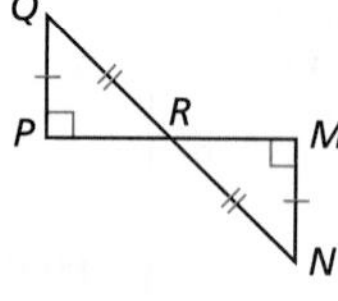

Statements	Reasons
1. $\angle P$ and $\angle M$ are rt. ∡	1. Given
2. $\angle P \cong \angle M$	2. Rt. $\angle \cong$ Thm.
3. $\angle PRQ \cong \angle MRN$	3. Vert. ∡ Thm.
4. $\angle Q \cong \angle N$	4. Third ∡ Thm.
5. R is the mdpt. of $\overline{PM}$.	5. Given
6. $\overline{PR} \cong \overline{MR}$	6. Def. of mdpt.
7. $\overline{PQ} \cong \overline{MN}$; $\overline{QR} \cong \overline{NR}$	7. Given
8. $\triangle PQR \cong \triangle MNR$	8. Def. of $\cong$ ▵

3. Given: $\overline{AD}$ bisects $\overline{BE}$.
$\overline{BE}$ bisects $\overline{AD}$.
$\overline{AB} \cong \overline{DE}$, $\angle A \cong \angle D$

Prove: $\triangle ABC \cong \triangle DEC$

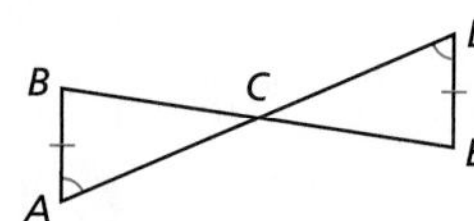

2 Teach

Guided Instruction

Show students how to name a polygon by writing the vertices in consecutive order. Discuss naming corresponding sides and angles of congruent polygons, including those that overlap.

Reading Math Explain that the everyday meaning of the word *consecutive* is "following one another without interruption."

ENGLISH LANGUAGE LEARNERS

Reaching All Learners

Through Visual Cues

Use two different-colored transparencies of congruent triangles. Demonstrate on an overhead projector or on a white board that if two triangles are congruent, you can slide one triangle exactly onto the other. Have students identify the corresponding sides and angles.

Student to Student *Overlapping Triangles*

Cecelia Medina
Lamar High School

"With overlapping triangles, it helps me to redraw the triangles separately. That way I can mark what I know about one triangle without getting confused by the other one."

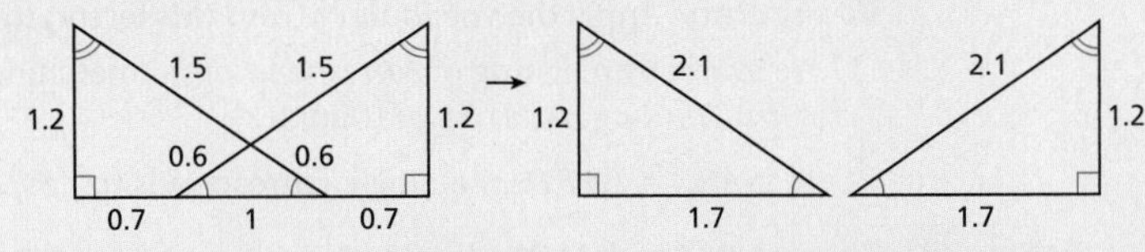

EXAMPLE 4 ***Engineering Application***

The bars that give structural support to a roller coaster form triangles. Since the angle measures and the lengths of the corresponding sides are the same, the triangles are congruent.

Given: $\overline{JK} \perp \overline{KL}$, $\overline{ML} \perp \overline{KL}$, $\angle KLJ \cong \angle LKM$, $\overline{JK} \cong \overline{ML}$, $\overline{JL} \cong \overline{MK}$

Prove: $\triangle JKL \cong \triangle MLK$

Proof:

Statements	Reasons
1. $\overline{JK} \perp \overline{KL}$, $\overline{ML} \perp \overline{KL}$	1. Given
2. $\angle JKL$ and $\angle MLK$ are rt. ∠s.	2. Def. of ⊥ lines
3. $\angle JKL \cong \angle MLK$	3. Rt. ∠ ≅ Thm.
4. $\angle KLJ \cong \angle LKM$	4. Given
5. $\angle KJL \cong \angle LMK$	5. Third ∠s Thm.
6. $\overline{JK} \cong \overline{ML}$, $\overline{JL} \cong \overline{MK}$	6. Given
7. $\overline{KL} \cong \overline{LK}$	7. Reflex. Prop. of ≅
8. $\triangle JKL \cong \triangle MLK$	8. Def. of ≅ △s

4. Use the diagram to prove the following.
Given: $\overline{MK}$ bisects $\overline{JL}$. $\overline{JL}$ bisects $\overline{MK}$. $\overline{JK} \cong \overline{ML}$, $\overline{JK} \parallel \overline{ML}$
Prove: $\triangle JKN \cong \triangle LMN$

THINK AND DISCUSS

1. A roof truss is a triangular structure that supports a roof. How can you be sure that two roof trusses are the same size and shape?

2. GET ORGANIZED Copy and complete the graphic organizer. In each box, name the congruent corresponding parts.

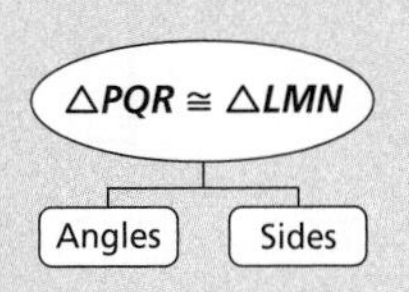

3 Close

Summarize

Review how to name corresponding angles and sides of congruent polygons. Remind students that to prove two triangles congruent, you must show all three pairs of sides and all three pairs of angles are congruent.

ONGOING ASSESSMENT

and INTERVENTION

***Diagnose Before* the Lesson**
4-3 Warm Up, TE p. 231

***Monitor During* the Lesson**
Check It Out! Exercises, SE pp. 231–233
Questioning Strategies, TE pp. 232–233

***Assess After* the Lesson**
4-3 Lesson Quiz, TE p. 237
Alternative Assessment, TE p. 237

COMMON ERROR ALERT

In **Example 4,** students may write $\triangle JKL = \triangle MLK$ instead of $\triangle JKL \cong \triangle MLK$. Stress the difference between the meanings of *equal* and *congruent*.

Power Presentations with PowerPoint®

Additional Examples

Example 4

The diagonal bars across a gate give it support. Since the angle measures and the lengths of the corresponding sides are the same, the triangles are congruent.

Given: $\overline{PR}$ and $\overline{QT}$ bisect each other. $\angle PQS \cong \angle RTS$, $\overline{QP} \cong \overline{RT}$
Prove: $\triangle QPS \cong \triangle TRS$

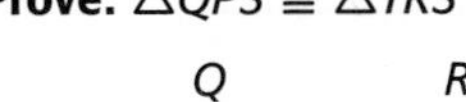

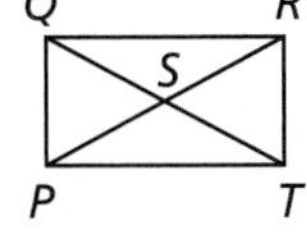

1. $\overline{QP} \cong \overline{RT}$ (Given)
2. $\angle PQS \cong \angle RTS$ (Given)
3. $\overline{PR}$ and $\overline{QT}$ bisect each other. (Given)
4. $\overline{QS} \cong \overline{TS}$, $\overline{PS} \cong \overline{RS}$ (Def. of bisector)
5. $\angle QSP \cong \angle TSR$ (Vert. ∠s Thm.)
6. $\angle QPS \cong \angle TRS$ (Third ∠s Thm.)
7. $\triangle QPS \cong \triangle TRS$ (Def. of ≅ △s)

INTERVENTION
Questioning Strategies

EXAMPLE 

- What all do you need to know for this proof? Explain.

Answers to *Check It Out!*

3–4. See p. A15.

Answers to *Think and Discuss*

1. Measure all the sides and all the ∠s.
   The trusses are the same size and shape if all the corr. sides and ∠s are ≅.
2. See p. A4.

4-3 Exercises

go.hrw.com
Homework Help Online
KEYWORD: MG7 4-3
Parent Resources Online
KEYWORD: MG7 Parent

Assignment Guide

Assign *Guided Practice* exercises as necessary.

If you finished Examples **1–2**
Basic 13–18, 21, 23–25
Average 13–18, 21, 22–25
Advanced 13–18, 21, 22–25, 36

If you finished Examples **1–4**
Basic 13–20, 23–26, 29, 31–34, 38–45
Average 13–26, 28–35, 38–45
Advanced 13–20, 22–28, 30–45

Homework Quick Check
Quickly check key concepts.
Exercises: 13, 18, 19, 20, 24

Answers

1. You find the ∠s and sides that are in the same, or matching, places in the 2 △s.

GUIDED PRACTICE

Vocabulary **Apply the vocabulary from this lesson to answer each question.**

1. An everyday meaning of *corresponding* is "matching." How can this help you find the *corresponding* parts of two triangles?
2. If $\triangle ABC \cong \triangle RST$, what angle corresponds to $\angle S$? **∠B**

SEE EXAMPLE 1 p. 231

Given: $\triangle RST \cong \triangle LMN$. Identify the congruent corresponding parts.

3. $\overline{RS} \cong$ __?__ $\overline{LM}$
4. $\overline{LN} \cong$ __?__ $\overline{RT}$
5. $\angle S \cong$ __?__ $\angle M$
6. $\overline{TS} \cong$ __?__ $\overline{NM}$
7. $\angle L \cong$ __?__ $\angle R$
8. $\angle N \cong$ __?__ $\angle T$

SEE EXAMPLE 2 p. 232

Given: $\triangle FGH \cong \triangle JKL$. Find each value.

9. KL **9**
10. x **32**

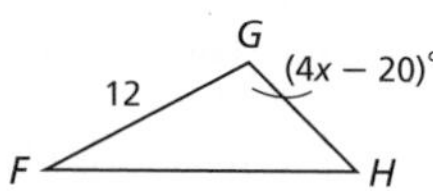

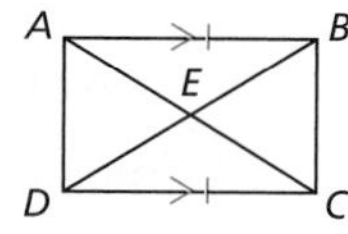

SEE EXAMPLE 3 p. 232

11. **Given:** E is the midpoint of $\overline{AC}$ and $\overline{BD}$. $\overline{AB} \cong \overline{CD}$, $\overline{AB} \parallel \overline{CD}$
Prove: $\triangle ABE \cong \triangle CDE$
Proof:

A B E D C

Statements	Reasons
1. $\overline{AB} \parallel \overline{CD}$	1. a. __?__
2. $\angle ABE \cong \angle CDE$, $\angle BAE \cong \angle DCE$	2. b. __?__
3. $\overline{AB} \cong \overline{CD}$	3. c. __?__
4. E is the mdpt. of $\overline{AC}$ and $\overline{BD}$.	4. d. __?__
5. e. __?__	5. Def. of mdpt.
6. $\angle AEB \cong \angle CED$	6. f. __?__
7. $\triangle ABE \cong \triangle CDE$	7. g. __?__

a. Given
b. Alt. Int. ∠s Thm.
c. Given
d. Given
e. $\overline{AE} \cong \overline{CE}$, $\overline{DE} \cong \overline{BE}$
f. Vert. ∠s Thm.
g. Def. of ≅ △s

SEE EXAMPLE 4 p. 233

12. **Engineering** The geodesic dome shown is a 14-story building that models Earth. Use the given information to prove that the triangles that make up the sphere are congruent.
Given: $\overline{SU} \cong \overline{ST} \cong \overline{SR}$, $\overline{TU} \cong \overline{TR}$, $\angle UST \cong \angle RST$, and $\angle U \cong \angle R$
Prove: $\triangle RTS \cong \triangle UTS$

U S T R

12.
1. $\angle UST \cong \angle RST$, $\angle U \cong \angle R$ (Given)
2. $\angle STU \cong \angle STR$ (Third ∠s Thm.)
3. $\overline{SU} \cong \overline{SR}$ (Given) 4. $\overline{ST} \cong \overline{ST}$ (Reflex. Prop. of ≅)
5. $\overline{TU} \cong \overline{TR}$ (Given) 6. $\triangle RTS \cong \triangle UTS$ (Def. of ≅ △s)

State Resources

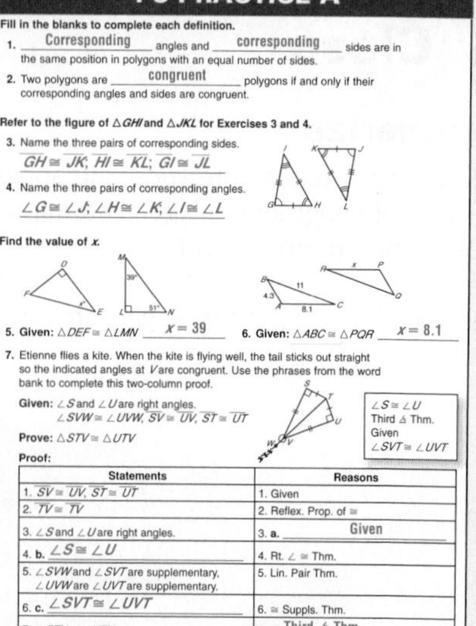

4-3 PRACTICE A

Fill in the blanks to complete each definition.

1. Corresponding angles and corresponding sides are in the same position in polygons with an equal number of sides.
2. Two polygons are congruent polygons if and only if their corresponding angles and sides are congruent.

Refer to the figure of △GHI and △JKL for Exercises 3 and 4.

3. Name the three pairs of corresponding sides.
$\overline{GH} \cong \overline{JK}$; $\overline{HI} \cong \overline{KL}$; $\overline{GI} \cong \overline{JL}$
4. Name the three pairs of corresponding angles.
$\angle G \cong \angle J$; $\angle H \cong \angle K$; $\angle I \cong \angle L$

Find the value of x.

5. **Given:** $\triangle DEF \cong \triangle LMN$ $x = 39$
6. **Given:** $\triangle ABC \cong \triangle PQR$ $x = 8.1$
7. Etienne flies a kite. When the kite is flying well, the tail sticks out straight so the indicated angles at V are congruent. Use the phrases from the word bank to complete this two-column proof.

Given: $\angle S$ and $\angle U$ are right angles. $\angle SVW \cong \angle UVW$, $\overline{SV} \cong \overline{UV}$, $\overline{ST} \cong \overline{UT}$
Prove: $\triangle STV \cong \triangle UTV$

$\angle S \cong \angle U$
Third ∠s Thm.
Given
$\angle SVT \cong \angle UVT$

Proof:

Statements	Reasons
1. $\overline{SV} \cong \overline{UV}$, $\overline{ST} \cong \overline{UT}$	1. Given
2. $\overline{TV} \cong \overline{TV}$	2. Reflex. Prop. of ≅
3. $\angle S$ and $\angle U$ are right angles.	3. a. Given
4. b. $\angle S \cong \angle U$	4. Rt. ∠ ≅ Thm.
5. $\angle SVW$ and $\angle SVT$ are supplementary, $\angle UVW$ are $\angle UVT$ are supplementary.	5. Lin. Pair Thm.
6. c. $\angle SVT \cong \angle UVT$	6. ≅ Suppls. Thm.
7. $\angle STV \cong \angle UTV$	7. d. Third ∠s Thm.
8. $\triangle STV \cong \triangle UTV$	8. Def. of ≅ △s

PRACTICE AND PROBLEM SOLVING

Independent Practice	
For Exercises	See Example
13–16	1
17–18	2
19	3
20	4

Extra Practice
Skills Practice p. S10
Application Practice p. S31

Given: Polygon $CDEF \cong$ polygon $KLMN$. Identify the congruent corresponding parts.

13. $\overline{DE} \cong$ ___?___ $\overline{LM}$
14. $\overline{KN} \cong$ ___?___ $\overline{CF}$
15. $\angle F \cong$ ___?___ $\angle N$
16. $\angle L \cong$ ___?___ $\angle D$

Given: $\triangle ABD \cong \triangle CBD$. Find each value.

17. $m\angle C$ **31°**
18. y **19**

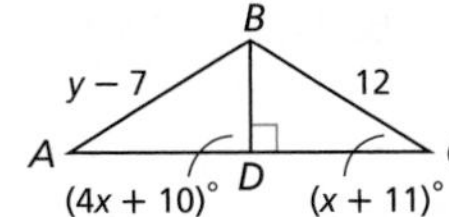

19. **Given:** $\overline{MP}$ bisects $\angle NMR$. P is the midpoint of $\overline{NR}$. $\overline{MN} \cong \overline{MR}$, $\angle N \cong \angle R$
Prove: $\triangle MNP \cong \triangle MRP$

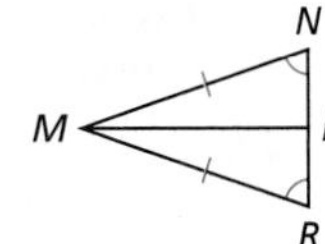

Proof:

Statements	Reasons
1. $\angle N \cong \angle R$	1. a. ___?___
2. $\overline{MP}$ bisects $\angle NMR$.	2. b. ___?___
3. c. ___?___	3. Def. of ∠ bisector
4. d. ___?___	4. Third ⩟ Thm.
5. P is the mdpt. of $\overline{NR}$.	5. e. ___?___
6. f. ___?___	6. Def. of mdpt.
7. $\overline{MN} \cong \overline{MR}$	7. g. ___?___
8. $\overline{MP} \cong \overline{MP}$	8. h. ___?___
9. $\triangle MNP \cong \triangle MRP$	9. Def. of ≅ ⩟

a. Given
b. Given
c. $\angle NMP \cong \angle RMP$
d. $\angle NPM \cong \angle RPM$
e. Given
f. $\overline{PN} \cong \overline{PR}$
g. Given
h. Reflex. Prop. of ≅

20. **Hobbies** In a garden, triangular flower beds are separated by straight rows of grass as shown.
Given: $\angle ADC$ and $\angle BCD$ are right angles. $\overline{AC} \cong \overline{BD}$, $\overline{AD} \cong \overline{BC}$, $\angle DAC \cong \angle CBD$
Prove: $\triangle ADC \cong \triangle BCD$

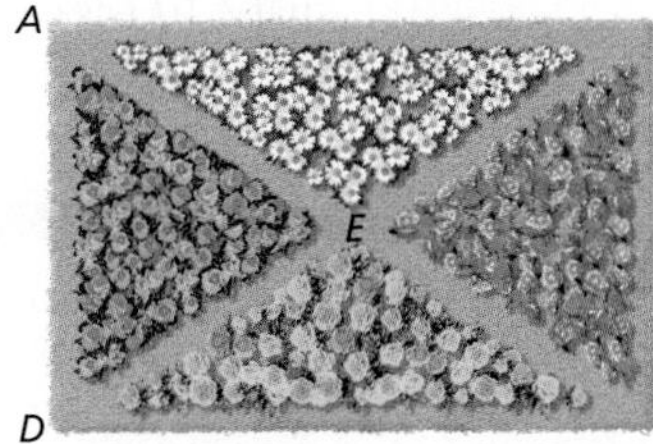

21. For two triangles, the following corresponding parts are given: $\overline{GS} \cong \overline{KP}$, $\overline{GR} \cong \overline{KH}$, $\overline{SR} \cong \overline{PH}$, $\angle S \cong \angle P$, $\angle G \cong \angle K$, and $\angle R \cong \angle H$. Write three different congruence statements.
$\triangle GSR \cong \triangle KPH$; $\triangle SRG \cong \triangle PHK$; $\triangle RGS \cong \triangle HKP$

22. The two polygons in the diagram are congruent. Complete the following congruence statement for the polygons.
polygon R ___?___ $\cong$ polygon V ___?___
Possible answer: $RVUTS \cong VWXZY$

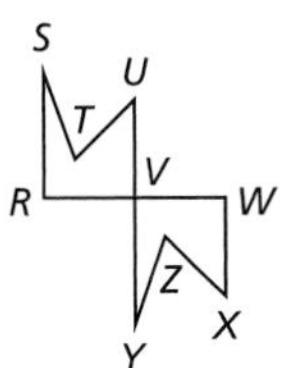

Write and solve an equation for each of the following.

23. $\triangle ABC \cong \triangle DEF$. $AB = 2x - 10$, and $DE = x + 20$. Find the value of x and AB. **$x = 30$; $AB = 50$**

24. $\triangle JKL \cong \triangle MNP$. $m\angle L = (x^2 + 10)^\circ$, and $m\angle P = (2x^2 + 1)^\circ$. What is $m\angle L$? **19°**

25. Polygon $ABCD \cong$ polygon $PQRS$. $BC = 6x + 5$, and $QR = 5x + 7$. Find the value of x and BC. **$x = 2$; $BC = 17$**

COMMON ERROR ALERT

In **Exercise 19,** be sure students understand that the order in which vertices are written is important. In line 3, if they name the angle $\angle NMP$, then it must be congruent to $\angle RMP$.

Teaching Tip **Visual** Have students draw and color code two congruent polygons so corresponding sides and angles are the same color. Then have students identify the corresponding parts.

Teaching Tip **Inclusion** In **Exercises 19** and **20,** have students write an *S* or an *A* next to each statement that states the congruence of a pair of sides or a pair of angles. Then they can see if they have listed enough parts to conclude that the triangles are congruent.

Answers

20. 1. $\angle ADC$ and $\angle BCD$ are rt. ⩟. (Given)
2. $\angle ADC \cong \angle BCD$ (Rt. ∠ ≅ Thm.)
3. $\angle DAC \cong \angle CBD$ (Given)
4. $\angle ACD \cong \angle BDC$ (Third ⩟ Thm.)
5. $\overline{AC} \cong \overline{BD}$, $\overline{AD} \cong \overline{BC}$ (Given)
6. $\overline{DC} \cong \overline{DC}$ (Reflex. Prop. of ≅)
7. $\triangle ADC \cong \triangle BCD$ (Def. of ≅ ⩟)

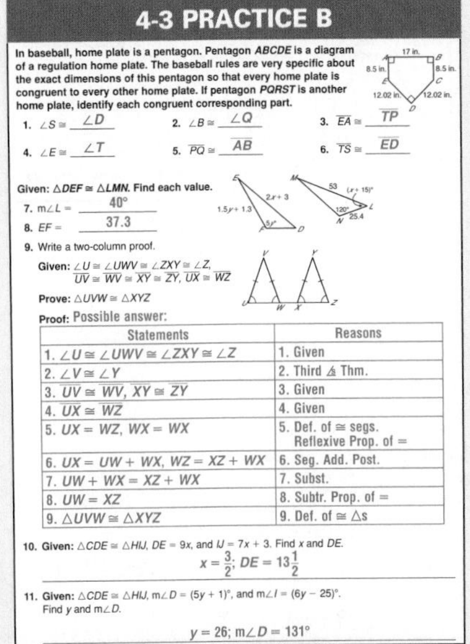

4-3 PRACTICE B

In baseball, home plate is a pentagon. Pentagon *ABCDE* is a diagram of a regulation home plate. The baseball rules are very specific about the exact dimensions of this pentagon so that every home plate is congruent to every other home plate. If pentagon *PQRST* is another home plate, identify each congruent corresponding part.

1. $\angle S \cong$ $\angle D$
2. $\angle B \cong$ $\angle Q$
3. $\overline{EA} \cong$ $\overline{TP}$
4. $\angle E \cong$ $\angle T$
5. $\overline{PQ} \cong$ $\overline{AB}$
6. $\overline{TS} \cong$ $\overline{ED}$

Given: $\triangle DEF \cong \triangle LMN$. Find each value.

7. $m\angle L =$ 40°
8. $EF =$ 37.3

9. Write a two-column proof.
Given: $\angle U \cong \angle UWV \cong \angle ZXY \cong \angle Z$, $\overline{UV} \cong \overline{WV} \cong \overline{XY} \cong \overline{ZY}$, $\overline{UX} \cong \overline{WZ}$
Prove: $\triangle UVW \cong \triangle XYZ$
Proof: Possible answer:

Statements	Reasons
1. $\angle U \cong \angle UWV \cong \angle ZXY \cong \angle Z$	1. Given
2. $\angle V \cong \angle Y$	2. Third ⩟ Thm.
3. $\overline{UV} \cong \overline{WV}$, $\overline{XY} \cong \overline{ZY}$	3. Given
4. $\overline{UX} \cong \overline{WZ}$	4. Given
5. $UX = WZ$, $WX = WX$	5. Def. of ≅ segs. Reflexive Prop. of =
6. $UX = UW + WX$, $WZ = XZ + WX$	6. Seg. Add. Post.
7. $UW + WX = XZ + WX$	7. Subst.
8. $UW = XZ$	8. Subtr. Prop. of =
9. $\triangle UVW \cong \triangle XYZ$	9. Def. of ≅ △s

10. Given: $\triangle CDE \cong \triangle HIJ$, $DE = 9x$, and $IJ = 7x + 3$. Find x and DE.
$x = \frac{3}{2}$; $DE = 13\frac{1}{2}$

11. Given: $\triangle CDE \cong \triangle HIJ$, $m\angle D = (5y + 1)^\circ$, and $m\angle I = (6y - 25)^\circ$. Find y and $m\angle D$.
$y = 26$; $m\angle D = 131^\circ$

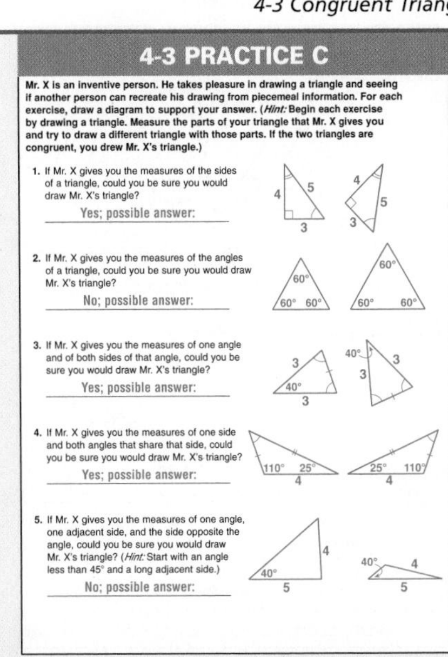

4-3 PRACTICE C

Mr. X is an inventive person. He takes pleasure in drawing a triangle and seeing if another person can recreate his drawing from piecemeal information. For each exercise, draw a diagram to support your answer. (*Hint:* Begin each exercise by drawing a triangle. Measure the parts of your triangle that Mr. X gives you and try to draw a different triangle with those parts. If the two triangles are congruent, you drew Mr. X's triangle.)

1. If Mr. X gives you the measures of the sides of a triangle, could you be sure you would draw Mr. X's triangle?
Yes; possible answer:

2. If Mr. X gives you the measures of the angles of a triangle, could you be sure you would draw Mr. X's triangle?
No; possible answer:

3. If Mr. X gives you the measures of one angle and of both sides of that angle, could you be sure you would draw Mr. X's triangle?
Yes; possible answer:

4. If Mr. X gives you the measures of one side and both angles that share that side, could you be sure you would draw Mr. X's triangle?
Yes; possible answer:

5. If Mr. X gives you the measures of one angle, one adjacent side, and the side opposite the angle, could you be sure you would draw Mr. X's triangle? (*Hint:* Start with an angle less than 45° and a long adjacent side.)
No; possible answer:

MULTI-STEP TEST PREP **Exercise 26** involves proving triangles congruent when they are formed by folding paper. This prepares students for the Multi-Step Test Prep on page 238.

TEST PREP DOCTOR In **Exercise 33**, if students chose **A**, they have made the measure of ∠*Y* equal to the measure of ∠*C* instead of ∠*B*.

Answers

26a. $\overline{KL} \cong \overline{ML}$ by the def. of a square.

b. 1. *JKLM* is a square. (Given)
2. $\overline{KL} \cong \overline{ML}$ (Def. of a square)
3. $\overline{JL}$ and $\overline{MK}$ are ⊥ bisectors of each other. (Given)
4. $\overline{MN} \cong \overline{KN}$ (Def. of bisect)
5. $\overline{NL} \cong \overline{NL}$ (Reflex. Prop. of ≅)
6. ∠*MNL* and ∠*KNL* are rt. ∡. (Def. of ⊥)
7. ∠*MNL* ≅ ∠*KNL* (Rt. ∠ ≅ Thm.)
8. ∠*NML* ≅ ∠*NKL* (Given)
9. ∠*NLM* ≅ ∠*NLK* (Third ∡ Thm.)
10. △*NML* ≅ △*NKL* (Def. of ≅ ▲)

27.

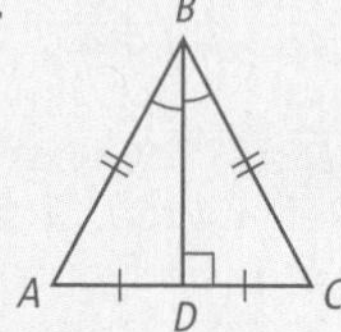

1. $\overline{BD} \perp \overline{AC}$ (Given)
2. ∠*ADB* and ∠*CDB* are rt. ∡. (Def. of ⊥)
3. ∠*ADB* ≅ ∠*CDB* (Rt. ∠ ≅ Thm.)
4. $\overline{BD}$ bisects ∠*ABC*. (Given)
5. ∠*ABD* ≅ ∠*CBD* (Def. of bisect)
6. ∠*A* ≅ ∠*C* (Third ∡ Thm.)
7. $\overline{AB} \cong \overline{CB}$ (Given)
8. $\overline{BD} \cong \overline{DB}$ (Reflex. Prop. of ≅)
9. *D* is the mdpt. of $\overline{AC}$. (Given)
10. $\overline{AD} \cong \overline{CD}$ (Def. of mdpt.)
11. △*ABD* ≅ △*CBD* (Def of ≅ ▲)

28. Possible answer:

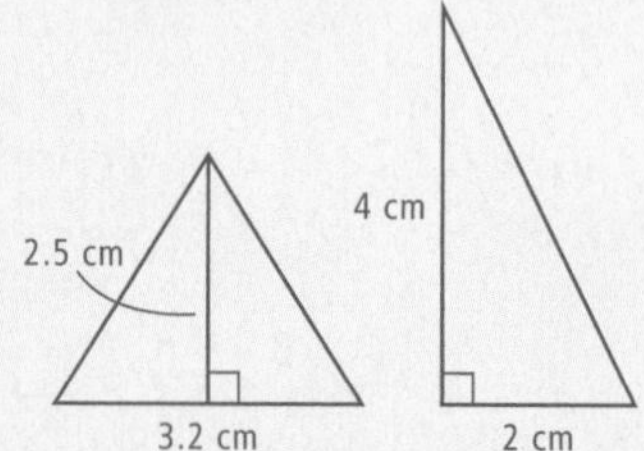

30. Yes; by the Third ∡ Thm., ∠*K* ≅ ∠*W*, so all 6 pairs of corr. parts are ≅. Therefore the ▲ are ≅.

26. This problem will prepare you for the Multi-Step Test Prep on page 238. Many origami models begin with a square piece of paper, *JKLM*, that is folded along both diagonals to make the creases shown. $\overline{JL}$ and $\overline{MK}$ are perpendicular bisectors of each other, and ∠*NML* ≅ ∠*NKL*.

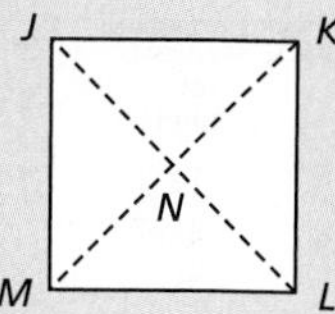

   a. Explain how you know that $\overline{KL}$ and $\overline{ML}$ are congruent.
   b. Prove △*NML* ≅ △*NKL*.

27. Draw a diagram and then write a proof.
Given: $\overline{BD} \perp \overline{AC}$. *D* is the midpoint of $\overline{AC}$. $\overline{AB} \cong \overline{CB}$, and $\overline{BD}$ bisects ∠*ABC*.
Prove: △*ABD* ≅ △*CBD*

28. **Critical Thinking** Draw two triangles that are not congruent but have an area of 4 cm^2 each.

29. **ERROR ANALYSIS** Given △*MPQ* ≅ △*EDF*. Two solutions for finding m∠*E* are shown. Which is incorrect? Explain the error.

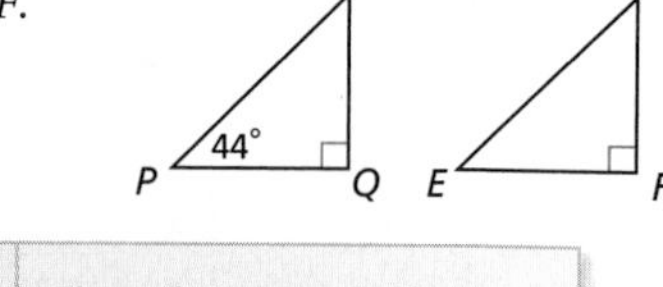

Solution A is incorrect.
∠*E* ≅ ∠*M*, so m∠*E* = 46°.

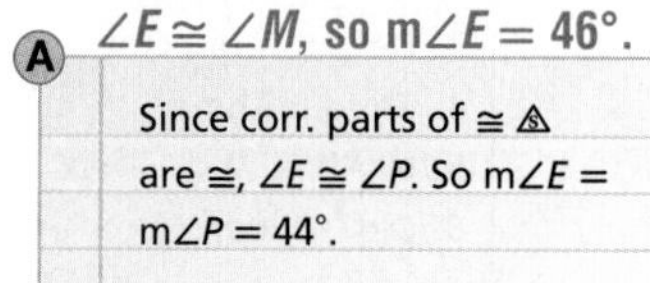

A
Since corr. parts of ≅ ▲ are ≅, ∠E ≅ ∠P. So m∠E = m∠P = 44°.

B: Since the acute ∡ of a rt. △ are comp., m∠*M* = 46°. ∠*E* ≅ ∠*M*, so m∠*E* = 46°.

30. **Write About It** Given the diagram of the triangles, is there enough information to prove that △*HKL* is congruent to △*YWX*? Explain.

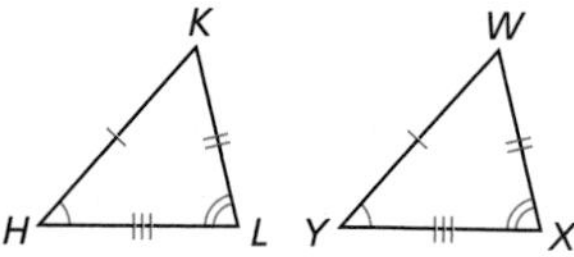

31. Which congruence statement correctly indicates that the two given triangles are congruent?

   Ⓐ △*ABC* ≅ △*EFD* Ⓒ △*ABC* ≅ △*DEF*
   Ⓑ △*ABC* ≅ △*FDE* (circled) Ⓓ △*ABC* ≅ △*FED*

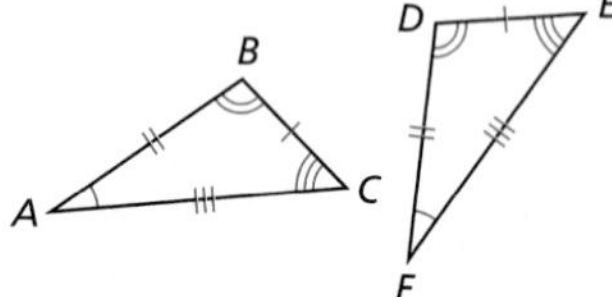

32. △*MNP* ≅ △*RST*. What are the values of *x* and *y*?

   Ⓕ $x = 26, y = 21\frac{1}{3}$ Ⓗ $x = 25, y = 20\frac{2}{3}$
   Ⓖ $x = 27, y = 20$ (circled) Ⓙ $x = 30\frac{1}{3}, y = 16\frac{2}{3}$

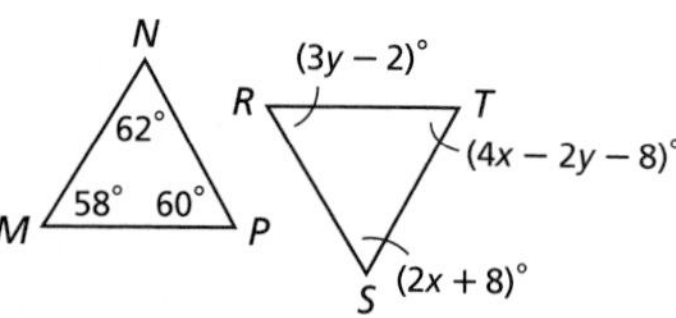

33. △*ABC* ≅ △*XYZ*. m∠*A* = 47.1°, and m∠*C* = 13.8°. Find m∠*Y*.

   Ⓐ 13.8 Ⓒ 76.2
   Ⓑ 42.9 **Ⓓ 119.1** (circled)

34. △*MNR* ≅ △*SPQ*, *NL* = 18, *SP* = 33, *SR* = 10, *RQ* = 24, and *QP* = 30. What is the perimeter of △*MNR*?

   Ⓕ 79 Ⓗ 87
   Ⓖ 85 **Ⓙ 97** (circled)

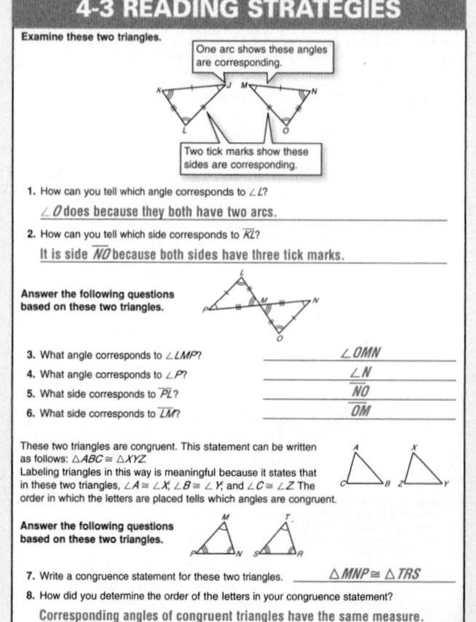

4-3 READING STRATEGIES

Examine these two triangles.

1. How can you tell which angle corresponds to ∠*L*?
   ∠*O* does because they both have two arcs.
2. How can you tell which side corresponds to $\overline{KL}$?
   It is side $\overline{NO}$ because both sides have three tick marks.

Answer the following questions based on these two triangles.

3. What angle corresponds to ∠*LMP*? ∠*OMN*
4. What angle corresponds to ∠*P*? ∠*N*
5. What side corresponds to $\overline{PL}$? $\overline{NO}$
6. What side corresponds to $\overline{LM}$? $\overline{OM}$

These two triangles are congruent. This statement can be written as follows: △*ABC* ≅ △*XYZ*.
Labeling triangles in this way is meaningful because it states that in these two triangles, ∠*A* ≅ ∠*X*, ∠*B* ≅ ∠*Y*, and ∠*C* ≅ ∠*Z*. The order in which the letters are placed tells which angles are congruent.

Answer the following questions based on these two triangles.

7. Write a congruence statement for these two triangles. △*MNP* ≅ △*TRS*
8. How did you determine the order of the letters in your congruence statement?
   Corresponding angles of congruent triangles have the same measure.

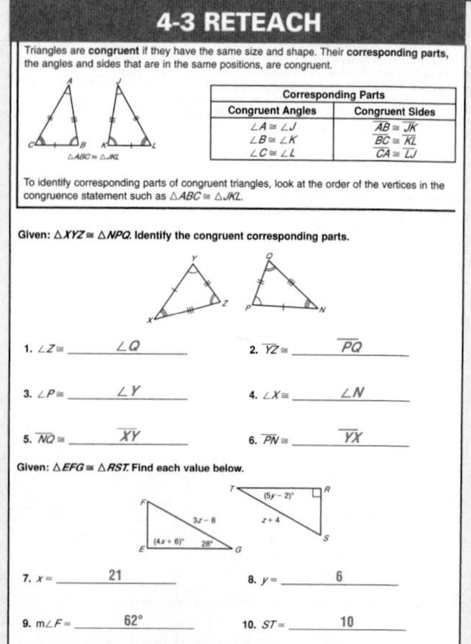

4-3 RETEACH

Triangles are **congruent** if they have the same size and shape. Their **corresponding parts**, the angles and sides that are in the same positions, are congruent.

△*ABC* ≅ △*JKL*

Corresponding Parts	
Congruent Angles	Congruent Sides
∠*A* ≅ ∠*J*	$\overline{AB} \cong \overline{JK}$
∠*B* ≅ ∠*K*	$\overline{BC} \cong \overline{KL}$
∠*C* ≅ ∠*L*	$\overline{CA} \cong \overline{LJ}$

To identify corresponding parts of congruent triangles, look at the order of the vertices in the congruence statement such as △*ABC* ≅ △*JKL*.

Given: △*XYZ* ≅ △*NPQ*. Identify the congruent corresponding parts.

1. ∠*Z* ≅ ∠*Q* 2. $\overline{YZ} \cong$ $\overline{PQ}$
3. ∠*P* ≅ ∠*Y* 4. ∠*X* ≅ ∠*N*
5. $\overline{NQ} \cong$ $\overline{XY}$ 6. $\overline{PN} \cong$ $\overline{YX}$

Given: △*EFG* ≅ △*RST*. Find each value below.

7. *x* = 21 8. *y* = 6
9. m∠*F* = 62° 10. *ST* = 10

CHALLENGE AND EXTEND

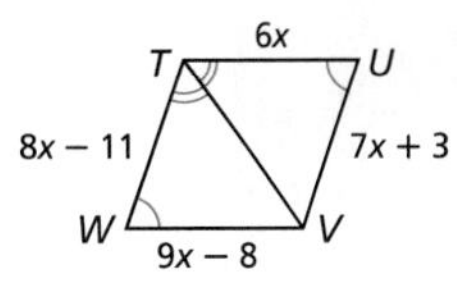

35. **Multi-Step** Given that the perimeter of $TUVW$ is 149 units, find the value of x. Is $\triangle TUV \cong \triangle TWV$? Explain.

36. **Multi-Step** Polygon $ABCD \cong$ polygon $EFGH$. $\angle A$ is a right angle. $m\angle E = (y^2 - 10)°$, and $m\angle H = (2y^2 - 132)°$. Find $m\angle D$. **68°**

37. **Given:** $\overline{RS} \cong \overline{RT}$, $\angle S \cong \angle T$
Prove: $\triangle RST \cong \triangle RTS$

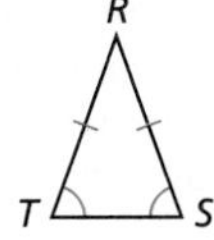

SPIRAL REVIEW

Two number cubes are rolled. Find the probability of each outcome. *(Previous course)*

38. Both numbers rolled are even. $\frac{1}{4}$

39. The sum of the numbers rolled is 5. $\frac{1}{9}$

Classify each angle by its measure. *(Lesson 1-3)*

40. $m\angle DOC = 40°$ **acute**

41. $m\angle BOA = 90°$ **rt.**

42. $m\angle COA = 140°$ **obtuse**

Find each angle measure. *(Lesson 4-2)*

43. $\angle Q$ **72°**

44. $\angle P$ **74°**

45. $\angle QRS$ **146°**

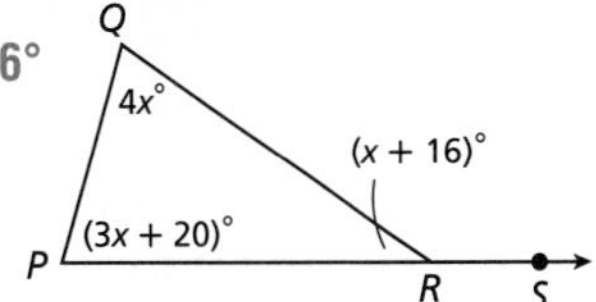

Career Path

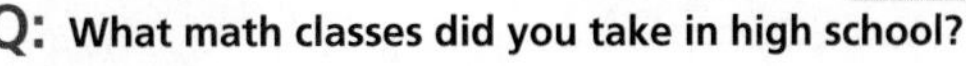

Jordan Carter
Emergency Medical Services Program

Q: **What math classes did you take in high school?**
A: Algebra 1 and 2, Geometry, Precalculus

Q: **What kind of degree or certification will you receive?**
A: I will receive an associate's degree in applied science. Then I will take an exam to be certified as an EMT or paramedic.

Q: **How do you use math in your hands-on training?**
A: I calculate dosages based on body weight and age. I also calculate drug doses in milligrams per kilogram per hour or set up an IV drip to deliver medications at the correct rate.

Q: **What are your future career plans?**
A: When I am certified, I can work for a private ambulance service or with a fire department. I could also work in a hospital, transporting critically ill patients by ambulance or helicopter.

Teaching Tip

Visual For **Exercise 37,** suggest that students draw two separate triangles.

Answers

35. $x = 5.5$; yes; $UV = WV = 41.5$, and $UT = WT = 33$. $TV = TV$ by the Reflex. Prop. of =. It is given that $\angle VWT \cong \angle VUT$ and $\angle WTV \cong \angle UTV$. $\angle WVT \cong \angle UVT$ by the Third ∠ Thm. Thus $\triangle TUV \cong \triangle TWV$ by the def. of ≅ △.

37.
1. $\overline{RS} \cong \overline{RT}$; $\angle S \cong \angle T$ (Given)
2. $\overline{ST} \cong \overline{TS}$ (Reflex. Prop. of ≅)
3. $\angle T \cong \angle S$ (Sym. Prop. of ≅)
4. $\angle R \cong \angle R$ (Reflex. Prop of ≅)
5. $\triangle RST \cong \triangle RTS$ (Def. of ≅ △)

Journal

Have students explain why the order of vertices is important in congruence statements.

ALTERNATIVE ASSESSMENT

Have students create a booklet for elementary school students that explains what it means for two real-world objects to be congruent. They should identify the corresponding angles and sides of each.

Power Presentations with PowerPoint®

4-3 Lesson Quiz

1. $\triangle ABC \cong \triangle JKL$ and $AB = 2x + 12$. $JK = 4x - 50$. Find x and AB. 31, 74

Given that polygon $MNOP \cong$ polygon $QRST$, identify the congruent corresponding part.

2. $\overline{NO} \cong$ __?__ $\overline{RS}$

3. $\angle T \cong$ __?__ $\angle P$

4. **Given:** C is the midpoint of $\overline{BD}$ and $\overline{AE}$. $\angle A \cong \angle E$, $\overline{AB} \cong \overline{ED}$
Prove: $\triangle ABC \cong \triangle EDC$

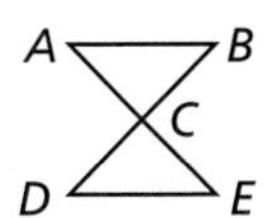

1. $\angle A \cong \angle E$ (Given)
2. C is mdpt. of $\overline{BD}$ and $\overline{AE}$. (Given)
3. $\overline{AC} \cong \overline{EC}$; $\overline{BC} \cong \overline{DC}$ (Def. of mdpt.)
4. $\overline{AB} \cong \overline{ED}$ (Given)
5. $\angle ACB \cong \angle ECD$ (Vert. ∠ Thm.)
6. $\angle B \cong \angle D$ (Third ∠ Thm.)
7. $\triangle ABC \cong \triangle EDC$ (Def. of ≅ △)

Also available on transparency

4-3 PROBLEM SOLVING

Use the diagram of the fence for Exercises 1 and 2.

$\triangle RQW \cong \triangle TVW$

1. If $m\angle RWQ = 36°$ and $m\angle TWV = (2x + 5)°$, what is the value of x?
15.5°

2. If $RW = (3y - 1)$ feet and $TW = (y + 5)$ feet, what is the length of $\overline{RW}$?
8 ft

Use the diagram of a section of the Bank of China Tower for Exercises 3 and 4.

$\triangle JKL \cong \triangle LHJ$

3. What is the value of x?
$x = 19$

4. Find $m\angle JHL$.
72°

Choose the best answer.

5. Chairs with triangular seats were popular in the Middle Ages. Suppose a chair has a seat that is an isosceles triangle and the congruent sides measure $1\frac{1}{2}$ feet. A second chair has a triangular seat with a perimeter of $5\frac{1}{10}$ feet, and it is congruent to the first seat. What is a side length of the second seat?
A $1\frac{4}{5}$ ft
(B) $2\frac{1}{10}$ ft
C 3 ft
D $3\frac{3}{5}$ ft

Use the diagram for Exercises 6 and 7.

6. C is the midpoint of $\overline{EB}$ and $\overline{AD}$. What additional information would allow you to prove $\triangle ABC \cong \triangle DEC$?
F $\overline{EB} \cong \overline{AD}$
G $\overline{DE} \cong \overline{AB}$
H $\angle ECD \cong \angle ACB$
(J) $\angle A \cong \angle D$, $\angle B \cong \angle E$

7. If $\triangle ABC \cong \triangle DEC$, $ED = 4y + 2$, and $AB = 6y - 4$, what is the length of $\overline{AB}$?
A 3
B 12
(C) 14
D 18

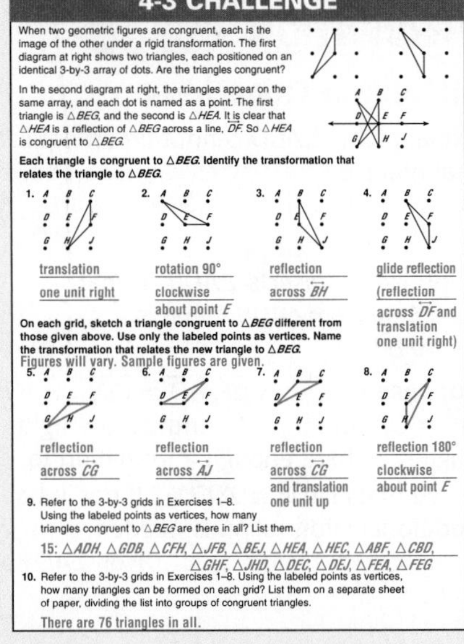

4-3 CHALLENGE

When two geometric figures are congruent, each is the image of the other under a rigid transformation. The first diagram at right shows two triangles, each positioned on an identical 3-by-3 array of dots. Are the triangles congruent?

In the second diagram at right, the triangles appear on the same array, and each dot is named as a point. The first triangle is $\triangle BEG$, and the second is $\triangle HEA$. It is clear that $\triangle HEA$ is a reflection of $\triangle BEG$ across a line, $\overleftrightarrow{DF}$. So $\triangle HEA$ is congruent to $\triangle BEG$.

Each triangle is congruent to $\triangle BEG$. Identify the transformation that relates the triangle to $\triangle BEG$.

1. translation one unit right
2. rotation 90° clockwise about point E
3. reflection across $\overleftrightarrow{BH}$
4. glide reflection (reflection across $\overleftrightarrow{DF}$ and translation one unit right)

On each grid, sketch a triangle congruent to $\triangle BEG$ different from those given above. Use only the labeled points as vertices. Name the transformation that relates the new triangle to $\triangle BEG$.

Figures will vary. Sample figures are given.

5. reflection across $\overleftrightarrow{CG}$
6. reflection across $\overleftrightarrow{AJ}$
7. reflection across $\overleftrightarrow{CG}$ and translation one unit up
8. reflection 180° clockwise about point E

9. Refer to the 3-by-3 grids in Exercises 1–8. Using the labeled points as vertices, how many triangles congruent to $\triangle BEG$ are there in all? List them.
15: $\triangle ADH$, $\triangle GDB$, $\triangle CFH$, $\triangle JFB$, $\triangle BEJ$, $\triangle HEA$, $\triangle HEC$, $\triangle ABF$, $\triangle CBD$, $\triangle GHF$, $\triangle JHD$, $\triangle DEC$, $\triangle DEJ$, $\triangle FEA$, $\triangle FEG$

10. Refer to the 3-by-3 grids in Exercises 1–8. Using the labeled points as vertices, how many triangles can be formed on each grid? List them on a separate sheet of paper, dividing the list into groups of congruent triangles.
There are 76 triangles in all.

Organizer

Objective: Assess students' ability to apply concepts and skills in Lessons 4-1 through 4-3 in a real-world format.

Online Edition

Resources

Geometry Assessments
www.mathtekstoolkit.org

Problem	Text Reference
1	Lesson 4-1
2	Lesson 4-2
3	Lesson 4-3

Answers

2. m$\angle EBD = 45°$ ($\overline{DB}$ bisects rt. $\angle ABC$.) m$\angle BDE = 22.5°$ ($\overline{DE}$ bisects $\angle ADB$.) m$\angle DEB = 112.5°$ ($\triangle$ Sum Thm.)
3. 1. $\overline{DB}$ bisects $\angle ABC$ and $\angle EDF$. (Given)
   2. $\angle EBD \cong \angle FBD$; $\angle EDB \cong \angle FDB$ (Def. of $\angle$ bisector)
   3. $\angle DEB \cong \angle DFB$ (Third $\angle$ Thm.)
   4. $\overline{BE} \cong \overline{BF}$; $\overline{DE} \cong \overline{DF}$ (Given)
   5. $\overline{DB} \cong \overline{DB}$ (Reflex. Prop. of $\cong$)
   6. $\triangle EDB \cong \triangle FDB$ (Def. of $\cong$ $\triangle$s)

State Resources

State Resources Online
KEYWORD: MG7 Resources

MULTI-STEP TEST PREP

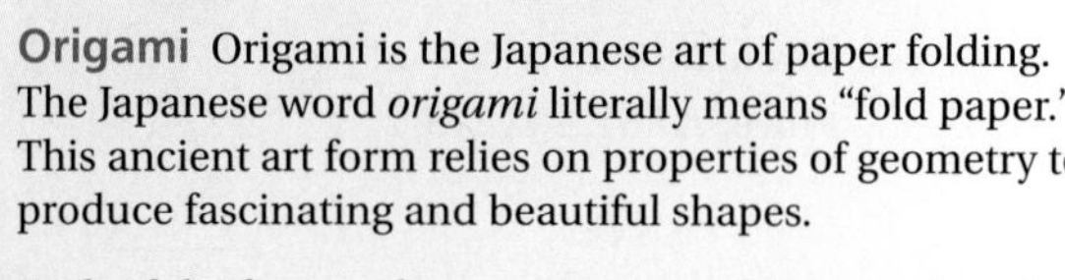

Triangles and Congruence

Origami Origami is the Japanese art of paper folding. The Japanese word *origami* literally means "fold paper." This ancient art form relies on properties of geometry to produce fascinating and beautiful shapes.

Each of the figures shows a step in making an origami swan from a square piece of paper. The final figure shows the creases of an origami swan that has been unfolded.

Step 1

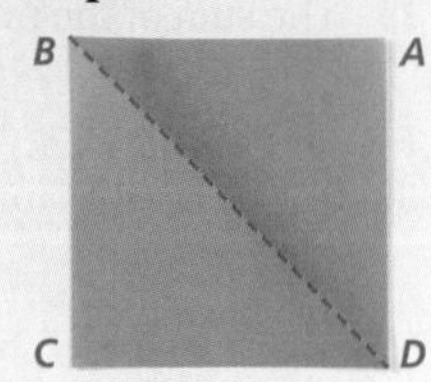

Fold the paper in half diagonally and crease it. Turn it over.

Step 2

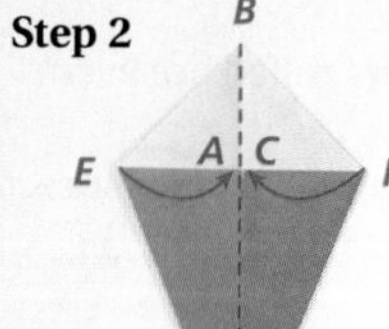

Fold corners A and C to the center line and crease. Turn it over.

Step 3

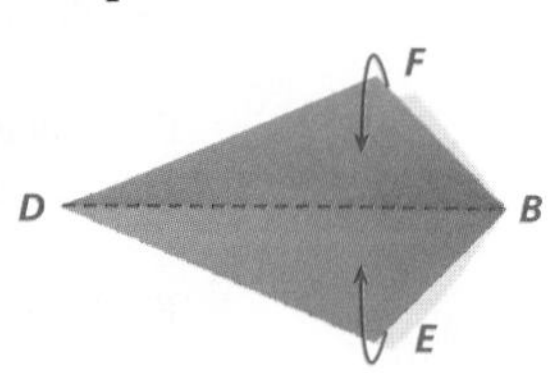

Fold in half along the center crease so that $\overline{DE}$ and $\overline{DF}$ are together.

Step 4

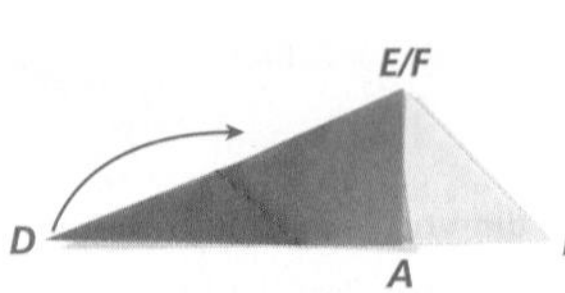

Fold the narrow point upward at a 90° angle and crease. Push in the fold so that the neck is inside the body.

Step 5

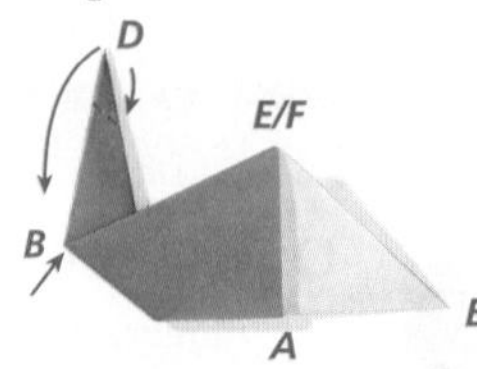

Fold the tip downward and crease. Push in the fold so that the head is inside the neck.

Step 6

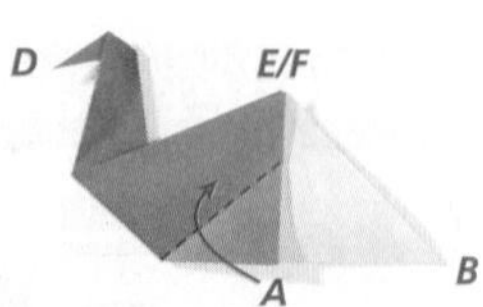

Fold up the flap to form the wing.

isosc. $\triangle$; rt. $\triangle$

1. Use the fact that $ABCD$ is a square to classify $\triangle ABD$ by its side lengths and by its angle measures.
2. $\overline{DB}$ bisects $\angle ABC$ and $\angle ADC$. $\overline{DE}$ bisects $\angle ADB$. Find the measures of the angles in $\triangle EDB$. Explain how you found the measures.
3. Given that $\overline{DB}$ bisects $\angle ABC$ and $\angle EDF$, $\overline{BE} \cong \overline{BF}$, and $\overline{DE} \cong \overline{DF}$, prove that $\triangle EDB \cong \triangle FDB$.

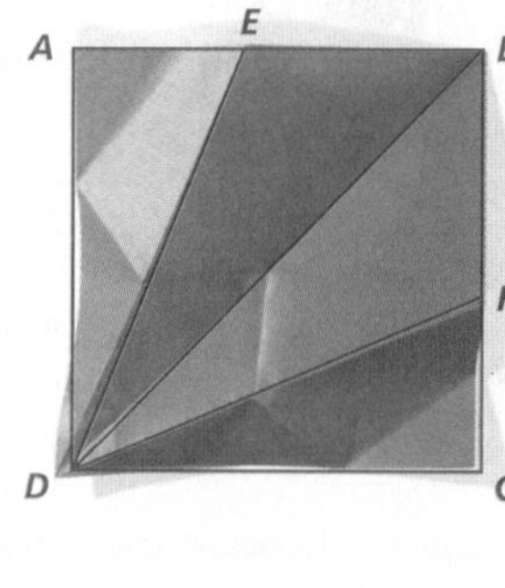

INTERVENTION

Scaffolding Questions

1. Explain why $\triangle ABD$ cannot be an equilateral triangle. The 3 sides cannot all have equal lengths since $DB^2 = AB^2 + AD^2$ by the Pyth. Thm.
2. Suppose $\overline{DE}$ trisects $\angle ADB$ so that m$\angle EDB = \frac{1}{3}$m$\angle ADB$. What is m$\angle AED$? 60°
3. Suppose that $\overline{AE} \cong \overline{CF}$, $\overline{AD} \cong \overline{CD}$, $\overline{DE} \cong \overline{DF}$, and that $\angle A$ and $\angle C$ are right angles. Is there enough information to prove that $\triangle ADE \cong \triangle CDF$? If not, what additional information is needed? No; you need to know $\angle ADE \cong \angle CDF$ or $\angle AED \cong \angle CFD$.

Extension

Draw a large scalene $\triangle ABC$. Then construct equilateral $\triangle ABC'$ outward from side $\overline{AB}$. Similarly construct equilateral $\triangle BCA'$ and $\triangle ACB'$. Bisect each angle of the three equilateral triangles. Where the bisectors meet label the points D, E, and F. How would you classify $\triangle DEF$? equilateral

SECTION 4A

Quiz for Lessons 4-1 Through 4-3

4-1 Classifying Triangles

Classify each triangle by its angle measures.

1. $\triangle ACD$ rt.
2. $\triangle ABD$ equiangular
3. $\triangle ADE$ obtuse

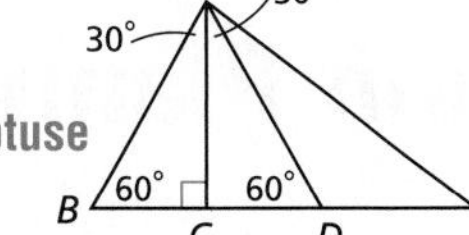

Classify each triangle by its side lengths.

4. $\triangle PQR$ isosc.
5. $\triangle PRS$ equil.
6. $\triangle PQS$ scalene

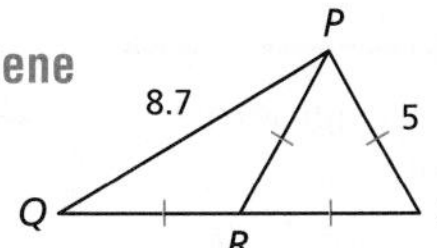

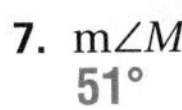

4-2 Angle Relationships in Triangles

Find each angle measure.

7. $m\angle M$ 51°

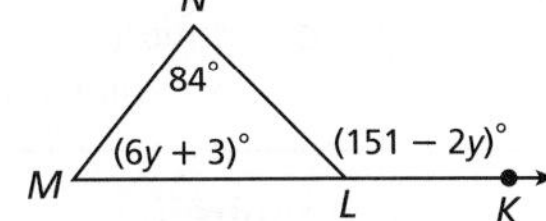

8. $m\angle ABC$ 125°

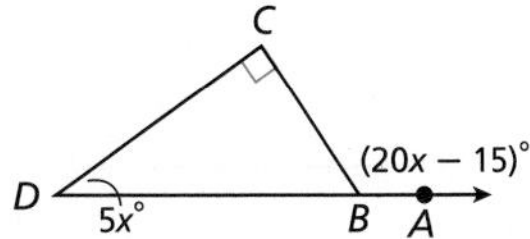

9. A carpenter built a triangular support structure for a roof. Two of the angles of the structure measure 37° and 55°. Find the measure of $\angle RTP$, the angle formed by the roof of the house and the roof of the patio. 92°

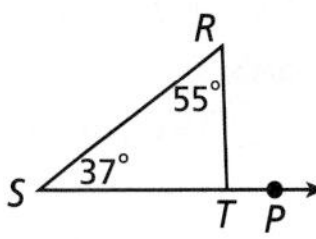

4-3 Congruent Triangles

Given: $\triangle JKL \cong \triangle DEF$. Identify the congruent corresponding parts.

10. $\overline{KL} \cong$ __?__ $\overline{EF}$
11. $\overline{DF} \cong$ __?__ $\overline{JL}$
12. $\angle K \cong$ __?__ $\angle E$
13. $\angle F \cong$ __?__ $\angle L$

Given: $\triangle PQR \cong \triangle STU$. Find each value.

14. PQ 9
15. y 23

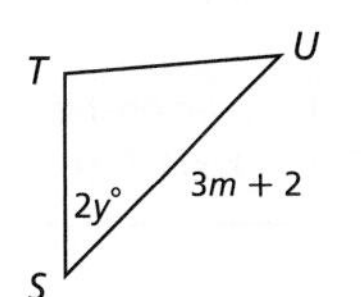

16. Given: $\overleftrightarrow{AB} \parallel \overleftrightarrow{CD}$, $\overline{AB} \cong \overline{CD}$, $\overline{AC} \cong \overline{BD}$, $\overline{AC} \perp \overline{CD}$, $\overline{DB} \perp \overline{AB}$

Prove: $\triangle ACD \cong \triangle DBA$

Proof:

Statements	Reasons
1. $\overleftrightarrow{AB} \parallel \overleftrightarrow{CD}$	1. a. __?__
2. $\angle BAD \cong \angle CDA$	2. b. __?__
3. $\overline{AC} \perp \overline{CD}$, $\overline{DB} \perp \overline{AB}$	3. c. __?__
4. $\angle ACD$ and $\angle DBA$ are rt. ∠s	4. d. __?__
5. e. __?__	5. Rt. ∠ ≅ Thm.
6. f. __?__	6. Third ∠s Thm.
7. $\overline{AB} \cong \overline{CD}$, $\overline{AC} \cong \overline{BD}$	7. g. __?__
8. h. __?__	8. Reflex Prop. of ≅
9. $\triangle ACD \cong \triangle DBA$	9. i. __?__

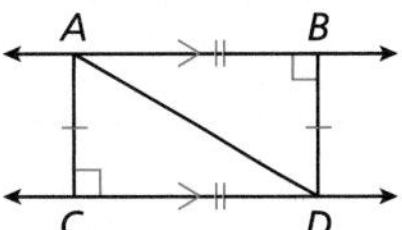

a. Given
b. Alt. Int. ∠s Thm.
c. Given
d. Def. of ⊥
e. $\angle ACD \cong \angle DBA$
f. $\angle CAD \cong \angle BDA$
g. Given
h. $\overline{AD} \cong \overline{DA}$
i. Def. of ≅ △s

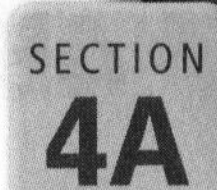

READY TO GO ON?

Organizer

Objective: Assess students' mastery of concepts and skills in Lessons 4-1 through 4-3.

Resources

Assessment Resources
Section 4A Quiz

Teacher One Stop™
Test & Practice Generator

INTERVENTION

Resources

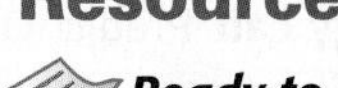
Ready to Go On? Intervention and Enrichment Worksheets

***Ready to Go On?* CD-ROM**

***Ready to Go On?* Online**

READY TO GO ON? Diagnose and Prescribe

Ready to Go On? Intervention	*Ready to Go On? Intervention*, Section 4A: Worksheets	CD-ROM	Online
Lesson 4-1	4-1 Intervention	Activity 4-1	Diagnose and Prescribe Online
Lesson 4-2	4-2 Intervention	Activity 4-2	
Lesson 4-3	4-3 Intervention	Activity 4-3	

Ready to Go On? Enrichment, Section 4A
Worksheets
CD-ROM
Online

SECTION **4B**

Proving Triangle Congruence

One-Minute Section Planner

Lesson	Lab Resources	Materials
4-4 Geometry Lab Explore SSS and SAS Triangle Congruence • Discover shortcuts for proving triangles are congruent. ☐ SAT-10 ☑ NAEP ☐ ACT ☐ SAT ☐ SAT Subject Tests	***Geometry Lab Activities*** 4-4 Lab Recording Sheet	**Required** straws, string, paper clip, and protractor (MK) **Optional** envelopes with three descriptions of parts of a triangle, ruler, protractor (MK)
Lesson 4-4 Triangle Congruence: SSS and SAS • Apply SSS and SAS to construct triangles and solve problems. • Prove triangles congruent by using SSS and SAS. ☐ SAT-10 ☑ NAEP ☐ ACT ☐ SAT ☐ SAT Subject Tests	***Geometry Lab Activities*** 4-4 Geometry Lab	**Required** straightedge, compass (MK), geometry software **Optional** magazine pictures showing triangle congruence, ruler, protractor (MK)
4-5 Technology Lab Predict Other Triangle Congruence Relationships • Use geometry software to explore triangle congruence relationships. ☐ SAT-10 ☐ NAEP ☐ ACT ☑ SAT ☑ SAT Subject Tests	***Technology Lab Activities*** 4-5 Lab Recording Sheet	**Required** geometry software
Lesson 4-5 Triangle Congruence: ASA, AAS, and HL • Apply ASA, AAS, and HL to construct triangles and solve problems. • Prove triangles congruent by using ASA, AAS, and HL. ☐ SAT-10 ☑ NAEP ☐ ACT ☐ SAT ☐ SAT Subject Tests		**Required** straightedge, compass (MK) **Optional** map of the area that contains your school, paper and scissors
Lesson 4-6 Triangle Congruence: CPCTC • Use CPCTC to prove parts of triangles are congruent. ☐ SAT-10 ☑ NAEP ☐ ACT ☐ SAT ☐ SAT Subject Tests		**Optional** designs by M. C. Escher
Lesson 4-7 Introduction to Coordinate Proof • Position figures in the coordinate plane for use in coordinate proofs. • Prove geometric concepts by using coordinate proofs. ☑ SAT-10 ☑ NAEP ☑ ACT ☑ SAT ☐ SAT Subject Tests		**Required** graph paper **Optional** scissors
Lesson 4-8 Isosceles and Equilateral Triangles • Prove theorems about isosceles and equilateral triangles. • Apply properties of isosceles and equilateral triangles. ☐ SAT-10 ☑ NAEP ☑ ACT ☑ SAT ☑ SAT Subject Tests		**Required** graph paper **Optional** different examples of isosceles and equilateral triangles, poster board, ruler (MK)
Extension Proving Constructions Valid • Use congruent triangles to prove constructions valid. ☐ SAT-10 ☑ NAEP ☑ ACT ☐ SAT ☐ SAT Subject Tests		

MK = *Manipulatives Kit*

Math Background

CONGRUENCE POSTULATES AND THEOREMS

Lessons 4-4, 4-5

To show that two triangles are congruent by using the definition of congruence, one must demonstrate that three pairs of corresponding sides are congruent and that three pairs of corresponding angles are congruent. However, it is possible to conclude that two triangles are congruent by verifying the congruence of certain subsets of the six pairs of corresponding sides and angles. The congruence postulates and theorems of Lessons 4-4 and 4-5 describe such shortcuts.

Note that SSS Congruence and SAS Congruence are presented in this book as postulates. Strictly speaking, only one of SSS, SAS, or ASA needs to be taken as a postulate. In other words, any one of these may be assumed to be true, and the other two may then be proved as theorems.

Euclid actually proved all three results (SSS, SAS, and ASA) as theorems. However, he did so through the use of a "superposition" postulate that allowed one triangle to be placed on top of another. Modern mathematicians consider this type of motion to be invalid within the logical system of classical Euclidean geometry, and for this reason one of the three statements is generally taken as a postulate.

COORDINATE PROOF

Lesson 4-7

The development of analytic geometry by Descartes and other mathematicians offered a new approach to proving theorems: coordinate proofs. Because analytic geometry brings an algebraic perspective to geometry, coordinate proofs can be especially efficient for proving theorems that deal with properties that can be quantified, such as lengths, midpoints, and slopes.

There are two essential points about coordinate proofs that should be emphasized to students from the beginning.

1. **Maintain the generality of figures.** It is important to assign coordinates in such a way that no more is assumed about a figure than necessary. For example, when using a coordinate proof to demonstrate a property of triangles, the triangle must be positioned on the coordinate plane so that it can represent *any* triangle. To that end, the following figure shows one way to assign coordinates to the vertices of a general triangle.

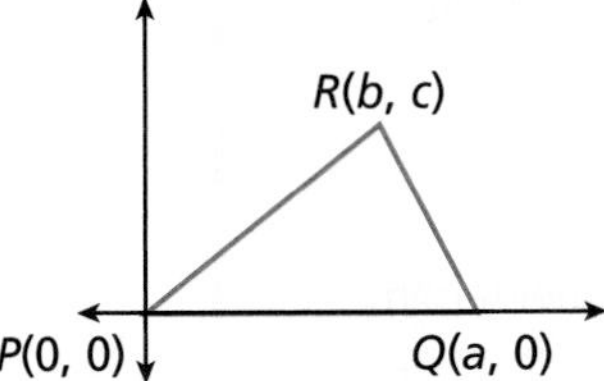

By way of contrast, the figure below shows a triangle with coordinates that may be easier to work with. However, this figure assumes that the triangle is a right triangle. The figure cannot be used to prove a property that holds for all triangles; it can only be used to prove a property of right triangles.

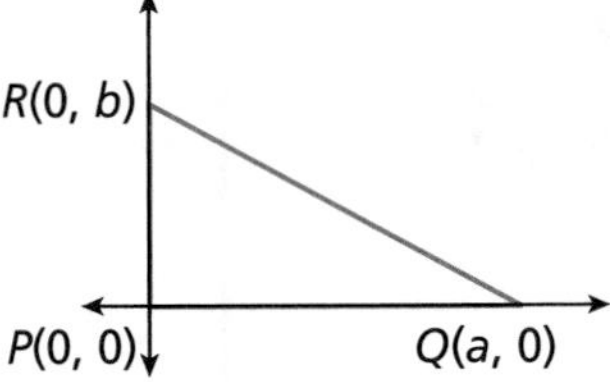

2. **Do not assume what is to be proved.** When setting up a coordinate proof, students should be careful that they are not inadvertently using the very fact that they are trying to prove. For example, the figure below shows one way to assign coordinates to a parallelogram, based on the fact that opposite sides of a parallelogram are congruent. The figure can therefore be used to prove any property of parallelograms, except for the property that opposite sides are congruent!

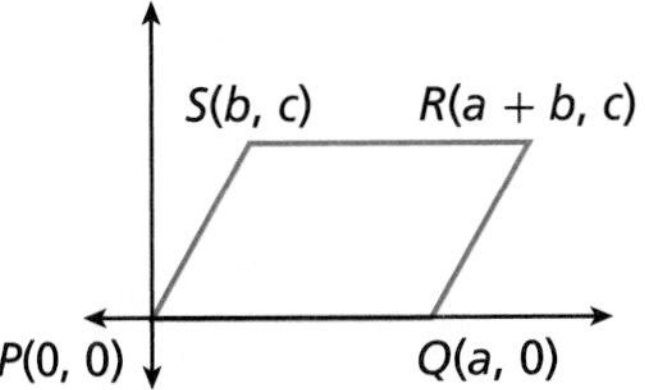

Organizer

Use with Lesson 4-4

Pacing:
Traditional 1 day
Block $\frac{1}{2}$ day

Objective: Discover shortcuts for proving triangles are congruent.

Materials: straws, string, paperclip, protractor

Online Edition

Countdown Week 8

Resources

Geometry Lab Activities
4-4 Lab Recording Sheet

Teach

Discuss

Discuss with students their attempts to make a second triangle using the same side lengths as the first triangle. Lead them to the conjecture that two triangles with three pairs of congruent corresponding sides are congruent.

In the second activity, discuss with students which combinations of sides and angles form congruent triangles. Lead them to the conclusion that the angle must be "between" the two sides. If two corresponding sides and their included angles are congruent, then the triangles are congruent.

State Resources

go.hrw.com
State Resources Online
KEYWORD: MG7 Resources

4-4

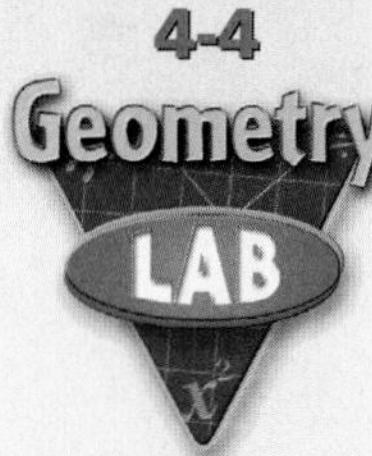

Use with Lesson 4-4

Explore SSS and SAS Triangle Congruence

In Lesson 4-3, you used the definition of congruent triangles to prove triangles congruent. To use the definition, you need to prove that all three pairs of corresponding sides and all three pairs of corresponding angles are congruent.

In this lab, you will discover some shortcuts for proving triangles congruent.

Activity 1

1. Measure and cut six pieces from the straws: two that are 2 inches long, two that are 4 inches long, and two that are 5 inches long.
2. Cut two pieces of string that are each about 20 inches long.
3. Thread one piece of each size of straw onto a piece of string. Tie the ends of the string together so that the pieces of straw form a triangle.
4. Using the remaining pieces, try to make another triangle with the same side lengths that is *not* congruent to the first triangle.

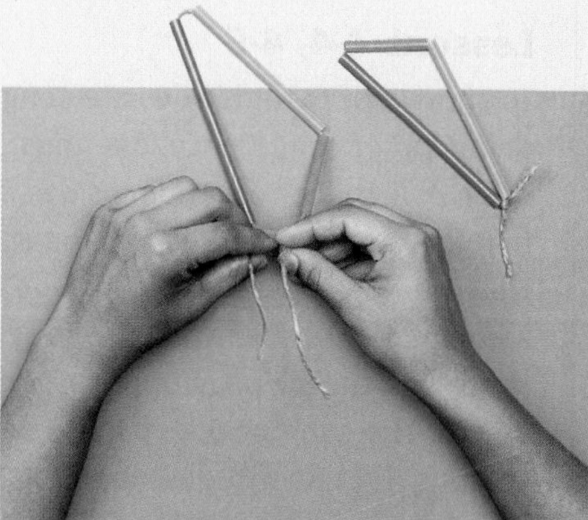

2. It is not possible. Once the lengths of the 3 straws are determined, only 1 △ can be formed.

3. To prove that 2 ⚠ are ≅, check to see if the 3 pairs of corr. sides are ≅.

Try This

1. Repeat Activity 1 using side lengths of your choice. Are your results the same? **yes**
2. Do you think it is possible to make two triangles that have the same side lengths but that are not congruent? Why or why not?
3. How does your answer to Problem 2 provide a shortcut for proving triangles congruent?
4. Complete the following conjecture based on your results. Two triangles are congruent if ____?____. **three sides of 1 △ are ≅ to 3 sides of the other △**

Activity 2

1. Measure and cut two pieces from the straws: one that is 4 inches long and one that is 5 inches long.

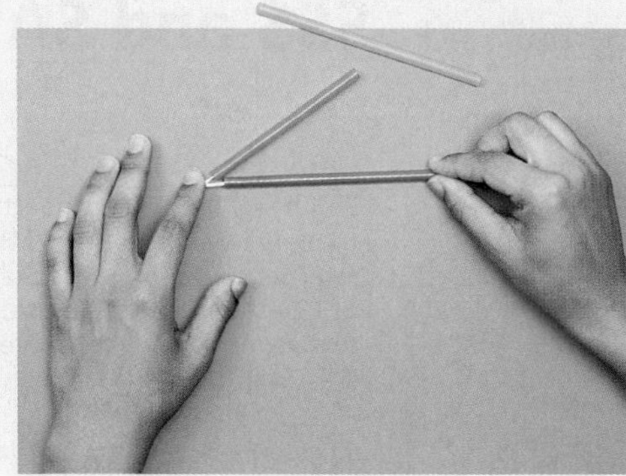

2. Use a protractor to help you bend a paper clip to form a 30° angle.

3. Place the pieces of straw on the sides of the 30° angle. The straws will form two sides of your triangle.

4. Without changing the angle formed by the paper clip, use a piece of straw to make a third side for your triangle, cutting it to fit as necessary. Use additional paper clips or string to hold the straws together in a triangle.

6. No; once 2 side lengths and the included ∠ measure are determined, only 1 length is possible for the remaining side.

Try This

7. To prove that 2 △s are ≅, check to see if there are 2 pairs of ≅ corr. sides and that their included ∠s are ≅.

5. Repeat Activity 2 using side lengths and an angle measure of your choice. Are your results the same? **yes**

6. Suppose you know two side lengths of a triangle and the measure of the angle between these sides. Can the length of the third side be any measure? Explain.

7. How does your answer to Problem 6 provide a shortcut for proving triangles congruent?

8. Use the two given sides and the given angle from Activity 2 to form a triangle that is not congruent to the triangle you formed. (*Hint:* One of the given sides does not have to be adjacent to the given angle.) **Check students' work.**

9. Complete the following conjecture based on your results. Two triangles are congruent if ___?___.
2 sides and the included ∠ of 1 △ are ≅ to 2 sides and the included ∠ of the other △

Alternative Approach

Place students in small groups. Give each student in the group an envelope containing three descriptions of parts of a triangle. For example, AB is 4 in., $m\angle A = 32°$, and $m\angle B = 48°$. At least one envelope should have the same characteristics as another envelope given to the group. The group should determine how many of the triangles are congruent and why.

Close

Key Concept

You do not need all six pairs of congruent corresponding parts to prove triangles congruent. If you know three pairs of corresponding sides are congruent (SSS) or two pairs of corresponding sides and the included angles are congruent (SAS), then you know the triangles are congruent.

Assessment

Journal Have students compare and contrast the SSS and SAS postulates and support their answers with a sketch that illustrates each postulate.

4-4 Organizer

Pacing: Traditional 2 days
Block 1 day

Objectives: Apply SSS and SAS to construct triangles and solve problems.

Prove triangles congruent by using SSS and SAS.

Geometry Lab
In *Geometry Lab Activities*

Online Edition
Tutorial Videos

Countdown Week 8

Power Presentations with PowerPoint®

Warm Up

1. Name the angle formed by $\overrightarrow{AB}$ and $\overrightarrow{AC}$. Possible answer: $\angle A$
2. Name the three sides of $\triangle ABC$. $\overline{AB}, \overline{AC}, \overline{BC}$
3. $\triangle QRS \cong \triangle LMN$. Name all pairs of congruent corresponding parts. $\overline{QR} \cong \overline{LM}$, $\overline{RS} \cong \overline{MN}$, $\overline{QS} \cong \overline{LN}$, $\angle Q \cong \angle L$, $\angle R \cong \angle M$, $\angle S \cong \angle N$

Also available on transparency

Math Humor

Q: Why did the greeting card come after your birthday?

A: Postulate!

4-4 Triangle Congruence: SSS and SAS

Objectives
Apply SSS and SAS to construct triangles and to solve problems.

Prove triangles congruent by using SSS and SAS.

Vocabulary
triangle rigidity
included angle

Who uses this?
Engineers used the property of triangle rigidity to design the internal support for the Statue of Liberty and to build bridges, towers, and other structures. (See Example 2.)

In Lesson 4-3, you proved triangles congruent by showing that all six pairs of corresponding parts were congruent.

The property of **triangle rigidity** gives you a shortcut for proving two triangles congruent. It states that if the side lengths of a triangle are given, the triangle can have only one shape.

For example, you only need to know that two triangles have three pairs of congruent corresponding sides. This can be expressed as the following postulate.

Know it! Note

Postulate 4-4-1 Side-Side-Side (SSS) Congruence

POSTULATE	HYPOTHESIS	CONCLUSION
If three sides of one triangle are congruent to three sides of another triangle, then the triangles are congruent.	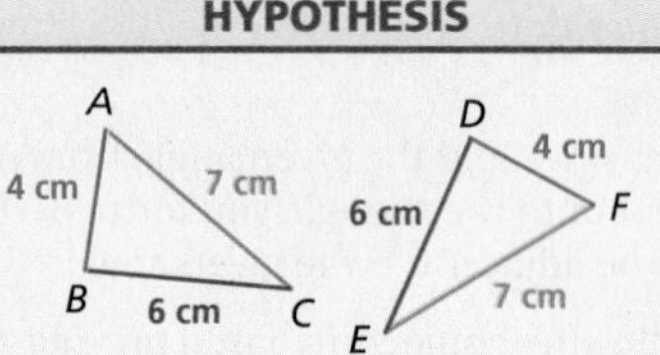	$\triangle ABC \cong \triangle FDE$

EXAMPLE 1 Using SSS to Prove Triangle Congruence

Use SSS to explain why $\triangle PQR \cong \triangle PSR$.

It is given that $\overline{PQ} \cong \overline{PS}$ and that $\overline{QR} \cong \overline{SR}$. By the Reflexive Property of Congruence, $\overline{PR} \cong \overline{PR}$. Therefore $\triangle PQR \cong \triangle PSR$ by SSS.

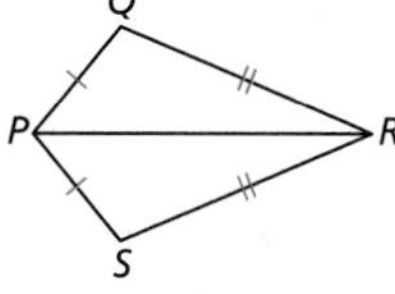

Remember!
Adjacent triangles share a side, so you can apply the Reflexive Property to get a pair of congruent parts.

1. Use SSS to explain why $\triangle ABC \cong \triangle CDA$.

It is given that $\overline{AB} \cong \overline{CD}$ and $\overline{BC} \cong \overline{DA}$. By the Reflex. Prop. of $\cong$, $\overline{AC} \cong \overline{CA}$. So $\triangle ABC \cong \triangle CDA$ by SSS.

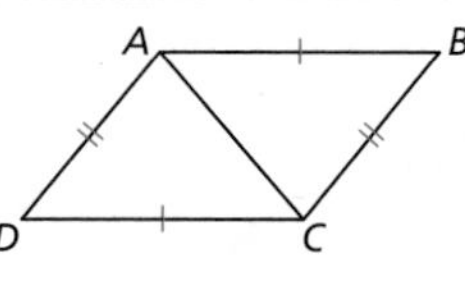

An **included angle** is an angle formed by two adjacent sides of a polygon. $\angle B$ is the included angle between sides $\overline{AB}$ and $\overline{BC}$.

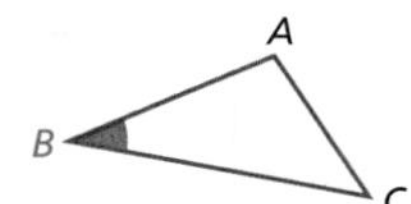

State Resources

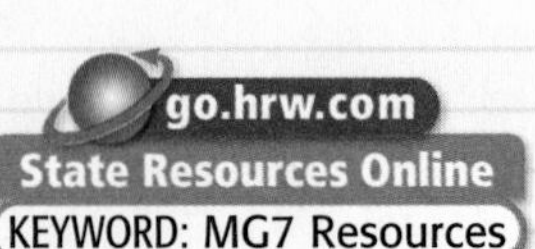

1 Introduce

EXPLORATION

4-4 Triangle Congruence: SSS and SAS

You will need a ruler and protractor for this Exploration.

1. Draw $\triangle ABC$ with the given measurements. (*Hint:* First draw an angle with the given measure and label it $\angle A$. Then draw $\overline{AB}$ and $\overline{AC}$ on the sides of this angle. Finally, draw $\overline{BC}$.)

$\triangle ABC$	
AB	2 in.
AC	3.5 in.
$m\angle A$	40°

2. Draw $\triangle DEF$ with the given measurements.

$\triangle DEF$	
DE	2 in.
DF	3.5 in.
$m\angle D$	40°

3. What do you notice about the two triangles you drew?
4. Is it possible to draw $\triangle DEF$ so that it is NOT congruent to $\triangle ABC$? If so, how?
5. Repeat Steps 1–4, choosing your own measures so that $AB = DE$, $AC = DF$, and $m\angle A = m\angle D$. Do you get the same results?
6. An *included angle* is an angle formed by two adjacent sides of a polygon. Complete the following conjecture: If two sides and the included angle of one triangle are congruent to two sides and the included angle of another triangle, then __?__.

THINK AND DISCUSS

7. Explain how you could use the above

Motivate

Use pictures from magazines to show students that triangle congruence is important in designing and building structures. Triangles can be proved congruent without using all three pairs of angles and all three pairs of sides. Explain to students that this lesson will show them how to prove triangles congruent using three pairs of congruent corresponding parts.

Explorations and answers are provided in *Alternate Openers: Explorations Transparencies.*

It can also be shown that only two pairs of congruent corresponding sides are needed to prove the congruence of two triangles if the included angles are also congruent.

Postulate 4-4-2 Side-Angle-Side (SAS) Congruence

POSTULATE	HYPOTHESIS	CONCLUSION
If two sides and the included angle of one triangle are congruent to two sides and the included angle of another triangle, then the triangles are congruent.	A, B, C; D, E, F	$\triangle ABC \cong \triangle EFD$

EXAMPLE 2 ***Engineering Application***

The figure shows part of the support structure of the Statue of Liberty. Use SAS to explain why $\triangle KPN \cong \triangle LPM$.

It is given that $\overline{KP} \cong \overline{LP}$ and that $\overline{NP} \cong \overline{MP}$. By the Vertical Angles Theorem, $\angle KPN \cong \angle LPM$. Therefore $\triangle KPN \cong \triangle LPM$ by SAS.

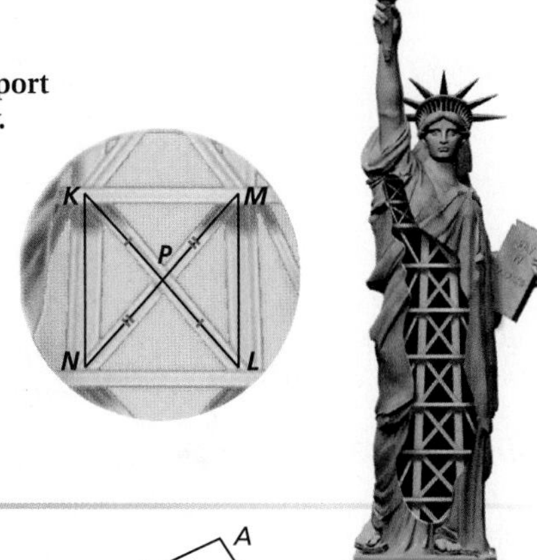

Caution!

The letters SAS are written in that order because the congruent angles must be between pairs of congruent corresponding sides.

CHECK IT OUT! **2.** Use SAS to explain why $\triangle ABC \cong \triangle DBC$.

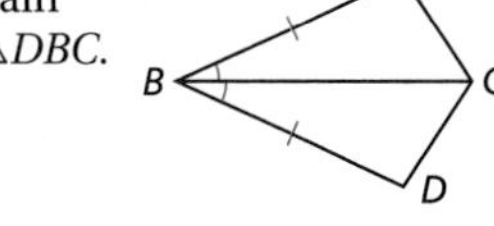

2. It is given that $\overline{BA} \cong \overline{BD}$ and $\angle ABC \cong \angle DBC$. By the Reflex. Prop. of $\cong$, $\overline{BC} \cong \overline{BC}$. So $\triangle ABC \cong \triangle DBC$ by SAS.

The SAS Postulate guarantees that if you are given the lengths of two sides and the measure of the included angle, you can construct one and only one triangle.

Construction Congruent Triangles Using SAS

Use a straightedge to draw two segments and one angle, or copy the given segments and angle.

1

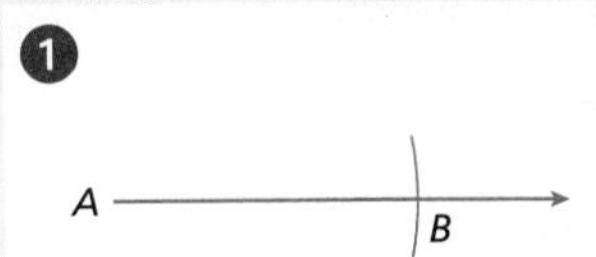

Construct $\overline{AB}$ congruent to one of the segments.

2

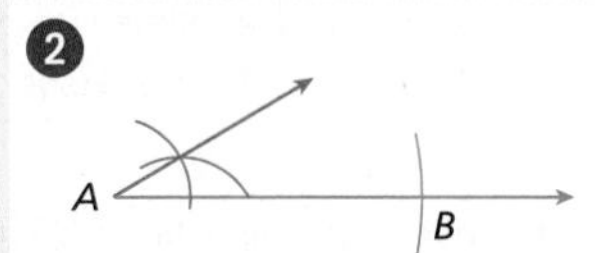

Construct $\angle A$ congruent to the given angle.

3

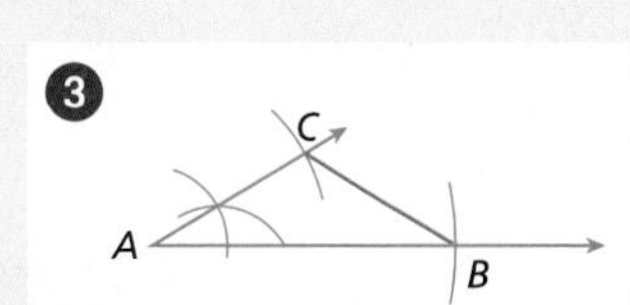

Construct $\overline{AC}$ congruent to the other segment. Draw $\overline{CB}$ to complete $\triangle ABC$.

COMMON ERROR ALERT

Students may choose the wrong angle when SAS is used to prove triangles congruent. Explain that the angle must be formed by the sides. The included angle is named by the letter the segments share.

Teaching Tip **Transformations** Lead students to recognize when reflection is modeled in the examples. You can do this with a mirror (MK) or Mira.

Power Presentations with PowerPoint®

Additional Examples

Example 1

Use SSS to explain why $\triangle ABC \cong \triangle DBC$.

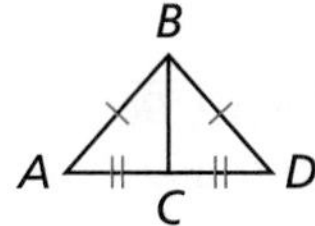

It is given that $\overline{AC} \cong \overline{DC}$ and that $\overline{AB} \cong \overline{DB}$. By the Reflex. Prop. of $\cong$, $\overline{BC} \cong \overline{BC}$. Therefore $\triangle ABC \cong \triangle DBC$ by SSS.

Example 2

The diagram shows part of the support structure for a tower. Use SAS to explain why $\triangle XYZ \cong \triangle VWZ$.

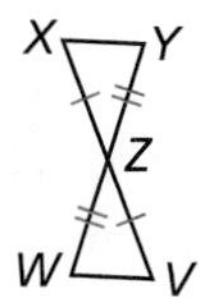

It is given that $\overline{XZ} \cong \overline{VZ}$ and that $\overline{YZ} \cong \overline{WZ}$. By the Vert. ⦣ Thm. $\angle XZY \cong \angle VZW$. Therefore $\triangle XYZ \cong \triangle VWZ$ by SAS.

2 Teach

Guided Instruction

Review with students how to write congruence statements based on corresponding parts. Explain that the SSS and the SAS congruence postulates are shortcuts to verifying all six corresponding parts congruent. Draw triangles with the following measures: one side 7 cm, one side 10 cm, and a 40° angle. Explain that the triangles are not necessarily congruent. The triangles drawn with the 40° angle included between the given sides are congruent.

Reaching All Learners

Through Modeling

Introduce the SSS postulate with the following activity. Have the students draw three line segments of given lengths. Using one of the three lengths as a base and one endpoint of the base as center, draw an arc with a radius equal to a second length. Draw an arc with a radius equal to the third length, using the other endpoint as center. Join the endpoints with the intersection of the arcs. Have students compare their triangles and make a conjecture.

INTERVENTION

Questioning Strategies

EXAMPLE 1

- What do the tick marks on the triangles show? What additional information do you need to prove the triangles congruent by SSS?

EXAMPLE 2

- Is enough information given to prove the triangles congruent by SAS? What additional information do you need?

Power Presentations with PowerPoint®

Additional Examples

Example 3

Show that the triangles are congruent for the given value of the variable.

A. $\triangle MNO \cong \triangle PQR$, when $x = 5$.

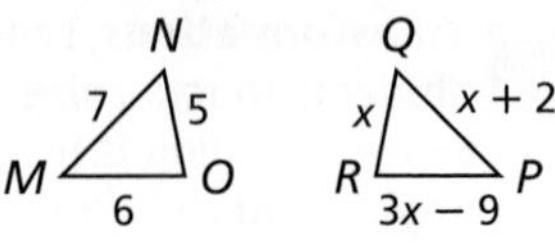

$\triangle MNO \cong \triangle PQR$ by SSS.

B. $\triangle STU \cong \triangle VWX$, when $y = 4$

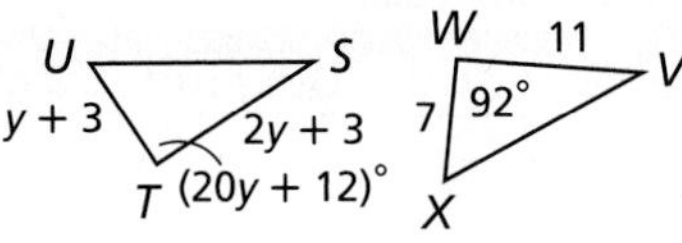

$\triangle STU \cong \triangle VWX$ by SAS.

Example 4

Given: $\overline{BC} \parallel \overline{AD}$, $\overline{BC} \cong \overline{AD}$
Prove: $\triangle ABD \cong \triangle CDB$

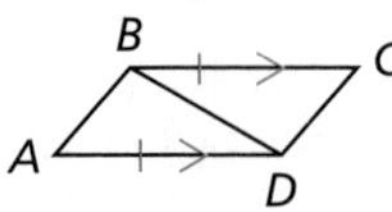

1. $\overline{BC} \parallel \overline{AD}$ (Given)
2. $\angle CBD \cong \angle ADB$ (Alt. Int. ∠s Thm.)
3. $\overline{BC} \cong \overline{AD}$ (Given)
4. $\overline{BD} \cong \overline{BD}$ (Reflex. Prop. of ≅)
5. $\triangle ABD \cong \triangle CDB$ (SAS *Steps 3, 2, 4*)

INTERVENTION

Questioning Strategies

EXAMPLE 3

- How do you find the lengths of the sides of both triangles?

EXAMPLE 4

- How do parallel lines help you verify congruent angles?

EXAMPLE 3 Verifying Triangle Congruence

Algebra

Show that the triangles are congruent for the given value of the variable.

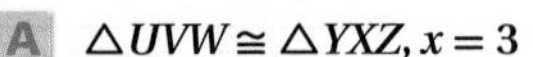

A $\triangle UVW \cong \triangle YXZ, x = 3$

$ZY = x - 1$
$= 3 - 1 = 2$
$XZ = x = 3$
$XY = 3x - 5$
$= 3(3) - 5 = 4$

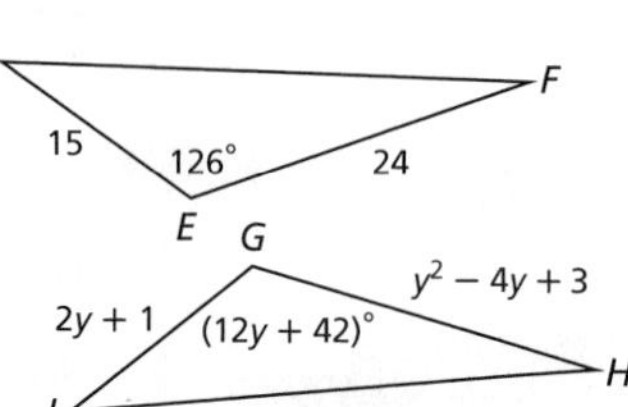

$\overline{UV} \cong \overline{YX}$. $\overline{VW} \cong \overline{XZ}$, and $\overline{UW} \cong \overline{YZ}$.
So $\triangle UVW \cong \triangle YXZ$ by SSS.

B $\triangle DEF \cong \triangle JGH, y = 7$

$JG = 2y + 1$
$= 2(7) + 1$
$= 15$
$GH = y^2 - 4y + 3$
$= (7)^2 - 4(7) + 3$
$= 24$
$m\angle G = 12y + 42$
$= 12(7) + 42$
$= 126°$

D, F, E, 15, 126°, 24, G, 2y + 1, (12y + 42)°, $y^2 - 4y + 3$, J, H

$\overline{DE} \cong \overline{JG}$. $\overline{EF} \cong \overline{GH}$, and $\angle E \cong \angle G$.
So $\triangle DEF \cong \triangle JGH$ by SAS.

3. Show that $\triangle ADB \cong \triangle CDB$ when $t = 4$.

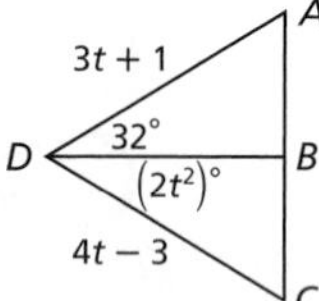

3. $DA = DC = 13$, so $\overline{DA} \cong \overline{DC}$ by def. of ≅. $m\angle ADB = m\angle CDB = 32°$, so $\angle ADB \cong \angle CDB$ by def. of ≅. $\overline{DB} \cong \overline{DB}$ by the Reflex. Prop. of ≅. Therefore $\triangle ADB \cong \triangle CDB$ by SAS.

EXAMPLE 4 Proving Triangles Congruent

Given: $\ell \parallel m$, $\overline{EG} \cong \overline{HF}$
Prove: $\triangle EGF \cong \triangle HFG$
Proof:

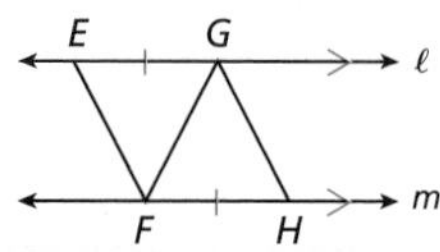

Statements	Reasons
1. $\overline{EG} \cong \overline{HF}$	1. Given
2. $\ell \parallel m$	2. Given
3. $\angle EGF \cong \angle HFG$	3. Alt. Int. ∠s Thm.
4. $\overline{FG} \cong \overline{GF}$	4. Reflex Prop. of ≅
5. $\triangle EGF \cong \triangle HFG$	5. SAS *Steps 1, 3, 4*

4. Given: $\overrightarrow{QP}$ bisects $\angle RQS$. $\overline{QR} \cong \overline{QS}$
Prove: $\triangle RQP \cong \triangle SQP$

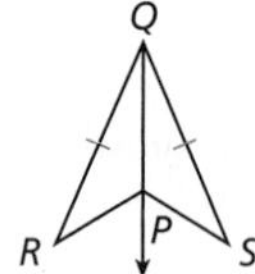

1. $\overline{QR} \cong \overline{QS}$ (Given)
2. $\overrightarrow{QP}$ bisects $\angle RQS$. (Given)
3. $\angle RQP \cong \angle SQP$ (Def. of bisector)
4. $\overline{QP} \cong \overline{QP}$ (Reflex. Prop. of ≅)
5. $\triangle RQP \cong \triangle SQP$ (SAS *Steps 1, 3, 4*)

3 Close

Summarize

Review the SSS and SAS postulates for proving triangles congruent, and give examples of each. Remind students of the importance of the order of the letters in a congruence statement.

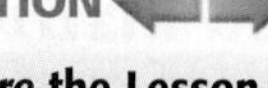

ONGOING ASSESSMENT and INTERVENTION

Diagnose Before **the Lesson**
4-4 Warm Up, TE p. 242

Monitor During **the Lesson**
Check It Out! Exercises, SE pp. 242–244
Questioning Strategies, TE pp. 243–244

Assess After **the Lesson**
4-4 Lesson Quiz, TE p. 249
Alternative Assessment, TE p. 249

THINK AND DISCUSS

1. Describe three ways you could prove that $\triangle ABC \cong \triangle DEF$.
2. Explain why the SSS and SAS Postulates are shortcuts for proving triangles congruent.
3. **GET ORGANIZED** Copy and complete the graphic organizer. Use it to compare the SSS and SAS postulates.

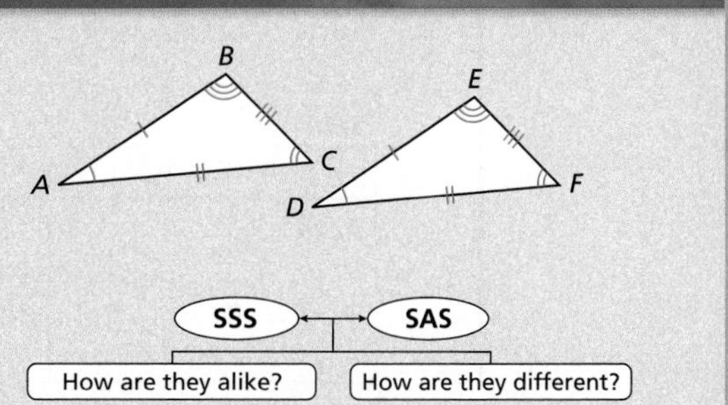

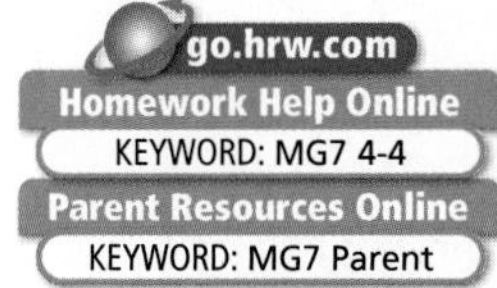

Answers to *Think and Discuss*

1. Show that all six pairs of corr. parts are ≅; SSS; SAS
2. The SSS and SAS Post. are methods for proving ⚠ ≅ without having to prove the congruence of all 6 corr. parts.
3. See p. A4.

4-4 Exercises

go.hrw.com
Homework Help Online
KEYWORD: MG7 4-4
Parent Resources Online
KEYWORD: MG7 Parent

GUIDED PRACTICE

1. **Vocabulary** In $\triangle RST$ which angle is the included angle of sides $\overline{ST}$ and $\overline{TR}$? $\angle T$

SEE EXAMPLE 1 p. 242

Use SSS to explain why the triangles in each pair are congruent.

2. $\triangle ABD \cong \triangle CDB$

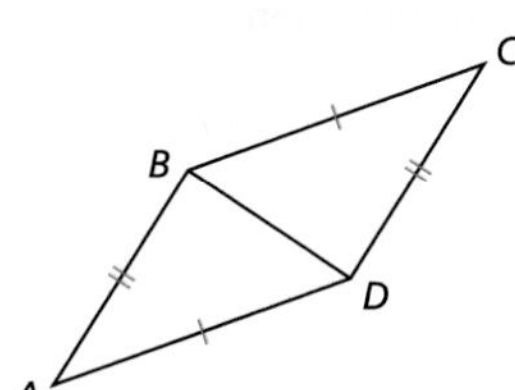

3. $\triangle MNP \cong \triangle MQP$

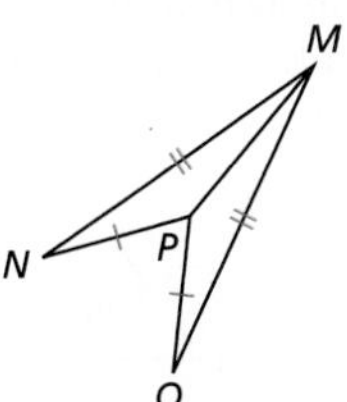

SEE EXAMPLE 2 p. 243

4. **Sailing** Signal flags are used to communicate messages when radio silence is required. The Zulu signal flag means, "I require a tug." $GJ = GH = GL = GK = 20$ in. Use SAS to explain why $\triangle JGK \cong \triangle LGH$.

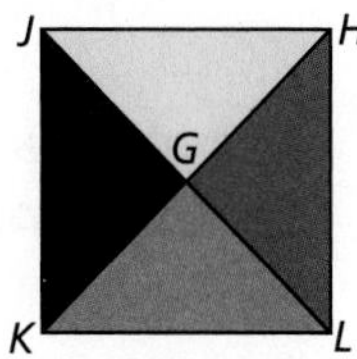

SEE EXAMPLE 3 p. 244

Show that the triangles are congruent for the given value of the variable.

5. $\triangle GHJ \cong \triangle IHJ$, $x = 4$

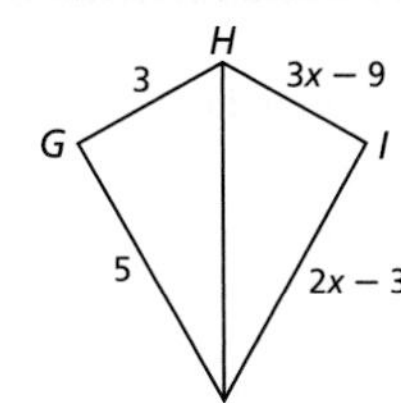

When $x = 4$, $HI = GH = 3$, and $IJ = GJ = 5$. $\overline{HJ} \cong \overline{HJ}$ by the Reflex. Prop. of ≅. Therefore $\triangle GHJ \cong \triangle IHJ$ by SSS.

6. $\triangle RST \cong \triangle TUR$, $x = 18$

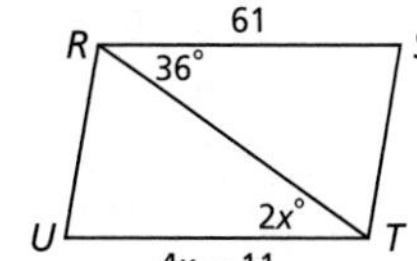

When $x = 18$, $RS = UT = 61$, and $m\angle SRT = m\angle UTR = 36°$. $\overline{RT} \cong \overline{TR}$ by the Reflex. Prop. of ≅. So $\triangle RST \cong \triangle TUR$ by SAS.

4-4 Exercises

Assignment Guide

Assign *Guided Practice* exercises as necessary.

If you finished Examples **1–2**
- **Basic** 8–10, 14–18, 27
- **Average** 8–10, 14–18, 24, 27
- **Advanced** 8–10, 14–18, 24–27

If you finished Examples **1–4**
- **Basic** 8–18, 21, 23, 25, 26, 28–32, 37–45
- **Average** 8–19, 21, 22–31, 33, 36–44
- **Advanced** 8–14, 19–44

Homework Quick Check
Quickly check key concepts.
Exercises: 8, 10, 12, 13, 14, 25

Teaching Tip **Critical Thinking** In **Exercises 5** and **6**, have students consider how they can find the value of the variable if the triangles are given as congruent.

Answers

2. It is given that $\overline{DA} \cong \overline{BC}$ and $\overline{AB} \cong \overline{CD}$. $\overline{BD} \cong \overline{DB}$ by the Reflex. Prop. of ≅. Thus $\triangle ABD \cong \triangle CDB$ by SSS.
3. It is given that $\overline{MN} \cong \overline{MQ}$ and $\overline{NP} \cong \overline{QP}$. $\overline{MP} \cong \overline{MP}$ by the Reflex. Prop. of ≅. Thus $\triangle MNP \cong \triangle MQP$ by SSS.
4. It is given that $\overline{JG} \cong \overline{LG}$ and $\overline{GK} \cong \overline{GH}$. $\angle JGK \cong \angle LGH$ by the Vert. ⚠ Thm. So $\triangle JGK \cong \triangle LGH$ by SAS.

State Resources

go.hrw.com
State Resources Online
KEYWORD: MG7 Resources

Visual In **Exercises 11** and **12,** have students label the congruent corresponding sides with *S* and the congruent corresponding angles with *A*.

Answers

8. It is given that $BC = ED = 4$ in. and $BD = EC = 3$ in. So by the def. of ≅, $\overline{BC} \cong \overline{ED}$, and $\overline{BD} \cong \overline{EC}$. $\overline{CD} \cong \overline{DC}$ by the Reflex. Prop. of ≅. Thus $\triangle BCD \cong \triangle EDC$ by SSS.
9. It is given that $\overline{KJ} \cong \overline{LJ}$ and $\overline{GK} \cong \overline{GL}$. $\overline{GJ} \cong \overline{GJ}$ by the Reflex. Prop. of ≅. So $\triangle GJK \cong \triangle GJL$ by SSS.
10. It is given that $\angle C$ and $\angle B$ are rt. ∡ and $\overline{EC} \cong \overline{DB}$. $\angle C \cong \angle B$ by the Rt. ∠ ≅ Thm. $\overline{CB} \cong \overline{BC}$ by the Reflex. Prop. of ≅. So $\triangle ECB \cong \triangle DBC$ by SAS.
11. When $y = 3$, $NQ = NM = 3$, and $QP = MP = 4$. So by the def. of ≅, $\overline{NQ} \cong \overline{NM}$, and $\overline{QP} \cong \overline{MP}$. $m\angle M = m\angle Q = 90°$, so $\angle M \cong \angle Q$ by the def. of ≅. Thus $\triangle MNP \cong \triangle QNP$ by SAS.
12. When $t = 5$, $YZ = 24$, $ST = 20$, and $SU = 22$. So by the def. of ≅, $\overline{XY} \cong \overline{ST}$, $\overline{YZ} \cong \overline{TU}$, and $\overline{XZ} \cong \overline{SU}$. Thus $\triangle XYZ \cong \triangle STU$ by SSS.

SEE EXAMPLE 4 p. 244

7. **Given:** $\overline{JK} \cong \overline{ML}$, $\angle JKL \cong \angle MLK$
Prove: $\triangle JKL \cong \triangle MLK$

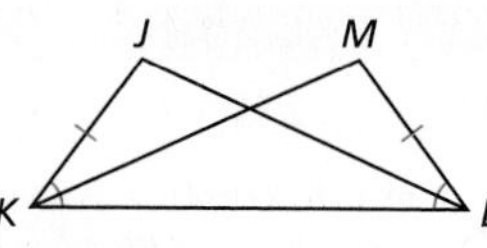

Proof:

Statements	Reasons
1. $\overline{JK} \cong \overline{ML}$	1. a. ?
2. b. ?	2. Given
3. $\overline{KL} \cong \overline{LK}$	3. c. ?
4. $\triangle JKL \cong \triangle MLK$	4. d. ?

a. Given
b. $\angle JKL \cong \angle MLK$
c. Reflex. Prop. of ≅
d. SAS *Steps 1, 2, 3*

PRACTICE AND PROBLEM SOLVING

Independent Practice	
For Exercises	See Example
8–9	1
10	2
11–12	3
13	4

Extra Practice
Skills Practice p. S11
Application Practice p. S31

Use SSS to explain why the triangles in each pair are congruent.

8. $\triangle BCD \cong \triangle EDC$

B, C, D, E; 4 in., 3 in., 3 in., 4 in.

9. $\triangle GJK \cong \triangle GJL$

G, K, J, L

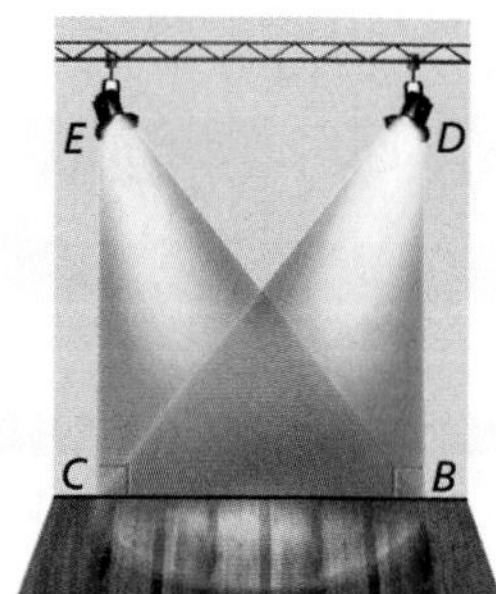

10. **Theater** The lights shining on a stage appear to form two congruent right triangles. Given $\overline{EC} \cong \overline{DB}$, use SAS to explain why $\triangle ECB \cong \triangle DBC$.

Show that the triangles are congruent for the given value of the variable.

11. $\triangle MNP \cong \triangle QNP$, $y = 3$

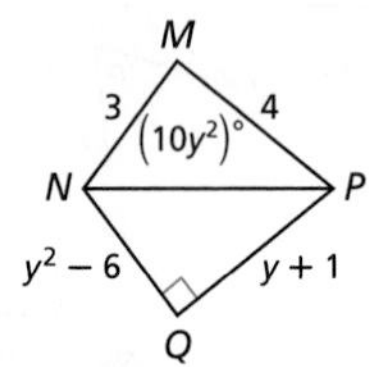

12. $\triangle XYZ \cong \triangle STU$, $t = 5$

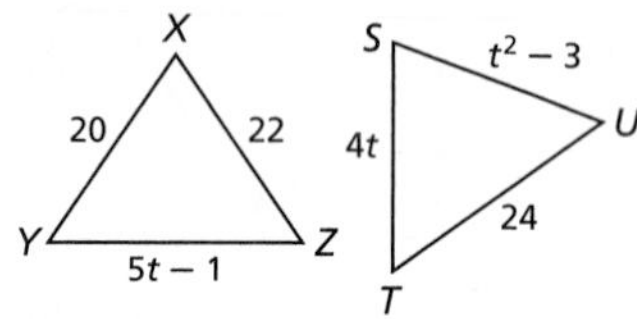

13. **Given:** B is the midpoint of $\overline{DC}$. $\overline{AB} \perp \overline{DC}$
Prove: $\triangle ABD \cong \triangle ABC$

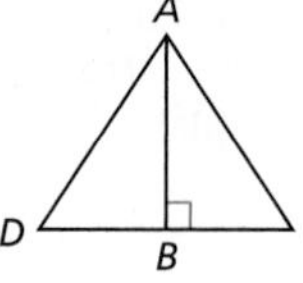

Proof:

Statements	Reasons
1. B is the mdpt. of $\overline{DC}$.	1. a. ?
2. b. ?	2. Def. of mdpt.
3. c. ?	3. Given
4. $\angle ABD$ and $\angle ABC$ are rt. ∡.	4. d. ?
5. $\angle ABD \cong \angle ABC$	5. e. ?
6. f. ?	6. Reflex. Prop. of ≅
7. $\triangle ABD \cong \triangle ABC$	7. g. ?

a. Given
b. $\overline{DB} \cong \overline{CB}$
c. $\overline{AB} \perp \overline{DC}$
d. Def. of ⊥
e. Rt. ∠ ≅ Thm.
f. $\overline{AB} \cong \overline{AB}$
g. SAS *Steps 2, 5, 6*

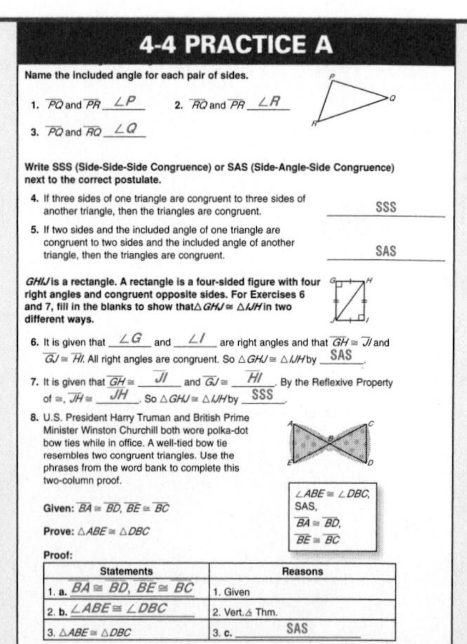

4-4 PRACTICE A

Name the included angle for each pair of sides.

1. $\overline{PQ}$ and $\overline{PR}$ $\angle P$
2. $\overline{RQ}$ and $\overline{PR}$ $\angle R$
3. $\overline{PQ}$ and $\overline{RQ}$ $\angle Q$

Write SSS (Side-Side-Side Congruence) or SAS (Side-Angle-Side Congruence) next to the correct postulate.

4. If three sides of one triangle are congruent to three sides of another triangle, then the triangles are congruent. SSS
5. If two sides and the included angle of one triangle are congruent to two sides and the included angle of another triangle, then the triangles are congruent. SAS

***GHIJ* is a rectangle. A rectangle is a four-sided figure with four right angles and congruent opposite sides. For Exercises 6 and 7, fill in the blanks to show that $\triangle GHJ \cong \triangle IJH$ in two different ways.**

6. It is given that $\angle G$ and $\angle I$ are right angles and that $\overline{GH} \cong \overline{JI}$ and $\overline{GJ} \cong \overline{HI}$. All right angles are congruent. So $\triangle GHJ \cong \triangle IJH$ by SAS.
7. It is given that $\overline{GH} \cong \overline{JI}$ and $\overline{GJ} \cong \overline{HI}$. By the Reflexive Property of ≅, $\overline{JH} \cong \overline{JH}$. So $\triangle GHJ \cong \triangle IJH$ by SSS.
8. U.S. President Harry Truman and British Prime Minister Winston Churchill both wore polka-dot bow ties while in office. A well-tied bow tie resembles two congruent triangles. Use the phrases from the word bank to complete this two-column proof.

$\angle ABE \cong \angle DBC$, SAS, $\overline{BA} \cong \overline{BD}$, $\overline{BE} \cong \overline{BC}$

Given: $\overline{BA} \cong \overline{BD}$, $\overline{BE} \cong \overline{BC}$
Prove: $\triangle ABE \cong \triangle DBC$

Proof:

Statements	Reasons
1. a. $\overline{BA} \cong \overline{BD}$, $\overline{BE} \cong \overline{BC}$	1. Given
2. b. $\angle ABE \cong \angle DBC$	2. Vert. ∡ Thm.
3. $\triangle ABE \cong \triangle DBC$	3. c. SAS

Which postulate, if any, can be used to prove the triangles congruent?

14. 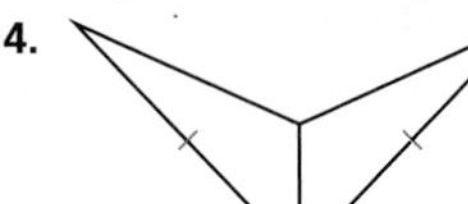 SAS

15. 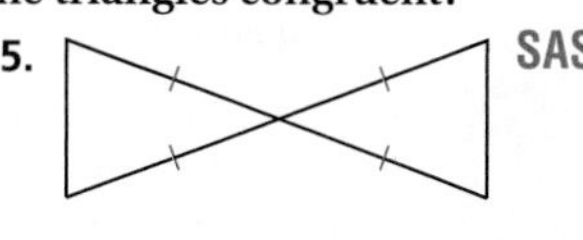 SAS

16. 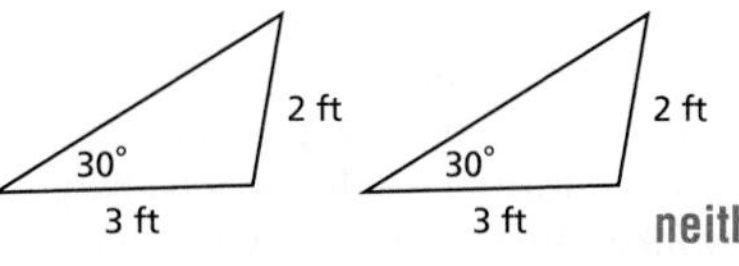

neither

17.  neither

18. Explain what additional information, if any, you would need to prove $\triangle ABC \cong \triangle DEC$ by each postulate.
   a. SSS   b. SAS

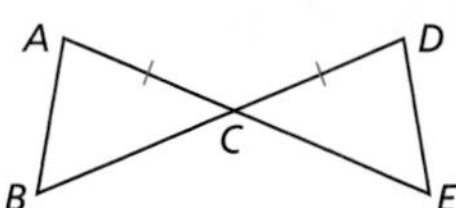

18a. To use SSS, you need to know that $\overline{AB} \cong \overline{DE}$ and $\overline{CB} \cong \overline{CE}$.
b. To use SAS, you need to know that $\overline{CB} \cong \overline{CE}$.

Multi-Step Graph each triangle. Then use the Distance Formula and the SSS Postulate to determine whether the triangles are congruent.

19. $\triangle QRS$ and $\triangle TUV$
   $Q(-2, 0)$, $R(1, -2)$, $S(-3, -2)$
   $T(5, 1)$, $U(3, -2)$, $V(3, 2)$

20. $\triangle ABC$ and $\triangle DEF$
   $A(2, 3)$, $B(3, -1)$, $C(7, 2)$
   $D(-3, 1)$, $E(1, 2)$, $F(-3, 5)$

21. Given: $\angle ZVY \cong \angle WYV$, $\angle ZVW \cong \angle WYZ$, $\overline{VW} \cong \overline{YZ}$
   Prove: $\triangle ZVY \cong \triangle WYV$
   Proof:

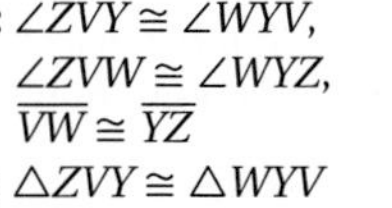

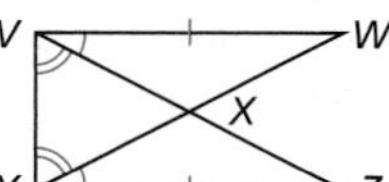

Statements	Reasons
1. $\angle ZVY \cong \angle WYV$, $\angle ZVW \cong WYZ$	1. a. ___?___
2. $m\angle ZVY = m\angle WYV$, $m\angle ZVW = m\angle WYZ$	2. b. ___?___
3. $m\angle ZVY + m\angle ZVW = m\angle WYV + m\angle WYZ$	3. Add. Prop. of =
4. c. ___?___	4. ∠ Add. Post.
5. $\angle WVY \cong \angle ZYV$	5. d. ___?___
6. $\overline{VW} \cong \overline{YZ}$	6. e. ___?___
7. f. ___?___	7. Reflex. Prop. of ≅
8. $\triangle ZVY \cong \triangle WYV$	8. g. ___?___

21a. Given
b. Def. of ≅
c. $m\angle WVY = m\angle ZYV$
d. Def. of ≅
e. Given
f. $\overline{VY} \cong \overline{YV}$
g. SAS *Steps 6, 5, 7*

MULTI-STEP TEST PREP

22. This problem will prepare you for the Multi-Step Test Prep on page 280. The diagram shows two triangular trusses that were built for the roof of a doghouse.
   a. You can use a protractor to check that $\angle A$ and $\angle D$ are right angles. Explain how you could make just two additional measurements on each truss to ensure that the trusses are congruent.
   b. You verify that the trusses are congruent and find that $AB = AC = 2.5$ ft. Find the length of $\overline{EF}$ to the nearest tenth. Explain.

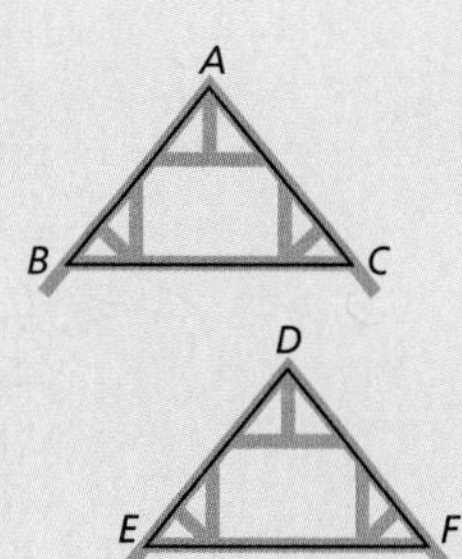

Teaching Tip **Visual** In **Exercise 15,** students may forget that they can use the vertical angles even though they are not marked congruent. Remind them to look for common sides, common angles, and vertical angles in a diagram.

Teaching Tip **Algebra** For **Exercises 19** and **20,** review the Distance Formula.

$$d = \sqrt{(x_2 - x_1)^2 + (y_2 - y_1)^2}$$

MULTI-STEP TEST PREP **Exercise 23** involves proving triangles congruent. This exercise prepares students for the Multi-Step Test Prep on page 280.

Answers

19. Check students' graphs. $QS = TV = \sqrt{5}$. $SR = VU = 4$. $QR = TU = \sqrt{13}$. The △s are ≅ by SSS.

20. Check students' graphs. $AB = \sqrt{17}$, $BC = 5$, $AC = \sqrt{26}$; $DE = \sqrt{17}$, $EF = 5$, and $DF = 4$. The △s are not ≅.

22a. Measure $\overline{AB}$ and $\overline{AC}$ on 1 truss and measure $\overline{DE}$ and $\overline{DF}$ on the other. If $\overline{AB} \cong \overline{DE}$ and $\overline{AC} \cong \overline{DF}$, then the trusses are ≅ by SAS.
b. 3.5 ft; by the Pyth. Thm., $BC \approx 3.5$ ft. Since the △s are congruent, $\overline{EF} \cong \overline{BC}$.

4-4 PRACTICE B

Write which of the SSS or SAS postulates, if either, can be used to prove the triangles congruent.

1. neither
2. SAS
3. neither
4. SSS

Find the value of x so that the triangles are congruent.

5. $x =$ 1.8
6. $x =$ 17

The Hatfield and McCoy families are feuding over some land. Neither family will be satisfied unless the two triangular fields are exactly the same size. You know that C is the midpoint of each of the intersecting segments. Write a two-column proof that will settle the dispute.

7. Given: C is the midpoint of $\overline{AD}$ and $\overline{BE}$.
   Prove: $\triangle ABC \cong \triangle DEC$
   Proof: Possible answer:

Statements	Reasons
1. C is the midpoint of $\overline{AD}$ and $\overline{BE}$.	1. Given
2. $AC = CD$, $BC = CE$	2. Def. of mdpt.
3. $\overline{AC} \cong \overline{CD}$, $\overline{BC} \cong \overline{CE}$	3. Def. of ≅ Segs.
4. $\angle ACB \cong \angle DCE$	4. Vert. △s Thm.
5. $\triangle ABC \cong \triangle DEC$	5. SAS

4-4 PRACTICE C

For each definition, tell what angle measures or side lengths of the quadrilateral must be given in order to determine a specific figure. (*Hint:* Think in terms of congruent triangles.)

1. A *square* is a quadrilateral with four congruent sides and four right angles.
   any side length
2. A *rectangle* is a quadrilateral with congruent pairs of opposite sides and four right angles.
   lengths of two adjacent sides
3. A *rhombus* is a quadrilateral with four congruent sides and parallel pairs of opposite sides.
   any angle measure and any side length
4. A *parallelogram* is a quadrilateral with congruent and parallel pairs of opposite sides.
   any angle measure and the lengths of two adjacent sides
5. Can a square be determined given only the length of a diagonal? Explain your answer.
   Yes; possible answer: The diagonal is the hypotenuse of an isosceles right triangle. The length of one side can be found by using the Pythagorean Theorem, and knowing one side is enough to draw a specific square.
6. Find the total area of the figure.
   540 ft^2

Write a paragraph proof .

7. Given: $\overline{BA} \cong \overline{BC}$, $\overline{BE} \cong \overline{BF}$, $\overline{AG} \cong \overline{CD}$, $\overline{GF} \cong \overline{DE}$
   Prove: $\triangle AEG \cong \triangle CFD$

Possible answer: It is given that $\overline{BA} \cong \overline{BC}$ and $\overline{BE} \cong \overline{BF}$, so by the definition of congruent segments, $BA = BC$ and $BE = BF$. Adding these together gives $BA + BE = BC + BF$, and from the figure and the Segment Addition Postulate, $AE = BA + BE$ and $CF = BC + BF$. It is clear by the Transitive Property that $AE = CF$, hence $\overline{AE} \cong \overline{CF}$. It is given that $\overline{GF} \cong \overline{DE}$ and the Reflexive Property shows that $\overline{FE} \cong \overline{FE}$. So by the Common Segments Theorem, $\overline{GE} \cong \overline{DF}$. The final pair of sides is given congruent, so $\triangle AEG \cong \triangle CFD$ by the Side-Side-Side Congruence Postulate.

Construction

To help students construct the triangle in **Exercise 27,** have them construct $\overline{AB}$ congruent to one of the segments. Then set their compasses to the length of another segment. Have them make an arc centered at *A*. Next set their compasses to the length of the third segment and draw an arc centered at *B*. They should label the intersection of the arcs *C*. Finally have them draw $\triangle ABC$.

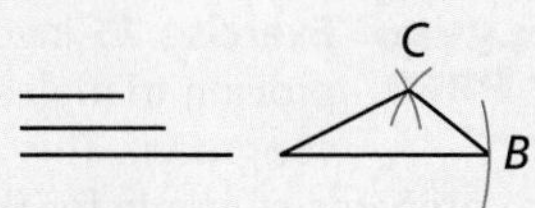

If students chose **H** for **Exercise 29,** they included the length of $\overline{AC}$ in the perimeter.

Answers

23.

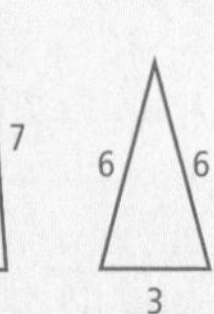

24. $x = 5.5$; by the def. of $\cong$, $\overline{AB} \cong \overline{BD}$, and $\overline{BC} \cong \overline{DC}$. $\overline{AC} \cong \overline{AC}$ by the Reflex. Prop. of $\cong$. Thus $\triangle ABC \cong \triangle ADC$ by SSS.

25. Measure the lengths of the logs. If the lengths of the logs in 1 wing deflector match the lengths of the logs in the other wing deflector, the ⚠ will be $\cong$ by SAS or SSS.

26. Yes; if the ⚠ have the same 2 side lengths and the same included $\angle$ measure, the ⚠ are $\cong$ by SAS.

27. Check students' constructions; yes; if each side is $\cong$ to the corr. side of the second $\triangle$, they can be in any order.

32.
1. Draw $\overline{DB}$. (Through any 2 pts. there is exactly 1 line.)
2. $\angle ADC$ and $\angle BCD$ are supp. (Given)
3. $\overline{AD} \parallel \overline{CB}$ (conv. of Same-Side Int. ∠s Thm.)
4. $\angle ADB \cong \angle CBD$ (Alt. Int. ∠s Thm.)
5. $\overline{AD} \cong \overline{CB}$ (Given)
6. $\overline{DB} \cong \overline{BD}$ (Reflex. Prop. of $\cong$)
7. $\triangle ADB \cong \triangle CBD$ (SAS *Steps 5, 4, 6*)

33.
1. $\angle QPS \cong \angle TPR$ (Given)
2. $\angle RPS \cong \angle RPS$ (Reflex. Prop. of $\cong$)
3. $\angle QPR \cong \angle TPS$ (Subtr. Prop. of $\cong$)
4. $\overline{PQ} \cong \overline{PT}$, $\overline{PR} \cong \overline{PS}$ (Given)
5. $\triangle PQR \cong \triangle PTS$ (SAS *Steps 3, 4*)

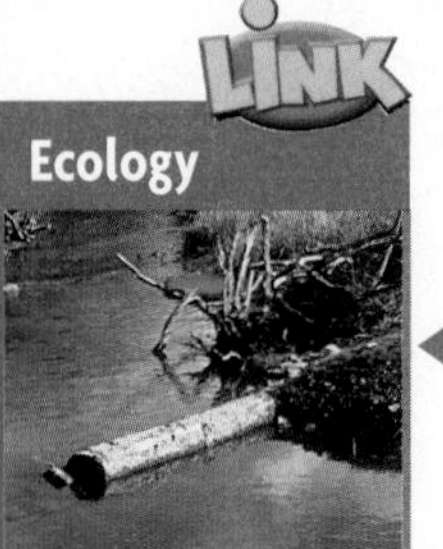

Wing deflectors are designed to reduce the width-to-depth ratio of a stream. Reducing the width increases the velocity of the stream.

23. **Critical Thinking** Draw two isosceles triangles that are not congruent but that have a perimeter of 15 cm each.

24. $\triangle ABC \cong \triangle ADC$ for what value of *x*? Explain why the SSS Postulate can be used to prove the two triangles congruent.

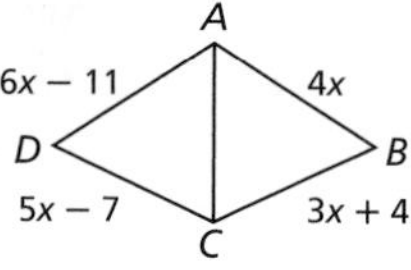

25. **Ecology** A *wing deflector* is a triangular structure made of logs that is filled with large rocks and placed in a stream to guide the current or prevent erosion. Wing deflectors are often used in pairs. Suppose an engineer wants to build two wing deflectors. The logs that form the sides of each wing deflector are perpendicular. How can the engineer make sure that the two wing deflectors are congruent?

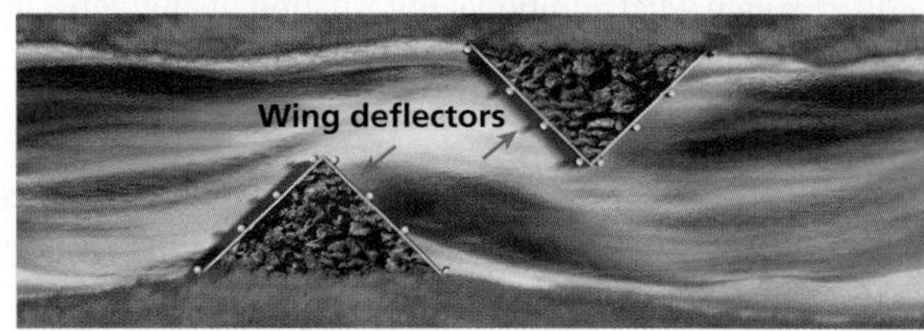

26. **Write About It** If you use the same two sides and included angle to repeat the construction of a triangle, are your two constructed triangles congruent? Explain.

27. **Construction** Use three segments (SSS) to construct a scalene triangle. Suppose you then use the same segments in a different order to construct a second triangle. Will the result be the same? Explain.

28. Which of the three triangles below can be proven congruent by SSS or SAS?

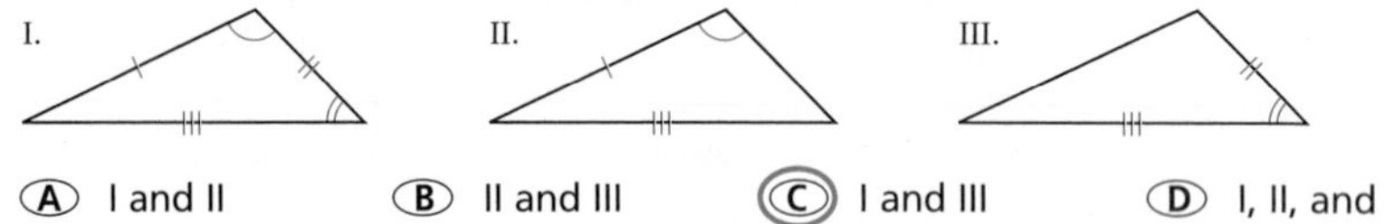

Ⓐ I and II　Ⓑ II and III　Ⓒ I and III　Ⓓ I, II, and III

29. What is the perimeter of polygon *ABCD*?

Ⓕ 29.9 cm　Ⓗ 49.8 cm
Ⓖ 39.8 cm　Ⓙ 59.8 cm

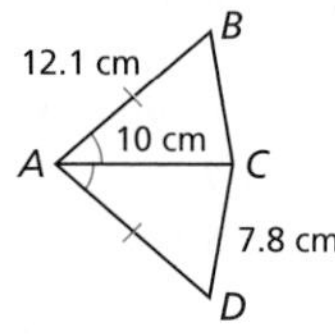

30. Jacob wants to prove that $\triangle FGH \cong \triangle JKL$ using SAS. He knows that $\overline{FG} \cong \overline{JK}$ and $\overline{FH} \cong \overline{JL}$. What additional piece of information does he need?

Ⓐ $\angle F \cong \angle J$　Ⓒ $\angle H \cong \angle L$
Ⓑ $\angle G \cong \angle K$　Ⓓ $\angle F \cong \angle G$

31. What must the value of *x* be in order to prove that $\triangle EFG \cong \triangle EHG$ by SSS?

Ⓕ 1.5　Ⓗ 4.67
Ⓖ 4.25　Ⓙ 5.5

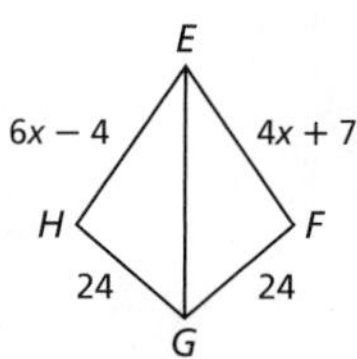

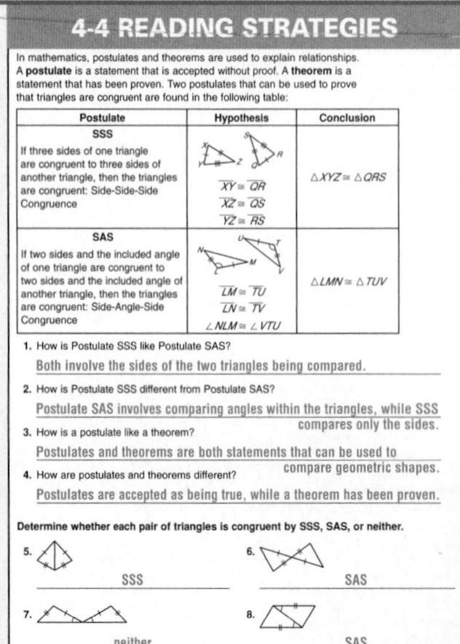

4-4 READING STRATEGIES

In mathematics, postulates and theorems are used to explain relationships. A **postulate** is a statement that is accepted without proof. A **theorem** is a statement that has been proven. Two postulates that can be used to prove that triangles are congruent are found in the following table:

Postulate	Hypothesis	Conclusion
SSS If three sides of one triangle are congruent to three sides of another triangle, then the triangles are congruent: Side-Side-Side Congruence	$\overline{XY} \cong \overline{QR}$, $\overline{XZ} \cong \overline{QS}$, $\overline{YZ} \cong \overline{RS}$	$\triangle XYZ \cong \triangle QRS$
SAS If two sides and the included angle of one triangle are congruent to two sides and the included angle of another triangle, then the triangles are congruent: Side-Angle-Side Congruence	$\overline{LM} \cong \overline{TU}$, $\overline{LN} \cong \overline{TV}$, $\angle NLM \cong \angle VTU$	$\triangle LMN \cong \triangle TUV$

1. How is Postulate SSS like Postulate SAS?
Both involve the sides of the two triangles being compared.
2. How is Postulate SSS different from Postulate SAS?
Postulate SAS involves comparing angles within the triangles, while SSS compares only the sides.
3. How is a postulate like a theorem?
Postulates and theorems are both statements that can be used to compare geometric shapes.
4. How are postulates and theorems different?
Postulates are accepted as being true, while a theorem has been proven.

Determine whether each pair of triangles is congruent by SSS, SAS, or neither.

5. SSS
6. SAS
7. neither
8. SAS

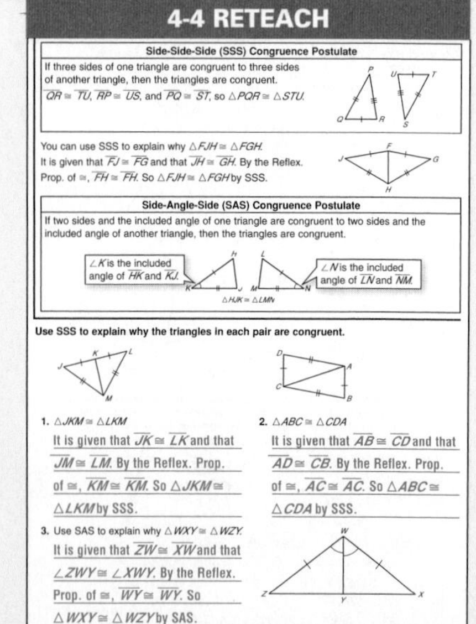

4-4 RETEACH

Side-Side-Side (SSS) Congruence Postulate

If three sides of one triangle are congruent to three sides of another triangle, then the triangles are congruent.
$\overline{QR} \cong \overline{TU}$, $\overline{RP} \cong \overline{US}$, and $\overline{PQ} \cong \overline{ST}$, so $\triangle PQR \cong \triangle STU$.

You can use SSS to explain why $\triangle FJH \cong \triangle FGH$.
It is given that $\overline{FJ} \cong \overline{FG}$ and that $\overline{JH} \cong \overline{GH}$. By the Reflex. Prop. of $\cong$, $\overline{FH} \cong \overline{FH}$. So $\triangle FJH \cong \triangle FGH$ by SSS.

Side-Angle-Side (SAS) Congruence Postulate

If two sides and the included angle of one triangle are congruent to two sides and the included angle of another triangle, then the triangles are congruent.

$\angle K$ is the included angle of $\overline{HK}$ and $\overline{KJ}$.
$\angle N$ is the included angle of $\overline{LN}$ and $\overline{NM}$.
$\triangle HJK \cong \triangle LMN$

Use SSS to explain why the triangles in each pair are congruent.

1. $\triangle JKM \cong \triangle LKM$
It is given that $\overline{JK} \cong \overline{LK}$ and that $\overline{JM} \cong \overline{LM}$. By the Reflex. Prop. of $\cong$, $\overline{KM} \cong \overline{KM}$. So $\triangle JKM \cong \triangle LKM$ by SSS.
2. $\triangle ABC \cong \triangle CDA$
It is given that $\overline{AB} \cong \overline{CD}$ and that $\overline{AD} \cong \overline{CB}$. By the Reflex. Prop. of $\cong$, $\overline{AC} \cong \overline{AC}$. So $\triangle ABC \cong \triangle CDA$ by SSS.
3. Use SAS to explain why $\triangle WXY \cong \triangle WZY$.
It is given that $\overline{ZW} \cong \overline{XW}$ and that $\angle ZWY \cong \angle XWY$. By the Reflex. Prop. of $\cong$, $\overline{WY} \cong \overline{WY}$. So $\triangle WXY \cong \triangle WZY$ by SAS.

CHALLENGE AND EXTEND

32. Given: $\angle ADC$ and $\angle BCD$ are supplementary. $\overline{AD} \cong \overline{CB}$
Prove: $\triangle ADB \cong \triangle CBD$
(*Hint:* Draw an auxiliary line.)

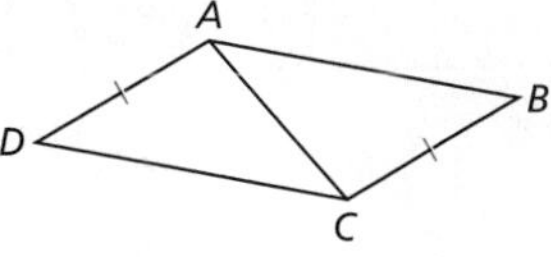

33. Given: $\angle QPS \cong \angle TPR$, $\overline{PQ} \cong \overline{PT}$, $\overline{PR} \cong \overline{PS}$
Prove: $\triangle PQR \cong \triangle PTS$

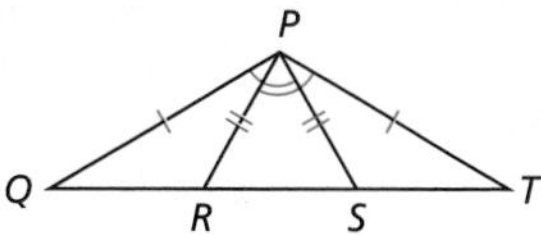

Algebra Use the following information for Exercises 34 and 35. Find the value of x. Then use SSS or SAS to write a paragraph proof showing that two of the triangles are congruent.

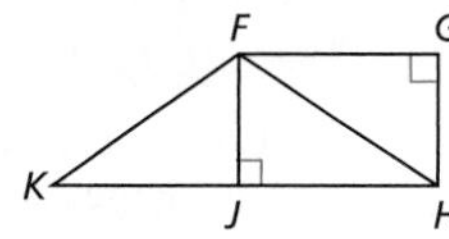

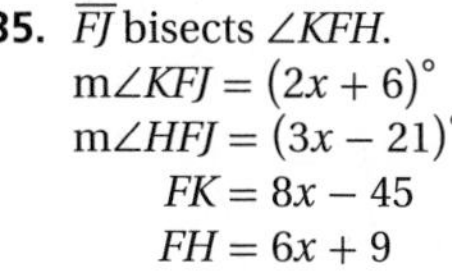

34. $m\angle FKJ = 2x°$
$m\angle KFJ = (3x + 10)°$
$KJ = 4x + 8$
$HJ = 6(x - 4)$

$x = 16$; $KJ = HJ = 72$, so $\overline{KJ} \cong \overline{HJ}$ by def. of $\cong$. $\angle FJK \cong \angle FJH$ by the Rt. $\angle \cong$ Thm. $\overline{FJ} \cong \overline{FJ}$ by the Reflex. Prop. of $\cong$. So $\triangle FJK \cong \triangle FJH$ by SAS.

35. $\overline{FJ}$ bisects $\angle KFH$.
$m\angle KFJ = (2x + 6)°$
$m\angle HFJ = (3x - 21)°$
$FK = 8x - 45$
$FH = 6x + 9$

$x = 27$; $FK = FH = 171$, so $\overline{FK} \cong \overline{FH}$ by the def of $\cong$. $\angle KFJ \cong \angle HFJ$ by the def. of $\angle$ bisector. $\overline{FJ} \cong \overline{FJ}$ by the Reflex. Prop. of $\cong$. So $\triangle FJK \cong \triangle FJH$ by SAS.

SPIRAL REVIEW

Solve and graph each inequality. *(Previous course)*

36. $\frac{x}{2} - 8 \leq 5$ $x \leq 26$
37. $2a + 4 > 3a$ $a < 4$
38. $-6m - 1 \leq -13$ $m \geq 2$

Solve each equation. Write a justification for each step. *(Lesson 2-5)*

39. $4x - 7 = 21$
40. $\frac{a}{4} + 5 = -8$
41. $6r = 4r + 10$

Given: $\triangle EFG \cong \triangle GHE$. Find each value. *(Lesson 4-3)*

42. x 86
43. $m\angle FEG$ 34°
44. $m\angle FGH$ 70°

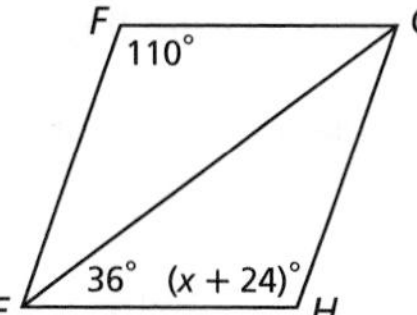

Using Technology

Use geometry software to complete the following. 1. Check students' drawings.

1. Draw a triangle and label the vertices A, B, and C. Draw a point and label it D. Mark a vector from A to B and translate D by the marked vector. Label the image E. Draw $\overleftrightarrow{DE}$. Mark $\angle BAC$ and rotate $\overleftrightarrow{DE}$ about D by the marked angle. Mark $\angle ABC$ and rotate $\overleftrightarrow{DE}$ about E by the marked angle. Label the intersection F.
2. Drag A, B, and C to different locations. What do you notice about the two triangles?
3. Write a conjecture about $\triangle ABC$ and $\triangle DEF$. $\triangle ABC \cong \triangle DEF$
4. Test your conjecture by measuring the sides and angles of $\triangle ABC$ and $\triangle DEF$. Check students' measurements.

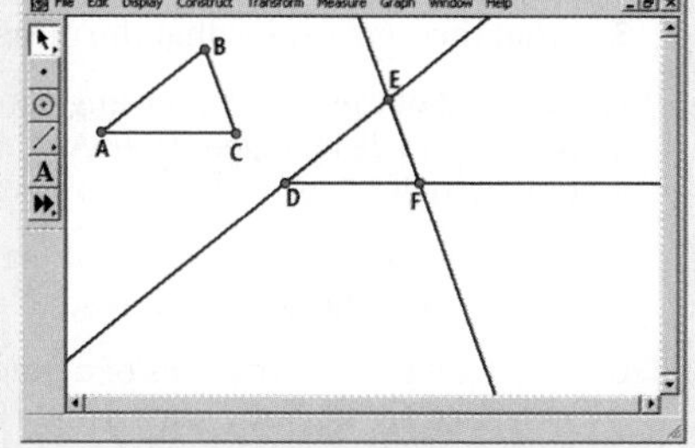

2. They stay the same size and shape.

4-4 PROBLEM SOLVING

Use the diagram for Exercises 1 and 2.
A shed door appears to be divided into congruent right triangles.

1. Suppose $\overline{AB} \cong \overline{CD}$. Use SAS to show $\triangle ABD \cong \triangle DCA$.
We know that $\overline{AB} \cong \overline{DC}$. $\angle ADC$ and $\angle DAB$ are right angles, so $\angle ADC \cong \angle DAB$ by Rt. $\angle \cong$ Thm. $\overline{AD} \cong \overline{DA}$ by Reflex. Prop. of $\cong$. So $\triangle ABD \cong \triangle DCA$ by SAS.
2. J is the midpoint of AB and $AK \cong BK$. Use SSS to explain why $\triangle AKJ \cong \triangle BKJ$.
We know that $\overline{AK} \cong \overline{BK}$. Since J is the midpoint of $\overline{AB}$, $\overline{AJ} \cong \overline{BJ}$ by def. of midpoint. $\overline{JK} \cong \overline{JK}$ by Reflex. Prop. of $\cong$. So $\triangle AKJ \cong \triangle BKJ$ by SSS.
3. A *balalaika* is a Russian stringed instrument. Show that the triangular parts of the two balalaikas are congruent for $x = 6$.
By the $\triangle$ Sum Thm., $m\angle H = 54°$. For $x = 6$, $WY = FH = 10$ in., $m\angle Y = m\angle H = 54°$, and $XY = HG = 12$ in. So $\triangle WXY \cong \triangle FHG$ by SAS.

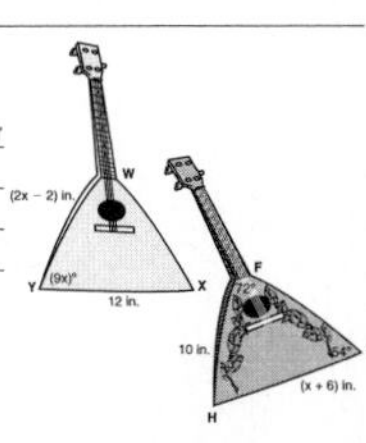

A quilt pattern of a dog is shown. Choose the best answer.

4. $ML = MP = MN = MQ = 1$ inch. Which statement is correct?
   - (A) $\triangle LMN \cong \triangle QMP$ by SAS.
   - B $\triangle LMN \cong \triangle QMP$ by SSS.
   - C $\triangle LMN \cong \triangle MQP$ by SAS.
   - D $\triangle LMN \cong \triangle MQP$ by SSS.
5. P is the midpoint of $\overline{TS}$ and $TR = SR = 1.4$ inches. What can you conclude about $\triangle TRP$ and $\triangle SRP$?
   - F $\triangle TRP \cong \triangle SRP$ by SAS.
   - (G) $\triangle TRP \cong \triangle SRP$ by SAS.
   - H $\triangle TRP \cong \triangle SRP$ by SAS.
   - J $\triangle TRP \cong \triangle SRP$ by SSS.

Answers

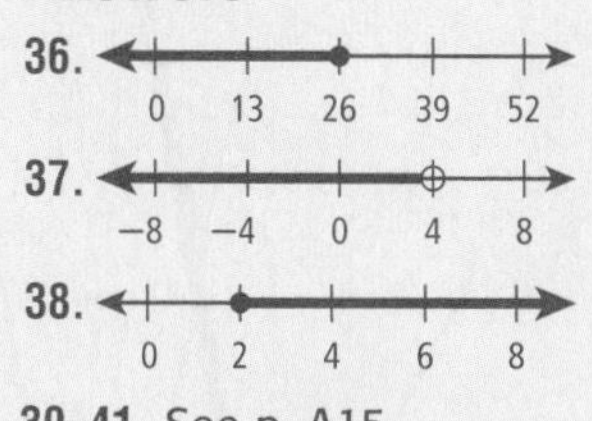

39–41. See p. A15.

Journal

Have students describe how they can use color coding to help them recognize the postulates SSS and SAS. Have them support their descriptions with colored sketches.

ALTERNATIVE ASSESSMENT

Have students work in pairs. One student should draw the diagrams and write the *Given* and *Prove* statements. The second student should write the proof. Then have students reverse roles. One proof should be an example of SSS and the other SAS.

Power Presentations with PowerPoint®

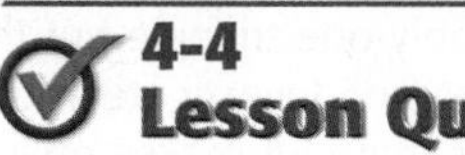

4-4 Lesson Quiz

1. Show that $\triangle ABC \cong \triangle DBC$, when $x = 6$.

B, 26°, $(x + 20)°$, $3x + 10$, $4x + 4$, A, D, C

$\angle ABC \cong \angle DBC$, $\overline{BC} \cong \overline{BC}$, and $\overline{AB} \cong \overline{DB}$. So $\triangle ABC \cong \triangle DBC$ by SAS.

Which postulate, if any, can be used to prove the triangles congruent?

2. none

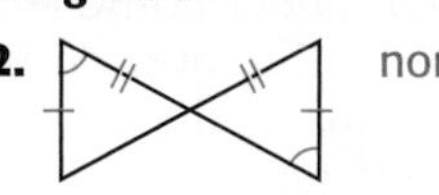

3. SSS

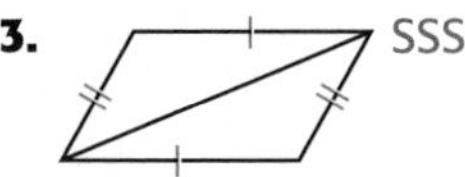

4. **Given:** $\overline{PN}$ bisects $\overline{MO}$. $\overline{PN} \perp \overline{MO}$
Prove: $\triangle MNP \cong \triangle ONP$

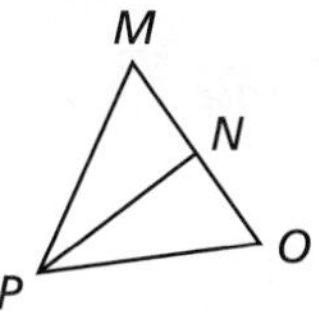

1. $\overline{PN}$ bisects $\overline{MO}$. (Given)
2. $\overline{MN} \cong \overline{ON}$ (Def. of bisect)
3. $\overline{PN} \cong \overline{PN}$ (Reflex. Prop. of $\cong$)
4. $\overline{PN} \perp \overline{MO}$ (Given)
5. $\angle PNM$ and $\angle PNO$ are rt. $\angle$s. (Def. of $\perp$)
6. $\angle PNM \cong \angle PNO$ (Rt. $\angle \cong$ Thm.)
7. $\triangle MNP \cong \triangle ONP$ (SAS *Steps 2, 6, 3*)

Also available on transparency

Organizer

Use with Lesson 4-5

Pacing:
Traditional 1 day
Block $\frac{1}{2}$ day

Objective: Use geometry software to explore triangle congruence relationships.

Materials: geometry software

 **Online Edition**

Resources

Technology Lab Activities
4-5 Lab Recording Sheet

Teach

Discuss

Discuss with students that ASA makes only one triangle but that SSA does not. Investigate and show students that SSA makes only one triangle for the special case when there is a right angle. Also explain that AAA does not make only one triangle.

Alternative Approach

Have students work in small groups. Each person in the group should draw a different triangle and label it $\triangle ABC$. Have students construct $\overline{DF} \cong \overline{AC}$. Students should construct an angle congruent to $\angle A$ at $\angle D$ and construct an angle congruent to $\angle C$ at F, and label their intersection E. Then have them cut out $\triangle ABC$ and $\triangle DEF$ and place $\triangle ABC$ over $\triangle DEF$. Have students compare the results and make a conjecture.

State Resources

State Resources Online
KEYWORD: MG7 Resources

Use with Lesson 4-5

Predict Other Triangle Congruence Relationships

Geometry software can help you investigate whether certain combinations of triangle parts will make only one triangle. If a combination makes only one triangle, then this arrangement can be used to prove two triangles congruent.

Activity 1

1. Construct $\angle CAB$ measuring 45° and $\angle EDF$ measuring 110°.

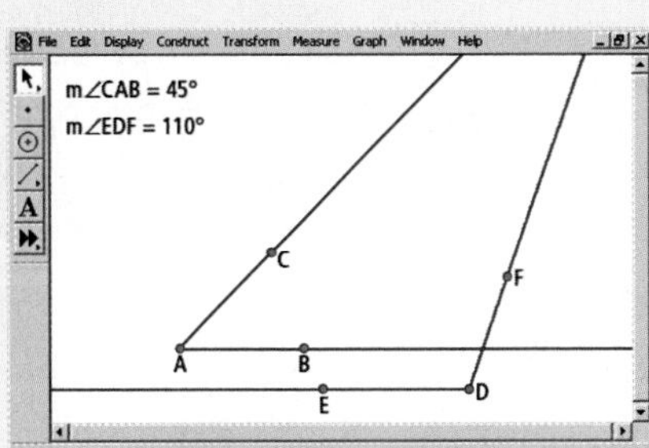

Check students' constructions.

2. Move $\angle EDF$ so that $\overrightarrow{DE}$ overlays $\overrightarrow{BA}$. Where $\overrightarrow{DF}$ and $\overrightarrow{AC}$ intersect, label the point G. Measure $\angle DGA$.

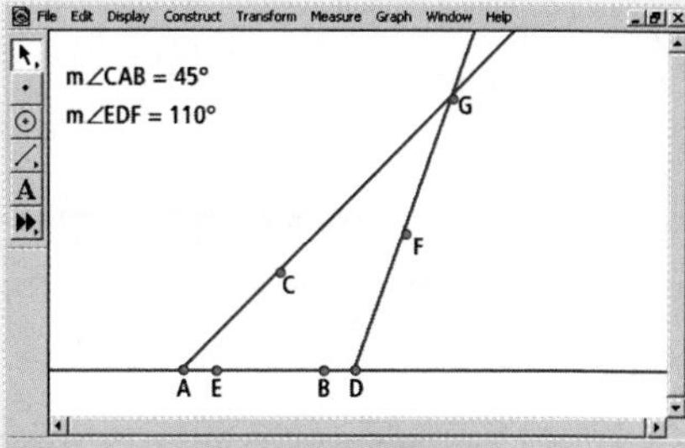

Check students' constructions.

3. Move $\angle CAB$ to the left and right without changing the measures of the angles. Observe what happens to the size of $\angle DGA$. It stays the same.

4. Measure the distance from A to D. Try to change the shape of the triangle without changing AD and the measures of $\angle A$ and $\angle D$. Check students' work.

Try This

1. Repeat Activity 1 using angle measures of your choice. Are your results the same? Explain. Yes; the $\triangle$ stays the same shape if you do not change AD or the measures of $\angle A$ and $\angle D$.
2. Do the results change if one of the given angles measures 90°? no
3. What theorem proves that the measure of $\angle DGA$ in Step 2 will always be the same? Third $\angle$s Thm.
4. In Step 3 of the activity, the angle measures in $\triangle ADG$ stayed the same as the size of the triangle changed. Does Angle-Angle-Angle, like Side-Side-Side, make only one triangle? Explain. No; the $\angle$ measures may stay the same, but the side lengths can vary.
5. Repeat Step 4 of the activity but measure the length of $\overline{AG}$ instead of $\overline{AD}$. Are your results the same? Does this lead to a new congruence postulate or theorem? Check students' constructions; yes; yes; AAS.
6. If you are given two angles of a triangle, what additional piece of information is needed so that only one triangle is made? Make a conjecture based on your findings in Step 5. You need the length of 1 side of the $\triangle$. In an AAS combination, if 2 corr. $\angle$s and sides are $\cong$, then only 1 $\triangle$ is made.

Activity 2

1. Construct $\overline{YZ}$ with a length of 6.5 cm.

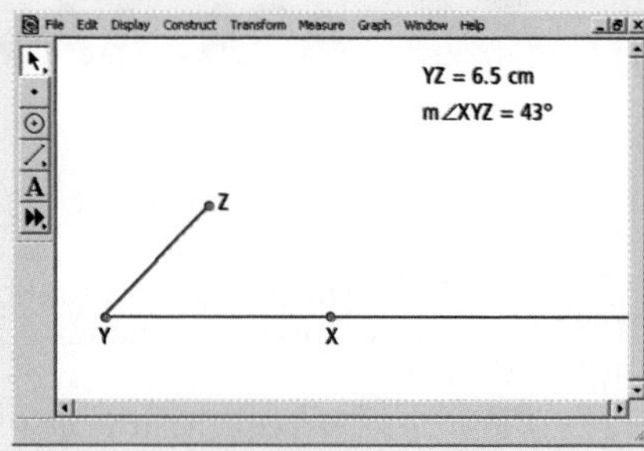

2. Using $\overline{YZ}$ as a side, construct $\angle XYZ$ measuring 43°.

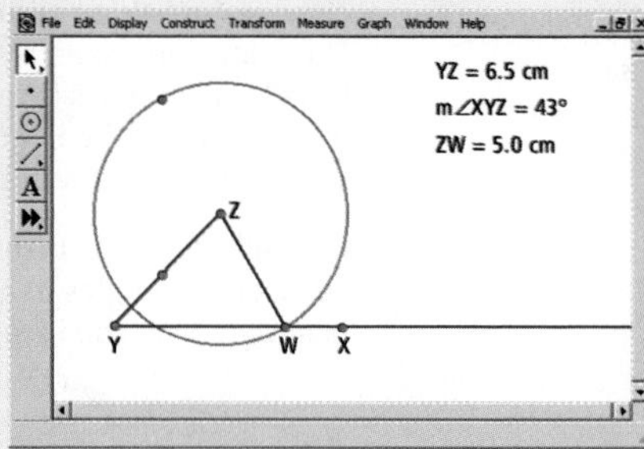

3. Draw a circle at Z with a radius of 5 cm. Construct $\overline{ZW}$, a radius of circle Z.

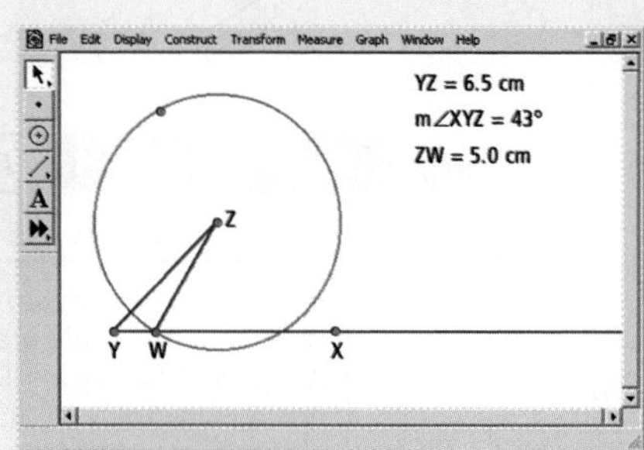

4. Move W around circle Z. Observe the possible shapes of $\triangle YZW$.

Try This

7. In Step 4 of the activity, how many different triangles were possible? Does Side-Side-Angle make only one triangle? **many; no**
8. Repeat Activity 2 using an angle measure of 90° in Step 2 and a circle with a radius of 7 cm in Step 3. How many different triangles are possible in Step 4? **1**
9. Repeat the activity again using a measure of 90° in Step 2 and a circle with a radius of 8.25 cm in Step 3. Classify the resulting triangle by its angle measures. **rt.**
10. Based on your results, complete the following conjecture. In a Side-Side-Angle combination, if the corresponding nonincluded angles are __?__, then only one triangle is possible. **rt. △**

Close

Key Concept

Triangles can be proved congruent by ASA, but not by SSA or AAA. These last two methods do not always form a unique triangle. Remind students that they need to find only one counterexample. That is, students should find one triangle with the same SSA or AAA that is not congruent to the original triangle.

Assessment

Journal Have students compare and contrast ASA, AAA, and SSA. Have them show examples, including where SSA forms only one triangle.

4-5 Organizer

Pacing: Traditional 2 days
Block 1 day

Objectives: Apply ASA, AAS, and HL to construct triangles and solve problems.

Prove triangles congruent by using ASA, AAS, and HL.

Online Edition
Tutorial Videos

Countdown Week 8

Power Presentations with PowerPoint®

Warm Up

1. What are sides $\overline{AC}$ and $\overline{BC}$ called? side $\overline{AB}$?
legs; hypotenuse

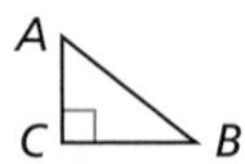

2. Which side is between $\angle A$ and $\angle C$? $\overline{AC}$

3. Given $\triangle DEF$ and $\triangle GHI$, if $\angle D \cong \angle G$ and $\angle E \cong \angle H$, why is $\angle F \cong \angle I$? Third ∡ Thm.

Also available on transparency

Math Fact !!!

SSS, SAS, and ASA are usually presented as postulates in high school texts, but in fact any one of them can be chosen as a postulate and used to prove the other two as theorems.

4-5 Triangle Congruence: ASA, AAS, and HL

Objectives
Apply ASA, AAS, and HL to construct triangles and to solve problems.

Prove triangles congruent by using ASA, AAS, and HL.

Vocabulary
included side

Why use this?
Bearings are used to convey direction, helping people find their way to specific locations.

Participants in an *orienteering* race use a map and a compass to find their way to checkpoints along an unfamiliar course. Directions are given by *bearings*, which are based on compass headings. For example, to travel along the bearing S 43° E, you face south and then turn 43° to the east.

An **included side** is the common side of two consecutive angles in a polygon. The following postulate uses the idea of an *included side*.

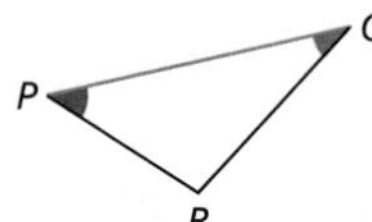

$\overline{PQ}$ is the included side of $\angle P$ and $\angle Q$.

Know it! Note

Postulate 4-5-1 **Angle-Side-Angle (ASA) Congruence**

POSTULATE	HYPOTHESIS	CONCLUSION
If two angles and the included side of one triangle are congruent to two angles and the included side of another triangle, then the triangles are congruent.	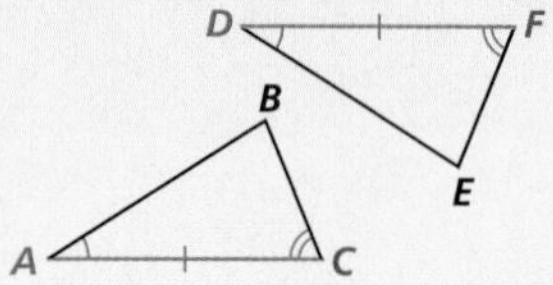 (triangles ABC and DEF)	$\triangle ABC \cong \triangle DEF$

EXAMPLE 1 ***Problem-Solving Application***

PROBLEM SOLVING

Organizers of an orienteering race are planning a course with checkpoints *A*, *B*, and *C*. Does the table give enough information to determine the location of the checkpoints?

	Bearing	Distance
A* to *B	N 55° E	7.6 km
B* to *C	N 26° W	
C* to *A	S 20° W	

1 Understand the Problem

The **answer** is whether the information in the table can be used to find the position of checkpoints *A*, *B*, and *C*. List the **important information:** The bearing from *A* to *B* is N 55° E. From *B* to *C* is N 26° W, and from *C* to *A* is S 20° W. The distance from *A* to *B* is 7.6 km.

State Resources

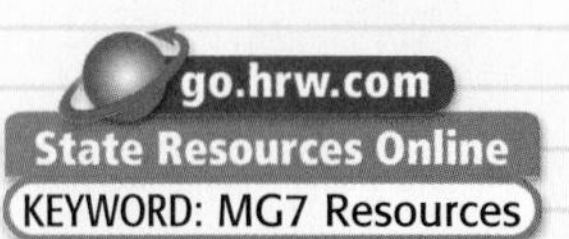

1 Introduce

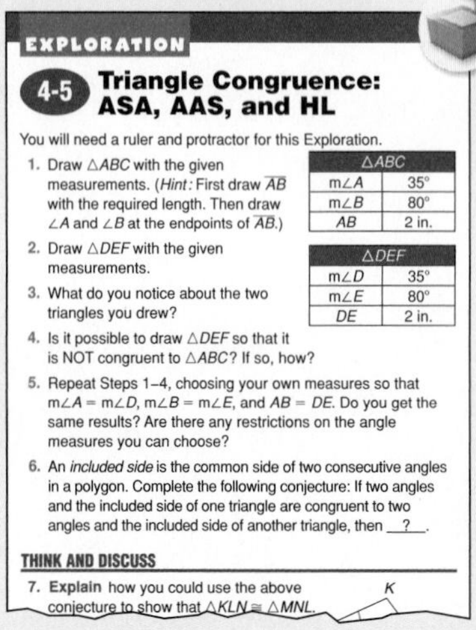

EXPLORATION

4-5 Triangle Congruence: ASA, AAS, and HL

You will need a ruler and protractor for this Exploration.

1. Draw $\triangle ABC$ with the given measurements. (*Hint:* First draw $\overline{AB}$ with the required length. Then draw $\angle A$ and $\angle B$ at the endpoints of $\overline{AB}$.)

$\triangle ABC$	
m∠A	35°
m∠B	80°
AB	2 in.

2. Draw $\triangle DEF$ with the given measurements.

$\triangle DEF$	
m∠D	35°
m∠E	80°
DE	2 in.

3. What do you notice about the two triangles you drew?
4. Is it possible to draw $\triangle DEF$ so that it is NOT congruent to $\triangle ABC$? If so, how?
5. Repeat Steps 1–4, choosing your own measures so that $m\angle A = m\angle D$, $m\angle B = m\angle E$, and $AB = DE$. Do you get the same results? Are there any restrictions on the angle measures you can choose?
6. An *included side* is the common side of two consecutive angles in a polygon. Complete the following conjecture: If two angles and the included side of one triangle are congruent to two angles and the included side of another triangle, then __?__.

THINK AND DISCUSS

7. **Explain** how you could use the above conjecture to show that $\triangle KLN \cong \triangle MNL$.

Motivate

Give students a map of the area that contains their school. Have them plot a triangle, using the school, their house, and another location as vertices. Ask them to calculate the measures of the angles of the triangle. Explain to students that angles are important in navigation where directions are given by bearings.

Explorations and answers are provided in *Alternate Openers: Explorations Transparencies.*

 **Make a Plan**

Draw the course using vertical lines to show north-south directions. Then use these parallel lines and the alternate interior angles to help find angle measures of $\triangle ABC$.

 **Solve**

$m\angle CAB = 55° - 20° = 35°$

$m\angle CBA = 180° - (26° + 55°) = 99°$

You know the measures of $\angle CAB$ and $\angle CBA$ and the length of the included side $\overline{AB}$. Therefore by ASA, a unique triangle ABC is determined.

4 Look Back

One and only one triangle can be made using the information in the table, so the table does give enough information to determine the location of all the checkpoints.

1. **What if...?** If 7.6 km is the distance from B to C, is there enough information to determine the location of all the checkpoints? Explain.
   Yes; the △ is uniquely determined by AAS.

EXAMPLE 2 Applying ASA Congruence

Determine if you can use ASA to prove $\triangle UVX \cong \triangle WVX$. Explain.

$\angle UXV \cong \angle WXV$ as given. Since $\angle WVX$ is a right angle that forms a linear pair with $\angle UVX$, $\angle WVX \cong \angle UVX$. Also $\overline{VX} \cong \overline{VX}$ by the Reflexive Property. Therefore $\triangle UVX \cong \triangle WVX$ by ASA.

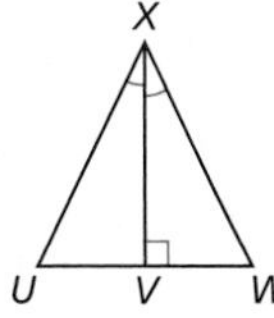

2. Determine if you can use ASA to prove $\triangle NKL \cong \triangle LMN$. Explain.

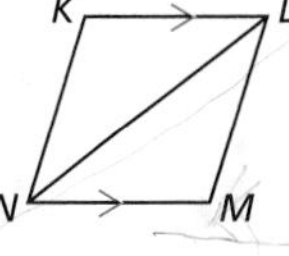

By the Alt. Int. ∠s Thm., $\angle KLN \cong \angle MNL$. $\overline{NL} \cong \overline{LN}$ by the Reflex. Prop. No other congruence relationships can be determined, so ASA cannot be applied.

Construction Congruent Triangles Using ASA

Use a straightedge to draw a segment and two angles, or copy the given segment and angles.

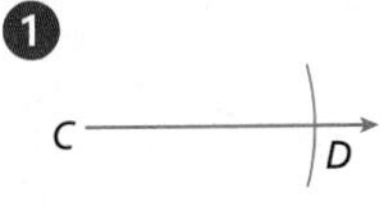

1. Construct $\overline{CD}$ congruent to the given segment.

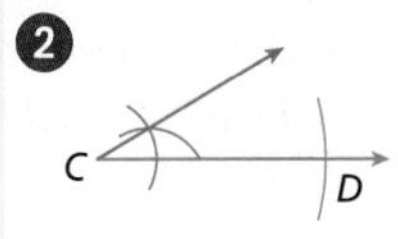

2. Construct $\angle C$ congruent to one of the angles.

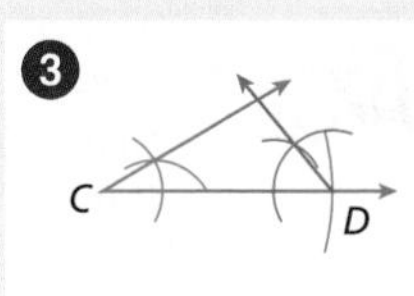

3. Construct $\angle D$ congruent to the other angle.

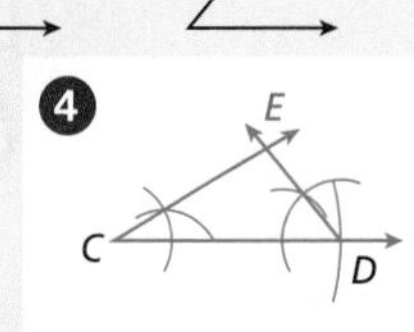

4. $\triangle CDE$ Label the intersection of the rays as E.

2 Teach

Guided Instruction

Review with students how to read bearings before presenting examples. If more explanation is needed for the drawing in Example 1, give students the following directions:

1. Draw A.
2. Find B.
3. Use a straightedge and draw $\overrightarrow{AC}$ with the bearing from A being N 20° E.

With students, practice identifying ASA, AAS, and HL from diagrams before writing proofs.

Reaching All Learners

Through Auditory Cues

As students work through the lesson have them identify orally whether the triangles are congruent by HL, ASA, AAS, SAS, or SSS. Then have them work with a partner to identify the congruent parts and to determine if the congruent pairs of angles or sides are corresponding parts.

Teaching Tip **Inclusion** Explain that the included side is named by the two vertices of the angles.

Power Presentations with PowerPoint®

Additional Examples

Example 1

A mailman has to collect mail from mailboxes at A and B and drop it off at the post office at C. Does the table give enough information to determine the location of the mailboxes and the post office? yes

	Bearing	Distance
A* to *B	N 65° E	8 mi
B* to *C	N 24° W	
C* to *A	S 20° W	

Example 2

Determine if you can use ASA to prove the triangles congruent. Explain.

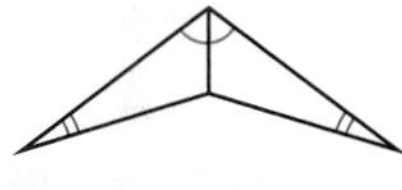

no; no included side

INTERVENTION

Questioning Strategies

EXAMPLE 1

- How are bearings used when finding the distance between two points?

EXAMPLE 2

- What transformation take place to change position from one triangle to the orientation of the second triangle?

Teaching Tip **Reading Math** Mark the given information on the diagram before starting a proof. Put an S or an A next to each step in the proof to indicate which side or angle is given.

English Language Learners

Additional Examples

Example 3

Use AAS to prove the triangles congruent.

Given: $\angle X \cong \angle V$, $\angle YZW \cong \angle YWZ$, $\overline{XY} \cong \overline{VY}$

Prove: $\triangle XYZ \cong \triangle VYW$

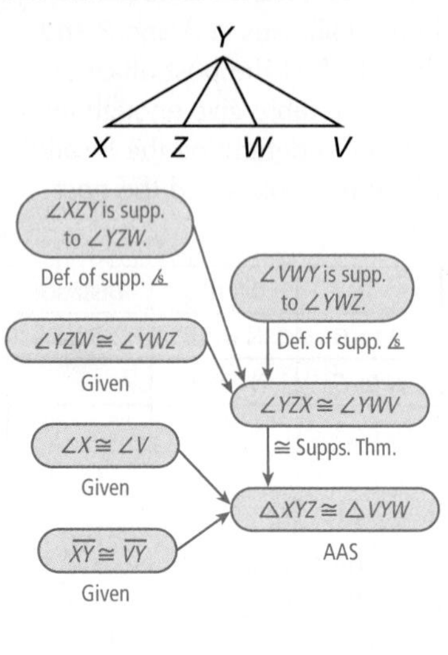

INTERVENTION

Questioning Strategies

EXAMPLE 3

- If AAS is used as the method of proof, can the triangles also be proved congruent using ASA?

Answers to *Check It Out!*

3.

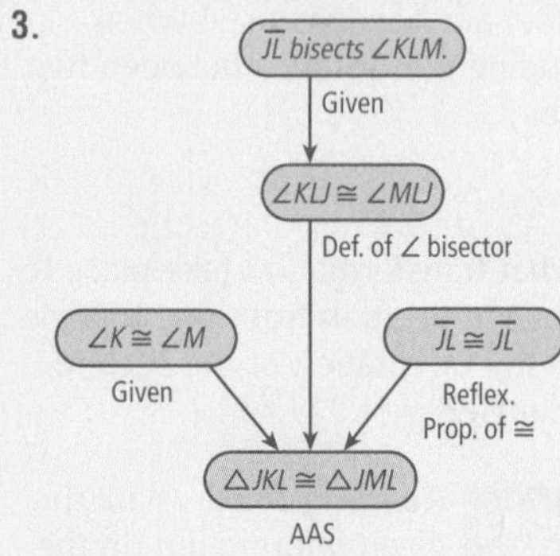

You can use the Third Angles Theorem to prove another congruence relationship based on ASA. This theorem is Angle-Angle-Side (AAS).

Theorem 4-5-2 Angle-Angle-Side (AAS) Congruence

THEOREM	HYPOTHESIS	CONCLUSION
If two angles and a nonincluded side of one triangle are congruent to the corresponding angles and nonincluded side of another triangle, then the triangles are congruent.	G, H, J; L, M, K	$\triangle GHJ \cong \triangle KLM$

PROOF **Angle-Angle-Side Congruence**

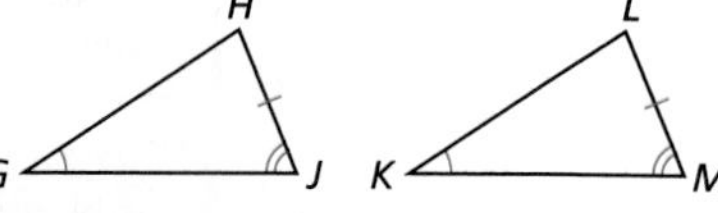

Given: $\angle G \cong \angle K$, $\angle J \cong \angle M$, $\overline{HJ} \cong \overline{LM}$

Prove: $\triangle GHJ \cong \triangle KLM$

Proof:

Statements	Reasons
1. $\angle G \cong \angle K$, $\angle J \cong \angle M$	1. Given
2. $\angle H \cong \angle L$	2. Third ∠s Thm.
3. $\overline{HJ} \cong \overline{LM}$	3. Given
4. $\triangle GHJ \cong \triangle KLM$	4. ASA *Steps 1, 3, and 2*

EXAMPLE 3 **Using AAS to Prove Triangles Congruent**

Use AAS to prove the triangles congruent.

Given: $\overline{AB} \parallel \overline{ED}$, $\overline{BC} \cong \overline{DC}$

Prove: $\triangle ABC \cong \triangle EDC$

Proof:

$\overline{BC} \cong \overline{DC}$ (Given)

$\overline{AB} \parallel \overline{ED}$ (Given) → $\angle B \cong \angle D$ (Alt. Int. ∠s Thm.); $\angle A \cong \angle E$ (Alt. Int. ∠s Thm.)

→ $\triangle ABC \cong \triangle EDC$ (AAS)

3. Use AAS to prove the triangles congruent.
   Given: $\overline{JL}$ bisects $\angle KLM$. $\angle K \cong \angle M$
   Prove: $\triangle JKL \cong \triangle JML$

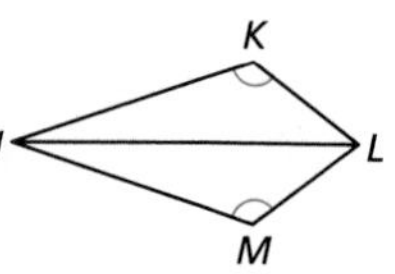

There are four theorems for right triangles that are not used for acute or obtuse triangles. They are Leg-Leg (LL), Hypotenuse-Angle (HA), Leg-Angle (LA), and Hypotenuse-Leg (HL). You will prove LL, HA, and LA in Exercises 21, 23, and 33.

Theorem 4-5-3 Hypotenuse-Leg (HL) Congruence

THEOREM	HYPOTHESIS	CONCLUSION
If the hypotenuse and a leg of a right triangle are congruent to the hypotenuse and a leg of another right triangle, then the triangles are congruent.		$\triangle ABC \cong \triangle DEF$

You will prove the Hypotenuse-Leg Theorem in Lesson 4-8.

EXAMPLE 4 **Applying HL Congruence**

Determine if you can use the HL Congruence Theorem to prove the triangles congruent. If not, tell what else you need to know.

A $\triangle VWX$ **and** $\triangle YXW$

According to the diagram, $\triangle VWX$ and $\triangle YXW$ are right triangles that share hypotenuse $\overline{WX}$. $\overline{WX} \cong \overline{XW}$ by the Reflexive Property. It is given that $\overline{WV} \cong \overline{XY}$, therefore $\triangle VWX \cong \triangle YXW$ by HL.

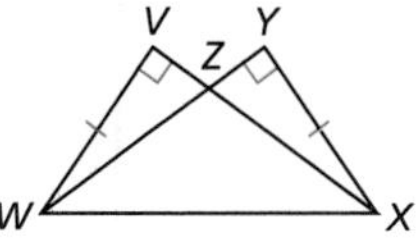

B $\triangle VWZ$ **and** $\triangle YXZ$

This conclusion cannot be proved by HL. According to the diagram, $\triangle VWZ$ and $\triangle YXZ$ are right triangles, and $\overline{WV} \cong \overline{XY}$. You do not know that hypotenuse $\overline{WZ}$ is congruent to hypotenuse $\overline{XZ}$.

4. Determine if you can use the HL Congruence Theorem to prove $\triangle ABC \cong \triangle DCB$. If not, tell what else you need to know.

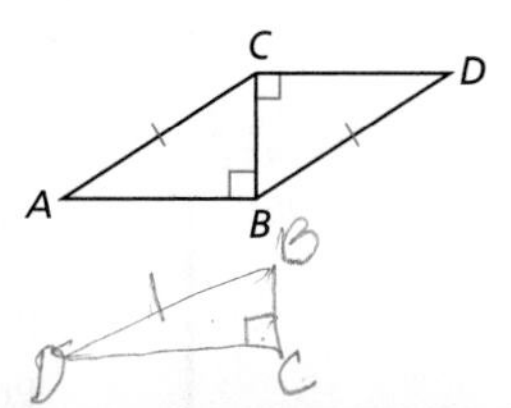

4. Yes; it is given that $\overline{AC} \cong \overline{DB}$. $\overline{BC} \cong \overline{CB}$ by the Reflex. Prop. of $\cong$. Since $\angle ABC$ and $\angle DCB$ are rt. ∠s, $\triangle ABC$ and $\triangle DCB$ are rt. △s. $\triangle ABC \cong \triangle DCB$ by *HL*.

THINK AND DISCUSS

1. Could you use AAS to prove that these two triangles are congruent? Explain.

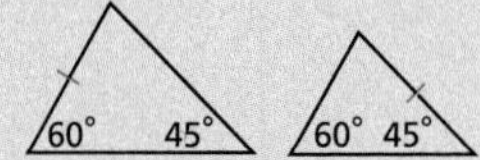

2. The arrangement of the letters in ASA matches the arrangement of what parts of congruent triangles? Include a sketch to support your answer.

3. GET ORGANIZED Copy and complete the graphic organizer. In each column, write a description of the method and then sketch two triangles, marking the appropriate congruent parts.

Proving Triangles Congruent						
	Def. of △ ≅	SSS	SAS	ASA	AAS	HL
Words						
Pictures						

Teaching Tip **Visual** For **Example 4,** it may be less confusing if students redraw the triangles separately and then carefully label the triangles and mark the congruent corresponding parts.

Teaching Tip **Inclusion** For **Example 4** show that AAS could be used as the method of proof. Include an illustration showing why SSA cannot be used to prove two triangles congruent. If the triangles are right triangles, then you would use HL.

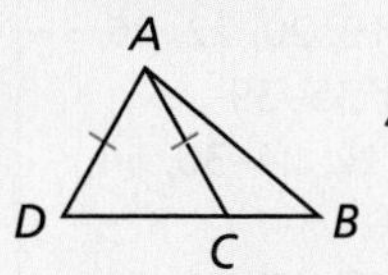

$\triangle DAB \not\cong \triangle CAB$

Power Presentations with PowerPoint®

Additional Examples

Example 4

Determine if you can use the HL Congruence Theorem to prove the triangles congruent. If not, tell what else you need to know.

A.

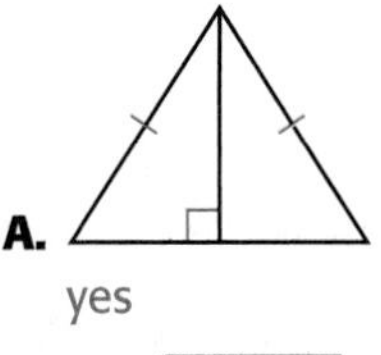

yes

B.

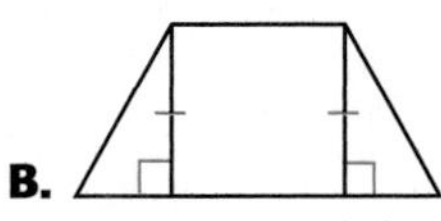

No; you need the hyp. ≅.

INTERVENTION

Questioning Strategies

EXAMPLE 4

- What type of triangle must be given to use HL as a method of proof?

3 Close

Summarize

Review how to identify when you should use AAS, HL, or ASA to prove triangles congruent. Remind students that three pairs of congruent corresponding parts are necessary for AAS and ASA. For HL they first must prove that the triangles are right triangles.

ONGOING ASSESSMENT and INTERVENTION

***Diagnose Before* the Lesson**
4-5 Warm Up, TE p. 252

***Monitor During* the Lesson**
Check It Out! Exercises, SE pp. 253–255
Questioning Strategies, TE pp. 253–255

***Assess After* the Lesson**
4-5 Lesson Quiz, TE p. 259
Alternative Assessment, TE p. 259

Answers to *Think and Discuss*

1. No; the ≅ sides are not corr. sides.
2. Possible answer: corr. ∠s and sides

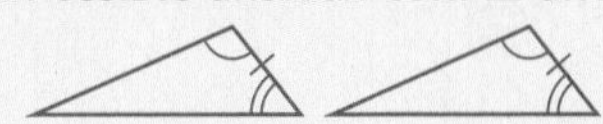

3. See p. A4.

4-5 Exercises

Assignment Guide

Assign *Guided Practice* exercises as necessary.

If you finished Examples **1–2**
Basic 9–12, 17, 25
Average 9–12, 17, 21, 25
Advanced 9–12, 17, 21, 25, 32

If you finished Examples **1–4**
Basic 9–17, 19, 20, 22, 25, 26–30, 35–39
Average 9–20, 22, 24–30, 34, 35–39
Advanced 9–16, 18, 19, 21–39

Homework Quick Check
Quickly check key concepts.
Exercises: 10, 12, 13, 14, 16, 22

Answers

1. The included side $\overline{BC}$ is enclosed between $\angle ABC$ and $\angle ACB$.

2. 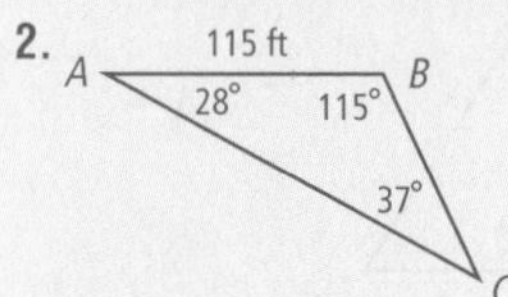

4. Yes; by the def. of bisector, $\angle TSV \cong \angle RSV$, and $\angle TVS \cong \angle RVS$. $\overline{SV} \cong \overline{SV}$ by the Reflex. Prop. of $\cong$. So $\triangle VRS \cong \triangle VTS$ by ASA.

7. Yes; it is given that $\angle D$ and $\angle B$ are rt. $\angle$s and $\overline{AD} \cong \overline{BC}$. $\triangle ABC$ and $\triangle CDA$ are rt. $\triangle$s by def. $\overline{AC} \cong \overline{CA}$ by the Reflex. Prop. of $\cong$. So $\triangle ABC \cong \triangle CDA$ by HL.

State Resources

4-5 Exercises

go.hrw.com
Homework Help Online
KEYWORD: MG7 4-5
Parent Resources Online
KEYWORD: MG7 Parent

GUIDED PRACTICE

1. **Vocabulary** A triangle contains $\angle ABC$ and $\angle ACB$ with $\overline{BC}$ "closed in" between them. How would this help you remember the definition of *included side*?

SEE EXAMPLE 1 p. 252

Surveying **Use the table for Exercises 2 and 3.** A landscape designer surveyed the boundaries of a triangular park. She made the following table for the dimensions of the land.

A
115 ft
B
C

	A to B	B to C	C to A
Bearing	E	S 25° E	N 62° W
Distance	115 ft	?	?

2. Draw the plot of land described by the table. Label the measures of the angles in the triangle.

3. Does the table have enough information to determine the locations of points A, B, and C? Explain.
Yes, the $\triangle$ is determined by AAS.

SEE EXAMPLE 2 p. 253

Determine if you can use ASA to prove the triangles congruent. Explain.

4. $\triangle VRS$ and $\triangle VTS$, given that $\overline{VS}$ bisects $\angle RST$ and $\angle RVT$

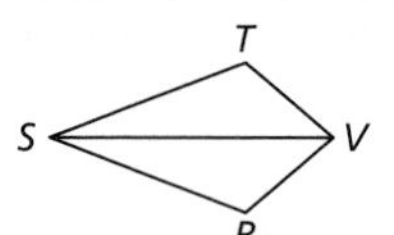

5. $\triangle DEH$ and $\triangle FGH$

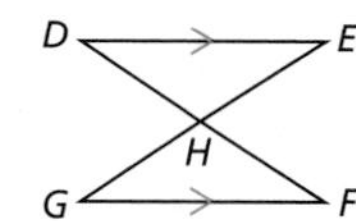

No; you need to know that a pair of corr. sides are $\cong$.

SEE EXAMPLE 3 p. 254

6. Use AAS to prove the triangles congruent.
Given: $\angle R$ and $\angle P$ are right angles. $\overline{QR} \parallel \overline{SP}$
Prove: $\triangle QPS \cong \triangle SRQ$
Proof:

Q R P S

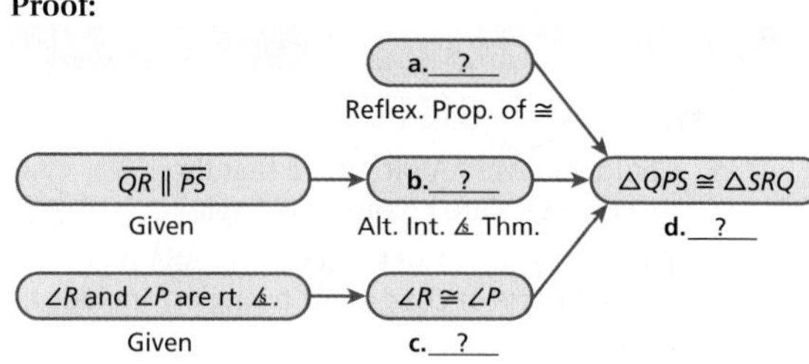

a. $\overline{QS} \cong \overline{SQ}$
b. $\angle RQS \cong \angle PSQ$
c. Rt $\angle \cong$ Thm.
d. AAS

SEE EXAMPLE 4 p. 255

Determine if you can use the HL Congruence Theorem to prove the triangles congruent. If not, tell what else you need to know.

7. $\triangle ABC$ and $\triangle CDA$

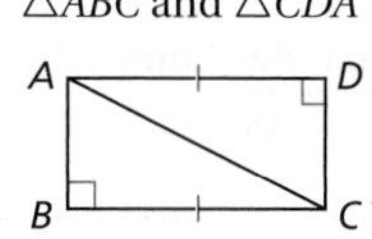

8. $\triangle XYV$ and $\triangle ZYV$

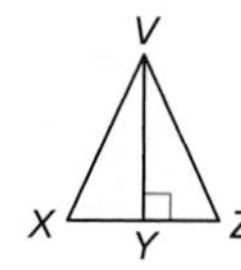

No; you need to know that $\overline{VX} \cong \overline{VZ}$.

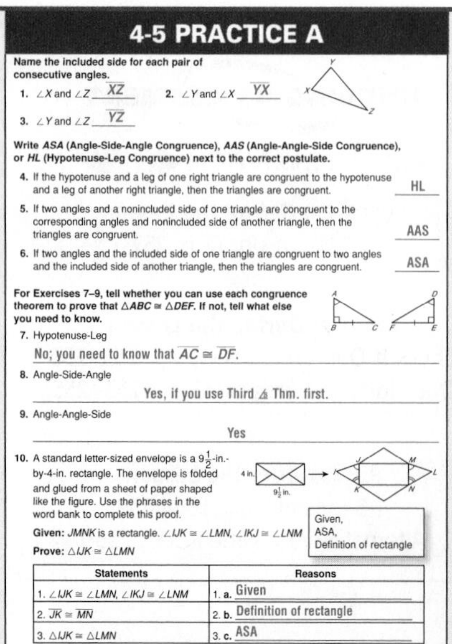

4-5 PRACTICE A

Name the included side for each pair of consecutive angles.

1. $\angle X$ and $\angle Z$ $\overline{XZ}$
2. $\angle Y$ and $\angle X$ $\overline{YX}$
3. $\angle Y$ and $\angle Z$ $\overline{YZ}$

Write *ASA* (Angle-Side-Angle Congruence), *AAS* (Angle-Angle-Side Congruence), or *HL* (Hypotenuse-Leg Congruence) next to the correct postulate.

4. If the hypotenuse and a leg of one right triangle are congruent to the hypotenuse and a leg of another right triangle, then the triangles are congruent. HL
5. If two angles and a nonincluded side of one triangle are congruent to the corresponding angles and nonincluded side of another triangle, then the triangles are congruent. AAS
6. If two angles and the included side of one triangle are congruent to two angles and the included side of another triangle, then the triangles are congruent. ASA

For Exercises 7–9, tell whether you can use each congruence theorem to prove that $\triangle ABC \cong \triangle DEF$. If not, tell what else you need to know.

7. Hypotenuse-Leg
No; you need to know that $\overline{AC} \cong \overline{DF}$.
8. Angle-Side-Angle
Yes, if you use Third $\angle$s Thm. first.
9. Angle-Angle-Side
Yes

10. A standard letter-sized envelope is a $9\frac{1}{2}$-in.-by-4-in. rectangle. The envelope is folded and glued from a sheet of paper shaped like the figure. Use the phrases in the word bank to complete this proof.

4 in. $9\frac{1}{2}$ in.

Given, ASA, Definition of rectangle

Given: *JMNK* is a rectangle. $\angle IJK \cong \angle LMN$, $\angle IKJ \cong \angle LNM$
Prove: $\triangle IJK \cong \triangle LMN$

Statements	Reasons
1. $\angle IJK \cong \angle LMN$, $\angle IKJ \cong \angle LNM$	1. a. Given
2. $\overline{JK} \cong \overline{MN}$	2. b. Definition of rectangle
3. $\triangle IJK \cong \triangle LMN$	3. c. ASA

PRACTICE AND PROBLEM SOLVING

Independent Practice	
For Exercises	See Example
9–10	1
11–12	2
13	3
14–15	4

Extra Practice
Skills Practice p. S11
Application Practice p. S31

Surveying **Use the table for Exercises 9 and 10.**
From two different observation towers a fire is sighted. The locations of the towers are given in the following table.

	X to Y	X to F	Y to F
Bearing	E	N 53° E	N 16° W
Distance	6 km	?	?

9. Draw the diagram formed by observation tower *X*, observation tower *Y*, and the fire *F*. Label the measures of the angles.

10. Is there enough information given in the table to pinpoint the location of the fire? Explain. **Yes; the △ is uniquely determined by ASA.**

LINK
Math History

Euclid wrote the mathematical text *The Elements* around 2300 years ago. It may be the second most reprinted book in history.

Determine if you can use ASA to prove the triangles congruent. Explain.

11. $\triangle MKJ$ and $\triangle MKL$ **No; you need to know that $\angle MKJ \cong \angle MKL$.**

12. $\triangle RST$ and $\triangle TUR$

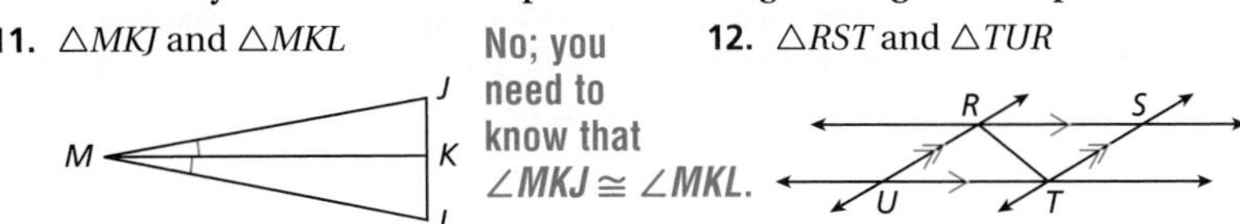

13. **Given:** $\overline{AB} \cong \overline{DE}$, $\angle C \cong \angle F$
Prove: $\triangle ABC \cong \triangle DEF$

Proof:

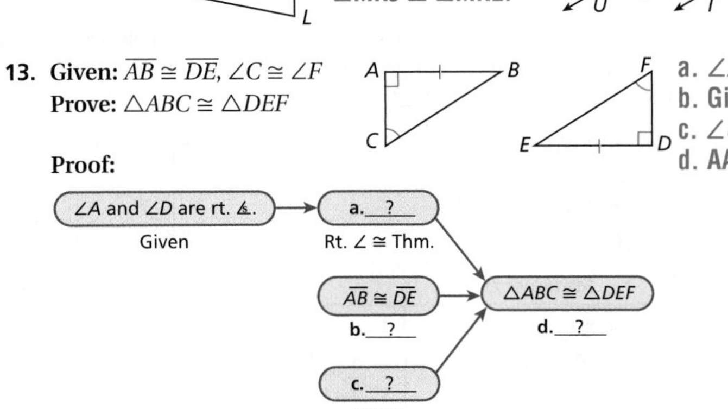

a. $\angle A \cong \angle D$
b. Given
c. $\angle C \cong \angle F$
d. AAS

Determine if you can use the HL Congruence Theorem to prove the triangles congruent. If not, tell what else you need to know.

14. $\triangle GHJ$ and $\triangle JKG$ **No; you need to know that $\angle K$ and $\angle H$ are rt. ⦣.**

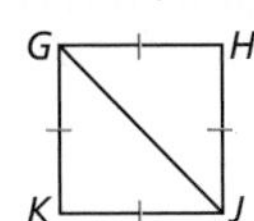

15. $\triangle ABE$ and $\triangle DCE$, given that E is the midpoint of $\overline{AD}$ and $\overline{BC}$

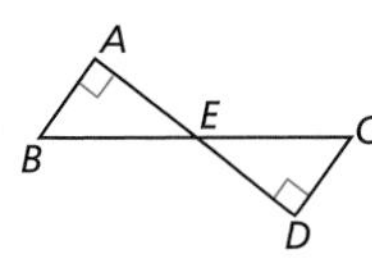

Multi-Step **For each pair of triangles write a triangle congruence statement. Identify the transformation that moves one triangle to the position of the other triangle.**

16. 17.

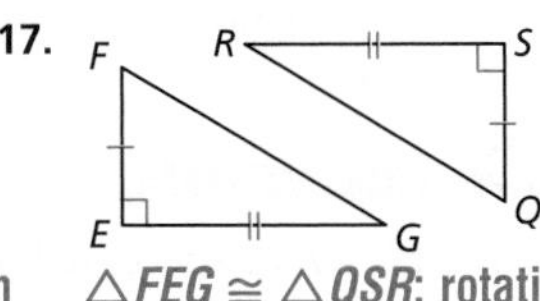

16. **$\triangle ADB \cong \triangle CDB$; reflection**
17. **$\triangle FEG \cong \triangle QSR$; rotation**

18. **Critical Thinking** Side-Side-Angle (SSA) cannot be used to prove two triangles congruent. Draw a diagram that shows why this is true.

COMMON ERROR ALERT

For **Exercise 9**, students may label the wrong angles 53° and 16°. Review that N 53° E means 53° east of north, instead of 53° north of east.

Teaching Tip

Transformations For **Exercises 16** and **17,** it helps students increase their visual discrimination if they can rotate, reflect, and slide figures mentally to determine what transformations would make the triangles' orientations identical.

Answers

9.

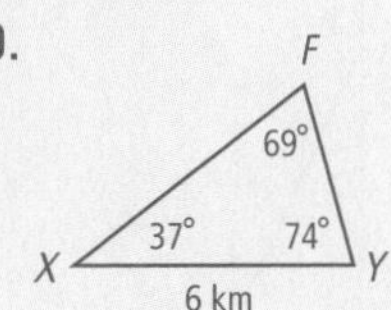

12. Yes; by the Alt. Int. ⦣ Thm. $\angle SRT \cong \angle UTR$, and $\angle STR \cong \angle URT$. $\overline{RT} \cong \overline{TR}$ by the Reflex. Prop. of ≅. So $\triangle RST \cong \triangle TUR$ by ASA.

15. Yes; E is a mdpt. So by def., $\overline{BE} \cong \overline{CE}$, and $\overline{AE} \cong \overline{DE}$. $\angle A$ and $\angle D$ are ≅ by the Rt. ∠ ≅ Thm. By def., $\triangle ABE$ and $\triangle DCE$ are rt. ⦣. So $\triangle ABE \cong \triangle DCE$ by HL.

18.

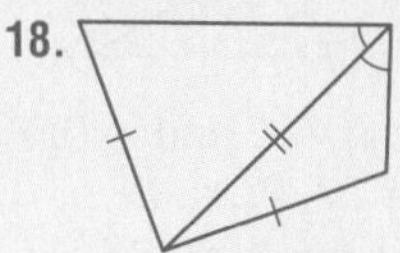

4-5 PRACTICE B

Students in Mrs. Marquez's class are watching a film on the uses of geometry in architecture. The film projector casts the image on a flat screen as shown in the figure. The dotted line is the bisector of $\angle ABC$. Tell whether you can use each congruence theorem to prove that $\triangle ABD \cong \triangle CBD$. If not, tell what else you need to know.

1. Hypotenuse-Leg
No; you need to know that $\overline{AB} \cong \overline{CB}$.

2. Angle-Side-Angle
Yes

3. Angle-Angle-Side
Yes

Write which postulate, if any, can be used to prove the pair of triangles congruent.

4. HL
5. ASA
6. none
7. AAS

Write a paragraph proof.

8. **Given:** $\angle PQU \cong \angle TSU$, $\angle QUR$ and $\angle SUR$ are right angles.
Prove: $\triangle RUQ \cong \triangle RUS$

Possible answer: All right angles are congruent, so $\angle QUR \cong \angle SUR$. $\angle RQU$ and $\angle PQU$ are supplementary and $\angle RSU$ and $\angle TSU$ are supplementary by the Linear Pair Theorem. But it is given that $\angle PQU \cong \angle TSU$, so by the Congruent Supplements Theorem, $\angle RQU \cong \angle RSU$. $\overline{RU} \cong \overline{RU}$ by the Reflexive Property of ≅, so $\angle RUQ \cong \angle RUS$ by AAS.

4-5 PRACTICE C

1. In what case is knowing three parts (side lengths or angle measures) of a triangle not sufficient information to determine a specific triangle?
If the three parts are one non-right angle, one adjacent side, and the side opposite the angle, then you might not have enough information to draw the triangle.

2. Describe how the Leg-Leg (LL), Hypotenuse Angle (HA), and Leg-Angle (LA) theorems of right-triangle congruence are related to the theorems and postulates of congruence that apply to all triangles. Possible answer:
In right triangles, one of the three angles is known, and all right angles are congruent. This means that fewer parts must be shown congruent to prove two right triangles congruent. LL is a special case of SAS in which the A is the right angle. HA is a special case of AAS in which the first A is the right angle. LA is a special case of ASA in which one A is a right angle.

3. You know that a triangle is a right triangle. You are given two more parts. Is it possible that you do not have sufficient information to determine a specific triangle? Explain your answer.
Yes; possible answer: If the two parts given are both angles, then the angle measures are set, but the side lengths are not.

Write a paragraph proof. Remember that if triangles are congruent, their matching parts are congruent.

4. **Given:** $\overline{GB}$, $\overline{GD}$, and $\overline{GF}$ are radii of the circle centered at G and are perpendicular to the sides of $\triangle ACE$.
Prove: $\triangle ACE$ is equilateral.

Possible answer: $\overline{GB}$, $\overline{GD}$, and $\overline{GF}$ all have the same length, by the definition of the radius of a circle, and so they are all congruent. Each radius is perpendicular to its side of the triangle, so all those angles are right angles, and they are all congruent. GE is congruent to GE by the Reflexive Property, and thus the conditions for HL congruence between $\triangle FGE$ and $\triangle DGE$ have been met. Similar reasoning shows that $\triangle FGA$ is congruent to $\triangle BGA$ and that $\triangle BGC$ is congruent to $\triangle DGC$. $\angle EGD$ and $\angle AGB$ are vertical angles, so they are congruent. This fact, and the congruencies already shown, meet the conditions for ASA congruence between $\triangle EGD$ and $\triangle BGA$. Similar reasoning shows that $\triangle FGE$ is congruent to $\triangle BGC$. The Transitive Property of Congruence can now be used to show that all the triangles within $\triangle ACE$ are congruent. When triangles have been proven congruent, it is known that each matching part of the triangles is congruent. Hence $AB = BC = CD = DE = EF = FA$. By the Addition Property of Equality and the Segment Addition Postulate, $AC = CE = EA$ and thus $\triangle ACE$ is equilateral.

Exercise 19 involves proving that the triangles that form a truss are congruent. This exercise prepares students for the Multi-Step Test Prep on page 280.

Construction For **Exercise 25,** have students draw a 5 cm segment and a 10 cm segment. Have them construct $\overline{AB}$ congruent to the 5 cm segment and $\overrightarrow{AX}$ perpendicular to $\overline{AB}$ at *A*. Then have them set their compasses to the length of the 10 cm segment and draw an arc centered at *A*. Have them label the intersection of the arc and $\overrightarrow{AX}$ as *C*. Finally, have them draw right $\triangle ABC$.

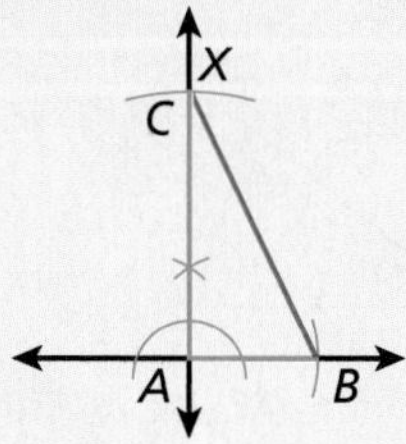

Answers

19a. No; there is not enough information given to use any of the congruence theorems.

21.  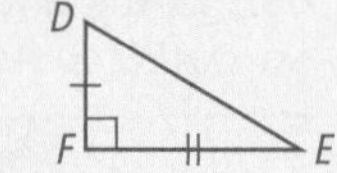

It is given that $\triangle ABC$ and $\triangle DEF$ are rt. ⊿s. $\overline{AC} \cong \overline{DF}$, $\overline{BC} \cong \overline{EF}$, and $\angle C$ and $\angle F$ are rt. ∠s. $\angle C \cong \angle F$ by the Rt. ∠ ≅ Thm. Thus $\triangle ABC \cong \triangle DEF$ by SAS.

23. 1. $\overline{KM} \perp \overline{JL}$ (Given)
2. $\angle JKM$ and $\angle LKM$ are rt. ∠s. (Def. of ⊥)
3. $\angle JKM \cong \angle LKM$ (Rt. ∠ ≅ Thm.)
4. $\overline{JM} \cong \overline{LM}$, $\angle JMK \cong \angle LMK$ (Given)
5. $\triangle JKM \cong \triangle LKM$ (AAS *Steps 3, 4*)

24. Since 2 sides and the included ∠ are equal in measure and therefore ≅, you could prove the ⊿s ≅ using SAS. You could also use HL since the ⊿s are rt. ⊿s.

31. Yes; the sum of the ∠ measures in each △ must be 180°, which makes it possible to solve for *x* and *y*. The value of *x* is 15, and the value of *y* is 12. Each △ has ∠s measuring 82°, 68°, and 30°. $\overline{VU} \cong \overline{VU}$ by the Reflex. Prop. of ≅. So $\triangle VSU \cong \triangle VTU$ by ASA or AAS.

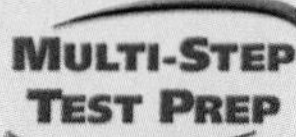

19. This problem will prepare you for the Multi-Step Test Prep on page 280. A carpenter built a truss to support the roof of a doghouse.
    a. The carpenter knows that $\overline{KJ} \cong \overline{MJ}$. Can the carpenter conclude that $\triangle KJL \cong \triangle MJL$? Why or why not?
    b. Suppose the carpenter also knows that $\angle JLK$ is a right angle. Which theorem can be used to show that $\triangle KJL \cong \triangle MJL$? **HL**

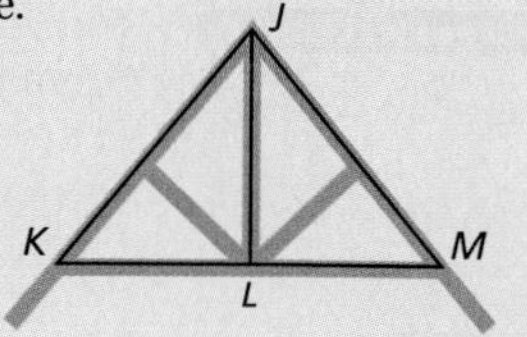

20. **ERROR ANALYSIS** Two proofs that $\triangle EFH \cong \triangle GHF$ are given. Which is incorrect? Explain the error.

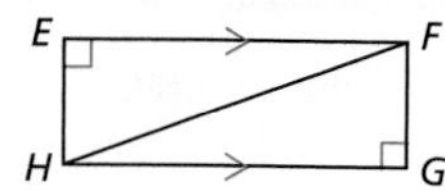

20. Proof B is incorrect. The corr. sides are not in the correct order.

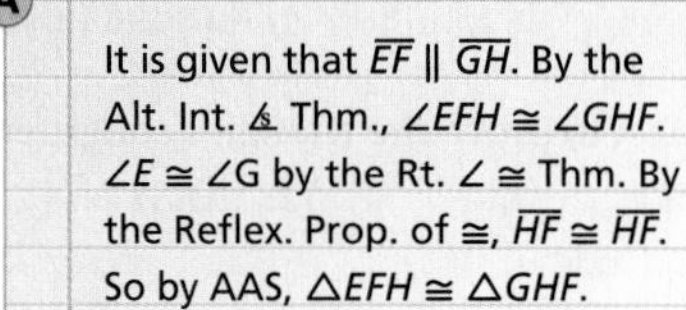

A It is given that $\overline{EF} \parallel \overline{GH}$. By the Alt. Int. ∠s Thm., $\angle EFH \cong \angle GHF$. $\angle E \cong \angle G$ by the Rt. ∠ ≅ Thm. By the Reflex. Prop. of ≅, $\overline{HF} \cong \overline{HF}$. So by AAS, $\triangle EFH \cong \triangle GHF$.

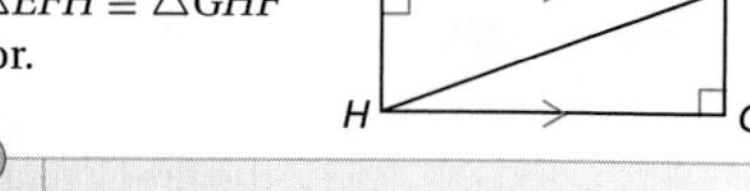

B $\overline{HF}$ is the hyp. of both rt. ⊿s. $\overline{HF} \cong \overline{HF}$ by the Reflex. Prop. of ≅. Since the opp. sides of a rect. are ≅, $\overline{EF} \cong \overline{GH}$. So by HL, $\triangle EFH \cong \triangle FHG$.

21. Write a paragraph proof of the Leg-Leg (LL) Congruence Theorem. If the legs of one right triangle are congruent to the corresponding legs of another right triangle, the triangles are congruent.

22. Use AAS to prove the triangles congruent.
Given: $\overline{AD} \parallel \overline{BC}$, $\overline{AD} \cong \overline{CB}$
Prove: $\triangle AED \cong \triangle CEB$

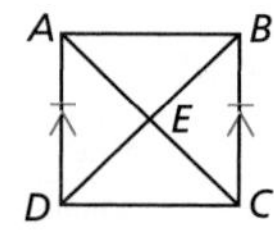

Proof:

Statements	Reasons
1. $\overline{AD} \parallel \overline{BC}$	1. a. ___?___
2. $\angle DAE \cong \angle BCE$	2. b. ___?___
3. c. ___?___	3. Vert. ∠s Thm.
4. d. ___?___	3. Given
5. e. ___?___	4. f. ___?___

a. Given
b. Alt. Int. ∠s Thm.
c. $\angle AED \cong \angle CEB$
d. $\overline{AD} \cong \overline{CB}$
e. $\triangle AED \cong \triangle CEB$
f. AAS *Steps 2, 3, 4*

23. Prove the Hypotenuse-Angle (HA) Theorem.
Given: $\overline{KM} \perp \overline{JL}$, $\overline{JM} \cong \overline{LM}$, $\angle JMK \cong \angle LMK$
Prove: $\triangle JKM \cong \triangle LKM$

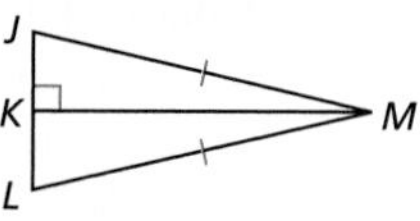

24. **Write About It** The legs of both right $\triangle DEF$ and right $\triangle RST$ are 3 cm and 4 cm. They each have a hypotenuse 5 cm in length. Describe two different ways you could prove that $\triangle DEF \cong \triangle RST$.

25. **Construction** Use the method for constructing perpendicular lines to construct a right triangle. **Check students' constructions.**

26. What additional congruence statement is necessary to prove $\triangle XWY \cong \triangle XVZ$ by ASA?
    (A) $\angle XVZ \cong \angle XWY$
    (B) $\angle VUY \cong \angle WUZ$
    (C) $\overline{VZ} \cong \overline{WY}$
    (D) $\overline{XZ} \cong \overline{XY}$

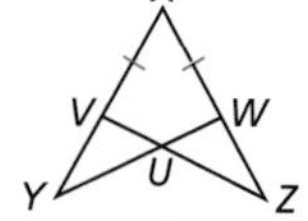

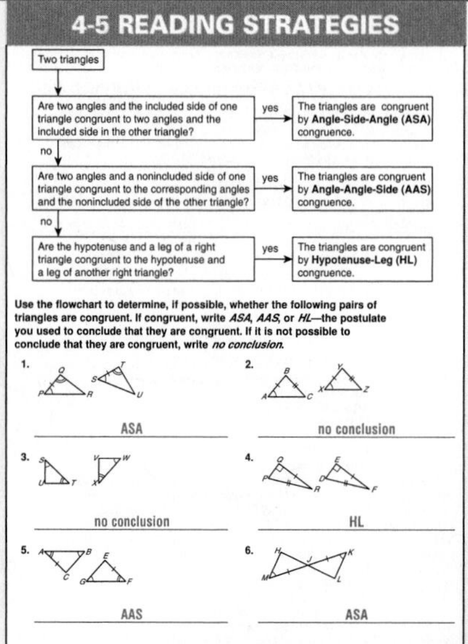

4-5 READING STRATEGIES

Two triangles

Are two angles and the included side of one triangle congruent to two angles and the included side in the other triangle? — yes → The triangles are congruent by **Angle-Side-Angle (ASA)** congruence.

no ↓

Are two angles and a nonincluded side of one triangle congruent to the corresponding angles and the nonincluded side of the other triangle? — yes → The triangles are congruent by **Angle-Angle-Side (AAS)** congruence.

no ↓

Are the hypotenuse and a leg of a right triangle congruent to the hypotenuse and a leg of another right triangle? — yes → The triangles are congruent by **Hypotenuse-Leg (HL)** congruence.

Use the flowchart to determine, if possible, whether the following pairs of triangles are congruent. If congruent, write *ASA*, *AAS*, or *HL*—the postulate you used to conclude that they are congruent. If it is not possible to conclude that they are congruent, write *no conclusion*.

1. ASA
2. no conclusion
3. no conclusion
4. HL
5. AAS
6. ASA

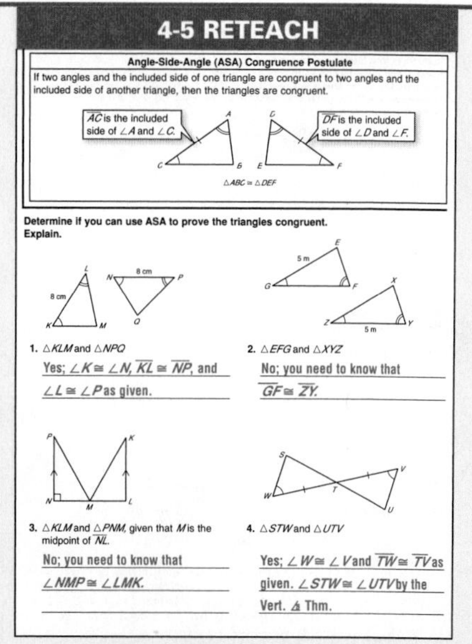

4-5 RETEACH

Angle-Side-Angle (ASA) Congruence Postulate

If two angles and the included side of one triangle are congruent to two angles and the included side of another triangle, then the triangles are congruent.

$\overline{AC}$ is the included side of ∠A and ∠C.

$\overline{DF}$ is the included side of ∠D and ∠F.

△ABC ≅ △DEF

Determine if you can use ASA to prove the triangles congruent. Explain.

1. △KLM and △NPQ
Yes; ∠K ≅ ∠N, $\overline{KL} \cong \overline{NP}$, and ∠L ≅ ∠P as given.

2. △EFG and △XYZ
No; you need to know that $\overline{GF} \cong \overline{ZY}$.

3. △KLM and △PNM, given that *M* is the midpoint of $\overline{NL}$.
No; you need to know that ∠NMP ≅ ∠LMK.

4. △STW and △UTV
Yes; ∠W ≅ ∠V and $\overline{TW} \cong \overline{TV}$ as given. ∠STW ≅ ∠UTV by the Vert. ∠s Thm.

27. Which postulate or theorem justifies the congruence statement $\triangle STU \cong \triangle VUT$?

Ⓕ ASA Ⓗ HL

Ⓖ SSS Ⓙ SAS

TEST PREP DOCTOR For **Exercise 27,** students may assume that the hypotenuses are congruent. Since $\overline{TU}$ is a common side, the triangles are congruent by SAS, not HL.

28. Which of the following congruence statements is true?

Ⓐ $\angle A \cong \angle B$ Ⓒ $\triangle AED \cong \triangle CEB$

Ⓑ $\overline{CE} \cong \overline{DE}$ Ⓓ $\triangle AED \cong \triangle BEC$

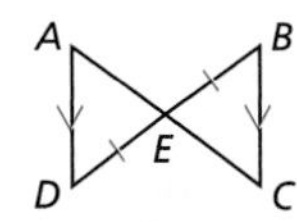

29. In $\triangle RST$, $RT = 6y - 2$. In $\triangle UVW$, $UW = 2y + 7$. $\angle R \cong \angle U$, and $\angle S \cong \angle V$. What must be the value of y in order to prove that $\triangle RST \cong \triangle UVW$?

Ⓕ 1.25 Ⓖ 2.25 Ⓗ 9.0 Ⓙ 11.5

30. **Extended Response** Draw a triangle. Construct a second triangle that has the same angle measures but is not congruent. Compare the lengths of each pair of corresponding sides. Consider the relationship between the lengths of the sides and the measures of the angles. Explain why Angle-Angle-Angle (AAA) is not a congruence principle.

30. Check students' drawings and constructions; since the lengths of the corr. sides of the 2 △ are not equal, the 2 △ are not ≅ even if the corr. ∠ have the same measure.

CHALLENGE AND EXTEND

31. **Sports** This bicycle frame includes $\triangle VSU$ and $\triangle VTU$, which lie in intersecting planes. From the given angle measures, can you conclude that $\triangle VSU \cong \triangle VTU$? Explain.

$m\angle VUS = (7y - 2)°$ $m\angle VUT = \left(5\frac{1}{2}x - \frac{1}{2}\right)°$

$m\angle USV = 5\frac{2}{3}y°$ $m\angle UTV = (4x + 8)°$

$m\angle SVU = (3y - 6)°$ $m\angle TVU = 2x°$

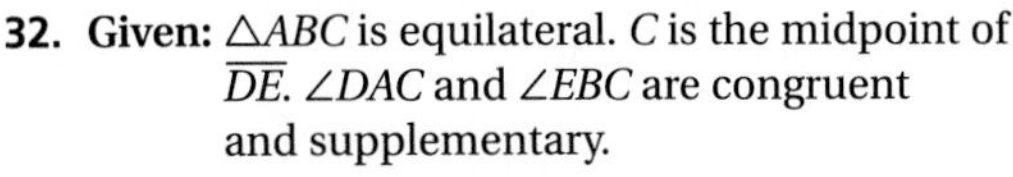

32. **Given:** $\triangle ABC$ is equilateral. C is the midpoint of $\overline{DE}$. $\angle DAC$ and $\angle EBC$ are congruent and supplementary.

Prove: $\triangle DAC \cong \triangle EBC$

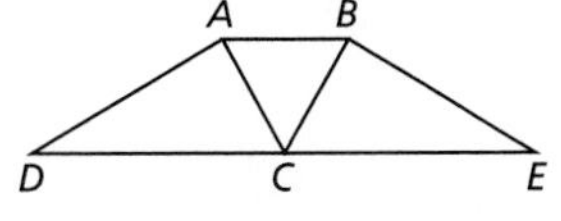

33. Write a two-column proof of the Leg-Angle (LA) Congruence Theorem. If a leg and an acute angle of one right triangle are congruent to the corresponding parts of another right triangle, the triangles are congruent. (*Hint:* There are two cases to consider.)

34. If two triangles are congruent by ASA, what theorem could you use to prove that the triangles are also congruent by AAS? Explain.

34. Third ∠ Thm.; if the third pair of ∠ are ≅, then the △ are also ≅ by AAS.

SPIRAL REVIEW

Identify the *x*- and *y*-intercepts. Use them to graph each line. *(Previous course)*

35. $y = 3x - 6$ **2; −6** 36. $y = -\frac{1}{2}x + 4$ **8; 4** 37. $y = -5x + 5$ **1; 5**

38. Find AB and BC if $AC = 10$. *(Lesson 1-6)* **$AB = 6$; $BC = 8$**

39. Find $m\angle C$. *(Lesson 4-2)* **36.9°**

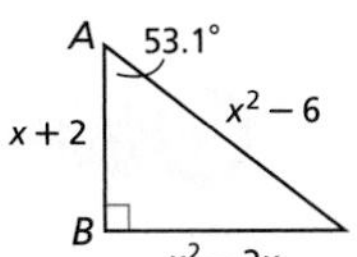

Journal

Have students describe how proving two triangles congruent by HL is different from the SAS method.

ALTERNATIVE ASSESSMENT

Group students in pairs and have each student cut out three large triangles. Have them then fold each over to create two congruent triangles. Each student should mark off given information on the triangles and then give them to their partner to decide if the triangles are congruent by AAS, ASA, or HL.

Power Presentations with PowerPoint®

4-5 Lesson Quiz

Identify the postulate or theorem that proves the triangles congruent.

1\. ASA

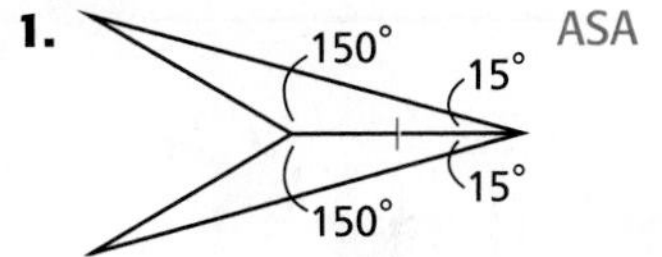

2\. HL

3\. SAS or SSS

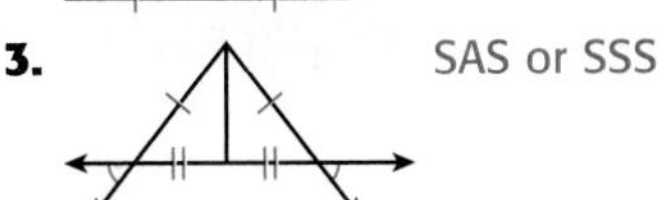

4\. **Given:** $\angle FAB \cong \angle GED$, $\angle ACB \cong \angle DCE$, $\overline{AC} \cong \overline{EC}$

Prove: $\triangle ABC \cong \triangle EDC$

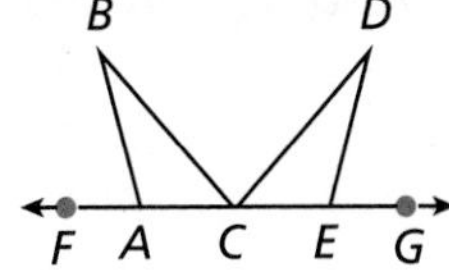

Proof:

1. $\angle FAB \cong \angle GED$ (Given)
2. $\angle BAC$ is a supp. of $\angle FAB$; $\angle DEC$ is a supp. of $\angle GED$. (Def. of supp. ∠)
3. $\angle BAC \cong \angle DEC$ (≅ Supp. Thm.)
4. $\angle ACB \cong \angle DCE$; $\overline{AC} \cong \overline{EC}$ (Given)
5. $\triangle ABC \cong \triangle EDC$ (ASA Steps 3, 4)

Also available on transparency

4-5 PROBLEM SOLVING

Use the following information for Exercises 1 and 2.

Melanie is at hole 6 on a miniature golf course. She walks east 7.5 meters to hole 7. She then faces south, turns 67° west, and walks to hole 8. From hole 8, she faces north, turns 35° west, and walks to hole 6.

Possible drawing: 6, 7.5 m, 7, 23°, 67°, 35°, 67°, 8

1. Draw the section of the golf course described. Label the measures of the angles in the triangle.

2. Is there enough information given to determine the location of holes 6, 7, and 8? Explain.

Yes; the △ is uniquely determined by AAS.

3. A section of the front of an English Tudor home is shown in the diagram. If you know that $\overline{KN} \cong \overline{LN}$ and $\overline{JN} \cong \overline{MN}$, can you use HL to conclude that $\triangle JKN \cong \triangle MLN$? Explain.

No; you need to know that ∠KJN and ∠LMN are rt. ∠.

Use the diagram of a kite for Exercises 4 and 5.

$\overline{AE}$ is the angle bisector of ∠DAF and ∠DEF.

4. What can you conclude about △DEA and △FEA?

A △DEA ≅ △FEA by HL.

B △DEA ≅ △FEA by AAA.

Ⓒ △DEA ≅ △FEA by ASA.

D △DEA ≅ △FEA by SAS.

5. Based on the diagram, what can you conclude about △BCA and △HGA?

F △BCA ≅ △HGA by HL.

G △BCA ≅ △HGA by AAS.

H △BCA ≅ △HGA by ASA.

Ⓙ It cannot be shown using the given information that △BCA ≅ △HGA.

Answers

32\.
1. $\triangle ABC$ is equil. (Given)
2. $\overline{AC} \cong \overline{BC}$ (Def. of equil.)
3. C is the mdpt. of $\overline{DE}$. (Given)
4. $\overline{DC} \cong \overline{EC}$ (Def. of mdpt.)
5. $\angle DAC$ and $\angle EBC$ are ≅ and supp. (Given)
6. $\angle DAC$ and $\angle EBC$ are rt. ∠. (∠ that are ≅ and supp. are rt. ∠.)
7. $\triangle DAC$ and $\triangle EBC$ are rt. △. (Def. of rt. △)
8. $\triangle DAC \cong \triangle EBC$ (HL *Steps 4, 2*)

33, 35–37. See pp. A15–A16.

4-6 Organizer

Pacing: Traditional $\frac{1}{2}$ day
Block $\frac{1}{4}$ day

Objective: Use CPCTC to prove parts of triangles are congruent.

Online Edition
Tutorial Videos

Countdown Week 8

Power Presentations with PowerPoint®

Warm Up

1. If $\triangle ABC \cong \triangle DEF$, then $\angle A \cong$ ___?___ and $\overline{BC} \cong$ ___?___. $\angle D$, $\overline{EF}$
2. What is the distance between (3, 4) and (–1, 5)? $\sqrt{17}$
3. If $\angle 1 \cong \angle 2$, why is $a \parallel b$? Conv. of Alt. Int. ∠s Thm.

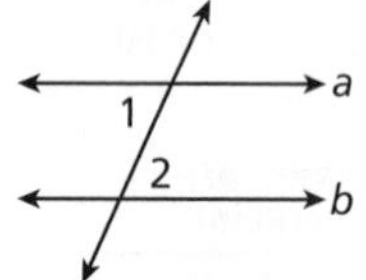

4. List methods used to prove two triangles congruent. SSS, SAS, ASA, AAS, HL

Also available on transparency

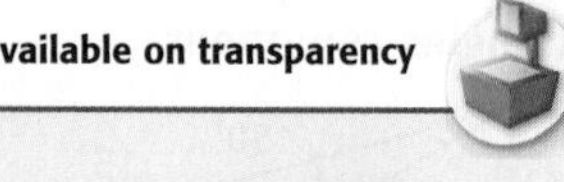

Q: What do you write as the reason when using corresponding parts of congruent triangles in a proof?

A: See Peas Eat Easy! (CPCTC)

4-6 Triangle Congruence: CPCTC

Objective
Use CPCTC to prove parts of triangles are congruent.

Vocabulary
CPCTC

Why learn this?
You can use congruent triangles to estimate distances.

CPCTC is an abbreviation for the phrase "Corresponding Parts of Congruent Triangles are Congruent." It can be used as a justification in a proof after you have proven two triangles congruent.

Remember!
SSS, SAS, ASA, AAS, and HL use corresponding parts to prove triangles congruent. CPCTC uses congruent triangles to prove corresponding parts congruent.

EXAMPLE 1 *Engineering Application*

To design a bridge across a canyon, you need to find the distance from A to B. Locate points C, D, and E as shown in the figure. If $DE = 600$ ft, what is AB?

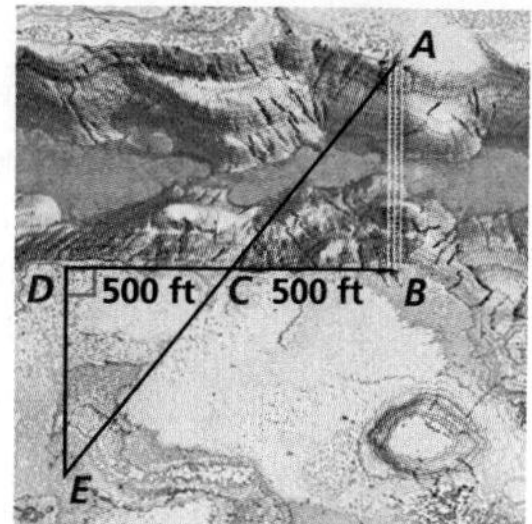

$\angle D \cong \angle B$, because they are both right angles.
$\overline{DC} \cong \overline{CB}$, because $DC = CB = 500$ ft.
$\angle DCE \cong \angle BCA$, because vertical angles are congruent. Therefore $\triangle DCE \cong \triangle BCA$ by ASA or LA. By CPCTC, $\overline{ED} \cong \overline{AB}$, so $AB = ED = 600$ ft.

1. A landscape architect sets up the triangles shown in the figure to find the distance JK across a pond. What is JK? **41 ft**

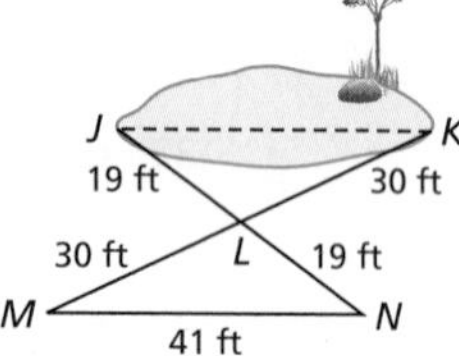

EXAMPLE 2 Proving Corresponding Parts Congruent

Given: $\overline{AB} \cong \overline{DC}$, $\angle ABC \cong \angle DCB$
Prove: $\angle A \cong \angle D$

A, D, B, C (figure)

Proof:

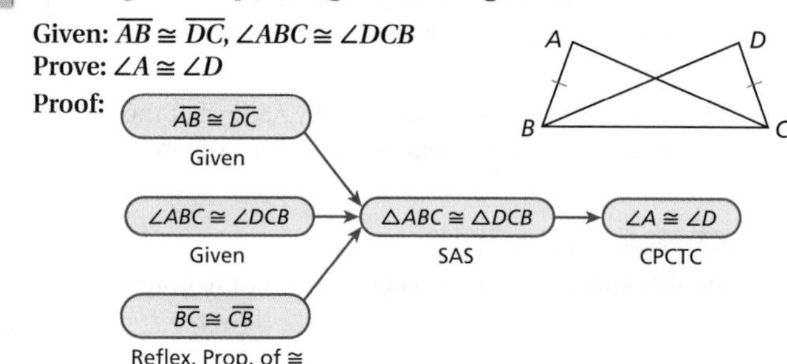

2. **Given:** $\overline{PR}$ bisects $\angle QPS$ and $\angle QRS$.
Prove: $\overline{PQ} \cong \overline{PS}$

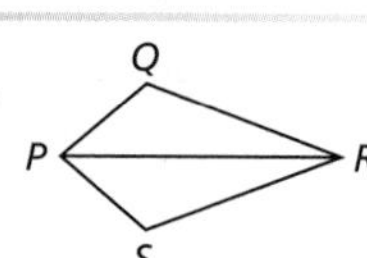

State Resources

1 Introduce

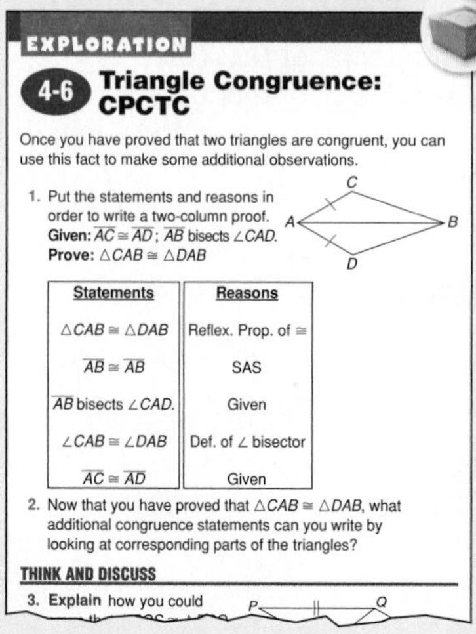

EXPLORATION

4-6 Triangle Congruence: CPCTC

Once you have proved that two triangles are congruent, you can use this fact to make some additional observations.

1. Put the statements and reasons in order to write a two-column proof.
Given: $\overline{AC} \cong \overline{AD}$; $\overline{AB}$ bisects $\angle CAD$.
Prove: $\triangle CAB \cong \triangle DAB$

Statements	Reasons
$\triangle CAB \cong \triangle DAB$	Reflex. Prop. of ≅
$\overline{AB} \cong \overline{AB}$	SAS
$\overline{AB}$ bisects $\angle CAD$.	Given
$\angle CAB \cong \angle DAB$	Def. of ∠ bisector
$\overline{AC} \cong \overline{AD}$	Given

2. Now that you have proved that $\triangle CAB \cong \triangle DAB$, what additional congruence statements can you write by looking at corresponding parts of the triangles?

THINK AND DISCUSS

3. **Explain** how you could

Motivate

Point out that congruent triangles can be used to find the distance between two points that is difficult to measure, such as the distance across a lake. Show designs by M. C. Escher to demonstrate that the size of one part determines the size of another. Students will learn that you can base assumptions about parts of a triangles on information about other parts.

Explorations and answers are provided in *Alternate Openers: Explorations Transparencies.*

EXAMPLE 3 Using CPCTC in a Proof

Helpful Hint

Work backward when planning a proof. To show that $\overline{ED} \parallel \overline{GF}$, look for a pair of angles that are congruent. Then look for triangles that contain these angles.

Given: $\overline{EG} \parallel \overline{DF}$, $\overline{EG} \cong \overline{DF}$
Prove: $\overline{ED} \parallel \overline{GF}$
Proof:

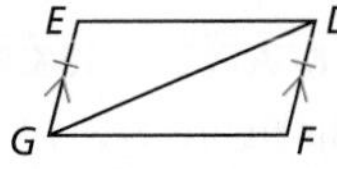

Statements	Reasons
1. $\overline{EG} \cong \overline{DF}$	1. Given
2. $\overline{EG} \parallel \overline{DF}$	2. Given
3. $\angle EGD \cong \angle FDG$	3. Alt. Int. ∠s Thm.
4. $\overline{GD} \cong \overline{DG}$	4. Reflex. Prop. of ≅
5. $\triangle EGD \cong \triangle FDG$	5. SAS *Steps 1, 3, and 4*
6. $\angle EDG \cong \angle FGD$	6. CPCTC
7. $\overline{ED} \parallel \overline{GF}$	7. Converse of Alt. Int. ∠s Thm.

CHECK IT OUT! 3. Given: J is the midpoint of $\overline{KM}$ and $\overline{NL}$.
Prove: $\overline{KL} \parallel \overline{MN}$

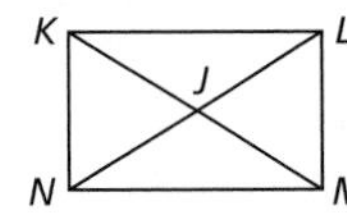

You can also use CPCTC when triangles are on a coordinate plane. You use the Distance Formula to find the lengths of the sides of each triangle. Then, after showing that the triangles are congruent, you can make conclusions about their corresponding parts.

EXAMPLE 4 Using CPCTC in the Coordinate Plane

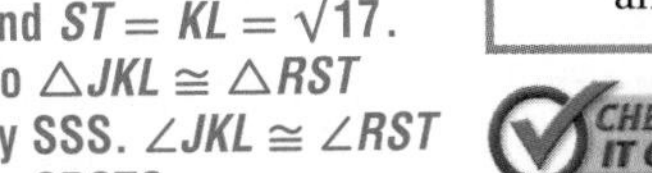

Algebra

Given: $A(2, 3), B(5, -1), C(1, 0),$
$D(-4, -1), E(0, 2), F(-1, -2)$
Prove: $\angle ABC \cong \angle DEF$

Step 1 Plot the points on a coordinate plane.

Step 2 Use the Distance Formula to find the lengths of the sides of each triangle.

$$D = \sqrt{(x_2 - x_1)^2 + (y_2 - y_1)^2}$$

$$AB = \sqrt{(5-2)^2 + (-1-3)^2} = \sqrt{9+16} = \sqrt{25} = 5$$

$$DE = \sqrt{(0-(-4))^2 + (2-(-1))^2} = \sqrt{16+9} = \sqrt{25} = 5$$

$$BC = \sqrt{(1-5)^2 + (0-(-1))^2} = \sqrt{16+1} = \sqrt{17}$$

$$EF = \sqrt{(-1-0)^2 + (-2-2)^2} = \sqrt{1+16} = \sqrt{17}$$

$$AC = \sqrt{(1-2)^2 + (0-3)^2} = \sqrt{1+9} = \sqrt{10}$$

$$DF = \sqrt{(-1-(-4))^2 + (-2-(-1))^2} = \sqrt{9+1} = \sqrt{10}$$

So $\overline{AB} \cong \overline{DE}$, $\overline{BC} \cong \overline{EF}$, and $\overline{AC} \cong \overline{DF}$. Therefore $\triangle ABC \cong \triangle DEF$ by SSS, and $\angle ABC \cong \angle DEF$ by CPCTC.

CHECK IT OUT! 4. Given: $J(-1, -2), K(2, -1), L(-2, 0), R(2, 3), S(5, 2), T(1, 1)$
Prove: $\angle JKL \cong \angle RST$

4. $RT = JL = \sqrt{5}$, $RS = JK = \sqrt{10}$, and $ST = KL = \sqrt{17}$. So $\triangle JKL \cong \triangle RST$ by SSS. $\angle JKL \cong \angle RST$ by CPCTC.

2 Teach

Guided Instruction

Present CPCTC as a way to use congruent triangles to prove corresponding parts congruent. Have students complete fill-in-the-blank proofs using CPCTC. Be sure students know the importance of first proving triangle congruence before using CPCTC to prove parts congruent. Review the Distance Formula before Example 4.

Auditory Have students recite the meaning of CPCTC with emphasis on the words congruent triangles.

3 Close

Summarize

Remind students what CPCTC means. Point out that the middle of this statement implies that students first prove triangles congruent and then make conclusions about the corresponding parts. Remind students that they can use the Distance Formula when proving triangle congruence in the coordinate plane.

Answers to *Check It Out!*

2–3. See p. A16.

Power Presentations with PowerPoint®

Additional Examples

Example 1

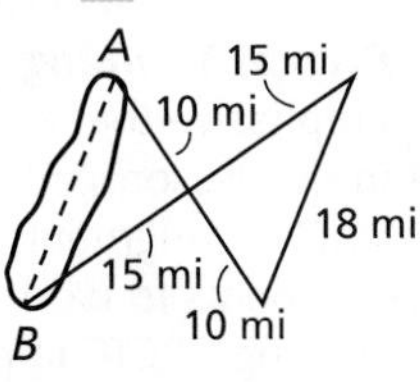

A and B are on the edges of a ravine. What is AB? 18 mi

Example 2

Given: $\overline{YW}$ bisects $\overline{XZ}$. $\overline{XY} \cong \overline{YZ}$.

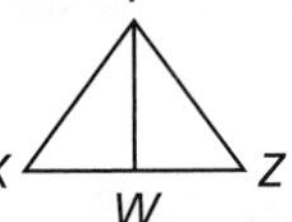

Prove: $\angle XYW \cong \angle ZYW$

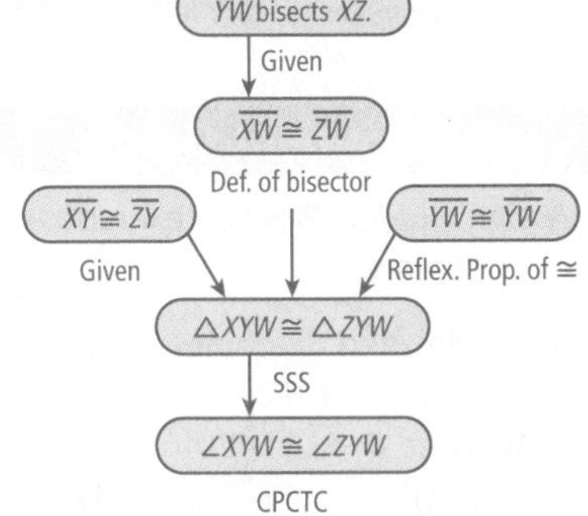

Example 3

Given: $\overline{NO} \parallel \overline{MP}$, $\angle N \cong \angle P$

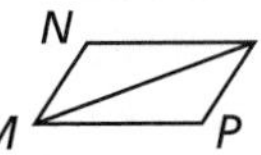

Prove: $\overline{MN} \parallel \overline{OP}$

1. $\angle N \cong \angle P$; $\overline{NO} \parallel \overline{MP}$ (Given)
2. $\angle NOM \cong \angle PMO$ (Alt. Int. ∠s Thm.)
3. $\overline{MO} \cong \overline{MO}$ (Reflex. Prop of ≅)
4. $\triangle MNO \cong \triangle OPM$ (AAS)
5. $\angle NMO \cong \angle POM$ (CPCTC)
6. $\overline{MN} \parallel \overline{OP}$ (Conv. of Alt. Int. ∠s Thm.)

Example 4

Given: $D(-5, -5), E(-3, -1), F(-2, -3), G(-2, 1), H(0, 5)$, and $I(1, 3)$

Prove: $\angle DEF \cong \angle GHI$

$DE = GH = 2\sqrt{5}$, $EF = HI = \sqrt{5}$, $DF = GI = \sqrt{13}$. Therefore $\triangle DEF \cong \triangle GHI$ by SSS, and $\angle DEF \cong \angle GHI$ by CPCTC.

INTERVENTION
Questioning Strategies

EXAMPLES 1–4

- What transformations are used to change each triangle into the second congruent triangle?

Answers to *Think and Discuss*

1. SAS; $\overline{UW} \cong \overline{XZ}$; $\angle U \cong \angle X$; $\angle W \cong \angle Z$
2. See p. A4.

Critical Thinking Emphasize that proofs in this lesson go beyond proving triangles congruent. Encourage students to work backward when using CPCTC in proofs. Remind students to first locate which triangles they need to prove congruent and then find the angles or sides needed.

THINK AND DISCUSS

1. In the figure, $\overline{UV} \cong \overline{XY}$, $\overline{VW} \cong \overline{YZ}$, and $\angle V \cong \angle Y$. Explain why $\triangle UVW \cong \triangle XYZ$. By CPCTC, which additional parts are congruent?

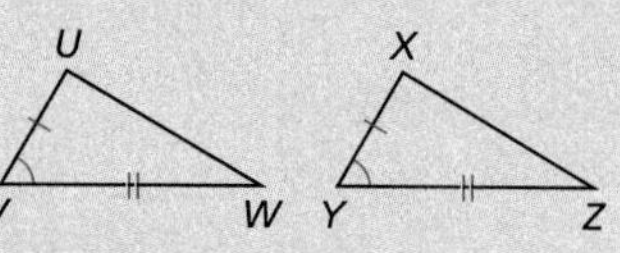

2. **GET ORGANIZED** Copy and complete the graphic organizer. Write all conclusions you can make using CPCTC.

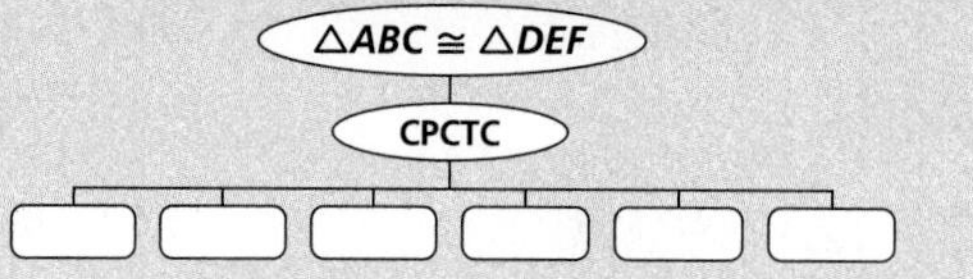

4-6 Exercises

4-6 Exercises

go.hrw.com
Homework Help Online
KEYWORD: MG7 4-6
Parent Resources Online
KEYWORD: MG7 Parent

Assignment Guide

Assign *Guided Practice* exercises as necessary.

If you finished Examples 1–2
Basic 7–9, 17–19
Average 7–9, 17–20
Advanced 7–9, 17–20, 29, 32

If you finished Examples 1–4
Basic 7–19, 24–28, 33–37
Average 7–16, 20–28, 30, 33–37
Advanced 7–16, 19–37

Homework Quick Check
Quickly check key concepts.
Exercises: 7, 8, 10, 12, 14

GUIDED PRACTICE

1. **Vocabulary** You use CPCTC after proving triangles are congruent. Which parts of congruent triangles are referred to as corresponding parts? **corr. ∡ and corr. sides**

SEE EXAMPLE 1 p. 260

2. **Archaeology** An archaeologist wants to find the height AB of a rock formation. She places a marker at C and steps off the distance from C to B. Then she walks the same distance from C and places a marker at D. If $DE = 6.3$ m, what is AB? **6.3 m**

SEE EXAMPLE 2 p. 260

3. **Given:** X is the midpoint of $\overline{ST}$. $\overline{RX} \perp \overline{ST}$
Prove: $\overline{RS} \cong \overline{RT}$

Proof:

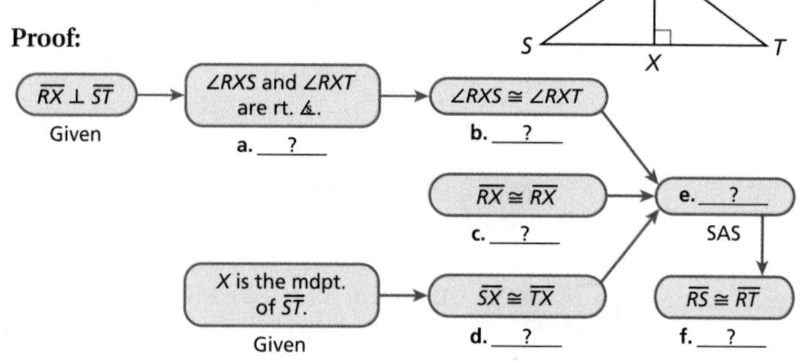

State Resources

ONGOING ASSESSMENT and INTERVENTION

Diagnose Before **the Lesson**
4-6 Warm Up, TE p. 260

Monitor During **the Lesson**
Check It Out! Exercises, SE pp. 260–261
Questioning Strategies, TE p. 261

Assess After **the Lesson**
4-6 Lesson Quiz, TE p. 265
Alternative Assessment, TE p. 265

Answers

3a. Def. of ⊥
b. Rt. ∠ ≅ Thm.
c. Reflex. Prop. of ≅
d. Def. of mdpt.
e. $\triangle RXS \cong \triangle RXT$
f. CPCTC

SEE EXAMPLE 3
p. 261

4. **Given:** $\overline{AC} \cong \overline{AD}$, $\overline{CB} \cong \overline{DB}$
Prove: $\overline{AB}$ bisects $\angle CAD$.

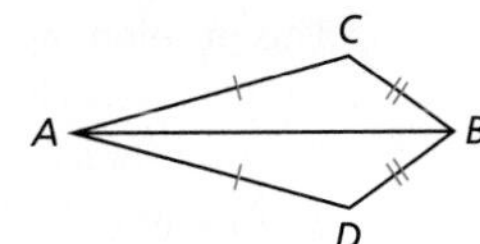

Proof:

Statements	Reasons
1. $\overline{AC} \cong \overline{AD}$, $\overline{CB} \cong \overline{DB}$	1. a. ___?___
2. b. ___?___	2. Reflex. Prop. of $\cong$
3. $\triangle ACB \cong \triangle ADB$	3. c. ___?___
4. $\angle CAB \cong \angle DAB$	4. d. ___?___
5. $\overline{AB}$ bisects $\angle CAD$	5. e. ___?___

a. Given
b. $\overline{AB} \cong \overline{AB}$
c. SSS *Steps 1, 2*
d. CPCTC
e. Def. of $\angle$ bisect

SEE EXAMPLE 4
p. 261

Multi-Step Use the given set of points to prove each congruence statement.

5. $E(-3, 3)$, $F(-1, 3)$, $G(-2, 0)$, $J(0, -1)$, $K(2, -1)$, $L(1, 2)$; $\angle EFG \cong \angle JKL$
6. $A(2, 3)$, $B(4, 1)$, $C(1, -1)$, $R(-1, 0)$, $S(-3, -2)$, $T(0, -4)$; $\angle ACB \cong \angle RTS$

PRACTICE AND PROBLEM SOLVING

Independent Practice

For Exercises	See Example
7	1
8–9	2
10–11	3
12–13	4

Extra Practice
Skills Practice p. S11
Application Practice p. S31

7. **Surveying** To find the distance AB across a river, a surveyor first locates point C. He measures the distance from C to B. Then he locates point D the same distance east of C. If $DE = 420$ ft, what is AB? **420 ft**

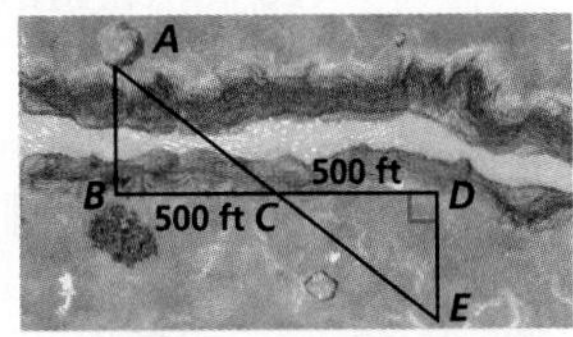

8. **Given:** M is the midpoint of $\overline{PQ}$ and $\overline{RS}$.
Prove: $\overline{QR} \cong \overline{PS}$

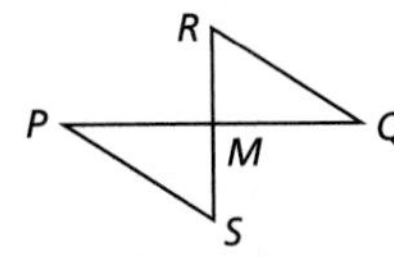

9. **Given:** $\overline{WX} \cong \overline{XY} \cong \overline{YZ} \cong \overline{ZW}$
Prove: $\angle W \cong \angle Y$

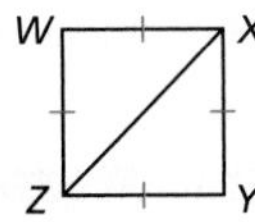

10. **Given:** G is the midpoint of $\overline{FH}$. $\overline{EF} \cong \overline{EH}$
Prove: $\angle 1 \cong \angle 2$

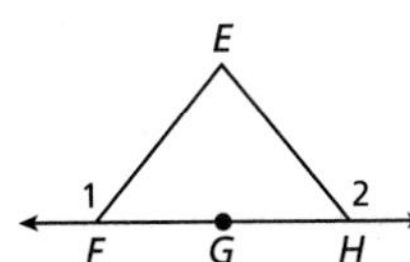

11. **Given:** $\overline{LM}$ bisects $\angle JLK$. $\overline{JL} \cong \overline{KL}$
Prove: M is the midpoint of $\overline{JK}$.

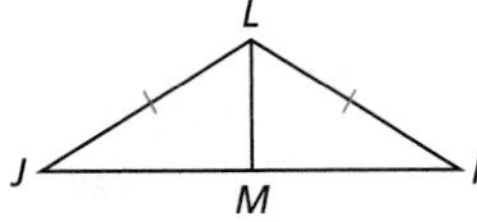

Multi-Step Use the given set of points to prove each congruence statement.

12. $R(0, 0)$, $S(2, 4)$, $T(-1, 3)$, $U(-1, 0)$, $V(-3, -4)$, $W(-4, -1)$; $\angle RST \cong \angle UVW$
13. $A(-1, 1)$, $B(2, 3)$, $C(2, -2)$, $D(2, -3)$, $E(-1, -5)$, $F(-1, 0)$; $\angle BAC \cong \angle EDF$
14. **Given:** $\triangle QRS$ is adjacent to $\triangle QTS$. $\overline{QS}$ bisects $\angle RQT$. $\angle R \cong \angle T$
Prove: $\overline{QS}$ bisects $\overline{RT}$.
15. **Given:** $\triangle ABE$ and $\triangle CDE$ with E the midpoint of $\overline{AC}$ and $\overline{BD}$
Prove: $\overline{AB} \parallel \overline{CD}$

12. $ST = VW = RT = UW = \sqrt{10}$. $RS = UV = 2\sqrt{5}$. So $\triangle RST \cong \triangle UVW$ by SSS. $\angle RST \cong \angle UVW$ by CPCTC.

COMMON ERROR ALERT

In **Exercise 11,** students may think that if a ray bisects an angle of a triangle then it also bisects the side opposite the angle. Explain that this is only true for some triangles.

Technology For **Exercises 5, 6, 12,** and **13,** use geometry software to graph the points and to demonstrate that the corresponding angle measures in each proof statement are the same. Also address transformations after triangles are graphed.

Answers

5. $EF = JK = 2$, and $EG = FG = JL = KL = \sqrt{10}$. So $\triangle EFG \cong \triangle JKL$ by SSS. $\angle EFG \cong \angle JKL$ by CPCTC.

6. $AB = RS = 2\sqrt{2}$, $BC = ST = \sqrt{13}$, and $RT = AC = \sqrt{17}$. So $\triangle ABC \cong \triangle RST$ by SSS. $\angle ACB \cong \angle RTS$ by CPCTC.

8. 1. M is the mdpt. of $\overline{PQ}$ and $\overline{RS}$. (Given)
   2. $\overline{PM} \cong \overline{QM}$, $\overline{RM} \cong \overline{SM}$ (Def. of mdpt.)
   3. $\angle PMS \cong \angle QMR$ (Vert. ∠s Thm.)
   4. $\triangle PMS \cong \triangle QMR$ (SAS, *Steps 2, 3*)
   5. $\overline{QR} \cong \overline{PS}$ (CPCTC)

9. 1. $\overline{WX} \cong \overline{XY} \cong \overline{YZ} \cong \overline{ZW}$ (Given)
   2. $\overline{ZX} \cong \overline{ZX}$ (Reflex. Prop. of $\cong$)
   3. $\triangle WXZ \cong \triangle YZX$ (SSS)
   4. $\angle W \cong \angle Y$ (CPCTC)

10. 1. G is the mdpt. of $\overline{FH}$. (Given)
    2. $FG = HG$ (Def. of mdpt.)
    3. $\overline{FG} \cong \overline{HG}$ (Def. of $\cong$)
    4. Draw $\overline{EG}$. (Through any 2 pts. there is exactly 1 line.)
    5. $\overline{EG} \cong \overline{EG}$ (Reflex. Prop. of $\cong$)
    6. $\overline{EF} \cong \overline{EH}$ (Given)
    7. $\triangle EGF \cong \triangle EGH$ (SSS *Steps 3, 5, 6*)
    8. $\angle EFG \cong \angle EHG$ (CPCTC)
    9. $\angle 1 \cong \angle 2$ ($\cong$ Supp. Thm.)

11. 1. $\overline{LM}$ bisects $\angle JLK$. (Given)
    2. $\angle JLM \cong \angle KLM$ (Def. of $\angle$ bisect)
    3. $\overline{JL} \cong \overline{KL}$ (Given)
    4. $\overline{LM} \cong \overline{LM}$ (Reflex. Prop. of $\cong$)
    5. $\triangle JLM \cong \triangle KLM$ (SAS *Steps 3, 2, 4*)
    6. $\overline{JM} \cong \overline{KM}$ (CPCTC)
    7. M is the mdpt. of $\overline{JK}$. (Def. of mdpt.)

Answers

13. $AB = DE = \sqrt{13}$, $BC = EF = 5$, and $AC = DF = \sqrt{18} = 3\sqrt{2}$. So $\triangle ABC \cong \triangle DEF$ by SSS. $\angle BAC \cong \angle EDF$ by CPCTC.

14. 1. $\triangle QRS$ is adj. to $\triangle QTS$. $\overline{QS}$ bisects $\angle RQT$. $\angle R \cong \angle T$ (Given)
    2. $\angle RQS \cong \angle TQS$ (Def. of $\angle$ bisect)
    3. $\overline{QS} \cong \overline{QS}$ (Reflex. Prop. of $\cong$)
    4. $\triangle RSQ \cong \triangle TSQ$ (AAS *Steps 1, 2, 3*)
    5. $\overline{RS} \cong \overline{TS}$ (CPCTC)
    6. $\overline{QS}$ bisects $\overline{RT}$. (Def. of bisect)

15. 1. E is the mdpt. of $\overline{AC}$ and $\overline{BD}$. (Given)
    2. $\overline{AE} \cong \overline{CE}$; $\overline{BE} \cong \overline{DE}$ (Def. of mdpt.)
    3. $\angle AEB \cong \angle CED$ (Vert. ∠s Thm.)
    4. $\triangle AEB \cong \triangle CED$ (SAS *Steps 2, 3*)
    5. $\angle A \cong \angle C$ (CPCTC)
    6. $\overline{AB} \parallel \overline{CD}$ (Conv. of Alt. Int. ∠s Thm.)

Exercise 16 involves using CPCTC to prove corresponding sides of a triangle are congruent. This exercise prepares students for the Multi-Step Test Prep on page 280.

If students chose **J** in **Exercise 25,** they might be assuming that the quadrilateral is a rectangle with all angles congruent. If they chose **F** or **H,** they might be assuming that the diagonals bisect the angles.

Answers

16b. 1. $\overline{AD} \perp \overline{BC}$ (Given)
2. $\angle ADB$ and $\angle ADC$ are rt. $\angle$s. (Def. of $\perp$)
3. $\triangle ADB$ and $\triangle ADC$ are rt. $\triangle$s. (Def. of rt. $\triangle$)
4. $AB = AC = 20$ in. (Given)
5. $\overline{AB} \cong \overline{AC}$ (Def. of $\cong$)
6. $\overline{AD} \cong \overline{AD}$ (Reflex. Prop. of $\cong$)
7. $\triangle ADB \cong \triangle ADC$ (HL *Steps 5, 6*)
8. $\overline{BD} = \overline{CD}$ (CPCTC)

19. 1. $PS = RQ$ (Given)
2. $\overline{PS} \cong \overline{RQ}$ (Def. of $\cong$)
3. $m\angle 1 = m\angle 4$ (Given)
4. $\angle 1 \cong \angle 4$ (Def. of $\cong$)
5. $\overline{SQ} \cong \overline{QS}$ (Reflex. Prop. of $\cong$)
6. $\triangle PSQ \cong \triangle RQS$ (SAS *Steps 2, 4, 5*)
7. $\angle 3 \cong \angle 2$ (CPCTC)
8. $m\angle 3 = m\angle 2$ (Def. of $\cong$)

20. 1. $m\angle 1 = m\angle 2$, $m\angle 3 = m\angle 4$ (Given)
2. $\angle 1 \cong \angle 2$, $\angle 3 \cong \angle 4$ (Def. of $\cong$)
3. $\overline{SQ} \cong \overline{SQ}$ (Reflex. Prop. of $\cong$)
4. $\triangle PSQ \cong \triangle RSQ$ (ASA *Steps 2,3*)
5. $\overline{PS} \cong \overline{RS}$ (CPCTC)
6. $PS = RS$ (Def. of $\cong$)

21, 23. See p. A16.

4-6 PRACTICE A

4-6 PRACTICE C

4-6 PRACTICE B

1. Heike Drescher set the Woman's World Junior Record for the long jump in 1983. She jumped about 23.4 feet. The diagram shows two triangles and a pond. Explain whether Heike could have jumped the pond along path *BA* or along path *CA*. Possible answer:

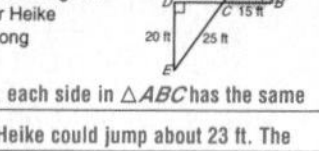

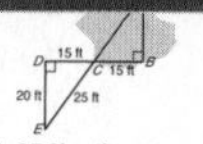

Because the triangles are congruent by ASA, each side in $\triangle ABC$ has the same length as its corresponding side in $\triangle EDC$. Heike could jump about 23 ft. The distance along path *BA* is 20 ft, so Heike could have jumped this distance. The distance along path *CA* is 25 ft, so Heike could not have jumped this distance.

Write a flowchart proof.

2. **Given:** $\angle L \cong \angle J$, $\overline{KJ} \parallel \overline{LM}$
Prove: $\angle LKM \cong \angle JMK$

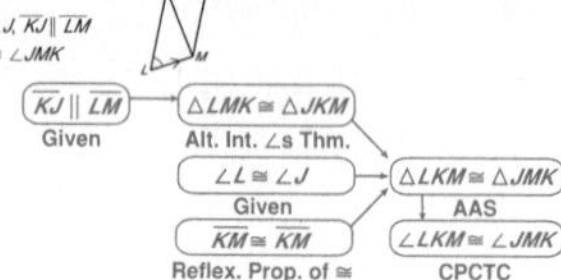

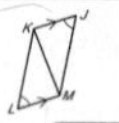

Write a two-column proof.

3. **Given:** *FGHI* is a rectangle. 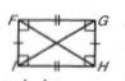
Prove: The diagonals of a rectangle have equal lengths. Possible answer:

Statements	Reasons
1. *FGHI* is a rectangle.	1. Given
2. $\overline{FI} \cong \overline{GH}$, $\angle I$ and $\angle H$ are right angles.	2. Def. of rectangle
3. $\angle I \cong \angle H$	3. Rt. $\angle \cong$ Thm.
4. $\overline{IH} \cong \overline{IH}$	4. Reflex. Prop. of $\cong$
5. $\triangle FIH \cong \triangle GHI$	5. SAS
6. $\overline{FH} \cong \overline{GI}$	6. CPCTC
7. $FH = GI$	7. Def. of $\cong$ segs.

16. This problem will prepare you for the Multi-Step Test Prep on page 280.
The front of a doghouse has the dimensions shown.
 a. How can you prove that $\triangle ADB \cong \triangle ADC$? **HL**
 b. Prove that $\overline{BD} \cong \overline{CD}$.
 c. What is the length of $\overline{BD}$ and $\overline{BC}$ to the nearest tenth? **17.3 in.; 34.6 in.**

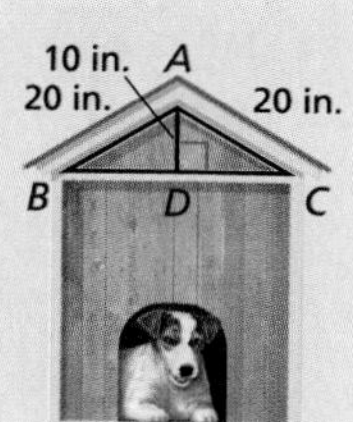

Multi-Step Find the value of *x*.

17. **14**

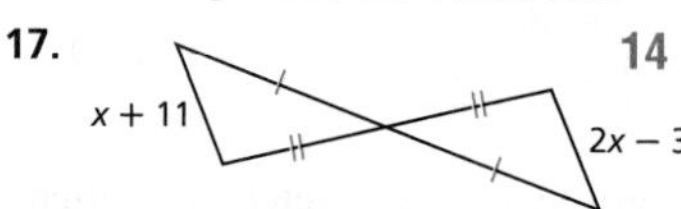

18. **21**

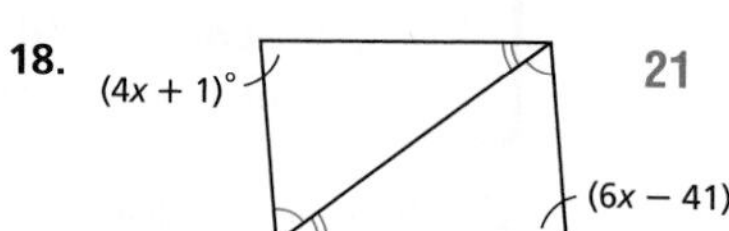

Use the diagram for Exercises 19–21.

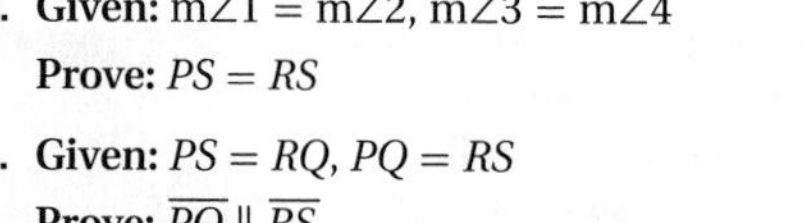

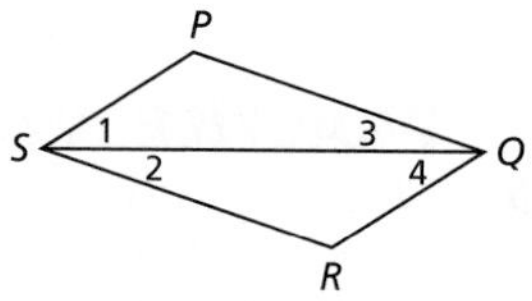

19. **Given:** $PS = RQ$, $m\angle 1 = m\angle 4$
Prove: $m\angle 3 = m\angle 2$

20. **Given:** $m\angle 1 = m\angle 2$, $m\angle 3 = m\angle 4$
Prove: $PS = RS$

21. **Given:** $PS = RQ$, $PQ = RS$
Prove: $\overline{PQ} \parallel \overline{RS}$

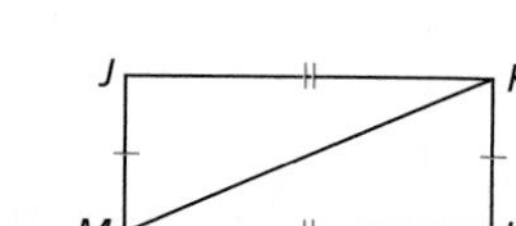

22. **Critical Thinking** Does the diagram contain enough information to allow you to conclude that $\overline{JK} \parallel \overline{ML}$? Explain.

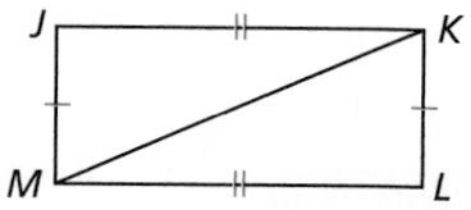

22. Yes; $\triangle JKM \cong \triangle LMK$ by SSS, so $\angle JKM \cong \angle LMK$ by CPCTC. Therefore $\overline{JK} \parallel \overline{ML}$ by the Conv. of the Alt. Int. $\angle$s Thm.

23. **Write About It** Draw a diagram and explain how a surveyor can set up triangles to find the distance across a lake. Label each part of your diagram. List which sides or angles must be congruent.

24. Which of these will NOT be used as a reason in a proof of $\overline{AC} \cong \overline{AD}$?
 (A) SAS
 (B) CPCTC
 (C) ASA
 (D) Reflexive Property

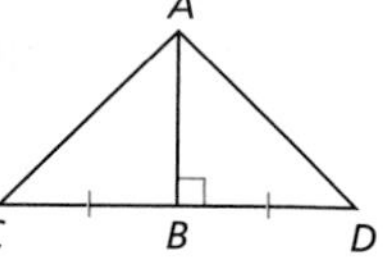

25. Given the points $K(1, 2)$, $L(0, -4)$, $M(-2, -3)$, and $N(-1, 3)$, which of these is true?
 (F) $\angle KNL \cong \angle MNL$
 (G) $\angle LNK \cong \angle NLM$
 (H) $\angle MLN \cong \angle KLN$
 (J) $\angle MNK \cong \angle NKL$

26. What is the value of *y*? 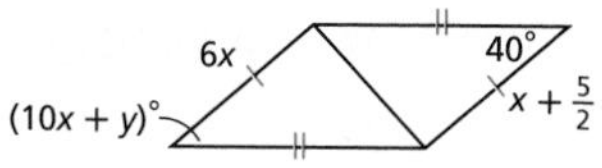
 (A) 10
 (B) 20
 (C) 35
 (D) 85

6x
40°
$(10x + y)°$
$x + \frac{5}{2}$

27. Which of these are NOT used to prove angles congruent?
 (F) congruent triangles
 (G) noncorresponding parts
 (H) parallel lines
 (J) perpendicular lines

4-6 READING STRATEGIES

An **acronym** is a word formed from the first letters of a phrase. For example, ASAP stands for "As Soon As Possible." Acronyms can also combine the first letters or series of letters in a series of words, as in *radar*, which stands for **ra**dio **d**etecting **a**nd **r**anging.

One acronym used in geometry is CPCTC.
Look at the breakdown of this acronym:

C P C T C

Corresponding
Parts of
Congruent
Triangles are
Congruent

1. What are some reasons you would use an acronym?
to abbreviate or make a statement simpler to understand or remember

2. What are some other acronyms you have used in your everyday life?
Answers will vary. Students may mention FBI, IRS, RSVP, FAQ, or others that are popular in text messaging.

Examine the figure and answer the question.

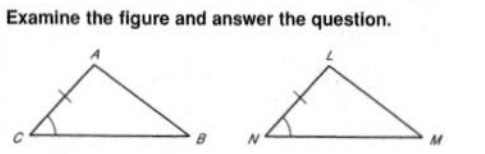

3. In this triangle, $\angle C \cong \angle N$ and $\overline{AC} \cong \overline{LN}$. Assume that $\triangle ABC \cong \triangle LMN$. Name four other parts that are congruent using CPCTC.
$\angle B \cong \angle M$; $\angle A \cong \angle L$; $\overline{CB} \cong \overline{NM}$; $\overline{AB} \cong \overline{LM}$

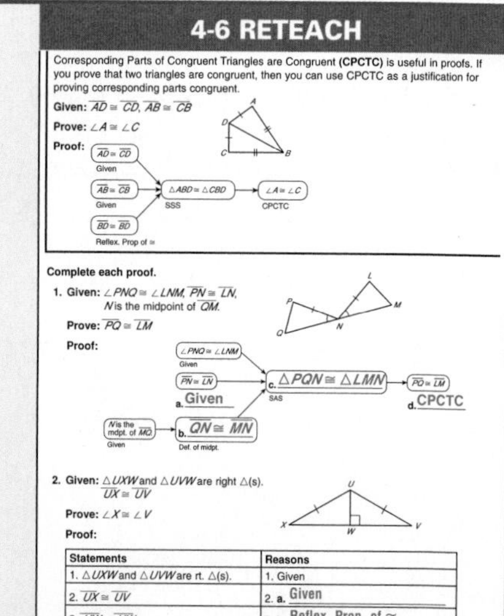

4-6 RETEACH

Corresponding Parts of Congruent Triangles are Congruent **(CPCTC)** is useful in proofs. If you prove that two triangles are congruent, then you can use CPCTC as a justification for proving corresponding parts congruent.

Given: $\overline{AD} \cong \overline{CD}$, $\overline{AB} \cong \overline{CB}$
Prove: $\angle A \cong \angle C$
Proof: $\overline{AD} \cong \overline{CD}$ (Given); $\overline{AB} \cong \overline{CB}$ (Given); $\overline{BD} \cong \overline{BD}$ (Reflex. Prop of $\cong$) → $\triangle ABD \cong \triangle CBD$ (SSS) → $\angle A \cong \angle C$ (CPCTC)

Complete each proof.

1. **Given:** $\angle PNQ \cong \angle LNM$, $\overline{PN} \cong \overline{LN}$, *N* is the midpoint of $\overline{QM}$.
Prove: $\overline{PQ} \cong \overline{LM}$
Proof: $\angle PNQ \cong \angle LNM$ (Given); $\overline{PN} \cong \overline{LN}$ (a. Given); *N* is the mdpt. of $\overline{MQ}$ (Given) → b. $\overline{QN} \cong \overline{MN}$ (Def. of mdpt.) → c. $\triangle PQN \cong \triangle LMN$ (SAS) → $\overline{PQ} \cong \overline{LM}$ (d. CPCTC)

2. **Given:** $\triangle UXW$ and $\triangle UVW$ are right $\triangle$(s). $\overline{UX} \cong \overline{UV}$
Prove: $\angle X \cong \angle V$
Proof:

Statements	Reasons
1. $\triangle UXW$ and $\triangle UVW$ are rt. $\triangle$(s).	1. Given
2. $\overline{UX} \cong \overline{UV}$	2. a. Given
3. $\overline{UW} \cong \overline{UW}$	3. b. Reflex. Prop. of $\cong$
4. c. $\triangle UXM \cong \triangle UVW$	4. d. HL
5. $\angle X \cong \angle V$	5. e. CPCTC

28. Which set of coordinates represents the vertices of a triangle congruent to $\triangle RST$? (*Hint:* Find the lengths of the sides of $\triangle RST$.)

Ⓐ (3, 4), (3, 0), (0, 0) Ⓒ (3, 1), (3, 3), (4, 6)
Ⓑ (3, 3), (0, 4), (0, 0) Ⓓ (3, 0), (4, 4), (0, 6)

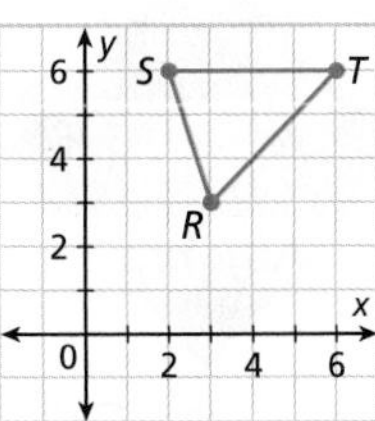

CHALLENGE AND EXTEND

29. Any diag. on any face of the cube is the hyp. of a rt. △ whose legs are edges of the cube. Any 2 of these △ are ≅ by SAS. Therefore any 2 diags. are ≅ by CPCTC.

29. All of the edges of a cube are congruent. All of the angles on each face of a cube are right angles. Use CPCTC to explain why any two diagonals on the faces of a cube (for example, $\overline{AC}$ and $\overline{AF}$) must be congruent.

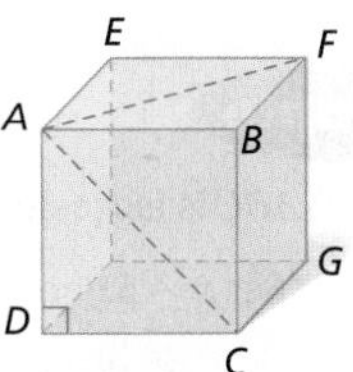

30. **Given:** $\overline{JK} \cong \overline{ML}$, $\overline{JM} \cong \overline{KL}$
Prove: $\angle J \cong \angle L$
(*Hint:* Draw an auxiliary line.)

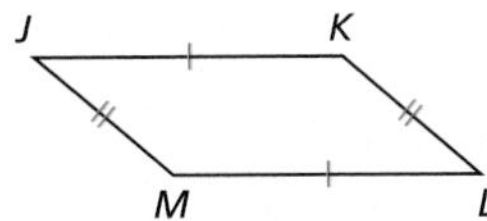

31. **Given:** R is the midpoint of $\overline{AB}$.
S is the midpoint of $\overline{DC}$.
$\overline{RS} \perp \overline{AB}$, $\angle ASD \cong \angle BSC$
Prove: $\triangle ASD \cong \triangle BSC$

32. $\triangle ABC$ is in plane $\mathcal{M}$. $\triangle CDE$ is in plane $\mathcal{P}$. Both planes have C in common and $\angle A \cong \angle E$. What is the height AB to the nearest foot? **18 ft**

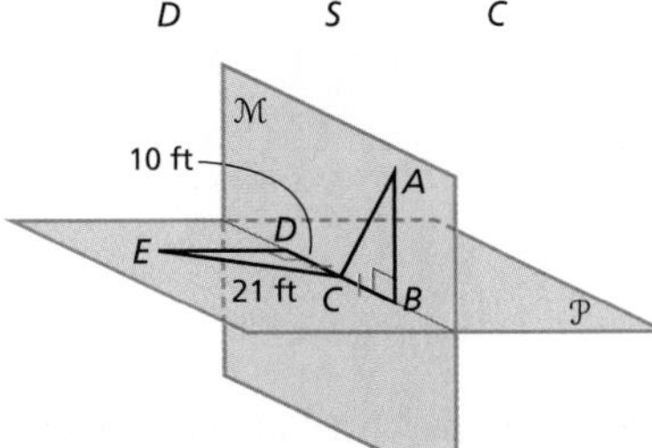

SPIRAL REVIEW

33. Lina's test scores in her history class are 90, 84, 93, 88, and 91. What is the minimum score Lina must make on her next test to have an average test score of 90? *(Previous course)* **94**

34. One long-distance phone plan costs \$3.95 per month plus \$0.08 per minute of use. A second long-distance plan costs \$0.10 per minute for the first 50 minutes used each month and then \$0.15 per minute after that. Which plan is cheaper if you use an average of 75 long-distance minutes per month? *(Previous course)*
The second plan is cheaper.

A figure has vertices at (1, 3), (2, 2), (3, 2), and (4, 3). Identify the transformation of the figure that produces an image with each set of vertices. *(Lesson 1-7)*

35. (1, −3), (2, −2), (3, −2), (4, −3)

36. (−2, −1), (−1, −2), (0, −2), (1, −1)

37. Determine if you can use ASA to prove $\triangle ACB \cong \triangle ECD$. Explain. *(Lesson 4-5)*

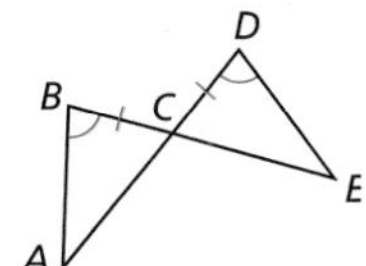

35. reflection across the x-axis

36. translation $(x, y) \rightarrow (x - 3, y - 4)$

37. Yes; it is given that $\angle B \cong \angle D$ and $\overline{BC} \cong \overline{DC}$. By the Vert. ∠ Thm., $\angle BCA \cong \angle DCE$. Therefore $\triangle ABC \cong \triangle EDC$ by ASA.

Answers

30. 1. Draw $\overline{MK}$. (Through any 2 pts. there is exactly 1 line.)
2. $\overline{KM} \cong \overline{MK}$ (Reflex. Prop. of ≅)
3. $\overline{JK} \cong \overline{LM}$, $\overline{JM} = \overline{LK}$ (Given)
4. $\triangle JKM = \triangle LMK$ (SSS *Steps 2, 3*)
5. $\angle J \cong \angle L$ (CPCTC)

Journal

Have students explain what CPCTC means. They should include an example with their explanation.

ALTERNATIVE ASSESSMENT

Have students work in small groups to create an example where they must first prove triangles congruent in order to reach a required conclusion.

Power Presentations with PowerPoint®

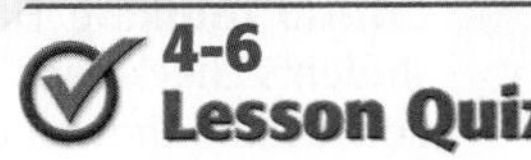

4-6 Lesson Quiz

1. **Given:** Isosceles $\triangle PQR$, base $\overline{QR}$, $\overline{PA} \cong \overline{PB}$
Prove: $\overline{AR} \cong \overline{BQ}$

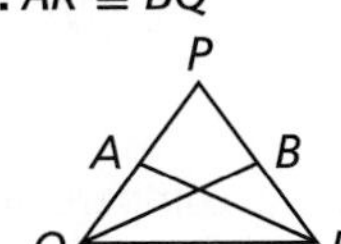

1. Isosc. $\triangle PQR$, base $\overline{QR}$ (Given)
2. $PQ = PR$ (Def. of Isosc. △)
3. $PA = PB$ (Given)
4. $\angle P \cong \angle P$ (Reflex. Prop. of ≅)
5. $\triangle QPB \cong \triangle RPA$ (SAS *Steps 2, 4, 3*)
6. $AR = BQ$ (CPCTC)

2. **Given:** X is the midpoint of $\overline{AC}$. $\angle 1 \cong \angle 2$
Prove: X is the midpoint of $\overline{BD}$.

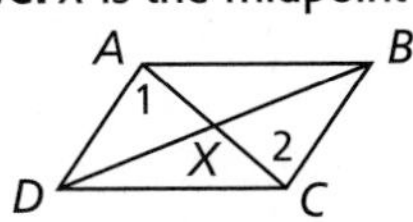

1. X is mdpt. of $\overline{AC}$. $\angle 1 \cong \angle 2$ (Given)
2. $AX = CX$ (Def. of mdpt.)
3. $\overline{AX} \cong \overline{CX}$ (Def. of ≅)
4. $\angle AXD \cong \angle CXB$ (Vert. ∠s Thm.)
5. $\triangle AXD \cong \triangle CXB$ (ASA *Steps 1, 4, 5*)
6. $\overline{DX} \cong \overline{BX}$ (CPCTC)
7. $DX = BX$ (Def. of ≅)
8. X is mdpt. of $\overline{BD}$. (Def. of mdpt.)

3. Use the given set of points to prove $\triangle DEF \cong \triangle GHJ$: $D(-4, 4)$, $E(-2, 1)$, $F(-6, 1)$, $G(3, 1)$, $H(5, -2)$, $J(1, -2)$.
$DE = GH = \sqrt{13}$, $DF = GJ = \sqrt{13}$, $EF = HJ = 4$, and $\triangle DEF \cong \triangle GHJ$ by SSS.

Also available on transparency

4-6 PROBLEM SOLVING

1. Two triangular plates are congruent. The area of one of the plates is 60 square inches. What is the area of the other plate? Explain.
$60\ in^2$; Since the triangles are ≅, they have the same measures. So, the triangles also have the same areas.

2. An archaeologist draws the triangles to find the distance XY across a ravine. What is XY? Explain.
82 m; $\triangle UVW \cong \triangle XYW$ by SAS, so $\overline{UV} \cong \overline{XY}$ by CPCTC. Therefore $UV = XY = 82$ m.

3. A city planner sets up the triangles to find the distance RS across a river. Describe the steps that she can use to find RS.
$\angle P \cong \angle R$ because they are both rt. △. $\overline{PQ} \cong \overline{RQ}$ because $PQ = RQ = 65$ ft. $\angle NQP \cong \angle SQR$ because vert. △ are ≅. Therefore $\angle NPQ \cong \angle SRQ$ by ASA. By CPCTC, $\overline{NP} \cong \overline{SR}$. So $SR = NP = 40$ ft.

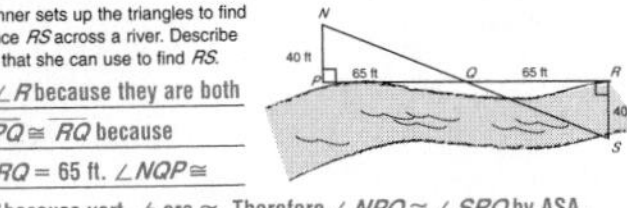

Choose the best answer.

4. A lighthouse and the range of its shining light are shown. What can you conclude?
Ⓐ $x = y$ by CPCTC C $\angle AED \cong \angle ADE$ by CPCTC
B $x = 2y$ D $\angle AED \cong \angle ACB$

5. A rectangular piece of cloth 15 centimeters long is cut along a diagonal to form two triangles. One of the triangles has a side length of 9 centimeters. Which is a true statement?
F The second triangle has an angle measure of 15° by CPCTC.
Ⓖ The second triangle has a side length of 9 centimeters by CPCTC.
H You cannot make a conclusion about the side length of the second triangle.
J The triangles are not congruent.

6. Small sandwiches are cut in the shape of right triangles. The longest sides of all the sandwiches are 3 inches. One sandwich has a side length of 2 inches. Which is a true statement?
A All the sandwiches have a side length of 2 inches by CPCTC.
B All the sandwiches are isosceles triangles with side lengths of 2 inches.
C None of the other sandwiches have side lengths of 2 inches.
Ⓓ You cannot make a conclusion using CPCTC.

Answers

31. 1. R is the mdpt. of $\overline{AB}$. (Given)
2. $\overline{AR} \cong \overline{BR}$ (Def. of mdpt.)
3. $\overline{RS} \perp \overline{AB}$ (Given)
4. $\angle ARS$ and $\angle BRS$ are rt. ∠s. (Def. of ⊥)
5. $\angle ARS \cong \angle BRS$ (Rt. ∠ ≅ Thm.)
6. $\overline{RS} \cong \overline{RS}$ (Reflex. Prop. of ≅)
7. $\triangle ARS \cong \triangle BRS$ (SAS *Steps 2, 5, 6*)
8. $\overline{AS} \cong \overline{BS}$ (CPCTC)
9. $\angle ASD \cong \angle BSC$ (Given)
10. S is the mdpt. of $\overline{DC}$. (Given)
11. $\overline{DS} = \overline{CS}$ (Def. of mdpt.)
12. $\triangle ASD \cong \triangle BSC$ (SAS *Steps 8, 9, 11*)

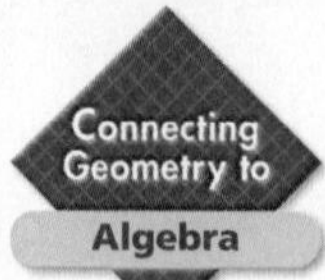

Organizer

Pacing:
Traditional $\frac{1}{2}$ day
Block $\frac{1}{4}$ day

Objective: Solve quadratic equations to find the length of a side of a triangle.

 **Online Edition**

 **Countdown Week 9**

Teach

Remember

Students review and apply the methods of solving quadratic equations.

 **Critical Thinking** Have students check each solution. Even if the value of x is negative, a length of the side cannot be negative.

Close

Assess

Have students compare and contrast the two methods used for finding the value of the variable.

State Resources

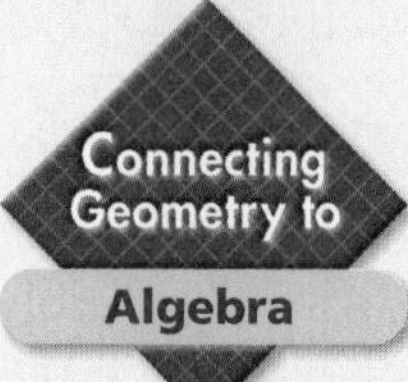

Quadratic Equations

A quadratic equation is an equation that can be written in the form $ax^2 + bx + c = 0$.

Example

Given: $\triangle ABC$ is isosceles with $\overline{AB} \cong \overline{AC}$. Solve for x.

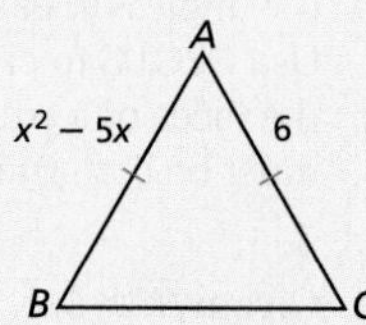

Step 1 Set $x^2 - 5x$ equal to 6 to get $x^2 - 5x = 6$.

Step 2 Rewrite the quadratic equation by subtracting 6 from each side to get $x^2 - 5x - 6 = 0$.

Step 3 Solve for x.

Method 1: Factoring		Method 2: Quadratic Formula	
$x^2 - 5x - 6 = 0$		$x = \frac{-b \pm \sqrt{b^2 - 4ac}}{2a}$	
$(x-6)(x+1) = 0$	*Factor.*	$x = \frac{-(-5) \pm \sqrt{(-5)^2 - 4(1)(-6)}}{2(1)}$	*Substitute 1 for a, −5 for b, and −6 for c.*
$x - 6 = 0$ or $x + 1 = 0$	*Set each factor equal to 0.*	$x = \frac{5 \pm \sqrt{49}}{2}$	*Simplify.*
$x = 6$ or $x = -1$	*Solve.*	$x = \frac{5 \pm 7}{2}$	*Find the square root.*
		$x = \frac{12}{2}$ or $x = \frac{-2}{2}$	*Simplify.*
		$x = 6$ or $x = -1$	

Step 4 Check each solution in the original equation.

$x^2 - 5x$	$= 6$
$(6)^2 - 5(6)$	6
$36 - 30$	6
6	6 ✓

$x^2 - 5x$	$= 6$
$(-1)^2 - 5(-1)$	6
$1 + 5$	6
6	6 ✓

Try This

Solve for x in each isosceles triangle.

1. **Given: $\overline{FE} \cong \overline{FG}$**
   6 or −3

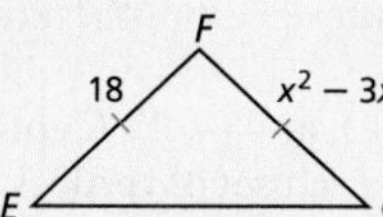

2. **Given: $\overline{JK} \cong \overline{JL}$**
   −6 or 2

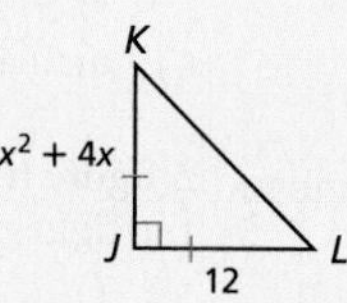

3. **Given: $\overline{YX} \cong \overline{YZ}$**
   6 or −2

Y
12
Z
$x^2 - 4x$
X

4. **Given: $\overline{QP} \cong \overline{QR}$**
   −3 or 1

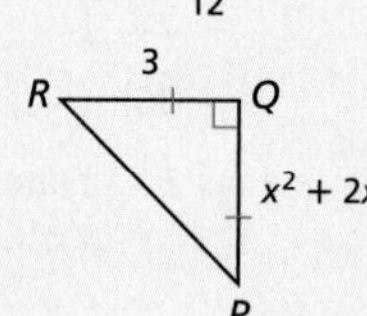

4-7 Introduction to Coordinate Proof

Objectives
Position figures in the coordinate plane for use in coordinate proofs.

Prove geometric concepts by using coordinate proof.

Vocabulary
coordinate proof

Who uses this?
The Bushmen in South Africa use the Global Positioning System to transmit data about endangered animals to conservationists. (See Exercise 24.)

You have used coordinate geometry to find the midpoint of a line segment and to find the distance between two points. Coordinate geometry can also be used to prove conjectures.

A **coordinate proof** is a style of proof that uses coordinate geometry and algebra. The first step of a coordinate proof is to position the given figure in the plane. You can use any position, but some strategies can make the steps of the proof simpler.

Strategies for Positioning Figures in the Coordinate Plane

- Use the origin as a vertex, keeping the figure in Quadrant I.
- Center the figure at the origin.
- Center a side of the figure at the origin.
- Use one or both axes as sides of the figure.

EXAMPLE 1 Positioning a Figure in the Coordinate Plane

Position a rectangle with a length of 8 units and a width of 3 units in the coordinate plane.

Method 1 You can center the longer side of the rectangle at the origin.

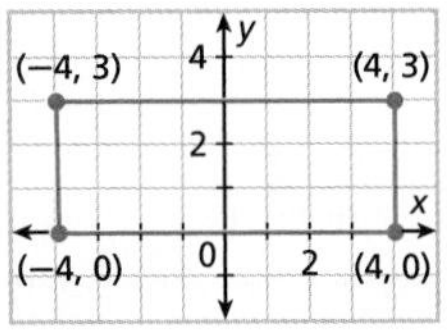

(−4, 3) (4, 3) (−4, 0) (4, 0)

Method 2 You can use the origin as a vertex of the rectangle.

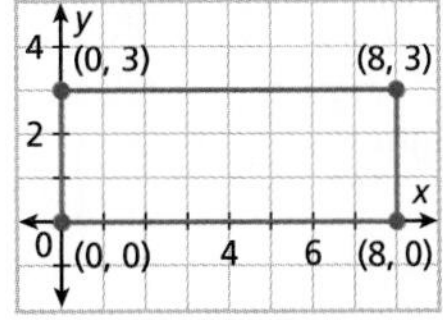

Depending on what you are using the figure to prove, one solution may be better than the other. For example, if you need to find the midpoint of the longer side, use the first solution.

1. Position a right triangle with leg lengths of 2 and 4 units in the coordinate plane. (*Hint:* Use the origin as the vertex of the right angle.)

4-7 Organizer

Pacing: Traditional 2 days
Block 1 day

Objectives: Position figures in the coordinate plane for use in coordinate proofs.

Prove geometric concepts by using coordinate proof.

Online Edition
Tutorial Videos

Countdown Week 9

Power Presentations with PowerPoint®

Warm Up

Evaluate.

1. Find the midpoint between $(0, 2x)$ and $(2y, 2z)$. $(y, x + z)$
2. One leg of a right triangle has length 12, and the hypotenuse has length 13. What is the length of the other leg? 5
3. Find the distance between $(0, a)$ and $(0, b)$, where $b > a$. $b - a$

Also available on transparency

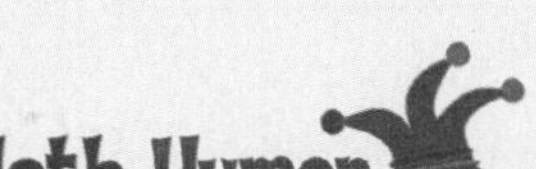

Q: What do you call a broken angle?

A: A rectangle!

Answers to *Check it Out!*

1. See p. A16.

1 Introduce

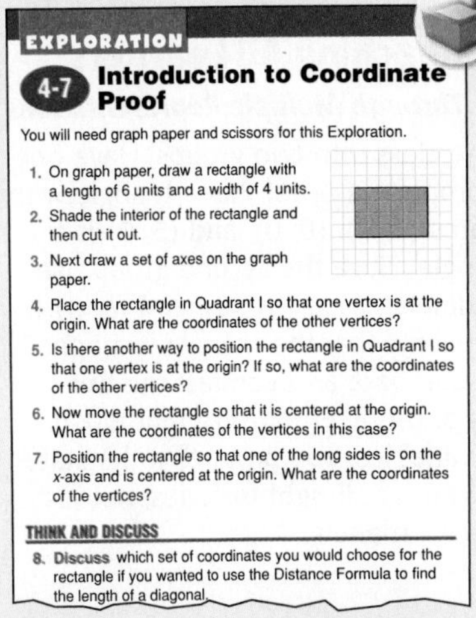

EXPLORATION

4-7 Introduction to Coordinate Proof

You will need graph paper and scissors for this Exploration.

1. On graph paper, draw a rectangle with a length of 6 units and a width of 4 units.
2. Shade the interior of the rectangle and then cut it out.
3. Next draw a set of axes on the graph paper.
4. Place the rectangle in Quadrant I so that one vertex is at the origin. What are the coordinates of the other vertices?
5. Is there another way to position the rectangle in Quadrant I so that one vertex is at the origin? If so, what are the coordinates of the other vertices?
6. Now move the rectangle so that it is centered at the origin. What are the coordinates of the vertices in this case?
7. Position the rectangle so that one of the long sides is on the x-axis and is centered at the origin. What are the coordinates of the vertices?

THINK AND DISCUSS

8. **Discuss** which set of coordinates you would choose for the rectangle if you wanted to use the Distance Formula to find the length of a diagonal.

Motivate

Relate coordinate proofs to other methods of proofs students have used. Point out that they will use algebra and what they already know about triangles in the coordinate plane in this geometric proof. Make transparencies of graph paper so students can display their work on the overhead projector as they discuss coordinate proofs.

Explorations and answers are provided in *Alternate Openers: Explorations Transparencies.*

State Resources

go.hrw.com
State Resources Online
KEYWORD: MG7 Resources

Power Presentations with PowerPoint®

Additional Examples

Example 1

Position a square with a side length of 6 units in the coordinate plane. Possible answer:

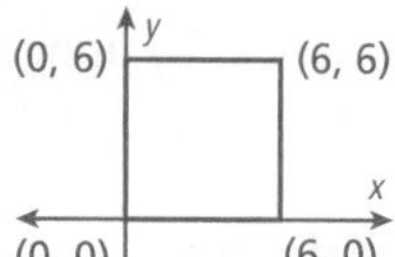

Example 2

Write a coordinate proof.

Given: Rectangle $ABCD$ with $A(0, 0)$, $B(4, 0)$, $C(4, 10)$, and $D(0, 10)$

Prove: The diagonals bisect each other.

Mdpt. of $\overline{AC}$ is (2, 5). Mdpt. of $\overline{BD}$ is also (2, 5). Therefore the diags. bisect each other.

Example 3

Position each figure in the coordinate plane and give the coordinates of each vertex.

A. rectangle with width m and length twice the width

Possible answer:

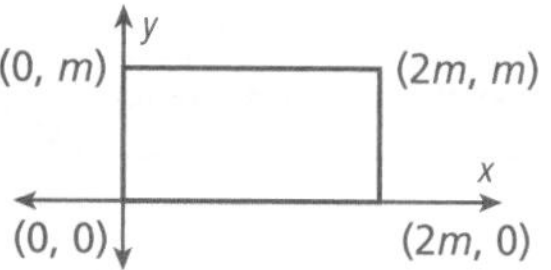

B. right triangle with legs of lengths s and t

Possible answer:

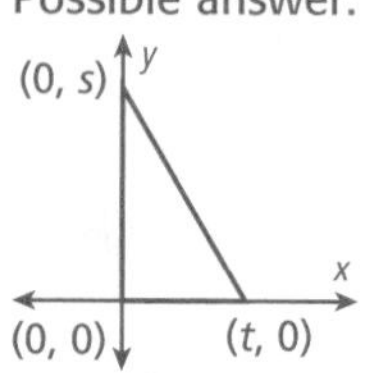

Once the figure is placed in the coordinate plane, you can use slope, the coordinates of the vertices, the Distance Formula, or the Midpoint Formula to prove statements about the figure.

EXAMPLE 2 Writing a Proof Using Coordinate Geometry

Write a coordinate proof.

Given: Right $\triangle ABC$ has vertices $A(0, 6)$, $B(0, 0)$, and $C(4, 0)$. D is the midpoint of $\overline{AC}$.

Prove: The area of $\triangle DBC$ is one half the area of $\triangle ABC$.

Proof: $\triangle ABC$ is a right triangle with height AB and base BC.

area of $\triangle ABC = \frac{1}{2}bh$

$= \frac{1}{2}(4)(6) = 12$ square units

By the Midpoint Formula, the coordinates of $D = \left(\frac{0+4}{2}, \frac{6+0}{2}\right) = (2, 3)$. The y-coordinate of D is the height of $\triangle DBC$, and the base is 4 units.

area of $\triangle DBC = \frac{1}{2}bh$

$= \frac{1}{2}(4)(3) = 6$ square units

Since $6 = \frac{1}{2}(12)$, the area of $\triangle DBC$ is one half the area of $\triangle ABC$.

2. Use the information in Example 2 to write a coordinate proof showing that the area of $\triangle ADB$ is one half the area of $\triangle ABC$.

A coordinate proof can also be used to prove that a certain relationship is always true. You can prove that a statement is true for all right triangles without knowing the side lengths. To do this, assign variables as the coordinates of the vertices.

EXAMPLE 3 Assigning Coordinates to Vertices

Caution!

Do not use both axes when positioning a figure unless you know the figure has a right angle.

Position each figure in the coordinate plane and give the coordinates of each vertex.

A a right triangle with leg lengths a and b

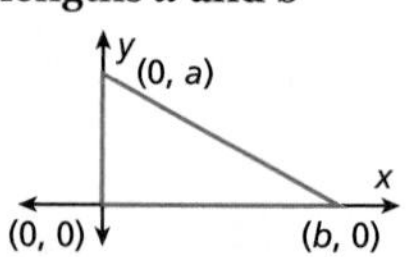

B a rectangle with length c and width d

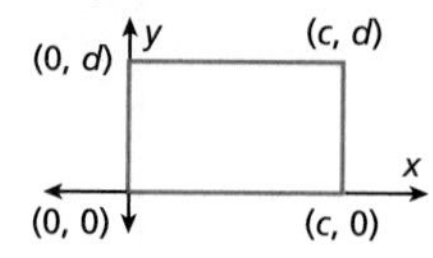

3. Position a square with side length $4p$ in the coordinate plane and give the coordinates of each vertex.

If a coordinate proof requires calculations with fractions, choose coordinates that make the calculations simpler. For example, use multiples of 2 when you are to find coordinates of a midpoint. Once you have assigned the coordinates of the vertices, the procedure for the proof is the same, except that your calculations will involve variables.

INTERVENTION

Questioning Strategies

EXAMPLES 1–3

- How do you decide which strategy to use to position a figure in a coordinate plane? What are the advantages of each position?

Answers to Check it Out!

2–3. See p. A16.

2 Teach

Guided Instruction

Discuss how to position figures in the coordinate plane. Show students how to assign convenient variable coordinates to vertices. Have students review the Distance and Midpoint Formulas before using them in coordinate proofs.

Social Studies René Descartes, a 17th century mathematician and philosopher, first developed the coordinate plane to make it easier to describe the position of objects.

Reaching All Learners

Through Multiple Representations

Divide the class into two groups. Have one group complete a proof that a triangle with coordinates (0, 4), (0, 0), and (3, 0) is a right triangle. Have the second group use the coordinates (0, a), (0, 0), and (b, 0) and then verify that the triangle is a right triangle. Compare and contrast the two methods of proof. Emphasize that when you use variables, you prove that the statement is true for all right triangles, not just for a specific triangle.

EXAMPLE 4 Writing a Coordinate Proof

Given: $\angle B$ is a right angle in $\triangle ABC$. D is the midpoint of $\overline{AC}$.
Prove: The area of $\triangle DBC$ is one half the area of $\triangle ABC$.

Step 1 Assign coordinates to each vertex.
The coordinates of A are $(0, 2j)$,
the coordinates of B are $(0, 0)$,
and the coordinates of C are $(2n, 0)$.

Since you will use the Midpoint Formula to find the coordinates of D, use multiples of 2 for the leg lengths.

Step 2 Position the figure in the coordinate plane.

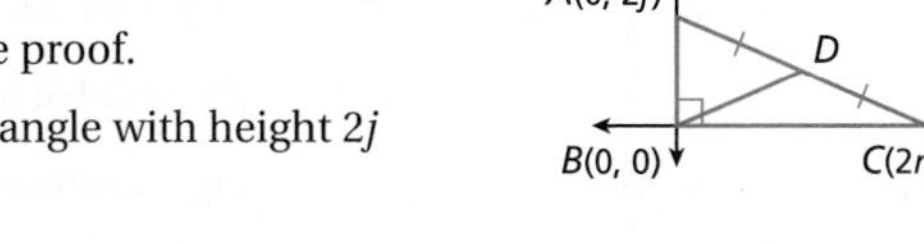

Step 3 Write a coordinate proof.

Proof: $\triangle ABC$ is a right triangle with height $2j$ and base $2n$.

$$\text{area of } \triangle ABC = \frac{1}{2}bh$$
$$= \frac{1}{2}(2n)(2j)$$
$$= 2nj \text{ square units}$$

By the Midpoint Formula, the coordinates of $D = \left(\frac{0 + 2n}{2}, \frac{2j + 0}{2}\right) = (n, j)$.

The height of $\triangle DBC$ is j units, and the base is $2n$ units.

$$\text{area of } \triangle DBC = \frac{1}{2}bh$$
$$= \frac{1}{2}(2n)(j)$$
$$= nj \text{ square units}$$

Since $nj = \frac{1}{2}(2nj)$, the area of $\triangle DBC$ is one half the area of $\triangle ABC$.

Remember!

Because the x- and y-axes intersect at right angles, they can be used to form the sides of a right triangle.

4. Use the information in Example 4 to write a coordinate proof showing that the area of $\triangle ADB$ is one half the area of $\triangle ABC$.

THINK AND DISCUSS

1. When writing a coordinate proof why are variables used instead of numbers as coordinates for the vertices of a figure?
2. How does the way you position a figure in the coordinate plane affect your calculations in a coordinate proof?
3. Explain why it might be useful to assign $2p$ as a coordinate instead of just p.

4. **GET ORGANIZED** Copy and complete the graphic organizer. In each row, draw an example of each strategy that might be used when positioning a figure for a coordinate proof.

Positioning Strategy	Example
Use origin as a vertex.	
Center figure at origin.	
Center side of figure at origin.	
Use axes as sides of figure.	

COMMON ERROR ALERT

In **Example 2,** students may want to use $\overline{AC}$ as the base and $\overline{BD}$ as the height. Remind students that in a right triangle, either leg can be the base and the other leg the height.

Algebra Remind students that when finding the midpoint, they can simplify by factoring. For example, $\frac{2a + 2b}{2} = \frac{2(a + b)}{2} = a + b$.

Inclusion Point out that students are not to choose coordinates that are "special" when doing proofs. For example, they should not choose the vertices of a rectangle so that it is a square. They should use coordinates that make the figure a nonsquare rectangle.

Power Presentations with PowerPoint®

Additional Examples

Example 4

Given: Rectangle $PQRS$
Prove: The diagonals are $\cong$.

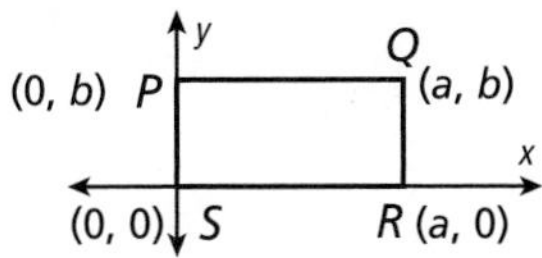

$PR = \sqrt{a^2 + b^2}$, and $QS = \sqrt{a^2 + b^2}$. Thus the diagonals are $\cong$.

INTERVENTION
Questioning Strategies

EXAMPLE 4

- How is the figure placed in the coordinate plane? Why?

3 Close

Summarize

Review the strategies for positioning figures in the coordinate plane. Remind students to choose coordinates that make calculations simpler. Advise students to use variables instead of numbers as coordinates for the vertices of a figure when doing a proof.

ONGOING ASSESSMENT

and INTERVENTION

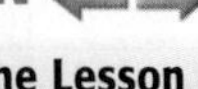

Diagnose ***Before*** **the Lesson**
4-7 Warm Up, TE p. 267

Monitor ***During*** **the Lesson**
Check It Out! Exercises, SE pp. 267–269
Questioning Strategies, TE pp. 268–269

Assess ***After*** **the Lesson**
4-7 Lesson Quiz, TE p. 272
Alternative Assessment, TE p. 272

Answers to *Check it Out!*

4. See p. A16.

Answers to *Think and Discuss*

1. Possible answer: By using variables, your results are not limited to specific numbers.
2. Possible answer: The way you position the figure will affect the coords. assigned to the vertices and therefore your calculations.
3. Possible answer: If you need to calculate the coords. of a mdpt., assigning $2p$ allows you to avoid using fractions.
4. See p. A4.

4-7 Exercises

Assignment Guide

Assign *Guided Practice* exercises as necessary.

If you finished Examples **1–2**
Basic 8–10, 15–17, 21
Average 8–10, 15–17, 20–22
Advanced 8–10, 15–17, 20–24

If you finished Examples **1–4**
Basic 8–13, 15–21, 26–30, 35–40
Average 8–15, 21, 22, 25–32, 35–40
Advanced 8–15, 21–40

Homework Quick Check
Quickly check key concepts.
Exercises: 8, 10, 12, 13, 15

Answers

2. Possible answer:

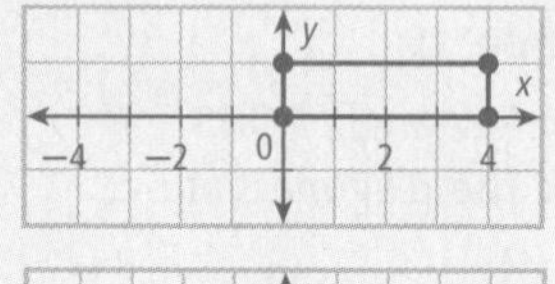

3.

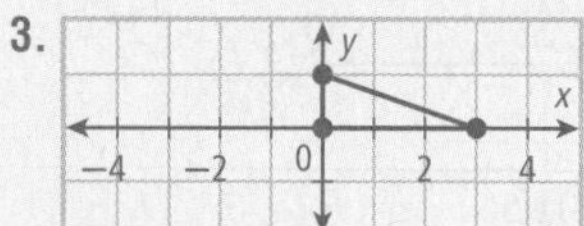

5. Possible answer:

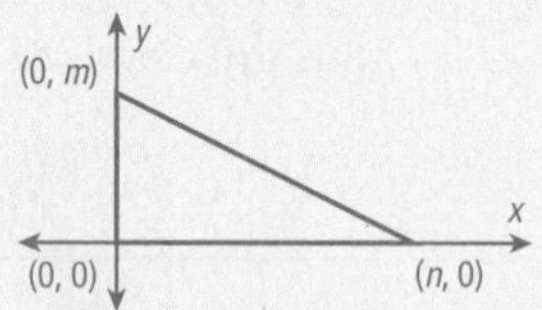

4, 6–13. See pp. A16–A17.

State Resources

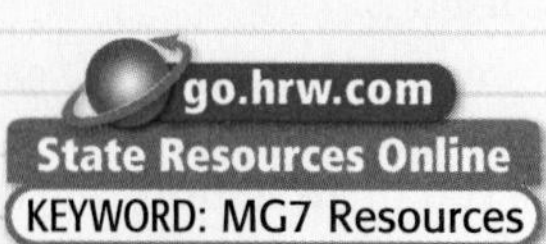

4-7 Exercises

go.hrw.com
Homework Help Online
KEYWORD: MG7 4-7
Parent Resources Online
KEYWORD: MG7 Parent

GUIDED PRACTICE

1. **Vocabulary** What is the relationship between *coordinate geometry, coordinate plane,* and *coordinate proof*? Possible answer: In coord. geometry, a coord. proof is a proof in which you place figures in the coord. plane to prove a result.

SEE EXAMPLE 1 p. 267

Position each figure in the coordinate plane.

2. a rectangle with a length of 4 units and width of 1 unit
3. a right triangle with leg lengths of 1 unit and 3 units

SEE EXAMPLE 2 p. 268

Write a proof using coordinate geometry.

4. **Given:** Right $\triangle PQR$ has coordinates $P(0, 6)$, $Q(8, 0)$, and $R(0, 0)$. A is the midpoint of $\overline{PR}$. B is the midpoint of $\overline{QR}$.
Prove: $AB = \frac{1}{2}PQ$

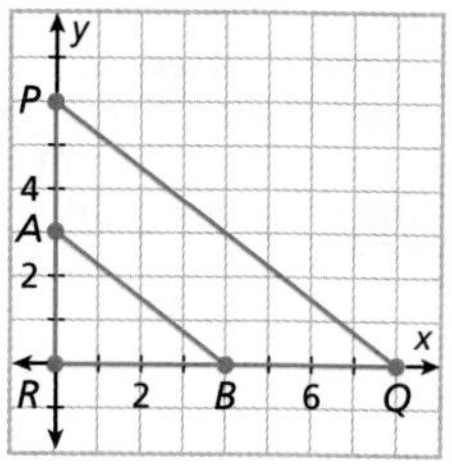

SEE EXAMPLE 3 p. 268

Position each figure in the coordinate plane and give the coordinates of each vertex.

5. a right triangle with leg lengths m and n
6. a rectangle with length a and width b

SEE EXAMPLE 4 p. 269

Multi-Step **Assign coordinates to each vertex and write a coordinate proof.**

7. **Given:** $\angle R$ is a right angle in $\triangle PQR$. A is the midpoint of $\overline{PR}$. B is the midpoint of $\overline{QR}$.
Prove: $AB = \frac{1}{2}PQ$

PRACTICE AND PROBLEM SOLVING

Independent Practice

For Exercises	See Example
8–9	1
10	2
11–12	3
13	4

Extra Practice
Skills Practice p. S11
Application Practice p. S31

Position each figure in the coordinate plane.

8. a square with side lengths of 2 units
9. a right triangle with leg lengths of 1 unit and 5 units

Write a proof using coordinate geometry.

10. **Given:** Rectangle $ABCD$ has coordinates $A(0, 0)$, $B(0, 10)$, $C(6, 10)$, and $D(6, 0)$. E is the midpoint of $\overline{AB}$, and F is the midpoint of $\overline{CD}$.
Prove: $EF = BC$

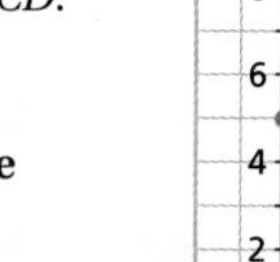

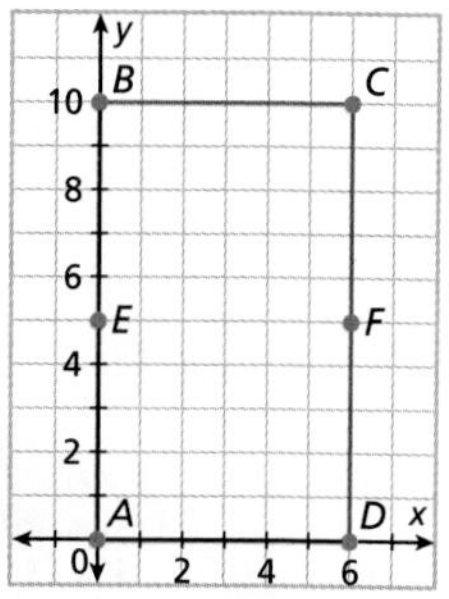

Position each figure in the coordinate plane and give the coordinates of each vertex.

11. a square with side length $2m$
12. a rectangle with dimensions x and $3x$

Multi-Step **Assign coordinates to each vertex and write a coordinate proof.**

13. **Given:** E is the midpoint of $\overline{AB}$ in rectangle $ABCD$. F is the midpoint of $\overline{CD}$.
Prove: $EF = AD$

14. **Critical Thinking** Use variables to write the general form of the endpoints of a segment whose midpoint is $(0, 0)$. (x, y) and $(-x, -y)$

4-7 READING STRATEGIES

Figures can be positioned in a coordinate plane in one of four ways:

- **Use the origin as a vertex,** which may keep the figure in Quadrant I.
- **Center the figure** at the origin of the coordinate plane.
- **Center a side** of the figure at the origin of the coordinate plane.
- **Use one or both axes** as sides of the figure.

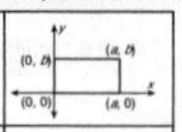

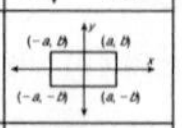

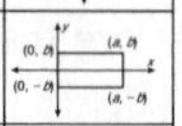

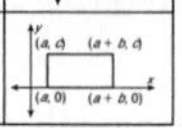

Using the given information, position the figure on the coordinate plane provided and answer the following questions.

1. Where would you position the triangle on the coordinate plane if you want to find the area of $\triangle ABC$? with one leg along one of the axes
2. Where would you position the triangle to find the midpoint of $\overline{AB}$? with one leg running through the origin

Indicate where on a coordinate plane each figure should be placed in order to find the following measurement.

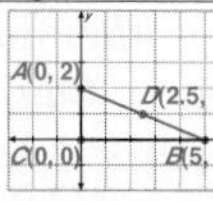

3. the area of $\triangle ABC$ — so that one side is along each axis
4. the midpoint of $\overline{AB}$ — so that the side straddles the origin
5. the area of $\triangle ADC$ — so that one vertex is at the origin
6. the area of $\triangle CDB$ — so that one side crosses through the origin

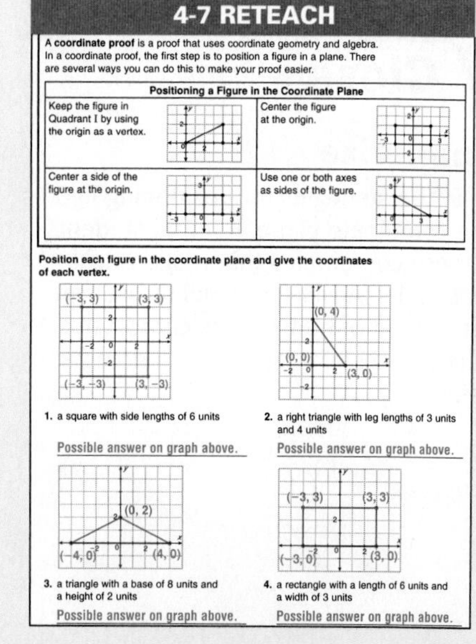
4-7 RETEACH

A **coordinate proof** is a proof that uses coordinate geometry and algebra. In a coordinate proof, the first step is to position a figure in a plane. There are several ways you can do this to make your proof easier.

Positioning a Figure in the Coordinate Plane

Keep the figure in Quadrant I by using the origin as a vertex.	Center the figure at the origin.
Center a side of the figure at the origin.	Use one or both axes as sides of the figure.

Position each figure in the coordinate plane and give the coordinates of each vertex.

1. a square with side lengths of 6 units — Possible answer on graph above.
2. a right triangle with leg lengths of 3 units and 4 units — Possible answer on graph above.
3. a triangle with a base of 8 units and a height of 2 units — Possible answer on graph above.
4. a rectangle with a length of 6 units and a width of 3 units — Possible answer on graph above.

15. **Recreation** A hiking trail begins at $E(0, 0)$. Bryan hikes from the start of the trail to a waterfall at $W(3, 3)$ and then makes a 90° turn to a campsite at $C(6, 0)$.

a. Draw Bryan's route in the coordinate plane.

b. If one grid unit represents 1 mile, what is the total distance Bryan hiked? Round to the nearest tenth. **8.5 mi**

Find the perimeter and area of each figure.

16. a right triangle with leg lengths of a and $2a$ units **$a(3 + \sqrt{5})$ units; a^2 square units**

17. a rectangle with dimensions s and t units **$2s + 2t$ units; st square units**

Find the missing coordinates for each figure.

18. 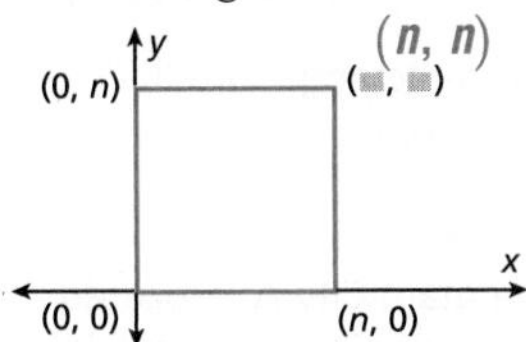

19. 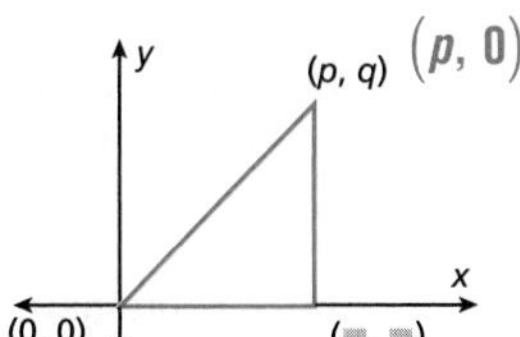

LINK Conservation

The origin of the springbok's name may come from its habit of *pronking*, or bouncing. When pronking, a springbok can leap up to 13 feet in the air. Springboks can run up to 53 miles per hour.

20. **Conservation** The Bushmen have sighted animals at the following coordinates: $(-25, 31.5)$, $(-23.2, 31.4)$, and $(-24, 31.1)$. Prove that the distance between two of these locations is approximately twice the distance between two other.

21. **Navigation** Two ships depart from a port at $P(20, 10)$. The first ship travels to a location at $A(-30, 50)$, and the second ship travels to a location at $B(70, -30)$. Each unit represents one nautical mile. Find the distance to the nearest nautical mile between the two ships. Verify that the port is at the midpoint between the two.

Write a coordinate proof.

22. **Given:** Rectangle $PQRS$ has coordinates $P(0, 2)$, $Q(3, 2)$, $R(3, 0)$, and $S(0, 0)$. $\overline{PR}$ and $\overline{QS}$ intersect at $T(1.5, 1)$.
Prove: The area of $\triangle RST$ is $\frac{1}{4}$ of the area of the rectangle.

23. **Given:** $A(x_1, y_1)$, $B(x_2, y_2)$, with midpoint $M\left(\frac{x_1 + x_2}{2}, \frac{y_1 + y_2}{2}\right)$
Prove: $AM = \frac{1}{2}AB$

24. Plot the points on a coordinate plane and connect them to form $\triangle KLM$ and $\triangle MPK$. Write a coordinate proof.
Given: $K(-2, 1)$, $L(-2, 3)$, $M(1, 3)$, $P(1, 1)$
Prove: $\triangle KLM \cong \triangle MPK$

25. **Write About It** When you place two sides of a figure on the coordinate axes, what are you assuming about the figure? **You are assuming the figure has a rt. ∠.**

MULTI-STEP TEST PREP

26. This problem will prepare you for the Multi-Step Test Prep on page 280.

Paul designed a doghouse to fit against the side of his house. His plan consisted of a right triangle on top of a rectangle.

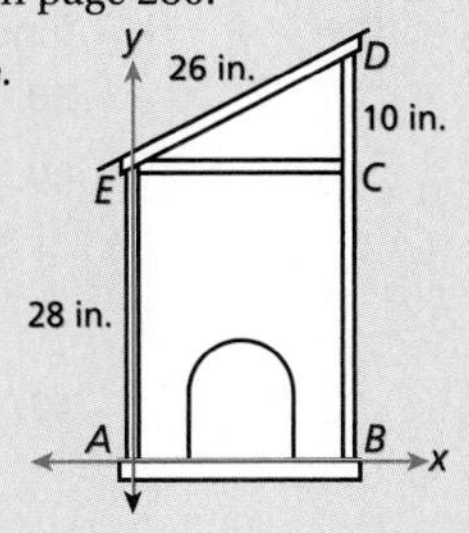

a. Find BD and CE. **$BD = 38$ in.; $CE = 24$ in.**

b. Before building the doghouse, Paul sketched his plan on a coordinate plane. He placed A at the origin and $\overline{AB}$ on the x-axis. Find the coordinates of B, C, D, and E, assuming that each unit of the coordinate plane represents one inch.
$B(24, 0)$; $C(24, 28)$; $D(24, 38)$; $E(0, 28)$

COMMON ERROR ALERT

In **Exercise 19,** students may give the missing coordinates as $(0, p)$ instead of $(p, 0)$. Review with students the order of coordinates.

MULTI-STEP TEST PREP **Exercise 26** involves using the Pythagorean Theorem to find the length of a missing side of a right triangle. This exercise prepares students for the Multi-Step Test Prep on page 280.

Answers

15a. 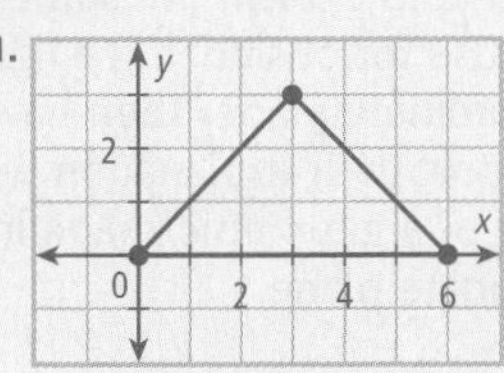

20. $\sqrt{(-25 + 23.2)^2 + (31.5 - 31.4)^2} \approx 1.8$

$\sqrt{(-23.2 + 24)^2 + (31.4 - 31.1)^2} \approx 0.9$

$\sqrt{(-24 + 25)^2 + (31.1 - 31.5)^2} \approx 1.1$

1.8 is twice 0.9. The dist. between 2 of the locations is approximately twice the dist. between 2 of the other.

21. $AB \approx 128$ nautical miles; $AP = BP \approx 64$ nautical miles; so P is the mdpt. of $\overline{AB}$.

4-7 PROBLEM SOLVING

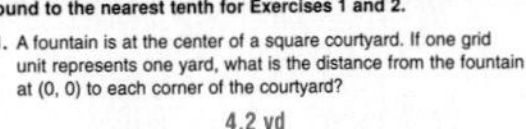

Round to the nearest tenth for Exercises 1 and 2.

1. A fountain is at the center of a square courtyard. If one grid unit represents one yard, what is the distance from the fountain at (0, 0) to each corner of the courtyard?
4.2 yd

2. Noah started at his home at $A(0, 0)$, walked with his dog to the park at $B(4, 2)$, walked to his friend's house at $C(8, 0)$, then walked home. If one grid unit represents 20 meters, what is the distance that Noah and his dog walked?
338.9 m

Use the following information for Exercises 3 and 4.

Rachel started her cycling trip at $G(0, 7)$. Malik started his trip at $J(0, 0)$. Their paths crossed at $H(4, 2)$.

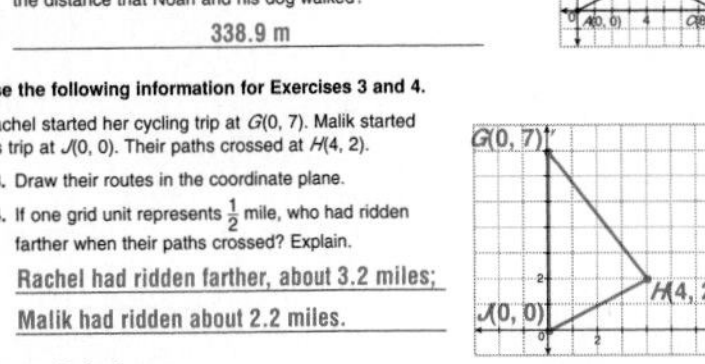

3. Draw their routes in the coordinate plane.

4. If one grid unit represents $\frac{1}{2}$ mile, who had ridden farther when their paths crossed? Explain.
Rachel had ridden farther, about 3.2 miles; Malik had ridden about 2.2 miles.

Choose the best answer.

5. Two airplanes depart from an airport at $A(9, 11)$. The first airplane travels to a location at $N(-250, 80)$, and the second airplane travels to a location at $P(105, -400)$. Each unit represents 1 mile. What is the distance, to the nearest mile, between the two airplanes?

(A) 335.3 mi
B 477.9 mi
C 490.3 mi
D 597.0 mi

6. A corner garden has vertices at $Q(0, 0)$, $R(0, 2d)$, and $S(2c, 0)$. A brick walkway runs from point Q to the midpoint M of $\overline{RS}$. What is QM?

F (c, d)
G $c^2 + d^2$
H $\sqrt{c + d}$
(J) $\sqrt{c^2 + d^2}$

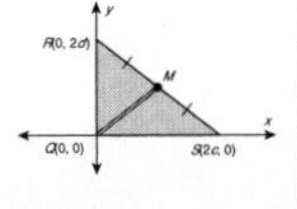

Answers

22.
The area of the rect. is $A = \ell w = 3(2) = 6$ square units. For $\triangle RST$, the base is 3 units, and the height is 1 unit. So the area of $\triangle RST = \frac{1}{2}bh = \frac{1}{2}(3)(1) = 1.5$ square units. Since $\frac{1}{4}(6) = 1.5$, the area of $\triangle RST$ is $\frac{1}{4}$ the area of the rect.

23–24. See p. A17.

4-7 PRACTICE A

4-7 PRACTICE C

4-7 PRACTICE B

Position an isosceles triangle with sides of 8 units, 5 units, and 5 units in the coordinate plane. Label the coordinates of each vertex. (*Hint:* Use the Pythagorean Theorem.)

1. Center the long side on the x-axis at the origin.

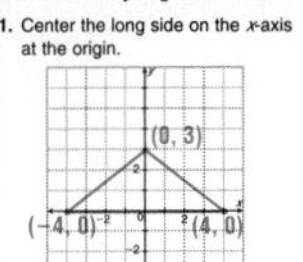

2. Place the long side on the y-axis centered at the origin.

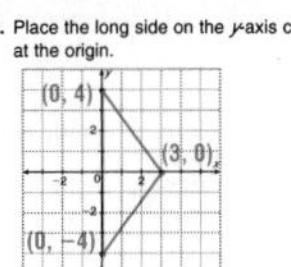

Write a coordinate proof.

3. **Given:** Rectangle $ABCD$ has vertices $A(0, 4)$, $B(6, 4)$, $C(6, 0)$, and $D(0, 0)$. E is the midpoint of $\overline{DC}$. F is the midpoint of $\overline{DA}$.
Prove: The area of rectangle $DEGF$ is one-fourth the area of rectangle $ABCD$.

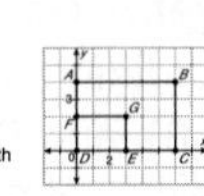

Possible answer: $ABCD$ is a rectangle with width AD and length DC. The area of $ABCD$ is $(AD)(DC)$ or $(4)(6) = 24$ square units. By the Midpoint Formula, the coordinates of E are $\left(\frac{0+6}{2}, \frac{0+0}{2}\right) = (3, 0)$ and the coordinates of F are $\left(\frac{0+0}{2}, \frac{0+4}{2}\right) = (0, 2)$. The x-coordinate of E is the length of rectangle $DEGF$, and the y-coordinate of F is the width. So the area of $DEGF$ is $(3)(2) = 6$ square coordinates. Since $6 = \frac{1}{4}(24)$, the area of rectangle $DEGF$ is one-fourth the area of rectangle $ABCD$.

TEST PREP DOCTOR For **Exercise 28,** discuss that the vertices of a rectangle do not have to be in the first quadrant.

If students chose **F** for **Exercise 30,** they found the midpoint between *A* and *C,* not the midpoint between *A* and *B.*

Journal

Ask students to explain the strategies they use for positioning a figure in the coordinate plane. Then have them support their explanation with a drawing of a geometric shape in the coordinate plane.

ALTERNATIVE ASSESSMENT

Have students place a rectangle in a coordinate plane so that the length is twice the width. Then ask them to make a conjecture about the area of the rectangle and to write a coordinate proof.

Power Presentations with PowerPoint®

4-7 Lesson Quiz

Position each figure in the coordinate plane.

1. rectangle with a length of 6 units and a width of 3 units
   Possible answer:

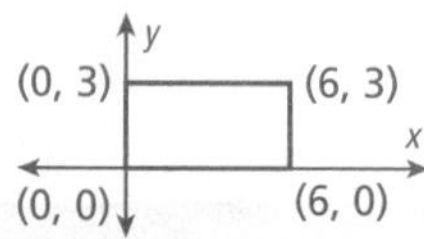

2. square with side lengths of $5a$ units. Possible answer:

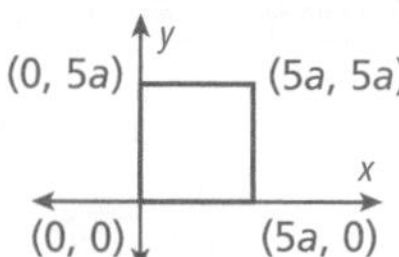

3. **Given:** Rectangle *ABCD* with coordinates $A(0, 0)$, $B(0, 8)$, $C(5, 8)$, and $D(5, 0)$. *E* is mdpt. of $\overline{BC}$, and *F* is mdpt. of $\overline{AD}$.
   Prove: $EF = AB$
   By the Midpoint Formula, the coordinates of *E* are $\left(\frac{5}{2}, 8\right)$ and *F* are $\left(\frac{5}{2}, 0\right)$.
   Then $EF = 8$, and $AB = 8$.
   Thus $EF = AB$.

Also available on transparency

TEST PREP

27. The coordinates of the vertices of a right triangle are (0, 0), (4, 0), and (0, 2). Which is a true statement?
    Ⓐ The vertex of the right angle is at (4, 2).
    Ⓑ The midpoints of the two legs are at (2, 0) and (0, 1).
    Ⓒ The hypotenuse of the triangle is $\sqrt{6}$ units.
    Ⓓ The shortest side of the triangle is positioned on the *x*-axis.

28. A rectangle has dimensions of $2g$ and $2f$ units. If one vertex is at the origin, which coordinates could NOT represent another vertex?
    Ⓕ $(2f, g)$ Ⓖ $(2f, 0)$ Ⓗ $(2g, 2f)$ Ⓙ $(-2f, 2g)$

29. The coordinates of the vertices of a rectangle are (0, 0), (*a*, 0), (*a*, *b*), and (0, *b*). What is the perimeter of the rectangle?
    Ⓐ $a + b$ Ⓑ ab Ⓒ $\frac{1}{2}ab$ Ⓓ $2a + 2b$

30. A coordinate grid is placed over a map. City A is located at (−1, 2) and city C is located at (3, 5). If city C is at the midpoint between city A and city B, what are the coordinates of city B?
    Ⓕ (1, 3.5) Ⓖ (−5, −1) Ⓗ (7, 8) Ⓙ (2, 7)

CHALLENGE AND EXTEND

Find the missing coordinates for each figure.

31. $(a + c, b)$

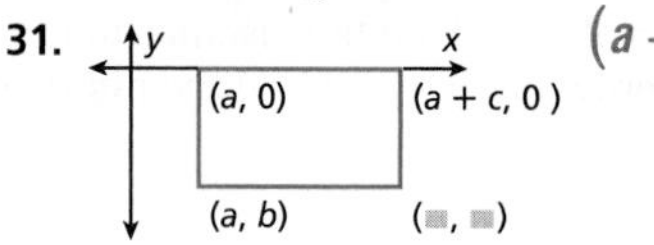

32. $(p, 0)$

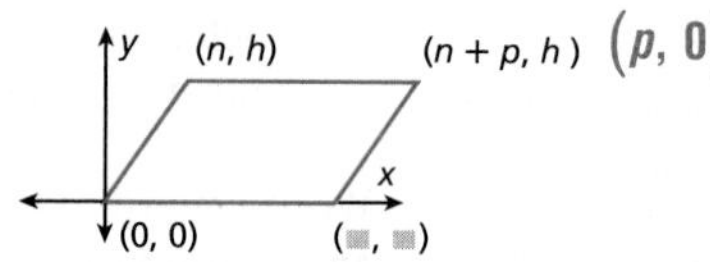

33. The vertices of a right triangle are at $(-2s, 2s)$, $(0, 2s)$, and $(0, 0)$. What coordinates could be used so that a coordinate proof would be easier to complete?

33. Possible answer: Rotate the △ 180° and translate it vertically $2s$ units. The new coords. would be $(0, 0)$, $(0, 2s)$, and $(2s, 0)$.

34. Rectangle *ABCD* has dimensions of $2f$ and $2g$ units. The equation of the line containing $\overline{BD}$ is $y = \frac{g}{f}x$, and the equation of the line containing $\overline{AC}$ is $y = -\frac{g}{f}x + 2g$. Use algebra to show that the coordinates of *E* are (f, g).

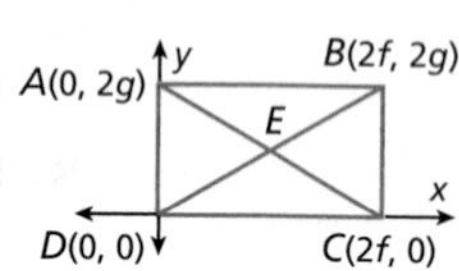

SPIRAL REVIEW

Use the quadratic formula to solve for *x*. Round to the nearest hundredth if necessary. *(Previous course)*

35. $0 = 8x^2 + 18x - 5$ −2.5 or 0.25
36. $0 = x^2 + 3x - 5$ 1.19 or −4.19
37. $0 = 3x^2 - x - 10$ 2 or −1.67

Find each value. *(Lesson 3-2)*

38. x 112
39. y 22

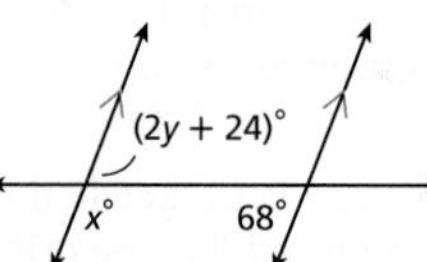

40. Use $A(-4, 3)$, $B(-1, 3)$, $C(-3, 1)$, $D(0, -2)$, $E(3, -2)$, and $F(2, -4)$ to prove $\angle ABC \cong \angle EDF$. *(Lesson 4-6)*.

Answers

34.

$\frac{g}{f}x = -\frac{g}{f}x + 2g$	Set eqns. = to each other.
$\frac{2g}{f}x = 2g$	Combine like terms.
$x = f$	Simplify.
$y = \frac{g}{f}x$	Given
$y = \frac{g}{f}(f)$	Subst.
$y = g$	Simplify.

40. $AB = 3$, $BC = 2\sqrt{2}$, $AC = \sqrt{5}$
$ED = 3$, $DF = 2\sqrt{2}$, $EF = \sqrt{5}$
$\overline{AB} \cong \overline{ED}$, $\overline{BC} \cong \overline{DF}$, and $\overline{AC} \cong \overline{EF}$.
Therefore $\triangle ABC \cong \triangle EDF$ by SSS, and $\angle ABC \cong \angle EDF$ by CPCTC.

4-8 Isosceles and Equilateral Triangles

Objectives
Prove theorems about isosceles and equilateral triangles.

Apply properties of isosceles and equilateral triangles.

Vocabulary
legs of an isosceles triangle
vertex angle
base
base angles

Who uses this?
Astronomers use geometric methods. (See Example 1.)

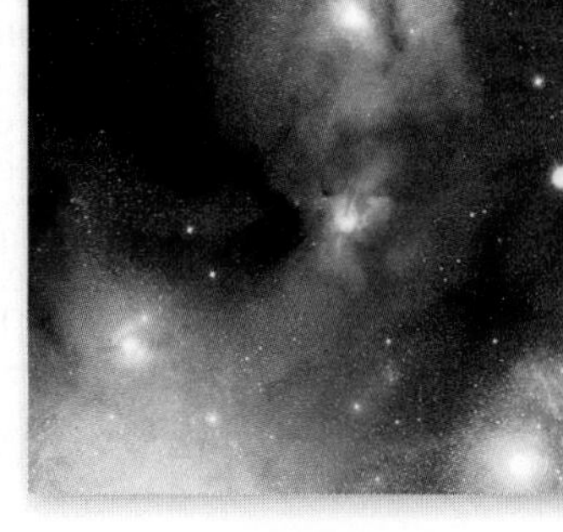

Recall that an isosceles triangle has at least two congruent sides. The congruent sides are called the **legs**. The **vertex angle** is the angle formed by the legs. The side opposite the vertex angle is called the **base**, and the **base angles** are the two angles that have the base as a side.

∠3 is the vertex angle.
∠1 and ∠2 are the base angles.

Know it! Note

Theorems Isosceles Triangle

THEOREM	HYPOTHESIS	CONCLUSION
4-8-1 Isosceles Triangle Theorem If two sides of a triangle are congruent, then the angles opposite the sides are congruent.	$\triangle ABC$	$\angle B \cong \angle C$
4-8-2 Converse of Isosceles Triangle Theorem If two angles of a triangle are congruent, then the sides opposite those angles are congruent.	$\triangle DEF$	$\overline{DE} \cong \overline{DF}$

Theorem 4-8-1 is proven below. You will prove Theorem 4-8-2 in Exercise 35.

PROOF **Isosceles Triangle Theorem**

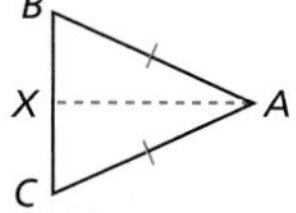

Given: $\overline{AB} \cong \overline{AC}$
Prove: $\angle B \cong \angle C$
Proof:

Statements	Reasons
1. Draw X, the mdpt. of $\overline{BC}$.	1. Every seg. has a unique mdpt.
2. Draw the auxiliary line $\overline{AX}$.	2. Through two pts. there is exactly one line.
3. $\overline{BX} \cong \overline{CX}$	3. Def. of mdpt.
4. $\overline{AB} \cong \overline{AC}$	4. Given
5. $\overline{AX} \cong \overline{AX}$	5. Reflex. Prop. of ≅
6. $\triangle ABX \cong \triangle ACX$	6. SSS *Steps 3, 4, 5*
7. $\angle B \cong \angle C$	7. CPCTC

Reading Math
The Isosceles Triangle Theorem is sometimes stated as "Base angles of an isosceles triangle are congruent."

4-8 Organizer

Pacing: Traditional 1 day
Block $\frac{1}{2}$ day

Objectives: Prove theorems about isosceles and equilateral triangles.

Apply properties of isosceles and equilateral triangles.

Online Edition
Tutorial Videos, Interactivity

Countdown Week 9

Power Presentations with PowerPoint®

Warm Up

1. Find each angle measure.
   60°; 60°; 60°

True or False. If false explain.

2. Every equilateral triangle is isosceles. T
3. Every isosceles triangle is equilateral. F; an isosc. △ has only 2 ≅ sides.

Also available on transparency

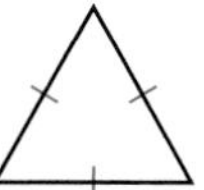

Q: What did the frowning student say to his teacher?
A: "I've got more problems than a math book."

1 Introduce

EXPLORATION

4-8 Isosceles and Equilateral Triangles

You can use paper folding to explore properties of isosceles triangles.

1. Use a ruler to draw $\overline{AB}$. Then draw $\overline{AC}$ so that it is the same length as $\overline{AB}$.
2. Complete the triangle by drawing the segment with endpoints B and C.
3. Now fold the paper so that $\overline{AB}$ matches up with $\overline{AC}$. What do you notice about $\angle B$ and $\angle C$?
4. Repeat the process by drawing several more isosceles triangles with different shapes and sizes. Do you get the same results?
5. State a conjecture based on your results.

THINK AND DISCUSS

6. **Explain** how you can use your conjecture to find $m\angle J$ and $m\angle K$.
7. **Describe** how you could use paper folding to find out if the converse of your conjecture is true.

Motivate

Give small groups of students different examples of isosceles and equilateral triangles. Have each group measure the lengths of the three sides and the three angles of their triangles. Then ask them to make as many conjectures about isosceles and equilateral triangles as they can. For example, students should recognize that the base angles of an isosceles triangle are congruent.

Explorations and answers are provided in *Alternate Openers: Explorations Transparencies.*

State Resources

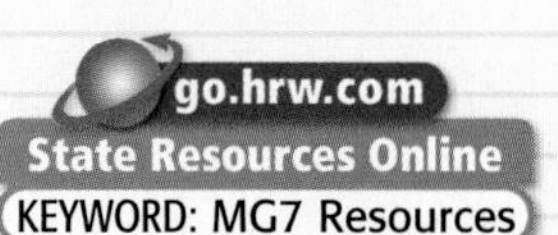

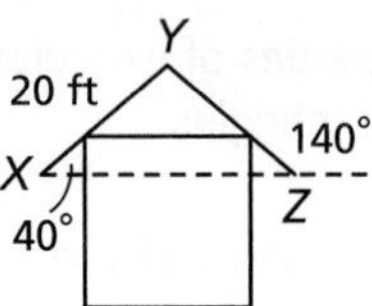

Additional Examples

Example 1

The length of $\overline{YX}$ is 20 feet. Explain why the length of $\overline{YZ}$ is the same.

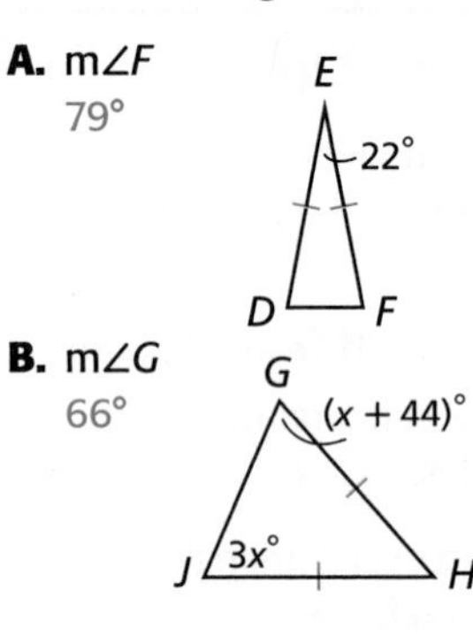

$m\angle YZX = 40°$, so $\overline{XY} \cong \overline{YZ}$ by Conv. of Isosc. △ Thm. Thus $YZ = 20$ ft.

Example 2

Find each angle measure.

A. $m\angle F$
79°

B. $m\angle G$
66°

INTERVENTION 

Questioning Strategies

EXAMPLE 1

- How is the Converse of the Isosceles Triangle Theorem used?

EXAMPLE 2

- When you find the value of x, is this the answer to the problem? Explain.

EXAMPLE 1 Astronomy Application

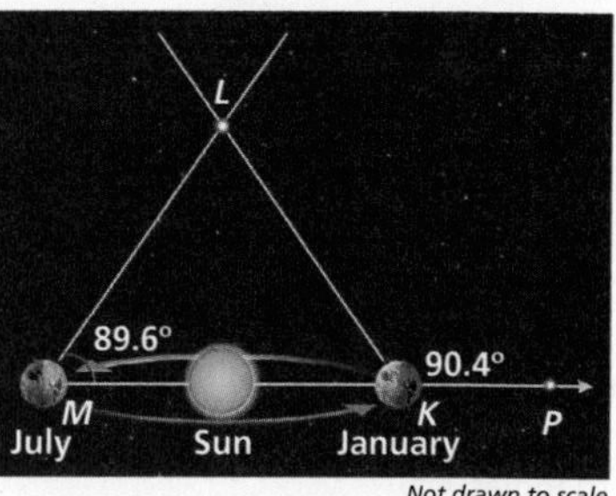

The distance from Earth to nearby stars can be measured using the parallax method, which requires observing the positions of a star 6 months apart. If the distance LM to a star in July is 4.0×10^{13} km, explain why the distance LK to the star in January is the same. (Assume the distance from Earth to the Sun does not change.)

$m\angle LKM = 180 - 90.4$, so $m\angle LKM = 89.6°$. Since $\angle LKM \cong \angle M$, $\triangle LMK$ is isosceles by the Converse of the Isosceles Triangle Theorem. Thus $LK = LM = 4.0 \times 10^{13}$ km.

1. If the distance from Earth to a star in September is 4.2×10^{13} km, what is the distance from Earth to the star in March? Explain.

EXAMPLE 2 Finding the Measure of an Angle

Algebra

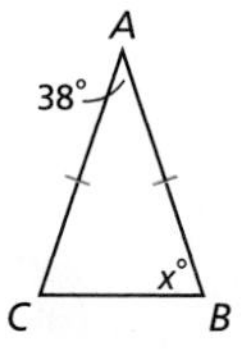

Find each angle measure.

A $m\angle C$

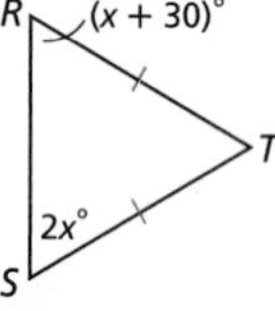

$m\angle C = m\angle B = x°$	*Isosc. △ Thm.*
$m\angle C + m\angle B + m\angle A = 180$	*△ Sum Thm.*
$x + x + 38 = 180$	*Substitute the given values.*
$2x = 142$	*Simplify and subtract 38 from both sides.*
$x = 71$	*Divide both sides by 2.*

Thus $m\angle C = 71°$.

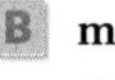

B $m\angle S$

$m\angle S = m\angle R$	*Isosc. △ Thm.*
$2x° = (x + 30)°$	*Substitute the given values.*
$x = 30$	*Subtract x from both sides.*

Thus $m\angle S = 2x° = 2(30) = 60°$.

Find each angle measure.

2a. $m\angle H$ **66°** **2b.** $m\angle N$ **48°**

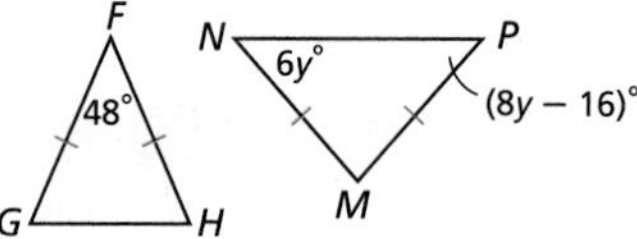

The following corollary and its converse show the connection between equilateral triangles and equiangular triangles.

Corollary 4-8-3 Equilateral Triangle

COROLLARY	HYPOTHESIS	CONCLUSION
If a triangle is equilateral, then it is equiangular. (equilateral △ → equiangular △)	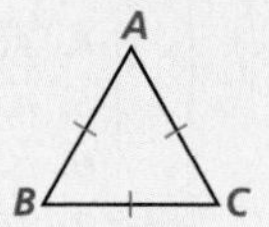 (triangle ABC with congruent sides)	$\angle A \cong \angle B \cong \angle C$

You will prove Corollary 4-8-3 in Exercise 36.

2 Teach

Guided Instruction

Have students practice finding angle measures of isosceles and equilateral triangles using natural numbers before using algebraic expressions. Review the most efficient way to name the vertices of a triangle before doing a coordinate proof.

Reaching All Learners

Through Visual Cues

Represent the Isosceles Triangle Theorem as:

If then

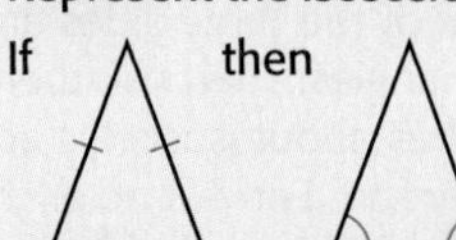

and the Converse of Isosceles Triangle Theorem as:

If 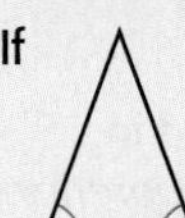 then 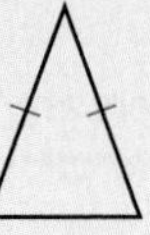

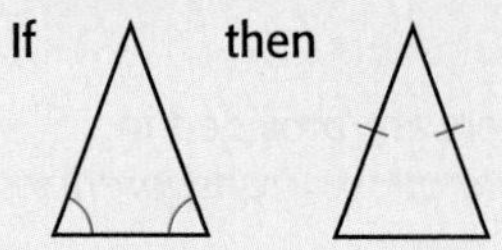

Answers to *Check It Out!*

1. 4.2×10^{13}; since there are 6 months between September and March, the ∠ measures will be approximately the same between Earth and the star. By the Conv. of the Isosc. △ Thm., the △s created are isosc., and the dist. is the same.

Corollary 4-8-4 Equiangular Triangle

COROLLARY	HYPOTHESIS	CONCLUSION
If a triangle is equiangular, then it is equilateral. (equiangular △ → equilateral △)	D, E, F	$\overline{DE} \cong \overline{DF} \cong \overline{EF}$

You will prove Corollary 4-8-4 in Exercise 37.

EXAMPLE 3 Using Properties of Equilateral Triangles

Find each value.

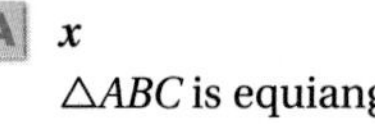

A x

$\triangle ABC$ is equiangular.	*Equilateral △ → equiangular △*
$(3x + 15)^\circ = 60^\circ$	*The measure of each ∠ of an equiangular △ is 60°.*
$3x = 45$	*Subtract 15 from both sides.*
$x = 15$	*Divide both sides by 3.*

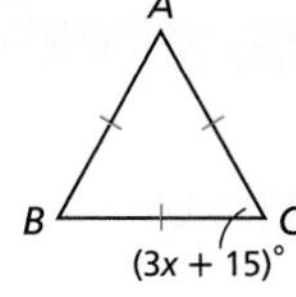

B t

$\triangle JKL$ is equilateral.	*Equiangular △ → equilateral △*
$4t - 8 = 2t + 1$	*Def. of equilateral △*
$2t = 9$	*Subtract 2t and add 8 to both sides.*
$t = 4.5$	*Divide both sides by 2.*

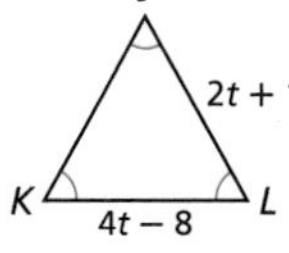

3. Use the diagram to find JL. 10

EXAMPLE 4 Using Coordinate Proof

Remember!

A coordinate proof may be easier if you place one side of the triangle along the x-axis and locate a vertex at the origin or on the y-axis.

Prove that the triangle whose vertices are the midpoints of the sides of an isosceles triangle is also isosceles.

Given: $\triangle ABC$ is isosceles. X is the mdpt. of $\overline{AB}$. Y is the mdpt. of $\overline{AC}$. Z is the mdpt. of $\overline{BC}$.

Prove: $\triangle XYZ$ is isosceles.

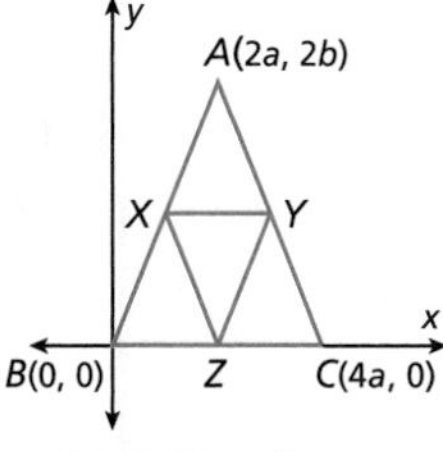

Proof:

Draw a diagram and place the coordinates of $\triangle ABC$ and $\triangle XYZ$ as shown.

By the Midpoint Formula, the coordinates of X are $\left(\frac{2a+0}{2}, \frac{2b+0}{2}\right) = (a, b)$, the coordinates of Y are $\left(\frac{2a+4a}{2}, \frac{2b+0}{2}\right) = (3a, b)$, and the coordinates of Z are $\left(\frac{4a+0}{2}, \frac{0+0}{2}\right) = (2a, 0)$.

By the Distance Formula, $XZ = \sqrt{(2a-a)^2 + (0-b)^2} = \sqrt{a^2+b^2}$, and $YZ = \sqrt{(2a-3a)^2 + (0-b)^2} = \sqrt{a^2+b^2}$.

Since $XZ = YZ$, $\overline{XZ} \cong \overline{YZ}$ by definition. So $\triangle XYZ$ is isosceles.

4. **What if...?** The coordinates of $\triangle ABC$ are $A(0, 2b)$, $B(-2a, 0)$, and $C(2a, 0)$. Prove $\triangle XYZ$ is isosceles.

4. By the Mdpt. Formula, the coords. of X are $(-a, b)$, the coords. of Y are (a, b), and the coords. of Z are $(0, 0)$. By the Dist. Formula, $XZ = YZ = \sqrt{a^2 + b^2}$. So $\overline{XZ} \cong \overline{YZ}$ and $\triangle XYZ$ is isosc.

Power Presentations with PowerPoint®

Additional Examples

Example 3

Find each value.

A. x 14

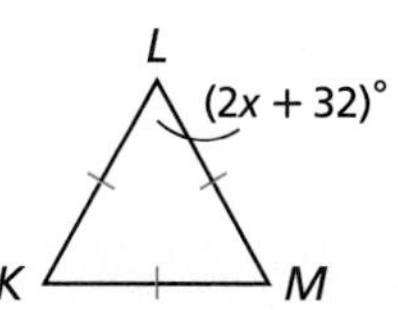

B. y 18

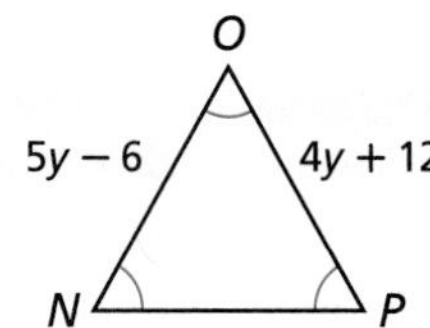

Example 4

Prove that the segment joining the Mdpt. of two sides of an isosceles triangle is half the base.

Given: In isosceles $\triangle ABC$, X is the Mdpt. of $\overline{AB}$, and Y is the Mdpt. of $\overline{AC}$.

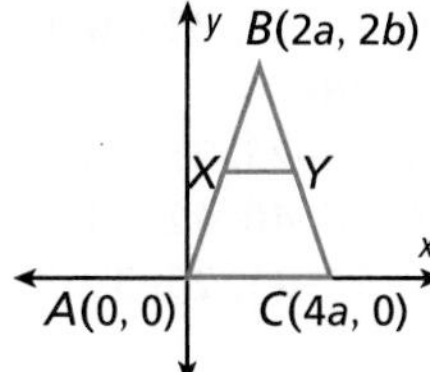

Prove: $XY = \frac{1}{2}AC$.

By the Mdpt. Formula, the coords. of X are (a, b), and Y are $(3a, b)$. By the Dist. Formula, $XY = \sqrt{4a^2} = 2a$, and $AC = 4a$. Therefore $XY = \frac{1}{2}AC$.

3 Close

Summarize

Remind students that an isosceles triangle has at least two congruent sides, and its properties can be used to prove that it also has at least two congruent angles. Emphasize that an equilateral triangle has three congruent sides and angles. Review the best methods of naming the vertices of an isosceles and equilateral triangle in the coordinate plane.

ONGOING ASSESSMENT and INTERVENTION

***Diagnose Before* the Lesson**
4-8 Warm Up, TE p. 273

***Monitor During* the Lesson**
Check It Out! Exercises, SE pp. 274–275
Questioning Strategies, TE pp. 274–275

***Assess After* the Lesson**
4-8 Lesson Quiz, TE p. 279
Alternative Assessment, TE p. 279

INTERVENTION

Questioning Strategies

EXAMPLE 3

- If the triangle is equiangular, how do you find the measure of one of its angles?

EXAMPLE 4

- Why is it not suggested that you use numerical values for the vertices in a coordinate proof?

Multiple Representations For **Example 4,** you could also place the triangle's vertices at $(2a, 0)$, $(-2a, 0)$, and $(0, 2b)$.

Answers to *Think and Discuss*

1. An equil. △ is also an equiangular △, so the 3 ∠s have the same measure. They must add up to 180° by the △ Sum Thm. So each ∠ must measure 60°.
2. See p. A4.

THINK AND DISCUSS

1. Explain why each of the angles in an equilateral triangle measures 60°.
2. **GET ORGANIZED** Copy and complete the graphic organizer. In each box, draw and mark a diagram for each type of triangle.

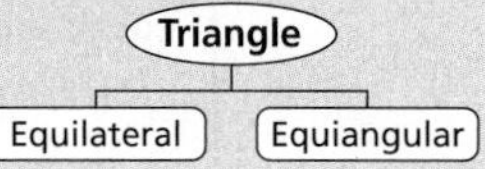

4-8 Exercises

4-8 Exercises

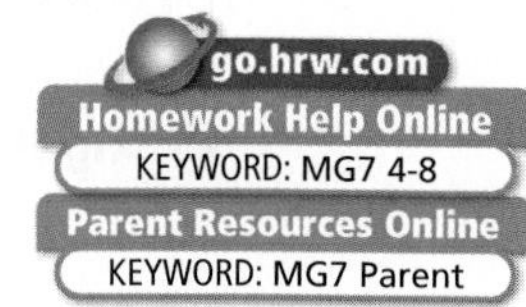

go.hrw.com
Homework Help Online
KEYWORD: MG7 4-8
Parent Resources Online
KEYWORD: MG7 Parent

Assignment Guide

Assign *Guided Practice* exercises as necessary.

If you finished Examples **1–2**
- **Basic** 12–16, 22–25, 28, 29, 32–34
- **Average** 12–16, 22–25, 28, 29, 32–39
- **Advanced** 12–16, 22–25, 28, 29, 32–39, 41, 45

If you finished Examples **1–4**
- **Basic** 12–25, 28–30, 42–44, 48–54
- **Average** 12–23, 26–31, 33, 35, 36, 40, 42–44, 47–54
- **Advanced** 12–21, 26–33, 35–54

Homework Quick Check
Quickly check key concepts.
Exercises: 12, 14, 18, 21, 28, 30

Teaching Tip

Algebra In **Exercise 11,** show students that $\sqrt{a^2 + a^2} \neq a + a$, or $2a$.

GUIDED PRACTICE

1. **Vocabulary** Draw isosceles △*JKL* with ∠*K* as the vertex angle. Name the legs, base, and base angles of the triangle.

SEE EXAMPLE 1 p. 274

2. **Surveying** To find the distance *QR* across a river, a surveyor locates three points *Q*, *R*, and *S*. *QS* = 41 m, and m∠*S* = 35°. The measure of exterior ∠*PQS* = 70°. Draw a diagram and explain how you can find *QR*.

SEE EXAMPLE 2 p. 274

Find each angle measure.

3. m∠*ECD* **118°**
4. m∠*K* **49°**
5. m∠*X* **27°**
6. m∠*A* **90°**

SEE EXAMPLE 3 p. 275

Find each value.

7. *y* **5**
8. *x* **4**

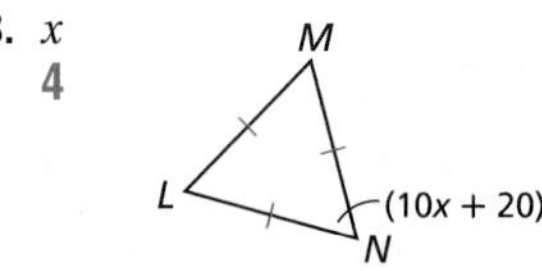

9. *BC* **20**
10. *JK* **50**

SEE EXAMPLE 4 p. 275

11. **Given:** △*ABC* is right isosceles. *X* is the midpoint of $\overline{AC}$. $\overline{AB} \cong \overline{BC}$
    Prove: △*AXB* is isosceles.

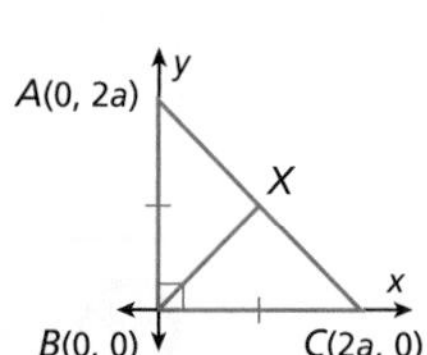

Answers

1. legs: $\overline{KJ}$ and $\overline{KL}$
   base: $\overline{JL}$
   base ∠s: ∠*J*; ∠*L*

2. By the Ext. ∠ Thm., m∠*R* = 35°. Since m∠*R* = m∠*S* by the Conv. of the Isosc. △ Thm., *QR* = *QS* = 41 m.

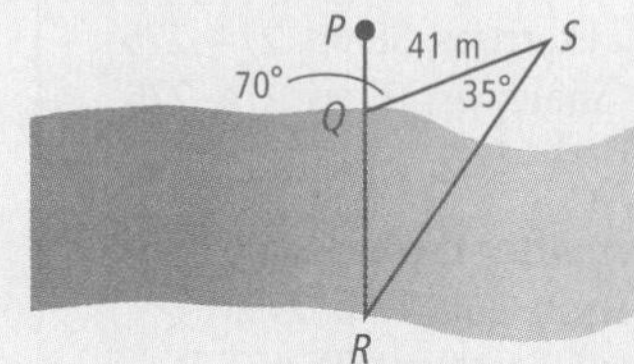

11. It is given that △*ABC* is rt. isosc., $\overline{AB} \cong \overline{BC}$, and *X* is the mdpt. of $\overline{AC}$. By the Mdpt. Formula, the coords. of *X* are (a, a). By the Dist. Formula, $AX = BX = a\sqrt{2}$. So △*AXB* is isosc. by def. of an isosc. △.

State Resources

go.hrw.com
State Resources Online
KEYWORD: MG7 Resources

PRACTICE AND PROBLEM SOLVING

Independent Practice

For Exercises	See Example
12	1
13–16	2
17–20	3
21	4

Extra Practice

Skills Practice p. S11
Application Practice p. S31

12. **Aviation** A plane is flying parallel to the ground along $\overrightarrow{AC}$. When the plane is at A, an air-traffic controller in tower T measures the angle to the plane as 40°. After the plane has traveled 2.4 mi to B, the angle to the plane is 80°. How can you find BT?

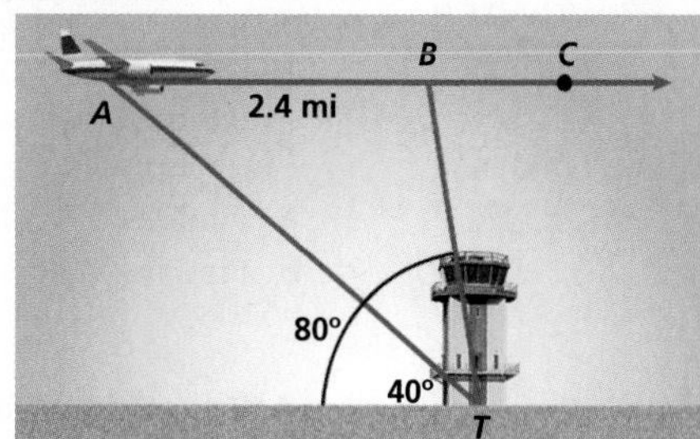

Find each angle measure.

13. m∠E **69°**

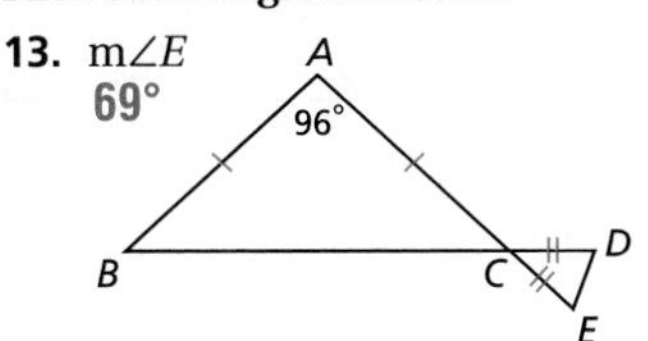

14. m∠TRU **33°**

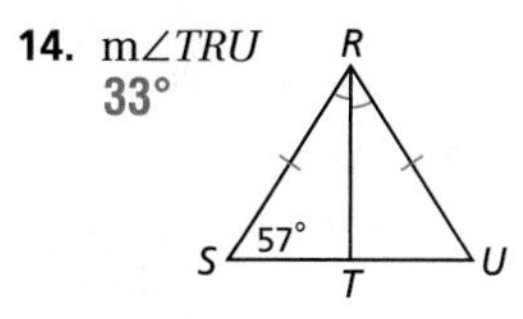

15. m∠F **130° or 172°**

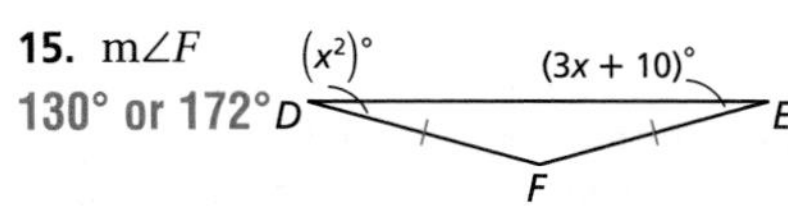

16. m∠A **31°**

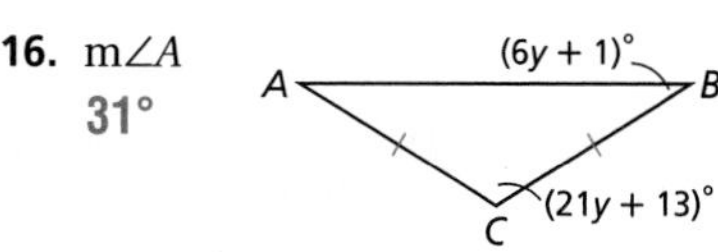

Find each value.

17. z **92**

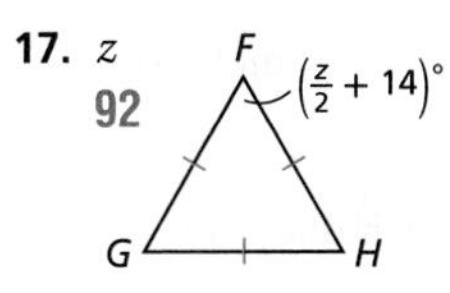

18. y **48**

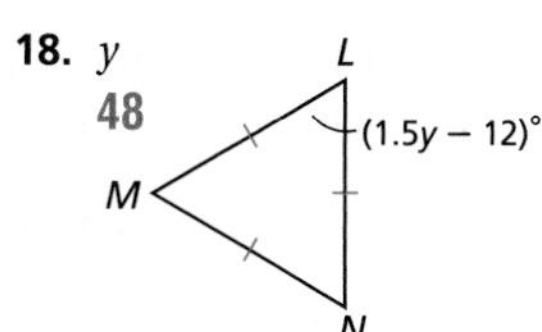

19. BC **26**

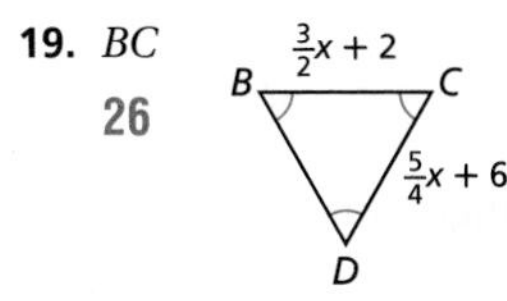

20. XZ **20**

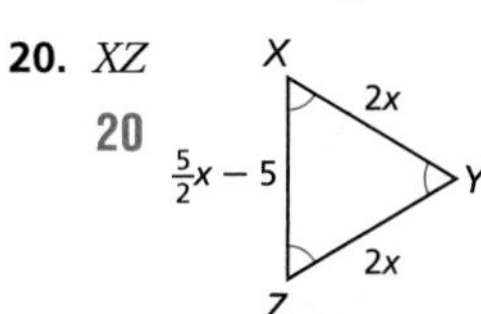

21. **Given:** $\triangle ABC$ is isosceles. P is the midpoint of $\overline{AB}$. Q is the midpoint of $\overline{AC}$. $\overline{AB} \cong \overline{AC}$
Prove: $\overline{PC} \cong \overline{QB}$

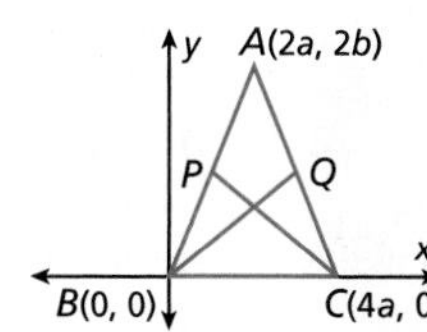

Tell whether each statement is sometimes, always, or never true. Support your answer with a sketch.

22. An equilateral triangle is an isosceles triangle. **A**
23. The vertex angle of an isosceles triangle is congruent to the base angles. **S**
24. An isosceles triangle is a right triangle. **S**
25. An equilateral triangle and an obtuse triangle are congruent. **N**
26. **Critical Thinking** Can a base angle of an isosceles triangle be an obtuse angle? Why or why not?

COMMON ERROR ALERT

In **Exercises 5, 6, 9,** and **10,** students may forget to substitute the value of the variable back in the equation to determine the answer to the problem. Have them check their answers as a way to avoid this.

Answers

12. By the ∠ Add. Post., m∠ATB = 40°. m∠BAT = 40° by the Alt. Int. ∠s Thm. ∠ATB ≅ ∠BAT by def. of ≅. Since △ABT is isosc. by the Converse of the Isosc. △ Thm., $BT = BA = 2.4$ mi.

21. It is given that △ABC is isosc. $\overline{AB} \cong \overline{AC}$, P is the mdpt. of $\overline{AB}$, and Q is the mdpt. of $\overline{AC}$. By the Mdpt. Formula, the coords. of P are (a, b), and the coords. of Q are $(3a, b)$ By the Dist. Formula, $PC = QB = \sqrt{9a^2 + b^2}$, so $\overline{PC} \cong \overline{QB}$ by the def. of ≅.

4-8 PRACTICE A

4-8 PRACTICE C

4-8 PRACTICE B

An altitude of a triangle is a perpendicular segment from a vertex to the line containing the opposite side. Write a paragraph proof that the altitude to the base of an isosceles triangle bisects the base.

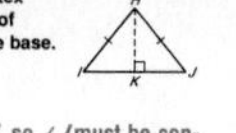

1. Given: $\overline{HI} \cong \overline{HJ}$, $\overline{HK} \perp \overline{IJ}$
Prove: $\overline{HK}$ bisects $\overline{IJ}$.
Possible answer: It is given that $\overline{HI}$ is congruent to $\overline{HJ}$, so ∠I must be congruent to ∠J by the Isosceles Triangle Theorem. ∠IKH and ∠JKH are both right angles by the definition of perpendicular, and all right angles are congruent. Thus by AAS, △HKI is congruent to △HKJ. $\overline{IK}$ is congruent to $\overline{KJ}$ by CPCTC, so $\overline{HK}$ bisects $\overline{IJ}$ by the definition of segment bisector.

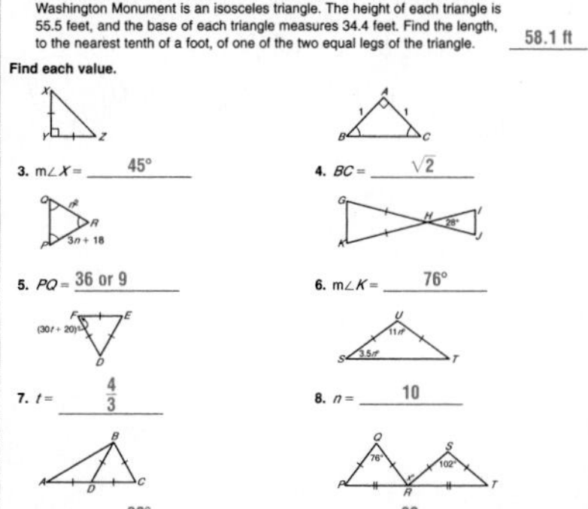

2. An *obelisk* is a tall, thin, four-sided monument that tapers to a pyramidal top. The most well-known obelisk to Americans is the Washington Monument on the National Mall in Washington, D.C. Each face of the pyramidal top of the Washington Monument is an isosceles triangle. The height of each triangle is 55.5 feet, and the base of each triangle measures 34.4 feet. Find the length, to the nearest tenth of a foot, of one of the two equal legs of the triangle. 58.1 ft

Find each value.

3. m∠X = 45°
4. BC = $\sqrt{2}$
5. PQ = 36 or 9
6. m∠K = 76°
7. t = $\frac{4}{3}$
8. n = 10
9. m∠A = 30°
10. x = 89

Answers

22.

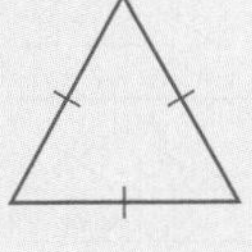

23.

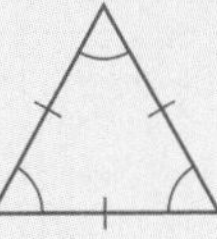

24.

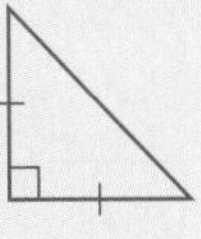

25. Possible answer:

26. No; if a base ∠ is obtuse, then the other base ∠ would also have to be obtuse since they are ≅. The sum of the measures of the ∠s of the △ cannot be greater than 180°.

Exercise 27 involves finding angle measures of an isosceles triangle. This exercise prepares students for the Multi-Step Test Prep on page 280.

Answers

30. It is given that $\triangle ABC$ is isosc. $\overline{BA} \cong \overline{BC}$, and X is the mdpt. of $\overline{AC}$. Assign the coords. $A(0, 2a)$, $B(0, 0)$ and $C(2a, 0)$. By the Mdpt. Formula, the coords. of X are (a, a). By the Dist. Formula, $AX = XB = XC = a\sqrt{2}$. So $\triangle AXB \cong \triangle CXB$ by SSS.

31. Check students' drawings. The ∡ are approximately 34°, 34°, and 112°. The conjecture should be that the △ is isosc. The conjecture is correct since there are 2 ≅ ∡.

35. 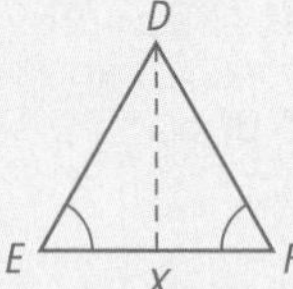

1. $\triangle DEF$ (Given)
2. Draw the bisector of $\angle EDF$ so that it intersects $\overline{EF}$ at X. (Every ∠ has a unique bisector.)
3. $\angle EDX \cong \angle FDX$ (Def. of ∠ bisector)
4. $\overline{DX} \cong \overline{DX}$ (Reflex. Prop. of ≅)
5. $\angle E \cong \angle F$ (Given)
6. $\triangle EDX \cong \triangle FDX$ (AAS *Steps 3, 5, 4*)
7. $\overline{DE} \cong \overline{DF}$ (CPCTC)

36a. $\angle B \cong \angle C$
b. Isosc. △ Thm.
c. Trans. Prop. of ≅

37. $\triangle DEF$ with $\angle D \cong \angle E \cong \angle F$ is given. Since $\angle E \cong \angle F$, $\overline{DE} \cong \overline{DF}$ by the Conv. of the Isosc. △ Thm. Similarly, since $\angle D \cong \angle F$, $\overline{EF} \cong \overline{DE}$. By the Trans. Prop. of ≅, $\overline{EF} \cong \overline{DF}$. Combining the ≅ statements, $\overline{DE} \cong \overline{DF} \cong \overline{EF}$, and $\triangle DEF$ is equil. by def.

38. By the Ext. ∠ Thm., $m\angle C = 45°$, so $\angle A \cong \angle C$. $BC = AB$ by the Conv. of the Isosc. △ Thm. So the distance to island C is the same as the distance traveled from A to B.

39. 1. $\triangle ABC \cong \triangle CBA$ (Given)
2. $\overline{AB} \cong \overline{CB}$ (CPCTC)
3. $\triangle ABC$ is isosceles (Def. of Isosc. △)

27. This problem will prepare you for the Multi-Step Test Prep on page 280.
The diagram shows the inside view of the support structure of the back of a doghouse. $\overline{PQ} \cong \overline{PR}$, $\overline{PS} \cong \overline{PT}$, $m\angle PST = 71°$, and $m\angle QPS = m\angle RPT = 18°$.
a. Find $m\angle SPT$. **38°**
b. Find $m\angle PQR$ and $m\angle PRQ$. **53°**

Multi-Step Find the measure of each numbered angle.

28. 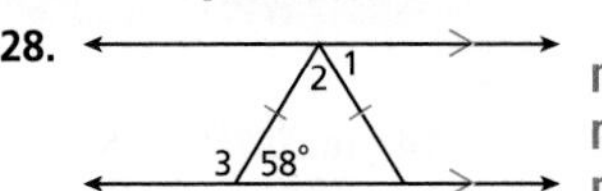

$m\angle 1 = 58°$; $m\angle 2 = 64°$; $m\angle 3 = 122°$

29. 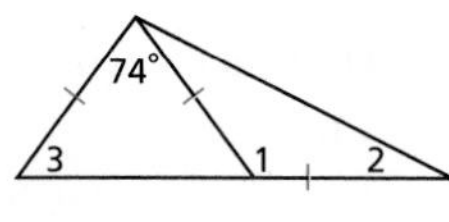

$m\angle 1 = 127°$; $m\angle 2 = 26.5°$; $m\angle 3 = 53°$

30. Write a coordinate proof.
Given: $\angle B$ is a right angle in isosceles right $\triangle ABC$. X is the midpoint of $\overline{AC}$. $\overline{BA} \cong \overline{BC}$
Prove: $\triangle AXB \cong \triangle CXB$

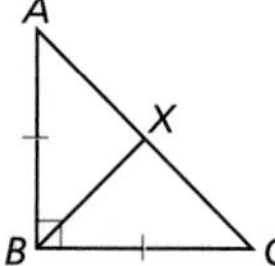

31. **Estimation** Draw the figure formed by $(-2, 1)$, $(5, 5)$, and $(-1, -7)$. Estimate the measure of each angle and make a conjecture about the classification of the figure. Then use a protractor to measure each angle. Was your conjecture correct? Why or why not?

32. How many different isosceles triangles have a perimeter of 18 and sides whose lengths are natural numbers? Explain. **4 ∡: 5, 5, 8; 6, 6, 6; 7, 7, 4; 8, 8, 2**

Multi-Step Find the value of the variable in each diagram.

33. 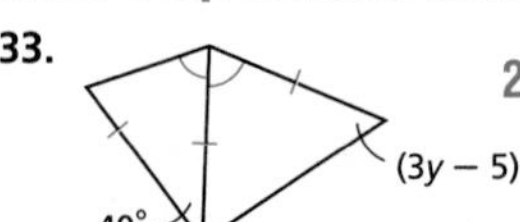

20

34. 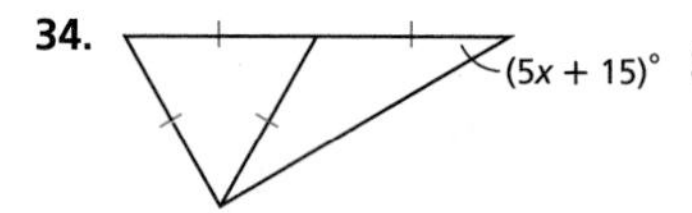

3

LINK

Navigation

The taffrail log is dragged from the stern of a vessel to measure the speed or distance traveled during a voyage. The log consists of a rotator, recording device, and governor.

35. Prove the Converse of the Isosceles Triangle Theorem.

36. Complete the proof of Corollary 4-8-3.
Given: $\overline{AB} \cong \overline{AC} \cong \overline{BC}$
Prove: $\angle A \cong \angle B \cong \angle C$

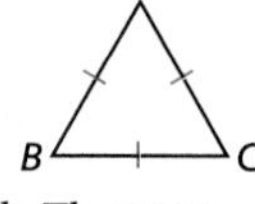

Proof: Since $\overline{AB} \cong \overline{AC}$, **a.** ___?___ by the Isosceles Triangle Theorem. Since $\overline{AC} \cong \overline{BC}$, $\angle A \cong \angle B$ by **b.** ___?___. Therefore $\angle A \cong \angle C$ by **c.** ___?___. By the Transitive Property of ≅, $\angle A \cong \angle B \cong \angle C$.

37. Prove Corollary 4-8-4.

38. **Navigation** The captain of a ship traveling along $\overrightarrow{AB}$ sights an island C at an angle of 45°. The captain measures the distance the ship covers until it reaches B, where the angle to the island is 90°. Explain how to find the distance BC to the island.

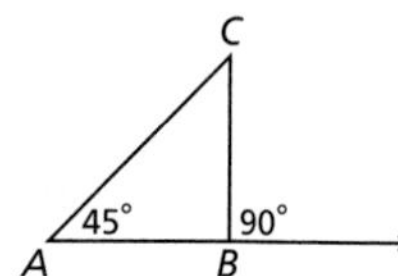

39. **Given:** $\triangle ABC \cong \triangle CBA$
Prove: $\triangle ABC$ is isosceles.

40. **Write About It** Write the Isosceles Triangle Theorem and its converse as a biconditional. **Two sides of a △ are ≅ if and only if the ∡ opp. those sides are ≅.**

4-8 READING STRATEGIES

Isosceles and equilateral triangles can be described in the following ways.

Theorem or Corollary	Hypothesis and Conclusion	Example
Isosceles Triangle Theorem If two sides of a triangle are congruent, then the angles opposite those sides are congruent.	If $\overline{XZ} \cong \overline{XY}$, then $\angle Y \cong \angle Z$.	X, Z, Y
Converse of Isosceles Triangle Theorem If two angles of a triangle are congruent, then the sides opposite those angles are congruent.	If $\angle N \cong \angle M$, then $\overline{LM} \cong \overline{LN}$.	L, N, M
Equilateral Triangle Corollary If a triangle is equilateral, then it is equiangular. (equilateral △ → equiangular △)	If $\overline{QR} \cong \overline{RS} \cong \overline{SQ}$, then $\angle Q \cong \angle R \cong \angle S$.	Q, S, R
Equiangular Triangle Corollary If a triangle is equiangular, then it is equilateral. (equilateral △ → equiangular △)	If $\angle E \cong \angle F \cong \angle G$, then $\overline{EF} \cong \overline{FG} \cong \overline{GE}$.	E, G, F

Find each value and indicate which theorem you used in determining the answer.

1. (H, J, I; 12, 12) JI 12; if a triangle is equiangular, then it is equilateral.

2. (A, C, B; 5, 5, 5; 60°) $m\angle A$ 60°; if a triangle is equilateral, then it is equiangular.

3. (X, Z, Y; 7, 7; 45°) $m\angle Z$ 45°; if two sides of a triangle are congruent, then the angles opposite the sides are congruent.

4. (Q, S, R; 10; 15) QR 10; if two angles of a triangle are congruent, then the sides opposite those angles are congruent.

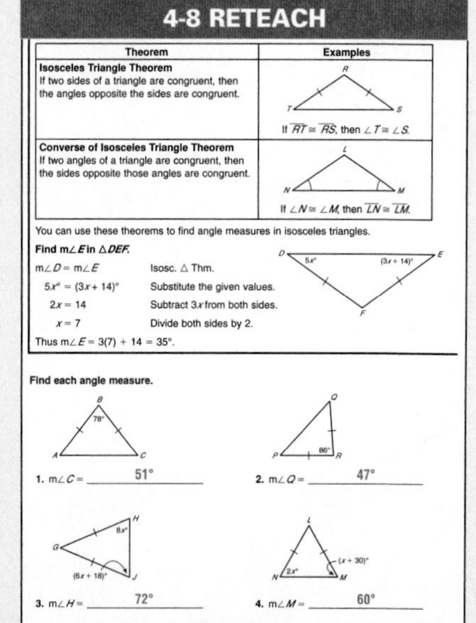

4-8 RETEACH

Theorem	Examples
Isosceles Triangle Theorem If two sides of a triangle are congruent, then the angles opposite the sides are congruent.	If $\overline{RT} \cong \overline{RS}$, then $\angle T \cong \angle S$.
Converse of Isosceles Triangle Theorem If two angles of a triangle are congruent, then the sides opposite those angles are congruent.	If $\angle N \cong \angle M$, then $\overline{LN} \cong \overline{LM}$.

You can use these theorems to find angle measures in isosceles triangles.

Find $m\angle E$ in $\triangle DEF$.

$m\angle D = m\angle E$	Isosc. △ Thm.
$5x° = (3x + 14)°$	Substitute the given values.
$2x = 14$	Subtract $3x$ from both sides.
$x = 7$	Divide both sides by 2.

Thus $m\angle E = 3(7) + 14 = 35°$.

Find each angle measure.

1. $m\angle C =$ 51°
2. $m\angle Q =$ 47°
3. $m\angle H =$ 72°
4. $m\angle M =$ 60°

41. Rewrite the paragraph proof of the Hypotenuse-Leg (HL) Congruence Theorem as a two-column proof.

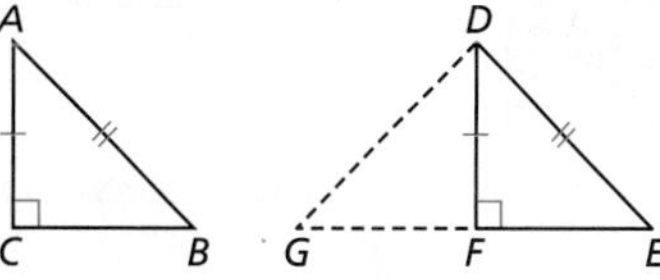

Given: $\triangle ABC$ and $\triangle DEF$ are right triangles.
$\angle C$ and $\angle F$ are right angles.
$\overline{AC} \cong \overline{DF}$, and $\overline{AB} \cong \overline{DE}$.
Prove: $\triangle ABC \cong \triangle DEF$

Proof: On $\triangle DEF$ draw $\overrightarrow{EF}$. Mark G so that $FG = CB$. Thus $\overline{FG} \cong \overline{CB}$. From the diagram, $\overline{AC} \cong \overline{DF}$ and $\angle C$ and $\angle F$ are right angles. $\overline{DF} \perp \overline{EG}$ by definition of perpendicular lines. Thus $\angle DFG$ is a right angle, and $\angle DFG \cong \angle C$. $\triangle ABC \cong \triangle DGF$ by SAS. $\overline{DG} \cong \overline{AB}$ by CPCTC. $\overline{AB} \cong \overline{DE}$ as given. $\overline{DG} \cong \overline{DE}$ by the Transitive Property. By the Isosceles Triangle Theorem $\angle G \cong \angle E$. $\angle DFG \cong \angle DFE$ since right angles are congruent. So $\triangle DGF \cong \triangle DEF$ by AAS. Therefore $\triangle ABC \cong \triangle DEF$ by the Transitive Property.

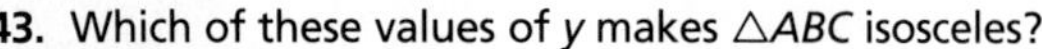

42. Lorena is designing a window so that $\angle R$, $\angle S$, $\angle T$, and $\angle U$ are right angles, $\overline{VU} \cong \overline{VT}$, and $m\angle UVT = 20°$. What is $m\angle RUV$?

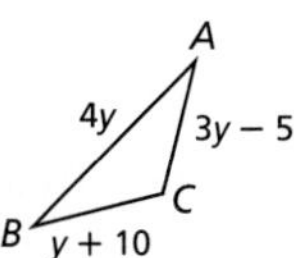

Ⓐ 10° (circled)   Ⓒ 20°
Ⓑ 70°   Ⓓ 80°

43. Which of these values of y makes $\triangle ABC$ isosceles?

Ⓕ $1\frac{1}{4}$ Ⓗ $7\frac{1}{2}$ (circled)
Ⓖ $2\frac{1}{2}$ Ⓙ $15\frac{1}{2}$

A; B; C; $4y$; $3y - 5$; $y + 10$

44. **Gridded Response** The vertex angle of an isosceles triangle measures $(6t - 9)°$, and one of the base angles measures $(4t)°$. Find t. 13.5

CHALLENGE AND EXTEND

45. In the figure, $\overline{JK} \cong \overline{JL}$, and $\overline{KM} \cong \overline{KL}$. Let $m\angle J = x°$. Prove $m\angle MKL$ must also be $x°$.

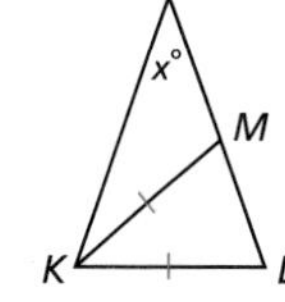

46. An equilateral $\triangle ABC$ is placed on a coordinate plane. Each side length measures $2a$. B is at the origin, and C is at $(2a, 0)$. Find the coordinates of A. $(a, a\sqrt{3})$

47. An isosceles triangle has coordinates $A(0, 0)$ and $B(a, b)$. What are all possible coordinates of the third vertex?
$(2a, 0)$, $(0, 2b)$, or any pt. on the $\perp$ bisector of $\overline{AB}$

SPIRAL REVIEW

Find the solutions for each equation. *(Previous course)*

48. $x^2 + 5x + 4 = 0$ -4 or -1
49. $x^2 - 4x + 3 = 0$ 3 or 1
50. $x^2 - 2x + 1 = 0$ 1

Find the slope of the line that passes through each pair of points. *(Lesson 3-5)*

51. $(2, -1)$ and $(0, 5)$ -3
52. $(-5, -10)$ and $(20, -10)$ 0
53. $(4, 7)$ and $(10, 11)$ $\frac{2}{3}$
54. Position a square with a perimeter of $4s$ in the coordinate plane and give the coordinates of each vertex. *(Lesson 4-7)*

54. Possible answer:
$(0, s)$, (s, s), $(0, 0)$, $(s, 0)$; x; y

In **Exercise 34,** students may write the equation $5x + 15 = 60$. Encourage them to label all angle measures before writing an equation.

TEST PREP DOCTOR If students have difficulty with **Exercise 43,** remind them that they cannot assume which two sides are congruent, so they must try all possibilities.

Journal

Compare the hypothesis and the conclusion of the Isosceles Triangle Theorem with its converse. Support your comparison with a sketch.

ALTERNATIVE ASSESSMENT

Have students create a poster to present examples of how to find missing parts of an isosceles and an equilateral triangle, when given the measure of one angle or an algebraic expression.

Power Presentations with PowerPoint®

4-8 Lesson Quiz

Find each angle measure.

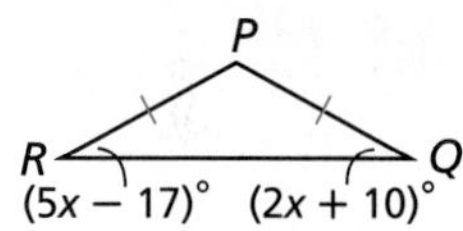

1. $m\angle R$ 28°   2. $m\angle P$ 124°

Find each value.

3. x 20

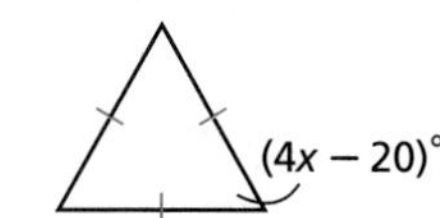

4. y 6

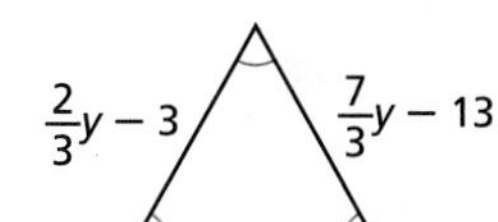

5. x 26°

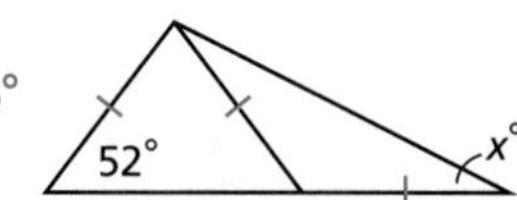

6. The vertex angle of an isosceles triangle measures $(a + 15)°$, and one of the base angles measures $7a°$. Find a and each angle measure.
$a = 11$; 26°; 77°; 77°

Also available on transparency

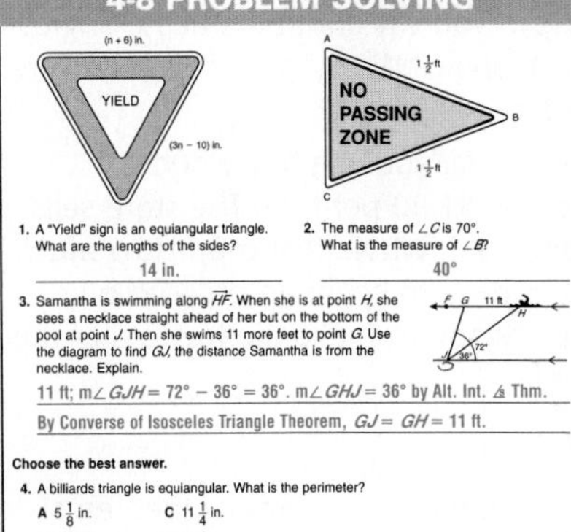

(n + 6) in.; YIELD; (3n – 10) in.; A; NO PASSING ZONE; $1\frac{1}{2}$ ft; B; $1\frac{1}{2}$ ft; C

1. A "Yield" sign is an equiangular triangle. What are the lengths of the sides? 14 in.

2. The measure of $\angle C$ is 70°. What is the measure of $\angle B$? 40°

3. Samantha is swimming along $\overrightarrow{HF}$. When she is at point H, she sees a necklace straight ahead of her but on the bottom of the pool at point J. Then she swims 11 more feet to point G. Use the diagram to find GJ, the distance Samantha is from the necklace. Explain.
11 ft; $m\angle GJH = 72° - 36° = 36°$. $m\angle GHJ = 36°$ by Alt. Int. ∠s Thm. By Converse of Isosceles Triangle Theorem, $GJ = GH = 11$ ft.

Choose the best answer.

4. A billiards triangle is equiangular. What is the perimeter?
A $5\frac{1}{8}$ in.   C $11\frac{1}{4}$ in.
B $10\frac{1}{4}$ in.   Ⓓ $33\frac{3}{4}$ in.

5. A triangular shaped trellis has angles R, S, and T that measure 73°, 73°, and 34°, respectively. If $ST = 4y + 6$ and $TR = 7y - 21$, what is the value of y?
F 5   H 11
Ⓖ 9   J 15

6. Two triangular tiles each have two sides measuring 4 inches. Which is a true statement?
A Their corresponding angles are congruent.   Ⓒ The triangles may be congruent.
B The triangles are congruent.   D The triangles cannot be congruent.

7. What is the value of x in the figure?
F 42°   Ⓗ 96°
G 90°   J 106°

Answers

41. See p. A17.

45. It is given that $\overline{JK} \cong \overline{JL}$, $\overline{KM} \cong \overline{KL}$, and $m\angle J = x°$. By the $\triangle$ Sum Thm., $m\angle JKL + m\angle JLK + x° = 180°$. By the Isosc. $\triangle$ Thm., $m\angle JKL = m\angle JLK$. So $2(m\angle JLK) + x° = 180°$ or $m\angle JLK = \left(\frac{180 - x}{2}\right)°$. Since $m\angle KML = m\angle JLK$, $m\angle KML = \left(\frac{180 - x}{2}\right)°$ by the Isosc. $\triangle$ Thm. By the $\triangle$ Sum Thm., $m\angle MKL + m\angle JLK + m\angle KML = 180°$ or $m\angle MKL = 180° - \left(\frac{180 - x}{2}\right)° - \left(\frac{180 - x}{2}\right)°$. Simplifying gives $m\angle MKL = x°$.

Organizer

Objective: Assess students' ability to apply concepts and skills in Lessons 4-4 through Lesson 4-8 in a real-world format.

Online Edition

Resources

Geometry Assessments
www.mathtekstoolkit.org

Problem	Text Reference
1	Lesson 4-4
2	Lesson 4-5
3	Lesson 4-6
4	Lesson 4-7
5	Lesson 4-8
6	Lessons 4-4 to 4-8

Answers

2. 1. $\overline{CD} \perp \overline{AB}$ (Given)
   2. $\angle CDA$ and $\angle CDB$ are rt. ∠s. (Def. of ⊥)
   3. $\triangle CDA$ and $\triangle CDB$ are rt. △s. (Def. of rt. △)
   4. $\overline{AC} \cong \overline{BC}$ (Given)
   5. $\overline{CD} \cong \overline{CD}$ (Reflex. Prop. of ≅)
   6. $\triangle CDA \cong \triangle CDB$ (HL *Steps 4, 5*)

State Resources

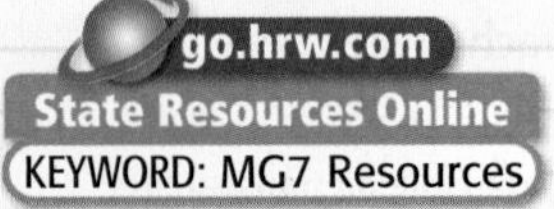

MULTI-STEP TEST PREP

SECTION 4B

Proving Triangles Congruent

Gone to the Dogs You are planning to build a doghouse for your dog. The pitched roof of the doghouse will be supported by four trusses. Each truss will be an isosceles triangle with the dimensions shown. To determine the materials you need to purchase and how you will construct the trusses, you must first plan carefully.

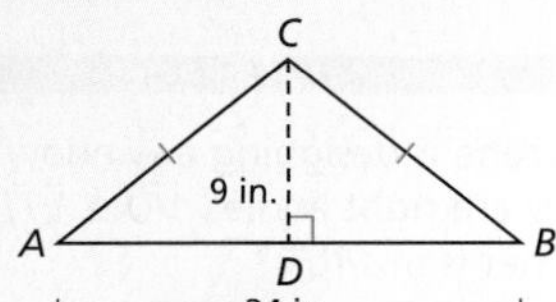

1. You want to be sure that all four trusses are exactly the same size and shape. Explain how you could measure three lengths on each truss to ensure this. Which postulate or theorem are you using?
   1. Measure $\overline{AB}$, $\overline{BC}$, and $\overline{CA}$. If these 3 lengths are the same for every truss, then the trusses all have the same size and shape by SSS.
2. Prove that the two triangular halves of the truss are congruent.
3. What can you say about $\overline{AD}$ and $\overline{DB}$? Why is this true? Use this to help you find the lengths of $\overline{AD}$, $\overline{DB}$, $\overline{AC}$, and $\overline{BC}$.
   3. $\overline{AD} \cong \overline{DB}$ by CPCTC. $AD = DB = 12$ in. and $AC = BC = 15$ in.
4. You want to make careful plans on a coordinate plane before you begin your construction of the trusses. Each unit of the coordinate plane represents 1 inch. How could you assign coordinates to vertices *A*, *B*, and *C*?
   4. Possible answer: $A(0, 0)$, $B(24, 0)$, $C(12, 9)$
5. $m\angle ACB = 106°$. What is the measure of each of the acute angles in the truss? Explain how you found your answer.
   5. $m\angle A = m\angle B = 37°$; the base ∠s of an isosc. △ are ≅, so $2m\angle A + 106° = 180°$.
6. You can buy the wood for the trusses at the building supply store for \$0.80 a foot. The store sells the wood in 6-foot lengths only. How much will you have to spend to get enough wood for the 4 trusses of the doghouse? **\$14.40**

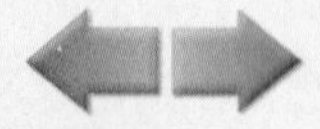

INTERVENTION

Scaffolding Questions

1. Which postulate or theorem applies if you know that three sides of one triangle are congruent to three sides of another triangle? SSS
2. What type of triangle is formed by each half of the truss? rt.
3. Can you conclude that $\overline{AD} \cong \overline{DB}$? If so, why? Yes; CPCTC Once you know *AD*, how can you find *AC*? Pyth. Thm.
4. If you place *A* at the origin and $\overline{AB}$ along the *x*-axis, what are the coordinates of *B*? Why? $B(24, 0)$; $AB = 24$
5. What can you say about the acute angles of the triangle? Why? They are ≅; they are base ∠s of an isosc. △.
6. Suppose that you can buy wooden boards for \$1.80 per foot. The store sells the boards in whole feet only. How much will you have to spend in order to buy enough wood to make the trusses for the doghouse? \$9

Extension

Which congruence postulates or theorems involve only one pair of congruent sides? ASA; AAS Can they be applied to prove $\triangle ACD \cong \triangle BCD$? Yes

SECTION 4B

Quiz for Lessons 4-4 Through 4-8

4-4 Triangle Congruence: SSS and SAS

1. The figure shows one tower and the cables of a suspension bridge. Given that $\overline{AC} \cong \overline{BC}$, use SAS to explain why $\triangle ACD \cong \triangle BCD$.

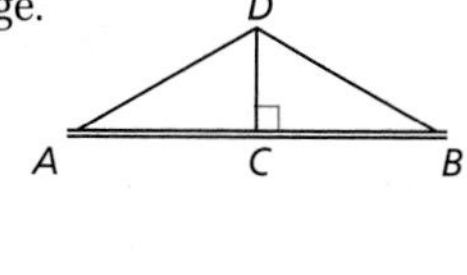

2. **Given:** $\overline{JK}$ bisects $\angle MJN$. $\overline{MJ} \cong \overline{NJ}$
   Prove: $\triangle MJK \cong \triangle NJK$

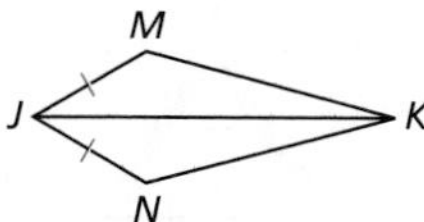

4-5 Triangle Congruence: ASA, AAS, and HL

Determine if you can use the HL Congruence Theorem to prove the triangles congruent. If not, tell what else you need to know.

3. $\triangle RSU$ and $\triangle TUS$
   yes

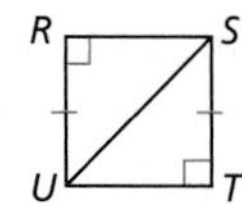

4. $\triangle ABC$ and $\triangle DCB$
   no; $\overline{AC} \cong \overline{DB}$

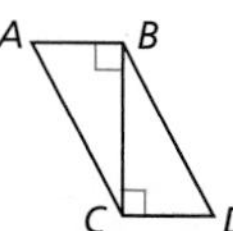

Observers in two lighthouses K and L spot a ship S.

5. Draw a diagram of the triangle formed by the lighthouses and the ship. Label each measure.
6. Is there enough data in the table to pinpoint the location of the ship? Why?
   Yes; the △ is uniquely determined by ASA.

	K to L	K to S	L to S
Bearing	E	N 58° E	N 77° W
Distance	12 km	?	?

5.

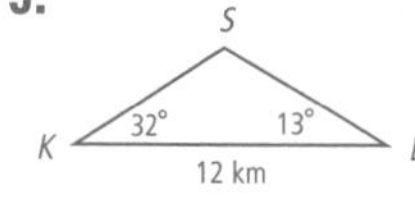

4-6 Triangle Congruence: CPCTC

7. **Given:** $\overline{CD} \parallel \overline{BE}$, $\overline{DE} \parallel \overline{CB}$
   Prove: $\angle D \cong \angle B$

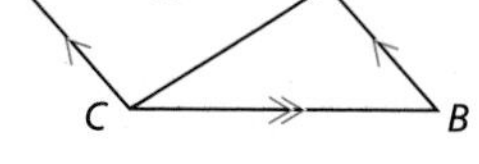

4-7 Introduction to Coordinate Proof

Check students' work; possible answer: vertices at (0, 0), (9, 0), (9, 9), and (0, 9).

8. Position a square with side lengths of 9 units in the coordinate plane
9. Assign coordinates to each vertex and write a coordinate proof.
   Given: $ABCD$ is a rectangle with M as the midpoint of $\overline{AB}$. N is the midpoint of $\overline{AD}$.
   Prove: The area of $\triangle AMN$ is $\frac{1}{8}$ the area of rectangle $ABCD$.

4-8 Isosceles and Equilateral Triangles

Find each value.

10. m∠C
    100°

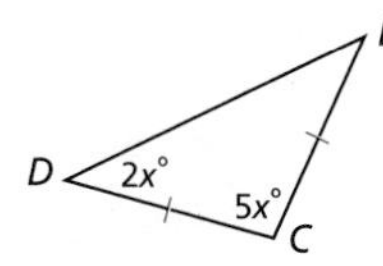

11. ST
    6

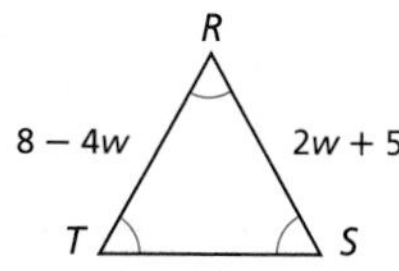

12. **Given:** Isosceles $\triangle JKL$ has coordinates $J(0, 0)$, $K(2a, 2b)$, and $L(4a, 0)$. M is the midpoint of $\overline{JK}$, and N is the midpoint of $\overline{KL}$.
    Prove: $\triangle KMN$ is isosceles.

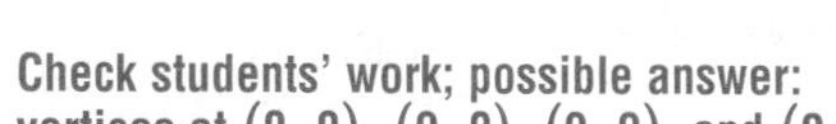

READY TO GO ON?

SECTION 4B

Organizer

Objective: Assess students' mastery of concepts and skills in Lessons 4-4 through 4-8.

Resources

Assessment Resources
Section 4B Quiz

Teacher One Stop™
Test & Practice Generator

INTERVENTION

Resources

Ready to Go On? Intervention and Enrichment Worksheets

***Ready to Go On?* CD-ROM**

***Ready to Go On?* Online**

my.hrw.com

Answers

1, 2, 7, 9, 12. See p. A17.

READY TO GO ON?
Diagnose and Prescribe

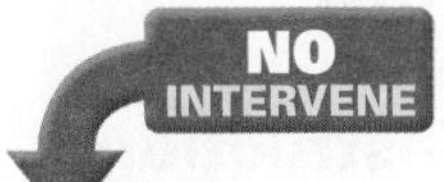

Ready to Go On? Intervention	READY TO GO ON? Intervention, Section 4B: Worksheets	CD-ROM	Online
Lesson 4-4	4-4 Intervention	Activity 4-4	Diagnose and Prescribe Online
Lesson 4-5	4-5 Intervention	Activity 4-5	
Lesson 4-6	4-6 Intervention	Activity 4-6	
Lesson 4-7	4-7 Intervention	Activity 4-7	
Lesson 4-8	4-8 Intervention	Activity 4-8	

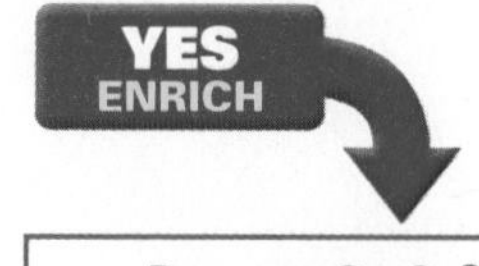

READY TO GO ON? Enrichment, Section 4B
Worksheets
CD-ROM
Online

CHAPTER 4 Organizer

Pacing: Traditional 1 day
Block $\frac{1}{2}$ day

Objective: Use congruent triangles to prove constructions valid.

Using the Extension

In Chapter 4, students learn to prove triangles congruent and to use properties of congruent triangles in other proofs. In this extension, students use the properties of congruent triangles to prove constructions valid.

Answers to *Check It Out!*

1. 1. Draw $\overline{AC}$, $\overline{BC}$, $\overline{AD}$, and $\overline{BD}$. (Through any 2 pts. there is exactly 1 line.)
   2. $\overline{AC} \cong \overline{BC} \cong \overline{AD} \cong \overline{BD}$ (Same compass setting used)
   3. $\overline{CD} \cong \overline{CD}$ (Reflex. Prop. of $\cong$)
   4. $\triangle ACD \cong \triangle BCD$ (SSS *Steps 2, 3*)
   5. $\angle ACD \cong \angle BCD$ (CPCTC)
   6. $\overline{CM} \cong \overline{CM}$ (Reflex. Prop. of $\cong$)
   7. $\triangle ACM \cong \triangle BCM$ (SAS *Steps 2, 5, 6*)
   8. $\angle AMC \cong \angle BMC$ (CPCTC)
   9. $\angle AMC$ and $\angle BMC$ are rt. $\angle$s. ($\cong$ $\angle$s supp. $\rightarrow$ rt. $\angle$s)
   10. $\overline{CD} \perp \overline{AB}$ (Def. of $\perp$)
   11. $\overline{AM} \cong \overline{BM}$ (CPCTC)
   12. $\overleftrightarrow{CD}$ bisects $\overline{AB}$. (Def. of bisector)

State Resources

EXTENSION Proving Constructions Valid

Objective
Use congruent triangles to prove constructions valid.

When performing a compass and straight edge construction, the compass setting remains the same width until you change it. This fact allows you to construct a segment congruent to a given segment. You can assume that two distances constructed with the same compass setting are congruent.

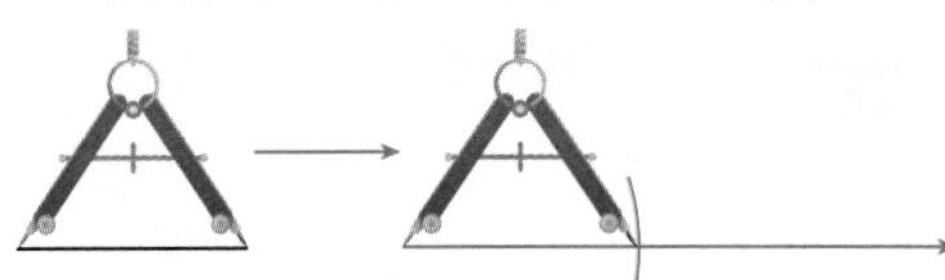

The steps in the construction of a figure can be justified by combining the assumptions of compass and straightedge constructions and the postulates and theorems that are used for proving triangles congruent.

You have learned that there exists exactly one midpoint on any line segment. The proof below justifies the construction of a midpoint.

EXAMPLE 1 Proving the Construction of a Midpoint

Given: diagram showing the steps in the construction
Prove: M is the midpoint of $\overline{AB}$.

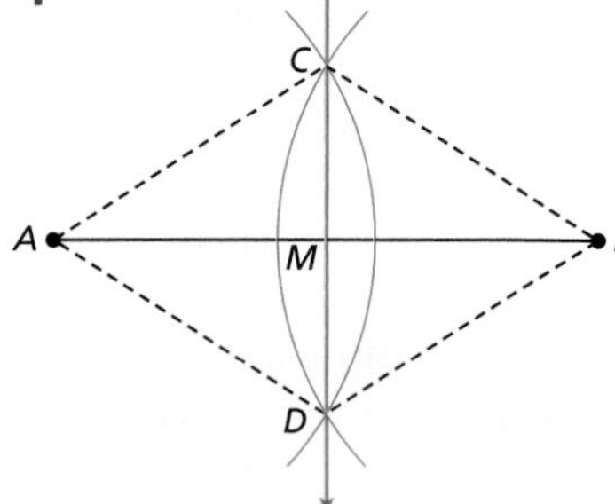

To construct a midpoint, see the construction of a perpendicular bisector on p. 172.

Proof:

Statements	Reasons
1. Draw $\overline{AC}$, $\overline{BC}$, $\overline{AD}$, and $\overline{BD}$.	1. Through any two pts. there is exactly one line.
2. $\overline{AC} \cong \overline{BC} \cong \overline{AD} \cong \overline{BD}$	2. Same compass setting used
3. $\overline{CD} \cong \overline{CD}$	3. Reflex. Prop. of $\cong$
4. $\triangle ACD \cong \triangle BCD$	4. SSS *Steps 2, 3*
5. $\angle ACD \cong \angle BCD$	5. CPCTC
6. $\overline{CM} \cong \overline{CM}$	6. Reflex. Prop. of $\cong$
7. $\triangle ACM \cong \triangle BCM$	7. SAS *Steps 2, 5, 6*
8. $\overline{AM} \cong \overline{BM}$	8. CPCTC
9. M is the midpt. of $\overline{AB}$.	9. Def. of mdpt.

CHECK IT OUT! 1. **Given:** above diagram
Prove: $\overleftrightarrow{CD}$ is the perpendicular bisector of $\overline{AB}$.

1 Introduce

Motivate

Point out to students that some assumptions made about their construction tools, such as a compass setting being fixed, could make their constructions inaccurate. Discuss what characteristics of their construction tools might make their constructions invalid. Possible answer: Compass does not hold its setting; compass does not hold the pencil firmly; straightedge is cracked or broken.

2 Teach

Guided Instruction

Explain that steps in a construction contain given information much like the tick marks in a diagram show that segments are congruent. Have students practice identifying what information is given from the construction marks in a diagram. Explain to students that justifying their constructions can provide a review of concepts from previous lessons.

Inclusion Remind students to make their constructions big enough for easy use of their compass.

EXAMPLE 2 **Proving the Construction of an Angle**

Given: diagram showing the steps in the construction

Prove: $\angle A \cong \angle D$

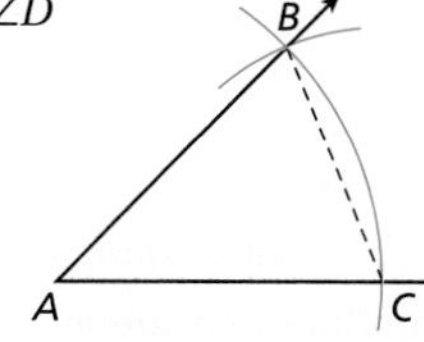

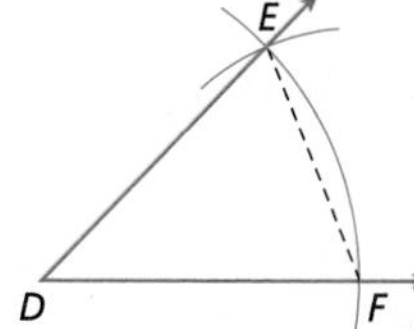

Proof: Since there is a straight line through any two points, you can draw $\overline{BC}$ and $\overline{EF}$. The same compass setting was used to construct $\overline{AC}, \overline{AB}, \overline{DF}$, and $\overline{DE}$, so $\overline{AC} \cong \overline{AB} \cong \overline{DF} \cong \overline{DE}$. The same compass setting was used to construct $\overline{BC}$ and $\overline{EF}$, so $\overline{BC} \cong \overline{EF}$. Therefore $\triangle BAC \cong \triangle EDF$ by SSS, and $\angle A \cong \angle D$ by CPCTC.

Remember!

To review the construction of an angle congruent to another angle, see page 22.

2. Prove the construction for bisecting an angle. (See page 23.)

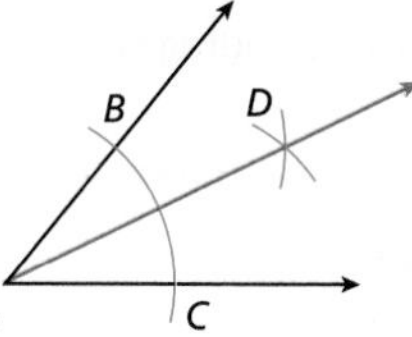

Draw $\overline{BD}$ and $\overline{CD}$ (through any 2 pts. there is exactly 1 line). Since the same compass setting was used, $\overline{AB} \cong \overline{AC}$ and $\overline{BD} \cong \overline{CD}$. $\overline{AD} \cong \overline{AD}$ by the Reflex. Prop. of $\cong$. So $\triangle ABD \cong \triangle ACD$ by SSS, and $\angle BAD \cong \angle CAD$ by CPCTC. Therefore $\overrightarrow{AD}$ bisects $\angle BAC$ by the def. of $\angle$ bisector.

EXTENSION Exercises

Use each diagram to prove the construction valid.

1. parallel lines (See page 163 and page 170.)

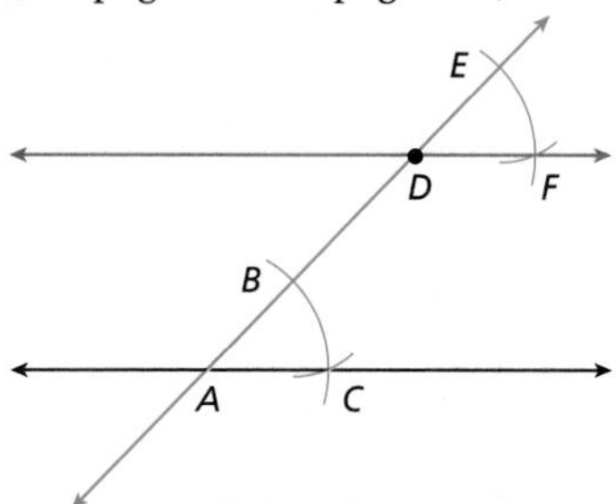

2. a perpendicular through a point not on the line (See page 179.)

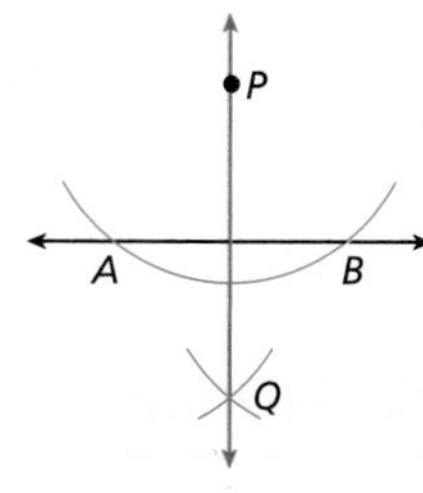

3. constructing a triangle using SAS (See page 243.)

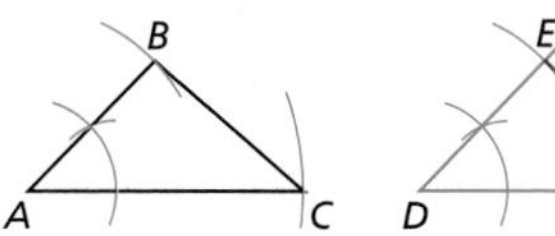

4. constructing a triangle using ASA (See page 253.)

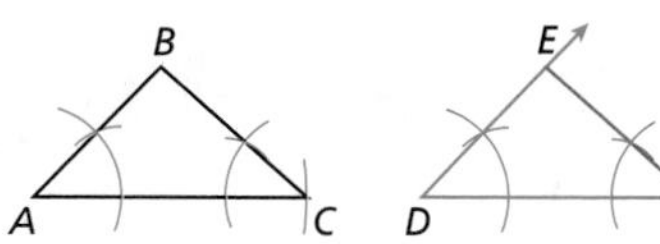

Power Presentations with PowerPoint®

Additional Examples

Example 1

Given: Diagram showing the steps in the construction

Prove: $\overline{CD} \perp \overline{AB}$.

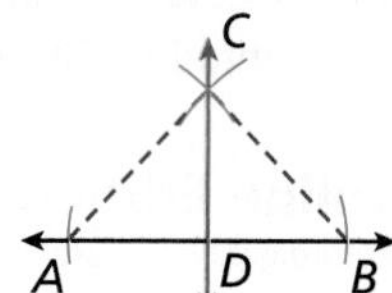

1. Draw $\overline{AC}, \overline{BC}$. (Through any two pts. there is exactly one line.)
2. $\overline{AC} \cong \overline{BC}$ (Same compass setting used)
3. $\overline{AD} \cong \overline{BD}$ (Same compass setting used)
4. $\overline{CD} \cong \overline{CD}$ (Reflex. Prop. of $\cong$)
5. $\triangle ADC \cong \triangle BDC$ (SSS *Steps 2, 3, 4*)
6. $\angle ADC \cong \angle BDC$ (CPCTC)
7. $\angle ADC$ and $\angle BDC$ are rt. $\angle$s. ($\cong \angle$s that form a lin. pair are rt. $\angle$s.)
8. $\overline{CD} \perp \overline{AB}$ (Def. of $\perp$)

Example 2

Given: Diagram showing the steps in the construction

Prove: $\angle D \cong \angle A$

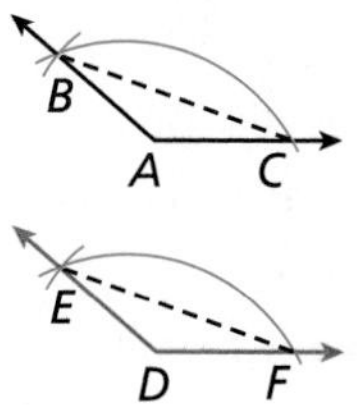

Since there is a straight line through any two points, you can draw $\overline{BC}$ and $\overline{EF}$. The same compass setting was used to construct $\overline{AC}, \overline{AB}, \overline{DF}$, and $\overline{DE}$, so $\overline{AC} \cong \overline{AB} \cong \overline{DF} \cong \overline{DE}$. The same compass setting was used to construct $\overline{BC}$ and $\overline{EF}$, so $\overline{BC} \cong \overline{EF}$. Therefore $\triangle ABC \cong \triangle DEF$ by SSS, and $\angle D \cong \angle A$ by CPCTC.

3 Close

Summarize

Review the steps for proving a construction valid.

- Identify congruent segments constructed with the same compass setting.
- Use triangle congruence and CPCTC (or other theorems and postulates) to complete the proof.

Answers

1. Draw auxiliary segments $\overline{BC}$ and $\overline{EF}$. (Through any 2 pts. there is exactly 1 line.) Since the same compass setting was used, $\overline{AB} \cong \overline{AC} \cong \overline{DE} \cong \overline{DF}$ and $\overline{BC} \cong \overline{EF}$. $\triangle BAC \cong \triangle EDF$ by SSS. $\angle BAC \cong \angle EDF$ by CPCTC. Therefore $\overleftrightarrow{DF} \parallel \overleftrightarrow{AC}$ by the Conv. of the Corr. $\angle$s Thm.

2–4. See p. A17.

INTERVENTION

Questioning Strategies

EXAMPLES 1–2

- Why is it necessary to first prove congruent triangles when proving constructions valid?

Study Guide: Review

Organizer

Objective: Help students organize and review key concepts and skills presented in Chapter 4.

Online Edition
Multilingual Glossary

Countdown Week 9

Resources

Teacher One Stop™
PuzzleView
Test & Practice Generator

Multilingual Glossary **Online**
go.hrw.com
KEYWORD: MG7 Glossary

Lesson Tutorial Videos
CD-ROM

Answers

1. isosceles triangle
2. corresponding angles
3. included side
4. equiangular; equil.
5. obtuse; scalene
6. 60°
7. 66.5°

CHAPTER 4 Study Guide: Review

For a complete list of the postulates and theorems in this chapter, see p. PS12.

Vocabulary

Complete the sentences below with vocabulary words from the list above.

1. A(n) __?__ is a triangle with at least two congruent sides.
2. A name given to matching angles of congruent triangles is __?__ .
3. A(n) __?__ is the common side of two consecutive angles in a polygon.

4-1 Classifying Triangles *(pp. 216–221)*

EXAMPLE

- **Classify the triangle by its angle measures and side lengths.**

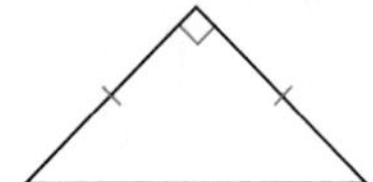

isosceles right triangle

EXERCISES

Classify each triangle by its angle measures and side lengths.

4. 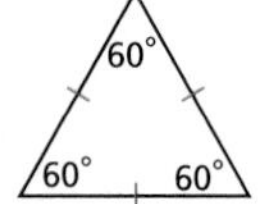

5.

4-2 Angle Relationships in Triangles *(pp. 223–230)*

EXAMPLE

- **Find m∠S.**

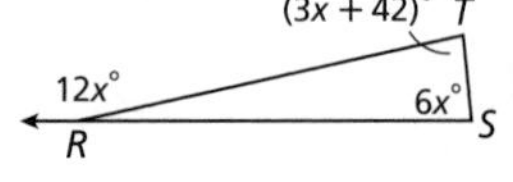

$12x = 3x + 42 + 6x$
$12x = 9x + 42$
$3x = 42$
$x = 14$
$m\angle S = 6(14) = 84°$

EXERCISES

Find m∠N.

6. 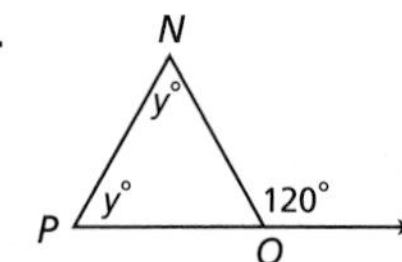

7. In $\triangle LMN$, $m\angle L = 8x°$, $m\angle M = (2x + 1)°$, and $m\angle N = (6x - 1)°$.

4-3 Congruent Triangles *(pp. 231–237)*

EXAMPLE

- **Given: $\triangle DEF \cong \triangle JKL$. Identify all pairs of congruent corresponding parts. Then find the value of x.**

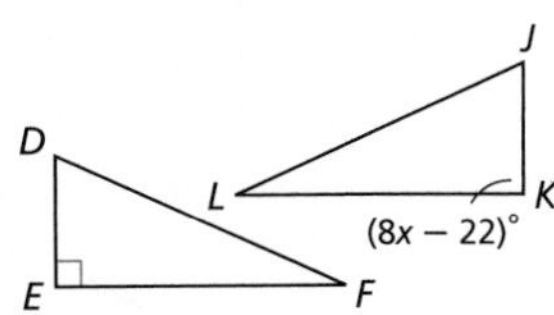

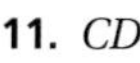

The congruent pairs follow: $\angle D \cong \angle J$, $\angle E \cong \angle K$, $\angle F \cong \angle L$, $\overline{DE} \cong \overline{JK}$, $\overline{EF} \cong \overline{KL}$, and $\overline{DF} \cong \overline{JL}$.

Since $m\angle E = m\angle K$, $90 = 8x - 22$. After 22 is added to both sides, $112 = 8x$. So $x = 14$.

EXERCISES

Given: $\triangle PQR \cong \triangle XYZ$. Identify the congruent corresponding parts.

8. $\overline{PR} \cong$ ___?___ **9.** $\angle Y \cong$ ___?___

Given: $\triangle ABC \cong \triangle CDA$ Find each value.

10. x

11. CD

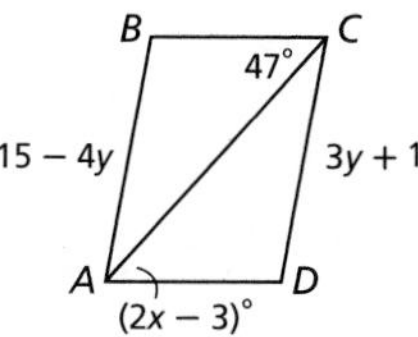

4-4 Triangle Congruence: SSS and SAS *(pp. 242–249)*

EXAMPLES

- **Given: $\overline{RS} \cong \overline{UT}$, and $\overline{VS} \cong \overline{VT}$. V is the midpoint of $\overline{RU}$.**

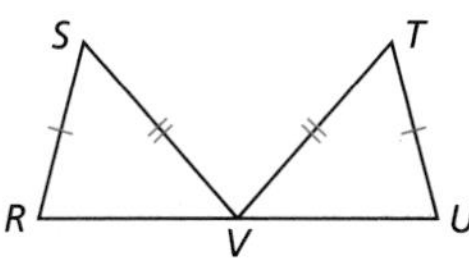

Prove: $\triangle RSV \cong \triangle UTV$

Proof:

Statements	Reasons
1. $\overline{RS} \cong \overline{UT}$	1. Given
2. $\overline{VS} \cong \overline{VT}$	2. Given
3. *V is the mdpt. of* $\overline{RU}$.	3. Given
4. $\overline{RV} \cong \overline{UV}$	4. Def. of mdpt.
5. $\triangle RSV \cong \triangle UTV$	5. SSS *Steps 1, 2, 4*

- **Show that $\triangle ADB \cong \triangle CDB$ when s = 5.**

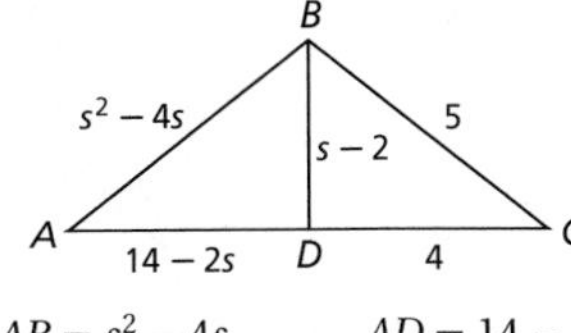

$AB = s^2 - 4s$ $\quad AD = 14 - 2s$
$= 5^2 - 4(5)$ $\quad = 14 - 2(5)$
$= 5$ $\quad = 4$

$\overline{BD} \cong \overline{BD}$ by the Reflexive Property. $\overline{AD} \cong \overline{CD}$ and $\overline{AB} \cong \overline{CB}$. So $\triangle ADB \cong \triangle CDB$ by SSS.

EXERCISES

12. Given: $\overline{AB} \cong \overline{DE}$, $\overline{DB} \cong \overline{AE}$
Prove: $\triangle ADB \cong \triangle DAE$

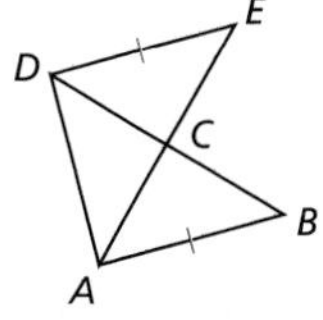

13. Given: $\overline{GJ}$ bisects $\overline{FH}$, and $\overline{FH}$ bisects $\overline{GJ}$.
Prove: $\triangle FGK \cong \triangle HJK$

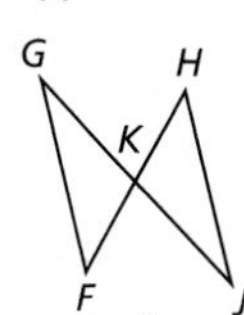

14. Show that $\triangle ABC \cong \triangle XYZ$ when $x = -6$.

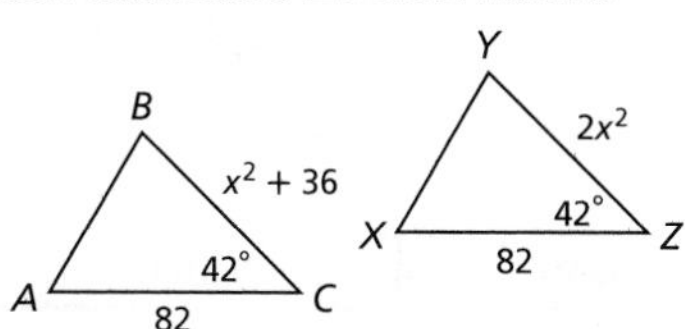

15. Show that $\triangle LMN \cong \triangle PQR$ when $y = 25$.

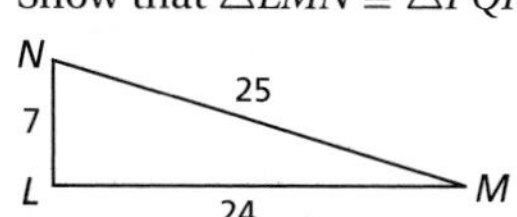

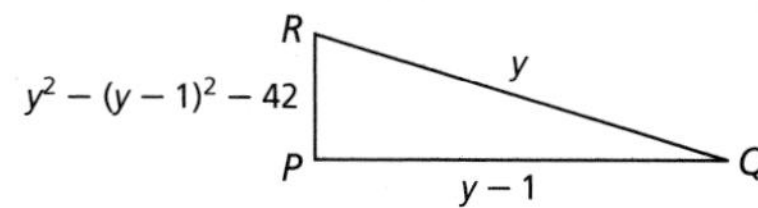

8. $\overline{XZ}$
9. $\angle Q$
10. 25
11. 7
12. 1. $\overline{AB} \cong \overline{DE}$, $\overline{DB} \cong \overline{AE}$ (Given)
    2. $\overline{DA} \cong \overline{DA}$ (Reflex. Prop. of $\cong$)
    3. $\triangle ADB \cong \triangle DAE$ (SSS *Steps 1, 2*)
13. 1. $\overline{GJ}$ bisects $\overline{FH}$, and $\overline{FH}$ bisects $\overline{GJ}$. (Given)
    2. $\overline{GK} \cong \overline{JK}$, $\overline{FK} \cong \overline{HK}$ (Def. of seg. bisect)
    3. $\angle GKF \cong \angle JKH$ (Vert. ∡ Thm.)
    4. $\triangle FGK \cong \triangle HJK$ (SAS *Steps 2, 3*)
14. $BC = (-6)^2 + 36 = 72$; $YZ = 2(-6)^2 = 72$; $\overline{BC} \cong \overline{YZ}$; $\angle C \cong \angle Z$; $\overline{AC} \cong \overline{XZ}$. So $\triangle ABC \cong \triangle XYZ$ by SAS.
15. $PQ = 25 - 1 = 24$; $QR = 25$; and $PR = 25^2 - (25 - 1)^2 - 42 = 7$; $\overline{LM} \cong \overline{PQ}$; $\overline{MN} \cong \overline{QR}$; $\overline{LN} \cong \overline{PR}$; so $\triangle LMN \cong \triangle PQR$ by SSS.

Answers

16. 1. C is the mdpt. of $\overline{AG}$. (Given)
    2. $\overline{GC} \cong \overline{AC}$ (Def. of mdpt.)
    3. $\overline{HA} \parallel \overline{GB}$ (Given)
    4. $\angle HAC \cong \angle BGC$ (Alt. Int. ∠s Thm.)
    5. $\angle HCA \cong \angle BCG$ (Vert. ∠s Thm.)
    6. $\triangle HAC \cong \triangle BGC$ (ASA *Steps 4, 2, 5*)
17. 1. $\overline{WX} \perp \overline{XZ}$, $\overline{YZ} \perp \overline{ZX}$ (Given)
    2. $\angle WXZ$ and $\angle YZX$ are rt. ∠s. (Def. of ⊥)
    3. $\triangle WZX$ and $\triangle YXZ$ are rt. △s. (Def. of rt. △)
    4. $\overline{XZ} \cong \overline{XZ}$ (Reflex. Prop. of ≅)
    5. $\overline{WZ} \cong \overline{YX}$ (Given)
    6. $\triangle WZX \cong \triangle YXZ$ (HL *Steps 5, 4*)
18. 1. $\angle S$ and $\angle V$ are rt. ∠s. (Given)
    2. $\angle S \cong \angle V$ (Rt. ∠ ≅ Thm.)
    3. $RT = UW$ (Given)
    4. $\overline{RT} \cong \overline{UW}$ (Def. of ≅)
    5. $m\angle T = m\angle W$ (Given)
    6. $\angle T \cong \angle W$ (Def. of ≅)
    7. $\triangle RST \cong \triangle UVW$ (AAS *Steps 2, 6, 4*)
19. 1. M is the mdpt. of $\overline{BD}$. (Given)
    2. $\overline{MB} \cong \overline{DM}$ (Def. of mdpt.)
    3. $\overline{BC} \cong \overline{DC}$ (Given)
    4. $\overline{CM} \cong \overline{CM}$ (Reflex. Prop. of ≅)
    5. $\triangle CBM \cong \triangle CDM$ (SSS *Steps 2, 3, 4*)
    6. $\angle 1 \cong \angle 2$ (CPCTC)
20. 1. $\overline{PQ} \cong \overline{RQ}$ (Given)
    2. $\overline{PS} \cong \overline{RS}$ (Given)
    3. $\overline{QS} \cong \overline{QS}$ (Reflex. Prop. of ≅)
    4. $\triangle PQS \cong \triangle RQS$ (SSS *Steps 1, 2, 3*)
    5. $\angle PQS \cong \angle RQS$ (CPCTC)
    6. $\overline{QS}$ bisects $\angle PQR$. (Def. of bisect)
21. 1. H is mdpt. of $\overline{GJ}$, and L is mdpt. of $\overline{MK}$. (Given)
    2. $GH = JH$, $ML = KL$ (Def. of mdpt.)
    3. $\overline{GH} \cong \overline{JH}$, $\overline{ML} \cong \overline{KL}$ (Def. of ≅)
    4. $\overline{GJ} \cong \overline{KM}$ (Given)
    5. $\overline{GH} \cong \overline{KL}$ (Div. Prop. of ≅)
    6. $\overline{GM} \cong \overline{KJ}$, $\angle G \cong \angle K$ (Given)
    7. $\triangle GMH \cong \triangle KJL$ (SAS *Steps 5, 6*)
    8. $\angle GMH \cong \angle KJL$ (CPCTC)

4-5 Triangle Congruence: ASA, AAS, and HL *(pp. 252–259)*

EXAMPLES

■ **Given:** B is the midpoint of $\overline{AE}$.
$\angle A \cong \angle E$,
$\angle ABC \cong \angle EBD$

Prove: $\triangle ABC \cong \triangle EBD$

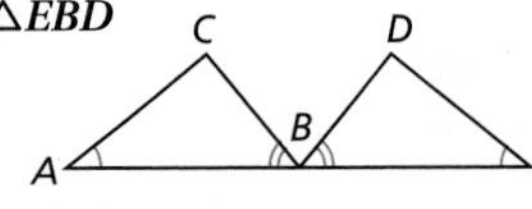

Proof:

Statements	Reasons
1. $\angle A \cong \angle E$	1. Given
2. $\angle ABC \cong \angle EBD$	2. Given
3. B is the mdpt. of $\overline{AE}$.	3. Given
4. $\overline{AB} \cong \overline{EB}$	4. Def. of mdpt.
5. $\triangle ABC \cong \triangle EBD$	5. ASA *Steps 1, 4, 2*

EXERCISES

16. **Given:** C is the midpoint of $\overline{AG}$. $\overline{HA} \parallel \overline{GB}$
Prove: $\triangle HAC \cong \triangle BGC$

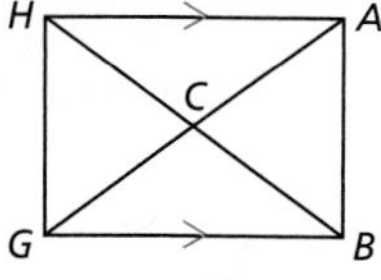

17. **Given:** $\overline{WX} \perp \overline{XZ}$, $\overline{YZ} \perp \overline{ZX}$, $\overline{WZ} \cong \overline{YX}$
Prove: $\triangle WZX \cong \triangle YXZ$

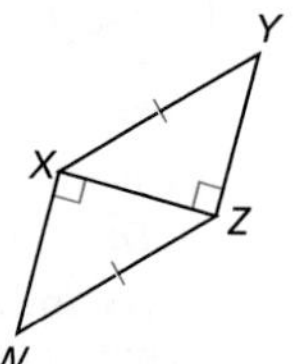

18. **Given:** $\angle S$ and $\angle V$ are right angles. $RT = UW$. $m\angle T = m\angle W$
Prove: $\triangle RST \cong \triangle UVW$

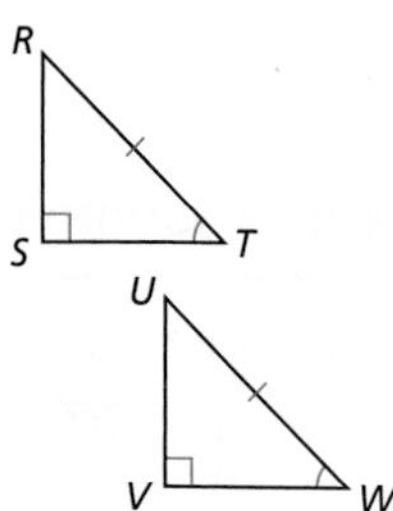

4-6 Triangle Congruence: CPCTC *(pp. 260–265)*

EXAMPLES

■ **Given:** $\overline{JL}$ and $\overline{HK}$ bisect each other.

Prove: $\angle JHG \cong \angle LKG$

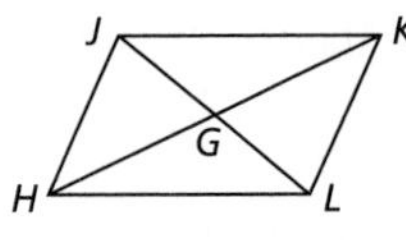

Proof:

Statements	Reasons
1. $\overline{JL}$ and $\overline{HK}$ bisect each other.	1. Given
2. $\overline{JG} \cong \overline{LG}$, and $\overline{HG} \cong \overline{KG}$.	2. Def. of bisect
3. $\angle JGH \cong \angle LGK$	3. Vert. ∠s Thm.
4. $\triangle JHG \cong \triangle LKG$	4. SAS *Steps 2, 3*
5. $\angle JHG \cong \angle LKG$	5. CPCTC

EXERCISES

19. **Given:** M is the midpoint of $\overline{BD}$. $\overline{BC} \cong \overline{DC}$
Prove: $\angle 1 \cong \angle 2$

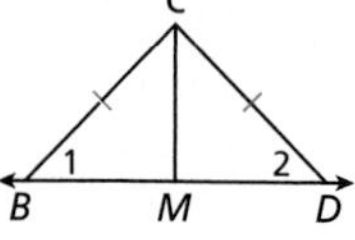

20. **Given:** $\overline{PQ} \cong \overline{RQ}$, $\overline{PS} \cong \overline{RS}$
Prove: $\overline{QS}$ bisects $\angle PQR$.

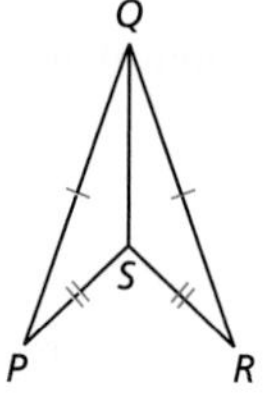

21. **Given:** H is the midpoint of $\overline{GL}$. L is the midpoint of $\overline{MK}$. $\overline{GM} \cong \overline{KJ}$, $\overline{GJ} \cong \overline{KM}$, $\angle G \cong \angle K$
Prove: $\angle GMH \cong \angle KJL$

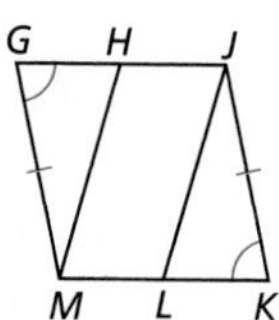

4-7 Introduction to Coordinate Proof *(pp. 267–272)*

EXAMPLES

- **Given: $\angle B$ is a right angle in isosceles right $\triangle ABC$. E is the midpoint of $\overline{AB}$. D is the midpoint of $\overline{CB}$. $\overline{AB} \cong \overline{CB}$**

Prove: $\overline{CE} \cong \overline{AD}$

Proof: Use the coordinates $A(0, 2a)$, $B(0, 0)$, and $C(2a, 0)$. Draw $\overline{AD}$ and $\overline{CE}$.

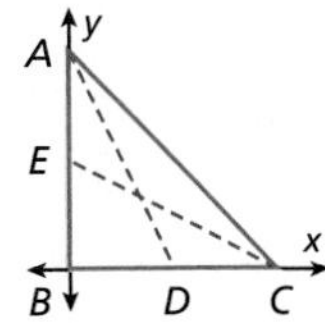

By the Midpoint Formula,

$E = \left(\frac{0+0}{2}, \frac{2a+0}{2}\right) = (0, a)$ and

$D = \left(\frac{0+2a}{2}, \frac{0+0}{2}\right) = (a, 0)$

By the Distance Formula,

$CE = \sqrt{(2a-0)^2 + (0-a)^2}$

$= \sqrt{4a^2 + a^2} = a\sqrt{5}$

$AD = \sqrt{(a-0)^2 + (0-2a)^2}$

$= \sqrt{a^2 + 4a^2} = a\sqrt{5}$

Thus $\overline{CE} \cong \overline{AD}$ by the definition of congruence.

EXERCISES

Position each figure in the coordinate plane and give the coordinates of each vertex.

22. a right triangle with leg lengths r and s
23. a rectangle with length $2p$ and width p
24. a square with side length $8m$

For exercises 25 and 26 assign coordinates to each vertex and write a coordinate proof.

25. **Given:** In rectangle $ABCD$, E is the midpoint of $\overline{AB}$, F is the midpoint of $\overline{BC}$, G is the midpoint of $\overline{CD}$, and H is the midpoint of $\overline{AD}$.
Prove: $\overline{EF} \cong \overline{GH}$
26. **Given:** $\triangle PQR$ has a right $\angle Q$. M is the midpoint of $\overline{PR}$.
Prove: $MP = MQ = MR$
27. Show that a triangle with vertices at $(3, 5)$, $(3, 2)$, and $(2, 5)$ is a right triangle.

4-8 Isosceles and Equilateral Triangles *(pp. 273–279)*

EXAMPLE

- **Find the value of x.**

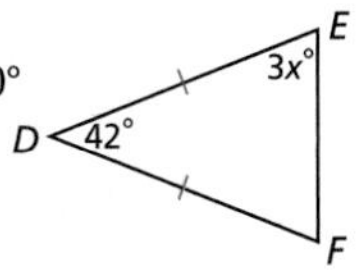

$m\angle D + m\angle E + m\angle F = 180°$ by the Triangle Sum Theorem. $m\angle E = m\angle F$ by the Isosceles Triangle Theorem.

(Figure: triangle DEF with $\angle D = 42°$, $\angle E = 3x°$.)

$m\angle D + 2m\angle E = 180°$	*Substitution*
$42 + 2(3x) = 180$	*Substitute the given values.*
$6x = 138$	*Simplify.*
$x = 23$	*Divide both sides by 6.*

EXERCISES

Find each value.

28. x

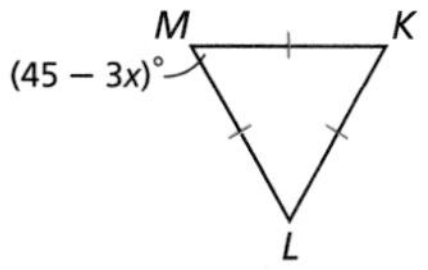

(Figure: triangle MKL, angle at M labeled $(45 - 3x)°$.)

29. RS

(Figure: triangle RST with $RT = 2y - 4.5$, $RS = 1.5y$.)

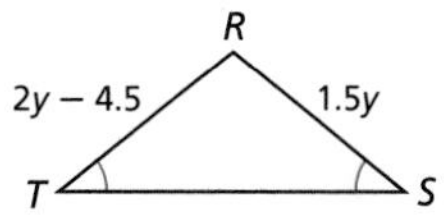

30. **Given:** $\triangle ACD$ is isosceles with $\angle D$ as the vertex angle. B is the midpoint of $\overline{AC}$. $AB = x + 5$, $BC = 2x - 3$, and $CD = 2x + 6$. Find the perimeter of $\triangle ACD$.

Answers

22. $(0, 0)$, $(r, 0)$, $(0, s)$

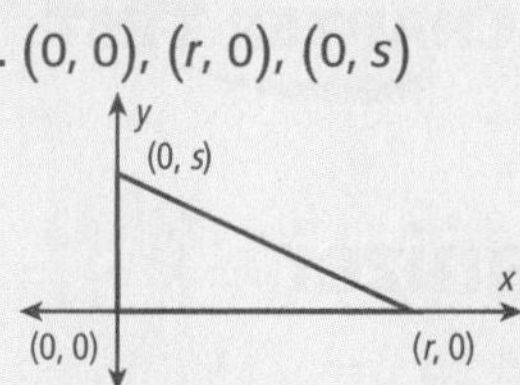

23. $(0, 0)$, $(2p, 0)$, $(2p, p)$, $(0, p)$

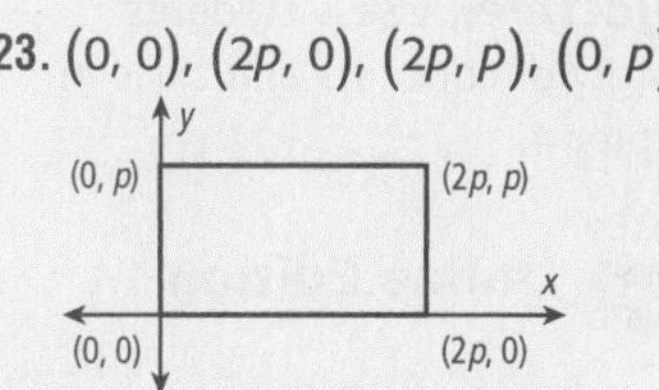

24. $(0, 0)$, $(8m, 0)$, $(8m, 8m)$, $(0, 8m)$

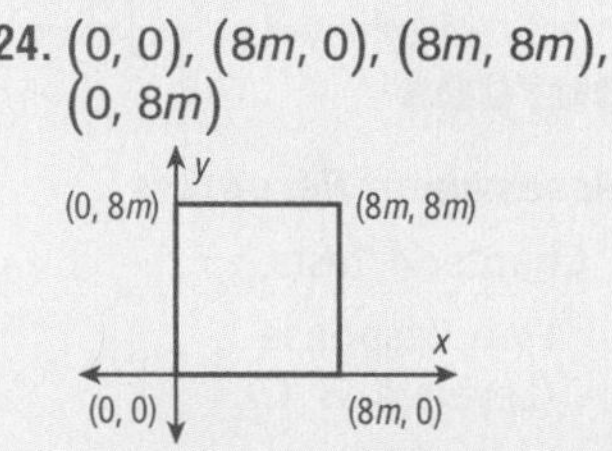

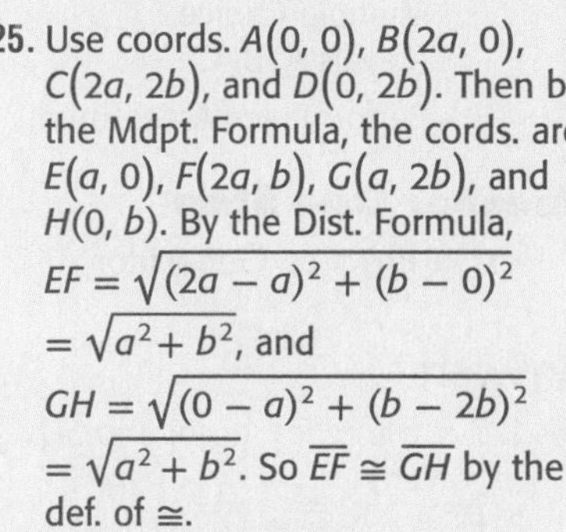

25. Use coords. $A(0, 0)$, $B(2a, 0)$, $C(2a, 2b)$, and $D(0, 2b)$. Then by the Mdpt. Formula, the cords. are $E(a, 0)$, $F(2a, b)$, $G(a, 2b)$, and $H(0, b)$. By the Dist. Formula, $EF = \sqrt{(2a-a)^2 + (b-0)^2}$ $= \sqrt{a^2 + b^2}$, and $GH = \sqrt{(0-a)^2 + (b-2b)^2}$ $= \sqrt{a^2 + b^2}$. So $\overline{EF} \cong \overline{GH}$ by the def. of $\cong$.

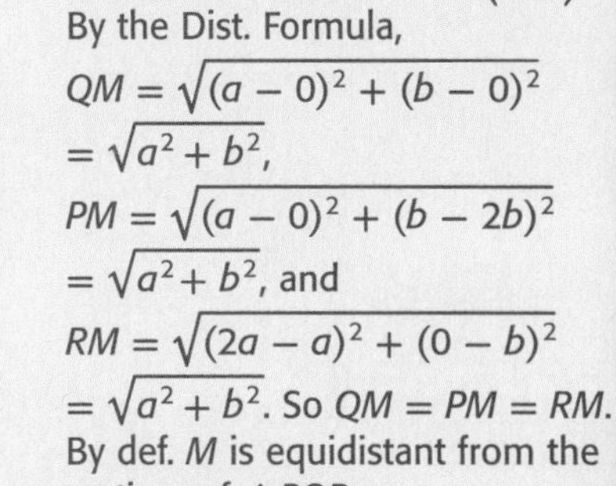

26. Use coords. $P(0, 2b)$, $Q(0, 0)$, and $R(2a, 0)$. Then by the Mdpt. Formula, the cords. are $M(a, b)$. By the Dist. Formula, $QM = \sqrt{(a-0)^2 + (b-0)^2}$ $= \sqrt{a^2 + b^2}$, $PM = \sqrt{(a-0)^2 + (b-2b)^2}$ $= \sqrt{a^2 + b^2}$, and $RM = \sqrt{(2a-a)^2 + (0-b)^2}$ $= \sqrt{a^2 + b^2}$. So $QM = PM = RM$. By def. M is equidistant from the vertices of $\triangle PQR$.
27. In a rt. $\triangle$, $a^2 + b^2 = c^2$. $\sqrt{(3-3)^2 + (5-2)^2} = 3$, $\sqrt{(3-2)^2 + (2-5)^2} = \sqrt{10}$, $\sqrt{(2-3)^2 + (5-5)^2} = 1$, and $3^2 + 1^2 = (\sqrt{10})^2$. Since $9 + 1 = 10$, it is a rt. $\triangle$.
28. -5
29. 13.5
30. 70 units

Organizer

Objective: Assess students' mastery of concepts and skills in Chapter 4.

Online Edition

Resources

Assessment Resources

Chapter 4 Tests

- Free Response (Levels A, B, C)
- Multiple Choice (Levels A, B, C)
- Performance Assessment

Teacher One Stop™

Test & Practice Generator

Answers

10.
1. T is the mdpt. of $\overline{PR}$ and $\overline{SQ}$. (Given)
2. $\overline{PT} \cong \overline{RT}$, $\overline{ST} \cong \overline{QT}$ (Def. of mdpt.)
3. $\angle PTS \cong \angle RTQ$ (Vert. ∠s Thm.)
4. $\triangle PTS \cong \triangle RTQ$ (SAS *Steps 2, 3*)

State Resources

1. Classify $\triangle ACD$ by its angle measures. **rt.**

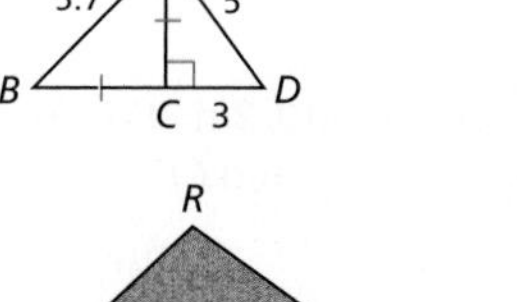

Classify each triangle by its side lengths.

2. $\triangle ACD$ **scalene**
3. $\triangle ABC$ **isosc.**
4. $\triangle ABD$ **scalene**

5. While surveying the triangular plot of land shown, a surveyor finds that $m\angle S = 43°$. The measure of $\angle RTP$ is twice that of $\angle RTS$. What is $m\angle R$? **77°**

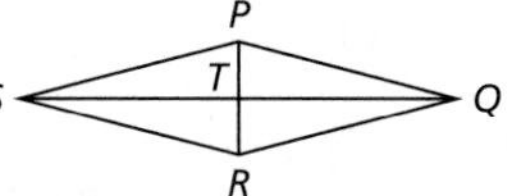

Given: $\triangle XYZ \cong \triangle JKL$
Identify the congruent corresponding parts.

6. $\overline{JL} \cong$ __?__ $\overline{XZ}$
7. $\angle Y \cong$ __?__ $\angle K$
8. $\angle L \cong$ __?__ $\angle Z$
9. $\overline{YZ} \cong$ __?__ $\overline{KL}$

10. **Given:** T is the midpoint of $\overline{PR}$ and $\overline{SQ}$.
Prove: $\triangle PTS \cong \triangle RTQ$

11. The figure represents a walkway with triangular supports. Given that $\overline{GJ}$ bisects $\angle HGK$ and $\angle H \cong \angle K$, use AAS to prove $\triangle HGJ \cong \triangle KGJ$

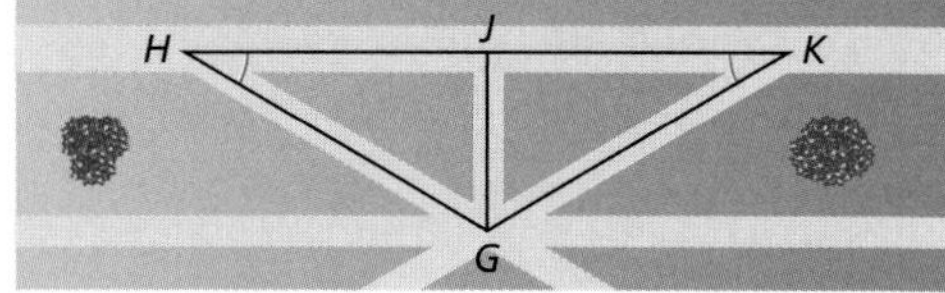

12. **Given:** $\overline{AB} \cong \overline{DC}$, $\overline{AB} \perp \overline{AC}$, $\overline{DC} \perp \overline{DB}$
Prove: $\triangle ABC \cong \triangle DCB$

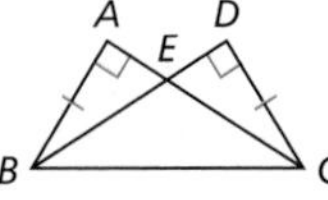

13. **Given:** $\overline{PQ} \parallel \overline{SR}$, $\angle S \cong \angle Q$
Prove: $\overline{PS} \parallel \overline{QR}$

14. Position a right triangle with legs 3 m and 4 m long in the coordinate plane. Give the coordinates of each vertex.

15. Assign coordinates to each vertex and write a coordinate proof.
Given: Square $ABCD$
Prove: $\overline{AC} \cong \overline{BD}$

Find each value.

16. y **−5**

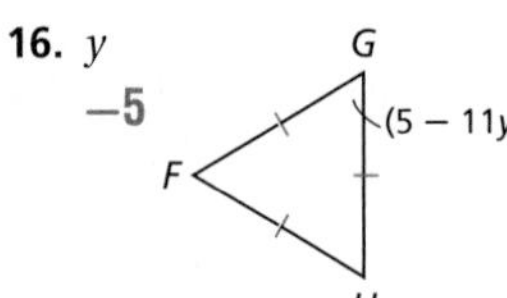

17. $m\angle S$ **44°**

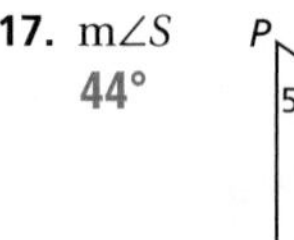
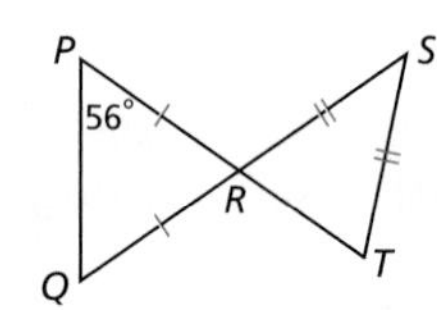

18. **Given:** Isosceles $\triangle ABC$ has coordinates $A(2a, 0)$, $B(0, 2b)$, and $C(-2a, 0)$. D is the midpoint of $\overline{AC}$, and E is the midpoint of $\overline{AB}$.
Prove: $\triangle AED$ is isosceles.

Answers

11.
1. $\angle H \cong \angle K$ (Given)
2. $\overline{GJ}$ bisects $\angle HGK$. (Given)
3. $\angle HGJ \cong \angle KGJ$ (Def. of bisect)
4. $\overline{JG} \cong \overline{JG}$ (Reflex. Prop. of ≅)
5. $\triangle HGJ \cong \triangle KGJ$ (AAS *Steps 1, 3, 4*)

12.
1. $\overline{AB} \perp \overline{AC}$, $\overline{DC} \perp \overline{DB}$ (Given)
2. $\angle BAC$ and $\angle CDB$ are rt. ∠s. (Def. of ⊥)
3. $\triangle ABC$ and $\triangle DCB$ are rt. △s. (Def. of rt. △)
4. $\overline{AB} \cong \overline{DC}$ (Given)
5. $\overline{BC} \cong \overline{CB}$ (Reflex. Prop. of ≅)
6. $\triangle ABC \cong \triangle DCB$ (HL *Steps 5, 4*)

13.
1. $\overline{PQ} \parallel \overline{SR}$ (Given)
2. $\angle QPR \cong \angle SRP$ (Alt. Int. ∠s Thm.)
3. $\angle S \cong \angle Q$ (Given)
4. $\overline{PR} \cong \overline{RP}$ (Reflex. Prop. of ≅)
5. $\triangle QPR \cong \triangle SRP$ (AAS *Steps 2, 3, 4*)
6. $\angle SPR \cong \angle QRP$ (CPCTC)
7. $\overline{PS} \parallel \overline{QR}$ (Conv. of Alt. Int. ∠s Thm.)

14.

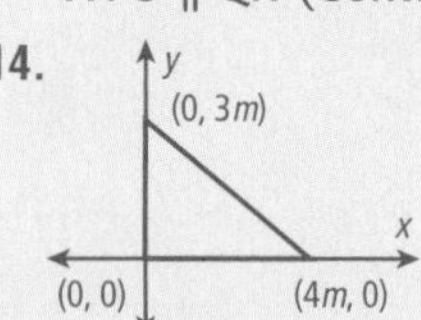

15, 18. See p. A17.

COLLEGE ENTRANCE EXAM PRACTICE

FOCUS ON ACT

The ACT Mathematics Test is one of four tests in the ACT. You are given 60 minutes to answer 60 multiple-choice questions. The questions cover material typically taught through the end of eleventh grade. You will need to know basic formulas but nothing too difficult.

There is no penalty for guessing on the ACT. If you are unsure of the correct answer, eliminate as many answer choices as possible and make your best guess. Make sure you have entered an answer for every question before time runs out.

You may want to time yourself as you take this practice test. It should take you about 5 minutes to complete.

---

1. For the figure below, which of the following must be true?

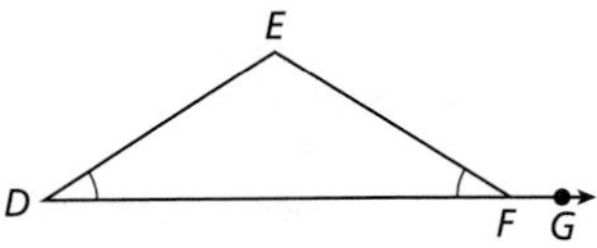

I. $m\angle EFG > m\angle DEF$

II. $m\angle EDF = m\angle EFD$

III. $m\angle DEF + m\angle EDF > m\angle EFG$

(A) I only

(B) II only

(C) I and II only

(D) II and III only

(E) I, II, and III

---

2. In the figure below, $\triangle ABD \cong \triangle CDB$, $m\angle A = (2x + 14)°$, $m\angle C = (3x - 15)°$, and $m\angle DBA = 49°$. What is the measure of $\angle BDA$?

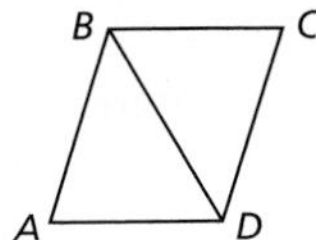

(F) 29°

(G) 49°

(H) 59°

(J) 72°

(K) 101°

---

3. Which of the following best describes a triangle with vertices having coordinates $(-1, 0)$, $(0, 3)$, and $(1, -4)$?

(A) Equilateral

(B) Isosceles

(C) Right

(D) Scalene

(E) Equiangular

---

4. In the figure below, what is the value of y?

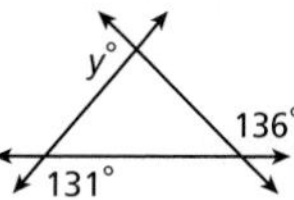

(F) 49

(G) 87

(H) 93

(J) 131

(K) 136

---

5. In $\triangle RST$, $RS = 2x + 10$, $ST = 3x - 2$, and $RT = \frac{1}{2}x + 28$. If $\triangle RST$ is equiangular, what is the value of x?

(A) 2

(B) $5\frac{1}{3}$

(C) 6

(D) 12

(E) 34

COLLEGE ENTRANCE EXAM PRACTICE CHAPTER 4

Organizer

Objective: Provide practice for college entrance exams such as the ACT.

Online Edition

Resources

College Entrance Exam Practice

Questions on the ACT represent the following content areas:

Pre-Algebra, 23%
Elementary Algebra, 17%
Intermediate Algebra, 15%
Coordinate Geometry, 15%
Plane Geometry, 23%
Trigonometry, 7%

Items on this page focus on:
- Elementary Algebra
- Coordinate Geometry
- Plane Geometry

Text References:

Item	1	2	3	4	5
Lesson	4-2	4-3	4-7	4-2	4-8

TEST PREP DOCTOR

1. Remind students that the sum of the angle measures of a triangle is 180° and that the measure of an exterior angle is equal to the sum of the measures of its remote interior angles. These facts, along with the diagram, lead to the conclusion that statements **I** and **II** are true but **III** is false.

2. Students may choose **G** because they mislabeled the figure or misinterpreted the names of the angles. Students may choose **F** because they only solved for x. Remind students to read each test item completely.

3. Encourage students to draw a rough sketch of the triangle to estimate the position of the vertices. This should eliminate choices **A** and **E**. Using the coordinates, slope, and the Distance Formula eliminates choices **B** and **C**.

4. Students may choose answer **G** because they found the measures of the remote interior angles and subtracted their sum from 180. The result is the measure of the third interior angle instead of the exterior angle labeled y.

5. Students may choose answer **D** because they did not answer the question being asked. Remind students to read each test item carefully.

Organizer

Objective: Provide opportunities to learn and practice common test-taking strategies.

 **Online Edition**

 This Test Tackler explains how extended-response test items are scored and demonstrates how to create a response that is deserving of full credit. Explain to students that extended response questions are longer and more complex than short-response questions. The scoring rubric used is based on a 4-point scale rather than a 2-point scale. Point out how these types of questions may have different parts. For full credit, each part of the question has to be completed correctly and explained thoroughly.

Standardized Test Strategies

Extended Response: Write Extended Responses

Extended-response questions are designed to assess your ability to apply and explain what you have learned. These test items are graded using a 4-point scoring rubric.

Scoring Rubric

4 points: The student shows an understanding of properties relating to parallel lines, triangle congruence, and the differences between ASA, SSS, and SAS.

3 points: The student correctly chooses which theorem to use but does not completely defend the choice or leaves out crucial understanding of parallel lines.

2 points: The student chooses the correct theorem but only defends part of it.

1 point: The student does not follow directions or does not provide any explanation for the answer.

0 points: The student does not attempt to answer.

EXAMPLE 1

Extended Response Given $p \parallel q$, state which theorem, AAS, ASA, SSS, or SAS, you would use to prove that $\triangle ABC \cong \triangle DCB$. Explain your reasoning.

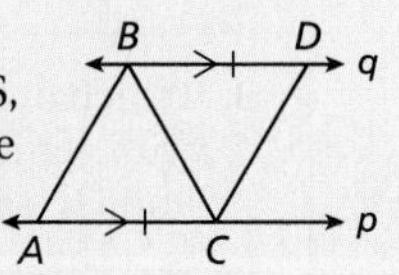

4-point response:

The correct theorem to use is SAS. According to the figure, $\overline{AC} \cong \overline{DB}$. By the Reflexive Property, $\overline{BC} \cong \overline{BC}$. So it just needs to be shown that $\angle BCA \cong \angle CBD$. Since $p \parallel q$ and they are cut by transversal $\overline{BC}$, $\angle BCA \cong \angle CBD$ by the Alternate Interior Angles Theorem. So by SAS, $\triangle ABC \cong \triangle DCB$. SSS cannot be used to prove that $\triangle ABC \cong \triangle DCB$ because it cannot be proven that $\overline{AB} \cong \overline{DC}$. ASA cannot be used because it cannot be proven that $\angle BAC \cong \angle CDB$. AAS cannot be used because it cannot be proven that $\angle ABC \cong \angle DCB$.

The student gave a complete, correct response to the question and provided an explanation as to why the other theorems could not be used.

3-point response:

The theorem to use is SAS because, according to the figure, two sides and their included angle in each triangle can be shown to be congruent. Side 1: $\overline{AC} \cong \overline{DB}$ according to the figure. Side 2: $\overline{BC} \cong \overline{BC}$ because of the Reflexive Property. $\angle BCA \cong \angle CBD$ because of the Alternate Interior Angles Theorem.

The reasoning is correct, but the student did not explain why other theorems could not be used.

2-point response:

You can use SAS because the picture shows that the triangles share one side. There are congruence marks on $\overline{AC}$ and $\overline{BD}$, so these sides are congruent.

The answer is correct, but the student did not explain why the included angles are congruent.

1-point response:

You can use SAS.

The student did not provide any reasoning.

To receive full credit, make sure all parts of the problem are answered. Be sure to provide a complete explanation for your reasoning.

Read each test item and answer the questions that follow.

Scoring Rubric:

4 points: The student demonstrates a thorough understanding of the concept, correctly answers the question, and provides a complete explanation.

3 points: The student correctly answers the question but does not show all work or does not provide an explanation.

2 points: The student makes minor errors resulting in an incorrect solution but shows and explains an understanding of the concept.

1 point: The student gives a response showing no work or explanation.

0 points: The student gives no response.

Item A

What theorem(s) can you use, other than the HL Theorem, to prove that $\triangle MNP \cong \triangle XYZ$? Explain your reasoning.

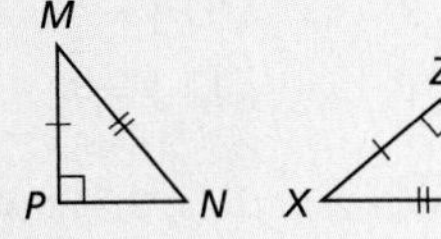

1. What should a full-credit response to this test item include?
2. A student wrote this response:

   You can use the Pythagorean Theorem.

   What score should this response receive? Why?
3. Write a list of the ways to prove triangles congruent. Is the Pythagorean Theorem on your list?
4. Add to the response so that it receives a score of 4-points.

Item B

Can an equilateral triangle be an obtuse triangle? Explain your answer. Include a sketch to support your reasoning.

5. What should a full-credit response to this test item include?
6. A student wrote this response:

   No, an equilateral triangle cannot be an obtuse triangle because an equilateral triangle has three congruent sides and three congruent acute angles. An acute angle has a measure less than 90°. By definition, an obtuse triangle has one obtuse angle, which is an angle with a measure greater than 90°.

   Why will this response not receive a score of 4 points?
7. Correct the response so that it receives full credit.

Item C

An isosceles right triangle has two sides, each with length $y + 4$.

Describe how you would find the length of the hypotenuse. Provide a sketch in your explanation.

8. A student began trying to find the length of the hypotenuse by writing the following:

   $$(y+4)^2 + (y+4)^2 = (\text{hypotenuse})^2$$
   $$(y^2 + 8y + 16) + (y^2 + 8y + 16) = (\text{hypotenuse})^2$$
   $$2y^2 + 16y + 32 = (\text{hypotenuse})^2$$
   $$\sqrt{2y^2 + 16y + 32} = \text{hypotenuse}$$

   Is the student on his way to receiving a 4-point response? Explain.
9. Describe a different method the student could use for this response.

Answers

Possible answers:

1. the name of each thm. used and why
2. 1 pt.; although the student provided a partial correct response, no reasoning is provided.
3. all 6 pairs of corr. parts; SSS; SAS; ASA; AAS; HL; no
4. You can use the Pyth. Thm. to prove $\overline{NP} \cong \overline{YZ}$. Then once you have shown that corr. sides of each △ are ≅, you can use SSS to prove $\triangle MNP \cong \triangle XYZ$.
5. an explanation of the answer to the question and a sketch of an equil. △ and an obtuse △
6. The response is not complete, and there is no sketch provided.
7. Since an obtuse △ must include an obtuse ∠, and an equil. △ contains only acute ∠s, it cannot possibly be an obtuse △.

8. No; the question asks for the student to describe how to find the length of the hyp., not to actually do the calculation.
9. I would draw a sketch of an isosc. rt. △ with side lengths labeled and then describe, using the Pyth. Thm., how to find the length of the hyp.

State Resources

go.hrw.com
State Resources Online
KEYWORD: MG7 Resources

Organizer

Objective: Provide review and practice for Chapters 1–4 and standardized tests.

Online Edition

Resources

Assessment Resources

Chapter 4 Cumulative Test

go.hrw.com
KEYWORD: MG7 TestPrep

Answers

1. D
2. H
3. B
4. F
5. A
6. H
7. A
8. G
9. B
10. J
11. A
12. J
13. A
14. 3
15. 450
16. 16
17. 90
18. 44
19. 70

State Resources

CUMULATIVE ASSESSMENT, CHAPTERS 1–4

Multiple Choice

Use the diagram for Items 1 and 2.

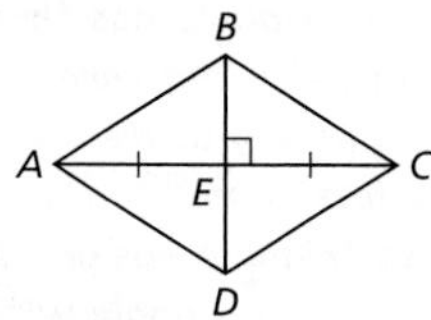

1. Which of these congruence statements can be proved from the information given in the figure?

Ⓐ $\triangle AEB \cong \triangle CED$
Ⓑ $\triangle BAC \cong \triangle DAC$
Ⓒ $\triangle ABD \cong \triangle BCA$
Ⓓ $\triangle DEC \cong \triangle DEA$

2. What other information is needed to prove that $\triangle CEB \cong \triangle AED$ by the HL Congruence Theorem?

Ⓕ $\overline{AD} \cong \overline{AB}$
Ⓖ $\overline{BE} \cong \overline{AE}$
Ⓗ $\overline{CB} \cong \overline{AD}$
Ⓙ $\overline{DE} \cong \overline{CE}$

3. Which biconditional statement is true?

Ⓐ Tomorrow is Monday if and only if today is not Saturday.
Ⓑ Next month is January if and only if this month is December.
Ⓒ Today is a weekend day if and only if yesterday was Friday.
Ⓓ This month had 31 days if and only if last month had 30 days.

4. What must be true if $\overleftrightarrow{PQ}$ intersects $\overleftrightarrow{ST}$ at more than one point?

Ⓕ P, Q, S, and T are collinear.
Ⓖ P, Q, S, and T are noncoplanar.
Ⓗ $\overrightarrow{PQ}$ and $\overrightarrow{ST}$ are opposite rays.
Ⓙ $\overleftrightarrow{PQ}$ and $\overleftrightarrow{ST}$ are perpendicular.

5. $\triangle ABC \cong \triangle DEF$, $EF = x^2 - 7$, and $BC = 4x - 2$. Find the values of x.

Ⓐ −1 and 5
Ⓑ −1 and 6
Ⓒ 1 and 5
Ⓓ 2 and 3

6. Which conditional statement has the same truth value as its inverse?

Ⓕ If $n < 0$, then $n^2 > 0$.
Ⓖ If a triangle has three congruent sides, then it is an isosceles triangle.
Ⓗ If an angle measures less than 90°, then it is an acute angle.
Ⓙ If n is a negative integer, then $n < 0$.

7. On a map, an island has coordinates (3, 5), and a reef has coordinates (6, 8). If each map unit represents 1 mile, what is the distance between the island and the reef to the nearest tenth of a mile?

Ⓐ 4.2 miles
Ⓑ 6.0 miles
Ⓒ 9.0 miles
Ⓓ 15.8 miles

8. A line has an x-intercept of −8 and a y-intercept of 3. What is the equation of the line?

Ⓕ $y = -8x + 3$
Ⓖ $y = \frac{3}{8}x + 3$
Ⓗ $y = \frac{8}{3}x - 8$
Ⓙ $y = 3x - 8$

9. $\overleftrightarrow{JK}$ passes through points $J(1, 3)$ and $K(-3, 11)$. Which of these lines is perpendicular to $\overleftrightarrow{JK}$?

Ⓐ $y = -\frac{1}{2}x + \frac{1}{3}$
Ⓑ $y = \frac{1}{2}x + 6$
Ⓒ $y = -2x - \frac{1}{5}$
Ⓓ $y = 2x - 4$

10. If $PQ = 2(RS) + 4$ and $RS = TU + 1$, which equation is true by the Substitution Property of Equality?

Ⓕ $PQ = TU + 5$
Ⓖ $PQ = TU + 6$
Ⓗ $PQ = 2(TU) + 5$
Ⓙ $PQ = 2(TU) + 6$

11. Which of the following is NOT valid for proving that triangles are congruent?

Ⓐ AAA
Ⓑ ASA
Ⓒ SAS
Ⓓ HL

Answers

20. Possible answer: Because the acute ∠s of a rt. △ are comp., ∠1 is comp. to ∠2. By the Corr. ∠s Post., ∠1 ≅ ∠3. Therefore ∠3 is also comp. to ∠2 by the ≅ Comps. Thm.

21a.
$$\begin{aligned} 2x + 12 + x &= 180 \\ 3x + 12 &= 180 \quad \text{(Simplify.)} \\ 3x + 12 - 12 &= 180 - 12 \quad \text{(Subtr. Prop. of =)} \\ 3x &= 168 \quad \text{(Simplify.)} \\ \frac{3x}{3} &= \frac{168}{3} \quad \text{(Div. Prop. of =)} \\ x &= 56 \quad \text{(Simplify.)} \end{aligned}$$

21b. Possible answer: The sum of the measures of an ∠ and its comp. is 90°. Therefore any ∠ that measures 90° or greater does not have a comp. Because $m\angle H = x° = 56°$, the ∠ does have a comp. Because $m\angle G = (2x + 12)° = [2(56) + 12]° = 124°$, ∠G does not have a comp.

22a. 90; based on the conjecture, 60 out of 1000 parts will be defective. Express this ratio as a percent: $\frac{60}{1000} = \frac{6}{100} = 6\%$. Find 6% of 1500. $1500 \times 6\% = 1500 \times 0.06 = 90$. Based on the conjecture, 90 out of 1500 parts will be defective.

Use this diagram for Items 12 and 13.

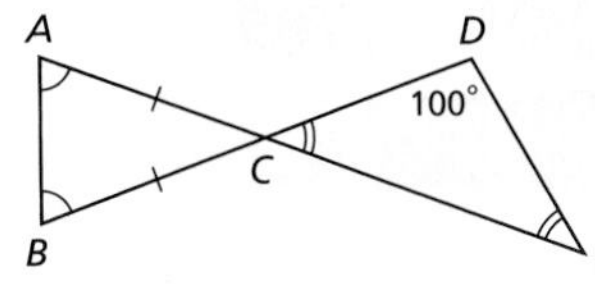

12. What is the measure of $\angle ACD$?

(F) 40° (H) 100°
(G) 80° (J) 140°

13. What type of triangle is $\triangle ABC$?

(A) Isosceles acute
(B) Equilateral acute
(C) Isosceles obtuse
(D) Scalene acute

Take some time to learn the directions for filling in a grid. Check and recheck to make sure you are filling in the grid properly. You will only get credit if the ovals below the boxes are filled in correctly. To check your answer, solve the problem using a different method from the one you originally used. If you made a mistake the first time, you are unlikely to make the same mistake when you solve a different way.

Gridded Response

14. $\triangle CDE \cong \triangle JKL$. $m\angle E = (3x + 4)°$, and $m\angle L = (6x - 5)°$. What is the value of x?

15. Lucy, Eduardo, Carmen, and Frank live on the same street. Eduardo's house is halfway between Lucy's house and Frank's house. Lucy's house is halfway between Carmen's house and Frank's house. If the distance between Eduardo's house and Lucy's house is 150 ft, what is the distance in feet between Carmen's house and Eduardo's house?

16. $\triangle JKL \cong \triangle XYZ$, and $JK = 10 - 2n$. $XY = 2$, and $YZ = n^2$. Find KL.

17. An angle is its own supplement. What is its measure?

18. The area of a circle is 154 square inches. What is its circumference to the nearest inch?

19. The measure of $\angle P$ is $3\frac{1}{2}$ times the measure of $\angle Q$. If $\angle P$ and $\angle Q$ are complementary, what is $m\angle P$ in degrees?

Short Response

20. Given $\ell \parallel m$ with transversal n, explain why $\angle 2$ and $\angle 3$ are complementary.

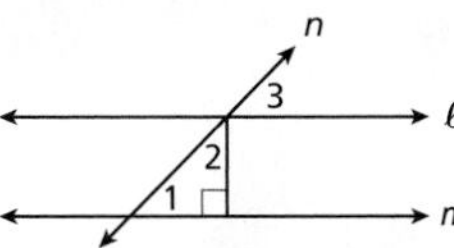

21. $\angle G$ and $\angle H$ are supplementary angles. $m\angle G = (2x + 12)°$, and $m\angle H = x°$.

    a. Write an equation that can be used to determine the value of x. Solve the equation and justify each step.

    b. Explain why $\angle H$ has a complement but $\angle G$ does not.

22. A manager conjectures that for every 1000 parts a factory produces, 60 are defective.

    a. If the factory produces 1500 parts in one day, how many of them can be expected to be defective based on the manager's conjecture? Explain how you found your answer.

    b. Use the data in the table below to show that the manager's conjecture is false.

Day	1	2	3	4	5
Parts	1000	2000	500	1500	2500
Defective Parts	60	150	30	90	150

23. $\overline{BD}$ is the perpendicular bisector of $\overline{AC}$.

    a. What are the conclusions you can make from this statement?

    b. Suppose $\overline{BD}$ intersects $\overline{AC}$ at D. Explain why $\overline{BD}$ is the shortest path from B to $\overline{AC}$.

Extended Response

24. $\triangle ABC$ and $\triangle DEF$ are isosceles triangles. $\overline{BC} \cong \overline{EF}$, and $\overline{AC} \cong \overline{DF}$. $m\angle C = 42.5°$, and $m\angle E = 95°$.

    a. What is $m\angle D$? Explain how you determined your answer.

    b. Show that $\triangle ABC$ and $\triangle DEF$ are congruent.

    c. Given that $EF = 2x + 7$ and $AB = 3x + 2$, find the value for x. Explain how you determined your answer.

Short-Response Rubric

Items 20–23

2 Points = The student's answer is an accurate and complete execution of the task or tasks.

1 Point = The student's answer contains attributes of an appropriate response but is flawed.

0 Points = The student's answer contains no attributes of an appropriate response.

Extended-Response Rubric

Item 24

4 Points = The student correctly draws three different rectangles in part **a,** lists five more different rectangles in part **b,** answers and explains part **c,** and answers part **d,** showing all work.

3 Points = The student correctly draws some rectangles in part **a** and lists some rectangles in part **b** but does not identify eight different possibilities, or the student correctly answers parts **a, b,** and **c** but does not correctly answer part **d.**

2 Points = The student answers all parts correctly but does not show any work or explanation, or the student correctly answers parts **a** and **b** but does not correctly answer parts **c** and **d.**

1 Point = The student finds four or fewer rectangles to fit the situation but does not correctly answer other parts of the problem, or the student attempts to answer all parts of the problem but does not correctly answer any part.

0 Points = The student does not answer correctly and does not attempt all parts of the problem.

Answers

22b. Possible answer: Based on the manager's conjecture, 120 parts should be defective if 2000 parts are produced. However, the table shows that 150 out of 2000 parts were defective on day 2. Therefore the data for day 2 is a counterexample to the manager's conjecture. This shows that the conjecture is false.

23a. Possible answer: $\angle BDA$ is a rt. $\angle$; $\angle BDC$ is a rt. $\angle$; $AD = DC$; D is the mdpt. of $\overline{AC}$.

23b. The shortest dist. from a pt. to a line is measured along the $\perp$ from the pt. to the line.

24a. 42.5°
Possible answer: Because $\triangle DEF$ is an isosc. $\triangle$, 2 of its sides are $\cong$, and the $\angle$s opp. these sides are $\cong$. $\angle E$ is an obtuse $\angle$. Because a $\triangle$ cannot have more than 1 obtuse $\angle$, the 2 $\cong$ $\angle$s in $\triangle DEF$ must be $\angle D$ and $\angle F$. Use this information to find $m\angle D$. $m\angle D + m\angle E + m\angle F = 180°$ by the $\triangle$ Sum Thm. $x + 95° + x = 180°$. Substitute x for $m\angle D$ and $m\angle F$, and 95° for $m\angle E$. $2x = 85°$. Simplify and then subtract 95° from both sides. $x = 42.5°$. Divide both sides by 2. Thus $m\angle D = 42.5°$.

24b. Possible answer: From part **a**, $\angle F \cong \angle D$. Therefore $m\angle F = m\angle D = 42.5°$. It is given that $m\angle C = 42.5°$. Therefore $\angle C \cong \angle F$. It is also given that $\overline{BC} \cong \overline{EF}$ and $\overline{AC} \cong \overline{DF}$. Therefore $\triangle ABC \cong \triangle DEF$ by SAS.

24c. 5; possible answer: because $\angle D \cong \angle F$, $\overline{DE} \cong \overline{EF}$ by the Conv. of the Isosc. $\triangle$ Thm.

$\overline{AB} \cong \overline{DE}$	CPCTC
$\overline{AB} \cong \overline{EF}$	Trans. Prop. of $\cong$
$AB = EF$	Def. of $\cong$ Segs.
$3x + 2 = 2x + 7$	Subst. Prop. of =
$x = 5$	Subtr. Prop. of =

Organizer

Objective: Choose appropriate problem-solving strategies and use them with skills from Chapters 3 and 4 to solve real-world problems.

Online Edition

The Queen's Cup

Reading Strategies

ENGLISH LANGUAGE LEARNERS

Have students read **Problem 2.** Then suggest that they reread the problem, this time jotting down the given information as they read.

Using Data The table on this page uses bearings. Have one or more students explain how bearings are measured. As they do so, ask them to sketch some examples on the board.

State Resources

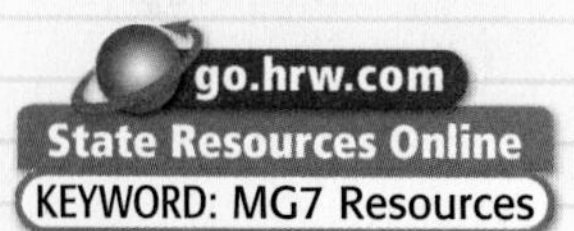

go.hrw.com
State Resources Online
KEYWORD: MG7 Resources

The Queen's Cup

The annual Queen's Cup race is one of the most exciting sailing events of the year. Traditionally held at the end of June, the race attracts hundreds of yachts that compete to cross Lake Michigan—at night—in the fastest time possible.

Choose one or more strategies to solve each problem.

1. The race starts in Milwaukee, Wisconsin, and ends in Grand Haven, Michigan. The boats don't sail from the start to the finish in a straight line. They follow a zigzag course to take advantage of the wind. Suppose one of the boats leaves Milwaukee at a bearing of N 50° E and follows the course shown. At what bearing does the boat approach Grand Haven? **S 20° E**

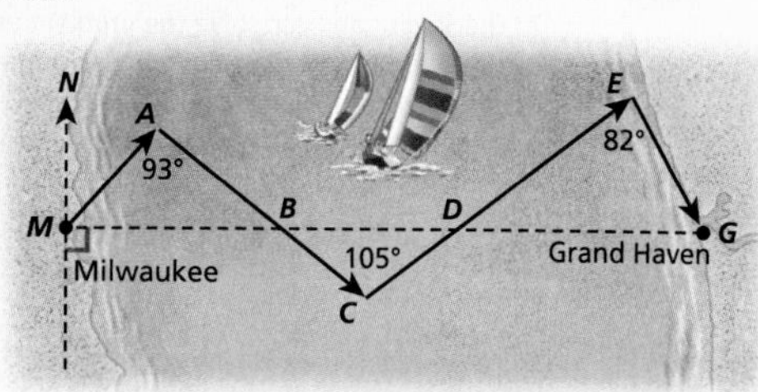

2. The Queen's Cup race is 78.75 miles long. In 2004, the winning sailboat completed the first 29.4 miles in about 3 hours and the first 49 miles in about 5 hours. Suppose it had continued at this rate. What would the winning time have been? **8 h**

3. During the race one of the boats leaves Milwaukee *M*, sails to *X*, and then sails to *Y*. The team discovers a problem with the boat so it has to return directly to Milwaukee. Does the table contain enough information to determine the course to return to *M*? Explain.

	Bearing	Distance (mi)
M to *X*	N 42° E	3.1
X to *Y*	S 59° E	2.4
Y to *M*		

Problem-Solving Focus

Ask students what strategy they would use to solve **Problem 2.** The strategy Make a Table may be especially useful in organizing the given information.

Discuss with students different ways they might find the winning time. Some students may find it helpful to use proportional reasoning. To foster this type of thinking, encourage students to rephrase the problem in if-then form. If it takes 3 hours to go 29.4 miles and 5 hours to 49 miles, then it takes x hours to go 29.4 miles. Other students may benefit from thinking about this problem in terms of slope. Ask them what ordered pairs they could use to find the slope of the line that represents the boat's distance at a given time. (3,29.4) and (5,49)

Answers

3. Yes; there is enough information to find $m\angle MXY$ (101°). MX and MY are known, so a unique $\triangle MXY$ is determined by SAS.

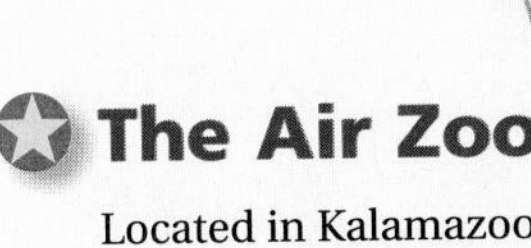

The Air Zoo

Located in Kalamazoo, Michigan, the Air Zoo offers visitors a thrilling, interactive voyage through the history of flight. It features full-motion flight simulators, a "4-D" theater, and more than 80 rare aircraft. The Air Zoo is also home to *The Century of Flight*, the world's largest indoor mural.

Choose one or more strategies to solve each problem.

1. *The Century of Flight* mural measures 28,800 square feet—approximately the size of three football fields! The table gives data on the rate at which the mural was painted. How many months did it take to complete the mural? ≈ **11 mo**

Painting *The Century of Flight*

Months of Work	Amount Completed (ft^2)
2	5,236
5	13,091
7	18,327

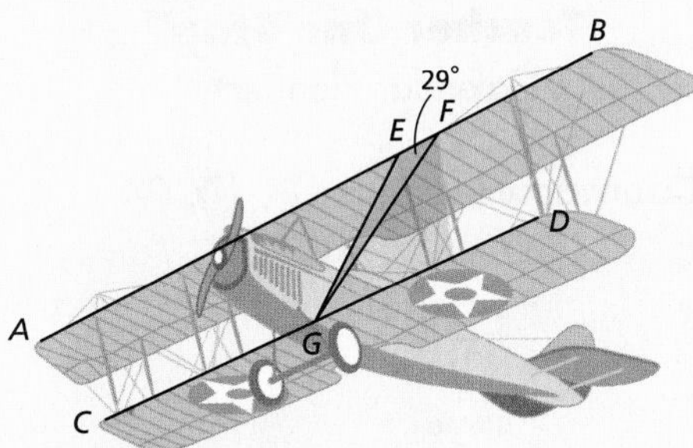

2. Visitors to the Air Zoo can see a replica of a Curtiss JN-4 "Jenny," the plane that flew the first official U.S. airmail route in 1918. The plane has two parallel wings $\overline{AB}$ and $\overline{CD}$ that are connected by bracing wires. The wires are arranged so that $m\angle EFG = 29°$ and $\overline{GF}$ bisects $\angle EGD$. What is $m\angle AEG$? **58°**

3. The Air Zoo's flight simulators let visitors practice takeoffs and landings. To determine the position of a plane during takeoff, an airport uses two cameras mounted 1000 ft apart. What is the distance d that the plane has moved along the runway since it passed camera 1? **850 ft**

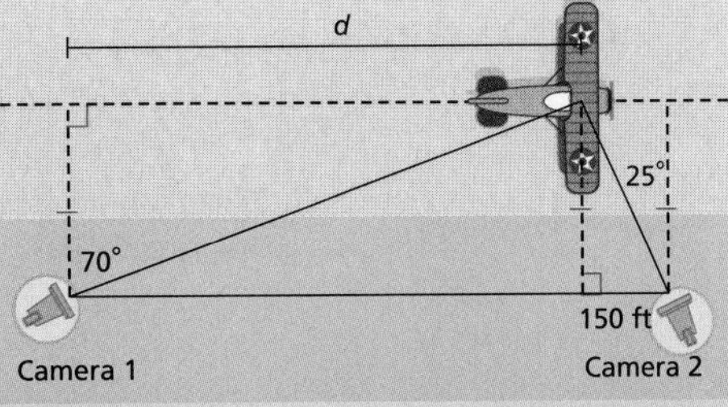

Real-World Connections 295

The Air Zoo

Reading Strategies

ENGLISH LANGUAGE LEARNERS

Make sure that students know what a mural is. Spanish-speaking ELL students may recognize the similarity of the word *mural* to *muro,* the Spanish word for *wall.*

Using Data Before students begin **Problem 1,** have a brief discussion about the data in the table. Ask students to estimate the number of months it took to complete the mural. approximately 11 Later they can compare their calculated values to these initial estimates.

Problem-Solving Focus

Encourage students to use the four-step problem-solving process for the problems. Focus on the third step: **(3) Plan.** In particular, ask students to consider the information that is given in the statement of **Problem 2,** and in the accompanying diagram.

Discuss Ask students to decide which pieces of information are essential in solving the problem. $\overline{AB} \parallel \overline{CD}$; $m\angle EFG = 29°$; $\overline{GF}$ bisects $\angle EGD$ Then have students describe a sequence of steps they can use to find $m\angle AEG$. First find the $m\angle FGD$. Then add $m\angle FGD$ and $m\angle EGF$. Finally use the Alt. Int. ∠ Thm.

Properties and Attributes of Triangles

Section 5A

Segments in Triangles

5-1 Perpendicular and Angle Bisectors
5-2 Bisectors of Triangles
5-3 Medians and Altitudes of Triangles
5-3 Technology Lab Explore Special Points in Triangles
5-4 The Triangle Midsegment Theorem

Section 5B

Relationships in Triangles

Connecting Geometry to Algebra Solving Compound Inequalities
5-5 Geometry Lab Explore Triangle Inequalities
5-5 Indirect Proof and Inequalities in One Triangle
5-6 Inequalities in Two Triangles
Connecting Geometry to Algebra Simplest Radical Form
5-7 Geometry Lab Hands-on Proof of the Pythagorean Theorem
5-7 The Pythagorean Theorem
5-8 Applying Special Right Triangles
5-8 Geometry Lab Graph Irrational Numbers

Pacing Guide for 45-Minute Classes

Teacher One Stop™
Calendar Planner®

Chapter 5

Countdown Weeks 10, 11, 12

DAY 1	DAY 2	DAY 3	DAY 4	DAY 5
5-1 Lesson	5-2 Lesson	5-3 Lesson	5-3 Technology Lab	5-4 Lesson
DAY 6	**DAY 7**	**DAY 8**	**DAY 9**	**DAY 10**
Multi-Step Test Prep Ready to Go On?	Connecting Geometry to Algebra 5-5 Geometry Lab	5-5 Lesson	5-6 Lesson	Connecting Geometry to Algebra 5-7 Geometry Lab
DAY 11	**DAY 12**	**DAY 13**	**DAY 14**	**DAY 15**
5-7 Lesson	5-8 Lesson	5-8 Geometry Lab	Multi-Step Test Prep Ready to Go On?	Chapter 5 Review
DAY 16				
Chapter 5 Test				

Pacing Guide for 90-Minute Classes

Teacher One Stop™
Calendar Planner®

Chapter 5

DAY 1	DAY 2	DAY 3	DAY 4	DAY 5
Chapter 4 Test 5-1 Lesson	5-2 Lesson 5-3 Lesson	5-3 Technology Lab 5-4 Lesson	Multi-Step Test Prep Ready to Go On? Connecting Geometry to Algebra 5-5 Geometry Lab	5-5 Lesson 5-6 Lesson
DAY 6	**DAY 7**	**DAY 8**	**DAY 9**	
Connecting Geometry to Algebra 5-7 Geometry Lab 5-7 Lesson	5-8 Lesson 5-8 Geometry Lab	Multi-Step Test Prep Ready to Go On? Chapter 5 Review	Chapter 5 Test 6-1 Geometry Lab	

ONGOING ASSESSMENT and INTERVENTION

	DIAGNOSE	PRESCRIBE
Assess Prior Knowledge	**Before Chapter 5**	
	Diagnose readiness for the chapter. 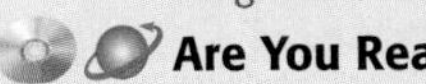 **Are You Ready?** SE p. 297	Prescribe intervention. ***Are You Ready? Intervention***
Formative Assessment	**Before Every Lesson**	
	Diagnose readiness for the lesson. **Warm Up** TE	Prescribe intervention. **Reteach** CRB
	During Every Lesson	
	Diagnose understanding of lesson concepts. **Check It Out!** SE **Questioning Strategies** TE **Think and Discuss** SE **Write About It** SE **Journal** TE	Prescribe intervention. **Reading Strategies** CRB ***Success for Every Learner*** ***Lesson Tutorial Videos***
	After Every Lesson	
	Diagnose mastery of lesson concepts. **Lesson Quiz** TE **Test Prep** SE ***Test and Practice Generator***	Prescribe intervention. **Reteach** CRB **Test Prep Doctor** TE ***Homework Help* Online**
	Before Chapter 5 Testing	
	Diagnose mastery of concepts in chapter. **Ready to Go On?** SE pp. 329, 365 **Multi-Step Test Prep** SE pp. 328, 364 **Section Quizzes** AR ***Test and Practice Generator***	Prescribe intervention. ***Ready to Go On? Intervention*** **Scaffolding Questions** TE pp. 328, 364 **Reteach** CRB ***Lesson Tutorial Videos***
	Before High Stakes Testing 	
	Diagnose mastery of benchmark concepts. **College Entrance Exam Practice** SE p. 371 **Standardized Test Prep** SE pp. 374–375	Prescribe intervention. ***College Entrance Exam Practice***
Summative Assessment	**After Chapter 5**	
	Check mastery of chapter concepts. **Multiple-Choice Tests (Forms A, B, C)** **Free-Response Tests (Forms A, B, C)** **Performance Assessment** AR **Cumulative Test** AR ***Test and Practice Generator***	Prescribe intervention. **Reteach** CRB ***Lesson Tutorial Videos***

KEY: **SE** = *Student Edition* **TE** = *Teacher's Edition* **CRB** = *Chapter Resource Book* **AR** = *Assessment Resources* 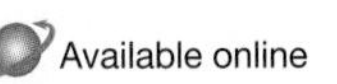 Available online Available on CD- or DVD-ROM

Lesson Resources

Before the Lesson

Prepare *Teacher One Stop* SPANISH 
- Editable lesson plans
- Calendar Planner
- Easy access to all chapter resources

Lesson Transparencies
- Teacher Tools

Teach the Lesson

Introduce *Alternate Openers: Explorations*

Lesson Transparencies
- Warm Up
- Problem of the Day

Teach *Lesson Transparencies*
- Teaching Transparencies

Know-It Notebook™
- Vocabulary
- Key Concepts

Power Presentations 

Lesson Tutorial Videos SPANISH 

Interactive Online Edition 
- Lesson Activities
- Lesson Tutorial Videos

Lab Activities

Lab Resources Online 

Online Interactivities SPANISH 

TechKeys 

Practice the Lesson

Practice *Chapter Resources*
- Practice A, B, C

Practice and Problem Solving Workbook

IDEA Works!® Modified Worksheets and Tests

ExamView Test and Practice Generator

Homework Help Online

Online Interactivities SPANISH

Interactive Online Edition
- Homework Help

Apply *Chapter Resources*
- Problem Solving

Practice and Problem Solving Workbook

Interactive Online Edition
- Chapter Project

Project Teacher Support

After the Lesson

Reteach *Chapter Resources*
- Reteach
- Reading Strategies ELL

Success for Every Learner

Review *Interactive Answers and Solutions*

Solutions Key

Know-It Notebook™
- Big Ideas
- Chapter Review

Extend *Chapter Resources*
- Challenge

Technology Highlights for the Teacher

Power Presentations

Dynamic presentations to engage students. Complete PowerPoint® presentations for every lesson in Chapter 5.

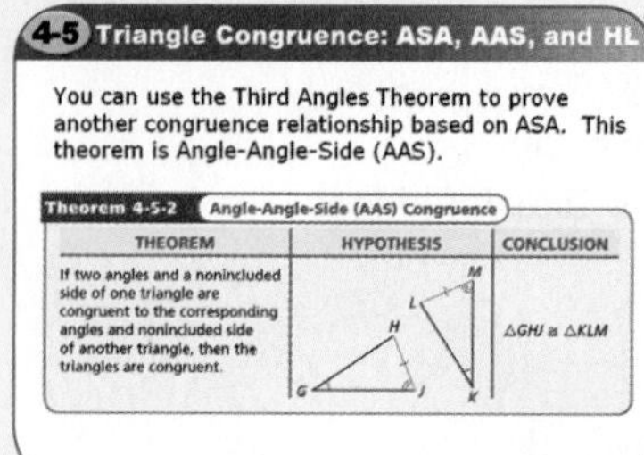

Teacher One Stop SPANISH

Easy access to Chapter 5 resources and assessments. Includes lesson planning, test generation, and puzzle creation software.

Premier Online Edition SPANISH

Chapter 5 includes Tutorial Videos, Lesson Activities, Lesson Quizzes, Homework Help, and Chapter Project.

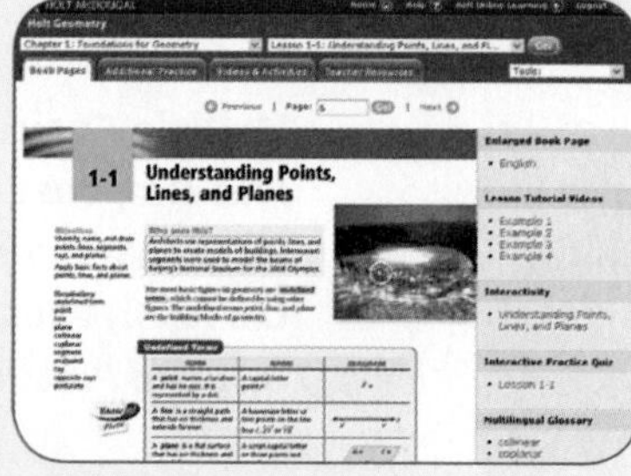

KEY: **SE** = *Student Edition* **TE** = *Teacher's Edition* ELL English Language Learners  SPANISH Spanish version available  Available online  Available on CD- or DVD-ROM 

Reaching All Learners

Teaching tips to help all learners appear throughout the chapter. A few that target specific students are included in the lists below.

All Learners

Lab Activities
Practice and Problem Solving Workbook
Know-It Notebook

Special Needs Students

Practice A	CRB
Reteach	CRB
Reading Strategies	CRB
Are You Ready?	SE p. 297
Inclusion	TE pp. 303, 316, 323, 353, 360

IDEA Works!® Modified Worksheets and Tests
Ready to Go On? Intervention SPANISH
Know-It Notebook
Online Interactivities  SPANISH
Lesson Tutorial Videos  SPANISH

Developing Learners

Practice A	CRB
Reteach	CRB
Reading Strategies	CRB
Are You Ready?	SE p. 297
Vocabulary Connections	SE p. 298
Questioning Strategies	TE

Ready to Go On? Intervention SPANISH
Know-It Notebook
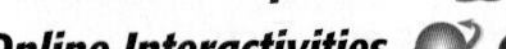
Homework Help Online
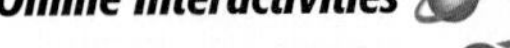
Online Interactivities  SPANISH

Lesson Tutorial Videos SPANISH

On-Level Learners

Practice B	CRB
Problem Solving	CRB
Vocabulary Connections	SE p. 298
Questioning Strategies	TE

Ready to Go On? Intervention SPANISH
Know-It Notebook
Homework Help Online
Online Interactivities  SPANISH

Advanced Learners

Practice C	CRB
Challenge	CRB
Challenge Exercises	SE
Reading and Writing Math *Extend*	TE p. 299
Critical Thinking	TE pp. 302, 316, 350, 358

Are You Ready? Enrichment SPANISH
Ready To Go On? Enrichment SPANISH

English Language Learners

ENGLISH LANGUAGE LEARNERS

Reading Strategies	CRB
Are You Ready? Vocabulary	SE p. 297
Vocabulary Connections	SE p. 298
Vocabulary Review	SE p. 366
English Language Learners	TE pp. 299, 308, 315

Success for Every Learner
Know-It Notebook
Spanish Study Guide (Resumen y Repaso)
Multilingual Glossary
Lesson Tutorial Videos  

Technology Highlights for Reaching All Learners

Lesson Tutorial Videos SPANISH

Starring Holt authors Ed Burger and Freddie Renfro! Live tutorials to support every lesson in Chapter 5.

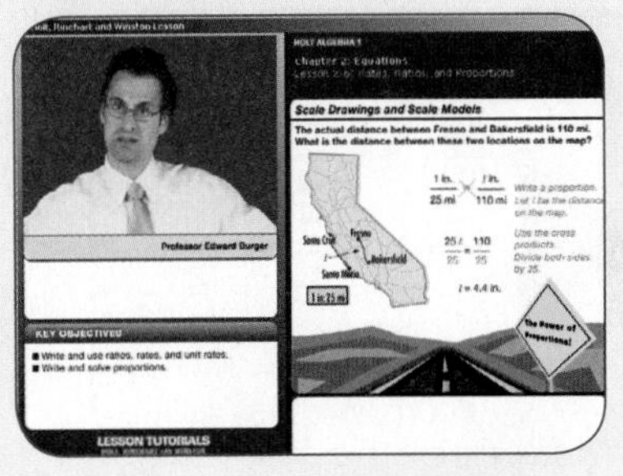

Multilingual Glossary

Searchable glossary includes definitions in English, Spanish, Vietnamese, Chinese, Hmong, Korean, and 4 other languages.

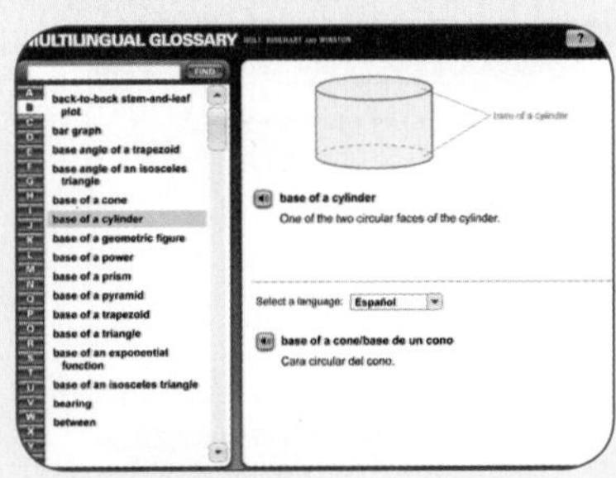

Online Interactivities

Interactive tutorials provide visually engaging alternative opportunities to learn concepts and master skills.

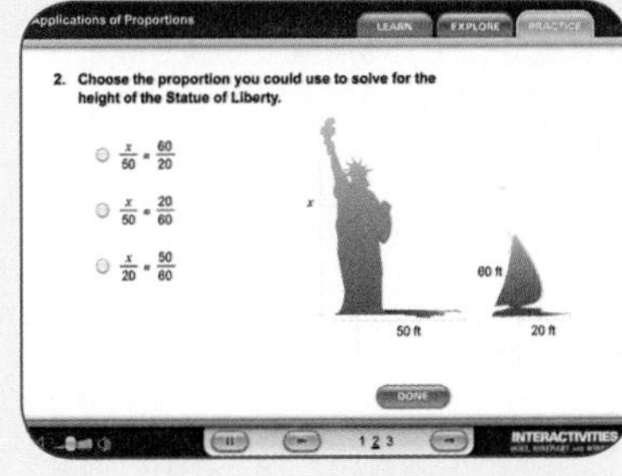

KEY: **SE** = *Student Edition* **TE** = *Teacher's Edition* **CRB** = *Chapter Resource Book* SPANISH Spanish version available; Available online; Available on CD- or DVD-ROM

Ongoing Assessment

Assessing Prior Knowledge

Determine whether students have the prerequisite concepts and skills for success in Chapter 5.

Are You Ready? SPANISH .... SE p. 297
Warm Up .... TE

Test Preparation

Provide review and practice for Chapter 5 and standardized tests.

Multi-Step Test Prep .... SE pp. 328, 364
Study Guide: Review .... SE pp. 366–369
Test Tackler .... SE pp. 372–373
Standardized Test Prep .... SE pp. 374–375
College Entrance Exam Practice .... SE p. 371
Countdown to Testing .... SE pp. C4-C27
IDEA Works!® Modified Worksheets and Tests

Alternative Assessment

Assess students' understanding of Chapter 5 concepts and combined problem-solving skills.

Chapter 5 Project .... SE p. 296
Alternative Assessment .... TE
Performance Assessment .... AR
Portfolio Assessment .... AR

Lesson Assessment

Provide formative assessment for each lesson of Chapter 5.

Questioning Strategies .... TE
Think and Discuss .... SE
Check It Out! Exercises .... SE
Write About It .... SE
Journal .... TE
Lesson Quiz .... TE
Alternative Assessment .... TE
IDEA Works!® Modified Worksheets and Tests

Weekly Assessment

Provide formative assessment for each section of Chapter 5.

Multi-Step Test Prep .... SE pp. 328, 364
Ready to Go On? SPANISH .... SE pp. 329, 365
Section Quizzes .... AR
Test and Practice Generator .... *Teacher One Stop*

Chapter Assessment

Provide summative assessment of Chapter 5 mastery.

Chapter 5 Test .... SE p. 370
Chapter Test (Levels A, B, C) .... AR
• Multiple Choice • Free Response
Cumulative Test .... AR
Test and Practice Generator .... *Teacher One Stop*
IDEA Works!® Modified Worksheets and Tests

Technology Highlights for Assessment

 Are You Ready? 

Automatically assess readiness and prescribe intervention for Chapter 5 prerequisite skills.

Ready to Go On?

Automatically assess understanding of and prescribe intervention for Sections 5A and 5B.

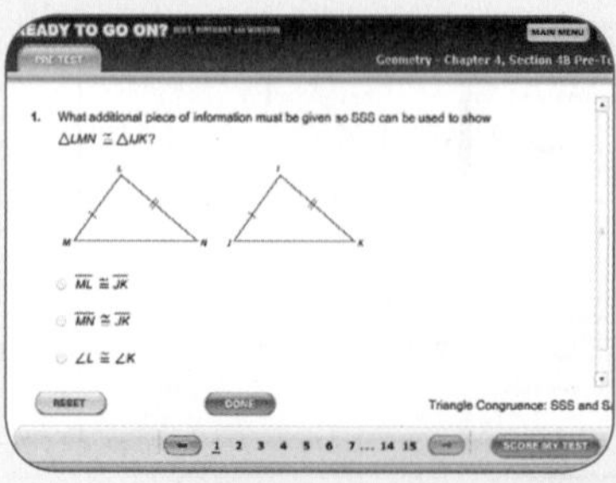

Test and Practice Generator

Use Chapter 5 problem banks to create assessments and worksheets to print out or deliver online. Includes dynamic problems.

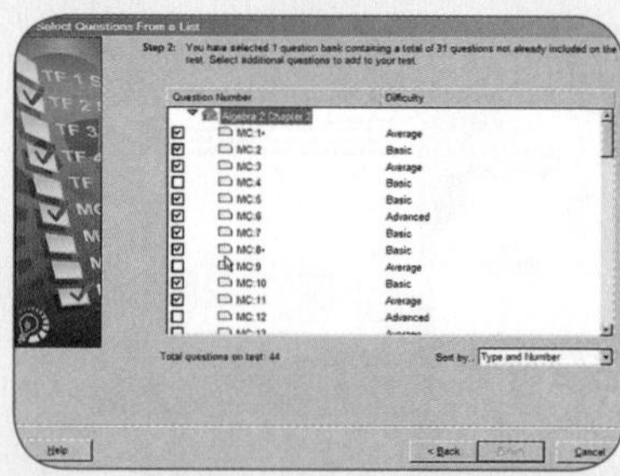

KEY: **SE** = *Student Edition* **TE** = *Teacher's Edition* **AR** = *Assessment Resources*  Spanish version available  Available online  Available on CD- or DVD-ROM

Three levels (A, B, C) of multiple-choice and free-response chapter tests, along with a performance assessment, are available in the *Assessment Resources.*

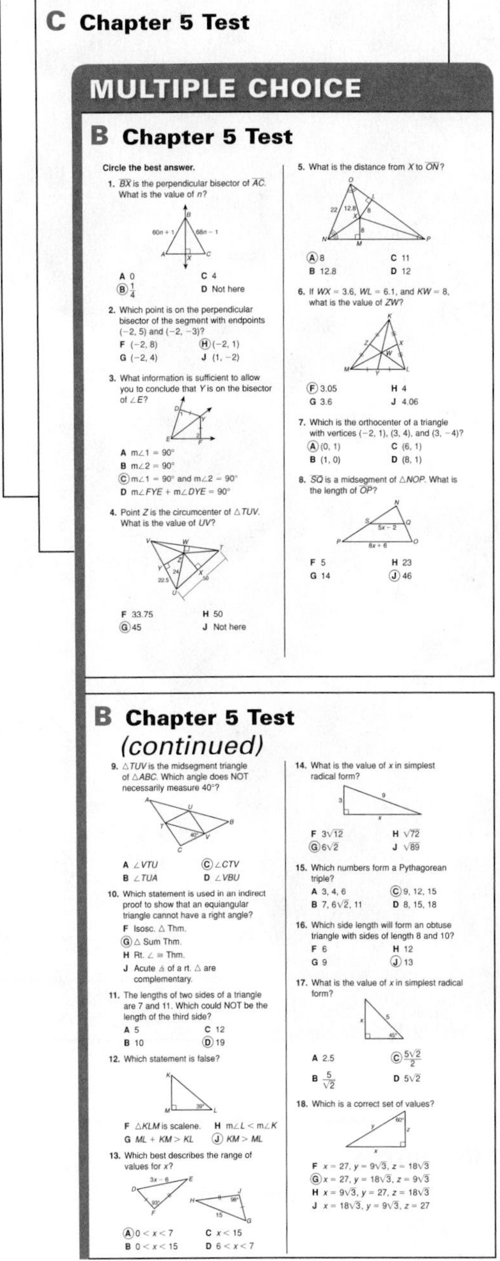

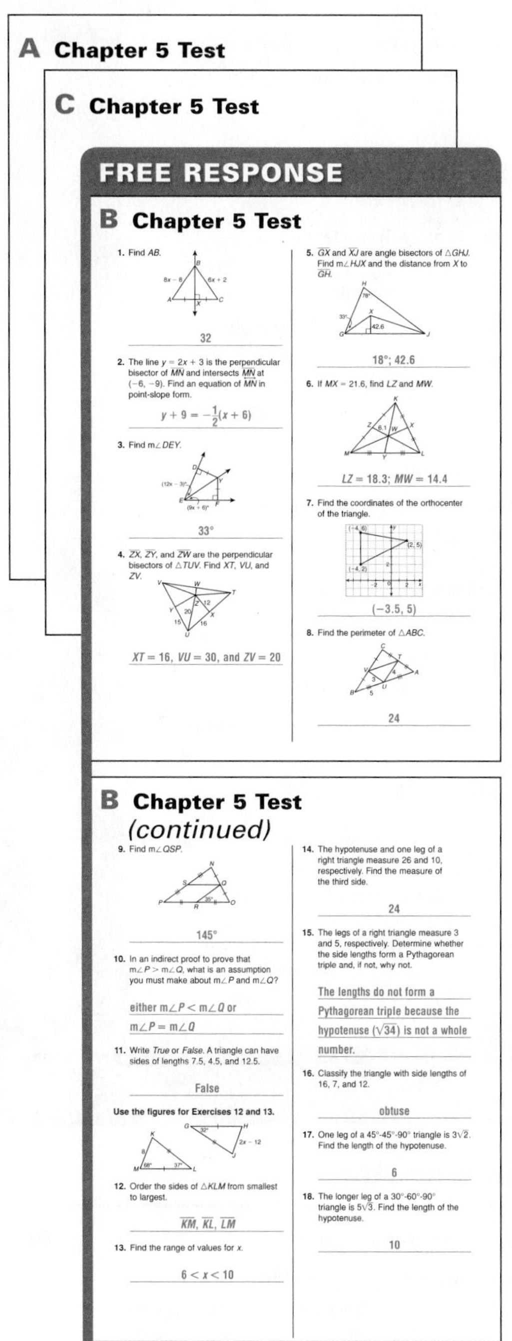

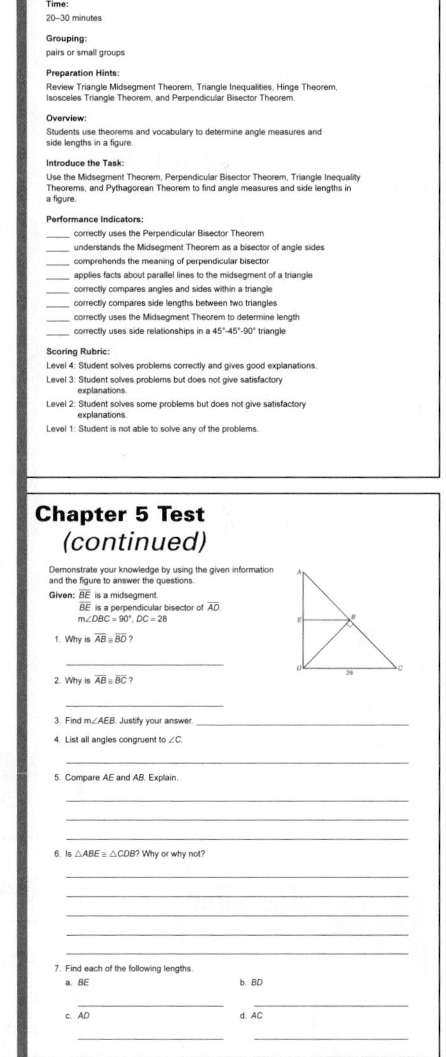

Teacher One Stop™

Test & Practice Generator

Create and customize Chapter 5 Tests. Instantly generate multiple test versions, answer keys, and practice versions of test items.

Modified chapter tests that address special learning needs are available in *IDEA Works!® Modified Worksheets and Tests.*

CHAPTER 5

SECTION 5A
Segments in Triangles

On page 328, students use special points in triangles to find possible locations for a music distribution warehouse.

Exercises designed to prepare students for success on the Multi-Step Test Prep can be found on pages 305, 312, 319, and 326.

SECTION 5B
Relationships in Triangles

On page 364, students use relationships in triangles to analyze the possible locations for a new airport.

Exercises designed to prepare students for success on the Multi-Step Test Prep can be found on pages 338, 344, 354, and 361.

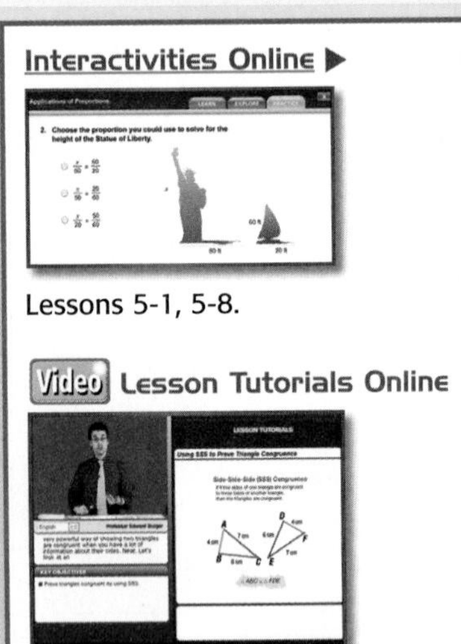

Lessons 5-1, 5-8.

Lesson Tutorial Videos are available for EVERY example.

CHAPTER 5 Properties and Attributes of Triangles

Chapter Focus

- Apply the properties of special triangle segments to solve real-world problems.
- Justify and apply inequality relationships in triangles.

Balancing Act

Sculptures and mobiles often include carefully balanced shapes. You can use medians to find the point at which a triangular shape will balance.

296 *Chapter 5*

Balancing Act

About the Project

In the Chapter Project, students use theorems about perpendicular bisectors to build a stand that will support a balanced triangle. Then students cut out a cardboard triangle, locate its centroid, and check to see whether the triangle will balance at this point.

Project Resources

All project resources for teachers and students are provided online.

Materials:

- cardboard
- scissors
- string
- tape

ARE YOU READY?

Vocabulary

Match each term on the left with a definition on the right.

1. angle bisector **E**
2. conclusion **C**
3. hypotenuse **A**
4. leg of a right triangle **D**
5. perpendicular bisector of a segment **B**

A. the side opposite the right angle in a right triangle
B. a line that is perpendicular to a segment at its midpoint
C. the phrase following the word *then* in a conditional statement
D. one of the two sides that form the right angle in a right triangle
E. a line or ray that divides an angle into two congruent angles
F. the phrase following the word *if* in a conditional statement

Classify Triangles

Tell whether each triangle is acute, right, or obtuse.

6. 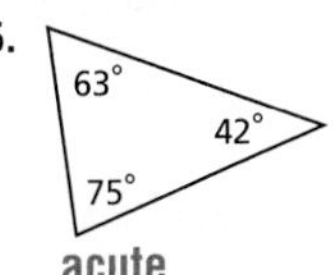

acute

7. 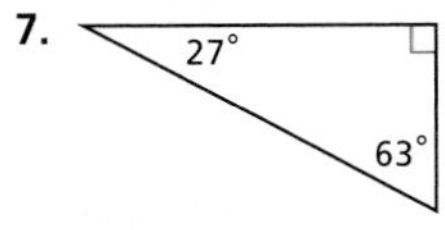

right

8. 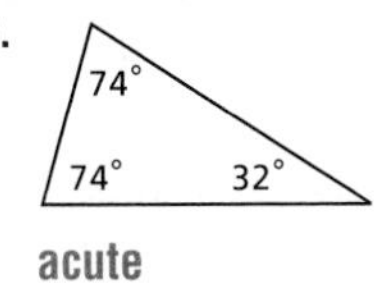

acute

9. 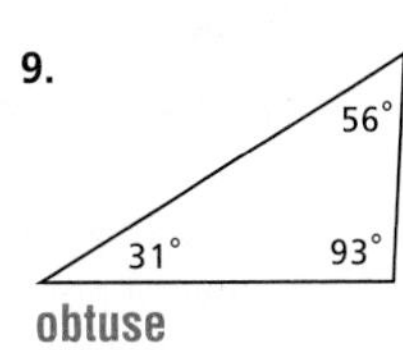

obtuse

Squares and Square Roots

Simplify each expression.

10. 8^2 **64**
11. $(-12)^2$ **144**
12. $\sqrt{49}$ **7**
13. $-\sqrt{36}$ **−6**

Simplify Radical Expressions

Simplify each expression.

14. $\sqrt{9+16}$ **5**
15. $\sqrt{100-36}$ **8**
16. $\sqrt{\frac{81}{25}}$ $\frac{9}{5}$
17. $\sqrt{2^2}$ **2**

Solve and Graph Inequalities

Solve each inequality. Graph the solutions on a number line.

18. $d+5<1$ $d<-4$
19. $-4 \le w-7$ $w \ge 3$
20. $-3s \ge 6$ $s \le -2$
21. $-2 > \frac{m}{10}$ $m < -20$

Logical Reasoning

Draw a conclusion from each set of true statements.

22. If two lines intersect, then they are not parallel. Lines ℓ and m intersect at P. **Lines ℓ and m are not parallel.**
23. If M is the midpoint of $\overline{AB}$, then $AM = MB$. If $AM = MB$, then $AM = \frac{1}{2}AB$ and $MB = \frac{1}{2}AB$. **If M is the mdpt. of $\overline{AB}$, then $AM = \frac{1}{2}AB$ and $MB = \frac{1}{2}AB$.**

ARE YOU READY?

Organizer

Objective: Use properties of congruent triangles.

Prerequisite Skills

Classify Triangles
Squares and Square Roots
Simplify Radical Expressions
Solve and Graph Inequalities
Logical Reasoning

Assessing Prior Knowledge

INTERVENTION

Diagnose and Prescribe

Use this page to determine whether intervention is necessary or whether enrichment is appropriate.

Resources

 ***Are You Ready? Intervention and Enrichment*** **Worksheets**

 ***Are You Ready?*** **CD-ROM**

 ***Are You Ready?*** **Online**

my.hrw.com

Answers

18–21. For graphs, see p. A18.

ARE YOU READY?

Diagnose and Prescribe

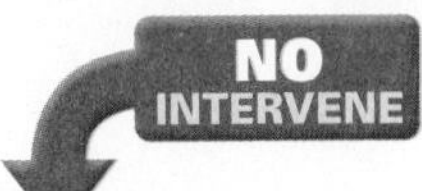

NO INTERVENE

Prerequisite Skill	*Are You Ready? Intervention,* Chapter 5 — Worksheets	CD-ROM	Online
Classify Triangles	Skill 29	Activity 29	Diagnose and Prescribe Online
Squares and Square Roots	Skill 6	Activity 6	
Simplify Radical Expressions	Skill 53	Activity 53	
Solve and Graph Inequalities	Skill 74	Activity 74	
Logical Reasoning	Skill 87	Activity 87	

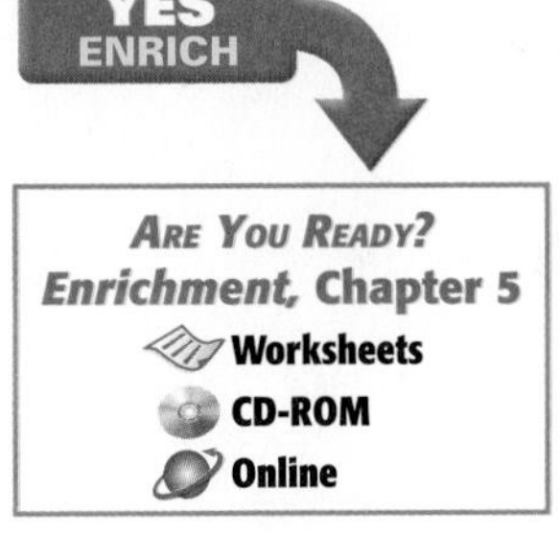

YES ENRICH

Are You Ready? Enrichment, Chapter 5
Worksheets
CD-ROM
Online

CHAPTER 5

Study Guide: Preview

Organizer

Objective: Help students organize the new concepts they will learn in Chapter 5.

Resources

Teacher One Stop™
PuzzleView

***Multilingual Glossary* Online**
go.hrw.com
KEYWORD: MG7 Glossary

Answers to *Vocabulary Connections*

Possible answers:

1. Lines that are concurrent "run together," or intersect, at one point.
2. Each endpoint of a midsegment of a triangle is the midpoint of one side of the triangle.
3. A median of a triangle is a segment whose endpoints are a vertex of the triangle and the midpoint of the opposite side.
4. equilateral–all sides equal in length; equilibrium–a state in which all things are balanced; equivalent–equal in value
5. The altitude of a triangle is the height of the triangle.

CHAPTER 5

Study Guide: Preview

Where You've Been

Previously, you

- studied points, lines, rays, segments, and angles.
- learned properties of triangles.
- identified congruent triangles.
- used the Pythagorean Theorem to find distances.
- used deductive reasoning to write proofs.

In This Chapter

You will study

- properties of perpendicular bisectors and angle bisectors.
- special points, segments, and lines related to triangles.
- inequalities in one triangle and in two triangles.
- Pythagorean inequalities and special right triangles.
- how to write an indirect proof.

Where You're Going

You can use the skills learned in this chapter

- to study trigonometry in geometry, algebra, and advanced math courses.
- to study motion and forces in physics courses.
- to estimate travel distances and to assess the validity of indirect arguments outside of school.

Key Vocabulary/Vocabulario

altitude of a triangle	altura de un triángulo
centroid of a triangle	centroide de un triángulo
circumcenter of a triangle	circuncentro de un triángulo
concurrent	concurrente
equidistant	equidistante
incenter of a triangle	incentro de un triángulo
median of a triangle	mediana de un triángulo
midsegment of a triangle	segmento medio de un triángulo
orthocenter of a triangle	orthocentro de un triángulo

Vocabulary Connections

To become familiar with some of the vocabulary terms in the chapter, consider the following. You may refer to the chapter, the glossary, or a dictionary if you like.

1. In Latin, *co* means "together with," and *currere* means "to run." How can you use these meanings to understand what **concurrent** lines are?
2. The endpoints of a **midsegment of a triangle** are on two sides of the triangle. Where on the sides do you think the endpoints are located?
3. The strip of concrete or grass in the middle of some roadways is called the *median*. What do you think the term **median of a triangle** means?
4. The word **equidistant** begins with *equi-*, which means "equal." List three other words that begin with *equi-*. What is the meaning of each word?
5. Think of the everyday meaning of *altitude*. What do you think the **altitude of a triangle** is?

298 Chapter 5

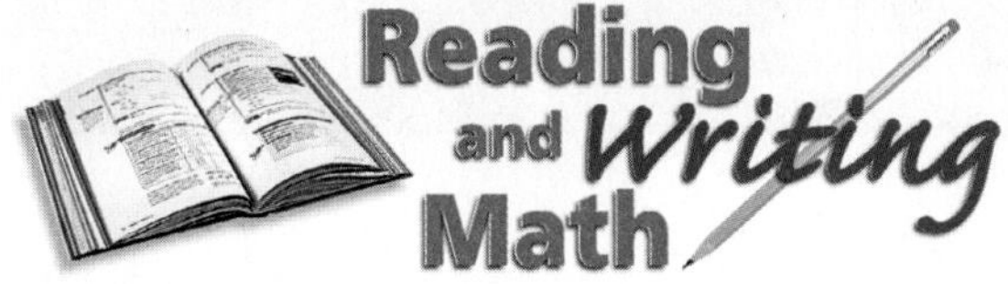

Reading Strategy: Learn Math Vocabulary

Mathematics has a vocabulary all its own. To learn and remember new vocabulary words, use the following study strategies.

- Try to figure out the meaning of a new word based on its context.
- Use a dictionary to look up the root word or prefix.
- Relate the new word to familiar everyday words.

Once you know what a word means, write its definition in your own words.

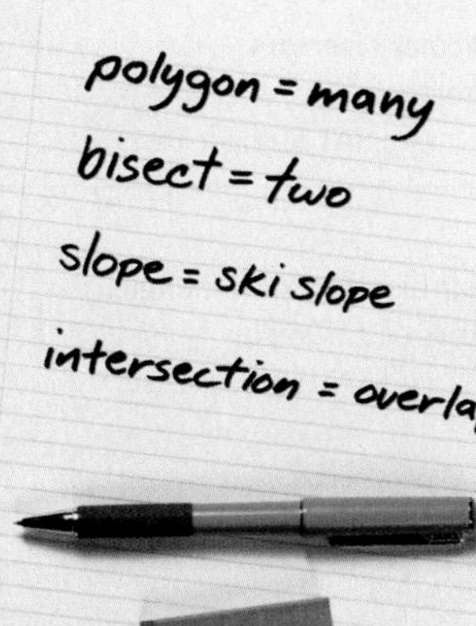

Term	Study Notes	Definition
Polygon	*The prefix poly means "many" or "several."*	*A closed plane figure formed by three or more line segments*
Bisect	*The prefix bi means "two."*	*Cuts or divides something into two equal parts*
Slope	*Think of a ski slope.*	*The measure of the steepness of a line*
Intersection	*The root word intersect means "to overlap." Think of the intersection of two roads.*	*The set of points that two or more lines have in common*

Complete the table below.

	Term	Study Notes	Definition
1.	Trinomial		
2.	Equiangular triangle		
3.	Perimeter		
4.	Deductive reasoning		

Use the given prefix and its meanings to write a definition for each vocabulary word.

5. *circum* (about, around); circumference

6. *co* (with, together); coplanar

7. *trans* (across, beyond, through); translation

Organizer

Objective: Help students apply strategies to understand and retain key concepts.

Resources

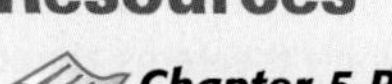
Chapter 5 Resource Book

Reading Strategies

Reading Strategy: Learn Math Vocabulary

ENGLISH LANGUAGE LEARNERS

Discuss Students will remember new vocabulary words better if they understand the meanings of prefixes and root words.

Extend Before each lesson, have students try to write a definition for each new term based on its prefix and/or root word.

Answers to *Try This*

Possible answers:

1. *Tri*: "three"; polynomial with 3 terms.
2. *Equi*: "equal"; *tri*: "three"; △ with 3 eq. ∠ meas.
3. *Peri*: "around"; *meter*: length; dist. around a fig.
4. *deduce*: "infer"; using logic to draw conclusions from facts, definitions, and properties.
5. distance around a circle
6. points in the same plane
7. movement across a plane

Reading Connection

Mathematicians Are People, Too Volume 1
by Luetta & Wilbert Reimer

Here are profiles of 15 mathematicians whose achievements span 2500 years. The authors tell the stories with an eye toward bringing out the human sides of these accomplished but sometimes misunderstood people.

Activity After students study the Pythagorean Theorem, have them read about the Pythagoreans in Chapter 2. Ask students to give reasons why Pythagoras is known as "the father of numbers."

SECTION 5A

Segments in Triangles

One-Minute Section Planner

Lesson	Lab Resources	Materials
Lesson 5-1 Perpendicular and Angle Bisectors • Prove and apply theorems about perpendicular bisectors. • Prove and apply theorems about angle bisectors. ☑ SAT-10 ☑ NAEP ☑ ACT ☑ SAT ☐ SAT Subject Tests	***Technology Lab Activities*** 5-1 Technology Lab	**Optional** ruler (MK), protractor (MK), compass (MK), straightedge (MK), local map, patty paper
Lesson 5-2 Bisectors of Triangles • Prove and apply properties of perpendicular bisectors of a triangle. • Prove and apply properties of angle bisectors of a triangle. ☑ SAT-10 ☑ NAEP ☑ ACT ☑ SAT ☐ SAT Subject Tests	***Technology Lab Activities*** 5-2 Technology Lab	**Required** patty paper **Optional** compass (MK), straightedge (MK), local map, geometry software
Lesson 5-3 Medians and Altitudes of Triangles • Apply properties of medians of a triangle. • Apply properties of altitudes of a triangle. ☐ SAT-10 ☑ NAEP ☑ ACT ☑ SAT ☐ SAT Subject Tests	***Geometry Lab Activities*** 5-3 Geometry Lab ***Technology Lab Activities*** 5-3 Technology Lab	**Required** compass (MK), straightedge (MK) **Optional** scissors, patty paper, cardboard triangles, string
5-3 Technology Lab Special Points in Triangles • Use special points in triangles to explore Euler's line. ☐ SAT-10 ☑ NAEP ☐ ACT ☐ SAT ☐ SAT Subject Tests	***Technology Lab Activities*** 5-3 Lab Recording Sheet	**Required** geometry software
Lesson 5-4 The Triangle Midsegment Theorem • Prove and use properties of triangle midsegments. ☐ SAT-10 ☑ NAEP ☑ ACT ☑ SAT ☑ SAT Subject Tests		**Optional** compass (MK), straightedge (MK), heavy paper, scissors, geometry software

MK = *Manipulatives Kit*

Math Background

THE CIRCUMCENTER

Lesson 5-2

By constructing the perpendicular bisectors of the sides of many different triangles, students can convince themselves that the following statement is likely to be true: the perpendicular bisectors of the sides of any triangle intersect in a point; in other words, the perpendicular bisectors are *concurrent*. The point of concurrency of the perpendicular bisectors of a triangle is called the *circumcenter* of the triangle.

As always, the inductive approach described above may be convincing, but it does not constitute a proof. The main steps in the proof of this concurrency theorem run as follows. Given $\triangle ABC$, let point P be the point of intersection of the perpendicular bisectors of sides $\overline{AB}$ and $\overline{BC}$. To prove the theorem, it is sufficient to show that point P also lies on the perpendicular bisector of $\overline{AC}$.

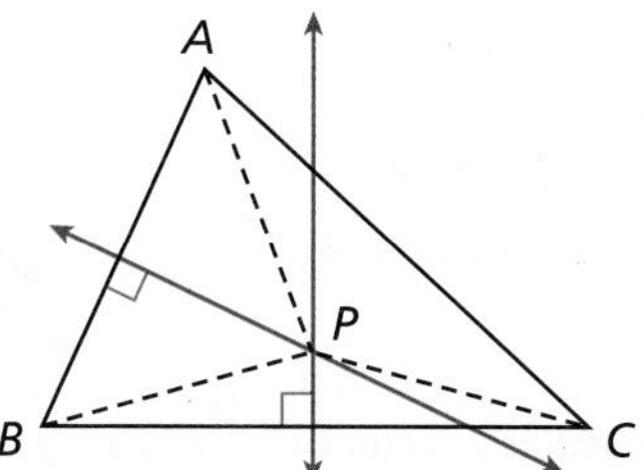

Since P lies on the perpendicular bisector of $\overline{AB}$, $\overline{PA} \cong \overline{PB}$ by the Perpendicular Bisector Theorem. Similarly, $\overline{PB} \cong \overline{PC}$. By transitivity, $\overline{PA} \cong \overline{PC}$ and therefore P lies on the perpendicular bisector of $\overline{AC}$ by the Converse of the Perpendicular Bisector Theorem.

Note that this concurrency theorem can also be demonstrated using a straightforward but somewhat tedious coordinate proof.

THE CENTROID

Lesson 5-3

The medians of a triangle are concurrent at a point called the *centroid* of the triangle. The centroid has important physical properties. For a triangle of uniform thickness and density, the centroid is the point at which the triangle will balance. In this sense, the centroid can be considered the "average" of all the points in the triangle.

The triangle will also balance along any line that passes through the centroid. In particular, this means that a median of a triangle divides the triangle into two smaller triangles with equal areas. For example, in the figure below, area($\triangle ABX$) = area($\triangle ACX$). This is easy to see since the two smaller triangles have equal bases and heights.

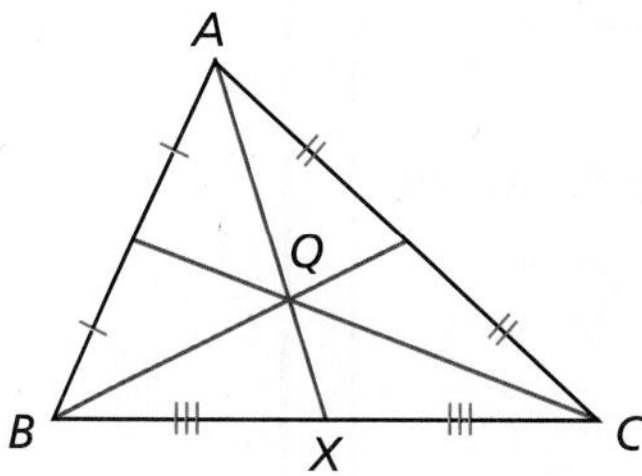

MIDSEGMENTS

Lesson 5-4

A *midsegment* of a triangle is a segment that joins the midpoints of two sides of the triangle. Together, the three midsegments of a triangle form the *midsegment triangle*, which is $\triangle XYZ$ in the figure.

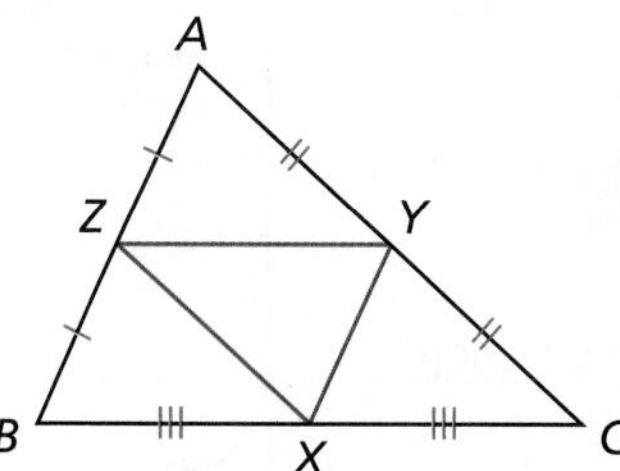

By the Triangle Midsegment Theorem, $XY = \frac{1}{2}AB$, $ZY = \frac{1}{2}BC$, and $XZ = \frac{1}{2}AC$. It follows by SSS Congruence that the four small triangles formed by the midsegments are congruent. Since the four triangles together form $\triangle ABC$, each small triangle has one-fourth the area of $\triangle ABC$.

The midsegment triangle will be revisited when students study similarity in Lesson 9-5.

5-1 Organizer

Pacing: Traditional 1 day
Block $\frac{1}{2}$ day

Objectives: Prove and apply theorems about perpendicular bisectors.

Prove and apply theorems about angle bisectors.

Technology Lab
In Technology Lab Activities

Online Edition
Tutorial Videos, Interactivity

Countdown Week 10

Power Presentations with PowerPoint®

Warm Up

Construct each of the following.

1. a perpendicular bisector **2.** an angle bisector

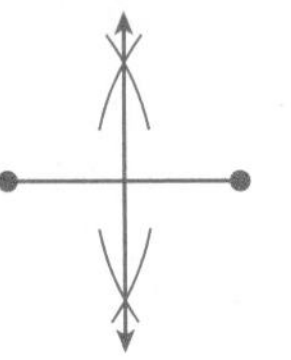

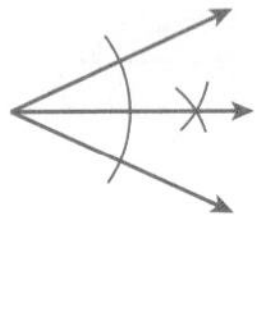

3. Find the midpoint and slope of the segment with endpoints (2, 8) and (−4, 6). $(-1, 7), \frac{1}{3}$

Also available on transparency

Math Humor

Q: Where do math teachers shop?

A: Deci-malls (decimals)!

5-1 Perpendicular and Angle Bisectors

Objectives
Prove and apply theorems about perpendicular bisectors.

Prove and apply theorems about angle bisectors.

Vocabulary
equidistant
locus

Who uses this?
The suspension and steering lines of a parachute keep the sky diver centered under the parachute. (See Example 3.)

When a point is the same distance from two or more objects, the point is said to be **equidistant** from the objects. Triangle congruence theorems can be used to prove theorems about equidistant points.

Know it! Note

Theorems Distance and Perpendicular Bisectors

	THEOREM	HYPOTHESIS	CONCLUSION
5-1-1	**Perpendicular Bisector Theorem** If a point is on the perpendicular bisector of a segment, then it is equidistant from the endpoints of the segment.	ℓ, X, A, Y, B $\overline{XY} \perp \overline{AB}$ $\overline{YA} \cong \overline{YB}$	$XA = XB$
5-1-2	**Converse of the Perpendicular Bisector Theorem** If a point is equidistant from the endpoints of a segment, then it is on the perpendicular bisector of the segment.	ℓ, X, A, Y, B $XA = XB$	$\overline{XY} \perp \overline{AB}$ $\overline{YA} \cong \overline{YB}$

You will prove Theorem 5-1-2 in Exercise 30.

PROOF **Perpendicular Bisector Theorem**

ℓ, X, A, Y, B

Given: ℓ is the perpendicular bisector of $\overline{AB}$.
Prove: $XA = XB$

Proof:

Since ℓ is the perpendicular bisector of $\overline{AB}$, $\ell \perp \overline{AB}$ and Y is the midpoint of $\overline{AB}$. By the definition of perpendicular, $\angle AYX$ and $\angle BYX$ are right angles and $\angle AYX \cong \angle BYX$. By the definition of midpoint, $\overline{AY} \cong \overline{BY}$. By the Reflexive Property of Congruence, $\overline{XY} \cong \overline{XY}$. So $\triangle AYX \cong \triangle BYX$ by SAS, and $\overline{XA} \cong \overline{XB}$ by CPCTC. Therefore $XA = XB$ by the definition of congruent segments.

Reading Math
The word *locus* comes from the Latin word for location. The plural of *locus* is *loci*, which is pronounced LOW-sigh.

A **locus** is a set of points that satisfies a given condition. The perpendicular bisector of a segment can be defined as the locus of points in a plane that are equidistant from the endpoints of the segment.

State Resources

go.hrw.com
State Resources Online
KEYWORD: MG7 Resources

1 Introduce

EXPLORATION

5-1 Perpendicular and Angle Bisectors

You can use a ruler and protractor to explore properties of perpendicular bisectors.

1. Draw a long segment on a sheet of paper and label it $\overline{AB}$.
2. Use a ruler to find the midpoint of $\overline{AB}$. Label it P.
3. Use a protractor to draw a line ℓ through P that is perpendicular to $\overline{AB}$.
4. Draw any point X on ℓ. Measure the distance from X to A and the distance from X to B. What do you notice?
5. Mark three more points on ℓ and measure the distance from each point to both endpoints. What do you find?
6. Complete the following conjecture: If a point is on the perpendicular bisector of a segment, then __?__ .

THINK AND DISCUSS

7. **Explain** how you can use your conjecture and the fact that line m is the perpendicular bisector of $\overline{QR}$ to classify $\triangle PQR$.

Motivate

Show students a local map marked with two locations, such as your school and a grocery store. Ask them to find places that are about the same distance from both locations. After they have found several, show them that all these places lie near the perpendicular bisector of the segment joining the two original locations. Explain that students will study properties like this in this lesson.

Explorations and answers are provided in *Alternate Openers: Explorations Transparencies.*

EXAMPLE 1 Applying the Perpendicular Bisector Theorem and Its Converse

Find each measure.

A YW

$YW = XW$	*⊥ Bisector Thm.*
$YW = 7.3$	*Substitute 7.3 for XW.*

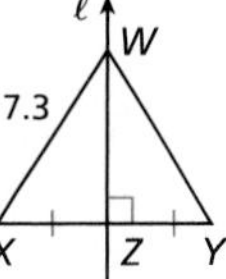

B BC

Since $AB = AC$ and $\ell \perp \overline{BC}$, ℓ is the perpendicular bisector of $\overline{BC}$ by the Converse of the Perpendicular Bisector Theorem.

$BC = 2CD$	*Def. of seg. bisector*
$BC = 2(16) = 32$	*Substitute 16 for CD.*

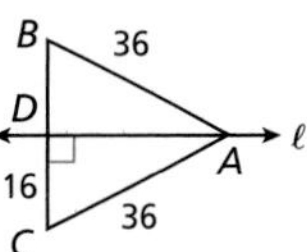

Algebra

C PR

$PR = RQ$	*⊥ Bisector Thm.*
$2n + 9 = 7n - 18$	*Substitute the given values.*
$9 = 5n - 18$	*Subtract 2n from both sides.*
$27 = 5n$	*Add 18 to both sides.*
$5.4 = n$	*Divide both sides by 5.*

So $PR = 2(5.4) + 9 = 19.8$.

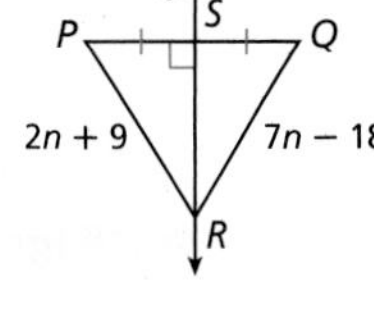

Find each measure.

1a. Given that line ℓ is the perpendicular bisector of $\overline{DE}$ and $EG = 14.6$, find DG. **14.6**

1b. Given that $DE = 20.8$, $DG = 36.4$, and $EG = 36.4$, find EF. **10.4**

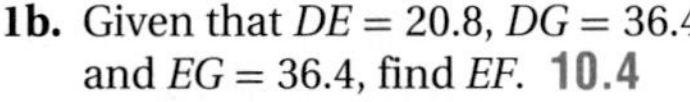

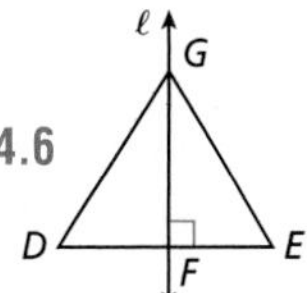

Remember that the distance between a point and a line is the length of the perpendicular segment from the point to the line.

Theorems — Distance and Angle Bisectors

	THEOREM	HYPOTHESIS	CONCLUSION
5-1-3	**Angle Bisector Theorem** If a point is on the bisector of an angle, then it is equidistant from the sides of the angle.	A, C, P, B; $\angle APC \cong \angle BPC$	$AC = BC$
5-1-4	**Converse of the Angle Bisector Theorem** If a point in the interior of an angle is equidistant from the sides of the angle, then it is on the bisector of the angle.	A, C, P, B; $AC = BC$	$\angle APC \cong \angle BPC$

You will prove these theorems in Exercises 31 and 40.

COMMON ERROR ALERT

Students sometimes confuse Theorems 5-1-1 and 5-1-2. To apply Theorem 5-1-1, they must be given a perpendicular bisector to conclude that a point on it is equidistant from the endpoints of the segment. To apply Theorem 5-1-2, they must have a point equidistant from the endpoints of a segment to conclude that the point is on the perpendicular bisector of that segment.

Power Presentations with PowerPoint®

Additional Examples

Example 1

Find each measure.

A. MN 2.6

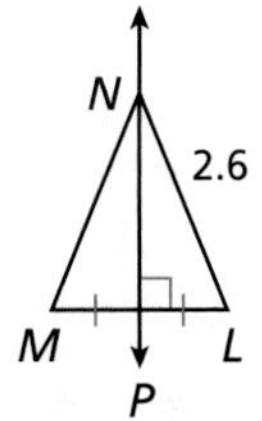

B. BC 24

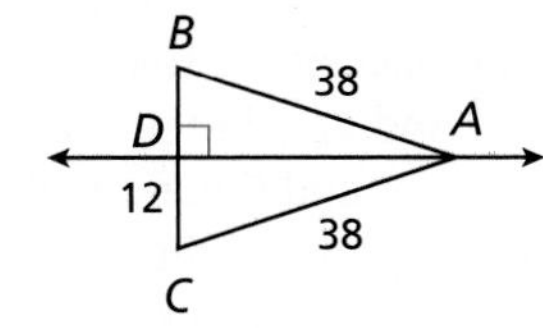

C. TU 28.5

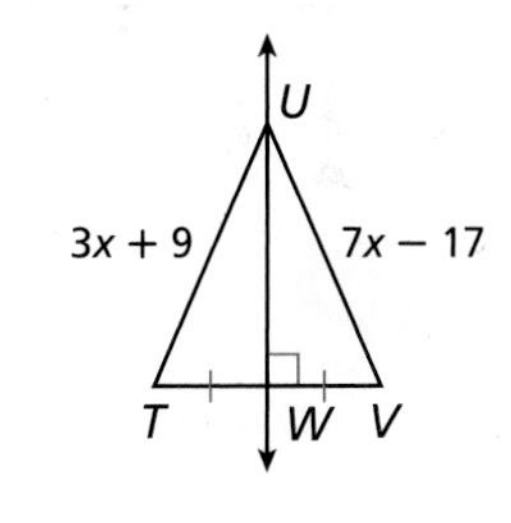

Guided Instruction

Review the definitions and constructions of perpendicular and angle bisectors. Discuss the Perpendicular Bisector Theorem and its converse, and illustrate them with algebraic examples. Discuss the Angle Bisector Theorem and its converse. Before covering **Example 4,** review how to find the midpoint and slope of a segment when given the coordinates of the endpoints, and then review the relationship between the slopes of perpendicular lines.

Reaching All Learners

Through Concrete Manipulatives

Have students draw a segment $\overline{AB}$ on a piece of patty paper and then fold the paper so that *A* and *B* coincide. Point out that the fold is the perpendicular bisector of the segment. Have students mark several points on the fold and measure the distance from each of these points to *A* and to *B*. Students should note that these distances are the same in each case. A similar exploration can be done with angle bisectors or by using a Mira.

INTERVENTION

Questioning Strategies

EXAMPLE 1

- How do you know which theorem to use in each part of the example?

Visual For **Example 1B,** draw counterexamples showing that $\overline{BC} \not\perp \overline{AD}$ to demonstrate why you must know that $\overline{BC} \perp \overline{AD}$ to conclude that ℓ is the perpendicular bisector.

Power Presentations with PowerPoint®

Additional Examples

Example 2

Find each measure.

A. BC 7.2

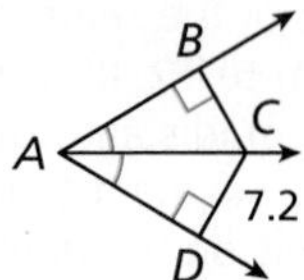

B. m∠EFH, given that m∠EFG = 50° 25°

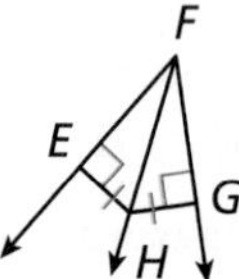

C. m∠MKL 38°

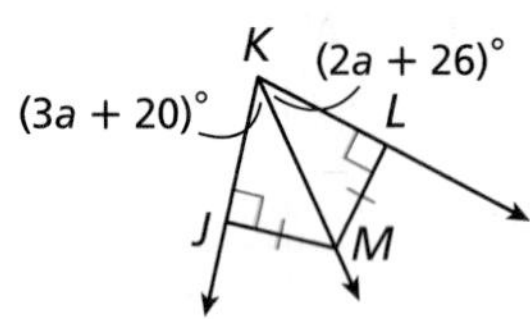

Example 3

John wants to hang a spotlight along the back of a display case. Wires $\overline{AD}$ and $\overline{CD}$ are the same length, and A and C are equidistant from B. How do the wires keep the spotlight centered?

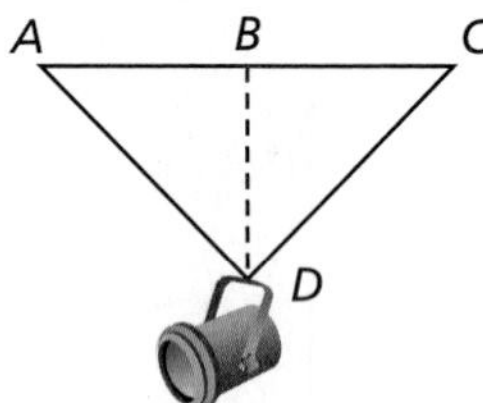

Since $\overline{AD} \cong \overline{CD}$, D is on the ⊥ bisector of $\overline{AC}$. B is the mdpt. of $\overline{AC}$, so $\overline{BD}$ is the ⊥ bisector of $\overline{AC}$. Thus D is centered below B.

Based on these theorems, an angle bisector can be defined as the locus of all points in the interior of the angle that are equidistant from the sides of the angle.

EXAMPLE 2 Applying the Angle Bisector Theorems

Find each measure.

A LM

$LM = JM$ ∠ Bisector Thm.

$LM = 12.8$ Substitute 12.8 for JM.

B **m∠ABD, given that m∠ABC = 112°**

Since $AD = DC$, $\overline{AD} \perp \overline{BA}$, and $\overline{DC} \perp \overline{BC}$, $\overrightarrow{BD}$ bisects ∠ABC by the Converse of the Angle Bisector Theorem.

$m\angle ABD = \frac{1}{2}m\angle ABC$ Def. of ∠ bisector

$m\angle ABD = \frac{1}{2}(112°) = 56°$ Substitute 112° for m∠ABC.

C **m∠TSU**

Since $RU = UT$, $\overline{RU} \perp \overline{SR}$, and $\overline{UT} \perp \overline{ST}$, $\overrightarrow{SU}$ bisects ∠RST by the Converse of the Angle Bisector Theorem.

$m\angle RSU = m\angle TSU$ Def. of ∠ bisector

$6z + 14 = 5z + 23$ Substitute the given values.

$z + 14 = 23$ Subtract 5z from both sides.

$z = 9$ Subtract 14 from both sides.

So $m\angle TSU = [5(9) + 23]° = 68°$.

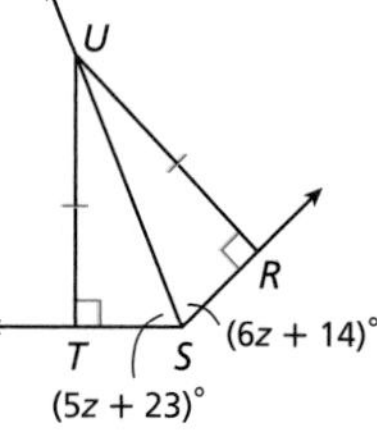

Find each measure.

2a. Given that $\overrightarrow{YW}$ bisects ∠XYZ and $WZ = 3.05$, find WX. **3.05**

2b. Given that m∠WYZ = 63°, $XW = 5.7$, and $ZW = 5.7$, find m∠XYZ. **126°**

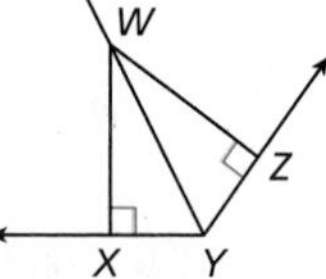

EXAMPLE 3 *Parachute Application*

Each pair of suspension lines on a parachute are the same length and are equally spaced from the center of the chute. How do these lines keep the sky diver centered under the parachute?

It is given that $\overline{PQ} \cong \overline{RQ}$. So Q is on the perpendicular bisector of $\overline{PR}$ by the Converse of the Perpendicular Bisector Theorem. Since S is the midpoint of $\overline{PR}$, $\overline{QS}$ is the perpendicular bisector of $\overline{PR}$. Therefore the sky diver remains centered under the chute.

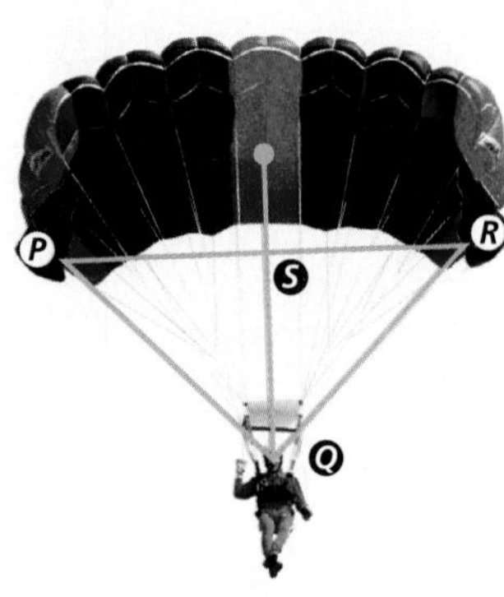

INTERVENTION Questioning Strategies

EXAMPLE 2

- How do you know which theorem to use in each part of the example?

EXAMPLE 3

- How can the Perpendicular Bisector Theorem be used to center a real-life object?

Teaching Tip **Critical Thinking** Ask students "Does the Converse of the Angle Bisector Theorem apply if the point is in the exterior of the angle?" Lead students to see that an angle bisector must be in the interior of the angle it bisects. Therefore a point equidistant from the sides must also be in the angle's interior in order to be on the bisector.

Teaching Tip **Reading Math** Remind students that in the converse of a statement, the hypothesis and conclusion are switched.

3. S is equidistant from each pair of suspension lines. What can you conclude about $\overrightarrow{QS}$? **$\overrightarrow{QS}$ bisects $\angle PQR$.**

EXAMPLE 4 Writing Equations of Bisectors in the Coordinate Plane

Algebra

Write an equation in point-slope form for the perpendicular bisector of the segment with endpoints $A(-1, 6)$ and $B(3, 4)$.

Step 1 Graph $\overline{AB}$.

The perpendicular bisector of $\overline{AB}$ is perpendicular to $\overline{AB}$ at its midpoint.

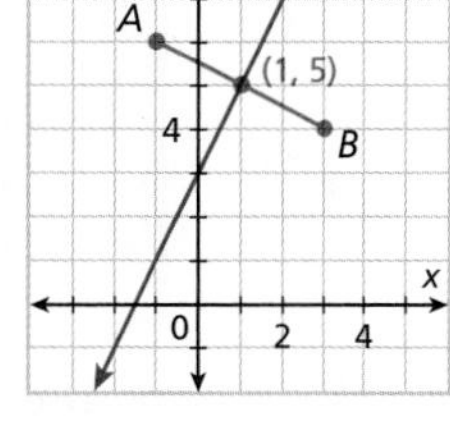

Step 2 Find the midpoint of $\overline{AB}$.

$\left(\frac{x_1 + x_2}{2}, \frac{y_1 + y_2}{2}\right)$ *Midpoint formula*

mdpt. of $\overline{AB} = \left(\frac{-1+3}{2}, \frac{6+4}{2}\right) = (1, 5)$

Step 3 Find the slope of the perpendicular bisector.

slope $= \frac{y_2 - y_1}{x_2 - x_1}$ *Slope formula*

slope of $\overline{AB} = \frac{4-6}{3-(-1)} = \frac{-2}{4} = -\frac{1}{2}$

Since the slopes of perpendicular lines are opposite reciprocals, the slope of the perpendicular bisector is 2.

Step 4 Use point-slope form to write an equation.

The perpendicular bisector of $\overline{AB}$ has slope 2 and passes through $(1, 5)$.

$y - y_1 = m(x - x_1)$ *Point-slope form*

$y - 5 = 2(x - 1)$ *Substitute 5 for y_1, 2 for m, and 1 for x_1.*

4. Write an equation in point-slope form for the perpendicular bisector of the segment with endpoints $P(5, 2)$ and $Q(1, -4)$. $y + 1 = -\frac{2}{3}(x - 3)$

THINK AND DISCUSS

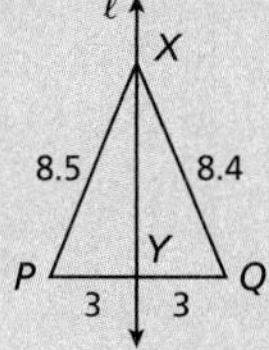

1. Is line ℓ a bisector of $\overline{PQ}$? Is it a perpendicular bisector of $\overline{PQ}$? Explain.
2. Suppose that M is in the interior of $\angle JKL$ and $MJ = ML$. Can you conclude that $\overrightarrow{KM}$ is the bisector of $\angle JKL$? Explain.

3. **GET ORGANIZED** Copy and complete the graphic organizer. In each box, write the theorem or its converse in your own words.

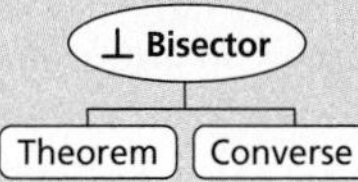

Teaching Tip **Inclusion** Before **Example 4,** review how to find the opposite reciprocal of a number. For example, the opposite reciprocal of 3 is $-\frac{1}{3}$.

Power Presentations with PowerPoint®

Additional Examples

Example 4

Write an equation in point-slope form for the perpendicular bisector of the segment with endpoints $C(6, -5)$ and $D(10, 1)$.

$y + 2 = -\frac{2}{3}(x - 8)$

INTERVENTION

Questioning Strategies

EXAMPLE 4

- How do you use the endpoints of the segment to write the equation of its perpendicular bisector?

3 Close

Summarize

Discuss how to construct a perpendicular bisector and an angle bisector. Review the theorems from the lesson, illustrating each with a diagram. Explain the method for writing the equation of the perpendicular bisector of a segment when given the coordinates of the endpoints.

ONGOING ASSESSMENT and INTERVENTION

Diagnose **Before** the Lesson
5-1 Warm Up, TE p. 300

Monitor **During** the Lesson
Check It Out! Exercises, SE pp. 301–303
Questioning Strategies, TE pp. 301–303

Assess **After** the Lesson
5-1 Lesson Quiz, TE p. 306
Alternative Assessment, TE p. 306

Answers to *Think and Discuss*

1. Yes; no; since $PY = QY = 3$, Y is the mdpt. of $\overline{PQ}$, and thus by the def. of bisect, ℓ is a bisector of $\overline{PQ}$. If ℓ were the ⊥ bisector of $\overline{PQ}$, then PX would equal QX by the ⊥ Bisector Thm. However, $PX = 8.5$ and $QX = 8.4$, so ℓ is not the ⊥ bisector of $\overline{PQ}$.
2. No; although $MJ = ML$, to apply the Conv. of the ∠ Bisector Thm., you must know that $\overline{MJ} \perp \overrightarrow{KJ}$ and $\overline{ML} \perp \overrightarrow{KL}$.
3. See p. A4.

5-1 Exercises

5-1 Exercises

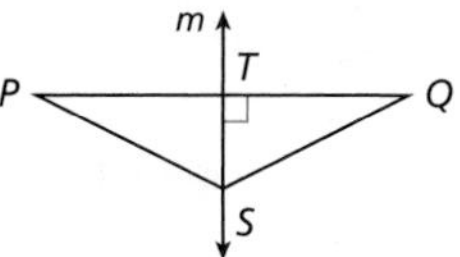

Assignment Guide

Assign *Guided Practice* exercises as necessary.

If you finished Examples **1–2**
- **Basic** 12–17, 23–28
- **Average** 12–17, 22–29
- **Advanced** 12–17, 22–30, 39, 41

If you finished Examples **1–4**
- **Basic** 12–29, 33, 35–37, 42–48
- **Average** 12–29, 32–38, 42–48
- **Advanced** 12–21, 24–28 even, 29–48

Homework Quick Check
Quickly check key concepts.
Exercises: 14, 16, 18, 20, 24, 26

Answers

8. The braces can be installed so that $\overline{PK} \perp \overline{JL}$, $\overline{PM} \perp \overline{NL}$, and $PK = PM$. Then by the Conv. of the ∠ Bisector Thm., P will be on the bisector of ∠JLN.
18. They can position Main St. so that the ∠ formed by Elm St. and Main St. is congruent to the ∠ formed by Grove St. and Main St. Then by the ∠ Bisector Thm., every point on Main St. will be equidistant from Elm St. and Grove St.
19. $y + 3 = -\frac{1}{2}(x + 2)$
20. $y - 2 = x + 4$
21. $y + 3 = \frac{5}{2}(x - 2)$

State Resources

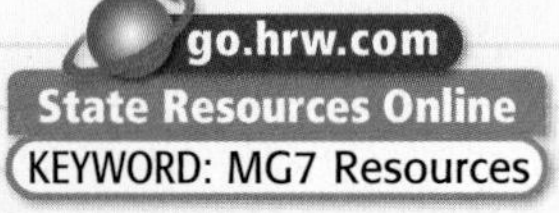

GUIDED PRACTICE

1. **Vocabulary** A __?__ is the *locus* of all points in a plane that are *equidistant* from the endpoints of a segment. *(perpendicular bisector* or *angle bisector)* **perpendicular bisector**

SEE EXAMPLE 1 p. 301

Use the diagram for Exercises 2–4.

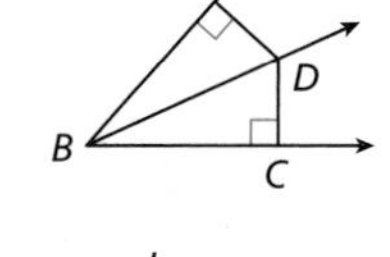

2. Given that $PS = 53.4$, $QT = 47.7$, and $QS = 53.4$, find PQ. **95.4**
3. Given that m is the perpendicular bisector of $\overline{PQ}$ and $SQ = 25.9$, find SP. **25.9**
4. Given that m is the perpendicular bisector of $\overline{PQ}$, $PS = 4a$, and $QS = 2a + 26$, find QS. **52**

SEE EXAMPLE 2 p. 302

Use the diagram for Exercises 5–7.

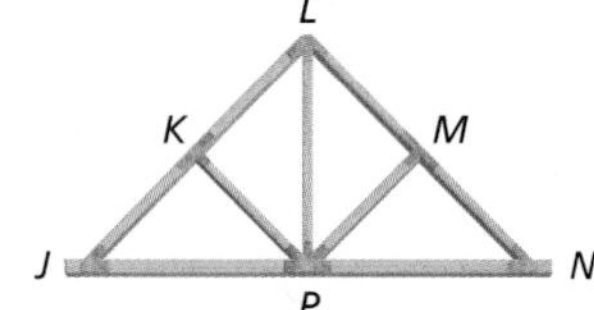

5. Given that $\overrightarrow{BD}$ bisects ∠ABC and $CD = 21.9$, find AD. **21.9**
6. Given that $AD = 61$, $CD = 61$, and m∠$ABC = 48°$, find m∠CBD. **24°**
7. Given that $DA = DC$, m∠$DBC = (10y + 3)°$, and m∠$DBA = (8y + 10)°$, find m∠DBC. **38°**

SEE EXAMPLE 3 p. 302

8. **Carpentry** For a king post truss to be constructed correctly, P must lie on the bisector of ∠JLN. How can braces $\overline{PK}$ and $\overline{PM}$ be used to ensure that P is in the proper location?

L K M J N P

SEE EXAMPLE 4 p. 303

Write an equation in point-slope form for the perpendicular bisector of the segment with the given endpoints.

9. $M(-5, 4)$, $N(1, -2)$ $y - 1 = x + 2$
10. $U(2, -6)$, $V(4, 0)$ $y + 3 = -\frac{1}{3}(x - 3)$
11. $J(-7, 5)$, $K(1, -1)$ $y - 2 = \frac{4}{3}(x + 3)$

PRACTICE AND PROBLEM SOLVING

Independent Practice

For Exercises	See Example
12–14	1
15–17	2
18	3
19–21	4

Extra Practice
Skills Practice p. S12
Application Practice p. S32

Use the diagram for Exercises 12–14.

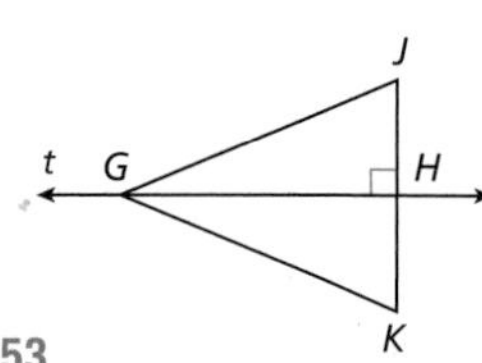

12. Given that line t is the perpendicular bisector of $\overline{JK}$ and $GK = 8.25$, find GJ. **8.25**
13. Given that line t is the perpendicular bisector of $\overline{JK}$, $JG = x + 12$, and $KG = 3x - 17$, find KG. **26.5**
14. Given that $GJ = 70.2$, $JH = 26.5$, and $GK = 70.2$, find JK. **53**

Use the diagram for Exercises 15–17.

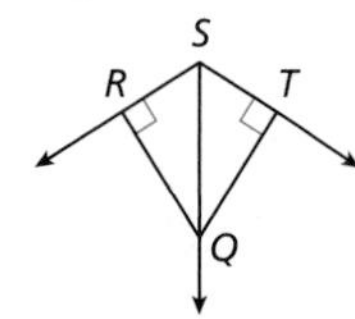

15. Given that m∠RSQ = m∠TSQ and $TQ = 1.3$, find RQ. **1.3**
16. Given that m∠$RSQ = 58°$, $RQ = 49$, and $TQ = 49$, find m∠RST. **116°**
17. Given that $RQ = TQ$, m∠$QSR = (9a + 48)°$, and m∠$QST = (6a + 50)°$, find m∠QST. **54°**

5-1 READING STRATEGIES

Triangle congruence theorems can be used to prove theorems about equidistant points.

Theorem	Example	Conclusion
Perpendicular Bisector Theorem If a point is on the perpendicular bisector of a segment, then it is equidistant from the endpoints of the segment.		$FT = FS$
Converse of the Perpendicular Bisector Theorem If a point is equidistant from the endpoints of a segment, then it is on the perpendicular bisector of the segment.		$\overline{FG} \perp \overline{TS}$ $\overline{TG} \cong \overline{SG}$
Angle Bisector Theorem If a point is on the bisector of an angle, then it is equidistant from the sides of the angle.		$MY = NY$
Converse of the Angle Bisector Theorem If a point in the interior of an angle is equidistant from the sides of the angle, then it is on the bisector of the angle.		∠$MZY \cong$ ∠NZY

Use the information in the chart to find the following values.

Given: = 6.3; = 8.7; ℓ is the perpendicular bisector of

1. What is the length of ? **12.6**
   How do you know? **Perpendicular Bisector Theorem**
2. What is the length of ? **8.7**
   How do you know? **Perpendicular Bisector Theorem**

Given: bisects ∠ M; = 17.3; m∠ M = 57°

3. What is m∠ M? **28.5°**
   How do you know? **Def. of angle bisector**
4. What is the length of M? **17.3**
   How do you know? **Angle Bisector Theorem**

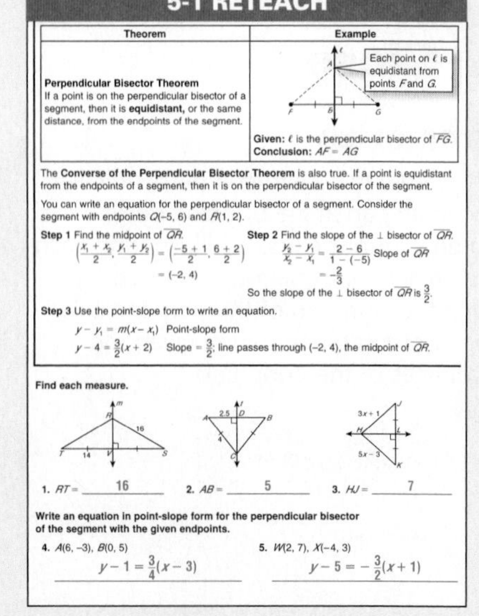

5-1 RETEACH

Theorem	Example
Perpendicular Bisector Theorem If a point is on the perpendicular bisector of a segment, then it is **equidistant,** or the same distance, from the endpoints of the segment.	Each point on ℓ is equidistant from points F and G. **Given:** ℓ is the perpendicular bisector of $\overline{FG}$. **Conclusion:** $AF = AG$

The **Converse of the Perpendicular Bisector Theorem** is also true. If a point is equidistant from the endpoints of a segment, then it is on the perpendicular bisector of the segment.

You can write an equation for the perpendicular bisector of a segment. Consider the segment with endpoints $Q(-5, 6)$ and $R(1, 2)$.

Step 1 Find the midpoint of $\overline{QR}$.
$\left(\frac{x_1 + x_2}{2}, \frac{y_1 + y_2}{2}\right) = \left(\frac{-5 + 1}{2}, \frac{6 + 2}{2}\right) = (-2, 4)$

Step 2 Find the slope of the ⊥ bisector of $\overline{QR}$.
$\frac{y_2 - y_1}{x_2 - x_1} = \frac{2 - 6}{1 - (-5)} = -\frac{2}{3}$ Slope of $\overline{QR}$
So the slope of the ⊥ bisector of $\overline{QR}$ is $\frac{3}{2}$.

Step 3 Use the point-slope form to write an equation.
$y - y_1 = m(x - x_1)$ Point-slope form
$y - 4 = \frac{3}{2}(x + 2)$ Slope $= \frac{3}{2}$; line passes through $(-2, 4)$, the midpoint of $\overline{QR}$.

Find each measure.

1. $RT =$ **16**
2. $AB =$ **5**
3. $HJ =$ **7**

Write an equation in point-slope form for the perpendicular bisector of the segment with the given endpoints.

4. $A(6, -3)$, $B(0, 5)$ $y - 1 = \frac{3}{4}(x - 3)$
5. $W(2, 7)$, $X(-4, 3)$ $y - 5 = -\frac{3}{2}(x + 1)$

18. **City Planning** The planners for a new section of the city want every location on Main Street to be equidistant from Elm Street and Grove Street. How can the planners ensure that this is the case?

Write an equation in point-slope form for the perpendicular bisector of the segment with the given endpoints.

19. $E(-4, -7), F(0, 1)$ 20. $X(-7, 5), Y(-1, -1)$ 21. $M(-3, -1), N(7, -5)$

22. $\overline{PQ}$ is the perpendicular bisector of $\overline{ST}$. Find the values of m and n. **$m = 11$; $n = 8.5$**

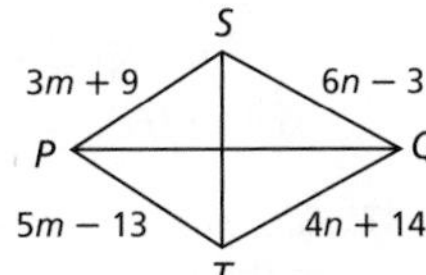

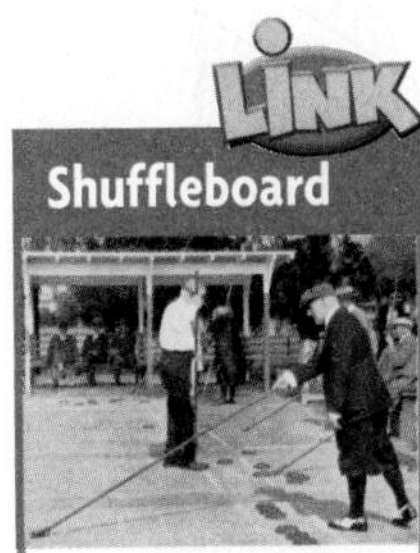

Shuffleboard

One of the first recorded shuffleboard games was played in England in 1532. In this game, Henry VIII supposedly lost £9 to Lord William.

Shuffleboard **Use the diagram of a shuffleboard and the following information to find each length in Exercises 23–28.**

$\overline{KZ}$ is the perpendicular bisector of $\overline{GN}$, $\overline{HM}$, and $\overline{JL}$.

23. JK **38** 24. GN **72** 25. ML **38**

26. HY **24** 27. JL **24** 28. NM **38**

29. **Multi-Step** The endpoints of $\overline{AB}$ are $A(-2, 1)$ and $B(4, -3)$. Find the coordinates of a point C other than the midpoint of $\overline{AB}$ that is on the perpendicular bisector of $\overline{AB}$. How do you know it is on the perpendicular bisector?

30. Write a paragraph proof of the Converse of the Perpendicular Bisector Theorem.

Given: $AX = BX$

Prove: X is on the perpendicular bisector of $\overline{AB}$.

Plan: Draw ℓ perpendicular to $\overline{AB}$ through X. Show that $\triangle AYX \cong \triangle BYX$ and thus $\overline{AY} \cong \overline{BY}$. By definition, ℓ is the perpendicular bisector of $\overline{AB}$.

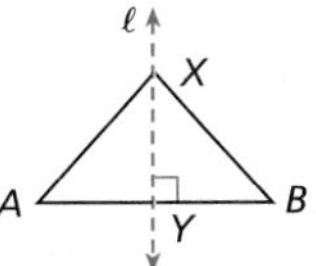

31. Write a two-column proof of the Angle Bisector Theorem.

Given: $\overrightarrow{PS}$ bisects $\angle QPR$. $\overline{SQ} \perp \overrightarrow{PQ}$, $\overline{SR} \perp \overrightarrow{PR}$

Prove: $SQ = SR$

Plan: Use the definitions of angle bisector and perpendicular to identify two pairs of congruent angles. Show that $\triangle PQS \cong \triangle PRS$ and thus $\overline{SQ} \cong \overline{SR}$.

32. **Critical Thinking** In the Converse of the Angle Bisector Theorem, why is it important to say that the point must be in the interior of the angle?

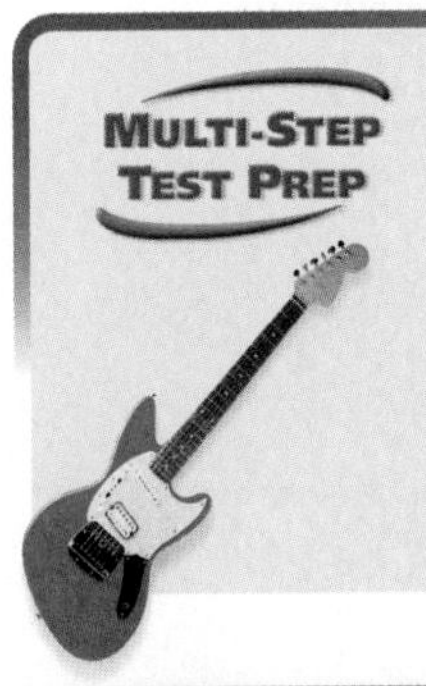

33. This problem will prepare you for the Multi-Step Test Prep on page 328.

A music company has stores in Abby $(-3, -2)$ and Cardenas $(3, 6)$. Each unit in the coordinate plane represents 1 mile.

a. The company president wants to build a warehouse that is equidistant from the two stores. Write an equation that describes the possible locations. **$y = -\frac{3}{4}x + 2$**

b. A straight road connects Abby and Cardenas. The warehouse will be located exactly 4 miles from the road. How many locations are possible? **2**

c. To the nearest tenth of a mile, how far will the warehouse be from each store? **6.4 mi**

In **Exercise 22,** students may solve the equations $3m + 9 = 6n - 3$ and $5m - 13 = 4n + 14$ instead of $3m + 9 = 5m - 13$ and $6n - 3 = 4n + 14$. Discuss which segments are equal when $\overline{PQ}$ is the perpendicular bisector of $\overline{ST}$.

Teaching Tip **Kinesthetic** For **Exercise 18,** have students copy the drawing and then fold their sketches so that Elm Street and Grove Street coincide. Show them that Main Street is on the fold and is therefore the bisector of the angle formed by Elm Street and Grove Street.

Exercise 33 involves using the equation of the perpendicular bisector of a segment when given the coordinates of the segment's endpoints. This exercise prepares students for the Multi-Step Test Prep on page 328.

Answers

29. Possible answer: $C(3, 2)$; $AC = \sqrt{26}$; $BC = \sqrt{26}$; so $AC = BC$, and by the Conv. of the ⊥ Bisector Thm., C is on the ⊥ bisector of $\overline{AB}$.

30–32. See p. A18.

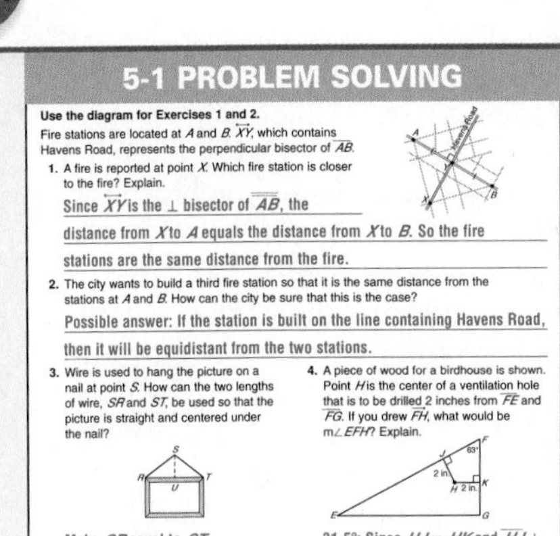

5-1 PROBLEM SOLVING

Use the diagram for Exercises 1 and 2.

Fire stations are located at A and B. $\overleftrightarrow{XY}$, which contains Havens Road, represents the perpendicular bisector of $\overline{AB}$.

1. A fire is reported at point X. Which fire station is closer to the fire? Explain.

Since $\overleftrightarrow{XY}$ is the ⊥ bisector of $\overline{AB}$, the distance from X to A equals the distance from X to B. So the fire stations are the same distance from the fire.

2. The city wants to build a third fire station so that it is the same distance from the stations at A and B. How can the city be sure that this is the case?

Possible answer: If the station is built on the line containing Havens Road, then it will be equidistant from the two stations.

3. Wire is used to hang the picture on a nail at point S. How can the two lengths of wire, SR and ST, be used so that the picture is straight and centered under the nail?

Make SR equal to ST.

4. A piece of wood for a birdhouse is shown. Point H is the center of a ventilation hole that is to be drilled 2 inches from $\overline{FE}$ and $\overline{FG}$. If you drew $\overrightarrow{FH}$, what would be $m\angle EFH$? Explain.

31.5°; Since $HJ = HK$ and $\overline{HJ} \perp \overline{EF}$ and $\overline{HK} \perp \overline{FG}$, $\overline{FH}$ bisects $\angle EFG$ by the Converse of the Angle Bisector Thm.

Choose the best answer.

The design at right was made by wrapping string around nails.

5. $\overline{PL}$ is the angle bisector of $\angle KPM$. Which can you conclude from this statement?

(A) $LN = 5$ in. C $m\angle K = 46°$
B $LK = 7$ in. D $m\angle JLK = 44°$

6. $\overline{LJ}$ is the perpendicular bisector of $\overline{KP}$. Which can you conclude?

F $m\angle K = 46°$ (H) $KL = 9$ in.
G $m\angle K = 44°$ J $KL = 7$ in.

5-1 CHALLENGE

1. $\overline{HJ}$ has endpoints $H(-5, 3)$ and $J(4, -3)$. What is the y-intercept of the line that is the perpendicular bisector of $\overline{HJ}$? **0.75**

2. $\overline{LM}$ has endpoints $L(6, 10)$ and $M(2, 8)$. What is the x-intercept of the line that is the perpendicular bisector of $\overline{LM}$? **6.5**

Use the graph of circle K for Exercises 3–6.

3. A **chord** is a segment whose endpoints are on a circle. Write an equation in slope-intercept form for the perpendicular bisector of chord $\overline{AB}$. **$y = x + 1$**

4. Point $C(1, 6)$ is also on circle K. Write an equation in slope-intercept form for the perpendicular bisector of $\overline{AC}$. **$y = -x + 11$**

5. Name the coordinates of the point where the perpendicular bisectors of chords $\overline{AB}$ and $\overline{AC}$ intersect. What does this point represent? **(5, 6); the center of the circle**

6. Find the coordinates of the center of a circle that contains the points $A(1, 8)$, $B(3, 4)$, and $C(-2, -1)$. Verify your solution. **(−2, 4)**

Use the figure for Exercises 7–10.

The lines containing $\overline{PQ}$ and $\overline{ST}$ form the sides of an angle.

7. Write equations in slope-intercept form of the lines containing $\overline{PQ}$ and $\overline{ST}$. **$\overline{PQ}$: $y = -2x$; $\overline{ST}$: $y = \frac{1}{2}x + 5$**

8. What is the equation of $\overline{UA}$ in slope-intercept form? What are the coordinates of the point A? **$y = \frac{1}{2}x$; (0, 0)**

9. What is the equation of $\overline{UB}$ in slope-intercept form? What are the coordinates of the point B? **$y = -2x + 10$; (2, 6)**

10. Show that U is on the bisector of the angle that is formed by $\overleftrightarrow{PQ}$ and $\overleftrightarrow{ST}$. **$UA = 2\sqrt{5}$ and $UB = 2\sqrt{5}$. So U is on the bisector of the angle that is formed.**

5-1 PRACTICE A

5-1 PRACTICE C

5-1 PRACTICE B

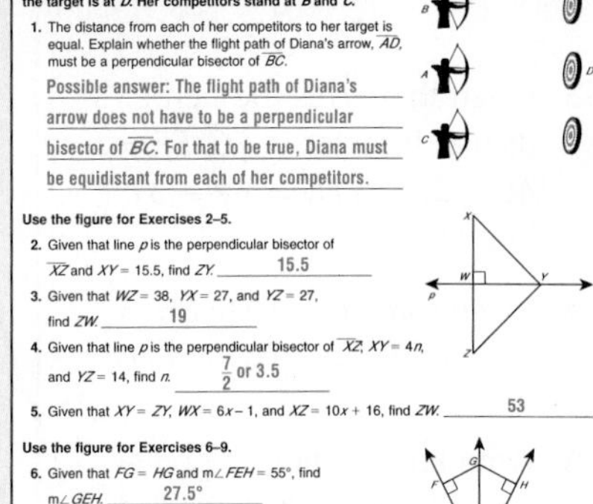

Diana is in an archery competition. She stands at A, and the target is at D. Her competitors stand at B and C.

1. The distance from each of her competitors to her target is equal. Explain whether the flight path of Diana's arrow, $\overline{AD}$, must be a perpendicular bisector of $\overline{BC}$.

Possible answer: The flight path of Diana's arrow does not have to be a perpendicular bisector of $\overline{BC}$. For that to be true, Diana must be equidistant from each of her competitors.

Use the figure for Exercises 2–5.

2. Given that line p is the perpendicular bisector of $\overline{XZ}$ and $XY = 15.5$, find ZY. **15.5**

3. Given that $WZ = 38$, $YX = 27$, and $YZ = 27$, find ZW. **19**

4. Given that line p is the perpendicular bisector of $\overline{XZ}$, $XY = 4n$, and $YZ = 14$, find n. **$\frac{7}{2}$ or 3.5**

5. Given that $XY = ZY$, $WX = 6x - 1$, and $XZ = 10x + 16$, find ZW. **53**

Use the figure for Exercises 6–9.

6. Given that $FG = HG$ and $m\angle FEH = 55°$, find $m\angle GEH$. **27.5°**

7. Given that $\overrightarrow{EG}$ bisects $\angle FEH$ and $GF = \sqrt{2}$, find GH. **$\sqrt{2}$**

8. Given that $\angle FEG \cong \angle GEH$, $FG = 10z - 30$, and $HG = 7z + 6$, find FG. **90**

9. Given that $GF = GH$, $m\angle GEF = \frac{8}{3}a°$, and $m\angle GEH = 24°$, find a. **9**

Write an equation in point-slope form for the perpendicular bisector of the segment with the given endpoints.

10. $L(4, 0), M(-2, 3)$ **$y - \frac{3}{2} = 2(x - 1)$**

11. $T(0, -3), U(0, 1)$ **$y + 1 = 0$**

12. $A(-1, 6), B(-3, -4)$ **$y - 1 = -\frac{1}{5}(x + 2)$**

TEST PREP DOCTOR If students have difficulty with **Exercises 35 and 36,** have them draw and label a diagram for each.

Journal

Have students write the Angle Bisector Theorem and its converse in their own words and explain the difference between the two, using examples.

ALTERNATIVE ASSESSMENT

Have students construct the perpendicular bisector of a segment and the bisector of an angle. Then have them illustrate that points on the perpendicular bisector are equidistant from the endpoints of the segment and that points on the angle bisector are equidistant from the sides of the angle.

Power Presentations with PowerPoint®

5-1 Lesson Quiz

Use the diagram for Items 1–2.

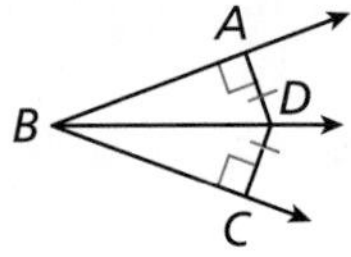

1. Given that $m\angle ABD = 16°$, find $m\angle ABC$. 32°
2. Given that $m\angle ABD = (2x + 12)°$ and $m\angle CBD = (6x - 18)°$, find $m\angle ABC$. 54°

Use the diagram for Items 3–4.

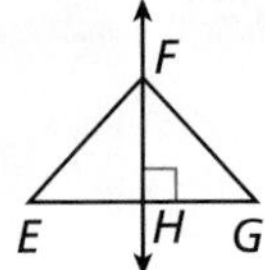

3. Given that $\overline{FH}$ is the perpendicular bisector of $\overline{EG}$, $EF = 4y - 3$, and $FG = 6y - 37$, find FG. 65
4. Given that $EF = 10.6$, $EH = 4.3$, and $FG = 10.6$, find EG. 8.6
5. Write an equation in point-slope form for the perpendicular bisector of the segment with endpoints $X(7, 9)$ and $Y(-3, 5)$. $y - 7 = -\frac{5}{2}(x - 2)$

Also available on transparency

34. **Write About It** How is the construction of the perpendicular bisector of a segment related to the Converse of the Perpendicular Bisector Theorem?

TEST PREP

35. If $\overleftrightarrow{JK}$ is perpendicular to $\overline{XY}$ at its midpoint M, which statement is true?
    Ⓐ $JX = KY$ Ⓑ $JX = KX$ Ⓒ $JM = KM$ Ⓓ $JX = JY$
36. What information is needed to conclude that $\overrightarrow{EF}$ is the bisector of $\angle DEG$?
    Ⓕ $m\angle DEF = m\angle DEG$ Ⓗ $m\angle GED = m\angle GEF$
    Ⓖ $m\angle FEG = m\angle DEF$ Ⓙ $m\angle DEF = m\angle EFG$
37. **Short Response** The city wants to build a visitor center in the park so that it is equidistant from Park Street and Washington Avenue. They also want the visitor center to be equidistant from the museum and the library. Find the point V where the visitor center should be built. Explain your answer.

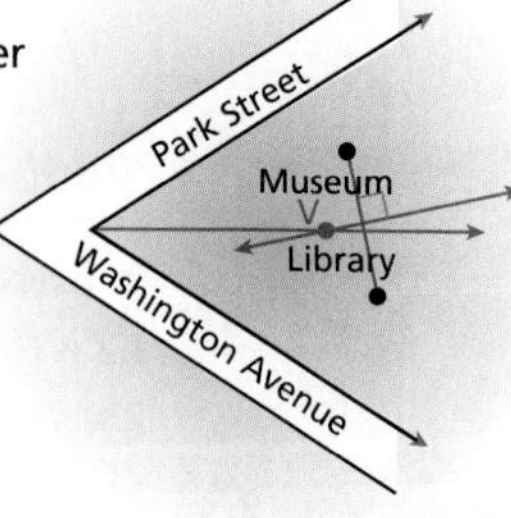

CHALLENGE AND EXTEND

38. Consider the points $P(2, 0)$, $A(-4, 2)$, $B(0, -6)$, and $C(6, -3)$.
    a. Show that P is on the bisector of $\angle ABC$.
    b. Write an equation of the line that contains the bisector of $\angle ABC$.
39. Find the locus of points that are equidistant from the x-axis and y-axis. the lines $y = x$ and $y = -x$
40. Write a two-column proof of the Converse of the Angle Bisector Theorem.
    Given: $\overline{VX} \perp \overrightarrow{YX}$, $\overline{VZ} \perp \overrightarrow{YZ}$, $VX = VZ$
    Prove: $\overrightarrow{YV}$ bisects $\angle XYZ$.

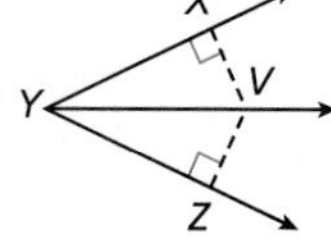

41. Write a paragraph proof.
    Given: $\overline{KN}$ is the perpendicular bisector of $\overline{JL}$.
    $\overline{LN}$ is the perpendicular bisector of $\overline{KM}$.
    $\overline{JR} \cong \overline{MT}$
    Prove: $\angle JKM \cong \angle MLJ$

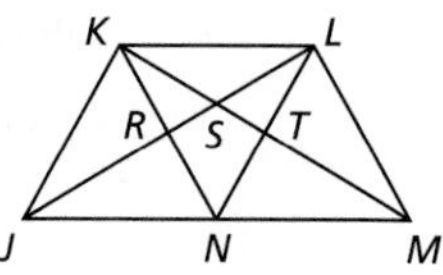

SPIRAL REVIEW

42. Lyn bought a sweater for \$16.95. The change c that she received can be described by $c = t - 16.95$, where t is the amount of money Lyn gave the cashier. What is the dependent variable? *(Previous course)* c

For the points $R(-4, 2)$, $S(1, 4)$, $T(3, -1)$, and $V(-7, -5)$, determine whether the lines are parallel, perpendicular, or neither. *(Lesson 3-5)*

43. $\overleftrightarrow{RS}$ and $\overleftrightarrow{VT}$ parallel
44. $\overleftrightarrow{RV}$ and $\overleftrightarrow{ST}$ neither
45. $\overleftrightarrow{RT}$ and $\overleftrightarrow{VR}$ perpendicular

Write the equation of each line in slope-intercept form. *(Lesson 3-6)*

46. the line through the points $(1, -1)$ and $(2, -9)$ $y = -8x + 7$
47. the line with slope -0.5 through $(10, -15)$ $y = -\frac{1}{2}x - 10$
48. the line with x-intercept -4 and y-intercept 5 $y = \frac{5}{4}x + 5$

Answers

34. In the construction of the ⊥ bisector of $\overline{AB}$, the same compass setting is used to draw an arc from each endpoint of the segment. So in the diagram, $AX = BX$ and $AY = BY$. By the Conv. of the ⊥ Bisector Thm., both X and Y lie on the ⊥ bisector of $\overline{AB}$. So ℓ is the ⊥ bisector of $\overline{AB}$.

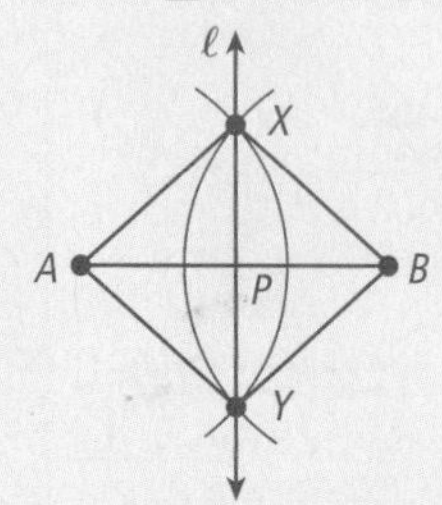

37. Possible answer: All locations that are equidistant from Park St. and Washington Ave. lie on the bisector of the ∠ formed by the 2 streets. All locations that are equidistant from the museum and the library lie on the ⊥ bisector of the seg. formed by the museum and the library. So the visitor center should be built at the point V, where the 2 bisectors intersect.

38a. The dist. from P to $\overrightarrow{BA}$ is $2\sqrt{5}$, and the dist. from P to $\overrightarrow{BC}$ is $2\sqrt{5}$. So P is equidistant from $\overrightarrow{BA}$ and $\overrightarrow{BC}$, and therefore, by the Conv. of the ∠ Bisector Thm., P is on the bisector of $\angle ABC$.

b. Possible answer: $y = 3x - 6$

40–41. See p. A18.

5-2 Bisectors of Triangles

Objectives
Prove and apply properties of perpendicular bisectors of a triangle.

Prove and apply properties of angle bisectors of a triangle.

Vocabulary
concurrent
point of concurrency
circumcenter of a triangle
circumscribed
incenter of a triangle
inscribed

Who uses this?
An event planner can use perpendicular bisectors of triangles to find the best location for a fireworks display. (See Example 4.)

Since a triangle has three sides, it has three perpendicular bisectors. When you construct the perpendicular bisectors, you find that they have an interesting property.

Construction Circumcenter of a Triangle

1. 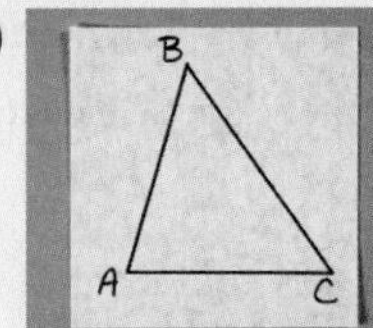

Draw a large scalene acute triangle ABC on a piece of patty paper.

2. 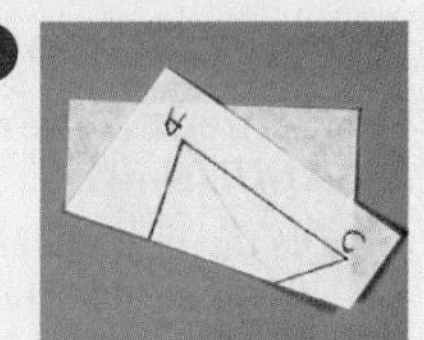
Fold the perpendicular bisector of each side.

3. 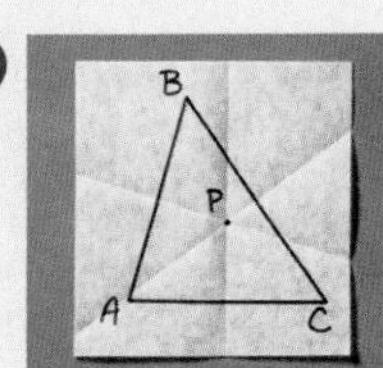

Label the point where the three perpendicular bisectors intersect as P.

Helpful Hint
The perpendicular bisector of a side of a triangle does not always pass through the opposite vertex.

When three or more lines intersect at one point, the lines are said to be **concurrent**. The **point of concurrency** is the point where they intersect. In the construction, you saw that the three perpendicular bisectors of a triangle are concurrent. This point of concurrency is the **circumcenter of the triangle**.

Theorem 5-2-1 Circumcenter Theorem

The circumcenter of a triangle is equidistant from the vertices of the triangle.

$PA = PB = PC$

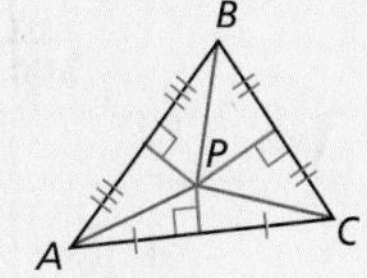

The circumcenter can be inside the triangle, outside the triangle, or on the triangle.

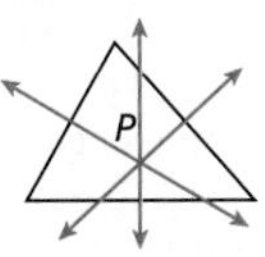

Acute triangle

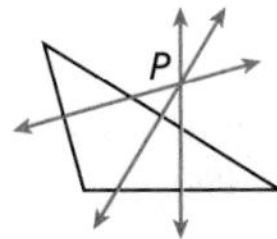

Obtuse triangle

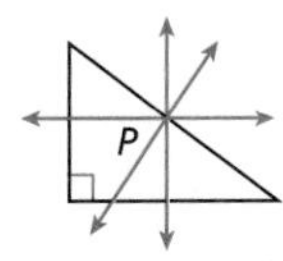

Right triangle

5-2 Organizer

Pacing: Traditional 1 day
Block $\frac{1}{2}$ day

Objectives: Prove and apply properties of perpendicular bisectors of a triangle.

Prove and apply properties of angle bisectors of a triangle.

Technology Lab
In *Technology Lab Activities*

Online Edition
Tutorial Videos

Countdown Week 10

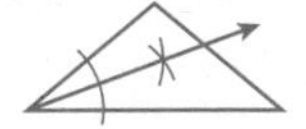

Warm Up

1. Draw a triangle and construct the bisector of one angle.

2. $\overline{JK}$ is perpendicular to $\overline{ML}$ at its midpoint K. List the congruent segments. $\overline{JM} \cong \overline{JL}$, $\overline{MK} \cong \overline{LK}$

Also available on transparency

Math Humor

Teacher: How many sides does a circle have?

Student: Two—inside and outside!

1 Introduce

EXPLORATION

5-2 Bisectors of Triangles

Use geometry software for this Exploration.

1. Construct a triangle. Label the vertices A, B, and C.	2. Select the vertices B, A, and C in that order. Then use the Construct menu to draw the angle bisector of ∠A.
3. Construct the bisectors of ∠B and ∠C.	4. What do you notice about the three angle bisectors? Drag the vertices of △ABC to change its size and shape. Do you get the same result?
5. Label the point of intersection of the angle bisectors X.	6. Measure the distance from X to each side of △ABC. What do you notice? As you change the shape of △ABC, do you get the same result?

Motivate

Give students a city map with three houses marked on it. Ask students to find a location equidistant from all three houses where three friends should meet. Explain that this point is the intersection of the perpendicular bisectors of the sides of the triangle formed by the three houses. It is called the circumcenter. Explain that in this lesson students will learn how to find the circumcenter and the incenter of a triangle.

Explorations and answers are provided in *Alternate Openers: Explorations Transparencies.*

Power Presentations with PowerPoint®

Additional Examples

Example 1

$\overline{DG}$, $\overline{EG}$, and $\overline{FG}$ are the perpendicular bisectors of $\triangle ABC$. Find GC. 13.4

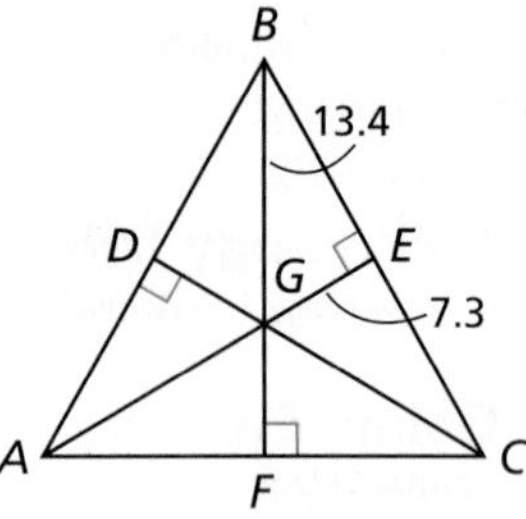

Example 2

Find the circumcenter of $\triangle HJK$ with vertices $H(0, 0)$, $J(10, 0)$, and $K(0, 6)$. (5, 3)

INTERVENTION

Questioning Strategies

EXAMPLE 1

- What is true of the circumcenter of a triangle?
- Which measure given for the triangle is unnecessary?

EXAMPLE 2

- How do you find the circumcenter of a triangle when given the coordinates of the three vertices?

Reading Math To help students remember the meanings of the words *incenter*, *inscribed*, *circumcenter*, and *circumscribed*, remind them of the meanings of the prefixes. The prefix *in-* means "inside" or "within," and the prefix *circum-* means "around." ENGLISH LANGUAGE LEARNERS

Kinesthetic Have students construct perpendicular bisectors to circumscribe a circle about a triangle. This will help students remember the meaning of *circumscribe*.

The circumcenter of $\triangle ABC$ is the center of its *circumscribed* circle. A circle that contains all the vertices of a polygon is **circumscribed** about the polygon.

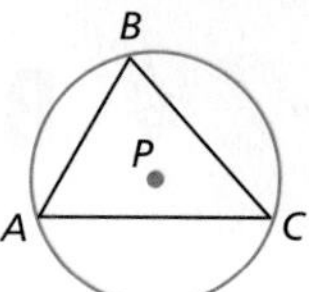

PROOF **Circumcenter Theorem**

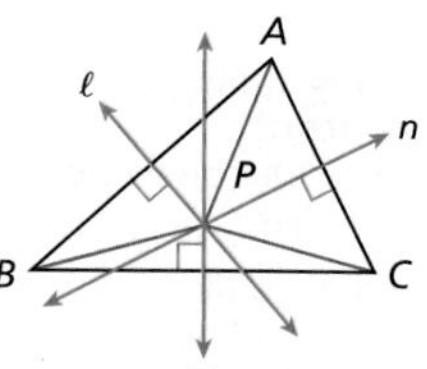

Given: Lines ℓ, m, and n are the perpendicular bisectors of $\overline{AB}$, $\overline{BC}$, and $\overline{AC}$, respectively.

Prove: $PA = PB = PC$

Proof:

P is the circumcenter of $\triangle ABC$. Since P lies on the perpendicular bisector of $\overline{AB}$, $PA = PB$ by the Perpendicular Bisector Theorem. Similarly, P also lies on the perpendicular bisector of $\overline{BC}$, so $PB = PC$. Therefore $PA = PB = PC$ by the Transitive Property of Equality.

EXAMPLE 1 Using Properties of Perpendicular Bisectors

$\overline{KZ}$, $\overline{LZ}$, and $\overline{MZ}$ are the perpendicular bisectors of $\triangle GHJ$. Find HZ.

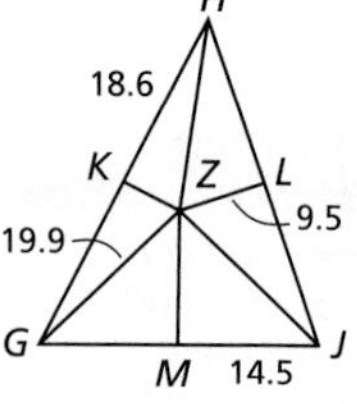

Z is the circumcenter of $\triangle GHJ$. By the Circumcenter Theorem, Z is equidistant from the vertices of $\triangle GHJ$.

$HZ = GZ$	*Circumcenter Thm.*
$HZ = 19.9$	*Substitute 19.9 for GZ.*

Use the diagram above. Find each length.

1a. GM 14.5 **1b.** GK 18.6 **1c.** JZ 19.9

EXAMPLE 2 Finding the Circumcenter of a Triangle

Algebra

Find the circumcenter of $\triangle RSO$ with vertices $R(-6, 0)$, $S(0, 4)$, and $O(0, 0)$.

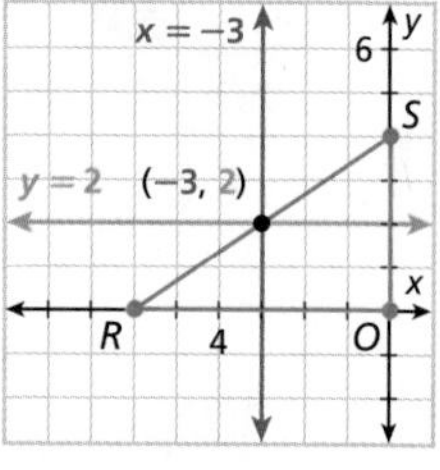

Step 1 Graph the triangle.

Step 2 Find equations for two perpendicular bisectors.

Since two sides of the triangle lie along the axes, use the graph to find the perpendicular bisectors of these two sides. The perpendicular bisector of $\overline{RO}$ is $x = -3$, and the perpendicular bisector of $\overline{OS}$ is $y = 2$.

Step 3 Find the intersection of the two equations.

The lines $x = -3$ and $y = 2$ intersect at $(-3, 2)$, the circumcenter of $\triangle RSO$.

2 Teach

Guided Instruction

Have students construct the circumcenter of a triangle by paper folding. Discuss the point of concurrency and the Circumcenter Theorem. Remind students of the properties of perpendicular bisectors from the previous lesson. Show them how to find the circumcenter of a triangle in the coordinate plane. Discuss the Incenter Theorem and explain how the properties of angle bisectors can be used to find segment lengths and angle measures in a triangle.

Reaching All Learners

Through Multiple Representations

Have students use geometry software to construct a triangle and the perpendicular bisectors of the sides. Have them drag a vertex of the triangle to change its shape and note that the perpendicular bisectors are still concurrent. Have them construct the circumscribed circle. Then have them construct the angle bisectors of the triangle. Have students drag a vertex to notice that the angle bisectors are still concurrent. Finally have students construct the inscribed circle.

2. Find the circumcenter of $\triangle GOH$ with vertices $G(0, -9)$, $O(0, 0)$, and $H(8, 0)$. $(4, -4.5)$

A triangle has three angles, so it has three angle bisectors. The angle bisectors of a triangle are also concurrent. This point of concurrency is the **incenter of the triangle**.

Theorem 5-2-2 **Incenter Theorem**

The incenter of a triangle is equidistant from the sides of the triangle.

$PX = PY = PZ$

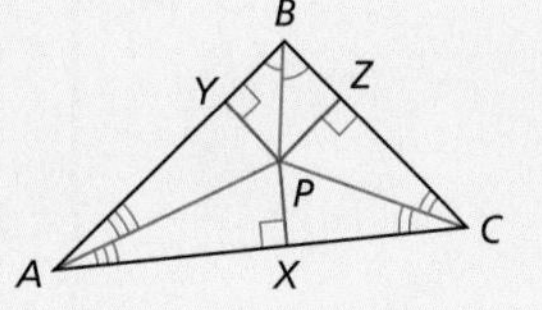

You will prove Theorem 5-2-2 in Exercise 35.

Remember!

The distance between a point and a line is the length of the perpendicular segment from the point to the line.

Unlike the circumcenter, the incenter is always inside the triangle.

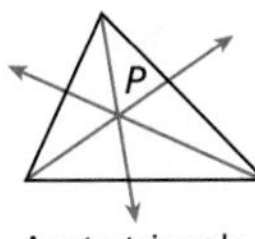

Acute triangle

Obtuse triangle

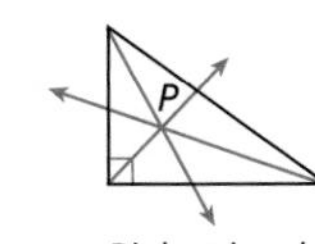

Right triangle

The incenter is the center of the triangle's *inscribed circle.* A circle **inscribed** in a polygon intersects each line that contains a side of the polygon at exactly one point.

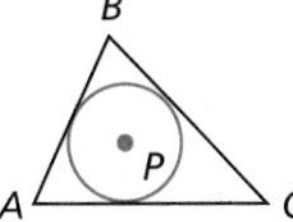

EXAMPLE 3 Using Properties of Angle Bisectors

$\overline{JV}$ and $\overline{KV}$ are angle bisectors of $\triangle JKL$. Find each measure.

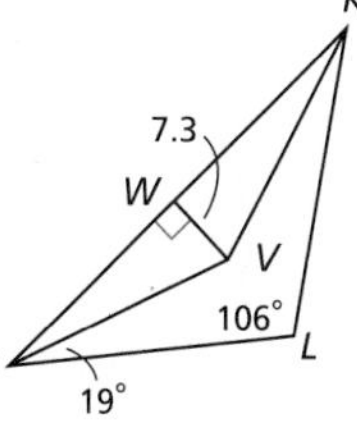

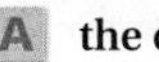

A **the distance from V to $\overline{KL}$**

V is the incenter of $\triangle JKL$. By the Incenter Theorem, V is equidistant from the sides of $\triangle JKL$.

The distance from V to $\overline{JK}$ is 7.3.
So the distance from V to $\overline{KL}$ is also 7.3.

B **$m\angle VKL$**

$m\angle KJL = 2m\angle VJL$	*$\overline{JV}$ is the bisector of $\angle KJL$.*
$m\angle KJL = 2(19°) = 38°$	*Substitute 19° for $m\angle VJL$.*
$m\angle KJL + m\angle JLK + m\angle JKL = 180°$	*△ Sum Thm.*
$38 + 106 + m\angle JKL = 180$	*Substitute the given values.*
$m\angle JKL = 36°$	*Subtract 144° from both sides.*
$m\angle VKL = \frac{1}{2}m\angle JKL$	*$\overline{KV}$ is the bisector of $\angle JKL$.*
$m\angle VKL = \frac{1}{2}(36°) = 18°$	*Substitute 36° for $m\angle JKL$.*

COMMON ERROR ALERT

When learning to find the circumcenter or incenter, students may use only an equilateral triangle. Encourage them to use other types of triangles to discover the various positions of the points of concurrency.

Power Presentations with PowerPoint®

Additional Examples

Example 3

$\overline{MP}$ and $\overline{LP}$ are angle bisectors of $\triangle LMN$. Find each measure.

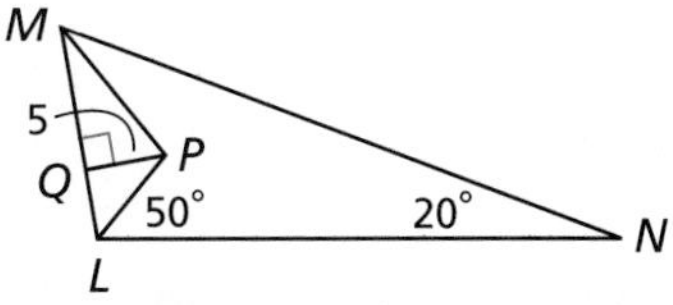

A. the distance from P to $\overline{MN}$ 5

B. $m\angle PMN$ 30°

INTERVENTION
Questioning Strategies

EXAMPLE 3

- How do you use the angle bisectors to find the indicated measures?

Technology Have students use geometry software to draw an angle, construct its bisector, and draw a point on the bisector. Have them construct perpendicular segments from the point to the sides of the angle. Then have them measure the distances and confirm that they are equal.

Power Presentations with PowerPoint®

Additional Examples

Example 4

A city planner wants to build a new library between a school, a post office, and a hospital. Draw a sketch to show where the library should be placed so it is the same distance from all three buildings.

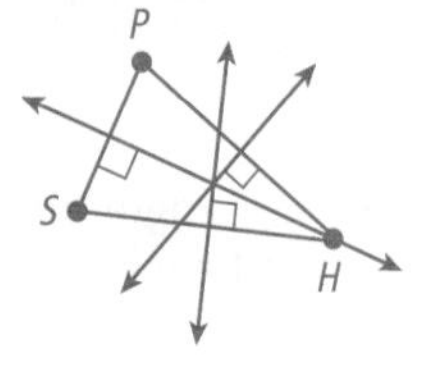

INTERVENTION

Questioning Strategies

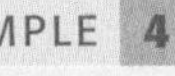

EXAMPLE 4

- How many perpendicular bisectors do you need to construct to find the circumcenter of a triangle?

$\overline{QX}$ **and** $\overline{RX}$ **are angle bisectors of** $\triangle PQR$**. Find each measure.**

3a. the distance from X to $\overline{PQ}$ **19.2**

3b. m$\angle PQX$ **52°**

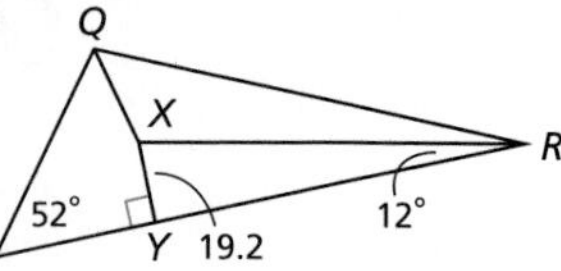

EXAMPLE 4 **Community Application**

For the next Fourth of July, the towns of Ashton, Bradford, and Clearview will launch a fireworks display from a boat in the lake. Draw a sketch to show where the boat should be positioned so that it is the same distance from all three towns. Justify your sketch.

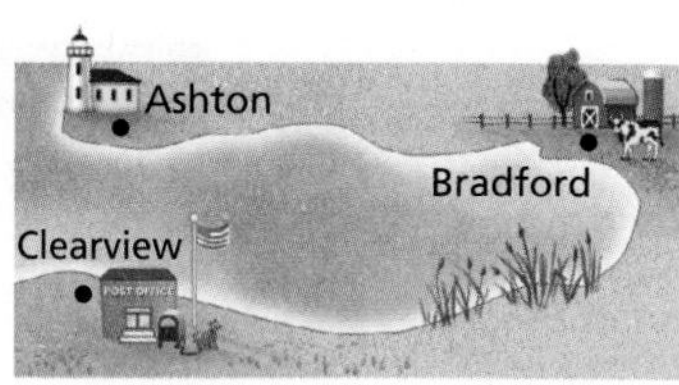

Let the three towns be vertices of a triangle. By the Circumcenter Theorem, the circumcenter of the triangle is equidistant from the vertices.

Trace the outline of the lake. Draw the triangle formed by the towns. To find the circumcenter, find the perpendicular bisectors of each side. The position of the boat is the circumcenter, *F*.

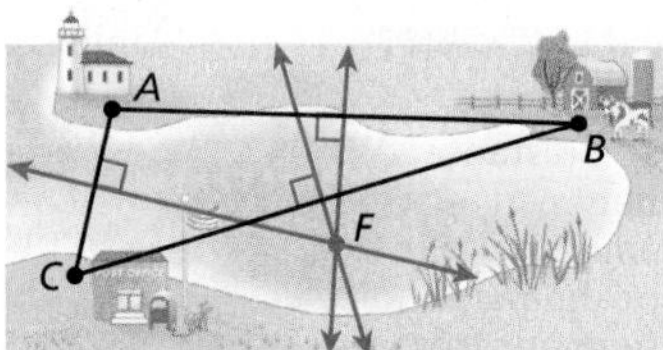

4. A city plans to build a firefighters' monument in the park between three streets. Draw a sketch to show where the city should place the monument so that it is the same distance from all three streets. Justify your sketch.

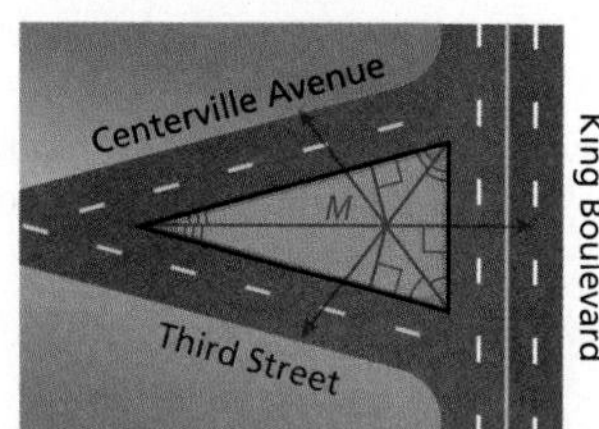

4. By the Incenter Thm., the incenter of a △ is equidistant from the sides of the △. Draw the △ formed by the streets and draw the ∠ bisectors to find the incenter, point *M*. The city should place the monument at point *M*.

THINK AND DISCUSS

1. Sketch three lines that are concurrent.

2. *P* and *Q* are the circumcenter and incenter of $\triangle RST$, but not necessarily in that order. Which point is the circumcenter? Which point is the incenter? Explain how you can tell without constructing any of the bisectors.

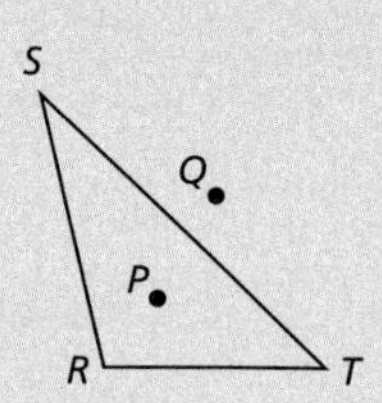

3. GET ORGANIZED Copy and complete the graphic organizer. Fill in the blanks to make each statement true.

	Circumcenter	Incenter
Definition	The point of concurrency of the _?_	The point of concurrency of the _?_
Distance	Equidistant from the _?_	Equidistant from the _?_
Location (Inside, Outside, or On)	Can be _?_ the triangle	_?_ the triangle

3 Close

Summarize

Discuss how to find the circumcenter and incenter of a triangle. Point out that the circumcenter is equidistant from the vertices of the triangle, while the incenter is equidistant from the sides. Illustrate the Circumcenter and Incenter Theorems with diagrams.

ONGOING ASSESSMENT and INTERVENTION

Diagnose ***Before*** *the Lesson*
5-2 Warm Up, TE p. 307

Monitor ***During*** *the Lesson*
Check It Out! Exercises, SE pp. 308–310
Questioning Strategies, TE pp. 308–310

Assess ***After*** *the Lesson*
5-2 Lesson Quiz, TE p. 313
Alternative Assessment, TE p. 313

Answers to *Think and Discuss*

1. Possible answer:

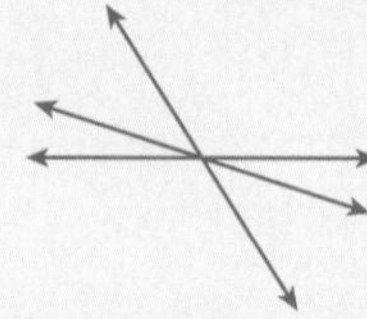

2. *Q*; *P*; possible answer: the incenter is always inside the △, so *Q* cannot be the incenter. Therefore *P* must be the incenter, and *Q* must be the circumcenter.

3. See p. A4.

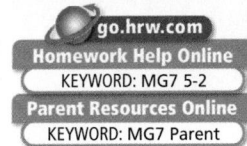

5-2 Exercises

go.hrw.com
Homework Help Online
KEYWORD: MG7 5-2
Parent Resources Online
KEYWORD: MG7 Parent

GUIDED PRACTICE

Vocabulary Apply the vocabulary from this lesson to answer each question.

1. Explain why lines ℓ, m, and n are NOT *concurrent*. **They do not intersect at a single point.**

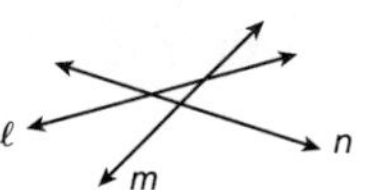

2. A circle that contains all the vertices of a polygon is ___?___ the polygon. (*circumscribed about* or *inscribed in*) **circumscribed about**

SEE EXAMPLE 1 p. 308

$\overline{SN}$, $\overline{TN}$, and $\overline{VN}$ are the perpendicular bisectors of $\triangle PQR$. Find each length.

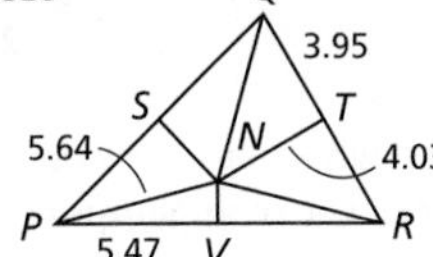

3. NR **5.64**
4. RV **5.47**
5. TR **3.95**
6. QN **5.64**

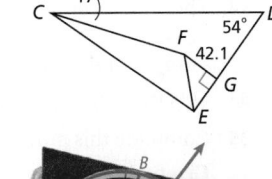

SEE EXAMPLE 2 p. 308

Multi-Step Find the circumcenter of a triangle with the given vertices.

7. $O(0, 0)$, $K(0, 12)$, $L(4, 0)$ **(2, 6)**
8. $A(-7, 0)$, $O(0, 0)$, $B(0, -10)$ **(−3.5, −5)**

SEE EXAMPLE 3 p. 309

$\overline{CF}$ and $\overline{EF}$ are angle bisectors of $\triangle CDE$. Find each measure.

9. the distance from F to $\overline{CD}$ **42.1**
10. $m\angle FED$ **46°**

SEE EXAMPLE 4 p. 310

11. **Design** The designer of the Newtown High School pennant wants the circle around the bear emblem to be as large as possible. Draw a sketch to show where the center of the circle should be located. Justify your sketch.

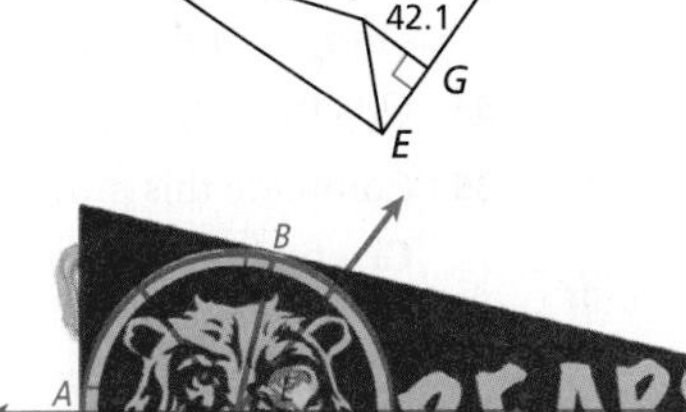

PRACTICE AND PROBLEM SOLVING

Independent Practice	
For Exercises	See Example
12–15	1
16–17	2
18–19	3
20	4

Extra Practice
Skills Practice p. S12
Application Practice p. S32

$\overline{DY}$, $\overline{EY}$, and $\overline{FY}$ are the perpendicular bisectors of $\triangle ABC$. Find each length.

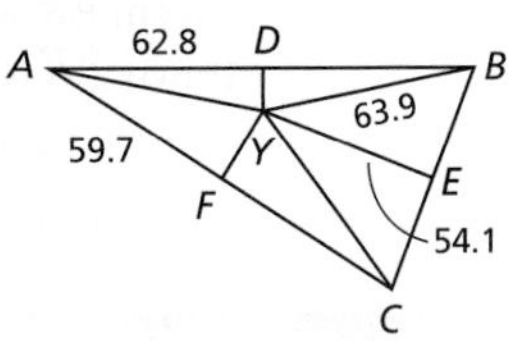

12. CF **59.7**
13. YC **63.9**
14. DB **62.8**
15. AY **63.9**

Multi-Step Find the circumcenter of a triangle with the given vertices.

16. $M(-5, 0)$, $N(0, 14)$, $O(0, 0)$ **(−2.5, 7)**
17. $O(0, 0)$, $V(0, 19)$, $W(-3, 0)$ **(−1.5, 9.5)**

$\overline{TJ}$ and $\overline{SJ}$ are angle bisectors of $\triangle RST$. Find each measure.

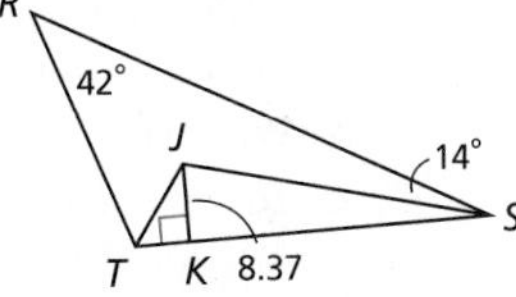

18. the distance from J to $\overline{RS}$ **8.37**
19. $m\angle RTJ$ **55°**

5-2 Exercises

Assignment Guide

Assign *Guided Practice* exercises as necessary.

If you finished Examples 1–2
Basic 12–17, 30, 32–34
Average 12–17, 30, 32–34, 36, 43
Advanced 12–17, 30, 32–34, 36, 43, 44

If you finished Examples 1–4
Basic 12–20, 22–35, 37, 40–42, 45–53
Average 12–21, 22–28 even, 30–43, 45–53
Advanced 12–21, 22–28 even, 29–53

Homework Quick Check
Quickly check key concepts.
Exercises: 12, 16, 18, 20, 22, 32

Answers

11. The largest possible ⊙ in the int. of the △ is its inscribed ⊙, and the center of the inscribed ⊙ is the incenter. Draw the △ and its ∠ bisectors. Center the ⊙ at *E*, the pt. of concurrency of the ∠ bisectors.

State Resources

go.hrw.com
State Resources Online
KEYWORD: MG7 Resources

Visual For **Exercises 28–32,** encourage students to try different types of triangles when testing the validity of each statement.

Algebra For **Exercises 33 and 34,** encourage students to graph the triangle first. Remind them that they need to find the equations of only two perpendicular bisectors of the triangle.

Exercise 37 involves using the perpendicular bisectors of a triangle to find its circumcenter. This exercise prepares students for the Multi-Step Test Prep on page 328.

Answers

20. By the Circumcenter Thm., the circumcenter of the △ is equidistant from the vertices. Draw the △ formed by the cities, and draw the ⊥ bisectors of the sides. The main office should be located at *M*, the circumcenter.

21. See p. A18.

29, 30, 32. For sketches, see p. A18.

36, 38, 43. See p. A18.

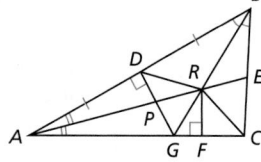

22. angle bisector; $m\angle BAE = m\angle EAC$

23. perpendicular bisector; $AD = BD$, $\overline{AD} \perp \overline{DG}$, and $\overline{BD} \perp \overline{DG}$

24. angle bisector; $m\angle ABG = m\angle GBC$

25. Angle bisector; since $\overline{AE}$ and $\overline{BG}$ are ∠ bisectors, *R* is the incenter. $\overline{CR}$ intersects the incenter, so it is an ∠ bisector.

35 a. ∠ Bisector Thm.
b. the bisector of ∠*B*
c. $PX = PZ$

20. Business A company repairs photocopiers in Harbury, Gaspar, and Knowlton. Draw a sketch to show where the company should locate its office so that it is the same distance from each city. Justify your sketch.

21. Critical Thinking If *M* is the incenter of △*JKL*, explain why ∠*JML* cannot be a right angle.

Tell whether each segment lies on a perpendicular bisector, an angle bisector, or neither. Justify your answer.

22. $\overline{AE}$	23. $\overline{DG}$	24. $\overline{BG}$
25. $\overline{CR}$	26. $\overline{FR}$ neither	27. $\overline{DR}$ neither

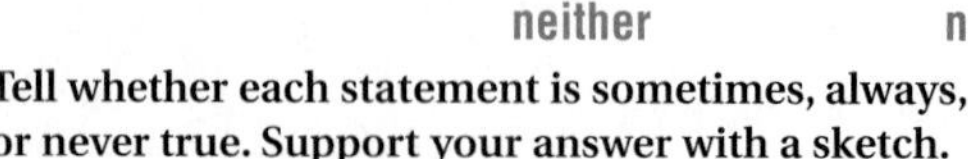

Tell whether each statement is sometimes, always, or never true. Support your answer with a sketch.

28. The angle bisectors of a triangle intersect at a point outside the triangle. N
29. An angle bisector of a triangle bisects the opposite side. S
30. A perpendicular bisector of a triangle passes through the opposite vertex. S
31. The incenter of a right triangle is on the triangle. N
32. The circumcenter of a scalene triangle is inside the triangle. S

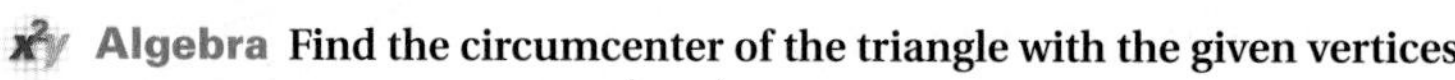

Algebra **Find the circumcenter of the triangle with the given vertices.**

33. $O(0, 0)$, $A(4, 8)$, $B(8, 0)$ $(4, 3)$
34. $O(0, 0)$, $Y(0, 12)$, $Z(6, 6)$ $(0, 6)$

35. Complete this proof of the Incenter Theorem by filling in the blanks.

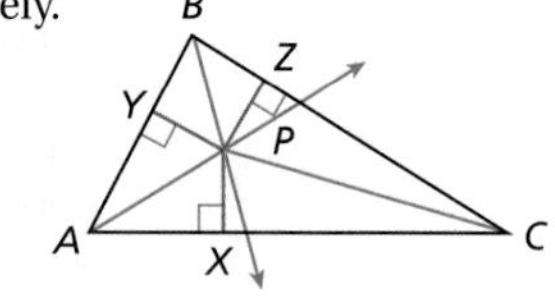

Given: $\overrightarrow{AP}$, $\overrightarrow{BP}$, and $\overrightarrow{CP}$ bisect ∠*A*, ∠*B*, and ∠*C*, respectively. $\overline{PX} \perp \overline{AC}$, $\overline{PY} \perp \overline{AB}$, $\overline{PZ} \perp \overline{BC}$

Prove: $PX = PY = PZ$

Proof: Let *P* be the incenter of △*ABC*. Since *P* lies on the bisector of ∠*A*, $PX = PY$ by **a.** __?__ . Similarly, *P* also lies on **b.** __?__ , so $PY = PZ$. Therefore **c.** __?__ by the Transitive Property of Equality.

36. Prove that the bisector of the vertex angle of an isosceles triangle is the perpendicular bisector of the base.

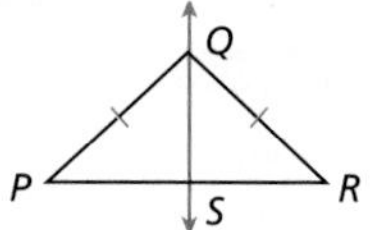

Given: $\overleftrightarrow{QS}$ bisects ∠*PQR*. $\overline{PQ} \cong \overline{RQ}$

Prove: $\overleftrightarrow{QS}$ is the perpendicular bisector of $\overline{PR}$.

Plan: Show that △*PQS* ≅ △*RQS*. Then use CPCTC to show that *S* is the midpoint of $\overline{PR}$ and that $\overleftrightarrow{QS} \perp \overline{PR}$.

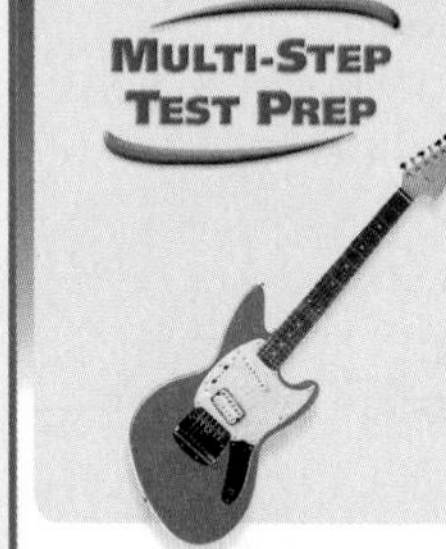

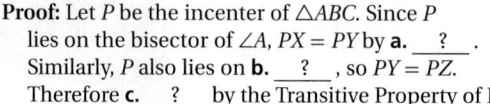

MULTI-STEP TEST PREP

37. This problem will prepare you for the Multi-Step Test Prep on page 328.
A music company has stores at $A(0, 0)$, $B(8, 0)$, and $C(4, 3)$, where each unit of the coordinate plane represents one mile.
 a. A new store will be built so that it is equidistant from the three existing stores. Find the coordinates of the new store's location. $\left(4, -\frac{7}{6}\right)$
 b. Where will the new store be located in relation to △*ABC*? outside
 c. To the nearest tenth of a mile, how far will the new store be from each of the existing stores? 4.2 mi

5-2 PRACTICE A
5-2 PRACTICE C
5-2 PRACTICE B

Use the figure for Exercises 1 and 2. $\overline{SV}$, $\overline{TV}$, and $\overline{UV}$ are perpendicular bisectors of the sides of △*PQR*. Find each length.

1. *RV* 26
2. *TR* 24

Find the circumcenter of the triangle with the given vertices.

3. $A(0, 0)$, $B(0, 5)$, $C(5, 0)$ (2.5, 2.5)
4. $D(0, 7)$, $E(-3, 1)$, $F(3, 1)$ (0, 3.25)

Use the figure for Exercises 7 and 8. $\overline{GJ}$ and $\overline{IJ}$ are angle bisectors of △*GHI*. Find each measure.

5. the distance from *J* to $\overline{GH}$ 64.3
6. m∠*JGK* 23°

Raleigh designs the interiors of cars. He is given two tasks to complete on a new production model.

7. A triangular surface as shown in the figure is molded into the driver's side door as an armrest. Raleigh thinks he can fit a cup holder into the triangle, but he'll have to put the largest possible circle into the triangle. Explain how Raleigh can do this. Sketch his design on the figure.
Possible answer: Raleigh needs to find the incircle of the triangle. The incircle just touches all three sides of the triangle, so it is the largest circle that will fit. The incenter can be found by drawing the angle bisector from each vertex of the triangle. The incircle is drawn from the incenter with a radius equal to the distance to one of the sides.

8. The car's logo is the triangle shown in the figure. Raleigh has to use this logo as the center of the steering wheel. Explain how Raleigh can do this. Sketch his design on the figure.
Possible answer: Raleigh needs to find the circumcircle of the triangle. The circumcircle just touches all three vertices of the triangle, so it fits just around it. The circumcenter can be found by drawing the perpendicular bisectors of the sides of the triangle. The circumcircle is drawn with the circumcenter as center and a radius equal to the distance to one of the vertices.

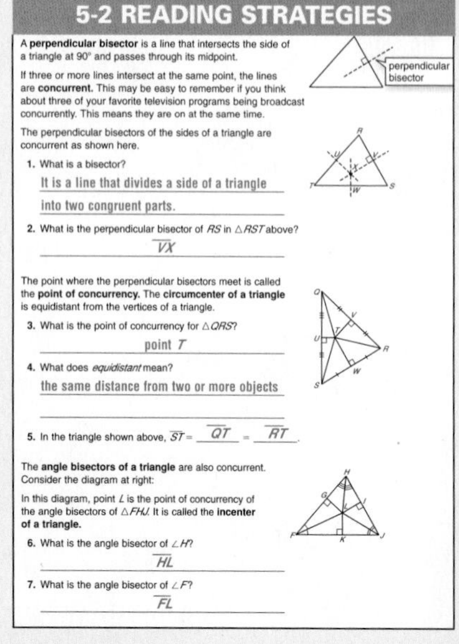

5-2 READING STRATEGIES

A **perpendicular bisector** is a line that intersects the side of a triangle at 90° and passes through its midpoint.

If three or more lines intersect at the same point, the lines are **concurrent.** This may be easy to remember if you think about three of your favorite television programs being broadcast concurrently. This means they are on at the same time.

The perpendicular bisectors of the sides of a triangle are concurrent as shown here.

1. What is a bisector?
It is a line that divides a side of a triangle into two congruent parts.

2. What is the perpendicular bisector of *RS* in △*RST* above?
$\overline{VX}$

The point where the perpendicular bisectors meet is called the **point of concurrency.** The **circumcenter of a triangle** is equidistant from the vertices of a triangle.

3. What is the point of concurrency for △*QRS*?
point *T*

4. What does *equidistant* mean?
the same distance from two or more objects

5. In the triangle shown above, $\overline{ST}$ = $\overline{QT}$ = $\overline{RT}$.

The **angle bisectors of a triangle** are also concurrent. Consider the diagram at right:

In this diagram, point *L* is the point of concurrency of the angle bisectors of △*FHJ*. It is called the **incenter of a triangle.**

6. What is the angle bisector of ∠*H*?
$\overline{HL}$

7. What is the angle bisector of ∠*F*?
$\overline{FL}$

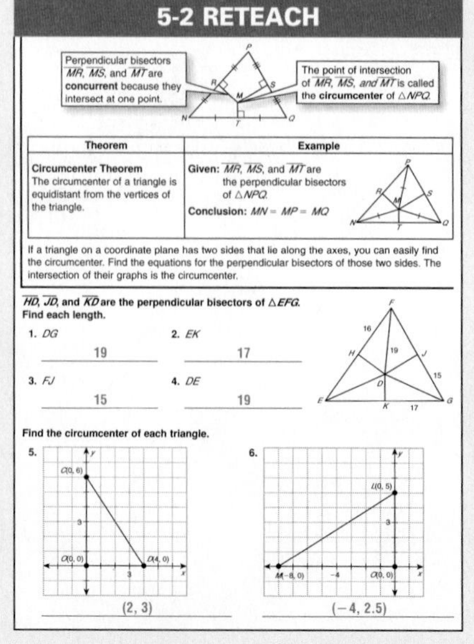

5-2 RETEACH

Perpendicular bisectors $\overline{MR}$, $\overline{MS}$, and $\overline{MT}$ are **concurrent** because they intersect at one point.

The point of intersection of $\overline{MR}$, $\overline{MS}$, and $\overline{MT}$ is called the **circumcenter** of △*NPQ*.

Theorem	Example
Circumcenter Theorem The circumcenter of a triangle is equidistant from the vertices of the triangle.	**Given:** $\overline{MR}$, $\overline{MS}$, and $\overline{MT}$ are the perpendicular bisectors of △*NPQ*. **Conclusion:** $MN = MP = MQ$

If a triangle on a coordinate plane has two sides that lie along the axes, you can easily find the circumcenter. Find the equations for the perpendicular bisectors of those two sides. The intersection of their graphs is the circumcenter.

$\overline{HD}$, $\overline{JD}$, and $\overline{KD}$ are the perpendicular bisectors of △*EFG*. Find each length.

1. *DG* 19
2. *EK* 17
3. *FJ* 15
4. *DE* 19

Find the circumcenter of each triangle.

5. (2, 3)
6. (−4, 2.5)

38. **Write About It** How are the inscribed circle and the circumscribed circle of a triangle alike? How are they different?

39. **Construction** Draw a large scalene acute triangle.
    a. Construct the angle bisectors to find the incenter. Inscribe a circle in the triangle. Check students' constructions.
    b. Construct the perpendicular bisectors to find the circumcenter. Circumscribe a circle around the triangle. Check students' constructions.

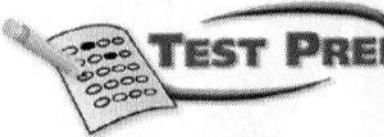

40. P is the incenter of $\triangle ABC$. Which must be true?
    (A) $PA = PB$ (C) $YA = YB$
    (B) $PX = PY$ (D) $AX = BZ$

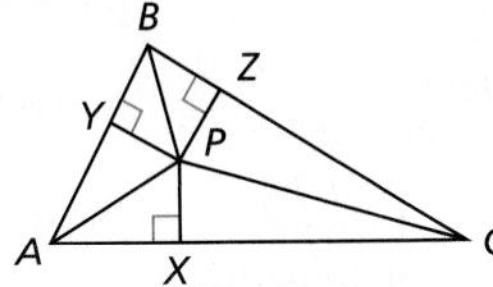

41. Lines r, s, and t are concurrent. The equation of line r is $x = 5$, and the equation of line s is $y = -2$. Which could be the equation of line t?
    (F) $y = x - 7$ (H) $y = x + 3$
    (G) $y = x - 3$ (J) $y = x + 7$

42. **Gridded Response** Lines a, b, and c are the perpendicular bisectors of $\triangle KLM$. Find LN. 14.75

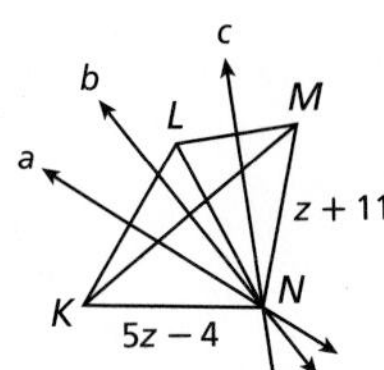

CHALLENGE AND EXTEND

43. Use the right triangle with the given coordinates.
    a. Prove that the midpoint of the hypotenuse of a right triangle is equidistant from all three vertices.
    b. Make a conjecture about the circumcenter of a right triangle.

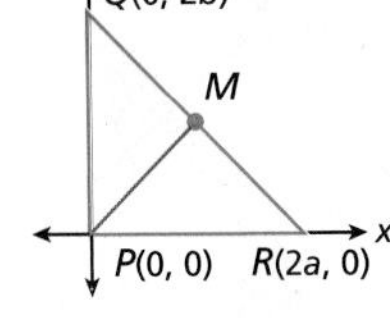

Design LINK

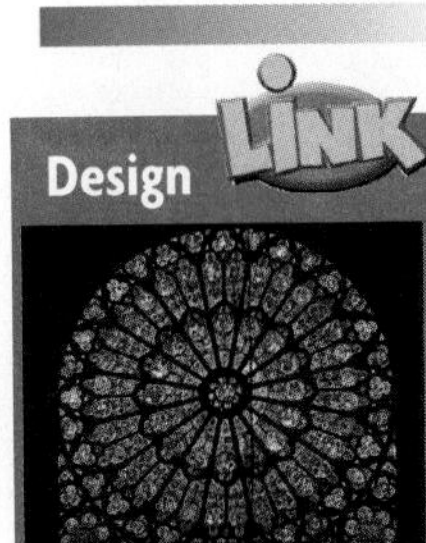

The trefoil shape, as seen in this stained glass window, has been used in design for centuries.

44. **Design** A *trefoil* is created by constructing three overlapping circles. In the figure, an equilateral triangle is inscribed inside a trefoil, and $\overline{AB}$ is a perpendicular bisector of the triangle. If the distance from one vertex to the circumcenter is 28 cm, what is the distance AB across the trefoil? 42 cm

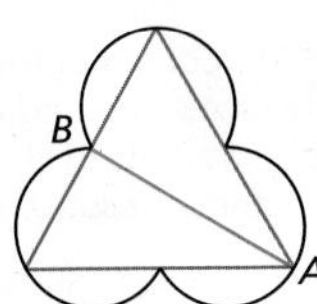

SPIRAL REVIEW

Solve each proportion. *(Previous course)*

45. $\frac{t}{26} = \frac{10}{65}$ $t = 4$
46. $\frac{2.5}{1.75} = \frac{6}{x}$ $x = 4.2$
47. $\frac{420}{y} = \frac{7}{2}$ $y = 120$

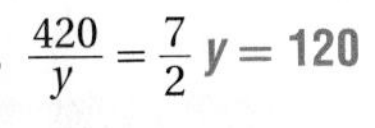

Find each angle measure. *(Lesson 1-3)*

48. $m\angle BFE$ 125°
49. $m\angle BFC$ 35°
50. $m\angle CFE$ 90°

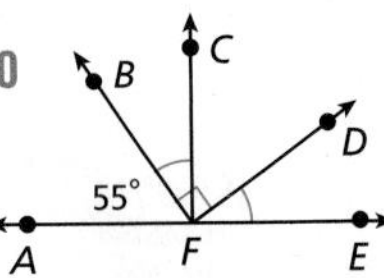

Determine whether each point is on the perpendicular bisector of the segment with endpoints $S(0, 8)$ and $T(4, 0)$. *(Lesson 5-1)*

51. $X(0, 3)$ yes
52. $Y(-4, 1)$ yes
53. $Z(-8, -2)$ no

TEST PREP DOCTOR If students have difficulty with Exercise 41, have them graph the two given lines and find the point of intersection. Then have them check each answer choice to see which equation is satisfied by that point.

Journal

Have students describe how they remember that the circumcenter is the intersection of the perpendicular bisectors and that the incenter is the intersection of the angle bisectors.

ALTERNATIVE ASSESSMENT

Give the students a map of your town. Have them mark their home and two other locations on the map to form a triangle. Have them use perpendicular bisectors to label the circumcenter and use angle bisectors to label the incenter.

Power Presentations with PowerPoint®

5-2 Lesson Quiz

1. $\overline{ED}$, $\overline{FD}$, and $\overline{GD}$ are the perpendicular bisectors of $\triangle ABC$. Find BD. 17

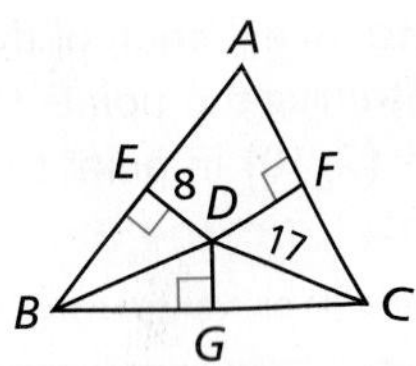

2. $\overline{JP}$, $\overline{KP}$, and $\overline{HP}$ are angle bisectors of $\triangle HJK$. Find the distance from P to HK. 3

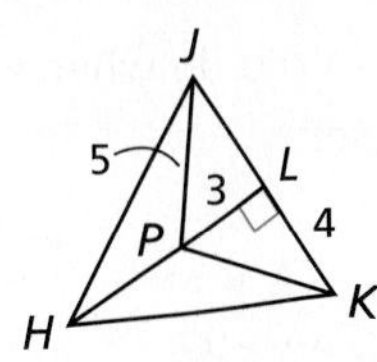

3. Lee's job requires him to travel to X, Y, and Z. Draw a sketch to show where he should buy a home so it is the same distance from all three places.

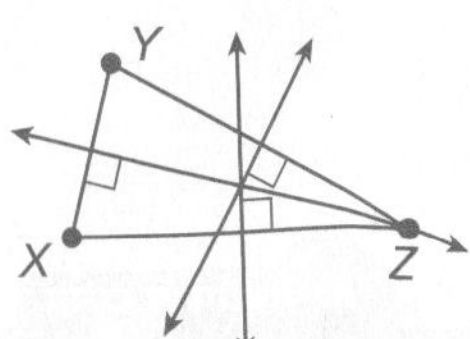

Also available on transparency

5-2 PROBLEM SOLVING

1. A new dog park is being planned. Describe how to find a location for the park so that it is the same distance from three suburbs.
   Draw a triangle that has the suburbs as its vertices. Find the circumcenter of the triangle by drawing the perpendicular bisector of each side.

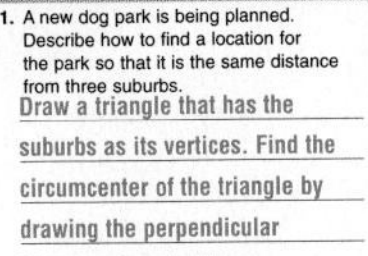

2. A fountain is in a triangular sitting area of a mall, $\triangle ABC$. A diagram shows that the fountain is at the point where the angle bisectors of $\triangle ABC$ are concurrent. If the distance from the fountain to one wall is 15 feet, what is the distance from the fountain to another wall? Explain.
   15 ft; By the Incenter Thm., the incenter of a triangle is equidistant from the sides of the triangle.

3. A water tower is to be built so that it is the same distance from the cities at X, Y, and Z. Draw a sketch on $\triangle XYZ$ to show the location W where the water tower should be built. Justify your sketch.
   Draw the perpendicular bisectors of $\overline{XY}$, $\overline{YZ}$, and $\overline{ZX}$. By the Circumcenter Thm., W is equidistant from X, Y, and Z.

Choose the best answer.

4. The circumcenter of $\triangle FGH$ is at $(4, -5)$. If G is at $(0, 0)$, which of the following are possible coordinates of F and H?
   A F(0, −8), H(10, 0)
   B F(0, 8), H(−10, 0)
   (C) F(0, −10), H(8, 0)
   D F(0, 10), H(−8, 0)

5. A triangle has vertices Q(−9, 10), R(0, 1), and S(8, 4). Which is a correct statement about the incenter and circumcenter of $\triangle QRS$?
   F Both points are on $\triangle QRS$.
   G Both points are inside $\triangle QRS$.
   H Both points are outside $\triangle QRS$.
   (J) One point is inside $\triangle QRS$, and one point is outside $\triangle QRS$.

6. $\overline{RT}$ and $\overline{TS}$ are perpendicular bisectors of $\triangle ABC$. What is the perimeter of $\triangle ATC$?
   A 17.2 units
   B 19.4 units
   C 20.9 units
   (D) 22.4 units

7. If $m\angle KPN = 44°$, find $m\angle JLP$.
   (F) 16° H 23°
   G 18° J 32°

5-2 CHALLENGE

In Lesson 5-2, you investigated the three perpendicular bisectors of the sides of a triangle and discovered some surprising facts about them. On this page, you will see how coordinate methods can help you prove those facts.

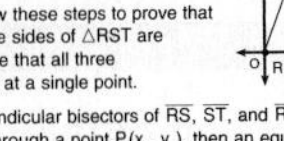

1. Refer to the figure at right. Follow these steps to prove that the perpendicular bisectors of the sides of $\triangle RST$ are concurrent. That is, you will prove that all three perpendicular bisectors intersect at a single point.
   a. Write equations for the perpendicular bisectors of $\overline{RS}$, $\overline{ST}$, and $\overline{RT}$. (Hint: If a line having slope m passes through a point $P(x_1, y_1)$, then an equation of the line is $y - y_1 = m(x - x_1)$.)
   $\overline{RS}$: $y - \frac{b}{2} = -\left(\frac{a}{b}\right)\left(x - \frac{a}{2}\right)$; $\overline{ST}$: $y - \frac{b}{2} = -\left(\frac{a-c}{b}\right)\left(x - \frac{a+c}{2}\right)$;
   $\overline{RT}$: $x = \frac{c}{2}$
   b. Use a system of equations to find the coordinates of the point where the perpendicular bisectors of $\overline{RS}$ and $\overline{RT}$ intersect.
   $\left(\frac{c}{2}, \frac{a^2 + b^2 - ac}{2b}\right)$
   c. Use a system of equations to find the coordinates of the point where the perpendicular bisectors of $\overline{ST}$ and $\overline{RT}$ intersect.
   $\left(\frac{c}{2}, \frac{a^2 + b^2 - ac}{2b}\right)$
   d. Use the results of parts b and c to complete the proof.
   Since the perpendicular bisectors of $\overline{RS}$ and $\overline{RT}$ intersect in the same point as the perpendicular bisectors of $\overline{ST}$ and $\overline{RT}$, all three lines intersect the same point. Thus the perpendicular bisectors of the sides of $\triangle RST$ are concurrent.

2. Let point Z be the point of concurrency of the three perpendicular bisectors of the sides of $\triangle RST$ above. Follow these steps to prove that point Z is equidistant from the vertices of $\triangle RST$. In other words, prove that RZ = SZ = TZ. Use the Distance Formula to write expressions for $(RZ)^2$, $(SZ)^2$, and $(TZ)^2$.
   $(RZ)^2$: $\left(\frac{c}{2}\right)^2 + \left(\frac{a^2 + b^2 - ac}{2b}\right)$;
   $(SZ)^2$: $\left(a - \frac{c}{2}\right)^2 + \left(b - \frac{a^2 + b^2 - ac}{2b}\right)^2$;
   $(TZ)^2$: $\left(c - \frac{c}{2}\right)^2 + \left(\frac{a^2 + b^2 - ac}{2b}\right)^2$

5-3 Organizer

Pacing: Traditional 1 day
Block $\frac{1}{2}$ day

Objectives: Apply properties of medians of a triangle.

Apply properties of altitudes of a triangle.

Geometry Lab
In Geometry Lab Activities

Online Edition
Tutorial Videos

Countdown Week 10

Power Presentations with PowerPoint®

Warm Up

1. What is the name of the point where the angle bisectors of a triangle intersect? incenter

Find the midpoint of the segment with the given endpoints.

2. (–1, 6) and (3, 0) (1, 3)
3. (–7, 2) and (–3, –8) (–5, –3)
4. Write an equation of the line containing the points (3, 1) and (2, 10) in point-slope form. $y - 1 = -9(x - 3)$

Also available on transparency

Math Humor

Q: What do you do when it rains?
A: Coincide!

State Resources

5-3 Medians and Altitudes of Triangles

Objectives
Apply properties of medians of a triangle.

Apply properties of altitudes of a triangle.

Vocabulary
median of a triangle
centroid of a triangle
altitude of a triangle
orthocenter of a triangle

Who uses this?
Sculptors who create mobiles of moving objects can use centers of gravity to balance the objects. (See Example 2.)

A **median of a triangle** is a segment whose endpoints are a vertex of the triangle and the midpoint of the opposite side.

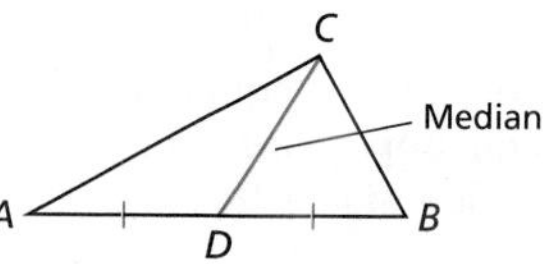

Every triangle has three medians, and the medians are concurrent, as shown in the construction below.

Construction Centroid of a Triangle

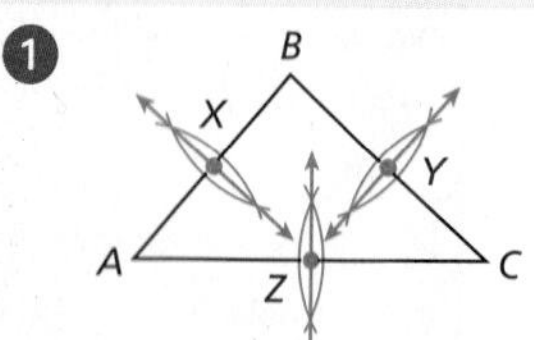

Draw $\triangle ABC$. Construct the midpoints of $\overline{AB}$, $\overline{BC}$, and $\overline{AC}$. Label the midpoints of the sides X, Y, and Z, respectively.

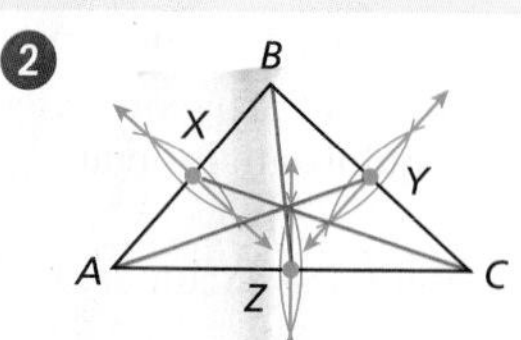

Draw $\overline{AY}$, $\overline{BZ}$, and $\overline{CX}$. These are the three medians of $\triangle ABC$.

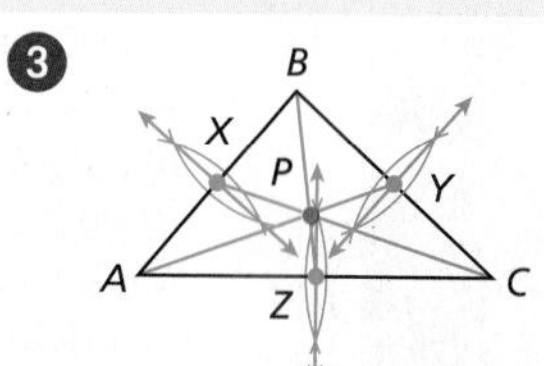

Label the point where $\overline{AY}$, $\overline{BZ}$, and $\overline{CX}$ intersect as P.

The point of concurrency of the medians of a triangle is the **centroid of the triangle**. The centroid is always inside the triangle. The centroid is also called the *center of gravity* because it is the point where a triangular region will balance.

Know it! Note

Theorem 5-3-1 **Centroid Theorem**

The centroid of a triangle is located $\frac{2}{3}$ of the distance from each vertex to the midpoint of the opposite side.

$AP = \frac{2}{3}AY$ $\quad BP = \frac{2}{3}BZ$ $\quad CP = \frac{2}{3}CX$

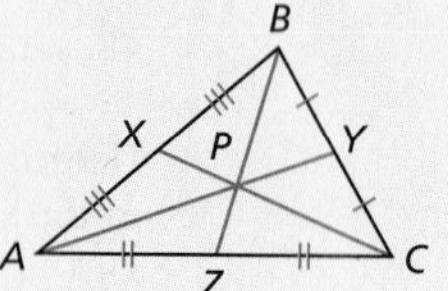

1 Introduce

EXPLORATION

5-3 Medians and Altitudes of Triangles

A *median of a triangle* is a segment whose endpoints are a vertex of the triangle and the midpoint of the opposite side.

1. Draw a large triangle on a sheet of paper. Then cut out the triangle.
2. Fold one side of the triangle onto itself so that two vertices meet. Make a short crease at the fold.
3. Unfold the triangle. Draw a segment from the end of the crease to the opposite vertex.
4. Repeat Steps 2 and 3 to draw the other two medians of the triangle.
5. What do you notice about the three medians? Does this result apply to your classmates' triangles?

THINK AND DISCUSS

6. Discuss whether the intersection of the medians of a triangle (which is called the *centroid*) can be located outside the

Motivate

Give groups of students triangles cut out of heavy construction paper. Have each group find the center of gravity of the triangular region by balancing it on the end of a pencil. Explain that this point is the *centroid* of the triangle and that in this lesson they will learn how to find two more points of concurrency—the centroid and the orthocenter.

Explorations and answers are provided in *Alternate Openers: Explorations Transparencies.*

EXAMPLE 1 Using the Centroid to Find Segment Lengths

In $\triangle ABC$, $AF = 9$, and $GE = 2.4$. Find each length.

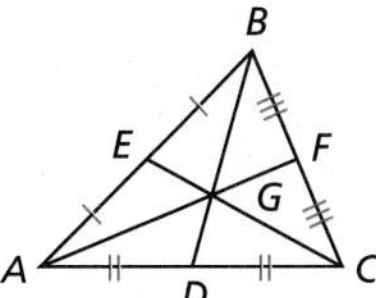

A AG

$AG = \frac{2}{3}AF$	*Centroid Thm.*
$AG = \frac{2}{3}(9)$	*Substitute 9 for AF.*
$AG = 6$	*Simplify.*

B CE

$CG = \frac{2}{3}CE$	*Centroid Thm.*
$CG + GE = CE$	*Seg. Add. Post.*
$\frac{2}{3}CE + GE = CE$	*Substitute $\frac{2}{3}CE$ for CG.*
$GE = \frac{1}{3}CE$	*Subtract $\frac{2}{3}CE$ from both sides.*
$2.4 = \frac{1}{3}CE$	*Substitute 2.4 for GE.*
$7.2 = CE$	*Multiply both sides by 3.*

In $\triangle JKL$, $ZW = 7$, and $LX = 8.1$. Find each length.

1a. KW 21

1b. LZ 5.4

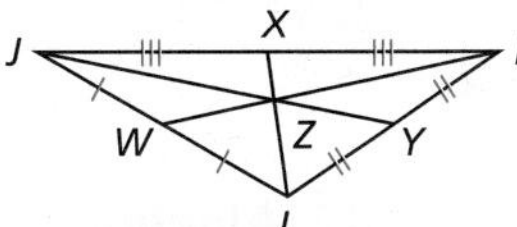

EXAMPLE 2 *Problem-Solving Application*

PROBLEM SOLVING

The diagram shows the plan for a triangular piece of a mobile. Where should the sculptor attach the support so that the triangle is balanced?

Understand the Problem

The **answer** will be the coordinates of the centroid of $\triangle PQR$. The **important information** is the location of the vertices, $P(3, 0)$, $Q(0, 8)$, and $R(6, 4)$.

2 Make a Plan

The centroid of the triangle is the point of intersection of the three medians. So write the equations for two medians and find their point of intersection.

Solve

Let M be the midpoint of $\overline{QR}$ and N be the midpoint of $\overline{QP}$.

$$M = \left(\frac{0+6}{2}, \frac{8+4}{2}\right) = (3, 6) \qquad N = \left(\frac{0+3}{2}, \frac{8+0}{2}\right) = (1.5, 4)$$

$\overline{PM}$ is vertical. Its equation is $x = 3$. $\overline{RN}$ is horizontal. Its equation is $y = 4$. The coordinates of the centroid are $S(3, 4)$.

2 Teach

Guided Instruction

Define the median of a triangle and discuss that every triangle has three medians, which intersect at the centroid. Explain that the centroid is also called the *center of gravity* and that the Centroid Theorem can be used to find segment lengths in triangles. Define the altitude of a triangle and explain how every triangle has three altitudes, which intersect at the orthocenter. Show students how to find the orthocenter of a triangle when given its vertices.

Reaching All Learners

Through Modeling

Have students cut out a large scalene acute triangle. Have them construct the centroid and the orthocenter. Then have students hang the triangle from string at each point to demonstrate which one allows the triangular region to balance.

When using the Centroid Theorem, students may identify the wrong part of the median as $\frac{2}{3}$ of the total length. Remind them that the centroid is closer to each side than to the vertex.

Power Presentations with PowerPoint®

Additional Examples

Example 1

In $\triangle LMN$, $RL = 21$, and $SQ = 4$. Find each length.

A. LS 14

B. NQ 12

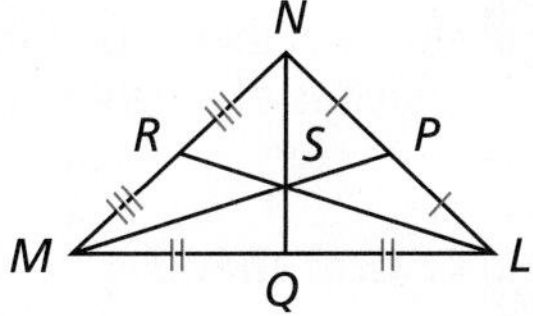

Example 2

A sculptor is shaping a triangular piece of iron that will balance on the point of a cone. At what coordinates will the triangular region balance? (8, 5)

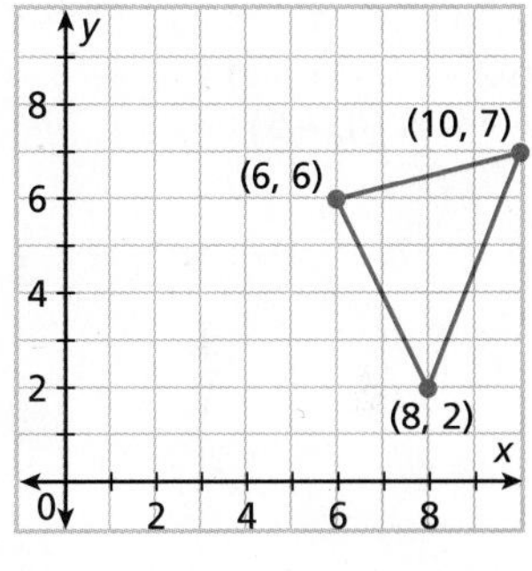

INTERVENTION

Questioning Strategies

EXAMPLE 1

- What is the ratio of the segment lengths of each median?

EXAMPLE 2

- How do you find the point at which a triangular region will balance?

Reading Math The prefix *ortho-* means "perpendicular" or "straight." To help students remember this, explain that an orthodontist straightens teeth with braces. The altitude of a triangle is straight (vertical) in relation to the side it is perpendicular to.

ENGLISH LANGUAGE LEARNERS

Power Presentations with PowerPoint®

Additional Examples

Example 3

Find the orthocenter of $\triangle XYZ$ with vertices $X(3, -2)$, $Y(3, 6)$, and $Z(7, 1)$. $(6.75, 1)$

INTERVENTION
Questioning Strategies

EXAMPLE 3

- How do you write the equations of a horizontal line and a vertical line?

Inclusion Remind students that two of the altitudes of a right triangle are its legs.

Critical Thinking To find the point that is $\frac{2}{3}$ of the distance from (2, 7) to (5, −11), find the difference between the x-coordinates (3) and the y-coordinates (−18). Multiply each difference by $\frac{2}{3}$ and add this to the coordinates of the first point. $\frac{2}{3}(3) = 2$, and $\frac{2}{3}(-18) = -12$. Since $2 + 2 = 4$ and $7 + -12 = -5$, the point is (4, −5).

Look Back

Let L be the midpoint of $\overline{PR}$. The equation for $\overline{QL}$ is $y = -\frac{4}{3}x + 8$, which intersects $x = 3$ at $S(3, 4)$.

2. Find the average of the x-coordinates and the average of the y-coordinates of the vertices of $\triangle PQR$. Make a conjecture about the centroid of a triangle.

Helpful Hint

The height of a triangle is the length of an altitude.

An **altitude of a triangle** is a perpendicular segment from a vertex to the line containing the opposite side. Every triangle has three altitudes. An altitude can be inside, outside, or on the triangle.

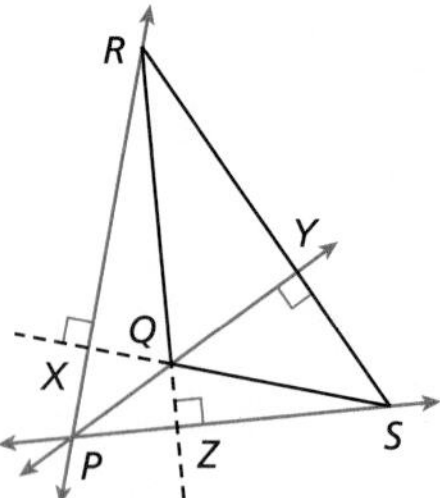

In $\triangle QRS$, altitude $\overline{QY}$ is inside the triangle, but $\overline{RX}$ and $\overline{SZ}$ are not. Notice that the lines containing the altitudes are concurrent at P. This point of concurrency is the **orthocenter of the triangle**.

EXAMPLE 3 Finding the Orthocenter

Algebra

Find the orthocenter of $\triangle JKL$ with vertices $J(-4, 2)$, $K(-2, 6)$, and $L(2, 2)$.

Step 1 Graph the triangle.

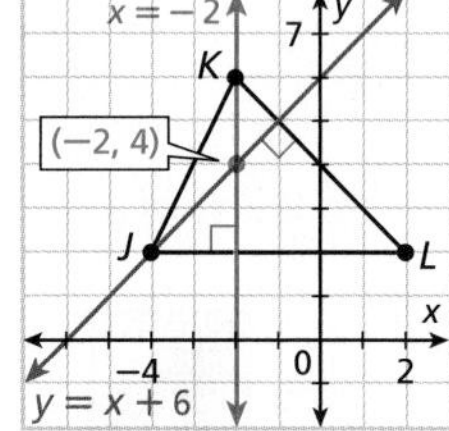

Step 2 Find an equation of the line containing the altitude from K to $\overline{JL}$.

Since $\overleftrightarrow{JL}$ is horizontal, the altitude is vertical. The line containing it must pass through $K(-2, 6)$, so the equation of the line is $x = -2$.

Step 3 Find an equation of the line containing the altitude from J to $\overline{KL}$.

$$\text{slope of } \overleftrightarrow{KL} = \frac{2 - 6}{2 - (-2)} = -1$$

The slope of a line perpendicular to $\overleftrightarrow{KL}$ is 1. This line must pass through $J(-4, 2)$.

$y - y_1 = m(x - x_1)$	*Point-slope form*
$y - 2 = 1[x - (-4)]$	*Substitute 2 for y_1, 1 for m, and −4 for x_1.*
$y - 2 = x + 4$	*Distribute 1.*
$y = x + 6$	*Add 2 to both sides.*

Step 4 Solve the system to find the coordinates of the orthocenter.

$$\begin{cases} x = -2 \\ y = x + 6 \end{cases}$$

$y = -2 + 6 = 4$ *Substitute −2 for x.*

The coordinates of the orthocenter are $(-2, 4)$.

3. Show that the altitude to $\overline{JK}$ passes through the orthocenter of $\triangle JKL$.

2. 3; 4; possible answer: the x-coordinate of the centroid is the average of the x-coordinates of the vertices of the △, and the y-coordinate of the centroid is the average of the y-coordinates of the vertices of the △.

3. Possible answer: An equation of the altitude to $\overline{JK}$ is $y = -\frac{1}{2}x + 3$. It is true that $4 = -\frac{1}{2}(-2) + 3$, so $(-2, 4)$ is a solution of this equation. Therefore this altitude passes through the orthocenter.

3 Close

Summarize

Review with students that the centroid of a triangle is the point of concurrency of the medians of the triangle. Remind students that by the Centroid Theorem, the centroid is located $\frac{2}{3}$ of the distance from each vertex to the midpoint of the opposite side. Discuss that the three altitudes of a triangle intersect at the orthocenter of the triangle.

ONGOING ASSESSMENT and INTERVENTION

Diagnose ***Before*** *the Lesson*
5-3 Warm Up, TE p. 314

Monitor ***During*** *the Lesson*
Check It Out! Exercises, SE pp. 315–316
Questioning Strategies, TE pp. 315–316

Assess ***After*** *the Lesson*
5-3 Lesson Quiz, TE p. 320
Alternative Assessment, TE p. 320

THINK AND DISCUSS

1. Draw a triangle in which a median and an altitude are the same segment. What type of triangle is it?
2. Draw a triangle in which an altitude is also a side of the triangle. What type of triangle is it?
3. The centroid of a triangle divides each median into two segments. What is the ratio of the two lengths of each median?
4. **GET ORGANIZED** Copy and complete the graphic organizer. Fill in the blanks to make each statement true.

	Centroid	Orthocenter
Definition	The point of concurrency of the ?	The point of concurrency of the ?
Location (Inside, Outside, or On)	? the triangle	Can be ? the triangle

Answers to *Think and Discuss*

1. Possible answer: The △ is isosc.

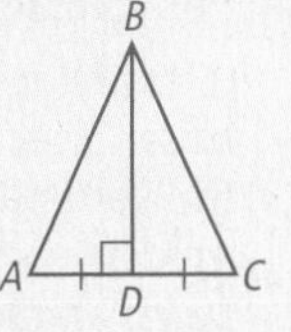

2. Possible answer: The △ is a rt △.

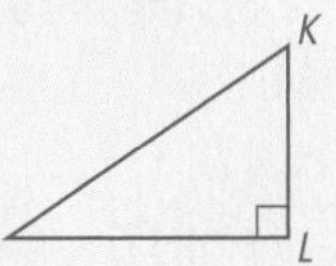

3. The ratio of the length of the longer seg. to the length of the shorter seg. is 2 : 1.
4. See p. A5.

5-3 Exercises

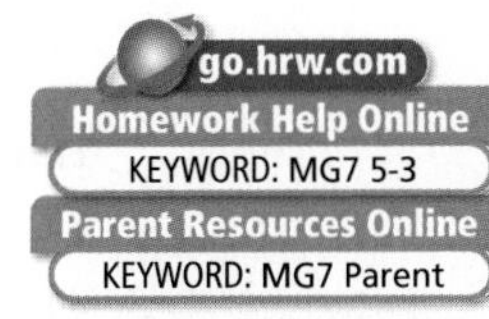

Homework Help Online
KEYWORD: MG7 5-3
Parent Resources Online
KEYWORD: MG7 Parent

Assignment Guide

Assign *Guided Practice* exercises as necessary.

If you finished Examples **1–3**
Basic 12–32, 34–37, 40–43, 46–51
Average 12–37, 39–43, 45–51
Advanced 12–51

Homework Quick Check
Quickly check key concepts.
Exercises: 12, 16, 18, 22, 28

GUIDED PRACTICE

Vocabulary **Apply the vocabulary from this lesson to answer each question.**

1. The ___?___ of a triangle is located $\frac{2}{3}$ of the distance from each vertex to the midpoint of the opposite side. (*centroid* or *orthocenter*) centroid
2. The ___?___ of a triangle is perpendicular to the line containing a side. (*altitude* or *median*) altitude

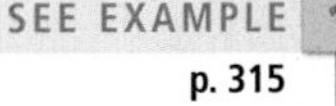

p. 315

VX **= 204, and** ***RW*** **= 104. Find each length.**

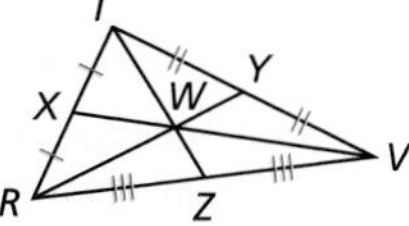

3. *VW* 136
4. *WX* 68
5. *RY* 156
6. *WY* 52

SEE EXAMPLE 2 p. 315

7. **Design** The diagram shows a plan for a piece of a mobile. A chain will hang from the centroid of the triangle. At what coordinates should the artist attach the chain? (4, 2)

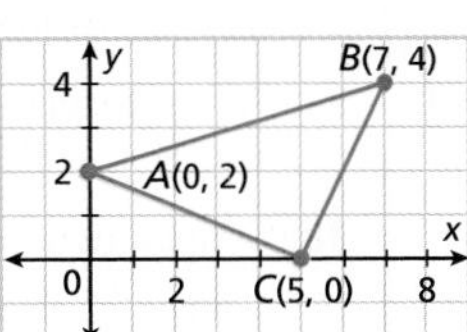

SEE EXAMPLE 3 p. 316

Multi-Step **Find the orthocenter of a triangle with the given vertices.**

8. $K(2, -2), L(4, 6), M(8, -2)$ (4, −1)
9. $U(-4, -9), V(-4, 6), W(5, -3)$ (2, −3)
10. $P(-5, 8), Q(4, 5), R(-2, 5)$ (−5, −4)
11. $C(-1, -3), D(-1, 2), E(9, 2)$ (−1, 2)

State Resources

go.hrw.com
State Resources Online
KEYWORD: MG7 Resources

Answers

33. Possible answer:

⊥ bisector of the base; bisector of the vertex ∠; median to the base; altitude to the base

34.

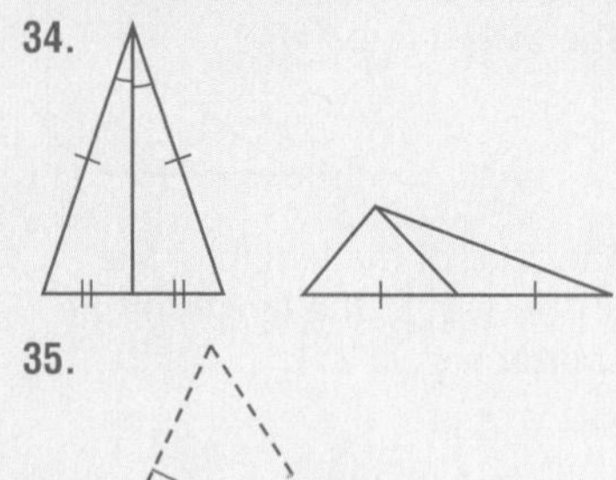

35.

37.

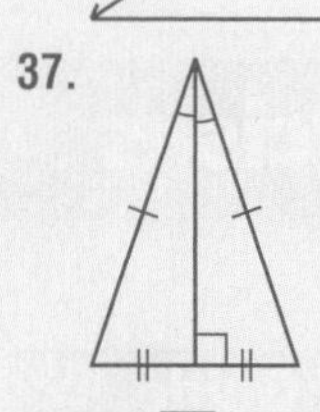

38. 1. $\overline{PS}$ and $\overline{RT}$ are medians of $\triangle PQR$. $\overline{PS} \cong \overline{RT}$ (Given)
2. $PS = RT$ (Def. of ≅ segs.)
3. $\frac{2}{3}PS = \frac{2}{3}RT$ (Mult. Prop. of =)
4. $PZ = \frac{2}{3}PS$, $RZ = \frac{2}{3}RT$ (Centroid Thm.)
5. $PZ = RZ$ (Subst.)
6. $\overline{PZ} \cong \overline{RZ}$ (Def. of ≅ segs.)
7. $\angle SPR \cong \angle TRP$ (Isosc. △ Thm.)
8. $\overline{PR} \cong \overline{PR}$ (Reflex. Prop. of ≅)
9. $\triangle PTR \cong \triangle RSP$ (SAS)
10. $\angle QPR \cong \angle QRP$ (CPCTC)
11. $\overline{PQ} \cong \overline{RQ}$ (Conv. of Isosc. △ Thm.)
12. $\triangle PQR$ is an isosc. △. (Def. of isosc. △)

39. See p. A19.

5-3 PRACTICE A

5-3 PRACTICE C

5-3 PRACTICE B

Use the figure for Exercises 1–4. $GB = 12\frac{2}{3}$ and $CD = 10$. Find each length.

1. FG $6\frac{1}{3}$
2. BF 19
3. GD $3\frac{1}{3}$
4. CG $6\frac{2}{3}$

5. A triangular compass needle will turn most easily if it is attached to the compass face through its centroid. Find the coordinates of the centroid. (1, 1.9)

Find the orthocenter of the triangle with the given vertices.

6. $X(-5, 4)$, $Y(2, -3)$, $Z(1, 4)$ (2, 5)
7. $A(0, -1)$, $B(2, -3)$, $C(4, -1)$ (2, −3)

Use the figure for Exercises 8 and 9. $\overline{HL}$, $\overline{IM}$, and $\overline{JK}$ are medians of $\triangle HIJ$.

8. Find the area of the triangle. $36\ m^2$
9. If the perimeter of the triangle is 49 meters, then find the length of $\overline{MH}$. (*Hint:* What kind of a triangle is it?) 10.25 m

10. Two medians of a triangle were cut apart at the centroid to make the four segments shown below. Use what you know about the Centroid Theorem to reconstruct the original triangle from the four segments shown. Measure the side lengths of your triangle to check that you constructed medians. (*Note:* There are many possible answers.)

Possible answer:

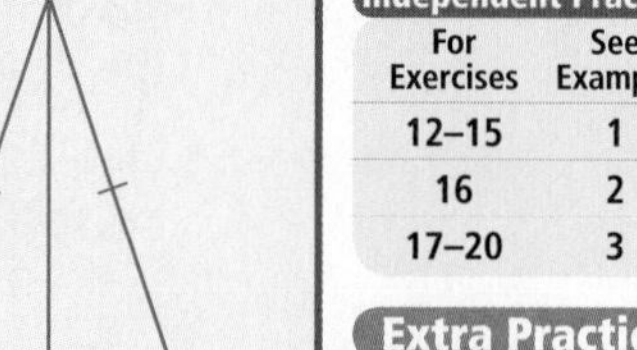

Independent Practice	
For Exercises	See Example
12–15	1
16	2
17–20	3

Extra Practice
Skills Practice p. S12
Application Practice p. S32

PRACTICE AND PROBLEM SOLVING

$PA = 2.9$, and $HC = 10.8$. Find each length.

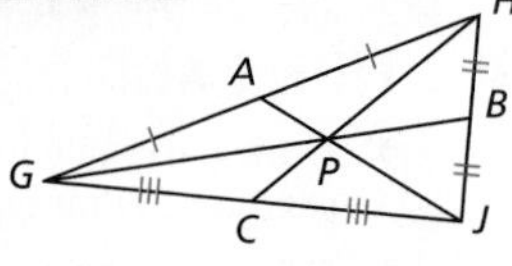

12. PC 3.6
13. HP 7.2
14. JA 8.7
15. JP 5.8

16. **Design** In the plan for a table, the triangular top has coordinates (0, 10), (4, 0), and (8, 14). The tabletop will rest on a single support placed beneath it. Where should the support be attached so that the table is balanced? **(4, 8)**

Multi-Step **Find the orthocenter of a triangle with the given vertices.**

17. $X(-2, -2)$, $Y(6, 10)$, $Z(6, -6)$ **(0, −2)**
18. $G(-2, 5)$, $H(6, 5)$, $J(4, -1)$ **(4, 3)**
19. $R(-8, 9)$, $S(-2, 9)$, $T(-2, 1)$ **(−2, 9)**
20. $A(4, -3)$, $B(8, 5)$, $C(8, -8)$ **(−2, −3)**

Find each measure.

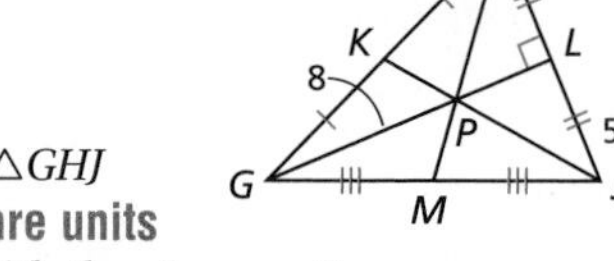

21. GL 12
22. PL 4
23. HL 5
24. GJ 13
25. perimeter of $\triangle GHJ$ 36 units
26. area of $\triangle GHJ$ 60 square units

Algebra **Find the centroid of a triangle with the given vertices.**

27. $A(0, -4)$, $B(14, 6)$, $C(16, -8)$ **(10, −2)**
28. $X(8, -1)$, $Y(2, 7)$, $Z(5, -3)$ **(5, 1)**

Find each length.

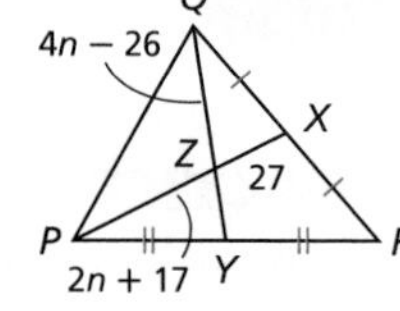

29. PZ 54
30. PX 81
31. QZ 48
32. YZ 24

LINK
Math History

In 1678, Giovanni Ceva published his famous theorem that states the conditions necessary for three *Cevians* (segments from a vertex of a triangle to the opposite side) to be concurrent. The medians and altitudes of a triangle meet these conditions.

33. **Critical Thinking** Draw an isosceles triangle and its line of symmetry. What are four other names for this segment?

Tell whether each statement is sometimes, always, or never true. Support your answer with a sketch.

34. A median of a triangle bisects one of the angles. **S**
35. If one altitude of a triangle is in the triangle's exterior, then a second altitude is also in the triangle's exterior. **A**
36. The centroid of a triangle lies in its exterior. **N**
37. In an isosceles triangle, the altitude and median from the vertex angle are the same line as the bisector of the vertex angle. **A**

38. Write a two-column proof.

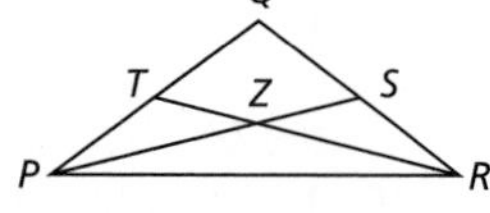

Given: $\overline{PS}$ and $\overline{RT}$ are medians of $\triangle PQR$. $\overline{PS} \cong \overline{RT}$
Prove: $\triangle PQR$ is an isosceles triangle.
Plan: Show that $\triangle PTR \cong \triangle RSP$ and use CPCTC to conclude that $\angle QPR \cong \angle QRP$.

39. **Write About It** Draw a large triangle on a sheet of paper and cut it out. Find the centroid by paper folding. Try to balance the shape on the tip of your pencil at a point other than the centroid. Now try to balance the shape at its centroid. Explain why the centroid is also called the center of gravity.

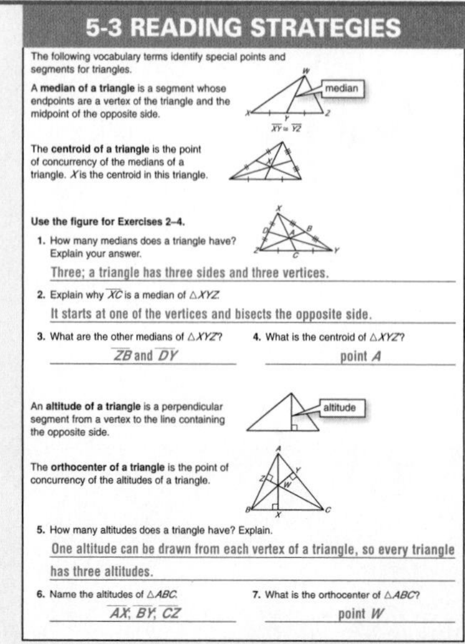

5-3 READING STRATEGIES

The following vocabulary terms identify special points and segments for triangles.

A **median of a triangle** is a segment whose endpoints are a vertex of the triangle and the midpoint of the opposite side.

The **centroid of a triangle** is the point of concurrency of the medians of a triangle. X is the centroid in this triangle.

Use the figure for Exercises 2–4.

1. How many medians does a triangle have? Explain your answer.
Three; a triangle has three sides and three vertices.
2. Explain why $\overline{XC}$ is a median of $\triangle XYZ$.
It starts at one of the vertices and bisects the opposite side.
3. What are the other medians of $\triangle XYZ$?
$\overline{ZB}$ and $\overline{DY}$
4. What is the centroid of $\triangle XYZ$?
point A

An **altitude of a triangle** is a perpendicular segment from a vertex to the line containing the opposite side.

The **orthocenter of a triangle** is the point of concurrency of the altitudes of a triangle.

5. How many altitudes does a triangle have? Explain.
One altitude can be drawn from each vertex of a triangle, so every triangle has three altitudes.
6. Name the altitudes of $\triangle ABC$.
$\overline{AX}$, $\overline{BY}$, $\overline{CZ}$
7. What is the orthocenter of $\triangle ABC$?
point W

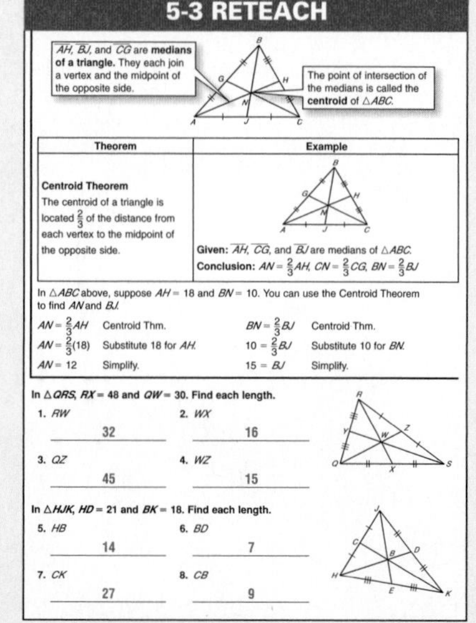

5-3 RETEACH

$\overline{AH}$, $\overline{BJ}$, and $\overline{CG}$ are **medians of a triangle.** They each join a vertex and the midpoint of the opposite side.

The point of intersection of the medians is called the **centroid** of $\triangle ABC$.

Theorem	Example
Centroid Theorem The centroid of a triangle is located $\frac{2}{3}$ of the distance from each vertex to the midpoint of the opposite side.	**Given:** $\overline{AH}$, $\overline{CG}$, and $\overline{BJ}$ are medians of $\triangle ABC$. **Conclusion:** $AN = \frac{2}{3}AH$, $CN = \frac{2}{3}CG$, $BN = \frac{2}{3}BJ$

In $\triangle ABC$ above, suppose $AH = 18$ and $BN = 10$. You can use the Centroid Theorem to find AN and BJ.

$AN = \frac{2}{3}AH$	Centroid Thm.	$BN = \frac{2}{3}BJ$	Centroid Thm.
$AN = \frac{2}{3}(18)$	Substitute 18 for AH.	$10 = \frac{2}{3}BJ$	Substitute 10 for BN.
$AN = 12$	Simplify.	$15 = BJ$	Simplify.

In $\triangle QRS$, $RX = 48$ and $QW = 30$. Find each length.

1. RW 32
2. WX 16
3. QZ 45
4. WZ 15

In $\triangle HJK$, $HD = 21$ and $BK = 18$. Find each length.

5. HB 14
6. BD 7
7. CK 27
8. CB 9

40. This problem will prepare you for the Multi-Step Test Prep on page 328.

The towns of Davis, El Monte, and Fairview have the coordinates shown in the table, where each unit of the coordinate plane represents one mile. A music company has stores in each city and a distribution warehouse at the centroid of $\triangle DEF$.

City	Location
Davis	$D(0, 0)$
El Monte	$E(0, 8)$
Fairview	$F(8, 0)$

a. What are the coordinates of the warehouse?

b. Find the distance from the warehouse to the Davis store. Round your answer to the nearest tenth of a mile. **3.8 mi**

c. A straight road connects El Monte and Fairview. What is the distance from the warehouse to the road? **1.9 mi**

a. $\left(2\frac{2}{3}, 2\frac{2}{3}\right)$

41. $\overline{QT}$, $\overline{RV}$, and $\overline{SW}$ are medians of $\triangle QRS$. Which statement is NOT necessarily true?

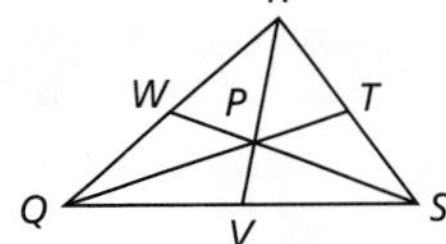

Ⓐ $QP = \frac{2}{3}QT$ Ⓒ $RT = ST$

Ⓑ $RP = 2PV$ **Ⓓ** $QT = SW$

42. Suppose that the orthocenter of a triangle lies outside the triangle. Which points of concurrency are inside the triangle?

I. incenter **II.** circumcenter **III.** centroid

Ⓕ I and II only Ⓗ II and III only

Ⓖ I and III only Ⓙ I, II, and III

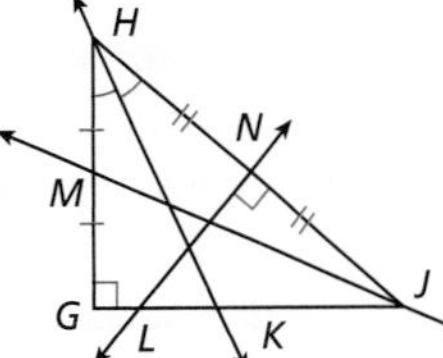

43. In the diagram, which of the following correctly describes $\overleftrightarrow{LN}$?

Ⓐ Altitude Ⓒ Median

Ⓑ Angle bisector **Ⓓ** Perpendicular bisector

CHALLENGE AND EXTEND

44. Draw an equilateral triangle.

a. Explain why the perpendicular bisector of any side contains the vertex opposite that side.

b. Explain why the perpendicular bisector through any vertex also contains the median, the altitude, and the angle bisector through that vertex.

c. Explain why the incenter, circumcenter, centroid, and orthocenter are the same point.

45. Use coordinates to show that the lines containing the altitudes of a triangle are concurrent.

a. Find the slopes of $\overline{RS}$, $\overline{ST}$, and $\overline{RT}$.

b. Find the slopes of lines ℓ, m, and n.

c. Write equations for lines ℓ, m, and n.

d. Solve a system of equations to find the point P where lines ℓ and m intersect.

e. Show that line n contains P.

f. What conclusion can you draw?

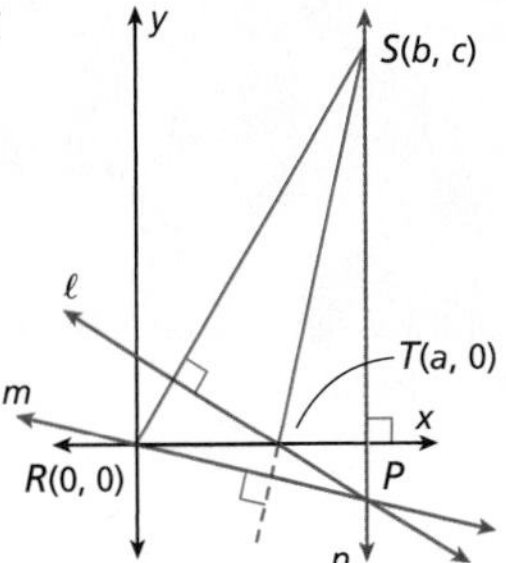

COMMON ERROR ALERT

For **Exercises 29–32,** students may assume that the medians $\overline{PX}$ and $\overline{QY}$ are congruent. Remind them that this is true only if $\overline{QR} \cong \overline{PR}$. They cannot assume from the diagram that the triangle is isosceles.

Exercise 40 involves finding the centroid of a triangle. This exercise prepares students for the Multi-Step Test Prep on page 328.

If students have difficulty with **Exercise 42,** have them draw a triangle whose orthocenter is in the exterior and then sketch the other points of concurrency.

Answers

44.

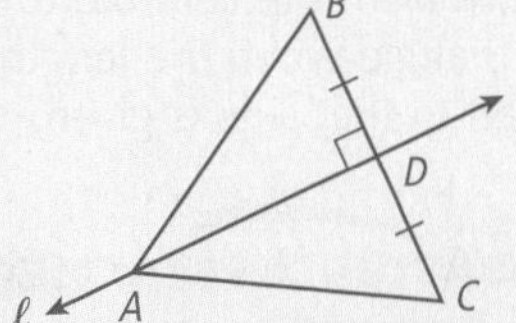

a. Possible answer: $\triangle ABC$ is equil., and ℓ is the $\perp$ bisector of $\overline{BC}$. Since $\triangle ABC$ is equil., $\overline{AB} \cong \overline{AC}$ by def. So $AB = AC$ by the def. of $\cong$ segs. Therefore by the Conv. of the $\perp$ Bisector Thm., A is on line ℓ. Similarly, B is on the $\perp$ bisector of $\overline{AC}$, and C is on the $\perp$ bisector of $\overline{AB}$.

b. Possible answer: By the def. of $\perp$ bisector, $\overline{BD} \cong \overline{CD}$. So D is the mdpt. of $\overline{BC}$ by def., and $\overline{AD}$ is a median of $\triangle ABC$ by the def. of median. Therefore ℓ contains the median of $\triangle ABC$ through A. Also by the def. of $\perp$ bisector, $\overline{AD} \perp \overline{BC}$. So $\overline{AD}$ is an altitude of $\triangle ABC$ by the def. Therefore ℓ contains the altitude of $\triangle ABC$ through A. Again by the def. of $\perp$ bisector, $\overline{BD} \cong \overline{CD}$. $\overline{AB} \cong \overline{AC}$ by the def. of equil., and $\overline{AD} \cong \overline{AD}$ by the Reflex. Prop. of $\cong$. So $\triangle ABD \cong \triangle ACD$ by SSS. Then $\angle DAB \cong \angle DAC$ by CPCTC, and $\overrightarrow{AD}$ is the bisector of $\angle BAC$ by the def. of $\angle$ bisector. Therefore ℓ contains the $\angle$ bisector of $\triangle ABC$ through A. The same reasoning can be applied to the other 2 $\perp$ bisectors.

44c, 45. See p. A19.

5-3 PROBLEM SOLVING

1. The diagram shows the coordinates of the vertices of a triangular patio umbrella. The umbrella will rest on a pole that will support it. Where should the pole be attached so that the umbrella is balanced?

$\left(4, \frac{14}{3}\right)$

2. In a plan for a triangular wind chime, the coordinates of the vertices are $J(10, 2)$, $K(7, 6)$, and $L(12, 10)$. At what coordinates should the manufacturer attach the chain from which it will hang in order for the chime to be balanced?

$\left(9\frac{2}{3}, 6\right)$

3. Triangle PQR has vertices at $P(-3, 5)$, $Q(-1, 7)$, and $R(3, 1)$. Find the coordinates of the orthocenter and the centroid.

$\left(-1\frac{4}{5}, 5\frac{4}{5}\right)$; $\left(-\frac{1}{3}, 4\frac{1}{3}\right)$

Choose the best answer.

4. A triangle has coordinates at $A(0, 6)$, $B(8, 6)$, and $C(5, 0)$. $\overline{CD}$ is a median of the triangle, and $\overline{CE}$ is an altitude of the triangle. Which is a true statement?

A The coordinates of D and E are the same.

Ⓑ The distance between D and E is 1 unit.

C The distance between D and E is 2 units.

D D is on the triangle, and E is outside the triangle.

5. Lines j and k contain medians of $\triangle DEF$. Find y and z.

F $y = 6$ $z = 4$ Ⓗ $y = 64$ $z = 4$.

G $y =$ $z = 4$ J $y =$ $z =$

6. An inflatable triangular raft is towed behind a boat. The raft is an equilateral triangle. To maintain balance, the seat is at the centroid B of the triangle. What is AB, the distance from the seat to the tow rope? Round to the nearest tenth.

A 18.7 in.

Ⓑ 37.4 in.

C 43.1 in.

D 56.0 in.

5-3 CHALLENGE

The **Fermat point,** named after seventeenth century mathematician Pierre de Fermat, is a special point in an acute triangle that can be found by using the following steps.

Step 1 Draw an acute triangle ABC.

Step 2 Construct an equilateral triangle on each side of $\triangle ABC$ and label the new vertices A', B', C' as shown.

Step 3 Connect the opposite vertices by drawing $\overline{AA'}$, $\overline{BB'}$, and $\overline{CC'}$.

Step 4 The point of concurrency of these segments is the Fermat point of $\triangle ABC$. Label this point F.

Use the figure above for Exercises 1 and 2.

1. Make a conjecture comparing the lengths of $\overline{AA'}$, $\overline{BB'}$, and $\overline{CC'}$. Verify your conjecture by measuring the segments.

The segments have equal lengths.

2. Find the sum of AF, BF, and CF. Compare this sum to the lengths of the segments that you found in Exercise 1.

The sum equals the segment lengths.

Point F is the Fermat point in $\triangle GHJ$.

3. Find the sum of the distances from the Fermat point to each vertex of $\triangle GHJ$. Round to the nearest tenth of a centimeter.

Possible answer: 5.8 cm

4. Draw two more points inside $\triangle GHJ$ and label the points X and Y. Then find each sum: $GX + HX + JX$ and $GY + HY + JY$. Compare the sums to the sum you found by using the Fermat point.

These sums are both greater than the sum found by using the Fermat point.

5. Make a conjecture about the sum of the distances from the Fermat point to the vertices of a triangle, compared to the sum of the distances from any point to the vertices of a triangle.

It is the least sum that is possible from any point in a triangle to each of the three vertices.

6. Draw an acute triangle. Locate the Fermat point. Repeat Exercises 3 and 4. How do the results compare to the conjecture you made in Exercise 5?

The sums found using X and Y are both greater than the sum found by using the Fermat point. This verifies the conjecture.

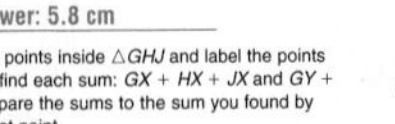

Communicating Math In Exercises 47 and 48, remind students that for a biconditional to be true, both the conditional and its converse must be true.

Journal

Have students explain how to find the distance from the centroid to the side of a triangle when the length of the median to that side is given.

ALTERNATIVE ASSESSMENT

Pair students. Have each student write the coordinates of the vertices of a right triangle. Have them exchange papers and find the coordinates of the centroid and orthocenter of their partner's triangle. Then have them use the coordinates to verify the Centroid Theorem.

Power Presentations with PowerPoint®

5-3 Lesson Quiz

Use the figure for Items 1–3. In $\triangle ABC$, $AE = 12$, $DG = 7$, and $BG = 9$. Find each length.

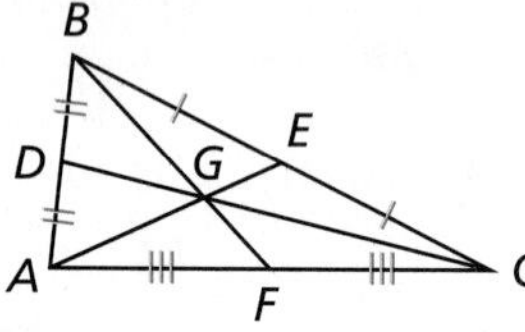

1. AG 8
2. GC 14
3. BF 13.5

For Items 4 and 5, use $\triangle MNP$ with vertices $M(-4, -2)$, $N(6, -2)$, and $P(-2, 10)$. Find the coordinates of each point.

4. the centroid $(0, 2)$
5. the orthocenter $\left(-2, -\frac{2}{3}\right)$

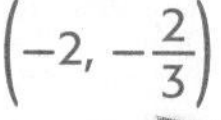

Also available on transparency

SPIRAL REVIEW

46. At a baseball game, a bag of peanuts costs \$0.75 more than a bag of popcorn. If a family purchases 5 bags of peanuts and 3 bags of popcorn for \$21.75, how much does one bag of peanuts cost? *(Previous course)* **\$3.00**

Determine if each biconditional is true. If false, give a counterexample. *(Lesson 2-4)*

47. The area of a rectangle is 40 cm^2 if and only if the length of the rectangle is 4 cm and the width of the rectangle is 10 cm.

48. A nonzero number n is positive if and only if $-n$ is negative. **T**

47. F; possible answer: a rectangle with width 5 and length 8

$\overline{NQ}$, $\overline{QP}$, and $\overline{QM}$ are perpendicular bisectors of $\triangle JKL$. Find each measure. *(Lesson 5-2)*

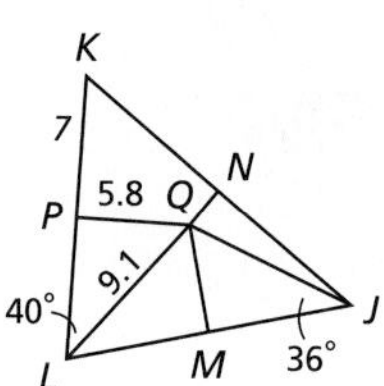

49. KL **14.0**
50. QJ **9.1**
51. $m\angle JQL$ **108°**

Construction Orthocenter of a Triangle

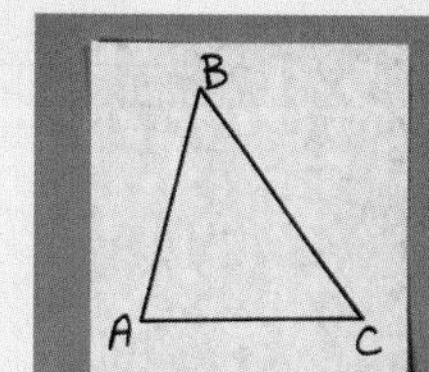

1. Draw a large scalene acute triangle ABC on a piece of patty paper.

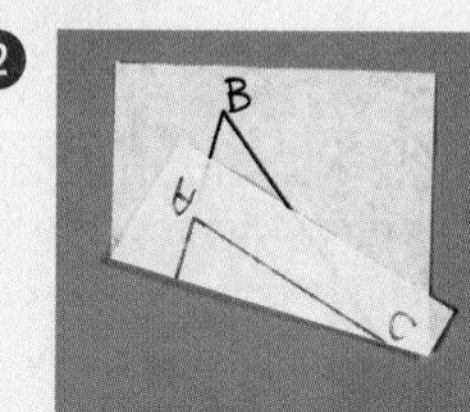

2. Find the altitude of each side by folding the side so that it overlaps itself and so that the fold intersects the opposite vertex.

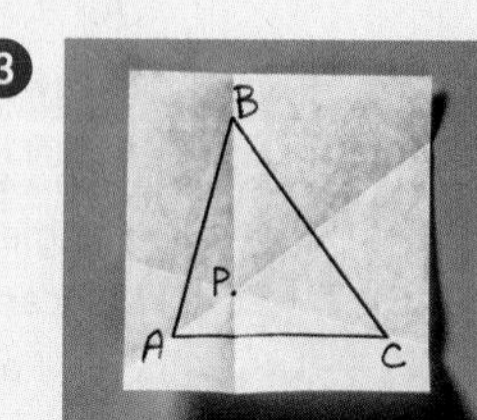

3. Mark the point where the three lines containing the altitudes intersect and label it P. P is the orthocenter of $\triangle ABC$.

1. Repeat the construction for a scalene obtuse triangle and a scalene right triangle. **Check students' constructions.**
2. Make a conjecture about the location of the orthocenter in an acute, an obtuse, and a right triangle.

Career Path

go.hrw.com
Career Resources Online
KEYWORD: MG7 Career

Alex Peralta
Electrician

Q: What high school math classes did you take?
A: Algebra 1, Geometry, and Statistics.

Q: What type of training did you receive?
A: In high school, I took classes in electricity, electronics, and drafting. I began an apprenticeship program last year to prepare for the exam to get my license.

Q: How do you use math?
A: Determining the locations of outlets and circuits on blueprints requires good spatial sense. I also use ratios and proportions, calculate distances, work with formulas, and estimate job costs.

Answers to *Construction*

2. Possible answer: The orthocenter of an acute △ is inside the △. The orthocenter of an obtuse △ is outside the △. The orthocenter of a rt. △ is the vertex of the rt. ∠.

Special Points in Triangles

In this lab you will use geometry software to explore properties of the four points of concurrency you have studied.

Use with Lesson 5-3

Activity

1. Construct a triangle.
2. Construct the perpendicular bisector of each side of the triangle. Construct the point of intersection of these three lines. This is the circumcenter of the triangle. Label it *U* and hide the perpendicular bisectors.

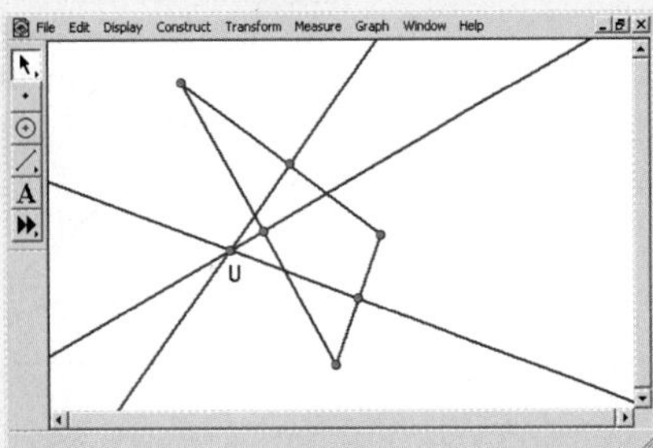

3. In the same triangle, construct the bisector of each angle. Construct the point of intersection of these three lines. This is the incenter of the triangle. Label it *I* and hide the angle bisectors.
4. In the same triangle, construct the midpoint of each side. Then construct the three medians. Construct the point of intersection of these three lines. Label the centroid *C* and hide the medians.

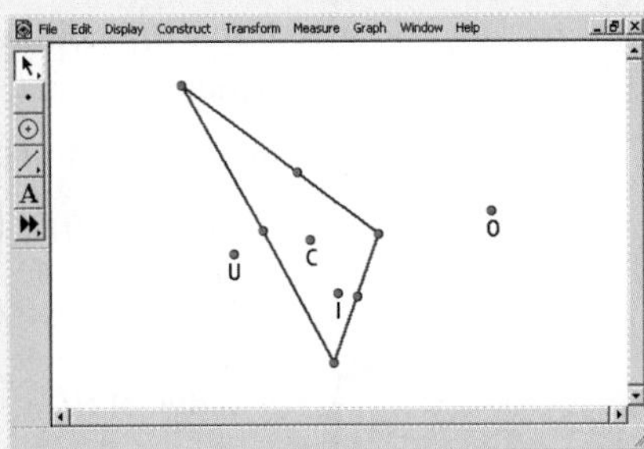

5. In the same triangle, construct the altitude to each side. Construct the point of intersection of these three lines. Label the orthocenter *O* and hide the altitudes.
6. Move a vertex of the triangle and observe the positions of the four points of concurrency. In 1765, Swiss mathematician Leonhard Euler showed that three of these points are always collinear. The line containing them is called the *Euler line*.

Try This

1. Which three points of concurrency lie on the Euler line? **the circumcenter, the orthocenter, and the centroid**
2. **Make a Conjecture** Which point on the Euler line is always between the other two? Measure the distances between the points. Make a conjecture about the relationship of the distances between these three points.
3. **Make a Conjecture** Move a vertex of the triangle until all four points of concurrency are collinear. In what type of triangle are all four points of concurrency on the Euler line? **isosceles triangle**
4. **Make a Conjecture** Find a triangle in which all four points of concurrency coincide. What type of triangle has this special property? **equilateral triangle**

Answers to *Try This*

2. The centroid; possible answer: the distance from the centroid to the orthocenter is twice the distance from the centroid to the circumcenter; that is, $CO = 2CU$.

Organizer

Use with Lesson 5-3

Pacing:
Traditional 1 day
Block $\frac{1}{2}$ day

Objective: Use special points in triangles to explore Euler's line.

Materials: geometry software

Online Edition
TechKeys

Countdown Week 10

Resources

Technology Lab Activities
5-3 Lab Recording Sheet

Teach

Discuss

Discuss what the four points of concurrency are and have students make a conjecture about which of them lie on the Euler line.

Close

Key Concept

The circumcenter, centroid, and orthocenter of a triangle are always collinear.

Assessment

Journal Have students explain which points of concurrency lie on the Euler line.

State Resources

5-4 Organizer

Pacing: Traditional 1 day
Block $\frac{1}{2}$ day

Objective: Prove and use properties of triangle midsegments.

Online Edition
Tutorial Videos

Countdown Week 11

Power Presentations with PowerPoint®

Warm Up

Use the points $A(2, 2)$, $B(12, 2)$, and $C(4, 8)$ for Exercises 1–5.

1. Find X and Y, the midpoints of $\overline{AC}$ and $\overline{CB}$. $(3, 5), (8, 5)$
2. Find XY. 5
3. Find AB. 10
4. Find the slope of $\overline{AB}$. 0
5. Find the slope of $\overline{XY}$. 0
6. What is the slope of a line parallel to $3x + 2y = 12$? $-\frac{3}{2}$

Also available on transparency

Math Humor

Q: What did the visitor from Planet Metric demand?

A: "Take me to your liter!"

5-4 The Triangle Midsegment Theorem

Objective
Prove and use properties of triangle midsegments.

Vocabulary
midsegment of a triangle

Why learn this?
You can use triangle midsegments to make indirect measurements of distances, such as the distance across a volcano. (See Example 3.)

A **midsegment of a triangle** is a segment that joins the midpoints of two sides of the triangle. Every triangle has three midsegments, which form the *midsegment triangle.*

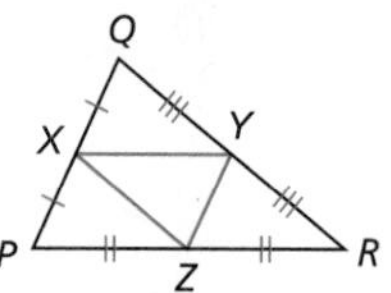

Midsegments: $\overline{XY}, \overline{YZ}, \overline{ZX}$
Midsegment triangle: $\triangle XYZ$

EXAMPLE 1 **Examining Midsegments in the Coordinate Plane**

In $\triangle GHJ$, show that midsegment $\overline{KL}$ is parallel to $\overline{GJ}$ and that $KL = \frac{1}{2}GJ$.

H(−5, 6), L, J(1, 2), K, G(−7, −2)

Step 1 Find the coordinates of K and L.

$$\text{mdpt. of } \overline{GH} = \left(\frac{-7 + (-5)}{2}, \frac{-2 + 6}{2}\right) = (-6, 2)$$

$$\text{mdpt. of } \overline{HJ} = \left(\frac{-5 + 1}{2}, \frac{6 + 2}{2}\right) = (-2, 4)$$

Step 2 Compare the slopes of $\overline{KL}$ and $\overline{GJ}$.

$$\text{slope of } \overline{KL} = \frac{4 - 2}{-2 - (-6)} = \frac{1}{2} \qquad \text{slope of } \overline{GJ} = \frac{2 - (-2)}{1 - (-7)} = \frac{1}{2}$$

Since the slopes are the same, $\overline{KL} \parallel \overline{GJ}$.

Step 3 Compare the lengths of $\overline{KL}$ and $\overline{GJ}$.

$$KL = \sqrt{\left[-2 - (-6)\right]^2 + (4 - 2)^2} = 2\sqrt{5}$$

$$GJ = \sqrt{\left[1 - (-7)\right]^2 + \left[2 - (-2)\right]^2} = 4\sqrt{5}$$

Since $2\sqrt{5} = \frac{1}{2}(4\sqrt{5})$, $KL = \frac{1}{2}GJ$.

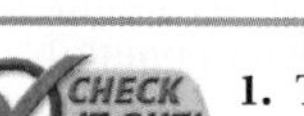

1. The vertices of $\triangle RST$ are $R(-7, 0)$, $S(-3, 6)$, and $T(9, 2)$. M is the midpoint of $\overline{RT}$, and N is the midpoint of $\overline{ST}$. Show that $\overline{MN} \parallel \overline{RS}$ and $MN = \frac{1}{2}RS$.

1. $M(1, 1)$; $N(3, 4)$; slope of $\overline{MN} = \frac{3}{2}$; slope of $\overline{RS} = \frac{3}{2}$; since the slopes are the same, $\overline{MN} \parallel \overline{RS}$. $MN = \sqrt{13}$; $RS = \sqrt{52} = 2\sqrt{13}$; the length of $\overline{MN}$ is half the length of $\overline{RS}$.

State Resources

go.hrw.com
State Resources Online
KEYWORD: MG7 Resources

1 Introduce

EXPLORATION

5-4 The Triangle Midsegment Theorem

A *midsegment* of a triangle is a segment that joins the midpoints of two sides of the triangle. Use geometry software to explore triangle midsegments.

1. Construct a triangle. Label the vertices A, B, and C.
2. Select $\overline{AB}$ and construct its midpoint. Do the same for $\overline{AC}$. Label the midpoints as shown.
3. Draw the midsegment $\overline{DE}$. Measure the lengths of $\overline{DE}$ and $\overline{BC}$.
4. Measure $\angle ADE$ and $\angle ABC$.
5. Drag the sides and vertices of $\triangle ABC$ to change its shape. How are the lengths of $\overline{DE}$ and $\overline{BC}$ related?
6. What do you notice about $m\angle ADE$ and $m\angle ABC$?

THINK AND DISCUSS

7. Describe how the length of a midsegment is related to the

Motivate

Have students cut a large scalene triangle from heavy paper. Have them construct the midpoints of two sides and connect them, forming a *midsegment.* Then have them cut along this segment to form a triangle and a trapezoid. Have them rotate the small triangle and place it next to the trapezoid to form a parallelogram. Ask students to make conjectures about the relationship between the midsegment and the base of the triangle.

Explorations and answers are provided in *Alternate Openers: Explorations Transparencies.*

The relationship shown in Example 1 is true for the three midsegments of every triangle.

Theorem 5-4-1 Triangle Midsegment Theorem

A midsegment of a triangle is parallel to a side of the triangle, and its length is half the length of that side.

$\overline{DE} \parallel \overline{AC}$, $DE = \frac{1}{2}AC$

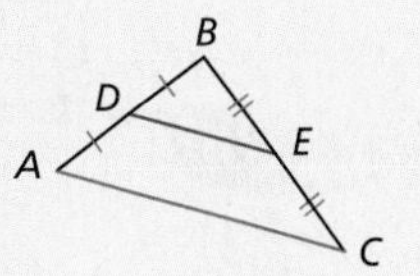

You will prove Theorem 5-4-1 in Exercise 38.

EXAMPLE 2 Using the Triangle Midsegment Theorem

Find each measure.

A UW

$UW = \frac{1}{2}ST$ — *△ Midsegment Thm.*

$UW = \frac{1}{2}(7.4)$ — *Substitute 7.4 for ST.*

$UW = 3.7$ — *Simplify.*

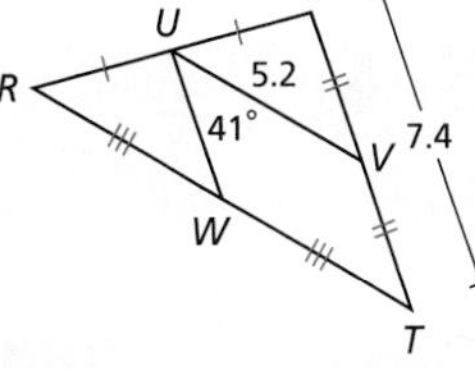

B $m\angle SVU$

$\overline{UW} \parallel \overline{ST}$ — *△ Midsegment Thm.*

$m\angle SVU = m\angle VUW$ — *Alt. Int. ∠s Thm.*

$m\angle SVU = 41°$ — *Substitute 41° for m∠VUW.*

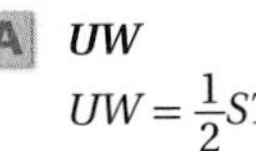

CHECK IT OUT! Find each measure.

2a. JL 72 **2b.** PM 48.5 **2c.** $m\angle MLK$ 102°

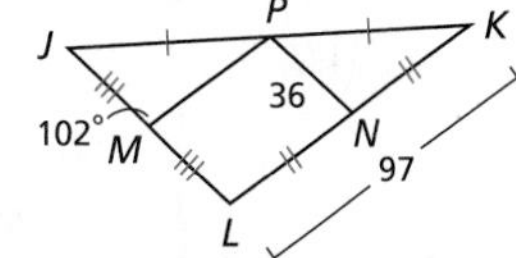

EXAMPLE 3 Indirect Measurement Application

Anna wants to find the distance across the base of Capulin Volcano, an extinct volcano in New Mexico. She measures a triangle at one side of the volcano as shown in the diagram. What is *AE*?

$BD = \frac{1}{2}AE$ — *△ Midsegment Thm.*

$775 = \frac{1}{2}AE$ — *Substitute 775 for BD.*

$1550 = AE$ — *Multiply both sides by 2.*

The distance AE across the base of the volcano is about 1550 meters.

CHECK IT OUT! **3. What if...?** Suppose Anna's result in Example 3 is correct. To check it, she measures a second triangle. How many meters will she measure between H and F? 775 m

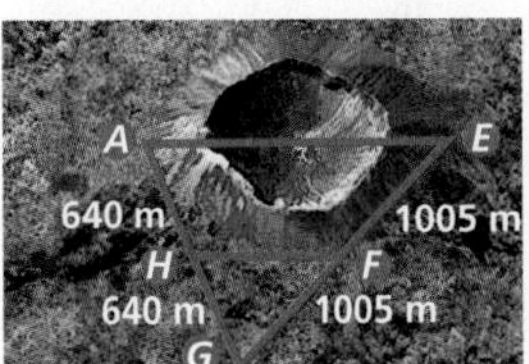

Power Presentations with PowerPoint®

Additional Examples

Example 1

The vertices of $\triangle XYZ$ are $X(-1, 8)$, $Y(9, 2)$, and $Z(3, -4)$. M and N are the midpoints of $\overline{XZ}$ and $\overline{YZ}$. Show that $\overline{MN} \parallel \overline{XY}$ and $MN = \frac{1}{2}XY$. $M(1, 2)$, $N(6, -1)$; slope of $\overline{MN} = -\frac{3}{5}$, slope of $\overline{XY} = -\frac{3}{5}$; $MN = \sqrt{34}$, $XY = 2\sqrt{34}$

Example 2

Find each measure.

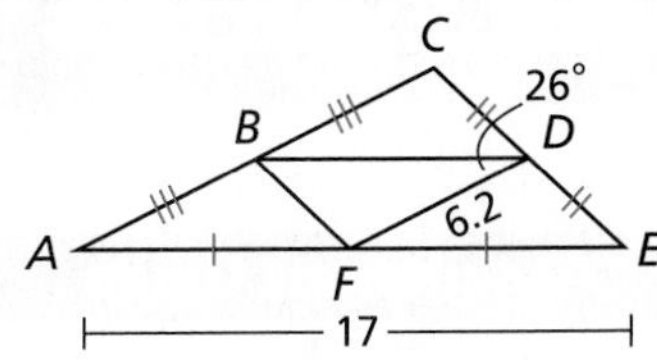

A. BD 8.5 **B.** $m\angle CBD$ 26°

Example 3

In an A-frame support, the distance PQ is 46 inches. What is the length of the support $\overline{ST}$ if S and T are at the midpoints of the sides? 23 in.

INTERVENTION
Questioning Strategies

EXAMPLES 1–2

- To which side of a triangle is a midsegment parallel?

EXAMPLE 3

- How do you know that you can use the Triangle Midsegment Theorem?

2 Teach

Guided Instruction

Define a midsegment of a triangle. Explain the Triangle Midsegment Theorem and how the theorem can be used to indirectly find the side lengths of a triangle.

Inclusion Remind students that two lines with equal slopes are parallel and that the slope of a segment is the difference of its *y*-coordinates divided by the difference of its *x*-coordinates. Also remind them to subtract the coordinates in the same order.

3 Close

Summarize

Ask students the following questions.

- How many midsegments does a triangle have? 3
- What is the relationship between a midsegment of a triangle and the sides of the triangle? Possible answer: The midsegment connects the mdpts. of 2 sides and is ∥ to the third side.

ONGOING ASSESSMENT and INTERVENTION

Diagnose ***Before*** **the Lesson**
5-4 Warm Up, TE p. 322

Monitor ***During*** **the Lesson**
Check It Out! Exercises, SE pp. 322–323
Questioning Strategies, TE p. 323

Assess ***After*** **the Lesson**
5-4 Lesson Quiz, TE p. 327
Alternative Assessment, TE p. 327

Answers to *Think and Discuss*

1. The endpoints of $\overline{XY}$ are not mdpts. of the sides of the $\triangle$.
2. See p. A5.

THINK AND DISCUSS

1. Explain why $\overline{XY}$ is NOT a midsegment of the triangle.

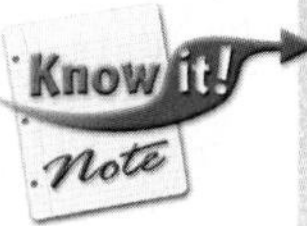

2. **GET ORGANIZED** Copy and complete the graphic organizer. Write the definition of a triangle midsegment and list its properties. Then draw an example and a nonexample.

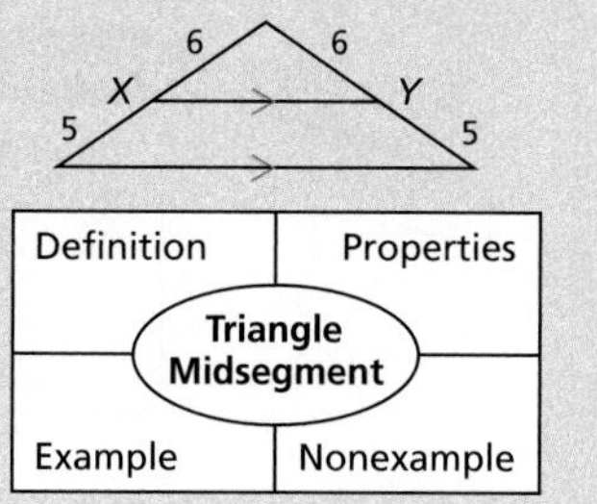

5-4 Exercises

5-4 Exercises

Assignment Guide

Assign *Guided Practice* exercises as necessary.

If you finished Examples **1–3**
Basic 10–27, 29–41, 48–55
Average 10–44, 47–55
Advanced 10–26, 28–55

Homework Quick Check
Quickly check key concepts.
Exercises: 10, 12, 17, 18, 22

Answers

2. $S(-1, 4)$; $T(4, 6)$; slope of $\overline{ST} = \frac{2}{5}$; slope of $\overline{PR} = \frac{2}{5}$; since the slopes are the same, $\overline{ST} \parallel \overline{PR}$. $ST = \sqrt{29}$; $PR = \sqrt{116} = 2\sqrt{29}$; the length of $\overline{ST}$ is half the length of $\overline{PR}$.

GUIDED PRACTICE

1. **Vocabulary** The *midsegment of a triangle* joins the ___?___ of two sides of the triangle. (*endpoints* or *midpoints*) **midpoints**

SEE EXAMPLE 1 p. 322

2. The vertices of $\triangle PQR$ are $P(-4, -1)$, $Q(2, 9)$, and $R(6, 3)$. S is the midpoint of $\overline{PQ}$, and T is the midpoint of $\overline{QR}$. Show that $\overline{ST} \parallel \overline{PR}$ and $ST = \frac{1}{2}PR$.

SEE EXAMPLE 2 p. 323

Find each measure.

3. NM **5.1**
4. XZ **11.2**
5. NZ **5.6**
6. $m\angle LMN$ **29°**
7. $m\angle YXZ$ **29°**
8. $m\angle XLM$ **151°**

X Y Z L M N 10.2 5.6 29°

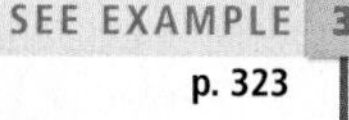

SEE EXAMPLE 3 p. 323

9. **Architecture** In this A-frame house, the width of the first floor $\overline{XZ}$ is 30 feet. The second floor $\overline{CD}$ is slightly above and parallel to the midsegment of $\triangle XYZ$. Is the width of the second floor more or less than 5 yards? Explain.

PRACTICE AND PROBLEM SOLVING

For Exercises	See Example
10	1
11–16	2
17	3

Independent Practice

Extra Practice
Skills Practice p. S12
Application Practice p. S32

10. The vertices of $\triangle ABC$ are $A(-6, 11)$, $B(6, -3)$, and $C(-2, -5)$. D is the midpoint of $\overline{AC}$, and E is the midpoint of $\overline{AB}$. Show that $\overline{DE} \parallel \overline{CB}$ and $DE = \frac{1}{2}CB$.

Find each measure.

11. GJ **38**
12. RQ **13.5**
13. RJ **19**
14. $m\angle PQR$ **55°**
15. $m\angle HGJ$ **55°**
16. $m\angle GPQ$ **125°**

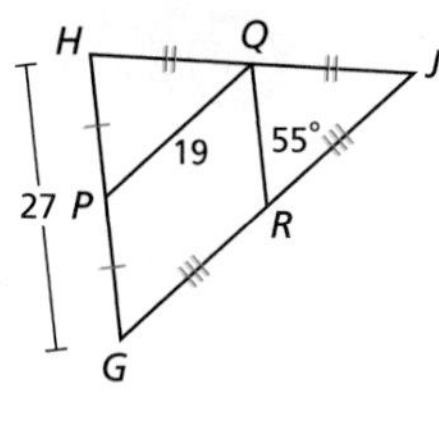

State Resources

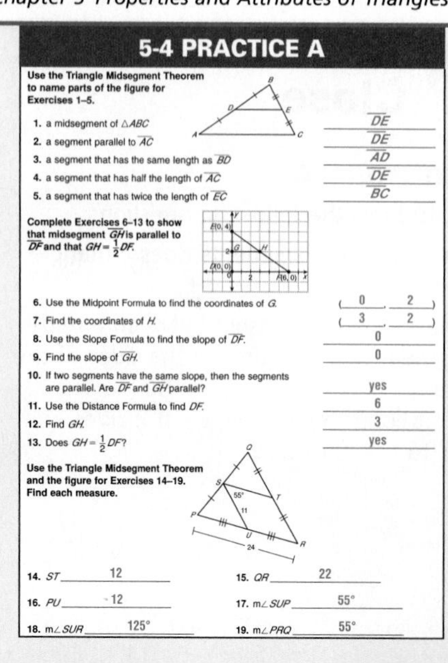

5-4 PRACTICE A

Use the Triangle Midsegment Theorem to name parts of the figure for Exercises 1–5.

1. a midsegment of $\triangle ABC$ $\overline{DE}$
2. a segment parallel to $\overline{AC}$ $\overline{DE}$
3. a segment that has the same length as $\overline{BD}$ $\overline{AD}$
4. a segment that has half the length of $\overline{AC}$ $\overline{DE}$
5. a segment that has twice the length of $\overline{EC}$ $\overline{BC}$

Complete Exercises 6–13 to show that midsegment $\overline{GH}$ is parallel to $\overline{DF}$ and that $GH = \frac{1}{2}DF$.

6. Use the Midpoint Formula to find the coordinates of G. (0, 2)
7. Find the coordinates of H. (3, 2)
8. Use the Slope Formula to find the slope of $\overline{DF}$. 0
9. Find the slope of $\overline{GH}$. 0
10. If two segments have the same slope, then the segments are parallel. Are $\overline{DF}$ and $\overline{GH}$ parallel? yes
11. Use the Distance Formula to find DF. 6
12. Find GH. 3
13. Does $GH = \frac{1}{2}DF$? yes

Use the Triangle Midsegment Theorem and the figure for Exercises 14–19. Find each measure.

14. ST 12
15. QR 22
16. PU 12
17. $m\angle SUP$ 55°
18. $m\angle SUR$ 125°
19. $m\angle PRQ$ 55°

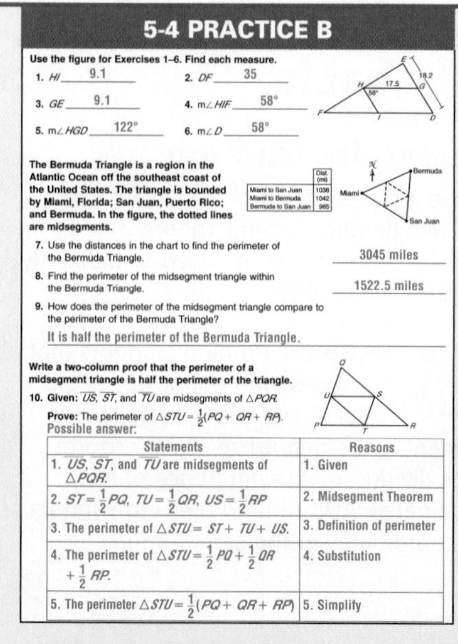

5-4 PRACTICE B

Use the figure for Exercises 1–6. Find each measure.

1. HI 9.1
2. DF 35
3. GE 9.1
4. $m\angle HIF$ 58°
5. $m\angle HGD$ 122°
6. $m\angle D$ 58°

The Bermuda Triangle is a region in the Atlantic Ocean off the southeast coast of the United States. The triangle is bounded by Miami, Florida; San Juan, Puerto Rico; and Bermuda. In the figure, the dotted lines are midsegments.

	Dist. (mi)
Miami to San Juan	1038
Miami to Bermuda	1042
Bermuda to San Juan	965

7. Use the distances in the chart to find the perimeter of the Bermuda Triangle. 3045 miles
8. Find the perimeter of the midsegment triangle within the Bermuda Triangle. 1522.5 miles
9. How does the perimeter of the midsegment triangle compare to the perimeter of the Bermuda Triangle? It is half the perimeter of the Bermuda Triangle.

Write a two-column proof that the perimeter of a midsegment triangle is half the perimeter of the triangle.

10. **Given:** $\overline{US}$, $\overline{ST}$, and $\overline{TU}$ are midsegments of $\triangle PQR$.
Prove: The perimeter of $\triangle STU = \frac{1}{2}(PQ + QR + RP)$.
Possible answer:

Statements	Reasons
1. $\overline{US}$, $\overline{ST}$, and $\overline{TU}$ are midsegments of $\triangle PQR$.	1. Given
2. $ST = \frac{1}{2}PQ$, $TU = \frac{1}{2}QR$, $US = \frac{1}{2}RP$	2. Midsegment Theorem
3. The perimeter of $\triangle STU = ST + TU + US$.	3. Definition of perimeter
4. The perimeter of $\triangle STU = \frac{1}{2}PQ + \frac{1}{2}QR + \frac{1}{2}RP$.	4. Substitution
5. The perimeter $\triangle STU = \frac{1}{2}(PQ + QR + RP)$	5. Simplify

17. Yes; $\overline{DE}$ is a midsegment of $\triangle ABC$, so its length is half of $4\frac{1}{2}$ ft, or $2\frac{1}{4}$ ft, which is 27 in. This is less than 30 in., so the carpenter can use the 30 in. timber to make the crossbar.

17. **Carpentry** In each support for the garden swing, the crossbar $\overline{DE}$ is attached at the midpoints of legs $\overline{BA}$ and $\overline{BC}$. The distance AC is $4\frac{1}{2}$ feet. The carpenter has a timber that is 30 inches long. Is this timber long enough to be used as one of the crossbars? Explain.

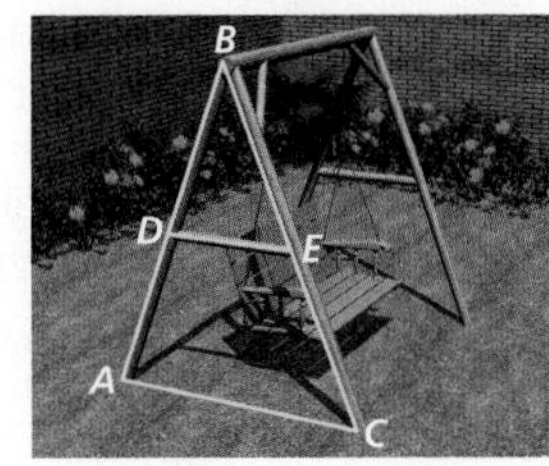

$\triangle KLM$ is the midsegment triangle of $\triangle GHJ$.

12, K, H, G, 7, L, M, 4, J

18. What is the perimeter of $\triangle GHJ$? 34

19. What is the perimeter of $\triangle KLM$? 17

20. What is the relationship between the perimeter of $\triangle GHJ$ and the perimeter of $\triangle KLM$?
The perimeter of $\triangle GHJ$ is twice the perimeter of $\triangle KLM$.

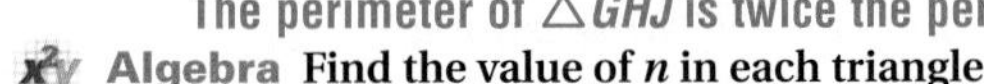

Algebra **Find the value of n in each triangle.**

21. 36

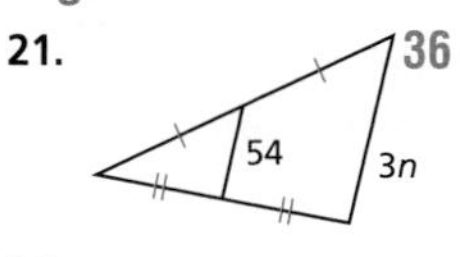

22. 26.5

$n - 9$, 35

23. 8

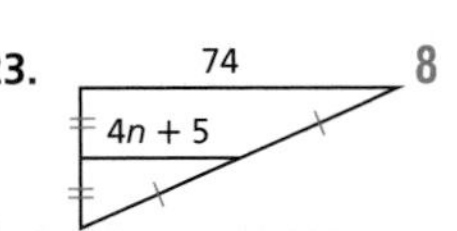

24. 21

9.5, $2n - 23$

25. 4

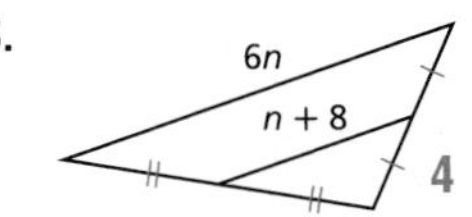

26. 5

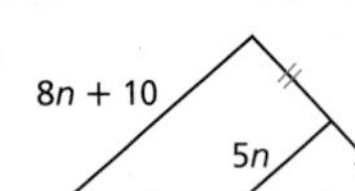

27. B; possible answer: in $\triangle ABC$, $\overline{DE}$ is a midsegment and $\overline{BC}$ is the side $\parallel$ to it. By the $\triangle$ Midsegment Thm., the length of a midsegment is half the length of the $\parallel$ side, so $DE = \frac{1}{2}BC$.

27. **/// ERROR ANALYSIS ///** Below are two solutions for finding BC. Which is incorrect? Explain the error.

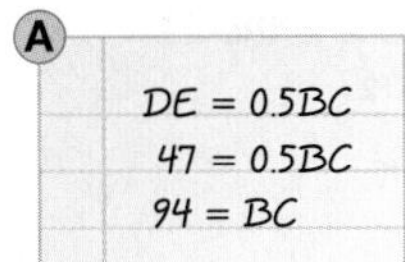

A

DE = 0.5BC
47 = 0.5BC
94 = BC

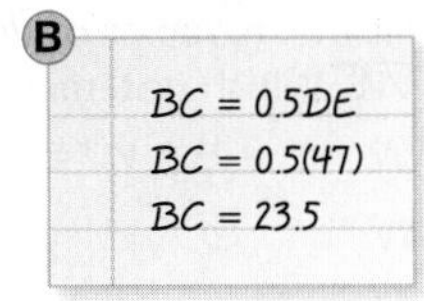

B

BC = 0.5DE
BC = 0.5(47)
BC = 23.5

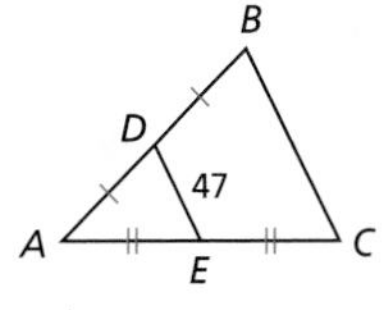

28. **Critical Thinking** Draw scalene $\triangle DEF$. Label X as the midpoint of $\overline{DE}$, Y as the midpoint of $\overline{EF}$, and Z as the midpoint of $\overline{DF}$. Connect the three midpoints. List all of the congruent angles in your drawing.

29. **Estimation** The diagram shows the sketch for a new street. Parallel parking spaces will be painted on both sides of the street. Each parallel parking space is 23 feet long. About how many parking spaces can the city accommodate on both sides of the new street? Explain your answer.

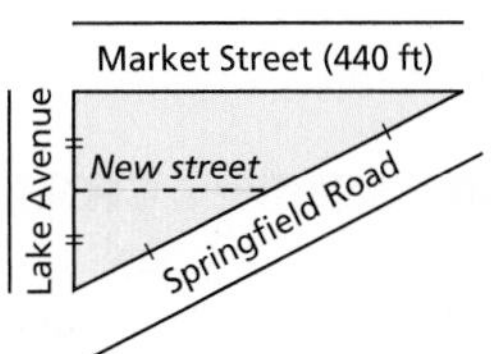

$\overline{CG}$, $\overline{EH}$, and $\overline{FJ}$ are midsegments of $\triangle ABD$, $\triangle GCD$, and $\triangle GHE$, respectively. Find each measure.

30. CG 16.5 31. EH 11 32. FJ 4.125

33. $m\angle DCG$ 57° 34. $m\angle GHE$ 57° 35. $m\angle FJH$ 123°

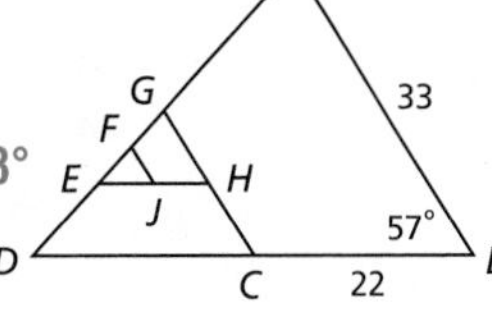

36. **Write About It** An isosceles triangle has two congruent sides. Does it also have two congruent midsegments? Explain.

5-4 PRACTICE C

Pedro has a hunch about the area of midsegment triangles. He is a careful student, so he investigates in a methodical manner. First Pedro draws a right triangle because he knows it will be easy to calculate the area.

B(0, 2b), E, D, A(0, 0), F, C(2a, 0)

1. Find the area of $\triangle ABC$. $2ab$
2. Find the coordinates of the midpoints D, E, and F. $D(0, b)$, $E(a, b)$, $F(a, 0)$
3. Pedro knows it will be easy to find the area of $\triangle EFD$ if $\angle DEF$ is a right angle. Write a proof that $\angle DEF \cong \angle A$.
Possible answer: F is the midpoint of $\overline{AC}$, so $AF = \frac{1}{2}AC$. $DE = \frac{1}{2}AC$ by the Midsegment Theorem, so $\overline{AF} \cong \overline{DE}$. $\overline{DE} \parallel \overline{AF}$ by the Midsegment Theorem and $\angle EDF$ and $\angle AFD$ are alternate interior angles, so $\angle EDF \cong \angle AFD$. $\overline{DF} \cong \overline{DF}$ by the Reflexive Property, thus $\triangle EFD \cong \triangle ADF$. By CPCTC, $\angle DEF \cong \angle A$.
4. Find the area of $\triangle EFD$. $\frac{1}{2}ab$
5. Compare the areas of $\triangle ABC$ and $\triangle EFD$.
$\triangle ABC$ has four times the area of $\triangle EFD$.
6. Pedro has already shown that $\triangle EFD \cong \triangle ADF$. Calculate the area of $\triangle ADF$. $\frac{1}{2}ab$
7. Write a conjecture about congruent triangles and area.
Possible answer: Congruent triangles have equal area.

Pedro already knows some things about the area of the midsegment triangle of a right triangle. But he thinks he can expand his theorem. Before he can get to that, however, he has to show another property of triangles and area.

X, 4, W, 3, Z, 5, Y

8. Find the area of $\triangle WXY$, $\triangle WXZ$, and $\triangle YXZ$.
16; 6; 10
9. Compare the total of the areas of $\triangle WXZ$ and $\triangle YXZ$ to the area of $\triangle WXY$.
Possible answer: The total of the areas of $\triangle WXZ$ and $\triangle YXZ$ is equal to the area of $\triangle WXY$.
10. Write a conjecture about the areas of triangles within a larger triangle.
Possible answer: The area of a larger triangle is the sum of areas of the triangles within it.

COMMON ERROR /// ALERT \\\

In **Exercise 26,** students may write $5n = \frac{1}{2} \cdot 8n + 10$ instead of $5n = \frac{1}{2}(8n + 10)$. Review the Distributive Property and remind students that the entire quantity $8n + 10$ is multiplied by $\frac{1}{2}$.

Algebra In **Exercise 22,** it may be easier to solve $2(n - 9) = 35$ rather than $n - 9 = \frac{1}{2}(35)$.

Answers

9. Less than 5 yd; possible answer: the length of the midsegment is half the length of $\overline{XZ}$. So the midsegment is 15 ft, or 5 yd. $\overline{CD}$ is shorter than the midsegment, so the width of the second floor will be less than 5 yd.

10. $D(-4, 3)$; $E(0, 4)$; slope of $\overline{DE} = \frac{1}{4}$; slope of $\overline{CB} = \frac{1}{4}$; since the slopes are the same, $\overline{DE} \parallel \overline{CB}$. $DE = \sqrt{17}$; $CB = \sqrt{68} = 2\sqrt{17}$; the length of $\overline{DE}$ is half the length of $\overline{CB}$.

28.

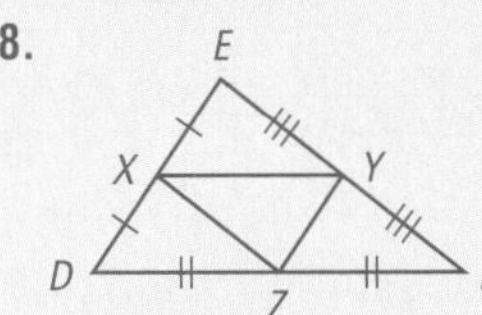

$\angle D \cong \angle FZY \cong \angle YXE \cong \angle ZYX$;
$\angle E \cong \angle ZYF \cong \angle DXZ \cong \angle XZY$;
$\angle F \cong \angle XYE \cong \angle DZX \cong \angle ZXY$

29. Possible answer: about 18 parking spaces; the new street is along the midsegment of the triangular plot of land. The length of the street is half of 440 ft, or 220 ft. Estimate the quotient $220 \div 23$ by rounding 220 to 225 and 23 to 25. Since $225 \div 25 = 9$, the city can put about 9 parking spaces on 1 side of the street. So the total number of parking spaces is about 2(9), or 18.

36. Yes; possible answer: let x be the length of each congruent side of an isosceles triangle. By the Triangle Midsegment Theorem, the length of the midsegment parallel to each of those sides is $\frac{1}{2}x$. Since these 2 midsegments are equal in length, they are congruent to each other.

MULTI-STEP TEST PREP **Exercise 37** involves finding the length of the midsegment of a triangle. This exercise prepares students for the Multi-Step Test Prep on page 328.

TEST PREP DOCTOR If students have difficulty with **Exercise 39,** have them write and solve the equation $2(x + 9) = 4x - 27$, and review the Distributive Property with them.

MULTI-STEP TEST PREP

37. This problem will prepare you for the Multi-Step Test Prep on page 328.

The figure shows the roads connecting towns A, B, and C. A music company has a store in each town and a distribution warehouse W at the midpoint of road $\overline{XY}$.

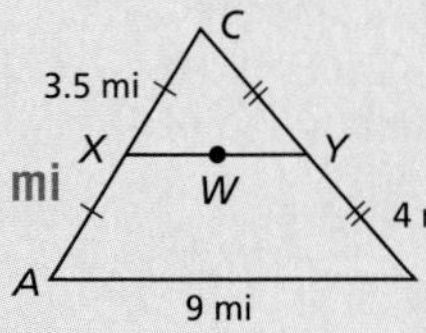

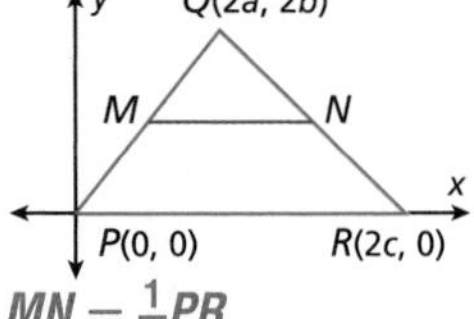

a. What is the distance from the warehouse to point X? **2.25 mi**

b. A truck starts at the warehouse, delivers instruments to the stores in towns A, B, and C (in this order) and then returns to the warehouse. What is the total length of the trip, assuming the driver takes the shortest possible route? **28.5 mi**

38. Use coordinates to prove the Triangle Midsegment Theorem.

a. M is the midpoint of $\overline{PQ}$. What are its coordinates? (a, b)

b. N is the midpoint of $\overline{QR}$. What are its coordinates? $(a + c, b)$

c. Find the slopes of $\overline{PR}$ and $\overline{MN}$. What can you conclude?

d. Find PR and MN. What can you conclude?

2c; c; the length of $\overline{PR}$ is twice the length of $\overline{MN}$, so $MN = \frac{1}{2}PR$.

38c. 0; 0; the slopes of $\overline{MN}$ and $\overline{PR}$ are equal, so $\overline{MN} \parallel \overline{PR}$.

y Q(2a, 2b) M N x P(0, 0) R(2c, 0)

TEST PREP

39. $\overline{PQ}$ is a midsegment of $\triangle RST$. What is the length of $\overline{RT}$?

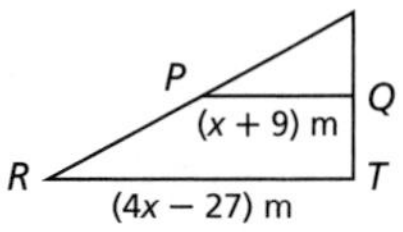

Ⓐ 9 meters

Ⓑ 21 meters

Ⓒ 45 meters

Ⓓ 63 meters

S P Q $(x + 9)$ m R T $(4x - 27)$ m

40. In $\triangle UVW$, M is the midpoint of $\overline{VU}$, and N is the midpoint of $\overline{VW}$. Which statement is true?

Ⓕ $VM = VN$ Ⓗ $VU = 2VM$

Ⓖ $MN = UV$ Ⓙ $VW = \frac{1}{2}VN$

41. $\triangle XYZ$ is the midsegment triangle of $\triangle JKL$, $XY = 8$, $YK = 14$, and $m\angle YKZ = 67°$. Which of the following measures CANNOT be determined?

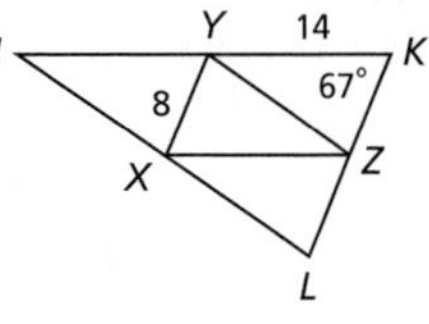

Ⓐ KL Ⓒ $m\angle XZL$

Ⓑ JY Ⓓ $m\angle KZY$

CHALLENGE AND EXTEND

42. **Multi-Step** The midpoints of the sides of a triangle are $A(-6, 3)$, $B(2, 1)$, and $C(0, -3)$. Find the coordinates of the vertices of the triangle. **$(-8, -1)$, $(-4, 7)$, $(8, -5)$**

43. **Critical Thinking** Classify the midsegment triangle of an equilateral triangle by its side lengths and angle measures. **equilateral and equiangular**

Algebra **Find the value of n in each triangle.**

44. **±9**

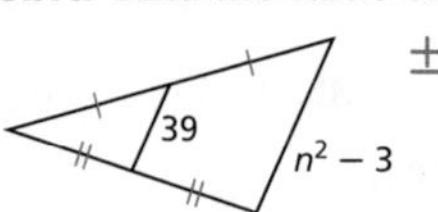

45. **7**

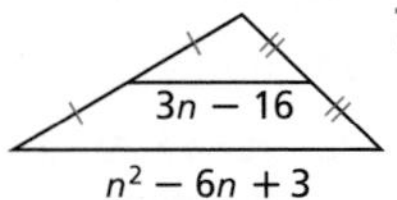

Answers to *Construction*

2. Possible answer: Find $m\angle BXY$ and $m\angle BAC$ and confirm that they are equal. This means the two segments are ∥ by the Conv. of the Corr. ∠s Post.

5-4 READING STRATEGIES

The **midsegment** of a triangle is a segment that joins the midpoints of two sides of the triangle.

A **midsegment triangle** is formed from the three midsegments of a triangle.

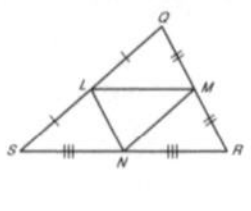

1. Name the midsegments in $\triangle QRS$. $\overline{LM}$, $\overline{MN}$, $\overline{NL}$
2. What is the midsegment triangle in $\triangle QRS$? $\triangle LMN$

The Triangle Midsegment Theorem: A midsegment of a triangle is parallel to a side of the triangle, and its length is half the length of that side.

3. Which midsegment is parallel to side $\overline{QS}$? $\overline{MN}$
4. If side $\overline{RS}$ is 12 cm, how long is $\overline{LM}$? 6 cm
5. $\overline{LN} \cong$ $\overline{NM}$ $\cong$ $\overline{ML}$
6. Draw the midsegments in $\triangle ABC$. 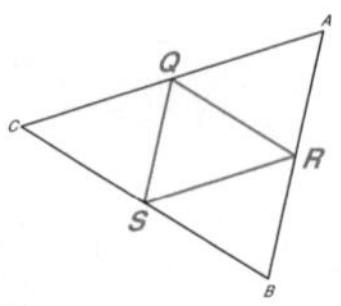
7. What are the names of the midsegments? Answers will vary based on students' choice of letters: $\overline{QR}$, $\overline{RS}$, $\overline{RQ}$.
8. What is the midsegment triangle? $\triangle QRS$

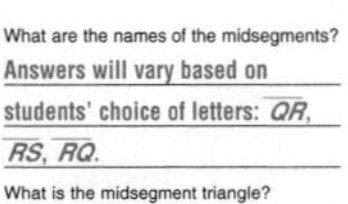

5-4 RETEACH

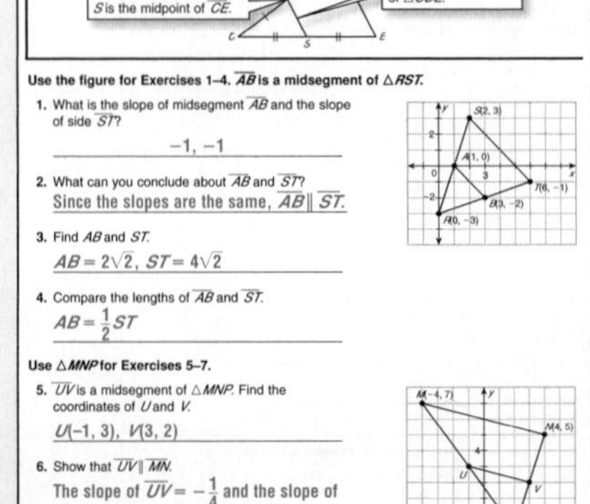

A **midsegment** of a triangle joins the midpoints of two sides of the triangle. Every triangle has three midsegments.

R is the midpoint of $\overline{CD}$.
S is the midpoint of $\overline{CE}$.

$\overline{RS}$ is a midsegment of $\triangle CDE$.

Use the figure for Exercises 1–4. $\overline{AB}$ is a midsegment of $\triangle RST$.

1. What is the slope of midsegment $\overline{AB}$ and the slope of side $\overline{ST}$? $-1, -1$
2. What can you conclude about $\overline{AB}$ and $\overline{ST}$? Since the slopes are the same, $\overline{AB} \parallel \overline{ST}$.
3. Find AB and ST. $AB = 2\sqrt{2}$, $ST = 4\sqrt{2}$
4. Compare the lengths of $\overline{AB}$ and $\overline{ST}$. $AB = \frac{1}{2}ST$

Use $\triangle MNP$ for Exercises 5–7.

5. $\overline{UV}$ is a midsegment of $\triangle MNP$. Find the coordinates of U and V. $U(-1, 3)$, $V(3, 2)$
6. Show that $\overline{UV} \parallel \overline{MN}$. The slope of $\overline{UV} = -\frac{1}{4}$ and the slope of $\overline{MN} = -\frac{1}{4}$. Since the slopes are the same, $\overline{UV} \parallel \overline{MN}$.

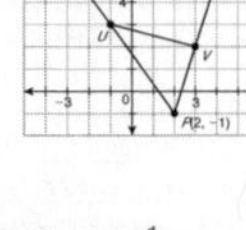

7. Show that $UV = \frac{1}{2}MN$. $UV = \sqrt{17}$ and $MN = 2\sqrt{17}$. Since $\sqrt{17} = \frac{1}{2}(2\sqrt{17})$, $UV = \frac{1}{2}MN$.

$\triangle QXY \cong \triangle XPZ \cong \triangle YZR \cong \triangle ZYX$; area of $\triangle XYZ = \frac{1}{4}$ (area of $\triangle PQR$)

46. $\triangle XYZ$ is the midsegment triangle of $\triangle PQR$. Write a congruence statement involving all four of the smaller triangles. What is the relationship between the area of $\triangle XYZ$ and $\triangle PQR$?

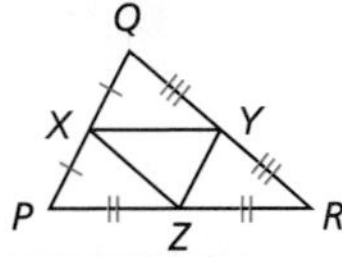

47. $\overline{AB}$ is a midsegment of $\triangle XYZ$. $\overline{CD}$ is a midsegment of $\triangle ABZ$. $\overline{EF}$ is a midsegment of $\triangle CDZ$, and $\overline{GH}$ is a midsegment of $\triangle EFZ$.

a. Copy and complete the table.

Number of Midsegment	1	2	3	4
Length of Midsegment	32	16	8	4

b. If this pattern continues, what will be the length of midsegment 8?

c. Write an algebraic expression to represent the length of midsegment n. (*Hint*: Think of the midsegment lengths as powers of 2.)

47b. $\frac{1}{4}$

47c. $64\left(\frac{1}{2}\right)^n = 2^{6-n}$

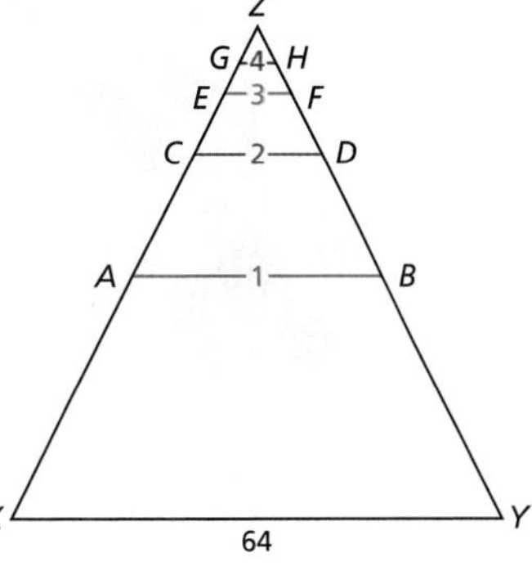

SPIRAL REVIEW

Suppose a 2% acid solution is mixed with a 3% acid solution. Find the percent of acid in each mixture. *(Previous course)*

48. a mixture that contains an equal amount of 2% acid solution and 3% acid solution 2.5%

49. a mixture that contains 3 times more 2% acid solution than 3% acid solution 2.25%

A figure has vertices $G(-3, -2)$, $H(0, 0)$, $J(4, 1)$, and $K(1, -2)$. Given the coordinates of the image of G under a translation, find the coordinates of the images of H, J, and K. *(Lesson 1-7)*

50. $(-3, 2)$ $(0, 4)$, $(4, 5)$, $(1, 2)$

51. $(1, -4)$ $(4, -2)$, $(8, -1)$, $(5, -4)$

52. $(3, 0)$ $(6, 2)$, $(10, 3)$, $(7, 0)$

Find each length. *(Lesson 5-3)*

53. NX 6

54. MR 8.25

55. NP 9

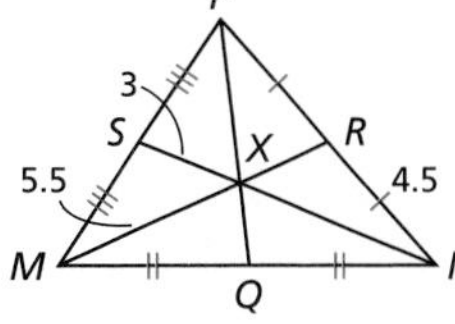

Construction Midsegment of a Triangle

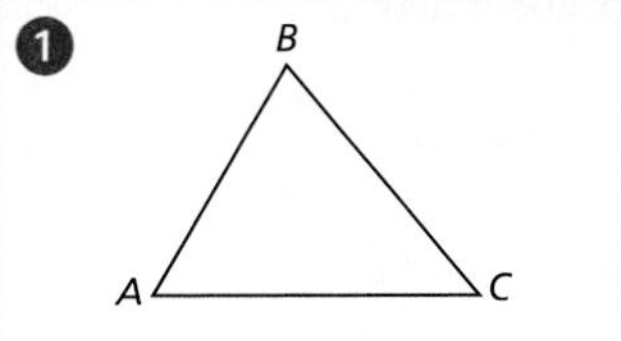

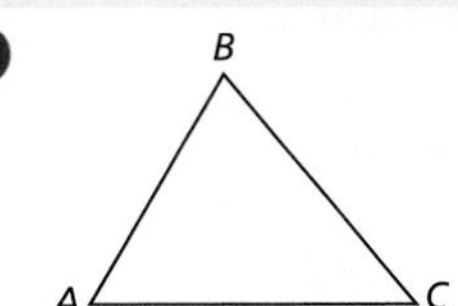

Draw a large triangle. Label the vertices A, B, and C.

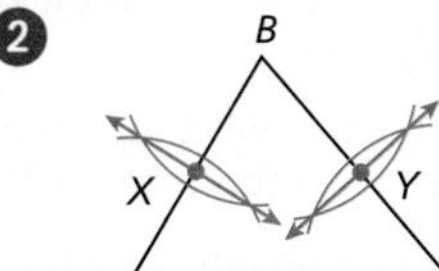

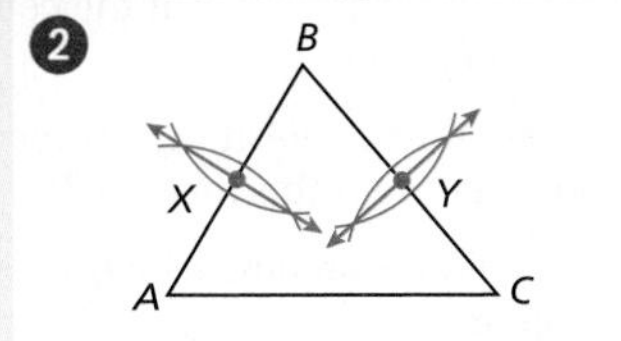

Construct the midpoints of $\overline{AB}$ and $\overline{BC}$. Label the midpoints X and Y, respectively.

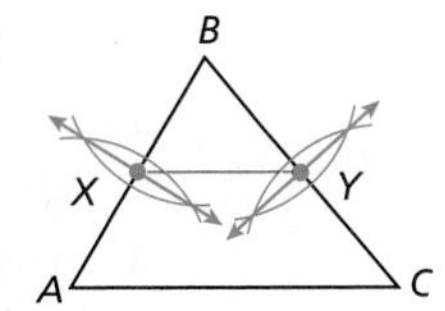

Draw the midsegment $\overline{XY}$.

1. Using a ruler, measure $\overline{XY}$ and $\overline{AC}$. How are the two lengths related? $XY = \frac{1}{2}AC$

2. How can you use a protractor to verify that $\overline{XY}$ is parallel to $\overline{AC}$?

5-4 PROBLEM SOLVING

1. The vertices of $\triangle JKL$ are $J(-9, 2)$, $K(10, 1)$, and $L(5, 6)$. $\overline{CD}$ is the midsegment parallel to $\overline{JK}$. What is the length of $\overline{CD}$? Round to the nearest tenth.

9.5

2. In $\triangle QRS$, $QR = 2x + 5$, $RS = 3x - 1$, and $SQ = 5x$. What is the perimeter of the midsegment triangle of $\triangle QRS$?

$5x + 2$

3. Is XY a midsegment of $\triangle LMN$ if its endpoints are $X(8, 2.5)$ and $Y(6.5, -2)$? Explain.

Yes; X is the midpoint of $\overline{LN}$, and Y is the midpoint of $\overline{ML}$.

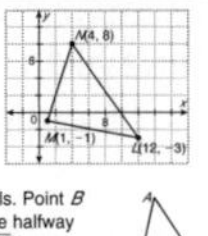

4. The diagram at right shows horseback riding trails. Point B is the halfway point along path $\overline{AC}$. Point D is the halfway point along path $\overline{CE}$. The paths along $\overline{BD}$ and $\overline{AE}$ are parallel. If riders travel from A to B to D to E, and then back to A, how far do they travel?

9.2 mi

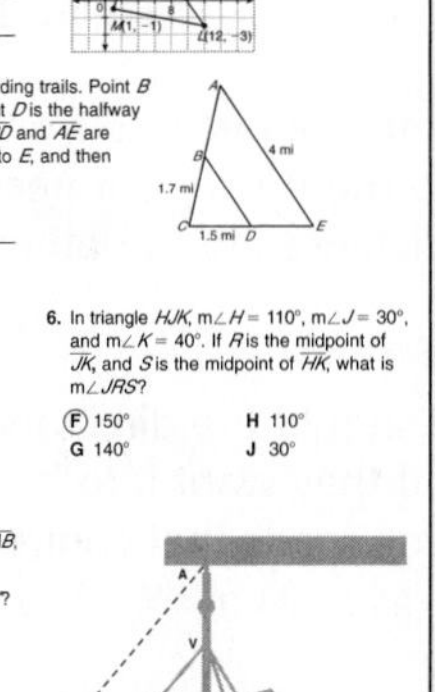

Choose the best answer.

5. Right triangle FGH has midsegments of length 10 centimeters, 24 centimeters, and 26 centimeters. What is the area of $\triangle FGH$?

A 60 cm² C 240 cm²
B 120 cm² (D) 480 cm²

6. In triangle HJK, $m\angle H = 110°$, $m\angle J = 30°$, and $m\angle K = 40°$. If R is the midpoint of $\overline{JK}$, and S is the midpoint of $\overline{HK}$, what is $m\angle JRS$?

(F) 150° H 110°
G 140° J 30°

Use the diagram for Exercises 7 and 8.

On the balance beam, V is the midpoint of $\overline{AB}$, and W is the midpoint of $\overline{YB}$.

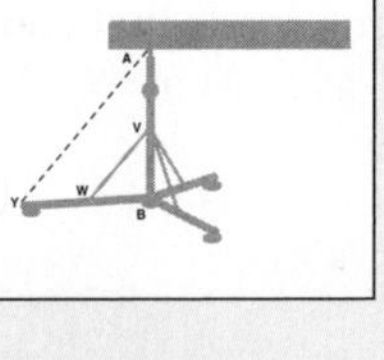

7. The length of $\overline{VW}$ is $1\frac{7}{8}$ feet. What is AY?

A $\frac{7}{8}$ ft (C) $3\frac{3}{4}$ ft
B $\frac{15}{16}$ ft D $7\frac{1}{2}$ ft

8. The measure of $\angle AYW$ is 50°. What is the measure of $\angle VWB$?

F 45° H 90°
(G) 50° J 130°

5-4 CHALLENGE

When solving a problem, it is sometimes necessary to consider more than one possible case. It is helpful to make a drawing of each case.

Triangle EFG is an isosceles triangle with $EF = FG$ and with the perimeter equal to 22 units. A midsegment, $\overline{QR}$, of $\triangle EFG$ is equal to 4 units.

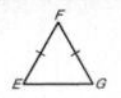

1. Describe two possible cases and make a drawing of each.

Case 1: The midsegment connects the two congruent sides $\overline{EF}$ and $\overline{FG}$.

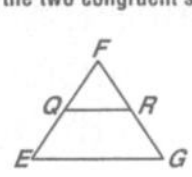

Case 2: The midsegment connects the base $\overline{EG}$ and one of the congruent sides of $\triangle EFG$.

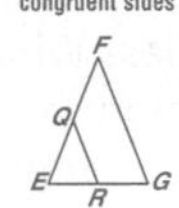

2. Find the lengths of the triangle's sides for each of the cases in Exercise 1.

case 1: $EF = FG = 7$ and $EG = 8$; case 2: $EF = FG = 8$ and $EG = 6$

Use $\triangle ABC$ for Exercises 4 and 5. A midsegment of the triangle is 9.

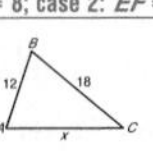

3. How many cases are there to consider when making a conclusion about the third side of the triangle? Explain.

Two cases; the midsegment joins the sides with lengths 12 and 18. The midsegment joins the side with lengths 12 and x.

4. Find the length of the third side of $\triangle ABC$ by considering both cases.

If the midsegment joins the sides with lengths 12 and 18, then the third side is 18. If the midsegment joins the side with lengths 12 and x, then it is impossible to find the length of the third side.

COMMON ERROR ALERT

In **Exercise 38,** students may think the slope of a horizontal line is undefined instead of 0. Remind them that a fraction with 0 in the numerator is equal to 0 but that the fraction is undefined when 0 is in the denominator.

Kinesthetic Have students use construction paper and cut out the four triangles in **Exercise 46.**

Journal

Have students explain how to find the length of a midsegment when given the length of the parallel side.

ALTERNATIVE ASSESSMENT

Have students use geometry software to construct the midsegment of a triangle. Have them measure the midsegment and the sides of the triangle. Ask them to use the angle measures to show that the midsegment is parallel to the third side of the triangle.

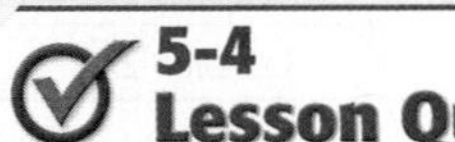

5-4 Lesson Quiz

Use the diagram for Items 1–3. Find each measure.

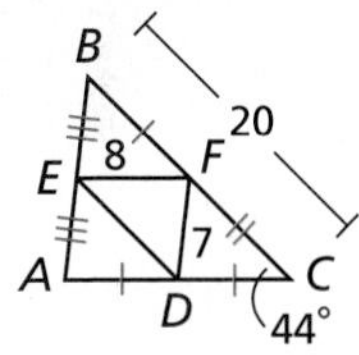

1. ED 10

2. AB 14

3. $m\angle BFE$ 44°

4. Find the value of n. 16

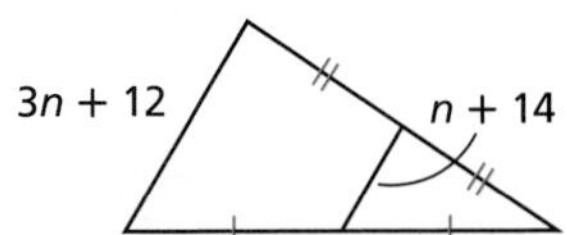

5. $\triangle XYZ$ is the midsegment triangle of $\triangle WUV$. What is the perimeter of $\triangle XYZ$? 11.5

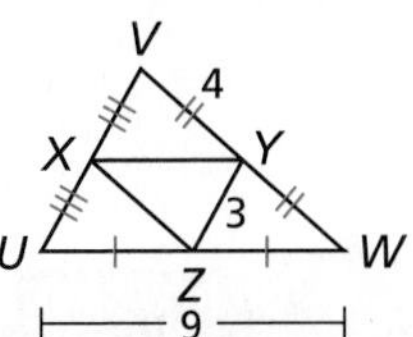

Also available on transparency

Organizer

Objective: Assess students' ability to apply concepts and skills in Lessons 5-1 through 5-4 in a real-world format.

 Online Edition

Resources

 ***Geometry Assessments***
www.mathtekstoolkit.org

Problem	Text Reference
1	Lesson 5-3
2	Lesson 5-3
3	Lesson 5-3
4	Lesson 5-3
5	Lesson 5-2
6	Lesson 5-2
7	Lesson 5-2

State Resources

CHAPTER 5

SECTION 5A

Segments in Triangles

Location Contemplation

A chain of music stores has locations in Ashville, Benton, and Carson. The directors of the company are using a coordinate plane to decide on the location for a new distribution warehouse. Each unit on the plane represents one mile.

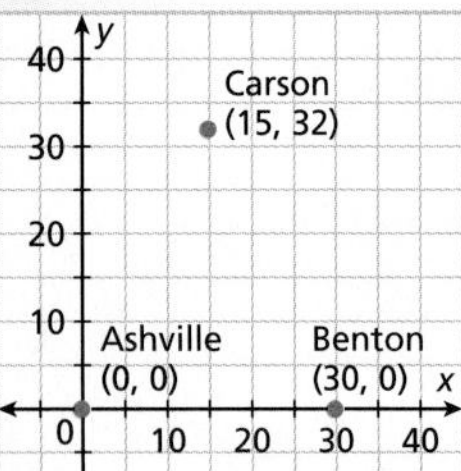

1. A plot of land is available at the centroid of the triangle formed by the three cities. What are the coordinates for this location? $\left(15, 10\frac{2}{3}\right)$
2. If the directors build the warehouse at the centroid, about how far will it be from each of the cities? **about 21.3 mi from Carson; about 18.4 mi from Benton and Ashville**
3. Another plot of land is available at the orthocenter of the triangle. What are the coordinates for this location? $\left(15, 7\frac{1}{32}\right)$
4. About how far would the warehouse be from each city if it were built at the orthocenter? **about 25 mi from Carson; about 16.6 mi from Benton and Ashville**
5. A third option is to build the warehouse at the circumcenter of the triangle. What are the coordinates for this location? $\left(15, 12\frac{31}{64}\right)$
6. About how far would the warehouse be from each city if it were built at the circumcenter? **about 19.5 mi from all 3 cities**
7. The directors decide that the warehouse should be equidistant from each city. Which location should they choose? **circumcenter**

INTERVENTION

Scaffolding Questions

1–2. What type of triangle is formed by the three cities? Which of the medians has an equation that is easy to find? isosc.; the median through Carson

3–4. What is the definition of orthocenter? Which of the altitudes has an equation that is easy to find? pt. of intersection of the altitudes; the altitude through Carson

5. How do you find the coordinates of the circumcenter? Find the pt. of intersection of the perp. bisectors of the sides.

6–7. What is always true about the circumcenter of a triangle? It is equidistant from the vertices of the △. Once you find the distance from the circumcenter to the origin, is it necessary to find the distances to the other vertices? No

Extension

Where should the directors place the warehouse if they want it to be equidistant from the three roads that connect the cities? at the incenter of the △

Quiz for Lessons 5-1 Through 5-4

5-1 Perpendicular and Angle Bisectors

Find each measure.

1. PQ 9.6

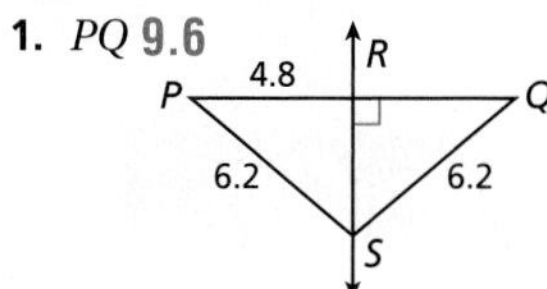

2. JM 58

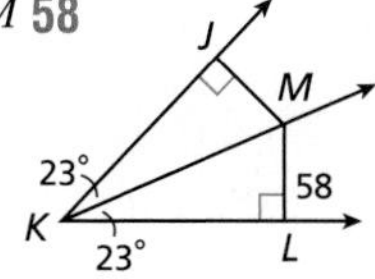

3. AC 51

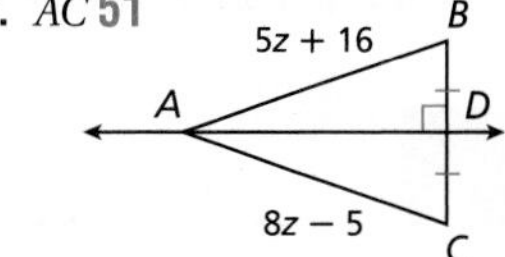

4. Write an equation in point-slope form for the perpendicular bisector of the segment with endpoints $M(-1, -3)$ and $N(7, 1)$. $y + 1 = -2(x - 3)$

5-2 Bisectors of Triangles

5. $\overline{PX}$, $\overline{PY}$, and $\overline{PZ}$ are the perpendicular bisectors of $\triangle RST$. Find PS and XT.

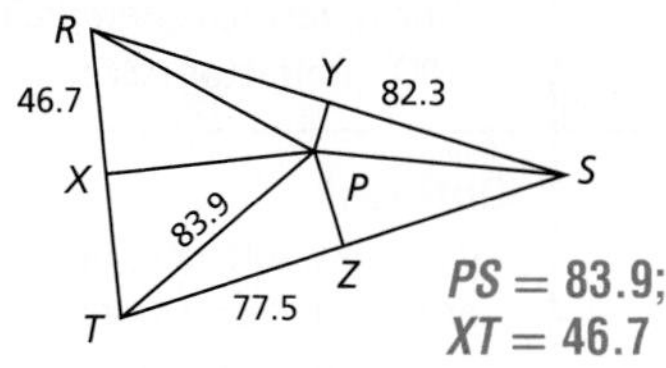

$PS = 83.9$; $XT = 46.7$

6. $\overline{JK}$ and $\overline{HK}$ are angle bisectors of $\triangle GHJ$. Find $m\angle GJK$ and the distance from K to $\overline{HJ}$.

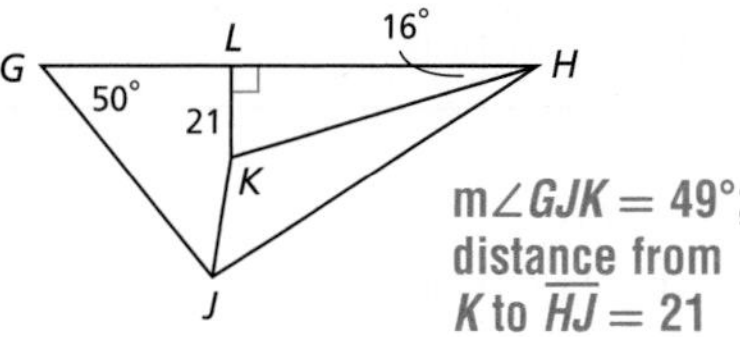

$m\angle GJK = 49°$; distance from K to $\overline{HJ} = 21$

7. Find the circumcenter of $\triangle TVO$ with vertices $T(9, 0)$, $V(0, -4)$, and $O(0, 0)$. $(4.5, -2)$

5-3 Medians and Altitudes of Triangles

8. In $\triangle DEF$, $BD = 87$, and $WE = 38$. Find BW, CW, and CE. $BW = 29$; $CW = 19$; $CE = 57$

9. Paula cuts a triangle with vertices at coordinates $(0, 4)$, $(8, 0)$, and $(10, 8)$ from grid paper. At what coordinates should she place the tip of a pencil to balance the triangle? $(6, 4)$

10. Find the orthocenter of $\triangle PSV$ with vertices $P(2, 4)$, $S(8, 4)$, and $V(4, 0)$. $(4, 2)$

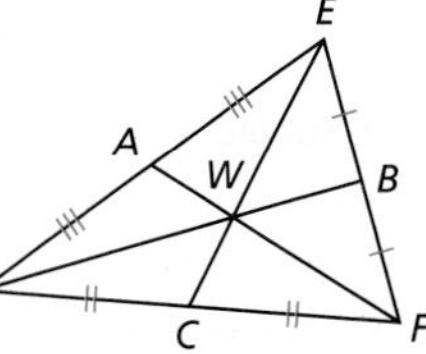

5-4 The Triangle Midsegment Theorem

11. Find ZV, PM, and $m\angle RZV$ in $\triangle JMP$. $ZV = 45$; $PM = 106$; $m\angle RZV = 36°$

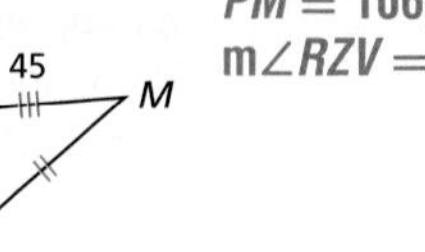

12. What is the distance XZ across the pond? 78 m

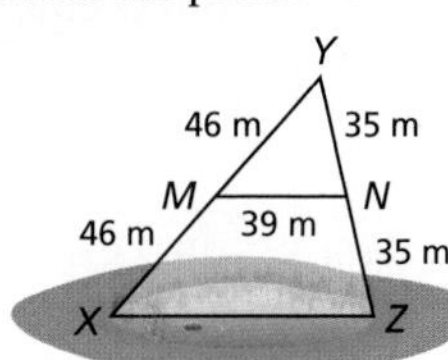

Organizer

Objective: Assess students' mastery of concepts and skills in Lessons 5-1 through 5-4.

Resources

 ***Assessment Resources***

Section 5A Quiz

Teacher One Stop™

Test & Practice Generator

INTERVENTION

Resources

 ***Ready to Go On? Intervention and Enrichment* Worksheets**

 ***Ready to Go On?* CD-ROM**

 ***Ready to Go On?* Online**

my.hrw.com

READY TO GO ON? Diagnose and Prescribe

NO — INTERVENE

Ready to Go On? Intervention	Ready to Go On? Intervention, Section 5A: Worksheets	CD-ROM	Online
Lesson 5-1	5-1 Intervention	Activity 5-1	Diagnose and Prescribe Online
Lesson 5-2	5-2 Intervention	Activity 5-2	
Lesson 5-3	5-3 Intervention	Activity 5-3	
Lesson 5-4	5-4 Intervention	Activity 5-4	

YES — ENRICH

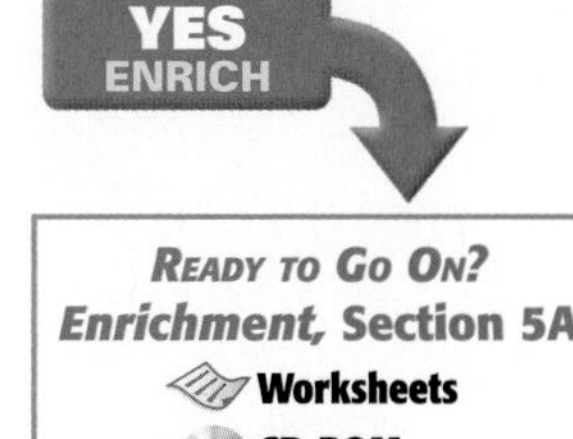

***Ready to Go On? Enrichment,* Section 5A**

Worksheets

CD-ROM

Online

SECTION 5B

Relationships in Triangles

One-Minute Section Planner

Lesson	Lab Resources	Materials
5-5 Geometry Lab Explore Triangle Inequalities • Explore the relationships between side lengths and angle measures in a triangle. ☐ SAT-10 ☑ NAEP ☑ ACT ☐ SAT ☐ SAT Subject Tests	***Geometry Lab Activities*** 5-5 Lab Recording Sheet	**Required** protractor (MK), ruler (MK), straws
Lesson 5-5 Indirect Proof and Inequalities in One Triangle • Write indirect proofs. • Apply inequalities in one triangle. ☐ SAT-10 ☑ NAEP ☑ ACT ☐ SAT ☐ SAT Subject Tests		**Optional** geometry software, colored pencils, raw spaghetti, ruler (MK), protractor (MK)
Lesson 5-6 Inequalities in Two Triangles • Apply inequalities in two triangles. ☐ SAT-10 ☑ NAEP ☑ ACT ☐ SAT ☐ SAT Subject Tests		**Optional** geometry software, book or scissors, straws or raw spaghetti, ruler (MK), protractor (MK), colored pencils
5-7 Geometry Lab Hands-on Proof of the Pythagorean Theorem • Use area to justify the Pythagorean Theorem. ☑ SAT-10 ☐ NAEP ☐ ACT ☑ SAT ☐ SAT Subject Tests	***Geometry Lab Activities*** 5-7 Lab Recording Sheet	**Required** graph paper, scissors **Optional** transparency
Lesson 5-7 The Pythagorean Theorem • Use the Pythagorean Theorem and its converse to solve problems. • Use Pythagorean inequalities to classify triangles. ☑ SAT-10 ☑ NAEP ☐ ACT ☑ SAT ☐ SAT Subject Tests	***Technology Lab Activities*** 5-7 Technology Lab	**Optional** geometry software, straws or raw spaghetti, protractor (MK), ruler (MK)
Lesson 5-8 Applying Special Right Triangles • Justify and apply properties of 45°-45°-90° triangles. • Justify and apply properties of 30°-60°-90° triangles. ☑ SAT-10 ☑ NAEP ☑ ACT ☑ SAT ☐ SAT Subject Tests	***Geometry Lab Activities*** 5-8 Geometry Lab	**Optional** 45°-45°-45° plastic triangle (MK), 30°-60°-90° plastic triangle (MK), geometry software, protractor (MK), ruler (MK)
5-8 Geometry Lab Graph Irrational Numbers • Graph irrational numbers on a number line. ☐ SAT-10 ☑ NAEP ☐ ACT ☐ SAT ☐ SAT Subject Tests	***Geometry Lab Activities*** 5-8 Lab Recording Sheet	**Required** compass (MK), straightedge (MK)

MK = *Manipulatives Kit*

Math Background

Professional Learning

THE TRIANGLE INEQUALITY

Lesson 5-5

The Triangle Inequality is the mathematical statement of a well-known fact: the shortest path between two points is a straight line. In the case of a triangle with vertices *A*, *B*, and *C*, the straight path from *A* to *B* is shorter than the path that includes a detour to point *C*. In other words, $AB < AC + BC$.

One can use the Triangle Inequality to find other useful results. For example, consider a triangle with sides of length *a*, *b*, and *c*.

$a < b + c$	*Triangle Inequality*
$2a < a + b + c$	*Addition Property of Equality*
$a < \dfrac{a+b+c}{2}$	*Division Property of Equality*

This last inequality demonstrates that the length of any side of a triangle is less than half the perimeter of the triangle.

A similar type of argument shows that the sum of the lengths of the diagonals of any quadrilateral is less than the perimeter of the quadrilateral. Specifically, in quadrilateral *ABCD*, four applications of the Triangle Inequality yield the four inequalities shown below.

$AC < AB + BC$

$AC < AD + CD$

$BD < AD + AB$

$BD < CD + BC$

Adding the four inequalities above gives $2(AC + BD) < 2AB + 2BC + 2CD + 2AD$, and dividing both sides of this inequality by 2 proves the result.

THE PYTHAGOREAN THEOREM

Lesson 5-7

The Pythagorean Theorem, one of the best-known relationships in mathematics, can be traced back almost as far as recorded history itself. Most of the early appearances of the theorem occur in the form of Pythagorean triples (sets of three nonzero whole numbers *a*, *b*, and *c* such that $a^2 + b^2 = c^2$). One example is the clay tablet known as Plimpton 322, which was written in Babylonia around 1800 B.C.E.; it contains 15 rows of numbers based on Pythagorean triples.

Such archaeological findings show that the relationship was known long before the time of the Greek mathematician Pythagoras (c. 582 B.C.E. – 507 B.C.E.); it is because of the work of later Greek and Roman historians that the theorem has come to bear Pythagoras's name. Regardless of its beginnings, the theorem has continued to inspire both professional and amateur mathematicians because of its elegance and adaptability to diverse methods of proof. In fact, *The Pythagorean Proposition* by Elisha Scott Loomis presents more than 350 different proofs of the Pythagorean Theorem!

The proof of the Pythagorean Theorem that is given in Chapter 5 of this text uses a standard area argument. It is worthwhile to revisit the proof once students have studied similarity. Drawing the altitude to the hypotenuse of a right triangle creates two smaller right triangles as shown. It is straightforward to prove that the small right triangles are similar to each other and to the original right triangle. By writing proportions that compare side lengths, it follows that $a^2 = xc$ and $b^2 = yc$. Thus, $a^2 + b^2 = xc + yc = (x + y)c = c^2$.

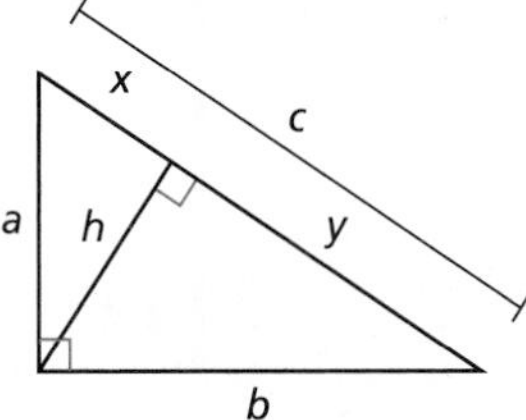

All proofs of the Pythagorean Theorem depend on the Parallel Postulate or on one of the consequences of the postulate. In fact, it can be shown that the Pythagorean Theorem is equivalent to the Parallel Postulate. That is, the Pythagorean Theorem may be taken as an axiom in place of the Parallel Postulate, and within this new logical system the Parallel Postulate may be proved as a theorem.

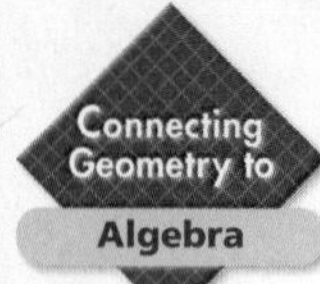

Organizer

Pacing:
Traditional $\frac{1}{2}$ day
Block $\frac{1}{4}$ day

Objective: Apply algebra skills to solving compound inequalities.

Online Edition

Countdown Week 11

Teach

Remember

Students review how to solve compound inequalities.

Number Sense Have students write a numeric inequality, such as 10 > 2. Have them add and subtract positive and negative numbers from each side. Repeat this exercise with multiplication and division so students can see that they must reverse the inequality symbol when multiplying or dividing by a negative number.

Close

Assess

Have students write a compound inequality and present their solutions to the class.

State Resources

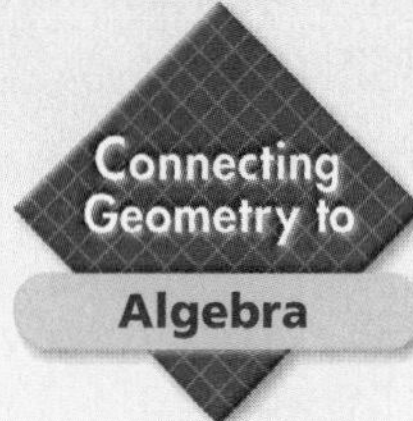

Solving Compound Inequalities

To solve an inequality, you use the Properties of Inequality and inverse operations to undo the operations in the inequality one at a time.

Properties of Inequality

PROPERTY	ALGEBRA
Addition Property	If $a < b$, then $a + c < b + c$.
Subtraction Property	If $a < b$, then $a - c < b - c$.
Multiplication Property	If $a < b$ and $c > 0$, then $ac < bc$. If $a < b$ and $c < 0$, then $ac > bc$.
Division Property	If $a < b$ and $c > 0$, then $\frac{a}{c} < \frac{b}{c}$. If $a < b$ and $c < 0$, then $\frac{a}{c} > \frac{b}{c}$.
Transitive Property	If $a < b$ and $b < c$, then $a < c$.
Comparison Property	If $a + b = c$ and $b > 0$, then $a < c$.

A compound inequality is formed when two simple inequalities are combined into one statement with the word *and* or *or*. To solve a compound inequality, solve each simple inequality and find the intersection or union of the solutions. The graph of a compound inequality may represent a line, a ray, two rays, or a segment.

Example

Solve the compound inequality $5 < 20 - 3a \leq 11$. What geometric figure does the graph represent?

$5 < 20 - 3a$	AND	$20 - 3a \leq 11$	*Rewrite the compound inequality as two simple inequalities.*
$-15 < -3a$	AND	$-3a \leq -9$	*Subtract 20 from both sides.*
$5 > a$	AND	$a \geq 3$	*Divide both sides by −3 and reverse the inequality symbols.*
	$3 \leq a < 5$		*Combine the two solutions into a single statement.*

The graph represents a segment.

Try This

Solve. What geometric figure does each graph represent?

1. $-4 + x > 1$ OR $-8 + 2x < -6$ **$x < 1$ OR $x > 5$; 2 rays**

2. $2x - 3 \geq -5$ OR $x - 4 > -1$ **$x \geq -1$; ray**

3. $-6 < 7 - x \leq 12$ **$-5 \leq x < 13$; segment**

4. $22 < -2 - 2x \leq 54$ **$-28 \leq x < -12$; segment**

5. $3x \geq 0$ OR $x + 5 < 7$ **all real numbers; line**

6. $2x - 3 \leq 5$ OR $-2x + 3 \leq -9$ **$x \leq 4$ OR $x \geq 6$; 2 rays**

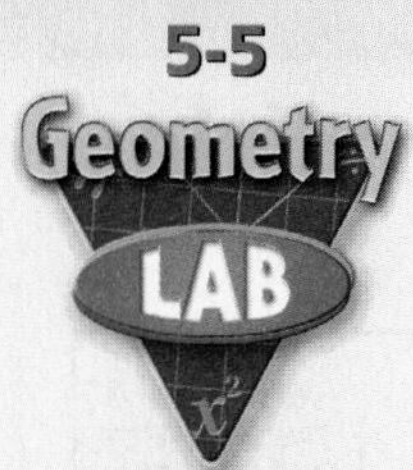

Explore Triangle Inequalities

Many of the triangle relationships you have learned so far involve a statement of equality. For example, the circumcenter of a triangle is equidistant from the vertices of the triangle, and the incenter is equidistant from the sides of the triangle. Now you will investigate some triangle relationships that involve inequalities.

Use with Lesson 5-5

Activity 1

1. Draw a large scalene triangle. Label the vertices *A*, *B*, and *C*.
2. Measure the sides and the angles. Copy the table below and record the measures in the first row.

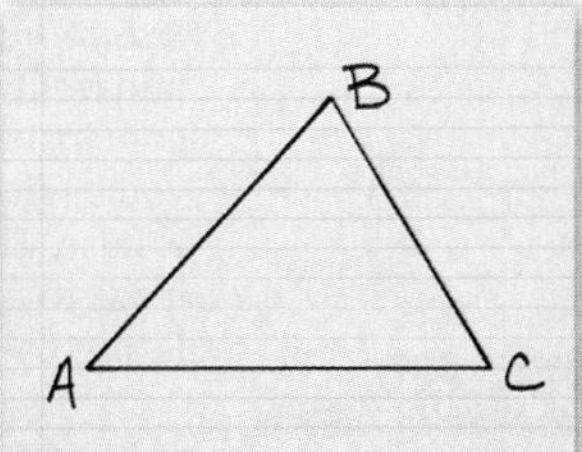

	BC	*AC*	*AB*	$m\angle A$	$m\angle B$	$m\angle C$
Triangle 1						
Triangle 2						
Triangle 3						
Triangle 4						

Try This

1. In the table, draw a circle around the longest side length, and draw a circle around the greatest angle measure of $\triangle ABC$. Draw a square around the shortest side length, and draw a square around the least angle measure. **Check students' work.**
2. **Make a Conjecture** Where is the longest side in relation to the largest angle? Where is the shortest side in relation to the smallest angle?
3. Draw three more scalene triangles and record the measures in the table. Does your conjecture hold? **Check students' work.**

Activity 2

1. Cut three sets of chenille stems to the following lengths.
   3 inches, 4 inches, 6 inches
   3 inches, 4 inches, 7 inches
   3 inches, 4 inches, 8 inches
2. Try to make a triangle with each set of chenille stems.

Try This

4. Which sets of chenille stems make a triangle? **only the set with lengths 3 in., 4 in., and 6 in.**
5. **Make a Conjecture** For each set of chenille stems, compare the sum of any two lengths with the third length. What is the relationship?
6. Select a different set of three lengths and test your conjecture. Does your conjecture hold? **Check students' work.**

Teacher to Teacher

For **Activity 2** of this lab, students can also use raw spaghetti. Have them break it into pieces of different lengths, figure out which sets of 3 pieces make a triangle, and then measure their lengths. Students can then find out which sets of 3 pieces *cannot* make a triangle and measure those lengths.

Another idea for this activity is to copy ruler markings onto paper strips and cut those into pieces. Then the lengths of the pieces are visible as students are trying to build the triangles.

Robert Brouhle
Huntington Beach, CA

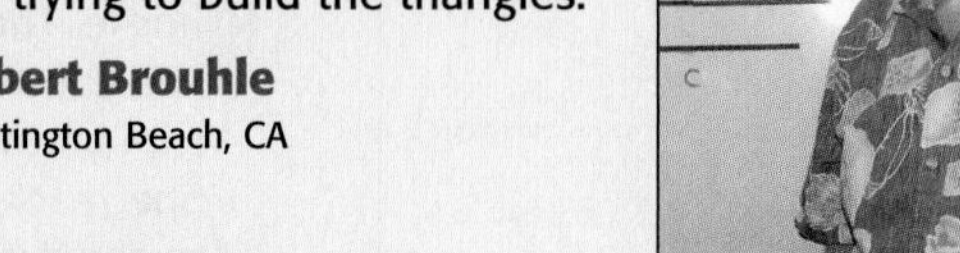

Organizer

Use with Lesson 5-5

Pacing:
Traditional $\frac{1}{2}$ day
Block $\frac{1}{4}$ day

Objective: Explore the relationships between side lengths and angle measures in a triangle.

Materials: protractor, ruler, straws

Online Edition

Resources

Geometry Lab Activities
5-5 Lab Recording Sheet

Teach

Discuss

Discuss with students how the side lengths of a triangle are related to the angle measures and to each other.

Close

Key Concept

The larger angle of a triangle is opposite the longer side and vice versa. The sum of any two sides of a triangle is greater than the third side.

Assessment

Journal Have students draw and label a triangle and then write three inequalities to represent the possible side lengths.

Answers to *Try This*

2, 5. See p. A19.

State Resources

5-5 Organizer

Pacing: Traditional 1 day
Block $\frac{1}{2}$ day

Objectives: Write indirect proofs.
Apply inequalities in one triangle.

Online Edition
Tutorial Videos

Countdown Week 11

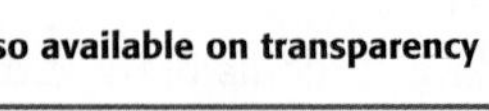

Power Presentations with PowerPoint®

Warm Up

1. Write a conditional from the sentence "An isosceles triangle has two congruent sides." If a △ is isosc., then it has 2 ≅ sides.
2. Write the contrapositive of the conditional "If it is Tuesday, then John has a piano lesson." If John does not have a piano lesson, then it is not Tuesday.
3. Show that the conjecture "If $x > 6$, then $2x > 14$" is false by finding a counterexample. $x = 7$

Also available on transparency

Math Humor

Q: What do you call a prisoner's poem?
A: A converse

5-5 Indirect Proof and Inequalities in One Triangle

Objectives
Write indirect proofs.
Apply inequalities in one triangle.

Vocabulary
indirect proof

Why learn this?
You can use a triangle inequality to find a reasonable range of values for an unknown distance. (See Example 5.)

Getting in shape for the Summer Olympics.

So far you have written proofs using *direct reasoning*. You began with a true hypothesis and built a logical argument to show that a conclusion was true. In an **indirect proof**, you begin by assuming that the conclusion is false. Then you show that this assumption leads to a contradiction. This type of proof is also called a *proof by contradiction*.

Helpful Hint
When writing an indirect proof, look for a contradiction of one of the following: the given information, a definition, a postulate, or a theorem.

Writing an Indirect Proof
1. Identify the conjecture to be proven.
2. Assume the opposite (the negation) of the conclusion is true.
3. Use direct reasoning to show that the assumption leads to a contradiction.
4. Conclude that since the assumption is false, the original conjecture must be true.

EXAMPLE 1 Writing an Indirect Proof

Write an indirect proof that a right triangle cannot have an obtuse angle.

Step 1 Identify the conjecture to be proven.
Given: $\triangle JKL$ is a right triangle.
Prove: $\triangle JKL$ does not have an obtuse angle.

Step 2 Assume the opposite of the conclusion.
Assume $\triangle JKL$ has an obtuse angle. Let $\angle K$ be obtuse.

Step 3 Use direct reasoning to lead to a contradiction.

$m\angle K + m\angle L = 90°$	*The acute ∠s of a rt. △ are comp.*
$m\angle K = 90° - m\angle L$	*Subtr. Prop. of =*
$m\angle K > 90°$	*Def. of obtuse ∠*
$90° - m\angle L > 90°$	*Substitute 90° − m∠L for m∠K.*
$m\angle L < 0°$	*Subtract 90° from both sides and solve for m∠L.*

However, by the Protractor Postulate, a triangle cannot have an angle with a measure less than 0°.

Step 4 Conclude that the original conjecture is true.
The assumption that $\triangle JKL$ has an obtuse angle is false.
Therefore $\triangle JKL$ does not have an obtuse angle.

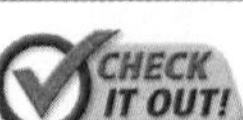

CHECK IT OUT! 1. Write an indirect proof that a triangle cannot have two right angles.

State Resources

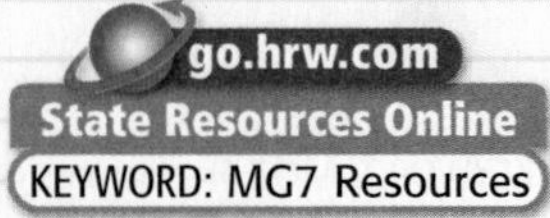

go.hrw.com
State Resources Online
KEYWORD: MG7 Resources

1 Introduce

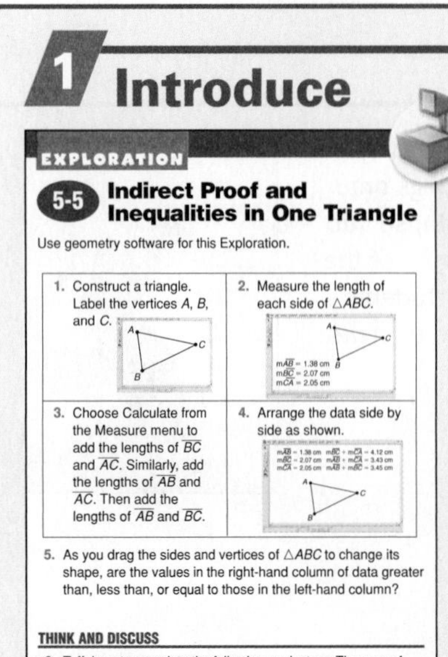

EXPLORATION
5-5 Indirect Proof and Inequalities in One Triangle
Use geometry software for this Exploration.
1. Construct a triangle. Label the vertices A, B, and C.
2. Measure the length of each side of △ABC.
3. Choose Calculate from the Measure menu to add the lengths of $\overline{BC}$ and $\overline{AC}$. Similarly, add the lengths of $\overline{AB}$ and $\overline{AC}$. Then add the lengths of $\overline{AB}$ and $\overline{BC}$.
4. Arrange the data side by side as shown.
5. As you drag the sides and vertices of △ABC to change its shape, are the values in the right-hand column of data greater than, less than, or equal to those in the left-hand column?
THINK AND DISCUSS

Motivate

Present the following scenario to students: Janet arrives home and wonders if her brother is already there. She knows that he always picks up the newspaper from the porch when he gets home. The newspaper is still on the porch, so she concludes that her brother is not yet home. Explain that Janet has used indirect reasoning. She reaches her conclusion without going inside to see if her brother is home.

Explorations and answers are provided in *Alternate Openers: Explorations Transparencies*.

The positions of the longest and shortest sides of a triangle are related to the positions of the largest and smallest angles.

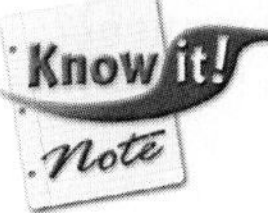

Theorems Angle-Side Relationships in Triangles

THEOREM	HYPOTHESIS	CONCLUSION
5-5-1 If two sides of a triangle are not congruent, then the larger angle is opposite the longer side. (In △, larger ∠ is opp. longer side.)	$AB > BC$	$m\angle C > m\angle A$
5-5-2 If two angles of a triangle are not congruent, then the longer side is opposite the larger angle. (In △, longer side is opp. larger ∠.)	$m\angle Z > m\angle Y$	$XY > XZ$

You will prove Theorem 5-5-1 in Exercise 67.

PROOF

Theorem 5-5-2

Given: $m\angle P > m\angle R$
Prove: $QR > QP$

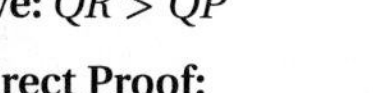

Indirect Proof:
Assume $QR \not> QP$. This means that either $QR < QP$ or $QR = QP$.

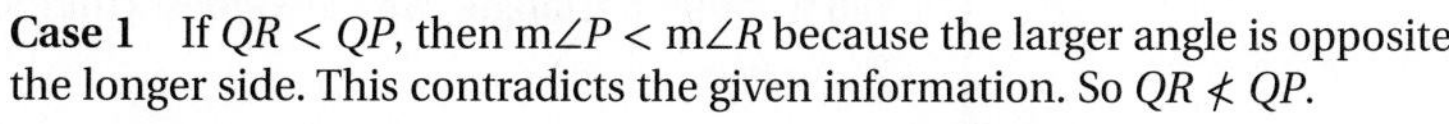

Case 1 If $QR < QP$, then $m\angle P < m\angle R$ because the larger angle is opposite the longer side. This contradicts the given information. So $QR \not< QP$.

Case 2 If $QR = QP$, then $m\angle P = m\angle R$ by the Isosceles Triangle Theorem. This also contradicts the given information, so $QR \neq QP$.

The assumption $QR \not> QP$ is false. Therefore $QR > QP$.

Caution!

Consider all cases when you assume the opposite. If the conclusion is $QR > QP$, the negation includes $QR < QP$ and $QR = QP$.

EXAMPLE 2 **Ordering Triangle Side Lengths and Angle Measures**

A **Write the angles in order from smallest to largest.**

The shortest side is $\overline{GJ}$, so the smallest angle is $\angle H$.
The longest side is $\overline{HJ}$, so the largest angle is $\angle G$.
The angles from smallest to largest are $\angle H$, $\angle J$, and $\angle G$.

B **Write the sides in order from shortest to longest.**

$m\angle M = 180° - (39° + 54°) = 87°$ *△ Sum Thm.*
The smallest angle is $\angle L$, so the shortest side is $\overline{KM}$.
The largest angle is $\angle M$, so the longest side is $\overline{KL}$.
The sides from shortest to longest are $\overline{KM}$, $\overline{LM}$, and $\overline{KL}$.

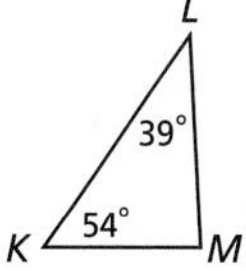

2a. Write the angles in order from smallest to largest.

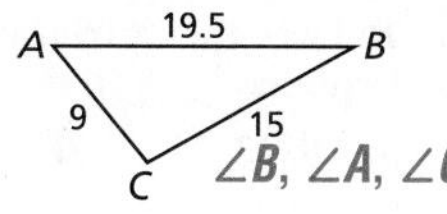

∠B, ∠A, ∠C

2b. Write the sides in order from shortest to longest.

$\overline{EF}$, $\overline{DF}$, $\overline{DE}$

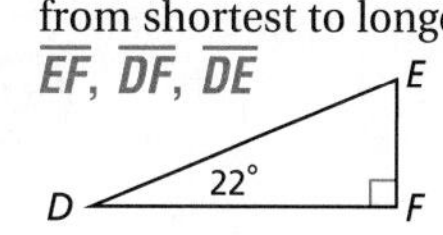

2 Teach

Guided Instruction

Remind students that a conditional statement is logically equivalent to its contrapositive. Have students practice writing negations and identifying statements that contradict each other. Explain the steps for an indirect proof. Point out that problems containing the word *not* are good candidates for an indirect proof. Discuss angle and side relationships in triangles and how to apply the Triangle Inequality Theorem.

Reaching All Learners

Through Visual Cues

Use colors to identify the steps in an indirect proof. Write each of the four steps on page 332 in a different color. Then place colored boxes around the parts of the proof that correspond to each step. For example, write the step "Assume the opposite of the conclusion is true" in blue and put a blue box around the assumption made in the indirect proof.

COMMON ERROR ALERT

Remind students not to assume the opposite of the Given statement. Carefully review what should be assumed when writing an indirect proof.

Power Presentations with PowerPoint®

Additional Examples

Example 1

Write an indirect proof that if $a > 0$, then $\frac{1}{a} > 0$.

Given: $a > 0$

Prove: $\frac{1}{a} > 0$

Proof: Assume $\frac{1}{a} \leq 0$. It is given that $a > 0$, so $a\left(\frac{1}{a}\right) \leq a(0)$. This simplifies to $1 \leq 0$, which is false. Therefore the assumption that $\frac{1}{a} \leq 0$ must be false, and thus $\frac{1}{a} > 0$.

Example 2

A. Write the angles in order from smallest to largest. *∠F, ∠H, ∠G*

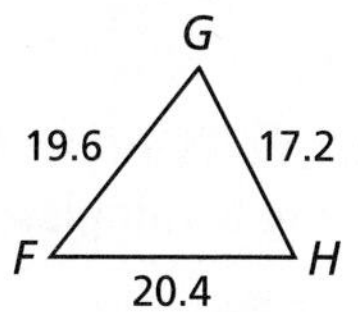

B. Write the sides in order from shortest to longest. *$\overline{PQ}$, $\overline{QR}$, $\overline{PR}$*

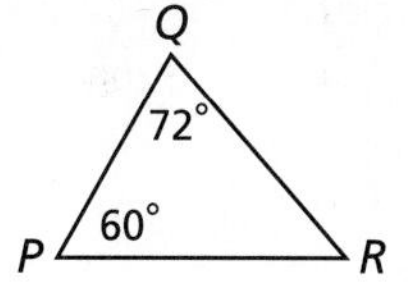

INTERVENTION

Questioning Strategies

EXAMPLE 1

- What is the negation?
- What is the contradiction?

EXAMPLE 2

- How do you order the sides or angles of a triangle?

Answers to Check It Out!

1. See p. A19.

Teaching Tip **Kinesthetic** Give students pieces of raw spaghetti and have them break three pieces of different lengths. Have them try to form a triangle with the pieces. Then have them apply the Triangle Inequality Theorem to their pieces.

Power Presentations with PowerPoint®

Additional Examples

Example 3

Tell whether a triangle can have sides with the given lengths. Explain.

A. 7, 10, 19 No; 7 + 10 is not greater than 19. By the △ Inequal. Thm., a △ cannot have these side lengths.

B. 2.3, 3.1, 4.6 Yes; the sum of each pair of 2 lengths is greater than the third length.

C. $n + 6$, $n^2 - 1$, $3n$, when $n = 4$ Yes; the sides are 10, 15, and 12. The sum of each pair of 2 lengths is greater than the third length.

INTERVENTION
Questioning Strategies

EXAMPLE 3

- How do you decide if three lengths can be the side lengths of a triangle?

A triangle is formed by three segments, but not every set of three segments can form a triangle.

Segments with lengths of 7, 4, and 4 can form a triangle.

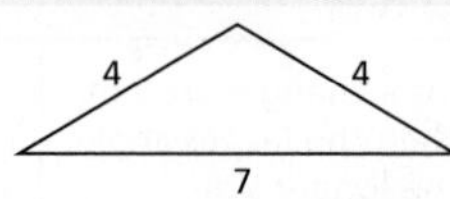

Segments with lengths of 7, 3, and 3 cannot form a triangle.

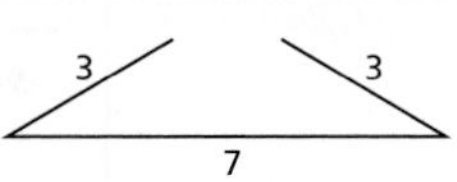

A certain relationship must exist among the lengths of three segments in order for them to form a triangle.

Theorem 5-5-3 **Triangle Inequality Theorem**

The sum of any two side lengths of a triangle is greater than the third side length.

$AB + BC > AC$
$BC + AC > AB$
$AC + AB > BC$

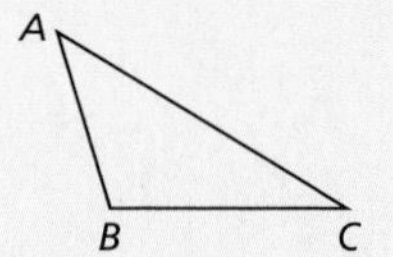

You will prove Theorem 5-5-3 in Exercise 68.

EXAMPLE 3 Applying the Triangle Inequality Theorem

Tell whether a triangle can have sides with the given lengths. Explain.

A 3, 5, 7

$3 + 5 \overset{?}{>} 7$ $8 > 7$ ✓
$3 + 7 \overset{?}{>} 5$ $10 > 5$ ✓
$5 + 7 \overset{?}{>} 3$ $12 > 3$ ✓

Yes—the sum of each pair of lengths is greater than the third length.

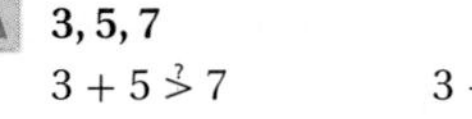

Helpful Hint

To show that three lengths cannot be the side lengths of a triangle, you only need to show that one of the three triangle inequalities is false.

B 4, 6.5, 11

$4 + 6.5 \overset{?}{>} 11$
$10.5 \not> 11$

No—by the Triangle Inequality Theorem, a triangle cannot have these side lengths.

C $n + 5$, n^2, $2n$, when $n = 3$

Step 1 Evaluate each expression when $n = 3$.

$n + 5$	n^2	$2n$
$3 + 5$	3^2	$2(3)$
8	9	6

Step 2 Compare the lengths.

$8 + 9 \overset{?}{>} 6$ $17 > 6$ ✓
$8 + 6 \overset{?}{>} 9$ $14 > 9$ ✓
$9 + 6 \overset{?}{>} 8$ $15 > 8$ ✓

Yes—the sum of each pair of lengths is greater than the third length.

CHECK IT OUT! **Tell whether a triangle can have sides with the given lengths. Explain.**

3a. 8, 13, 21 **3b.** 6.2, 7, 9 **3c.** $t - 2$, $4t$, $t^2 + 1$, when $t = 4$

3a. No; 8 + 13 = 21, which is not greater than the third side length.
3b. Yes; the sum of each pair of 2 lengths is greater than the third length.

Answers to *Check It Out!*

3c. Yes; when $t = 4$, the value of $t - 2$ is 2, the value of $4t$ is 16, and the value of $t^2 + 1$ is 17. The sum of each pair of 2 lengths is greater than the third length.

EXAMPLE 4 **Finding Side Lengths**

The lengths of two sides of a triangle are 6 centimeters and 11 centimeters. Find the range of possible lengths for the third side.

Let s represent the length of the third side. Then apply the Triangle Inequality Theorem.

$s + 6 > 11$	$s + 11 > 6$	$6 + 11 > s$
$s > 5$	$s > -5$	$17 > s$

Combine the inequalities. So $5 < s < 17$. The length of the third side is greater than 5 centimeters and less than 17 centimeters.

4. The lengths of two sides of a triangle are 22 inches and 17 inches. Find the range of possible lengths for the third side. **greater than 5 in. and less than 39 in.**

EXAMPLE 5 ***Travel Application***

The map shows the approximate distances from San Antonio to Mason and from San Antonio to Austin. What is the range of distances from Mason to Austin?

Let d be the distance from Mason to Austin.

$d + 111 > 78$	$d + 78 > 111$	$111 + 78 > d$	*△ Inequal. Thm.*
$d > -33$	$d > 33$	$189 > d$	*Subtr. Prop. of Inequal.*
	$33 < d < 189$		*Combine the inequalities.*

The distance from Mason to Austin is greater than 33 miles and less than 189 miles.

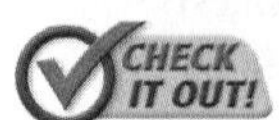

5. The distance from San Marcos to Johnson City is 50 miles, and the distance from Seguin to San Marcos is 22 miles. What is the range of distances from Seguin to Johnson City? **28 mi < d < 72 mi**

THINK AND DISCUSS

1. To write an indirect proof that an angle is obtuse, a student assumes that the angle is acute. Is this the correct assumption? Explain.

2. Give an example of three measures that can be the lengths of the sides of a triangle. Give an example of three lengths that cannot be the sides of a triangle.

3. GET ORGANIZED Copy and complete the graphic organizer. In each box, explain what you know about $\triangle ABC$ as a result of the theorem.

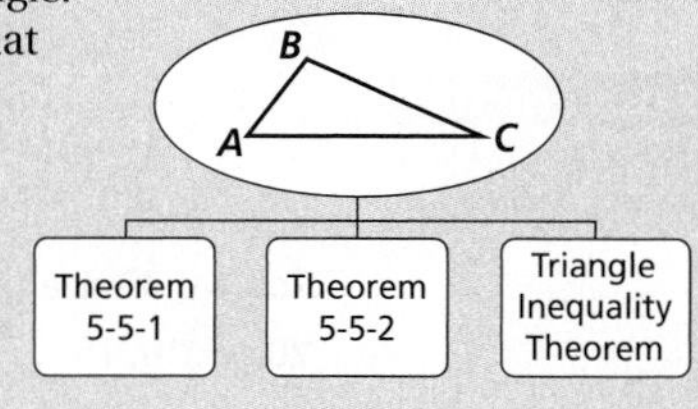

COMMON ERROR ALERT

If students have trouble with compound inequalities, have them write the inequalities separately and then use a number line to combine them into one.

Power Presentations with PowerPoint®

Additional Examples

Example 4

The lengths of two sides of a triangle are 8 in. and 13 in. Find the range of possible lengths for the third side. 5 in. < x < 21 in.

Example 5

The figure shows the approximate distances between cities in California. What is the range of distances from San Francisco to Oakland? 5 mi < x < 97 mi

San Francisco x Oakland
51 mi 46 mi
San Jose

INTERVENTION
Questioning Strategies

EXAMPLE 4

- How do you find the range for the length of the third side of a triangle?

EXAMPLE 5

- Could you find a range of distances between the cities if they were in a straight line? Explain.

3 Close

Summarize

Review the process of an indirect proof: You begin by assuming the opposite of the desired conclusion, and then you write the proof until you reach a contradiction. Review the angle and side relationships in a triangle and the Triangle Inequality Theorem.

and INTERVENTION

***Diagnose Before* the Lesson**
5-5 Warm Up, TE p. 332

***Monitor During* the Lesson**
Check It Out! Exercises, SE pp. 332–335
Questioning Strategies, TE pp. 333–335

***Assess After* the Lesson**
5-5 Lesson Quiz, TE p. 339
Alternative Assessment, TE p. 339

Answers to *Think and Discuss*

1. No; possible answer: the student must consider 2 cases and assume that either the ∠ is acute or the ∠ is rt.
2. Possible answers: 2 cm, 4 cm, 5 cm; 2 cm, 4 cm, 8 cm
3. See p. A5.

5-5 Exercises

Assignment Guide

Assign *Guided Practice* exercises as necessary.

If you finished Examples **1–3**
- **Basic** 16–25, 36–39, 42–57
- **Average** 16–25, 34, 36–57, 66, 67, 73
- **Advanced** 16–25, 34–57, 66–68, 73, 75

If you finished Examples **1–5**
- **Basic** 16–32, 36–39, 42–57, 59–65, 70–72, 76–81
- **Average** 16–34, 40–52, 54–73, 76–81
- **Advanced** 16–35, 40–52, 54–81

Homework Quick Check
Quickly check key concepts.
Exercises: 16, 18, 20, 26, 32, 48, 62

Answers

1–3. See p. A19.

6. Yes; the sum of each pair of 2 lengths is greater than the third length.

7. No; $2 + 9 = 11$, which is not greater than the third side length.

8. Yes; the sum of each pair of 2 lengths is greater than the third length.

9. No; $1.1 + 1.7 = 2.8$, which is not greater than the third side length.

10–17. See p. A19.

State Resources

go.hrw.com
State Resources Online
KEYWORD: MG7 Resources

5-5 Exercises

go.hrw.com
Homework Help Online
KEYWORD: MG7 5-5
Parent Resources Online
KEYWORD: MG7 Parent

GUIDED PRACTICE

1. **Vocabulary** Describe the process of an *indirect proof* in your own words.

SEE EXAMPLE 1 p. 332

Write an indirect proof of each statement.

2. A scalene triangle cannot have two congruent angles.
3. An isosceles triangle cannot have a base angle that is a right angle.

SEE EXAMPLE 2 p. 333

4. Write the angles in order from smallest to largest. $\angle R$, $\angle P$, $\angle Q$

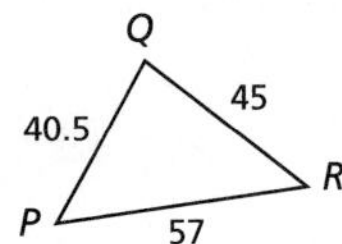

5. Write the sides in order from shortest to longest. $\overline{YZ}$, $\overline{XZ}$, $\overline{XY}$

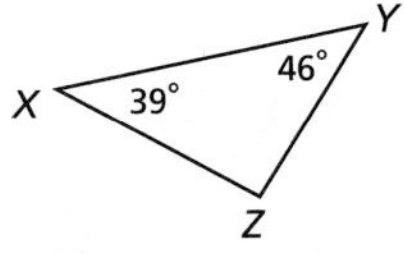

SEE EXAMPLE 3 p. 334

Tell whether a triangle can have sides with the given lengths. Explain.

6. 4, 7, 10
7. 2, 9, 12
8. $3\frac{1}{2}, 3\frac{1}{2}, 6$
9. 3, 1.1, 1.7
10. $3x, 2x - 1, x^2$, when $x = 5$
11. $7c + 6, 10c - 7, 3c^2$, when $c = 2$

SEE EXAMPLE 4 p. 335

The lengths of two sides of a triangle are given. Find the range of possible lengths for the third side.

12. 8 mm, 12 mm
13. 16 ft, 16 ft
14. 11.4 cm, 12 cm

SEE EXAMPLE 5 p. 335

15. **Design** The refrigerator, stove, and sink in a kitchen are at the vertices of a path called the work triangle.
    a. If the angle at the sink is the largest, which side of the work triangle will be the longest?
    b. The designer wants the longest side of this triangle to be 9 feet long. Can the lengths of the other sides be 5 feet and 4 feet? Explain.

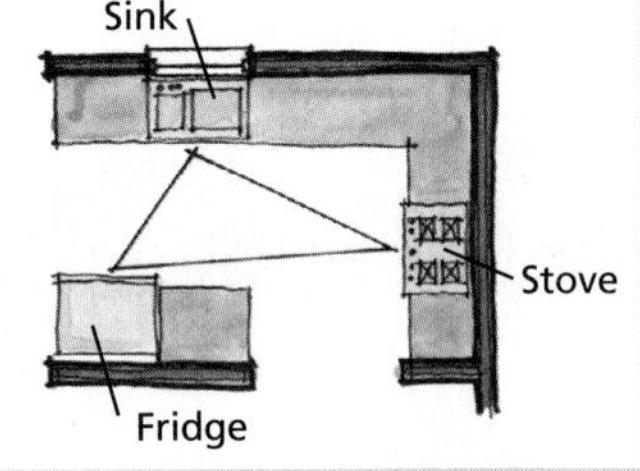

PRACTICE AND PROBLEM SOLVING

Independent Practice

For Exercises	See Example
16–17	1
18–19	2
20–25	3
26–31	4
32	5

Extra Practice
Skills Practice p. S13
Application Practice p. S32

Write an indirect proof of each statement.

16. A scalene triangle cannot have two congruent midsegments.
17. Two supplementary angles cannot both be obtuse angles.
18. Write the angles in order from smallest to largest. $\angle J$, $\angle L$, $\angle K$

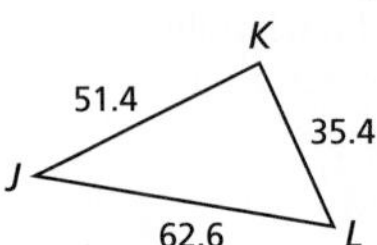

19. Write the sides in order from shortest to longest. $\overline{RS}$, $\overline{ST}$, $\overline{RT}$

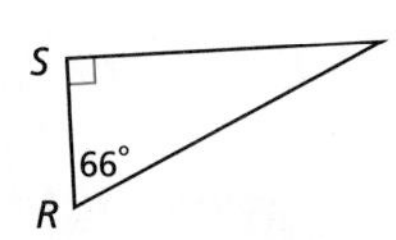

Tell whether a triangle can have sides with the given lengths. Explain.

20. 6, 10, 15
21. 14, 18, 32
22. 11.9, 5.8, 5.8
23. 103, 41.9, 62.5
24. $z + 8, 3z + 5, 4z - 11$, when $z = 6$
25. $m + 11, 8m, m^2 + 1$, when $m = 3$

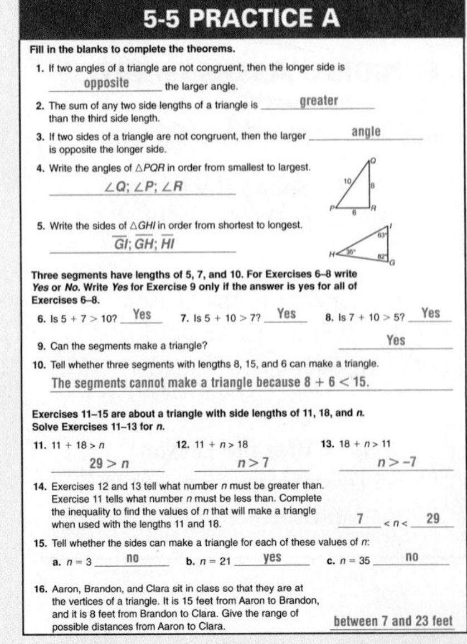

5-5 PRACTICE A

Fill in the blanks to complete the theorems.

1. If two angles of a triangle are not congruent, then the longer side is **opposite** the larger angle.
2. The sum of any two side lengths of a triangle is **greater** than the third side length.
3. If two sides of a triangle are not congruent, then the larger **angle** is opposite the longer side.
4. Write the angles of $\triangle PQR$ in order from smallest to largest. **$\angle Q$; $\angle P$; $\angle R$**
5. Write the sides of $\triangle GHI$ in order from shortest to longest. **$\overline{GI}$; $\overline{GH}$; $\overline{HI}$**

Three segments have lengths of 5, 7, and 10. For Exercises 6–8 write *Yes* or *No*. Write *Yes* for Exercise 9 only if the answer is yes for all of Exercises 6–8.

6. Is $5 + 7 > 10$? **Yes**
7. Is $5 + 10 > 7$? **Yes**
8. Is $7 + 10 > 5$? **Yes**
9. Can the segments make a triangle? **Yes**
10. Tell whether three segments with lengths 8, 15, and 6 can make a triangle. **The segments cannot make a triangle because $8 + 6 < 15$.**

Exercises 11–15 are about a triangle with side lengths of 11, 18, and *n*. Solve Exercises 11–13 for *n*.

11. $11 + 18 > n$ **$29 > n$**
12. $11 + n > 18$ **$n > 7$**
13. $18 + n > 11$ **$n > -7$**
14. Exercises 12 and 13 tell what number n must be greater than. Exercise 11 tells what number n must be less than. Complete the inequality to find the values of n that will make a triangle when used with the lengths 11 and 18. **7** $< n <$ **29**
15. Tell whether the sides can make a triangle for each of these values of n:
    a. $n = 3$ **no**
    b. $n = 21$ **yes**
    c. $n = 35$ **no**
16. Aaron, Brandon, and Clara sit in class so that they are at the vertices of a triangle. It is 15 feet from Aaron to Brandon, and it is 8 feet from Brandon to Clara. Give the range of possible distances from Aaron to Clara. **between 7 and 23 feet**

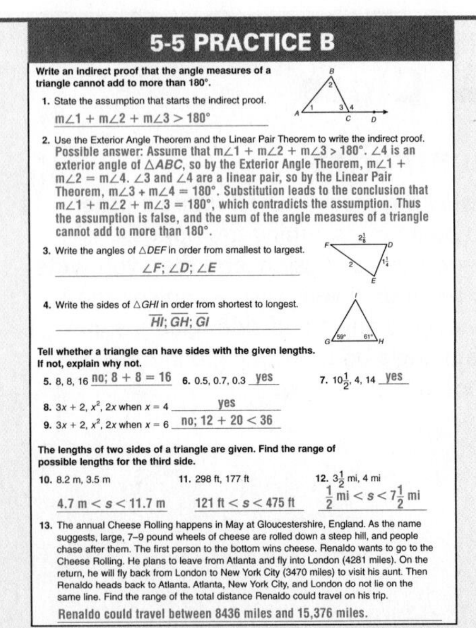

5-5 PRACTICE B

Write an indirect proof that the angle measures of a triangle cannot add to more than 180°.

1. State the assumption that starts the indirect proof. **$m\angle 1 + m\angle 2 + m\angle 3 > 180°$**
2. Use the Exterior Angle Theorem and the Linear Pair Theorem to write the indirect proof. **Possible answer: Assume that $m\angle 1 + m\angle 2 + m\angle 3 > 180°$. $\angle 4$ is an exterior angle of $\triangle ABC$, so by the Exterior Angle Theorem, $m\angle 1 + m\angle 2 = m\angle 4$. $\angle 3$ and $\angle 4$ are a linear pair, so by the Linear Pair Theorem, $m\angle 3 + m\angle 4 = 180°$. Substitution leads to the conclusion that $m\angle 1 + m\angle 2 + m\angle 3 = 180°$, which contradicts the assumption. Thus the assumption is false, and the sum of the angle measures of a triangle cannot add to more than 180°.**
3. Write the angles of $\triangle DEF$ in order from smallest to largest. **$\angle F$; $\angle D$; $\angle E$**
4. Write the sides of $\triangle GHI$ in order from shortest to longest. **$\overline{HI}$; $\overline{GH}$; $\overline{GI}$**

Tell whether a triangle can have sides with the given lengths. If not, explain why not.

5. 8, 8, 16 **no; $8 + 8 = 16$**
6. 0.5, 0.7, 0.3 **yes**
7. $10\frac{1}{2}$, 4, 14 **yes**
8. $3x + 2, x^2, 2x$ when $x = 4$ **yes**
9. $3x + 2, x^2, 2x$ when $x = 6$ **no; $12 + 20 < 36$**

The lengths of two sides of a triangle are given. Find the range of possible lengths for the third side.

10. 8.2 m, 3.5 m **$4.7 \text{ m} < s < 11.7 \text{ m}$**
11. 298 ft, 177 ft **$121 \text{ ft} < s < 475 \text{ ft}$**
12. $3\frac{1}{2}$ mi, 4 mi **$\frac{1}{2} \text{ mi} < s < 7\frac{1}{2} \text{ mi}$**
13. The annual Cheese Rolling happens in May at Gloucestershire, England. As the name suggests, large, 7–9 pound wheels of cheese are rolled down a steep hill, and people chase after them. The first person to the bottom wins cheese. Renaldo wants to go to the Cheese Rolling. He plans to leave from Atlanta and fly into London (4281 miles). On the return, he will fly back from London to New York City (3470 miles) to visit his aunt. Then Renaldo heads back to Atlanta. Atlanta, New York City, and London do not lie on the same line. Find the range of the total distance Renaldo could travel on his trip. **Renaldo could travel between 8436 miles and 15,376 miles.**

On June 26, 2004, Terry Goertzen of Winnipeg, Canada, attained the new Guinness world record for the tallest bicycle with his 5.5-meter-tall bike.

The lengths of two sides of a triangle are given. Find the range of possible lengths for the third side.

26. 4 yd, 19 yd **27.** 28 km, 23 km **28.** 9.2 cm, 3.8 cm

29. 3.07 m, 1.89 m **30.** $2\frac{1}{8}$ in., $3\frac{5}{8}$ in. **31.** $3\frac{5}{6}$ ft, $6\frac{1}{2}$ ft

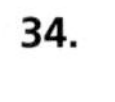

32. Bicycles The five steel tubes of this mountain bike frame form two triangles. List the five tubes in order from shortest to longest. Explain your answer.

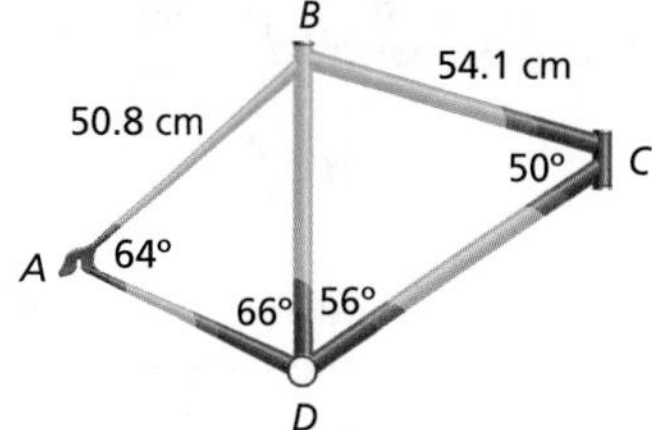

33. Critical Thinking The length of the base of an isosceles triangle is 15. What is the range of possible lengths for each leg? Explain.

List the sides of each triangle in order from shortest to longest.

34.

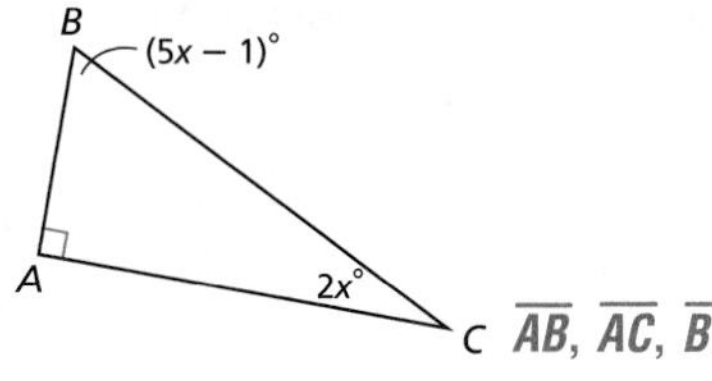

$\overline{AB}, \overline{AC}, \overline{BC}$

35.

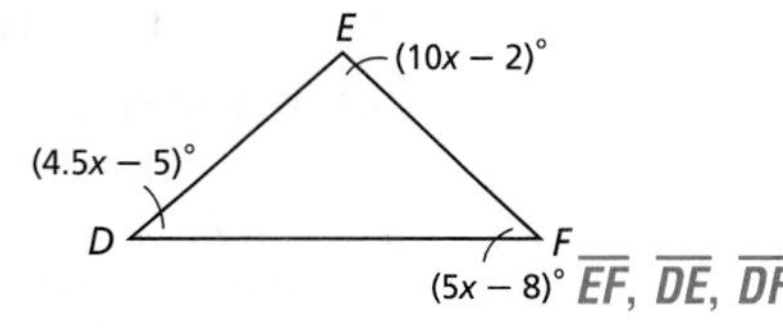

$\overline{EF}, \overline{DE}, \overline{DF}$

In each set of statements, name the two that contradict each other.

36. △*PQR* is a right triangle.
△*PQR* is a scalene triangle.
△*PQR* is an acute triangle.

37. ∠*Y* is supplementary to ∠*Z*.
m∠*Y* < 90°
∠*Y* is an obtuse angle.

38. △*JKL* is isosceles with base $\overline{JL}$.
In △*JKL*, m∠*K* > m∠*J*
In △*JKL*, *JK* > *LK*

39. $\overline{AB} \perp \overline{BC}$
$\overline{AB} \cong \overline{CD}$
$\overline{AB} \parallel \overline{BC}$

40. Figure *A* is a polygon.
Figure *A* is a triangle.
Figure *A* is a quadrilateral.

41. *x* is even.
x is a multiple of 4.
x is prime.

Compare. Write <, >, or =.

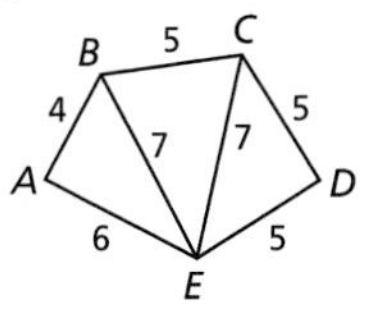

42. *QS* ▒ *PS* > **43.** *PQ* ▒ *QS* <

44. *QS* ▒ *QR* < **45.** *QS* ▒ *RS* =

46. *PQ* ▒ *RS* < **47.** *RS* ▒ *PS* >

48. m∠*ABE* ▒ m∠*BEA* > **49.** m∠*CBE* ▒ m∠*CEB* >

50. m∠*DCE* ▒ m∠*DEC* = **51.** m∠*DCE* ▒ m∠*CDE* <

52. m∠*ABE* ▒ m∠*EAB* < **53.** m∠*EBC* ▒ m∠*ECB* =

List the angles of △*JKL* in order from smallest to largest.

54. *J*(−3, −2), *K*(3, 6), *L*(8, −2) ∠*J*, ∠*L*, ∠*K* **55.** *J*(−5, −10), *K*(−5, 2), *L*(7, −5) ∠*L*, ∠*K*, ∠*J*

56. *J*(−4, 1), *K*(−3, 8), *L*(3, 4) ∠*L*, ∠*J*, ∠*K* **57.** *J*(−10, −4), *K*(0, 3), *L*(2, −8) ∠*J*, ∠*L*, ∠*K*

58. Critical Thinking An attorney argues that her client did not commit a burglary because a witness saw her client in a different city at the time of the burglary. Explain how this situation is an example of indirect reasoning.

COMMON ERROR ALERT

In **Exercise 32,** students may think $\overline{BD}$ is the shortest side because it is opposite the 50° angle, which is the smallest angle labeled in the figure. Have them order the sides in each triangle separately, using the given numeric measurements. This will help them see that $\overline{AD}$ is shorter than $\overline{BD}$, and $\overline{AD}$ is thus the shortest segment.

Answers

20. Yes; the sum of each pair of 2 lengths is greater than the third length.

21. No; 14 + 18 = 32, which is not greater than the third side length.

22. No; 5.8 + 5.8 = 11.6, which is not greater than the third side length.

23. Yes; the sum of each pair of 2 lengths is greater than the third length.

24. Yes; when $z = 6$, the value of $z + 8$ is 14, the value of $3z + 5$ is 23, and the value of $4z - 11$ is 13. The sum of each pair of 2 lengths is greater than the third length.

25. No; when $m = 3$, the value of $m + 11$ is 14, the value of $8m$ is 24, and the value of $m^2 + 1$ is 10. The sum of 14 and 10 is 24, which is not greater than the third side length.

26. greater than 15 yd and less than 23 yd

27. greater than 5 km and less than 51 km

28. greater than 5.4 cm and less than 13 cm

29. greater than 1.18 m and less than 4.96 m

30. greater than $1\frac{1}{2}$ in. and less than $5\frac{3}{4}$ in.

31. greater than $2\frac{2}{3}$ ft and less than $10\frac{1}{3}$ ft

32. $\overline{AD}, \overline{BD}, \overline{AB}, \overline{BC}, \overline{CD}$; possible answer: in △*ABD*, m∠*ABD* = 50°. In △*BCD*, m∠*DBC* = 74°. In △*ABD*, the order of the tubes from shortest to longest is $\overline{AD}$, $\overline{BD}$, $\overline{AB}$. In △*BCD*, the order of the tubes from shortest to longest is $\overline{BD}$, $\overline{BC}$, $\overline{CD}$. So $AD < BD < AB$, and $BD < BC < CD$. Since $AB = 50.8$ and $BC = 54.1$, it is also true that $AB < BC$. So $\overline{AD} < \overline{BD} < \overline{AB} < \overline{BC} < \overline{CD}$.

33. $a > 7.5$, where a is the length of a leg. Possible answer: By the △ Inequal. Thm., $a + a > 15$ and $a + 15 > a$. The solution of the first inequality is $a > 7.5$. The second inequality simplifies to $15 > 0$, which is always a true statement.

58. Possible answer: Assume that the client committed the burglary. A person who commits a burglary must be present at the scene at the time the crime is committed. However, a witness saw the client in a different city at the time the burglary was committed. This means the assumption that the client committed the burglary is false. Therefore the client did not commit the burglary.

5-5 PRACTICE C

Indirect proofs work by finding a contradiction that leads to the proof of a statement. For Exercises 1–7, rewrite each statement. Use the symbol → for an "if, then" statement and the symbol ~ for "not," the negation of a statement. Use *a* to stand for "The two angles are a linear pair." Use *b* to stand for "The two angles are supplementary."

Example: If the two angles are a linear pair, then the two angles are supplementary. $a \to b$

1. If the two angles are supplementary, then the two angles are a linear pair. $b \to a$
2. If the two angles are not supplementary, then the two angles are a linear pair. $\sim b \to a$
3. If the two angles are a linear pair, then the two angles are not supplementary. $a \to \sim b$
4. If the two angles are not a linear pair, then the two angles are not supplementary. $\sim a \to \sim b$
5. If the two angles are not supplementary, then the two angles are not a linear pair. $\sim b \to \sim a$
6. If the two angles are not a linear pair, then the two angles are supplementary. $\sim a \to b$
7. If the two angles are supplementary, then the two angles are not a linear pair. $b \to \sim a$
8. Suppose the example statement ($a \to b$) is to be proven. Give the number of the statement you would begin with (knowing it would lead to a contradiction) in order to prove the example statement by indirect proof. 2
9. Suppose then the contradiction negates the conclusion. Give the number of the statement that the contradiction leads you to believe must be true. 5
10. Name the logical relationship between the answer to Exercise 9 and the example statement. contrapositive
11. Name the shortest segment(s) in the figure and explain your reasoning. Do not use a ruler. (*Note:* The figure may not be drawn to scale.)

Possible answer: The shortest side in a triangle is opposite the shortest angle. The shortest side in △*AEF* is $\overline{AF}$. △*ABF* is equiangular, so $\overline{AF}$ has the same length as $\overline{BF}$. But $\overline{BG}$ is the shortest side in △*BGF*, so $\overline{AF}$, $\overline{AB}$, and $\overline{BF}$ cannot be the shortest segments in the figure. $\overline{CG}$ is the shortest segment in △*CHG*, but $\overline{BC}$ is the shortest segment in △*BCG*. So $\overline{BC}$ is shorter than $\overline{CG}$. The shortest segment in △*CDH* is $\overline{DH}$. $\overline{DH}$ has length *a* and $\overline{CG}$ has length $a - 2$, so $\overline{CG}$ is shorter than $\overline{DH}$. Therefore $\overline{BC}$ is the shortest segment in the figure.

MULTI-STEP TEST PREP Exercise 59 involves finding the range of values for the third side of a triangle when given the lengths of the other two sides. This exercise prepares students for the Multi-Step Test Prep on page 364.

Teaching Tip **Communicating Math** For **Exercise 66,** point out that since the conclusion is an inequality, the proof will probably use the Triangle Inequality Theorem.

Teaching Tip **Multiple Representations** Students may find it easier to write the proof for **Exercise 67** in a two-column format before filling in the blanks so it is easier to follow.

TEST PREP DOCTOR If students have difficulty with **Exercise 71,** have them find the measure of the third angle first.

For **Exercise 72,** have students consider the possible values for the other two angles. If m∠S = 92°, then the sum of ∠R and ∠T will be 88°, making each angle measure less than ∠S. This eliminates choices **A, B,** and **D.**

Teaching Tip **Probability** In **Exercise 73,** it may help students to make an organized list of all the combinations of three sticks and then determine which will form a triangle.

Answers

66. Possible answer:

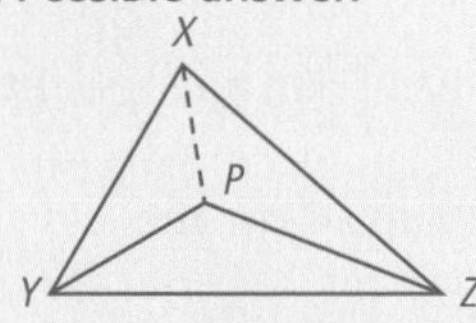

Given: P is in the int. of △XYZ.
Prove: XY + XP + PZ > YZ
Proof:
By the △ Inequal. Thm., PY + PZ > YZ and XY + XP > YP. Since PZ > 0, the second inequality is equivalent to XY + XP + PZ > YP + PZ. But then YP + PZ > YZ, so XY + XP + PZ > YZ by the Trans. Prop. of Inequal.

69, 75. See p. A20.

MULTI-STEP TEST PREP

59. This problem will prepare you for the Multi-Step Test Prep on page 364. The figure shows an airline's routes between four cities.

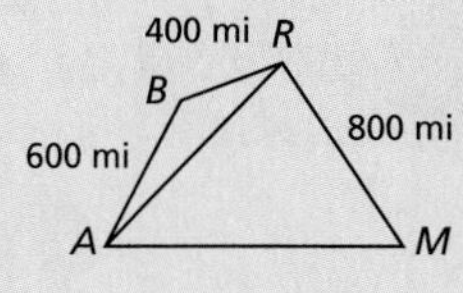

a. The airline's planes fly at an average speed of 500 mi/h. What is the range of time it might take to fly from Auburn (*A*) to Raymond (*R*)? **0.4 h < t < 2 h**

b. The airline offers one frequent-flier mile for every mile flown. Is it possible to earn 1800 miles by flying from Millford (*M*) to Auburn (*A*)? Explain. **No; AR < 1000, so by the △ Inequal. Thm., AM must be less than 1800.**

Multi-Step Each set of expressions represents the lengths of the sides of a triangle. Find the range of possible values of *n*.

60. $n, 6, 8$ **2 < n < 14**
61. $2n, 5, 7$ **1 < n < 6**
62. $n + 1, 3, 6$ **2 < n < 8**
63. $n + 1, n + 2, n + 3$ **n > 0**
64. $n + 2, n + 3, 3n - 2$ **1 < n < 7**
65. $n, n + 2, 2n + 1$ **n > 0.5**

66. Given that *P* is in the interior of △*XYZ*, prove that *XY* + *XP* + *PZ* > *YZ*.

67. Complete the proof of Theorem 5-5-1 by filling in the blanks.

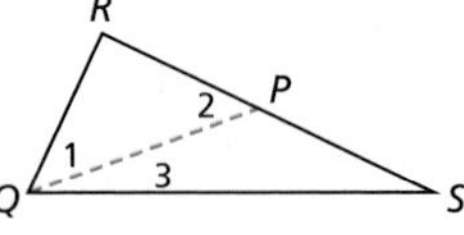

Given: *RS* > *RQ*
Prove: m∠*RQS* > m∠*S*

Proof:
Locate *P* on $\overline{RS}$ so that *RP* = *RQ*. So $\overline{RP} \cong \overline{RQ}$ by **a.** ___?___. Then ∠1 ≅ ∠2 by **b.** ___?___, and m∠1 = m∠2 by **c.** ___?___. By the Angle Addition Postulate, m∠*RQS* = **d.** ___?___. So m∠*RQS* > m∠1 by the Comparison Property of Inequality. Then m∠*RQS* > m∠2 by **e.** ___?___. By the Exterior Angle Theorem, m∠2 = m∠3 + **f.** ___?___. So m∠2 > m∠*S* by the Comparison Property of Inequality. Therefore m∠*RQS* > m∠*S* by **g.** ___?___.

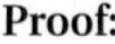

a. def. of ≅ segs.
b. Isosc. △ Thm.
c. def. of ≅ ∡
d. m∠1 + m∠3
e. subst.
f. m∠S
g. Trans. Prop. of Inequal.

68. Complete the proof of the Triangle Inequality Theorem.

Given: △*ABC*
Prove: *AB* + *BC* > *AC*, *AB* + *AC* > *BC*, *AC* + *BC* > *AB*

Proof:
One side of △*ABC* is as long as or longer than each of the other sides. Let this side be $\overline{AB}$. Then *AB* + *BC* > *AC*, and *AB* + *AC* > *BC*. Therefore what remains to be proved is *AC* + *BC* > *AB*.

Statements	Reasons
1. a. ___?___	1. Given
2. Locate *D* on $\overrightarrow{AC}$ so that *BC* = *DC*.	2. Ruler Post.
3. *AC* + *DC* = b. ___?___	3. Seg. Add. Post.
4. ∠1 ≅ ∠2	4. c. ___?___
5. m∠1 = m∠2	5. d. ___?___
6. m∠*ABD* = m∠2 + e. ___?___	6. ∠ Add. Post.
7. m∠*ABD* > m∠2	7. Comparison Prop. of Inequal.
8. m∠*ABD* > m∠1	8. f. ___?___
9. *AD* > *AB*	9. g. ___?___
10. *AC* + *DC* > *AB*	10. h. ___?___
11. i. ___?___	11. Subst.

a. △ABC
b. AD
c. Isosc. △ Thm.
d. Def. of ≅ ∡
e. m∠3
f. Subst.
g. In △, longer side is opp. larger ∠.
h. Subst.
i. AC + BC > AB

69. Write About It Explain why the hypotenuse is always the longest side of a right triangle. Explain why the diagonal of a square is longer than each side.

5-5 READING STRATEGIES

Indirect proofs can be written by following these steps:

1. Identify the conjecture to be proven.
2. Assume the opposite of the conclusion is true.
3. Use direct reasoning to show the assumption leads to a contradiction.
4. Conclude that since the assumption is false, the original conjecture must be true.

Find the two statements in each set that contradict each other or are opposites.

1. $\overline{XY} \parallel \overline{AB}$
$\overline{AB} \perp \overline{XY}$
$\overline{AB} \cong \overline{XZ}$
$\overline{XY} \parallel \overline{AB}$, $\overline{AB} \perp \overline{XY}$

2. In △*ABC*, m∠*A* > m∠*B*.
In △*ABC*, m∠*C* = 60°.
In △*ABC*, m∠*A* = 50° and m∠*B* = 70°.
In △*ABC*, m∠*A* > m∠*B*. In △*ABC*, m∠*A* = 50° and m∠*B* = 70°.

3. △*PQR* is a right triangle.
∠*P* is an acute angle.
∠*Q* is an obtuse angle.
△*PQR* is a right triangle. ∠*Q* is an obtuse angle.

Write True or False. Explain your answer.

4. Two supplementary angles can both be obtuse.
False; supplementary angles have measures that add up to be 180°, so both angles cannot be obtuse (greater than 90°).

5. A scalene triangle can have two congruent sides.
False; a scalene triangle has three unequal sides by definition.

5-5 RETEACH

In a direct proof, you begin with a true hypothesis and prove that a conclusion is true. In an **indirect proof,** you begin by assuming that the conclusion is false (that is, that the opposite of the conclusion is true). You then show that this assumption leads to a contradiction.

Consider the statement "Two acute angles do not form a linear pair."

Writing an Indirect Proof	
Steps	**Example**
1. Identify the conjecture to be proven.	**Given:** ∠1 and ∠2 are acute angles. **Prove:** ∠1 and ∠2 do not form a linear pair.
2. Assume the opposite of the conclusion is true.	Assume ∠1 and ∠2 form a linear pair.
3. Use direct reasoning to show that the assumption leads to a contradiction.	m∠1 + m∠2 = 180° by def. of linear pair. Since m∠1 < 90° and m∠2 < 90°, m∠1 + m∠2 < 180°. This is a contradiction.
4. Conclude that the assumption is false and hence that the original conjecture must be true.	The assumption that ∠1 and ∠2 form a linear pair is false. Therefore ∠1 and ∠2 do not form a linear pair.

Use the following statement for Exercises 1–4.

An obtuse triangle cannot have a right angle.

1. Identify the conjecture to be proven.
Given: △*ABC* is an obtuse △, ∠*B* is an obtuse angle; Prove: △*ABC* does not have a right angle.

2. Assume the opposite of the conclusion. Write this assumption.
Assume △*ABC* does have a right angle. Let ∠*A* be a right angle.

3. Use direct reasoning to arrive at a contradiction.
Possible answer: If ∠*A* is a right angle, then m∠*B* + m∠*C* = 90°. But m∠*B* > 90°, since ∠*B* is obtuse. So this is a contradiction.

4. What can you conclude?
The assumption that △*ABC* does have a right angle is false. Therefore △*ABC* does not have a right angle.

TEST PREP

70. The lengths of two sides of a triangle are 3 feet and 5 feet. Which could be the length of the third side?
(A) 3 feet (circled) B 8 feet C 15 feet D 16 feet

71. Which statement about $\triangle GHJ$ is false?
F $GH < GJ$ (H) $GH + HJ < GJ$ (circled)
G $m\angle H > m\angle J$ J $\triangle GHJ$ is a scalene triangle.

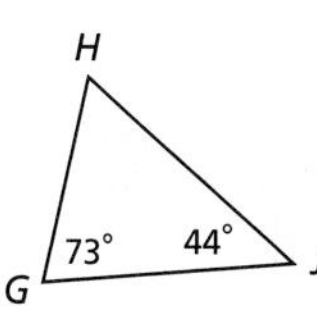

72. In $\triangle RST$, $m\angle S = 92°$. Which is the longest side of $\triangle RST$?
A $\overline{RS}$ (C) $\overline{RT}$ (circled)
B $\overline{ST}$ D Cannot be determined

CHALLENGE AND EXTEND

$\frac{3}{10}$, or 30%

73. **Probability** A bag contains five sticks. The lengths of the sticks are 1 inch, 3 inches, 5 inches, 7 inches, and 9 inches. Suppose you pick three sticks from the bag at random. What is the probability you can form a triangle with the three sticks?

a. $\sqrt{2}$ is rational
b. $\frac{p^2}{q^2}$
c. $2q^2$
d. $(2x)^2 = 4x^2$
e. $q^2 = \frac{1}{2}p^2$ and p^2 is divisible by 4

74. Complete this indirect argument that $\sqrt{2}$ is irrational. Assume that **a.** __?__. Then $\sqrt{2} = \frac{p}{q}$, where p and q are positive integers that have no common factors. Thus $2 =$ **b.** __?__, and $p^2 =$ **c.** __?__. This implies that p^2 is even, and thus p is even. Since p^2 is the square of an even number, p^2 is divisible by 4 because **d.** __?__. But then q^2 must be even because **e.** __?__, and so q is even. Then p and q have a common factor of 2, which contradicts the assumption that p and q have no common factors.

75. Prove that the perpendicular segment from a point to a line is the shortest segment from the point to the line.
Given: $\overline{PX} \perp \ell$. Y is any point on ℓ other than X.
Prove: $PY > PX$
Plan: Show that $\angle 2$ and $\angle P$ are complementary. Use the Comparison Property of Inequality to show that $90° > m\angle 2$. Then show that $m\angle 1 > m\angle 2$ and thus $PY > PX$.

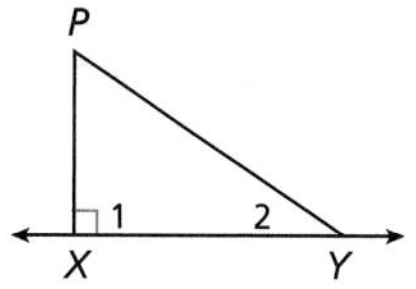

SPIRAL REVIEW

Write the equation of each line in standard form. *(Previous course)*

76. the line through points $(-3, 2)$ and $(-1, -2)$ $2x + y = -4$

77. the line with slope 2 and x-intercept of -3 $-2x + y = 6$

Show that the triangles are congruent for the given value of the variable. *(Lesson 4-4)*

78. $QP = 3$, $ST = 6$, and $SU = 4$, so $\triangle PQR \cong \triangle TUS$ by SSS.

79. $BC = 10$, $EF = 11$, and $m\angle ABC = 102°$, so $\triangle ABC \cong \triangle EFD$ by SAS.

78. $\triangle PQR \cong \triangle TUS$, when $x = -1$

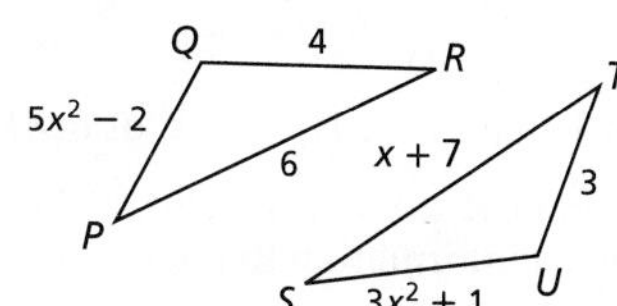

79. $\triangle ABC \cong \triangle EFD$, when $p = 6$

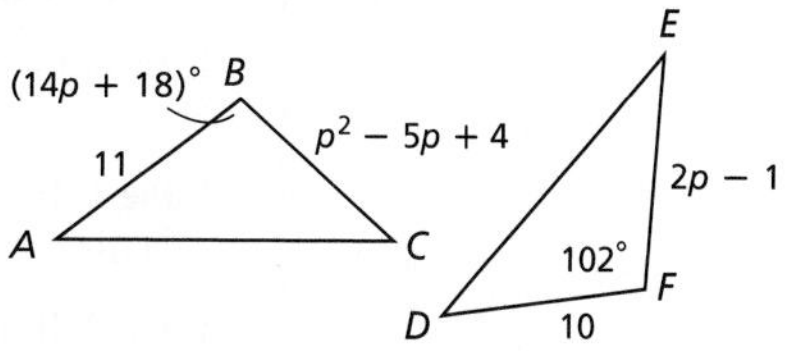

$(14p + 18)°$ B
11
$p^2 - 5p + 4$
A
C
E
$2p - 1$
102°
D
10
F

Find the orthocenter of a triangle with the given vertices. *(Lesson 5-3)*

80. $R(0, 5)$, $S(4, 3)$, $T(0, 1)$ $(1, 3)$

81. $M(0, 0)$, $N(3, 0)$, $P(0, 5)$ $(0, 0)$

5-5 PROBLEM SOLVING

1. A charter plane travels from Barrow, Alaska, to Fairbanks. From Fairbanks, it flies to Nome, and then back to its starting point in Barrow. Which of the three legs of the trip is the longest?
Fairbanks to Nome

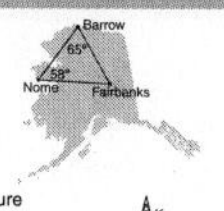

Barrow
65°
58°
Nome
Fairbanks

2. Three cell phone towers are shown at right. The measure of $\angle M$ is 10° less than the measure of $\angle K$. The measure of $\angle L$ is 1° greater than the measure of $\angle K$. Which two towers are closest together?
towers K and L

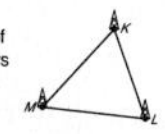

Use the figure for Exercises 3 and 4.

In disc golf, a player tries to throw a disc into a metal basket target. Four disc golf targets on a course are shown at right.

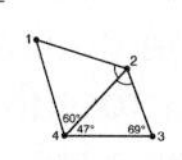

3. Which two targets are closest together?
targets 2 and 3

4. Which two targets are farthest apart?
targets 1 and 4

Choose the best answer.

5. The distance from Jacksonville to Tampa is 171 miles. The distance from Tampa to Miami is 206 miles. Use the Triangle Inequality Theorem to find the range for the distance from Jacksonville to Miami.
A 0 mi < d < 35 mi
B 0 mi < d < 377 mi
(C) 35 mi < d < 377 mi (circled)
D −35 mi < d < 377 mi

6. In Jessica's room, the distance from the door D to the closet C is 4 feet. The distance from the closet to the window W is 6 feet. The distance from the window to the door is 8 feet. On a floor plan of her room, $\triangle CDW$ is drawn. Order the angles from least to greatest measure.
F $\angle C, \angle D, \angle W$ H $\angle W, \angle C, \angle D$
G $\angle D, \angle C, \angle W$ (J) $\angle W, \angle D, \angle C$ (circled)

7. Walking paths at a park are shown. Which route represents the greatest distance?
(A) A to B to D (circled) C C to B to D
B A to D to B D C to D to B

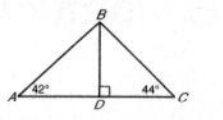

B
42°
44°
A
D
C

5-5 CHALLENGE

The Triangle Inequality Theorem describes a relationship among the lengths of the sides of a triangle. The following two theorems relate the lengths of the sides to the measures of the angles.

UNEQUAL SIDES THEOREM
If one side of a triangle is longer than another side, then the angle opposite the longer side is larger than the angle opposite the shorter side.

UNEQUAL ANGLES THEOREM
If one angle of a triangle is larger than another angle, then the side opposite the larger angle is longer than the side opposite the smaller angle.

1. In $\triangle XYZ$, $XY = 9.3$, $YZ = 7.6$, and $XZ = 8.05$. Name the largest and smallest angles of $\triangle XYZ$.
largest angle: $\angle Z$; smallest angle: $\angle X$

2. In $\triangle JKL$, $m\angle J = 62°$ and $m\angle K = 57°$. Name the longest and shortest sides of $\triangle JKL$.
longest side: $\overline{KL}$; shortest side: $\overline{JL}$

In each figure, list the segments in order from longest to shortest.

3. A, B, C, D; 57°, 58°, 44°
$\overline{CD}, \overline{BC}, \overline{BD}, \overline{AB}, \overline{AD}$

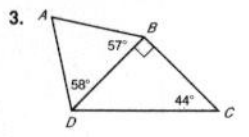

4.
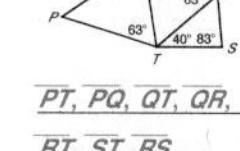

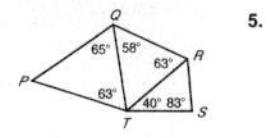

$\overline{PT}, \overline{PQ}, \overline{QT}, \overline{QR}, \overline{RT}, \overline{ST}, \overline{RS}$

5. W, X, V, Z, Y; 42°, 47°, 60°, 58°
$\overline{YZ}, \overline{XY}, \overline{XZ}, \overline{WX}, \overline{WZ}, \overline{VW}, \overline{VZ}$

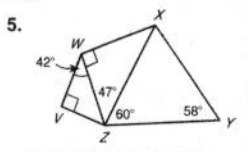

On a separate sheet of paper, write a proof of each theorem.

6. *Unequal Sides Theorem*
Given: $\triangle ABC$ with $BC > AB$
Prove: $m\angle BAC > m\angle C$. 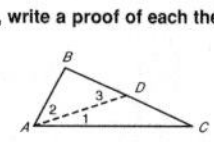
Plan for proof: Locate point D on $\overline{BC}$ such that $BD = BA$. Draw $\overline{AD}$. Explain why $m\angle BAC > m\angle 3$, $m\angle 3 > m\angle C$, and so $m\angle BAC > m\angle C$.

7. *Unequal Angles Theorem*
Given: $\triangle PQR$ with $m\angle P > m\angle R$
Prove: $QR > QP$ 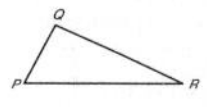
Plan for proof: The three possible relationships between QR and QP are $QR = QP$, $QR < QP$, and $QR > QP$. Show that the first two relationships listed are impossible.
Proofs may vary.

Journal

Have students describe in their own words how to write an indirect proof and have them explain what should be assumed when writing an indirect proof.

ALTERNATIVE ASSESSMENT

Have students draw two triangles. In one, have them measure the side lengths and then write the angle measures in order. In the other, have them measure two angles and then write the side lengths in order. Finally ask them to write one combination of lengths that will form a triangle and one combination that will not.

5-5 Lesson Quiz

1. Write the angles in order from smallest to largest. $\angle C, \angle B, \angle A$

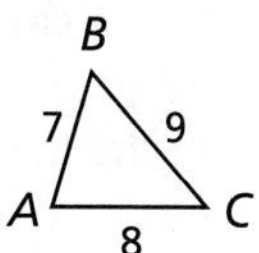

2. Write the sides in order from shortest to longest. $\overline{DE}, \overline{EF}, \overline{DF}$

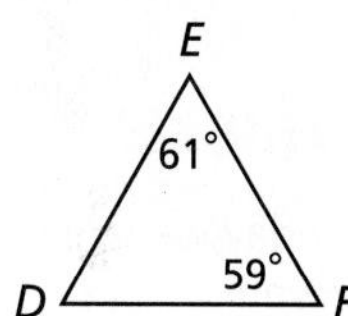

3. The lengths of two sides of a triangle are 17 cm and 12 cm. Find the range of possible lengths for the third side. 5 cm < x < 29 cm

4. Tell whether a triangle can have sides with lengths 2.7, 3.5, and 9.8. Explain. No; 2.7 + 3.5 is not greater than 9.8.

5. Ray wants to place a chair so it is 10 ft from his television set. Can the other two distances shown be 8 ft and 6 ft? Explain. Yes; the sum of any two lengths is greater than the third length.

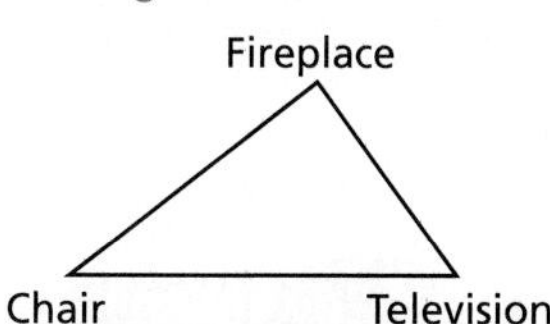

Also available on transparency

5-6 Organizer

Pacing: Traditional 1 day
Block $\frac{1}{2}$ day

Objective: Apply inequalities in two triangles.

Online Edition
Tutorial Videos

Countdown Week 11

Power Presentations with PowerPoint®

Warm Up

1. Write the angles in order from smallest to largest. ∠X, ∠Z, ∠Y

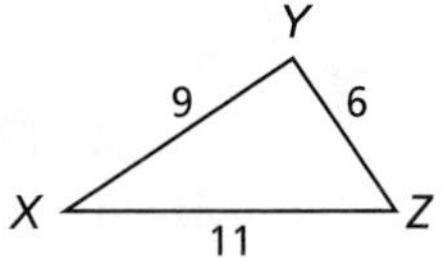

2. The lengths of two sides of a triangle are 12 cm and 9 cm. Find the range of possible lengths for the third side.
   3 cm < s < 21 cm

Also available on transparency

Math Humor

Teacher: Today we will study the Hinge Theorem.

Student: Do we need tools?

State Resources

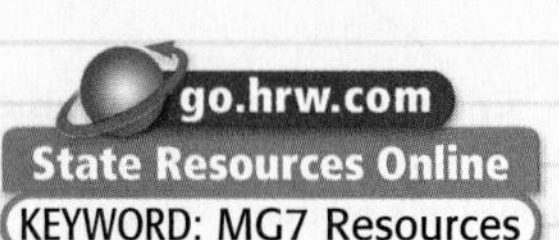

5-6 Inequalities in Two Triangles

Objective
Apply inequalities in two triangles.

Who uses this?
Designers of this circular swing ride can use the angle of the swings to determine how high the chairs will be at full speed. (See Example 2.)

In this lesson, you will apply inequality relationships between two triangles.

Theorems Inequalities in Two Triangles

THEOREM	HYPOTHESIS	CONCLUSION
5-6-1 Hinge Theorem If two sides of one triangle are congruent to two sides of another triangle and the included angles are not congruent, then the longer third side is across from the larger included angle.	m∠A > m∠D	BC > EF
5-6-2 Converse of the Hinge Theorem If two sides of one triangle are congruent to two sides of another triangle and the third sides are not congruent, then the larger included angle is across from the longer third side.	GH > KL	m∠J > m∠M

You will prove Theorem 5-6-1 in Exercise 35.

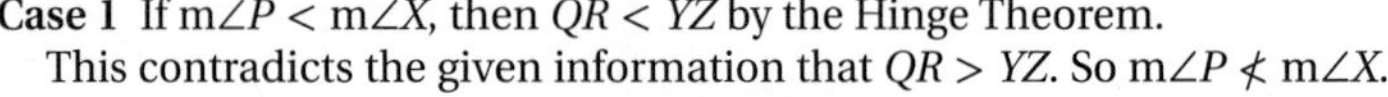

PROOF **Converse of the Hinge Theorem**

Given: $\overline{PQ} \cong \overline{XY}$, $\overline{PR} \cong \overline{XZ}$, $QR > YZ$
Prove: $m\angle P > m\angle X$

Indirect Proof:
Assume $m\angle P \not> m\angle X$. So either $m\angle P < m\angle X$, or $m\angle P = m\angle X$.

Case 1 If $m\angle P < m\angle X$, then $QR < YZ$ by the Hinge Theorem. This contradicts the given information that $QR > YZ$. So $m\angle P \not< m\angle X$.

Case 2 If $m\angle P = m\angle X$, then $\angle P \cong \angle X$. So $\triangle PQR \cong \triangle XYZ$ by SAS. Then $\overline{QR} \cong \overline{YZ}$ by CPCTC, and $QR = YZ$. This also contradicts the given information. So $m\angle P \neq m\angle X$.

The assumption $m\angle P \not> m\angle X$ is false. Therefore $m\angle P > m\angle X$.

1 Introduce

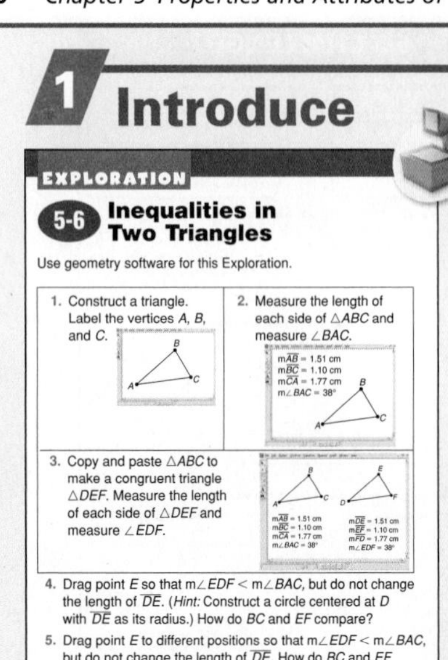

EXPLORATION

5-6 Inequalities in Two Triangles

Use geometry software for this Exploration.

1. Construct a triangle. Label the vertices A, B, and C.
2. Measure the length of each side of △ABC and measure ∠BAC.
   $m\overline{AB} = 1.51$ cm, $m\overline{BC} = 1.10$ cm, $m\overline{CA} = 1.77$ cm, $m\angle BAC = 38°$
3. Copy and paste △ABC to make a congruent triangle △DEF. Measure the length of each side of △DEF and measure ∠EDF.
   $m\overline{DE} = 1.51$ cm, $m\overline{EF} = 1.10$ cm, $m\overline{FD} = 1.77$ cm, $m\angle EDF = 38°$
4. Drag point E so that m∠EDF < m∠BAC, but do not change the length of $\overline{DE}$. (*Hint:* Construct a circle centered at D with $\overline{DE}$ as its radius.) How do BC and EF compare?
5. Drag point E to different positions so that m∠EDF < m∠BAC, but do not change the length of $\overline{DE}$. How do BC and EF compare?

Motivate

Open the classroom door and show students that as the angle between the door and the doorway increases, the distance across the floor from the door to the door jamb also increases. This geometric relationship is summarized in the Hinge Theorem and its converse. Explain that in this lesson, students will study inequality relationships in two triangles.

Explorations and answers are provided in *Alternate Openers: Explorations Transparencies.*

EXAMPLE 1 Using the Hinge Theorem and Its Converse

A **Compare m∠PQS and m∠RQS.**

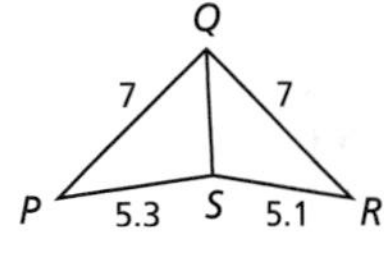

Compare the side lengths in △PQS and △RQS.

$PQ = RQ$ $QS = QS$ $PS > RS$

By the Converse of the Hinge Theorem, $m\angle PQS > m\angle RQS$.

B **Compare KL and MN.**

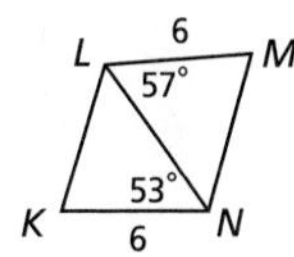

Compare the sides and angles in △KLN and △MNL.

$KN = ML$ $LN = LN$ $m\angle LNK < m\angle NLM$

By the Hinge Theorem, $KL < MN$.

Algebra

C **Find the range of values for z.**

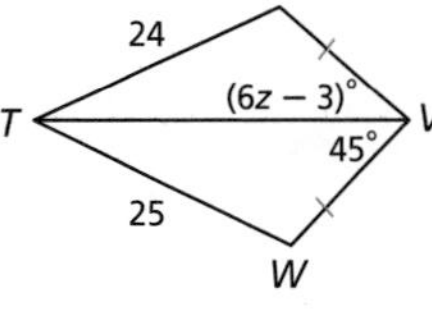

Step 1 Compare the side lengths in △TUV and △TWV.

$TV = TV$ $VU = VW$ $TU < TW$

By the Converse of the Hinge Theorem, $m\angle UVT < m\angle WVT$.

$6z - 3 < 45$ *Substitute the given values.*

$z < 8$ *Add 3 to both sides and divide both sides by 6.*

Step 2 Since ∠UVT is in a triangle, $m\angle UVT > 0°$.

$6z - 3 > 0$ *Substitute the given value.*

$z > 0.5$ *Add 3 to both sides and divide both sides by 6.*

Step 3 Combine the inequalities.

The range of values for z is $0.5 < z < 8$.

Compare the given measures.

1a. m∠EGH and m∠EGF

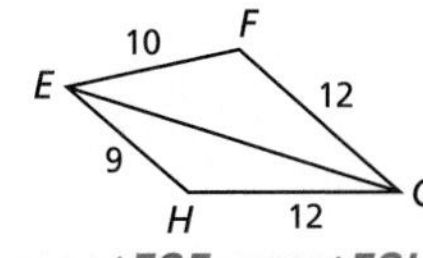

m∠EGF > m∠EGH

1b. BC and AB

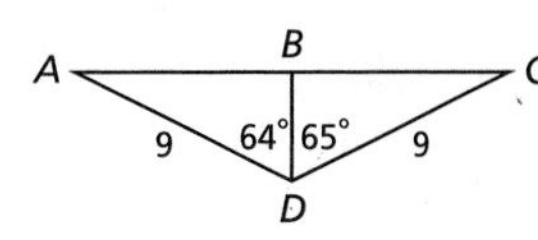

BC > AB

EXAMPLE 2 *Entertainment Application*

The angle of the swings in a circular swing ride changes with the speed of the ride. The diagram shows the position of one swing at two different speeds. Which rider is farther from the base of the swing tower? Explain.

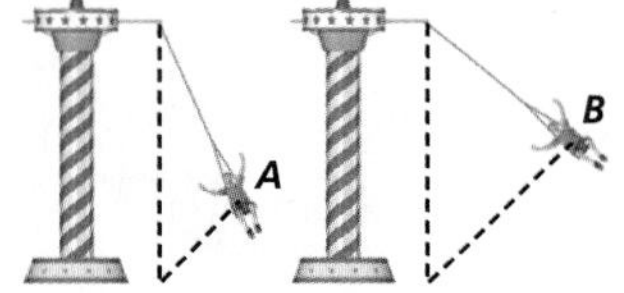

The height of the tower and the length of the cable holding the chair are the same in both triangles.

The angle formed by the swing in position A is smaller than the angle formed by the swing in position B. So rider B is farther from the base of the tower than rider A by the Hinge Theorem.

COMMON ERROR ALERT

In **Check It Out 1a,** students cannot compare m∠FEG and m∠HEG. Remind students that both pairs of sides including the angles must be congruent to compare the angle measures.

Power Presentations with PowerPoint®

Additional Examples

Example 1

A. Compare m∠BAC and m∠DAC. m∠BAC > m∠DAC

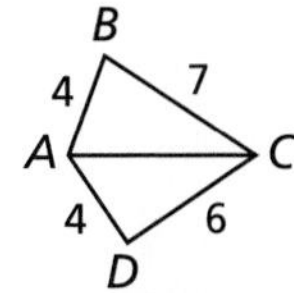

B. Compare EF and FG. EF < FG

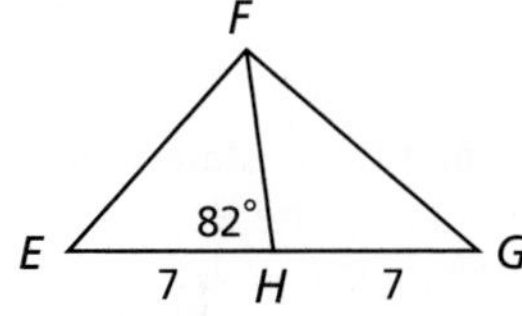

C. Find the range of values for k. $2.4 < k < 10$

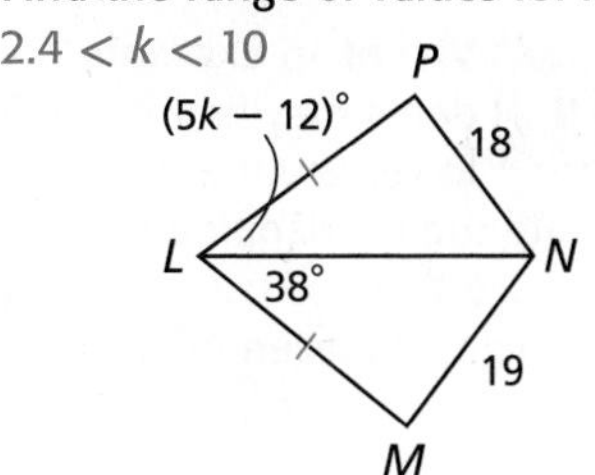

Example 2

John and Luke leave school at the same time. John rides his bike 3 blocks west and then 4 blocks north. Luke rides 4 blocks east and then 3 blocks at a bearing of N 10° E. Who is farther from school? Explain. The angle formed by John's route (90°) is less than the angle formed by Luke's route (100°), so Luke is farther from the school.

2 Teach

Guided Instruction

Explain the Hinge Theorem and its converse by using visual aids, such as a book or a pair of scissors. Show how the theorems are used to compare angle measures in two triangles by comparing their side lengths.

Kinesthetic Have students place the tips of their thumbs together in a line and touch their index fingers to form a triangle. Have them observe the angle at their index fingers as they pull their thumbs apart.

Reaching All Learners

Through Kinesthetic Experience

Have students use straws, raw spaghetti, or strips of paper to build triangles with side lengths of 4 in. and 5 in. and an included angle measure of 30°, 60°, and 80°. Have students measure and compare the lengths of the third sides of their triangles. Discuss how the third side increases as the angle increases.

INTERVENTION

Questioning Strategies

EXAMPLE 1

- Which theorem did you use for each example? Explain why.

EXAMPLE 2

- How do you know whether to use the Hinge Theorem or the Converse of the Hinge Theorem?

Power Presentations with PowerPoint®

Additional Examples

Example 3

Write a two-column proof.
Given: $\overline{AB} \cong \overline{CD}$, $m\angle ABD > m\angle CDB$
Prove: $AD > CB$

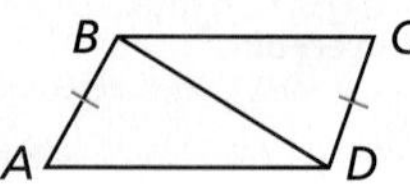

1. $\overline{AB} \cong \overline{CD}$, $m\angle ABD > m\angle CDB$ (Given)
2. $\overline{BD} \cong \overline{BD}$ (Reflex. Prop. of ≅)
3. $AD > CB$ (Hinge Thm.)

INTERVENTION

Questioning Strategies

EXAMPLE 3

- Why can't these statements be proved using the angle and side relationships learned in the previous lesson?

Visual In **Example 3,** students may find it helpful to redraw the diagram to separate the overlapping triangles. Encourage them to use colored pencils to highlight given information.

2. When the swing ride is at full speed, the chairs are farthest from the base of the swing tower. What can you conclude about the angles of the swings at full speed versus low speed? Explain. The ∠ of the swing at full speed is greater than the ∠ at low speed.

EXAMPLE 3 Proving Triangle Relationships

Write a two-column proof.
Given: $\overline{KL} \cong \overline{NL}$
Prove: $KM > NM$

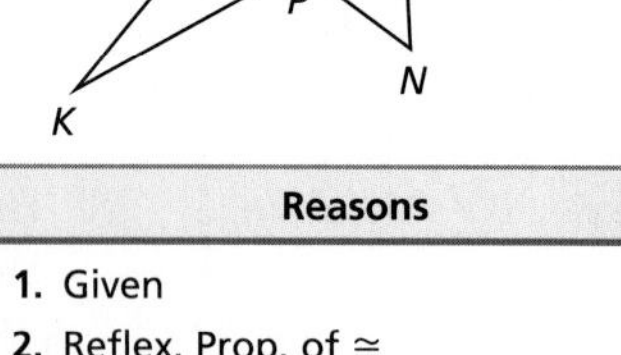

Proof:

Statements	Reasons
1. $\overline{KL} \cong \overline{NL}$	1. Given
2. $\overline{LM} \cong \overline{LM}$	2. Reflex. Prop. of ≅
3. $m\angle KLM = m\angle NLM + m\angle KLN$	3. ∠ Add. Post.
4. $m\angle KLM > m\angle NLM$	4. Comparison Prop. of Inequal.
5. $KM > NM$	5. Hinge Thm.

3a. 1. C is the mdpt. of $\overline{BD}$. $m\angle 1 = m\angle 2$, $m\angle 3 > m\angle 4$ (Given) 2. $\overline{BC} \cong \overline{DC}$ (Def. of mdpt.) 3. $\angle 1 \cong \angle 2$ (Def. of ≅ ∠s) 4. $\overline{AC} \cong \overline{EC}$ (Conv. of Isosc. △ Thm.) 5. $AB > ED$ (Hinge Thm.)

3b. 1. $\angle SRT \cong \angle STR$, $TU > RU$ (Given) 2. $\overline{ST} \cong \overline{SR}$ (Conv. of Isosc. △ Thm.) 3. $\overline{SU} \cong \overline{SU}$ (Reflex. Prop. of ≅) 4. $m\angle TSU > m\angle RSU$, (Conv. of Hinge Thm.)

CHECK IT OUT! Write a two-column proof.

3a. Given: C is the midpoint of $\overline{BD}$.
$m\angle 1 = m\angle 2$
$m\angle 3 > m\angle 4$
Prove: $AB > ED$

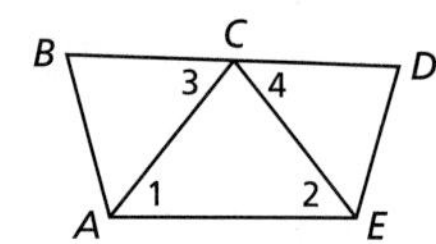

3b. Given: $\angle SRT \cong \angle STR$
$TU > RU$
Prove: $m\angle TSU > m\angle RSU$

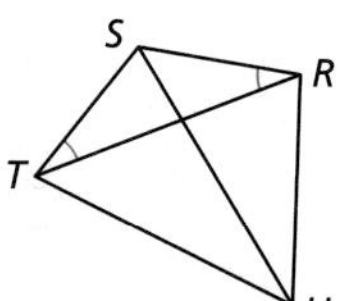

THINK AND DISCUSS

1. Describe a real-world object that shows the Hinge Theorem or its converse.
2. Can you make a conclusion about the triangles shown at right by applying the Hinge Theorem? Explain.
3. **GET ORGANIZED** Copy and complete the graphic organizer. In each box, use the given triangles to write a statement for the theorem.

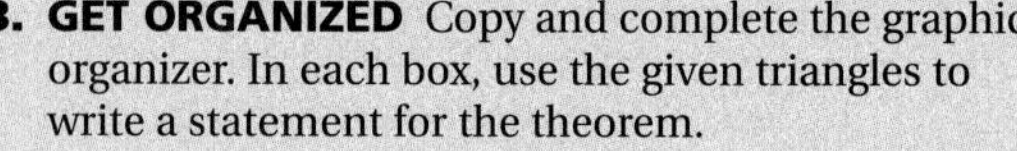

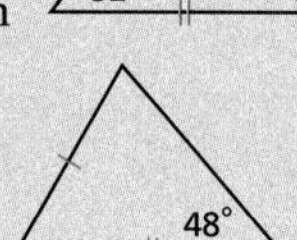

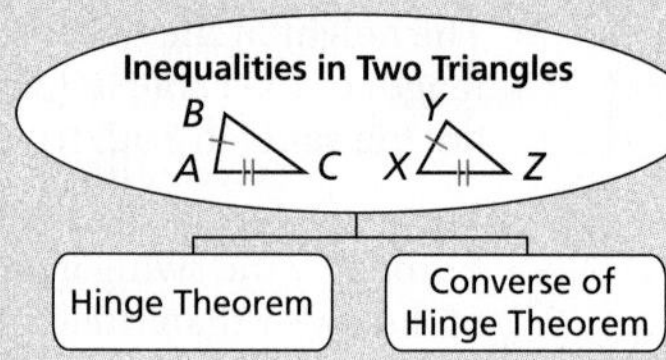

3 Close

Summarize

The Hinge Theorem and its converse establish inequalities involving two triangles in which two sides of one triangle are congruent to two sides of the other.

- If the included angles are not congruent, then the longer third side is across from the larger included angle.
- If the third sides are not congruent, then the larger included angle is across from the longer third side.

ONGOING ASSESSMENT and INTERVENTION

Diagnose ***Before*** **the Lesson**
5-6 Warm Up, TE p. 340

Monitor ***During*** **the Lesson**
Check It Out! Exercises, SE pp. 341–342
Questioning Strategies, TE pp. 341–342

Assess ***After*** **the Lesson**
5-6 Lesson Quiz, TE p. 345
Alternative Assessment, TE p. 345

Answers to *Think and Discuss*

1. Possible answer: kitchen tongs
2. No; in this case, 2 sides of one △ are ≅ to 2 sides of the second △, but the given ∠ measures are not the measures of the ∠s included between the ≅ sides. Thus you cannot apply the Hinge Thm.
3. See p. A5.

5-6 Exercises

go.hrw.com
Homework Help Online
KEYWORD: MG7 5-6
Parent Resources Online
KEYWORD: MG7 Parent

GUIDED PRACTICE

SEE EXAMPLE 1 p. 341

Compare the given measures.

1. AC and XZ

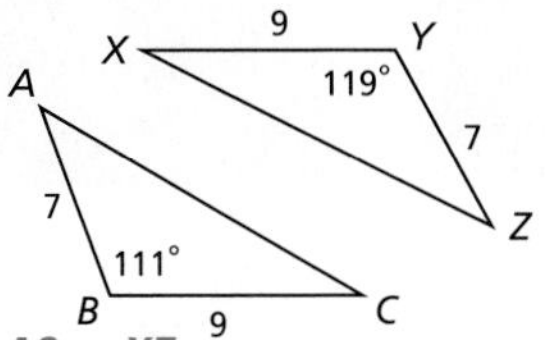

$AC < XZ$

2. $m\angle SRT$ and $m\angle QRT$

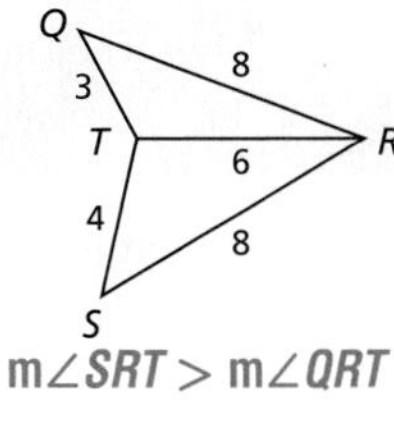

$m\angle SRT > m\angle QRT$

3. KL and KN

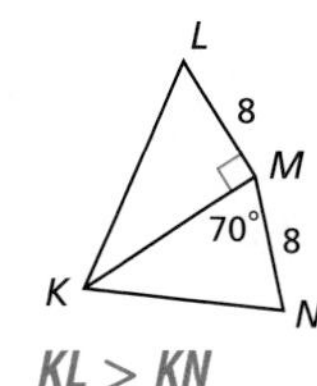

$KL > KN$

Find the range of values for x.

4. $-4 < x < 8.5$

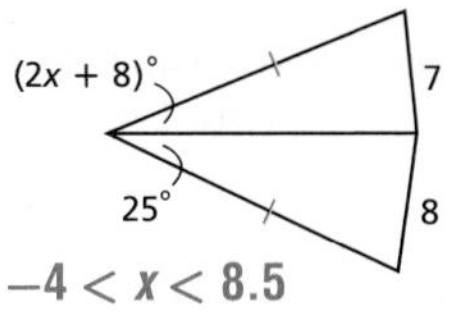

5. $1.2 < x < 3$

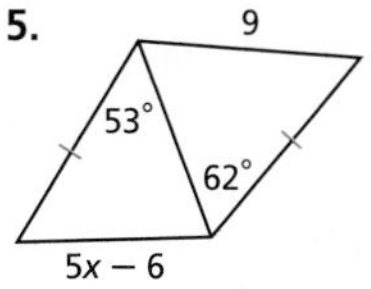

6.

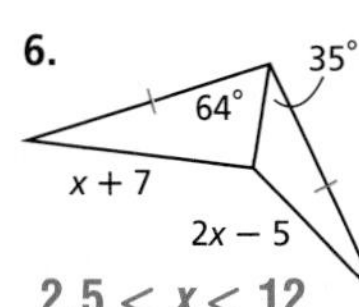

$2.5 < x < 12$

SEE EXAMPLE 2 p. 341

7. **Health** A therapist can take measurements to gauge the flexibility of a patient's elbow joint. In which position is the angle measure at the elbow joint greater? Explain.

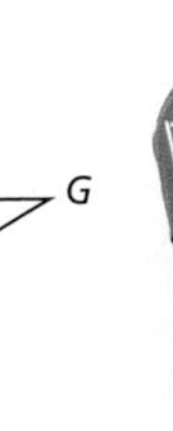

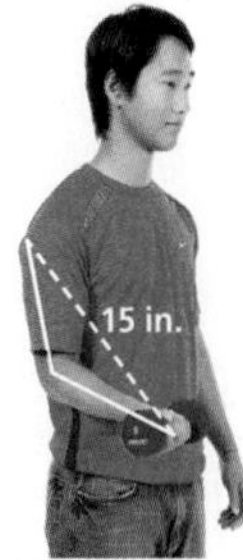

SEE EXAMPLE 3 p. 342

8. Write a two-column proof.
Given: $\overline{FH}$ is a median of $\triangle DFG$. $m\angle DHF > m\angle GHF$
Prove: $DF > GF$

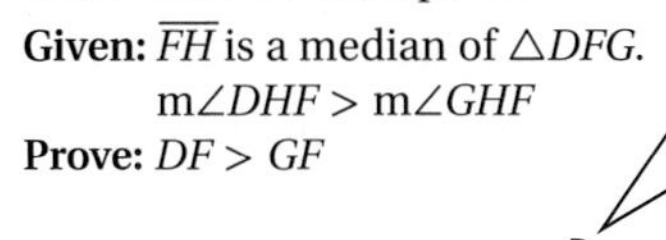

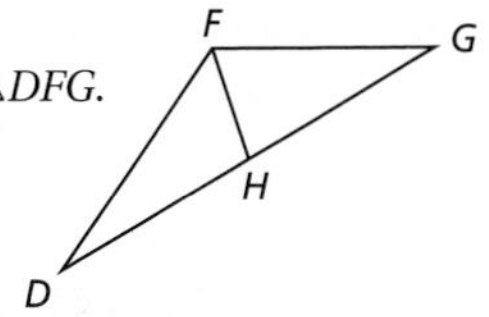

PRACTICE AND PROBLEM SOLVING

Independent Practice

For Exercises	See Example
9–14	1
15	2
16	3

Extra Practice
Skills Practice p. S13
Application Practice p. S32

Compare the given measures.

9. $m\angle DCA$ and $m\angle BCA$

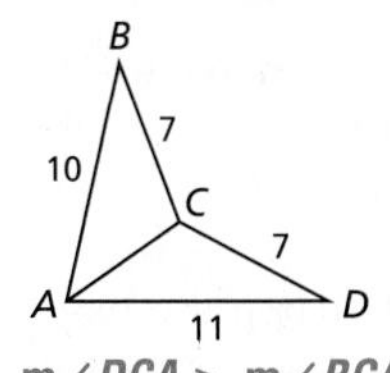

$m\angle DCA > m\angle BCA$

10. $m\angle GHJ$ and $m\angle KLM$

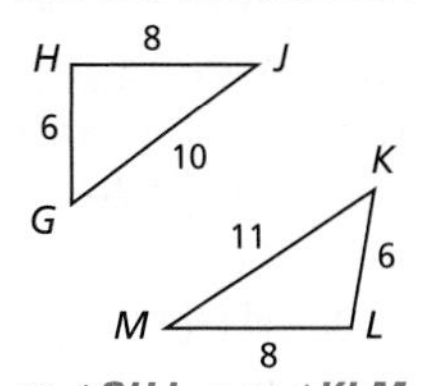

$m\angle GHJ < m\angle KLM$

11. TU and SV

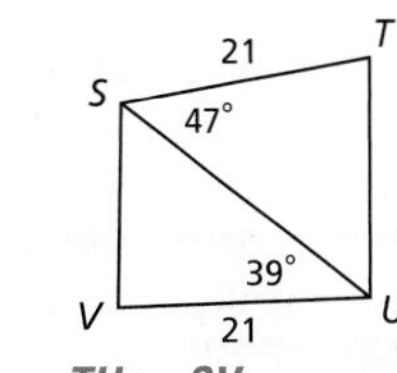

$TU > SV$

Find the range of values for z.

12.

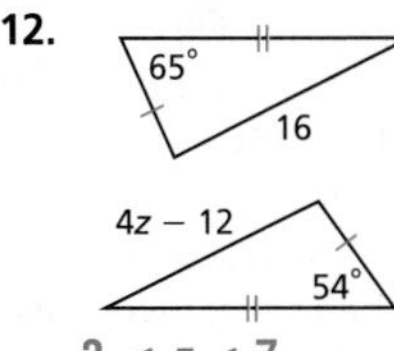

$3 < z < 7$

13.

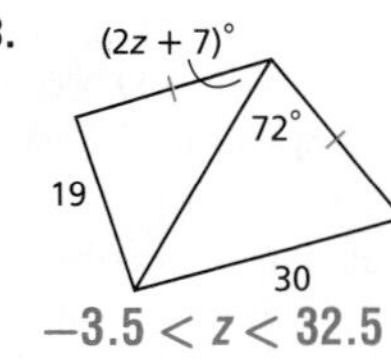

$-3.5 < z < 32.5$

14.

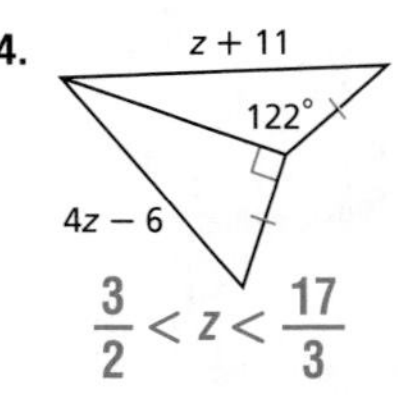

$\frac{3}{2} < z < \frac{17}{3}$

5-6 Exercises

Assignment Guide

Assign *Guided Practice* exercises as necessary.

If you finished Examples **1–3**
Basic 9–16, 18–28, 30–33, 36–43
Average 9–34, 36–43
Advanced 9–43

Homework Quick Check
Quickly check key concepts.
Exercises: 10, 15, 16, 18, 24

Answers

7. The second position; the lengths of the upper and lower arm are the same in both positions, but the distance from the shoulder to the wrist is greater in the second position. So the included ∠ measure is greater by the Conv. of the Hinge Thm.

8. 1. $\overline{FH}$ is a median of $\triangle DFG$. $m\angle DHF > m\angle GHF$ (Given)
   2. H is the midpoint of $\overline{DG}$. (Def. of median)
   3. $\overline{DH} \cong \overline{GH}$ (Def. of mdpt.)
   4. $\overline{FH} \cong \overline{FH}$ (Reflex. Prop. of ≅)
   5. $DF > GF$ (Hinge Thm.)

State Resources

Reading Math When the students are reading and writing the inequalities in **Exercises 18–23,** remind them not to confuse the less than symbol (<) with an angle symbol (∠).

Exercise 30 involves using the Hinge Theorem to find the minimum distance between cities. This exercise prepares students for the Multi-Step Test Prep on page 364.

Answers

15. The lengths of the arms are the same in both positions, but the included ∠ measure is greater in the second position. Therefore, by the Hinge Thm., the distance from the cab to the bucket is greater in the second position.

16. 1. $\overline{JK} \cong \overline{NM}$, $\overline{KP} \cong \overline{MQ}$, $JQ > NP$ (Given)
    2. $\overline{QP} \cong \overline{QP}$ (Reflex. Prop. of ≅)
    3. $QP = QP$ (Def. of ≅ segs.)
    4. $JQ + QP > NP + QP$ (Add. Prop. of Inequal.)
    5. $JQ + QP = JP$, $NP + QP = NQ$ (Seg. Add. Post.)
    6. $JP > NQ$ (Subst.)
    7. $m\angle K > m\angle M$ (Conv. of Hinge Thm.)

28, 29, 33, 35. See p. A20.

5-6 PRACTICE A

5-6 PRACTICE C

5-6 PRACTICE B

Compare the given measures.

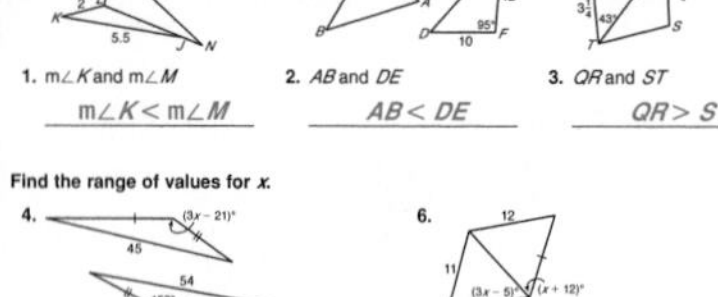

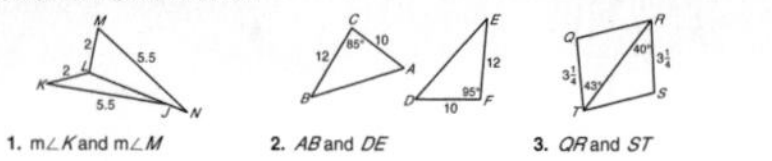

1. m∠K and m∠M — $m\angle K < m\angle M$
2. AB and DE — $AB < DE$
3. QR and ST — $QR > ST$

Find the range of values for x.

4. (figure: $(3x - 21)°$, 45, 54, 153°) — $7 < x < 58$
5. (figure: 37.5, 118°, 111°, $3x + 6$) — $-2 < x < 10.5$
6. (figure: 12, 11, $(3x - 5)°$, $(x + 12)°$) — $\frac{5}{3} < x < \frac{17}{2}$
7. (figure: 60°, $3x - 3$, 70°, $4x - 7$) — $1 < x < 4$

8. You have used a compass to copy and bisect segments and angles and to draw arcs and circles. A compass has a drawing leg, a pivot leg, and a hinge at the angle between the legs. Explain why and how the measure of the angle at the hinge changes if you draw two circles with different diameters.

Possible answer: The legs of a compass and the length spanned by it form a triangle, but the lengths of the legs cannot change. Therefore any two settings of the compass are subject to the Hinge Theorem. To draw a larger-diameter circle, the measure of the hinge angle must be made larger. To draw a smaller-diameter circle, the measure of the hinge angle must be made smaller.

15. **Industry** The operator of a backhoe changes the distance between the cab and the bucket by changing the angle formed by the arms. In which position is the distance from the cab to the bucket greater? Explain.

16. Write a two-column proof.
Given: $\overline{JK} \cong \overline{NM}$, $\overline{KP} \cong \overline{MQ}$, $JQ > NP$
Prove: $m\angle K > m\angle M$

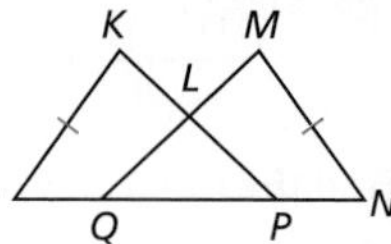

17. **Critical Thinking** *ABC* is an isosceles triangle with base $\overline{BC}$. *XYZ* is an isosceles triangle with base $\overline{YZ}$. Given that $\overline{AB} \cong \overline{XY}$ and $m\angle A = m\angle X$, compare *BC* and *YZ*. **$BC = YZ$**

Compare. Write <, >, or =.

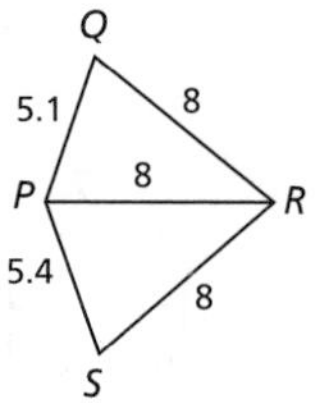

18. $m\angle QRP$ ▒ $m\angle SRP$ **<**
19. $m\angle QPR$ ▒ $m\angle QRP$ **>**
20. $m\angle PRS$ ▒ $m\angle RSP$ **<**
21. $m\angle RSP$ ▒ $m\angle RPS$ **=**
22. $m\angle QPR$ ▒ $m\angle RPS$ **>**
23. $m\angle PSR$ ▒ $m\angle PQR$ **<**

(Figure: Q, P, R, S; PQ = 5.1, QR = 8, PR = 8, PS = 5.4, SR = 8)

Make a conclusion based on the Hinge Theorem or its converse. (*Hint:* Draw a sketch.)

24. In △*ABC* and △*DEF*, $\overline{AB} \cong \overline{DE}$, $\overline{BC} \cong \overline{EF}$, $m\angle B = 59°$, and $m\angle E = 47°$. **$AC > DF$**

25. △*RST* is isosceles with base $\overline{RT}$. The endpoints of $\overline{SV}$ are vertex *S* and a point *V* on $\overline{RT}$. $RV = 4$, and $TV = 5$. **$m\angle RSV < m\angle TSV$**

26. In △*GHJ* and △*KLM*, $\overline{GH} \cong \overline{KL}$, and $\overline{GJ} \cong \overline{KM}$. ∠*G* is a right angle, and ∠*K* is an acute angle. **$HJ > LM$**

27. In △*XYZ*, $\overline{XM}$ is the median to $\overline{YZ}$, and $YX > ZX$. **$m\angle YMX > m\angle ZMX$**

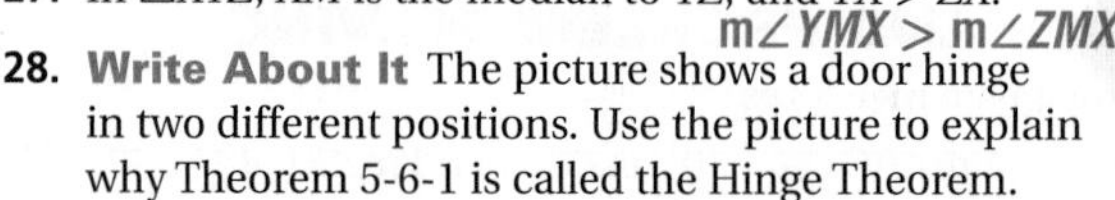

28. **Write About It** The picture shows a door hinge in two different positions. Use the picture to explain why Theorem 5-6-1 is called the Hinge Theorem.

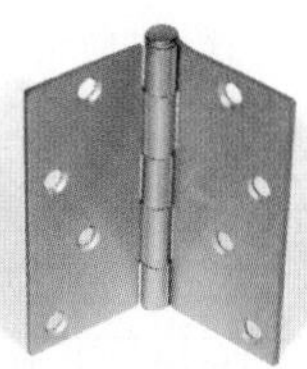

29. **Write About It** Compare the Hinge Theorem to the SAS Congruence Postulate. How are they alike? How are they different?

30a. Newton Springs; $NJ < JH$ by the Hinge Thm.

MULTI-STEP TEST PREP

30. This problem will prepare you for the Multi-Step Test Prep on page 364.
The solid lines in the figure show an airline's routes between four cities.
    a. A traveler wants to fly from Jackson (*J*) to Shelby (*S*), but there is no direct flight between these cities. Given that $m\angle NSJ < m\angle HSJ$, should the traveler first fly to Newton Springs (*N*) or to Hollis (*H*) if he wants to minimize the number of miles flown? Why?
    b. The distance from Shelby (*S*) to Jackson (*J*) is 182 mi. What is the minimum number of miles the traveler will have to fly? **418 mi**

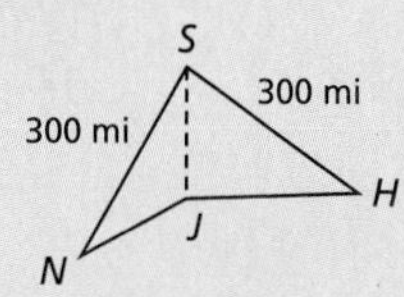

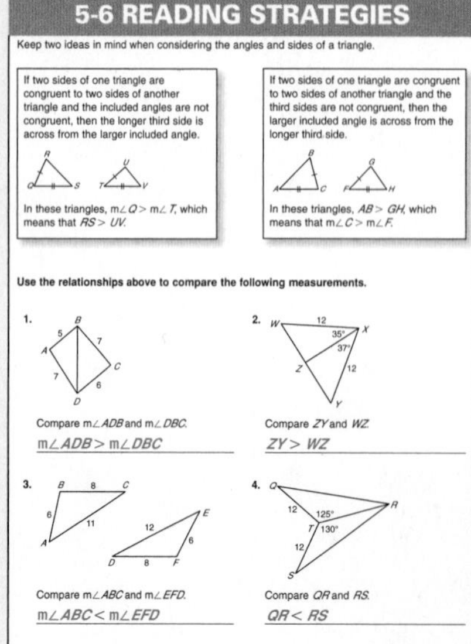

5-6 READING STRATEGIES

Keep two ideas in mind when considering the angles and sides of a triangle.

If two sides of one triangle are congruent to two sides of another triangle and the included angles are not congruent, then the longer third side is across from the larger included angle.

In these triangles, $m\angle Q > m\angle T$, which means that $RS > UV$.

If two sides of one triangle are congruent to two sides of another triangle and the third sides are not congruent, then the larger included angle is across from the longer third side.

In these triangles, $AB > GH$, which means that $m\angle C > m\angle F$.

Use the relationships above to compare the following measurements.

1. Compare m∠ADB and m∠DBC. — $m\angle ADB > m\angle DBC$
2. Compare ZY and WZ. — $ZY > WZ$
3. Compare m∠ABC and m∠EFD. — $m\angle ABC < m\angle EFD$
4. Compare QR and RS. — $QR < RS$

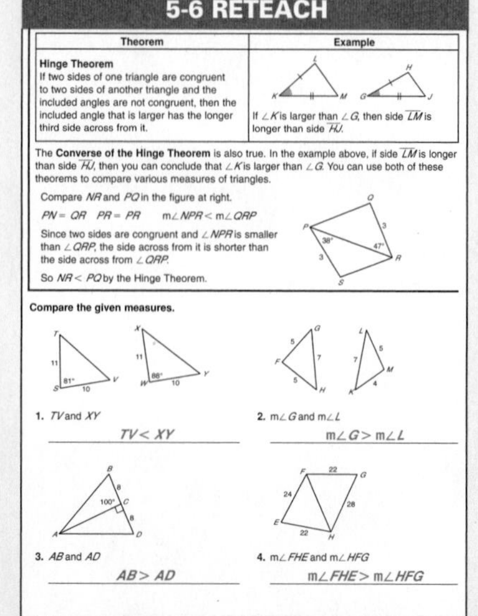

5-6 RETEACH

Theorem	Example
Hinge Theorem If two sides of one triangle are congruent to two sides of another triangle and the included angles are not congruent, then the included angle that is larger has the longer third side across from it.	If ∠K is larger than ∠G, then side $\overline{LM}$ is longer than side $\overline{HJ}$.

The **Converse of the Hinge Theorem** is also true. In the example above, if side $\overline{LM}$ is longer than side $\overline{HJ}$, then you can conclude that ∠K is larger than ∠G. You can use both of these theorems to compare various measures of triangles.

Compare NR and PQ in the figure at right.

$PN = QR$ $PR = PR$ $m\angle NPR < m\angle QRP$

Since two sides are congruent and ∠NPR is smaller than ∠QRP, the side across from it is shorter than the side across from ∠QRP.

So $NR < PQ$ by the Hinge Theorem.

Compare the given measures.

1. TV and XY — $TV < XY$
2. m∠G and m∠L — $m\angle G > m\angle L$
3. AB and AD — $AB > AD$
4. m∠FHE and m∠HFG — $m\angle FHE > m\angle HFG$

Test Prep

31. $\overline{ML}$ is a median of $\triangle JKL$. Which inequality best describes the range of values for x?

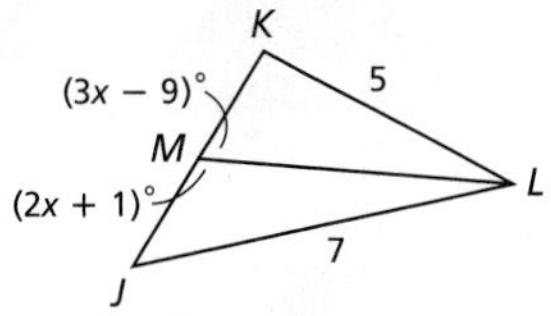

Ⓐ $x > 2$ Ⓒ $3 < x < 4\frac{2}{3}$

Ⓑ $x > 10$ Ⓓ $3 < x < 10$ (circled)

32. $\overline{DC}$ is a median of $\triangle ABC$. Which of the following statements is true?

Ⓕ $BC < AC$ Ⓖ $BC > AC$ Ⓗ $AD = DB$ (circled) Ⓙ $DC = AB$

33. **Short Response** Two groups start hiking from the same camp. Group A hikes 6.5 miles due west and then hikes 4 miles in the direction N 35° W. Group B hikes 6.5 miles due east and then hikes 4 miles in the direction N 45° E. At this point, which group is closer to the camp? Explain.

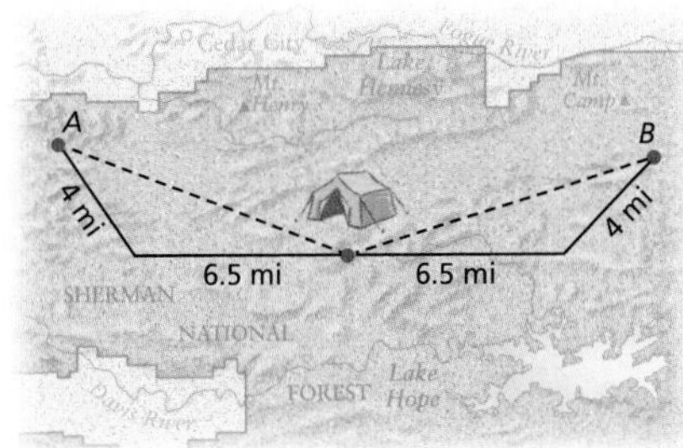

Challenge and Extend

34. **Multi-Step** In $\triangle XYZ$, $XZ = 5x + 15$, $XY = 8x - 6$, and $m\angle XVZ > m\angle XVY$. Find the range of values for x. **$0.75 < x < 7$**

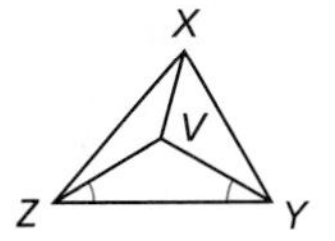

35. Use these steps to write a paragraph proof of the Hinge Theorem.

Given: $\overline{AB} \cong \overline{DE}$, $\overline{BC} \cong \overline{EF}$, $m\angle ABC > m\angle DEF$
Prove: $AC > DF$

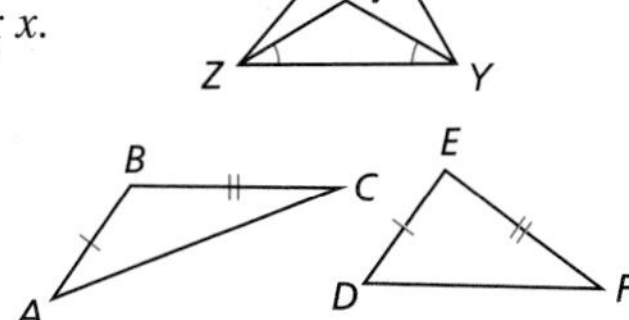

a. Locate P outside $\triangle ABC$ so that $\angle ABP \cong \angle DEF$ and $\overline{BP} \cong \overline{EF}$. Show that $\triangle ABP \cong \triangle DEF$ and thus $\overline{AP} \cong \overline{DF}$.

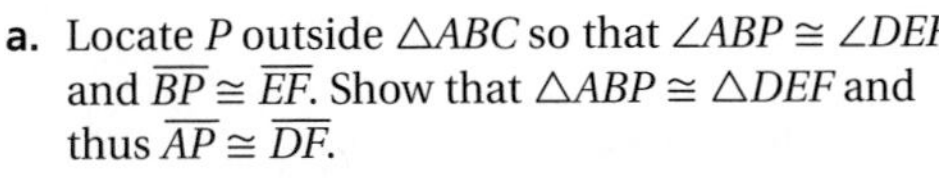

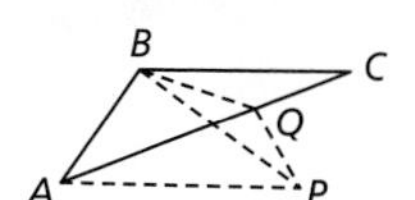

b. Locate Q on $\overline{AC}$ so that $\overline{BQ}$ bisects $\angle PBC$. Draw $\overline{QP}$. Show that $\triangle BQP \cong \triangle BQC$ and thus $\overline{QP} \cong \overline{QC}$.

c. Justify the statements $AQ + QP > AP$, $AQ + QC = AC$, $AQ + QC > AP$, $AC > AP$, and $AC > DF$.

Spiral Review

Find the range and mode, if any, of each set of data. *(Previous course)*

36. 2, 5, 1, 0.5, 0.75, 2 **4.5; 2**

37. 95, 97, 89, 87, 85, 99 **14; none**

38. 5, 5, 7, 9, 4, 4, 8, 7 **5; 4, 5, 7**

For the given information, show that $m \parallel n$. State any postulates or theorems used. *(Lesson 3-3)*

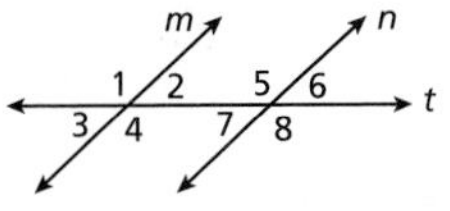

39. $m\angle 2 = (3x + 21)°$, $m\angle 6 = (7x + 1)°$, $x = 5$

40. $m\angle 4 = (2x + 34)°$, $m\angle 7 = (15x + 27)°$, $x = 7$

39. $m\angle 2 = m\angle 6 = 36°$; $m \parallel n$ by the Conv. of the Corr. ∠s Post.

40. $m\angle 4 = 48°$, $m\angle 7 = 132°$; $m \parallel n$ by the Conv. of the Same-Side Int. ∠s Thm.

Find each measure. *(Lesson 5-4)*

41. DF **2.5**

42. BC **4.6**

43. $m\angle BFD$ **85°**

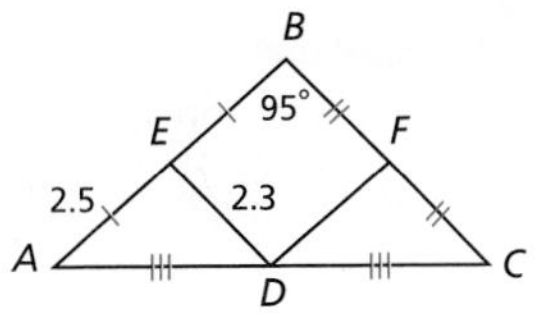

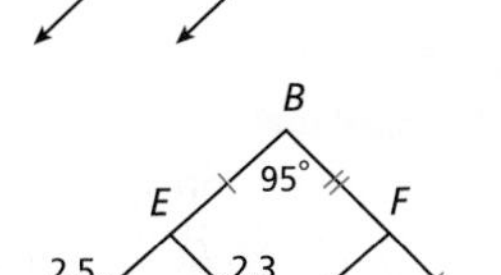

5-6 Problem Solving

1. The angle that a person makes as he or she is sitting changes with the task. The diagram shows the position of a student at his desk. In which position is the angle measure $a°$ at which he is sitting the greatest? The least? Explain.

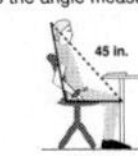

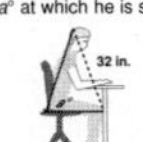

Greatest at relaxed position; least at writing position; the length of his leg and the length of his body are the same in all three triangles. So, by the Converse of the Hinge Thm., the larger included ∠ is across from the longer third side.

2. Two cyclists start from the same location and travel in opposite directions for 2 miles each. Then the first cyclist turns right 90° and continues for another mile. At the same time, the second cyclist turns 45° left and continues for another mile. At this point, which cyclist is closer to the original starting point?

the first cyclist

3. A compass is used to draw a circle. Then the compass is opened wider and another circle is drawn. Explain how this illustrates the Hinge Theorem.

The ∠ formed by the compass when drawing the first circle is smaller. So the distance between the points of the compass is greater for the second circle.

Choose the best answer.

4. Two sides of each triangle in the circle are formed from the radii of the circle. Compare EF and FG.

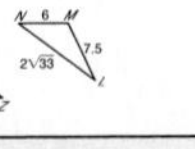

A $EF = FG$
Ⓑ $EF < FG$
C $EF > FG$
D Not enough information is given.

5. Compare $m\angle Y$ and $m\angle M$.

F $m\angle Y = m\angle M$
Ⓖ $m\angle Y > m\angle M$
H $m\angle Y < m\angle M$
J Not enough information is given.

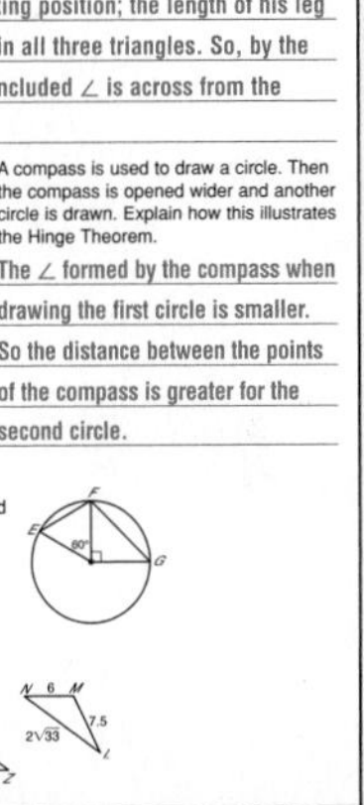

5-6 Challenge

1. **Concentric circles** are circles that have the same center and different radii. The circles at the right are concentric. The measure of $\angle BAC$ is 93°, and the measure of $\angle DAE$ is 60°. Explain why BC must be greater than DE.

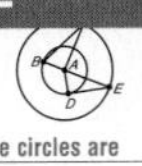

$\overline{AB} \cong \overline{AD}$ and $\overline{AC} \cong \overline{AE}$ because radii of the same circles are congruent. Since $m\angle BAC > m\angle DAE$, then by the Hinge Thm., $BC > DE$.

2. In $\triangle PQR$, $\angle SQR \cong \angle SRQ$, $PQ > PR$, $m\angle PSR = (4y + 9)°$, and $m\angle QSP = (6y - 24)°$. Find the range of values for y.

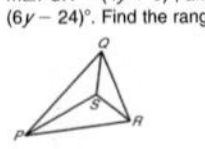

$16.5 < y < 34$

3. In $FGHJ$, $m\angle H < m\angle FJG$, $GH = 4z - 1$, and $FG = z + 8$. Find the range of values for z.

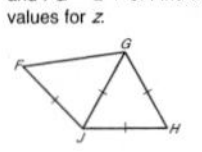

$0.25 < z < 3$

4. Write a two-column proof.

Given: $\overline{JK} \parallel \overline{HL}$
$\overline{JK} \cong \overline{HL}$
$m\angle KML > m\angle HML$

Prove: $KL > HL$

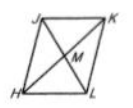

Statements	Reasons
1. $\overline{JK} \parallel \overline{HL}$, $\overline{JK} \cong \overline{HL}$, $m\angle KML > m\angle HML$	1. Given
2. $\angle JMK \cong \angle LMH$	2. Vert. ∠s Thm.
3. $\angle JKH \cong \angle LHK$	3. Alt. Int. ∠s Thm.
4. $\triangle JKM \cong \triangle LHM$	4. AAS
5. $\overline{MK} \cong \overline{MH}$	5. CPCTC
6. $\overline{ML} \cong \overline{ML}$	6. Reflex. Prop. of ≅
7. $KL > HL$	7. Hinge Thm.

Test Prep Doctor In **Exercise 31,** students may forget to switch the inequality sign in $-x > -10$ when solving $2x + 1 > 3x - 9$. Remind them that when they multiply or divide by a negative number, they must reverse the inequality sign.

For **Exercise 33,** review how bearings are written and that N 35° W means 35° west of north.

Journal

Have students describe a real-life example that helps them remember the Hinge Theorem.

Alternative Assessment

Have students create and explain a model demonstrating the Hinge Theorem and its converse. For example, they can use a plastic-foam ball and thin sticks so they can move the sticks to change the angle between them.

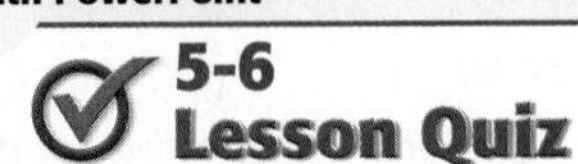

5-6 Lesson Quiz

1. Compare $m\angle ABC$ and $m\angle DEF$. $m\angle ABC > m\angle DEF$

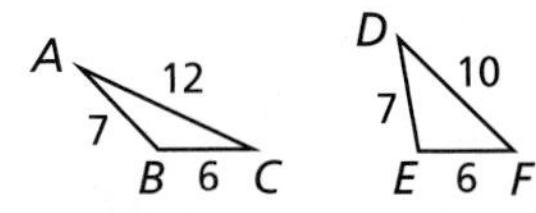

2. Compare PS and QR. $PS < QR$

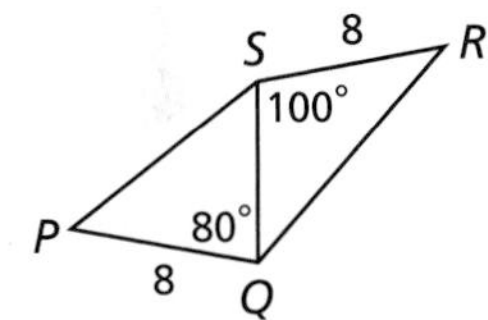

3. Find the range of values for z. $-3 < z < 7$

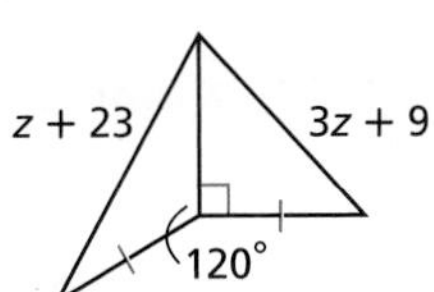

4. Write a two-column proof.

Given: $\overline{XY} \cong \overline{WZ}$, $XW < YZ$
Prove: $m\angle XYW < m\angle ZWY$

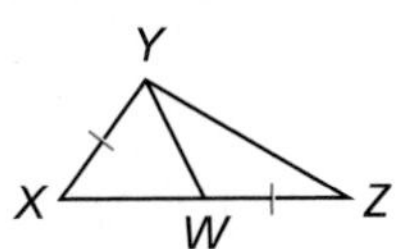

1. $\overline{XY} \cong \overline{WZ}$, $XW < YZ$ (Given)
2. $\overline{YW} \cong \overline{YW}$ (Reflex. Prop. of ≅)
3. $m\angle XYW < m\angle ZWY$ (Conv. of Hinge Thm.)

Also available on transparency

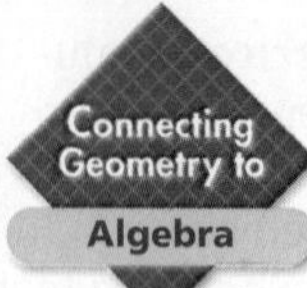

Organizer

Pacing:
Traditional $\frac{1}{2}$ day
Block $\frac{1}{4}$ day

Objective: Apply algebra skills to simplifying radical expressions.

Online Edition

Countdown Week 12

Teach

Remember

Students review how to simplify radical expressions.

Algebra Remind students that $(\sqrt{x})^2 = (\sqrt{x})(\sqrt{x}) = \sqrt{(x)(x)} = \sqrt{x^2} = x$. So $(\sqrt{3})^2 = 3$.

Close

Assess

Have students explain the conditions for simplest radical form of an expression.

State Resources

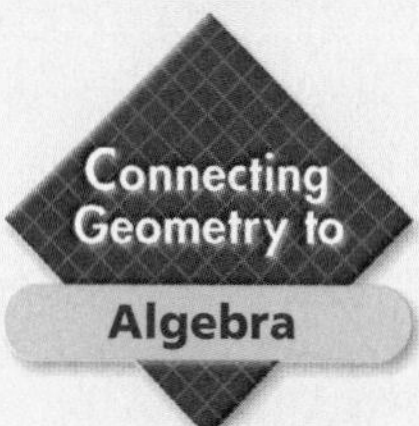

Simplest Radical Form

When a problem involves square roots, you may be asked to give the answer in simplest radical form. Recall that the radicand is the expression under the radical sign.

Simplest Form of a Square-Root Expression

An expression containing square roots is in simplest form when

- the radicand has no perfect square factors other than 1.
- the radicand has no fractions.
- there are no square roots in any denominator.

To simplify a radical expression, remember that the square root of a product is equal to the product of the square roots. Also, the square root of a quotient is equal to the quotient of the square roots.

$$\sqrt{ab} = \sqrt{a} \cdot \sqrt{b}, \text{ when } a \geq 0 \text{ and } b \geq 0$$

$$\sqrt{\frac{a}{b}} = \frac{\sqrt{a}}{\sqrt{b}}, \text{ when } a \geq 0 \text{ and } b > 0$$

Examples

Write each expression in simplest radical form.

A $\sqrt{216}$

$\sqrt{216}$	*216 has a perfect-square factor of 36, so the expression is not in simplest radical form.*
$\sqrt{(36)(6)}$	*Factor the radicand.*
$\sqrt{36} \cdot \sqrt{6}$	*Product Property of Square Roots*
$6\sqrt{6}$	*Simplify.*

B $\frac{6}{\sqrt{2}}$

$\frac{6}{\sqrt{2}}$	*There is a square root in the denominator, so the expression is not in simplest radical form.*
$\frac{6}{\sqrt{2}}\left(\frac{\sqrt{2}}{\sqrt{2}}\right)$	*Multiply by a form of 1 to eliminate the square root in the denominator.*
$\frac{6\sqrt{2}}{2}$	*Simplify.*
$3\sqrt{2}$	*Divide.*

Try This

Write each expression in simplest radical form.

1. $\sqrt{720}$ $12\sqrt{5}$ **2.** $\sqrt{\frac{3}{16}}$ $\frac{\sqrt{3}}{4}$ **3.** $\frac{10}{\sqrt{2}}$ $5\sqrt{2}$ **4.** $\sqrt{\frac{1}{3}}$ $\frac{\sqrt{3}}{3}$ **5.** $\sqrt{45}$ $3\sqrt{5}$

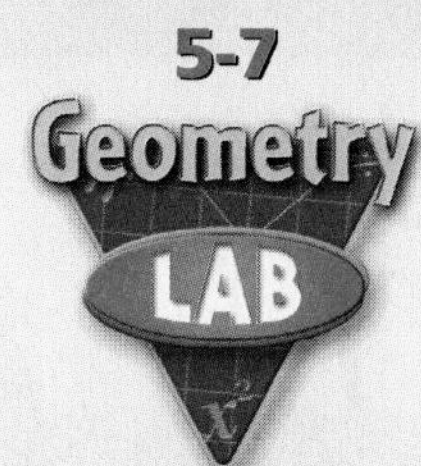

Hands-on Proof of the Pythagorean Theorem

Use with Lesson 5-7

In Lesson 1-6, you used the Pythagorean Theorem to find the distance between two points in the coordinate plane. In this activity, you will build figures and compare their areas to justify the Pythagorean Theorem.

Activity

1. Draw a large scalene right triangle on graph paper. Draw three copies of the triangle. On each triangle, label the shorter leg a, the longer leg b, and the hypotenuse c.

2. Draw a square with a side length of $b - a$. Label each side of the square.

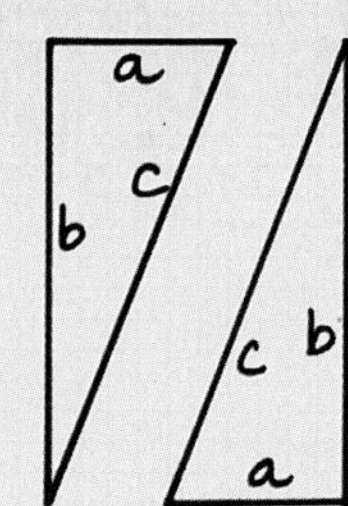

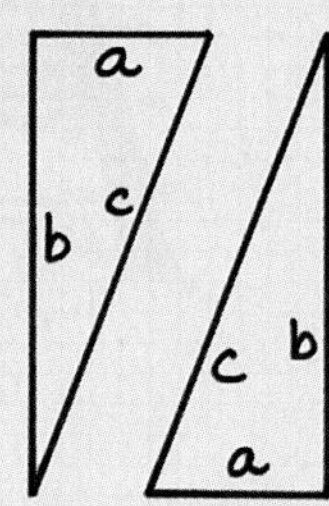

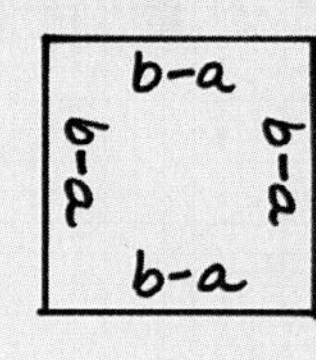

3. Cut out the five figures. Arrange them to make the composite figure shown at right.

4. You can think of this composite figure as being made of the two squares outlined in red. What are the side length and area of the small red square? of the large red square? a; a^2; b; b^2

5. Use your results from Step 4 to write an algebraic expression for the area of the composite figure. $a^2 + b^2$

6. Now rearrange the five figures to make a single square with side length c. Write an algebraic expression for the area of this square. area $= c^2$

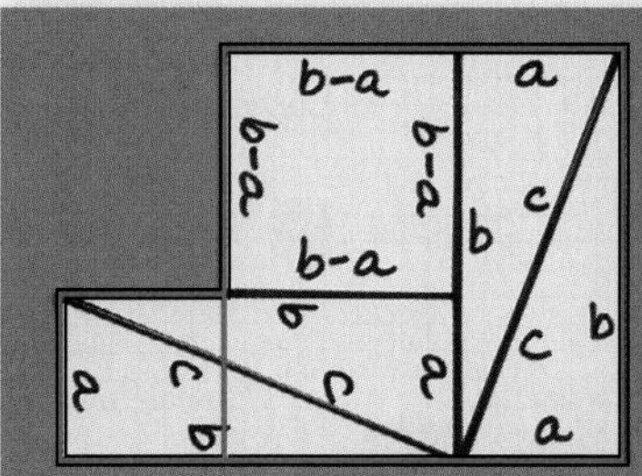

Try This

1. Since the composite figure and the square with side length c are made of the same five shapes, their areas are equal. Write and simplify an equation to represent this relationship. What conclusion can you make? $a^2 + b^2 = c^2$

2. Draw a scalene right triangle with different side lengths. Repeat the activity. Do you reach the same conclusion? Check students' work.

Answers to *Activity*

6.

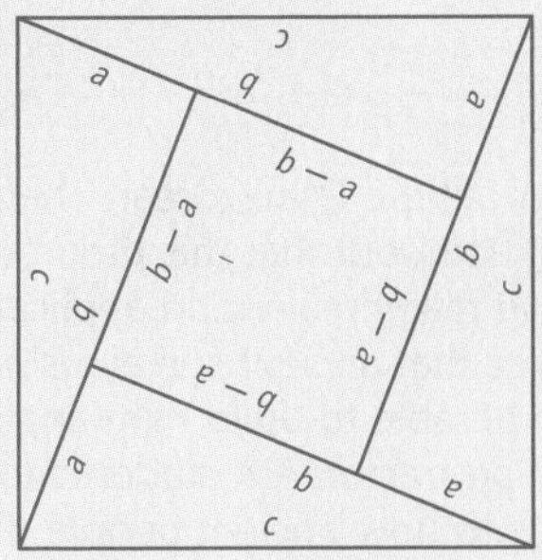

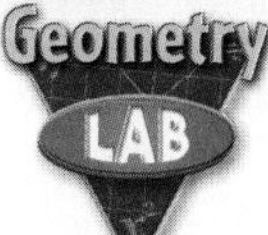

Organizer

Use with Lesson 5-7

Pacing:
Traditional $\frac{1}{2}$ day
Block $\frac{1}{4}$ day

Objective: Use area to justify the Pythagorean Theorem.

Materials: graph paper, scissors

Online Edition

Countdown Week 12

Resources

Geometry Lab Activities
5-7 Lab Recording Sheet

Teach

Discuss

Emphasize that the area of the composite figure students have made is equal to the sum of the areas of the five smaller figures. Remind students how to square a binomial.

Alternative Approach

Use pieces cut from a transparency to demonstrate this lab on an overhead projector.

Close

Key Concept

In a right triangle, the sum of the squares of the lengths of the legs equals the square of the hypotenuse.

Assessment

Journal Have students explain how they used area to justify the Pythagorean Theorem in this lab.

State Resources

5-7 Organizer

Pacing: Traditional 1 day
Block $\frac{1}{2}$ day

Objectives: Use the Pythagorean Theorem and its converse to solve problems.

Use Pythagorean inequalities to classify triangles.

Technology Lab
In *Technology Lab Activities*

Online Edition
Tutorial Videos

Countdown Week 12

Power Presentations with PowerPoint®

Warm Up

Classify each triangle by its angle measures.

1. (triangle with angles 80°, 70°) acute

2. 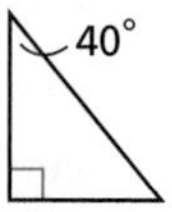 (right triangle with angle 40°) right

3. Simplify $(2\sqrt{3})^2$. 12

4. If $a = 6$, $b = 7$, and $c = 12$, find $a^2 + b^2$ and find c^2. Which value is greater? 85; 144; c^2

Also available on transparency

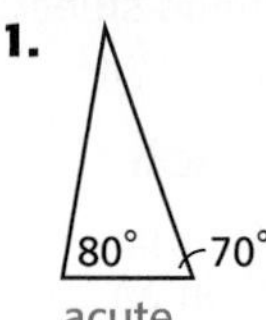

Math Humor

Q: What did the geometry teacher say to his student?

A: "Here's looking at Eu-Clid!" (you, kid)

State Resources

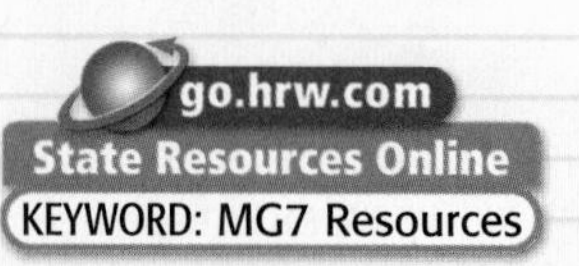

5-7 The Pythagorean Theorem

Objectives
Use the Pythagorean Theorem and its converse to solve problems.

Use Pythagorean inequalities to classify triangles.

Vocabulary
Pythagorean triple

Why learn this?
You can use the Pythagorean Theorem to determine whether a ladder is in a safe position. (See Example 2.)

The Pythagorean Theorem is probably the most famous mathematical relationship. As you learned in Lesson 1-6, it states that in a right triangle, the sum of the squares of the lengths of the legs equals the square of the length of the hypotenuse.

$$a^2 + b^2 = c^2$$

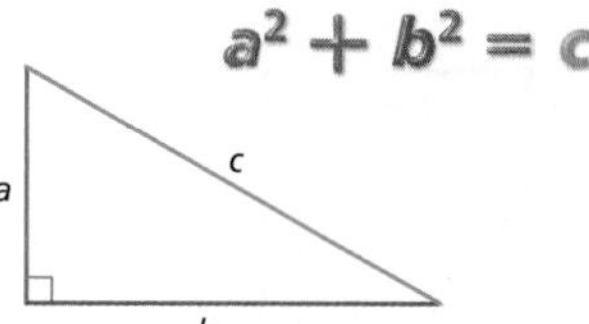

The Pythagorean Theorem is named for the Greek mathematician Pythagoras, who lived in the sixth century B.C.E. However, this relationship was known to earlier people, such as the Babylonians, Egyptians, and Chinese.

There are many different proofs of the Pythagorean Theorem. The one below uses area and algebra.

Remember!
The area A of a square with side length s is given by the formula $A = s^2$.
The area A of a triangle with base b and height h is given by the formula $A = \frac{1}{2}bh$.

PROOF **Pythagorean Theorem**

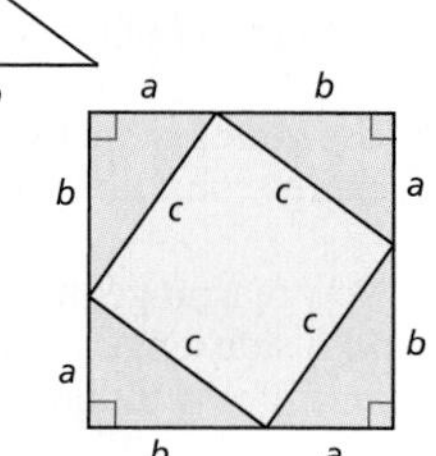

Given: A right triangle with leg lengths a and b and hypotenuse of length c

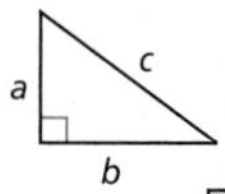

Prove: $a^2 + b^2 = c^2$

Proof: Arrange four copies of the triangle as shown. The sides of the triangles form two squares.

The area of the outer square is $(a + b)^2$. The area of the inner square is c^2. The area of each blue triangle is $\frac{1}{2}ab$.

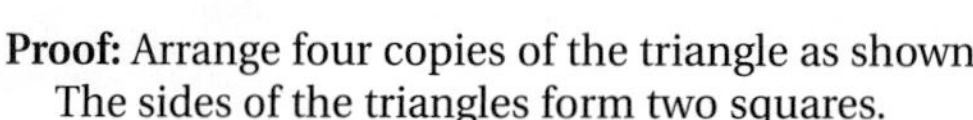

area of outer square = area of 4 blue triangles + area of inner square

$(a + b)^2 = 4\left(\frac{1}{2}ab\right) + c^2$ *Substitute the areas.*

$a^2 + 2ab + b^2 = 2ab + c^2$ *Simplify.*

$a^2 + b^2 = c^2$ *Subtract 2ab from both sides.*

The Pythagorean Theorem gives you a way to find unknown side lengths when you know a triangle is a right triangle.

1 Introduce

EXPLORATION

5-7 The Pythagorean Theorem

Use geometry software to explore some inequalities related to the Pythagorean Theorem.

1. Construct a triangle. Label its vertices A, B, and C.
2. Measure $\overline{AB}$, $\overline{CB}$, $\overline{CA}$, and $\angle BCA$. If necessary, drag the vertices so that $\overline{AB}$ is the longest side of the triangle.
3. Calculate AB^2 and $CB^2 + CA^2$. 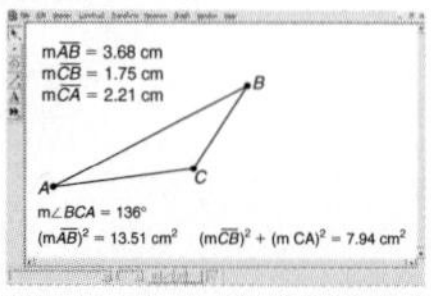
4. Drag point C to change the size of $\angle BCA$, keeping $\overline{AB}$ as the longest side of the triangle. When $AB^2 > CB^2 + CA^2$, what type of angle is $\angle BCA$?
5. When $AB^2 = CB^2 + CA^2$, what type of angle is $\angle BCA$?
6. When $AB^2 < CB^2 + CA^2$, what type of angle is $\angle BCA$?

Motivate

Ask students to recall the Pythagorean Theorem from Lesson 1-6. Point out that this theorem and its corollaries have many real-world applications. Explain to students that ancient surveyors and architects had to be able to build right angles without having a protractor. Ask students to brainstorm for ideas as to how ancient people might have done this. Explain that they will learn some methods in this lesson.

Explorations and answers are provided in *Alternate Openers: Explorations Transparencies.*

EXAMPLE 1 Using the Pythagorean Theorem

Find the value of x. Give your answer in simplest radical form.

A

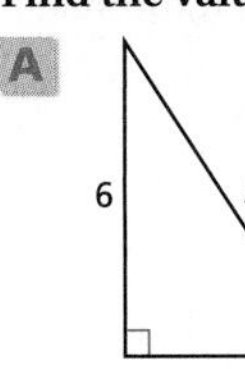

$a^2 + b^2 = c^2$ — *Pythagorean Theorem*

$6^2 + 4^2 = x^2$ — *Substitute 6 for a, 4 for b, and x for c.*

$52 = x^2$ — *Simplify.*

$\sqrt{52} = x$ — *Find the positive square root.*

$x = \sqrt{(4)(13)} = 2\sqrt{13}$ — *Simplify the radical.*

B

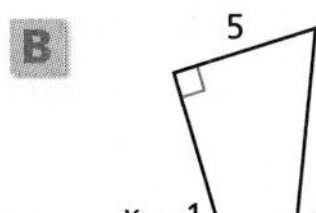

$a^2 + b^2 = c^2$ — *Pythagorean Theorem*

$5^2 + (x-1)^2 = x^2$ — *Substitute 5 for a, x − 1 for b, and x for c.*

$25 + x^2 - 2x + 1 = x^2$ — *Multiply.*

$-2x + 26 = 0$ — *Combine like terms.*

$26 = 2x$ — *Add 2x to both sides.*

$x = 13$ — *Divide both sides by 2.*

Find the value of x. Give your answer in simplest radical form.

1a.

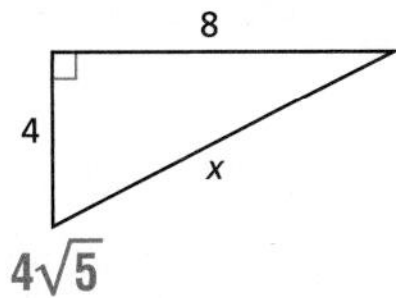

$4\sqrt{5}$

1b.

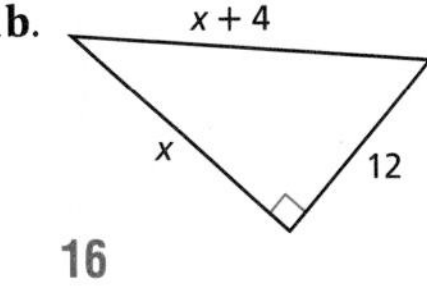

16

EXAMPLE 2 *Safety Application*

To prevent a ladder from shifting, safety experts recommend that the ratio of $a:b$ be 4 : 1. How far from the base of the wall should you place the foot of a 10-foot ladder? Round to the nearest inch.

Let x be the distance in feet from the foot of the ladder to the base of the wall. Then $4x$ is the distance in feet from the top of the ladder to the base of the wall.

$a^2 + b^2 = c^2$ — *Pythagorean Theorem*

$(4x)^2 + x^2 = 10^2$ — *Substitute.*

$17x^2 = 100$ — *Multiply and combine like terms.*

$x^2 = \frac{100}{17}$ — *Divide both sides by 17.*

$x = \sqrt{\frac{100}{17}} \approx 2 \text{ ft } 5 \text{ in.}$ — *Find the positive square root and round it.*

2. **What if...?** According to the recommended ratio, how high will a 30-foot ladder reach when placed against a wall? Round to the nearest inch. **29 ft 1 in.**

A set of three nonzero whole numbers a, b, and c such that $a^2 + b^2 = c^2$ is called a **Pythagorean triple**.

Common Pythagorean Triples			
3, 4, 5	5, 12, 13,	8, 15, 17	7, 24, 25

2 Teach

Guided Instruction

Review the Pythagorean Theorem and how to use it to find an unknown side length in a right triangle. Review how to simplify square roots and square radicals. Discuss Pythagorean triples and how to identify them by using the Converse of the Pythagorean Theorem. Then explain how to use the Pythagorean Inequalities Theorem to classify triangles by their angle measures.

Reaching All Learners

Through Concrete Manipulatives

Have students use raw spaghetti or straws to build triangles with side lengths of 3, 4, and 5 in., 3, 4, and 6 in., and 4, 5, and 6 in. Have them use a protractor (MK) to classify each triangle by its angle measures. right, obtuse, acute Then have them use the theorems from the lesson to classify the triangles mathematically.

COMMON ERROR ALERT

Students may have difficulty simplifying square roots. Review with students some common perfect squares, such as 25, 64, and 144. Review how to simplify a radical expression by factoring out perfect squares.

Power Presentations with PowerPoint®

Additional Examples

Example 1

Find the value of x. Give your answer in simplest radical form.

A. $2\sqrt{10}$

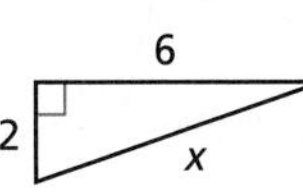

B. 5

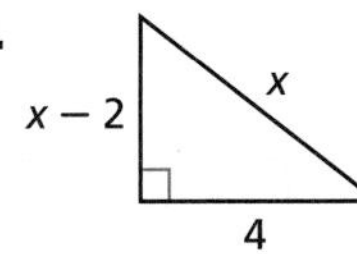

Example 2

Randy is building a rectangular picture frame. He wants the ratio of the length to the width to be 3:1 and the diagonal to be 12 cm. How wide should the frame be? Round to the nearest tenth of a centimeter. 3.8 cm

INTERVENTION

Questioning Strategies

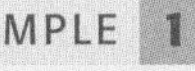

EXAMPLE 1

- How do you know which side length to substitute for *a, b,* and *c* in the Pythagorean Theorem?

EXAMPLE 2

- How do you solve for the hypotenuse when you are given the ratio of the side lengths?

Diversity The dimensions of an American football field are 100 yd by 53.3 yd. A Canadian football field is 110 yd by 65 yd. Have students calculate how much longer the diagonal of a Canadian field is than that of an American field. about 14.5 yd

Auditory As a class, write a short list of common Pythagorean triples. Have students recite them out loud so they will remember the values.

Power Presentations with PowerPoint®

Additional Examples

Example 3

Find the missing side length. Tell if the side lengths form a Pythagorean triple. Explain.

A.

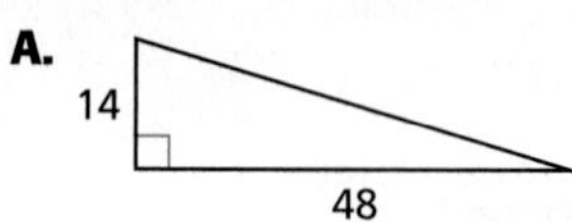

50; yes; the 3 side lengths are nonzero whole numbers that satisfy $a^2 + b^2 = c^2$, so they form a Pythagorean triple.

B.

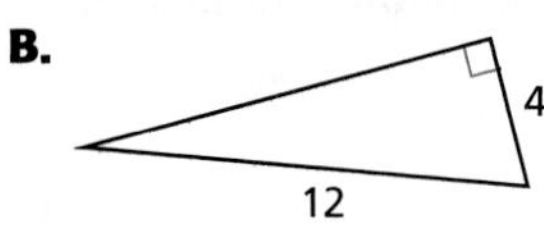

$8\sqrt{2}$; no; $8\sqrt{2}$ is not a whole number.

INTERVENTION

Questioning Strategies

EXAMPLE 3

- Do the values 0.3, 0.4, and 0.5 satisfy the Pythagorean Theorem? Do they form a Pythagorean triple? Explain.

EXAMPLE 3 Identifying Pythagorean Triples

Find the missing side length. Tell if the side lengths form a Pythagorean triple. Explain.

A

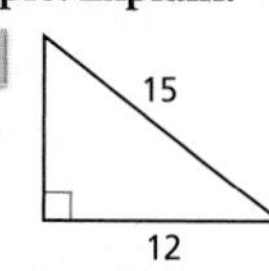

$a^2 + b^2 = c^2$	*Pythagorean Theorem*
$12^2 + b^2 = 15^2$	*Substitute 12 for a and 15 for c.*
$b^2 = 81$	*Multiply and subtract 144 from both sides.*
$b = 9$	*Find the positive square root.*

The side lengths are nonzero whole numbers that satisfy the equation $a^2 + b^2 = c^2$, so they form a Pythagorean triple.

B

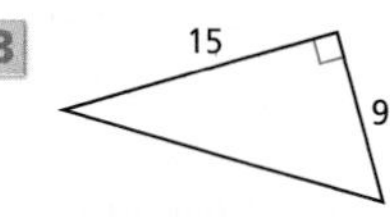

$a^2 + b^2 = c^2$	*Pythagorean Theorem*
$9^2 + 15^2 = c^2$	*Substitute 9 for a and 15 for b.*
$306 = c^2$	*Multiply and add.*
$c = \sqrt{306} = 3\sqrt{34}$	*Find the positive square root and simplify.*

The side lengths do not form a Pythagorean triple because $3\sqrt{34}$ is not a whole number.

3a. $2\sqrt{41}$; no; $2\sqrt{41}$ is not a whole number.

3b. 10; yes; the 3 side lengths are nonzero whole numbers that satisfy the equation $a^2 + b^2 = c^2$.

3c. 2.6; no; 2.4 and 2.6 are not whole numbers.

3d. 34; yes; the 3 side lengths are nonzero whole numbers that satisfy the equation $a^2 + b^2 = c^2$.

Find the missing side length. Tell if the side lengths form a Pythagorean triple. Explain.

3a.

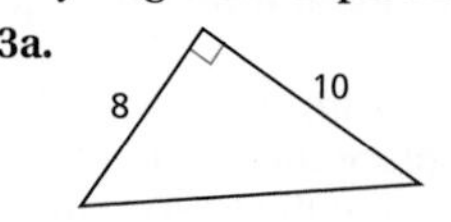

3b.

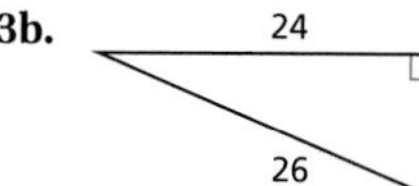

3c.

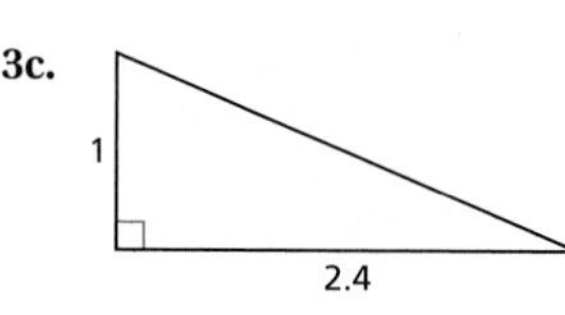

3d.

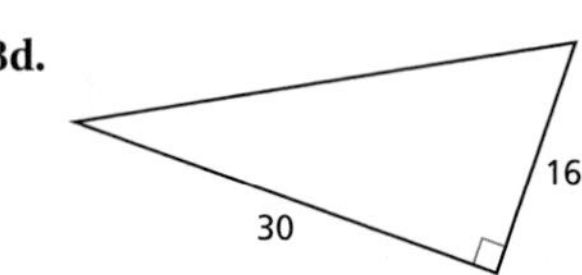

The converse of the Pythagorean Theorem gives you a way to tell if a triangle is a right triangle when you know the side lengths.

Know it! Note

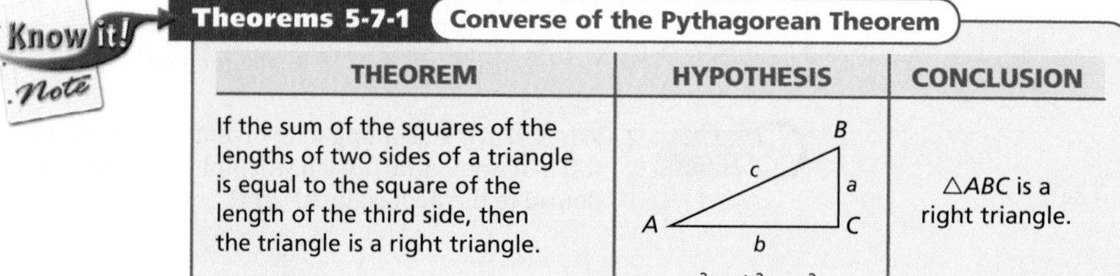

Theorems 5-7-1 Converse of the Pythagorean Theorem

THEOREM	HYPOTHESIS	CONCLUSION
If the sum of the squares of the lengths of two sides of a triangle is equal to the square of the length of the third side, then the triangle is a right triangle.	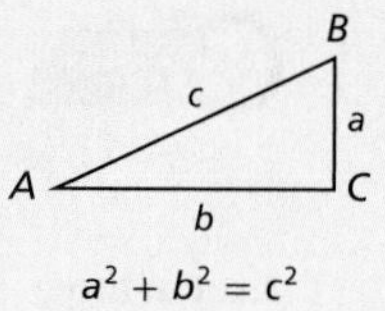 (triangle ABC with sides a, b, c) $a^2 + b^2 = c^2$	$\triangle ABC$ is a right triangle.

You will prove Theorem 5-7-1 in Exercise 45.

Teaching Tip

Social Studies Link Pythagoras was born around 569 B.C.E. on the Greek island of Samos. He studied mathematics, astronomy, and philosophy. Though it is believed that he did in fact prove the Pythagorean Theorem, the ancient Egyptians were familiar with the relationship long before Pythagoras's lifetime.

Critical Thinking Ask students "If you multiply each value in a Pythagorean triple by 5, what is true of the resulting values?" They also form a Pythagorean triple.

You can also use side lengths to classify a triangle as acute or obtuse.

Theorems 5-7-2 Pythagorean Inequalities Theorem

In $\triangle ABC$, c is the length of the longest side.

If $c^2 > a^2 + b^2$, then $\triangle ABC$ is an obtuse triangle.	If $c^2 < a^2 + b^2$, then $\triangle ABC$ is an acute triangle.
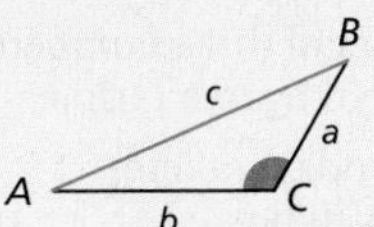	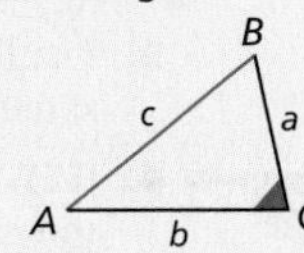

To understand why the Pythagorean inequalities are true, consider $\triangle ABC$.

If $c^2 = a^2 + b^2$, then $\triangle ABC$ is a right triangle by the Converse of the Pythagorean Theorem. So $m\angle C = 90°$.	If $c^2 > a^2 + b^2$, then c has increased. By the Converse of the Hinge Theorem, $m\angle C$ has also increased. So $m\angle C > 90°$.	If $c^2 < a^2 + b^2$, then c has decreased. By the Converse of the Hinge Theorem, $m\angle C$ has also decreased. So $m\angle C < 90°$.
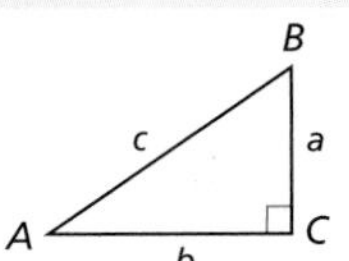	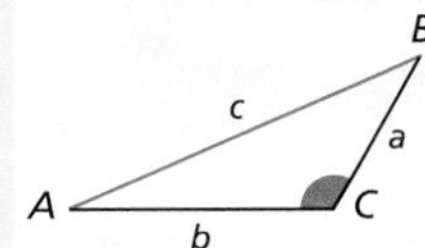	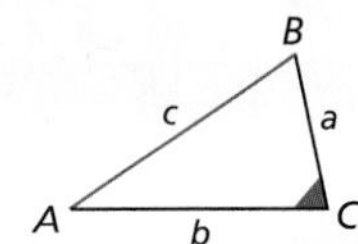

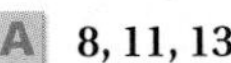

EXAMPLE 4 Classifying Triangles

Tell if the measures can be the side lengths of a triangle. If so, classify the triangle as acute, obtuse, or right.

A **8, 11, 13**

Step 1 Determine if the measures form a triangle.

By the Triangle Inequality Theorem, 8, 11, and 13 can be the side lengths of a triangle.

Step 2 Classify the triangle.

$c^2 \stackrel{?}{=} a^2 + b^2$	*Compare c^2 to $a^2 + b^2$.*
$13^2 \stackrel{?}{=} 8^2 + 11^2$	*Substitute the longest side length for c.*
$169 \stackrel{?}{=} 64 + 121$	*Multiply.*
$169 < 185$	*Add and compare.*

Since $c^2 < a^2 + b^2$, the triangle is acute.

Remember!

By the Triangle Inequality Theorem, the sum of any two side lengths of a triangle is greater than the third side length.

B **5.8, 9.3, 15.6**

Step 1 Determine if the measures form a triangle.

Since $5.8 + 9.3 = 15.1$ and $15.1 \not> 15.6$, these cannot be the side lengths of a triangle.

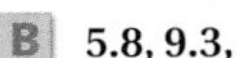

CHECK IT OUT! **Tell if the measures can be the side lengths of a triangle. If so, classify the triangle as acute, obtuse, or right.**

4a. 7, 12, 16 yes; obtuse **4b.** 11, 18, 34 no **4c.** 3.8, 4.1, 5.2 yes, acute

COMMON ERROR ALERT

Students may have difficulty squaring expressions involving square roots. Point out that $(2\sqrt{5})^2 = 20$, not $4\sqrt{5}$ or 10. Also point out that $\sqrt{3^2 + 4^2} = 5$, not 7.

Teaching Tip **Technology** Have students use geometry software to explore the Pythagorean Inequalities Theorem.

Power Presentations with PowerPoint®

Additional Examples

Example 4

Tell if the measures can be the side lengths of a triangle. If so, classify the triangle as acute, obtuse, or right.

A. 5, 7, 10 By the Triangle Inequality Theorem, 5, 7, and 10 can be the side lengths of a triangle; obtuse.

B. 5, 8, 17 Since $5 + 8 = 13$, which is not greater than 17, these cannot be the side lengths of a triangle.

INTERVENTION

Questioning Strategies

EXAMPLE 4

- How can you use the side lengths to classify a triangle by its angles?

3 Close

Summarize

Review the Pythagorean Theorem and some of the common Pythagorean triples. Explain the Converse of the Pythagorean Theorem and how the Pythagorean Inequalities Theorem can be used to classify a triangle. Ask students to classify a triangle with side lengths 5, 10, and 13. obtuse

ONGOING ASSESSMENT and INTERVENTION

***Diagnose Before* the Lesson**
5-7 Warm Up, TE p. 348

***Monitor During* the Lesson**
Check It Out! Exercises, SE pp. 349–351
Questioning Strategies, TE pp. 349–351

***Assess After* the Lesson**
5-7 Lesson Quiz, TE p. 355
Alternative Assessment, TE p. 355

Answers to *Think and Discuss*

1. The greatest number is substituted for c. The other 2 numbers are substituted for a and b in any order.
2. Possible answer: The sum of the areas of the 2 smaller squares equals the area of the largest square. So $3^2 + 4^2 = 5^2$, or $9 + 16 = 25$.
3. must be nonzero whole numbers and must satisfy the equation $a^2 + b^2 = c^2$
4. See p. A5.

THINK AND DISCUSS

1. How do you know which numbers to substitute for c, a, and b when using the Pythagorean Inequalities?
2. Explain how the figure at right demonstrates the Pythagorean Theorem.

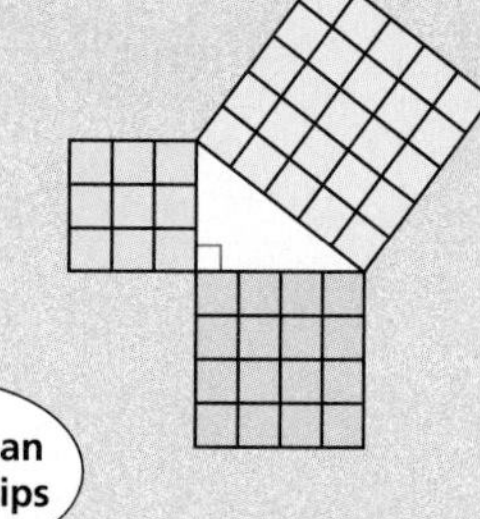

3. List the conditions that a set of three numbers must satisfy in order to form a Pythagorean triple.
4. **GET ORGANIZED** Copy and complete the graphic organizer. In each box, summarize the Pythagorean relationship.

Know it! Note

Pythagorean Relationships

Pythagorean Theorem	Converse of the Pythagorean Theorem	Pythagorean Inequalities Theorem

5-7 Exercises

Assignment Guide

Assign *Guided Practice* exercises as necessary.

If you finished Examples **1–2**
- **Basic** 15–18, 30–36, 38–40
- **Average** 15–18, 30–36, 38–43, 45, 46
- **Advanced** 15–18, 30–36, 38–43, 45, 46, 53, 54

If you finished Examples **1–4**
- **Basic** 15–36, 38–44, 47–51, 56–61
- **Average** 15–51, 55–61
- **Advanced** 15–28, 30–61

Homework Quick Check
Quickly check key concepts.
Exercises: 16, 18, 20, 22, 30, 36

State Resources

5-7 Exercises

GUIDED PRACTICE

1. **Vocabulary** Do the numbers 2.7, 3.6, and 4.5 form a *Pythagorean triple*? Explain why or why not.

SEE EXAMPLE 1 p. 349

Find the value of x. Give your answer in simplest radical form.

2. 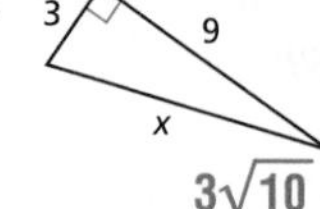

$3\sqrt{10}$

3. 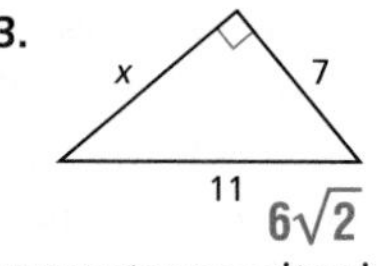

$6\sqrt{2}$

4. 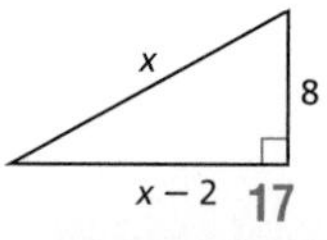

17

SEE EXAMPLE 2 p. 349

5. **Computers** The size of a computer monitor is usually given by the length of its diagonal. A monitor's aspect ratio is the ratio of its width to its height. This monitor has a diagonal length of 19 inches and an aspect ratio of 5:4. What are the width and height of the monitor? Round to the nearest tenth of an inch.
width: 14.8 in.; height: 11.9 in.

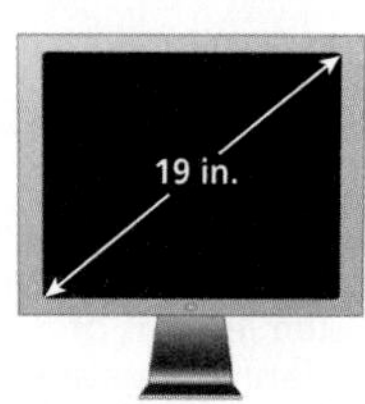

SEE EXAMPLE 3 p. 350

Find the missing side length. Tell if the side lengths form a Pythagorean triple. Explain.

6. 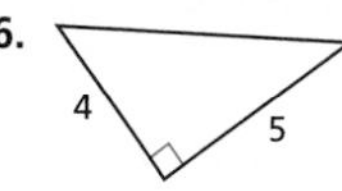

7. 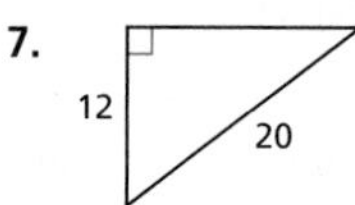

8. 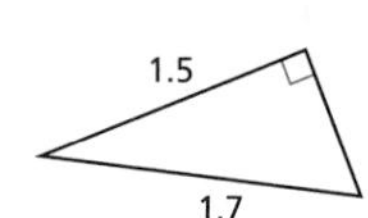

SEE EXAMPLE 4 p. 351

Multi-Step **Tell if the measures can be the side lengths of a triangle. If so, classify the triangle as acute, obtuse, or right.**

9. 7, 10, 12 **triangle; acute**
10. 9, 11, 15 **triangle; obtuse**
11. 9, 40, 41 **triangle; right**
12. $1\frac{1}{2}, 1\frac{3}{4}, 3\frac{1}{4}$ **not a triangle**
13. 5.9, 6, 8.4 **triangle; acute**
14. 11, 13, $7\sqrt{6}$ **triangle; obtuse**

Answers

1. No; although it is true that $(2.7)^2 + (3.6)^2 = (4.5)^2$, the numbers 2.7, 3.6, and 4.5 are not whole numbers.
6. $\sqrt{41}$; no; $\sqrt{41}$ is not a whole number.
7. 16; yes; the 3 side lengths are nonzero whole numbers that satisfy the equation $a^2 + b^2 = c^2$.
8. 0.8; no; the 3 side lengths are not whole numbers.

PRACTICE AND PROBLEM SOLVING

Independent Practice

For Exercises	See Example
15–17	1
18	2
19–21	3
22–27	4

Extra Practice

Skills Practice p. S13
Application Practice p. S32

Find the value of x. Give your answer in simplest radical form.

15. 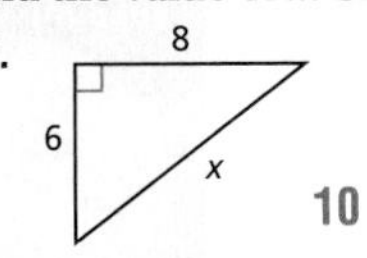

10

16. 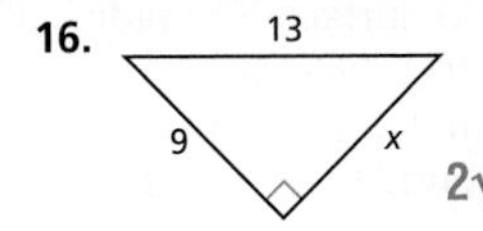

$2\sqrt{22}$

17. 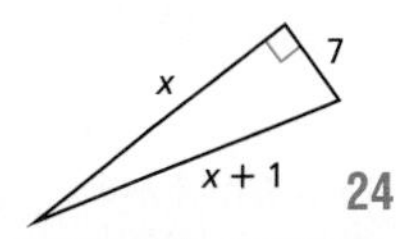

24

18. Safety The safety rules for a playground state that the height of the slide and the distance from the base of the ladder to the front of the slide must be in a ratio of 3:5. If a slide is about 8 feet long, what are the height of the slide and the distance from the base of the ladder to the front of the slide? Round to the nearest inch.
4 ft 1 in.; 6 ft 10 in.

Find the missing side length. Tell if the side lengths form a Pythagorean triple. Explain.

19. 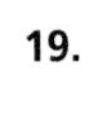 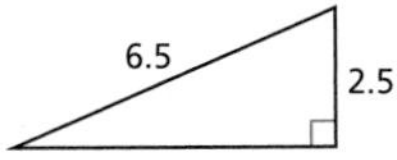

20. 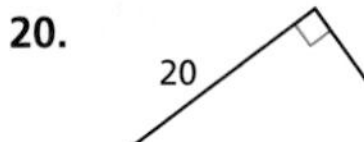 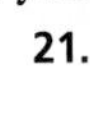

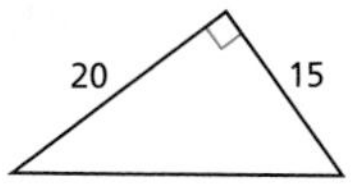

21. 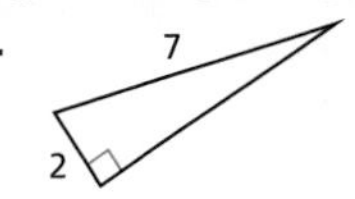

LINK

Surveying

Ancient Egyptian surveyors were referred to as *rope-stretchers*. The standard surveying rope was 100 royal cubits. A cubit is 52.4 cm long.

Multi-Step Tell if the measures can be the side lengths of a triangle. If so, classify the triangle as acute, obtuse, or right.

22. 10, 12, 15 triangle; acute
23. 8, 13, 23 not a triangle
24. 9, 14, 17 triangle; obtuse
25. $1\frac{1}{2}, 2, 2\frac{1}{2}$ triangle; right
26. 0.7, 1.1, 1.7 triangle; obtuse
27. 7, 12, $6\sqrt{5}$ triangle; acute

28. Surveying It is believed that surveyors in ancient Egypt laid out right angles using a rope divided into twelve sections by eleven equally spaced knots. How could the surveyors use this rope to make a right angle?

29. ERROR ANALYSIS Below are two solutions for finding x. Which is incorrect? Explain the error.

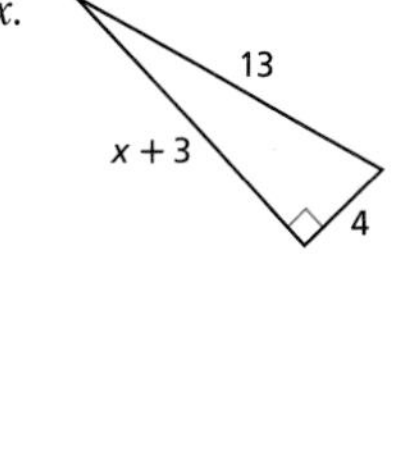

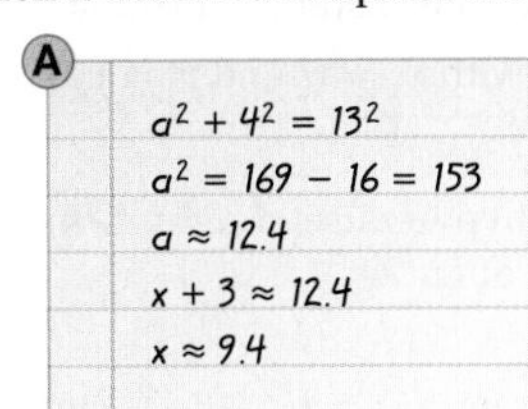

A

$a^2 + 4^2 = 13^2$
$a^2 = 169 - 16 = 153$
$a \approx 12.4$
$x + 3 \approx 12.4$
$x \approx 9.4$

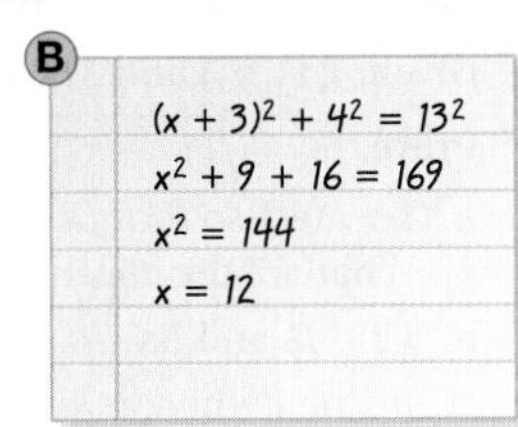

B

$(x + 3)^2 + 4^2 = 13^2$
$x^2 + 9 + 16 = 169$
$x^2 = 144$
$x = 12$

Find the value of x. Give your answer in simplest radical form.

30. 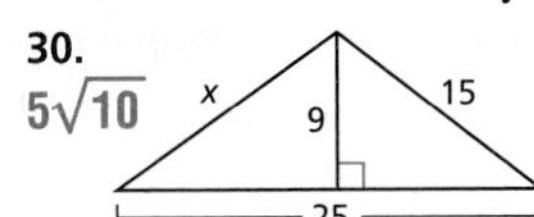

$5\sqrt{10}$

31. 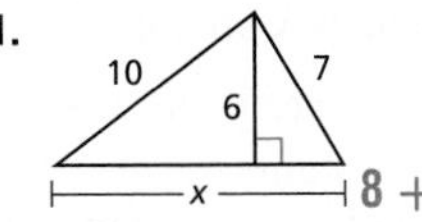 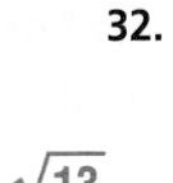

$8 + \sqrt{13}$

32. 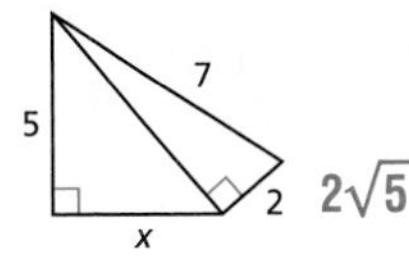

$2\sqrt{5}$

33. 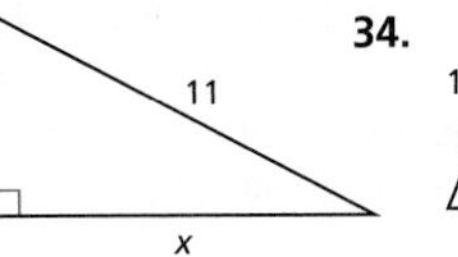

34.
13
20
5
x

35. 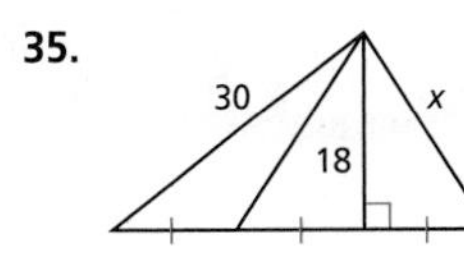

33. $4\sqrt{6}$ 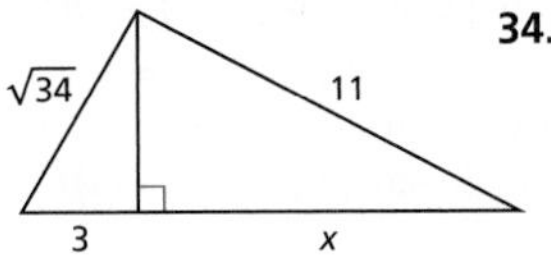
34. 11 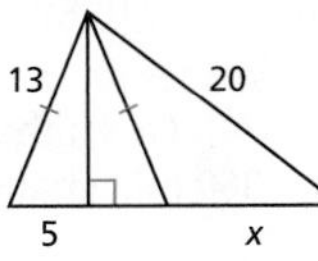
35. $6\sqrt{13}$

COMMON ERROR ALERT

In **Exercise 25,** students may have difficulty squaring the mixed numbers. Suggest that they first change these numbers to decimals or improper fractions.

Teaching Tip

Inclusion In **Exercise 18,** the slide length is given in feet, but the answer is to be rounded to the nearest inch. Advise students either to convert the slide measurement to inches first or to convert the decimal part of their answers in feet to inches after applying the Pythagorean Theorem.

Answers

19. 6; no; 2.5 and 6.5 are not whole numbers.
20. 25; yes; the 3 side lengths are nonzero whole numbers that satisfy the equation $a^2 + b^2 = c^2$.
21. $3\sqrt{5}$; no; $3\sqrt{5}$ is not a whole number.
28. Possible answer: Shape the rope into a △ with side lengths of 3, 4, and 5. Because $3^2 + 4^2 = 5^2$, the △ is a rt. △ with the rt. ∠ across from the side with length 5.
29. B; $(x + 3)^2 + 4^2 = (x^2 + 6x + 9) + 16$. In the solution shown, the $6x$ term was omitted.

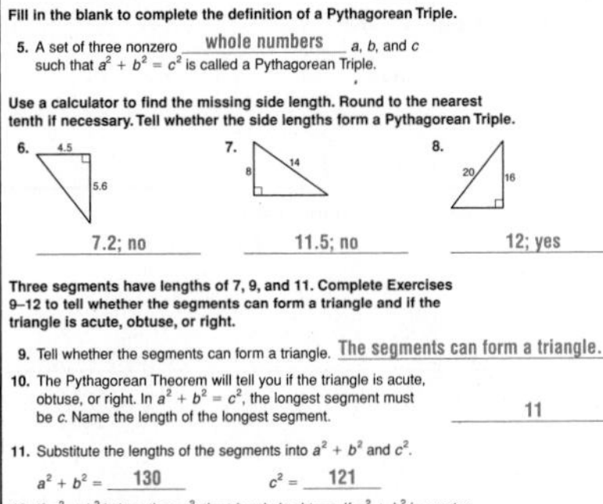

5-7 PRACTICE A

Use the Pythagorean Theorem and a calculator to find the value of x. Round to the nearest tenth if necessary.

1. (triangle: 10, 24, x) 26
2. (triangle: x, 30, 34) 16
3. (triangle: 12, x, 8) 8.9

4. A home builder is designing the braces for a roof. She wants the length of the brace to be six times its height. Refer to the figure to find the height of the brace to the nearest inch. (152 in., x, 3x) 48 in.

Fill in the blank to complete the definition of a Pythagorean Triple.

5. A set of three nonzero whole numbers a, b, and c such that $a^2 + b^2 = c^2$ is called a Pythagorean Triple.

Use a calculator to find the missing side length. Round to the nearest tenth if necessary. Tell whether the side lengths form a Pythagorean Triple.

6. (4.5, 5.6) 7.2; no
7. (8, 14) 11.5; no
8. (20, 16) 12; yes

Three segments have lengths of 7, 9, and 11. Complete Exercises 9–12 to tell whether the segments can form a triangle and if the triangle is acute, obtuse, or right.

9. Tell whether the segments can form a triangle. The segments can form a triangle.
10. The Pythagorean Theorem will tell you if the triangle is acute, obtuse, or right. In $a^2 + b^2 = c^2$, the longest segment must be c. Name the length of the longest segment. 11
11. Substitute the lengths of the segments into $a^2 + b^2$ and c^2.
$a^2 + b^2 =$ 130 $c^2 =$ 121
12. If $a^2 + b^2$ is less than c^2, the triangle is obtuse. If $a^2 + b^2$ is greater than c^2, the triangle is acute. If $a^2 + b^2$ is equal to c^2, the triangle is right. What kind of triangle is made with segments of lengths 7, 9, and 11? acute

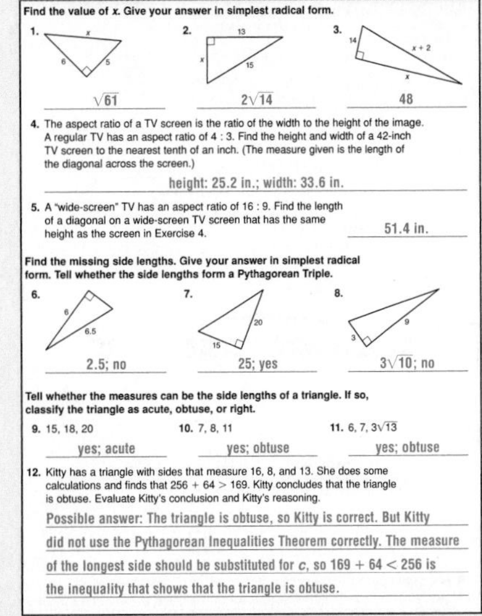

5-7 PRACTICE B

Find the value of x. Give your answer in simplest radical form.

1. (6, 5, x) $\sqrt{61}$
2. (13, x, 15) $2\sqrt{14}$
3. (14, x + 2, x) 48

4. The aspect ratio of a TV screen is the ratio of the width to the height of the image. A regular TV has an aspect ratio of 4 : 3. Find the height and width of a 42-inch TV screen to the nearest tenth of an inch. (The measure given is the length of the diagonal across the screen.)
height: 25.2 in.; width: 33.6 in.

5. A "wide-screen" TV has an aspect ratio of 16 : 9. Find the length of a diagonal on a wide-screen TV screen that has the same height as the screen in Exercise 4. 51.4 in.

Find the missing side lengths. Give your answer in simplest radical form. Tell whether the side lengths form a Pythagorean Triple.

6. (6, 6.5) 2.5; no
7. (20, 15) 25; yes
8. (9, 3) $3\sqrt{10}$; no

Tell whether the measures can be the side lengths of a triangle. If so, classify the triangle as acute, obtuse, or right.

9. 15, 18, 20 yes; acute
10. 7, 8, 11 yes; obtuse
11. 6, 7, $3\sqrt{13}$ yes; obtuse

12. Kitty has a triangle with sides that measure 16, 8, and 13. She does some calculations and finds that 256 + 64 > 169. Kitty concludes that the triangle is obtuse. Evaluate Kitty's conclusion and Kitty's reasoning.
Possible answer: The triangle is obtuse, so Kitty is correct. But Kitty did not use the Pythagorean Inequalities Theorem correctly. The measure of the longest side should be substituted for c, so 169 + 64 < 256 is the inequality that shows that the triangle is obtuse.

5-7 PRACTICE C

1. For a triangle to be obtuse, only one of the angles must be shown to be obtuse. (In fact, only one of the angles can possibly be obtuse.) But for a triangle to be acute, all three angles must be shown to be acute. Explain why determining one acute angle with the Pythagorean Inequalities Theorem shows that the triangle is acute.
Possible answer: When using the Pythagorean Inequalities Theorem, the longest side of the triangle is substituted for c, and the angle opposite that side is determined as right, acute, or obtuse. The longest side in a triangle is opposite the largest angle. So if the angle opposite the longest side is acute, then the other two angles must also be acute.
2. What values of x satisfy the equation $x^2 = 13$? $\sqrt{13}, -\sqrt{13}$
3. In light of your answer to Exercise 2, explain why there is only one correct value for x in this figure. (2, 3, x)
Possible answer: Segments must have positive lengths. A negative length does not make sense. In geometry, only positive square roots are used.
4. A builder has to surmount a rise in elevation from 1260 feet to 1930 feet with a straight road. He has only been granted funding to build a mile-long section of road, and regulations state that the road cannot have a slope of more than $\frac{1}{8}$. Can he complete his task? If so, give the horizontal distance from the start of the road to the end of the road to the nearest inch. If not, give the slope to the nearest thousandth that would allow him to build the road. no; 0.127

Use the figure for Exercise 5.

5. Find the missing side length in each triangle. (5, 3; 9, 15) $\sqrt{34}$; $3\sqrt{34}$

Use what you learned from Exercise 5 to find the missing side lengths below without using a calculator.

6. (126, 72) $18\sqrt{65}$
7. (13,000, 12,000) 5000
8. (2.5, 2) $\frac{\sqrt{41}}{2}$

Math Background For **Exercises 38–43,** review how to find the area and perimeter of a triangle and a trapezoid.

Exercise 47 involves using the Pythagorean Theorem to find distances between cities. This exercise prepares students for the Multi-Step Test Prep on page 364.

Answers

37. Possible answer: Outer figure: The length of each side is $a + b$, so the outer figure has 4 ≅ sides. Each ∠ is a rt. ∠ from 1 of the rt. ⊿s, so the outer figure has 4 rt. ∠s. By def., it is a square. Inner figure: The length of each side is c, so the inner figure has 4 ≅ sides. The 2 acute ∠s of a rt. △ are comp., so the measure of each ∠ in the inner figure is 90°. Therefore the inner figure has 4 rt. ∠s. By def., it is a square.
44. Possible answer: When you use the Pythagorean Theorem, you know that the triangle is a right triangle. You substitute the known values into $a^2 + b^2 = c^2$ and solve for the unknown side length. When you use the Converse of the Pythagorean Theorem, you are trying to find out whether a given triangle is a right triangle. Usually all the side lengths are known. You substitute all the values into $a^2 + b^2 = c^2$ to determine whether the resulting equation is true. If it is true, then you know that the triangle is a right triangle.
45. Draw △PQR with ∠R as the rt. ∠, leg lengths of a and b, and hyp. length of x. In △ABC, it is given that $a^2 + b^2 = c^2$. In △PQR, $a^2 + b^2 = x^2$ by the Pyth. Thm. Since $a^2 + b^2 = c^2$ and $a^2 + b^2 = x^2$, it follows by subst. that $x^2 = c^2$. Take the positive square root of both sides, and $x = c$. So $AB = PQ$, $BC = QR$, and $AC = PR$. By the def. of ≅ segs., $\overline{AB} \cong \overline{PQ}$, $\overline{BC} \cong \overline{QR}$, and $\overline{AC} \cong \overline{PR}$. Then △ABC ≅ △PQR by SSS, and ∠C ≅ ∠R by CPCTC. By the def. of rt. ∠, m∠R = 90°. So by the def. of ≅ ∠s, m∠C = 90°. Therefore ∠C is a rt. ∠ by def., and △ABC is a rt. △ by def.

51, 53, 55, 59. See p. A20.

38. perimeter: 40 units; area: 60 square units
39. perimeter: $16 + 4\sqrt{7}$ units; area: $12\sqrt{7}$ square units
40. perimeter: 32 units; area: $32\sqrt{2}$ square units
41. perimeter: $14 + 2\sqrt{13}$ units; area: 18 square units
42. perimeter: $30 + 6\sqrt{5}$ units; area: 90 square units
43. perimeter: 22 units; area: 26 square units

36. **Space Exploration** The International Space Station orbits at an altitude of about 250 miles above Earth's surface. The radius of Earth is approximately 3963 miles. How far can an astronaut in the space station see to the horizon? Round to the nearest mile. **1430 mi**

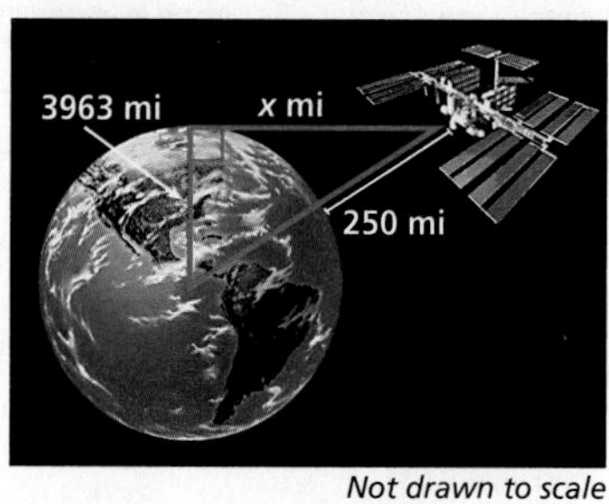

Not drawn to scale

37. **Critical Thinking** In the proof of the Pythagorean Theorem on page 348, how do you know the outer figure is a square? How do you know the inner figure is a square?

Multi-Step Find the perimeter and the area of each figure. Give your answer in simplest radical form.

38. 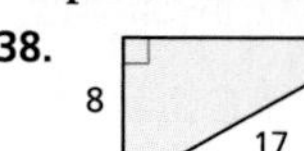

39. 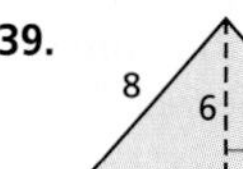

40. 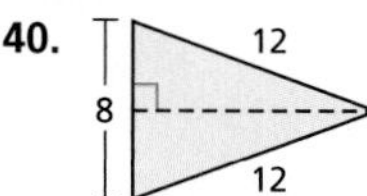

41. 5, 3, 6

42. 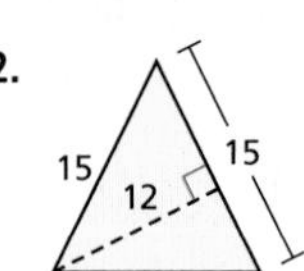

43. 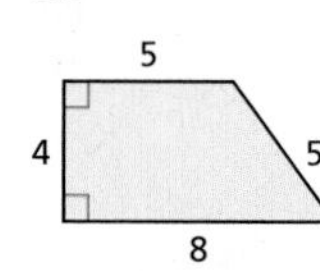

44. **Write About It** When you apply both the Pythagorean Theorem and its converse, you use the equation $a^2 + b^2 = c^2$. Explain in your own words how the two theorems are different.

45. Use this plan to write a paragraph proof of the Converse of the Pythagorean Theorem.

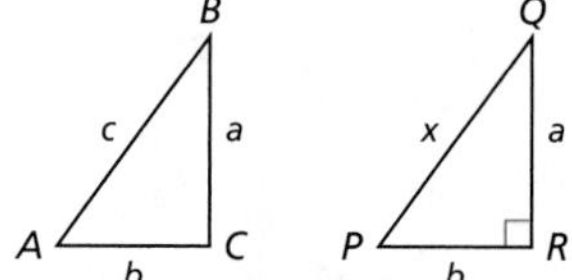

Given: △ABC with $a^2 + b^2 = c^2$
Prove: △ABC is a right triangle.
Plan: Draw △PQR with ∠R as the right angle, leg lengths of a and b, and a hypotenuse of length x. By the Pythagorean Theorem, $a^2 + b^2 = x^2$. Use substitution to compare x and c. Show that △ABC ≅ △PQR and thus ∠C is a right angle.

46. Complete these steps to prove the Distance Formula.
Given: $J(x_1, y_1)$ and $K(x_2, y_2)$ with $x_1 \neq x_2$ and $y_1 \neq y_2$
Prove: $JK = \sqrt{(x_2 - x_1)^2 + (y_2 - y_1)^2}$
a. Locate L so that $\overline{JK}$ is the hypotenuse of right △JKL. What are the coordinates of L? (x_2, y_1)
b. Find JL and LK. $JL = x_2 - x_1$, $LK = y_2 - y_1$
c. By the Pythagorean Theorem, $JK^2 = JL^2 + LK^2$. Find JK.
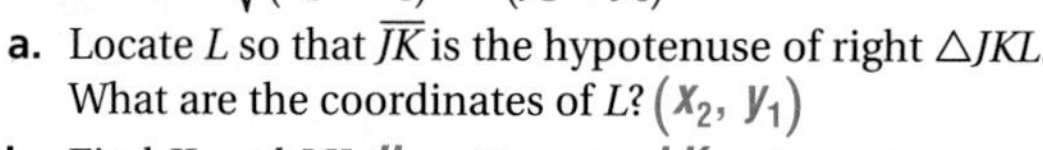
$JK = \sqrt{(x_2 - x_1)^2 + (y_2 - y_1)^2}$

y, $K(x_2, y_2)$, $J(x_1, y_1)$, L, x

MULTI-STEP TEST PREP

47. This problem will prepare you for the Multi-Step Test Prep on page 364.
The figure shows an airline's routes between four cities.
a. A traveler wants to go from Sanak (S) to Manitou (M). To minimize the total number of miles traveled, should she first fly to King City (K) or to Rice Lake (R)?
b. The airline decides to offer a direct flight from Sanak (S) to Manitou (M). Given that the length of this flight is more than 1360 mi, what can you say about m∠SRM? m∠SRM > 90°

S, 1300 mi, 500 mi, K, R, 390 mi, M

5-7 READING STRATEGIES

The Pythagorean Theorem states that in a right triangle, $a^2 + b^2 = c^2$, given a and b are the lengths of the legs and c is the length of the hypotenuse.

1. What is the length of each side of the triangle?
One side has a length of 3 units, one a length of 4 units, and the last a length of 5 units.

2. What is the area of the large square on each side of the triangle?
One square has an area of 9 square units, one has an area of 16 square units, and the last one has an area of 25 square units.

3. How does the length of each side of the triangle relate to the area of the corresponding square?
The length of the side of the triangle is the square root of the area of the square.

Another example of the Pythagorean Theorem can be shown using the same technique.

4. Substitute the side lengths of △PQR into the Pythagorean Theorem and show that the Pythagorean Theorem is true using these side lengths.
$PQ^2 + QR^2 = PR^2$
$(6)^2 + (8)^2 = (10)^2$
$36 + 64 = 100$
$100 = 100$

5. Explain how to place the squares on this triangle to show another example of the Pythagorean Theorem.

6. How do the areas of the squares relate to the lengths of the sides of this triangle?
The length of the side of the triangle is the square root of the area of the square.

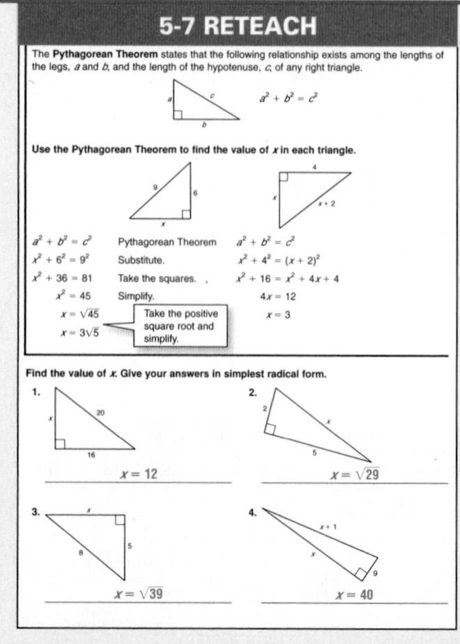

5-7 RETEACH

The **Pythagorean Theorem** states that the following relationship exists among the lengths of the legs, a and b, and the length of the hypotenuse, c, of any right triangle.

$a^2 + b^2 = c^2$

Use the Pythagorean Theorem to find the value of x in each triangle.

$a^2 + b^2 = c^2$	Pythagorean Theorem	$a^2 + b^2 = c^2$
$x^2 + 6^2 = 9^2$	Substitute.	$x^2 + 4^2 = (x + 2)^2$
$x^2 + 36 = 81$	Take the squares.	$x^2 + 16 = x^2 + 4x + 4$
$x^2 = 45$	Simplify.	$4x = 12$
$x = \sqrt{45}$		$x = 3$
$x = 3\sqrt{5}$	Take the positive square root and simplify.	

Find the value of x. Give your answers in simplest radical form.

1. $x = 12$
2. $x = \sqrt{29}$
3. $x = \sqrt{39}$
4. $x = 40$

TEST PREP

48. **Gridded Response** $\overline{KX}$, $\overline{LX}$, and $\overline{MX}$ are the perpendicular bisectors of $\triangle GHJ$. Find GJ to the nearest tenth of a unit. **8.9**

49. Which number forms a Pythagorean triple with 24 and 25?
   Ⓐ 1   **Ⓑ 7**   Ⓒ 26   Ⓓ 49

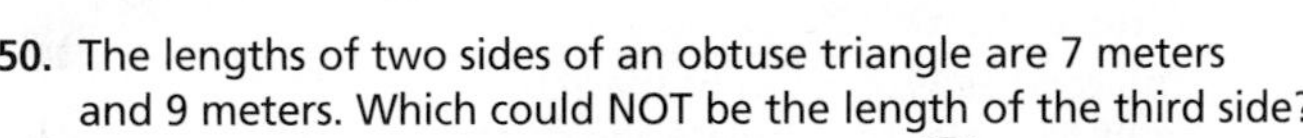

50. The lengths of two sides of an obtuse triangle are 7 meters and 9 meters. Which could NOT be the length of the third side?
   Ⓕ 4 meters   Ⓖ 5 meters   **Ⓗ 11 meters**   Ⓙ 12 meters

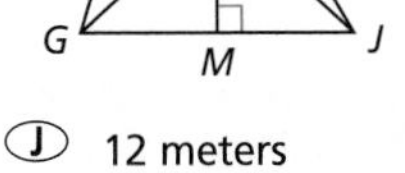

51. **Extended Response** The figure shows the first six triangles in a pattern of triangles.
   a. Find PA, PB, PC, PD, PE, and PF in simplest radical form.
   b. If the pattern continues, what would be the length of the hypotenuse of the ninth triangle? Explain your answer.
   c. Write a rule for finding the length of the hypotenuse of the nth triangle in the pattern. Explain your answer.

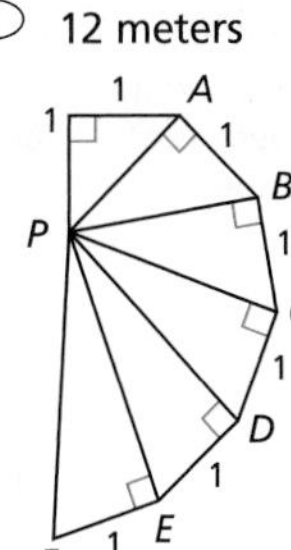

CHALLENGE AND EXTEND

52. **Algebra** Find all values of k so that $(-1, 2)$, $(-10, 5)$, and $(-4, k)$ are the vertices of a right triangle. $k = -7, -1, 8,$ or 23

53. **Critical Thinking** Use a diagram of a right triangle to explain why $a + b > \sqrt{a^2 + b^2}$ for any positive numbers a and b.

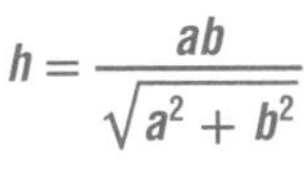

$h = \dfrac{ab}{\sqrt{a^2 + b^2}}$

54. In a right triangle, the leg lengths are a and b, and the length of the altitude to the hypotenuse is h. Write an expression for h in terms of a and b. (*Hint*: Think of the area of the triangle.)

55. **Critical Thinking** Suppose the numbers a, b, and c form a Pythagorean triple. Is each of the following also a Pythagorean triple? Explain.
   a. $a + 1, b + 1, c + 1$ b. $2a, 2b, 2c$
   c. a^2, b^2, c^2 d. $\sqrt{a}, \sqrt{b}, \sqrt{c}$

SPIRAL REVIEW

Solve each equation. *(Previous course)*

56. $(4 + x)12 - (4x + 1)6 = 0$ $x = 3.5$

57. $\dfrac{2x - 5}{3} = x$ $x = -5$

58. $4x + 3(x + 2) = -3(x + 3)$ $x = -\dfrac{3}{2}$

Write a coordinate proof. *(Lesson 4-7)*

59. **Given:** $ABCD$ is a rectangle with $A(0, 0)$, $B(0, 2b)$, $C(2a, 2b)$, and $D(2a, 0)$. M is the midpoint of $\overline{AC}$.
   Prove: $AM = MB$

Find the range of values for x. *(Lesson 5-6)*

60.

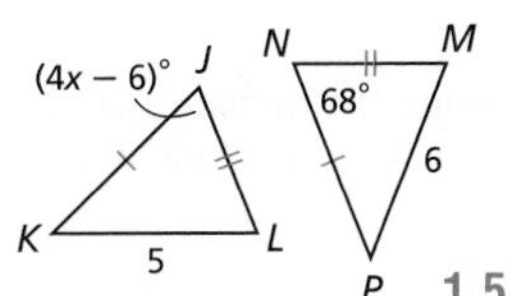

$1.5 < x < 18.5$

61.

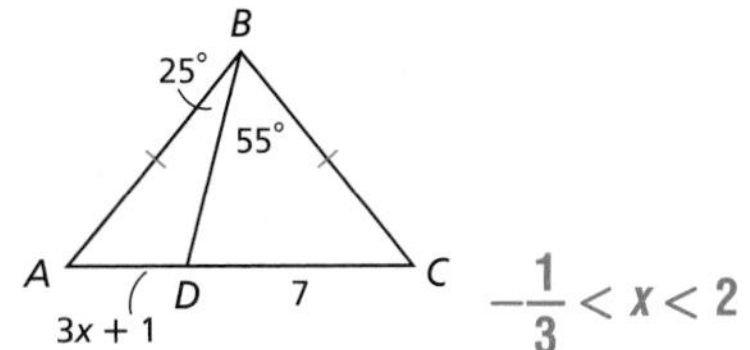

$-\dfrac{1}{3} < x < 2$

5-7 PROBLEM SOLVING

1. It is recommended that for a height of 20 inches, a wheelchair ramp be 19 feet long. What is the value of x to the nearest tenth? **18.9 ft**

2. Find x, the length of the weight-lifting incline bench. Round to the nearest tenth. **4.1 ft**

3. A ladder 15 feet from the base of a building reaches a window that is 35 feet high. What is the length of the ladder to the nearest foot? **38 ft**

4. In a wide-screen television, the ratio of width to height is 16:9. What are the width and height of a television that has a diagonal measure of 42 inches? Round to the nearest tenth. **length = 36.6 in.; width = 20.6 in.**

Choose the best answer.

5. The distance from Austin to San Antonio is about 74 miles, and the distance from San Antonio to Victoria is about 102 miles. Find the approximate distance from Austin to Victoria.
   A 28 mi   C 126 mi
   Ⓑ 70 mi   D 176 mi

6. What is the approximate perimeter of $\triangle DEC$ if rectangle $ABCD$ has a length of 4.6 centimeters?
   F 5.1 cm
   G 6.5 cm
   H 9.8 cm
   Ⓙ 11.1 cm

7. The legs of a right triangle measure $3x$ and 15. If the hypotenuse measures $3x + 3$, what is the value of x?
   Ⓐ 12   C 36
   B 16   D 221

8. A cube has edge lengths of 6 inches. What is the approximate length of a diagonal d of the cube?
   F 6 in.   **Ⓗ 10.4 in.**
   G 8.4 in.   J 12 in.

5-7 CHALLENGE

At right is shown a segment, $\overline{AB}$. Consider its length to be 1 unit.

Suppose that you construct a right triangle with legs of length 1 unit, as shown at right. Then, by the Pythagorean Theorem, the length of the hypotenuse is $\sqrt{2}$ units. If you then construct an adjacent right triangle as shown, with legs of length $\sqrt{2}$ units and 1 unit, then the length of its hypotenuse is $\sqrt{3}$ units.

Continuing this process, you can construct segments of length $\sqrt{4}$ units, $\sqrt{5}$ units, $\sqrt{6}$ units, and so on. The resulting construction is called the *wheel of Theodorus*. It is named for the Greek philosopher Theodorus of Cyrene (465–398 B.C.), who is known for his contributions to the understanding of irrational numbers. Before his work, $\sqrt{2}$ was the only known irrational number. Theodorus showed that $\sqrt{3}, \sqrt{5}, \sqrt{6}, \sqrt{7}, \sqrt{8}, \sqrt{10}, \sqrt{11}, \sqrt{12}, \sqrt{13}, \sqrt{14}, \sqrt{15}$, and $\sqrt{17}$ are also irrational.

1. In the figure below, the wheel of Theodorus has been constructed through $\sqrt{5}$. Using compass and straightedge, continue the construction through $\sqrt{17}$.

2. To construct a segment of length $\sqrt{24}$ units, you could continue constructing the wheel through $\sqrt{24}$. Describe an alternative method. (*Hint:* How can you use algebra to simplify $\sqrt{24}$?)
   You can simplify $\sqrt{24}$ as $\sqrt{4 \cdot 6}$, or $2\sqrt{6}$. So you can construct a segment of length $\sqrt{24}$ units by copying the segment with length $\sqrt{6}$ units twice in succession along the same straight line.

COMMON ERROR ALERT

For **Exercise 53,** remind students that $\sqrt{a^2 + b^2} \neq a + b$.

TEST PREP DOCTOR If students have difficulty with **Exercise 48,** explain that $\triangle HXK \cong \triangle GXK$, so $GX = 6$. They can find GM by using the Pythagorean Theorem and then calculate GJ by doubling GM.

Journal

Have students explain how the Pythagorean inequalities are used to classify a triangle as obtuse, acute, or right.

ALTERNATIVE ASSESSMENT

Have students draw a right triangle and measure two side lengths. Have them calculate the unknown side length using the Pythagorean Theorem. Ask them to tell if the side lengths of their triangles form a Pythagorean triple. Finally have students give three lengths that form an acute triangle and three that form an obtuse triangle.

5-7 Lesson Quiz

1. Find the value of x.   12

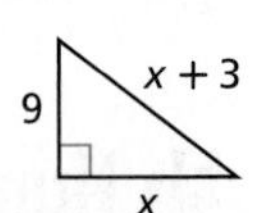

2. An entertainment center is 52 in. wide and 40 in. high. Will a TV with a 60 in. diagonal fit in it? Explain.
   yes; $\sqrt{40^2 + 52^2} \approx 65.6 > 60$

3. Find the missing side length. Tell if the side lengths form a Pythagorean triple. Explain.

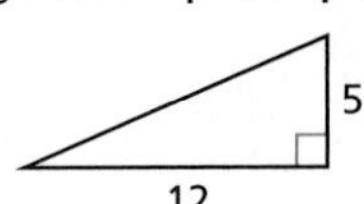

   13; yes; the side lengths are nonzero whole numbers that satisfy $a^2 + b^2 = c^2$.

4. Tell if the measures 7, 11, and 15 can be the side lengths of a triangle. If so, classify the triangle as acute, obtuse, or right.   yes; obtuse

Also available on transparency

5-8 Organizer

Pacing: Traditional 1 day
Block $\frac{1}{2}$ day

Objectives: Justify and apply properties of 45°-45°-90° triangles.

Justify and apply properties of 30°-60°-90° triangles.

Geometry Lab
In Geometry Lab Activities

Online Edition
Tutorial Videos, Interactivity

Countdown Week 12

Power Presentations with PowerPoint®

Warm Up

For Exercises 1 and 2, find the value of *x*. Give your answer in simplest radical form.

1. 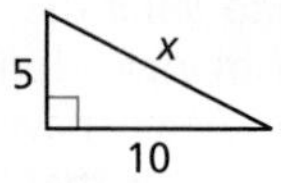 (right triangle with legs 5 and 10, hypotenuse *x*) $5\sqrt{5}$

2. 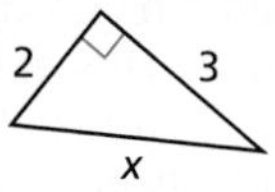 (right triangle with legs 2 and 3, hypotenuse *x*) $\sqrt{13}$

Simplify each expression.

3. $\frac{12}{\sqrt{3}}$ $4\sqrt{3}$ **4.** $\frac{\sqrt{20}}{2}$ $\sqrt{5}$

Also available on transparency

Math Humor

Q: How do you rationalize a denominator?

A: Ask it to be reasonable.

5-8 Applying Special Right Triangles

Objectives
Justify and apply properties of 45°-45°-90° triangles.

Justify and apply properties of 30°-60°-90° triangles.

Who uses this?
You can use properties of special right triangles to calculate the correct size of a bandana for your dog. (See Example 2.)

A diagonal of a square divides it into two congruent isosceles right triangles. Since the base angles of an isosceles triangle are congruent, the measure of each acute angle is 45°. So another name for an isosceles right triangle is a 45°-45°-90° triangle.

A 45°-45°-90° triangle is one type of *special right triangle*. You can use the Pythagorean Theorem to find a relationship among the side lengths of a 45°-45°-90° triangle.

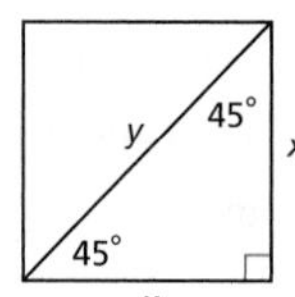

$a^2 + b^2 = c^2$	*Pythagorean Theorem*
$x^2 + x^2 = y^2$	*Substitute the given values.*
$2x^2 = y^2$	*Simplify.*
$\sqrt{2x^2} = \sqrt{y^2}$	*Find the square root of both sides.*
$x\sqrt{2} = y$	*Simplify.*

Theorem 5-8-1 45°-45°-90° Triangle Theorem

In a 45°-45°-90° triangle, both legs are congruent, and the length of the hypotenuse is the length of a leg times $\sqrt{2}$.

$AC = BC = \ell$ $AB = \ell\sqrt{2}$

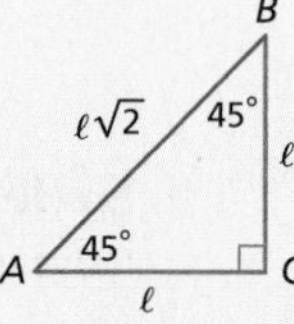

EXAMPLE  **Finding Side Lengths in a 45°-45°-90° Triangle**

Find the value of *x*. Give your answer in simplest radical form.

A

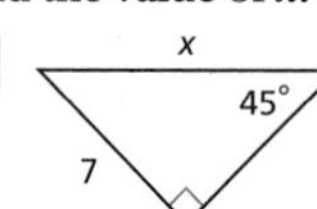

By the Triangle Sum Theorem, the measure of the third angle of the triangle is 45°. So it is a 45°-45°-90° triangle with a leg length of 7.

$x = 7\sqrt{2}$ *Hypotenuse = leg$\sqrt{2}$*

State Resources

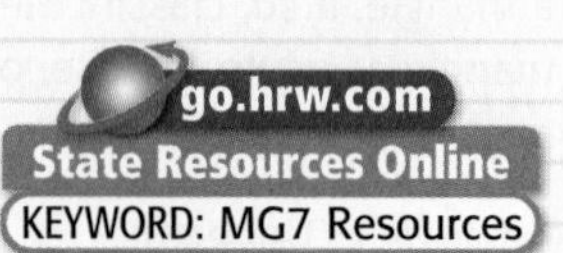

go.hrw.com
State Resources Online
KEYWORD: MG7 Resources

1 Introduce

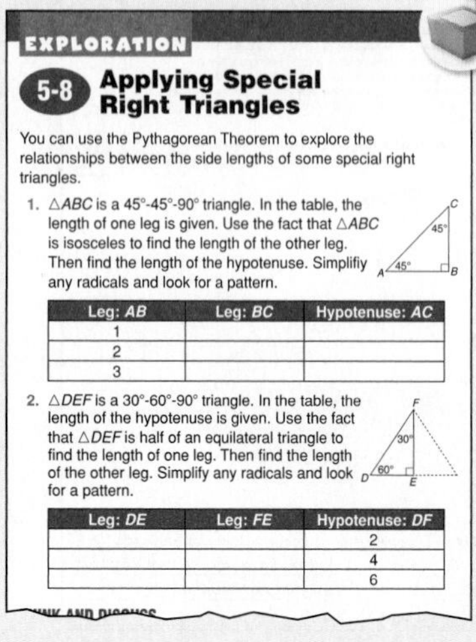

EXPLORATION

5-8 Applying Special Right Triangles

You can use the Pythagorean Theorem to explore the relationships between the side lengths of some special right triangles.

1. △*ABC* is a 45°-45°-90° triangle. In the table, the length of one leg is given. Use the fact that △*ABC* is isosceles to find the length of the other leg. Then find the length of the hypotenuse. Simplify any radicals and look for a pattern.

Leg: *AB*	Leg: *BC*	Hypotenuse: *AC*
1		
2		
3		

2. △*DEF* is a 30°-60°-90° triangle. In the table, the length of the hypotenuse is given. Use the fact that △*DEF* is half of an equilateral triangle to find the length of one leg. Then find the length of the other leg. Simplify any radicals and look for a pattern.

Leg: *DE*	Leg: *FE*	Hypotenuse: *DF*
		2
		4
		6

Motivate

Special right triangles appear in squares, equilateral triangles, hexagons, and other figures. They are used in three-dimensional shapes and also in trigonometry. Explain to students that they will learn about side relationships in special right triangles. The theorems covered in this lesson can be used to find unknown lengths without having to use the Pythagorean Theorem.

Explorations and answers are provided in *Alternate Openers: Explorations Transparencies*.

Find the value of x. Give your answer in simplest radical form.

B

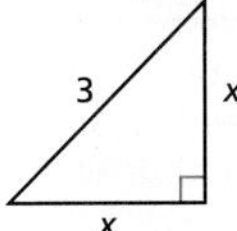

The triangle is an isosceles right triangle, which is a 45°-45°-90° triangle. The length of the hypotenuse is 3.

$3 = x\sqrt{2}$ *Hypotenuse = leg$\sqrt{2}$*

$\frac{3}{\sqrt{2}} = x$ *Divide both sides by $\sqrt{2}$.*

$\frac{3\sqrt{2}}{2} = x$ *Rationalize the denominator.*

CHECK IT OUT! Find the value of x. Give your answer in simplest radical form.

1a.

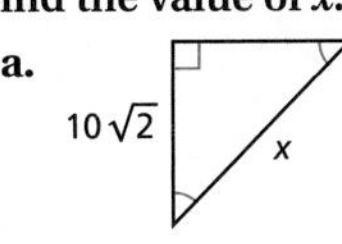

20

1b.

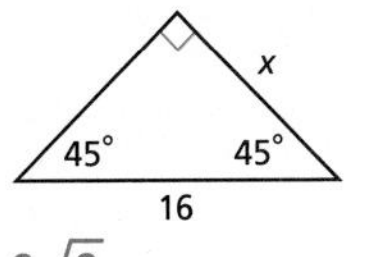

$8\sqrt{2}$

EXAMPLE 2 ***Craft Application***

Tessa wants to make a bandana for her dog by folding a square of cloth into a 45°-45°-90° triangle. Her dog's neck has a circumference of about 32 cm. The folded bandana needs to be an extra 16 cm long so Tessa can tie it around her dog's neck. What should the side length of the square be? Round to the nearest centimeter.

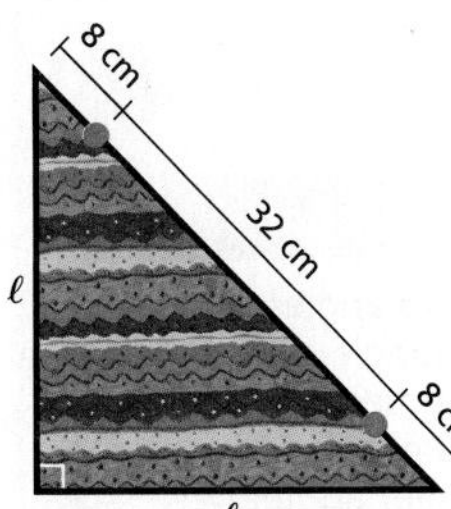

Tessa needs a 45°-45°-90° triangle with a hypotenuse of 48 cm.

$48 = \ell\sqrt{2}$ *Hypotenuse = leg$\sqrt{2}$*

$\ell = \frac{48}{\sqrt{2}} \approx 34$ cm *Divide by $\sqrt{2}$ and round.*

CHECK IT OUT! **2. What if...?** Tessa's other dog is wearing a square bandana with a side length of 42 cm. What would you expect the circumference of the other dog's neck to be? Round to the nearest centimeter. 43 cm

A 30°-60°-90° triangle is another special right triangle. You can use an equilateral triangle to find a relationship between its side lengths.

Draw an altitude in $\triangle PQR$. Since $\triangle PQS \cong \triangle RQS$, $\overline{PS} \cong \overline{RS}$. Label the side lengths in terms of x, and use the Pythagorean Theorem to find y.

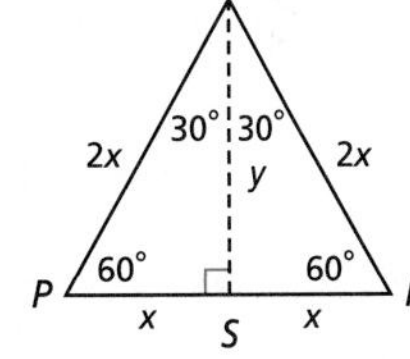

$a^2 + b^2 = c^2$ *Pythagorean Theorem*

$x^2 + y^2 = (2x)^2$ *Substitute x for a, y for b, and 2x for c.*

$y^2 = 3x^2$ *Multiply and combine like terms.*

$\sqrt{y^2} = \sqrt{3x^2}$ *Find the square root of both sides.*

$y = x\sqrt{3}$ *Simplify.*

COMMON ERROR ALERT

Students may assume that a length of $\sqrt{3}$ is always across from the 60° angle. Show them a 30°-60°-90° triangle with side lengths of $\sqrt{3}$, 3, and $2\sqrt{3}$. In this case, $\sqrt{3}$ is opposite the 30° angle. Suggest that they use a calculator to order the side lengths from shortest to longest.

Teaching Tip **Algebra** Review adding and multiplying square roots with the following examples:

- $3\sqrt{2} + 3\sqrt{2} = 6\sqrt{2}$
- $3\sqrt{2} + 6$ is simplified.
- $(3\sqrt{2})(3\sqrt{2}) = 9\sqrt{4} = 18$
- $3(3\sqrt{2}) = 9\sqrt{2}$

Power Presentations with PowerPoint®

Additional Examples

Example 1

Find the value of x. Give your answer in simplest radical form.

A. $8\sqrt{2}$

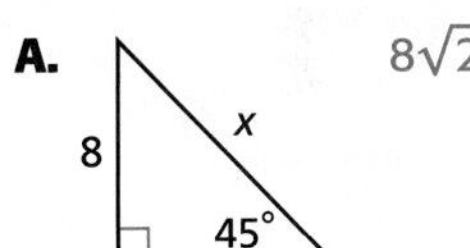

B. $\frac{5\sqrt{2}}{2}$

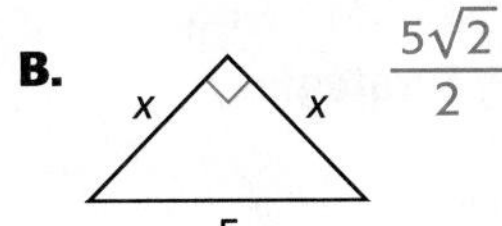

Example 2

Jana is cutting a square of material for a tablecloth. The table's diagonal is 36 in. She wants the diagonal of the tablecloth to be an extra 10 in. so it will hang over the edges of the table. What size square should Jana cut to make the tablecloth? Round to the nearest inch. 33 in.

2 Teach

Guided Instruction

Discuss the relationships between the side lengths of a 45°-45°-90° and a 30°-60°-90° triangle by using the Pythagorean Theorem. Show students how they can use these relationships to find unknown side lengths of special right triangles.

Teaching Tip **Visual** Remind students to draw and label a diagram if they forget the formulas for the side lengths of a special right triangle (MK).

Reaching All Learners

Through Auditory Cues

Have students practice the formulas for the side lengths of special right triangles by quizzing each other out loud. For example, have them fill in the blanks in the following statements. "The side of a 45°-45°-90° triangle is $8\sqrt{2}$ if the hypotenuse is __?__." 16 "In a 30°-60°-90° triangle, the side opposite the 60° angle is $6\sqrt{3}$ if the side opposite the 30° angle is __?__." 6

INTERVENTION

Questioning Strategies

EXAMPLE 1

- What is the relationship between the side lengths of a 45°-45°-90° triangle?

EXAMPLE 2

- What type of special right triangle is formed by the diagonal of a square?

Technology Have students use geometry software to construct a 45°-45°-90° and a 30°-60°-90° triangle. Then have them measure the sides and explore the relationships between them.

Power Presentations with PowerPoint®

Additional Examples

Example 3

Find the values of x and y. Give your answers in simplest radical form.

A.

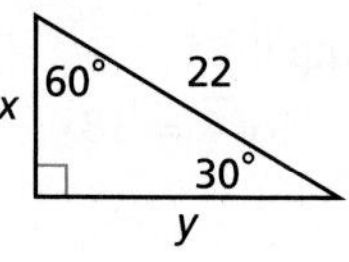

$x = 11; y = 11\sqrt{3}$

B.

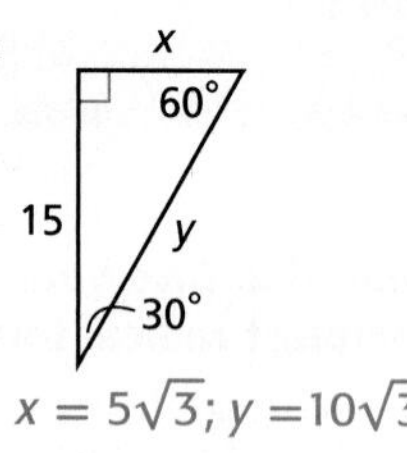

$x = 5\sqrt{3}; y = 10\sqrt{3}$

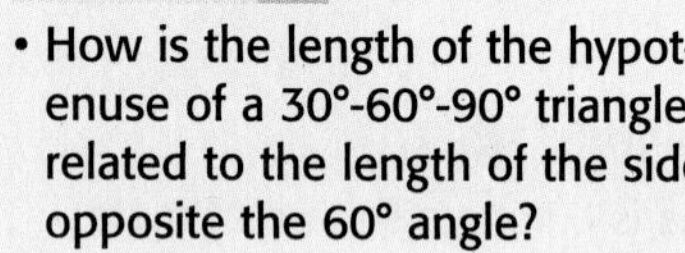

INTERVENTION

Questioning Strategies

EXAMPLE 3

- How is the length of the hypotenuse of a 30°-60°-90° triangle related to the length of the side opposite the 60° angle?

Theorem 5-8-2 30°-60°-90° Triangle Theorem

In a 30°-60°-90° triangle, the length of the hypotenuse is is 2 times the length of the shorter leg, and the length of the longer leg is the length of the shorter leg times $\sqrt{3}$.

$AC = s$ $AB = 2s$ $BC = s\sqrt{3}$

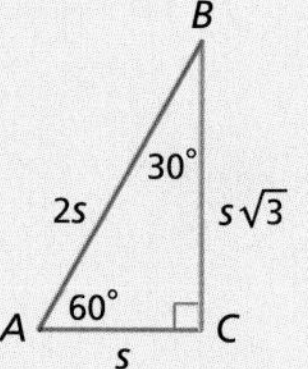

EXAMPLE 3 Finding Side Lengths in a 30°-60°-90° Triangle

Find the values of x and y. Give your answers in simplest radical form.

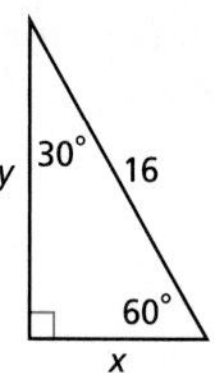

$16 = 2x$ *Hypotenuse = 2(shorter leg)*

$8 = x$ *Divide both sides by 2.*

$y = x\sqrt{3}$ *Longer leg = (shorter leg)$\sqrt{3}$*

$y = 8\sqrt{3}$ *Substitute 8 for x.*

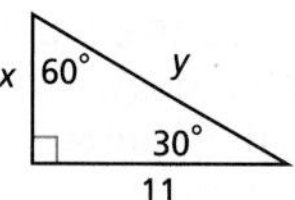

$11 = x\sqrt{3}$ *Longer leg = (shorter leg)$\sqrt{3}$*

$\frac{11}{\sqrt{3}} = x$ *Divide both sides by $\sqrt{3}$.*

$\frac{11\sqrt{3}}{3} = x$ *Rationalize the denominator.*

$y = 2x$ *Hypotenuse = 2(shorter leg)*

$y = 2\left(\frac{11\sqrt{3}}{3}\right)$ *Substitute $\frac{11\sqrt{3}}{3}$ for x.*

$y = \frac{22\sqrt{3}}{3}$ *Simplify.*

Remember!

If two angles of a triangle are not congruent, the shorter side lies opposite the smaller angle.

Find the values of x and y. Give your answers in simplest radical form.

3a.

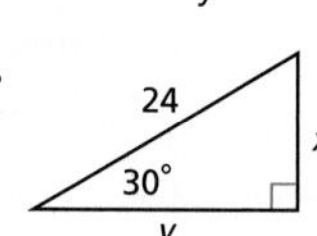

3b.

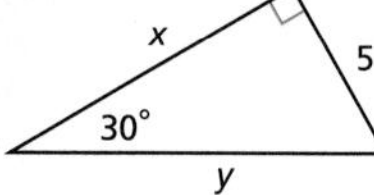

3c.

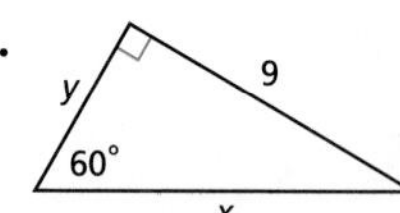

3d.

3a. $x = 9\sqrt{3}$; $y = 27$

3b. $x = 5\sqrt{3}$; $y = 10$

3c. $x = 12$; $y = 12\sqrt{3}$

3d. $x = 6\sqrt{3}$; $y = 3\sqrt{3}$

Teaching Tip

Auditory Encourage the class to think of a mnemonic, verse, song, or short story to help them remember the relationships between the sides of special right triangles.

Teaching Tip

Critical Thinking Point out that if students know the Pythagorean Theorem, they can figure out the formulas for the side lengths of special right triangles. In a 45°-45°-90° triangle, the two legs are equal. In a 30°-60°-90° triangle, the hypotenuse is twice the shorter leg.

Student to Student

30°-60°-90° Triangles

Marcus Maiello
Johnson High School

To remember the side relationships in a 30°-60°-90° triangle, I draw a simple "1-2-$\sqrt{3}$" triangle like this.

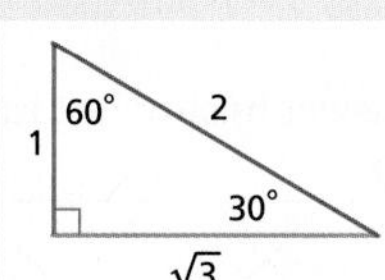

$2 = 2(1)$, so
hypotenuse = 2(shorter leg).

$\sqrt{3} = \sqrt{3}(1)$, so
longer leg = $\sqrt{3}$(shorter leg).

EXAMPLE 4 **Using the 30°-60°-90° Triangle Theorem**

The frame of the clock shown is an equilateral triangle. The length of one side of the frame is 20 cm. Will the clock fit on a shelf that is 18 cm below the shelf above it?

Step 1 Divide the equilateral triangle into two 30°-60°-90° triangles.
The height of the frame is the length of the longer leg.

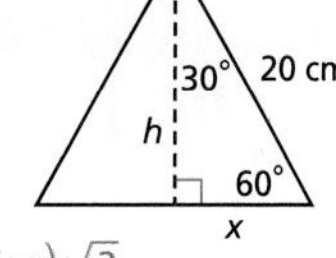

Step 2 Find the length x of the shorter leg.

$20 = 2x$ *Hypotenuse = 2(shorter leg)*
$10 = x$ *Divide both sides by 2.*

Step 3 Find the length h of the longer leg.

$h = 10\sqrt{3} \approx 17.3$ cm *Longer leg = (shorter leg)$\sqrt{3}$*

The frame is approximately 17.3 centimeters tall.
So the clock will fit on the shelf.

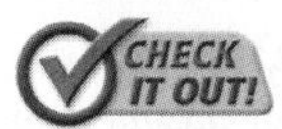

4. What if...? A manufacturer wants to make a larger clock with a height of 30 centimeters. What is the length of each side of the frame? Round to the nearest tenth. **34.6 cm**

THINK AND DISCUSS

1. Explain why an isosceles right triangle is a 45°-45°-90° triangle.

2. Describe how finding x in triangle I is different from finding x in triangle II.

I.

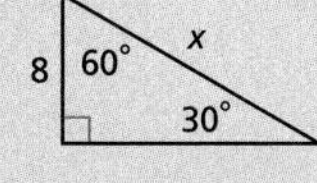

II.

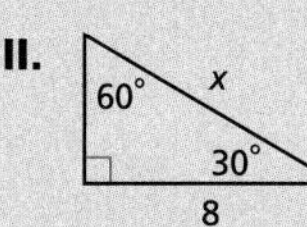

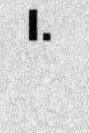

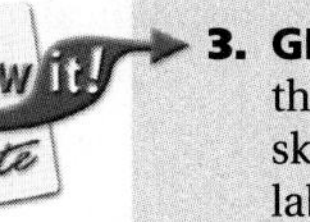

3. GET ORGANIZED Copy and complete the graphic organizer. In each box, sketch the special right triangle and label its side lengths in terms of s.

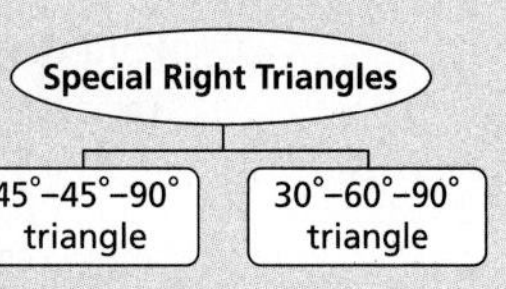

COMMON ERROR ALERT

Students may attempt to apply the formulas from the lesson to any right triangle. Remind them that these relationships only work when the angles are 30°, 60°, and 90° or 45°, 45°, and 90°.

Power Presentations with PowerPoint®

Additional Examples

Example 4

An ornamental pin is in the shape of an equilateral triangle. The length of each side is 6 cm. Josh will attach the fastener to the back along $\overline{AB}$. Will the fastener fit if it is 4 cm long? Yes; $AB = 3\sqrt{3}$ cm, which is greater than 4 cm.

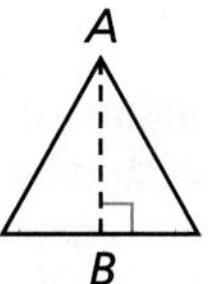

INTERVENTION 
Questioning Strategies

EXAMPLE 4

- What kind of special right triangles are formed when an equilateral triangle is divided in half by a median?

3 Close

Summarize

Review with students the 45°-45°-90° and 30°-60°-90° Triangle Theorems, illustrating each with a diagram and numeric example. Emphasize that these relationships between the side lengths apply only to these two special right triangles.

ONGOING ASSESSMENT and INTERVENTION

***Diagnose Before* the Lesson**
5-8 Warm Up, TE p. 356

***Monitor During* the Lesson**
Check It Out! Exercises, SE pp. 357–359
Questioning Strategies, TE pp. 357–359

***Assess After* the Lesson**
5-8 Lesson Quiz, TE p. 362
Alternative Assessment, TE p. 362

Answers to *Think and Discuss*

1. Possible answer: The △ is a rt. △, so the measure of 1 ∠ is 90°, and the other 2 acute ∠s are comp. The △ is isosc., so its base ∠s are ≅. So the measure of each of the base ∠s is 45°.
2. In figure I, use the relationship $x = 2(8)$. In figure II, first use the relationship $8 = \sqrt{3}$(shorter leg), and then use the relationship $x = 2$(shorter leg).
3. See p. A5.

Assignment Guide

Assign *Guided Practice* exercises as necessary.

If you finished Examples **1–2**
Basic 9–12, 17, 19, 22
Average 9–12, 17, 19, 22, 24, 25
Advanced 9–12, 17, 19, 22, 24, 25, 34

If you finished Examples **1–4**
Basic 9–22, 24–33, 38–46
Average 9–35, 38–46
Advanced 9–46

Homework Quick Check
Quickly check key concepts.
Exercises: 10, 12, 14, 16, 17, 18

Inclusion In **Exercise 15,** some students may find it easier to solve the equation $x\sqrt{3} = 2$ by multiplying both sides by $\sqrt{3}$ first. So $3x = 2\sqrt{3}$, and thus $x = \frac{2\sqrt{3}}{3}$.

State Resources

5-8 Exercises

go.hrw.com
Homework Help Online
KEYWORD: MG7 5-8
Parent Resources Online
KEYWORD: MG7 Parent

GUIDED PRACTICE

SEE EXAMPLE 1 p. 356

Find the value of x. Give your answer in simplest radical form.

1. 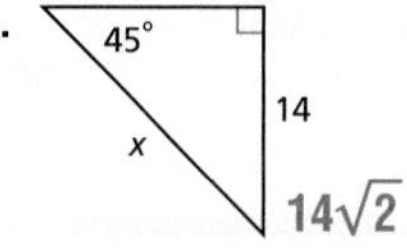

$14\sqrt{2}$

2. 12; x; x $6\sqrt{2}$

3. 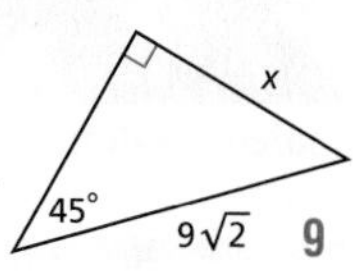

9

SEE EXAMPLE 2 p. 357

4. **Transportation** The two arms of the railroad sign are perpendicular bisectors of each other. In Pennsylvania, the lengths marked in red must be 19.5 inches. What is the distance labeled d? Round to the nearest tenth of an inch. **27.6 in.**

SEE EXAMPLE 3 p. 358

Find the values of x and y. Give your answers in simplest radical form.

5. 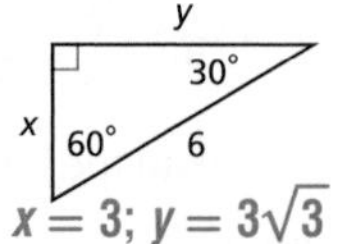

$x = 3$; $y = 3\sqrt{3}$

6. y; x; 30°; 15 $x = 5\sqrt{3}$; $y = 10\sqrt{3}$

7. 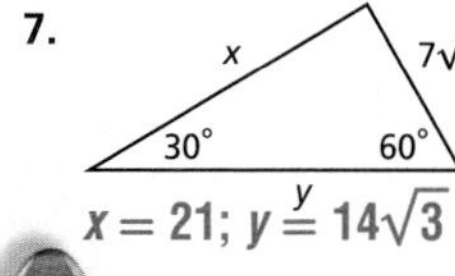

$x = 21$; $y = 14\sqrt{3}$

SEE EXAMPLE 4 p. 359

8. **Entertainment** Regulation billiard balls are $2\frac{1}{4}$ inches in diameter. The rack used to group 15 billiard balls is in the shape of an equilateral triangle. What is the approximate height of the triangle formed by the rack? Round to the nearest quarter of an inch. **9.75 in.**

PRACTICE AND PROBLEM SOLVING

Independent Practice	
For Exercises	See Example
9–11	1
12	2
13–15	3
16	4

Extra Practice
Skills Practice p. S13
Application Practice p. S32

Find the value of x. Give your answer in simplest radical form.

9. 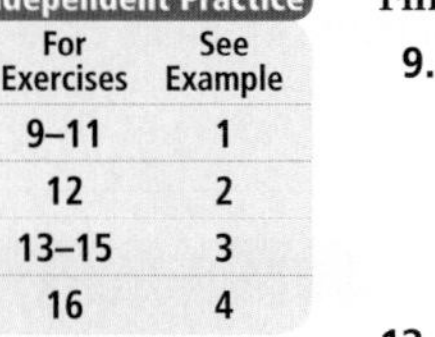

$\frac{15\sqrt{2}}{2}$

10. 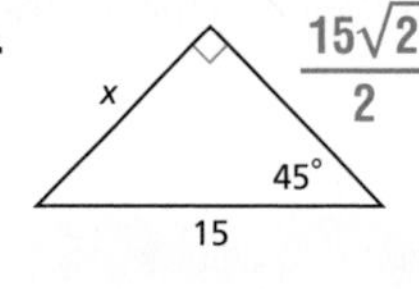

8

11. x; $18\sqrt{2}$ **18**

12. **Design** This tabletop is an isosceles right triangle. The length of the front edge of the table is 48 inches. What is the length w of each side edge? Round to the nearest tenth of an inch. **33.9 in.**

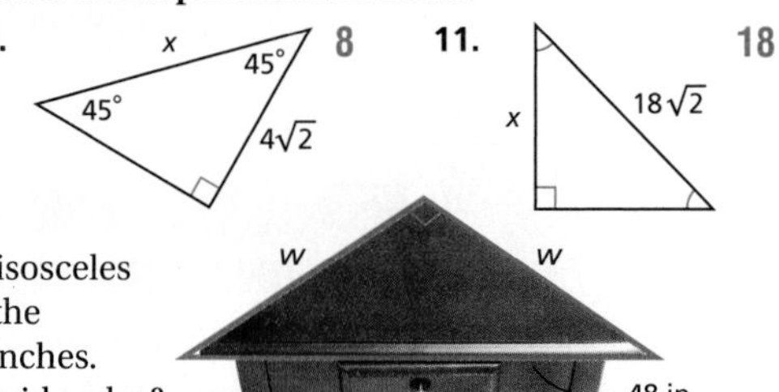

Find the value of x and y. Give your answers in simplest radical form.

13. 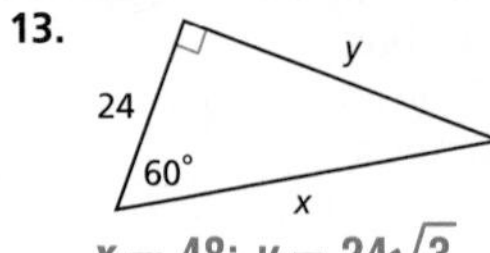

$x = 48$; $y = 24\sqrt{3}$

14. 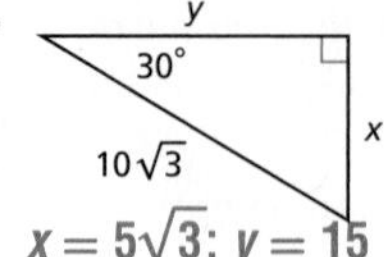

$x = 5\sqrt{3}$; $y = 15$

15. 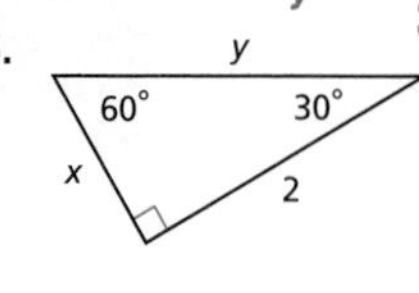

$x = \frac{2\sqrt{3}}{3}$; $y = \frac{4\sqrt{3}}{3}$

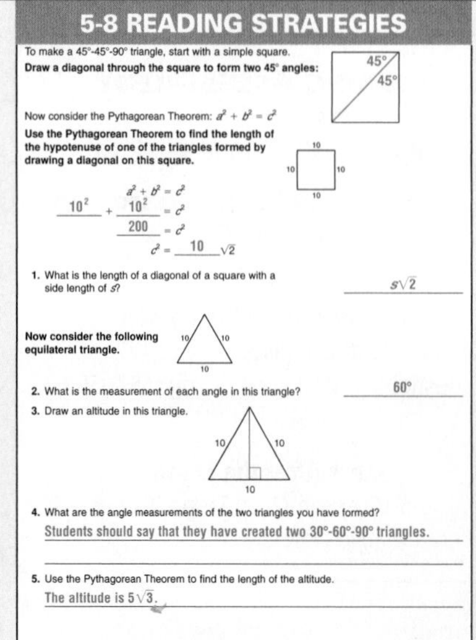

5-8 READING STRATEGIES

To make a 45°-45°-90° triangle, start with a simple square.
Draw a diagonal through the square to form two 45° angles:

Now consider the Pythagorean Theorem: $a^2 + b^2 = c^2$
Use the Pythagorean Theorem to find the length of the hypotenuse of one of the triangles formed by drawing a diagonal on this square.

$a^2 + b^2 = c^2$
$10^2 + 10^2 = c^2$
$200 = c^2$
$c = 10\sqrt{2}$

1. What is the length of a diagonal of a square with a side length of s? $s\sqrt{2}$

Now consider the following equilateral triangle.

2. What is the measurement of each angle in this triangle? 60°
3. Draw an altitude in this triangle.
4. What are the angle measurements of the two triangles you have formed? Students should say that they have created two 30°-60°-90° triangles.
5. Use the Pythagorean Theorem to find the length of the altitude. The altitude is $5\sqrt{3}$.

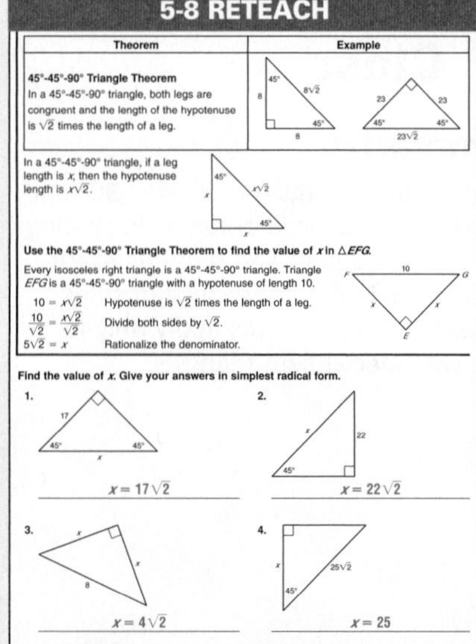

5-8 RETEACH

Theorem	Example
45°-45°-90° Triangle Theorem In a 45°-45°-90° triangle, both legs are congruent and the length of the hypotenuse is $\sqrt{2}$ times the length of a leg.	

In a 45°-45°-90° triangle, if a leg length is x, then the hypotenuse length is $x\sqrt{2}$.

Use the 45°-45°-90° Triangle Theorem to find the value of x in $\triangle EFG$.

Every isosceles right triangle is a 45°-45°-90° triangle. Triangle EFG is a 45°-45°-90° triangle with a hypotenuse of length 10.

$10 = x\sqrt{2}$ Hypotenuse is $\sqrt{2}$ times the length of a leg.
$\frac{10}{\sqrt{2}} = \frac{x\sqrt{2}}{\sqrt{2}}$ Divide both sides by $\sqrt{2}$.
$5\sqrt{2} = x$ Rationalize the denominator.

Find the value of x. Give your answers in simplest radical form.

1. $x = 17\sqrt{2}$
2. $x = 22\sqrt{2}$
3. $x = 4\sqrt{2}$
4. $x = 25$

16. **Pets** A dog walk is used in dog agility competitions. In this dog walk, each ramp makes an angle of 30° with the ground.

a. How long is one ramp? **9 ft**

b. How long is the entire dog walk, including both ramps? **30 ft**

Multi-Step Find the perimeter and area of each figure. Give your answers in simplest radical form.

17. a 45°-45°-90° triangle with hypotenuse length 12 inches

18. a 30°-60°-90° triangle with hypotenuse length 28 centimeters

19. a square with diagonal length 18 meters

20. an equilateral triangle with side length 4 feet

21. an equilateral triangle with height 30 yards

22. **Estimation** The triangle loom is made from wood strips shaped into a 45°-45°-90° triangle. Pegs are placed every $\frac{1}{2}$ inch along the hypotenuse and every $\frac{1}{4}$ inch along each leg. Suppose you make a loom with an 18-inch hypotenuse. Approximately how many pegs will you need? **about 138 nails**

23. **Critical Thinking** The angle measures of a triangle are in the ratio 1:2:3. Are the side lengths also in the ratio 1:2:3? Explain your answer.

17. perimeter: $(12 + 12\sqrt{2})$ in.; area: 36 in^2

18. perimeter: $(42 + 14\sqrt{3})$ cm; area: $98\sqrt{3}$ cm^2

19. perimeter: $(36\sqrt{2})$ m; area: 162 m^2

20. perimeter: 12 ft; area: $4\sqrt{3}$ ft^2

21. perimeter: $60\sqrt{3}$ yd; area: $300\sqrt{3}$ yd^2

Find the coordinates of point P under the given conditions. Give your answers in simplest radical form.

24. $\triangle PQR$ is a 45°-45°-90° triangle with vertices $Q(4, 6)$ and $R(-6, -4)$, and $m\angle P = 90°$. P is in Quadrant II. $(-6, 6)$

25. $\triangle PST$ is a 45°-45°-90° triangle with vertices $S(4, -3)$ and $T(-2, 3)$, and $m\angle S = 90°$. P is in Quadrant I. $(10, 3)$

26. $\triangle PWX$ is a 30°-60°-90° triangle with vertices $W(-1, -4)$ and $X(4, -4)$, and $m\angle W = 90°$. P is in Quadrant II. $(-1, -4 + 5\sqrt{3})$

27. $\triangle PYZ$ is a 30°-60°-90° triangle with vertices $Y(-7, 10)$ and $Z(5, 10)$, and $m\angle Z = 90°$. P is in Quadrant IV. $(5, 10 - 12\sqrt{3})$

28. **Write About It** Why do you think 30°-60°-90° triangles and 45°-45°-90° triangles are called *special right triangles*?

MULTI-STEP TEST PREP

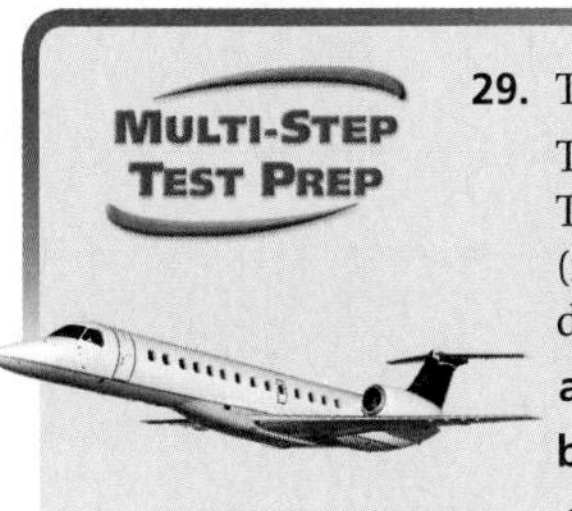

29. This problem will prepare you for the Multi-Step Test Prep on page 364.

The figure shows an airline's routes among four cities. The airline offers one frequent-flier mile for each mile flown (rounded to the nearest mile). How many frequent-flier miles do you earn for each flight?

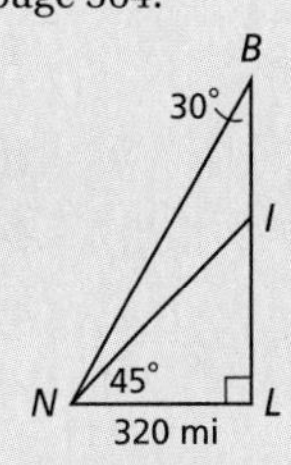

a. Nelson (N) to Belton (B) **640 mi**

b. Idria (I) to Nelson (N) **453 mi**

c. Belton (B) to Idria (I) **234 mi**

In **Exercise 17,** the perimeter is $6\sqrt{2} + 6\sqrt{2} + 12 = 12\sqrt{2} + 12$. Students may add the terms incorrectly to get an answer of $24\sqrt{2}$. Remind them that $12\sqrt{2}$ and 12 are not like terms and cannot be added.

Teaching Tip

Math Background For **Exercises 24–27,** remind students that the quadrants are numbered counterclockwise from the one in which both the *x*-values and *y*-values are positive.

MULTI-STEP TEST PREP **Exercise 29** involves finding the lengths of sides of special right triangles. This exercise prepares students for the Multi-Step Test Prep on page 364.

Answers

23. No; possible answer: if the ∠ measures are in the ratio 1:2:3, then the measures of the ∠s are 30°, 60°, and 90°, and the △ is a 30°-60°-90° △. Assume the length of the shortest leg is 1. Then the length of the hyp. is 2, and the length of the longer leg is $\sqrt{3}$. So the side lengths would be in the ratio $1:\sqrt{3}:2$.

28. Possible answer: Both types of triangles are right triangles. In each 1, there is a unique relationship among the side lengths. For each type of triangle, if you know 1 side length, you can find the other 2.

5-8 PROBLEM SOLVING

For Exercises 1–6, give your answers in simplest radical form.

1. In bowling, the pins are arranged in a pattern based on equilateral triangles. What is the distance between pins 1 and 5?

$12\sqrt{3}$ in. or about 20.8 in.

2. To secure an outdoor canopy, a 64-inch cord is extended from the top of a vertical pole to the ground. If the cord makes a 60° angle with the ground, how tall is the pole?

$32\sqrt{3}$ in. or about 55.4 in.

Find the length of $\overline{AB}$ in each quilt pattern.

3. $3\sqrt{2}$ in. or about 4.2 in.

4. $\frac{8\sqrt{3}}{3}$ in. or about 4.6 in.

Choose the best answer.

5. An equilateral triangle has an altitude of 21 inches. What is the side length of the triangle?

$14\sqrt{3}$ in.

6. A shelf is an isosceles right triangle, and the longest side is 38 centimeters. What is the length of each of the other two sides?

$19\sqrt{2}$ cm

Use the figure for Exercises 7 and 8.
Assume $\triangle JKL$ is in the first quadrant, with $m\angle K = 90°$.

7. Suppose that $\overline{JK}$ is a leg of $\triangle JKL$, a 45°-45°-90° triangle. What are possible coordinates of point L?

A (6, 4.5) C (6, 2)
(B) (7, 2) D (8, 7)

8. Suppose $\triangle JKL$ is a 30°-60°-90° triangle and $\overline{JK}$ is the side opposite the 60° angle. What are the approximate coordinates of point L?

(F) (4.9, 2) H (8.7, 2)
G (4.5, 2) J (7.1, 2)

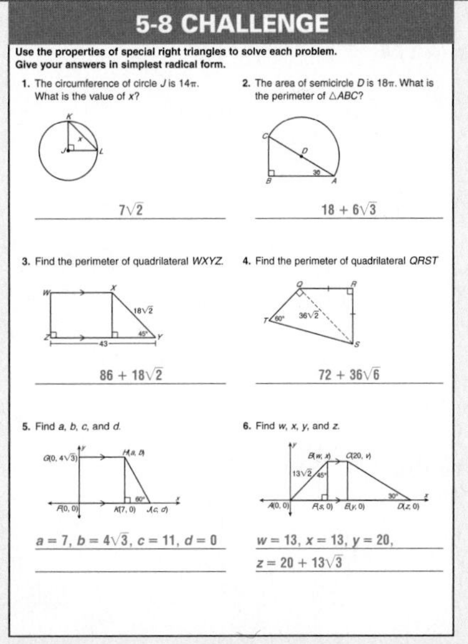

5-8 CHALLENGE

Use the properties of special right triangles to solve each problem. Give your answers in simplest radical form.

1. The circumference of circle J is 14π. What is the value of x?

$7\sqrt{2}$

2. The area of semicircle D is 18π. What is the perimeter of $\triangle ABC$?

$18 + 6\sqrt{3}$

3. Find the perimeter of quadrilateral $WXYZ$.

$86 + 18\sqrt{2}$

4. Find the perimeter of quadrilateral $QRST$

$72 + 36\sqrt{6}$

5. Find a, b, c, and d.

$a = 7$, $b = 4\sqrt{3}$, $c = 11$, $d = 0$

6. Find w, x, y, and z.

$w = 13$, $x = 13$, $y = 20$, $z = 20 + 13\sqrt{3}$

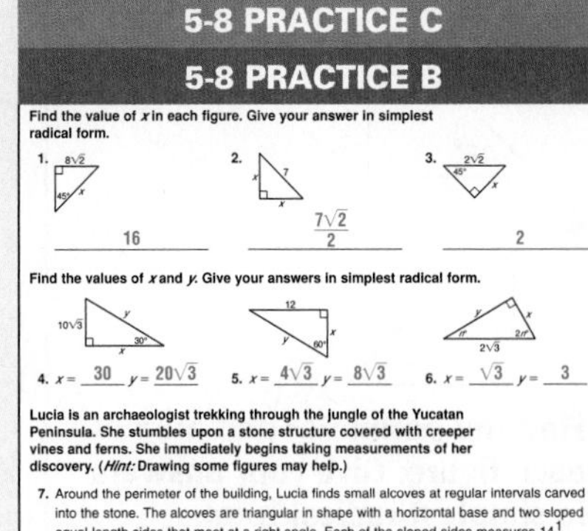

5-8 PRACTICE A
5-8 PRACTICE C
5-8 PRACTICE B

Find the value of x in each figure. Give your answer in simplest radical form.

1. 16

2. $\frac{7\sqrt{2}}{2}$

3. 2

Find the values of x and y. Give your answers in simplest radical form.

4. $x =$ 30 $y =$ $20\sqrt{3}$

5. $x =$ $4\sqrt{3}$ $y =$ $8\sqrt{3}$

6. $x =$ $\sqrt{3}$ $y =$ 3

Lucia is an archaeologist trekking through the jungle of the Yucatan Peninsula. She stumbles upon a stone structure covered with creeper vines and ferns. She immediately begins taking measurements of her discovery. (*Hint:* Drawing some figures may help.)

7. Around the perimeter of the building, Lucia finds small alcoves at regular intervals carved into the stone. The alcoves are triangular in shape with a horizontal base and two sloped equal-length sides that meet at a right angle. Each of the sloped sides measures $14\frac{1}{4}$ inches. Lucia has also found several stone tablets inscribed with characters. The stone tablets measure $22\frac{1}{8}$ inches long. Lucia hypothesizes that the alcoves once held the stone tablets. Tell whether Lucia's hypothesis may be correct. Explain your answer.

Possible answer: Lucia's hypothesis cannot be correct. The base of the alcove is just over 20 inches long, so a $22\frac{1}{8}$-inch tablet could not fit.

8. Lucia also finds several statues around the building. The statues measure $9\frac{7}{16}$ inches tall. She wonders whether the statues might have been placed in the alcoves. Tell whether this is possible. Explain your answer.

Possible answer: To find the height of a 45°-45°-90° triangle, draw a perpendicular to the hypotenuse. This makes another smaller 45°-45°-90° triangle whose hypotenuse is the length of one of the legs of the larger triangle. The height of the alcove is about 10 inches, so the statues could have been placed in the alcoves.

TEST PREP DOCTOR If students have difficulty with **Exercise 33,** have them draw one of the triangles formed, label the angles, and find the lengths of both sides. Remind students how to find the area of a rectangle and how to multiply 16 by $16\sqrt{3}$.

Journal

Have students describe how they remember the relationship between the side lengths of a 45°-45°-90° and a 30°-60°-90° triangle.

ALTERNATIVE ASSESSMENT

Have students draw a 45°-45°-90° triangle and a 30°-60°-90° triangle. Have them measure the hypotenuse and then use the theorems from the lesson to find the other lengths. Then have them verify the lengths by measuring.

Power Presentations with PowerPoint®

5-8 Lesson Quiz

Find the values of the variables. Give your answers in simplest radical form.

1.

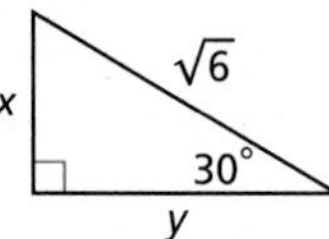

$x = \frac{\sqrt{6}}{2}$; $y = \frac{3\sqrt{2}}{2}$

2.

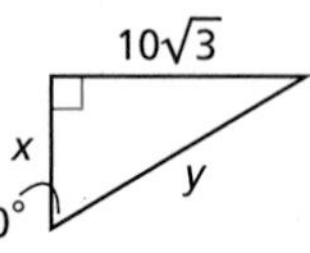

$x = 10$; $y = 20$

3.

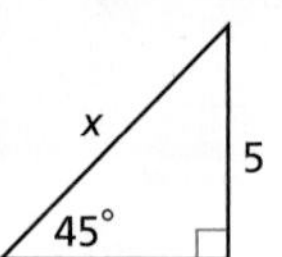

$5\sqrt{2}$

4.

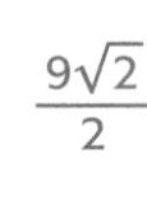

$\frac{9\sqrt{2}}{2}$

Find the perimeter and area of each figure. Give your answers in simplest radical form.

5. a square with diagonal length 20 cm $40\sqrt{2}$ cm; 200 cm^2
6. an equilateral triangle with height 24 in. $48\sqrt{3}$ in.; $192\sqrt{3}$ in^2

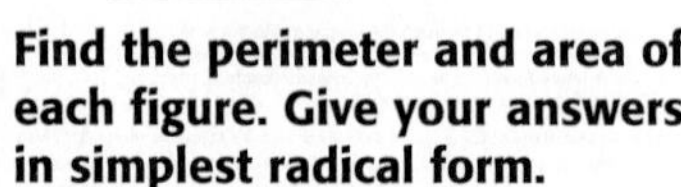

Also available on transparency

TEST PREP

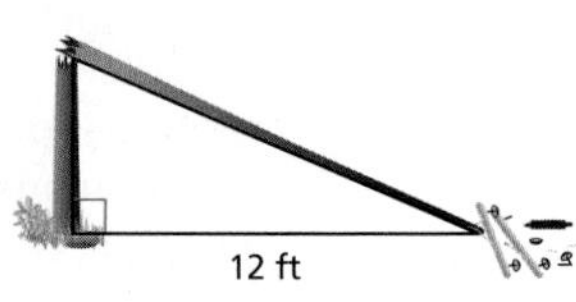

30. Which is a true statement?
    - (A) $AB = BC\sqrt{2}$
    - (B) $AB = BC\sqrt{3}$
    - **(C) $AC = BC\sqrt{3}$**
    - (D) $AC = AB\sqrt{2}$

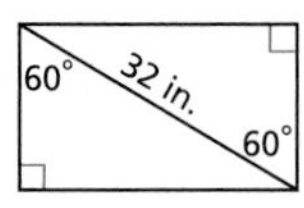

31. An 18-foot pole is broken during a storm. The top of the pole touches the ground 12 feet from the base of the pole. How tall is the part of the pole left standing?
    - **(F) 5 feet**
    - (G) 6 feet
    - (H) 13 feet
    - (J) 22 feet

32. The length of the hypotenuse of an isosceles right triangle is 24 inches. What is the length of one leg of the triangle, rounded to the nearest tenth of an inch?
    - (A) 13.9 inches
    - **(B) 17.0 inches**
    - (C) 33.9 inches
    - (D) 41.6 inches

33. **Gridded Response** Find the area of the rectangle to the nearest tenth of a square inch. **443.4**

CHALLENGE AND EXTEND

Multi-Step Find the value of x in each figure.

34. **1**

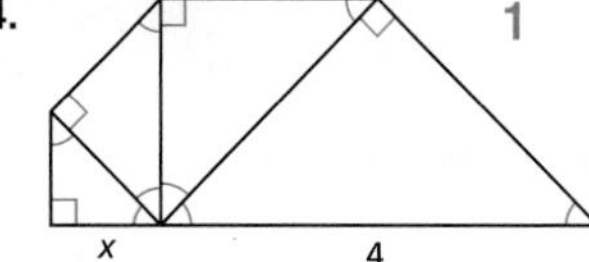

35. $\frac{32}{9}$

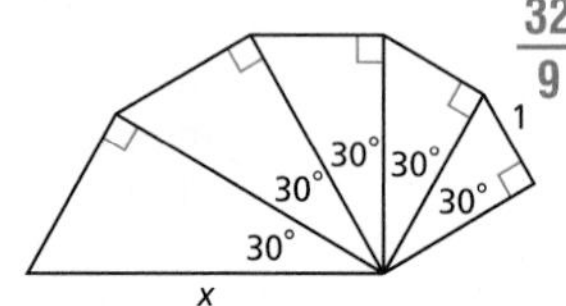

36. Each edge of the cube has length e.
    a. Find the diagonal length d when $e = 1$, $e = 2$, and $e = 3$. Give the answers in simplest radical form.
    b. Write a formula for d for any positive value of e.

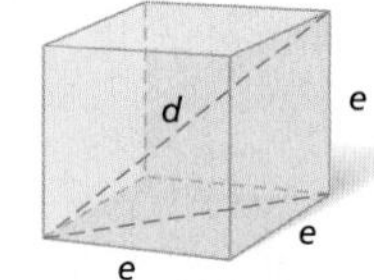

36a. When $e = 1$, $d = \sqrt{3}$. When $e = 2$, $d = 2\sqrt{3}$. When $e = 3$, $d = 3\sqrt{3}$.

36b. $d = e\sqrt{3}$

37. Write a paragraph proof to show that the altitude to the hypotenuse of a 30°-60°-90° triangle divides the hypotenuse into two segments, one of which is 3 times as long as the other.

SPIRAL REVIEW

Rewrite each function in the form $y = a(x - h)^2 - k$ and find the axis of symmetry. *(Previous course)*

38. $y = x^2 + 4x$
39. $y = x^2 - 10x - 2$
40. $y = x^2 + 7x + 15$

38. $y = (x + 2)^2 - 4$; $x = -2$

39. $y = (x - 5)^2 - 27$; $x = 5$

40. $y = (x + 3.5)^2 + 2.75$; $x = -3.5$

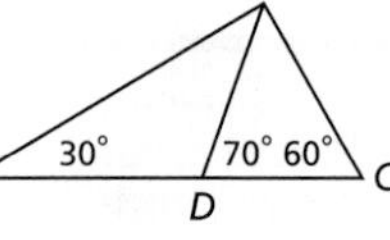

Classify each triangle by its angle measures. *(Lesson 4-1)*

41. $\triangle ADB$ **obtuse**
42. $\triangle BDC$ **acute**
43. $\triangle ABC$ **right**

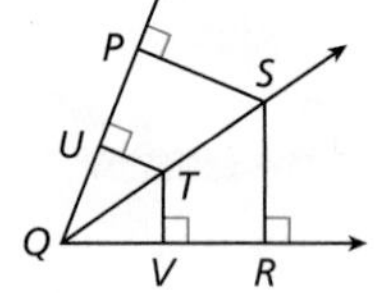

Use the diagram for Exercises 44–46. *(Lesson 5-1)*

44. Given that $PS = SR$ and $m\angle PSQ = 65°$, find $m\angle PQR$. **50°**
45. Given that $UT = TV$ and $m\angle PQS = 42°$, find $m\angle VTS$. **132°**
46. Given that $\angle PQS \cong \angle SQR$, $SR = 3TU$, and $PS = 7.5$, find TV. **2.5**

Answers

37. Possible answer:

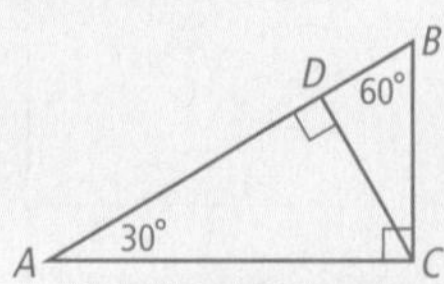

Given: $\triangle ABC$ is a 30°-60°-90° $\triangle$ with $m\angle A = 30°$ and $m\angle B = 60°$. $\overline{CD}$ is the altitude to the hyp.

Prove: $AD = 3DB$

Proof: It is given that $\overline{CD}$ is the altitude to the hyp. Thus $\overline{CD} \perp \overline{AB}$ by the def. of altitude. So $\angle ADC$ and $\angle BDC$ are rt. ∠s by the def. of ⊥, and $\triangle ADC$ and $\triangle BDC$ are rt. △s by def. It is given that $m\angle A = 30°$ and $m\angle B = 60°$. Since the acute ∠s of a rt. △ are comp., $m\angle DCA = 60°$ and $m\angle DCB = 30°$ by the Subtr. Prop. of =. So $\triangle ADC$ and $\triangle BDC$ are both 30°-60°-90° △s. By the 30°-60°-90° △ Thm., $AD = \sqrt{3}(DC)$ and $DC = \sqrt{3}(DB)$. By subst., $AD = \sqrt{3}[\sqrt{3}(DB)]$. This simplifies to $AD = 3DB$.

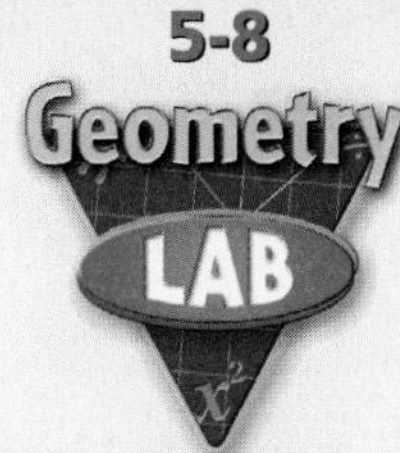

Graph Irrational Numbers

Numbers such as $\sqrt{2}$ and $\sqrt{3}$ are irrational. That is, they cannot be written as the ratio of two integers. In decimal form, they are infinite nonrepeating decimals. You can round the decimal form to estimate the location of these numbers on a number line, or you can use right triangles to construct their locations exactly.

Use with Lesson 5-8

Activity

1. Draw a line. Mark two points near the left side of the line and label them 0 and 1. The distance from 0 to 1 is 1 unit.

2. Set your compass to 1 unit and mark increments at 2, 3, 4, and 5 units to construct a number line.

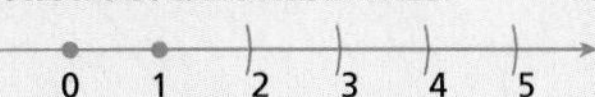

3. Construct a perpendicular to the line through 1.

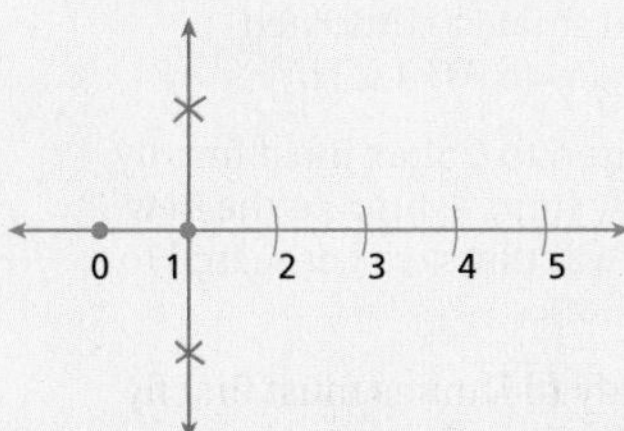

4. Using your compass, mark 1 unit up from the number line and then draw a right triangle. The legs both have length 1, so by the Pythagorean Theorem, the hypotenuse has a length of $\sqrt{2}$.

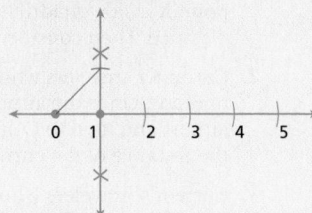

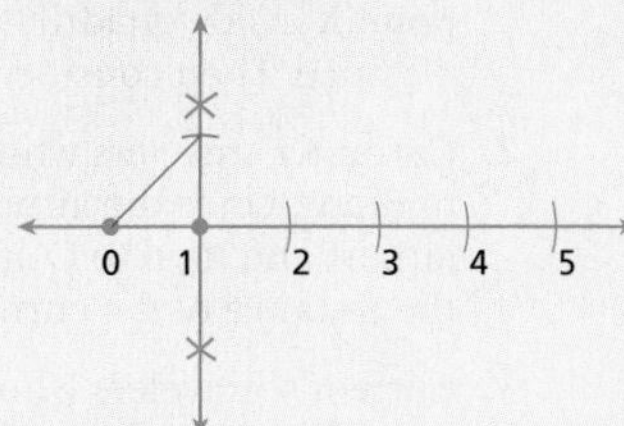

5. Set your compass to the length of the hypotenuse. Draw an arc centered at 0 that intersects the number line at $\sqrt{2}$.

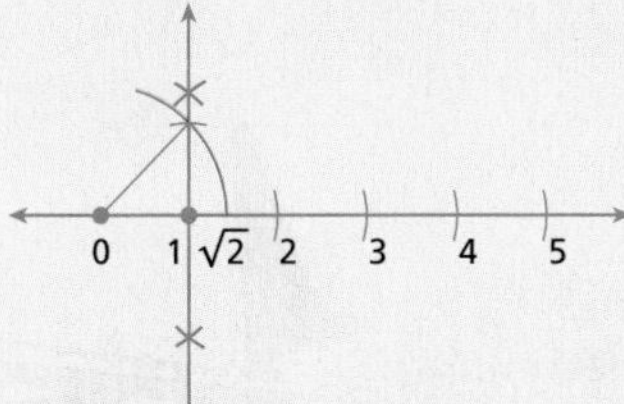

6. Repeat Steps 3 through 5, starting at $\sqrt{2}$, to construct a segment of length $\sqrt{3}$.

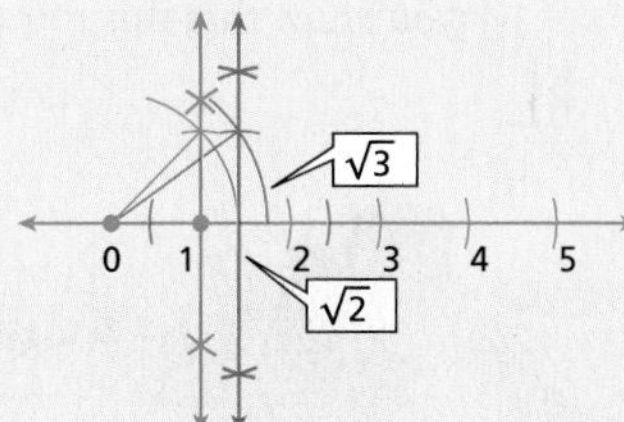

Try This

1. Sketch the two right triangles from Step 6. Label the side lengths and use the Pythagorean Theorem to show why the construction is correct.
2. Construct $\sqrt{4}$ and verify that it is equal to 2.
3. Construct $\sqrt{5}$ through $\sqrt{9}$ and verify that $\sqrt{9}$ is equal to 3.
4. Set your compass to the length of the segment from 0 to $\sqrt{2}$. Mark off another segment of length $\sqrt{2}$ to show that $\sqrt{8}$ is equal to $2\sqrt{2}$.

Answers to *Try This*

1.

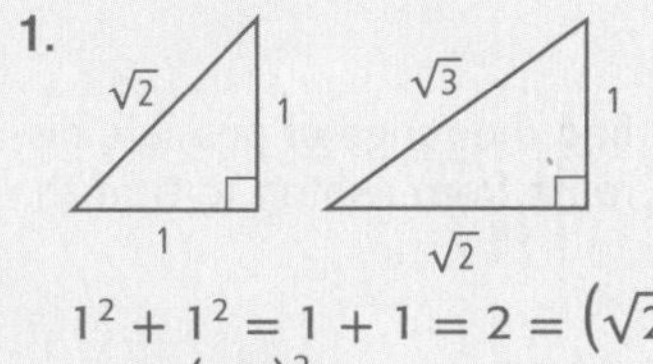

$1^2 + 1^2 = 1 + 1 = 2 = \left(\sqrt{2}\right)^2$

$1^2 + \left(\sqrt{2}\right)^2 = 1 + 2 = 3 = \left(\sqrt{3}\right)^2$

2. Check students' constructions to confirm that $\sqrt{4}$ lies at 2 on the number line.
3. Check students' constructions to confirm that $\sqrt{9}$ lies at 3 on the number line.
4. Check students' constructions to confirm that $2\sqrt{2}$ lies at $\sqrt{8}$ on the number line.

Organizer

Use with Lesson 5-8

Pacing:
Traditional 1 day
Block $\frac{1}{2}$ day

Objective: Graph irrational numbers on a number line.

Materials: compass, straightedge

Online Edition

Countdown Week 12

Resources

Geometry Lab Activities
5-8 Lab Recording Sheet

Teach

Discuss

By using a 45°-45°-90° triangle with a side length of 1, you can construct a segment of length $\sqrt{2}$. This segment can then be used to construct other irrational lengths.

Alternative Approach

After **Step 5,** put students in groups and have each group construct a different irrational length and present their construction to the class.

Close

Key Concept

The Pythagorean Theorem can be used to construct segments of irrational lengths.

Assessment

Journal Have students describe how to construct a segment of length $\sqrt{2}$.

State Resources

go.hrw.com
State Resources Online
KEYWORD: MG7 Resources

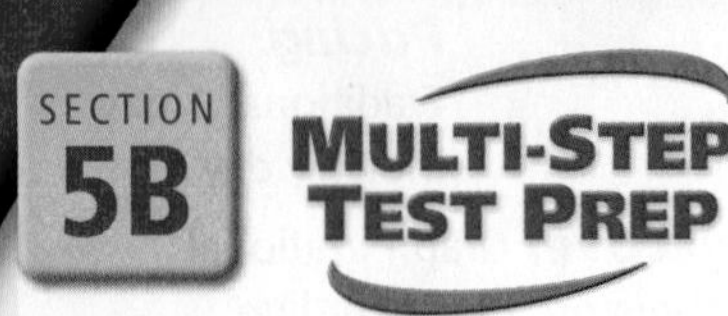

Organizer

Objective: Assess students' ability to apply concepts and skills in Lessons 5-5 through 5-8 in a real-world format.

Online Edition

Resources

Geometry Assessments
www.mathtekstoolkit.org

Problem	Text Reference
1	Lesson 5-5
2	Lesson 5-8
3	Lesson 5-8
4	Lesson 5-5, 5-6

Answers

1, 4. See p. A21.

State Resources

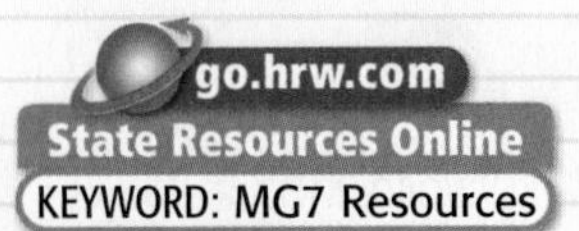

MULTI-STEP TEST PREP

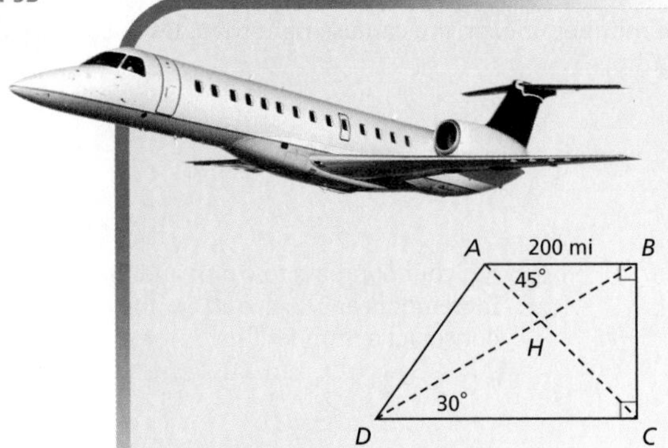

Relationships in Triangles

Fly Away! A commuter airline serves the four cities of Ashton, Brady, Colfax, and Dumas, located at points A, B, C, and D, respectively. The solid lines in the figure show the airline's existing routes. The airline is building an airport at H, which will serve as a hub. This will add four new routes to their schedule: $\overline{AH}$, $\overline{BH}$, $\overline{CH}$, and $\overline{DH}$.

1. The airline wants to locate the airport so that the combined distance to the cities $(AH + BH + CH + DH)$ is as small as possible. Give an indirect argument to explain why the airline should locate the airport at the intersection of the diagonals $\overline{AC}$ and $\overline{BD}$. (*Hint*: Assume that a different point X inside quadrilateral $ABCD$ results in a smaller combined distance. Then consider how $AX + CX$ compares to $AH + CH$.)
2. Currently, travelers who want to go from Ashton to Colfax must first fly to Brady. Once the airport is built, they will fly from Ashton to the new airport and then to Colfax. How many miles will this save compared to the distance of the current trip? **about 117.2 mi**
3. Currently, travelers who want to go from Brady to Dumas must first fly to Colfax. Once the airport is built, they will fly from Brady to the new airport and then to Dumas. How many miles will this save? **about 146.4 mi**
4. Once the airport is built, the airline plans to serve a meal only on its longest flight. On which route should they serve the meal? How do you know that this route is the longest?

INTERVENTION

Scaffolding Questions

1. How can you use the Triangle Inequality Theorem to write an inequality involving AX and CX? $AX + CX > AC$ How can you rewrite this inequality to include AH and CH? $AX + CX > AH + CH$
2. How can you find AC? It is the hyp. of a 45°-45°-90° triangle with leg length 200. So multiply 200 by $\sqrt{2}$.
3. How are $\overline{DB}$ and $\overline{DC}$ related? They are the hyp. and longer leg of a 30°-60°-90° triangle with a shorter leg length of 200.
4. Which route appears to be the longest? $\overline{DC}$ How can you show that this route is longer than $\overline{AD}$? Hinge Thm.

Extension

Use $\triangle ACD$ to find the range of possible distances for the route from Ashton to Dumas. about 63.6 mi to 629.2 mi

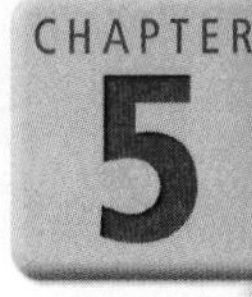

SECTION 5B

Quiz for Lessons 5-5 Through 5-8

5-5 Indirect Proof and Inequalities in One Triangle

1. Write an indirect proof that the supplement of an acute angle cannot be an acute angle.
2. Write the angles of $\triangle KLM$ in order from smallest to largest. $\angle L$, $\angle K$, $\angle M$

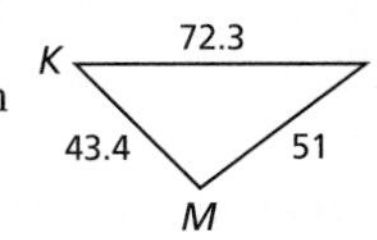

3. Write the sides of $\triangle DEF$ in order from shortest to longest. $\overline{EF}$, $\overline{DE}$, $\overline{DF}$

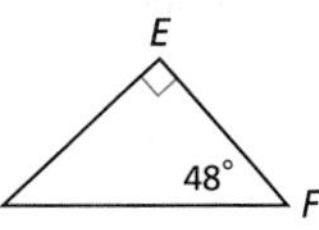

Tell whether a triangle can have sides with the given lengths. Explain.

4. 8.3, 10.5, 18.8
5. $4s$, $s + 10$, s^2, when $s = 4$
6. The distance from Kara's school to the theater is 9 km. The distance from her school to the zoo is 16 km. If the three locations form a triangle, what is the range of distances from the theater to the zoo? **greater than 7 km and less than 25 km**

5-6 Inequalities in Two Triangles

7. Compare PR and SV.

V 5.6 T, 102°, 3.8, P, 3.8, 127°, Q 5.6 R, S

$PR > SV$

8. Compare $m\angle KJL$ and $m\angle MJL$.

K, 14, 4, L, 12, 6, J 14 M

$m\angle KJL < m\angle MJL$

9. Find the range of values for x.

A $4x - 13$ B, 68°, 55°, D 15 C

$3.25 < x < 7$

5-7 The Pythagorean Theorem

10. Find the value of x. Give the answer in simplest radical form. $\sqrt{106}$

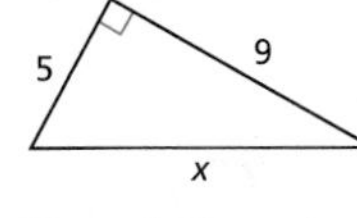

11. Find the missing side length. Tell if the side lengths form a Pythagorean triple. Explain.

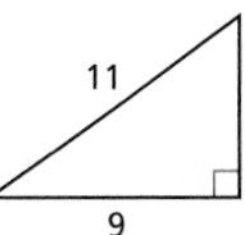

12. Tell if the measures 10, 12, and 16 can be the side lengths of a triangle. If so, classify the triangle as acute, obtuse, or right. **triangle; obtuse**
13. A landscaper wants to place a stone walkway from one corner of the rectangular lawn to the opposite corner. What will be the length of the walkway? Round to the nearest inch. **94 ft 4 in.**

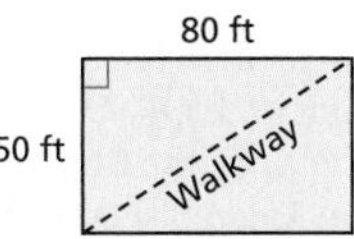

5-8 Applying Special Right Triangles

14. A yield sign is an equilateral triangle with a side length of 36 inches. What is the height h of the sign? Round to the nearest inch. **31 in.**

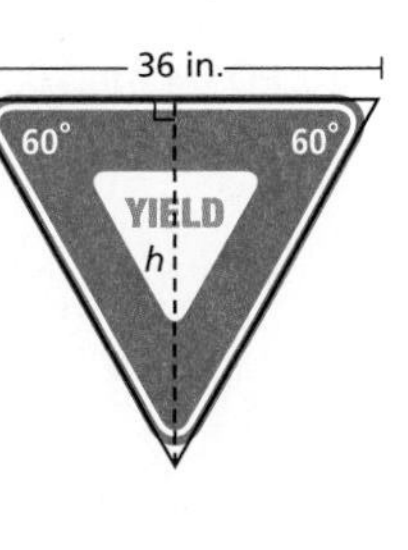

Find the values of the variables. Give your answers in simplest radical form.

15.

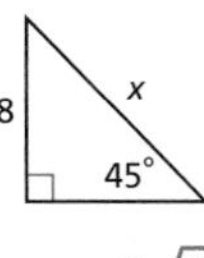

$x = 8\sqrt{2}$

16.

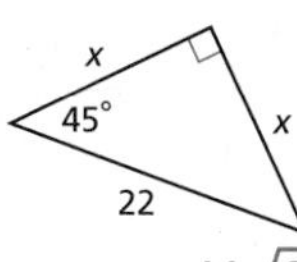

$x = 11\sqrt{2}$

17.

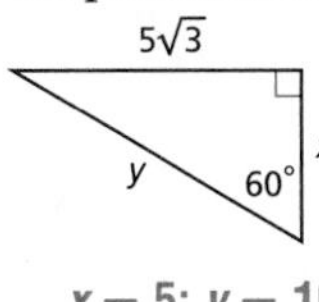

$x = 5$; $y = 10$

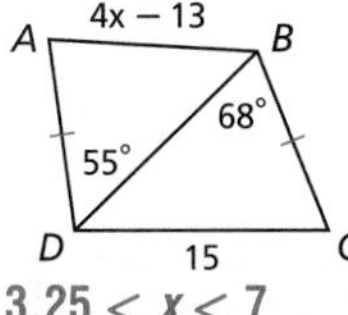

READY TO GO ON? SECTION 5B

Organizer

Objective: Assess students' mastery of concepts and skills in Lessons 5-5 through 5-8.

Resources

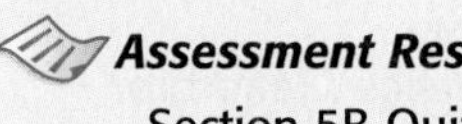
Assessment Resources
Section 5B Quiz

Teacher One Stop™
Test & Practice Generator

INTERVENTION

Resources

***Ready to Go On? Intervention and Enrichment* Worksheets**

***Ready to Go On?* CD-ROM**

***Ready to Go On?* Online**

my.hrw.com

Answers

1, 4, 5, 11. See p. A21.

READY TO GO ON?
Diagnose and Prescribe

NO — INTERVENE

Ready to Go On? Intervention	Ready to Go On? Intervention, Section 5B: Worksheets	CD-ROM	Online
Lesson 5-5	5-5 Intervention	Activity 5-5	Diagnose and Prescribe Online
Lesson 5-6	5-6 Intervention	Activity 5-6	
Lesson 5-7	5-7 Intervention	Activity 5-7	
Lesson 5-8	5-8 Intervention	Activity 5-8	

YES — ENRICH

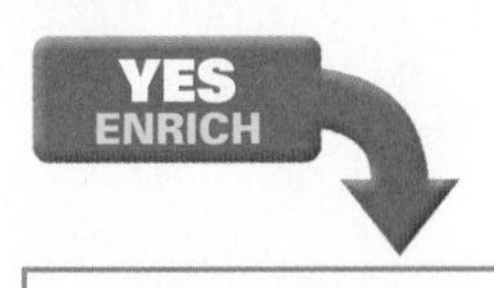
Ready to Go On? Enrichment, Section 5B
Worksheets
CD-ROM
Online

CHAPTER 5 Study Guide: Review

Organizer

Objective: Help students organize and review key concepts and skills presented in Chapter 5.

PREMIER **Online Edition**
Multilingual Glossary

Resources

Teacher One Stop™
PuzzleView
Test & Practice Generator

Multilingual Glossary **Online**
go.hrw.com
KEYWORD: MG7 Glossary

Lesson Tutorial Videos **CD-ROM**

Answers

1. equidistant
2. midsegment
3. incenter
4. locus
5. 7.4
6. 13.4
7. 5.8
8. 52°
9. $y = x - 1$
10. $y - 6 = -0.25(x - 4)$
11. No; to apply the Conv. of the ∠ Bisector Thm., you need to know that $\overline{AP} \perp \overline{AB}$ and $\overline{CP} \perp \overline{CB}$.
12. Yes; because $\overline{AP} \perp \overline{AB}$, $\overline{CP} \perp \overline{CB}$, and $\overline{AP} \cong \overline{CP}$, P is on the bisector of $\angle ABC$ by the Conv. of the ∠ Bisector Thm.

CHAPTER 5 Study Guide: Review

For a complete list of the postulates and theorems in this chapter, see p. PS12.

Vocabulary

Complete the sentences below with vocabulary words from the list above.

1. A point that is the same distance from two or more objects is __?__ from the objects.
2. A __?__ is a segment that joins the midpoints of two sides of the triangle.
3. The point of concurrency of the angle bisectors of a triangle is the __?__ .
4. A __?__ is a set of points that satisfies a given condition.

5-1 Perpendicular and Angle Bisectors *(pp. 300–306)*

EXAMPLES

Find each measure.

■ JL

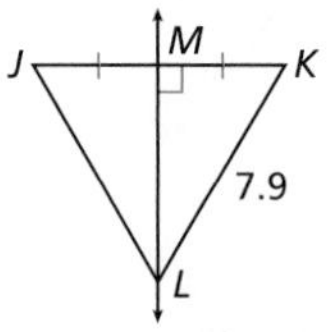

Because $\overline{JM} \cong \overline{MK}$ and $\overline{ML} \perp \overline{JK}$, $\overline{ML}$ is the perpendicular bisector of $\overline{JK}$.

$JL = KL$ *⊥ Bisector Thm.*

$JL = 7.9$ *Substitute 7.9 for KL.*

■ $m\angle PQS$, given that $m\angle PQR = 68°$

Since $SP = SR$, $\overline{SP} \perp \overline{QP}$, and $\overline{SR} \perp \overline{QR}$, $\overrightarrow{QS}$ bisects $\angle PQR$ by the Converse of the Angle Bisector Theorem.

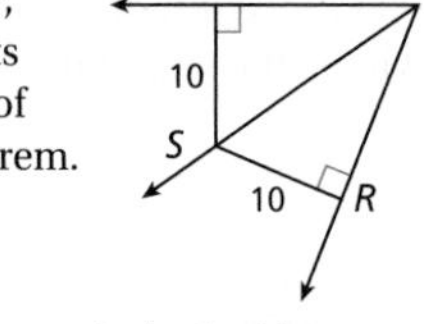

$m\angle PQS = \frac{1}{2}m\angle PQR$ *Def. of ∠ bisector*

$m\angle PQS = \frac{1}{2}(68°) = 34°$ *Substitute 68° for m∠PQR.*

EXERCISES

Find each measure.

5. BD

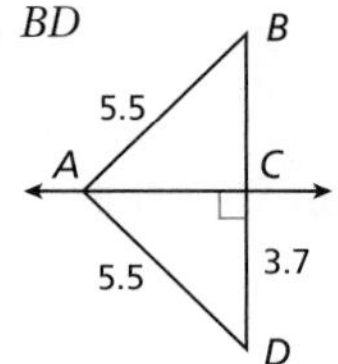

6. YZ

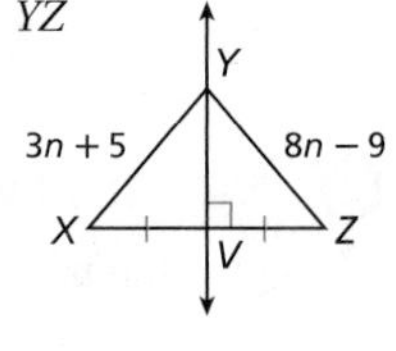

7. HT

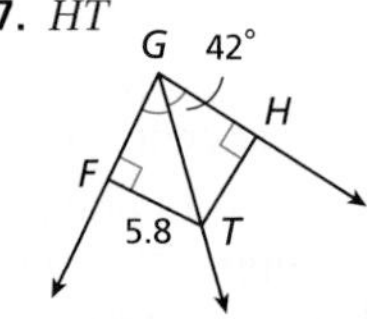

8. $m\angle MNP$

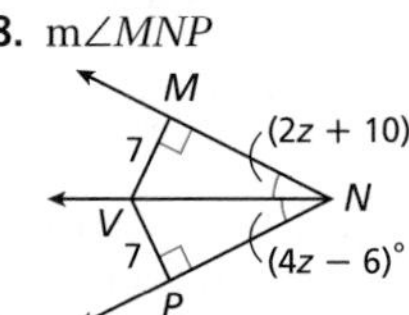

Write an equation in point-slope form for the perpendicular bisector of the segment with the given endpoints.

9. $A(-4, 5)$, $B(6, -5)$
10. $X(3, 2)$, $Y(5, 10)$

Tell whether the given information allows you to conclude that P is on the bisector of $\angle ABC$.

11.

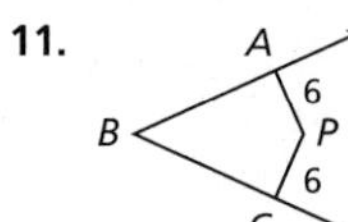

12.

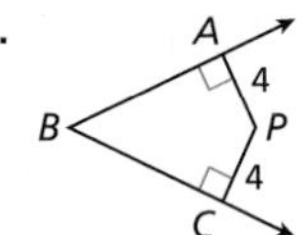

5-2 Bisectors of Triangles (pp. 307–313)

EXAMPLES

- $\overline{DG}$, $\overline{EG}$, and $\overline{FG}$ are the perpendicular bisectors of $\triangle ABC$. Find AG.

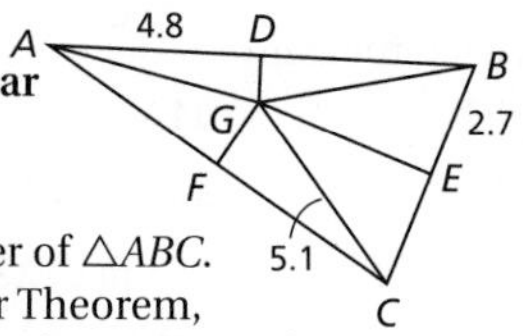

G is the circumcenter of $\triangle ABC$. By the Circumcenter Theorem, G is equidistant from the vertices of $\triangle ABC$.

$AG = CG$ *Circumcenter Thm.*

$AG = 5.1$ *Substitute 5.1 for CG.*

- $\overline{QS}$ and $\overline{RS}$ are angle bisectors of $\triangle PQR$. Find the distance from S to $\overline{PR}$.

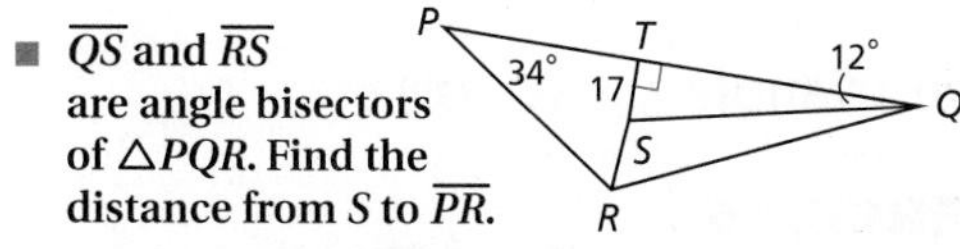

S is the incenter of $\triangle PQR$. By the Incenter Theorem, S is equidistant from the sides of $\triangle PQR$. The distance from S to $\overline{PQ}$ is 17, so the distance from S to $\overline{PR}$ is also 17.

EXERCISES

$\overline{PX}$, $\overline{PY}$, and $\overline{PZ}$ are the perpendicular bisectors of $\triangle GHJ$. Find each length.

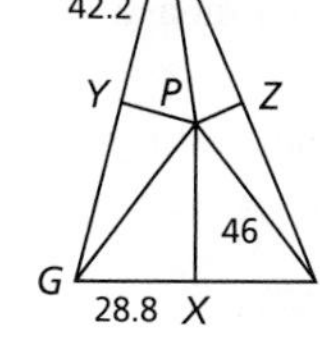

13. GY **14.** GP

15. GJ **16.** PH

$\overline{UA}$ and $\overline{VA}$ are angle bisectors of $\triangle UVW$. Find each measure.

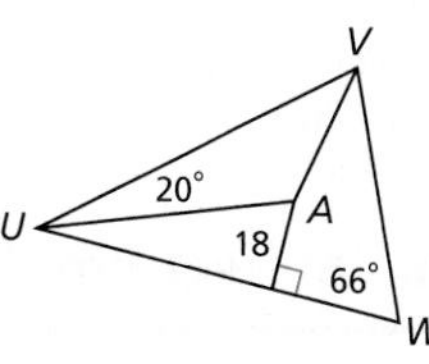

17. the distance from A to $\overline{UV}$

18. $m\angle WVA$

Find the circumcenter of a triangle with the given vertices.

19. $M(0, 6)$, $N(8, 0)$, $O(0, 0)$

20. $O(0, 0)$, $R(0, -7)$, $S(-12, 0)$

5-3 Medians and Altitudes of Triangles (pp. 314–320)

EXAMPLES

- In $\triangle JKL$, $JP = 42$. Find JQ.

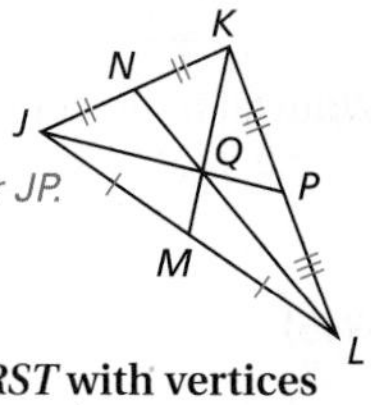

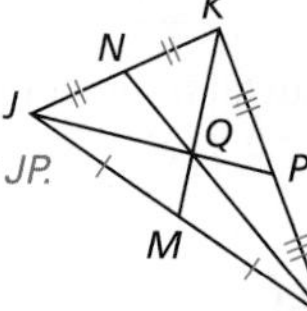

$JQ = \frac{2}{3}JP$ *Centroid Thm.*

$JQ = \frac{2}{3}(42)$ *Substitute 42 for JP.*

$JQ = 28$ *Multiply.*

- Find the orthocenter of $\triangle RST$ with vertices $R(-5, 3)$, $S(-2, 5)$, and $T(-2, 0)$.

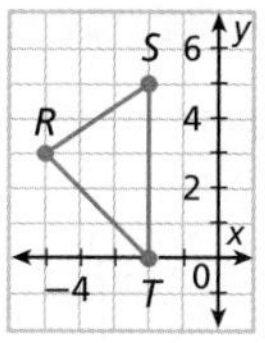

Since $\overline{ST}$ is vertical, the equation of the line containing the altitude from R to $\overline{ST}$ is $y = 3$.

slope of $\overline{RT} = \frac{3 - 0}{-5 - (-2)} = -1$

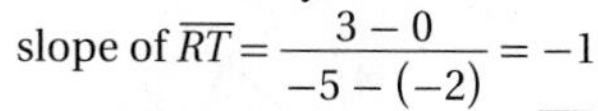

The slope of the altitude to $\overline{RT}$ is 1. This line must pass through $S(-2, 5)$.

$y - y_1 = m(x - x_1)$ *Point-slope form*

$y - 5 = 1(x + 2)$ *Substitution*

Solve the system $\begin{cases} y = 3 \\ y = x + 7 \end{cases}$ to find that the coordinates of the orthocenter are $(-4, 3)$.

EXERCISES

In $\triangle DEF$, $DB = 24.6$, and $EZ = 11.6$. Find each length.

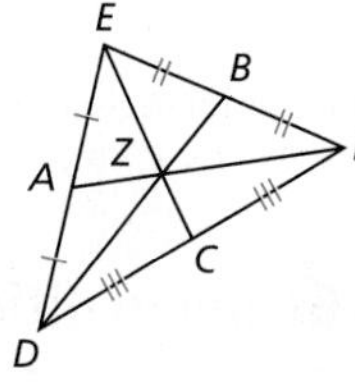

21. DZ **22.** ZB

23. ZC **24.** EC

Find the orthocenter of a triangle with the given vertices.

25. $J(-6, 7)$, $K(-6, 0)$, $L(-11, 0)$

26. $A(1, 2)$, $B(6, 2)$, $C(1, -8)$

27. $R(2, 3)$, $S(7, 8)$, $T(8, 3)$

28. $X(-3, 2)$, $Y(5, 2)$, $Z(3, -4)$

29. The coordinates of a triangular piece of a mobile are $(0, 4)$, $(3, 8)$, and $(6, 0)$. The piece will hang from a chain so that it is balanced. At what coordinates should the chain be attached?

Answers

13. 42.2
14. 46
15. 57.6
16. 46
17. 18
18. 37°
19. (4, 3)
20. (−6, −3.5)
21. 16.4
22. 8.2
23. 5.8
24. 17.4
25. (−6, 0)
26. (1, 2)
27. (7, 4)
28. (3, 0)
29. (3, 4)

Study Guide: Review 367

Answers

30. 35.1
31. 64.8
32. 32.4
33. 42°
34. 138°
35. 42°
36. $V(-1, -1)$; $W(6, 1)$; slope of $\overline{VW} = \frac{2}{7}$; slope of $\overline{GJ} = \frac{2}{7}$; since the slopes are the same, $\overline{VW} \parallel \overline{GJ}$. $VW = \sqrt{53}$; $GJ = 2\sqrt{53}$; since $\sqrt{53} = \frac{1}{2}(2\sqrt{53})$, $VW = \frac{1}{2}GJ$.
37. $\overline{BC}, \overline{AC}, \overline{AB}$
38. ∠F, ∠H, ∠G
39. greater than 9 cm and less than 18 cm
40. Yes; possible answer: the sum of each pair of 2 lengths is greater than the third length.
41. No; possible answer: when $z = 5$, the value of $3z$ is 15. So the 3 lengths are 5, 5, and 15. The sum of 5 and 5 is 10, which is not greater than 15. By the △ Inequality Thm., a △ cannot have these side lengths.
42. Possible answer:
Given: △ABC
Prove: △ABC cannot have 2 obtuse ∠s.
Proof: Assume that △ABC has 2 obtuse ∠s. Let ∠A and ∠B be the obtuse ∠s. By the def. of obtuse, $m\angle A > 90°$ and $m\angle B > 90°$. If the 2 inequalities are added, $m\angle A + m\angle B > 180°$. However, by the △ Sum Thm., $m\angle A + m\angle B + m\angle C = 180°$. So $m\angle A + m\angle B = 180° - m\angle C$. But then $180° - m\angle C > 180°$ by subst., and thus $m\angle C < 0°$. A △ cannot have an ∠ with a measure less than 0°. So the assumption that △ABC has 2 obtuse ∠s is false. Therefore a △ cannot have 2 obtuse ∠s.
43. $PS < RS$
44. $m\angle BCA < m\angle DCA$
45. $-1.4 < n < 3$
46. $2.75 < n < 12.5$

5-4 The Triangle Midsegment Theorem *(pp. 322–327)*

EXAMPLES

Find each measure.

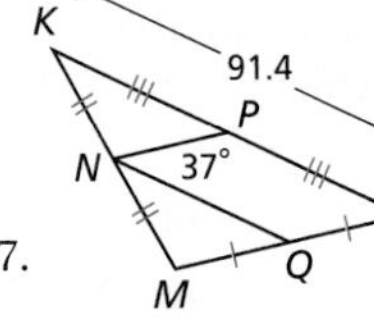

- NQ

By the △ Midsegment Thm., $NQ = \frac{1}{2}KL = 45.7$.

- $m\angle NQM$

$\overline{NP} \parallel \overline{ML}$	*△ Midsegment Thm.*
$m\angle NQM = m\angle PNQ$	*Alt. Int. ∠s Thm.*
$m\angle NQM = 37°$	*Substitution*

EXERCISES

Find each measure.

30. BC 31. XZ
32. XC 33. $m\angle BCZ$
34. $m\angle BAX$ 35. $m\angle YXZ$

36. The vertices of △GHJ are $G(-4, -7)$, $H(2, 5)$, and $J(10, -3)$. V is the midpoint of $\overline{GH}$, and W is the midpoint of $\overline{HJ}$. Show that $\overline{VW} \parallel \overline{GJ}$ and $VW = \frac{1}{2}GJ$.

5-5 Indirect Proof and Inequalities in One Triangle *(pp. 332–339)*

EXAMPLES

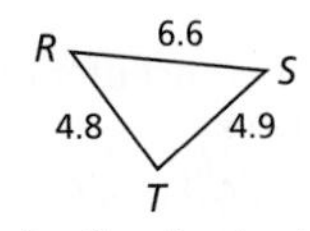

- **Write the angles of △RST in order from smallest to largest.**

The smallest angle is opposite the shortest side. In order, the angles are ∠S, ∠R, and ∠T.

- **The lengths of two sides of a triangle are 15 inches and 12 inches. Find the range of possible lengths for the third side.**

Let s be the length of the third side.

$s + 15 > 12$	$s + 12 > 15$	$15 + 12 > s$
$s > -3$	$s > 3$	$27 > s$

By the Triangle Inequality Theorem, 3 in. $< s <$ 27 in.

EXERCISES

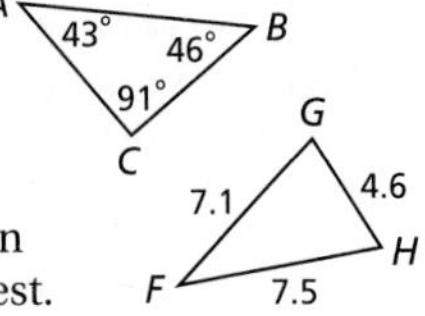

37. Write the sides of △ABC in order from shortest to longest.
38. Write the angles of △FGH in order from smallest to largest.
39. The lengths of two sides of a triangle are 13.5 centimeters and 4.5 centimeters. Find the range of possible lengths for the third side.

Tell whether a triangle can have sides with the given lengths. Explain.

40. 6.2, 8.1, 14.2
41. $z, z, 3z$, when $z = 5$
42. Write an indirect proof that a triangle cannot have two obtuse angles.

5-6 Inequalities in Two Triangles *(pp. 340–345)*

EXAMPLES

Compare the given measures.

- KL and ST

$KJ = RS$, $JL = RT$, and $m\angle J > m\angle R$. By the Hinge Theorem, $KL > ST$.

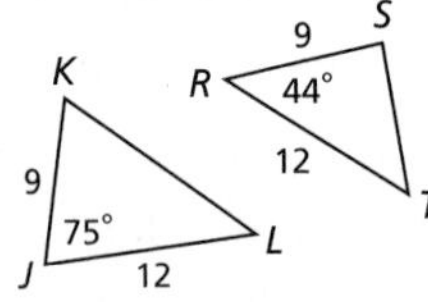

- $m\angle ZXY$ and $m\angle XZW$

$XY = WZ$, $XZ = XZ$, and $YZ < XW$. By the Converse of the Hinge Theorem, $m\angle ZXY < m\angle XZW$.

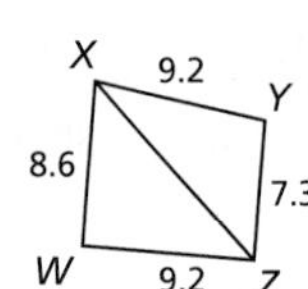

EXERCISES

Compare the given measures.

43. PS and RS
44. $m\angle BCA$ and $m\angle DCA$

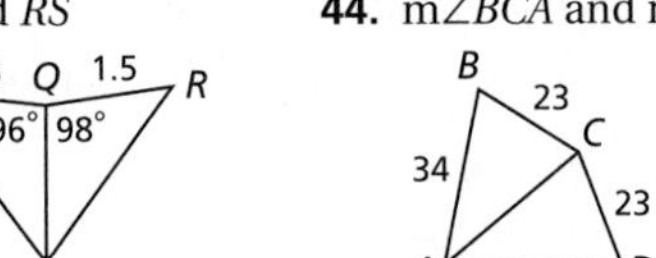

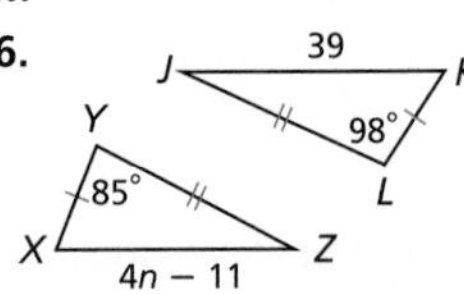

Find the range of values for n.

45.
46.

5-7 The Pythagorean Theorem *(pp. 348–355)*

EXAMPLES

- **Find the value of x. Give your answer in simplest radical form.**

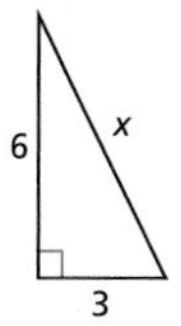

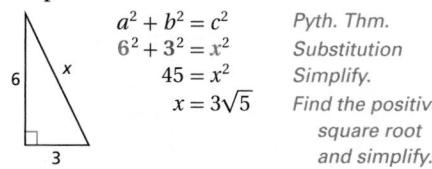

$a^2 + b^2 = c^2$	*Pyth. Thm.*
$6^2 + 3^2 = x^2$	*Substitution*
$45 = x^2$	*Simplify.*
$x = 3\sqrt{5}$	*Find the positive square root and simplify.*

- **Find the missing side length. Tell if the sides form a Pythagorean triple. Explain.**

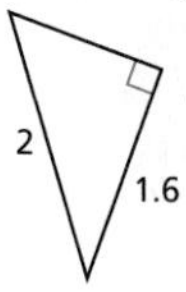

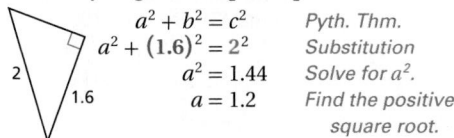

$a^2 + b^2 = c^2$	*Pyth. Thm.*
$a^2 + (1.6)^2 = 2^2$	*Substitution*
$a^2 = 1.44$	*Solve for a^2.*
$a = 1.2$	*Find the positive square root.*

The side lengths do not form a Pythagorean triple because 1.2 and 1.6 are not whole numbers.

EXERCISES

Find the value of x. Give your answer in simplest radical form.

47.

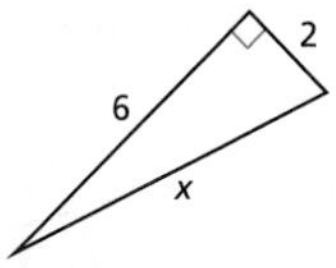

48.

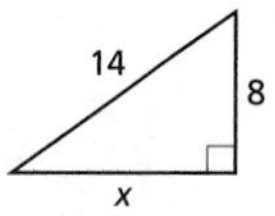

Find the missing side length. Tell if the sides form a Pythagorean triple. Explain.

49.

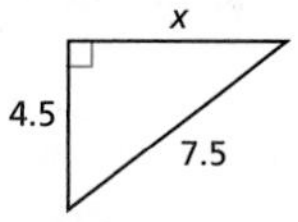

50.

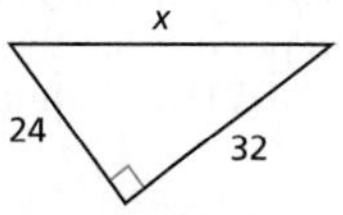

Tell if the measures can be the side lengths of a triangle. If so, classify the triangle as acute, obtuse, or right.

51. 9, 12, 16

52. 11, 14, 27

53. 1.5, 3.6, 3.9

54. 2, 3.7, 4.1

5-8 Applying Special Right Triangles *(pp. 356–362)*

EXAMPLES

Find the values of the variables. Give your answers in simplest radical form.

- 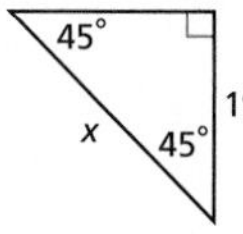

This is a 45°-45°-90° triangle.

$x = 19\sqrt{2}$ *Hyp. = leg$\sqrt{2}$*

- 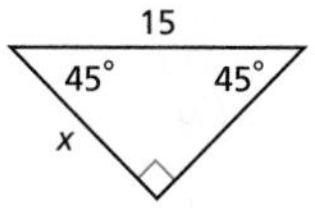

This is a 45°-45°-90° triangle.

$15 = x\sqrt{2}$ *Hyp. = leg$\sqrt{2}$*

$\frac{15}{\sqrt{2}} = x$ *Divide both sides by $\sqrt{2}$.*

$\frac{15\sqrt{2}}{2} = x$ *Rationalize the denominator.*

- 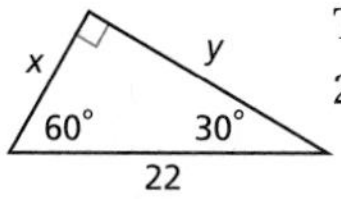

This is a 30°-60°-90° triangle.

$22 = 2x$ *Hyp. = 2(shorter leg)*

$11 = x$ *Divide both sides by 2.*

$y = 11\sqrt{3}$ *Longer leg = (shorter leg)$\sqrt{3}$*

EXERCISES

Find the values of the variables. Give your answers in simplest radical form.

55.

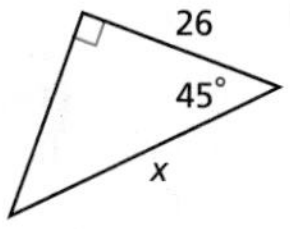

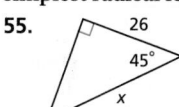

56.

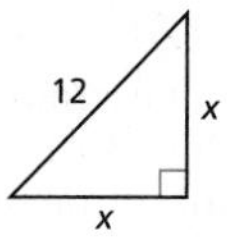

57.

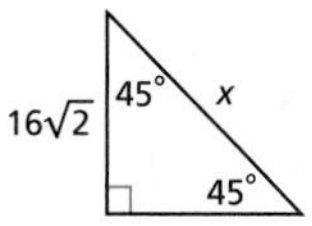

58.

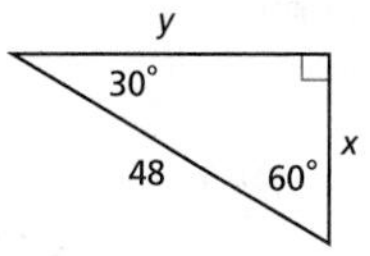

59.

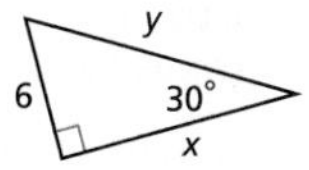

60.

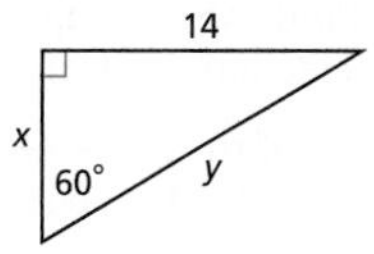

Find the value of each variable. Round to the nearest inch.

61.

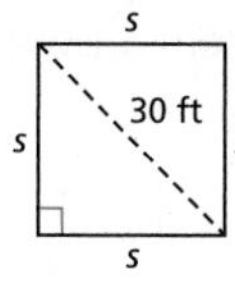

62.

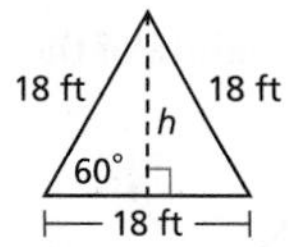

Answers

47. $x = 2\sqrt{10}$
48. $x = 2\sqrt{33}$
49. 6; the lengths do not form a Pythagorean triple because 4.5 and 7.5 are not whole numbers.
50. 40; the lengths do form a Pythagorean triple because they are nonzero whole numbers that satisfy the equation $a^2 + b^2 = c^2$.
51. triangle; obtuse
52. not a triangle
53. triangle; right
54. triangle; acute
55. $x = 26\sqrt{2}$
56. $x = 6\sqrt{2}$
57. $x = 32$
58. $x = 24$; $y = 24\sqrt{3}$
59. $x = 6\sqrt{3}$; $y = 12$
60. $x = \frac{14\sqrt{3}}{3}$; $y = \frac{28\sqrt{3}}{3}$
61. 21 ft 3 in.
62. 15 ft 7 in.

Study Guide: Review 369

Organizer

Objective: Assess students' mastery of concepts and skills in Chapter 5.

Online Edition

Resources

Assessment Resources

Chapter 5 Tests
- Free Response (Levels A, B, C)
- Multiple Choice (Levels A, B, C)
- Performance Assessment

Teacher One Stop™
Test & Practice Generator

State Resources

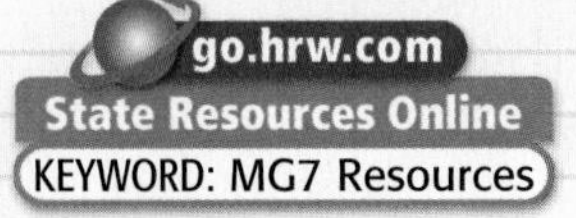
go.hrw.com
State Resources Online
KEYWORD: MG7 Resources

Find each measure.

1. KL **9.8**

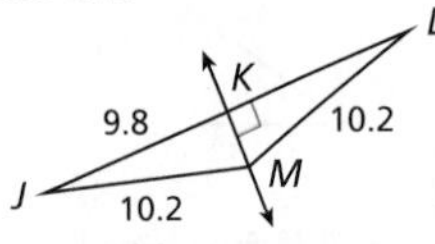

2. $m\angle WXY$ **34°**

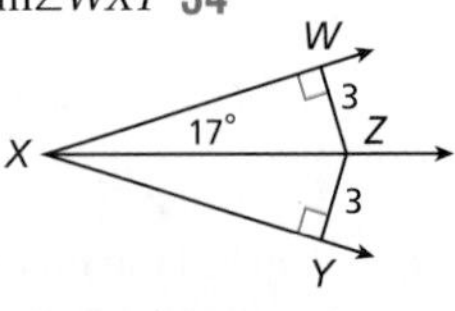

3. BC **21**

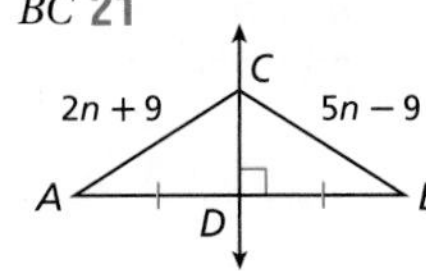

4. $\overline{MQ}$, $\overline{NQ}$, and $\overline{PQ}$ are the perpendicular bisectors of $\triangle RST$. Find RS and RQ.

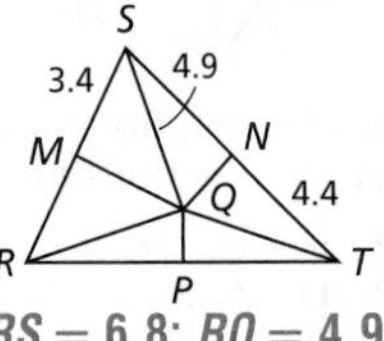

$RS = 6.8$; $RQ = 4.9$

5. $\overline{EG}$ and $\overline{FG}$ are angle bisectors of $\triangle DEF$. Find $m\angle GEF$ and the distance from G to $\overline{DF}$. **$m\angle GEF = 44°$; distance from G to $\overline{DF} = 3.7$**

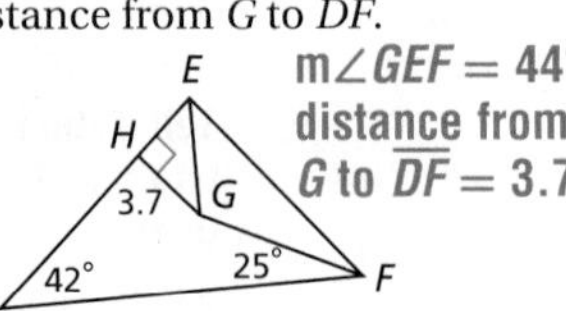

6. In $\triangle XYZ$, $XC = 261$, and $ZW = 118$. Find XW, BW, and BZ. **$XW = 174$; $BW = 59$; $BZ = 177$**

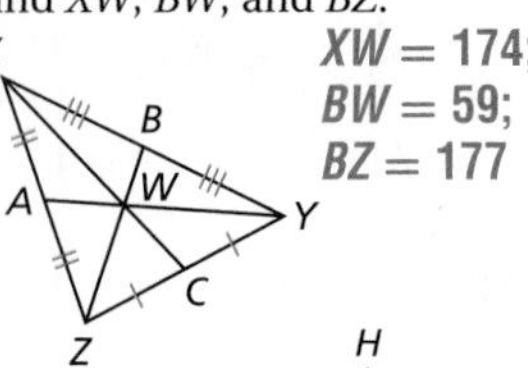

7. Find the orthocenter of $\triangle JKL$ with vertices $J(-5, 2)$, $K(-5, 10)$, and $L(1, 4)$. **$(-3, 4)$**
8. In $\triangle GHJ$ at right, find PR, GJ, and $m\angle GRP$. **$PR = 51$; $GJ = 148$; $m\angle GRP = 71°$**

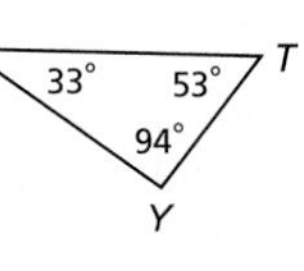

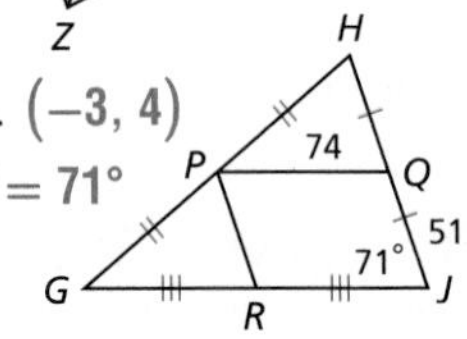

9. Write an indirect proof that two obtuse angles cannot form a linear pair.
10. Write the angles of $\triangle BEH$ in order from smallest to largest. **$\angle E$, $\angle B$, $\angle H$**

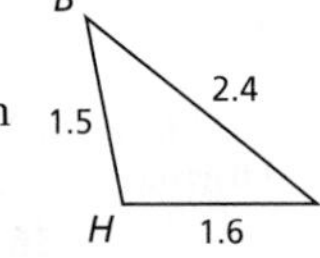

11. Write the sides of $\triangle RTY$ in order from shortest to longest. **$\overline{TY}$, $\overline{RY}$, $\overline{RT}$**

12. The distance from Arville to Branton is 114 miles. The distance from Branton to Camford is 247 miles. If the three towns form a triangle, what is the range of distances from Arville to Camford?
13. Compare $m\angle SPV$ and $m\angle ZPV$.

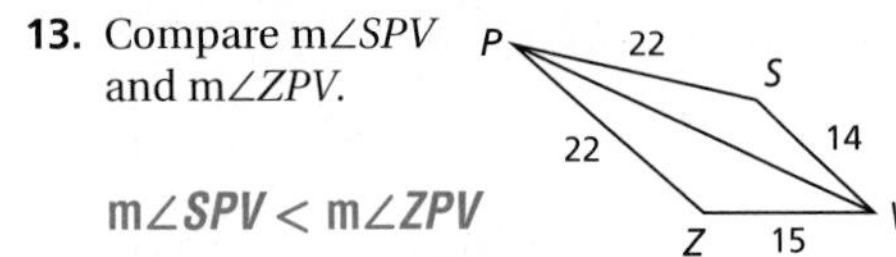

$m\angle SPV < m\angle ZPV$

14. Find the range of values for x.

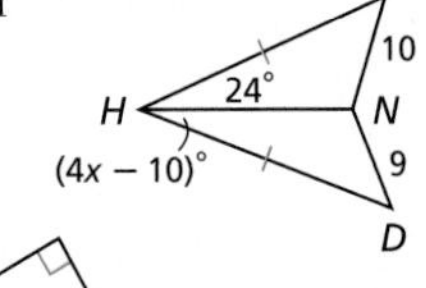

$2.5 < x < 8.5$

15. Find the missing side length in the triangle. Tell if the side lengths form a Pythagorean triple. Explain.

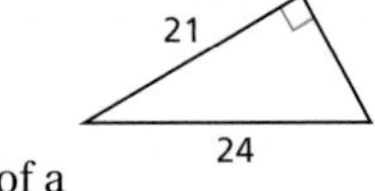

16. Tell if the measures 18, 20, and 27 can be the side lengths of a triangle. If so, classify the triangle as acute, obtuse, or right. **triangle; obtuse**
17. An IMAX screen is 62 feet tall and 82 feet wide. What is the length of the screen's diagonal? Round to the nearest inch. **102 ft 10 in.**

Find the values of the variables. Give your answers in simplest radical form.

18. (triangle: 20, 45°, x) **$x = 10\sqrt{2}$** 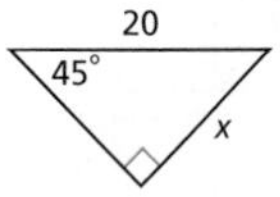
19. (triangle: x, 60°, 32, y) **$x = 16$; $y = 16\sqrt{3}$** 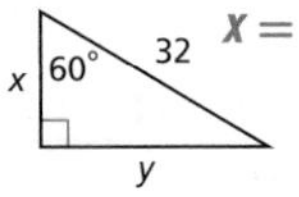
20. **$x = \dfrac{8\sqrt{3}}{3}$; $y = \dfrac{16\sqrt{3}}{3}$**

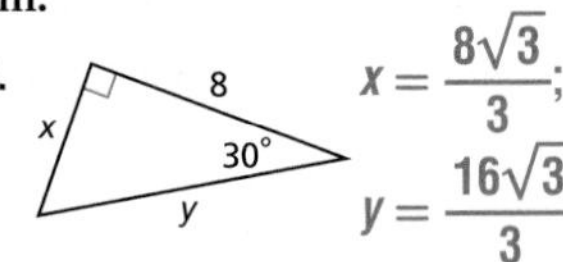

Answers

9. Possible answer:
Given: $\angle 1$ and $\angle 2$ form a lin. pair.
Prove: $\angle 1$ and $\angle 2$ cannot both be obtuse $\angle$s.
Proof: Assume $\angle 1$ and $\angle 2$ are both obtuse $\angle$s. By the def. of obtuse, $m\angle 1 > 90°$ and $m\angle 2 > 90°$. If the 2 inequalities are added, $m\angle 1 + m\angle 2 > 180°$. However, by the Lin. Pair Thm., $\angle 1$ and $\angle 2$ are supp. By the def. of supp. $\angle$s, this means that $m\angle 1 + m\angle 2 = 180°$. So $m\angle 1 + m\angle 2 > 180°$ contradicts the given information. The assumption that $\angle 1$ and $\angle 2$ are both obtuse $\angle$s is false. Therefore $\angle 1$ and $\angle 2$ cannot both be obtuse.

12. greater than 133 mi and less than 361 mi

15. $3\sqrt{15}$; the side lengths do not form a Pythagorean triple because $3\sqrt{15}$ is not a whole number.

COLLEGE ENTRANCE EXAM PRACTICE

FOCUS ON SAT MATHEMATICS SUBJECT TESTS

Some questions on the SAT Mathematics Subject Tests require the use of a calculator. You can take the test without one, but it is not recommended. The calculator you use must meet certain criteria. For example, calculators that make noise or have typewriter-like keypads are not allowed.

If you have both a scientific and a graphing calculator, bring the graphing calculator to the test. Make sure you spend time getting used to a new calculator before the day of the test.

You may want to time yourself as you take this practice test. It should take you about 6 minutes to complete.

1. In $\triangle ABC$, $m\angle C = 2m\angle A$, and $CB = 3$ units. What is AB to the nearest hundredth unit?

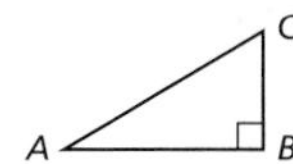

(A) 1.73 units

(B) 4.24 units

(C) 5.20 units

(D) 8.49 units

(E) 10.39 units

2. What is the perimeter of $\triangle ABC$ if D is the midpoint of $\overline{AB}$, E is the midpoint of $\overline{BC}$, and F is the midpoint of $\overline{AC}$?

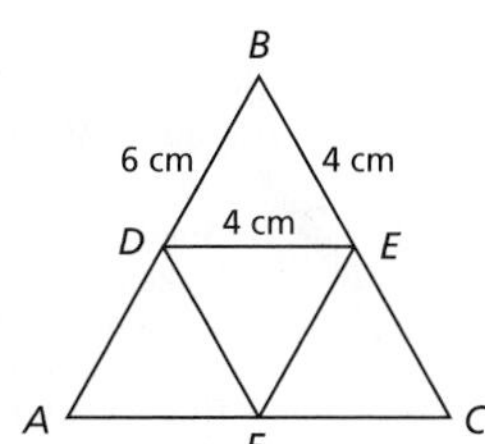

Note: Figure not drawn to scale.

(A) 8 centimeters

(B) 14 centimeters

(C) 20 centimeters

(D) 28 centimeters

(E) 35 centimeters

3. The side lengths of a right triangle are 2, 5, and c, where $c > 5$. What is the value of c?

(A) $\sqrt{21}$

(B) $\sqrt{29}$

(C) 7

(D) 9

(E) $\sqrt{145}$

4. In the triangle below, which of the following CANNOT be the length of the unknown side?

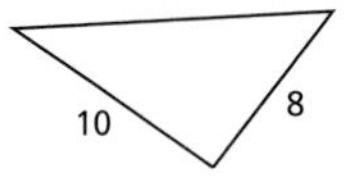

10 8

(A) 2.2

(B) 6

(C) 12.8

(D) 17.2

(E) 18.1

5. Which of the following points is on the perpendicular bisector of the segment with endpoints $(3, 4)$ and $(9, 4)$?

(A) $(4, 2)$

(B) $(4, 5)$

(C) $(5, 4)$

(D) $(6, -1)$

(E) $(7, 4)$

COLLEGE ENTRANCE EXAM PRACTICE CHAPTER 5

Organizer

Objective: Provide practice for college entrance exams such as the SAT Mathematics Subject Tests.

Resources

Questions on the SAT Mathematics Subject Tests Levels 1 and 2 represent the following math content areas:

	Level	
	1	2
Number and Operations	10–14%	10–14%
Algebra and Functions	38–42%	48–52%
Geometry and Measurement	38–42%	28–32%
Plane Euclidean	18–22%	0%
Coordinate	8–12%	10–14%
Three-Dimensional	4–6%	4–6%
Trigonometry	6–8%	12–16%
Data Analysis and Statistics	6–10%	6–10%

Items on this page focus on:

- Plane Euclidean Geometry
- Coordinate Geometry

Text References:

Item	1	2	3	4	5
Lesson	5-8	5-4	5-7	5-5	5-1

TEST PREP DOCTOR

1. Students who chose **E** applied the properties of a 30°-60°-90° triangle incorrectly and found the value of $6\sqrt{3}$. Students who chose **B** applied the properties of a 45°-45°-90° triangle and found the value of $3\sqrt{2}$.

2. Students who chose **A** found *AC* but did not answer the question. Students who chose **B** found the perimeter of $\triangle DEF$. Students who chose **E** might have confused properties of midsegments and centroids and used a factor of $\frac{2}{3}$.

3. Students who chose **A** did not consider the given fact that $c > 5$. They used the Pythagorean Theorem with 5 as the hypotenuse. Remind students to read test items carefully.

4. Students who did not choose **E** did not apply the Triangle Inequality Theorem. Remind students not to rely on the relative lengths in the diagram.

5. Suggest that students graph the given points on a coordinate plane. They should quickly see that the segment is horizontal, so its perpendicular bisector is vertical through the midpoint. This should allow students to quickly find the correct answer, **D.**

Organizer

Objective: Provide opportunities to learn and practice common test-taking strategies.

 This Test Tackler focuses on using a different method to check the answer to a test problem. If students work a problem two ways and get the same answer both times, they can be fairly certain that their work is correct. Review with students the various problem-solving methods they have learned, as summarized in the table on the student page.

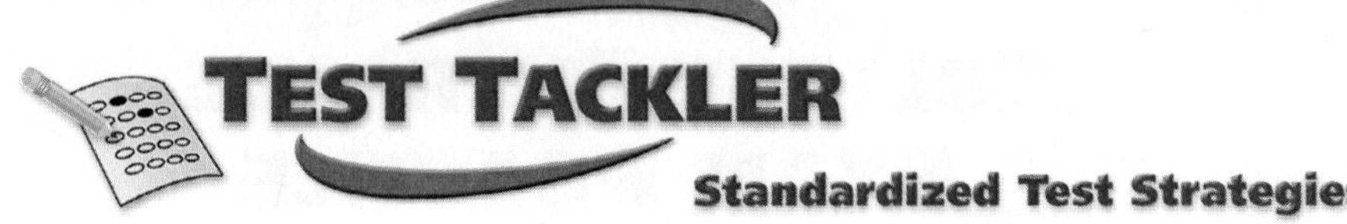

Standardized Test Strategies

Any Question Type: Check with a Different Method

It is important to check all of your answers on a test. An effective way to do this is to use a different method to answer the question a second time. If you get the same answer with two different methods, then your answer is probably correct.

EXAMPLE 1

Short Response What are the coordinates of the centroid of $\triangle ABC$ with $A(-2, 4)$, $B(4, 6)$, and $C(1, -1)$? Show your work.

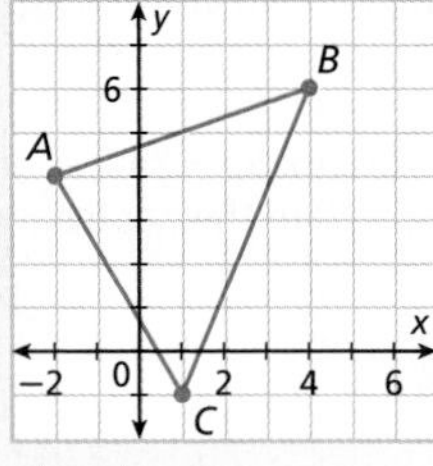

Method 1: *The centroid of a triangle is the point of concurrency of the medians. Write the equations of two medians and find their point of intersection.*

Let D be the midpoint of $\overline{AB}$ and let E be the midpoint of $\overline{BC}$.

$$D = \left(\frac{-2+4}{2}, \frac{4+6}{2}\right) = (1, 5) \quad E = \left(\frac{4+1}{2}, \frac{6+(-1)}{2}\right) = (2.5, 2.5)$$

The median from C to D contains $C(1, -1)$ and $D(1, 5)$. It is vertical, so its equation is $x = 1$.

The median from A to E contains $A(-2, 4)$ and $E(2.5, 2.5)$.

$$\text{slope of } \overline{AE} = \frac{4-2.5}{-2-2.5} = \frac{1.5}{-4.5} = -\frac{1}{3}$$

$y - y_1 = m(x - x_1)$ — *Point-slope form*

$y - 4 = -\frac{1}{3}(x + 2)$ — *Substitute 4 for y_1, $-\frac{1}{3}$ for m, and −2 for x_1.*

Solve the system $\begin{cases} x = 1 \\ y - 4 = -\frac{1}{3}(x + 2) \end{cases}$ *to find the point of intersection.*

$y - 4 = -\frac{1}{3}(1 + 2)$ — *Substitute 1 for x.*

$y = 3$ — *Simplify.*

The coordinates of the centroid are $(1, 3)$.

Method 2: *To check this answer, use a different method. By the Centroid Theorem, the centroid of a triangle is $\frac{2}{3}$ of the distance from each vertex to the midpoint of the opposite side. $\overline{CD}$ is vertical with a length of 6 units. $\frac{2}{3}(6) = 4$, and the coordinates of the point that is 4 units up from C is $(1, 3)$.*

This method confirms the first answer.

Problem Solving Strategies

- Draw a Diagram
- Make a Model
- Guess and Test
- Work Backward
- Find a Pattern
- Make a Table
- Solve a Simpler Problem
- Use Logical Reasoning
- Use a Venn Diagram
- Make an Organized List

If you can't think of a different method to use to check your answer, circle the question and come back to it later.

Read each test item and answer the questions that follow.

Item A
Multiple Choice **Given that ℓ is the perpendicular bisector of $\overline{AB}$, $AC = 3n + 1$, and $BC = 6n - 11$, what is the value of n?**

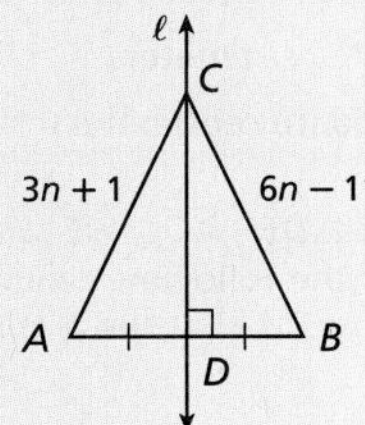

Ⓐ −4
Ⓑ $\frac{3}{4}$
Ⓒ $\frac{4}{3}$
Ⓓ 4

1. How can you use the given answer choices to solve this problem?
2. Describe how to solve this problem differently.

Item B
Multiple Choice **Which number forms a Pythagorean triple with 15 and 17?**

Ⓕ 5
Ⓖ 7
Ⓗ 8
Ⓙ 10

3. How can you use the given answer choices to find the answer?
4. Describe a different method you can use to check your answer.

Item C
Gridded Response **Find the area of the square in square centimeters.**

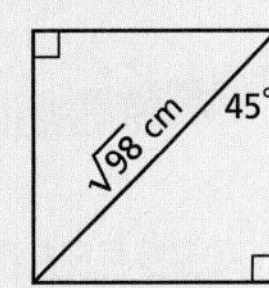

5. How can you use special right triangles to answer this question?
6. Explain how you can check your answer by using the Pythagorean Theorem.

Item D
Short Response **Do the ordered pairs $A(-8, 4)$, $B(0, -2)$, and $C(8, 4)$ form a right triangle? Explain your answer.**

7. Explain how to use slope to determine if $\triangle ABC$ is a right triangle.
8. How can you use the Converse of the Pythagorean Theorem to check your answer?

Item E
Short Response **Find the orthocenter of $\triangle RST$. Show your work.**

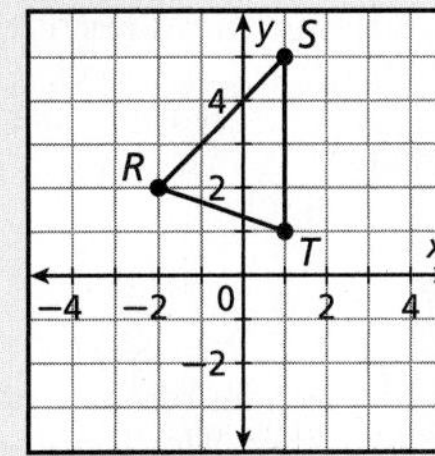

9. Describe how you would solve this problem.
10. How can you use the third altitude of the triangle to confirm that your answer is correct?

Answers

Possible answers:

1. Substitute each answer choice into the equation $3n + 1 = 6n - 11$ to determine which choice makes the equation true.
2. Solve the equation $3n + 1 = 6n - 11$ for n.
3. Substitute each answer choice into the Pyth. Thm. as a leg length, along with a leg length of 15 and hypotenuse of 17, to determine which answer choice results in a true equation.
4. Solve the equation $x^2 + (15)^2 = (17)^2$ for x.
5. Since this is a 45°-45°-90° △, the hyp. is equal to the product of the side length and $\sqrt{2}$. Solve $\sqrt{98} = s\sqrt{2}$ for s, and then use the formula $A = s^2$ to find the area.
6. Confirm that $s^2 + s^2 = 98$.
7. Find the slope of each of the 3 sides and determine if any 2 slopes are negative reciprocals of each other.
8. Find AB, BC, and AC and check whether these 3 lengths satisfy the equation $a^2 + b^2 = c^2$.
9. Write equations for 2 of the altitudes of the △, and find their point of intersection.
10. Write the equation for the third altitude of the △, and confirm that it passes through the point of intersection of the first 2 altitudes.

Answers to Test Items

A. D
B. H
C. 49
D. no
E. (0, 2)

State Resources

go.hrw.com
State Resources Online
KEYWORD: MG7 Resources

Organizer

Objective: Provide review and practice for Chapters 1–5 and standardized tests.

Online Edition

Resources

Assessment Resources

Chapter 5 Cumulative Test

go.hrw.com
KEYWORD: MG7 TestPrep

Answers

1. B
2. F
3. A
4. H
5. B
6. G
7. C
8. J
9. D
10. F
11. B
12. J
13. 2
14. 8
15. 71
16. 5

State Resources

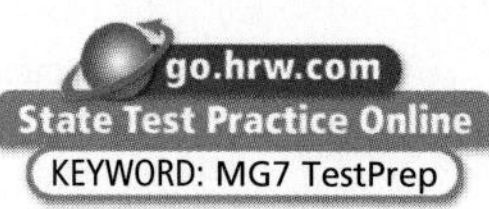

CUMULATIVE ASSESSMENT, CHAPTERS 1–5

Multiple Choice

1. $\overline{GJ}$ is a midsegment of $\triangle DEF$, and $\overline{HK}$ is a midsegment of $\triangle GFJ$. What is the length of $\overline{HK}$?

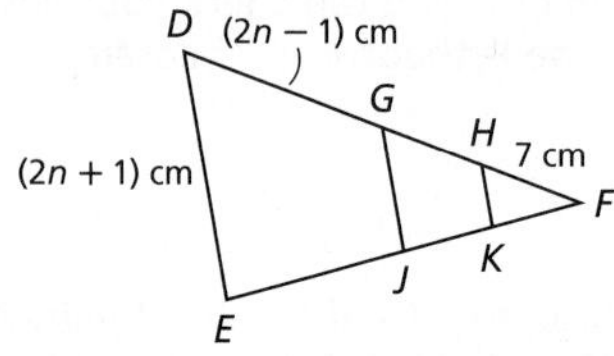

Ⓐ 2.25 centimeters
Ⓑ 4 centimeters
Ⓒ 7.5 centimeters
Ⓓ 9 centimeters

2. In $\triangle RST$, $SR < ST$, and $RT > ST$. If $m\angle R = (2x + 10)°$ and $m\angle T = (3x - 25)°$, which is a possible value of x?

Ⓕ 25　Ⓗ 35
Ⓖ 30　Ⓙ 40

3. The vertex angle of an isosceles triangle measures $(7a - 2)°$, and one of the base angles measures $(4a + 1)°$. Which term best describes this triangle?

Ⓐ Acute
Ⓑ Equiangular
Ⓒ Right
Ⓓ Obtuse

4. The lengths of two sides of an acute triangle are 8 inches and 10 inches. Which of the following could be the length of the third side?

Ⓕ 5 inches　Ⓗ 12 inches
Ⓖ 6 inches　Ⓙ 13 inches

5. For the coordinates $M(-1, 0)$, $N(-2, 2)$, $P(10, y)$, and $Q(4, 6)$, $\overline{MN} \parallel \overline{PQ}$. What is the value of y?

Ⓐ −18　Ⓒ 6
Ⓑ −6　Ⓓ 18

6. What is the area of an equilateral triangle that has a perimeter of 18 centimeters?

Ⓕ 9 square centimeters
Ⓖ $9\sqrt{3}$ square centimeters
Ⓗ 18 square centimeters
Ⓙ $18\sqrt{3}$ square centimeters

7. In $\triangle ABC$ and $\triangle DEF$, $\overline{AC} \cong \overline{DE}$, and $\angle A \cong \angle E$. Which of the following would allow you to conclude by SAS that these triangles are congruent?

Ⓐ $\overline{AB} \cong \overline{DF}$
Ⓑ $\overline{AC} \cong \overline{EF}$
Ⓒ $\overline{BA} \cong \overline{FE}$
Ⓓ $\overline{CB} \cong \overline{DF}$

8. For the segment below, $AB = \frac{1}{2}AC$, and $CD = 2BC$. Which expression is equal to the length of $\overline{AD}$?

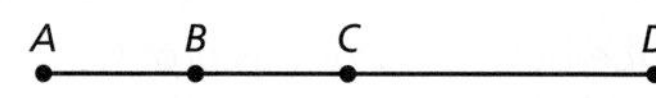

Ⓕ $2AB + BC$
Ⓖ $2AC + AB$
Ⓗ $3AB$
Ⓙ $4BC$

9. In $\triangle DEF$, $m\angle D = 2(m\angle E + m\angle F)$. Which term best describes $\triangle DEF$?

Ⓐ Acute
Ⓑ Equiangular
Ⓒ Right
Ⓓ Obtuse

10. Which point of concurrency is always located inside the triangle?

Ⓕ The centroid of an obtuse triangle
Ⓖ The circumcenter of an obtuse triangle
Ⓗ The circumcenter of a right triangle
Ⓙ The orthocenter of a right triangle

Answers

17. 42°; since S is on the ⊥ bisector of $\overline{RT}$, $RS = TS$. By the Isosc. △ Thm., $\angle R \cong \angle T$, so $m\angle R = m\angle T$. By the △ Sum Thm., $(4n + 16) + 2(3n - 18) = 180$, and thus $n = 20$. So $m\angle R = 3(20) - 18 = 42°$.

18. Since $\overline{BD} \parallel \overline{AC}$, $\angle BCA \cong \angle DBC$ by the Alt. Int. ∠s Thm. So $m\angle BCA = m\angle DBC = 84°$. By the △ Sum Thm., $m\angle ABC = 50°$. Since $\overline{AB} \cong \overline{BD}$, $\overline{BC} \cong \overline{BC}$, and $m\angle ABC < m\angle DBC$, by the Hinge Thm., $AC < DC$.

19. Assume the opposite, that $\triangle XYZ$ has a pair of comp. ∠s. Let $\angle X$ and $\angle Y$ be comp. So $m\angle X + m\angle Y = 90°$ by the def. of comp. ∠s. By the △ Sum Thm., $m\angle X + m\angle Y + m\angle Z = 180°$. But then by the Subtr. Prop. of =, $m\angle Z = 90°$. This contradicts the given information that $\triangle XYZ$ is acute. So the assumption is false, and $\triangle XYZ$ cannot contain a pair of comp. ∠s.

If a diagram is not provided, draw your own. Use the given information to label the diagram.

11. The length of one leg of a right triangle is 3 times the length of the other, and the length of the hypotenuse is 10. What is the length of the longest leg?

   Ⓐ 3 Ⓒ $\sqrt{10}$
   Ⓑ $3\sqrt{10}$ Ⓓ $12\sqrt{5}$

12. Which statement is true by the Transitive Property of Congruence?

   Ⓕ If $\angle A \cong \angle T$, then $\angle T \cong \angle A$.
   Ⓖ If $m\angle L = m\angle S$, then $\angle L \cong \angle S$.
   Ⓗ $5QR + 10 = 5(QR + 2)$
   Ⓙ If $\overline{BD} \cong \overline{DE}$ and $\overline{DE} \cong \overline{EF}$, then $\overline{BD} \cong \overline{EF}$.

Gridded Response

13. P is the incenter of $\triangle JKL$. The distance from P to $\overline{KL}$ is $2y - 9$. What is the distance from P to $\overline{JK}$?

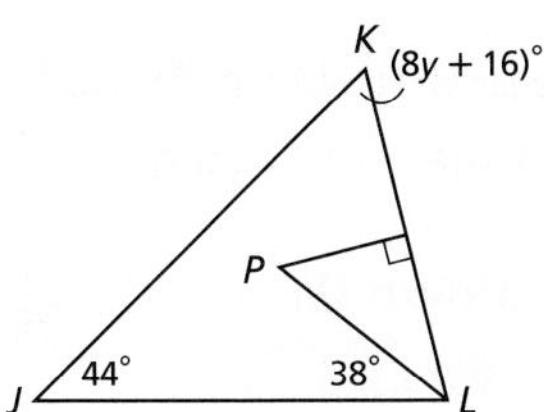

14. In a plane, $r \parallel s$, and $s \perp t$. How many right angles are formed by the lines r, s, and t?

15. What is the measure, in degrees, of $\angle H$?

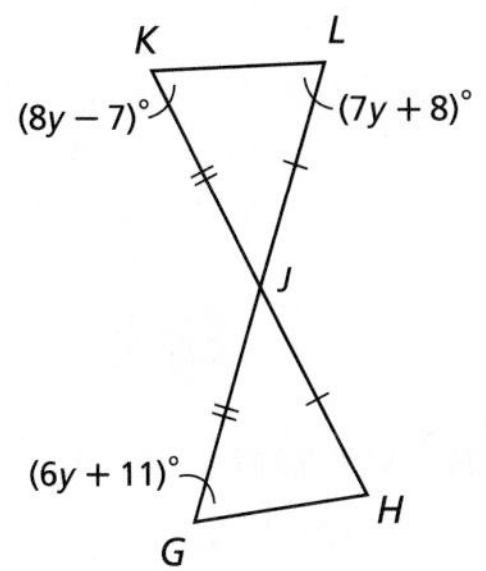

16. The point T is in the interior of $\angle XYZ$. If $m\angle XYZ = (25x + 10)°$, $m\angle XYT = 90°$, and $m\angle TYZ = (9x)°$, what is the value of x?

Short Response

17. In $\triangle RST$, S is on the perpendicular bisector of $\overline{RT}$, $m\angle S = (4n + 16)°$, and $m\angle R = (3n - 18)°$. Find $m\angle R$. Show your work and explain how you determined your answer.

18. Given that $\overline{BD} \parallel \overline{AC}$ and $\overline{AB} \cong \overline{BD}$, explain why $AC < DC$.

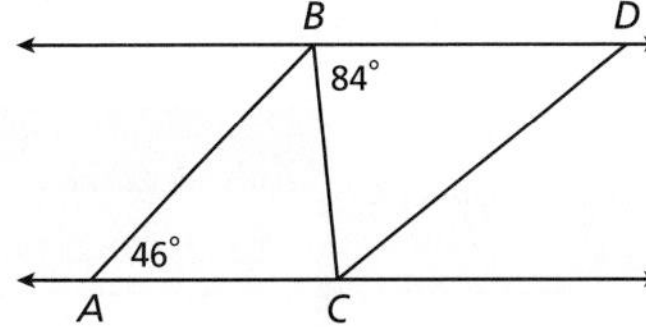

19. Write an indirect proof that an acute triangle cannot contain a pair of complementary angles.

   Given: $\triangle XYZ$ is an acute triangle.

   Prove: $\triangle XYZ$ does not contain a pair of complementary angles.

20. Find the coordinates of the orthocenter of $\triangle JKL$. Show your work and explain how you found your answer.

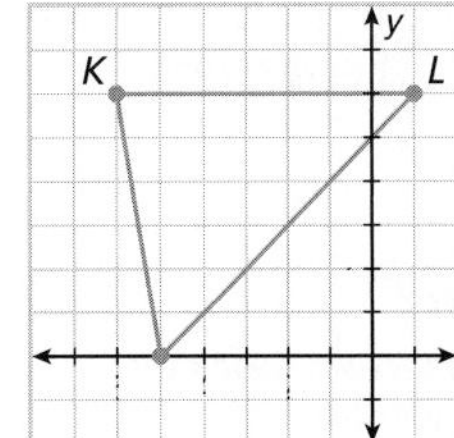

Extended Response

21. Consider the statement "If a triangle is equiangular, then it is acute."

   a. Write the converse, inverse, and contrapositive of this conditional statement.

   b. Write a biconditional statement from the conditional statement.

   c. Determine the truth value of the biconditional statement. If it is false, give a counterexample.

   d. Determine the truth value of each statement below. Give an example or counterexample to justify your reasoning.

   "For any conditional, if the inverse and contrapositive are true, then the biconditional is true."

   "For any conditional, if the inverse and converse are true, then the biconditional is true."

Short-Response Rubric

Items 17–20

2 Points = The student's answer is an accurate and complete execution of the task or tasks.

1 Point = The student's answer contains attributes of an appropriate response but is flawed.

0 Points = The student's answer contains no attributes of an appropriate response.

Extended-Response Rubric

Item 21

4 Points = The student's answers and counterexamples are correct, and explanations are complete. Work demonstrates a thorough understanding of concepts related to conditional statements, biconditional statements, and their truth values.

3 Points = The student correctly answers parts a, b, and c, but explanations or counterexamples may contain minor flaws. Work demonstrates an understanding of major concepts.

2 Points = The student answers correctly, but explanations are missing or incomplete. Work demonstrates a limited understanding of concepts related to conditional and biconditional statements.

1 Point = The student answers incorrectly but makes a reasonable attempt to explain the answers.

0 Points = The student does not answer correctly and does not attempt all parts of the problem.

20. Since $\overline{KL}$ is horizontal, the altitude from J to $\overline{KL}$ is vertical. It must pass through $J(-5, 0)$. So the equation of the altitude is $x = -5$. The slope of $\overline{JL}$ is $\frac{6}{1-(-5)} = 1$, so the slope of a line $\perp$ to $\overline{JL}$ is -1. This line must pass through $K(-6, 6)$. In point-slope form, the equation of the line is $y - 6 = -1[x - (-6)]$, which simplifies to $y = -x$. The intersection of $x = -5$ and $y = -x$ is $(-5, 5)$, which is the orthocenter of $\triangle JKL$.

21a. Converse: If a △ is acute, then it is equiangular. Inverse: If a △ is not equiangular, then it is not acute. Contrapositive: If a △ is not acute, then it is not equiangular.

b. A △ is equiangular if and only if it is acute.

c. F; a △ with angle measures of 50°, 60°, and 70° is acute, but not equiangular.

d. T; if the inverse is true, then the converse is also true. If the contrapositive is true, then the original conditional is true. Since the conditional and its converse are true, the biconditional must be true. F; if the inverse is true, then the converse is also true. Nothing is known about the original conditional, so the truth value of the biconditional is not determined. The statement "If a triangle is acute, then it is equiangular" is a counterexample. The inverse and converse are true, but the biconditional is false.

Polygons and Quadrilaterals

Section 6A

Polygons and Parallelograms

Section 6B

Other Special Quadrilaterals

Pacing Guide for 45-Minute Classes

Teacher One Stop™
Calendar Planner®

Chapter 6

Countdown Weeks 13, 14

DAY 1	DAY 2	DAY 3	DAY 4	DAY 5
6-1 Geometry Lab	6-1 Lesson	Connecting Geometry to Algebra 6-2 Geometry Lab	6-2 Lesson	6-3 Lesson
DAY 6	**DAY 7**	**DAY 8**	**DAY 9**	**DAY 10**
Multi-Step Test Prep Ready to Go On?	6-4 Lesson	6-5 Technology Lab	6-5 Lesson	6-6 Technology Lab
DAY 11	**DAY 12**	**DAY 13**	**DAY 14**	
6-6 Lesson	Multi-Step Test Prep Ready to Go On?	Chapter 6 Review	Chapter 6 Test	

Pacing Guide for 90-Minute Classes

Teacher One Stop™
Calendar Planner®

Chapter 6

DAY 1	DAY 2	DAY 3	DAY 4	DAY 5
Chapter 5 Test 6-1 Geometry Lab	6-1 Lesson Connecting Geometry to Algebra 6-2 Geometry Lab	6-2 Lesson 6-3 Lesson	Multi-Step Test Prep Ready to Go On? 6-4 Lesson	6-5 Technology Lab 6-5 Lesson
DAY 6	**DAY 7**	**DAY 8**		
6-6 Technology Lab 6-6 Lesson	Multi-Step Test Prep Ready to Go On? Chapter 6 Review	Chapter 6 Test 7-1 Lesson		

ONGOING ASSESSMENT and INTERVENTION

Assess Prior Knowledge

Before Chapter 6

DIAGNOSE	PRESCRIBE
Diagnose readiness for the chapter.	Prescribe intervention.
Are You Ready? SE p. 377	  ***Are You Ready? Intervention***

Formative Assessment

Before Every Lesson

DIAGNOSE	PRESCRIBE
Diagnose readiness for the lesson.	Prescribe intervention.
Warm Up TE	**Reteach** CRB

During Every Lesson

DIAGNOSE	PRESCRIBE
Diagnose understanding of lesson concepts.	Prescribe intervention.
Check It Out! SE	**Reading Strategies** CRB
Questioning Strategies TE	***Success for Every Learner***
Think and Discuss SE	***Lesson Tutorial Videos***
Write About It SE	
Journal TE	

After Every Lesson

DIAGNOSE	PRESCRIBE
Diagnose mastery of lesson concepts.	Prescribe intervention.
Lesson Quiz TE	**Reteach** CRB
Test Prep SE	**Test Prep Doctor** TE
Test and Practice Generator	***Homework Help* Online**

Before Chapter 6 Testing

DIAGNOSE	PRESCRIBE
Diagnose mastery of concepts in chapter.	Prescribe intervention.
Ready to Go On? SE pp. 407, 437	***Ready to Go On? Intervention***
Multi-Step Test Prep SE pp. 406, 436	**Scaffolding Questions** TE pp. 406, 436
Section Quizzes AR	**Reteach** CRB
Test and Practice Generator	***Lesson Tutorial Videos***

Before High Stakes Testing

DIAGNOSE	PRESCRIBE
Diagnose mastery of benchmark concepts.	Prescribe intervention.
College Entrance Exam Practice SE p. 443	***College Entrance Exam Practice***
Standardized Test Prep SE pp. 446–447	

Summative Assessment

After Chapter 6

DIAGNOSE	PRESCRIBE
Check mastery of chapter concepts.	Prescribe intervention.
Multiple-Choice Tests (Forms A, B, C)	**Reteach** CRB
Free-Response Tests (Forms A, B, C)	***Lesson Tutorial Videos***
Performance Assessment AR	
Cumulative Test AR	
Test and Practice Generator	

KEY: **SE** = *Student Edition* **TE** = *Teacher's Edition* **CRB** = *Chapter Resource Book* **AR** = *Assessment Resources* 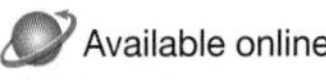 Available online Available on CD- or DVD-ROM

Lesson Resources

Before the Lesson

Prepare *Teacher One Stop*  
- Editable lesson plans
- Calendar Planner
- Easy access to all chapter resources

Lesson Transparencies
- Teacher Tools

Teach the Lesson

Introduce *Alternate Openers: Explorations*

Lesson Transparencies
- Warm Up
- Problem of the Day

Teach *Lesson Transparencies*
- Teaching Transparencies

Know-It Notebook™
- Vocabulary
- Key Concepts

Power Presentations 

 *Lesson Tutorial Videos* SPANISH

Interactive Online Edition 
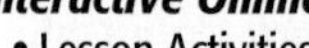 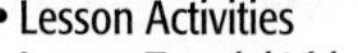
- Lesson Activities
- Lesson Tutorial Videos

Lab Activities

Lab Resources Online 

Online Interactivities  SPANISH

TechKeys 

Practice the Lesson

Practice *Chapter Resources*
- Practice A, B, C

Practice and Problem Solving Workbook

IDEA Works!® Modified Worksheets and Tests

ExamView Test and Practice Generator

Homework Help Online

Online Interactivities SPANISH

Interactive Online Edition
- Homework Help

Apply *Chapter Resources*
- Problem Solving

Practice and Problem Solving Workbook

Interactive Online Edition
- Chapter Project

Project Teacher Support

After the Lesson

Reteach *Chapter Resources*
- Reteach
- Reading Strategies 

Success for Every Learner

Review *Interactive Answers and Solutions*

Solutions Key

Know-It Notebook™
- Big Ideas
- Chapter Review

Extend *Chapter Resources*
- Challenge

Technology Highlights for the Teacher

 **Power Presentations**

Dynamic presentations to engage students. Complete PowerPoint® presentations for every lesson in Chapter 6.

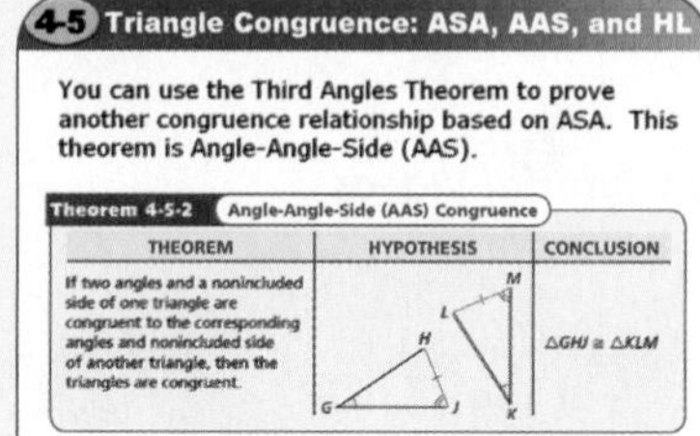

 **Teacher One Stop** SPANISH

Easy access to Chapter 6 resources and assessments. Includes lesson planning, test generation, and puzzle creation software.

 **Premier Online Edition** SPANISH

Chapter 6 includes Tutorial Videos, Lesson Activities, Lesson Quizzes, Homework Help, and Chapter Project.

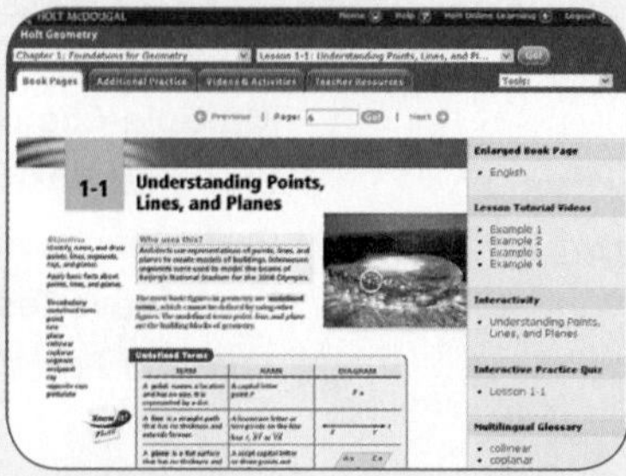

KEY: **SE** = *Student Edition* **TE** = *Teacher's Edition*  English Language Learners  Spanish version available  Available online  Available on CD- or DVD-ROM

CHAPTER 6

Reaching All Learners

Teaching tips to help all learners appear throughout the chapter. A few that target specific students are included in the lists below.

All Learners

Lab Activities
Practice and Problem Solving Workbook
Know-It Notebook

Special Needs Students

Practice A .... CRB
Reteach .... CRB
Reading Strategies .... CRB
Are You Ready? .... SE p. 377
Inclusion .... TE p. 384
IDEA Works!® Modified Worksheets and Tests
Ready to Go On? Intervention SPANISH
Know-It Notebook
Online Interactivities  SPANISH
Lesson Tutorial Videos  SPANISH

Developing Learners

Practice A .... CRB
Reteach .... CRB
Reading Strategies .... CRB
Are You Ready? .... SE p. 377
Vocabulary Connections .... SE p. 378
Questioning Strategies .... TE
Ready to Go On? Intervention SPANISH
Know-It Notebook
Homework Help Online 
Online Interactivities SPANISH
Lesson Tutorial Videos  

On-Level Learners

Practice B .... CRB
Problem Solving .... CRB
Vocabulary Connections .... SE p. 378
Questioning Strategies .... TE
Ready to Go On? Intervention SPANISH
Know-It Notebook
Homework Help Online
Online Interactivities   SPANISH

Advanced Learners

Practice C .... CRB
Challenge .... CRB
Challenge Exercises .... SE
Reading and Writing Math *Extend* .... TE p. 379
Critical Thinking .... TE pp. 383, 395, 419, 421, 431
Are You Ready? Enrichment SPANISH
Ready To Go On? Enrichment SPANISH

English Language Learners

ENGLISH LANGUAGE LEARNERS

Reading Strategies .... CRB
Are You Ready? Vocabulary .... SE p. 377
Vocabulary Connections .... SE p. 378
Vocabulary Review .... SE p. 438
English Language Learners .... TE pp. 399, 419, 431, 449
Success for Every Learner
Know-It Notebook
Spanish Study Guide (Resumen y Repaso)
Multilingual Glossary
Lesson Tutorial Videos  SPANISH

Technology Highlights for Reaching All Learners

Lesson Tutorial Videos SPANISH

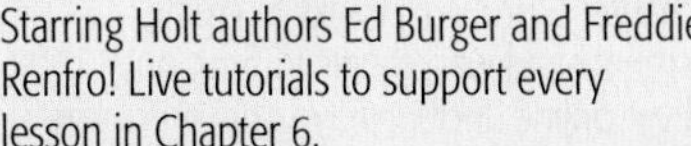

Starring Holt authors Ed Burger and Freddie Renfro! Live tutorials to support every lesson in Chapter 6.

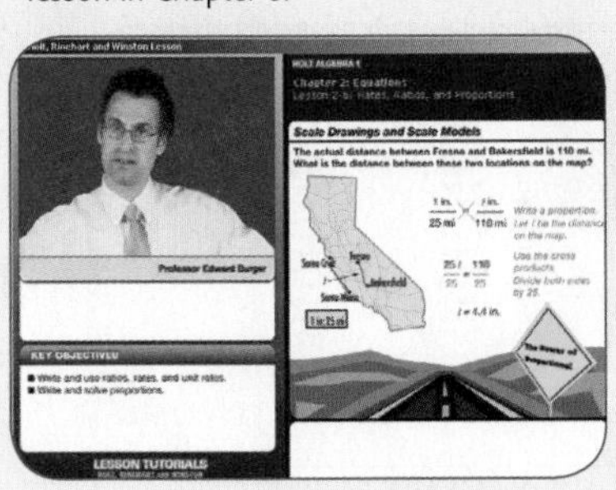

Multilingual Glossary

Searchable glossary includes definitions in English, Spanish, Vietnamese, Chinese, Hmong, Korean, and 4 other languages.

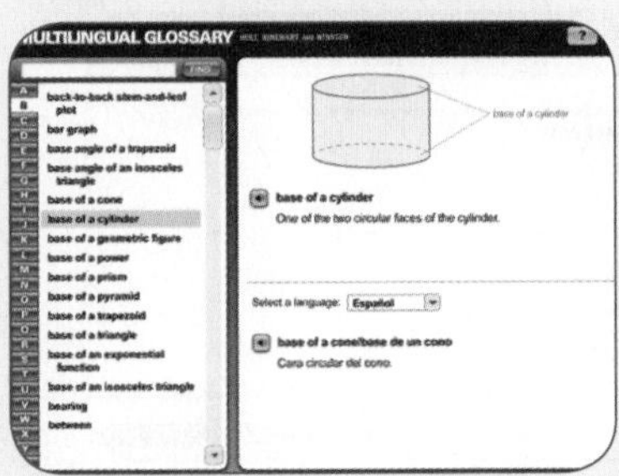

Online Interactivities

Interactive tutorials provide visually engaging alternative opportunities to learn concepts and master skills.

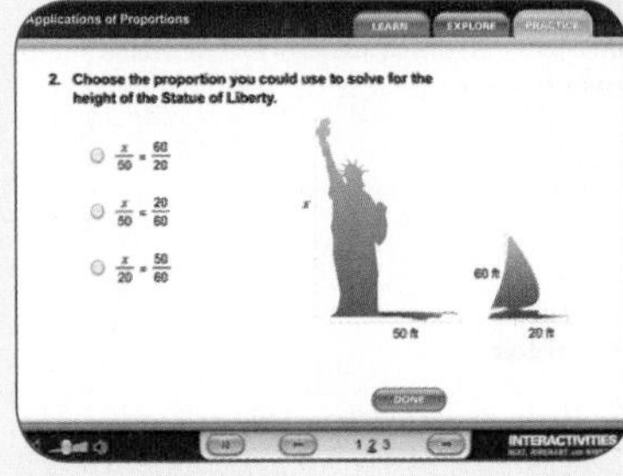

KEY: **SE** = *Student Edition* **TE** = *Teacher's Edition* **CRB** = *Chapter Resource Book*  Spanish version available  Available online Available on CD- or DVD-ROM

Ongoing Assessment

Assessing Prior Knowledge

Determine whether students have the prerequisite concepts and skills for success in Chapter 6.

Are You Ready? SPANISH .... SE p. 377
Warm Up .... TE

Test Preparation

Provide review and practice for Chapter 6 and standardized tests.

Multi-Step Test Prep .... SE pp. 406, 436
Study Guide: Review .... SE pp. 438–441
Test Tackler .... SE pp. 444–445
Standardized Test Prep .... SE pp. 446–447
College Entrance Exam Practice .... SE p. 443
Countdown to Testing .... SE pp. C4-C27
IDEA Works!® Modified Worksheets and Tests

Alternative Assessment

Assess students' understanding of Chapter 6 concepts and combined problem-solving skills.

Chapter 6 Project .... SE p. 376
Alternative Assessment .... TE
Performance Assessment .... AR
Portfolio Assessment .... AR

Lesson Assessment

Provide formative assessment for each lesson of Chapter 6.

Questioning Strategies .... TE
Think and Discuss .... SE
Check It Out! Exercises .... SE
Write About It .... SE
Journal .... TE
Lesson Quiz .... TE
Alternative Assessment .... TE
IDEA Works!® Modified Worksheets and Tests

Weekly Assessment

Provide formative assessment for each section of Chapter 6.

Multi-Step Test Prep .... SE pp. 406, 436
Ready to Go On? SPANISH .... SE pp. 407, 437
Section Quizzes .... AR
Test and Practice Generator .... *Teacher One Stop*

Chapter Assessment

Provide summative assessment of Chapter 6 mastery.

Chapter 6 Test .... SE p. 442
Chapter Test (Levels A, B, C) .... AR
• Multiple Choice • Free Response
Cumulative Test .... AR
Test and Practice Generator .... *Teacher One Stop*
IDEA Works!® Modified Worksheets and Tests

Technology Highlights for Assessment

 **Are You Ready?** 

Automatically assess readiness and prescribe intervention for Chapter 6 prerequisite skills.

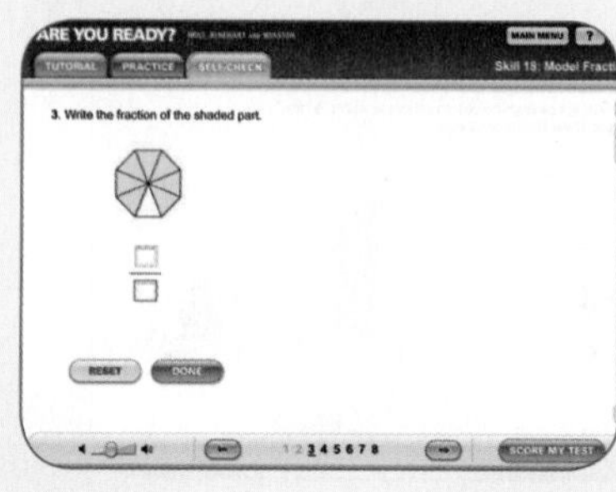

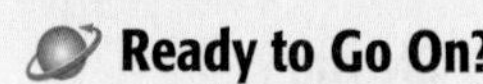

Ready to Go On?

Automatically assess understanding of and prescribe intervention for Sections 6A and 6B.

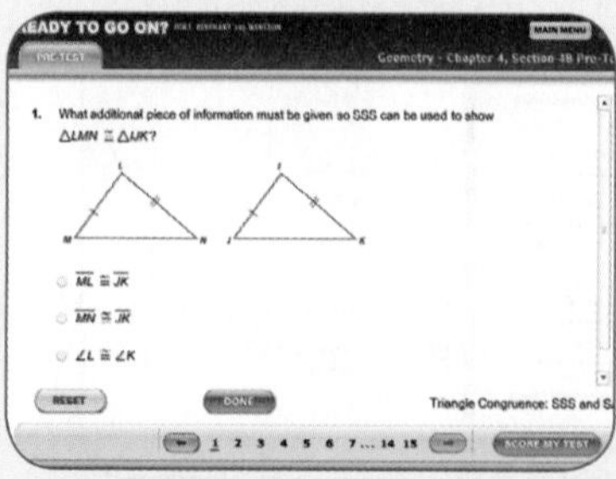

Test and Practice Generator

Use Chapter 6 problem banks to create assessments and worksheets to print out or deliver online. Includes dynamic problems.

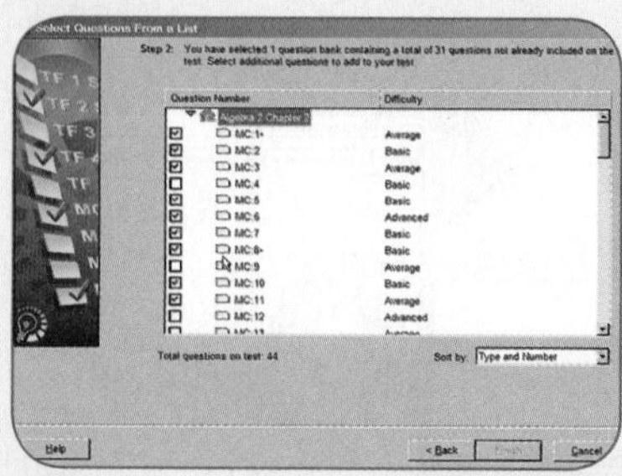

KEY: **SE** = *Student Edition* **TE** = *Teacher's Edition* **AR** = *Assessment Resources*  Spanish version available  Available online  Available on CD- or DVD-ROM

Formal Assessment

Three levels (A, B, C) of multiple-choice and free-response chapter tests, along with a performance assessment, are available in the *Assessment Resources.*

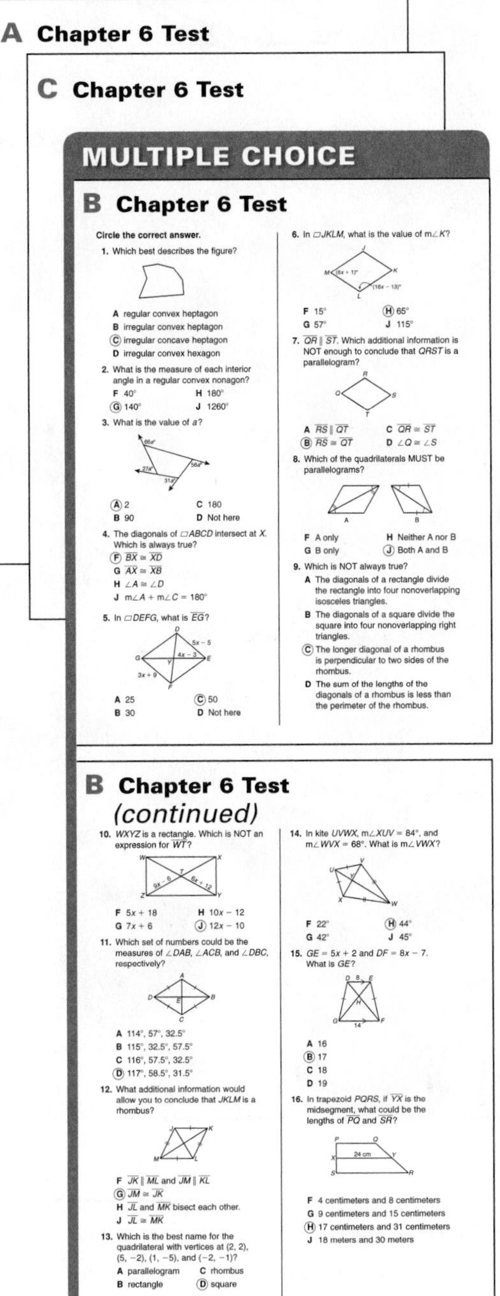

A Chapter 6 Test

C Chapter 6 Test

MULTIPLE CHOICE

B Chapter 6 Test

Circle the correct answer.

1. Which best describes the figure?
   A regular convex heptagon
   B irregular convex heptagon
   Ⓒ irregular concave heptagon
   D irregular convex hexagon
2. What is the measure of each interior angle in a regular convex nonagon?
   F 40° H 180°
   Ⓖ 140° J 1260°
3. What is the value of *a*?
   Ⓐ 2 C 180
   B 90 D Not here
4. The diagonals of ▱*ABCD* intersect at *X*. Which is always true?
   Ⓕ $\overline{BX} \cong \overline{XD}$
   G $\overline{AX} \cong \overline{XB}$
   H $\angle A \cong \angle D$
   J $m\angle A + m\angle C = 180°$
5. In ▱*DEFG*, what is *EG*?
   A 25 Ⓒ 50
   B 30 D Not here
6. In ▱*JKLM*, what is the value of $m\angle K$?
   F 15° Ⓗ 65°
   G 57° J 115°
7. $\overline{QR} \parallel \overline{ST}$. Which additional information is NOT enough to conclude that *QRST* is a parallelogram?
   A $\overline{RS} \parallel \overline{QT}$ C $\overline{QR} \cong \overline{ST}$
   Ⓑ $\overline{RS} \cong \overline{QT}$ D $\angle Q \cong \angle S$
8. Which of the quadrilaterals MUST be parallelograms?
   F A only H Neither A nor B
   G B only Ⓙ Both A and B
9. Which is NOT always true?
   A The diagonals of a rectangle divide the rectangle into four nonoverlapping isosceles triangles.
   B The diagonals of a square divide the square into four nonoverlapping right triangles.
   Ⓒ The longer diagonal of a rhombus is perpendicular to two sides of the rhombus.
   D The sum of the lengths of the diagonals of a rhombus is less than the perimeter of the rhombus.

B Chapter 6 Test (continued)

10. *WXYZ* is a rectangle. Which is NOT an expression for *WT*?
    F 5x + 18 H 10x − 12
    G 7x + 6 Ⓙ 12x − 10
11. Which set of numbers could be the measures of ∠*DAB*, ∠*ACB*, and ∠*DBC*, respectively?
    A 114°, 57°, 32.5°
    B 115°, 32.5°, 57.5°
    C 116°, 57.5°, 32.5°
    Ⓓ 117°, 58.5°, 31.5°
12. What additional information would allow you to conclude that *JKLM* is a rhombus?
    F $\overline{JK} \parallel \overline{ML}$ and $\overline{JM} \parallel \overline{KL}$
    Ⓖ $\overline{JM} \cong \overline{JK}$
    H $\overline{JL}$ and $\overline{MK}$ bisect each other.
    J $\overline{JL} \cong \overline{MK}$
13. Which is the best name for the quadrilateral with vertices at (2, 2), (5, −2), (1, −5), and (−2, −1)?
    A parallelogram C rhombus
    B rectangle Ⓓ square
14. In kite *UVWX*, $m\angle XUV = 84°$, and $m\angle WVX = 68°$. What is $m\angle VWX$?
    F 22° Ⓗ 44°
    G 42° J 45°
15. *GE* = 5x + 2 and *DF* = 8x − 7. What is *GE*?
    A 16
    Ⓑ 17
    C 18
    D 19
16. In trapezoid *PQRS*, if $\overline{YX}$ is the midsegment, what could be the lengths of $\overline{PQ}$ and $\overline{SR}$?
    F 4 centimeters and 8 centimeters
    G 9 centimeters and 15 centimeters
    Ⓗ 17 centimeters and 31 centimeters
    J 18 meters and 30 meters

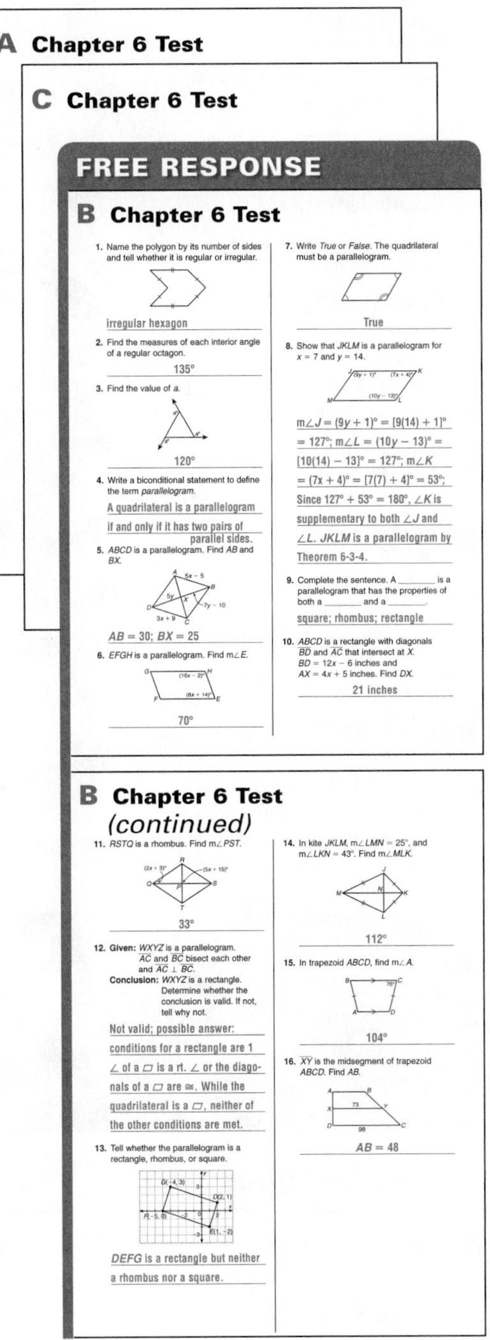

A Chapter 6 Test

C Chapter 6 Test

FREE RESPONSE

B Chapter 6 Test

1. Name the polygon by its number of sides and tell whether it is regular or irregular.
   irregular hexagon
2. Find the measures of each interior angle of a regular octagon.
   135°
3. Find the value of *a*.
   120°
4. Write a biconditional statement to define the term *parallelogram*.
   A quadrilateral is a parallelogram if and only if it has two pairs of parallel sides.
5. *ABCD* is a parallelogram. Find *AB* and *BX*.
   AB = 30; *BX* = 25
6. *EFGH* is a parallelogram. Find $m\angle E$.
   70°
7. Write *True* or *False*. The quadrilateral must be a parallelogram.
   True
8. Show that *JKLM* is a parallelogram for *x* = 7 and *y* = 14.
   $m\angle J = (9y + 1)° = [9(14) + 1]° = 127°$; $m\angle L = (10y − 13)° = [10(14) − 13]° = 127°$; $m\angle K = (7x + 4)° = [7(7) + 4]° = 53°$; Since 127° + 53° = 180°, ∠*K* is supplementary to both ∠*J* and ∠*L*. *JKLM* is a parallelogram by Theorem 6-3-4.
9. Complete the sentence. A ______ is a parallelogram that has the properties of both a ______ and a ______.
   square; rhombus; rectangle
10. *ABCD* is a rectangle with diagonals $\overline{BD}$ and $\overline{AC}$ that intersect at *X*. *BD* = 12x − 6 inches and *AX* = 4x + 5 inches. Find *DX*.
    21 inches

B Chapter 6 Test (continued)

11. *RSTQ* is a rhombus. Find $m\angle PST$.
    33°
12. Given: *WXYZ* is a parallelogram. $\overline{AC}$ and $\overline{BC}$ bisect each other and $\overline{AC} \perp \overline{BC}$.
    Conclusion: *WXYZ* is a rectangle. Determine whether the conclusion is valid. If not, tell why not.
    Not valid; possible answer: conditions for a rectangle are 1 ∠ of a ▱ is a rt. ∠ or the diagonals of a ▱ are ≅. While the quadrilateral is a ▱, neither of the other conditions are met.
13. Tell whether the parallelogram is a rectangle, rhombus, or square.
    DEFG is a rectangle but neither a rhombus nor a square.
14. In kite *JKLM*, $m\angle LMN = 25°$, and $m\angle LKN = 43°$. Find $m\angle MLK$.
    112°
15. In trapezoid *ABCD*, find $m\angle A$.
    104°
16. $\overline{XY}$ is the midsegment of trapezoid *ABCD*. Find *AB*.
    AB = 48

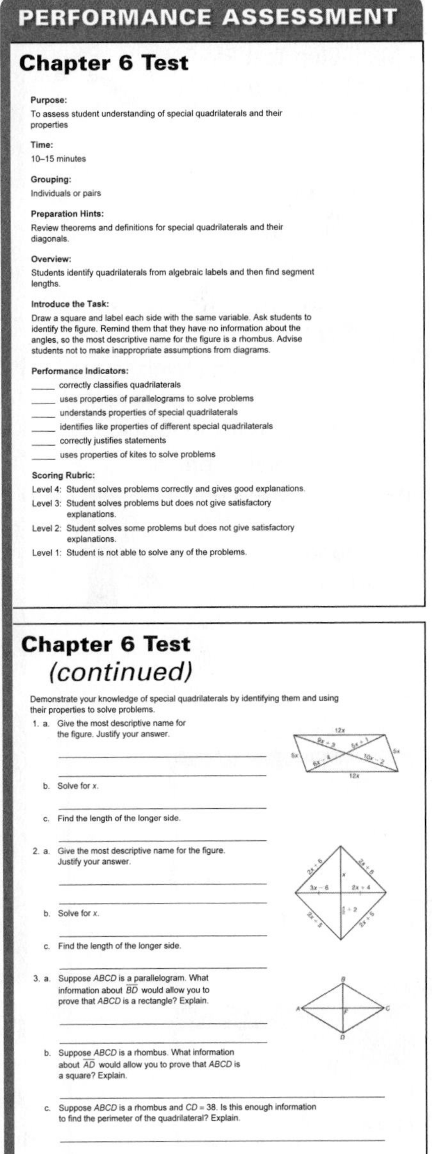

PERFORMANCE ASSESSMENT

Chapter 6 Test

Purpose: To assess student understanding of special quadrilaterals and their properties

Time: 10–15 minutes

Grouping: Individuals or pairs

Preparation Hints: Review theorems and definitions for special quadrilaterals and their diagonals.

Overview: Students identify quadrilaterals from algebraic labels and then find segment lengths.

Introduce the Task: Draw a square and label each side with the same variable. Ask students to identify the figure. Remind them that they have no information about the angles, so the most descriptive name for the figure is a rhombus. Advise students not to make inappropriate assumptions from diagrams.

Performance Indicators:
____ correctly classifies quadrilaterals
____ uses properties of parallelograms to solve problems
____ understands properties of special quadrilaterals
____ identifies like properties of different special quadrilaterals
____ correctly justifies statements
____ uses properties of kites to solve problems

Scoring Rubric:
Level 4: Student solves problems correctly and gives good explanations.
Level 3: Student solves problems but does not give satisfactory explanations.
Level 2: Student solves some problems but does not give satisfactory explanations.
Level 1: Student is not able to solve any of the problems.

Chapter 6 Test (continued)

Demonstrate your knowledge of special quadrilaterals by identifying them and using their properties to solve problems.

1. a. Give the most descriptive name for the figure. Justify your answer.
   b. Solve for *x*.
   c. Find the length of the longer side.
2. a. Give the most descriptive name for the figure. Justify your answer.
   b. Solve for *x*.
   c. Find the length of the longer side.
3. a. Suppose *ABCD* is a parallelogram. What information about $\overline{BD}$ would allow you to prove that *ABCD* is a rectangle? Explain.
   b. Suppose *ABCD* is a rhombus. What information about $\overline{AD}$ would allow you to prove that *ABCD* is a square? Explain.
   c. Suppose *ABCD* is a rhombus and *CD* = 38. Is this enough information to find the perimeter of the quadrilateral? Explain.

Teacher One Stop™
Test & Practice Generator

Create and customize Chapter 6 Tests. Instantly generate multiple test versions, answer keys, and practice versions of test items.

Modified chapter tests that address special learning needs are available in *IDEA Works!*® *Modified Worksheets and Tests.*

CHAPTER 6

SECTION 6A
Polygons and Parallelograms

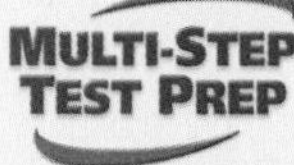

MULTI-STEP TEST PREP On page 406, students use the properties of polygons and parallelograms to investigate the faces of crystals.

Exercises designed to prepare students for success on the Multi-Step Test Prep can be found on pages 387, 396, and 404.

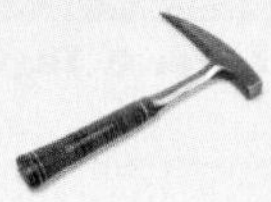

SECTION 6B
Other Special Quadrilaterals

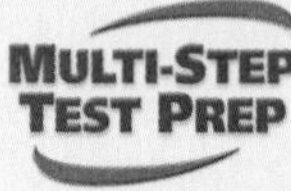

MULTI-STEP TEST PREP On page 436, students use special quadrilaterals in the coordinate plane to plan the layout for a county fair.

Exercises designed to prepare students for success on the Multi-Step Test Prep can be found on pages 414, 424, and 434.

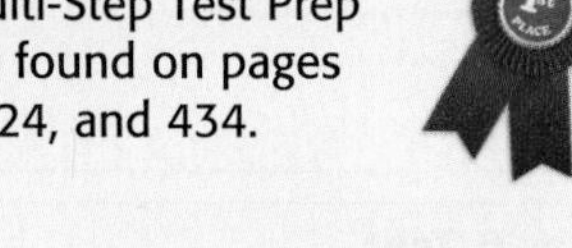

Interactivities Online ▶

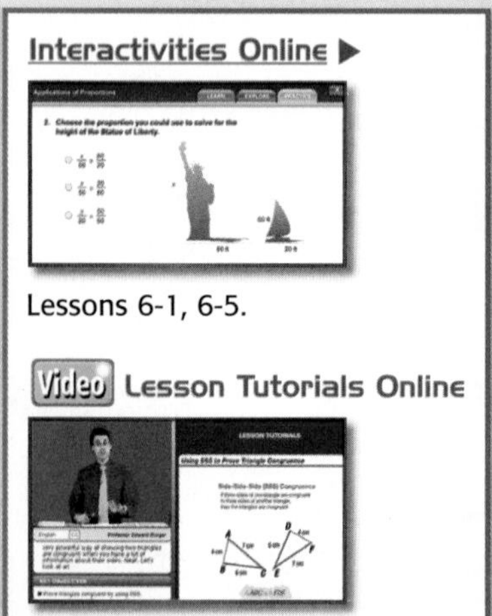

Lessons 6-1, 6-5.

Video Lesson Tutorials Online

Lesson Tutorial Videos are available for EVERY example.

CHAPTER 6

Polygons and Quadrilaterals

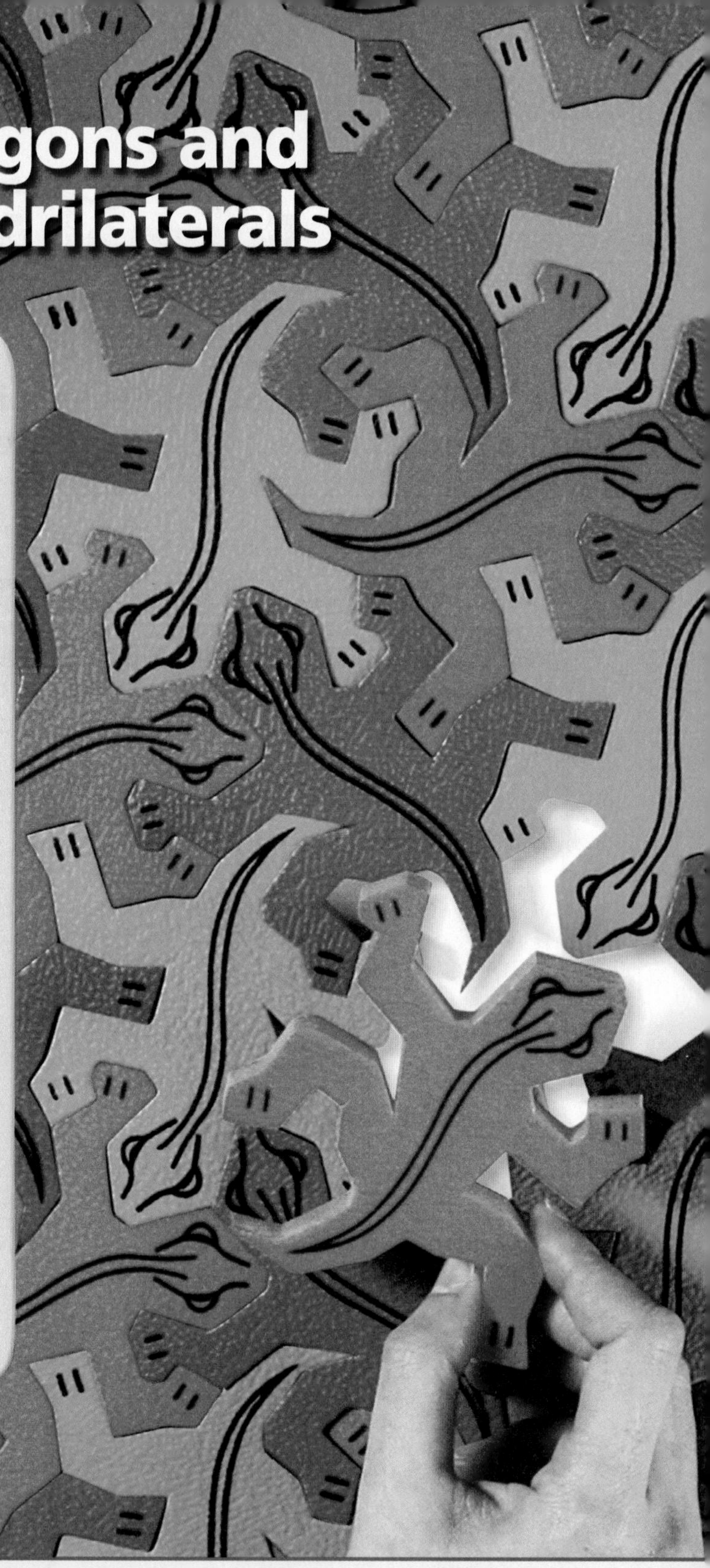

Chapter Focus

- Apply the properties of regular polygons to solve real-world problems.
- Justify and apply the properties of special parallelograms.

Divide and Conquer

Some of the trickiest puzzles are based on simple polygonal shapes. You can use polygons to solve and create a variety of puzzles.

go.hrw.com
Chapter Project Online
KEYWORD: MG7 ChProj

Divide and Conquer

About the Project

In the Chapter Project, students use their knowledge of polygons to find ways to divide squares and hexagons according to given rules. Students also use squares, rectangles, parallelograms, trapezoids, and triangles to make a puzzle of their own.

Project Resources

All project resources for teachers and students are provided online.

Materials:
- graph paper
- isometric dot paper
- patterned wrapping paper or magazine photo
- scissors
- glue

go.hrw.com
Project Teacher Support
KEYWORD: MG7 ProjectTS

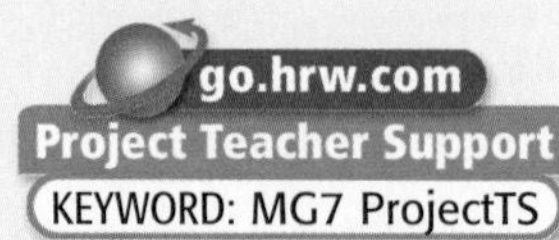

CHAPTER 6

ARE YOU READY?

Vocabulary

Match each term on the left with a definition on the right.

1. exterior angle F
2. parallel lines B
3. perpendicular lines A
4. polygon D
5. quadrilateral E

A. lines that intersect to form right angles
B. lines in the same plane that do not intersect
C. two angles of a polygon that share a side
D. a closed plane figure formed by three or more segments that intersect only at their endpoints
E. a four-sided polygon
F. an angle formed by one side of a polygon and the extension of a consecutive side

Triangle Sum Theorem

Find the value of x.

6. 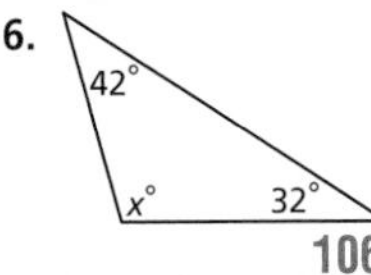

106

7. 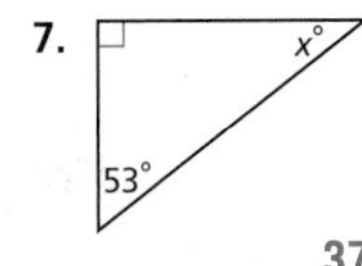

37

8. 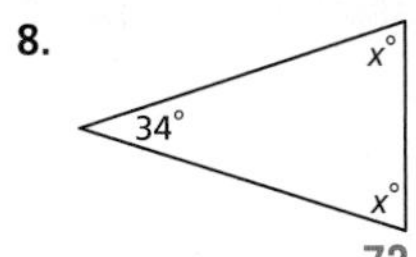

73

9. 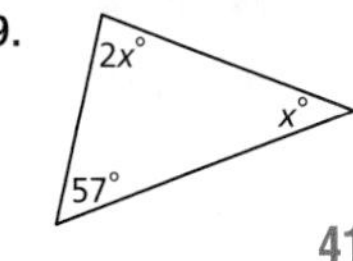

41

Parallel Lines and Transversals

Find the measure of each numbered angle.

10. 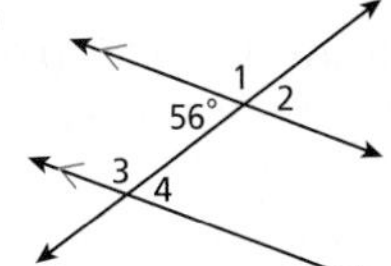

11. 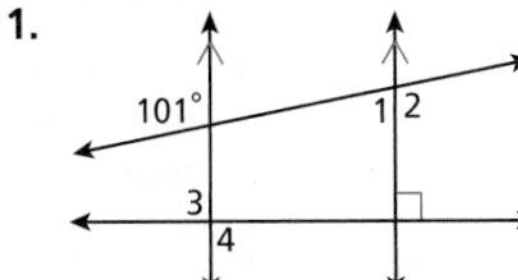

12. 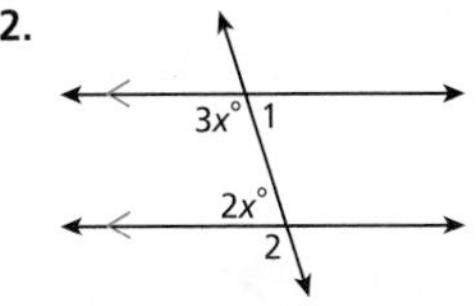

Special Right Triangles

Find the value of x. Give the answer in simplest radical form.

13. 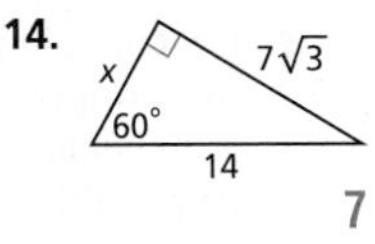

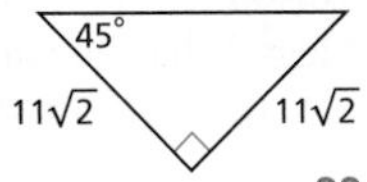

22

14. 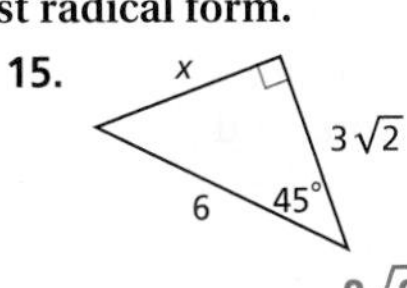

7

15. 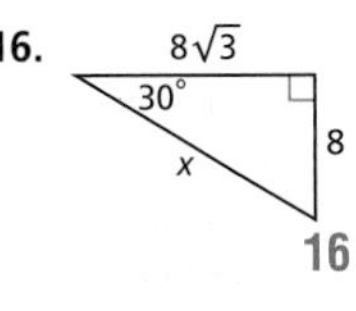

$3\sqrt{2}$

16.
16

Conditional Statements

Tell whether the given statement is true or false. Write the converse. Tell whether the converse is true or false.

17. If two angles form a linear pair, then they are supplementary.
T; if 2 ∠s are supp., then they form a lin. pair; F.
18. If two angles are congruent, then they are right angles.
F; if 2 ∠s are rt. ∠s, then they are ≅; T.
19. If a triangle is a scalene triangle, then it is an acute triangle.
F; if a △ is an acute △, then it is a scalene △; F.

ARE YOU READY?

Organizer

Objective: Assess students' understanding of prerequisite skills.

Prerequisite Skills

- Triangle Sum Theorem
- Parallel Lines and Transversals
- Special Right Triangles
- Conditional Statements

Assessing Prior Knowledge

INTERVENTION

Diagnose and Prescribe

Use this page to determine whether intervention is necessary or whether enrichment is appropriate.

Resources

 ***Are You Ready? Intervention and Enrichment* Worksheets**

 ***Are You Ready?* CD-ROM**

 ***Are You Ready?* Online**

my.hrw.com

Answers

10–12. See p. A21.

ARE YOU READY?
Diagnose and Prescribe

NO — INTERVENE

Prerequisite Skill	*Are You Ready? Intervention*, Chapter 6 — Worksheets	CD-ROM	Online
Triangle Sum Theorem	Skill 30	Activity 30	Diagnose and Prescribe Online
Parallel Lines and Transversals	Skill 26	Activity 26	
Special Right Triangles	Skill 32	Activity 32	
Conditional Statements	Skill 88	Activity 88	

YES — ENRICH

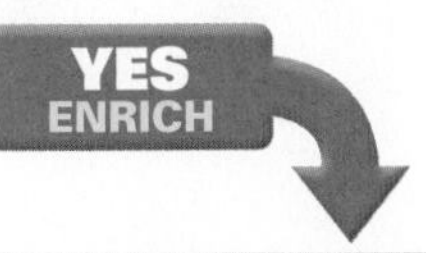

***Are You Ready? Enrichment*, Chapter 6**
- Worksheets
- CD-ROM
- Online

CHAPTER 6

Study Guide: Preview

Organizer

Objective: Help students organize the new concepts they will learn in Chapter 6.

Online Edition
Multilingual Glossary

Resources

Teacher One Stop™
PuzzleView

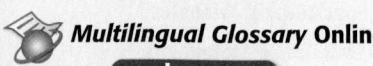

***Multilingual Glossary* Online**

go.hrw.com
KEYWORD: MG7 Glossary

Answers to *Vocabulary Connections*

Possible answers:

1. 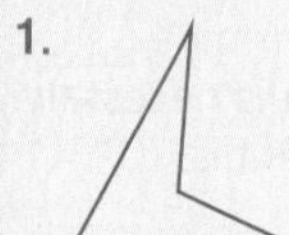
2. A diag. is a seg. that goes across a polygon from ∠ to ∠.
3. It has 2 ≅ legs.
4. The sides that do not intersect are ∥.
5. A reg. polygon is an "orderly" polygon, in which all the ∡ are ≅ and all the sides are ≅.

CHAPTER 6

Study Guide: Preview

Where You've Been

Previously, you

- learned properties of triangles.
- studied properties of parallel and perpendicular lines.
- classified triangles based on their side lengths and angle measures.
- wrote proofs involving congruent triangles.

In This Chapter

You will study

- properties of polygons.
- properties of special quadrilaterals.
- how to show that a polygon is a special quadrilateral.
- how to write proofs involving special quadrilaterals.

Where You're Going

You can use the skills learned in this chapter

- to find areas and volumes in geometry, algebra, and advanced math courses.
- to study motion and mechanics in physics courses.
- to use devices such as cameras and binoculars and to work on hobbies and craft projects outside of school.

Key Vocabulary/Vocabulario

concave	cóncavo
diagonal	diagonal
isosceles trapezoid	trapecio isósceles
kite	cometa
parallelogram	paralelogramo
rectangle	rectángulo
regular polygon	polígono regular
rhombus	rombo
square	cuadrado
trapezoid	trapecio

Vocabulary Connections

To become familiar with some of the vocabulary terms in the chapter, consider the following. You may refer to the chapter, the glossary, or a dictionary if you like.

1. The word **concave** is made up of two parts: *con* and *cave*. Sketch a polygon that looks like it caves in.
2. In Greek, *dia* means "through" or "across," and *gonia* means "angle" or "corner." How can you use these meanings to understand the term **diagonal**?
3. If a triangle is *isosceles*, then it has two congruent legs. What do you think is a special property of an **isosceles trapezoid**?
4. A **parallelogram** has four sides. What do you think is a special property of the sides of a parallelogram?
5. One of the meanings of the word *regular* is "orderly." What do you think the term **regular polygon** means?

378 Chapter 6

Writing Strategy: Write a Convincing Argument

Throughout this book, the icon identifies exercises that require you to write an explanation or argument to support an idea. Your response to a Write About It exercise shows that you have a solid understanding of the mathematical concept.

To be effective, a written argument should contain

- a clear statement of your mathematical claim.
- evidence or reasoning that supports your claim.

From Lesson 5-4

36. Write About It An isosceles triangle has two congruent sides. Does it also have two congruent midsegments? Explain.

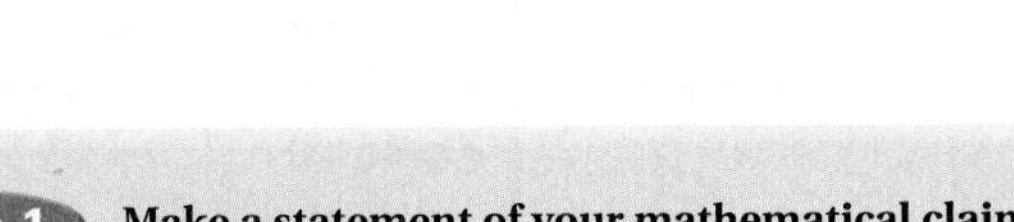

Step 1 **Make a statement of your mathematical claim.**

Draw a sketch to investigate the properties of the midsegments of an isosceles triangle. You will find that the midsegments parallel to the legs of the isosceles triangle are congruent.

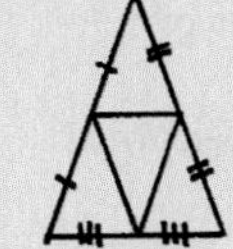

Claim: The midsegments parallel to the legs of an isosceles triangle are congruent.

Step 2 **Give evidence to support your claim.**

Identify any properties or theorems that support your claim. In this case, the Triangle Midsegment Theorem states that the length of a midsegment of a triangle is $\frac{1}{2}$ the length of the parallel side.

To clarify your argument, label your diagram and use it in your response.

Step 3 **Write a complete response.**

Yes, the two midsegments parallel to the legs of an isosceles triangle are congruent. Suppose $\triangle ABC$ is isosceles with $\overline{AB} \cong \overline{AC}$. $\overline{XZ}$ and $\overline{YZ}$ are midsegments of $\triangle ABC$. By the Triangle Midsegment Theorem, $XZ = \frac{1}{2}AC$ and $YZ = \frac{1}{2}AB$. Since $\overline{AB} \cong \overline{AC}$, $AB = AC$. So $\frac{1}{2}AB = \frac{1}{2}AC$ by the Multiplication Property of Equality. By substitution, $XZ = YZ$, so $\overline{XZ} \cong \overline{YZ}$.

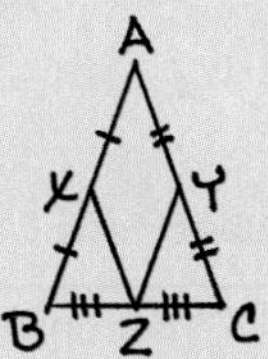

Try This

Write a convincing argument.

1. Compare the circumcenter and the incenter of a triangle.
2. If you know the side lengths of a triangle, how do you determine which angle is the largest?

Reading and Writing Math

Organizer

Objective: Help students apply strategies to understand and retain key concepts.

Online Edition

Resources

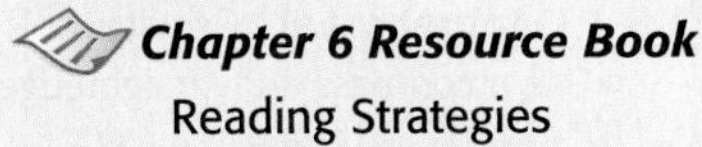

Chapter 6 Resource Book

Reading Strategies

Writing Strategy: Write a Convincing Argument

Discuss By writing a clear, convincing argument, students demonstrate mastery of new concepts.

Extend After each lesson, have students present their responses to the Write About It exercises and ask for feedback.

Answers to *Try This*

Possible answers:

1. Both are pts. of concurrency in a triangle. The circumcenter is the pt. of concurrency of the perp. bisectors. The incenter is the pt. of concurrency of the angle bisectors. The circumcenter is equidistant from the vertices of the triangle. The incenter is equidistant from the sides of the triangle. The circumcenter is the center of the circumscribed circle, and the incenter is the center of the inscribed circle.
2. Apply angle-side relationships to conclude that the largest angle is opp. the longest side.

Reading Connection

***Islamic Geometric Patterns* by Eric Broug**

This book presents 20 stunning geometric patterns from Islamic sites around the world, plus detailed instructions on how to draw them. Students learn to construct the basic polygons on which all of the patterns are based, and then proceed to more complex designs.

Activity Have students identify pentagons, hexagons, heptagons, and octagons in the book. Then have them learn to draw a pentagon using compass and straightedge and demonstrate to the class.

SECTION 6A

Polygons and Parallelograms

One-Minute Section Planner

Lesson	Lab Resources	Materials
6-1 Geometry Lab Construct Regular Polygons • Use a compass and straightedge to construct regular polygons. ☑ SAT-10 ☑ NAEP ☐ ACT ☑ SAT ☐ SAT Subject Tests	***Geometry Lab Activities*** 6-1 Lab Recording Sheet	**Required** compass (MK), straightedge (MK), protractor (MK) **Optional** geometry software
Lesson 6-1 Properties and Attributes of Polygons • Classify polygons based on their sides and angles. • Find and use the measures of interior and exterior angles of polygons. ☑ SAT-10 ☑ NAEP ☐ ACT ☑ SAT ☐ SAT Subject Tests		**Optional** straightedge (MK), protractor (MK), picture frame, hexagonal nut, pennant, paper plate, ball, polygons cut out of construction paper
6-2 Geometry Lab Explore Properties of Parallelograms • Explore properties of parallelograms. ☐ SAT-10 ☑ NAEP ☑ ACT ☑ SAT ☐ SAT Subject Tests	***Geometry Lab Activities*** 6-2 Lab Recording Sheet	**Required** index cards, patty paper, ruler (MK) **Optional** cutouts of congruent parallelograms
Lesson 6-2 Properties of Parallelograms • Prove and apply properties of parallelograms. • Use properties of parallelograms to solve problems. ☐ SAT-10 ☑ NAEP ☑ ACT ☐ SAT ☐ SAT Subject Tests	***Technology Lab Activities*** 6-2 Technology Lab	**Optional** geometry software, tangram puzzle (MK), colored pencils
Lesson 6-3 Conditions for Parallelograms • Prove that a given quadrilateral is a parallelogram. ☐ SAT-10 ☑ NAEP ☑ ACT ☐ SAT ☐ SAT Subject Tests	***Geometry Lab Activities*** 6-3 Geometry Lab	**Optional** scissors, ruler (MK), chenile stems, compass (MK), straightedge (MK), heavy construction paper, hole punch, brads, raw spaghetti, straws

MK = *Manipulatives Kit*

Math Background

POLYGONS

Lesson 6-1

A *polygon* is a closed plane figure formed by three or more line segments such that:

(1) each segment intersects exactly two other segments only at their endpoints, and

(2) no two segments with a common endpoint are collinear.

The first condition prevents a polygon from intersecting itself, as shown at right.

The second condition guarantees that a polygon that appears to have *n* vertices actually has *n* vertices! If a polygon's segments were allowed to be collinear, the triangle below could be considered to have 7 vertices.

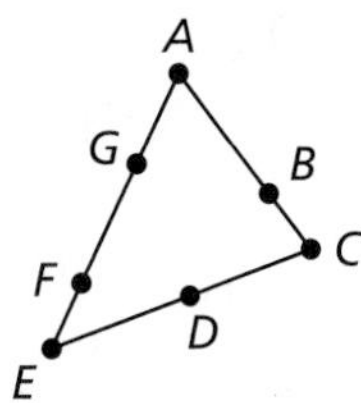

A *convex polygon* is a polygon for which no diagonal contains points in the exterior of the polygon. The figure below shows a polygon that is not convex; the indicated diagonal lies outside the polygon.

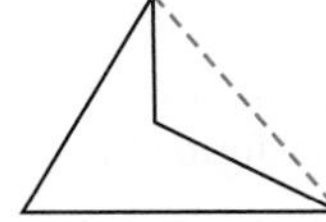

The two essential theorems of Lesson 6-1 concern the angles of polygons.

- The Polygon Angle Sum Theorem states that the sum of the measures of the interior angles of a convex *n*-gon is $(n - 2)180°$. This leads to an immediate corollary for regular polygons: each interior angle of a regular *n*-gon measures $\frac{(n - 2)180°}{n}$.
- The Polygon Exterior Angle Sum Theorem asserts that the sum of the exterior angle measures, one at each vertex, for any convex polygon is 360°. Thus, for a regular polygon, each exterior angle measures $\frac{360°}{n}$.

To verify the Polygon Angle Sum Theorem, we first notice that in a convex *n*-gon, there are $(n - 3)$ diagonals that can be drawn from a single vertex. These diagonals divide the polygon into $(n - 2)$ triangles, as shown below.

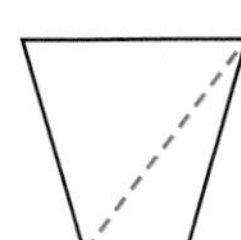

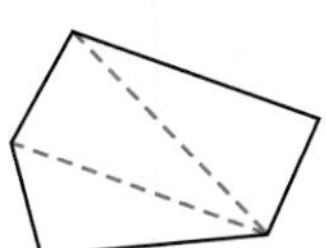

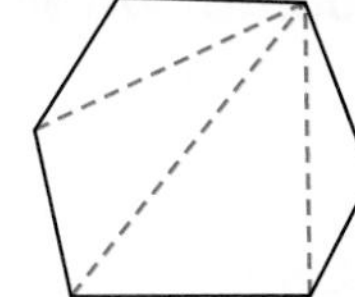

Each triangle has 180°, hence the total of the angle measures is $(n - 2)180°$.

The figures below lend informal visual support to the Polygon Exterior Angle Sum Theorem. Beginning with the figure on the left, the convex polygon is "scaled down" until it has been contracted to a single point. This leaves the exterior angles, which fit perfectly around the point. Hence the sum of their measures is 360°.

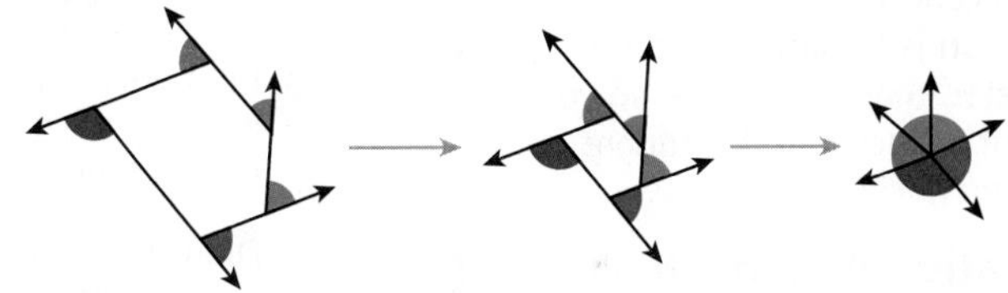

PARALLELOGRAMS

Lessons 6-2, 6-3

A *parallelogram* is a quadrilateral whose opposite sides are parallel. Like every polygon, parallelograms are named by listing consecutive vertices. Because of this convention, the pairs of parallel sides can be identified from the parallelogram's name. For example, ▱*JKLM* has sides $\overline{JK}$, $\overline{KL}$, $\overline{LM}$, and $\overline{MJ}$ with $\overline{JK} \parallel \overline{LM}$ and $\overline{KL} \parallel \overline{MJ}$. This relationship is easily verified by sketching a parallelogram with consecutive vertices *J*, *K*, *L*, and *M*.

It is worth emphasizing to students that the theorems of Lesson 6-2 all have the form "If a quadrilateral is a parallelogram, then [property]." In contrast, the theorems in Lesson 6-3 consider the converse situation. In other words, the theorems of Lesson 6-3 all have the form, "If [condition], then the quadrilateral is a parallelogram."

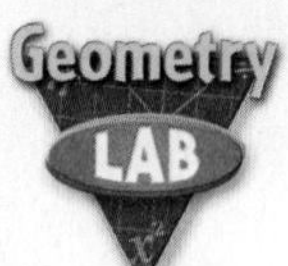

Organizer

Use with Lesson 6-1

Pacing:

Traditional 1 day

Block $\frac{1}{2}$ day

Objective: Use a compass and straightedge to construct regular polygons.

Materials: compass, straightedge, protractor

Online Edition

Countdown Week 13

Resources

Geometry Lab Activities

6-1 Lab Recording Sheet

Teach

Discuss

Discuss with students the different procedures that are used to construct each regular polygon. Ask students to draw connections between the construction procedure and the number of sides of the polygon. The justification for the pentagon construction is significantly more complicated than the others, so you may want to focus on the square and hexagon.

Alternative Approach

Use geometry software to construct the regular polygons in the lab and investigate their angle measures.

State Resources

6-1

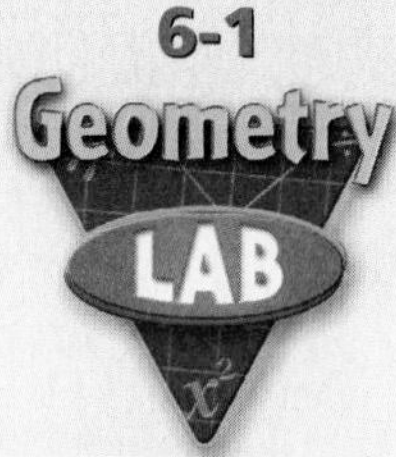

Use with Lesson 6-1

Construct Regular Polygons

In Chapter 4, you learned that an equilateral triangle is a triangle with three congruent sides. You also learned that an equilateral triangle is equiangular, meaning that all its angles are congruent.

In this lab, you will construct polygons that are both equilateral and equiangular by inscribing them in circles.

Activity 1

1. Construct circle *P*. Draw a diameter $\overline{AC}$.
2. Construct the perpendicular bisector of $\overline{AC}$. Label the intersections of the bisector and the circle as *B* and *D*.
3. Draw $\overline{AB}$, $\overline{BC}$, $\overline{CD}$, and $\overline{DA}$. The polygon *ABCD* is a *regular quadrilateral.* This means it is a four-sided polygon that has four congruent sides and four congruent angles.

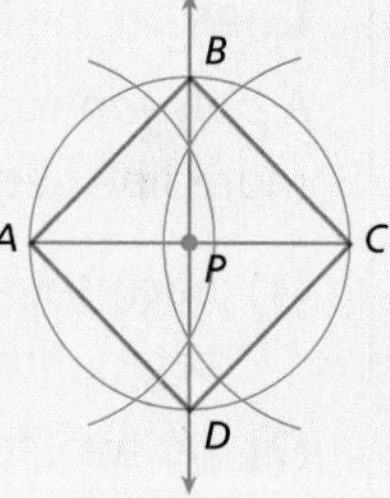

Try This

1. Describe a different method for constructing a regular quadrilateral.
2. The regular quadrilateral in Activity 1 is inscribed in the circle. What is the relationship between the circle and the regular quadrilateral?
3. A *regular octagon* is an eight-sided polygon that has eight congruent sides and eight congruent angles. Use angle bisectors to construct a regular octagon from a regular quadrilateral.

Activity 2

1. Construct circle *P*. Draw a point *A* on the circle.
2. Use the same compass setting. Starting at *A*, draw arcs to mark off equal parts along the circle. Label the other points where the arcs intersect the circle as *B, C, D, E,* and *F.*
3. Draw $\overline{AB}$, $\overline{BC}$, $\overline{CD}$, $\overline{DE}$, $\overline{EF}$, and $\overline{FA}$. The polygon *ABCDEF* is a *regular hexagon.* This means it is a six-sided polygon that has six congruent sides and six congruent angles.

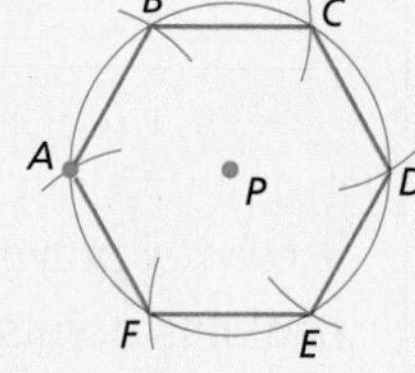

Try This

4. Justify the conclusion that *ABCDEF* is a regular hexagon. (*Hint:* Draw diameters $\overline{AD}$, $\overline{BE}$, and $\overline{CF}$. What types of triangles are formed?)
5. A *regular dodecagon* is a 12-sided polygon that has 12 congruent sides and 12 congruent angles. Use the construction of a regular hexagon to construct a regular dodecagon. Explain your method.

Answers to *Try This*

1. Possible answer: Draw a line ℓ. Draw *A* and *D* on ℓ. Construct *m* ⊥ to ℓ through *A*. Construct *n* ⊥ to ℓ through *D*. Set the compass to the length *AD*. With the compass point at *A*, draw an arc that intersects *m* above ℓ. Label the pt. of intersection *B*. With the compass point at *D*, draw an arc that intersects *n* above ℓ. Label the pt. of intersection C. Draw $\overline{BC}$. The polygon *ABCD* is a reg. quad.

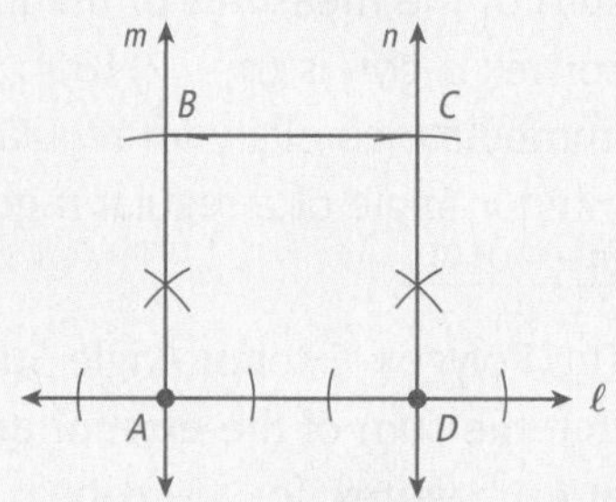

2. The circle is circumscribed about the polygon.

1. Construct circle P. Draw a diameter $\overline{AB}$.
2. Construct the perpendicular bisector of $\overline{AB}$. Label one point where the bisector intersects the circle as point E.
3. Construct the midpoint of radius $\overline{PB}$. Label it as point C.
4. Set your compass to the length CE. Place the compass point at C and draw an arc that intersects $\overline{AB}$. Label the point of intersection D.
5. Set the compass to the length ED. Starting at E, draw arcs to mark off equal parts along the circle. Label the other points where the arcs intersect the circle as F, G, H, and J.
6. Draw $\overline{EF}$, $\overline{FG}$, $\overline{GH}$, $\overline{HJ}$, and $\overline{JE}$. The polygon $EFGHJ$ is a *regular pentagon*. This means it is a five-sided polygon that has five congruent sides and five congruent angles.

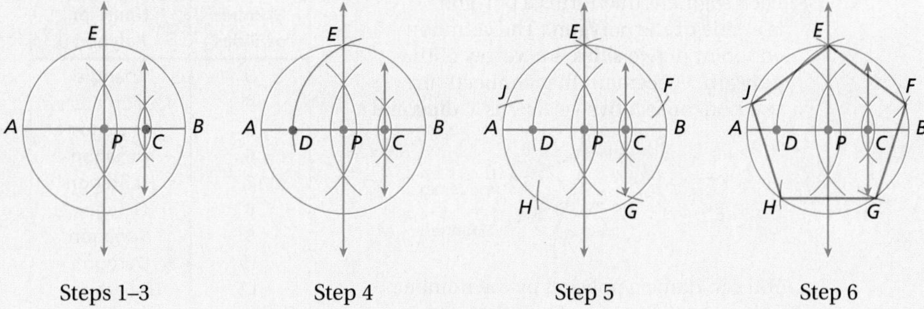

Steps 1–3 | Step 4 | Step 5 | Step 6

Try This

6. A *regular decagon* is a ten-sided polygon that has ten congruent sides and ten congruent angles. Use the construction of a regular pentagon to construct a regular decagon. Explain your method.
7. Measure each angle of the regular polygons in Activities 1–3 and complete the following table.

REGULAR POLYGONS				
Number of Sides	3	4	5	6
Measure of Each Angle	60°	**90°**	**108°**	**120°**
Sum of Angle Measures	180°	**360°**	**540°**	**720°**

8. **Make a Conjecture** What is a general rule for finding the sum of the angle measures in a regular polygon with n sides? $(n-2)180°$
9. **Make a Conjecture** What is a general rule for finding the measure of each angle in a regular polygon with n sides? $\frac{(n-2)180°}{n}$

Close

Key Concept

Students should recognize that there is a relationship between the number of sides a polygon has and the sum of the angle measures of the polygon.

Assessment

Journal Have students explain how to use a compass and straightedge to construct regular polygons with 4, 6, and 8 sides.

Answers to *Try This*

3. Check students' work. Possible answer:

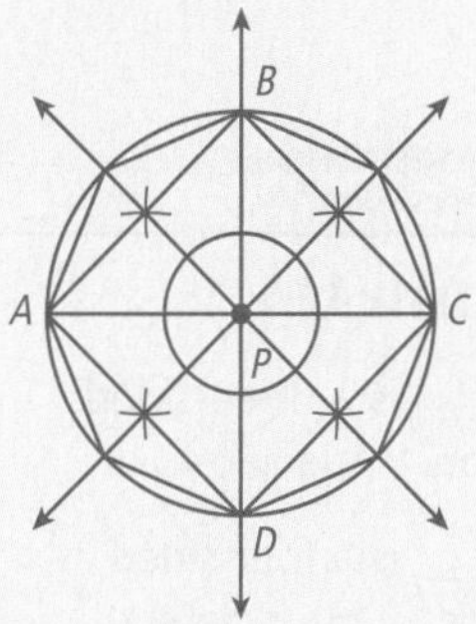

4. Possible answer: The 6 sides of *ABCDEF* were marked off with the same compass setting, so they are ≅. When $\overline{AD}$, $\overline{BE}$, and $\overline{CF}$ are drawn, the 6 △ formed are ≅ and equil. The measure of each ∠ of an equil. △ is 60°. Each ∠ of the hexagon is formed by 2 of these 60° ∠, so the 6 ∠ of *ABCDEF* are ≅. Since it has 6 ≅ sides and 6 ≅ ∠, *ABCDEF* is a reg. hexagon.

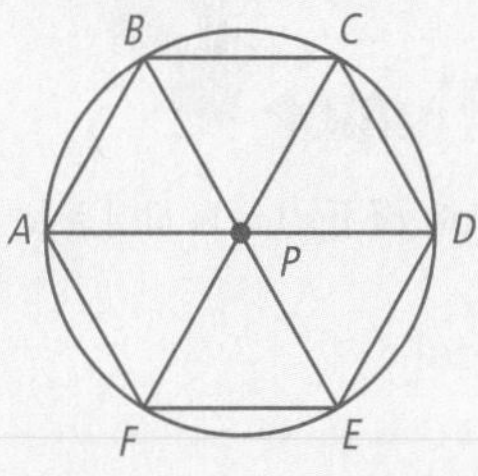

5. Check students' work. Possible answer: Draw $\overline{AD}$, $\overline{BE}$, and $\overline{CF}$. Construct the bisectors of ∠*APB*, ∠*BPC*, ∠*CPD*, ∠*DPE*, ∠*EPF*, and ∠*FPA*. Connect the 6 pts. where the ∠ bisectors intersect the circle to pts. *A*, *B*, *C*, *D*, *E*, and *F* in order around the circle.

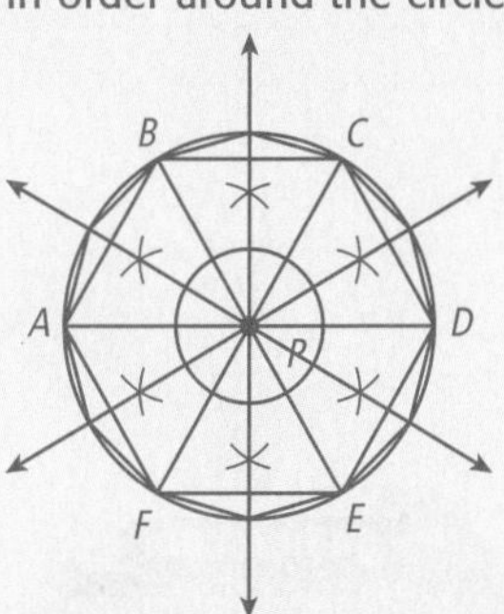

6. See p. A21.

Teacher to Teacher

I like the emphasis on traditional construction in this lab, but I think that technology can be used to complement compass-and-straightedge construction methods. For example, when students use geometry software for one or more of these activities, they can make the polygon larger or smaller and see that the angle measures remain the same.

Loralea Wright
Mauldin, SC

6-1 Organizer

Pacing: Traditional 1 day
Block $\frac{1}{2}$ day

Objectives: Classify polygons based on their sides and angles.

Find and use the measures of interior and exterior angles of polygons.

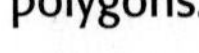

Online Edition
Tutorial Videos, Interactivity

Countdown Week 13

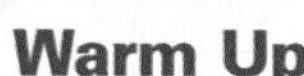

Power Presentations with PowerPoint®

Warm Up

1. A __?__ is a three-sided polygon. triangle
2. A __?__ is a four-sided polygon. quadrilateral

Evaluate each expression for $n = 6$.

3. $(n - 4)12$ 24
4. $(n - 3)90$ 270

Solve for a.

5. $12a + 4a + 9a = 100$ 4

Also available on transparency

Math Humor

Q: What type of figure is like a lost parrot?

A: A polygon!

6-1 Properties and Attributes of Polygons

Objectives
Classify polygons based on their sides and angles.

Find and use the measures of interior and exterior angles of polygons.

Vocabulary
side of a polygon
vertex of a polygon
diagonal
regular polygon
concave
convex

Why learn this?
The opening that lets light into a camera lens is created by an aperture, a set of blades whose edges may form a polygon. (See Example 5.)

In Lesson 2-4, you learned the definition of a polygon. Now you will learn about the parts of a polygon and about ways to classify polygons.

Each segment that forms a polygon is a **side of the polygon**. The common endpoint of two sides is a **vertex of the polygon**. A segment that connects any two nonconsecutive vertices is a **diagonal**.

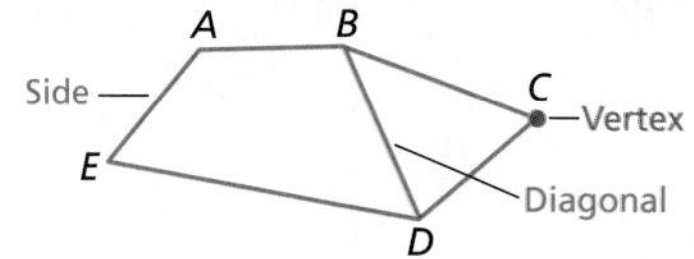

You can name a polygon by the number of its sides. The table shows the names of some common polygons. Polygon *ABCDE* is a pentagon.

Number of Sides	Name of Polygon
3	Triangle
4	Quadrilateral
5	Pentagon
6	Hexagon
7	Heptagon
8	Octagon
9	Nonagon
10	Decagon
12	Dodecagon
n	n-gon

EXAMPLE 1 Identifying Polygons

Remember!
A polygon is a closed plane figure formed by three or more segments that intersect only at their endpoints.

Tell whether each figure is a polygon. If it is a polygon, name it by the number of its sides.

A

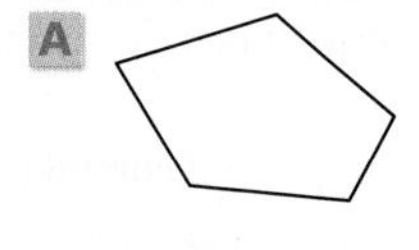

polygon, pentagon

B

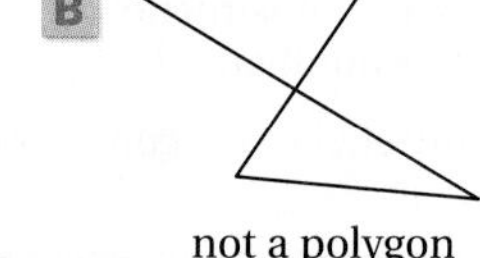

not a polygon

C

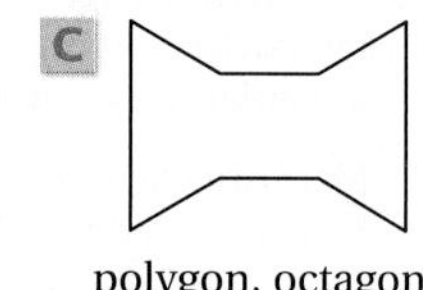

polygon, octagon

Tell whether each figure is a polygon. If it is a polygon, name it by the number of its sides.

1a. **1b.**

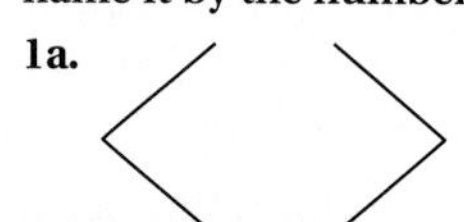

not a polygon polygon, nonagon

1c.

not a polygon

All the sides are congruent in an equilateral polygon. All the angles are congruent in an equiangular polygon. A **regular polygon** is one that is both equilateral and equiangular. If a polygon is not regular, it is called irregular.

State Resources

go.hrw.com
State Resources Online
KEYWORD: MG7 Resources

1 Introduce

EXPLORATION

6-1 Properties and Attributes of Polygons

A *convex polygon* is a polygon in which no diagonal contains points in the exterior of the polygon.

Convex Not Convex

1. Use a straightedge to draw a convex polygon with five sides.
2. Use the straightedge to extend consecutive sides of the polygon, as shown. This forms five exterior angles, ∠1 through ∠5.
3. Use a protractor to measure the exterior angles. What is the sum of the measures of the exterior angles?
4. Repeat the process with convex polygons that have 3, 4, and 6 sides. Record your results in the table.

Number of Sides	3	4	5	6
Sum of Exterior Angle Measures				

5. Compare your results with those of other students. What do you notice?

THINK AND DISCUSS

Motivate

Bring objects to class that show polygons, such as a picture frame, a hexagonal nut, or a pennant. Also bring items with shapes that are not polygons, such as a paper plate or a ball. Ask students to compare both sets of objects. Explain that students will learn properties of polygons in this lesson.

Explorations and answers are provided in *Alternate Openers: Explorations Transparencies.*

A polygon is **concave** if any part of a diagonal contains points in the exterior of the polygon. If no diagonal contains points in the exterior, then the polygon is **convex**. A regular polygon is always convex.

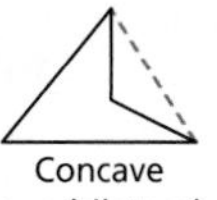
Concave quadrilateral

Convex quadrilateral

EXAMPLE 2 Classifying Polygons

Tell whether each polygon is regular or irregular. Tell whether it is concave or convex.

A
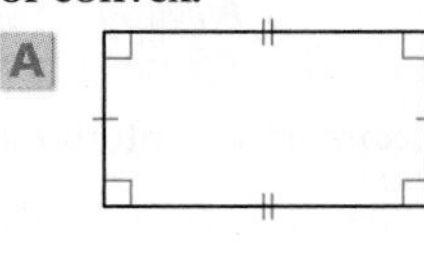
irregular, convex

B
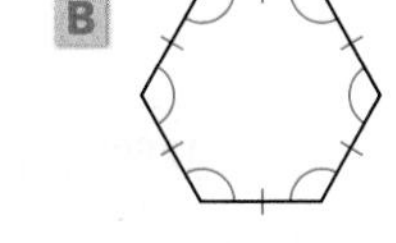
regular, convex

C
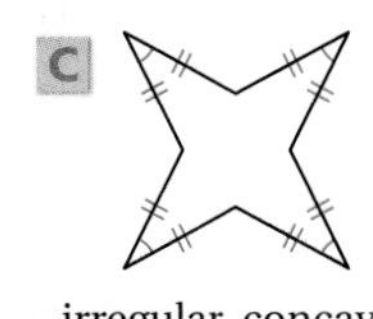
irregular, concave

CHECK IT OUT! **Tell whether each polygon is regular or irregular. Tell whether it is concave or convex.**

2a.
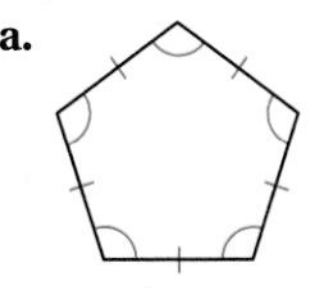
regular, convex

2b.
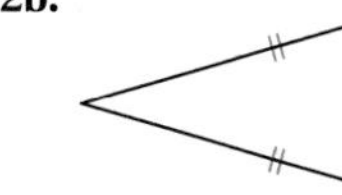
irregular, concave

To find the sum of the interior angle measures of a convex polygon, draw all possible diagonals from one vertex of the polygon. This creates a set of triangles. The sum of the angle measures of all the triangles equals the sum of the angle measures of the polygon.

Remember!
By the Triangle Sum Theorem, the sum of the interior angle measures of a triangle is 180°.

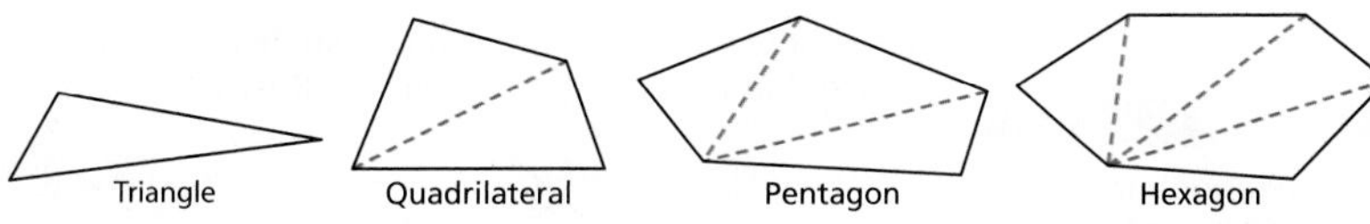

Polygon	Number of Sides	Number of Triangles	Sum of Interior Angle Measures
Triangle	3	1	$(1)180° = 180°$
Quadrilateral	4	2	$(2)180° = 360°$
Pentagon	5	3	$(3)180° = 540°$
Hexagon	6	4	$(4)180° = 720°$
n-gon	n	$n - 2$	$(n - 2)180°$

In each convex polygon, the number of triangles formed is two less than the number of sides n. So the sum of the angle measures of all these triangles is $(n - 2)180°$.

Theorem 6-1-1 **Polygon Angle Sum Theorem**

The sum of the interior angle measures of a convex polygon with n sides is $(n - 2)180°$.

Power Presentations with PowerPoint®

Additional Examples

Example 1

Tell whether each figure is a polygon. If it is a polygon, name it by the number of sides.

A.
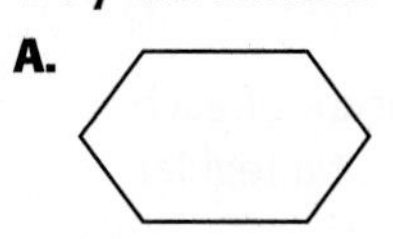
polygon, hexagon

B.
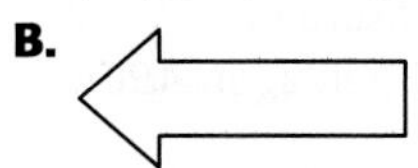
polygon, heptagon

C.
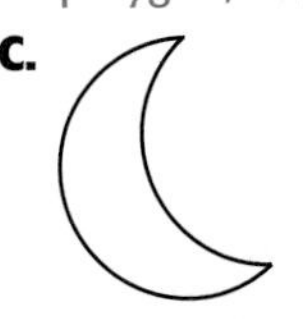
not a polygon

Example 2

Tell whether each polygon is regular or irregular. Tell whether it is concave or convex.

A.
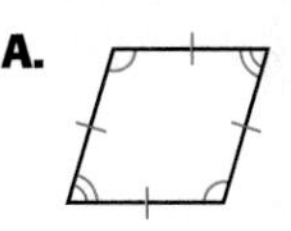
irregular, convex

B.
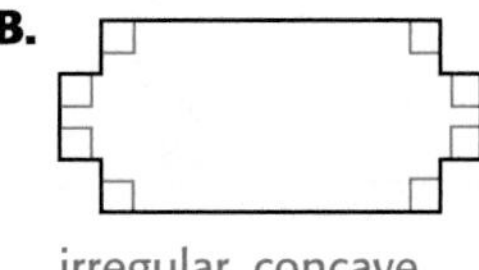
irregular, concave

C.
regular, convex

2 Teach

Guided Instruction

Review the definition of *polygon,* and discuss with students why the figures in Example 1 are or are not polygons. Walk students through the development of both sum formulas, while having them verify the given angle measures with a protractor (MK).

Algebra Review with students how to evaluate algebraic expressions and how to use inverse operations to solve equations.

Reaching All Learners

Through Concrete Manipulatives

Have students fold and crease the four corners of a sheet of paper. Next, ask them to open the folds to reveal a creased polygon shape. Have students classify the polygon. octagon Ask them to find the sum of the interior and exterior angle measures. 1080°; 360° Then have students measure the interior and exterior angles to verify their sums.

INTERVENTION

Questioning Strategies

EXAMPLE 1

- How can you tell whether a figure is a polygon?

EXAMPLE 2

- Explain how you know if a polygon is regular, irregular, concave, or convex.

Critical Thinking Point out the angles larger than 180° in the figure in **Example 2C.**

Power Presentations with PowerPoint®

Additional Examples

Example 3

A. Find the sum of the interior angle measures of a convex heptagon. 900°

B. Find the measure of each interior angle of a regular 16-gon. 157.5°

C. Find the measure of each interior angle of pentagon *ABCDE*.

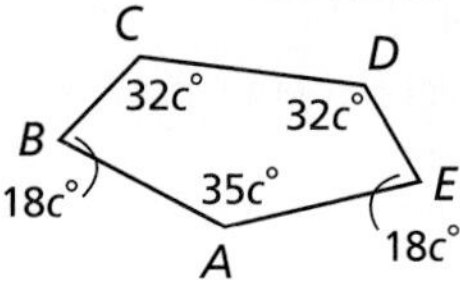

$m\angle A = 140°$; $m\angle B = m\angle E = 72°$; $m\angle C = m\angle D = 128°$

Example 4

A. Find the measure of each exterior angle of a regular 20-gon. 18°

B. Find the value of b in polygon *FGHJKL*.

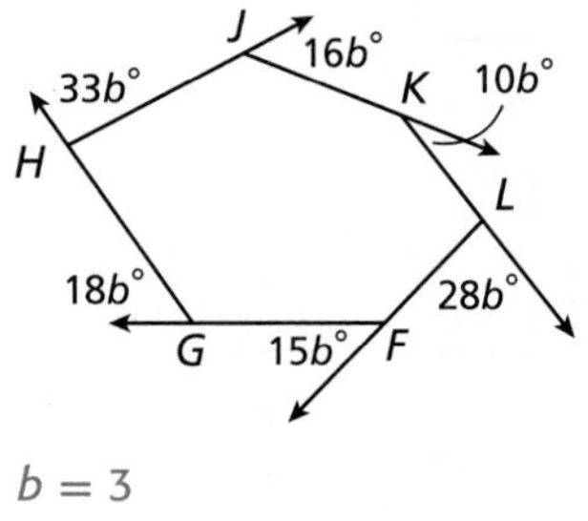

$b = 3$

INTERVENTION

Questioning Strategies

EXAMPLE 3

- How do you use the sum of the interior angle measures of a regular polygon to find the measure of each interior angle?

EXAMPLE 4

- How does finding the measure of an exterior angle differ from finding the measure of an interior angle?

EXAMPLE 3 Finding Interior Angle Measures and Sums in Polygons

A **Find the sum of the interior angle measures of a convex octagon.**

$(n - 2)180°$	*Polygon ∠ Sum Thm.*
$(8 - 2)180°$	*An octagon has 8 sides, so substitute 8 for n.*
$1080°$	*Simplify.*

B **Find the measure of each interior angle of a regular nonagon.**

Step 1 Find the sum of the interior angle measures.

$(n - 2)180°$	*Polygon ∠ Sum Thm.*
$(9 - 2)180° = \mathbf{1260°}$	*Substitute 9 for n and simplify.*

Step 2 Find the measure of one interior angle.

$\frac{1260°}{9} = 140°$ *The int. ∠s are ≅, so divide by 9.*

Algebra

C **Find the measure of each interior angle of quadrilateral *PQRS*.**

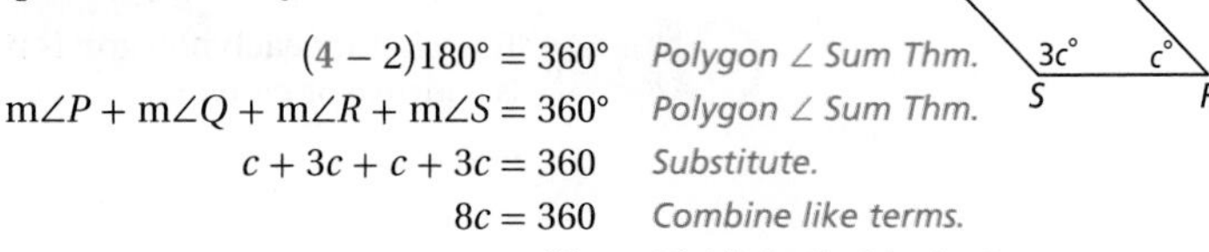

$(4 - 2)180° = 360°$	*Polygon ∠ Sum Thm.*
$m\angle P + m\angle Q + m\angle R + m\angle S = 360°$	*Polygon ∠ Sum Thm.*
$c + 3c + c + 3c = 360$	*Substitute.*
$8c = 360$	*Combine like terms.*
$c = 45$	*Divide both sides by 8.*

$m\angle P = m\angle R = 45°$

$m\angle Q = m\angle S = 3(45°) = 135°$

3a. 2340°

3a. Find the sum of the interior angle measures of a convex 15-gon.

3b. Find the measure of each interior angle of a regular decagon. 144°

In the polygons below, an exterior angle has been measured at each vertex. Notice that in each case, the sum of the exterior angle measures is 360°.

Remember!

An exterior angle is formed by one side of a polygon and the extension of a consecutive side.

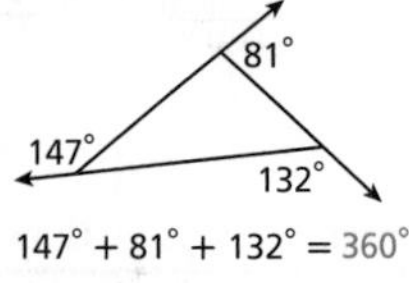

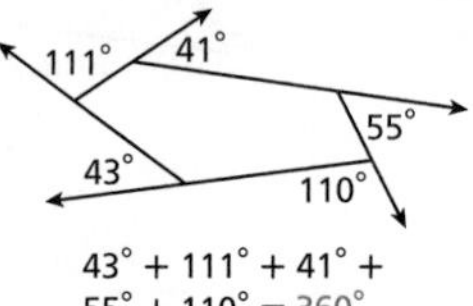

Theorem 6-1-2 Polygon Exterior Angle Sum Theorem

The sum of the exterior angle measures, one angle at each vertex, of a convex polygon is 360°.

EXAMPLE 4 Finding Exterior Angle Measures in Polygons

A **Find the measure of each exterior angle of a regular hexagon.**

A hexagon has 6 sides and 6 vertices.

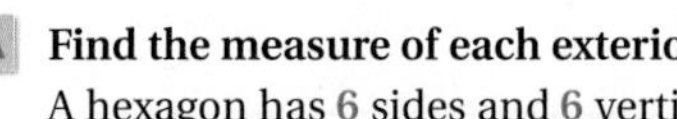

sum of ext. ∠s = **360°**	*Polygon Ext. ∠ Sum Thm.*
measure of one ext. $\angle = \frac{360°}{6} = 60°$	*A regular hexagon has 6 ≅ ext. ∠s, so divide the sum by 6.*

The measure of each exterior angle of a regular hexagon is 60°.

Teaching Tip

Inclusion To clarify the words *concave* and *convex,* provide the class with several polygons cut out of heavyweight construction paper. Have students use a straightedge (MK) as a diagonal to determine if the polygons are *concave* or *convex*.

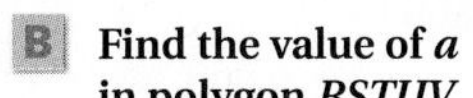

Algebra

B **Find the value of *a* in polygon *RSTUV*.**

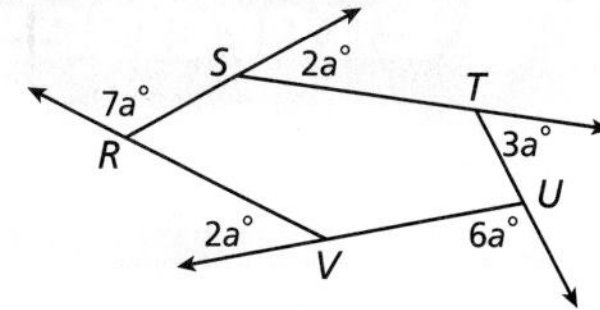

$$7a° + 2a° + 3a° + 6a° + 2a° = 360°$$ *Polygon Ext. ∠ Sum Thm.*

$$20a = 360$$ *Combine like terms.*

$$a = 18$$ *Divide both sides by 20.*

CHECK IT OUT!

4a. Find the measure of each exterior angle of a regular dodecagon. **30°**

4b. Find the value of *r* in polygon *JKLM*. **$r = 15$**

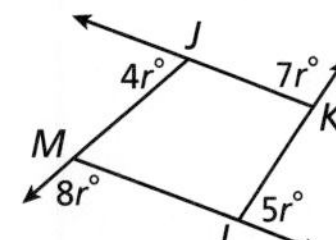

EXAMPLE **5** ***Photography Application***

The aperture of the camera is formed by ten blades. The blades overlap to form a regular decagon. What is the measure of ∠*CBD*?

∠*CBD* is an exterior angle of a regular decagon. By the Polygon Exterior Angle Sum Theorem, the sum of the exterior angle measures is 360°.

$$m\angle CBD = \frac{360°}{10} = 36°$$ *A regular decagon has 10 ≅ ext. ∡, so divide the sum by 10.*

CHECK IT OUT!

5. What if...? Suppose the shutter were formed by 8 blades. What would the measure of each exterior angle be? **45°**

THINK AND DISCUSS

1. Draw a concave pentagon and a convex pentagon. Explain the difference between the two figures.
2. Explain why you cannot use the expression $\frac{360°}{n}$ to find the measure of an exterior angle of an irregular *n*-gon.
3. **GET ORGANIZED** Copy and complete the graphic organizer. In each cell, write the formula for finding the indicated value for a regular convex polygon with *n* sides.

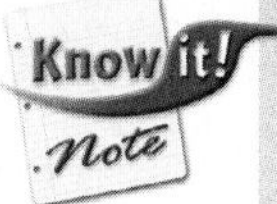

	Interior Angles	Exterior Angles
Sum of Angle Measures		
One Angle Measure		

COMMON ERROR ALERT

Some students may confuse the two theorems in this lesson and incorrectly assume that the sum of the interior angles of a polygon is 360°. Remind students of the Triangle Sum Theorem from Lesson 4-2. Have them draw an equilateral triangle and show that its interior angle measures add to 180° and its exterior angle measures add to 360°.

Power Presentations with PowerPoint®

Additional Examples

Example 5

Ann is making paper stars for party decorations. What is the measure of ∠1? 72°

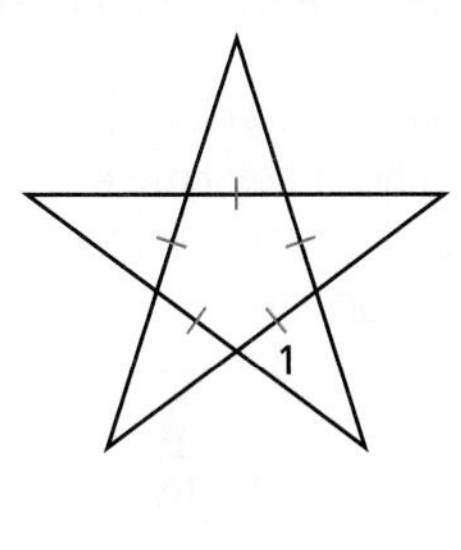

INTERVENTION

Questioning Strategies

EXAMPLE 5

- What happens to the measure of each exterior angle as the number of sides of a regular polygon increases?

3 Close

Summarize

Review the naming of polygons, as shown on page 382. Discuss the difference between irregular and regular polygons, and concave and convex polygons. To review the Polygon Angle Sum Theorem and the Polygon Exterior Angle Sum Theorem, draw a regular pentagon and show how to find its interior and exterior angle measures. 108° and 72°

ONGOING ASSESSMENT and INTERVENTION

***Diagnose Before* the Lesson**
6-1 Warm Up, TE p. 382

***Monitor During* the Lesson**
Check It Out! Exercises, SE pp. 382–385
Questioning Strategies, TE pp. 383–385

***Assess After* the Lesson**
6-1 Lesson Quiz, TE p. 388
Alternative Assessment, TE p. 388

Answers to *Think and Discuss*

1. Possible answers:

Concave pentagon Convex pentagon

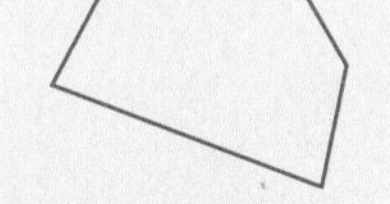

A concave polygon seems to "cave in" or have a dent. A convex polygon does not have a dent.

2. Since the polygon is not reg., you cannot assume that each of the ext. ∡ has the same measure.
3. See p. A5.

6-1 Exercises

6-1 Exercises

go.hrw.com
Homework Help Online
KEYWORD: MG7 6-1
Parent Resources Online
KEYWORD: MG7 Parent

Assignment Guide

Assign *Guided Practice* exercises as necessary.

If you finished Examples **1–3**
- **Basic** 16–24, 29, 30, 35–38, 46–50
- **Average** 16–24, 29, 30, 35–38, 44, 46–50
- **Advanced** 16–24, 29, 30, 35–38, 44, 46–50, 56, 57

If you finished Examples **1–5**
- **Basic** 16–31, 32–42 even, 43, 45–50, 53–55, 60–67
- **Average** 16–46, 51–56, 60–67
- **Advanced** 16–42, 44, 45, 51–67

Homework Quick Check
Quickly check key concepts.
Exercises: 16, 20, 24, 26, 28, 30, 36

Answers

1. Possible answer: If a polygon is equil., all its sides are ≅, but all its ∡ are not necessarily ≅. For a polygon to be reg., all its sides must be ≅, and all its ∡ must be ≅.
9. $m\angle A = m\angle D = 81°$; $m\angle B = 108°$; $m\angle C = m\angle E = 135°$

State Resources

GUIDED PRACTICE

1. **Vocabulary** Explain why an equilateral polygon is not necessarily a *regular* polygon.

SEE EXAMPLE 1 p. 382

Tell whether each outlined shape is a polygon. If it is a polygon, name it by the number of its sides.

2.  polygon, decagon
3. not a polygon
4. polygon, quadrilateral
5. 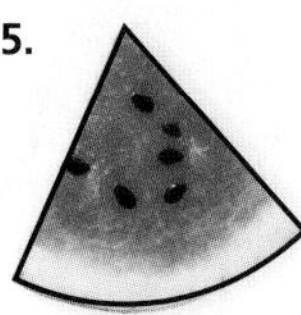 not a polygon

SEE EXAMPLE 2 p. 383

Tell whether each polygon is regular or irregular. Tell whether it is concave or convex.

6. regular, convex
7. irregular, concave
8. irregular, convex

SEE EXAMPLE 3 p. 384

9. Find the measure of each interior angle of pentagon *ABCDE*.
10. Find the measure of each interior angle of a regular dodecagon. 150°
11. Find the sum of the interior angle measures of a convex 20-gon. 3240°

SEE EXAMPLE 4 p. 384

12. Find the value of *y* in polygon *JKLM*. $y = 22.5$
13. Find the measure of each exterior angle of a regular pentagon. 72°

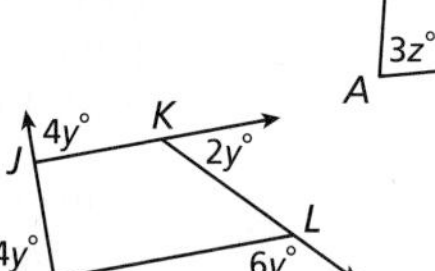

SEE EXAMPLE 5 p. 385

Safety **Use the photograph of the traffic sign for Exercises 14 and 15.**

14. Name the polygon by the number of its sides. pentagon
15. In the polygon, $\angle P$, $\angle R$, and $\angle T$ are right angles, and $\angle Q \cong \angle S$. What are $m\angle Q$ and $m\angle S$? $m\angle Q = m\angle S = 135°$

PRACTICE AND PROBLEM SOLVING

Independent Practice	
For Exercises	See Example
16–18	1
19–21	2
22–24	3
25–26	4
27–28	5

Extra Practice
Skills Practice p. S14
Application Practice p. S33

Tell whether each figure is a polygon. If it is a polygon, name it by the number of its sides.

16. polygon, hexagon
17. not a polygon
18. polygon, quadrilateral

Tell whether each polygon is regular or irregular. Tell whether it is concave or convex.

19. irregular, concave
20. regular, convex
21. irregular, convex

6-1 READING STRATEGIES

Triangle Quadrilateral Pentagon Hexagon Heptagon Octagon Nonagon Decagon Dodecagon

Diagonal
Vertex
Side

1. How many sides does a pentagon have? five
2. Give some examples of pentagons in real life.
   Sample answer: pedestrian crossing street signs
3. How many vertices does a quadrilateral have? four
4. How does the number of vertices of a polygon compare to the number of sides of the same polygon?
   There is an equal number of sides and vertices in polygons.
5. What is the name of a polygon with eight sides? octagon
6. How many diagonals can be drawn from one vertex of a hexagon? three

concave—any part of a diagonal contains points in the exterior of the polygon
convex—no diagonal contains points in the exterior of the polygon

Draw an example of each polygon.

7. convex heptagon
   Sample answer:
8. concave quadrilateral
   Sample answer:

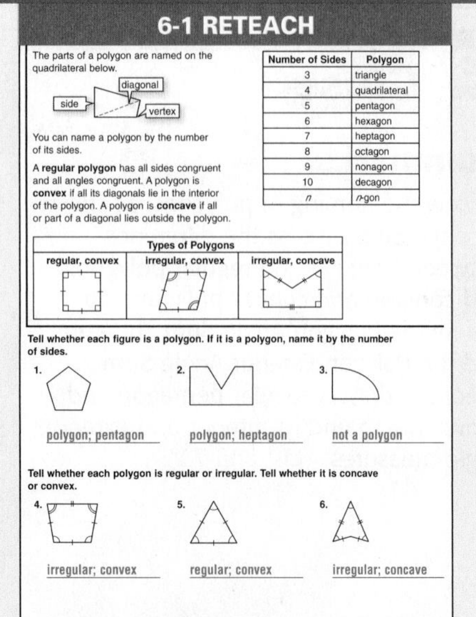

6-1 RETEACH

The parts of a polygon are named on the quadrilateral below.

diagonal
side
vertex

You can name a polygon by the number of its sides.

A **regular polygon** has all sides congruent and all angles congruent. A polygon is **convex** if all its diagonals lie in the interior of the polygon. A polygon is **concave** if all or part of a diagonal lies outside the polygon.

Number of Sides	Polygon
3	triangle
4	quadrilateral
5	pentagon
6	hexagon
7	heptagon
8	octagon
9	nonagon
10	decagon
n	*n*-gon

Types of Polygons		
regular, convex	irregular, convex	irregular, concave

Tell whether each figure is a polygon. If it is a polygon, name it by the number of sides.

1. polygon; pentagon
2. polygon; heptagon
3. not a polygon

Tell whether each polygon is regular or irregular. Tell whether it is concave or convex.

4. irregular; convex
5. regular; convex
6. irregular; concave

22. Find the measure of each interior angle of quadrilateral *RSTV*.

23. Find the measure of each interior angle of a regular 18-gon. **160°**

24. Find the sum of the interior angle measures of a convex heptagon. **900°**

25. Find the measure of each exterior angle of a regular nonagon. **40°**

26. A pentagon has exterior angle measures of $5a°$, $4a°$, $10a°$, $3a°$, and $8a°$. Find the value of a. **12**

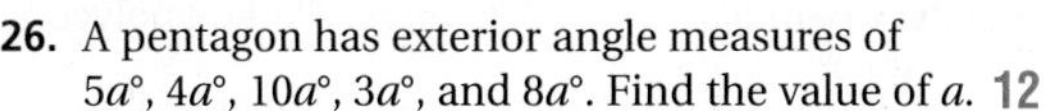

Crafts The folds on the lid of the gift box form a regular hexagon. Find each measure.

27. $m\angle JKM$ **120°**

28. $m\angle MKL$ **60°**

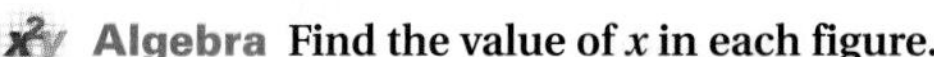

Algebra **Find the value of x in each figure.**

29. 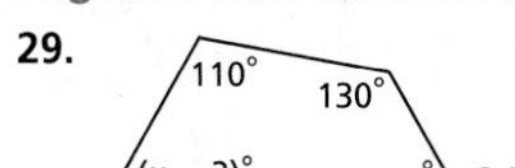

61.5

30. 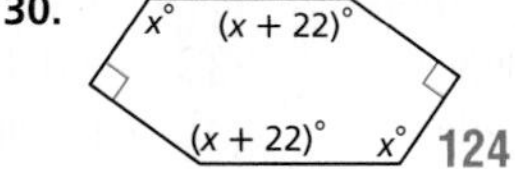

124

31. 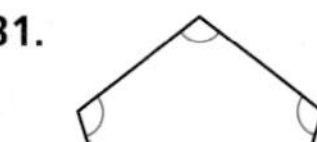

72

Find the number of sides a regular polygon must have to meet each condition.

32. Each interior angle measure equals each exterior angle measure. **4**

33. Each interior angle measure is four times the measure of each exterior angle. **10**

34. Each exterior angle measure is one eighth the measure of each interior angle. **18**

Name the convex polygon whose interior angle measures have each given sum.

35. 540° **pentagon** **36.** 900° **heptagon** **37.** 1800° **dodecagon** **38.** 2520° **16-gon**

Multi-Step **An exterior angle measure of a regular polygon is given. Find the number of its sides and the measure of each interior angle.**

39. 120° **3; 60°** **40.** 72° **5; 108°** **41.** 36° **10; 144°** **42.** 24° **15; 156°**

43. **ERROR ANALYSIS** Which conclusion is incorrect? Explain the error.

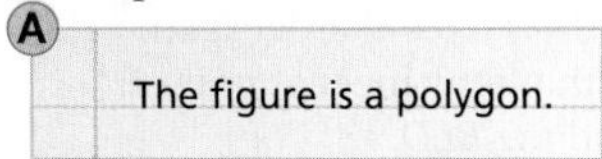

A
The figure is a polygon.

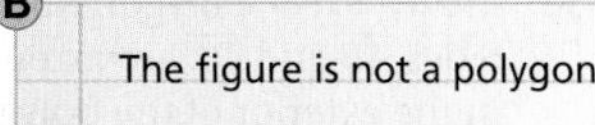

B
The figure is not a polygon.

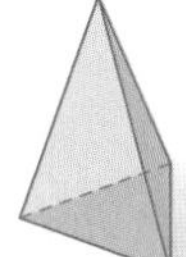

44. **Estimation** Graph the polygon formed by the points $A(-2, -6)$, $B(-4, -1)$, $C(-1, 2)$, $D(4, 0)$, and $E(3, -5)$. Estimate the measure of each interior angle. Make a conjecture about whether the polygon is equiangular. Now measure each interior angle with a protractor. Was your conjecture correct?

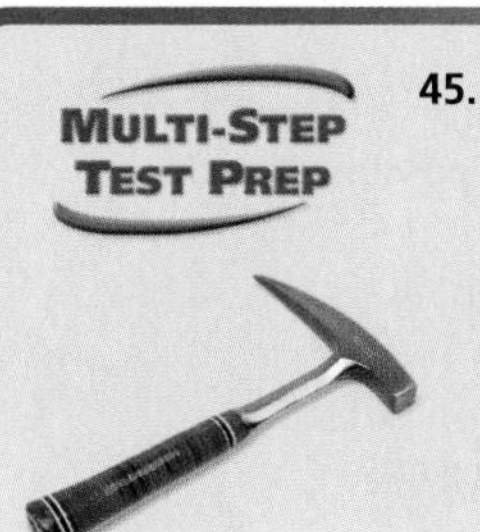

MULTI-STEP TEST PREP

45. This problem will prepare you for the Multi-Step Test Prep on page 406.

In this quartz crystal, $m\angle A = 95°$, $m\angle B = 125°$, $m\angle E = m\angle D = 130°$, and $\angle C \cong \angle F \cong \angle G$.

a. Name polygon *ABCDEFG* by the number of sides. **heptagon**

b. What is the sum of the interior angle measures of *ABCDEFG*? **900°**

c. Find $m\angle F$. **140°**

COMMON ERROR ALERT

If a diagram is not provided, suggest that students draw the polygon themselves. In **Exercises 39–42,** point out that the word *regular* is necessary to solve these problems.

MULTI-STEP TEST PREP **Exercise 45** involves classifying polygons in crystals and finding interior angle measures. This exercise prepares students for the Multi-Step Test Prep on page 406.

Answers

22. $m\angle R = m\angle T = 48°$; $m\angle S = 144°$; $m\angle V = 120°$

43. A; possible answer: this is not a plane figure, so it cannot be a polygon.

44. 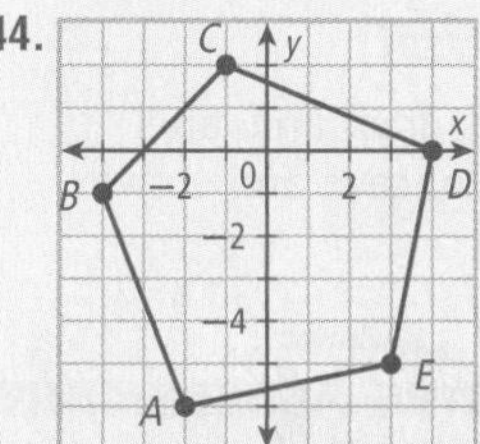

Check students' estimates; possible answer: the pentagon is not equiangular; $m\angle A = 100°$; $m\angle B = 113°$; $m\angle C = 113°$; $m\angle D = 101°$; $m\angle E = 113°$; yes, the pentagon is not equiangular.

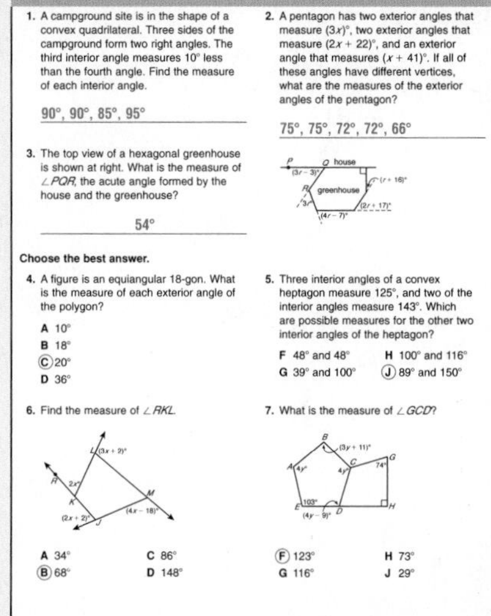

6-1 PROBLEM SOLVING

1. A campground site is in the shape of a convex quadrilateral. Three sides of the campground form two right angles. The third interior angle measures 10° less than the fourth angle. Find the measure of each interior angle. **90°, 90°, 85°, 95°**

2. A pentagon has two exterior angles that measure $(3x)°$, two exterior angles that measure $(2x + 22)°$, and an exterior angle that measures $(x + 41)°$. If all of these angles have different vertices, what are the measures of the exterior angles of the pentagon? **75°, 75°, 72°, 72°, 66°**

3. The top view of a hexagonal greenhouse is shown at right. What is the measure of $\angle PQR$, the acute angle formed by the house and the greenhouse? **54°**

Choose the best answer.

4. A figure is an equiangular 18-gon. What is the measure of each exterior angle of the polygon?
A 10°
B 18°
(C) 20°
D 36°

5. Three interior angles of a convex heptagon measure 125°, and two of the interior angles measure 143°. Which are possible measures for the other two interior angles of the heptagon?
F 48° and 48°
H 100° and 116°
G 39° and 100°
(J) 89° and 150°

6. Find the measure of $\angle RKL$.
A 34°
C 86°
(B) 68°
D 148°

7. What is the measure of $\angle GCD$?
(F) 123°
H 73°
G 116°
J 29°

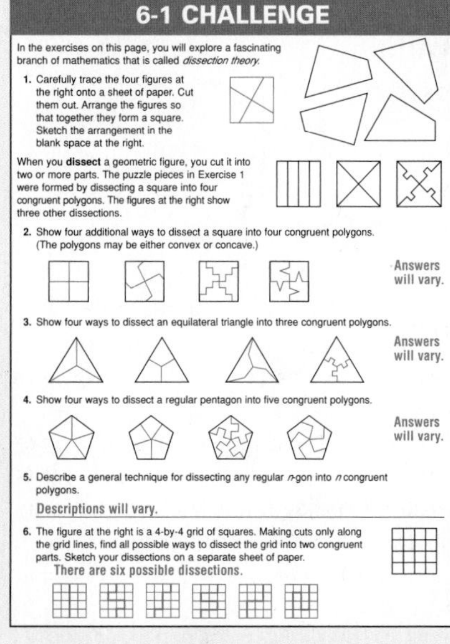

6-1 CHALLENGE

In the exercises on this page, you will explore a fascinating branch of mathematics that is called *dissection theory*.

1. Carefully trace the four figures at the right onto a sheet of paper. Cut them out. Arrange the figures so that together they form a square. Sketch the arrangement in the blank space at the right.

When you **dissect** a geometric figure, you cut it into two or more parts. The puzzle pieces in Exercise 1 were formed by dissecting a square into four congruent polygons. The figures at the right show three other dissections.

2. Show four additional ways to dissect a square into four congruent polygons. (The polygons may be either convex or concave.) **Answers will vary.**

3. Show four ways to dissect an equilateral triangle into three congruent polygons. **Answers will vary.**

4. Show four ways to dissect a regular pentagon into five congruent polygons. **Answers will vary.**

5. Describe a general technique for dissecting any regular n-gon into n congruent polygons. **Descriptions will vary.**

6. The figure at the right is a 4-by-4 grid of squares. Making cuts only along the grid lines, find all possible ways to dissect the grid into two congruent parts. Sketch your dissections on a separate sheet of paper. **There are six possible dissections.**

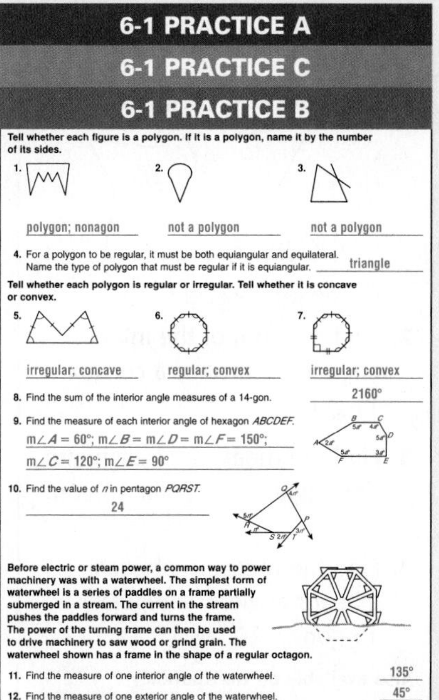

6-1 PRACTICE A
6-1 PRACTICE C
6-1 PRACTICE B

Tell whether each figure is a polygon. If it is a polygon, name it by the number of its sides.

1. **polygon; nonagon**
2. **not a polygon**
3. **not a polygon**

4. For a polygon to be regular, it must be both equiangular and equilateral. Name the type of polygon that must be regular if it is equiangular. **triangle**

Tell whether each polygon is regular or irregular. Tell whether it is concave or convex.

5. **irregular; concave**
6. **regular; convex**
7. **irregular; convex**

8. Find the sum of the interior angle measures of a 14-gon. **2160°**

9. Find the measure of each interior angle of hexagon *ABCDEF*.
$m\angle A = 60°$; $m\angle B = m\angle D = m\angle F = 150°$; $m\angle C = 120°$; $m\angle E = 90°$

10. Find the value of n in pentagon *PQRST*. **24**

Before electric or steam power, a common way to power machinery was with a waterwheel. The simplest form of waterwheel is a series of paddles on a frame partially submerged in a stream. The current in the stream pushes the paddles forward and turns the frame. The power of the turning frame can then be used to drive machinery to saw wood or grind grain. The waterwheel shown has a frame in the shape of a regular octagon.

11. Find the measure of one interior angle of the waterwheel. **135°**

12. Find the measure of one exterior angle of the waterwheel. **45°**

For **Exercise 55,** encourage students to write an equation to organize the information in the problem. If students chose **C,** they may have assumed that $m\angle C = m\angle D$, instead of $m\angle C = 2m\angle D$. If students chose **B,** they may have found $m\angle D$ instead of $m\angle C$.

Answers

47. Possible answer:

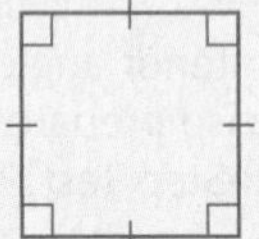

48. Possible answer:

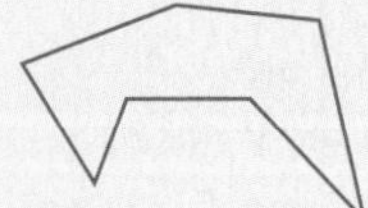

Journal

Have students draw and label examples of concave and convex polygons.

ALTERNATIVE ASSESSMENT

Have students cut out two polygons and name them based on the number of sides. Then have students cut out a convex pentagon. Have them find the sum of its interior and exterior angle measures. Have students use a protractor to verify their sums.

Power Presentations with PowerPoint®

6-1 Lesson Quiz

1. Name the polygon by the number of its sides. Then tell whether the polygon is regular or irregular, concave or convex.

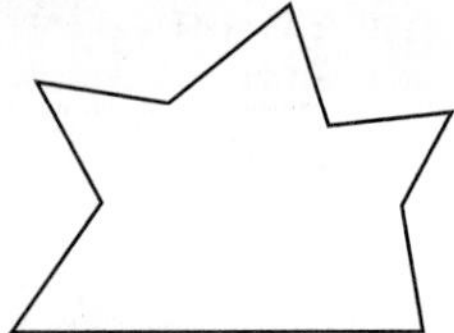

nonagon; irregular; concave

2. Find the sum of the interior angle measures of a convex 11-gon. 1620°
3. Find the measure of each interior angle of a regular 18-gon. 160°
4. Find the measure of each exterior angle of a regular 15-gon. 24°

Also available on transparency

46. The perimeter of a regular polygon is 45 inches. The length of one side is 7.5 inches. Name the polygon by the number of its sides. **hexagon**

Draw an example of each figure.

47. a regular quadrilateral
48. an irregular concave heptagon
49. an irregular convex pentagon
50. an equilateral polygon that is not equiangular

51. **Write About It** Use the terms from the lesson to describe the figure as specifically as possible.

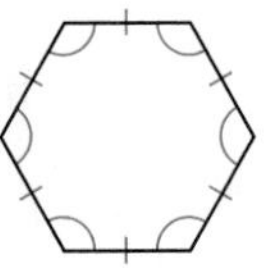

52. **Critical Thinking** What geometric figure does a regular polygon begin to resemble as the number of sides increases? **circle**

TEST PREP

53. Which terms describe the figure shown?
I. quadrilateral II. concave III. regular
(A) I only (C) I and II
(B) II only (D) I and III

54. Which statement is NOT true about a regular 16-gon?
(F) It is a convex polygon.
(G) It has 16 congruent sides.
(H) The sum of the interior angle measures is 2880°.
(J) The sum of the exterior angles, one at each vertex, is 360°.

55. In polygon $ABCD$, $m\angle A = 49°$, $m\angle B = 107°$, and $m\angle C = 2m\angle D$. What is $m\angle C$?
(A) 24° (B) 68° (C) 102° (D) 136°

CHALLENGE AND EXTEND

56. The interior angle measures of a convex pentagon are consecutive multiples of 4. Find the measure of each interior angle. **100°; 104°; 108°; 112°; 116°**

57. Polygon $PQRST$ is a regular pentagon. Find the values of x, y, and z. $x = 36$; $y = 36$; $z = 72$

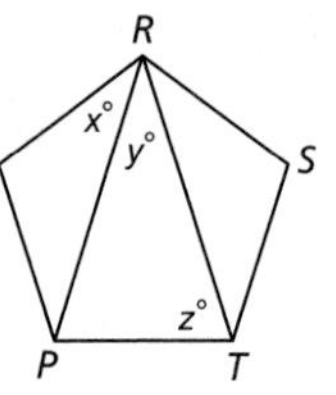

58. **Multi-Step** Polygon $ABCDEFGHJK$ is a regular decagon. Sides $\overline{AB}$ and $\overline{DE}$ are extended so that they meet at point L in the exterior of the polygon. Find $m\angle BLD$. **72°**

59. **Critical Thinking** Does the Polygon Angle Sum Theorem work for concave polygons? Draw a sketch to support your answer. **Yes, if you allow for ∠ measures greater than 180°.**

SPIRAL REVIEW

Solve by factoring. *(Previous course)*

60. $x^2 + 3x - 10 = 0$ $x = -5$ or $x = 2$
61. $x^2 - x - 12 = 0$ $x = -3$ or $x = 4$
62. $x^2 - 12x = -35$ $x = 5$ or $x = 7$

The lengths of two sides of a triangle are given. Find the range of possible lengths for the third side. *(Lesson 5-5)*

63. 4, 4 $0 < x < 8$
64. 6, 12 $6 < x < 18$
65. 3, 7 $4 < x < 10$

Find each side length for a 30°-60°-90° triangle. *(Lesson 5-8)*

66. the length of the hypotenuse when the length of the shorter leg is 6 **12**
67. the length of the longer leg when the length of the hypotenuse is 10 $5\sqrt{3}$

Answers

49. Possible answer:

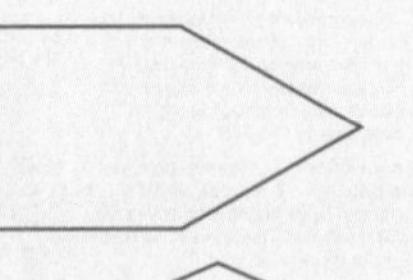

50. Possible answer:

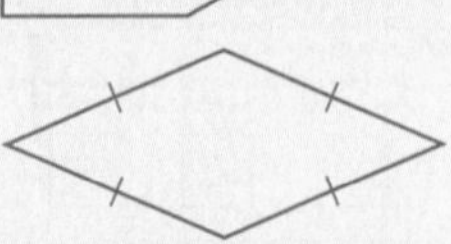

51. The figure has 6 sides, so it is a hexagon. The 6 sides are ≅, so the hexagon is equilateral. The 6 ∠s are ≅, so the hexagon is equiangular. Since the hexagon is equilateral and equiangular, it is regular. No diagonal contains points in the exterior, so it is convex.

59. Possible answer:

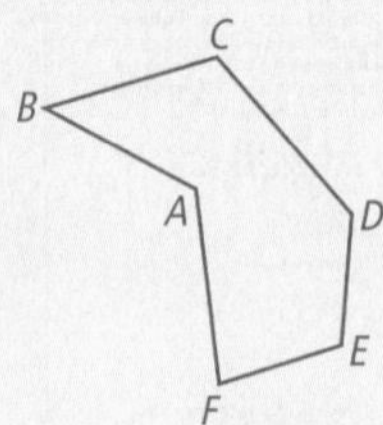

$m\angle A + m\angle B + m\angle C + m\angle D + m\angle E + m\angle F = 720°$

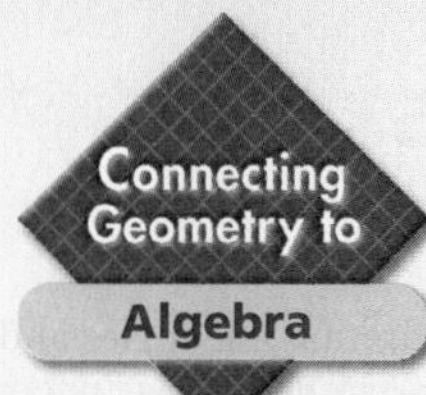

Relations and Functions

Many numeric relationships in geometry can be represented by algebraic relations. These relations may or may not be functions, depending on their domain and range.

A *relation* is a set of ordered pairs. All the first coordinates in the set of ordered pairs are the *domain* of the relation. All the second coordinates are the *range* of the relation.

A *function* is a type of relation that pairs each element in the domain with exactly one element in the range.

Example

Give the domain and range of the relation $y = \frac{6}{x-6}$. Tell whether the relation is a function.

Step 1 Make a table of values for the relation.

x	−6	0	5	6	7	12
y	−0.5	−1	−6	Undefined	6	1

Step 2 Plot the points and connect them with smooth curves.

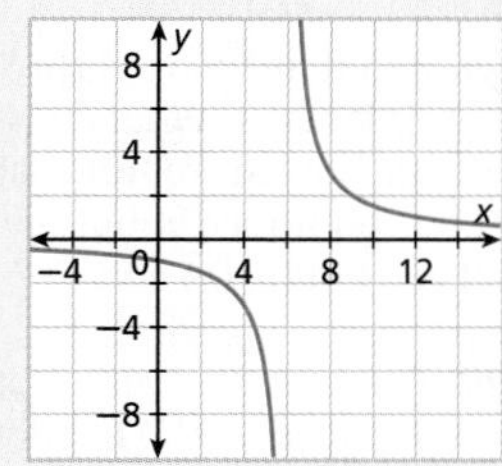

Step 3 Identify the domain and range.
Since y is undefined at $x = 6$, the domain of the relation is the set of all real numbers except 6. Since there is no x-value such that $y = 0$, the range of the relation is the set of all real numbers except 0.

Step 4 Determine whether the relation is a function.
From the graph, you can see that only one y-value exists for each x-value, so the relation is a function.

Try This

Give the domain and range of each relation. Tell whether the relation is a function.

1. $y = (x - 2)180$
2. $y = 360$
3. $y = \frac{(x-2)180}{x}$
4. $y = \frac{360}{x}$
5. $x = 3y - 10$
6. $x^2 + y^2 = 9$
7. $x = -2$
8. $y = x^2 + 4$
9. $-x + 8y = 5$

Answers to *Try This*

1. D: all real numbers; R: all real numbers; function
2. D: all real numbers; R: 360; function
3. D: all real numbers except 0; R: all real numbers except 180; function
4. D: all real numbers except 0; R: all real numbers except 0; function
5. D: all real numbers; R: all real numbers; function
6. D: $-3 \le x \le 3$; R: $-3 \le y \le 3$; not a function
7. D: −2; R: all real numbers; not a function
8. D: all real numbers; R: $y \ge 4$; function
9. D: all real numbers; R: all real numbers; function

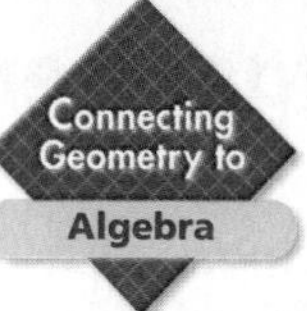

Organizer

Pacing:
Traditional $\frac{1}{2}$ day
Block $\frac{1}{4}$ day

Objective: Apply the polygon formulas learned in Lesson 6-1 to identifying relations, functions, domain, and range.

Teach

Remember

Students compare relations and functions and review the concepts of domain and range.

Visual In the example, $x = 6$ and $y = 0$ are both asymptotes. Remind students that an asymptote is a line the graph approaches as the absolute value of the variable increases.

Close

Assess

Ask students to use domain and range to explain whether the relation $y = \frac{-5x + 9}{3}$ is a function. D: all real numbers; R: all real numbers; function

State Resources

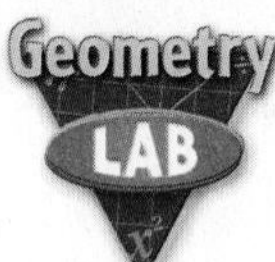

Organizer

Use with Lesson 6-2

Pacing:
Traditional $\frac{1}{2}$ day
Block $\frac{1}{4}$ day

Objective: Explore properties of parallelograms.

Materials: index cards, patty paper, ruler

Online Edition

Countdown Week 13

Resources

Geometry Lab Activities
6-2 Lab Recording Sheet

Teach

Discuss

Point out to students that if they have drawn their parallelograms correctly, each overlay involves a simple translation of ▱*QRST*.

Alternative Approach

Provide students with cutouts of congruent parallelograms to use.

Close

Key Concept

The opposite sides and opposite angles of a parallelogram are congruent. Consecutive angles are supplementary, and the diagonals bisect each other.

Assessment

Journal Have students summarize the relationships they discovered about parallelograms.

State Resources

6-2

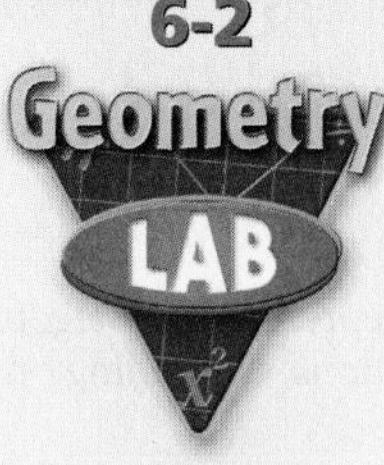

Use with Lesson 6-2

Explore Properties of Parallelograms

In this lab you will investigate the relationships among the angles and sides of a special type of quadrilateral called a *parallelogram*. You will need to apply the Transitive Property of Congruence. That is, if figure $A \cong$ figure B and figure $B \cong$ figure C, then figure $A \cong$ figure C.

Activity

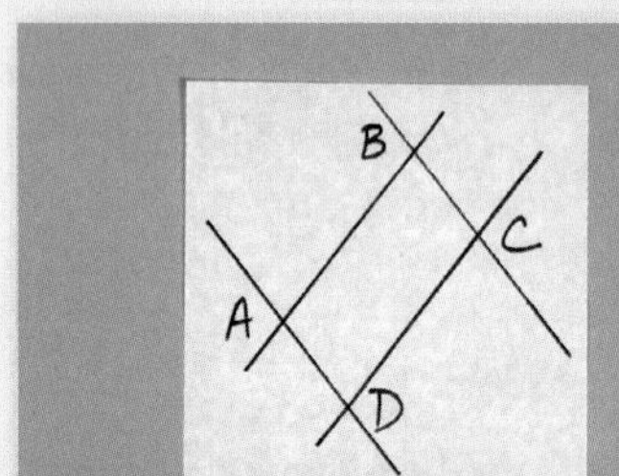

1. Use opposite sides of an index card to draw a set of parallel lines on a piece of patty paper. Then use opposite sides of a ruler to draw a second set of parallel lines that intersects the first. Label the points of intersection *A*, *B*, *C*, and *D*, in that order. Quadrilateral *ABCD* has two pairs of parallel sides. It is a *parallelogram*.
   Check students' work.
2. Place a second piece of patty paper over the first and trace *ABCD*. Label the points that correspond to *A*, *B*, *C*, and *D* as *Q*, *R*, *S*, and *T*, in that order. The parallelograms *ABCD* and *QRST* are congruent. Name all the pairs of congruent corresponding sides and angles.

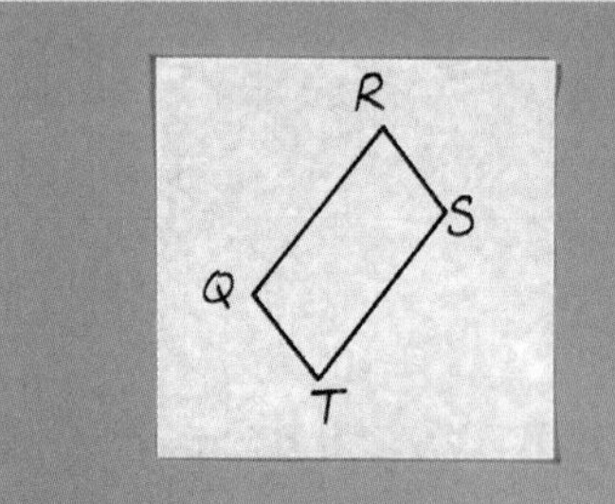

3. Lay *ABCD* over *QRST* so that $\overline{AB}$ overlays $\overline{ST}$. What do you notice about their lengths? What does this tell you about $\overline{AB}$ and $\overline{CD}$? Now move *ABCD* so that $\overline{DA}$ overlays $\overline{RS}$. What do you notice about their lengths? What does this tell you about $\overline{DA}$ and $\overline{BC}$?
   $AB = ST$; $\overline{AB} \cong \overline{CD}$; $DA = RS$; $\overline{DA} \cong \overline{BC}$
4. Lay *ABCD* over *QRST* so that $\angle A$ overlays $\angle S$. What do you notice about their measures? What does this tell you about $\angle A$ and $\angle C$? Now move *ABCD* so that $\angle B$ overlays $\angle T$. What do you notice about their measures? What does this tell you about $\angle B$ and $\angle D$?
   $m\angle A = m\angle S$; $\angle A \cong \angle C$; $m\angle B = m\angle T$; $\angle B \cong \angle D$
5. Arrange the pieces of patty paper so that $\overline{RS}$ overlays $\overline{AD}$. What do you notice about $\overline{QR}$ and $\overline{AB}$? What does this tell you about $\angle A$ and $\angle R$? What can you conclude about $\angle A$ and $\angle B$?
6. Draw diagonals $\overline{AC}$ and $\overline{BD}$. Fold *ABCD* so that *A* matches *C*, making a crease. Unfold the paper and fold it again so that *B* matches *D*, making another crease. What do you notice about the creases? What can you conclude about the diagonals?
   The creases intersect at the same pt. where $\overline{AC}$ and $\overline{BD}$ intersect. So the diags. intersect at the mdpt. of each, and therefore the diags. bisect each other.

Try This

1. Repeat the above steps with a different parallelogram. Do you get the same results? **Check students' work. They should obtain the same results.**
2. **Make a Conjecture** How do you think the sides of a parallelogram are related to each other? the angles? the diagonals? Write your conjectures as conditional statements.

Answers to *Activity*

2. $\overline{QR} \cong \overline{AB}$; $\overline{RS} \cong \overline{BC}$; $\overline{ST} \cong \overline{CD}$; $\overline{TQ} \cong \overline{DA}$; $\angle Q \cong \angle A$; $\angle R \cong \angle B$; $\angle S \cong \angle C$; $\angle T \cong \angle D$
5. $\overline{QR}$ and $\overline{AB}$ are collinear. $\angle A$ and $\angle R$ form a lin. pair, so $\angle A$ is supp. to $\angle R$. Since $\angle R \cong \angle B$, $\angle A$ is supp. to $\angle B$.

Answers to *Try This*

2. Possible answers: If a quad. is a ▱, then its opp. sides are ≅. If a quad. is a ▱, then its opp. ∠s are ≅. If a quad. is a ▱, then its cons. ∠s are supp. If a quad. is a ▱, then its diags. intersect at their mdpts.

6-2 Properties of Parallelograms

Objectives
Prove and apply properties of parallelograms.
Use properties of parallelograms to solve problems.

Vocabulary
parallelogram

Who uses this?
Race car designers can use a parallelogram-shaped linkage to keep the wheels of the car vertical on uneven surfaces. (See Example 1.)

Any polygon with four sides is a quadrilateral. However, some quadrilaterals have special properties. These *special quadrilaterals* are given their own names.

Helpful Hint
Opposite sides of a quadrilateral do not share a vertex. Opposite angles do not share a side.

A quadrilateral with two pairs of parallel sides is a **parallelogram**. To write the name of a parallelogram, you use the symbol ▱.

Parallelogram *ABCD*
▱*ABCD*

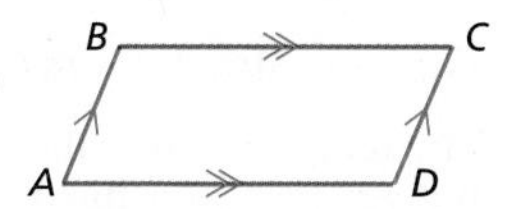

$\overline{AB} \parallel \overline{CD}$, $\overline{BC} \parallel \overline{DA}$

Theorem 6-2-1 Properties of Parallelograms

THEOREM	HYPOTHESIS	CONCLUSION
If a quadrilateral is a parallelogram, then its opposite sides are congruent. (▱ → opp. sides ≅)	B, C, A, D	$\overline{AB} \cong \overline{CD}$ $\overline{BC} \cong \overline{DA}$

PROOF

Theorem 6-2-1

Given: *JKLM* is a parallelogram.
Prove: $\overline{JK} \cong \overline{LM}$, $\overline{KL} \cong \overline{MJ}$

Proof:

Statements	Reasons
1. *JKLM* is a parallelogram.	**1.** Given
2. $\overline{JK} \parallel \overline{LM}$, $\overline{KL} \parallel \overline{MJ}$	**2.** Def. of ▱
3. $\angle 1 \cong \angle 2$, $\angle 3 \cong \angle 4$	**3.** Alt. Int. ∠s Thm.
4. $\overline{JL} \cong \overline{JL}$	**4.** Reflex. Prop. of ≅
5. $\triangle JKL \cong \triangle LMJ$	**5.** ASA *Steps 3, 4*
6. $\overline{JK} \cong \overline{LM}$, $\overline{KL} \cong \overline{MJ}$	**6.** CPCTC

6-2 Organizer

Pacing: Traditional 1 day
Block $\frac{1}{2}$ day

Objectives: Prove and apply properties of parallelograms.
Use properties of parallelograms to solve problems.

Technology Lab
In *Technology Lab Activities*

Online Edition
Tutorial Videos

Countdown Week 13

Power Presentations with PowerPoint®

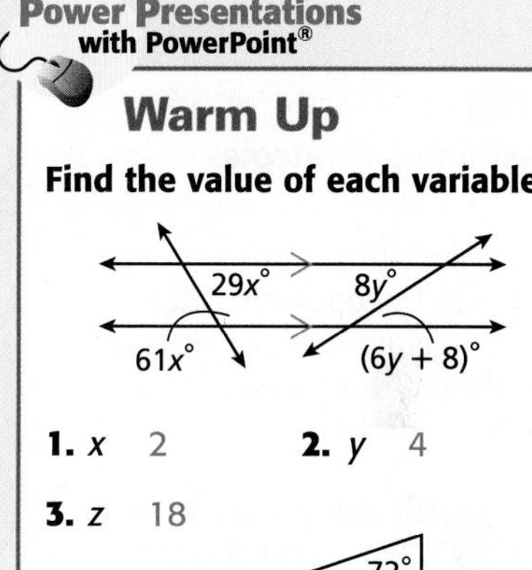

Q: What do you call an urgent message sent across a parallel network?
A: A parallelogram.

1 Introduce

EXPLORATION

6-2 Properties of Parallelograms

A *parallelogram* is a quadrilateral with two pairs of parallel sides. Use geometry software to explore the properties of parallelograms.

1. Draw a line and a point not on the line.	2. Use the Construct menu to draw a line through the point that is parallel to the first line.
3. Repeat Steps 1 and 2 to draw another pair of parallel lines.	4. Construct the intersections of the lines. Label the points of intersection *A*, *B*, *C*, and *D*.

5. Measure the angles of parallelogram *ABCD*. What do you notice? Drag the vertices of *ABCD* to see if the same relationships hold for parallelograms with different shapes.
6. Measure the sides of parallelogram *ABCD*. What do you

Motivate

Draw two parallel lines cut by two parallel transversals. Explain that the resulting figure is a parallelogram. Ask students to locate examples of parallelograms in the classroom, such as the wall, the tile on the floor, or the door.

Explorations and answers are provided in *Alternate Openers: Explorations Transparencies.*

Power Presentations with PowerPoint®

Additional Examples

Example 1

In ▱CDEF, DE = 74 mm, DG = 31 mm, and m∠FCD = 42°. Find each measure.

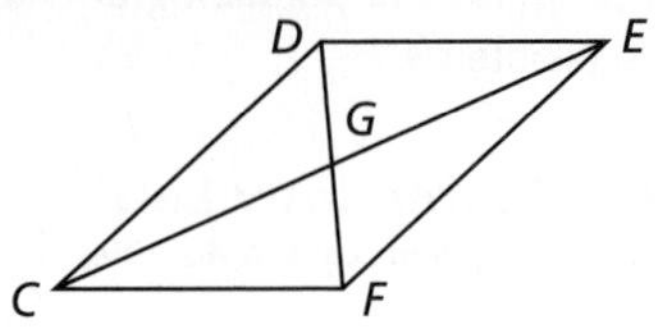

A. *CF* 74 mm

B. m∠*EFC* 138°

C. *DF* 62 mm

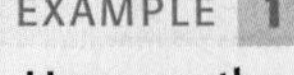

INTERVENTION

Questioning Strategies

EXAMPLE 1

- How are the opposite sides of a parallelogram related? How are the diagonals of a parallelogram related?

Teaching Tip **Diversity** Explain that a *tangram* (MK) is an ancient Chinese puzzle made up of seven polygons that fit together in a square. It always includes a parallelogram as one piece. Point out that the key to solving the puzzle is often the correct placement of the parallelogram.

Know it! Note

Theorems Properties of Parallelograms

THEOREM		HYPOTHESIS	CONCLUSION
6-2-2	If a quadrilateral is a parallelogram, then its opposite angles are congruent. (▱ → opp. ∠s ≅)	Parallelogram ABCD	∠A ≅ ∠C ∠B ≅ ∠D
6-2-3	If a quadrilateral is a parallelogram, then its consecutive angles are supplementary. (▱ → cons. ∠s supp.)	Parallelogram ABCD	m∠A + m∠B = 180° m∠B + m∠C = 180° m∠C + m∠D = 180° m∠D + m∠A = 180°
6-2-4	If a quadrilateral is a parallelogram, then its diagonals bisect each other. (▱ → diags. bisect each other)	Parallelogram ABCD with diagonals meeting at Z	$\overline{AZ} \cong \overline{CZ}$ $\overline{BZ} \cong \overline{DZ}$

You will prove Theorems 6-2-3 and 6-2-4 in Exercises 45 and 44.

EXAMPLE 1 *Racing Application*

The diagram shows the parallelogram-shaped linkage that joins the frame of a race car to one wheel of the car. In ▱PQRS, QR = 48 cm, RT = 30 cm, and m∠QPS = 73°. Find each measure.

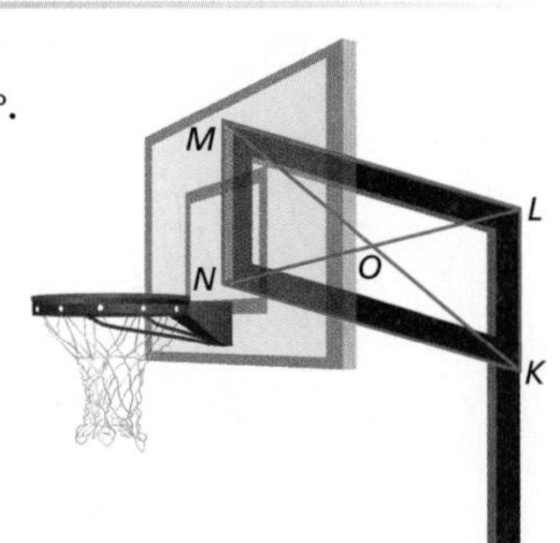

A *PS*

$\overline{PS} \cong \overline{QR}$	*▱ → opp. sides ≅*
$PS = QR$	*Def. of ≅ segs.*
$PS = 48$ cm	*Substitute 48 for QR.*

B m∠*PQR*

$m\angle PQR + m\angle QPS = 180°$	*▱ → cons. ∠s supp.*
$m\angle PQR + 73 = 180$	*Substitute 73 for m∠QPS.*
$m\angle PQR = 107°$	*Subtract 73 from both sides.*

C *PT*

$\overline{PT} \cong \overline{RT}$	*▱ → diags. bisect each other*
$PT = RT$	*Def. of ≅ segs.*
$PT = 30$ cm	*Substitute 30 for RT.*

CHECK IT OUT! **In ▱KLMN, LM = 28 in., LN = 26 in., and m∠LKN = 74°. Find each measure.**

1a. *KN* 28 in.

1b. m∠*NML* 74°

1c. *LO* 13 in.

M, L, N, O, K

2 Teach

Guided Instruction

Review the relationships among angle pairs formed by parallel lines and a transversal. As you discuss the four theorems in the lesson, explain that their proofs use CPCTC or these angle pairs.

Reaching All Learners

Through Visual Cues

Have students draw three parallelograms. Then have them use colored pencils to mark the pairs of congruent sides on one parallelogram, the pairs of congruent angles on the second parallelogram, and the pairs of supplementary angles on the third parallelogram.

EXAMPLE 2 Using Properties of Parallelograms to Find Measures

x^2y Algebra

ABCD is a parallelogram. Find each measure.

A AD

$\overline{AD} \cong \overline{BC}$	*▱ → opp. sides ≅*
$AD = BC$	*Def. of ≅ segs.*
$7x = 5x + 19$	*Substitute the given values.*
$2x = 19$	*Subtract 5x from both sides.*
$x = 9.5$	*Divide both sides by 2.*

$AD = 7x = 7(9.5) = 66.5$

B: $5x + 19$, C, $(6y + 5)°$, $(10y - 1)°$, A, $7x$, D

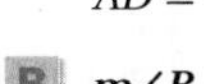

B $m\angle B$

$m\angle A + m\angle B = 180°$	*▱ → cons. ∡ supp.*
$(10y - 1) + (6y + 5) = 180$	*Substitute the given values.*
$16y + 4 = 180$	*Combine like terms.*
$16y = 176$	*Subtract 4 from both sides.*
$y = 11$	*Divide both sides by 16.*

$m\angle B = (6y + 5)° = [6(11) + 5]° = 71°$

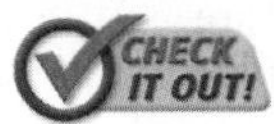

CHECK IT OUT!

EFGH is a parallelogram. Find each measure.

2a. JG 12

2b. FH 18

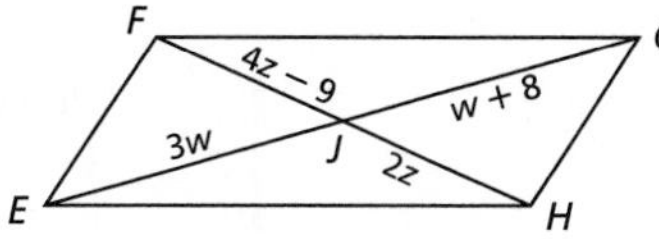

EXAMPLE 3 Parallelograms in the Coordinate Plane

Three vertices of ▱ABCD are $A(1, -2)$, $B(-2, 3)$, and $D(5, -1)$. Find the coordinates of vertex C.

Since $ABCD$ is a parallelogram, both pairs of opposite sides must be parallel.

Step 1 Graph the given points.

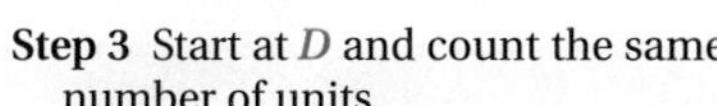

Step 2 Find the slope of $\overline{AB}$ by counting the units from A to B.
The rise from -2 to 3 is 5.
The run from 1 to -2 is -3.

Step 3 Start at D and count the same number of units.
A rise of 5 from -1 is 4.
A run of -3 from 5 is 2. Label $(2, 4)$ as vertex C.

Step 4 Use the slope formula to verify that $\overline{BC} \parallel \overline{AD}$.

$$\text{slope of } \overline{BC} = \frac{4 - 3}{2 - (-2)} = \frac{1}{4}$$

$$\text{slope of } \overline{AD} = \frac{-1 - (-2)}{5 - 1} = \frac{1}{4}$$

The coordinates of vertex C are $(2, 4)$.

Remember!

When you are drawing a figure in the coordinate plane, the name *ABCD* gives the order of the vertices.

CHECK IT OUT!

3. Three vertices of ▱$PQRS$ are $P(-3, -2)$, $Q(-1, 4)$, and $S(5, 0)$. Find the coordinates of vertex R. (7, 6)

COMMON ERROR ALERT

Advise students to pay close attention to the markings on a diagram, especially when writing a proof. Explain that a quadrilateral with only one set of parallel lines is not necessarily a parallelogram.

Power Presentations with PowerPoint®

Additional Examples

Example 2

***WXYZ* is a parallelogram. Find each measure.**

W, $6a + 10$, X, $(18b - 11)°$, $(9b + 2)°$, Z, $8a - 4$, Y

A. YZ 52

B. $m\angle Z$ 65°

Example 3

Three vertices of ▱$JKLM$ are $J(3, -8)$, $K(-2, 2)$, and $L(2, 6)$. Find the coordinates of vertex M. $(7, -4)$

INTERVENTION

Questioning Strategies

EXAMPLE 2

- How are algebra and the definition of supplementary angles used to find the angle measure in this example?

EXAMPLE 3

- How are the slopes of the sides of a parallelogram related?

Power Presentations with PowerPoint®

Additional Examples

Example 4

A. Use the figure in Example 4A to write a two-column proof.
Given: *ABCD* is a parallelogram.
Prove: $\triangle AEB \cong \triangle CED$

1. *ABCD* is a ▱. (Given)
2. $\overline{AB} \cong \overline{CD}$ (▱ → opp. sides ≅)
3. $\overline{AE} \cong \overline{CE}$, $\overline{BE} \cong \overline{DE}$ (▱ → diags. bisect each other)
4. $\triangle AEB \cong \triangle CED$ (SSS)

B. Use the figure in Example 4B to write a two-column proof.
Given: *GHJN* and *JKLM* are parallelograms. *H* and *M* are collinear. *N* and *K* are collinear.
Prove: $\angle H \cong \angle M$

1. *GHJN* and *JKLM* are ▱s. (Given)
2. $\angle H$ and $\angle HJN$ are supp.; $\angle M$ and $\angle MJK$ are supp. (▱ → cons. ∠s supp.)
3. $\angle HJN \cong \angle MJK$ (Vert. ∠s Thm.)
4. $\angle H \cong \angle M$ (≅ Supps. Thm.)

INTERVENTION

Questioning Strategies

EXAMPLE 4

- Can you think of another way to prove the same result in each example? Explain.

EXAMPLE 4 Using Properties of Parallelograms in a Proof

Write a two-column proof.

A Theorem 6-2-2

Given: *ABCD* is a parallelogram.
Prove: $\angle BAD \cong \angle DCB$, $\angle ABC \cong \angle CDA$
Proof:

Statements	Reasons
1. *ABCD* is a parallelogram.	1. Given
2. $\overline{AB} \cong \overline{CD}$, $\overline{DA} \cong \overline{BC}$	2. ▱ → opp. sides ≅
3. $\overline{BD} \cong \overline{BD}$	3. Reflex. Prop. of ≅
4. $\triangle BAD \cong \triangle DCB$	4. SSS *Steps 2, 3*
5. $\angle BAD \cong \angle DCB$	5. CPCTC
6. $\overline{AC} \cong \overline{AC}$	6. Reflex. Prop. of ≅
7. $\triangle ABC \cong \triangle CDA$	7. SSS *Steps 2, 6*
8. $\angle ABC \cong \angle CDA$	8. CPCTC

B **Given:** *GHJN* and *JKLM* are parallelograms. *H* and *M* are collinear. *N* and *K* are collinear.

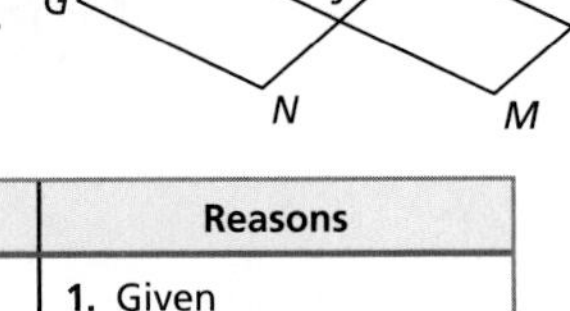

Prove: $\angle G \cong \angle L$
Proof:

Statements	Reasons
1. *GHJN* and *JKLM* are parallelograms.	1. Given
2. $\angle HJN \cong \angle G$, $\angle MJK \cong \angle L$	2. ▱ → opp. ∠s ≅
3. $\angle HJN \cong \angle MJK$	3. Vert. ∠s Thm.
4. $\angle G \cong \angle L$	4. Trans. Prop. of ≅

4. Use the figure in Example 4B to write a two-column proof.
Given: *GHJN* and *JKLM* are parallelograms. *H* and *M* are collinear. *N* and *K* are collinear.
Prove: $\angle N \cong \angle K$

4. 1. *GHJN* and *JKLM* are ▱s. (Given)
2. $\angle N$ and $\angle HJN$ are supp. $\angle K$ and $\angle MJK$ are supp. (▱ → cons. ∠s supp.)
3. $\angle HJN \cong \angle MJK$ (Vert. ∠s Thm.)
4. $\angle N \cong \angle K$ (≅ Supps. Thm.)

THINK AND DISCUSS

1. The measure of one angle of a parallelogram is 71°. What are the measures of the other angles?
2. In ▱*VWXY*, $VW = 21$, and $WY = 36$. Find as many other measures as you can. Justify your answers.

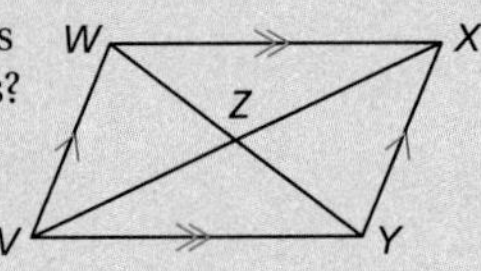

Know it! Note

3. **GET ORGANIZED** Copy and complete the graphic organizer. In each cell, draw a figure with markings that represents the given property.

Properties of Parallelograms				
Opp. sides ∥	Opp. sides ≅	Opp. ∠s ≅	Cons. ∠s supp.	Diags. bisect each other.

3 Close

Summarize

Review the five properties of parallelograms covered in the lesson.

- Opposite sides are parallel.
- Opposite sides are congruent.
- Opposite angles are congruent.
- Consecutive angles are supplementary.
- Diagonals bisect each other.

Draw a sketch on the board to illustrate each property.

ONGOING ASSESSMENT and INTERVENTION

Diagnose **Before the Lesson**
6-2 Warm Up, TE p. 391

Monitor **During the Lesson**
Check It Out! Exercises, SE pp. 392–394
Questioning Strategies, TE pp. 392–394

Assess **After the Lesson**
6-2 Lesson Quiz, TE p. 397
Alternative Assessment, TE p. 397

Answers to *Think and Discuss*

1. The measure of the opp. ∠ is 71°. The measure of each cons. ∠ is 109°.
2. $XY = 21$, $WZ = 18$, and $YZ = 18$. Possible answer: Since *VWXY* is a ▱, its opp. sides are ≅. So $XY = VW = 21$. $\overline{WY}$ is one of its diags., and by Thm. 6-2-4, the other diag. bisects it, so $WZ = YZ = \frac{1}{2}(WY) = 18$.
3. See p. A5.

go.hrw.com
Homework Help Online
KEYWORD: MG7 6-2
Parent Resources Online
KEYWORD: MG7 Parent

GUIDED PRACTICE

1. Only 1 pair of sides are ∥. By def., a ▱ has 2 pairs of ∥ sides.

Vocabulary Apply the vocabulary from this lesson to answer each question.

1. Explain why the figure at right is NOT a *parallelogram*.
2. Draw ▱*PQRS*. Name the opposite sides and opposite angles.

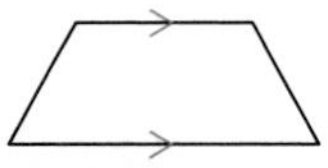

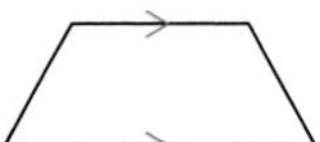

SEE EXAMPLE 1 p. 392

Safety The handrail is made from congruent parallelograms. In ▱*ABCD*, $AB = 17.5$, $DE = 18$, and $m\angle BCD = 110°$. Find each measure.

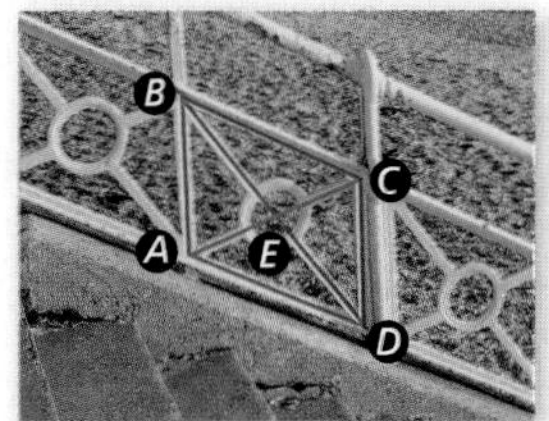

3. *BD* 36
4. *CD* 17.5
5. *BE* 18
6. m∠*ABC* 70°
7. m∠*ADC* 70°
8. m∠*DAB* 110°

SEE EXAMPLE 2 p. 393

JKLM is a parallelogram. Find each measure.

K, L, J, M; 7x; $(2z - 3)°$; $3x + 14$; $(5z - 6)°$

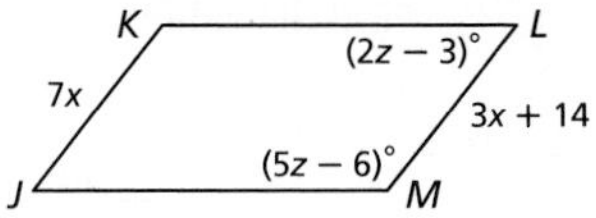

9. *JK* 24.5
10. *LM* 24.5
11. m∠*L* 51°
12. m∠*M* 129°

SEE EXAMPLE 3 p. 393

13. **Multi-Step** Three vertices of ▱*DFGH* are $D(-9, 4)$, $F(-1, 5)$, and $G(2, 0)$. Find the coordinates of vertex *H*. $(-6, -1)$

SEE EXAMPLE 4 p. 394

14. Write a two-column proof.
Given: *PSTV* is a parallelogram. $\overline{PQ} \cong \overline{RQ}$
Prove: $\angle STV \cong \angle R$

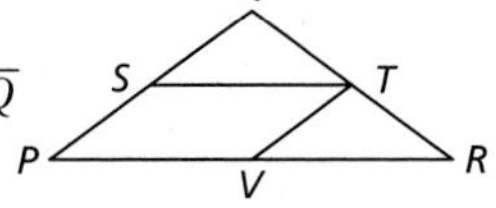

PRACTICE AND PROBLEM SOLVING

Independent Practice	
For Exercises	See Example
15–20	1
21–24	2
25	3
26	4

Extra Practice
Skills Practice p. S14
Application Practice p. S33

Shipping Cranes can be used to load cargo onto ships. In ▱*JKLM*, $JL = 165.8$, $JK = 110$, and $m\angle JML = 50°$. Find the measure of each part of the crane.

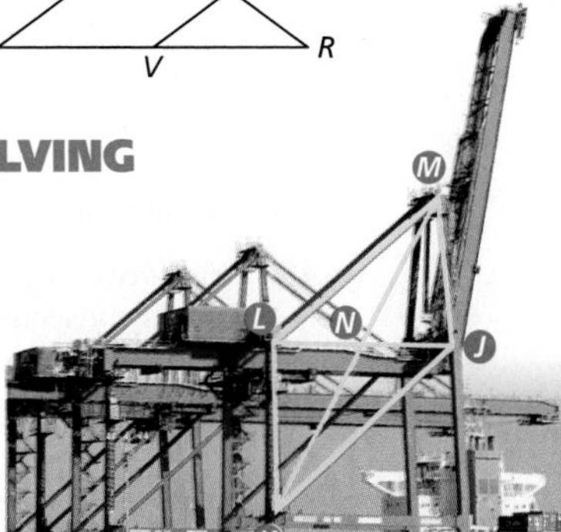

15. *JN* 82.9
16. *LM* 110
17. *LN* 82.9
18. m∠*JKL* 50°
19. m∠*KLM* 130°
20. m∠*MJK* 130°

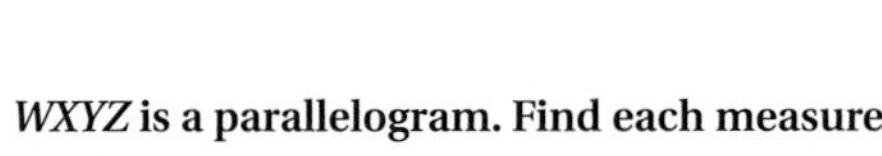

WXYZ is a parallelogram. Find each measure.

X, Y, W, Z, V; $3a - 7$; $5b$; $b + 8$; $2a$

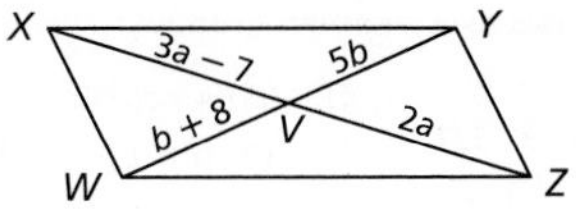

21. *WV* 10
22. *YW* 20
23. *XZ* 28
24. *ZV* 14

25. **Multi-Step** Three vertices of ▱*PRTV* are $P(-4, -4)$, $R(-10, 0)$, and $V(5, -1)$. Find the coordinates of vertex *T*. $(-1, 3)$

26. Write a two-column proof.
Given: *ABCD* and *AFGH* are parallelograms.
Prove: $\angle C \cong \angle G$

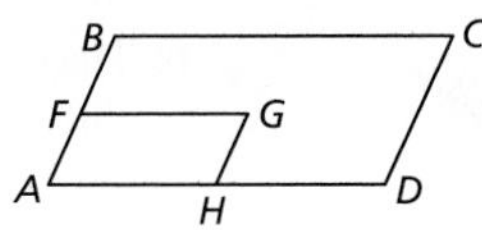

Assignment Guide

Assign *Guided Practice* exercises as necessary.

If you finished Examples 1–2
Basic 15–24, 27–30, 32–42 even
Average 15–24, 27–31, 32–40 even, 41–43, 46, 47
Advanced 15–24, 27–31, 32–40 even, 41–43, 46, 47, 56

If you finished Examples 1–4
Basic 15–30, 32–40, 42, 46, 48, 51–53, 58–66
Average 15–26, 29, 30, 32–40 even, 41–54, 58–66
Advanced 15–31, 32–42 even, 44–66

Homework Quick Check
Quickly check key concepts.
Exercises: 16, 22, 25, 26, 32, 42

Teaching Tip **Critical Thinking** For **Exercise 25,** explain that while there are 3 points that would complete the parallelogram, only one point $(-1, 3)$ completes ▱*PRTV*. Challenge students to find the other two points that would form a parallelogram if the order of the vertices were not important. $(11, -5)$ and $(-19, -3)$

Answers

2. Possible answer:

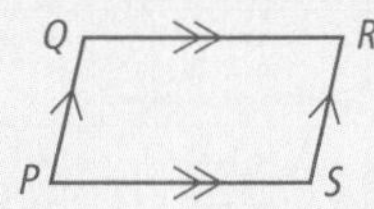

opposite sides: $\overline{PQ}$ and $\overline{RS}$, $\overline{QR}$ and $\overline{SP}$
opposite angles: ∠*P* and ∠*R*, ∠*Q* and ∠*S*

14. 1. *PSTV* is a ▱. $\overline{PQ} \cong \overline{RQ}$ (Given)
2. $\angle STV \cong \angle P$ (▱ → opp. ∠s ≅)
3. $\angle P \cong \angle R$ (Isosc. △ Thm.)
4. $\angle STV \cong \angle R$ (Trans. Prop. of ≅)

26. 1. *ABCD* and *AFGH* are ▱s. (Given)
2. $\angle C \cong \angle A$, $\angle A \cong \angle G$ (▱ → opp. ∠s ≅)
3. $\angle C \cong \angle G$ (Trans. Prop. of ≅)

State Resources

go.hrw.com
State Resources Online
KEYWORD: MG7 Resources

Teaching Tip **Visual** For **Exercises 32–40,** encourage students to copy ▱*KMPR* and use colored pencils to keep track of the congruent angles and segments.

MULTI-STEP TEST PREP **Exercise 48** involves using the properties of parallelograms to find angle measures. This exercise prepares students for the Multi-Step Test Prep on page 406.

Answers

27. $PQ = QR = RS = SP = 21$
28. $PQ = RS = 10.5$; $QR = SP = 31.5$
29. $PQ = RS = 17.5$; $QR = SP = 24.5$
30. $PQ = RS = 6$; $QR = SP = 36$

31b. ∠2 is supp. to ∠1 (▱ → cons. ∠s supp.); ∠4 is supp. to ∠1 (▱ → cons. ∠s supp.); ∠5 is supp. to ∠1 (▱ → cons. ∠s supp.); ∠7 is supp. to ∠1 (Subst.)

45.

Given: *ABCD* is a ▱.
Prove: ∠*A* and ∠*B* are supp. ∠*B* and ∠*C* are supp. ∠*C* and ∠*D* are supp. ∠*D* and ∠*A* are supp.

1. *ABCD* is a ▱. (Given)
2. $\overline{AB} \parallel \overline{CD}$, $\overline{BC} \parallel \overline{DA}$ (Def. of ▱)
3. ∠*A* and ∠*B* are supp. ∠*B* and ∠*C* are supp. ∠*C* and ∠*D* are supp. ∠*D* and ∠*A* are supp. (Same-Side Int. ∠s Thm.)

49, 50, 56, 57. See p. A21.

31a. ∠3 ≅ ∠1 (Corr. ∠s Post.); ∠6 ≅ ∠1 (▱ → opp. ∠s ≅); ∠8 ≅ ∠1 (▱ → opp. ∠s ≅)

32. ∠*RKM* (▱ → opp. ∠s ≅)

33. ∠*KMP* (▱ → opp. ∠s ≅)

34. $\overline{RT}$ (▱ → diags. bisect each other)

35. $\overline{KM}$ (▱ → opp. sides ≅)

36. $\overline{RK}$ (Def. of ▱)

37. $\overline{RP}$ (Def. of ▱)

38. ∠*RKP* (Alt. Int. ∠s Thm.)

39. ∠*RTP* (Vert. ∠s Thm.)

41. $x = 119$; $y = 61$; $z = 119$

42. $x = 90$; $y = 37$; $z = 53$

43. $x = 24$; $y = 50$; $z = 50$

44d. opp. sides of a ▱ are ≅
e. ASA
f. CPCTC

Algebra The perimeter of ▱*PQRS* is 84. Find the length of each side of ▱*PQRS* under the given conditions.

27. $PQ = QR$ 28. $QR = 3(RS)$ 29. $RS = SP - 7$ 30. $SP = RS^2$

31. **Cars** To repair a large truck, a mechanic might use a *parallelogram lift*. In the lift, $\overline{FG} \cong \overline{GH} \cong \overline{LK} \cong \overline{KJ}$, and $\overline{FL} \cong \overline{GK} \cong \overline{HJ}$.
    a. Which angles are congruent to ∠1? Justify your answer.
    b. What is the relationship between ∠1 and each of the remaining labeled angles? Justify your answer.

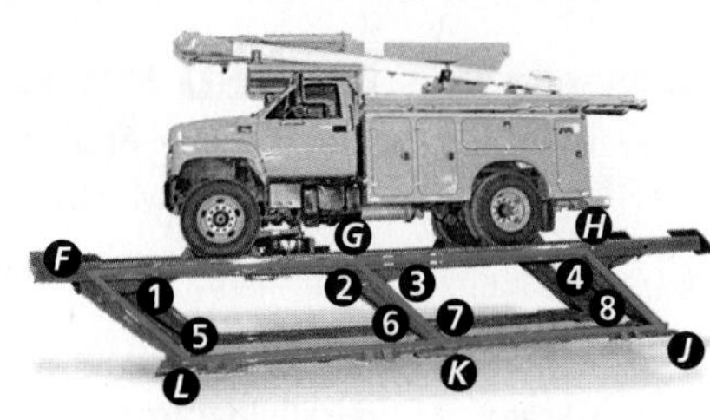

Complete each statement about ▱*KMPR*. Justify your answer.

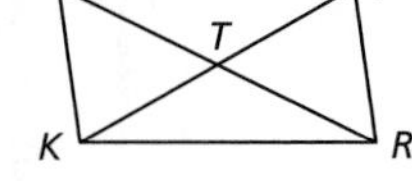

32. ∠*MPR* ≅ ___?___ 33. ∠*PRK* ≅ ___?___ 34. $\overline{MT}$ ≅ ___?___
35. $\overline{PR}$ ≅ ___?___ 36. $\overline{MP}$ ∥ ___?___ 37. $\overline{MK}$ ∥ ___?___
38. ∠*MPK* ≅ ___?___ 39. ∠*MTK* ≅ ___?___ 40. m∠*MKR* + m∠*PRK* = ___?___
180° (▱ → cons. ∠s supp.)

Find the values of *x*, *y*, and *z* in each parallelogram.

41.

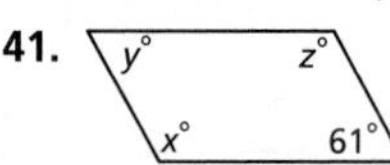

42.

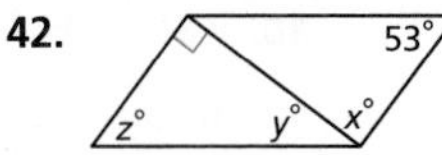

43.

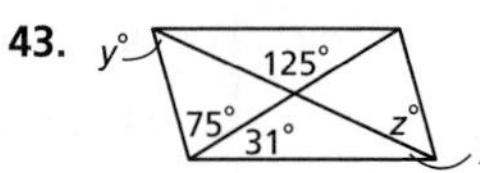

44. Complete the paragraph proof of Theorem 6-2-4 by filling in the blanks.

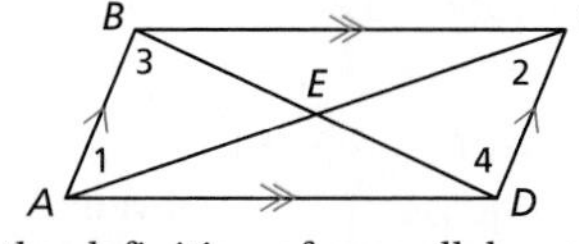

Given: *ABCD* is a parallelogram.
Prove: $\overline{AC}$ and $\overline{BD}$ bisect each other at *E*.

Proof: It is given that *ABCD* is a parallelogram. By the definition of a parallelogram, $\overline{AB} \parallel$ **a.** ___?$\overline{CD}$___. By the Alternate Interior Angles Theorem, ∠1 ≅ **b.** ___?∠2___, and ∠3 ≅ **c.** ___?∠4___. $\overline{AB} \cong \overline{CD}$ because **d.** ___?___. This means that △*ABE* ≅ △*CDE* by **e.** ___?___. So by **f.** ___?___, $\overline{AE} \cong \overline{CE}$, and $\overline{BE} \cong \overline{DE}$. Therefore $\overline{AC}$ and $\overline{BD}$ bisect each other at *E* by the definition of **g.** ___?___. bisect

45. Write a two-column proof of Theorem 6-2-3: If a quadrilateral is a parallelogram, then its consecutive angles are supplementary.

Algebra **Find the values of *x* and *y* in each parallelogram.**

46. 2*x*, *x*, 2*y* − 9, *y*
$x = 3$; $y = 6$

47.

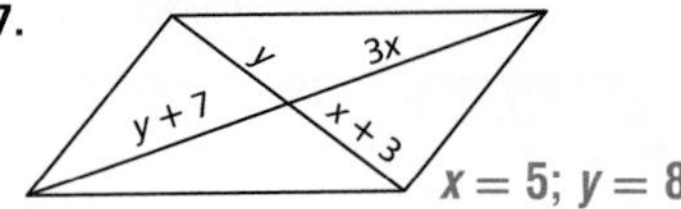

$x = 5$; $y = 8$

MULTI-STEP TEST PREP

48. This problem will prepare you for the Multi-Step Test Prep on page 406.
    In this calcite crystal, the face *ABCD* is a parallelogram.
    a. In ▱*ABCD*, $m\angle B = (6x + 12)°$, and $m\angle D = (9x - 33)°$. Find m∠*B*. 102°
    b. Find m∠*A* and m∠*C*. Which theorem or theorems did you use to find these angle measures?
    78° (▱ → cons. ∠s supp.)

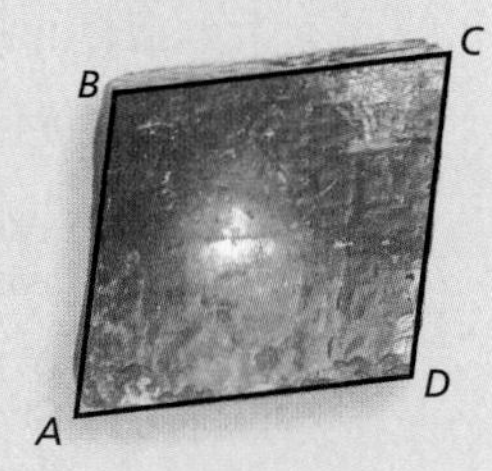

6-2 PRACTICE A
6-2 PRACTICE C
6-2 PRACTICE B

A gurney is a wheeled cot or stretcher used in hospitals. Many gurneys are made so that the base will fold up for easy storage in an ambulance. When partially folded, the base forms a parallelogram. In ▱*STUV*, *VU* = 91 centimeters, *UW* = 108.8 centimeters, and m∠*TSV* = 57°. Find each measure.

1. *SW* 108.8 cm 2. *TS* 91 cm 3. *US* 217.6 cm
4. m∠*SVU* 123° 5. m∠*STU* 123° 6. m∠*TUV* 57°

JKLM is a parallelogram. Find each measure.

7. m∠*L* 117° 8. m∠*K* 63° 9. *MJ* 71

VWXY is a parallelogram. Find each measure.

10. *VX* 21 11. *XZ* 10.5
12. *ZW* 15 13. *WY* 30

14. Three vertices of ▱*ABCD* are *B*(−3, 3), *C*(2, 7), and *D*(5, 1). Find the coordinates of vertex *A*. (0, −3)

Write a two-column proof.

15. **Given:** *DEFG* is a parallelogram.
Prove: m∠*DHG* = m∠*EDH* + m∠*FGH* Possible answer:

Statements	Reasons
1. *DEFG* is a parallelogram.	1. Given
2. m∠*EDG* = m∠*EDH* + m∠*GDH*, m∠*FGD* = m∠*FGH* + m∠*DGH*	2. Angle Add. Post.
3. m∠*EDG* + m∠*FGD* = 180°	3. ▱ → cons. ∠s supp.
4. m∠*EDH* + m∠*GDH* + m∠*FGH* + m∠*DGH* = 180°	4. Subst. (Steps 2, 3)
5. m∠*GDH* + m∠*DGH* + m∠*DHG* = 180°	5. Triangle Sum Thm.
6. m∠*GDH* + m∠*DGH* + m∠*DHG* = m∠*EDH* + m∠*GDH* + m∠*FGH* + m∠*DGH*	6. Trans. Prop. of =
7. m∠*DHG* = m∠*EDH* + m∠*FGH*	7. Subtr. Prop. of =

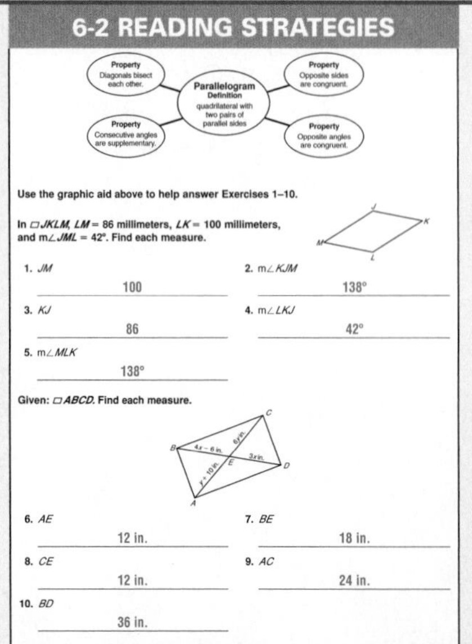

6-2 READING STRATEGIES

Use the graphic aid above to help answer Exercises 1–10.

In ▱*JKLM*, *LM* = 86 millimeters, *LK* = 100 millimeters, and m∠*JML* = 42°. Find each measure.

1. *JM* 100 2. m∠*KJM* 138°
3. *KJ* 86 4. m∠*LKJ* 42°
5. m∠*MLK* 138°

Given: ▱*ABCD*. Find each measure.

6. *AE* 12 in. 7. *BE* 18 in.
8. *CE* 12 in. 9. *AC* 24 in.
10. *BD* 36 in.

6-2 RETEACH

A parallelogram is a quadrilateral with two pairs of parallel sides. All parallelograms, such as ▱*FGHJ*, have the following properties.

Properties of Parallelograms	
$\overline{FG} \cong \overline{HJ}$, $\overline{GH} \cong \overline{JF}$ Opposite sides are congruent.	∠*F* ≅ ∠*H*, ∠*G* ≅ ∠*J* Opposite angles are congruent.
m∠*F* + m∠*G* = 180°, m∠*G* + m∠*H* = 180°, m∠*H* + m∠*J* = 180°, m∠*J* + m∠*F* = 180° Consecutive angles are supplementary.	$\overline{FP} \cong \overline{HP}$, $\overline{GP} \cong \overline{JP}$ The diagonals bisect each other.

Find each measure.

1. *AB* 10 cm 2. m∠*D* 70°

Find each measure in ▱*LMNP*.

3. *ML* 12 m 4. *LP* 10 m
5. m∠*LPM* 53° 6. *LN* 18 m
7. m∠*MLN* 32° 8. *QN* 9 m

49. **Critical Thinking** Draw any parallelogram. Draw a second parallelogram whose corresponding sides are congruent to the sides of the first parallelogram but whose corresponding angles are not congruent to the angles of the first.

a. Is there an SSSS congruence postulate for parallelograms? Explain. no

b. Remember the meaning of triangle rigidity. Is a parallelogram rigid? Explain. no

50. **Write About It** Explain why every parallelogram is a quadrilateral but every quadrilateral is not necessarily a parallelogram.

TEST PREP

51. What is the value of x in ▱$PQRS$?

Ⓐ 15 (B) 20 (C) 30 (D) 70

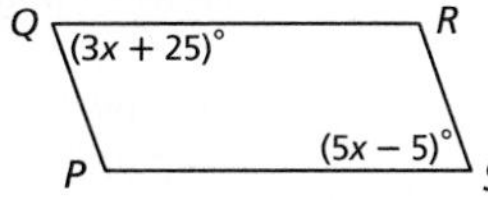

52. The diagonals of ▱$JKLM$ intersect at Z. Which statement is true?

(F) $JL = KM$ (G) $JL = \frac{1}{2}KM$ (H) $JL = \frac{1}{2}JZ$ Ⓙ $JL = 2JZ$

53. **Gridded Response** In ▱$ABCD$, $BC = 8.2$, and $CD = 5$. What is the perimeter of ▱$ABCD$? 26.4

CHALLENGE AND EXTEND

The coordinates of three vertices of a parallelogram are given. Give the coordinates for all possible locations of the fourth vertex.

54. (0, 5), (4, 0), (8, 5)   55. (−2, 1), (3, −1), (−1, −4)

54. (12, 0), (−4, 0), (4, 10)
55. (2, 4), (4, −6), (−6, −2)

56. The feathers on an arrow form two congruent parallelograms that share a common side. Each parallelogram is the reflection of the other across the line they share. Show that $y = 2x$.

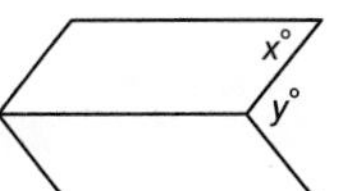

57. Prove that the bisectors of two consecutive angles of a parallelogram are perpendicular.

SPIRAL REVIEW

Describe the correlation shown in each scatter plot as positive, negative, or no correlation. *(Previous course)*

58. 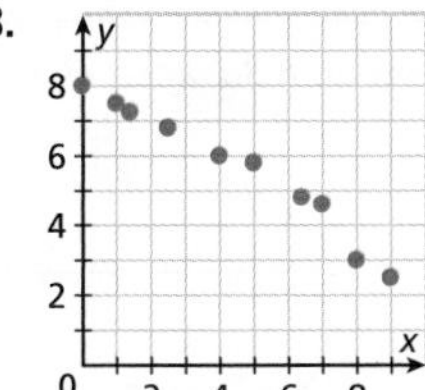

negative correlation

59. 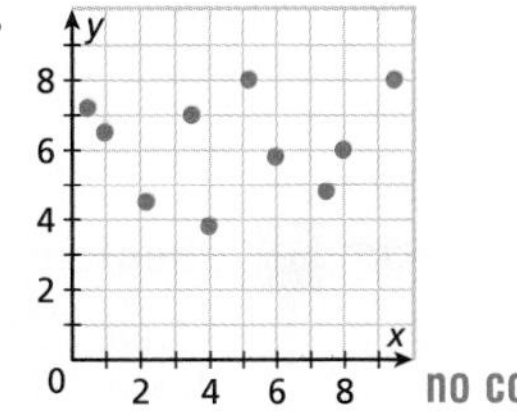

no correlation

Classify each angle pair. *(Lesson 3-1)*

60. ∠2 and ∠7   61. ∠5 and ∠4

62. ∠6 and ∠7 same-side int. ∠s   63. ∠1 and ∠3 corr. ∠s

60. alt. int. ∠s
61. alt. ext. ∠s

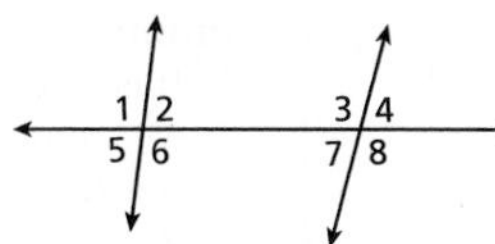

An interior angle measure of a regular polygon is given. Find the number of sides and the measure of each exterior angle. *(Lesson 6-1)*

64. 120° 6 sides; 60°   65. 135° 8 sides; 45°   66. 156° 15 sides; 24°

6-2 PROBLEM SOLVING

Use the diagram for Exercises 1 and 2.
The wall frames on the staircase wall form parallelograms $ABCD$ and $EFGH$.

1. In ▱$ABCD$, the measure of ∠A is three times the measure of ∠B. What are the measures of ∠C and ∠D?

m∠C = 135°; m∠D = 45°

2. In ▱$EFGH$, $FH = 5x$ inches, $EG = (2x + 4)$ inches, and $JG = 8$ inches. What is the length of JH?

15 in.

3. The diagram shows a section of the support structure of a roller coaster. In ▱$JKLM$, $JK = (3z - 0.9)$ feet, and $LM = (z + 2.7)$ feet. Find JK.

4. In ▱$TUVW$, part of a ceramic tile pattern, m∠$TUV = (8x + 1)°$ and m∠$UVW = (12x + 19)°$. Find m∠TUV.

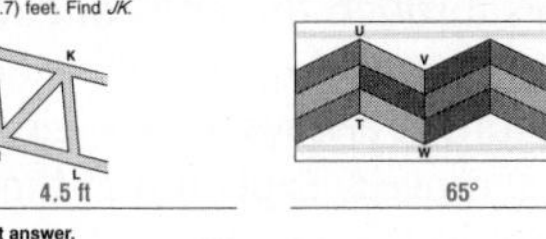

4.5 ft   65°

Choose the best answer.

5. What is the measure of ∠Z in parallelogram $WXYZ$?

A 18°
Ⓑ 74°
C 106°
D 108°

6. The perimeter of ▱$CDEF$ is 54 centimeters. Find the length of $\overline{FC}$ if $\overline{DE}$ is 5 centimeters longer than $\overline{EF}$.

F 11 cm
G 14 cm
Ⓗ 16 cm
J 44 cm

7. In ▱$PQRS$, $QT = 7x$, $TS = 2x + 2.5$, $RT = 2y$, and $TP = y + 3$. Find the perimeter of △PTS.

A 6   C 12
B 9.5   Ⓓ 17.3

6-2 CHALLENGE

In the game of air hockey, a puck glides on a thin layer of air above a rectangular table that is 4 feet wide and 8 feet long. The object of the game is to hit the puck into your opponent's goal. The movement of the puck is confined to the table by walls at the edges of the table. Because of a physical principle, the *law of reflection*, the angle at which the puck bounces off a wall is congruent to the angle at which it strikes the wall.

In the figure at right, a puck has been hit in such a way that it bounces off each wall of the table exactly once. Complete the following proof that the path shown is a parallelogram.

Given: $WXYZ$ is a rectangle; m∠1 = m∠2; m∠3 = m∠4; m∠5 = m∠6; m∠7 = m∠8

Prove: $ABCD$ is a parallelogram.

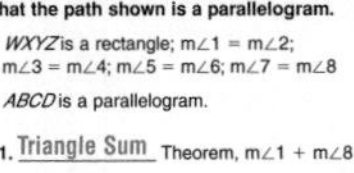

By the 1. Triangle Sum Theorem, m∠1 + m∠8 + m∠X = 180° and m∠6 + m∠7 + m∠W = 180°. So m∠1 = 180° − m∠8 − m∠X and m∠6 = 180° − m∠7 − m∠W. It is given that m∠8 = 2. m∠7. Because $WXYZ$ is a rectangle, m∠X = m∠W = 3. 90°. So, using properties of equality, m∠1 = m∠6. By similar reasoning, m∠2 = 4. m∠5. You know that m∠1 + m∠ABC + m∠2 = 5. 180° and that m∠5 + m∠CDA + m∠6 = 6. 180°. So m∠ABC = 180° − m∠1 − m∠2 and m∠CDA = 180° − m∠6 − m∠5. Using properties of equality, it follows that m∠ABC = 7. m∠CDA. By similar reasoning, m∠BCD = 8. m∠DAB. You know that m∠ABC + m∠BCD + m∠CDA + m∠DAB = 9. 360°. So, using properties of equality, m∠ABC + m∠BCD + m∠ABC + m∠BCD = 360°, or 2(m∠ABC) + 2(m∠BCD) = 360°. It follows that 2(m∠ABC + m∠BCD) = 360°, or m∠ABC + m∠BCD = 180°. This means that ∠ABC and ∠BCD are a pair of 10. supplementary angles. Similarly, ∠BCD and ∠CDA are a pair of 11. supplementary angles. So $\overline{AB} \parallel \overline{DC}$ and $\overline{BC} \parallel \overline{AD}$ by the 12. Converse of the Same-Side Interior Angles Theorem. Therefore, $ABCD$ is a parallelogram by the 13. definition of a parallelogram.

Can the path of a puck have the given shape? Write an explanation on a separate sheet of paper.

14. rhombus Yes; explanations will vary   15. rectangle No; explanations will vary   16. kite No; explanations will vary

TEST PREP DOCTOR If students chose **D for Exercise 51,** remind them that the answer is the value of x and not m∠Q or m∠S.

Journal

Ask students to describe how they remember which parts of a parallelogram are congruent and which parts are supplementary.

ALTERNATIVE ASSESSMENT

Have students draw a parallelogram and write algebraic expressions for a pair of congruent sides and a pair of supplementary angles. Have students exchange papers and solve for the measures of the labeled sides and all four angles.

Power Presentations with PowerPoint®

6-2 Lesson Quiz

In ▱$PNWL$, $NW = 12$, $PM = 9$, and m∠$WLP = 144°$. Find each measure.

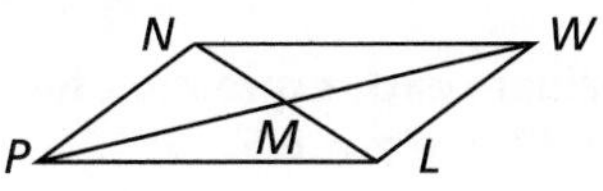

1. PW 18   2. m∠PNW 144°

$QRST$ is a parallelogram. Find each measure.

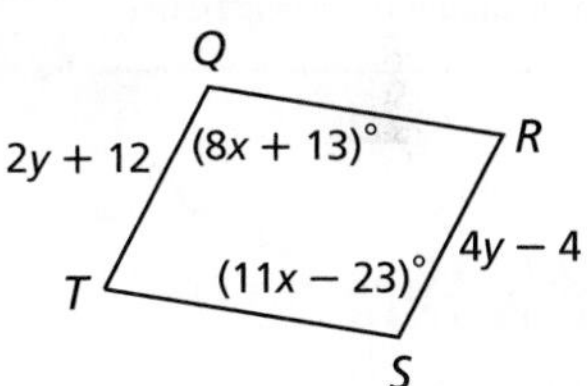

3. TQ 28   4. m∠T 71°

5. Three vertices of ▱$ABCD$ are $A(2, -6)$, $B(-1, 2)$, and $C(5, 3)$. Find the coordinates of vertex D. (8, −5)

6. Write a two-column proof.
Given: $RSTU$ is a parallelogram.
Prove: △RSU ≅ △TUS

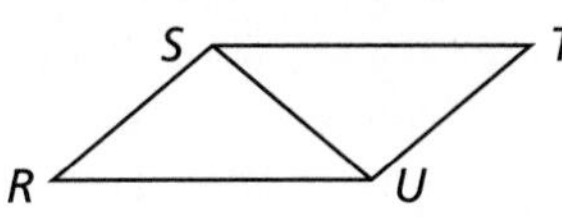

1. $RSTU$ is a ▱. (Given)
2. $\overline{RU} \cong \overline{TS}$, $\overline{RS} \cong \overline{UT}$ (▱ → opp. sides ≅)
3. ∠R ≅ ∠T (▱ → opp. ∠s ≅)
4. △RSU ≅ △TUS (SAS)

Also available on transparency

6-3 Organizer

Pacing: Traditional 1 day
Block $\frac{1}{2}$ day

Objective: Prove that a given quadrilateral is a parallelogram.

Geometry Lab
In Geometry Lab Activities

Online Edition
Tutorial Videos

Countdown Week 13

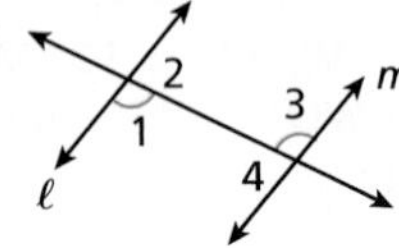
Power Presentations with PowerPoint®

Warm Up

Justify each statement.

1. $\overline{QR} \cong \overline{QR}$ Reflex. Prop. of $\cong$
2. $\ell \parallel m$ Conv. of the Alt. Int. ∡ Thm.

Evaluate each expression for $x = 12$ and $y = 8.5$.

3. $2x + 7$ 31
4. $16x - 9$ 183
5. $(8y + 5)°$ 73°

Also available on transparency

Math Humor

Q: Did you hear about the quadrilateral who wanted to be a parallelogram?

A: Yes, his opposite angles weren't quite up to par.

State Resources

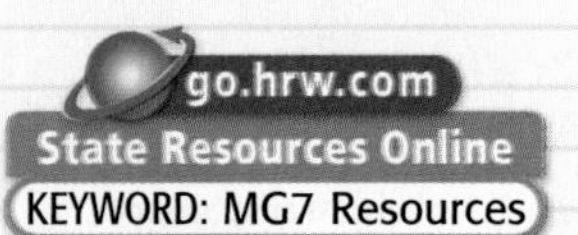

6-3 Conditions for Parallelograms

Objective
Prove that a given quadrilateral is a parallelogram.

Who uses this?
A bird watcher can use a *parallelogram mount* to adjust the height of a pair of binoculars without changing the viewing angle. (See Example 4.)

You have learned to identify the properties of a parallelogram. Now you will be given the properties of a quadrilateral and will have to tell if the quadrilateral is a parallelogram. To do this, you can use the definition of a parallelogram or the conditions below.

Know it! Note

Remember!
In the converse of a theorem, the hypothesis and conclusion are exchanged.

Theorems Conditions for Parallelograms

	THEOREM	EXAMPLE
6-3-1	If one pair of opposite sides of a quadrilateral are parallel and congruent, then the quadrilateral is a parallelogram. (quad. with pair of opp. sides ∥ and $\cong \rightarrow ▱$)	Parallelogram ABCD
6-3-2	If both pairs of opposite sides of a quadrilateral are congruent, then the quadrilateral is a parallelogram. (quad. with opp. sides $\cong \rightarrow ▱$)	Parallelogram ABCD
6-3-3	If both pairs of opposite angles of a quadrilateral are congruent, then the quadrilateral is a parallelogram. (quad. with opp. ∡ $\cong \rightarrow ▱$)	Parallelogram ABCD

You will prove Theorems 6-3-2 and 6-3-3 in Exercises 26 and 29.

PROOF

Theorem 6-3-1

Given: $\overline{KL} \parallel \overline{MJ}$, $\overline{KL} \cong \overline{MJ}$
Prove: *JKLM* is a parallelogram.

Proof:
It is given that $\overline{KL} \cong \overline{MJ}$. Since $\overline{KL} \parallel \overline{MJ}$, $\angle 1 \cong \angle 2$ by the Alternate Interior Angles Theorem. By the Reflexive Property of Congruence, $\overline{JL} \cong \overline{JL}$. So $\triangle JKL \cong \triangle LMJ$ by SAS. By CPCTC, $\angle 3 \cong \angle 4$, and $\overline{JK} \parallel \overline{LM}$ by the Converse of the Alternate Interior Angles Theorem. Since the opposite sides of *JKLM* are parallel, *JKLM* is a parallelogram by definition.

1 Introduce

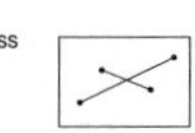

EXPLORATION
6-3 Conditions for Parallelograms

For this Exploration you will need scissors, a ruler, and several chenille stems.

1. Cut two stems so that they are different lengths. Mark the midpoint of each stem.
2. Place the stems on a sheet of paper. Cross the stems so they intersect at their midpoints. Mark a point on the paper at each endpoint of the stems.
3. Remove the stems and connect the points to form a quadrilateral. What type of quadrilateral does it appear to be?
4. Repeat the process, but arrange the stems so that they intersect at their midpoints at a different angle. Do you get the same result?
5. Repeat Steps 1–4, using stems of different lengths. Do you get the same results?

THINK AND DISCUSS

6. Explain how you can use your observations to make a conjecture about quadrilaterals whose diagonals bisect each other.

Motivate

Have students cut two short strips of equal length and two long strips of equal length out of heavy paper. Punch holes through the ends of each and use brads to make a parallelogram. Ask students if they think the figure is always a parallelogram, no matter how it is moved. Explain that they will explore this concept in this lesson.

Explorations and answers are provided in *Alternate Openers: Explorations Transparencies.*

The two theorems below can also be used to show that a given quadrilateral is a parallelogram.

Theorems Conditions for Parallelograms

	THEOREM	EXAMPLE
6-3-4	If an angle of a quadrilateral is supplementary to both of its consecutive angles, then the quadrilateral is a parallelogram. (quad. with ∠ supp. to cons. ∡ → ▱)	B (180 − x)° C; A x° (180 − x)° D
6-3-5	If the diagonals of a quadrilateral bisect each other, then the quadrilateral is a parallelogram. (quad. with diags. bisecting each other → ▱)	B C Z A D

You will prove Theorems 6-3-4 and 6-3-5 in Exercises 27 and 30.

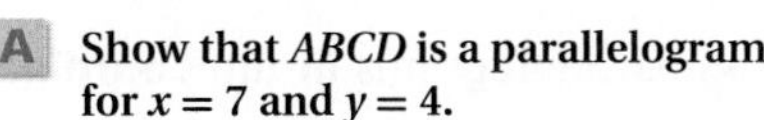

EXAMPLE 1 Verifying Figures are Parallelograms

Algebra

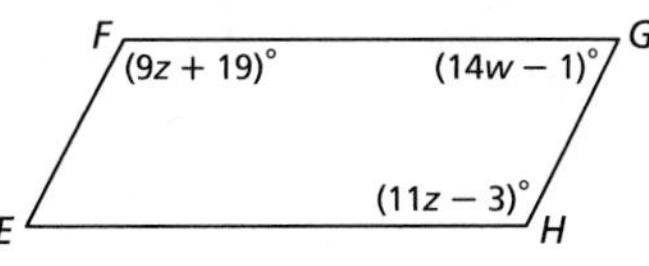

A **Show that $ABCD$ is a parallelogram for $x = 7$ and $y = 4$.**

Step 1 Find BC and DA.

$BC = x + 14$	*Given*	$DA = 3x$
$BC = 7 + 14 = 21$	*Substitute and simplify.*	$DA = 3x = 3(7) = 21$

Step 2 Find AB and CD.

$AB = 5y - 4$	*Given*	$CD = 2y + 8$
$AB = 5(4) - 4 = 16$	*Substitute and simplify.*	$CD = 2(4) + 8 = 16$

Since $BC = DA$ and $AB = CD$, $ABCD$ is a parallelogram by Theorem 6-3-2.

B **Show that $EFGH$ is a parallelogram for $z = 11$ and $w = 4.5$.**

F (9z + 19)° (14w − 1)° G; E (11z − 3)° H

$m\angle F = (9z + 19)°$	*Given*
$m\angle F = [9(11) + 19]° = 118°$	*Substitute 11 for z and simplify.*
$m\angle H = (11z - 3)°$	*Given*
$m\angle H = [11(11) - 3]° = 118°$	*Substitute 11 for z and simplify.*
$m\angle G = (14w - 1)°$	*Given*
$m\angle G = [14(4.5) - 1]° = 62°$	*Substitute 4.5 for w and simplify.*

Since $118° + 62° = 180°$, $\angle G$ is supplementary to both $\angle F$ and $\angle H$. $EFGH$ is a parallelogram by Theorem 6-3-4.

1. Show that $PQRS$ is a parallelogram for $a = 2.4$ and $b = 9$.

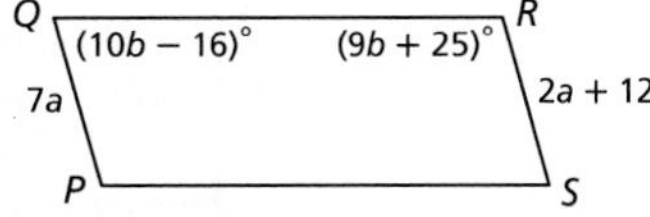

1. $\overline{PQ} = \overline{RS} = 16.8$, so $\overline{PQ} \cong \overline{RS}$. $m\angle Q = 74°$, and $m\angle R = 106°$, so $\angle Q$ and $\angle R$ are supp., which means that $\overline{PQ} \parallel \overline{RS}$. So 1 pair of opp. sides of $PQRS$ are $\parallel$ and $\cong$. By Thm. 6-3-1, $PQRS$ is a ▱.

COMMON ERROR ALERT

When students are proving that a figure in the coordinate plane is a parallelogram, advise them to plot the points first so that the order of the vertices will be obvious. This will prevent them from confusing the diagonals with the sides.

Power Presentations with PowerPoint®

Additional Examples

Example 1

A. Show that $JKLM$ is a parallelogram for $a = 3$ and $b = 9$.

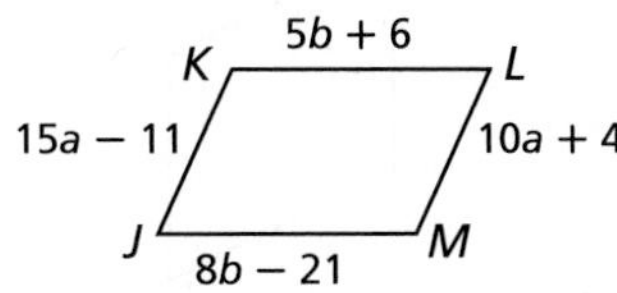

$JK = LM = 34$, and $KL = JM = 51$, so $JKLM$ is a ▱ by Thm. 6-3-2.

B. Show that $PQRS$ is a parallelogram for $x = 10$ and $y = 6.5$.

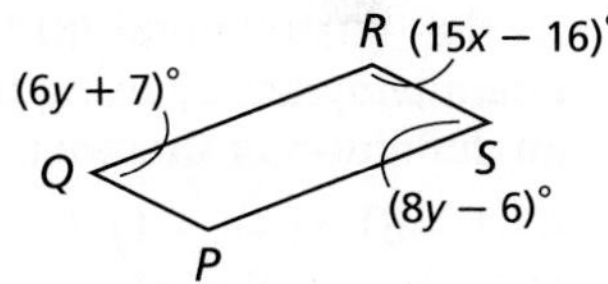

$m\angle Q = m\angle S = 46°$; $m\angle R = 134°$. Since $134° + 46° = 180°$, $\angle R$ is supp. to $\angle Q$ and $\angle S$. $PQRS$ is a ▱ by Thm. 6-3-4.

INTERVENTION Questioning Strategies

EXAMPLE 1

- How is Theorem 6-3-2 used to show that the given quadrilateral is a parallelogram in Example 1A?
- How is Theorem 6-3-4 used to show that the given quadrilateral is a parallelogram in Example 1B?

2 Teach

Guided Instruction

Review the properties of a parallelogram. Explain that students will now work with the converse situation; they will determine if a quadrilateral with certain properties is a parallelogram.

Reading Math Encourage students to pay close attention to the key words in each theorem, such as *opposite, parallel,* and *congruent*. Have them write the theorems and highlight these key words.

ENGLISH LANGUAGE LEARNERS

Reaching All Learners

Through Kinesthetic Experience

Have students use raw spaghetti to demonstrate the theorems in the lesson. For example, ask them to try to form a parallelogram with opposite sides that are congruent but not parallel, or vice versa. This should emphasize that in Theorem 6-3-1, the same pair of opposite sides must be congruent *and* parallel.

Power Presentations with PowerPoint®

Additional Examples

Example 2

Determine if each quadrilateral must be a parallelogram. Justify your answer.

A.

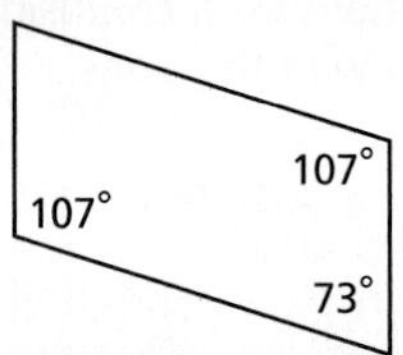

Yes; the 73° ∠ is supp. to both of its cons. ∡. By Thm. 6-3-4, the quad. is a ▱.

B.

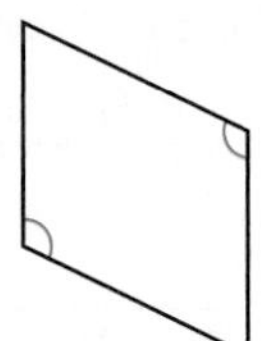

No; 1 pair of opp. ∡ are ≅. The other pair are not. The conditions for a ▱ are not met.

Example 3

Show that quadrilateral *JKLM* is a parallelogram by using the given definition or theorem.

A. $J(-1, -6)$, $K(-4, -1)$, $L(4, 5)$, $M(7, 0)$; definition of parallelogram Slope of $\overline{JK}$ = slope of $\overline{LM} = -\frac{5}{3}$; slope of $\overline{KL}$ = slope of $\overline{MJ} = \frac{3}{4}$; both pairs of opp. sides are ‖, so *JKLM* is a ▱ by def.

B. $A(2, 3)$, $B(6, 2)$, $C(5, 0)$, $D(1, 1)$; Theorem 6-3-1 Slope of $\overline{DA}$ = slope of $\overline{BC}$ = 2; $DA = BC = \sqrt{5}$; so $\overline{DA} \parallel \overline{BC}$ and $\overline{DA} \cong \overline{BC}$. By Thm. 6-3-1, *ABCD* is a ▱.

EXAMPLE 2 Applying Conditions for Parallelograms

Determine if each quadrilateral must be a parallelogram. Justify your answer.

A

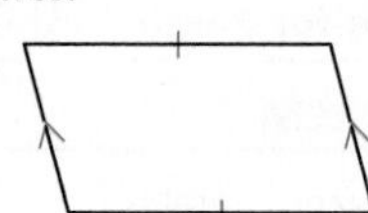

No. One pair of opposite sides are parallel. A different pair of opposite sides are congruent. The conditions for a parallelogram are not met.

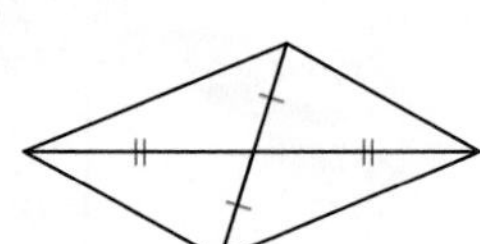

Yes. The diagonals bisect each other. By Theorem 6-3-5, the quadrilateral is a parallelogram.

CHECK IT OUT! **Determine if each quadrilateral must be a parallelogram. Justify your answer.**

2a.

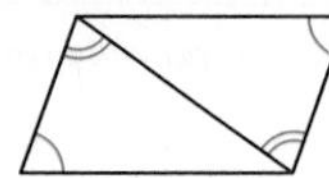

2b.

2a. Yes; possible answer: the diag. of the quad. forms 2 ⚠s. 2 ∡ of 1 △ are ≅ to 2 ∡ of the other, so the third pair of ∡ are ≅ by the Third ∡ Thm. So both pairs of opp. ∡ of the quad. are ≅. By Thm. 6-3-3, the quad. is a ▱.

2b. No; 2 pairs of cons. sides are ≅. None of the sets of conditions for a ▱ are met.

EXAMPLE 3 Proving Parallelograms in the Coordinate Plane

Show that quadrilateral *ABCD* is a parallelogram by using the given definition or theorem.

A $A(-3, 2)$, $B(-2, 7)$, $C(2, 4)$, $D(1, -1)$; **definition of parallelogram**

Find the slopes of both pairs of opposite sides.

$$\text{slope of } \overline{AB} = \frac{7-2}{-2-(-3)} = \frac{5}{1} = 5$$

$$\text{slope of } \overline{CD} = \frac{-1-4}{1-2} = \frac{-5}{-1} = 5$$

$$\text{slope of } \overline{BC} = \frac{4-7}{2-(-2)} = \frac{-3}{4} = -\frac{3}{4}$$

$$\text{slope of } \overline{DA} = \frac{2-(-1)}{-3-1} = \frac{3}{-4} = -\frac{3}{4}$$

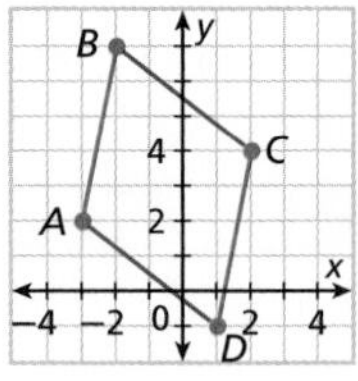

Since both pairs of opposite sides are parallel, *ABCD* is a parallelogram by definition.

Helpful Hint

To say that a quadrilateral is a parallelogram *by definition*, you must show that both pairs of opposite sides are parallel.

B $F(-4, -2)$, $G(-2, 2)$, $H(4, 3)$, $J(2, -1)$; **Theorem 6-3-1**

Find the slopes and lengths of one pair of opposite sides.

$$\text{slope of } \overline{GH} = \frac{3-2}{4-(-2)} = \frac{1}{6}$$

$$\text{slope of } \overline{JF} = \frac{-2-(-1)}{-4-2} = \frac{-1}{-6} = \frac{1}{6}$$

$$GH = \sqrt{[4-(-2)]^2 + (3-2)^2} = \sqrt{37}$$

$$JF = \sqrt{(-4-2)^2 + [-2-(-1)]^2} = \sqrt{37}$$

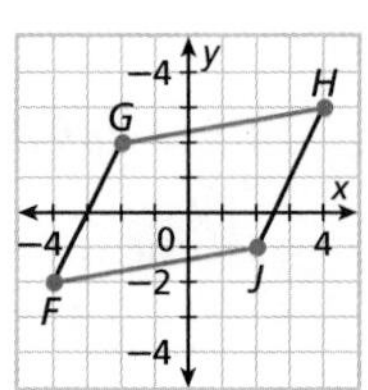

$\overline{GH}$ and $\overline{JF}$ have the same slope, so $\overline{GH} \parallel \overline{JF}$. Since $GH = JF$, $\overline{GH} \cong \overline{JF}$. So by Theorem 6-3-1, *FGHJ* is a parallelogram.

INTERVENTION

Questioning Strategies

EXAMPLE 2

- What conditions must a quadrilateral satisfy to be a parallelogram? Explain.

EXAMPLE 3

- How can you use the diagonals to show that a quadrilateral in the coordinate plane is a parallelogram?

3. Use the definition of a parallelogram to show that the quadrilateral with vertices $K(-3, 0)$, $L(-5, 7)$, $M(3, 5)$, and $N(5, -2)$ is a parallelogram.

You have learned several ways to determine whether a quadrilateral is a parallelogram. You can use the given information about a figure to decide which condition is best to apply.

Helpful Hint 

To show that a quadrilateral is a parallelogram, you only have to show that it satisfies one of these sets of conditions.

Conditions for Parallelograms
Both pairs of opposite sides are parallel. (definition)
One pair of opposite sides are parallel and congruent. (Theorem 6-3-1)
Both pairs of opposite sides are congruent. (Theorem 6-3-2)
Both pairs of opposite angles are congruent. (Theorem 6-3-3)
One angle is supplementary to both of its consecutive angles. (Theorem 6-3-4)
The diagonals bisect each other. (Theorem 6-3-5)

EXAMPLE 4 *Bird-Watching Application*

In the parallelogram mount, there are bolts at *P*, *Q*, *R*, and *S* such that $PQ = RS$ and $QR = SP$. The frame *PQRS* moves when you raise or lower the binoculars. Why is *PQRS* always a parallelogram?

When you move the binoculars, the angle measures change, but *PQ*, *QR*, *RS*, and *SP* stay the same. So it is always true that $PQ = RS$ and $QR = SP$. Since both pairs of opposite sides of the quadrilateral are congruent, *PQRS* is always a parallelogram.

4. The frame is attached to the tripod at points *A* and *B* such that $AB = RS$ and $BR = SA$. So *ABRS* is also a parallelogram. How does this ensure that the angle of the binoculars stays the same?

THINK AND DISCUSS

1. What do all the theorems in this lesson have in common?
2. How are the theorems in this lesson different from the theorems in Lesson 6-2?

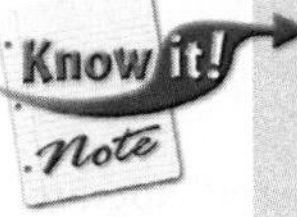

3. **GET ORGANIZED** Copy and complete the graphic organizer. In each box, write one of the six conditions for a parallelogram. Then sketch a parallelogram and label it to show how it meets the condition.

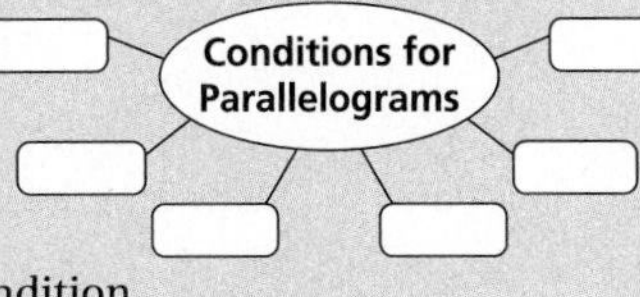

Power Presentations with PowerPoint®

Additional Examples

Example 4

The legs of a keyboard tray are connected by a bolt at their midpoints, which allows the tray to be raised or lowered. Why is *PQRS* always a parallelogram?

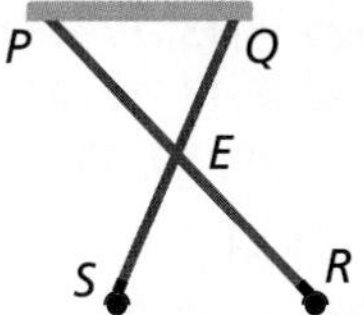

Since the bolt is at the mdpt. of both legs, $PE = ER$ and $SE = EQ$. So the diags. of *PQRS* bisect each other, and by Thm. 6-3-5, *PQRS* is a ▱.

INTERVENTION 

Questioning Strategies

EXAMPLE 4

- How could you prove that the opposite angles of *PQRS* are congruent?
- Why are parallelograms useful in mechanical structures?

Answers to *Check It Out!*

3. Possible answer: slope of $\overline{KL}$ = slope of $\overline{MN} = -\frac{7}{2}$; slope of $\overline{LM}$ = slope of $\overline{NK} = -\frac{1}{4}$; both pairs of opp. sides have the same slope, so $\overline{KL} \parallel \overline{MN}$ and $\overline{LM} \parallel \overline{NK}$; by def., *KLMN* is a ▱.
4. Possible answer: Since *ABRS* is a ▱, it is always true that $\overline{AB} \parallel \overline{RS}$. Since $\overline{AB}$ stays vert., $\overline{RS}$ also remains vert. no matter how the frame is adjusted. Therefore the viewing ∠ never changes.

3 Close

Summarize

Ask students the following: "A pair of opposite angles in a quadrilateral each measure 103°. Can you conclude that this quadrilateral is a parallelogram? Explain why or draw a counterexample." No, since only 1 pair of opp. ∠s are ≅. Possible counterexample:

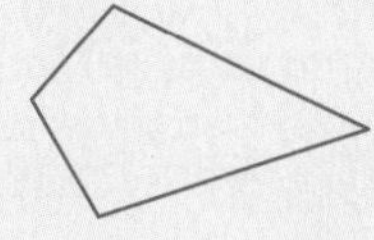

ONGOING ASSESSMENT and INTERVENTION 

***Diagnose Before* the Lesson**
6-3 Warm Up, TE p. 398

***Monitor During* the Lesson**
Check It Out! Exercises, SE pp. 399–401
Questioning Strategies, TE pp. 399–401

***Assess After* the Lesson**
6-3 Lesson Quiz, TE p. 405
Alternative Assessment, TE p. 405

Answers to *Think and Discuss*

1. Possible answer: The conclusion of each thm. is "The quad. is a ▱."
2. Possible answer: In Lesson 6-2, "A quad. is a ▱" is the hypothesis of each thm. rather than the conclusion.
3. See p. A5.

Assignment Guide

Assign *Guided Practice* exercises as necessary.

If you finished Examples **1–2**
- **Basic** 9–13, 17–20, 26, 27
- **Average** 9–13, 17–23, 26, 29
- **Advanced** 9–13, 17–23, 25–27, 29, 30, 33, 40

If you finished Examples **1–4**
- **Basic** 9–20, 26, 27, 34–37, 41–49
- **Average** 9–23, 24–32 even, 33–38, 41–49
- **Advanced** 9–16, 18, 20–49

Homework Quick Check
Quickly check key concepts.
Exercises: 10, 12, 14, 16, 18, 20

Answers

1. $FJ = HJ = 10$, so $\overline{FJ} \cong \overline{HJ}$. Thus $\overline{EG}$ bisects $\overline{FH}$. $EJ = GJ = 18$, so $\overline{EJ} \cong \overline{GJ}$. Thus $\overline{FH}$ bisects $\overline{EG}$. So the diags. of *EFGH* bisect each other. By Thm. 6-3-5, *EFGH* is a ▱.
2. $m\angle L = m\angle Q = 106°$, and $m\angle P = 74°$. So $\angle P$ is supp. to $\angle L$ and to $\angle Q$. So 1 ∠ of *KLPQ* is supp. to both of its cons. ∠s. By Thm. 6-3-4, *KLPQ* is a ▱.
3. Both pairs of opp. ∠s of the quad. are ≅. By Thm. 6-3-3, the quad. is a ▱.
4. 1 pair of opp. sides of the quad. are ≅. 1 diag. is bisected by the other diag. None of the conditions for a ▱ are met.

State Resources

6-3 Exercises

go.hrw.com
Homework Help Online
KEYWORD: MG7 6-3
Parent Resources Online
KEYWORD: MG7 Parent

GUIDED PRACTICE

SEE EXAMPLE 1 p. 399

1. Show that *EFGH* is a parallelogram for $s = 5$ and $t = 6$.

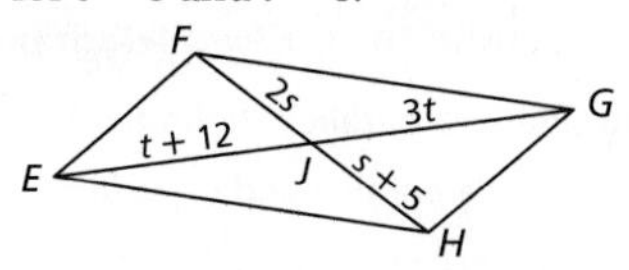

2. Show that *KLPQ* is a parallelogram for $m = 14$ and $n = 12.5$.

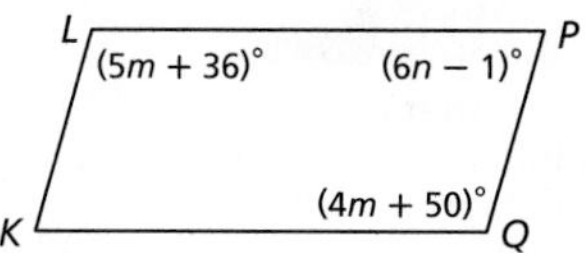

SEE EXAMPLE 2 p. 400

Determine if each quadrilateral must be a parallelogram. Justify your answer.

3. 

4. 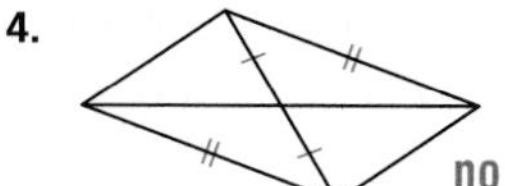

5. 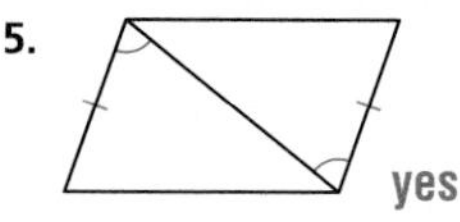

SEE EXAMPLE 3 p. 400

Show that the quadrilateral with the given vertices is a parallelogram.

6. $W(-5, -2)$, $X(-3, 3)$, $Y(3, 5)$, $Z(1, 0)$
7. $R(-1, -5)$, $S(-2, -1)$, $T(4, -1)$, $U(5, -5)$

SEE EXAMPLE 4 p. 401

8. **Navigation** A parallel rule can be used to plot a course on a navigation chart. The tool is made of two rulers connected at hinges to two congruent crossbars $\overline{AD}$ and $\overline{BC}$. You place the edge of one ruler on your desired course and then move the second ruler over the compass rose on the chart to read the bearing for your course. If $\overline{AD} \parallel \overline{BC}$, why is $\overline{AB}$ always parallel to $\overline{CD}$?

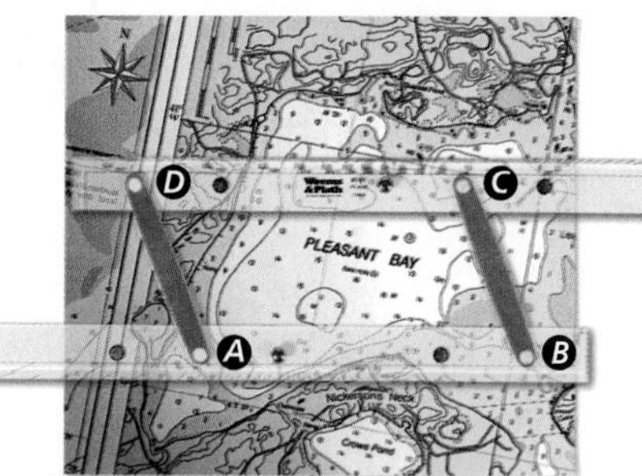

PRACTICE AND PROBLEM SOLVING

Independent Practice	
For Exercises	See Example
9–10	1
11–13	2
14–15	3
16	4

Extra Practice
Skills Practice p. S14
Application Practice p. S33

9. Show that *BCGH* is a parallelogram for $x = 3.2$ and $y = 7$.

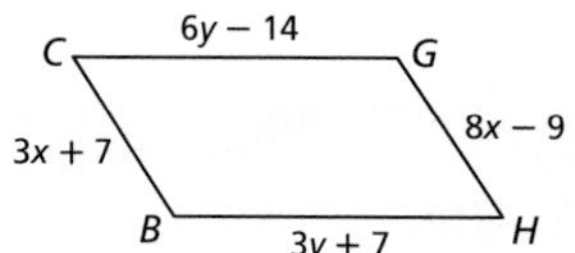

10. Show that *TUVW* is a parallelogram for $a = 19.5$ and $b = 22$.

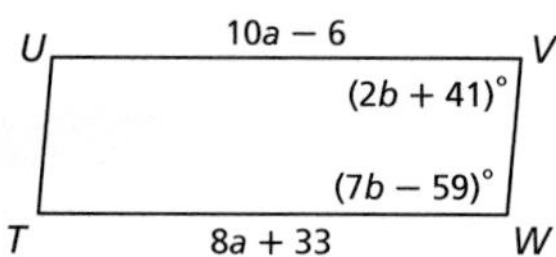

Determine if each quadrilateral must be a parallelogram. Justify your answer.

11. 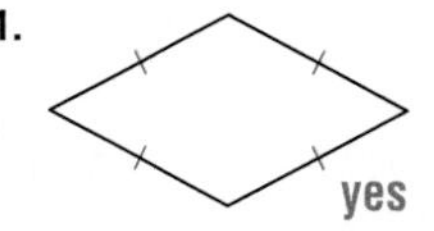

12. 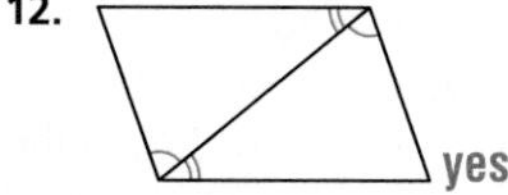

13. 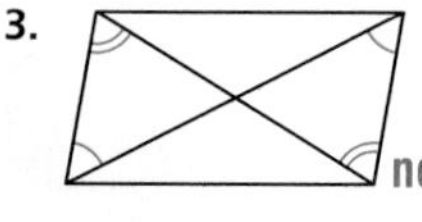

Show that the quadrilateral with the given vertices is a parallelogram.

14. $J(-1, 0)$, $K(-3, 7)$, $L(2, 6)$, $M(4, -1)$
15. $P(-8, -4)$, $Q(-5, 1)$, $R(1, -5)$, $S(-2, -10)$

5. Possible answer: A pair of alt. int. ∠s are ≅, so 1 pair of opp. sides are ∥. The same pair of opp. sides are ≅. By Thm. 6-3-1, the quad. is a ▱.
6. Possible answer: slope of $\overline{WX}$ = slope of $\overline{YZ} = \frac{5}{2}$; slope of $\overline{XY}$ = slope of $\overline{ZW} = \frac{1}{3}$; both pairs of opp. sides have the same slope, so $\overline{WX} \parallel \overline{YZ}$, and $\overline{XY} \parallel \overline{ZW}$; by def., *WXYZ* is a ▱.
7. Possible answer: slope of $\overline{ST}$ = slope of $\overline{UR} = 0$; $\overline{ST}$ and $\overline{UR}$ have the same slope, so $\overline{ST} \parallel \overline{UR}$; $ST = UR = 6$; 1 pair of opp. sides are ∥ and ≅; by Thm. 6-3-1, *RSTU* is a ▱.
8. Possible answer: $\overline{BC}$ and $\overline{AD}$ are opp. sides of quad. *ABCD*. It is given that $\overline{AD} \parallel \overline{BC}$ and $\overline{AD} \cong \overline{BC}$. By Thm. 6-3-1, if 1 pair of opp. sides of a quad. are ∥ and ≅, then the quad. is a ▱. So *ABCD* is a ▱. By the def. of a ▱, both pairs of opp. sides are ∥, so $\overline{AB}$ is always ∥ to $\overline{CD}$.
9. $BC = GH = 16.6$, so $\overline{BC} \cong \overline{GH}$. $CG = HB = 28$, so $\overline{CG} \cong \overline{HB}$. Since both pairs of opp. sides of *BCGH* are ≅, *BCGH* is a ▱ by Thm. 6-3-2.
10. $UV = WT = 189$, so $\overline{UV} \cong \overline{WT}$. $m\angle V = 85°$, and $m\angle W = 95°$, so $\angle V$ is supp. to $\angle W$. Therefore $\overline{UV} \parallel \overline{WT}$. By Thm. 6-3-1, *TUVW* is a ▱.

18. No; you are only given the measures of the 4 ∠s formed by the intersecting diags. of the quad. None of the sets of conditions for a ▱ are met.

19. Yes; the diags. of the quad. bisect each other. By Thm. 6-3-5, the quad. is a ▱.

16. **Design** The toolbox has cantilever trays that pull away from the box so that you can reach the items beneath them. Two congruent brackets connect each tray to the box. Given that $AD = BC$, how do the brackets $\overline{AB}$ and $\overline{CD}$ keep the tray horizontal?

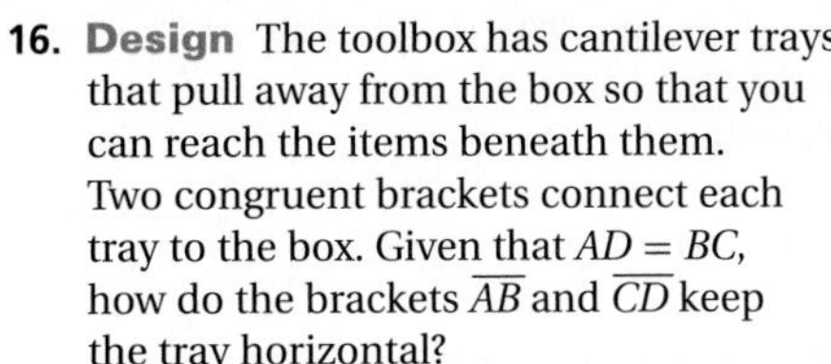

Determine if each quadrilateral must be a parallelogram. Justify your answer.

17. 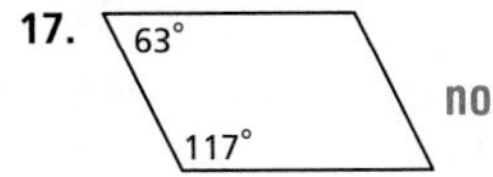

no

18. 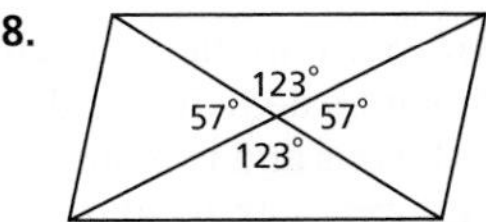

19. 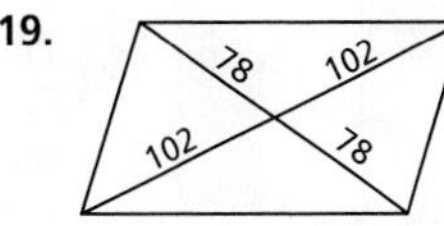

Algebra **Find the values of a and b that would make the quadrilateral a parallelogram.**

20. 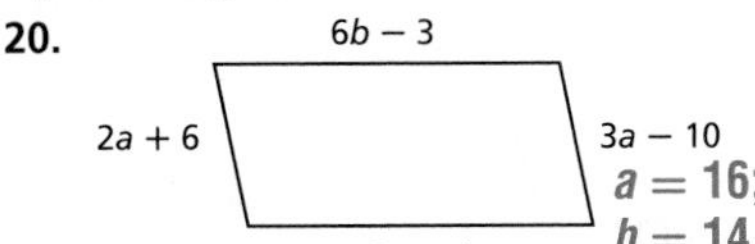

$a = 16$; $b = 14$

21. 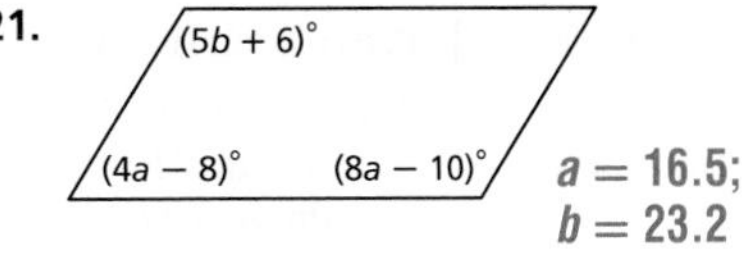

$a = 16.5$; $b = 23.2$

22. 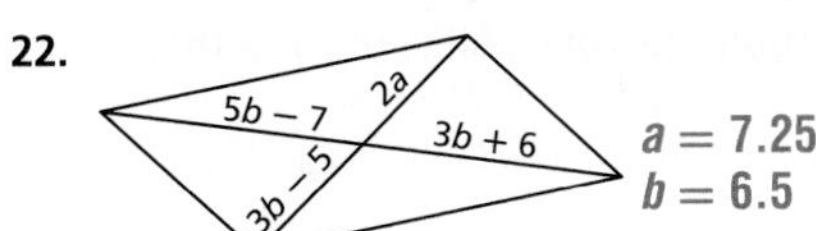

$a = 7.25$; $b = 6.5$

23. 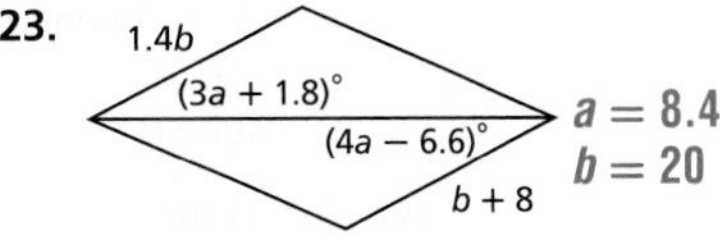

$a = 8.4$; $b = 20$

25. Possible answer: The red and green △s are isosc. rt. △s, so the measure of each acute ∠ of the △s is 45°. Each of the smaller ∠s of the yellow stripe is comp. to 1 of the acute ∠s of the rt. △s, so the measure of each of the smaller ∠s of the yellow stripe is 90° − 45° = 45°. Each of the larger ∠s of the yellow stripe is supp. to 1 of the acute ∠s of the rt. △s, so the measure of each of the larger ∠s of the yellow stripe is 180° − 45° = 135°. So the yellow stripe is a quad. in which both pairs of opp. ∠s are ≅. By Thm. 6-3-3, the shape of the yellow stripe is a ▱.

24. **Critical Thinking** Draw a quadrilateral that has congruent diagonals but is not a parallelogram. What can you conclude about using congruent diagonals as a condition for a parallelogram?

25. **Social Studies** The angles at the corners of the flag of the Republic of the Congo are right angles. The red and green triangles are congruent isosceles right triangles. Why is the shape of the yellow stripe a parallelogram?

26. Complete the two-column proof of Theorem 6-3-2 by filling in the blanks.

Given: $\overline{AB} \cong \overline{CD}$, $\overline{BC} \cong \overline{DA}$

Prove: $ABCD$ is a parallelogram.

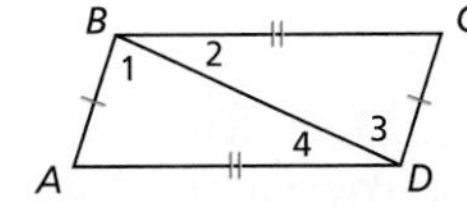

Proof:

Statements	Reasons
1. $\overline{AB} \cong \overline{CD}$, $\overline{BC} \cong \overline{DA}$	1. Given
2. $\overline{BD} \cong \overline{BD}$	2. a. ___?___
3. $\triangle DAB \cong$ b. ___?___ $\triangle BCD$	3. c. ___?___ SSS
4. $\angle 1 \cong$ d. ___?___, $\angle 4 \cong$ e. ___?___	4. CPCTC
5. $\overline{AB} \parallel \overline{CD}$, $\overline{BC} \parallel \overline{DA}$	5. f. ___?___
6. $ABCD$ is a parallelogram.	6. g. ___?___ Def. of ▱

d. ∠3
e. ∠2

a. Reflex. Prop. of ≅

f. Conv. of Alt. Int. ∠s Thm.

COMMON ERROR ALERT

In **Exercise 24,** some students may incorrectly draw diagonals that bisect each other. Other students might draw congruent diagonals that also bisect each other. Remind students to draw diagonals that are congruent but *do not* bisect each other.

Auditory For **Exercises 11–13** and **17–19,** ask students to state the properties represented by each diagram. Then state the six conditions for parallelograms and have the students decide if any of these are met.

Answers

16. Possible answer: The brackets are always the same length, so it is always true that $AB = CD$. The bolts are always the same distance apart, so it is always true that $BC = DA$. By Thm. 6-3-2, $ABCD$ is always a ▱. The side $\overline{AD}$ stays horiz. no matter how you move the tray. Since $\overline{BC} \parallel \overline{AD}$, $\overline{BC}$ stays horiz. Since $\overline{BC}$ holds the tray in position, the tray will stay horiz. no matter how it is moved.

17. The given ∠ measures only indicate that 1 ∠ of the quad. is supp. to 1 of its cons. ∠s. By Thm. 6-3-4, you must know that 1 ∠ is supp. to both of its cons. ∠s in order to conclude that the quad. is a ▱.

24. Possible answer:

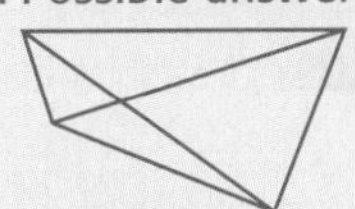

If the diags. of a quad. are ≅, you cannot necessarily conclude that the quad. is a ▱.

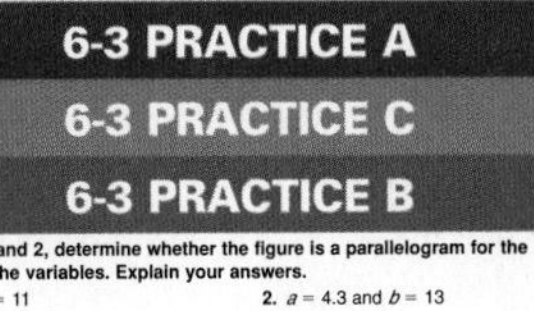

For Exercises 1 and 2, determine whether the figure is a parallelogram for the given values of the variables. Explain your answers.

1. $x = 9$ and $y = 11$
2. $a = 4.3$ and $b = 13$

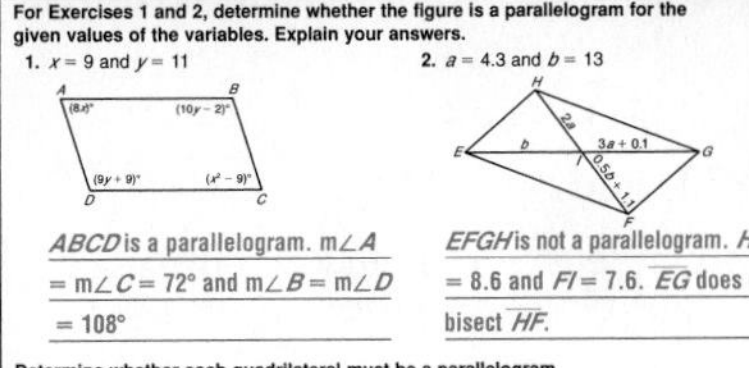

1. $ABCD$ is a parallelogram. m∠A = m∠C = 72° and m∠B = m∠D = 108°
2. $EFGH$ is not a parallelogram. HI = 8.6 and FI = 7.6. $\overline{EG}$ does not bisect $\overline{HF}$.

Determine whether each quadrilateral must be a parallelogram. Justify your answers.

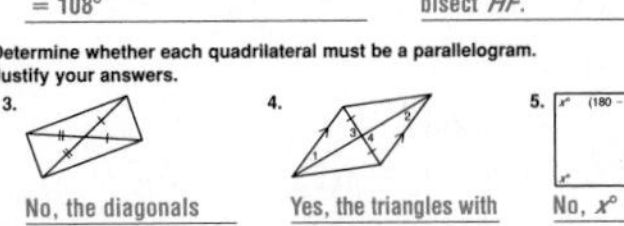

3. No, the diagonals do not necessarily bisect each other.
4. Yes, the triangles with numbered angles are ≅ by AAS. By CPCTC, the parallel sides are congruent.
5. No, $x° + x°$ may not be 180°.

Use the given method to determine whether the quadrilateral with the given vertices is a parallelogram.

6. Find the slopes of all four sides: $J(-4, -1)$, $K(-7, -4)$, $L(2, -10)$, $M(5, -7)$
   $JKLM$ is a parallelogram.
7. Find the lengths of all four sides: $P(2, 2)$, $Q(1, -3)$, $R(-4, 2)$, $S(-3, 7)$
   $PQRS$ is a parallelogram.
8. Find the slopes and lengths of one pair of opposite sides: $T\left(\frac{3}{2}, -2\right)$, $U\left(\frac{3}{2}, 4\right)$, $V\left(-\frac{1}{2}, 0\right)$, $W\left(-\frac{1}{2}, -6\right)$
   $TUVW$ is a parallelogram.

Answers

11. All the sides are ≅ to each other. So both pairs of opp. sides are ≅. By Thm. 6-3-2, the quad. is a ▱.

12. Each pair of ≅ ∠s is a pair of alt. int. ∠s. So both pairs of opp. sides of the quad. are ∥. The quad. is a ▱ by def.

13. Each pair of ≅ ∠s is a pair of alt. int. ∠s. Each pair indicates that the same set of opp. sides of the quad. are ∥. If only 1 set of opp. sides are ∥, you cannot conclude that the quad. is a ▱.

14. Possible answer: slope of $\overline{JK}$ = slope of $\overline{LM} = -\frac{7}{2}$; slope of $\overline{KL}$ = slope of $\overline{MJ} = -\frac{1}{5}$; both pairs of opp. sides have the same slope, so $\overline{JK} \parallel \overline{LM}$ and $\overline{KL} \parallel \overline{MJ}$; by def., $JKLM$ is a ▱.

15. Possible answer: slope of $\overline{PQ}$ = slope of $\overline{RS} = \frac{5}{3}$; $\overline{PQ}$ and $\overline{RS}$ have the same slope, so $\overline{PQ} \parallel \overline{RS}$; $PQ = RS = \sqrt{34}$; 1 pair of opp. sides are ∥ and ≅; by Thm. 6-3-1, $PQRS$ is a ▱.

Exercise 34 involves determining if a given quadrilateral is a parallelogram. This exercise prepares students for the Multi-Step Test Prep on page 406.

Answers

28. Given: $ABCD$ is a ▱. E is the mdpt. of $\overline{AB}$, and F is the mdpt. of $\overline{DC}$.
Prove: $AEFD$ and $EBCF$ are ▱s.
Proof: Since $ABCD$ is a ▱, $\overline{AB} \parallel \overline{CD}$, so $\overline{AE} \parallel \overline{DF}$ and $\overline{EB} \parallel \overline{FC}$. Since opp. sides of a ▱ are ≅, $\overline{AB} \cong \overline{DC}$. It is given that E is the mdpt. of $\overline{AB}$ and F is the mdpt. of $\overline{DC}$. Because these two segs. are ≅, it follows that $\overline{AE} \cong \overline{EB} \cong \overline{DF} \cong \overline{FC}$. Since $\overline{AE} \parallel \overline{DF}$ and $\overline{AE} \cong \overline{DF}$, $AEFD$ is a ▱. Similarly, $EBCF$ is a ▱.

29. Possible answer:
1. $\angle E \cong \angle G$, $\angle F \cong \angle H$ (Given)
2. $m\angle E = m\angle G$, $m\angle F = m\angle H$ (Def. of ≅ ∠s)
3. $m\angle E + m\angle F + m\angle G + m\angle H = 360°$ (Polygon Sum Thm.)
4. $m\angle E + m\angle F + m\angle E + m\angle F = 360°$, $m\angle E + m\angle H + m\angle E + m\angle H = 360°$ (Subst.)
5. $2m\angle E + 2m\angle F = 360°$, $2m\angle E + 2m\angle H = 360°$ (Distrib. Prop.)
6. $m\angle E + m\angle F = 180°$, $m\angle E + m\angle H = 180°$ (Div. Prop. of =)
7. $\angle E$ is supp. to $\angle F$. $\angle E$ is supp. to $\angle H$. (Def. of supp. ∠s)
8. $\overline{EF} \parallel \overline{GH}$, $\overline{FG} \parallel \overline{HE}$ (Conv. of Same-Side Int. ∠s Thm.)
9. $EFGH$ is a ▱. (Def. of ▱)

30.
1. $\overline{JL}$ and $\overline{KM}$ bisect each other. (Given)
2. $\overline{JN} \cong \overline{LN}$, $\overline{KN} \cong \overline{MN}$ (Def. of bisect)
3. $\angle JNK \cong \angle LNM$, $\angle KNL \cong \angle MNJ$ (Vert. ∠s Thm.)
4. $\triangle JNK \cong \triangle LNM$, $\triangle KNL \cong \triangle MNJ$ (SAS)
5. $\angle JKN \cong \angle LMN$, $\angle KLN \cong \angle MJN$ (CPCTC)
6. $\overline{JK} \parallel \overline{LM}$, $\overline{KL} \parallel \overline{MJ}$ (Conv. of Alt. Int. ∠s Thm.)
7. $JKLM$ is a ▱. (Def. of ▱)

31–33. See pp. A21–22.

34b. Since $\angle S$ and $\angle R$ are supp., $\overline{PS} \parallel \overline{QR}$. Thus $PQRS$ is a ▱ by Thm. 6-3-1.

c. Draw $\overline{PR}$. $\angle QPR \cong \angle SRP$ (Alt. Int. ∠s Thm.), and $\overline{PR} \cong \overline{PR}$ (Reflex. Prop. of ≅). So $\triangle QPR \cong \triangle SRP$ by AAS, and $\overline{PQ} \cong \overline{SR}$ (CPCTC). Since $\overline{PQ} \parallel \overline{SR}$ and $\overline{PQ} \cong \overline{SR}$, $PQRS$ is a ▱ by Thm. 6-3-1.

37, 38, 40–43, 45. See p. A22.

---

a. $\angle Q$ b. $\angle S$ c. $\overline{SP}$ d. $\overline{RS}$ e. ▱

27. Complete the paragraph proof of Theorem 6-3-4 by filling in the blanks.
Given: $\angle P$ is supplementary to $\angle Q$.
$\angle P$ is supplementary to $\angle S$.
Prove: $PQRS$ is a parallelogram.
Proof:
It is given that $\angle P$ is supplementary to **a.** ___?___ and **b.** ___?___. By the Converse of the Same-Side Interior Angles Theorem, $\overline{QR} \parallel$ **c.** ___?___ and $\overline{PQ} \parallel$ **d.** ___?___. So $PQRS$ is a parallelogram by the definition of **e.** ___?___.

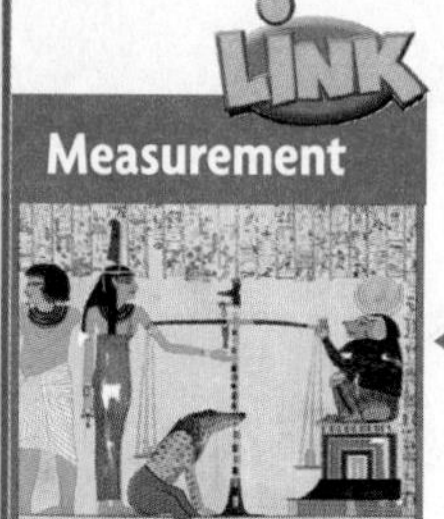

LINK Measurement

Ancient balance scales had one beam that moved on a single hinge. The stress on the hinge often made the scale imprecise.

28. **Measurement** In the eighteenth century, Gilles Personne de Roberval designed a scale with two beams and two hinges. In ▱$ABCD$, E is the midpoint of $\overline{AB}$, and F is the midpoint of $\overline{CD}$. Write a paragraph proof that $AEFD$ and $EBCF$ are parallelograms.

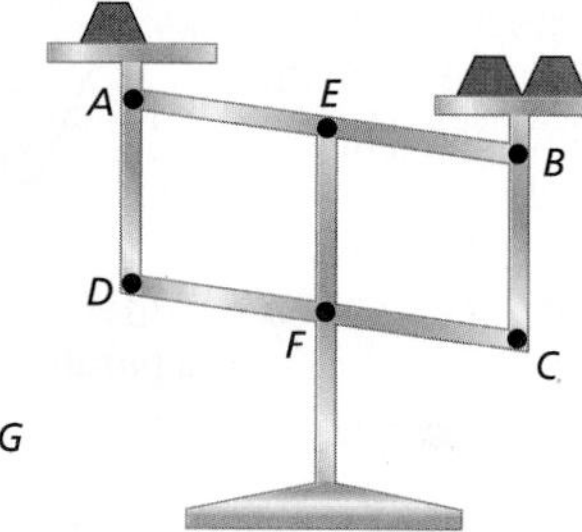

Prove each theorem.

29. Theorem 6-3-3
Given: $\angle E \cong \angle G$, $\angle F \cong \angle H$
Prove: $EFGH$ is a parallelogram.

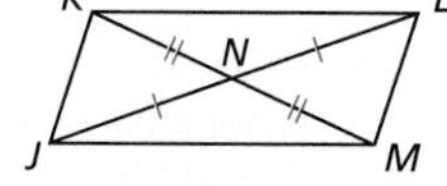

Plan: Show that the sum of the interior angles of $EFGH$ is 360°. Then apply properties of equality to show that $m\angle E + m\angle F = 180°$ and $m\angle E + m\angle H = 180°$. Then you can conclude that $\overline{EF} \parallel \overline{GH}$ and $\overline{FG} \parallel \overline{HE}$.

30. Theorem 6-3-5
Given: $\overline{JL}$ and $\overline{KM}$ bisect each other.
Prove: $JKLM$ is a parallelogram.
Plan: Show that $\triangle JNK \cong \triangle LNM$ and $\triangle KNL \cong \triangle MNJ$. Then use the fact that the corresponding angles are congruent to show $\overline{JK} \parallel \overline{LM}$ and $\overline{KL} \parallel \overline{MJ}$.

31. Prove that the figure formed by two midsegments of a triangle and their corresponding bases is a parallelogram.

32. **Write About It** Use the theorems from Lessons 6-2 and 6-3 to write three biconditional statements about parallelograms.

33. **Construction** Explain how you can construct a parallelogram based on the conditions of Theorem 6-3-1. Use your method to construct a parallelogram.

MULTI-STEP TEST PREP

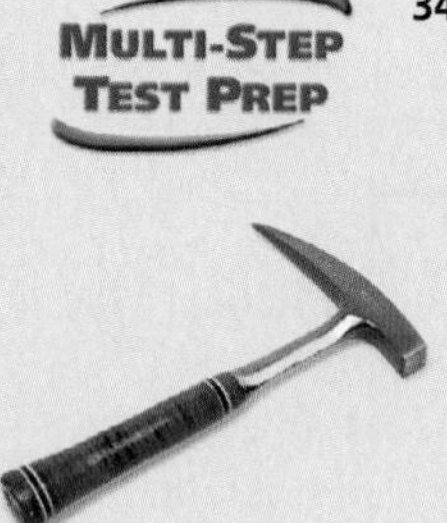

34. This problem will prepare you for the Multi-Step Test Prep on page 406.
A geologist made the following observations while examining this amethyst crystal. Tell whether each set of observations allows the geologist to conclude that $PQRS$ is a parallelogram. If so, explain why.

a. $\overline{PQ} \cong \overline{SR}$, and $\overline{PS} \parallel \overline{QR}$. no
b. $\angle S$ and $\angle R$ are supplementary, and $\overline{PS} \cong \overline{QR}$. yes
c. $\angle S \cong \angle Q$, and $\overline{PQ} \parallel \overline{SR}$. yes

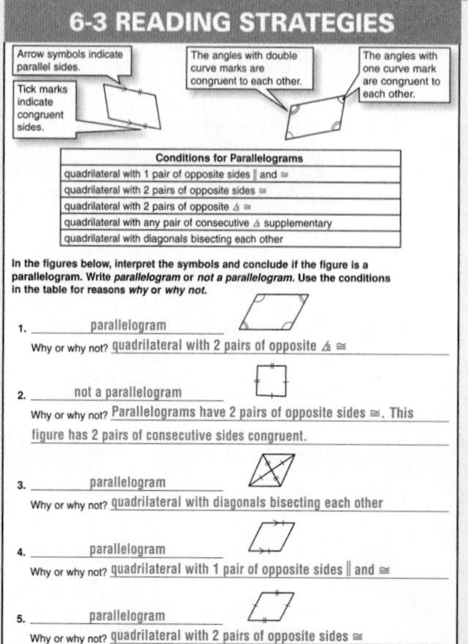

6-3 READING STRATEGIES

Arrow symbols indicate parallel sides.
Tick marks indicate congruent sides.
The angles with double curve marks are congruent to each other.
The angles with one curve mark are congruent to each other.

Conditions for Parallelograms
quadrilateral with 1 pair of opposite sides ∥ and ≅
quadrilateral with 2 pairs of opposite sides ≅
quadrilateral with 2 pairs of opposite ∠s ≅
quadrilateral with any pair of consecutive ∠s supplementary
quadrilateral with diagonals bisecting each other

In the figures below, interpret the symbols and conclude if the figure is a parallelogram. Write *parallelogram* or *not a parallelogram*. Use the conditions in the table for reasons *why* or *why not*.

1. parallelogram
Why or why not? quadrilateral with 2 pairs of opposite ∠s ≅

2. not a parallelogram
Why or why not? Parallelograms have 2 pairs of opposite sides ≅. This figure has 2 pairs of consecutive sides congruent.

3. parallelogram
Why or why not? quadrilateral with diagonals bisecting each other

4. parallelogram
Why or why not? quadrilateral with 1 pair of opposite sides ∥ and ≅

5. parallelogram
Why or why not? quadrilateral with 2 pairs of opposite sides ≅

6-3 RETEACH

You can use the following conditions to determine whether a quadrilateral such as $PQRS$ is a parallelogram.

Conditions for Parallelograms	
$\overline{QR} \parallel \overline{SP}$, $\overline{QR} \cong \overline{SP}$ If one pair of opposite sides is ∥ and ≅, then $PQRS$ is a parallelogram.	$\overline{QR} \cong \overline{SP}$, $\overline{PQ} \cong \overline{RS}$ If both pairs of opposite sides are ≅, then $PQRS$ is a parallelogram.
$\angle P \cong \angle R$, $\angle Q \cong \angle S$ If both pairs of opposite angles are ≅, then $PQRS$ is a parallelogram.	$\overline{PT} \cong \overline{RT}$, $\overline{QT} \cong \overline{ST}$ If the diagonals bisect each other, then $PQRS$ is a parallelogram.

A quadrilateral is also a parallelogram if one of the angles is supplementary to both of its consecutive angles.

$65° + 115° = 180°$, so $\angle A$ is supplementary to $\angle B$ and $\angle D$.

Therefore, $ABCD$ is a parallelogram.

Show that each quadrilateral is a parallelogram for the given values. Explain.

1. **Given:** $x = 9$ and $y = 4$
$QR = ST = 12$; $RS = TQ = 16$; both pairs of opp. sides are ≅.

2. **Given:** $w = 3$ and $z = 31$
$DE = FC = 10$; $m\angle E = 118°$ and $m\angle F = 62°$, so $\angle E$, $\angle F$ are supp. and $\overline{DE} \parallel \overline{FC}$; one pair of opposite sides are ∥ and ≅.

TEST PREP

35. What additional information would allow you to conclude that $WXYZ$ is a parallelogram?

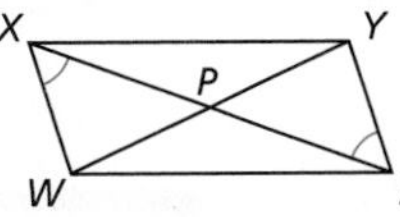

Ⓐ $\overline{XY} \cong \overline{ZW}$ Ⓒ $\overline{WY} \cong \overline{WZ}$
Ⓑ (circled) $\overline{WX} \cong \overline{YZ}$ Ⓓ $\angle XWY \cong \angle ZYW$

36. Which could be the coordinates of the fourth vertex of ▱$ABCD$ with $A(-1, -1)$, $B(1, 3)$, and $C(6, 1)$?

Ⓕ $D(8, 5)$ Ⓖ (circled) $D(4, -3)$ Ⓗ $D(13, 3)$ Ⓙ $D(3, 7)$

37. **Short Response** The vertices of quadrilateral $RSTV$ are $R(-5, 0)$, $S(-1, 3)$, $T(5, 1)$, and $V(2, -2)$. Is $RSTV$ a parallelogram? Justify your answer. no

CHALLENGE AND EXTEND

38. **Write About It** As the upper platform of the movable staircase is raised and lowered, the height of each step changes. How does the upper platform remain parallel to the ground?

$(3, 1)$; $(-6, -3.5)$ 39. **Multi-Step** The diagonals of a parallelogram intersect at $(-2, 1.5)$. Two vertices are located at $(-7, 2)$ and $(2, 6.5)$. Find the coordinates of the other two vertices.

40. **Given:** D is the midpoint of $\overline{AC}$, and E is the midpoint of $\overline{BC}$.
Prove: $\overline{DE} \parallel \overline{AB}$, $DE = \frac{1}{2}AB$
(*Hint:* Extend $\overline{DE}$ to form $\overline{DF}$ so that $\overline{EF} \cong \overline{DE}$. Then show that $DFBA$ is a parallelogram.)

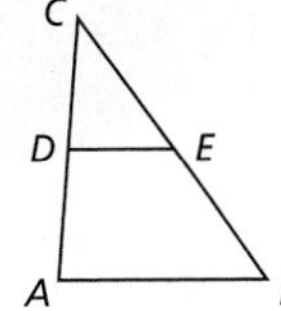

SPIRAL REVIEW

Complete a table of values for each function. Use the domain $\{-5, -2, 0, 0.5\}$. *(Previous course)*

41. $f(x) = 7x - 3$ 42. $f(x) = \dfrac{x+2}{2}$ 43. $f(x) = 3x^2 + 2$

Use SAS to explain why each pair of triangles are congruent. *(Lesson 4-4)*

44. $\triangle ABD \cong \triangle CDB$

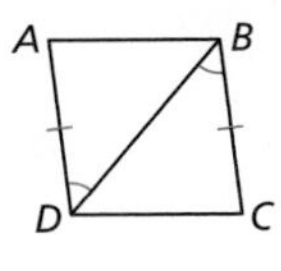

45. $\triangle TUW \cong \triangle VUW$

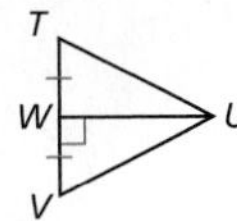

44. It is given that $\overline{BC} \cong \overline{DA}$ and that $\angle DBC \cong \angle BDA$. By the Reflex. Prop. of $\cong$, $\overline{DB} \cong \overline{DB}$. Therefore, $\triangle ABD \cong \triangle CDB$ by SAS.

For ▱$JKLM$, find each measure. *(Lesson 6-2)*

46. NM 14 47. LM 12
48. JL 16 49. JK 12

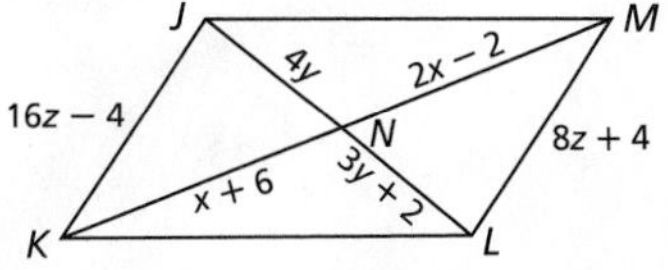

TEST PREP DOCTOR For **Exercise 35,** ask students which sides of $WXYZ$ are parallel by the Converse of the Alternate Interior Angles Theorem.

Students who chose **F** for **Exercise 36** did not consider the order of the vertices. Remind students that the problem specifies this order.

Journal

Have students describe how to use the measures of the sides of a quadrilateral to determine if it is a parallelogram.

ALTERNATIVE ASSESSMENT

Have pairs of students use straws or spaghetti to create parallelograms by using three different methods (e.g., opposite sides are congruent, or diagonals bisect each other). Have students use the theorems from the lesson to explain why each construction is valid.

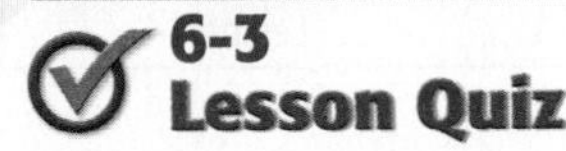

6-3 Lesson Quiz

1. Show that $JKLM$ is a parallelogram for $a = 4$ and $b = 5$.

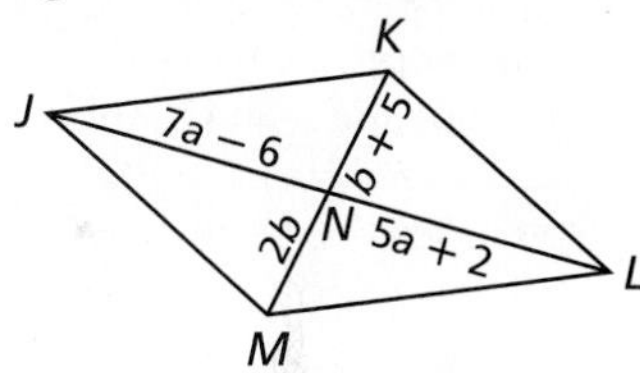

$JN = LN = 22$; $KN = MN = 10$; so $JKLM$ is a ▱ by Thm. 6-3-5.

2. Determine if $QWRT$ must be a parallelogram. Justify your answer.

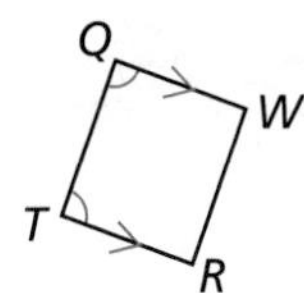

No; 1 pair of cons. ∠s are ≅, and 1 pair of opp. sides are ∥. The conditions for a ▱ are not met.

3. Show that the quadrilateral with vertices $E(-1, 5)$, $F(2, 4)$, $G(0, -3)$, and $H(-3, -2)$ is a parallelogram. Slope of $\overline{EF}$ = slope of $\overline{GH} = -\frac{1}{3}$; $EF = GH = \sqrt{10}$; since 1 pair of opp. sides are ∥ and ≅, $EFGH$ is a ▱ by Thm. 6-3-1.

Also available on transparency

6-3 PROBLEM SOLVING

Use the diagram for Exercises 1 and 2.
A *pantograph* is a drawing instrument used to magnify figures.

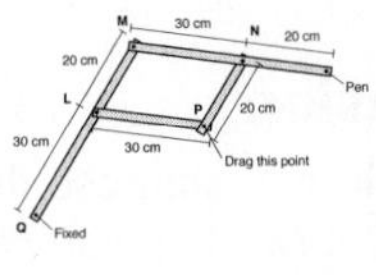

M
30 cm
N
20 cm
20 cm
Pen
L
P
20 cm
30 cm
30 cm
Drag this point
Q
Fixed

1. If you drag the point at P so that the angle measures change, will $LMNP$ continue to be a parallelogram? Explain.

Yes; both pairs of opposite sides of quadrilateral $LMNP$ remain congruent, so $LMNP$ is always a ▱.

2. If you drag the point at P so that $m\angle LMN = 56°$, what will be the measure of $\angle QLP$?

56°

3. In the state flag of Maryland, $m\angle G = 60°$ and $m\angle H = 120°$. Name one more condition that would allow you to conclude that $EFGH$ is a parallelogram.

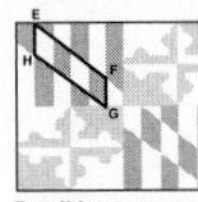

E
H
F
G

Possible answer: $m\angle F = 120°$

4. The graphs of $y = 2x$, $y = 2x - 5$, and $y = -x$ in the coordinate plane contain three sides of a quadrilateral. Give an equation of a line whose graph contains a segment that can complete the quadrilateral to form a parallelogram. Explain.

Possible answer: $y = -x + 1$; both pairs of opposite sides have the same slope, so they are parallel.

Choose the best answer.

5. For which value of n is $QRST$ a parallelogram?

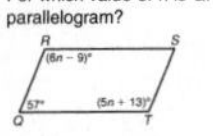

R
S
$(8n - 9)°$
57°
$(5n + 13)°$
Q
T

A 15.5
B 20.6
Ⓒ 22
D 25

6. Under what conditions must $ABCD$ be a parallelogram?

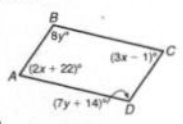

B
$8y°$
$(3x - 1)°$
C
A
$(2x + 22)°$
$(7y + 14)°$
D

F $x = 23$
G $y = 14$
Ⓗ $x = 23$ and $y = 14$
J $x = 14$ and $y = 23$

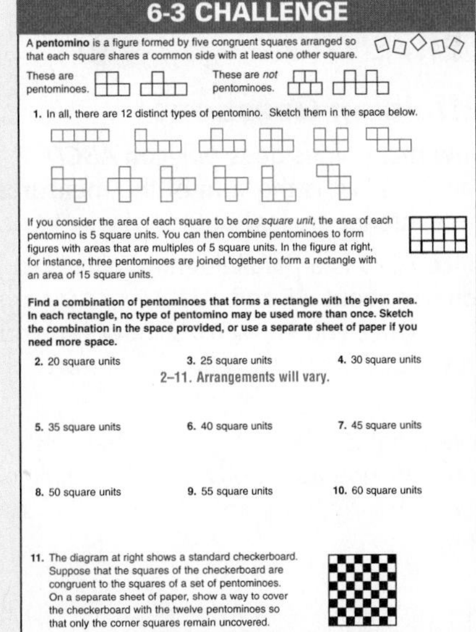

6-3 CHALLENGE

A **pentomino** is a figure formed by five congruent squares arranged so that each square shares a common side with at least one other square.

These are pentominoes. These are *not* pentominoes.

1. In all, there are 12 distinct types of pentomino. Sketch them in the space below.

If you consider the area of each square to be *one square unit*, the area of each pentomino is 5 square units. You can then combine pentominoes to form figures with areas that are multiples of 5 square units. In the figure at right, for instance, three pentominoes are joined together to form a rectangle with an area of 15 square units.

Find a combination of pentominoes that forms a rectangle with the given area. In each rectangle, no type of pentomino may be used more than once. Sketch the combination in the space provided, or use a separate sheet of paper if you need more space.

2. 20 square units 3. 25 square units 4. 30 square units

2–11. Arrangements will vary.

5. 35 square units 6. 40 square units 7. 45 square units

8. 50 square units 9. 55 square units 10. 60 square units

11. The diagram at right shows a standard checkerboard. Suppose that the squares of the checkerboard are congruent to the squares of a set of pentominoes. On a separate sheet of paper, show a way to cover the checkerboard with the twelve pentominoes so that only the corner squares remain uncovered.

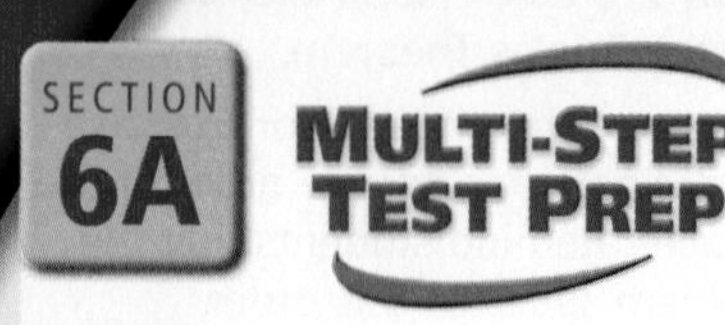

Organizer

Objective: Assess students' ability to apply concepts and skills in Lessons 6-1 through 6-3 in a real-world format.

Resources

Geometry Assessments
www.mathtekstoolkit.org

Problem	Text Reference
1	Lesson 6-1
2	Lesson 6-2
3	Lesson 6-3

Answers

2. 85°; since *FGHJ* is a ▱, $\angle F$ and $\angle J$ are supp. So $9x - 13 + 7x + 1 = 180$, and $x = 12$. Thus $m\angle J = (7)12 + 1 = 85°$. Opp. ∡ are ≅, so $m\angle G = 85°$.

State Resources

SECTION 6A

Polygons and Parallelograms

Crystal Clear A crystal is a mineral formation that has polygonal faces. Geologists classify crystals based on the types of polygons that the faces form.

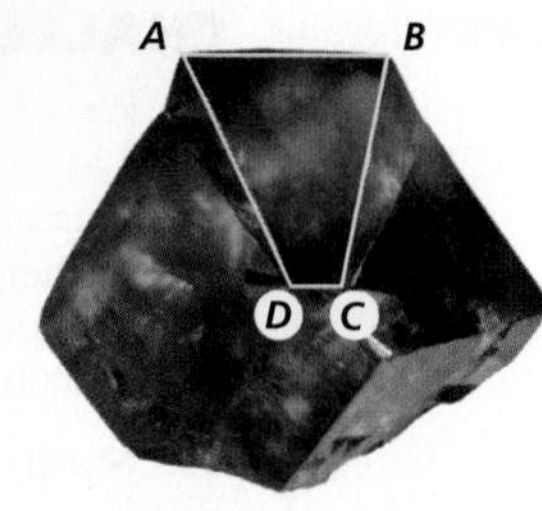

1. What type of polygon is *ABCD* in the fluorite crystal? Given that $\overline{AB} \parallel \overline{DC}$, $m\angle B = 82°$, $m\angle D = 116°$, find $m\angle A$. **quadrilateral; 64°**

2. The red crystals are called rhodochrosite. The face *FGHJ* is a parallelogram. Given that $m\angle F = (9x - 13)°$ and $m\angle J = (7x + 1)°$, find $m\angle G$. Explain how you found this angle measure.

3. While studying the amazonite crystal, a geologist found that $\overline{MN} \cong \overline{QP}$ and $\angle NQP \cong \angle QNM$. Can the geologist conclude that *MNPQ* is a parallelogram? Why or why not? Justify your answer.

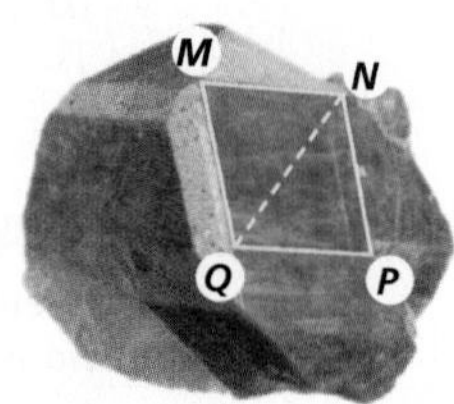

3. **Yes; $\angle NQP \cong \angle QNM$, so $\overline{MN} \parallel \overline{QP}$ by the Conv. of the Alt. Int. ∡ Thm. So *MNPQ* is a ▱ by Thm. 6-3-1.**

INTERVENTION

Scaffolding Questions

1. How many sides does polygon *ABCD* have? 4 What is the sum of the measures of its interior angles? 360°
2. Since *FGHJ* is a parallelogram, what can you say about $\angle F$ and $\angle J$? $\angle F$ and $\angle J$ are supp. Once you know $m\angle J$, how can you find $m\angle G$? $\angle J$ and $\angle G$ are ≅, so $m\angle G = m\angle J$.
3. Given that $\angle NQP \cong \angle QNM$, what can you conclude about $\overline{MN}$ and $\overline{QP}$? Explain. They are ∥ by the Conv. of the Alt. Int. ∡ Thm.

Extension

In **Problem 3,** suppose that $\overline{MN} \cong \overline{QP}$ and $\overline{MQ} \parallel \overline{NP}$. Can you conclude that *MNPQ* is a parallelogram? If so, explain why. If not, draw a counterexample. no

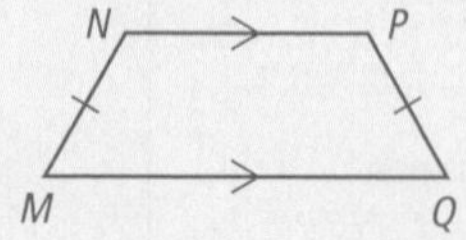

SECTION 6A

Quiz for Lessons 6-1 Through 6-3

6-1 Properties and Attributes of Polygons

Tell whether each figure is a polygon. If it is a polygon, name it by the number of its sides.

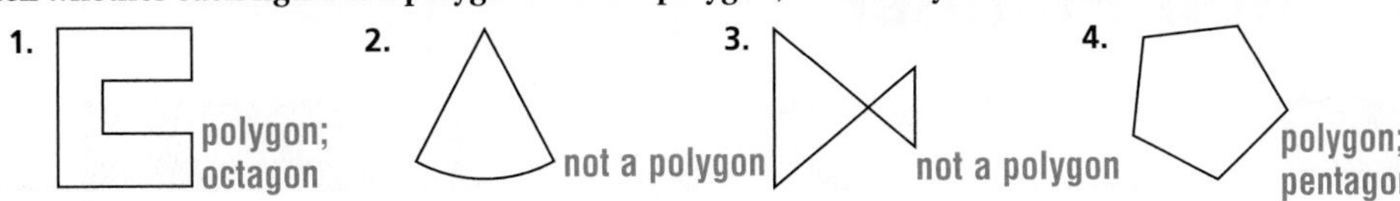

5. Find the sum of the interior angle measures of a convex 16-gon. 2520°
6. The surface of a trampoline is in the shape of a regular hexagon. Find the measure of each interior angle of the trampoline. 120°
7. A park in the shape of quadrilateral $PQRS$ is bordered by four sidewalks. Find the measure of each exterior angle of the park.
8. Find the measure of each exterior angle of a regular decagon. 36°

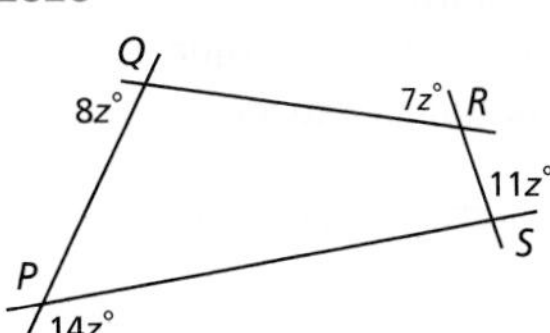

7. 126°; 72°; 63°; 99°

6-2 Properties of Parallelograms

A pantograph is used to copy drawings. Its legs form a parallelogram. In ▱$JKLM$, $LM = 17$ cm, $KN = 13.5$ cm, and $m\angle KJM = 102°$. Find each measure.

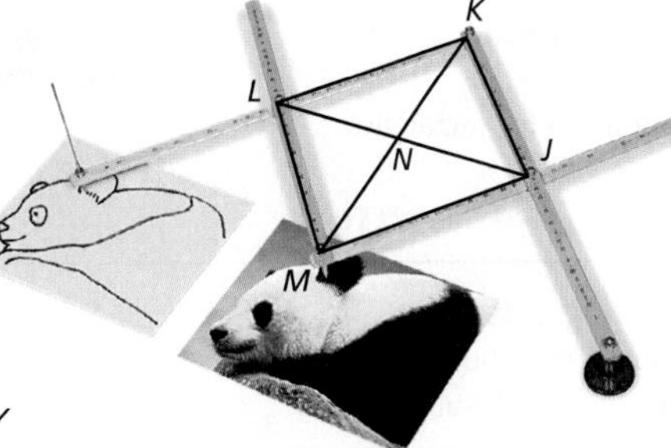

9. KM 27 cm
10. KJ 17 cm
11. MN 13.5 cm
12. $m\angle JKL$ 78°
13. $m\angle JML$ 78°
14. $m\angle KLM$ 102°
15. Three vertices of ▱$ABCD$ are $A(-3, 1)$, $B(5, 7)$, and $C(6, 2)$. Find the coordinates of vertex D. $(-2, -4)$

$WXYZ$ is a parallelogram. Find each measure.

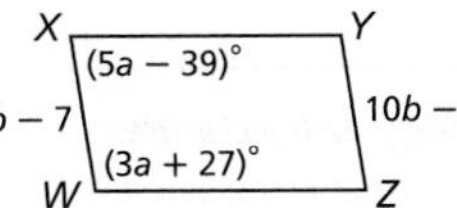

16. WX 11
17. YZ 11
18. $m\angle X$ 81°
19. $m\angle W$ 99°

6-3 Conditions for Parallelograms

20. Show that $RSTV$ is a parallelogram for $x = 6$ and $y = 4.5$.

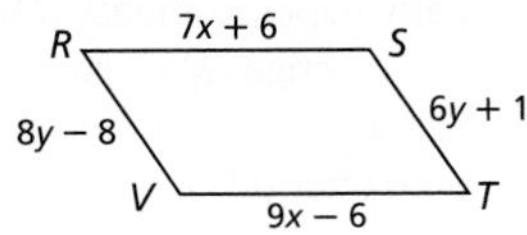

21. Show that $GHJK$ is a parallelogram for $m = 12$ and $n = 9.5$.

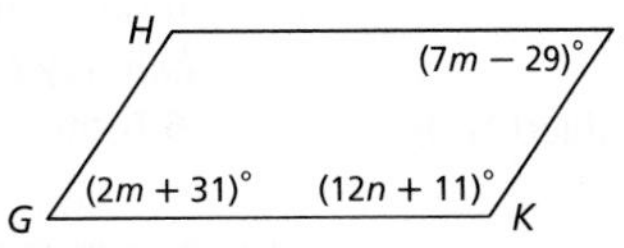

Determine if each quadrilateral must be a parallelogram. Justify your answer.

22. 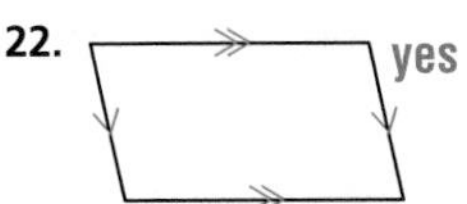 yes
23. 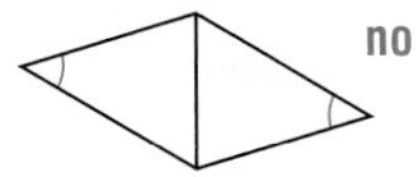 no
24. 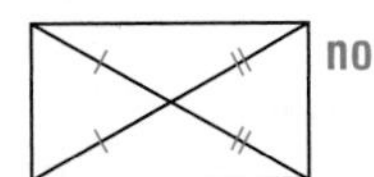 no

25. Show that a quadrilateral with vertices $C(-9, 4)$, $D(-4, 8)$, $E(2, 6)$, and $F(-3, 2)$ is a parallelogram.

Organizer

Objective: Assess students' mastery of concepts and skills in Lessons 6-1 through 6-3.

Resources

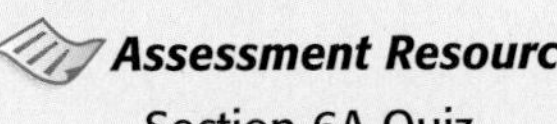
Section 6A Quiz

Teacher One Stop™
Test & Practice Generator

Resources

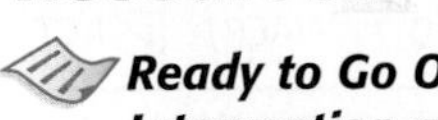

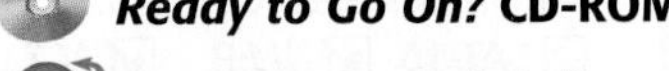

Answers

20–25. See p. A22.

READY TO GO ON? Diagnose and Prescribe

NO INTERVENE

Ready to Go On? Intervention	*Ready to Go On? Intervention,* Section 6A: Worksheets	CD-ROM	Online
Lesson 6-1	6-1 Intervention	Activity 6-1	Diagnose and Prescribe Online
Lesson 6-2	6-2 Intervention	Activity 6-2	
Lesson 6-3	6-3 Intervention	Activity 6-3	

YES ENRICH

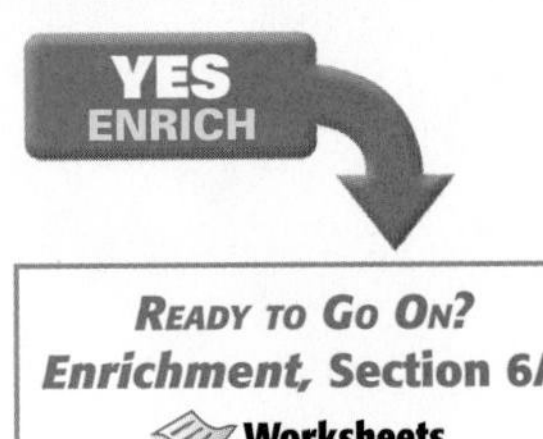

SECTION 6B

Other Special Quadrilaterals

One-Minute Section Planner

Lesson	Lab Resources	Materials
Lesson 6-4 Properties of Special Parallelograms • Prove and apply properties of rectangles, rhombuses, and squares. • Use properties of rectangles, rhombuses, and squares to solve problems. ☐ SAT-10 ☑ NAEP ☑ ACT ☐ SAT ☐ SAT Subject Tests	***Geometry Lab Activities*** 6-4 Geometry Lab	**Optional** toothpicks, compass (MK), straightedge (MK), magazine photos of rectangles, rhombuses, and squares, paper strips, brads, construction paper, scissors, protractor (MK), ruler (MK)
6-5 Technology Lab Predict Conditions for Special Parallelograms • Use geometry software to predict the conditions for rectangles, rhombuses, and squares. ☐ SAT-10 ☑ NAEP ☐ ACT ☐ SAT ☐ SAT Subject Tests	***Technology Lab Activities*** 6-5 Lab Recording Sheet	**Required** geometry software
Lesson 6-5 Conditions for Special Parallelograms • Prove that a given quadrilateral is a rectangle, rhombus, or square. ☐ SAT-10 ☑ NAEP ☑ ACT ☐ SAT ☐ SAT Subject Tests		**Optional** compass (MK), straightedge (MK)
6-6 Technology Lab Explore Isosceles Trapezoids • Use geometry software to investigate the properties and conditions of an isosceles trapezoid. ☐ SAT-10 ☑ NAEP ☑ ACT ☑ SAT ☑ SAT Subject Tests	***Technology Lab Activities*** 6-6 Lab Recording Sheet	**Required** geometry software
Lesson 6-6 Properties of Kites and Trapezoids • Use properties of kites to solve problems. • Use properties of trapezoids to solve problems. ☐ SAT-10 ☑ NAEP ☑ ACT ☑ SAT ☑ SAT Subject Tests	***Geometry Lab Activities*** 6-6 Geometry Lab ***Technology Lab Activities*** 6-6 Technology Lab	**Optional** patty paper, compass (MK), straightedge (MK), geometry software, colored pencils, protractor (MK)

MK = *Manipulatives Kit*

Math Background

OTHER SPECIAL QUADRILATERALS AND THEIR PROPERTIES

Lesson 6-4

Three special quadrilaterals are introduced in Lesson 6-4: the *rectangle*, the *rhombus*, and the *square*. Each is defined to be a quadrilateral with specific properties.

- **Rectangle:** a quadrilateral with four congruent (right) angles
- **Rhombus:** a quadrilateral with four congruent sides
- **Square:** a quadrilateral with four congruent (right) angles and four congruent sides

The first order of business is to demonstrate that each of these special quadrilaterals is a parallelogram. In general, the proofs are straightforward, because the properties that define the special quadrilaterals readily fit one or more of the conditions for parallelograms discussed in Lesson 6-3.

Once you know that the special quadrilaterals are parallelograms, you can conclude that the special quadrilaterals inherit all of the properties of parallelograms. This is a good application of the Law of Detachment (if $p \rightarrow q$ is true and p is true, then q is true). For example, Theorem 6-2-1 states that if a quadrilateral is a parallelogram, then its opposite sides are congruent. A rectangle is a parallelogram. Therefore, the opposite sides of a rectangle are congruent.

The special quadrilaterals have additional properties beyond those of parallelograms. Students can discover these properties by using inductive reasoning and can then prove the properties via coordinate or synthetic proofs. Such proofs can be instructive because they often draw upon triangle congruence theorems.

It is also useful to step back and consider the relationships among the special quadrilaterals and their properties. To that end, students can organize their findings in a Venn diagram (as on page 431) or in a flowchart. The following table of properties also illustrates the connections among the quadrilaterals.

Properties of Quadrilaterals

Property	▱	▭	◇	□
Opposite sides congruent	•	•	•	•
Opposite angles congruent	•	•	•	•
Consecutive angles supp.	•	•	•	•
Diagonals bisect each other	•	•	•	•
Diagonals congruent		•		•
Diagonals perpendicular			•	•
Diags. bisect opp. angles			•	•

The first four rows show that any property of a parallelogram is a property of all special quadrilaterals. The table also shows that any property that is true for parallelograms, rectangles, or rhombuses is true for squares. This makes sense because a square is also a parallelogram, rectangle, and rhombus; a property of any of these quadrilaterals thus applies to squares.

KITES AND TRAPEZOIDS

Lesson 6-6

A *kite* is a quadrilateral with exactly two pairs of congruent consecutive sides. A *trapezoid* is a quadrilateral with exactly one pair of parallel sides. Note that both definitions use the word *exactly* to exclude the possibility of a rhombus being considered a kite or a parallelogram being considered a trapezoid.

Such decisions about definitions are somewhat arbitrary. In other instances, inclusive definitions are used. For example, an isosceles triangle is a triangle with (at least) two congruent sides. This definition includes the possibility that all three sides may be congruent and, as such, equilateral triangles are also considered to be isosceles.

In fact, other sources may use the inclusive definitions of kite and trapezoid. For example, a trapezoid is sometimes defined as a quadrilateral with (at least) one pair of parallel sides. The result is that parallelograms are considered trapezoids. Note that variations of definitions do not change the facts of mathematics, but they do change the way the facts are expressed.

It is interesting to explore the properties of kites and trapezoids by adding columns for these quadrilaterals to the above table. The extended table makes it clear that these quadrilaterals do not inherit the properties of parallelograms.

6-4 Organizer

Pacing: Traditional 1 day
Block $\frac{1}{2}$ day

Objectives: Prove and apply properties of rectangles, rhombuses, and squares.

Use properties of rectangles, rhombuses, and squares to solve problems.

Geometry Lab
In *Geometry Lab Activities*

Online Edition
Tutorial Videos

Countdown Week 14

Power Presentations with PowerPoint®

Warm Up

Solve for *x*.

1. $16x - 3 = 12x + 13$ 4
2. $2x - 4 = 90$ 47

***ABCD* is a parallelogram. Find each measure.**

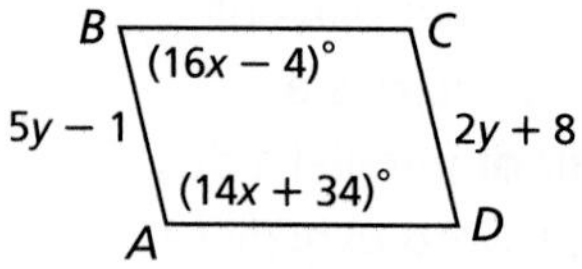

(Parallelogram ABCD with angle B = $(16x - 4)°$, angle A = $(14x + 34)°$, AB = $5y - 1$, CD = $2y + 8$)

3. *CD* 14
4. $m\angle C$ 104°

Also available on transparency

Math Humor

Q: What did the rhombus say to the square?

A: Lean on me, friend!

State Resources

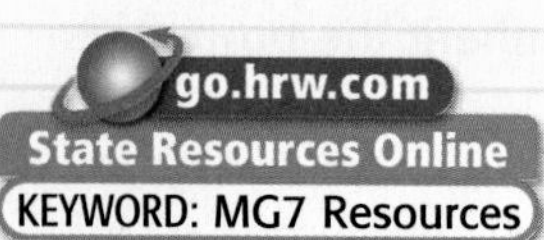

go.hrw.com
State Resources Online
KEYWORD: MG7 Resources

6-4 Properties of Special Parallelograms

Objectives
Prove and apply properties of rectangles, rhombuses, and squares.

Use properties of rectangles, rhombuses, and squares to solve problems.

Vocabulary
rectangle
rhombus
square

Who uses this?
Artists who work with stained glass can use properties of rectangles to cut materials to the correct sizes.

A second type of special quadrilateral is a *rectangle.* A **rectangle** is a quadrilateral with four right angles.

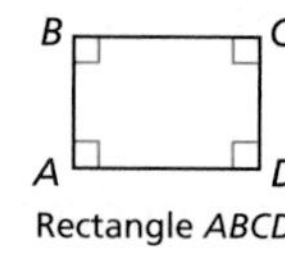

Rectangle *ABCD*

Know it! Note

Theorems Properties of Rectangles

	THEOREM	HYPOTHESIS	CONCLUSION
6-4-1	If a quadrilateral is a rectangle, then it is a parallelogram. (rect. → ▱)	Rectangle ABCD	*ABCD* is a parallelogram.
6-4-2	If a parallelogram is a rectangle, then its diagonals are congruent. (rect. → diags. ≅)	Rectangle ABCD with diagonals	$\overline{AC} \cong \overline{BD}$

You will prove Theorems 6-4-1 and 6-4-2 in Exercises 38 and 35.

Since a rectangle is a parallelogram by Theorem 6-4-1, a rectangle "inherits" all the properties of parallelograms that you learned in Lesson 6-2.

EXAMPLE 1 Craft Application

An artist connects stained glass pieces with lead strips. In this rectangular window, the strips are cut so that $FG = 24$ in. and $FH = 34$ in. Find *JG*.

$\overline{EG} \cong \overline{FH}$	*Rect. → diags. ≅*
$EG = FH = 34$	*Def. of ≅ segs.*
$JG = \frac{1}{2}EG$	*▱ → diags. bisect each other*
$JG = \frac{1}{2}(34) = 17$ in.	*Substitute and simplify.*

Carpentry The rectangular gate has diagonal braces. Find each length.

1a. *HJ* **48 in.**

1b. *HK* **61.6 in.**

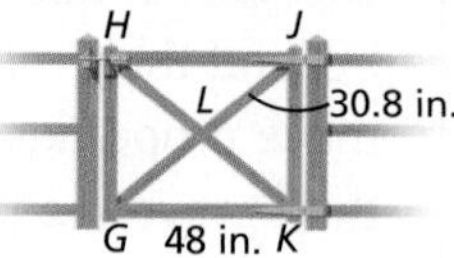

1 Introduce

EXPLORATION

6-4 Properties of Special Parallelograms

A *rhombus* is a quadrilateral with four congruent sides. Use toothpicks to explore properties of rhombuses.

1. Arrange four congruent toothpicks to form a quadrilateral. Since the toothpicks are congruent, the quadrilateral is a rhombus.
2. Form different rhombuses by changing the angles between the toothpicks. What do you notice about the opposite sides of every rhombus you make? What can you conclude?
3. Use toothpicks to form a rhombus on a sheet of paper. Mark the vertices on the paper and remove the toothpicks. Connect the vertices to draw the rhombus and its diagonals. What do you notice about the angle of intersection of the diagonals?
4. Repeat Step 3 with a different rhombus. Do you get the same result?

THINK AND DISCUSS

5. Explain how you can use your findings to state a conjecture about the diagonals of a rhombus.

Motivate

Look through magazines or books to find pictures of rectangles, rhombuses, and squares. Group the pictures based on the type of figure. Then show the pictures to the class and ask students to describe the identifying characteristics of each type of figure.

Explorations and answers are provided in *Alternate Openers: Explorations Transparencies.*

A *rhombus* is another special quadrilateral. A **rhombus** is a quadrilateral with four congruent sides.

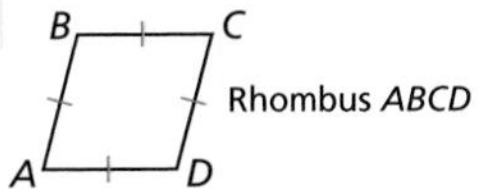

Theorems **Properties of Rhombuses**

	THEOREM	HYPOTHESIS	CONCLUSION
6-4-3	If a quadrilateral is a rhombus, then it is a parallelogram. (rhombus → ▱)		$ABCD$ is a parallelogram.
6-4-4	If a parallelogram is a rhombus, then its diagonals are perpendicular. (rhombus → diags. ⊥)		$\overline{AC} \perp \overline{BD}$
6-4-5	If a parallelogram is a rhombus, then each diagonal bisects a pair of opposite angles. (rhombus → each diag. bisects opp. ∠s)		$\angle 1 \cong \angle 2$ $\angle 3 \cong \angle 4$ $\angle 5 \cong \angle 6$ $\angle 7 \cong \angle 8$

You will prove Theorems 6-4-3 and 6-4-4 in Exercises 34 and 37.

PROOF **Theorem 6-4-5**

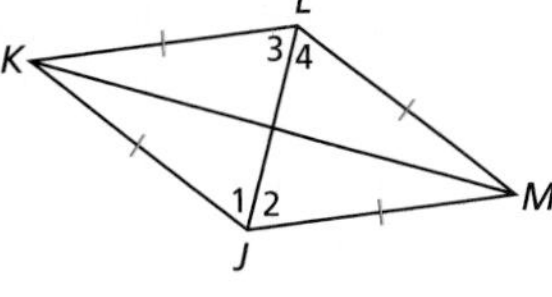

Given: $JKLM$ is a rhombus.
Prove: $\overline{JL}$ bisects $\angle KJM$ and $\angle KLM$.
$\overline{KM}$ bisects $\angle JKL$ and $\angle JML$.

Proof:
Since $JKLM$ is a rhombus, $\overline{JK} \cong \overline{JM}$, and $\overline{KL} \cong \overline{ML}$ by the definition of a rhombus. By the Reflexive Property of Congruence, $\overline{JL} \cong \overline{JL}$. Thus $\triangle JKL \cong \triangle JML$ by SSS. Then $\angle 1 \cong \angle 2$, and $\angle 3 \cong \angle 4$ by CPCTC. So $\overline{JL}$ bisects $\angle KJM$ and $\angle KLM$ by the definition of an angle bisector. By similar reasoning, $\overline{KM}$ bisects $\angle JKL$ and $\angle JML$.

Like a rectangle, a rhombus is a parallelogram. So you can apply the properties of parallelograms to rhombuses.

EXAMPLE 2 **Using Properties of Rhombuses to Find Measures**

$RSTV$ is a rhombus. Find each measure.

S, T, R, V, W; $4x + 7$; $9x - 11$

A VT

$ST = SR$	*Def. of rhombus*
$4x + 7 = 9x - 11$	*Substitute the given values.*
$18 = 5x$	*Subtract 4x from both sides and add 11 to both sides.*
$3.6 = x$	*Divide both sides by 5.*
$VT = ST$	*Def. of rhombus*
$VT = 4x + 7$	*Substitute 4x + 7 for ST.*
$VT = 4(3.6) + 7 = 21.4$	*Substitute 3.6 for x and simplify.*

Power Presentations with PowerPoint®

Additional Examples

Example 1

A woodworker constructs a rectangular picture frame so that $JK = 50$ cm and $JL = 86$ cm. Find HM. 43 cm

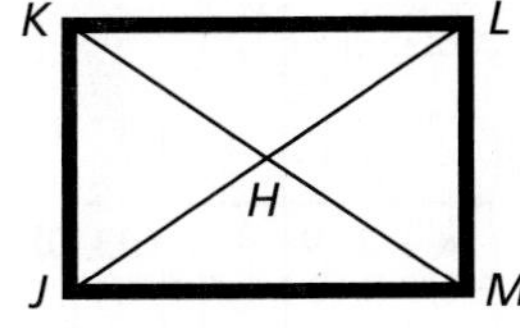

Example 2

***TVWX* is a rhombus. Find each measure.**

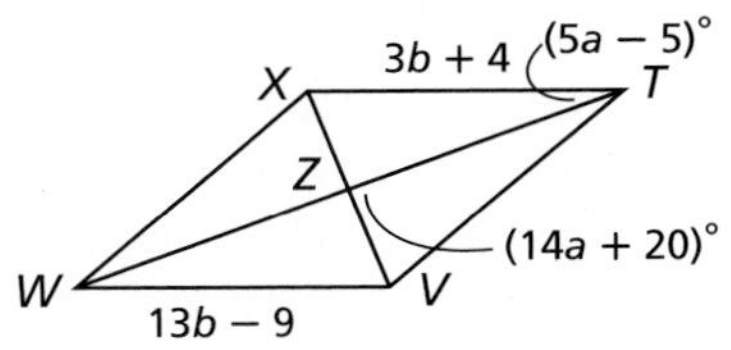

A. TV 7.9

B. $m\angle VTZ$ 20°

INTERVENTION
Questioning Strategies

EXAMPLE 1

- In a rectangle, how do you know that $\frac{1}{2}$ of one diagonal is congruent to $\frac{1}{2}$ of the other diagonal?

EXAMPLE 2

- What type of angles do the diagonals of a rhombus form?

Reading Math Remind students that the sides and angles marked in the figure are not necessarily the ones asked for in the problem. Have students copy the figure and circle the length or measure they are asked to find as soon as they read the problem.

2 Teach

Guided Instruction

Review the properties of parallelograms from Lesson 6-2. Then discuss the properties of rectangles and rhombuses. Point out that these figures are also parallelograms. Explain that a square has all the properties of a parallelogram, a rectangle, and a rhombus.

Teaching Tip **Kinesthetic** Have students make a physical model of a parallelogram with paper strips and brads. Ask them to adjust the model until it is a rectangle and then measure its diagonals.

Reaching All Learners

Through Modeling

Divide students into groups. Have each group cut out models of a rectangle, a rhombus, and a square from construction paper. Then have students use a protractor (MK) and a ruler (MK) to verify the properties in Theorems 6-4-1 through 6-4-5.

Power Presentations with PowerPoint®

Additional Examples

Example 3

Show that the diagonals of square $EFGH$ are congruent perpendicular bisectors of each other.

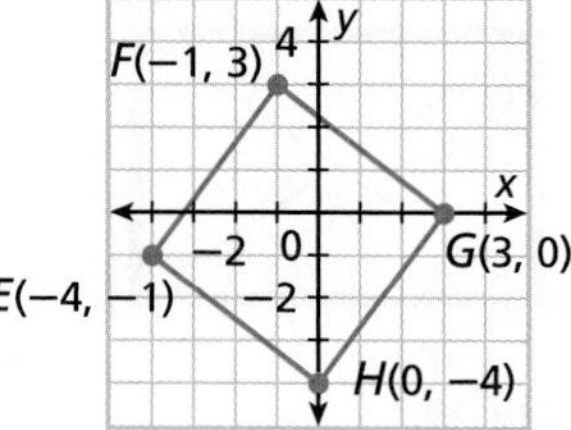

$EG = FH = \sqrt{50}$, so $\overline{EG} \cong \overline{FH}$. Slope of $\overline{EG} = \frac{1}{7}$, and slope of $\overline{FH} = -7$, so $\overline{EG} \perp \overline{FH}$. $\left(-\frac{1}{2}, -\frac{1}{2}\right)$ is the midpoint of $\overline{EG}$ and $\overline{FH}$, so $\overline{EG}$ and $\overline{FH}$ bisect each other. Thus the diags. of $EFGH$ are $\cong \perp$ bisectors of each other.

INTERVENTION

Questioning Strategies

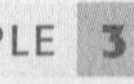

EXAMPLE 3

- Does the order in which you show that the diagonals are congruent, are perpendicular, and share a midpoint matter?
- How does showing that the diagonals have the same midpoint prove that they bisect each other?

$RSTV$ **is a rhombus. Find each measure.**

B $m\angle WSR$

$m\angle SWT = 90°$	*Rhombus → diags. ⊥*
$2y + 10 = 90$	*Substitute $2y + 10$ for $m\angle SWT$.*
$y = 40$	*Subtract 10 from both sides and divide both sides by 2.*
$m\angle WSR = m\angle TSW$	*Rhombus → each diag. bisects opp. ∠s*
$m\angle WSR = (y + 2)°$	*Substitute $y + 2$ for $m\angle TSW$.*
$m\angle WSR = (40 + 2)° = 42°$	*Substitute 40 for y and simplify.*

$CDFG$ **is a rhombus. Find each measure.**

2a. CD **42.5**

2b. $m\angle GCH$ if $m\angle GCD = (b + 3)°$ and $m\angle CDF = (6b - 40)°$ **17°**

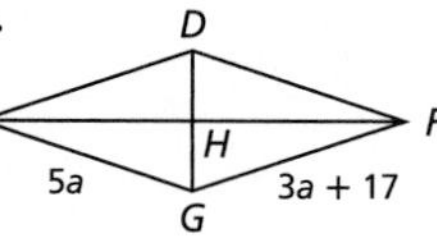

Helpful Hint

Rectangles, rhombuses, and squares are sometimes referred to as *special parallelograms.*

A **square** is a quadrilateral with four right angles and four congruent sides. In the exercises, you will show that a square is a parallelogram, a rectangle, and a rhombus. So a square has the properties of all three.

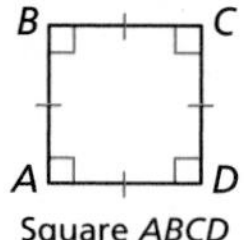

Square $ABCD$

EXAMPLE 3 Verifying Properties of Squares

Show that the diagonals of square $ABCD$ are congruent perpendicular bisectors of each other.

Step 1 Show that $\overline{AC}$ and $\overline{BD}$ are congruent.

$$AC = \sqrt{[2-(-1)]^2 + (7-0)^2} = \sqrt{58}$$

$$BD = \sqrt{[4-(-3)]^2 + (2-5)^2} = \sqrt{58}$$

Since $AC = BD$, $\overline{AC} \cong \overline{BD}$.

Step 2 Show that $\overline{AC}$ and $\overline{BD}$ are perpendicular.

$$\text{slope of } \overline{AC} = \frac{7-0}{2-(-1)} = \frac{7}{3}$$

$$\text{slope of } \overline{BD} = \frac{2-5}{4-(-3)} = \frac{-3}{7} = -\frac{3}{7}$$

Since $\left(\frac{7}{3}\right)\left(-\frac{3}{7}\right) = -1$, $\overline{AC} \perp \overline{BD}$.

Step 3 Show that $\overline{AC}$ and $\overline{BD}$ bisect each other.

$$\text{mdpt. of } \overline{AC}: \left(\frac{-1+2}{2}, \frac{0+7}{2}\right) = \left(\frac{1}{2}, \frac{7}{2}\right)$$

$$\text{mdpt. of } \overline{BD}: \left(\frac{-3+4}{2}, \frac{5+2}{2}\right) = \left(\frac{1}{2}, \frac{7}{2}\right)$$

Since $\overline{AC}$ and $\overline{BD}$ have the same midpoint, they bisect each other. The diagonals are congruent perpendicular bisectors of each other.

3. The vertices of square $STVW$ are $S(-5, -4)$, $T(0, 2)$, $V(6, -3)$, and $W(1, -9)$. Show that the diagonals of square $STVW$ are congruent perpendicular bisectors of each other.

3. $SV = TW = \sqrt{122}$, so $\overline{SV} \cong \overline{TW}$. Slope of $\overline{SV} = \frac{1}{11}$, and slope of $\overline{TW} = -11$, so $\overline{SV} \perp \overline{TW}$. The coordinates of the mdpt. of $\overline{SV}$ and $\overline{TW}$ are $\left(\frac{1}{2}, -\frac{7}{2}\right)$, so $\overline{SV}$ and $\overline{TW}$ bisect each other. So the diags. of $STVW$ are $\cong \perp$ bisectors of each other.

Student to Student

Special Parallelograms

Taylor Gallinghouse
Central High School

*To remember the properties of rectangles, rhombuses, and squares, I start with a **square**, which has all the properties of the others.*

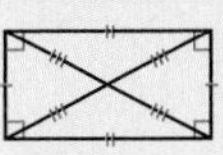

*To get a **rectangle** that is not a square, I stretch the square in one direction. Its diagonals are still congruent, but they are no longer perpendicular.*

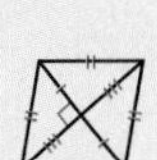

*To get a **rhombus** that is not a square, I go back to the square and slide the top in one direction. Its diagonals are still perpendicular and bisect the opposite angles, but they aren't congruent.*

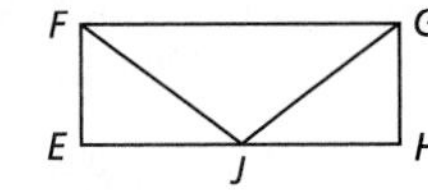

EXAMPLE 4 **Using Properties of Special Parallelograms in Proofs**

Given: $EFGH$ is a rectangle. J is the midpoint of $\overline{EH}$.
Prove: $\triangle FJG$ is isosceles.

Proof:

Statements	Reasons
1. $EFGH$ is a rectangle. J is the midpoint of $\overline{EH}$.	1. Given
2. $\angle E$ and $\angle H$ are right angles.	2. Def. of rect.
3. $\angle E \cong \angle H$	3. Rt. $\angle \cong$ Thm.
4. $EFGH$ is a parallelogram.	4. Rect. → ▱
5. $\overline{EF} \cong \overline{HG}$	5. ▱ → opp. sides $\cong$
6. $\overline{EJ} \cong \overline{HJ}$	6. Def. of mdpt.
7. $\triangle FJE \cong \triangle GJH$	7. SAS *Steps 3, 5, 6*
8. $\overline{FJ} \cong \overline{GJ}$	8. CPCTC
9. $\triangle FJG$ is isosceles.	9. Def. of isos. △

4. Possible answer:
1. $PQTS$ is a rhombus. (Given)
2. $\overline{PT}$ bisects $\angle QPS$. (Rhombus → each diag. bisects opp. ∠s)
3. $\angle QPR \cong \angle SPR$ (Def. of ∠ bisector)
4. $\overline{PQ} \cong \overline{PS}$ (Def. of rhombus)
5. $\overline{PR} \cong \overline{PR}$ (Reflex. Prop. of $\cong$)
6. $\triangle QPR \cong \triangle SPR$ (SAS)
7. $\overline{RQ} \cong \overline{RS}$ (CPCTC)

CHECK IT OUT! **4.** Given: $PQTS$ is a rhombus with diagonal $\overline{PR}$.
Prove: $\overline{RQ} \cong \overline{RS}$

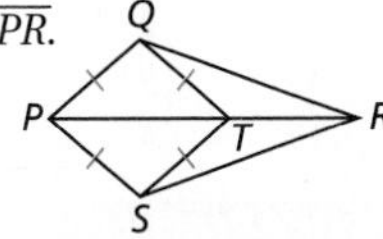

THINK AND DISCUSS

1. Which theorem means "The diagonals of a rectangle are congruent"? Why do you think the theorem is written as a conditional?
2. What properties of a rhombus are the same as the properties of all parallelograms? What special properties does a rhombus have?
3. **GET ORGANIZED** Copy and complete the graphic organizer. Write the missing terms in the three unlabeled sections. Then write a definition of each term.

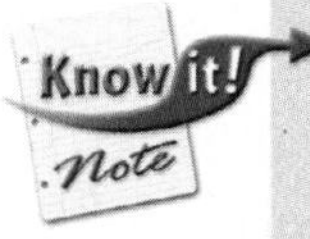

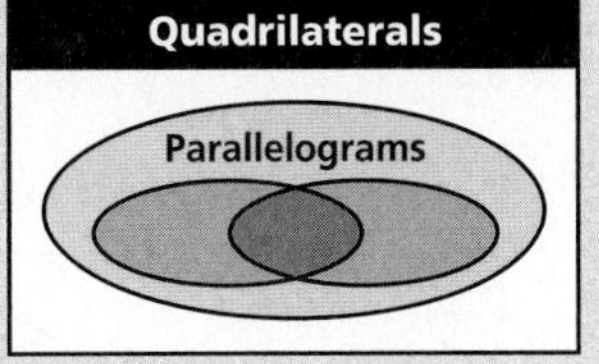

COMMON ERROR ALERT

Students might expect to use only the current lesson's properties and theorems when writing proofs. Point out that proofs often build on previous knowledge and thus use concepts learned in earlier lessons.

Power Presentations with PowerPoint®

Additional Examples

Example 4

Given: $ABCD$ is a rhombus. E is the midpoint of $\overline{AB}$, and F is the midpoint of $\overline{CD}$.
Prove: $AEFD$ is a parallelogram.

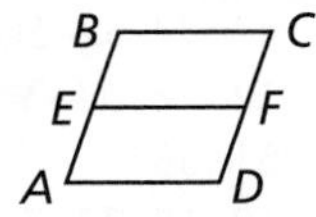

1. $ABCD$ is a rhombus. E is the mdpt. of $\overline{AB}$. F is the mdpt. of $\overline{CD}$. (Given)
2. $ABCD$ is a ▱. (Rhombus → ▱)
3. $\overline{AE} \parallel \overline{FD}$ (Def. of ▱)
4. $\overline{AB} \cong \overline{CD}$ (▱ → opp. sides $\cong$)
5. $AB = CD$ (Def. of $\cong$)
6. $AE = \frac{1}{2}AB$, $FD = \frac{1}{2}CD$ (Def. of mdpt.)
7. $FD = \frac{1}{2}AB$ (Subst.)
8. $AE = FD$ (Trans. Prop. of =)
9. $\overline{AE} \cong \overline{FD}$ (Def. of $\cong$)
10. $AEFD$ is a ▱. (Quad. with 1 pair of opp. sides $\cong$ and $\parallel$ → ▱)

INTERVENTION

Questioning Strategies

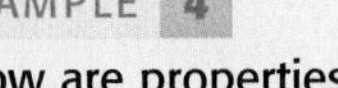

EXAMPLE 4

- How are properties of parallelograms used in these proofs?

3 Close

Summarize

Draw a rectangle, rhombus, and square on the board, and list the properties of each. Mark the properties on the figures as you review each one. For example, look at the Section Overview on page 408B.

ONGOING ASSESSMENT and INTERVENTION

Diagnose **Before** the Lesson
6-4 Warm Up, TE p. 408

Monitor **During** the Lesson
Check It Out! Exercises, SE pp. 408–411
Questioning Strategies, TE pp. 409–411

Assess **After** the Lesson
6-4 Lesson Quiz, TE p. 415
Alternative Assessment, TE p. 415

Answers to *Think and Discuss*

1. Thm. 6-4-2; possible answer: when the thm. is written as a conditional statement, it is easier to identify the hypothesis and the conclusion.
2. same properties: 2 pairs of $\parallel$ sides, opp. sides $\cong$, opp. ∠s $\cong$, cons. ∠s supp., diags. bisect each other; special properties: 4 $\cong$ sides, $\perp$ diags., each diag. bisects a pair of opp. ∠s
3. See p. A6.

6-4 Exercises

Assignment Guide

Assign *Guided Practice* exercises as necessary.

If you finished Examples **1–2**
- **Basic** 10–15, 18–21, 24–30 even, 40–42
- **Average** 10–15, 18–30 even, 40–42, 51
- **Advanced** 10–15, 18–30 even, 33, 40–42, 48, 51

If you finished Examples **1–4**
- **Basic** 10–23, 24–28 even, 29, 31, 34–36, 40–42, 44–47, 52–56
- **Average** 10–28, 34–36, 39–48, 51–56
- **Advanced** 10–19, 22–32 even, 33, 35–56

Homework Quick Check
Quickly check key concepts.
Exercises: 10, 14, 16, 17, 22, 24

Answers

8. $JL = KM = \sqrt{74}$, so $\overline{JL} \cong \overline{KM}$. Slope of $\overline{JL} = \frac{7}{5}$, and slope of $\overline{KM} = -\frac{5}{7}$, so $\overline{JL} \perp \overline{KM}$. The coordinates of the mdpt. of $\overline{JL}$ and $\overline{KM}$ are $\left(-\frac{1}{2}, -\frac{3}{2}\right)$, so $\overline{JL}$ and $\overline{KM}$ bisect each other. So the diags. of *JKLM* are ≅ ⊥ bisectors of each other.

State Resources

go.hrw.com
State Resources Online
KEYWORD: MG7 Resources

6-4 Exercises

go.hrw.com
Homework Help Online
KEYWORD: MG7 6-4
Parent Resources Online
KEYWORD: MG7 Parent

GUIDED PRACTICE

1. **Vocabulary** What is another name for an *equilateral quadrilateral*? an *equiangular quadrilateral*? a *regular quadrilateral*? **rhombus; rectangle; square**

SEE EXAMPLE 1 p. 408

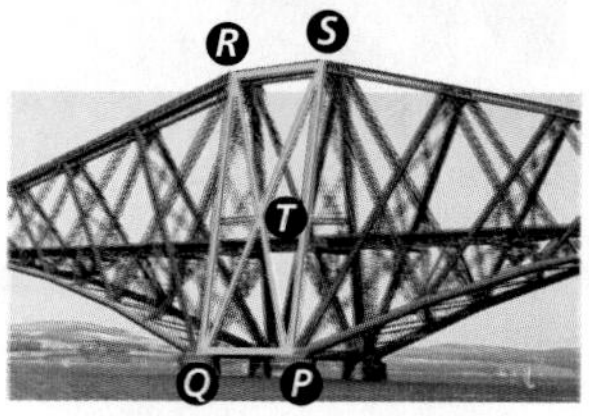

Engineering The braces of the bridge support lie along the diagonals of rectangle *PQRS*. $RS = 160$ ft, and $QS = 380$ ft. Find each length.

2. TQ **190 ft**
3. PQ **160 ft**
4. ST **190 ft**
5. PR **380 ft**

SEE EXAMPLE 2 p. 409

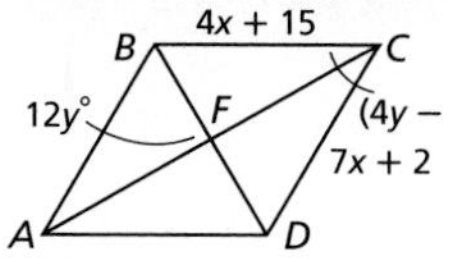

***ABCD* is a rhombus. Find each measure.**

6. AB **$32\frac{1}{3}$**
7. $m\angle ABC$ **122°**

SEE EXAMPLE 3 p. 410

8. **Multi-Step** The vertices of square *JKLM* are $J(-3, -5)$, $K(-4, 1)$, $L(2, 2)$, and $M(3, -4)$. Show that the diagonals of square *JKLM* are congruent perpendicular bisectors of each other.

SEE EXAMPLE 4 p. 411

9. **Given:** *RECT* is a rectangle. $\overline{RX} \cong \overline{TY}$
Prove: $\triangle REY \cong \triangle TCX$

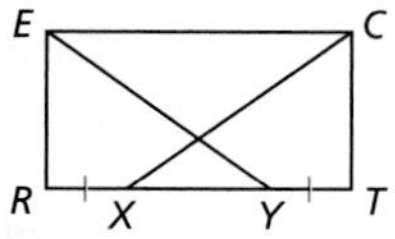

PRACTICE AND PROBLEM SOLVING

Independent Practice	
For Exercises	See Example
10–13	1
14–15	2
16	3
17	4

Extra Practice
Skills Practice p. S15
Application Practice p. S33

Carpentry A carpenter measures the diagonals of a piece of wood. In rectangle *JKLM*, $JM = 25$ in., and $JP = 14\frac{1}{2}$ in. Find each length.

10. JL **29**
11. KL **25**
12. KM **29**
13. MP **$14\frac{1}{2}$**

***VWXY* is a rhombus. Find each measure.**

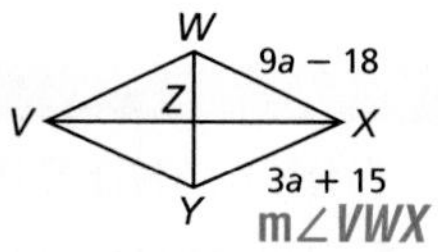

14. VW **31.5**
15. $m\angle VWX$ and $m\angle WYX$ if $m\angle WVY = (4b + 10)^\circ$ and $m\angle XZW = (10b - 5)^\circ$ **$m\angle VWX = 132°$; $m\angle WYX = 66°$**

16. **Multi-Step** The vertices of square *PQRS* are $P(-4, 0)$, $Q(4, 3)$, $R(7, -5)$, and $S(-1, -8)$. Show that the diagonals of square *PQRS* are congruent perpendicular bisectors of each other.

17. **Given:** *RHMB* is a rhombus with diagonal $\overline{HB}$.
Prove: $\angle HMX \cong \angle HRX$

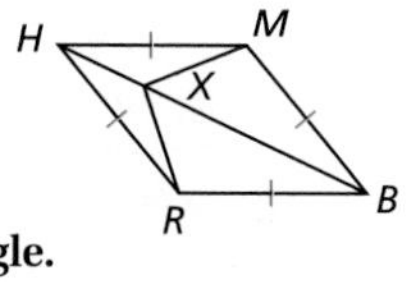

Find the measures of the numbered angles in each rectangle.

18.
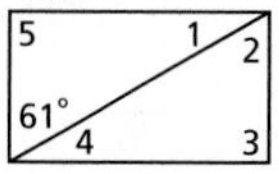

19.
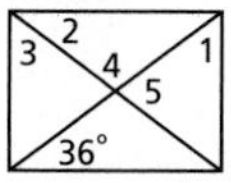

20.
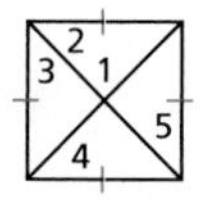

18. $m\angle 1 = 29°$; $m\angle 2 = 61°$; $m\angle 3 = 90°$; $m\angle 4 = 29°$; $m\angle 5 = 90°$.

19. $m\angle 1 = 54°$; $m\angle 2 = 36°$; $m\angle 3 = 54°$; $m\angle 4 = 108°$; $m\angle 5 = 72°$

6-4 PRACTICE A

Match each figure with the letter of one of the vocabulary terms. Use each term once.

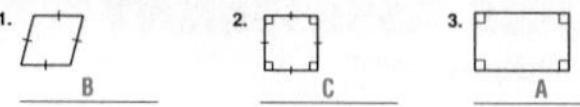

1. B
2. C
3. A

A. rectangle
B. rhombus
C. square

Fill in the blanks to complete each theorem.

4. If a parallelogram is a rhombus, then its diagonals are perpendicular.
5. If a parallelogram is a rectangle, then its diagonals are congruent.
6. If a quadrilateral is a rectangle, then it is a parallelogram.
7. If a parallelogram is a rhombus, then each diagonal bisects a pair of opposite angles.
8. If a quadrilateral is a rhombus, then it is a parallelogram.

The part of a ruler shown is a rectangle with $AB = 3$ inches and $BD = 3\frac{1}{4}$ inches. Find each length.

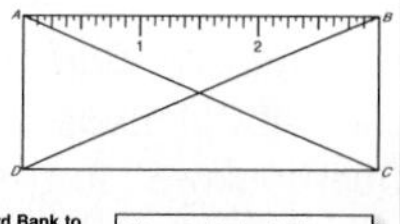

9. $DC =$ 3 inches
10. $AC =$ $3\frac{1}{4}$ inches

Use the phrases and theorems from the Word Bank to complete this two-column proof.

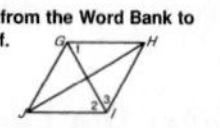

Alternate Interior ∠s Thm.
GHIJ is a parallelogram.
Trans. Prop. of ≅
∠2 ≅ ∠3

11. **Given:** *GHIJ* is a rhombus.
Prove: ∠1 ≅ ∠3

Statements	Reasons
1. *GHIJ* is a rhombus.	1. Given
2. **a.** *GHIJ* is a parallelogram.	2. rhomb. → ▱
3. $\overline{GH} \parallel \overline{JI}$	3. ▱ → opp. sides ∥
4. ∠1 ≅ ∠2	4. **b.** Alternate Interior ∠s Thm.
5. **c.** ∠2 ≅ ∠3	5. rhomb. → each diag. bisects opp. ∠s
6. ∠1 ≅ ∠3	6. **d.** Trans. Prop. of ≅

6-4 PRACTICE B

Tell whether each figure must be a rectangle, rhombus, or square based on the information given. Use the most specific name possible.

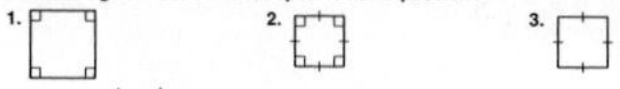

1. rectangle
2. square
3. rhombus

A modern artist's sculpture has rectangular faces. The face shown here is 9 feet long and 4 feet wide. Find each measure in simplest radical form. (*Hint:* Use the Pythagorean Theorem.)

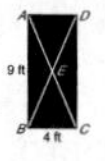

4. $DC =$ 9 feet
5. $AD =$ 4 feet
6. $DB =$ $\sqrt{97}$ feet
7. $AE =$ $\frac{\sqrt{97}}{2}$ feet

***VWXY* is a rhombus. Find each measure.**

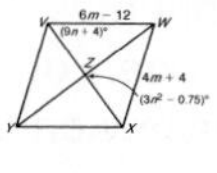

8. $XY =$ 36
9. $m\angle YVW =$ 107°
10. $m\angle VYX =$ 73°
11. $m\angle XYZ =$ 36.5°

12. The vertices of square *JKLM* are $J(-2, 4)$, $K(-3, -1)$, $L(2, -2)$, and $M(3, 3)$. Find each of the following to show that the diagonals of square *JKLM* are congruent perpendicular bisectors of each other.

$JL =$ $2\sqrt{13}$ $KM =$ $2\sqrt{13}$
slope of $\overline{JL} =$ $-\frac{3}{2}$ slope of $\overline{KM} =$ $\frac{2}{3}$
midpoint of $\overline{JL} =$ (0, 1) midpoint of $\overline{KM} =$ (0, 1)

Write a paragraph proof.

13. **Given:** *ABCD* is a rectangle.
Prove: ∠EDC ≅ ∠ECD

Possible answer: *ABCD* is a rectangle, so $\overline{AC}$ is congruent to $\overline{BD}$. Because *ABCD* is a rectangle, it is also a parallelogram. Because *ABCD* is a parallelogram, its diagonals bisect each other. By the definition of bisector, $EC = \frac{1}{2}AC$ and $ED = \frac{1}{2}BD$. But by the definition of congruent segments, $AC = BD$. So substitution and the Transitive Property of Equality show that $EC = ED$. Because $\overline{EC} \cong \overline{ED}$, $\triangle ECD$ is an isosceles triangle. The base angles of an isosceles triangle are congruent, so $\angle EDC \cong \angle ECD$.

Find the measures of the numbered angles in each rhombus.

21. 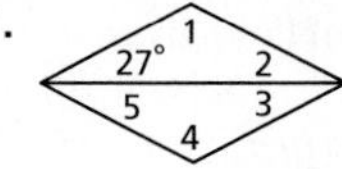

22. 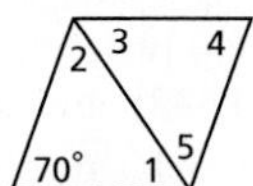

23. 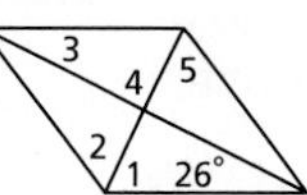

Tell whether each statement is sometimes, always, or never true.
(*Hint:* Refer to your graphic organizer for this lesson.)

24. A rectangle is a parallelogram. **A**
25. A rhombus is a square. **S**
26. A parallelogram is a rhombus. **S**
27. A rhombus is a rectangle. **S**
28. A square is a rhombus. **A**
29. A rectangle is a quadrilateral. **A**
30. A square is a rectangle. **A**
31. A rectangle is a square. **S**
32. **Critical Thinking** A triangle is equilateral if and only if the triangle is equiangular. Can you make a similar statement about a quadrilateral? Explain your answer.
33. **History** There are five shapes of clay tiles in this tile mosaic from the ruins of Pompeii.
    a. Make a sketch of each shape of tile and tell whether the shape is a polygon.
    b. Name each polygon by its number of sides. Does each shape appear to be regular or irregular?
    c. Do any of the shapes appear to be special parallelograms? If so, identify them by name.
    d. Find the measure of each interior angle of the center polygon. **120°**

34. You cannot use Thm. 6-2-1 to justify the final statement because you do not know that *JKLM* is a ▱. That is what is being proven. Instead, Thm. 6-3-2 states that if both pairs of opp. sides of a quad. are ≅, then the quad. is a ▱. So *JKLM* is a ▱ by Thm. 6-3-2.

34. **/// ERROR ANALYSIS ///** Find and correct the error in this proof of Theorem 6-4-3.
    Given: *JKLM* is a rhombus.
    Prove: *JKLM* is a parallelogram.
    Proof:

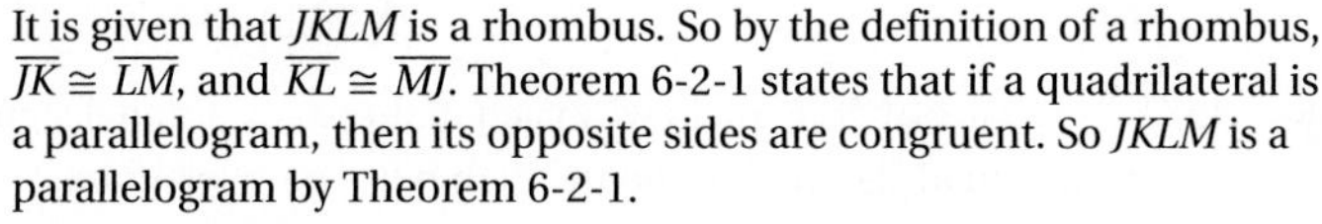
It is given that *JKLM* is a rhombus. So by the definition of a rhombus, $\overline{JK} \cong \overline{LM}$, and $\overline{KL} \cong \overline{MJ}$. Theorem 6-2-1 states that if a quadrilateral is a parallelogram, then its opposite sides are congruent. So *JKLM* is a parallelogram by Theorem 6-2-1.

35. Complete the two-column proof of Theorem 6-4-2 by filling in the blanks.
    Given: *EFGH* is a rectangle.
    Prove: $\overline{FH} \cong \overline{GE}$
    Proof:

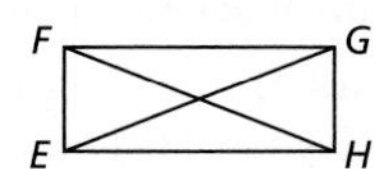

Statements	Reasons
1. *EFGH* is a rectangle.	1. Given
2. *EFGH* is a parallelogram.	2. a. __?__ **Rect. → ▱**
3. $\overline{EF} \cong$ b. __?__ **$\overline{HG}$**	3. ▱ → opp. sides ≅
4. $\overline{EH} \cong \overline{EH}$	4. c. __?__ **Reflex. Prop. of ≅**
5. ∠*FEH* and ∠*GHE* are right angles.	5. d. __?__ **Def. of rect.**
6. ∠*FEH* ≅ e. __?__ **∠*GHE***	6. Rt. ∠ ≅ Thm.
7. △*FEH* ≅ △*GHE*	7. f. __?__ **SAS**
8. $\overline{FH} \cong \overline{GE}$	8. g. __?__ **CPCTC**

Some students may have difficulty determining whether a statement is *sometimes* or *always* true in **Exercises 24–31.** Suggest that they rewrite each sentence as a conditional statement before trying to assess its truth value.

Teaching Tip **Social Studies Link** The tile mosaic in **Exercise 33** was used as a street sign in ancient Pompeii. Explain that when written histories do not exist, archaeologists work with the ruins and remains of ancient cultures to learn how these people lived.

6-4 PRACTICE C

For Exercises 1–5, give your answers in simplest radical form.

1. Find the length of the diagonals of a rectangle with sides of lengths a and b. $\sqrt{a^2 + b^2}$
2. Find the length of the diagonals of a square with sides of length a. $\sqrt{2}a$
3. Find the length of the sides of a square with diagonals of length a. $\frac{\sqrt{2}}{2}a$
4. Find the length of the sides of a rhombus with diagonals of lengths a and b. $\frac{\sqrt{a^2 + b^2}}{2}$
5. Find the length of a rectangle with width x and a diagonal of length 2x. $\sqrt{3}x$
6. Find the measures of the angles in the triangles formed by one diagonal of the rectangle in Exercise 5. 30°-60°-90°

The figure shows a kind of quadrilateral called a kite. A kite is a quadrilateral with exactly two pairs of congruent consecutive sides. Use the figure to write paragraph proofs for Exercises 7 and 8.

7. **Prove:** ∠CBA ≅ ∠CDA
   Possible answer: It is given that $\overline{CB} \cong \overline{CD}$ and $\overline{AB} \cong \overline{AD}$. $\overline{CA}$ is congruent to $\overline{CA}$ by the Reflexive Property of Congruence. Thus △ABC is congruent to △ADC by SSS. By CPCTC, ∠CBA ≅ ∠CDA.
8. **Prove:** $\overline{AC}$ is the perpendicular bisector of $\overline{BD}$.
   Possible answer: It is given that $\overline{CB} \cong \overline{CD}$ and $\overline{AB} \cong \overline{AD}$. So C and A are on the perpendicular bisector of $\overline{BD}$ by the Conv. of the Perpendicular Bisector Thm. So, since two points determine a line, $\overline{AC}$ is the perpendicular bisector of $\overline{BD}$.

For Exercises 9–11, name all the types of quadrilaterals (kite, parallelogram, rectangle, rhombus, or square) that satisfy the given conditions.

9. The diagonals bisect each other.
   parallelogram, rectangle, rhombus, square
10. The diagonals are perpendicular.
   kite, rhombus, square
11. The diagonals are congruent.
   rectangle, square

33a. 1. △ Polygon
2. □ Polygon
3. ⬡ Polygon
4. ◇ Polygon
5. Not a polygon

b. 1. triangle; reg.
2. quad.; reg.
3. hexagon; reg.
4. quad.; irregular

c. Shape 2 appears to be a square. Shape 4 appears to be a rhombus.

Answers

9. Possible answer:
   1. *RECT* is a rect. $\overline{RX} \cong \overline{TY}$ (Given)
   2. $\overline{XY} \cong \overline{XY}$ (Reflex. Prop. of ≅)
   3. $RX = TY$, $XY = XY$ (Def. of ≅ segs.)
   4. $RX + XY = TY + XY$ (Add. Prop. of =)
   5. $RX + XY = RY$, $TY + XY = TX$ (Seg. Add. Post.)
   6. $RY = TX$ (Subst.)
   7. $\overline{RY} \cong \overline{TX}$ (Def. of ≅ segs.)
   8. ∠*R* and ∠*T* are rt. ∠s. (Def. of rect.)
   9. ∠*R* ≅ ∠*T* (Rt. ∠ ≅ Thm.)
   10. *RECT* is a ▱. (Rect. → ▱)
   11. $\overline{RE} \cong \overline{TC}$ (▱ → opp. sides ≅)
   12. △*REY* ≅ △*TCX* (SAS)

16. $PR = QS = \sqrt{146}$, so $\overline{PR} \cong \overline{QS}$. Slope of $\overline{PR} = -\frac{5}{11}$, and slope of $\overline{QS} = \frac{11}{5}$, so $\overline{PR} \perp \overline{QS}$. The coordinates of the mdpt. of $\overline{PR}$ and $\overline{QS}$ are $\left(\frac{3}{2}, -\frac{5}{2}\right)$, so $\overline{PR}$ and $\overline{QS}$ bisect each other. So the diags. of *PQRS* are ≅ ⊥ bisectors of each other.

17. Possible answer:
   1. *RHMB* is a rhombus. $\overline{HB}$ is a diag. of *RHMB*. (Given)
   2. $\overline{MH} \cong \overline{RH}$ (Def. of rhombus)
   3. $\overline{HB}$ bisects ∠*RHM*. (Rhombus → each diag. bisects opp. ∠s)
   4. ∠*MHX* ≅ ∠*RHX* (Def. of ∠ bisector)
   5. $\overline{HX} \cong \overline{HX}$ (Reflex. Prop. of ≅)
   6. △*MHX* ≅ △*RHX* (SAS)
   7. ∠*HMX* ≅ ∠*HRX* (CPCTC)

20. m∠1 = 90°; m∠2 = 45°; m∠3 = 45°; m∠4 = 45°; m∠5 = 45°
21. m∠1 = 126°; m∠2 = 27°; m∠3 = 27°; m∠4 = 126°; m∠5 = 27°
22. m∠1 = 55°; m∠2 = 55°; m∠3 = 55°; m∠4 = 70°; m∠5 = 55°
23. m∠1 = 64°; m∠2 = 64°; m∠3 = 26°; m∠4 = 90°; m∠5 = 64°
32. See p. A22.

MULTI-STEP TEST PREP **Exercise 36** involves applying the properties of a rectangle in a coordinate plane. This exercise prepares students for the Multi-Step Test Prep on page 436.

TEST PREP DOCTOR If students have difficulty with **Exercise 45,** have them label each angle of the figure in terms of $x°$. Remind them to use the properties of parallelograms.

In **Exercise 46,** advise students to draw and label the figure carefully before trying to find the perimeter. Students may want to use colored pencils to mark the sides of $\triangle RST$.

Answers

37. Possible answer:
    1. $VWXY$ is a rhombus. (Given)
    2. $\overline{WX} \cong \overline{YX}$ (Def. of rhombus)
    3. $VWXY$ is a ▱. (Rhombus → ▱)
    4. $\overline{WZ} \cong \overline{YZ}$ (▱ → diags. bisect each other)
    5. $\overline{XZ} \cong \overline{XZ}$ (Reflex. Prop. of ≅)
    6. $\triangle WZX \cong \triangle YZX$ (SSS)
    7. $\angle WZX \cong \angle YZX$ (CPCTC)
    8. $\angle WZX$ and $\angle YZX$ are supp. (Lin. Pair Thm.)
    9. $\angle WZX$ and $\angle YZX$ are rt. ∠s. (≅ ∠s supp. → rt. ∠s)
    10. $m\angle WZX = m\angle YZX = 90°$ (Def. of rt. ∠)
    11. $\overline{VX} \perp \overline{WY}$ (Def. of ⊥)

38. Possible answer: It is given that $ABCD$ is a rect. By the def. of a rect., $\angle A$, $\angle B$, $\angle C$, and $\angle D$ are rt. ∠s. So $\angle A \cong \angle C$ and $\angle B \cong \angle D$ because all rt. ∠s are ≅. Thm. 6-3-3 states that if both pairs of opp. ∠s of a quad. are ≅, then the quad. is a ▱. So $ABCD$ is a ▱.

39. Possible answer:
    1. $ABCD$ is a rhombus. (Given)
    2. $ABCD$ is a ▱. (Rhombus → ▱)
    3. $\angle B \cong \angle D$, $\angle A \cong \angle C$ (▱ → opp. ∠s ≅)
    4. $\overline{AB} \cong \overline{BC} \cong \overline{CD} \cong \overline{DA}$ (Def. of rhombus)
    5. E, F, G, and H are the mdpts. of the sides. (Given)
    6. $\overline{EB} \cong \overline{BF} \cong \overline{HD} \cong \overline{DG}$, $\overline{EA} \cong \overline{AH} \cong \overline{FC} \cong \overline{CG}$ (Def. of mdpt.)
    7. $\triangle BEF \cong \triangle DGH$, $\triangle AEH \cong \triangle CGF$ (SAS)
    8. $\overline{EF} \cong \overline{GH}$, $\overline{EH} \cong \overline{GF}$ (CPCTC)
    9. $EFGH$ is a ▱. (Quad. with opp. sides ≅ → ▱)

43, 44, 46, 49, 50, 54. See p. A22.

36. This problem will prepare you for the Multi-Step Test Prep on page 436.
    The organizers of a fair plan to fence off a plot of land given by the coordinates $A(2, 4)$, $B(4, 2)$, $C(-1, -3)$, and $D(-3, -1)$.
    a. Find the slope of each side of quadrilateral $ABCD$. **slope of $\overline{AB}$ = slope of $\overline{CD} = -1$; slope of $\overline{BC}$ = slope of $\overline{DA} = 1$**
    b. What type of quadrilateral is formed by the fences? Justify your answer.
    c. The organizers plan to build a straight path connecting A and C and another path connecting B and D. Explain why these two paths will have the same length. **By Thm. 6-4-2, the diags. of a rect. are ≅.**

36b. Rect.; adj. sides are ⊥.

37. Use this plan to write a proof of Theorem 6-4-4.
    Given: $VWXY$ is a rhombus.
    Prove: $\overline{VX} \perp \overline{WY}$
    Plan: Use the definition of a rhombus and the properties of parallelograms to show that $\triangle WZX \cong \triangle YZX$. Then use CPCTC to show that $\angle WZX$ and $\angle YZX$ are right angles.

38. Write a paragraph proof of Theorem 6-4-1.
    Given: $ABCD$ is a rectangle.
    Prove: $ABCD$ is a parallelogram.

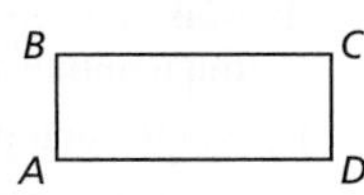

39. Write a two-column proof.
    Given: $ABCD$ is a rhombus. E, F, G, and H are the midpoints of the sides.
    Prove: $EFGH$ is a parallelogram.

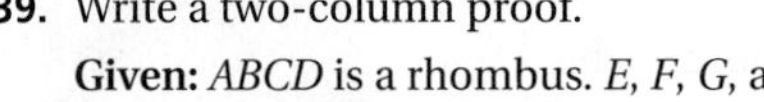

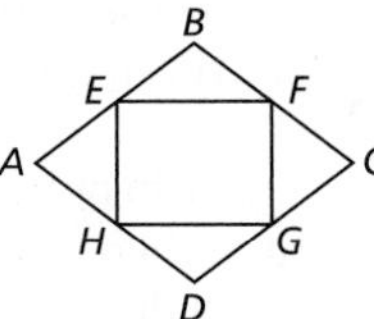

Multi-Step Find the perimeter and area of each figure. Round to the nearest hundredth, if necessary.

40. 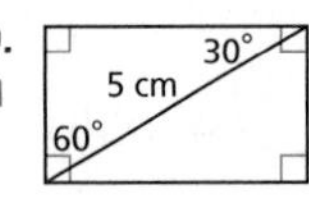

$(5 + 5\sqrt{3})$ cm ≈ 13.66 cm; $6.25\sqrt{3}$ cm^2 ≈ 10.83 cm^2

41. 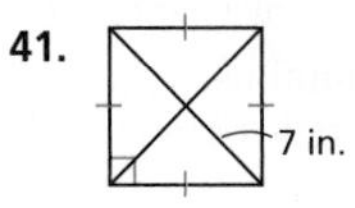

$28\sqrt{2}$ in. ≈ 39.60 in.; 98 in^2

42. 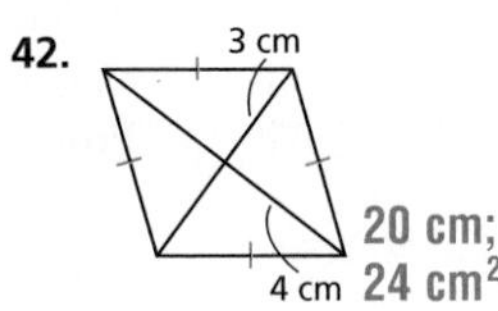

20 cm; 24 cm^2

43. **Write About It** Explain why each of these conditional statements is true.
    a. If a quadrilateral is a square, then it is a parallelogram.
    b. If a quadrilateral is a square, then it is a rectangle.
    c. If a quadrilateral is a square, then it is a rhombus.

44. **Write About It** List the properties that a square "inherits" because it is (1) a parallelogram, (2) a rectangle, and (3) a rhombus.

45. Which expression represents the measure of $\angle J$ in rhombus $JKLM$?
    (A) $x°$
    (B) $2x°$
    (C) $(180 - x)°$
    (D) $(180 - 2x)°$

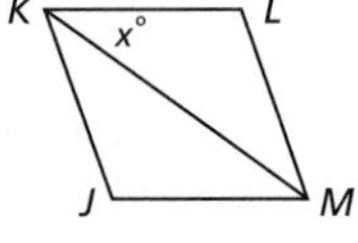

46. **Short Response** The diagonals of rectangle $QRST$ intersect at point P. If $QR = 1.8$ cm, $QP = 1.5$ cm, and $QT = 2.4$ cm, find the perimeter of $\triangle RST$. Explain how you found your answer.

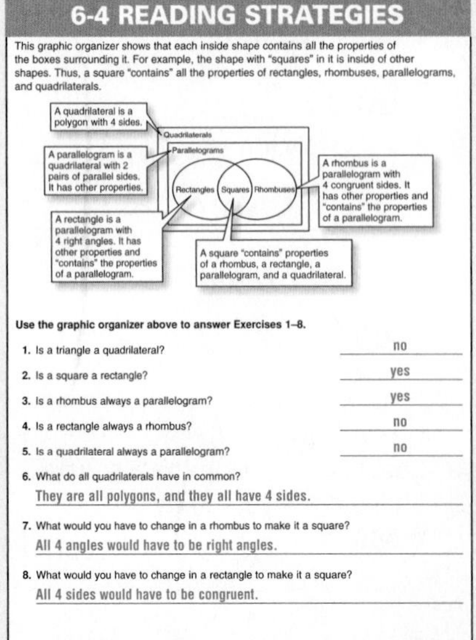

6-4 READING STRATEGIES

This graphic organizer shows that each inside shape contains all the properties of the boxes surrounding it. For example, the shape with "squares" in it is inside of other shapes. Thus, a square "contains" all the properties of rectangles, rhombuses, parallelograms, and quadrilaterals.

Use the graphic organizer above to answer Exercises 1–8.

1. Is a triangle a quadrilateral? **no**
2. Is a square a rectangle? **yes**
3. Is a rhombus always a parallelogram? **yes**
4. Is a rectangle always a rhombus? **no**
5. Is a quadrilateral always a parallelogram? **no**
6. What do all quadrilaterals have in common?
   They are all polygons, and they all have 4 sides.
7. What would you have to change in a rhombus to make it a square?
   All 4 angles would have to be right angles.
8. What would you have to change in a rectangle to make it a square?
   All 4 sides would have to be congruent.

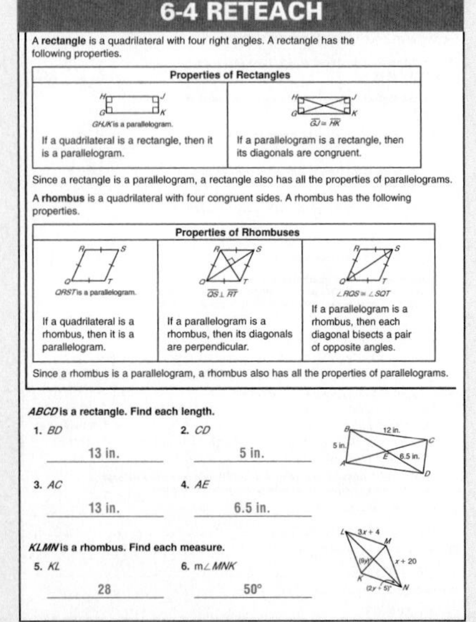

6-4 RETEACH

A **rectangle** is a quadrilateral with four right angles. A rectangle has the following properties.

Properties of Rectangles	
$GHJK$ is a parallelogram. If a quadrilateral is a rectangle, then it is a parallelogram.	$\overline{GJ} \cong \overline{HK}$ If a parallelogram is a rectangle, then its diagonals are congruent.

Since a rectangle is a parallelogram, a rectangle also has all the properties of parallelograms.

A **rhombus** is a quadrilateral with four congruent sides. A rhombus has the following properties.

Properties of Rhombuses		
$QRST$ is a parallelogram. If a quadrilateral is a rhombus, then it is a parallelogram.	$\overline{QS} \perp \overline{RT}$ If a parallelogram is a rhombus, then its diagonals are perpendicular.	$\angle RQS \cong \angle SQT$ If a parallelogram is a rhombus, then each diagonal bisects a pair of opposite angles.

Since a rhombus is a parallelogram, a rhombus also has all the properties of parallelograms.

***ABCD* is a rectangle. Find each length.**

1. BD **13 in.**
2. CD **5 in.**
3. AC **13 in.**
4. AE **6.5 in.**

***KLMN* is a rhombus. Find each measure.**

5. KL **28**
6. $m\angle MNK$ **50°**

47. Which statement is NOT true of a rectangle?
 F Both pairs of opposite sides are congruent and parallel.
 G Both pairs of opposite angles are congruent and supplementary.
 (H) All pairs of consecutive sides are congruent and perpendicular.
 J All pairs of consecutive angles are congruent and supplementary.

CHALLENGE AND EXTEND

48. **Algebra** Find the value of x in the rhombus. $x = 5$ or $x = -5.25$

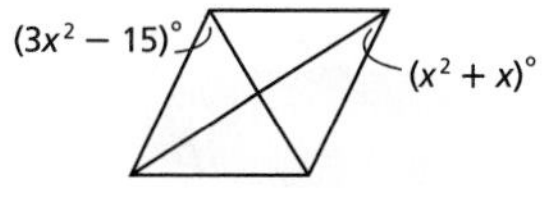

49. Prove that the segment joining the midpoints of two consecutive sides of a rhombus is perpendicular to one diagonal and parallel to the other.

50. Extend the definition of a triangle midsegment to write a definition for the midsegment of a rectangle. Prove that a midsegment of a rectangle divides the rectangle into two congruent rectangles.

51. The figure is formed by joining eleven congruent squares. How many rectangles are in the figure?

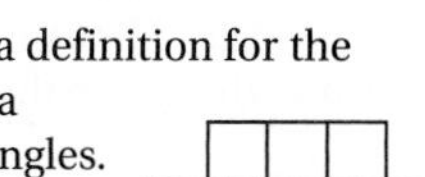

SPIRAL REVIEW

51. 45 (11 1-by-1's, 8 1-by-2's, 5 1-by-3's, 2 1-by-4's, 1 1-by-5, 6 2-by-1's, 4 2-by-2's, 2 2-by-3's, 3 3-by-1's, 2 3-by-2's, 1 3-by-3)

52. The cost c of a taxi ride is given by $c = 2 + 1.8(m - 1)$, where m is the length of the trip in miles. Mr. Hatch takes a 6-mile taxi ride. How much change should he get if he pays with a \$20 bill and leaves a 10% tip? *(Previous course)* **\$7.90**

Determine if each conditional is true. If false, give a counterexample. *(Lesson 2-2)*

53. If a number is divisible by -3, then it is divisible by 3. T

54. If the diameter of a circle is doubled, then the area of the circle will double. F

Determine if each quadrilateral must be a parallelogram. Justify your answer. *(Lesson 6-3)*

55. 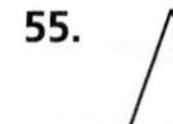 No; none of the conditions for a ▱ are met.

56. 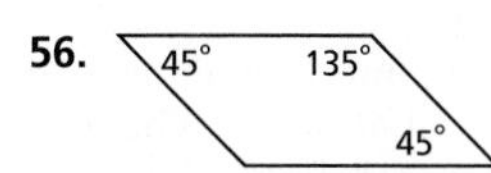

Yes; 1 ∠ is supp. to both of its cons. ∠s, so the quad. is a ▱.

Construction Rhombus

Check students' constructions.

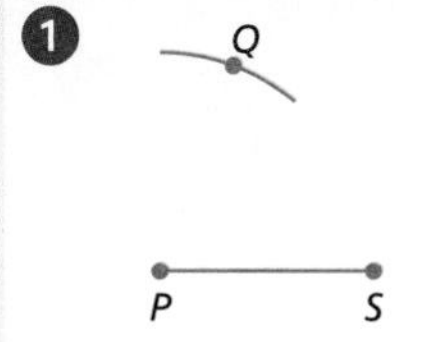

Draw $\overline{PS}$. Set the compass to the length of $\overline{PS}$. Place the compass point at P and draw an arc above $\overline{PS}$. Label a point Q on the arc.

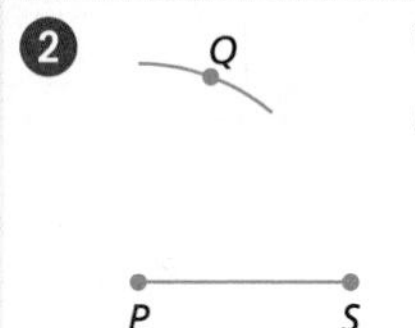

Place the compass point at Q and draw an arc to the right of Q.

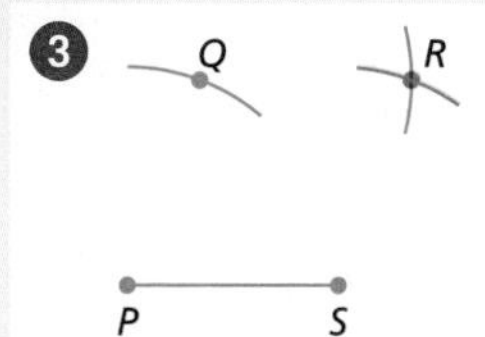

Place the compass point at S and draw an arc that intersects the arc drawn from Q. Label the point of intersection R.

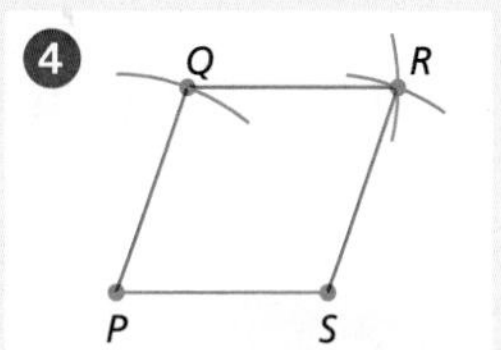

Draw $\overline{PQ}$, $\overline{QR}$, and $\overline{RS}$.

6-4 PROBLEM SOLVING

Use the diagram for Exercises 1 and 2.
The soccer goalposts determine rectangle *ABCD*.

1. The distance between goalposts, *BC*, is three times the distance from the top of the goalpost to the ground. If the perimeter of *ABCD* is $21\frac{1}{3}$ yards, what is the length of $\overline{BC}$?
 8 yd

2. The distance from *B* to *D* is approximately $(x + 10)$ feet, and the distance from *A* to *C* is approximately $(2x - 5.3)$ feet. What is the approximate distance from *A* to *C*?
 25.3 ft

3. *MNPQ* is a rhombus. The measure of $\angle MRQ$ is $(13t - 1)°$, and the measure of $\angle PQR$ is $(7t + 4)°$. What is the measure of $\angle PQM$?
 106°

4. The *scissor lift* forms rhombus *PQRS* with $PQ = (7b - 5)$ meters and $QR = (2b - 0.5)$ meters. If *S* is the midpoint of $\overline{RT}$, what is the length of $\overline{RT}$?
 2.6 m

5. The diagram shows the lid of a rectangular case that holds 80 CDs. What are the dimensions of the case?
 $(b + 9)$ in., $(2a - 1)$ in., $(a + 6)$ in., $(4b - \frac{3}{4})$ in.
 13 in. by $12\frac{1}{4}$ in.

Choose the best answer.

6. What is the measure of ∠1 in the rectangle?
 A 34°
 (B) 68°
 C 90°
 D 146°

7. A square graphed on the coordinate plane has a diagonal with endpoints $E(2, 3)$ and $F(0, -3)$. What are the coordinates of the endpoints of the other diagonal?
 (F) $(4, -1)$ and $(-2, 1)$
 G $(4, 0)$ and $(-2, 1)$
 H $(4, -1)$ and $(-3, 1)$
 J $(3, -1)$ and $(-2, 1)$

6-4 CHALLENGE

The figure at right shows a Chinese puzzle called the *tangram*. No one is certain how old the puzzle is, but it was unquestionably one of the most popular puzzles of the nineteenth century. The seven puzzle pieces are called tans. To make your own tans, fold a large square sheet of paper in half four times as shown below. Unfold the paper, draw the segments shown, then cut along the segments.

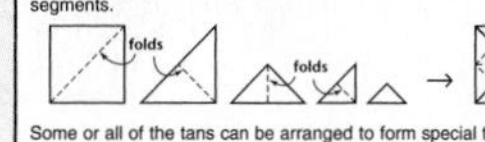

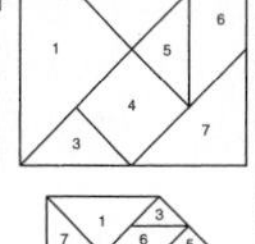

Some or all of the tans can be arranged to form special types of quadrilaterals. For instance, the figure at right shows how tans 1, 3, 5, 6, and 7 can be arranged to form a trapezoid.

Complete the table below by arranging the given number of tans to form each figure. If it is not possible to make the figure, enter an *X* in the table.

	Number of tans	Square	Rectangle (not square)	Isosceles trapezoid	Trapezoid (not isosceles)	Rhombus (not square)	Parallelogram (not rhombus or rectangle)
1.	2		X			X	
2.	3					X	
3.	4					X	
4.	5					X	
5.	6	X				X	X
6.	7					X	

7. Tangram puzzles arise from the countless silhouetes of people, animals, and objects that can be formed by arrangements of the tans. Find an arrangement of the tans that forms the silhouette of a bird, as shown at right. Sketch your answer on a separate sheet of paper.

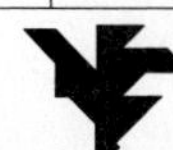

Journal

Have students describe the properties of a rectangle and a rhombus, and then have them draw and label examples of each type of figure.

ALTERNATIVE ASSESSMENT

Have students draw and label diagrams to represent the hypothesis and conclusion of each theorem in the lesson.

Power Presentations with PowerPoint®

6-4 Lesson Quiz

A slab of concrete is poured with diagonal spacers. In rectangle *CNRT*, *CN* = 35 ft, and *NT* = 58 ft. Find each length.

1. *TR* 35 ft 2. *CE* 29 ft

***PQRS* is a rhombus. Find each measure.**

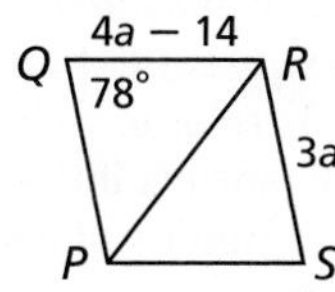

3. *QP* 42 4. m∠*QRP* 51°

5. The vertices of square *ABCD* are $A(1, 3)$, $B(3, 2)$, $C(4, 4)$, and $D(2, 5)$. Show that its diagonals are congruent perpendicular bisectors of each other. $AC = BD = \sqrt{10}$, so $\overline{AC} \cong \overline{BD}$. Slope of $\overline{AC} = \frac{1}{3}$, and slope of $\overline{BD} = -3$, so $\overline{AC} \perp \overline{BD}$. (2.5, 3.5) is the mdpt. of $\overline{AC}$ and $\overline{BD}$, so $\overline{AC}$ and $\overline{BD}$ bisect each other.

6. **Given:** *ABCD* is a rhombus.
 Prove: $\triangle ABE \cong \triangle CDF$

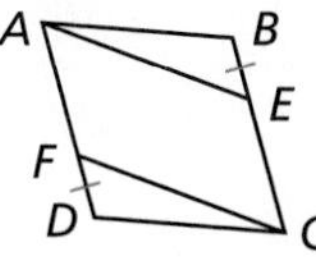

1. *ABCD* is a rhombus. (Given)
2. $\overline{AB} \cong \overline{CD}$ (Def. of rhombus)
3. *ABCD* is a ▱ (Rhombus → ▱)
4. ∠*B* ≅ ∠*D* (▱ → opp. ∠s ≅)
5. $\overline{DF} \cong \overline{BE}$ (Given)
6. $\triangle ABE \cong \triangle CDF$ (SAS)

Also available on transparency

Organizer

Use with Lesson 6-5

Pacing:
Traditional 1 day
Block $\frac{1}{2}$ day

Objective: Use geometry software to predict the conditions for rectangles, rhombuses, and squares.

Materials: geometry software

Online Edition
TechKeys

Countdown Week 14

Resources

Technology Lab Activities
6-5 Lab Recording Sheet

Teach

Discuss

Guide students through the construction of the parallelogram given in **Steps 1** and **2.** Then ask students to predict the answers to the questions in the activities before they follow each subsequent instruction. Have students refer to their journals or graphic organizers if they need to review the properties of each special parallelogram.

State Resources

6-5

Predict Conditions for Special Parallelograms

In this lab, you will use geometry software to predict the conditions that are sufficient to prove that a parallelogram is a rectangle, rhombus, or square.

Use with Lesson 6-5

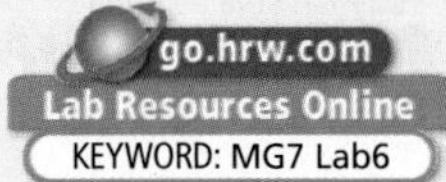

go.hrw.com
Lab Resources Online
KEYWORD: MG7 Lab6

Activity 1

1. Construct $\overline{AB}$ and $\overline{AD}$ with a common endpoint A. Construct a line through D parallel to $\overline{AB}$. Construct a line through B parallel to $\overline{AD}$. **Check students' work.**

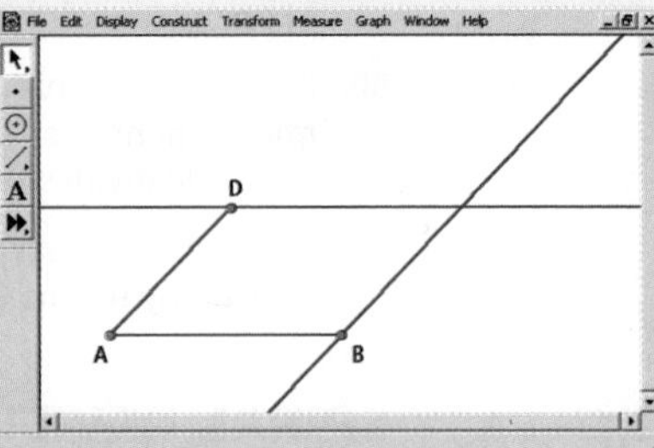

2. Construct point C at the intersection of the two lines. Hide the lines and construct $\overline{BC}$ and $\overline{CD}$ to complete the parallelogram. **Check students' work.**
3. Measure the four sides and angles of the parallelogram. **Check students' work.**
4. Move A so that $m\angle ABC = 90°$. What type of special parallelogram results? **rect.**
5. Move A so that $m\angle ABC \neq 90°$. **Check students' work.**

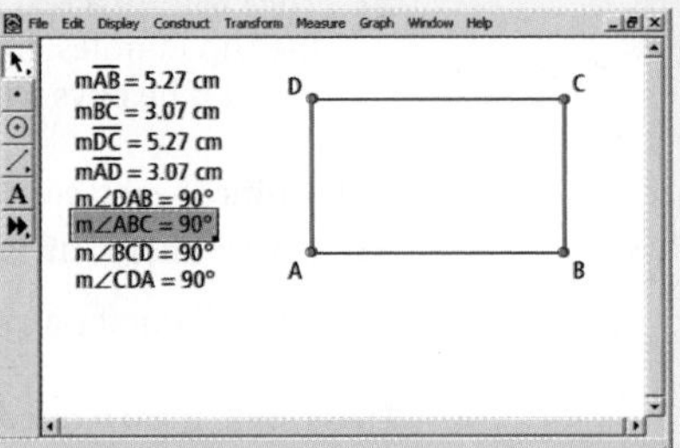

6. Construct $\overline{AC}$ and $\overline{BD}$ and measure their lengths. Move A so that $AC = BD$. What type of special parallelogram results? **rect.**

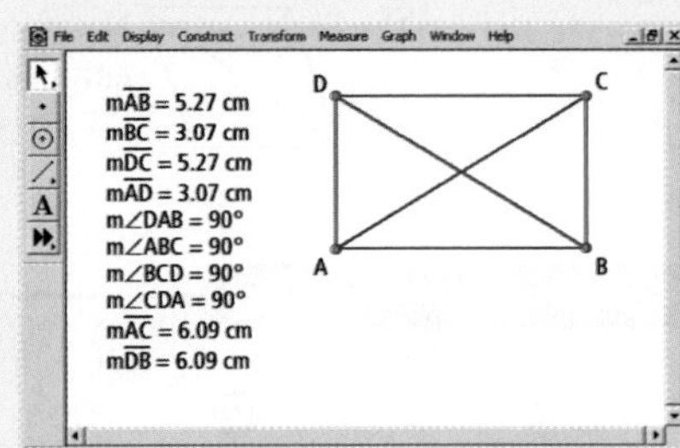

Try This

1. How does the method of constructing $ABCD$ in Steps 1 and 2 guarantee that the quadrilateral is a parallelogram? **Both pairs of opp. sides are ∥, so *ABCD* is a ▱ by def.**
2. **Make a Conjecture** What are two conditions for a rectangle? Write your conjectures as conditional statements. **Possible answers: If a ▱ has a rt. ∠, then it is a rect. If a ▱ has ≅ diags., then it is a rect.**

Activity 2

1. Use the parallelogram you constructed in Activity 1. Move A so that $AB = BC$. What type of special parallelogram results? **rhombus**

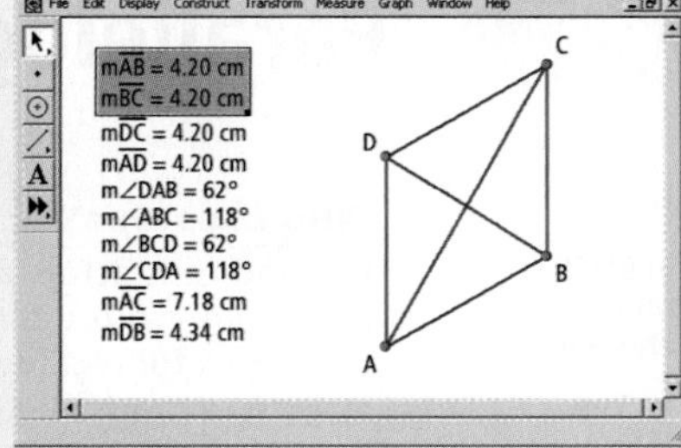

2. Move A so that $AB \neq BC$. **Check students' work.**

3. Label the intersection of the diagonals as E. Measure $\angle AEB$. **Check students' work.**

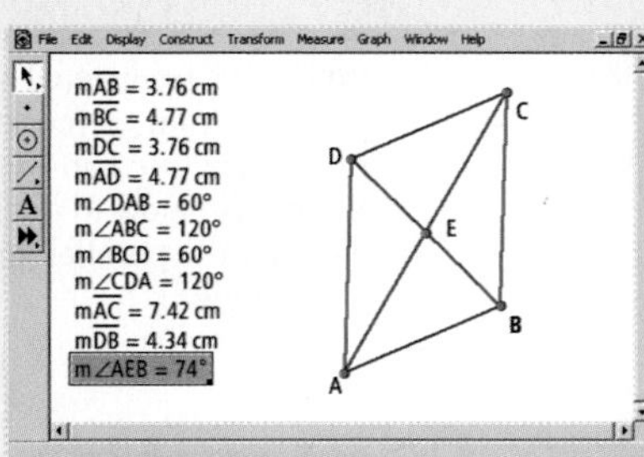

4. Move A so that $m\angle AEB = 90°$. What type of special parallelogram results? **rhombus**

5. Move A so that $m\angle AEB \neq 90°$. **Check students' work.**

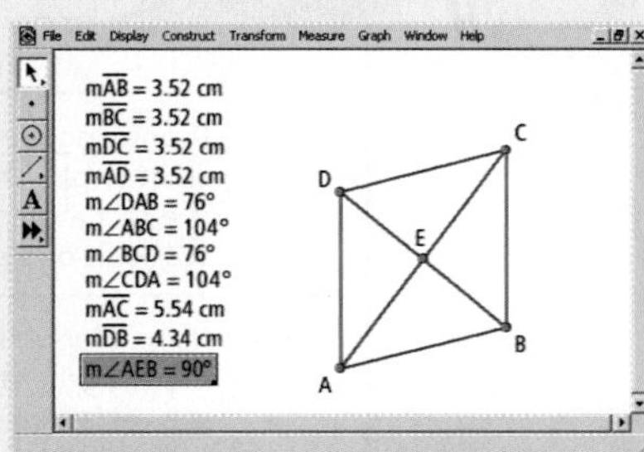

6. Measure $\angle ABD$ and $\angle CBD$. Move A so that $m\angle ABD = m\angle CBD$. What type of special parallelogram results? **rhombus**

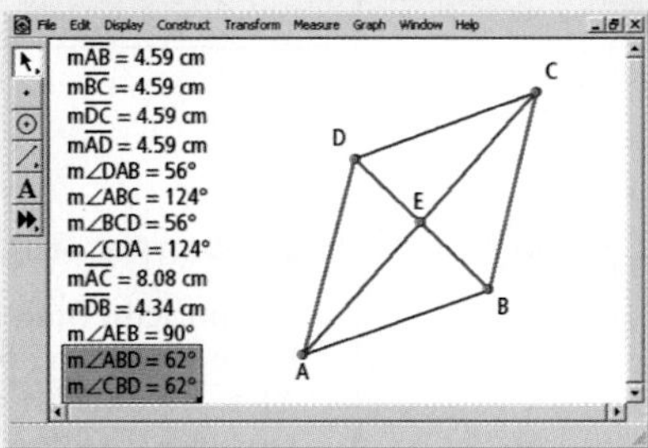

Try This

3. **Make a Conjecture** What are three conditions for a rhombus? Write your conjectures as conditional statements.
4. **Make a Conjecture** A square is both a rectangle and a rhombus. What conditions do you think must hold for a parallelogram to be a square?

Close

Key Concept

By manipulating the side lengths and angle measures in a parallelogram, you can discover the conditions for a rectangle, rhombus, or square.

Assessment

Journal Have students summarize the conditions for a rectangle, rhombus, and square.

Answers to *Try This*

3. Possible answers: If a pair of cons. sides of a ▱ are ≅, then the ▱ is a rhombus. If the diags. of a ▱ are ⊥, then the ▱ is a rhombus. If a diag. of a ▱ bisects opp. ∡, then the ▱ is a rhombus.
4. Possible answers: If a ▱ is a rect. and a rhombus, then the ▱ is a square.

6-5 Organizer

Pacing: Traditional 1 day
Block $\frac{1}{2}$ day

Objective: Prove that a given quadrilateral is a rectangle, rhombus, or square.

Online Edition
Tutorial Videos, Interactivity

Countdown Week 14

Power Presentations with PowerPoint®

Warm Up

1. Find AB for $A(-3, 5)$ and $B(1, 2)$. 5
2. Find the slope of $\overline{JK}$ for $J(-4, 4)$ and $K(3, -3)$. -1

***ABCD* is a parallelogram. Justify each statement.**

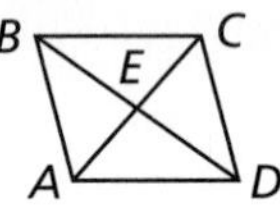

3. $\angle ABC \cong \angle CDA$ ▱ → opp. ∠s ≅
4. $\angle AEB \cong \angle CED$ Vert. ∠s Thm.

Also available on transparency

Parent: Your geometry teacher thinks you need extra homework.
Student: Tell her I want proof!

6-5 Conditions for Special Parallelograms

Objective
Prove that a given quadrilateral is a rectangle, rhombus, or square.

Who uses this?
Building contractors and carpenters can use the conditions for rectangles to make sure the frame for a house has the correct shape.

When you are given a parallelogram with certain properties, you can use the theorems below to determine whether the parallelogram is a rectangle.

Know it! Note

Theorems Conditions for Rectangles

	THEOREM	EXAMPLE
6-5-1	If one angle of a parallelogram is a right angle, then the parallelogram is a rectangle. (▱ with one rt. ∠ → rect.)	Rectangle $ABCD$ with right angle at A
6-5-2	If the diagonals of a parallelogram are congruent, then the parallelogram is a rectangle. (▱ with diags. ≅ → rect.)	Rectangle $ABCD$ with diagonals; $\overline{AC} \cong \overline{BD}$

You will prove Theorems 6-5-1 and 6-5-2 in Exercises 31 and 28.

EXAMPLE 1 ***Carpentry Application***

A contractor built a wood frame for the side of a house so that $\overline{XY} \cong \overline{WZ}$ and $\overline{XW} \cong \overline{YZ}$. Using a tape measure, the contractor found that $XZ = WY$. Why must the frame be a rectangle?

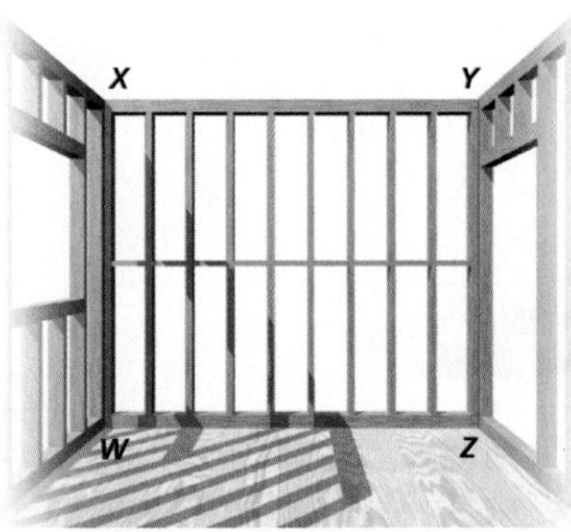

Both pairs of opposite sides of $WXYZ$ are congruent, so $WXYZ$ is a parallelogram. Since $XZ = WY$, the diagonals of ▱$WXYZ$ are congruent. Therefore the frame is a rectangle by Theorem 6-5-2.

1 Introduce

EXPLORATION

6-5 Conditions for Special Parallelograms

Recall that if the diagonals of a quadrilateral bisect each other, then the quadrilateral is a parallelogram.

1. The figures show quadrilaterals with diagonals that bisect each other, so the quadrilaterals are parallelograms. The diagonals are also perpendicular. What type of parallelograms do $ABCD$, $EFGH$, and $JKLM$ appear to be?
2. The figures show three more quadrilaterals with diagonals that bisect each other. Their diagonals are also congruent to each other. What type of parallelograms do $NPQR$, $STUV$, and $WXYZ$ appear to be?
3. Based on the above, describe some conditions that allow you to conclude that a parallelogram is a rhombus or a rectangle.

Motivate

Remind students that in the previous lesson they were introduced to the properties of rectangles, rhombuses, and squares. Explain that in this lesson, they will be given a quadrilateral and will learn what conditions can be used to classify it as a rectangle, rhombus, or square.

Explorations and answers are provided in *Alternate Openers: Explorations Transparencies.*

State Resources

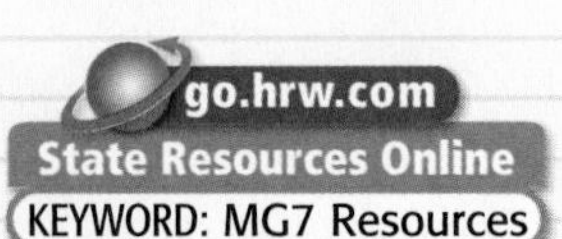

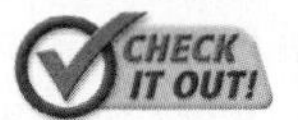

1. A carpenter's square can be used to test that an angle is a right angle. How could the contractor use a carpenter's square to check that the frame is a rectangle?

Below are some conditions you can use to determine whether a parallelogram is a rhombus.

Caution!

In order to apply Theorems 6-5-1 through 6-5-5, the quadrilateral must be a parallelogram.

Theorems **Conditions for Rhombuses**

	THEOREM	EXAMPLE
6-5-3	If one pair of consecutive sides of a parallelogram are congruent, then the parallelogram is a rhombus. (▱ with one pair cons. sides ≅ → rhombus)	F G E H
6-5-4	If the diagonals of a parallelogram are perpendicular, then the parallelogram is a rhombus. (▱ with diags. ⊥ → rhombus)	F G E H
6-5-5	If one diagonal of a parallelogram bisects a pair of opposite angles, then the parallelogram is a rhombus. (▱ with diag. bisecting opp. ∠s → rhombus)	F G E H

You will prove Theorems 6-5-3 and 6-5-4 in Exercises 32 and 30.

PROOF **Theorem 6-5-5**

Given: *JKLM* is a parallelogram. $\overline{JL}$ bisects ∠*KJM* and ∠*KLM*.
Prove: *JKLM* is a rhombus.
Proof:

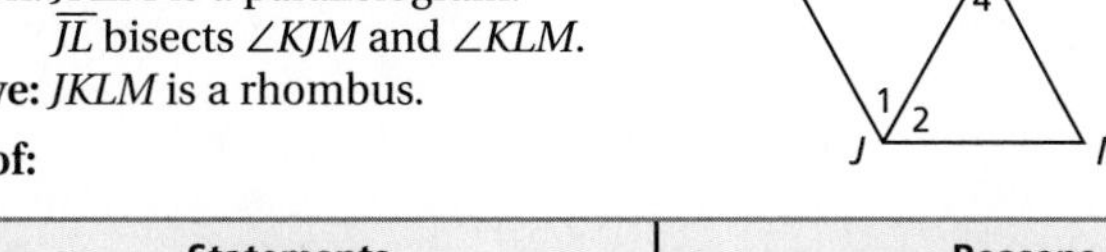

Statements	Reasons
1. *JKLM* is a parallelogram. $\overline{JL}$ bisects ∠*KJM* and ∠*KLM*.	1. Given
2. ∠1 ≅ ∠2, ∠3 ≅ ∠4	2. Def. of ∠ bisector
3. $\overline{JL} \cong \overline{JL}$	3. Reflex. Prop. of ≅
4. △*JKL* ≅ △*JML*	4. ASA *Steps 2, 3*
5. $\overline{JK} \cong \overline{JM}$	5. CPCTC
6. *JKLM* is a rhombus.	6. ▱ with one pair cons. sides ≅ → rhombus

To prove that a given quadrilateral is a square, it is sufficient to show that the figure is both a rectangle and a rhombus. You will explain why this is true in Exercise 43.

Power Presentations with PowerPoint®

Additional Examples

Example 1

A manufacturer builds a mold for a desktop so that $\overline{AB} \cong \overline{CD}$, $\overline{BC} \cong \overline{DA}$, and m∠*ABC* = 90°. Why must *ABCD* be a rectangle?

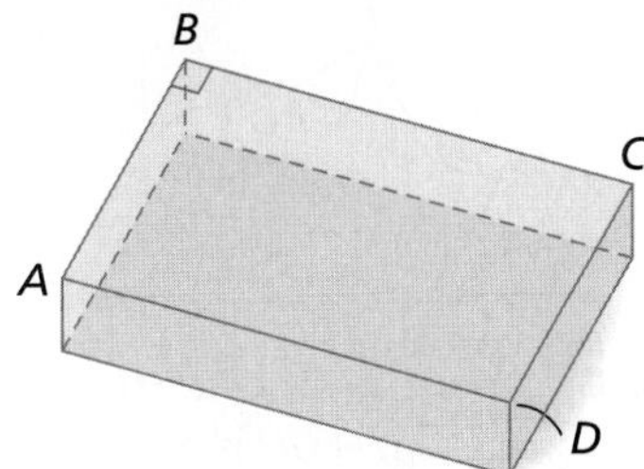

Both pairs of opp. sides of *ABCD* are ≅, so *ABCD* is a ▱. Since m∠*ABC* = 90°, 1 ∠ of ▱*ABCD* is a rt. ∠. *ABCD* is a rect. by Thm. 6-5-1.

2 Teach

Guided Instruction

Review the conditions for rectangles, rhombuses, and squares. In particular, if a parallelogram

- has one right angle, it is a rectangle.
- has congruent diagonals, it is a rectangle.
- has congruent consecutive sides, it is a rhombus.
- has perpendicular diagonals, it is a rhombus.
- is a rectangle and a rhombus, it is a square.

Reaching All Learners

Through Communication

Have a student list aloud four words, one of which does not fit with the other three. Have another student identify which word does not belong and explain to the class why. For example, the first student might say, "rhombus, rectangle, square, equilateral triangle." A possible response is that the rectangle does not belong because it does not necessarily have all congruent sides.

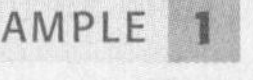

INTERVENTION

Questioning Strategies

EXAMPLE 1

- Is a four-sided object with congruent opposite sides always a rectangle? Explain.
- How do you know when you have enough information to classify an object as a rectangle?

Critical Thinking Some math textbooks define a rectangle as a parallelogram with one right angle. Point out to students that this definition is equivalent to "a quadrilateral with four right angles," because of Theorems 6-4-1 and 6-5-1.

Auditory Call on students to read each theorem aloud. Then ask them to explain the theorem in their own words. Challenge students to come up with unique ways to explain the theorems. ENGLISH LANGUAGE LEARNERS

Answers to Check It Out!

1. Both pairs of opp. sides of *WXYZ* are ≅, so *WXYZ* is a ▱. The contractor can use the carpenter's square to see if 1 ∠ of *WXYZ* is a rt. ∠. If 1 ∠ is a rt. ∠, then by Thm. 6-5-1 the frame is a rect.

Power Presentations with PowerPoint®

Additional Examples

Example 2

Determine if the conclusion is valid. If not, tell what additional information is needed to make it valid.

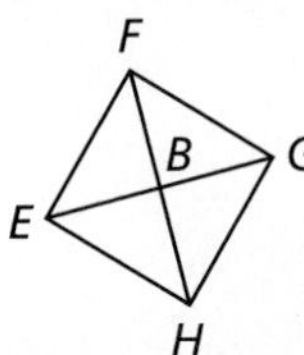

A. Given: $\overline{EF} \cong \overline{FG}$, $\overline{EG} \perp \overline{FH}$
Conclusion: *EFGH* is a rhombus.
Not valid. You must first know that *EFGH* is a ▱.

B. Given: $\overline{EB} \cong \overline{BG}$, $\overline{FB} \cong \overline{BH}$, $\overline{EG} \cong \overline{FH}$, $\triangle EBF \cong \triangle EBH$
Conclusion: *EFGH* is a square.
valid

Example 3

Use the diagonals to determine whether a parallelogram with the given vertices is a rectangle, rhombus, or square. Give all the names that apply.

A. $P(-1, 4)$, $Q(2, 6)$, $R(4, 3)$, $S(1, 1)$ rect., rhombus, square

B. $W(0, 1)$, $X(4, 2)$, $Y(3, -2)$, $Z(-1, -3)$ rhombus

INTERVENTION
Questioning Strategies

EXAMPLE 2

- How do you determine what additional information is needed to make a conclusion valid?
- Can there be more than one way to demonstrate that a conclusion is valid? Explain.

EXAMPLE 3

- How can you use the diagonals of a parallelogram to classify a figure as a rectangle, rhombus, or square?

EXAMPLE 2 Applying Conditions for Special Parallelograms

Determine if the conclusion is valid. If not, tell what additional information is needed to make it valid.

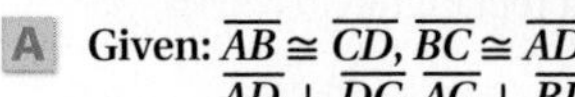

A **Given:** $\overline{AB} \cong \overline{CD}$, $\overline{BC} \cong \overline{AD}$, $\overline{AD} \perp \overline{DC}$, $\overline{AC} \perp \overline{BD}$
Conclusion: *ABCD* **is a square.**

Step 1 Determine if *ABCD* is a parallelogram.
$\overline{AB} \cong \overline{CD}$, $\overline{BC} \cong \overline{AD}$ — *Given*
ABCD is a parallelogram. — *Quad. with opp. sides ≅ → ▱*

Step 2 Determine if *ABCD* is a rectangle.
$\overline{AD} \perp \overline{DC}$, so $\angle ADC$ is a right angle. — *Def. of ⊥*
ABCD is a rectangle. — *▱ with one rt. ∠ → rect.*

Step 3 Determine if *ABCD* is a rhombus.
$\overline{AC} \perp \overline{BD}$ — *Given*
ABCD is a rhombus. — *▱ with diags. ⊥ → rhombus*

Step 4 Determine if *ABCD* is a square.
Since *ABCD* is a rectangle and a rhombus, it has four right angles and four congruent sides. So *ABCD* is a square by definition.
The conclusion is valid.

B **Given:** $\overline{AB} \cong \overline{BC}$
Conclusion: *ABCD* **is a rhombus.**
The conclusion is not valid. By Theorem 6-5-3, if one pair of consecutive sides of a parallelogram are congruent, then the parallelogram is a rhombus. To apply this theorem, you must first know that *ABCD* is a parallelogram.

Remember!
You can also prove that a given quadrilateral is a rectangle, rhombus, or square by using the definitions of the special quadrilaterals.

2. Determine if the conclusion is valid. If not, tell what additional information is needed to make it valid.
Given: $\angle ABC$ is a right angle.
Conclusion: *ABCD* is a rectangle.

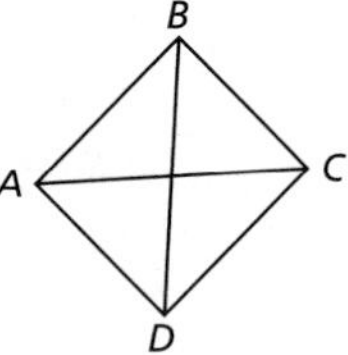

2. Not valid; by Thm. 6-5-1, if 1 ∠ of a ▱ is a rt. ∠, then the ▱ is a rect. To apply this thm., you need to know that *ABCD* is a ▱.

EXAMPLE 3 Identifying Special Parallelograms in the Coordinate Plane

Use the diagonals to determine whether a parallelogram with the given vertices is a rectangle, rhombus, or square. Give all the names that apply.

A $A(0, 2)$, $B(3, 6)$, $C(8, 6)$, $D(5, 2)$

Step 1 Graph ▱*ABCD*.

Step 2 Determine if *ABCD* is a rectangle.

$$AC = \sqrt{(8-0)^2 + (6-2)^2} = \sqrt{80} = 4\sqrt{5}$$

$$BD = \sqrt{(5-3)^2 + (2-6)^2} = \sqrt{20} = 2\sqrt{5}$$

Since $4\sqrt{5} \neq 2\sqrt{5}$, *ABCD* is not a rectangle.
Thus *ABCD* is not a square.

Step 3 Determine if *ABCD* is a rhombus.

slope of $\overline{AC} = \frac{6-2}{8-0} = \frac{1}{2}$ slope of $\overline{BD} = \frac{2-6}{5-3} = -2$

Since $\left(\frac{1}{2}\right)(-2) = -1$, $\overline{AC} \perp \overline{BD}$. *ABCD* is a rhombus.

B $E(-4, -1), F(-3, 2), G(3, 0), H(2, -3)$

Step 1 Graph ▱*EFGH*.

Step 2 Determine if *EFGH* is a rectangle.

$EG = \sqrt{[3-(-4)]^2 + [0-(-1)]^2}$
$= \sqrt{50} = 5\sqrt{2}$

$FH = \sqrt{[2-(-3)]^2 + (-3-2)^2}$
$= \sqrt{50} = 5\sqrt{2}$

Since $5\sqrt{2} = 5\sqrt{2}$, the diagonals are congruent. *EFGH* is a rectangle.

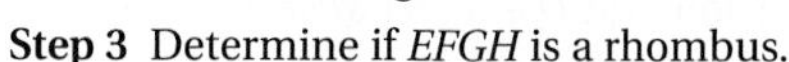

Step 3 Determine if *EFGH* is a rhombus.

slope of $\overline{EG} = \frac{0-(-1)}{3-(-4)} = \frac{1}{7}$

slope of $\overline{FH} = \frac{-3-2}{2-(-3)} = \frac{-5}{5} = -1$

Since $\left(\frac{1}{7}\right)(-1) \neq -1$, $\overline{EG} \not\perp \overline{FH}$.

So *EFGH* is a not a rhombus and cannot be a square.

Use the diagonals to determine whether a parallelogram with the given vertices is a rectangle, rhombus, or square. Give all the names that apply.

3a. $K(-5, -1), L(-2, 4), M(3, 1), N(0, -4)$ **rect., rhombus, square**

3b. $P(-4, 6), Q(2, 5), R(3, -1), S(-3, 0)$ **rhombus**

THINK AND DISCUSS

1. What special parallelogram is formed when the diagonals of a parallelogram are congruent? when the diagonals are perpendicular? when the diagonals are both congruent and perpendicular?
2. Draw a figure that shows why this statement is not necessarily true: If one angle of a quadrilateral is a right angle, then the quadrilateral is a rectangle.
3. A rectangle can also be defined as a parallelogram with a right angle. Explain why this definition is accurate.

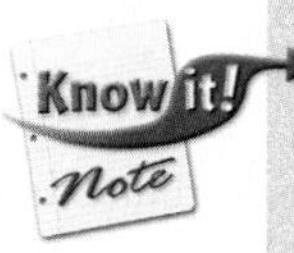

4. **GET ORGANIZED** Copy and complete the graphic organizer. In each box, write at least three conditions for the given parallelogram.

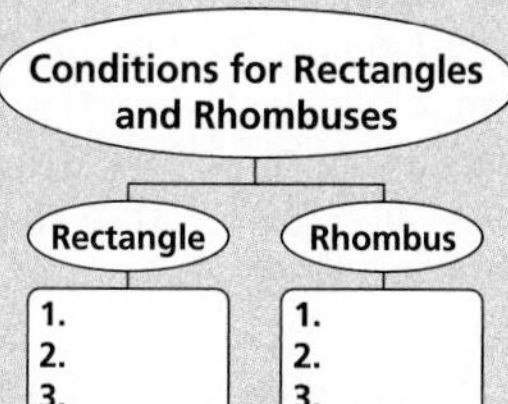

COMMON ERROR ALERT

Some students may have trouble identifying a piece of additional information that is sufficient to make a conclusion valid. Suggest that once they have an answer, they write a complete statement of the given information, sketch the figure, mark it with this information, and then recheck their work.

Teaching Tip **Critical Thinking** Explain how some of the theorems in the lesson can be used as alternate definitions. For example, some people define a rectangle as a parallelogram with one right angle. In this case, the remaining properties and our definition as a quadrilateral with four right angles follow.

3 Close

Summarize

Ask students to classify the figure below.

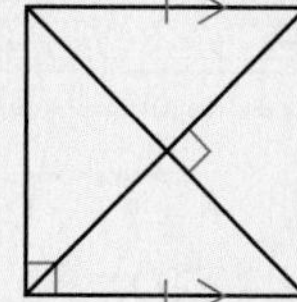

1 pair of opp. sides are ≅ and ||, so it is a ▱. It has 1 rt. ∠, so it is a rect. Its diags. are ⊥, so it is a rhombus. Since it is a rect. and a rhombus, it is also a square.

ONGOING ASSESSMENT and INTERVENTION

Diagnose ***Before*** **the Lesson**
6-5 Warm Up, TE p. 418

Monitor ***During*** **the Lesson**
Check It Out! Exercises, SE pp. 419–421
Questioning Strategies, TE pp. 419–420

Assess ***After*** **the Lesson**
6-5 Lesson Quiz, TE p. 425
Alternative Assessment, TE p. 425

Answers to *Think and Discuss*

1. rect.; rhombus; square
2. Possible answer:

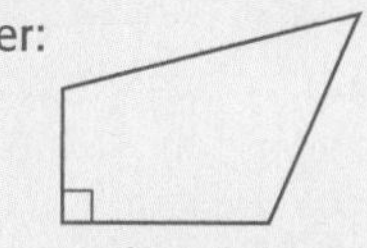

3. If a quad. is a rect., then it is a ▱. If a ▱ has 1 rt. ∠, then it is a rect. Thus these defs. are equivalent.
4. See p. A6.

6-5 Exercises

Assignment Guide

Assign *Guided Practice* exercises as necessary.

If you finished Examples **1–3**

Basic 6–17, 19, 20, 22, 28–30, 33, 35, 39–41, 45–52

Average 6–10, 12–16 even, 17, 18, 20–24, 26–29, 31, 33, 35–41, 44–52

Advanced 6–10, 12–24 even, 25–27, 29–52

Homework Quick Check

Quickly check key concepts.
Exercises: 6, 8, 10, 12, 20, 22

Answers

1. Possible answer: If *WXYZ* is both a rhombus and a rect., then it is a square. All 4 sides of *WXYZ* are ≅, so *WXYZ* is a rhombus. A rhombus is a ▱. If the diags. of a ▱ are ≅, then by Thm. 6-5-2 the ▱ is a rect. So the club members can measure the diags., and if they are equal, *WXYZ* is both a rhombus and a rect. Therefore it is a square.
2. By Thm. 6-5-2, if the diags. of a ▱ are ≅, then the ▱ is a rect. To apply this thm., you need to know that *ABCD* is a ▱.
6. Both pairs of opp. sides of *PQRS* are ≅, so *PQRS* is a ▱. Since $PZ = QZ$ and $RZ = SZ$, it follows that $PR = QS$ by the Segment Addition Postulate. Thus $\overline{PR} \cong \overline{QS}$. So the diags. of ▱*PQRS* are ≅. The frame is a rect. by Thm. 6-5-2.

State Resources

6-5 Exercises

go.hrw.com
Homework Help Online
KEYWORD: MG7 6-5
Parent Resources Online
KEYWORD: MG7 Parent

GUIDED PRACTICE

SEE EXAMPLE 1 p. 418

1. **Gardening** A city garden club is planting a square garden. They drive pegs into the ground at each corner and tie strings between each pair. The pegs are spaced so that $\overline{WX} \cong \overline{XY} \cong \overline{YZ} \cong \overline{ZW}$. How can the garden club use the diagonal strings to verify that the garden is a square?

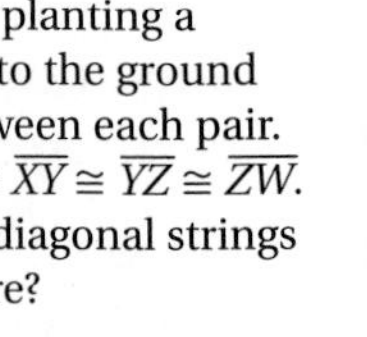

SEE EXAMPLE 2 p. 420

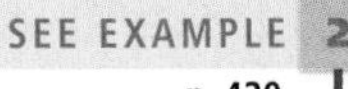

Determine if the conclusion is valid. If not, tell what additional information is needed to make it valid.

2. Given: $\overline{AC} \cong \overline{BD}$
   Conclusion: *ABCD* is a rectangle. **not valid**
3. Given: $\overline{AB} \parallel \overline{CD}$, $\overline{AB} \cong \overline{CD}$, $\overline{AB} \perp \overline{BC}$
   Conclusion: *ABCD* is a rectangle. **valid**

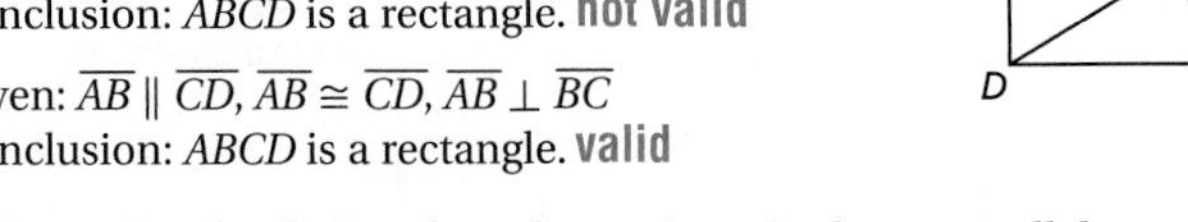

SEE EXAMPLE 3 p. 420

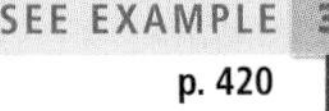

Multi-Step **Use the diagonals to determine whether a parallelogram with the given vertices is a rectangle, rhombus, or square. Give all the names that apply.**

4. $P(-5, 2)$, $Q(4, 5)$, $R(6, -1)$, $S(-3, -4)$ **rect.**
5. $W(-6, 0)$, $X(1, 4)$, $Y(2, -4)$, $Z(-5, -8)$ **rhombus**

PRACTICE AND PROBLEM SOLVING

Independent Practice	
For Exercises	See Example
6	1
7–8	2
9–10	3

Extra Practice
Skills Practice p. S15
Application Practice p. S33

6. **Crafts** A framer uses a clamp to hold together the pieces of a picture frame. The pieces are cut so that $\overline{PQ} \cong \overline{RS}$ and $\overline{QR} \cong \overline{SP}$. The clamp is adjusted so that PZ, QZ, RZ, and SZ are all equal. Why must the frame be a rectangle?

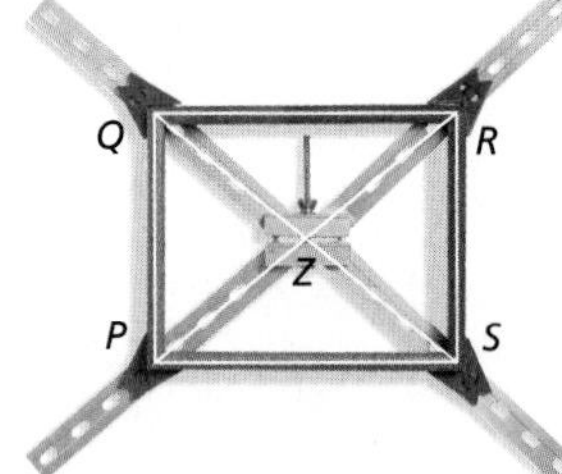

Determine if the conclusion is valid. If not, tell what additional information is needed to make it valid.

7. Given: $\overline{EG}$ and $\overline{FH}$ bisect each other. $\overline{EG} \perp \overline{FH}$
   Conclusion: *EFGH* is a rhombus. **valid**
8. Given: $\overline{FH}$ bisects ∠*EFG* and ∠*EHG*.
   Conclusion: *EFGH* is a rhombus.

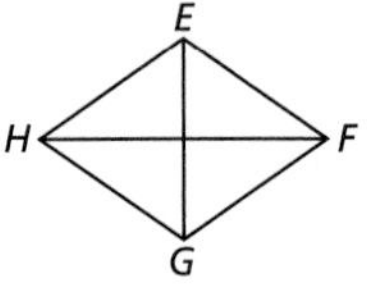

8. Not valid; by Thm. 6-5-5, if 1 diag. of a ▱ bisects a pair of opp. ∠s, then the ▱ is a rhombus. To apply this thm., you need to know that *EFGH* is a ▱.

Multi-Step **Use the diagonals to determine whether a parallelogram with the given vertices is a rectangle, rhombus, or square. Give all the names that apply.**

9. $A(-10, 4)$, $B(-2, 10)$, $C(4, 2)$, $D(-4, -4)$ **square, rect., rhombus**
10. $J(-9, -7)$, $K(-4, -2)$, $L(3, -3)$, $M(-2, -8)$ **rhombus**

Tell whether each quadrilateral is a parallelogram, rectangle, rhombus, or square. Give all the names that apply.

11. 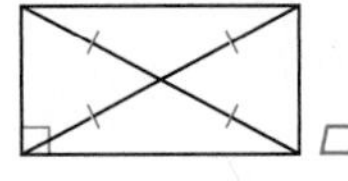 **▱, rect.**

12. 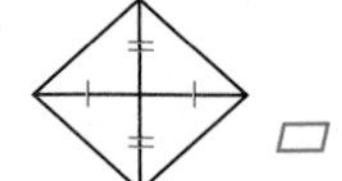 **▱**

13.  **▱, rect., rhombus, square**

6-5 READING STRATEGIES

Theorem	Example
If one angle of a parallelogram is a right angle, then the parallelogram is a rectangle.	R S V T
If the diagonals of a parallelogram are congruent, then the parallelogram is a rectangle.	R S V T
If one pair of consecutive sides of a parallelogram is congruent, then the parallelogram is a rhombus.	J K M L
If the diagonals of a parallelogram are perpendicular, then the parallelogram is a rhombus.	J K M L
If one diagonal of a parallelogram bisects a pair of opposite angles, then the parallelogram is a rhombus.	J K M L
If a parallelogram is both a rectangle and a rhombus, then the parallelogram is a square.	J K M L

In the table below, write the name of the quadrilateral that BEST matches the information that is checked. Choose from the following list:

rectangle rhombus square

Quadrilateral that BEST matches the information	Parallelogram with one right angle	Parallelogram with a diagonal that bisects a pair of opposite angles	Parallelogram with congruent diagonals	Parallelogram with one pair of congruent consecutive sides	Parallelogram with perpendicular diagonals
1. rectangle	X				
2. rhombus		X			
3. square	X	X			
4. rectangle			X		
5. square			X	X	
6. rhombus				X	
7. rhombus					X

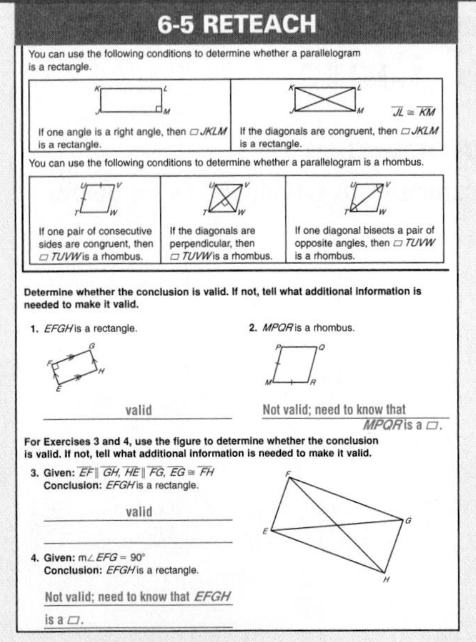

6-5 RETEACH

You can use the following conditions to determine whether a parallelogram is a rectangle.

If one angle is a right angle, then ▱*JKLM* is a rectangle.	If the diagonals are congruent, then ▱*JKLM* is a rectangle. ($\overline{JL} \cong \overline{KM}$)

You can use the following conditions to determine whether a parallelogram is a rhombus.

If one pair of consecutive sides are congruent, then ▱*TUVW* is a rhombus.	If the diagonals are perpendicular, then ▱*TUVW* is a rhombus.	If one diagonal bisects a pair of opposite angles, then ▱*TUVW* is a rhombus.

Determine whether the conclusion is valid. If not, tell what additional information is needed to make it valid.

1. *EFGH* is a rectangle.
   valid
2. *MPQR* is a rhombus.
   Not valid; need to know that *MPQR* is a ▱.

For Exercises 3 and 4, use the figure to determine whether the conclusion is valid. If not, tell what additional information is needed to make it valid.

3. **Given:** $\overline{EF} \parallel \overline{GH}$, $\overline{HE} \parallel \overline{FG}$, $\overline{EG} \cong \overline{FH}$
   Conclusion: *EFGH* is a rectangle.
   valid
4. **Given:** $m\angle EFG = 90°$
   Conclusion: *EFGH* is a rectangle.
   Not valid; need to know that *EFGH* is a ▱.

Tell whether each quadrilateral is a parallelogram, rectangle, rhombus, or square. Give all the names that apply.

14. 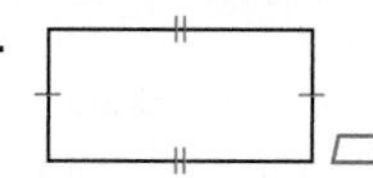 ▱

15. ▱, rect., rhombus, square

16. 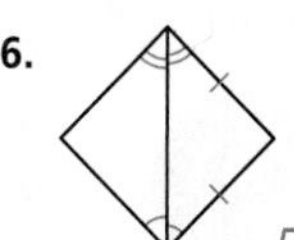 ▱, rhombus

17. B; possible answer: it is given that $\overline{ABCD}$ is a ▱. $\overline{AC}$ and $\overline{BD}$ are its diags. By Thm. 6-5-2, if the diags. of a ▱ are ≅, you can conclude that the ▱ is a rect. There is not enough information to conclude that *ABCD* is a square.

17. **/// ERROR ANALYSIS ///** In ▱*ABCD*, $\overline{AC} \cong \overline{BD}$. Which conclusion is incorrect? Explain the error.

Ⓐ *ABCD* is a rectangle.

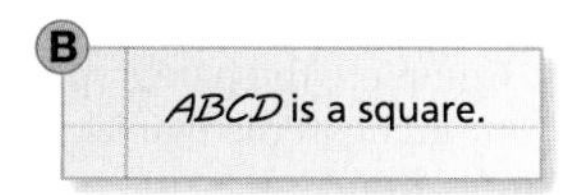
Ⓑ *ABCD* is a square.

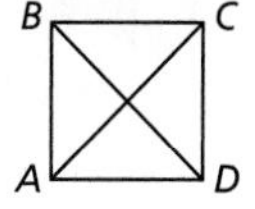

Give one characteristic of the diagonals of each figure that would make the conclusion valid.

18. Conclusion: *JKLM* is a rhombus.

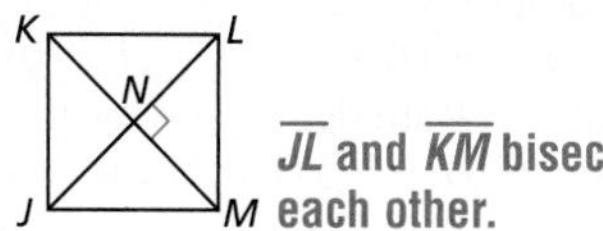

$\overline{JL}$ and $\overline{KM}$ bisect each other.

19. Conclusion: *PQRS* is a square.

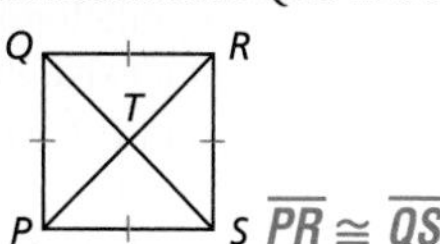

$\overline{PR} \cong \overline{QS}$

The coordinates of three vertices of ▱*ABCD* are given. Find the coordinates of *D* so that the given type of figure is formed.

20. $(-5, 4)$
21. $(2, 6)$
22. $(-4, -2)$
23. $(-2, -2)$

20. $A(4, -2)$, $B(-5, -2)$, $C(4, 4)$; rectangle **21.** $A(-5, 5)$, $B(0, 0)$, $C(7, 1)$; rhombus

22. $A(0, 2)$, $B(4, -2)$, $C(0, -6)$; square **23.** $A(2, 1)$, $B(-1, 5)$, $C(-5, 2)$; square

Find the value of *x* that makes each parallelogram the given type.

24. rectangle **25.** rhombus **26.** square

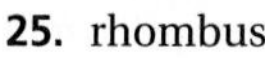

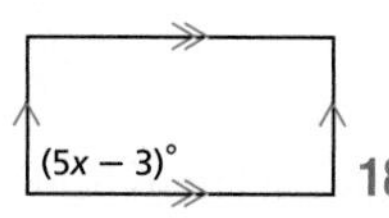

18.6

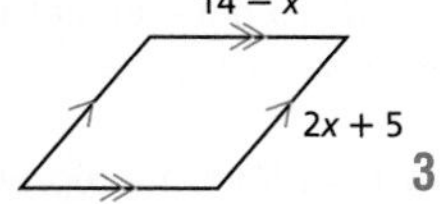

3

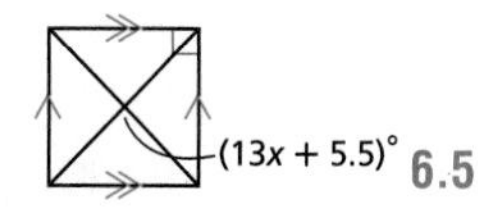

6.5

27. Rhombus; since the diags. bisect each other, the quad. is a ▱. Since the diags. of the ▱ are ⊥, the quad. is a rhombus.

27. **Critical Thinking** The diagonals of a quadrilateral are perpendicular bisectors of each other. What is the best name for this quadrilateral? Explain your answer.

28. Complete the two-column proof of Theorem 6-5-2 by filling in the blanks.

Given: *EFGH* is a parallelogram.
$\overline{EG} \cong \overline{HF}$

Prove: *EFGH* is a rectangle.

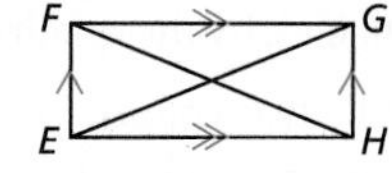

Proof:

Statements	Reasons
1. *EFGH* is a parallelogram. $\overline{EG} \cong \overline{HF}$	1. Given
2. $\overline{EF} \cong \overline{HG}$	2. a. __?__ ▱ → opp. sides ≅
3. b. __?__ $\overline{EH} \cong \overline{EH}$	3. Reflex. Prop. of ≅
4. △*EFH* ≅ △*HGE*	4. c. __?__ SSS
5. ∠*FEH* ≅ d. __?__ ∠*GHE*	5. e. __?__ CPCTC
6. ∠*FEH* and ∠*GHE* are supplementary.	6. f. __?__ ▱ → cons. ∠s supp.
7. g. __?__ ∠*FEH* and ∠*GHE* are rt. ∠s.	7. ≅ ∠s supp. → rt. ∠s
8. *EFGH* is a rectangle.	8. h. __?__ h. ▱ with 1 rt. ∠ → rect.

Teaching Tip **Communicating Math** When students work **Exercises 18 and 19,** encourage them to write a complete statement of the given information and then compare it with the theorems in the lesson.

6-5 PROBLEM SOLVING

1. An amusement park has a rectangular observation deck with walkways above the bungee jumping and sky jumping. The distance from the center of the deck to points *E*, *F*, *G*, and *H* is 15 meters. Explain why *EFGH* must be a rectangle.
   Diagonals bisect each other, so the quad. is a ▱. The diagonals are ≅, so *EFGH* is a rect. because ▱ with diags. ≅ → rect.

2. In the mosaic, $\overline{AB} \parallel \overline{CD}$ and $\overline{BC} \parallel \overline{DA}$. If $AB = 4$ inches and $BC = 4$ inches, can you conclude that *ABCD* is a square? Explain.
   No; from the given information, you can conclude only that *ABCD* is a rhombus.

3. If $\overline{TV} \cong \overline{US}$, explain why the basketball backboard must be a rectangle.
   Both pairs of opposite sides are ≅, so *STUV* is a ▱. *STUV* is a rectangle because ▱ with diags. ≅ → rect.

Choose the best answer.

4. The vertices of a parallelogram are $M(0, -4)$, $P(6, -1)$, $Q(4, 3)$, and $R(-2, 0)$. Classify the parallelogram as specifically as possible.
   Ⓐ rectangle only
   B square
   C rhombus only
   D quadrilateral

5. Choose the best description for the quadrilateral.
   Ⓕ parallelogram
   G parallelogram and rectangle
   H parallelogram and rhombus
   J parallelogram and square

6. In parallelogram *KLMN*, $m\angle L = (4w + 5)°$. Choose the value of *w* that makes *KLMN* a rectangle.
   A 90 C 43.75
   B 85 Ⓓ 21.25

7. The coordinates of three vertices of quadrilateral *ABCD* are $A(3, -1)$, $B(10, 0)$, and $C(5, 5)$. For which coordinates of *D* will the quadrilateral be a rhombus?
   F $(-1, 4)$ H $(-1, 3)$
   Ⓖ $(-2, 4)$ J $(-2, 3)$

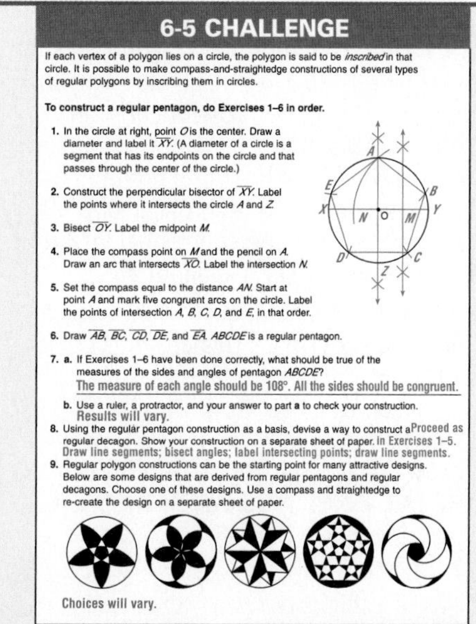

6-5 CHALLENGE

If each vertex of a polygon lies on a circle, the polygon is said to be *inscribed* in that circle. It is possible to make compass-and-straightedge constructions of several types of regular polygons by inscribing them in circles.

To construct a regular pentagon, do Exercises 1–6 in order.

1. In the circle at right, point *O* is the center. Draw a diameter and label it $\overline{XY}$. (A diameter of a circle is a segment that has its endpoints on the circle and that passes through the center of the circle.)
2. Construct the perpendicular bisector of $\overline{XY}$. Label the points where it intersects the circle *A* and *Z*.
3. Bisect $\overline{OY}$. Label the midpoint *M*.
4. Place the compass point on *M* and the pencil on *A*. Draw an arc that intersects $\overline{XO}$. Label the intersection *N*.
5. Set the compass equal to the distance *AN*. Start at point *A* and mark five congruent arcs on the circle. Label the points of intersection *A*, *B*, *C*, *D*, and *E*, in that order.
6. Draw $\overline{AB}$, $\overline{BC}$, $\overline{CD}$, $\overline{DE}$, and $\overline{EA}$. *ABCDE* is a regular pentagon.
7. a. If Exercises 1–6 have been done correctly, what should be true of the measures of the sides and angles of pentagon *ABCDE*?
   The measure of each angle should be 108°. All the sides should be congruent.
   b. Use a ruler, a protractor, and your answer to part **a** to check your construction.
   Results will vary.
8. Using the regular pentagon construction as a basis, devise a way to construct a regular decagon. Show your construction on a separate sheet of paper. Proceed as in Exercises 1–5. Draw line segments; bisect angles; label intersecting points; draw line segments.
9. Regular polygon constructions can be the starting point for many attractive designs. Below are some designs that are derived from regular pentagons and regular decagons. Choose one of these designs. Use a compass and straightedge to re-create the design on a separate sheet of paper.

Choices will vary.

6-5 PRACTICE A
6-5 PRACTICE C
6-5 PRACTICE B

1. On the National Mall in Washington, D.C., a reflecting pool lies between the Lincoln Memorial and the World War II Memorial. The pool has two 2300-foot-long sides and two 150-foot-long sides. Tell what additional information you need to know in order to determine whether the reflecting pool is a rectangle. (*Hint:* Remember that you have to show it is a parallelogram first.)
   Possible answer: To know that the reflecting pool is a parallelogram, the congruent sides must be opposite each other. If this is true, then knowing that one angle in the pool is a right angle or that the diagonals are congruent proves that the pool is a rectangle.

Use the figure for Exercises 2–5. Determine whether each conclusion is valid. If not, tell what additional information is needed to make it valid.

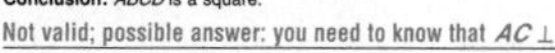

2. **Given:** *AC* and *BD* bisect each other. *AC* ≅ *BD*
   Conclusion: *ABCD* is a square.
   Not valid; possible answer: you need to know that *AC* ⊥ *BD*.
3. **Given:** *AC* ⊥ *BD*, *AB* ≅ *BC*
   Conclusion: *ABCD* is a rhombus. Not valid; possible answer: you need to know that *AC* and *BD* bisect each other.
4. **Given:** *AB* ≅ *DC*, *AD* ≅ *BC*, $m\angle ADB = m\angle ABD = 45°$
   Conclusion: *ABCD* is a square.
   valid
5. **Given:** *AB* ∥ *DC*, *AD* ≅ *BC*, *AC* ≅ *BD*
   Conclusion: *ABCD* is a rectangle.
   Not valid; possible answer: you need to know that *AD* ∥ *BC*.

Find the lengths and slopes of the diagonals to determine whether a parallelogram with the given vertices is a rectangle, rhombus, or square. Give all names that apply.

6. $(-2, -4)$, $(0, -1)$, $(-3, 1)$, $(-5, -2)$ — rectangle, rhombus, square
   $= \sqrt{26}$ $= \sqrt{26}$
   slope of $= -5$ slope of $= \frac{1}{5}$
7. $(-1, 3)$, $(-2, 5)$, $(0, 4)$, $(1, 2)$ — rhombus
   $= \sqrt{2}$ $= 3\sqrt{2}$
   slope of $= 1$ slope of $= -1$

Exercise 29 involves identifying special parallelograms in the coordinate plane. This exercise prepares students for the Multi-Step Test Prep on page 436.

Answers

29a. slope of $\overline{AB}$ = slope of $\overline{CD}$ = $-\frac{1}{3}$; slope of $\overline{AD}$ = slope of $\overline{CB} = -3$

b. Slope of $\overline{AC} = -1$; slope of $\overline{BD}$ = 1; the slopes are negative reciprocals of each other, so $\overline{AC} \perp \overline{BD}$.

c. $ABCD$ is a rhombus, since it is a ▱ and its diags. are ⊥ (Thm. 6-5-4).

31. Possible answer:
1. $ABCD$ is a ▱. ∠A is a rt. ∠. (Given)
2. m∠A = 90° (Def. of rt. ∠)
3. ∠A and ∠B are supp. (▱ → cons. ∠s supp.)
4. m∠A + m∠B = 180° (Def. of supp. ∠s)
5. 90° + m∠B = 180° (Subst.)
6. m∠B = 90° (Subtr. Prop. of =)
7. ∠C ≅ ∠A, ∠D ≅ ∠B (▱ → opp. ∠s ≅)
8. m∠C = m∠A, m∠D = m∠B (Def. of ≅ ∠s)
9. m∠C = 90°, m∠D = 90° (Trans. Prop. of =)
10. ∠B, ∠C, and ∠D are rt. ∠s. (Def. of rt. ∠)
11. $ABCD$ is a rect. (Def. of rect.)

32. Possible answer: It is given that $\overline{JK} \cong \overline{KL}$. Since opp. sides of a ▱ are ≅, $\overline{JK} \cong \overline{LM}$, and $\overline{KL} \cong \overline{MJ}$. By the Trans. Prop. of ≅, $\overline{JK} \cong \overline{MJ}$. So $\overline{JK}$ is ≅ to each of the other 3 sides of $JKLM$. Therefore $JKLM$ is a rhombus by def.

33a. 

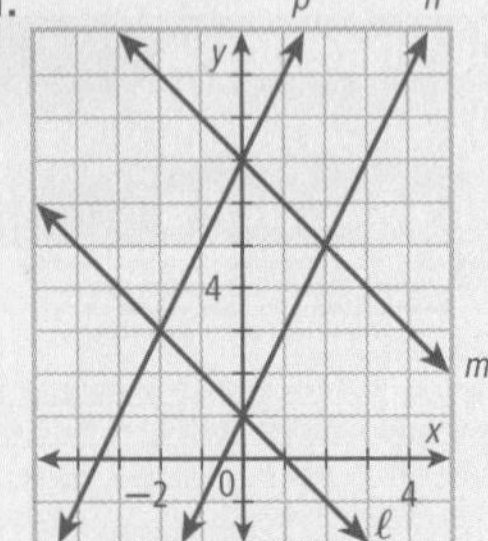

34. Possible answer:
1. $FHJN$ and $GLMF$ are ▱s. $\overline{FG} \cong \overline{FN}$ (Given)
2. $\overline{FH} \parallel \overline{NJ}$, $\overline{GL} \parallel \overline{FM}$ (Def. of ▱)
3. $FGKN$ is a ▱. (Def. of ▱)
4. $FGKN$ is a rhombus. (▱ with 1 pair cons. sides ≅ → rhombus)

29. This problem will prepare you for the Multi-Step Test Prep on page 436.

A state fair takes place on a plot of land given by the coordinates $A(-2, 3)$, $B(1, 2)$, $C(2, -1)$, and $D(-1, 0)$.

a. Show that the opposite sides of quadrilateral $ABCD$ are parallel.

b. A straight path connects A and C, and another path connects B and D. Use slopes to prove that these two paths are perpendicular.

c. What can you conclude about $ABCD$? Explain your answer.

30. Complete the paragraph proof of Theorem 6-5-4 by filling in the blanks.

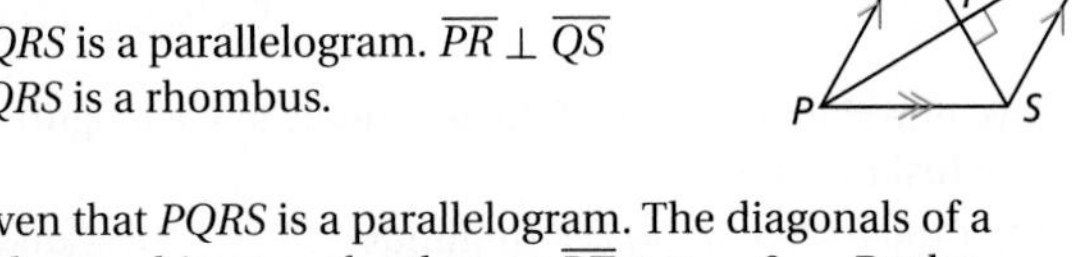

Given: $PQRS$ is a parallelogram. $\overline{PR} \perp \overline{QS}$

Prove: $PQRS$ is a rhombus.

Proof:

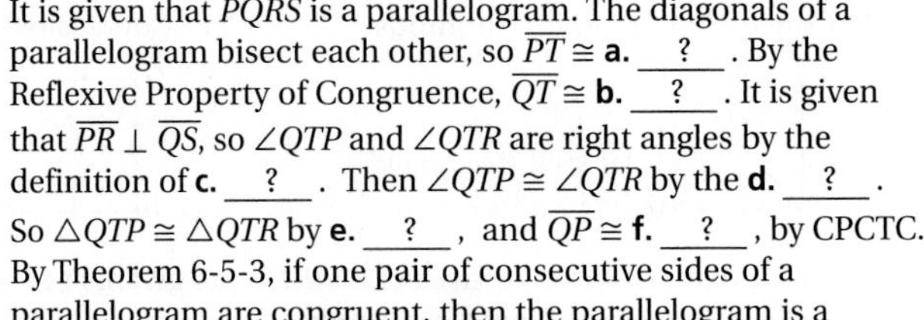

It is given that $PQRS$ is a parallelogram. The diagonals of a parallelogram bisect each other, so $\overline{PT} \cong$ **a.** __?__. By the Reflexive Property of Congruence, $\overline{QT} \cong$ **b.** __?__. It is given that $\overline{PR} \perp \overline{QS}$, so ∠$QTP$ and ∠QTR are right angles by the definition of **c.** __?__. Then ∠QTP ≅ ∠QTR by the **d.** __?__. So △QTP ≅ △QTR by **e.** __?__, and $\overline{QP} \cong$ **f.** __?__, by CPCTC. By Theorem 6-5-3, if one pair of consecutive sides of a parallelogram are congruent, then the parallelogram is a **g.** __?__. Therefore $PQRS$ is rhombus.

a. $\overline{RT}$
b. $\overline{QT}$
c. ⊥ lines
d. Rt. ∠ ≅ Thm.
e. SAS
f. $\overline{QR}$
g. rhombus

31. Write a two-column proof of Theorem 6-5-1.

Given: $ABCD$ is a parallelogram. ∠A is a right angle.

Prove: $ABCD$ is a rectangle.

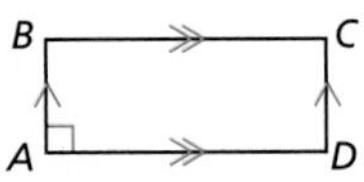

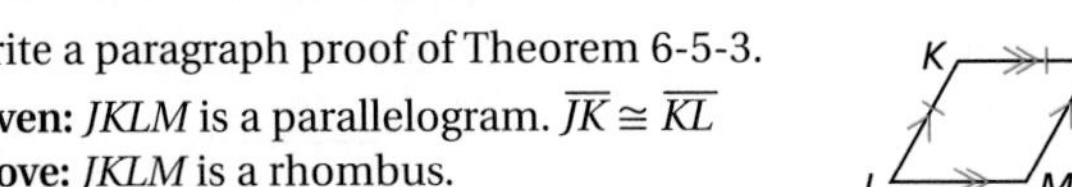

32. Write a paragraph proof of Theorem 6-5-3.

Given: $JKLM$ is a parallelogram. $\overline{JK} \cong \overline{KL}$

Prove: $JKLM$ is a rhombus.

33. **Algebra** Four lines are represented by the equations below.

ℓ: $y = -x + 1$ m: $y = -x + 7$ n: $y = 2x + 1$ p: $y = 2x + 7$

a. Graph the four lines in the coordinate plane.

b. Classify the quadrilateral formed by the lines. ▱

c. **What if...?** Suppose the slopes of lines n and p change to 1. Reclassify the quadrilateral. square

34. Write a two-column proof.

Given: $FHJN$ and $GLMF$ are parallelograms. $\overline{FG} \cong \overline{FN}$

Prove: $FGKN$ is a rhombus.

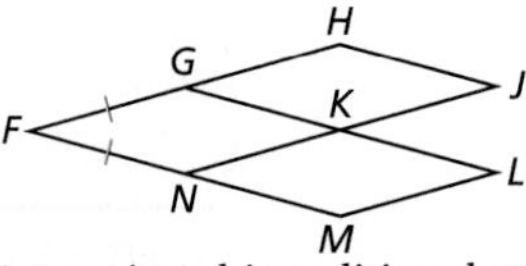

35. **Write About It** Use Theorems 6-4-2 and 6-5-2 to write a biconditional statement about rectangles. Use Theorems 6-4-4 and 6-5-4 to write a biconditional statement about rhombuses. Can you combine Theorems 6-4-5 and 6-5-5 to write a biconditional statement? Explain your answer.

Construction Use the diagonals to construct each figure. Then use the theorems from this lesson to explain why your method works.

36. rectangle 37. rhombus 38. square

36–38. Check students' work. Answers will vary.

35. A ▱ is a rect. if and only if its diags. are ≅; a ▱ is a rhombus if and only if its diags. are ⊥; no; possible answer: Thms. 6-4-5 and 6-5-5 are not converses. The conclusion of the conditional in Thm. 6-4-5 refers to both diags. of a ▱. The hypothesis of the conditional in Thm. 6-5-5 refers to only 1 diag. of a ▱.

41b. m∠JKM = m∠LMK, so $\overline{JK} \parallel \overline{LM}$. Since both pairs of opp. sides are ∥, $JKLM$ is a ▱.

c. By subst., Lin. Pair Thm., and Rt. ∠ ≅ Thm., all 4 ∠s at N are rt. ∠s. Since $JKLM$ is a ▱, N is mdpt. of both diags. By SAS, △KNL ≅ △KNJ, so by CPCTC, ∠LKN ≅ ∠JKN. Therefore m∠JKL = 2m∠JKN = 2(36) = 72° ≠ 90°.

d. m∠KNL = 90°, so the diags. are ⊥, and $JKLM$ is a rhombus.

42. Possible answer:
1. $\overline{AC} \cong \overline{DF}$, $\overline{AB} \cong \overline{DE}$, $\overline{AB} \perp \overline{BC}$, $\overline{DE} \perp \overline{EF}$, $\overline{BE} \perp \overline{EF}$, $\overline{BC} \parallel \overline{EF}$ (Given)
2. m∠ABC = 90°, m∠DEF = 90°, m∠BEF = 90° (Def. of ⊥)
3. ∠ABC, ∠DEF, and ∠BEF are rt. ∠s. (Def. of rt. ∠)
4. △ABC and △DEF are rt. △s. (Def. of rt. △)
5. △ABC ≅ △DEF (HL)
6. $\overline{BC} \cong \overline{EF}$ (CPCTC)
7. $EBCF$ is a ▱. (Quad. with pair of opp. sides ≅ and ∥ → ▱)
8. $EBCF$ is a rect. (▱ with 1 rt. ∠ → rect.)

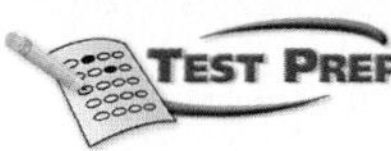

39. In $\square PQRS$, $\overline{PR}$ and $\overline{QS}$ intersect at T. What additional information is needed to conclude that $PQRS$ is a rectangle?

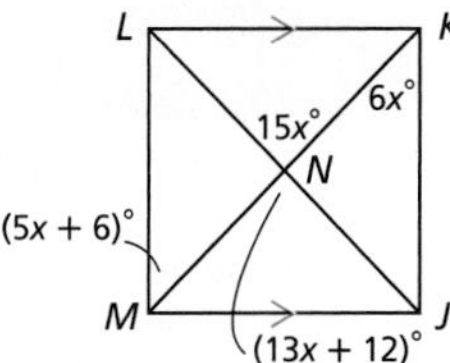

Ⓐ $\overline{PT} \cong \overline{QT}$ Ⓒ $\overline{PT} \perp \overline{QT}$

Ⓑ $\overline{PT} \cong \overline{RT}$ Ⓓ $\overline{PT}$ bisects $\angle QPS$.

40. Which of the following is the best name for figure $WXYZ$ with vertices $W(-3, 1)$, $X(1, 5)$, $Y(8, -2)$, and $Z(4, -6)$?

Ⓕ Parallelogram Ⓖ Rectangle Ⓗ Rhombus Ⓙ Square

41. **Extended Response** $15x = 13x + 12;\ x = 6$

a. Write and solve an equation to find the value of x.

b. Is $JKLM$ a parallelogram? Explain. yes

c. Is $JKLM$ a rectangle? Explain. no

d. Is $JKLM$ a rhombus? Explain. yes

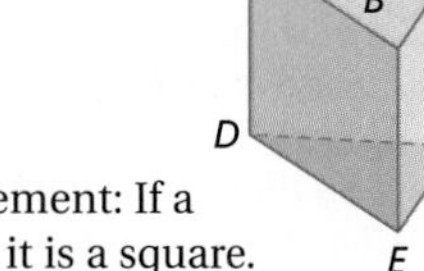

CHALLENGE AND EXTEND

42. Given: $\overline{AC} \cong \overline{DF}$, $\overline{AB} \cong \overline{DE}$, $\overline{AB} \perp \overline{BC}$, $\overline{DE} \perp \overline{EF}$, $\overline{BE} \perp \overline{EF}$, $\overline{BC} \parallel \overline{EF}$

Prove: $EBCF$ is a rectangle.

43. **Critical Thinking** Consider the following statement: If a quadrilateral is a rectangle and a rhombus, then it is a square.

a. Explain why the statement is true.

b. If a quadrilateral is a rectangle, is it necessary to show that all four sides are congruent in order to conclude that it is a square? Explain. no

c. If a quadrilateral is a rhombus, is it necessary to show that all four angles are right angles in order to conclude that it is a square? Explain. no

44. The diags. of the $\square$ are $\perp$, so it is a rhombus.

44. **Cars** As you turn the crank of a car jack, the platform that supports the car rises. Use the diagonals of the parallelogram to explain whether the jack forms a rectangle, rhombus, or square.

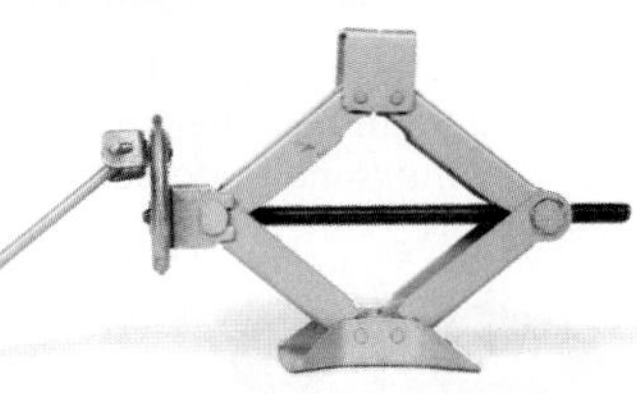

SPIRAL REVIEW

Sketch the graph of each function. State whether the function is linear or nonlinear. *(Previous course)*

45. $y = -3x + 1$ linear

46. $y = x^2 - 4$ nonlinear

47. $y = 3$ linear

Find the perimeter of each figure. Round to the nearest tenth. *(Lesson 5-7)*

48. $20 + 4\sqrt{41} \approx 45.6$

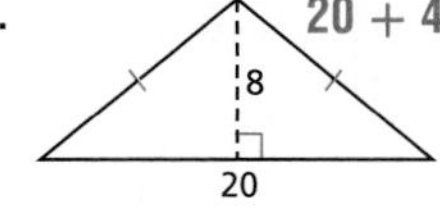

49. $31 + \sqrt{61} \approx 38.8$

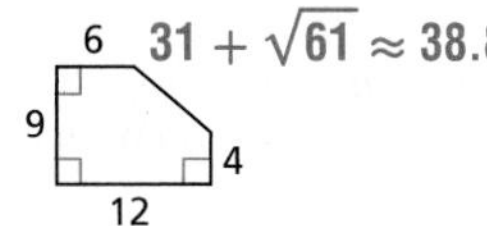

Find the value of each variable that would make the quadrilateral a parallelogram. *(Lesson 6-3)*

50. x 7

51. y 4

52. z 2

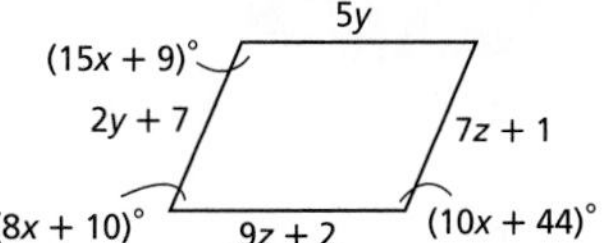

43a. Possible answer: If a quad. is a rect., then it has 4 rt. ∠s. If a quad. is a rhombus, then it has 4 ≅ sides. By def., a quad. with 4 ≅ sides and 4 rt. ∠s is a square. Therefore the statement is true.

b. Possible answer: If a quad. is a rect., then it is a $\square$. By Thm. 6-5-3, if 1 pair of cons. sides of a $\square$ are ≅, then the $\square$ is a rhombus. So if 1 pair of cons. sides of a rect. are ≅, it is a rhombus. If a quad. is a rect. and a rhombus, then it is a square.

c. Possible answer: If a quad. is a rhombus, then it is a $\square$. By Thm. 6-5-1, if 1 ∠ of a $\square$ is a rt. ∠, then the $\square$ is a rect. So if 1 ∠ of a rhombus is a rt. ∠, it is a rect. If a quad. is a rhombus and a rect., then it is a square.

45.

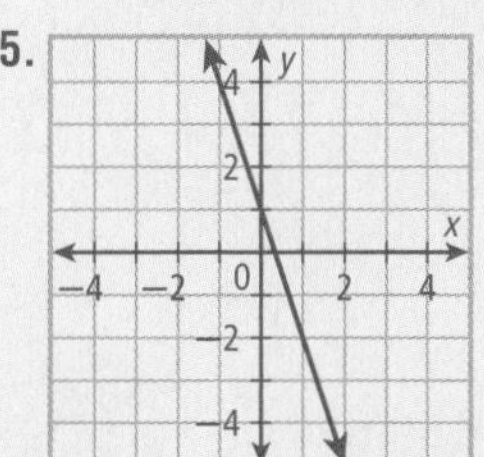

46, 47. For graphs, see p. A23.

TEST PREP DOCTOR  If students have difficulty with **Exercise 39,** point out that $PQRS$ is a parallelogram and that the diagonals of a parallelogram bisect each other. Tell students who chose **C** that they can conclude that $PQRS$ is a rhombus, but not a rectangle.

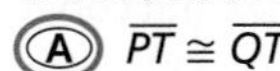

Journal

Have students draw a graphic organizer showing the relationship between a parallelogram, rectangle, rhombus, and square.

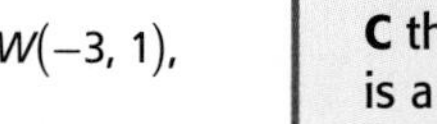

ALTERNATIVE ASSESSMENT

Have each student draw three parallelograms and mark some given characteristics on each. Have students exchange papers and explain whether each figure is a rectangle, rhombus, square, or none of these.

Power Presentations with PowerPoint®

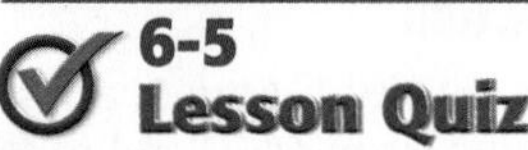

6-5 Lesson Quiz

1. Given that $AB = BC = CD = DA$, what additional information is needed to conclude that $ABCD$ is a square? $\overline{AC} \cong \overline{BD}$

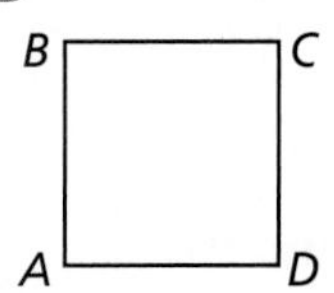

2. Determine if the conclusion is valid. If not, tell what additional information is needed to make it valid.

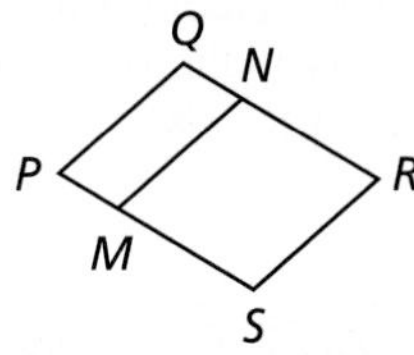

Given: $PQRS$ and $PQNM$ are ▭. $\overline{MN} \cong \overline{NR}$

Conclusion: $MNRS$ is a rhombus. valid

3. Use the diagonals to determine whether a parallelogram with vertices $A(2, 7)$, $B(7, 9)$, $C(5, 4)$, and $D(0, 2)$ is a rectangle, rhombus, or square. Give all the names that apply. $AC \neq BD$, so $ABCD$ is not a rect. or a square. The slope of $AC = -1$, and the slope of $BD = 1$, so $\overline{AC} \perp \overline{BD}$. $ABCD$ is a rhombus.

Also available on transparency 

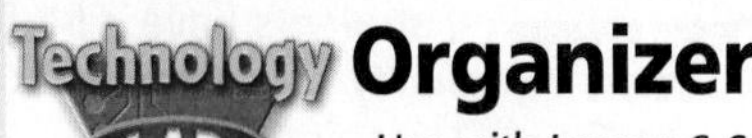

Organizer

Use with Lesson 6-6

Pacing:
Traditional 1 day
Block $\frac{1}{2}$ day

Objective: Use geometry software to investigate the properties and conditions of an isosceles trapezoid.

Materials: geometry software

Online Edition
TechKeys

Countdown Week 14

Resources

Technology Lab Activities
6-6 Lab Recording Sheet

Teach

Discuss

After **Activity 1, Step 5,** ask students to compare m∠*ACD* and m∠*BDC*. Explain to students that in order to prove that a trapezoid is isosceles, you only have to show that one pair of base angles is congruent. Ask students to discuss why the other pair is necessarily congruent.

Close

Key Concept

An isosceles trapezoid has congruent pairs of base angles and congruent diagonals.

Assessment

Journal Have students describe the properties they discovered about isosceles trapezoids.

State Resources

Explore Isosceles Trapezoids

Use with Lesson 6-6

In this lab you will investigate the properties and conditions of an *isosceles trapezoid*. A *trapezoid* is a quadrilateral with one pair of parallel sides, called *bases*. The sides that are not parallel are called *legs*. In an isosceles trapezoid, the legs are congruent.

Activity 1

1. Draw $\overline{AB}$ and a point C not on $\overline{AB}$. Construct a parallel line ℓ through C. **Check students' work.**
2. Draw point D on line ℓ. Construct $\overline{AC}$ and $\overline{BD}$. **Check students' work.**
3. Measure AC, BD, $\angle CAB$, $\angle ABD$, $\angle ACD$, and $\angle CDB$. **Check students' work.**
4. Move D until $AC = BD$. What do you notice about $m\angle CAB$ and $m\angle ABD$? What do you notice about $m\angle ACD$ and $m\angle CDB$? **$m\angle CAB = m\angle ABD$; $m\angle ACD = m\angle CDB$**
5. Move D so that $AC \neq BD$. Now move D so that $m\angle CAB = m\angle ABD$. What do you notice about AC and BD? **$AC = BD$**

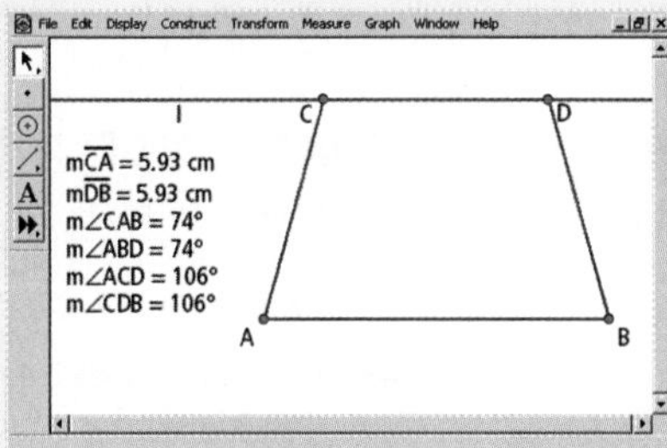

Try This

1. **Make a Conjecture** What is true about the base angles of an isosceles trapezoid? Write your conjecture as a conditional statement. **Possible answer: If a trap. is isosc., then its base ∠s are ≅.**
2. **Make a Conjecture** How can the base angles of a trapezoid be used to determine if the trapezoid is isosceles? Write your conjecture as a conditional statement. **Possible answer: If 1 pair of base ∠s of a trap. are ≅, then the trap. is isosc.**

Activity 2

1. Construct $\overline{AD}$ and $\overline{CB}$. **Check students' work.**
2. Measure AD and CB. **Check students' work.**
3. Move D until $AC = BD$. What do you notice about AD and CB? **$AD = CB$**
4. Move D so that $AC \neq BD$. Now move D so that $AD = BC$. What do you notice about AC and BD? **$AC = BD$**

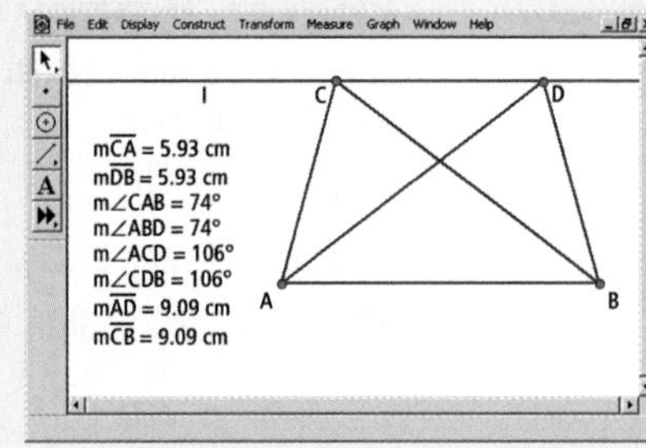

Try This

3. **Make a Conjecture** What is true about the diagonals of an isosceles trapezoid? Write your conjecture as a conditional statement. **Possible answer: If a trap. is isosc., then its diags. are ≅.**
4. **Make a Conjecture** How can the diagonals of a trapezoid be used to determine if the trapezoid is isosceles? Write your conjecture as a conditional statement. **Possible answer: If the diags. of a trap. are ≅, then the trap. is isosc.**

6-6 Properties of Kites and Trapezoids

Objectives

Use properties of kites to solve problems.

Use properties of trapezoids to solve problems.

Vocabulary

kite
trapezoid
base of a trapezoid
leg of a trapezoid
base angle of a trapezoid
isosceles trapezoid
midsegment of a trapezoid

Why learn this?

The design of a simple kite flown at the beach shares the properties of the geometric figure called a *kite*.

A **kite** is a quadrilateral with exactly two pairs of congruent consecutive sides.

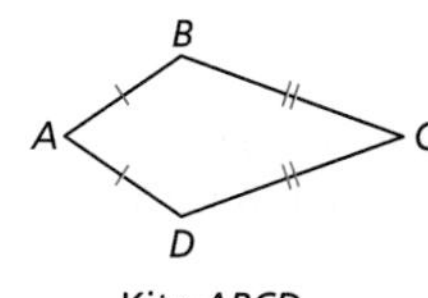

Kite *ABCD*

Theorems Properties of Kites

THEOREM		HYPOTHESIS	CONCLUSION
6-6-1	If a quadrilateral is a kite, then its diagonals are perpendicular. (kite → diags. ⊥)	Kite ABCD with diagonals	$\overline{AC} \perp \overline{BD}$
6-6-2	If a quadrilateral is a kite, then exactly one pair of opposite angles are congruent. (kite → one pair opp. ∠s ≅)	Kite ABCD with ∠B and ∠D marked	$\angle B \cong \angle D$ $\angle A \ncong \angle C$

You will prove Theorem 6-6-1 in Exercise 39.

PROOF **Theorem 6-6-2**

Given: *JKLM* is a kite with $\overline{JK} \cong \overline{JM}$ and $\overline{KL} \cong \overline{ML}$.
Prove: $\angle K \cong \angle M$, $\angle KJM \ncong \angle KLM$

Proof:

Step 1 Prove $\angle K \cong \angle M$.

It is given that $\overline{JK} \cong \overline{JM}$ and $\overline{KL} \cong \overline{ML}$. By the Reflexive Property of Congruence, $\overline{JL} \cong \overline{JL}$. This means that $\triangle JKL \cong \triangle JML$ by SSS. So $\angle K \cong \angle M$ by CPCTC.

Step 2 Prove $\angle KJM \ncong \angle KLM$.

If $\angle KJM \cong \angle KLM$, then both pairs of opposite angles of *JKLM* are congruent. This would mean that *JKLM* is a parallelogram. But this contradicts the given fact that *JKLM* is a kite. Therefore $\angle KJM \ncong \angle KLM$.

6-6 Organizer

Pacing: Traditional 1 day
Block $\frac{1}{2}$ day

Objectives: Use properties of kites to solve problems.

Use properties of trapezoids to solve problems.

Geometry Lab
In *Geometry Lab Activities*

Technology Lab
In *Technology Lab Activities*

Online Edition
Tutorial Videos

Countdown Week 14

Power Presentations with PowerPoint®

Warm Up

Solve for *x*.

1. $x^2 + 38 = 3x^2 - 12$ 5 or −5
2. $137 + x = 180$ 43
3. $42 = \frac{1}{4}(12 + x)$ 156
4. Find *FE*. $6\sqrt{11}$ in.

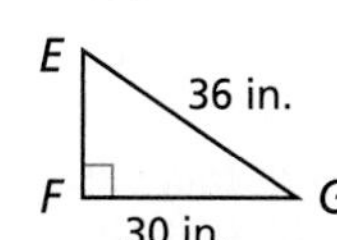

Also available on transparency

Math Humor

Q: Do geometry teachers have any special talents?

A: I hear they can fly kites well.

1 Introduce

EXPLORATION

6-6 Properties of Kites and Trapezoids

A *kite* is a quadrilateral with exactly two pairs of congruent consecutive sides.

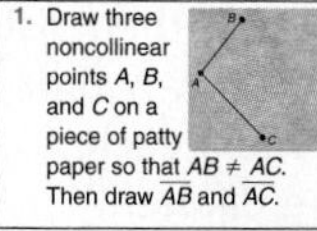

1. Draw three noncollinear points *A*, *B*, and *C* on a piece of patty paper so that *AB* ≠ *AC*. Then draw $\overline{AB}$ and $\overline{AC}$.
2. Fold the paper so that the fold passes through points *B* and *C*. Use the point of a pencil to make a small hole through point *A*.
3. Unfold the paper. Label the hole across from point *A* as point *D*.
4. Draw $\overline{BD}$ and $\overline{CD}$. What type of quadrilateral is *ABDC*?
5. Draw the diagonals of quadrilateral *ABDC*. Do they bisect each other? Are they perpendicular?
6. Repeat the process starting with a new set of points. Do you get the same results?

THINK AND DISCUSS

7. Explain how to use your findings to make a conjecture about

Motivate

Challenge students to draw a counterexample for these statements.

A quadrilateral with one pair of consecutive congruent sides is a rhombus. A quadrilateral with congruent diagonals is a rectangle.

Then draw a kite and an isosceles trapezoid for students. Explain that they will learn the properties of these quadrilaterals in this lesson.

Explorations and answers are provided in *Alternate Openers: Explorations Transparencies.*

State Resources

go.hrw.com
State Resources Online
KEYWORD: MG7 Resources

Power Presentations with PowerPoint®

Additional Examples

Example 1

Lucy is framing a kite with wooden dowels. She uses two dowels that measure 18 cm, one dowel that measures 30 cm, and two dowels that measure 27 cm. To complete the kite, she needs a dowel to place along $\overline{KL}$. She has a dowel that is 36 cm long. About how much wood will she have left over after cutting the last dowel? ≈ 3.6 cm

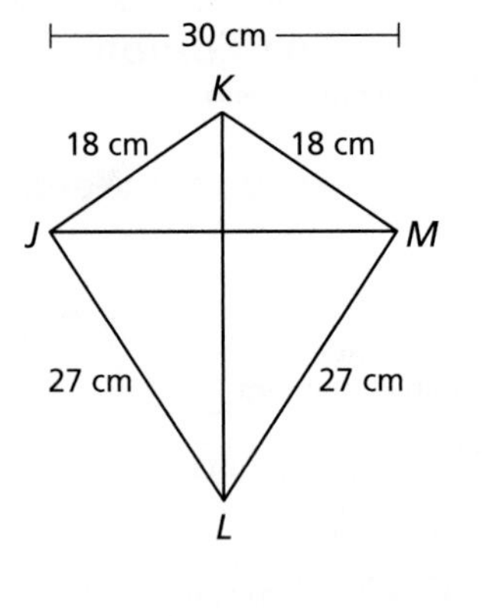

INTERVENTION

Questioning Strategies

- What kind of triangles do the diagonals of a kite form? Are any of these triangles congruent? Explain.

EXAMPLE 1 ***Problem-Solving Application***

Alicia is using a pattern to make a kite. She has made the frame of the kite by placing wooden sticks along the diagonals. She also has cut four triangular pieces of fabric and has attached them to the frame. To finish the kite, Alicia must cover the outer edges with a cloth binding. There are 2 yards of binding in one package. What is the total amount of binding needed to cover the edges of the kite? How many packages of binding must Alicia buy?

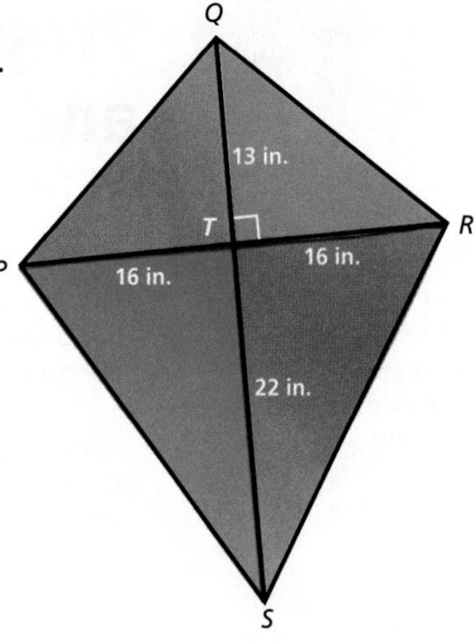

 **Understand the Problem**

The **answer** has two parts.

- the total length of binding Alicia needs
- the number of packages of binding Alicia must buy

 **Make a Plan**

The diagonals of a kite are perpendicular, so the four triangles are right triangles. Use the Pythagorean Theorem and the properties of kites to find the unknown side lengths. Add these lengths to find the perimeter of the kite.

 **Solve**

$PQ = \sqrt{16^2 + 13^2}$ *Pyth. Thm.*

$= \sqrt{425} = 5\sqrt{17}$ in.

$RQ = PQ = 5\sqrt{17}$ in. $\overline{PQ} \cong \overline{RQ}$

$PS = \sqrt{16^2 + 22^2}$ *Pyth. Thm.*

$= \sqrt{740} = 2\sqrt{185}$ in.

$RS = PS = 2\sqrt{185}$ in. $\overline{RS} \cong \overline{PS}$

perimeter of $PQRS = 5\sqrt{17} + 5\sqrt{17} + 2\sqrt{185} + 2\sqrt{185} \approx 95.6$ in.

Alicia needs approximately 95.6 inches of binding.

One package of binding contains 2 yards, or 72 inches.

$\frac{95.6}{72} \approx 1.3$ packages of binding

In order to have enough, Alicia must buy 2 packages of binding.

 **Look Back**

To estimate the perimeter, change the side lengths into decimals and round. $5\sqrt{17} \approx 21$, and $2\sqrt{185} \approx 27$. The perimeter of the kite is approximately $2(21) + 2(27) = 96$. So 95.6 is a reasonable answer.

1. **What if...?** Daryl is going to make a kite by doubling all the measures in the kite above. What is the total amount of binding needed to cover the edges of his kite? How many packages of binding must Daryl buy?

2 Teach

Guided Instruction

Draw a kite and an isosceles trapezoid on the board. As you discuss the properties of each type of figure, label the diagrams accordingly. For kites, include that their diagonals are perpendicular and that they have one pair of congruent opposite angles. For isosceles trapezoids, include that each pair of base angles is congruent and that the diagonals are congruent.

Reaching All Learners

Through Multiple Representations

Have students make a table of the properties of kites and trapezoids. Have them list the properties of each in their own words and draw a diagram to represent each. Then have students compare different types of quadrilaterals. For example, ask "How are kites and squares alike?" Possible answer: Both are quadrilaterals, and both have perpendicular diagonals. "How are trapezoids and parallelograms alike?" Possible answer: Both have a pair of parallel sides.

EXAMPLE 2 Using Properties of Kites

In kite $EFGH$, $m\angle FEJ = 25°$, and $m\angle FGJ = 57°$. Find each measure.

A $m\angle GFJ$

$m\angle FJG = 90°$	*Kite → diags. ⊥*
$m\angle GFJ + m\angle FGJ = 90$	*Acute ∠s of rt. △ are comp.*
$m\angle GFJ + 57 = 90$	*Substitute 57 for m∠FGJ.*
$m\angle GFJ = 33°$	*Subtract 57 from both sides.*

B $m\angle JFE$

$\triangle FJE$ is also a right triangle, so $m\angle JFE + m\angle FEJ = 90°$. By substituting 25° for $m\angle FEJ$, you find that $m\angle JFE = 65°$.

C $m\angle GHE$

$\angle GHE \cong \angle GFE$	*Kite → one pair opp. ∠s ≅*
$m\angle GHE = m\angle GFE$	*Def. of ≅ ∠s*
$m\angle GFE = m\angle GFJ + m\angle JFE$	*∠ Add. Post.*
$m\angle GHE = 33° + 65° = 98°$	*Substitute.*

In kite $PQRS$, $m\angle PQR = 78°$, and $m\angle TRS = 59°$. Find each measure.

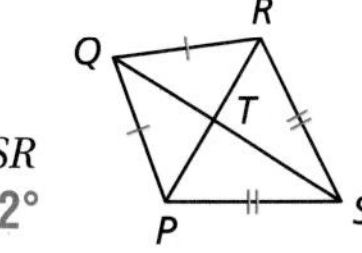

2a. $m\angle QRT$ 51° **2b.** $m\angle QPS$ 110° **2c.** $m\angle PSR$ 62°

A **trapezoid** is a quadrilateral with exactly one pair of parallel sides. Each of the parallel sides is called a **base**. The nonparallel sides are called **legs**. **Base angles** of a trapezoid are two consecutive angles whose common side is a base.

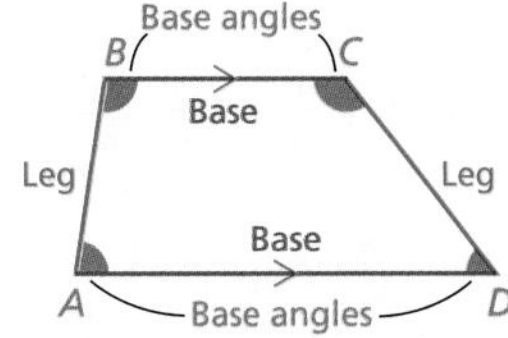

If the legs of a trapezoid are congruent, the trapezoid is an **isosceles trapezoid**. The following theorems state the properties of an isosceles trapezoid.

Know it! Note

Theorems Isosceles Trapezoids

	THEOREM	DIAGRAM	EXAMPLE
6-6-3	If a quadrilateral is an isosceles trapezoid, then each pair of base angles are congruent. (isosc. trap. → base ∠s ≅)		$\angle A \cong \angle D$ $\angle B \cong \angle C$
6-6-4	If a trapezoid has one pair of congruent base angles, then the trapezoid is isosceles. (trap. with pair base ∠s ≅ → isosc. trap.)		$ABCD$ is isosceles.
6-6-5	A trapezoid is isosceles if and only if its diagonals are congruent. (isosc. trap. ↔ diags. ≅)		$\overline{AC} \cong \overline{DB}$ ↔ $ABCD$ is isosceles.

Remember!

Theorem 6-6-5 is a biconditional statement. So it is true both "forward" and "backward."

Power Presentations with PowerPoint®

Additional Examples

Example 2

In kite $ABCD$, $m\angle DAB = 54°$, and $m\angle CDF = 52°$. Find each measure.

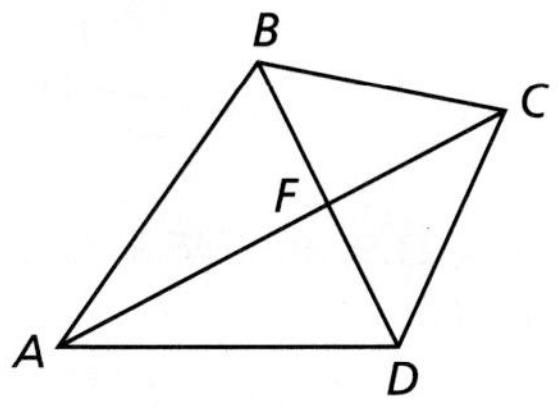

A. $m\angle BCD$ 76°

B. $m\angle ABC$ 115°

C. $m\angle FDA$ 63°

INTERVENTION

Questioning Strategies

EXAMPLE 2

- How do you use the properties of a kite to find the measures of its angles?

Technology Have students use geometry software to draw the figures in some of the examples. This will allow them to check their answers.

Power Presentations with PowerPoint®

Additional Examples

Example 3

A. Find m∠A. 80°

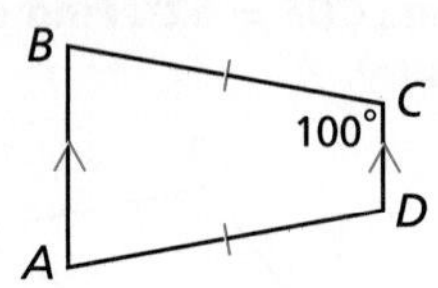

B. $KB = 21.9$, and $MF = 32.7$. Find FB. 10.8

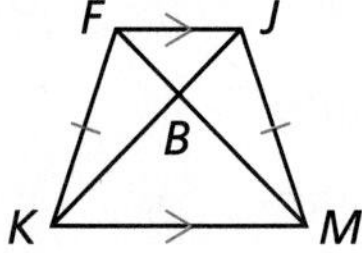

Example 4

A. Find the value of a so that $PQRS$ is isosceles. 9 or −9

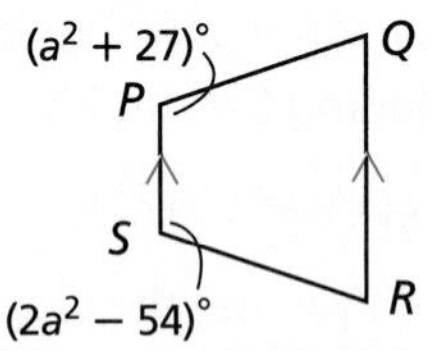

B. $AD = 12x - 11$, and $BC = 9x - 2$. Find the value of x so that $ABCD$ is isosceles. 3

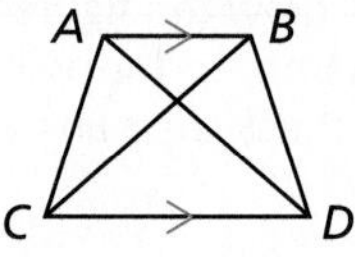

INTERVENTION
Questioning Strategies

EXAMPLE 3

- If you are trying to find the length of one part of a diagonal of an isosceles trapezoid, what information do you need?
- Can the bases of a trapezoid be congruent? Explain.

EXAMPLE 4

- What is the relationship between base angles in an isosceles trapezoid?

EXAMPLE 3 Using Properties of Isosceles Trapezoids

A **Find m∠Y.**

$m\angle W + m\angle X = 180°$	*Same-Side Int. ∠s Thm.*
$117 + m\angle X = 180$	*Substitute 117 for m∠W.*
$m\angle X = 63°$	*Subtract 117 from both sides.*
$\angle Y \cong \angle X$	*Isosc. trap. → base ∠s ≅*
$m\angle Y = m\angle X$	*Def. of ≅ ∠s*
$m\angle Y = 63°$	*Substitute 63 for m∠X.*

B **$RT = 24.1$, and $QP = 9.6$. Find PS.**

$\overline{QS} \cong \overline{RT}$	*Isosc. trap. → diags. ≅*
$QS = RT$	*Def. of ≅ segs.*
$QS = 24.1$	*Substitute 24.1 for RT.*
$QP + PS = QS$	*Seg. Add. Post.*
$9.6 + PS = 24.1$	*Substitute 9.6 for QP and 24.1 for QS.*
$PS = 14.5$	*Subtract 9.6 from both sides.*

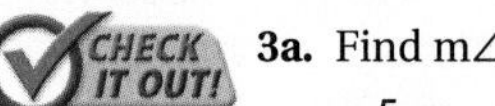

CHECK IT OUT! **3a.** Find m∠F. 131° **3b.** $JN = 10.6$, and $NL = 14.8$. Find KM. 25.4

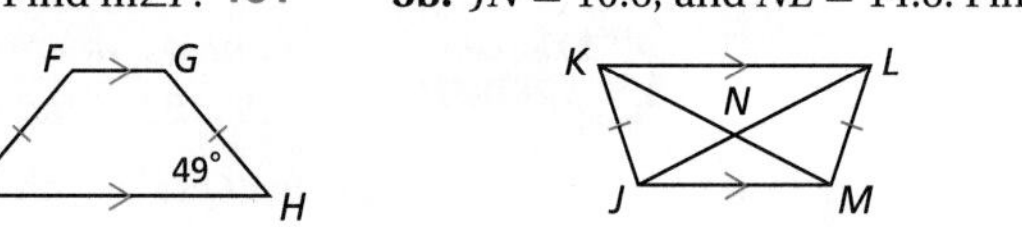

EXAMPLE 4 Applying Conditions for Isosceles Trapezoids

Algebra

A **Find the value of y so that $EFGH$ is isosceles.**

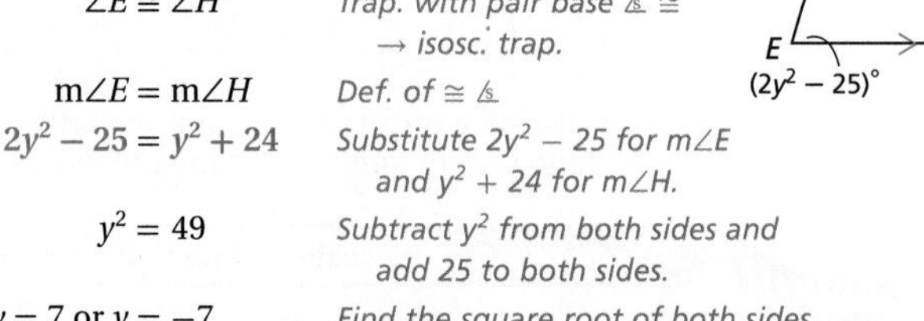

$\angle E \cong \angle H$	*Trap. with pair base ∠s ≅ → isosc. trap.*
$m\angle E = m\angle H$	*Def. of ≅ ∠s*
$2y^2 - 25 = y^2 + 24$	*Substitute $2y^2 - 25$ for m∠E and $y^2 + 24$ for m∠H.*
$y^2 = 49$	*Subtract y^2 from both sides and add 25 to both sides.*
$y = 7$ or $y = -7$	*Find the square root of both sides.*

B **$JL = 5z + 3$, and $KM = 9z - 12$. Find the value of z so that $JKLM$ is isosceles.**

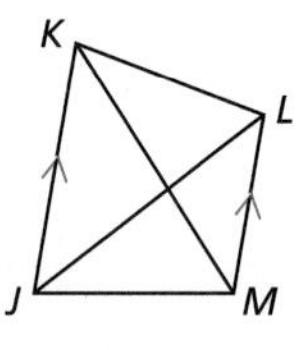

$\overline{JL} \cong \overline{KM}$	*Diags. ≅ → isosc. trap.*
$JL = KM$	*Def. of ≅ segs.*
$5z + 3 = 9z - 12$	*Substitute $5z + 3$ for JL and $9z - 12$ for KM.*
$15 = 4z$	*Subtract 5z from both sides and add 12 to both sides.*
$3.75 = z$	*Divide both sides by 4.*

CHECK IT OUT! **4.** Find the value of x so that $PQST$ is isosceles. $x = 4$ or $x = -4$

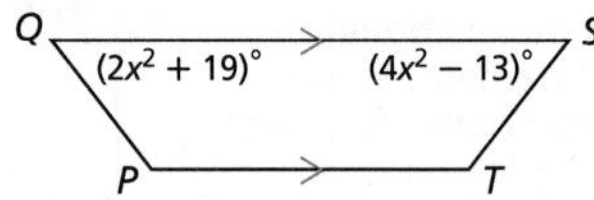

Teaching Tip

Algebra In **Example 4A,** some students might think the value of the variable cannot be negative, since they are working with positive angles. Point out that since the variable is squared, the angle measure is positive.

The **midsegment of a trapezoid** is the segment whose endpoints are the midpoints of the legs. In Lesson 5-4, you studied the Triangle Midsegment Theorem. The Trapezoid Midsegment Theorem is similar to it.

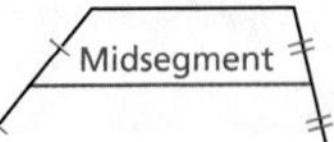

Theorem 6-6-6 Trapezoid Midsegment Theorem

The midsegment of a trapezoid is parallel to each base, and its length is one half the sum of the lengths of the bases.

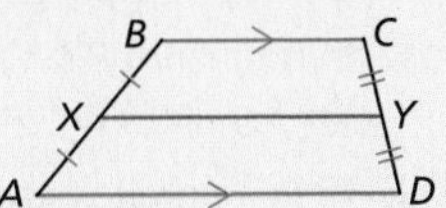

$\overline{XY} \parallel \overline{BC}$, $\overline{XY} \parallel \overline{AD}$

$XY = \frac{1}{2}(BC + AD)$

You will prove the Trapezoid Midsegment Theorem in Exercise 46.

EXAMPLE 5 Finding Lengths Using Midsegments

Find *ST*.

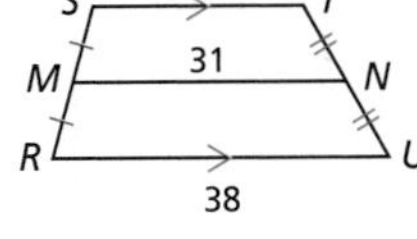

$MN = \frac{1}{2}(ST + RU)$	*Trap. Midsegment Thm.*
$31 = \frac{1}{2}(ST + 38)$	*Substitute the given values.*
$62 = ST + 38$	*Multiply both sides by 2.*
$24 = ST$	*Subtract 38 from both sides.*

5. Find *EH*. 8

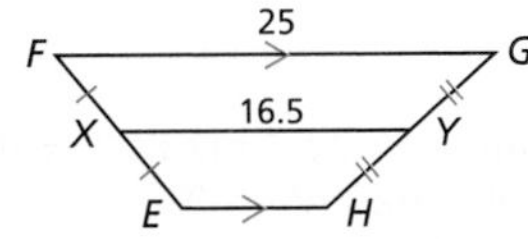

THINK AND DISCUSS

1. Is it possible for the legs of a trapezoid to be parallel? Explain.
2. How is the midsegment of a trapezoid similar to a midsegment of a triangle? How is it different?

3. **GET ORGANIZED** Copy and complete the graphic organizer. Write the missing terms in the unlabeled sections. Then write a definition of each term. (*Hint:* This completes the Venn diagram you started in Lesson 6-4.)

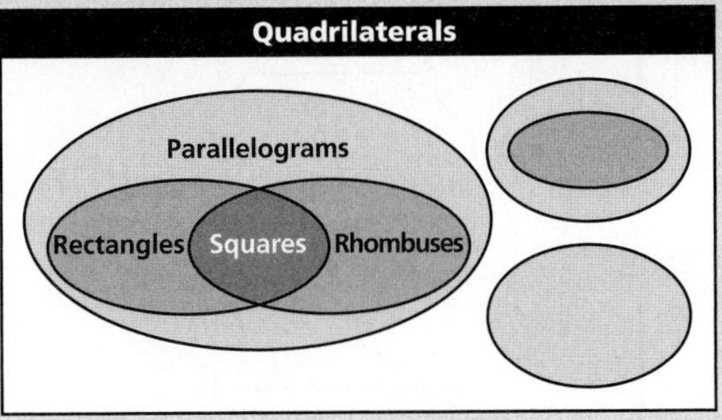

COMMON ERROR ALERT

Students may have trouble keeping track of given information, especially when algebraic expressions are involved. Encourage students to color code measures on each diagram. This may help students identify the information needed for their calculations.

Power Presentations with PowerPoint®

Additional Examples

Example 5

Find *EF*. 10.75

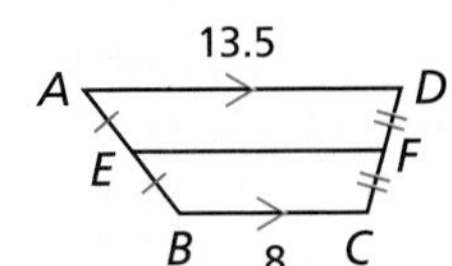

INTERVENTION

Questioning Strategies

EXAMPLE 5

- In the formula for the length of the midsegment, how do you know which segment lengths to substitute where?

Reading Math Tell students that the midsegment of a trapezoid can also be called a *median*.

ENGLISH LANGUAGE LEARNERS

Critical Thinking Show students how the length of a midsegment of a triangle can be found by using a second base length of 0 in the formula for a trapezoid midsegment.

3 Close

Summarize

Review the properties of kites and trapezoids and the difference between a trapezoid and an isosceles trapezoid. Review the Trapezoid Midsegment Theorem, and remind students that the midsegment of a trapezoid is the segment whose endpoints are the midpoints of the legs.

ONGOING ASSESSMENT and INTERVENTION

Diagnose ***Before*** **the Lesson**
6-6 Warm Up, TE p. 427

Monitor ***During*** **the Lesson**
Check It Out! Exercises, SE pp. 428–431
Questioning Strategies, TE pp. 428–431

Assess ***After*** **the Lesson**
6-6 Lesson Quiz, TE p. 435
Alternative Assessment, TE p. 435

Answers to *Think and Discuss*

1. No; possible answer: if the legs are ∥, then the trap. has 2 pairs of ∥ sides. By def., the figure would be a ▱, not a trap.
2. Possible answer: Similarities: The endpoints of both are the mdpts. of 2 sides. Both are ∥ to another side. Differences: A △ has 3 midsegments, while a trap. has just 1. To find the length of a midsegment of a △, you find half the measure of just 1 side; to find the length of the midsegment of a trap., you must average the lengths of 2 sides.
3. See p. A6.

6-6 Exercises

Assignment Guide

Assign *Guided Practice* exercises as necessary.

If you finished Examples **1–2**
- **Basic** 13–16, 24, 25, 28, 29, 31
- **Average** 13–16, 24, 25, 28, 29, 31, 37, 38
- **Advanced** 13–16, 24, 25, 28, 29, 31, 37–39

If you finished Examples **1–5**
- **Basic** 13–34, 40–42, 45, 47–49, 52–56
- **Average** 13–23, 24–32 even, 33–36, 38–42 even, 43–45, 47–49, 52–56
- **Advanced** 13–23, 28–32 even, 33, 35–42, 44–56

Homework Quick Check
Quickly check key concepts.
Exercises: 13, 14, 18, 20, 22, 28, 32

Answers

2. Possible answer: In a ▱, 2 pairs of opp. sides are ≅. In a kite, exactly 2 distinct pairs of cons. sides are ≅.

State Resources

6-6 Exercises

go.hrw.com
Homework Help Online
KEYWORD: MG7 6-6
Parent Resources Online
KEYWORD: MG7 Parent

GUIDED PRACTICE

Vocabulary Apply the vocabulary from this lesson to answer each question.

bases: $\overline{RS}$ and $\overline{PV}$; legs: $\overline{PR}$ and $\overline{VS}$; midsegment: $\overline{QT}$

1. In trapezoid *PRSV*, name the *bases*, the *legs*, and the *midsegment.*

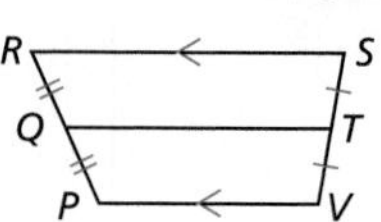

2. Both a parallelogram and a *kite* have two pairs of congruent sides. How are the congruent sides of a kite different from the congruent sides of a parallelogram?

SEE EXAMPLE 1 p. 428

3. **Crafts** The edges of the kite-shaped glass in the sun catcher are sealed with lead strips. *JH*, *KH*, and *LH* are 2.75 inches, and *MH* is 5.5 inches. How much lead is needed to seal the edges of the sun catcher? If the craftsperson has two 3-foot lengths of lead, how many sun catchers can be sealed? about 20.1 in.; 3 sun catchers

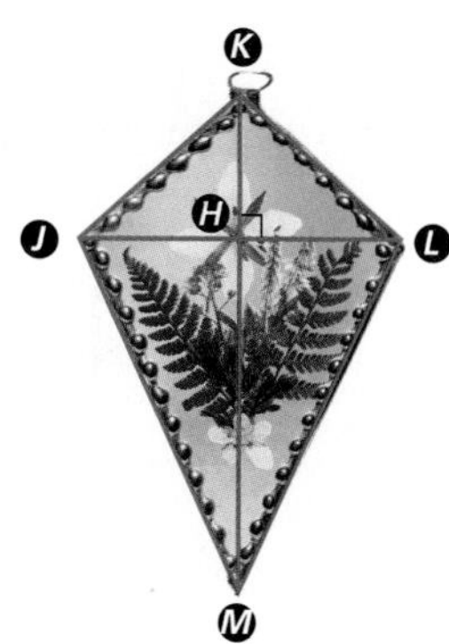

SEE EXAMPLE 2 p. 429

In kite *WXYZ*, m∠*WXY* = 104°, and m∠*VYZ* = 49°. Find each measure.

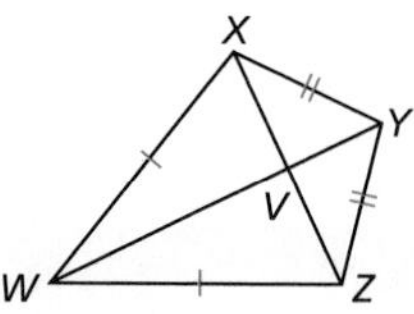

4. m∠*VZY* 41°
5. m∠*VXW* 63°
6. m∠*XWZ* 54°

SEE EXAMPLE 3 p. 430

7. Find m∠*A*. 106°

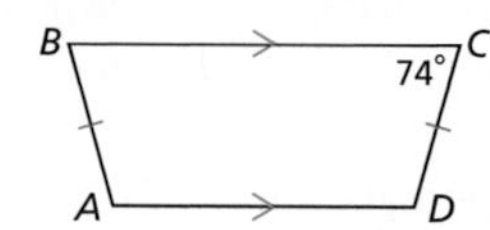

8. *RW* = 17.7, and *SV* = 23.3. Find *TW*. 5.6

SEE EXAMPLE 4 p. 430

9. Find the value of *z* so that *EFGH* is isosceles. 2 or −2

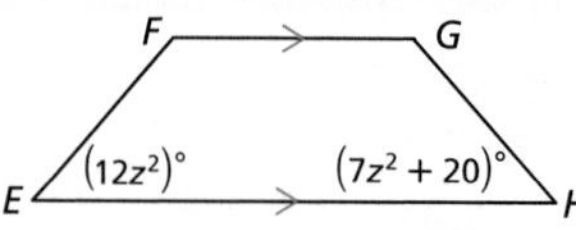

10. *MQ* = 7*y* − 6, and *LP* = 4*y* + 11. Find the value of *y* so that *LMPQ* is isosceles. $\frac{17}{3} = 5\frac{2}{3}$

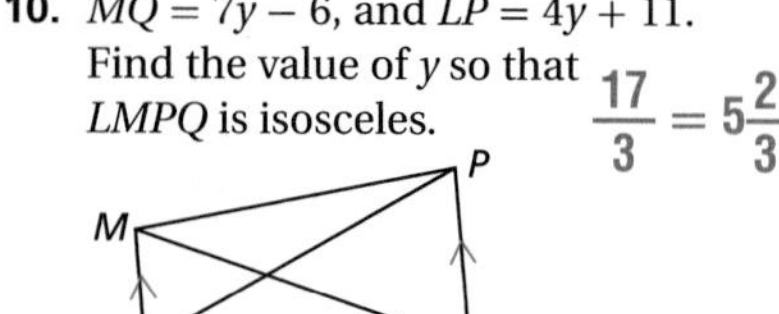

SEE EXAMPLE 5 p. 431

11. Find *QR*. 14

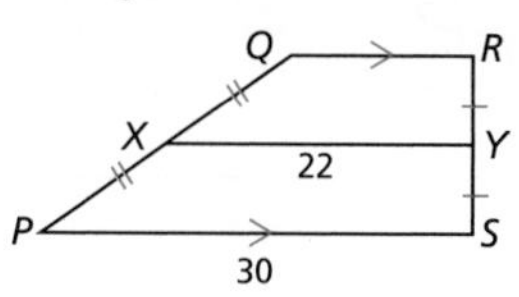

12. Find *AZ*. 9.5

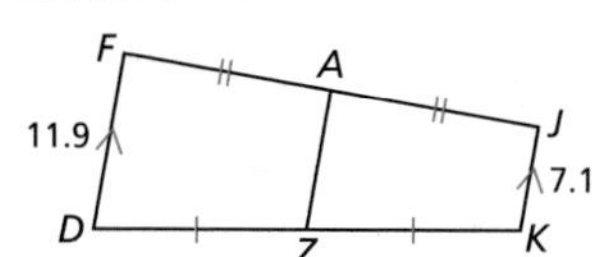

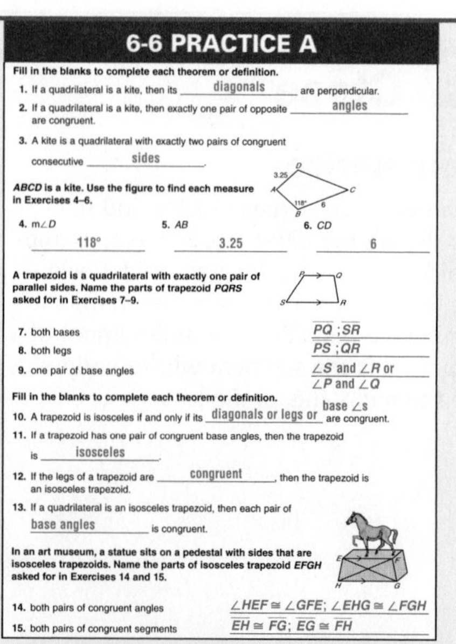

6-6 PRACTICE A

Fill in the blanks to complete each theorem or definition.

1. If a quadrilateral is a kite, then its diagonals are perpendicular.
2. If a quadrilateral is a kite, then exactly one pair of opposite angles are congruent.
3. A kite is a quadrilateral with exactly two pairs of congruent consecutive sides.

***ABCD* is a kite. Use the figure to find each measure in Exercises 4–6.**

4. m∠*D* 118°
5. *AB* 3.25
6. *CD* 6

A trapezoid is a quadrilateral with exactly one pair of parallel sides. Name the parts of trapezoid *PQRS* asked for in Exercises 7–9.

7. both bases $\overline{PQ}$; $\overline{SR}$
8. both legs $\overline{PS}$; $\overline{QR}$
9. one pair of base angles ∠*S* and ∠*R* or ∠*P* and ∠*Q*

Fill in the blanks to complete each theorem or definition.

10. A trapezoid is isosceles if and only if its diagonals or legs or base ∠s are congruent.
11. If a trapezoid has one pair of congruent base angles, then the trapezoid is isosceles.
12. If the legs of a trapezoid are congruent, then the trapezoid is an isosceles trapezoid.
13. If a quadrilateral is an isosceles trapezoid, then each pair of base angles is congruent.

In an art museum, a statue sits on a pedestal with sides that are isosceles trapezoids. Name the parts of isosceles trapezoid *EFGH* asked for in Exercises 14 and 15.

14. both pairs of congruent angles ∠*HEF* ≅ ∠*GFE*; ∠*EHG* ≅ ∠*FGH*
15. both pairs of congruent segments $\overline{EH} \cong \overline{FG}$; $\overline{EG} \cong \overline{FH}$

Independent Practice	
For Exercises	See Example
13	1
14–16	2
17–18	3
19–20	4
21–22	5

Extra Practice
Skills Practice p. S15
Application Practice p. S33

PRACTICE AND PROBLEM SOLVING

13. Design Each square section in the iron railing contains four small kites. The figure shows the dimensions of one kite. What length of iron is needed to outline one small kite? How much iron is needed to outline one complete section, including the square? about 56.6 in.; about 418.3 in.

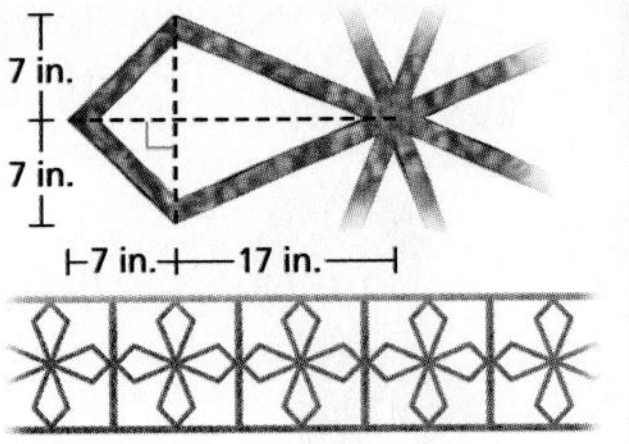

In kite $ABCD$, $m\angle DAX = 32°$, and $m\angle XDC = 64°$. Find each measure.

14. $m\angle XDA$ 58° **15.** $m\angle ABC$ 122° **16.** $m\angle BCD$ 52°

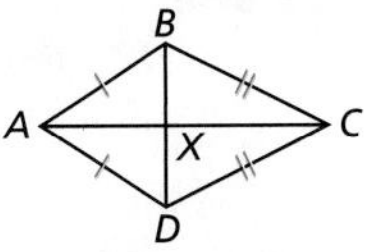

17. Find $m\angle Q$. 62°

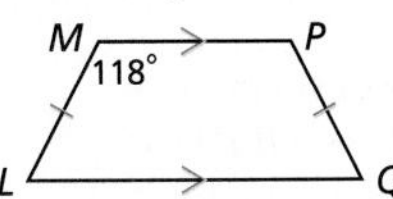

18. $SZ = 62.6$, and $KZ = 34$. Find RJ. 96.6

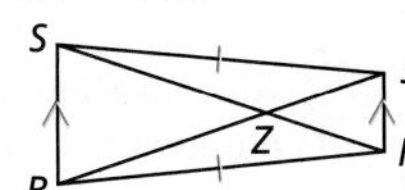

19. Algebra Find the value of a so that $XYZW$ is isosceles. Give your answer as a simplified radical. $\pm 4\sqrt{5}$

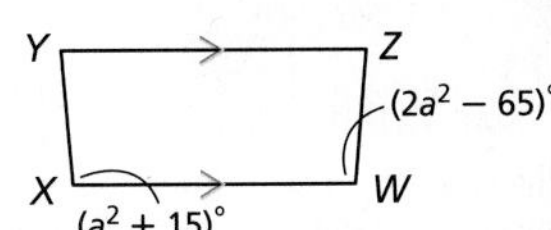

20. Algebra $GJ = 4x - 1$, and $FH = 9x - 15$. Find the value of x so that $FGHJ$ is isosceles. 2.8

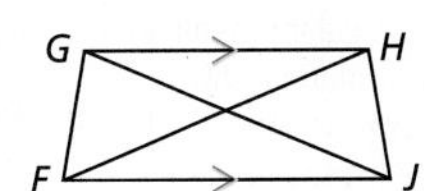

21. Find PQ. 3.6

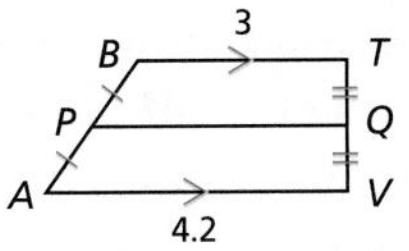

22. Find KR. 72.5

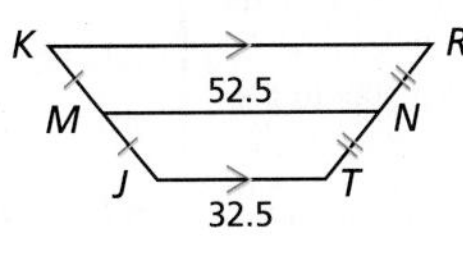

Tell whether each statement is sometimes, always, or never true.

23. The opposite angles of a trapezoid are supplementary. S

24. The opposite angles of a kite are supplementary. S

25. A pair of consecutive angles in a kite are supplementary. N

26. Estimation Hal is building a trapezoid-shaped frame for a flower bed. The lumber costs \$1.29 per foot. Based on Hal's sketch, estimate the cost of the lumber. (*Hint:* Find the angle measures in the triangle formed by the dashed line.) Possible answer: about \$60

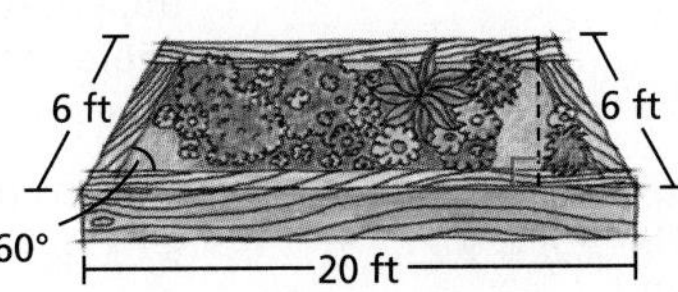

Find the measure of each numbered angle.

27.

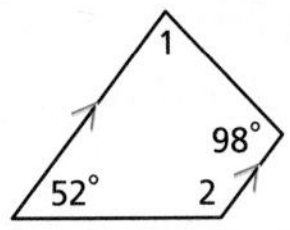

28. $m\angle 1 = 82°$; $m\angle 2 = 128°$

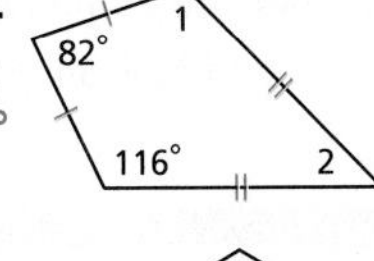

29.

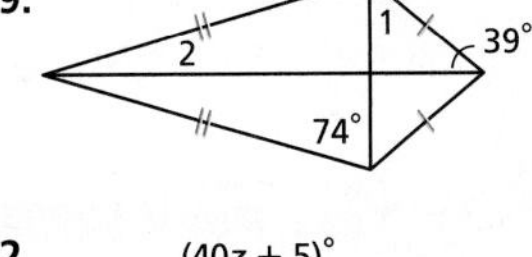

28. $m\angle 1 = 116°$; $m\angle 2 = 46°$

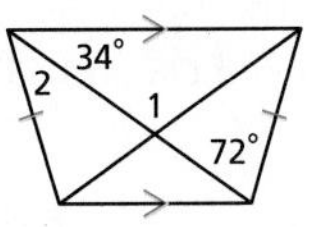

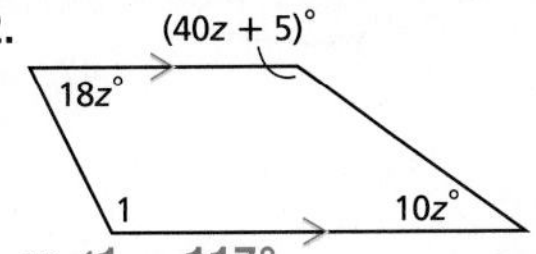

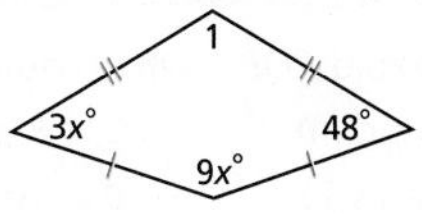

29. $m\angle 1 = 51°$; $m\angle 2 = 16°$

30. $m\angle 1 = 112°$; $m\angle 2 = 40°$

30.

31.

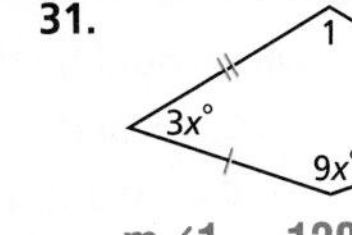

$m\angle 1 = 120°$

32. $m\angle 1 = 117°$

COMMON ERROR ALERT

In **Exercises 27–32,** students may not be sure how to begin solving the problem. Point out that they must first determine if the figure is a kite, a trapezoid, or an isosceles trapezoid. Then suggest that they redraw each figure, marking known properties for that type of quadrilateral.

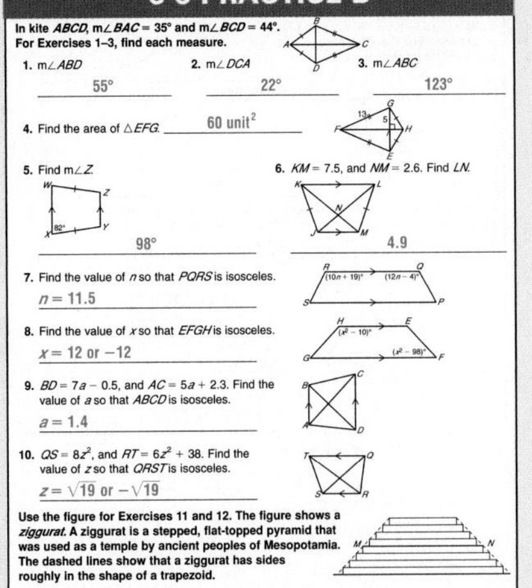

6-6 PRACTICE B

In kite $ABCD$, $m\angle BAC = 35°$ and $m\angle BCD = 44°$. For Exercises 1–3, find each measure.

1. $m\angle ABD$ 55°
2. $m\angle DCA$ 22°
3. $m\angle ABC$ 123°
4. Find the area of $\triangle EFG$. 60 unit²
5. Find $m\angle Z$. 98°
6. $KM = 7.5$, and $NM = 2.6$. Find LN. 4.9
7. Find the value of n so that $PQRS$ is isosceles. $n = 11.5$
8. Find the value of x so that $EFGH$ is isosceles. $x = 12$ or -12
9. $BD = 7a - 0.5$, and $AC = 5a + 2.3$. Find the value of a so that $ABCD$ is isosceles. $a = 1.4$
10. $QS = 8z^2$, and $RT = 6z^2 + 38$. Find the value of z so that $QRST$ is isosceles. $z = \sqrt{19}$ or $-\sqrt{19}$

Use the figure for Exercises 11 and 12. The figure shows a *ziggurat.* A ziggurat is a stepped, flat-topped pyramid that was used as a temple by ancient peoples of Mesopotamia. The dashed lines show that a ziggurat has sides roughly in the shape of a trapezoid.

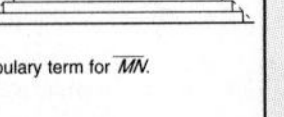

11. Each "step" in the ziggurat has equal height. Give the vocabulary term for $\overline{MN}$. trapezoid midsegment
12. The bottom of the ziggurat is 27.3 meters long, and the top of the ziggurat is 11.6 meters long. Find MN. 19.45 m

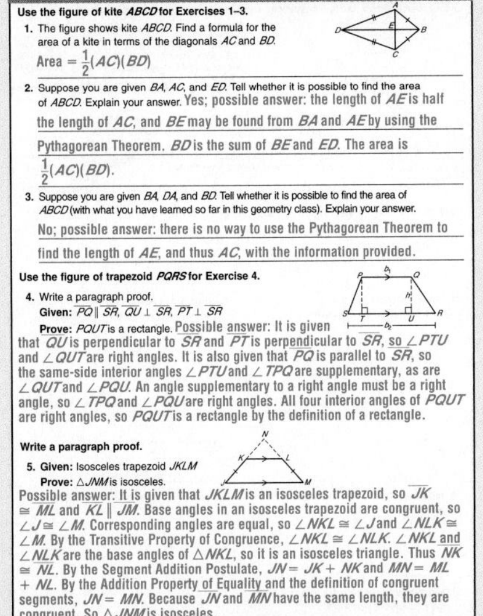

6-6 PRACTICE C

Use the figure of kite $ABCD$ for Exercises 1–3.

1. The figure shows kite $ABCD$. Find a formula for the area of a kite in terms of the diagonals AC and BD. Area $= \frac{1}{2}(AC)(BD)$
2. Suppose you are given BA, AC, and ED. Tell whether it is possible to find the area of $ABCD$. Explain your answer. Yes; possible answer: the length of AE is half the length of AC, and BE may be found from BA and AE by using the Pythagorean Theorem. BD is the sum of BE and ED. The area is $\frac{1}{2}(AC)(BD)$.
3. Suppose you are given BA, DA, and BD. Tell whether it is possible to find the area of $ABCD$ (with what you have learned so far in this geometry class). Explain your answer. No; possible answer: there is no way to use the Pythagorean Theorem to find the length of AE, and thus AC, with the information provided.

Use the figure of trapezoid $PQRS$ for Exercise 4.

4. Write a paragraph proof.
Given: $\overline{PQ} \parallel \overline{SR}$, $\overline{QU} \perp \overline{SR}$, $\overline{PT} \perp \overline{SR}$
Prove: $PQUT$ is a rectangle. Possible answer: It is given that $\overline{QU}$ is perpendicular to $\overline{SR}$ and $\overline{PT}$ is perpendicular to $\overline{SR}$, so $\angle PTU$ and $\angle QUT$ are right angles. It is also given that $\overline{PQ}$ is parallel to $\overline{SR}$, so the same-side interior angles $\angle PTU$ and $\angle TPQ$ are supplementary, as are $\angle QUT$ and $\angle PQU$. An angle supplementary to a right angle must be a right angle, so $\angle TPQ$ and $\angle PQU$ are right angles. All four interior angles of $PQUT$ are right angles, so $PQUT$ is a rectangle by the definition of a rectangle.

Write a paragraph proof.

5. Given: Isosceles trapezoid $JKLM$
Prove: $\triangle JNM$ is isosceles.
Possible answer: It is given that $JKLM$ is an isosceles trapezoid, so $\overline{JK} \cong \overline{ML}$ and $\overline{KL} \parallel \overline{JM}$. Base angles in an isosceles trapezoid are congruent, so $\angle J \cong \angle M$. Corresponding angles are equal, so $\angle NKL \cong \angle J$ and $\angle NLK \cong \angle M$. By the Transitive Property of Congruence, $\angle NKL \cong \angle NLK$. $\angle NKL$ and $\angle NLK$ are the base angles of $\triangle NKL$, so it is an isosceles triangle. Thus $\overline{NK} \cong \overline{NL}$. By the Segment Addition Postulate, $JN = JK + NK$ and $MN = ML + NL$. By the Addition Property of Equality and the definition of congruent segments, $JN = MN$. Because $\overline{JN}$ and $\overline{MN}$ have the same length, they are congruent. So $\triangle JNM$ is isosceles.

Exercise 33 involves applying the properties of kites in the coordinate plane. This exercise prepares students for the Multi-Step Test Prep on page 436.

If students have difficulty with **Exercise 47,** suggest that they work backward to find out which answer choices have an average of 16.

For **Exercise 48,** encourage students to begin by eliminating the choices that describe properties of kites.

In **Exercise 49,** have students draw the midsegment of the trapezoid before working the problem.

Answers

33a. $EF = FG = \sqrt{17}$ and $GH = HE = \sqrt{29}$, so $\overline{EF} \cong \overline{FG}$ and $\overline{GH} \cong \overline{HE}$. Thus $EFGH$ is a kite, since it has exactly 2 pairs of $\cong$ cons. sides.

b. $m\angle E = m\angle G = 126°$

37. $m\angle PAQ = 108°$; $m\angle OAQ = 130°$; $m\angle OBP = 22°$

38. Possible answer:

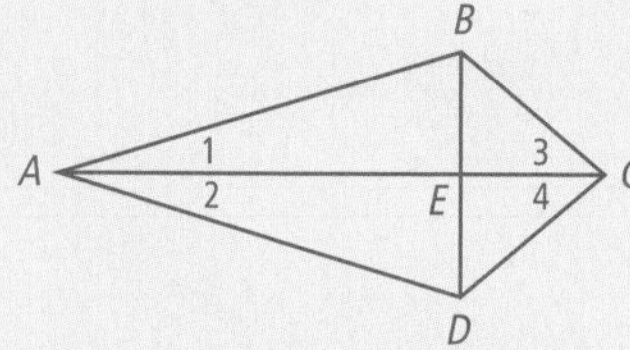

Given: $ABCD$ is a kite with $\overline{AB} \cong \overline{AD}$ and $\overline{CB} \cong \overline{CD}$.
Prove: $\overline{AC}$ bisects $\angle DAB$ and $\angle DCB$. $\overline{AC}$ bisects $\overline{BD}$.

1. $ABCD$ is a kite with $\overline{AB} \cong \overline{AD}$ and $\overline{CB} \cong \overline{CD}$. (Given)
2. $\overline{AC} \cong \overline{AC}$ (Reflex. Prop. of $\cong$)
3. $\triangle ABC \cong \triangle ADC$ (SSS)
4. $\angle 1 \cong \angle 2$, $\angle 3 \cong \angle 4$ (CPCTC)
5. $\overline{AC}$ bisects $\angle DAB$ and $\angle DCB$. (Def. of $\angle$ bisector)
6. $\overline{AE} \cong \overline{AE}$ (Reflex. Prop. of $\cong$)
7. $\triangle ABE \cong \triangle ADE$ (SAS)
8. $\overline{BE} \cong \overline{DE}$ (CPCTC)
9. $\overline{AC}$ bisects $\overline{BD}$. (Def. of seg. bisector)

39. See p. A23.

44. $m\angle A = m\angle D = 112.5°$; $m\angle B = m\angle C = 67.5°$

45. Possible answer: Common properties: exactly 1 pair of $\parallel$ sides; 2 pairs of cons. $\angle$s supp.; length of midsegment is the average of the lengths of the bases; special properties of isosc. trap.: $\cong$ legs; 2 pairs of $\cong$ base $\angle$s; $\cong$ diags.

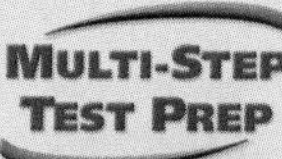

33. This problem will prepare you for the Multi-Step Test Prep on page 436.
The boundary of a fairground is a quadrilateral with vertices at $E(-1, 3)$, $F(3, 4)$, $G(2, 0)$, and $H(-3, -2)$.
- **a.** Use the Distance Formula to show that $EFGH$ is a kite.
- **b.** The organizers need to know the angle measure at each vertex. Given that $m\angle H = 46°$ and $m\angle F = 62°$, find $m\angle E$ and $m\angle G$.

Algebra **Find the length of the midsegment of each trapezoid.**

34. 15

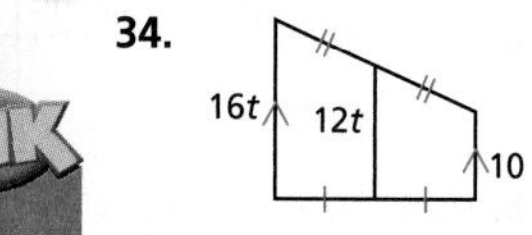

35. 13

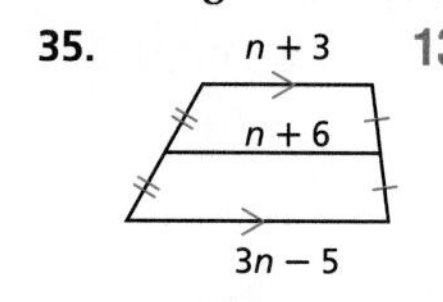

36. 8

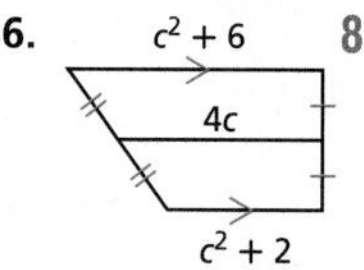

LINK Mechanics

The Peaucellier cell, invented in 1864, converts circular motion into linear motion. This type of linkage was supposedly used in the fans that ventilated the Houses of Parliament in London prior to the invention of electric fans.

The Granger Collection, New York

37. Mechanics A *Peaucellier cell* is made of seven rods connected by joints at the labeled points. $AQBP$ is a rhombus, and $\overline{OA} \cong \overline{OB}$. As P moves along a circular path, Q moves along a linear path. In the position shown, $m\angle AQB = 72°$, and $m\angle AOB = 28°$. What are $m\angle PAQ$, $m\angle OAQ$, and $m\angle OBP$?

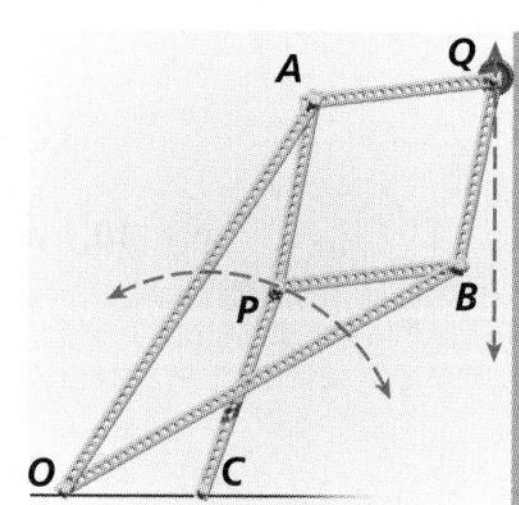

38. Prove that one diagonal of a kite bisects a pair of opposite angles and the other diagonal.

39. Prove Theorem 6-6-1: If a quadrilateral is a kite, then its diagonals are perpendicular.

Multi-Step **Give the best name for a quadrilateral with the given vertices.**

40. $(-4, -1)$, $(-4, 6)$, $(2, 6)$, $(2, -4)$ trap.

41. $(-5, 2)$, $(-5, 6)$, $(-1, 6)$, $(2, -1)$ kite

42. $(-2, -2)$, $(1, 7)$, $(4, 4)$, $(1, -5)$ ▱

43. $(-4, -3)$, $(0, 3)$, $(4, 3)$, $(8, -3)$ isosc. trap.

44. Carpentry The window frame is a regular octagon. It is made from eight pieces of wood shaped like congruent isosceles trapezoids. What are $m\angle A$, $m\angle B$, $m\angle C$, and $m\angle D$?

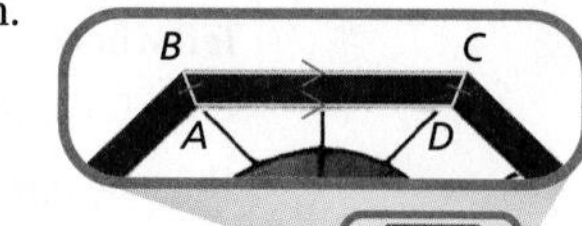

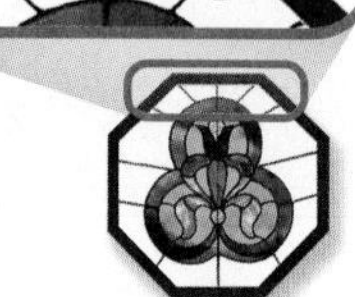

45. Write About It Compare an isosceles trapezoid to a trapezoid that is not isosceles. What properties do the figures have in common? What properties does one have that the other does not?

46. Use coordinates to verify the Trapezoid Midsegment Theorem.
- **a.** M is the midpoint of $\overline{QP}$. What are its coordinates? (a, b)
- **b.** N is the midpoint of $\overline{RS}$. What are its coordinates? $(c + d, b)$
- **c.** Find the slopes of $\overline{QR}$, $\overline{PS}$, and $\overline{MN}$. What can you conclude? The slopes equal 0, so all 3 segs. are $\parallel$.
- **d.** Find QR, PS, and MN. Show that $MN = \frac{1}{2}(PS + QR)$.

46d. $QR = c - 2a$; $PS = c + 2d$; $MN = c + d - a$; $c + d - a = \frac{1}{2}(c + 2d + c - 2a)$, so $MN = \frac{1}{2}(PS + QR)$.

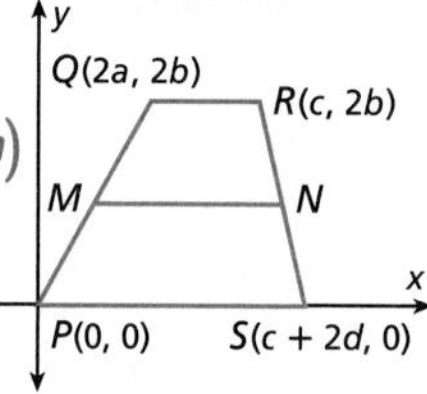

47. In trapezoid $PQRS$, what could be the lengths of $\overline{QR}$ and $\overline{PS}$?

Ⓐ 6 and 10
Ⓑ 6 and 26
Ⓒ 8 and 32
Ⓓ 10 and 24

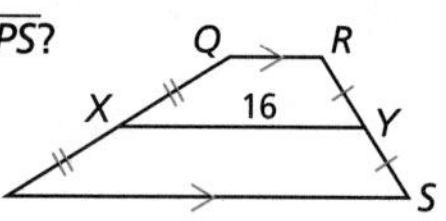

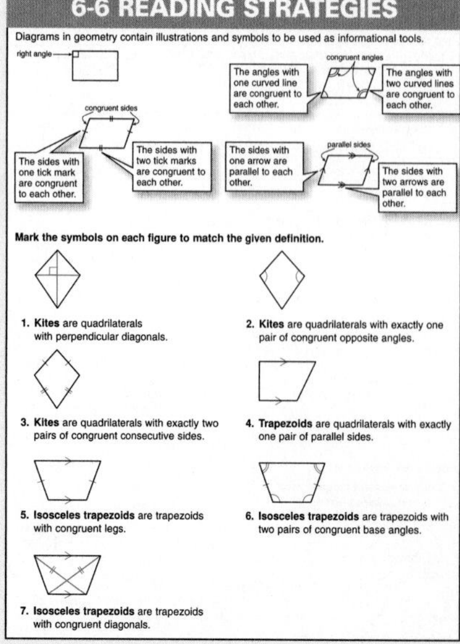

6-6 READING STRATEGIES

Diagrams in geometry contain illustrations and symbols to be used as informational tools.

right angle

congruent angles

The angles with one curved line are congruent to each other.

The angles with two curved lines are congruent to each other.

congruent sides

The sides with one tick mark are congruent to each other.

The sides with two tick marks are congruent to each other.

The sides with one arrow are parallel to each other.

parallel sides

The sides with two arrows are parallel to each other.

Mark the symbols on each figure to match the given definition.

1. **Kites** are quadrilaterals with perpendicular diagonals.
2. **Kites** are quadrilaterals with exactly one pair of congruent opposite angles.
3. **Kites** are quadrilaterals with exactly two pairs of congruent consecutive sides.
4. **Trapezoids** are quadrilaterals with exactly one pair of parallel sides.
5. **Isosceles trapezoids** are trapezoids with congruent legs.
6. **Isosceles trapezoids** are trapezoids with two pairs of congruent base angles.
7. **Isosceles trapezoids** are trapezoids with congruent diagonals.

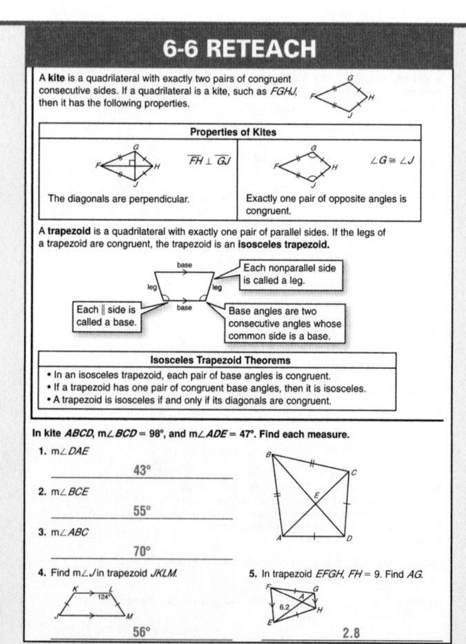

6-6 RETEACH

A **kite** is a quadrilateral with exactly two pairs of congruent consecutive sides. If a quadrilateral is a kite, such as $FGHJ$, then it has the following properties.

Properties of Kites	
$\overline{FH} \perp \overline{GJ}$ The diagonals are perpendicular.	$\angle G \cong \angle J$ Exactly one pair of opposite angles is congruent.

A **trapezoid** is a quadrilateral with exactly one pair of parallel sides. If the legs of a trapezoid are congruent, the trapezoid is an **isosceles trapezoid.**

base, leg, leg, base

Each nonparallel side is called a leg.

Each $\parallel$ side is called a base.

Base angles are two consecutive angles whose common side is a base.

Isosceles Trapezoid Theorems
• In an isosceles trapezoid, each pair of base angles is congruent. • If a trapezoid has one pair of congruent base angles, then it is isosceles. • A trapezoid is isosceles if and only if its diagonals are congruent.

In kite $ABCD$, $m\angle BCD = 98°$, and $m\angle ADE = 47°$. Find each measure.

1. $m\angle DAE$ 43°
2. $m\angle BCE$ 55°
3. $m\angle ABC$ 70°
4. Find $m\angle J$ in trapezoid $JKLM$. 56°
5. In trapezoid $EFGH$, $FH = 9$. Find AG. 2.8

48. Which statement is never true for a kite?

Ⓕ The diagonals are perpendicular.

Ⓖ One pair of opposite angles are congruent.

Ⓗ (circled) One pair of opposite sides are parallel.

Ⓙ Two pairs of consecutive sides are congruent.

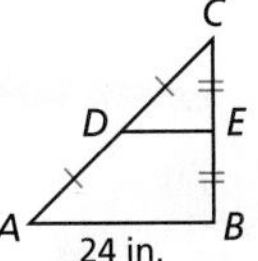

49. **Gridded Response** What is the length of the midsegment of trapezoid $ADEB$ in inches? 18

CHALLENGE AND EXTEND

50. Write a two-column proof. (*Hint:* If there is a line and a point not on the line, then there is exactly one line through the point perpendicular to the given line. Use this fact to draw auxiliary lines $\overline{UX}$ and $\overline{VY}$ so that $\overline{UX} \perp \overline{WZ}$ and $\overline{VY} \perp \overline{WZ}$.)

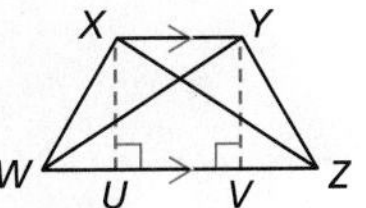

Given: $WXYZ$ is a trapezoid with $\overline{XZ} \cong \overline{YW}$.
Prove: $WXYZ$ is an isosceles trapezoid.

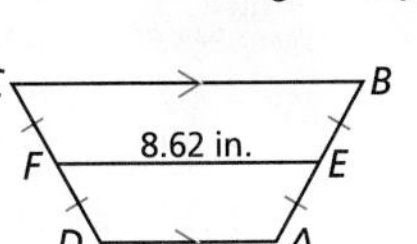

51. The perimeter of isosceles trapezoid $ABCD$ is 27.4 inches. If $BC = 2(AB)$, find AD, AB, BC, and CD.
$AD = 7.08$ in.; $AB = CD = 5.08$ in.; $BC = 10.16$ in.

SPIRAL REVIEW

52. An empty pool is being filled with water. After 10 hours, 20% of the pool is full. If the pool is filled at a constant rate, what fraction of the pool will be full after 25 hours? *(Previous course)* $\frac{1}{2}$

Write and solve an inequality for *x*. *(Lesson 3-4)*

53.

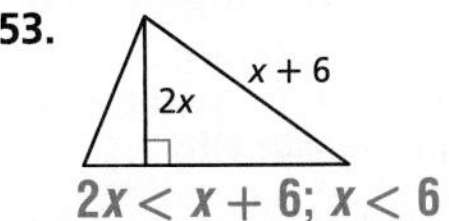

$2x < x + 6$; $x < 6$

54.

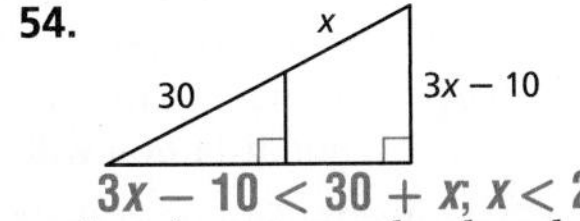

$3x - 10 < 30 + x$; $x < 20$

Tell whether a parallelogram with the given vertices is a rectangle, rhombus, or square. Give all the names that apply. *(Lesson 6-5)*

55. $(-3, 1)$, $(-1, 3)$, $(1, 1)$, and $(-1, -1)$
rect., rhombus, square

56. $(1, 1)$, $(4, 5)$, $(4, 0)$, and $(1, -4)$
rhombus

Construction Kite

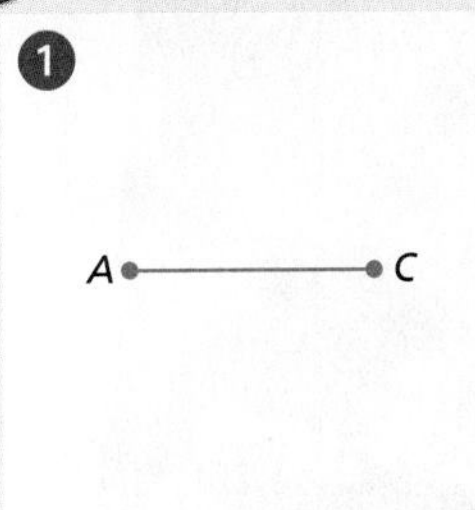

Draw a segment $\overline{AC}$.

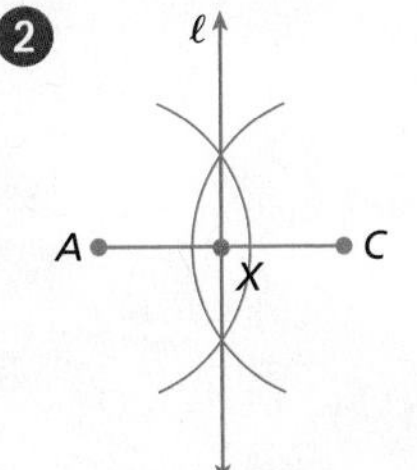

Construct line ℓ as the perpendicular bisector of $\overline{AC}$. Label the intersection as X.

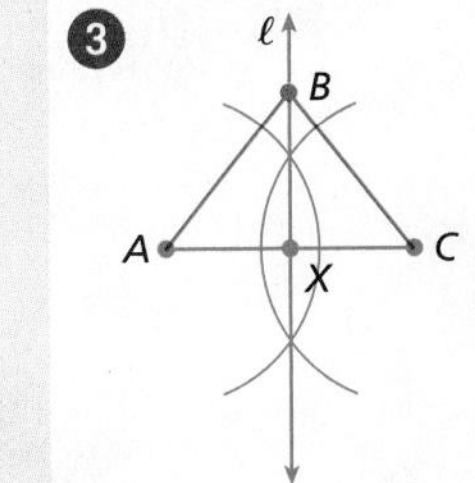

Draw a point B on ℓ above $\overline{AC}$. Draw $\overline{AB}$ and $\overline{CB}$.

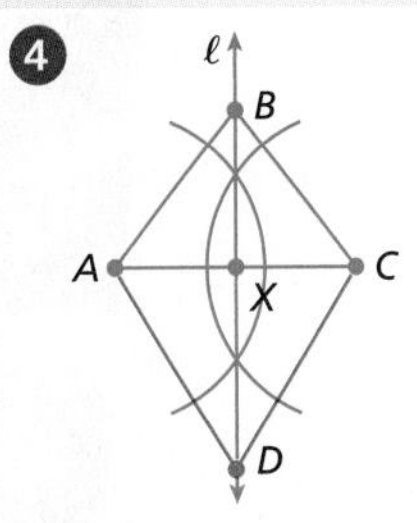

Draw a point D on ℓ below $\overline{AC}$ so that $DX \neq BX$. Draw $\overline{AD}$ and $\overline{CD}$.

1. **Critical Thinking** How would you modify the construction above so that $ABCD$ is a concave kite?

Answers

50, Construction. See p. A23.

Journal

Have students draw an isosceles trapezoid. Have them label the angle measures in terms of x and write a justification for each measure.

ALTERNATIVE ASSESSMENT

Have students construct a kite and an isosceles trapezoid. Have them measure one angle in each figure and then use the properties in the lesson to find the other three angle measures.

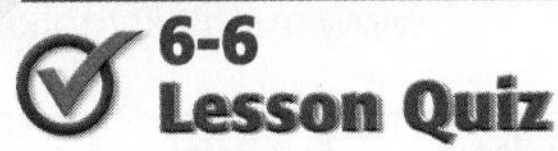

6-6 Lesson Quiz

1. Erin is making a kite based on the pattern below. About how much binding does Erin need to cover the edges of the kite? about 191.2 in.

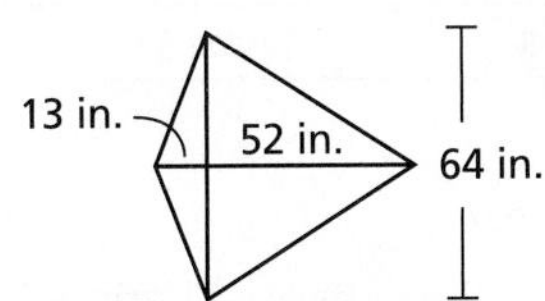

In kite $HJKL$, $m\angle KLP = 72°$, and $m\angle HJP = 49.5°$. Find each measure.

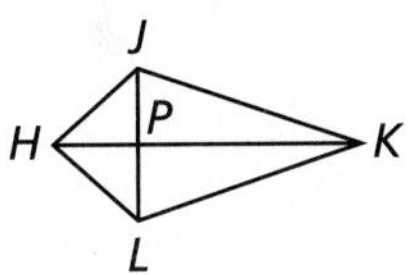

2. $m\angle LHJ$ 81°
3. $m\angle PKL$ 18°

Use the diagram for Items 4 and 5.

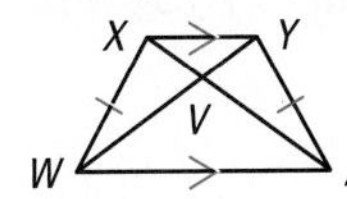

4. $m\angle WZY = 61°$. Find $m\angle WXY$. 119°

5. $XV = 4.6$, and $WY = 14.2$. Find VZ. 9.6

6. Find LP. 18

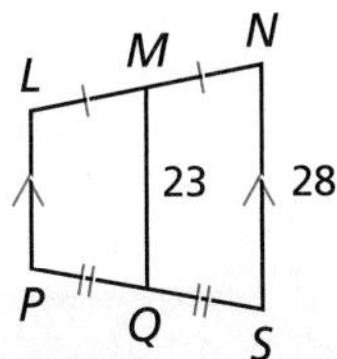

Also available on transparency

6-6 PROBLEM SOLVING

Use the figure of the kite for Exercises 1 and 2.

1. What is AD to the nearest tenth?
23.1

2. What is the perimeter of the kite to the nearest tenth?
74.0

3. In kite $STUV$, $m\angle TUW = 35°$ and $m\angle WSV = 21°$. What is the measure of $\angle UVS$?
124°

4. A car window is in the shape of a trapezoid. When the window is halfway down, the top is $\overline{KL}$, the midsegment of $FGHJ$. If $KL = 23$ inches, what is GH?
18 in.

Choose the best answer.

5. Trapezoid $PQRS$ has base angles that measure $(9r + 21)°$ and $(15r - 21)°$. Find the value of r so that $PQRS$ is isosceles.
A 3
B 5
Ⓒ 7
D 14

6. In kite $KLMN$, find the measure of $\angle M$.
F 100.5°
Ⓖ 101°
H 122°
J 130°

7. In the design, eight isosceles trapezoids surround a regular octagon. What is the measure of $\angle B$ in trapezoid $ABCD$?
A 35°
Ⓑ 45°
C 55°
D 65°

6-6 CHALLENGE

A **dart** is another type of geometric figure. Examples of darts are shown in the table.

Darts	Not Darts

1. Based on your observations of the figures in the table, write a definition of the term *dart*.
Possible answer: A dart is a concave quadrilateral with exactly two pairs of congruent consecutive sides.

2. Describe the similarities and differences between the properties of darts and kites.
Darts and kites both have exactly two pairs of congruent consecutive sides. Darts are concave, and kites are convex.

3. Find the values of x and y so that $GHJK$ is a dart.
$x = 11$; $y = 2$

4. Make a conjecture about the line that contains the diagonal from the tip to the vertex of the tail of a dart and the diagonal that joins the fin angles.
Possible answer: The lines are perpendicular. The line containing the first diagonal bisects the diagonal that joins the fin angles.

5. Make a conjecture about the two triangles formed by the tip-to-tail diagonal.
Possible answer: The triangles are congruent and obtuse.

6. Write a paragraph proof.
Given: $ABCD$ is a dart with $\overline{AB} \cong \overline{AD}$ and $\overline{BC} \cong \overline{DC}$.
Prove: $\angle B \cong \angle D$ Possible answer:
It is given that $\overline{AB} \cong \overline{AD}$ and $\overline{BC} \cong \overline{DC}$. By the Reflex. Prop. of $\cong$, $\overline{AC} \cong \overline{AC}$. This means that $\triangle ABC \cong \triangle ADC$ by SSS. So $\angle B \cong \angle D$ by CPCTC.

MULTI-STEP TEST PREP

Organizer

Objective: Assess students' ability to apply concepts and skills in Lessons 6-4 through 6-6 in a real-world format.

Resources

Geometry Assessments
www.mathtekstoolkit.org

Problem	Text Reference
1	Lesson 6-4
2	Lesson 6-3
3	Lesson 6-5
4	Lesson 6-6
5	Lesson 6-6

Answers

1. By the Distance Formula, $AB = BC = CD = DA = 4\sqrt{5}$. Since the 4 sides of $ABCD$ are $\cong$, $ABCD$ is a rhombus. $\overline{AC}$ and $\overline{BD}$ are the diags. of the rhombus, so by Thm. 6-4-4, $\overline{AC} \perp \overline{BD}$.
2. Slope of $\overline{SP}$ = slope of $\overline{RQ} = 1$, and slope of $\overline{SR}$ = slope of $\overline{PQ} = -1$, so opp. sides are $\parallel$, and $PQRS$ is a ▱ by def.
3. See p. A23.

State Resources

go.hrw.com
State Resources Online
KEYWORD: MG7 Resources

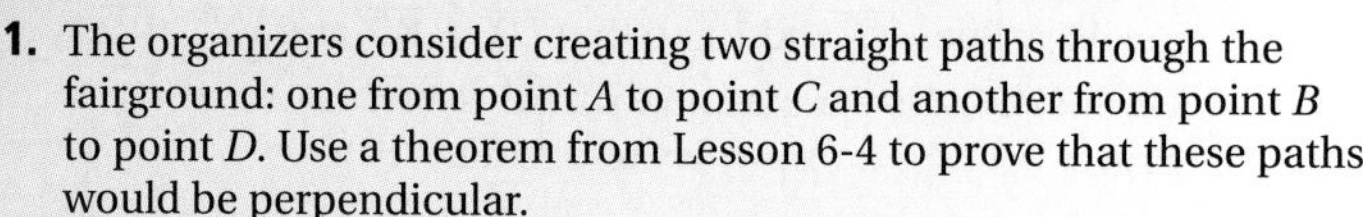

Other Special Quadrilaterals

A Fair Arrangement The organizers of a county fair are using a coordinate plane to plan the layout of the fairground. The fence that surrounds the fairground will have vertices at $A(-1, 4)$, $B(7, 8)$, $C(3, 0)$, and $D(-5, -4)$.

1. The organizers consider creating two straight paths through the fairground: one from point A to point C and another from point B to point D. Use a theorem from Lesson 6-4 to prove that these paths would be perpendicular.
2. The organizers instead decide to put an entry gate at the midpoint of each side of the fence, as shown. They plan to create straight paths that connect the gates. Show that the paths $\overline{PQ}$, $\overline{QR}$, $\overline{RS}$, and $\overline{SP}$ form a parallelogram.
3. Use the paths $\overline{PR}$ and $\overline{SQ}$ to tell whether ▱$PQRS$ is a rhombus, rectangle, or square.
4. One section of the fair will contain all the rides and games. The organizers will fence off this area within the fairground by using the existing fences along $\overline{AB}$ and $\overline{BC}$ and adding fences along $\overline{AE}$ and $\overline{CE}$, where E has coordinates $(-1, 0)$. What type of quadrilateral will be formed by these four fences? **kite**
5. To construct the fences, the organizers need to know the angle measures at each vertex. Given that $m\angle B = 37°$, find the measures of the other angles in quadrilateral $ABCE$.
$m\angle E = 90°$; $m\angle BAE = m\angle BCE = 116.5°$

INTERVENTION

Scaffolding Questions

1. What type of quadrilateral is $ABCD$? rhombus What is true about its diagonals? They are $\perp$.

2–3. How do $\overline{PR}$ and $\overline{SQ}$ relate to ▱$PQRS$? They are diags. of $PQRS$. How can you show that $\overline{PR} \cong \overline{SQ}$? Use the Distance Formula to find PR and SQ. What can you conclude about a parallelogram with congruent diagonals? The ▱ is a rect.

4–5. Which sides of $ABCE$ are congruent? $\overline{AE} \cong \overline{CE}$; $\overline{AB} \cong \overline{BC}$ Which angles of $ABCE$ must be congruent? $\angle BAE \cong \angle BCE$

Extension

Suppose the coordinates of B are $(3, 4)$, with P, Q, R, and S as the midpoints of the sides of $ABCD$. Classify the quadrilaterals $ABCD$, $PQRS$, and $ABCE$. kite; rectangle; square

READY TO GO ON?

CHAPTER 6

SECTION 6B

Quiz for Lessons 6-4 Through 6-6

6-4 Properties of Special Parallelograms

The flag of Jamaica is a rectangle with stripes along the diagonals. In rectangle $QRST$, $QS = 80.5$, and $RS = 36$. Find each length.

1. SP 40.25
2. QT 36
3. TR 80.5
4. TP 40.25

$GHJK$ is a rhombus. Find each measure.

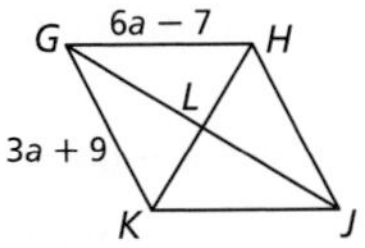

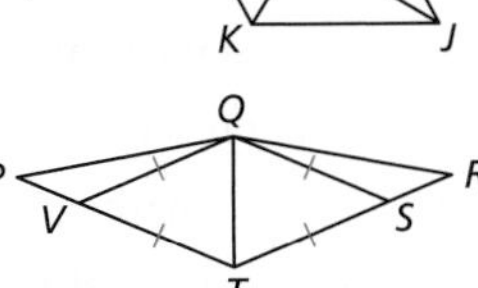

5. HJ 25
6. $m\angle HJG$ and $m\angle GHJ$ if $m\angle JLH = (4b - 6)°$ and $m\angle JKH = (2b + 11)°$
   $m\angle HJG = 31°$; $m\angle GHJ = 118°$
7. **Given:** $QSTV$ is a rhombus. $\overline{PT} \cong \overline{RT}$
   Prove: $\overline{PQ} \cong \overline{RQ}$

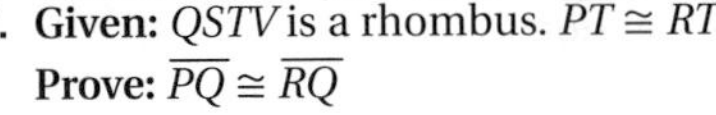

6-5 Conditions for Special Parallelograms

Determine if the conclusion is valid. If not, tell what additional information is needed to make it valid.

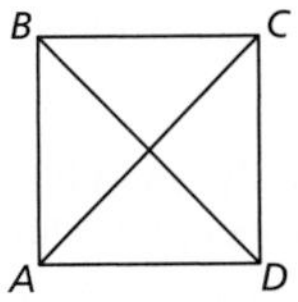

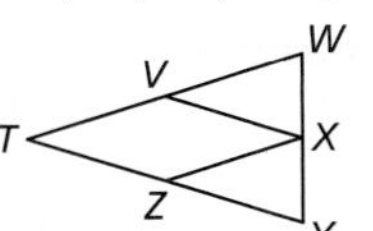

8. Given: $\overline{AC} \perp \overline{BD}$ not valid
   Conclusion: $ABCD$ is a rhombus.
9. Given: $\overline{AB} \cong \overline{CD}$, $\overline{AC} \cong \overline{BD}$, $\overline{AB} \parallel \overline{CD}$
   Conclusion: $ABCD$ is a rectangle. valid

Use the diagonals to determine whether a parallelogram with the given vertices is a rectangle, rhombus, or square. Give all the names that apply.

10. $W(-2, 2)$, $X(1, 5)$, $Y(7, -1)$, $Z(4, -4)$ rect.
11. $M(-4, 5)$, $N(1, 7)$, $P(3, 2)$, $Q(-2, 0)$ rect., rhombus, square
12. **Given:** $\overline{VX}$ and $\overline{ZX}$ are midsegments of $\triangle TWY$. $\overline{TW} \cong \overline{TY}$
    Prove: $TVXZ$ is a rhombus.

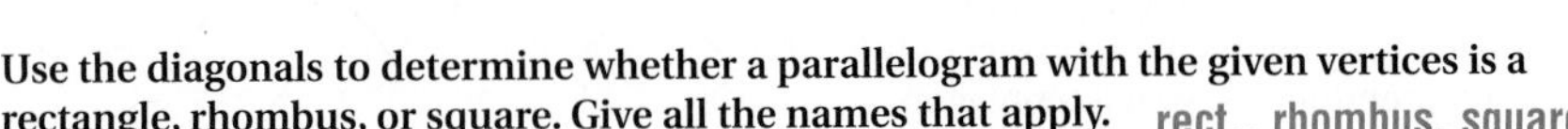

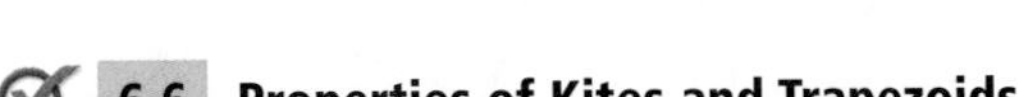

6-6 Properties of Kites and Trapezoids

In kite $EFGH$, $m\angle FHG = 68°$, and $m\angle FEH = 62°$. Find each measure.

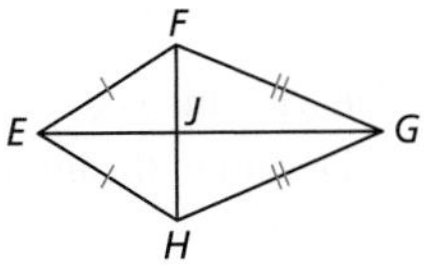

13. $m\angle FEJ$ 31°
14. $m\angle EHJ$ 59°
15. $m\angle FGJ$ 22°
16. $m\angle EHG$ 127°
17. Find $m\angle R$. 103°
18. $YZ = 34.2$, and $VX = 53.4$. Find WZ. 19.2

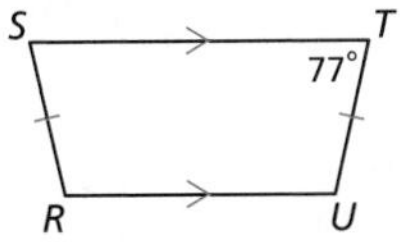

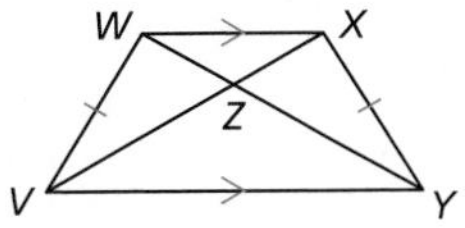

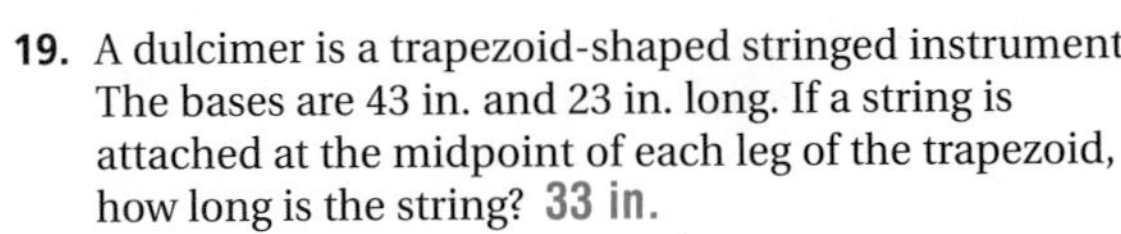

19. A dulcimer is a trapezoid-shaped stringed instrument. The bases are 43 in. and 23 in. long. If a string is attached at the midpoint of each leg of the trapezoid, how long is the string? 33 in.

READY TO GO ON? SECTION 6B

Organizer

Objective: Assess students' mastery of concepts and skills in Lessons 6-4 through 6-6.

Resources

Assessment Resources
Section 6B Quiz

Teacher One Stop™
Test & Practice Generator

INTERVENTION

Resources

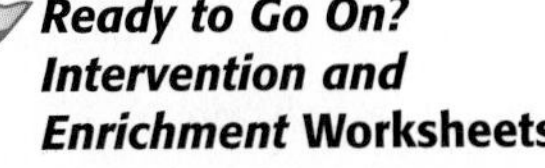

Ready to Go On? Intervention and Enrichment **Worksheets**

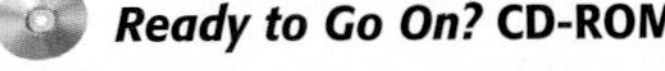

Ready to Go On? **CD-ROM**

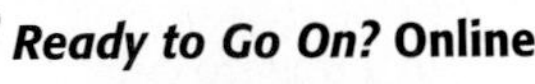

Ready to Go On? **Online**

my.hrw.com

Answers

7, 8, 12. See p. A23.

READY TO GO ON?
Diagnose and Prescribe

NO — INTERVENE

Ready to Go On? Intervention	Ready to Go On? Intervention, Section 6B: Worksheets	CD-ROM	Online
Lesson 6-4	6-4 Intervention	Activity 6-4	Diagnose and Prescribe Online
Lesson 6-5	6-5 Intervention	Activity 6-5	
Lesson 6-6	6-6 Intervention	Activity 6-6	

YES — ENRICH

Ready to Go On? Enrichment, **Section 6B**
Worksheets
CD-ROM
Online

CHAPTER 6

Study Guide: Review

Organizer

Objective: Help students organize and review key concepts and skills presented in Chapter 6.

Resources

Teacher One Stop™

PuzzleView
Test & Practice Generator

***Multilingual Glossary* Online**
go.hrw.com
KEYWORD: MG7 Glossary

Lesson Tutorial Videos
CD-ROM

Answers

1. vertex of a polygon
2. convex
3. rhombus
4. base of a trapezoid
5. not a polygon
6. polygon; triangle
7. polygon; dodecagon
8. irregular; concave
9. irregular; convex
10. reg.; convex
11. 1800°
12. 162°
13. 90°
14. m∠A = m∠D = 144°; m∠B = m∠E = 126°; m∠C = m∠F = 90°

CHAPTER 6

Study Guide: Review

For a complete list of the postulates and theorems in this chapter, see p. PS12.

Vocabulary

Complete the sentences below with vocabulary words from the list above.

1. The common endpoint of two sides of a polygon is a(n) __?__ .
2. A polygon is __?__ if no diagonal contains points in the exterior.
3. A(n) __?__ is a quadrilateral with four congruent sides.
4. Each of the parallel sides of a trapezoid is called a(n) __?__ .

6-1 Properties and Attributes of Polygons *(pp. 382–388)*

EXAMPLES

■ **Tell whether the figure is a polygon. If it is a polygon, name it by the number of its sides.**

The figure is a closed plane figure made of segments that intersect only at their endpoints, so it is a polygon. It has six sides, so it is a hexagon.

■ **Tell whether the polygon is regular or irregular. Tell whether it is concave or convex.**

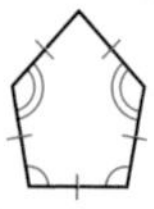

The polygon is equilateral, but it is not equiangular. So it is not regular. No diagonal contains points in the exterior, so it is convex.

Find each measure.

■ the sum of the interior angle measures of a convex 11-gon

$(n - 2)180°$ *Polygon ∠ Sum Thm.*

$(11 - 2)180° = 1620°$ *Substitute 11 for n.*

■ the measure of each exterior angle of a regular pentagon

sum of ext. ∠s = 360° *Polygon Ext. ∠ Sum Thm.*

measure of one ext. $\angle = \frac{360°}{5} = 72°$

EXERCISES

Tell whether each figure is a polygon. If it is a polygon, name it by the number of its sides.

5. 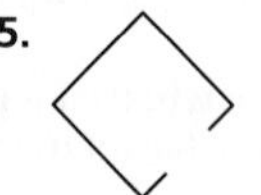
6. 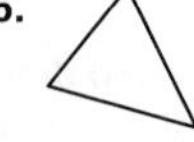
7. 

Tell whether each polygon is regular or irregular. Tell whether it is concave or convex.

8. 
9. 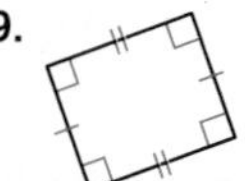
10. 

Find each measure.

11. the sum of the interior angle measures of a convex dodecagon
12. the measure of each interior angle of a regular 20-gon
13. the measure of each exterior angle of a regular quadrilateral
14. the measure of each interior angle of hexagon *ABCDEF*

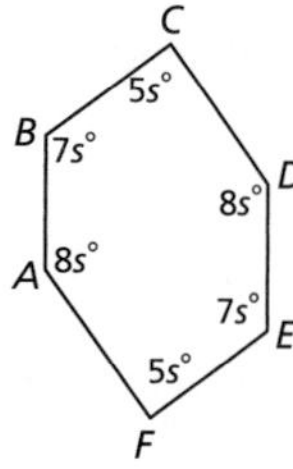

6-2 Properties of Parallelograms *(pp. 391–397)*

EXAMPLES

- **In ▱$PQRS$, $m\angle RSP = 99°$, $PQ = 19.8$, and $RT = 12.3$. Find PT.**

$\overline{PT} \cong \overline{RT}$ *▱ → diags. bisect each other*
$PT = RT$ *Def. of ≅ segs.*
$PT = 12.3$ *Substitute 12.3 for RT.*

$JKLM$ is a parallelogram. Find each measure.

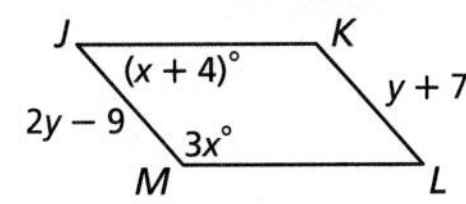

- LK

$\overline{JM} \cong \overline{LK}$ *▱ → opp. sides ≅*
$JM = LK$ *Def. of ≅ segs.*
$2y - 9 = y + 7$ *Substitute the given values.*
$y = 16$ *Solve for y.*
$LK = 16 + 7 = 23$

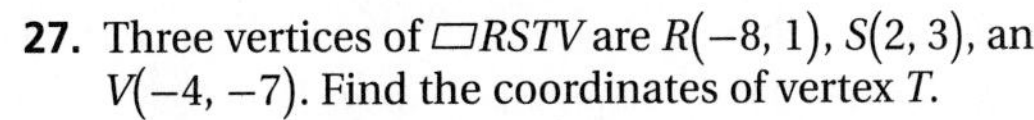

- $m\angle M$

$m\angle J + m\angle M = 180°$ *▱ → cons. ∠s supp.*
$(x + 4) + 3x = 180$ *Substitute the given values.*
$x = 44$ *Solve for x.*
$m\angle M = 3(44) = 132°$

EXERCISES

In ▱$ABCD$, $m\angle ABC = 79°$, $BC = 62.4$, and $BD = 75$. Find each measure.

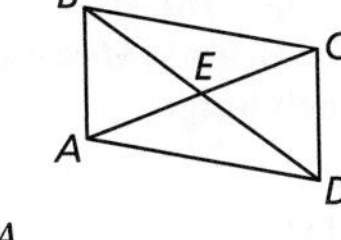

15. BE **16.** AD
17. ED **18.** $m\angle CDA$
19. $m\angle BCD$ **20.** $m\angle DAB$

$WXYZ$ is a parallelogram. Find each measure.

21. WX **22.** YZ
23. $m\angle W$ **24.** $m\angle X$
25. $m\angle Y$ **26.** $m\angle Z$

27. Three vertices of ▱$RSTV$ are $R(-8, 1)$, $S(2, 3)$, and $V(-4, -7)$. Find the coordinates of vertex T.

28. Write a two-column proof.
Given: $GHLM$ is a parallelogram. $\angle L \cong \angle JMG$
Prove: $\triangle GJM$ is isosceles.

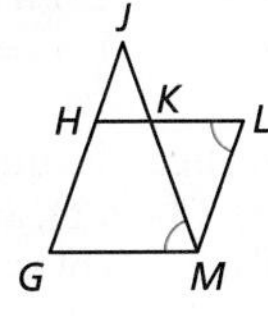

6-3 Conditions for Parallelograms *(pp. 398–405)*

EXAMPLES

- **Show that $MNPQ$ is a parallelogram for $a = 6$ and $b = 1.6$.**

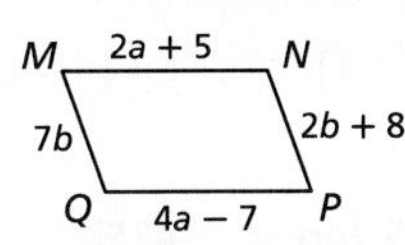

$MN = 2a + 5$ $QP = 4a - 7$
$MN = 2(6) + 5 = 17$ $QP = 4(6) - 7 = 17$
$MQ = 7b$ $NP = 2b + 8$
$MQ = 7(1.6) = 11.2$ $NP = 2(1.6) + 8 = 11.2$

Since its opposite sides are congruent, $MNPQ$ is a parallelogram.

- **Determine if the quadrilateral must be a parallelogram. Justify your answer.**

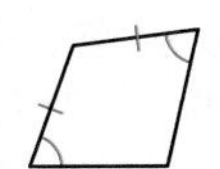

No. One pair of opposite angles are congruent, and one pair of consecutive sides are congruent. None of the conditions for a parallelogram are met.

EXERCISES

Show that the quadrilateral is a parallelogram for the given values of the variables.

29. $m = 13, n = 27$ **30.** $x = 25, y = 7$

Determine if the quadrilateral must be a parallelogram. Justify your answer.

31.   **32.**

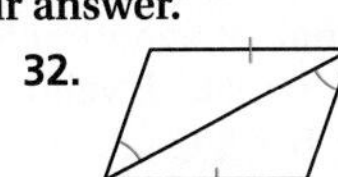

33. Show that the quadrilateral with vertices $B(-4, 3)$, $D(6, 5)$, $F(7, -1)$, and $H(-3, -3)$ is a parallelogram.

Answers

15. 37.5
16. 62.4
17. 37.5
18. 79°
19. 101°
20. 101°
21. 9.5
22. 9.5
23. 54°
24. 126°
25. 54°
26. 126°
27. $T(6, -5)$
28. **1.** $GHLM$ is a ▱. $\angle L \cong \angle JMG$ (Given)
2. $\angle G \cong \angle L$ (▱ → opp. ∠s ≅)
3. $\angle G \cong \angle JMG$ (Trans. Prop. of ≅)
4. $\overline{GJ} \cong \overline{MJ}$ (Conv. of Isosc. △ Thm.)
5. $\triangle GJM$ is isosc. (Def. of isosc. △)
29. $m\angle A = m\angle E = 63°$; $m\angle G = 117°$; since $117° + 63° = 180°$, $\angle G$ is supp. to $\angle A$ and to $\angle E$. So 1 ∠ of $ACEG$ is supp. to both of its cons. ∠s. By Thm. 6-3-4, $ACEG$ is a ▱.
30. $RS = QT = 25$, so $\overline{RS} \cong \overline{QT}$. $m\angle R = 76°$, $m\angle Q = 104°$, and $m\angle R + m\angle Q = 180°$, so $\angle R$ is supp. to $\angle Q$. Since $\angle R$ and $\angle Q$ are a pair of same-side int. ∠s, and they are supp., $\overline{RS} \parallel \overline{QT}$. So 1 pair of opp. sides of $QRST$ are ∥ and ≅. By Thm. 6-3-1, $QRST$ is a ▱.
31. Yes; the diags. of the quad. bisect each other. By Thm. 6-3-5, the quad. is a ▱.
32. No; a pair of alt. int. ∠s are ≅, so 1 pair of opp. sides are ∥. A different pair of opp. sides are ≅. None of the conditions for a ▱ are met.
33. slope of $\overline{BD}$ = slope of $\overline{FH} = \frac{1}{5}$; slope of $\overline{BH}$ = slope of $\overline{DF} = -6$; both pairs of opp. sides have the same slope, so $\overline{BD} \parallel \overline{FH}$ and $\overline{BH} \parallel \overline{DF}$; by def., $BDFH$ is a ▱.

Answers

34. 18
35. 39.6
36. 39.6
37. 19.8
38. 25.5
39. 10.5
40. 25.5
41. 21
42. 41°
43. 49°
44. 82°
45. 98°
46. $m\angle 1 = 57°$; $m\angle 2 = 66°$; $m\angle 3 = 33°$; $m\angle 4 = 114°$; $m\angle 5 = 57°$
47. $m\angle 1 = 37°$; $m\angle 2 = 53°$; $m\angle 3 = 90°$; $m\angle 4 = 37°$; $m\angle 5 = 53°$
48. $RT = SU = 2\sqrt{10}$, so $\overline{RT} \cong \overline{SU}$. Slope of $\overline{RT} = -3$, and slope of $\overline{SU} = \frac{1}{3}$, so $\overline{RT} \perp \overline{SU}$. The coordinates of the mdpt. of $\overline{RT}$ and $\overline{SU}$ are $(-4, -3)$, so $\overline{RT}$ and $\overline{SU}$ bisect each other. So the diags. of $RSTU$ are $\cong$ $\perp$ bisectors of each other.
49. $EG = FH = 3\sqrt{2}$, so $\overline{EG} \cong \overline{FH}$. Slope of $\overline{EG} = -1$, and slope of $\overline{FH} = 1$, so $\overline{EG} \perp \overline{FH}$. The coordinates of the mdpt. of $\overline{EG}$ and $\overline{FH}$ are $\left(\frac{7}{2}, -\frac{1}{2}\right)$, so $\overline{EG}$ and $\overline{FH}$ bisect each other. So the diags. of $EFGH$ are $\cong$ $\perp$ bisectors of each other.
50. Not valid; by Thm. 6-5-2, if the diags. of a ▱ are ≅, then the ▱ is a rect. By Thm. 6-5-4, if the diags. of a ▱ are ⊥, then the ▱ is a rhombus. If a ▱ is both a rect. and a rhombus, then the ▱ is a square. To apply this chain of reasoning, you must first know that EFRS is a ▱.
51. valid
52. valid

6-4 Properties of Special Parallelograms *(pp. 408–415)*

EXAMPLES

In rectangle $JKLM$, $KM = 52.8$, and $JM = 45.6$. Find each length.

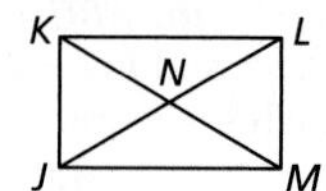

- **KL**

$JKLM$ is a ▱. — *Rect. → ▱*
$KL = JM = 45.6$ — *▱ → opp. sides ≅*

- **NL**

$JL = KM = 52.8$ — *Rect. → diags. ≅*
$NL = \frac{1}{2}JL = 26.4$ — *▱ → diags. bisect each other*

- **$PQRS$ is a rhombus. Find $m\angle QPR$, given that $m\angle QTR = (6y + 6)°$ and $m\angle SPR = 3y°$.**

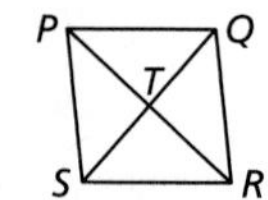

$m\angle QTR = 90°$ — *Rhombus → diags. ⊥*
$6y + 6 = 90$ — *Substitute the given value.*
$y = 14$ — *Solve for y.*
$m\angle QPR = m\angle SPR$ — *Rhombus → each diag. bisects opp. ∠s*
$m\angle QPR = 3(14)° = 42°$

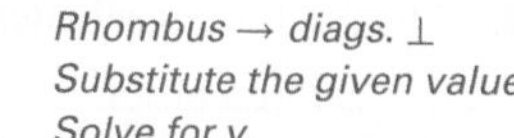

- **The vertices of square $ABCD$ are $A(5, 0)$, $B(2, 4)$, $C(-2, 1)$, and $D(1, -3)$. Show that the diagonals of square $ABCD$ are congruent perpendicular bisectors of each other.**

$AC = BD = 5\sqrt{2}$ — *Diags. are ≅.*
slope of $\overline{AC} = -\frac{1}{7}$
slope of $\overline{BD} = 7$ — *Product of slopes is −1, so diags. are ⊥.*
mdpt. of $\overline{AC}$ = mdpt. of $\overline{BD} = \left(\frac{3}{2}, \frac{1}{2}\right)$ — *Diags. bisect each other.*

EXERCISES

In rectangle $ABCD$, $CD = 18$, and $CE = 19.8$. Find each length.

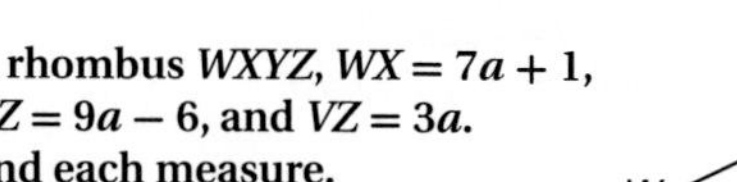

34. AB **35.** AC
36. BD **37.** BE

In rhombus $WXYZ$, $WX = 7a + 1$, $WZ = 9a - 6$, and $VZ = 3a$. Find each measure.

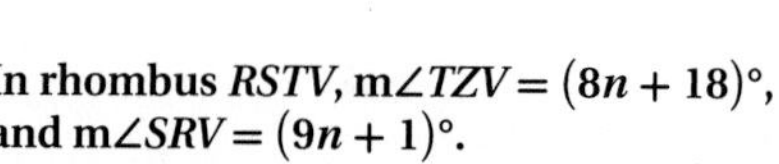

38. WZ **39.** XV
40. XY **41.** XZ

In rhombus $RSTV$, $m\angle TZV = (8n + 18)°$, and $m\angle SRV = (9n + 1)°$. Find each measure.

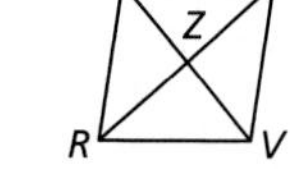

42. $m\angle TRS$ **43.** $m\angle RSV$
44. $m\angle STV$ **45.** $m\angle TVR$

Find the measures of the numbered angles in each figure.

46. rectangle $MNPQ$

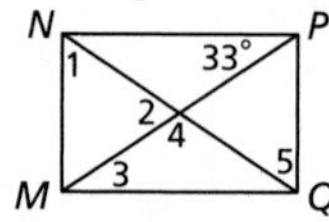

47. rhombus $CDGH$

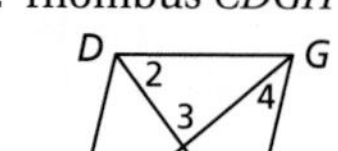

Show that the diagonals of the square with the given vertices are congruent perpendicular bisectors of each other.

48. $R(-5, 0)$, $S(-1, -2)$, $T(-3, -6)$, and $U(-7, -4)$
49. $E(2, 1)$, $F(5, 1)$, $G(5, -2)$, and $H(2, -2)$

6-5 Conditions for Special Parallelograms *(pp. 418–425)*

EXAMPLES

- **Determine if the conclusion is valid. If not, tell what additional information is needed to make it valid.**
Given: $\overline{LP} \perp \overline{KN}$
Conclusion: $KLNP$ is a rhombus.

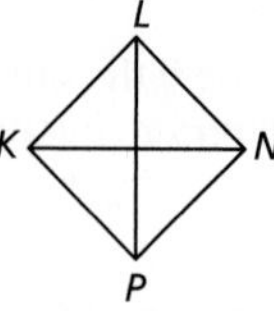

The conclusion is not valid.
If the diagonals of a parallelogram are perpendicular, then the parallelogram is a rhombus. To apply this theorem, you must first know that $KLNP$ is a parallelogram.

EXERCISES

Determine if the conclusion is valid. If not, tell what additional information is needed to make it valid.

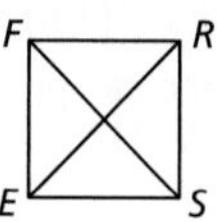

50. Given: $\overline{ER} \perp \overline{FS}$, $\overline{ER} \cong \overline{FS}$
Conclusion: $EFRS$ is a square.

51. Given: $\overline{ER}$ and $\overline{FS}$ bisect each other. $\overline{ER} \cong \overline{FS}$
Conclusion: $EFRS$ is a rectangle.

52. Given: $\overline{EF} \parallel \overline{RS}$, $\overline{FR} \parallel \overline{ES}$, $\overline{EF} \cong \overline{ES}$
Conclusion: $EFRS$ is a rhombus.

- **Use the diagonals to tell whether a parallelogram with vertices $P(-5, 3)$, $Q(0, 1)$, $R(2, -4)$, and $S(-3, -2)$ is a rectangle, rhombus, or square. Give all the names that apply.**

  $PR = \sqrt{98} = 7\sqrt{2}$ *Distance Formula*
  $QS = \sqrt{18} = 3\sqrt{2}$ *Distance Formula*

  Since $PR \neq QS$, $PQRS$ is not a rectangle and not a square.

  slope of $\overline{PR} = \frac{7}{-7} = -1$ *Slope Formula*

  slope of $\overline{QS} = \frac{3}{3} = 1$ *Slope Formula*

  Since the product of the slopes is -1, the diagonals are perpendicular. $PQRS$ is a rhombus.

Use the diagonals to tell whether a parallelogram with the given vertices is a rectangle, rhombus, or square. Give all the names that apply.

53. $B(-3, 0)$, $F(-2, 7)$, $J(5, 8)$, $N(4, 1)$

54. $D(-4, -3)$, $H(5, 6)$, $L(8, 3)$, $P(-1, -6)$

55. $Q(-8, -2)$, $T(-6, 8)$, $W(4, 6)$, $Z(2, -4)$

6-6 Properties of Kites and Trapezoids *(pp. 427–435)*

EXAMPLES

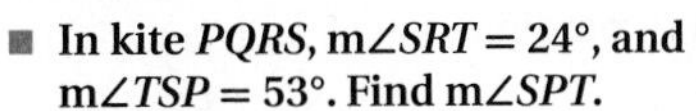
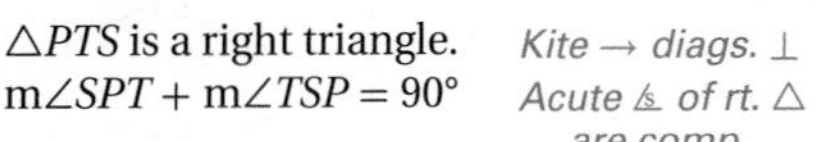

- **In kite $PQRS$, $m\angle SRT = 24°$, and $m\angle TSP = 53°$. Find $m\angle SPT$.**

  $\triangle PTS$ is a right triangle. *Kite → diags. ⊥*
  $m\angle SPT + m\angle TSP = 90°$ *Acute ∠s of rt. △ are comp.*
  $m\angle SPT + 53 = 90$ *Substitute 53 for m∠TSP.*
  $m\angle SPT = 37°$ *Subtract 53 from both sides.*

- **Find $m\angle D$.**

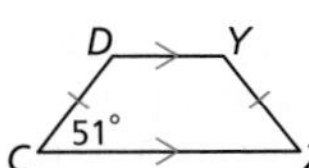

  $m\angle C + m\angle D = 180°$ *Same-Side Int. ∠s Thm.*
  $51 + m\angle D = 180$ *Substitute 51 for m∠C.*
  $m\angle D = 129°$ *Subtract.*

- **In trapezoid $HJLN$, $JP = 32.5$, and $HL = 50$. Find PN.**

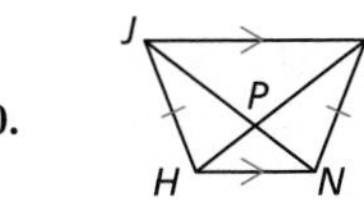

  $\overline{JN} \cong \overline{HL}$ *Isosc. trap. → diags. ≅*
  $JN = HL = 50$ *Def. of ≅ segs.*
  $JP + PN = JN$ *Seg. Add. Post.*
  $32.5 + PN = 50$ *Substitute.*
  $PN = 17.5$ *Subtract 32.5 from both sides.*

- **Find WZ.**

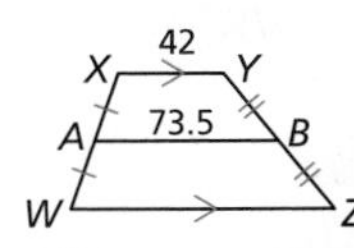

  $AB = \frac{1}{2}(XY + WZ)$ *Trap. Midsegment Thm.*
  $73.5 = \frac{1}{2}(42 + WZ)$ *Substitute.*
  $147 = 42 + WZ$ *Multiply both sides by 2.*
  $105 = WZ$ *Solve for WZ.*

EXERCISES

In kite $WXYZ$, $m\angle VXY = 58°$, and $m\angle ZWX = 50°$. Find each measure.

56. $m\angle XYZ$ **57.** $m\angle ZWV$

58. $m\angle VZW$ **59.** $m\angle WZY$

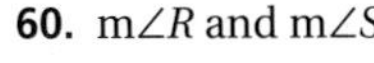

Find each measure.

60. $m\angle R$ and $m\angle S$

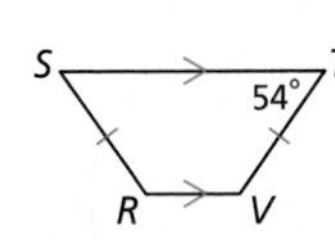

61. BZ if $ZH = 70$ and $EK = 121.6$

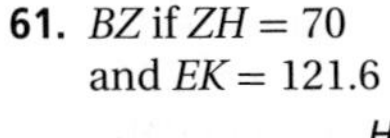
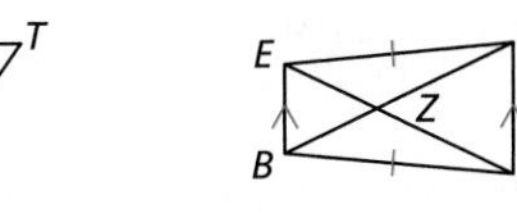

62. MN

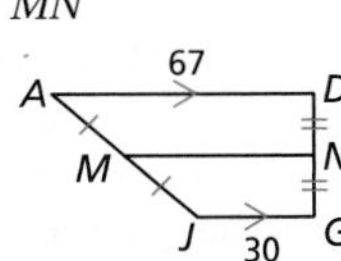

63. EQ

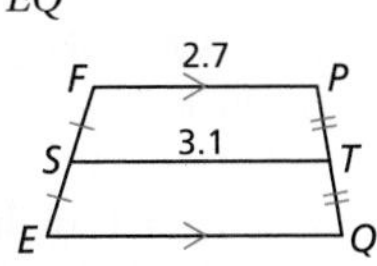

64. Find the value of n so that $PQXY$ is isosceles.

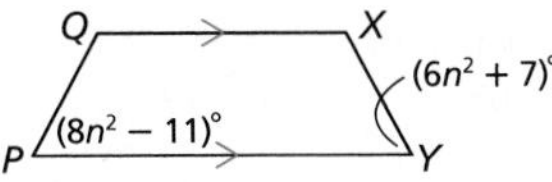

Give the best name for a quadrilateral whose vertices have the given coordinates.

65. $(-4, 5)$, $(-1, 8)$, $(5, 5)$, $(-1, 2)$

66. $(1, 4)$, $(5, 4)$, $(5, -4)$, $(1, -1)$

67. $(-6, -1)$, $(-4, 2)$, $(0, 2)$, $(2, -1)$

Answers

53. rhombus
54. rect.
55. rect., rhombus, square
56. 64°
57. 25°
58. 65°
59. 123°
60. $m\angle R = 126°$; $m\angle S = 54°$
61. 51.6
62. 48.5
63. 3.5
64. $n = 3$ or $n = -3$
65. kite
66. trap.
67. isosc. trap.

Organizer

Objective: Assess students' mastery of concepts and skills in Chapter 6.

Online Edition

Resources

Assessment Resources

Chapter 6 Tests

- Free Response (Levels A, B, C)
- Multiple Choice (Levels A, B, C)
- Performance Assessment

Teacher One Stop™
Test & Practice Generator

State Resources

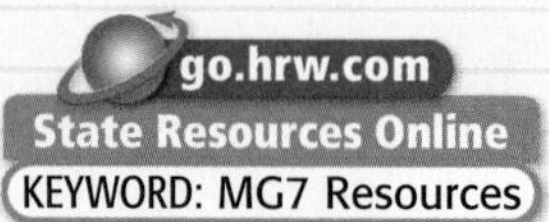

Tell whether each figure is a polygon. If it is a polygon, name it by the number of its sides.

1.  not a polygon
2. 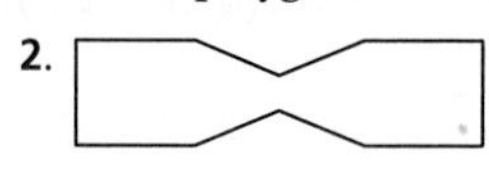 polygon; decagon

3. The base of a fountain is in the shape of a quadrilateral, as shown. Find the measure of each interior angle of the fountain.
4. Find the sum of the interior angle measures of a convex nonagon. 1260°
5. Find the measure of each exterior angle of a regular 15-gon. 24°

3. $m\angle A = 96°$; $m\angle B = 112°$; $m\angle C = 64°$; $m\angle D = 88°$

6. In $\square EFGH$, $EH = 28$, $HZ = 9$, and $m\angle EHG = 145°$. Find FH and $m\angle FEH$. $FH = 18$; $m\angle FEH = 35°$

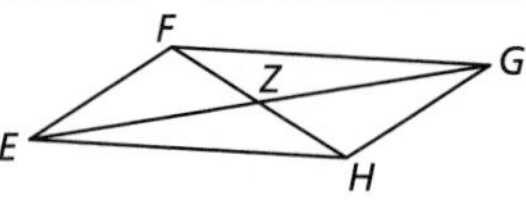

7. $JKLM$ is a parallelogram. Find KL and $m\angle L$. $KL = 17$; $m\angle L = 52°$

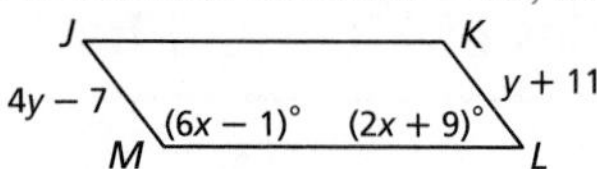

8. Three vertices of $\square PQRS$ are $P(-2, -3)$, $R(7, 5)$, and $S(6, 1)$. Find the coordinates of Q. $(-1, 1)$

9. Show that $WXYZ$ is a parallelogram for $a = 4$ and $b = 3$.

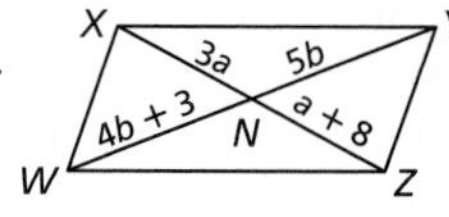

10. Determine if $CDGH$ must be a parallelogram. Justify your answer.

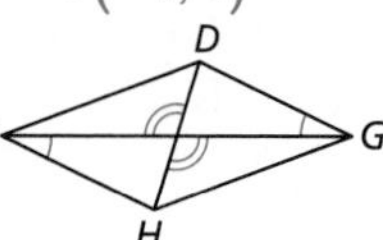

11. Show that a quadrilateral with vertices $K(-7, -3)$, $L(2, 0)$, $S(5, -4)$, and $T(-4, -7)$ is a parallelogram.

12. In rectangle $PLCM$, $LC = 19$, and $LM = 23$. Find PT and PM. $PT = 11.5$; $PM = 19$

13. In rhombus $EHKN$, $m\angle NQK = (7z + 6)°$, and $m\angle ENQ = (5z + 1)°$. Find $m\angle HEQ$ and $m\angle EHK$. $m\angle HEQ = 29°$; $m\angle EHK = 122°$

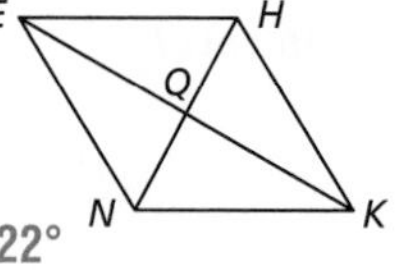

Determine if the conclusion is valid. If not, tell what additional information is needed to make it valid.

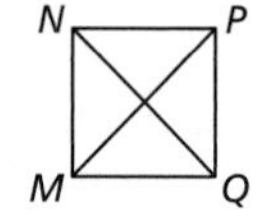

14. Given: $\overline{NP} \cong \overline{PQ} \cong \overline{QM} \cong \overline{MN}$
Conclusion: $MNPQ$ is a square. not valid

15. Given: $\overline{NP} \cong \overline{MQ}$, $\overline{NM} \cong \overline{PQ}$, $\overline{NQ} \cong \overline{MP}$
Conclusion: $MNPQ$ is a rectangle. valid

Use the diagonals to determine whether a parallelogram with the given vertices is a rectangle, rhombus, or square. Give all the names that apply.

16. $A(-5, 7)$, $C(3, 6)$, $E(7, -1)$, $G(-1, 0)$ rhombus
17. $P(4, 1)$, $Q(3, 4)$, $R(-3, 2)$, $S(-2, -1)$ rect.

18. $m\angle JFR = 43°$, and $m\angle JNB = 68°$. Find $m\angle FBN$. 103°

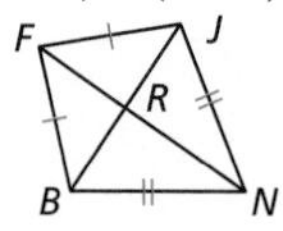

19. $PV = 61.1$, and $YS = 24.7$. Find MY. 36.4

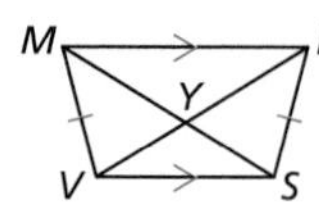

20. Find HR. 27 in.

Answers

9. $XN = ZN = 12$, so $\overline{XN} \cong \overline{ZN}$. Thus $\overline{WY}$ bisects $\overline{XZ}$. $WN = YN = 15$, so $\overline{WN} \cong \overline{YN}$. Thus $\overline{XZ}$ bisects $\overline{WY}$. The diags. of $WXYZ$ bisect each other. By Thm. 6-3-5, $WXYZ$ is a $\square$.

10. No; 1 pair of opp. sides of the quad. are ∥. A pair of vert. ∠s formed by the diags. are ≅. None of the conditions for a $\square$ are met.

11. Possible answer: slope of $\overline{KL}$ = slope of $\overline{ST} = \frac{1}{3}$; slope of $\overline{KT}$ = slope of $\overline{LS} = -\frac{4}{3}$; both pairs of opp. sides have the same slope, so $\overline{KL} \parallel \overline{ST}$ and $\overline{KT} \parallel \overline{LS}$; by def., $KLST$ is a $\square$.

14. Possible answer: $MNPQ$ is a rhombus by def. because its 4 sides are ≅. To show that $MNPQ$ is a square, you need to know that $MNPQ$ is also a rect.

COLLEGE ENTRANCE EXAM PRACTICE

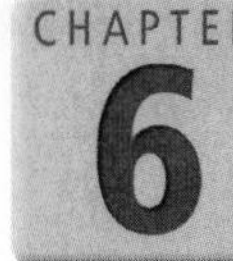

FOCUS ON SAT

The scores for each SAT section range from 200 to 800. Your score is calculated by subtracting a fraction for each incorrect multiple-choice answer from the total number of correct answers. No points are deducted for incorrect grid-in answers or items you left blank.

If you have time, go back through each section of the test and check as many of your answers as possible. Try to use a different method of solving the problem than you used the first time.

You may want to time yourself as you take this practice test. It should take you about 6 minutes to complete.

1. Given the quadrilateral below, what value of x would allow you to conclude that the figure is a parallelogram?

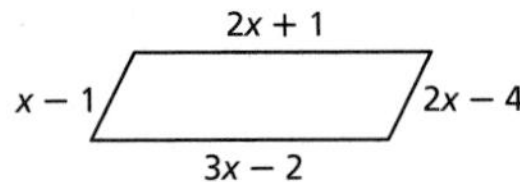

(A) −2

(B) 0

(C) 1

(D) 2

(E) 3

2. In the figure below, if *ABCD* is a rectangle, what type of triangle must $\triangle ABE$ be?

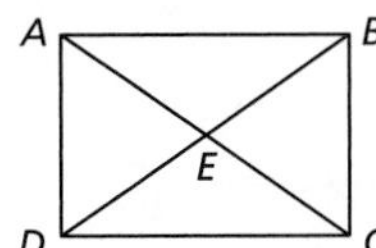

(A) Equilateral

(B) Right

(C) Equiangular

(D) Isosceles

(E) Scalene

3. Which of the following terms best describes the figure below?

(A) Rhombus

(B) Trapezoid

(C) Quadrilateral

(D) Square

(E) Parallelogram

4. Three vertices of ▱*MNPQ* are $M(3, 1)$, $N(0, 6)$, and $P(4, 7)$. Which of the following could be the coordinates of vertex *Q*?

(A) $(7, 0)$

(B) $(-1, 1)$

(C) $(7, 2)$

(D) $(11, 3)$

(E) $(9, 4)$

5. If *ABCDE* is a regular pentagon, what is the measure of $\angle C$?

(A) 45°

(B) 60°

(C) 90°

(D) 108°

(E) 120°

COLLEGE ENTRANCE EXAM PRACTICE

CHAPTER 6

Organizer

Objective: Provide practice for college entrance exams such as the SAT.

Resources

Questions on the SAT represent the following math strands:

Number and Operation, 20–25%

Algebra and Functions, 35–40%

Geometry and Measurement, 25–30%

Data Analysis, Statistics, and Probability, 10–15%

Items on this page focus on:

- Geometry and Measurement

Text References:

Item	1	2	3	4	5
Lesson	6-3	6-4	6-6	6-2	6-1

TEST PREP DOCTOR

1. Students who chose **A** may have set the lengths of adjacent sides equal to each other. Remind students that any quadrilateral in which both pairs of opposite sides are congruent must be a parallelogram.

2. Students who chose **B** may be thinking of the properties of a rhombus, in which the diagonals are perpendicular. Remind students that the diagonals of a rectangle bisect each other, and ask students what that means about the sides of $\triangle ABE$.

3. Students who did not choose **B** should review the vocabulary from this chapter. Ask students to review their graphic organizer from page 431, which shows the relationships between the quadrilaterals studied in this chapter.

4. Students who chose **A** or **E** may have found the correct slopes but applied them incorrectly. Suggest that students graph the points in the coordinate plane to make sure they understand their relative locations.

5. Remind students that the sum of the measures of the interior angles of a convex polygon with n sides is $(n - 2)180$ and that a pentagon has 5 sides.

Organizer

Objective: Provide opportunities to learn and practice common test-taking strategies.

This Test Tackler focuses on using logic and estimation to eliminate answer choices to multiple-choice test items. While this strategy may not always give students the specific answer, it may save students time by eliminating some of the choices. Encourage students to read a multiple-choice test item carefully. Then, before they begin to solve the problem, have them determine if any of the answer choices can be eliminated.

TEST TACKLER
Standardized Test Strategies

Multiple Choice: Eliminate Answer Choices

For some multiple-choice test items, you can eliminate one or more of the answer choices without having to do many calculations. Use estimation or logic to help you decide which answer choices can be eliminated.

EXAMPLE 1

What is the value of x in the figure?

Ⓐ 3° Ⓒ 83°

Ⓑ 63° Ⓓ 153°

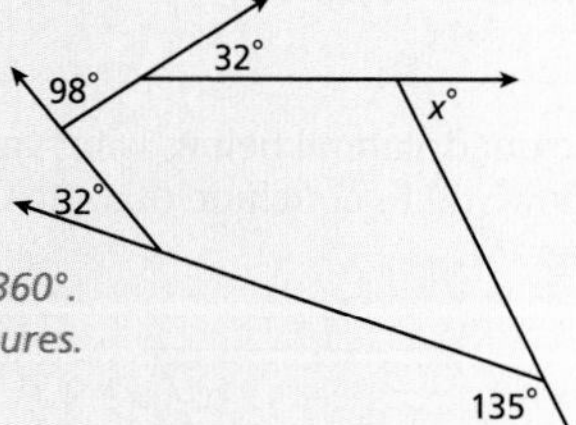

The sum of the exterior angle measures of a convex polygon is 360°. By rounding, you can estimate the sum of the given angle measures.

$100° + 30° + 140° + 30° = 300°$

If $x = 153°$, the sum of the angle measures would be far greater than 360°. So eliminate D.

If $x = 3°$, the sum would be far less than 360°. So eliminate A.

From your estimate, it seems likely that the correct choice is B, 63°. Confirm that this is correct by doing the actual calculation.

$98° + 32° + 63° + 135° + 32° = 360°$

The correct answer is B, 63°.

EXAMPLE 2

What is $m\angle B$ in the isosceles trapezoid?

Ⓕ 216° Ⓗ 72°

Ⓖ 108° Ⓙ 58°

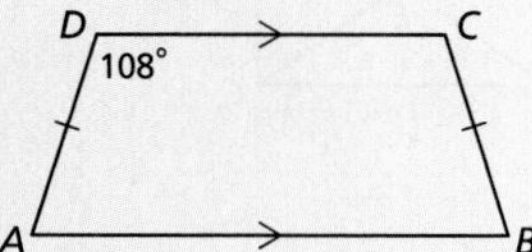

Base angles of an isosceles trapezoid are congruent. Since $\angle D$ and $\angle B$ are not a pair of base angles, their measures are not equal. Eliminate G, 108°.

$\angle D$ and $\angle C$ are base angles, so $m\angle C = 108°$. $\angle B$ and $\angle C$ are same-side interior angles formed by parallel lines. So they are supplementary angles. Therefore the measure of angle B cannot be greater than 180°. You can eliminate F.

$m\angle B = 180° - 108° = 72°$

The correct answer is H, 72°.

Try to eliminate unreasonable answer choices. Some choices may be too large or too small or may have incorrect units.

Read each test item and answer the questions that follow.

Item A

The diagonals of rectangle $MNPQ$ intersect at S. If $MN = 4.1$ meters, $MS = 2.35$ meters, and $MQ = 2.3$ meters, what is the area of $\triangle MPQ$ to the nearest tenth?

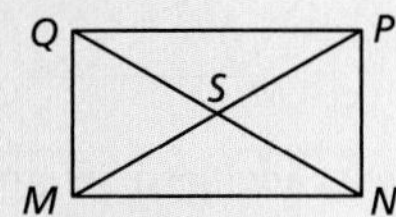

Ⓐ 4.7 square meters

Ⓑ 5.4 meters

Ⓒ 9.4 square meters

Ⓓ 12.8 meters

1. Are there any answer choices you can eliminate immediately? If so, which choices and why?
2. Describe how to use estimation to eliminate at least one more answer choice.

Item B

What is the sum of the interior angles of a convex hexagon?

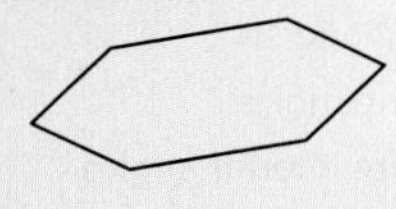

Ⓕ 180° Ⓗ 720°

Ⓖ 500° Ⓙ 1080°

3. Can any of the answer choices be eliminated immediately? If so, which choices and why?
4. How can you use the fact that 500 is not a multiple of 180 to eliminate choice G?
5. A student answered this problem with J. Explain the mistake the student made.

Item C

In isosceles trapezoid $ABCD$, $AC = 18.2$, and $DG = 6.3$. What is GB?

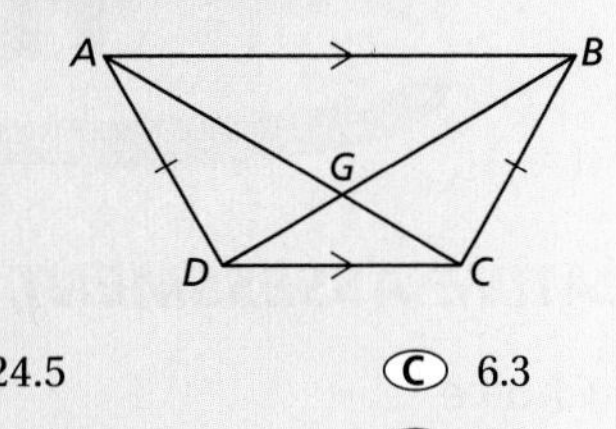

Ⓐ 24.5 Ⓒ 6.3

Ⓑ 11.9 Ⓓ 2.9

6. Will the measure of $\overline{GB}$ be more than, less than, or equal to the measure of $\overline{AC}$? What answer choices can you eliminate and why?
7. Explain how to use estimation to answer this problem.

Item D

In trapezoid $LMNP$, $XY = 25$ feet. What are two possible lengths for $\overline{LM}$ and $\overline{PN}$?

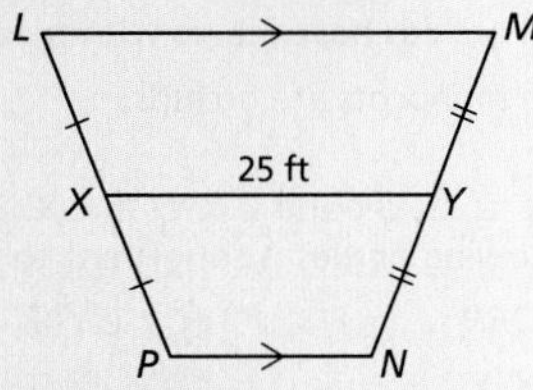
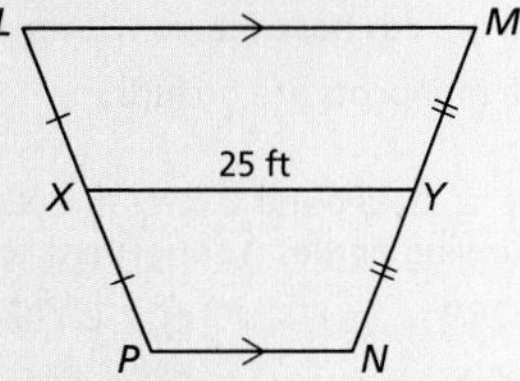

Ⓕ 18 feet and 32 feet

Ⓖ 49 feet and 2 feet

Ⓗ 10 feet and 15 feet

Ⓙ 7 inches and 43 inches

8. Which answer choice can you eliminate immediately? Why?
9. A student used logic to eliminate choice H. Do you agree with the student's decision? Explain.
10. A student used estimation and answered this problem with G. Explain the mistake the student made.

Answers

Possible answers:

1. Yes; **D;** the units are incorrect.
2. Use the formula for the area of a △ and substitute 4 for the height and 2 for the base: $A = \frac{1}{2}bh = \frac{1}{2}(4)(2) = 4$. Eliminate **C** because it is much greater than 4.
3. Yes; **F;** 180° is the sum of the int. ∡ of a △, and because a hexagon has 3 more sides than a △, the sum of its int. ∡ must be much greater than 180°.
4. The sum of the int. ∡ of a convex polygon must be a multiple of 180°. Because 500 is not a multiple of 180, it can be eliminated.
5. The student did not subtract 2 from the number of sides before multiplying by 180.
6. Less than; **A** can be eliminated because $24.5 > 18.2$.
7. Use compatible numbers and subtract: $18 - 6 = 12$. GB is about 12, so select **B** as the answer.
8. **J;** the units are incorrect.
9. Yes; the midsegment of a trap. has a measure less than that of the longest base and greater than that of the shortest base. Because 10 and 15 are both less than 25, it cannot be the correct answer.
10. The student used numbers compatible with 50 and 0: $\frac{1}{2}(50 + 0) = 25$. However, the student should have checked the answer, because $\frac{1}{2}(49 + 2) = 25.5 \neq 25$.

Answers to Test Items

A. A

B. H

C. B

D. F

State Resources

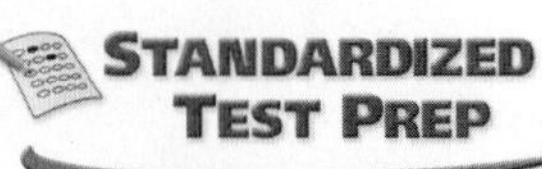

Organizer

Objective: Provide review and practice for Chapters 1–6 and standardized tests.

Online Edition

Resources

Assessment Resources

Chapter 6 Cumulative Test

State Resources

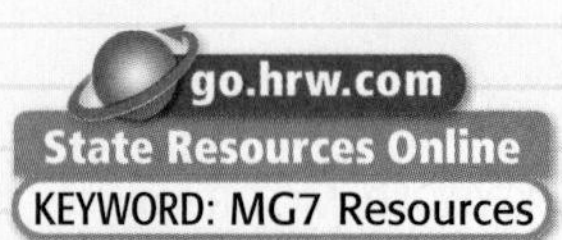

CUMULATIVE ASSESSMENT, CHAPTERS 1–6

Multiple Choice

1. The exterior angles of a triangle have measures of $(x + 10)°$, $(2x + 20)°$, and $3x°$. What is the measure of the smallest interior angle of the triangle?

Ⓐ 15° Ⓒ 55°

Ⓑ 35° Ⓓ 65°

2. If a plant is a monocot, then its leaves have parallel veins. If a plant is an orchid, then it is a monocot. A Mexican vanilla plant is an orchid. Based on this information, which conclusion is NOT valid?

Ⓕ The leaves of a Mexican vanilla plant have parallel veins.

Ⓖ A Mexican vanilla plant is a monocot.

Ⓗ All orchids have leaves with parallel veins.

Ⓙ All monocots are orchids.

3. If $\triangle ABC \cong \triangle PQR$ and $\triangle RPQ \cong \triangle XYZ$, which of the following angles is congruent to $\angle CAB$?

Ⓐ $\angle QRP$ Ⓒ $\angle YXZ$

Ⓑ $\angle XZY$ Ⓓ $\angle XYZ$

4. Which line coincides with the line $2y + 3x = 4$?

Ⓕ $3y + 2x = 4$

Ⓖ $y = \frac{2}{3}x + 2$

Ⓗ a line through $(-1, 1)$ and $(2, 3)$

Ⓙ a line through $(0, 2)$ and $(4, -4)$

5. What is the value of x in polygon $ABCDEF$?

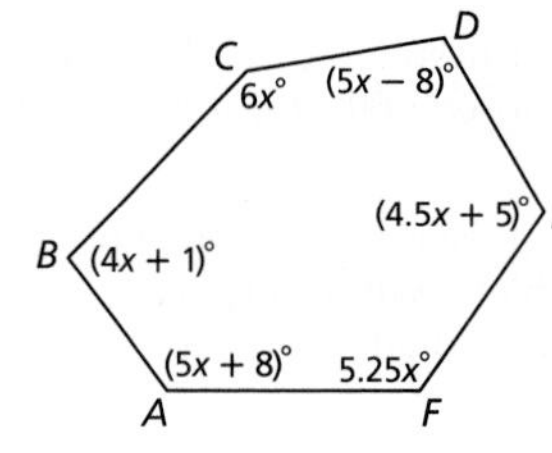

Ⓐ 12 Ⓒ 24

Ⓑ 18 Ⓓ 36

Use the figure below for Items 6 and 7.

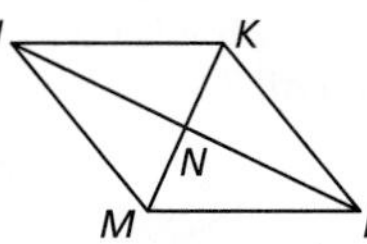

6. If $\overline{JK} \parallel \overline{ML}$, what additional information do you need to prove that quadrilateral $JKLM$ is a parallelogram?

Ⓕ $\overline{JM} \cong \overline{KL}$

Ⓖ $\overline{MN} \cong \overline{LN}$

Ⓗ $\angle MLK$ and $\angle LKJ$ are right angles.

Ⓙ $\angle JML$ and $\angle KLM$ are supplementary.

7. Given that $JKLM$ is a parallelogram and that $m\angle KLN = 25°$, $m\angle JMN = 65°$, and $m\angle JML = 130°$, which term best describes quadrilateral $JKLM$?

Ⓐ Rectangle

Ⓑ Rhombus

Ⓒ Square

Ⓓ Trapezoid

8. For two lines and a transversal, $\angle 1$ and $\angle 2$ are same-side interior angles, $\angle 2$ and $\angle 3$ are vertical angles, and $\angle 3$ and $\angle 4$ are alternate exterior angles. Which classification best describes the angle pair $\angle 2$ and $\angle 4$?

Ⓕ Adjacent angles

Ⓖ Alternate interior angles

Ⓗ Corresponding angles

Ⓙ Vertical angles

9. For $\triangle ABC$ and $\triangle DEF$, $\angle A \cong \angle F$, and $\overline{AC} \cong \overline{EF}$. Which of the following would allow you to conclude that these triangles are congruent by AAS?

Ⓐ $\angle ABC \cong \angle EDF$

Ⓑ $\angle ACB \cong \angle EDF$

Ⓒ $\angle BAC \cong \angle FDE$

Ⓓ $\angle CBA \cong \angle FED$

Answers

1. A
2. J
3. D
4. J
5. C
6. J
7. B
8. H
9. A
10. H
11. C
12. H
13. B
14. 36
15. 15
16. 13.5

10. The vertices of ▱$ABCD$ are $A(1, 4)$, $B(4, y)$, $C(3, -2)$, and $D(0, -3)$. What is the value of y?

Ⓕ 3 Ⓗ 5

Ⓖ 4 Ⓙ 6

11. Quadrilateral $RSTU$ is a kite. What is the length of $\overline{RV}$?

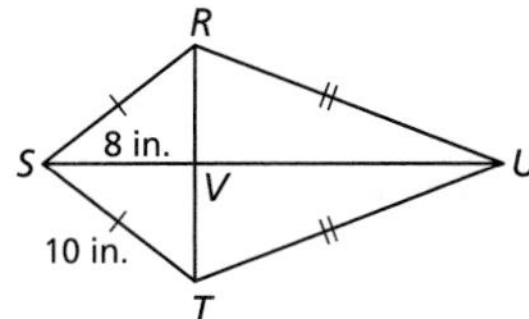

Ⓐ 4 inches Ⓒ 6 inches

Ⓑ 5 inches Ⓓ 13 inches

12. What is the measure of each interior angle in a regular dodecagon?

Ⓕ 30° Ⓗ 150°

Ⓖ 144° Ⓙ 162°

13. The coordinates of the vertices of quadrilateral $RSTU$ are $R(1, 3)$, $S(2, 7)$, $T(10, 5)$, and $U(9, 1)$. Which term best describes quadrilateral $RSTU$?

Ⓐ Parallelogram Ⓒ Rhombus

Ⓑ Rectangle Ⓓ Trapezoid

Mixed numbers cannot be entered into the grid for gridded-response questions. For example, if you get an answer of $7\frac{1}{4}$, you must grid either 7.25 or $\frac{29}{4}$.

Gridded Response

14. If quadrilateral $MNPQ$ is a parallelogram, what is the value of x?

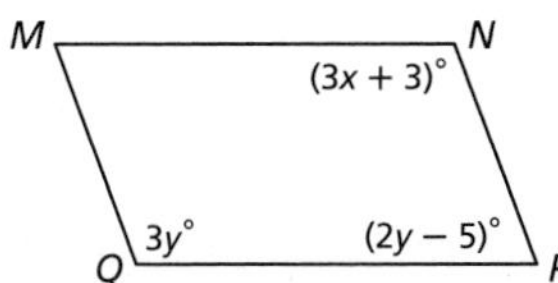

15. What is the greatest number of line segments determined by six coplanar points when no three are collinear?

16. Quadrilateral $RSTU$ is a rectangle with diagonals $\overline{RT}$ and $\overline{SU}$. If $RT = 4a + 2$ and $SU = 6a - 25$, what is the value of a?

Short Response

17. In △ABC, $AE = 9x - 11.25$, and $AF = x + 4$.

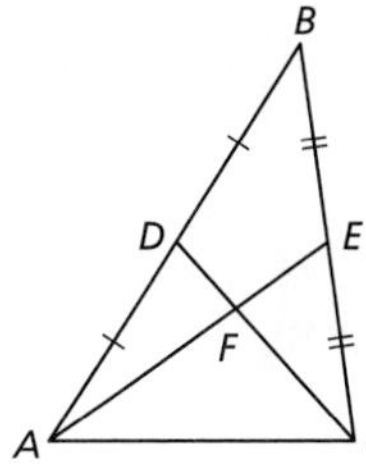

a. Find the value of x. Show your work and explain how you found your answer.

b. If $\overline{DF} \cong \overline{EF}$, show that △$AFD \cong$ △CFE. State any theorems or postulates used.

18. Consider quadrilateral $ABCD$.

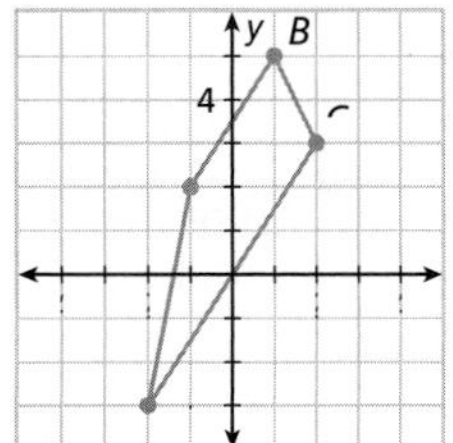

a. Show th[illegible] Justify your answer.

b. What are the coordinates for the endpoints of the midsegment of trapezoid $ABCD$?

19. Suppose that ∠M is complementary to ∠N and ∠N is complementary to ∠P. Explain why the measurements of these three angles cannot be the angle measurements of a triangle.

Extended Response

20. Given △ABC and △XYZ, suppose that $\overline{AB} \cong \overline{XY}$ and $\overline{BC} \cong \overline{YZ}$.

a. If $AB = 5$, $BC = 6$, $AC = 8$, and $m\angle B < m\angle Y$, explain why △XYZ is obtuse. Justify your reasoning and state any theorems or postulates used.

b. If $AB = 3$, $BC = 5$, $AC = 5$, and $m\angle B > m\angle Y$, find the length of $\overline{XZ}$ so that △XYZ is a right triangle. Justify your reasoning and state any theorems or postulates used.

c. If $AB = 8$ and $BC = 4$, find the range of possible values for the length of $\overline{AC}$. Justify your answer.

Short-Response Rubric

Items 17–19

2 Points = The student's answer is an accurate and complete execution of the task or tasks.

1 Point = The student's answer contains attributes of an appropriate response but is flawed.

0 Points = The student's answer contains no attributes of an appropriate response.

Extended-Response Rubric

Item 20

4 Points = The student correctly finds XZ and the range for AC. Explanations are complete, and work demonstrates a thorough understanding of concepts related to triangle inequality theorems.

3 Points = The student's answers are correct, but explanations may contain minor flaws. Work demonstrates an understanding of major concepts related to triangle inequality theorems.

2 Points = The student answers correctly, but explanations are missing or incomplete. Work demonstrates a limited understanding of triangle inequality theorems.

1 Point = The student answers incorrectly but makes a reasonable attempt to show work.

0 Points = The student answers incorrectly and does not attempt all parts of the problem.

Answers

17a. By the Centroid Thm., $\frac{2}{3}(9x - 11.25) = x + 4$. So $6x - 7.5 = x + 4$, $-11.5 = -5x$, and $x = 2.3$.

b. Possible answer: By the Centroid Thm., $FC = \frac{2}{3}DC$. It is given that $\overline{DF} \cong \overline{EF}$, so $DF = EF$. From part **a**, $EF = 3.15$, and $AF = 6.3$. So $DF = 3.15$. $FC = \frac{2}{3}(DF + FC) = \frac{2}{3}(3.15 + FC)$, so $FC = 6.3$. Thus $AF = FC$, and $\overline{AF} \cong \overline{FC}$. ∠$DFA \cong$ ∠EFC by the Vert. ∡ Thm. Thus △$AFD \cong$ △CFE by SAS.

18a. Slope of $\overline{AB} = \frac{3}{2}$, and slope of $\overline{CD} = \frac{3}{2}$, so $\overline{AB} \parallel \overline{CD}$. Slope of $\overline{BC} = -2$, and slope of $\overline{AD} = 5$. So $\overline{BC}$ is not ∥ to $\overline{AD}$. $ABCD$ is a trap. by def.

b. $\left(-1\frac{1}{2}, -\frac{1}{2}\right)$, $\left(1\frac{1}{2}, 4\right)$

19. ∠$M \cong$ ∠P by the ≅ Comps. Thm, and thus $m\angle M = m\angle P$. Also, $m\angle N = 90° - m\angle P$ by the def. of comp. ∡. If these ∡ were ∡ of a △, $m\angle M + m\angle N + m\angle P = 180°$ by the △ Sum Thm. By subst., $m\angle P + (90° - m\angle P) + m\angle P = 180°$. Thus, $m\angle P = 90°$. But $m\angle P < 90°$ because ∠N is comp. to ∠P. So there is a contradiction, and therefore, these ∡ cannot be the ∡ of a △.

20a. Since $m\angle B < m\angle Y$, $\overline{AB} \cong \overline{XY}$, and $\overline{BC} \cong \overline{YZ}$, it follows by the Hinge Thm. that $XZ > AC = 8$. Since $64 > 25 + 36$, △ABC is obtuse by the Pyth. Inequals. Thm. Since the longer side lies opp. the greater ∠, ∠B is the largest ∠ in △ABC. Since △ABC is obtuse, ∠B must be obtuse. Since $m\angle B < m\angle Y$, $m\angle Y$ must also be obtuse, so △XYZ is obtuse.

b. Since $m\angle B > m\angle Y$, $\overline{AB} \cong \overline{XY}$, and $\overline{BC} \cong \overline{YZ}$, it follows by the Hinge Thm. that $XZ < AC = 5$. So the hyp. of △XYZ would be $\overline{YZ}$, the longest side. According to the Pyth. Thm., $XY^2 + XZ^2 = YZ^2$, $3^2 + XZ^2 = 5^2$, $XZ^2 = 25 - 9 = 16$, and $XZ = 4$.

c. $4 < AC < 12$. By the △ Inequal. Thm., $AB + AC > BC$. By subst. $8 + AC > 4$. This is true when $AC > 0$. $AB + BC > AC$, so $8 + 4 = 12 > AC$. Also, $AC + BC > AB$, so $AC + 4 > 8$, and $AC > 4$.

Organizer

Objective: Choose appropriate problem-solving strategies and use them with skills from Chapters 5 and 6 to solve real-world problems.

Handmade Tiles

Reading Strategies

Have students write down the important information as they read **Problem 1.** Then have them summarize the problem in their own words.

Using Data Ask students what else they need to know about the tile to solve **Problem 1.** the height of the ▱ Ask them to describe how they can find this information. Find the shorter leg of the 30°-60°-90° △ formed by the height of the ▱. (2 in.)

Handmade Tiles

During the nineteenth century, an important industry developed in east central Ohio thanks to an "earthy" discovery—clay! The region's rich soil and easy access to river transportation helped establish Ohio as the pottery and ceramic capital of the United States. Today the majority of the earthenware clay used in handmade tiles is still mined in Ohio.

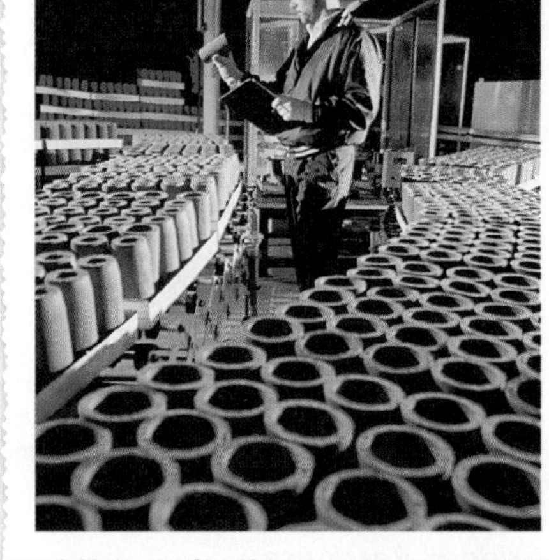

Choose one or more strategies to solve each problem.

1. In tile making, soft clay is pressed into long rectangular wooden trays. After the clay has dried, tiles are cut from the rectangular slab. A tile manufacturer wants to make parallelogram-shaped tiles with the dimensions shown. What is the maximum number of such tiles that can be cut from a 12 in. by 40 in. slab of clay? **36 tiles**

2. An interior designer is buying tiles that are in the shape of isosceles trapezoids. Each tile has bases that are 1 in. and 3 in. long, and the tiles can be arranged as shown to form a rectangle. How many tiles should the designer buy in order to frame a 25 in. by 49 in. window? **76 tiles**

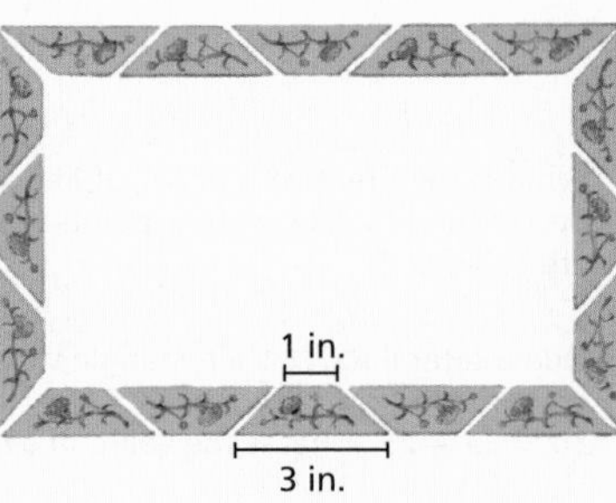

3. A tile manufacturer wants to make a tile in the shape of a rhombus where one diagonal is twice the length of the other diagonal. What should the lengths of the diagonals be in order to make a tile with sides 7 cm long? Round to the nearest hundredth. **6.26 cm, 12.52 cm**

Problem-Solving Focus

For **Problem 2,** ask students which problem-solving strategies might be helpful. Possible answer: Find a pattern. For each side, the corner tile gives 1 in. of length. After that, every 2 tiles provide another 4 in. of length. So it takes $1 + \frac{\ell - 1}{2}$ tiles to make a side that is ℓ inches long.

Discuss different strategies that could be used to solve **Problem 2.** Some students might make a table that shows the number of tiles and the corresponding distance. Others might start by solving a simpler problem, such as the number of tiles needed for a 5 in. by 9 in. window.

The Millennium Force Roller Coaster

When it opened in May 2000, the Millennium Force roller coaster broke all previous records and became the tallest and fastest roller coaster in the world. One of 16 roller coasters at Cedar Point in Sandusky, Ohio, the Millennium Force takes riders on a wild journey that features 1.25 miles of track, a top speed of 93 miles per hour, and a breathtaking 310-foot drop!

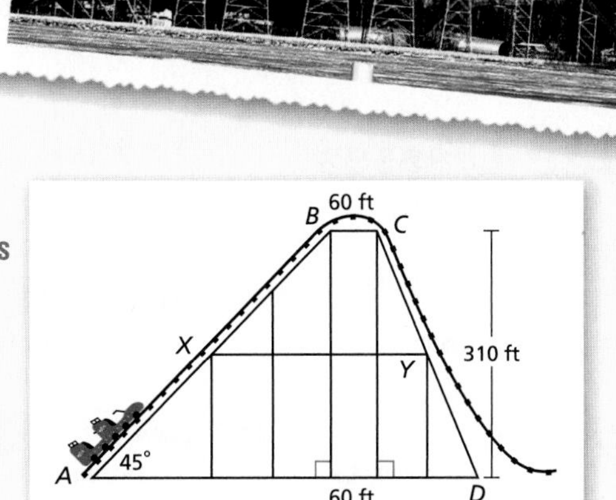

Choose one or more strategies to solve each problem.

1. The first hill of the Millennium Force is 310 ft tall. The ascent to the top of the hill is at a 45° angle. What is the length of the ascent to the nearest tenth of a foot? 438.4 ft
2. The Millennium Force was the first coaster in which an elevator lift system was used to pull the trains to the top of the first hill. The system pulls the trains at a speed of 20 ft/s. How long does it take a train to reach the top of the hill? 22 s

The figure shows the support structure for the first hill of the Millennium Force. For 3 and 4, use the figure.

3. The length of the first descent $\overline{CD}$ is 314.8 ft. To the nearest foot, what is the total horizontal distance AD that the train covers as it goes over the first hill? 425 ft
4. Engineers designed the support beam $\overline{XY}$ so that X is the midpoint of the ascent $\overline{AB}$ and Y is the midpoint of the descent $\overline{CD}$. What is the length of the beam to the nearest foot? 242 ft

Real-World Connections

The Millennium Force Roller Coaster

Reading Strategies

ENGLISH LANGUAGE LEARNERS

Make sure that students understand what the words *ascent* and *descent* mean. If students are unfamiliar with the terms, ask them if they can guess their meanings from context clues in the problems.

Using Data Have students identify the segments in the figure that represent the ascent and descent. $\overline{AB}$; $\overline{CD}$ Ask students to identify a 45°-45°-90° right triangle in the figure. the rt. △ with $\overline{AB}$ as its hyp.

Problem-Solving Focus

For **Problem 2,** focus on the final step of the problem-solving process: **(4) Look Back.** In particular, ask students if their answer seems reasonable. Based on their experiences with roller coasters, does the amount of time for the ascent seem realistic? If not, encourage students to check their work for errors.

Similarity

Section 7A	Section 7B
Similarity Relationships	**Applying Similarity**
7-1 Ratio and Proportion	**7-4 Technology Lab** Investigate Angle Bisectors of a Triangle
7-2 Technology Lab Explore the Golden Ratio	**7-4 Applying Properties of Similar Triangles**
7-2 Ratios in Similar Polygons	**7-5 Using Proportional Relationships**
7-3 Technology Lab Predict Triangle Similarity Relationships	**7-6 Dilations and Similarity in the Coordinate Plane**
7-3 Triangle Similarity: AA, SSS, and SAS	**Connecting Geometry to Algebra** Direct Variation

Pacing Guide for 45-Minute Classes

Teacher One Stop™
Calendar Planner®

Chapter 7

Countdown Weeks 15, 16

DAY 1	DAY 2	DAY 3	DAY 4	DAY 5
7-1 Lesson	7-1 Technology Lab	7-2 Lesson	7-3 Technology Lab	7-3 Lesson
DAY 6	**DAY 7**	**DAY 8**	**DAY 9**	**DAY 10**
7-3 Lesson	Multi-Step Test Prep Ready to Go On?	7-4 Technology Lab 7-4 Lesson	7-4 Lesson	7-5 Lesson
DAY 11	**DAY 12**	**DAY 13**	**DAY 14**	**DAY 15**
7-6 Lesson	7-6 Lesson Connecting Geometry to Algebra	Multi-Step Test Prep Ready to Go On?	Chapter 7 Review	Chapter 7 Test

Pacing Guide for 90-Minute Classes

Teacher One Stop™
Calendar Planner®

Chapter 7

DAY 1	DAY 2	DAY 3	DAY 4	DAY 5
Chapter 6 Test 7-1 Lesson	7-1 Technology Lab 7-2 Lesson	7-3 Technology Lab 7-3 Lesson	7-3 Lesson Multi-Step Test Prep Ready to Go On?	7-4 Technology Lab 7-4 Lesson
DAY 6	**DAY 7**	**DAY 8**		
7-5 Lesson 7-6 Lesson	7-6 Lesson Connecting Geometry to Algebra Multi-Step Test Prep Ready to Go On?	Chapter 7 Review Chapter 7 Test		

ONGOING ASSESSMENT and INTERVENTION

Assess Prior Knowledge

Before Chapter 7

DIAGNOSE	PRESCRIBE
Diagnose readiness for the chapter.	Prescribe intervention.
Are You Ready? SE p. 451	 ***Are You Ready? Intervention***

Formative Assessment

Before Every Lesson

DIAGNOSE	PRESCRIBE
Diagnose readiness for the lesson.	Prescribe intervention.
Warm Up TE	**Reteach** CRB

During Every Lesson

DIAGNOSE	PRESCRIBE
Diagnose understanding of lesson concepts.	Prescribe intervention.
Check It Out! SE	**Reading Strategies** CRB
Questioning Strategies TE	***Success for Every Learner***
Think and Discuss SE	***Lesson Tutorial Videos***
Write About It SE	
Journal TE	

After Every Lesson

DIAGNOSE	PRESCRIBE
Diagnose mastery of lesson concepts.	Prescribe intervention.
Lesson Quiz TE	**Reteach** CRB
Test Prep SE	**Test Prep Doctor** TE
Test and Practice Generator	***Homework Help* Online**

Before Chapter 7 Testing

DIAGNOSE	PRESCRIBE
Diagnose mastery of concepts in chapter.	Prescribe intervention.
Ready to Go On? SE pp. 479, 503	***Ready to Go On? Intervention***
Multi-Step Test Prep SE pp. 478, 502	**Scaffolding Questions** TE pp. 478, 502
Section Quizzes AR	**Reteach** CRB
Test and Practice Generator	***Lesson Tutorial Videos***

Before High Stakes Testing

DIAGNOSE	PRESCRIBE
Diagnose mastery of benchmark concepts.	Prescribe intervention.
College Entrance Exam Practice SE p. 509	***College Entrance Exam Practice***
Standardized Test Prep SE pp. 512–513	

Summative Assessment

After Chapter 7

DIAGNOSE	PRESCRIBE
Check mastery of chapter concepts.	Prescribe intervention.
Multiple-Choice Tests (Forms A, B, C)	**Reteach** CRB
Free-Response Tests (Forms A, B, C)	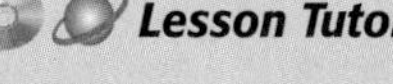 ***Lesson Tutorial Videos***
Performance Assessment AR	
Cumulative Test AR	
Test and Practice Generator	

KEY: **SE** = *Student Edition* **TE** = *Teacher's Edition* **CRB** = *Chapter Resource Book* **AR** = *Assessment Resources* Available online 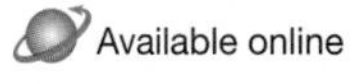 Available on CD- or DVD-ROM

Lesson Resources

Before the Lesson

Prepare ***Teacher One Stop***  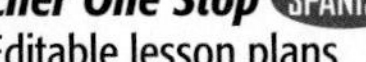
- Editable lesson plans
- Calendar Planner
- Easy access to all chapter resources

Lesson Transparencies
- Teacher Tools

Teach the Lesson

Introduce ***Alternate Openers: Explorations***

Lesson Transparencies
- Warm Up
- Problem of the Day

Teach ***Lesson Transparencies***
- Teaching Transparencies

Know-It Notebook™
- Vocabulary
- Key Concepts

Power Presentations

Lesson Tutorial Videos  SPANISH

Interactive Online Edition 
- Lesson Activities
- Lesson Tutorial Videos

Lab Activities

Lab Resources Online

Online Interactivities  SPANISH

TechKeys  

Practice the Lesson

Practice ***Chapter Resources***
- Practice A, B, C

Practice and Problem Solving Workbook

IDEA Works!® Modified Worksheets and Tests

ExamView Test and Practice Generator

Homework Help Online

Online Interactivities SPANISH

Interactive Online Edition 
- Homework Help

Apply ***Chapter Resources***
- Problem Solving

Practice and Problem Solving Workbook

Interactive Online Edition
- Chapter Project

Project Teacher Support 

After the Lesson

Reteach ***Chapter Resources***
- Reteach
- Reading Strategies  ELL

Success for Every Learner

Review ***Interactive Answers and Solutions***

Solutions Key

Know-It Notebook™
- Big Ideas
- Chapter Review

Extend ***Chapter Resources***
- Challenge

Technology Highlights for the Teacher

 **Power Presentations**

Dynamic presentations to engage students. Complete PowerPoint® presentations for every lesson in Chapter 7.

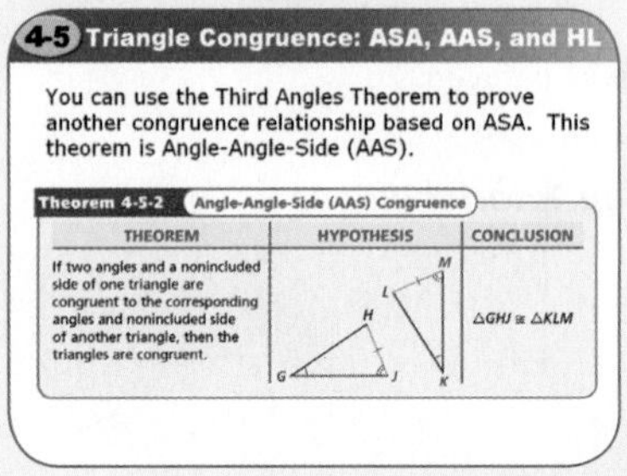

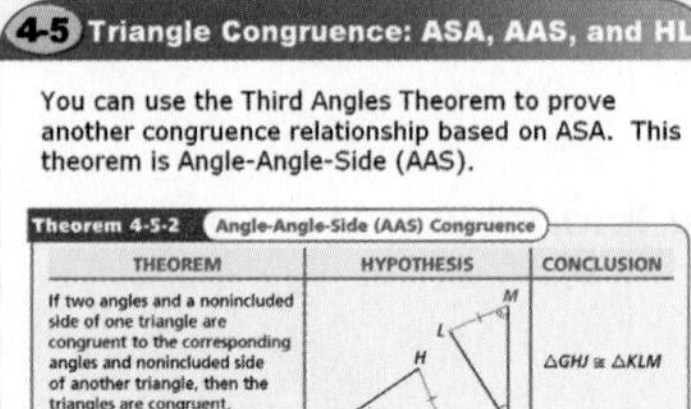

 **Teacher One Stop** SPANISH

Easy access to Chapter 7 resources and assessments. Includes lesson planning, test generation, and puzzle creation software.

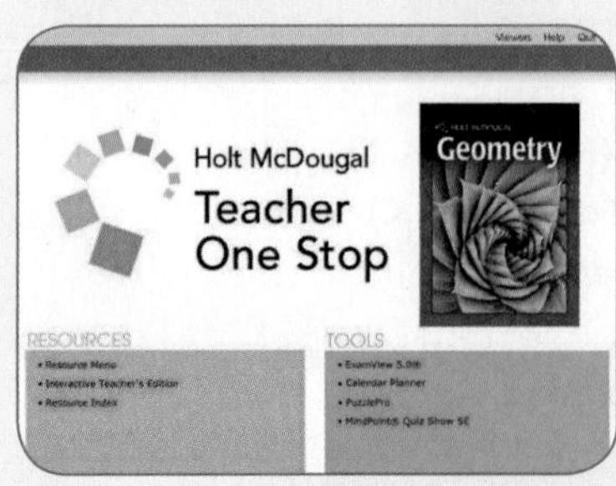

 **Premier Online Edition** 

Chapter 7 includes Tutorial Videos, Lesson Activities, Lesson Quizzes, Homework Help, and Chapter Project.

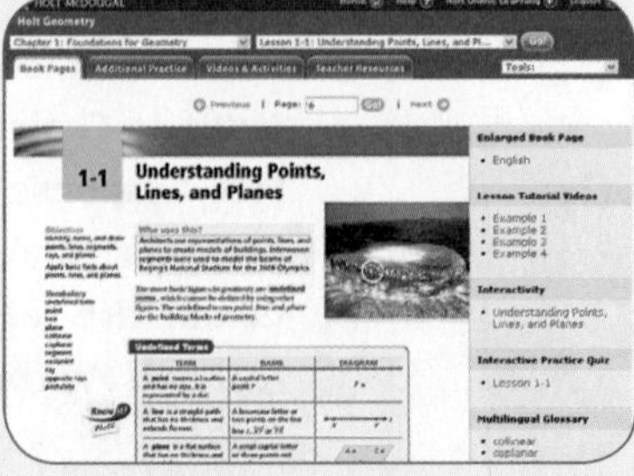

KEY: **SE** = *Student Edition* **TE** = *Teacher's Edition* 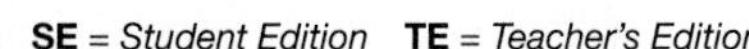 ELL English Language Learners  SPANISH Spanish version available   Available online  Available on CD- or DVD-ROM

Reaching All Learners

Teaching tips to help all learners appear throughout the chapter. A few that target specific students are included in the lists below.

All Learners

Lab Activities
Practice and Problem Solving Workbook
Know-It Notebook

Special Needs Students

Practice A .... CRB
Reteach .... CRB
Reading Strategies .... CRB
Are You Ready? .... SE p. 451
Inclusion .... TE pp. 456, 463, 471, 473, 491
IDEA Works!® Modified Worksheets and Tests
Ready to Go On? Intervention SPANISH
Know-It Notebook
Online Interactivities 
Lesson Tutorial Videos 

Developing Learners

Practice A .... CRB
Reteach .... CRB
Reading Strategies .... CRB
Are You Ready? .... SE p. 451
Vocabulary Connections .... SE p. 452
Questioning Strategies .... TE
Ready to Go On? Intervention SPANISH
Know-It Notebook
Homework Help Online 
Online Interactivities 
Lesson Tutorial Videos 

On-Level Learners

Practice B .... CRB
Problem Solving .... CRB
Vocabulary Connections .... SE p. 452
Questioning Strategies .... TE
Ready to Go On? Intervention SPANISH
Know-It Notebook
Homework Help Online 
Online Interactivities SPANISH

Advanced Learners

Practice C .... CRB
Challenge .... CRB
Challenge Exercises .... SE
Reading and Writing Math *Extend* .... TE p. 453
Critical Thinking .... TE pp. 482, 485, 494, 496
Are You Ready? Enrichment SPANISH
Ready To Go On? Enrichment 

English Language Learners

ENGLISH LANGUAGE LEARNERS

Reading Strategies .... CRB
Are You Ready? Vocabulary .... SE p. 451
Vocabulary Connections .... SE p. 452
Vocabulary Review .... SE p. 504
English Language Learners .... TE pp. 483, 496
Success for Every Learner
Know-It Notebook
Spanish Study Guide (Resumen y Repaso)
Multilingual Glossary
Lesson Tutorial Videos  

Technology Highlights for Reaching All Learners

Lesson Tutorial Videos 

Starring Holt authors Ed Burger and Freddie Renfro! Live tutorials to support every lesson in Chapter 7.

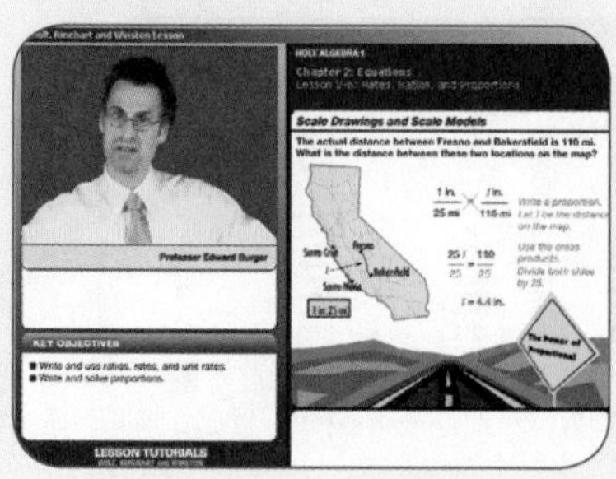

Multilingual Glossary

Searchable glossary includes definitions in English, Spanish, Vietnamese, Chinese, Hmong, Korean, and 4 other languages.

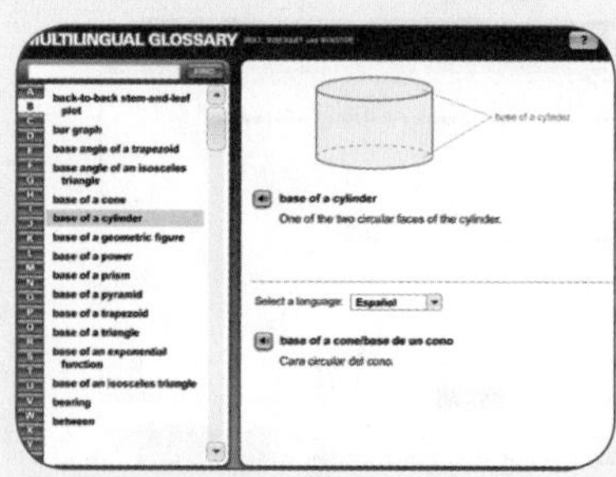

Online Interactivities

Interactive tutorials provide visually engaging alternative opportunities to learn concepts and master skills.

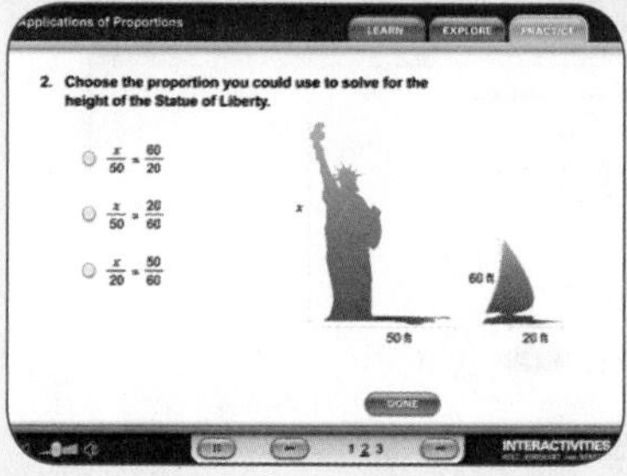

KEY: **SE** = *Student Edition* **TE** = *Teacher's Edition* **CRB** = *Chapter Resource Book* SPANISH Spanish version available · Available online · Available on CD- or DVD-ROM

CHAPTER 7

Ongoing Assessment

Assessing Prior Knowledge

Determine whether students have the prerequisite concepts and skills for success in Chapter 7.

Are You Ready? SPANISH .... SE p. 451
Warm Up .... TE

Test Preparation

Provide review and practice for Chapter 7 and standardized tests.

Multi-Step Test Prep .... SE pp. 478, 502
Study Guide: Review .... SE pp. 504–507
Test Tackler .... SE pp. 510–511
Standardized Test Prep .... SE pp. 512–513
College Entrance Exam Practice .... SE p. 509
Countdown to Testing .... SE pp. C4-C27
IDEA Works!® Modified Worksheets and Tests

Alternative Assessment

Assess students' understanding of Chapter 7 concepts and combined problem-solving skills.

Chapter 7 Project .... SE p. 450
Alternative Assessment .... TE
Performance Assessment .... AR
Portfolio Assessment .... AR

Lesson Assessment

Provide formative assessment for each lesson of Chapter 7.

Questioning Strategies .... TE
Think and Discuss .... SE
Check It Out! Exercises .... SE
Write About It .... SE
Journal .... TE
Lesson Quiz .... TE
Alternative Assessment .... TE
IDEA Works!® Modified Worksheets and Tests

Weekly Assessment

Provide formative assessment for each section of Chapter 7.

Multi-Step Test Prep .... SE pp. 478, 502
Ready to Go On? SPANISH .... SE pp. 479, 503
Section Quizzes .... AR
Test and Practice Generator .... *Teacher One Stop*

Chapter Assessment

Provide summative assessment of Chapter 7 mastery.

Chapter 7 Test .... SE p. 508
Chapter Test (Levels A, B, C) .... AR
- Multiple Choice
- Free Response

Cumulative Test .... AR
Test and Practice Generator .... *Teacher One Stop*
IDEA Works!® Modified Worksheets and Tests

Technology Highlights for Assessment

 **Are You Ready?** 

Automatically assess readiness and prescribe intervention for Chapter 7 prerequisite skills.

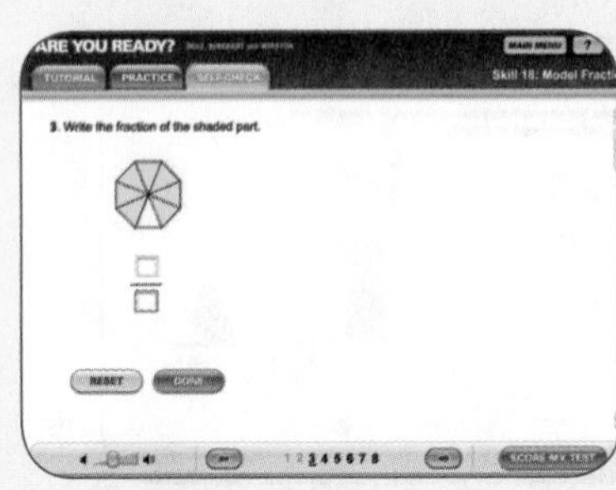

Ready to Go On?

Automatically assess understanding of and prescribe intervention for Sections 7A and 7B.

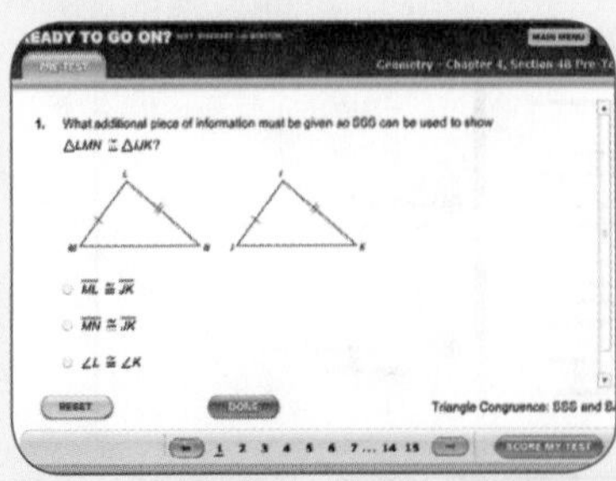

Test and Practice Generator

Use Chapter 7 problem banks to create assessments and worksheets to print out or deliver online. Includes dynamic problems.

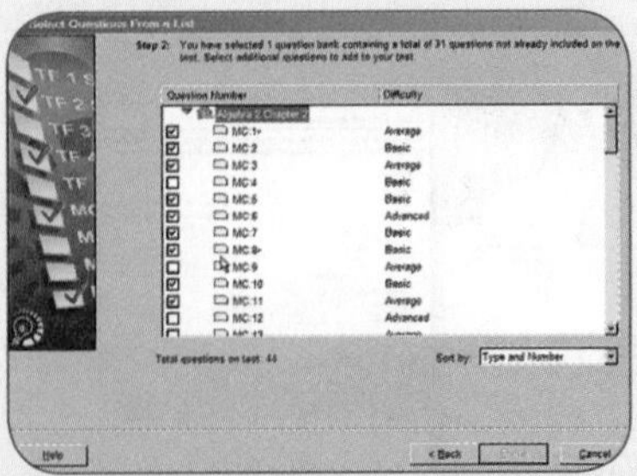

KEY: **SE** = *Student Edition* **TE** = *Teacher's Edition* **AR** = *Assessment Resources* SPANISH Spanish version available  Available online  Available on CD- or DVD-ROM

Formal Assessment

Three levels (A, B, C) of multiple-choice and free-response chapter tests, along with a performance assessment, are available in the *Assessment Resources.*

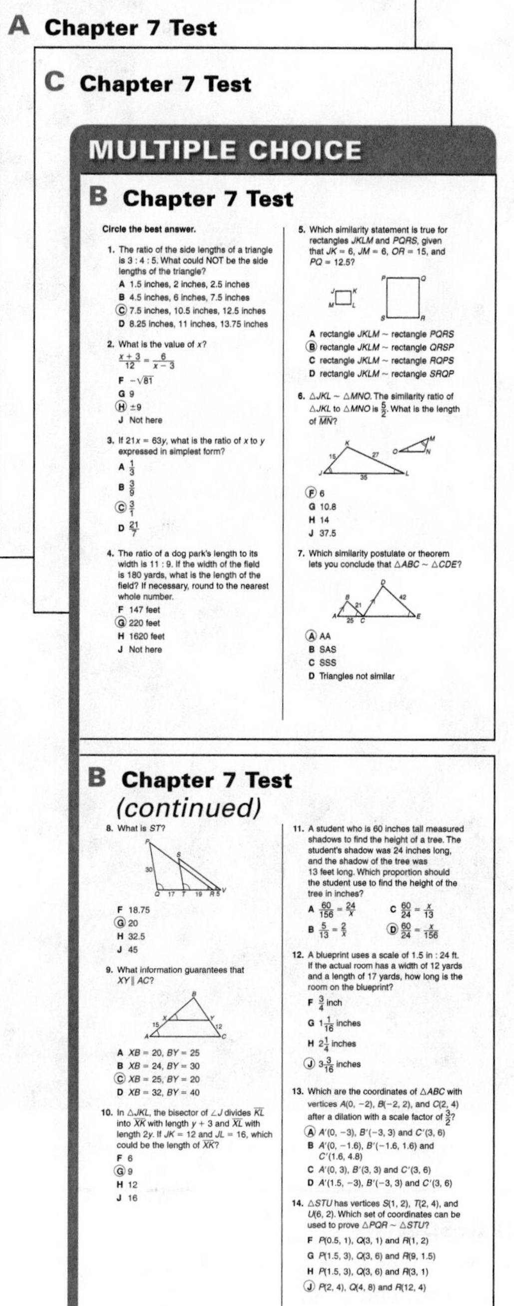

A Chapter 7 Test

C Chapter 7 Test

MULTIPLE CHOICE

B Chapter 7 Test

Circle the best answer.

1. The ratio of the side lengths of a triangle is 3 : 4 : 5. What could NOT be the side lengths of the triangle?
   A 1.5 inches, 2 inches, 2.5 inches
   B 4.5 inches, 6 inches, 7.5 inches
   (C) 7.5 inches, 10.5 inches, 12.5 inches
   D 8.25 inches, 11 inches, 13.75 inches

2. What is the value of x?
   $\frac{x+3}{12} = \frac{6}{x-3}$
   F $-\sqrt{81}$
   G 9
   (H) ± 9
   J Not here

3. If $21x = 63y$, what is the ratio of x to y expressed in simplest form?
   A $\frac{1}{3}$
   B $\frac{3}{9}$
   (C) $\frac{3}{1}$
   D $\frac{21}{7}$

4. The ratio of a dog park's length to its width is 11 : 9. If the width of the field is 180 yards, what is the length of the field? If necessary, round to the nearest whole number.
   F 147 feet
   (G) 220 feet
   H 1620 feet
   J Not here

5. Which similarity statement is true for rectangles $JKLM$ and $PQRS$, given that $JK = 6$, $JM = 6$, $QR = 15$, and $PQ = 12.5$?
   A rectangle $JKLM \sim$ rectangle $PQRS$
   (B) rectangle $JKLM \sim$ rectangle $QRSP$
   C rectangle $JKLM \sim$ rectangle $RQPS$
   D rectangle $JKLM \sim$ rectangle $SRQP$

6. $\triangle JKL \sim \triangle MNO$. The similarity ratio of $\triangle JKL$ to $\triangle MNO$ is $\frac{5}{2}$. What is the length of $\overline{MN}$?
   (F) 6
   G 10.8
   H 14
   J 37.5

7. Which similarity postulate or theorem lets you conclude that $\triangle ABC \sim \triangle CDE$?
   (A) AA
   B SAS
   C SSS
   D Triangles not similar

B Chapter 7 Test (continued)

8. What is ST?
   F 18.75
   (G) 20
   H 32.5
   J 45

9. What information guarantees that $XY \parallel AC$?
   A $XB = 20$, $BY = 25$
   B $XB = 24$, $BY = 30$
   (C) $XB = 25$, $BY = 20$
   D $XB = 32$, $BY = 40$

10. In $\triangle JKL$, the bisector of $\angle J$ divides $\overline{KL}$ into $\overline{XK}$ with length $y + 3$ and $\overline{XL}$ with length $2y$. If $JK = 12$ and $JL = 16$, which could be the length of $\overline{XK}$?
    F 6
    (G) 9
    H 12
    J 16

11. A student who is 60 inches tall measured shadows to find the height of a tree. The student's shadow was 24 inches long, and the shadow of the tree was 13 feet long. Which proportion should the student use to find the height of the tree in inches?
    A $\frac{60}{156} = \frac{24}{x}$
    B $\frac{5}{13} = \frac{2}{x}$
    C $\frac{60}{24} = \frac{x}{13}$
    (D) $\frac{60}{24} = \frac{x}{156}$

12. A blueprint uses a scale of 1.5 in : 24 ft. If the actual room has a width of 12 yards and a length of 17 yards, how long is the room on the blueprint?
    F $\frac{3}{4}$ inch
    G $1\frac{1}{16}$ inches
    H $2\frac{1}{4}$ inches
    (J) $3\frac{3}{16}$ inches

13. Which are the coordinates of $\triangle ABC$ with vertices $A(0, -2)$, $B(-2, 2)$, and $C(2, 4)$ after a dilation with a scale factor of $\frac{3}{2}$?
    (A) $A'(0, -3)$, $B'(-3, 3)$ and $C'(3, 6)$
    B $A'(0, -1.6)$, $B'(-1.6, 1.6)$ and $C'(1.6, 4.8)$
    C $A'(0, 3)$, $B'(3, 3)$ and $C'(3, 6)$
    D $A'(1.5, -3)$, $B'(-3, 3)$ and $C'(3, 6)$

14. $\triangle STU$ has vertices $S(1, 2)$, $T(2, 4)$, and $U(6, 2)$. Which set of coordinates can be used to prove $\triangle PQR \sim \triangle STU$?
    F $P(0.5, 1)$, $Q(3, 1)$ and $R(1, 2)$
    G $P(1.5, 3)$, $Q(3, 6)$ and $R(9, 1.5)$
    H $P(1.5, 3)$, $Q(3, 6)$ and $R(3, 1)$
    (J) $P(2, 4)$, $Q(4, 8)$ and $R(12, 4)$

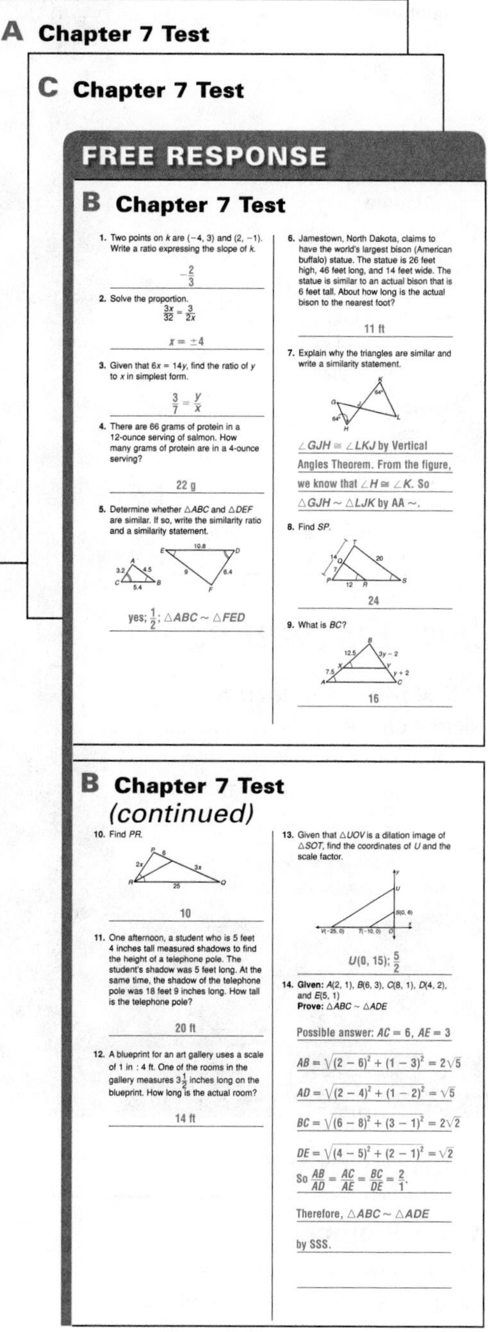

A Chapter 7 Test

C Chapter 7 Test

FREE RESPONSE

B Chapter 7 Test

1. Two points on k are $(-4, 3)$ and $(2, -1)$. Write a ratio expressing the slope of k.
   $-\frac{2}{3}$

2. Solve the proportion.
   $\frac{3x}{32} = \frac{3}{2x}$
   $x = \pm 4$

3. Given that $6x = 14y$, find the ratio of y to x in simplest form.
   $\frac{3}{7} = \frac{y}{x}$

4. There are 66 grams of protein in a 12-ounce serving of salmon. How many grams of protein are in a 4-ounce serving?
   22 g

5. Determine whether $\triangle ABC$ and $\triangle DEF$ are similar. If so, write the similarity ratio and a similarity statement.
   yes; $\frac{1}{2}$; $\triangle ABC \sim \triangle FED$

6. Jamestown, North Dakota, claims to have the world's largest bison (American buffalo) statue. The statue is 26 feet high, 46 feet long, and 14 feet wide. The statue is similar to an actual bison that is 6 feet tall. About how long is the actual bison to the nearest foot?
   11 ft

7. Explain why the triangles are similar and write a similarity statement.
   $\angle GJH \cong \angle LKJ$ by Vertical Angles Theorem. From the figure, we know that $\angle H \cong \angle K$. So $\triangle GJH \sim \triangle LJK$ by AA ~.

8. Find SP.
   24

9. What is BC?
   16

B Chapter 7 Test (continued)

10. Find PR.
    10

11. One afternoon, a student who is 5 feet 4 inches tall measured shadows to find the height of a telephone pole. The student's shadow was 5 feet long. At the same time, the shadow of the telephone pole was 18 feet 9 inches long. How tall is the telephone pole?
    20 ft

12. A blueprint for an art gallery uses a scale of 1 in : 4 ft. One of the rooms in the gallery measures $3\frac{1}{2}$ inches long on the blueprint. How long is the actual room?
    14 ft

13. Given that $\triangle UOV$ is a dilation image of $\triangle SOT$, find the coordinates of U and the scale factor.
    $U(0, 15)$; $\frac{5}{2}$

14. **Given:** $A(2, 1)$, $B(6, 3)$, $C(8, 1)$, $D(4, 2)$, and $E(5, 1)$
    Prove: $\triangle ABC \sim \triangle ADE$
    Possible answer: $AC = 6$, $AE = 3$
    $AB = \sqrt{(2-6)^2 + (1-3)^2} = 2\sqrt{5}$
    $AD = \sqrt{(2-4)^2 + (1-2)^2} = \sqrt{5}$
    $BC = \sqrt{(6-8)^2 + (3-1)^2} = 2\sqrt{2}$
    $DE = \sqrt{(4-5)^2 + (2-1)^2} = \sqrt{2}$
    So $\frac{AB}{AD} = \frac{AC}{AE} = \frac{BC}{DE} = \frac{2}{1}$.
    Therefore, $\triangle ABC \sim \triangle ADE$ by SSS.

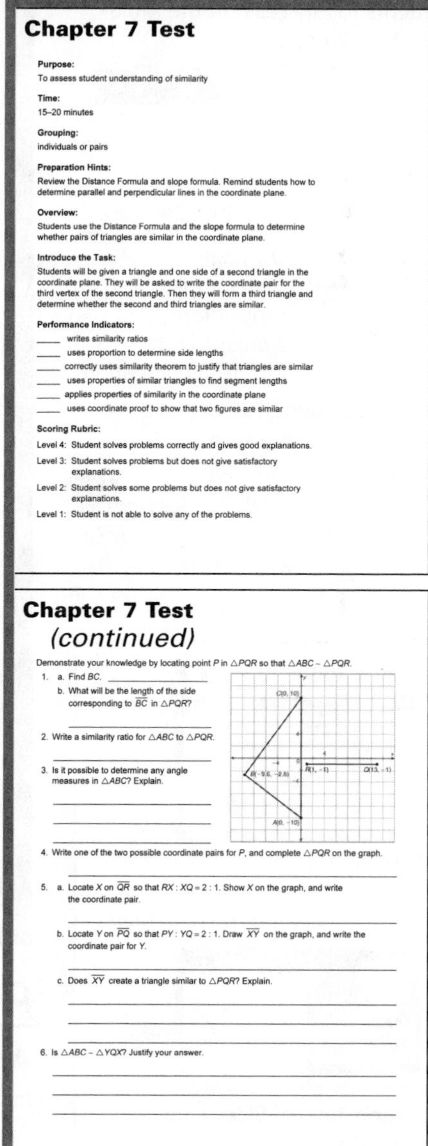

PERFORMANCE ASSESSMENT

Chapter 7 Test

Purpose:
To assess student understanding of similarity

Time:
15–20 minutes

Grouping:
individuals or pairs

Preparation Hints:
Review the Distance Formula and slope formula. Remind students how to determine parallel and perpendicular lines in the coordinate plane.

Overview:
Students use the Distance Formula and the slope formula to determine whether pairs of triangles are similar in the coordinate plane.

Introduce the Task:
Students will be given a triangle and one side of a second triangle in the coordinate plane. They will be asked to write the coordinate pair for the third vertex of the second triangle. Then they will form a third triangle and determine whether the second and third triangles are similar.

Performance Indicators:
_____ writes similarity ratios
_____ uses proportion to determine side lengths
_____ correctly uses similarity theorem to justify that triangles are similar
_____ uses properties of similar triangles to find segment lengths
_____ applies properties of similarity in the coordinate plane
_____ uses coordinate proof to show that two figures are similar

Scoring Rubric:
Level 4: Student solves problems correctly and gives good explanations.
Level 3: Student solves problems but does not give satisfactory explanations.
Level 2: Student solves some problems but does not give satisfactory explanations.
Level 1: Student is not able to solve any of the problems.

Chapter 7 Test (continued)

Demonstrate your knowledge by locating point P in $\triangle PQR$ so that $\triangle ABC \sim \triangle PQR$.

1. a. Find BC. _____
   b. What will be the length of the side corresponding to $\overline{BC}$ in $\triangle PQR$? _____
2. Write a similarity ratio for $\triangle ABC$ to $\triangle PQR$. _____
3. Is it possible to determine any angle measures in $\triangle ABC$? Explain. _____
4. Write one of the two possible coordinate pairs for P, and complete $\triangle PQR$ on the graph. _____
5. a. Locate X on $\overline{QR}$ so that $RX : XQ = 2 : 1$. Show X on the graph, and write the coordinate pair. _____
   b. Locate Y on $\overline{PQ}$ so that $PY : YQ = 2 : 1$. Draw $\overline{XY}$ on the graph, and write the coordinate pair for Y. _____
   c. Does $\overline{XY}$ create a triangle similar to $\triangle PQR$? Explain. _____
6. Is $\triangle ABC \sim \triangle YQX$? Justify your answer. _____

Teacher One Stop™
Test & Practice Generator

Create and customize Chapter 7 Tests. Instantly generate multiple test versions, answer keys, and practice versions of test items.

Modified chapter tests that address special learning needs are available in *IDEA Works!® Modified Worksheets and Tests.*

CHAPTER 7

SECTION 7A
Similarity Relationships

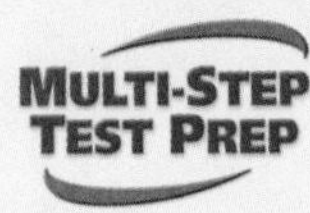

MULTI-STEP TEST PREP On page 478, students apply similarity concepts to solve real-world problems. They use ratios, proportions, and similar triangles to model building a set for a video project.

Exercises designed to prepare students for success on the Multi-Step Test Prep can be found on pages 458, 466, and 476.

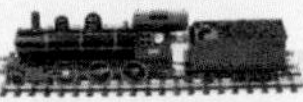

SECTION 7B
Applying Similarity

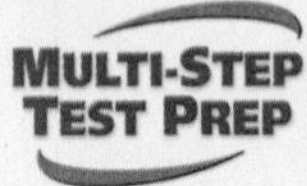

MULTI-STEP TEST PREP On page 502, students apply ratios, proportions, and similar triangles to model a real-world design situation.

Exercises designed to prepare students for success on the Multi-Step Test Prep can be found on pages 486, 492, and 499.

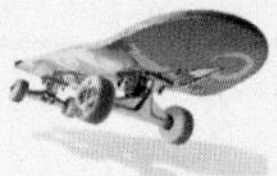

Interactivities Online ▶

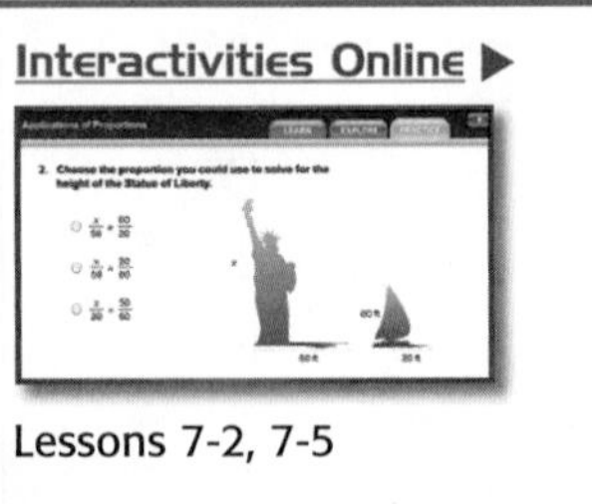

Lessons 7-2, 7-5

Video Lesson Tutorials Online

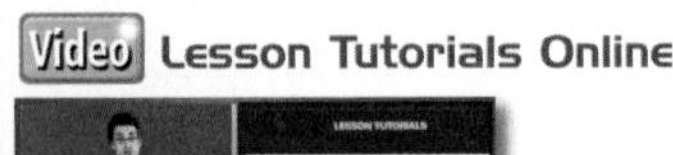

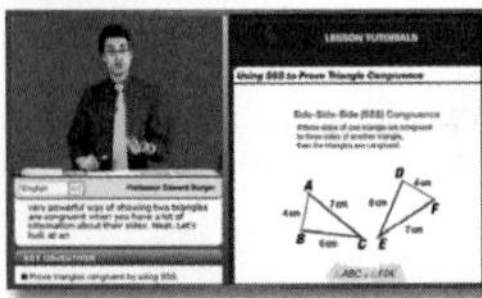

Lesson Tutorial Videos are available for EVERY example.

CHAPTER 7

Similarity

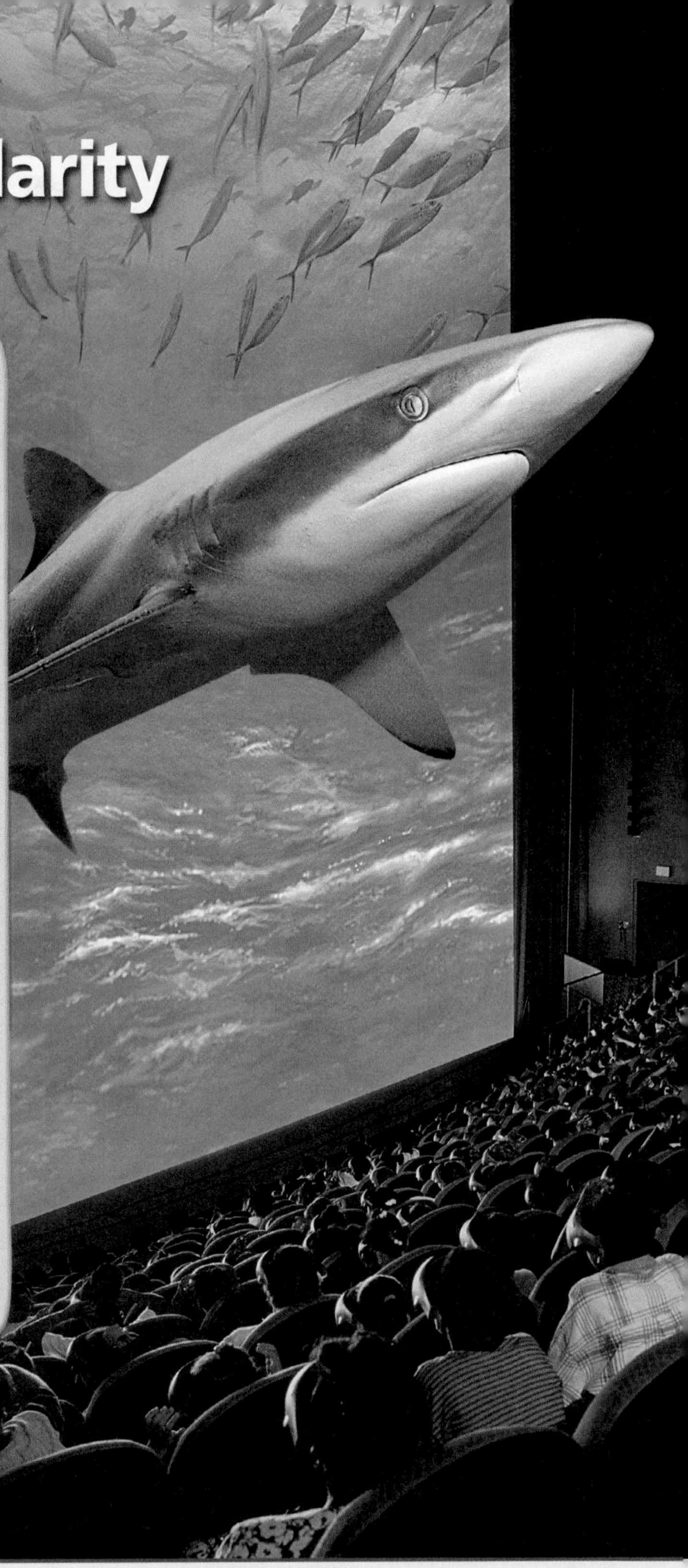

Chapter Focus

- Justify conditions for triangle similarity.
- Apply similarity and proportion to solve real-world problems.

Close Encounters

IMAX films use a wide array of modern technology. The mathematics of similarity and perspective are key to making realistic movie images.

go.hrw.com
Chapter Project Online
KEYWORD: MG7 ChProj

Close Encounters

About the Project

In the Chapter Project, students use everyday materials to construct their own pinhole camera. Then they use similar triangles, ratios, and proportions to understand the mathematics behind the pinhole camera.

Project Resources

All project resources for teachers and students are provided online.

Materials:

- empty coffee can, hammer, nail, cardboard, tape, pin, waxed paper, scissors, rubber band
- meterstick or tape measure

go.hrw.com
Project Teacher Support
KEYWORD: MG7 ProjectTS

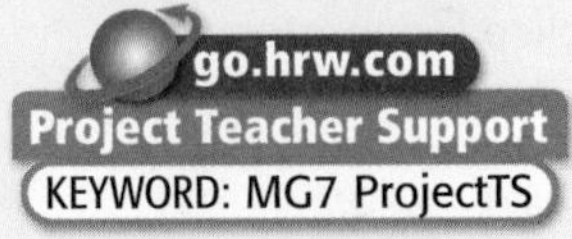

ARE YOU READY?

Vocabulary

Match each term on the left with a definition on the right.

1. side of a polygon E
2. denominator F
3. numerator B
4. vertex of a polygon D
5. vertical angles A

A. two nonadjacent angles formed by two intersecting lines
B. the top number of a fraction, which tells how many parts of a whole are being considered
C. a point that corresponds to one and only one number
D. the intersection of two sides of a polygon
E. one of the segments that form a polygon
F. the bottom number of a fraction, which tells how many equal parts are in the whole

Simplify Fractions

Write each fraction in simplest form.

6. $\frac{16}{20}$ $\frac{4}{5}$
7. $\frac{14}{21}$ $\frac{2}{3}$
8. $\frac{33}{121}$ $\frac{3}{11}$
9. $\frac{56}{80}$ $\frac{7}{10}$

Ratios

Use the table to write each ratio in simplest form.

10. jazz CDs to country CDs 3 to 4
11. hip-hop CDs to jazz CDs 17 to 9
12. rock CDs to total CDs 9 to 28
13. total CDs to country CDs 14 to 3

Ryan's CD Collection	
Rock	36
Jazz	18
Hip-hop	34
Country	24

Identify Polygons

Determine whether each figure is a polygon. If so, name it by the number of sides.

14. 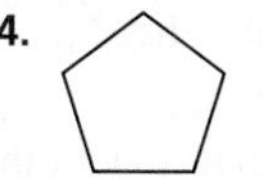 yes; pentagon
15. 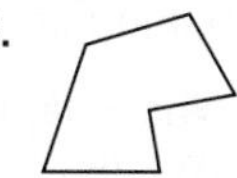 yes; hexagon
16. 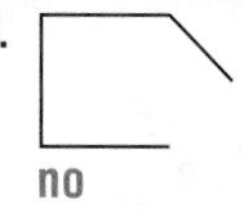 no
17. 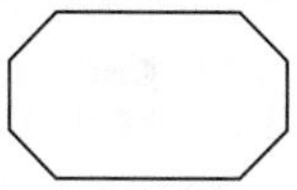  yes; octagon

Find Perimeter

Find the perimeter of each figure.

18. rectangle *PQRS* 25 ft

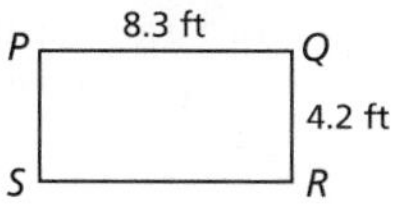

19. regular hexagon *ABCDEF* 180 cm

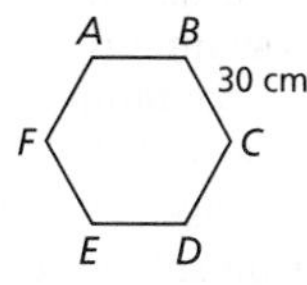

20. rhombus *JKLM* 45.6 m

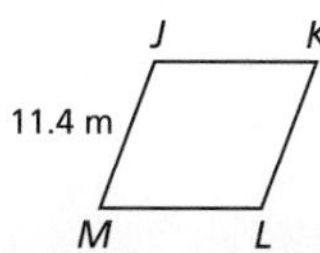

21. regular pentagon *UVWXY* 19.5 in.

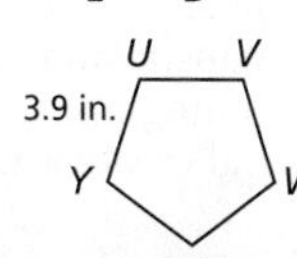

7 ARE YOU READY?

Organizer

Objective: Assess students' understanding of prerequisite skills.

Prerequisite Skills

Simplify Fractions
Ratios
Identify Polygons
Find Perimeter

Assessing Prior Knowledge

INTERVENTION

Diagnose and Prescribe

Use this page to determine whether intervention is necessary or whether enrichment is appropriate.

Resources

 ***Are You Ready? Intervention and Enrichment* Worksheets**

 ***Are You Ready?* CD-ROM**

 ***Are You Ready?* Online**

my.hrw.com

ARE YOU READY?

Diagnose and Prescribe

Prerequisite Skill	*Are You Ready? Intervention*, Chapter 7 Worksheets	CD-ROM	Online
Simply Fractions	Skill 10	Activity 10	Diagnose and Prescribe Online
Ratios	Skill 12	Activity 12	
Identify Polygons	Skill 27	Activity 27	
Find Perimeter	Skill 36	Activity 36	

***Are You Ready? Enrichment*, Chapter 7**
Worksheets
CD-ROM
Online

Study Guide: Preview

Organizer

Objective: Help students organize the new concepts they will learn in Chapter 7.

Online Edition
Multilingual Glossary

Resources

Teacher One Stop™
PuzzleView

***Multilingual Glossary* Online**
go.hrw.com
KEYWORD: MG7 Glossary

Answers to *Vocabulary Connections*

1. One figure is an enlargement (or reduction) of the other.
2. A scale drawing is a drawing that represents an enlargement or reduction of an object.
3. The word *similar* means "alike." Similar polygons are polygons that have the same shape.
4. Possible answer: win/loss ratio, and the aspect ratio of a television screen; both involve a comparison of one quantity to another by means of division.

CHAPTER 7

Study Guide: Preview

Where You've Been

Previously, you

- classified polygons based on their sides and angles.
- used properties of polygons.
- wrote proofs about polygons.

In This Chapter

You will study

- verifying that polygons are similar using corresponding angles and sides.
- using properties of similar polygons.
- writing proofs about similar polygons.

Where You're Going

You can use the skills learned in this chapter

- in Algebra 2 and Precalculus.
- in other classes, such as in Physics when you study the symmetries of nature, in Geography when you look at the symmetry of many natural formations, and in Art.
- outside of school to read maps, plan trips, enlarge photographs, build models, and create art.

Key Vocabulary/Vocabulario

dilation	dilatación
proportion	proporción
ratio	razón
scale	escala
scale drawing	dibujo a escala
scale factor	factor de escala
similar	semejante
similar polygons	polígonos semejantes
similarity ratio	razón de semejanza

Vocabulary Connections

To become familiar with some of the vocabulary terms in the chapter, consider the following. You may refer to the chapter, the glossary, or a dictionary if you like.

1. When an eye doctor dilates your eyes, the pupils become enlarged. What might it mean for one geometric figure to be a **dilation** of another figure?
2. A blueprint is a scale drawing of a building. What do you think is the definition of a **scale drawing**?
3. What does the word *similar* mean in everyday language? What do you think the term **similar polygons** means?
4. Bike riders often talk about gear ratios. Give examples of situations where the word **ratio** is used. What do these examples have in common?

452 Chapter 7

Reading Strategy: Read and Understand the Problem

Many of the concepts you are learning are used in real-world situations. Throughout the text, there are examples and exercises that are real-world word problems. Listed below are strategies for solving word problems.

Problem Solving Strategies

- Read slowly and carefully. Determine what information is given and what you are asked to find.
- If a diagram is provided, read the labels and make sure that you understand the information. If you do not, resketch and relabel the diagram so it makes sense to you. If a diagram is not provided, make a quick sketch and label it.
- Use the given information to set up and solve the problem.
- Decide whether your answer makes sense.

From Lesson 6-1: Look at how the Polygon Exterior Angle Theorem is used in photography.

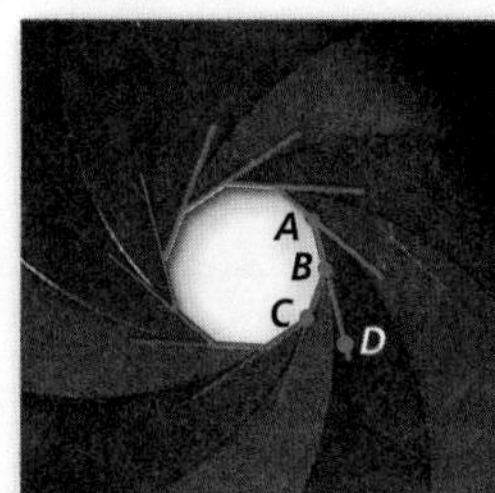

Photography Application

The aperture of the camera shown is formed by ten blades. The blades overlap to form a regular decagon. What is the measure of $\angle CBD$?

Step	Procedure	Result
Understand the Problem	• List the **important information.** • The **answer** will be the measure of $\angle CBD$.	$\angle CBD$ is one of the exterior angles of the regular decagon formed by the apeture.
Make a Plan	• A **diagram** is provided, and it is labeled accurately.	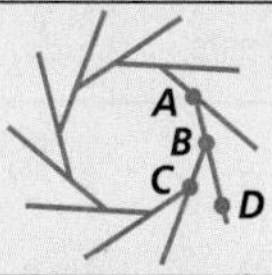 A, B, C, D (diagram)
Solve	• You can use the **Polygon Exterior Angle Theorem.** Then divide to find the measure of **one** of the exterior angles.	$m\angle CBD = \frac{360°}{10} = 36°$
Look Back	• The **answer** is reasonable since a decagon has 10 angles.	$10(36°) = 360°$

Try This

Use the problem-solving strategies for the following problem.

1. A painter's scaffold is constructed so that the braces lie along the diagonals of rectangle *PQRS*. Given $RS = 28$ and $QS = 85$, find QT.

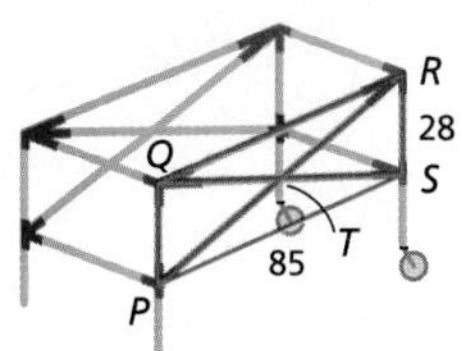

Reading and Writing Math

Organizer

Objective: Help students apply strategies to understand and retain key concepts.

Resources

Chapter 7 Resource Book
Reading Strategies

Reading Strategy: Read and Understand the Problem

Discuss Students benefit from a planned approach to problem-solving.

Extend As students work through Chapter 7, encourage them to list the important information when they begin a problem.

Answers to *Try This*

1. (1) The ans. will be the meas. of $\overline{QT}$. *PQRS* is a rect. with diags. $\overline{RP}$ and $\overline{QS}$.
   (2) The diags. of a rect. bisect each other. So $QT = \frac{1}{2}QS$.
   (3) $QT = \frac{1}{2}(85) = 42.5$
   (4) The answer is reasonable, since $2(42.5) = 85$.

Reading Connection

***Leonardo da Vinci for Kids* by Janis Herbert**

How long is your foot? One-half the distance from your heel to your knee, according to Leonardo da Vinci. This book combines a congenial biography of Da Vinci with 21 activities based on Da Vinci's ideas and experiments. Students will come away impressed not only by Da Vinci's genius but also by the sheer volume of his accomplishments.

Activity Have students carry out the activity "Measuring Up." They'll compare their own body proportions with proportions Da Vinci worked out through scrupulous measurement.

SECTION 7A

Similarity Relationships

One-Minute Section Planner

Lesson	Lab Resources	Materials
Lesson 7-1 Ratio and Proportion • Write and simplify ratios. • Use proportions to solve problems. ☑ SAT-10 ☑ NAEP ☐ ACT ☑ SAT ☑ SAT Subject Tests		**Optional** scale models (e.g., road map, globe, blueprint, replica of building or other structure), rulers (MK)
7-2 Technology Lab Explore the Golden Ratio • Use geometry software to explore the golden ratio and the golden rectangle. ☑ SAT-10 ☑ NAEP ☐ ACT ☐ SAT ☐ SAT Subject Tests	***Technology Lab Activities*** 7-2 Lab Recording Sheet	**Required** rulers (MK), geometry software
Lesson 7-2 Ratios in Similar Polygons • Identify similar polygons. • Apply properties of similar polygons to solve problems. ☑ SAT-10 ☑ NAEP ☐ ACT ☑ SAT ☐ SAT Subject Tests	***Geometry Lab Activities*** 7-2 Geometry Lab	**Optional** pattern blocks (MK), transparency sheets, rulers (MK), graph paper, protractor (MK)
7-3 Technology Lab Predict Triangle Similarity Relationships • Use geometry software to find ways to determine that triangles are similar. ☐ SAT-10 ☑ NAEP ☐ ACT ☐ SAT ☐ SAT Subject Tests	***Technology Lab Activities*** 7-3 Lab Recording Sheet	**Required** geometry software
Lesson 7-3 Triangle Similarity: AA, SSS, SAS • Prove certain triangles are similar by using AA, SSS, and SAS. • Use triangle similarity to solve problems. ☐ SAT-10 ☑ NAEP ☐ ACT ☐ SAT ☐ SAT Subject Tests		**Optional** colored pencils, highlighters, tangrams (MK), protractor (MK)

MK = *Manipulatives Kit*

Math Background

Professional Learning

PROPORTIONS

Lesson 7-1

A *proportion* is an equation that states that two ratios are equal. Students should realize that the steps for solving a proportion such as $\frac{x}{3} = \frac{5}{8}$ are the same as those for solving any other type of equation; that is, the equation must be transformed into simpler equivalent equations with the goal of isolating the variable on one side of the equation. A possible first step in solving $\frac{x}{3} = \frac{5}{8}$ is to clear the fractions by multiplying both sides of the equation by $3 \cdot 8$ or 24. This results in the equivalent equation $8x = 15$, which may be solved by dividing both sides by 8.

Performing the initial multiplication on a general proportion leads to an important short cut—the Cross Product Property. This property states that if $\frac{a}{b} = \frac{c}{d}$, where $b \neq 0$ and $d \neq 0$, then $ad = bc$. To see why the Cross Product Property is true, begin by multiplying both sides of the proportion $\frac{a}{b} = \frac{c}{d}$ by bd.

$$\frac{a}{b} = \frac{c}{d},$$

$$(bd)\frac{a}{b} = (bd)\frac{c}{d}, \quad \textit{Multiplication Property of Equality}$$

$$\frac{bda}{b} = \frac{bdc}{d} \quad \textit{Multiply.}$$

$$da = bc \quad \textit{Simplify.}$$

$$ad = bc \quad \textit{Commutative Property of Mult.}$$

Note that the Cross Product Property may be stated as a biconditional: $\frac{a}{b} = \frac{c}{d}$ if and only if $ad = bc$, where $b \neq 0$ and $d \neq 0$.

SIMILARITY

Lessons 7-2, 7-3

We often describe two figures as *similar* if they have the same shape but not necessarily the same size. Although this gives an intuitive idea of what is meant by the term *similar,* the statement is not a mathematical definition because it does not specify what is meant by *same shape.* For polygons, the formal definition is as follows. Two polygons are similar if and only if their corresponding angles are congruent and their corresponding sides are proportional.

Notice that the definition specifies that two conditions must be met in order to state that two polygons are similar. The following examples of nonsimilar polygons clarify why both conditions are important.

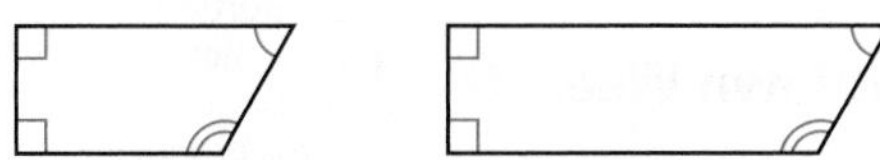

Corresponding angles congruent
Corresponding sides not proportional

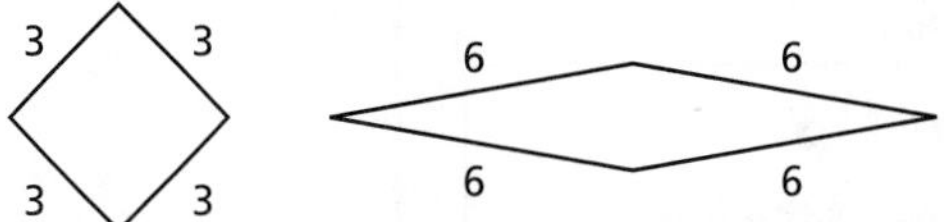

Corresponding sides proportional
Corresponding angles not congruent

For triangles, the situation is simpler. Either one of the two conditions is enough to guarantee that two triangles are similar. This is precisely what is stated in the AA Similarity Postulate and the SSS Similarity Theorem. (Note that an AAA Similarity Postulate is not required because of the Third Angles Theorem. Given two triangles, if two pairs of corresponding angles are congruent, then the remaining pair of corresponding angles must also be congruent.)

Recall that two figures can be defined as *congruent* if there is a sequence of isometries—reflections, translations, and/or rotations—that maps one figure onto the other. Likewise, similarity may be defined in terms of transformations. In particular, two figures are similar if one may be obtained from the other through a combination of a dilation and one or more isometries. Dilations, which transform figures by enlarging or reducing them, are introduced in Lesson 7-6.

Finally, it is worth noting that similarity is an equivalence relation; that is, similarity is reflexive, symmetric, and transitive. For figures F_1, F_2, and F_3, $F_1 \sim F_1$ (reflexivity); if $F_1 \sim F_2$, then $F_2 \sim F_1$ (symmetry); and if $F_1 \sim F_2$ and $F_2 \sim F_3$, then $F_1 \sim F_3$ (transitivity).

7-1 Organizer

Pacing: Traditional 1 day
Block $\frac{1}{2}$ day

Objectives: Write and simplify ratios.

Use proportions to solve problems.

Online Edition
Tutorial Videos

Countdown Week 15

Power Presentations with PowerPoint®

Warm Up

Find the slope of the line through each pair of points.

1. $(1, 5)$ and $(3, 9)$ 2
2. $(-6, 4)$ and $(6, -2)$ $-\frac{1}{2}$

Solve each equation.

3. $4x + 5x + 6x = 45$ $x = 3$
4. $(x - 5)^2 = 81$ $x = 14$ or $x = -4$
5. Write $\frac{16}{24}$ in simplest form. $\frac{2}{3}$

Also available on transparency

Q: Who invented fractions?

A: Henry the $\frac{1}{8}$!

7-1 Ratio and Proportion

Objectives
Write and simplify ratios.

Use proportions to solve problems.

Vocabulary
ratio
proportion
extremes
means
cross products

Who uses this?
Filmmakers use ratios and proportions when creating special effects. (See Example 5.)

The *Lord of the Rings* movies transport viewers to the fantasy world of Middle Earth. Many scenes feature vast fortresses, sprawling cities, and bottomless mines. To film these images, the moviemakers used *ratios* to help them build highly detailed miniature models.

A **ratio** compares two numbers by division. The ratio of two numbers a and b can be written as a to b, $a:b$, or $\frac{a}{b}$, where $b \neq 0$. For example, the ratios 1 to 2, 1:2, and $\frac{1}{2}$ all represent the same comparison.

Remember!
In a ratio, the denominator of the fraction cannot be zero because division by zero is undefined.

EXAMPLE 1 Writing Ratios

Write a ratio expressing the slope of ℓ.

$$\text{Slope} = \frac{\text{rise}}{\text{run}} = \frac{y_2 - y_1}{x_2 - x_1}$$

$$= \frac{3 - (-1)}{4 - (-2)} \quad \text{Substitute the given values.}$$

$$= \frac{4}{6} = \frac{2}{3} \quad \text{Simplify.}$$

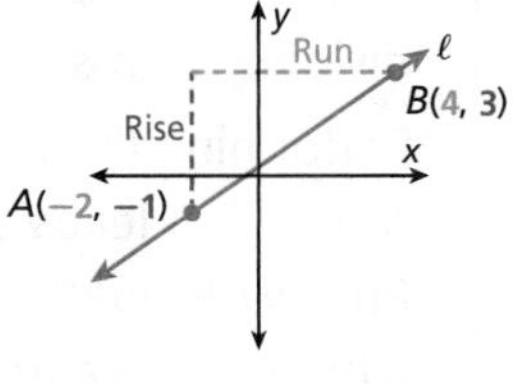

1. Given that two points on m are $C(-2, 3)$ and $D(6, 5)$, write a ratio expressing the slope of m. $\frac{1}{4}$

A ratio can involve more than two numbers. For the rectangle, the ratio of the side lengths may be written as 3:7:3:7.

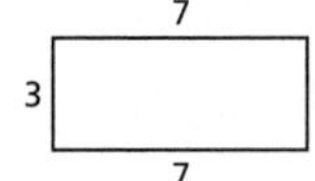

EXAMPLE 2 Using Ratios

The ratio of the side lengths of a quadrilateral is 2:3:5:7, and its perimeter is 85 ft. What is the length of the longest side?

Let the side lengths be $2x$, $3x$, $5x$, and $7x$. Then $2x + 3x + 5x + 7x = 85$. After like terms are combined, $17x = 85$. So $x = 5$. The length of the longest side is $7x = 7(5) = 35$ ft.

2. The ratio of the angle measures in a triangle is 1:6:13. What is the measure of each angle? 9°; 54°; 117°

State Resources

go.hrw.com
State Resources Online
KEYWORD: MG7 Resources

1 Introduce

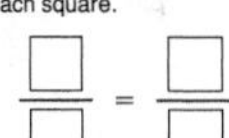

EXPLORATION

7-1 Ratio and Proportion

A *proportion* is an equation stating that two ratios are equal.

1. Use the numbers 1, 3, 4, and 12 to write a proportion. Write one number in each square.
2. There are other ways to use these numbers to fill in the squares. Write as many different proportions as possible.
3. Use the same numbers to write an equation by filling in the circles.
4. All of the equations that you wrote in Steps 1–3 are equivalent. Write the proportion $\frac{a}{b} = \frac{c}{d}$ in as many equivalent forms as you can.

THINK AND DISCUSS

5. **Discuss** whether the proportion $\frac{a}{b} = \frac{c}{d}$ is equivalent to $\frac{a}{d} = \frac{c}{b}$. Give an example using numbers to support your

Motivate

Bring in several items that are scale models, including a two-dimensional and a three-dimensional object. These might consist of a road map for your state, a globe, a blueprint for a house or a school in your district, and a replica of a famous building. Ask students what these *scale models* have in common. same proportions as the original Have students bring in scale models from their art or design classes to present to the class.

Explorations and answers are provided in *Alternate Openers: Explorations Transparencies.*

A **proportion** is an equation stating that two ratios are equal. In the proportion $\frac{a}{b} = \frac{c}{d}$, the values a and d are the **extremes**. The values b and c are the **means**. When the proportion is written as $a:b = c:d$, the extremes are in the first and last positions. The means are in the two middle positions.

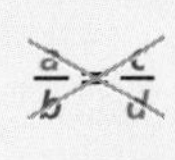

Reading Math

The Cross Products Property can also be stated as, "In a proportion, the product of the extremes is equal to the product of the means."

In Algebra 1 you learned the Cross Products Property. The product of the extremes ad and the product of the means bc are called the **cross products**.

Cross Products Property

In a proportion, if $\frac{a}{b} = \frac{c}{d}$ and b and $d \neq 0$, then $ad = bc$.

$\frac{a}{b} \times \frac{c}{d}$

$ad = bc$

EXAMPLE 3 Solving Proportions

Solve each proportion.

A $\frac{5}{y} = \frac{45}{63}$

$5(63) = y(45)$	*Cross Products Prop.*
$315 = 45y$	*Simplify.*
$y = 7$	*Divide both sides by 45.*

B $\frac{x+2}{6} = \frac{24}{x+2}$

$(x+2)^2 = 6(24)$	*Cross Products Prop.*
$(x+2)^2 = 144$	*Simplify.*
$x + 2 = \pm 12$	*Find the square root of both sides.*
$x + 2 = 12$ or $x + 2 = -12$	*Rewrite as two eqns.*
$x = 10$ or $x = -14$	*Subtract 2 from both sides.*

CHECK IT OUT! Solve each proportion.

3a. $\frac{3}{8} = \frac{x}{56}$ 21 **3b.** $\frac{2y}{9} = \frac{8}{4y}$ ± 3

3c. $\frac{d}{3} = \frac{6}{2}$ 9 **3d.** $\frac{x+3}{4} = \frac{9}{x+3}$ 3 or -9

The following table shows equivalent forms of the Cross Products Property.

Know it! Note

Properties of Proportions

ALGEBRA	NUMBERS
The proportion $\frac{a}{b} = \frac{c}{d}$ is equivalent to the following:	The proportion $\frac{1}{3} = \frac{2}{6}$ is equivalent to the following:
$ad = bc$	$1(6) = 3(2)$
$\frac{b}{a} = \frac{d}{c}$	$\frac{3}{1} = \frac{6}{2}$
$\frac{a}{c} = \frac{b}{d}$	$\frac{1}{2} = \frac{3}{6}$

Power Presentations with PowerPoint®

Additional Examples

Example 1

Write a ratio expressing the slope of ℓ. $-\frac{5}{3}$

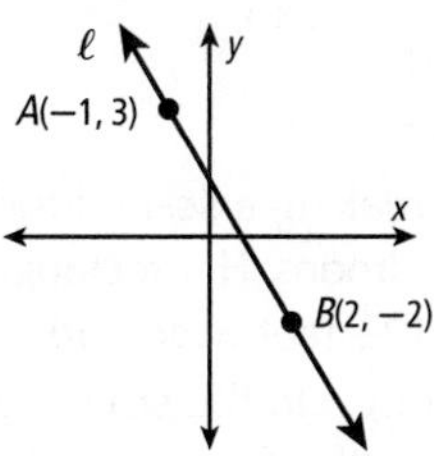

Example 2

The ratio of the side lengths of a triangle is 4:7:5, and its perimeter is 96 cm. What is the length of the shortest side? 24 cm

Example 3

Solve each proportion.

A. $\frac{7}{x} = \frac{56}{72}$ $x = 9$

B. $\frac{z-4}{5} = \frac{20}{z-4}$ $z = 14$ or $z = -6$

INTERVENTION Questioning Strategies

EXAMPLE 1

- How do you know which way to subtract the coordinates when finding the slope?

EXAMPLE 2

- If the ratio of the side lengths of a quadrilateral is 1:1:1:1, what kind of special quadrilateral is it?
- How do you use a ratio of side lengths to write an algebraic expression for perimeter?

EXAMPLE 3

- How can you solve an equation when the variable expression is squared?
- How can you check your solution to a proportion?

2 Teach

Guided Instruction

Explain that a ratio compares two numbers by division. Show why a proportion is an equation that states that two ratios are equal and uses the Cross Products Property to solve. Review the properties of proportions and discuss how to use the properties to solve equations.

Teaching Tip **Algebra** Show students that once the Cross Products Property has been applied, the result is either a linear or a simple quadratic equation that they can solve algebraically.

Reaching All Learners

Through Kinesthetic Experience

Explain to students that the scale on a map gives the ratio of the map distance to the actual distance. Students should use a ruler to measure the distance between two cities. Then estimate the distance between the cities. Emphasize the importance of making accurate measurements and using the correct scale. Rulers can be found in the Manipulatives Kit (MK).

Power Presentations with PowerPoint®

Additional Examples

Example 4

Given that $18c = 24d$, find the ratio of d to c in simplest form. $\frac{3}{4}$ or 3:4

Example 5

Marta is making a scale drawing of her bedroom. Her rectangular room is $12\frac{1}{2}$ feet wide and 15 feet long. On the scale drawing, the width of her room is 5 inches. What is the length? 6 in.

INTERVENTION

Questioning Strategies

EXAMPLE 4

- Did you expect the result of Example 4 to be the reciprocal? Explain.

EXAMPLE 5

- How is algebra used in this application of ratio and proportion?

Teaching Tip **Inclusion** If students make errors in writing proportions in problem-solving applications, show them that it may be easier to write the proportion in words first, and then place the numbers in the ratios.

EXAMPLE 4 Using Properties of Proportions

Reading Math

Since x comes before y in the sentence, x will be in the numerator of the fraction.

Given that $4x = 10y$, find the ratio of x to y in simplest form.

$4x = 10y$

$\frac{x}{y} = \frac{10}{4}$ *Divide both sides by 4y.*

$\frac{x}{y} = \frac{5}{2}$ *Simplify.*

CHECK IT OUT! 4. Given that $16s = 20t$, find the ratio $t:s$ in simplest form. 4:5

EXAMPLE 5 *Problem-Solving Application*

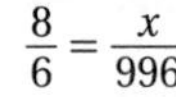

PROBLEM SOLVING

During the filming of *The Lord of the Rings*, the special-effects team built a model of Sauron's tower with a height of 8 m and a width of 6 m. If the width of the full-size tower is 996 m, what is its height?

1 Understand the Problem

The **answer** will be the height of the tower.

2 Make a Plan

Let x be the height of the tower. Write a proportion that compares the ratios of the height to the width.

$$\frac{\text{height of model tower}}{\text{width of model tower}} = \frac{\text{height of full-size tower}}{\text{width of full-size tower}}$$

$$\frac{8}{6} = \frac{x}{996}$$

3 Solve

$\frac{8}{6} = \frac{x}{996}$

$6x = 8(996)$ *Cross Products Prop.*

$6x = 7968$ *Simplify.*

$x = 1328$ *Divide both sides by 6.*

The height of the full-size tower is 1328 m.

4 Look Back

Check the answer in the original problem. The ratio of the height to the width of the model is 8:6, or 4:3. The ratio of the height to the width of the tower is 1328:996. In simplest form, this ratio is also 4:3. So the ratios are equal, and the answer is correct.

CHECK IT OUT! 5. **What if...?** Suppose the special-effects team made a different model with a height of 9.2 m and a width of 6 m. What is the height of the actual tower? 1527.2 m

3 Close

Summarize

To summarize the lesson, lead a discussion based on these questions: "What is the difference between a ratio and a proportion?" Possible answer: A ratio is an expression that compares two quantities, while a proportion is an equation that states that two ratios are equal. "What method can be used to solve any proportion?" Possible answer: Use the Cross Products Property to write an equation, which may be linear or quadratic. Then solve the resulting equation.

ONGOING ASSESSMENT and INTERVENTION

***Diagnose Before* the Lesson**
7-1 Warm Up, TE p. 454

***Monitor During* the Lesson**
Check It Out! Exercises, SE pp. 454–456
Questioning Strategies, TE pp. 455–456

***Assess After* the Lesson**
7-1 Lesson Quiz, TE p. 459
Alternative Assessment, TE p. 459

THINK AND DISCUSS

1. Is the ratio 6 : 7 the same ratio as 7 : 6? Why or why not?
2. Susan wants to know if the fractions $\frac{3}{7}$ and $\frac{12}{28}$ are equivalent. Explain how she can use the properties of proportions to find out.

3. **GET ORGANIZED** Copy and complete the graphic organizer. In the boxes, write the definition of a proportion, the properties of proportions, and examples and nonexamples of a proportion.

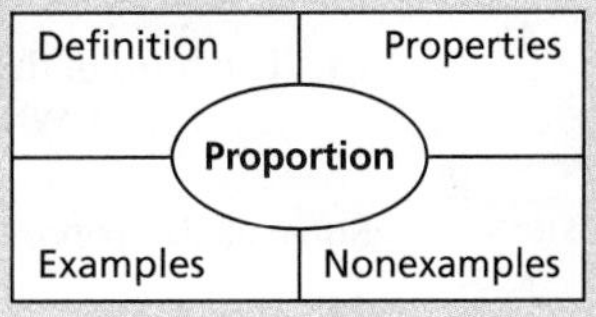

Answers to *Think and Discuss*

1. No; the ratio 6 : 7 is less than 1; the ratio 7 : 6 is greater than 1.
2. She can see if the cross products are =. Since 3(28) = 7(12), the ratios do form a proportion. Therefore the ratios are = and the fractions are equivalent.
3. See p. A6.

7-1 Exercises

go.hrw.com
Homework Help Online
KEYWORD: MG7 7-1
Parent Resources Online
KEYWORD: MG7 Parent

GUIDED PRACTICE

Vocabulary Apply the vocabulary from this lesson to answer each question.

1. Name the means and extremes in the proportion $\frac{1}{3} = \frac{2}{6}$. **means: 3 and 2; extremes: 1 and 6**
2. Write the cross products for the proportion $\frac{s}{t} = \frac{u}{v}$. **sv; tu**

SEE EXAMPLE 1 p. 454

Write a ratio expressing the slope of each line.

3. ℓ $\frac{1}{2}$
4. m $\frac{1}{1}$
5. n $-\frac{2}{3}$

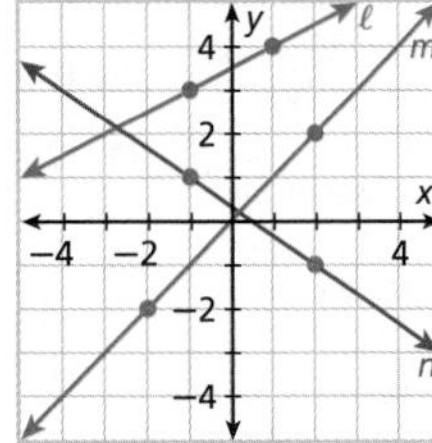

SEE EXAMPLE 2 p. 454

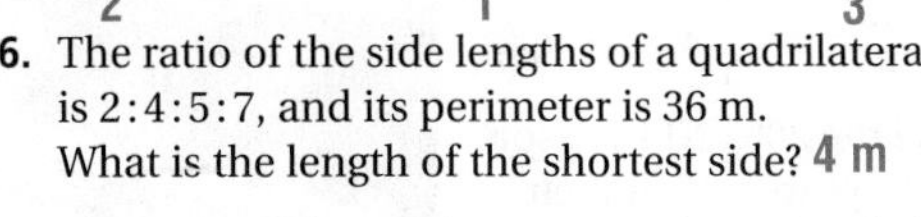

6. The ratio of the side lengths of a quadrilateral is 2 : 4 : 5 : 7, and its perimeter is 36 m. What is the length of the shortest side? **4 m**

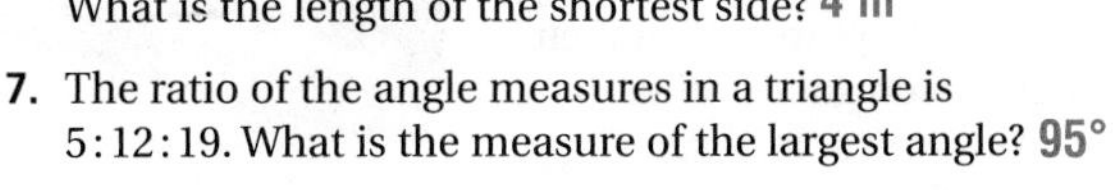

7. The ratio of the angle measures in a triangle is 5 : 12 : 19. What is the measure of the largest angle? **95°**

SEE EXAMPLE 3 p. 455

Solve each proportion.

8. $\frac{x}{2} = \frac{40}{16}$ **5**
9. $\frac{7}{y} = \frac{21}{27}$ **9**
10. $\frac{6}{58} = \frac{t}{29}$ **3**
11. $\frac{y}{3} = \frac{27}{y}$ **±9**
12. $\frac{16}{x-1} = \frac{x-1}{4}$ **9 or −7**
13. $\frac{x^2}{18} = \frac{x}{6}$ **0 or 3**

SEE EXAMPLE 4 p. 456

14. Given that $2a = 8b$, find the ratio of a to b in simplest form. **4 to 1**
15. Given that $6x = 27y$, find the ratio $y : x$ in simplest form. **2 : 9**

SEE EXAMPLE 5 p. 456

16. **Architecture** The Arkansas State Capitol Building is a smaller version of the U.S. Capitol Building. The U.S. Capitol is 752 ft long and 288 ft tall. The Arkansas State Capitol is 564 ft long. What is the height of the Arkansas State Capitol? **216 ft**

7-1 Exercises

Assignment Guide

Assign *Guided Practice* exercises as necessary.

If you finished Examples **1–3**
Basic 17–27, 34–38
Average 17–27, 34–38, 40, 47
Advanced 17–27, 34–37, 41, 51

If you finished Examples **1–5**
Basic 17–32, 35–40, 42–47, 52–59
Average 17–30, 32–36, 39–48, 51–59
Advanced 17–33, 37–59

Homework Quick Check
Quickly check key concepts.
Exercises: 18, 20, 26, 28, 30, 32

State Resources

go.hrw.com
State Resources Online
KEYWORD: MG7 Resources

Visual Help students multiply the correct factors in **Exercises 22–27** by encouraging them to draw two arrows, one through the means and another through the extremes.

Algebra In **Exercise 25,** students may have difficulty solving the proportion if they expand the binomial square. Remind them to leave the product as a square $(2m + 2)^2$ and solve the problem by taking the square root of each side.

Exercise 39 involves setting up a proportion to solve a real-world problem. This exercise prepares students for the Multi-Step Test Prep on page 478.

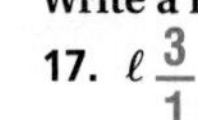

PRACTICE AND PROBLEM SOLVING

Independent Practice

For Exercises	See Example
17–19	1
20–21	2
22–27	3
28–29	4
30	5

Extra Practice
Skills Practice p. S16
Application Practice p. S34

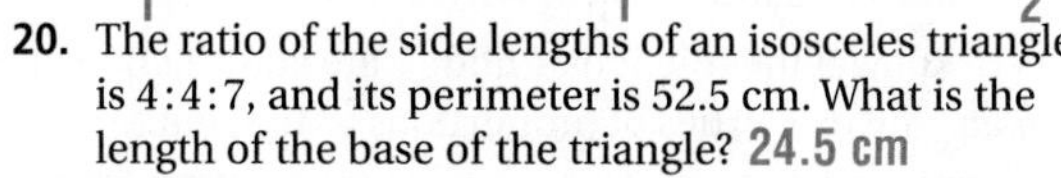

Write a ratio expressing the slope of each line.

17. ℓ $\frac{3}{1}$
18. m $\frac{-1}{1}$
19. n $\frac{3}{2}$

20. The ratio of the side lengths of an isosceles triangle is 4 : 4 : 7, and its perimeter is 52.5 cm. What is the length of the base of the triangle? **24.5 cm**

21. The ratio of the angle measures in a parallelogram is 2 : 3 : 2 : 3. What is the measure of each angle? **72°; 108°; 72°; 108°**

Solve each proportion.

22. $\frac{6}{8} = \frac{9}{y}$ **12**
23. $\frac{x}{14} = \frac{50}{35}$ **20**
24. $\frac{z}{12} = \frac{3}{8}$ **4.5**
25. $\frac{2m+2}{3} = \frac{12}{2m+2}$ **2 or −4**
26. $\frac{5y}{16} = \frac{125}{y}$ **±20**
27. $\frac{x+2}{12} = \frac{5}{x-2}$ **±8**

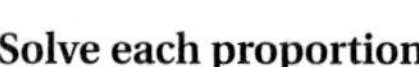

28. Given that $5y = 25x$, find the ratio of x to y in simplest form. $\frac{1}{5}$
29. Given that $35b = 21c$, find the ratio $b : c$ in simplest form. **3 : 5**

Travel

For more than 50 years, Madurodam has been Holland's smallest city. The canal houses, market, airplanes, and windmills are all replicated on a 1 : 25 scale.

Source: madurodam.nl

30. **Travel** Madurodam is a park in the Netherlands that contains a complete Dutch city built entirely of miniature models. One of the models of a windmill is 1.2 m tall and 0.8 m wide. The width of the actual windmill is 20 m. What is its height? **30 m**

Given that $\frac{a}{b} = \frac{5}{7}$, complete each of the following equations.

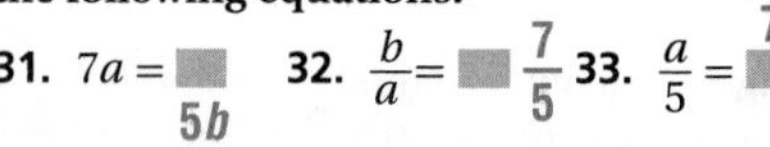

31. $7a = $ ■ **5b**
32. $\frac{b}{a} = $ ■ $\frac{7}{5}$
33. $\frac{a}{5} = $ ■ $\frac{b}{7}$

34. **Sports** During the 2003 NFL season, the Dallas Cowboys won 10 of their 16 regular-season games. What is their ratio of wins to losses in simplest form? **5 : 3**

Write a ratio expressing the slope of the line through each pair of points.

35. $(-6, -4)$ and $(21, 5)$ $\frac{1}{3}$
36. $(16, -5)$ and $(6, 1)$ $-\frac{3}{5}$
37. $\left(6\frac{1}{2}, -2\right)$ and $\left(4, 5\frac{1}{2}\right)$ -3
38. $(-6, 1)$ and $(-2, 0)$ $-\frac{1}{4}$

MULTI-STEP TEST PREP

39. This problem will prepare you for the Multi-Step Test Prep on page 478.
A claymation film is shot on a set that is a scale model of an actual city. On the set, a skyscraper is 1.25 in. wide and 15 in. tall. The actual skyscraper is 800 ft tall.
    a. Write a proportion that you can use to find the width of the actual skyscraper.
    b. Solve the proportion from part **a**. What is the width of the actual skyscraper?

a. $\frac{1.25 \text{ in.}}{15 \text{ in.}} = \frac{x \text{ in.}}{9600 \text{ in.}}$ **b.** $x = 800$ in., or 66 ft 8 in.

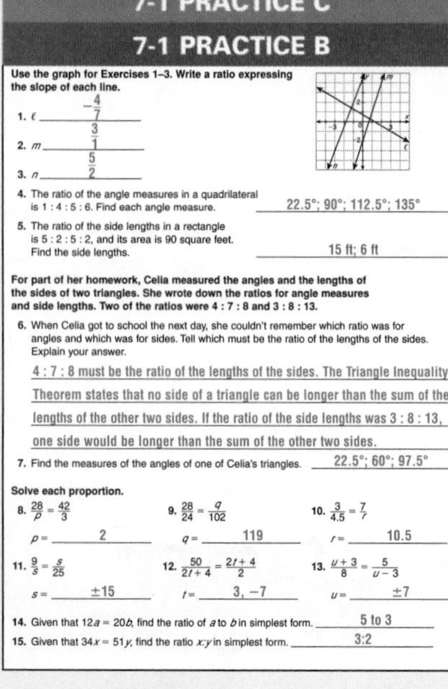

7-1 PRACTICE A
7-1 PRACTICE C
7-1 PRACTICE B

Use the graph for Exercises 1–3. Write a ratio expressing the slope of each line.

1. ℓ $-\frac{4}{7}$
2. m $\frac{3}{1}$
3. n $\frac{5}{2}$

4. The ratio of the angle measures in a quadrilateral is 1 : 4 : 5 : 6. Find each angle measure. 22.5°; 90°; 112.5°; 135°
5. The ratio of the side lengths in a rectangle is 5 : 2 : 5 : 2, and its area is 90 square feet. Find the side lengths. 15 ft; 6 ft

For part of her homework, Celia measured the angles and the lengths of the sides of two triangles. She wrote down the ratios for angle measures and side lengths. Two of the ratios were 4 : 7 : 8 and 3 : 8 : 13.

6. When Celia got to school the next day, she couldn't remember which ratio was for angles and which was for sides. Tell which must be the ratio of the lengths of the sides. Explain your answer.
4 : 7 : 8 must be the ratio of the lengths of the sides. The Triangle Inequality Theorem states that no side of a triangle can be longer than the sum of the lengths of the other two sides. If the ratio of the side lengths was 3 : 8 : 13, one side would be longer than the sum of the other two sides.
7. Find the measures of the angles of one of Celia's triangles. 22.5°; 60°; 97.5°

Solve each proportion.

8. $\frac{28}{p} = \frac{42}{3}$ $p = $ 2
9. $\frac{28}{24} = \frac{q}{102}$ $q = $ 119
10. $\frac{3}{4.5} = \frac{7}{r}$ $r = $ 10.5
11. $\frac{9}{s} = \frac{s}{25}$ $s = $ ±15
12. $\frac{50}{2t+4} = \frac{2t+4}{2}$ $t = $ 3, −7
13. $\frac{u+3}{8} = \frac{5}{u-3}$ $u = $ ±7
14. Given that $12a = 20b$, find the ratio of a to b in simplest form. 5 to 3
15. Given that $34x = 51y$, find the ratio $x:y$ in simplest form. 3:2

7-1 READING STRATEGIES

A **proportion** is an equation showing two equal ratios. The procedure below tells how to write and solve a proportion to find a missing dimension in similar rectangles.

Step 1: Figure out what you need to know. This is the unknown dimension. Make this x.

Step 2: Use x and the other dimensions from the problem to write a proportion comparing length and width.

First figure $\frac{length}{width}$ = Second figure $\frac{length}{width}$

Step 3: Cross multiply the proportion.

$\frac{length}{width} \times \frac{length}{width}$

Step 4: Solve for x.

Step 5: Answer the question in the problem.

A painter is making a smaller version of the painting at right. It will be proportional to the original painting. The original painting is 36 inches long and 30 inches wide. The smaller painting will be 4 inches wide. How long will the smaller painting be? Use the procedure to solve the problem.

30 in.
36 in.
4 in.
?

1. What do you want to find out? the length of the smaller painting
2. Write a proportion.

Original painting / Smaller painting

$\frac{length}{width} \rightarrow \frac{36 \text{ in.}}{30 \text{ in.}} = \frac{x}{4 \text{ in.}}$

3. Cross multiply. Write the resulting equation. (36 in.)(4 in.) = (30 in.)(x)
4. Solve for x. $x = 4.8$ in.
5. What is the length of the smaller painting? 4.8 in.

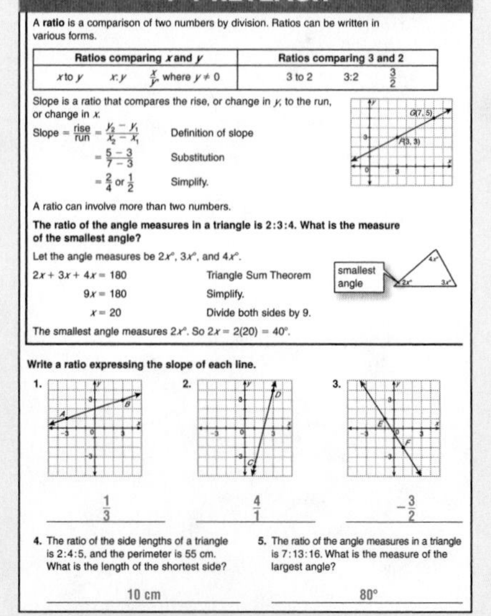

7-1 RETEACH

A **ratio** is a comparison of two numbers by division. Ratios can be written in various forms.

Ratios comparing x and y	Ratios comparing 3 and 2
x to y $\quad x:y \quad \frac{x}{y}$, where $y \neq 0$	3 to 2 $\quad$ 3:2 $\quad \frac{3}{2}$

Slope is a ratio that compares the rise, or change in y, to the run, or change in x.

$\text{Slope} = \frac{\text{rise}}{\text{run}} = \frac{y_2 - y_1}{x_2 - x_1}$ Definition of slope

$= \frac{5-3}{7-3}$ Substitution

$= \frac{2}{4}$ or $\frac{1}{2}$ Simplify.

A ratio can involve more than two numbers.

The ratio of the angle measures in a triangle is 2:3:4. What is the measure of the smallest angle?

Let the angle measures be $2x°$, $3x°$, and $4x°$.

$2x + 3x + 4x = 180$ Triangle Sum Theorem

$9x = 180$ Simplify.

$x = 20$ Divide both sides by 9.

The smallest angle measures $2x°$. So $2x = 2(20) = 40°$.

Write a ratio expressing the slope of each line.

1. $\frac{1}{3}$
2. $\frac{4}{1}$
3. $-\frac{3}{2}$

4. The ratio of the side lengths of a triangle is 2:4:5, and the perimeter is 55 cm. What is the length of the shortest side? 10 cm
5. The ratio of the angle measures in a triangle is 7:13:16. What is the measure of the largest angle? 80°

40. The quad. is a rect. because opp. sides are ≅ and the diags. are ≅.

40. Critical Thinking The ratio of the lengths of a quadrilateral's consecutive sides is 2:5:2:5. The ratio of the lengths of the quadrilateral's diagonals is 1:1. What type of quadrilateral is this? Explain.

41. Multi-Step One square has sides 6 cm long. Another has sides 9 cm long. Find the ratio of the areas of the squares. $\frac{4}{9}$

42. Photography A photo shop makes prints of photographs in a variety of sizes. Every print has a length-to-width ratio of 5:3.5 regardless of its size. A customer wants a print that is 20 in. long. What is the width of this print? 14 in.

43. Write About It What is the difference between a ratio and a proportion?

TEST PREP

44. An 18-inch stick breaks into three pieces. The ratio of the lengths of the pieces is 1:4:5. Which of these is NOT a length of one of the pieces?

(A) 1.8 inches (B) 3.6 inches (C) 7.2 inches (D) 9 inches

45. Which of the following is equivalent to $\frac{3}{5} = \frac{x}{y}$?

(F) $\frac{3}{y} = \frac{5}{x}$ (G) $3x = 5y$ (H) $\frac{x}{3} = \frac{y}{5}$ (J) $3(5) = xy$

46. A recipe for salad dressing calls for oil and vinegar in a ratio of 5 parts oil to 2 parts vinegar. If you use $1\frac{1}{4}$ cups of oil, how many cups of vinegar will you need?

(A) $\frac{1}{2}$ (B) $\frac{5}{8}$ (C) $2\frac{1}{2}$ (D) $6\frac{1}{4}$

47. **Short Response** Explain how to solve the proportion $\frac{36}{72} = \frac{15}{x}$ for x. Tell what you must assume about x in order to solve the proportion.

47. First, cross multiply: $36x = 15(72)$, or $36x = 1080$. Then divide both sides by 36: $\frac{36x}{36} = \frac{1080}{36}$. Finally, simplify: $x = 30$. You must assume that $x \neq 0$.

CHALLENGE AND EXTEND

48. The ratio of the perimeter of rectangle $ABCD$ to the perimeter of rectangle $EFGH$ is 4:7. Find x. 10

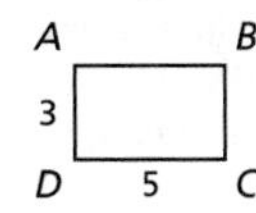

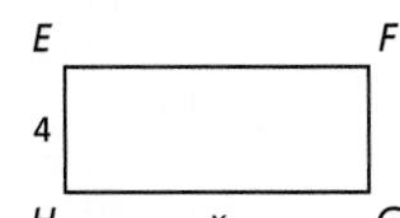

49. Explain why $\frac{a}{b} = \frac{c}{d}$ and $\frac{a+b}{b} = \frac{c+d}{d}$ are equivalent proportions.

49. Given $\frac{a}{b} = \frac{c}{d}$, add 1 to both sides of the eqn. as shown: $\frac{a}{b} + \frac{b}{b} = \frac{c}{d} + \frac{d}{d}$. Adding the fractions on both sides of the eqn. gives $\frac{a+b}{b} = \frac{c+d}{d}$.

50. **Probability** The numbers 1, 2, 3, and 6 are randomly placed in these four boxes: $\frac{\blacksquare}{\blacksquare} ? \frac{\blacksquare}{\blacksquare}$. What is the probability that the two ratios will form a proportion? $\frac{1}{3}$

51. Express the ratio $\frac{x^2 + 9x + 18}{x^2 - 36}$ in simplest form. $\frac{x+3}{x-6}$, where $x \neq \pm 6$

SPIRAL REVIEW

Complete each ordered pair so that it is a solution to $y - 6x = -3$. *(Previous course)*

52. (0, ■) −3
53. (■, 3) 1
54. (−4, ■) −27

Find each angle measure. *(Lesson 3-2)*

55. m∠ABD 96°
56. m∠CDB 84°

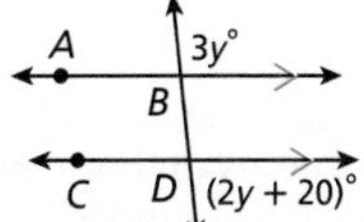

Each set of numbers represents the side lengths of a triangle. Classify each triangle as acute, right, or obtuse. *(Lesson 5-7)*

57. 5, 8, 9 acute
58. 8, 15, 20 obtuse
59. 7, 24, 25 right

7-1 PROBLEM SOLVING

1. For a certain type of tropical fish, it is recommended that you have no more than 2 fish per 10 gallons of water. How many fish could you have in a fish tank that holds 35 gallons of water? 7 fish

2. A library is being expanded, and the new wing's length is to be 50 feet greater than its width. A diagram of the new wing is shown. What are the actual dimensions of the new wing? 220 ft by 270 ft

22 in.
27 in.

3. The *Titanic* was 882 feet 9 inches long. You can build a model of the ship that is 2 feet 6 inches long and 6 inches high. What was the approximate height of the *Titanic* to the nearest inch? 176 ft 7 in.

4. The *aspect ratio,* or ratio of length to width of the viewing area, of a wide-screen 42-inch television is 16:9. What are the dimensions of the rectangular viewing area to the nearest tenth? 36.6 in. by 20.6 in.

viewing area
42 in.

Choose the best answer.

5. In a museum gift shop, a miniature *Acrocanthosaurus* is 22.8 centimeters long and 15.9 centimeters tall. The package says that the actual dinosaur was approximately 9 meters long. About how tall was the dinosaur?

(A) 6.3 m C 12.9 m
B 7.7 m D 40.3 m

6. A model airplane has a wingspan of about 15 inches. The actual airplane has a wingspan of 30 feet and a length of 42 feet. How long is the model?

F 11 in. (H) 21 in.
G 14 in. J 30 in.

7. Write a ratio expressing the slope of the hypotenuse in right triangle *MNP.*

M(−4, 6) y
P(3, 2)
x
N(−1, 0) 0

A $-\frac{7}{4}$ C $-\frac{1}{2}$
(B) $-\frac{4}{7}$ D $\frac{1}{4}$

8. The ratio of the interior angle measures of a pentagon is 2:2:3:4:6. What is the measure of the smallest angle to the nearest degree?

F 32° H 95°
(G) 64° J 191°

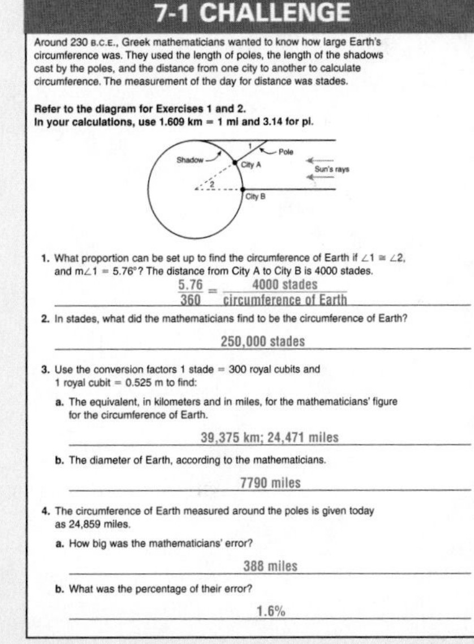

7-1 CHALLENGE

Around 230 B.C.E., Greek mathematicians wanted to know how large Earth's circumference was. They used the length of poles, the length of the shadows cast by the poles, and the distance from one city to another to calculate circumference. The measurement of the day for distance was stades.

Refer to the diagram for Exercises 1 and 2.
In your calculations, use 1.609 km = 1 mi and 3.14 for pi.

Shadow
1
Pole
City A
Sun's rays
2
City B

1. What proportion can be set up to find the circumference of Earth if ∠1 ≅ ∠2, and m∠1 = 5.76°? The distance from City A to City B is 4000 stades.

$\frac{5.76}{360} = \frac{4000 \text{ stades}}{\text{circumference of Earth}}$

2. In stades, what did the mathematicians find to be the circumference of Earth?

250,000 stades

3. Use the conversion factors 1 stade = 300 royal cubits and 1 royal cubit = 0.525 m to find:

a. The equivalent, in kilometers and in miles, for the mathematicians' figure for the circumference of Earth.

39,375 km; 24,471 miles

b. The diameter of Earth, according to the mathematicians.

7790 miles

4. The circumference of Earth measured around the poles is given today as 24,859 miles.

a. How big was the mathematicians' error?

388 miles

b. What was the percentage of their error?

1.6%

TEST PREP DOCTOR If students answered **Exercise 46** incorrectly, they may be having trouble setting up the proportion correctly or trouble working with the fractions. If they chose **C** or **D,** have them reread the question carefully to see that there will be less vinegar than oil. If they chose **B,** have them check their work to find the step in which they made an error.

Answers

43. A ratio is a comparison of 2 numbers by div. A proportion is an eqn. stating that 2 ratios are =.

Journal

Given that $\frac{w}{x} = \frac{y}{z}$, have students write four proportions using numbers to represent the variables. Explain why these proportions are all equivalent. Then write a nonexample of a proportion using these same numbers.

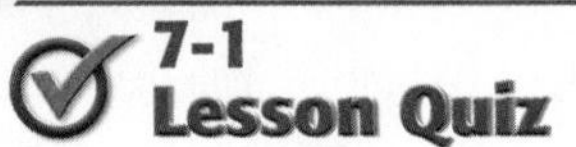

Have students work with a road map of your state. Give them a list of pairs of cities in the state. Ask them to measure the distance between each pair on the map and calculate the actual distances. Finally, ask them to check the accuracy of their answers using distances listed on the map or on the Internet.

Power Presentations with PowerPoint®

7-1 Lesson Quiz

1. The ratio of the angle measures in a triangle is 1:5:6. What is the measure of each angle? 15°, 75°, 90°

Solve each proportion.

2. $\frac{80}{120} = \frac{2}{x}$ 3

3. $\frac{x+3}{8} = \frac{5}{x-3}$ ±7

4. Given that $14a = 35b$, find the ratio of a to b in simplest form. $\frac{5}{2}$

5. An apartment building is 90 ft tall and 55 ft wide. If a scale model of this building is 11 in. wide, how tall is the scale model of the building? 18 in.

Also available on transparency

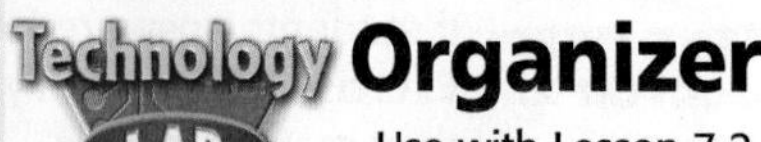

Organizer

Use with Lesson 7-2

Pacing:
Traditional 1 day
Block $\frac{1}{2}$ day

Objective: Use geometry software to explore the golden ratio and the golden rectangle.

Materials: geometry software

Online Edition
TechKeys

Countdown Week 15

Resources

Technology Lab Activities
7-2 Lab Recording Sheet

Teach

Discuss

Throughout history, the golden ratio has been said to appear in many works of art, in paintings, and in architecture. It also appears in the structures of some plants. Explain to students that they will be using geometry software to explore the golden ratio. Since the value of the golden ratio is $\frac{1+\sqrt{5}}{2} \approx 1.618$ you may want to review irrational numbers and their decimal approximations.

State Resources

go.hrw.com
State Resources Online
KEYWORD: MG7 Resources

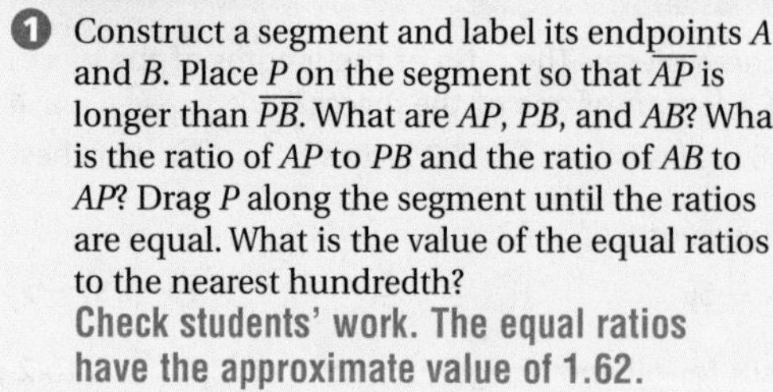

7-2 Technology LAB

Use with Lesson 7-2

Explore the Golden Ratio

In about 300 B.C.E., Euclid showed in his book *Elements* how to calculate the *golden ratio.* It is claimed that this ratio was used in many works of art and architecture to produce rectangles of pleasing proportions. The *golden ratio* also appears in the natural world and it is said even in the human face. If the ratio of a rectangle's length to its width is equal to the golden ratio, it is called a *golden rectangle.*

go.hrw.com
Lab Resources Online
KEYWORD: MG7 Lab7

Activity 1

1. Construct a segment and label its endpoints A and B. Place P on the segment so that $\overline{AP}$ is longer than $\overline{PB}$. What are AP, PB, and AB? What is the ratio of AP to PB and the ratio of AB to AP? Drag P along the segment until the ratios are equal. What is the value of the equal ratios to the nearest hundredth?
Check students' work. The equal ratios have the approximate value of 1.62.

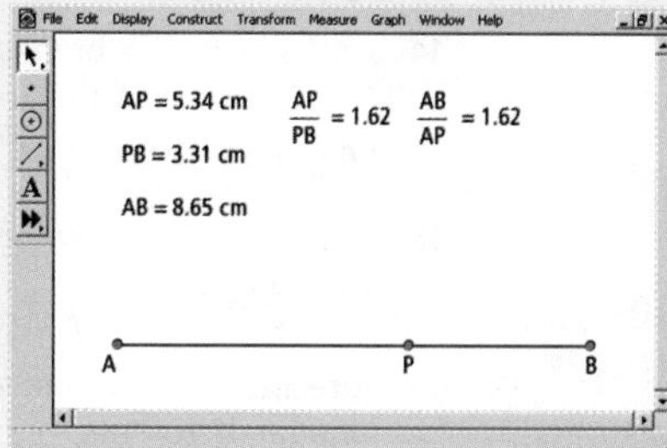

2. Construct a *golden rectangle* beginning with a square. Create $\overline{AB}$. Then construct a circle with its center at A and a radius of $\overline{AB}$. Construct a line perpendicular to $\overline{AB}$ through A. Where the circle and the perpendicular line intersect, label the point D. Construct perpendicular lines through B and D and label their intersection C. Hide the lines and the circle, leaving only the segments to complete the square.

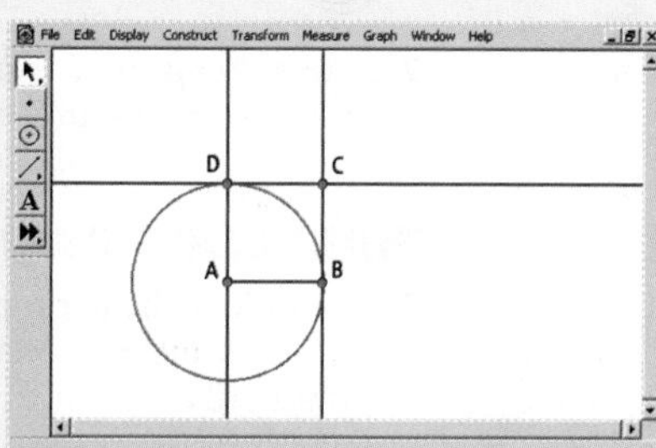

3. Find the midpoint of $\overline{AB}$ and label it M. Create a segment from M to C. Construct a circle with its center at M and radius of $\overline{MC}$. Construct a ray with endpoint A through B. Where the circle and the ray intersect, label the point E. Create a line through E that is perpendicular to $\overrightarrow{AB}$. Show the previously hidden line through D and C. Label the point of intersection of these two lines F. Hide the lines and circle and create segments to complete golden rectangle $AEFD$.

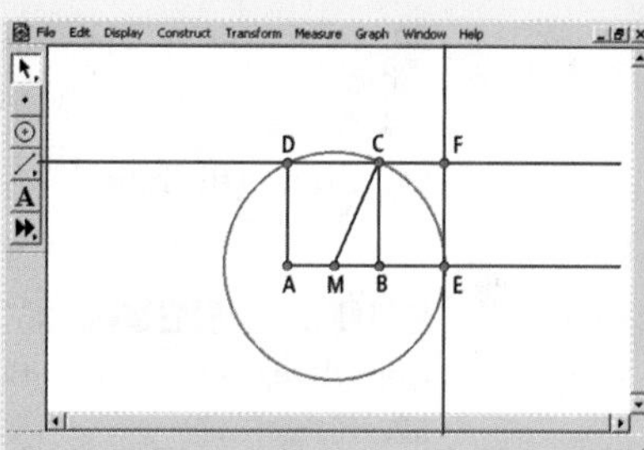

4. Measure $\overline{AE}$, $\overline{EF}$, and $\overline{BE}$. Find the ratio of AE to EF and the ratio of EF to BE. Compare these ratios to those found in Step 1. What do you notice? **The ratios have the same value as the ratios in step 1.**

Try This

1. Adjust your construction from Step 2 so that the side of the original square is 2 units long. Use the Pythagorean Theorem to find the length of $\overline{MC}$. Calculate the length of $\overline{AE}$. Write the ratio of AE to EF as a fraction and as a decimal rounded to the nearest thousandth.
2. Find the length of $\overline{BE}$ in your construction from Step 3. Write the ratio of EF to BE as a fraction and as a decimal rounded to the nearest thousandth. Compare your results to those from Try This Problem 1. What do you notice?
3. Each number in the Fibonacci sequence $(1, 1, 2, 3, 5, 8, 13 \ldots)$ is created by adding the two preceding numbers together. That is, $1 + 1 = 2$, $1 + 2 = 3$, $2 + 3 = 5$, and so on. Investigate the ratios of the numbers in the sequence by finding the quotients. $\frac{1}{1} = 1$, $\frac{2}{1} = 2$, $\frac{3}{2} = 1.5$, $\frac{5}{3} = 1.\overline{666}$, $\frac{8}{5} = 1.6$, and so on. What do you notice as you continue to find the quotients? **The quotients have values that approach 1.618.**

Tell why each of the following is an example of the appearance of the Fibonacci sequence in nature.

4. 

There are $1 + 1 = 2$ rabbits.

5. 

There are $8 + 13 = 21$ petals on the daisy.

Determine whether each picture is an example of an application of the golden rectangle. Measure the length and the width of each and decide whether the ratio of the length to the width is approximately the golden ratio.

6. 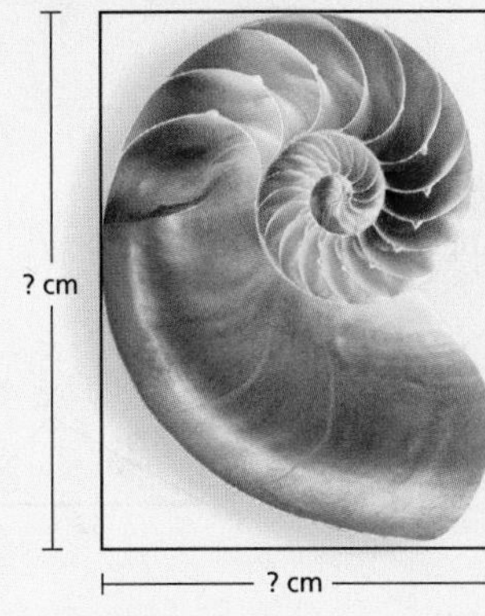

no; $\frac{5.4}{4} \approx 1.4$

7. 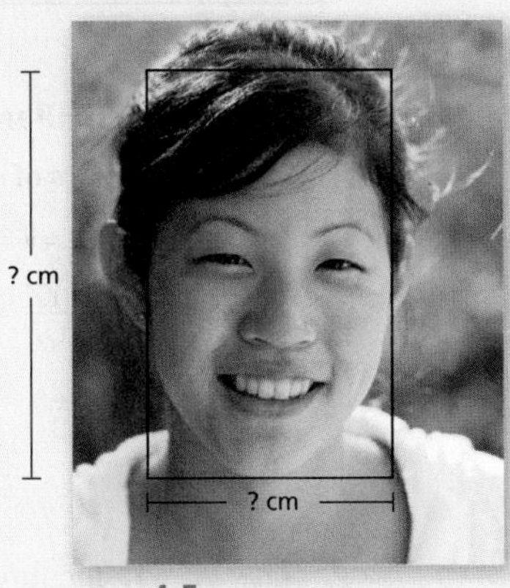

yes; $\frac{4.5}{2.8} \approx 1.6$

Close

Key Concept

The golden ratio is a ratio between lengths of line segments that is revealed in many different ways, both in the natural world and in man-made objects. Rectangular objects are called golden rectangles if the ratio of their length to their width is the golden ratio.

Assessment

Journal Have students create their own drawing using golden rectangles. Then explain how they know it is an example of a golden rectangle.

Answers to *Try This*

1. If the side length of the square is 2 units, then $MB = 1$ unit, and $BC = 2$ units. $\overline{MC}$ is the hyp. of the rt. △ formed by $\overline{MB}$ and $\overline{BC}$. By the Pyth. Thm., $\overline{MC}$ has length $\sqrt{5}$ units. $\overline{AE}$ has length $\sqrt{5} + 1$ units. $\frac{AE}{EF} = \frac{\sqrt{5}+1}{2} \approx 1.618$.
2. BE has length $\sqrt{5} - 1$ units. $\frac{BE}{EF} = \frac{\sqrt{5}-1}{2} \approx 0.618$. The sign of the numerator in this fraction is different from that of the fraction in Try This **Problem 1.**

7-2 Organizer

Pacing: Traditional 1 day
Block $\frac{1}{2}$ day

Objectives: Identify similar polygons.

Apply properties of similar polygons to solve problems.

Geometry Lab
In *Geometry Lab Activities*

Online Edition
Tutorial Videos, Interactivity

Countdown Week 15

Power Presentations with PowerPoint®

Warm Up

1. If $\triangle QRS \cong \triangle ZYX$, identify the pairs of congruent angles and the pairs of congruent sides. $\angle Q \cong \angle Z$; $\angle R \cong \angle Y$; $\angle S \cong X$; $\overline{QR} \cong \overline{ZY}$; $\overline{RS} \cong \overline{YX}$; $\overline{QS} \cong \overline{ZX}$

Solve each proportion.

2. $\frac{2}{x-3} = \frac{8}{3x-3}$ $\quad x = 9$
3. $\frac{x-6}{42} = \frac{2x-14}{77}$ $\quad x = 18$

Also available on transparency

Math Humor

Q: What does the zero say to the eight?

A: Nice belt!

7-2 Ratios in Similar Polygons

Objectives
Identify similar polygons.

Apply properties of similar polygons to solve problems.

Vocabulary
similar
similar polygons
similarity ratio

Why learn this?
Similar polygons are used to build models of actual objects. (See Example 3.)

Figures that are **similar** (~) have the same shape but not necessarily the same size.

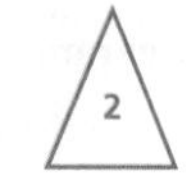

$\triangle 1$ is similar to $\triangle 2$ ($\triangle 1 \sim \triangle 2$).

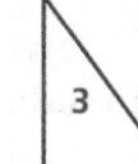

$\triangle 1$ is not similar to $\triangle 3$ ($\triangle 1 \nsim \triangle 3$).

Know it! Note — **Similar Polygons**

DEFINITION	DIAGRAM	STATEMENTS
Two polygons are **similar polygons** if and only if their corresponding angles are congruent and their corresponding side lengths are proportional.	Quadrilateral ABCD (AB = 6, BC = 5.4, CD = 4, DA = 5) and quadrilateral EFGH (EF = 12, FG = 10.8, GH = 8, HE = 10) $ABCD \sim EFGH$	$\angle A \cong \angle E$ $\angle B \cong \angle F$ $\angle C \cong \angle G$ $\angle D \cong \angle H$ $\frac{AB}{EF} = \frac{BC}{FG} = \frac{CD}{GH} = \frac{DA}{HE} = \frac{1}{2}$

EXAMPLE 1 **Describing Similar Polygons**

Identify the pairs of congruent angles and corresponding sides.

$\angle Z \cong \angle R$ and $\angle Y \cong \angle Q$. By the Third Angles Theorem, $\angle X \cong \angle S$.

$\frac{XY}{SQ} = \frac{6}{9} = \frac{2}{3}, \frac{YZ}{QR} = \frac{12}{18} = \frac{2}{3},$

$\frac{XZ}{SR} = \frac{9}{13.5} = \frac{2}{3}$

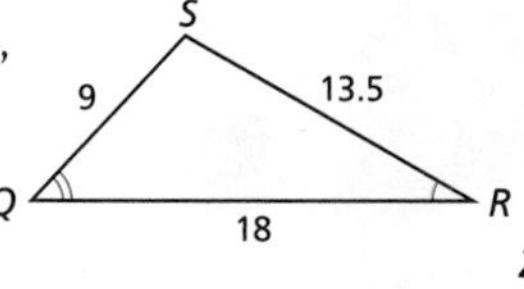

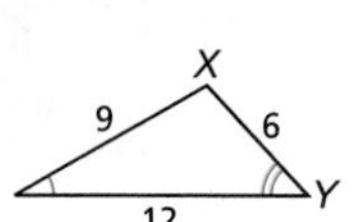

1. Identify the pairs of congruent angles and corresponding sides.
$\angle A \cong \angle J$; $\angle B \cong \angle G$; $\angle C \cong \angle H$;
$\frac{AB}{JG} = \frac{BC}{GH} = \frac{AC}{JH} = 2$

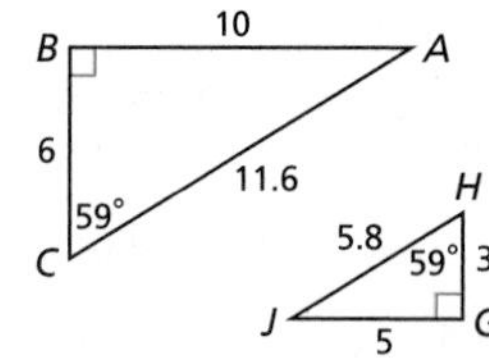

State Resources

go.hrw.com
State Resources Online
KEYWORD: MG7 Resources

1 Introduce

EXPLORATION

7-2 Ratios in Similar Polygons

Figures that are *similar* have the same shape but not necessarily the same size. Use graph paper to explore similar figures.

1. Copy $\triangle ABC$ on a piece of graph paper.
2. Draw another $\triangle DEF$ that has the same shape as $\triangle ABC$ but is a different size.
3. Explain how you know that $\triangle DEF$ has the same shape as $\triangle ABC$.
4. Use a protractor to measure the angles of $\triangle ABC$ and $\triangle DEF$. What do you notice?
5. How do the side lengths of $\triangle ABC$ and $\triangle DEF$ compare?
6. Complete the following conjecture: Two polygons are similar polygons if and only if their corresponding angles are __?__ and their corresponding sides are __?__.

THINK AND DISCUSS

7. Discuss whether the two rectangles are similar. Explain why or why not.

Motivate

Draw three or more similar triangles, each a different size and color, on separate transparencies. Show on the overhead that by superimposing the triangles so that the angles coincide, all the triangles have three pairs of congruent angles. Explain to students that they will learn how to determine if polygons are similar by identifying corresponding congruent angles and comparing corresponding side lengths.

Explorations and answers are provided in *Alternate Openers: Explorations Transparencies.*

A **similarity ratio** is the ratio of the lengths of the corresponding sides of two similar polygons. The similarity ratio of $\triangle ABC$ to $\triangle DEF$ is $\frac{3}{6}$, or $\frac{1}{2}$. The similarity ratio of $\triangle DEF$ to $\triangle ABC$ is $\frac{6}{3}$, or 2.

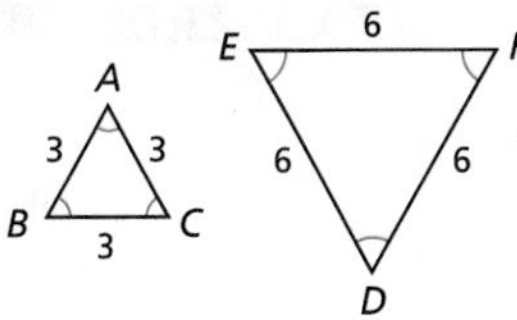

EXAMPLE 2 **Identifying Similar Polygons**

Determine whether the polygons are similar. If so, write the similarity ratio and a similarity statement.

A rectangles *PQRS* and *TUVW*

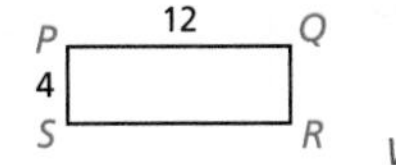

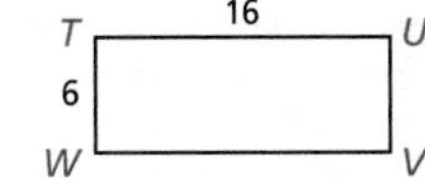

Step 1 Identify pairs of congruent angles.

$\angle P \cong \angle T, \angle Q \cong \angle U,$
$\angle R \cong \angle V,$ and $\angle S \cong \angle W$ *All ∡ of a rect. are rt. ∡ and are ≅.*

Step 2 Compare corresponding sides.

$\frac{PQ}{TU} = \frac{12}{16} = \frac{3}{4}, \frac{PS}{TW} = \frac{4}{6} = \frac{2}{3}$

Since corresponding sides are not proportional, the rectangles are not similar.

Writing Math

Writing a similarity statement is like writing a congruence statement—be sure to list corresponding vertices in the same order.

B $\triangle ABC$ and $\triangle DEF$

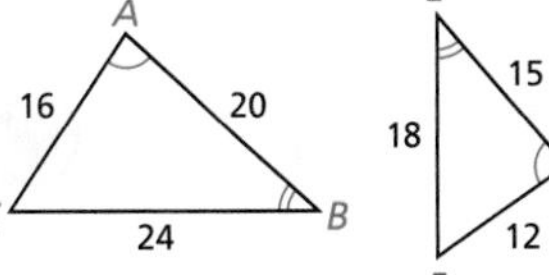

Step 1 Identify pairs of congruent angles.

$\angle A \cong \angle D, \angle B \cong \angle E$ *Given*

$\angle C \cong \angle F$ *Third ∡ Thm.*

Step 2 Compare corresponding sides.

$\frac{AB}{DE} = \frac{20}{15} = \frac{4}{3}, \frac{BC}{EF} = \frac{24}{18} = \frac{4}{3}, \frac{AC}{DF} = \frac{16}{12} = \frac{4}{3}$

Thus the similarity ratio is $\frac{4}{3}$, and $\triangle ABC \sim \triangle DEF$.

2. Determine if $\triangle JLM \sim \triangle NPS$. If so, write the similarity ratio and a similarity statement.

yes; $\frac{5}{2}$; $\triangle LMJ \sim \triangle PNS$

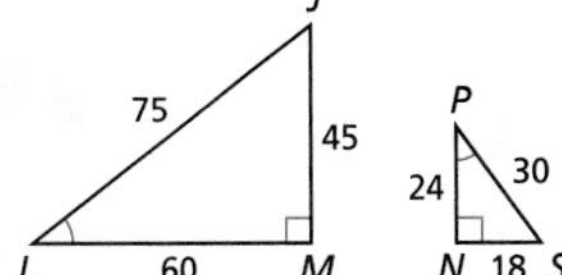

Student to Student *Proportions with Similar Figures*

Anna Woods
Westwood High School

When I set up a proportion, I make sure each ratio compares the figures in the same order. To find x, I wrote $\frac{10}{4} = \frac{6}{x}$. This will work because the first ratio compares the lengths starting with rectangle ABCD. The second ratio compares the widths, also starting with rectangle ABCD.

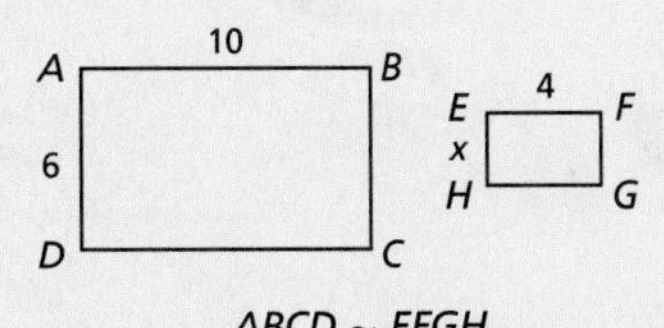

COMMON ERROR ALERT

Students may invert one of the fractions when writing a proportion comparing the side lengths of similar polygons. Help them establish the habit of choosing either the numerator or denominator for all side lengths from the same triangle.

Power Presentations with PowerPoint®

Additional Examples

Example 1

Identify the pairs of congruent angles and corresponding sides.

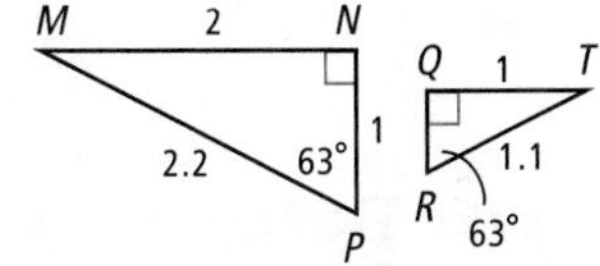

$\angle M \cong \angle T, \angle N \cong \angle Q, \angle P \cong \angle R$

$\frac{MN}{TQ} = \frac{NP}{QR} = \frac{MP}{TR} = \frac{2}{1}$

Example 2

Determine whether the polygons are similar. If so, write the similarity ratio and a similarity statement.

A.

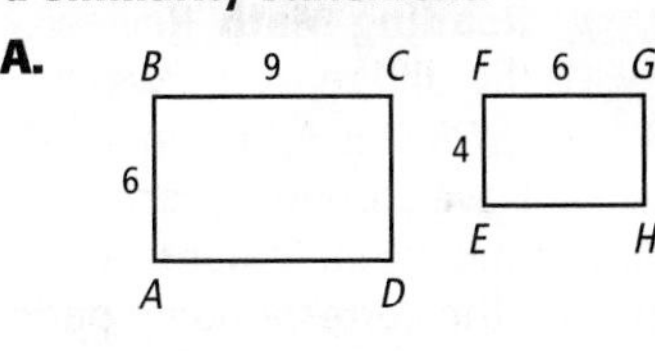

yes; $\frac{3}{2}$; rectangle *ABCD* ~ rectangle *EFGH*

B.

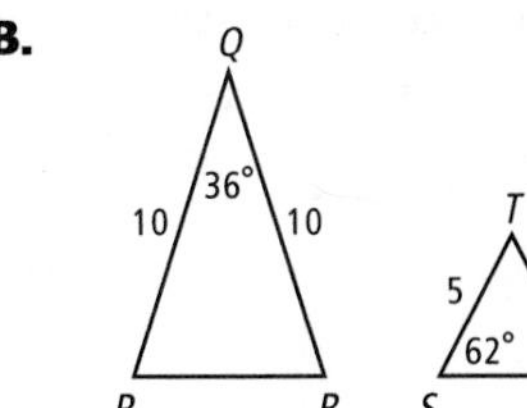

no

2 Teach

Guided Instruction

Review how to identify corresponding angles and corresponding sides of congruent polygons. Compare and contrast the definitions of similar and congruent. Show students how to use similarity ratios to find the unknown lengths of corresponding sides in similar polygons.

Inclusion Remind students that when polygons are named in the problem, the order of the vertices can help identify corresponding sides and vertices.

Reaching All Learners

Through Concrete Manipulatives

Have students work with pattern blocks (MK) to explore the concept of similarity. Students can work in pairs, with one student creating a block design and the other creating a figure that is similar, but not congruent, to the first one. For more sets of pattern blocks there are websites that feature "virtual pattern blocks," allowing students to select, combine, and rearrange blocks on a computer screen.

INTERVENTION
Questioning Strategies

EXAMPLE 1

- How can you use the congruent angles to help you determine the corresponding sides?

EXAMPLE 2

- What is the least amount of information necessary to determine that two isosceles triangles are similar? Explain.

Power Presentations with PowerPoint®

Additional Examples

Example 3

Find the length of the model to the nearest tenth of a centimeter.

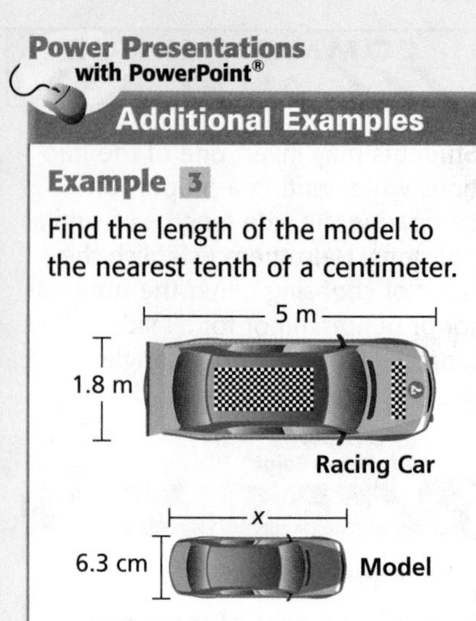

$x \approx 17.5$ cm

INTERVENTION

Questioning Strategies

EXAMPLE 3

- When solving a proportion about a scale model, do you need to use the same units for the dimensions of the original object and the scale model?

Reading Math Review the difference between $\triangle QRS \cong \triangle ZYX$ and $\triangle QRS \sim \triangle ZYX$. Have students practice reading similarity statements and identifying the corresponding parts. For example, $\triangle QRS \sim \triangle ZYX$ means that triangle QRS is similar to triangle ZYX. Q corresponds to Z, R corresponds to Y, and S corresponds to X.

EXAMPLE  **Hobby Application**

A Railbox boxcar can be used to transport auto parts. If the length of the actual boxcar is 50 ft, find the width of the actual boxcar to the nearest tenth of a foot.

Let x be the width of the actual boxcar in feet. The rectangular model of a boxcar is similar to the rectangular boxcar, so the corresponding lengths are proportional.

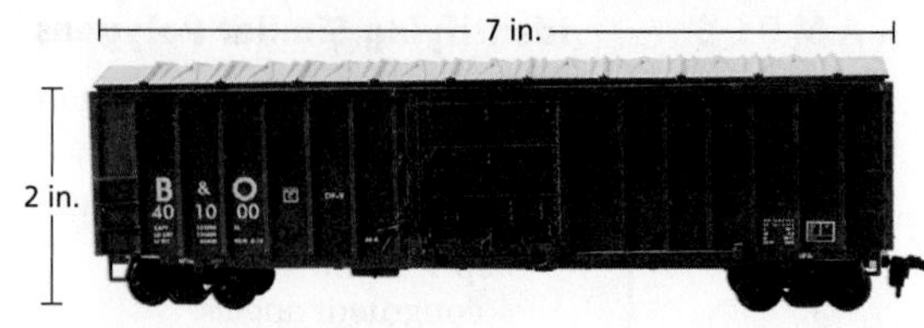

$$\frac{\text{length of boxcar}}{\text{length of model}} = \frac{\text{width of boxcar}}{\text{width of model}}$$

$$\frac{50}{7} = \frac{x}{2}$$

$7x = (50)(2)$ *Cross Products Prop.*

$7x = 100$ *Simplify.*

$x \approx 14.3$ *Divide both sides by 7.*

The width of the model is approximately 14.3 ft.

Helpful Hint

When you work with proportions, be sure the ratios compare corresponding measures.

CHECK IT OUT! **3.** A boxcar has the dimensions shown. A model of the boxcar is 1.25 in. wide. Find the length of the model to the nearest inch. **5 in.**

36.25 ft | 9 ft | Boxcar | x in. | Model | 1.25 in.

THINK AND DISCUSS

1. If you combine the symbol for similarity with the equal sign, what symbol is formed?
2. The similarity ratio of rectangle $ABCD$ to rectangle $EFGH$ is $\frac{1}{9}$. How do the side lengths of rectangle $ABCD$ compare to the corresponding side lengths of rectangle $EFGH$?
3. What shape(s) are always similar?

4. **GET ORGANIZED** Copy and complete the graphic organizer. Write the definition of similar polygons, and a similarity statement. Then draw examples and nonexamples of similar polygons.

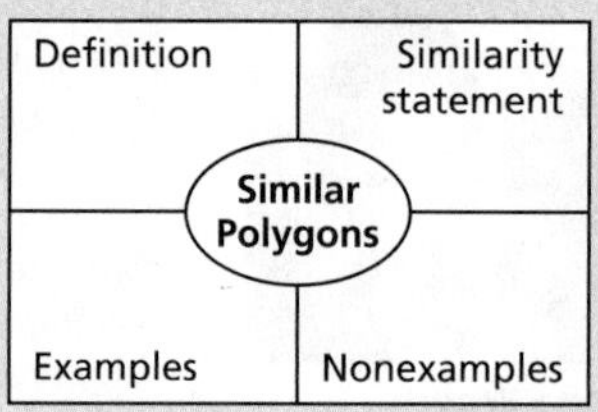

3 Close

Summarize

Review the concepts of similarity, same shape; and congruence, same shape and same size. Point out that only when the similarity ratio is 1 : 1 are similar polygons congruent. Write proportions comparing corresponding sides for $\triangle ABC \sim \triangle DEF$ $\left(\frac{AB}{DE} = \frac{AC}{DF} = \frac{BC}{EF}\right)$, and identify the congruent angles ($\angle A \cong \angle D$, $\angle B \cong \angle E$, $\angle C \cong \angle F$).

ONGOING ASSESSMENT and INTERVENTION

Diagnose ***Before*** **the Lesson**
7-2 Warm Up, TE p. 462

Monitor ***During*** **the Lesson**
Check It Out! Exercises, SE pp. 462–464
Questioning Strategies, TE pp. 463–464

Assess ***After*** **the Lesson**
7-2 Lesson Quiz, TE p. 467
Alternative Assessment, TE p. 467

Answers to *Think and Discuss*

1. ≅
2. The sides of rect. $EFGH$ are 9 times as long as the corr. sides of rect. $ABCD$.
3. Possible answers: reg. polygons of the same type; circles
4. See p. A6.

7-2 Exercises

go.hrw.com
Homework Help Online
KEYWORD: MG7 7-2
Parent Resources Online
KEYWORD: MG7 Parent

GUIDED PRACTICE

1. **Vocabulary** Give an example of similar figures in your classroom. **Possible answer: students' desks**

SEE EXAMPLE 1 p. 462

Identify the pairs of congruent angles and corresponding sides.

2. △MNP with MN = 4, MP = 3, NP = 2; △WUV with VW = 4, WU = 6, VU = 8

3. 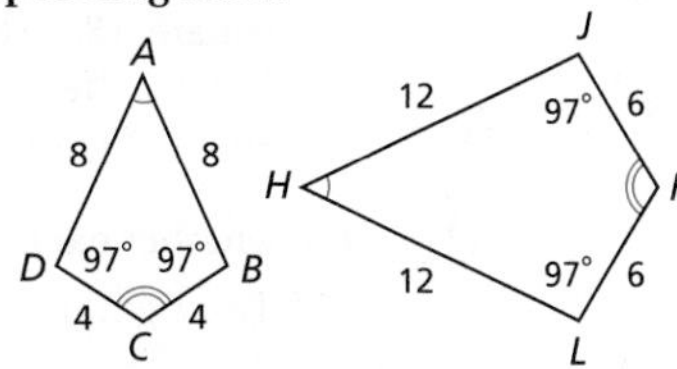

SEE EXAMPLE 2 p. 463

Multi-Step **Determine whether the polygons are similar. If so, write the similarity ratio and a similarity statement.**

4. rectangles $ABCD$ and $EFGH$

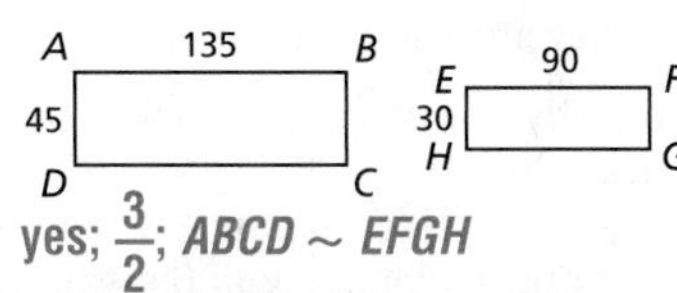

yes; $\frac{3}{2}$; $ABCD \sim EFGH$

5. $\triangle RMP$ and $\triangle UWX$

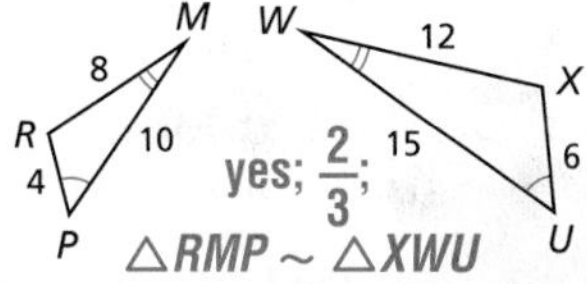

yes; $\frac{2}{3}$; $\triangle RMP \sim \triangle XWU$

SEE EXAMPLE 3 p. 464

6. **Art** The town of Goodland, Kansas, claims that it has one of the world's largest easels. It holds an enlargement of a van Gogh painting that is 24 ft wide. The original painting is 58 cm wide and 73 cm tall. If the reproduction is similar to the original, what is the height of the reproduction to the nearest foot? **30 ft**

PRACTICE AND PROBLEM SOLVING

Independent Practice	
For Exercises	See Example
7–8	1
9–10	2
11	3

Extra Practice
Skills Practice p. S16
Application Practice p. S34

Identify the pairs of congruent angles and corresponding sides.

7. 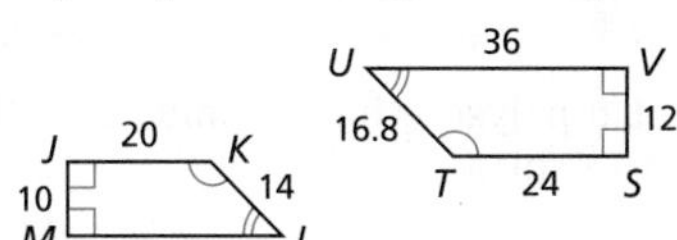

8. △ABC with AC = 12, AB = 8, CB = 6; 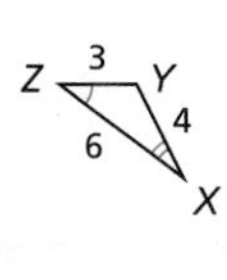

Multi-Step **Determine whether the polygons are similar. If so, write the similarity ratio and a similarity statement.**

9. $\triangle RSQ$ and $\triangle UXZ$

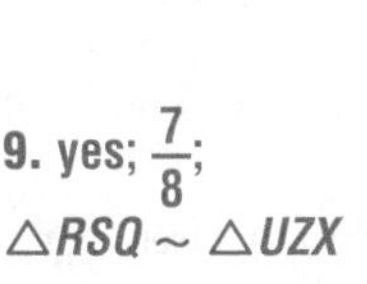

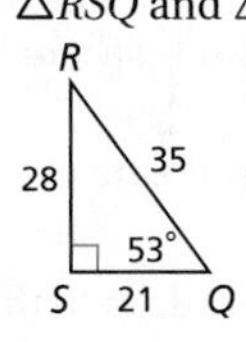

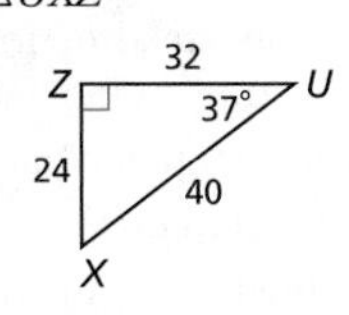

9. yes; $\frac{7}{8}$; $\triangle RSQ \sim \triangle UZX$

10. rectangles $ABCD$ and $JKLM$

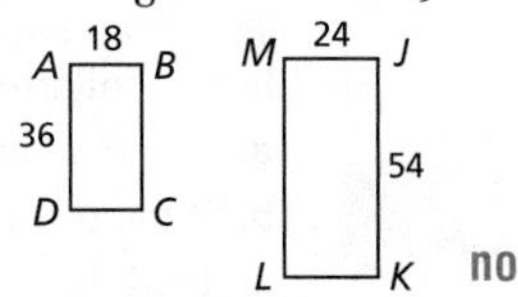

no

Teacher to Teacher

Corresponding vertices in similar figures are usually named in alphabetical order. However, this could enable a student to solve problems using only the letters' order instead of the desired geometric reasons. Think about naming figures by beginning the sequence of letters at different corresponding vertices.

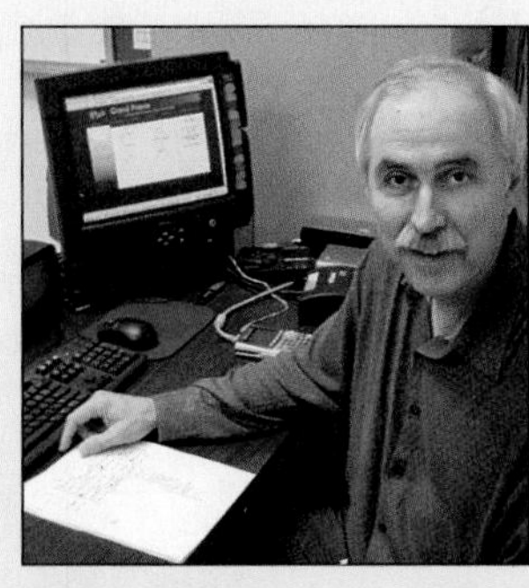

Roger Fuller
Grand Prairie, TX

7-2 Exercises

Assignment Guide

Assign *Guided Practice* exercises as necessary.

If you finished Examples **1–3**
Basic 7–17, 19–21, 25–29, 34–40
Average 7–15, 18–20, 22–30, 34–40
Advanced 7–11, 12–20 even, 21–40

Homework Quick Check
Quickly check key concepts.
Exercises: 8, 10, 11, 14, 20

Answers

2. $\angle M \cong \angle U$; $\angle N \cong \angle V$; $\angle P \cong \angle W$; $\frac{MN}{UV} = \frac{NP}{VW} = \frac{PM}{WU} = \frac{1}{2}$

3. $\angle A \cong \angle H$; $\angle B \cong \angle J$; $\angle C \cong \angle K$; $\angle D \cong \angle L$; $\frac{AB}{HJ} = \frac{BC}{JK} = \frac{CD}{KL} = \frac{DA}{LH} = \frac{2}{3}$

7. $\angle J \cong \angle S$; $\angle K \cong \angle T$; $\angle L \cong \angle U$; $\angle M \cong \angle V$; $\frac{JK}{ST} = \frac{KL}{TU} = \frac{LM}{UV} = \frac{MJ}{VS} = \frac{5}{6}$

8. $\angle A \cong \angle X$; $\angle B \cong \angle Y$; $\angle C \cong \angle Z$; $\frac{AB}{XY} = \frac{BC}{YZ} = \frac{CA}{ZX} = 2$

State Resources

go.hrw.com
State Resources Online
KEYWORD: MG7 Resources

Teaching Tip **Kinesthetic** For **Exercise 13,** have students demonstrate that the answer is "sometimes." They can use rulers (MK) and yardsticks to create two right triangles that are similar and two that are not similar.

Teaching Tip **Visual** For **Exercises 13–17,** have students work in small groups and draw a diagram to illustrate each statement. Point out that they may need to draw different pairs of figures for some statements to illustrate the different cases. Students should be prepared to justify their answers.

MULTI-STEP TEST PREP **Exercise 26** involves working with similarity ratios and perspective to give the illusion of distance on a stage set. This exercise prepares students for the Multi-Step Test Prep on page 478.

Answers

22. If 2 polygons are ~, then their corr. ∡ are ≅ and their corr. sides are proportional. If the corr. ∡ of 2 polygons are ≅ and their corr. sides are proportional, then the polygons are ~.

25. The polygons must be ≅. Since the polygons are ~, their corr. ∡ must be ≅. Since the similarity ratio is 1, the corr. sides must have the same length.

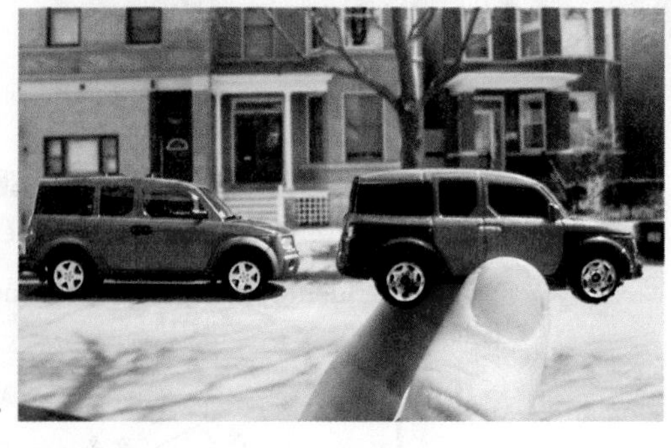

11. **Hobbies** The ratio of the model car's dimensions to the actual car's dimensions is $\frac{1}{56}$. The model has a length of 3 in. What is the length of the actual car? **14 ft**

12. Square $ABCD$ has an area of 4 m^2. Square $PQRS$ has an area of 36 m^2. What is the similarity ratio of square $ABCD$ to square $PQRS$? What is the similarity ratio of square $PQRS$ to square $ABCD$? **$\frac{1}{3}$; $\frac{3}{1}$**

Tell whether each statement is sometimes, always, or never true.

13. Two right triangles are similar. **S**

14. Two squares are similar. **A**

15. A parallelogram and a trapezoid are similar. **N**

16. If two polygons are congruent, they are also similar. **A**

17. If two polygons are similar, they are also congruent. **S**

18. **Critical Thinking** Explain why any two regular polygons having the same number of sides are similar. **By def. of reg. polygons, the corr. int. ∡ are ≅, and the side lengths are ≅ and proportional. So any 2 reg. polygons with the same number of sides are ~.**

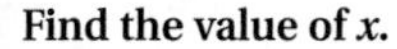

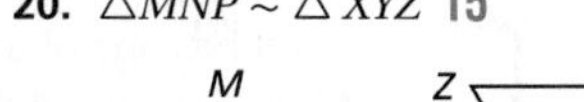

Find the value of x.

19. $ABCD \sim EFGH$ **5**

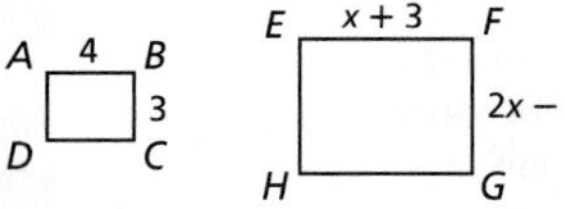

20. $\triangle MNP \sim \triangle XYZ$ **15**

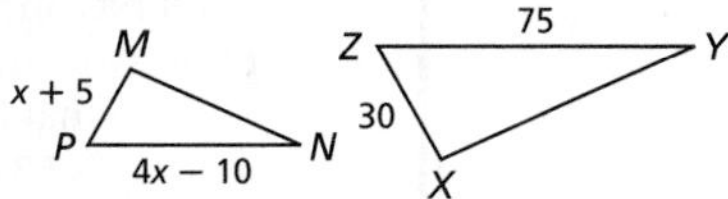

LINK Monument

The height of the Statue of Liberty from the foundation of the pedestal to the torch is 305 ft. Her index finger measures 8 ft, and the fingernail is 13 in. by 10 in.

Source: libertystatepark.org

21. **Estimation** The Statue of Liberty's hand is 16.4 ft long. Assume that your own body is similar to that of the Statue of Liberty and estimate the length of the Statue of Liberty's nose. (*Hint:* Use a ruler to measure your own hand and nose. Then set up a proportion.) **Possible answer: 4.5 ft**

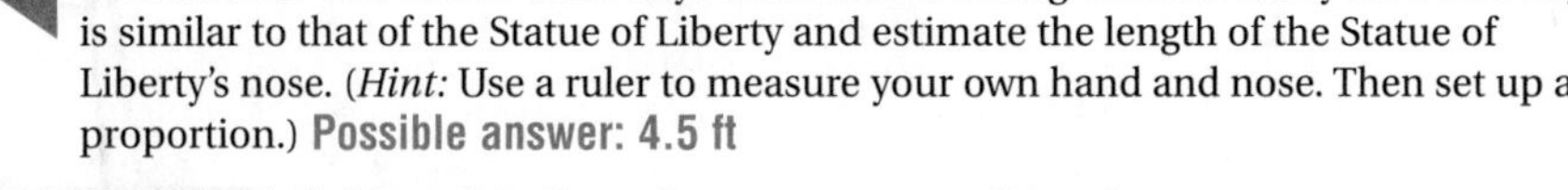

22. Write the definition of similar polygons as two conditional statements.

23. ▱$JKLM \sim$ ▱$NOPQ$. If $m\angle K = 75°$, name two 75° angles in ▱$NOPQ$. **∠O; ∠Q**

24. A dining room is 18 ft long and 14 ft wide. On a blueprint for the house, the dining room is 3.5 in. long. To the nearest tenth of an inch, what is the width of the dining room on the blueprint? **2.7 in.**

25. **Write About It** Two similar polygons have a similarity ratio of 1 : 1. What can you say about the two polygons? Explain.

MULTI-STEP TEST PREP

26. This problem will prepare you for the Multi-Step Test Prep on page 478.
A stage set consists of a painted backdrop with some wooden flats in front of it. One of the flats shows a tree that has a similarity ratio of $\frac{1}{2}$ to an actual tree. To give an illusion of distance, the backdrop includes a small painted tree that has a similarity ratio of $\frac{1}{10}$ to the tree on the flat.
    a. The tree on the backdrop is 0.9 ft tall. What is the height of the tree on the flat? **9 ft**
    b. What is the height of the actual tree? **18 ft**
    c. Find the similarity ratio of the tree on the backdrop to the actual tree. **$\frac{1}{20}$**

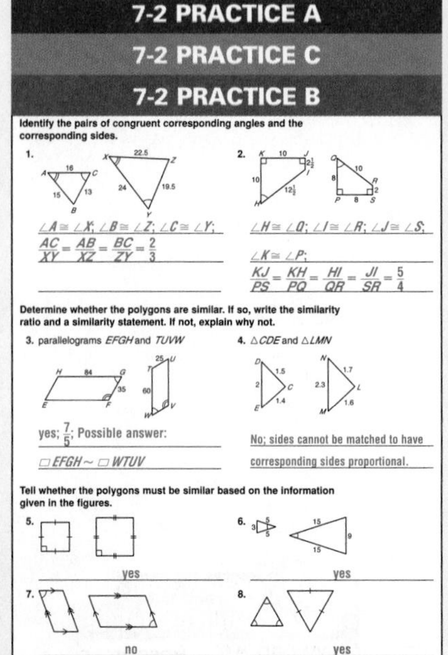

7-2 PRACTICE A
7-2 PRACTICE C
7-2 PRACTICE B

Identify the pairs of congruent corresponding angles and the corresponding sides.

1. ∠A ≅ ∠X; ∠B ≅ ∠Z; ∠C ≅ ∠Y; $\frac{AC}{XY} = \frac{AB}{XZ} = \frac{BC}{ZY} = \frac{2}{3}$

2. ∠H ≅ ∠Q; ∠I ≅ ∠R; ∠J ≅ ∠S; ∠K ≅ ∠P; $\frac{KJ}{PS} = \frac{KH}{PQ} = \frac{HI}{QR} = \frac{JI}{SR} = \frac{5}{4}$

Determine whether the polygons are similar. If so, write the similarity ratio and a similarity statement. If not, explain why not.

3. parallelograms $EFGH$ and $TUVW$
yes; $\frac{7}{5}$; Possible answer: ▱$EFGH \sim$ ▱$WTUV$

4. $\triangle CDE$ and $\triangle LMN$
No; sides cannot be matched to have corresponding sides proportional.

Tell whether the polygons must be similar based on the information given in the figures.

5. yes
6. yes
7. no
8. yes

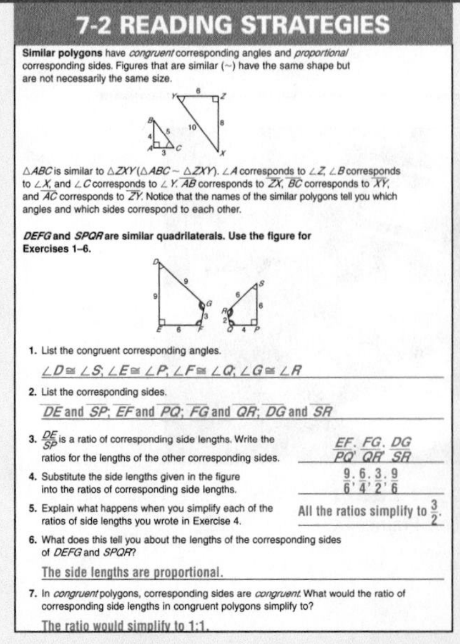

7-2 READING STRATEGIES

Similar polygons have *congruent* corresponding angles and *proportional* corresponding sides. Figures that are similar (~) have the same shape but are not necessarily the same size.

$\triangle ABC$ is similar to $\triangle ZXY$ ($\triangle ABC \sim \triangle ZXY$). ∠A corresponds to ∠Z, ∠B corresponds to ∠X, and ∠C corresponds to ∠Y. $\overline{AB}$ corresponds to $\overline{ZX}$, $\overline{BC}$ corresponds to $\overline{XY}$, and $\overline{AC}$ corresponds to $\overline{ZY}$. Notice that the names of the similar polygons tell you which angles and which sides correspond to each other.

DEFG and *SPQR* are similar quadrilaterals. Use the figure for Exercises 1–6.

1. List the congruent corresponding angles.
∠D ≅ ∠S, ∠E ≅ ∠P, ∠F ≅ ∠Q, ∠G ≅ ∠R

2. List the corresponding sides.
$\overline{DE}$ and $\overline{SP}$; $\overline{EF}$ and $\overline{PQ}$; $\overline{FG}$ and $\overline{QR}$; $\overline{DG}$ and $\overline{SR}$

3. $\frac{DE}{SP}$ is a ratio of corresponding side lengths. Write the ratios for the lengths of the other corresponding sides. $\frac{EF}{PQ}$; $\frac{FG}{QR}$; $\frac{DG}{SR}$

4. Substitute the side lengths given in the figure into the ratios of corresponding side lengths. $\frac{9}{6}$; $\frac{6}{4}$; $\frac{3}{2}$; $\frac{9}{6}$

5. Explain what happens when you simplify each of the ratios of side lengths you wrote in Exercise 4. All the ratios simplify to $\frac{3}{2}$.

6. What does this tell you about the lengths of the corresponding sides of *DEFG* and *SPQR*?
The side lengths are proportional.

7. In *congruent* polygons, corresponding sides are *congruent*. What would the ratio of corresponding side lengths in congruent polygons simplify to?
The ratio would simplify to 1:1.

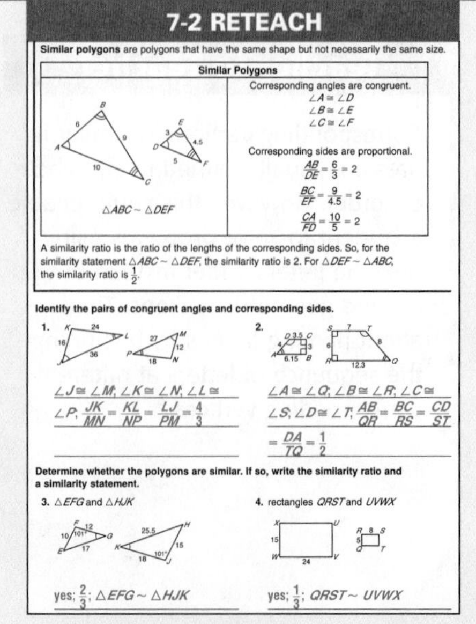

7-2 RETEACH

Similar polygons are polygons that have the same shape but not necessarily the same size.

Similar Polygons	
$\triangle ABC \sim \triangle DEF$	Corresponding angles are congruent. ∠A ≅ ∠D, ∠B ≅ ∠E, ∠C ≅ ∠F Corresponding sides are proportional. $\frac{AB}{DE} = \frac{6}{3} = 2$, $\frac{BC}{EF} = \frac{9}{4.5} = 2$, $\frac{CA}{FD} = \frac{10}{5} = 2$

A similarity ratio is the ratio of the lengths of the corresponding sides. So, for the similarity statement $\triangle ABC \sim \triangle DEF$, the similarity ratio is 2. For $\triangle DEF \sim \triangle ABC$, the similarity ratio is $\frac{1}{2}$.

Identify the pairs of congruent angles and corresponding sides.

1. ∠J ≅ ∠M, ∠K ≅ ∠N, ∠L ≅ ∠P; $\frac{JK}{MN} = \frac{KL}{NP} = \frac{LJ}{PM} = \frac{4}{3}$

2. ∠A ≅ ∠Q, ∠B ≅ ∠R, ∠C ≅ ∠S, ∠D ≅ ∠T; $\frac{AB}{QR} = \frac{BC}{RS} = \frac{CD}{ST} = \frac{DA}{TQ} = \frac{1}{2}$

Determine whether the polygons are similar. If so, write the similarity ratio and a similarity statement.

3. $\triangle EFG$ and $\triangle HJK$
yes; $\frac{2}{3}$; $\triangle EFG \sim \triangle HJK$

4. rectangles $QRST$ and $UVWX$
yes; $\frac{1}{3}$; $QRST \sim UVWX$

TEST PREP

27. Which value of y makes the two rectangles similar?

Ⓐ 3   Ⓒ 25.2 (circled)
Ⓑ 8.2   Ⓓ 28.8

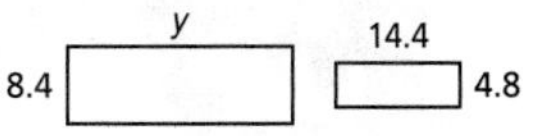

(Rectangles: y by 8.4; 14.4 by 4.8)

28. $\triangle CGL \sim \triangle MPS$. The similarity ratio of $\triangle CGL$ to $\triangle MPS$ is $\frac{5}{2}$. What is the length of $\overline{PS}$?

Ⓕ 8 (circled)   Ⓗ 50
Ⓖ 12   Ⓙ 75

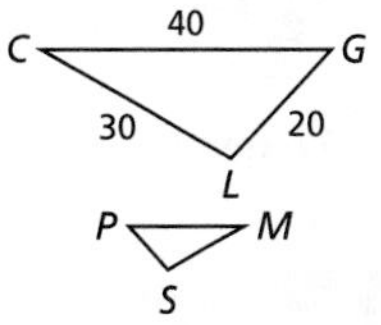

(Triangle CGL: $CG = 40$, $CL = 30$, $GL = 20$; triangle PMS)

29. **Short Response** Explain why 1.5, 2.5, 3.5 and 6, 10, 12 cannot be corresponding sides of similar triangles.
The ratios of the sides are not the same; $\frac{12}{3.5} = \frac{24}{7}$; $\frac{10}{2.5} = 4$; $\frac{6}{1.5} = 4$.

CHALLENGE AND EXTEND

30. **Architecture** An architect is designing a building that is 200 ft long and 140 ft wide. She builds a model so that the similarity ratio of the model to the building is $\frac{1}{500}$. What is the length and width of the model in inches? 4.8 in. long; 3.36 in. wide

31. Write a paragraph proof.
Given: $\overline{QR} \parallel \overline{ST}$
Prove: $\triangle PQR \sim \triangle PST$

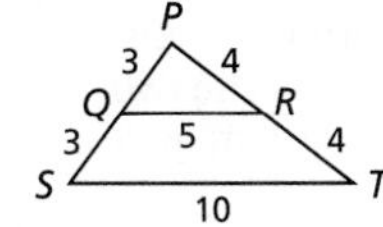

32. In the figure, D is the midpoint of $\overline{AC}$.
  a. Find AC, DC, and DB.
  b. Use your results from part **a** to help you explain why $\triangle ABC \sim \triangle CDB$.

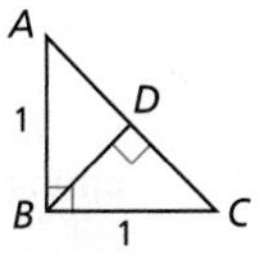

33. A golden rectangle has the following property: If a square is cut from one end of the rectangle, the rectangle that remains is similar to the original rectangle.
  a. Rectangle $ABCD$ is a golden rectangle. Write a similarity statement for rectangle $ABCD$ and rectangle $BCFE$.
  b. Write a proportion using the corresponding sides of these rectangles.
  c. Solve the proportion for ℓ. (*Hint:* Use the Quadratic Formula.)
  d. The value of ℓ is known as the golden ratio. Use a calculator to find ℓ to the nearest tenth.

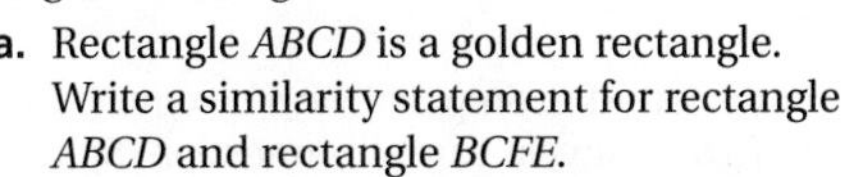
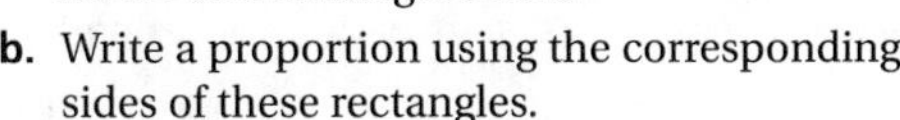

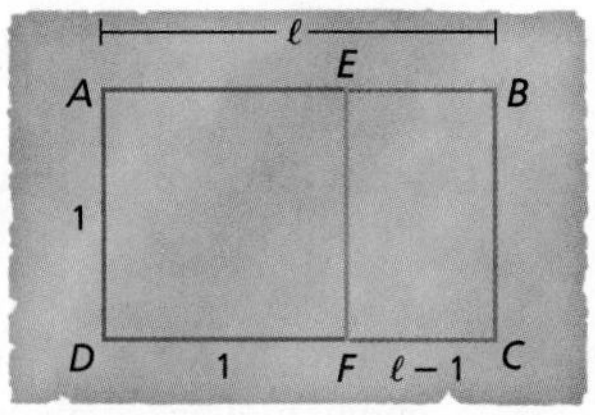

33a. rect. $ABCD \sim$ rect. $BCFE$
b. $\frac{\ell}{1} = \frac{1}{\ell - 1}$
c. $\ell = \frac{1 + \sqrt{5}}{2}$
d. $\ell \approx 1.6$

SPIRAL REVIEW

34. There are four runners in a 200-meter race. Assuming there are no ties, in how many different orders can the runners finish the race? *(Previous course)* 24

In kite $PQRS$, $\overline{PS} \cong \overline{RS}$, $\overline{QR} \cong \overline{QP}$, $m\angle QPT = 45°$, and $m\angle RST = 20°$. Find each angle measure. *(Lesson 6-6)*

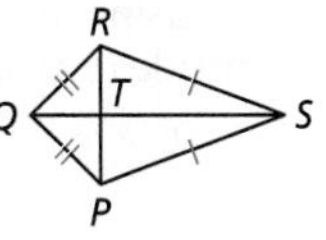

35. $m\angle QTR$ 90°   36. $m\angle PST$ 20°   37. $m\angle TPS$ 70°

Complete each of the following equations, given that $\frac{x}{4} = \frac{y}{10}$. *(Lesson 7-1)*

38. $10x = \blacksquare$ 4y   39. $\frac{10}{y} = \blacksquare$ $\frac{4}{x}$ 40. $\frac{x}{y} = \blacksquare$ $\frac{4}{10}$, or $\frac{2}{5}$

TEST PREP DOCTOR In **Exercise 28,** choices **H** and **J** can be eliminated because the similarity ratio is greater than 1, so the lengths of each side of $\triangle CGL$ must be longer. Students who chose **G** are using $\overline{CL}$ rather than $\overline{GL}$ as the side corresponding to $\overline{PS}$.

Journal

Ask students to explain what a scale on a map means, how it is used, and how it is related to the concept of a similarity ratio.

ALTERNATIVE ASSESSMENT

Have students draw an obtuse triangle, measure its angles and sides, and write the measurements on the triangle. Ask them to draw two more triangles similar to the original, using similarity ratios of $\frac{2}{1}$ and $\frac{1}{2}$. Then calculate what the side lengths of the new triangles should be, and compare these to the results they get by measuring.

Power Presentations with PowerPoint®

7-2 Lesson Quiz

1. Determine whether the polygons are similar. If so, write the similarity ratio and a similarity statement. no

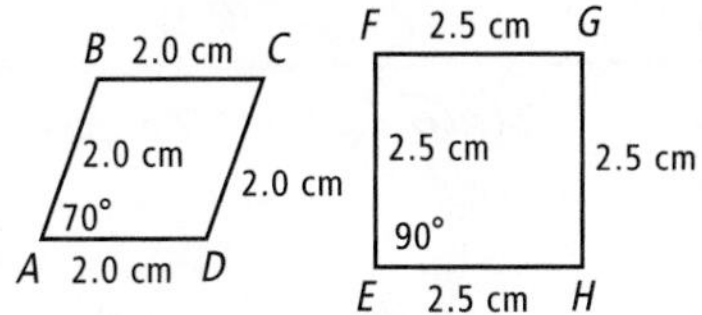

2. The ratio of a model sailboat's dimensions to the actual boat's dimensions is $\frac{1}{30}$. If the length of the model is 10 inches, what is the length of the actual sailboat in feet? 25 ft

3. Tell whether the following statement is sometimes, always, or never true.
Two equilateral triangles are similar. Always

Also available on transparency

7-2 PROBLEM SOLVING

1. $EFGH \sim JKLM$. What is the value of x? 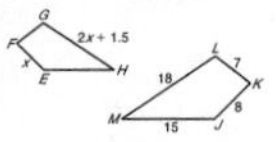
(Figure: $EFGH$ with $EF = x$, $GH = 2x + 1.5$; $JKLM$ with $ML = 18$, $LK = 7$, $KJ = 8$, $MJ = 15$)
6

2. The ratio of a model scale die cast motorcycle is 1:18. The model is $5\frac{1}{4}$ inches long. What is the length of the actual motorcycle in feet and inches?
7 ft 10.5 in.

3. A diagram of a new competition swimming pool is shown. If the width of the pool is 25 meters, find the length of the actual pool. 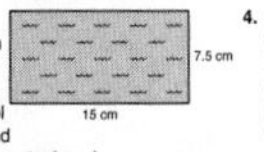
(Diagram: 15 cm by 7.5 cm)
50 m

4. Rectangle A has side lengths 16.4 centimeters and 10.8 centimeters. Rectangle B has side lengths 10.25 centimeters and 6.75 centimeters. Determine whether the rectangles are similar. If so, write the similarity ratio.
yes; $\frac{8}{5}$

Choose the best answer.

5. A pet store has various sizes of guinea pig cages. A diagram of the top view of one of the cages is shown. What are possible dimensions of this cage? 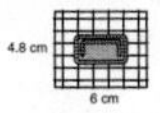
(Diagram: 6 cm by 4.8 cm)
A 28 in. by 24 in.   Ⓒ 30 in. by 24 in.
B 28 in. by 18 in.   D 30 in. by 18 in.

6. A gymnasium is 96 feet long and 75 feet wide. On a blueprint, the gymnasium is 5.5 inches long. To the nearest tenth of an inch, what is the width of the gymnasium on the blueprint?
F 3.7 in.   H 7.0 in.
Ⓖ 4.3 in.   J 13.6 in.

7. $\triangle QRS \sim \triangle TUV$. Find the value of y. 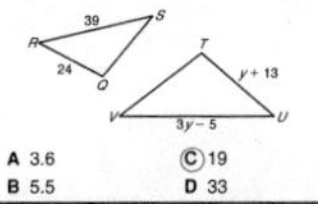
(Figure: $RS = 39$, $RQ = 24$; $TU = y + 13$, $VU = 3y - 5$)
A 3.6   Ⓒ 19
B 5.5   D 33

8. $\triangle ABC$ has side lengths 14, 8, and 10.4. What are possible side lengths of $\triangle DEF$ if $\triangle ABC \sim \triangle DEF$?
F 28, 20, 20.8
G 35, 16, 20.8
H 28, 20, 26
Ⓙ 35, 20, 26

Answers

31. Since $\overline{QR} \parallel \overline{ST}$, $\angle PQR \cong \angle PST$, and $\angle PRQ \cong \angle PTS$ by the Alt. Int. $\angle$s Thm. $\angle P \cong \angle P$ by the Reflex. Prop. of $\cong$. Thus the corr. $\angle$s of $\triangle PQR$ and $\triangle PST$ are $\cong$. It is easy to see that $PS = 6$ and $PT = 8$, so $\frac{PQ}{PS} = \frac{PR}{PT} = \frac{QR}{ST} = \frac{1}{2}$. Therefore $\triangle PQR \sim \triangle PST$ by the def. of $\sim$ polygons.

32a. $AC = \sqrt{2}$, $DC = BD = \frac{\sqrt{2}}{2}$

b. By the Isosc. $\triangle$ Thm., $\angle A \cong \angle C$, so $m\angle A = m\angle C = 45°$. Also $\angle DBC \cong \angle C$, so $m\angle DBC = 45°$. Thus the corr. $\angle$s of $\triangle ABC$ and $\triangle BDC$ are $\cong$. $\frac{AB}{BD} = \frac{BC}{DC} = \frac{AC}{BC} = \sqrt{2}$. By the def. of similarity, $\triangle ABC \sim \triangle CDB$.

Technology LAB Organizer

Use with Lesson 7-3

Pacing:
Traditional 1 day
Block $\frac{1}{2}$ day

Objective: Use geometry software to find ways to determine that triangles are similar.

Materials: geometry software

Online Edition
TechKeys

Countdown Week 15

Resources

Technology Lab Activities
7-3 Lab Recording Sheet

Teach

Discuss

Review with students that SAS, ASA, and SSS guarantee congruent triangles, and explain that in this lab, students will be using geometry software to discover if there are similar conditions that guarantee similar triangles. Also review the definitions of *similar* and *congruent* triangles and make sure that students understand how these two concepts differ.

State Resources

Use with Lesson 7-3

Predict Triangle Similarity Relationships

In Chapter 4, you found shortcuts for determining that two triangles are congruent. Now you will use geometry software to find ways to determine that triangles are similar.

go.hrw.com
Lab Resources Online
KEYWORD: MG7 Lab7

Activity 1

1. Construct $\triangle ABC$. Construct $\overline{DE}$ longer than any of the sides of $\triangle ABC$. Rotate $\overline{DE}$ around D by rotation $\angle BAC$. Rotate $\overline{DE}$ around E by rotation $\angle ABC$. Label the intersection point of the two rotated segments as F.

2. Measure angles to confirm that $\angle BAC \cong \angle EDF$ and $\angle ABC \cong \angle DEF$. Drag a vertex of $\triangle ABC$ or an endpoint of $\overline{DE}$ to show that the two triangles have two pairs of congruent angles.

3. Measure the side lengths of both triangles. Divide each side length of $\triangle ABC$ by the corresponding side length of $\triangle DEF$. Compare the resulting ratios. What do you notice? **The ratios of corr. side lengths are =.**

Try This

1. What theorem guarantees that the third pair of angles in the triangles are also congruent? **△ Sum Thm.**
2. Will the ratios of corresponding sides found in Step 3 always be equal? Drag a vertex of $\triangle ABC$ or an endpoint of $\overline{DE}$ to investigate this question. State a conjecture based on your results. **Yes; in ~ △s, corr. sides are proportional.**

Activity 2

1. Construct a new $\triangle ABC$. Create P in the interior of the triangle. Create $\triangle DEF$ by enlarging $\triangle ABC$ around P by a multiple of 2 using the Dilation command. Drag P outside of $\triangle ABC$ to separate the triangles.

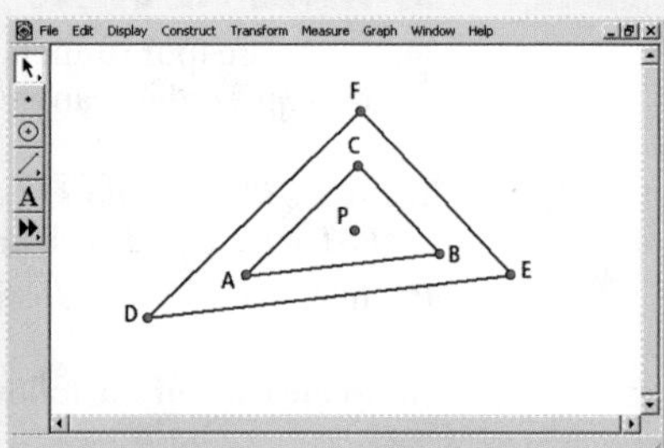

2. Measure the side lengths of $\triangle DEF$ to confirm that each side is twice as long as the corresponding side of $\triangle ABC$. Drag a vertex of $\triangle ABC$ to verify that this relationship is true.

3. Measure the angles of both triangles. What do you notice? **Corr. $\angle$s are $\cong$.**

Try This

3. Did the construction of the triangles with three pairs of sides in the same ratio guarantee that the corresponding angles would be congruent? State a conjecture based on these results. **Yes; if 2 $\triangle$s have their corr. sides in the same ratio, then the $\triangle$s are $\sim$.**
4. Compare your conjecture to the SSS Congruence Theorem from Chapter 4. How are they similar and how are they different?
They are similar in that both allow you to conclude that corr. $\angle$s are $\cong$. They are different in that the conjecture suggests that $\triangle$s with corr. sides in the same ratio have the same shape, but the SSS $\cong$ Thm. allows you to conclude that the $\triangle$s have both the same shape and the same size.

1. Construct a different $\triangle ABC$. Create P in the interior of the triangle. Expand $\overline{AB}$ and $\overline{AC}$ around P by a multiple of 2 using the Dilation command. Create an angle congruent to $\angle BAC$ with sides that are each twice as long as $\overline{AB}$ and $\overline{AC}$.

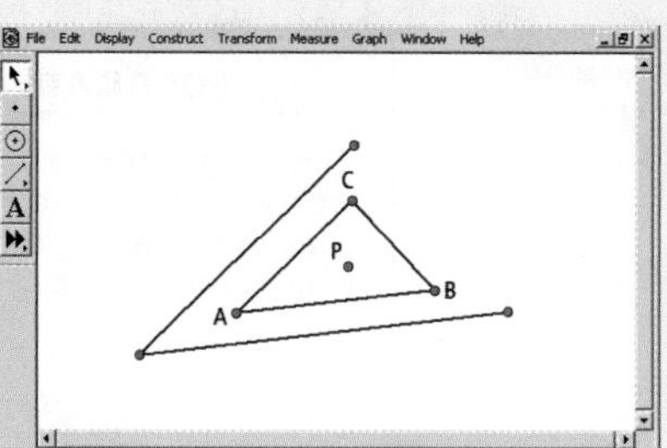

2. Use a segment to create the third side of a new triangle and label it $\triangle DEF$. Drag P outside of $\triangle ABC$ to separate the triangles.

3. Measure each side length and determine the relationship between corresponding sides of $\triangle ABC$ and $\triangle DEF$. **The ratio of the corr. sides of $\triangle ABC$ and $\triangle DEF$ are proportional.**

4. Measure the angles of both triangles. What do you notice? **The corr. $\angle$s of the $\triangle$s are $\cong$.**

Try This

5. Tell whether $\triangle ABC$ is similar to $\triangle DEF$. Explain your reasoning. **Yes; corr. sides are proportional and corr. $\angle$s are $\cong$.**
6. Write a conjecture based on the activity. What congruency theorem is related to your conjecture?
If $\triangle$s have 2 pairs of corr. sides in proportion and the included $\angle$s are $\cong$, then the $\triangle$s are $\sim$. This is related to the SAS $\cong$ Thm.

Close

Key Concept

Triangles can be proved similar by AA, SSS, and SAS, where corresponding angles are congruent and pairs of corresponding sides are proportional.

Assessment

Journal Have students compare and contrast the conditions that guarantee similar triangles with those that guarantee congruence.

7-3 Organizer

Pacing: Traditional 2 day
Block 1 day

Objectives: Prove certain triangles are similar by using AA, SSS, and SAS.

Use triangle similarity to solve problems.

Online Edition
Tutorial Videos

Countdown Week 15

Power Presentations with PowerPoint®

Warm Up

Solve each proportion.

1. $\frac{6}{11} = \frac{8}{b}$ $b = \frac{44}{3}$ or $14\frac{2}{3}$
2. $\frac{5}{z} = \frac{z}{20}$ $z = \pm 10$
3. $\frac{3}{10} = \frac{6}{x + 12}$ $x = 8$
4. If $\triangle QRS \sim \triangle XYZ$, identify the pairs of congruent angles and write 3 proportions using pairs of corresponding sides.
   $\angle Q \cong \angle X$; $\angle R \cong \angle Y$; $\angle S \cong \angle Z$; $\frac{QR}{XY} = \frac{RS}{YZ}$; $\frac{RS}{YZ} = \frac{QS}{XZ}$; $\frac{QS}{XZ} = \frac{QR}{XY}$

Also available on transparency

Math Humor

Q: What do you call a fierce beast?

A: A line

7-3 Triangle Similarity: AA, SSS, and SAS

Objectives
Prove certain triangles are similar by using AA, SSS, and SAS.

Use triangle similarity to solve problems.

Who uses this?
Engineers use similar triangles when designing buildings, such as the Pyramid Building in San Diego, California. (See Example 5.)

There are several ways to prove certain triangles are similar. The following postulate, as well as the SSS and SAS Similarity Theorems, will be used in proofs just as SSS, SAS, ASA, HL, and AAS were used to prove triangles congruent.

Know it! Note

Postulate 7-3-1 Angle-Angle (AA) Similarity

POSTULATE	HYPOTHESIS	CONCLUSION
If two angles of one triangle are congruent to two angles of another triangle, then the triangles are similar.		$\triangle ABC \sim \triangle DEF$

EXAMPLE 1 Using the AA Similarity Postulate

Explain why the triangles are similar and write a similarity statement.

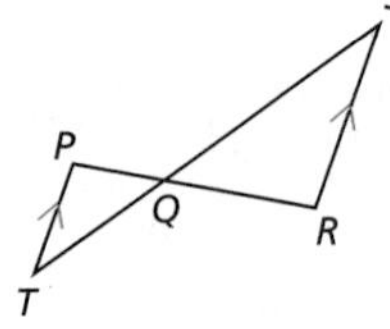

Since $\overline{PT} \parallel \overline{SR}$, $\angle P \cong \angle R$, and $\angle T \cong \angle S$ by the Alternate Interior Angles Theorem. Therefore $\triangle PQT \sim \triangle RQS$ by AA $\sim$.

1. Explain why the triangles are similar and write a similarity statement.

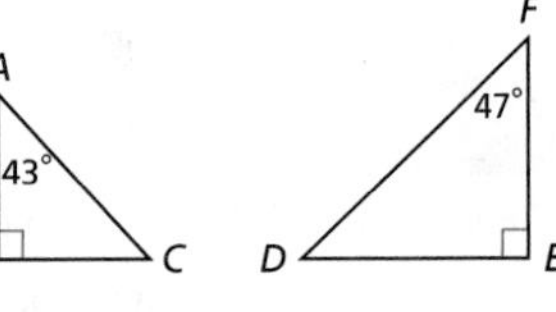

By the $\triangle$ Sum Thm., $m\angle C = 47°$, so $\angle C \cong \angle F$. $\angle B \cong \angle E$ by the Rt. $\angle \cong$ Thm. Therefore $\triangle ABC \sim \triangle DEF$ by AA $\sim$.

Theorem 7-3-2 Side-Side-Side (SSS) Similarity

THEOREM	HYPOTHESIS	CONCLUSION
If the three sides of one triangle are proportional to the three corresponding sides of another triangle, then the triangles are similar.		$\triangle ABC \sim \triangle DEF$

You will prove Theorem 7-3-2 in Exercise 38.

State Resources

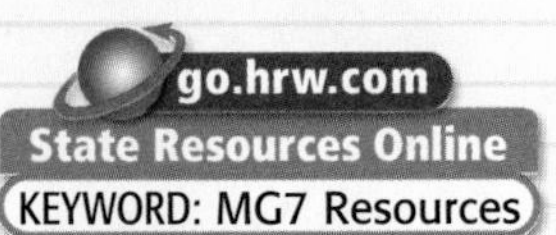

State Resources Online
KEYWORD: MG7 Resources

1 Introduce

EXPLORATION

7-3 Triangle Similarity: AA, SSS, and SAS

Explore a shortcut for proving that two triangles are similar.

1. Draw $\triangle ABC$ with the given measurements. (*Hint:* First draw $\overline{AB}$. Then use a protractor to draw $\angle A$ and $\angle B$ at each endpoint of $\overline{AB}$.)
2. Draw $\triangle DEF$ with the given measurements so that $\triangle DEF$ is **NOT** congruent to $\triangle ABC$. (*Hint:* First draw $\overline{DE}$ so that $DE \neq AB$.)
3. What can you say about $\angle C$ and $\angle F$? Why?
4. Measure the lengths of the sides of each triangle. Then calculate $\frac{AB}{DE}$, $\frac{BC}{EF}$, and $\frac{AC}{DF}$. What do you notice about these values?
5. What can you conclude about $\triangle ABC$ and $\triangle DEF$? Why?
6. Repeat Steps 1–5, choosing your own measures so that $m\angle A = m\angle D$ and $m\angle B = m\angle E$. Do you get the same results?

$\triangle ABC$	
$m\angle A$	45°
$m\angle B$	60°

$\triangle DEF$	
$m\angle D$	45°
$m\angle E$	60°

THINK AND DISCUSS

7. **Describe** a shortcut, based on your results, for showing that two triangles are similar.
8. **Explain** how you can use your shortcut

Motivate

Review the triangle congruence postulates SSS, SAS, and ASA. Point out that in this lesson, postulates and theorems will be used as shortcuts to prove that two triangles are similar. Given a set of tangrams (MK) or other objects, students should categorize and describe the pieces that are similar, and those that are congruent to each other.

Explorations and answers are provided in *Alternate Openers: Explorations Transparencies.*

Theorem 7-3-3 Side-Angle-Side (SAS) Similarity

THEOREM	HYPOTHESIS	CONCLUSION
If two sides of one triangle are proportional to two sides of another triangle and their included angles are congruent, then the triangles are similar.	$\angle B \cong \angle E$	$\triangle ABC \sim \triangle DEF$

You will prove Theorem 7-3-3 in Exercise 39.

EXAMPLE 2 Verifying Triangle Similarity

Verify that the triangles are similar.

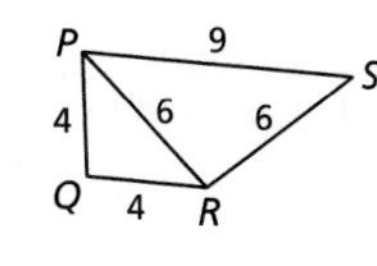

A $\triangle PQR$ **and** $\triangle PRS$

$\frac{PQ}{PR} = \frac{4}{6} = \frac{2}{3}, \frac{QR}{RS} = \frac{4}{6} = \frac{2}{3}, \frac{PR}{PS} = \frac{6}{9} = \frac{2}{3}$

Therefore $\triangle PQR \sim \triangle PRS$ by SSS ~.

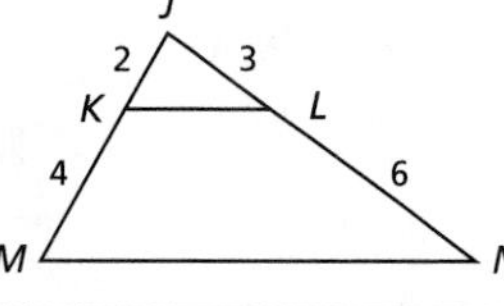

B $\triangle JKL$ **and** $\triangle JMN$

$\angle J \cong \angle J$ by the Reflexive Property of $\cong$.

$\frac{JK}{JM} = \frac{2}{6} = \frac{1}{3}, \frac{JL}{JN} = \frac{3}{9} = \frac{1}{3}$

Therefore $\triangle JKL \sim \triangle JMN$ by SAS ~.

2. Verify that $\triangle TXU \sim \triangle VXW$.

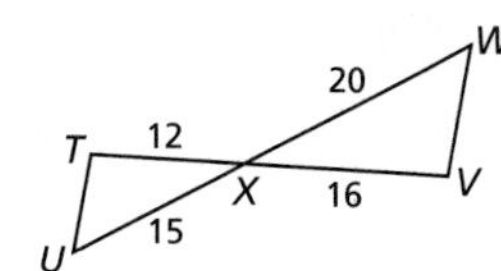

$\angle TXU \cong \angle VXW$ by the Vert. $\angle$s Thm. $\frac{TX}{VX} = \frac{12}{16} = \frac{3}{4}$, and $\frac{XU}{XW} = \frac{15}{20} = \frac{3}{4}$. Therefore $\triangle TXU \sim \triangle VXW$ by SAS ~.

EXAMPLE 3 Finding Lengths in Similar Triangles

Explain why $\triangle ABC \sim \triangle DBE$ and then find BE.

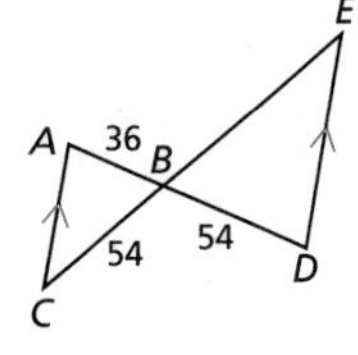

Step 1 Prove triangles are similar.

As shown $\overline{AC} \parallel \overline{ED}$, $\angle A \cong \angle D$, and $\angle C \cong \angle E$ by the Alternate Interior Angles Theorem. Therefore $\triangle ABC \sim \triangle DBE$ by AA ~.

Step 2 Find BE.

$\frac{AB}{DB} = \frac{BC}{BE}$	*Corr. sides are proportional.*
$\frac{36}{54} = \frac{54}{BE}$	*Substitute 36 for AB, 54 for DB, and 54 for BC.*
$36(BE) = 54^2$	*Cross Products Prop.*
$36(BE) = 2916$	*Simplify.*
$BE = 81$	*Divide both sides by 36.*

3. Explain why $\triangle RSV \sim \triangle RTU$ and then find RT.

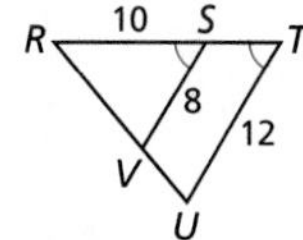

3. It is given that $\angle RSV \cong \angle T$. By the Reflex. Prop. of $\cong$, $\angle R \cong \angle R$. Therefore $\triangle RSV \sim \triangle RTU$ by AA ~. $RT = 15$.

2 Teach

Guided Instruction

Introduce the AA Similarity Postulate and the SSS and SAS Similarity Theorems, illustrating each with an example. Remind students that in triangle similarity, they should identify sides that are *proportional*, rather than congruent. Finally, discuss the Properties of Similarity and give an example of each.

Inclusion Remind students that similarity statements indicate corresponding parts in the same way as in congruence statements.

Reaching All Learners

Through Visual Cues

When working with similar triangles, some students have trouble identifying the corresponding sides. Point out that tick marks should not be used, because they imply congruent segments. Instead, encourage students to use different colored pencils or highlighters to mark the segments that make up each corresponding pair.

Power Presentations with PowerPoint®

Additional Examples

Example 1

Explain why the triangles are similar and write a similarity statement.

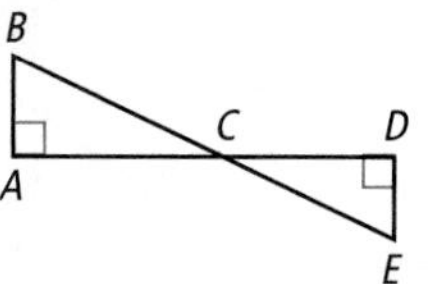

$\angle A \cong \angle D$ by the Rt. $\angle \cong$ Thm. $\angle ACB \cong \angle DCE$ by the Vert. $\angle$s Thm. Therefore $\triangle ACB \sim \triangle DEC$ by AA ~.

Example 2

Verify that the triangles are similar.

A. $\triangle PQR$ and $\triangle STU$

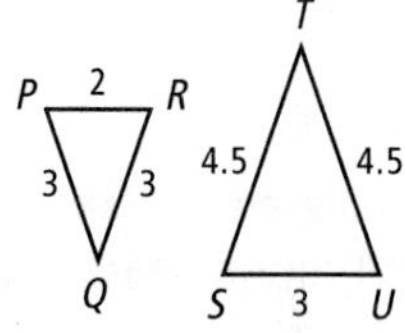

$\frac{PQ}{ST} = \frac{QR}{TU} = \frac{PR}{SU} = \frac{2}{3}$. Therefore $\triangle PQR \sim \triangle STU$ by SSS ~.

B. $\triangle DEF$ and $\triangle HJK$

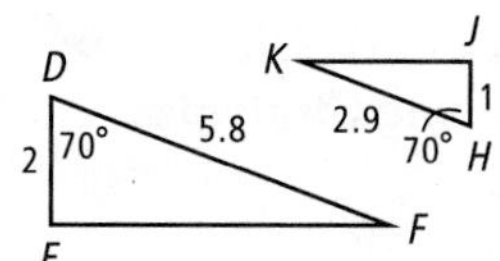

$m\angle D = m\angle H = 70°$, so $\angle D \cong \angle H$. $\frac{DE}{JH} = \frac{2}{1}$ and $\frac{DF}{HK} = \frac{5.8}{2.9} = \frac{2}{1}$. Therefore $\triangle DEF \sim \triangle HJK$ by SAS ~.

Example 3

Explain why $\triangle ABE \sim \triangle ACD$, and then find CD.

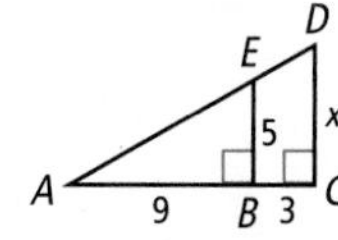

$\angle A \cong \angle A$ by the Reflex. Prop. of $\cong$. $\angle ABE \cong \angle ACD$ by the Rt. $\angle \cong$ Thm. Therefore $\triangle ABE \sim \triangle ACD$ by AA ~. $CD = \frac{60}{9} = \frac{20}{3}$, or $6\frac{2}{3}$.

INTERVENTION

Questioning Strategies

EXAMPLES 1–3

- Why are ASA and AAS not similarity theorems?

Power Presentations with PowerPoint®

Additional Examples

Example 4

Given: $3UT = 5RT$ and $3VT = 5ST$

Prove: $\triangle UVT \sim \triangle RST$

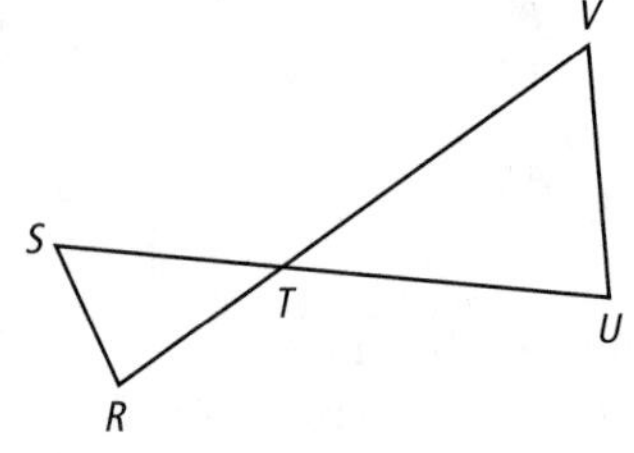

Proof:

1. $3UT = 5RT$ and $3VT = 5ST$ (Given)
2. $\frac{UT}{RT} = \frac{5}{3}, \frac{VT}{ST} = \frac{5}{3}$ (Div. Prop. of =)
3. $\frac{UT}{RT} = \frac{VT}{ST}$ (Trans. Prop. of =)
4. $\angle UTV \cong \angle RTS$ (Vert. ∠s Thm.)
5. $\triangle UVT \sim \triangle RST$ (SAS ~)

Example 5

Use the diagram in **Example 5** to find BA to the nearest tenth.

23.3 ft

INTERVENTION

Questioning Strategies

EXAMPLE 4

- Can you use just two pairs of corresponding sides when proving triangles similar? Explain.

EXAMPLE 5

- How can the Triangle Midsegment Theorem be applied to find the lengths of some of the segments in the diagram in Example 5?

EXAMPLE 4 Writing Proofs with Similar Triangles

Given: A is the midpoint of $\overline{BC}$.
D is the midpoint of $\overline{BE}$.

Prove: $\triangle BDA \sim \triangle BEC$

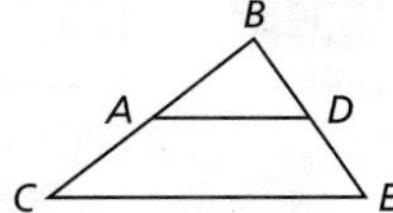

Proof:

Statements	Reasons
1. A is the mdpt. of $\overline{BC}$. D is the mdpt. of $\overline{BE}$.	1. Given
2. $\overline{BA} \cong \overline{AC}$, $\overline{BD} \cong \overline{DE}$	2. Def. of mdpt.
3. $BA = AC$, $BD = DE$	3. Def. of ≅ seg.
4. $BC = BA + AC$, $BE = BD + DE$	4. Seg. Add. Post.
5. $BC = BA + BA$, $BE = BD + BD$	5. Subst. Prop.
6. $BC = 2BA$, $BE = 2BD$	6. Simplify.
7. $\frac{BC}{BA} = 2$, $\frac{BE}{BD} = 2$	7. Div. Prop. of =
8. $\frac{BC}{BA} = \frac{BE}{BD}$	8. Trans. Prop. of =
9. $\angle B \cong \angle B$	9. Reflex. Prop. of ≅
10. $\triangle BDA \sim \triangle BEC$	10. SAS ~ *Steps 8, 9*

4\. 1. M is the mdpt. of $\overline{JK}$, N is the mdpt. of $\overline{KL}$, and P is the mdpt. of $\overline{JL}$. (Given)
2\. $MP = \frac{1}{2}KL$, $MN = \frac{1}{2}JL$, $NP = \frac{1}{2}KJ$ (△ Midsegs. Thm.)
3\. $\frac{MP}{KL} = \frac{MN}{JL} = \frac{NP}{KJ} = \frac{1}{2}$ (Div. Prop. of =)
4\. $\triangle JKL \sim \triangle NPM$ (SSS ~ *Step 3*)

CHECK IT OUT! 4. **Given:** M is the midpoint of $\overline{JK}$. N is the midpoint of $\overline{KL}$, and P is the midpoint of $\overline{JL}$.

Prove: $\triangle JKL \sim \triangle NPM$

(*Hint:* Use the Triangle Midsegment Theorem and SSS ~.)

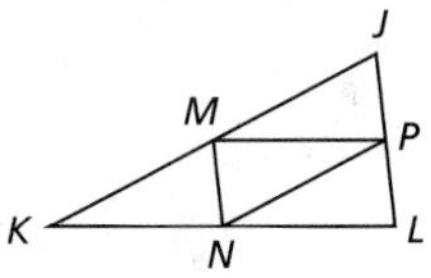

EXAMPLE 5 Engineering Application

The photo shows a gable roof. $\overline{AC} \parallel \overline{FG}$. Use similar triangles to prove $\triangle ABC \sim \triangle FBG$ and then find BF to the nearest tenth of a foot.

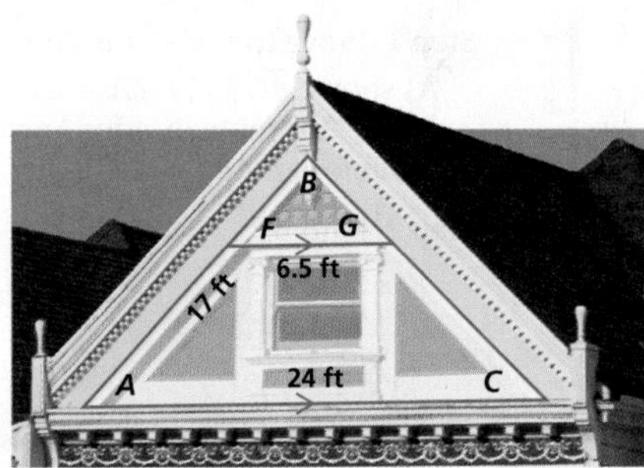

Step 1 Prove the triangles are similar.

$\overline{AC} \parallel \overline{FG}$	*Given*
$\angle BFG \cong \angle BAC$	*Corr. ∠s Thm.*
$\angle B \cong \angle B$	*Reflex. Prop. of ≅*

Therefore $\triangle ABC \sim \triangle FBG$ by AA ~.

Step 2 Find *BF*.

$$\frac{BA}{AC} = \frac{BF}{FG} \quad \textit{Corr. sides are proportional.}$$
$$\frac{x+17}{24} = \frac{x}{6.5} \quad \textit{Substitute the given values.}$$
$$6.5(x+17) = 24x \quad \textit{Cross Products Prop.}$$
$$6.5x + 110.5 = 24x \quad \textit{Distrib. Prop.}$$
$$110.5 = 17.5x \quad \textit{Subtract 6.5x from both sides.}$$
$$6.3 \approx x \text{ or } BF \quad \textit{Divide both sides by 17.5.}$$

5. What if...? If $AB = 4x$, $AC = 5x$, and $BF = 4$, find FG. 5

You learned in Chapter 2 that the Reflexive, Symmetric, and Transitive Properties of Equality have corresponding properties of congruence. These properties also hold true for similarity of triangles.

Properties of Similarity

Reflexive Property of Similarity

$\triangle ABC \sim \triangle ABC$ (Reflex. Prop. of $\sim$)

Symmetric Property of Similarity

If $\triangle ABC \sim \triangle DEF$, then $\triangle DEF \sim \triangle ABC$. (Sym. Prop. of $\sim$)

Transitive Property of Similarity

If $\triangle ABC \sim \triangle DEF$ and $\triangle DEF \sim \triangle XYZ$, then $\triangle ABC \sim \triangle XYZ$. (Trans. Prop. of $\sim$)

THINK AND DISCUSS

1. What additional information, if any, would you you need in order to show that $\triangle ABC \sim \triangle DEF$ by the AA Similarity Postulate?
2. What additional information, if any, would you need in order to show that $\triangle ABC \sim \triangle DEF$ by the SAS Similarity Theorem?
3. Do corresponding sides of similar triangles need to be proportional and congruent? Explain.
4. **GET ORGANIZED** Copy and complete the graphic organizer. If possible, write a congruence or similarity theorem or postulate in each section of the table. Include a marked diagram for each.

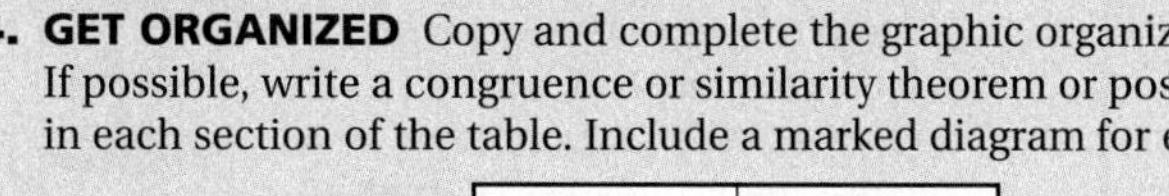

	Congruence	Similarity
SSS		
SAS		
AA		

If you only need to know that two angles of two triangles are congruent in order to prove similarity, students might think you only need to know three angles of two quadrilaterals to do the same. Students will inaccurately compare the ratios of the sides as in SSS similarity for any *n*-gon. Use counterexamples to show that this is incorrect. Stress that triangles are a special case because they are rigid structures.

Kinesthetic Some students may have difficulty identifying corresponding sides in similar triangles because of the orientation of the figures. Show these students how they can copy one of the triangles onto a piece of paper, then cut it out and rotate it, so that the two triangles have the same orientation.

Inclusion When using the SSS and SAS Similarity Theorems, some students have difficulty matching up the corresponding sides. Tell these students to match up small to small sides, medium to medium sides, and large to large sides.

3 Close

Summarize

Review the three ways that students have learned to prove triangles similar: AA, SSS, and SAS. Go over how to find the lengths of missing sides in similar triangles. Review the Reflexive, Symmetric, and Transitive Properties of Similarity.

ONGOING ASSESSMENT and INTERVENTION

***Diagnose Before* the Lesson**
7-3 Warm Up, TE p. 470

***Monitor During* the Lesson**
Check It Out! Exercises, SE pp. 470–473
Questioning Strategies, TE pp. 471–472

***Assess After* the Lesson**
7-3 Lesson Quiz, TE p. 477
Alternative Assessment, TE p. 477

Answers to *Think and Discuss*

1. $\angle A \cong \angle D$ or $\angle C \cong \angle F$
2. $\frac{BA}{ED} = \frac{3}{5}$
3. No; the corr. sides need to be proportional but not necessarily $\cong$ for the $\triangle$s to be $\sim$.
4. See p. A6.

7-3 Exercises

Assignment Guide

Assign *Guided Practice* exercises as necessary.

If you finished Examples **1–3**
- **Basic** 11–16, 20–24, 31
- **Average** 11–16, 19–24, 27, 31
- **Advanced** 11–16, 20–24, 27, 31, 37, 40

If you finished Examples **1–5**
- **Basic** 11–19, 23–25, 32–37, 41–46
- **Average** 11–25, 29–37, 41–46
- **Advanced** 11–20, 23–28, 30, 31, 33–46

Homework Quick Check
Quickly check key concepts.
Exercises: 11, 12, 14, 16, 18, 23

Answers

1. By the △ Sum Thm., m∠A = 47°. So by the def. of ≅, ∠A ≅ ∠F, and ∠C ≅ ∠H. Therefore △ABC ~ △FGH by AA ~.
2. It is given that ∠P ≅ ∠T. ∠QST is a rt. ∠ by the Lin. Pair Thm., so ∠QST ≅ ∠RSP. Therefore △QST ~ △RSP by AA ~.
3. $\frac{DF}{JL} = \frac{DE}{JK} = \frac{EF}{KL} = \frac{1}{2}$, so △DEF ~ △JKL by SSS ~.
4. It is given that ∠NMP ≅ ∠RMQ. $\frac{MN}{MR} = \frac{MP}{MQ} = \frac{2}{3}$. Therefore △MNP ~ △MRQ by SAS ~.
5. It is given that ∠AED ≅ ∠ACB. ∠A ≅ ∠A by the Reflex. Prop. of ≅. Therefore △AED ~ △ACB by AA ~. AB = 10

6–8. See p. A23.

State Resources

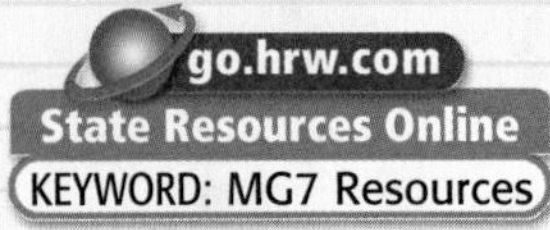

7-3 Exercises

go.hrw.com
Homework Help Online
KEYWORD: MG7 7-3
Parent Resources Online
KEYWORD: MG7 Parent

GUIDED PRACTICE

SEE EXAMPLE 1 p. 470

Explain why the triangles are similar and write a similarity statement.

1. 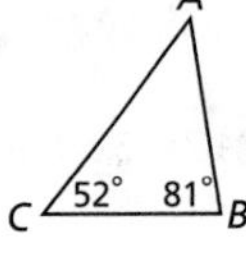

2.

SEE EXAMPLE 2 p. 471

Verify that the triangles are similar.

3. △DEF and △JKL

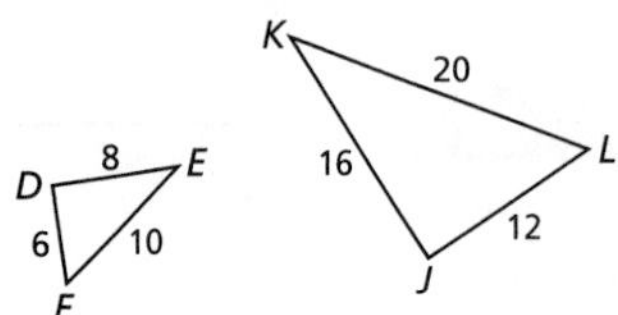

4. △MNP and △MRQ

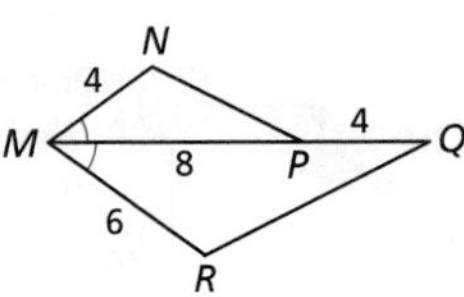

SEE EXAMPLE 3 p. 471

Multi-Step Explain why the triangles are similar and then find each length.

5. AB

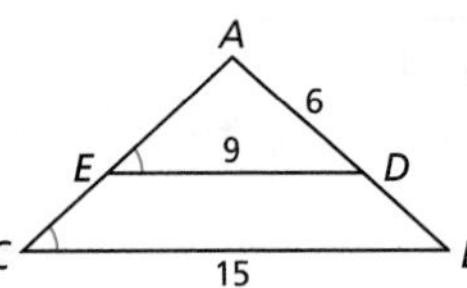

6. WY

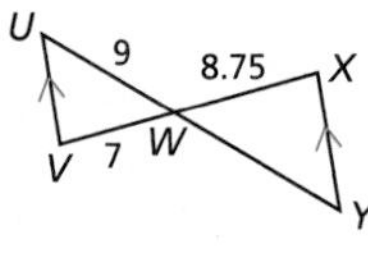

SEE EXAMPLE 4 p. 472

7. **Given:** $\overleftrightarrow{MN} \parallel \overline{KL}$
Prove: △JMN ~ △JKL

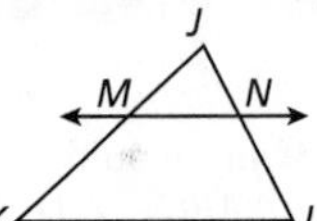

8. **Given:** SQ = 2QP, TR = 2RP
Prove: △PQR ~ △PST

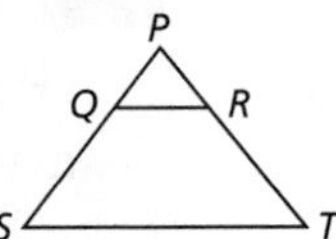

9. The coordinates of A, B, and C are A(0, 0), B(2, 6), and C(8, −2). What theorem or postulate justifies the statement △ABC ~ △ADE, if the coordinates of D and E are twice the coordinates of B and C? **SAS or SSS ~ Thm.**

SEE EXAMPLE 5 p. 472

10. **Surveying** In order to measure the distance AB across the meteorite crater, a surveyor at S locates points A, B, C, and D as shown. What is AB to the nearest meter? nearest kilometer? **1200 m, or 1.2 km**

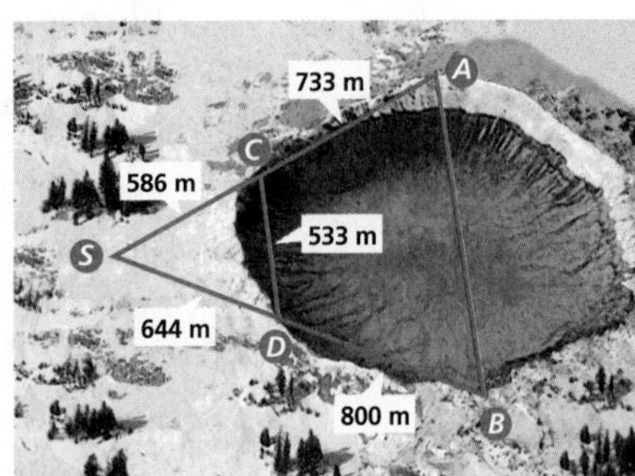

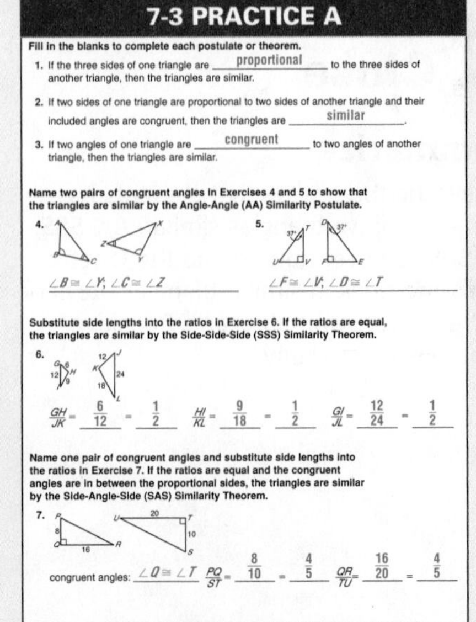

7-3 PRACTICE A

Fill in the blanks to complete each postulate or theorem.

1. If the three sides of one triangle are **proportional** to the three sides of another triangle, then the triangles are similar.
2. If two sides of one triangle are proportional to two sides of another triangle and their included angles are congruent, then the triangles are **similar**.
3. If two angles of one triangle are **congruent** to two angles of another triangle, then the triangles are similar.

Name two pairs of congruent angles in Exercises 4 and 5 to show that the triangles are similar by the Angle-Angle (AA) Similarity Postulate.

4. ∠B ≅ ∠Y; ∠C ≅ ∠Z

5. ∠F ≅ ∠V; ∠D ≅ ∠T

Substitute side lengths into the ratios in Exercise 6. If the ratios are equal, the triangles are similar by the Side-Side-Side (SSS) Similarity Theorem.

6. $\frac{GH}{JK} = \frac{6}{12} = \frac{1}{2}$ $\frac{HI}{KL} = \frac{9}{18} = \frac{1}{2}$ $\frac{GI}{JL} = \frac{12}{24} = \frac{1}{2}$

Name one pair of congruent angles and substitute side lengths into the ratios in Exercise 7. If the ratios are equal and the congruent angles are in between the proportional sides, the triangles are similar by the Side-Angle-Side (SAS) Similarity Theorem.

7. congruent angles: ∠Q ≅ ∠T $\frac{PQ}{ST} = \frac{8}{10} = \frac{4}{5}$ $\frac{QR}{TU} = \frac{16}{20} = \frac{4}{5}$

Independent Practice

For Exercises	See Example
11–12	1
13–14	2
15–16	3
17–18	4
19	5

Extra Practice

Skills Practice p. S16
Application Practice p. S34

PRACTICE AND PROBLEM SOLVING

Explain why the triangles are similar and write a similarity statement.

11.

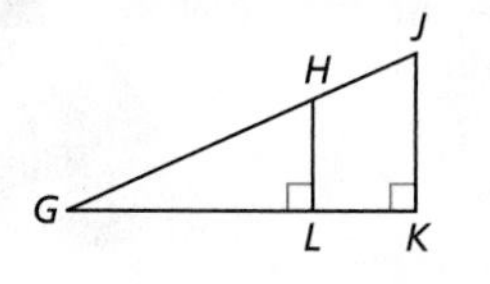

12.

Verify that the given triangles are similar.

13. $\triangle KLM$ and $\triangle KNL$

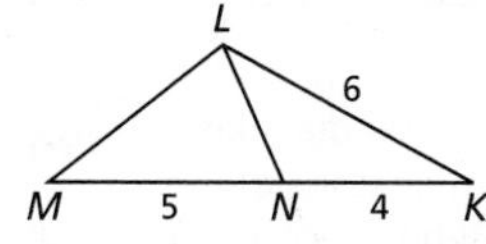

14. $\triangle UVW$ and $\triangle XYZ$

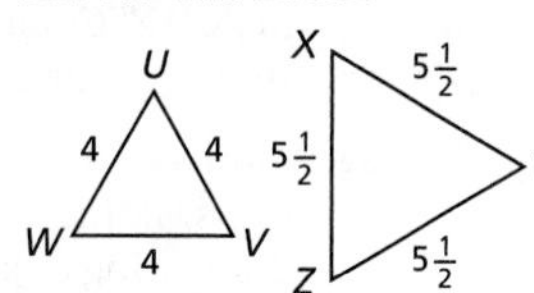

Multi-Step Explain why the triangles are similar and then find each length.

15. AB

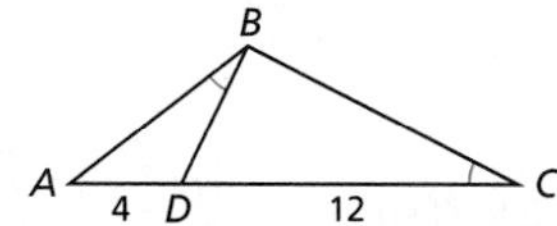

16. PS

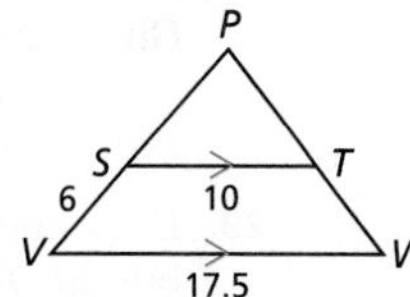

17. **Given:** $CD = 3AC$, $CE = 3BC$
Prove: $\triangle ABC \sim \triangle DEC$

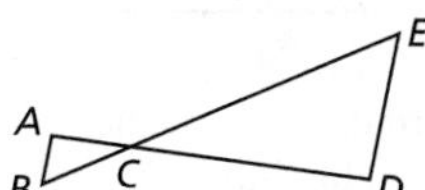

18. **Given:** $\frac{PR}{MR} = \frac{QR}{NR}$
Prove: $\angle 1 \cong \angle 2$

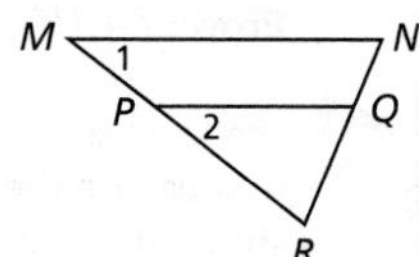

19. Photography The picture shows a person taking a pinhole photograph of himself. Light entering the opening reflects his image on the wall, forming similar triangles. What is the height of the image to the nearest tenth of a foot? 1.5 ft

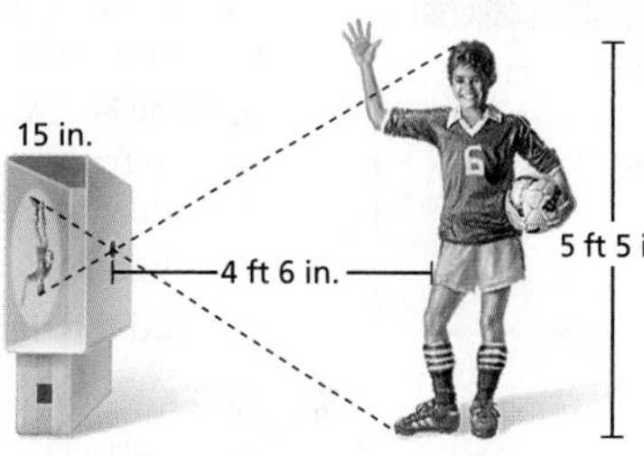

Draw $\triangle JKL$ and $\triangle MNP$. Determine if you can conclude that $\triangle JKL \sim \triangle MNP$ based on the given information. If so, which postulate or theorem justifies your response?

20. $\angle K \cong \angle N$, $\frac{JK}{MN} = \frac{KL}{NP}$ yes; SAS ~

21. $\frac{JK}{MN} = \frac{KL}{NP} = \frac{JL}{MP}$ yes; SSS ~

22. $\angle J \cong \angle M$, $\frac{JL}{MP} = \frac{KL}{NP}$ no

Find the value of x.

23. 3

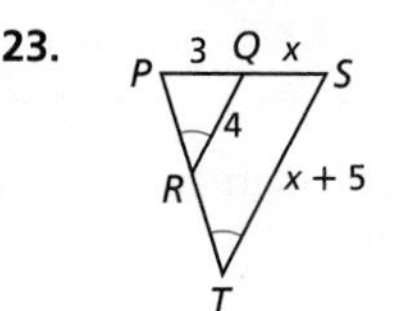

24. 7

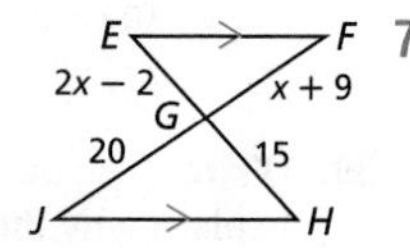

11. It is given that $\angle GLH \cong \angle K$. $\angle G \cong \angle G$ by the Reflex. Prop. of $\cong$. Therefore $\triangle HLG \sim \triangle JKG$ by AA ~.

12. By the Isosc. $\triangle$ Thm., $\angle C \cong \angle B$. By the $\triangle$ Sum Thm. $m\angle C = m\angle B = 74°$. In the same way, $m\angle F = 74°$. So by the def. of $\cong$, $\angle B \cong \angle E$ and $\angle C \cong \angle F$. Therefore $\triangle ABC \sim \triangle DEF$ by AA ~.

13. $\angle K \cong \angle K$ by the Reflex. Prop. of $\cong$. $\frac{KL}{KN} = \frac{KM}{KL} = \frac{3}{2}$. Therefore $\triangle KLM \sim \triangle KNL$ by SAS ~.

14. $\frac{UV}{XY} = \frac{VW}{YZ} = \frac{WU}{ZX} = \frac{8}{11}$. Therefore $\triangle UVW \sim \triangle XYZ$ by SSS ~.

COMMON ERROR ALERT

A common error in **Exercise 16** is to let $PS = x$ and then to write and solve the proportion $\frac{x}{6} = \frac{10}{17.5}$. Point out that 6 is not the length of a side of any triangle, so it cannot be used in the proportion. Encourage students to draw $\triangle PST$ and $\triangle PVW$ separately and then write the correct proportion, $\frac{x}{x+6} = \frac{10}{17.5}$.

Teaching Tip

Algebra In **Exercise 16,** remind students that in any proportion such as $\frac{x}{x+6} = \frac{10}{17.5}$, they should use parentheses to write the product as $10(x + 6)$. Then use the Distributive Property to remove the parentheses.

Answers

15. It is given that $\angle ABD \cong \angle C$. $\angle A \cong \angle A$ by the Reflex. Prop. of $\cong$. Therefore $\triangle ABD \sim \triangle ACB$ by AA ~. $AB = 8$

16. Since $\overline{ST} \parallel \overline{VW}$, $\angle PST \cong \angle V$ by the Corr. ∠s Post. $\angle P \cong \angle P$ by the Reflex. Prop. of $\cong$. Therefore $\triangle PST \sim \triangle PVW$ by AA ~. $PS = 8$

17.
1. $CD = 3AC$, $CE = 3BC$ (Given)
2. $\frac{CD}{AC} = 3$, $\frac{CE}{BC} = 3$ (Div. Prop. of =)
3. $\angle ACB \cong \angle DCE$ (Vert. ∠s Thm.)
4. $\triangle ABC \sim \triangle DEC$ (SAS ~ *Steps 2, 3*)

18.
1. $\frac{PR}{MR} = \frac{QR}{NR}$ (Given)
2. $\angle R \cong \angle R$ (Reflex. Prop. of $\cong$)
3. $\triangle PQR \sim \triangle MNR$ (SAS ~ *Steps 1, 2*)
4. $\angle 1 \cong \angle 2$ (Def. of ~ △s)

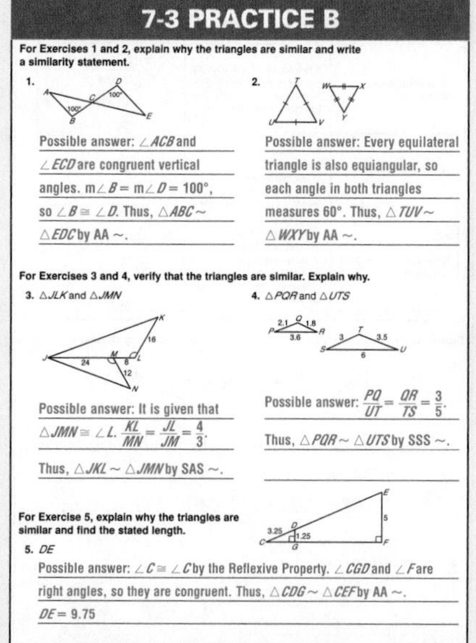

7-3 PRACTICE B

For Exercises 1 and 2, explain why the triangles are similar and write a similarity statement.

1. Possible answer: $\angle ACB$ and $\angle ECD$ are congruent vertical angles. $m\angle B = m\angle D = 100°$, so $\angle B \cong \angle D$. Thus, $\triangle ABC \sim \triangle EDC$ by AA ~.

2. Possible answer: Every equilateral triangle is also equiangular, so each angle in both triangles measures 60°. Thus, $\triangle TUV \sim \triangle WXY$ by AA ~.

For Exercises 3 and 4, verify that the triangles are similar. Explain why.

3. $\triangle JLK$ and $\triangle JMN$
Possible answer: It is given that $\triangle JMN \cong \angle L$. $\frac{KL}{MN} = \frac{JL}{JM} = \frac{4}{3}$. Thus, $\triangle JKL \sim \triangle JMN$ by SAS ~.

4. $\triangle PQR$ and $\triangle UTS$
Possible answer: $\frac{PQ}{UT} = \frac{QR}{TS} = \frac{3}{5}$. Thus, $\triangle PQR \sim \triangle UTS$ by SSS ~.

For Exercise 5, explain why the triangles are similar and find the stated length.

5. DE
Possible answer: $\angle C \cong \angle C$ by the Reflexive Property. $\angle CGD$ and $\angle F$ are right angles, so they are congruent. Thus, $\triangle CDG \sim \triangle CEF$ by AA ~.
$DE = 9.75$

7-3 PRACTICE C

Use the figure for Exercises 1–3.

1. Prove similarity relationships between triangles in the figure. Give a similarity ratio for each relationship you find.
Possible answer: $\triangle ABC$ and $\triangle ADB$ share $\angle A$. They also each have a right angle, so $\triangle ABC \sim \triangle ADB$ by AA ~. They have a similarity ratio of $\frac{2}{1}$. $\triangle ABC$ and $\triangle BDC$ share $\angle C$. They also each have a right angle, so $\triangle ABC \sim \triangle BDC$ by AA ~. They have a similarity ratio of $\frac{2\sqrt{3}}{3}$. By the Transitive Property of Similarity, $\triangle ADB \sim \triangle BDC$. They have a similarity ratio of $\frac{\sqrt{3}}{3}$.

2. $AD = 1$ and $DC = 3$. Find the perimeter of $\triangle ABC$. $6 + 2\sqrt{3}$

3. Use the similarity ratios you found in Exercise 1 and the answer to Exercise 2 to find the perimeters of $\triangle ADB$ and $\triangle BDC$. $3 + \sqrt{3}; 3 + 3\sqrt{3}$

4. Find ST. $\frac{13}{3}$

5. Use triangle similarity to prove that $GHIJK \sim PQRST$.
Possible answer: Draw diagonals $\overline{HK}$, $\overline{HJ}$, $\overline{QS}$, and $\overline{QT}$. $\angle G$ and $\angle P$ are right angles, so they are congruent. $\frac{GK}{PT} = \frac{GH}{PQ} = \frac{3}{2}$, so $\triangle GHK \sim \triangle PQT$ by SAS. It is given that $\angle I \cong \angle R$. $\frac{HI}{QR} = \frac{IJ}{RS} = \frac{3}{2}$, so $\triangle HIJ \sim \triangle QRS$ by SAS. Because $\triangle GHK \sim \triangle PQT$, $\frac{HK}{QT} = \frac{3}{2}$ and $\angle GHK \cong \angle PQT$. Because $\triangle HIJ \sim \triangle QRS$, $\frac{HJ}{QS} = \frac{3}{2}$ and $\angle IHJ \cong \angle RQS$. It is given that $\angle H \cong \angle Q$. So by the Angle Addition Postulate, $\angle KHJ \cong \angle TQS$. $\frac{HK}{QT} = \frac{HJ}{QS} = \frac{3}{2}$, so $\triangle KHJ \sim \triangle TQS$ by SAS. Because $\triangle KHJ \sim \triangle TQS$, $\frac{KJ}{ST} = \frac{HK}{QT} = \frac{3}{2}$. All the corresponding angles are congruent; all the corresponding sides are proportional. Thus, $GHIJK \sim PQRST$.

Exercise 25 involves determining which of three isosceles triangles are similar, and finding a similarity ratio. This exercise prepares students for the Multi-Step Test Prep on page 478.

Answers

26. Possible answer: Yes; if corr. ∠s are ≅ and corr. sides are proportional, $\triangle ABC \sim \triangle XYZ$.

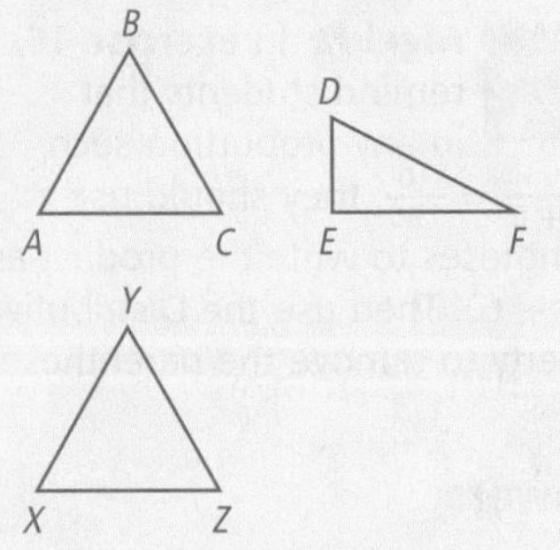

28. Since $\triangle ABC \sim \triangle DEF$, by the def. of ~ △s, $\angle A \cong \angle D$, and $\angle B \cong \angle E$. Similarly, since $\triangle DEF \sim \triangle XYZ$, $\angle D \cong \angle X$, and $\angle E \cong \angle Y$. Thus by the Trans. Prop. of ≅, $\angle A \cong \angle X$, and $\angle B \cong \angle Y$. $\triangle ABC \sim \triangle XYZ$ by AA ~.

29. Possible answer:

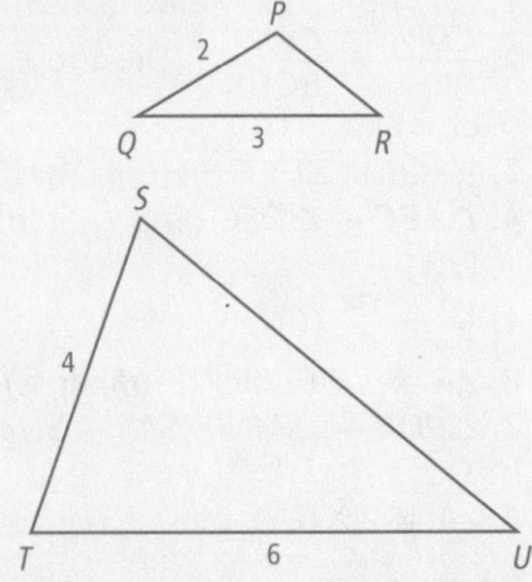

30. Since $\triangle KNJ$ is isosc. with vertex $\angle N$, $\overline{KN} \cong \overline{JN}$ by def. of an isosc. △. $\angle NKJ \cong \angle NJK$ by the Isosc. △ Thm. It is given that $\angle H \cong \angle L$, so $\triangle GHJ \sim \triangle MLK$ by AA ~.

31a. The △s are ~ by AA ~ if you assume that the camera is ∥ to the hurricane (that is, $\overline{YX} \parallel \overline{AB}$).

b. $\triangle YWZ \sim \triangle BCZ$, and $\triangle XWZ \sim \triangle ACZ$, also by AA ~.

c. 105 mi

33. Let the measure of the vertex ∠s be $x°$. Then by the Isosc. △ Thm., the base ∠s in each of the △s must measure $\left(\frac{180 - x}{2}\right)°$. So the △s are ~ by AA ~.

25. This problem will prepare you for the Multi-Step Taks Prep on page 478.
The set for an animated film includes three small triangles that represent pyramids.
a. Which pyramids are similar? Why?
b. What is the similarity ratio of the similar pyramids? $\frac{5}{4}$

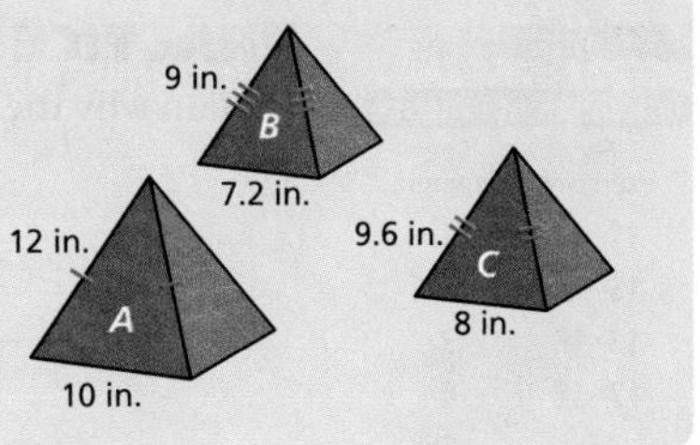

25a. Pyramids *A* and *C* are ~ because the ratios of their corr. sides lengths are =.

26. **Critical Thinking** $\triangle ABC$ is not similar to $\triangle DEF$, and $\triangle DEF$ is not similar to $\triangle XYZ$. Could $\triangle ABC$ be similar to $\triangle XYZ$? Why or why not? Make a sketch to support your answer.

27. **Recreation** To play shuffleboard, two teams take turns sliding disks on a court. The dimensions of the scoring area for a standard shuffleboard court are shown. What are *JK* and *MN*? 2 ft; 4 ft

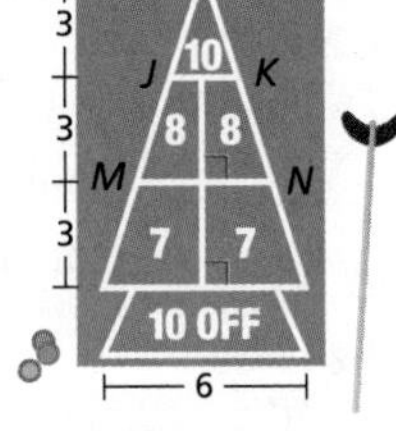

28. Prove the Transitive Property of Similarity.
Given: $\triangle ABC \sim \triangle DEF$, $\triangle DEF \sim \triangle XYZ$
Prove: $\triangle ABC \sim \triangle XYZ$

29. Draw and label $\triangle PQR$ and $\triangle STU$ such that $\frac{PQ}{ST} = \frac{QR}{TU}$ but $\triangle PQR$ is NOT similar to $\triangle STU$.

30. **Given:** $\triangle KNJ$ is isosceles with $\angle N$ as the vertex angle. $\angle H \cong \angle L$
Prove: $\triangle GHJ \sim \triangle MLK$

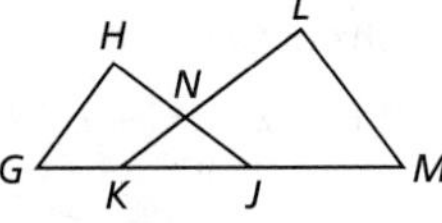

LINK Meteorology

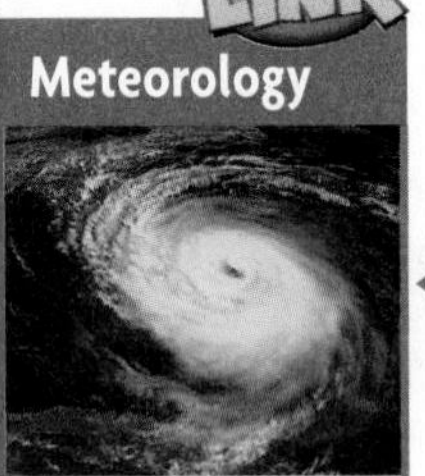

A tropical storm is classified as a hurricane if its winds reach a speed of at least 74 mi/h.
Source: http://www.nhc.noaa.gov

31. **Meteorology** Satellite photography makes it possible to measure the diameter of a hurricane. The figure shows that a camera's aperture *YX* is 35 mm and its focal length *WZ* is 50 mm. The satellite *W* holding the camera is 150 mi above the hurricane, centered at *C*.
a. Why is $\triangle XYZ \sim \triangle ABZ$? What assumption must you make about the position of the camera in order to make this conclusion?
b. What other triangles in the figure must be similar? Why?
c. Find the diameter *AB* of the hurricane.

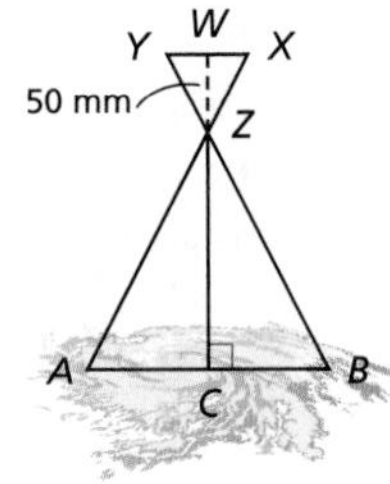

32. **ERROR ANALYSIS** Which solution for the value of *y* is incorrect? Explain the error.

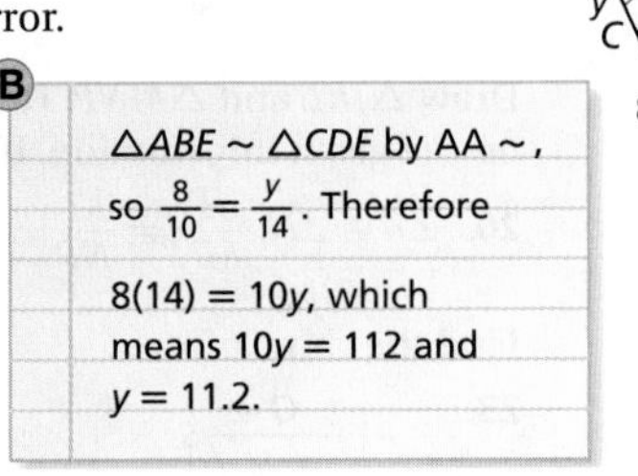

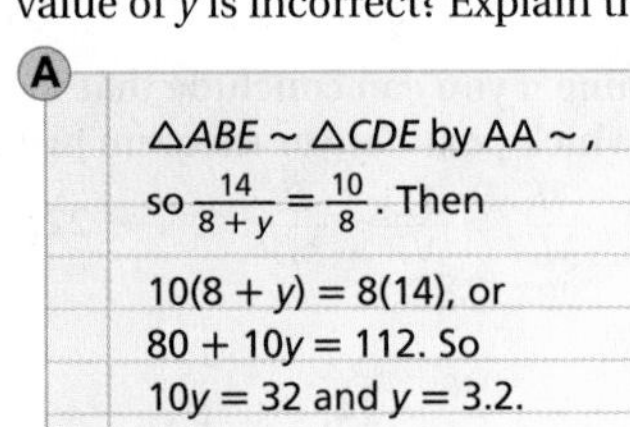

A
$\triangle ABE \sim \triangle CDE$ by AA ~, so $\frac{14}{8+y} = \frac{10}{8}$. Then $10(8 + y) = 8(14)$, or $80 + 10y = 112$. So $10y = 32$ and $y = 3.2$.

B
$\triangle ABE \sim \triangle CDE$ by AA ~, so $\frac{8}{10} = \frac{y}{14}$. Therefore $8(14) = 10y$, which means $10y = 112$ and $y = 11.2$.

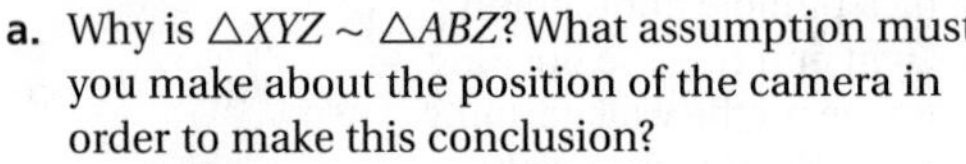
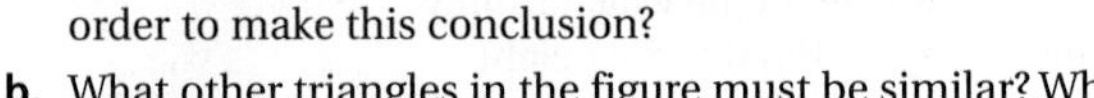
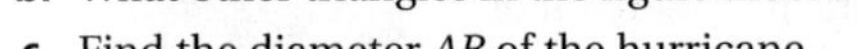

32. Solution B is incorrect. The proportion should be $\frac{8}{10} = \frac{8+y}{14}$.

33. **Write About It** Two isosceles triangles have congruent vertex angles. Explain why the two triangles must be similar.

476 *Chapter 7 Similarity*

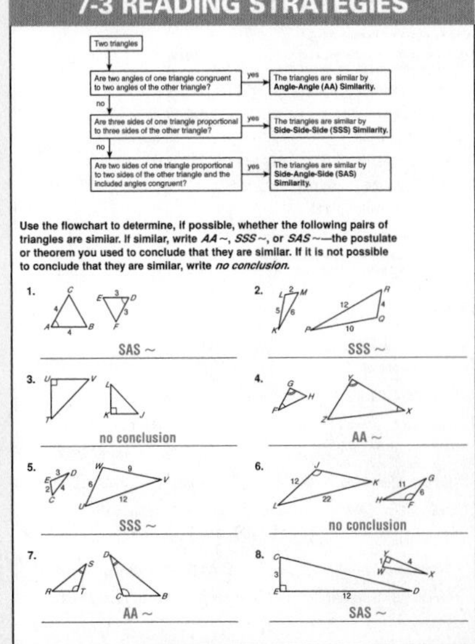

7-3 READING STRATEGIES

Two triangles
Are two angles of one triangle congruent to two angles of the other triangle? yes → The triangles are similar by Angle-Angle (AA) Similarity.
no
Are three sides of one triangle proportional to three sides of the other triangle? yes → The triangles are similar by Side-Side-Side (SSS) Similarity.
no
Are two sides of one triangle proportional to two sides of the other triangle and the included angles congruent? yes → The triangles are similar by Side-Angle-Side (SAS) Similarity.

Use the flowchart to determine, if possible, whether the following pairs of triangles are similar. If similar, write *AA ~*, *SSS ~*, or *SAS ~*—the postulate or theorem you used to conclude that they are similar. If it is not possible to conclude that they are similar, write *no conclusion.*

1. SAS ~
2. SSS ~
3. no conclusion
4. AA ~
5. SSS ~
6. no conclusion
7. AA ~
8. SAS ~

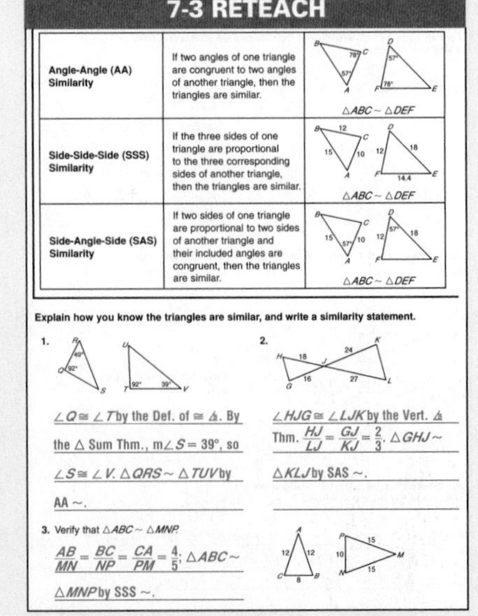

7-3 RETEACH

Angle-Angle (AA) Similarity	If two angles of one triangle are congruent to two angles of another triangle, then the triangles are similar.	$\triangle ABC \sim \triangle DEF$
Side-Side-Side (SSS) Similarity	If the three sides of one triangle are proportional to the three corresponding sides of another triangle, then the triangles are similar.	$\triangle ABC \sim \triangle DEF$
Side-Angle-Side (SAS) Similarity	If two sides of one triangle are proportional to two sides of another triangle and their included angles are congruent, then the triangles are similar.	$\triangle ABC \sim \triangle DEF$

Explain how you know the triangles are similar, and write a similarity statement.

1. $\angle Q \cong \angle T$ by the Def. of ≅ ∠s. By the △ Sum Thm., m∠S = 39°, so $\angle S \cong \angle V$. $\triangle QRS \sim \triangle TUV$ by AA ~.

2. $\angle HJG \cong \angle LJK$ by the Vert. ∠s Thm. $\frac{HJ}{LJ} = \frac{GJ}{KJ} = \frac{2}{3}$. $\triangle GHJ \sim \triangle KLJ$ by SAS ~.

3. Verify that $\triangle ABC \sim \triangle MNP$.
$\frac{AB}{MN} = \frac{BC}{NP} = \frac{CA}{PM} = \frac{4}{5}$; $\triangle ABC \sim \triangle MNP$ by SSS ~.

34. What is the length of $\overline{TU}$?

Ⓐ 36 　 Ⓒ 48 (circled)
Ⓑ 40 　 Ⓓ 90

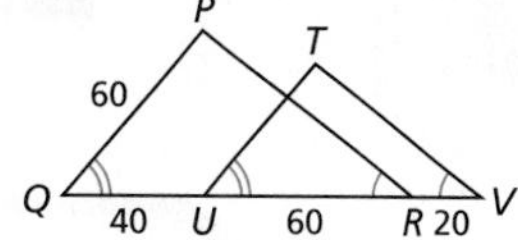

35. Which dimensions guarantee that $\triangle BCD \sim \triangle FGH$?

Ⓕ $FG = 11.6$, $GH = 8.4$
Ⓖ $FG = 12$, $GH = 14$
Ⓗ $FG = 11.4$, $GH = 11.4$
Ⓙ (circled) $FG = 10.5$, $GH = 14.5$

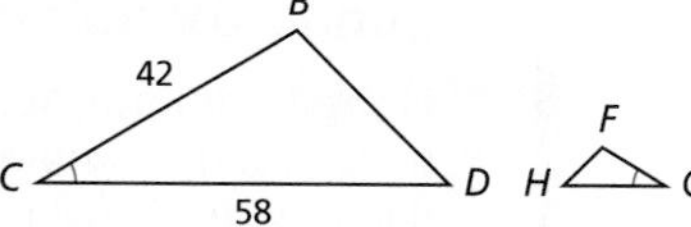

36. $\square ABCD \sim \square EFGH$. Which similarity postulate or theorem lets you conclude that $\triangle BCD \sim \triangle FGH$?

Ⓐ AA 　 Ⓒ (circled) SAS
Ⓑ SSS 　 Ⓓ None of these

37. **Gridded Response** If 6, 8, and 12 and 15, 20, and x are the lengths of the corresponding sides of two similar triangles, what is the value of x? **30**

CHALLENGE AND EXTEND

38. Prove the SSS Similarity Theorem.
Given: $\frac{AB}{DE} = \frac{BC}{EF} = \frac{AC}{DF}$
Prove: $\triangle ABC \sim \triangle DEF$
(*Hint:* Assume that $AB < DE$ and choose point X on $\overline{DE}$ so that $\overline{AB} \cong \overline{DX}$. Then choose point Y on $\overline{DF}$ so that $\overleftrightarrow{XY} \parallel \overline{EF}$. Show that $\triangle DXY \sim \triangle DEF$ and that $\triangle ABC \cong \triangle DXY$.)

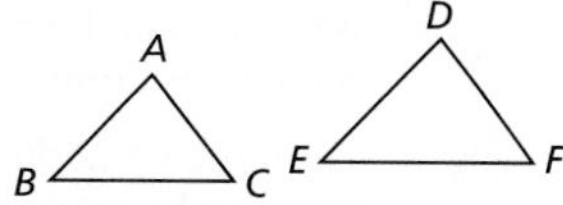

39. Prove the SAS Similarity Theorem.
Given: $\angle B \cong \angle E$, $\frac{AB}{DE} = \frac{BC}{EF}$
Prove: $\triangle ABC \sim \triangle DEF$
(*Hint:* Assume that $AB < DE$ and choose point X on $\overline{DE}$ so that $\overline{EX} \cong \overline{BA}$. Then choose point Y on $\overline{EF}$ so that $\angle EXY \cong \angle EDF$. Show that $\triangle XEY \sim \triangle DEF$ and that $\triangle ABC \cong \triangle XEF$.)

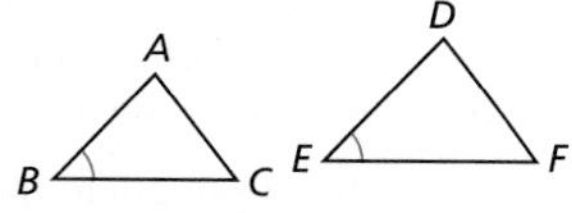

40. Given $\triangle ABC \sim \triangle XYZ$, $m\angle A = 50°$, $m\angle X = (2x + 5y)°$, $m\angle Z = (5x + y)°$, and that $m\angle B = (102 - x)°$, find $m\angle Z$. **33°**

SPIRAL REVIEW

41. Jessika's scores in her last six rounds of golf were 96, 99, 105, 105, 94, and 107. What score must Jessika make on her next round to make her mean score 100? *(Previous course)* **94**

Position each figure in the coordinate plane and give possible coordinates of each vertex. *(Lesson 4-7)*

42. a right triangle with leg lengths of 4 units and 2 units **Possible answer: (0, 4), (0, 0), (2, 0)**

43. a rectangle with length $2k$ and width k **Possible answer: (0, k), (2k, k), (2k, 0), (0, 0)**

Solve each proportion. Check your answer. *(Lesson 7-1)*

44. $\frac{2x}{10} = \frac{35}{25}$ **7**

45. $\frac{5y}{450} = \frac{25}{10y}$ **±15**

46. $\frac{b-5}{28} = \frac{7}{b-5}$ **19 or −9**

TEST PREP DOCTOR In **Exercise 35,** since $CD > BC$, students should see that $GH > FG$, which eliminates choices **F** and **H**. Then use mental math to see that only choice **J** gives proportional sides.

Journal

Have students make two columns, one with examples of triangles that are similar, and one with examples of triangles that are not similar. Then compare and contrast the columns.

ALTERNATIVE ASSESSMENT

Have students make two lists, one of all the triangle congruence postulates and theorems, and another of all the similarity postulates and theorems. Then ask them to draw and label examples of each.

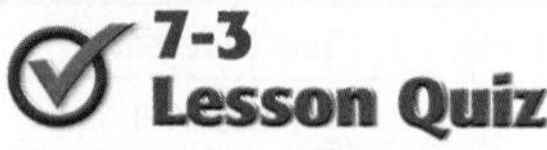

7-3 Lesson Quiz

1. Explain why the triangles are similar and write a similarity statement.

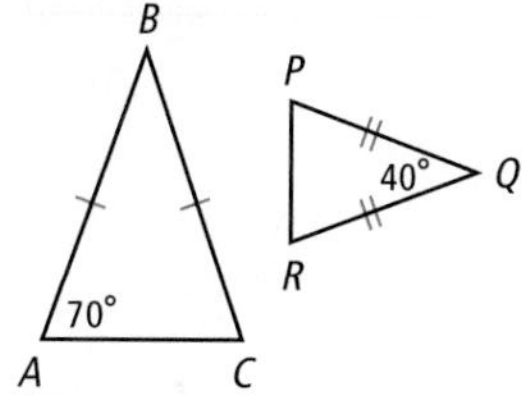

By the Isosc. △ Thm., $\angle A \cong \angle C$, so by the def. of ≅, $m\angle C = m\angle A$. Thus $m\angle C = 70°$ by subst. By the △ Sum Thm., $m\angle B = 40°$. Apply the Isosc. △ Thm. and the △ Sum Thm. to $\triangle PQR$. $m\angle R = m\angle P = 70°$. So by the def. of ≅, $\angle A \cong \angle P$, and $\angle C \cong \angle R$. Therefore $\triangle ABC \sim \triangle PQR$ by AA ~.

2. Explain why the triangles are similar, then find BE and CD.

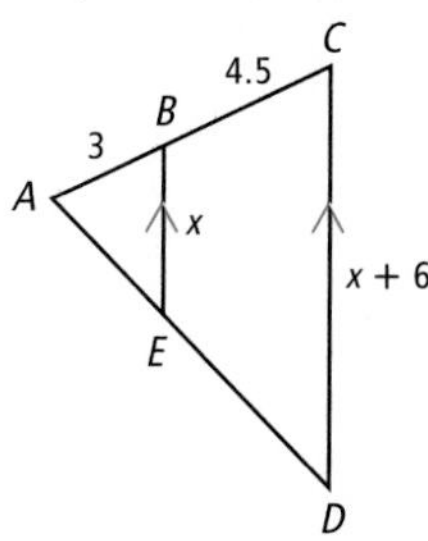

$\angle A \cong \angle A$ by the Reflex. Prop. of ≅. Since $\overline{BE} \parallel \overline{CD}$, $\angle ABE \cong \angle ACD$ by the Corr. ∠s Post. Therefore $\triangle ABE \sim \triangle ACD$ by AA ~. $BE = 4$ and $CD = 10$.

Also available on transparency

7-3 PROBLEM SOLVING

Use the diagram for Exercises 1 and 2.

In the diagram of the tandem bike, $\overline{AE} \parallel \overline{BD}$.

1. Explain why $\triangle CBD \sim \triangle CAE$.
$\angle CBD \cong \angle CAE$ by Corr. ∠s Thm. and $\angle C \cong \angle C$ by the Reflex. Prop. of ≅. So $\triangle CBD \sim \triangle CAE$ by AA ~.

2. Find CE to the nearest tenth. 46.7 in.

3. Is $\triangle WXZ \sim \triangle XYZ$? Explain.
No; $\frac{WX}{XY} \neq \frac{XZ}{YZ}$

4. Find RQ. Explain how you found it.
15; $\triangle MNP \sim \triangle RQP$ by SAS ~. Corr. sides of ~ ∠s are proportional.

Choose the best answer.

5. Find the value of x that makes $\triangle FGH \sim \triangle JKL$.
A 8 　 C 12
Ⓑ 9 　 D 16

6. Triangle STU has vertices at $S(0, 0)$, $T(2, 6)$, and $U(8, 2)$. If $\triangle STU \sim \triangle WXY$ and the coordinates of W are (0, 0), what are possible coordinates of X and Y?
Ⓕ $X(1, 3)$ and $Y(4, 1)$
G $X(1, 3)$ and $Y(2, 0)$
H $X(3, 1)$ and $Y(2, 4)$
J $X(0, 3)$ and $Y(4, 0)$

7. To measure the distance EF across the lake, a surveyor at S locates points E, F, G, and H as shown. What is EF?
A 25 m 　 Ⓒ 45 m
B 36 m 　 D 90 m

Answers

38. Assume that $AB < DE$ and choose X on $\overline{DE}$ so that $\overline{AB} \cong \overline{DX}$. Then choose Y on $\overline{DF}$ so that $\overleftrightarrow{XY} \parallel \overline{EF}$. By the Corr. ∠s Post., $\angle DXY \cong \angle DEF$, and $\angle DYX \cong \angle DFE$. Therefore $\triangle DXY \sim \triangle DEF$ by AA ~. By the def. of ~ △s, $\frac{DX}{DE} = \frac{XY}{EF} = \frac{DY}{DF}$. By the def. of ≅, $AB = DX$. So $\frac{AB}{DE} = \frac{XY}{EF}$. It is given that $\frac{AB}{DE} = \frac{BC}{EF}$, so $XY = BC$. $\overline{XY} \cong \overline{BC}$ by the def. of ≅. Similarly, $\overline{DY} \cong \overline{AC}$, so $\triangle ABC \cong \triangle DXY$ by SSS ≅ Thm. It follows that $\triangle ABC \sim \triangle DXY$. Then by the Trans. Prop. of ~, $\triangle ABC \sim \triangle DEF$.

39. See pp. A23–24.

Organizer

Objective: Assess students' ability to apply concepts and skills in Lessons 7-1 through 7-3 in a real-world format.

Online Edition

Resources

Geometry Assessments
www.mathtekstoolkit.org

Problem	Text Reference
1	Lesson 7-1
2	Lesson 7-1
3	Lesson 7-2
4	Lesson 7-3

State Resources

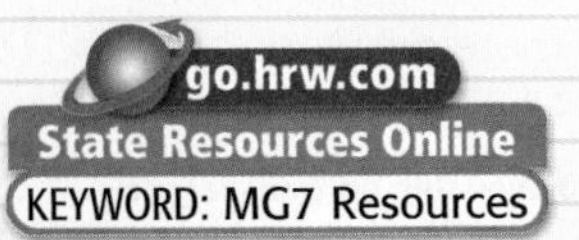

go.hrw.com
State Resources Online
KEYWORD: MG7 Resources

CHAPTER 7

MULTI-STEP TEST PREP

SECTION 7A

Similarity Relationships

Lights! Camera! Action! Lorenzo, Maria, Sam, and Tia are working on a video project for their history class. They decide to film a scene where the characters in the scene are on a train arriving at a town. Since Lorenzo collects model trains, they decide to use one of his trains and to build a set behind it. To create the set, they use a film technique called forced perspective. They want to use small objects to create an illusion of great distance in a very small space.

1. Lorenzo's model train is $\frac{1}{87}$ the size of the original train. He measures the engine of the model train and finds that it is $2\frac{1}{2}$ in. tall. What is the height of the real engine to the nearest foot? **18 ft**

2. The closest building to the train needs to be made using the same scale as the train. Maria and Sam estimate that the height of an actual station is 20 ft. How tall would they need to build their model of the train station to the nearest $\frac{1}{4}$ in.? **$2\frac{3}{4}$ in.**

3. To give depth to their scene, they want to construct partial buildings behind the train station. Lorenzo decided to build a restaurant. If the height of the restaurant is actually 24 ft, how tall would they need to build their model of the restaurant to the nearest inch? **3 in.**

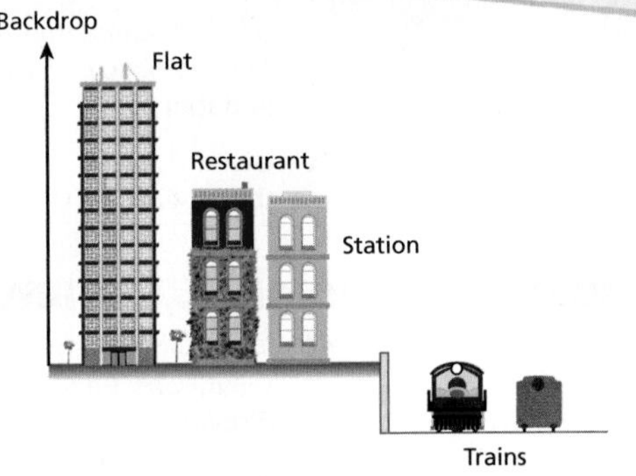

4. The other buildings on the set will have triangular roofs. Which of the roofs are similar to each other? Why? **4. the bank's and the hotel's; by SSS~**

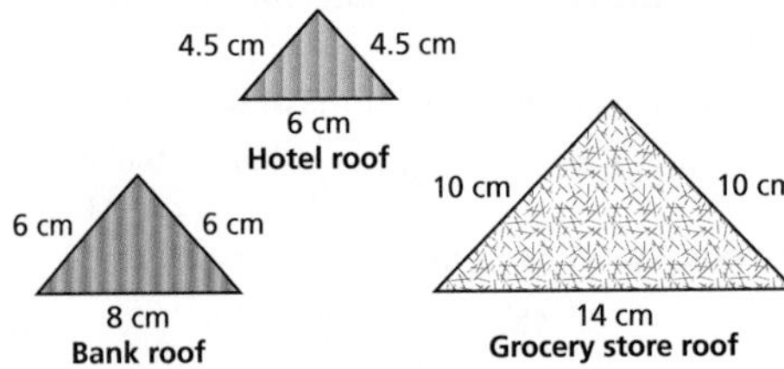

INTERVENTION

Scaffolding Questions

1. How many times the size of the model is the real locomotive? 87
2. What is the actual height of the caboose in inches? What is the ratio of the model's height to the actual height? 174 in.; 2:174 or 1:87
3. What proportion do you use to find the height of a model of a partial building, if you know the building's actual height? $\frac{x}{\text{actual height}} = \frac{1}{87}$
4. The roof of the sheriff's office has sides of length 5 cm, 5 cm, and 6.5 cm. Is the sheriff's office similar to any of the other buildings? Why or why not? No; the sides of this roof are not proportional to the sides of any of the other roofs.

Extension

What is the similarity ratio of the model train to the actual train? A train painted on a backdrop has a similarity ratio of $\frac{1}{2}$ to the model train. What is the similarity ratio of the painted train to the actual train? $\frac{1}{87}$; $\frac{1}{174}$

READY TO GO ON?

Quiz for Lessons 7-1 Through 7-3

7-1 Ratio and Proportion

Write a ratio expressing the slope of each line.

1. ℓ $\frac{1}{5}$
2. m $-\frac{2}{1}$
3. n $-\frac{1}{4}$
4. x-axis 0

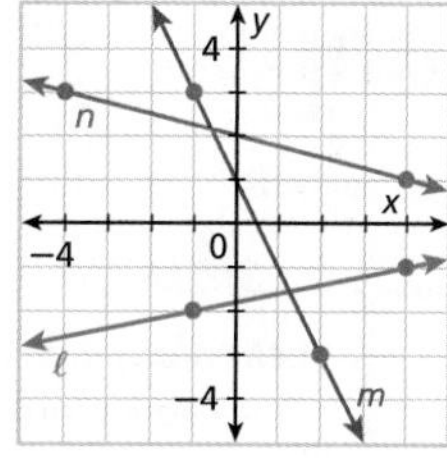

Solve each proportion.

5. $\frac{y}{6} = \frac{12}{9}$ 8
6. $\frac{16}{24} = \frac{20}{t}$ 30
7. $\frac{x-2}{4} = \frac{9}{x-2}$ −4 or 8
8. $\frac{2}{3y} = \frac{y}{24}$ ±4

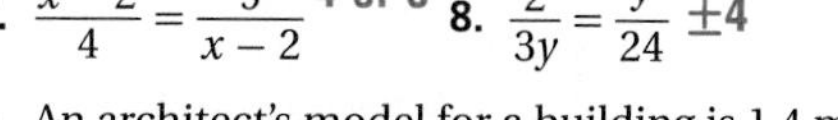

9. An architect's model for a building is 1.4 m long and 0.8 m wide. The actual building is 240 m wide. What is the length of the building? 420 m

7-2 Ratios in Similar Polygons

Determine whether the two polygons are similar. If so, write the similarity ratio and a similarity statement.

10. rectangles $ABCD$ and $WXYZ$ no

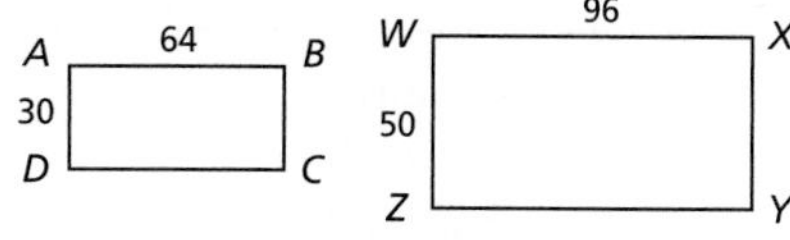

11. $\triangle JMR$ and $\triangle KNP$ yes; $\frac{2}{3}$; $\triangle JMR \sim \triangle NPK$

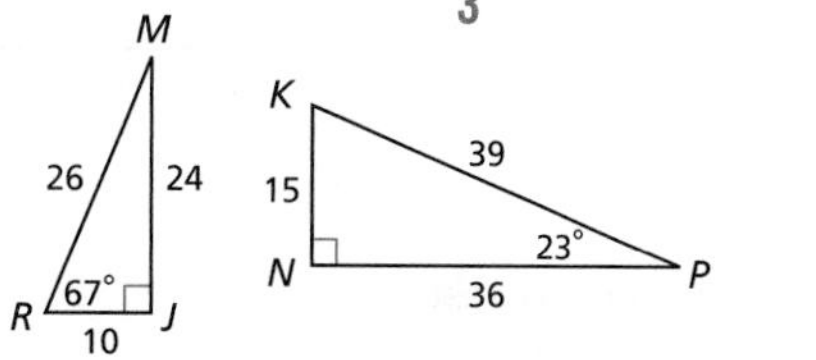

12. Leonardo da Vinci's famous portrait the *Mona Lisa* is 30 in. long and 21 in. wide. Janelle has a refrigerator magnet of the painting that is 3.5 cm wide. What is the length of the magnet? 5 cm

7-3 Triangle Similarity: AA, SSS, and SAS

13. Given: ▱$ABCD$
Prove: $\triangle EDG \sim \triangle FBG$

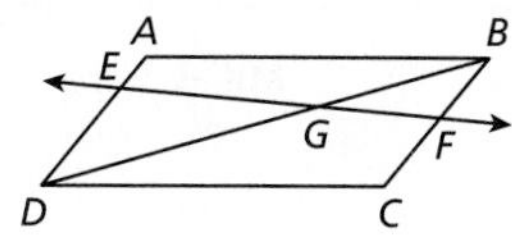

14. Given: $MQ = \frac{1}{3}MN$, $MR = \frac{1}{3}MP$
Prove: $\triangle MQR \sim \triangle MNP$

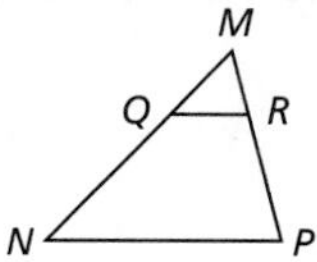

15. A geologist wants to measure the length XY of a rock formation. To do so, she locates points U, V, X, Y, and Z as shown. What is XY? 40 ft

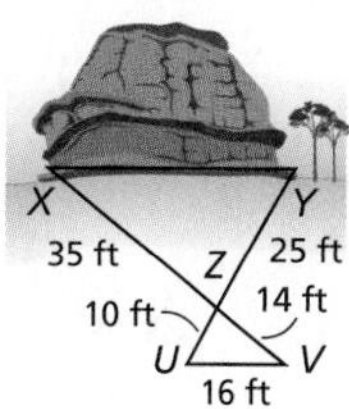

READY TO GO ON? SECTION 7A

Organizer

Objective: Assess students' mastery of concepts and skills in Lessons 7-1 through 7-3.

Resources

Assessment Resources
Section 7A Quiz

Teacher One Stop™
Test & Practice Generator

INTERVENTION

Resources

Ready to Go On? Intervention and Enrichment **Worksheets**

Ready to Go On? **CD-ROM**

Ready to Go On? **Online**

my.hrw.com

Answers

13–14. See p. A24.

READY TO GO ON?

Diagnose and Prescribe

Ready to Go On? Intervention	*Ready to Go On? Intervention,* Section 7A		
	Worksheets	CD-ROM	Online
Lesson 7-1	7-1 Intervention	Activity 7-1	Diagnose and Prescribe Online
Lesson 7-2	7-2 Intervention	Activity 7-2	
Lesson 7-3	7-3 Intervention	Activity 7-3	

Ready to Go On? Enrichment, **Section 7A**

Worksheets
CD-ROM

Online

SECTION 7B

Applying Similarity

One-Minute Section Planner

Lesson	Lab Resources	Materials
7-4 Technology Lab Investigate Angle Bisectors of a Triangle • Explore the relationship between the two segments into which an angle bisector divides the opposite side of a triangle. ☐ SAT-10 ☑ NAEP ☐ ACT ☑ SAT ☑ SAT Subject Tests	***Technology Lab Activities*** 7-4 Lab Recording Sheet	**Required** geometry software
Lesson 7-4 Applying Properties of Similar Triangles • Use properties of similar triangles to find segment lengths. • Apply proportionality and triangle angle bisector theorems. ☑ SAT-10 ☑ NAEP ☑ ACT ☑ SAT ☑ SAT Subject Tests		**Required** compass (MK), straightedge **Optional** city maps, transparency sheets, rulers (MK), straightedges, geometry software
Lesson 7-5 Using Proportional Relationships • Use ratios to make indirect measurements. • Use scale drawings to solve problems. ☑ SAT-10 ☑ NAEP ☐ ACT ☑ SAT ☑ SAT Subject Tests		**Required** rulers (MK) **Optional** miniature objects (e.g., toy car, model train, miniature tea set, doll house furniture), yardsticks or metersticks (MK)
Lesson 7-6 Dilations and Similarity in the Coordinate Plane • Apply similarity properties in the coordinate plane. • Use coordinate proof to prove figures similar. ☐ SAT-10 ☑ NAEP ☑ ACT ☑ SAT ☑ SAT Subject Tests	***Geometry Lab Activities*** 7-6 Geometry Lab	**Optional** computer projector, $\frac{1}{4}$ in. graph paper, rulers (MK), geometry software

MK = *Manipulatives Kit*

TRIANGLE PROPORTIONALITY

Lesson 7-4

The Triangle Proportionality Theorem states that if a line is parallel to a side of a triangle and intersects the other two sides, then it divides those sides proportionally. In the figure, $\overleftrightarrow{EF} \parallel \overline{BC}$. Therefore, $\frac{AE}{EB} = \frac{AF}{FC}$.

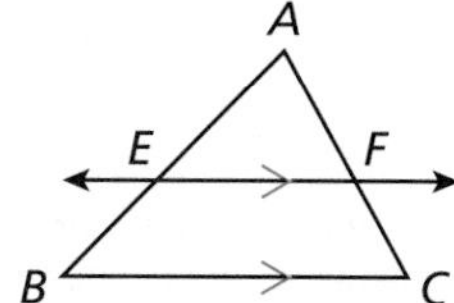

The proof, which uses similarity and facts about proportions, runs as follows. Because they are corresponding angles, $\angle AEF \cong \angle ABC$. Since $\angle A \cong \angle A$, $\triangle AEF \sim \triangle ABC$ by AA Similarity. Thus, $\frac{AE}{AB} = \frac{AF}{AC}$, which is equivalent to the proportion $\frac{AB}{AE} = \frac{AC}{AF}$. By the Segment Addition Postulate, $AB = AE + EB$ and $AC = AF + FC$. By substitution, $\frac{AE + EB}{AE} = \frac{AF + FC}{AF}$ or $1 + \frac{EB}{AE} = 1 + \frac{FC}{AF}$. Therefore, $\frac{EB}{AE} = \frac{FC}{AF}$, which is equivalent to the required proportion.

INDIRECT MEASUREMENT

Lesson 7-5

When you place a ruler or measuring tape next to an object, you are measuring it directly. *Indirect measurement* is used when an object is difficult or impossible to measure directly. Many of the myriad techniques that fall under the category of indirect measurement date to ancient times. Legend has it that during a visit to Egypt, the Greek engineer and mathematician Thales (c. 624 B.C.E.–547 B.C.E.) determined the height of the Great Pyramid by measuring the length of its shadow at a time of day when the length of his own shadow was equal to his own height.

The indirect measurement problems in Lesson 7-5 use a generalization of Thales's method. All are based on finding the length of an unknown side in a pair of similar triangles. It is worth discussing some of the underlying assumptions that are used to set up the similar triangles. For example, in problems based on the length of shadows, it is assumed that the rays of the sun are parallel lines. Given the great distance of the sun from Earth, this assumption poses no difficulties. Also, it is assumed that the object whose height is being measured is perpendicular to the ground and that the ground is level. While these conditions may not always be met in the real world, they are not unreasonable and they show that, given modest assumptions, indirect measurement can be a powerful problem-solving technique.

For many students, the main difficulty in solving indirect measurement problems is in setting up an appropriate proportion. While there are many equivalent ways to write any proportion, the essential principle is that each ratio should compare corresponding quantities in the same order. For example, for the situation below, the proportion $\frac{x}{6} = \frac{24}{8}$ is correct because the ratio on the left compares heights, starting with the flagpole, and the ratio on the right compares shadows, also starting with the flagpole.

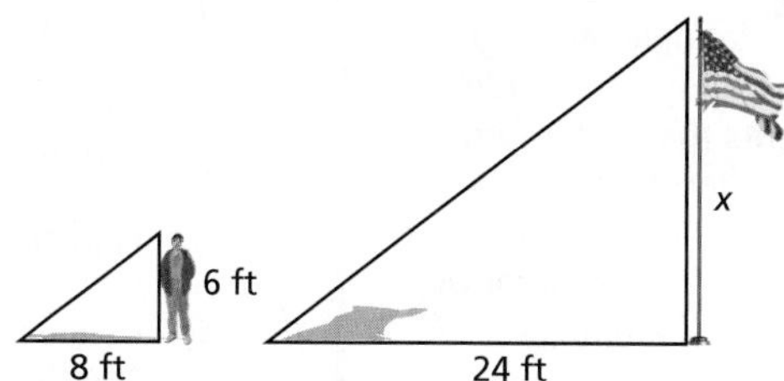

CHANGING DIMENSIONS

Lesson 7-5

If the similarity ratio of two similar figures is k, then the ratio of the figures' perimeters is also k and the ratio of their areas is k^2. Students should understand that they can use this principle to find the perimeter or area of a figure for which they do not know all of the dimensions. For instance, suppose that $\triangle ABC$ has an area of 60 cm^2 and that all of the dimensions of $\triangle ABC$ are doubled to create $\triangle XYZ$. Then, the similarity ratio of $\triangle ABC$ to $\triangle XYZ$ is $\frac{1}{2}$, and the ratio of the triangles' areas is $\left(\frac{1}{2}\right)^2 = \frac{1}{4}$. Thus, $\frac{area(\triangle ABC)}{area(\triangle XYZ)} = \frac{1}{4}$ and $\frac{60}{area(\triangle XYZ)} = \frac{1}{4}$, so the area of $\triangle XYZ$ is 240 cm^2.

Organizer

Use with Lesson 7-4

Pacing:
Traditional $\frac{1}{2}$ day
Block $\frac{1}{4}$ day

Objective: Explore the relationship between the two segments into which an angle bisector divides the opposite side of a triangle.

Materials: geometry software

Online Edition
TechKeys

Countdown Week 16

Resources

Technology Lab Activities
7-4 Lab Recording Sheet

Teach

Discuss

Discuss that in a triangle, an angle bisector divides the opposite side into two segments that are in proportion to their adjacent sides. For Activity 2, remind students that the incenter is the intersection point of the angle bisectors of a triangle.

Close

Key Concept

This lab leads to the Triangle Angle Bisector Theorem in Lesson 7-4.

Assessment

Journal Have students make a conjecture from what they learned by doing this lab. Ask them to support their conjecture with a diagram.

State Resources

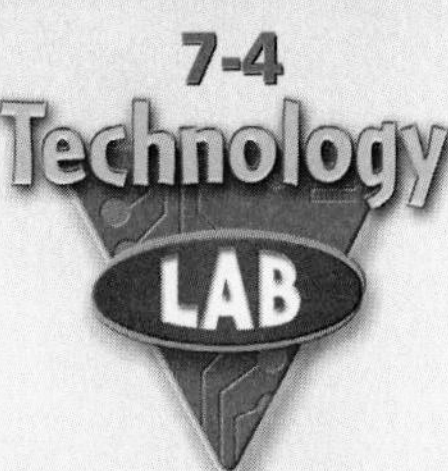

Investigate Angle Bisectors of a Triangle

Use with Lesson 7-4

In a triangle, an angle bisector divides the opposite side into two segments. You will use geometry software to explore the relationships between these segments.

go.hrw.com
Lab Resources Online
KEYWORD: MG7 Lab7

Activity 1

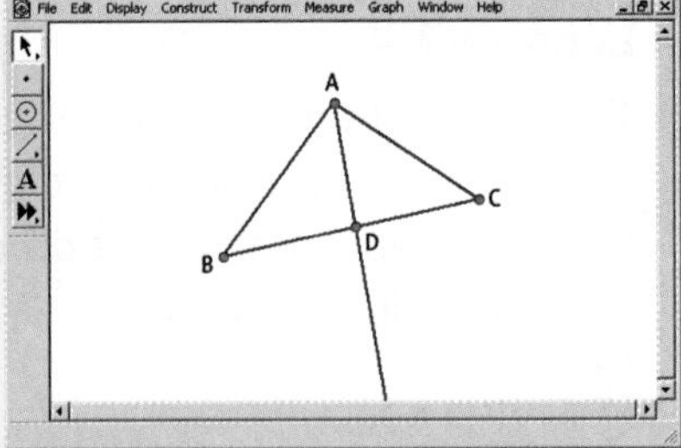

1. Construct $\triangle ABC$. Bisect $\angle BAC$ and create the point of intersection of the angle bisector and $\overline{BC}$. Label the intersection D.
2. Measure $\overline{AB}$, $\overline{AC}$, $\overline{BD}$, and $\overline{CD}$. Use these measurements to write ratios. What are the results? Drag a vertex of $\triangle ABC$ and examine the ratios again. What do you notice? $\frac{BD}{AB} = \frac{CD}{AC}$ or $\frac{BD}{CD} = \frac{AB}{AC}$

Try This

1. Choose Tabulate and create a table using the four lengths and the ratios from Step 2. Drag a vertex of $\triangle ABC$ and add the new measurements to the table. What conjecture can you make about the segments created by an angle bisector?
2. Write a proportion based on your conjecture. $\frac{BD}{CD} = \frac{AB}{AC}$ or $\frac{BD}{AB} = \frac{CD}{AC}$

Activity 2

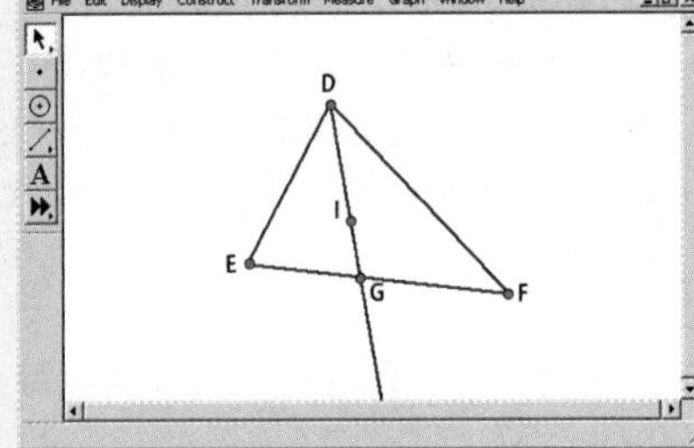

1. Construct $\triangle DEF$. Create the *incenter* of the triangle and label it I. Hide the angle bisectors of $\angle E$ and $\angle F$. Find the point of intersection of $\overline{EF}$ and the bisector of $\angle D$. Label the intersection G.
2. Find DI, DG, and the perimeter of $\triangle DEF$. Check students' work.
3. Divide the length of $\overline{DI}$ by the length of DG. Add the lengths of $\overline{DE}$ and $\overline{DF}$. Then divide this sum by the perimeter of $\triangle DEF$. Compare the two quotients. Drag a vertex of $\triangle DEF$ and examine the quotients again. What do you notice? $\frac{DI}{DG} = \frac{DE + DF}{\text{perimeter } \triangle DEF}$
4. Write a proportion based on your quotients. What conjecture can you make about this relationship?

Try This

3. Show the hidden angle bisector of $\angle E$ or $\angle F$. Confirm that your conjecture is true for this bisector. Drag a vertex of $\triangle DEF$ and observe the results. Check students' work.
4. Choose Tabulate and create a table with the measurements you used in your proportion in Step 4. Check students' work.

Answers to *Try This*

1. Check students' work; the segs. created by an $\angle$ bisector will be in proportion to the adj. sides.

Answers to *Activity 2*

4. $\frac{DI}{DG} = \frac{DE + DF}{DE + DF + EF}$; the length of the seg. from the vertex of the bisected $\angle$ to the incenter divided by the length of the seg. from the vertex to the opp. side is = to the sum of the sides of the bisected $\angle$ divided by the perimeter of the $\triangle$.

7-4 Applying Properties of Similar Triangles

Objectives

Use properties of similar triangles to find segment lengths.

Apply proportionality and triangle angle bisector theorems.

Who uses this?

Artists use similarity and proportionality to give paintings an illusion of depth. (See Example 3.)

Artists use mathematical techniques to make two-dimensional paintings appear three-dimensional. The invention of *perspective* was based on the observation that far away objects look smaller and closer objects look larger.

Mathematical theorems like the Triangle Proportionality Theorem are important in making perspective drawings.

Theorem 7-4-1 Triangle Proportionality Theorem

THEOREM	HYPOTHESIS	CONCLUSION
If a line parallel to a side of a triangle intersects the other two sides, then it divides those sides proportionally.	$\overline{EF} \parallel \overline{BC}$	$\frac{AE}{EB} = \frac{AF}{FC}$

You can use a compass-and-straightedge construction to verify this theorem. Although the construction is not a proof, it should help convince you that the theorem is true. After you have completed the construction, use a ruler to measure $\overline{AE}$, $\overline{EB}$, $\overline{AF}$, and $\overline{FC}$ to see that $\frac{AE}{EB} = \frac{AF}{FC}$.

Construction Triangle Proportionality Theorem

Construct a line parallel to a side of a triangle.

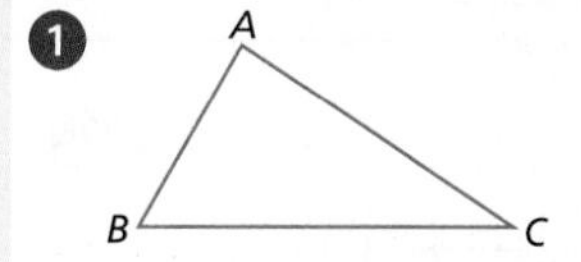

1. Use a straightedge to draw $\triangle ABC$.

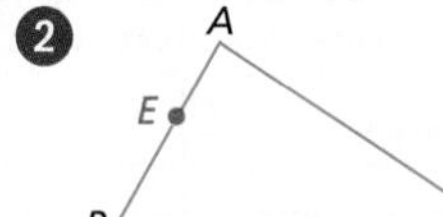

2. Label E on AB.

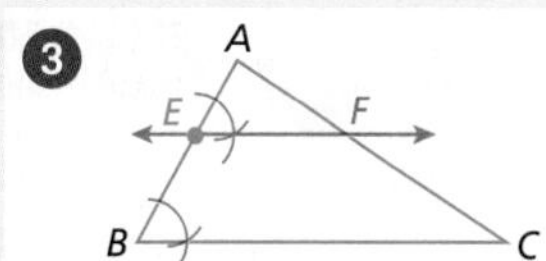

3. Construct $\angle E \cong \angle B$. Label the intersection of $\overleftrightarrow{EF}$ and $\overline{AC}$ as F. $\overleftrightarrow{EF} \parallel \overline{BC}$ by the Converse of the Corresponding Angles Postulate.

7-4 Organizer

Pacing: Traditional $1\frac{1}{2}$ day
Block $\frac{3}{4}$ day

Objectives: Use properties of similar triangles to find segment lengths.

Apply proportionality and triangle angle bisector theorems.

Online Edition
Tutorial Videos

Countdown Week 16

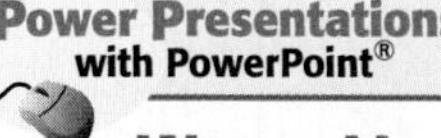

Power Presentations with PowerPoint®

Warm Up

Solve each proportion.

1. $\frac{12}{15} = \frac{AB}{20}$ $AB = 16$
2. $\frac{9.5}{QR} = \frac{3.8}{4.2}$ $QR = 10.5$
3. $\frac{x-5}{20} = \frac{x+3}{30}$ $x = 21$
4. $\frac{y+7}{2y-4} = \frac{3.5}{2.8}$ $y = 8$

Also available on transparency

Math Humor

Q: What do you call two L's?
A: A parallel

1 Introduce

EXPLORATION

7-4 Applying Properties of Similar Triangles

Use geometry software for this Exploration.

1. Draw $\triangle ABC$. Then place a point D on $\overline{AB}$.
2. Construct the line through D parallel to $\overline{BC}$. Then construct the intersection of the line with $\overline{AC}$. Label the intersection E.
3. Measure $\overline{AD}$, $\overline{DB}$, $\overline{AE}$, and $\overline{EC}$.
4. Calculate $\frac{AD}{DB}$ and $\frac{AE}{EC}$.
5. Drag the vertices of $\triangle ABC$. Move point D along $\overline{AB}$. What do you notice about $\frac{AD}{DB}$ and $\frac{AE}{EC}$?

THINK AND DISCUSS

6. Explain how you can use your findings to

Motivate

Explain to students that this lesson will show how properties of similar triangles can be used to find distances or segment lengths. Point out to students that these properties are often used in art. Use one or more sets of hand-drawn similar polygons. Have students create a sense of space by arranging the polygons from largest to smallest moving toward a *horizon,* as in **Example 3.**

Explorations and answers are provided in *Alternate Openers: Explorations Transparencies.*

State Resources

go.hrw.com
State Resources Online
KEYWORD: MG7 Resources

Critical Thinking Show students how to prove the Triangle Proportionality Theorem using similar triangles. Because $\overleftrightarrow{EF} \parallel \overline{BC}$, $\angle AEF \cong \angle ABC$ by the Corr. ∠s Post. $\angle A \cong \angle A$ by the Reflex. Prop. of ≅. So $\triangle ABC \sim \triangle AEF$ by AA ~. If the △s are ~, then $\frac{AB}{AE} = \frac{AC}{AF}$, or $\frac{AE + EB}{AE} = \frac{AF + FC}{AF}$. Simplifying, $1 + \frac{EB}{AE} = 1 + \frac{FC}{AF}$. By the Subtr. Prop. of =, $\frac{EB}{AE} = \frac{FC}{AF}$. Thus $\frac{AE}{EB} = \frac{AF}{FC}$.

Power Presentations with PowerPoint®

Additional Examples

Example 1

Find *US*.

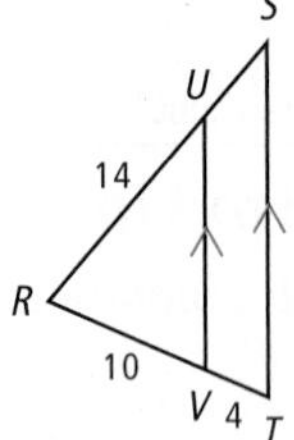

$US = \frac{28}{5}$ or $5\frac{3}{5}$

Example 2

Verify that $\overline{DE} \parallel \overline{BC}$.

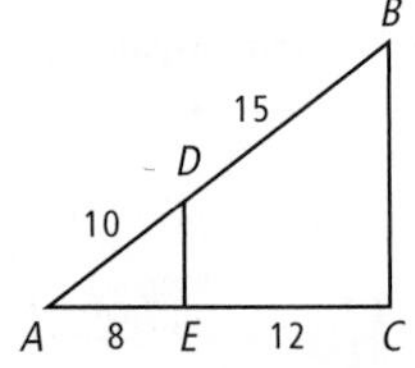

$\frac{AD}{DB} = \frac{10}{15} = \frac{2}{3}$ and $\frac{AE}{EC} = \frac{8}{12} = \frac{2}{3}$.

Since $\frac{AD}{DB} = \frac{AE}{EC}$, $\overline{DE} \parallel \overline{BC}$ by the Conv. of the △ Proportionality Thm.

INTERVENTION

Questioning Strategies

EXAMPLE 1

- What are two different ways you can set up your proportions?

EXAMPLE 2

- What other proportions can you use to verify that the segments are parallel?

EXAMPLE 1 **Finding the Length of a Segment**

Find *CY*.

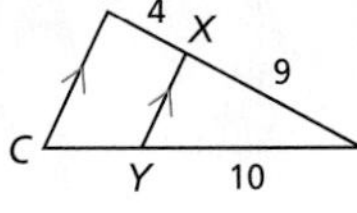

It is given that $\overline{XY} \parallel \overline{BC}$, so $\frac{AX}{XB} = \frac{AY}{YC}$ by the Triangle Proportionality Theorem.

$\frac{9}{4} = \frac{10}{CY}$ — *Substitute 9 for AX, 4 for XB, and 10 for AY.*

$9(CY) = 40$ — *Cross Products Prop.*

$CY = \frac{40}{9}$, or $4\frac{4}{9}$ — *Divide both sides by 9.*

1. Find *PN*. 7.5

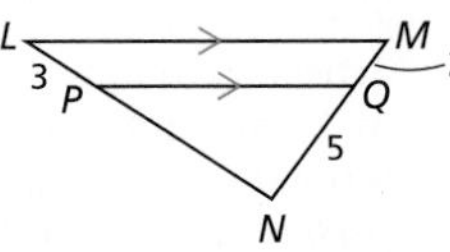

Know it! Note

Theorem 7-4-2 **Converse of the Triangle Proportionality Theorem**

THEOREM	HYPOTHESIS	CONCLUSION
If a line divides two sides of a triangle proportionally, then it is parallel to the third side.	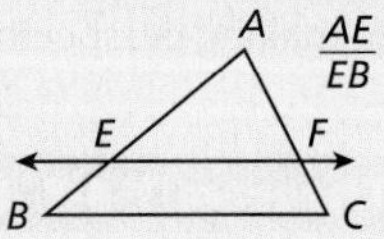 $\frac{AE}{EB} = \frac{AF}{FC}$ (triangle ABC with E on AB, F on AC)	$\overleftrightarrow{EF} \parallel \overline{BC}$

You will prove Theorem 7-4-2 in Exercise 23.

EXAMPLE 2 **Verifying Segments are Parallel**

Verify that $\overline{MN} \parallel \overline{KL}$.

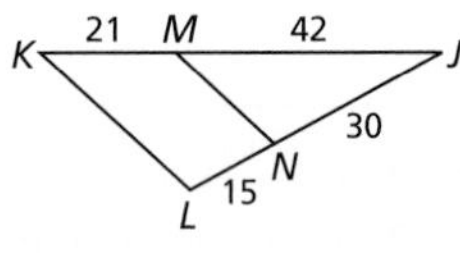

$\frac{JM}{MK} = \frac{42}{21} = 2$

$\frac{JN}{NL} = \frac{30}{15} = 2$

Since $\frac{JM}{MK} = \frac{JN}{NL}$, $\overline{MN} \parallel \overline{KL}$ by the Converse of the Triangle Proportionality Theorem.

2. $AD = 16$, and $BE = 12$, so $\frac{DC}{AD} = \frac{20}{16} = \frac{5}{4}$, and $\frac{EC}{BE} = \frac{15}{12} = \frac{5}{4}$. Since $\frac{DC}{AD} = \frac{EC}{BE}$, $\overline{DE} \parallel \overline{AB}$ by the Conv. of the △ Proportionality Thm.

2. $AC = 36$ cm, and $BC = 27$ cm. Verify that $\overline{DE} \parallel \overline{AB}$.

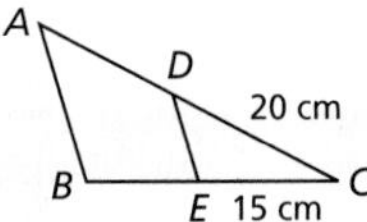

Corollary 7-4-3 **Two-Transversal Proportionality**

COROLLARY	HYPOTHESIS	CONCLUSION
If three or more parallel lines intersect two transversals, then they divide the transversals proportionally.	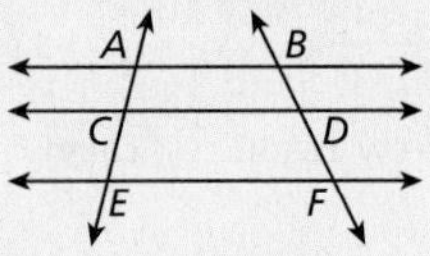 (parallel lines cut by transversals at A, B, C, D, E, F)	$\frac{AC}{CE} = \frac{BD}{DF}$

You will prove Corollary 7-4-3 in Exercise 24.

2 Teach

Guided Instruction

Use transparencies to explain the Triangle Proportionality Theorem. Put $\overleftrightarrow{EF}$ on a separate transparency from the diagram of $\triangle ABC$. Slide $\overleftrightarrow{EF}$ up and down relative to the triangle to show that regardless of its position, $\overline{AB}$ and $\overline{AC}$ will be divided proportionally. Use transparencies again to illustrate the Two-Transversal Proportionality Theorem and the Triangle Angle Bisector Theorem. Measure the angles and sides to verify the theorems.

Reaching All Learners

Through Kinesthetic Experience

Give small groups of students a sheet with three parallel lines cut by a transversal. Have students measure the segments of the transversal and verify the ratio formed. Then have them draw another transversal across the parallel lines and measure the resulting segments. Have students try to form a conjecture based on their results.

EXAMPLE 3 Art Application

An artist used perspective to draw guidelines to help her sketch a row of parallel trees. She then checked the drawing by measuring the distances between the trees. What is LN?

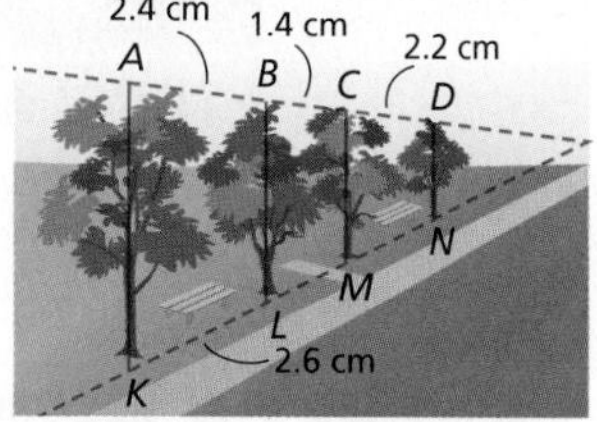

$\overline{AK} \parallel \overline{BL} \parallel \overline{CM} \parallel \overline{DN}$	*Given*
$\frac{KL}{LN} = \frac{AB}{BD}$	*2-Transv. Proportionality Corollary*
$BD = BC + CD$	*Seg. Add. Post.*
$BD = 1.4 + 2.2 = 3.6$ cm	*Substitute 1.4 for BC and 2.2 for CD.*
$\frac{2.6}{LN} = \frac{2.4}{3.6}$	*Substitute the given values.*
$2.4(LN) = 3.6(2.6)$	*Cross Products Prop.*
$LN = 3.9$ cm	*Divide both sides by 2.4.*

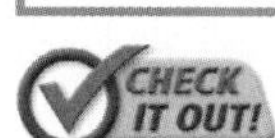
CHECK IT OUT!

3. Use the diagram to find LM and MN to the nearest tenth.
$LM \approx 1.5$ cm; $MN \approx 2.4$ cm

The previous theorems and corollary lead to the following conclusion.

Know it! Note

Theorem 7-4-4 Triangle Angle Bisector Theorem

THEOREM	HYPOTHESIS	CONCLUSION
An angle bisector of a triangle divides the opposite side into two segments whose lengths are proportional to the lengths of the other two sides. ($\triangle \angle$ Bisector Thm.)	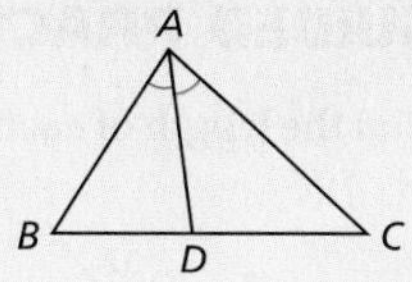 Triangle ABC with $\overline{AD}$ bisecting $\angle A$, D on $\overline{BC}$	$\frac{BD}{DC} = \frac{AB}{AC}$

You will prove Theorem 7-4-4 in Exercise 38.

EXAMPLE 4 Using the Triangle Angle Bisector Theorem

Algebra

Find RV and VT.

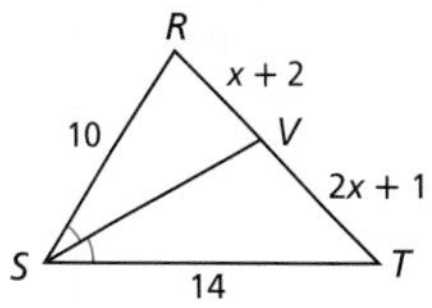

$\frac{RV}{VT} = \frac{SR}{ST}$ by the $\triangle \angle$ Bisector Thm.

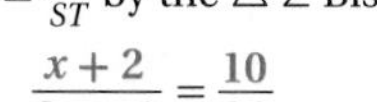

$\frac{x+2}{2x+1} = \frac{10}{14}$	*Substitute the given values.*
$14(x+2) = 10(2x+1)$	*Cross Products Prop.*
$14x + 28 = 20x + 10$	*Dist. Prop.*
$18 = 6x$	*Simplify.*
$x = 3$	*Divide both sides by 6.*

$RV = x + 2 = 3 + 2 = 5$ $\quad VT = 2x + 1 = 2(3) + 1 = 7$ *Substitute 3 for x.*

Helpful Hint

You can check your answer by substituting the values into the proportion.

$\frac{RV}{VT} = \frac{SR}{ST}$

$\frac{5}{7} = \frac{10}{14}$

$\frac{5}{7} = \frac{5}{7}$

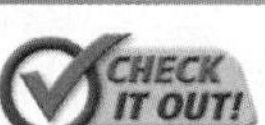
CHECK IT OUT!

4. Find AC and DC.
$AC = 16$; $DC = 9$

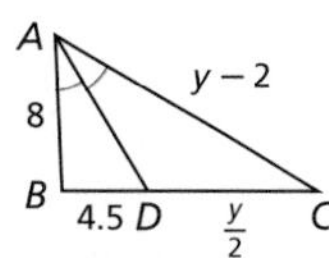

COMMON ERROR ALERT

Some students may mistake the Triangle Proportionality Theorem to mean that a line parallel to one side of a triangle divides the other two sides into *congruent* segments rather than *proportional* ones. Show these students that you get congruent segments only in the special case where the line intersects the two sides at their midpoints.

Teaching Tip **Reading Math** Some students may have difficulty identifying the transversal in **Example 3** before applying the Two-Transversal Proportionality Corollary. Remind them that the prefix *trans* means "across," as in *transportation, transfer,* and *transatlantic. Transverse* means "situated or lying across." Therefore the *transversal* is the line that lies across other lines. ENGLISH LANGUAGE LEARNERS

Power Presentations with PowerPoint®

Additional Examples

Example 3

Suppose that the artist in **Example 3** decided to make a larger sketch of the trees. In the figure, if $AB = 4.5$ in., $BC = 2.6$ in., $CD = 4.1$ in., and $KL = 4.9$ in., find LM and MN to the nearest tenth of an inch.

$LM \approx 2.8$ in., $MN \approx 4.5$ in.

Example 4

Find PS and SR.

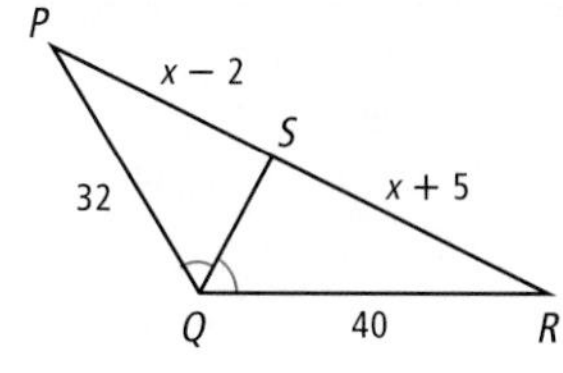

$PS = 28$, $SR = 35$

3 Close

Summarize

Point out that properties of similar triangles are based on proportion. Remind students that *proportional* means having the same or a constant ratio, and its meaning differs from *congruence*. Review the three theorems and the corollary from this lesson, illustrating each with a diagram.

ONGOING ASSESSMENT and INTERVENTION

***Diagnose Before* the Lesson**
7-4 Warm Up, TE p. 481

***Monitor During* the Lesson**
Check It Out! Exercises, SE pp. 482–483
Questioning Strategies, TE pp. 482–483

***Assess After* the Lesson**
7-4 Lesson Quiz, TE p. 487
Alternative Assessment, TE p. 487

INTERVENTION
Questioning Strategies

EXAMPLE 3

- How is the Two-Transversal Proportionality Corollary used in this example?

EXAMPLE 4

- How can you check your answers?

Answers to *Think and Discuss*

1. Possible answer: $\frac{AX}{XB} = \frac{AY}{YC}$; $\frac{AX}{AB} = \frac{XY}{BC}$; $\frac{AY}{AC} = \frac{XY}{BC}$
2. See p. A6.

THINK AND DISCUSS

1. $\overline{XY} \parallel \overline{BC}$. Use what you know about similarity and proportionality to state as many different proportions as possible.

2. **GET ORGANIZED** Copy and complete the graphic organizer. Draw a figure for each proportionality theorem or corollary and then measure it. Use your measurements to write an if-then statement about each figure.

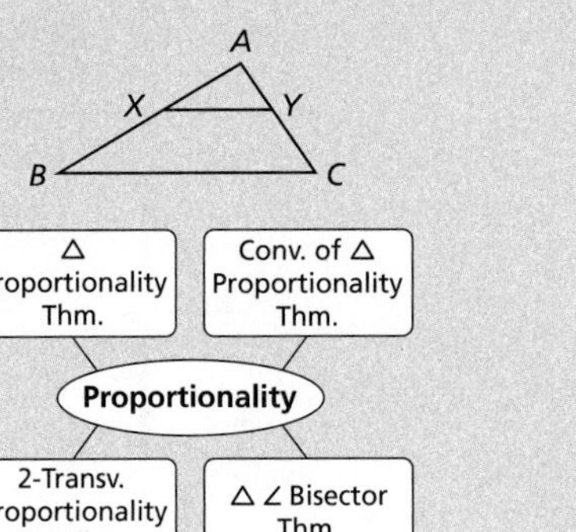

7-4 Exercises

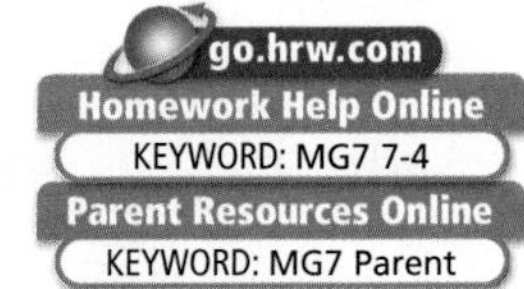

Assignment Guide

Assign *Guided Practice* exercises as necessary.

If you finished Examples **1–2**
- **Basic** 8–11, 23
- **Average** 8–11, 23, 30
- **Advanced** 8–11, 23, 30

If you finished Examples **1–4**
- **Basic** 8–20, 22, 26, 28, 30, 32–35, 40–45
- **Average** 8–18, 21–23, 25–27, 29–36, 40–45
- **Advanced** 8–16, 21–45

Homework Quick Check
Quickly check key concepts.
Exercises: 8, 10, 12, 14, 16, 26

GUIDED PRACTICE

SEE EXAMPLE 1 p. 482

Find the length of each segment.

1. $\overline{DG}$ **30**

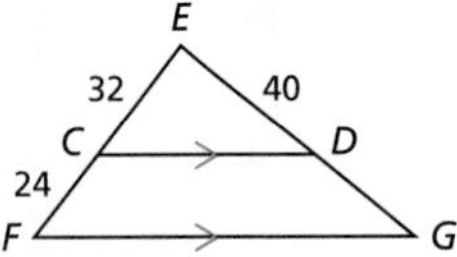

2. $\overline{RN}$ **6.25**

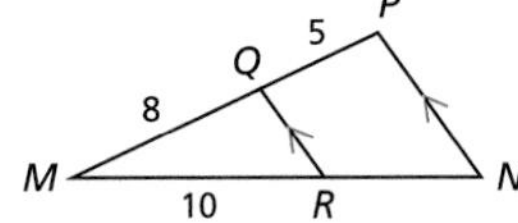

SEE EXAMPLE 2 p. 482

Verify that the given segments are parallel.

3. $\overline{AB}$ and $\overline{CD}$

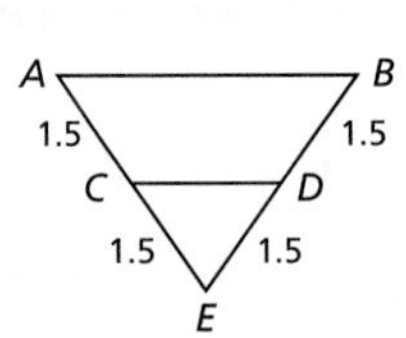

4. $\overline{TU}$ and $\overline{RS}$

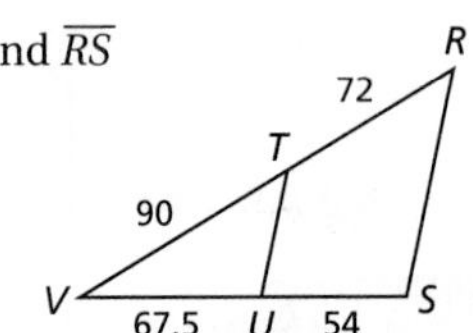

SEE EXAMPLE 3 p. 483

5. **Travel** The map shows the area around Herald Square in Manhattan, New York, and the approximate length of several streets. If the numbered streets are parallel, what is the length of Broadway between 34th St. and 35th St. to the nearest foot? **286 ft**

State Resources

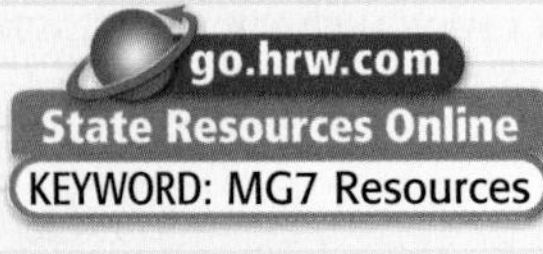

Answers

3. $\frac{EC}{AC} = 1$, and $\frac{ED}{DB} = 1$. Since $\frac{EC}{AC} = \frac{ED}{DB}$, $\overline{AB} \parallel \overline{CD}$ by the Conv. of the △ Proportionality Thm.

4. $\frac{VU}{US} = \frac{67.5}{54} = \frac{5}{4}$, and $\frac{VT}{TR} = \frac{90}{72} = \frac{5}{4}$. Since $\frac{VU}{US} = \frac{VT}{TR}$, $\overline{TU} \parallel \overline{RS}$ by the Conv. of the △ Proportionality Thm.

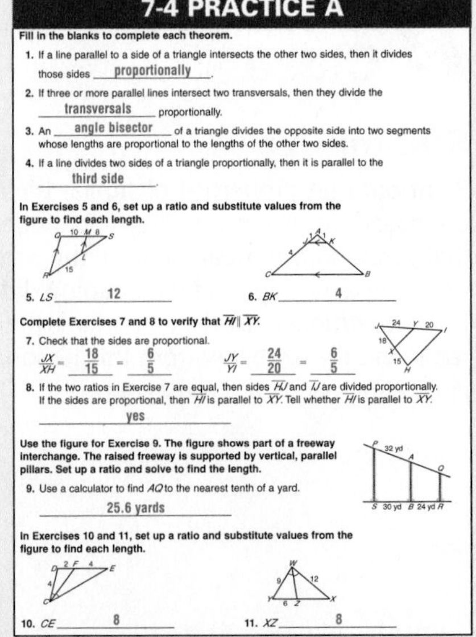

7-4 PRACTICE A

Fill in the blanks to complete each theorem.

1. If a line parallel to a side of a triangle intersects the other two sides, then it divides those sides **proportionally**.
2. If three or more parallel lines intersect two transversals, then they divide the **transversals** proportionally.
3. An **angle bisector** of a triangle divides the opposite side into two segments whose lengths are proportional to the lengths of the other two sides.
4. If a line divides two sides of a triangle proportionally, then it is parallel to the **third side**.

In Exercises 5 and 6, set up a ratio and substitute values from the figure to find each length.

5. LS **12**
6. BK **4**

Complete Exercises 7 and 8 to verify that $\overline{HI} \parallel \overline{XY}$.

7. Check that the sides are proportional.
$\frac{JX}{XH} = \frac{18}{15} = \frac{6}{5}$ $\frac{JY}{YI} = \frac{24}{20} = \frac{6}{5}$
8. If the two ratios in Exercise 7 are equal, then sides $\overline{HJ}$ and $\overline{IJ}$ are divided proportionally. If the sides are proportional, then $\overline{HI}$ is parallel to $\overline{XY}$. Tell whether $\overline{HI}$ is parallel to $\overline{XY}$. **yes**

Use the figure for Exercise 9. The figure shows part of a freeway interchange. The raised freeway is supported by vertical, parallel pillars. Set up a ratio and solve to find the length.

9. Use a calculator to find AQ to the nearest tenth of a yard. **25.6 yards**

In Exercises 10 and 11, set up a ratio and substitute values from the figure to find each length.

10. CE **8**
11. XZ **8**

SEE EXAMPLE 4 p. 483

Find the length of each segment.

6. $\overline{QR}$ and $\overline{RS}$ **$QR = 9$; $RS = 12$**

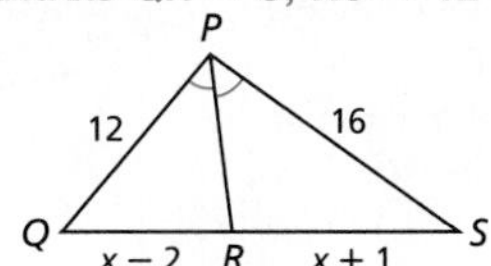

7. $\overline{CD}$ and $\overline{AD}$ **$CD = 4$; $AD = 6$**

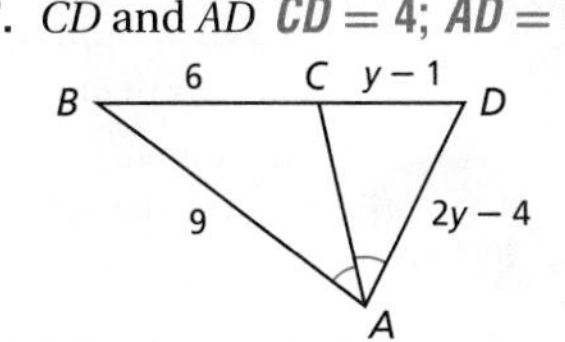

PRACTICE AND PROBLEM SOLVING

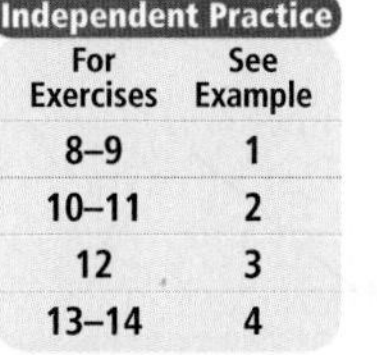

Independent Practice	
For Exercises	See Example
8–9	1
10–11	2
12	3
13–14	4

Extra Practice

Skills Practice p. S17
Application Practice p. S34

Find the length of each segment.

8. $\overline{KL}$ **$5\frac{1}{3}$**

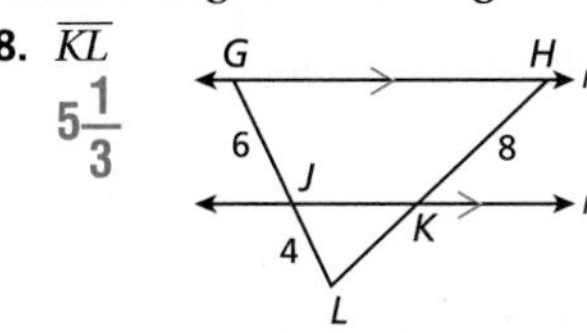

9. $\overline{XZ}$ **20**

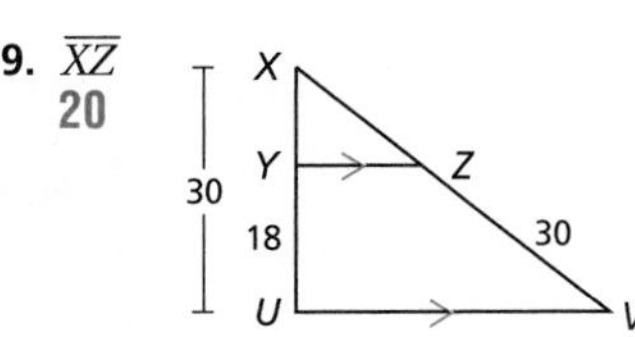

Verify that the given segments are parallel.

10. $\overline{AB}$ and $\overline{CD}$

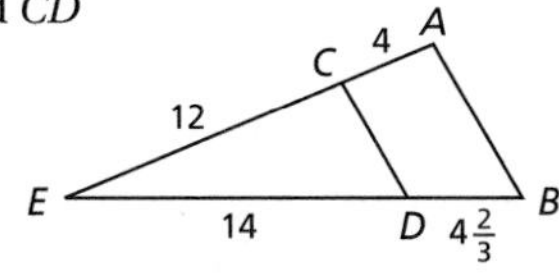

11. $\overline{MN}$ and $\overline{QR}$

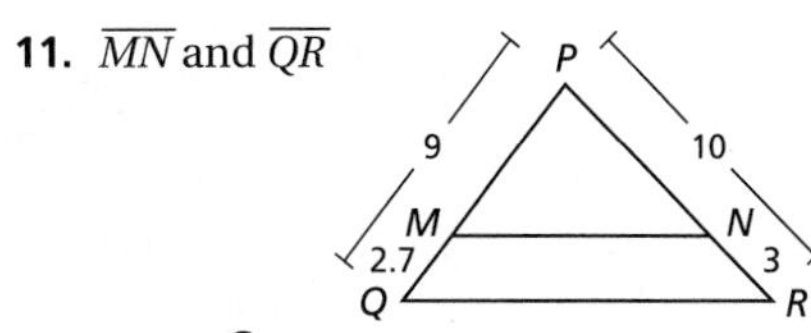

10. $\frac{EC}{CA} = \frac{12}{4} = 3$, and $\frac{ED}{DB} = \frac{14}{4\frac{2}{3}} = 3$. Since $\frac{EC}{CA} = \frac{ED}{DB}$, $\overline{AB} \parallel \overline{CD}$ by the Conv. of the △ Proportionality Thm.

11. $\frac{PM}{MQ} = \frac{6.3}{2.7} = 2\frac{1}{3}$, and $\frac{PN}{NR} = \frac{7}{3} = 2\frac{1}{3}$. Since $\frac{PM}{MQ} = \frac{PN}{NR}$, $\overline{MN} \parallel \overline{QR}$ by the Conv. of the △ Proportionality Thm.

12. **Architecture** The wooden treehouse has horizontal siding that is parallel to the base. What are *LM* and *MN* to the nearest hundredth?
$LM = 2.83$ ft; $MN = 2.39$ ft

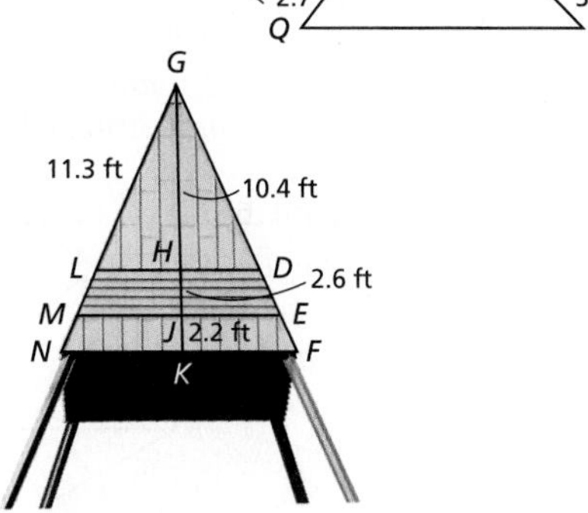

Find the length of each segment.

13. $\overline{BC}$ and $\overline{CD}$ **$BC = 6$; $CD = 5$**

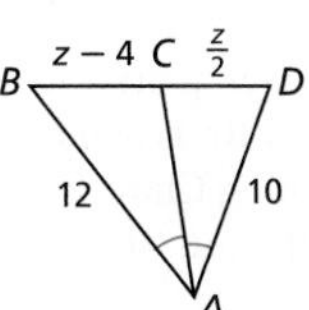

14. $\overline{ST}$ and $\overline{TU}$ **$ST = 10$; $TU = 6$**

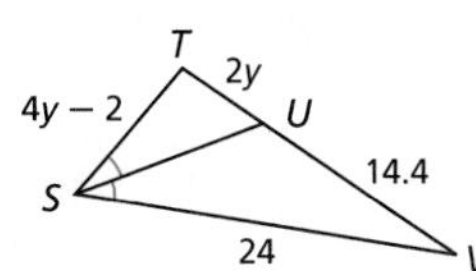

In the figure, $\overleftrightarrow{BC} \parallel \overleftrightarrow{DE} \parallel \overleftrightarrow{FG}$. Complete each proportion.

15. $\frac{AB}{BD} = \frac{AC}{\blacksquare}$ **CE**

16. $\frac{\blacksquare}{DF} = \frac{AE}{EG}$ **AD**

17. $\frac{DF}{\blacksquare} = \frac{EG}{CE}$ **BD**

18. $\frac{AF}{AB} = \frac{\blacksquare}{AC}$ **AG**

19. $\frac{BD}{CE} = \frac{\blacksquare}{EG}$ **DF**

20. $\frac{AB}{AC} = \frac{BF}{\blacksquare}$ **CG**

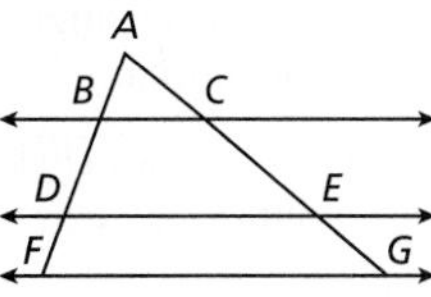

21. The bisector of an angle of a triangle divides the opposite side of the triangle into segments that are 12 in. and 16 in. long. Another side of the triangle is 20 in. long. What are two possible lengths for the third side?
15 in. or $26\frac{2}{3}$ in.

COMMON ERROR ALERT

In exercises similar to **Exercise 6,** a common error is to give the value of the variable as the answer. Remind students they need to use the value to evaluate the expressions. They should see that they need to substitute 11 for *x* in the expressions $x - 2$ and $x + 1$ to find the segment lengths.

Critical Thinking In **Exercise 9,** show students that they can find the required length by using similar triangles rather than the Triangle Proportionality Theorem. Encourage them to draw the two triangles separately to identify corresponding parts.

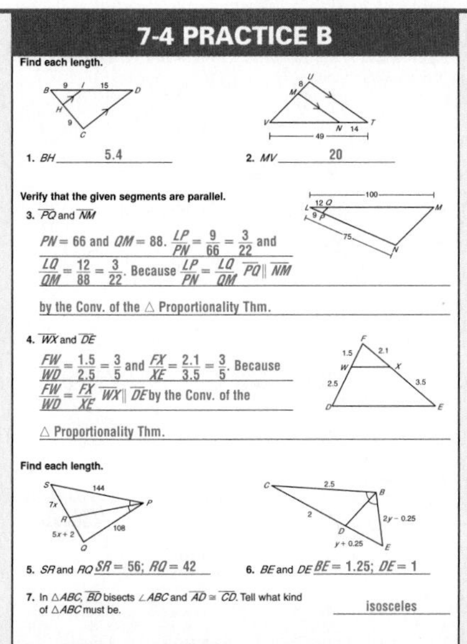

7-4 PRACTICE B

Find each length.

1. BH 5.4

2. MV 20

Verify that the given segments are parallel.

3. $\overline{PQ}$ and $\overline{NM}$

$PN = 66$ and $QM = 88$. $\frac{LP}{PN} = \frac{9}{66} = \frac{3}{22}$ and $\frac{LQ}{QM} = \frac{12}{88} = \frac{3}{22}$. Because $\frac{LP}{PN} = \frac{LQ}{QM}$, $\overline{PQ} \parallel \overline{NM}$ by the Conv. of the △ Proportionality Thm.

4. $\overline{WX}$ and $\overline{DE}$

$\frac{FW}{WD} = \frac{1.5}{2.5} = \frac{3}{5}$ and $\frac{FX}{XE} = \frac{2.1}{3.5} = \frac{3}{5}$. Because $\frac{FW}{WD} = \frac{FX}{XE}$, $\overline{WX} \parallel \overline{DE}$ by the Conv. of the △ Proportionality Thm.

Find each length.

5. SR and RQ $SR = 56$; $RQ = 42$

6. BE and DE $BE = 1.25$; $DE = 1$

7. In △ABC, $\overline{BD}$ bisects ∠ABC and $\overline{AD} \cong \overline{CD}$. Tell what kind of △ABC must be. isosceles

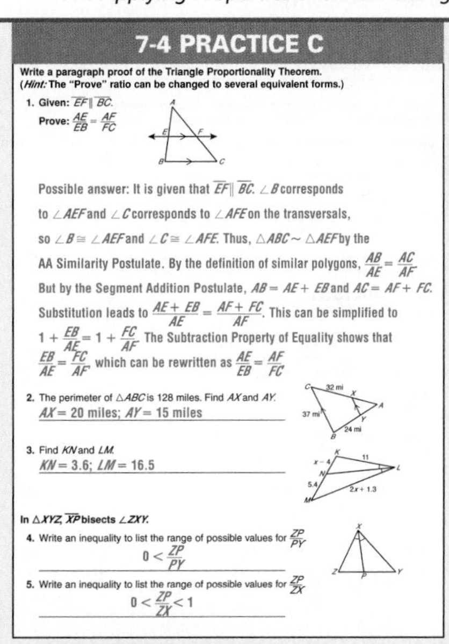

7-4 PRACTICE C

Write a paragraph proof of the Triangle Proportionality Theorem. (*Hint:* The "Prove" ratio can be changed to several equivalent forms.)

1. Given: $\overline{EF} \parallel \overline{BC}$.
Prove: $\frac{AE}{EB} = \frac{AF}{FC}$

Possible answer: It is given that $\overline{EF} \parallel \overline{BC}$. ∠B corresponds to ∠AEF and ∠C corresponds to ∠AFE on the transversals, so ∠B ≅ ∠AEF and ∠C ≅ ∠AFE. Thus, △ABC ~ △AEF by the AA Similarity Postulate. By the definition of similar polygons, $\frac{AB}{AE} = \frac{AC}{AF}$. But by the Segment Addition Postulate, $AB = AE + EB$ and $AC = AF + FC$. Substitution leads to $\frac{AE + EB}{AE} = \frac{AF + FC}{AF}$. This can be simplified to $1 + \frac{EB}{AE} = 1 + \frac{FC}{AF}$. The Subtraction Property of Equality shows that $\frac{EB}{AE} = \frac{FC}{AF}$, which can be rewritten as $\frac{AE}{EB} = \frac{AF}{FC}$.

2. The perimeter of △ABC is 128 miles. Find AX and AY.
$AX = 20$ miles; $AY = 15$ miles

3. Find KN and LM.
$KN = 3.6$; $LM = 16.5$

In △XYZ, $\overline{XP}$ bisects ∠ZXY.

4. Write an inequality to list the range of possible values for $\frac{ZP}{PY}$.
$0 < \frac{ZP}{PY}$

5. Write an inequality to list the range of possible values for $\frac{ZP}{ZX}$.
$0 < \frac{ZP}{ZX} < 1$

MULTI-STEP TEST PREP **Exercise 22** involves applying the Two-Transversal Proportionality Corollary to find an unknown length of a slide rail for a skateboard park. This exercise prepares students for the Multi-Step Test Prep on page 502.

Answers

23\. 1. $\frac{AE}{EB} = \frac{AF}{FC}$ (Given)
2\. $\angle A \cong \angle A$ (Reflex. Prop. of $\cong$)
3\. $\triangle AEF \sim \triangle ABC$ (SAS $\sim$ *Steps 1, 2*)
4\. $\angle AEF \cong \angle ABC$ (Def. of $\sim \triangle$)
5\. $\overleftrightarrow{EF} \parallel \overleftrightarrow{BC}$ (Conv. of Corr. $\angle$s Post.)

24\. 1. $\overleftrightarrow{AB} \parallel \overleftrightarrow{CD}$, $\overleftrightarrow{CD} \parallel \overleftrightarrow{EF}$ (Given)
2\. Draw $\overleftrightarrow{EB}$ intersecting $\overline{CD}$ at X. (2 pts. determine a line.)
3\. $\frac{AC}{CE} = \frac{BX}{XE}$ ($\triangle$ Proportionality Thm.)
4\. $\frac{BX}{XE} = \frac{BD}{DF}$ ($\triangle$ Proportionality Thm.)
5\. $\frac{AC}{CE} = \frac{BD}{DF}$ (Trans. Prop. of =)

29\. Draw a seg. on tracing paper whose length is = to the vert. dist. from line 1 to line 6 or no greater than the diag. dist. from line 1 to line 6 of the notebook paper. Place the tracing paper over the notebook paper so that the seg. spans exactly 6 of the lines on the notebook paper. Then mark the spots where the tracing-paper seg. crosses the lines on the notebook paper. The method works by the 2-Transv. Proportionality Corollary.

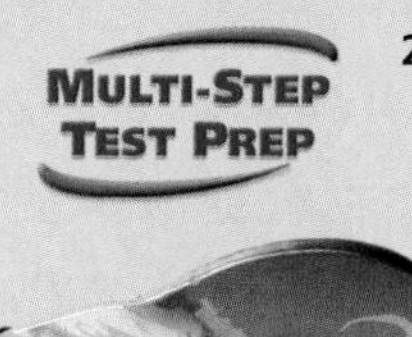

MULTI-STEP TEST PREP

22\. This problem will prepare you for the Multi-Step Test Prep on page 502.
Jaclyn is building a slide rail, the narrow, slanted beam found in skateboard parks.
a. Write a proportion that Jaclyn can use to calculate the length of $\overline{CE}$. $\frac{AC}{BD} = \frac{CE}{DF}$
b. Find *CE*. **71.4 cm**
c. What is the overall length of the slide rail *AJ*? **255 cm**

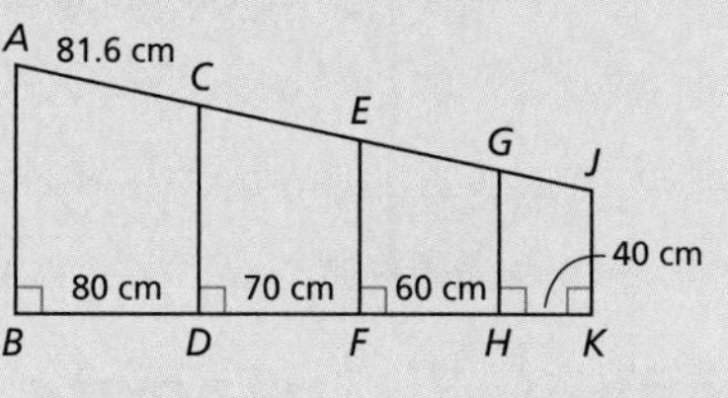

23\. Prove the Converse of the Triangle Proportionality Theorem.
Given: $\frac{AE}{EB} = \frac{AF}{FC}$
Prove: $\overleftrightarrow{EF} \parallel \overleftrightarrow{BC}$

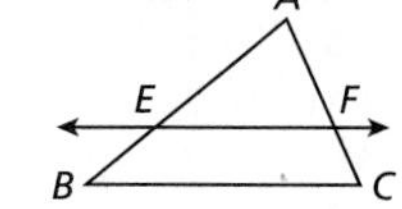

24\. Prove the Two-Transversal Proportionality Corollary.
Given: $\overleftrightarrow{AB} \parallel \overleftrightarrow{CD}$, $\overleftrightarrow{CD} \parallel \overleftrightarrow{EF}$
Prove: $\frac{AC}{CE} = \frac{BD}{DF}$
(*Hint:* Draw $\overleftrightarrow{BE}$ through *X*.)

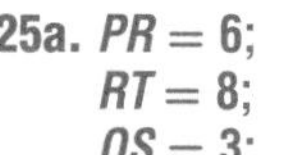

25a. $PR = 6$; $RT = 8$; $QS = 3$; $SU = 4$
25b. $\frac{PR}{RT} = \frac{QS}{SU}$, or $\frac{6}{8} = \frac{3}{4}$

25\. Given that $\overleftrightarrow{PQ} \parallel \overleftrightarrow{RS} \parallel \overleftrightarrow{TU}$
a. Find *PR*, *RT*, *QS*, and *SU*.
b. Use your results from part **b** to write a proportion relating the segment lengths.

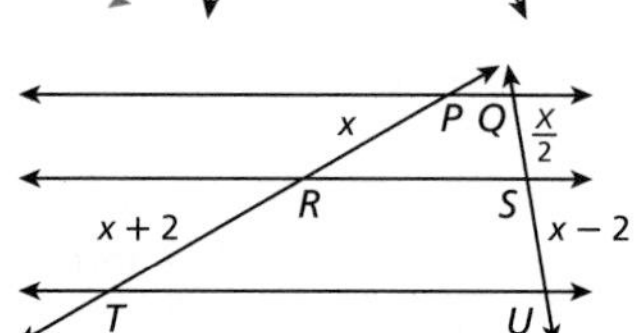

Find the length of each segment.

26\. $\overline{EF}$ $13\frac{1}{3}$

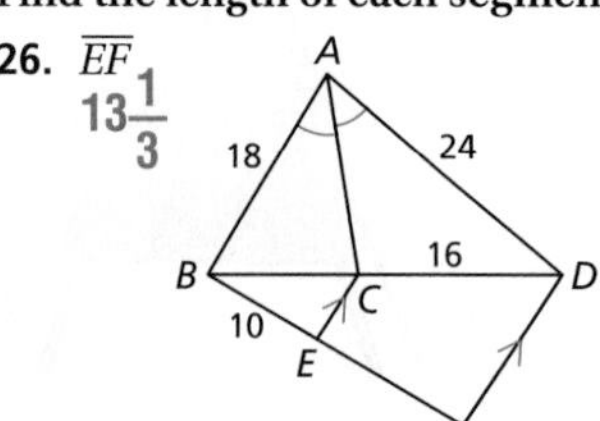

27\. $\overline{ST}$ 15

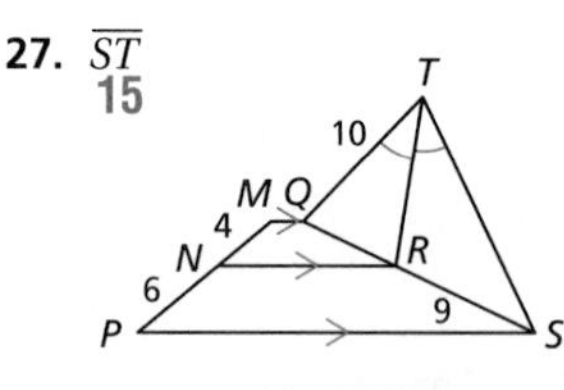

28\. **Real Estate** A developer is laying out lots along Grant Rd. whose total width is 500 ft. Given the width of each lot along Chavez St., what is the width of each of the lots along Grant Rd. to the nearest foot? **176 ft; 235 ft; 88 ft**

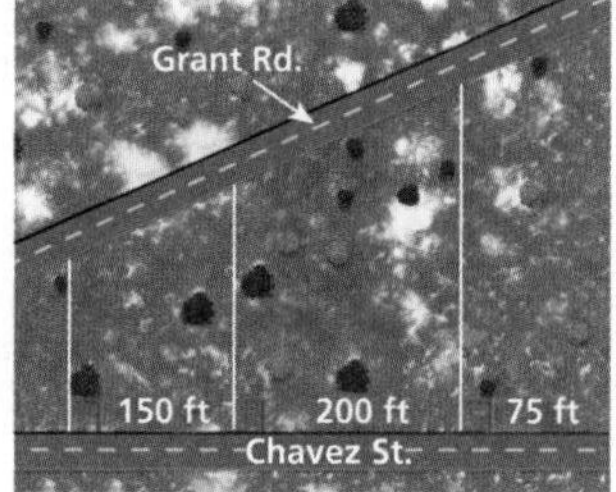

29\. **Critical Thinking** Explain how to use a sheet of lined notebook paper to divide a segment into five congruent segments. Which theorem or corollary do you use?

30\. Given that $\overline{DE} \parallel \overline{BC}$, $\overline{XY} \parallel \overline{AD}$ Find *EC*. $16\frac{1}{18}$

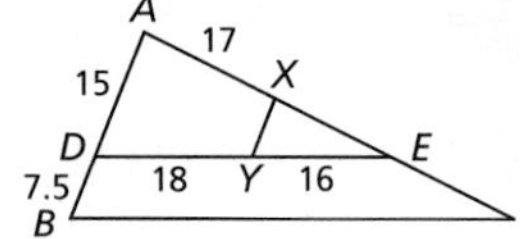

31\. $\frac{CD}{AC} = \frac{DB}{AB}$; $\triangle$ $\angle$ Bisector Thm.

31\. **Write About It** In $\triangle ABC$, $\overrightarrow{AD}$ bisects $\angle BAC$. Write a proportionality statement for the triangle. What theorem supports your conclusion?

7-4 READING STRATEGIES

A proportion shows two equal ratios. Consider the three theorems below.

Triangle Proportionality Theorem: If a line parallel to a side of a triangle intersects two sides, then it divides those sides proportionally.

Use the figure for Exercises 1 and 2.

1. Draw a line parallel to $\overline{EF}$ that intersects $\overline{DF}$ and $\overline{DE}$. Label the intersection point of the line and $\overline{DF}$ point *A*, and label the intersection point of the line and $\overline{DE}$ point *B*.
2. Write a proportion for the figure based on the Triangle Proportionality Theorem. $\frac{DA}{AF} = \frac{DB}{BE}$

Two-Transversal Proportionality Theorem: If three or more parallel lines intersect two transversals, then they divide the transversals proportionally.

Use the figure for Exercises 3 and 4. Lines ℓ, *m*, and *n* are parallel lines.

3. Draw two transversals that intersect lines ℓ, *m*, and *n*. Label the intersection points with ℓ points *P* and *Q*. Label the intersection points with *m* points *R* and *S*. Label the intersection points with *n* points *T* and *U*.
4. Write a proportion for the figure based on the Two-Transversal Proportionality Theorem. $\frac{PR}{RT} = \frac{QS}{SU}$

Triangle Angle Bisector Theorem: An angle bisector of a triangle divides the opposite side into two segments whose lengths are proportional to the lengths of the other two sides.

Use the figure for Exercises 5–7. m∠*J* = 100°.

5. Use a protractor to draw ∠*LJM* so that *M* is on $\overline{LK}$ and m∠*LJM* = 50°.
6. What is m∠*KJM*? 50°
7. Write a proportion for the figure based on the Triangle Angle Bisector Theorem. $\frac{LM}{MK} = \frac{LJ}{JK}$

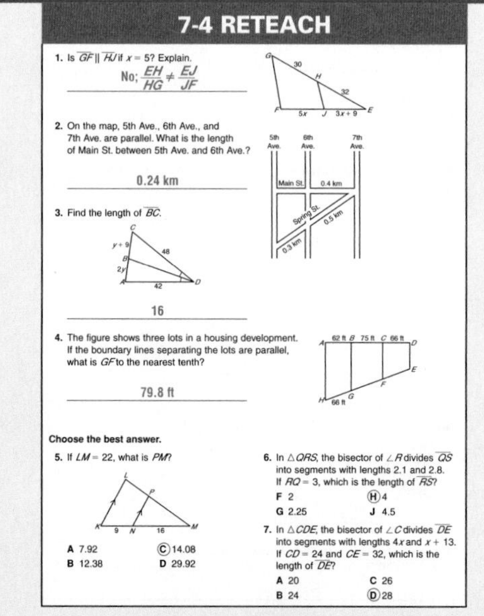

7-4 RETEACH

1. Is $\overline{GF} \parallel \overline{HJ}$ if $x = 5$? Explain.
No; $\frac{EH}{HG} \neq \frac{EJ}{JF}$

2. On the map, 5th Ave., 6th Ave., and 7th Ave. are parallel. What is the length of Main St. between 5th Ave. and 6th Ave.?
0.24 km

3. Find the length of $\overline{BC}$.
16

4. The figure shows three lots in a housing development. If the boundary lines separating the lots are parallel, what is *GF* to the nearest tenth?
79.8 ft

Choose the best answer.

5. If $LM = 22$, what is *PM*?
A 7.92
B 12.38
Ⓒ 14.08
D 29.92

6. In △*QRS*, the bisector of ∠*R* divides $\overline{QS}$ into segments with lengths 2.1 and 2.8. If $RQ = 3$, which is the length of $\overline{RS}$?
F 2
G 2.25
Ⓗ 4
J 4.5

7. In △*CDE*, the bisector of ∠*C* divides $\overline{DE}$ into segments with lengths $4x$ and $x + 13$. If $CD = 24$ and $CE = 32$, which is the length of $\overline{DE}$?
A 20
B 24
C 26
Ⓓ 28

TEST PREP

32. Which dimensions let you conclude that $\overline{UV} \parallel \overline{ST}$?

Ⓐ $SR = 12, TR = 9$ Ⓒ $SR = 35, TR = 28$
Ⓑ $SR = 16, TR = 20$ Ⓓ $SR = 50, TR = 48$

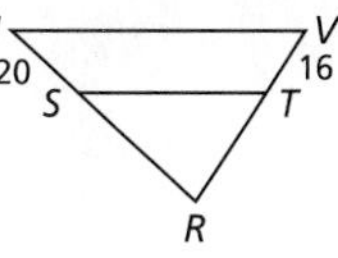

33. In $\triangle ABC$, the bisector of $\angle A$ divides $\overline{BC}$ into segments with lengths 16 and 20. $AC = 25$. Which of these could be the length of $\overline{AB}$?

Ⓕ 12.8 Ⓖ 16 Ⓗ 18.75 Ⓙ 20

34. On the map, 1st St. and 2nd St. are parallel. What is the distance from City Hall to 2nd St. along Cedar Rd.?

Ⓐ 1.8 mi Ⓒ 4.2 mi
Ⓑ 3.2 mi Ⓓ 5.6 mi

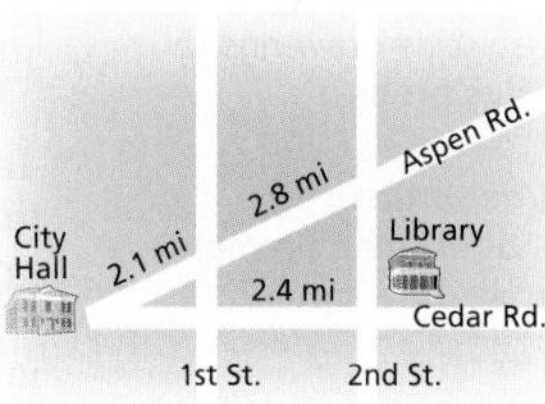

35. **Extended Response** Two segments are divided proportionally. The first segment is divided into lengths 20, 15, and x. The corresponding lengths in the second segment are 16, y, and 24. Find the value of x and y. Use these values and write six proportions.

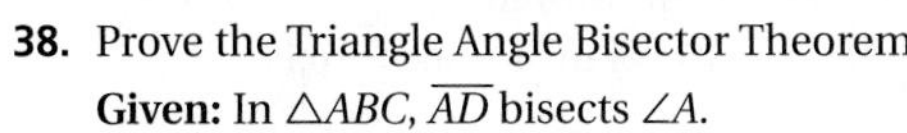

CHALLENGE AND EXTEND

36. The perimeter of $\triangle ABC$ is 29 m. $\overline{AD}$ bisects $\angle A$. Find AB and AC. $AB = 8\frac{8}{9}$; $AC = 11\frac{1}{9}$

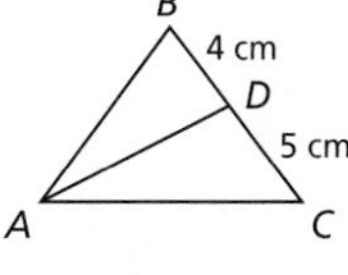

37. Prove that if two triangles are similar, then the ratio of their corresponding angle bisectors is the same as the ratio of their corresponding sides.

38. Prove the Triangle Angle Bisector Theorem.

Given: In $\triangle ABC$, $\overline{AD}$ bisects $\angle A$.

Prove: $\frac{BD}{DC} = \frac{AB}{AC}$

Plan: Draw $\overline{BX} \parallel \overline{AD}$ and extend $\overline{AC}$ to X. Use properties of parallel lines and the Converse of the Isosceles Triangle Theorem to show that $\overline{AX} \cong \overline{AB}$. Then apply the Triangle Proportionality Theorem.

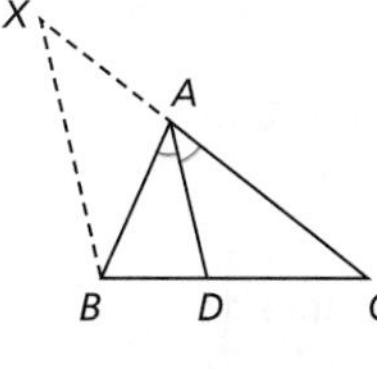

39. **Construction** Construct three parallel lines cut by a transversal. Construct a second transversal that forms line segments twice the length of the corresponding segments on the first transversal. **Check students' work.**

SPIRAL REVIEW

Write an algebraic expression that can be used to find the nth term of each sequence. *(Previous course)*

40. 5, 6, 7, 8,... $n + 4$ 41. 3, 6, 9, 12,... $3n$ 42. 1, 4, 9, 16,... n^2

43. B is the midpoint of $\overline{AC}$. A has coordinates $(1, 4)$, and B has coordinates $(3, -7)$. Find the coordinates of C. *(Lesson 1-6)* $(5, -18)$

Verify that the given triangles are similar. *(Lesson 7-3)*

44. $\triangle ABC$ and $\triangle ADE$

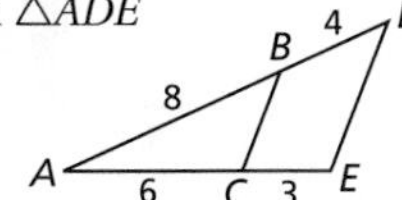

45. $\triangle JKL$ and $\triangle MLN$

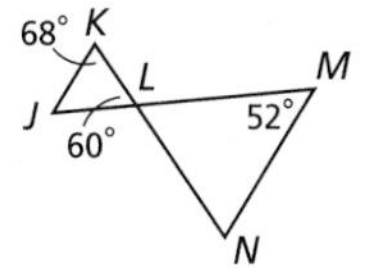

45. $\angle KLJ \cong \angle NLM$ by the Vert. ∡ Thm. By the △ Sum Thm., $m\angle MNL = 68°$. So $\angle JKL \cong \angle MNL$. Therefore $\triangle JKL \sim \triangle MLN$ by AA ~.

7-4 PROBLEM SOLVING

A streetlight is mounted at the top of a 15-foot pole. A 6-foot tall man walks away from the pole along a straight path. How long is his shadow when he is 40 feet from the pole?

1. In the space provided, draw two triangles that represent this problem. Label the smaller triangle $\triangle ABC$ and the larger triangle $\triangle DBE$. What is the name of the resulting diagram?

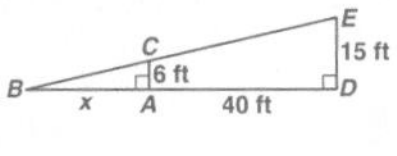

(Diagram labels: E, C, 15 ft, 6 ft, B, D, x, A, 40 ft)

overlapping right triangles

2. What is the relationship between $\triangle ABC$ and $\triangle DBE$?

similar triangles

3. Prove that $\triangle ABC \sim \triangle DBE$.

1. $\triangle ABC$ and $\triangle DBE$ are overlapping right triangles; Given. 2. $\angle B \sim \angle B$; Reflexive Property of Congruence. 3. $\triangle CAB \sim \triangle EDB$; All right triangles are congruent (Right Angle Congruence Theorem). 4. $\triangle ABC \sim \triangle DBE$; AA Similarity (Angle-Angle Similarity Postulate).

4. Set up a proportion that can be used to find x, the length of the man's shadow.

$\frac{15}{x + 40} = \frac{6}{x}$

5. Solve for x. Round to the nearest tenth.

26.7 ft

Draw two 30°-60°-90° right triangles. Label one $\triangle ABC$ with $\angle C$ as the right angle. Label the other one $\triangle DEF$ with $\angle F$ as the right angle. Let $m\angle A = m\angle D = 30°$. If $AB = FE = 8$ cm, find the missing sides.

6. CB 4 cm
7. AC $4\sqrt{3}$ cm
8. DE 16 cm
9. DF $8\sqrt{3}$ cm

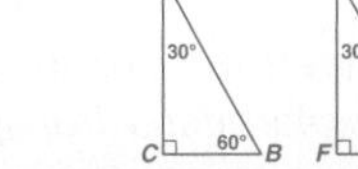

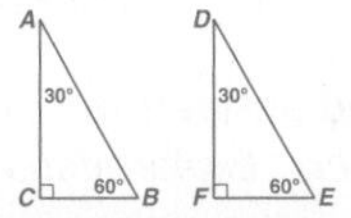

Answers

35. Possible answer: If $\frac{20}{16} = \frac{15}{y}$, then $y = 12$. If $\frac{20}{16} = \frac{x}{24}$, then $x = 30$; $\frac{20}{16} = \frac{15}{12}$; $\frac{20}{16} = \frac{30}{24}$; $\frac{15}{12} = \frac{30}{24}$; $\frac{20 + 15}{30} = \frac{16 + 12}{24}$; $\frac{20}{15 + 30} = \frac{16}{12 + 24}$; $\frac{20}{20 + 15 + 30} = \frac{16}{16 + 12 + 24}$.

37–38. See p. A24.

44. $\angle A \cong \angle A$ by the Reflex. Prop. of ≅. $\frac{AB}{AD} = \frac{8}{12} = \frac{2}{3}$, and $\frac{AC}{AE} = \frac{6}{9} = \frac{2}{3}$. Therefore $\triangle ABC \sim \triangle ADE$ by SAS ~.

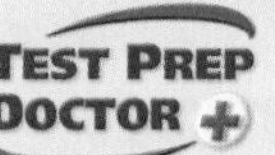

TEST PREP DOCTOR In **Exercise 34,** students who chose **A** have correctly found the distance from City Hall to 1st St., but they have forgotten that they must add this distance to 2.4 mi to find the required distance. Choice **D** can be eliminated. The diagram shows that the distance from City Hall to 2nd St. is longer along Aspen Rd than along Cedar Rd.

Journal

Have students compare and contrast the three theorems used to establish proportionality.

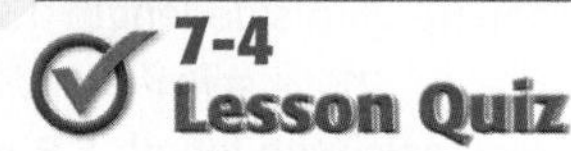

ALTERNATIVE ASSESSMENT

Ask students to bring in a city map that shows a rectangular street grid with one or more diagonal streets. Have students use the streets to illustrate the Two-Transversal Proportionality Corollary.

Power Presentations with PowerPoint®

7-4 Lesson Quiz

Find the length of each segment.

1. $\overline{JG}$ $\frac{33}{2}$ or $16\frac{1}{2}$

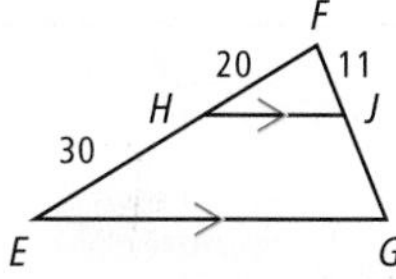

2. $\overline{SR}$ and $\overline{ST}$ $SR = 25$, $ST = 15$

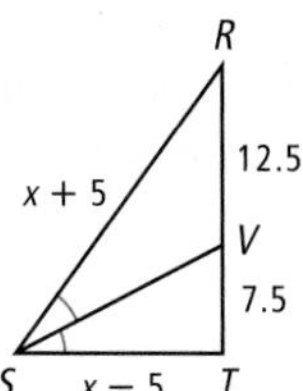

3. Verify that $\overline{BE}$ and $\overline{CD}$ are parallel.

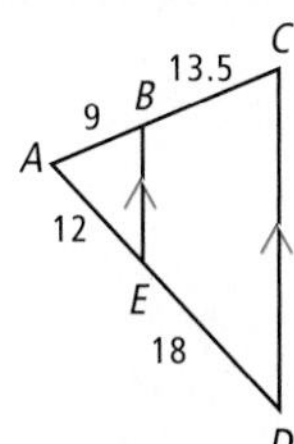

$\frac{BC}{AB} = \frac{13.5}{9} = 1.5$; $\frac{ED}{AE} = \frac{18}{12} = 1.5$; since $\frac{BC}{AB} = \frac{ED}{AE}$, $\overline{BE} \parallel \overline{CD}$ by the Converse of the △ Proportionality Thm.

Also available on transparency

7-5 Organizer

Pacing: Traditional 1 day
Block $\frac{1}{2}$ day

Objectives: Use ratios to make indirect measurements.

Use scale drawings to solve problems.

Online Edition
Tutorial Videos, Interactivity

Countdown Week 16

Power Presentations with PowerPoint®

Warm Up

Convert each measurement.

1. 6 ft 3 in. to inches 75 in.
2. 5 m 38 cm to centimeters 538 cm

Find the perimeter and area of each polygon.

3. square with side length 13 cm $P = 52$ cm, $A = 169$ cm^2
4. rectangle with length 5.8 m and width 2.5 m $P = 16.6$ m, $A = 14.5$ m^2

Also available on transparency

Math Humor

Q: How many seconds are there in a year?

A: Twelve: January second, February second, March second, … .

7-5 Using Proportional Relationships

Objectives
Use ratios to make indirect measurements.

Use scale drawings to solve problems.

Vocabulary
indirect measurement
scale drawing
scale

Why learn this?
Proportional relationships help you find distances that cannot be measured directly.

"Now that's what I call a big tree!"

Indirect measurement is any method that uses formulas, similar figures, and/or proportions to measure an object. The following example shows one indirect measurement technique.

EXAMPLE 1 *Measurement Application*

A student wanted to find the height of a statue of a pineapple in Nambour, Australia. She measured the pineapple's shadow and her own shadow. The student's height is 5 ft 4 in. What is the height of the pineapple?

Step 1 Convert the measurements to inches.

$AC = 5$ ft 4 in. $= (5 \cdot 12)$ in. $+ 4$ in. $= 64$ in.
$BC = 2$ ft $= (2 \cdot 12)$ in. $= 24$ in.
$EF = 8$ ft 9 in. $= (8 \cdot 12)$ in. $+ 9$ in. $= 105$ in.

Step 2 Find similar triangles.

Because the sun's rays are parallel, $\angle 1 \cong \angle 2$. Therefore $\triangle ABC \sim \triangle DEF$ by $AA \sim$.

Step 3 Find DF.

$\frac{AC}{DF} = \frac{BC}{EF}$ *Corr. sides are proportional.*

$\frac{64}{DF} = \frac{24}{105}$ *Substitute 64 for AC, 24 for BC, and 105 for EF.*

$24(DF) = 64 \cdot 105$ *Cross Products Prop.*

$DF = 280$ *Divide both sides by 24.*

The height of the pineapple is 280 in., or 23 ft 4 in.

Helpful Hint
Whenever dimensions are given in both feet and inches, you must convert them to either feet or inches before doing any calculations.

1. A student who is 5 ft 6 in. tall measured shadows to find the height LM of a flagpole. What is LM?
15 ft 7 in.

State Resources

1 Introduce

EXPLORATION

7-5 Using Proportional Relationships

Explore the relationships among the perimeters and areas of similar polygons.

1. *ABCD* and *EFGH* are rectangles. Explain why *ABCD* ~ *EFGH*.
2. Find the similarity ratio of *ABCD* to *EFGH*.
3. Find the perimeter and area of each rectangle. Fill in the table.

	Rectangle *ABCD*	Rectangle *EFGH*
Perimeter		
Area		

4. What is the ratio of the perimeters? What is the ratio of the areas?
5. How do the ratios in Step 4 compare to the similarity ratio?
6. Repeat Steps 1–5 by drawing your own similar rectangles and assigning lengths to the sides. Do the same relationships apply?

THINK AND DISCUSS

7. **Explain** how to find the ratio of the perimeters of two polygons whose similarity ratio is $\frac{a}{b}$.

Motivate

Show students a miniature object such as a toy car, a model train carriage, a miniature tea set, or furniture from a dollhouse. Encourage students to think of hobbies or collections that involve scale models such as model trains, model airplanes, and souvenirs of buildings. Explain to students that miniature objects have been made to scale based on proportional relationships.

Explorations and answers are provided in *Alternate Openers: Explorations Transparencies.*

A **scale drawing** represents an object as smaller than or larger than its actual size. The drawing's **scale** is the ratio of any length in the drawing to the corresponding actual length. For example, on a map with a scale of 1 cm:1500 m, one centimeter on the map represents 1500 m in actual distance.

EXAMPLE 2 Solving for a Dimension

The scale of this map of downtown Dallas is 1.5 cm:300 m. Find the actual distance between Union Station and the Dallas Public Library.

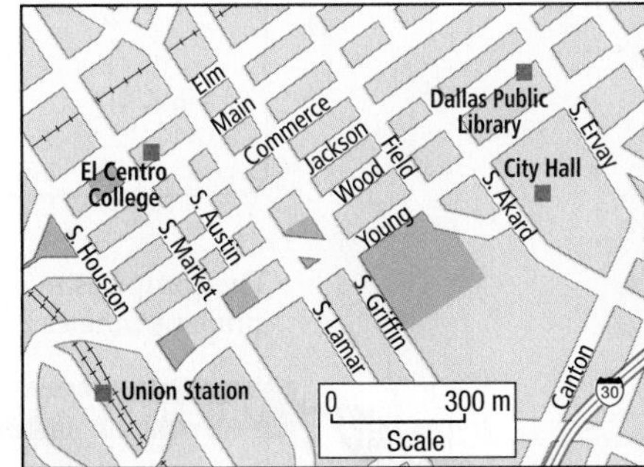

Remember!

A proportion may compare measurements that have different units.

Use a ruler to measure the distance between Union Station and the Dallas Public Library. The distance is 6 cm.

To find the actual distance x write a proportion comparing the map distance to the actual distance.

$$\frac{6}{x} = \frac{1.5}{300}$$

$1.5x = 6(300)$ *Cross Products Prop.*

$1.5x = 1800$ *Simplify.*

$x = 1200$ *Divide both sides by 1.5.*

The actual distance is 1200 m, or 1.2 km.

2. Find the actual distance between City Hall and El Centro College. **900 m, or 0.9 km**

EXAMPLE 3 Making a Scale Drawing

The Lincoln Memorial in Washington, D.C., is approximately 57 m long and 36 m wide. Make a scale drawing of the base of the building using a scale of 1 cm:15 m.

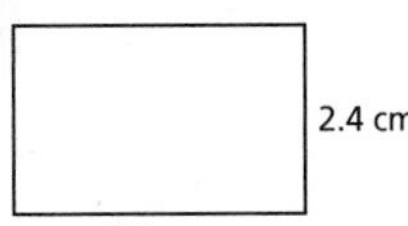

Step 1 Set up proportions to find the length ℓ and width w of the scale drawing.

$$\frac{\ell}{57} = \frac{1}{15} \qquad \frac{w}{36} = \frac{1}{15}$$

$15\ell = 57 \qquad 15w = 36$

$\ell = 3.8 \text{ m} \qquad w = 2.4 \text{ cm}$

Step 2 Use a ruler to draw a rectangle with these dimensions.

2.4 cm

3.8 cm

3. The rectangular central chamber of the Lincoln Memorial is 74 ft long and 60 ft wide. Make a scale drawing of the floor of the chamber using a scale of 1 in.:20 ft.

Check students' work. The drawing should be 3.7 in. by 3 in.

COMMON ERROR ALERT

Some students may confuse the three ratios involving similar figures given on p. 490. Remind them that the *similarity ratio* refers only to the ratio of the lengths of the sides. It is equal to the perimeter ratio and the square root of the area ratio.

Power Presentations with PowerPoint®

Additional Examples

Example 1

Tyler wants to find the height of a telephone pole. He measured the pole's shadow and his own shadow and then made a diagram. What is the height h of the pole? 28 ft 9 in.

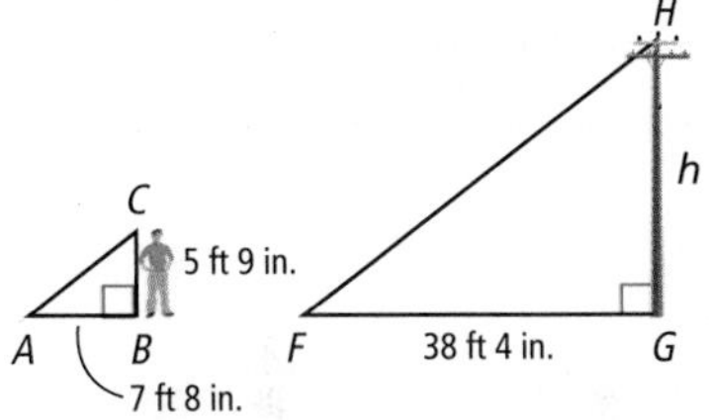

Example 2

On a Wisconsin road map, Kristin measured a distance of $11\frac{1}{8}$ in. from Madison to Wausau. The scale of this map is 1 inch:13 miles. What is the actual distance between Madison and Wausau to the nearest mile? 145 mi

Example 3

Lady Liberty holds a tablet in her left hand. The tablet is 7.19 m long and 4.14 m wide. If you made a scale drawing using the scale 1 cm:0.75 m, what would be the dimensions to the nearest tenth? ℓ: 9.6 cm; w: 5.5 cm

2 Teach

Guided Instruction

Review how to convert measurements. Show how to set up a proportion to solve an indirect measurement problem using a scale on a map. Remind students that a proportion can be set up in different ways. **Example 1** can also be written as man:shadow = tree:shadow. Review the Proportional Perimeters and Areas Theorem and explain that these ratios apply to any pair of similar polygons, not just triangles.

Reaching All Learners

Through Cooperative Learning

Have students work in groups to draw or build a scale model of a famous building, monument, or local landmark. Ask them to choose their object and to make a list of the different tasks required. Then divide these tasks among the group members. These tasks should include finding out the measurements of the actual object, choosing a suitable scale, calculating the measurements needed to make the model, and then drawing or constructing it.

INTERVENTION

Questioning Strategies

EXAMPLE 1

- Explain how a right triangle models the relationship between the shadow of an object and its height.

EXAMPLES 2–3

- How can you set up proportions using measures in different units?

Auditory To make it easier for students to remember Theorem 7-5-1, explain the theorem as "The ratio of the perimeters of similar figures is the same as the ratio of the corresponding sides. The ratio of the areas is the square of the ratio of the corresponding sides."

Power Presentations with PowerPoint®

Additional Examples

Example 4

Given that $\triangle LMN \sim \triangle QRS$, find the perimeter P and area A of $\triangle QRS$.

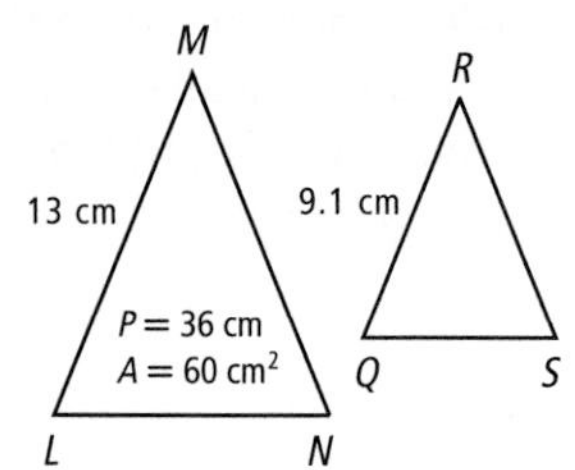

$P = 25.2$ cm, $A = 29.4$ cm^2

INTERVENTION

Questioning Strategies

EXAMPLE 4

- What is an easy way to remember that the ratio of the areas of similar figures is the square of the similarity ratio?
- How are the perimeter ratio and the area ratio related to the similarity ratio?

Similar Triangles — **Similarity, Perimeter, and Area Ratios**

STATEMENT	RATIO
$\triangle ABC \sim \triangle DEF$ 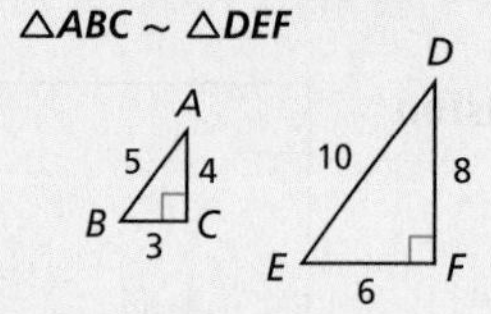 (triangle ABC with sides 5, 4, 3; triangle DEF with sides 10, 8, 6)	**Similarity ratio:** $\frac{AB}{DE} = \frac{AC}{DF} = \frac{BC}{EF} = \frac{1}{2}$ **Perimeter ratio:** $\frac{\text{perimeter } \triangle ABC}{\text{perimeter } \triangle DEF} = \frac{12}{24} = \frac{1}{2}$ **Area ratio:** $\frac{\text{area } \triangle ABC}{\text{area } \triangle DEF} = \frac{6}{24} = \frac{1}{4} = \left(\frac{1}{2}\right)^2$

The comparison of the similarity ratio and the ratio of perimeters and areas of similar triangles leads to the following theorem.

Theorem 7-5-1 — **Proportional Perimeters and Areas Theorem**

If the similarity ratio of two similar figures is $\frac{a}{b}$, then the ratio of their perimeters is $\frac{a}{b}$, and the ratio of their areas is $\frac{a^2}{b^2}$, or $\left(\frac{a}{b}\right)^2$.

You will prove Theorem 7-5-1 in Exercises 44 and 45.

EXAMPLE 4 Using Ratios to Find Perimeters and Areas

Given that $\triangle RST \sim \triangle UVW$, find the perimeter P and area A of $\triangle UVW$.

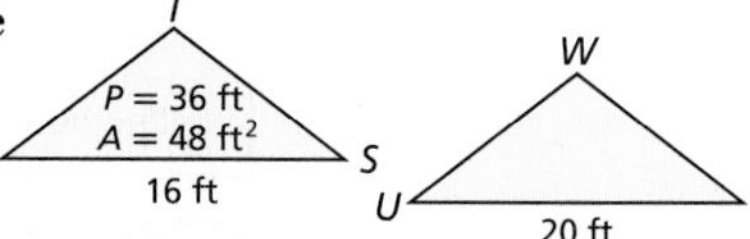

The similarity ratio of $\triangle RST$ to $\triangle UVW$ is $\frac{16}{20}$, or $\frac{4}{5}$.

By the Proportional Perimeters and Areas Theorem, the ratio of the triangles' perimeters is also $\frac{4}{5}$, and the ratio of the triangles' areas is $\left(\frac{4}{5}\right)^2$, or $\frac{16}{25}$.

Perimeter	Area
$\frac{36}{P} = \frac{4}{5}$	$\frac{48}{A} = \frac{16}{25}$
$4P = 5(36)$	$16A = 25 \cdot 48$
$P = 45$ ft	$A = 75$ ft^2

The perimeter of $\triangle UVW$ is 45 ft, and the area is 75 ft^2.

4. $\triangle ABC \sim \triangle DEF$, $BC = 4$ mm, and $EF = 12$ mm. If $P = 42$ mm and $A = 96$ mm^2 for $\triangle DEF$, find the perimeter and area of $\triangle ABC$. $P = 14$ mm; $A = 10\frac{2}{3}$ mm^2

THINK AND DISCUSS

1. Explain how to find the actual distance between two cities 5.5 in. apart on a map that has a scale of 1 in.:25 mi.

2. **GET ORGANIZED** Copy and complete the graphic organizer. Draw and measure two similar figures. Then write their ratios.

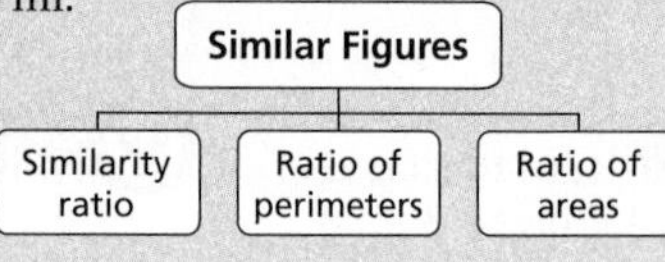

3 Close

Summarize

Remind students that indirect measurement and scale drawings are among the many real-world applications of similarity, such as maps and blueprints. Review that if the similarity ratio of two similar figures is $\frac{a}{b}$, then the ratio of the perimeters is also $\frac{a}{b}$, and the ratio of the areas is $\frac{a^2}{b^2}$. Also remind students to always simplify their ratios.

ONGOING ASSESSMENT and INTERVENTION

Diagnose ***Before*** **the Lesson**
7-5 Warm Up, TE p. 488

Monitor ***During*** **the Lesson**
Check It Out! Exercises, SE pp. 488–490
Questioning Strategies, TE pp. 489–490

Assess ***After*** **the Lesson**
7-5 Lesson Quiz, TE p. 494
Alternative Assessment, TE p. 494

Answers to *Think and Discuss*

1. Set up a proportion: $\frac{5.5}{x} = \frac{1}{25}$. Then solve for x to find the actual dist. of 137.5 mi.
2. See p. A6.

7-5 Exercises

go.hrw.com
Homework Help Online
KEYWORD: MG7 7-5
Parent Resources Online
KEYWORD: MG7 Parent

GUIDED PRACTICE

1. **Vocabulary** Finding distances using similar triangles is called __?__. (*indirect measurement* or *scale drawing*) **indirect measurement**

SEE EXAMPLE 1 p. 488

2. **Measurement** To find the height of a dinosaur in a museum, Amir placed a mirror on the ground 40 ft from its base. Then he stepped back 4 ft so that he could see the top of the dinosaur in the mirror. Amir's eyes were approximately 5 ft 6 in. above the ground. What is the height of the dinosaur? **55 ft**

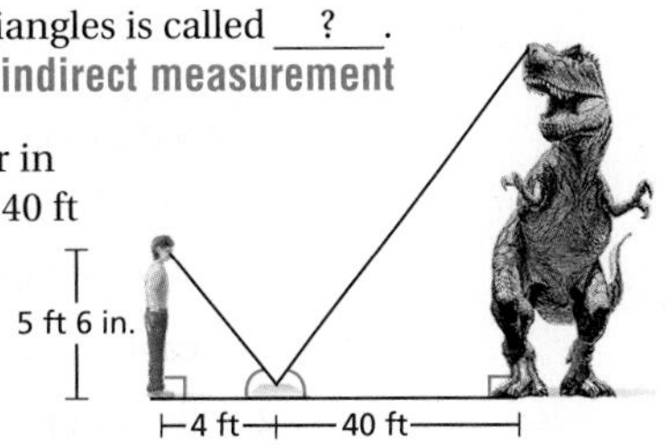

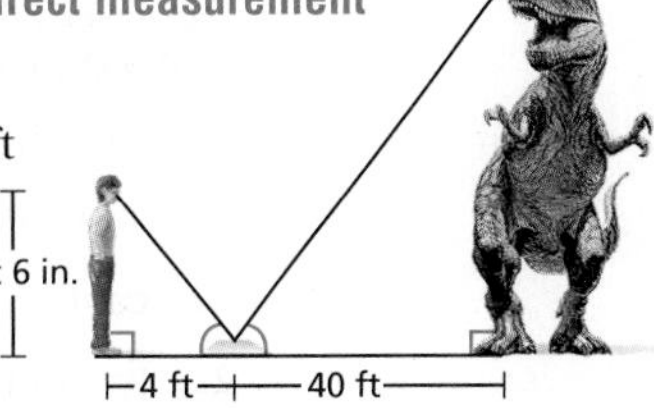

SEE EXAMPLE 2 p. 489

The scale of this blueprint of an art gallery is 1 in.:48 ft. Find the actual lengths of the following walls.

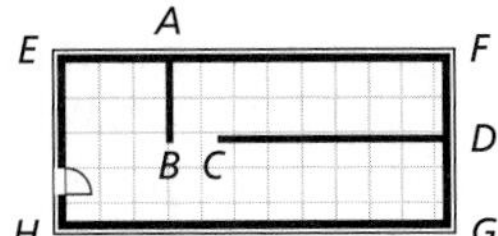

3. $\overline{AB}$ **12 ft**
4. $\overline{CD}$ **36 ft**
5. $\overline{EF}$ **60 ft**
6. $\overline{FG}$ **24 ft**

SEE EXAMPLE 3 p. 489

Multi-Step A rectangular classroom is 10 m long and 4.6 m wide. Make a scale drawing of the classroom using the following scales.

7. 1 cm:1 m
8. 1 cm:2 m
9. 1 cm:2.3 m

SEE EXAMPLE 4 p. 490

Given: rectangle $MNPQ \sim$ rectangle $RSTU$

10. Find the perimeter of rectangle $RSTU$. **21 cm**
11. Find the area of rectangle $RSTU$. **27 cm^2**

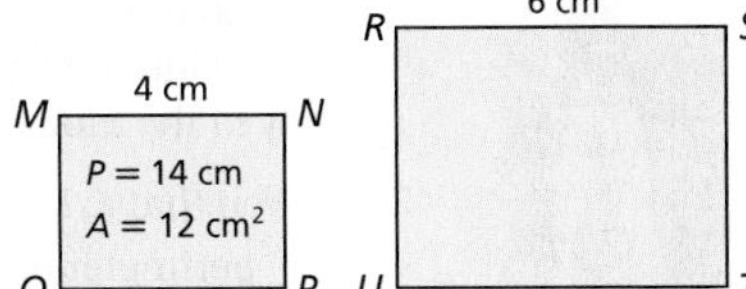

PRACTICE AND PROBLEM SOLVING

Independent Practice

For Exercises	See Example
12	1
13–14	2
15–17	3
18–19	4

Extra Practice
Skills Practice p. S17
Application Practice p. S34

12. **Measurement** Jenny is 5 ft 2 in. tall. To find the height of a light pole, she measured her shadow and the pole's shadow. What is the height of the pole? **$10\frac{1}{3}$ ft**

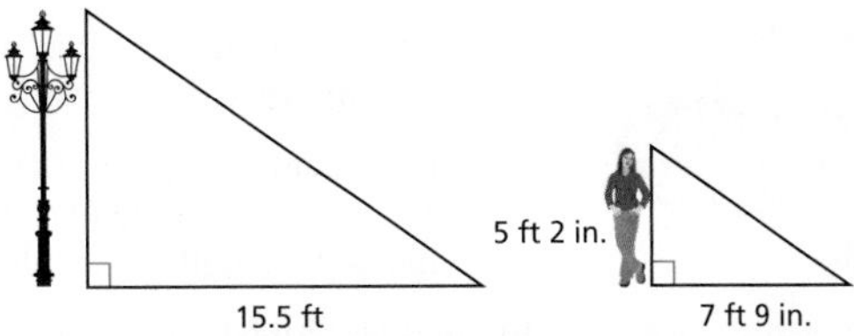

Space Exploration Use the following information for Exercises 13 and 14.

This is a map of the Mars Exploration Rover *Opportunity's* predicted landing site on Mars. The scale is 1 cm:9.4 km. What are the approximate measures of the actual length and width of the ellipse?

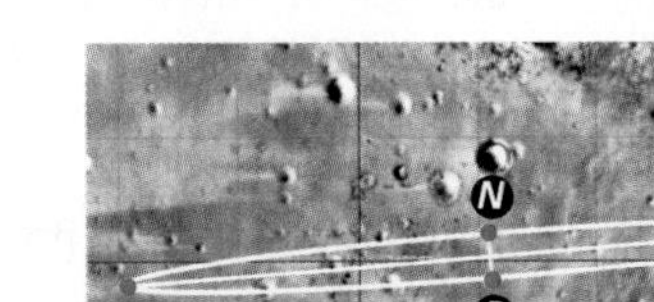
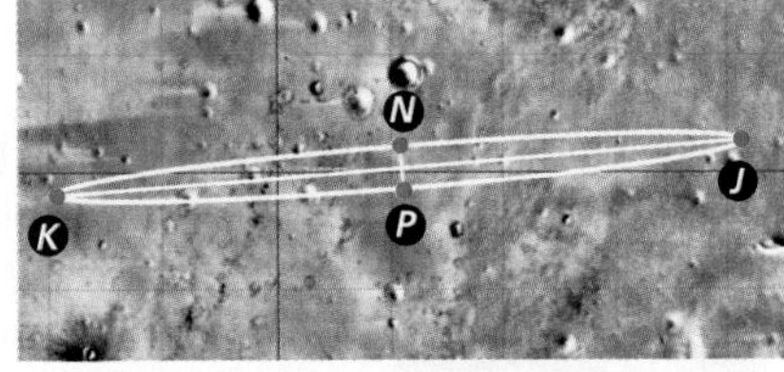

13. $KJ \approx$ **57 km**
14. $NP \approx$ **4 km**

Multi-Step A park at the end of a city block is a right triangle with legs 150 ft and 200 ft long. Make a scale drawing of the park using the following scales.

15. 1.5 in.:100 ft
16. 1 in.:300 ft
17. 1 in.:150 ft

Answers

7–9, 15–17. Check students' drawings. Approximate dimensions are given.

7. 10 cm by 4.6 cm
8. 5 cm by 2.3 cm
9. 4.3 cm by 2 cm
15. 2.25 in. by 3 in.
16. 0.5 in. by 0.67 in.
17. 1 in. by 1.3 in.

7-5 Exercises

Assignment Guide

Assign *Guided Practice* exercises as necessary.

If you finished Examples 1–2
Basic 12–15, 20–23, 27, 32
Average 12–15, 20–23, 27, 32
Advanced 12–15, 20–23, 27, 32, 33, 43

If you finished Examples 1–4
Basic 12–31, 36, 37, 39–42, 47–52
Average 12–31, 35–43, 47–52
Advanced 12–22, 26–52

Homework Quick Check
Quickly check key concepts.
Exercises: 12, 14, 16, 18, 20, 28

Teaching Tip

Inclusion For **Exercise 12,** prompt students to convert all measurements to the same unit. Remind them that 7 ft 9 in. is not 7.9 ft. Since there are 12 inches in a foot, 7 ft 9 in. is $7\frac{9}{12}$ ft or $7\frac{3}{4}$ ft.

State Resources

go.hrw.com
State Resources Online
KEYWORD: MG7 Resources

Visual To help students with exercises involving areas of similar figures such as **Exercises 25, 26, 28,** and **29,** draw a square measuring 1 unit on each side. Then draw a second square measuring 3 units on each side. Split the larger square into 9 smaller squares. It is easier to see the relationship between the ratio of sides and ratios of areas with a square than with a triangle.

Exercise 31 involves using similarity ratios to find the area of a skateboard ramp. This exercise prepares students for the Multi-Step Test Prep on page 502.

Answers

28c. The ratio of the areas is the square of the ratio of the perimeters.

Given that pentagon $ABCDE \sim$ pentagon $FGHJK$, find each of the following.

18. perimeter of pentagon $FGHJK$ **254 m**
19. area of pentagon $FGHJK$ **864 m²**

Estimation Use the scale on the map for Exercises 20–23. Give the approximate distance of the shortest route between each pair of sites.

20. campfire and the lake $\approx$ **38 ft**
21. lookout point and the campfire $\approx$ **25 ft**
22. cabins and the dining hall $\approx$ **32 ft**
23. lookout point and the lake $\approx$ **39 ft**

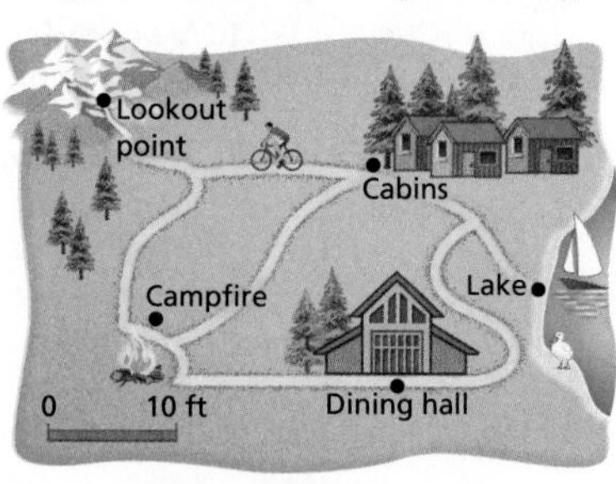

Given: $\triangle ABC \sim \triangle DEF$

24. The ratio of the perimeter of $\triangle ABC$ to the perimeter of $\triangle DEF$ is $\frac{8}{9}$. What is the similarity ratio of $\triangle ABC$ to $\triangle DEF$? $\mathbf{\frac{8}{9}}$
25. The ratio of the area of $\triangle ABC$ to the area of $\triangle DEF$ is $\frac{16}{25}$. What is the similarity ratio of $\triangle ABC$ to $\triangle DEF$? $\mathbf{\frac{4}{5}}$
26. The ratio of the area of $\triangle ABC$ to the area of $\triangle DEF$ is $\frac{4}{81}$. What is the ratio of the perimeter of $\triangle ABC$ to the perimeter of $\triangle DEF$? $\mathbf{\frac{2}{9}}$
27. **Space Exploration** The scale of this model of the space shuttle is 1 ft:50 ft. In the actual space shuttle, the main cargo bay measures 15 ft wide by 60 ft long. What are the dimensions of the cargo bay in the model? **0.3 ft by 1.2 ft**

28. Given that $\triangle PQR \sim \triangle WXY$, find each ratio.
    a. $\frac{\text{perimeter of } \triangle PQR}{\text{perimeter of } \triangle WXY}$ $\mathbf{\frac{1}{2}}$
    b. $\frac{\text{area of } \triangle PQR}{\text{area of } \triangle WXY}$ $\mathbf{\frac{1}{4}}$
    c. How does the result in part **a** compare with the result in part **b**?

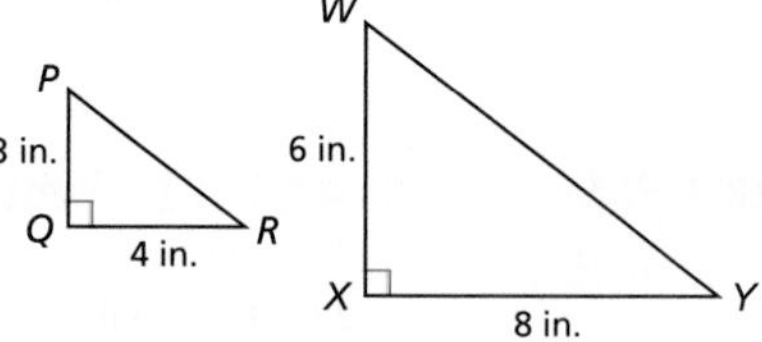

29. Given that rectangle $ABCD \sim EFGH$. The area of rectangle $ABCD$ is 135 in². The area of rectangle $EFGH$ is 240 in². If the width of rectangle $ABCD$ is 9 in., what is the length and width of rectangle $EFGH$? **20 in.; 12 in.**
30. **Sports** An NBA basketball court is 94 ft long and 50 ft wide. Make a scale drawing of a court using a scale of $\frac{1}{4}$ in.:10 ft. **Check students' work. The drawing should be 2.35 in. by 1.25 in.**

MULTI-STEP TEST PREP

31. This problem will prepare you for the Multi-Step Test Prep on page 502.
    A blueprint for a skateboard ramp has a scale of 1 in.:2 ft. On the blueprint, the rectangular piece of wood that forms the ramp measures 2 in. by 3 in.
    a. What is the similarity ratio of the blueprint to the actual ramp? $\mathbf{\frac{1}{24}}$
    b. What is the ratio of the area of the ramp on the blueprint to its actual area? $\mathbf{\frac{1}{576}}$
    c. Find the area of the actual ramp. **24 ft²**

7-5 PRACTICE A
7-5 PRACTICE C
7-5 PRACTICE B

Refer to the figure for Exercises 1–3. A city is planning an outdoor concert for an Independence Day celebration. To hold speakers and lights, a crew of technicians sets up a scaffold with two platforms by the stage. The first platform is 8 feet 2 inches off the ground. The second platform is 7 feet 6 inches above the first platform. The shadow of the first platform stretches 6 feet 3 inches across the ground.

7 ft 6 in.
8 ft 2 in.
A 6 ft 3 in. B

1. Explain why $\triangle ABC$ is similar to $\triangle ADE$. (*Hint:* The sun's rays are parallel.)
   Possible answer: Because the sun's rays are parallel, $\overline{BC} \parallel \overline{DE}$. $\angle ABC$ and $\angle ADE$ are congruent corresponding angles, and $\angle A$ is common to both triangles. So $\triangle ABC \sim \triangle ADE$ by AA $\sim$.
2. Find the length of the shadow of the second platform in feet and inches to the nearest inch. 12 feet
3. A 5-foot-8-inch-tall technician is standing on top of the second platform. Find the length of the shadow the scaffold and the technician cast in feet and inches to the nearest inch. 16 feet 4 inches

Refer to the figure for Exercises 4–6. Ramona wants to renovate the kitchen in her house. The figure shows a blueprint of the new kitchen drawn to a scale of 1 cm : 2 ft. Use a centimeter ruler and the figure to find each actual measure in feet.

Sink
Stove
Pantry

4. width of the kitchen 10 feet
5. length of the kitchen 14 feet
6. width of the sink $2\frac{1}{2}$ feet
7. area of the pantry 12 ft²

Given that $DEFG \sim WXYZ$, find each of the following.

$P = 28$ mm
$A = 40$ mm²
10 mm
15 mm

8. perimeter of $WXYZ$ 42 mm
9. area of $WXYZ$ 90 mm²

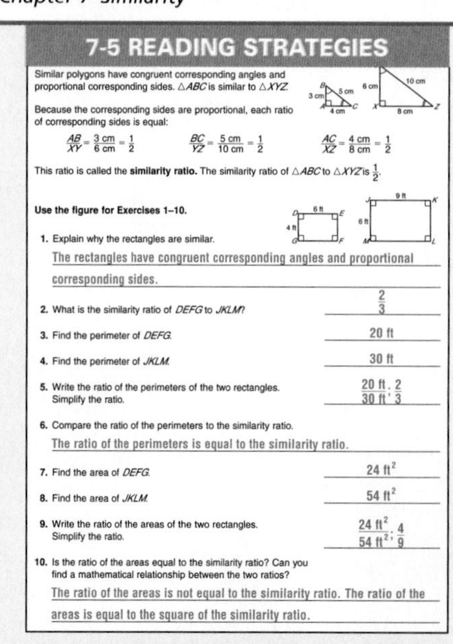

7-5 READING STRATEGIES

Similar polygons have congruent corresponding angles and proportional corresponding sides. $\triangle ABC$ is similar to $\triangle XYZ$.

3 cm, 5 cm, 4 cm; 6 cm, 10 cm, 8 cm

Because the corresponding sides are proportional, each ratio of corresponding sides is equal:

$\frac{AB}{XY} = \frac{3\text{ cm}}{6\text{ cm}} = \frac{1}{2}$ $\quad \frac{BC}{YZ} = \frac{5\text{ cm}}{10\text{ cm}} = \frac{1}{2}$ $\quad \frac{AC}{XZ} = \frac{4\text{ cm}}{8\text{ cm}} = \frac{1}{2}$

This ratio is called the **similarity ratio.** The similarity ratio of $\triangle ABC$ to $\triangle XYZ$ is $\frac{1}{2}$.

Use the figure for Exercises 1–10.

6 ft, 4 ft; 9 ft, 6 ft

1. Explain why the rectangles are similar.
   The rectangles have congruent corresponding angles and proportional corresponding sides.
2. What is the similarity ratio of $DEFG$ to $JKLM$? $\frac{2}{3}$
3. Find the perimeter of $DEFG$. 20 ft
4. Find the perimeter of $JKLM$. 30 ft
5. Write the ratio of the perimeters of the two rectangles. Simplify the ratio. $\frac{20\text{ ft}}{30\text{ ft}}; \frac{2}{3}$
6. Compare the ratio of the perimeters to the similarity ratio.
   The ratio of the perimeters is equal to the similarity ratio.
7. Find the area of $DEFG$. 24 ft²
8. Find the area of $JKLM$. 54 ft²
9. Write the ratio of the areas of the two rectangles. Simplify the ratio. $\frac{24\text{ ft}^2}{54\text{ ft}^2}; \frac{4}{9}$
10. Is the ratio of the areas equal to the similarity ratio? Can you find a mathematical relationship between the two ratios?
    The ratio of the areas is not equal to the similarity ratio. The ratio of the areas is equal to the square of the similarity ratio.

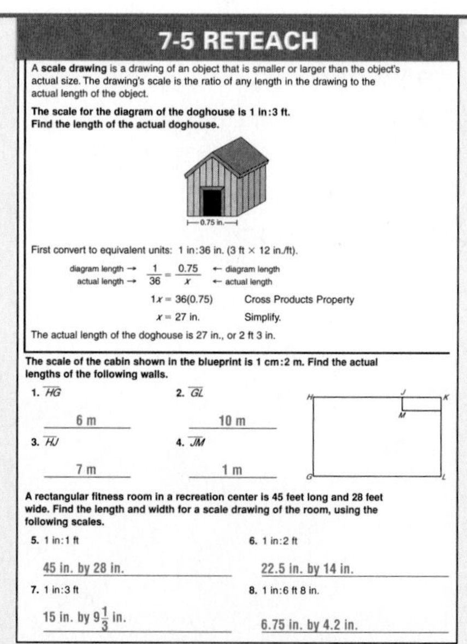

7-5 RETEACH

A **scale drawing** is a drawing of an object that is smaller or larger than the object's actual size. The drawing's scale is the ratio of any length in the drawing to the actual length of the object.

The scale for the diagram of the doghouse is 1 in:3 ft. Find the length of the actual doghouse.

0.75 in.

First convert to equivalent units: 1 in:36 in. (3 ft × 12 in./ft).

diagram length → $\frac{1}{36} = \frac{0.75}{x}$ ← diagram length
actual length → ← actual length

$1x = 36(0.75)$ Cross Products Property
$x = 27$ in. Simplify.

The actual length of the doghouse is 27 in., or 2 ft 3 in.

The scale of the cabin shown in the blueprint is 1 cm:2 m. Find the actual lengths of the following walls.

1. $\overline{HG}$ 6 m
2. $\overline{GL}$ 10 m
3. $\overline{HJ}$ 7 m
4. $\overline{JM}$ 1 m

A rectangular fitness room in a recreation center is 45 feet long and 28 feet wide. Find the length and width for a scale drawing of the room, using the following scales.

5. 1 in:1 ft 45 in. by 28 in.
6. 1 in:2 ft 22.5 in. by 14 in.
7. 1 in:3 ft 15 in. by $9\frac{1}{3}$ in.
8. 1 in:6 ft 8 in. 6.75 in. by 4.2 in.

32. **Estimation** The photo shows a person who is 5 ft 1 in. tall standing by a statue in Jamestown, North Dakota. Estimate the actual height of the head of the statue by using a ruler to measure her height and the height of the head of the statuein the photo. **16 ft**

33. **Math History** In A.D. 1076, the mathematician Shen Kua was asked by the emperor of China to produce maps of all Chinese territories. Shen created 23 maps, each drawn with a scale of 1 cm:900,000 cm. How many centimeters long would a 1 km road be on such a map? $\frac{1}{9}$ **cm**

34. Points X, Y, and Z are the midpoints of $\overline{JK}$, $\overline{KL}$, and $\overline{LJ}$, respectively. What is the ratio of the area of $\triangle JKL$ to the area of $\triangle XYZ$? $\frac{4}{1}$

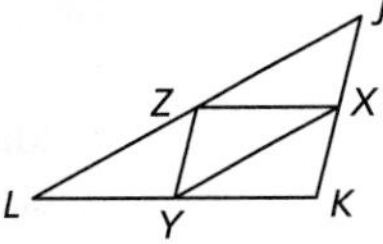

35. **Critical Thinking** Keisha is making two scale drawings of her school. In one drawing, she uses a scale of 1 cm:1 m. In the other drawing, she uses a scale of 1 cm:5 m. Which of these scales will produce a smaller drawing? Explain.

36. $AB = 16$ **units;** $HE = 36$ **units**

36. The ratio of the perimeter of square $ABCD$ to the perimeter of square $EFGH$ is $\frac{4}{9}$. Find the side lengths of each square.

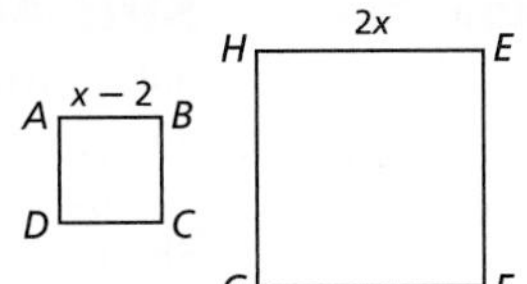

37. **Write About It** Explain what it would mean to make a scale drawing with a scale of 1:1.

38. **Write About It** One square has twice the area of another square. Explain why it is impossible for both squares to have side lengths that are whole numbers.

39. $\triangle ABC \sim \triangle RST$, and the area of $\triangle ABC$ is 24 m². What is the area of $\triangle RST$?

Ⓐ 16 m² Ⓑ 29 m² Ⓒ 36 m² **Ⓓ 54 m²**

40. A blueprint for a museum uses a scale of $\frac{1}{4}$ in.:1 ft. One of the rooms on the blueprint is $3\frac{3}{4}$ in. long. How long is the actual room?

Ⓕ 4 ft **Ⓖ 15 ft** Ⓗ 45 ft Ⓙ 180 ft

41. The similarity ratio of two similar pentagons is $\frac{9}{4}$. What is the ratio of the perimeters of the pentagons?

Ⓐ $\frac{2}{3}$ Ⓑ $\frac{3}{2}$ **Ⓒ $\frac{9}{4}$** Ⓓ $\frac{81}{16}$

42. Of two similar triangles, the second triangle has sides half the length of the first. Given that the area of the first triangle is 16 ft², find the area of the second.

Ⓕ 4 ft² Ⓖ 8 ft² Ⓗ 16 ft² Ⓙ 32 ft²

COMMON ERROR ALERT

In **Exercises 24–26,** some students may not think they can find the similarity ratio of $\triangle ABC$ to $\triangle DEF$ without knowing the lengths of the sides. Remind them that the perimeters have the same similarity ratio as the corresponding sides, and the areas have the same ratio as the squares of the corresponding sides.

In **Exercise 42,** since the first triangle has longer sides, it must have the larger area, so choices **H** and **J** can be eliminated right away. Students who chose **G** neglected to square the ratio of sides to get the ratio of areas.

Answers

35. 1 cm:5 m; since each cm will equal 5 m, this drawing will be $\frac{1}{5}$ the size of the drawing with a scale of 1 cm:1 m.

37. With a scale of 1:1, the drawing is the same size as the actual object.

38. Suppose x is a whole-number side length of the smaller square and y is a whole-number side length of the larger square. Then $2x^2 = y^2$. Thus $x\sqrt{2} = y$ or $x = \frac{y}{\sqrt{2}}$. A whole number that is divided by or multiplied by $\sqrt{2}$ cannot equal a whole number, since $\sqrt{2}$ is irrational.

7-5 PROBLEM SOLVING

1. A student is standing next to a sculpture. The figure shows the shadows that they cast. What is the height of the sculpture?

9 ft $7\frac{1}{2}$ in.

2. At the halftime show during a football game, a marching band is to form a rectangle 50 yards by 16 yards. The conductor wants to plan out the band members' positions using a 14- by 8.5-in. sheet of paper. What scale should she use to fit both dimensions of the rectangle on the page? (Use whole inches and yards.)

1 in.: 4 yd

3. An artist makes a scale drawing of a new lion enclosure at the zoo. The scale is 1 in.:25 ft. On the drawing, the length of the enclosure is $7\frac{1}{4}$ inches. What is the actual length of the lion enclosure?

$181\frac{1}{4}$ ft

4. A room is 14 feet long and 11 feet wide. If you made a scale drawing of the top view of the room using the scale $\frac{1}{2}$ in = 2 ft, what would be the length and width of the room in your drawing?

$3\frac{1}{2}$ in. by $2\frac{3}{4}$ in.

Choose the best answer.

5. A visual-effects model maker for a movie draws a spaceship using a ratio of 1:24. The drawing of the spaceship is 22 inches long. What is the length of the spaceship in the movie?

A 4 ft **Ⓒ 44 ft**
B 8 ft D 528 ft

6. A free-fall ride at an amusement park casts a shadow $43\frac{2}{3}$ feet long. At the same time, a 6-foot-tall person standing in line casts a shadow 2 feet long. What is the height of the ride?

F $21\frac{5}{6}$ ft H $98\frac{1}{4}$ ft
G $65\frac{1}{2}$ ft **Ⓙ 131 ft**

7. The scale of the park map is 1.5 cm = 60 m. Which is the best estimate for the actual distance between the horse stables and the picnic area?

A 21.4 m **Ⓒ 168.0 m**
B 90.0 m D 288.0 m

8. A hot-air balloon is 26.8 meters tall. Use the scale drawing to find the actual distance across the hot-air balloon.

Ⓕ 23.45 m H 75.0 m
G 30.6 m J 85.8 m

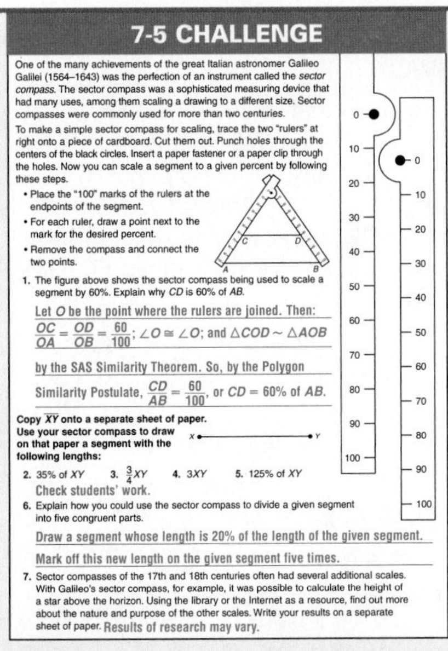

7-5 CHALLENGE

One of the many achievements of the great Italian astronomer Galileo Galilei (1564–1643) was the perfection of an instrument called the *sector compass*. The sector compass was a sophisticated measuring device that had many uses, among them scaling a drawing to a different size. Sector compasses were commonly used for more than two centuries.

To make a simple sector compass for scaling, trace the two "rulers" at right onto a piece of cardboard. Cut them out. Punch holes through the centers of the black circles. Insert a paper fastener or a paper clip through the holes. Now you can scale a segment to a given percent by following these steps.

- Place the "100" marks of the rulers at the endpoints of the segment.
- For each ruler, draw a point next to the mark for the desired percent.
- Remove the compass and connect the two points.

1. The figure above shows the sector compass being used to scale a segment by 60%. Explain why CD is 60% of AB.

Let O be the point where the rulers are joined. Then: $\frac{OC}{OA} = \frac{OD}{OB} = \frac{60}{100}$; $\angle O \cong \angle O$; and $\triangle COD \sim \triangle AOB$ by the SAS Similarity Theorem. So, by the Polygon Similarity Postulate, $\frac{CD}{AB} = \frac{60}{100}$, or CD = 60% of AB.

Copy $\overline{XY}$ onto a separate sheet of paper. Use your sector compass to draw on that paper a segment with the following lengths:

2. 35% of XY 3. $\frac{3}{4}XY$ 4. $3XY$ 5. 125% of XY

Check students' work.

6. Explain how you could use the sector compass to divide a given segment into five congruent parts.

Draw a segment whose length is 20% of the length of the given segment. Mark off this new length on the given segment five times.

7. Sector compasses of the 17th and 18th centuries often had several additional scales. With Galileo's sector compass, for example, it was possible to calculate the height of a star above the horizon. Using the library or the Internet as a resource, find out more about the nature and purpose of the other scales. Write your results on a separate sheet of paper. **Results of research may vary.**

Critical Thinking In **Exercise 45,** encourage students to first prove $\frac{h_1}{h_2} = \frac{PR}{WY}$. Then use similar triangles and substitution to prove that $\frac{\text{Area } \triangle PQR}{\text{Area } \triangle WXY} = \frac{PR^2}{WY^2}$.

Journal

Have students estimate the size of something in the school building that would be difficult to measure. Examples include the height of a stairwell or a flagpole. Then describe a way of actually measuring the structure.

ALTERNATIVE ASSESSMENT

Have students select a two-dimensional object in the classroom, such as the top of a desk or a table. Have them measure the object with a yardstick and record the measurements. Then have them select a suitable scale and create a scale drawing. Finally, have them calculate the similarity ratio and the perimeters and areas of the actual object and of the scale model.

Power Presentations with PowerPoint®

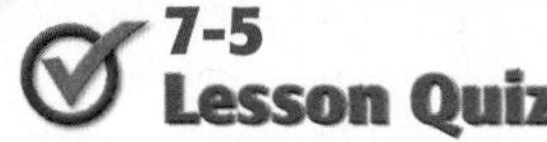

7-5 Lesson Quiz

1. Maria is 4 ft 2 in. tall. To find the height of a flagpole, she measured her shadow and the pole's shadow. What is the height h of the flagpole?

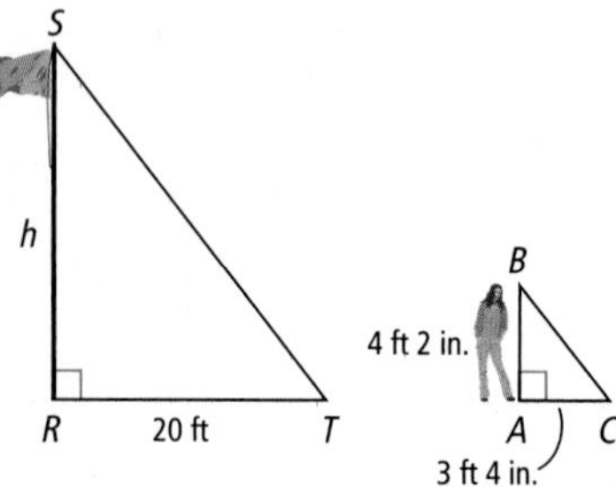

25 ft

2. A blueprint for Latisha's bedroom uses a scale of 1 in.:4 ft. Her bedroom on the blueprint is 3 in. long. How long is the actual room? 12 feet

3. $\triangle ABC \sim \triangle DEF$. Find the perimeter and area of $\triangle ABC$.

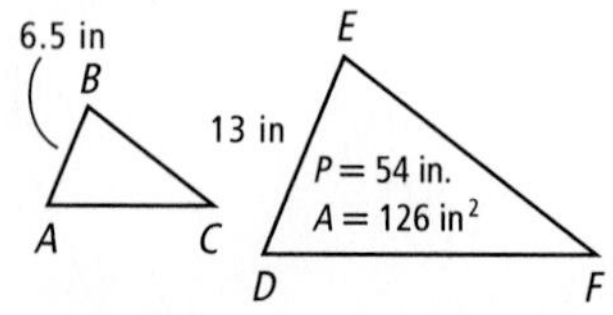

$P = 27$ in., $A = 31.5$ in^2

Also available on transparency

CHALLENGE AND EXTEND

43. **Astronomy** The Falkland Islands has a scale model of the solar system nearly 6 km long. The model's scale is 1 km : 1 billion km.
    a. Earth is 150,000,000 km from the Sun. How many meters apart are Earth and the Sun in the model? **150 m**
    b. The diameter of Earth is 12,800 km. What is the diameter, in centimeters, of Earth in the model? **1.28 cm**

44. **Given:** $\triangle ABC \sim \triangle DEF$
    Prove: $\frac{AB + BC + AC}{DE + EF + DF} = \frac{AB}{DE}$

45. **Given:** $\triangle PQR \sim \triangle WXY$
    Prove: $\frac{\text{Area } \triangle PQR}{\text{Area } \triangle WXY} = \frac{PR^2}{WY^2}$

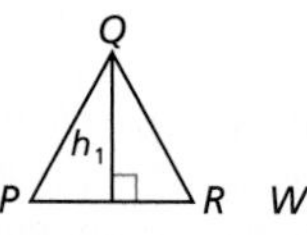

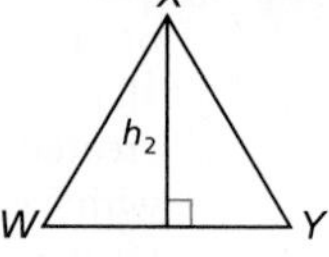

46. Quadrilateral $PQRS$ has side lengths of 6 m, 7 m, 10 m, and 12 m. The similarity ratio of quadrilateral $PQRS$ to quadrilateral $WXYZ$ is 1:2.
    a. Find the lengths of the sides of quadrilateral $WXYZ$. **a. $WX = 12$; $XY = 14$; $YZ = 20$; $WZ = 24$**
    b. Make a table of the lengths of the sides of both figures.
    c. Graph the data in the table.
    d. Determine an equation that relates the lengths of the sides of quadrilateral $PQRS$ to the lengths of the sides of quadrilateral $WXYZ$. **$y = 2x$**

SPIRAL REVIEW

Solve each equation. Round to the nearest hundredth if necessary. *(Previous course)*

47. $(x - 3)^2 = 49$ **−4 or 10**
48. $(x + 1)^2 - 4 = 0$ **−3 or 1**
49. $4(x + 2)^2 - 28 = 0$ **≈ 0.65 or ≈ −4.65**

Show that the quadrilateral with the given vertices is a parallelogram. *(Lesson 6-3)*

50. $A(-2, -2)$, $B(1, 0)$, $C(5, 0)$, $D(2, -2)$
51. $J(1, 3)$, $K(3, 5)$, $L(6, 2)$, $M(4, 0)$

52. Given that $58x = 26y$, find the ratio $y:x$ in simplest form. *(Lesson 7-1)* **29 : 13**

Career Path

go.hrw.com
Career Resources Online
KEYWORD: MG7 Career

Elaine Koch
Photogrammetrist

Q: What math classes did you take in high school?
A: Algebra, Geometry, and Probability and Statistics

Q: What math-related classes did you take in college?
A: Trigonometry, Precalculus, Drafting, and System Design

Q: How do photogrammetrists use math?
A: Photogrammetrists use aerial photographs to make detailed maps. To prepare maps, I use computers and perform a lot of scale measures to make sure the maps are accurate.

Q: What are your future plans?
A: My favorite part of making maps is designing scale drawings. Someday I'd like to apply these skills toward architectural work.

Answers

44. It is given that $\triangle ABC \sim \triangle DEF$. Let $\frac{AB}{DE} = x$. Then $AB = DEx$ by the Mult. Prop. of =. Similarly, $BC = EFx$, and $AC = DFx$. By the Add. Prop. of =, $AB + BC + AC = DEx + EFx + DFx$. Thus $AB + BC + AC = x(DE + EF + DF)$. By the Div. Prop. of =, $\frac{AB + BC + AC}{DE + EF + DF} = x$. By Subst., $\frac{AB + BC + AC}{DE + EF + DF} = \frac{AB}{DE}$.

45. It is given that $\triangle PQR \sim \triangle WXY$. Draw a ⊥ from Q and X to meet $\overline{PR}$ at S and $\overline{WY}$ at Z. By the def. of ∼ polygons, $\frac{PQ}{WX} = \frac{QR}{XY} = \frac{PR}{WY}$, and $\angle P \cong \angle W$. In $\triangle PQS$ and $\triangle WXZ$, $\angle PSQ \cong \angle WZX$. Thus $\triangle PQS \sim \triangle WXZ$ by AA ∼. $\frac{PQ}{WX} = \frac{QS}{XZ} = \frac{SP}{ZW}$ by def. of ∼ polygons. $\frac{QR}{XY} = \frac{SP}{ZW}$ by subst. $\frac{\text{Area } \triangle PQR}{\text{Area } \triangle WXY} = \frac{PR}{WY} \cdot \frac{QS}{XZ}$. By subst. $\frac{QS}{XZ} = \frac{PR}{WY}$, so $\frac{PR}{WY} \cdot \frac{PR}{WY} = \frac{PR^2}{WY^2}$. Therefore $\frac{\text{area } \triangle PQR}{\text{area } \triangle WXY} = \frac{PR^2}{WY^2}$.

46b–c, 50, 51. See p. A24.

7-6 Dilations and Similarity in the Coordinate Plane

Objectives
Apply similarity properties in the coordinate plane.
Use coordinate proof to prove figures similar.

Vocabulary
dilation
scale factor

Who uses this?
Computer programmers use coordinates to enlarge or reduce images.

Many photographs on the Web are in JPEG format, which is short for Joint Photographic Experts Group. When you drag a corner of a JPEG image in order to enlarge it or reduce it, the underlying program uses coordinates and similarity to change the image's size.

A **dilation** is a transformation that changes the size of a figure but not its shape. The preimage and the image are always similar. A **scale factor** describes how much the figure is enlarged or reduced. For a dilation with scale factor k, you can find the image of a point by multiplying each coordinate by k: $(a, b) \rightarrow (ka, kb)$.

EXAMPLE 1 ***Computer Graphics Application***

The figure shows the position of a JPEG photo. Draw the border of the photo after a dilation with scale factor $\frac{3}{2}$.

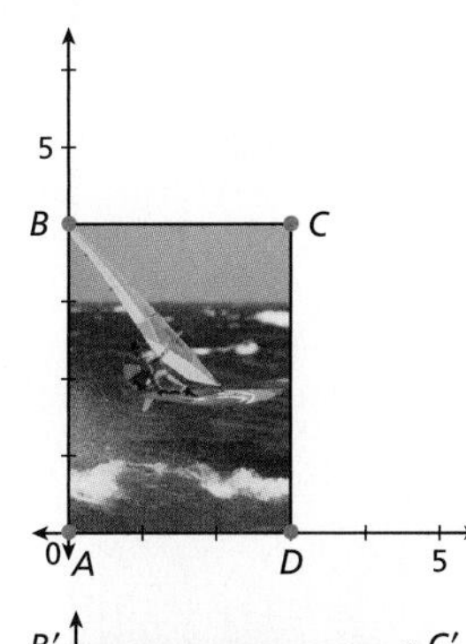

Step 1 Multiply the vertices of the photo $A(0, 0)$, $B(0, 4)$, $C(3, 4)$, and $D(3, 0)$ by $\frac{3}{2}$.

Rectangle *ABCD*	Rectangle *A′B′C′D′*
$A(0, 0) \rightarrow A'\left(0 \cdot \frac{3}{2}, 0 \cdot \frac{3}{2}\right) \rightarrow A'(0, 0)$	
$B(0, 4) \rightarrow B'\left(0 \cdot \frac{3}{2}, 4 \cdot \frac{3}{2}\right) \rightarrow B'(0, 6)$	
$C(3, 4) \rightarrow C'\left(3 \cdot \frac{3}{2}, 4 \cdot \frac{3}{2}\right) \rightarrow C'(4.5, 6)$	
$D(3, 0) \rightarrow D'\left(3 \cdot \frac{3}{2}, 0 \cdot \frac{3}{2}\right) \rightarrow D'(4.5, 0)$	

Step 2 Plot points $A'(0, 0)$, $B'(0, 6)$, $C'(4.5, 6)$, and $D'(4.5, 0)$. Draw the rectangle.

Helpful Hint

If the scale factor of a dilation is greater than 1 ($k > 1$), it is an *enlargement*.
If the scale factor is less than 1 ($k < 1$), it is a *reduction*.

1. **What if...?** Draw the border of the original photo after a dilation with scale factor $\frac{1}{2}$.

1. Check students' work. The photo should have vertices $A'(0, 0)$, $B'(0, 2)$, $C'(1.5, 2)$, and $D'(1.5, 0)$

7-6 Organizer

Pacing: Traditional $1\frac{1}{2}$ day
Block $\frac{3}{4}$ day

Objectives: Apply similarity properties in the coordinate plane.
Use coordinate proof to prove figures similar.

Geometry Lab
In *Geometry Lab Activities*

Online Edition
Tutorial Videos

Countdown Week 16

Power Presentations with PowerPoint®

Warm Up

Simplify each radical.

1. $\sqrt{12}$ $2\sqrt{3}$
2. $\sqrt{50}$ $5\sqrt{2}$
3. $\sqrt{75}$ $5\sqrt{3}$

Find the distance between each pair of points. Write your answer in simplest radical form.

4. $C(1, 6)$ and $D(-2, 0)$ $3\sqrt{5}$
5. $E(-7, -1)$ and $F(-1, -5)$ $2\sqrt{13}$

Also available on transparency

Q: What do you get when you double a triangle?
A: A try-again angle!

1 Introduce

EXPLORATION

7-6 Dilations and Similarity in the Coordinate Plane

Use graph paper to explore similarity in the coordinate plane.

1. Write down the vertices of $\triangle PQR$.
2. Multiply each coordinate of each vertex of $\triangle PQR$ by 3. Then graph $\triangle P'Q'R'$ with these new vertices. How is $\triangle P'Q'R'$ related to $\triangle PQR$?
3. Now multiply each coordinate of each vertex of $\triangle PQR$ by $\frac{1}{2}$. Then graph $\triangle P''Q''R''$ with these new vertices. How is $\triangle P''Q''R''$ related to $\triangle PQR$?
4. A *dilation* is a transformation that changes the size of a figure but not its shape. For a dilation with a *scale factor* of k, you can find the image of a point by multiplying each coordinate by k: $(a, b) \rightarrow (ka, kb)$. What is the scale factor of the dilation that mapped $\triangle PQR$ to $\triangle P'Q'R'$?
5. What is the scale factor of the dilation that mapped $\triangle PQR$ to $\triangle P''Q''R''$?

THINK AND DISCUSS

Motivate

Use a projector and a computer to do a class demonstration using a digital photo. Show how the photo can be enlarged and reduced without changing its shape. Then show how cropping the photo may change its shape. Explain to students that they will learn how transformations can enlarge or reduce a figure. An alternative would be to use microscopes and prepared slides or photocopied images to demonstrate dilated figures.

Explorations and answers are provided in *Alternate Openers: Explorations Transparencies.*

State Resources

go.hrw.com
State Resources Online
KEYWORD: MG7 Resources

Power Presentations with PowerPoint®

Additional Examples

Example 1

Use the photo in **Example 1.** Draw the border of the photo after a dilation with scale factor $\frac{5}{2}$. The new vertices are $A'(0, 0)$, $B'(0, 10)$, $C'(7.5, 10)$, and $D'(7.5, 0)$.

Example 2

Given that $\triangle TUO \sim \triangle RSO$, find the coordinates of U and the scale factor. $U(0, 12)$; $\frac{3}{4}$

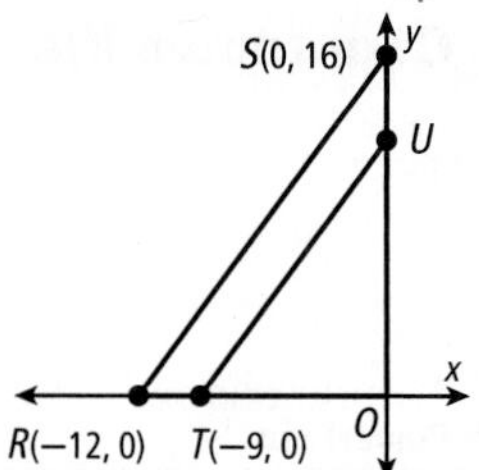

Example 3

Given: $E(-2, -6)$, $F(-3, -2)$, $G(2, -2)$, $H(-4, 2)$, and $J(6, 2)$.

Prove: $\triangle EHJ \sim \triangle EFG$.

By the Dist. Formula, $EH = 2\sqrt{17}$ and $EF = \sqrt{17}$, so $\frac{EH}{EF} = 2$. $EJ = 8\sqrt{2}$ and $EG = 4\sqrt{2}$, so $\frac{EJ}{EG} = 2$. The similarity ratio is 2, and $\frac{EH}{EF} = \frac{EJ}{EG}$. $\angle E \cong \angle E$ by the Reflex. Prop. of $\cong$. Therefore $\triangle EHJ \sim \triangle EFG$ by SAS~.

INTERVENTION

Questioning Strategies

EXAMPLES 1–2

- What is the difference between the terms "scale factor" and "similarity ratio"?

EXAMPLE 3

- What are two other ways besides SAS~ to prove that the triangles are similar?

Critical Thinking Help students recognize that the similarity ratio and the scale factor are reciprocals of each other. Similarity ratio = $\frac{\text{preimage}}{\text{image}}$, and scale factor = $\frac{\text{image}}{\text{preimage}}$.

EXAMPLE 2 Finding Coordinates of Similar Triangles

Given that $\triangle AOB \sim \triangle COD$, find the coordinates of D and the scale factor.

Since $\triangle AOB \sim \triangle COD$,

$$\frac{AO}{CO} = \frac{OB}{OD}$$

$$\frac{2}{4} = \frac{3}{OD}$$ *Substitute 2 for AO, 4 for CO, and 3 for OB.*

$$2OD = 12$$ *Cross Products Prop.*

$$OD = 6$$ *Divide both sides by 2.*

D lies on the x-axis, so its y-coordinate is 0. Since $OD = 6$, its x-coordinate must be 6. The coordinates of D are $(6, 0)$. $(3, 0) \rightarrow (3 \cdot 2, 0 \cdot 2) \rightarrow (6, 0)$, so the scale factor is 2.

2. Given that $\triangle MON \sim \triangle POQ$ and coordinates $P(-15, 0)$, $M(-10, 0)$, and $Q(0, -30)$, find the coordinates of N and the scale factor.
$N(0, -20)$; $\frac{2}{3}$

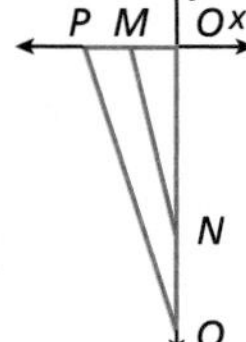

EXAMPLE 3 Proving Triangles Are Similar

Given: $A(1, 5)$, $B(-1, 3)$, $C(3, 4)$, $D(-3, 1)$, and $E(5, 3)$

Prove: $\triangle ABC \sim \triangle ADE$

Step 1 Plot the points and draw the triangles.

Step 2 Use the Distance Formula to find the side lengths.

$$AB = \sqrt{(-1 - 1)^2 + (3 - 5)^2} = \sqrt{8} = 2\sqrt{2}$$

$$AC = \sqrt{(3 - 1)^2 + (4 - 5)^2} = \sqrt{5}$$

$$AD = \sqrt{(-3 - 1)^2 + (1 - 5)^2} = \sqrt{32} = 4\sqrt{2}$$

$$AE = \sqrt{(5 - 1)^2 + (3 - 5)^2} = \sqrt{20} = 2\sqrt{5}$$

Step 3 Find the similarity ratio.

$$\frac{AB}{AD} = \frac{2\sqrt{2}}{4\sqrt{2}} = \frac{2}{4} = \frac{1}{2}$$

$$\frac{AC}{AE} = \frac{\sqrt{5}}{2\sqrt{5}} = \frac{1}{2}$$

Since $\frac{AB}{AD} = \frac{AC}{AE}$ and $\angle A \cong \angle A$ by the Reflexive Property, $\triangle ABC \sim \triangle ADE$ by SAS ~.

3. **Given:** $R(-2, 0)$, $S(-3, 1)$, $T(0, 1)$, $U(-5, 3)$, and $V(4, 3)$
Prove: $\triangle RST \sim \triangle RUV$

3. $RS = \sqrt{2}$, $RU = 3\sqrt{2}$, $RT = \sqrt{5}$, and $RV = 3\sqrt{5}$, so $\frac{RS}{RU} = \frac{RT}{RV} = \frac{1}{3}$. $\angle R \cong \angle R$ by the Reflex. Prop. of $\cong$. So $\triangle RST \sim \triangle RUV$ by SAS ~.

2 Teach

Guided Instruction

Explain that dilations are transformations that produce an image that is similar to the preimage. Discuss how the scale factor can be used to find coordinates of similar triangles. Review the Distance Formula and the SAS and SSS Similarity Theorems.

Reading Math The word *dilation* means "to expand." When a person's pupils *dilate*, they open wide.

ENGLISH LANGUAGE LEARNERS

Reaching All Learners

Through Kinesthetic Experience

Have students make a design or choose a cartoon or photo to enlarge. Use a ruler to draw a grid of $\frac{1}{8}$ in. squares on the design. Use $\frac{1}{4}$ in. graph paper and copy the pattern that appears in each square of the first grid onto the corresponding square of the graph paper. Once all the squares are copied, the students can see that they have an accurate enlargement of the design.

7-6 Dilations and Similarity in the Coordinate Plane

Objectives
Apply similarity properties in the coordinate plane.

Use coordinate proof to prove figures similar.

Vocabulary
dilation
scale factor

Who uses this?
Computer programmers use coordinates to enlarge or reduce images.

Many photographs on the Web are in JPEG format, which is short for Joint Photographic Experts Group. When you drag a corner of a JPEG image in order to enlarge it or reduce it, the underlying program uses coordinates and similarity to change the image's size.

A **dilation** is a transformation that changes the size of a figure but not its shape. The preimage and the image are always similar. A **scale factor** describes how much the figure is enlarged or reduced. For a dilation with scale factor k, you can find the image of a point by multiplying each coordinate by k: $(a, b) \rightarrow (ka, kb)$.

EXAMPLE 1 *Computer Graphics Application*

The figure shows the position of a JPEG photo. Draw the border of the photo after a dilation with scale factor $\frac{3}{2}$.

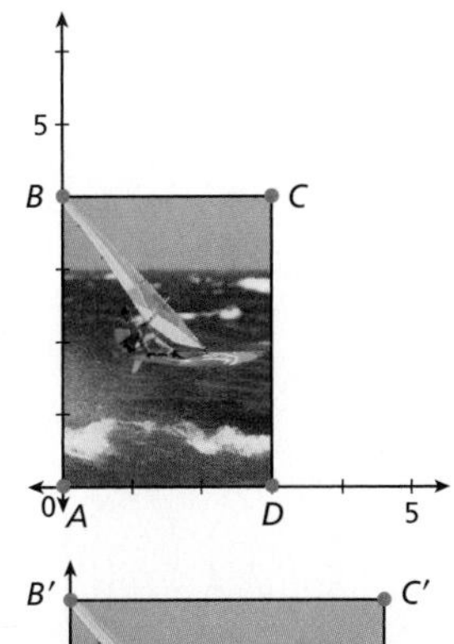

Step 1 Multiply the vertices of the photo $A(0, 0)$, $B(0, 4)$, $C(3, 4)$, and $D(3, 0)$ by $\frac{3}{2}$.

Rectangle $ABCD$		Rectangle $A'B'C'D'$
$A(0, 0) \rightarrow A'\left(0 \cdot \frac{3}{2}, 0 \cdot \frac{3}{2}\right)$	$\rightarrow$	$A'(0, 0)$
$B(0, 4) \rightarrow B'\left(0 \cdot \frac{3}{2}, 4 \cdot \frac{3}{2}\right)$	$\rightarrow$	$B'(0, 6)$
$C(3, 4) \rightarrow C'\left(3 \cdot \frac{3}{2}, 4 \cdot \frac{3}{2}\right)$	$\rightarrow$	$C'(4.5, 6)$
$D(3, 0) \rightarrow D'\left(3 \cdot \frac{3}{2}, 0 \cdot \frac{3}{2}\right)$	$\rightarrow$	$D'(4.5, 0)$

Step 2 Plot points $A'(0, 0)$, $B'(0, 6)$, $C'(4.5, 6)$, and $D'(4.5, 0)$. Draw the rectangle.

Helpful Hint

If the scale factor of a dilation is greater than 1 ($k > 1$), it is an *enlargement*. If the scale factor is less than 1 ($k < 1$), it is a *reduction*.

1. What if...? Draw the border of the original photo after a dilation with scale factor $\frac{1}{2}$.

1. Check students' work. The photo should have vertices $A'(0, 0)$, $B'(0, 2)$, $C'(1.5, 2)$, and $D'(1.5, 0)$

7-6 Organizer

Pacing: Traditional $1\frac{1}{2}$ day
Block $\frac{3}{4}$ day

Objectives: Apply similarity properties in the coordinate plane.

Use coordinate proof to prove figures similar.

Geometry Lab
In Geometry Lab Activities

Online Edition
Tutorial Videos

Countdown Week 16

Power Presentations with PowerPoint®

Warm Up

Simplify each radical.

1. $\sqrt{12}$ $2\sqrt{3}$

2. $\sqrt{50}$ $5\sqrt{2}$

3. $\sqrt{75}$ $5\sqrt{3}$

Find the distance between each pair of points. Write your answer in simplest radical form.

4. $C(1, 6)$ and $D(-2, 0)$ $3\sqrt{5}$

5. $E(-7, -1)$ and $F(-1, -5)$ $2\sqrt{13}$

Also available on transparency

Math Humor

Q: What do you get when you double a triangle?

A: A try-again angle!

1 Introduce

EXPLORATION

7-6 Dilations and Similarity in the Coordinate Plane

Use graph paper to explore similarity in the coordinate plane.

1. Write down the vertices of $\triangle PQR$.
2. Multiply each coordinate of each vertex of $\triangle PQR$ by 3. Then graph $\triangle P'Q'R'$ with these new vertices. How is $\triangle P'Q'R'$ related to $\triangle PQR$?
3. Now multiply each coordinate of each vertex of $\triangle PQR$ by $\frac{1}{2}$. Then graph $\triangle P''Q''R''$ with these new vertices. How is $\triangle P''Q''R''$ related to $\triangle PQR$?
4. A *dilation* is a transformation that changes the size of a figure but not its shape. For a dilation with a *scale factor* of k, you can find the image of a point by multiplying each coordinate by k: $(a, b) \rightarrow (ka, kb)$. What is the scale factor of the dilation that mapped $\triangle PQR$ to $\triangle P'Q'R'$?
5. What is the scale factor of the dilation that mapped $\triangle PQR$ to $\triangle P''Q''R''$?

THINK AND DISCUSS

Motivate

Use a projector and a computer to do a class demonstration using a digital photo. Show how the photo can be enlarged and reduced without changing its shape. Then show how cropping the photo may change its shape. Explain to students that they will learn how transformations can enlarge or reduce a figure. An alternative would be to use microscopes and prepared slides or photocopied images to demonstrate dilated figures.

Explorations and answers are provided in *Alternate Openers: Explorations Transparencies.*

State Resources

go.hrw.com
State Resources Online
KEYWORD: MG7 Resources

Power Presentations with PowerPoint®

Additional Examples

Example 1

Use the photo in **Example 1.** Draw the border of the photo after a dilation with scale factor $\frac{5}{2}$. The new vertices are $A'(0, 0)$, $B'(0, 10)$, $C'(7.5, 10)$, and $D'(7.5, 0)$.

Example 2

Given that $\triangle TUO \sim \triangle RSO$, find the coordinates of U and the scale factor. $U(0, 12)$; $\frac{3}{4}$

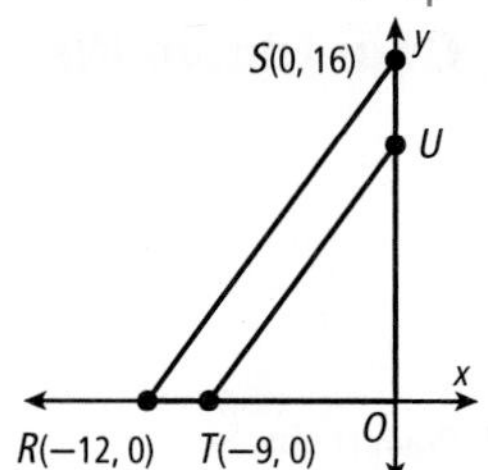

Example 3

Given: $E(-2, -6)$, $F(-3, -2)$, $G(2, -2)$, $H(-4, 2)$, and $J(6, 2)$.

Prove: $\triangle EHJ \sim \triangle EFG$.

By the Dist. Formula, $EH = 2\sqrt{17}$ and $EF = \sqrt{17}$, so $\frac{EH}{EF} = 2$. $EJ = 8\sqrt{2}$ and $EG = 4\sqrt{2}$, so $\frac{EJ}{EG} = 2$. The similarity ratio is 2, and $\frac{EH}{EF} = \frac{EJ}{EG}$. $\angle E \cong \angle E$ by the Reflex. Prop. of $\cong$. Therefore $\triangle EHJ \sim \triangle EFG$ by SAS~.

INTERVENTION

Questioning Strategies

EXAMPLES 1–2

- What is the difference between the terms "scale factor" and "similarity ratio"?

EXAMPLE 3

- What are two other ways besides SAS~ to prove that the triangles are similar?

Critical Thinking Help students recognize that the similarity ratio and the scale factor are reciprocals of each other. Similarity ratio $= \frac{\text{preimage}}{\text{image}}$, and scale factor $= \frac{\text{image}}{\text{preimage}}$.

EXAMPLE 2 **Finding Coordinates of Similar Triangles**

Given that $\triangle AOB \sim \triangle COD$, find the coordinates of D and the scale factor.

Since $\triangle AOB \sim \triangle COD$,

$$\frac{AO}{CO} = \frac{OB}{OD}$$

$$\frac{2}{4} = \frac{3}{OD}$$ *Substitute 2 for AO, 4 for CO, and 3 for OB.*

$$2OD = 12$$ *Cross Products Prop.*

$$OD = 6$$ *Divide both sides by 2.*

D lies on the x-axis, so its y-coordinate is 0. Since $OD = 6$, its x-coordinate must be 6. The coordinates of D are $(6, 0)$.

$(3, 0) \rightarrow (3 \cdot 2, 0 \cdot 2) \rightarrow (6, 0)$, so the scale factor is 2.

2. Given that $\triangle MON \sim \triangle POQ$ and coordinates $P(-15, 0)$, $M(-10, 0)$, and $Q(0, -30)$, find the coordinates of N and the scale factor.

$N(0, -20)$; $\frac{2}{3}$

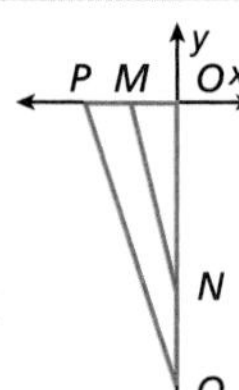

EXAMPLE 3 **Proving Triangles Are Similar**

Given: $A(1, 5)$, $B(-1, 3)$, $C(3, 4)$, $D(-3, 1)$, and $E(5, 3)$

Prove: $\triangle ABC \sim \triangle ADE$

Step 1 Plot the points and draw the triangles.

Step 2 Use the Distance Formula to find the side lengths.

$$AB = \sqrt{(-1-1)^2 + (3-5)^2} = \sqrt{8} = 2\sqrt{2}$$

$$AC = \sqrt{(3-1)^2 + (4-5)^2} = \sqrt{5}$$

$$AD = \sqrt{(-3-1)^2 + (1-5)^2} = \sqrt{32} = 4\sqrt{2}$$

$$AE = \sqrt{(5-1)^2 + (3-5)^2} = \sqrt{20} = 2\sqrt{5}$$

Step 3 Find the similarity ratio.

$$\frac{AB}{AD} = \frac{2\sqrt{2}}{4\sqrt{2}} = \frac{2}{4} = \frac{1}{2}$$

$$\frac{AC}{AE} = \frac{\sqrt{5}}{2\sqrt{5}} = \frac{1}{2}$$

Since $\frac{AB}{AD} = \frac{AC}{AE}$ and $\angle A \cong \angle A$ by the Reflexive Property, $\triangle ABC \sim \triangle ADE$ by SAS ~.

3. **Given:** $R(-2, 0)$, $S(-3, 1)$, $T(0, 1)$, $U(-5, 3)$, and $V(4, 3)$
Prove: $\triangle RST \sim \triangle RUV$

3. $RS = \sqrt{2}$, $RU = 3\sqrt{2}$, $RT = \sqrt{5}$, and $RV = 3\sqrt{5}$, so $\frac{RS}{RU} = \frac{RT}{RV} = \frac{1}{3}$. $\angle R \cong \angle R$ by the Reflex. Prop. of $\cong$. So $\triangle RST \sim \triangle RUV$ by SAS ~.

2 Teach

Guided Instruction

Explain that dilations are transformations that produce an image that is similar to the preimage. Discuss how the scale factor can be used to find coordinates of similar triangles. Review the Distance Formula and the SAS and SSS Similarity Theorems.

Reading Math The word *dilation* means "to expand." When a person's pupils *dilate*, they open wide.

Reaching All Learners

Through Kinesthetic Experience

Have students make a design or choose a cartoon or photo to enlarge. Use a ruler to draw a grid of $\frac{1}{8}$ in. squares on the design. Use $\frac{1}{4}$ in. graph paper and copy the pattern that appears in each square of the first grid onto the corresponding square of the graph paper. Once all the squares are copied, the students can see that they have an accurate enlargement of the design.

EXAMPLE 4 Using the SSS Similarity Theorem

Graph the image of $\triangle ABC$ after a dilation with scale factor 2. Verify that $\triangle A'B'C' \sim \triangle ABC$.

Step 1 Multiply each coordinate by 2 to find the coordinates of the vertices of $\triangle A'B'C'$.

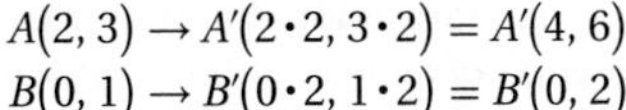

$A(2, 3) \rightarrow A'(2 \cdot 2, 3 \cdot 2) = A'(4, 6)$
$B(0, 1) \rightarrow B'(0 \cdot 2, 1 \cdot 2) = B'(0, 2)$
$C(3, 0) \rightarrow C'(3 \cdot 2, 0 \cdot 2) = C'(6, 0)$

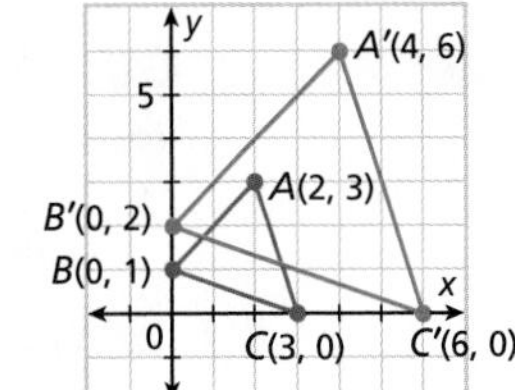

Step 2 Graph $\triangle A'B'C'$.

Step 3 Use the Distance Formula to find the side lengths.

$AB = \sqrt{(2-0)^2 + (3-1)^2} = \sqrt{8} = 2\sqrt{2}$ $A'B' = \sqrt{(4-0)^2 + (6-2)^2} = \sqrt{32} = 4\sqrt{2}$

$BC = \sqrt{(3-0)^2 + (0-1)^2} = \sqrt{10}$ $B'C' = \sqrt{(6-0)^2 + (0-2)^2} = \sqrt{40} = 2\sqrt{10}$

$AC = \sqrt{(3-2)^2 + (0-3)^2} = \sqrt{10}$ $A'C' = \sqrt{(6-4)^2 + (0-6)^2} = \sqrt{40} = 2\sqrt{10}$

Step 4 Find the similarity ratio.

$$\frac{A'B'}{AB} = \frac{4\sqrt{2}}{2\sqrt{2}} = 2, \quad \frac{B'C'}{BC} = \frac{2\sqrt{10}}{\sqrt{10}} = 2, \quad \frac{A'C'}{AC} = \frac{2\sqrt{10}}{\sqrt{10}} = 2$$

Since $\frac{A'B'}{AB} = \frac{B'C'}{BC} = \frac{A'C'}{AC}$, $\triangle ABC \sim \triangle A'B'C'$ by SSS $\sim$.

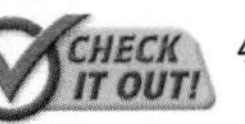

4. Graph the image of $\triangle MNP$ after a dilation with scale factor 3. Verify that $\triangle M'N'P' \sim \triangle MNP$.

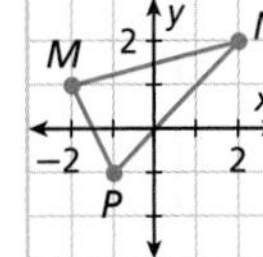

4. Check students' work. The image of $\triangle MNP$ has vertices $M'(-6, 3)$, $N'(6, 6)$, and $P'(-3, -3)$. $MP = \sqrt{5}$, $MN = \sqrt{17}$, and $PN = 3\sqrt{2}$. $M'P' = 3\sqrt{5}$, $M'N' = 3\sqrt{17}$, and $P'N' = 9\sqrt{2}$. $\frac{M'P'}{MP} = \frac{M'N'}{MN} = \frac{P'N'}{PN} = 3$. So $\triangle M'N'P' \sim \triangle MNP$ by SSS $\sim$.

THINK AND DISCUSS

1. $\triangle JKL$ has coordinates $J(0, 0)$, $K(0, 2)$, and $L(3, 0)$. Its image after a dilation has coordinates $J'(0, 0)$, $K'(0, 8)$, and $L'(12, 0)$. Explain how to find the scale factor of the dilation.

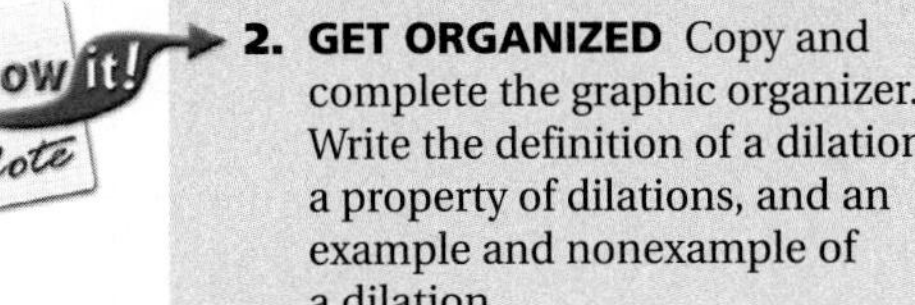

2. GET ORGANIZED Copy and complete the graphic organizer. Write the definition of a dilation, a property of dilations, and an example and nonexample of a dilation.

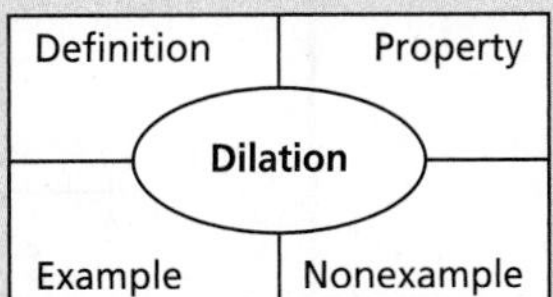

Power Presentations with PowerPoint®

Additional Examples

Example 4

Graph the image of $\triangle ABC$ after a dilation with scale factor $\frac{2}{3}$. Verify that $\triangle A'B'C' \sim \triangle ABC$.

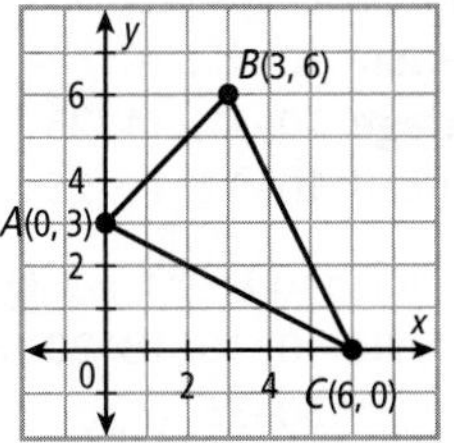

The image of $\triangle ABC$ has vertices $A'(0, 2)$, $B'(2, 4)$, and $C'(4, 0)$. By the Dist. Formula, $AB = 3\sqrt{2}$, $BC = 3\sqrt{5}$, and $AC = 3\sqrt{5}$. Also, $A'B' = 2\sqrt{2}$, $B'C' = 2\sqrt{5}$, and $A'C' = 2\sqrt{5}$. Thus $\frac{A'B'}{AB} = \frac{B'C'}{BC} = \frac{A'C'}{AC} = \frac{2}{3}$. Therefore $\triangle A'B'C' \sim \triangle ABC$ by SSS $\sim$.

INTERVENTION
Questioning Strategies

EXAMPLE 4

- Is it likely that you will get whole number answers when you calculate the ratio of the sides? Explain.
- How do you use a scale factor to find the vertices of a dilation?

Multiple Representations Another way to record the coordinates for **Example 4** is to place them in a table.

x	y	$2x$	$2y$
0	1	0	2

3 Close

Summarize

Review with students that a dilation is a proportional enlargement or reduction of a figure through a point called the center of dilation. In this lesson, all dilations in the coordinate plane were centered at the origin. Tell students that the center of a dilation will be discussed in more detail in Chapter 12. The size of the enlargement or reduction is called the scale factor of the dilation. When similar triangles are drawn in the coordinate plane, a combination of the Distance Formula and one of the similarity theorems can be used to prove that the triangles are similar.

ONGOING ASSESSMENT and INTERVENTION

Diagnose ***Before*** **the Lesson**
7-6 Warm Up, TE p. 495

Monitor ***During*** **the Lesson**
Check It Out! Exercises, SE pp. 495–497
Questioning Strategies, TE pp. 496–497

Assess ***After*** **the Lesson**
7-6 Lesson Quiz, TE p. 500
Alternative Assessment, TE p. 500

Answers to *Think and Discuss*

1. The scale factor is 4, since each coord. of the preimage is multiplied by 4 in order to get the coords. of the image.
2. See p. A6.

7-6 Exercises

Assignment Guide

Assign *Guided Practice* exercises as necessary.

If you finished Examples **1–2**
Basic 10–12, 14
Average 10–12, 14, 25
Advanced 10–12, 14, 25, 26

If you finished Examples **1–4**
Basic 10–16, 18, 20–24, 30–35
Average 10–24, 29–35
Advanced 10–35

Homework Quick Check
Quickly check key concepts.
Exercises: 10, 11, 13, 14, 18

Answers

3.

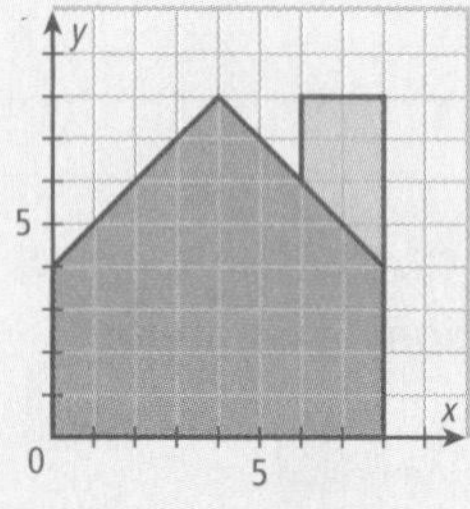

6. $AB = \sqrt{2}, AD = 2\sqrt{2}, AC = \sqrt{13}$, and $AE = 2\sqrt{13}$, so $\frac{AB}{AD} = \frac{AC}{AE} = \frac{1}{2}$. $\angle A \cong \angle A$ by the Reflex. Prop. of $\cong$. So $\triangle ABC \sim \triangle ADE$ by SAS $\sim$.

7. $JK = 2\sqrt{5}, JM = 3\sqrt{5}, JL = 2\sqrt{5}$, and $JN = 3\sqrt{5}$, so $\frac{JK}{JM} = \frac{JL}{JN} = \frac{2}{3}$. $\angle J \cong \angle J$ by the Reflex. Prop. of $\cong$. So $\triangle JKL \sim \triangle JMN$ by SAS $\sim$.

8–9. See p. A24.

State Resources

7-6 Exercises

go.hrw.com
Homework Help Online
KEYWORD: MG7 7-6
Parent Resources Online
KEYWORD: MG7 Parent

GUIDED PRACTICE

Vocabulary **Apply the vocabulary from this lesson to answer each question.**

1. A ___?___ is a transformation that proportionally reduces or enlarges a figure, such as the pupil of an eye. (*dilation* or *scale factor*) **dilation**

2. A ratio that describes or determines the dimensional relationship of a figure to that which it represents, such as a map scale of 1 in. : 45 ft, is called a ___?___. (*dilation* or *scale factor*) **scale factor**

SEE EXAMPLE 1 p. 495

3. **Graphic Design** A designer created this logo for a real estate agent but needs to make the logo twice as large for use on a sign. Draw the logo after a dilation with scale factor 2.

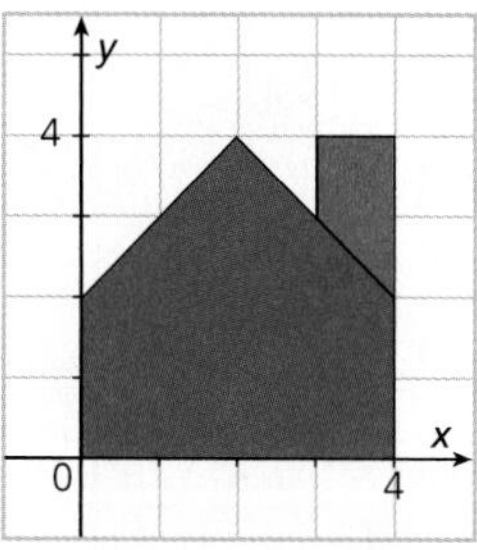

SEE EXAMPLE 2 p. 496

4. Given that $\triangle AOB \sim \triangle COD$, find the coordinates of C and the scale factor. $C(25, 0); \frac{5}{2}$

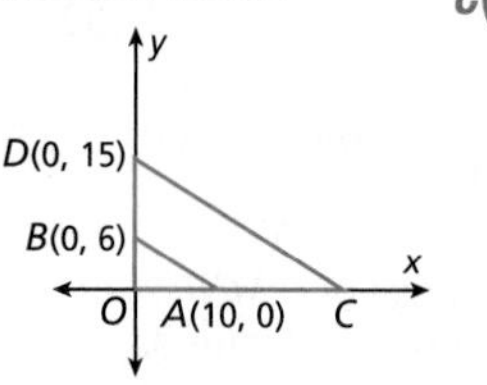

5. Given that $\triangle ROS \sim \triangle POQ$, find the coordinates of S and the scale factor. $S(0, -8); \frac{5}{2}$

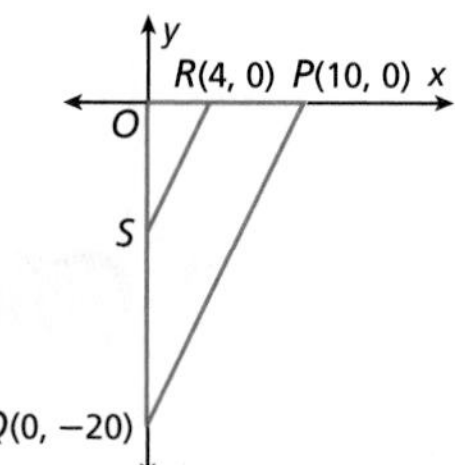

SEE EXAMPLE 3 p. 496

6. **Given:** $A(0, 0)$, $B(-1, 1)$, $C(3, 2)$, $D(-2, 2)$, and $E(6, 4)$
Prove: $\triangle ABC \sim \triangle ADE$

7. **Given:** $J(-1, 0)$, $K(-3, -4)$, $L(3, -2)$, $M(-4, -6)$, and $N(5, -3)$
Prove: $\triangle JKL \sim \triangle JMN$

SEE EXAMPLE 4 p. 497

Multi-Step **Graph the image of each triangle after a dilation with the given scale factor. Then verify that the image is similar to the given triangle.**

8. scale factor 2

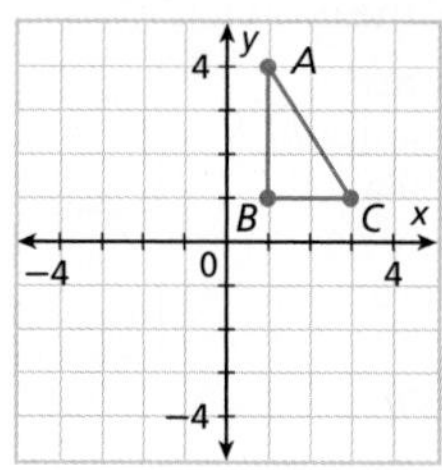

9. scale factor $\frac{3}{2}$

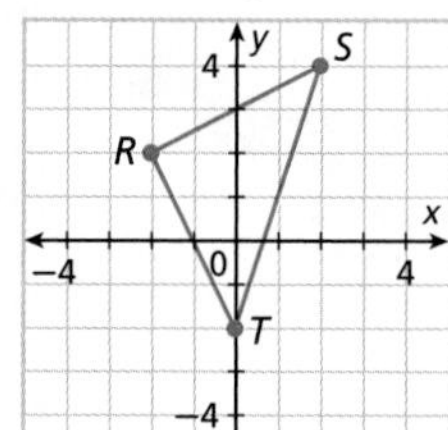

7-6 READING STRATEGIES

A **dilation** is a transformation that enlarges or reduces a figure. The original figure and the dilated figure are similar.

A **scale factor** is a ratio that describes how much a figure is enlarged or reduced. The scale factor is equal to the similarity ratio of the original figure to the dilated figure.

Consider the dilation of $\triangle ABC$ below.

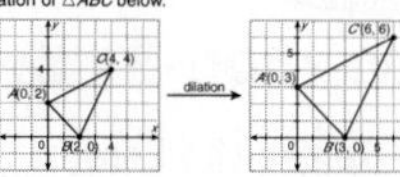

The scale factor in this dilation is $\frac{3}{2}$. To find the coordinates of the vertices of a dilated figure, each coordinate is multiplied by the scale factor. For instance, A has coordinates (0, 2).

$$0 \cdot \frac{3}{2} = 0 \qquad 2 \cdot \frac{3}{2} = 3$$

So the coordinates of A' are (0, 3).

Use the figure for Exercises 1–6.

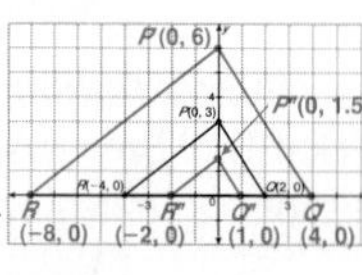

1. Multiply each coordinate of the vertices of $\triangle PQR$ by 2 to find the coordinates of $\triangle P'Q'R'$ that is a dilation of $\triangle PQR$ with a scale factor of 2. List the coordinates of the vertices of $\triangle P'Q'R'$. Draw $\triangle P'Q'R'$.
$P'(0, 6), Q'(4, 0), R'(-8, 0)$

2. Compare the size of $\triangle P'Q'R'$ and $\triangle PQR$.
$\triangle P'Q'R'$ is larger than $\triangle PQR$.

3. The scale factor for the dilation was 2. Is 2 greater than or less than 1?
greater than 1

4. Multiply each coordinate of the vertices of $\triangle PQR$ by $\frac{1}{2}$ to find the coordinates of $\triangle P''Q''R''$ that is a dilation of $\triangle PQR$ with a scale factor of $\frac{1}{2}$. List the coordinates of the vertices of $\triangle P''Q''R''$.
$P''(0, 1.5), Q''(1, 0), R''(-2, 0)$

5. Draw $\triangle P''Q''R''$. Compare the size of $\triangle P''Q''R''$ and $\triangle PQR$.
$\triangle P''Q''R''$ is smaller than $\triangle PQR$.

6. The scale factor for the dilation was $\frac{1}{2}$. Is $\frac{1}{2}$ greater than or less than 1? less than 1

7-6 RETEACH

A **dilation** is a transformation that changes the size of a figure but not its shape. The preimage and image are always similar. A **scale factor** describes how much a figure is enlarged or reduced.

Triangle ABC has vertices $A(0, 0)$, $B(2, 6)$, and $C(6, 4)$. Find the coordinates of the vertices of the image after a dilation with a scale factor $\frac{1}{2}$.

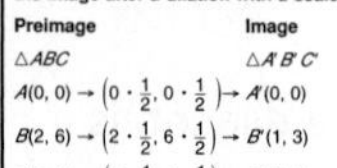

Preimage	**Image**
$\triangle ABC$	$\triangle A'B'C'$

$A(0, 0) \to \left(0 \cdot \frac{1}{2}, 0 \cdot \frac{1}{2}\right) \to A'(0, 0)$

$B(2, 6) \to \left(2 \cdot \frac{1}{2}, 6 \cdot \frac{1}{2}\right) \to B'(1, 3)$

$C(6, 4) \to \left(6 \cdot \frac{1}{2}, 4 \cdot \frac{1}{2}\right) \to C'(3, 2)$

$\triangle FEG \sim \triangle HEJ$. Find the coordinates of F and the scale factor.

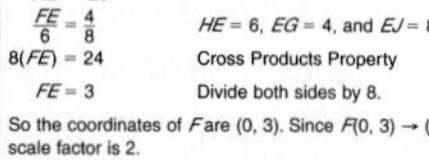

$\frac{FE}{HE} = \frac{EG}{EJ}$	Write a proportion.
$\frac{FE}{6} = \frac{4}{8}$	$HE = 6$, $EG = 4$, and $EJ = 8$.
$8(FE) = 24$	Cross Products Property
$FE = 3$	Divide both sides by 8.

So the coordinates of F are (0, 3). Since $F(0, 3) \to (0 \cdot 2, 3 \cdot 2) \to H(0, 6)$, the scale factor is 2.

1. Triangle EFG has vertices $E(0, 0)$, $F(1, 5)$, and $G(7, 2)$. Find the coordinates of the image after a dilation with a scale factor 2.
$E'(0, 0), F'(2, 10), G'(14, 4)$

2. Rectangle $LMNP$ has vertices $L(-6, 0)$, $M(6, 0)$, $N(6, -3)$, and $P(-6, -3)$. Find the coordinates of the image after a dilation with a scale factor $\frac{1}{3}$.
$L'(-2, 0), M'(2, 0), N'(2, -1), P'(-2, -1)$

3. Given that $\triangle AEB \sim \triangle CED$, find the coordinates of C and the scale factor.
(0, 6); 3

4. Given that $\triangle LKM \sim \triangle NKP$, find the coordinates of P and the scale factor.
$(8, 0); \frac{4}{3}$

PRACTICE AND PROBLEM SOLVING

Independent Practice

For Exercises	See Example
10	1
11–12	2
13–14	3
15–16	4

Extra Practice

Skills Practice p. S17
Application Practice p. S34

10. **Advertising** A promoter produced this design for a street festival. She now wants to make the design smaller to use on postcards. Sketch the design after a dilation with scale factor $\frac{1}{2}$.

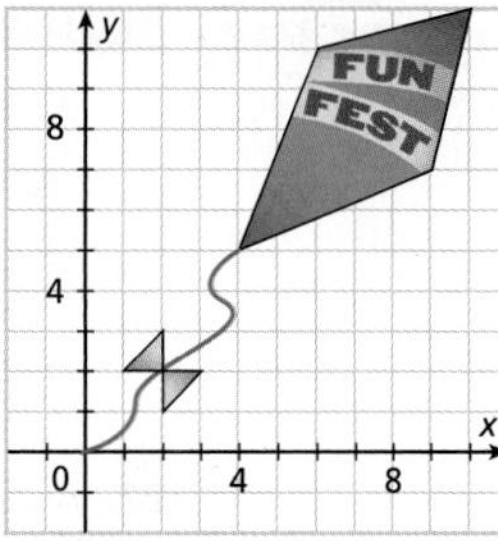

11. Given that $\triangle UOV \sim \triangle XOY$, find the coordinates of X and the scale factor.

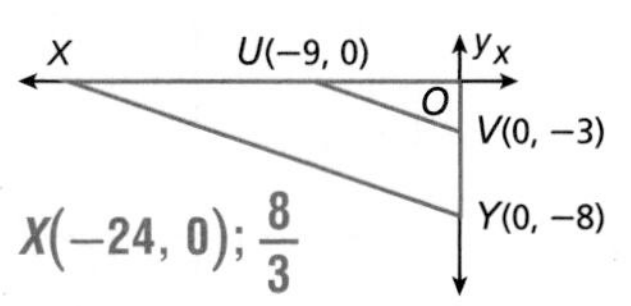

$X(-24, 0); \frac{8}{3}$

12. Given that $\triangle MON \sim \triangle KOL$, find the coordinates of K and the scale factor.

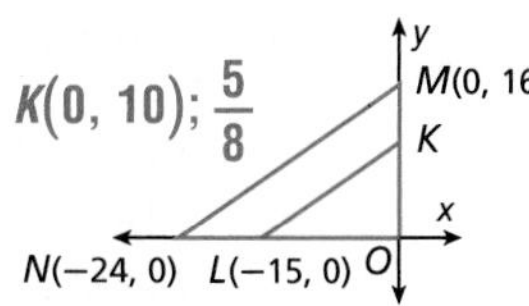

$K(0, 10); \frac{5}{8}$

13. **Given:** $D(-1, 3)$, $E(-3, -1)$, $F(3, -1)$, $G(-4, -3)$, and $H(5, -3)$
Prove: $\triangle DEF \sim \triangle DGH$

14. **Given:** $M(0, 10)$, $N(5, 0)$, $P(15, 15)$, $Q(10, -10)$, and $R(30, 20)$
Prove: $\triangle MNP \sim \triangle MQR$

Multi-Step Graph the image of each triangle after a dilation with the given scale factor. Then verify that the image is similar to the given triangle.

15. $J(-2, 0)$ and $K(-1, -1)$, and $L(-3, -2)$ with scale factor 3

16. $M(0, 4)$, $N(4, 2)$, and $P(2, -2)$ with scale factor $\frac{1}{2}$

17. **Critical Thinking** Consider the transformation given by the mapping $(x, y) \rightarrow (2x, 4y)$. Is this transformation a dilation? Why or why not?

17. It is not a dilation; because it changes the shape of the figure.

18. **ERROR ANALYSIS** Which solution to find the scale factor of the dilation that maps $\triangle RST$ to $\triangle UVW$ is incorrect? Explain the error.

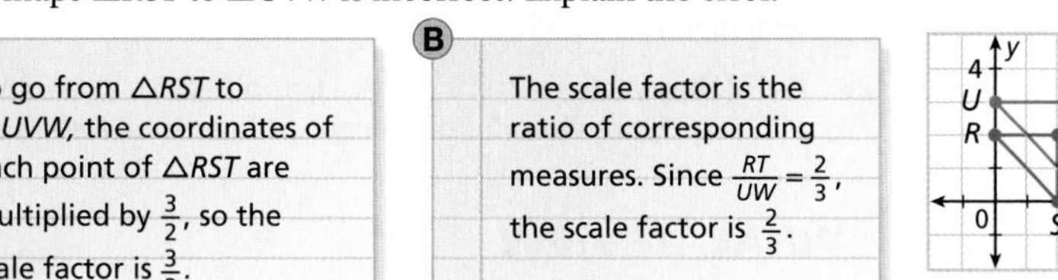

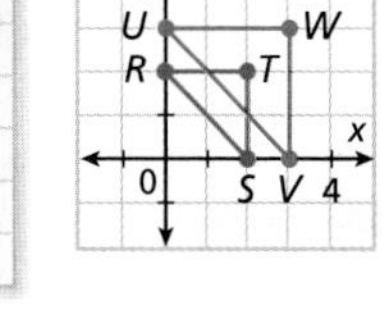

18. Solution B is incorrect. The scale factor is the ratio of a lin. measure of the image to the corr. lin. measure of the preimage, so the scale factor is $\frac{UW}{RT} = \frac{3}{2}$.

19. **Write About It** A dilation maps $\triangle ABC$ to $\triangle A'B'C'$. How is the scale factor of the dilation related to the similarity ratio of $\triangle ABC$ to $\triangle A'B'C'$? Explain.
They are reciprocals. The similarity ratio is $\frac{AB}{A'B'}$. The scale factor is $\frac{A'B'}{AB}$.

MULTI-STEP TEST PREP

20. This problem will prepare you for the Multi-Step Test Prep on page 502.
 a. In order to build a skateboard ramp, Miles draws $\triangle JKL$ on a coordinate plane. One unit on the drawing represents 60 cm of actual distance. Explain how he should assign coordinates for the vertices of $\triangle JKL$.
 b. Graph the image of $\triangle JKL$ after a dilation with scale factor 3.

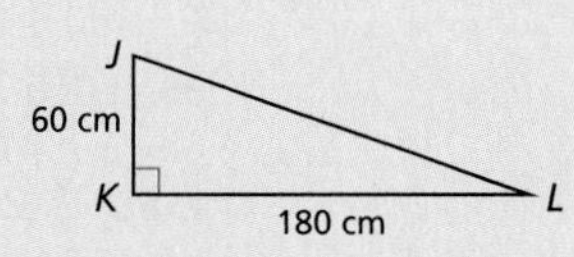

COMMON ERROR ALERT

In **Exercise 17,** some students may assume that the mapping is a dilation because the coordinates have been doubled. Encourage students to draw the figures on graph paper before answering the problem.

Teaching Tip

Technology Remind students that if the scale factor is greater than 1, the dilation is an enlargement. If the scale factor is less than 1, the dilation is a reduction. This can be demonstrated using geometry software for **Exercises 8, 9, 15,** and **16.**

MULTI-STEP TEST PREP **Exercise 20** involves assigning coordinates to the vertices of a triangle, and enlarging the triangle with a dilation. This exercise prepares students for the Multi-Step Test Prep on page 502.

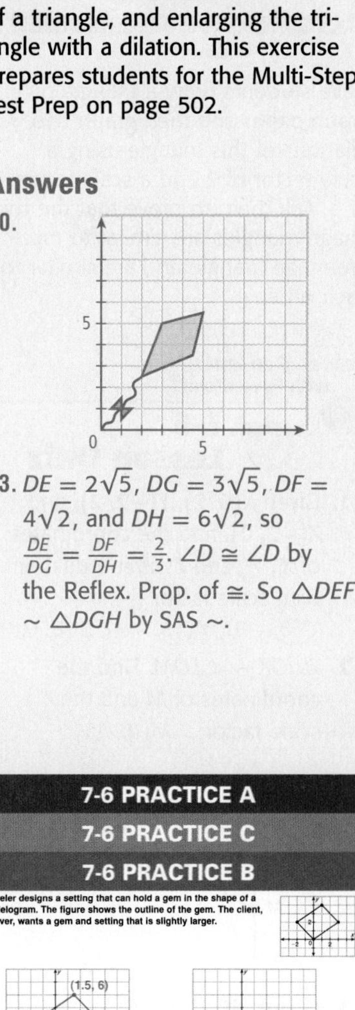

Answers

10.

13. $DE = 2\sqrt{5}$, $DG = 3\sqrt{5}$, $DF = 4\sqrt{2}$, and $DH = 6\sqrt{2}$, so $\frac{DE}{DG} = \frac{DF}{DH} = \frac{2}{3}$. $\angle D \cong \angle D$ by the Reflex. Prop. of $\cong$. So $\triangle DEF \sim \triangle DGH$ by SAS $\sim$.

7-6 PROBLEM SOLVING

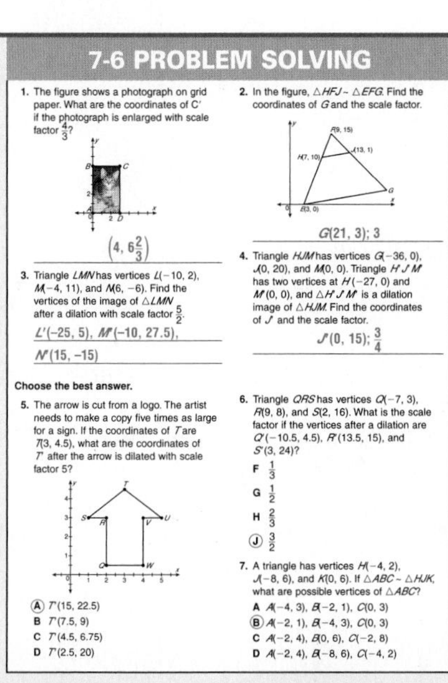

1. The figure shows a photograph on grid paper. What are the coordinates of C′ if the photograph is enlarged with scale factor $\frac{4}{3}$?
$(4, 6\frac{2}{3})$

2. In the figure, $\triangle HFJ \sim \triangle EFG$. Find the coordinates of G and the scale factor.
$G(21, 3); 3$

3. Triangle LMN has vertices $L(-10, 2)$, $M(-4, 11)$, and $N(6, -6)$. Find the vertices of the image of $\triangle LMN$ after a dilation with scale factor $\frac{5}{2}$.
$L'(-25, 5)$, $M'(-10, 27.5)$, $N'(15, -15)$

4. Triangle HJM has vertices $G(-36, 0)$, $J(0, 20)$, and $M(0, 0)$. Triangle H′J′M′ has two vertices at $H'(-27, 0)$ and $M'(0, 0)$, and $\triangle H'J'M'$ is a dilation image of $\triangle HJM$. Find the coordinates of J′ and the scale factor.
$J'(0, 15); \frac{3}{4}$

Choose the best answer.

5. The arrow is cut from a logo. The artist needs to make a copy five times as large for a sign. If the coordinates of T are $T(3, 4.5)$, what are the coordinates of T′ after the arrow is dilated with scale factor 5?
Ⓐ $T'(15, 22.5)$
B $T'(7.5, 9)$
C $T'(4.5, 6.75)$
D $T'(2.5, 20)$

6. Triangle QRS has vertices $Q(-7, 3)$, $R(9, 8)$, and $S(2, 16)$. What is the scale factor if the vertices after a dilation are $Q'(-10.5, 4.5)$, $R'(13.5, 15)$, and $S'(3, 24)$?
F $\frac{1}{3}$
G $\frac{1}{2}$
H $\frac{2}{3}$
Ⓙ $\frac{3}{2}$

7. A triangle has vertices $H(-4, 2)$, $J(-8, 6)$, and $K(0, 6)$. If $\triangle ABC \sim \triangle HJK$, what are possible vertices of $\triangle ABC$?
A $A(-4, 3)$, $B(-2, 1)$, $C(0, 3)$
Ⓑ $A(-2, 1)$, $B(-4, 3)$, $C(0, 3)$
C $A(-2, 4)$, $B(0, 6)$, $C(-2, 8)$
D $A(-2, 4)$, $B(-8, 6)$, $C(-4, 2)$

Answers

14. $MN = 5\sqrt{5}$, $MQ = 10\sqrt{5}$, $MP = 5\sqrt{10}$, and $MR = 10\sqrt{10}$, so $\frac{MN}{MQ} = \frac{MP}{MR} = \frac{1}{2}$. $\angle M \cong \angle M$ by the Reflex. Prop. of $\cong$. So $\triangle MNP \sim \triangle MQR$ by SAS $\sim$.

15. Check students' work. The image of $\triangle JKL$ has vertices $J'(-6, 0)$, $K'(-3, -3)$, and $L'(-9, -6)$. $JK = \sqrt{2}$, $JL = \sqrt{5}$, and $LK = \sqrt{5}$. $J'K' = 3\sqrt{2}$, $J'L' = 3\sqrt{5}$, and $L'K' = 3\sqrt{5}$. $\frac{J'K'}{JK} = \frac{J'L'}{JL} = \frac{L'K'}{LK} = 3$. So $\triangle JKL \sim \triangle J'K'L'$ by SSS $\sim$.

16, 20. See p. A24.

7-6 PRACTICE A

7-6 PRACTICE C

7-6 PRACTICE B

A jeweler designs a setting that can hold a gem in the shape of a parallelogram. The figure shows the outline of the gem. The client, however, wants a gem and setting that is slightly larger.

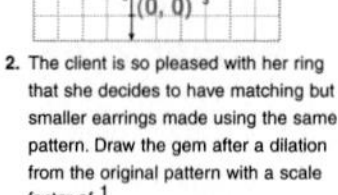

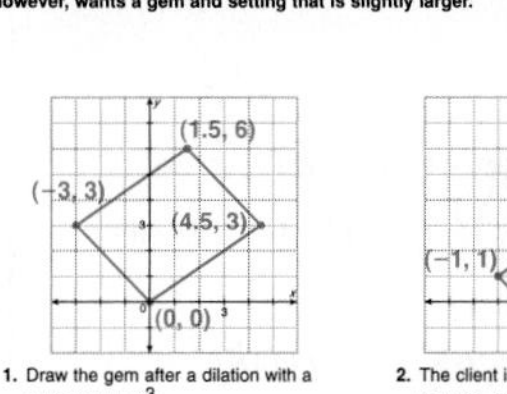

1. Draw the gem after a dilation with a scale factor of $\frac{3}{2}$.

2. The client is so pleased with her ring that she decides to have matching but smaller earrings made using the same pattern. Draw the gem after a dilation from the original pattern with a scale factor of $\frac{1}{2}$.

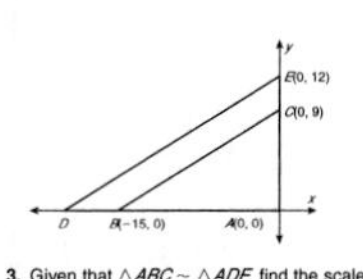

3. Given that $\triangle ABC \sim \triangle ADE$, find the scale factor and the coordinates of D.
$\frac{4}{3}$; $(-20, 0)$

4. Given that $\triangle PQR \sim \triangle PST$, find the scale factor and the coordinates of S.
$3; (8, 0)$

TEST PREP DOCTOR In **Exercise 22,** students who chose **J** have incorrectly applied the Proportional Perimeters and Areas Theorem, using the rule for areas rather than for perimeters. If they understand that $\triangle R'S'T'$ is larger than $\triangle RST$, they will know that choices **F** and **G** can be eliminated.

Journal

Have students compare and contrast the similarity ratio and the scale factor.

ALTERNATIVE ASSESSMENT

Have students draw a triangle on graph paper and then graph two dilations of this triangle using a scale factor of 2 and a scale factor of $\frac{1}{2}$. Ask them to prove that the two image triangles are similar to the preimage triangle and are similar to each other.

Power Presentations with PowerPoint®

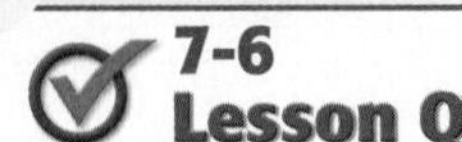

7-6 Lesson Quiz

1. Given $X(0, 2)$, $Y(-2, 2)$, and $Z(-2, 0)$, find the coordinates of X', Y', and Z' after a dilation with scale factor -4.
   $X'(0, -8)$; $Y'((8, -8)$; $Z'(8, 0)$
2. $\triangle JOK \sim \triangle LOM$. Find the coordinates of M and the scale factor. $M(0, -5)$; $\frac{5}{2}$

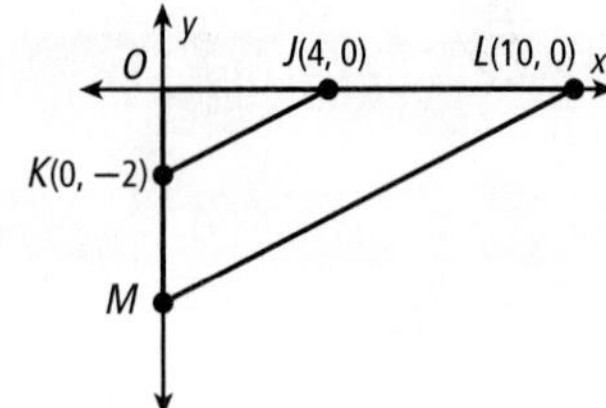

3. **Given:** $A(-1, 0)$, $B(-4, 5)$, $C(2, 2)$, $D(2, -1)$, $E(-4, 9)$, and $F(8, 3)$
   Prove: $\triangle ABC \sim \triangle DEF$
   By the Dist. Formula, $AB = \sqrt{34}$, $AC = \sqrt{13}$, and $BC = 3\sqrt{5}$. Also, $DE = 2\sqrt{34}$, $DF = 2\sqrt{13}$, and $EF = 6\sqrt{5}$. Therefore $\frac{AB}{DE} = \frac{AC}{DF} = \frac{BC}{EF} = \frac{1}{2}$, and $\triangle ABC \sim \triangle DEF$ by SSS $\sim$.

Also available on transparency

TEST PREP

21. Which coordinates for C make $\triangle COD$ similar to $\triangle AOB$?
    (A) (0, 2.4) (C) (0, 3)
    (B) (0, 2.5) (D) (0, 3.6)

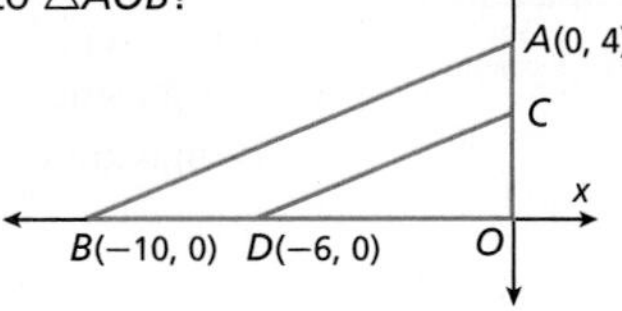

22. A dilation with scale factor 2 maps $\triangle RST$ to $\triangle R'S'T'$. The perimeter of $\triangle RST$ is 60. What is the perimeter of $\triangle R'S'T'$?
    (F) 30 (G) 60 (H) 120 (J) 240

23. Which triangle with vertices D, E, and F is similar to $\triangle ABC$?
    (A) $D(1, 2)$, $E(3, 2)$, $F(2, 0)$
    (B) $D(-1, -2)$, $E(2, -2)$, $F(1, -5)$
    (C) $D(1, 2)$, $E(5, 2)$, $F(3, 0)$
    (D) $D(-2, -2)$, $E(0, 2)$, $F(-1, 0)$

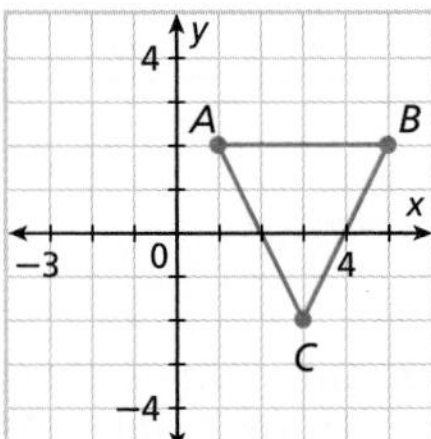

24. **Gridded Resonse** $\overline{AB}$ with endpoints $A(3, 2)$ and $B(7, 5)$ is dilated by a scale factor of 3. Find the length of $\overline{A'B'}$. 15

CHALLENGE AND EXTEND

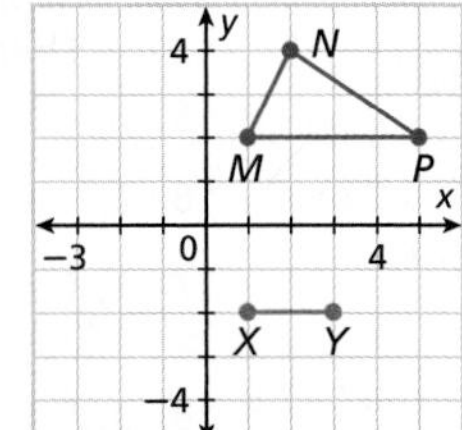

25. How many different triangles having $\overline{XY}$ as a side are similar to $\triangle MNP$? 12
26. $\triangle XYZ \sim \triangle MPN$. Find the coordinates of Z.
    26. $\left(1\frac{1}{2}, -1\right)$ or $\left(1\frac{1}{2}, -3\right)$
27. A rectangle has two of its sides on the x- and y-axes, a vertex at the origin, and a vertex on the line $y = 2x$. Prove that any two such rectangles are similar.
28. $\triangle ABC$ has vertices $A(0, 1)$, $B(3, 1)$, and $C(1, 3)$. $\triangle DEF$ has vertices $D(1, -1)$ and $E(7, -1)$. Find two different locations for vertex F so that $\triangle ABC \sim \triangle DEF$. $(3, 3)$; $(3, -5)$

SPIRAL REVIEW

Write an inequality to represent the situation. *(Previous course)*

29. A weight lifter must lift at least 250 pounds. There are two 50-pound weights on a bar that weighs 5 pounds. Let w represent the additional weight that must be added to the bar. Possible answer: $105 + w \geq 250$

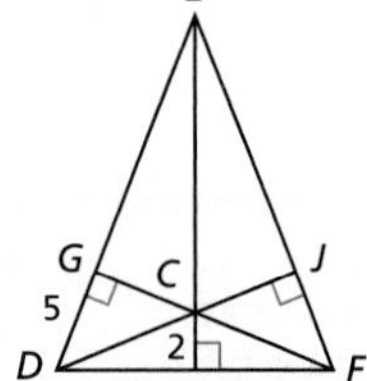

Find the length of each segment, given that $\overline{DE} \cong \overline{FE}$. *(Lesson 5-2)*

30. $\overline{HF}$ 6.71
31. $\overline{JF}$ 5
32. $\overline{CF}$ 7

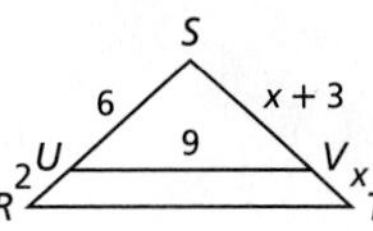

$\triangle SUV \sim \triangle SRT$. Find the length of each segment. *(Lesson 7-4)*

33. $\overline{RT}$ 12
34. $\overline{VT}$ 1.5
35. $\overline{ST}$ 6

Answers

27. All the corr. ∠s of the rects. are ≅ because they are all rt. ∠s. It must only be shown that the corr. sides are proportional. Suppose the first rect. has its vertex on the line $y = 2x$ at (a, b). Since this pt. is on the line, it is a solution to the eqn., so $b = 2a$, and the coords. of this vertex must be $(a, 2a)$. Similarly, for the other rect., the coords. of the vertex that lies on the line must be of the form $(c, 2c)$.

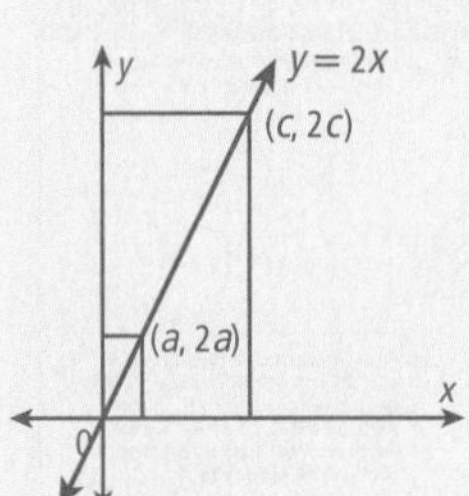

One of the rects. has dimensions a and $2a$, and the other has dimensions c and $2c$. So all the ratios of corr. sides equal $\frac{c}{a}$. Therefore the rects. are $\sim$.

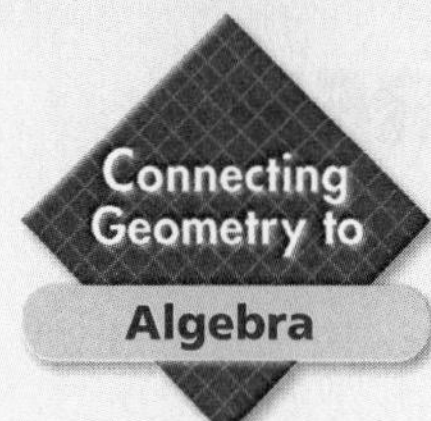

Direct Variation

In Lesson 7-6 you learned that for two similar figures, the measure of each point was multiplied by the same scale factor. Is the relationship between the scale factor and the perimeter of the figure a direct variation?

Recall from algebra that if y varies directly as x, then $y = kx$, or $\frac{y}{x} = k$, where k is the constant of variation.

Example

A rectangle has a length of 4 ft and a width of 2 ft. Find the relationship between the scale factors of similar rectangles and their corresponding perimeters. If the relationship is a direct variation, find the constant of variation.

Step 1 Make a table to record data.

Scale Factor x	Length $\ell = x(4)$	Width $w = x(2)$	Perimeter $P = 2\ell + 2w$
$\frac{1}{2}$	$\ell = \frac{1}{2}(4) = 2$	$w = \frac{1}{2}(2) = 1$	$2(2) + 2(1) = 6$
2	8	4	24
3	12	6	36
4	16	8	48
5	20	10	60

Step 2 Graph the points $\left(\frac{1}{2}, 6\right)$, (2, 24), (3, 36), (4, 48), and (5, 60).

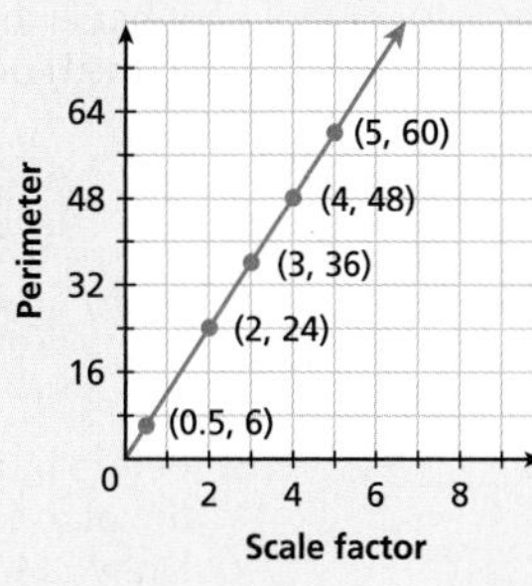

Since the points are collinear and the line that contains them includes the origin, the relationship is a direct variation.

Step 3 Find the equation of direct variation.

$y = kx$

$60 = k(5)$ *Substitute 60 for y and 5 for x.*

$12 = k$ *Divide both sides by 5.*

$y = 12x$ *Substitute 12 for k.*

Thus the constant of variation is 12.

Try This

Use the scale factors given in the above table. Find the relationship between the scale factors of similar figures and their corresponding perimeters. If the relationship is a direct variation, find the constant of variation.

1. regular hexagon with side length 6 $k = 36$
2. triangle with side lengths 3, 6, and 7 $k = 16$
3. square with side length 3 $k = 12$

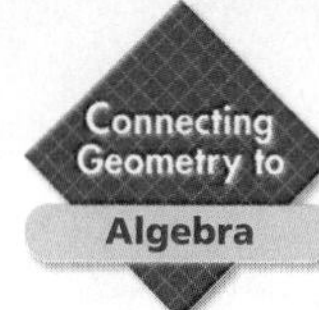

Organizer

Pacing:
Traditional $\frac{1}{2}$ day
Block $\frac{1}{4}$ day

Objective: Determine whether there is a direct variation between scale factor and perimeter.

 **Online Edition**

 **Countdown Week 16**

Teach

Remember

Students review and apply direct variation to perimeters of similar polygons.

Teaching Tip **Visual** Remind students that the graph of a direct variation always passes through the origin.

Close

Assess

Ask students for another name for the constant of variation. slope Have them use algebra to find the slope of the graph of the line.

State Resources

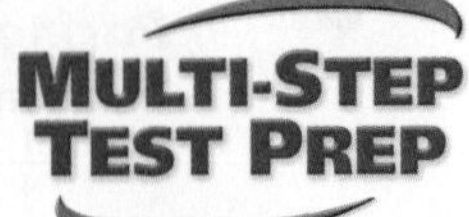

Organizer

Objective: Assess students' ability to apply concepts and skills in Lessons 7-4 through 7-6 in a real-world format.

 **Online Edition**

Resources

 ***Geometry Assessments***
www.mathtekstoolkit.org

Problem	Text Reference
1	Lesson 7-4
2	Lesson 7-5
3	Lesson 7-6

Answers

3.

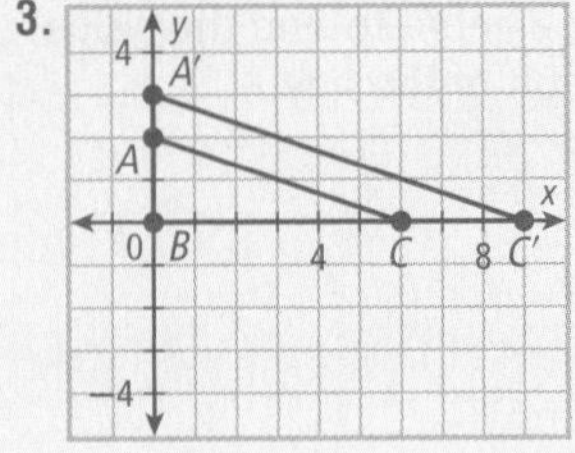

State Resources

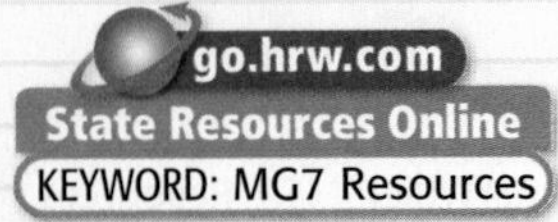

CHAPTER 7

MULTI-STEP TEST PREP

SECTION 7B

Applying Similarity

Ramp It Up Many companies sell plans for build-it-yourself skateboard ramps. The figures below show a ramp and the plan for the triangular support structure at the side of the ramp. In the plan, $\overline{AB}$, $\overline{EF}$, $\overline{GH}$, and $\overline{JK}$ are perpendicular to the base $\overline{BC}$.

1. The instructions call for extra pieces of wood to reinforce $\overline{AE}$, $\overline{EG}$, $\overline{GJ}$, and $\overline{JC}$. Given $AE = 42.2$ cm, find EG, GJ, and JC to the nearest tenth. **$EG = 42.2$ cm; $GJ \approx JC \approx 36.9$ cm**

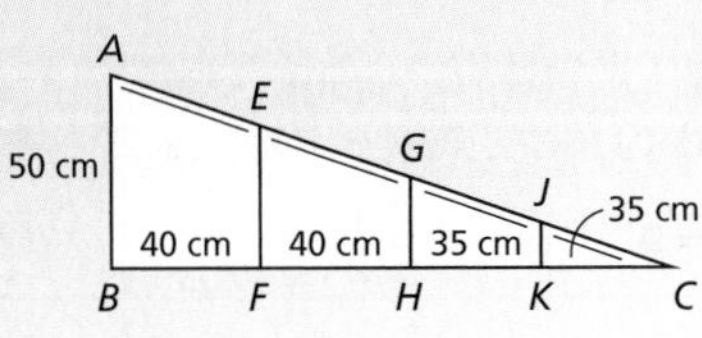

2. Once the support structure is built, it is covered with a triangular piece of plywood. Find the area of the piece of wood needed to cover $\triangle ABC$. A separate blueprint for the ramp uses a scale of 1 cm:25 cm. What is the area of $\triangle ABC$ in the blueprint? **3750 cm^2; 6 cm^2**

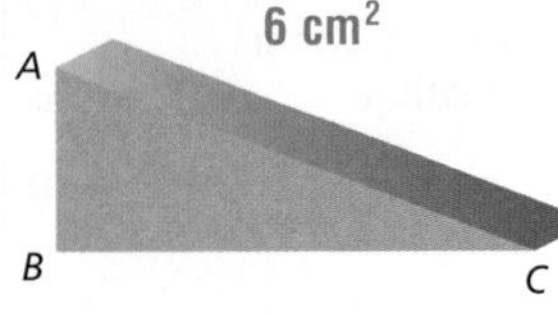

3. Before building the ramp, you transfer the plan to a coordinate plane. Draw $\triangle ABC$ on a coordinate plane so that 1 unit represents 25 cm and B is at the origin. Then draw the image of $\triangle ABC$ after a dilation with scale factor $\frac{3}{2}$.

INTERVENTION

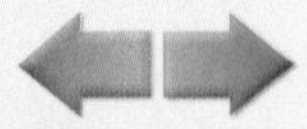

Scaffolding Questions

1. What proportion can you use to find EG? Once you've found EG, what proportion can you use to find GJ? $\frac{EG}{AE} = \frac{FH}{BF}$; $\frac{GJ}{AG} = \frac{HK}{BH}$
2. What formula can you use to find the area of $\triangle ABC$? What is the similarity ratio of the support structure to the blueprint? What is the ratio of the area of the support structure to the area of the triangle in the blueprint? $A = \frac{1}{2}bh$; $\frac{1}{25}$; $\left(\frac{1}{25}\right)^2 = \frac{1}{625}$
3. If point B is at the origin, what are the coordinates of A and C? $A(0, 2)$ and $C(6, 0)$

Extension

What scale factor should you use so that the image of point C after the dilation has coordinates $(14, 0)$? $\frac{7}{3}$

Quiz for Lessons 7-4 Through 7-6

7-4 Applying Properties of Similar Triangles

Find the length of each segment.

1. $\overline{ST}$ $18\frac{2}{3}$

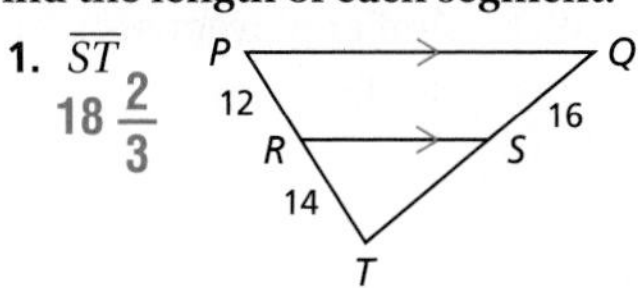

2. $\overline{AB}$ and $\overline{AC}$ 15; 20

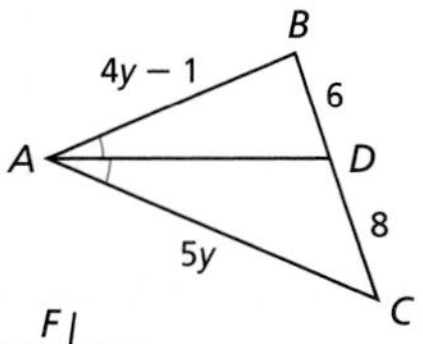

3. An artist drew a picture of railroad tracks such that the ties $\overline{EF}$, $\overline{GH}$, and $\overline{JK}$ are parallel. What is the length of $\overline{FH}$? 3 cm

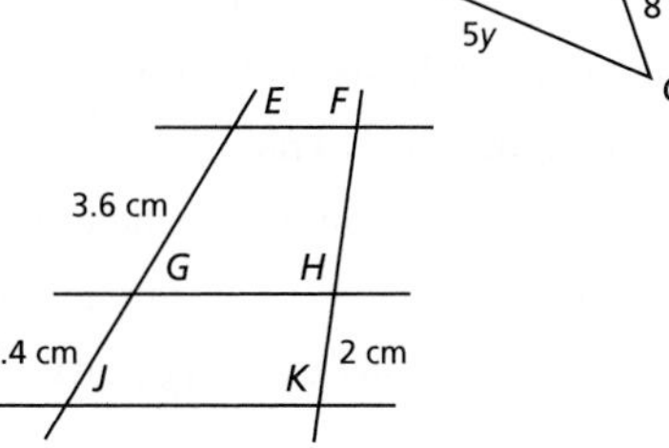

7-5 Using Proportional Relationships

The plan for a restaurant uses the scale of 1.5 in.:60 ft. Find the actual length of the following walls.

4. $\overline{AB}$ 10 ft
5. $\overline{BC}$ 30 ft
6. $\overline{CD}$ 40 ft
7. $\overline{EF}$ 20 ft

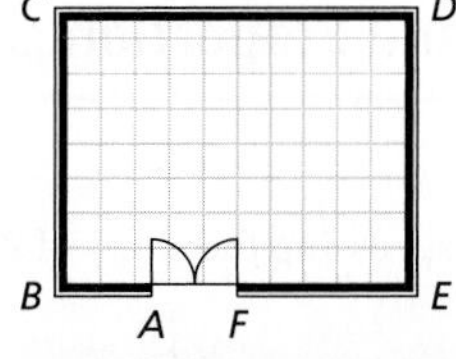

8. A student who is 5 ft 3 in. tall measured her shadow and the shadow cast by a water tower shaped like a golf ball. What is the height of the tower? 36 ft

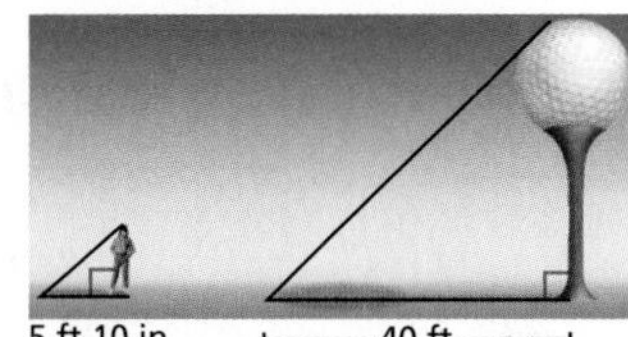

7-6 Dilations and Similarity in the Coordinate Plane

9. Given: $A(-1, 2)$, $B(-3, -2)$, $C(3, 0)$, $D(-2, 0)$, and $E(1, 1)$
   Prove: $\triangle ADE \sim \triangle ABC$
10. Given: $R(0, 0)$, $S(-2, -1)$, $T(0, -3)$, $U(4, 2)$, and $V(0, 6)$
    Prove: $\triangle RST \sim \triangle RUV$

Graph the image of each triangle after a dilation with the given scale factor. Then verify that the image is similar to the given triangle.

11. scale factor 3

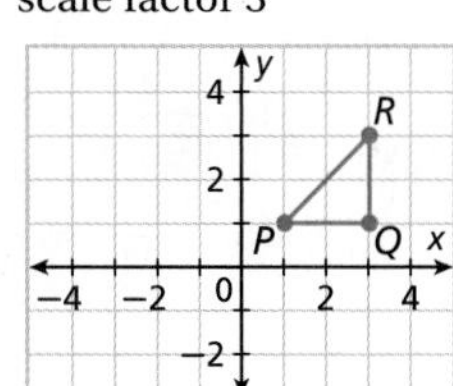

12. scale factor 1.5

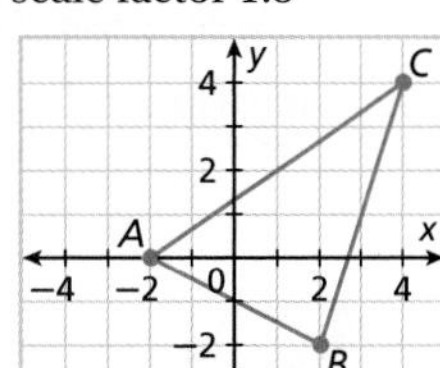

READY TO GO ON? SECTION 7B

Organizer

Objective: Assess students' mastery of concepts and skills in Lessons 7-4 through 7-6.

Resources

Assessment Resources
Section 7B Quiz

Teacher One Stop™
Test & Practice Generator

INTERVENTION

Resources

Ready to Go On? Intervention and Enrichment **Worksheets**

Ready to Go On? **CD-ROM**

Ready to Go On? **Online**

my.hrw.com

Answers

9–12. See p. A24.

READY TO GO ON? Diagnose and Prescribe

NO INTERVENE

Ready to Go On? Intervention	READY TO GO ON? Intervention, Section 7B: Worksheets	CD-ROM	Online
Lesson 7-4	7-4 Intervention	Activity 7-4	Diagnose and Prescribe Online
Lesson 7-5	7-5 Intervention	Activity 7-5	
Lesson 7-6	7-6 Intervention	Activity 7-6	

READY TO GO ON? Enrichment, Section 7B
Worksheets

CD-ROM
Online

CHAPTER 7 Study Guide: Review

Organizer

Objective: Help students organize and review key concepts and skills presented in Chapter 7.

Online Edition
Multilingual Glossary

Resources

Teacher One Stop™
PuzzleView
Test & Practice Generator

***Multilingual Glossary* Online**
go.hrw.com
KEYWORD: MG7 Glossary

Lesson Tutorial Videos
CD-ROM

Answers

1. proportion
2. dilation
3. means
4. ratio
5. $\frac{1}{5}$
6. $-\frac{1}{2}$
7. $\frac{3}{2}$
8. 54
9. 17.5; 30; 17.5; 30
10. $y = 21$
11. $s = 10$
12. $x = \pm 6$
13. $z = 13$ or $z = -11$
14. $x = \pm 8$
15. $y = 3$ or $y = -5$

CHAPTER 7 Study Guide: Review

For a complete list of the postulates and theorems in this chapter, see p. PS12.

Vocabulary

Complete the sentences below with vocabulary words from the list above.

1. An equation stating that two ratios are equal is called a(n) __?__ .
2. A(n) __?__ is a transformation that changes the size of a figure but not its shape.
3. In the proportion $\frac{u}{v} = \frac{x}{y}$, the __?__ are v and x.
4. A(n) __?__ compares two numbers by division.

7-1 Ratio and Proportion *(pp. 454–459)*

EXAMPLES

■ **Write a ratio expressing the slope of ℓ.**

$$\text{slope} = \frac{\text{rise}}{\text{run}} = \frac{y_2 - y_1}{x_2 - x_1} = \frac{4-2}{-1-3} = \frac{2}{-4} = -\frac{1}{2}$$

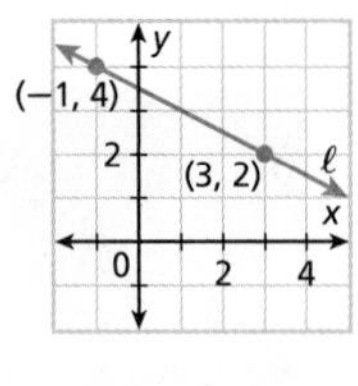

■ **Solve the proportion.**

$$\frac{2}{4(x-3)} = \frac{x-3}{50}$$

$4(x-3)^2 = 2(50)$	*Cross Products Prop.*
$4(x-3)^2 = 100$	*Simplify.*
$(x-3)^2 = 25$	*Divide both sides by 4.*
$x - 3 = \pm 5$	*Find the square root of both sides.*
$x - 3 = 5$ or $x - 3 = -5$	*Rewrite as two eqns.*
$x = 8$ or $x = -2$	*Add 3 to both sides.*

EXERCISES

Write a ratio expressing the slope of each line.

5. m
6. n
7. p

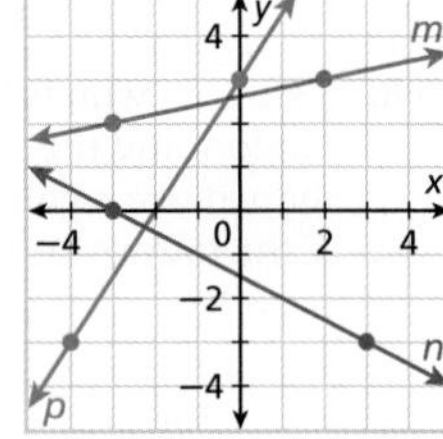

8. If 84 is divided into three parts in the ratio 3 : 5 : 6, what is the sum of the smallest and the largest part?
9. The ratio of the measures of a pair of sides of a rectangle is 7 : 12. If the perimeter of the rectangle is 95, what is the length of each side?

Solve each proportion.

10. $\frac{y}{7} = \frac{9}{3}$
11. $\frac{10}{4} = \frac{25}{s}$
12. $\frac{x}{4} = \frac{9}{x}$
13. $\frac{4}{z-1} = \frac{z-1}{36}$
14. $\frac{12}{2x} = \frac{3x}{32}$
15. $\frac{y+1}{24} = \frac{2}{3(y+1)}$

7-2 Ratios in Similar Polygons *(pp. 462–467)*

EXAMPLE

- **Determine whether $\triangle ABC$ and $\triangle DEF$ are similar. If so, write the similarity ratio and a similarity statement.**

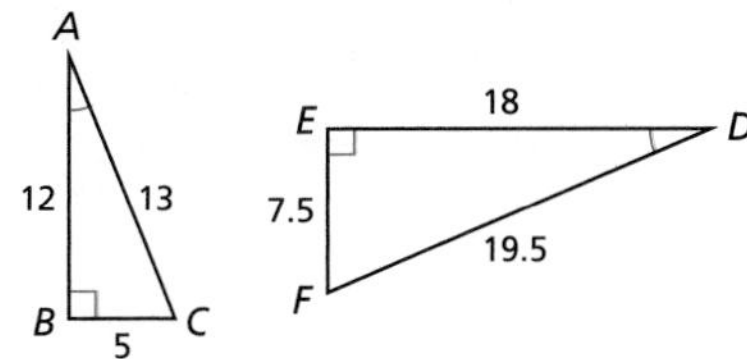

It is given that $\angle A \cong \angle D$ and $\angle B \cong \angle E$. $\angle C \cong \angle F$ by the Third Angles Theorem. $\frac{AB}{DE} = \frac{BC}{EF} = \frac{AC}{DF} = \frac{2}{3}$. Thus the similarity ratio is $\frac{2}{3}$, and $\triangle ABC \sim \triangle DEF$.

EXERCISES

Determine whether the polygons are similar. If so, write the similarity ratio and a similarity statement.

16. rectangles *JKLM* and *PQRS*

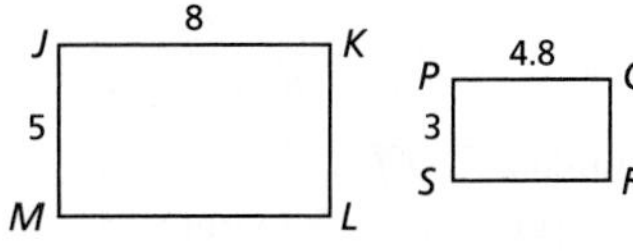

17. $\triangle TUV$ and $\triangle WXY$

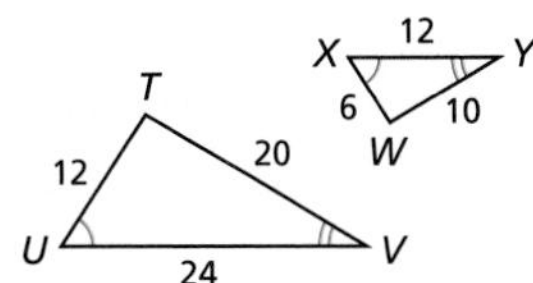

7-3 Triangle Similarity: AA, SSS, and SAS *(pp. 470–477)*

EXAMPLE

- **Given: $\overline{AB} \parallel \overline{CD}$, $AB = 2CD$, $AC = 2CE$**
  Prove: $\triangle ABC \sim \triangle CDE$

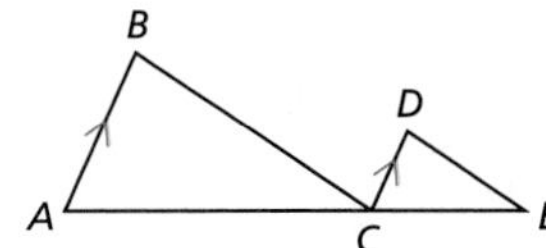

Proof:

Statements	Reasons
1. $\overline{AB} \parallel \overline{CD}$	1. Given
2. $\angle BAC \cong \angle DCE$	2. Corr. ∠s Post.
3. $AB = 2CD$, $AC = 2CE$	3. Given
4. $\frac{AB}{CD} = 2$, $\frac{AC}{CE} = 2$	4. Division Prop.
5. $\frac{AB}{CD} = \frac{AC}{CE}$	5. Trans. Prop. of =
6. $\triangle ABC \sim \triangle CDE$	6. SAS ~ *(Steps 2, 5)*

EXERCISES

18. Given: $JL = \frac{1}{3}JN$, $JK = \frac{1}{3}JM$
Prove: $\triangle JKL \sim \triangle JMN$

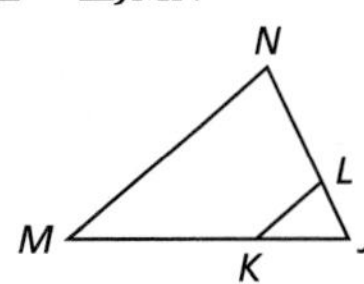

19. Given: $\overline{QR} \parallel \overline{ST}$
Prove: $\triangle PQR \sim \triangle PTS$

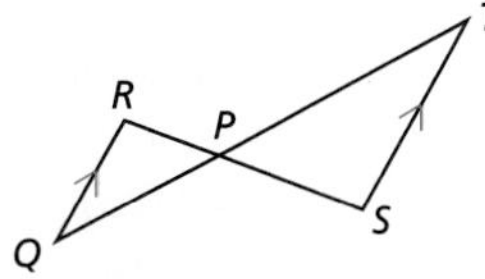

20. Given: $\overline{BD} \parallel \overline{CE}$
Prove: $AB(CE) = AC(BD)$

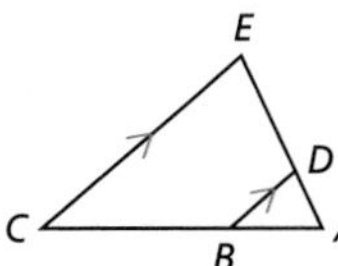

(*Hint:* After you have proved the triangles similar, look for a proportion using *AB*, *AC*, *CE*, and *BD*, the lengths of corresponding sides.)

Answers

16. yes; $\frac{5}{3}$; $JKLM \sim PQRS$
17. yes; 2; $\triangle TUV \sim \triangle WXY$
18. 1. $JL = \frac{1}{3}JN$, $JK = \frac{1}{3}JM$ (Given)
    2. $\frac{JL}{JN} = \frac{1}{3}$, $\frac{JK}{JM} = \frac{1}{3}$ (Div. Prop. of =)
    3. $\frac{JL}{JN} = \frac{JK}{JM}$ (Trans. Prop. of =)
    4. $\angle J \cong \angle J$ (Reflex. Prop. of ≅)
    5. $\triangle JKL \sim \triangle JMN$ (SAS ~ *Steps 3, 4*)
19. 1. $\overline{QR} \parallel \overline{ST}$ (Given)
    2. $\angle RQP \cong \angle STP$ (Alt. Int. ∠ Thm.)
    3. $\angle RPQ \cong \angle SPT$ (Vert. ∠s Thm.)
    4. $\triangle PQR \sim \triangle PTS$ (AA ~ *Steps 2, 3*)
20. 1. $\overline{BC} \parallel \overline{CE}$ (Given)
    2. $\angle ABD \cong \angle C$ (Corr. ∠ Post.)
    3. $\angle ADB \cong \angle E$ (Corr. ∠ Post.)
    4. $\triangle ABD \sim \triangle ACE$ (AA ~ *Steps 2, 3*)
    5. $\frac{AB}{AC} = \frac{BD}{CE}$ (Def. of ~ polygons)
    6. $AB(CE) = AC(BD)$ (Cross Products Prop.)

Study Guide: Review **505**

Answers

21. 10

22. $3\frac{1}{3}$

23. $\frac{JK}{JM} = \frac{JL}{JN} = \frac{1}{2}$. Since $\frac{JK}{JM} = \frac{JL}{JN}$, $\overline{KL} \parallel \overline{MN}$ by the Conv. of the △ Proportionality Thm.

24. $\frac{EC}{EA} = \frac{ED}{EB} = \frac{3}{7}$. Since $\frac{EC}{EA} = \frac{ED}{EB}$, $\overline{AB} \parallel \overline{CD}$ by the Conv. of the △ Proportionality Thm.

25. $SU = 4$; $SV = 6$

26. 18

27. $4x + 8$

7-4 Applying Properties of Similar Triangles *(pp. 481–487)*

EXAMPLES

■ **Find PQ.**

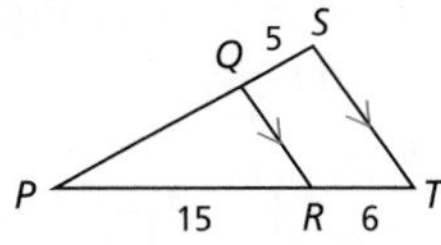

It is given that $\overline{QR} \parallel \overline{ST}$, so $\frac{PQ}{QS} = \frac{PR}{RT}$ by the Triangle Proportionality Theorem.

$\frac{PQ}{5} = \frac{15}{6}$	*Substitute 5 for QS, 15 for PR, and 6 for RT.*
$6(PQ) = 75$	*Cross Products Prop.*
$PQ = 12.5$	*Divide both sides by 6.*

■ **Verify that $\overline{AB} \parallel \overline{CD}$.**

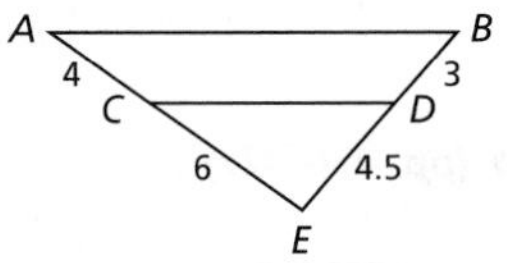

$\frac{EC}{CA} = \frac{6}{4} = 1.5$

$\frac{ED}{DB} = \frac{4.5}{3} = 1.5$

Since $\frac{EC}{CA} = \frac{ED}{DB}$, $\overline{AB} \parallel \overline{CD}$ by the Converse of the Triangle Proportionality Theorem.

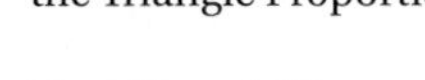

■ **Find JL and LK.**

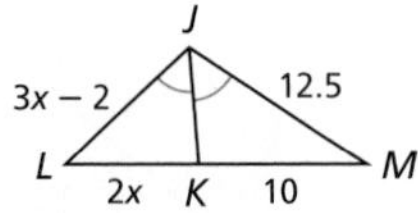

Since $\overline{JK}$ bisects $\angle LJM$, $\frac{JL}{LK} = \frac{JM}{MK}$ by the Triangle Angle Bisector Theorem.

$\frac{3x - 2}{2x} = \frac{12.5}{10}$	*Substitute the given values.*
$10(3x - 2) = 12.5(2x)$	*Cross Products Prop.*
$30x - 20 = 25x$	*Simplify.*
$30x = 25x + 20$	*Add 20 to both sides.*
$5x = 20$	*Subtract 25x from both sides.*
$x = 4$	*Divide both sides by 5.*

$JL = 3x - 2$

$= 3(4) - 2 = 10$

$LK = 2x$

$= 2(4) = 8$

EXERCISES

Find each length.

21. CE

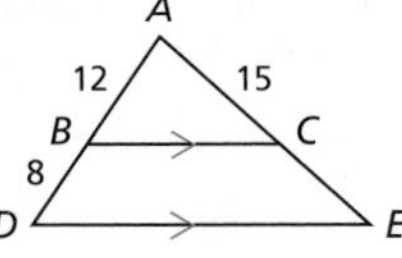

22. ST

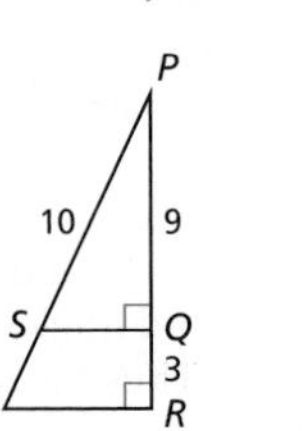

Verify that the given segments are parallel.

23. $\overline{KL}$ and $\overline{MN}$

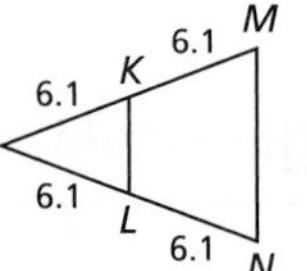

24. $\overline{AB}$ and $\overline{CD}$

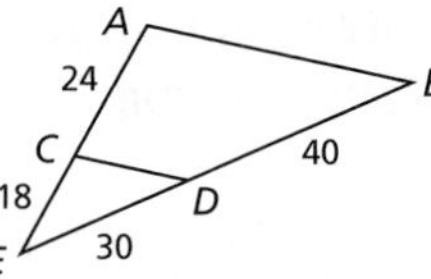

25. Find SU and SV.

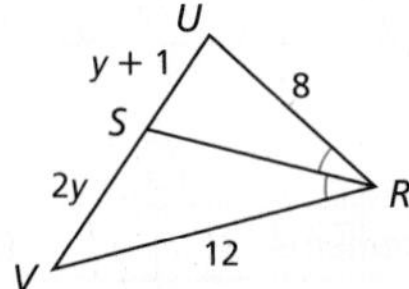

26. Find the length of the third side of $\triangle ABC$.

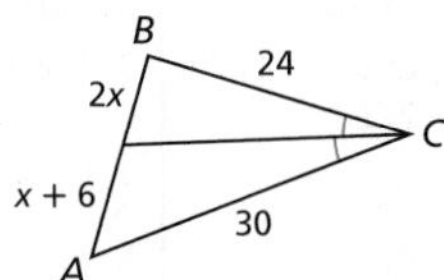

27. One side of a triangle is x inches longer than another side. The ray bisecting the angle formed by these sides divides the opposite side into 3-inch and 5-inch segments. Find the perimeter of the triangle in terms of x.

7-5 Using Proportional Relationships *(pp. 488–494)*

EXAMPLE

- **Use the dimensions in the diagram to find the height h of the tower.**

A student who is 5 ft 5 in. tall measured his shadow and a tower's shadow to find the height of the tower.

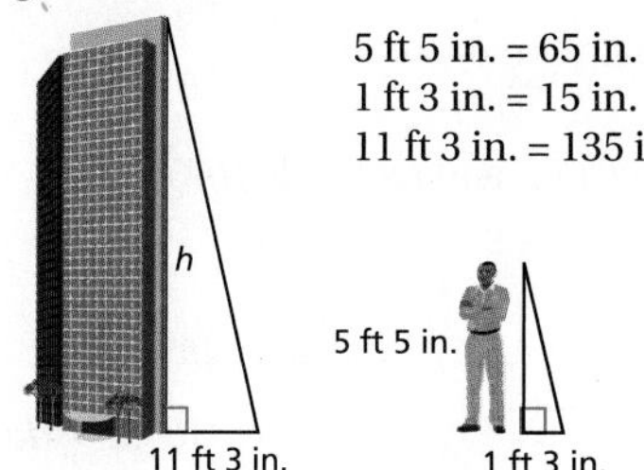

5 ft 5 in. = 65 in.
1 ft 3 in. = 15 in.
11 ft 3 in. = 135 in.

$\frac{h}{135} = \frac{65}{15}$ *Corr. sides are proportional.*

$15h = 65(135)$ *Cross Products Prop.*

$15h = 8775$ *Simplify.*

$h = 585$ in. *Divide both sides by 15.*

The height of the tower is 48 ft 9 in.

EXERCISES

28. To find the height of a flagpole, Casey measured her own shadow and the flagpole's shadow. Given that Casey's height is 5 ft 4 in., what is the height x of the flagpole?

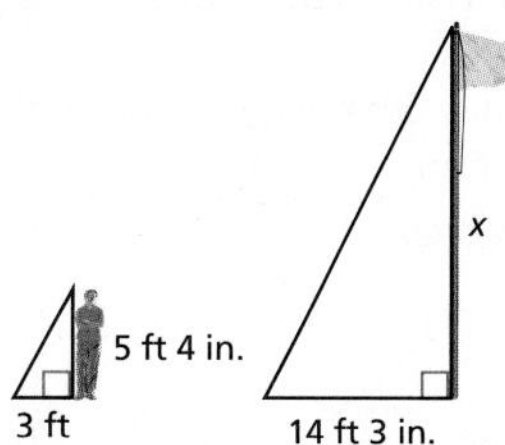

29. Jonathan is 3 ft from a lamppost that is 12 ft high. The lamppost and its shadow form the legs of a right triangle. Jonathan is 6 ft tall and is standing parallel to the lamppost. How long is Jonathan's shadow?

7-6 Dilations and Similarity in the Coordinate Plane *(pp. 495–500)*

EXAMPLE

- **Given:** $A(5, -4), B(-1, -2), C(3, 0), D(-4, -1)$ and $E(2, 2)$

Prove: $\triangle ABC \sim \triangle ADE$

Proof: Plot the points and draw the triangles.

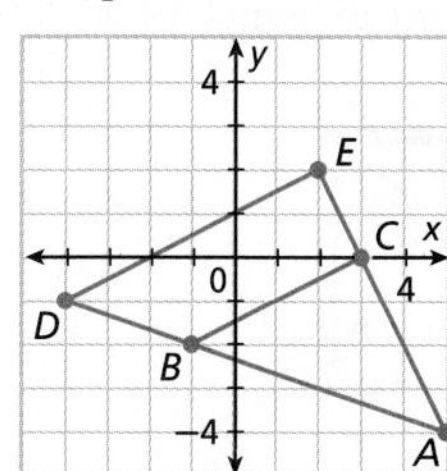

Use the Distance Formula to find the side lengths.

$AC = 2\sqrt{5}, AE = 3\sqrt{5}$

$AB = 2\sqrt{10}, AD = 3\sqrt{10}$

Therefore $\frac{AB}{AD} = \frac{AC}{AE} = \frac{2}{3}$.

Since corresponding sides are proportional and $\angle A \cong \angle A$ by the Reflexive Property, $\triangle ABC \sim \triangle ADE$ by SAS $\sim$.

EXERCISES

30. Given: $R(1, -3), S(-1, -1), T(2, 0), U(-3, 1)$, and $V(3, 3)$

Prove: $\triangle RST \sim \triangle RUV$

31. Given: $J(4, 4), K(2, 3), L(4, 2), M(-4, 0)$, and $N(4, -4)$

Prove: $\triangle JKL \sim \triangle JMN$

32. Given that $\triangle AOB \sim \triangle COD$, find the coordinates of B and the scale factor.

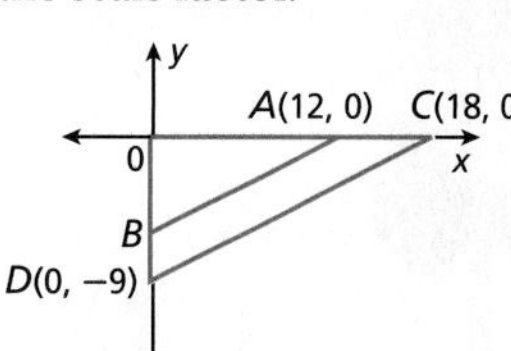

33. Graph the image of the triangle after a dilation with the given scale factor. Then verify that the image is similar to the given triangle. $K(0, 3), L(0, 0)$, and $M(4, 0)$ with scale factor 3.

Answers

28. 25 ft 4 in.
29. 3 ft
30. By the Dist. Formula, $RS = 2\sqrt{2}$, $RU = 4\sqrt{2}$, $RT = \sqrt{10}$, and $RV = 2\sqrt{10}$. $\frac{RS}{RU} = \frac{RT}{RV} = \frac{1}{2}$. $\angle R \cong \angle R$ by the Reflex. Prop. of $\cong$. So $\triangle RST \sim \triangle RUV$ by SAS $\sim$.
31. By the Dist. Formula, $JK = \sqrt{5}$, $JM = 4\sqrt{5}$, $JL = 2$, and $JN = 8$. $\frac{JK}{JM} = \frac{JL}{JN} = \frac{1}{4}$. $\angle J \cong \angle J$ by the Reflex. Prop. of $\cong$. So $\triangle JKL \sim \triangle JMN$ by SAS $\sim$.
32. $(0, -6); \frac{2}{3}$
33. The image of $\triangle KLM$ has vertices $K'(0, 9)$, $L'(0, 0)$, and $M'(12, 0)$. By the Dist. Formula, $KL = 3$, $LM = 4$, $KM = 5$, $K'L' = 9$, $L'M' = 12$, and $K'M' = 15$. $\frac{K'L'}{KL} = \frac{L'M'}{LM} = \frac{K'M'}{KM} = \frac{3}{1}$. Therefore $\triangle KLM \sim \triangle K'L'M'$ by SSS $\sim$.

Organizer

Objective: Assess students' mastery of concepts and skills in Chapter 7.

 **Online Edition**

Resources

 ***Assessment Resources***

Chapter 7 Tests
- Free Response (Levels A, B, C)
- Multiple Choice (Levels A, B, C)
- Performance Assessment

Teacher One Stop™

Test & Practice Generator

State Resources

1. Two points on ℓ are $A(-6, 4)$ and $B(10, -6)$. Write a ratio expressing the slope of ℓ. $-\frac{5}{8}$
2. Alana has a photograph that is 5 in. long and 3.5 in. wide. She enlarges it so that its length is 8 in. What is the width of the enlarged photograph? **5.6 in.**

Determine whether the polygons are similar. If so, write the similarity ratio and a similarity statement.

3. $\triangle ABC$ and $\triangle MNP$

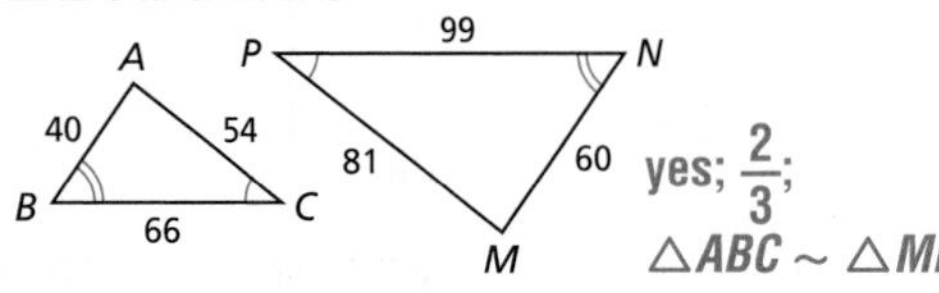

yes; $\frac{2}{3}$; $\triangle ABC \sim \triangle MNP$

4. rectangle $DEFG$ and rectangle $HJKL$

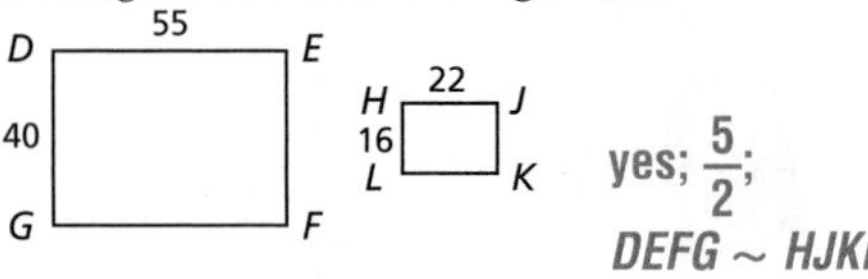

yes; $\frac{5}{2}$; $DEFG \sim HJKL$

5. **Given:** $\square RSTU$
Prove: $\triangle RWV \sim \triangle SWT$

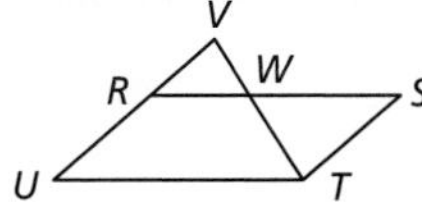

6. Derrick is building a skateboard ramp as shown. Given that $BD = DF = FG = 3$ ft, find CD and EF to the nearest tenth. **1.7 ft; 0.8 ft**

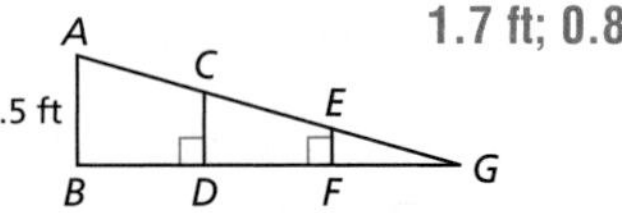

Find the length of each segment.

7. $\overline{PR}$ $11\frac{2}{3}$

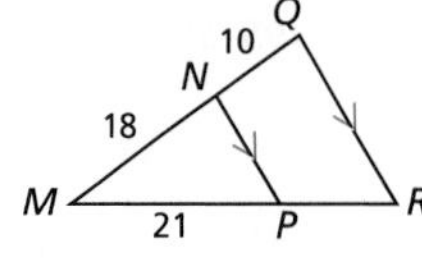

8. $\overline{YW}$ and $\overline{WZ}$ $YW = 5$; $WZ = 8$

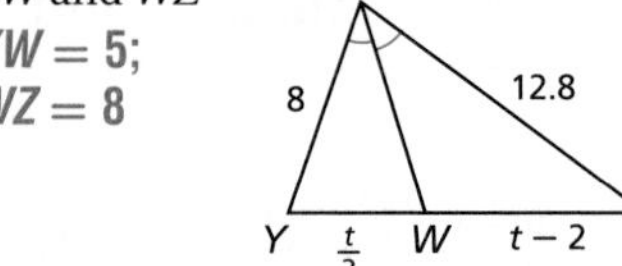

9. To find the height of a tree, a student measured the tree's shadow and her own shadow. If the student's height is 5 ft 8 in., what is the height of the tree? **51 ft**

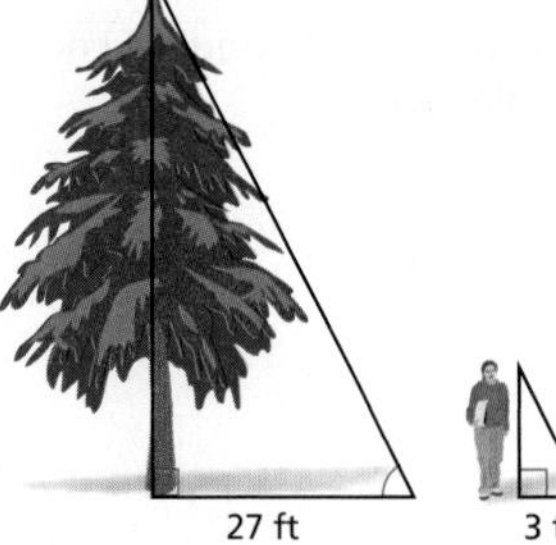

10. The plan for a living room uses the scale of 1.5 in.:30 ft. Use a ruler and find the length of the actual room's diagonal $\overline{AB}$. **25 ft**

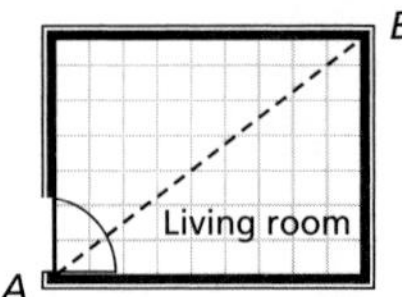

11. **Given:** $A(6, 5)$, $B(3, 4)$, $C(6, 3)$, $D(-3, 2)$, and $E(6, -1)$
Prove: $\triangle ABC \sim \triangle ADE$

12. A quilter designed this patch for a quilt but needs a larger version for a different project. Draw the quilt patch after a dilation with scale factor $\frac{3}{2}$.

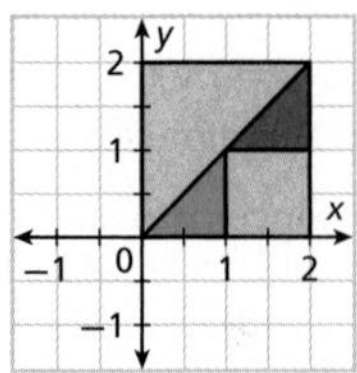

Answers

5. 1. $RSTU$ is a $\square$. (Given)
2. $\overline{RU} \parallel \overline{ST}$ (Def. of $\square$)
3. $\angle VRW \cong \angle TSW$ (Alt. Int. ∠s Thm.)
4. $\angle RWV \cong \angle SWT$ (Vert. ∠s Thm.)
5. $\triangle RWV \sim \triangle SWT$ (AA ~ *Steps 3, 4*)

11. By the Dist. Formula, $AB = \sqrt{10}$, $AD = 3\sqrt{10}$, $AC = 2$, and $AE = 6$. $\frac{AB}{AD} = \frac{AC}{AE} = \frac{1}{3}$. $\angle A \cong \angle A$ by the Reflex. Prop. of ≅. So $\triangle ABC \sim \triangle ADE$ by SAS ~.

12. 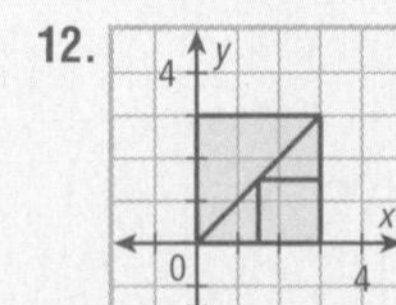

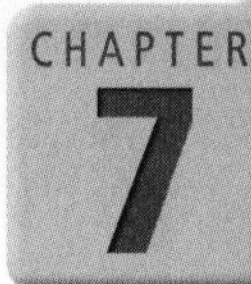

FOCUS ON SAT

The SAT consists of seven test sections: three verbal, three math, and one more verbal or math section not used to compute your final score. The "extra" section is used to try out questions for future tests and to compare your score to previous tests.

Read each question carefully and make sure you answer the question being asked. Check that your answer makes sense in the context of the problem. If you have time, check your work.

You may want to time yourself as you take this practice test. It should take you about 8 minutes to complete.

1. In the figure below, the coordinates of the vertices are $A(1, 5)$, $B(1, 1)$, $D(10, 1)$, and $E(10, -7)$. If the length of $\overline{CE}$ is 10, what are the coordinates of C?

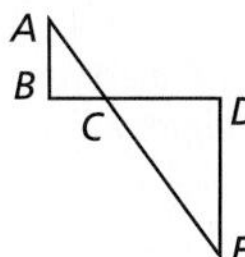

Note: Figure not drawn to scale.

(A) (4, 1)

(B) (1, 4)

(C) (7, 1)

(D) (1, 7)

(E) (6, 1)

2. In the figure below, triangles JKL and MKN are similar, and ℓ is parallel to segment JL. What is the length of $\overline{KM}$?

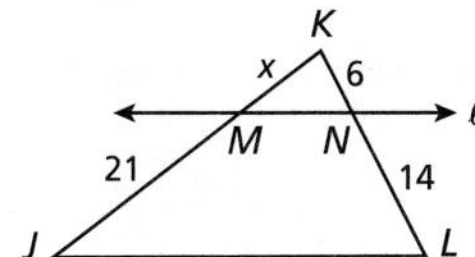

Note: Figure not drawn to scale.

(A) 4

(B) 8

(C) 9

(D) 13

(E) 18

3. Three siblings are to share an inheritance of $750,000 in the ratio 4:5:6. What is the amount of the greatest share?

(A) $125,000

(B) $187,500

(C) $250,000

(D) $300,000

(E) $450,000

4. A 35-foot flagpole casts a 9-foot shadow at the same time that a girl casts a 1.2-foot shadow. How tall is the girl?

(A) 3 feet 8 inches

(B) 4 feet 6 inches

(C) 4 feet 7 inches

(D) 4 feet 8 inches

(E) 5 feet 6 inches

5. What polygon is similar to every other polygon of the same name?

(A) Triangle

(B) Parallelogram

(C) Rectangle

(D) Square

(E) Trapezoid

CHAPTER 7

Organizer

Objective: Provide practice for college entrance exams such as the SAT.

Online Edition

Resources

College Entrance Exam Practice

Questions on the SAT represent the following math strands:

Number and Operation, 20–25%

Algebra and Functions, 35–40%

Geometry and Measurement, 25–30%

Data Analysis, Statistics, and Probability, 10–15%

Items on this page focus on:

- Number and Operation
- Geometry and Measurement

Text References:

Item	1	2	3	4	5	6
Lesson	7-3	7-4	7-1	7-5	7-6	7-2

TEST PREP DOCTOR

1. Students may not know how to approach this test item. Suggest that students label the figure with the coordinates of each point and determine the lengths of line segments from the coordinates. Ask students if the triangles are similar and to justify their responses.

2. Students who chose **A** did not set up a proportion of corresponding lengths correctly.

3. Students who chose **A** did not set up a proportion and simply divided the inheritance by 6. Remind students that the ratio gives the relative magnitude of the parts of the whole, but a variable is needed to determine the exact amount of each part.

4. Students who chose **B** or **C** did not convert feet to inches correctly.

5. Students who did not choose **D** have not considered all possibilities for the selected polygon. Provide counterexamples for the other polygons to show students what the differences could be.

Organizer

Objective: Provide opportunities to learn and practice common test-taking strategies.

TEST PREP DOCTOR This Test Tackler explains how figures and diagrams can mislead students. If students assume information from a diagram based on "what they see," they will likely misinterpret the information. Advise students that figures and diagrams are not always drawn to scale, and they should not rely solely on the appearance of the drawing to answer the question. Students need to look at how the drawing is labeled.

Remind students to also look at the positioning of figures. The triangles in the test item above **Problem 10** are similar, but they are situated in different directions. Students may set up the similarity ratios incorrectly. Advise students to redraw the figures so that they are positioned the same.

TEST TACKLER
Standardized Test Strategies

Any Question Type: Interpret A Diagram

When a diagram is included as part of a test question, do not make any assumptions about the diagram. Diagrams are not always drawn to scale and can be misleading if you are not careful.

EXAMPLE 1

Multiple Choice What is *DE*?

Ⓐ 3.6 Ⓒ 4.8

Ⓑ 4 Ⓓ 9

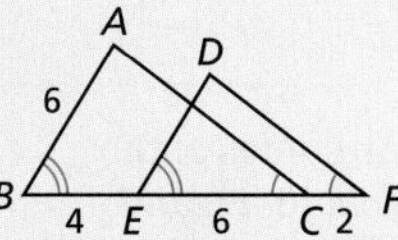

Make your own sketch of the diagram. Separate the two triangles so that you are able to find the side length measures.

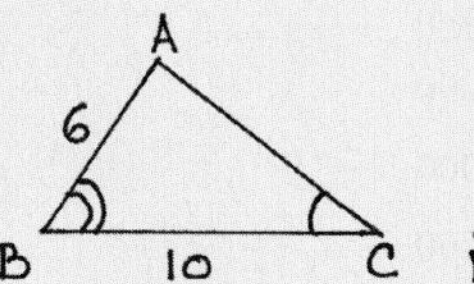

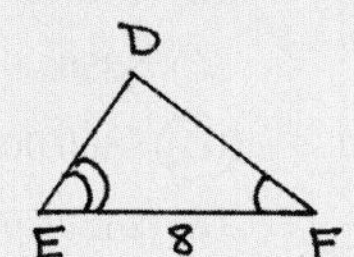

By redrawing the diagram, it is clear that the two triangles are similar. Set up a proportion to find DE.

$$\frac{AB}{BC} = \frac{DE}{EF}$$

$$\frac{6}{10} = \frac{DE}{8}$$

$$\frac{48}{10} = DE$$

$$DE = 4.8$$

The correct choice is C.

EXAMPLE 2

Gridded Response $\triangle X'Y'Z'$ is the image of $\triangle XYZ$ after a dilation with scale factor $\frac{1}{2}$. Find $X'Z'$.

Before you begin, look at the scale of both the x-axis and the y-axis. Do not assume that the scale is always 1.

At first glance, you might assume that XZ is 4. But by looking closely at the x-axis, notice that each increment represents 2 units. So XZ is actually 8.

When $\triangle XYZ$ is dilated by a factor of $\frac{1}{2}$, $X'Z'$ will be half of XZ.

$$X'Z' = \frac{1}{2}XZ = \frac{1}{2}(8) = 4$$

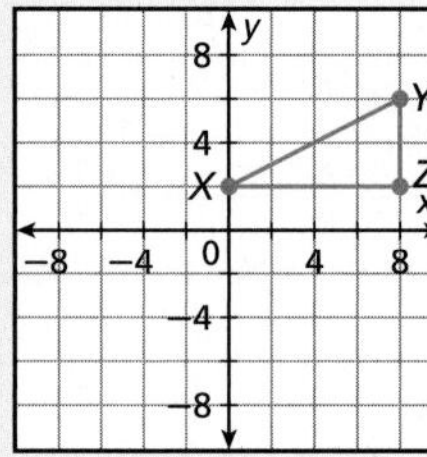

If the diagram does not match the given information, draw one that is more accurate.

Read each test item and answer the questions that follow.

Item A

Multiple Choice **Which ratio is the slope of m?**

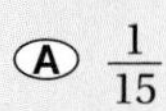

Ⓐ $\frac{1}{15}$

Ⓑ $\frac{1}{3}$

Ⓒ 3

Ⓓ 15

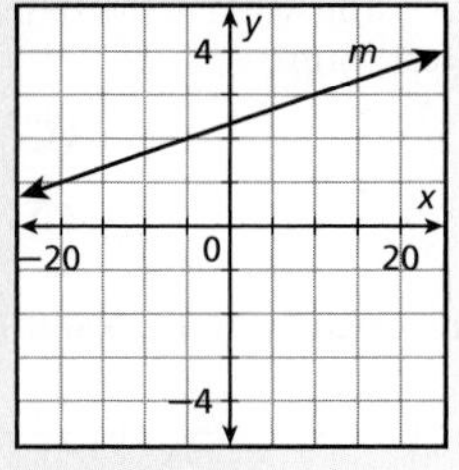

1. What is the scale of the y-axis? Use this scale to determine the rise of the slope.
2. What is the scale of the x-axis? Use this scale to determine the run of the slope.
3. Write the ratio that represents the slope of m.
4. Anna selected choice B as her answer. Is she correct? If not, what do you think she did wrong?

Item B

Gridded Response **If $ABDC \sim MNPO$ and AC is 6, what is AB?**

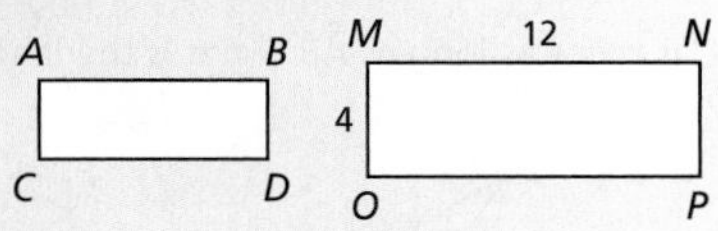

5. Examine the figures. Do you think $\overline{AB}$ is longer or shorter than $\overline{MN}$?
6. Do you think the drawings actually represent the given information? If not, explain why.
7. Create your own sketch of the figures to more accurately match the given information.

Item C

Short Response **Find the measure of MN and PR.**

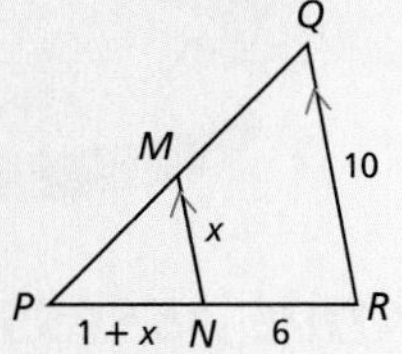

8. Describe how redrawing the figure can help you better understand the given information.
9. After reading this test question, a student redrew the figure as shown below. Explain if it is a correct interpretation of the original figure. If it is not, redraw and/or relabel it so that it is correct.

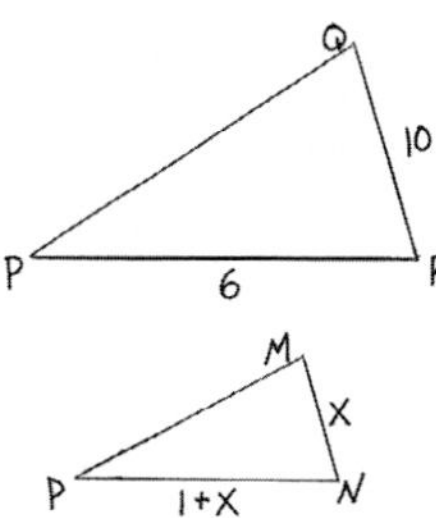

Item D

Multiple Choice **Which is a similarity ratio for the triangles shown?**

Ⓐ $\frac{20}{1}$

Ⓑ $\frac{10}{1}$

Ⓒ $\frac{2}{1}$

Ⓓ $\frac{15}{1}$

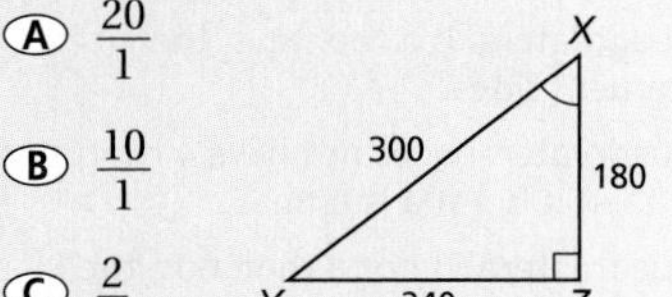

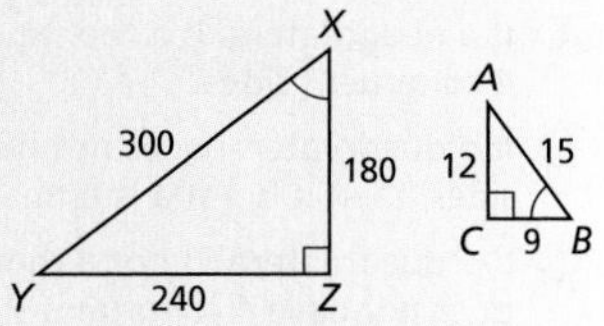

10. Chad determined that choice D was correct. Do you agree? If not, what do you think he did wrong?
11. Redraw the figures so that they are easier to understand. Write three statements that describe which vertices correspond to each other and three statements that describe which sides correspond to each other.

Answers

Possible answers:

1. 1 unit; 1 unit
2. 5 units; 15 units
3. $\frac{1}{15}$
4. No; she assumed the axes both had a scale of 1.
5. $\overline{AB}$ should be longer.
6. No; it appears that $\overline{AC}$ is shorter than $\overline{MO}$, and this is not consistent with the dimensions that are given.
7. 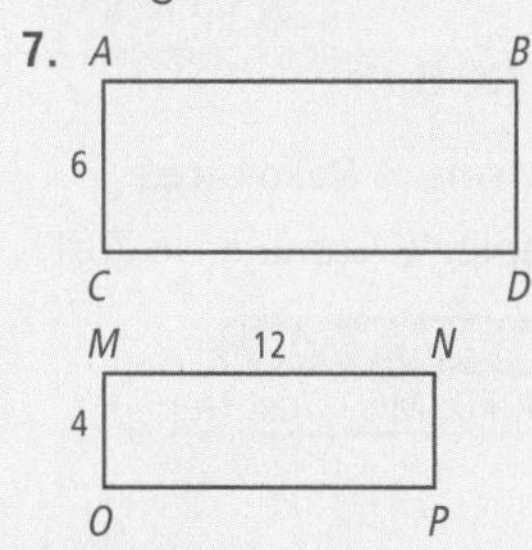

8. By redrawing the figure into 2 separate △s, I can see the measures of each side length. This will help me set up a proportion correctly.
9. No, it is not correct. The student mislabeled the length of $\overline{PR}$. It should be labeled as $(1 + x) + 6$, or $7 + x$.
10. No; he misinterpreted the diagram and assumed that $\overline{XZ}$ and $\overline{AC}$ were proportional.
11. 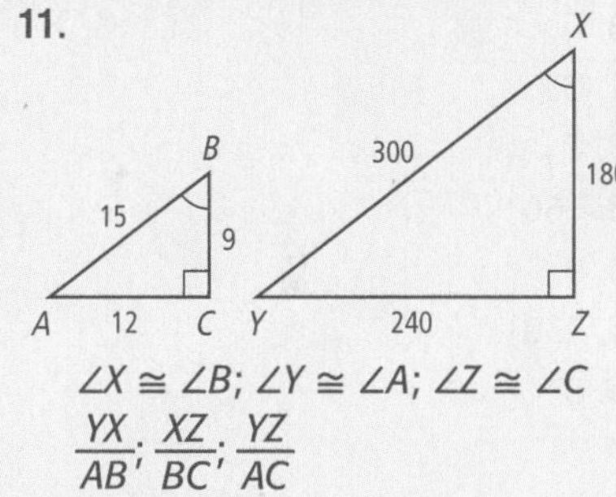

$\angle X \cong \angle B$; $\angle Y \cong \angle A$; $\angle Z \cong \angle C$

$\frac{YX}{AB}$, $\frac{XZ}{BC}$, $\frac{YZ}{AC}$

State Resources

go.hrw.com
State Resources Online
KEYWORD: MG7 Resources

Answers to Test Items

A. A

B. 18

C. $MN = 5$; $PR = 12$

D. A

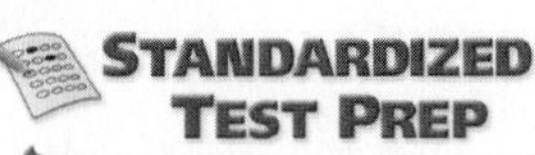

Organizer

Objective: Provide review and practice for Chapters 1–7 and standardized tests.

 Online Edition

Resources

 **Assessment Resources**

Chapter 7 Cumulative Test

go.hrw.com
KEYWORD: MG7 TestPrep

Answers

1. D
2. G
3. A
4. J
5. C
6. F
7. B
8. H
9. A
10. G
11. D
12. F
13. 160
14. 9
15. 130
16. 8

State Resources

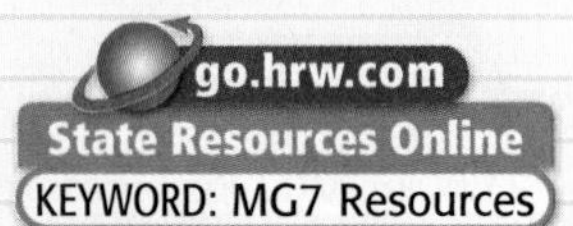

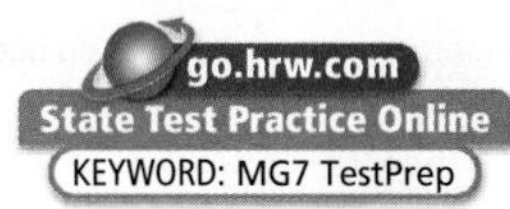

CUMULATIVE ASSESSMENT, CHAPTERS 1–7

Multiple Choice

1. Which similarity statement is true for rectangles $ABCD$ and $MNPQ$, given that $AB = 3$, $AD = 4$, $MN = 6$, and $NP = 4.5$?

- (A) Rectangle $ABCD \sim$ rectangle $MNPQ$
- (B) Rectangle $ABCD \sim$ rectangle $PQMN$
- (C) Rectangle $ABCD \sim$ rectangle $MPNQ$
- (D) Rectangle $ABCD \sim$ rectangle $QMNP$

2. $\triangle ABC$ has perpendicular bisectors $\overline{XP}$, $\overline{YP}$, and $\overline{ZP}$. If $AP = 6$ and $ZP = 4.5$, what is the length of $\overline{BC}$ to the nearest tenth?

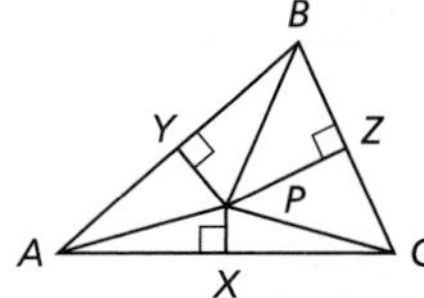

- (F) 4.0
- (G) 7.9
- (H) 9.0
- (J) 12.7

3. What is the converse of the statement "If a quadrilateral has 4 congruent sides, then it is a rhombus"?

- (A) If a quadrilateral is a rhombus, then it has 4 congruent sides.
- (B) If a quadrilateral does not have 4 congruent sides, then it is not a rhombus.
- (C) If a quadrilateral is not a rhombus, then it does not have 4 congruent sides.
- (D) If a rhombus has 4 congruent sides, then it is a quadrilateral.

4. A blueprint for a hotel uses a scale of 3 in. : 100 ft. On the blueprint, the lobby has a width of 1.5 in. and a length of 2.25 in. If the carpeting for the lobby costs \$1.25 per square foot, how much will the carpeting for the entire lobby cost?

- (F) \$312.50
- (G) \$1406.25
- (H) \$3000.00
- (J) \$4687.50

5. If $12x = 16y$, what is the ratio of x to y in simplest form?

- (A) $\frac{1}{4}$
- (B) $\frac{3}{4}$
- (C) $\frac{4}{3}$
- (D) $\frac{4}{1}$

Use the diagram for Items 6 and 7.

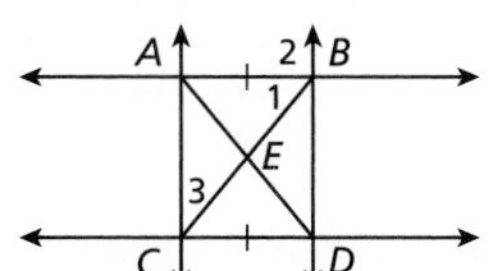

6. Given that $\overline{AB} \cong \overline{CD}$, which additional information would be sufficient to prove that $ABCD$ is a parallelogram?

- (F) $\overline{AB} \parallel \overline{CD}$
- (G) $\overline{AC} \parallel \overline{BD}$
- (H) $\angle CAB \cong \angle CDB$
- (J) E is the midpoint of $\overline{AD}$.

7. If $\overleftrightarrow{AC}$ is parallel to $\overleftrightarrow{BD}$ and $m\angle 1 + m\angle 2 = 140°$, what is the measure of $\angle 3$?

- (A) 20°
- (B) 40°
- (C) 50°
- (D) 70°

8. If $\overline{AC}$ is twice as long as $\overline{AB}$, what is the length of $\overline{DC}$?

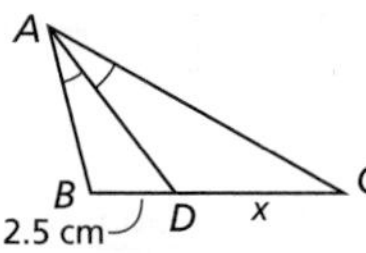

- (F) 2.5 centimeters
- (G) 3.75 centimeters
- (H) 5 centimeters
- (J) 15 centimeters

Answers

17. By the Dist. Formula, $BC = 4$, $EC = 2$, $AC = 2\sqrt{5}$, and $DC = \sqrt{5}$. $\frac{BC}{EC} = \frac{4}{2} = \frac{2}{1}$, and $\frac{AC}{DC} = \frac{2\sqrt{5}}{\sqrt{5}} = \frac{2}{1}$. Thus $\frac{BC}{EC} = \frac{AC}{DC}$. $\angle C \cong \angle C$ by the Reflex. Prop. of $\cong$. Therefore $\triangle ABC \sim \triangle DEC$ by SAS.

18. Possible answer: $48° < m\angle TUW < 108°$;

1. $90° < m\angle TUV < 180°$ (Def. of obtuse $\angle$)
2. $m\angle TUV = m\angle TUW + m\angle WUV$ ($\angle$ Add. Post.)
3. $90° < m\angle TUW + m\angle WUV < 180°$ (Subst.)
4. $90° < 2x° + (x + 18)° < 180°$ (Subst.)
5. $90° < (3x + 18)° < 180°$ (Simplify.)
6. $72° < 3x° < 162°$ (Subtr. Prop. of =)
7. $24° < x° < 54°$ (Div. Prop. of =)
8. $48° < 2x° < 108°$ (Mult. Prop. of =)
9. $48° < m\angle TUW < 108°$ (Subst.)

19. Possible answer: Because $\triangle ABC \sim \triangle ABD$, their corr. $\angle$s are $\cong$. Therefore $\angle BAC \cong \angle BAD$, and $\angle C \cong \angle D$. $\overline{AB} \cong \overline{AB}$ by the Reflex. Prop. of $\cong$. Because 2 $\angle$s and a side of $\triangle ABC$ are $\cong$ to 2 corr. $\angle$s and a side of $\triangle ABD$, the 2 $\triangle$s are $\cong$ by AAS.

When writing proportions for similar figures, make sure that each ratio compares corresponding side lengths in each figure.

9. What type of triangle has angles that measure $(2x)°$, $(3x - 9)°$, and $(x + 27)°$?
   - (A) Isosceles acute triangle
   - (B) Isosceles right triangle
   - (C) Scalene acute triangle
   - (D) Scalene obtuse triangle

Use the diagram for Items 10 and 11.

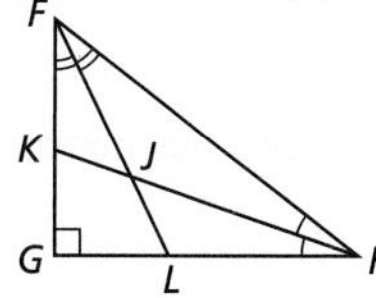

10. Which of these points is the orthocenter of $\triangle FGH$?
    - (F) F
    - (G) G
    - (H) H
    - (J) J

11. Which of the following could be the side lengths of $\triangle FGH$?
    - (A) $FG = 2$, $GH = 3$, and $FH = 4$
    - (B) $FG = 4$, $GH = 5$, and $FH = 6$
    - (C) $FG = 5$, $GH = 4$, and $FH = 3$
    - (D) $FG = 6$, $GH = 8$, and $FH = 10$

12. The measure of one of the exterior angles of a right triangle is 120°. What are the measures of the acute interior angles of the triangle?
    - (F) 30° and 60°
    - (G) 40° and 50°
    - (H) 40° and 80°
    - (J) 60° and 60°

Gridded Response

13. The ratio of a football field's length to its width is 9:4. If the length of the field is 360 ft, what is the width of the field in feet?

14. The sum of the measures of the interior angles of a convex polygon is 1260°. How many sides does the polygon have?

15. In kite $PQRS$, $\angle P$ and $\angle R$ are opposite angles. If $m\angle P = 25°$ and $m\angle R = 75°$, what is the measure of $\angle Q$ in degrees?

16. Heather is 1.6 m tall and casts a shadow of 3.5 m. At the same time, a barn casts a shadow of 17.5 m. Find the height of the barn in meters.

Short Response

17. $\triangle ABC$ has vertices $A(-2, 0)$, $B(2, 2)$, and $C(2, -2)$. $\triangle DEC$ has vertices $D(0, -1)$, $E(2, 0)$, and $C(2, -2)$. Prove that $\triangle ABC \sim \triangle DEC$.

18. $\angle TUV$ in the diagram below is an obtuse angle.

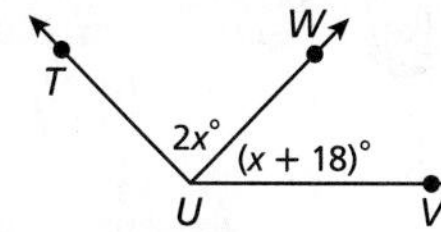

Write an inequality showing the range of possible measurements for $\angle TUW$. Show your work or explain your answer.

19. $\triangle ABC$ and $\triangle ABD$ share side $\overline{AB}$. Given that $\triangle ABC \sim \triangle ABD$, use AAS to explain why these two triangles must also be congruent.

20. Rectangle $ABCD$ has a length of 2.6 cm and a width of 1.8 cm. Rectangle $WXYZ$ has a length of 7.8 cm and a width of 5.4 cm. Determine whether rectangle $ABCD$ is similar to rectangle $WXYZ$. Explain your reasoning.

21. If $\triangle ABC$ and $\triangle XYZ$ are similar triangles, there are six possible similarity statements.
    - **a.** What is the probability that $\triangle ABC \sim \triangle XYZ$ is correct?
    - **b.** If $\triangle ABC$ and $\triangle XYZ$ are isosceles, what is the probability that $\triangle ABC \sim \triangle XYZ$?
    - **c.** If $\triangle ABC$ and $\triangle XYZ$ are equilateral, what is the probability that $\triangle ABC \sim \triangle XYZ$? Explain.

Extended Response

22. **a.** Explain in words how you determine the possible values for x and y that would make the two triangles below similar.

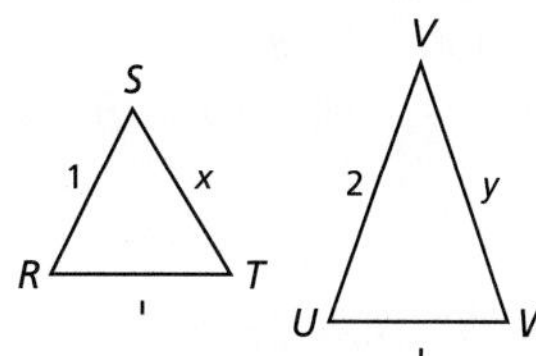

Note: Triangles not drawn to scale.

b. Pick values for x and y that satisfy the conditions you found in part a. Given those values, write a proof that the triangles are similar.

c. Explain why x cannot have a value of 1 if the two triangles in the diagram above are similar.

Short-Response Rubric

Items 17–21

2 Points = The student's answer is an accurate and complete execution of the task or tasks.

1 Point = The student's answer contains attributes of an appropriate response but is flawed.

0 Points = The student's answer contains no attributes of an appropriate response.

Extended-Response Rubric

Item 22

4 Points = The student's answers are correct, the proof and explanations are complete, and all work is shown. Work demonstrates a thorough understanding of concepts related to similar triangles and similarity ratios.

3 Points = The student's answers are correct, but explanations may contain minor flaws. Work demonstrates an understanding of major concepts related to similar triangles and similarity ratios.

2 Points = The student answers correctly, but explanations or steps of the proof are missing or incomplete. Work demonstrates a limited understanding of concepts.

1 Point = The student answers incorrectly, but makes a reasonable attempt to show work and offer explanation.

0 Points = The student answers incorrectly and does not attempt all parts of the problem.

Answers

20. Since every ∠ is rt., corr. ∠s are ≅. $\frac{2.6}{7.8} = \frac{1.8}{5.4}$, so corr. sides are proportional. $ABCD \sim WXYZ$

21a. $\frac{1}{6}$

b. $\frac{1}{3}$

c. 1; all equil. △s are ~.

22a. Possible answer: Because $\triangle RST$ is isosc., the second △ must also be isosc. if the 2 △s are ~. Because $\triangle UVW$ must be isosc., the only possible values for y are 1 and 2. If $y = 1$, then $\overline{ST}$ corresponds to $\overline{UV}$, and $\overline{RS}$ and $\overline{RT}$ correspond to $\overline{WU}$ and $\overline{WV}$. Therefore $\frac{ST}{UV} = \frac{RS}{WV}$. Substituting the values of the side lengths results in the eqn. $\frac{x}{2} = \frac{1}{1}$. So if $y = 1$, $x = 2$. If $y = 2$, then $\overline{ST}$ corresponds to $\overline{UW}$, and $\overline{RS}$ and $\overline{RT}$ correspond to $\overline{VU}$ and $\overline{VW}$. Therefore $\frac{ST}{UW} = \frac{RS}{VU}$. Substituting the values of the side lengths results in the eqn. $\frac{x}{1} = \frac{1}{2}$. So if $y = 2$, $x = 0.5$.

b. Proofs may vary depending on values students choose for x and y. Sample: In TRS we are given $RS = 1, ST = 0.5$, and $TR = 1$. In $\triangle UVW$ we are given $UV = 2$, $VW = 2$, and $WU = 1$. Therefore $\frac{TR}{UV} = \frac{1}{2}, \frac{RS}{VW} = \frac{1}{2}$, and $\frac{ST}{WU} = \frac{1}{2}$. $\frac{TR}{UV} = \frac{RS}{VW} = \frac{ST}{WU}$ by the Trans. Prop. of =, and $\triangle TRS \sim \triangle UVW$ by SSS.

c. Possible answer: If $x = 1$, then $\triangle RST$ is equil. As a result, $\triangle UVW$ can only be ~ to $\triangle RST$ if it is also equil. However $\triangle UVW$ is not equil. because at least 2 of its sides have different lengths. Therefore the 2 △s are ≁ if $x = 1$.

Right Triangles and Trigonometry

Section 8A
Trigonometric Ratios

- **8-1 Similarity in Right Triangles**
- **8-2 Technology Lab** Explore Trigonometric Ratios
- **8-2 Trigonometric Ratios**
- **Connecting Geometry to Algebra** Inverse Functions
- **8-3 Solving Right Triangles**

Section 8B
Applying Trigonometric Ratios

- **8-4 Angles of Elevation and Depression**
- **8-4 Geometry Lab** Indirect Measurement Using Trigonometry
- **8-5 Law of Sines and Law of Cosines**
- **8-6 Vectors**
- **EXTENSION Trigonometry and the Unit Circle**

Pacing Guide for 45-Minute Classes

Teacher One Stop™
Calendar Planner®

Countdown Weeks 17, 18, 19

Chapter 8

DAY 1	DAY 2	DAY 3	DAY 4	DAY 5
8-1 Lesson	8-2 Technology Lab	8-2 Lesson	Connecting Geometry to Algebra	8-3 Lesson
DAY 6	**DAY 7**	**DAY 8**	**DAY 9**	**DAY 10**
Multi-Step Test Prep Ready to Go On?	8-4 Lesson	8-4 Geometry Lab	8-5 Lesson	8-5 Lesson
DAY 11	**DAY 12**	**DAY 13**	**DAY 14**	**DAY 15**
8-6 Lesson	EXTENSION	Multi-Step Test Prep Ready to Go On?	Chapter 8 Review	Chapter 8 Test

Pacing Guide for 90-Minute Classes

Teacher One Stop™
Calendar Planner®

Chapter 8

DAY 1	DAY 2	DAY 3	DAY 4	DAY 5
8-1 Lesson 8-2 Technology Lab	8-2 Lesson Connecting Geometry to Algebra	8-3 Lesson Multi-Step Test Prep Ready to Go On?	8-4 Lesson 8-4 Geometry Lab	8-5 Lesson
DAY 6	**DAY 7**	**DAY 8**		
8-6 Lesson EXTENSION	Multi-Step Test Prep Ready to Go On? Chapter 8 Review	Chapter 8 Test Connecting Geometry to Algebra		

ONGOING ASSESSMENT and INTERVENTION

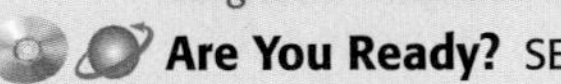

	DIAGNOSE	PRESCRIBE
Assess Prior Knowledge	**Before Chapter 8**	
	Diagnose readiness for the chapter.	Prescribe intervention.
	Are You Ready? SE p. 515	***Are You Ready? Intervention***
Formative Assessment	**Before Every Lesson**	
	Diagnose readiness for the lesson.	Prescribe intervention.
	Warm Up TE	**Reteach** CRB
	During Every Lesson	
	Diagnose understanding of lesson concepts.	Prescribe intervention.
	Check It Out! SE	**Reading Strategies** CRB
	Questioning Strategies TE	***Success for Every Learner***
	Think and Discuss SE	***Lesson Tutorial Videos***
	Write About It SE	
	Journal TE	
	After Every Lesson	
	Diagnose mastery of lesson concepts.	Prescribe intervention.
	Lesson Quiz TE	**Reteach** CRB
	Test Prep SE	**Test Prep Doctor** TE
	Test and Practice Generator	***Homework Help*** **Online**
	Before Chapter 8 Testing	
	Diagnose mastery of concepts in chapter.	Prescribe intervention.
	Ready to Go On? SE pp. 543, 569	***Ready to Go On? Intervention***
	Multi-Step Test Prep SE pp. 542, 568	**Scaffolding Questions** TE pp. 542, 568
	Section Quizzes AR	**Reteach** CRB
	Test and Practice Generator	***Lesson Tutorial Videos***
	Before High Stakes Testing	
	Diagnose mastery of benchmark concepts.	Prescribe intervention.
	College Entrance Exam Practice SE p. 577	***College Entrance Exam Practice***
	Standardized Test Prep SE pp. 580–581	
Summative Assessment	**After Chapter 8**	
	Check mastery of chapter concepts.	Prescribe intervention.
	Multiple-Choice Tests (Forms A, B, C)	**Reteach** CRB
	Free-Response Tests (Forms A, B, C)	***Lesson Tutorial Videos***
	Performance Assessment AR	
	Cumulative Test AR	
	Test and Practice Generator	

KEY: **SE** = *Student Edition* **TE** = *Teacher's Edition* **CRB** = *Chapter Resource Book* **AR** = *Assessment Resources* 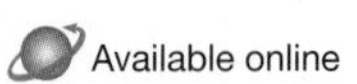 Available online Available on CD- or DVD-ROM

Lesson Resources

Before the Lesson

Prepare ***Teacher One Stop*** SPANISH
- Editable lesson plans
- Calendar Planner
- Easy access to all chapter resources

Lesson Transparencies
- Teacher Tools

Teach the Lesson

Introduce ***Alternate Openers: Explorations***

Lesson Transparencies
- Warm Up
- Problem of the Day

Teach ***Lesson Transparencies***
- Teaching Transparencies

Know-It Notebook™
- Vocabulary
- Key Concepts

Power Presentations

Lesson Tutorial Videos SPANISH 

Interactive Online Edition
- Lesson Activities
- Lesson Tutorial Videos

Lab Activities

Lab Resources Online

Online Interactivities  SPANISH  

TechKeys

Practice the Lesson

Practice ***Chapter Resources***
- Practice A, B, C

Practice and Problem Solving Workbook

IDEA Works!® Modified Worksheets and Tests

ExamView Test and Practice Generator

Homework Help Online

Online Interactivities SPANISH 

Interactive Online Edition
- Homework Help

Apply ***Chapter Resources***
- Problem Solving

Practice and Problem Solving Workbook

Interactive Online Edition
- Chapter Project

Project Teacher Support 

After the Lesson

Reteach ***Chapter Resources***
- Reteach
- Reading Strategies ELL 

Success for Every Learner

Review ***Interactive Answers and Solutions*** 

Solutions Key

Know-It Notebook™
- Big Ideas
- Chapter Review

Extend ***Chapter Resources***
- Challenge

Technology Highlights for the Teacher

Power Presentations

Dynamic presentations to engage students. Complete PowerPoint® presentations for every lesson in Chapter 8.

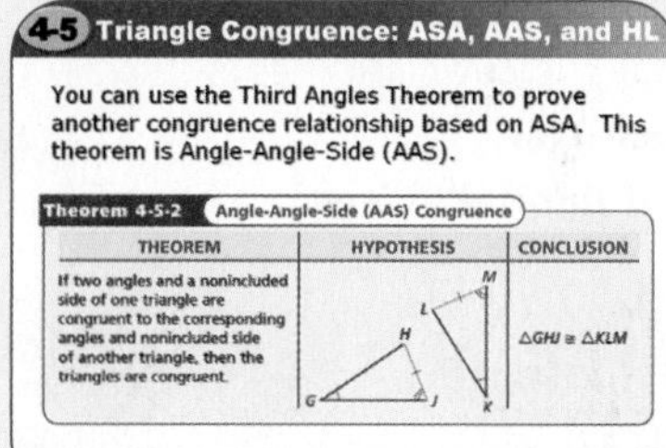

Teacher One Stop SPANISH

Easy access to Chapter 8 resources and assessments. Includes lesson planning, test generation, and puzzle creation software.

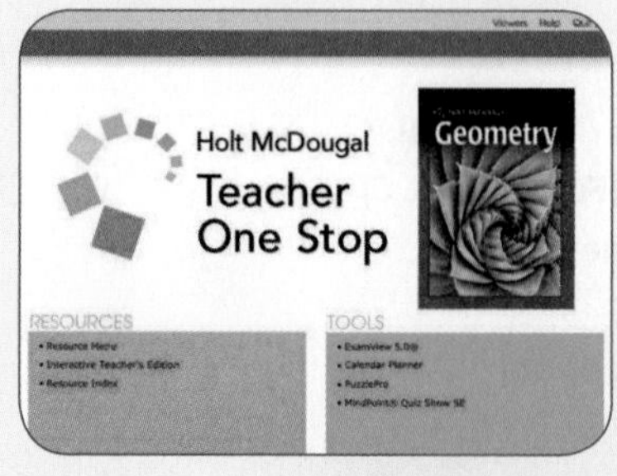

Premier Online Edition SPANISH

Chapter 8 includes Tutorial Videos, Lesson Activities, Lesson Quizzes, Homework Help, and Chapter Project.

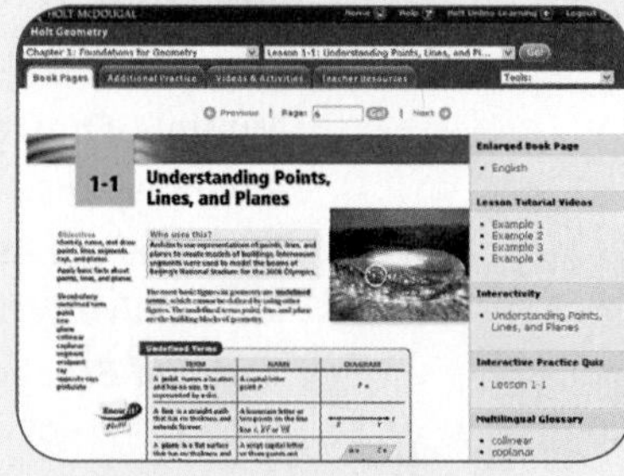

KEY: **SE** = *Student Edition* **TE** = *Teacher's Edition*  English Language Learners  Spanish version available  Available online  Available on CD- or DVD-ROM

Reaching All Learners

Teaching tips to help all learners appear throughout the chapter. A few that target specific students are included in the lists below.

All Learners

Lab Activities
Practice and Problem Solving Workbook
Know-It Notebook

Special Needs Students

- **Practice A** .... CRB
- **Reteach** .... CRB
- **Reading Strategies** .... CRB
- **Are You Ready?** .... SE p. 515
- **Inclusion** .... TE pp. 521, 526, 528, 536, 538, 555, 562
- ***IDEA Works!® Modified Worksheets and Tests***
- ***Ready to Go On? Intervention*** SPANISH
- ***Know-It Notebook***
- ***Online Interactivities***  SPANISH
- ***Lesson Tutorial Videos*** SPANISH

Developing Learners

- **Practice A** .... CRB
- **Reteach** .... CRB
- **Reading Strategies** .... CRB
- **Are You Ready?** .... SE p. 515
- **Vocabulary Connections** .... SE p. 516
- **Questioning Strategies** .... TE
- ***Ready to Go On? Intervention*** SPANISH
- ***Know-It Notebook***
- ***Homework Help Online***
- ***Online Interactivities*** SPANISH
- ***Lesson Tutorial Videos***   SPANISH

On-Level Learners

- **Practice B** .... CRB
- **Problem Solving** .... CRB
- **Vocabulary Connections** .... SE p. 516
- **Questioning Strategies** .... TE
- ***Ready to Go On? Intervention*** SPANISH
- ***Know-It Notebook***
- ***Homework Help Online***
- ***Online Interactivities***  SPANISH

Advanced Learners

- **Practice C** .... CRB
- **Challenge** .... CRB
- **Challenge Exercises** .... SE
- **Reading and Writing Math** *Extend* .... TE p. 517
- **Critical Thinking** .... TE pp. 526, 540
- ***Are You Ready? Enrichment*** SPANISH
- ***Ready To Go On? Enrichment*** SPANISH

English Language Learners

ENGLISH LANGUAGE LEARNERS

- **Reading Strategies** .... CRB
- **Are You Ready? Vocabulary** .... SE p. 515
- **Vocabulary Connections** .... SE p. 516
- **Vocabulary Review** .... SE p. 572
- **English Language Learners** .... TE pp. 517, 526, 535, 545, 552, 561, 583
- ***Success for Every Learner***
- ***Know-It Notebook***
- ***Spanish Study Guide (Resumen y Repaso)***
- ***Multilingual Glossary***
- ***Lesson Tutorial Videos***  SPANISH 

Technology Highlights for Reaching All Learners

Lesson Tutorial Videos SPANISH

Starring Holt authors Ed Burger and Freddie Renfro! Live tutorials to support every lesson in Chapter 8.

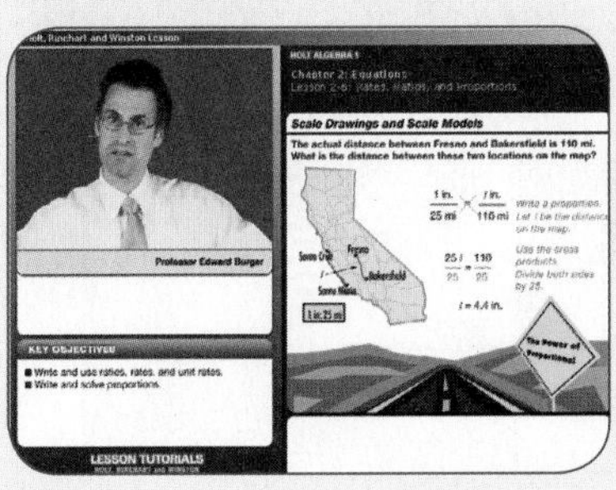

Multilingual Glossary

Searchable glossary includes definitions in English, Spanish, Vietnamese, Chinese, Hmong, Korean, and 4 other languages.

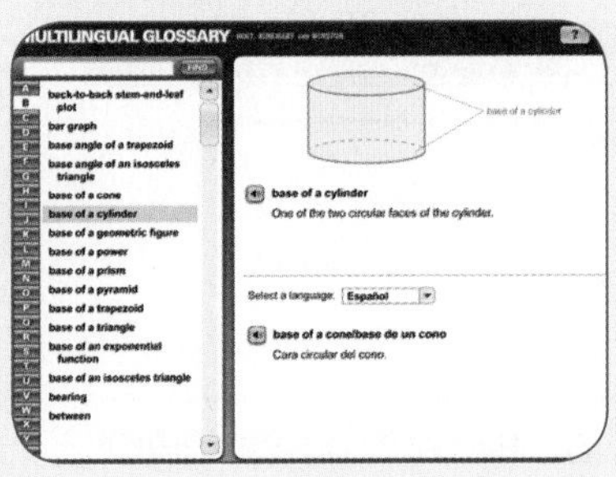

Online Interactivities

Interactive tutorials provide visually engaging alternative opportunities to learn concepts and master skills.

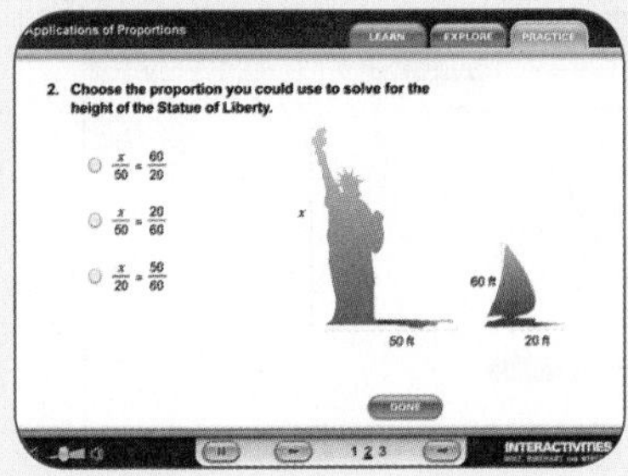

KEY: **SE** = *Student Edition* **TE** = *Teacher's Edition* **CRB** = *Chapter Resource Book* SPANISH Spanish version available; Available online; Available on CD- or DVD-ROM

Ongoing Assessment

Assessing Prior Knowledge

Determine whether students have the prerequisite concepts and skills for success in Chapter 8.

Are You Ready? SPANISH .... SE p. 515
Warm Up .... TE

Test Preparation

Provide review and practice for Chapter 8 and standardized tests.

Multi-Step Test Prep .... SE pp. 542, 568
Study Guide: Review .... SE pp. 572–575
Test Tackler .... SE pp. 578–579
Standardized Test Prep .... SE pp. 580–581
College Entrance Exam Practice .... SE p. 577
Countdown to Testing .... SE pp. C4-C27
IDEA Works!® Modified Worksheets and Tests

Alternative Assessment

Assess students' understanding of Chapter 8 concepts and combined problem-solving skills.

Chapter 8 Project .... SE p. 514
Alternative Assessment .... TE
Performance Assessment .... AR
Portfolio Assessment .... AR

Lesson Assessment

Provide formative assessment for each lesson of Chapter 8.

Questioning Strategies .... TE
Think and Discuss .... SE
Check It Out! Exercises .... SE
Write About It .... SE
Journal .... TE
Lesson Quiz .... TE
Alternative Assessment .... TE
IDEA Works!® Modified Worksheets and Tests

Weekly Assessment

Provide formative assessment for each section of Chapter 8.

Multi-Step Test Prep .... SE pp. 542, 568
Ready to Go On? SPANISH .... SE pp. 543, 569
Section Quizzes .... AR
Test and Practice Generator .... *Teacher One Stop*

Chapter Assessment

Provide summative assessment of Chapter 8 mastery.

Chapter 8 Test .... SE p. 576
Chapter Test (Levels A, B, C) .... AR
• Multiple Choice • Free Response
Cumulative Test .... AR
Test and Practice Generator .... *Teacher One Stop*
IDEA Works!® Modified Worksheets and Tests

Technology Highlights for Assessment

Are You Ready? 

Automatically assess readiness and prescribe intervention for Chapter 8 prerequisite skills.

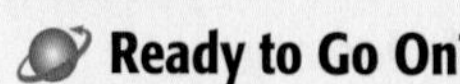

Ready to Go On?

Automatically assess understanding of and prescribe intervention for Sections 8A and 8B.

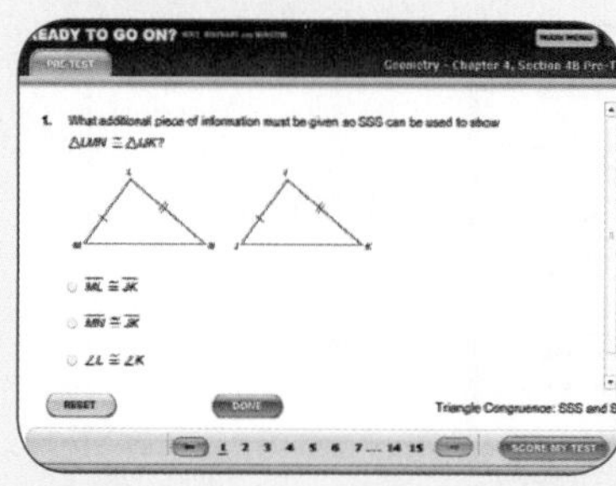

Test and Practice Generator

Use Chapter 8 problem banks to create assessments and worksheets to print out or deliver online. Includes dynamic problems.

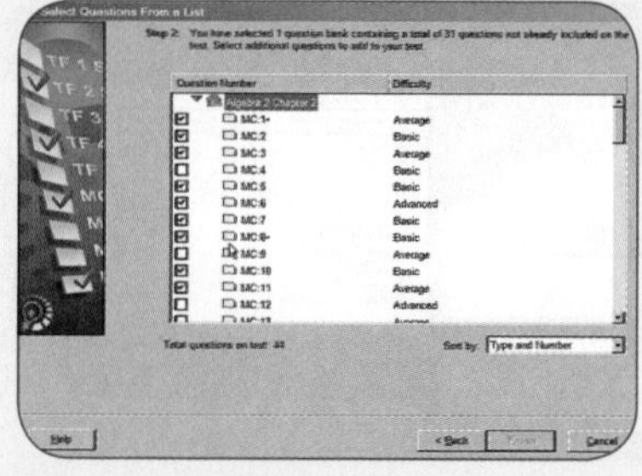

KEY: **SE** = *Student Edition* **TE** = *Teacher's Edition* **AR** = *Assessment Resources* SPANISH Spanish version available Available online  Available on CD- or DVD-ROM

Formal Assessment

Three levels (A, B, C) of multiple-choice and free-response chapter tests, along with a performance assessment, are available in the *Assessment Resources.*

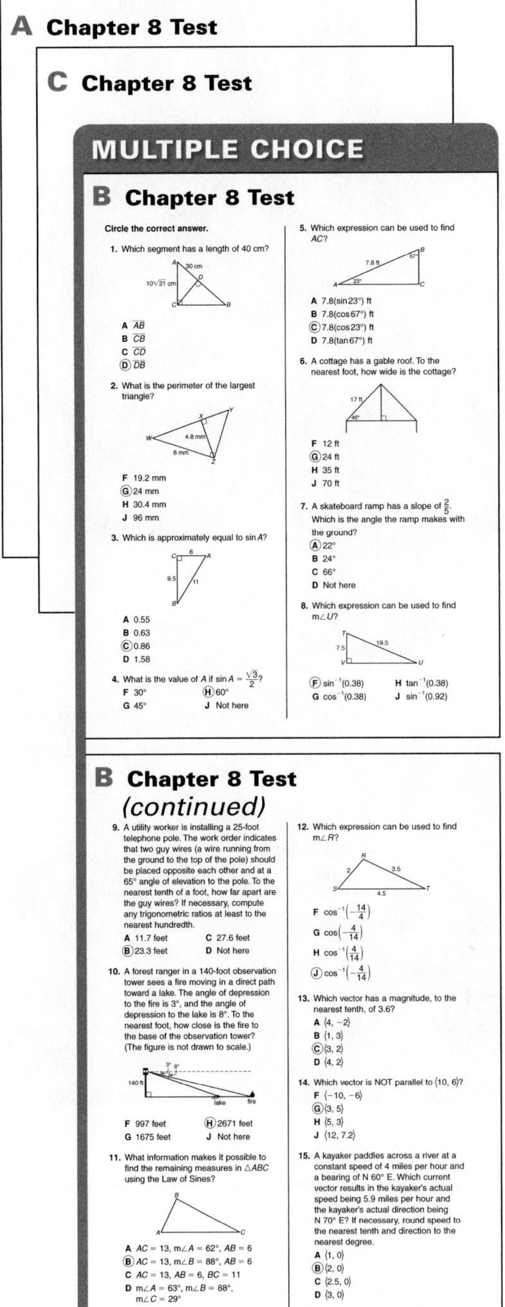

A Chapter 8 Test

C Chapter 8 Test

MULTIPLE CHOICE

B Chapter 8 Test

Circle the correct answer.

1. Which segment has a length of 40 cm?
A $\overline{AB}$
B $\overline{CB}$
C $\overline{CD}$
(D) $\overline{DB}$

2. What is the perimeter of the largest triangle?
F 19.2 mm
(G) 24 mm
H 30.4 mm
J 96 mm

3. Which is approximately equal to sin *A*?
A 0.55
B 0.63
(C) 0.86
D 1.58

4. What is the value of *A* if $\sin A = \frac{\sqrt{3}}{2}$?
F 30°
G 45°
(H) 60°
J Not here

5. Which expression can be used to find *AC*?
A 7.8(sin 23°) ft
B 7.8(cos 67°) ft
(C) 7.8(cos 23°) ft
D 7.8(tan 67°) ft

6. A cottage has a gable roof. To the nearest foot, how wide is the cottage?
F 12 ft
(G) 24 ft
H 35 ft
J 70 ft

7. A skateboard ramp has a slope of $\frac{2}{5}$. Which is the angle the ramp makes with the ground?
(A) 22°
B 24°
C 66°
D Not here

8. Which expression can be used to find m∠*U*?
(F) $\sin^{-1}(0.38)$
G $\cos^{-1}(0.38)$
H $\tan^{-1}(0.38)$
J $\sin^{-1}(0.92)$

B Chapter 8 Test (continued)

9. A utility worker is installing a 25-foot telephone pole. The work order indicates that two guy wires (a wire running from the ground to the top of the pole) should be placed opposite each other and at a 65° angle of elevation to the pole. To the nearest tenth of a foot, how far apart are the guy wires? If necessary, compute any trigonometric ratios at least to the nearest hundredth.
A 11.7 feet
(B) 23.3 feet
C 27.6 feet
D Not here

10. A forest ranger in a 140-foot observation tower sees a fire moving in a direct path toward a lake. The angle of depression to the fire is 3°, and the angle of depression to the lake is 8°. To the nearest foot, how close is the fire to the base of the observation tower? (The figure is not drawn to scale.)
F 997 feet
G 1675 feet
(H) 2671 feet
J Not here

11. What information makes it possible to find the remaining measures in △*ABC* using the Law of Sines?
A *AC* = 13, m∠*A* = 62°, *AB* = 6
(B) *AC* = 13, m∠*B* = 88°, *AB* = 6
C *AC* = 13, *AB* = 6, *BC* = 11
D m∠*A* = 63°, m∠*B* = 88°, m∠*C* = 29°

12. Which expression can be used to find m∠*R*?
F $\cos^{-1}\left(-\frac{14}{4}\right)$
G $\cos\left(-\frac{4}{14}\right)$
H $\cos^{-1}\left(\frac{4}{14}\right)$
(J) $\cos^{-1}\left(-\frac{4}{14}\right)$

13. Which vector has a magnitude, to the nearest tenth, of 3.6?
A ⟨4, −2⟩
B ⟨1, 3⟩
(C) ⟨3, 2⟩
D ⟨4, 2⟩

14. Which vector is NOT parallel to ⟨10, 6⟩?
F ⟨−10, −6⟩
(G) ⟨3, 5⟩
H ⟨5, 3⟩
J ⟨12, 7.2⟩

15. A kayaker paddles across a river at a constant speed of 4 miles per hour and a bearing of N 60° E. Which current vector results in the kayaker's actual speed being 5.9 miles per hour and the kayaker's actual direction being N 70° E? If necessary, round speed to the nearest tenth and direction to the nearest degree.
A ⟨1, 0⟩
(B) ⟨2, 0⟩
C ⟨2.5, 0⟩
D ⟨3, 0⟩

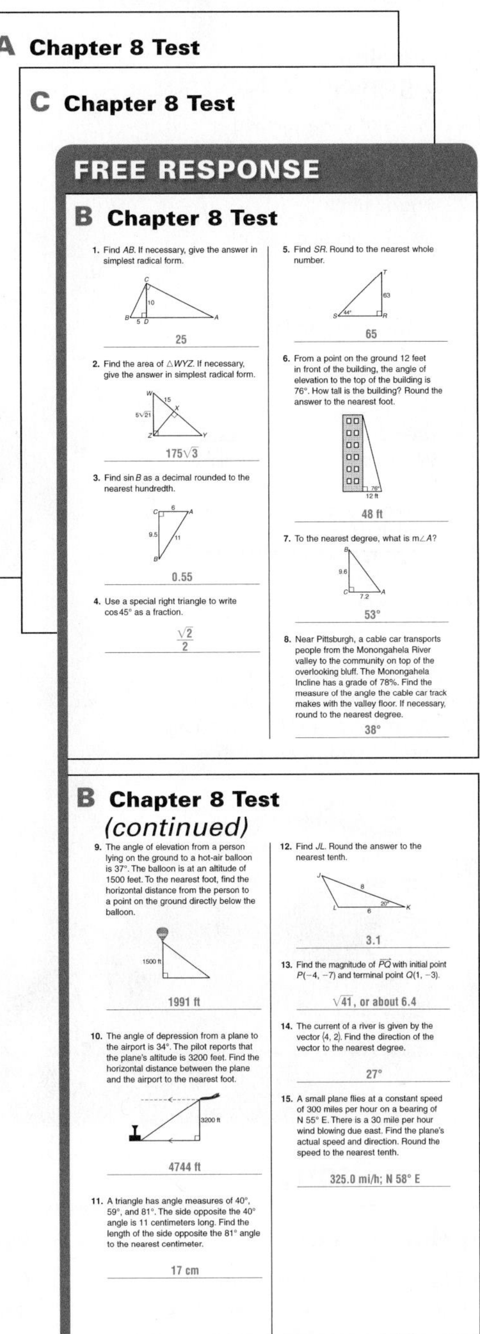

A Chapter 8 Test

C Chapter 8 Test

FREE RESPONSE

B Chapter 8 Test

1. Find *AB*. If necessary, give the answer in simplest radical form.
25

2. Find the area of △*WYZ*. If necessary, give the answer in simplest radical form.
$175\sqrt{3}$

3. Find sin *B* as a decimal rounded to the nearest hundredth.
0.55

4. Use a special right triangle to write cos 45° as a fraction.
$\frac{\sqrt{2}}{2}$

5. Find *SR*. Round to the nearest whole number.
65

6. From a point on the ground 12 feet in front of the building, the angle of elevation to the top of the building is 76°. How tall is the building? Round the answer to the nearest foot.
48 ft

7. To the nearest degree, what is m∠*A*?
53°

8. Near Pittsburgh, a cable car transports people from the Monongahela River valley to the community on top of the overlooking bluff. The Monongahela Incline has a grade of 78%. Find the measure of the angle the cable car track makes with the valley floor. If necessary, round to the nearest degree.
38°

B Chapter 8 Test (continued)

9. The angle of elevation from a person lying on the ground to a hot-air balloon is 37°. The balloon is at an altitude of 1500 feet. To the nearest foot, find the horizontal distance from the person to a point on the ground directly below the balloon.
1991 ft

10. The angle of depression from a plane to the airport is 34°. The pilot reports that the plane's altitude is 3200 feet. Find the horizontal distance between the plane and the airport to the nearest foot.
4744 ft

11. A triangle has angle measures of 40°, 59°, and 81°. The side opposite the 40° angle is 11 centimeters long. Find the length of the side opposite the 81° angle to the nearest centimeter.
17 cm

12. Find *JL*. Round the answer to the nearest tenth.
3.1

13. Find the magnitude of $\vec{PQ}$ with initial point *P*(−4, −7) and terminal point *Q*(1, −3).
$\sqrt{41}$, or about 6.4

14. The current of a river is given by the vector ⟨4, 2⟩. Find the direction of the vector to the nearest degree.
27°

15. A small plane flies at a constant speed of 300 miles per hour on a bearing of N 55° E. There is a 30 mile per hour wind blowing due east. Find the plane's actual speed and direction. Round the speed to the nearest tenth.
325.0 mi/h; N 58° E

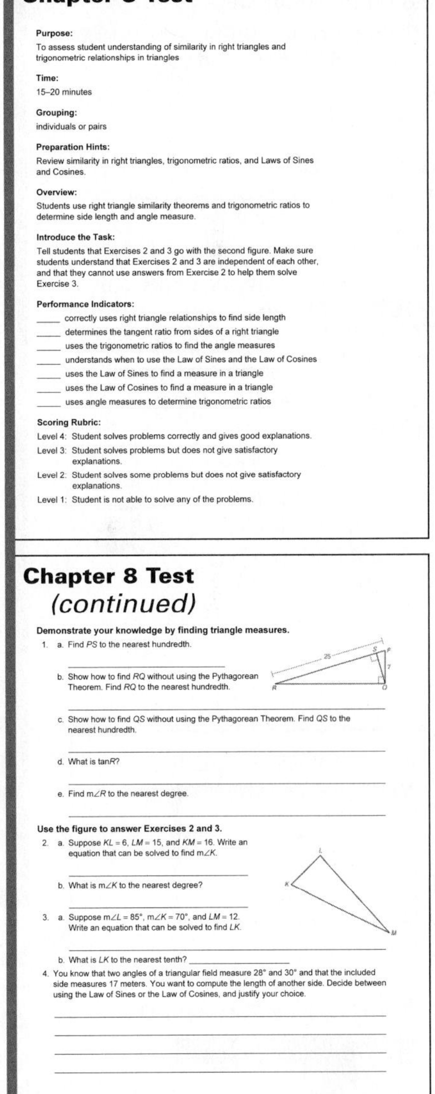

PERFORMANCE ASSESSMENT

Chapter 8 Test

Purpose:
To assess student understanding of similarity in right triangles and trigonometric relationships in triangles

Time:
15–20 minutes

Grouping:
individuals or pairs

Preparation Hints:
Review similarity in right triangles, trigonometric ratios, and Laws of Sines and Cosines.

Overview:
Students use right triangle similarity theorems and trigonometric ratios to determine side length and angle measure.

Introduce the Task:
Tell students that Exercises 2 and 3 go with the second figure. Make sure students understand that Exercises 2 and 3 are independent of each other, and that they cannot use answers from Exercise 2 to help them solve Exercise 3.

Performance Indicators:
____ correctly uses right triangle relationships to find side length
____ determines the tangent ratio from sides of a right triangle
____ uses the trigonometric ratios to find the angle measures
____ understands when to use the Law of Sines and the Law of Cosines
____ uses the Law of Sines to find a measure in a triangle
____ uses the Law of Cosines to find a measure in a triangle
____ uses angle measures to determine trigonometric ratios

Scoring Rubric:
Level 4: Student solves problems correctly and gives good explanations.
Level 3: Student solves problems but does not give satisfactory explanations.
Level 2: Student solves some problems but does not give satisfactory explanations.
Level 1: Student is not able to solve any of the problems.

Chapter 8 Test (continued)

Demonstrate your knowledge by finding triangle measures.

1. a. Find *PS* to the nearest hundredth.
b. Show how to find *RQ* without using the Pythagorean Theorem. Find *RQ* to the nearest hundredth.
c. Show how to find *QS* without using the Pythagorean Theorem. Find *QS* to the nearest hundredth.
d. What is tan*R*?
e. Find m∠*R* to the nearest degree.

Use the figure to answer Exercises 2 and 3.

2. a. Suppose *KL* = 6, *LM* = 15, and *KM* = 16. Write an equation that can be solved to find m∠*K*.
b. What is m∠*K* to the nearest degree?

3. a. Suppose m∠*L* = 85°, m∠*K* = 70°, and *LM* = 12. Write an equation that can be solved to find *LK*.
b. What is *LK* to the nearest tenth?

4. You know that two angles of a triangular field measure 28° and 30° and that the included side measures 17 meters. You want to compute the length of another side. Decide between using the Law of Sines or the Law of Cosines, and justify your choice.

Teacher One Stop™

Test & Practice Generator

Create and customize Chapter 8 Tests. Instantly generate multiple test versions, answer keys, and practice versions of test items.

Modified chapter tests that address special learning needs are available in *IDEA Works!*® *Modified Worksheets and Tests.*

CHAPTER 8

SECTION 8A
Trigonometric Ratios

MULTI-STEP TEST PREP On page 542, students use geometric means and trigonometric ratios to calculate distances and angles created by utility poles and electrical lines.

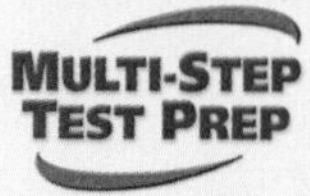

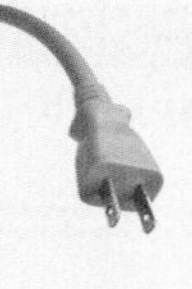

Exercises designed to prepare students for success on the Multi-Step Test Prep can be found on pages 522, 530, and 539.

SECTION 8B
Applying Trigonometric Ratios

MULTI-STEP TEST PREP On page 568, students apply trigonometric ratios and vectors to model a real-world search-and-rescue situation.

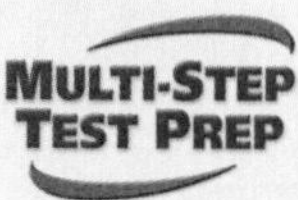

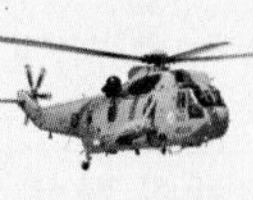

Exercises designed to prepare students for success on the Multi-Step Test Prep can be found on pages 548, 557, and 565.

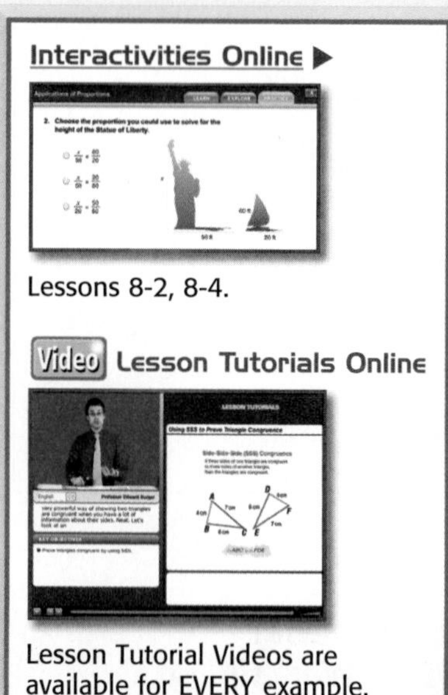

Interactivities Online ▶

Lessons 8-2, 8-4.

Video Lesson Tutorials Online

Lesson Tutorial Videos are available for EVERY example.

CHAPTER 8

Right Triangles and Trigonometry

Chapter Focus
- Solve problems using the similarity relationships of right triangles.
- Apply trigonometric ratios to real-world situations.

Written in Stone

Plimpton 322, a 4000-year-old Babylonian tablet, lists columns of numbers based on Pythagorean triples and trigonometric ratios.

go.hrw.com
Chapter Project Online
KEYWORD: MG7 ChProj

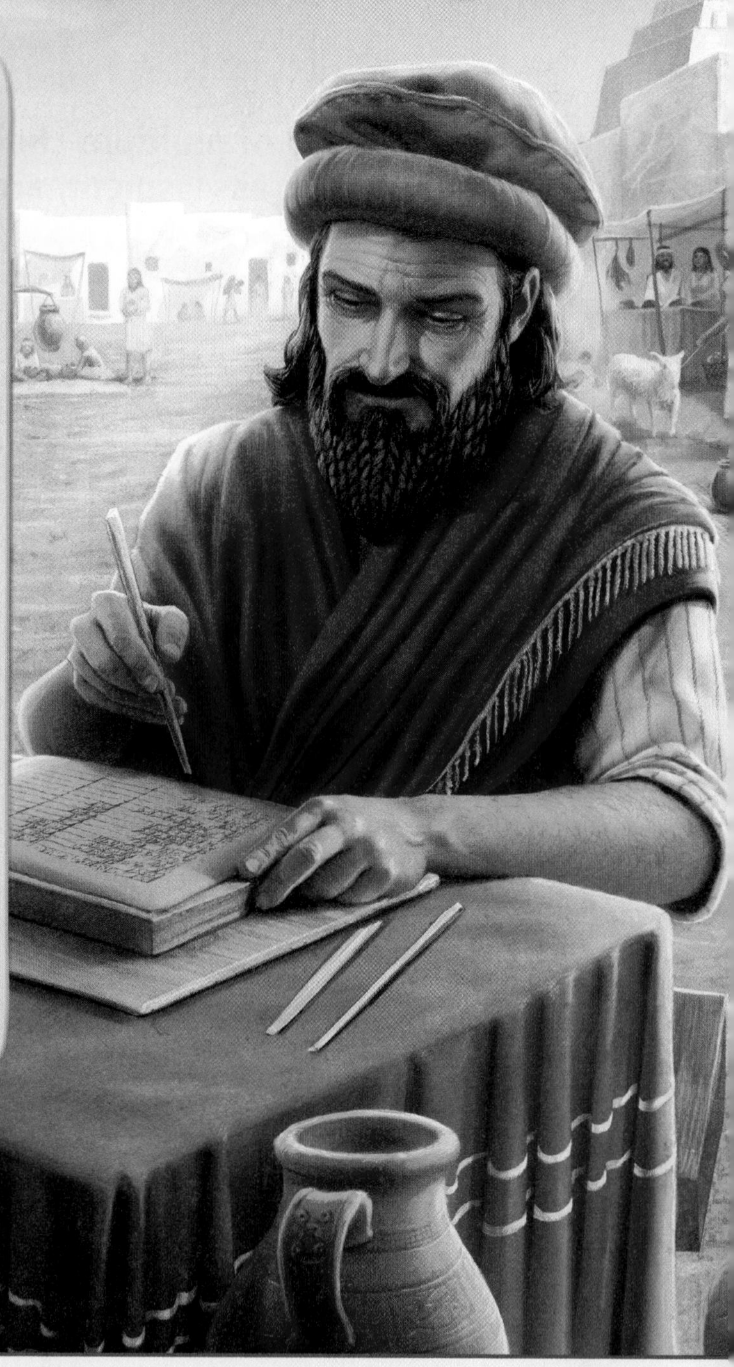

514 Chapter 8

Written in Stone

About the Project

In the Chapter Project, students calculate trigonometric ratios and angle measures from Plimpton 322, a 4000-year-old Babylonian clay tablet. The ancient tablet lists columns of Pythagorean triples, providing evidence that the Babylonians knew the relationship between the side lengths in a right triangle more than a thousand years before the birth of Pythagoras, the teacher to whom the discovery is traditionally credited.

Project Resources

All project resources for teachers and students are provided online.

go.hrw.com
Project Teacher Support
KEYWORD: MG7 ProjectTS

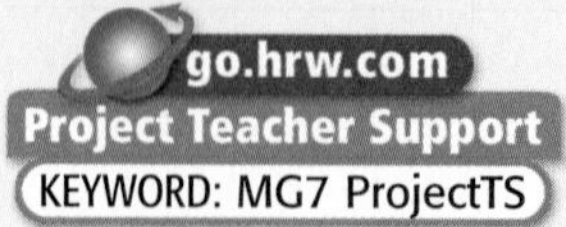

Vocabulary

Match each term on the left with a definition on the right.

1. altitude D
2. proportion C
3. ratio A
4. right triangle E

A. a comparison of two numbers by division
B. a segment from a vertex to the midpoint of the opposite side of a triangle
C. an equation stating that two ratios are equal
D. a perpendicular segment from the vertex of a triangle to a line containing the base
E. a triangle that contains a right angle

Identify Similar Figures

Determine if the two triangles are similar.

5.
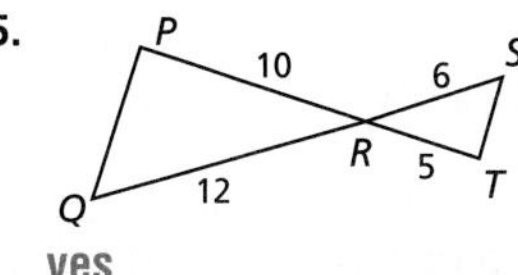

yes

6.
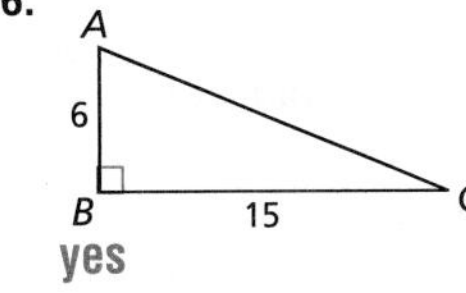

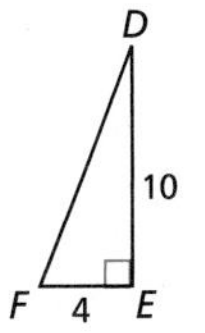

yes

Special Right Triangles

Find the value of x. Give the answer in simplest radical form.

7. J, x, 5, K, 45°, L — $5\sqrt{2}$

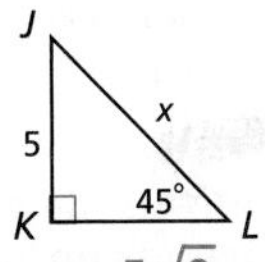

8.
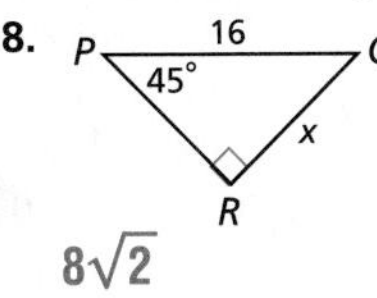

$8\sqrt{2}$

9.
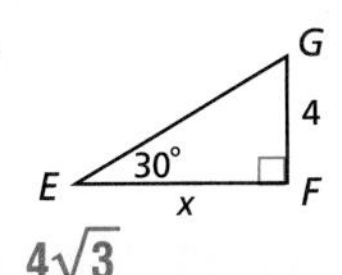

$4\sqrt{3}$

10.
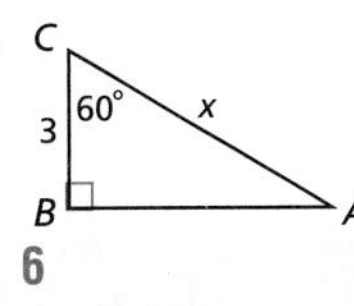

6

Solve Multi-Step Equations

Solve each equation.

11. $3(x-1)=12$ 5
12. $-2(y+5)=-1$ -4.5
13. $6=8(x-3)$ 3.75
14. $2=-1(z+4)$ -6

Solve Proportions

Solve each proportion.

15. $\frac{4}{y}=\frac{6}{18}$ 12
16. $\frac{5}{8}=\frac{x}{32}$ 20
17. $\frac{m}{9}=\frac{8}{12}$ 6
18. $\frac{y}{4}=\frac{9}{y}$ ± 6

Rounding and Estimation

Round each decimal to the indicated place value.

19. 13.118; hundredth 13.12
20. 37.91; tenth 37.9
21. 15.992; tenth 16.0
22. 173.05; whole number 173

ARE YOU READY?

Organizer

Objective: Assess students' understanding of prerequisite skills.

Prerequisite Skills

Identify Similar Figures
Special Right Triangles
Solve Multi-Step Equations
Solve Proportions
Rounding and Estimation

Assessing Prior Knowledge

INTERVENTION

Diagnose and Prescribe

Use this page to determine whether intervention is necessary or whether enrichment is appropriate.

Resources

Are You Ready? Intervention and Enrichment **Worksheets**

Are You Ready? **CD-ROM**

Are You Ready? **Online**

my.hrw.com

ARE YOU READY?

Diagnose and Prescribe

NO INTERVENE

Prerequisite Skill	*Are You Ready? Intervention,* Chapter 8 — Worksheets	CD-ROM	Online
Identify Similar Figures	Skill 34	Activity 34	Diagnose and Prescribe Online
Special Right Triangles	Skill 32	Activity 32	
Solve Multi-Step Equations	Skill 69	Activity 69	
Solve Proportions	Skill 77	Activity 77	
Rounding and Estimation	Skill 9	Activity 9	

***Are You Ready? Enrichment,* Chapter 8**

Worksheets
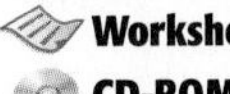
CD-ROM

Online

CHAPTER 8 Study Guide: Preview

Organizer

Objective: Help students organize the new concepts they will learn in Chapter 8.

Online Edition
Multilingual Glossary

Resources

Teacher One Stop™
PuzzleView

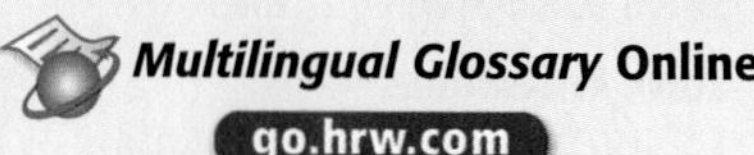

***Multilingual Glossary* Online**
go.hrw.com
KEYWORD: MG7 Glossary

Answers to *Vocabulary Connections*

Possible answers:

1. *Elevate* means "to lift." An ∠ of elevation is the ∠ of the line of sight from a horizontal line to a point above the horizontal line.
2. The term *depression* refers to something that has been lowered. An ∠ of depression is the ∠ of the line of sight from a horizontal line to a point below the horizontal line.
3. A vector is a quantity that has size, or length, like a line segment, but it also has direction.
4. A trigonometric ratio can be used to find the side lengths and ∠ measures in △.

CHAPTER 8 Study Guide: Preview

Where You've Been

Previously, you

- identified similar polygons and proved that triangles are similar.
- used ratios and proportions.
- solved real-world problems using similarity.

In This Chapter

You will study

- similarity of right triangles.
- how to use ratios and proportions to find missing side lengths in right triangles.
- how to use trigonometric ratios to solve real-world problems.

Where You're Going

You can use the skills learned in this chapter

- in your future math classes, especially Trigonometry.
- in other classes, such as Physics and Physical Education.
- outside of school to measure distances, to estimate heights, or to plan a course for hiking or kayaking.

Key Vocabulary/Vocabulario

angle of depression	ángulo de depresión
angle of elevation	ángulo de elevación
cosine	coseno
geometric mean	media geométrica
sine	seno
tangent	tangente
trigonometric ratio	razón trigonométrica
vector	vector

Vocabulary Connections

To become familiar with some of the vocabulary terms in the chapter, consider the following. You may refer to the chapter, the glossary, or a dictionary if you like.

1. The term **angle of elevation** includes the word *elevation*. What does *elevate* mean in everyday usage? What do you think an angle of elevation might be?
2. What is a *depression*? What do you think the term **angle of depression** means?
3. A **vector** is sometimes defined as "a directed line segment." How can you use this definition to understand this term?
4. The word *trigonometric* comes from the Greek word *trigonon*, which means "triangle," and the suffix *metric*, which means "measurement." Based on this, how do you think you might use a **trigonometric ratio**?

Reading Strategy: Read to Understand

As you read a lesson, read with a purpose. Lessons are about one or two specific objectives. These objectives are at the top of the first page of every lesson. Reading with the objectives in mind can help you understand the lesson.

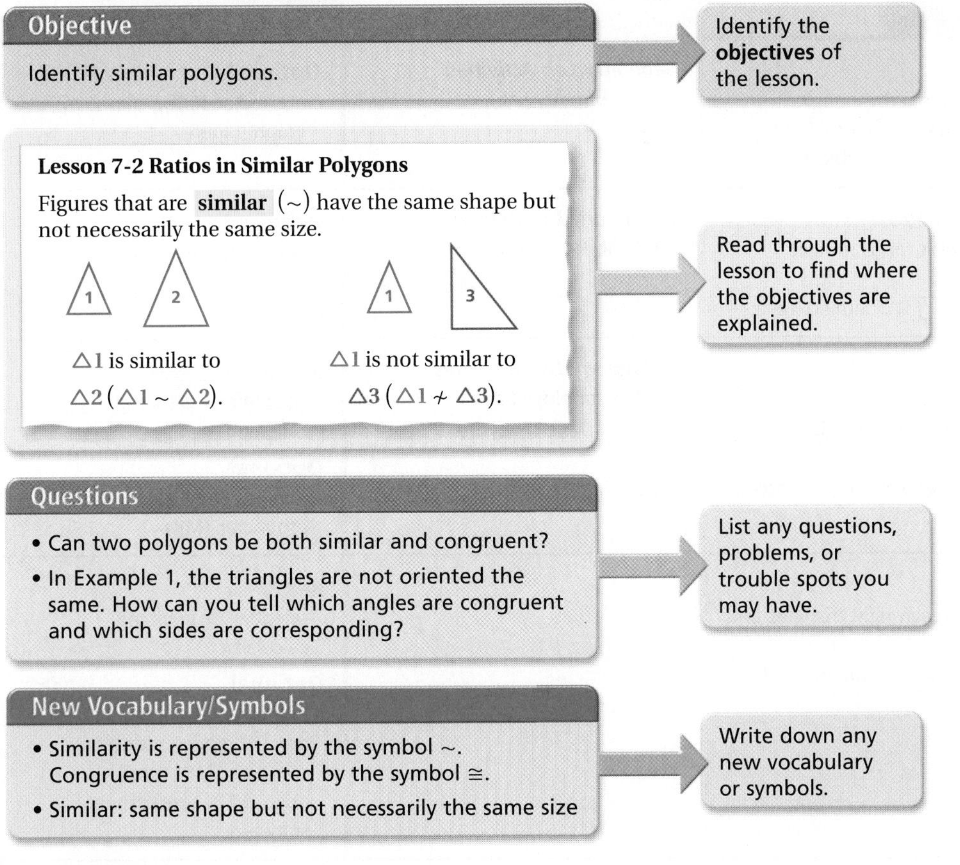

Objective
Identify similar polygons.
Identify the objectives of the lesson.
Lesson 7-2 Ratios in Similar Polygons
Figures that are similar (~) have the same shape but not necessarily the same size.
△1 is similar to △2 (△1 ~ △2).
△1 is not similar to △3 (△1 ≁ △3).
Read through the lesson to find where the objectives are explained.
Questions
• Can two polygons be both similar and congruent?
• In Example 1, the triangles are not oriented the same. How can you tell which angles are congruent and which sides are corresponding?
List any questions, problems, or trouble spots you may have.
New Vocabulary/Symbols
• Similarity is represented by the symbol ~. Congruence is represented by the symbol ≅.
• Similar: same shape but not necessarily the same size
Write down any new vocabulary or symbols.

Try This

Use Lesson 8-1 to complete each of the following.

1. What are the objectives of the lesson?
2. Identify any new vocabulary, formulas, and symbols.
3. Identify any examples that you need clarified.
4. Make a list of questions you need answered during class.

Organizer

Objective: Help students apply strategies to understand and retain key concepts.

English Language Learners

Reading Strategy: Read to Understand

Discuss Students who read the content of the lesson before class can identify which parts of the lesson might be difficult.

Extend Ask students to make a list of familiar and unfamiliar topics as they read each lesson in Chapter 8. After a lesson is presented in class, students should check that each of the unfamiliar topics they listed does not need further clarification.

Answers to *Try This*

1. Use geometric mean to find segment lengths in right triangles. Apply similarity relationships in right triangles to solve problems.
2. Possible answer: geometric mean
3. Answers will vary.
4. Possible answer: How does geometric mean differ from the mean of a set of data?

Reading Connection

***Trigonometric Delights* by Eli Maor**

This is one of the few books that treats the history of trigonometry in a manner accessible to high school students. The early chapters on the Babylonians and Egyptians will be of greatest interest.

Activity After students study the tangent ratio, have them read about Ahmes the Scribe and Problem 56 of the Rhind Papyrus. Ask students to define the *seked* of a pyramid, which is the reciprocal of the tangent of the angle between the base of the pyramid and its face.

SECTION
8A Trigonometric Ratios

One-Minute Section Planner

Lesson	Lab Resources	Materials
Lesson 8-1 Similarity in Right Triangles • Use geometric mean to find segment lengths in right triangles. • Apply similarity relationships in right triangles to solve problems. ☐ SAT-10 ☑ NAEP ☑ ACT ☑ SAT ☑ SAT Subject Tests	***Geometry Lab Activities*** 8-1 Geometry Lab	**Optional** protractor (MK), ruler (MK), graph paper
8-2 Technology Lab Explore Trigonometric Ratios • Use geometry software to explore trigonometric ratios in right triangles. ☐ SAT-10 ☑ NAEP ☐ ACT ☐ SAT ☐ SAT Subject Tests	***Technology Lab Activities*** 8-2 Lab Recording Sheet	**Required** geometry software
Lesson 8-2 Trigonometric Ratios • Find the sine, cosine, and tangent of an acute angle. • Use trigonometric ratios to find side lengths in right triangles and to solve real-world problems. ☐ SAT-10 ☑ NAEP ☐ ACT ☑ SAT ☑ SAT Subject Tests	***Technology Lab Activities*** 8-2 Technology Lab	**Required** scientific or graphing calculator **Optional** masking tape, ruler (MK), protractor (MK)
Lesson 8-3 Solving Right Triangles • Use trigonometric ratios to find angle measures in right triangles and to solve real-world problems. ☐ SAT-10 ☑ NAEP ☐ ACT ☑ SAT ☑ SAT Subject Tests		**Required** scientific or graphing calculator **Optional** highway signs showing percent grade, ruler (MK), compass (MK), straightedge (MK), spreadsheet software

MK = *Manipulatives Kit*

Math Background

Professional Learning

TRIGONOMETRY

Lesson 8-2

Trigonometry comes from the Greek words *trigonon* (triangle) and *metron* (measure). As a branch of mathematics, trigonometry dates to ancient times. Its first recorded use is attributed to the Greek astronomer Hipparchus (c. 190 B.C.E. – 120 B.C.E.), who prepared a table of values for the sine function.

The foundation of trigonometry is the observation that all right triangles with a given acute angle are similar by the AA Similarity Postulate. For the triangles shown below, this means that the ratios $\frac{AB}{AC}$, $\frac{JK}{JL}$, and $\frac{PQ}{PR}$ are all equal.

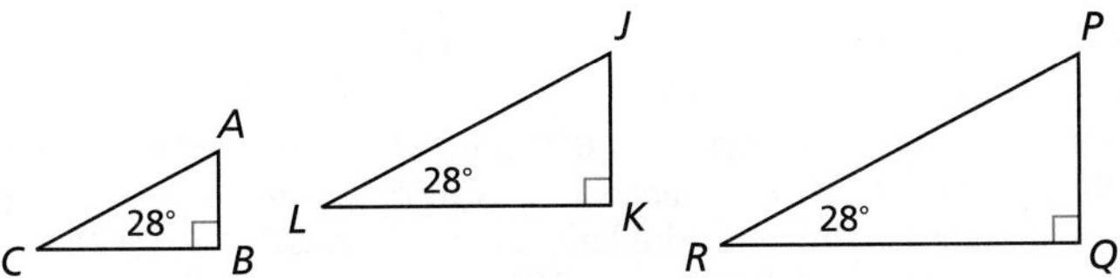

Thus, given a 28° angle in a right triangle, the ratio of the length of the leg opposite the angle to the length of the hypotenuse is well defined. That is, the ratio does not depend upon the size of the triangle. This ratio is defined to be the *sine* of 28°, written sin 28°.

Students sometimes regard trigonometric ratios as random numbers that are mysteriously assigned to angle measures. They should recognize that they can estimate trigonometric ratios by using basic drawing tools or geometry software. For example, it may be worthwhile to have students use a protractor to draw right triangles with 28° angles as shown above and then use a ruler to measure the side lengths. Calculating the ratios $\frac{AB}{AC}$, $\frac{JK}{JL}$, and $\frac{PQ}{PR}$ shows that the three ratios are all equal to approximately 0.47, which is the value of sin 28°. This is the same value that can be found in a trigonometric table or by using a calculator.

Other trigonometric ratios are defined by considering the ratios of other combinations of side lengths. The *cosine* of an angle is the ratio of the length of the leg adjacent to the angle to the length of the hypotenuse. The *tangent* of an angle is the ratio of the length of the leg opposite the angle to the length of the leg adjacent to the angle. Again, students should understand that these ratios can be approximated by drawing a right triangle that contains the given angle, measuring the side lengths, and calculating the desired ratio.

SOLVING RIGHT TRIANGLES

Lesson 8-3

Solving a right triangle is the process of using given measures in the triangle to find unknown side lengths or angle measures. Note that a right triangle is uniquely determined given either of the following sets of information.

- The measure of an acute angle and the length of any side
- The length of any two sides

In the first case, it is possible to show that the triangle is uniquely determined by ASA Congruence. In the second case, the Pythagorean Theorem may be used to find the third side length and the triangle is uniquely determined by SSS Congruence. In either case, it is possible to use trigonometry to determine all of the unknown side lengths and angle measures.

In order to solve a right triangle, it is sometimes necessary to know the measure of an angle given the value of the angle's sine, cosine, or tangent. This is possible because, for angle measures between 0° and 90°, the trigonometric ratios are one-to-one functions. For example, given that the cosine of an angle is 0.3907, the fact that the cosine is a one-to-one function means that there is exactly one angle whose measure is between 0° and 90° that has this cosine. This angle measure is written as $\cos^{-1}(0.3907)$, and a calculator can be used to determine that the angle measures 67°.

When introducing the notation for inverse trigonometric functions, students must understand the meaning of the exponent −1. In the context of functions, $f^{-1}(x)$ represents the inverse of the function $f(x)$, rather than a reciprocal.

8-1 Organizer

Pacing: Traditional 1 day
Block $\frac{1}{2}$ day

Objectives: Use geometric mean to find segment lengths in right triangles.

Apply similarity relationships in right triangles to solve problems.

Geometry Lab
In *Geometry Lab Activities*

Online Edition
Tutorial Videos

Countdown Week 17

Power Presentations with PowerPoint®

Warm Up

1. Write a similarity statement comparing the two triangles.

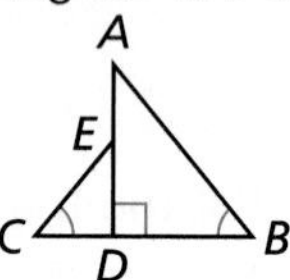

$\triangle ADB \sim \triangle EDC$

Simplify.

2. $\sqrt{72}$ $6\sqrt{2}$ 3. $\sqrt{27}$ $3\sqrt{3}$

Solve each equation.

4. $\frac{3}{x} = \frac{5}{8}$ $\frac{24}{5}$ 5. $2x^2 = 50$ ± 5

Also available on transparency

Q: Why was the bluebird suspicious of his neighbor's gift?

A: Adjacent (a jay sent) it

State Resources

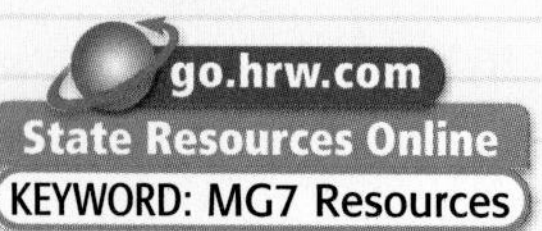

8-1 Similarity in Right Triangles

Objectives
Use geometric mean to find segment lengths in right triangles.

Apply similarity relationships in right triangles to solve problems.

Vocabulary
geometric mean

Why learn this?
You can use similarity relationships in right triangles to find the height of Big Tex.

Twisted Texas/Wesley Treat

Big Tex debuted as the official symbol of the State Fair of Texas in 1952. This 6000-pound cowboy wears size 70 boots and a 75-gallon hat. In this lesson, you will learn how to use right triangle relationships to find Big Tex's height.

In a right triangle, an altitude drawn from the vertex of the right angle to the hypotenuse forms two right triangles.

Know it! Note

Theorem 8-1-1

The altitude to the hypotenuse of a right triangle forms two triangles that are similar to each other and to the original triangle.

$\triangle ABC \sim \triangle ACD \sim \triangle CBD$

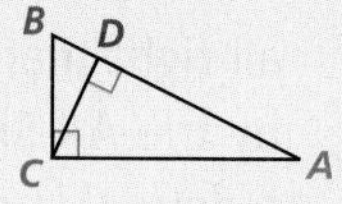

PROOF **Theorem 8-1-1**

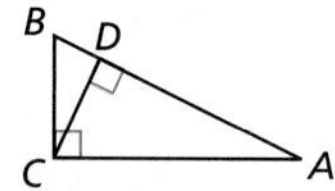

Given: $\triangle ABC$ is a right triangle with altitude $\overline{CD}$.
Prove: $\triangle ABC \sim \triangle ACD \sim \triangle CBD$

Proof: The right angles in $\triangle ABC$, $\triangle ACD$, and $\triangle CBD$ are all congruent. By the Reflexive Property of Congruence, $\angle A \cong \angle A$. Therefore $\triangle ABC \sim \triangle ACD$ by the AA Similarity Theorem. Similarly, $\angle B \cong \angle B$, so $\triangle ABC \sim \triangle CBD$. By the Transitive Property of Similarity, $\triangle ABC \sim \triangle ACD \sim \triangle CBD$.

EXAMPLE 1 **Identifying Similar Right Triangles**

Write a similarity statement comparing the three triangles.

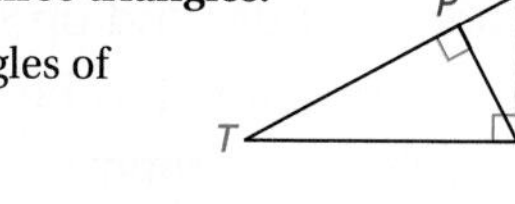

Sketch the three right triangles with the angles of the triangles in corresponding positions.

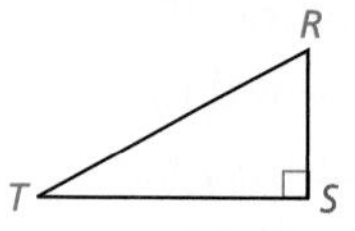

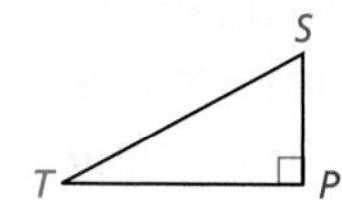

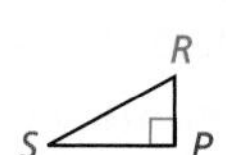

By Theorem 8-1-1, $\triangle RST \sim \triangle SPT \sim \triangle RPS$.

1. Write a similarity statement comparing the three triangles.
$\triangle LJK \sim \triangle JMK \sim \triangle LMJ$

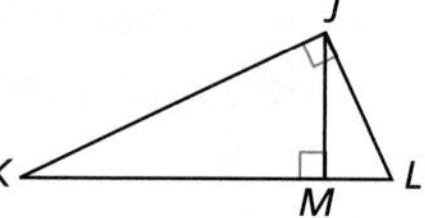

1 Introduce

8-1 Similarity in Right Triangles

The *geometric mean* of two positive numbers is the positive square root of their product. The geometric mean of positive numbers a and b is $\sqrt{ab}$.

1. Complete the table by finding the geometric mean of each pair of numbers. Write each geometric mean in simplified radical form, rounded to the nearest tenth.

a	b	Geometric Mean	
		Simplified Radical Form	Rounded to the Nearest Tenth
2	3		
6	10		
4	9		
2	32		
12	18		
50	60		

2. How does the geometric mean of a and b compare to a and b? Assuming that $a < b$, do you think the geometric mean can ever be less than a or greater than b?

THINK AND DISCUSS

3. **Explain** why x is the geometric mean of a and b in the proportion $\frac{a}{x} = \frac{x}{b}$.

Motivate

Ask students to draw a right triangle and then draw the altitude to the hypotenuse. Have them measure the altitude and the lengths of the two segments of the hypotenuse. Explain to students that they will learn how to use similarity relationships to relate the length of the altitude to the product of the segment lengths.

Explorations and answers are provided in *Alternate Openers: Explorations Transparencies.*

Consider the proportion $\frac{a}{x} = \frac{x}{b}$. In this case, the means of the proportion are the same number, and that number is the *geometric mean* of the extremes. The **geometric mean** of two positive numbers is the positive square root of their product. So the geometric mean of a and b is the positive number x such that $x = \sqrt{ab}$, or $x^2 = ab$.

EXAMPLE 2 Finding Geometric Means

Find the geometric mean of each pair of numbers. If necessary, give the answer in simplest radical form.

A **4 and 9**

Let x be the geometric mean.

$x^2 = (4)(9) = 36$ *Def. of geometric mean*

$x = 6$ *Find the positive square root.*

B **6 and 15**

Let x be the geometric mean.

$x^2 = (6)(15) = 90$ *Def. of geometric mean*

$x = \sqrt{90} = 3\sqrt{10}$ *Find the positive square root.*

Find the geometric mean of each pair of numbers. If necessary, give the answer in simplest radical form.

2a. 2 and 8 **4**
2b. 10 and 30 $10\sqrt{3}$
2c. 8 and 9 $6\sqrt{2}$

You can use Theorem 8-1-1 to write proportions comparing the side lengths of the triangles formed by the altitude to the hypotenuse of a right triangle. All the relationships in red involve geometric means.

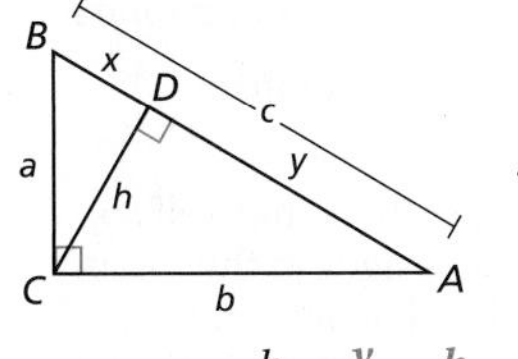

~

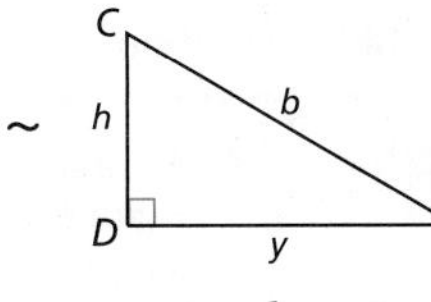

~

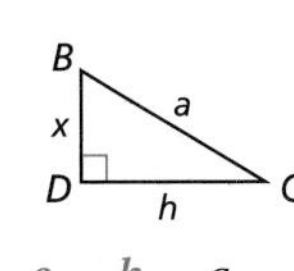

$\frac{b}{a} = \frac{y}{h} = \frac{h}{x}$ $\frac{c}{a} = \frac{b}{h} = \frac{a}{x}$ $\frac{c}{b} = \frac{b}{y} = \frac{a}{h}$

Corollaries Geometric Means

	COROLLARY	EXAMPLE	DIAGRAM
8-1-2	The length of the altitude to the hypotenuse of a right triangle is the geometric mean of the lengths of the two segments of the hypotenuse.	$h^2 = xy$	x, c, y, a, h, b
8-1-3	The length of a leg of a right triangle is the geometric mean of the lengths of the hypotenuse and the segment of the hypotenuse adjacent to that leg.	$a^2 = xc$ $b^2 = yc$	

2 Teach

Guided Instruction

Discuss how the altitude to the hypotenuse of a right triangle forms two triangles that are similar to each other and to the original triangle. Before introducing the concept of geometric mean, remind students that in a proportion, the product of the means equals the product of the extremes. Though there are two solutions to a proportion with equal means, point out that only the positive solution can represent the length of a segment. Go through the steps for the derivation of the corollaries on page 519.

Reaching All Learners

Through Concrete Manipulatives

Have students cut a 15-20-25 unit right triangle out of a sheet of graph paper. Ask them to draw the altitude to the hypotenuse, forming a 12-16-20 unit right triangle and a 9-12-15 unit right triangle. Then have students use the side lengths in these triangles to verify the relationships in the Geometric Mean Corollaries as you discuss their derivation on page 519.

COMMON ERROR ALERT

In **Example 2,** students may incorrectly solve the equation $x^2 = a$ by taking half of both sides instead of the positive square root of both sides. Review the meaning of x^2 and suggest that students check their answers using a proportion.

Power Presentations with PowerPoint®

Additional Examples

Example 1

Write a similarity statement comparing the three triangles.

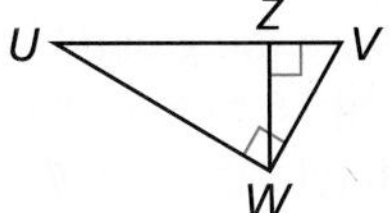

$\triangle UVW \sim \triangle UWZ \sim \triangle WVZ$

Example 2

Find the geometric mean of each pair of numbers. If necessary, give the answer in simplest radical form.

A. 4 and 25 10

B. 5 and 30 $5\sqrt{6}$

INTERVENTION

Questioning Strategies

EXAMPLE 1

- How do you determine the corresponding positions for the three triangles?

EXAMPLE 2

- How is the geometric mean of two numbers, a and b, related to a proportion involving a and b?
- Can a geometric mean ever be negative?

Math Background In mathematics, the word *mean* describes a relationship between numbers. Remind students that the *arithmetic mean* of two numbers is the average of the numbers. This is different from the *geometric mean* of two numbers. In later math courses, students may also study *harmonic means*.

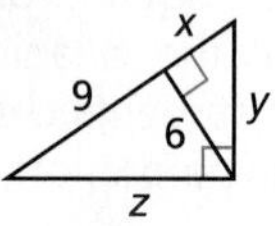

Power Presentations with PowerPoint®

Additional Examples

Example 3

Find x, y and z.

$x = 4$; $y = 2\sqrt{13}$; $z = 3\sqrt{13}$

Example 4

To estimate the height of a Douglas fir, Jan positions herself so that her lines of sight to the top and bottom of the tree form a 90° angle. Her eyes are about 1.6 m above the ground, and she is standing 7.8 m from the tree. What is the height of the tree to the nearest meter? 40 m

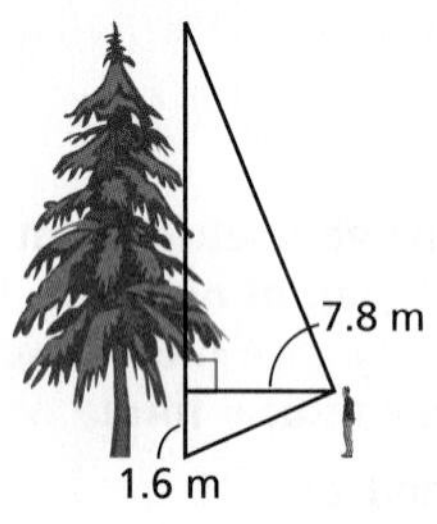

INTERVENTION

Questioning Strategies

EXAMPLE 3

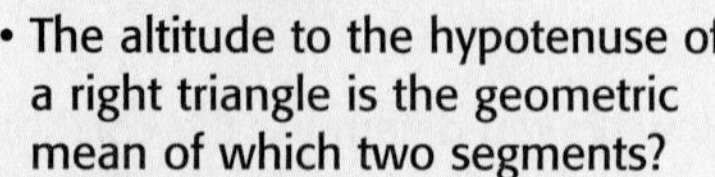

- The altitude to the hypotenuse of a right triangle is the geometric mean of which two segments?

EXAMPLE 4

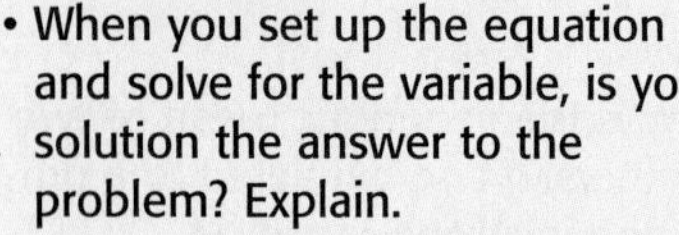

- When you set up the equation and solve for the variable, is your solution the answer to the problem? Explain.

EXAMPLE 3 Finding Side Lengths in Right Triangles

Helpful Hint

Once you've found the unknown side lengths, you can use the Pythagorean Theorem to check your answers.

Find x, y, and z.

$x^2 = (2)(10) = 20$	*x is the geometric mean of 2 and 10.*
$x = \sqrt{20} = 2\sqrt{5}$	*Find the positive square root.*
$y^2 = (12)(10) = 120$	*y is the geometric mean of 12 and 10.*
$y = \sqrt{120} = 2\sqrt{30}$	*Find the positive square root.*
$z^2 = (12)(2) = 24$	*z is the geometric mean of 12 and 2.*
$z = \sqrt{24} = 2\sqrt{6}$	*Find the positive square root.*

CHECK IT OUT! **3.** Find u, v, and w. **27; $3\sqrt{10}$; $9\sqrt{10}$**

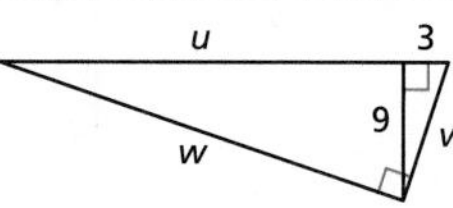

EXAMPLE 4 *Measurement Application*

To estimate the height of Big Tex at the State Fair of Texas, Michael steps away from the statue until his line of sight to the top of the statue and his line of sight to the bottom of the statue form a 90° angle. His eyes are 5 ft above the ground, and he is standing 15 ft 3 in. from Big Tex. How tall is Big Tex to the nearest foot?

Not drawn to scale

Let x be the height of Big Tex above eye level.

15 ft 3 in. = 15.25 ft	*Convert 3 in. to 0.25 ft.*
$(15.25)^2 = 5x$	*15.25 is the geometric mean of 5 and x.*
$x = 46.5125 \approx 47$	*Solve for x and round.*

Big Tex is about 47 + 5, or 52 ft tall.

CHECK IT OUT! **4.** A surveyor positions himself so that his line of sight to the top of a cliff and his line of sight to the bottom form a right angle as shown. What is the height of the cliff to the nearest foot? **148 ft**

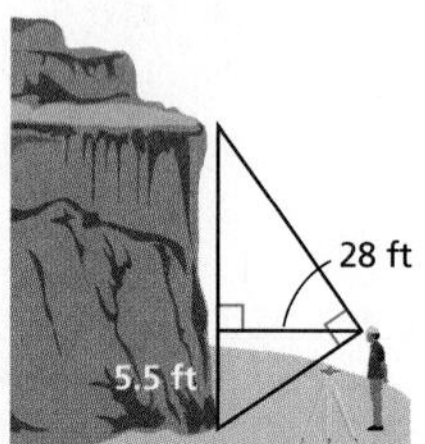

THINK AND DISCUSS

1. Explain how to find the geometric mean of 7 and 21.

2. GET ORGANIZED Copy and complete the graphic organizer. Label the right triangle and draw the altitude to the hypotenuse. In each box, write a proportion in which the given segment is a geometric mean.

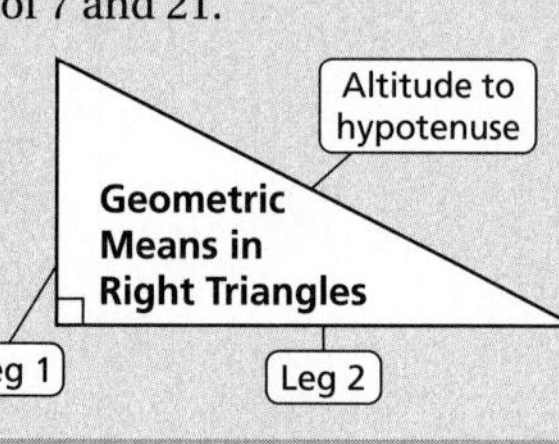

3 Close

Summarize

When the altitude to the hypotenuse of a right triangle is drawn, the following relationships are true:

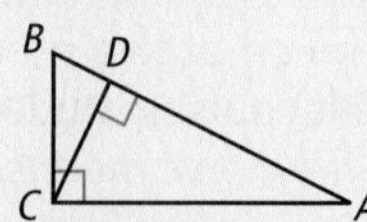

- $\triangle ABC \sim \triangle ACD \sim \triangle CBD$
- $(CD)^2 = (BD)(AD)$
- $(BC)^2 = (BD)(AB)$
- $(AC)^2 = (AD)(AB)$

ONGOING ASSESSMENT and INTERVENTION

***Diagnose Before* the Lesson**
8-1 Warm Up, TE p. 518

***Monitor During* the Lesson**
Check It Out! Exercises, SE pp. 518–520
Questioning Strategies, TE pp. 519–520

***Assess After* the Lesson**
8-1 Lesson Quiz, TE p. 523
Alternative Assessment, TE p. 523

Answers to *Think and Discuss*

1. Set up the proportion $\frac{7}{x} = \frac{x}{21}$, and solve for x. $x = 7\sqrt{3}$
2. See p. A7.

8-1 Exercises

go.hrw.com
Homework Help Online
KEYWORD: MG7 8-1
Parent Resources Online
KEYWORD: MG7 Parent

GUIDED PRACTICE

1. **Vocabulary** In the proportion $\frac{2}{8} = \frac{8}{32}$, which number is the *geometric mean* of the other two numbers? 8 is the geometric mean of 2 and 32.

SEE EXAMPLE 1 p. 518

Write a similarity statement comparing the three triangles in each diagram.

2. 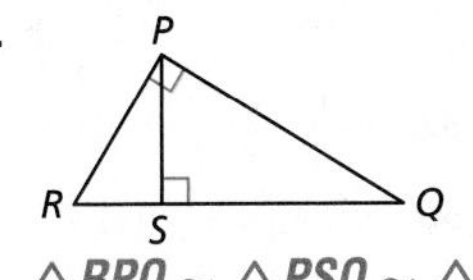

$\triangle RPQ \sim \triangle PSQ \sim \triangle RSP$

3. 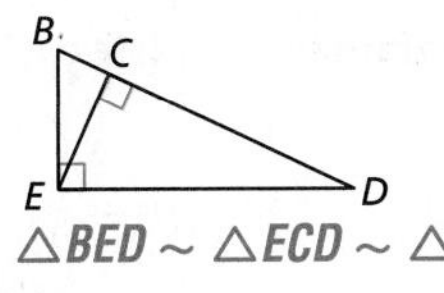

$\triangle BED \sim \triangle ECD \sim \triangle BCE$

4. 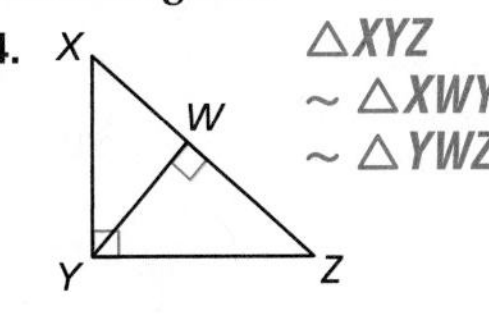

$\triangle XYZ \sim \triangle XWY \sim \triangle YWZ$

SEE EXAMPLE 2 p. 519

Find the geometric mean of each pair of numbers. If necessary, give the answer in simplest radical form.

5. 2 and 50 10
6. 4 and 16 8
7. $\frac{1}{2}$ and 8 2
8. 9 and 12 $6\sqrt{3}$
9. 16 and 25 20
10. 7 and 11 $\sqrt{77}$

SEE EXAMPLE 3 p. 520

Find x, y, and z.

11. 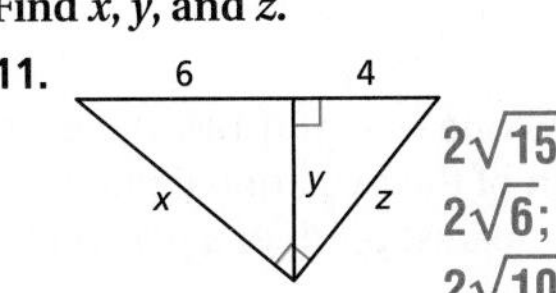

$2\sqrt{15}$; $2\sqrt{6}$; $2\sqrt{10}$

12. 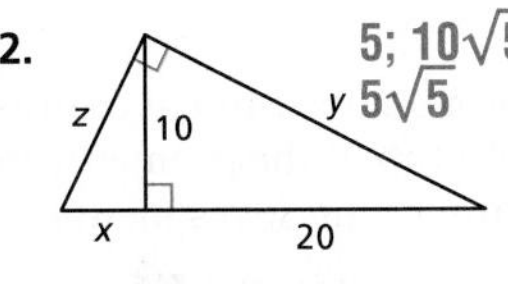

5; $10\sqrt{5}$; $5\sqrt{5}$

13. 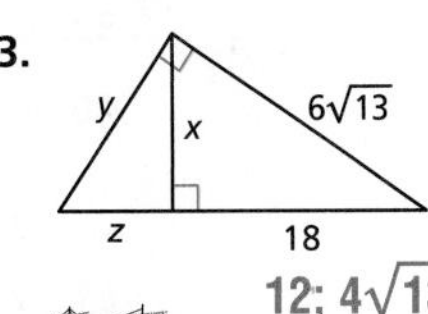

12; $4\sqrt{13}$; 8

SEE EXAMPLE 4 p. 520

14. **Measurement** To estimate the length of the USS *Constitution* in Boston harbor, a student locates points T and U as shown. What is RS to the nearest tenth? 62.0 m

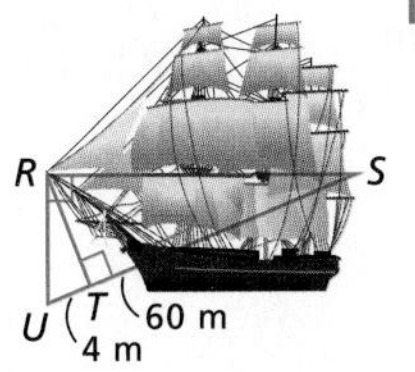

PRACTICE AND PROBLEM SOLVING

Independent Practice	
For Exercises	See Example
15–17	1
18–23	2
24–26	3
27	4

Extra Practice
Skills Practice p. S18
Application Practice p. S35

Write a similarity statement comparing the three triangles in each diagram.

15. 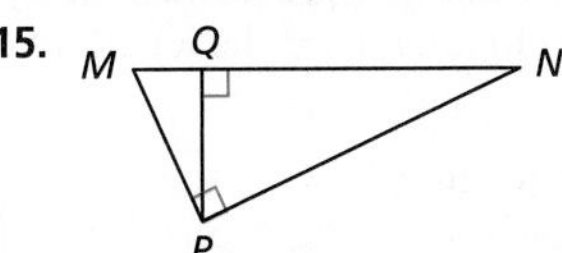

$\triangle MPN \sim \triangle PQN \sim \triangle MQP$

16. 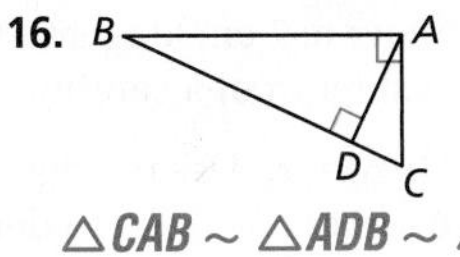

$\triangle CAB \sim \triangle ADB \sim \triangle CDA$

17. 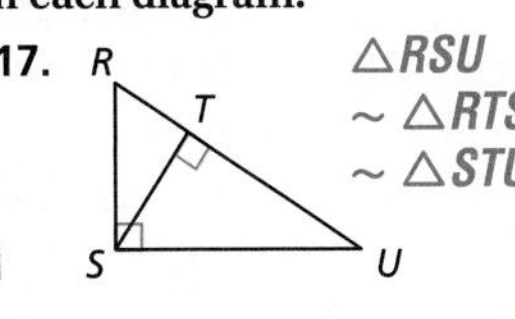

$\triangle RSU \sim \triangle RTS \sim \triangle STU$

Find the geometric mean of each pair of numbers. If necessary, give the answer in simplest radical form.

18. 5 and 45 15
19. 3 and 15 $3\sqrt{5}$
20. 5 and 8 $2\sqrt{10}$
21. $\frac{1}{4}$ and 80 $2\sqrt{5}$
22. 1.5 and 12 $3\sqrt{2}$
23. $\frac{2}{3}$ and $\frac{27}{40}$ $\frac{3\sqrt{5}}{10}$

Find x, y, and z.

24. 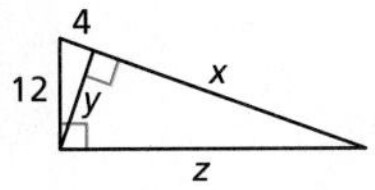 4, 12, x, y, z
32; $8\sqrt{2}$; $24\sqrt{2}$

25. 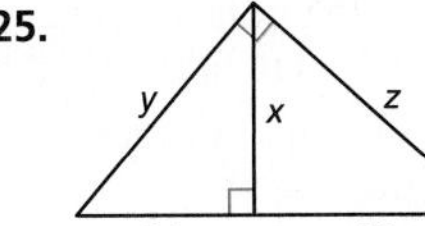

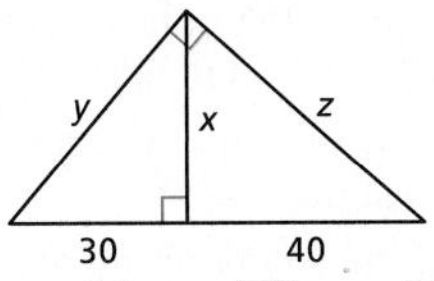

$20\sqrt{3}$; $10\sqrt{21}$; $20\sqrt{7}$

26. 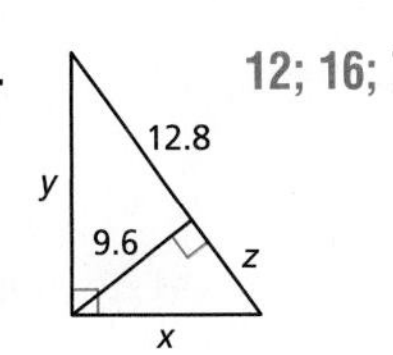

12; 16; 7.2

8-1 Exercises

Assignment Guide

Assign *Guided Practice* exercises as necessary.

If you finished Examples 1–2
Basic 15–23, 28, 29
Average 15–23, 28, 29, 45
Advanced 15–23, 28, 29, 45, 46

If you finished Examples 1–4
Basic 15–37, 41, 44, 47–49, 54–62
Average 15–27, 30–38 even, 39–50, 54–62
Advanced 15–27, 28–40 even, 42–62

Homework Quick Check
Quickly check key concepts.
Exercises: 16, 18, 24, 27, 36

Teaching Tip

Visual In Exercises **2–4** and **15–17,** some students may have difficulty visualizing the corresponding angles in the overlapping triangles. Suggest that they redraw the diagram to separate the three triangles.

Inclusion Remind students not to rely on the given diagram for scale in **Exercises 14** and **27.**

State Resources

Algebra Before students begin **Exercise 29,** you may want to review the properties of exponents. That is, $(a\sqrt{x})^2 = a^2(\sqrt{x})^2 = a^2x$, for $x > 0$.

Number Sense If the average rate of return in **Exercise 40** were the arithmetic mean, it would be 6.5%. Unfortunately for the consumer, the geometric mean of two numbers is always smaller than the arithmetic mean.

Exercise 44 involves using the geometric mean corollaries to find the lengths of a guy wire anchor. This exercise prepares students for the Multi-Step Test Prep on page 542.

Answers

45. The area of the rect. is ab, and the area of the square is s^2. It is given that $s^2 = ab$, so s is the geometric mean of a and b.
46. Let z be the geometric mean of x and y, where $x = a^2$ and $y = b^2$. So $z = \sqrt{a^2b^2} = ab$, which is a whole number.
52. Let $AD = DC = a$. By Corollary 8-1-3, $AB^2 = (a)(2a) = 2a^2$, and $BC^2 = (a)(2a) = 2a^2$. So $AB = BC = a\sqrt{2}$. Therefore $\triangle ABC$ is isosceles, so it is a 45°-45°-90° triangle.

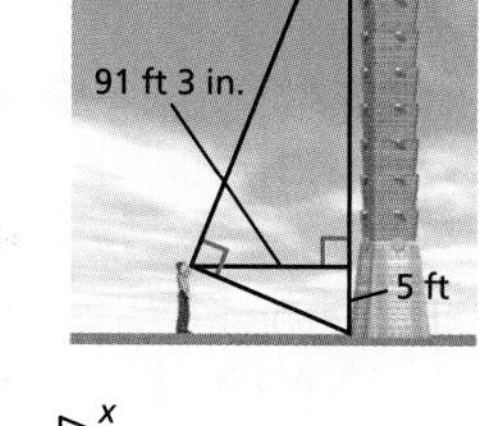

27. **Measurement** To estimate the height of the Taipei 101 tower, Andrew stands so that his lines of sight to the top and bottom of the tower form a 90° angle. What is the height of the tower to the nearest foot? **1670 ft**
28. The geometric mean of two numbers is 8. One of the numbers is 2. Find the other number. **32**
29. The geometric mean of two numbers is $2\sqrt{5}$. One of the numbers is 6. Find the other number. $\mathbf{\frac{10}{3}}$**, or** $\mathbf{3\frac{1}{3}}$

Use the diagram to complete each equation.

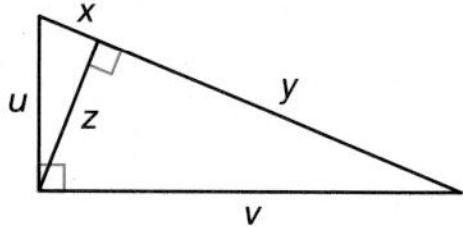

30. $\frac{x}{z} = \frac{z}{?}$ **y**
31. $\frac{?}{u} = \frac{u}{x + y}$ **x + y**
32. $\frac{x + y}{v} = \frac{v}{?}$ **y**
33. $\frac{y}{?} = \frac{z}{x}$ **z**
34. $(?)^2 = y(x + y)$ **v**
35. $u^2 = (x + y)(?)$ **x**

Give each answer in simplest radical form.

36. $AD = 12$, and $CD = 8$. Find BD. $\mathbf{4\sqrt{6}}$
37. $AC = 16$, and $CD = 5$. Find BC. $\mathbf{4\sqrt{5}}$
38. $AD = CD = \sqrt{2}$. Find BD. $\mathbf{\sqrt{2}}$
39. $BC = \sqrt{5}$, and $AC = \sqrt{10}$. Find CD. $\mathbf{\frac{\sqrt{10}}{2}}$
40. **Finance** An investment returns 3% one year and 10% the next year. The average rate of return is the geometric mean of the two annual rates. What is the average rate of return for this investment to the nearest tenth of a percent? **5.5%**

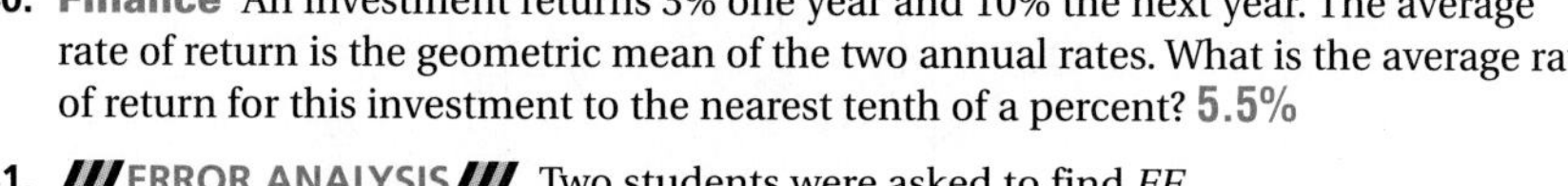

41. **ERROR ANALYSIS** Two students were asked to find EF. Which solution is incorrect? Explain the error.

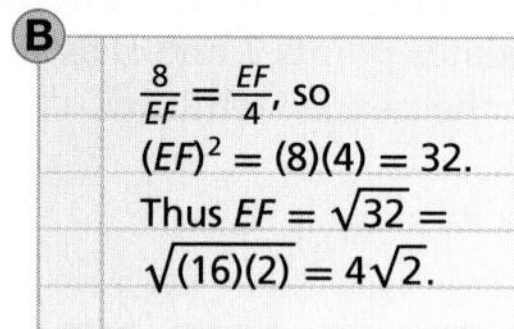

A
$\frac{12}{EF} = \frac{EF}{8}$, so
$(EF)^2 = (12)(8) = 96.$
Thus $EF = \sqrt{96} = \sqrt{(16)(6)} = 4\sqrt{6}.$

B
$\frac{8}{EF} = \frac{EF}{4}$, so
$(EF)^2 = (8)(4) = 32.$
Thus $EF = \sqrt{32} = \sqrt{(16)(2)} = 4\sqrt{2}.$

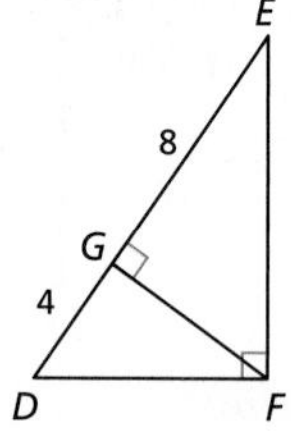

41. B; the proportion should be $\frac{12}{EF} = \frac{EF}{8}$.

42. The altitude to the hypotenuse of a right triangle divides the hypotenuse into segments that are 2 cm long and 5 cm long. Find the length of the altitude to the nearest tenth of a centimeter. **3.2 cm**
43. **Critical Thinking** Use the figure to show how Corollary 8-1-3 can be used to derive the Pythagorean Theorem. (*Hint:* Use the corollary to write expressions for a^2 and b^2. Then add the expressions.)

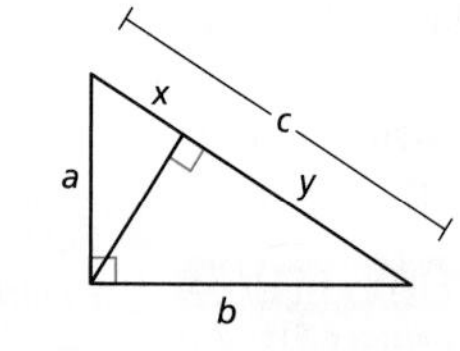

43. By Corollary 8-1-3, $a^2 = x(x + y)$, and $b^2 = y(x + y)$. So $a^2 + b^2 = x(x + y) + y(x + y)$. By the Distrib. Prop., this expression simplifies to $(x + y)(x + y) = (x + y)^2 = c^2$. So $a^2 + b^2 = c^2$.

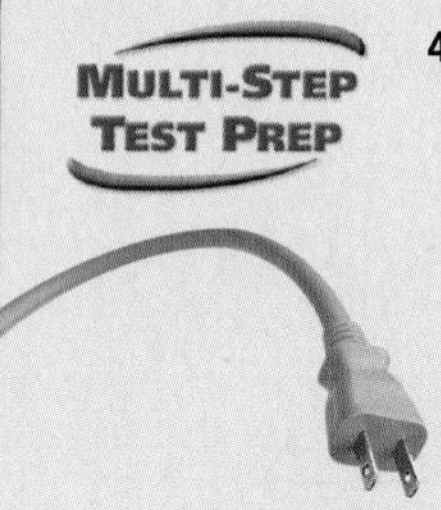

MULTI-STEP TEST PREP

44. This problem will prepare you for the Multi-Step Test Prep on page 542.

    Before installing a utility pole, a crew must first dig a hole and install the anchor for the guy wire that supports the pole. In the diagram, $\overline{SW} \perp \overline{RT}$, $\overline{RW} \perp \overline{WT}$, $RS = 4$ ft, and $ST = 3$ ft.

    a. Find the depth of the anchor $\overline{SW}$ to the nearest inch. **3 ft 6 in.**

    b. Find the length of the rod $\overline{RW}$ to the nearest inch. **5 ft 3 in.**

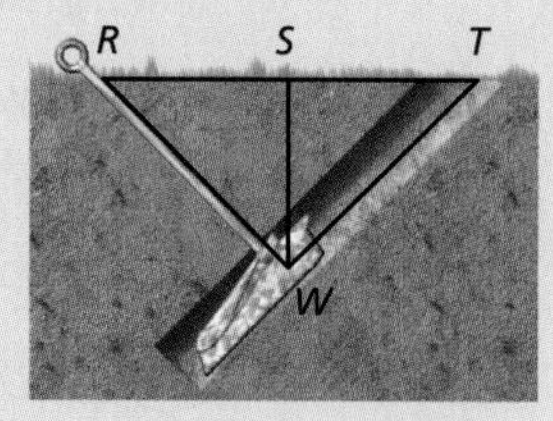

8-1 PRACTICE A

8-1 PRACTICE C

8-1 PRACTICE B

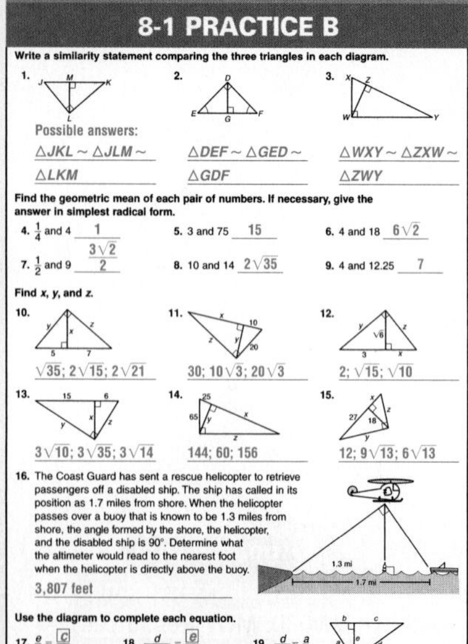

Write a similarity statement comparing the three triangles in each diagram.

Possible answers:
1. $\triangle JKL \sim \triangle JLM \sim \triangle LKM$
2. $\triangle DEF \sim \triangle GED \sim \triangle GDF$
3. $\triangle WXY \sim \triangle ZXW \sim \triangle ZWY$

Find the geometric mean of each pair of numbers. If necessary, give the answer in simplest radical form.

4. $\frac{1}{4}$ and 4 — 1
5. 3 and 75 — 15
6. 4 and 18 — $6\sqrt{2}$
7. $\frac{1}{2}$ and 9 — $\frac{3\sqrt{2}}{2}$
8. 10 and 14 — $2\sqrt{35}$
9. 4 and 12.25 — 7

Find x, y, and z.

10. $\sqrt{35}$; $2\sqrt{15}$; $2\sqrt{21}$
11. 30; $10\sqrt{3}$; $20\sqrt{3}$
12. 2; $\sqrt{15}$; $\sqrt{10}$
13. $3\sqrt{10}$; $3\sqrt{35}$; $3\sqrt{14}$
14. 144; 60; 156
15. 12; $9\sqrt{13}$; $6\sqrt{13}$

16. The Coast Guard has sent a rescue helicopter to retrieve passengers off a disabled ship. The ship has called in its position as 1.7 miles from shore. When the helicopter passes over a buoy that is known to be 1.3 miles from shore, the angle formed by the shore, the helicopter, and the disabled ship is 90°. Determine what the altimeter would read to the nearest foot when the helicopter is directly above the buoy. 3,807 feet

Use the diagram to complete each equation.

17. $\frac{a}{b} = \frac{c}{e}$
18. $\frac{d}{b + c} = \frac{e}{a}$
19. $\frac{d}{c} = \frac{a}{e}$

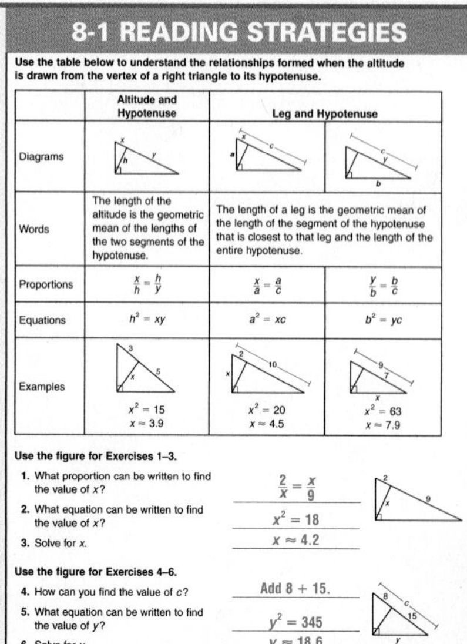

8-1 READING STRATEGIES

Use the table below to understand the relationships formed when the altitude is drawn from the vertex of a right triangle to its hypotenuse.

	Altitude and Hypotenuse	Leg and Hypotenuse	
Diagrams			
Words	The length of the altitude is the geometric mean of the lengths of the two segments of the hypotenuse.	The length of a leg is the geometric mean of the length of the segment of the hypotenuse that is closest to that leg and the length of the entire hypotenuse.	
Proportions	$\frac{x}{h} = \frac{h}{y}$	$\frac{x}{a} = \frac{a}{c}$	$\frac{y}{b} = \frac{b}{c}$
Equations	$h^2 = xy$	$a^2 = xc$	$b^2 = yc$
Examples	$x^2 = 15$, $x \approx 3.9$	$x^2 = 20$, $x \approx 4.5$	$x^2 = 63$, $x \approx 7.9$

Use the figure for Exercises 1–3.

1. What proportion can be written to find the value of x? $\frac{2}{x} = \frac{x}{9}$
2. What equation can be written to find the value of x? $x^2 = 18$
3. Solve for x. $x \approx 4.2$

Use the figure for Exercises 4–6.

4. How can you find the value of c? Add 8 + 15.
5. What equation can be written to find the value of y? $y^2 = 345$
6. Solve for y. $y \approx 18.6$

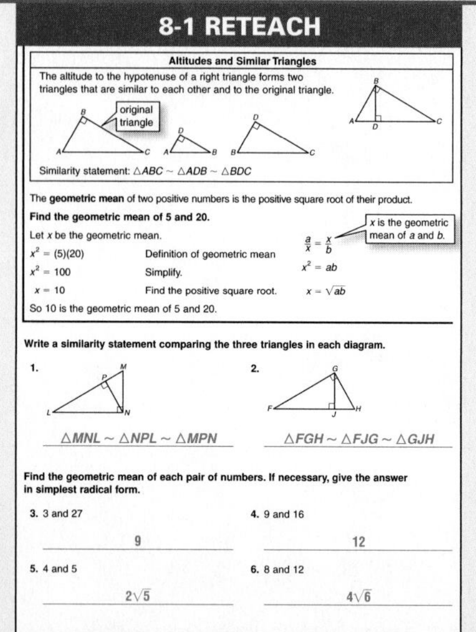

8-1 RETEACH

Altitudes and Similar Triangles

The altitude to the hypotenuse of a right triangle forms two triangles that are similar to each other and to the original triangle.

Similarity statement: $\triangle ABC \sim \triangle ADB \sim \triangle BDC$

The **geometric mean** of two positive numbers is the positive square root of their product.

Find the geometric mean of 5 and 20.

Let x be the geometric mean.

$x^2 = (5)(20)$ — Definition of geometric mean
$x^2 = 100$ — Simplify.
$x = 10$ — Find the positive square root.

So 10 is the geometric mean of 5 and 20.

$\frac{a}{x} = \frac{x}{b}$, $x^2 = ab$, $x = \sqrt{ab}$ — x is the geometric mean of a and b.

Write a similarity statement comparing the three triangles in each diagram.

1. $\triangle MNL \sim \triangle NPL \sim \triangle MPN$
2. $\triangle FGH \sim \triangle FJG \sim \triangle GJH$

Find the geometric mean of each pair of numbers. If necessary, give the answer in simplest radical form.

3. 3 and 27 — 9
4. 9 and 16 — 12
5. 4 and 5 — $2\sqrt{5}$
6. 8 and 12 — $4\sqrt{6}$

45. **Write About It** Suppose the rectangle and square have the same area. Explain why s must be the geometric mean of a and b.

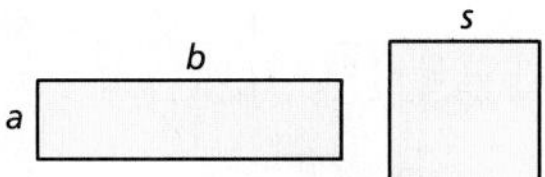

46. **Write About It** Explain why the geometric mean of two perfect squares must be a whole number.

TEST PREP

47. Lee is building a skateboard ramp based on the plan shown. Which is closest to the length of the ramp from point X to point Y?

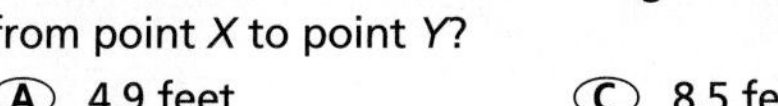
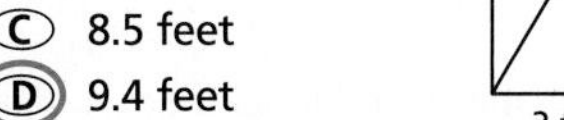

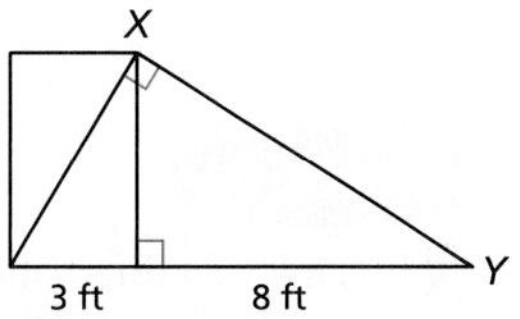

Ⓐ 4.9 feet　Ⓒ 8.5 feet
Ⓑ 5.7 feet　Ⓓ 9.4 feet (circled)

48. What is the area of $\triangle ABC$?

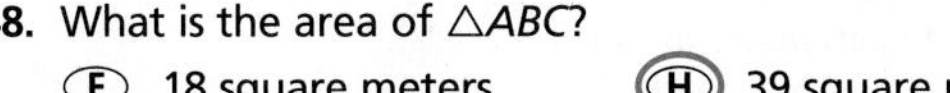

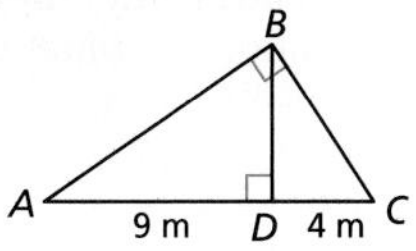

Ⓕ 18 square meters　Ⓗ 39 square meters (circled)
Ⓖ 36 square meters　Ⓙ 78 square meters

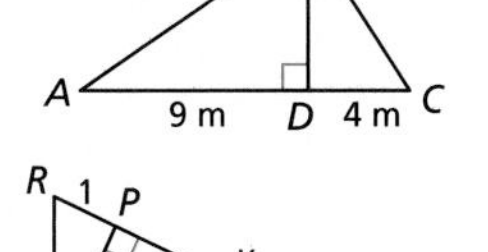

49. Which expression represents the length of $\overline{RS}$?

Ⓐ $\sqrt{y+1}$ (circled)　Ⓒ y^2
Ⓑ $\sqrt{y}$　Ⓓ $y(y+1)$

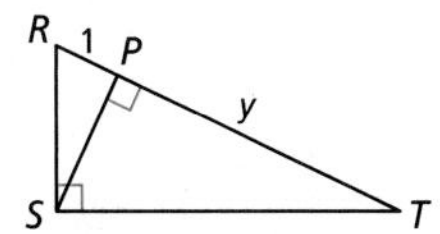

CHALLENGE AND EXTEND

50. **Algebra** An 8-inch-long altitude of a right triangle divides the hypotenuse into two segments. One segment is 4 times as long as the other. What are the lengths of the segments of the hypotenuse? **4 in.; 16 in.**

51. Use similarity in right triangles to find x, y, and z. **$7; \sqrt{35}; 2\sqrt{15}$**

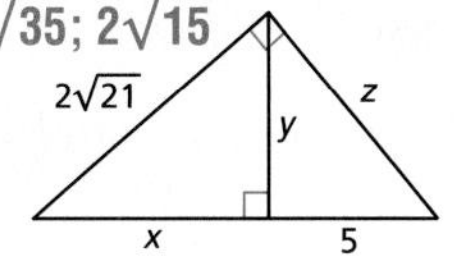

52. Prove the following. If the altitude to the hypotenuse of a right triangle bisects the hypotenuse, then the triangle is a 45°-45°-90° right triangle.

53. **Multi-Step** Find AC and AB to the nearest hundredth. **$AC \approx 15.26$ cm; $AB \approx 8.53$ cm**

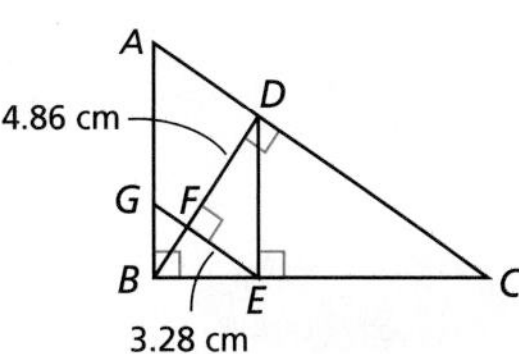

SPIRAL REVIEW

Find the x-intercept and y-intercept for each equation. *(Previous course)*

54. $3y + 4 = 6x$ **$\frac{2}{3}; -\frac{4}{3}$**　55. $x + 4 = 2y$ **−4; 2**　56. $3y - 15 = 15x$ **−1; 5**

The leg lengths of a 30°-60°-90° triangle are given. Find the length of the hypotenuse. *(Lesson 5-8)*

57. 3 and $\sqrt{27}$ **6**　58. 7 and $7\sqrt{3}$ **14**　59. 2 and $2\sqrt{3}$ **4**

For rhombus $ABCD$, find each measure, given that $m\angle DEC = 30y°$, $m\angle EDC = (8y + 15)°$, $AB = 2x + 8$, and $BC = 4x$. *(Lesson 6-4)*

60. $m\angle EDC$ **39°**　61. $m\angle EDA$ **39°**　62. AB **16**

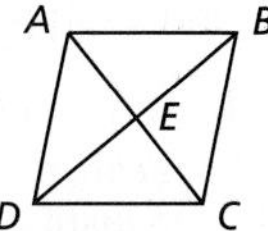

TEST PREP DOCTOR In **Exercise 49,** students who chose **B** found *PS*. Students who chose **C** may have multiplied the lengths of the hypotenuse segments instead of adding them. Students who chose **D** did not use the segment of the hypotenuse adjacent to $\overline{RS}$.

Journal

Have students write the proportional relationships from the geometric mean corollaries in words.

ALTERNATIVE ASSESSMENT

Have students draw and label a right triangle with the altitude drawn to the hypotenuse. Have them identify three similar triangles. Ask them to write three different proportions involving a geometric mean.

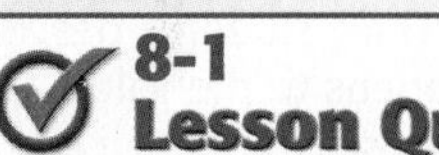

8-1 Lesson Quiz

Find the geometric mean of each pair of numbers. If necessary, give the answer in simplest radical form.

1. 8 and 18　12
2. 6 and 15　$3\sqrt{10}$

For Items 3–6, use $\triangle RST$.

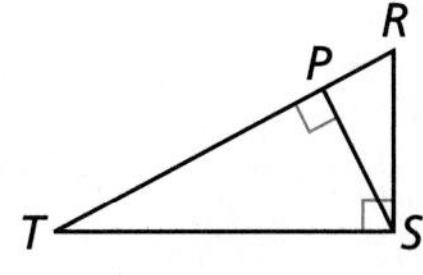

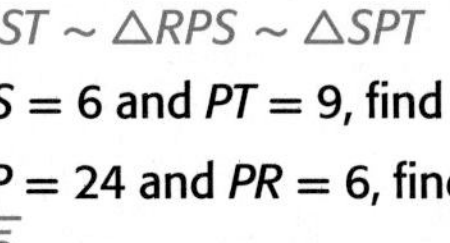

3. Write a similarity statement comparing the three triangles. $\triangle RST \sim \triangle RPS \sim \triangle SPT$
4. If $PS = 6$ and $PT = 9$, find PR. 4
5. If $TP = 24$ and $PR = 6$, find RS. $6\sqrt{5}$
6. Complete the equation $(ST)^2 = (TP + PR)(?)$. TP

Also available on transparency

8-1 PROBLEM SOLVING

1. A sculpture is 10 feet long and 6 feet wide. The artist made the sculpture so that the height is the geometric mean of the length and the width. What is the height of the sculpture to the nearest tenth of a foot?
7.7 ft

2. The altitude to the hypotenuse of a right triangle divides the hypotenuse into two segments that are 12 mm long and 27 mm long. What is the area of the triangle?
351 mm²

3. The perimeter of $\triangle ABC$ is 56.4 cm, and the perimeter of $\triangle GHJ$ is 14.1 cm. The perimeter of $\triangle DEF$ is the geometric mean of these two perimeters. What is the perimeter of $\triangle DEF$?

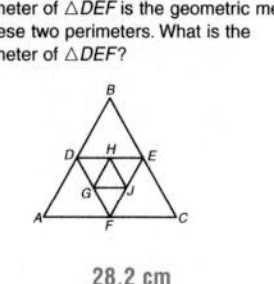

28.2 cm

4. Tamara stands facing a painting in a museum. Her lines of sight to the top and bottom of the painting form a 90° angle. How tall is the painting?

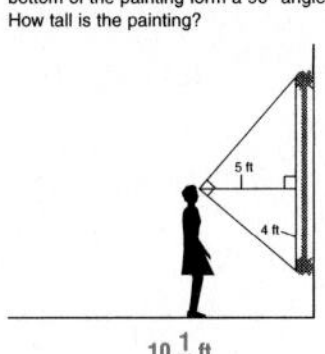

$10\frac{1}{4}$ ft

Choose the best answer.

5. The altitude to the hypotenuse of a right triangle divides the hypotenuse into two segments that are x cm and $4x$ cm, respectively. What is the length of the altitude?
Ⓐ $2x$ (circled)　C $5x$
B $2.5x$　D $4x^2$

6. Jack stands 9 feet from the primate enclosure at the zoo. His lines of sight to the top and bottom of the enclosure form a 90° angle. When he looks straight ahead at the enclosure, the vertical distance between his line of sight and the bottom of the enclosure is 5 feet. What is the height of the enclosure?
F 16.2 ft　H 23.8 ft
Ⓖ 21.2 ft (circled)　J 28.8 ft

7. A surveyor sketched the diagram at right to calculate the distance across a ravine. What is x, the distance across the ravine, to the nearest tenth of a meter? (Diagram labels: N, P, M, 4.2 m, 8.3 m, L)
A 6.2 m　C 16.4 m
Ⓑ 12.2 m (circled)　D 64.7 m

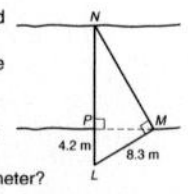

8-1 CHALLENGE

The **geometric mean** can be used to find the maximum area of a rectangle if the perimeter is known. The arithmetic mean–geometric mean theorem (GM-AM theorem) states that the geometric mean of two positive numbers is less than or equal to their arithmetic mean, with equality holding if and only if the two numbers are equal.

Grant has 142 feet of fencing for a rectangular garden. Find the maximum area of the garden he can enclose.

The GM-AM theorem lets us find the maximum area of the garden.

(Rectangle with sides ℓ and w)

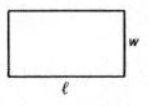

Using the variables ℓ for length and w for width, the arithmetic mean of the two dimensions of a rectangle can be written as $\frac{\ell + w}{2}$ and the geometric mean can be written as $\sqrt{\ell w}$.

The perimeter formula is $P = 2\ell + 2w$. Using the information given about Grant's garden, the perimeter formula gives

$2\ell + 2w = 142$　Substitute 142 feet for perimeter.
$\ell + w = 71$　Simplify by dividing all terms by 2.

The arithmetic mean of the dimensions is $\frac{71}{2} = 35.5$.

The GM-AM theorem states that the geometric mean, $\sqrt{\ell w}$, is less than or equal to 35.5. That can be written

$\text{GM} \le 35.5$
$\sqrt{\ell w} \le 35.5$　GM-AM theorem
$\ell w \le 35.5^2$　Square both sides.
$\ell w \le 1260.25 \text{ ft}^2$　Simplify, substitute for ℓw.

The maximum area of the rectangular garden with perimeter 142 is 1260.25 ft². This area is attained when $\ell = w$, that is, when the garden is a square.

Using this method, find the maximum area of rectangles with the given perimeter P.

1. $P = 44$ ft　maximum area **121 ft²**
2. $P = 95$ ft　maximum area **564.0625 ft²**
3. Tell how to quickly find the maximum area of a rectangle with a given perimeter.
Divide the perimeter by 4 and square the quotient.

Organizer

Use with Lesson 8-2

Pacing:
Traditional 1 day
Block $\frac{1}{2}$ day

Objective: Use geometry software to explore trigonometric ratios in right triangles.

Materials: geometry software

Online Edition
TechKeys

Countdown Week 17

Resources

Technology Lab Activities
8-2 Lab Recording Sheet

Teach

Discuss

Explain that the ratios students are calculating are associated with the measure of an acute angle of a right triangle—in this case, $\triangle ADE$.

Close

Key Concept

A given acute angle measure has the same trigonometric ratios regardless of the exact size of the right triangle it is a part of.

Assessment

Journal Have students describe what happens to the value $\frac{DE}{AD}$ as $\angle A$ gets closer to 90°.

State Resources

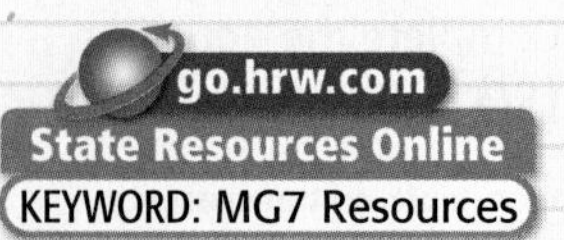

go.hrw.com
State Resources Online
KEYWORD: MG7 Resources

8-2 Technology LAB

Explore Trigonometric Ratios

In a right triangle, the ratio of two side lengths is known as a *trigonometric ratio.*

Use with Lesson 8-2

go.hrw.com
Lab Resources Online
KEYWORD: MG7 Lab8

Activity

1. Construct three points and label them *A*, *B*, and *C*. Construct rays $\overrightarrow{AB}$ and $\overrightarrow{AC}$ with common endpoint *A*. Move *C* so that $\angle A$ is an acute angle.

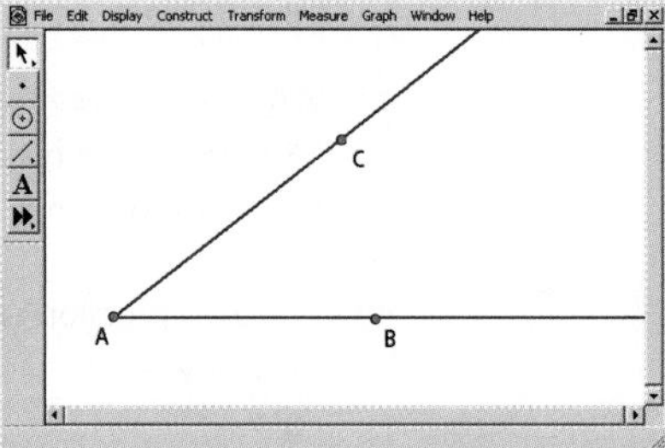

2. Construct point *D* on $\overrightarrow{AC}$. Construct a line through *D* perpendicular to $\overrightarrow{AB}$. Label the intersection of the perpendicular line and $\overrightarrow{AB}$ as *E*.

3. Measure $\angle A$. Measure *DE*, *AE*, and *AD*, the side lengths of $\triangle AED$.

4. Calculate the ratios $\frac{DE}{AD}$, $\frac{AE}{AD}$, and $\frac{DE}{AE}$.

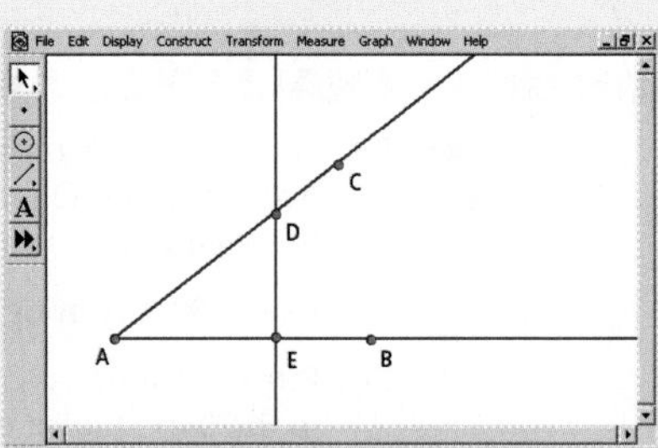

Try This

1. Drag *D* along $\overrightarrow{AC}$. What happens to the measure of $\angle A$ as *D* moves? What postulate or theorem guarantees that the different triangles formed are similar to each other?
2. As you move *D*, what happens to the values of the three ratios you calculated? Use the properties of similar triangles to explain this result.
3. Move *C*. What happens to the measure of $\angle A$? With a new value for $m\angle A$, note the values of the three ratios. What happens to the ratios if you drag *D*?
4. Move *C* until $\frac{DE}{AD} = \frac{AE}{AD}$. What is the value of $\frac{DE}{AE}$? What is the measure of $\angle A$? Use the properties of special right triangles to justify this result.

4. $\frac{DE}{AE} = 1$, **and** $m\angle A = 45°$. **If** $\frac{DE}{AD} = \frac{AE}{AD}$, **then** $DE = AE$, **so** $\frac{DE}{AE} = 1$. **Since 2 sides are equal,** $\triangle DEA$ **is an isosc.** $\triangle$**. It is also a rt.** $\triangle$**. Thus** $\triangle DEA$ **must be a 45°-45°-90° special rt.** $\triangle$**, so** $m\angle A = 45°$**.**

Answers to *Try This*

1. $m\angle A$ stays the same. Each $\triangle$ will have 2 ∡ ($\angle DEA$ and $\angle A$) $\cong$ to 2 ∡ in every other $\triangle$, so by the AA Similarity Post., these △ are similar to each other.
2. The values of the ratios do not change, because the ratios of the side lengths are equal in similar △.
3. As *C* moves, $m\angle A$ changes. Once *C* is in a new position, moving *D* does not change the ratios.

8-2 Trigonometric Ratios

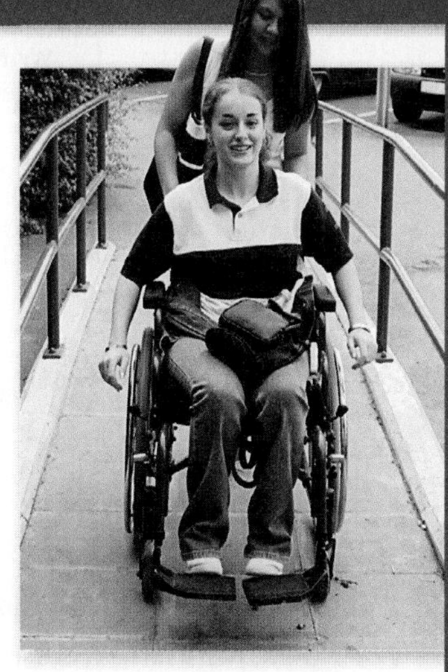

Objectives
Find the sine, cosine, and tangent of an acute angle.

Use trigonometric ratios to find side lengths in right triangles and to solve real-world problems.

Vocabulary
trigonometric ratio
sine
cosine
tangent

Who uses this?
Contractors use trigonometric ratios to build ramps that meet legal requirements.

According to the Americans with Disabilities Act (ADA), the maximum slope allowed for a wheelchair ramp is $\frac{1}{12}$, which is an angle of about 4.8°. Properties of right triangles help builders construct ramps that meet this requirement.

By the AA Similarity Postulate, a right triangle with a given acute angle is similar to every other right triangle with that same acute angle measure. So $\triangle ABC \sim \triangle DEF \sim \triangle XYZ$, and $\frac{BC}{AC} = \frac{EF}{DF} = \frac{YZ}{XZ}$. These are *trigonometric ratios*. A **trigonometric ratio** is a ratio of two sides of a right triangle.

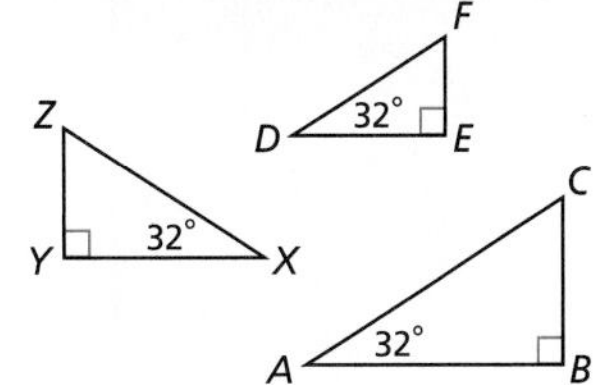

Know it! Note

Writing Math
In trigonometry, the letter of the vertex of the angle is often used to represent the measure of that angle. For example, the sine of $\angle A$ is written as $\sin A$.

Trigonometric Ratios

DEFINITION	SYMBOLS	DIAGRAM
The **sine** of an angle is the ratio of the length of the leg opposite the angle to the length of the hypotenuse.	$\sin A = \frac{\text{opposite leg}}{\text{hypotenuse}} = \frac{a}{c}$ $\sin B = \frac{\text{opposite leg}}{\text{hypotenuse}} = \frac{b}{c}$	
The **cosine** of an angle is the ratio of the length of the leg adjacent to the angle to the length of the hypotenuse.	$\cos A = \frac{\text{adjacent leg}}{\text{hypotenuse}} = \frac{b}{c}$ $\cos B = \frac{\text{adjacent leg}}{\text{hypotenuse}} = \frac{a}{c}$	B, c, a, A, b, C
The **tangent** of an angle is the ratio of the length of the leg opposite the angle to the length of the leg adjacent to the angle.	$\tan A = \frac{\text{opposite leg}}{\text{adjacent leg}} = \frac{a}{b}$ $\tan B = \frac{\text{opposite leg}}{\text{adjacent leg}} = \frac{b}{a}$	

EXAMPLE 1 **Finding Trigonometric Ratios**

Write each trigonometric ratio as a fraction and as a decimal rounded to the nearest hundredth.

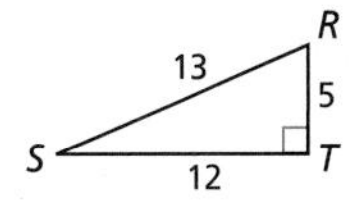

A $\sin R$

$\sin R = \frac{12}{13} \approx 0.92$ *The sine of an ∠ is $\frac{\text{opp. leg}}{\text{hyp.}}$.*

8-2 Organizer

Pacing: Traditional 1 day
Block $\frac{1}{2}$ day

Objectives: Find the sine, cosine, and tangent of an acute angle.

Use trigonometric ratios to find side lengths in right triangles and to solve real-world problems.

Technology Lab
In *Technology Lab Activities*

Online Edition
Tutorial Videos, Interactivity

Countdown Week 17

Power Presentations with PowerPoint®

Warm Up

Write each fraction as a decimal rounded to the nearest hundredth.

1. $\frac{2}{3}$ 0.67 **2.** $\frac{7}{24}$ 0.29

Solve each equation.

3. $0.8 = \frac{5.8}{x}$ $x = 7.25$

4. $0.94 = \frac{x}{8.5}$ $x = 7.99$

Also available on transparency

Math Humor

Q: What happened to the geometry student who went to the beach to catch some rays?

A: He became a tangent!

Introduce

EXPLORATION

8-2 Trigonometric Ratios

Use a ruler and protractor for this Exploration.

1. Carefully draw right triangle $\triangle ABC$ so that $\angle B$ is a right angle and $m\angle A = 35°$.
2. Compare your triangle to those drawn by your classmates. What is the relationship between all of the triangles? Why?
3. Measure the three sides of your trangle to the nearest millimeter.
4. Calculate the ratios $\frac{AB}{AC}$, $\frac{BC}{AC}$, and $\frac{BC}{AB}$. Round to the nearest hundredth.
5. Compare your ratios to those calculated by classmates. How do the ratios compare?
6. A *trigonometric ratio* is a ratio of two sides of a right triangle. You calculated three trigonometric ratios for a 35° angle. Explain why you also calculated three trigonometric ratios for a 55° angle.

THINK AND DISCUSS

7. **Discuss** how you can find $m\angle J$ if you know

Motivate

This lesson introduces *trigonometry*, the branch of mathematics concerned with angle relationships in triangles. Explain to students that the ancient Egyptians used trigonometry to reset land boundaries after the Nile River flooded each year. The Babylonians used trigonometry to measure distances to nearby stars. Trigonometry is used in modern engineering, cartography, medical imaging, and many other fields.

Explorations and answers are provided in *Alternate Openers: Explorations Transparencies*.

State Resources

go.hrw.com
State Resources Online
KEYWORD: MG7 Resources

Power Presentations with PowerPoint®

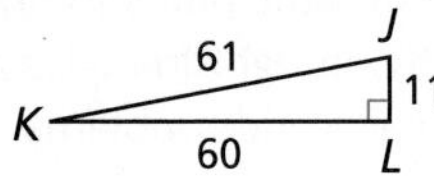

Additional Examples

Example 1

Write each trigonometric ratio as a fraction and as a decimal rounded to the nearest hundredth.

K, J, L; 61, 60, 11

A. $\sin J$ $\frac{60}{61} \approx 0.98$

B. $\cos J$ $\frac{11}{61} \approx 0.18$

C. $\tan K$ $\frac{11}{60} \approx 0.18$

Example 2

Use a special right triangle to write cos 30° as a fraction.

$\cos 30° = \frac{\sqrt{3}}{2}$

Example 3

Use your calculator to find each trigonometric ratio. Round to the nearest hundredth.

A. sin 52° 0.79

B. cos 19° 0.95

C. tan 65° 2.14

INTERVENTION

Questioning Strategies

EXAMPLE 1

- How are the sine and cosine ratios alike, and how are they different?

EXAMPLE 2

- If you use a variable to label the side lengths of the special right triangle, what happens to the variable in the trigonometric ratio?

EXAMPLE 3

- How is this example similar to **Example 1**?

Inclusion Suggest to students that they repeat **Example 3** using their own calculator to learn the correct sequence of keystrokes.

Write each trigonometric ratio as a fraction and as a decimal rounded to the nearest hundredth.

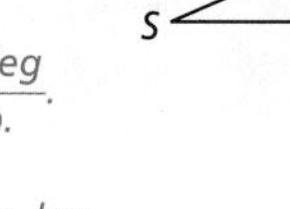

B $\cos R$

$\cos R = \frac{5}{13} \approx 0.38$ *The cosine of an ∠ is* $\frac{\text{adj. leg}}{\text{hyp.}}$.

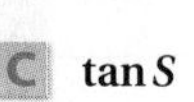

C $\tan S$

$\tan S = \frac{5}{12} \approx 0.42$ *The tangent of an ∠ is* $\frac{\text{opp. leg}}{\text{adj. leg}}$.

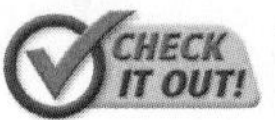

Write each trigonometric ratio as a fraction and as a decimal rounded to the nearest hundredth.

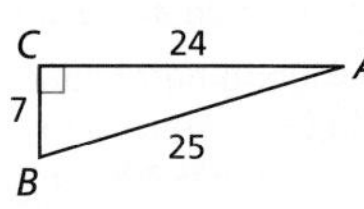

1a. $\cos A$ $\frac{24}{25} = 0.96$ **1b.** $\tan B$ $\frac{24}{7} \approx 3.43$ **1c.** $\sin B$ $\frac{24}{25} = 0.96$

EXAMPLE 2 Finding Trigonometric Ratios in Special Right Triangles

Use a special right triangle to write sin 60° as a fraction.

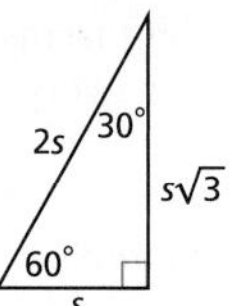

Draw and label a 30°-60°-90° △.

$\sin 60° = \frac{s\sqrt{3}}{2s} = \frac{\sqrt{3}}{2}$ *The sine of an ∠ is* $\frac{\text{opp. leg}}{\text{hyp.}}$.

2. Use a special right triangle to write tan 45° as a fraction. $\frac{s}{s} = 1$

EXAMPLE 3 Calculating Trigonometric Ratios

Use your calculator to find each trigonometric ratio. Round to the nearest hundredth.

Caution!

Be sure your calculator is in degree mode, not radian mode.

A cos 76° **B** sin 8° **C** tan 82°

$\cos 76° \approx 0.24$ $\sin 8° \approx 0.14$ $\tan 82° \approx 7.12$

Use your calculator to find each trigonometric ratio. Round to the nearest hundredth.

3a. tan 11° **0.19** **3b.** sin 62° **0.88** **3c.** cos 30° **0.87**

The hypotenuse is always the longest side of a right triangle. So the denominator of a sine or cosine ratio is always greater than the numerator. Therefore the sine and cosine of an acute angle are always positive numbers less than 1. Since the tangent of an acute angle is the ratio of the lengths of the legs, it can have any value greater than 0.

2 Teach

Guided Instruction

Review the side lengths of special right triangles. Identify the adjacent and opposite sides of an acute angle in a right triangle. Show students how to write the sine, cosine, and tangent ratios and how to use trigonometry to find a missing leg length in a right triangle.

Reading Math The abbreviations *sin*, *cos*, and *tan* are read "sine," "cosine," and "tangent".

ENGLISH LANGUAGE LEARNERS

Reaching All Learners

Through Kinesthetic Experience

To help students identify the opposite and adjacent legs, model a right triangle on the floor with masking tape. Have a student stand at one acute angle and walk to the leg next to, or touching, that angle. This is the adjacent leg. Then have the student walk from the acute angle to the leg opposite, or across from, the angle. This is the opposite leg.

EXAMPLE 4 Using Trigonometric Ratios to Find Lengths

Find each length. Round to the nearest hundredth.

A AB

$\overline{AB}$ is adjacent to the given angle, $\angle A$. You are given BC, which is opposite $\angle A$. Since the adjacent and opposite legs are involved, use a tangent ratio.

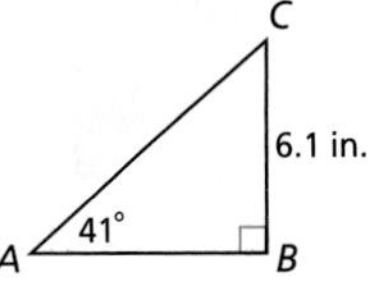

$\tan A = \frac{\text{opp. leg}}{\text{adj. leg}} = \frac{BC}{AB}$ *Write a trigonometric ratio.*

$\tan 41° = \frac{6.1}{AB}$ *Substitute the given values.*

$AB = \frac{6.1}{\tan 41°}$ *Multiply both sides by AB and divide by tan 41°.*

$AB \approx 7.02$ in. *Simplify the expression.*

B MP

$\overline{MP}$ is opposite the given angle, $\angle N$. You are given NP, which is the hypotenuse. Since the opposite side and hypotenuse are involved, use a sine ratio.

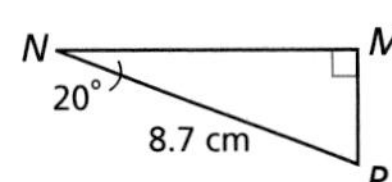

$\sin N = \frac{\text{opp. leg}}{\text{hyp.}} = \frac{MP}{NP}$ *Write a trigonometric ratio.*

$\sin 20° = \frac{MP}{8.7}$ *Substitute the given values.*

$8.7(\sin 20°) = MP$ *Multiply both sides by 8.7.*

$MP \approx 2.98$ cm *Simplify the expression.*

C YZ

YZ is the hypotenuse. You are given XZ, which is adjacent to the given angle, $\angle Z$. Since the adjacent side and hypotenuse are involved, use a cosine ratio.

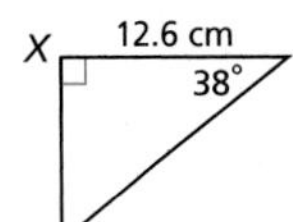
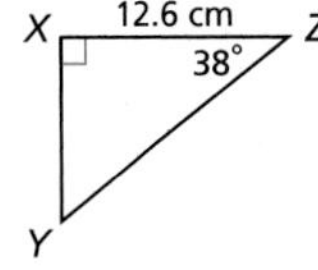

$\cos Z = \frac{\text{adj. leg}}{\text{hyp.}} = \frac{XZ}{YZ}$ *Write a trigonometric ratio.*

$\cos 38° = \frac{12.6}{YZ}$ *Substitute the given values.*

$YZ = \frac{12.6}{\cos 38°}$ *Multiply both sides by YZ and divide by cos 38°.*

$YZ \approx 15.99$ cm *Simplify the expression.*

Find each length. Round to the nearest hundredth.

4a. DF 21.87 m

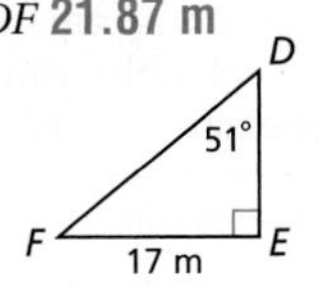

4b. ST 7.06 in.

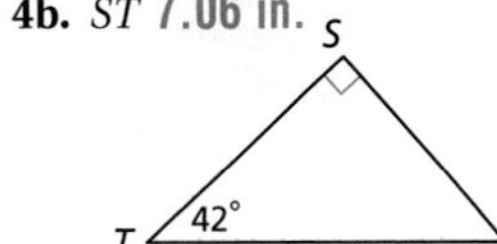

4c. BC 36.93 ft

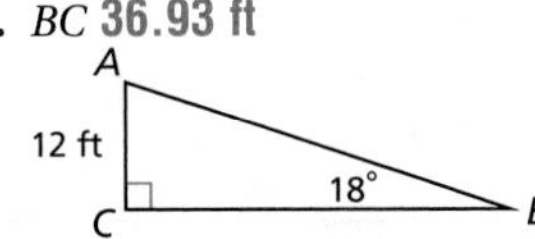

4d. JL 6.17 cm

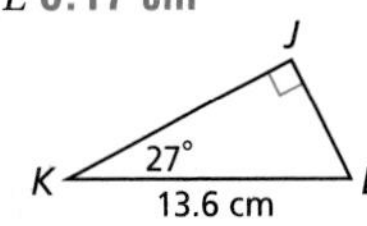

Caution!

Do not round until the final step of your answer. Use the values of the trigonometric ratios provided by your calculator.

COMMON ERROR ALERT

Students may have difficulty in **Example 4** applying the correct trigonometric ratio. Suggest that they label the triangle with the given measurements and a variable for the unknown side. Point out that the sine and cosine ratios should not be used if the hypotenuse is unlabeled.

Power Presentations with PowerPoint®

Additional Examples

Example 4

Find each length. Round to the nearest hundredth.

A. BC 38.07 ft

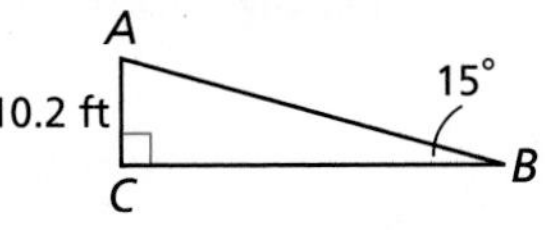

B. QR 11.49 cm

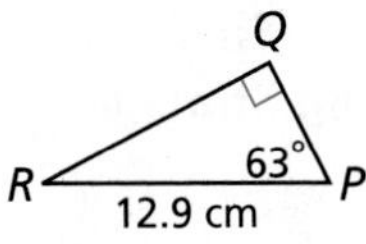

C. FD 25.74 m

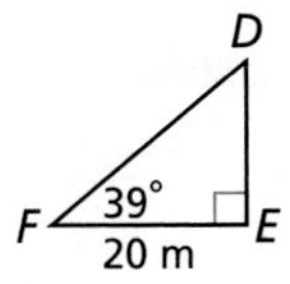

INTERVENTION
Questioning Strategies

EXAMPLE 4

- How do you decide which trigonometric ratio to use to find a missing side length in a right triangle?

Auditory Students can use the mnemonic **soh-cah-toa** to remember that

$\sin A = \frac{\text{opposite leg}}{\text{hypotenuse}}$,

$\cos A = \frac{\text{adjacent leg}}{\text{hypotenuse}}$, and

$\tan A = \frac{\text{opposite leg}}{\text{adjacent leg}}$.

Inclusion If students are using a trig table instead of a calculator for this lesson, instruct them to round the angle measure in **Example 5** to 5°. In this case, the answer is 13.72 ft. The Check It Out answer is 13.77 ft.

Power Presentations with PowerPoint®

Additional Examples

Example 5

The Pilatusbahn in Switzerland is the world's steepest cog railway. Its steepest section makes an angle of about 25.6° with the horizontal and rises about 0.9 km. To the nearest hundredth of a kilometer, how long is this section of the railway track?

2.08 km

INTERVENTION

Questioning Strategies

EXAMPLE 5

- How do you solve $\tan A = \frac{y}{x}$ for x?
- How do you solve $\tan A = \frac{y}{x}$ for y?

EXAMPLE 5 ***Problem Solving Application***

A contractor is building a wheelchair ramp for a doorway that is 1.2 ft above the ground. To meet ADA guidelines, the ramp will make an angle of 4.8° with the ground. To the nearest hundredth of a foot, what is the horizontal distance covered by the ramp?

1 Understand the Problem

Make a sketch. The **answer** is BC.

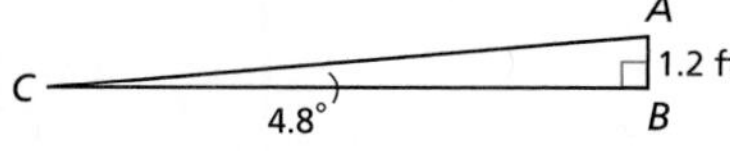

2 Make a Plan

$\overline{BC}$ is the leg adjacent to $\angle C$. You are given AB, which is the leg opposite $\angle C$. Since the opposite and adjacent legs are involved, write an equation using the tangent ratio.

3 Solve

$\tan C = \frac{AB}{BC}$ *Write a trigonometric ratio.*

$\tan 4.8° = \frac{1.2}{BC}$ *Substitute the given values.*

$BC = \frac{1.2}{\tan 4.8°}$ *Multiply both sides by BC and divide by tan 4.8°.*

$BC \approx 14.2904$ ft *Simplify the expression.*

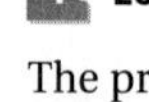

4 Look Back

The problem asks for BC rounded to the nearest hundredth, so round the length to 14.29. The ramp covers a horizontal distance of 14.29 ft.

5. Find AC, the length of the ramp in Example 5, to the nearest hundredth of a foot. **14.34 ft**

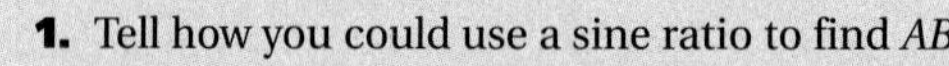
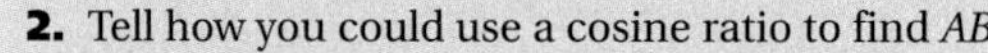
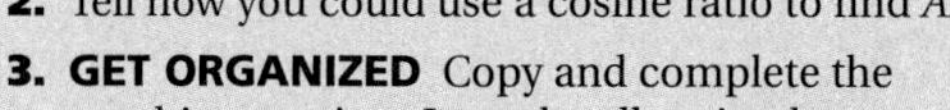

THINK AND DISCUSS

1. Tell how you could use a sine ratio to find AB.
2. Tell how you could use a cosine ratio to find AB.
3. **GET ORGANIZED** Copy and complete the graphic organizer. In each cell, write the meaning of each abbreviation and draw a diagram for each.

Know It! Note

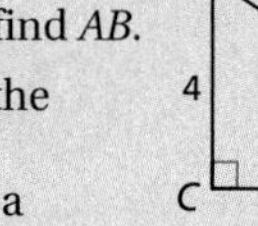

Abbreviation	Words	Diagram
$\sin = \frac{\text{opp. leg}}{\text{hyp.}}$		
$\cos = \frac{\text{adj. leg}}{\text{hyp.}}$		
$\tan = \frac{\text{opp. leg}}{\text{adj. leg}}$		

3 Close

Summarize

Review the sine, cosine, and tangent ratios with students. Be sure they understand how to solve for a variable when it is in the denominator.

Have students write all the trigonometric ratios they can from $\triangle ABC$.

A, c, b, B, a, C

$\sin A = \frac{a}{c}$, $\cos A = \frac{b}{c}$, $\tan A = \frac{a}{b}$,

$\sin B = \frac{b}{c}$, $\cos B = \frac{a}{c}$, $\tan B = \frac{b}{a}$

ONGOING ASSESSMENT and INTERVENTION

***Diagnose Before* the Lesson**
8-2 Warm Up, TE p. 525

***Monitor During* the Lesson**
Check It Out! Exercises, SE pp. 526–528
Questioning Strategies, TE pp. 526–528

***Assess After* the Lesson**
8-2 Lesson Quiz, TE p. 532
Alternative Assessment, TE p. 532

Answers to *Think and Discuss*

1. Solve $\sin 32° = \frac{4}{AB}$.
2. Solve $\cos 32° = \frac{6.4}{AB}$.
3. See p. A7.

8-2 Exercises

go.hrw.com
Homework Help Online
KEYWORD: MG7 8-2
Parent Resources Online
KEYWORD: MG7 Parent

GUIDED PRACTICE

Vocabulary Apply the vocabulary from this lesson to answer each question.

1. In $\triangle JKL$, $\angle K$ is a right angle. Write the *sine* of $\angle J$ as a ratio of side lengths. $\frac{LK}{JL}$
2. In $\triangle MNP$, $\angle M$ is a right angle. Write the *tangent* of $\angle N$ as a ratio of side lengths. $\frac{MP}{MN}$

SEE EXAMPLE 1 p. 525

Write each trigonometric ratio as a fraction and as a decimal rounded to the nearest hundredth.

3. $\sin C$ $\frac{4}{5} = 0.80$
4. $\tan A$ $\frac{3}{4} = 0.75$
5. $\cos A$ $\frac{4}{5} = 0.80$
6. $\cos C$ $\frac{3}{5} = 0.60$
7. $\tan C$ $\frac{4}{3} \approx 1.33$
8. $\sin A$ $\frac{3}{5} = 0.60$

SEE EXAMPLE 2 p. 526

Use a special right triangle to write each trigonometric ratio as a fraction.

9. $\cos 60°$ $\frac{1}{2}$
10. $\tan 30°$ $\frac{\sqrt{3}}{3}$
11. $\sin 45°$ $\frac{\sqrt{2}}{2}$

SEE EXAMPLE 3 p. 526

Use your calculator to find each trigonometric ratio. Round to the nearest hundredth.

12. $\tan 67°$ 2.36
13. $\sin 23°$ 0.39
14. $\sin 49°$ 0.75
15. $\cos 88°$ 0.03
16. $\cos 12°$ 0.98
17. $\tan 9°$ 0.16

SEE EXAMPLE 4 p. 527

Find each length. Round to the nearest hundredth.

18. *BC*

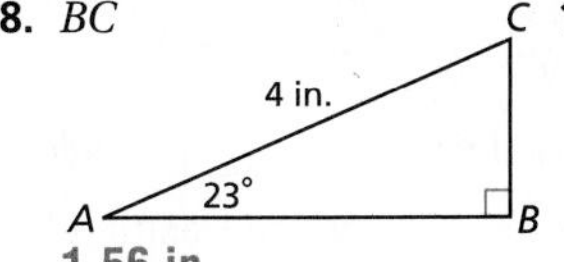

1.56 in.

19. *QR* 9.65 m

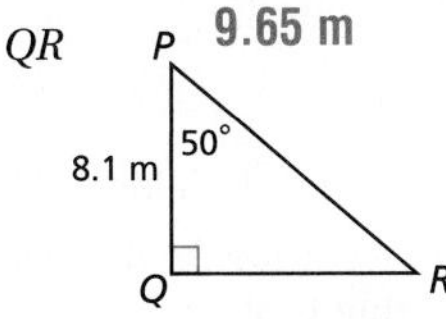

20. *KL*

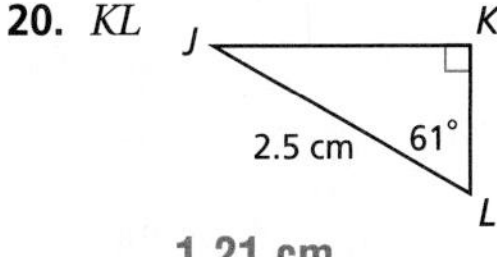

1.21 cm

SEE EXAMPLE 5 p. 528

21. **Architecture** A pediment has a pitch of 15°, as shown. If the width of the pediment, *WZ*, is 56 ft, what is *XY* to the nearest inch? 7 ft 6 in.

PRACTICE AND PROBLEM SOLVING

Independent Practice

For Exercises	See Example
22–27	1
28–30	2
31–36	3
37–42	4
43	5

Extra Practice
Skills Practice p. S18
Application Practice p. S35

Write each trigonometric ratio as a fraction and as a decimal rounded to the nearest hundredth.

22. $\cos D$ $\frac{8}{17} \approx 0.47$
23. $\tan D$ $\frac{15}{8} \approx 1.88$
24. $\tan F$ $\frac{8}{15} \approx 0.53$
25. $\cos F$ $\frac{15}{17} \approx 0.88$
26. $\sin F$ $\frac{8}{17} \approx 0.47$
27. $\sin D$ $\frac{15}{17} \approx 0.88$

Use a special right triangle to write each trigonometric ratio as a fraction.

28. $\tan 60°$ $\sqrt{3}$
29. $\sin 30°$ $\frac{1}{2}$
30. $\cos 45°$ $\frac{\sqrt{2}}{2}$

Use your calculator to find each trigonometric ratio. Round to the nearest hundredth.

31. $\tan 51°$ 1.23
32. $\sin 80°$ 0.98
33. $\cos 77°$ 0.22
34. $\tan 14°$ 0.25
35. $\sin 55°$ 0.82
36. $\cos 48°$ 0.67

Teaching Tip **Multiple Representations** Use **Exercises 31–36** to reinforce the fact that each trigonometric ratio is associated with an angle measure. For example, in **Exercise 31,** have students draw a right triangle with an acute angle measure of 51°. Have them measure the opposite and adjacent legs and confirm that $\frac{\text{opp.}}{\text{adj.}} \approx 1.23 \approx \tan 51°$.

8-2 Exercises

Assignment Guide

Assign *Guided Practice* exercises as necessary.

If you finished Examples **1–3**
Basic 22–36, 44–47, 56
Average 22–36, 44–47, 56–61
Advanced 22–36, 44–47, 56–61, 75–77

If you finished Examples **1–5**
Basic 22–43, 48–50, 52, 53, 56, 58, 62–65, 68–70, 78–86
Average 22–43, 44–50 even, 51, 52, 57–72, 78–86
Advanced 22–43, 45, 47–86

Homework Quick Check
Quickly check key concepts.
Exercises: 22, 28, 32, 40, 43, 48, 50

Teaching Tip **Critical Thinking** In **Exercise 21,** some students may incorrectly use the equation $\tan 15° = \frac{XY}{56}$ to find the length of $\overline{XY}$. Remind students that the altitude to the base of an isosceles triangle bisects the base.

State Resources

go.hrw.com
State Resources Online
KEYWORD: MG7 Resources

MULTI-STEP TEST PREP **Exercise 52** involves using trigonometric ratios to find unknown lengths. This exercise prepares students for the Multi-Step Test Prep on page 542.

Answers

51. The tangent ratio is less than 1 for ∡ measuring less than 45°. The tangent ratio is greater than 1 for ∡ measuring greater than 45°. In a 45°-45°-90° triangle, both legs have the same length, so tan 45° = 1. If the acute ∠ measure increases, the opposite leg length also increases, so the tangent ratio is greater than 1. If the acute ∠ measure decreases, the opposite leg length decreases, so the tangent ratio is less than 1.

Find each length. Round to the nearest hundredth.

37. *PQ* **3.58 cm**

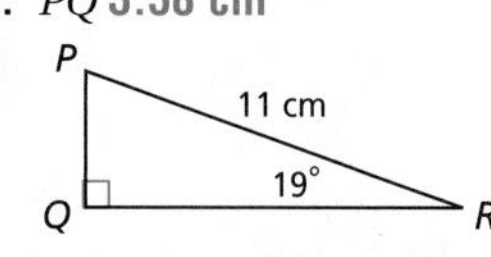

38. *AC* **27.64 in.**

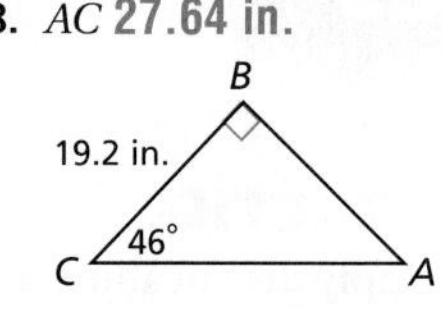

39. *GH* **19.67 ft**

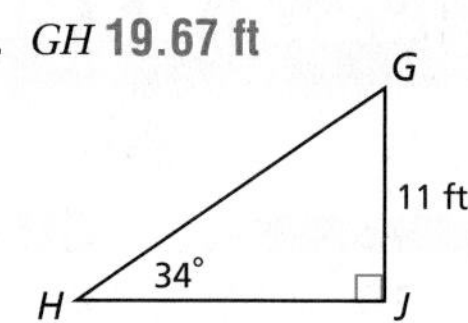

40. *XZ* **36.41 in.**

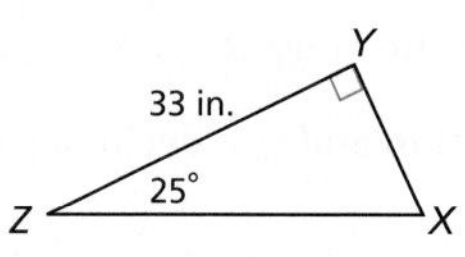

41. *KL* **5.27 ft**

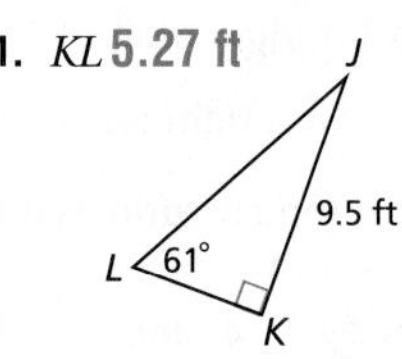

42. *EF* **17.66 m**

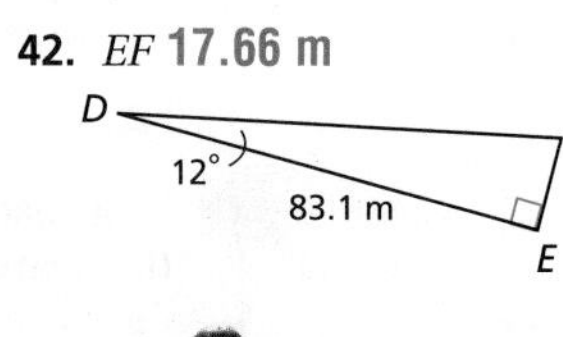

43. **Sports** A jump ramp for waterskiing makes an angle of 15° with the surface of the water. The ramp rises 1.58 m above the surface. What is the length of the ramp to the nearest hundredth of a meter? **6.10 m**

Use special right triangles to complete each statement.

44. An angle that measures __?__ has a tangent of 1. **45°**
45. For a 45° angle, the __?__ and __?__ ratios are equal. **sine; cosine**
46. The sine of a __?__ angle is 0.5. **30°**
47. The cosine of a 30° angle is equal to the sine of a __?__ angle. **60°**
48. **Safety** According to the Occupational Safety and Health Administration (OSHA), a ladder that is placed against a wall should make a 75.5° angle with the ground for optimal safety. To the nearest tenth of a foot, what is the maximum height that a 10-ft ladder can safely reach? **9.7 ft**

Find the indicated length in each rectangle. Round to the nearest tenth.

49. *BC* **1.2 ft**

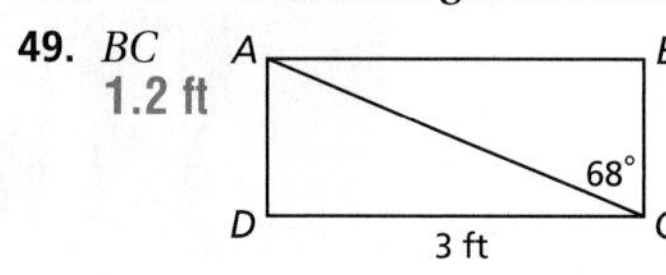

50. *SU* **14.3 in.**

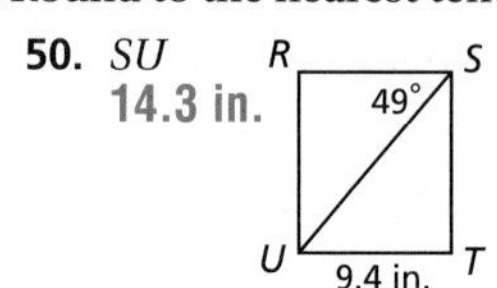

51. **Critical Thinking** For what angle measures is the tangent ratio less than 1? greater than 1? Explain.

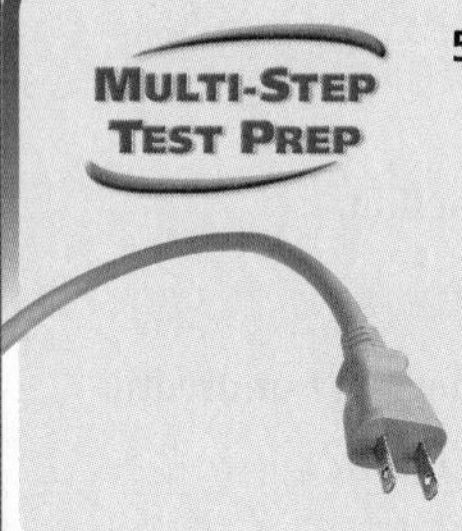

MULTI-STEP TEST PREP

52. This problem will prepare you for the Multi-Step Test Prep on page 542.

A utility worker is installing a 25-foot pole $\overline{AB}$ at the foot of a hill. Two guy wires, $\overline{AC}$ and $\overline{AD}$, will help keep the pole vertical.

a. To the nearest inch, how long should $\overline{AC}$ be? **27 ft 7 in.**

b. $\overline{AD}$ is perpendicular to the hill, which makes an angle of 28° with a horizontal line. To the nearest inch, how long should this guy wire be? **22 ft 1 in.**

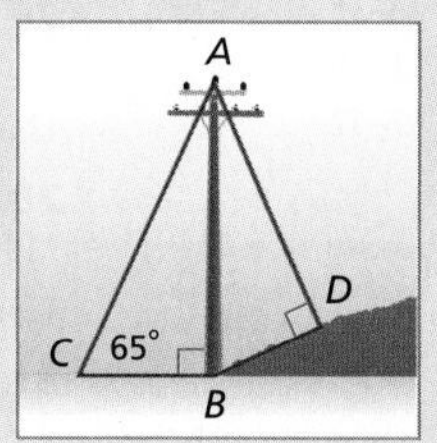

8-2 PRACTICE A

8-2 PRACTICE C

8-2 PRACTICE B

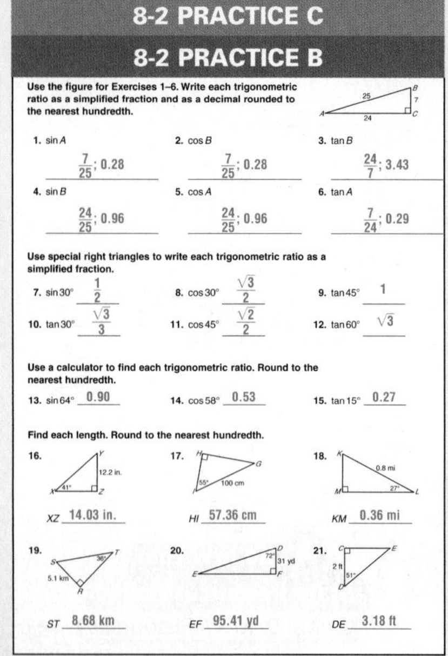

Use the figure for Exercises 1–6. Write each trigonometric ratio as a simplified fraction and as a decimal rounded to the nearest hundredth.

1. sin *A* $\frac{7}{25}$; 0.28
2. cos *B* $\frac{7}{25}$; 0.28
3. tan *B* $\frac{24}{7}$; 3.43
4. sin *B* $\frac{24}{25}$; 0.96
5. cos *A* $\frac{24}{25}$; 0.96
6. tan *A* $\frac{7}{24}$; 0.29

Use special right triangles to write each trigonometric ratio as a simplified fraction.

7. sin 30° $\frac{1}{2}$
8. cos 30° $\frac{\sqrt{3}}{2}$
9. tan 45° 1
10. tan 30° $\frac{\sqrt{3}}{3}$
11. cos 45° $\frac{\sqrt{2}}{2}$
12. tan 60° $\sqrt{3}$

Use a calculator to find each trigonometric ratio. Round to the nearest hundredth.

13. sin 64° 0.90
14. cos 58° 0.53
15. tan 15° 0.27

Find each length. Round to the nearest hundredth.

16. *XZ* 14.03 in.
17. *HI* 57.36 cm
18. *KM* 0.36 mi
19. *ST* 8.68 km
20. *EF* 95.41 yd
21. *DE* 3.18 ft

8-2 READING STRATEGIES

You can remember the trigonometric ratios by using a mnemonic: one word for the first letter of each word in the equations. Here is a sample mnemonic and examples for the triangle at right.

Such **O**utrageous **H**ats — Sine = $\frac{\text{Opposite}}{\text{Hypotenuse}}$ — Example: $\sin B = \frac{24}{26}$

Can **A**ttract **H**orses — Cosine = $\frac{\text{Adjacent}}{\text{Hypotenuse}}$ — Example: $\cos B = \frac{10}{26}$

Tigers **O**r **A**lligators — Tangent = $\frac{\text{Opposite}}{\text{Adjacent}}$ — Example: $\tan B = \frac{24}{10}$

1. Make up your own mnemonic for remembering the ratios.

S Answers will vary.
O
H
C
A
H
T
O
A

2. How are the ratios for sine and cosine alike?

Both ratios have *Hypotenuse* in the denominator.

3. Which side is not used when finding the tangent of an angle? hypotenuse

4. Use the triangle above to find the following. Write the ratios both as a fraction and as a decimal rounded to the nearest hundredth.

a. $\sin A = \frac{10}{26}$ 0.38
b. $\cos A = \frac{24}{26}$ 0.92
c. $\tan A = \frac{10}{24}$ 0.42

8-2 RETEACH

Trigonometric Ratios

$\sin A = \frac{\text{leg opposite } \angle A}{\text{hypotenuse}} = \frac{4}{5} = 0.8$

$\cos A = \frac{\text{leg adjacent to } \angle A}{\text{hypotenuse}} = \frac{3}{5} = 0.6$

$\tan A = \frac{\text{leg opposite } \angle A}{\text{leg adjacent to } \angle A} = \frac{4}{3} \approx 1.33$

hypotenuse — leg opposite ∠A — leg adjacent to ∠A

You can use special right triangles to write trigonometric ratios as fractions.

$\sin 45° = \sin Q = \frac{\text{leg opposite } \angle Q}{\text{hypotenuse}} = \frac{x\sqrt{2}}{x} = \frac{\sqrt{2}}{2}$

So $\sin 45° = \frac{\sqrt{2}}{2}$.

Write each trigonometric ratio as a fraction and as a decimal rounded to the nearest hundredth.

1. sin *K* $\frac{15}{17} \approx 0.88$
2. cos *H* $\frac{15}{17} \approx 0.88$
3. cos *K* $\frac{8}{17} \approx 0.47$
4. tan *H* $\frac{8}{15} \approx 0.53$

Use a special right triangle to write each trigonometric ratio as a fraction.

5. cos 45° $\frac{\sqrt{2}}{2}$
6. tan 45° $\frac{1}{1} = 1$
7. sin 60° $\frac{\sqrt{3}}{2}$
8. tan 30° $\frac{\sqrt{3}}{3}$

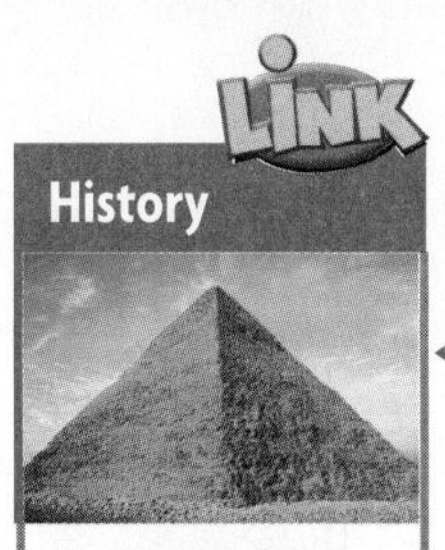

The Pyramid of Cheops consists of more than 2,000,000 blocks of stone with an average weight of 2.5 tons each.

53. Find the sine of the smaller acute angle in a triangle with side lengths of 3, 4, and 5 inches. **0.6**

54. Find the tangent of the greater acute angle in a triangle with side lengths of 7, 24, and 25 centimeters. $\frac{24}{7} \approx 3.43$

55. History The Great Pyramid of Cheops in Giza, Egypt, was completed around 2566 B.C.E. Its original height was 482 ft. Each face of the pyramid forms a 52° angle with the ground. To the nearest foot, how long is the base of the pyramid? **753 ft**

56. Measurement Follow these steps to calculate trigonometric ratios.

a. Use a centimeter ruler to find AB, BC, and AC. **Check students' work.**

b. Use your measurements from part **a** to find the sine, cosine, and tangent of $\angle A$. **Check students' work.**

c. Use a protractor to find $m\angle A$. **20°**

d. Use a calculator to find the sine, cosine, and tangent of $\angle A$. **0.34, 0.94, 0.36**

e. How do the values in part **d** compare to the ones you found in part **b**?

57. Algebra Recall from Algebra I that an *identity* is an equation that is true for all values of the variables.

a. Show that the identity $\tan A = \frac{\sin A}{\cos A}$ is true when $m\angle A = 30°$.

b. Write $\tan A$, $\sin A$, and $\cos A$ in terms of a, b, and c.

c. Use your results from part **b** to prove the identity $\tan A = \frac{\sin A}{\cos A}$.

Verify that $(\sin A)^2 + (\cos A)^2 = 1$ for each angle measure.

58. $m\angle A = 45°$ **59.** $m\angle A = 30°$ **60.** $m\angle A = 60°$

61. Multi-Step The equation $(\sin A)^2 + (\cos A)^2 = 1$ is known as a Pythagorean Identity.

a. Write $\sin A$ and $\cos A$ in terms of a, b, and c.

b. Use your results from part **a** to prove the identity $(\sin A)^2 + (\cos A)^2 = 1$.

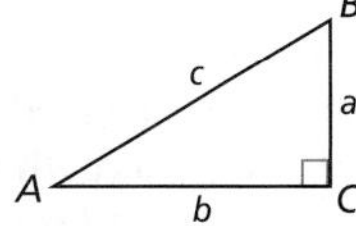

c. **Write About It** Why do you think this identity is called a Pythagorean identity?

Find the perimeter and area of each triangle. Round to the nearest hundredth.

62. **5.08 m; 0.89 m²**

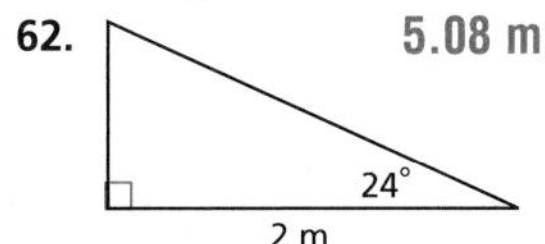

63. **18.64 cm; 16.00 cm²**

51°
7.2 cm

64. **11.22 ft; 5.00 ft²**

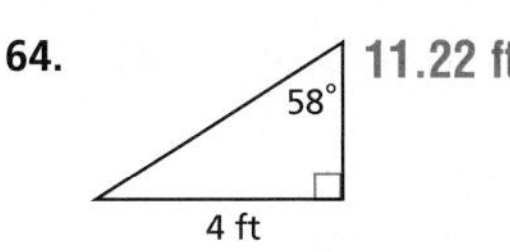

65. **22.60 in.; 14.69 in²**

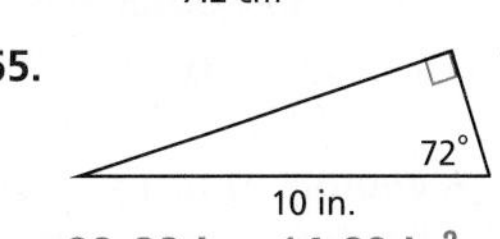

66. Critical Thinking Draw $\triangle ABC$ with $\angle C$ a right angle. Write $\sin A$ and $\cos B$ in terms of the side lengths of the triangle. What do you notice? How are $\angle A$ and $\angle B$ related? Make a conjecture based on your observations.

67. Write About It Explain how the tangent of an acute angle changes as the angle measure increases. **The tangent of an ∠ increases as the measure of the ∠ increases.**

COMMON ERROR ALERT

Some students may incorrectly assume that the angle included between the two congruent sides in **Exercise 63** is a right angle. Remind them of the properties of isosceles triangles, and have them calculate this angle measure. Then have them draw an altitude to the base to form a right triangle.

Algebra Remind students who are unsure how to complete **Exercise 57c** that $\frac{\frac{a}{b}}{\frac{c}{d}} = \frac{a}{b} \div \frac{c}{d} = \frac{a}{b} \times \frac{d}{c} = \frac{ad}{bc}$.

Answers

56. Note: Figure is reduced in TE.

e. The values in part **d** should be close to the estimated values in part **b**.

57a. $\tan 30° = \frac{\sqrt{3}}{3}$, $\sin 30° = \frac{1}{2}$, $\cos 30° = \frac{\sqrt{3}}{2}$, and $\frac{\frac{1}{2}}{\frac{\sqrt{3}}{2}} = \left(\frac{1}{2}\right)\left(\frac{2}{\sqrt{3}}\right) = \frac{1}{\sqrt{3}} = \frac{\sqrt{3}}{3}$, so $\tan 30° = \frac{\sin 30°}{\cos 30°}$.

b. $\tan A = \frac{a}{b}$; $\sin A = \frac{a}{c}$; $\cos A = \frac{b}{c}$

c. $\frac{\sin A}{\cos A} = \frac{\frac{a}{c}}{\frac{b}{c}} = \left(\frac{a}{c}\right)\left(\frac{c}{b}\right) = \frac{a}{b} = \tan A$

58. $\left(\frac{\sqrt{2}}{2}\right)^2 + \left(\frac{\sqrt{2}}{2}\right)^2 = \frac{2}{4} + \frac{2}{4} = 1$

59. $\left(\frac{1}{2}\right)^2 + \left(\frac{\sqrt{3}}{2}\right)^2 = \frac{1}{4} + \frac{3}{4} = 1$

60. $\left(\frac{\sqrt{3}}{2}\right)^2 + \left(\frac{1}{2}\right)^2 = \frac{3}{4} + \frac{1}{4} = 1$

61a. $\sin A = \frac{a}{c}$; $\cos A = \frac{b}{c}$

b. $(\sin A)^2 + (\cos A)^2 = \left(\frac{a}{c}\right)^2 + \left(\frac{b}{c}\right)^2 = \frac{a^2}{c^2} + \frac{b^2}{c^2} = \frac{a^2 + b^2}{c^2} = \frac{c^2}{c^2} = 1$

c. The derivation of the identity uses the fact that in a rt. △, $a^2 + b^2 = c^2$, which is the Pyth. Thm.

66. $\sin A = \frac{BC}{AB}$; $\cos B = \frac{BC}{AB}$; $\sin A = \cos B$; $\angle A$ and $\angle B$ are comp.; the sine of an ∠ is equal to the cosine of its comp.

8-2 PROBLEM SOLVING

1. A ramp is used to load a 4-wheeler onto a truck bed that is 3 feet above the ground. The angle that the ramp makes with the ground is 32°. What is the horizontal distance covered by the ramp? Round to the nearest hundredth.
4.80 ft

2. Find the perimeter of the triangle. Round to the nearest hundredth.
L, M, K, 18°, 4.2 cm
9.49 cm

3. A right triangle has an angle that measures 55°. The leg adjacent to this angle has a length of 43 cm. What is the length of the other leg of the triangle? Round to the nearest tenth.
61.4 cm

4. The hypotenuse of a right triangle measures 9 inches, and one of the acute angles measures 36°. What is the area of the triangle? Round to the nearest square inch.
19 in²

Choose the best answer.

5. A 14-foot ladder makes a 62° angle with the ground. To the nearest foot, how far up the house does the ladder reach?
A 6 ft
B 7 ft
Ⓒ 12 ft
D 16 ft

6. To the nearest inch, what is the length of the springboard shown below?
16°, 35 in.
F 24 in.
Ⓖ 36 in.
H 38 in.
J 127 in.

7. What is EF, the measure of the longest side of the sail on the model? Round to the nearest inch.
F, 28 in., E, 65°, G
Ⓐ 31 in.
B 35 in.
C 40 in.
D 60 in.

8. Right triangle ABC is graphed on the coordinate plane and has vertices at $A(-1, 3)$, $B(0, 5)$, and $C(4, 3)$. Which is a true trigonometric ratio for the measure of $\angle C$?
Ⓕ $\tan C = \frac{1}{2}$
G $\tan C = 2$
H $\sin C = \frac{\sqrt{5}}{3}$
J $\cos C = 2$

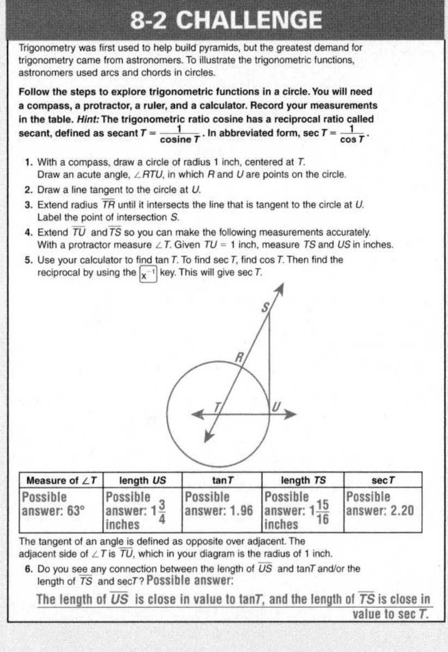

8-2 CHALLENGE

Trigonometry was first used to help build pyramids, but the greatest demand for trigonometry came from astronomers. To illustrate the trigonometric functions, astronomers used arcs and chords in circles.

Follow the steps to explore trigonometric functions in a circle. You will need a compass, a protractor, a ruler, and a calculator. Record your measurements in the table. *Hint:* The trigonometric ratio cosine has a reciprocal ratio called secant, defined as secant $T = \frac{1}{\text{cosine } T}$. In abbreviated form, $\sec T = \frac{1}{\cos T}$.

1. With a compass, draw a circle of radius 1 inch, centered at T. Draw an acute angle, $\angle RTU$, in which R and U are points on the circle.
2. Draw a line tangent to the circle at U.
3. Extend radius $\overline{TR}$ until it intersects the line that is tangent to the circle at U. Label the point of intersection S.
4. Extend $\overline{TU}$ and $\overline{TS}$ so you can make the following measurements accurately. With a protractor measure $\angle T$. Given $TU = 1$ inch, measure TS and US in inches.
5. Use your calculator to find $\tan T$. To find $\sec T$, find $\cos T$. Then find the reciprocal by using the x^{-1} key. This will give $\sec T$.

S, R, T, U

Measure of ∠T	length US	tan T	length TS	sec T
Possible answer: 63°	Possible answer: $1\frac{3}{4}$ inches	Possible answer: 1.96	Possible answer: $1\frac{15}{16}$ inches	Possible answer: 2.20

The tangent of an angle is defined as opposite over adjacent. The adjacent side of $\angle T$ is $\overline{TU}$, which in your diagram is the radius of 1 inch.

6. Do you see any connection between the length of $\overline{US}$ and $\tan T$ and/or the length of $\overline{TS}$ and $\sec T$? **Possible answer:**
The length of $\overline{US}$ is close in value to $\tan T$, and the length of $\overline{TS}$ is close in value to $\sec T$.

TEST PREP DOCTOR For **Exercise 68,** point out that the values of choices **B** and **C** are the same. The value of choice **D** is larger than *AC* and is therefore not a possible measure for *AB*.

In **Exercise 70,** students can check their answers by assigning angle measures to ∠*M* and ∠*N* and substituting the values into the expressions in the answer choices.

Journal

Have students describe how they remember the difference between the sine, cosine, and tangent ratios.

ALTERNATIVE ASSESSMENT

Have students draw a right triangle and measure one side length and one acute angle measure. Have them use a trigonometric ratio to find a second side length. Then have them use a ruler to measure this side length and compare the results to their calculated value.

Power Presentations with PowerPoint®

8-2 Lesson Quiz

Use a special right triangle to write each trigonometric ratio as a fraction.

1. sin 60° $\frac{\sqrt{3}}{2}$ **2.** cos 45° $\frac{\sqrt{2}}{2}$

Use your calculator to find each trigonometric ratio. Round to the nearest hundredth.

3. tan 84° 9.51 **4.** cos 13° 0.97

Find each length. Round to the nearest tenth.

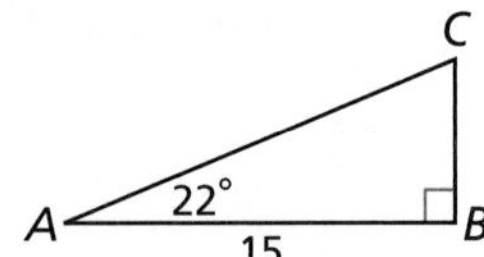

5. *CB* 6.1 **6.** *AC* 16.2

Use your answers from Items 5 and 6 to write each trigonometric ratio as a fraction and as a decimal rounded to the nearest hundredth.

7. sin *A* $\frac{6.1}{16.2} \approx 0.38$

8. cos *A* $\frac{15}{16.2} \approx 0.93$

9. tan *A* $\frac{6.1}{15} \approx 0.41$

Also available on transparency

TEST PREP

68. Which expression can be used to find *AB*?
Ⓐ 7.1(sin 25°) Ⓒ 7.1(sin 65°)
Ⓑ 7.1(cos 25°) Ⓓ 7.1(tan 65°)

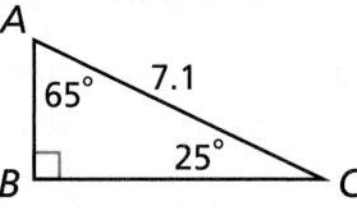

69. A steel cable supports an electrical tower as shown. The cable makes a 65° angle with the ground. The base of the cable is 17 ft from the tower. What is the height of the tower to the nearest foot?
Ⓕ 8 feet Ⓗ 36 feet
Ⓖ 15 feet Ⓙ 40 feet

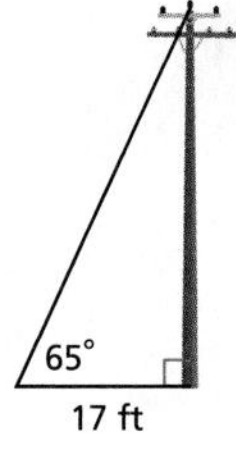

70. Which of the following has the same value as sin *M*?
Ⓐ sin *N* Ⓒ cos *N*
Ⓑ tan *M* Ⓓ cos *M*

CHALLENGE AND EXTEND

Algebra Find the value of *x*. Then find *AB*, *BC*, and *AC*. Round each to the nearest unit.

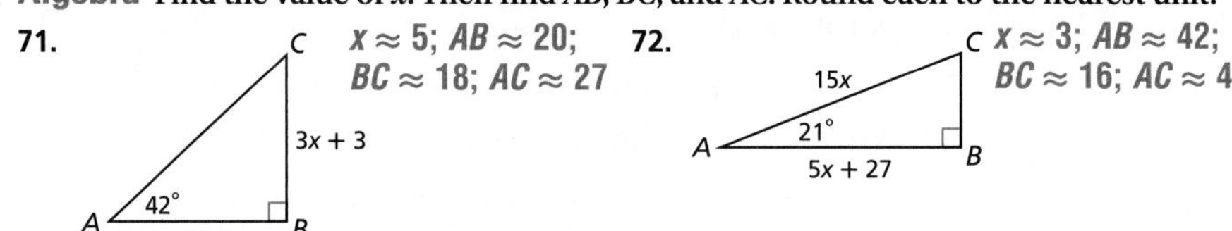

71. $x \approx 5$; $AB \approx 20$; $BC \approx 18$; $AC \approx 27$

72. $x \approx 3$; $AB \approx 42$; $BC \approx 16$; $AC \approx 45$

73. Multi-Step Prove the identity $(\tan A)^2 + 1 = \frac{1}{(\cos A)^2}$.

74. A regular pentagon with 1 in. sides is inscribed in a circle. Find the radius of the circle rounded to the nearest hundredth. **0.85 in.**

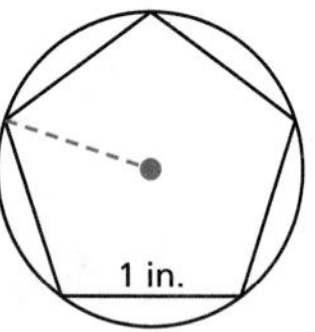

Each of the three trigonometric ratios has a reciprocal ratio, as defined below. These ratios are *cosecant* (csc), *secant* (sec), and *cotangent* (cot).

$\csc A = \frac{1}{\sin A}$ $\sec A = \frac{1}{\cos A}$ $\cot A = \frac{1}{\tan A}$

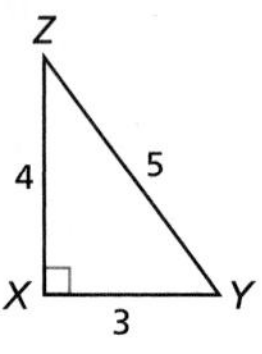

Find each trigonometric ratio to the nearest hundredth.

75. csc *Y* **1.25** **76.** sec *Z* **1.25** **77.** cot *Y* **0.75**

SPIRAL REVIEW

78–80. Possible answers given.

Find three ordered pairs that satisfy each function. *(Previous course)*

78. $f(x) = 3x - 6$ **(−3, −15); (−1, −9); (0, −6)**

79. $f(x) = -0.5x + 10$ **(−2, 11); (0, 10); (2, 9)**

80. $f(x) = x^2 - 4x + 2$ **(−2, 14); (0, 2); (4, 2)**

Identify the property that justifies each statement. *(Lesson 2-5)*

81. $\overline{AB} \cong \overline{CD}$, and $\overline{CD} \cong \overline{DE}$. So $\overline{AB} \cong \overline{DE}$. **Trans. Prop. of ≅**

82. $\overline{AB} \cong \overline{AB}$ **Reflex. Prop. of ≅**

83. If ∠*JKM* ≅ ∠*MLK*, then ∠*MLK* ≅ ∠*JKM*. **Sym. Prop. of ≅**

Find the geometric mean of each pair of numbers. *(Lesson 8-1)*

84. 3 and 27 **9** **85.** 6 and 24 **12** **86.** 8 and 32 **16**

Answers

73. $(\tan A)^2 + 1 = \left(\frac{\sin A}{\cos A}\right)^2 + 1$

$= \frac{(\sin A)^2}{(\cos A)^2} + 1 = \frac{(\sin A)^2}{(\cos A)^2}$

$+ \frac{(\cos A)^2}{(\cos A)^2} = \frac{(\sin A)^2 + (\cos A)^2}{(\cos A)^2}$

$= \frac{1}{(\cos A)^2}$

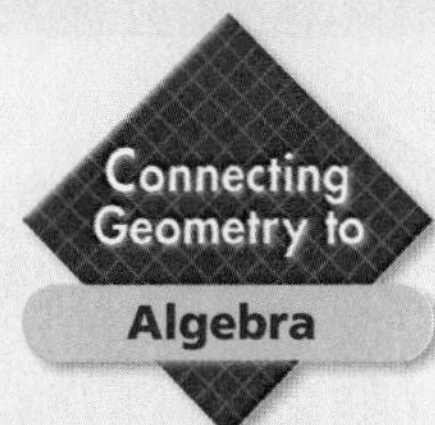

Inverse Functions

In Algebra, you learned that a function is a relation in which each element of the domain is paired with exactly one element of the range. If you switch the domain and range of a one-to-one function, you create an *inverse function.*

The function $y = \sin^{-1} x$ is the inverse of the function $y = \sin x$.

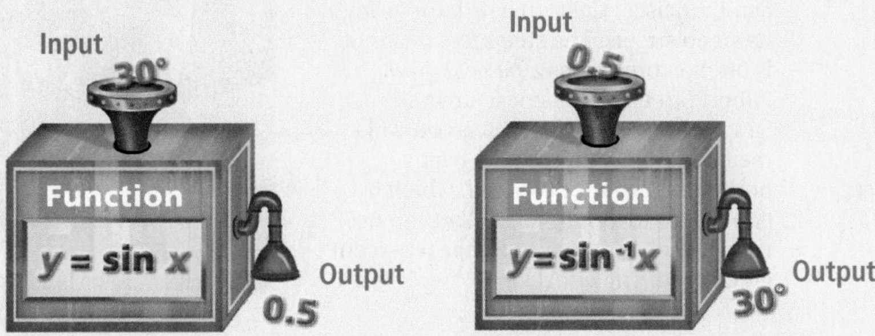

If you know the value of a trigonometric ratio, you can use the inverse trigonometric function to find the angle measure. You can do this either with a calculator or by looking at the graph of the function.

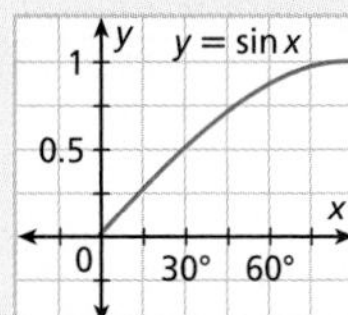

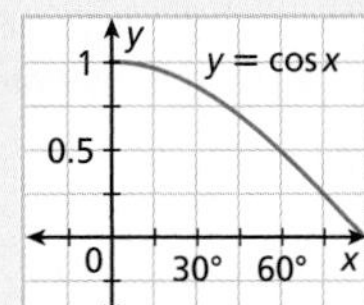

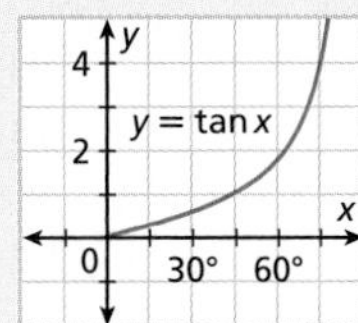

Example

Use the graphs above to find the value of x for $1 = \sin x$. Then write this expression using an inverse trigonometric function.

$1 = \sin x$ — *Look at the graph of $y = \sin x$. Find where the graph intersects the line $y = 1$ and read the corresponding x-coordinate.*

$x = 90°$

$90° = \sin^{-1}(1)$ — *Switch the x- and y-values.*

Try This

Use the graphs above to find the value of x for each of the following. Then write each expression using an inverse trigonometric function.

1. $0 = \sin x$
   $0°$; $\sin^{-1}(0) = 0°$
2. $\frac{1}{2} = \cos x$
   $60°$; $\cos^{-1}\left(\frac{1}{2}\right) = 60°$
3. $1 = \tan x$
   $45°$; $\tan^{-1}(1) = 45°$
4. $0 = \cos x$
   $90°$; $\cos^{-1}(0) = 90°$
5. $0 = \tan x$
   $0°$; $\tan^{-1}(0) = 0°$
6. $\frac{1}{2} = \sin x$
   $30°$; $\sin^{-1}\left(\frac{1}{2}\right) = 30°$

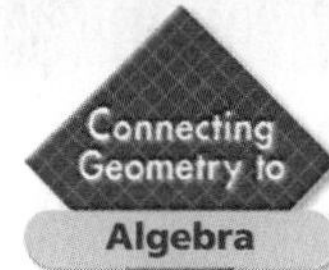

Organizer

Pacing:
Traditional 1 day
Block $\frac{1}{2}$ day

Objective: Apply properties of inverses to trigonometric functions.

Online Edition

Countdown Week 17

Teach

Remember

Students use the graphs of trigonometric functions to review inverse functions.

Teaching Tip **Multiple Representations** For **Exercises 2** and **3,** have students draw a right triangle with the given ratio and use special right triangles to find the angle measure.

Close

Assess

For $y = \tan x$, y is the trigonometric ratio, and x is the angle measure. Ask students what x and y represent in the equation $y = \tan^{-1}x$. x is the trigonometric ratio, and y is the angle measure.

State Resources

8-3 Organizer

Pacing: Traditional 1 day
Block $\frac{1}{2}$ day

Objective: Use trigonometric ratios to find angle measures in right triangles and to solve real-world problems.

Online Edition
Tutorial Videos

Countdown Week 18

Power Presentations with PowerPoint®

Warm Up

Use $\triangle ABC$ for Exercises 1–3.

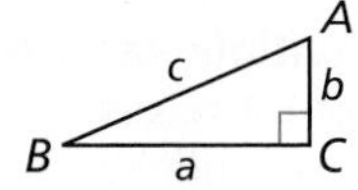

1. If $a = 8$ and $b = 5$, find c. $\sqrt{89}$
2. If $a = 60$ and $c = 61$, find b. 11
3. If $b = 6$ and $c = 10$, find $\sin B$. 0.6

Find *AB*.

4. $A(8, 10)$, $B(3, 0)$ $5\sqrt{5}$
5. $A(1, -2)$, $B(2, 6)$ $\sqrt{65}$

Also available on transparency

Math Humor

Q: Why are you reading that sign backwards?

A: It's an *inverse sine*!

8-3 Solving Right Triangles

Objective
Use trigonometric ratios to find angle measures in right triangles and to solve real-world problems.

Why learn this?
You can convert the percent grade of a road to an angle measure by solving a right triangle.

San Francisco, California, is famous for its steep streets. The steepness of a road is often expressed as a *percent grade.* Filbert Street, the steepest street in San Francisco, has a 31.5% grade. This means the road rises 31.5 ft over a horizontal distance of 100 ft, which is equivalent to a 17.5° angle. You can use trigonometric ratios to change a percent grade to an angle measure.

EXAMPLE 1 Identifying Angles from Trigonometric Ratios

Use the trigonometric ratio $\cos A = 0.6$ to determine which angle of the triangle is $\angle A$.

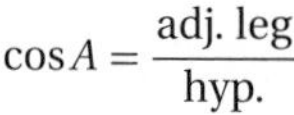

6 cm, 4.8 cm, 3.6 cm, angles 1 and 2

$\cos A = \frac{\text{adj. leg}}{\text{hyp.}}$ *Cosine is the ratio of the adjacent leg to the hypotenuse.*

$\cos \angle 1 = \frac{3.6}{6} = 0.6$ *The leg adjacent to ∠1 is 3.6. The hypotenuse is 6.*

$\cos \angle 2 = \frac{4.8}{6} = 0.8$ *The leg adjacent to ∠2 is 4.8. The hypotenuse is 6.*

Since $\cos A = \cos \angle 1$, $\angle 1$ is $\angle A$.

CHECK IT OUT! **Use the given trigonometric ratio to determine which angle of the triangle is $\angle A$.**

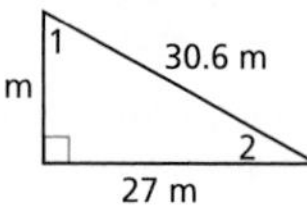

1a. $\sin A = \frac{8}{17}$ $\angle 2$ **1b.** $\tan A = 1.875$ $\angle 1$

In Lesson 8-2, you learned that $\sin 30° = 0.5$. Conversely, if you know that the sine of an acute angle is 0.5, you can conclude that the angle measures 30°. This is written as $\sin^{-1}(0.5) = 30°$.

Reading Math
The expression $\sin^{-1}x$ is read "the inverse sine of x." It does *not* mean $\frac{1}{\sin x}$. You can think of $\sin^{-1}x$ as "the angle whose sine is x."

If you know the sine, cosine, or tangent of an acute angle measure, you can use the inverse trigonometric functions to find the measure of the angle.

Inverse Trigonometric Functions
If $\sin A = x$, then $\sin^{-1}x = m\angle A$.
If $\cos A = x$, then $\cos^{-1}x = m\angle A$.
If $\tan A = x$, then $\tan^{-1}x = m\angle A$.

State Resources

go.hrw.com
State Resources Online
KEYWORD: MG7 Resources

1 Introduce

EXPLORATION

8-3 Solving Right Triangles

The tangent of a 45° angle is 1, so you can write $\tan 45° = 1$. You can use an *inverse trigonometric function* to write $\tan^{-1}(1) = 45°$. This means that the angle whose tangent is 1 measures 45°.

1. Use the figure to complete the table.

Trigonometric Function	Inverse Trigonometric Function
$\tan 22.6° =$ ____	$\tan^{-1}\left(\frac{5}{12}\right) =$ ____
$\tan 67.4° =$ ____	$\tan^{-1}\left(\frac{12}{5}\right) =$ ____

13, 5, 12, 67.4°, 22.6°

2. Similar notation is used for the inverse sine and inverse cosine. For example, $\sin 30° = \frac{1}{2}$, so $\sin^{-1}\left(\frac{1}{2}\right) = 30°$. Use the figure above to complete the table.

Trigonometric Function	Inverse Trigonometric Function
$\sin 22.6° =$ ____	$\sin^{-1}\left(\frac{5}{13}\right) =$ ____
$\sin 67.4° =$ ____	$\sin^{-1}\left(\frac{12}{13}\right) =$ ____
$\cos 22.6° =$ ____	$\cos^{-1}\left(\frac{12}{13}\right) =$ ____

Motivate

Show students pictures of percent grade signs from a highway. Explain that many highways include runaway truck ramps near the bottom of these grades in case a truck's brakes fail. The grade of the ramp affects the truck's stopping distance and can be found by using a trigonometric ratio. Explain that students will learn how to find the acute angle measure of a right triangle in this lesson.

Explorations and answers are provided in *Alternate Openers: Explorations Transparencies.*

EXAMPLE 2 Calculating Angle Measures from Trigonometric Ratios

> **Helpful Hint**
>
> When using your calculator to find the value of an inverse trigonometric expression, you may need to press the [arc], [inv], or [2nd] key.

Use your calculator to find each angle measure to the nearest degree.

A $\cos^{-1}(0.5)$ **B** $\sin^{-1}(0.45)$ **C** $\tan^{-1}(3.2)$

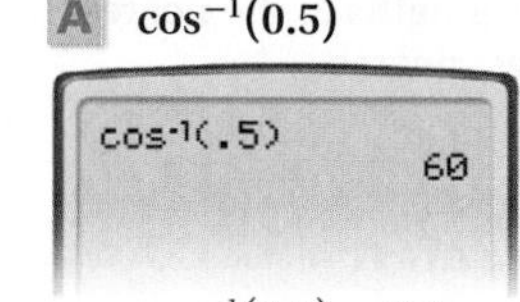

$\cos^{-1}(0.5) = 60°$

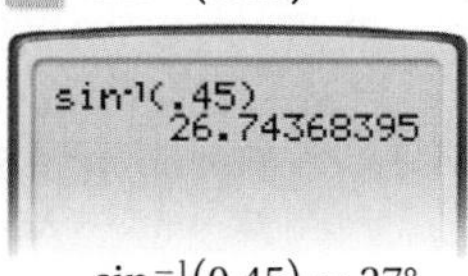

$\sin^{-1}(0.45) \approx 27°$

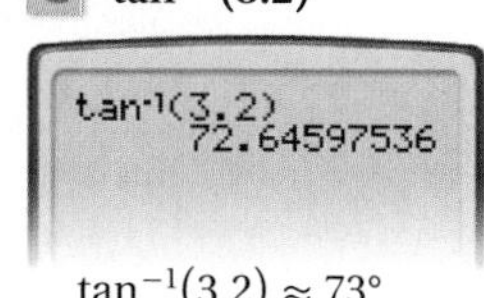

$\tan^{-1}(3.2) \approx 73°$

Use your calculator to find each angle measure to the nearest degree.

2a. $\tan^{-1}(0.75)$ **37°** **2b.** $\cos^{-1}(0.05)$ **87°** **2c.** $\sin^{-1}(0.67)$ **42°**

Using given measures to find the unknown angle measures or side lengths of a triangle is known as *solving a triangle.* To solve a right triangle, you need to know two side lengths or one side length and an acute angle measure.

EXAMPLE 3 Solving Right Triangles

Find the unknown measures. Round lengths to the nearest hundredth and angle measures to the nearest degree.

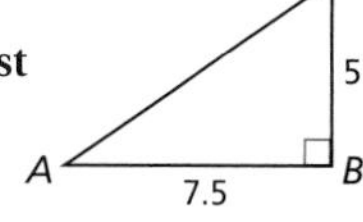

Method 1:

By the Pythagorean Theorem,

$AC^2 = AB^2 + BC^2.$

$= (7.5)^2 + 5^2 = 81.25$

So $AC = \sqrt{81.25} \approx 9.01.$

$m\angle A = \tan^{-1}\left(\frac{5}{7.5}\right) \approx 34°$

Since the acute angles of a right triangle are complementary, $m\angle C \approx 90° - 34° \approx 56°.$

Method 2:

$m\angle A = \tan^{-1}\left(\frac{5}{7.5}\right) \approx 34°$

Since the acute angles of a right triangle are complementary, $m\angle C \approx 90° - 34° \approx 56°.$

$\sin A = \frac{5}{AC}$, so $AC = \frac{5}{\sin A}.$

$$AC \approx \frac{5}{\sin\left[\tan^{-1}\left(\frac{5}{7.5}\right)\right]} \approx 9.01$$

3. Find the unknown measures. Round lengths to the nearest hundredth and angle measures to the nearest degree.

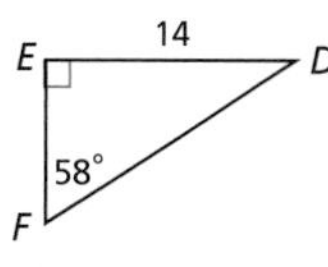

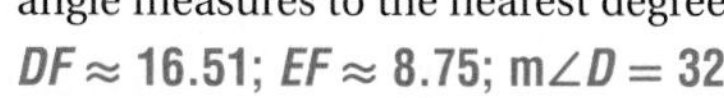

***DF* ≈ 16.51; *EF* ≈ 8.75; m∠*D* = 32°**

Student to Student — *Solving Right Triangles*

Kendell Waters
Marshall High School

Rounding can really make a difference! To find AC, I used the Pythagorean Theorem and got 15.62.

Then I did it a different way. I used $m\angle A = \tan^{-1}\left(\frac{10}{12}\right)$ *to find* $m\angle A = 39.8056°$*, which I rounded to 40°.* $\sin 40° = \frac{10}{AC}$*, so* $AC = \frac{10}{\sin 40°} \approx 15.56.$

The difference in the two answers reminded me not to round values until the last step.

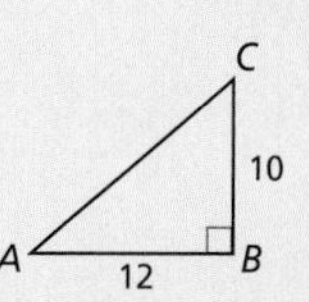

2 Teach

Guided Instruction

Review with students how to use trigonometric ratios to find the side lengths in a right triangle. Then discuss how to use an inverse trigonometric function to find an angle measure when the ratio is known. Review the Distance Formula. Discuss how to solve a right triangle in the coordinate plane. Be sure that students realize that sine and cosine ratios never have values greater than 1.

Reaching All Learners
Through Auditory Cues

Display the expressions $\sin^{-1} x$, $\cos^{-1} x$, and $\tan^{-1} x$. Have students point to the corresponding expression as they practice reading the following aloud:

- The inverse sine of *x* is the angle whose sine equals *x*.
- The inverse cosine of *x* is the angle whose cosine equals *x*.
- The inverse tangent of *x* is the angle whose tangent equals *x*.

ENGLISH LANGUAGE LEARNERS

Power Presentations with PowerPoint®

Additional Examples

Example 1

Use the trigonometric ratio $\cos A = \frac{24}{25}$ to determine which angle of the triangle is $\angle A$. ∠2

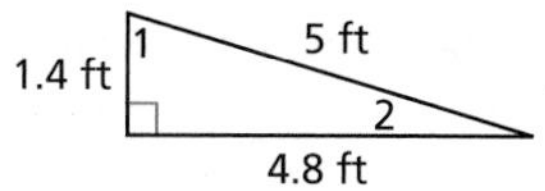

Example 2

Use your calculator to find each angle measure to the nearest degree.

A. $\cos^{-1}(0.87)$ 30°

B. $\sin^{-1}(0.85)$ 58°

C. $\tan^{-1}(0.71)$ 35°

Example 3

Find the unknown measures. Round lengths to the nearest hundredth and angle measures to the nearest degree. $m\angle R \approx 29°$; $m\angle T \approx 61°$; $ST \approx 2.74$

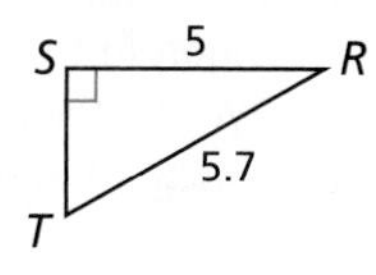

INTERVENTION
Questioning Strategies

EXAMPLE 1

- How do you determine from a diagram which angle has a given trigonometric ratio?

EXAMPLE 2

- How do you use your calculator to find what angle has a given trigonometric ratio?

EXAMPLE 3

- What information do you need to solve a right triangle?

Teaching Tip **Technology** Pushing the SIN key on some calculators displays "sin(" on the screen. When students are calculating $(\sin A)(x)$, remind them to close the parentheses before entering the multiplication symbol and the value of *x*. This applies to expressions involving cosine or tangent as well.

Power Presentations with PowerPoint®

Additional Examples

Example 4

The coordinates of the vertices of $\triangle PQR$ are $P(-3, 3)$, $Q(2, 3)$, and $R(-3, -4)$. Find the side lengths to the nearest hundredth and the angle measures to the nearest degree. $PQ = 5$; $PR = 7$; $QR \approx 8.60$; $m\angle P = 90°$; $m\angle Q \approx 54°$; $m\angle R \approx 36°$

Example 5

A highway sign warns that a section of road ahead has a 7% grade. To the nearest degree, what angle does the road make with a horizontal line? 4°

INTERVENTION

Questioning Strategies

EXAMPLE 4

- How could you use the Pythagorean Theorem to find the length of the hypotenuse?
- How could you use a tangent ratio to find the acute angle measures?

EXAMPLE 5

- How do you change a percent grade to an angle measure?
- What happens to the acute angle that is made with the horizontal as the percent grade of a road decreases?

Teaching Tip **Algebra** Since the sine and cosine ratios are never greater than 1, the range of the graphs of $y = \sin x$ and $y = \cos x$ do not include values greater than 1.

Teaching Tip **Inclusion** For greater accuracy, remind students to use given measurements instead of calculated values in the later steps of solving a right triangle.

EXAMPLE 4 Solving a Right Triangle in the Coordinate Plane

The coordinates of the vertices of $\triangle JKL$ are $J(-1, 2)$, $K(-1, -3)$, and $L(3, -3)$. Find the side lengths to the nearest hundredth and the angle measures to the nearest degree.

Step 1 Find the side lengths.

Plot points J, K, and L.

$JK = 5 \quad KL = 4$

By the Distance Formula,

$$JL = \sqrt{[3-(-1)]^2 + (-3-2)^2}.$$
$$= \sqrt{4^2 + (-5)^2}$$
$$= \sqrt{16+25} = \sqrt{41} \approx 6.40$$

Step 2 Find the angle measures.

$m\angle K = 90°$ — *$\overline{JK}$ and $\overline{KL}$ are ⊥.*

$m\angle J = \tan^{-1}\left(\frac{4}{5}\right) \approx 39°$ — *$\overline{KL}$ is opp. ∠J, and $\overline{JK}$ is adj. to ∠J.*

$m\angle L \approx 90° - 39° \approx 51°$ — *The acute ∠s of a rt. △ are comp.*

4. The coordinates of the vertices of $\triangle RST$ are $R(-3, 5)$, $S(4, 5)$, and $T(4, -2)$. Find the side lengths to the nearest hundredth and the angle measures to the nearest degree. **$RS = ST = 7$; $RT \approx 9.90$; $m\angle S = 90°$; $m\angle R = m\angle T = 45°$**

EXAMPLE 5 *Travel Application*

San Francisco's Lombard Street is known as one of "the crookedest streets in the world." The road's eight switchbacks were built in the 1920s to make the steep hill passable by cars. If the hill has a percent grade of 84%, what angle does the hill make with a horizontal line? Round to the nearest degree.

$84\% = \frac{84}{100}$ — *Change the percent grade to a fraction.*

An 84% grade means the hill rises 84 ft for every 100 ft of horizontal distance.

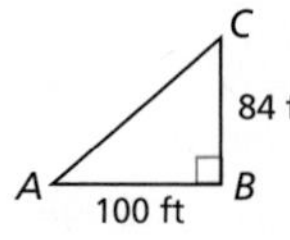

Draw a right triangle to represent the hill. ∠A is the angle the hill makes with a horizontal line.

$m\angle A = \tan^{-1}\left(\frac{84}{100}\right) \approx 40°$

5. Baldwin St. in Dunedin, New Zealand, is the steepest street in the world. It has a grade of 38%. To the nearest degree, what angle does Baldwin St. make with a horizontal line? **21°**

3 Close

Summarize

Review the definitions of the three trigonometric ratios covered in the previous lesson. Review how the related inverse trigonometric functions can be used to find the acute angle measures of a right triangle.

ONGOING ASSESSMENT and INTERVENTION

***Diagnose Before* the Lesson**
8-3 Warm Up, TE p. 534

***Monitor During* the Lesson**
Check It Out! Exercises, SE pp. 534–536
Questioning Strategies, TE pp. 535–536

***Assess After* the Lesson**
8-3 Lesson Quiz, TE p. 541
Alternative Assessment, TE p. 541

THINK AND DISCUSS

1. Describe the steps you would use to solve $\triangle RST$.
2. Given that $\cos Z = 0.35$, write an equivalent statement using an inverse trigonometric function.

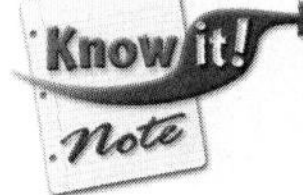

3. **GET ORGANIZED** Copy and complete the graphic organizer. In each box, write a trigonometric ratio for $\angle A$. Then write an equivalent statement using an inverse trigonometric function.

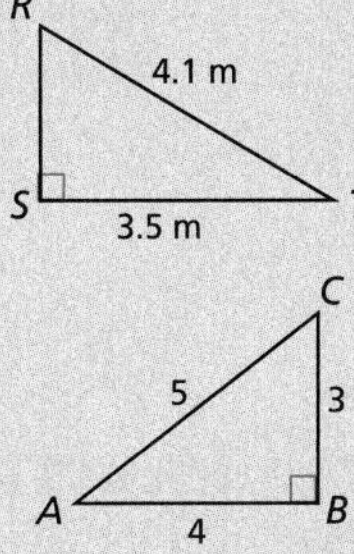

	Trigonometric Ratio	Inverse Trigonometric Function
Sine		
Cosine		
Tangent		

Answers to *Think and Discuss*

1. Find *RS* using the Pyth. Thm. Then find $m\angle R$ using $m\angle R = \sin^{-1}\left(\frac{3.5}{4.1}\right)$ and find $m\angle T$ using $m\angle T = \cos^{-1}\left(\frac{3.5}{4.1}\right)$.
2. $\cos^{-1}(0.35) = m\angle Z$
3. See p. A7.

8-3 Exercises

GUIDED PRACTICE

SEE EXAMPLE 1 p. 534

Use the given trigonometric ratio to determine which angle of the triangle is $\angle A$.

1. $\sin A = \frac{4}{5}$ ∠1
2. $\tan A = 1\frac{1}{3}$ ∠1
3. $\cos A = 0.6$ ∠1
4. $\cos A = 0.8$ ∠2
5. $\tan A = 0.75$ ∠2
6. $\sin A = 0.6$ ∠2

SEE EXAMPLE 2 p. 535

Use your calculator to find each angle measure to the nearest degree.

7. $\tan^{-1}(2.1)$ **65°**
8. $\cos^{-1}\left(\frac{1}{3}\right)$ **71°**
9. $\cos^{-1}\left(\frac{5}{6}\right)$ **34°**
10. $\sin^{-1}(0.5)$ **30°**
11. $\sin^{-1}(0.61)$ **38°**
12. $\tan^{-1}(0.09)$ **5°**

SEE EXAMPLE 3 p. 535

Multi-Step Find the unknown measures. Round lengths to the nearest hundredth and angle measures to the nearest degree.

13. 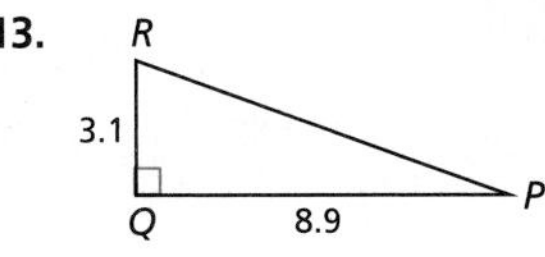

14. 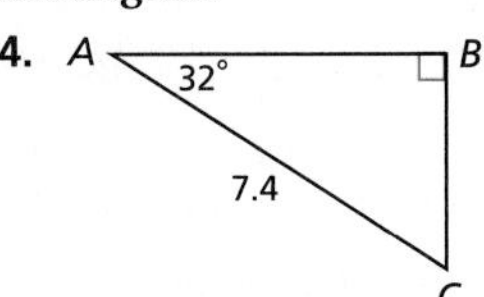

15. 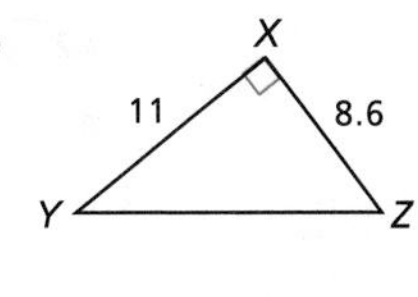

SEE EXAMPLE 4 p. 536

Multi-Step For each triangle, find the side lengths to the nearest hundredth and the angle measures to the nearest degree.

16. $D(4, 1), E(4, -2), F(-2, -2)$
17. $R(3, 3), S(-2, 3), T(-2, -3)$
18. $X(4, -6), Y(-3, 1), Z(-3, -6)$
19. $A(-1, 1), B(1, 1), C(1, 5)$

8-3 Exercises

Assignment Guide

Assign *Guided Practice* exercises as necessary.

If you finished Examples **1–3**

Basic 21–35, 39–44, 48–50

Average 21–35, 39–44, 48–50, 54, 56

Advanced 21–35, 39–44, 48–50, 54, 56, 69, 76

If you finished Examples **1–5**

Basic 21–39, 42, 47–57, 59, 62, 63, 65–68, 77–85

Average 21–39, 42, 45–49, 53–63, 65–69, 74, 77–85

Advanced 21–47, 51–54, 56, 58, 60, 61, 63–85

Homework Quick Check

Quickly check key concepts.
Exercises: 22, 28, 34, 36, 38, 54

Answers

13. $RP \approx 9.42$; $m\angle P \approx 19°$; $m\angle R \approx 71°$
14. $AB \approx 6.28$; $BC \approx 3.92$; $m\angle C = 58°$
15. $YZ \approx 13.96$; $m\angle Y \approx 38°$; $m\angle Z \approx 52°$
16. $DE = 3$; $EF = 6$; $DF \approx 6.71$; $m\angle E = 90°$; $m\angle D \approx 63°$; $m\angle F \approx 27°$
17. $RS = 5$; $ST = 6$; $RT \approx 7.81$; $m\angle S = 90°$; $m\angle R \approx 50°$; $m\angle T \approx 40°$
18. $XZ = YZ = 7$; $XY \approx 9.90$; $m\angle Z = 90°$; $m\angle X = m\angle Y = 45°$
19. $AB = 2$; $BC = 4$; $AC \approx 4.47$; $m\angle B = 90°$; $m\angle A \approx 63°$; $m\angle C \approx 27°$

State Resources

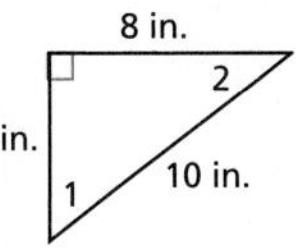

Communicating Math Encourage students to communicate their understanding of the relationship between the trigonometric ratios and their inverses as they work through **Exercises 27–32.** For example, using their answer to **Exercise 27,** students can write $\sin 18° \approx 0.31$, and then use their calculator to check their equation.

Inclusion Students may find **Exercises 39–44** easier if they first identify whether they are looking for a ratio or an angle measure. If they are looking for a ratio, they should use sin, cos, or tan. If they are looking for an angle measure, they should use $\sin^{-1}$, $\cos^{-1}$, or $\tan^{-1}$.

Answers

45. Assume the square has sides of length a. Then the rt. △ formed by a diag. has legs of length a. The measure of the ∠ formed by the diag. and a side is $\tan^{-1}\left(\frac{a}{a}\right) = \tan^{-1}(1) = 45°$.

46. Note: Figure is reduced in TE.

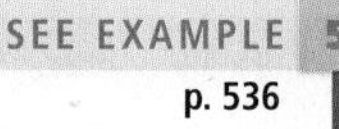

p. 536

20. **Cycling** A hill in the Tour de France bike race has a grade of 8%. To the nearest degree, what is the angle that this hill makes with a horizontal line? **5°**

PRACTICE AND PROBLEM SOLVING

Independent Practice

For Exercises	See Example
21–26	1
27–32	2
33–35	3
36–37	4
38	5

Extra Practice

Skills Practice p. S18
Application Practice p. S35

Use the given trigonometric ratio to determine which angle of the triangle is ∠A.

7.5 cm, 18 cm, 19.5 cm, 1, 2

21. $\tan A = \frac{5}{12}$ **∠2**
22. $\tan A = 2.4$ **∠1**
23. $\sin A = \frac{12}{13}$ **∠1**
24. $\sin A = \frac{5}{13}$ **∠2**
25. $\cos A = \frac{12}{13}$ **∠2**
26. $\cos A = \frac{5}{13}$ **∠1**

Use your calculator to find each angle measure to the nearest degree.

27. $\sin^{-1}(0.31)$ **18°**
28. $\tan^{-1}(1)$ **45°**
29. $\cos^{-1}(0.8)$ **37°**
30. $\cos^{-1}(0.72)$ **44°**
31. $\tan^{-1}(1.55)$ **57°**
32. $\sin^{-1}\left(\frac{9}{17}\right)$ **32°**

Multi-Step Find the unknown measures. Round lengths to the nearest hundredth and angle measures to the nearest degree.

33. 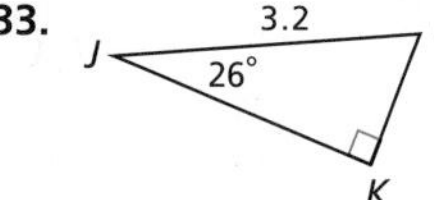

34. 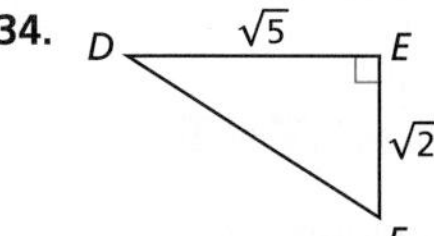

35. 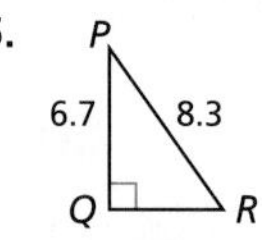

Multi-Step For each triangle, find the side lengths to the nearest hundredth and the angle measures to the nearest degree.

36. $A(2, 0)$, $B(2, -5)$, $C(1, -5)$
37. $M(3, 2)$, $N(3, -2)$, $P(-1, -2)$

38. **Building** For maximum accessibility, a wheelchair ramp should have a slope between $\frac{1}{16}$ and $\frac{1}{20}$. What is the range of angle measures that a ramp should make with a horizontal line? Round to the nearest degree. **3° to 4°**

Complete each statement. If necessary, round angle measures to the nearest degree. Round other values to the nearest hundredth.

39. tan ___?___ ≈ 3.5 **74°**
40. sin ___?___ $\approx \frac{2}{3}$ **42°**
41. ___?___ 42° ≈ 0.74 **cos**
42. $\cos^{-1}$(___?___) ≈ 12° **0.98**
43. $\sin^{-1}$(___?___) ≈ 69° **0.93**
44. ___?___ 60° = $\frac{1}{2}$ **cos**

45. **Critical Thinking** Use trigonometric ratios to explain why the diagonal of a square forms a 45° angle with each of the sides.

46. **Estimation** You can use trigonometry to find angle measures when a protractor is not available.
    a. Estimate the measure of ∠P. **Possible answer: 40°**
    b. Use a centimeter ruler to find RQ and PQ.
    c. Use your measurements from part **b** and an inverse trigonometric function to find m∠P to the nearest degree.
    d. How does your result in part **c** compare to your estimate in part **a**? **Answers will vary.**

R, P, Q

33. $JK \approx 2.88$; $LK \approx 1.40$; $m\angle L = 64°$

34. $DF \approx 2.65$; $m\angle D \approx 32°$; $m\angle F \approx 58°$

35. $QR \approx 4.90$; $m\angle P \approx 36°$; $m\angle R \approx 54°$

36. $AB = 5$; $BC = 1$; $AC \approx 5.10$; $m\angle B = 90°$; $m\angle A \approx 11°$; $m\angle C \approx 79°$

37. $MN = NP = 4$; $MP \approx 5.66$; $m\angle N = 90°$; $m\angle M = m\angle P = 45°$

46b. $RQ \approx 2.2$ cm; $PQ \approx 3.1$ cm

c. 35°

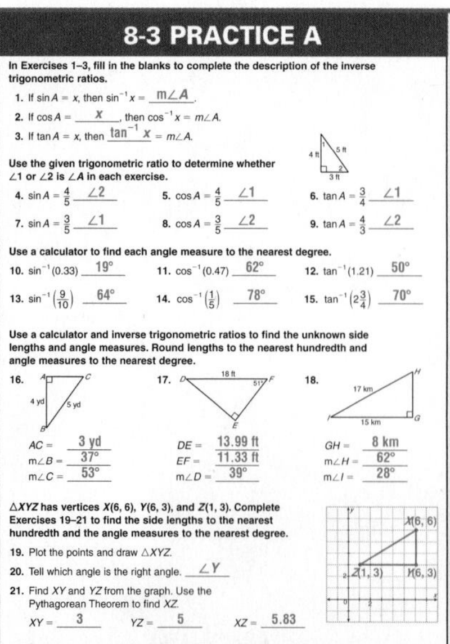

8-3 PRACTICE A

In Exercises 1–3, fill in the blanks to complete the description of the inverse trigonometric ratios.

1. If $\sin A = x$, then $\sin^{-1} x =$ **m∠A**.
2. If $\cos A =$ **x**, then $\cos^{-1} x = m\angle A$.
3. If $\tan A = x$, then **$\tan^{-1} x$** $= m\angle A$.

Use the given trigonometric ratio to determine whether ∠1 or ∠2 is ∠A in each exercise.

4 ft, 5 ft, 3 ft, 1, 2

4. $\sin A = \frac{4}{5}$ **∠2**
5. $\cos A = \frac{4}{5}$ **∠1**
6. $\tan A = \frac{3}{4}$ **∠1**
7. $\sin A = \frac{3}{5}$ **∠1**
8. $\cos A = \frac{3}{5}$ **∠2**
9. $\tan A = \frac{4}{3}$ **∠2**

Use a calculator to find each angle measure to the nearest degree.

10. $\sin^{-1}(0.33)$ **19°**
11. $\cos^{-1}(0.47)$ **62°**
12. $\tan^{-1}(1.21)$ **50°**
13. $\sin^{-1}\left(\frac{9}{10}\right)$ **64°**
14. $\cos^{-1}\left(\frac{1}{5}\right)$ **78°**
15. $\tan^{-1}\left(2\frac{3}{4}\right)$ **70°**

Use a calculator and inverse trigonometric ratios to find the unknown side lengths and angle measures. Round lengths to the nearest hundredth and angle measures to the nearest degree.

16. A, C, B; 4 yd, 5 yd
AC = **3 yd**
m∠B = **37°**
m∠C = **53°**

17. D, F, E; 18 ft, 51°
DE = **13.99 ft**
EF = **11.33 ft**
m∠D = **39°**

18. H, I, G; 17 km, 15 km
GH = **8 km**
m∠H = **62°**
m∠I = **28°**

△XYZ has vertices X(6, 6), Y(6, 3), and Z(1, 3). Complete Exercises 19–21 to find the side lengths to the nearest hundredth and the angle measures to the nearest degree.

19. Plot the points and draw △XYZ.
20. Tell which angle is the right angle. **∠Y**
21. Find XY and YZ from the graph. Use the Pythagorean Theorem to find XZ.
XY = **3** YZ = **5** XZ = **5.83**

X(6, 6), Z(1, 3), Y(6, 3)

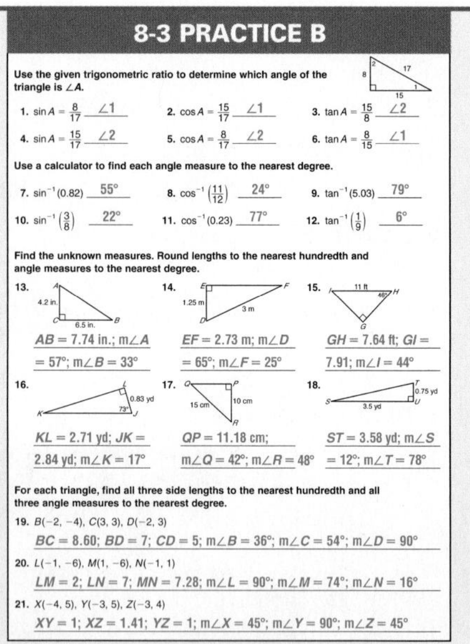

8-3 PRACTICE B

Use the given trigonometric ratio to determine which angle of the triangle is ∠A.

8, 17, 15, 1, 2

1. $\sin A = \frac{8}{17}$ **∠1**
2. $\cos A = \frac{15}{17}$ **∠1**
3. $\tan A = \frac{15}{8}$ **∠2**
4. $\sin A = \frac{15}{17}$ **∠2**
5. $\cos A = \frac{8}{17}$ **∠2**
6. $\tan A = \frac{8}{15}$ **∠1**

Use a calculator to find each angle measure to the nearest degree.

7. $\sin^{-1}(0.82)$ **55°**
8. $\cos^{-1}\left(\frac{11}{12}\right)$ **24°**
9. $\tan^{-1}(5.03)$ **79°**
10. $\sin^{-1}\left(\frac{3}{8}\right)$ **22°**
11. $\cos^{-1}(0.23)$ **77°**
12. $\tan^{-1}\left(\frac{1}{9}\right)$ **6°**

Find the unknown measures. Round lengths to the nearest hundredth and angle measures to the nearest degree.

13. A, C, B; 4.2 in., 6.5 in.
AB = 7.74 in.; m∠A = 57°; m∠B = 33°

14. E, F, D; 1.25 m, 3 m
EF = 2.73 m; m∠D = 65°; m∠F = 25°

15. I, H, G; 11 ft, 46°
GH = 7.64 ft; GI = 7.91; m∠I = 44°

16. L, K, J; 0.83 yd, 73°
KL = 2.71 yd; JK = 2.84 yd; m∠K = 17°

17. Q, P, R; 15 cm, 10 cm
QP = 11.18 cm; m∠Q = 42°; m∠R = 48°

18. T, S, U; 0.75 yd, 3.5 yd
ST = 3.58 yd; m∠S = 12°; m∠T = 78°

For each triangle, find all three side lengths to the nearest hundredth and all three angle measures to the nearest degree.

19. B(−2, −4), C(3, 3), D(−2, 3)
BC = 8.60; BD = 7; CD = 5; m∠B = 36°; m∠C = 54°; m∠D = 90°

20. L(−1, −6), M(1, −6), N(−1, 1)
LM = 2; LN = 7; MN = 7.28; m∠L = 90°; m∠M = 74°; m∠N = 16°

21. X(−4, 5), Y(−3, 5), Z(−3, 4)
XY = 1; XZ = 1.41; YZ = 1; m∠X = 45°; m∠Y = 90°; m∠Z = 45°

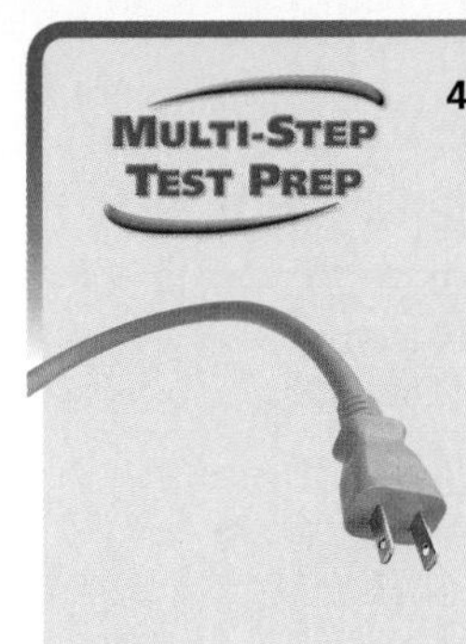

MULTI-STEP TEST PREP

47. This problem will prepare you for the Multi-Step Test Prep on page 542.

An electric company wants to install a vertical utility pole at the base of a hill that has an 8% grade.

a. To the nearest degree, what angle does the hill make with a horizontal line? **5°**

b. What is the measure of the angle between the pole and the hill? Round to the nearest degree. **85°**

c. A utility worker installs a 31-foot guy wire from the top of the pole to the hill. Given that the guy wire is perpendicular to the hill, find the height of the pole to the nearest inch. **31 ft 1 in.**

The side lengths of a right triangle are given below. Find the measures of the acute angles in the triangle. Round to the nearest degree.

48. 3, 4, 5 **37°; 53°** **49.** 5, 12, 13 **23°; 67°** **50.** 8, 15, 17 **28°; 62°**

51. What if...? A right triangle has leg lengths of 28 and 45 inches. Suppose the length of the longer leg doubles. What happens to the measure of the acute angle opposite that leg?

52. Fitness As part of off-season training, the Houston Texans football team must sprint up a ramp with a 28% grade. To the nearest degree, what angle does this ramp make with a horizontal line? **16°**

53. The coordinates of the vertices of a triangle are $A(-1, 0)$, $B(6, 1)$, and $C(0, 3)$.

a. Use the Distance Formula to find AB, BC, and AC.

b. Use the Converse of the Pythagorean Theorem to show that $\triangle ABC$ is a right triangle. Identify the right angle.

c. Find the measures of the acute angles of $\triangle ABC$. Round to the nearest degree. **$m\angle A = 63°$; $m\angle B = 27°$**

Find the indicated measure in each rectangle. Round to the nearest degree.

54. $m\angle BDC$ **16°**

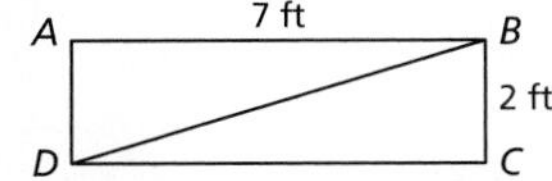

55. $m\angle STV$ **35°**

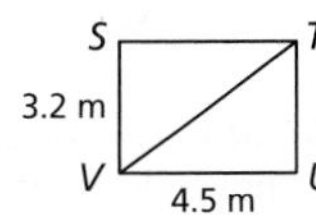

Find the indicated measure in each rhombus. Round to the nearest degree.

56. $m\angle DGF$ **66°**

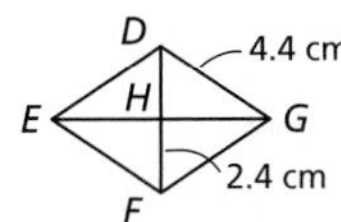

57. $m\angle LKN$ **62°**

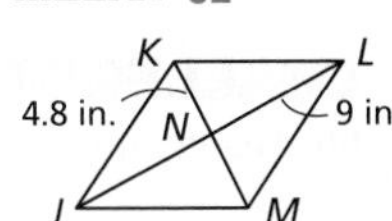

58. Critical Thinking Without using a calculator, compare the values of tan 60° and tan 70°. Explain your reasoning.

The measure of an acute angle formed by a line with slope m and the x-axis can be found by using the expression $\tan^{-1}(m)$. Find the measure of the acute angle that each line makes with the x-axis. Round to the nearest degree.

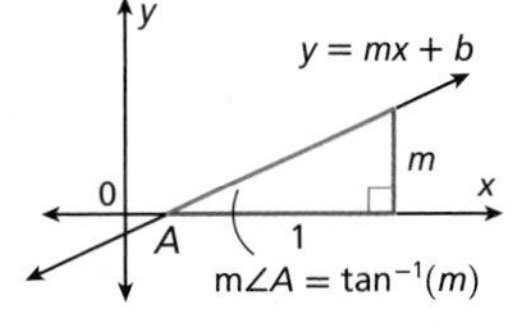

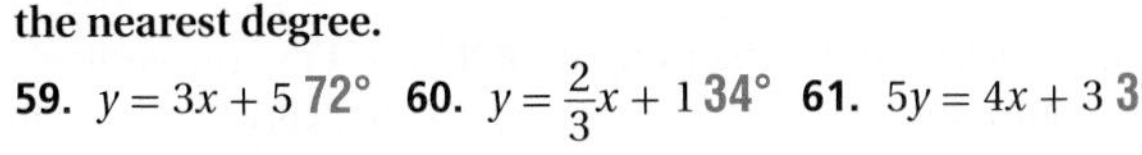

59. $y = 3x + 5$ **72°** **60.** $y = \frac{2}{3}x + 1$ **34°** **61.** $5y = 4x + 3$ **39°**

LINK Fitness

Running on a treadmill is slightly easier than running outdoors, since you don't have to overcome wind resistance. Set the treadmill to a 1% grade to match the intensity of an outdoor run.

51. The acute ∠ measure changes from about 58° to about 73°, an increase by a factor of 1.26.

53a. $AB = 5\sqrt{2}$; $BC = 2\sqrt{10}$; $AC = \sqrt{10}$

b. $AC^2 + BC^2 = AB^2$, so $\triangle ABC$ is a rt. △, and $\angle C$ is the rt. ∠.

COMMON ERROR ALERT

Students may assume that the angle measure in **Exercise 51** should double because the length of the leg doubled. Encourage students to confirm their conjectures by drawing a diagram and using the inverse tangent function.

MULTI-STEP TEST PREP **Exercise 47** involves solving a right triangle to determine angle measures. This exercise prepares students for the Multi-Step Test Prep on page 542.

Teaching Tip **Math Background** For **Exercises 56–57**, remind students that all four sides of a rhombus are congruent and that the diagonals of a rhombus are perpendicular.

Answers

58. tan 70° > tan 60°; possible answer: consider 2 rt. △s, 1 with a 60° ∠ and 1 with a 70° ∠. Suppose that the legs adj. to these △s have a length of 1 unit. The leg opp. the 70° ∠ will be longer than the leg opp. the 60° ∠. So tan 70° is greater than tan 60°.

8-3 PRACTICE C

A Pythagorean triple is a set of whole numbers that satisfies the Pythagorean Theorem. Exercises 1–4 show Pythagorean triples. Find the measures of the two acute angles, to the nearest degree, in triangles with sides of these lengths.

1. 3, 4, 5 **37°; 53°**
2. 5, 12, 13 **23°; 67°**
3. 8, 15, 17 **28°; 62°**
4. 7, 24, 25 **16°; 74°**

5. In the United States, common units used for measuring length are inches, feet, and miles. Most of the rest of the world uses centimeters, meters, and kilometers. Would a 20% grade in America be equal to a 20% grade elsewhere? Explain why or why not.

Yes, a 20% grade in the United States is equal to a 20% grade elsewhere. Possible answer: A 20% grade in the United States means a rise in elevation of 20 feet over 100 horizontal feet. A 20% grade elsewhere means a rise in elevation of 20 meters over 100 meters. But a grade is a ratio: $\frac{20 \text{ ft}}{100 \text{ ft}} = \frac{20 \text{ m}}{100 \text{ m}}$. The units cancel out, and either way a 20% grade simplifies to $\frac{1}{5}$, or an angle with the horizontal that measures about 11°.

Use the law of sines to find the unknown measures. Round lengths to the nearest hundredth and angle measures to the nearest degree.

6. (E, F, G; 35 cm; 49°) **$EF = 24.75$ cm; $FG = 24.75$ cm; $m\angle E = 45°$**

7. (K, M, L; $15\sqrt{3}$ m; 30°) **$ML = 15$ m; $KL = 30$ m; $m\angle L = 60°$**

8. (D, C, B; 42°; 12.5 in.) **$DC = 13.88$ in.; $DB = 18.68$ in.; $m\angle B = 48°$**

9. (U, V, T; $2\sqrt{5}$ ft; 28°) **$TV = 8.41$ ft; $UT = 9.53$ ft; $m\angle T = 62°$**

10. (J, I, H; 28°; 4.7 yd; 2.5 yd) **$IJ = 5.32$ yd; $m\angle H = 90°$; $m\angle I = 62°$**

11. (S, R, T; 62°; 30 m) **$RS = 26.49$ m; $ST = 14.08$ m; $m\angle R = 28°$**

Teaching Tip **Critical Thinking** For **Exercise 62,** review the Pythagorean Theorem and its converse from Lesson 5-7. Since $\triangle ABC$ is not a right triangle, you cannot use trigonometric ratios to solve it.

TEST PREP DOCTOR If students answered **Exercise 65** incorrectly, have them write the three possible trigonometric ratios for $\angle A$ and then use these equations to find the correct answer.

Remind students who chose **B** or **C** for **Exercise 67** that the sine and cosine ratios involve the hypotenuse of the triangle. The measurements given in the diagram are the leg lengths, so students should use a tangent ratio.

Answers

63. No; possible answer: it is only necessary to know 2 side lengths. You can use the Pyth. Thm. to find the third side length or use trigonometric ratios to find the acute $\angle$ measures.

75. Possible answer: the expression $\sin^{-1}(1.5)$ represents an $\angle$ measure that has a sine of 1.5. The sine of an acute $\angle$ of a rt. $\triangle$ must be between 0 and 1, so the expression $\sin^{-1}(1.5)$ is undefined.

76. Let h be the length of the altitude from B to $\overline{AC}$. Then $\sin A = \frac{h}{c}$, so $h = c\sin A$. The area of the $\triangle$ is $\frac{1}{2}bh = \frac{1}{2}bc\sin A$.

62. **ERROR ANALYSIS** A student was asked to find m$\angle C$. Explain the error in the student's solution.

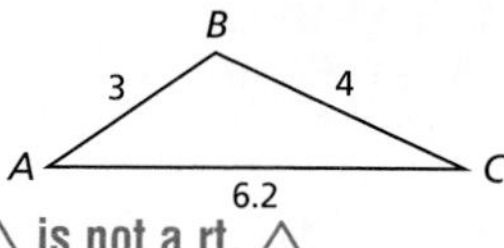

> Since $\tan C = \frac{3}{4}$, $m\angle C = \tan^{-1}\left(\frac{3}{4}\right)$, and $\tan^{-1}(0.75) \approx 37°$. So $m\angle C \approx 37°$.

Since the $\triangle$ is not a rt. $\triangle$, the trig. ratios do not apply.

63. **Write About It** A student claims that you must know the three side lengths of a right triangle before you can use trigonometric ratios to find the measures of the acute angles. Do you agree? Why or why not?

64. $\overline{DC}$ is an altitude of right $\triangle ABC$. Use trigonometric ratios to find the missing lengths in the figure. Then use these lengths to verify the three relationships in the Geometric Mean Corollaries from Lesson 8-1.

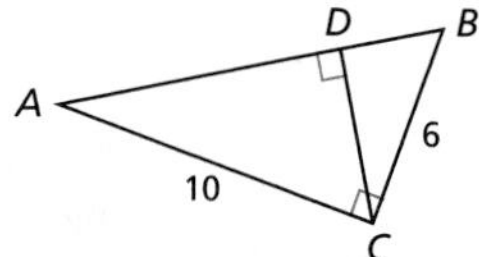

64. $AD \approx 8.57$; $BD \approx 3.09$; $CD \approx 5.14$; $(8.57)(3.09) \approx 26 \approx (5.14)^2$; $(8.57)(8.57 + 3.09) \approx 100 = (10)^2$; $(3.09)(8.57 + 3.09) \approx 36 = (6)^2$

65. Which expression can be used to find m$\angle A$?

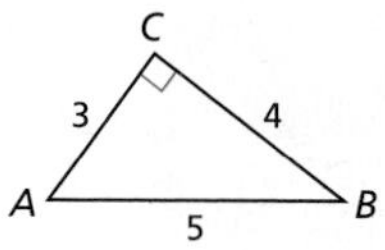

Ⓐ $\tan^{-1}(0.75)$ Ⓒ $\cos^{-1}(0.8)$
Ⓑ $\sin^{-1}\left(\frac{3}{5}\right)$ **Ⓓ** $\tan^{-1}\left(\frac{4}{3}\right)$

C, 3, 4, A, 5, B

66. Which expression is NOT equivalent to $\cos 60°$?

Ⓕ $\frac{1}{2}$ Ⓗ $\frac{\sin 60°}{\tan 60°}$
Ⓖ $\sin 30°$ **Ⓙ** $\cos^{-1}\left(\frac{1}{2}\right)$

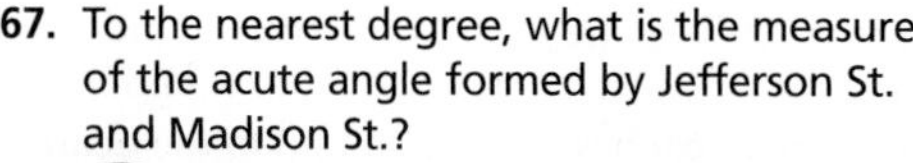

67. To the nearest degree, what is the measure of the acute angle formed by Jefferson St. and Madison St.?

Ⓐ 27° Ⓒ 59°
Ⓑ 31° Ⓓ 63°

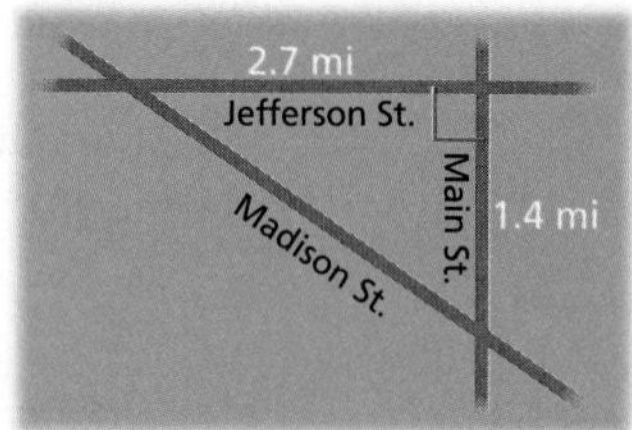

68. **Gridded Response** A highway exit ramp has a slope of $\frac{3}{20}$. To the nearest degree, find the angle that the ramp makes with a horizontal line. **9°**

CHALLENGE AND EXTEND

Find each angle measure. Round to the nearest degree.

69. m$\angle J$ **58°**

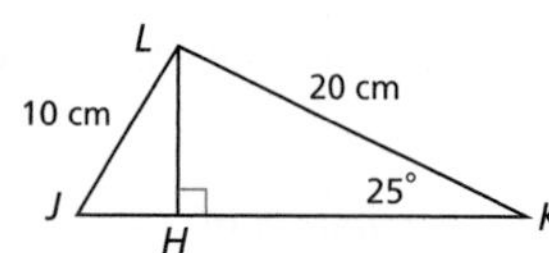

70. m$\angle A$ **48°**

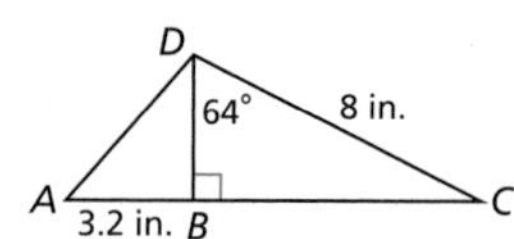

Simply each expression.

71. $\cos^{-1}(\cos 34°)$ **34°**
72. $\tan\left[\tan^{-1}(1.5)\right]$ **1.5**
73. $\sin\left(\sin^{-1} x\right)$ **x**

74. A ramp has a 6% grade. The ramp is 40 ft long. Find the vertical distance that the ramp rises. Round your answer to the nearest hundredth. **2.40 ft**

8-3 READING STRATEGIES

Solving a right triangle means finding the measures of all its unknown sides and angles.

(Triangle: B, C, A; 4, 9)

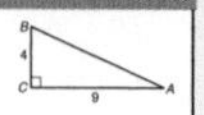

Solve the right triangle at right.

Step 1 Use an *inverse* trigonometric function to find an unknown angle.

$m\angle A = \tan^{-1}\left(\frac{4}{9}\right) \approx 24°$ $m\angle A \approx 24°$

> If $\sin A = x$, then $\sin^{-1} x = m\angle A$.
> If $\cos A = x$, then $\cos^{-1} x = m\angle A$.
> If $\tan A = x$, then $\tan^{-1} x = m\angle A$.

Step 2 Subtract to find the other angle.

$90° - 24° = 66°$ $m\angle B \approx 66°$

Step 3 Find the unknown side.

$4^2 + 9^2 = AB^2$ Use the Pythagorean Theorem.
$16 + 81 = AB^2$
$97 = AB^2$
$\sqrt{97} = AB^2$
$9.85 \approx AB$ $AB \approx 9.85$

Answer each of the following.

1. What does it mean to solve a right triangle?
finding the measures of all unknown sides and angles of the triangle

2. Look at Step 1 above. Write the expression you would use if you wanted to find m$\angle B$ first.
$m\angle B = \tan^{-1}\left(\frac{9}{4}\right)$

3. Step 3 could also be solved by writing a trigonometric expression. Complete this expression that could be used to find AB: $\sin 24° = \frac{4}{AB}$.

4. Solve the triangle at right. Round lengths to the nearest hundredth and angles to the nearest degree.

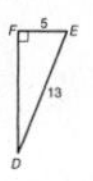

(Triangle: F, E, D; 5, 13)

m$\angle E$ **67°**
m$\angle D$ **23°**
FD **12**

8-3 RETEACH

Use the trigonometric ratio $\sin A = 0.8$ to determine which angle of the triangle is $\angle A$.

$\sin\angle 1 = \frac{\text{leg opposite } \angle 1}{\text{hypotenuse}} = \frac{6}{10} = 0.6$ $\sin\angle 2 = \frac{\text{leg opposite } \angle 2}{\text{hypotenuse}} = \frac{8}{10} = 0.8$

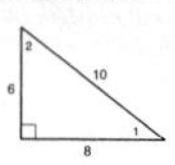

(Triangle: 2, 10, 6, 1, 8)

Since $\sin A = \sin\angle 2$, $\angle 2$ is $\angle A$.

If you know the sine, cosine, or tangent of an acute angle measure, then you can use your calculator to find the measure of the angle.

Inverse Trigonometric Functions	
Symbols	**Examples**
$\sin A = x \Rightarrow \sin^{-1} x = m\angle A$	$\sin 30° = \frac{1}{2} \Rightarrow \sin^{-1}\frac{1}{2} = 30°$
$\cos B = x \Rightarrow \cos^{-1} x = m\angle B$	$\cos 45° = \frac{\sqrt{2}}{2} \Rightarrow \cos^{-1}\frac{\sqrt{2}}{2} = 45°$
$\tan C = x \Rightarrow \tan^{-1} x = m\angle C$	$\tan 76° \approx 4.01 \Rightarrow \tan^{-1} 4.01 \approx 76°$

Use the given trigonometric ratio to determine which angle of the triangle is $\angle A$.

(Triangle: 5.2, 2, 3, 6, 1)

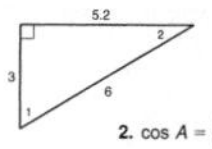

1. $\sin A = \frac{1}{2}$ **$\angle 2$**
2. $\cos A = \frac{13}{15}$ **$\angle 2$**
3. $\cos A = 0.5$ **$\angle 1$**
4. $\tan A = \frac{15}{26}$ **$\angle 2$**

Use your calculator to find each angle measure to the nearest degree.

5. $\sin^{-1}(0.8)$ **53°**
6. $\cos^{-1}(0.19)$ **79°**
7. $\tan^{-1}(3.4)$ **74°**
8. $\sin^{-1}\left(\frac{1}{5}\right)$ **12°**

75. **Critical Thinking** Explain why the expression $\sin^{-1}(1.5)$ does not make sense.

76. If you are given the lengths of two sides of $\triangle ABC$ and the measure of the included angle, you can use the formula $\frac{1}{2}bc\sin A$ to find the area of the triangle. Derive this formula. (*Hint:* Draw an altitude from B to $\overline{AC}$. Use trigonometric ratios to find the length of this altitude.)

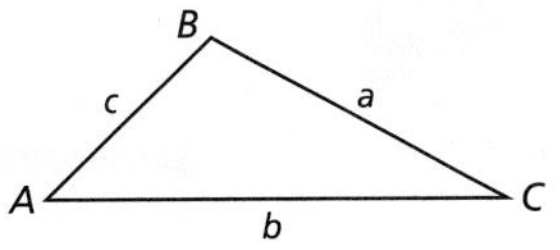

SPIRAL REVIEW

The graph shows the amount of rainfall in a city for the first five months of the year. Determine whether each statement is true or false. *(Previous course)*

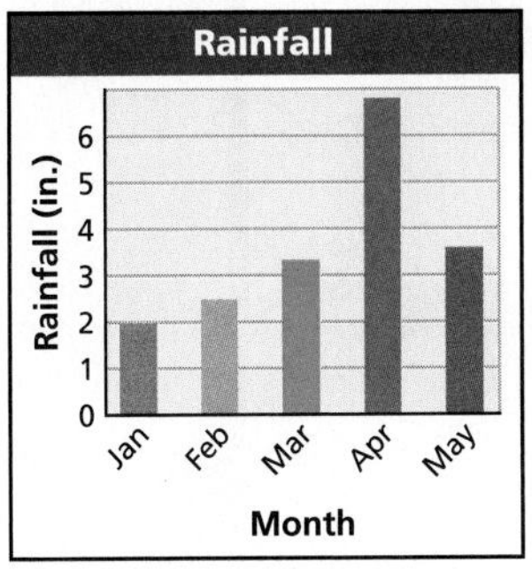

77. It rained more in April than it did in January, February, and March combined. **F**

78. The average monthly rainfall for this five-month period was approximately 3.5 inches. **T**

79. The rainfall amount increased at a constant rate each month over the five-month period. **F**

Use the diagram to find each value, given that $\triangle ABC \cong \triangle DEF$. *(Lesson 4-3)*

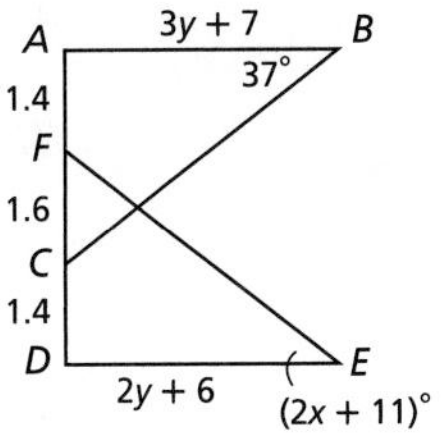

80. x **13**
81. y **−1**
82. DF **3**

Use your calculator to find each trigonometric ratio. Round to the nearest hundredth. *(Lesson 8-2)*

83. $\sin 63°$ **0.89**
84. $\cos 27°$ **0.89**
85. $\tan 64°$ **2.05**

Using Technology

Use a spreadsheet to complete the following.

	A	B	C	D	E
1	a	b	c	m(angle A)	m(angle B)
2					

= SQRT(A2^2 + B2^2)

= DEGREES(ATAN(A2/B2))

= DEGREES(ATAN(B2/A2))

1–5. Check students' work.

1. In cells A2 and B2, enter values for the leg lengths of a right triangle.
2. In cell C2, write a formula to calculate c, the length of the hypotenuse.
3. Write a formula to calculate the measure of $\angle A$ in cell D2. Be sure to use the Degrees function so that the answer is given in degrees. Format the value to include no decimal places.
4. Write a formula to calculate the measure of $\angle B$ in cell E2. Again, be sure to use the Degrees function and format the value to include no decimal places.
5. Use your spreadsheet to check your answers for Exercises 48–50.

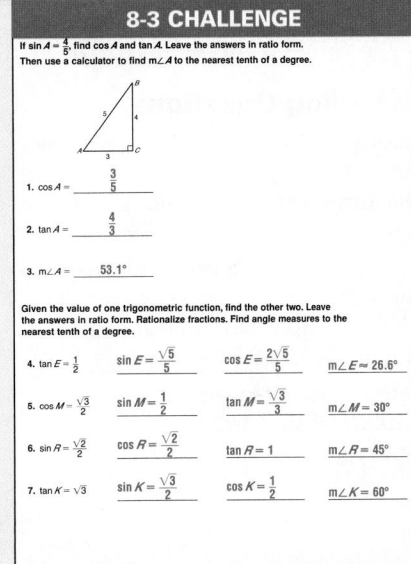

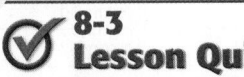

Journal

Have students explain when they would use the sin, cos, or tan buttons on their calculator and when they would use $\sin^{-1}$, $\cos^{-1}$, or $\tan^{-1}$.

ALTERNATIVE ASSESSMENT

Have students construct a right triangle and measure the lengths of two sides. Ask students to find the length of the third side and the acute angle measures without using the Pythagorean Theorem or a protractor. Have students construct a second right triangle and measure one acute angle and a side. Have them find the other acute angle measure and the lengths of the other two sides.

Power Presentations with PowerPoint®

8-3 Lesson Quiz

Use your calculator to find each angle measure to the nearest degree.

1. $\cos^{-1}(0.97)$ 14°
2. $\tan^{-1}(2)$ 63°
3. $\sin^{-1}(0.59)$ 36°

Find the unknown measures. Round lengths to the nearest hundredth and angle measures to the nearest degree.

4. 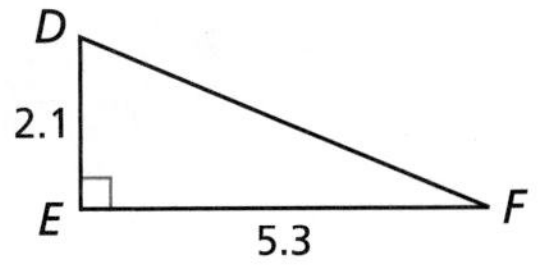

$DF \approx 5.7$; $m\angle D \approx 68°$; $m\angle F \approx 22°$

5. 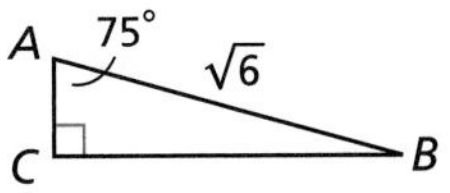

$AC \approx 0.63$; $BC \approx 2.37$; $m\angle B = 15°$

6. The coordinates of the vertices of $\triangle MNP$ are $M(-3, -2)$, $N(-3, 5)$, and $P(6, 5)$. Find the side lengths to the nearest hundredth and the angle measures to the nearest degree.
$MN = 7$; $NP = 9$; $MP \approx 11.40$; $m\angle N = 90°$; $m\angle M \approx 52°$; $m\angle P \approx 38°$

Also available on transparency

8-3 PROBLEM SOLVING

1. A road has a grade of 28.4%. This means that the road rises 28.4 ft over a horizontal distance of 100 ft. What angle does the hill make with a horizontal line? Round to the nearest degree.
16°

2. Pet ramps for loading larger dogs into vehicles usually have slopes between $\frac{2}{5}$ and $\frac{1}{2}$. What is the range of angle measures that most pet ramps make with a horizontal line? Round to the nearest degree.
22° to 27°

Use the side view of a water slide for Exercises 3 and 4.

The ladder, represented by $\overline{AB}$, is 17 feet long.

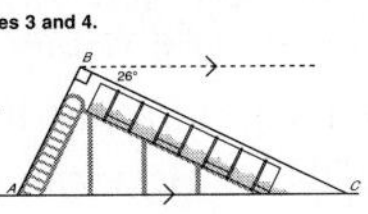

3. What is the measure of angle A, the angle that the ladder makes with a horizontal line?
64°

4. What is BC, the length of the slide? Round to the nearest tenth of a foot.
34.9 ft

Choose the best answer.

5. Janelle sets her treadmill grade to 6%. What is the angle that the treadmill surface makes with a horizontal line? Round to the nearest degree.
(A) 3° C 12°
B 4° D 31°

6. The coordinates of the vertices of $\triangle RST$ are $R(3, 3)$, $S(8, 3)$, and $T(8, -6)$. What is the measures of angle T? Round to the nearest degree.
F 18° H 61°
(G) 29° J 65°

7. If $\cos A = 0.28$, which angle in the triangles below is $\angle A$?

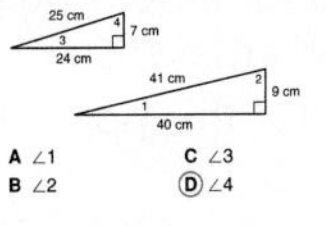

A ∠1 C ∠3
B ∠2 (D) ∠4

8. Find the measure of the acute angle formed by the graph of $y = \frac{3}{4}x$ and the x-axis. Round to the nearest degree.

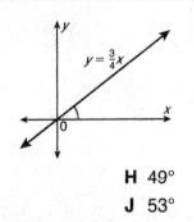

(F) 37° H 49°
G 41° J 53°

8-3 CHALLENGE

If $\sin A = \frac{4}{5}$, find $\cos A$ and $\tan A$. Leave the answers in ratio form. Then use a calculator to find $m\angle A$ to the nearest tenth of a degree.

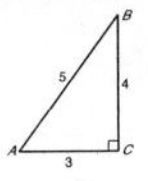

1. $\cos A =$ **$\frac{3}{5}$**
2. $\tan A =$ **$\frac{4}{3}$**
3. $m\angle A =$ **53.1°**

Given the value of one trigonometric function, find the other two. Leave the answers in ratio form. Rationalize fractions. Find angle measures to the nearest tenth of a degree.

4. $\tan E = \frac{1}{2}$ — $\sin E = \frac{\sqrt{5}}{5}$ — $\cos E = \frac{2\sqrt{5}}{5}$ — $m\angle E \approx 26.6°$
5. $\cos M = \frac{\sqrt{3}}{2}$ — $\sin M = \frac{1}{2}$ — $\tan M = \frac{\sqrt{3}}{3}$ — $m\angle M = 30°$
6. $\sin R = \frac{\sqrt{2}}{2}$ — $\cos R = \frac{\sqrt{2}}{2}$ — $\tan R = 1$ — $m\angle R = 45°$
7. $\tan K = \sqrt{3}$ — $\sin K = \frac{\sqrt{3}}{2}$ — $\cos K = \frac{1}{2}$ — $m\angle K = 60°$

MULTI-STEP TEST PREP

Organizer

Objective: Assess students' ability to apply concepts and skills in Lessons 8-1 through 8-3 in a real-world format.

 Online Edition

Resources

 ***Geometry Assessments***
www.mathtekstoolkit.org

Problem	Text Reference
1	Lesson 8-1
2	Lesson 8-1
3	Lesson 8-3
4	Lesson 8-3
5	Lesson 8-3

State Resources

go.hrw.com
State Resources Online
KEYWORD: MG7 Resources

CHAPTER 8

MULTI-STEP TEST PREP

SECTION 8A

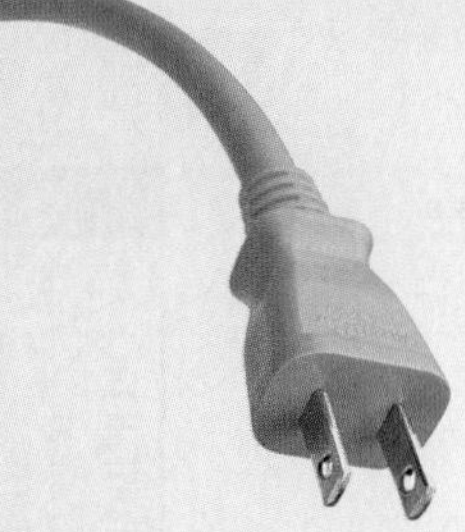

Trigonometric Ratios

It's Electrifying! Utility workers install and repair the utility poles and wires that carry electricity from generating stations to consumers. As shown in the figure, a crew of workers plans to install a vertical utility pole $\overline{AC}$ and a supporting guy wire $\overline{AB}$ that is perpendicular to the ground.

1. The utility pole is 30 ft tall. The crew finds that $DC = 6$ ft. What is the distance DB from the pole to the anchor point of the guy wire? **12 ft**
2. How long is the guy wire? Round to the nearest inch. **26 ft 10 in.**
3. In the figure, $\angle ABD$ is called the *line angle*. In order to choose the correct weight of the cable for the guy wire, the crew needs to know the measure of the line angle. Find $m\angle ABD$ to the nearest degree. **63°**
4. To the nearest degree, what is the measure of the angle formed by the pole and the guy wire? **27°**
5. What is the percent grade of the hill on which the crew is working? **50%**

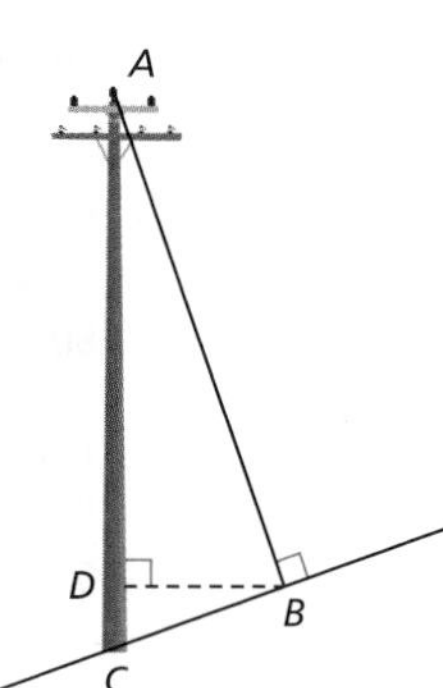

INTERVENTION

Scaffolding Questions

1. Classify $\triangle ABC$, $\triangle ABD$ and $\triangle BDC$ by their angle measures. All 3 are rt. What relationship can you use to find DB? DB is the geometric mean of AD and DC.
2. How can you use a geometric mean to find AB? Use the relationship $AB^2 = (AD)(AC)$. How can you use right $\triangle ADB$ to find this length? Use the Pyth. Thm.
3. Can you use a tangent ratio to find $m\angle ABD$? If so, how? Yes, $m\angle ABD = \tan^{-1}\left(\frac{AD}{DB}\right)$.
4. How are the two acute angle measures in a right triangle related? They are comp.
5. Which segment has the same slope as the hill? $\overline{BC}$ How can you find the slope of this segment? $\frac{DC}{DB}$ How can you convert this to a percent grade? Multiply it by 100.

Extension

While installing the guy wire for a 30 ft pole on another hill, the crew finds that $DC = 10$ ft. What is the line angle for this pole? 55°

SECTION 8A

Quiz for Lessons 8-1 Through 8-3

8-1 Similarity in Right Triangles

Find the geometric mean of each pair of numbers. If necessary, give the answer in simplest radical form.

1. 5 and 12 $2\sqrt{15}$
2. 2.75 and 44 11
3. $\frac{5}{2}$ and $\frac{15}{8}$ $\frac{5\sqrt{3}}{4}$

Find *x*, *y*, and *z*.

4. $x = 4\sqrt{2}$; $y = 4\sqrt{3}$; $z = 4\sqrt{6}$

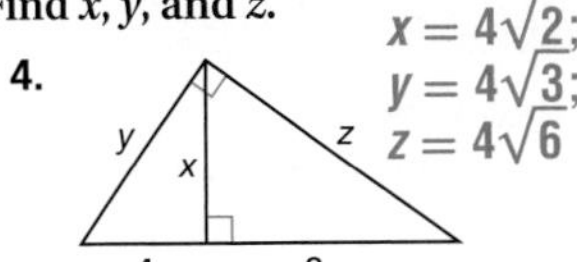

5. $x = 6$; $y = 12$; $z = 6\sqrt{5}$

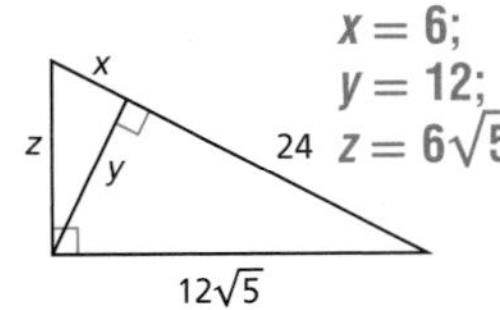

6. $x = 3$; $y = 6\sqrt{5}$; $z = 3\sqrt{5}$

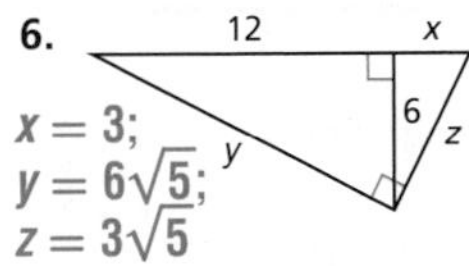

7. A land developer needs to know the distance across a pond on a piece of property. What is *AB* to the nearest tenth of a meter? 25.7 m

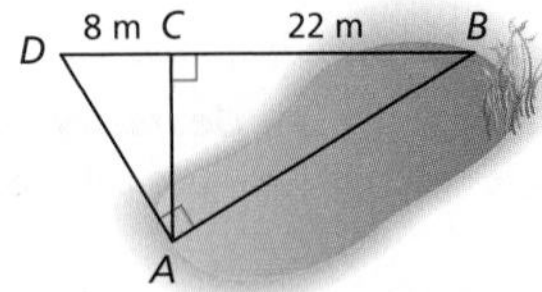

8-2 Trigonometric Ratios

Use a special right triangle to write each trigonometric ratio as a fraction.

8. $\tan 45°$ 1
9. $\sin 30°$ $\frac{1}{2}$
10. $\cos 30°$ $\frac{\sqrt{3}}{2}$

Use your calculator to find each trigonometric ratio. Round to the nearest hundredth.

11. $\sin 16°$ 0.28
12. $\cos 79°$ 0.19
13. $\tan 27°$ 0.51

Find each length. Round to the nearest hundredth.

14. *QR* 23.30 in.

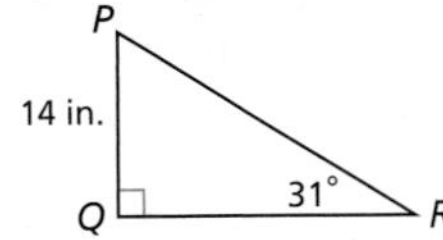

15. *AB* 3.86 m

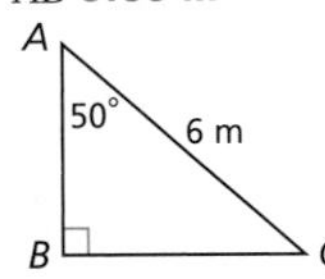

16. *LM* 3.71 cm

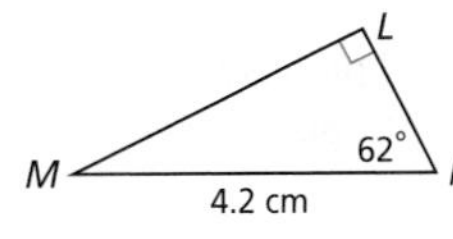

8-3 Solving Right Triangles

Find the unknown measures. Round lengths to the nearest hundredth and angle measures to the nearest degree.

17.

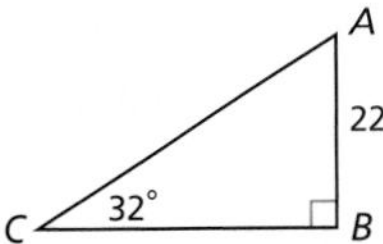

18.

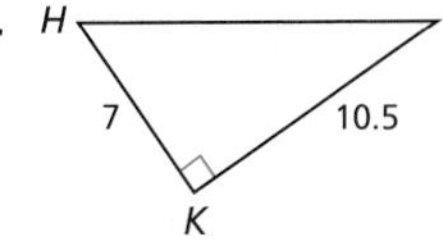

19.

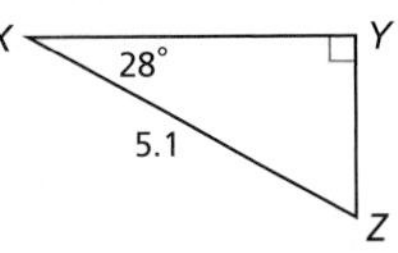

20. The wheelchair ramp at the entrance of the Mission Bay Library has a slope of $\frac{1}{18}$. What angle does the ramp make with the sidewalk? Round to the nearest degree. 3°

Ready to Go On? **543**

READY TO GO ON? SECTION **8A**

Organizer

Objective: Assess students' mastery of concepts and skills in Lessons 8-1 through 8-3.

Resources

Assessment Resources

Section 8A Quiz

Teacher One Stop™

Test & Practice Generator

INTERVENTION

Resources

***Ready to Go On? Intervention and Enrichment* Worksheets**

***Ready to Go On?* CD-ROM**

***Ready to Go On?* Online**

my.hrw.com

Answers

17. m∠A = 58°; $BC \approx 35.21$; $AC \approx 41.52$

18. $HJ \approx 12.62$; m∠H ≈ 56°; m∠J ≈ 34°

19. m∠Z = 62°; $XY \approx 4.50$; $YZ \approx 2.39$

READY TO GO ON? Diagnose and Prescribe

NO INTERVENE

Ready to Go On? Intervention	*Ready to Go On? Intervention,* Section 8A: Worksheets	CD-ROM	Online
Lesson 8-1	8-1 Intervention	Activity 8-1	Diagnose and Prescribe Online
Lesson 8-2	8-2 Intervention	Activity 8-2	
Lesson 8-3	8-3 Intervention	Activity 8-3	

***Ready to Go On? Enrichment,* Section 8A**

Worksheets

CD-ROM

Online

SECTION 8B

Applying Trigonometric Ratios

One-Minute Section Planner

Lesson	Lab Resources	Materials
Lesson 8-4 Angles of Elevation and Depression • Solve problems involving angles of elevation and angles of depression. ☐ SAT-10 ☑ NAEP ☐ ACT ☑ SAT ☐ SAT Subject Tests		**Required** scientific or graphing calculator **Optional** string
8-4 Geometry Lab Indirect Measurement Using Trigonometry • Make a clinometer and use trigonometry to measure objects indirectly. ☐ SAT-10 ☑ NAEP ☐ ACT ☑ SAT ☑ SAT Subject Tests	***Geometry Lab Activities*** 8-4 Lab Recording Sheet	**Required** scientific or graphing calculator, washer or paper clip, 6-inch string, tape, protractor (MK), straw, tape measure
Lesson 8-5 Law of Sines and Law of Cosines • Use the Law of Sines and the Law of Cosines to solve triangles. ☐ SAT-10 ☐ NAEP ☐ ACT ☑ SAT ☑ SAT Subject Tests		**Required** scientific or graphing calculator **Optional** geometry software
Lesson 8-6 Vectors • Find the magnitude and direction of a vector. • Use vectors and vector addition to solve real-world problems. ☐ SAT-10 ☑ NAEP ☐ ACT ☐ SAT ☑ SAT Subject Tests		**Required** graph paper, scientific or graphing calculator **Optional** protractor (MK)
Extension Trigonometry and the Unit Circle • Define trigonometric ratios for angle measures greater than or equal to 90°. ☐ SAT-10 ☐ NAEP ☐ ACT ☐ SAT ☐ SAT Subject Tests	***Technology Lab Activities*** Extension Technology Lab	**Optional** heavy paper, compass (MK), straightedge (MK), chenille stems

MK = *Manipulatives Kit*

LAW OF SINES

Lesson 8-5

The Law of Sines may be used to solve a triangle given either of the following.

- Two angle measures and any side length
- Two side lengths and a non-included angle measure

Note that in the second case, two side lengths and a non-included angle measure are known (SSA) and that this is generally not enough information to uniquely determine a triangle. (Thus, there is no SSA Congruence Theorem.) The ambiguity arises when you are given an acute angle measure and the side opposite the known angle is shorter than the other side. As the figures show, this situation may result in no triangle or two triangles.

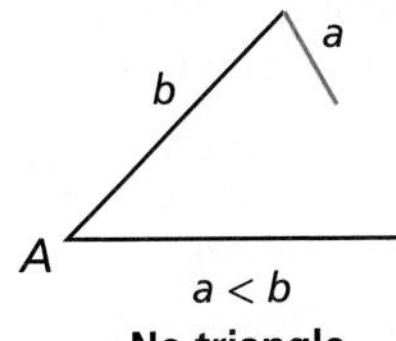

$a < b$
No triangle

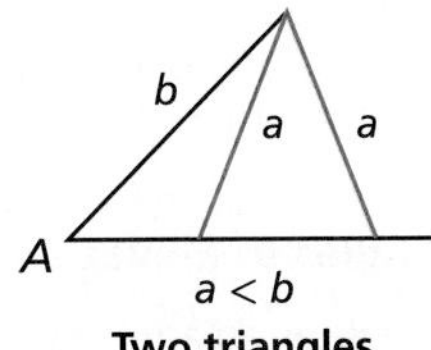

$a < b$
Two triangles

Similarly, when the given angle is right or obtuse, there will be no triangle if the side opposite the given angle is shorter than the other side. All of the situations described here are known as the *ambiguous case* of the Law of Sines.

LAW OF COSINES

Lesson 8-5

The Law of Cosines may be used to solve a triangle given either of the following.

- Two sides lengths and the included angle measure
- Three side lengths

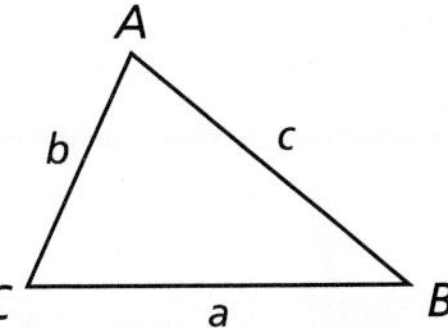

The Law of Cosines may be considered to be a generalization of the Pythagorean Theorem. For the triangle at right, the Law of Cosines states that $c^2 = a^2 + b^2 - 2ab\cos C$. In the case that $\angle C$ is a right angle, $\cos C = \cos 90° = 0$, and the Law of Cosines reduces to $c^2 = a^2 + b^2 - 2ab(0)$ or $c^2 = a^2 + b^2$, which is the Pythagorean Theorem.

VECTORS

Lesson 8-6

Vectors are one of the central concepts of physics. A *vector* is a quantity that has both magnitude and direction. A typical example is velocity, for which a magnitude (50 mi/h) and a direction (due north) must be specified. By contrast, a quantity that has only a magnitude, such as length, is sometimes called a *scalar*.

Vectors are often represented as directed line segments, and it is convenient to write vectors in the plane by using the component form, $\langle x, y \rangle$. The x-component represents the horizontal change from the vector's initial point to its terminal point; the y-component represents the vertical change.

Although component form resembles the use of coordinates to name a point, it is important to understand that a vector's name in component form does not depend on the vector's location on a coordinate plane. All of the vectors shown below have component form $\langle 4, 2 \rangle$, and they may be considered to be representations of the same vector. For this reason, vectors are often shown on a coordinate grid without axes.

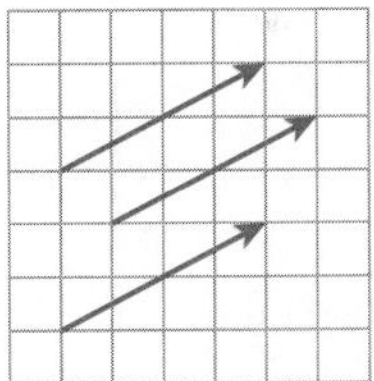

The *magnitude* of a vector is the vector's length. A simple application of the Distance Formula shows that the magnitude of vector $\langle a, b \rangle$ is $\sqrt{a^2 + b^2}$. A vector with magnitude 1 is called a *unit vector*.

The *direction* of a vector is the angle the vector makes with a horizontal line. The direction of $\langle a, b \rangle$ may be found by drawing the vector on a coordinate plane so that the initial point is at the origin. Then, a right triangle can be formed with the vector as the hypotenuse, and the inverse tangent function can be used to find the measure of the required angle, $\arctan \frac{b}{a}$.

8-4 Organizer

Pacing: Traditional 1 day
Block $\frac{1}{2}$ day

Objective: Solve problems involving angles of elevation and angles of depression.

Online Edition
Tutorial Videos, Interactivity

Countdown Week 18

Power Presentations with PowerPoint®

Warm Up

1. Identify the pairs of alternate interior angles. $\angle 2$ and $\angle 7$; $\angle 3$ and $\angle 6$

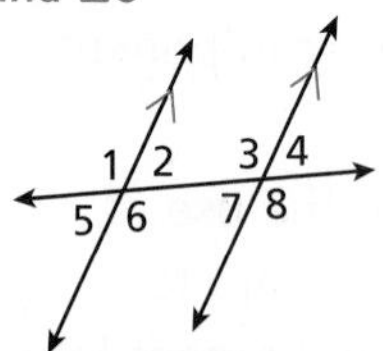

2. Use your calculator to find tan 30° to the nearest hundredth. 0.58
3. Solve $\tan 54° = \frac{2500}{x}$. Round to the nearest hundredth. 1816.36

Also available on transparency

Math Humor

Q: Why do mathematicians dislike the beach?

A: Because they have to sine and cosine to get a tan!

8-4 Angles of Elevation and Depression

Objective
Solve problems involving angles of elevation and angles of depression.

Vocabulary
angle of elevation
angle of depression

Who uses this?
Pilots and air traffic controllers use angles of depression to calculate distances.

An **angle of elevation** is the angle formed by a horizontal line and a line of sight to a point *above* the line. In the diagram, $\angle 1$ is the angle of elevation from the tower T to the plane P.

An **angle of depression** is the angle formed by a horizontal line and a line of sight to a point *below* the line. $\angle 2$ is the angle of depression from the plane to the tower.

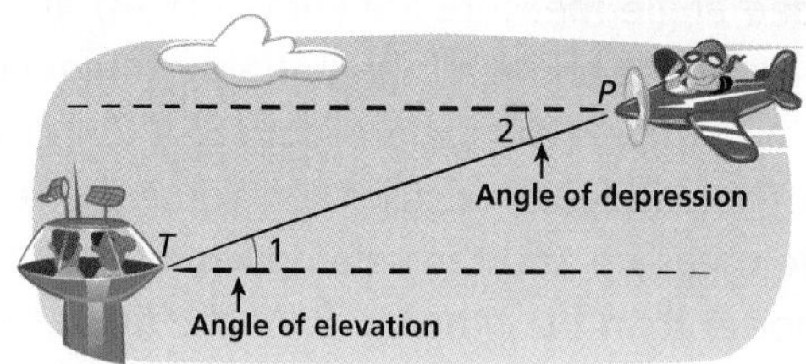

Since horizontal lines are parallel, $\angle 1 \cong \angle 2$ by the Alternate Interior Angles Theorem. Therefore the angle of elevation from one point is congruent to the angle of depression from the other point.

EXAMPLE 1 Classifying Angles of Elevation and Depression

Classify each angle as an angle of elevation or angle of depression.

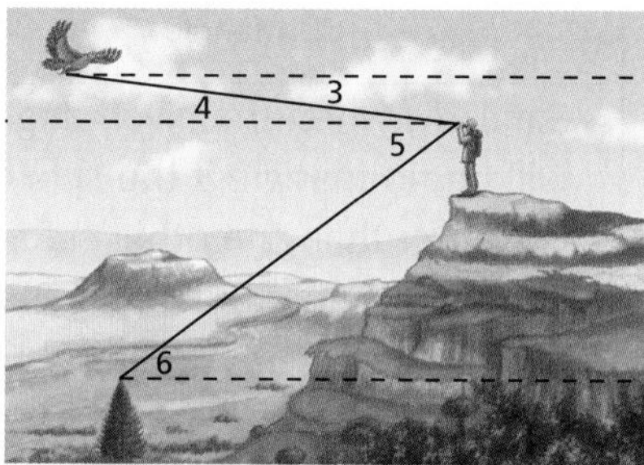

A $\angle 3$

$\angle 3$ is formed by a horizontal line and a line of sight to a point below the line. It is an angle of depression.

B $\angle 4$

$\angle 4$ is formed by a horizontal line and a line of sight to a point above the line. It is an angle of elevation.

CHECK IT OUT! **Use the diagram above to classify each angle as an angle of elevation or angle of depression.**

1a. $\angle 5$ angle of depression **1b.** $\angle 6$ angle of elevation

State Resources

State Resources Online
KEYWORD: MG7 Resources

1 Introduce

EXPLORATION

8-4 Angles of Elevation and Depression

An *angle of elevation* is an angle formed by a horizontal line and a line of sight to a point above the line. An *angle of depression* is an angle formed by a horizontal line and a line of sight to a point below the line.

1. In each row of the table, put an X in the appropriate column to indicate whether the situation describes an angle of elevation or an angle of depression.

	Angle of Elevation	Angle of Depression
From Jogger to Helicopter		
From Helicopter to Hot Air Balloon		
From Hot Air Balloon to Jogger		
From Jogger to Hot Air Balloon		

THINK AND DISCUSS

Motivate

Sketch a pair of parallel lines cut by a transversal. Label the alternate interior angles and ask students how the measures of these angles are related. Explain that students will learn how they can combine their understanding of alternate interior angles with their knowledge of trigonometry to find distances, such as the vertical drop of a ski slope.

Explorations and answers are provided in *Alternate Openers: Explorations Transparencies.*

EXAMPLE 2 Finding Distance by Using Angle of Elevation

An air traffic controller at an airport sights a plane at an angle of elevation of 41°. The pilot reports that the plane's altitude is 4000 ft. What is the horizontal distance between the plane and the airport? Round to the nearest foot.

Draw a sketch to represent the given information. Let A represent the airport and let P represent the plane. Let x be the horizontal distance between the plane and the airport.

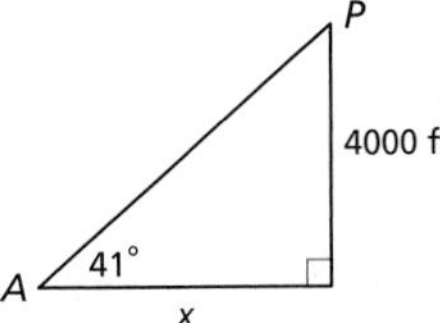

$\tan 41° = \frac{4000}{x}$ *You are given the side opposite ∠A, and x is the side adjacent to ∠A. So write a tangent ratio.*

$x = \frac{4000}{\tan 41°}$ *Multiply both sides by x and divide both sides by tan 41°.*

$x \approx 4601$ ft *Simplify the expression.*

2. **What if...?** Suppose the plane is at an altitude of 3500 ft and the angle of elevation from the airport to the plane is 29°. What is the horizontal distance between the plane and the airport? Round to the nearest foot. **6314 ft**

EXAMPLE 3 Finding Distance by Using Angle of Depression

A forest ranger in a 90-foot observation tower sees a fire. The angle of depression to the fire is 7°. What is the horizontal distance between the tower and the fire? Round to the nearest foot.

Draw a sketch to represent the given information. Let T represent the top of the tower and let F represent the fire. Let x be the horizontal distance between the tower and the fire.

Caution!

The angle of depression may not be one of the angles in the triangle you are solving. It may be the complement of one of the angles in the triangle.

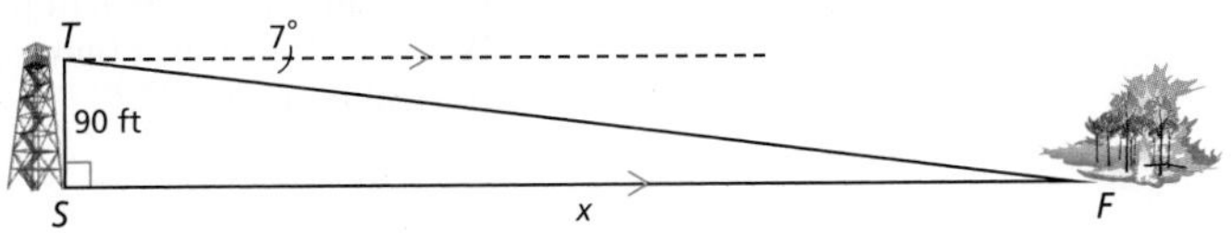

By the Alternate Interior Angles Theorem, $m\angle F = 7°$.

$\tan 7° = \frac{90}{x}$ *Write a tangent ratio.*

$x = \frac{90}{\tan 7°}$ *Multiply both sides by x and divide both sides by tan 7°.*

$x \approx 733$ ft *Simplify the expression.*

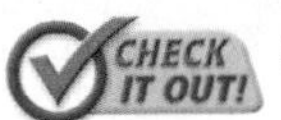

3. **What if...?** Suppose the ranger sees another fire and the angle of depression to the fire is 3°. What is the horizontal distance to this fire? Round to the nearest foot. **1717 ft**

2 Teach

Guided Instruction

Review how to identify pairs of alternate interior angles, and make sure students know that these angles are congruent when formed by parallel lines. Point out that a horizontal line can be used to form an angle of elevation or an angle of depression from any point. Discuss how students can identify these angles. Remind students how to find a side length in a right triangle when one acute angle measure and another side length are known.

Reaching All Learners

Through Modeling

Use string to model angles of elevation and depression. Hold one end of the string while standing on a chair. Have a student hold the other end of the string at the floor, away from the chair. Ask the class to identify the angles formed by you, the floor, and the string, and to classify each angle as an angle of elevation, depression, or neither.

Power Presentations with PowerPoint®

Additional Examples

Example 1

Classify each angle as an angle of elevation or angle of depression.

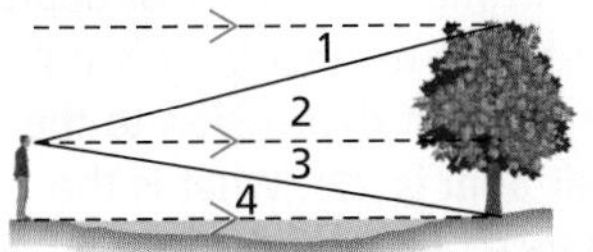

A. ∠1 angle of depression

B. ∠4 angle of elevation

Example 2

The Seattle Space Needle casts a 67 m shadow. If the angle of elevation from the tip of the shadow to the top of the Space Needle is 70°, how tall is the Space Needle? Round to the nearest meter. 184 m

Example 3

An ice climber stands at the edge of a crevasse that is 115 ft wide. The angle of depression from the edge where she stands to the bottom of the opposite side is 52°. How deep is the crevasse at this point? Round to the nearest foot. 147 ft

INTERVENTION

Questioning Strategies

EXAMPLE 1

- How can you distinguish between an angle of elevation and an angle of depression?

EXAMPLE 2

- Why should you use the tangent ratio to solve **Example 2**?

EXAMPLE 3

- How do you know whether to use the given angle or its complement when solving a problem that involves an angle of depression?

Reading Math The root of *elevation* is *elevate*, which means "to raise." The root of *depression* is *depress*, which means "down." Students can use these root words to remember the difference between an angle of elevation and an angle of depression. ENGLISH LANGUAGE LEARNERS

Power Presentations with PowerPoint®

Additional Examples

Example 4

An observer in a lighthouse is 69 ft above the water. He sights two boats in the water directly in front of him. The angle of depression to the nearest boat is 48°. The angle of depression to the other boat is 22°. What is the distance between the two boats? Round to the nearest foot. 109 ft

INTERVENTION

Questioning Strategies

EXAMPLE 4

- Why do you have to use two tangent ratios to solve this problem?
- How do you know where to place the angles in your sketch?

Visual Some students may find if easier to work **Example 4** if they first draw the two triangles formed by the towers separately.

EXAMPLE 4 Aviation Application

A pilot flying at an altitude of 2.7 km sights two control towers directly in front of her. The angle of depression to the base of one tower is 37°. The angle of depression to the base of the other tower is 58°. What is the distance between the two towers? Round to the nearest tenth of a kilometer.

Helpful Hint

Always make a sketch to help you correctly place the given angle measure.

Step 1 Draw a sketch. Let P represent the plane and let A and B represent the two towers. Let x be the distance between the towers.

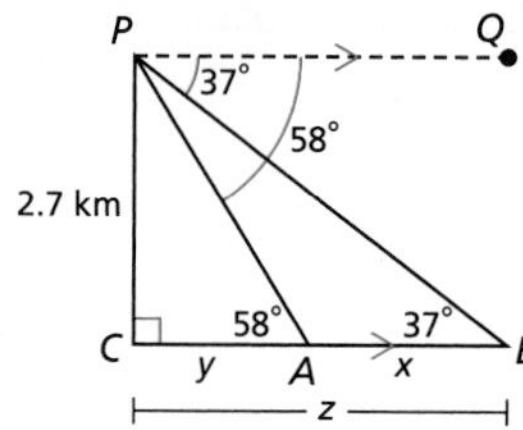

Step 2 Find y.

By the Alternate Interior Angles Theorem, $m\angle CAP = 58°$.

In $\triangle APC$, $\tan 58° = \frac{2.7}{y}$.

So $y = \frac{2.7}{\tan 58°} \approx 1.6871$ km.

Step 3 Find z.

By the Alternate Interior Angles Theorem, $m\angle CBP = 37°$.

In $\triangle BPC$, $\tan 37° = \frac{2.7}{z}$.

So $z = \frac{2.7}{\tan 37°} \approx 3.5830$ km.

Step 4 Find x.

$x = z - y$

$x \approx 3.5830 - 1.6871 \approx 1.9$ km

So the two towers are about 1.9 km apart.

4. A pilot flying at an altitude of 12,000 ft sights two airports directly in front of him. The angle of depression to one airport is 78°, and the angle of depression to the second airport is 19°. What is the distance between the two airports? Round to the nearest foot. **32,300 ft**

THINK AND DISCUSS

1. Explain what happens to the angle of elevation from your eye to the top of a skyscraper as you walk toward the skyscraper.
2. **GET ORGANIZED** Copy and complete the graphic organizer below. In each box, write a definition or make a sketch.

Know it! Note

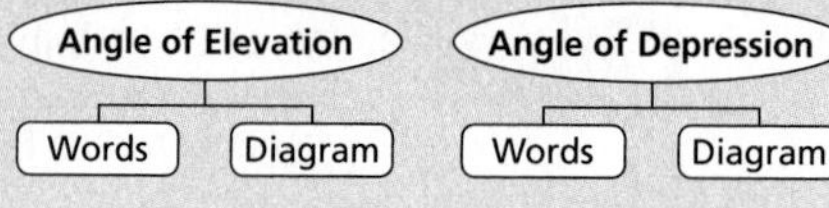

3 Close

Summarize

Review the classification of angles as angles of depression or angles of elevation. Emphasize that alternate interior angles are congruent for parallel lines, and therefore the angle of elevation from one point is congruent to the angle of depression from the other point. Point out that angles of depression can be used to find the distance between objects you see when you look down.

ONGOING ASSESSMENT and INTERVENTION

***Diagnose Before* the Lesson**
8-4 Warm Up, TE p. 544

***Monitor During* the Lesson**
Check It Out! Exercises, SE pp. 544–546
Questioning Strategies, TE pp. 545–546

***Assess After* the Lesson**
8-4 Lesson Quiz, TE p. 549
Alternative Assessment, TE p. 549

Answers to *Think and Discuss*

1. It increases.
2. See p. A7.

8-4 Exercises

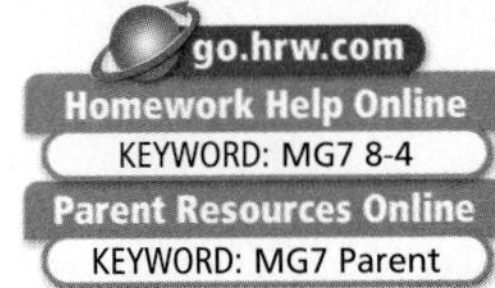

GUIDED PRACTICE

Vocabulary Apply the vocabulary from this lesson to answer each question.

1. An angle of __?__ is measured from a horizontal line to a point above that line. (*elevation* or *depression*) **elevation**

2. An angle of __?__ is measured from a horizontal line to a point below that line. (*elevation* or *depression*) **depression**

SEE EXAMPLE 1 p. 544

Classify each angle as an angle of elevation or angle of depression.

3. ∠1
4. ∠2
5. ∠3
6. ∠4

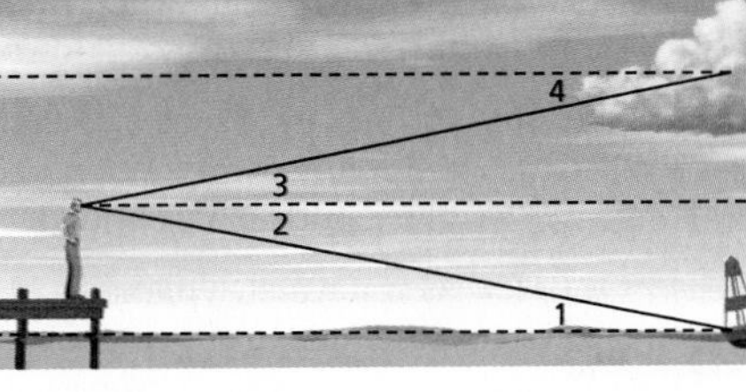

SEE EXAMPLE 2 p. 545

7. **Measurement** When the angle of elevation to the sun is 37°, a flagpole casts a shadow that is 24.2 ft long. What is the height of the flagpole to the nearest foot? **18 ft**

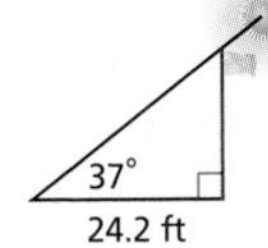

SEE EXAMPLE 3 p. 545

8. **Aviation** The pilot of a traffic helicopter sights an accident at an angle of depression of 18°. The helicopter's altitude is 1560 ft. What is the horizontal distance from the helicopter to the accident? Round to the nearest foot. **4801 ft**

SEE EXAMPLE 4 p. 546

9. **Surveying** From the top of a canyon, the angle of depression to the far side of the river is 58°, and the angle of depression to the near side of the river is 74°. The depth of the canyon is 191 m. What is the width of the river at the bottom of the canyon? Round to the nearest tenth of a meter. **64.6 m**

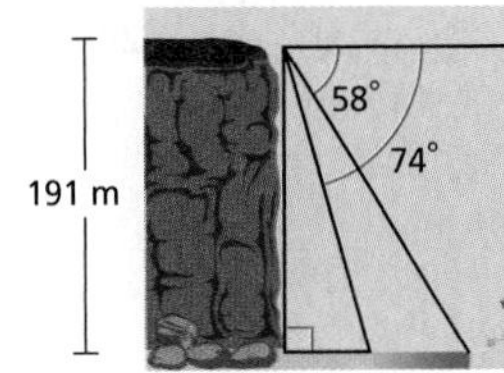

PRACTICE AND PROBLEM SOLVING

Independent Practice

For Exercises	See Example
10–13	1
14	2
15	3
16	4

Extra Practice
Skills Practice p. S19
Application Practice p. S35

Classify each angle as an angle of elevation or angle of depression.

10. ∠1
11. ∠2
12. ∠3
13. ∠4

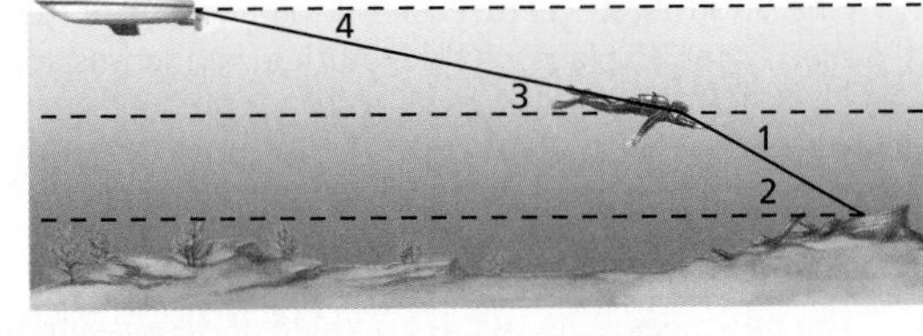

14. **Geology** To measure the height of a rock formation, a surveyor places her transit 100 m from its base and focuses the transit on the top of the formation. The angle of elevation is 67°. The transit is 1.5 m above the ground. What is the height of the rock formation? Round to the nearest meter. **237 m**

8-4 Exercises

Assignment Guide

Assign *Guided Practice* exercises as necessary.

If you finished Examples **1–2**
Basic 10–14, 17, 21, 22
Average 10–14, 17–19, 21, 22
Advanced 10–14, 17–19, 21, 22, 25

If you finished Examples **1–4**
Basic 10–22, 24, 27–30, 35–43
Average 10–31, 35–43
Advanced 10–43

Homework Quick Check
Quickly check key concepts.
Exercises: 10, 14–16, 20, 24

Auditory For exercises that do not have a diagram provided, such as **Exercise 8,** pair students and have one student read the text while another student sketches a diagram of the situation.

Science Link For **Exercises 10–13,** explain that trigonometry is used in many modern applications, such as radar and sonar technology. Sonar, satellite tracking, and deep-sea technology helped locate the remains of the *Titanic* in 1985, 73 years after it sank.

Answers

3. angle of elevation
4. angle of depression
5. angle of elevation
6. angle of depression
10. angle of depression
11. angle of elevation
12. angle of elevation
13. angle of depression

State Resources

go.hrw.com
State Resources Online
KEYWORD: MG7 Resources

Kinesthetic Students may have difficulty visualizing the scenarios described in **Exercises 17–20.** Encourage students to act out the scenarios by using objects in the classroom.

Communicating Math Have students share their situations in **Exercise 23** with the class.

MULTI-STEP TEST PREP **Exercise 27** involves using an angle of depression to find a distance. This exercise prepares students for the Multi-Step Test Prep on page 568.

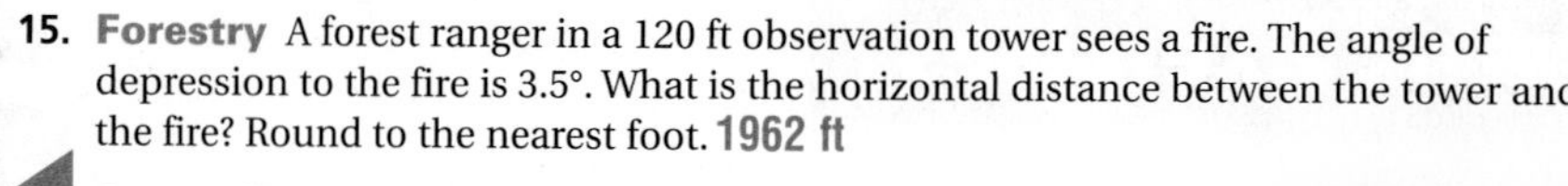

LINK Space Shuttle

During its launch, a space shuttle accelerates to more than 27,359 km/h in just over 8 minutes. So the shuttle travels 3219 km/h faster each minute.

15. **Forestry** A forest ranger in a 120 ft observation tower sees a fire. The angle of depression to the fire is 3.5°. What is the horizontal distance between the tower and the fire? Round to the nearest foot. **1962 ft**

16. **Space Shuttle** Marion is observing the launch of a space shuttle from the command center. When she first sees the shuttle, the angle of elevation to it is 16°. Later, the angle of elevation is 74°. If the command center is 1 mi from the launch pad, how far did the shuttle travel while Marion was watching? Round to the nearest tenth of a mile. **3.2 mi**

16° 74° 1 mi

Tell whether each statement is true or false. If false, explain why.

17. The angle of elevation from your eye to the top of a tree increases as you walk toward the tree. **T**

18. If you stand at street level, the angle of elevation to a building's tenth-story window is greater than the angle of elevation to one of its ninth-story windows. **T**

19. As you watch a plane fly above you, the angle of elevation to the plane gets closer to 0° as the plane approaches the point directly overhead. **F; the angle of elevation gets closer to 90°.**

20. An angle of depression can never be more than 90°. **T**

Use the diagram for Exercises 21 and 22.

21. Which angles are not angles of elevation or angles of depression? **∠1 and ∠3**

22. The angle of depression from the helicopter to the car is 30°. Find m∠1, m∠2, m∠3, and m∠4. **m∠1 = m∠3 = 60°; m∠2 = m∠4 = 30°**

23. **Critical Thinking** Describe a situation in which the angle of depression to an object is decreasing.

23. Possible answer: as a hot air balloon descends vertically, the ∠ of depression to an object on the ground decreases.

24. An observer in a hot-air balloon sights a building that is 50 m from the balloon's launch point. The balloon has risen 165 m. What is the angle of depression from the balloon to the building? Round to the nearest degree. **73°**

165 m 50 m

25. **Multi-Step** A surveyor finds that the angle of elevation to the top of a 1000 ft tower is 67°.
    a. To the nearest foot, how far is the surveyor from the base of the tower? **424 ft**
    b. How far back would the surveyor have to move so that the angle of elevation to the top of the tower is 55°? Round to the nearest foot. **276 ft**

26. **Write About It** Two students are using shadows to calculate the height of a pole. One says that it will be easier if they wait until the angle of elevation to the sun is exactly 45°. Explain why the student made this suggestion.

26. When the ∠ of elevation of the sun is exactly 45°, the length of the shadow will be the same as the length of the telephone pole, since an isosc. rt. △ is formed and tan 45° = 1.

MULTI-STEP TEST PREP

27. This problem will prepare you for the Multi-Step Test Prep on page 568.
    The pilot of a rescue helicopter is flying over the ocean at an altitude of 1250 ft. The pilot sees a life raft at an angle of depression of 31°.
    a. What is the horizontal distance from the helicopter to the life raft, rounded to the nearest foot? **2080 ft**
    b. The helicopter travels at 150 ft/s. To the nearest second, how long will it take until the helicopter is directly over the raft? **14 s**

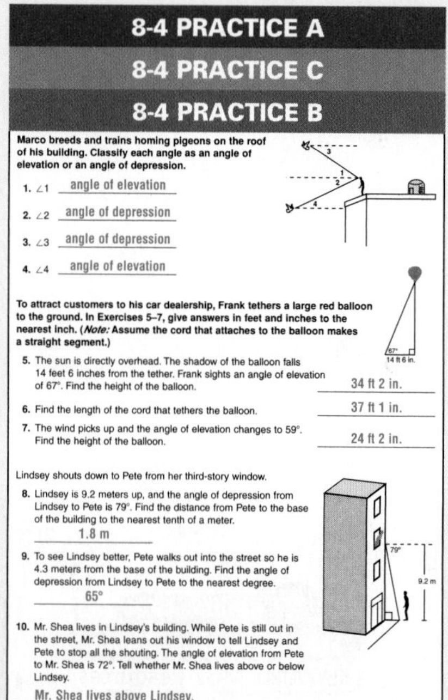

8-4 PRACTICE A
8-4 PRACTICE C
8-4 PRACTICE B

Marco breeds and trains homing pigeons on the roof of his building. Classify each angle as an angle of elevation or an angle of depression.

1. ∠1 angle of elevation
2. ∠2 angle of depression
3. ∠3 angle of depression
4. ∠4 angle of elevation

To attract customers to his car dealership, Frank tethers a large red balloon to the ground. In Exercises 5–7, give answers in feet and inches to the nearest inch. (*Note:* Assume the cord that attaches to the balloon makes a straight segment.)

5. The sun is directly overhead. The shadow of the balloon falls 14 feet 6 inches from the tether. Frank sights an angle of elevation of 67°. Find the height of the balloon. 34 ft 2 in.
6. Find the length of the cord that tethers the balloon. 37 ft 1 in.
7. The wind picks up and the angle of elevation changes to 59°. Find the height of the balloon. 24 ft 2 in.

Lindsey shouts down to Pete from her third-story window.

8. Lindsey is 9.2 meters up, and the angle of depression from Lindsey to Pete is 79°. Find the distance from Pete to the base of the building to the nearest tenth of a meter. 1.8 m
9. To see Lindsey better, Pete walks out into the street so he is 4.3 meters from the base of the building. Find the angle of depression from Lindsey to Pete to the nearest degree. 65°
10. Mr. Shea lives in Lindsey's building. While Pete is still out in the street, Mr. Shea leans out his window to tell Lindsey and Pete to stop all the shouting. The angle of elevation from Pete to Mr. Shea is 72°. Tell whether Mr. Shea lives above or below Lindsey. Mr. Shea lives above Lindsey.

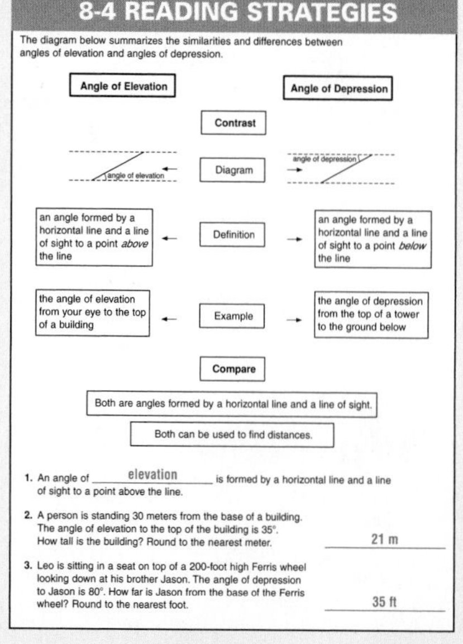

8-4 READING STRATEGIES

The diagram below summarizes the similarities and differences between angles of elevation and angles of depression.

Angle of Elevation		Angle of Depression
	Contrast	
angle of elevation	Diagram	angle of depression
an angle formed by a horizontal line and a line of sight to a point *above* the line	Definition	an angle formed by a horizontal line and a line of sight to a point *below* the line
the angle of elevation from your eye to the top of a building	Example	the angle of depression from the top of a tower to the ground below
	Compare	

Both are angles formed by a horizontal line and a line of sight.

Both can be used to find distances.

1. An angle of elevation is formed by a horizontal line and a line of sight to a point above the line.
2. A person is standing 30 meters from the base of a building. The angle of elevation to the top of the building is 35°. How tall is the building? Round to the nearest meter. 21 m
3. Leo is sitting in a seat on top of a 200-foot high Ferris wheel looking down at his brother Jason. The angle of depression to Jason is 80°. How far is Jason from the base of the Ferris wheel? Round to the nearest foot. 35 ft

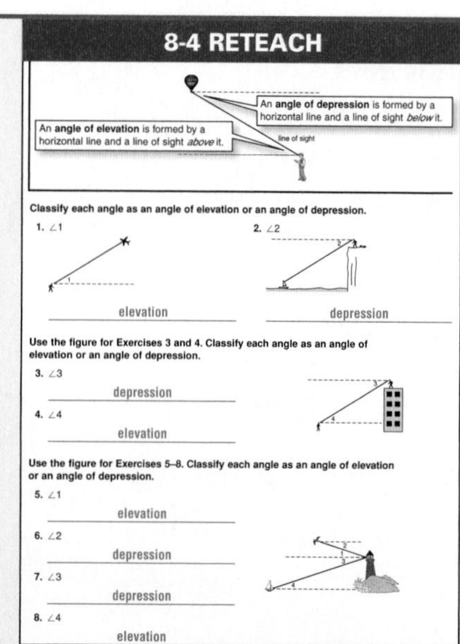

8-4 RETEACH

An angle of elevation is formed by a horizontal line and a line of sight *above* it.

An **angle of depression** is formed by a horizontal line and a line of sight *below* it.

Classify each angle as an angle of elevation or an angle of depression.

1. ∠1 elevation
2. ∠2 depression

Use the figure for Exercises 3 and 4. Classify each angle as an angle of elevation or an angle of depression.

3. ∠3 depression
4. ∠4 elevation

Use the figure for Exercises 5–8. Classify each angle as an angle of elevation or an angle of depression.

5. ∠1 elevation
6. ∠2 depression
7. ∠3 depression
8. ∠4 elevation

28. Mai is flying a plane at an altitude of 1600 ft. She sights a stadium at an angle of depression of 35°. What is Mai's approximate horizontal distance from the stadium?

Ⓐ 676 feet Ⓒ 1450 feet
Ⓑ 1120 feet ⒹD 2285 feet

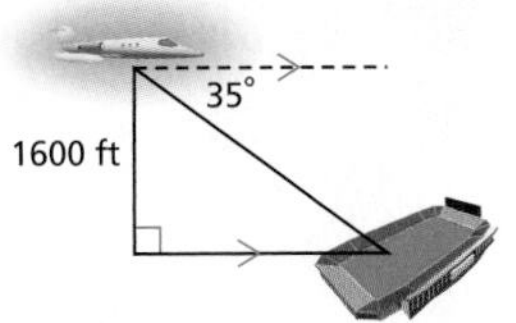

29. Jeff finds that an office building casts a shadow that is 93 ft long when the angle of elevation to the sun is 60°. What is the height of the building?

Ⓕ 54 feet Ⓖ 81 feet Ⓗ 107 feet Ⓙ 161 feet

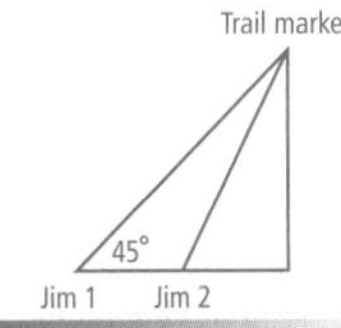

30. **Short Response** Jim is rafting down a river that runs through a canyon. He sees a trail marker ahead at the top of the canyon and estimates the angle of elevation from the raft to the marker as 45°. Draw a sketch to represent the situation. Explain what happens to the angle of elevation as Jim moves closer to the marker.
The ∠ of elevation increases as Jim moves closer to the trail marker.

CHALLENGE AND EXTEND

31. Susan and Jorge stand 38 m apart. From Susan's position, the angle of elevation to the top of Big Ben is 65°. From Jorge's position, the angle of elevation to the top of Big Ben is 49.5°. To the nearest meter, how tall is Big Ben? **98 m**

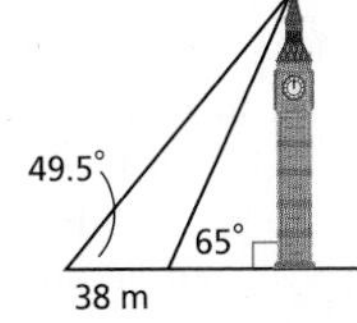

32. A plane is flying at a constant altitude of 14,000 ft and a constant speed of 500 mi/h. The angle of depression from the plane to a lake is 6°. To the nearest minute, how much time will pass before the plane is directly over the lake? **3 min**

33. A skyscraper stands between two school buildings. The two schools are 10 mi apart. From school A, the angle of elevation to the top of the skyscraper is 5°. From school B, the angle of elevation is 2°. What is the height of the skyscraper to the nearest foot? **1318 ft**

34. Katie and Kim are attending a theater performance. Katie's seat is at floor level. She looks down at an angle of 18° to see the orchestra pit. Kim's seat is in the balcony directly above Katie. Kim looks down at an angle of 42° to see the pit. The horizontal distance from Katie's seat to the pit is 46 ft. What is the vertical distance between Katie's seat and Kim's seat? Round to the nearest inch. **26 ft 6 in.**

SPIRAL REVIEW

35. Emma and her mother jog along a mile-long circular path in opposite directions. They begin at the same place and time. Emma jogs at a pace of 4 mi/h, and her mother runs at 6 mi/h. In how many minutes will they meet? *(Previous course)* **6 min**

36. Greg bought a shirt that was discounted 30%. He used a coupon for an additional 15% discount. What was the original price of the shirt if Greg paid $17.85? **$30** *(Previous course)*

Tell which special parallelograms have each given property. *(Lesson 6-5)*

37. The diagonals are perpendicular.
38. The diagonals are congruent.
39. The diagonals bisect each other.
40. Opposite angles are congruent.

37. rhombus and square
38. rectangle and square
39. rectangle, rhombus, and square
40. rectangle, rhombus, and square

Find each length. *(Lesson 8-1)*

41. x **4** 42. y $\frac{20}{3}$ 43. z $\frac{16}{3}$

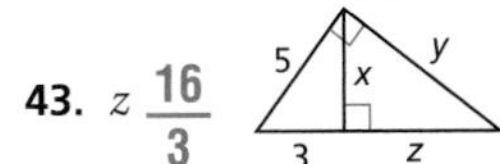

8-4 PROBLEM SOLVING

1. Mayuko is sitting 30 feet high in a football stadium. The angle of depression to the center of the field is 14°. What is the horizontal distance between Mayuko and the center of the field? Round to the nearest foot.
120 ft

2. A surveyor 50 meters from the base of a cliff measures the angle of elevation to the top of the cliff as 72°. What is the height of the cliff? Round to the nearest meter.
154 m

3. Shane is 61 feet high on a ride at an amusement park. The angle of depression to the park entrance is 42°, and the angle of depression to his friends standing below is 80°. How far from the entrance are his friends standing? Round to the nearest foot.
57 ft

42° 80° 61 ft Friends Entrance

Choose the best answer.

4. The figure shows a person parasailing. What is x, the height of the parasailer, to the nearest foot?

36° 400 ft x

Ⓐ 235 ft C 290 ft
B 245 ft D 323 ft

5. The elevation angle from the ground to the object to which the satellite dish is pointed is 32°. If x = 2.5 meters, which is the best estimate for y, the height of the satellite stand?

elevation angle x

F 0.8 m Ⓗ 1.6 m
G 1.3 m J 2.1 m

6. A lifeguard is in an observation chair and spots a person who needs help. The angle of depression to the person is 22°. The eye level of the lifeguard is 10 feet above the ground. What is the horizontal distance between the lifeguard and the person? Round to the nearest foot.

A 4 ft Ⓒ 25 ft
B 11 ft D 27 ft

7. At a topiary garden, Emily is 8 feet from a shrub that is shaped like a dolphin. From where she is looking, the angle of elevation to the top of the shrub is 46°. If she is 5 feet tall, which is the best estimate for the height of the shrub?

F 6 ft H 10 ft
G 8 ft Ⓙ 13 ft

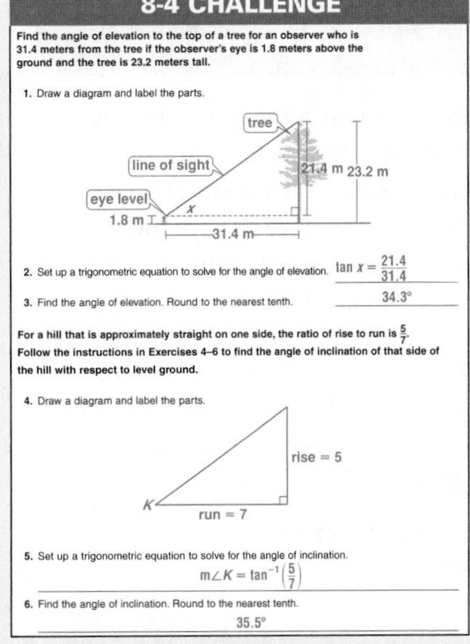

8-4 CHALLENGE

Find the angle of elevation to the top of a tree for an observer who is 31.4 meters from the tree if the observer's eye is 1.8 meters above the ground and the tree is 23.2 meters tall.

1. Draw a diagram and label the parts.

2. Set up a trigonometric equation to solve for the angle of elevation. $\tan x = \frac{21.4}{31.4}$

3. Find the angle of elevation. Round to the nearest tenth. **34.3°**

For a hill that is approximately straight on one side, the ratio of rise to run is $\frac{5}{7}$. Follow the instructions in Exercises 4–6 to find the angle of inclination of that side of the hill with respect to level ground.

4. Draw a diagram and label the parts.

5. Set up a trigonometric equation to solve for the angle of inclination.
$m\angle K = \tan^{-1}\left(\frac{5}{7}\right)$

6. Find the angle of inclination. Round to the nearest tenth.
35.5°

COMMON ERROR ALERT

Some students may be confused by the vertical lines drawn in **Exercise 21,** causing them to see ∠1 and ∠3 as angles of elevation or depression. Remind them that angles of elevation and depression are formed from a horizontal line.

TEST PREP DOCTOR + If students chose **B** in **Exercise 28,** ask them to identify the angle whose adjacent side length is 1600.

Journal

Have students describe situations involving an angle of elevation and an angle of depression, and support each situation with a diagram.

ALTERNATIVE ASSESSMENT

Have students work in pairs. Ask one student to write a situation involving an angle of elevation, and the other, an angle of depression. Have them trade papers and solve for the missing distance. Then have them trade back and check each other's work.

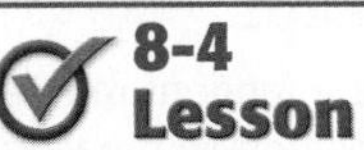

8-4 Lesson Quiz

Classify each angle as an angle of elevation or angle of depression.

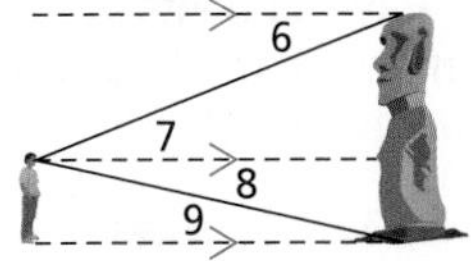

1. ∠6 angle of depression
2. ∠9 angle of elevation
3. A plane is flying at an altitude of 14,500 ft. The angle of depression from the plane to a control tower is 15°. What is the horizontal distance from the plane to the tower? Round to the nearest foot. 54,115 ft
4. A woman is standing 12 ft from a sculpture. The angle of elevation from her eye to the top of the sculpture is 30°, and the angle of depression to its base is 22°. How tall is the sculpture to the nearest foot? 12 ft

Also available on transparency

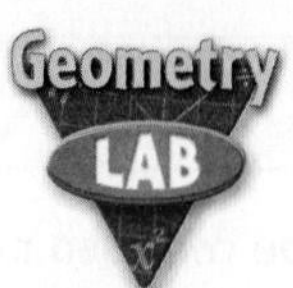

Organizer

Use with Lesson 8-4

Pacing:
Traditional 1 day
Block $\frac{1}{2}$ day

Objective: Make a clinometer and use trigonometry to measure objects indirectly.

Materials: calculator, washer or paper clip, 6-inch string, tape, protractor, straw, tape measure

Online Edition

Countdown Week 18

Resources

Geometry Lab Activities
8-4 Lab Recording Sheet

Teach

Discuss

Have students describe the measurements in their diagrams in terms of variables. Discuss why students of different heights get different angles of elevation for the same object.

Close

Key Concept

You can use a tangent ratio and an angle of elevation to measure the height of an object indirectly.

Assessment

Journal Have students describe how to measure the height of a tall object indirectly with a clinometer.

Answers to *Try This*

1, 3–5. See p. A25.

State Resources

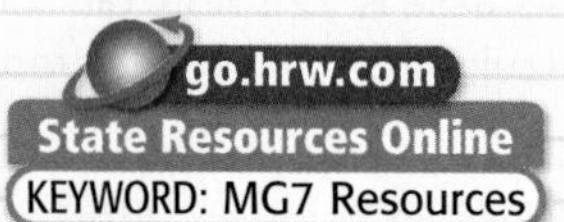

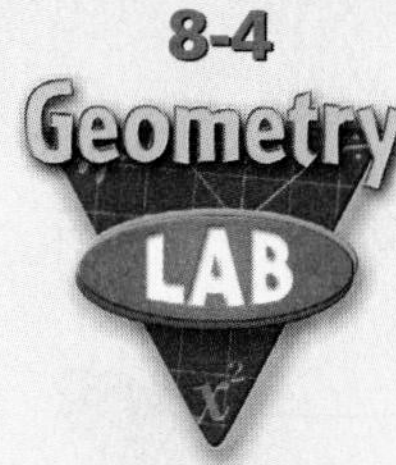

8-4

Use with Lesson 8-4

Indirect Measurement Using Trigonometry

A *clinometer* is a surveying tool that is used to measure angles of elevation and angles of depression. In this lab, you will make a simple clinometer and use it to find indirect measurements. Choose a tall object, such as a flagpole or tree, whose height you will measure.

Activity

1. Follow these instructions to make a clinometer.
   a. Tie a washer or paper clip to the end of a 6-inch string.
   b. Tape the string's other end to the midpoint of the straight edge of a protractor.
   c. Tape a straw along the straight edge of the protractor.

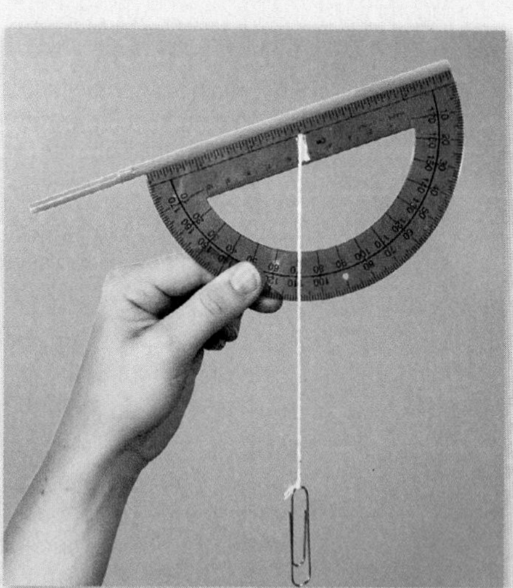

2. Stand back from the object you want to measure. Use a tape measure to measure and record the distance from your feet to the base of the object. Also measure the height of your eyes above the ground.

3. Hold the clinometer steady and look through the straw to sight the top of the object you are measuring. When the string stops moving, pinch it against the protractor and record the acute angle measure.

Try This

1. How is the angle reading from the clinometer related to the angle of elevation from your eye to the top of the object you are measuring?
2. Draw and label a diagram showing the object and the measurements you made. Then use trigonometric ratios to find the height of the object. **Check students' work.**
3. Repeat the activity, measuring the angle of elevation to the object from a different distance. How does your result compare to the previous one?
4. Describe possible measurement errors that can be made in the activity.
5. Explain why this method of indirect measurement is useful in real-world situations.

Teacher to Teacher

This activity is a great way to put mathematics into students' hands. I have used it in my geometry classes for years and have always found it to be a great way for students to use, and better understand, right triangle trigonometry. My students have always liked it because it allows them an opportunity to get out of the textbook, as well as the classroom, for a lesson.

Mike Kingery
Las Cruces, NM

8-5 Law of Sines and Law of Cosines

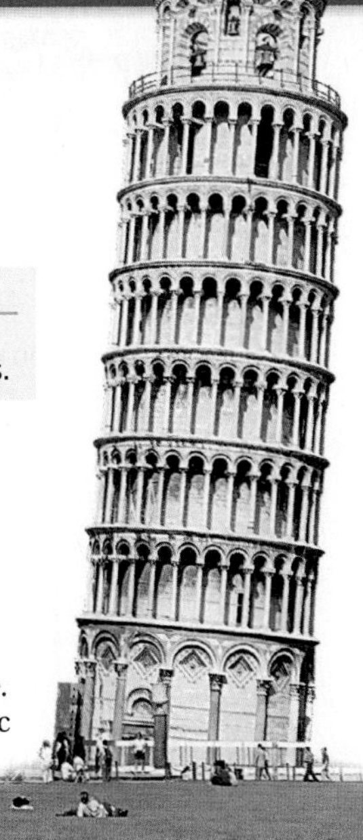

Objective
Use the Law of Sines and the Law of Cosines to solve triangles.

Who uses this?
Engineers can use the Law of Sines and the Law of Cosines to solve construction problems.

Since its completion in 1370, engineers have proposed many solutions for lessening the tilt of the Leaning Tower of Pisa. The tower does not form a right angle with the ground, so the engineers have to work with triangles that are not right triangles.

In this lesson, you will learn to solve *any* triangle. To do so, you will need to calculate trigonometric ratios for angle measures up to 180°. You can use a calculator to find these values.

EXAMPLE 1 Finding Trigonometric Ratios for Obtuse Angles

Helpful Hint
You will learn more about trigonometric ratios of angle measures greater than or equal to 90° in the Chapter Extension.

Use a calculator to find each trigonometric ratio. Round to the nearest hundredth.

A sin 135° **B** tan 98° **C** cos 108°

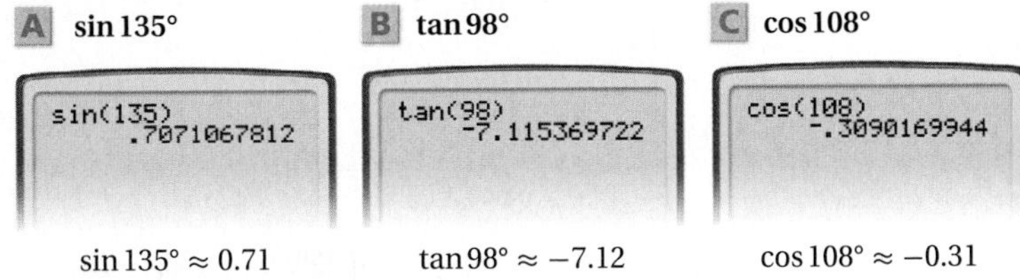

$\sin 135° \approx 0.71$ $\tan 98° \approx -7.12$ $\cos 108° \approx -0.31$

Use a calculator to find each trigonometric ratio. Round to the nearest hundredth.

1a. tan 175° **−0.09** **1b.** cos 92° **−0.03** **1c.** sin 160° **0.34**

You can use the altitude of a triangle to find a relationship between the triangle's side lengths.

In $\triangle ABC$, let h represent the length of the altitude from C to $\overline{AB}$.

From the diagram, $\sin A = \frac{h}{b}$, and $\sin B = \frac{h}{a}$.

By solving for h, you find that $h = b\sin A$ and $h = a\sin B$. So $b\sin A = a\sin B$, and $\frac{\sin A}{a} = \frac{\sin B}{b}$.

You can use another altitude to show that these ratios equal $\frac{\sin C}{c}$.

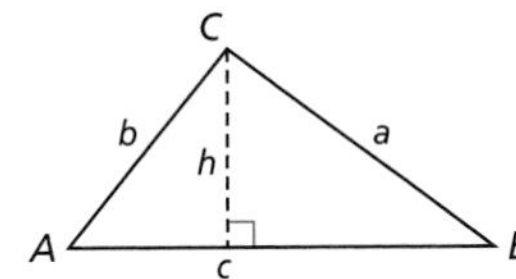

8-5 Organizer

Pacing: Traditional 2 days
Block 1 day

Objective: Use the Law of Sines and the Law of Cosines to solve triangles.

Online Edition
Tutorial Videos

Countdown Week 18

Power Presentations with PowerPoint®

Warm Up

1. What is the third angle measure in a triangle with angles measuring 65° and 43°? 72°

Find each value. Round trigonometric ratios to the nearest hundredth and angle measures to the nearest degree.

2. sin 73° 0.96

3. cos 18° 0.95

4. tan 82° 7.12

5. $\sin^{-1}(0.34)$ 20°

6. $\cos^{-1}(0.63)$ 51°

7. $\tan^{-1}(2.75)$ 70°

Also available on transparency

Math Humor

Q: What's the difference between a teacher and a triangle?

A: A teacher is always right!

1 Introduce

EXPLORATION

8-5 Law of Sines and Law of Cosines

You can use certain trigonometric relationships to solve any triangle. To do so, you will need to find trigonometric ratios for angle measures up to 180°.

1. Use your calculator to find the trigonometric ratios in the table. Round to the nearest hundredth.

	90°	110°	139°	164°	174°
Sine					
Cosine					
Tangent					

2. What happened when you used your calculator to find tan 90°? Why do you think this happened?

3. For angles between 90° and 180°, how is the sine ratio different from the cosine and tangent ratios?

4. Which trigonometric ratio increases as the angle measures increase from 90° to 180°?

THINK AND DISCUSS

5. **Discuss** whether you think there is an angle measure between 90° and 180° whose sine and cosine ratios are equal.

Motivate

So far students have used trigonometry with right triangles and acute angles only. Explain to students that real-world applications in electronics, surveying, and other fields require solving triangles that are not right triangles. In this lesson, students will learn how to solve any triangle using the sine and cosine ratios.

Explorations and answers are provided in *Alternate Openers: Explorations Transparencies.*

State Resources

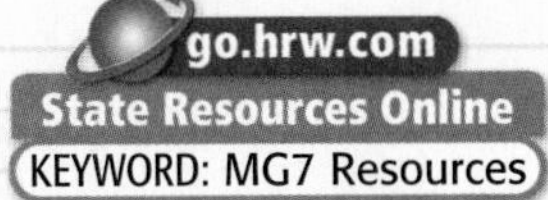

Critical Thinking Some students might ask why trigonometric ratios of obtuse angles are sometimes negative. You may wish to refer these students to the extension on pages 570–571, where the unit circle is shown.

Power Presentations with PowerPoint®

Additional Examples

Example 1

Use a calculator to find each trigonometric ratio. Round to the nearest hundredth.

A. tan 103° −4.33

B. cos 165° −0.97

C. sin 93° 1.00

Example 2

Find each measure. Round lengths to the nearest tenth and angle measures to the nearest degree.

A. *FG* 33.7

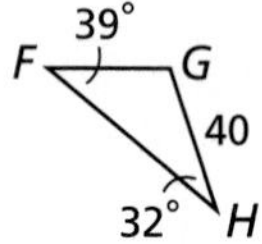

B. m∠Q 36°

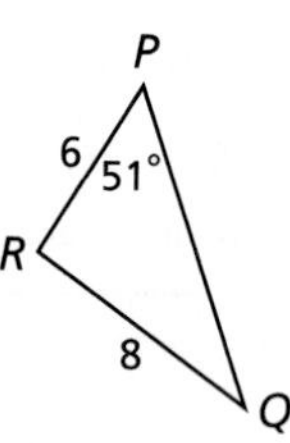

INTERVENTION
Questioning Strategies

EXAMPLE 1

- Do only acute angles have trigonometric ratios?
- Are all trigonometric ratios greater than zero?

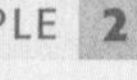

EXAMPLE 2

- Suppose you know the measures of two angles and their included side in a triangle. What do you have to do before you can apply the Law of Sines to find another side length?

Theorem 8-5-1 The Law of Sines

For any $\triangle ABC$ with side lengths a, b, and c,

$$\frac{\sin A}{a} = \frac{\sin B}{b} = \frac{\sin C}{c}.$$

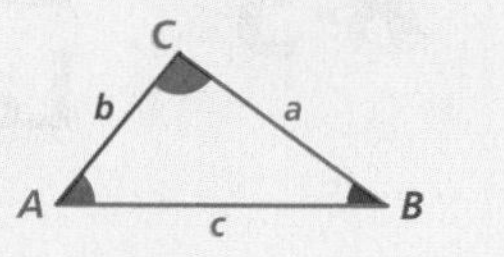

You can use the Law of Sines to solve a triangle if you are given
- two angle measures and any side length (ASA or AAS) or
- two side lengths and a non-included angle measure (SSA).

EXAMPLE 2 Using the Law of Sines

Find each measure. Round lengths to the nearest tenth and angle measures to the nearest degree.

A DF

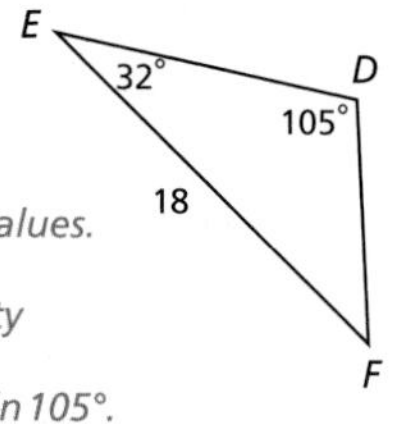

$\frac{\sin D}{EF} = \frac{\sin E}{DF}$ *Law of Sines*

$\frac{\sin 105°}{18} = \frac{\sin 32°}{DF}$ *Substitute the given values.*

$DF \sin 105° = 18 \sin 32°$ *Cross Products Property*

$DF = \frac{18 \sin 32°}{\sin 105°} \approx 9.9$ *Divide both sides by sin 105°.*

(Figure: E, D, F; 32°, 105°, 18)

Remember!

In a proportion with three parts, you can use any of the two parts together.

B $m\angle S$

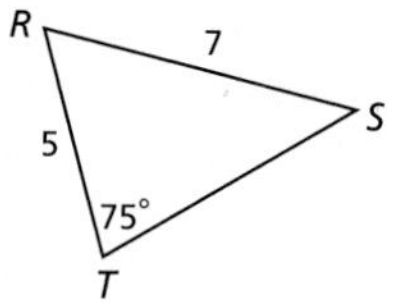

$\frac{\sin T}{RS} = \frac{\sin S}{RT}$ *Law of Sines*

$\frac{\sin 75°}{7} = \frac{\sin S}{5}$ *Substitute the given values.*

$\sin S = \frac{5 \sin 75°}{7}$ *Multiply both sides by 5.*

$m\angle S \approx \sin^{-1}\left(\frac{5 \sin 75°}{7}\right) \approx 44°$ *Use the inverse sine function to find m∠S.*

(Figure: R, S, T; 7, 5, 75°)

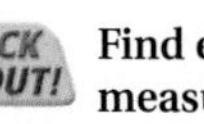

Find each measure. Round lengths to the nearest tenth and angle measures to the nearest degree.

2a. NP **34.9**

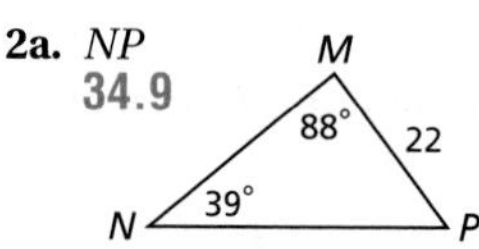

2b. $m\angle L$ **29°** (Figure: J, L, K; 10, 6, 125°)

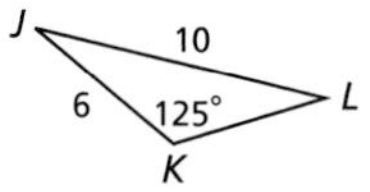

2c. $m\angle X$ **26°**

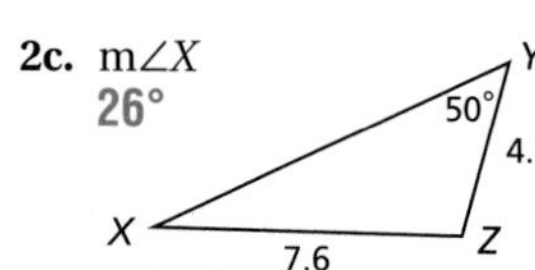

2d. AC **17.7**

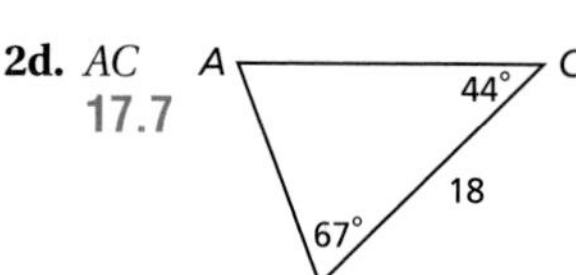

The Law of Sines cannot be used to solve every triangle. If you know two side lengths and the included angle measure or if you know all three side lengths, you cannot use the Law of Sines. Instead, you can apply the Law of Cosines.

2 Teach

Guided Instruction

Review with students the definitions of acute and obtuse triangles. Discuss why trigonometric ratios cannot be used directly to solve such triangles. Go through the steps for the derivation of the Law of Sines on page 551. Present the Law of Cosines. Explain when students should apply the Law of Sines versus the Law of Cosines.

Reaching All Learners
Through Cognitive Strategies

The Law of Sines can also be derived from the formula for the area of a triangle. In any $\triangle ABC$ with side lengths a, b, and c, draw the altitude to each side. The area can be found in three ways, by using each side as the base. This yields the equation $\frac{1}{2}bc \sin A = \frac{1}{2}ac \sin B = \frac{1}{2}ab \sin C$. Divide each expression by $\frac{1}{2}abc$, and it follows that $\frac{\sin A}{a} = \frac{\sin B}{b} = \frac{\sin C}{c}$.

Theorem 8-5-2 The Law of Cosines

For any $\triangle ABC$ with side lengths a, b, and c:

$$a^2 = b^2 + c^2 - 2bc\cos A$$
$$b^2 = a^2 + c^2 - 2ac\cos B$$
$$c^2 = a^2 + b^2 - 2ab\cos C$$

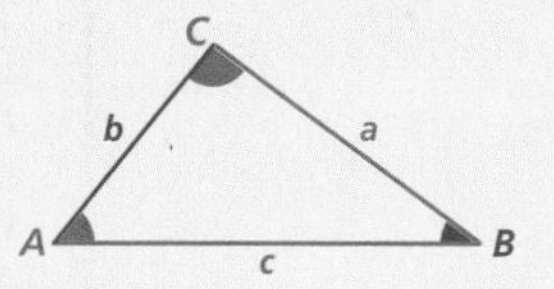

You will prove one case of the Law of Cosines in Exercise 57.

Helpful Hint

The angle referenced in the Law of Cosines is across the equal sign from its corresponding side.

You can use the Law of Cosines to solve a triangle if you are given

- two side lengths and the included angle measure (SAS) or
- three side lengths (SSS).

EXAMPLE 3 Using the Law of Cosines

Find each measure. Round lengths to the nearest tenth and angle measures to the nearest degree.

A BC

$BC^2 = AB^2 + AC^2 - 2(AB)(AC)\cos A$	*Law of Cosines*
$= 14^2 + 9^2 - 2(14)(9)\cos 62°$	*Substitute the given values.*
$BC^2 \approx 158.6932$	*Simplify.*
$BC \approx 12.6$	*Find the square root of both sides.*

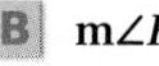

B $m\angle R$

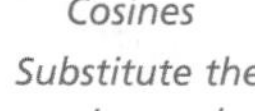

$ST^2 = RS^2 + RT^2 - 2(RS)(RT)\cos R$	*Law of Cosines*
$9^2 = 4^2 + 7^2 - 2(4)(7)\cos R$	*Substitute the given values.*
$81 = 65 - 56\cos R$	*Simplify.*
$16 = -56\cos R$	*Subtract 65 from both sides.*
$\cos R = -\frac{16}{56}$	*Solve for cos R.*
$m\angle R = \cos^{-1}\left(-\frac{16}{56}\right) \approx 107°$	*Use the inverse cosine function to find m∠R.*

CHECK IT OUT! Find each measure. Round lengths to the nearest tenth and angle measures to the nearest degree.

3a. DE 6.5

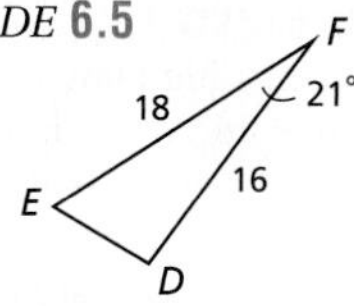

3b. $m\angle K$ 30°

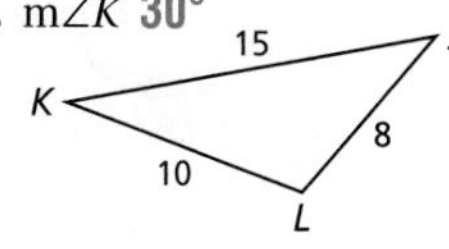

3c. YZ 7.0

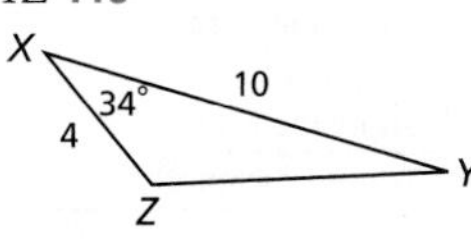

3d. $m\angle R$ 65°

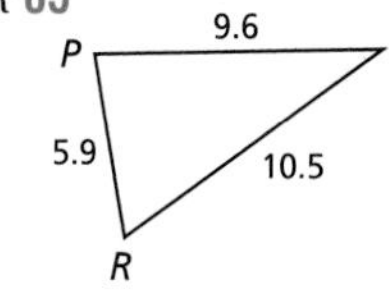

COMMON ERROR ALERT

When using the Law of Cosines, students may end up with a negative cosine ratio and mistakenly assume that $\cos^{-1}(-x) = -\cos^{-1}(x)$. Remind students to always check their answers by finding all three angle measures in the triangle and confirming that their sum is 180°.

Power Presentations with PowerPoint®

Additional Examples

Example 3

Find each measure. Round lengths to the nearest tenth and angle measures to the nearest degree.

A. XZ 53.3

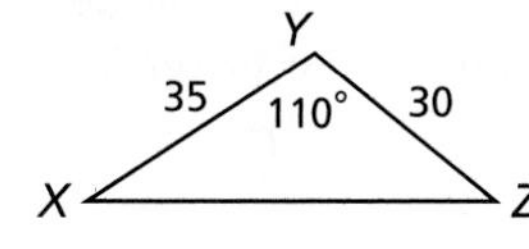

B. $m\angle T$ 33°

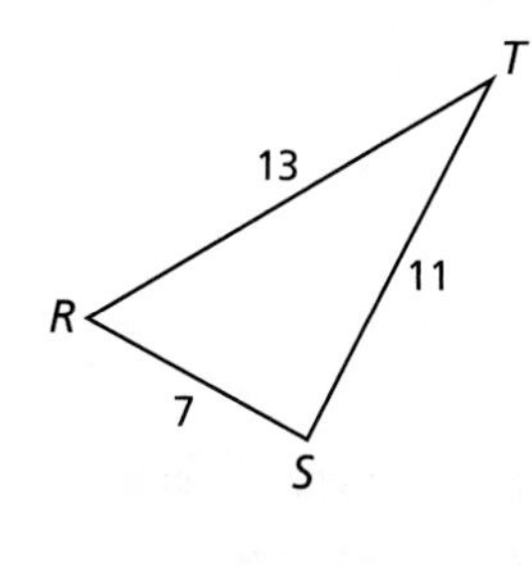

INTERVENTION

Questioning Strategies

EXAMPLE 3

- How is **Example 3A** different from **Example 2B**?
- When is it necessary to use the inverse cosine function when applying the Law of Cosines?

Teaching Tip

Auditory Pair students. Have the first student verbalize when to use the Law of Sines, and have the other verbalize when to use the Law of Cosines. Have the students ask each other questions until both have a clear understanding of how to use these laws.

Teaching Tip **Science Link** The interaction of complex layers of soil and water are probably responsible for the tilt of the Leaning Tower of Pisa. Today soil scientists in the United States and other countries conduct extensive tests of soil characteristics to determine the feasibility of erecting buildings on a particular site.

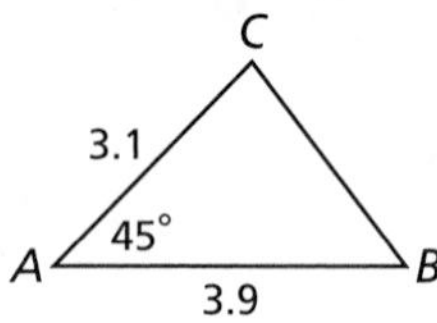

Power Presentations with PowerPoint®

Additional Examples

Example 4

A sailing club has planned a triangular racecourse, as shown in the diagram. How long is the leg of the race along $\overline{BC}$? How many degrees must competitors turn at point C? Round the length to the nearest tenth and the angle measure to the nearest degree.

C

3.1

45°

A B

3.9

2.8 miles; 83°

INTERVENTION

Questioning Strategies

EXAMPLE 4

- How do you know when to use the Law of Sines or the Law of Cosines?

EXAMPLE 4 Engineering Application

The Leaning Tower of Pisa is 56 m tall. In 1999, the tower made a 100° angle with the ground. To stabilize the tower, an engineer considered attaching a cable from the top of the tower to a point that is 40 m from the base. How long would the cable be, and what angle would it make with the ground? Round the length to the nearest tenth and the angle measure to the nearest degree.

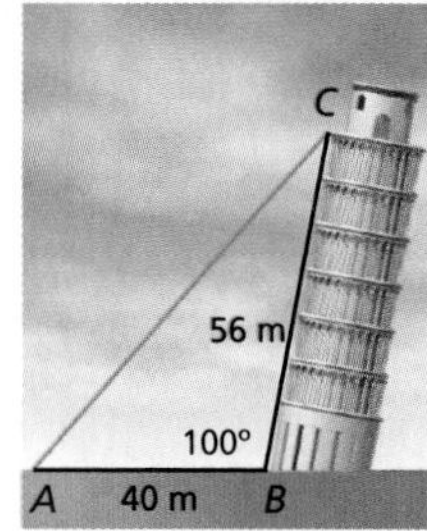

Step 1 Find the length of the cable.

$AC^2 = AB^2 + BC^2 - 2(AB)(BC)\cos B$ *Law of Cosines*

$= 40^2 + 56^2 - 2(40)(56)\cos 100°$ *Substitute the given values.*

$AC^2 \approx 5513.9438$ *Simplify.*

$AC \approx 74.3 \text{ m}$ *Find the square root of both sides.*

Step 2 Find the measure of the angle the cable would make with the ground.

$\frac{\sin A}{BC} = \frac{\sin B}{AC}$ *Law of Sines*

$\frac{\sin A}{56} \approx \frac{\sin 100°}{74.2559}$ *Substitute the calculated value for AC.*

$\sin A \approx \frac{56 \sin 100°}{74.2559}$ *Multiply both sides by 56.*

$m\angle A \approx \sin^{-1}\left(\frac{56 \sin 100°}{74.2559}\right) \approx 48°$ *Use the inverse sine function to find m∠A.*

Helpful Hint

Do not round your answer until the final step of the computation. If a problem has multiple steps, store the calculated answers to each part in your calculator.

CHECK IT OUT! **4. What if...?** Another engineer suggested using a cable attached from the top of the tower to a point 31 m from the base. How long would this cable be, and what angle would it make with the ground? Round the length to the nearest tenth and the angle measure to the nearest degree. **68.6 m; 54°**

THINK AND DISCUSS

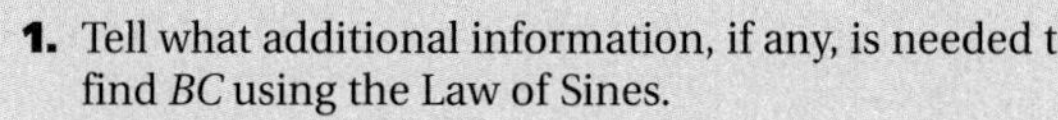

1. Tell what additional information, if any, is needed to find *BC* using the Law of Sines.

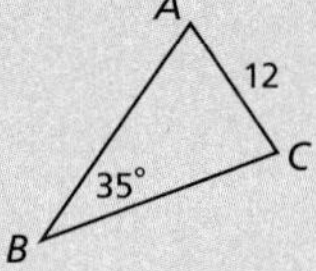

Know it! Note **2. GET ORGANIZED** Copy and complete the graphic organizer. Tell which law you would use to solve each given triangle and then draw an example.

Given	Law	Example
Two angle measures and any side length		
Two side lengths and a nonincluded angle measure		
Two side lengths and the included angle measure		
Three side lengths		

3 Close

Summarize

Review with students the Law of Sines and the Law of Cosines. Ask students, "To the nearest tenth of a degree, what are the angle measures in a triangle with side lengths of 5, 6, and 7?" 44.4°; 57.1°; 78.5°

ONGOING ASSESSMENT and INTERVENTION

***Diagnose Before* the Lesson**
8-5 Warm Up, TE p. 551

***Monitor During* the Lesson**
Check It Out! Exercises, SE pp. 551–554
Questioning Strategies, TE pp. 552–554

***Assess After* the Lesson**
8-5 Lesson Quiz, TE p. 558
Alternative Assessment, TE p. 558

Answers to *Think and Discuss*

1. m∠A
2. See p. A7.

8-5 Exercises

GUIDED PRACTICE

SEE EXAMPLE 1 p. 551

Use a calculator to find each trigonometric ratio. Round to the nearest hundredth.

1. sin 100° **0.98** **2.** cos 167° **−0.97** **3.** tan 92° **−28.64**

4. tan 141° **−0.81** **5.** cos 133° **−0.68** **6.** sin 150° **0.5**

7. sin 147° **0.54** **8.** tan 164° **−0.29** **9.** cos 156° **−0.91**

SEE EXAMPLE 2 p. 552

Find each measure. Round lengths to the nearest tenth and angle measures to the nearest degree.

10. *RT* **24.0**

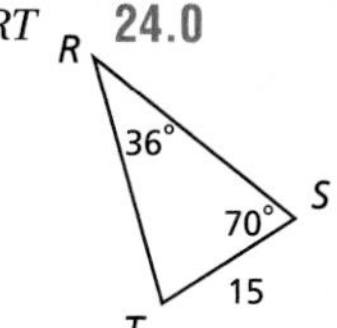

11. m∠*B* **43°**

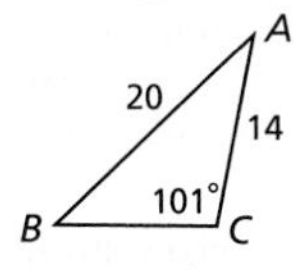

12. m∠*F* **40°**

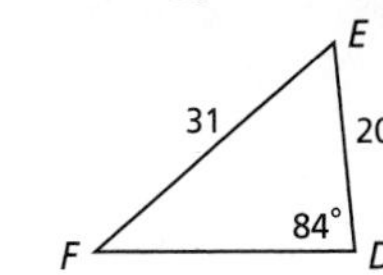

SEE EXAMPLE 3 p. 553

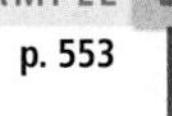

13. m∠*Q* **44°**

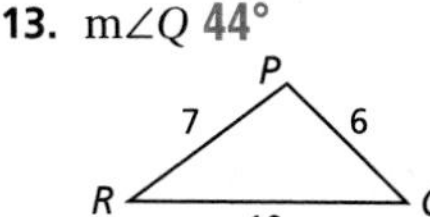

14. *MN* **34.5**

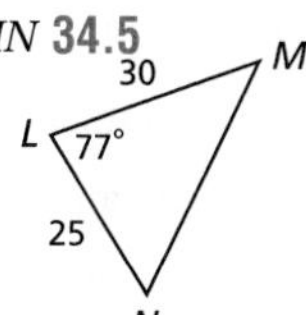

15. *AB* **17.3**

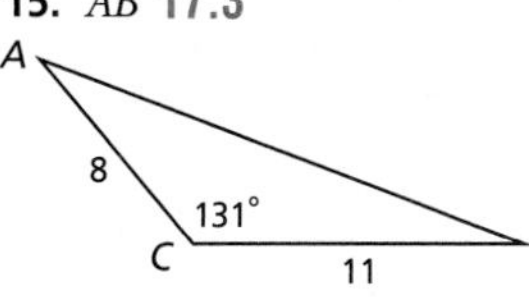

SEE EXAMPLE 4 p. 554

16. Carpentry A carpenter makes a triangular frame by joining three pieces of wood that are 20 cm, 24 cm, and 30 cm long. What are the measures of the angles of the triangle? Round to the nearest degree. **42°; 53°; 85°**

PRACTICE AND PROBLEM SOLVING

Independent Practice

For Exercises	See Example
17–25	1
26–31	2
32–37	3
38	4

Extra Practice
Skills Practice p. S19
Application Practice p. S35

Use a calculator to find each trigonometric ratio. Round to the nearest hundredth.

17. cos 95° **−0.09** **18.** tan 178° **−0.03** **19.** tan 118° **−1.88**

20. sin 132° **0.74** **21.** sin 98° **0.99** **22.** cos 124° **−0.56**

23. tan 139° **−0.87** **24.** cos 145° **−0.82** **25.** sin 128° **0.79**

Find each measure. Round lengths to the nearest tenth and angle measures to the nearest degree.

26. m∠*C* **34°**

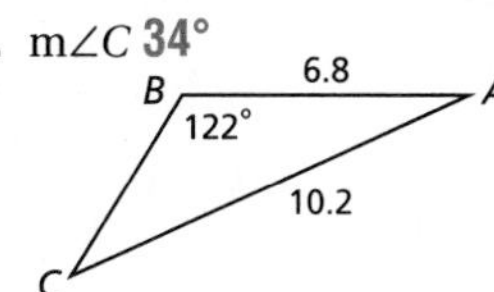

27. *PR* **20.6**

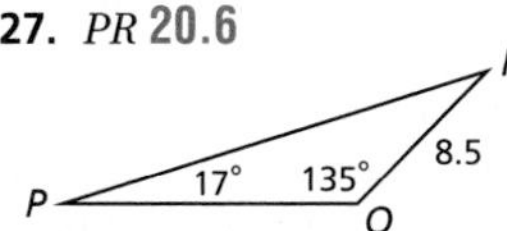

28. *JL* **4.8**

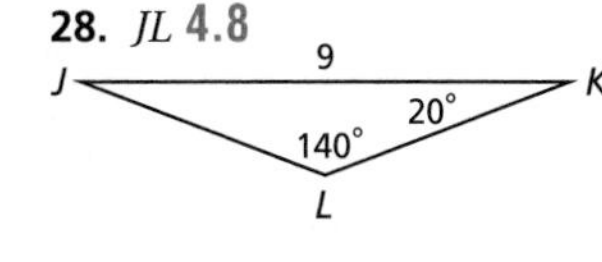

29. *EF* **10.4**

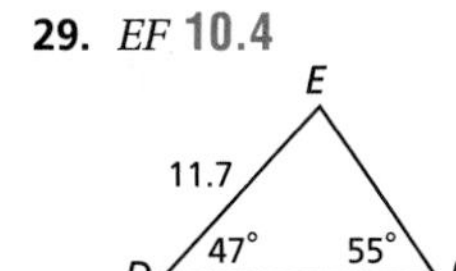

30. m∠*J* **37°**

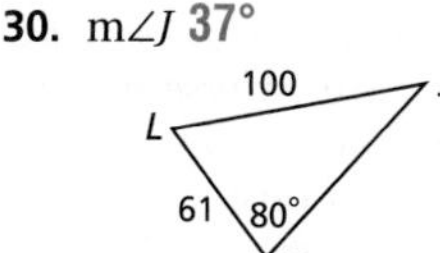

31. m∠*X* **65°**

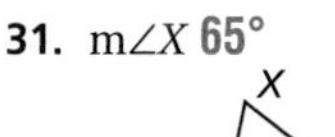

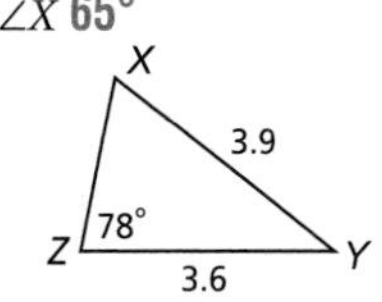

8-5 Exercises

Assignment Guide

Assign *Guided Practice* exercises as necessary.

If you finished Examples **1–2**
Basic 14–31, 39, 42
Average 14–31, 39, 42, 47,
Advanced 14–31, 39, 42, 47, 48

If you finished Examples **1–4**
Basic 14–42, 46–48, 50–54, 56, 58–61, 65–74
Average 14–51, 56, 58–61, 64–74
Advanced 14–50, 54, 55, 57–74

Homework Quick Check
Quickly check key concepts.
Exercises: 18, 26, 32, 38, 42, 46

Teaching Tip

Inclusion For **Exercises 10–12,** have students write all three possible Law of Sines ratios that could be applied to each triangle.

State Resources

Teaching Tip **Visual** Have students draw and label a separate triangle for each exercise in **Exercises 39–42.**

Teaching Tip **Math Background** As students explore the ambiguous case of the Law of Sines in **Exercise 49,** refer them to the exploration of SSA congruence in **Activity 2** of the lab on page 251. Also remind students that the longest side of a triangle is opposite the largest angle.

Teaching Tip **Technology** After students have completed **Exercise 49,** have them use geometry software to explore the ambiguous case of the Law of Sines. Have them construct $\overrightarrow{AC}$ and $\overline{AB}$ of length 12 so that $m\angle BAC = 30°$. Then have them construct a circle at B with a radius of 9. Students can then see that the circle intersects $\overline{AC}$ in two locations. Have them measure $\angle ACB$ in both cases to check their answer.

LINK — Surveying

Many modern surveys are done with GPS (Global Positioning System) technology. GPS uses orbiting satellites as reference points from which other locations are established.

Find each measure. Round lengths to the nearest tenth and angle measures to the nearest degree.

32. AB **12.0**

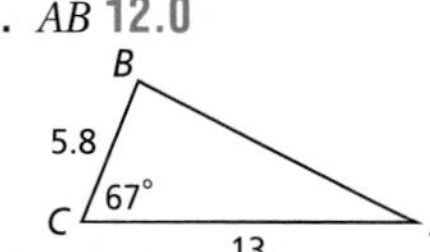

33. $m\angle Z$ **33°**

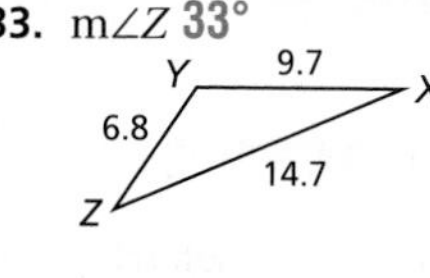

34. $m\angle R$ **23°**

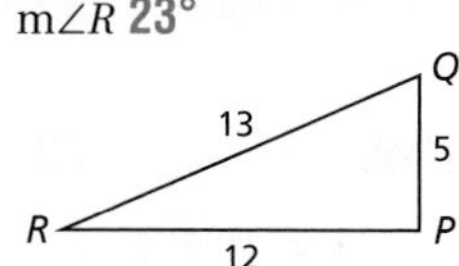

35. EF **8.4**

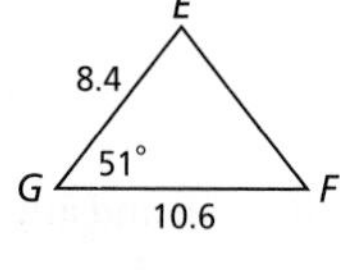

36. LM **19.1**

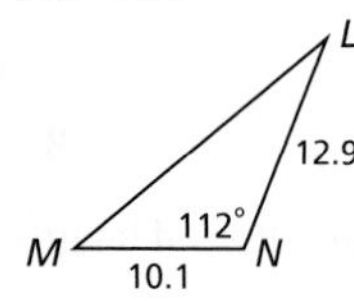

37. $m\angle G$ **21°**

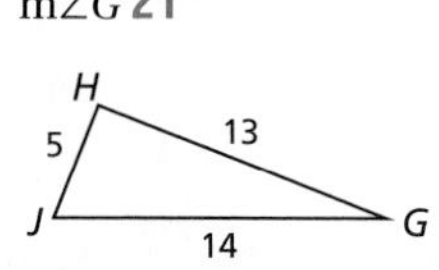

38. Surveying To find the distance across a lake, a surveyor locates points A, B, and C as shown. What is AB to the nearest tenth of a meter, and what is $m\angle B$ to the nearest degree? **92.6 m; 31°**

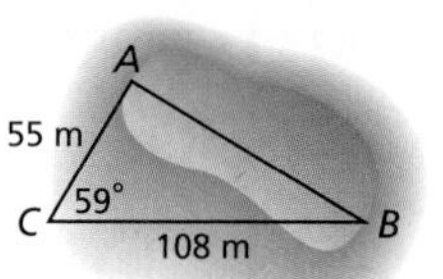

Use the figure for Exercises 39–42. Round lengths to the nearest tenth and angle measures to the nearest degree.

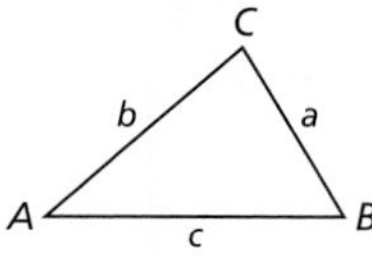

39. $m\angle A = 74°$, $m\angle B = 22°$, and $b = 3.2$ cm. Find a. **8.2 cm**

40. $m\angle C = 100°$, $a = 9.5$ in., and $b = 7.1$ in. Find c. **12.8 in.**

41. $a = 2.2$ m, $b = 3.1$ m, and $c = 4$ m. Find $m\angle B$. **50°**

42. $a = 10.3$ cm, $c = 8.4$ cm, and $m\angle A = 45°$. Find $m\angle C$. **35°**

43. Critical Thinking Suppose you are given the three angle measures of a triangle. Can you use the Law of Sines or the Law of Cosines to find the lengths of the sides? Why or why not?

43. No; 3 ∠ measures do not uniquely determine a △. There is not enough information to use either the Law of Sines or the Law of Cosines.

44. What if...? What does the Law of Cosines simplify to when the given angle is a right angle?

44. Pyth. Thm.

45. Orienteering The map of a beginning orienteering course is shown at right. To the nearest degree, at what angle should a team turn in order to go from the first checkpoint to the second checkpoint? **63°**

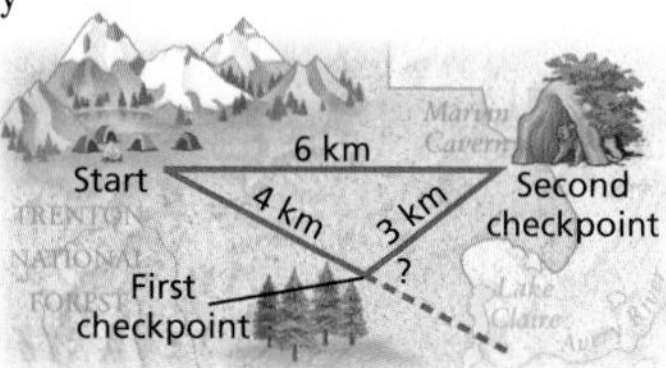

Multi-Step **Find the perimeter of each triangle. Round to the nearest tenth.**

46.

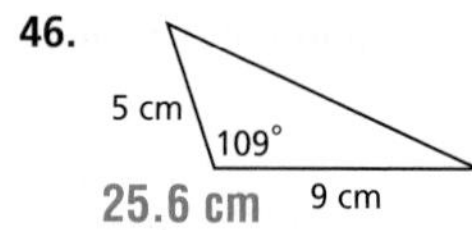

25.6 cm

47.

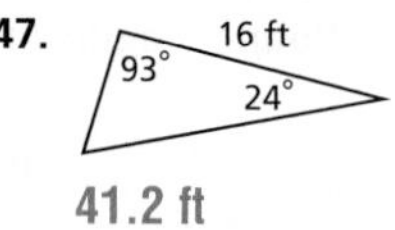

41.2 ft

48. **20.2 in.**

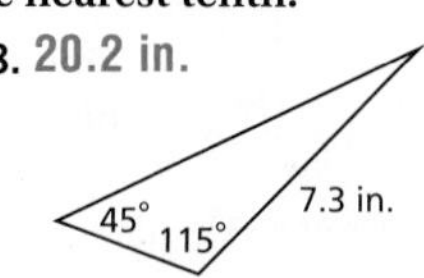

49. The *ambiguous case* of the Law of Sines occurs when you are given an acute angle measure and when the side opposite this angle is shorter than the other given side. In this case, there are two possible triangles.

Find two possible values for $m\angle C$ to the nearest degree. (*Hint:* The inverse sine function on your calculator gives you only acute angle measures. Consider this angle *and* its supplement.) **42°; 138°**

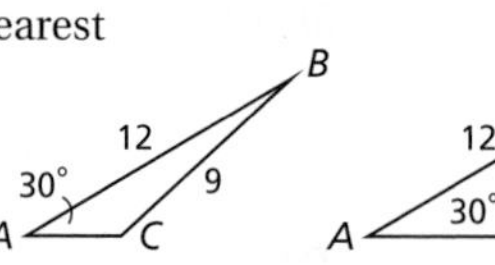

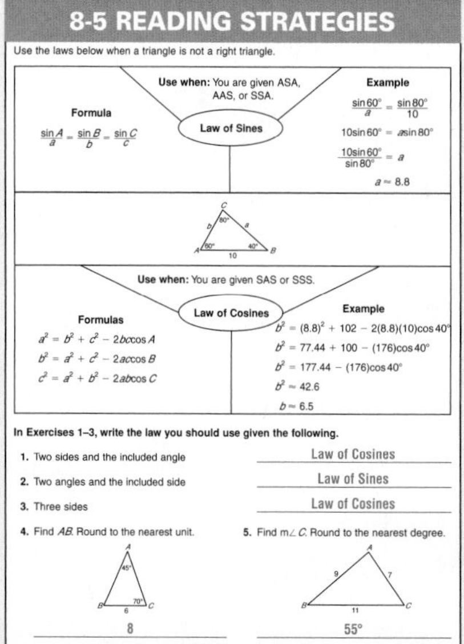

8-5 READING STRATEGIES

Use the laws below when a triangle is not a right triangle.

Law of Sines — Use when: You are given ASA, AAS, or SSA.

Formula: $\frac{\sin A}{a} = \frac{\sin B}{b} = \frac{\sin C}{c}$

Example: $\frac{\sin 60°}{a} = \frac{\sin 80°}{10}$; $10\sin 60° = a\sin 80°$; $\frac{10\sin 60°}{\sin 80°} = a$; $a \approx 8.8$

Law of Cosines — Use when: You are given SAS or SSS.

Formulas: $a^2 = b^2 + c^2 - 2bc\cos A$; $b^2 = a^2 + c^2 - 2ac\cos B$; $c^2 = a^2 + b^2 - 2ab\cos C$

Example: $b^2 = (8.8)^2 + 10^2 - 2(8.8)(10)\cos 40°$; $b^2 = 77.44 + 100 - (176)\cos 40°$; $b^2 = 177.44 - (176)\cos 40°$; $b^2 \approx 42.6$; $b \approx 6.5$

In Exercises 1–3, write the law you should use given the following.

1. Two sides and the included angle — Law of Cosines
2. Two angles and the included side — Law of Sines
3. Three sides — Law of Cosines
4. Find AB. Round to the nearest unit. — 8
5. Find $m\angle C$. Round to the nearest degree. — 55°

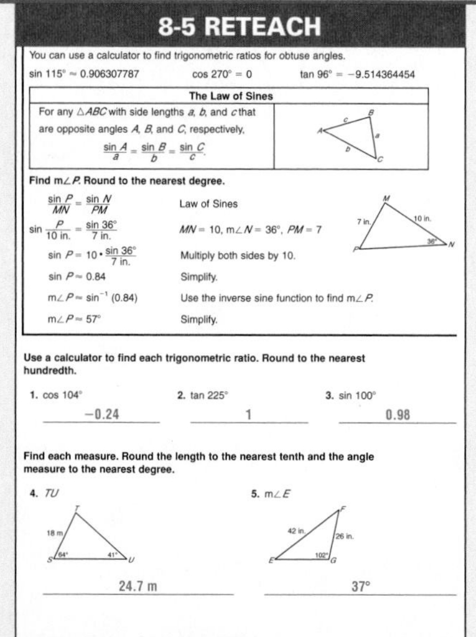

8-5 RETEACH

You can use a calculator to find trigonometric ratios for obtuse angles.

sin 115° ≈ 0.906307787 cos 270° = 0 tan 96° ≈ −9.514364454

The Law of Sines

For any △ABC with side lengths a, b, and c that are opposite angles A, B, and C, respectively, $\frac{\sin A}{a} = \frac{\sin B}{b} = \frac{\sin C}{c}$.

Find $m\angle P$. Round to the nearest degree.

$\frac{\sin P}{MN} = \frac{\sin N}{PM}$	Law of Sines
$\frac{\sin P}{10 \text{ in.}} = \frac{\sin 36°}{7 \text{ in.}}$	$MN = 10$, $m\angle N = 36°$, $PM = 7$
$\sin P = 10 \cdot \frac{\sin 36°}{7 \text{ in.}}$	Multiply both sides by 10.
$\sin P \approx 0.84$	Simplify.
$m\angle P \approx \sin^{-1}(0.84)$	Use the inverse sine function to find $m\angle P$.
$m\angle P \approx 57°$	Simplify.

Use a calculator to find each trigonometric ratio. Round to the nearest hundredth.

1. cos 104° −0.24
2. tan 225° 1
3. sin 100° 0.98

Find each measure. Round the length to the nearest tenth and the angle measure to the nearest degree.

4. TU 24.7 m
5. $m\angle E$ 37°

MULTI-STEP TEST PREP

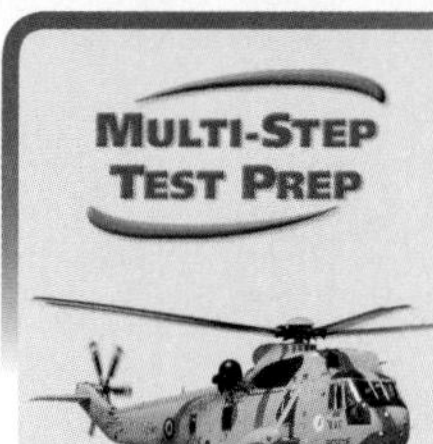

50. This problem will prepare you for the Multi-Step Test Prep on page 568.
Rescue teams at two heliports, *A* and *B*, receive word of a fire at *F*.

a. What is m∠*AFB*? **91°**

b. To the nearest mile, what are the distances from each heliport to the fire? **11 mi; 14 mi**

c. If a helicopter travels 150 mi/h, how much time is saved by sending a helicopter from *A* rather than *B*? **1.2 min**

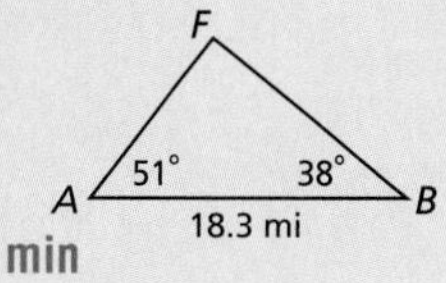

F
A
51°
38°
B
18.3 mi

COMMON ERROR ALERT

For **Exercise 50,** some students may incorrectly use the equations $\tan A = \frac{FB}{18.3}$ and $\tan B = \frac{AF}{18.3}$. Ask them to verify that ∠*F* is not a right angle.

MULTI-STEP TEST PREP **Exercise 50** involves using the Law of Sines and the Law of Cosines. This exercise prepares students for the Multi-Step Test Prep on page 568.

54b. ∠*R*, because it is opposite the longest side

55. $BC \approx 10.73$; $AB \approx 10.34$; $m\angle ABC \approx 50°$

56. A; possible answer: the fraction on the right side of the proportion is incorrect. It should be $\frac{\sin 70°}{12} = \frac{\sin 85°}{x}$, as in B.

57a. $y^2 + h^2$
b. b^2
c. $a^2 = c^2 - 2cx + x^2 + h^2$
d. $a^2 = c^2 + b^2 - 2cx$
e. $b\cos A$
f. Subst.

58. No; possible answer: to use the Law of Sines, you need to know at least 1 side length and the ∠ measure opp. that side.

Identify whether you would use the Law of Sines or Law of Cosines as the first step when solving the given triangle.

51.

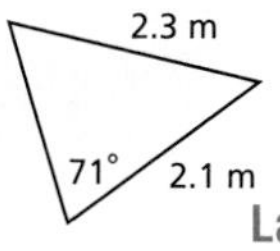

2.3 m
71°
2.1 m

Law of Sines

52.

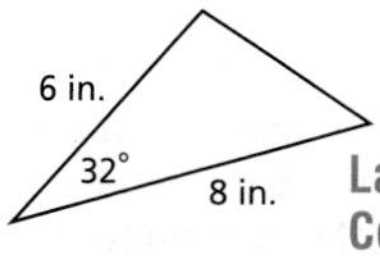

6 in.
32°
8 in.

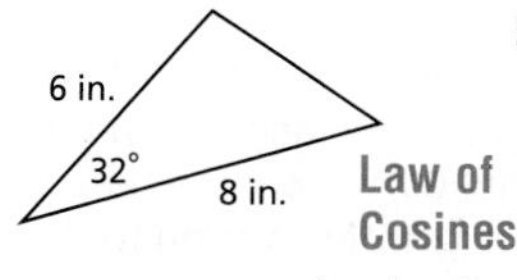

Law of Cosines

53.

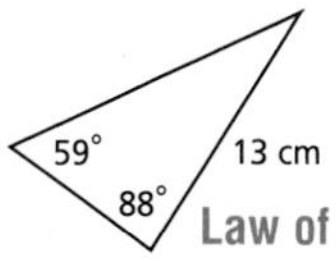

59°
88°
13 cm

Law of Sines

54. The coordinates of the vertices of △*RST* are *R*(0, 3), *S*(3, 1), and *T*(−3, −1).

a. Find *RS*, *ST*, and *RT*. $RS = \sqrt{13} \approx 3.6$; $ST = 2\sqrt{10} \approx 6.3$; $RT = 5$

b. Which angle of △*RST* is the largest? Why?

c. Find the measure of the largest angle in △*RST* to the nearest degree. **93°**

55. Art Jessika is creating a pattern for a piece of stained glass. Find *BC*, *AB*, and m∠*ABC*. Round lengths to the nearest hundredth and angle measures to the nearest degree.

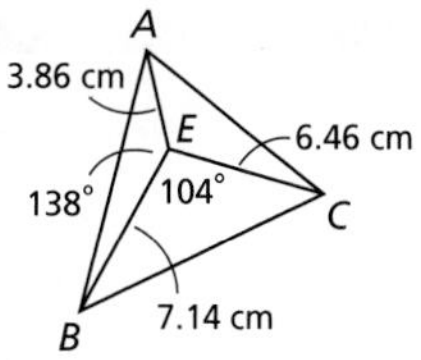

A
3.86 cm
E
6.46 cm
138°
104°
C
B
7.14 cm

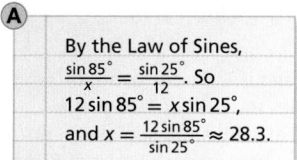

56. ///ERROR ANALYSIS/// Two students were asked to find *x* in △*DEF*. Which solution is incorrect? Explain the error.

A

By the Law of Sines,
$\frac{\sin 85°}{x} = \frac{\sin 25°}{12}$. So
$12\sin 85° = x\sin 25°$,
and $x = \frac{12\sin 85°}{\sin 25°} \approx 28.3$.

B

By the Law of Sines,
$\frac{\sin 85°}{x} = \frac{\sin 70°}{12}$. So
$12\sin 85° = x\sin 70°$,
and $x = \frac{12\sin 85°}{\sin 70°} \approx 12.7$.

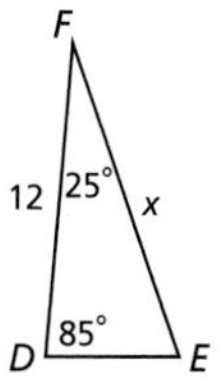

F
12
25°
x
D
85°
E

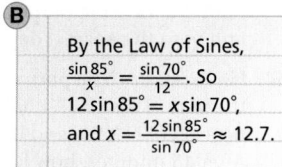

57. Complete the proof of the Law of Cosines for the case when △*ABC* is an acute triangle.
Given: △*ABC* is acute with side lengths *a*, *b*, and *c*.
Prove: $a^2 = b^2 + c^2 - 2bc\cos A$

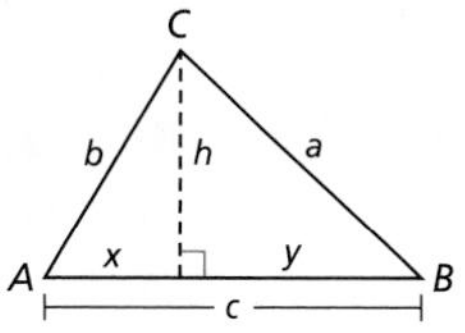

C
b
h
a
A
x
y
B
c

Proof: Draw the altitude from *C* to $\overline{AB}$. Let *h* be the length of this altitude. It divides $\overline{AB}$ into segments of lengths *x* and *y*. By the Pythagorean Theorem, $a^2 =$ **a.** ___?___ , and **b.** ___?___ $= h^2 + x^2$. Substitute $y = c - x$ into the first equation to get **c.** ___?___ . Rearrange the terms to get $a^2 = (h^2 + x^2) + c^2 - 2cx$. Substitute the expression for b^2 to get **d.** ___?___ . From the diagram, $\cos A = \frac{x}{b}$. So $x =$ **e.** ___?___ . Therefore $a^2 = b^2 + c^2 - 2bc\cos A$ by **f.** ___?___ .

58. Write About It Can you use the Law of Sines to solve △*EFG*? Explain why or why not.

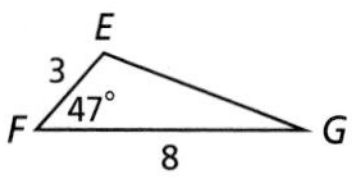

E
3
F
47°
8
G

8-5 PROBLEM SOLVING

1. The map shows three earthquake centers for one week in California. How far apart were the earthquake centers at points *A* and *C*? Round to the nearest tenth.

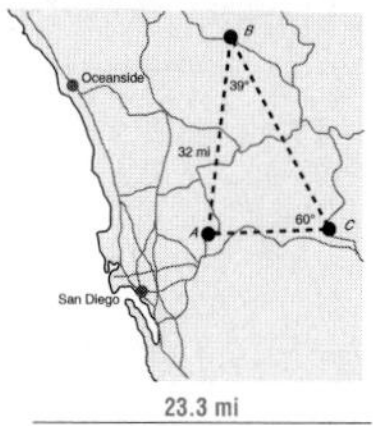

Oceanside
B
39°
32 mi
60°
A
C
San Diego

23.3 mi

2. A BMX track has a starting hill as shown in the diagram. What is the length of the hill, *WY*? Round to the nearest tenth.

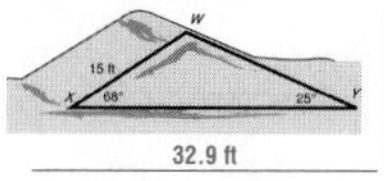

W
15 ft
X
68°
25°
Y

32.9 ft

3. The edges of a triangular cushion measure 8 inches, 3 inches, and 6 inches. What is the measure of the largest angle of the cushion to the nearest degree?

122°

4. The coordinates of the vertices of △*HJK* are *H*(0, 4), *J*(5, 7), and *K*(9, −1). Find the measure of ∠*H* to the nearest degree.

60°

Choose the best answer. Use the following information and diagram for Exercises 5 and 6.

To find the distance across a bay, a surveyor locates points *Q*, *R*, and *S* as shown.

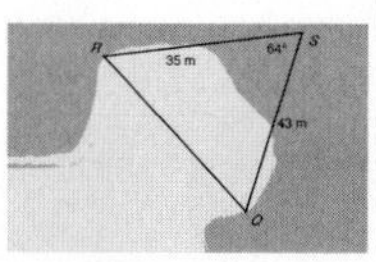

R
35 m
64°
S
43 m
Q

5. What is *QR* to the nearest tenth?
A 8 m
Ⓒ 41.9 m
B 35.2 m
D 55.4 m

6. What is m∠*Q* to the nearest degree?
F 43°
H 67°
Ⓖ 49°
J 107°

7. Two angles of a triangle measure 56° and 77°. The side opposite the 56° angle is 29 cm long. What is the measure of the shortest side? Round to the nearest tenth.
A 23.4 cm
C 32.9 cm
Ⓑ 25.6 cm
D 34.1 cm

8. Which is the best estimate for the perimeter of a triangle if two sides measure 7 inches and 10 inches, and the included angle between the two sides is 82°?
F 11.4 in.
Ⓗ 28.4 in.
G 12.2 in.
J 39.9 in.

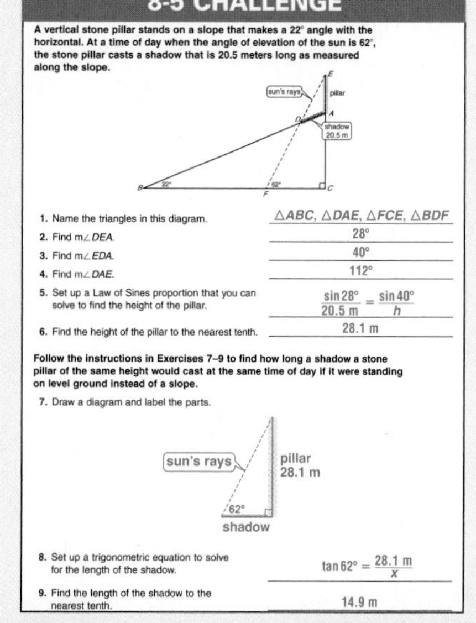

8-5 CHALLENGE

A vertical stone pillar stands on a slope that makes a 22° angle with the horizontal. At a time of day when the angle of elevation of the sun is 62°, the stone pillar casts a shadow that is 20.5 meters long as measured along the slope.

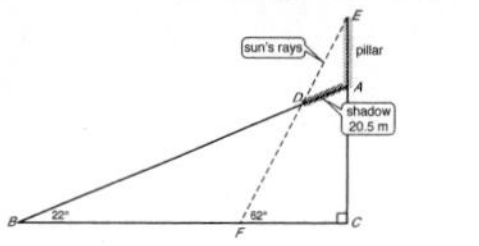

E
sun's rays
pillar
D
A
shadow
20.5 m
B
22°
62°
F
C

1. Name the triangles in this diagram. △*ABC*, △*DAE*, △*FCE*, △*BDF*
2. Find m∠*DEA*. 28°
3. Find m∠*EDA*. 40°
4. Find m∠*DAE*. 112°
5. Set up a Law of Sines proportion that you can solve to find the height of the pillar. $\frac{\sin 28°}{20.5 \text{ m}} = \frac{\sin 40°}{h}$
6. Find the height of the pillar to the nearest tenth. 28.1 m

Follow the instructions in Exercises 7–9 to find how long a shadow a stone pillar of the same height would cast at the same time of day if it were standing on level ground instead of a slope.

7. Draw a diagram and label the parts.

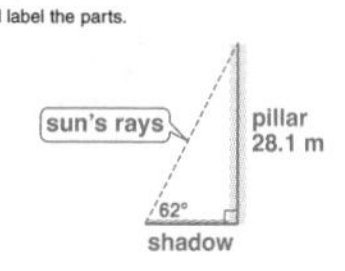

sun's rays
pillar
28.1 m
62°
shadow

8. Set up a trigonometric equation to solve for the length of the shadow. $\tan 62° = \frac{28.1 \text{ m}}{x}$
9. Find the length of the shadow to the nearest tenth. 14.9 m

8-5 PRACTICE A
8-5 PRACTICE C
8-5 PRACTICE B

Use a calculator to find each trigonometric ratio. Round to the nearest hundredth.

1. sin 111° 0.93
2. cos 150° −0.87
3. tan 163° −0.31
4. sin 92° 1.00
5. cos 129° −0.63
6. tan 99° −6.31
7. sin 170° 0.17
8. cos 96° −0.10
9. tan 117° −1.96

Use the Law of Sines to find each measure. Round lengths to the nearest tenth and angle measures to the nearest degree.

10.

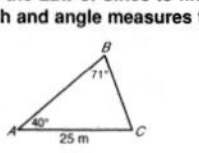

B
71°
A
40°
25 m
C

BC 17.0 m

11.

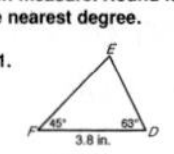

E
F
45°
63°
D
3.8 in.

DE 2.8 in.

12.

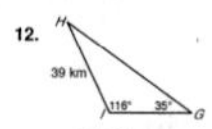

H
39 km
I
116°
35°
G

GH 61.1 km

13.

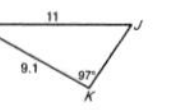

L
11
J
9.1
97°
K

m∠*J* 55°

14.

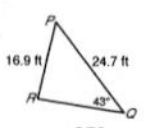

P
16.9 ft
24.7 ft
R
43°
Q

m∠*R* 85°

15.

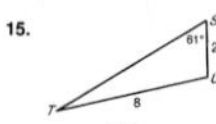

S
61°
2.8
U
T
8

m∠*T* 18°

Use the Law of Cosines to find each measure. Round lengths to the nearest tenth and angle measures to the nearest degree.

16.

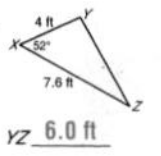

4 ft
Y
X
52°
7.6 ft
Z

YZ 6.0 ft

17.

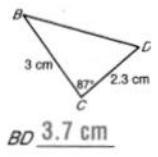

B
D
3 cm
87°
2.3 cm
C

BD 3.7 cm

18.

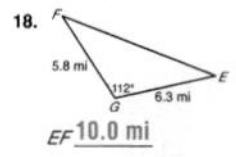

F
5.8 mi
112°
E
G
6.3 mi

EF 10.0 mi

19.

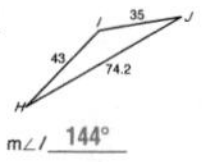

I
35
J
43
74.2
H

m∠*I* 144°

20.

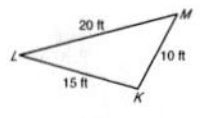

20 ft
M
L
10 ft
15 ft
K

m∠*M* 47°

21.

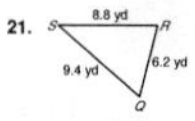

S
8.8 yd
R
9.4 yd
6.2 yd
Q

m∠*S* 40°

TEST PREP

59. Which of these is closest to the length of $\overline{AB}$?
   - (A) 5.5 centimeters (circled)
   - (B) 7.5 centimeters
   - (C) 14.4 centimeters
   - (D) 22.2 centimeters

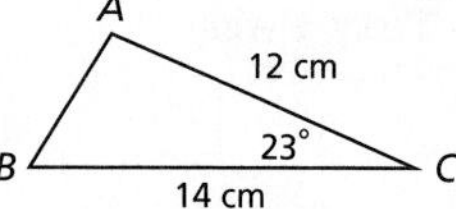

60. Which set of given information makes it possible to find x using the Law of Sines?
   - (F) $m\angle T = 38°$, $RS = 8.1$, $ST = 15.3$
   - (G) $RS = 4$, $m\angle S = 40°$, $ST = 9$
   - (H) $m\angle R = 92°$, $m\angle S = 34°$, $ST = 7$ (circled)
   - (J) $m\angle R = 105°$, $m\angle S = 44°$, $m\angle T = 31°$

61. A surveyor finds that the face of a pyramid makes a 135° angle with the ground. From a point 100 m from the base of the pyramid, the angle of elevation to the top is 25°. How long is the face of the pyramid, $\overline{XY}$?
   - (A) 48 meters
   - (B) 81 meters
   - (C) 124 meters (circled)
   - (D) 207 meters

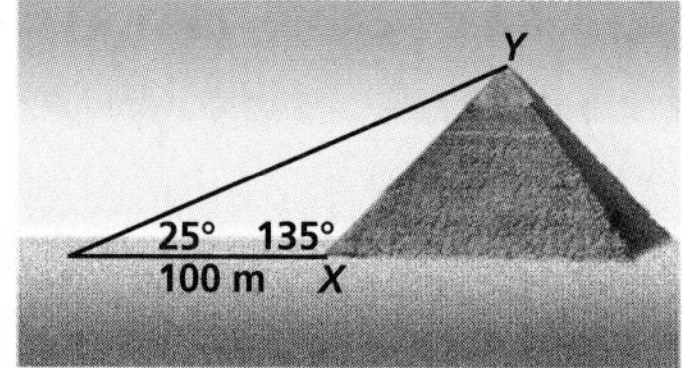

CHALLENGE AND EXTEND

62. **Multi-Step** Three circular disks are placed next to each other as shown. The disks have radii of 2 cm, 3 cm, and 4 cm. The centers of the disks form $\triangle ABC$. Find $m\angle ACB$ to the nearest degree. **44°**

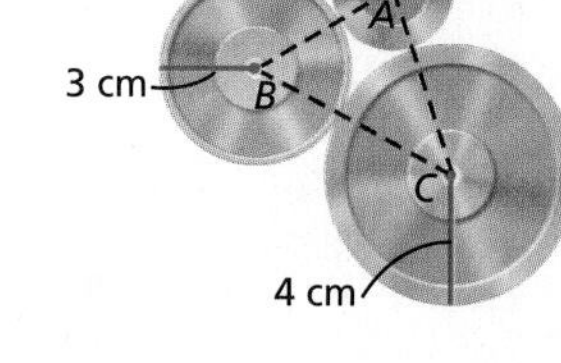

63. Line ℓ passes through points $(-1, 1)$ and $(1, 3)$. Line m passes through points $(-1, 1)$ and $(3, 2)$. Find the measure of the acute angle formed by ℓ and m to the nearest degree. **31°**

64. **Navigation** The port of Bonner is 5 mi due south of the port of Alston. A boat leaves the port of Alston at a bearing of N 32° E and travels at a constant speed of 6 mi/h. After 45 minutes, how far is the boat from the port of Bonner? Round to the nearest tenth of a mile. **9.1 mi**

SPIRAL REVIEW

Write a rule for the nth term in each sequence. *(Previous course)*

65. 3, 6, 9, 12, 15, … **$3n$**
66. 3, 5, 7, 9, 11, … **$2n + 1$**
67. 4, 6, 8, 10, 12, … **$2n + 2$**

State the theorem or postulate that justifies each statement. *(Lesson 3-2)*

68. $\angle 1 \cong \angle 8$ **Alt. Ext. ∠s Thm.**
69. $\angle 4 \cong \angle 5$ **Alt. Int. ∠s Thm.**
70. $m\angle 4 + m\angle 6 = 180°$ **Same-Side Int. ∠s Thm.**
71. $\angle 2 \cong \angle 7$ **Alt. Ext. ∠s Thm.**

Use the given trigonometric ratio to determine which angle of the triangle is $\angle A$. *(Lesson 8-3)*

72. $\cos A = \frac{15}{17}$ **∠2**
73. $\sin A = \frac{15}{17}$ **∠1**
74. $\tan A = 1.875$ **∠1**

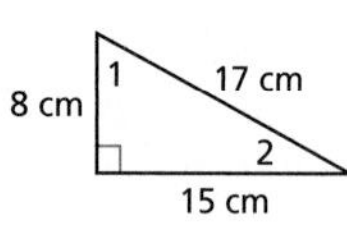

TEST PREP DOCTOR For **Exercise 59,** remind students not to rely on the drawing to estimate AB.

In **Exercise 61,** students should recognize that choices **A** and **B** are not possible values for XY. Since the smallest angle in the triangle is 20°, 100 m is the shortest side, and thus $XY > 100$.

Journal

Have students explain how they remember which law to use—the Law of Sines or the Law of Cosines.

ALTERNATIVE ASSESSMENT

Have students draw and label two triangles—one that requires the Law of Sines to solve, and another that requires the Law of Cosines. Then have them solve each triangle.

Power Presentations with PowerPoint®

8-5 Lesson Quiz

Use a calculator to find each trigonometric ratio. Round to the nearest hundredth.

1. tan 154° −0.49
2. cos 124° −0.56
3. sin 162° 0.31

Use $\triangle ABC$ for Items 4–6. Round lengths to the nearest tenth and angle measures to the nearest degree.

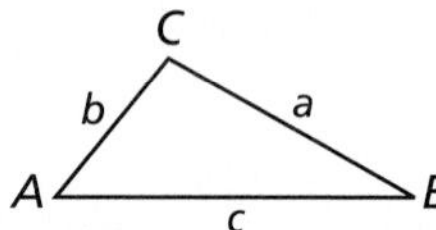

4. $m\angle B = 20°$, $m\angle C = 31°$, and $b = 210$. Find a. 477.2
5. $a = 16$, $b = 10$, and $m\angle C = 110°$. Find c. 21.6
6. $a = 20$, $b = 15$, and $c = 8.3$. Find $m\angle A$. 115°
7. An observer in tower A sees a fire 1554 ft away at an angle of depression of 28°. To the nearest foot, how far is the fire from an observer in tower B? To the nearest degree, what is the angle of depression to the fire from tower B? 1212 ft; 37°

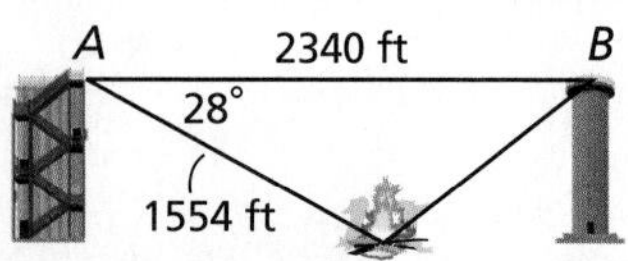

Also available on transparency

8-6 Vectors

Objectives
Find the magnitude and direction of a vector.

Use vectors and vector addition to solve real-world problems.

Vocabulary
vector
component form
magnitude
direction
equal vectors
parallel vectors
resultant vector

Who uses this?
By using vectors, a kayaker can take water currents into account when planning a course. (See Example 5.)

The speed and direction an object moves can be represented by a *vector*. A **vector** is a quantity that has both length and direction.

You can think of a vector as a directed line segment. The vector below may be named $\overrightarrow{AB}$ or $\vec{v}$.

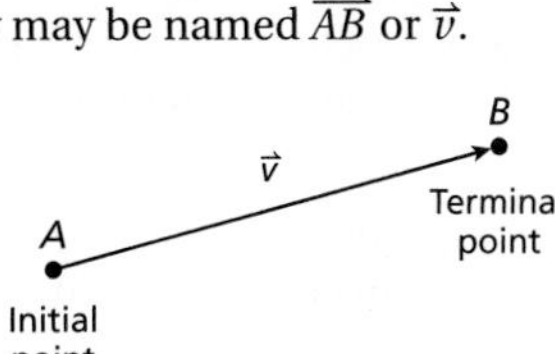

A vector can also be named using *component form*. The **component form** $\langle x, y\rangle$ of a vector lists the horizontal and vertical change from the initial point to the terminal point. The component form of $\overrightarrow{CD}$ is $\langle 2, 3\rangle$.

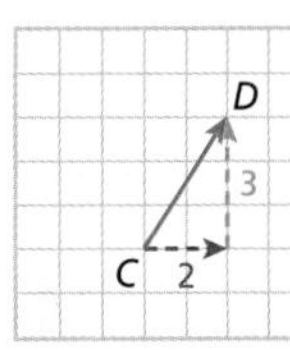

EXAMPLE 1 Writing Vectors in Component Form

Write each vector in component form.

A $\overrightarrow{EF}$

The horizontal change from E to F is 4 units.
The vertical change from E to F is −3 units.
So the component form of $\overrightarrow{EF}$ is $\langle 4, -3\rangle$.

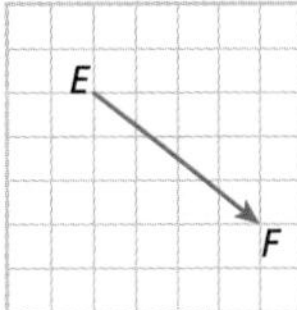

B $\overrightarrow{PQ}$ **with** $P(7, -5)$ **and** $Q(4, 3)$

$\overrightarrow{PQ} = \langle x_2 - x_1, y_2 - y_1\rangle$ *Subtract the coordinates of the initial point from the coordinates of the terminal point.*

$\overrightarrow{PQ} = \langle 4 - 7, 3 - (-5)\rangle$ *Substitute the coordinates of the given points.*

$\overrightarrow{PQ} = \langle -3, 8\rangle$ *Simplify.*

CHECK IT OUT! **Write each vector in component form.**

1a. $\vec{u}$ $\langle -3, -4\rangle$

1b. the vector with initial point $L(-1, 1)$ and terminal point $M(6, 2)$ $\langle 7, 1\rangle$

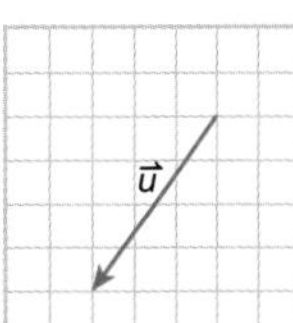

8-6 Organizer

Pacing: Traditional 1 day
Block $\frac{1}{2}$ day

Objectives: Find the magnitude and direction of a vector.

Use vectors and vector addition to solve real-world problems.

Online Edition
Tutorial Videos

Countdown Week 18

Power Presentations with PowerPoint®

Warm Up

Find *AB*.

1. $A(0, 15), B(17, 0)$ $\sqrt{514}$

2. $A(-4, 2), B(4, -2)$ $4\sqrt{5}$

Solve each equation. Round to the nearest tenth or nearest degree.

3. $\cos 26° = \frac{x}{7}$ 6.3

4. $\sin 26° = \frac{y}{7}$ 3.1

5. $\tan P = \frac{41}{53}$ 38°

6. $\tan Q = \frac{13}{11}$ 50°

Also available on transparency

Math Humor

Q: Which trigonometric ratios do pig farmers use?

A: Swine (sine) and coswine (cosine)!

1 Introduce

EXPLORATION

8-6 Vectors

A *vector* is a quantity that has both length and direction. You can think of a vector as a line segment with a direction. The figure shows vector *v*, which can be written $\vec{v}$. The vector can also be named $\overrightarrow{PQ}$.

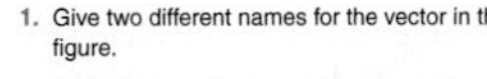

1. Give two different names for the vector in the figure.

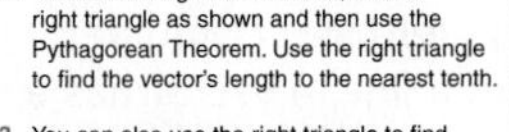

2. To find the length of the vector, draw a right triangle as shown and then use the Pythagorean Theorem. Use the right triangle to find the vector's length to the nearest tenth.

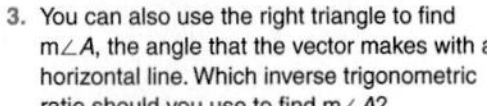

3. You can also use the right triangle to find m∠*A*, the angle that the vector makes with a horizontal line. Which inverse trigonometric ratio should you use to find m∠*A*?

4. Find m∠*A* to the nearest degree.

THINK AND DISCUSS

5. **Describe** how the vector $\overrightarrow{MN}$ is different from the vector $\overrightarrow{NM}$.

6. **Explain** the difference between a vector and a ray.

Motivate

Using $A(2, 3)$ and $B(-3, 1)$, have students draw $\overline{AB}$ and $\overline{BA}$ on one grid, and $\overrightarrow{AB}$ and $\overrightarrow{BA}$ on a second grid. Ask "What is the relationship between $\overline{AB}$ and $\overline{BA}$?" They are ≅. Ask "What is the relationship between $\overrightarrow{AB}$ and $\overrightarrow{BA}$?" They are opp. rays. Explain that students will work with quantities called vectors, which have both a length and a direction.

Explorations and answers are provided in *Alternate Openers: Explorations Transparencies.*

State Resources

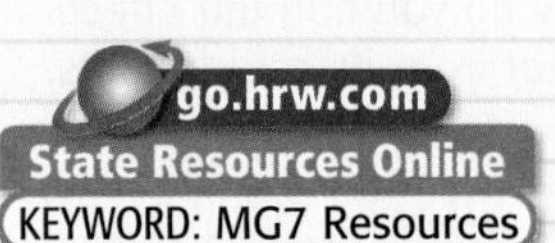

The **magnitude** of a vector is its length. The magnitude of a vector is written $|\overrightarrow{AB}|$ or $|\vec{v}|$.

When a vector is used to represent speed in a given direction, the magnitude of the vector equals the speed. For example, if a vector represents the course a kayaker paddles, the magnitude of the vector is the kayaker's speed.

EXAMPLE 2 Finding the Magnitude of a Vector

Draw the vector $\langle 4, -2\rangle$ on a coordinate plane. Find its magnitude to the nearest tenth.

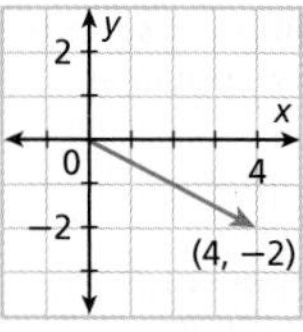

Step 1 Draw the vector on a coordinate plane.
Use the origin as the initial point. Then $(4, -2)$ is the terminal point.

Step 2 Find the magnitude.
Use the Distance Formula.

$$|\langle 4, -2\rangle| = \sqrt{(4-0)^2 + (-2-0)^2} = \sqrt{20} \approx 4.5$$

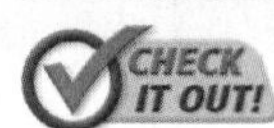

2. Draw the vector $\langle -3, 1\rangle$ on a coordinate plane. Find its magnitude to the nearest tenth. 3.2

The **direction** of a vector is the angle that it makes with a horizontal line. This angle is measured counterclockwise from the positive x-axis. The direction of $\overrightarrow{AB}$ is 60°.

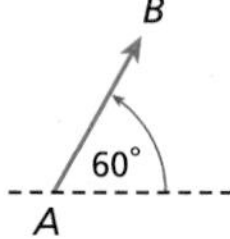

Remember!
See Lesson 4-5, page 252, to review bearings.

The direction of a vector can also be given as a bearing relative to the compass directions *north, south, east,* and *west.* $\overrightarrow{AB}$ has a bearing of N 30° E.

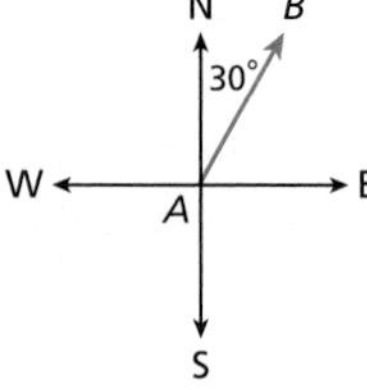

EXAMPLE 3 Finding the Direction of a Vector

A wind velocity is given by the vector $\langle 2, 5\rangle$. Draw the vector on a coordinate plane. Find the direction of the vector to the nearest degree.

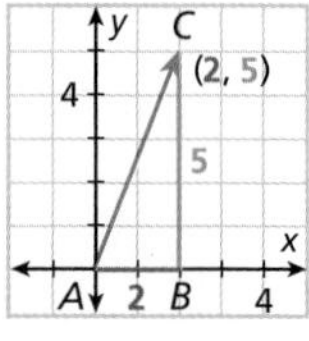

Step 1 Draw the vector on a coordinate plane.
Use the origin as the initial point.

Step 2 Find the direction.
Draw right triangle ABC as shown. $\angle A$ is the angle formed by the vector and the x-axis, and $\tan A = \frac{5}{2}$. So $m\angle A = \tan^{-1}\left(\frac{5}{2}\right) \approx 68°$.

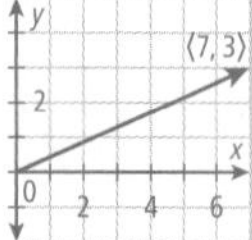

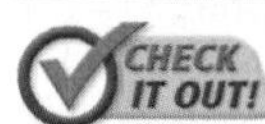

3. The force exerted by a tugboat is given by the vector $\langle 7, 3\rangle$. Draw the vector on a coordinate plane. Find the direction of the vector to the nearest degree. 23°

Power Presentations with PowerPoint®

Additional Examples

Example 1

Write each vector in component form.

A. $\overrightarrow{HG}$ $\langle -3, 5\rangle$

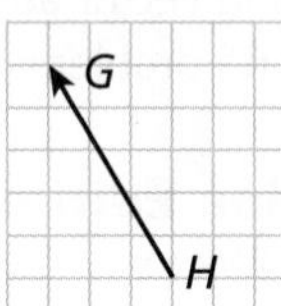

B. $\overrightarrow{MN}$ with $M(-8, 1)$ and $N(2, -7)$ $\langle 10, -8\rangle$

Example 2

Draw the vector $\langle -1, 5\rangle$ on a coordinate plane. Find its magnitude to the nearest tenth.

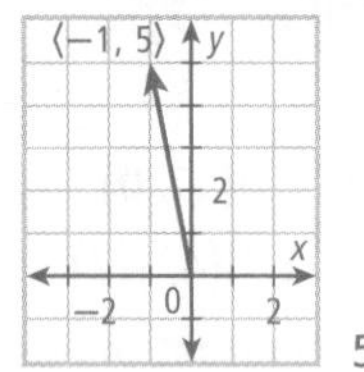

5.1

Example 3

The force exerted by a skier is given by the vector $\langle 1, 4\rangle$. Draw the vector on a coordinate plane. Find the direction of the vector to the nearest degree.

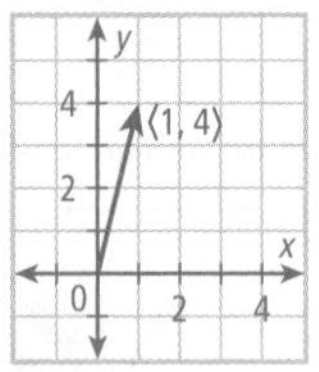

76°

INTERVENTION

Questioning Strategies

EXAMPLE 1

- How do you find the components of a vector sketched on a coordinate grid?
- How do you find the components of a vector from its initial and terminal points?

EXAMPLE 2

- What formula can you use to find the magnitude of a vector when you know its components?

EXAMPLE 3

- How do you find the direction of a vector from its components?

2 Teach

Guided Instruction

Compare quantities described by a single number, such as area or speed, and quantities that have both magnitude and direction, such as a northwest wind at 15 mi/h. Explain that the latter can be represented by vectors. Show students how to write a vector in component form and how to find its magnitude and direction. Discuss equal and parallel vectors, and explain how vectors are added to find a resultant vector.

Reaching All Learners

Through Multiple Representations

Discuss with students how the components of a vector are related to the slope of the line containing the vector. The vertical and horizontal components of a vector represent the rise and run of the vector from its initial point to its terminal point. Remind students that unlike a line, a vector has a finite magnitude.

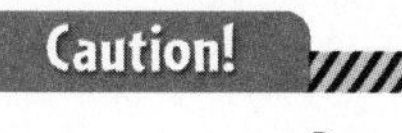

Note that $\overrightarrow{AB} \neq \overrightarrow{BA}$ since these vectors do not have the same direction.

Two vectors are **equal vectors** if they have the same magnitude and the same direction. For example, $\vec{u} = \vec{v}$. Equal vectors do not have to have the same initial point and terminal point.

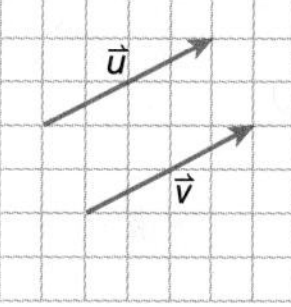

$|\vec{u}| = |\vec{v}| = 2\sqrt{5}$

Two vectors are **parallel vectors** if they have the same direction or if they have opposite directions. They may have different magnitudes. For example, $\vec{w} \parallel \vec{x}$. Equal vectors are always parallel vectors.

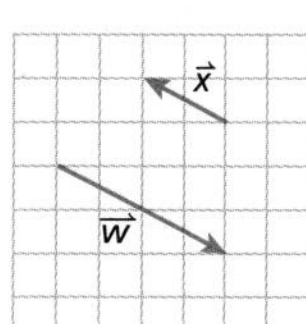

$|\vec{w}| = 2\sqrt{5}$
$|\vec{x}| = \sqrt{5}$

EXAMPLE 4 **Identifying Equal and Parallel Vectors**

Identify each of the following.

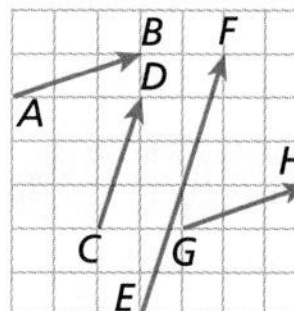

A **equal vectors**
$\overrightarrow{AB} = \overrightarrow{GH}$ *Identify vectors with the same magnitude and direction.*

B **parallel vectors**
$\overrightarrow{AB} \parallel \overrightarrow{GH}$ and $\overrightarrow{CD} \parallel \overrightarrow{EF}$ *Identify vectors with the same or opposite directions.*

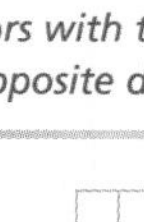

CHECK IT OUT! **Identify each of the following.**

4a. equal vectors $\overrightarrow{PQ} = \overrightarrow{RS}$

4b. parallel vectors
$\overrightarrow{PQ} \parallel \overrightarrow{RS}$; $\overrightarrow{XY} \parallel \overrightarrow{MN}$

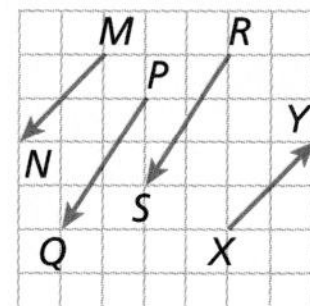

The **resultant vector** is the vector that represents the sum of two given vectors. To add two vectors geometrically, you can use the head-to-tail method or the parallelogram method.

Vector Addition

METHOD	EXAMPLE
Head-to-Tail Method Place the initial point (tail) of the second vector on the terminal point (head) of the first vector. The resultant is the vector that joins the initial point of the first vector to the terminal point of the second vector.	$\vec{u} + \vec{v}$, $\vec{v}$, $\vec{u}$
Parallelogram Method Use the same initial point for both of the given vectors. Create a parallelogram by adding a copy of each vector at the terminal point (head) of the other vector. The resultant vector is a diagonal of the parallelogram formed.	$\vec{u} + \vec{v}$, $\vec{v}$, $\vec{u}$

Students might assume that vectors must have the same direction to be parallel. Remind them that opposite vectors are parallel. However, equal vectors must have the same magnitude and the same direction. So opposite vectors cannot be equal.

Power Presentations with PowerPoint®

Additional Examples

Example 4

Identify each of the following.

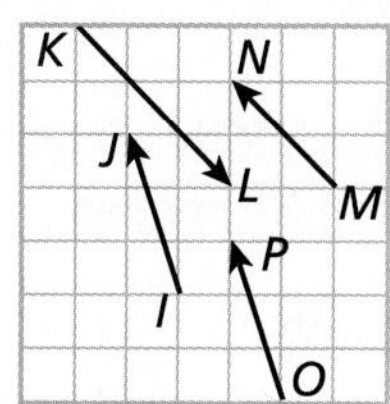

A. equal vectors $\overrightarrow{IJ} = \overrightarrow{OP}$

B. parallel vectors $\overrightarrow{IJ} \parallel \overrightarrow{OP}$; $\overrightarrow{KL} \parallel \overrightarrow{MN}$

INTERVENTION
Questioning Strategies

EXAMPLE 4

- Suppose two vectors have the same magnitude and the same horizontal component, but opposite vertical components. Are the vectors equal? Are they parallel?

Reading Math The word *resultant* is also an adjective, meaning "issuing or following as a consequence or result." A resultant vector "follows from" two vectors; it is their sum.

ENGLISH LANGUAGE LEARNERS

Power Presentations with PowerPoint®

Additional Examples

Example 5

An airplane is flying at a constant speed of 400 mi/h at a bearing of N 70° E. A 60 mi/h wind is blowing due north. What are the plane's actual speed and direction? Round the speed to the nearest tenth and the direction to the nearest degree.

424.3 mi/h; N 62° E

INTERVENTION
Questioning Strategies

EXAMPLE 5

- How does wind speed or water current affect the speed of a plane or a boat?
- How do you draw a vector to represent a northeast wind?

Inclusion Remind students not to round calculated values in intermediate steps. When working **Example 5,** students should store the values in Steps 2 and 4 in their calculators.

To add vectors numerically, add their components. If $\vec{u} = \langle x_1, y_1\rangle$ and $\vec{v} = \langle x_2, y_2\rangle$, then $\vec{u} + \vec{v} = \langle x_1 + x_2, y_1 + y_2\rangle$.

EXAMPLE 5 *Sports Application*

A kayaker leaves shore at a bearing of N 55° E and paddles at a constant speed of 3 mi/h. There is a 1 mi/h current moving due east. What are the kayak's actual speed and direction? Round the speed to the nearest tenth and the direction to the nearest degree.

Step 1 Sketch vectors for the kayaker and the current.

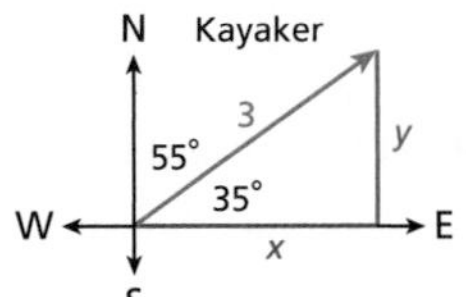

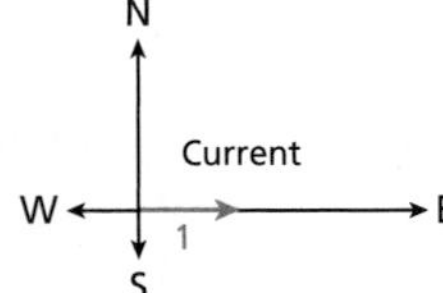

Remember!

Component form gives the horizontal and vertical change from the initial point to the terminal point of the vector.

Step 2 Write the vector for the kayaker in component form.

The kayaker's vector has a magnitude of 3 mi/h and makes an angle of 35° with the x-axis.

$\cos 35° = \frac{x}{3}$, so $x = 3\cos 35° \approx 2.5$.

$\sin 35° = \frac{y}{3}$, so $y = 3\sin 35° \approx 1.7$.

The kayaker's vector is $\langle 2.5, 1.7\rangle$.

Step 3 Write the vector for the current in component form.

Since the current moves 1 mi/h in the direction of the x-axis, it has a horizontal component of 1 and a vertical component of 0. So its vector is $\langle 1, 0\rangle$.

Step 4 Find and sketch the resultant vector $\overrightarrow{AB}$.

Add the components of the kayaker's vector and the current's vector.

$\langle 2.5, 1.7\rangle + \langle 1, 0\rangle = \langle 3.5, 1.7\rangle$

The resultant vector in component form is $\langle 3.5, 1.7\rangle$.

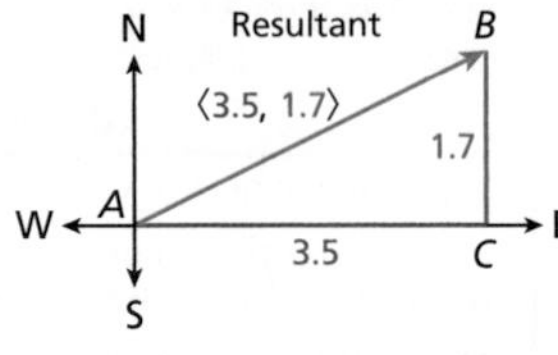

Step 5 Find the magnitude and direction of the resultant vector.

The magnitude of the resultant vector is the kayak's actual speed.

$|\langle 3.5, 1.7\rangle| = \sqrt{(3.5 - 0)^2 + (1.7 - 0)^2} \approx 3.9$ mi/h

The angle measure formed by the resultant vector gives the kayak's actual direction.

$\tan A = \frac{1.7}{3.5}$, so $A = \tan^{-1}\left(\frac{1.7}{3.5}\right) \approx 26°$, or N 64° E.

4.4 mi/h; 58°, or N 32° E

5. What if...? Suppose the kayaker in Example 5 instead paddles at 4 mi/h at a bearing of N 20° E. What are the kayak's actual speed and direction? Round the speed to the nearest tenth and the direction to the nearest degree.

3 Close

Summarize

Quantities that have magnitude and direction are called vectors. Vectors have an initial point and a terminal point. The component form of a vector shows the horizontal and vertical change from the initial point to the terminal point. Two vectors can be added, and the sum is called a resultant vector.

ONGOING ASSESSMENT and INTERVENTION

***Diagnose Before* the Lesson**
8-6 Warm Up, TE p. 559

***Monitor During* the Lesson**
Check It Out! Exercises, SE pp. 559–562
Questioning Strategies, TE pp. 560–562

***Assess After* the Lesson**
8-6 Lesson Quiz, TE p. 567
Alternative Assessment, TE p. 567

THINK AND DISCUSS

1. Explain why the segment with endpoints (0, 0) and (1, 4) is not a vector.
2. Assume you are given a vector in component form. Other than the Distance Formula, what theorem can you use to find the vector's magnitude?
3. Describe how to add two vectors numerically.

4. **GET ORGANIZED** Copy and complete the graphic organizer.

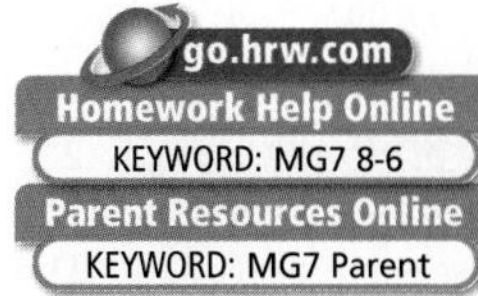

Answers to *Think and Discuss*

1. It does not have a direction.
2. Pyth. Thm.
3. Possible answer: Write each vector in component form and add their horizontal and vertical components.
4. See p. A7.

8-6 Exercises

GUIDED PRACTICE

Vocabulary **Apply the vocabulary from this lesson to answer each question.**

equal 1. ___?___ vectors have the same magnitude and direction. (*equal*, *parallel*, or *resultant*)

parallel 2. ___?___ vectors have the same or opposite directions. (*equal*, *parallel*, or *resultant*)

magnitude 3. The ___?___ of a vector indicates the vector's size. (*magnitude* or *direction*)

SEE EXAMPLE 1 p. 559

Write each vector in component form.

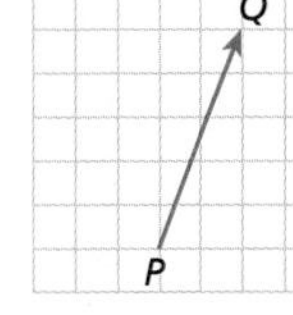

4. $\overrightarrow{AC}$ with $A(1, 2)$ and $C(6, 5)$ **⟨5, 3⟩**
5. the vector with initial point $M(-4, 5)$ and terminal point $N(4, -3)$ **⟨8, −8⟩**
6. $\overrightarrow{PQ}$ **⟨2, 5⟩**

SEE EXAMPLE 2 p. 560

Draw each vector on a coordinate plane. Find its magnitude to the nearest tenth.

7. ⟨1, 4⟩ **4.1**
8. ⟨−3, −2⟩ **3.6**
9. ⟨5, −3⟩ **5.8**

SEE EXAMPLE 3 p. 560

Draw each vector on a coordinate plane. Find the direction of the vector to the nearest degree.

10. A river's current is given by the vector ⟨4, 6⟩. **56°**
11. The velocity of a plane is given by the vector ⟨5, 1⟩. **11°**
12. The path of a hiker is given by the vector ⟨6, 3⟩. **27°**

SEE EXAMPLE 4 p. 561

Identify each of the following.

13. equal vectors in diagram 1 — **13.** $\overrightarrow{CD} = \overrightarrow{EF}$
14. parallel vectors in diagram 1 — **14.** $\overrightarrow{CD} \parallel \overrightarrow{EF}$; $\overrightarrow{AB} \parallel \overrightarrow{GH}$
15. equal vectors in diagram 2 — **15.** $\overrightarrow{RS} = \overrightarrow{XY}$
16. parallel vectors in diagram 2 — $\overrightarrow{RS} \parallel \overrightarrow{XY}$; $\overrightarrow{MN} \parallel \overrightarrow{PQ}$

Diagram 1

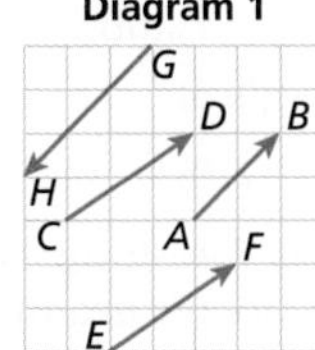

Diagram 2

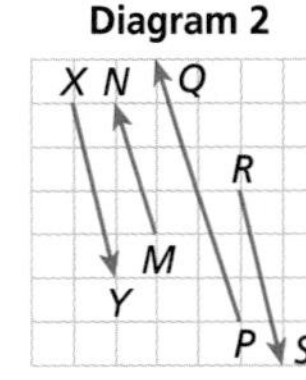

8-6 Exercises

Assignment Guide

Assign *Guided Practice* exercises as necessary.

If you finished Examples **1–3**
- **Basic** 18–26, 38–41, 45–48
- **Average** 18–26, 38–41, 44–48, 64
- **Advanced** 18–26, 38–41, 44–48, 64, 65

If you finished Examples **1–5**
- **Basic** 18–32, 34, 37–41, 44–48, 50, 53, 54, 59–63, 69–76
- **Average** 18–32, 34, 36–40, 43, 44, 50–56, 58–64, 69–76
- **Advanced** 18–39, 42–44, 46, 48–50, 54, 56–76

Homework Quick Check

Quickly check key concepts.

Exercises: 18, 22, 24, 28, 31, 40, 54

Teaching Tip **Multiple Representations** The initial point of the vectors in **Exercises 7–12** does not have to be the origin. Remind students that an infinite number of vectors are equal to a given vector with initial point at (0, 0).

Answers

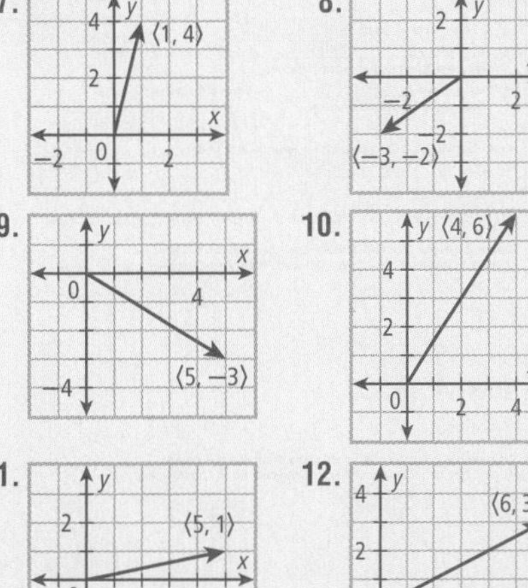

State Resources

Diversity Students who have flown across the United States may be able to relate their personal experience to **Exercise 31.** Since the prevailing winds in the continental United States are from west to east, flights from the east coast to the west coast generally have a "headwind," and those from the west coast to the east coast are likely to have a "tailwind." Consequently, a flight from west to east can take less time than a flight of the same distance from east to west.

Answers

21. 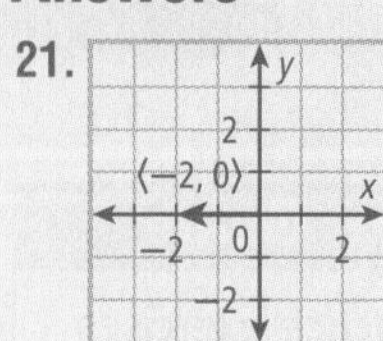

22. 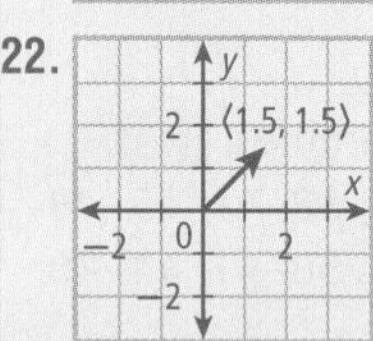

23. 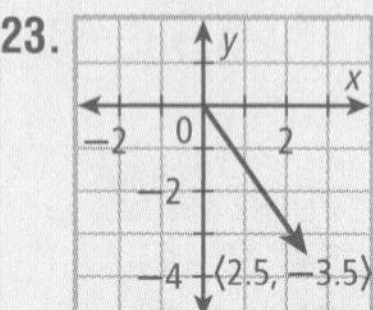

24. 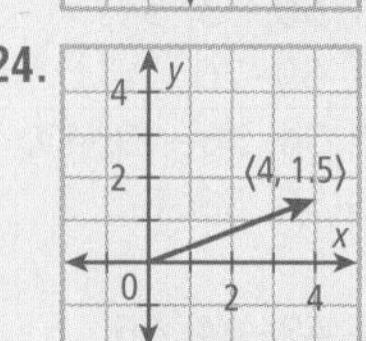

25. 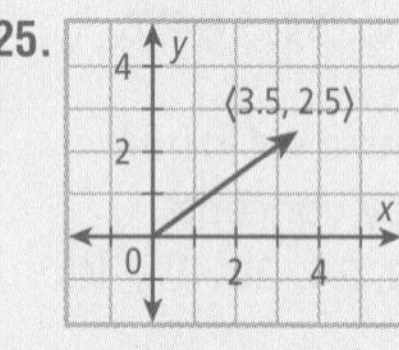

26. 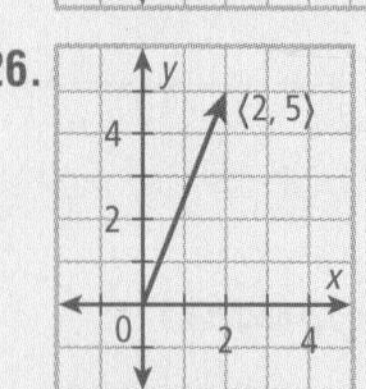

36. Yes; possible answer: if you use the head-to-tail method in both orders, you end up with a parallelogram and its diag. The resultant vector is the diag. See the figures below.

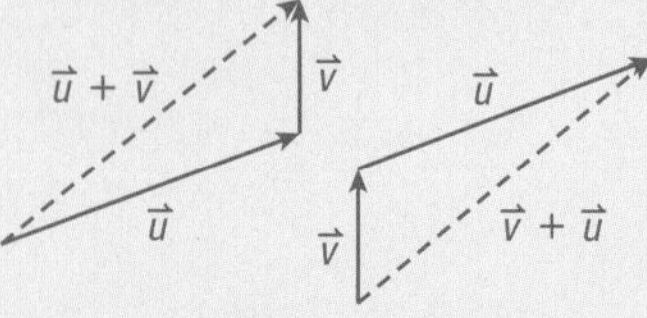
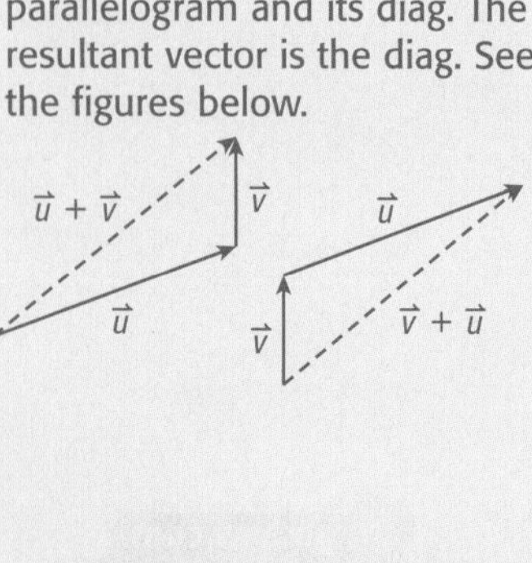

SEE EXAMPLE 5 p. 562

17. **Recreation** To reach a campsite, a hiker first walks for 2 mi at a bearing of N 40° E. Then he walks 3 mi due east. What are the magnitude and direction of his hike from his starting point to the campsite? Round the distance to the nearest tenth of a mile and the direction to the nearest degree.
4.6 mi; 20°, or N 70° E

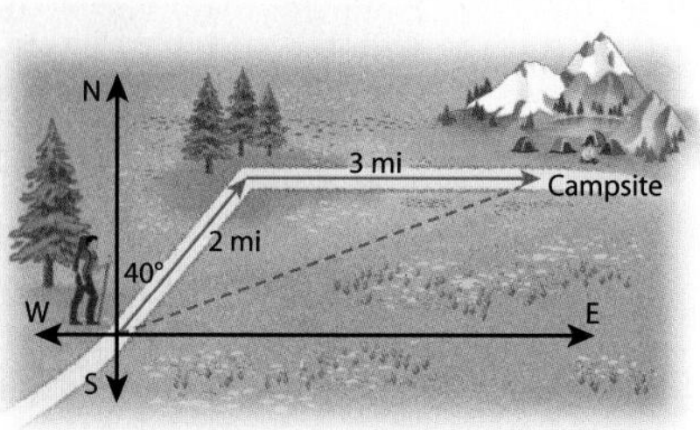

PRACTICE AND PROBLEM SOLVING

Independent Practice	
For Exercises	See Example
18–20	1
21–23	2
24–26	3
27–30	4
31	5

Extra Practice
Skills Practice p. S19
Application Practice p. S35

Write each vector in component form.

18. $\overrightarrow{JK}$ with $J(-6, -7)$ and $K(3, -5)$ **⟨9, 2⟩**
19. $\overrightarrow{EF}$ with $E(1.5, -3)$ and $F(-2, 2.5)$ **⟨−3.5, 5.5⟩**
20. $\vec{w}$ **⟨−4, −4⟩**

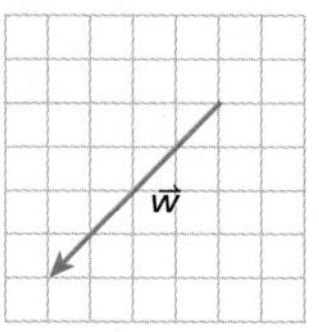

Draw each vector on a coordinate plane. Find its magnitude to the nearest tenth.

21. ⟨−2, 0⟩ **2.0**
22. ⟨1.5, 1.5⟩ **2.1**
23. ⟨2.5, −3.5⟩ **4.3**

Draw each vector on a coordinate plane. Find the direction of the vector to the nearest degree.

24. A boat's velocity is given by the vector ⟨4, 1.5⟩. **21°**
25. The path of a submarine is given by the vector ⟨3.5, 2.5⟩. **36°**
26. The path of a projectile is given by the vector ⟨2, 5⟩. **68°**

Identify each of the following.

27. equal vectors in diagram 1
28. parallel vectors in diagram 1
29. equal vectors in diagram 2
30. parallel vectors in diagram 2

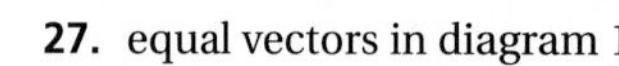
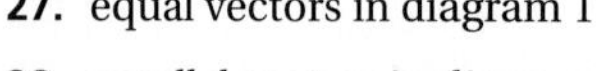
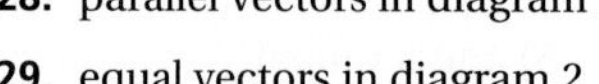

27. $\overrightarrow{DE} = \overrightarrow{LM}$
28. All four vectors are parallel.
29. $\overrightarrow{RS} = \overrightarrow{UV}$
30. $\overrightarrow{AB} \parallel \overrightarrow{UV} \parallel \overrightarrow{RS}$; $\overrightarrow{CD} \parallel \overrightarrow{XY}$

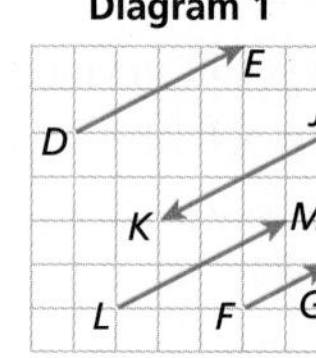

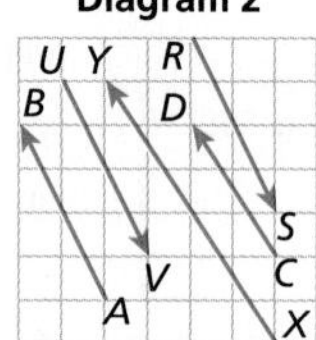

31. **Aviation** The pilot of a single-engine airplane flies at a constant speed of 200 km/h at a bearing of N 25° E. There is a 40 km/h crosswind blowing southeast (S 45° E). What are the plane's actual speed and direction? Round the speed to the nearest tenth and the direction to the nearest degree. **190.1 km/h; 54°, or N 36° E**

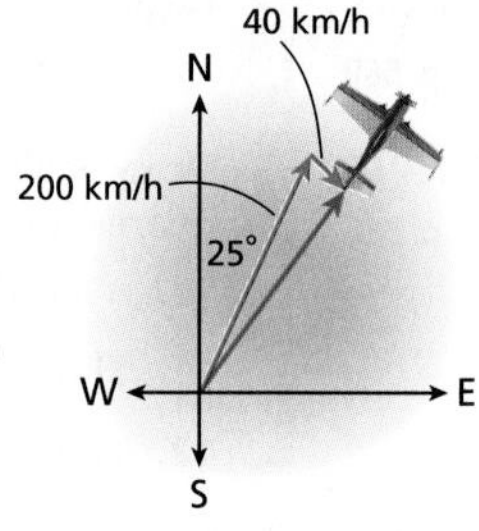

Find each vector sum.

32. ⟨1, 2⟩ + ⟨0, 6⟩ **⟨1, 8⟩**
33. ⟨−3, 4⟩ + ⟨5, −2⟩ **⟨2, 2⟩**
34. ⟨0, 1⟩ + ⟨7, 0⟩ **⟨7, 1⟩**
35. ⟨8, 3⟩ + ⟨−2, −1⟩ **⟨6, 2⟩**
36. **Critical Thinking** Is vector addition commutative? That is, is $\vec{u} + \vec{v}$ equal to $\vec{v} + \vec{u}$? Use the head-to-tail method of vector addition to explain why or why not.

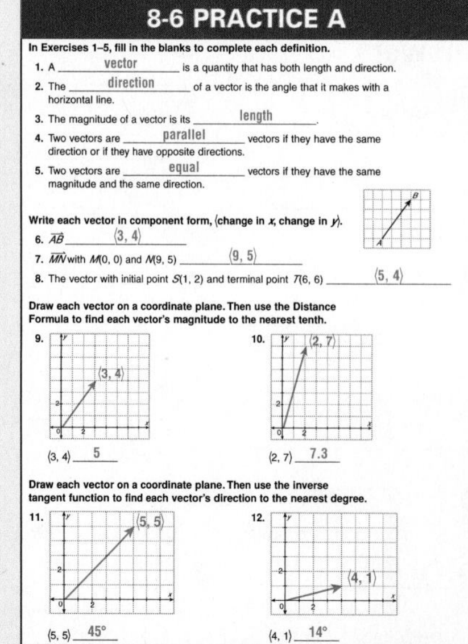

8-6 PRACTICE A

In Exercises 1–5, fill in the blanks to complete each definition.

1. A vector is a quantity that has both length and direction.
2. The direction of a vector is the angle that it makes with a horizontal line.
3. The magnitude of a vector is its length.
4. Two vectors are parallel vectors if they have the same direction or if they have opposite directions.
5. Two vectors are equal vectors if they have the same magnitude and the same direction.

Write each vector in component form, (change in x, change in y).

6. $\overrightarrow{AB}$ ⟨3, 4⟩
7. $\overrightarrow{MN}$ with M(0, 0) and N(9, 5) ⟨9, 5⟩
8. The vector with initial point S(1, 2) and terminal point T(6, 6) ⟨5, 4⟩

Draw each vector on a coordinate plane. Then use the Distance Formula to find each vector's magnitude to the nearest tenth.

9. ⟨3, 4⟩ 5
10. ⟨2, 7⟩ 7.3

Draw each vector on a coordinate plane. Then use the inverse tangent function to find each vector's direction to the nearest degree.

11. ⟨5, 5⟩ 45°
12. ⟨4, 1⟩ 14°

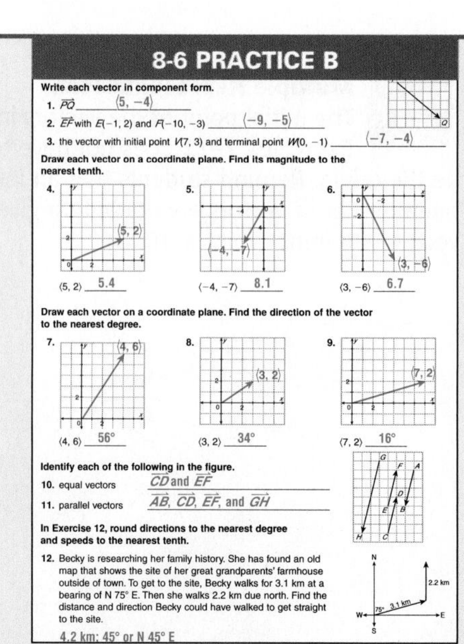

8-6 PRACTICE B

Write each vector in component form.

1. $\overrightarrow{PQ}$ ⟨5, −4⟩
2. $\overrightarrow{EF}$ with E(−1, 2) and F(−10, −3) ⟨−9, −5⟩
3. the vector with initial point V(7, 3) and terminal point W(0, −1) ⟨−7, −4⟩

Draw each vector on a coordinate plane. Find its magnitude to the nearest tenth.

4. ⟨5, 2⟩ 5.4
5. ⟨−4, −7⟩ 8.1
6. ⟨3, −6⟩ 6.7

Draw each vector on a coordinate plane. Find the direction of the vector to the nearest degree.

7. ⟨4, 6⟩ 56°
8. ⟨3, 2⟩ 34°
9. ⟨7, 2⟩ 16°

Identify each of the following in the figure.

10. equal vectors $\overrightarrow{CD}$ and $\overrightarrow{EF}$
11. parallel vectors $\overrightarrow{AB}$, $\overrightarrow{CD}$, $\overrightarrow{EF}$, and $\overrightarrow{GH}$

In Exercise 12, round directions to the nearest degree and speeds to the nearest tenth.

12. Becky is researching her family history. She has found an old map that shows the site of her great grandparents' farmhouse outside of town. To get to the site, Becky walks for 3.1 km at a bearing of N 75° E. Then she walks 2.2 km due north. Find the distance and direction Becky could have walked to get straight to the site.
4.2 km; 45° or N 45° E

37. This problem will prepare you for the Multi-Step Test Prep on page 568.
A helicopter at H must fly at 50 mi/h in the direction N 45° E to reach the site of a flood victim F. There is a 41 mi/h wind in the direction N 53° W. The pilot needs to the know the velocity vector $\overrightarrow{HX}$ he should use so that his resultant vector will be $\overrightarrow{HF}$.

a. What is m∠F? (*Hint:* Consider a vertical line through F.) **98°**
b. Use the Law of Cosines to find the magnitude of $\overrightarrow{HX}$ to the nearest tenth. **68.9 mi/h**
c. Use the Law of Sines to find m∠FHX to the nearest degree. **36°**
d. What is the direction of $\overrightarrow{HX}$? **N 81° E**

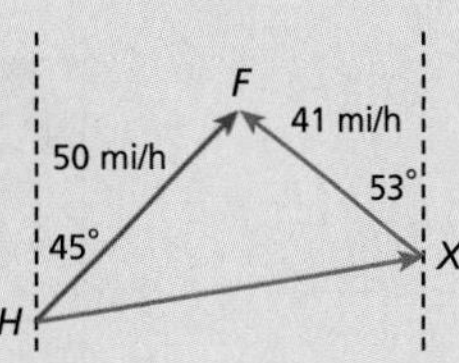

Write each vector in component form. Round values to the nearest tenth.

38. ⟨11.1, 10.0⟩
39. ⟨7.1, 1.1⟩
40. ⟨10.1, 6.6⟩
41. ⟨2.2, 5.4⟩

38. magnitude 15, direction 42°
39. magnitude 7.2, direction 9°
40. magnitude 12.1, direction N 57° E
41. magnitude 5.8, direction N 22° E

42. **Physics** A classroom has a window near the ceiling, and a long pole must be used to close it.
a. Carla holds the pole at a 45° angle to the floor and applies 10 lb of force to the upper edge of the window. Find the vertical component of the vector representing the force on the window. Round to the nearest tenth. **7.1 lb**
b. Taneka also applies 10 lb of force to close the window, but she holds the pole at a 75° angle to the floor. Find the vertical component of the force vector in this case. Round to the nearest tenth. **9.7 lb**
c. Who will have an easier time closing the window, Carla or Taneka? (*Hint:* Who applies more vertical force?) **Taneka; she applies more vert. force.**

43. **Probability** The numbers 1, 2, 3, and 4 are written on slips of paper and placed in a hat. Two different slips of paper are chosen at random to be the x- and y-components of a vector.
a. What is the probability that the vector will be equal to ⟨1, 2⟩? $\frac{1}{12}$
b. What is the probability that the vector will be parallel to ⟨1, 2⟩? $\frac{1}{6}$

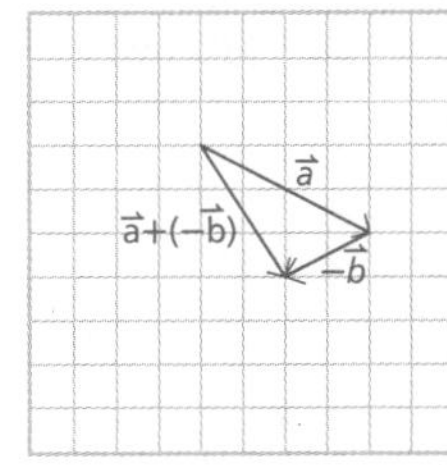

44. You can subtract one vector from another by subtracting the components of the second vector from the components of the first. If $\vec{a} = \langle x_1, y_1 \rangle$ and $\vec{b} = \langle x_2, y_2 \rangle$, then $\vec{a} - \vec{b} = \langle x_1 - x_2, y_1 - y_2 \rangle$
a. Find $\vec{a} - \vec{b}$ for $\vec{a} = \langle 4, -2 \rangle$ and $\vec{b} = \langle 2, -1 \rangle$. **⟨2, −3⟩**
b. You can also think of subtracting a vector as adding its opposite. In symbols, $\vec{a} - \vec{b} = \vec{a} + (-\vec{b})$ and $-\vec{b} = \langle -x_2, -y_2 \rangle$. Using the vectors given in part **a**, draw $\vec{a} + (-\vec{b})$ in the corrdinate plane using the head-to-tail method.

Multi-Step Find the magnitude of each vector to the nearest tenth and the direction of each vector to the nearest degree.

45. $\vec{u}$ **4; 0°**
46. $\vec{v}$ **3; 90°**
47. $\vec{w}$ **3.6; 56°**
48. $\vec{z}$ **4.1; 14°**

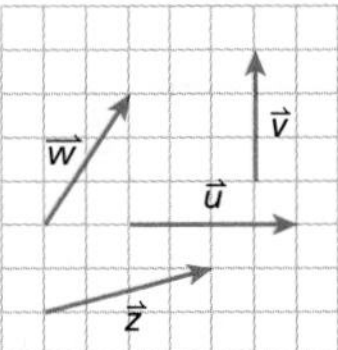

8-6 PRACTICE C

The figure shows coordinate axes. Each region bounded by the axes is called a *quadrant*. The quadrants are labeled I–IV. Think of a vector whose initial point is the origin and whose terminal point ends somewhere within the indicated quadrant. Tell whether the sine, cosine, and tangent ratios for this vector will be positive or negative.

90°
II I
180° 0° (360°)
III IV
270°

1. Quadrant I
sine positive
cosine positive
tangent positive

2. Quadrant II
sine positive
cosine negative
tangent negative

3. Quadrant III
sine negative
cosine negative
tangent positive

4. Quadrant IV
sine negative
cosine positive
tangent negative

For each given trigonometric ratio in Exercises 5–10, use a calculator and what you learned above to find both possible measures of ∠A. Round to the nearest degree. Measure angles from the positive x-axis in a counterclockwise direction. (*Hint:* If your calculator gives a negative answer, add 360° to find the equivalent positive angle measure.)

5. $\sin A = \frac{2}{5}$
24°; 156°

6. $\tan A = -1.4$
126°; 306°

7. $\cos A = -\frac{7}{13}$
123°; 237°

8. $\sin A = -\frac{3}{4}$
229°; 311°

9. $\tan A = 0.9$
42°; 222°

10. $\cos A = 0.33$
71°; 289°

11. A ferryboat carries passengers and cars across a river that runs from north to south. The river is 0.6 mile wide. The downstream dock is on the east side of the river and 0.15 mile south of the west side's upstream dock. The current in the river runs due south at 2.5 miles/hour. Find the speed and direction the ferryboat must take to make the crossing from the upstream dock to the downstream dock in 10 minutes.
3.9 mi/h; 24° or N 66° E

12. Find the speed and direction the ferryboat must take to make the crossing from the downstream dock to the upstream dock in 10 minutes.
5.0 mi/h; 137° or N 47° W

COMMON ERROR /// ALERT \\\

Students may forget to take the complement of the angle measures given in **Exercises 40–41.** Encourage them to draw a sketch of the vectors on a coordinate grid first.

Exercise 37 involves using vectors to find a flight direction. This exercise prepares students for the Multi-Step Test Prep on page 568.

Teaching Tip

Probability Before students begin **Exercise 43,** encourage them to list all possible outcomes in the sample. Then review the definition of theoretical probability. $P(E) = \frac{\text{number of favorable outcomes}}{\text{number of possible outcomes}}$.

Answers

49. $\langle 0, 10\rangle$, $\langle 10, 0\rangle$; $\langle 10, 10\rangle$; the magnitude of the resultant is $\sqrt{(10-0)^2+(0-10)^2} = 10\sqrt{2}$, and the direction of the resultant is $\tan^{-1}\left(\frac{10}{10}\right) = 45°$.

57a. $\langle 1, 3\rangle$; $\langle 2, 6\rangle$

b. $\sqrt{10}$; $2\sqrt{10}$; the magnitude of $2\vec{v}$ is twice the magnitude of $\vec{v}$.

c. 72°; 72°; the direction of $2\vec{v}$ is the same as the direction of $\vec{v}$.

d. Multiply each component by k.

e. $-\vec{v} = -1\vec{v} = -1\langle x, y\rangle = \langle -x, -y\rangle$

58. If $u > v$, the resultant points due west, with magnitude $u - v$. If $v > u$, the resultant points due east, with magnitude $v - u$. If $u = v$, the resultant is the vector $\langle 0, 0\rangle$.

59. A line segment has magnitude (or length), but no direction. A ray is a part of a line that continues indefinitely in one direction. Thus it has direction and infinite magnitude. A vector has both direction and magnitude.

53. $\langle 3.5, 1\rangle$; 3.6; 16°

54. $\langle 2.8, 3.9\rangle$; 4.8; 54°

55. $\langle 4, 4\rangle$; 5.7; 45°

56. $\langle 4, 5.9\rangle$; 7.1; 56°

49. Football Write two vectors in component form to represent the pass pattern that Jason is told to run. Find the resultant vector and show that Jason's move is equivalent to the vector.

FoxTrot
by Bill Amend
JASON, WHAT PATTERN DID I TELL YOU TO RUN?
YOU SAID TO GO 10 YARDS OUT, THEN 10 YARDS TO THE RIGHT.
AND WHAT PATTERN DID YOU RUN?
I WENT 10√2 YARDS AT A 45-DEGREE ANGLE.
AND ARE THEY THE SAME THING??
IF YOU ADD THE VECTORS, SURE.
THIS IS FOOTBALL, NOT MATH CLASS!
WHY DO YOU THINK I ROUNDED TO TWO DECIMAL PLACES?
www.foxtrot.com
© 1999 Bill Amend/Dist. by Universal Press Syndicate

For each given vector, find another vector that has the same magnitude but a different direction. Then find a vector that has the same direction but a different magnitude. 50–52. Possible answers given.

50. $\langle -3, 6\rangle$ — $\langle 3, 6\rangle$; $\langle -6, 12\rangle$

51. $\langle 12, 5\rangle$ — $\langle -12, -5\rangle$; $\langle 24, 10\rangle$

52. $\langle 8, -11\rangle$ — $\langle -8, 11\rangle$; $\langle 4, -5.5\rangle$

Multi-Step **Find the sum of each pair of vectors. Then find the magnitude and direction of the resultant vector. Round the magnitude to the nearest tenth and the direction to the nearest degree.**

53. $\vec{u} = \langle 1, 2\rangle$, $\vec{v} = \langle 2.5, -1\rangle$

54. $\vec{u} = \langle -2, 7\rangle$, $\vec{v} = \langle 4.8, -3.1\rangle$

55. $\vec{u} = \langle 6, 0\rangle$, $\vec{v} = \langle -2, 4\rangle$

56. $\vec{u} = \langle -1.2, 8\rangle$, $\vec{v} = \langle 5.2, -2.1\rangle$

LINK Math History

August Ferdinand Möbius is best known for experimenting with the Möbius strip, a three-dimensional figure that has only one side and one edge.

57. **Math History** In 1827, the mathematician August Ferdinand Möbius published a book in which he introduced directed line segments (what we now call vectors). He showed how to perform *scalar multiplication* of vectors. For example, consider a hiker who walks along a path given by the vector $\vec{v}$. The path of another hiker who walks twice as far in the same direction is given by the vector $2\vec{v}$.

a. Write the component form of the vectors $\vec{v}$ and $2\vec{v}$.

b. Find the magnitude of $\vec{v}$ and $2\vec{v}$. How do they compare?

c. Find the direction of $\vec{v}$ and $2\vec{v}$. How do they compare?

d. Given the component form of a vector, explain how to find the components of the vector $k\vec{v}$, where k is a constant.

e. Use scalar multiplication with $k = -1$ to write the *negation of a vector* $\vec{v}$ in component form.

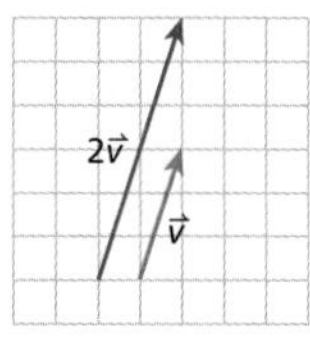

58. **Critical Thinking** A vector $\vec{u}$ points due west with a magnitude of u units. Another vector $\vec{v}$ points due east with a magnitude of v units. Describe three possible directions and magnitudes for the resultant vector.

59. **Write About It** Compare a line segment, a ray, and a vector.

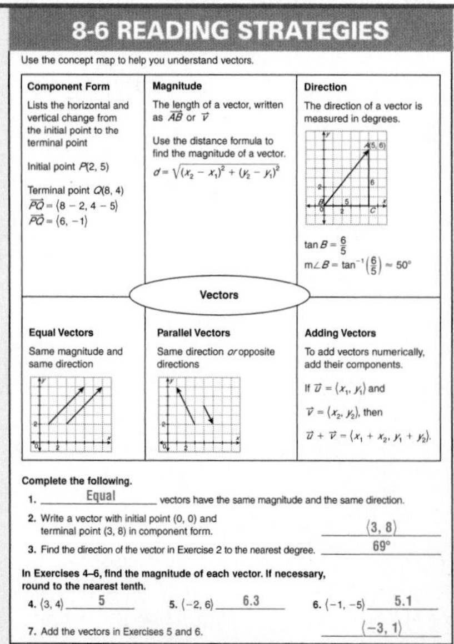

8-6 READING STRATEGIES

Use the concept map to help you understand vectors.

Vectors

Component Form
Lists the horizontal and vertical change from the initial point to the terminal point
Initial point $P(2, 5)$
Terminal point $Q(8, 4)$
$\overrightarrow{PQ} = \langle 8-2, 4-5\rangle$
$\overrightarrow{PQ} = \langle 6, -1\rangle$

Magnitude
The length of a vector, written as $|\overrightarrow{AB}|$ or $|\vec{v}|$
Use the distance formula to find the magnitude of a vector.
$d = \sqrt{(x_2-x_1)^2+(y_2-y_1)^2}$

Direction
The direction of a vector is measured in degrees.
$\tan B = \frac{6}{5}$
$m\angle B = \tan^{-1}\left(\frac{6}{5}\right) \approx 50°$

Equal Vectors
Same magnitude and same direction

Parallel Vectors
Same direction *or* opposite directions

Adding Vectors
To add vectors numerically, add their components.
If $\vec{u} = \langle x_1, y_1\rangle$ and $\vec{v} = \langle x_2, y_2\rangle$, then $\vec{u} + \vec{v} = \langle x_1 + x_2, y_1 + y_2\rangle$.

Complete the following.

1. Equal vectors have the same magnitude and the same direction.
2. Write a vector with initial point (0, 0) and terminal point (3, 8) in component form. $\langle 3, 8\rangle$
3. Find the direction of the vector in Exercise 2 to the nearest degree. 69°

In Exercises 4–6, find the magnitude of each vector. If necessary, round to the nearest tenth.

4. $\langle 3, 4\rangle$ 5
5. $\langle -2, 6\rangle$ 6.3
6. $\langle -1, -5\rangle$ 5.1
7. Add the vectors in Exercises 5 and 6. $\langle -3, 1\rangle$

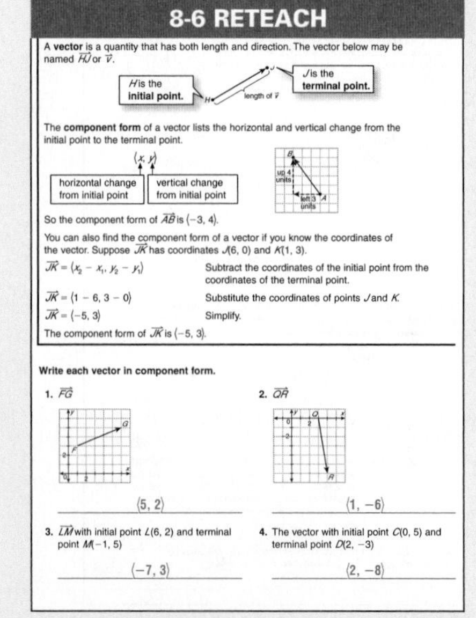

8-6 RETEACH

A **vector** is a quantity that has both length and direction. The vector below may be named $\overrightarrow{HJ}$ or $\vec{v}$.

H is the **initial point.** *J* is the **terminal point.** length of $\vec{v}$

The **component form** of a vector lists the horizontal and vertical change from the initial point to the terminal point.

$\langle x, y\rangle$ — horizontal change from initial point; vertical change from initial point

up 4 units; left 3 units

So the component form of $\overrightarrow{AB}$ is $\langle -3, 4\rangle$.

You can also find the component form of a vector if you know the coordinates of the vector. Suppose $\overrightarrow{JK}$ has coordinates $J(6, 0)$ and $K(1, 3)$.

$\overrightarrow{JK} = \langle x_2 - x_1, y_2 - y_1\rangle$	Subtract the coordinates of the initial point from the coordinates of the terminal point.
$\overrightarrow{JK} = \langle 1-6, 3-0\rangle$	Substitute the coordinates of points *J* and *K*.
$\overrightarrow{JK} = \langle -5, 3\rangle$	Simplify.

The component form of $\overrightarrow{JK}$ is $\langle -5, 3\rangle$.

Write each vector in component form.

1. $\overrightarrow{FG}$ — $\langle 5, 2\rangle$
2. $\overrightarrow{QR}$ — $\langle 1, -6\rangle$
3. $\overrightarrow{LM}$ with initial point $L(6, 2)$ and terminal point $M(-1, 5)$ — $\langle -7, 3\rangle$
4. The vector with initial point $C(0, 5)$ and terminal point $D(2, -3)$ — $\langle 2, -8\rangle$

TEST PREP

60. Which vector is parallel to $\langle 2, 1\rangle$?

Ⓐ $\vec{u}$ Ⓒ $\vec{w}$

Ⓑ $\vec{v}$ Ⓓ $\vec{z}$

61. The vector $\langle 7, 9\rangle$ represents the velocity of a helicopter. What is the direction of this vector to the nearest degree?

Ⓕ 38° Ⓖ 52° Ⓗ 128° Ⓙ 142°

62. A canoe sets out on a course given by the vector $\langle 5, 11\rangle$. What is the length of the canoe's course to the nearest unit?

Ⓐ 6 Ⓑ 8 Ⓒ 12 Ⓓ 16

63. **Gridded Response** $\overrightarrow{AB}$ has an initial point of $(-3, 6)$ and a terminal point of $(-5, -2)$. Find the magnitude of $\overrightarrow{AB}$ to the nearest tenth. **8.2**

CHALLENGE AND EXTEND

Recall that the angle of a vector's direction is measured counterclockwise from the positive x-axis. Find the direction of each vector to the nearest degree.

64. $\langle -2, 3\rangle$ **124°** 65. $\langle -4, 0\rangle$ **180°** 66. $\langle -5, -3\rangle$ **211°**

67. **Navigation** The captain of a ship is planning to sail in an area where there is a 4 mi/h current moving due east. What speed and bearing should the captain maintain so that the ship's actual course (taking the current into account) is 10 mi/h at a bearing of N 70° E? Round the speed to the nearest tenth and the direction to the nearest degree. **6.4 mi/h at a bearing of N 58° E**

68. Aaron hikes from his home to a park by walking 3 km at a bearing of N 30° E, then 6 km due east, and then 4 km at a bearing of N 50° E. What are the magnitude and direction of the vector that represents the straight path from Aaron's home to the park? Round the magnitude to the nearest tenth and the direction to the nearest degree. **11.8 km at a bearing of N 64° E**

SPIRAL REVIEW

Solve each system of equations by graphing. *(Previous course)*

69. $\begin{cases} x - y = -5 \\ y = 3x + 1 \end{cases}$ **(2, 7)** 70. $\begin{cases} x - 2y = 0 \\ 2y + x = 8 \end{cases}$ **(4, 2)** 71. $\begin{cases} x + y = 5 \\ 3y + 15 = 2x \end{cases}$ **(6, −1)**

Given that $\triangle JLM \sim \triangle NPS$, the perimeter of $\triangle JLM$ is 12 cm, and the area of $\triangle JLM$ is 6 cm², find each measure. *(Lesson 7-5)*

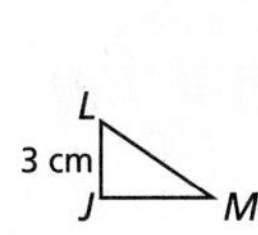

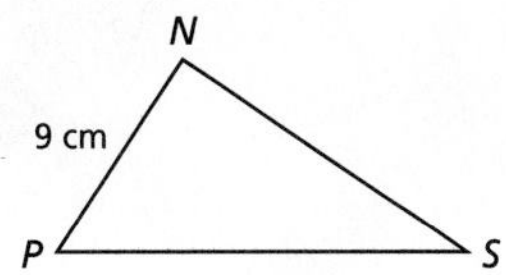

72. the perimeter of $\triangle NPS$ **36 cm** 73. the area of $\triangle NPS$ **54 cm²**

Find each measure. Round lengths to the nearest tenth and angle measures to the nearest degree. *(Lesson 8-5)*

74. BC **3.2** 75. $m\angle B$ **73°** 76. $m\angle C$ **57°**

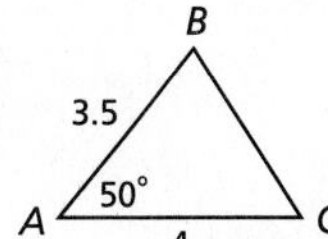

TEST PREP DOCTOR Students who chose **B** for **Exercise 60** switched the horizontal and vertical components of the given vector.

Students who chose **F** for **Exercise 61** chose the helicopter's bearing from north instead of its direction. Have students sketch the vector and label its direction.

Journal

Ask students to imagine that they are walking into a strong wind. Have them describe how the situation can be represented with vectors.

ALTERNATIVE ASSESSMENT

Have each student choose values for a and b, and then sketch a vector with horizontal component a and vertical component b. Ask them to compare this vector with $\langle -b, -a\rangle$ by finding the magnitude and direction of both vectors. Then have them add the two vectors and find the magnitude and direction of the resultant.

Power Presentations with PowerPoint®

8-6 Lesson Quiz

Round angles to the nearest degree and other values to the nearest tenth.

1. Write $\overrightarrow{ST}$ with $S(-5, 2)$ and $T(8, -4)$ in component form. $\langle 13, -6\rangle$
2. Write $\vec{v}$ with magnitude 12 and direction 36° in component form. $\langle 9.7, 7.1\rangle$
3. Find the magnitude and direction of the vector $\langle 4, 5\rangle$. 6.4; 51°
4. Find the sum of the vectors $\langle 2, -4\rangle$ and $\langle 3, 6\rangle$. Then find the magnitude and direction of the resultant vector. $\langle 5, 2\rangle$; 5.4; 22°
5. A boat is heading due east at a constant speed of 35 mi/h. There is an 8 mi/h current moving north. What is the boat's actual speed and direction? 35.9 mi/h; N 77° E

Also available on transparency

8-6 PROBLEM SOLVING

1. The velocity of a wave is given by the vector $\langle 7, 3\rangle$. Find the direction of the vector to the nearest degree. **23°**

2. Hikers set out on a course given by the vector $\langle 6, 11\rangle$. What is the length of the trip to the nearest unit? **13 units**

Use the following information for Exercises 3–5.

A sailboat is traveling in water with a current shown in the table.

	Direction	Rate
sailboat	due east	4 mi/h
current	N 60° E	1 mi/h

3. What is the resultant vector in component form? Round to the nearest tenth. **$\langle 4.9, 0.5\rangle$**

4. What is the sailboat's actual speed to the nearest tenth? **4.9 mi/h**

5. What is the sailboat's actual direction? Round to the nearest degree. **6° or N 84° E**

Choose the best answer.Use the following information for Exercises 6 and 7.

A small plane is flying with the conditions shown in the table.

	Direction	Rate
plane	due north	200 mi/h
wind	due east	28 mi/h

6. What is the plane's actual speed to the nearest mile per hour?

A 172 mi/h Ⓒ 202 mi/h
B 198 mi/h D 228 mi/h

7. What is the direction of the plane to the nearest degree?

Ⓕ 82° H 16°
G 41° J 8°

8. Find the direction of the resultant vector when you add the given vectors. Round to the nearest degree.

$\vec{u} = \langle -4, 3\rangle$ and $\vec{v} = \langle 1, 3\rangle$

A N 63° E C N 27° W
Ⓑ N 63° W D N 27° E

9. A person in a canoe leaves shore at a bearing of N 45° W and paddles at a constant speed of 2 mi/h. There is a 1.5 mi/h current moving due west. What is the canoe's actual speed?

F 0.5 mi/h Ⓗ 3.2 mi/h
G 0.8 mi/h J 3.5 mi/h

8-6 CHALLENGE

When a vector is on a coordinate plane, it can be represented by an ordered pair. If its tail, or **initial point,** has coordinates (x_1, y_1) and its head, or **terminal point,** has coordinates (x_2, y_2), then its component form is $\langle x_2 - x_1, y_2 - y_1\rangle$. For example, the component form for vector $\vec{m}$ on the coordinate plane at right is $\langle -4 - 5, 2 - (-3)\rangle$, or $\langle -9, 5\rangle$.

Find the component form of a vector with initial point J and terminal point K.

1. $J(5, 2)$, $K(9, 3)$ **$\langle 4, 1\rangle$** 2. $J(6, -8)$, $K(2, -1)$ **$\langle -4, 7\rangle$**

The **dot product** of two vectors $\vec{u} = \langle a_1, b_1\rangle$ and $\vec{v} = \langle a_2, b_2\rangle$ is denoted $\vec{u} \cdot \vec{v}$ and is defined by the rule $\vec{u} \cdot \vec{v} = a_1a_2 + b_1b_2$. For example, if $\vec{u} = \langle -3, 7\rangle$ and $\vec{v} = \langle -2, -1\rangle$, then the dot product $\vec{u} \cdot \vec{v}$ is $(-3)(-2) + 7(-1) = -1$. Notice that the dot product is a real number. It is *not* another vector.

Let $\vec{u} = \langle 1, 3\rangle$, $\vec{v} = \langle -2, 4\rangle$, and $\vec{w} = \langle -8, -4\rangle$. Find each dot product.

3. $\vec{u} \cdot \vec{v}$ **10** 4. $\vec{u} \cdot \vec{w}$ **−20** 5. $\vec{v} \cdot \vec{w}$ **0**

The dot product provides a method for calculating the angle between two vectors. For convenience, consider two vectors, $\vec{r}$ and $\vec{s}$, in *standard position,* that is, with their initial points at the origin. Let θ be the angle formed by $\vec{r}$ and $\vec{s}$. Then the Law of Cosines can be used to prove that $\cos\theta = \frac{\vec{r} \cdot \vec{s}}{\vec{r}\ \vec{s}}$. So $\theta = \cos^{-1}\frac{\vec{r} \cdot \vec{s}}{\vec{r}\ \vec{s}}$.

Referring to the figure at right, represent each expression below numerically. Round to the nearest tenth or whole degree.

6. $\vec{r}$ **$\langle 4, 3\rangle$** 7. $\vec{s}$ **$\langle 7, -3\rangle$** 8. $\vec{r} \cdot \vec{s}$ **19**

9. $\vec{r}$ **5** 10. $\vec{s}$ **$\sqrt{58}$, or 7.6** 11. $\vec{r}\ \vec{s}$ **$5\sqrt{58}$, or 38.1**

12. $\cos\theta$ **0.5** 13. $m\angle\theta$ **60°**

Find the angle between each pair of vectors.

14. $\vec{c} = \langle -3, 1\rangle$, $\vec{d} = \langle -6, -3\rangle$ **45°** 15. $\vec{p} = \langle -1, -2\rangle$, $\vec{q} = \langle 4, 2\rangle$ **143°**

16. The dot product of vectors $\vec{j}$ and $\vec{k}$ is 0. What is the relationship between $\vec{j}$ and $\vec{k}$? Explain.

They are perpendicular. If the dot product is 0, then the numerator of the expression $\frac{\vec{r} \cdot \vec{s}}{|\vec{r}||\vec{s}|}$ equals 0, and the value of the entire expression is 0. A calculator tells us that $\cos^{-1}0 = 90°$.

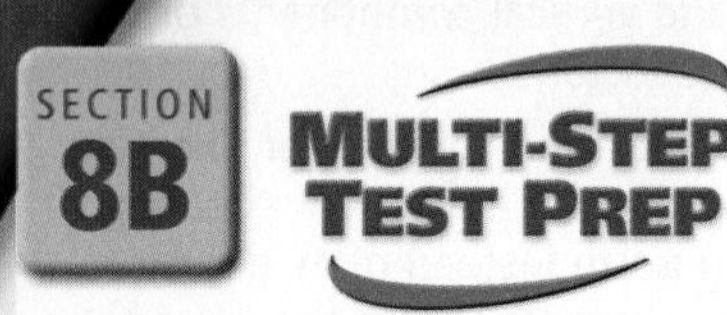

Organizer

Objective: Assess students' ability to apply concepts and skills in Lessons 8-4 through 8-6 in a real-world format.

Resources

Geometry Assessments
www.mathtekstoolkit.org

Problem	Text Reference
1	Lesson 8-4
2	Lessons 8-5, 8-6
3	Lesson 8-5

State Resources

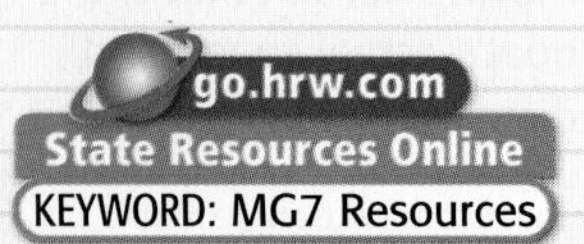

CHAPTER 8

SECTION 8B

Applying Trigonometric Ratios

Help Is on the Way! Rescue helicopters were first used in the 1950s during the Korean War. The helicopters made it possible to airlift wounded soldiers to medical stations. Today, helicopters are used to rescue injured hikers, flood victims, and people who are stranded at sea.

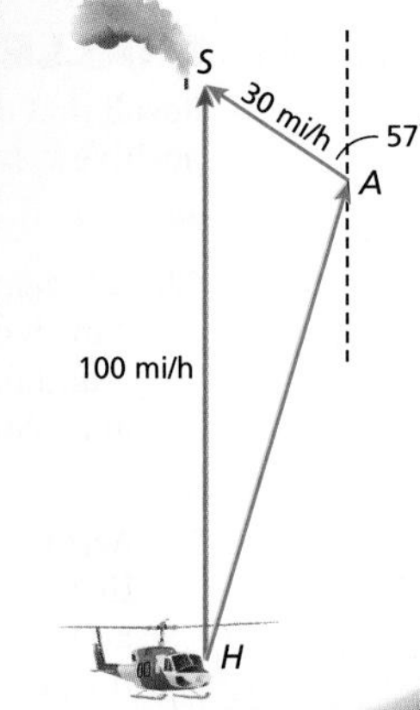

1. The pilot of a helicopter is searching for an injured hiker. While flying at an altitude of 1500 ft, the pilot sees smoke at an angle of depression of 14°. Assuming that the smoke is a distress signal from the hiker, what is the helicopter's horizontal distance to the hiker? Round to the nearest foot. **6016 ft**
2. The pilot plans to fly due north at 100 mi/h from the helicopter's current position H to the location of the smoke S. However there is a 30 mi/h wind in the direction N 57° W. The pilot needs to know the velocity vector $\overrightarrow{HA}$ that he should use so that his resultant vector will be $\overrightarrow{HS}$. Find m∠S and then use the Law of Cosines to find the magnitude of $\overrightarrow{HA}$ to the nearest mile per hour. **57°; 87 mi/h**
3. Use the Law of Sines to find the direction of $\overrightarrow{HA}$ to the nearest degree. **N 17° E**

INTERVENTION

Scaffolding Questions

1. Draw and label a right triangle to represent the situation. What trigonometric ratio can you use to solve the problem?

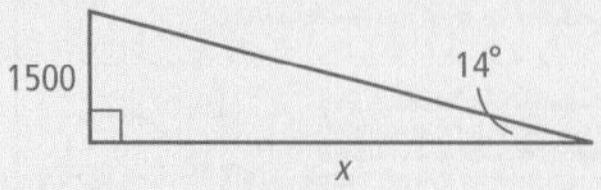

   (Right triangle: leg 1500, leg x, angle 14°)

   $\tan 14° = \frac{1500}{x}$
2. What side lengths and angle measures are known in △HSA? $HS = 100$; $SA = 30$; m∠S = 57° Which side length do you need to find? HA
3. What angle measure do you need to find? m∠H What proportion can you use to find it? $\frac{\sin H}{AS} = \frac{\sin S}{HA}$

Extension

How long will it take the helicopter to reach point S? 0.68 min, or 41 s

CHAPTER 8

SECTION 8B

Quiz for Lessons 8-4 Through 8-6

8-4 Angles of Elevation and Depression

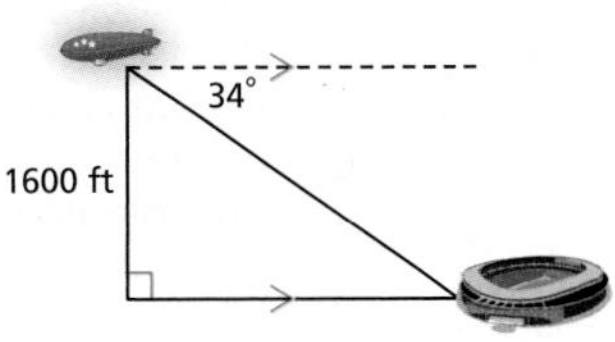

1. An observer in a blimp sights a football stadium at an angle of depression of 34°. The blimp's altitude is 1600 ft. What is the horizontal distance from the blimp to the stadium? Round to the nearest foot. **2372 ft**

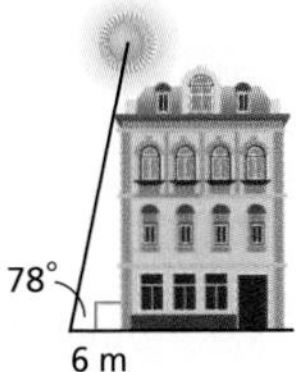

2. When the angle of elevation of the sun is 78°, a building casts a shadow that is 6 m long. What is the height of the building to the nearest tenth of a meter? **28.2 m**

8-5 Law of Sines and Law of Cosines

Find each measure. Round lengths to the nearest tenth and angle measures to the nearest degree.

3. m∠A **38°**

4. GH **10.6**

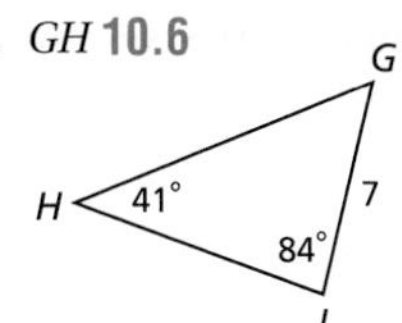

5. XZ **18.2**

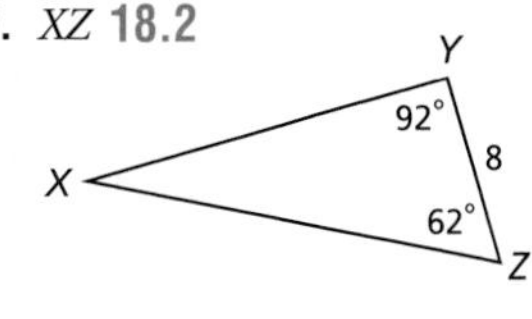

6. UV **6.9**

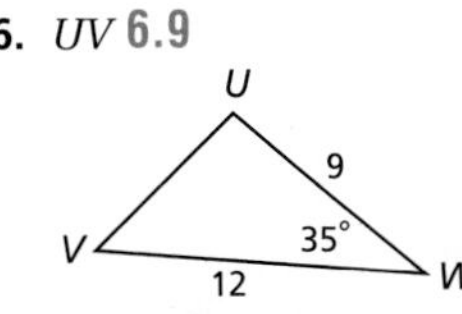

7. m∠F **41°**

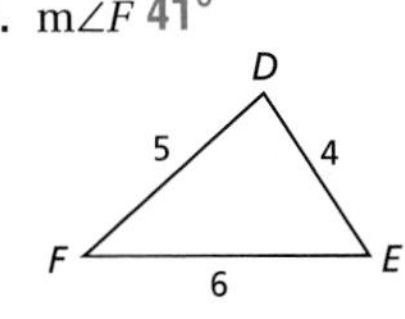

8. QS **7.0**

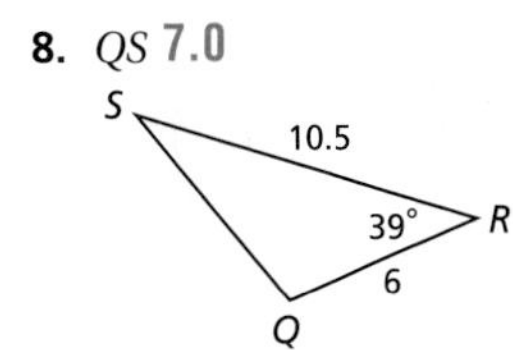

8-6 Vectors

Draw each vector on a coordinate plane. Find its magnitude to the nearest tenth.

9. ⟨3, 1⟩ **3.2**

10. ⟨−2, −4⟩ **4.5**

11. ⟨0, 5⟩ **5**

Draw each vector on a coordinate plane. Find the direction of the vector to the nearest degree.

12. A wind velocity is given by the vector ⟨2, 1⟩. **27°**
13. The current of a river is given by the vector ⟨5, 3⟩. **31°**
14. The force of a spring is given by the vector ⟨4, 4⟩. **45°**
15. To reach an island, a ship leaves port and sails for 6 km at a bearing of N 32° E. It then sails due east for 8 km. What are the magnitude and direction of the voyage directly from the port to the island? Round the distance to the nearest tenth of a kilometer and the direction to the nearest degree. **12.3 km; N 66° E**

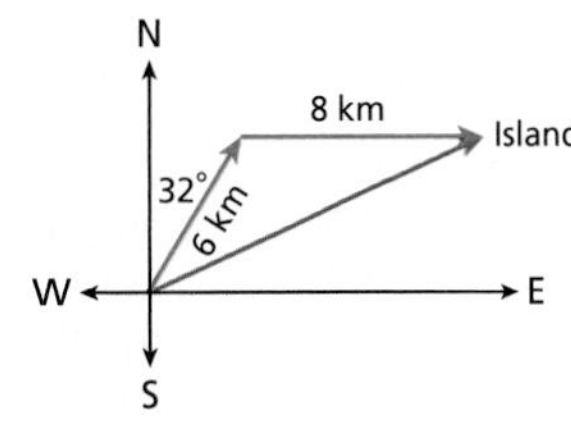

READY TO GO ON? SECTION 8B

Organizer

Objective: Assess students' mastery of concepts and skills in Lessons 8-4 through 8-6.

Resources

Assessment Resources
Section 8B Quiz

Teacher One Stop™
Test & Practice Generator

INTERVENTION

Resources

***Ready to Go On? Intervention and Enrichment* Worksheets**

***Ready to Go On?* CD-ROM**

***Ready to Go On?* Online**

my.hrw.com

Answers

9–14. For graphs, see p. A25.

READY TO GO ON? Diagnose and Prescribe

NO INTERVENE

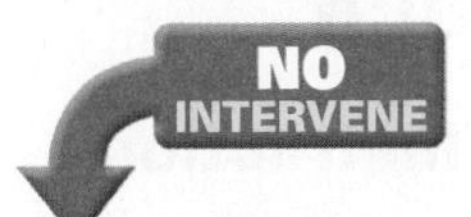

Ready to Go On? Intervention	Ready to Go On? Intervention, Section 8B: Worksheets	CD-ROM	Online
Lesson 8-4	8-4 Intervention	Activity 8-4	Diagnose and Prescribe Online
Lesson 8-5	8-5 Intervention	Activity 8-5	
Lesson 8-6	8-6 Intervention	Activity 8-6	

YES ENRICH

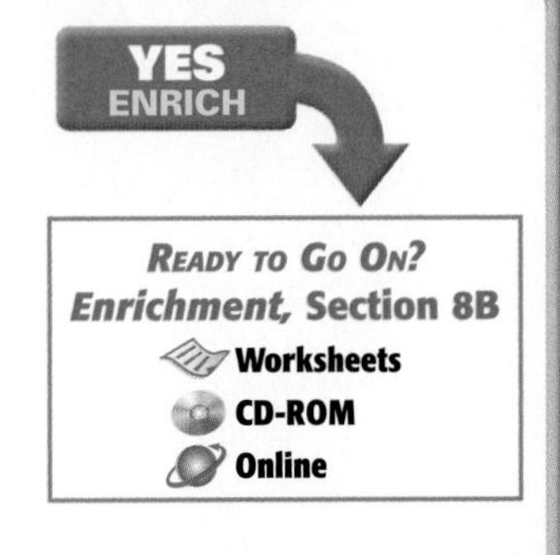

CHAPTER 8

Organizer

Pacing: Traditional 1 day
Block $\frac{1}{2}$ day

Objective: Define trigonometric ratios for angle measures greater than or equal to 90°.

Technology Lab
In *Technology Lab Activities*

Online Edition

Using the Extension

In Chapter 8, students learned to find the measures of acute angles in right triangles using trigonometric ratios. They used the Law of Sines and the Law of Cosines to find angle measures in any triangle. In this extension, they will explore how trigonometric ratios and angle measures are related to the concept of rotation on the unit circle.

Multiple Representations Angles on the unit circle can be used to express bearings. For example, 135° is equivalent to a bearing of N 45° W.

State Resources

State Resources Online
KEYWORD: MG7 Resources

EXTENSION

Trigonometry and the Unit Circle

Objective
Define trigonometric ratios for angle measures greater than or equal to 90°.

Vocabulary
reference angle
unit circle

Rotations are used to extend the concept of trigonometric ratios to angle measures greater than or equal to 90°. Consider a ray with its endpoint at the origin, pointing in the direction of the positive x-axis. Rotate the ray counterclockwise around the origin. The acute angle formed by the ray and the nearest part of the positive or negative x-axis is called the **reference angle**. The rotated ray is called the *terminal side* of that angle.

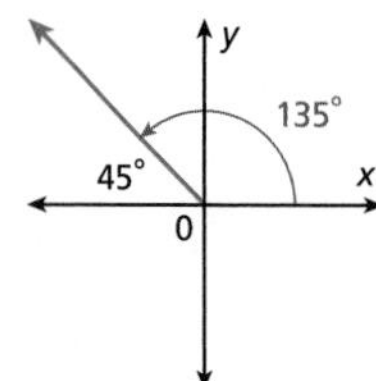

Angle measure: 135°
Reference angle: 45°

Angle measure: 345°
Reference angle: 15°

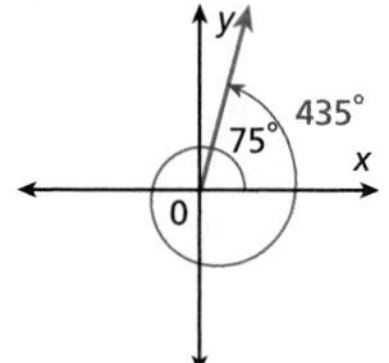

Angle measure: 435°
Reference angle: 75°

EXAMPLE 1 **Finding Reference Angles**

Sketch each angle on the coordinate plane. Find the measure of its reference angle.

A 102°

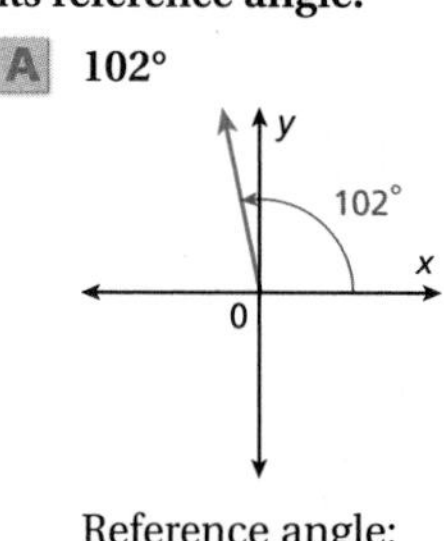

Reference angle:
$180° - 102° = 78°$

B 236°

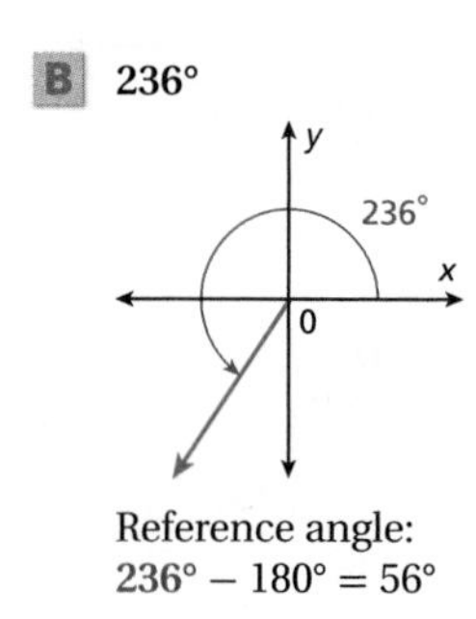

Reference angle:
$236° - 180° = 56°$

Sketch each angle on the coordinate plane. Find the measure of its reference angle.

1a. 309° **51°** **1b.** 410° **50°**

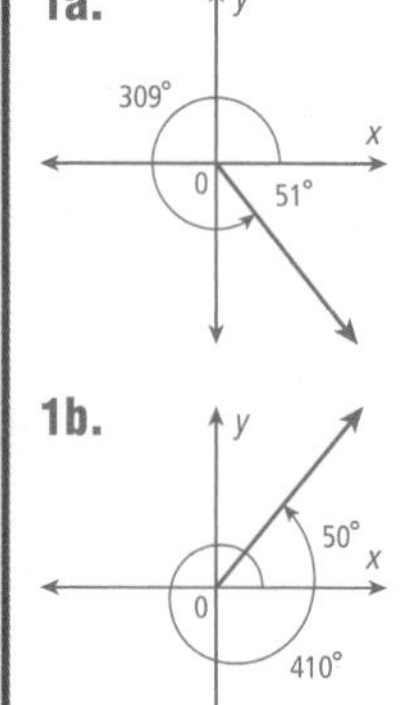

The **unit circle** is a circle with a radius of 1 unit, centered at the origin. It can be used to find the trigonometric ratios of an angle.

Consider the acute angle θ. Let $P(x, y)$ be the point where the terminal side of θ intersects the unit circle. Draw a vertical line from P to the x-axis. Since $\cos\theta = \frac{x}{1}$ and $\sin\theta = \frac{y}{1}$, the coordinates of P can be written as $(\cos\theta, \sin\theta)$. Thus if you know the coordinates of a point on the unit circle, you can find the trigonometric ratios for the associated angle.

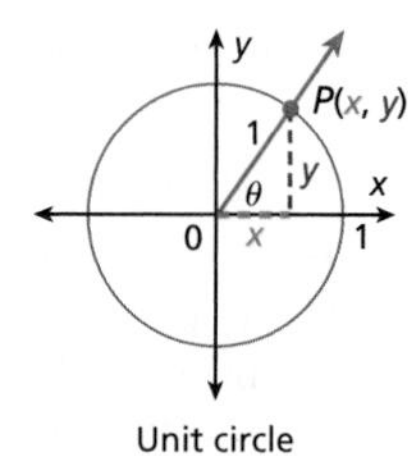

Unit circle

Reading Math
In trigonometry, the Greek letter *theta*, θ, is often used to represent angle measures.

1 Introduce

Motivate

Have students construct a large circle on heavy paper and then draw a set of coordinate axes with the origin at the center. Have them insert one end of a chenille stem through the center of the circle. Have them rotate the end of the stem to the second quadrant. Ask students to estimate the measures of the supplementary angles formed by the stem and the x-axis. Explain to students that they will use a unit circle to find trigonometric ratios for obtuse angles.

2 Teach

Guided Instruction

Discuss reference angles and show students how to find the reference angle for an angle measure greater than 90°. To find a trigonometric ratio of an angle measure greater than 90°, sketch the angle on the unit circle and use the signed (positive or negative) trigonometric ratios of the reference angle.

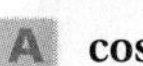

EXAMPLE 2 Finding Trigonometric Ratios

Find each trigonometric ratio.

A $\cos 150°$

Sketch the angle on the coordinate plane.
The reference angle is 30°.

$$\cos 30° = \frac{\sqrt{3}}{2} \qquad \sin 30° = \frac{1}{2}$$

Let $P(x, y)$ be the point where the terminal side of the angle intersects the unit circle. Since P is in Quadrant II, its x-coordinate is negative, and its y-coordinate is positive. So the coordinates of P are $\left(-\frac{\sqrt{3}}{2}, \frac{1}{2}\right)$.

The cosine of 150° is the x-coordinate of P, so $\cos 150° = -\frac{\sqrt{3}}{2}$.

B $\tan 315°$

Sketch the angle on the coordinate plane.
The reference angle is 45°.

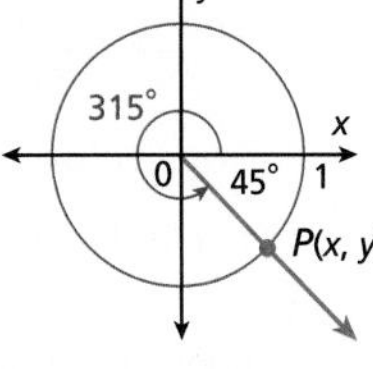

$$\cos 45° = \frac{\sqrt{2}}{2} \qquad \sin 45° = \frac{\sqrt{2}}{2}$$

Since $P(x, y)$ is in Quadrant IV, its y-coordinate is negative. So the coordinates of P are $\left(\frac{\sqrt{2}}{2}, -\frac{\sqrt{2}}{2}\right)$.

Remember that $\tan\theta = \frac{\sin\theta}{\cos\theta}$. So $\tan 315° = \frac{\sin 315°}{\cos 315°} = \frac{-\frac{\sqrt{2}}{2}}{\frac{\sqrt{2}}{2}} = -1$.

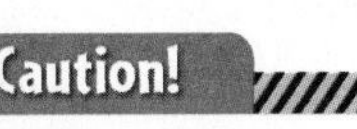

Be sure to use the correct sign when assigning coordinates to a point on the unit circle.

Find each trigonometric ratio.

2a. $\cos 240°$ $-\frac{1}{2}$ **2b.** $\sin 135°$ $\frac{\sqrt{2}}{2}$

EXTENSION Exercises

Sketch each angle on the coordinate plane. Find the measure of its reference angle.

1. 125° **55°**
2. 216° **36°**
3. 359° **1°**

Find each trigonometric ratio.

4. $\cos 225°$ $-\frac{\sqrt{2}}{2}$
5. $\sin 120°$ $\frac{\sqrt{3}}{2}$
6. $\cos 300°$ $\frac{1}{2}$
7. $\tan 135°$ -1
8. $\cos 420°$ $\frac{1}{2}$
9. $\tan 315°$ -1
10. $\sin 90°$ 1
11. $\cos 180°$ -1
12. $\sin 270°$ -1
13. **Critical Thinking** Given that $\cos\theta = 0.5$, what are the possible values for θ between 0° and 360°? **60° and 300°**

14. **Write About It** Explain how you can use the unit circle to find $\tan 180°$.
15. **Challenge** If $\sin\theta \approx -0.891$, what are two values of θ between 0° and 360°? **243° or 297°**

3 Close

Summarize

The unit circle is used to find trigonometric ratios for angle measures greater than or equal to 90°. Rotate a ray from the positive x-axis around the origin. The reference angle is the acute angle formed by the ray and the nearest part of the x-axis. If $P(x, y)$ is the point where the terminal side of a reference angle θ intersects the unit circle, the coordinates of P are $(\cos\theta, \sin\theta)$, and $\tan\theta = \frac{\sin\theta}{\cos\theta}$.

Answers

1–3. For graphs, see p. A25.

14. The terminal side of a 180° ∠ lies on the x-axis and intersects the unit circle at $(-1, 0)$. So $\cos 180° = -1$, and $\sin 180° = 0$. Thus $\tan 180° = \frac{\sin 180°}{\cos 180°} = \frac{0}{-1} = 0$.

COMMON ERROR ALERT

If students use a calculator to answer **Exercise 15,** they may conclude that there is only one angle whose sine is −0.891. Ask students in which quadrants $\sin\theta$ is negative. Explain that because it is negative in Quadrant III and Quadrant IV, there are two angles for which $\sin\theta \approx -0.891$.

Power Presentations with PowerPoint®

Additional Examples

Example 1

Sketch each angle on the coordinate plane. Find the measure of its reference angle.

A. 252° 72°

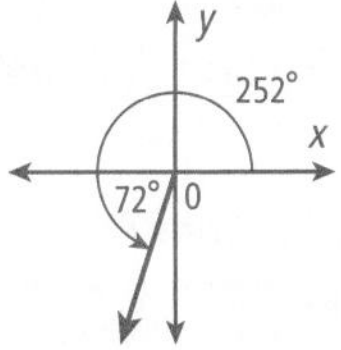

B. 297° 63°

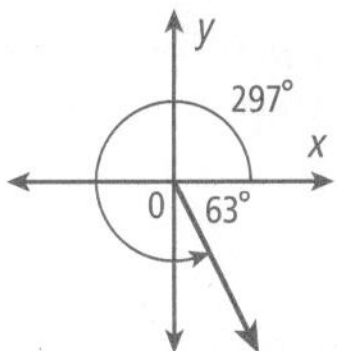

Example 2

Find each trigonometric ratio.

A. $\sin 240°$ $-\frac{\sqrt{3}}{2}$

B. $\tan 225°$ 1

Also available on transparency

INTERVENTION Questioning Strategies

EXAMPLE 1

- How do you find the reference angle for an angle in Quadrant II? in Quadrant III? in Quadrant IV?

EXAMPLE 2

- In which quadrants are a cosine ratio, sine ratio, and tangent ratio negative?

Organizer

Objective: Help students organize and review key concepts and skills presented in Chapter 8.

Online Edition
Multilingual Glossary

Countdown Week 19

Resources

Teacher One Stop™
PuzzleView
Test & Practice Generator

***Multilingual Glossary* Online**
go.hrw.com
KEYWORD: MG7 Glossary

Lesson Tutorial Videos
CD-ROM

Answers

1. component form
2. equal vectors
3. geometric mean
4. angle of elevation
5. trigonometric ratio
6. $\triangle PRQ \sim \triangle RSQ \sim \triangle PSR$
7. 5
8. $\sqrt{51}$
9. $x = \sqrt{35}$; $y = 2\sqrt{15}$; $z = 2\sqrt{21}$
10. $x = 3$; $y = 3\sqrt{5}$; $z = 6\sqrt{5}$
11. $x = 5$; $y = \sqrt{5}$; $z = \sqrt{30}$

CHAPTER 8 Study Guide: Review

For a complete list of the postulates and theorems in this chapter, see p. PS12.

Vocabulary

Complete the sentences below with vocabulary words from the list above.

1. The __?__ of a vector gives the horizontal and vertical change from the initial point to the terminal point.
2. Two vectors with the same magnitude and direction are called __?__ .
3. If a and b are positive numbers, then $\sqrt{ab}$ is the __?__ of a and b.
4. A(n) __?__ is the angle formed by a horizontal line and a line of sight to a point above the horizontal line.
5. The sine, cosine, and tangent are all examples of a(n) __?__ .

8-1 Similarity in Right Triangles *(pp. 518–523)*

EXAMPLES

- **Find the geometric mean of 5 and 30.**

  Let x be the geometric mean.

  $x^2 = (5)(30) = 150$ *Def. of geometric mean*

  $x = \sqrt{150} = 5\sqrt{6}$ *Find the positive square root.*

- **Find x, y, and z.**

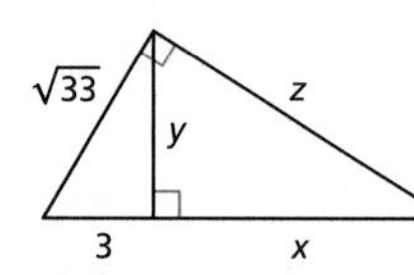

$(\sqrt{33})^2 = 3(3 + x)$ *$\sqrt{33}$ is the geometric mean of 3 and 3 + x.*

$33 = 9 + 3x$

$24 = 3x$

$x = 8$

$y^2 = (3)(8)$ *y is the geometric mean of 3 and 8.*

$y^2 = 24$

$y = \sqrt{24} = 2\sqrt{6}$

$z^2 = (8)(11)$ *z is the geometric mean of 8 and 11.*

$z^2 = 88$

$z = \sqrt{88} = 2\sqrt{22}$

EXERCISES

6. Write a similarity statement comparing the three triangles.

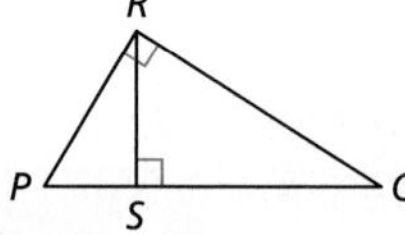

Find the geometric mean of each pair of numbers. If necessary, give the answer in simplest radical form.

7. $\frac{1}{4}$ and 100
8. 3 and 17

Find x, y, and z.

9.

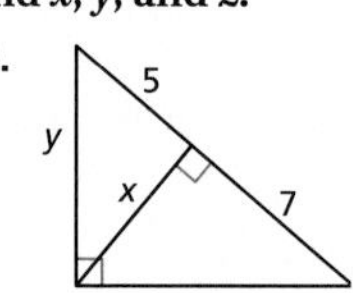

10.

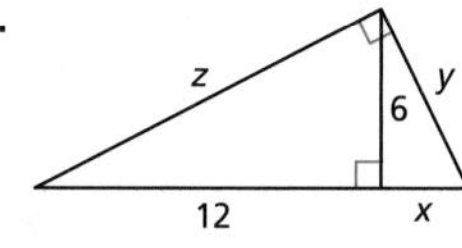

11.

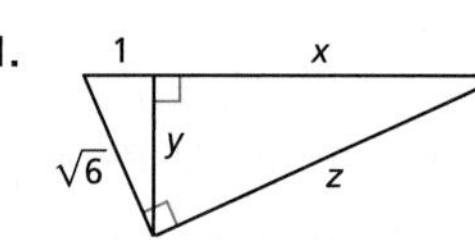

8-2 Trigonometric Ratios *(pp. 525–532)*

EXAMPLES

Find each length. Round to the nearest hundredth.

■ EF

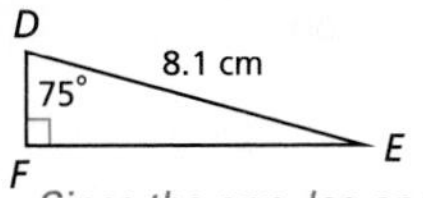

$\sin 75° = \frac{EF}{8.1}$

$EF = 8.1(\sin 75°)$

$EF \approx 7.82$ cm

Since the opp. leg and hyp. are involved, use a sine ratio.

■ AB

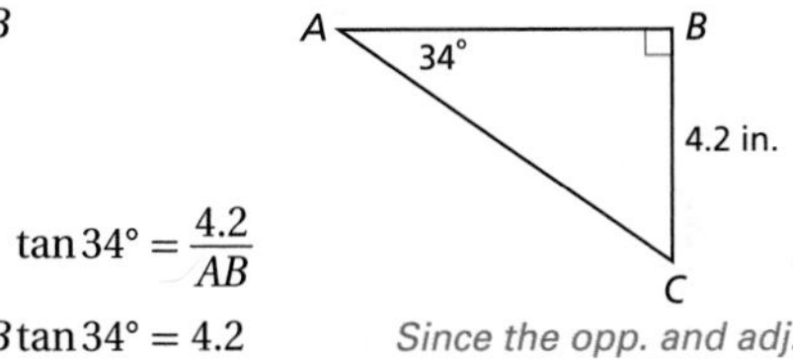

$\tan 34° = \frac{4.2}{AB}$

$AB \tan 34° = 4.2$

$AB = \frac{4.2}{\tan 34°}$

$AB \approx 6.23$ in.

Since the opp. and adj. legs are involved, use a tangent ratio.

EXERCISES

Find each length. Round to the nearest hundredth.

12. UV

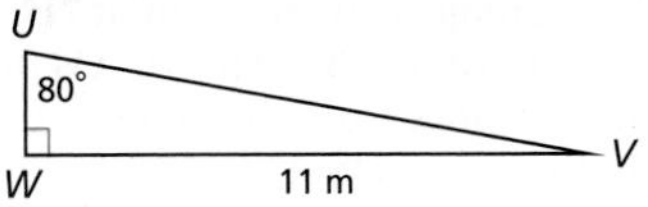

13. PR

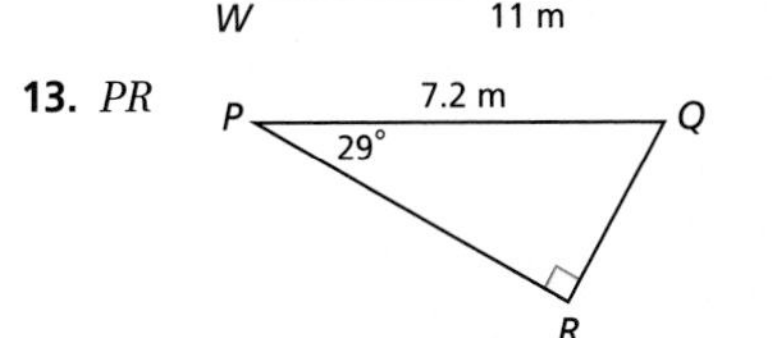

14. XY

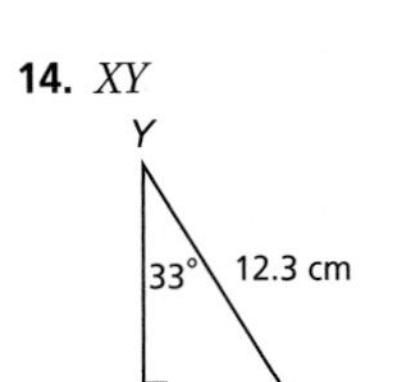

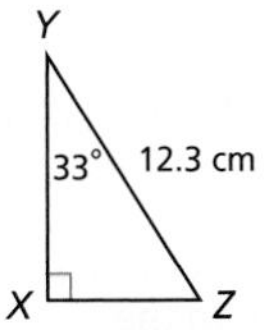

15. JL

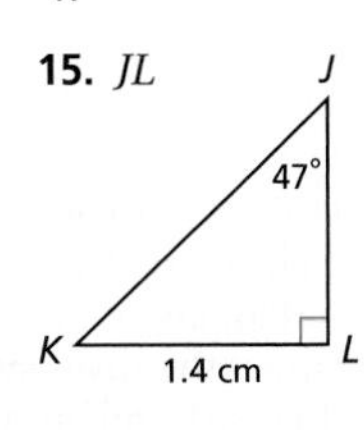

8-3 Solving Right Triangles *(pp. 534–541)*

EXAMPLE

■ **Find the unknown measures in $\triangle LMN$. Round lengths to the nearest hundredth and angle measures to the nearest degree.**

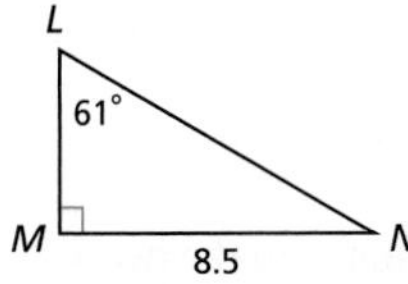

The acute angles of a right triangle are complementary. So $m\angle N = 90° - 61° = 29°$.

$\sin L = \frac{MN}{LN}$ *Write a trig. ratio.*

$\sin 61° = \frac{8.5}{LN}$ *Substitute the given values.*

$LN = \frac{8.5}{\sin 61°} \approx 9.72$ *Solve for LN.*

$\tan L = \frac{MN}{LM}$ *Write a trig. ratio.*

$\tan 61° = \frac{8.5}{LM}$ *Substitute the given values.*

$LM = \frac{8.5}{\tan 61°} \approx 4.71$ *Solve for LM.*

EXERCISES

Find the unknown measures. Round lengths to the nearest hundredth and angle measures to the nearest degree.

16.

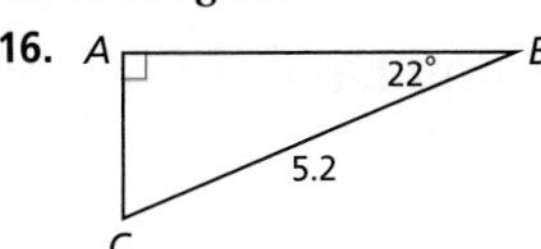

17.

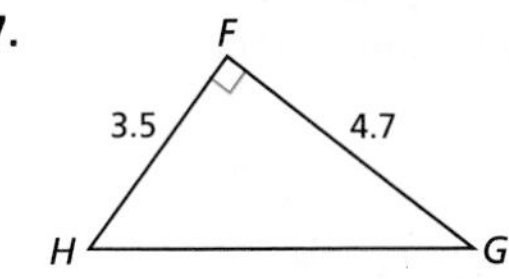

18.

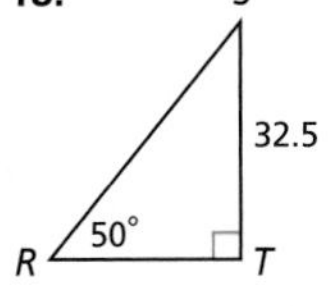

19.

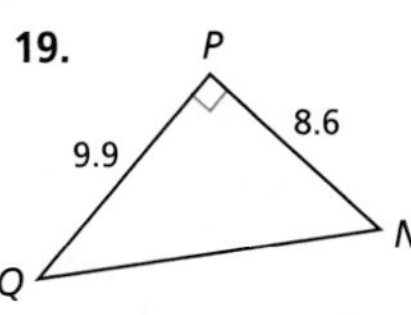

Answers

12. 11.17 m
13. 6.30 m
14. 10.32 cm
15. 1.31 cm
16. $m\angle C = 68°$; $AB \approx 4.82$; $AC \approx 1.95$
17. $m\angle H \approx 53°$; $m\angle G \approx 37°$; $HG \approx 5.86$
18. $m\angle S = 40°$; $RS \approx 42.43$; $RT \approx 27.27$
19. $m\angle Q \approx 41°$; $m\angle N \approx 49°$; $QN \approx 13.11$

Study Guide: Review 573

Answers

20. angle of depression
21. angle of elevation
22. 36 ft
23. 458 m
24. 22°
25. 31.4

8-4 Angles of Elevation and Depression *(pp. 544–549)*

EXAMPLES

- **A pilot in a plane spots a forest fire on the ground at an angle of depression of 71°. The plane's altitude is 3000 ft. What is the horizontal distance from the plane to the fire? Round to the nearest foot.**

$\tan 71° = \frac{3000}{XF}$

$XF = \frac{3000}{\tan 71°}$

$XF \approx 1033$ ft

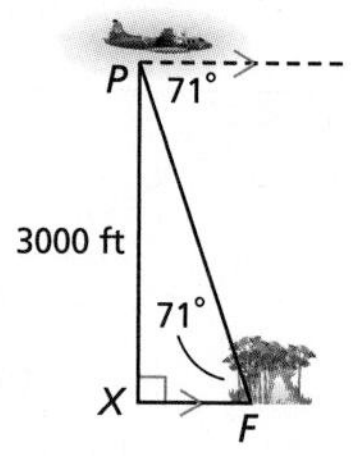

- **A diver is swimming at a depth of 63 ft below sea level. He sees a buoy floating at sea level at an angle of elevation of 47°. How far must the diver swim so that he is directly beneath the buoy? Round to the nearest foot.**

$\tan 47° = \frac{63}{XD}$

$XD = \frac{63}{\tan 47°}$

$XD \approx 59$ ft

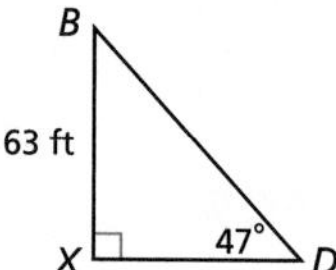

EXERCISES

Classify each angle as an angle of elevation or angle of depression.

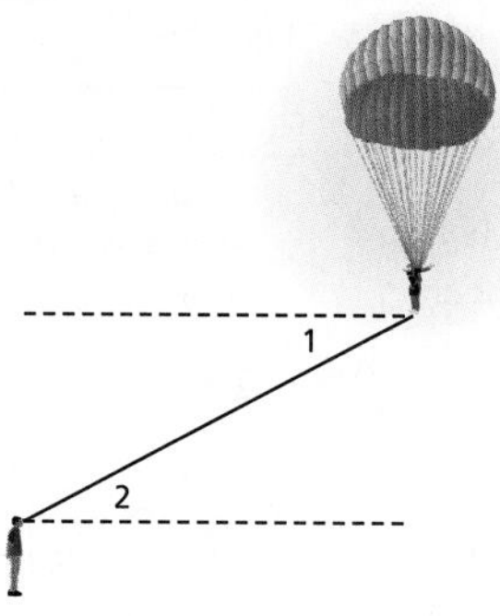

20. $\angle 1$

21. $\angle 2$

22. When the angle of elevation to the sun is 82°, a monument casts a shadow that is 5.1 ft long. What is the height of the monument to the nearest foot?

23. A ranger in a lookout tower spots a fire in the distance. The angle of depression to the fire is 4°, and the lookout tower is 32 m tall. What is the horizontal distance to the fire? Round to the nearest meter.

8-5 Law of Sines and Law of Cosines *(pp. 551–558)*

EXAMPLES

Find each measure. Round lengths to the nearest tenth and angle measures to the nearest degree.

- $m\angle B$

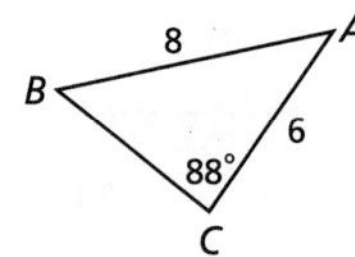

$\frac{\sin B}{AC} = \frac{\sin C}{AB}$ *Law of Sines*

$\frac{\sin B}{6} = \frac{\sin 88°}{8}$ *Substitute the given values.*

$\sin B = \frac{6 \sin 88°}{8}$ *Multiply both sides by 6.*

$m\angle B = \sin^{-1}\left(\frac{6 \sin 88°}{8}\right) \approx 49°$

EXERCISES

Find each measure. Round lengths to the nearest tenth and angle measures to the nearest degree.

24. $m\angle Z$

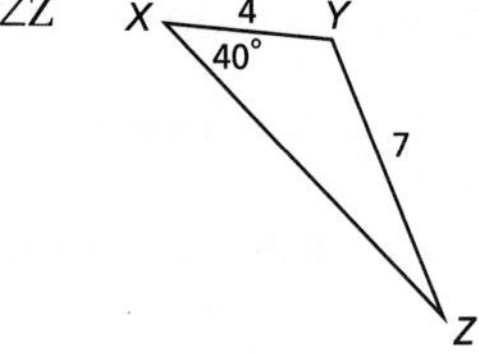

25. MN

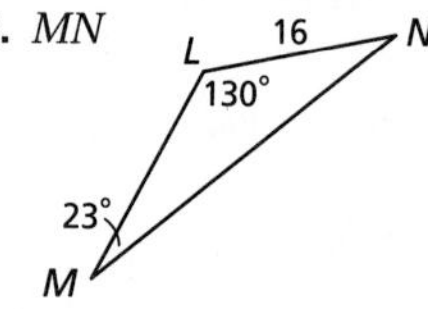

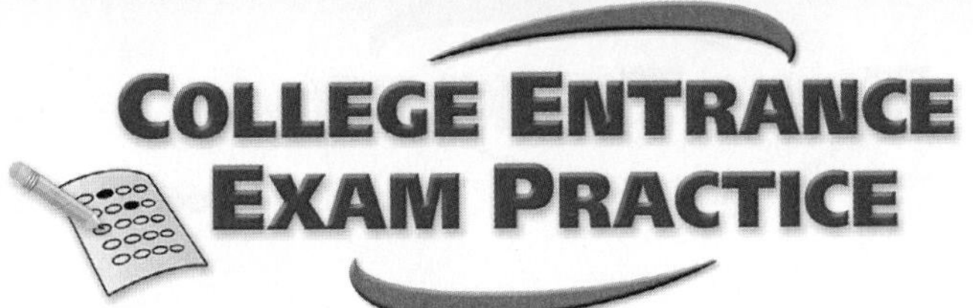

COLLEGE ENTRANCE EXAM PRACTICE

FOCUS ON SAT MATHEMATICS SUBJECT TESTS

The SAT Mathematics Subject Tests each consist of 50 multiple-choice questions. You are not expected to have studied every topic on the SAT Mathematics Subject Tests, so some questions may be unfamiliar.

Though you can use a calculator on the SAT Mathematics Subject Tests, it may be faster to answer some questions without one. Remember to use test-taking strategies before you press buttons!

You may want to time yourself as you take this practice test. It should take you about 6 minutes to complete.

1. Let P be the acute angle formed by the line $-x + 4y = 12$ and the x-axis. What is the approximate measure of $\angle P$?
   - (A) 14°
   - (B) 18°
   - (C) 72°
   - (D) 76°
   - (E) 85°

2. In right triangle DEF, $DE = 15$, $EF = 36$, and $DF = 39$. What is the cosine of $\angle F$?
   - (A) $\frac{5}{12}$
   - (B) $\frac{12}{5}$
   - (C) $\frac{5}{13}$
   - (D) $\frac{12}{13}$
   - (E) $\frac{13}{12}$

3. A triangle has angle measures of 19°, 61°, and 100°. What is the approximate length of the side opposite the 100° angle if the side opposite the 61° angle is 8 centimeters long?
   - (A) 2.5 centimeters
   - (B) 3 centimeters
   - (C) 9 centimeters
   - (D) 12 centimeters
   - (E) 13 centimeters

4. A swimmer jumps into a river and starts swimming directly across it at a constant velocity of 2 meters per second. The speed of the current is 7 meters per second. Given the current, what is the actual speed of the swimmer to the nearest tenth?
   - (A) 0.3 meters per second
   - (B) 1.7 meters per second
   - (C) 5.0 meters per second
   - (D) 7.3 meters per second
   - (E) 9.0 meters per second

5. What is the approximate measure of the vertex angle of the isosceles triangle below?

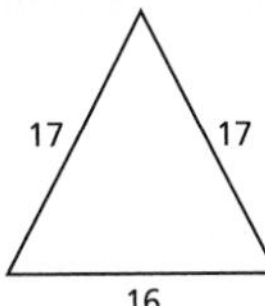

   - (A) 28.1°
   - (B) 56.1°
   - (C) 62.0°
   - (D) 112.2°
   - (E) 123.9°

COLLEGE ENTRANCE EXAM PRACTICE

CHAPTER 8

Organizer

Objective: Provide practice for college entrance exams such as the SAT Mathematics Subject Tests.

PREMIER Online Edition

Resources

College Entrance Exam Practice

Questions on the SAT Mathematics Subject Tests Levels 1 and 2 represent the following math content areas:

	Levels	
	1	2
Number and Operations	10–14%	10–14%
Algebra and Functions	38–42%	48–52%
Geometry and Measurement	38–42%	28–32%
Plane Euclidean	18–22%	0%
Coordinate	8–12%	10–14%
Three-Dimensional	4–6%	4–6%
Trigonometry	6–8%	12–16%
Data Analysis and Statistics	6–10%	6–10%

Items on this page focus on:
- Plane Euclidean Geometry
- Trigonometry

Text References:

Item	1	2	3	4	5
Lesson	8-3	8-2	8-5	8-6	8-3

TEST PREP DOCTOR

1. Students who chose **D** found the inverse tangent of 4 instead of $\frac{1}{4}$. Remind students that the acute angle formed by a line and the x-axis is equal to the inverse tangent of the slope. Suggest that they draw a right triangle on the coordinate plane to represent the rise and run of the line.
2. Suggest that students draw and label a triangle to figure out where $\angle F$ is in relation to the given side lengths. Students who did not choose answer **D** found the wrong trigonometric ratio or mislabeled the triangle.
3. Students who chose **B** found the side length opposite the 19° angle. Have students write all three proportions from the Law of Sines for the given triangle. Then ask them to point out which of the ratios is unnecessary.
4. Students who chose **E** simply added the velocities of the swimmer and the current. Remind students that they must account for the different directions of these two forces. Have students draw a sketch to represent the scenario.
5. Remind students that the altitude to the base of an isosceles triangle bisects the base. Students who chose answer **C** found the measure of one of the base angles. Students who chose answer **A** found one-half the measure of the vertex angle.

Organizer

Objective: Provide opportunities to learn and practice common test-taking strategies.

TEST PREP DOCTOR This Test Tackler focuses on using estimation to check answers. Emphasize to students that this strategy will either confirm that their answer is reasonable or alert them to a possible math error. Thus it is well worth the few extra moments spent on each test problem.

Standardized Test Strategies

Any Question Type: Estimate

Once you find the answer to a test problem, take a few moments to check your answer by using estimation strategies. By doing so, you can verify that your final answer is reasonable.

EXAMPLE 1

Gridded Response **Find the geometric mean of 38 and 12 to the nearest hundredth.**

Let x be the geometric mean.

$x^2 = (38)(12) = 456$	*Def. of geometric mean*
$x \approx 21.35$	*Find the positive square root.*

Now use estimation to check that this answer is reasonable.

$x^2 \approx (40)(10) = 400$	*Round 38 to 40 and round 12 to 10.*
$x \approx 20$	*Find the positive square root.*

The estimate is close to the calculated answer, so 21.35 is a reasonable answer.

EXAMPLE 2

Multiple Choice **Which of the following is equal to sin*X*?**

Ⓐ 0.02 Ⓒ 0.91

Ⓑ 0.41 Ⓓ 2.44

Y 9 Z
20.1 22
X

Use a trigonometric ratio to find the answer.

$\sin X = \frac{YZ}{XZ}$	*The sine of an ∠ is* $\frac{\text{opp. leg}}{\text{hyp.}}$.
$\sin X = \frac{9}{22} \approx 0.41$	*Substitute the given values and simplify.*

Now use estimation to check that this answer is reasonable.

$\sin X \approx \frac{10}{20} \approx 0.5$	*Round 9 to 10 and round 22 to 20.*

The estimate is close to the calculated answer, so B is a reasonable answer.

An extra minute spent checking your answers can result in a better test score.

Read each test item and answer the questions that follow.

Item A

Gridded Response **A cell phone tower casts a shadow that is 121 ft long when the angle of elevation to the sun is 48°. How tall is the cell phone tower? Round to the nearest foot.**

1. A student estimated that the answer should be slightly greater than 121 by comparing $\tan 48°$ and $\tan 45°$. Explain why this estimation strategy works.
2. Describe how to use the inverse tangent function to estimate whether an answer of 134 ft makes sense.

Item B

Short Response **$\overrightarrow{BC}$ has an initial point of $(-1, 0)$ and a terminal point of $(4, 2)$.**

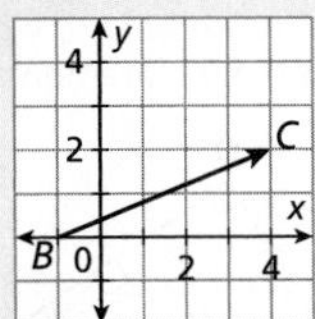

a. **Write $\overrightarrow{BC}$ in component form.**

b. **Find the magnitude of $\overrightarrow{BC}$. Round to the nearest hundredth.**

c. **Find the direction of $\overrightarrow{BC}$. Round to the nearest degree.**

3. A student correctly found the magnitude of $\overrightarrow{BC}$ as $\sqrt{29}$. The student then calculated the value of this radical as 6.39. Explain how to use perfect squares to estimate the value of $\sqrt{29}$. Is 6.39 a reasonable answer?
4. A student calculated the measure of the angle the vector forms with a horizontal line as 68°. Use estimation to explain why this answer is not reasonable.

Item C

Multiple Choice **In $\triangle QRS$, what is the measure of $\overline{SQ}$ to the nearest tenth of a centimeter?**

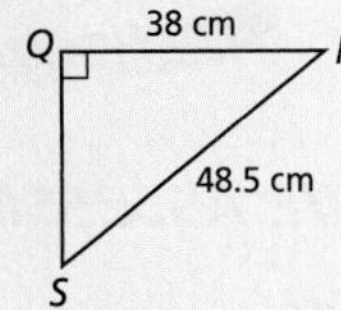

Ⓐ 9.3 centimeters

Ⓑ 10.5 centimeters

Ⓒ 30.1 centimeters

Ⓓ 61.7 centimeters

5. A student calculated the answer as 30.1 cm. The student then used the diagram to estimate that *SQ* is more than half of *RQ*. So the student decided that his answer was reasonable. Is this estimation method a good way to check your answer? Why or why not?
6. Describe how to use estimation and the Pythagorean Theorem to check your answer to this problem.

Item D

Multiple Choice **The McCleods have a variable interest rate on their mortgage. The rate is 2.625% the first year and 4% the following year. The average interest rate is the geometric mean of these two rates. To the nearest hundredth of a percent, what is the average interest rate for their mortgage?**

Ⓕ 1.38% Ⓗ 3.89%

Ⓖ 3.24% Ⓙ 10.50%

7. Describe how to use estimation to show that choices **F** and **J** are unreasonable.
8. To find the answer, a student uses the equation $x^2 = (2.625)(4)$. Which compatible numbers should the student use to quickly check the answer?

Answers

Possible answers:

1. The value of $\tan 48°$ is slightly greater than the value of $\tan 45°$, which equals 1. Since the height of the tower equals $121 \tan 48°$, and $\tan 48° > 1$, the height will be slightly greater than 121.
2. Find the value of the expression $\tan^{-1}\left(\frac{134}{121}\right)$. If it equals 48°, then 134 ft is a reasonable answer.
3. The 2 perfect squares closest to $\sqrt{29}$ are $\sqrt{25} = 5$ and $\sqrt{36} = 6$. Since $\sqrt{25} < \sqrt{29} < \sqrt{36}$, it is true that $5 < \sqrt{29} < 6$. Thus the value of $\sqrt{29}$ must be greater than 5 and less than 6. Since 6.39 is greater than 6, it is not a reasonable answer.
4. The ∠ the vector forms can be found with the expression $\tan^{-1}\left(\frac{2}{5}\right)$. Since the vert. component is less than the horiz. component, the ∠ is less than 45°, so an answer of 68° is not reasonable.
5. No; because diagrams are not always drawn to scale.
6. Round 48.5 to 50 and 38 to 40. By the Pyth. Thm., $b^2 \approx 50^2 - 40^2$, and $b^2 \approx 900$. Thus $b \approx 30$. Choice **C** is reasonable.
7. The geometric mean of 2.625% and 4% must lie somewhere between these 2 values. Choice **F** is less than 2.625%, and choice **J** is greater than 4%, so neither of these values is reasonable.
8. 3 and 4

Answers to Test Items

A. 134

Ba. ⟨5, 2⟩

b. 5.39

c. 22°

C. C

D. G

State Resources

go.hrw.com
State Resources Online
KEYWORD: MG7 Resources

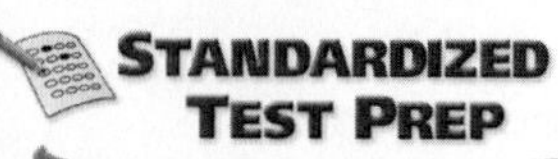

Organizer

Objective: Provide review and practice for Chapters 1–8 and standardized tests.

Resources

Assessment Resources

Chapter 8 Cumulative Test

go.hrw.com
KEYWORD: MG7 TestPrep

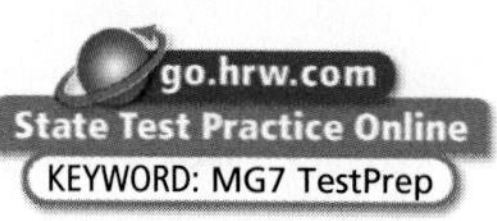

CUMULATIVE ASSESSMENT, CHAPTERS 1–8

Multiple Choice

1. What is the length of $\overline{UX}$ to the nearest centimeter?

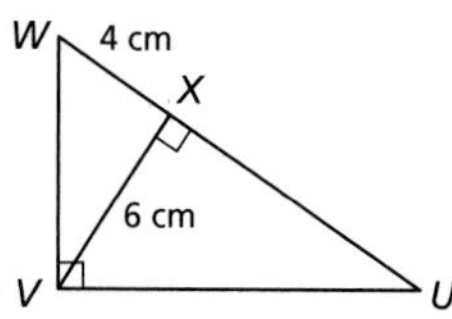

Ⓐ 3 centimeters
Ⓑ 7 centimeters
Ⓒ 9 centimeters
Ⓓ 13 centimeters

2. $\triangle ABC$ is a right triangle. $m\angle A = 20°$, $m\angle B = 90°$, $AC = 8$, and $AB = 3$. Which expression can be used to find BC?

Ⓕ $\dfrac{3}{\tan 70°}$
Ⓖ $\dfrac{8}{\sin 20°}$
Ⓗ $8 \tan 20°$
Ⓙ $3 \cos 70°$

3. A slide at a park is 25 ft long, and the top of the slide is 10 ft above the ground. What is the approximate measure of the angle the slide makes with the ground?

Ⓐ 21.8°
Ⓑ 23.6°
Ⓒ 66.4°
Ⓓ 68.2°

4. Which of the following vectors is equal to the vector with an initial point at $(2, -1)$ and a terminal point at $(-2, 4)$?

Ⓕ $\langle -4, -5 \rangle$
Ⓖ $\langle -4, 5 \rangle$
Ⓗ $\langle 5, -4 \rangle$
Ⓙ $\langle 5, 4 \rangle$

5. Which statement is true by the Addition Property of Equality?

Ⓐ If $3x + 6 = 9y$, then $x + 2 = 3y$.
Ⓑ If $t = 1$ and $s = t + 5$, then $s = 6$.
Ⓒ If $k + 1 = \ell + 2$, then $2k + 2 = 2\ell + 4$.
Ⓓ If $a + 2 = 3b$, then $a + 5 = 3b + 3$.

6. $\triangle ABC$ has vertices $A(-2, -2)$, $B(-3, 2)$, and $C(1, 3)$. Which translation produces an image with vertices at the coordinates $(-2, -2)$, $(2, -1)$, and $(-1, -6)$?

Ⓕ $(x, y) \rightarrow (x + 1, y - 4)$
Ⓖ $(x, y) \rightarrow (x + 2, y - 8)$
Ⓗ $(x, y) \rightarrow (x - 3, y - 5)$
Ⓙ $(x, y) \rightarrow (x - 4, y + 1)$

7. $\triangle ABC$ is a right triangle in which $m\angle A = 30°$ and $m\angle B = 60°$. Which of the following are possible lengths for the sides of this triangle?

Ⓐ $AB = \sqrt{3}$, $AC = \sqrt{2}$, and $BC = 1$
Ⓑ $AB = 4$, $AC = 2$, and $BC = 2\sqrt{3}$
Ⓒ $AB = 6\sqrt{3}$, $AC = 27$, and $BC = 3\sqrt{3}$
Ⓓ $AB = 8$, $AC = 4\sqrt{3}$, and $BC = 4$

8. Based on the figure below, which of the following similarity statements must be true?

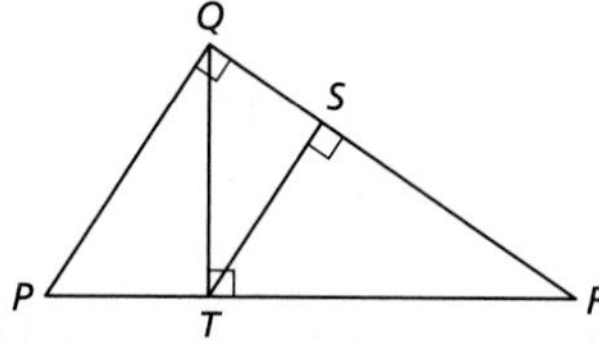

Ⓕ $\triangle PQR \sim \triangle TSR$
Ⓖ $\triangle PQR \sim \triangle RTQ$
Ⓗ $\triangle PQR \sim \triangle TSQ$
Ⓙ $\triangle PQR \sim \triangle TQP$

9. $ABCD$ is a rhombus with vertices $A(1, 1)$ and $C(3, 4)$. Which of the following lines is parallel to diagonal $\overline{BD}$?

Ⓐ $2x - 3y = 12$
Ⓑ $2x + 3y = 12$
Ⓒ $3x + 2y = 12$
Ⓓ $3x - 4y = 12$

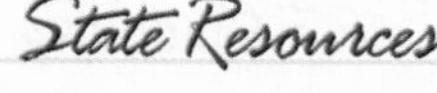

Answers

1. C
2. F
3. B
4. G
5. D
6. F
7. D
8. F
9. B
10. J
11. B
12. J
13. A
14. 31
15. 15
16. 2.25

10. Which of the following is NOT equivalent to $\sin 60°$?

Ⓕ $\cos 30°$ Ⓗ $(\cos 60°)(\tan 60°)$

Ⓖ $\frac{\sqrt{3}}{2}$ Ⓙ $\frac{\tan 30°}{\sin 30°}$

11. *ABCDE* is a convex pentagon. $\angle A \cong \angle B \cong \angle C$, $\angle D \cong \angle E$, and $m\angle A = 2m\angle D$. What is the measure of $\angle C$?

Ⓐ 67.5° Ⓒ 154.2°

Ⓑ 135° Ⓓ 225°

12. Which of the following sets of lengths can represent the side lengths of an obtuse triangle?

Ⓕ 4, 7.5, and 8.5

Ⓖ 7, 12, and 13

Ⓗ 9.5, 16.5, and 35

Ⓙ 36, 75, and 88

Be sure to correctly identify any pairs of parallel lines before using the Alternate Interior Angles Theorem or the Same-Side Interior Angles Theorem.

13. What is the value of *x*?

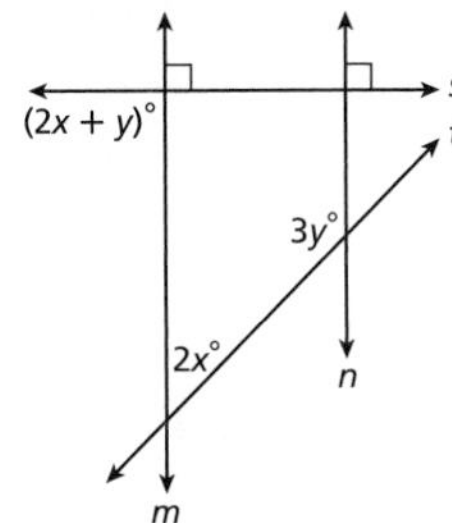

Ⓐ 22.5 Ⓒ 90

Ⓑ 45 Ⓓ 135

Gridded Response

14. Find the next item in the pattern below.

1, 3, 7, 13, 21, ...

15. In $\triangle XYZ$, $\angle X$ and $\angle Z$ are remote interior angles of exterior $\angle XYT$. If $m\angle X = (x + 15)°$, $m\angle Z = (50 - 3x)°$, and $m\angle XYT = (4x - 25)°$, what is the value of *x*?

16. In $\triangle ABC$ and $\triangle DEF$, $\angle A \cong \angle F$. If $EF = 4.5$, $DF = 3$, and $AC = 1.5$, what length for $\overline{AB}$ would let you conclude that $\triangle ABC \sim \triangle FED$?

Short Response

17. A building casts a shadow that is 85 ft long when the angle of elevation to the sun is 34°.

a. What is the height of the building? Round to the nearest inch and show your work.

b. What is the angle of elevation to the sun when the shadow is 42 ft 6 in. long? Round to the nearest tenth of a degree and show your work.

18. Use the figure to find each of the following. Round to the nearest tenth of a centimeter and show your work.

a. the length of $\overline{DC}$

b. the length of $\overline{AB}$

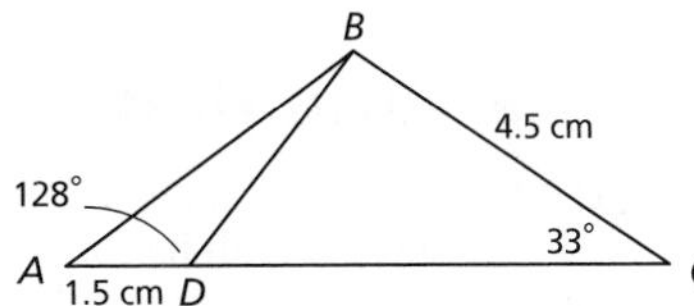

Extended Response

19. Tony and Paul are taking a vacation with their cousin, Greg. Tony and Paul live in the same house. Paul will go directly to the vacation spot, but Tony has to pick up Greg.

Tony travels 90 miles at a bearing of N 25° E to get to his cousin's house. He then travels due east for 50 miles to get to the vacation spot. Paul travels on one highway to get from his house to the vacation spot.

For each of the following, explain in words how you found your answer and round to the nearest tenth.

a. Write the vectors in component form for the route from Tony and Paul's house to their cousin's house and the route from their cousin's house to the vacation spot.

b. What are the direction and magnitude of Paul's direct route from his house to the vacation spot?

c. Tony and Paul leave the house at the same time and arrive at the vacation spot at the same time. If Tony traveled at an average speed of 50 mi/h, what was Paul's average speed?

Short-Response Rubric

Item 17–18

2 Points = The student's answer is an accurate and complete execution of the task or tasks.

1 Point = The student's answer contains attributes of an appropriate response but is flawed.

0 Points = The student's answer contains no attributes of an appropriate response.

Extended-Response Rubric

Item 19

4 Points = The student writes the correct vectors in part a, and the calculations and explanations in parts b and c are correct and complete. Work demonstrates a thorough understanding of vector concepts, including magnitude, direction, and resultant vectors.

3 Points = The student's answers in parts b and c are correct, but the explanations may contain minor flaws. Work demonstrates an understanding of major vector concepts.

2 Points = The student answers all parts correctly, but explanations are missing or incomplete, or the student answers only part of the problem. Work demonstrates a limited understanding of vector concepts.

1 Point = The student answers incorrectly but makes a reasonable attempt to show work.

0 Points = The student does not answer correctly and does not attempt all parts of the problem.

Answers

17a. $\tan 34° = \frac{\text{height}}{85 \text{ ft}}$, so the height ≈ 57 ft 4 in.

b. The ∠ of elevation of the sun is $\tan^{-1}\left(\frac{85 \tan 34°}{42.5}\right) \approx 53.5°$.

18a. $m\angle BDC = 180° - 128° = 52°$ and $m\angle DBC = 128° - 33° = 95°$. By the Law of Sines, $\frac{\sin 95°}{DC} = \frac{\sin 52°}{4.5}$. So $DC = \frac{4.5 \sin 95°}{\sin 52°} \approx 5.7$.

b. By the Seg. Add. Post., $AC = AD + DC = 1.5 + \frac{4.5 \sin 95°}{\sin 52°}$. By the Law of Cosines, $AB^2 = \left(1.5 + \frac{4.5 \sin 95°}{\sin 52°}\right)^2 + (4.5)^2 - 2\left(1.5 + \frac{4.5 \sin 95°}{\sin 52°}\right)(4.5)\cos 33° \approx 17.7$. So $AB \approx \sqrt{17.7} \approx 4.2$.

19a. The vector from Tony and Paul's house to Greg's house is ⟨38.0, 81.6⟩, since $90 \cos 65° \approx 38.0$, and $90 \sin 65° \approx 81.6$. The vector from Greg's house to the vacation spot is ⟨50, 0⟩, since the route has a horiz. change of 50 mi and a vert. change of 0 mi.

b. The vector for the direct route from Tony and Paul's house to the vacation spot is ⟨38.0, 81.6⟩ + ⟨50, 0⟩ = ⟨88.0, 81.6⟩. The magnitude is $\sqrt{88.0^2 + 81.6^2} = \sqrt{14{,}402.56} \approx 120.0$. The direction is $\tan^{-1}\left(\frac{81.6}{88.0}\right) \approx 42.8°$, or N 47.2° E.

c. Tony traveled a distance of 140 mi at 50 mi/h. He traveled for $\frac{140}{50} = 2.8$ h. Paul traveled for 2.8 h, covering a distance of 120 mi. So his speed was $\frac{120}{2.8} \approx 42.9$ mi/h.

Organizer

Objective: Choose appropriate problem-solving strategies and use them with skills from Chapters 7 and 8 to solve real-world problems.

The John Hancock Center

Reading Strategies

Students must use their answer from **Problem 2** to solve **Problems 3** and **4.** As they read **Problems 3** and **4,** ask students what information they need to answer the questions. Then ask them whether that information is in the chart or in the work they have already done.

Using Data Be sure students understand that the elevation of the sun presented in the chart represents an angle of elevation. Have students look for a trend within the data. Ask them if this trend matches their own observations about the sun's position in the sky at various times of the year.

State Resources

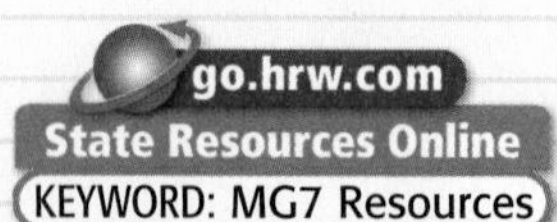

The John Hancock Center

The 100-story John Hancock Center is one of the most distinctive features of the Chicago skyline. With its combination of stores, offices, and 49 floors of apartments, the John Hancock Center is the world's tallest multifunctional skyscraper.

Choose one or more strategies to solve each problem.

1. The building's observation deck is on the 94th floor, 1000 ft above street level. The deck is equipped with telescopes that offer close-up views of the surrounding city. Using one of the telescopes, a visitor spots a ship on Lake Michigan. The angle of depression to the ship is 10°. To the nearest foot, how far is the ship from the base of the building? **5671 ft**

For 2–4, use the table.

2. At noon on May 15, the shadow of the John Hancock Center, including its antenna, is 818.2 ft long. Find the height of the building to the nearest foot. **1476 ft**
3. How long is the shadow of the building at noon on October 15? Round to the nearest foot. **1823 ft**
4. On which of the dates shown is the building's shadow the longest? What is the length of the shadow to the nearest foot? **Dec 15; 3165 ft**

Elevation of the Sun in Chicago, Illinois

Date	Angle of Elevation at Noon (°)
January 15	27
February 15	34
March 15	46
April 15	58
May 15	61
June 15	71
July 15	70
August 15	62
September 15	51
October 15	39
November 15	29
December 15	25

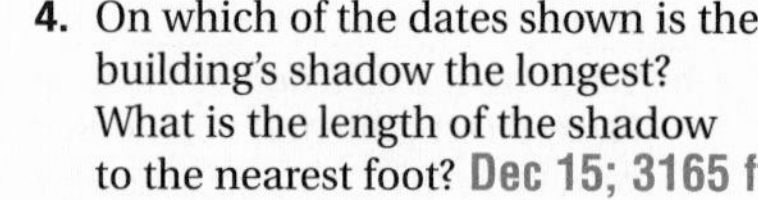

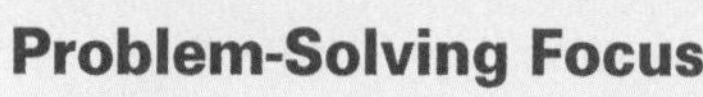

Problem-Solving Focus

For **Problem 1,** focus on the final step of the problem-solving process: **(4) Look Back.** Ask students if their answer seems reasonable. Remind students that 1 mile equals 5280 feet, and have them estimate the distance to the ship in miles.

Ernest Hemingway's Birthplace

The Nobel Prize-winning author Ernest Hemingway (1899–1961) was born in Oak Park, Illinois. Visitors to Oak Park, a suburb of Chicago, can tour the home where Hemingway was born and spent much of his childhood. Thanks to a recent restoration, the house appears just as it did when Hemingway lived there.

Choose one or more strategies to solve each problem.

1. The blueprint shown below was used during the restoration of the first floor of Hemingway's house. As part of the restoration project, a narrow border of wallpaper was placed along the edge of the ceiling around the perimeter of the dining room. Approximately how many feet of wallpaper were needed? **about 56 ft**
2. During the restoration, the floor of the parlor and living room was covered with red carpet. Estimate the number of square feet of carpet that were used. **Possible answer: 288 ft²**
3. Hemingway's childhood bedroom is located on the second floor of the house. The bedroom has a perimeter of 40 ft, and its length is 4 ft more than its width. Assuming the blueprint for the second floor uses the same scale as the blueprint below, what are the dimensions of the bedroom on the blueprint for the second floor? **$\frac{3}{4}$ in. by $\frac{1}{2}$ in.**

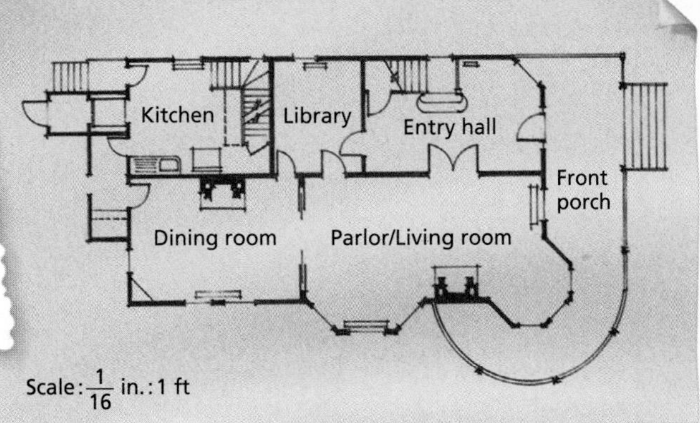

Real-World Connections

Ernest Hemingway's Birthplace

Reading Strategies

ENGLISH LANGUAGE LEARNERS

Have students read **Problem 1,** and then ask them to restate the problem in their own words. Have students identify the essential information in the problem. If students are unfamiliar with the word *restoration*, ask them to guess its meaning from the context or by considering its root, *restore*.

Using Data Ask students to identify and explain the scale of the blueprint. $\frac{1}{16}$ in. : 1 ft. Possible answer: $\frac{1}{16}$ in. on the blueprint represents 1 ft on the actual house. Make sure students understand what is meant by this scale. Tell students that a wall on the blueprint is 1 in. long, and ask them how long the actual wall would be. 16 ft

Problem-Solving Focus

Have students compare the different problem-solving strategies they used to solve **Problem 3.** Some students might have drawn a diagram of the bedroom to organize the given information. Others may have used a guess-and-test approach to determine the length and width of the room. Have students discuss the pros and cons of each strategy.

Discuss the effect of the scale on linear measurements, as in **Problem 1,** versus measurements of area, as in **Problem 2.** Remind students that each dimension must be multiplied by the scale factor.

Extending Perimeter, Circumference, and Area

Section 9A

Developing Geometric Formulas

- **Connecting Geometry to Algebra** Literal Equations
- **9-1 Developing Formulas for Triangles and Quadrilaterals**
- **9-2 Geometry Lab** Develop π
- **9-2 Developing Formulas for Circles and Regular Polygons**
- **9-3 Composite Figures**
- **Connecting Geometry to Trigonometry** Triangle Area Formulas

Section 9B

Applying Geometric Formulas

- **9-4 Perimeter and Area in the Coordinate Plane**
- **9-5 Effects of Changing Dimensions Proportionally**
- **Connecting Geometry to Probability** Probability
- **9-6 Geometric Probability**
- **9-6 Geometry Lab** Use Geometric Probability to Estimate π

Pacing Guide for 45-Minute Classes

Teacher One Stop™
Calendar Planner®

Chapter 9

Countdown Weeks 19, 20, 21

DAY 1	DAY 2	DAY 3	DAY 4	DAY 5
Connecting Geometry to Algebra	9-1 Lesson	9-1 Lesson	9-2 Geometry Lab	9-2 Lesson
DAY 6	**DAY 7**	**DAY 8**	**DAY 9**	**DAY 10**
9-3 Lesson	9-3 Geometry Lab	Multi-Step Test Prep Ready to Go On?	9-4 Lesson	9-5 Lesson
DAY 11	**DAY 12**	**DAY 13**	**DAY 14**	**DAY 15**
Connecting Geometry to Probability 9-6 Lesson	9-6 Lesson 9-6 Geometry Lab	Multi-Step Test Prep Ready to Go On?	Chapter 9 Review	Chapter 9 Test

Pacing Guide for 90-Minute Classes

Teacher One Stop™
Calendar Planner®

Chapter 9

DAY 1	DAY 2	DAY 3	DAY 4	DAY 5
Chapter 8 Test Connecting Geometry to Algebra	9-1 Lesson	9-2 Geometry Lab 9-2 Lesson	9-3 Lesson 9-3 Geometry Lab	Multi-Step Test Prep Ready to Go On? 9-4 Lesson
DAY 6	**DAY 7**	**DAY 8**		
9-5 Lesson Connecting Geometry to Probability 9-6 Lesson	9-6 Lesson 9-6 Geometry Lab Multi-Step Test Prep Ready to Go On?	Chapter 9 Review Chapter 9 Test		

ONGOING ASSESSMENT and INTERVENTION

Assess Prior Knowledge

Before Chapter 9

DIAGNOSE	PRESCRIBE
Diagnose readiness for the chapter.	Prescribe intervention.
Are You Ready? SE p. 585	 ***Are You Ready? Intervention***

Formative Assessment

Before Every Lesson

DIAGNOSE	PRESCRIBE
Diagnose readiness for the lesson.	Prescribe intervention.
Warm Up TE	**Reteach** CRB

During Every Lesson

DIAGNOSE	PRESCRIBE
Diagnose understanding of lesson concepts.	Prescribe intervention.
Check It Out! SE	**Reading Strategies** CRB
Questioning Strategies TE	***Success for Every Learner***
Think and Discuss SE	***Lesson Tutorial Videos***
Write About It SE	
Journal TE	

After Every Lesson

DIAGNOSE	PRESCRIBE
Diagnose mastery of lesson concepts.	Prescribe intervention.
Lesson Quiz TE	**Reteach** CRB
Test Prep SE	**Test Prep Doctor** TE
Test and Practice Generator	***Homework Help*** **Online**

Before Chapter 9 Testing

DIAGNOSE	PRESCRIBE
Diagnose mastery of concepts in chapter.	Prescribe intervention.
Ready to Go On? SE pp. 615, 639	***Ready to Go On? Intervention***
Multi-Step Test Prep SE pp. 614, 638	**Scaffolding Questions** TE pp. 614, 638
Section Quizzes AR	**Reteach** CRB
Test and Practice Generator	***Lesson Tutorial Videos***

Before High Stakes Testing

DIAGNOSE	PRESCRIBE
Diagnose mastery of benchmark concepts.	Prescribe intervention.
College Entrance Exam Practice SE p. 645	***College Entrance Exam Practice***
Standardized Test Prep SE pp. 648–649	

Summative Assessment

After Chapter 9

DIAGNOSE	PRESCRIBE
Check mastery of chapter concepts.	Prescribe intervention.
Multiple-Choice Tests (Forms A, B, C)	**Reteach** CRB
Free-Response Tests (Forms A, B, C)	 ***Lesson Tutorial Videos***
Performance Assessment AR	
Cumulative Test AR	
Test and Practice Generator	

KEY: **SE** = *Student Edition* **TE** = *Teacher's Edition* **CRB** = *Chapter Resource Book* **AR** = *Assessment Resources*  Available online Available on CD- or DVD-ROM

Lesson Resources

Before the Lesson

Prepare
- ***Teacher One Stop*** SPANISH
  - Editable lesson plans
  - Calendar Planner
  - Easy access to all chapter resources
- ***Lesson Transparencies***
  - Teacher Tools

Teach the Lesson

Introduce
- ***Alternate Openers: Explorations***
- ***Lesson Transparencies***
  - Warm Up
  - Problem of the Day

Teach
- ***Lesson Transparencies***
  - Teaching Transparencies
- ***Know-It Notebook™***
  - Vocabulary
  - Key Concepts
- ***Power Presentations***
- ***Lesson Tutorial Videos*** 
- ***Interactive Online Edition*** 
  - Lesson Activities
  - Lesson Tutorial Videos
- ***Lab Activities***
- ***Lab Resources Online***
- ***Online Interactivities*** 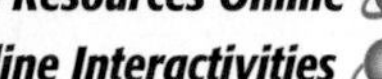 
- ***TechKeys***  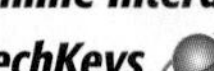

Practice the Lesson

Practice
- ***Chapter Resources***
  - Practice A, B, C
- ***Practice and Problem Solving Workbook***
- ***IDEA Works!® Modified Worksheets and Tests***
- ***ExamView Test and Practice Generator***
- ***Homework Help Online***
- ***Online Interactivities*** SPANISH
- ***Interactive Online Edition***
  - Homework Help

Apply
- ***Chapter Resources***
  - Problem Solving
- ***Practice and Problem Solving Workbook***
- ***Interactive Online Edition***
  - Chapter Project
- ***Project Teacher Support*** 

After the Lesson

Reteach
- ***Chapter Resources***
  - Reteach
  - Reading Strategies 
- ***Success for Every Learner***

Review
- ***Interactive Answers and Solutions***
- ***Solutions Key***
- ***Know-It Notebook™***
  - Big Ideas
  - Chapter Review

Extend
- ***Chapter Resources***
  - Challenge

Technology Highlights for the Teacher

 Power Presentations

Dynamic presentations to engage students. Complete PowerPoint® presentations for every lesson in Chapter 9.

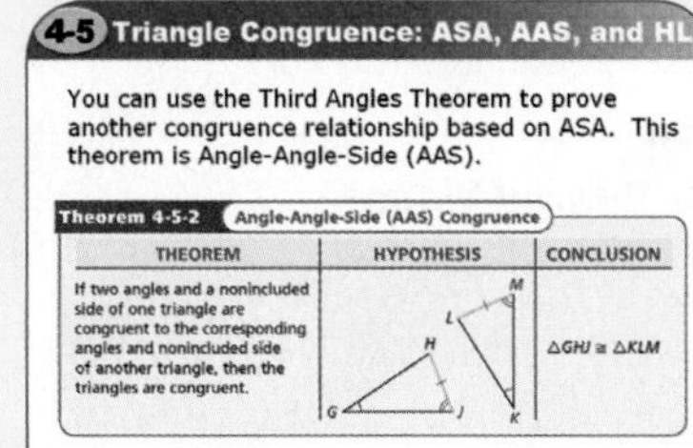

Teacher One Stop SPANISH

Easy access to Chapter 9 resources and assessments. Includes lesson planning, test generation, and puzzle creation software.

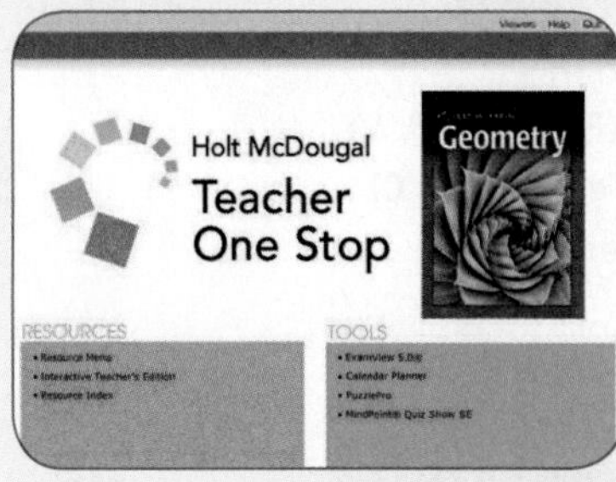

Premier Online Edition SPANISH

Chapter 9 includes Tutorial Videos, Lesson Activities, Lesson Quizzes, Homework Help, and Chapter Project.

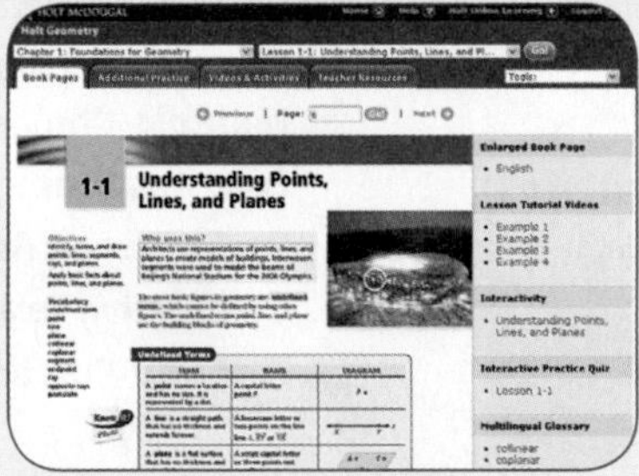

KEY: **SE** = *Student Edition* **TE** = *Teacher's Edition*  English Language Learners  Spanish version available  Available online  Available on CD- or DVD-ROM

Reaching All Learners

Teaching tips to help all learners appear throughout the chapter. A few that target specific students are included in the lists below.

All Learners

- ***Lab Activities***
- ***Practice and Problem Solving Workbook***
- ***Know-It Notebook***

Special Needs Students

- **Practice A** .... CRB
- **Reteach** .... CRB
- **Reading Strategies** .... CRB
- **Are You Ready?** .... SE p. 585
- **Inclusion** .... TE pp. 592, 596, 601, 613, 625
- ***IDEA Works!® Modified Worksheets and Tests***
- ***Ready to Go On? Intervention*** SPANISH
- ***Know-It Notebook***
- ***Online Interactivities***  SPANISH
- ***Lesson Tutorial Videos***  SPANISH

Developing Learners

- **Practice A** .... CRB
- **Reteach** .... CRB
- **Reading Strategies** .... CRB
- **Are You Ready?** .... SE p. 585
- **Vocabulary Connections** .... SE p. 586
- **Questioning Strategies** .... TE
- ***Ready to Go On? Intervention*** SPANISH
- ***Know-It Notebook***
- ***Homework Help Online*** 
- ***Online Interactivities***  SPANISH
- ***Lesson Tutorial Videos***  SPANISH

On-Level Learners

- **Practice B** .... CRB
- **Problem Solving** .... CRB
- **Vocabulary Connections** .... SE p. 586
- **Questioning Strategies** .... TE
- ***Ready to Go On? Intervention*** SPANISH
- ***Know-It Notebook***
- ***Homework Help Online***
- ***Online Interactivities***  SPANISH

Advanced Learners

- **Practice C** .... CRB
- **Challenge** .... CRB
- **Challenge Exercises** .... SE
- **Reading and Writing Math** *Extend* .... TE p. 587
- **Critical Thinking** .... TE pp. 603, 618, 623, 626
- ***Are You Ready? Enrichment*** SPANISH
- ***Ready To Go On? Enrichment*** SPANISH

English Language Learners

ENGLISH LANGUAGE LEARNERS

- **Reading Strategies** .... CRB
- **Are You Ready? Vocabulary** .... SE p. 585
- **Vocabulary Connections** .... SE p. 586
- **Vocabulary Review** .... SE p. 640
- **English Language Learners** .... TE pp. 587, 607, 611
- ***Success for Every Learner***
- ***Know-It Notebook***
- ***Spanish Study Guide (Resumen y Repaso)***
- ***Multilingual Glossary***
- ***Lesson Tutorial Videos***  

Technology Highlights for Reaching All Learners

 **Lesson Tutorial Videos** 

Starring Holt authors Ed Burger and Freddie Renfro! Live tutorials to support every lesson in Chapter 9.

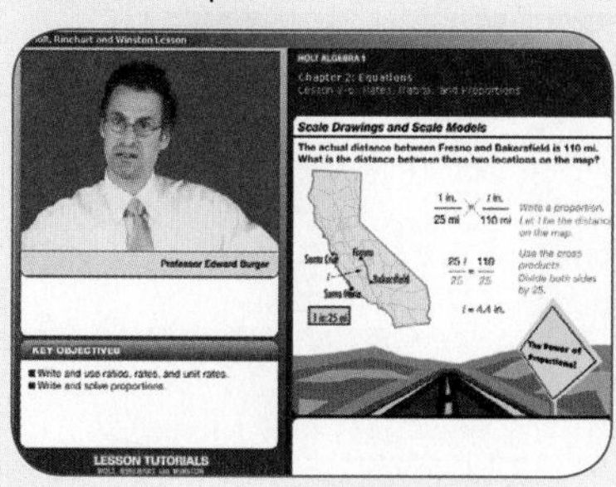

Multilingual Glossary

Searchable glossary includes definitions in English, Spanish, Vietnamese, Chinese, Hmong, Korean, and 4 other languages.

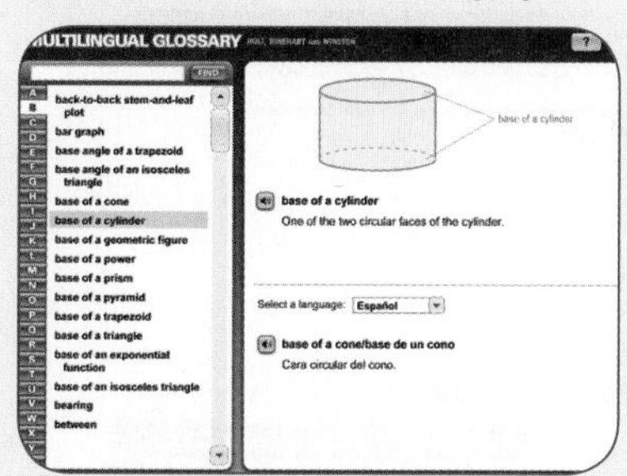

Online Interactivities

Interactive tutorials provide visually engaging alternative opportunities to learn concepts and master skills.

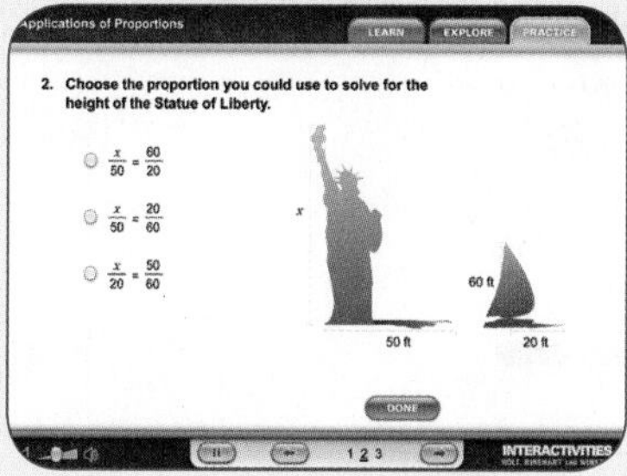

KEY: **SE** = *Student Edition* **TE** = *Teacher's Edition* **CRB** = *Chapter Resource Book* SPANISH Spanish version available · Available online · Available on CD- or DVD-ROM

Ongoing Assessment

Assessing Prior Knowledge

Determine whether students have the prerequisite concepts and skills for success in Chapter 9.

Are You Ready? SPANISH .... SE p. 585
Warm Up .... TE

Test Preparation

Provide review and practice for Chapter 9 and standardized tests.

Multi-Step Test Prep .... SE pp. 614, 638
Study Guide: Review .... SE pp. 642–643
Test Tackler .... SE pp. 646–647
Standardized Test Prep .... SE pp. 648–649
College Entrance Exam Practice .... SE p. 645
Countdown to Testing .... SE pp. C4-C27
IDEA Works!® Modified Worksheets and Tests

Alternative Assessment

Assess students' understanding of Chapter 9 concepts and combined problem-solving skills.

Chapter 9 Project .... SE p. 584
Alternative Assessment .... TE
Performance Assessment .... AR
Portfolio Assessment .... AR

Lesson Assessment

Provide formative assessment for each lesson of Chapter 9.

Questioning Strategies .... TE
Think and Discuss .... SE
Check It Out! Exercises .... SE
Write About It .... SE
Journal .... TE
Lesson Quiz .... TE
Alternative Assessment .... TE
IDEA Works!® Modified Worksheets and Tests

Weekly Assessment

Provide formative assessment for each section of Chapter 9.

Multi-Step Test Prep .... SE pp. 614, 638
Ready to Go On? SPANISH .... SE pp. 615, 639
Section Quizzes .... AR
Test and Practice Generator .... *Teacher One Stop*

Chapter Assessment

Provide summative assessment of Chapter 9 mastery.

Chapter 9 Test .... SE p. 644
Chapter Test (Levels A, B, C) .... AR
- Multiple Choice
- Free Response

Cumulative Test .... AR
Test and Practice Generator .... *Teacher One Stop*
IDEA Works!® Modified Worksheets and Tests

Technology Highlights for Assessment

Automatically assess readiness and prescribe intervention for Chapter 9 prerequisite skills.

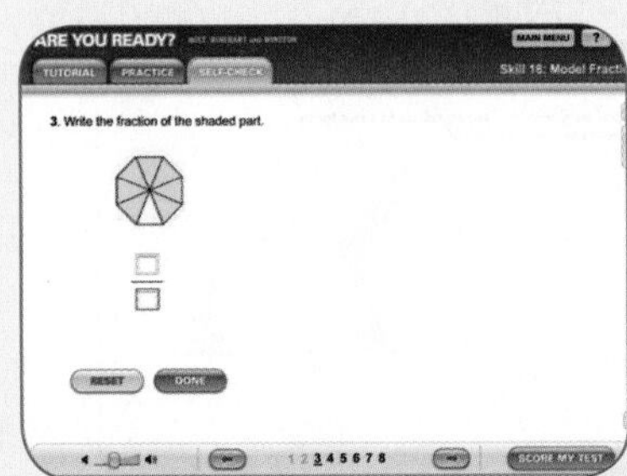

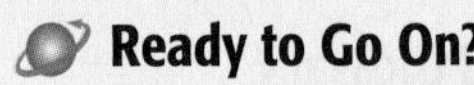

Automatically assess understanding of and prescribe intervention for Sections 9A and 9B.

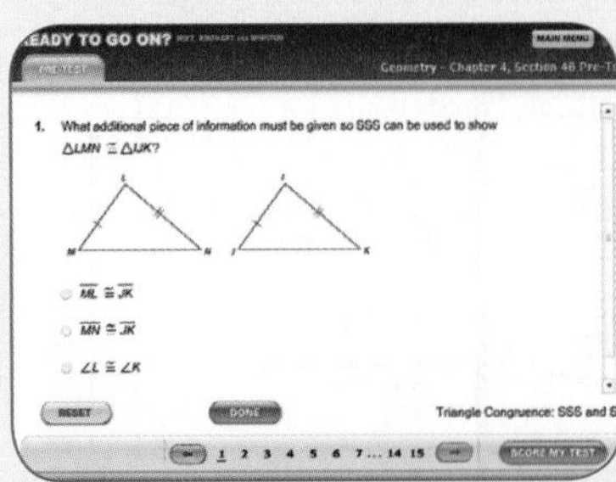

Test and Practice Generator

Use Chapter 9 problem banks to create assessments and worksheets to print out or deliver online. Includes dynamic problems.

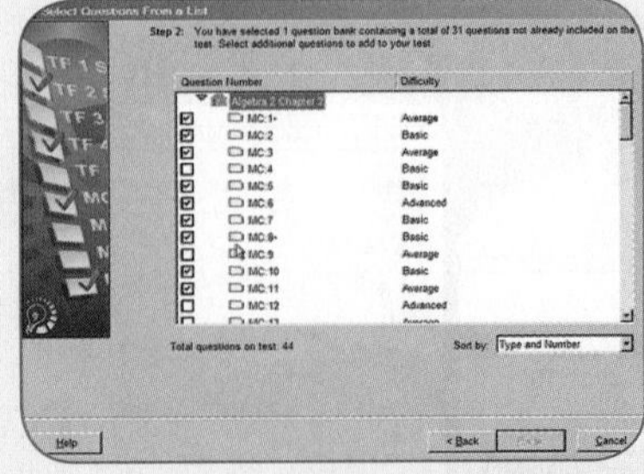

KEY: **SE** = *Student Edition* **TE** = *Teacher's Edition* **AR** = *Assessment Resources* SPANISH Spanish version available 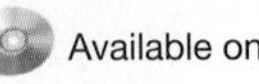 Available online Available on CD- or DVD-ROM

Three levels (A, B, C) of multiple-choice and free-response chapter tests, along with a performance assessment, are available in the *Assessment Resources.*

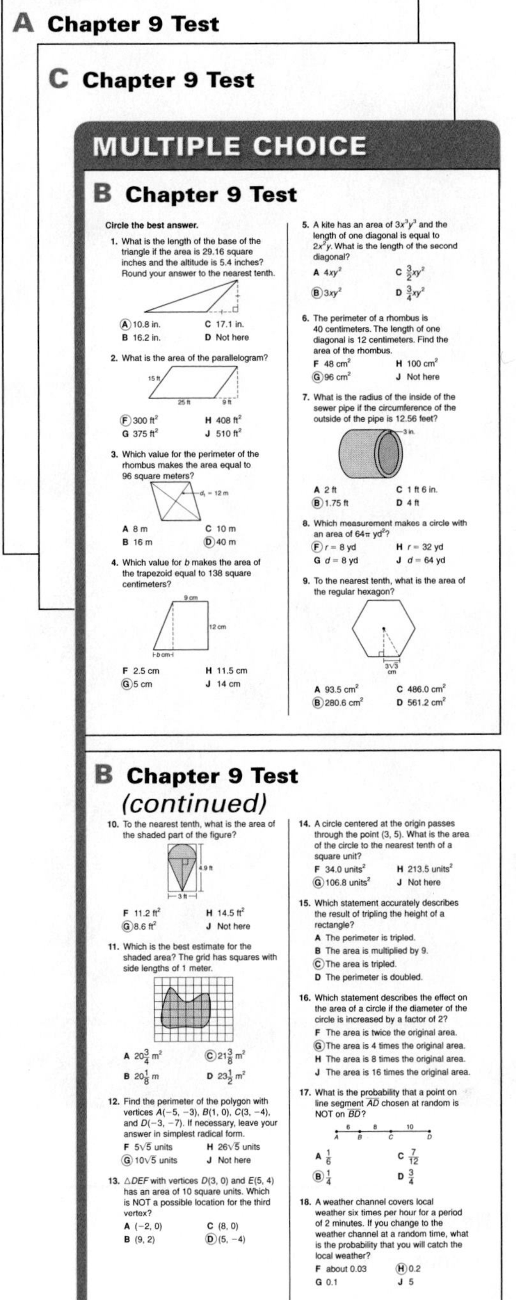

A Chapter 9 Test

C Chapter 9 Test

MULTIPLE CHOICE

B Chapter 9 Test

Circle the best answer.

1. What is the length of the base of the triangle if the area is 29.16 square inches and the altitude is 5.4 inches? Round your answer to the nearest tenth.
   (A) 10.8 in. C 17.1 in.
   B 16.2 in. D Not here
2. What is the area of the parallelogram?
   (F) 300 ft² H 408 ft²
   G 375 ft² J 510 ft²
3. Which value for the perimeter of the rhombus makes the area equal to 96 square meters?
   A 8 m C 10 m
   B 16 m (D) 40 m
4. Which value for b makes the area of the trapezoid equal to 138 square centimeters?
   F 2.5 cm H 11.5 cm
   (G) 5 cm J 14 cm
5. A kite has an area of $3x^3y^3$ and the length of one diagonal is equal to $2x^2y$. What is the length of the second diagonal?
   A $4xy^2$ C $\frac{3}{2}xy^2$
   (B) $3xy^2$ D $\frac{3}{4}xy^2$
6. The perimeter of a rhombus is 40 centimeters. The length of one diagonal is 12 centimeters. Find the area of the rhombus.
   F 48 cm² H 100 cm²
   (G) 96 cm² J Not here
7. What is the radius of the inside of the sewer pipe if the circumference of the outside of the pipe is 12.56 feet?
   A 2 ft C 1 ft 6 in.
   (B) 1.75 ft D 4 ft
8. Which measurement makes a circle with an area of 64π yd²?
   (F) $r = 8$ yd H $r = 32$ yd
   G $d = 8$ yd J $d = 64$ yd
9. To the nearest tenth, what is the area of the regular hexagon?
   A 93.5 cm² C 486.0 cm²
   (B) 280.6 cm² D 561.2 cm²

B Chapter 9 Test (continued)

10. To the nearest tenth, what is the area of the shaded part of the figure?
    F 11.2 ft² H 14.5 ft²
    (G) 8.6 ft² J Not here
11. Which is the best estimate for the shaded area? The grid has squares with side lengths of 1 meter.
    A $20\frac{3}{4}$ m² (C) $21\frac{3}{8}$ m²
    B $20\frac{1}{8}$ m D $23\frac{1}{4}$ m²
12. Find the perimeter of the polygon with vertices $A(-5, -3)$, $B(1, 0)$, $C(3, -4)$, and $D(-3, -7)$. If necessary, leave your answer in simplest radical form.
    F $5\sqrt{5}$ units H $26\sqrt{5}$ units
    (G) $10\sqrt{5}$ units J Not here
13. $\triangle DEF$ with vertices $D(3, 0)$ and $E(5, 4)$ has an area of 10 square units. Which is NOT a possible location for the third vertex?
    A (−2, 0) C (8, 0)
    B (9, 2) (D) (5, −4)
14. A circle centered at the origin passes through the point (3, 5). What is the area of the circle to the nearest tenth of a square unit?
    F 34.0 units² H 213.5 units²
    (G) 106.8 units² J Not here
15. Which statement accurately describes the result of tripling the height of a rectangle?
    A The perimeter is tripled.
    B The area is multiplied by 9.
    (C) The area is tripled.
    D The perimeter is doubled.
16. Which statement describes the effect on the area of a circle if the diameter of the circle is increased by a factor of 2?
    F The area is twice the original area.
    (G) The area is 4 times the original area.
    H The area is 8 times the original area.
    J The area is 16 times the original area.
17. What is the probability that a point on line segment $\overline{AD}$ chosen at random is NOT on $\overline{BD}$?
    A $\frac{1}{6}$ C $\frac{7}{12}$
    (B) $\frac{1}{4}$ D $\frac{3}{4}$
18. A weather channel covers local weather six times per hour for a period of 2 minutes. If you change to the weather channel at a random time, what is the probability that you will catch the local weather?
    F about 0.03 (H) 0.2
    G 0.1 J 5

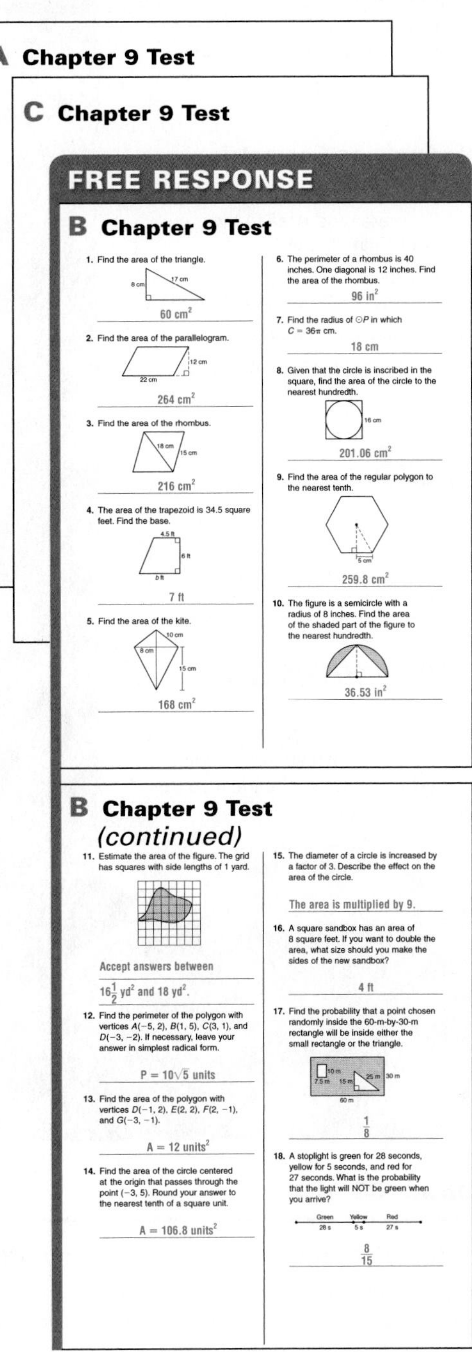

A Chapter 9 Test

C Chapter 9 Test

FREE RESPONSE

B Chapter 9 Test

1. Find the area of the triangle. 60 cm²
2. Find the area of the parallelogram. 264 cm²
3. Find the area of the rhombus. 216 cm²
4. The area of the trapezoid is 34.5 square feet. Find the base. 7 ft
5. Find the area of the kite. 168 cm²
6. The perimeter of a rhombus is 40 inches. One diagonal is 12 inches. Find the area of the rhombus. 96 in²
7. Find the radius of ⊙P in which $C = 36\pi$ cm. 18 cm
8. Given that the circle is inscribed in the square, find the area of the circle to the nearest hundredth. 201.06 cm²
9. Find the area of the regular polygon to the nearest tenth. 259.8 cm²
10. The figure is a semicircle with a radius of 8 inches. Find the area of the shaded part of the figure to the nearest hundredth. 36.53 in²

B Chapter 9 Test (continued)

11. Estimate the area of the figure. The grid has squares with side lengths of 1 yard. Accept answers between $16\frac{1}{2}$ yd² and 18 yd².
12. Find the perimeter of the polygon with vertices $A(-5, 2)$, $B(1, 5)$, $C(3, 1)$, and $D(-3, -2)$. If necessary, leave your answer in simplest radical form. $P = 10\sqrt{5}$ units
13. Find the area of the polygon with vertices $D(-1, 2)$, $E(2, 2)$, $F(2, -1)$, and $G(-3, -1)$. $A = 12$ units²
14. Find the area of the circle centered at the origin that passes through the point (−3, 5). Round your answer to the nearest tenth of a square unit. $A = 106.8$ units²
15. The diameter of a circle is increased by a factor of 3. Describe the effect on the area of the circle. The area is multiplied by 9.
16. A square sandbox has an area of 8 square feet. If you want to double the area, what size should you make the sides of the new sandbox? 4 ft
17. Find the probability that a point chosen randomly inside the 60-m-by-30-m rectangle will be inside either the small rectangle or the triangle. $\frac{1}{8}$
18. A stoplight is green for 28 seconds, yellow for 5 seconds, and red for 27 seconds. What is the probability that the light will NOT be green when you arrive? $\frac{8}{15}$

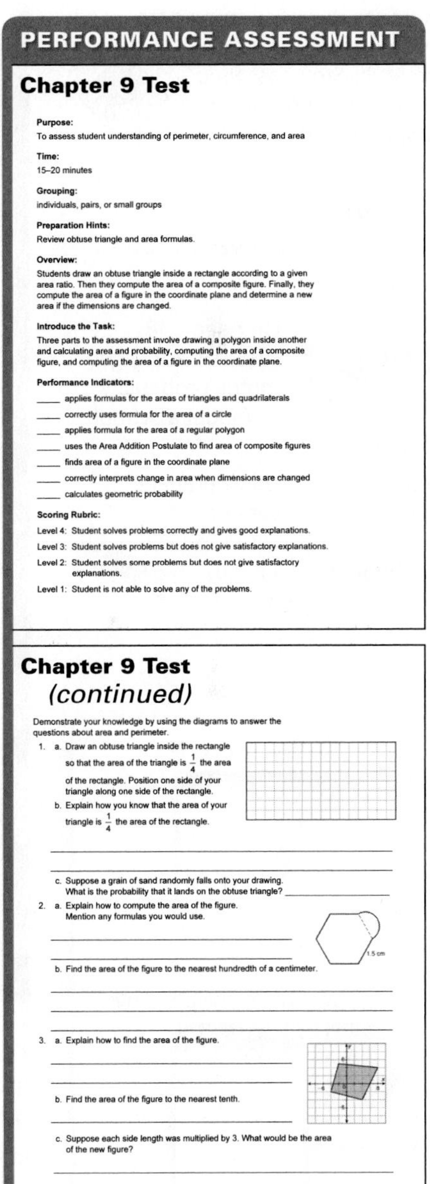

PERFORMANCE ASSESSMENT

Chapter 9 Test

Purpose: To assess student understanding of perimeter, circumference, and area

Time: 15–20 minutes

Grouping: individuals, pairs, or small groups

Preparation Hints: Review obtuse triangle and area formulas.

Overview: Students draw an obtuse triangle inside a rectangle according to a given area ratio. Then they compute the area of a composite figure. Finally, they compute the area of a figure in the coordinate plane and determine a new area if the dimensions are changed.

Introduce the Task: Three parts to the assessment involve drawing a polygon inside another and calculating area and probability, computing the area of a composite figure, and computing the area of a figure in the coordinate plane.

Performance Indicators:

- ____ applies formulas for the areas of triangles and quadrilaterals
- ____ correctly uses formula for the area of a circle
- ____ applies formula for the area of a regular polygon
- ____ uses the Area Addition Postulate to find area of composite figures
- ____ finds area of a figure in the coordinate plane
- ____ correctly interprets change in area when dimensions are changed
- ____ calculates geometric probability

Scoring Rubric:

Level 4: Student solves problems correctly and gives good explanations.

Level 3: Student solves problems but does not give satisfactory explanations.

Level 2: Student solves some problems but does not give satisfactory explanations.

Level 1: Student is not able to solve any of the problems.

Chapter 9 Test (continued)

Demonstrate your knowledge by using the diagrams to answer the questions about area and perimeter.

1. a. Draw an obtuse triangle inside the rectangle so that the area of the triangle is $\frac{1}{4}$ the area of the rectangle. Position one side of your triangle along one side of the rectangle.
   b. Explain how you know that the area of your triangle is $\frac{1}{4}$ the area of the rectangle.
   c. Suppose a grain of sand randomly falls onto your drawing. What is the probability that it lands on the obtuse triangle?
2. a. Explain how to compute the area of the figure. Mention any formulas you would use.
   b. Find the area of the figure to the nearest hundredth of a centimeter.
3. a. Explain how to find the area of the figure.
   b. Find the area of the figure to the nearest tenth.
   c. Suppose each side length was multiplied by 3. What would be the area of the new figure?

Modified chapter tests that address special learning needs are available in *IDEA Works!® Modified Worksheets and Tests.*

Teacher One Stop™

Test & Practice Generator

Create and customize Chapter 9 Tests. Instantly generate multiple test versions, answer keys, and practice versions of test items.

CHAPTER 9

SECTION 9A
Developing Geometric Formulas

MULTI-STEP TEST PREP On page 614, students use area formulas to model a real-world situation, the manufacturing of traffic signs.

Exercises designed to prepare students for success on the Multi-Step Test Prep can be found on pages 595, 604, and 610.

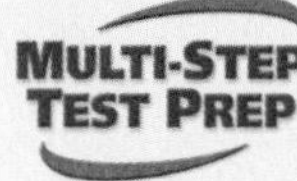

SECTION 9B
Applying Geometric Formulas

MULTI-STEP TEST PREP On page 638, students apply geometric probability to model a school carnival.

Exercises designed to prepare students for success on the Multi-Step Test Prep can be found on pages 620, 626, and 635.

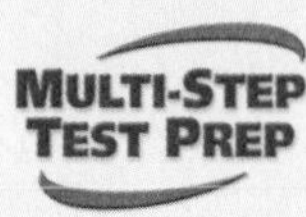

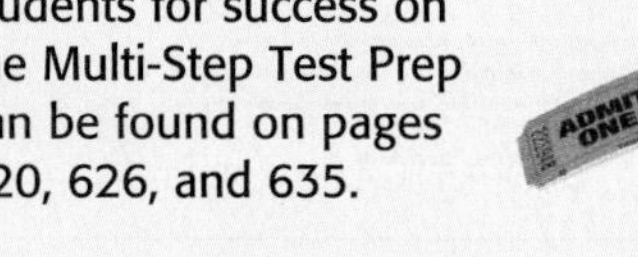

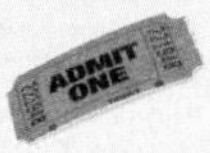

Interactivities Online ▶

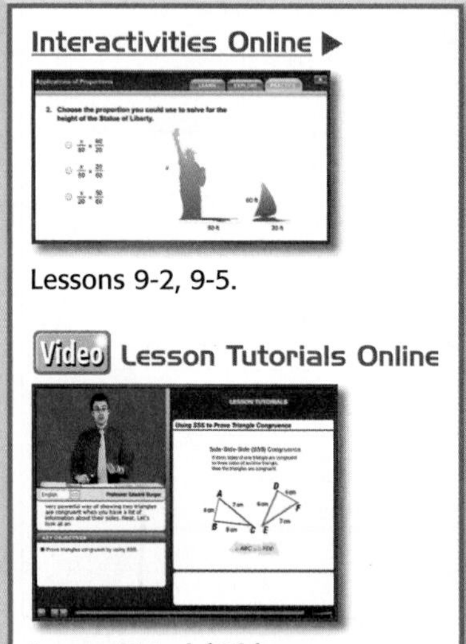

Lessons 9-2, 9-5.

Video Lesson Tutorials Online

Lesson Tutorial Videos are available for EVERY example.

CHAPTER 9

Extending Perimeter, Circumference, and Area

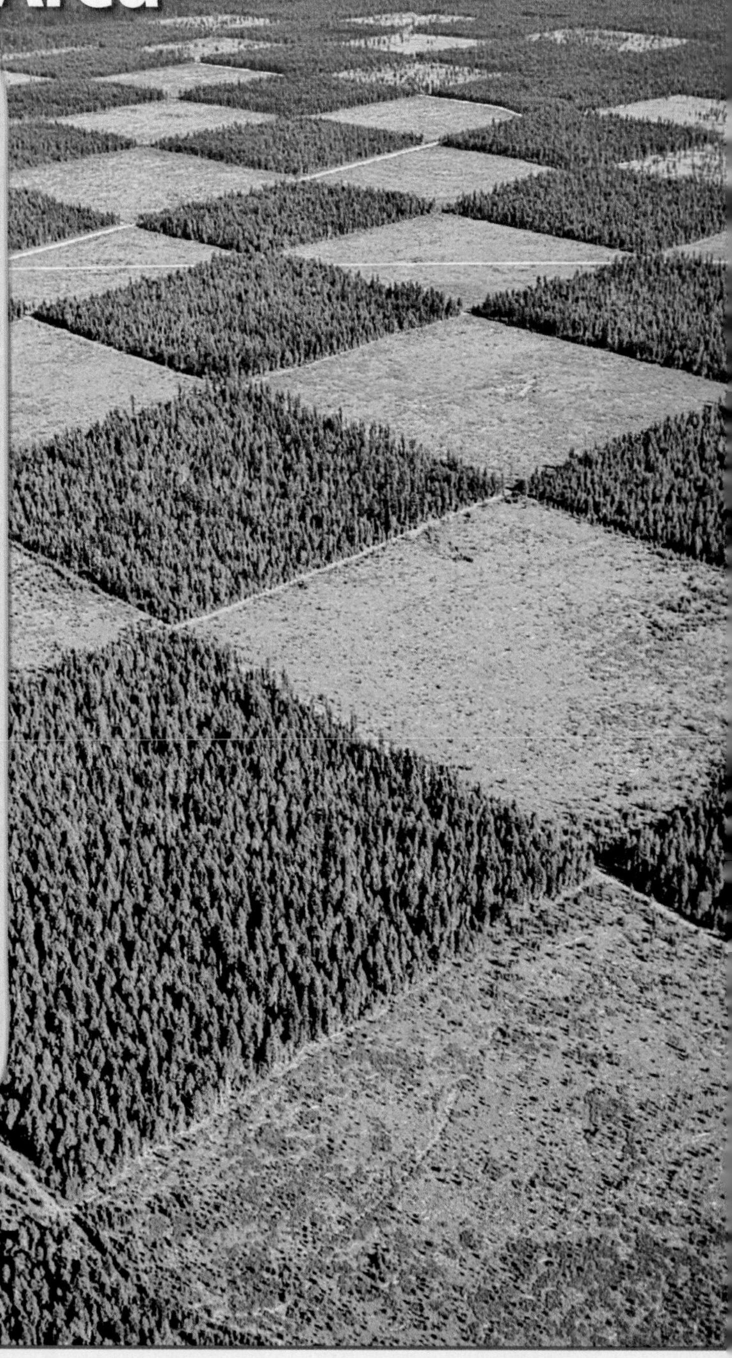

Chapter Focus

- Develop and apply area formulas for circles, polygons, and composite figures.
- Use area to solve geometric probability problems.

It measures up!

How would you find the area of a field or the floor of an irregularly shaped building? You can use the ideas in this chapter to find out!

go.hrw.com
Chapter Project Online
KEYWORD: MG7 ChProj

584 Chapter 9

It Measures Up

About the Project

In the Chapter Project, students begin by making their own trundle wheel. Then they choose an irregularly shaped plot of land near their school and use the trundle wheel to help them calculate the plot's perimeter and area.

Project Resources

All project resources for teachers and students are provided online.

Materials:

- corrugated cardboard, compass, ruler, string, scissors, hammer, nail, wooden stick

go.hrw.com
Project Teacher Support
KEYWORD: MG7 ProjectTS

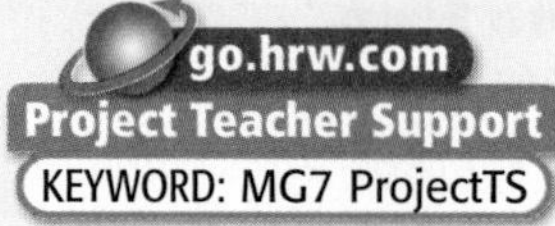

ARE YOU READY?

Vocabulary

Match each term on the left with a definition on the right.

1. area C
2. kite D
3. perimeter E
4. regular polygon A

A. a polygon that is both equilateral and equiangular
B. a quadrilateral with exactly one pair of parallel sides
C. the number of nonoverlapping unit squares of a given size that exactly cover the interior of a figure
D. a quadrilateral with exactly two pairs of adjacent congruent sides
E. the distance around a closed plane figure

Convert Units

Use multiplication or division to change from one unit of measure to another.

5. 12 mi = ▒ yd
6. 7.3 km = ▒ m
7. 6 in. = ▒ ft
8. 15 m = ▒ mm

5. 21,120 6. 7300
7. 0.5 8. 15,000

Length	
Metric	**Customary**
1 kilometer = 1000 meters 1 meter = 100 centimeters 1 centimeter = 10 millimeters	1 mile = 1760 yards 1 mile = 5280 feet 1 yard = 3 feet 1 foot = 12 inches

Pythagorean Theorem

Find x in each right triangle. Round to the nearest tenth, if necessary.

9.
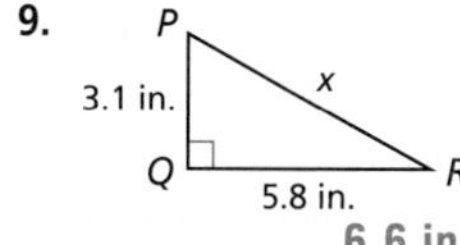

6.6 in.

10.

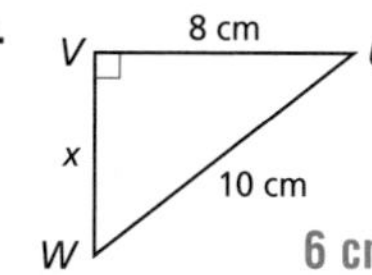

6 cm

11.
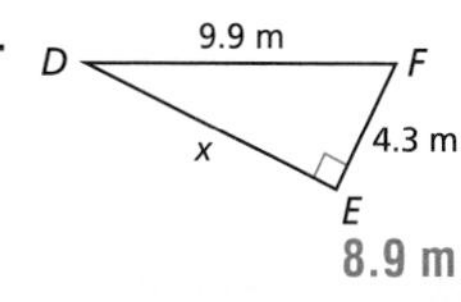

8.9 m

Measure with Customary and Metric Units

Measure each segment to the nearest eighth of an inch and to the nearest half of a centimeter. Note: Segments are reduced in TE.

12. $\frac{5}{8}$ in.; 1.5 cm

13. $1\frac{1}{8}$ in.; 3 cm

14.
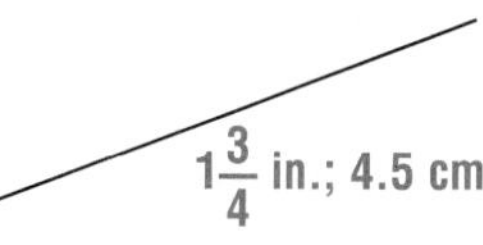
$1\frac{3}{4}$ in.; 4.5 cm

Solve for a Variable

Solve each equation for the indicated variable.

15. $A = \frac{1}{2}bh$ for b $b = \frac{2A}{h}$

16. $P = 2b + 2h$ for h $h = \frac{P - 2b}{2}$

17. $A = \frac{1}{2}(b_1 + b_2)h$ for b_1 $b_1 = \frac{2A}{h} - b_2$

18. $A = \frac{1}{2}d_1d_2$ for d_1 $d_1 = \frac{2A}{d_2}$

CHAPTER 9

ARE YOU READY?

Organizer

Objective: Assess students' understanding of prerequisite skills.

Prerequisite Skills

Convert Units
Pythagorean Theorem
Measure with Customary and Metric Units
Solve for a Variable

Assessing Prior Knowledge

INTERVENTION

Diagnose and Prescribe

Use this page to determine whether intervention is necessary or whether enrichment is appropriate.

Resources

Are You Ready? Intervention and Enrichment **Worksheets**

Are You Ready? **CD-ROM**

Are You Ready? **Online**

my.hrw.com

ARE YOU READY?

Diagnose and Prescribe

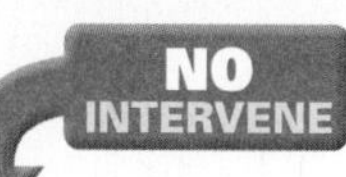

Prerequisite Skill	*Are You Ready? Intervention,* Chapter 9		
	Worksheets	**CD-ROM**	**Online**
Convert Units	Skill 21	Activity 21	Diagnose and Prescribe Online
Pythagorean Theorem	Skill 31	Activity 31	
Measure with Customary and Metric Units	Skill 20	Activity 20	
Solve for a Variable	Skill 72	Activity 72	

Are You Ready? Enrichment, Chapter 9
Worksheets
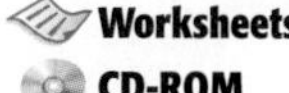
CD-ROM

Online

Study Guide: Preview

Organizer

Objective: Help students organize the new concepts they will learn in Chapter 9.

Online Edition
Multilingual Glossary

Resources

Teacher One Stop™
PuzzleView

Multilingual Glossary **Online**

go.hrw.com
KEYWORD: MG7 Glossary

Answers to *Vocabulary Connections*

1. The center is in the exact middle of the circle. It is the same distance from every point on the circle.
2. a figure made up of different shapes
3. A number that tells how likely an event is to occur; geometric probability is based on geometric properties of a figure, such as area.
4. The apothem is perpendicular to the side of the polygon.

CHAPTER 9

Study Guide: Preview

Where You've Been

Previously, you

- graphed ordered pairs.
- developed and used the Pythagorean Theorem.
- measured with customary and metric units.
- used formulas for area and perimeter.

In This Chapter

You will study

- areas and perimeters of figures whose vertices are given by ordered pairs.
- areas and perimeters of figures whose dimensions are found by using the Pythagorean Theorem.
- areas and perimeters of figures in customary and metric units.
- proofs of formulas for area and perimeter.

Where You're Going

You can use the skills learned in this chapter

- in your future math classes, such as Calculus, to find the area under a curve.
- in other classes, such as in Geography to find lengths of borders and areas of countries.
- outside of school to plan a garden, analyze data in the newspaper, and solve puzzles.

Key Vocabulary/Vocabulario

apothem	apotema
center of a circle	centro de un circulo
center of a regular polygon	centro de un poligono regular
central angle of a regular polygon	ángulo central de un poligono
circle	circulo
composite figure	figuras compuestas
geometric probability	probabilidad geométrica

Vocabulary Connections

To become familiar with some of the vocabulary terms in the chapter, consider the following. You may refer to the chapter, the glossary, or a dictionary if you like.

1. How can you use the everyday meaning of the word *center* to understand the term **center of a circle**?
2. The word *composite* means "of separate parts." What do you think the term **composite figure** means?
3. What does the word *probability* mean? How do you think **geometric probability** differs from theoretical probability?
4. The word **apothem** begins with the root *apo-*, which means "away from." The apothem of a regular polygon is measured "away from" the center to the midpoint of a side. What do you think is true about the apothem and the side of the polygon?

Study Strategy: Memorize Formulas

Throughout a geometry course, you will learn many formulas, theorems, postulates, and corollaries. You may be required to memorize some of these. In order not to become overwhelmed by the amount of information, it helps to use flash cards.

In a right triangle, the two sides that form the right angle are the **legs**. The side across from the right angle that stretches from one leg to the other is the **hypotenuse**. In the diagram, a and b are the lengths of the shorter sides, or legs, of the right triangle. The longest side is called the hypotenuse and has length c.

Know it! Note

Theorem 1-6-1 Pythagorean Theorem

In a right triangle, the sum of the squares of the lengths of the *legs* is equal to the square of the length of the *hypotenuse*.

$$a^2 + b^2 = c^2$$

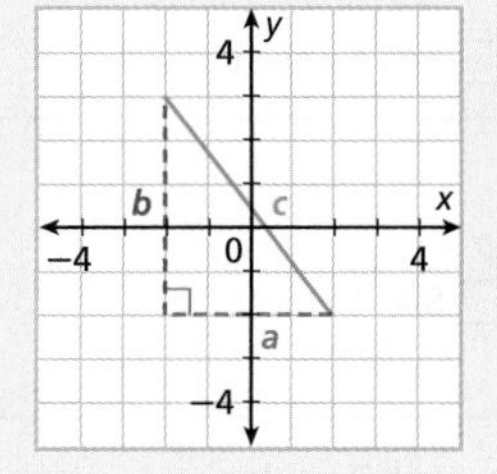

To create a flash card, write the name of the formula or theorem on the front of the card. Then clearly write the appropriate information on the back of the card. Be sure to include a labeled diagram.

Front — Pythagorean Theorem

Back — In a rt. △ with legs a and b and hypotenuse c, $a^2 + b^2 = c^2$ (c, b, a)

Try This

1. Choose a lesson from this book that you have already studied, and make flash cards of the formulas or theorems from the lesson.
2. Review your flash cards by looking at the front of each card and trying to recall the information on the back of the card.

Organizer

Objective: Help students apply strategies to understand and retain key concepts.

Online Edition

Resources

Chapter 9 Resource Book
Reading Strategies

ENGLISH LANGUAGE LEARNERS

Study Strategy: Memorize Formulas

Discuss Students benefit from simplifying difficult concepts on flash cards. Some calculators have a flash card feature that students can use to store information.

Extend As students work through Chapter 9, ask them to create flash cards for each type of problem. They can write the question on the front of the card and the procedure for solving it on the back.

Answers to *Try This*

1–2. Check students' work.

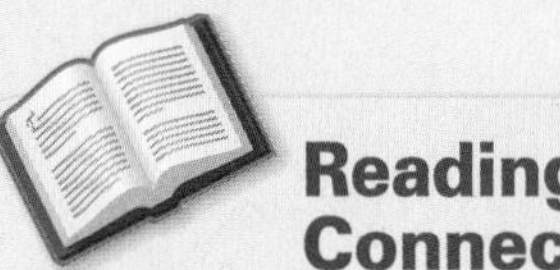

Reading Connection

The Joy of Pi
by David Blatner

Early in their schooling, students learn of a mysterious quantity called pi, a number imbued with many baffling properties. Here is the best explanation of these mysteries students are likely to find, a delightful compendium of stories, jokes, cartoons, and other ephemera relating to pi, including (over many pages) the first million digits of its decimal approximation.

Activity The author provides a series of mnemonic poems for memorizing pi. Have students make up their own such poems to lengths that you specify (e.g., to 20 places).

SECTION

9A Developing Geometric Formulas

One-Minute Section Planner

Lesson	Lab Resources	Materials
Lesson 9-1 Developing Formulas for Triangles and Quadrilaterals • Develop and apply the formulas for the areas of triangles and special quadrilaterals. • Solve problems involving perimeters and areas of triangles and special quadrilaterals. ☐ SAT-10 ☑ NAEP ☐ ACT ☑ SAT ☐ SAT Subject Tests	***Geometry Lab Activities*** 9-1 Geometry Lab	**Optional** scissors
9-2 Geometry Lab Develop π • Use construction and measurement to develop π. ☐ SAT-10 ☐ NAEP ☐ ACT ☐ SAT ☐ SAT Subject Tests	***Geometry Lab Activities*** 9-2 Lab Recording Sheet	**Required** compass (MK), cardboard, measuring tape (MK), scissors, ribbon, straightedge
Lesson 9-2 Developing Formulas for Circles and Regular Polygons • Develop and apply the formulas for the area and circumference of a circle. • Develop and apply the formula for the area of a regular polygon. ☑ SAT-10 ☑ NAEP ☐ ACT ☑ SAT ☑ SAT Subject Tests	***Technology Lab Activities*** 9-2 Technology Lab	**Optional** scissors
Lesson 9-3 Composite Figures • Use the Area Addition Postulate to find the areas of composite figures. • Use composite figures to estimate the areas of irregular shapes. ☐ SAT-10 ☑ NAEP ☐ ACT ☐ SAT ☑ SAT Subject Tests		**Optional** centimeter graph paper

MK = *Manipulatives Kit*

Math Background

Professional Learning

BASIC AREA FORMULAS

Lessons 9-1, 9-2

The fundamental idea in developing area formulas is the Area Addition Postulate: The area of a region is equal to the sum of the areas of the region's nonoverlapping parts. The postulate is analogous to the Segment Addition Postulate and the Angle Addition Postulate. The Area Addition Postulate makes it possible to find the area of a figure by partitioning it into simpler figures whose areas are known.

Another postulate not explicitly stated in the text asserts that the area of a square is the square of its side length. This postulate, plus the Area Addition Postulate, makes it possible to build a logically sound system of area formulas. For example, students may consider it obvious that the area of a rectangle is the product of its base b and height h, but it is interesting to consider the following proof of the familiar formula.

Beginning with a rectangle with base b and height h, let the area of the rectangle be A and construct the figure shown below.

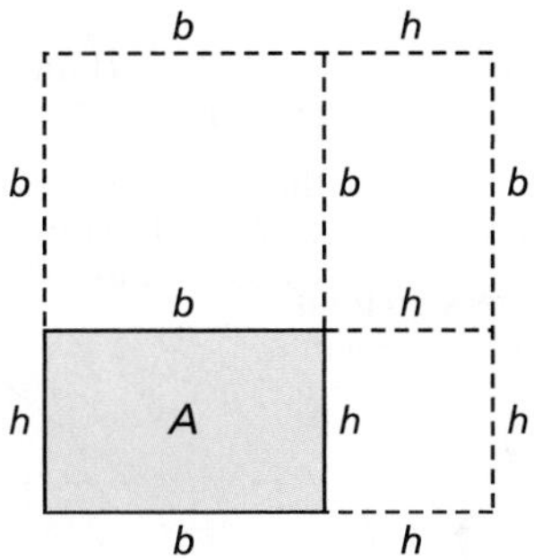

The area of the large square is $(b + h)^2$, but by the Area Addition Postulate, it is also $b^2 + 2A + h^2$ (note that the upper right rectangle has the same area, A, as the blue rectangle). Thus, $(b + h)^2 = b^2 + 2A + h^2$ and squaring the binomial on the left gives $b^2 + 2bh + h^2 = b^2 + 2A + h^2$, which shows that $A = bh$.

From these beginnings it is straightforward to use the Area Addition Postulate to develop formulas for the areas of parallelograms, trapezoids, triangles, rhombuses, kites, and finally, general regular polygons.

UNDERSTANDING PI

Lesson 9-2

The ratio of the circumference to the diameter of any circle is a constant. Ancient Egyptian, Babylonian, and Greek geometers all recognized that this constant ratio is a little greater than 3, with the Babylonians settling on the approximation $3\frac{1}{8}$, or 3.125. In 1706, the mathematician William Jones was the first to represent the constant by the Greek letter pi (π).

Pi is an irrational number, which means that its decimal representation neither terminates nor repeats. The first 20 digits to the right of the decimal point are shown below.

3.14159265358979323846...

For most practical purposes, 3.14 is a satisfactory approximation of pi, but whenever possible students should use the π key on their calculator and then round as needed in the last step of their solution.

One way to visualize the value of pi is to realize that the area of a circle with a radius of one unit (commonly called a unit circle) is pi.

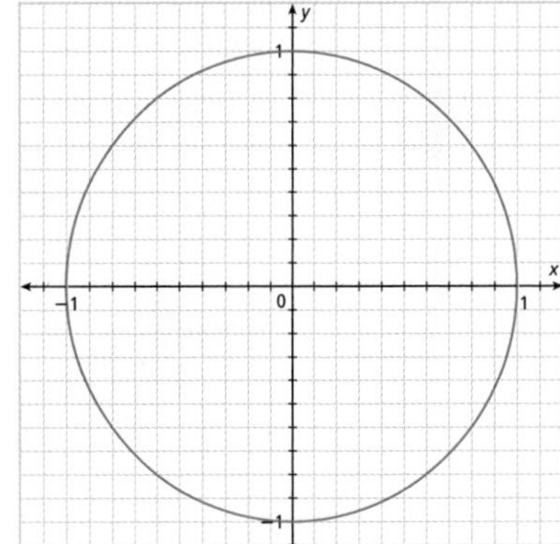

Each square on the grid represents $\frac{1}{100}$ of a square unit. You can count to find that there are about 314 squares inside the circle.

Another way to visualize the value of pi is to imagine a circle of diameter 1 sitting at the origin of a number line. As the circle rolls to the right, the point at the bottom of the circle that was originally touching the number line will next touch the number line again at π.

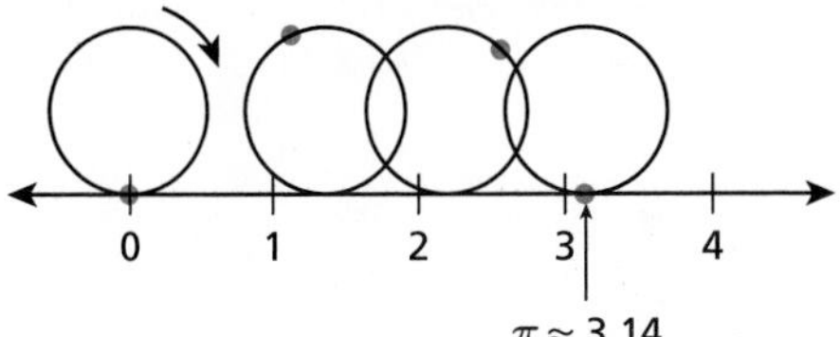

Organizer

Pacing:
Traditional 1 day
Block $\frac{1}{2}$ day

Objective: Apply geometry skills to solving formulas for a variable.

Online Edition

Countdown Week 19

Teach

Remember

Students review and apply solving equations for a variable and substituting values to evaluate an equation.

Algebra Have students look for patterns in their answers that they can use to check their work. For example, if the formula is linear, the answers should form an arithmetic sequence.

Close

Assess

Have students explain how to solve the formula $A = \pi r^2$ for r. Divide both sides by π. Then take the square root of the result.

State Resources

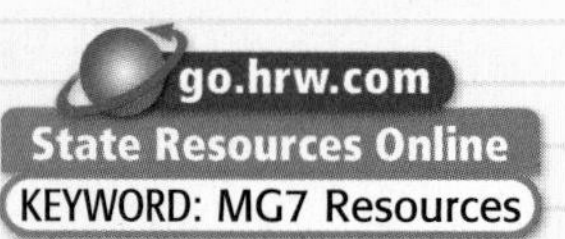

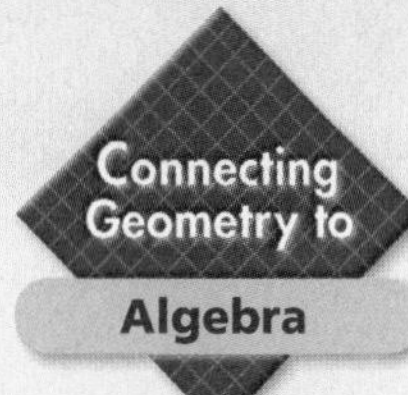

Literal Equations

A *literal equation* contains two or more variables. Formulas you have used to find perimeter, circumference, area, and side relationships of right triangles are examples of literal equations.

If you want to evaluate a formula for several different values of a given variable, it is helpful to solve for the variable first.

Example

Danielle plans to use 50 feet of fencing to build a dog run. Use the formula $P = 2\ell + 2w$ to find the length ℓ when the width w is 4, 5, 6, and 10 feet.

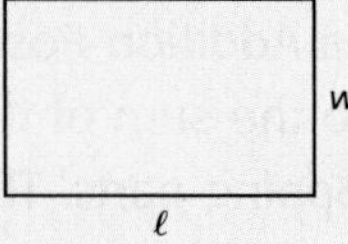

Solve the equation for ℓ.

First solve the formula for the variable.

$P = 2\ell + 2w$ *Write the original equation.*

$P - 2w = 2\ell$ *Subtract 2w from both sides.*

$\frac{P - 2w}{2} = \ell$ *Divide both sides by 2.*

Use your result to find ℓ for each value of w.

$\ell = \frac{P - 2w}{2} = \frac{50 - 2(4)}{2} = 21$ ft *Substitute 50 for P and 4 for w.*

$\ell = \frac{P - 2w}{2} = \frac{50 - 2(5)}{2} = 20$ ft *Substitute 50 for P and 5 for w.*

$\ell = \frac{P - 2w}{2} = \frac{50 - 2(6)}{2} = 19$ ft *Substitute 50 for P and 6 for w.*

$\ell = \frac{P - 2w}{2} = \frac{50 - 2(10)}{2} = 15$ ft *Substitute 50 for P and 10 for w.*

Try This

1. A rectangle has a perimeter of 24 cm. Use the formula $P = 2\ell + 2w$ to find the width when the length is 2, 3, 4, 6, and 8 cm. **w = 10, 9, 8, 6, and 4 cm**
2. A right triangle has a hypotenuse of length $c = 65$ ft. Use the Pythagorean Theorem to find the length of leg a when the length of leg b is 16, 25, 33, and 39 feet. **a = 63, 60, 56, and 52 ft**
3. The perimeter of $\triangle ABC$ is 112 in. Write an expression for a in terms of b and c, and use it to complete the following table. **$a = 112 - b - c$**

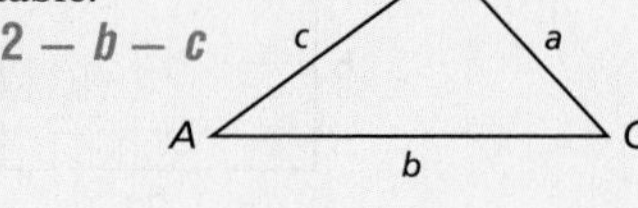

a	b	c
29	48	35
40	36	36
48	14	50

9-1 Developing Formulas for Triangles and Quadrilaterals

Objectives

Develop and apply the formulas for the areas of triangles and special quadrilaterals.

Solve problems involving perimeters and areas of triangles and special quadrilaterals.

Why learn this?

You can use formulas for area to help solve puzzles such as the tangram.

A tangram is an ancient Chinese puzzle made from a square. The pieces can be rearranged to form many different shapes. The area of a figure made with all the pieces is the sum of the areas of the pieces.

Know it! Note

Postulate 9-1-1 Area Addition Postulate

The area of a region is equal to the sum of the areas of its nonoverlapping parts.

Recall that a rectangle with base b and height h has an area of $A = bh$. You can use the Area Addition Postulate to see that a parallelogram has the same area as a rectangle with the same base and height.

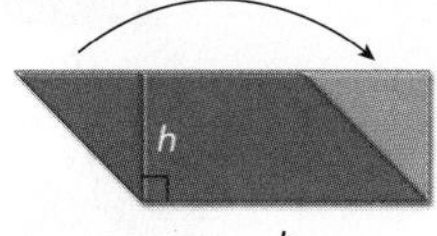

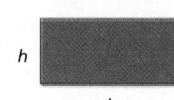

A triangle is cut off one side and translated to the other side.

Area Parallelogram

The area of a parallelogram with base b and height h is $A = bh$.

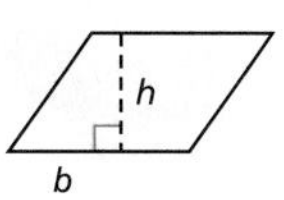

Remember that rectangles and squares are also parallelograms. The area of a square with side s is $A = s^2$, and the perimeter is $P = 4s$.

EXAMPLE  **Finding Measurements of Parallelograms**

Remember!

The height of a parallelogram is measured along a segment perpendicular to a line containing the base.

Find each measurement.

A the area of the parallelogram

Step 1 Use the Pythagorean Theorem to find the height h.

$3^2 + h^2 = 5^2$

$h = 4$

Step 2 Use h to find the area of the parallelogram.

$A = bh$	*Area of a parallelogram*
$A = 6(4)$	*Substitute 6 for b and 4 for h.*
$A = 24\text{ in}^2$	*Simplify.*

5 in. h 6 in. 3 in.

9-1 Organizer

Pacing: Traditional 2 days
Block 1 day

Objectives: Develop and apply the formulas for the areas of triangles and special quadrilaterals.

Solve problems involving perimeter and area of triangles and special quadrilaterals.

Geometry Lab
In *Geometry Lab Activities*

Online Edition
Tutorial Videos

Countdown Week 19

Power Presentations with PowerPoint®

Warm Up

Find the unknown side length in each right triangle with legs *a* and *b* and hypotenuse *c*.

1. $a = 20, b = 21$ $c = 29$

2. $b = 21, c = 35$ $a = 28$

3. $a = 20, c = 52$ $b = 48$

Also available on transparency

Photographer: What are you doing in my darkroom?

Math Student: I'm waiting for my formula to develop!

1 Introduce

EXPLORATION

9-1 Developing Formulas for Triangles and Quadrilaterals

The area of a rectangle is its length times its width. If a rectangle has base b and height h, its area is given by the formula $A = bh$. You can use this to derive the area formula for a parallelogram.

1. Place a ruler at a diagonal on a sheet of lined notebook paper. Draw lines on either side of the ruler. Use these lines and two parallel lines on the paper to draw a parallelogram.

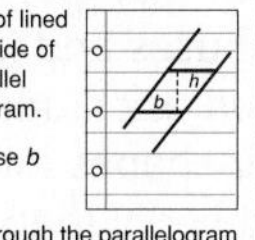

2. Cut out the parallelogram. Label its base b and its height h.
3. Find a way to make one straight cut through the parallelogram so that the two pieces of the parallelogram can be rearranged to form a rectangle.
4. How does the area of the rectangle compare to the area of the parallelogram?
5. What is the area of the rectangle in terms of b and h? What is the area of the parallelogram in terms of b and h?

THINK AND DISCUSS

6. Show how to write your results as a formula.

A B 4 cm D

Motivate

Have students copy the figure shown, cut out the pieces, and arrange them to form a rectangle. Discuss the relationship between the area of the original triangle and the area of the rectangle.

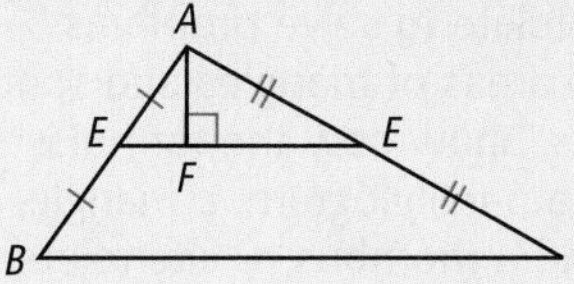

Explorations and answers are provided in *Alternate Openers: Explorations Transparencies.*

go.hrw.com
State Resources Online
KEYWORD: MG7 Resources

Power Presentations with PowerPoint®

Additional Examples

Example 1

Find each measurement.

A. the area of the parallelogram

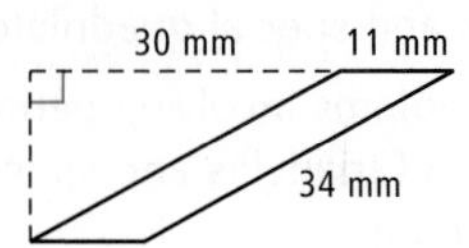

$A = 176 \text{ mm}^2$

B. the height of a rectangle in which $b = 3$ in. and $A = (6x^2 + 24x - 6) \text{ in}^2$

$h = (2x^2 + 8x - 2)$ in.

C. the perimeter of the rectangle, in which $A = (79.8x^2 - 42) \text{ cm}^2$

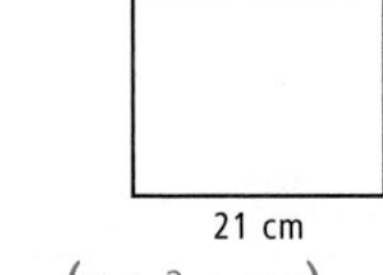

$P = (7.6x^2 + 38)$ cm

Example 2

Find each measurement.

A. the area of a trapezoid in which $b_1 = 8$ in., $b_2 = 5$ in., and $h = 6.2$ in. $A = 40.3 \text{ in}^2$

B. the base of the triangle, in which $A = (15x^2) \text{cm}^2$

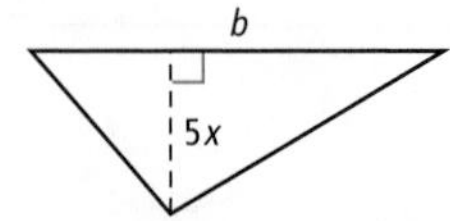

$b = 6x$ cm

C. b_2 of the trapezoid, in which $A = 231 \text{ mm}^2$

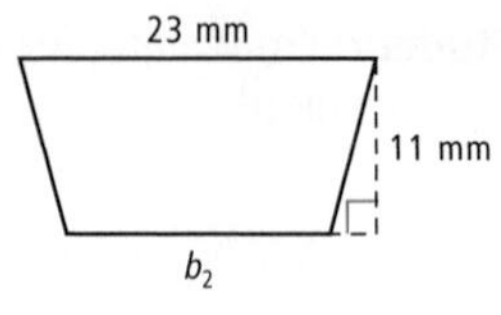

$b_2 = 19$ mm

Algebra

Find each measurement.

B the height of a rectangle in which $b = 5$ cm and $A = (5x^2 - 5x) \text{ cm}^2$

$A = bh$	*Area of a rectangle*
$5x^2 - 5x = 5h$	*Substitute $5x^2 - 5x$ for A and 5 for b.*
$5(x^2 - x) = 5h$	*Factor 5 out of the expression for A.*
$x^2 - x = h$	*Divide both sides by 5.*
$h = (x^2 - x)$ cm	*Sym. Prop. of =*

C the perimeter of the rectangle, in which $A = 12x \text{ ft}^2$

Step 1 Use the area and the height to find the base.

$A = bh$	*Area of a rectangle*
$12x = b(6)$	*Substitute 12x for A and 6 for h.*
$2x = b$	*Divide both sides by 6.*

Step 2 Use the base and the height to find the perimeter.

$P = 2b + 2h$	*Perimeter of a rectangle*
$P = 2(2x) + 2(6)$	*Substitute 2x for b and 6 for h.*
$P = (4x + 12)$ ft.	*Simplify.*

Remember!

The perimeter of a rectangle with base b and height h is $P = 2b + 2h$, or $P = 2(b + h)$.

CHECK IT OUT! **1.** Find the base of a parallelogram in which $h = 56$ yd and $A = 28 \text{ yd}^2$. $b = 0.5$ yd

To understand the formula for the area of a triangle or trapezoid, notice that two congruent triangles or two congruent trapezoids fit together to form a parallelogram. Thus the area of a triangle or trapezoid is half the area of the related parallelogram.

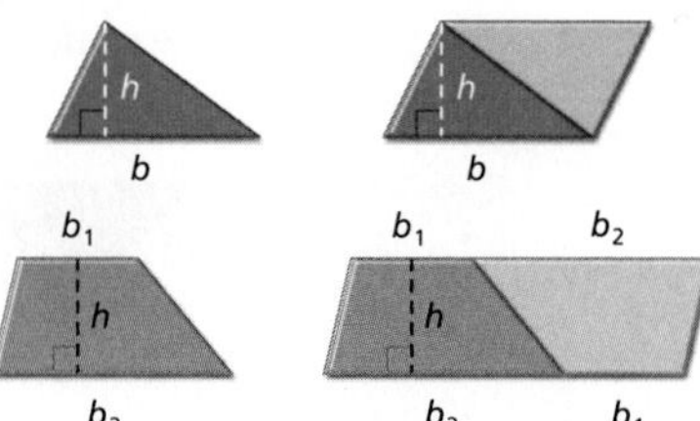

Know it! Note

Area Triangles and Trapezoids

The area of a triangle with base b and height h is $A = \frac{1}{2}bh$.

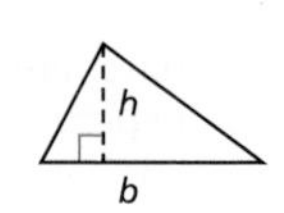

The area of a trapezoid with bases b_1 and b_2 and height h is $A = \frac{1}{2}(b_1 + b_2)h$, or $A = \frac{(b_1 + b_2)h}{2}$.

EXAMPLE 2 **Finding Measurements of Triangles and Trapezoids**

Find each measurement.

A the area of a trapezoid in which $b_1 = 9$ cm, $b_2 = 12$ cm, and $h = 3$ cm

$A = \frac{1}{2}(b_1 + b_2)h$	*Area of a trapezoid*
$A = \frac{1}{2}(9 + 12)3$	*Substitute 9 for b_1, 12 for b_2, and 3 for h.*
$A = 31.5 \text{ cm}^2$	*Simplify.*

2 Teach

Guided Instruction

Remind students that they previously learned how to find the length of a segment by finding the sum of its parts. Explain that they will apply the Area Addition Postulate to solve problems involving the areas of triangles and special quadrilaterals. Show how the formulas for the areas of a parallelogram, a triangle, a trapezoid, and a rhombus or kite relate to the formula for the area of a rectangle.

Reaching All Learners

Through Concrete Manipulatives

Have students cut out various shapes and sizes of triangles, trapezoids, kites, and rhombuses and find the area of each shape. Then ask students to cut and rearrange their shapes into rectangles and squares to verify their findings.

INTERVENTION

Questioning Strategies

EXAMPLE 1

- How are the area formulas for rectangles and parallelograms alike?
- Given the perimeter and height of a rectangle, how can you find its width?

EXAMPLE 2

- How are the area formulas for triangles and trapezoids alike?

Find each measurement.

B **the base of the triangle, in which $A = x^2$ in^2**

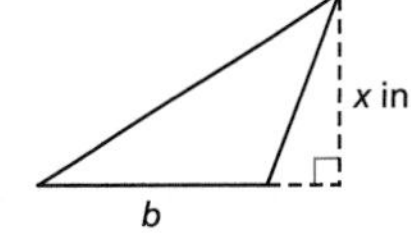

$A = \frac{1}{2}bh$	*Area of a triangle*
$x^2 = \frac{1}{2}bx$	*Substitute x^2 for A and x for h.*
$x = \frac{1}{2}b$	*Divide both sides by x.*
$2x = b$	*Multiply both sides by 2.*
$b = 2x$ in.	*Sym. Prop. of =*

C **b_2 of the trapezoid, in which $A = 8$ ft^2**

3 ft, 2 ft, b_2

$A = \frac{1}{2}(b_1 + b_2)h$	*Area of a trapezoid*
$8 = \frac{1}{2}(3 + b_2)(2)$	*Substitute 8 for A, 3 for b_1, and 2 for h.*
$8 = 3 + b_2$	*Multiply $\frac{1}{2}$ by 2.*
$5 = b_2$	*Subtract 3 from both sides.*
$b_2 = 5$ ft	*Sym. Prop. of =*

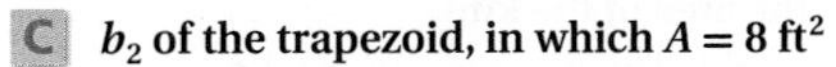

2. Find the area of the triangle.
$A = 96$ m^2

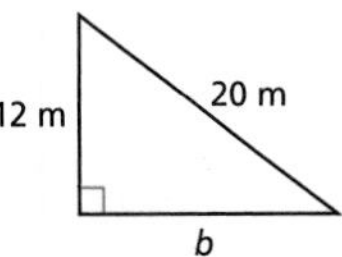

A kite or a rhombus with diagonals d_1 and d_2 can be divided into two congruent triangles with a base of d_1 and a height of $\frac{1}{2}d_2$.

area of each triangle: $A = \frac{1}{2}d_1\left(\frac{1}{2}d_2\right) = \frac{1}{4}d_1d_2$

total area: $A = 2\left(\frac{1}{4}d_1d_2\right) = \frac{1}{2}d_1d_2$

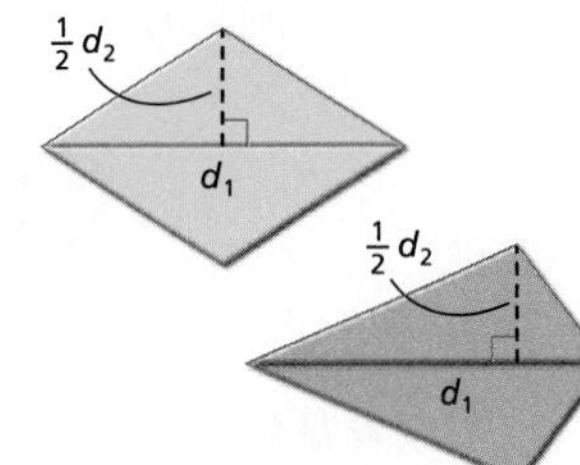

Know it! Note

Area **Rhombuses and Kites**

The area of a rhombus or kite with diagonals d_1 and d_2 is $A = \frac{1}{2}d_1d_2$.

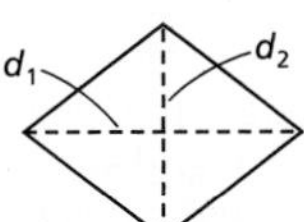

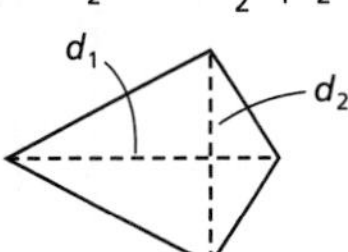

EXAMPLE 3 Finding Measurements of Rhombuses and Kites

Find each measurement.

A **d_2 of a kite in which $d_1 = 16$ cm and $A = 48$ cm^2**

$A = \frac{1}{2}d_1d_2$	*Area of a kite*
$48 = \frac{1}{2}(16)d_2$	*Substitute 48 for A and 16 for d_1.*
$6 = d_2$	*Solve for d_2.*
$d_2 = 6$ cm	*Sym. Prop. of =*

COMMON ERROR ALERT

Students may confuse any side length of a triangle with the height. Remind them that height is always measured along a segment perpendicular to the base.

Power Presentations with PowerPoint®

Additional Examples

Example 3

Find each measurement.

A. d_2 of a kite in which $d_1 =$ 14 in. and $A = 238$ in^2
$d_2 = 34$ in.

B. the area of the rhombus

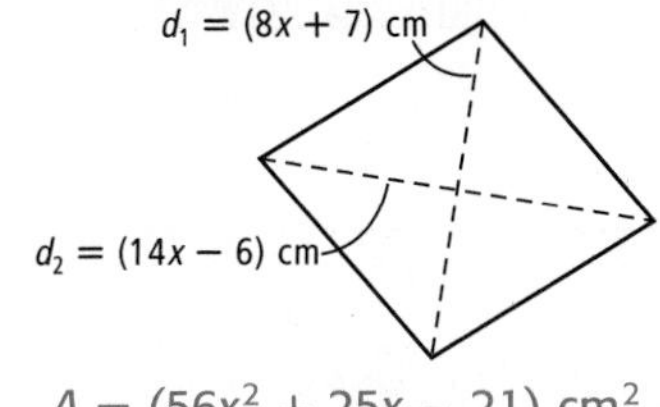

$A = (56x^2 + 25x - 21)$ cm^2

C. the area of the kite

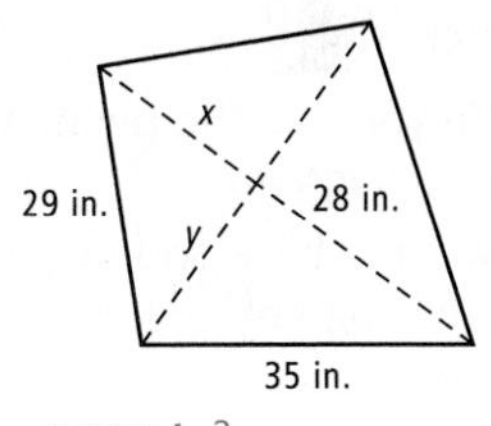

$A = 1008$ in^2

INTERVENTION
Questioning Strategies

EXAMPLE 3

- What steps would you use to find the area of a kite?

Teaching Tip

Auditory Students who have difficulty visualizing how the area formulas work may benefit from discussing them. Ask leading questions such as "How can you find the height?" and "Which segment is the base?" when you are presenting the area formulas so that students can express their reasoning aloud to one another.

Teaching Tip

Inclusion In **Example 4,** consider numbering each tangram shape or referring to the shapes by location for students who have trouble distinguishing colors.

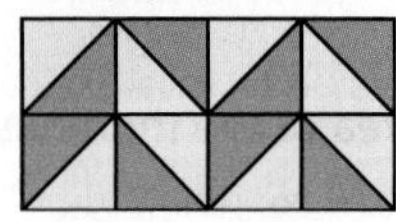

Power Presentations with PowerPoint®

Additional Examples

Example 4

The tile design shown is a rectangle with a base of 4 in. and a height of 2 in. Use the grid to find the perimeter and area of the leftmost shaded parallelogram.

$P = (2 + 2\sqrt{2})$ in.; $A = 1$ in^2

INTERVENTION

Questioning Strategies

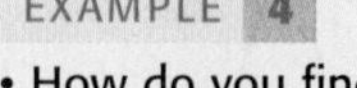

EXAMPLE 4

- How do you find the perimeter of the parallelogram?
- What are the base and height of the parallelogram?

Algebra

Find each measurement.

B **the area of the rhombus**

$A = \frac{1}{2}d_1d_2$

$A = \frac{1}{2}(6x + 4)(10x + 10)$ *Substitute (6x + 4) for d_1 and (10x + 10) for d_2.*

$A = \frac{1}{2}(60x^2 + 100x + 40)$ *Multiply the binomials (FOIL).*

$A = (30x^2 + 50x + 20)$ in^2 *Distrib. Prop.*

Remember!

The diagonals of a rhombus or kite are perpendicular, and the diagonals of a rhombus bisect each other.

C **the area of the kite**

Step 1 The diagonals d_1 and d_2 form four right triangles. Use the Pythagorean Theorem to find x and y.

$9^2 + x^2 = 41^2$ $\quad$ $9^2 + y^2 = 15^2$

$x^2 = 1600$ $\quad$ $y^2 = 144$

$x = 40$ $\quad$ $y = 12$

Step 2 Use d_1 and d_2 to find the area. d_1 is equal to $x + y$, which is 52. Half of d_2 is equal to 9, so d_2 is equal to 18.

$A = \frac{1}{2}d_1d_2$ *Area of a kite*

$A = \frac{1}{2}(52)(18)$ *Substitute 52 for d_1 and 18 for d_2.*

$A = 468$ ft^2 *Simplify.*

CHECK IT OUT! **3.** Find d_2 of a rhombus in which $d_1 = 3x$ m and $A = 12xy$ m^2. $d_2 = 8y$ m

EXAMPLE 4 ***Games Application***

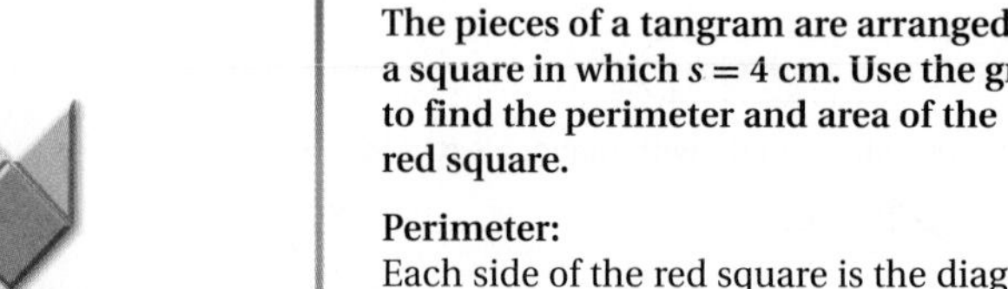

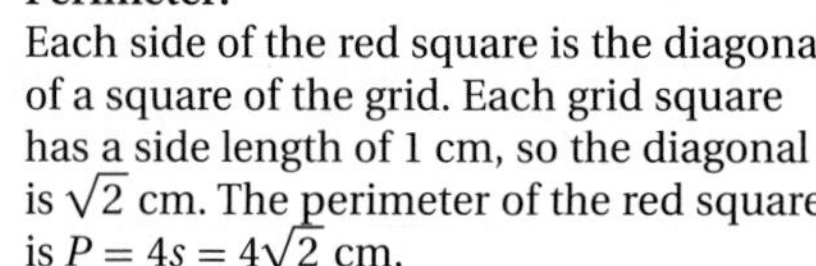

The pieces of a tangram are arranged in a square in which $s = 4$ cm. Use the grid to find the perimeter and area of the red square.

Perimeter:

Each side of the red square is the diagonal of a square of the grid. Each grid square has a side length of 1 cm, so the diagonal is $\sqrt{2}$ cm. The perimeter of the red square is $P = 4s = 4\sqrt{2}$ cm.

Area:

Method 1 The red square is also a rhombus. The diagonals d_1 and d_2 each measure 2 cm. So its area is

$A = \frac{1}{2}d_1d_2 = \frac{1}{2}(2)(2) = 2$ cm^2.

Method 2 The side length of the red square is $\sqrt{2}$ cm, so the area is

$A = s^2 = (\sqrt{2})^2 = 2$ cm.

CHECK IT OUT! **4.** In the tangram above, find the perimeter and area of the large green triangle. $P = (4 + 4\sqrt{2})$ cm; $A = 4$ cm^2

3 Close

Summarize

Remind students of the Area Addition Postulate and the area formulas for a parallelogram, a triangle, a trapezoid, and a rhombus or a kite.

ONGOING ASSESSMENT

and INTERVENTION

***Diagnose Before* the Lesson**
9-1 Warm Up, TE p. 589

***Monitor During* the Lesson**
Check It Out! Exercises, SE pp. 590–592
Questioning Strategies, TE pp. 590–592

***Assess After* the Lesson**
9-1 Lesson Quiz, TE p. 597
Alternative Assessment, TE p. 597

THINK AND DISCUSS

1. Explain why the area of a triangle is half the area of a parallelogram with the same base and height.
2. Compare the formula for the area of a trapezoid with the formula for the area of a rectangle.

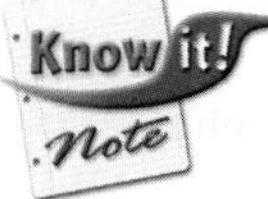

3. **GET ORGANIZED** Copy and complete the graphic organizer. Name all the shapes whose area is given by each area formula and sketch an example of each shape.

Area Formula	Shape(s)	Example(s)
$A = bh$		
$A = \frac{1}{2}bh$		
$A = \frac{1}{2}(b_1 + b_2)h$		
$A = \frac{1}{2}d_1d_2$		

Answers to *Think and Discuss*

1. because 2 ≅ copies of the triangle fit together to form a parallelogram with the same base and height as the triangle
2. The area of a rectangle is the base times the height, and the area of a trapezoid is the average of the bases times the height.
3. See p. A7.

9-1 Exercises

GUIDED PRACTICE

Find each measurement.

SEE EXAMPLE 1 p. 589

1. the area of the parallelogram **$A = 120\ \text{cm}^2$**

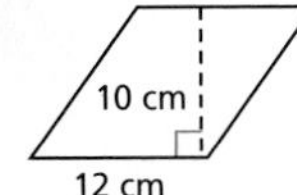

2. the height of the rectangle, in which $A = 10x^2\ \text{ft}^2$ **$h = 5x$ ft**

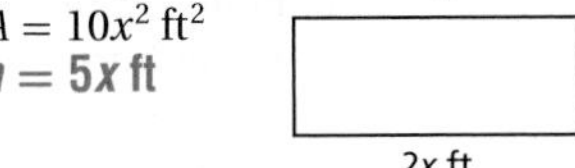

3. the perimeter of a square in which $A = 169\ \text{cm}^2$ **$P = 52$ cm**

SEE EXAMPLE 2 p. 590

4. the area of the trapezoid **$A = 240\ \text{m}^2$**

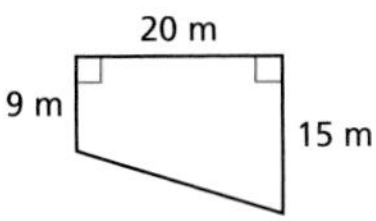

5. the base of the triangle, in which $A = 58.5\ \text{in}^2$ **$b = 13$ in.**

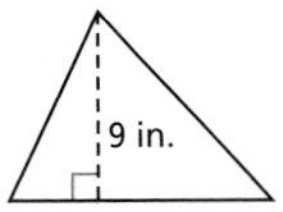

6. b_1 of a trapezoid in which $A = (48x + 68)\ \text{in}^2$, $h = 8$ in., and $b_2 = (9x + 12)$ in. **$b_1 = (3x + 5)$ in.**

SEE EXAMPLE 3 p. 591

7. the area of the rhombus **$A = 336\ \text{in}^2$**

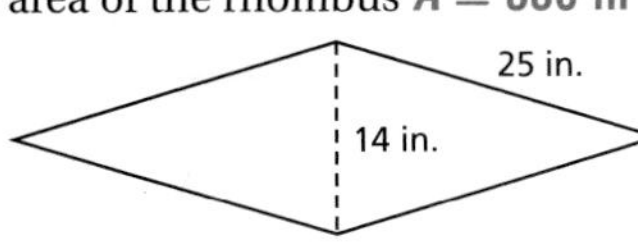

8. d_2 of the kite, in which $A = 187.5\ \text{m}^2$ **$d_2 = 25$ m**

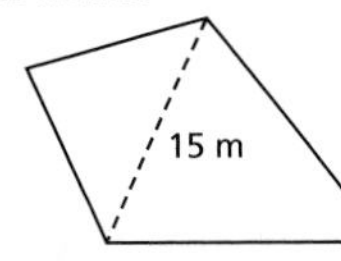

9. d_2 of a kite in which $A = 12x^2y^3\ \text{cm}^2$, $d_1 = 3xy$ cm **$d_2 = 8xy^2$ cm**

SEE EXAMPLE 4 p. 592

10. **Art** The stained-glass window shown is a rectangle with a base of 4 ft and a height of 3 ft. Use the grid to find the area of each piece.
parallelogram: 3 ft^2; rectangles: 2 ft^2; triangles: 1 ft^2; trapezoids: 1.5 ft^2

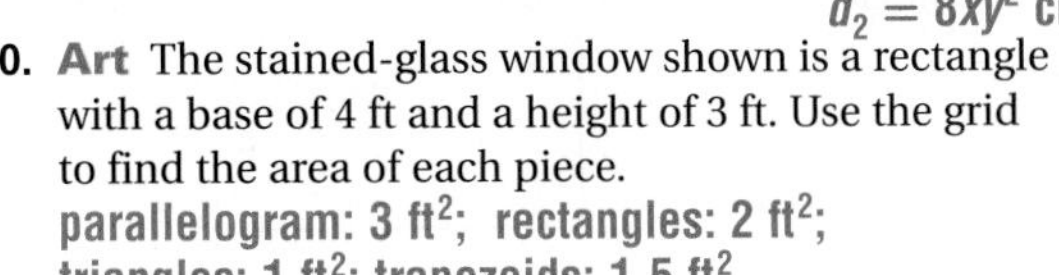

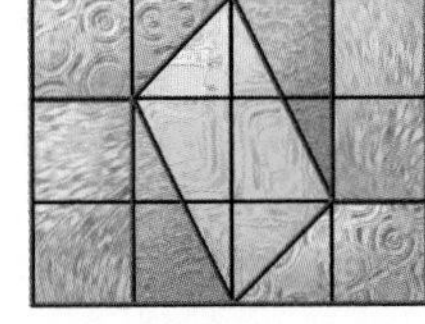

9-1 Exercises

Assignment Guide

Assign *Guided Practice* exercises as necessary.

If you finished Examples **1–2**
- **Basic** 11–16, 20–26, 28–39
- **Average** 11–16, 20–26, 28–39, 41, 43–45
- **Advanced** 11–16, 20–26, 28–39, 41, 43–45, 55–57

If you finished Examples **1–4**
- **Basic** 11–40, 46, 47, 50–54, 60–67
- **Average** 11–32, 37–41, 43, 46–55, 60–67
- **Advanced** 11–27, 28–36 even, 41–45, 48–67

Homework Quick Check
Quickly check key concepts.
Exercises: 12, 14, 18, 20, 24, 32

State Resources

go.hrw.com
State Resources Online
KEYWORD: MG7 Resources

Teaching Tip **Visual** In **Exercises 20–22,** have students redraw the figures and outline each shape so they can easily visualize the shapes before they try to find their areas.

Algebra In **Exercises 23–25,** point out that students will have to solve for unknown measures.

PRACTICE AND PROBLEM SOLVING

Independent Practice	
For Exercises	See Example
11–13	1
14–16	2
17–19	3
20–22	4

Extra Practice
Skills Practice p. S20
Application Practice p. S36

Find each measurement.

11. the height of the parallelogram, in which $A = 7.5\text{ m}^2$ $h = 1.25\text{ m}$

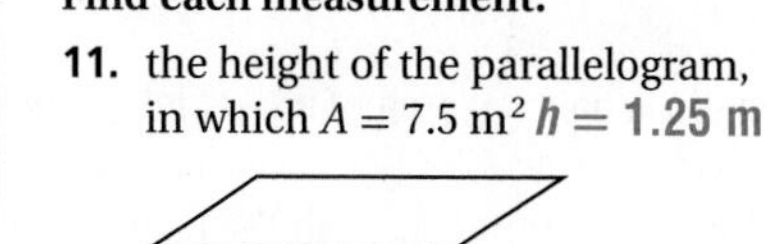

12. the perimeter of the rectangle $P = (4x + 2)\text{ in.}$

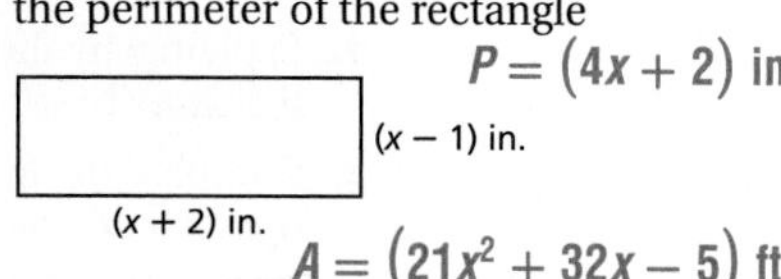

13. the area of a parallelogram in which $b = (3x + 5)$ ft and $h = (7x - 1)$ ft $A = (21x^2 + 32x - 5)\text{ ft}^2$

14. the area of the triangle $A = 210\text{ in}^2$

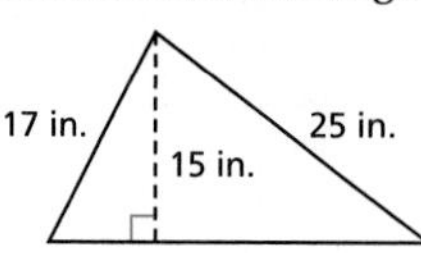

15. the height of the trapezoid, in which $A = 280\text{ cm}^2$ $h = 20\text{ cm}$

16. the area of a triangle in which $b = (x + 1)$ ft and $h = 8x$ ft $A = (4x^2 + 4x)\text{ ft}^2$

17. the area of the kite $A = 196\sqrt{3}\text{ in}^2$

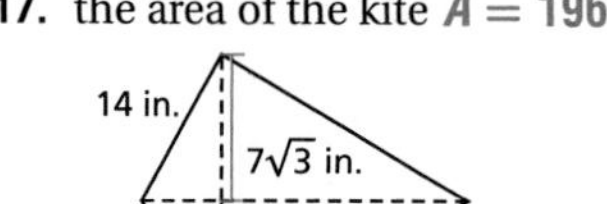

18. d_2 of the rhombus, in which $A = (3x^2 + 6x)\text{ m}^2$ $d_2 = 6x\text{ m}$

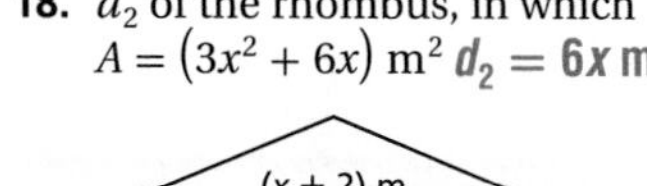

19. the area of a kite in which $d_1 = (6x + 5)$ ft and $d_2 = (4x + 8)$ ft $A = (12x^2 + 34x + 20)\text{ ft}$

Crafts In origami, a *square base* is the starting point for the creation of many figures, such as a crane. In the pattern for the square base, *ABCD* is a square, and *E, F, G,* and *H* are the midpoints of the sides. If $AB = 6$ in., find the area of each shape.

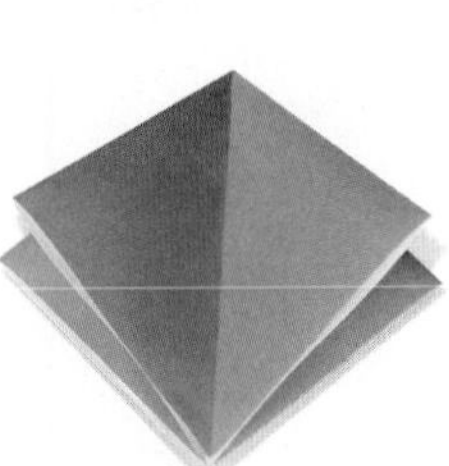

20. rectangle $ABFH$ $A = 18\text{ in}^2$
21. $\triangle AEJ$ $A = 4.5\text{ in}^2$
22. trapezoid $ABFJ$ $A = 13.5\text{ in}^2$

Multi-Step Find the area of each figure. Round to the nearest tenth, if necessary.

23. (10 cm, 6 cm, 60°) $A = 30\sqrt{3}\text{ cm}^2$

24. $A = 30\text{ m}^2$

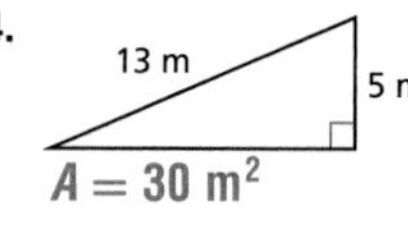

25. $A = 300\text{ in}^2$

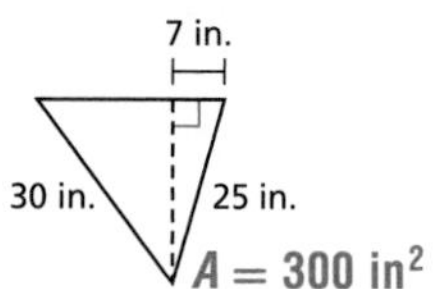

Write each area in terms of x.

26. equilateral triangle $A = \frac{x^2\sqrt{3}}{4}$

27. 30°-60°-90° triangle $A = \frac{x^2\sqrt{3}}{2}$

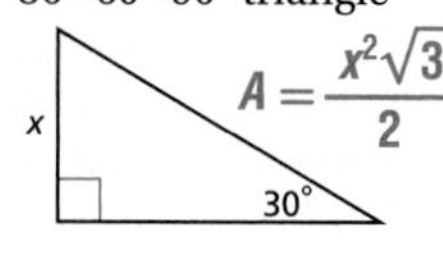

28. 45°-45°-90° triangle $A = \frac{x^2}{2}$

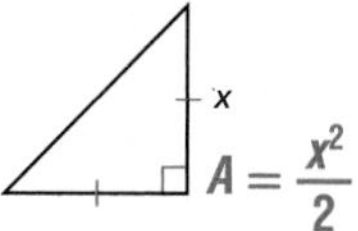

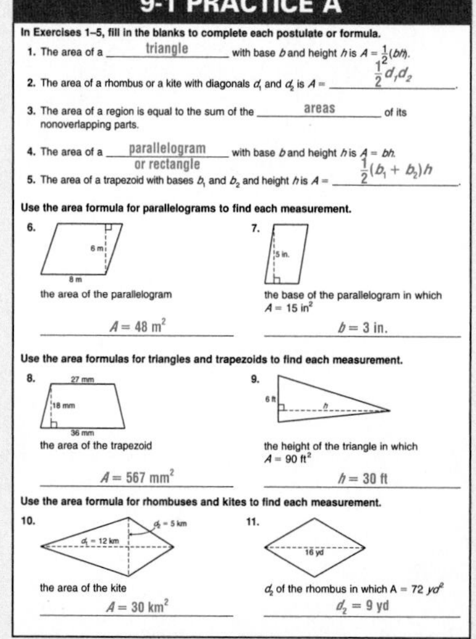

9-1 PRACTICE A

In Exercises 1–5, fill in the blanks to complete each postulate or formula.

1. The area of a triangle with base b and height h is $A = \frac{1}{2}(bh)$.
2. The area of a rhombus or a kite with diagonals d_1 and d_2 is $A = \frac{1}{2}d_1d_2$.
3. The area of a region is equal to the sum of the areas of its nonoverlapping parts.
4. The area of a parallelogram or rectangle with base b and height h is $A = bh$.
5. The area of a trapezoid with bases b_1 and b_2 and height h is $A = \frac{1}{2}(b_1 + b_2)h$.

Use the area formula for parallelograms to find each measurement.

6. (6 m, 8 m) the area of the parallelogram $A = 48\text{ m}^2$
7. (5 in.) the base of the parallelogram in which $A = 15\text{ in}^2$ $b = 3\text{ in.}$

Use the area formulas for triangles and trapezoids to find each measurement.

8. (27 mm, 18 mm, 36 mm) the area of the trapezoid $A = 567\text{ mm}^2$
9. (6 ft, h) the height of the triangle in which $A = 90\text{ ft}^2$ $h = 30\text{ ft}$

Use the area formula for rhombuses and kites to find each measurement.

10. ($d_1 = 12$ km, $d_2 = 5$ km) the area of the kite $A = 30\text{ km}^2$
11. (16 yd) d_2 of the rhombus in which $A = 72\text{ yd}^2$ $d_2 = 9\text{ yd}$

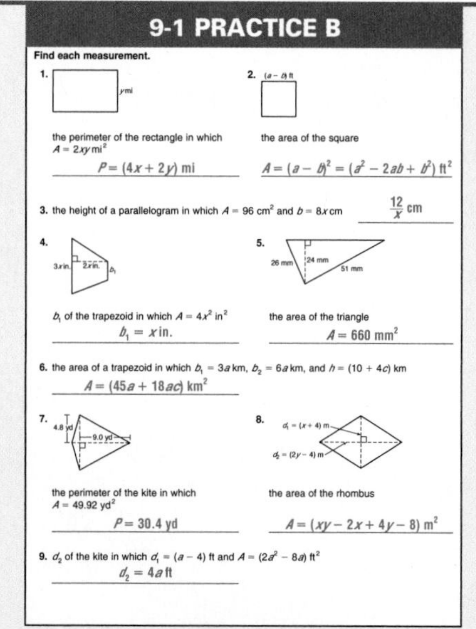

9-1 PRACTICE B

Find each measurement.

1. (y mi) the perimeter of the rectangle in which $A = 2xy\text{ mi}^2$ $P = (4x + 2y)\text{ mi}$
2. ($(a - b)$ ft) the area of the square $A = (a - b)^2 = (a^2 - 2ab + b^2)\text{ ft}^2$
3. the height of a parallelogram in which $A = 96\text{ cm}^2$ and $b = 8x$ cm $\frac{12}{x}\text{ cm}$
4. ($3x$ in., $2x$ in., b_1) b_1 of the trapezoid in which $A = 4x^2\text{ in}^2$ $b_1 = x\text{ in.}$
5. (26 mm, 24 mm, 51 mm) the area of the triangle $A = 660\text{ mm}^2$
6. the area of a trapezoid in which $b_1 = 3a$ km, $b_2 = 6a$ km, and $h = (10 + 4c)$ km $A = (45a + 18ac)\text{ km}^2$
7. (4.8 yd, 9.0 yd) the perimeter of the kite in which $A = 49.92\text{ yd}^2$ $P = 30.4\text{ yd}$
8. ($d_1 = (x + 4)$ m, $d_2 = (2y - 4)$ m) the area of the rhombus $A = (xy - 2x + 4y - 8)\text{ m}^2$
9. d_2 of the kite in which $d_1 = (a - 4)$ ft and $A = (2a^2 - 8a)\text{ ft}^2$ $d_2 = 4a\text{ ft}$

29. This problem will prepare you for the Multi-Step Test Prep on page 614.

A sign manufacturer makes yield signs by cutting an equilateral triangle from a square piece of aluminum with the dimensions shown. **$h = 31.2$ in.**

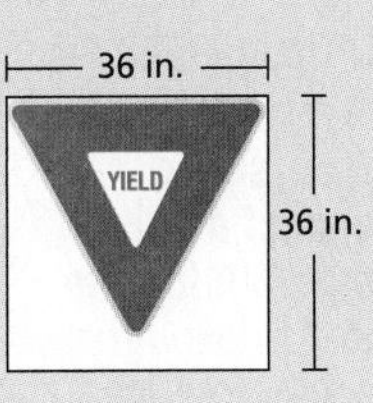

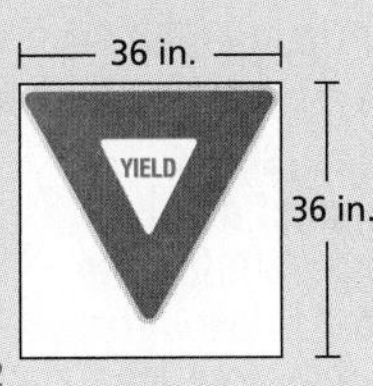

a. Find the height of the yield sign to the nearest tenth.

b. Find the area of the sign to the nearest tenth. **$A = 561.2\ \text{in}^2$**

c. How much material is left after a sign is made? **$734.8\ \text{in}^2$**

Find the missing measurements for each rectangle.

	Base b	Height h	Area A	Perimeter P
30.	12	16	**192**	**56**
31.	17	**8**	136	**50**
32.	**14**	11	**154**	50
33.	**9**	**24**	216	66

34. The perimeter of a rectangle is 72 in. The base is 3 times the height. Find the area of the rectangle. **$A = 243\ \text{in}^2$**

35. The area of a triangle is 50 cm^2. The base of the triangle is 4 times the height. Find the height of the triangle. **$h = 5$ cm**

36. The perimeter of an isosceles trapezoid is 40 ft. The bases of the trapezoid are 11 ft and 19 ft. Find the area of the trapezoid. **$A = 45\ \text{ft}^2$**

Use the conversion table for Exercises 37–42.

40. 4,014,489,600

37. 1 yd^2 = __**9**__ ft^2 **38.** 1 m^2 = __**10,000**__ cm^2

39. 1 cm^2 = __**100**__ mm^2 **40.** 1 mi^2 = __?__ in^2

Conversion Factors	
Metric	**Customary**
1 km = 1000 m	1 mi = 1760 yd
1 m = 100 cm	1 mi = 5280 ft
1 cm = 10 mm	1 yd = 3 ft
	1 ft = 12 in.

41. A triangle has a base of 3 yd and a height of 8 yd. Find the area in square feet. **$A = 108\ \text{ft}^2$**

LINK History

President James Garfield was a classics professor and a major general in the Union Army. He was assassinated in 1881.

Source: www.whitehouse.gov

The Granger Collection, New York

42. A rhombus has diagonals 500 yd and 800 yd in length. Find the area in square miles. **$A \approx 0.065\ \text{mi}^2$**

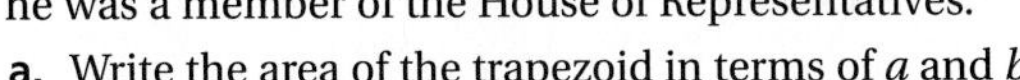

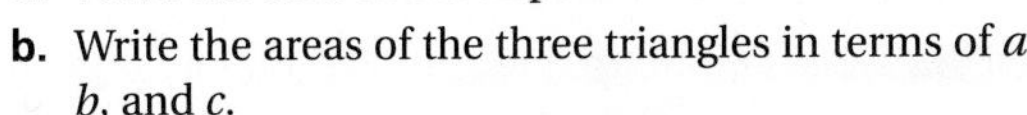

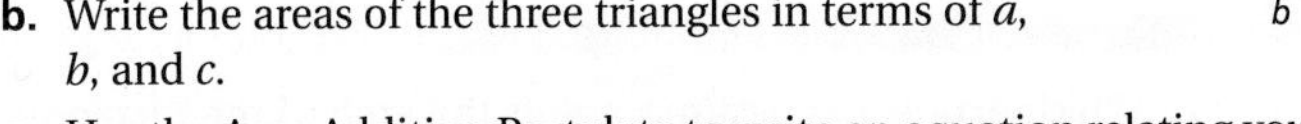

43. The following proof of the Pythagorean Theorem was discovered by President James Garfield in 1876 while he was a member of the House of Representatives.

a. Write the area of the trapezoid in terms of a and b.

b. Write the areas of the three triangles in terms of a, b, and c.

c. Use the Area Addition Postulate to write an equation relating your results from parts **a** and **b.** Simplify the equation to prove the Pythagorean Theorem.

44. Use the diagram to prove the formula for the area of a rectangle, given the formula for the area of a square.

Given: Rectangle with base b and height h

Prove: The area of the rectangle is $A = bh$.

Plan: Use the formula for the area of a square to find the areas of the outer square and the two squares inside the figure. Write and solve an equation for the area of the rectangle.

COMMON ERROR ALERT

Students may not recognize familiar shapes when they are rotated, such as the trapezoids in **Exercises 4** and **15.** Remind them that the bases of a trapezoid are always the two sides that are parallel.

MULTI-STEP TEST PREP **Exercise 29** involves finding the area of an equilateral triangle and subtracting this from the area of a rectangle to determine the amount of leftover material. This exercise prepares students for the Multi-Step Test Prep on page 614.

Answers

43a. $A = \dfrac{(a+b)}{2}(a+b)$
$= \dfrac{1}{2}(a+b)^2$

b. $\frac{1}{2}ab$; $\frac{1}{2}ab$; $\frac{1}{2}c^2$

c. $\frac{1}{2}(a+b)^2 = \frac{1}{2}ab + \frac{1}{2}ab + \frac{1}{2}c^2$

$(a+b)^2 = 2ab + c^2$

$a^2 + 2ab + b^2 = 2ab + c^2$

$a^2 + b^2 = c^2$

44. The area of the large square is $(b+h)^2$. The area of the medium square is b^2, and the area of the small square is h^2. The total area is the sum of the areas. Let A represent the area of the rectangle.

$(b+h)^2 = b^2 + h^2 + 2A$

$b^2 + 2bh + h^2 = b^2 + h^2 + 2A$

$2bh = 2A$

$bh = A$

9-1 PRACTICE C

1. The figure shows a parallelogram with side lengths b and c and known angle measure A. Develop a formula for the area of this parallelogram.
   Possible answer: Draw a segment showing the height from B to $\overline{AD}$ and label it h. The area of a parallelogram is bh. Since b is known and $h = c \sin A$, a formula for the area of the parallelogram is $A = bc \sin A$.
2. Use the formula you developed in Exercise 1 to prove the formula for the area of a rectangle.
   Possible answer: A rectangle is a parallelogram in which the measure of each angle is 90°. $\sin 90° = 1$. So $A = bc \sin A$ becomes $A = bc$, the product of the length and the width of the rectangle.

Find each measurement. Round to the nearest tenth.

3. (155°, 9 mm, 21 mm) the area of the parallelogram **$A \approx 79.9\ \text{mm}^2$**
4. (4 in., 121°, h, b_2) b_2 of the trapezoid in which $A = 20.8\ \text{in}^2$ **$b_2 \approx 6.4$ in.**
5. (10 mi, 60°, 75°, 20 mi) the area of the trapezoid **$A \approx 177.5\ \text{mi}^2$**
6. (12 yd, $x°$, 20 yd) x if the trapezoid has $A = 112\ \text{yd}^2$ **$x \approx 60.3$**
7. The figure shows two triangles and one rectangle. Sketch a way in which all three pieces can be put together without overlapping to form each of these shapes: a parallelogram, a rectangle, a square, and a trapezoid. **Possible answer:**

Parallelogram Square Rectangle Trapezoid

Inclusion For **Exercise 47,** review the rules for accuracy when multiplying numbers that have a given number of significant digits.

If students have difficulty with **Exercise 53,** point out that the given information from the exercise will be used for one equation, but the other equation is a formula that they will have used in this lesson. Students may find it easier to decide which formula to use if they draw and label the rectangle.

In **Exercise 55,** point out that they can use the Pythagorean Theorem to solve for JK^2 and then estimate the square root.

Answers

46. Both triangles have height h. The area of the upper triangle is $\frac{1}{2}b_1h$ and the area of the lower triangle is $\frac{1}{2}b_2h$. The area of the trapezoid is the sum of the areas of the triangles.
$$A = \frac{1}{2}b_1h + \frac{1}{2}b_2h$$
$$= \frac{1}{2}(b_1 + b_2)h$$

51. A square is a parallelogram and a rectangle in which $b = h = s$, so $A = bh = (s)(s) = s^2$.
A square is a rhombus in which $d_1 = d_2 = s\sqrt{2}$, so $A = \frac{1}{2}(s\sqrt{2})(s\sqrt{2}) = \frac{1}{2}s^2 2 = s^2$.

45. Opposite sides of a parallelogram are ≅, so the diagonal divides the parallelogram into 2 ≅ triangles. Let A represent the area of each triangle. The sum of the triangles' areas is the area of the parallelogram.

$2A = bh$

$A = \frac{1}{2}bh$

50. From the given measurements, the area is 12 cm^2. If the actual measurements were 5.9 cm and 1.9 cm, the area would be 11.21 cm^2. If the actual measurements were 6.1 cm and 2.1 cm, the area would be 12.81 cm^2. The maximum error is 0.81 cm^2.

Prove each area formula.

45. Given: Parallelogram with area $A = bh$
Prove: The area of the triangle is $A = \frac{1}{2}bh$.

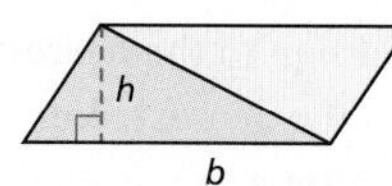

46. Given: Triangle with area $A = \frac{1}{2}bh$
Prove: The area of the trapezoid is $A = \frac{1}{2}(b_1 + b_2)h$.

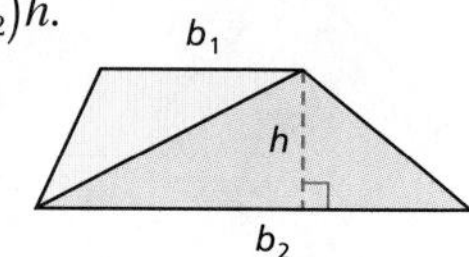

47. Measurement Choose an appropriate unit of measurement and measure the base and height of each parallelogram. **Note: Figures reduced in TE.**

a. Find the area of each parallelogram. Give your answer with the correct precision. **Possible answers: A: 4.2 cm^2; B: 3.8 cm^2; C: 4.3 cm^2**

b. Which has the greatest area? **C has the greatest area.**

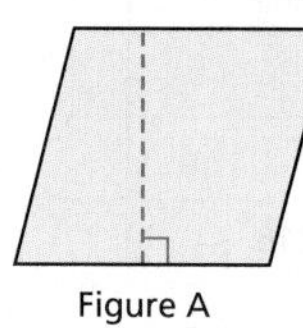

Figure A

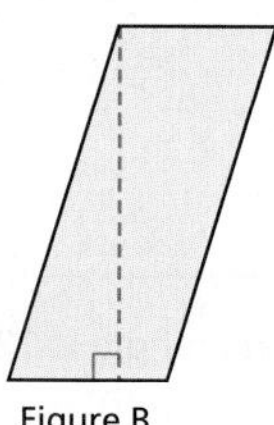

Figure B

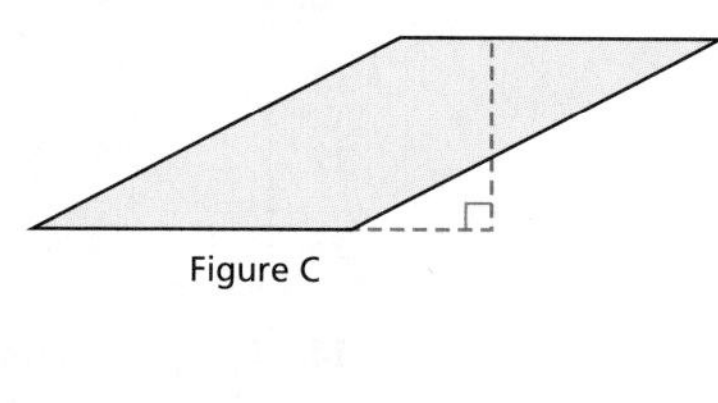

Figure C

48. Hobbies Tina is making a kite according to the plans at right. The fabric weighs about 40 grams per square meter. The diagonal braces, or *spars*, weigh about 20 grams per meter. Estimate the weight of the kite. **48.4 g**

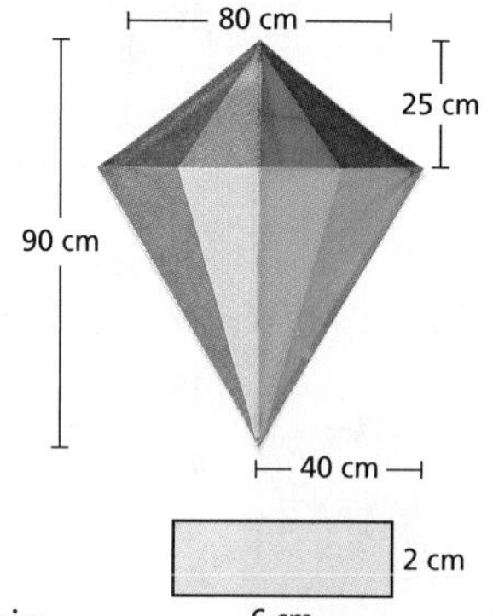

49. Home Improvement Tom is buying tile for a 12 ft by 18 ft rectangular kitchen floor. He needs to buy 15% extra in case some of the tiles break. The tiles are squares with 4 in. sides that come in cases of 100. How many cases should he buy? **23 cases**

50. Critical Thinking If the maximum error in the given measurements of the rectangle is 0.1 cm, what is the greatest possible error in the area? Explain.

2 cm

6 cm

51. Write About It A square is also a parallelogram, a rectangle, and a rhombus. Prove that the area formula for each shape gives the same result as the formula for the area of a square.

52. Which expression best represents the area of the rectangle?

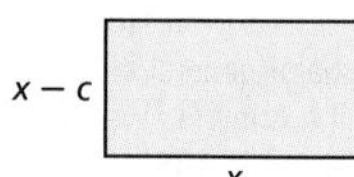

Ⓐ $2x + 2(x - c)$
Ⓑ $x(x - c)$
Ⓒ $x^2 + (x - c)^2$
Ⓓ $2x(x - c)$

53. The length of a rectangle is 3 times the width. The perimeter is 48 inches. Which system of equations can be used to find the dimensions of the rectangle?

Ⓕ $\ell = w + 3$, $2(\ell + w) = 48$
Ⓖ $\ell = 3w$, $2\ell + 6w = 48$
Ⓗ $\ell = 3w$, $2(\ell + w) = 48$
Ⓙ $\ell = w + 3$, $2\ell + 6w = 48$

9-1 READING STRATEGIES

Use the table below to help you find areas of triangles and quadrilaterals.

Figure	Diagram	Formula	Example
triangle		$A = \frac{1}{2}bh$	Find the area of a triangle with $b = 12$ cm and $h = 4$ cm. $A = \frac{1}{2}(12)(4)$ cm^2; $A = 24$ cm^2
parallelogram		$A = bh$	Find the height of a parallelogram with $A = 18$ in^2 and $b = 9$ in. $18 = (9)h$ in.; $h = 2$ in.
trapezoid		$A = \frac{1}{2}(b_1 + b_2)h$	Find the area of a trapezoid with $b_1 = 6$ ft, $b_2 = 8$ ft, and $h = 3$ ft. $A = \frac{1}{2}(6 + 8)(3)$ ft^2; $A = (7)(3)$ ft^2; $A = 21$ ft^2
rhombus or kite		$A = \frac{1}{2}d_1d_2$	Find the diagonal d_2 of a kite with $A = 36$ cm^2 and $d_1 = 8$ cm. $36 = \frac{1}{2}(8)d_2$ cm; $36 = 4d_2$ cm; $d_2 = 9$ cm

Find each measurement.

1. area of the parallelogram (12 cm, 9 cm) **$A = 108$ cm^2**
2. area of the triangle (7 yd, 10 yd) **$A = 35$ yd^2**
3. base of a triangle with $A = 150$ ft^2 and $h = 30$ ft **$b = 10$ ft**
4. area of a rhombus with $d_1 = 10$ mm and $d_2 = 30$ mm **$A = 150$ mm^2**
5. height of a trapezoid with $A = 60$ in^2, $b_1 = 3$ in., and $b_2 = 7$ in **$h = 12$ in.**
6. base of a parallelogram with $A = 28$ cm^2 and $h = 7$ cm **$b = 4$ cm**

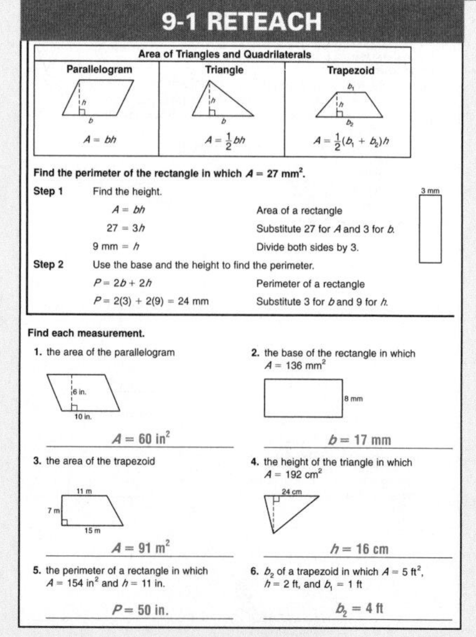

9-1 RETEACH

Area of Triangles and Quadrilaterals		
Parallelogram	Triangle	Trapezoid
$A = bh$	$A = \frac{1}{2}bh$	$A = \frac{1}{2}(b_1 + b_2)h$

Find the perimeter of the rectangle in which $A = 27$ mm^2.

Step 1 Find the height.

$A = bh$ — Area of a rectangle
$27 = 3h$ — Substitute 27 for A and 3 for b.
9 mm $= h$ — Divide both sides by 3.

Step 2 Use the base and the height to find the perimeter.

$P = 2b + 2h$ — Perimeter of a rectangle
$P = 2(3) + 2(9) = 24$ mm — Substitute 3 for b and 9 for h.

3 mm

Find each measurement.

1. the area of the parallelogram (6 in., 10 in.) **$A = 60$ in^2**
2. the base of the rectangle in which $A = 136$ mm^2 (8 mm) **$b = 17$ mm**
3. the area of the trapezoid (11 m, 7 m, 15 m) **$A = 91$ m^2**
4. the height of the triangle in which $A = 192$ cm^2 (24 cm) **$h = 16$ cm**
5. the perimeter of a rectangle in which $A = 154$ in^2 and $h = 11$ in. **$P = 50$ in.**
6. b_2 of a trapezoid in which $A = 5$ ft^2, $h = 2$ ft, and $b_1 = 1$ ft **$b_2 = 4$ ft**

54. A 16- by 18-foot rectangular section of a wall will be covered by square tiles that measure 2 feet on each side. If the tiles are not cut, how many of them will be needed to cover the section of the wall?

(A) 288 (B) 144 (C) 72 (circled) (D) 17

55. The area of trapezoid $HJKM$ is 90 square centimeters. Which is closest to the length of $\overline{JK}$?

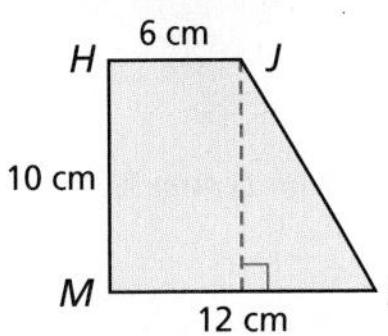

(F) 10 centimeters (H) 11.7 centimeters (circled)
(G) 10.5 centimeters (J) 16 centimeters

56. **Gridded Response** A driveway is shaped like a parallelogram with a base of 28 feet and a height of 17 feet. Covering the driveway with crushed stone will cost $2.75 per square foot. How much will it cost to cover the driveway with crushed stone? **$1309**

CHALLENGE AND EXTEND

Multi-Step **Find h in each parallelogram.**

57.

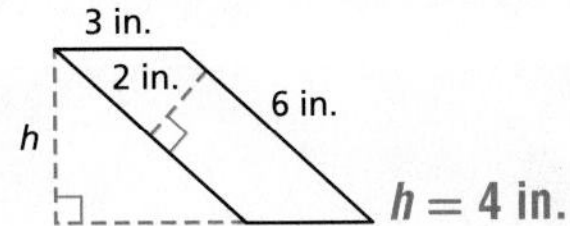

$h = 4$ in.

58.

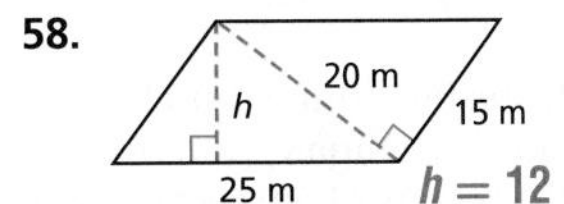

$h = 12$ m

59. $b = (7x + 5)$ cm
$h = (6x + 3)$ cm

59. **Algebra** A rectangle has a perimeter of $(26x + 16)$ cm and an area of $(42x^2 + 51x + 15)$ cm^2. Find the dimensions of the rectangle in terms of x.

60. Prove that the area of any quadrilateral with perpendicular diagonals is $\frac{1}{2}d_1d_2$.

61. **Gardening** A gardener has 24 feet of fencing to enclose a rectangular garden.

a. Let x and y represent the side lengths of the rectangle. Solve the perimeter formula $2x + 2y = 24$ for y, and substitute the expression into the area formula $A = xy$. $A = x(12 - x)$

61b. D: $0 < x < 12$
R: $0 < y \leq 36$

b. Graph the resulting function on a coordinate plane. What are the domain and range of the function?

c. What are the dimensions of the rectangle that will enclose the greatest area? **6 ft by 6 ft**

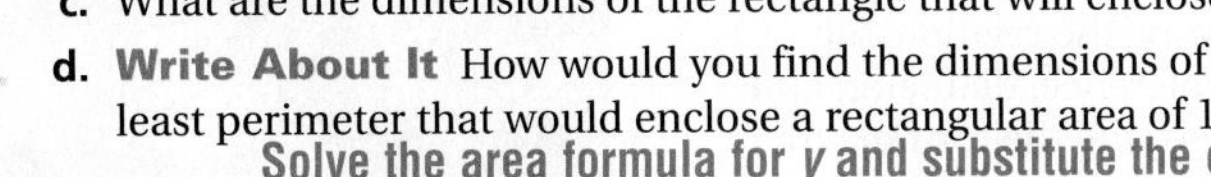

d. **Write About It** How would you find the dimensions of the rectangle with the least perimeter that would enclose a rectangular area of 100 square feet? **Solve the area formula for y and substitute the expression into the perimeter formula. Graph, and find the minimum value.**

SPIRAL REVIEW

Determine the range of each function for the given domain. *(Previous course)*

62. $f(x) = x - 3$, domain: $-4 \leq x \leq 6$ $\quad -7 \leq y \leq 3$

63. $f(x) = -x^2 + 2$, domain: $-2 \leq x \leq 2$ $\quad -2 \leq y \leq 2$

Find the perimeter and area of each figure. Express your answers in terms of x. *(Lesson 1-5)*

64.

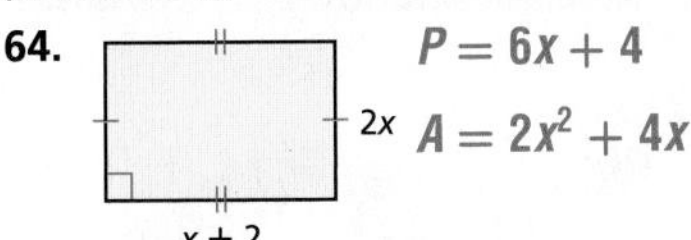

$P = 6x + 4$
$A = 2x^2 + 4x$

65.

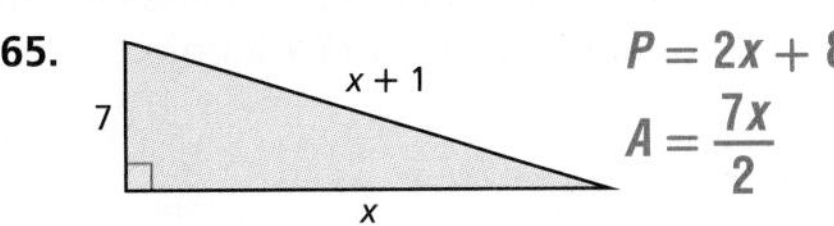

$P = 2x + 8$
$A = \dfrac{7x}{2}$

Write each vector in component form. *(Lesson 8-6)*

66. $\overrightarrow{LM}$ with $L(4, 3)$ and $M(5, 10)$ $\langle 1, 7 \rangle$

67. $\overrightarrow{ST}$ with $S(-2, -2)$ and $T(4, 6)$ $\langle 6, 8 \rangle$

Journal

Have students describe how they can use the formula for the area of a kite to build a kite of their own.

ALTERNATIVE ASSESSMENT

Have students make a tangram out of paper, arrange all the pieces to form a right triangle, and find its area and perimeter. Repeat this exercise for a parallelogram, a rhombus, a kite, a trapezoid, and a rectangle that is not a square. Then have students explain why it is not possible to form a square using one copy of each shape, omitting duplicates. (*Hint:* What would be the area?)

Power Presentations with PowerPoint®

9-1 Lesson Quiz

Find each measurement.

1. the height of the parallelogram, in which $A = 182x^2$ mm^2

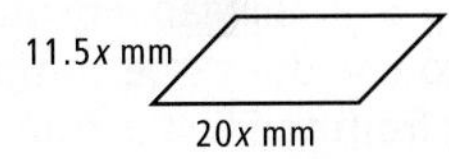

$h = 9.1x$ mm

2. the perimeter of a rectangle in which $h = 8$ in. and $A = 28x$ in^2 $\quad P = (16 + 7x)$ in.

3. the area of the trapezoid

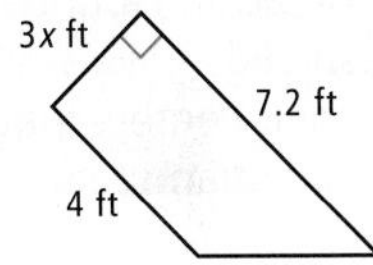

$A = 16.8x$ ft^2

4. the base of a triangle in which $h = 8$ cm and $A = (12x + 8)$ cm^2 $\quad b = (3x + 2)$ cm

5. the area of the rhombus

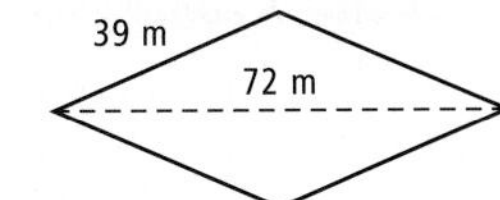

$A = 1080$ m^2

6. The wallpaper pattern shown is a rectangle with a base of 4 in. and a height of 3 in. Use the grid to find the area of the shaded kite.

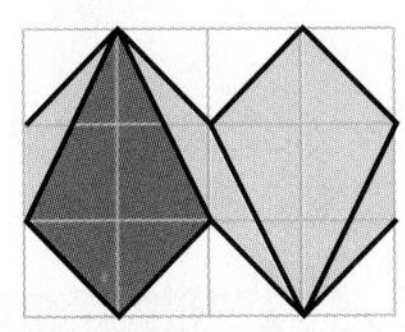

$A = 3$ in^2

Also available on transparency

9-1 PROBLEM SOLVING

1. The area of trapezoid $HJKL$ is 385 mm^2. Find LM to the nearest tenth.

K 32 mm L, J 23 mm H, 40°, M

21.8 mm

2. Samantha is buying stones for a 16 foot by 3 foot walkway. She needs to buy 10% extra for cutting stones for the corners and ends. The stones are rectangles 7 inches long and 4 inches wide and cost $0.97 each. About how much will the stones cost for her walkway?

about $263.84

3. The length of a rectangular pool is 2 feet less than twice the width. If the area of the pool is 264 ft^2, what are the dimensions of the pool?

12 ft by 22 ft

4. Find the area of the kite. Round to the nearest tenth.

8.5 cm, 2.3 cm, 4 cm

26.3 cm^2

Choose the best answer.

5. A parallelogram has sides of length 30 centimeters and 18 centimeters. One of its angles measures 58°. Which is the best estimate for the area of the parallelogram?

A 274.8 cm^2
B 286.2 cm^2
(C) 457.9 cm^2 (circled)
D 540.0 cm^2

6. Jamie is cutting out 32 right triangles from fabric for her quilt. The shortest side of each triangle is 2 inches, and the longest side is 5 inches. How much fabric will she use to cut out all the triangles?

(F) 146.6 in^2 (circled) H 366.6 in^2
G 293.3 in^2 J 672 in^2

7. In rhombus $ABCD$, the length of diagonal $\overline{BD}$ is $\frac{2}{3}$ the length of diagonal $\overline{AC}$. If the area of the figure is 75 cm^2, find BD.

A 7.1 cm C 10.6 cm
(B) 10 cm (circled) D 15 cm

8. The house is made from 7 puzzle pieces. The pieces are triangles and parallelograms. If the area of the chimney is $\frac{1}{8}$ in^2, what is the area of $\triangle LMN$?

F $\frac{9}{32}$ in^2 H $\frac{9}{2}$ in^2
(G) $\frac{9}{16}$ in^2 (circled) J 9 in^2

Answers

60. Let $ABCD$ be a quad. with $\perp$ diag. $\overline{AC}$ and $\overline{BD}$ that intersect at E. Let $d_1 = AC$, $d_2 = BD$, and $x = BE$. $\triangle ABC$ has $b = d_1$ and $h = x$, so $A = \frac{1}{2}d_1x$. $\triangle ADC$ has $b = d_1$ and $h = d_2 - x$, so $A = \frac{1}{2}d_1(d_2 - x)$. $ABCD$ has area $A = \frac{1}{2}d_1x + \frac{1}{2}d_1(d_2 - x) = \frac{1}{2}d_1(x + d_2 - x) = \frac{1}{2}d_1d_2$.

61b.

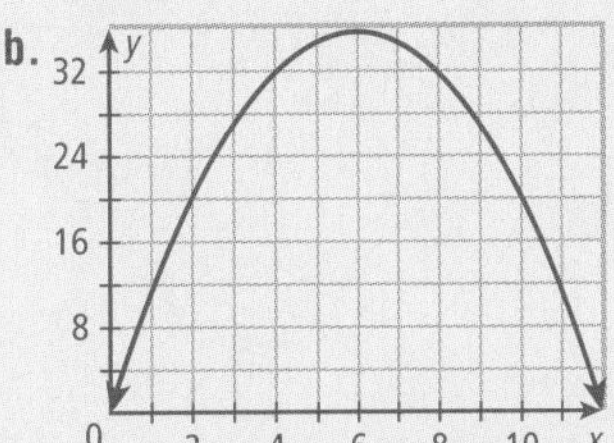

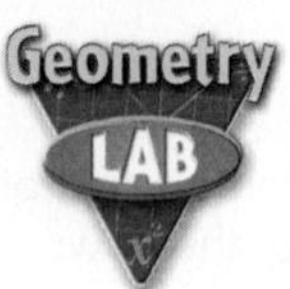

Organizer

Use with Lesson 9-2

Pacing:
Traditional 1 day
Block $\frac{1}{2}$ day

Objective: Use construction and measurement to develop π.

Materials: compass, cardboard, measuring tape, scissors, ribbon, straightedge

Online Edition

Countdown Week 20

Resources

Geometry Lab Activities
9-2 Lab Recording Sheet

Teach

Discuss

Explain to students that they will be using two different methods to develop π in this lab. Encourage them to use the same compass setting from the first activity to construct the square and the circle in the second activity, and then compare their results.

Alternative Approach

Use plastic lids or other circular objects instead of cardboard circles. Many plastic lids have small raised points at their centers that can be used to draw diameters.

State Resources

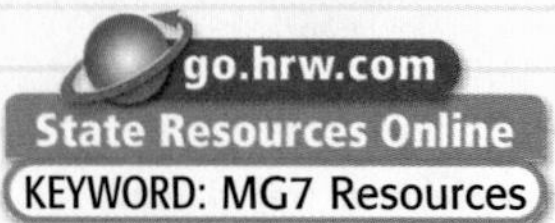

go.hrw.com
State Resources Online
KEYWORD: MG7 Resources

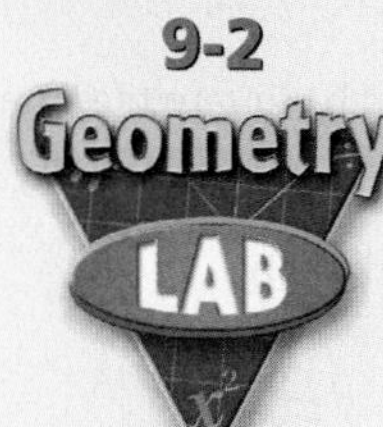

9-2 Geometry LAB

Use with Lesson 9-2

Develop π

The ratio of the circumference of a circle to its diameter is defined as π. All circles are similar, so this ratio is the same for all circles:

$$\pi = \frac{\text{circumference}}{\text{diameter}}.$$

Activity 1

1. Use your compass to draw a large circle on a piece of cardboard and then cut it out.
2. Use a measuring tape to measure the circle's diameter and circumference as accurately as possible.

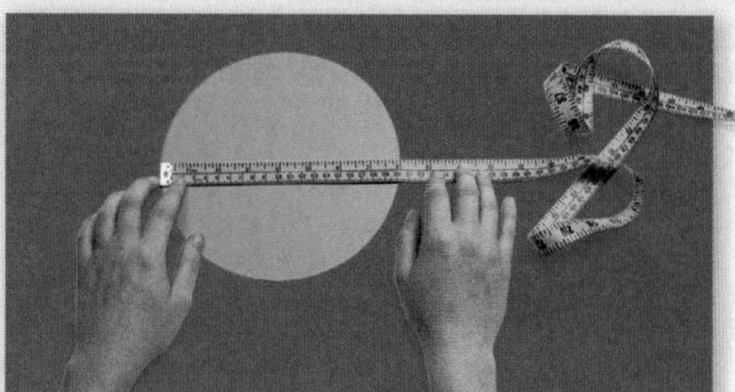

3. Use the results from your circle to estimate π. Compare your answers with the results of the rest of the class.

Try This

1. Do you think it is possible to draw a circle whose ratio of circumference to diameter is not π? Why or why not?
2. How does knowing the relationship between circumference, diameter, and π help you determine the formula for circumference?
3. Use a ribbon to make a π measuring tape. Mark off increments of π inches or π cm on your ribbon as accurately as possible. How could you use this π measuring tape to find the diameter of a circular object? Use your π measuring tape to measure 5 circular objects. Give the circumference and diameter of each object.

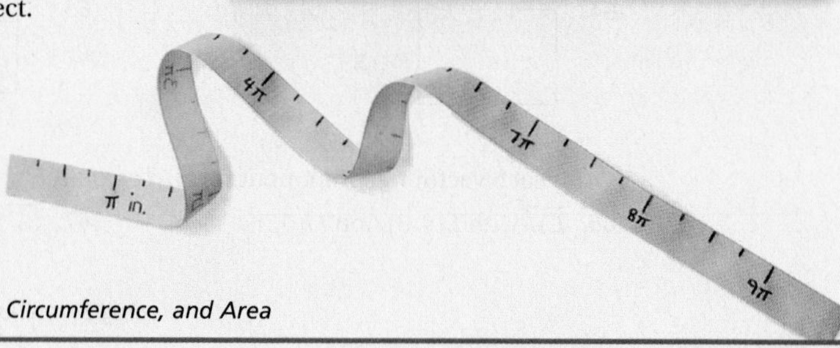

Answers to *Try This*

1. No; possible answer: all circles are similar, so the ratio of circumference to diameter is always the same.
2. Solving the relationship for C gives a formula in terms of d and π.
3. If the circumference is $n\pi$, then the diameter is n. Check students' measurements.

Archimedes used inscribed and circumscribed polygons to estimate the value of π. His "method of exhaustion" is considered to be an early version of calculus. In the figures below, the circumference of the circle is less than the perimeter of the larger polygon and greater than the perimeter of the smaller polygon. This fact is used to estimate π.

Activity 2

1–3. Check students' constructions.

1. Construct a large square. Construct the perpendicular bisectors of two adjacent sides.

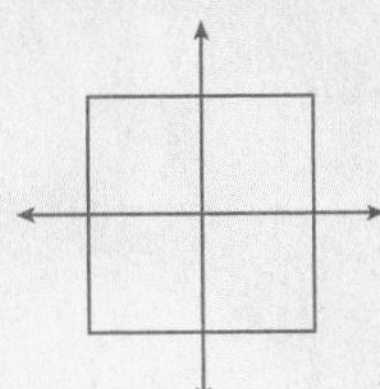

2. Use your compass to draw an inscribed circle as shown.

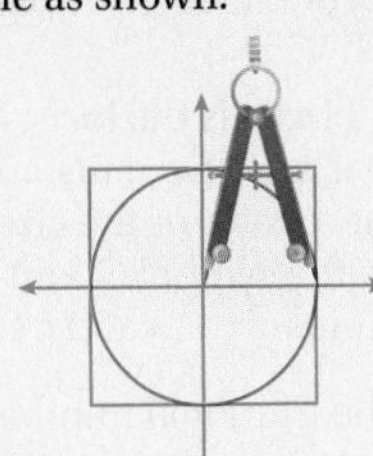

3. Connect the midpoints of the sides to form a square that is inscribed in the circle.

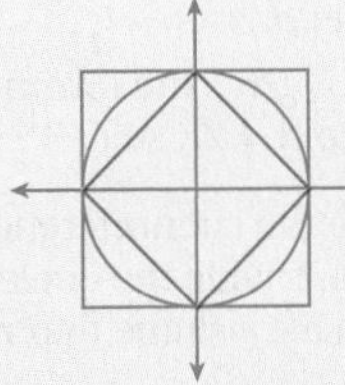

4. Let P_1 represent the perimeter of the smaller square, P_2 represent the perimeter of the larger square, and C represent the circumference of the circle. Measure the squares to find P_1 and P_2 and substitute the values into the inequality below.

$$P_1 < C < P_2$$ **Check students' measurements.**

5. Divide each expression in the inequality by the diameter of the circle. Why does this give you an inequality in terms of π? Complete the inequality below.

$\underline{\ ?\ } < \pi < \underline{\ ?\ }$ **because π is the ratio of the circumference to the diameter; possible answer: $2.8 < \pi < 4$**

Try This

4. Use the perimeters of the inscribed and circumscribed regular hexagons to write an inequality for π. Assume the diameter of each circle is 2 units.
$3 < \pi < 3.46$

5. Compare the inequalities you found for π. What do you think would be true about your inequality if you used regular polygons with more sides? How could you use inscribed and circumscribed regular polygons to estimate π?

6. An alternate definition of π is the area of a circle with radius 1. How could you use this definition and the figures above to estimate the value of π?
Possible answer: Average the areas of the inscribed and circumscribed polygons.

Close

Key Concept

You can use manipulatives to estimate and verify the value of π, which is the ratio of the circumference of a circle to its diameter.

Assessment

Journal Have students explain how to estimate π by using a compass and measuring tape and by using inscribed and circumscribed polygons.

Answers to *Try This*

5. Possible answer: The second inequality values are closer together. With more sides, the values would be even closer together. You can estimate π by averaging the upper and lower values.

Teacher to Teacher

A simple, inexpensive, and fun way to explore the relationship between circumference and diameter or radius is to use shoestring licorice and a circle.

Students can fold the circle twice to find the center, the intersection of two diameters. Have students draw a radius and a diameter of the circle.

Using the licorice as a bendable measuring device, students see that it takes a little more than 3 diameters or 6 radii to go around the circle, thus reinforcing the value of π and the formulas $C = \pi d$ and $C = 2\pi r$.

Denise Young
Overland Park, KS

9-2 Organizer

Pacing: Traditional 1 day
Block $\frac{1}{2}$ day

Objectives: Develop and apply the formulas for the area and circumference of a circle.

Develop and apply the formula for the area of a regular polygon.

Technology Lab
In *Technology Lab Activities*

Online Edition
Tutorial Videos, Interactivity

Countdown Week 20

Power Presentations with PowerPoint®

Warm Up

Find the unknown side lengths in each special right triangle.

1. a 30°-60°-90° triangle with hypotenuse 2 ft 1 ft; $\sqrt{3}$ ft
2. a 45°-45°-90° triangle with leg length 4 in. 4 in.; $4\sqrt{2}$ in.
3. a 30°-60°-90° triangle with longer leg length 3 m $\sqrt{3}$ m; $2\sqrt{3}$ m

Also available on transparency

Math Humor

Q: What do you get when you divide a jack-o'-lantern's circumference by its diameter?

A: Pumpkin pi.

9-2 Developing Formulas for Circles and Regular Polygons

Objectives
Develop and apply the formulas for the area and circumference of a circle.

Develop and apply the formula for the area of a regular polygon.

Vocabulary
circle
center of a circle
center of a regular polygon
apothem
central angle of a regular polygon

Who uses this?
Drummers use drums of different sizes to produce different notes. The pitch is related to the area of the top of the drum. (See Example 2.)

A **circle** is the locus of points in a plane that are a fixed distance from a point called the **center of the circle**. A circle is named by the symbol ⊙ and its center. ⊙*A* has radius $r = AB$ and diameter $d = CD$.

The irrational number π is defined as the ratio of the circumference C to the diameter d, or $\pi = \frac{C}{d}$. Solving for C gives the formula $C = \pi d$. Also $d = 2r$, so $C = 2\pi r$.

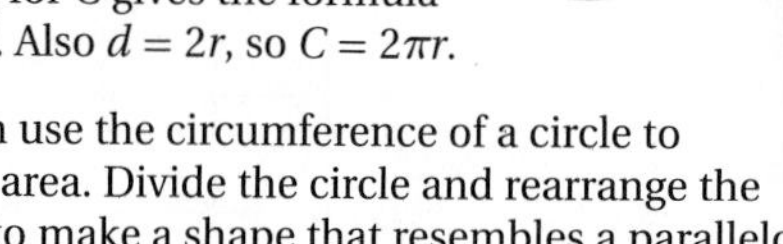

You can use the circumference of a circle to find its area. Divide the circle and rearrange the pieces to make a shape that resembles a parallelogram.

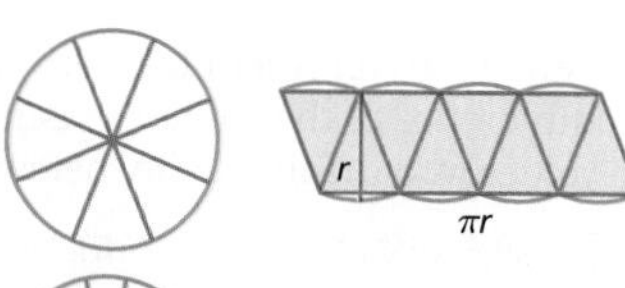

The base of the parallelogram is about half the circumference, or πr, and the height is close to the radius r. So $A \cong \pi r \cdot r = \pi r^2$.

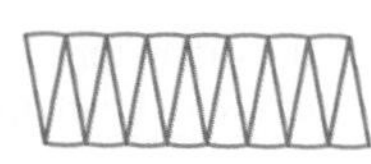

The more pieces you divide the circle into, the more accurate the estimate will be.

Circumference and Area — Circle

A circle with diameter d and radius r has circumference $C = \pi d$ or $C = 2\pi r$ and area $A = \pi r^2$.

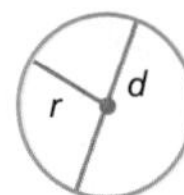

EXAMPLE 1 Finding Measurements of Circles

Find each measurement.

P
16 cm

A the area of ⊙*P* in terms of π

$A = \pi r^2$ *Area of a circle*
$A = \pi(8)^2$ *Divide the diameter by 2 to find the radius, 8.*
$A = 64\pi \text{ cm}^2$ *Simplify.*

1 Introduce

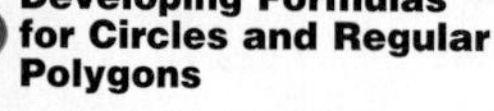

EXPLORATION
9-2 Developing Formulas for Circles and Regular Polygons

Recall the formula for the circumference of a circle, $C = \pi d$ or $C = 2\pi r$, where d is the circle's diameter and r is its radius. Use this to help you develop the formula for the area of a circle.

1. Use a compass to draw a circle on a sheet of paper. Cut out the circle.
2. Fold the circle in half three times, as shown.
3. Unfold the circle and cut along the creases to form eight pieces.
4. Arrange the pieces to make a figure that is close to a parallelogram.

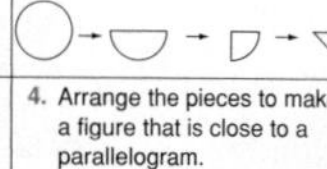

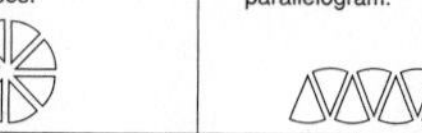

5. If your circle has radius r, what is the height of the figure?
6. How is the base of the figure related to the circumference of the circle? How can you express the base in terms of r?
7. What is the area of the figure?

Motivate

Cut a regular octagon out of paper and cut it into eight congruent isosceles triangles. Arrange the triangles to form a parallelogram as shown. The base of the parallelogram is half the perimeter, and the height is the apothem of the octagon.

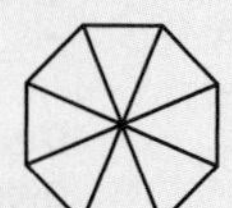

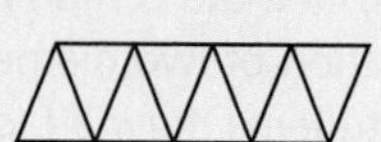

Explorations and answers are provided in *Alternate Openers: Explorations Transparencies.*

State Resources

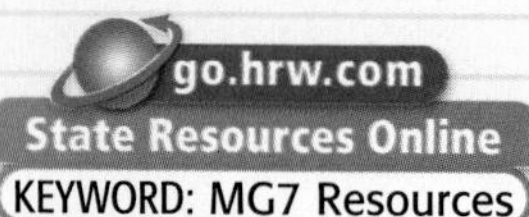

Find each measurement.

B the radius of $\odot X$ in which $C = 24\pi$ in.

$C = 2\pi r$ — *Circumference of a circle*

$24\pi = 2\pi r$ — *Substitute 24π for C.*

$r = 12$ in. — *Divide both sides by 2π.*

C the circumference of $\odot S$ in which $A = 9x^2\pi$ cm²

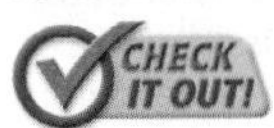
Algebra

Step 1 Use the given area to solve for r.

$A = \pi r^2$ — *Area of a circle*

$9x^2\pi = \pi r^2$ — *Substitute $9x^2\pi$ for A.*

$9x^2 = r^2$ — *Divide both sides by π.*

$3x = r$ — *Take the square root of both sides.*

Step 2 Use the value of r to find the circumference.

$C = 2\pi r$

$C = 2\pi(3x)$ — *Substitute 3x for r.*

$C = 6x\pi$ cm — *Simplify.*

CHECK IT OUT! 1. Find the area of $\odot A$ in terms of π in which $C = (4x - 6)\pi$ m. $A = (4x^2 - 12x + 9)\pi$ m²

EXAMPLE 2 **Music Application**

A drum kit contains three drums with diameters of 10 in., 12 in., and 14 in. Find the area of the top of each drum. Round to the nearest tenth.

10 in. diameter	12 in. diameter	14 in. diameter
$A = \pi(5^2)$ $r = \frac{10}{2} = 5$	$A = \pi(6^2)$ $r = \frac{12}{2} = 6$	$A = \pi(7)^2$ $r = \frac{14}{2} = 7$
$\cong 78.5$ in²	$\cong 113.1$ in²	$\cong 153.9$ in²

Helpful Hint

The π key gives the best possible approximation for π on your calculator. Always wait until the last step to round.

CHECK IT OUT! 2. Use the information above to find the circumference of each drum. $C \approx 31.4$ in.; $C \approx 37.7$ in.; $C \approx 44.0$ in.

The **center of a regular polygon** is equidistant from the vertices. The **apothem** is the distance from the center to a side. A **central angle of a regular polygon** has its vertex at the center, and its sides pass through consecutive vertices. Each central angle measure of a regular n-gon is $\frac{360°}{n}$.

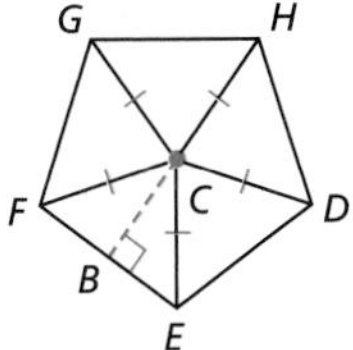

Regular pentagon DEFGH has center C, apothem BC, and central angle ∠DCE.

To find the area of a regular n-gon with side length s and apothem a, divide it into n congruent isosceles triangles.

area of each triangle: $\frac{1}{2}as$

total area of the polygon: $A = n\left(\frac{1}{2}as\right)$, or $A = \frac{1}{2}aP$ — *The perimeter is $P = ns$.*

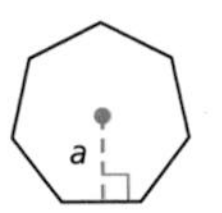

Know it! Note

Area Regular Polygon

The area of a regular polygon with apothem a and perimeter P is $A = \frac{1}{2}aP$.

COMMON ERROR ALERT

When working with π or irrational numbers, some students may introduce errors by rounding too soon. In **Example 3B,** if students round the apothem to 5.5 in Step 2, they will get a final answer of 110.0. Remind students not to round until the final step.

Power Presentations with PowerPoint®

Additional Examples

Example 1

Find each measurement.

A. the area of $\odot K$ in terms of π
$A = 9\pi$ in²

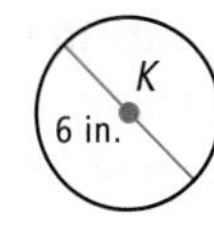

B. the radius of $\odot J$ if the circumference is $(65x + 14)\pi$ m
$r = (32.5x + 7)$ m

C. the circumference of $\odot M$ if the area is $25x^2\pi$ ft²
$C = 10x\pi$ ft

Example 2

A pizza-making kit contains three circular baking stones with diameters 24 cm, 36 cm, and 48 cm. Find the area of each stone. Round to the nearest tenth. $A_1 \approx 452.4$ cm²; $A_2 \approx 1017.9$ cm²; $A_3 \approx 1809.6$ cm²

2 Teach

Guided Instruction

Discuss the formulas for the circumference and area of a circle. Discuss different approximations for π and how they affect the accuracy of the answer. Show how the apothem is used to find the area of a regular polygon. Review the tangent ratio.

Teaching Tip **Inclusion** To remember the first five digits of π, count the letters in each word of this statement: "Wow, I made a great discovery!"

Reaching All Learners

Through Concrete Manipulatives

Have students construct a regular polygon and divide it into congruent isosceles triangles. Have them measure a central angle and compare with the result found by using the central angle formula. Instruct students to find the area of one triangle and multiply it by the number of sides of the polygon. Then have them use the formula for the area of a regular polygon and compare their results.

INTERVENTION

Questioning Strategies

EXAMPLE 1

- How can you find the area of a circle when given its circumference?
- How can you find the circumference of a circle when given its area?

EXAMPLE 2

- What happens if you use 3.14 instead of the π button on a calculator to find the area of a circle?

Power Presentations with PowerPoint®

Additional Examples

Example 3

Find the area of each regular polygon to the nearest tenth.

A. a regular heptagon with side length 2 ft $A \approx 14.5$ ft^2

B. a regular dodecagon with side length 5 cm $A \approx 279.9$ cm^2

INTERVENTION
Questioning Strategies

EXAMPLE 3

- How is the apothem used to find the area of a regular polygon?
- Why is the tangent ratio used in **Example 3B**?

Math Background Solve the tangent ratio for the apothem and substitute into the area formula to derive the alternate formula $A = \dfrac{ns^2}{4\tan\left(\frac{180}{n}\right)}$.

EXAMPLE 3 **Finding the Area of a Regular Polygon**

Find the area of each regular polygon. Round to the nearest tenth.

A a regular hexagon with side length 6 m

The perimeter is $6(6) = 36$ m. The hexagon can be divided into 6 equilateral triangles with side length 6 m. By the 30°-60°-90° Triangle Theorem, the apothem is $3\sqrt{3}$ m.

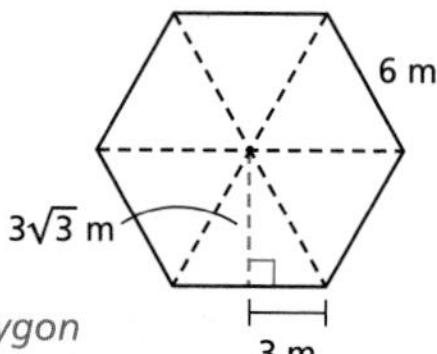

$A = \frac{1}{2}aP$ *Area of a regular polygon*

$A = \frac{1}{2}(3\sqrt{3})(36)$ *Substitute $3\sqrt{3}$ for a and 36 for P.*

$A = 54\sqrt{3} \cong 93.5$ m^2 *Simplify.*

Remember!

The tangent of an angle in a right triangle is the ratio of the opposite leg length to the adjacent leg length. See page 525.

B a regular pentagon with side length 8 in.

Step 1 Draw the pentagon. Draw an isosceles triangle with its vertex at the center of the pentagon. The central angle is $\frac{360°}{5} = 72°$. Draw a segment that bisects the central angle and the side of the polygon to form a right triangle.

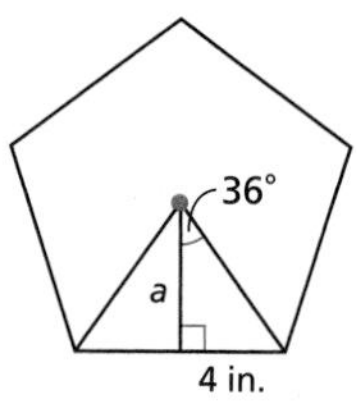

Step 2 Use the tangent ratio to find the apothem.

$\tan 36° = \frac{4}{a}$ *The tangent of an angle is $\frac{\text{opp. leg}}{\text{adj. leg}}$.*

$a = \frac{4}{\tan 36°}$ *Solve for a.*

Step 3 Use the apothem and the given side length to find the area.

$A = \frac{1}{2}aP$ *Area of a regular polygon*

$A = \frac{1}{2}\left(\frac{4}{\tan 36°}\right)(40)$ *The perimeter is $8(5) = 40$ in.*

$A \cong 110.1$ in^2 *Simplify. Round to the nearest tenth.*

CHECK IT OUT! **3.** Find the area of a regular octagon with a side length of 4 cm.
$A \approx 77.3$ cm^2

THINK AND DISCUSS

1. Describe the relationship between the circumference of a circle and π.

2. Explain how you would find the central angle of a regular polygon with n sides.

Know it! Note

3. GET ORGANIZED Copy and complete the graphic organizer.

Regular Polygons (Side Length = 1)					
Polygon	Number of Sides	Perimeter	Central Angle	Apothem	Area
Triangle					
Square					
Hexagon					

3 Close

Summarize

Draw a circle and an inscribed regular polygon on the board. Label the radius of the circle x and the apothem of the polygon y. Discuss the formulas that are used to find the area and circumference of the circle in terms of x and the area of the polygon in terms of y.

ONGOING ASSESSMENT and INTERVENTION

Diagnose ***Before*** **the Lesson**
9-2 Warm Up, TE p. 600

Monitor ***During*** **the Lesson**
Check It Out! Exercises, SE pp. 601–602
Questioning Strategies, TE pp. 601–602

Assess ***After*** **the Lesson**
9-2 Lesson Quiz, TE p. 605
Alternative Assessment, TE p. 605

Answers to *Think and Discuss*

1. The circumference of a circle is π times the diameter.
2. Divide 360° by n.
3. See p. A7.

9-2 Exercises

go.hrw.com
Homework Help Online
KEYWORD: MG7 9-2
Parent Resources Online
KEYWORD: MG7 Parent

GUIDED PRACTICE

1. Vocabulary Describe how to find the *apothem* of a square with side length *s*.
Draw a segment perpendicular to a side with one endpoint at the center. The apothem is $\frac{1}{2}s$.

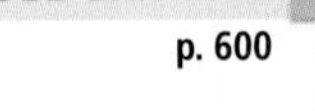

SEE EXAMPLE 1 p. 600

Find each measurement.

2. the circumference of $\odot C$

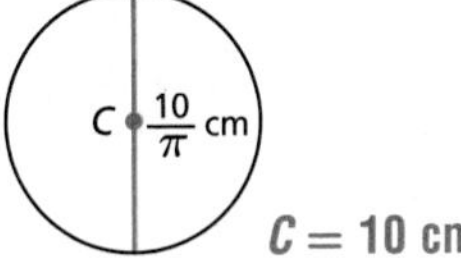

$C = 10$ cm

3. the area of $\odot A$ in terms of π

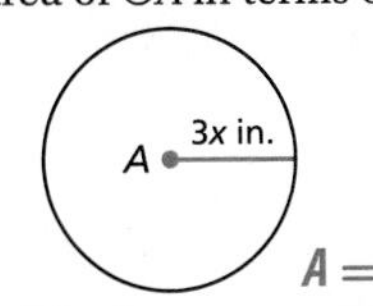

$A = 9x^2\pi$ in^2

4. the circumference of $\odot P$ in which $A = 36\pi$ in^2 $C = 12\pi$ in.

SEE EXAMPLE 2 p. 601

5. Food A pizza parlor offers pizzas with diameters of 8 in., 10 in., and 12 in. Find the area of each size pizza. Round to the nearest tenth. $A \approx 50.3$ in^2; $A \approx 78.5$ in^2; $A \approx 113.1$ in^2

SEE EXAMPLE 3 p. 602

Find the area of each regular polygon. Round to the nearest tenth.

6.

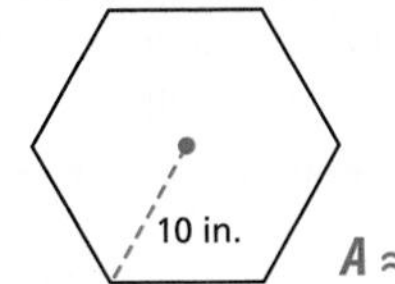

$A \approx 259.8$ in^2

7.

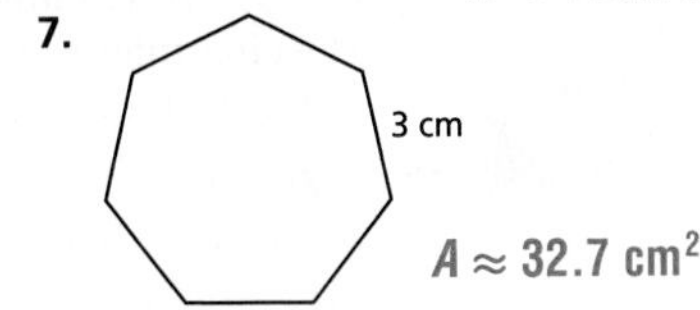

$A \approx 32.7$ cm^2

8. an equilateral triangle with an apothem of 2 ft $A \approx 20.8$ ft^2

9. a regular dodecagon with a side length of 5 m $A \approx 279.9$ m^2

PRACTICE AND PROBLEM SOLVING

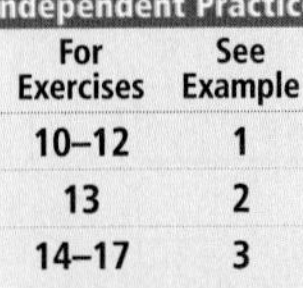

Independent Practice

For Exercises	See Example
10–12	1
13	2
14–17	3

Extra Practice
Skills Practice p. S20
Application Practice p. S36

Find each measurement. Give your answers in terms of π.

10. the area of $\odot M$ $A = 49\pi$ yd^2

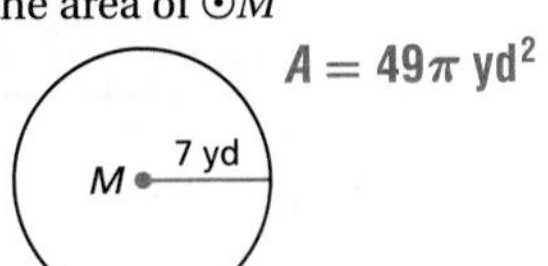

11. the circumference of $\odot Z$ $C = 5\pi$ m

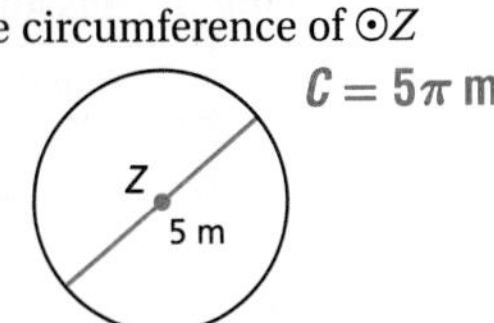

12. the diameter of $\odot G$ in which $C = 10$ ft. $d = \frac{10}{\pi}$ ft

13. Sports A horse trainer uses circular pens that are 35 ft, 50 ft, and 66 ft in diameter. Find the area of each pen. Round to the nearest tenth.
$A \approx 962.1$ ft^2; $A \approx 1963.5$ ft^2; $A \approx 3421.2$ ft^2

Find the area of each regular polygon. Round to the nearest tenth, if necessary.

14.

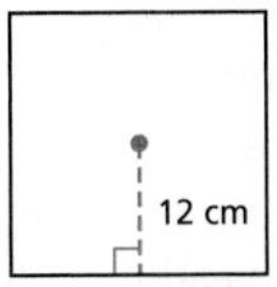

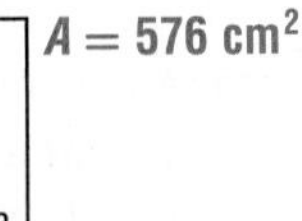

$A = 576$ cm^2

15.

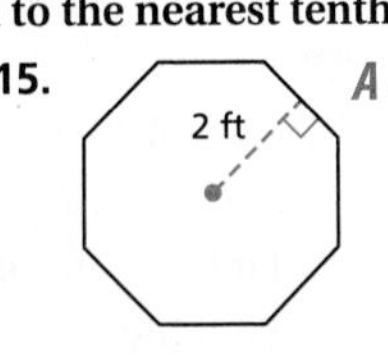

$A \approx 13.3$ ft^2

16. a regular nonagon with a perimeter of 144 in. $A \approx 1582.5$ in^2

17. a regular pentagon with an apothem of 2 ft. $A \approx 14.5$ ft^2

9-2 Exercises

Assignment Guide

Assign *Guided Practice* exercises as necessary.

If you finished Examples 1–3
Basic 10–26, 29–40, 43–45, 49–54
Average 10–17, 18–24 even, 26–46, 49–54
Advanced 10–17, 18–24 even, 26–32, 34–54

Homework Quick Check
Quickly check key concepts.
Exercises: 10, 13, 14, 22, 26

Critical Thinking In **Exercise 5,** have students estimate by using 3 for π to check whether their answers are reasonable.

State Resources

go.hrw.com
State Resources Online
KEYWORD: MG7 Resources

MULTI-STEP TEST PREP **Exercise 39** involves finding the area of an octagon. This exercise prepares students for the Multi-Step Test Prep on page 614.

Kinesthetic Have students make a mini trundle wheel to model **Exercise 40.** Have them use a compass to draw a circle on cardboard and then cut it out. Then have them place a brad through the center of the circle to attach a pencil as a handle.

Find the central angle measure of each regular polygon. (*Hint:* **To review polygon names, see page 382.)**

18. equilateral triangle **120°** **19.** square **90°** **20.** pentagon **72°** **21.** hexagon **60°**

22. heptagon $\approx$ **51.4°** **23.** octagon **45°** **24.** nonagon **40°** **25.** decagon **36°**

Find the area of each regular polygon. Round to the nearest tenth.

26.

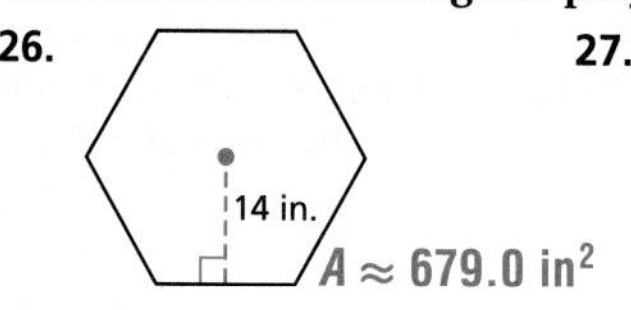

$A \approx 679.0$ in^2

27. 5 cm

$A \approx 84.3$ cm^2

28.

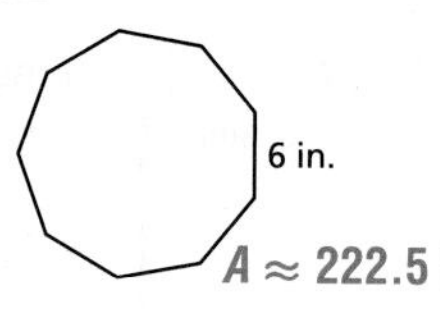

$A \approx 222.5$ in^2

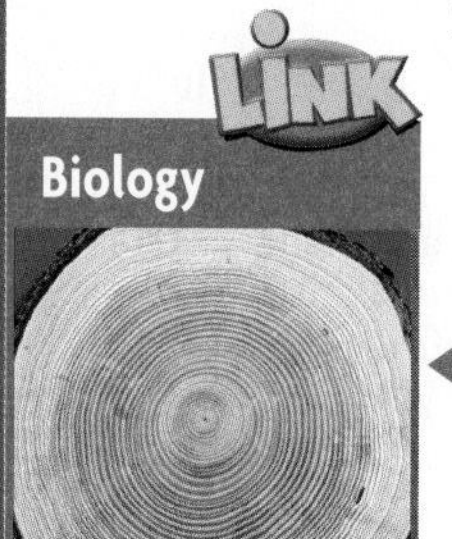

Biology

Dendroclimatologists study tree rings for evidence of changes in weather patterns over time.

29.

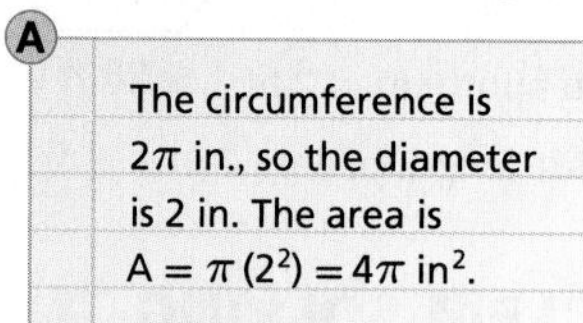

$A \approx 46.8$ m^2

30.

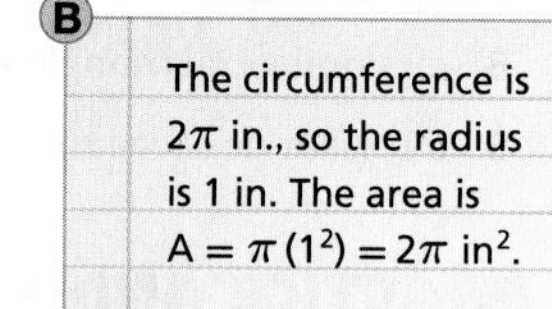

$A \approx 11.3$ cm^2

31. 5 ft

$A \approx 90.8$ ft^2

32. Biology You can estimate a tree's age in years by using the formula $a = \frac{r}{w}$, where r is the tree's radius without bark and w is the average thickness of the tree's rings. The circumference of a white oak tree is 100 in. The bark is 0.5 in. thick, and the average width of a ring is 0.2 in. Estimate the tree's age. **77 yr**

33. ERROR ANALYSIS A circle has a circumference of 2π in. Which calculation of the area is incorrect? Explain.

A The circumference is 2π in., so the diameter is 2 in. The area is $A = \pi(2^2) = 4\pi$ in^2.

B The circumference is 2π in., so the radius is 1 in. The area is $A = \pi(1^2) = 2\pi$ in^2.

The calculation shown in A is incorrect because the diameter, instead of the radius, is used to find the area.

Find the missing measurements for each circle. Give your answers in terms of π.

	Diameter d	Radius r	Area A	Circumference C
34.	6	3	9π	6π
35.			100	$20\sqrt{\pi}$
36.	34	17	289π	34π
37.	36	18	324π	36π

35. $20\frac{\sqrt{\pi}}{\pi}$; $10\frac{\sqrt{\pi}}{\pi}$

38. Multi-Step Janet is designing a garden around a gazebo that is a regular hexagon with side length 6 ft. The garden will be a circle that extends 10 feet from the vertices of the hexagon. What is the area of the garden? Round to the nearest square foot. $A \approx 711$ ft^2

39a. $A \approx 745.6$ in^2
b. $A \approx 1073.6$ in^2

39. This problem will prepare you for the Multi-Step Test Prep on page 614.

A stop sign is a regular octagon. The signs are available in two sizes: 30 in. or 36 in.

a. Find the area of a 30 in. sign. Round to the nearest tenth.

b. Find the area of a 36 in. sign. Round to the nearest tenth.

c. Find the percent increase in metal needed to make a 36 in. sign instead of a 30 in. sign. **44%**

9-2 PRACTICE A
9-2 PRACTICE C
9-2 PRACTICE B

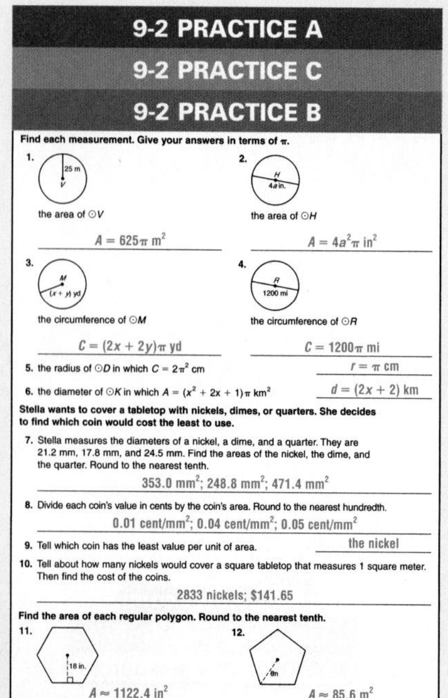

Find each measurement. Give your answers in terms of π.

1. the area of ⊙V — $A = 625\pi$ m^2
2. the area of ⊙H — $A = 4a^2\pi$ in^2
3. the circumference of ⊙M — $C = (2x + 2y)\pi$ yd
4. the circumference of ⊙R — $C = 1200\pi$ mi
5. the radius of ⊙D in which $C = 2\pi^2$ cm — $r = \pi$ cm
6. the diameter of ⊙K in which $A = (x^2 + 2x + 1)\pi$ km^2 — $d = (2x + 2)$ km

Stella wants to cover a tabletop with nickels, dimes, or quarters. She decides to find which coin would cost the least to use.

7. Stella measures the diameters of a nickel, a dime, and a quarter. They are 21.2 mm, 17.8 mm, and 24.5 mm. Find the areas of the nickel, the dime, and the quarter. Round to the nearest tenth. — 353.0 mm^2; 248.8 mm^2; 471.4 mm^2
8. Divide each coin's value in cents by the coin's area. Round to the nearest hundredth. — 0.01 cent/mm^2; 0.04 cent/mm^2; 0.05 cent/mm^2
9. Tell which coin has the least value per unit of area. — the nickel
10. Tell about how many nickels would cover a square tabletop that measures 1 square meter. Then find the cost of the coins. — 2833 nickels; $141.65

Find the area of each regular polygon. Round to the nearest tenth.

11. $A \approx 1122.4$ in^2
12. $A \approx 85.6$ m^2

9-2 READING STRATEGIES

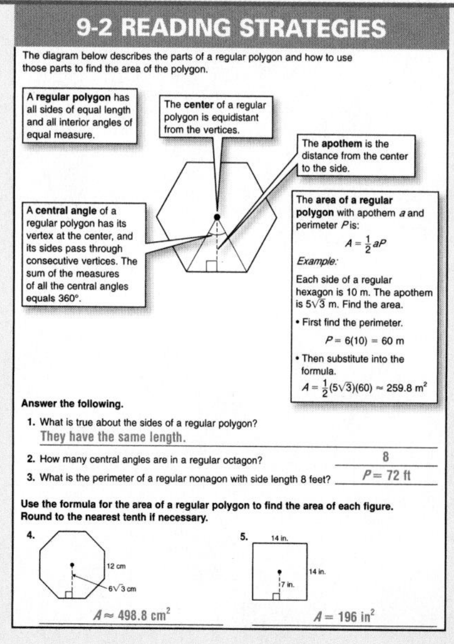

The diagram below describes the parts of a regular polygon and how to use those parts to find the area of the polygon.

A **regular polygon** has all sides of equal length and all interior angles of equal measure.

The **center** of a regular polygon is equidistant from the vertices.

The **apothem** is the distance from the center to the side.

A **central angle** of a regular polygon has its vertex at the center, and its sides pass through consecutive vertices. The sum of the measures of all the central angles equals 360°.

The **area of a regular polygon** with apothem a and perimeter P is: $A = \frac{1}{2}aP$

Example: Each side of a regular hexagon is 10 m. The apothem is $5\sqrt{3}$ m. Find the area.
• First find the perimeter. $P = 6(10) = 60$ m
• Then substitute into the formula. $A = \frac{1}{2}(5\sqrt{3})(60) \approx 259.8$ m^2

Answer the following.

1. What is true about the sides of a regular polygon? — They have the same length.
2. How many central angles are in a regular octagon? — 8
3. What is the perimeter of a regular nonagon with side length 8 feet? — $P = 72$ ft

Use the formula for the area of a regular polygon to find the area of each figure. Round to the nearest tenth if necessary.

4. $A \approx 498.8$ cm^2
5. $A = 196$ in^2

9-2 RETEACH

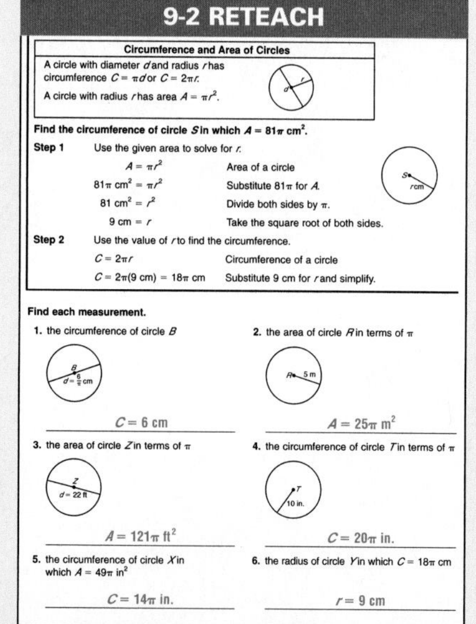

Circumference and Area of Circles

A circle with diameter d and radius r has circumference $C = \pi d$ or $C = 2\pi r$.
A circle with radius r has area $A = \pi r^2$.

Find the circumference of circle S in which $A = 81\pi$ cm^2.

Step 1 Use the given area to solve for r.
$A = \pi r^2$ — Area of a circle
81π cm^2 $= \pi r^2$ — Substitute 81π for A.
81 cm^2 $= r^2$ — Divide both sides by π.
9 cm $= r$ — Take the square root of both sides.

Step 2 Use the value of r to find the circumference.
$C = 2\pi r$ — Circumference of a circle
$C = 2\pi(9$ cm$) = 18\pi$ cm — Substitute 9 cm for r and simplify.

Find each measurement.

1. the circumference of circle B — $C = 6$ cm
2. the area of circle R in terms of π — $A = 25\pi$ m^2
3. the area of circle Z in terms of π — $A = 121\pi$ ft^2
4. the circumference of circle T in terms of π — $C = 20\pi$ in.
5. the circumference of circle X in which $A = 49\pi$ in^2 — $C = 14\pi$ in.
6. the radius of circle Y in which $C = 18\pi$ cm — $r = 9$ cm

40. **Measurement** A *trundle wheel* is used to measure distances by rolling it on the ground and counting its number of turns. If the circumference of a trundle wheel is 1 meter, what is its diameter? $d \approx 318$ mm, or 0.318 m

41. **Critical Thinking** Which do you think would seat more people, a 4 ft by 6 ft rectangular table or a circular table with a diameter of 6 ft? How many people would you sit at each table? Explain your reasoning.

42. **Write About It** The center of each circle in the figure lies on the number line. Describe the relationship between the circumference of the largest circle and the circumferences of the four smaller circles.
The circumference of the largest circle is equal to the sum of the circumferences of the four smaller circles.

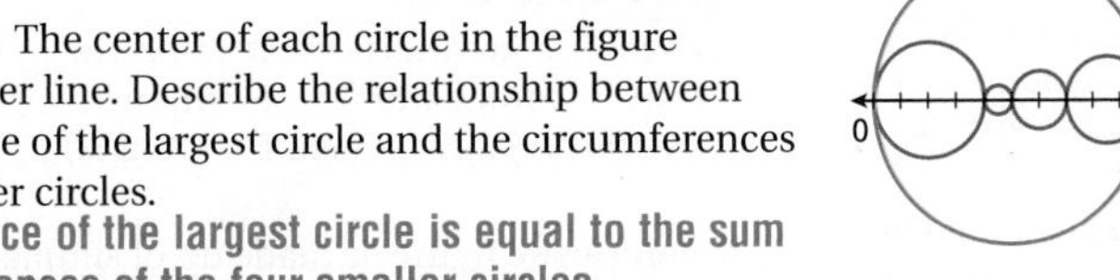

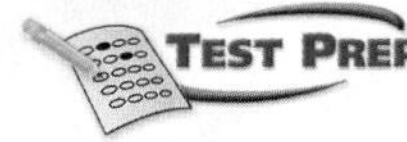

TEST PREP

43. Find the perimeter of the regular octagon to the nearest centimeter.
Ⓐ 5 Ⓑ 40 (circled) Ⓒ 20 Ⓓ 68

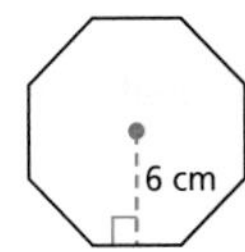

44. Which of the following ratios comparing a circle's circumference C to its diameter d gives the value of π?
Ⓕ $\frac{C}{d}$ (circled) Ⓖ $\frac{4C}{d^2}$ Ⓗ $\frac{d}{C}$ Ⓙ $\frac{d}{2C}$

48. As n gets very large, the n-gon begins to look like a circle with C close to P and a close to r. The area of the polygon can be written as $A = \frac{1}{2}aP$, which is close to $\frac{1}{2}rC$, or $\frac{1}{2}r(2\pi r) = \pi r^2$.

45. Alisa has a circular tabletop with a 2-foot diameter. She wants to paint a pattern on the table top that includes a 2-foot-by-1-foot rectangle and 4 squares with sides 0.5 foot long. Which information makes this scenario impossible?
Ⓐ There will be no room left on the tabletop after the rectangle has been painted.
Ⓑ A 2-foot-long rectangle will not fit on the circular tabletop. (circled)
Ⓒ Squares cannot be painted on the circle.
Ⓓ There will not be enough room on the table to fit all the 0.5-foot squares.

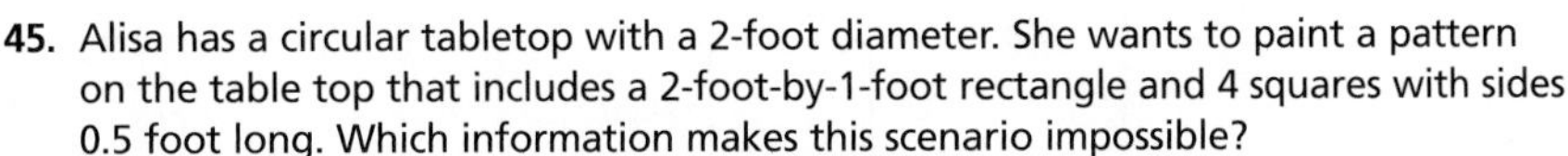

CHALLENGE AND EXTEND

46. Two circles have the same center. The radius of the larger circle is 5 units longer than the radius of the smaller circle. Find the difference in the circumferences of the two circles. 10π units

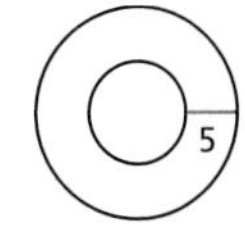

47. **Algebra** Write the formula for the area of a circle in terms of its circumference. $A = \frac{C^2}{4\pi}$

48. **Critical Thinking** Show that the formula for the area of a regular n-gon approaches the formula for the area of a circle as n gets very large.

SPIRAL REVIEW

Write an equation for the linear function represented by the table. *(Previous course)*

49.

x	−2	0	5	10
y	−19	−13	2	17

$y = 3x - 13$

50.

x	−3	0	4	9
y	2	−1	−5	−10

$y = -x - 1$

Find each value. *(Lesson 4-8)*

51. $m\angle B$ $m\angle B = 124°$

52. AB 30

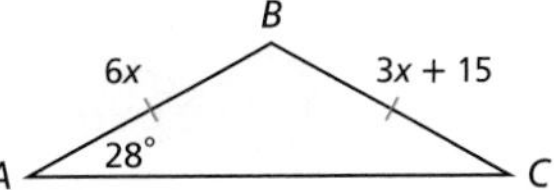

Find each measurement. *(Lesson 9-1)*

53. d_2 of a kite if $A = 14\text{ cm}^2$ and $d_1 = 20$ cm $d_2 = 1.4$ cm

54. the area of a trapezoid in which $b_1 = 3$ yd, $b_2 = 6$ yd, and $h = 4$ yd $A = 18\text{ yd}^2$

COMMON ERROR ALERT

In **Exercise 38,** students may think the radius of the circle is 10 ft. Have students read the problem carefully to see that the circle extends 10 ft from the vertices of the hexagon.

TEST PREP DOCTOR If students have difficulty with **Exercise 44,** encourage them to write the circumference formula and solve it for π.

For **Exercise 45,** students may find it difficult to visualize the pattern on the tabletop. Suggest that they sketch what the tabletop with the pattern might look like before choosing an answer.

Journal

Have students explain how to find the area of a regular polygon when given the apothem and the side length, and how to find the area when given the perimeter and the number of sides.

ALTERNATIVE ASSESSMENT

Have students make a table in which the first row contains figures from the lesson, the second row contains the formula for the area of each figure, and the third row contains the steps to find the area of each figure.

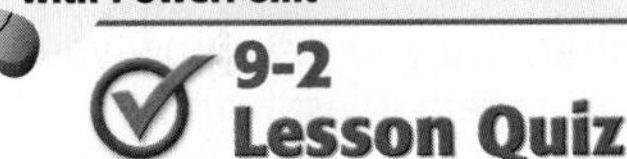

9-2 Lesson Quiz

Find each measurement.

1. the area of $\odot D$ in terms of π $A = 49\pi\text{ ft}^2$

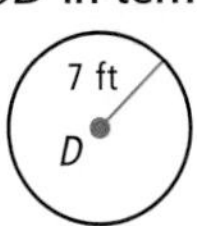

2. the circumference of $\odot T$ in which $A = 16\pi\text{ mm}^2$ $C = 8\pi$ mm

3. Speakers come in diameters of 4 in., 9 in., and 16 in. Find the area of each speaker to the nearest tenth. $A_1 \approx 12.6\text{ in}^2$; $A_2 \approx 63.6\text{ in}^2$; $A_3 \approx 201.1\text{ in}^2$

Find the area of each regular polygon to the nearest tenth.

4. a regular nonagon with side length 8 cm $A \approx 395.6\text{ cm}^2$

5. a regular octagon with side length 9 ft $A \approx 391.1\text{ ft}^2$

Also available on transparency

9-2 PROBLEM SOLVING

1. What is the area of the regular nonagon? Round to the nearest tenth.
8 cm
395.6 cm^2

2. The top view of a two-tiered wedding cake is shown. Each tier is a regular hexagon. What percent of the bottom tier is covered by the top tier? Round to the nearest percent.
5 in. 8 in. top tier bottom tier
39%

3. When diving and snorkeling, you should leave a "radius of approach," or a restricted area around certain animals that live in the waters where you are diving. How much greater is the restricted area around a monk seal than the restricted area around a sea turtle? Give your answer in terms of π.

Animal	Radius of Approach
sea turtle	20 ft
monk seal	100 ft

$9600\pi\text{ ft}^2$

4. A yield sign is a regular triangle and is available in two sizes: 30 inches or 36 inches. Find how much more metal is needed to make a 36 inch sign than a 30 inch sign. Answer to the nearest percent.
YIELD 30 in. or 36 in.
44%

Choose the best answer.

5. A regular hexagon has an apothem of 4.6 centimeters. Which is the best estimate for the area of the hexagon?
A 36.7 cm^2
B 63.5 cm^2
Ⓒ 73.3 cm^2
D 146.6 cm^2

6. An amusement park ride is made up of a large circular frame that holds 50 riders. The circumference of the frame is about 138 feet. What is the diameter of the ride to the nearest foot?
F 22 ft H 69 ft
Ⓖ 44 ft J 138 ft

7. A cyclist travels 50 feet after 7.34 rotations of her bicycle wheels. What is the approximate diameter of the wheels?
A 13 in. Ⓒ 26 in.
B 24 in. D 28 in.

8. A regular pentagon has side length 16 inches What is the area of the pentagon to the nearest square inch?
Ⓕ 440 in^2 H 544 in^2
G 369 in^2 J 881 in^2

Answers

41. Possible answer: The circular table would fit at least as many people as the rectangular table. At the rectangular table, 2 people would fit at each of the 4 ft sides and 3 people would fit at each of the 6 ft sides, for a total of 10 people. Each person would have 2 ft of space. If 11 people sat at the circular table, each person would have about 1 ft 9 in. of space.

9-3 Organizer

Pacing: Traditional 1 day
Block $\frac{1}{2}$ day

Objectives: Use the Area Addition Postulate to find the areas of composite figures.

Use composite figures to estimate the areas of irregular shapes.

Online Edition
Tutorial Videos

Countdown Week 20

Power Presentations with PowerPoint®

Warm Up

Find the area of each figure.

1. a rectangle in which $b = 14$ cm and $h = 5$ cm
   $A = 70 \text{ cm}^2$
2. a triangle in which $b = 6$ in. and $h = 18$ in. $A = 54 \text{ in}^2$
3. a trapezoid in which $b_1 = 7$ ft, $b_2 = 11$ ft, and $h = 3$ ft
   $A = 27 \text{ ft}^2$

Also available on transparency

Math Humor

Teacher: Did you just throw your art project together last night?

Student: Yes. I call it *Composite Art.*

9-3 Composite Figures

Objectives
Use the Area Addition Postulate to find the areas of composite figures.

Use composite figures to estimate the areas of irregular shapes.

Vocabulary
composite figure

Who uses this?
Landscape architects must compute areas of composite figures when designing gardens. (See Example 3.)

A **composite figure** is made up of simple shapes, such as triangles, rectangles, trapezoids, and circles. To find the area of a composite figure, find the areas of the simple shapes and then use the Area Addition Postulate.

EXAMPLE 1 Finding the Areas of Composite Figures by Adding

Find the shaded area. Round to the nearest tenth, if necessary.

A

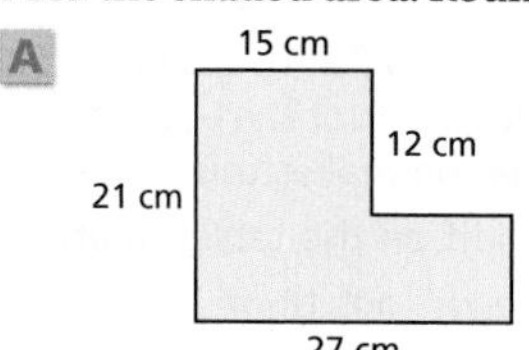

Divide the figure into rectangles.

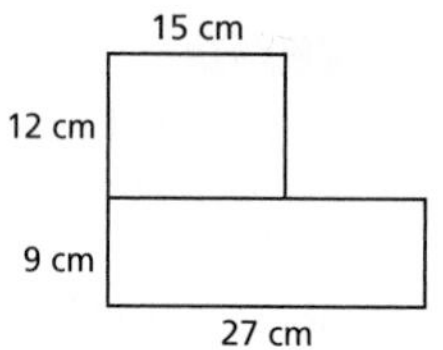

area of top rectangle:
$A = bh = 12(15) = 180 \text{ cm}^2$

area of bottom rectangle:
$A = bh = 9(27) = 243 \text{ cm}^2$

shaded area:
$180 + 243 = 423 \text{ cm}^2$

B

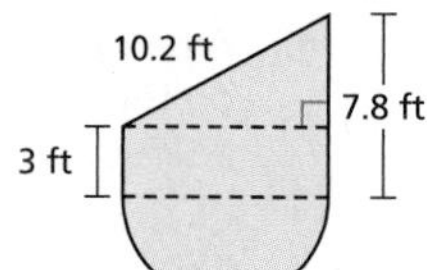

Divide the figure into parts. The base of the triangle is $\sqrt{10.2^2 - 4.8^2} = 9$ ft.

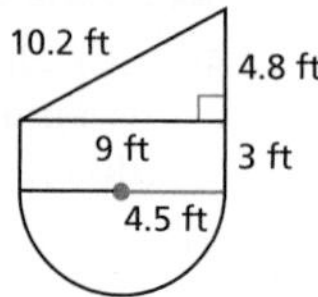

area of triangle:
$A = \frac{1}{2}bh = \frac{1}{2}(9)(4.8) = 21.6 \text{ ft}^2$

area of rectangle:
$A = bh = 9(3) = 27 \text{ ft}^2$

area of half circle:
$A = \frac{1}{2}\pi r^2 = \frac{1}{2}\pi(4.5^2) = 10.125\pi \text{ ft}^2$

shaded area:
$21.6 + 27 + 10.125\pi \approx 80.4 \text{ ft}^2$

CHECK IT OUT! 1. Find the shaded area. Round to the nearest tenth, if necessary.
$A = 1781.3 \text{ m}^2$

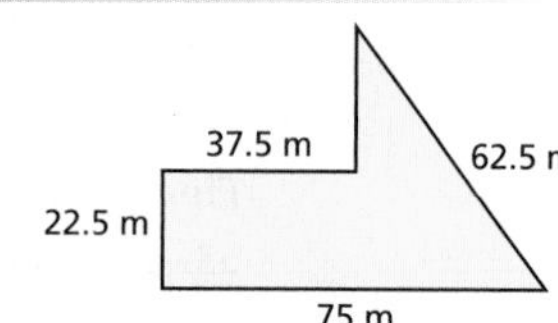

State Resources

go.hrw.com
State Resources Online
KEYWORD: MG7 Resources

1 Introduce

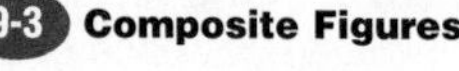

EXPLORATION

9-3 Composite Figures

Sometimes you can find the area of a complex figure by dividing it into simpler shapes such as triangles, rectangles, and trapezoids.

1. The figure shows the floor plan of an art gallery. The owner wants to divide the gallery into three smaller rooms. Each room must be a triangle, a rectangle, or a trapezoid. Copy the figure and show how the owner can divide the gallery.
2. Compare your work to that of other students. Are there different ways to divide the gallery? If so, sketch some of the other possibilities.
3. Suppose the owner wants to divide the gallery into four smaller rooms, each in the shape of either a trapezoid or a triangle. Show how the owner can do this.

THINK AND DISCUSS

4. **Explain** whether it is possible to divide the gallery so that all of the smaller rooms are

Motivate

Have each student trace the outside of one of his or her feet onto centimeter graph paper. Ask how they might find the area of this shape. In this lesson, students will learn to estimate the areas of irregular shapes by using composite figures.

Explorations and answers are provided in *Alternate Openers: Explorations Transparencies.*

Sometimes you need to subtract to find the area of a composite figure.

EXAMPLE 2 Finding the Areas of Composite Figures by Subtracting

Find the shaded area. Round to the nearest tenth, if necessary.

A

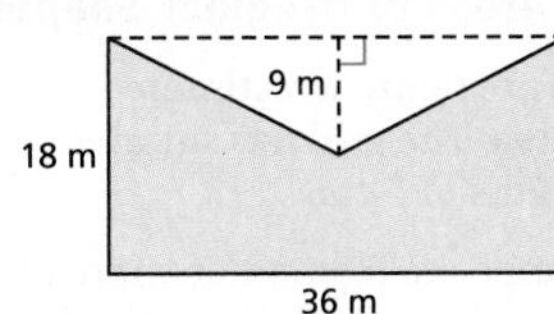

Subtract the area of the triangle from the area of the rectangle.

area of rectangle:
$A = bh = 18(36) = 648 \text{ m}^2$

area of triangle:
$A = \frac{1}{2}bh = \frac{1}{2}(36)(9) = 162 \text{ m}^2$

area of figure:
$A = 648 - 162 = 486 \text{ m}^2$

B

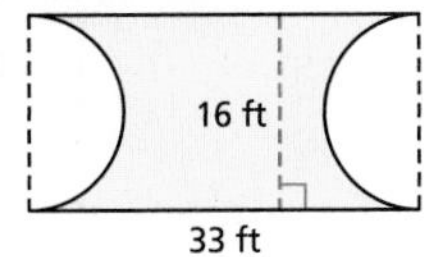

The two half circles have the same area as one circle. Subtract the area of the circle from the area of the rectangle.

area of the rectangle:
$A = bh = 33(16) = 528 \text{ ft}^2$

area of circle:
$A = \pi r^2 = \pi(8^2) = 64\pi \text{ ft}^2$

area of figure:
$A = 528 - 64\pi \approx 326.9 \text{ ft}^2$

2. Find the shaded area. Round to the nearest tenth, if necessary.
$A \approx 10.3 \text{ in}^2$

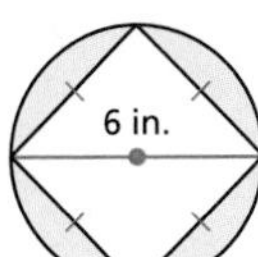

EXAMPLE 3 *Landscaping Application*

Katie is using the given plan to convert part of her lawn to a xeriscape garden. A newly planted xeriscape uses 17 gallons of water per square foot per year. How much water will the garden require in one year?

28.5 ft
7.5 ft
10.5 ft
19.5 ft
6 ft
12 ft

To find the area of the garden in square feet, divide the garden into parts.

The area of the top rectangle is $28.5(7.5) = 213.75 \text{ ft}^2$.

The area of the center trapezoid is $\frac{1}{2}(12 + 18)(6) = 90 \text{ ft}^2$.

The area of the bottom rectangle is $12(6) = 72 \text{ ft}^2$.

The total area of the garden is $213.75 + 90 + 72 = 375.75 \text{ ft}^2$.

The garden will use $375.75(17) = 6387.75$ gallons of water per year.

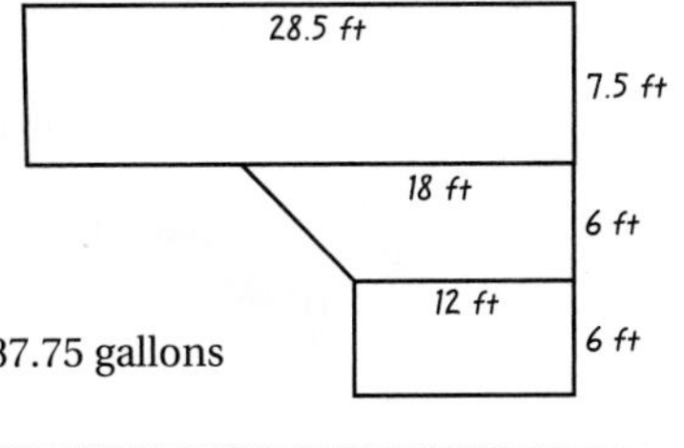

3. The lawn that Katie is replacing requires 79 gallons of water per square foot per year. How much water will Katie save by planting the xeriscape garden? **23,296.5 gal**

COMMON ERROR ALERT

Students may divide composite figures into shapes that they are unable to find the area of. Remind them that some figures can be divided in more than one way. If they are having difficulty, encourage them to divide the figures in a different way.

Power Presentations with PowerPoint®

Additional Examples

Example 1

Find the shaded area. Round to the nearest tenth, if necessary.

A. 521.1 mm²

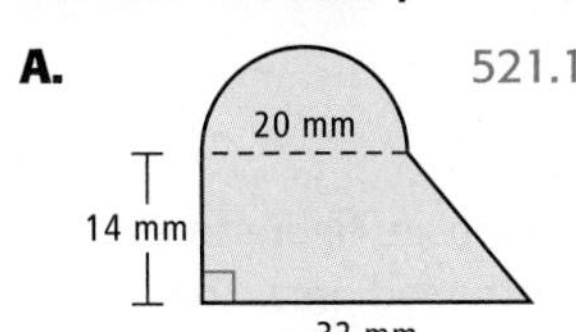

B. 65 ft²

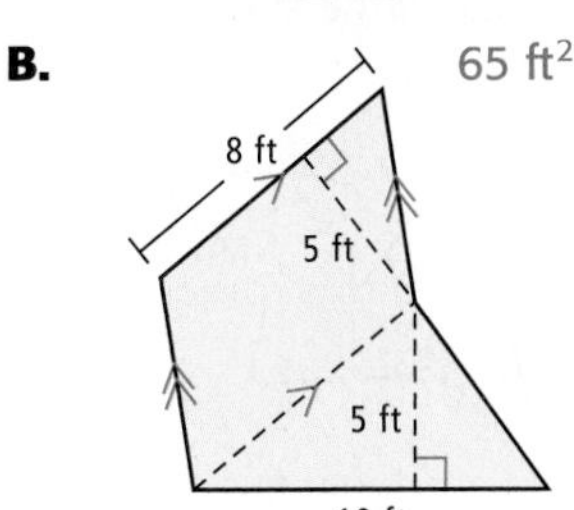

Example 2

Find the shaded area. Round to the nearest tenth, if necessary.

A. 202.2 ft²

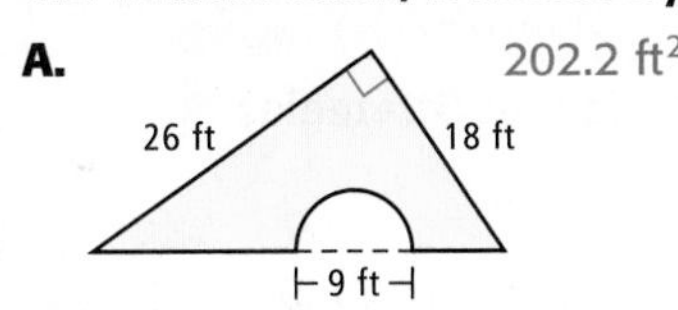

B. 186.2 cm²

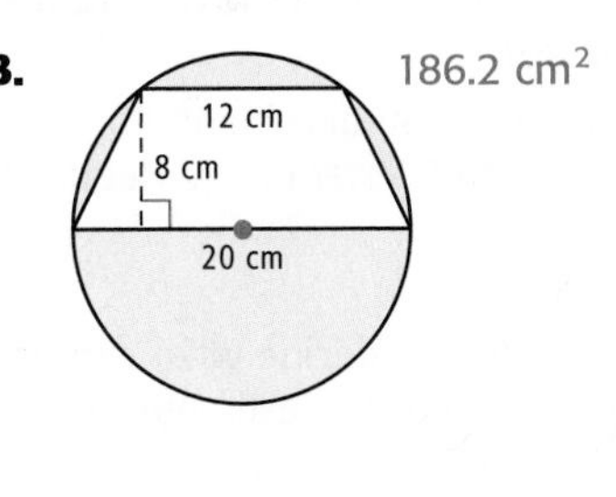

2 Teach

Guided Instruction

Review the Area Addition Postulate. Show how to find areas of composite figures by adding or subtracting areas and how to estimate areas of irregular shapes.

Reading Math To remember what a *composite figure* is, think of the word *compose*, which means "to form by putting together." A composite figure is formed by putting together simple shapes.

ENGLISH LANGUAGE LEARNERS

Reaching All Learners

Through Cooperative Learning

Divide students into groups. Have each group member find the area of one simple shape in a composite figure. Then they can add or subtract the areas as a group.

INTERVENTION 

Questioning Strategies

EXAMPLE 1

- What are some different ways that you can divide each composite figure?
- Will two different ways of dividing a figure give the same area?

EXAMPLE 2

- How do you know when to add areas and when to subtract areas?

Power Presentations with PowerPoint®

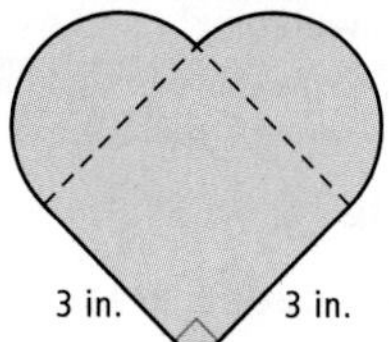

Example 3

A company receives an order for 65 pieces of fabric in the given shape. Each piece is to be dyed red. To dye 6 in^2 of fabric, 2 oz of dye is needed. How much dye is needed for the entire order?

348 oz

Example 4

Use a composite figure to estimate the shaded area. The grid has squares with a side length of 1 ft.

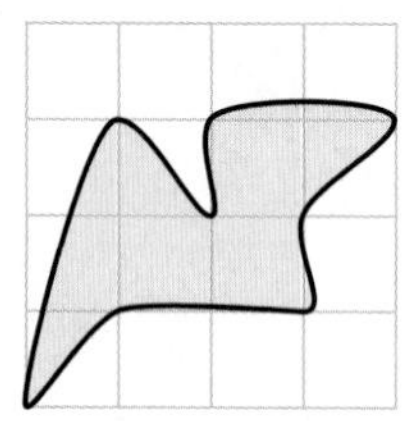

about 5.5 ft^2

INTERVENTION
Questioning Strategies

- How can you find the area of the figure?
- How can you determine the amount of water or dye needed?

- How do you decide what simple shapes to use to estimate the area of an irregular figure?

To estimate the area of an irregular shape, you can sometimes use a composite figure. First, draw a composite figure that resembles the irregular shape. Then divide the composite figure into simple shapes.

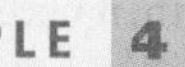

Estimating Areas of Irregular Shapes

Use a composite figure to estimate the shaded area. The grid has squares with side lengths of 1 cm.

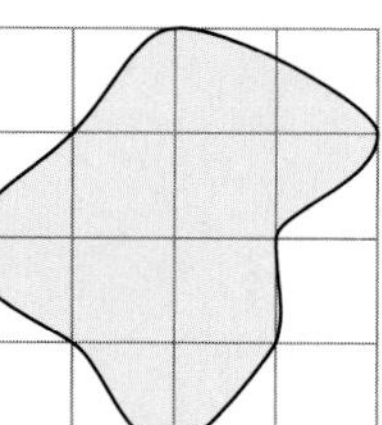

Draw a composite figure that approximates the irregular shape. Find the area of each part of the composite figure.

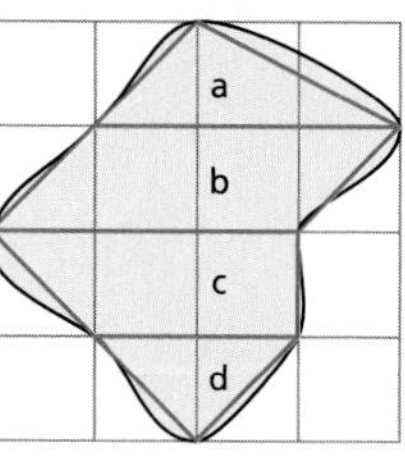

area of triangle a:

$A = \frac{1}{2}bh = \frac{1}{2}(3)(1) = 1.5 \text{ cm}^2$

area of parallelogram b:

$A = bh = 3(1) = 3 \text{ cm}^2$

area of trapezoid c:

$A = \frac{1}{2}(3 + 2)(1) = 2.5 \text{ cm}^2$

area of triangle d:

$A = \frac{1}{2}(2)(1) = 1 \text{ cm}^2$

area of composite figure:

$1.5 + 3 + 2.5 + 1 = 8 \text{ cm}^2$

The shaded area is about 8 cm^2.

4. Use a composite figure to estimate the shaded area. The grid has squares with side lengths of 1 ft.
$A \approx 12$ ft^2

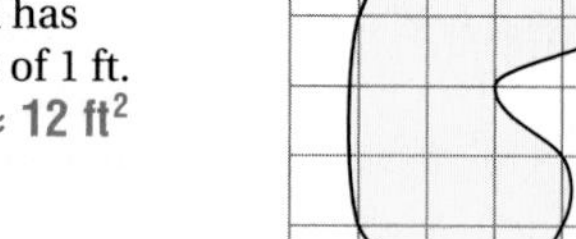

THINK AND DISCUSS

1. Describe a composite figure whose area you could find by using subtraction.
2. Explain how to find the area of an irregular shape by using a composite figure.

3. **GET ORGANIZED** Copy and complete the graphic organizer. Use the given composite figure.

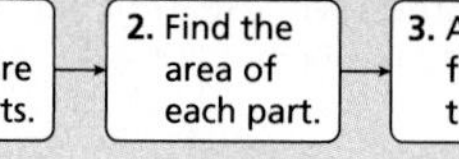

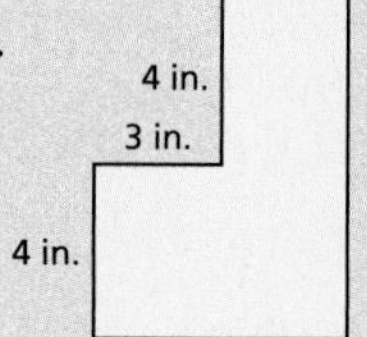

3 Close

Summarize

Review composite figures and remind students that they can find the area of a composite figure by dividing it into simple shapes. Explain that they can estimate the area of an irregular shape by drawing a composite figure that approximates the irregular shape and finding the area of the composite figure.

and INTERVENTION

Diagnose ***Before*** **the Lesson**
9-3 Warm Up, TE p. 606

Monitor ***During*** **the Lesson**
Check It Out! Exercises, SE pp. 606–608
Questioning Strategies, TE pp. 607–608

Assess ***After*** **the Lesson**
9-3 Lesson Quiz, TE p. 612
Alternative Assessment, TE p. 612

Answers to *Think and Discuss*

1. Possible answer: a figure with a hole in the middle
2. Draw a composite figure with an area close to the area of the irregular shape. Divide the composite figure into simpler shapes, such as triangles, rectangles, and trapezoids. Find the sum of the areas of the simpler shapes.
3. See p. A7.

9-3 Exercises

go.hrw.com
Homework Help Online
KEYWORD: MG7 9-3
Parent Resources Online
KEYWORD: MG7 Parent

GUIDED PRACTICE

1. **Vocabulary** Draw a *composite figure* that is made up of two rectangles.

SEE EXAMPLE 1
p. 606

Multi-Step Find the shaded area. Round to the nearest tenth, if necessary.

2. 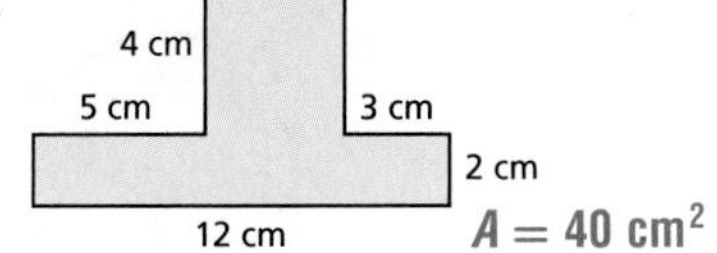

$A = 40 \text{ cm}^2$

3. 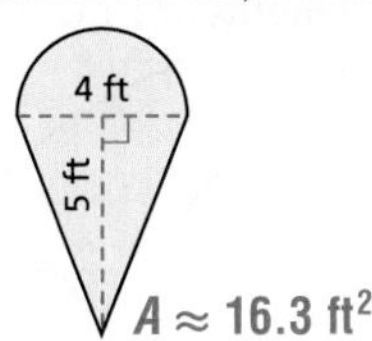

$A \approx 16.3 \text{ ft}^2$

SEE EXAMPLE 2
p. 607

4. 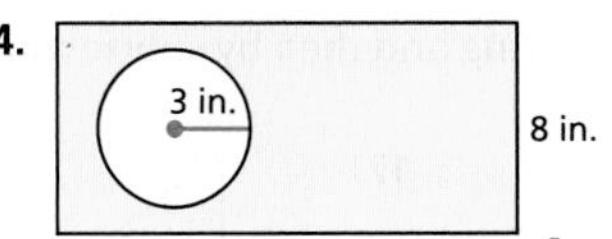

$A \approx 115.7 \text{ in}^2$

5. 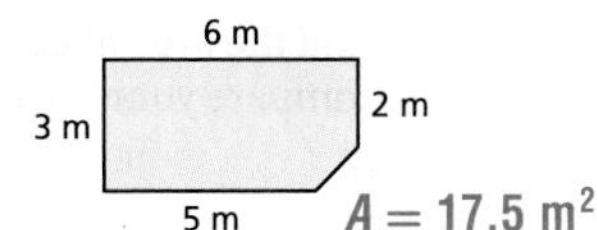

$A = 17.5 \text{ m}^2$

SEE EXAMPLE 3
p. 607

6. **Interior Decorating** Barbara is getting carpet installed in her living room and hallway. The cost of installation is $6 per square yard. What is the total cost of installing the carpet? **$270**

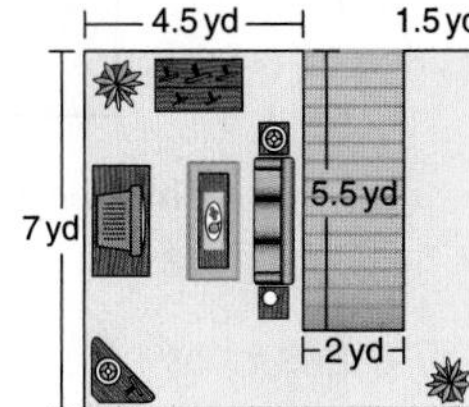

SEE EXAMPLE 4
p. 608

Use a composite figure to estimate each shaded area. The grid has squares with side lengths of 1 in.

7. 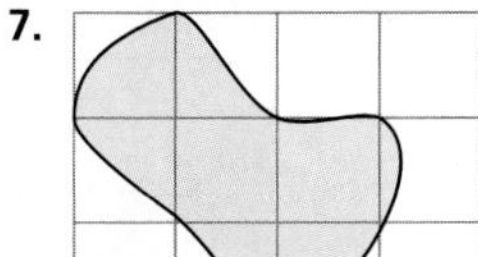
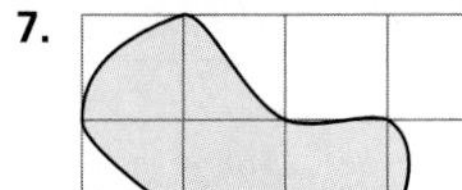

$A \approx 4.5 \text{ in}^2$

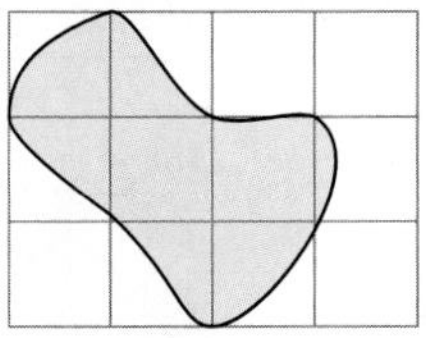

8. 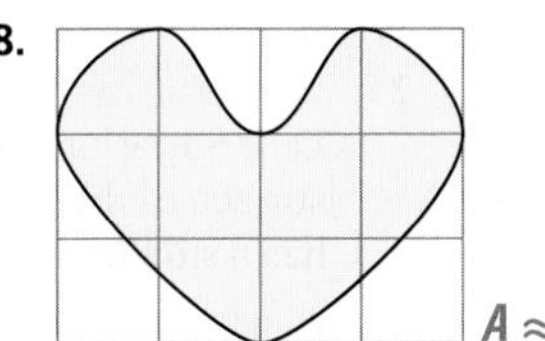
$A \approx 6 \text{ in}^2$

PRACTICE AND PROBLEM SOLVING

Independent Practice	
For Exercises	See Example
9–10	1
11–12	2
13	3
14–15	4

Extra Practice
Skills Practice p. S20
Application Practice p. S36

Multi-Step Find the shaded area. Round to the nearest tenth, if necessary.

9. 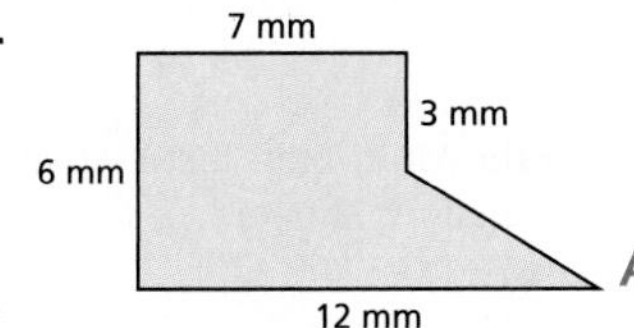

$A = 49.5 \text{ mm}^2$

10. 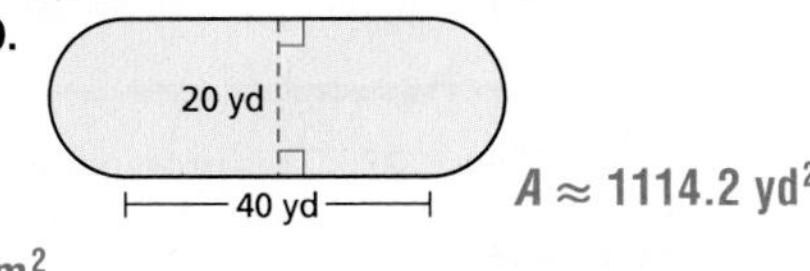

$A \approx 1114.2 \text{ yd}^2$

11. 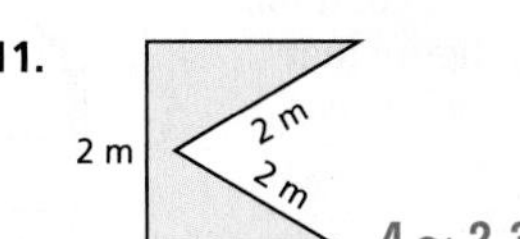

$A \approx 2.3 \text{ m}^2$

12. 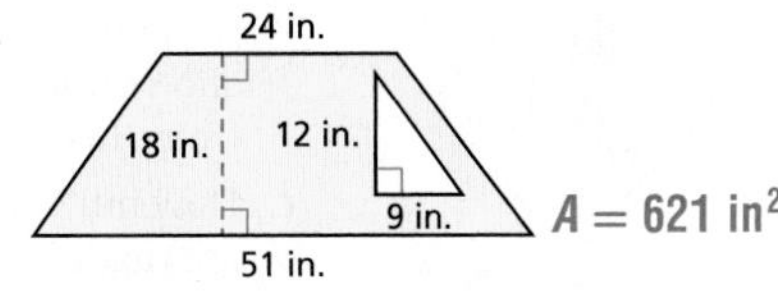

$A = 621 \text{ in}^2$

9-3 Exercises

Assignment Guide

Assign *Guided Practice* exercises as necessary.

If you finished Examples **1–2**
Basic 9–12, 16–19
Average 9–12, 16–20
Advanced 9–12, 16–20, 33

If you finished Examples **1–4**
Basic 9–21, 23–28, 31–33, 37–42
Average 9–34, 37–42
Advanced 9–42

Homework Quick Check
Quickly check key concepts.
Exercises: 10, 12, 13, 14, 16, 28

Answers

1. Possible answer:

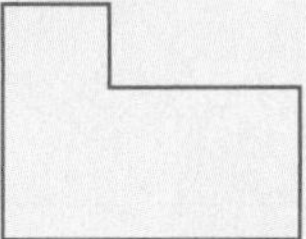

State Resources

Exercise 23 involves finding the area of a composite figure. This exercise prepares students for the Multi-Step Test Prep on page 614.

Answers

22.

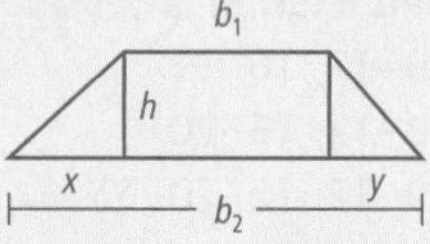

Let b_1 and b_2 be the bases of the trapezoid, h be the height of the trapezoid, triangles, and rectangle, and x and y be the bases of the triangles. Then $x + b_1 + y = b_2$. The area of the trapezoid is

$$A = \frac{1}{2}xh + b_1h + \frac{1}{2}yh$$
$$= \frac{1}{2}h(x + 2b_1 + y)$$
$$= \frac{1}{2}h(b_1 + x + b_1 + y)$$
$$= \frac{1}{2}h(b_1 + b_2)$$

23b.

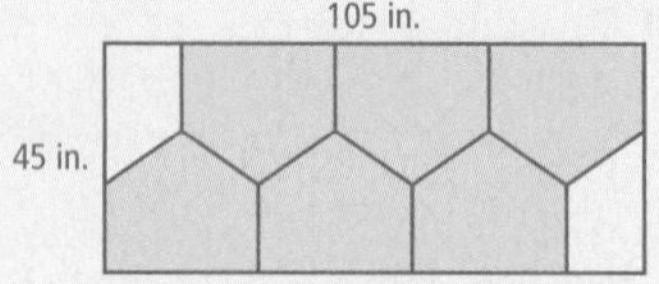

16. $A = 48 + 24 + 64 = 136\text{ cm}^2$; $A = 160 - 24 = 136\text{ cm}^2$; the answers are the same.

17. $A = 270 + 270 = 540\text{ in}^2$; $A = 756 - 216 = 540\text{ in}^2$; the answers are the same.

18. $A = (1440 + 289\pi)\text{ m}^2$

19. $A = \left(25\sqrt{3} + \frac{75\pi}{2}\right)\text{ in}^2$

21. Possible answer: $35{,}000\text{ mi}^2$

13. **Drama** Pat is painting a stage backdrop for a play. The paint he is using covers 90 square feet per quart. How many quarts of paint should Pat buy? 7 qt

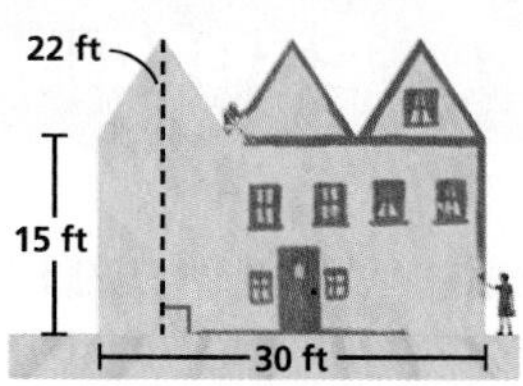

Use a composite figure to estimate each shaded area. The grid has squares with side lengths of 1 m.

14.

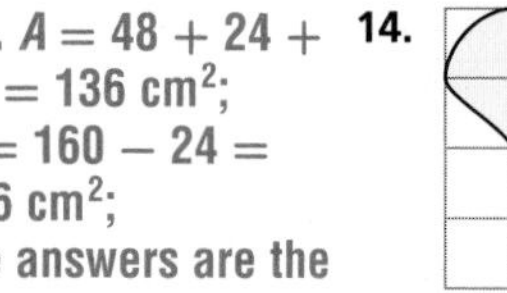

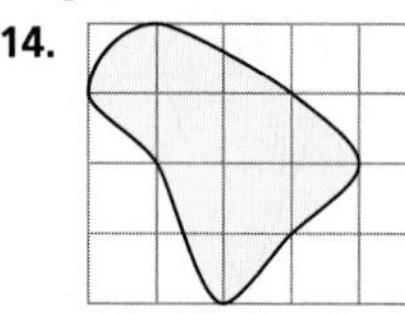

$A \approx 7.5\text{ m}^2$

15.

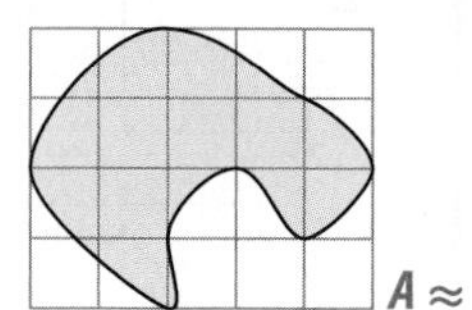

$A \approx 9\text{ m}^2$

Find the area of each figure first by adding and then by subtracting. Compare your answers.

16.

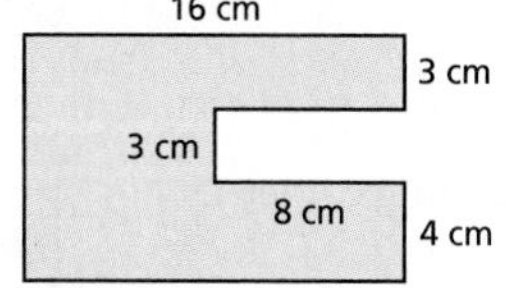

17.

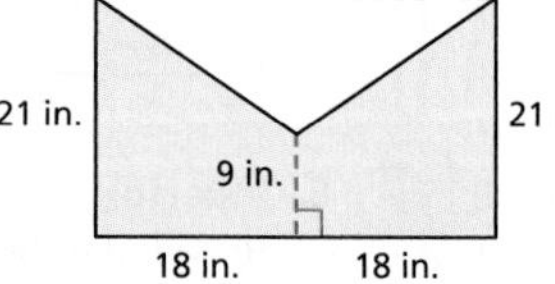

Find the area of each figure. Give your answers in terms of π.

18.

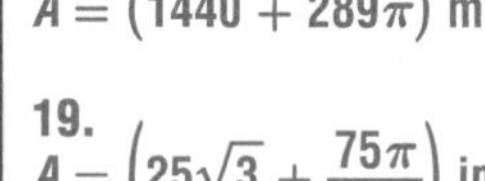

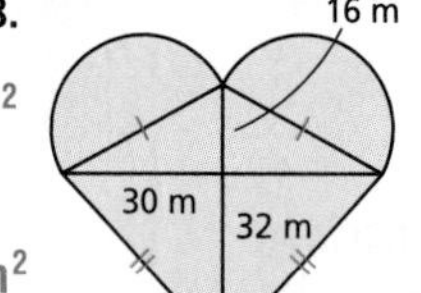

19.

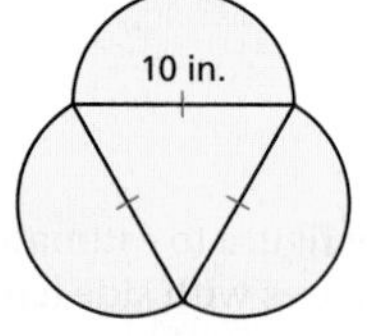

20. $A = 39\pi\text{ cm}^2$

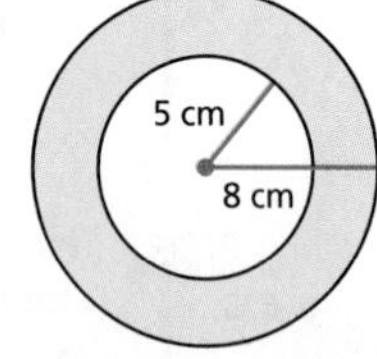

21. **Geography** Use the grid on the map of Lake Superior to estimate the area of the surface of the lake. Each square on the grid has a side length of 100 miles.

22. **Critical Thinking** A trapezoid can be divided into a rectangle and two triangles. Show that the area formula for a trapezoid gives the same result as the sum of the areas of the rectangle and triangles.

23. This problem will prepare you for the Multi-Step Test Prep on page 614. A school crossing sign has the dimensions shown.
    a. Find the area of the sign. $A = 675\text{ in}^2$
    b. A manufacturer has a rectangular sheet of metal measuring 45 in. by 105 in. Draw a figure that shows how 6 school crossing signs can be cut from this sheet of metal.
    c. How much metal will be left after the six signs are made? 675 in^2

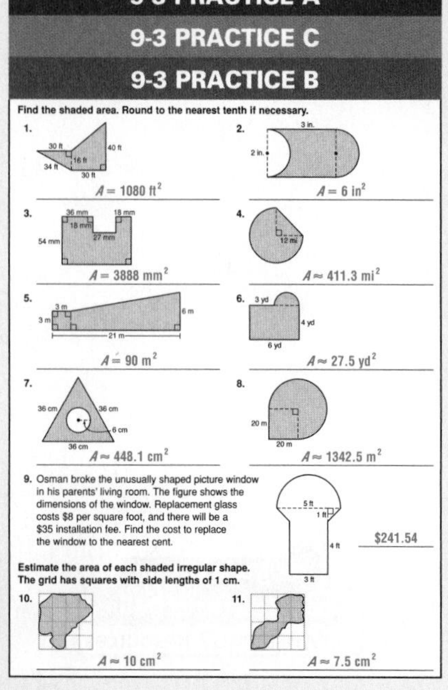

9-3 PRACTICE A
9-3 PRACTICE C
9-3 PRACTICE B

Find the shaded area. Round to the nearest tenth if necessary.

1. $A = 1080\text{ ft}^2$
2. $A = 6\text{ in}^2$
3. $A = 3888\text{ mm}^2$
4. $A \approx 411.3\text{ mi}^2$
5. $A = 90\text{ m}^2$
6. $A \approx 27.5\text{ yd}^2$
7. $A \approx 448.1\text{ cm}^2$
8. $A \approx 1342.5\text{ m}^2$
9. Osman broke the unusually shaped picture window in his parents' living room. The figure shows the dimensions of the window. Replacement glass costs \$8 per square foot, and there will be a \$35 installation fee. Find the cost to replace the window to the nearest cent. \$241.54

Estimate the area of each shaded irregular shape. The grid has squares with side lengths of 1 cm.

10. $A \approx 10\text{ cm}^2$
11. $A \approx 7.5\text{ cm}^2$

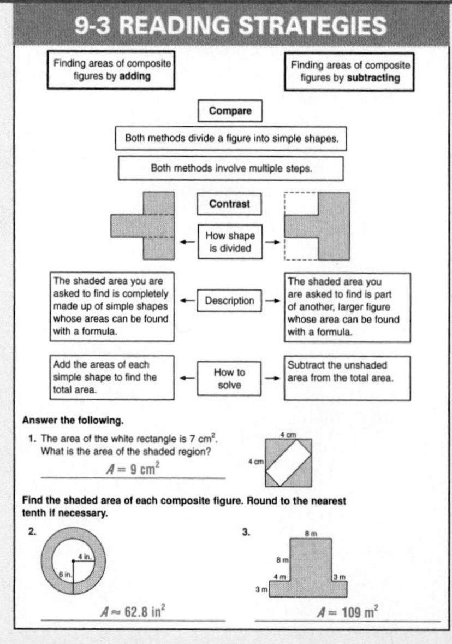

9-3 READING STRATEGIES

Finding areas of composite figures by **adding** | Finding areas of composite figures by **subtracting**

Compare

Both methods divide a figure into simple shapes.

Both methods involve multiple steps.

Contrast

How shape is divided

Description: The shaded area you are asked to find is completely made up of simple shapes whose areas can be found with a formula. | The shaded area you are asked to find is part of another, larger figure whose area can be found with a formula.

How to solve: Add the areas of each simple shape to find the total area. | Subtract the unshaded area from the total area.

Answer the following.

1. The area of the white rectangle is 7 cm^2. What is the area of the shaded region? $A = 9\text{ cm}^2$

Find the shaded area of each composite figure. Round to the nearest tenth if necessary.

2. $A \approx 62.8\text{ in}^2$
3. $A = 109\text{ m}^2$

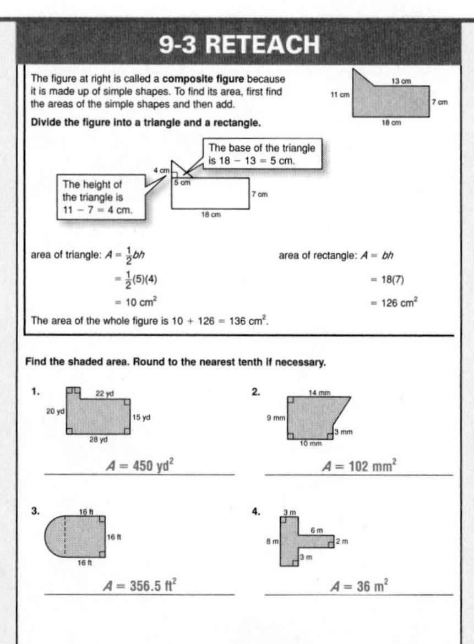

9-3 RETEACH

The figure at right is called a **composite figure** because it is made up of simple shapes. To find its area, first find the areas of the simple shapes and then add.

Divide the figure into a triangle and a rectangle.

The base of the triangle is $18 - 13 = 5$ cm.

The height of the triangle is $11 - 7 = 4$ cm.

area of triangle: $A = \frac{1}{2}bh = \frac{1}{2}(5)(4) = 10\text{ cm}^2$

area of rectangle: $A = bh = 18(7) = 126\text{ cm}^2$

The area of the whole figure is $10 + 126 = 136\text{ cm}^2$.

Find the shaded area. Round to the nearest tenth if necessary.

1. $A = 450\text{ yd}^2$
2. $A = 102\text{ mm}^2$
3. $A = 356.5\text{ ft}^2$
4. $A = 36\text{ m}^2$

Multi-Step **Use a ruler and compass to draw each figure and then find the area.**

24. A rectangle with a base length of $b = 3$ cm and a height of $h = 4$ cm has a circle with a radius of $r = 1$ cm removed from the interior. $A = (12 - \pi)$ cm^2

25. A square with a side length of $s = 4$ in. shares a side with a triangle with a height of $h = 5$ in. and a base length of $b = 4$ in. and shares another side with a half circle with $d = 4$ in. $A = (26 + 2\pi)$ in^2

26. A circle with a radius of $r = 5$ cm has a right triangle with a base of $b = 8$ cm and a height of $h = 6$ cm removed from its interior. $A = (25\pi - 24)$ cm^2

27. **Multi-Step** A lune is a crescent-shaped figure bounded by two intersecting circles. Find the shaded area in each of the first three diagrams, and then use your results to find the area of the lune. Note that AB is the diameter of the smaller circle.

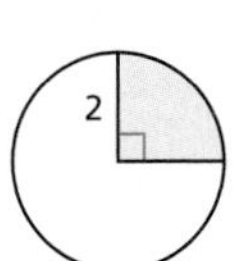

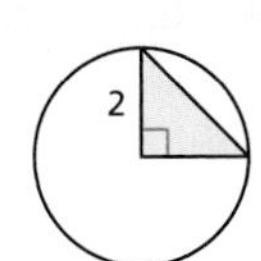

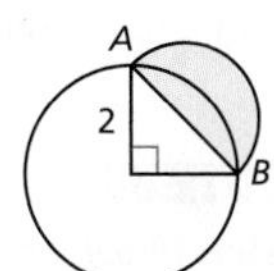

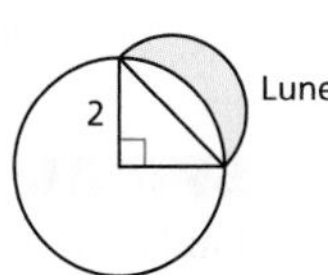

LINK

Math History

Hippocrates attempted to use lunes to solve a problem that has since been proven impossible: constructing a square with the same area as a given circle.

27. $A_1 = \pi$; $A_2 = 2$; $A_3 = \pi$; $A_4 = \pi - (\pi - 2) = 2$

Estimation **Trace each irregular shape and draw a composite figure that approximates it. Measure the composite figure and use it to estimate the area of the irregular shape.** Note: Figures are reduced in TE.

28.

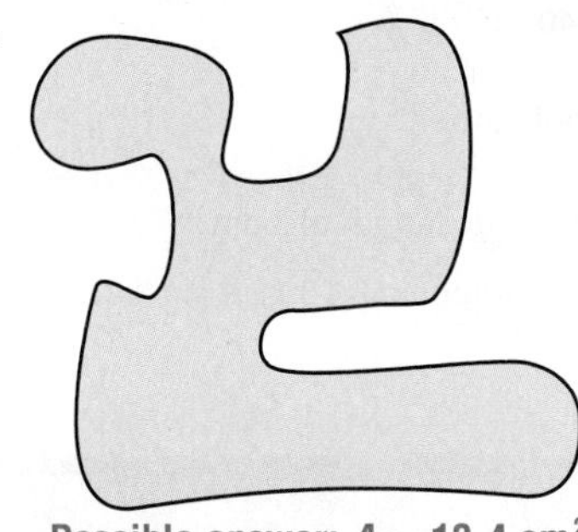

Possible answer: $A \approx 13.4$ cm^2

29.

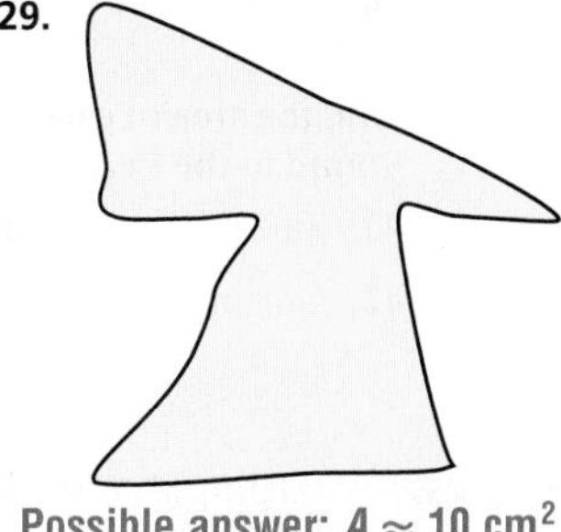

Possible answer: $A \approx 10$ cm^2

30. **Write About It** Explain when you would use addition to find the area of a composite figure and when you would use subtraction.

31. Which equation can be used to find the area of the composite figure?

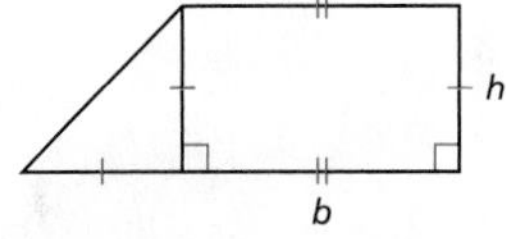

(A) $A = bh + \frac{1}{2}(h)^2$ (circled)
(B) $A = bh + h^2$
(C) $A = h + 2b + h^2$
(D) $A = h + 2b + \frac{1}{2}h^2$

32. Use a ruler to measure the dimensions of the composite figure to the nearest tenth of a centimeter.

Which of the following best represents the area of the composite figure?

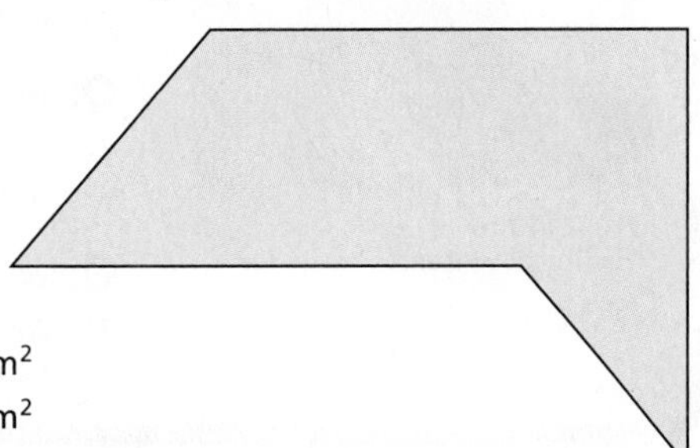

(F) 4 cm^2
(G) 19 cm^2 (circled)
(H) 22 cm^2
(J) 42 cm^2

9-3 PROBLEM SOLVING

1. Find the shaded area. Round to the nearest tenth.

12 cm, 4.5 cm, 9.5 cm

128.6 cm^2

2. Jessica is painting a bedroom wall shown by the shaded area below. The cost of paint is $6.90 per quart, and each quart covers 65 square feet. What is the total cost of the paint if she applies two coats of paint to the wall?

6 ft, 8 ft, 3 ft, 3 ft, 3 ft, 10 ft

$13.80

Choose the best answer.

3. Enchanted Rock State Natural Area in Fredericksburg, Texas, has a primitive camping area called Moss Lake. Which is the best estimate for this area if the length of each grid square is 10 meters?

(A) 1600 m^2
B 3200 m^2
C 6400 m^2
D 8000 m^2

Loop Trail
Moss Lake Primitive Camping Area

4. Find the area of the section of basketball court that is shown. Round to the nearest tenth.

F 612.7 ft^2
(G) 820.1 ft^2
H 1225.4 ft^2
J 2450.8 ft^2

39 ft 6 in.
5 ft 3 in.

5. Find the shaded area. Round to the nearest tenth.

18 mm, 12 mm, 15 mm, 7.2 mm

A 183.6 mm^2
B 194.4 mm^2
(C) 205.2 mm^2
D 216.0 mm^2

6. Which is the best estimate for the area of the pond? Each grid square represents 4 square feet.

F 24 ft^2
G 48 ft^2
(H) 96 ft^2
J 120 ft

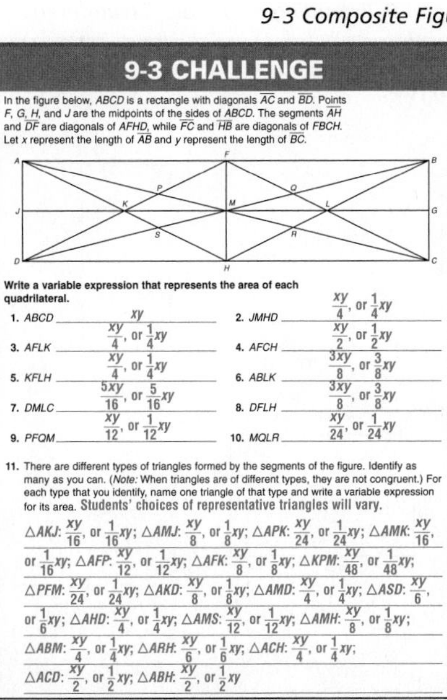

9-3 CHALLENGE

In the figure below, $ABCD$ is a rectangle with diagonals $\overline{AC}$ and $\overline{BD}$. Points F, G, H, and J are the midpoints of the sides of $ABCD$. The segments $\overline{AH}$ and $\overline{DF}$ are diagonals of $AFHD$, while $\overline{FC}$ and $\overline{HB}$ are diagonals of $FBCH$. Let x represent the length of $\overline{AB}$ and y represent the length of $\overline{BC}$.

Write a variable expression that represents the area of each quadrilateral.

1. $ABCD$ xy
2. $JMHD$ $\frac{xy}{4}$, or $\frac{1}{4}xy$
3. $AFLK$ $\frac{xy}{4}$, or $\frac{1}{4}xy$
4. $AFCH$ $\frac{xy}{2}$, or $\frac{1}{2}xy$
5. $KFLH$ $\frac{xy}{4}$, or $\frac{1}{4}xy$
6. $ABLK$ $\frac{3xy}{8}$, or $\frac{3}{8}xy$
7. $DMLC$ $\frac{5xy}{16}$, or $\frac{5}{16}xy$
8. $DFLH$ $\frac{3xy}{8}$, or $\frac{3}{8}xy$
9. $PFQM$ $\frac{xy}{12}$, or $\frac{1}{12}xy$
10. $MQLR$ $\frac{xy}{24}$, or $\frac{1}{24}xy$

11. There are different types of triangles formed by the segments of the figure. Identify as many as you can. (*Note:* When triangles are of different types, they are not congruent.) For each type that you identify, name one triangle of that type and write a variable expression for its area. Students' choices of representative triangles will vary.

$\triangle AKJ$: $\frac{xy}{16}$, or $\frac{1}{16}xy$; $\triangle AMJ$: $\frac{xy}{8}$, or $\frac{1}{8}xy$; $\triangle APK$: $\frac{xy}{24}$, or $\frac{1}{24}xy$; $\triangle AMK$: $\frac{xy}{16}$, or $\frac{1}{16}xy$; $\triangle AFP$: $\frac{xy}{12}$, or $\frac{1}{12}xy$; $\triangle AFK$: $\frac{xy}{8}$, or $\frac{1}{8}xy$; $\triangle KPM$: $\frac{xy}{48}$, or $\frac{1}{48}xy$; $\triangle PFM$: $\frac{xy}{24}$, or $\frac{1}{24}xy$; $\triangle AKD$: $\frac{xy}{8}$, or $\frac{1}{8}xy$; $\triangle AMD$: $\frac{xy}{4}$, or $\frac{1}{4}xy$; $\triangle ASD$: $\frac{xy}{6}$, or $\frac{1}{6}xy$; $\triangle AHD$: $\frac{xy}{4}$, or $\frac{1}{4}xy$; $\triangle AMS$: $\frac{xy}{12}$, or $\frac{1}{12}xy$; $\triangle AMH$: $\frac{xy}{8}$, or $\frac{1}{8}xy$; $\triangle ABM$: $\frac{xy}{4}$, or $\frac{1}{4}xy$; $\triangle ARH$: $\frac{xy}{6}$, or $\frac{1}{6}xy$; $\triangle ACH$: $\frac{xy}{4}$, or $\frac{1}{4}xy$; $\triangle ACD$: $\frac{xy}{2}$, or $\frac{1}{2}xy$; $\triangle ABH$: $\frac{xy}{2}$, or $\frac{1}{2}xy$

In **Exercise 27,** some students may not know how to solve for the area of a quarter of the circle. Ask students how to find the area of a semicircle, or $\frac{1}{2}$ of a circle, and ask them to extend this idea to find the area of $\frac{1}{4}$ of a circle.

Teaching Tip **Reading Math** For **Exercises 24–27,** you may want to review and explain expressions such as "intersecting circles," "removed from the interior," and "shares a side" to help students understand and draw figures from a written description. ENGLISH LANGUAGE LEARNERS

TEST PREP DOCTOR If students have difficulty with **Exercise 31,** remind them that all sides with one tick mark have length h and all sides with two tick marks have length b. Have them write the area formulas for the triangle and the rectangle separately and then add them.

In **Exercise 32,** remind students to measure carefully, and to use centimeters, since the answer choices are in centimeters. Encourage students to estimate the area before looking at the answer choices. This immediately eliminates choices **F** and **J.**

Answers

24.

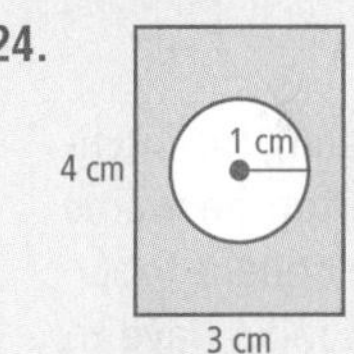

25.

5 in.
4 in.
4 in.

26.

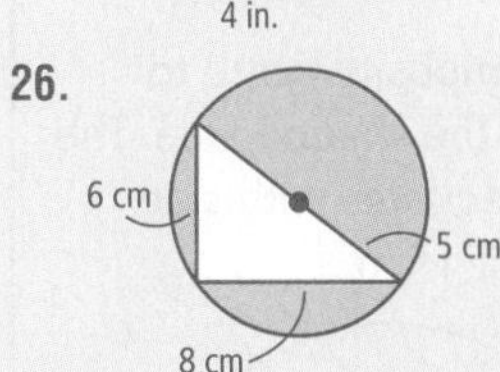

30. Possible answer: I would use addition to find the area of a figure that could be divided into triangles, rectangles, trapezoids, and semicircles. I would use subtraction to find the area of a figure that has a shape removed from the interior.

Journal

Have students explain how they would use a map and the scale of the map to estimate the area of their state.

ALTERNATIVE ASSESSMENT

Have students draw a composite figure with an area of 36 cm^2 that is made up of at least 3 simple shapes. Have them label the dimensions and area of each simple shape.

Power Presentations with PowerPoint®

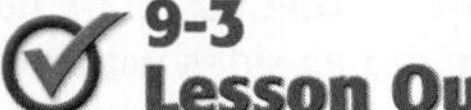

9-3 Lesson Quiz

Find the shaded area. Round to the nearest tenth, if necessary.

1. 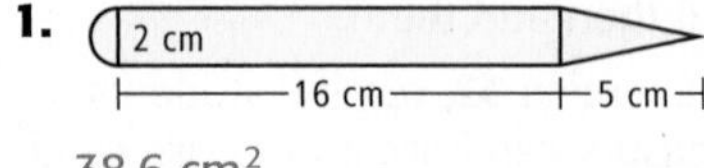

38.6 cm^2

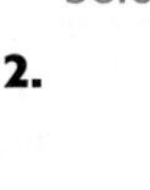

2. 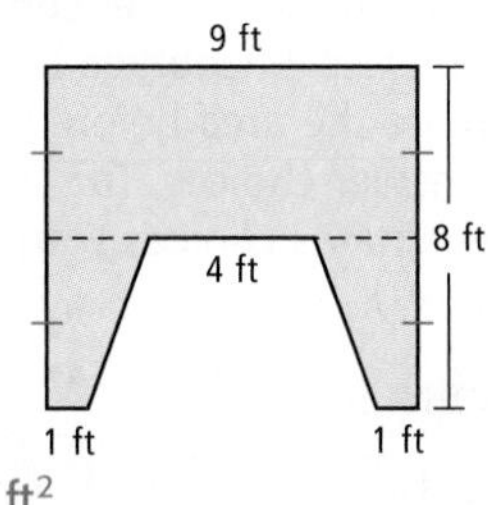

50 ft^2

3. Mike is remodeling his kitchen. The countertop he wants costs \$2.70 per square foot. How much will Mike have to spend on his remodeling project?

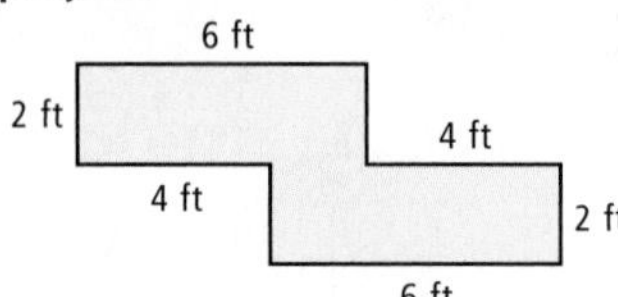

\$64.80

4. Use a composite figure to estimate the shaded area. The grid has squares with side lengths of 1 cm.

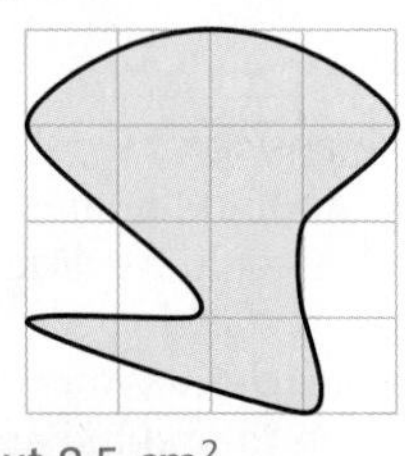

about 8.5 cm^2

Also available on transparency

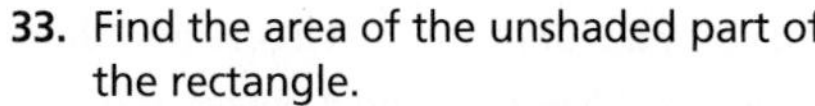

33. Find the area of the unshaded part of the rectangle.

Ⓐ 1800 m^2 Ⓒ 2925 m^2
Ⓑ 2250 m^2 Ⓓ 4725 m^2

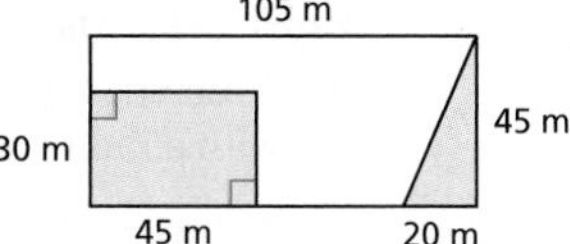

CHALLENGE AND EXTEND

$A = \pi(R^2 - r^2)$

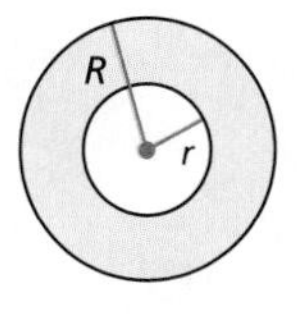

34. An *annulus* is the region between two circles that have the same center. Write the formula for the area of the annulus in terms of the outer radius *R* and the inner radius *r*.

35. Draw two composite figures with the same area: one made up of two rectangles and the other made up of a rectangle and a triangle.

36. Draw a composite figure that has a total area of 10π cm^2 and is made up of a rectangle and a half circle. Label the dimensions of your figure.

SPIRAL REVIEW

Find each sale price. *(Previous course)*

37. 20% off a regular price of \$19.95 **\$15.96**

38. 15% off a regular price of \$34.60 **\$29.41**

Find the length of each segment. *(Lesson 7-4)*

39. $\overline{BC}$ **1.4**

40. $\overline{CD}$ **0.7**

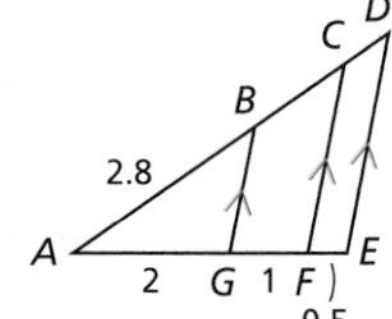

Find the area of each regular polygon. Round to the nearest tenth. *(Lesson 9-2)*

41. an equilateral triangle with a side length of 3 cm $A \approx 3.9$ cm^2

42. a regular hexagon with an apothem of $4\sqrt{3}$ m $A \approx 166.3$ cm^2

Career Path

go.hrw.com
Career Resources Online
KEYWORD: MG7 Career

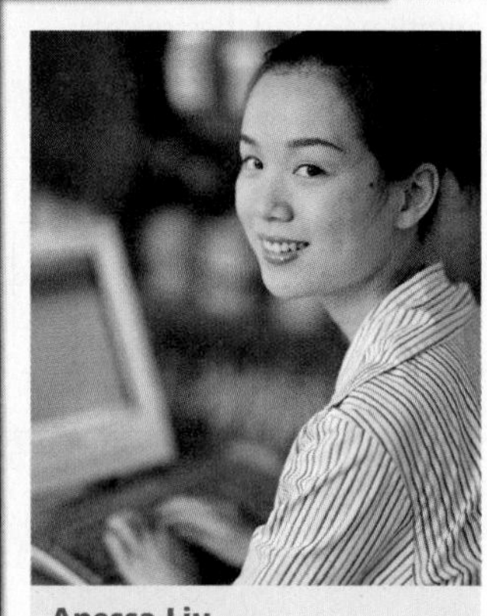

Anessa Liu
Technical writer

Q: What math classes did you take in high school?

A: In high school I took Algebra 1, Geometry, Algebra 2, and Trigonometry.

Q: What math classes did you take in college?

A: In college I took Precalculus, Calculus, and Statistics.

Q: What technical materials do you write?

A: I write training manuals for computer software packages.

Q: How do you use math?

A: Some manuals I write are for math programs, so I use a lot of formulas to describe patterns and measurements.

Q: What are your future plans?

A: After I get a few more years experience writing manuals, I would like to train others who use these programs.

Answers

35. Possible answer:

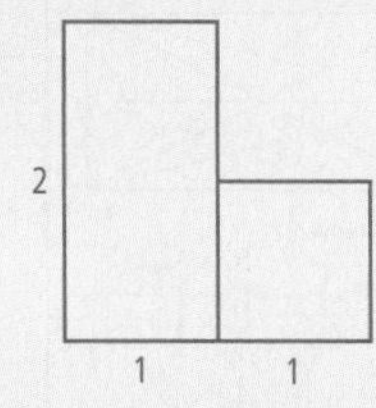

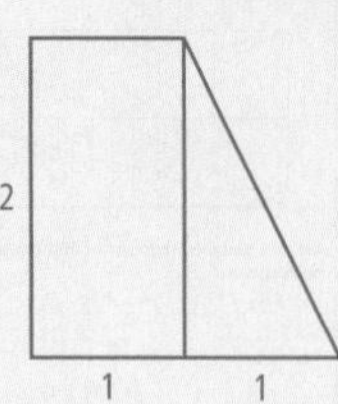

36. Possible answer:

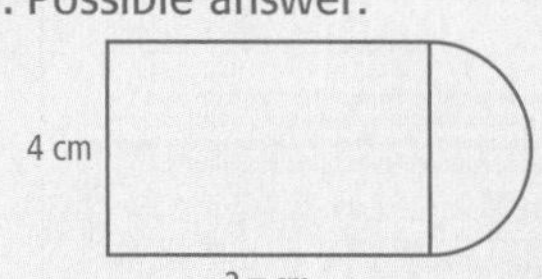

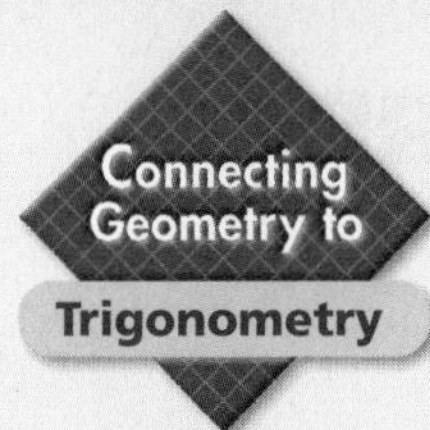

Triangle Area Formulas

You've used the formula $A = \frac{1}{2}bh$ to find the area of a triangle, and you've used trigonometric ratios to find missing lengths in right triangles. You can combine the two techniques to find the area of a triangle when you don't know the value of h.

If you are given the lengths of two sides and the included angle, you can use this information to find the area of the triangle

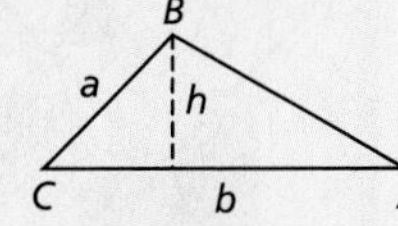

$\frac{h}{a} = \sin C$ *Write the sine of C in terms of h and a.*

$h = a \sin C$ *Multiply both sides by a to isolate h.*

$A = \frac{1}{2} ba \sin C$ *Substitute the expression for h into the area formula.*

Example

Find the area of the triangle shown.

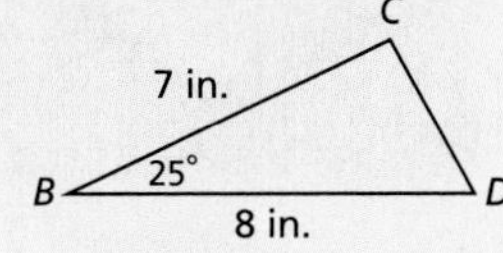

$A = \frac{1}{2} ba \sin B$

$A = \frac{1}{2}(7)(8)\sin 25°$ *Substitute the values for the side lengths and the measure of the included angle.*

$A \approx 11.8$ *Simplify.*

The area is approximately 11.8 in.^{2}.

Try This

Find the area of each triangle. Round to the nearest tenth.

1. R, S, T; 10 cm, 9.6 cm, 45°

33.9 cm²

2. 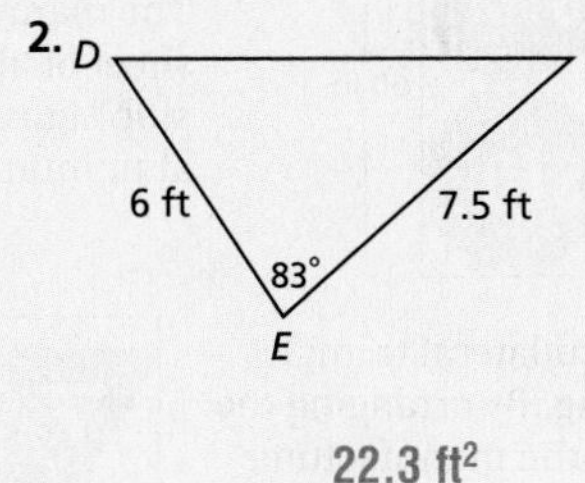

22.3 ft²

3. 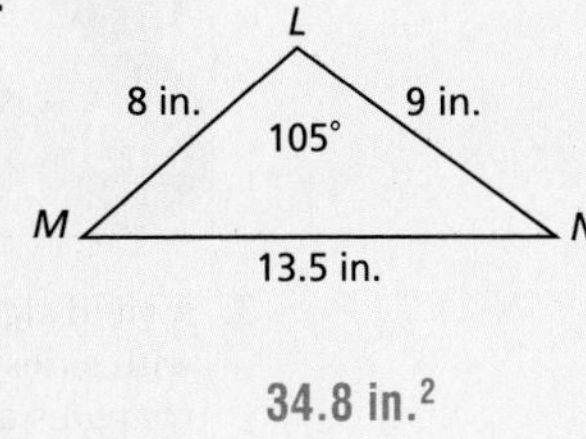

34.8 in.²

4. You can also find the area of a triangle if you only know the lengths of the sides. Heron's formula is $A = \sqrt{s(s-a)(s-b)(s-c)}$, where s is one-half of the perimeter of the triangle and a, b, and c are the side lengths of the triangle. Find s for the triangle in Exercise 3, and use Heron's formula to find the area. Round to the nearest tenth. **15.25 in.; 34.8 in.²**

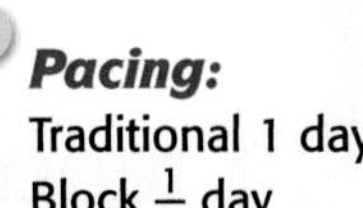

Organizer

Pacing:
Traditional 1 day
Block $\frac{1}{2}$ day

Objective: Develop and use the formula $A = \frac{1}{2} ba \sin\theta$ to find the area of a triangle.

Online Edition

Countdown Week 20

Teach

Remember

Students review the sine function and apply it to find the area of a triangle when given two side lengths and the measure of the included angle.

Critical Thinking Show students how the formula $A = \frac{1}{2} ba \sin\theta$ becomes the familiar formula $A = \frac{1}{2} bh$ when the triangle is a right triangle.

Close

Assess

Ask the students to explain what information they need to apply the formula $A = \frac{1}{2} ba \sin\theta$ and what information they need to apply Heron's formula. two side lengths and the included angle; all three side lengths

State Resources

Organizer

Objective: Assess students' ability to apply concepts and skills in Lessons 9-1 through 9-3 in a real-world format.

 **Online Edition**

Resources

 ***Geometry Assessments***
www.mathtekstoolkit.org

Problem	Text Reference
1	Lesson 9-2
2	Lesson 9-2
3	Lesson 9-1
4	Lessons 9-1, 9-2

State Resources

CHAPTER 9

MULTI-STEP TEST PREP

SECTION 9A

Developing Geometric Formulas

Traffic Signs Traffic signs are usually made of reflective aluminum. A manufacturer of traffic signs begins with a rectangular sheet of aluminum that measures 60 in. by 90 in.

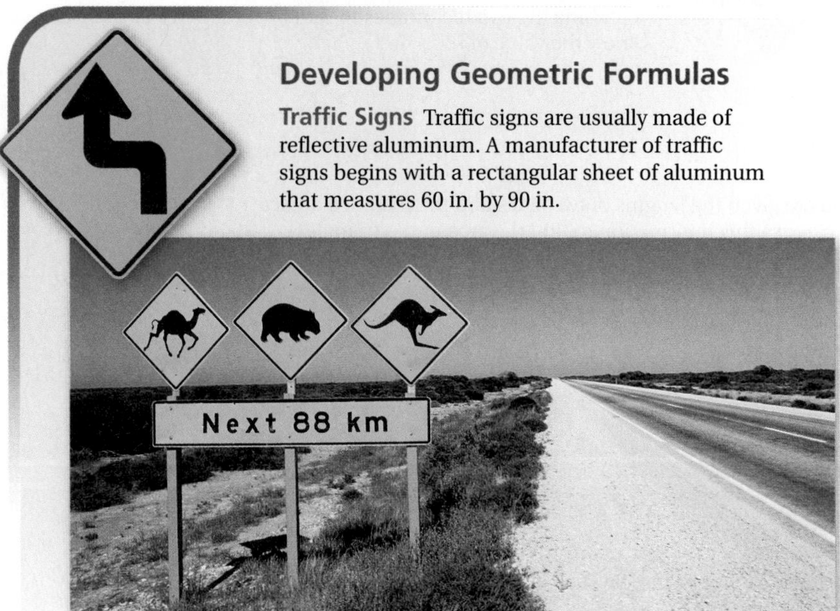

1. A railroad crossing sign is a circle with a diameter of 30 in. The manufacturer can make 6 of these signs from the sheet of aluminum by arranging the signs as shown. How much aluminum is left over once the signs have been made? **about 1159 in²**

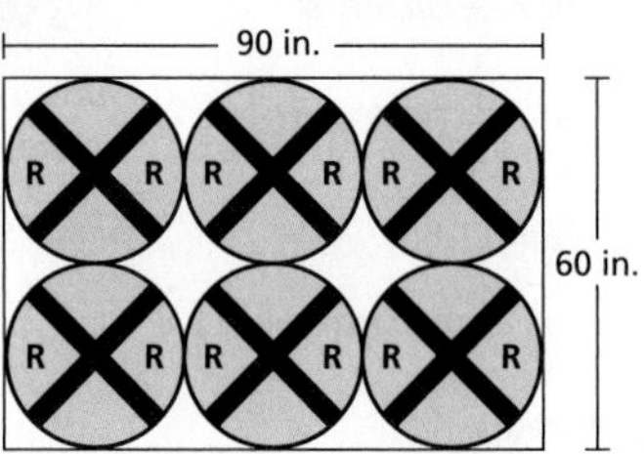

90 in. / 60 in. — STOP STOP STOP / STOP STOP STOP

2. A stop sign is a regular octagon. The manufacturer can use the sheet of aluminum to make 6 stop signs as shown. How much aluminum is left over in this case? **about 926 in²**

90 in. / 60 in. — YIELD

3. A yield sign is an equilateral triangle with sides 30 in. long. By arranging the triangles as shown, the manufacturer can use the sheet of aluminum to make 10 yield signs. How much aluminum is left over when yield signs are made? **about 1503 in²**

4. The making of which type of sign results in the least amount of waste? **stop sign**

INTERVENTION 

Scaffolding Questions

1. What is the area of the sheet of aluminum? 5400 in² What is the radius of each circular sign? 15 in. What formula can you use to find the area of each sign? $A = \pi r^2$
2. What is the apothem of each octagonal sign? 15 in. How can you set up a right triangle to find the side length of the octagon?

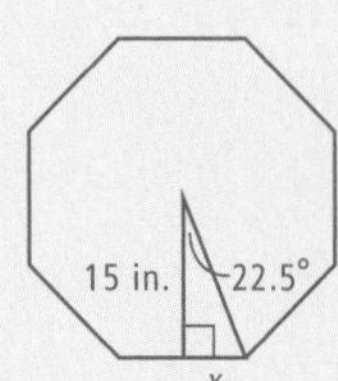

3. Given that the base of the equilateral triangle is 30 in., what is the height? $15\sqrt{3}$ in.
4. What does this problem ask you to compare? the amount of aluminum left over in **Problems 1, 2,** and **3**

Extension

A standard "one way" sign is a rectangle with dimensions 36 in. by 12 in. What is the maximum number of signs that can be made from the sheet of aluminum? 10 How much material is wasted in this case? 1080 in² Do one way signs use the aluminum more efficiently than stop signs? no

SECTION 9A

Quiz for Lessons 9-1 Through 9-3

9-1 Developing Formulas for Triangles and Quadrilaterals

Find each measurement.

1. the area of the parallelogram $A = 50 \text{ ft}^2$

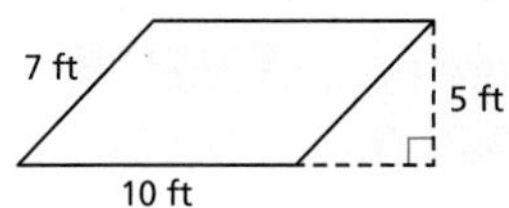

2. the base of the rectangle, in which $A = (24x^2 + 8x) \text{ m}^2$ $b = (6x + 2) \text{ m}$

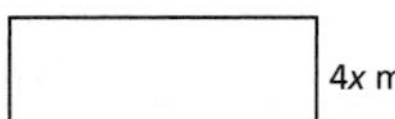

3. d_1 of the kite, in which $A = 126 \text{ ft}^2$ $d_1 = 21 \text{ ft}$

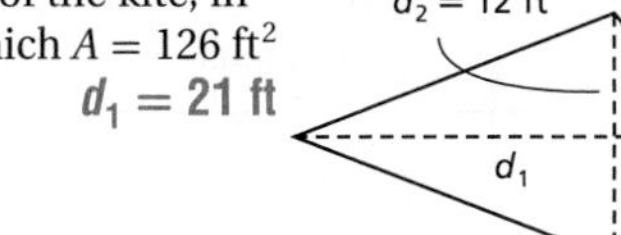

4. the area of the rhombus $A = 216 \text{ cm}^2$

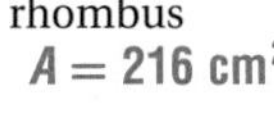

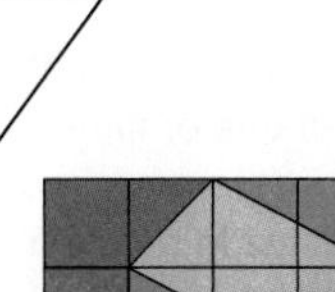

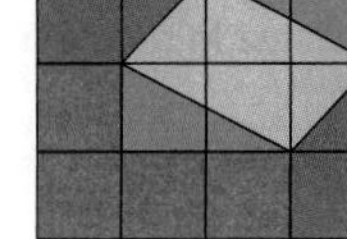

5. The tile mosaic shown is made up of 1 cm squares. Use the grid to find the perimeter and area of the green triangle, the blue trapezoid, and the yellow parallelogram.
$A = 1 \text{ cm}^2$; $P \approx 5.2 \text{ cm}$; $A = 1.5 \text{ cm}^2$; $P \approx 5.4 \text{ cm}$; $A = 3 \text{ cm}^2$; $P \approx 7.3 \text{ cm}$

9-2 Developing Formulas for Circles and Regular Polygons

Find each measurement.

6. the circumference of $\odot R$ in terms of π $C = 18\pi \text{ in.}$

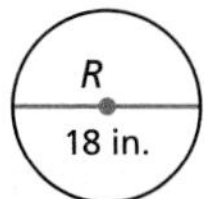

7. the area of $\odot E$ in terms of π $A = 36x^2\pi \text{ ft}^2$

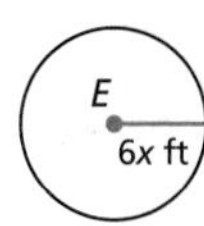

Find the area of each regular polygon. Round to the nearest tenth.

8. a regular hexagon with apothem 6 ft $A \approx 124.7 \text{ ft}^2$
9. a regular pentagon with side length 12 m $A \approx 247.7 \text{ m}^2$

9-3 Composite Figures

Find the shaded area. Round to the nearest tenth, if necessary.

10. 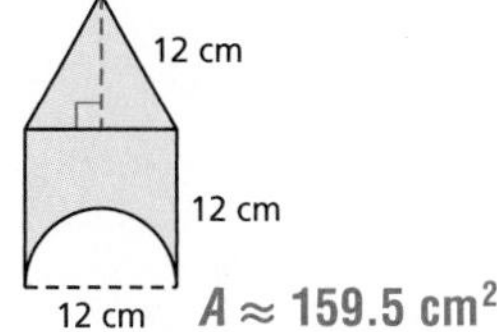

$A \approx 159.5 \text{ cm}^2$

11. 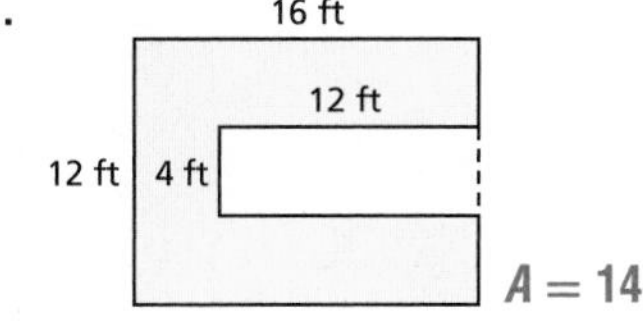

$A = 144 \text{ ft}^2$

12. Shelby is planting grass in an irregularly shaped garden as shown. The grid has squares with side lengths of 1 yd. Estimate the area of the garden. Given that grass cost \$6.50 per square yard, find the cost of the grass.
$A \approx 8.5 \text{ yd}^2$; about \$55

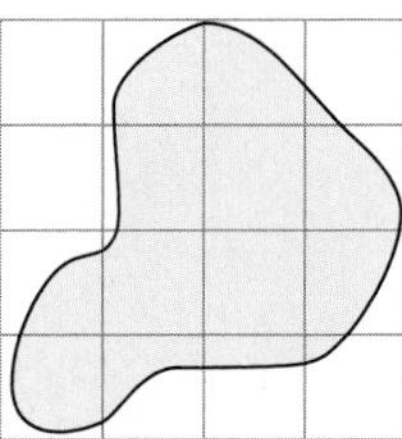

READY TO GO ON? SECTION 9A

Organizer

Objective: Assess students' mastery of concepts and skills in Lessons 9-1 through 9-3.

Resources

 ***Assessment Resources***
Section 9A Quiz

Teacher One Stop™
Test & Practice Generator

INTERVENTION

Resources

 ***Ready to Go On? Intervention and Enrichment* Worksheets**

 ***Ready to Go On?* CD-ROM**

 ***Ready to Go On?* Online**

my.hrw.com

READY TO GO ON? Diagnose and Prescribe

Ready to Go On? Intervention	*Ready to Go On? Intervention,* Section 9A Worksheets	CD-ROM	Online
Lesson 9-1	9-1 Intervention	Activity 9-1	Diagnose and Prescribe Online
Lesson 9-2	9-2 Intervention	Activity 9-2	
Lesson 9-3	9-3 Intervention	Activity 9-3	

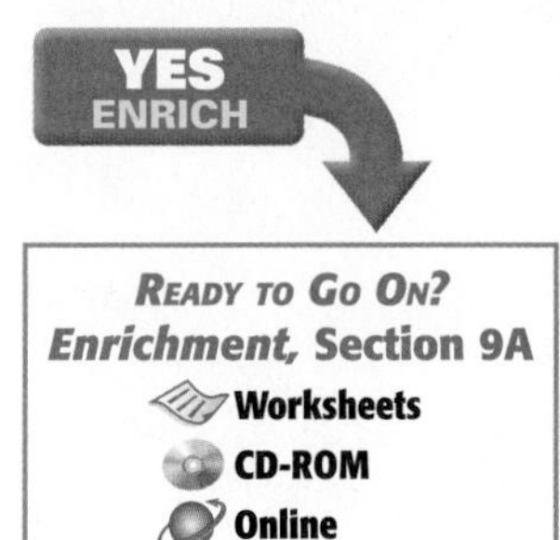

SECTION **9B**

Applying Geometric Formulas

One-Minute Section Planner

Lesson	Lab Resources	Materials
Lesson 9-4 Perimeter and Area in the Coordinate Plane • Find the perimeters and areas of figures in a coordinate plane. ☑ SAT-10 ☑ NAEP ☐ ACT ☑ SAT ☑ SAT Subject Tests		**Optional** transparency with 1 cm grid, graph paper
Lesson 9-5 Effects of Changing Dimensions Proportionally • Describe the effect on perimeter and area when one or more dimensions of a figure are changed. • Apply the relationship between perimeter and area in problem solving. ☑ SAT-10 ☑ NAEP ☐ ACT ☑ SAT ☑ SAT Subject Tests	***Technology Lab Activities*** 9-5 Technology Lab	**Optional** shrink plastic
Lesson 9-6 Geometric Probability • Calculate geometric probabilities. • Use geometric probability to predict results in real-world situations. ☐ SAT-10 ☑ NAEP ☐ ACT ☐ SAT ☑ SAT Subject Tests		**Optional** tape, compass (MK), protractor (MK), ruler (MK), colored pencils, rice
9-6 Geometry Lab Use Geometric Probability to Estimate π • Use geometric probability to estimate π. ☐ SAT-10 ☐ NAEP ☐ ACT ☐ SAT ☐ SAT Subject Tests	***Geometry Lab Activities*** 9-6 Lab Recording Sheet	**Required** pennies **Optional** grid with 0.75 in. squares

MK = *Manipulatives Kit*

Math Background

Professional Learning

CHANGING DIMENSIONS

Lesson 9-5

When all dimensions of a figure are multiplied by a nonzero constant k, the perimeter or circumference changes by a factor of k and the area changes by a factor of k^2. It is beyond the scope of this book to prove this principle in the most general terms, but it can be proved for various categories of figures by using established formulas.

Consider the case of a triangle, $\triangle ABC$, with sides of length a, b, and c. When all dimensions are multiplied by k ($k \neq 0$), the resulting triangle has sides of length ka, kb, and kc. The perimeter of the new triangle is therefore $ka + kb + kc$ or $k(a + b + c)$, which is k times the perimeter of $\triangle ABC$.

To show that the area of the triangle changes by a factor of k^2, let $\triangle A'B'C'$ be the triangle with sides of length ka, kb, and kc. As shown below, draw the altitude from B to the opposite side in $\triangle ABC$ and the altitude from B' to the opposite side in $\triangle A'B'C'$.

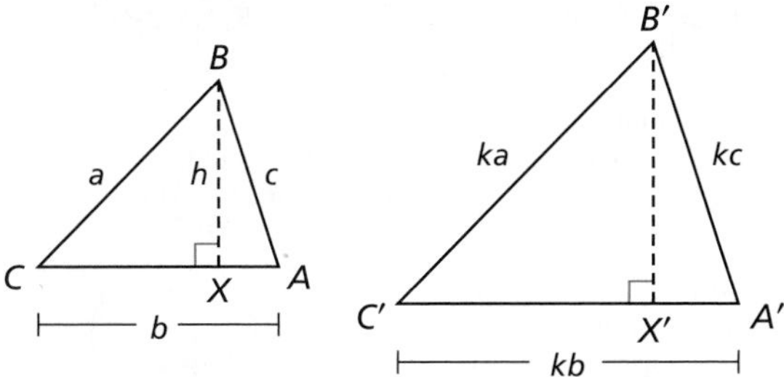

By SSS Similarity, $\triangle ABC \sim \triangle A'B'C'$, and so $\angle C \cong \angle C'$. Thus, by AA Similarity, $\triangle CBX \sim \triangle C'B'X'$. Because the sides of similar triangles are proportional, $\frac{B'X'}{BX} = \frac{B'C'}{BC}$ and so $\frac{B'X'}{h} = \frac{ka}{a}$. Therefore, $B'X' = kh$ and the area of $\triangle A'B'C'$ is $\frac{1}{2}(kb)(kh)$ or $\frac{1}{2}bh \cdot k^2$, which is k^2 times the area of $\triangle ABC$.

In Chapter 10, students will explore the three-dimensional analogue of this principle. Specifically, when all the dimensions of a three-dimensional figure are multiplied by a nonzero constant k, the surface area changes by a factor of k^2 and the volume changes by a factor of k^3.

GEOMETRIC PROBABILITY

Lesson 9-6

In general, the probability of an event is a ratio. Given a sample space in which every outcome is equally likely, the probability of an event is the ratio of the number of outcomes in the event to the number of outcomes in the sample space. In *geometric probability*, the probability of an event is based on a ratio of geometric measures, such as lengths or areas.

The history of geometric probability dates back at least as far as a famous problem that was first posed in 1777 by George Louis Leclerc, Comte de Buffon. At the time, a popular wagering game consisted of tossing a small coin onto a floor with square tiles. Players bet on whether or not the coin would land entirely within a tile. Buffon recognized that the probability of the coin landing inside a tile depended upon the location of the coin's center within the tile. In particular, a coin of radius r will land entirely within a square tile if the coin's center falls within the smaller, shaded square shown in the figure. In this way, Buffon reduced the problem to one that could be solved by calculating some areas.

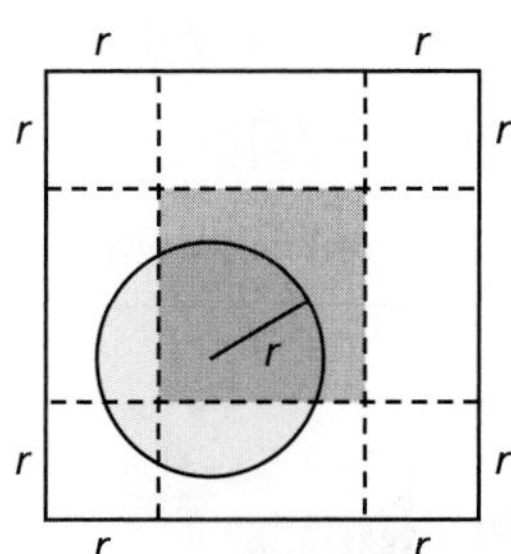

In a similar way, Buffon explored the probability that a needle tossed onto a surface that is marked with equidistant parallel lines will land across one of the lines. This is the well-known Buffon Needle Problem. If the length of the needle is equal to the distance between the lines, it is possible to show that the probability P of the needle landing across a line is $\frac{2}{\pi}$. This result provides an interesting method for estimating the value of pi. Toss a needle multiple times onto a surface that satisfies the above conditions and record the number of times the needle hits a line. Let P be the ratio of hits to the total number of tosses. Then, $\pi \approx \frac{2}{P}$. This approximation will become more accurate as the number of tosses increases.

9-4 Organizer

Pacing: Traditional 1 day
Block $\frac{1}{2}$ day

Objective: Find the perimeters and areas of figures in a coordinate plane.

Online Edition
Tutorial Videos

Countdown Week 20

Power Presentations with PowerPoint®

Warm Up

Use the slope formula to determine the slope of each line.

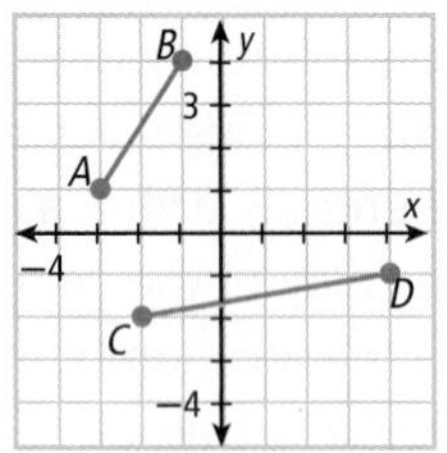

1. $\overline{AB}$ $\frac{3}{2}$ **2.** $\overline{CD}$ $\frac{1}{6}$

3. Simplify $(7\sqrt{3})(2\sqrt{3})$. 42

Also available on transparency

Math Humor

Q: What happened to the plant in the math classroom?

A: It grew square roots!

9-4 Perimeter and Area in the Coordinate Plane

Objective
Find the perimeters and areas of figures in a coordinate plane.

Why learn this?
You can use figures in a coordinate plane to solve puzzles like the one at right. (See Example 4.)

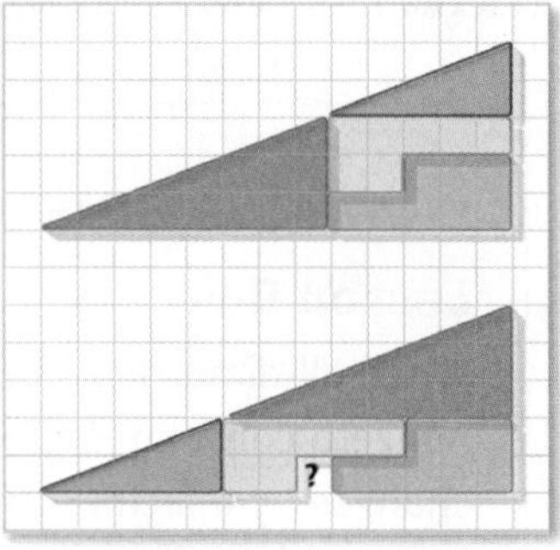

In Lesson 9-3, you estimated the area of irregular shapes by drawing composite figures that approximated the irregular shapes and by using area formulas.

Another method of estimating area is to use a grid and count the squares on the grid.

EXAMPLE 1 Estimating Areas of Irregular Shapes in the Coordinate Plane

Estimate the area of the irregular shape.

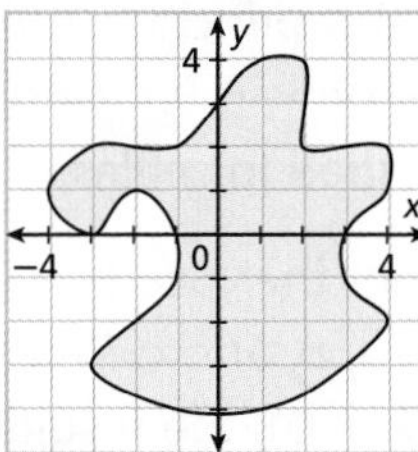

Method 1: Draw a composite figure that approximates the irregular shape and find the area of the composite figure.

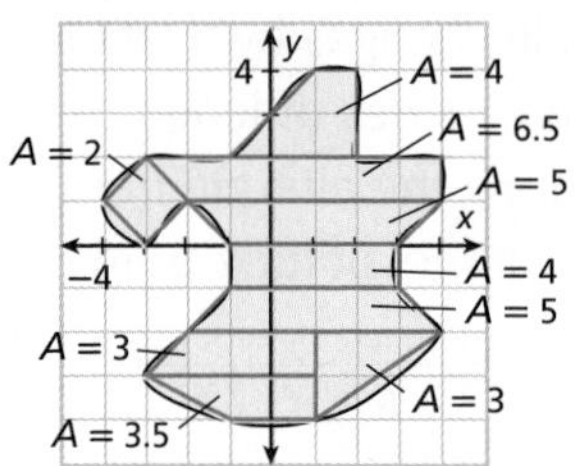

The area is approximately $4 + 6.5 + 5 + 4 + 5 + 3.5 + 3 + 3 + 2 = 36 \text{ units}^2$.

Method 2: Count the number of squares inside the figure, estimating half squares. Use a ■ for a whole square and a ◢ for a half square.

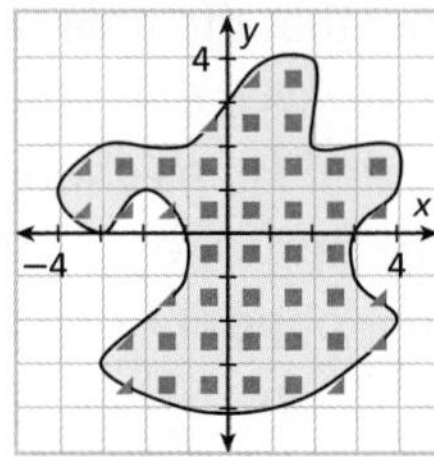

There are approximately 31 whole squares and 13 half squares, so the area is about $31 + \frac{1}{2}(13) = 37.5 \text{ units}^2$.

1. Estimate the area of the irregular shape.
$A \approx 38$ units²

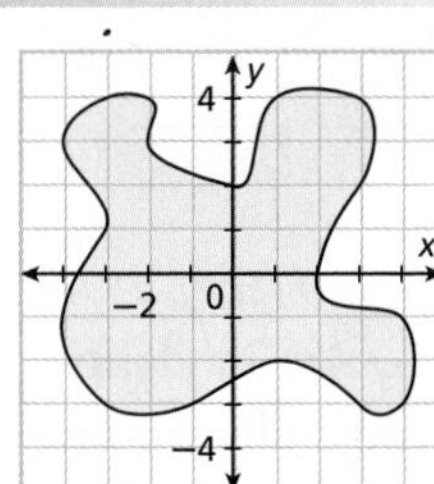

State Resources

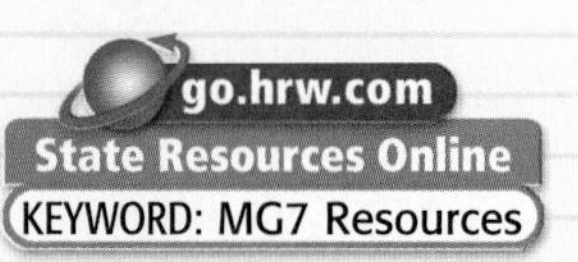

1 Introduce

EXPLORATION

9-4 Perimeter and Area in the Coordinate Plane

In this Exploration, you will investigate the areas of irregular shapes in the coordinate plane.

1. What is the area of the shaded square? Why?
2. What is the area of the shaded triangle? Why?
3. Find the area of each shape.
a. b. c.

THINK AND DISCUSS

4. Explain how you found the areas of the shapes in Problem 3.

Motivate

Discuss with students that figures in the coordinate plane can be used by graphic designers to find the perimeter and area of figures on a grid. Encourage students to think of some other professions that might use coordinate planes, such as engineering or surveying.

Explorations and answers are provided in *Alternate Openers: Explorations Transparencies.*

EXAMPLE 2

Finding Perimeter and Area in the Coordinate Plane

Algebra

Draw and classify the polygon with vertices $A(-4, 1)$, $B(2, 4)$, $C(4, 0)$, and $D(-2, -3)$. Find the perimeter and area of the polygon.

Step 1 Draw the polygon.

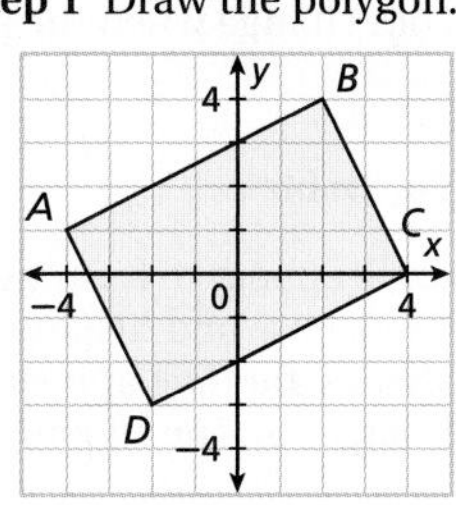

Step 2 *ABCD* appears to be a rectangle. To verify this, use slopes to show that the sides are perpendicular.

slope of $\overline{AB}$: $\frac{4-1}{2-(-4)} = \frac{3}{6} = \frac{1}{2}$

slope of $\overline{BC}$: $\frac{0-4}{4-2} = \frac{-4}{2} = -2$

slope of $\overline{CD}$: $\frac{-3-0}{-2-4} = \frac{-3}{-6} = \frac{1}{2}$

slope of $\overline{DA}$: $\frac{1-(-3)}{-4-(-2)} = \frac{4}{-2} = -2$

The consecutive sides are perpendicular, so *ABCD* is a rectangle.

Step 3 Let $\overline{CD}$ be the base and $\overline{BC}$ be the height of the rectangle. Use the Distance Formula to find each side length.

$b = CD = \sqrt{(-2-4)^2 + (-3-0)^2} = \sqrt{45} = 3\sqrt{5}$

$h = BC = \sqrt{(4-2)^2 + (0-4)^2} = \sqrt{20} = 2\sqrt{5}$

perimeter of *ABCD*: $P = 2b + 2h = 2(3\sqrt{5}) + 2(2\sqrt{5}) = 10\sqrt{5}$ units

area of *ABCD*: $A = bh = (3\sqrt{5})(2\sqrt{5}) = 30$ units^2.

Remember!

The distance from (x_1, y_1) to (x_2, y_2) in a coordinate plane is $d = \sqrt{(x_2 - x_1)^2 + (y_2 - y_1)^2}$, and the slope of the line containing the points is $m = \frac{y_2 - y_1}{x_2 - x_1}$. See pages 44 and 182.

2. Draw and classify the polygon with vertices $H(-3, 4)$, $J(2, 6)$, $K(2, 1)$, and $L(-3, -1)$. Find the perimeter and area of the polygon.

parallelogram; $A = 25$ units^2; $P \approx 20.8$ units

For a figure in a coordinate plane that does not have an area formula, it may be easier to enclose the figure in a rectangle and subtract the areas of the parts of the rectangle that are not included in the figure.

EXAMPLE 3

Finding Areas in the Coordinate Plane by Subtracting

Find the area of the polygon with vertices $W(1, 4)$, $X(4, 2)$, $Y(2, -3)$, and $Z(-4, 0)$.

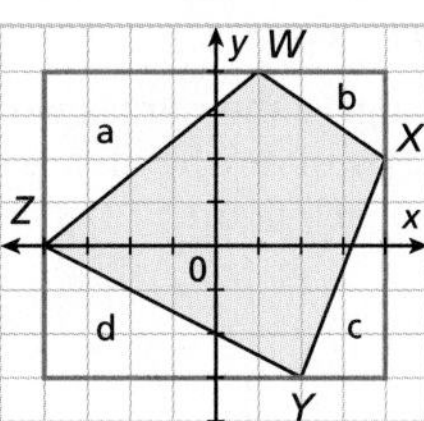

Draw the polygon and enclose it in a rectangle.

area of the rectangle: $A = bh = 8(7) = 56$ units^2

area of the triangles:

a: $A = \frac{1}{2}bh = \frac{1}{2}(5)(4) = 10$ units^2

b: $A = \frac{1}{2}bh = \frac{1}{2}(3)(2) = 3$ units^2

c: $A = \frac{1}{2}bh = \frac{1}{2}(2)(5) = 5$ units^2

d: $A = \frac{1}{2}bh = \frac{1}{2}(6)(3) = 9$ units^2

The area of the polygon is $56 - 10 - 3 - 5 - 9 = 29$ units^2.

3. Find the area of the polygon with vertices $K(-2, 4)$, $L(6, -2)$, $M(4, -4)$, and $N(-6, -2)$. **$A = 48$ units^2**

COMMON ERROR ALERT

Students might lose track as they try to count whole and half squares. Advise them to mark off the squares as they count them.

Power Presentations with PowerPoint®

Additional Examples

Example 1

Estimate the area of the irregular shape.

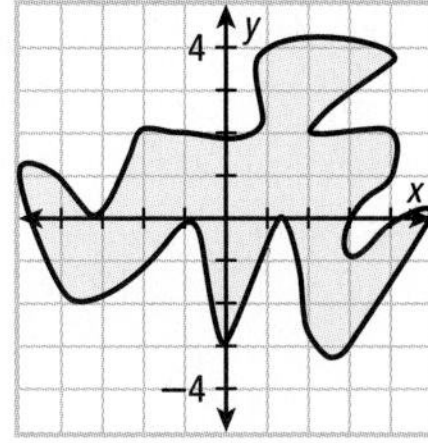

31 units^2

Example 2

Draw and classify the polygon with vertices $E(-1, -1)$, $F(2, -2)$, $G(-1, -4)$, and $H(-4, -3)$. Find the perimeter and area of the polygon.

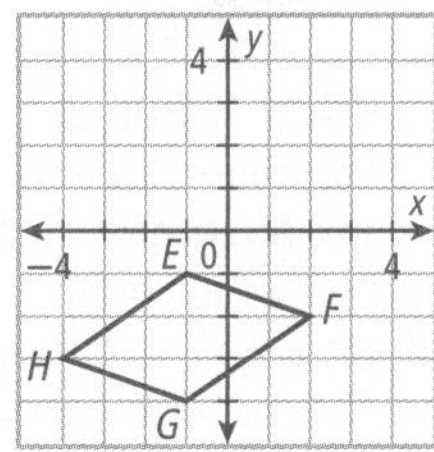

parallelogram; $P = 2\sqrt{10} + 2\sqrt{13}$ units; $A = 9$ units^2

Example 3

Find the area of the polygon with vertices $A(-4, 1)$, $B(2, 4)$, $C(4, 1)$, and $D(-2, -2)$.

$A = 24$ units^2

2 Teach

Guided Instruction

Use a composite figure from Lesson 9-3 to review the method for estimating the area of an irregular shape. Another method for estimating the area of an irregular shape in the coordinate plane is to count the squares in the figure, estimating half squares. Review the slope formula and the Distance Formula, and show how they can be used to classify polygons and to find their perimeters and areas.

Reaching All Learners

Through Modeling

Provide students with a 1 cm grid on a transparency. Ask them to draw an irregular shape, a triangle, and a composite figure. Have students place the grid over each figure and use the methods in this lesson to estimate the area.

Math Background In calculus, students will use methods of estimating areas between graphs in a coordinate plane to solve problems.

INTERVENTION

Questioning Strategies

EXAMPLE 1

- What method of estimation do you prefer?

EXAMPLE 2

- Why do you need to classify a figure before finding its area and perimeter?

EXAMPLE 3

- For what type of figure in the coordinate plane is it easier to find the area by subtracting?

Power Presentations with PowerPoint®

Additional Examples

Example 4

Show that the area does not change when the pieces are rearranged.

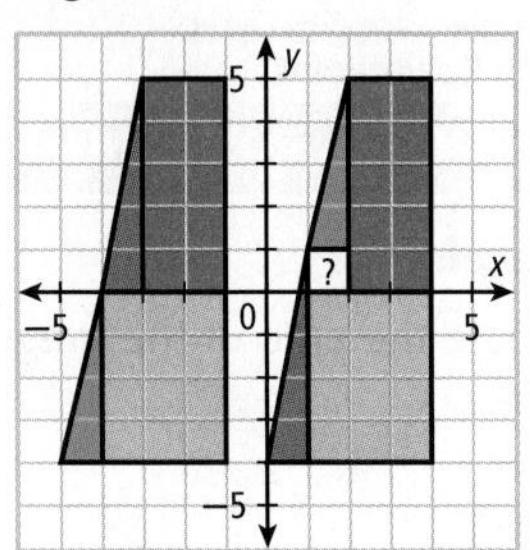

left figure: $A = 2.5 + 10 + 2 + 12 = 26.5$ units^2; right figure: $A = 2 + 10 + 2.5 + 12 = 26.5$ units^2

INTERVENTION 

Questioning Strategies

EXAMPLE 4

- Do the two figures really have the same outer shape?

Critical Thinking Encourage students to think of several methods to find the area of each figure. This will give them a way to check their answers as they work the exercises.

Teaching Tip

Visual Enlarge the puzzle in **Example 4** on an overhead projector. Overlay one figure on top of the other so that students can see that the two arrangements are not triangular.

EXAMPLE 4 ***Problem-Solving Application***

In the puzzle, the two figures are made up of the same pieces, but one figure appears to have a larger area. Use coordinates to show that the area does not change when the pieces are rearranged.

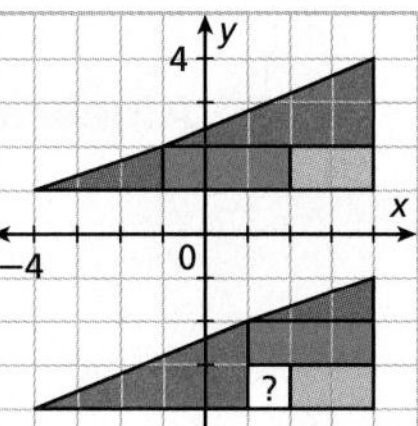

1 Understand the Problem

The parts of the puzzle appear to form two triangles with the same base and height that contain the same shapes, but one appears to have an area that is larger by one square unit.

2 Make a Plan

Find the areas of the shapes that make up each figure. If the corresponding areas are the same, then both figures have the same area by the Area Addition Postulate. To explain why the area appears to increase, consider the assumptions being made about the figure. Each figure is assumed to be a triangle with a base of 8 units and a height of 3 units. Both figures are divided into several smaller shapes.

3 Solve

Find the area of each shape.

Top figure	Bottom figure
red triangle: $A = \frac{1}{2}bh = \frac{1}{2}(5)(2) = 5$ units^2	red triangle: $A = \frac{1}{2}bh = \frac{1}{2}(5)(2) = 5$ units^2
blue triangle: $A = \frac{1}{2}bh = \frac{1}{2}(3)(1) = 1.5$ units^2	blue triangle: $A = \frac{1}{2}bh = \frac{1}{2}(3)(1) = 1.5$ units^2
green rectangle: $A = bh = (3)(1) = 3$ units^2	green rectangle: $A = bh = (3)(1) = 3$ units^2
yellow rectangle: $A = bh = (2)(1) = 2$ units^2	yellow rectangle: $A = bh = (2)(1) = 2$ units^2

The areas are the same. Both figures have an area of $5 + 1.5 + 3 + 2 = 11.5$ units^2.

If the figures were triangles, their areas would be $A = \frac{1}{2}(8)(3) = 12$ units^2. By the Area Addition Postulate, the area is only 11.5 units^2, so the figures must not be triangles. Each figure is a quadrilateral whose shape is very close to a triangle.

4 Look Back

The slope of the hypotenuse of the red triangle is $\frac{2}{5}$. The slope of the hypotenuse of the blue triangle is $\frac{1}{3}$. Since the slopes are unequal, the hypotenuses do not form a straight line. This means the overall shapes are not triangles.

4. Create a figure and divide it into pieces so that the area of the figure appears to increase when the pieces are rearranged. **Check students' work.**

3 Close

Summarize

Review the methods of estimating the area of an irregular figure in the coordinate plane. Remind students that to find the area of a polygon in the coordinate plane, you can classify the figure and use the area formula, divide it into simple shapes and add their areas, or enclose it in a rectangle and subtract the areas that are not part of the figure.

ONGOING ASSESSMENT

and INTERVENTION 

***Diagnose Before* the Lesson**
9-4 Warm Up, TE p. 616

***Monitor During* the Lesson**
Check It Out! Exercises, SE pp. 616–618
Questioning Strategies, TE pp. 617–618

***Assess After* the Lesson**
9-4 Lesson Quiz, TE p. 621
Alternative Assessment, TE p. 621

THINK AND DISCUSS

1. Describe two ways to estimate the area of an irregular shape in a coordinate plane.
2. Explain how you could use the Distance Formula to find the area of a special quadrilateral in a coordinate plane.

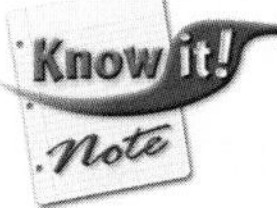

3. **GET ORGANIZED** Copy the graph and the graphic organizer. Complete the graphic organizer by writing the steps used to find the area of the parallelogram.

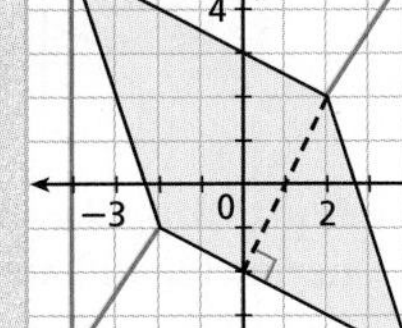

Finding the Area

By using the formula	By subtracting

Answers to *Think and Discuss*

1. One way is to draw a composite figure that approximates the irregular shape and then find its area. Another way is to count the grid squares, estimating half-squares.
2. If the quadrilateral is a parallelogram, rectangle, or trapezoid, you can use the Distance Formula to find the height and base or bases. If it is a rhombus or kite, you can use the Distance Formula to find the lengths of the diagonals.
3. See p. A8.

9-4 Exercises

GUIDED PRACTICE

SEE EXAMPLE 1 p. 616

Estimate the area of each irregular shape.

1. 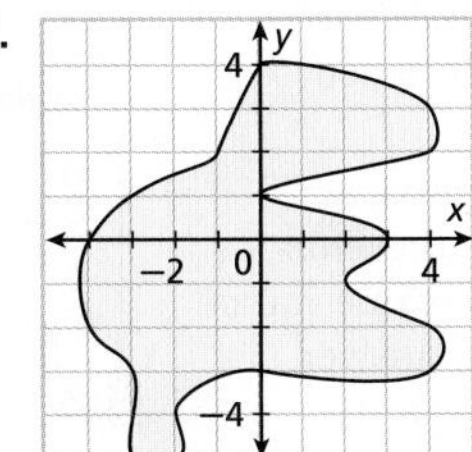
$A \approx 40.5$ units^2

2. 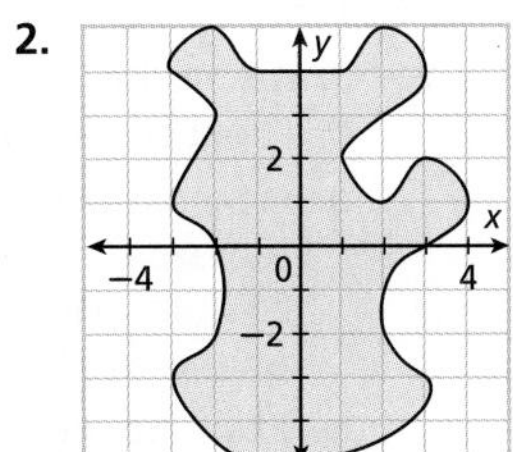
$A \approx 43$ units^2

SEE EXAMPLE 2 p. 617

Multi-Step Draw and classify the polygon with the given vertices. Find the perimeter and area of the polygon.

3. $V(-3, 0), W(3, 0), X(0, 3)$
4. $F(2, 8), G(4, 4), H(2, 0)$
5. $P(-2, 5), Q(8, 5), R(8, 1), S(-2, 1)$
6. $A(-4, 2), B(-2, 6), C(6, 6), D(8, 2)$

SEE EXAMPLE 3 p. 617

Find the area of each polygon with the given vertices.

7. $S(3, 8), T(8, 3), U(2, 1)$ $A = 20$ units^2
8. $L(3, 5), M(6, 8), N(9, 6), P(5, 0)$ $A = 23.5$ units^2

SEE EXAMPLE 4 p. 618

9. Find the area and perimeter of each polygon shown. Use your results to draw a polygon with a perimeter of 12 units and an area of 4 units^2 and a polygon with a perimeter of 12 units and an area of 3 units^2.

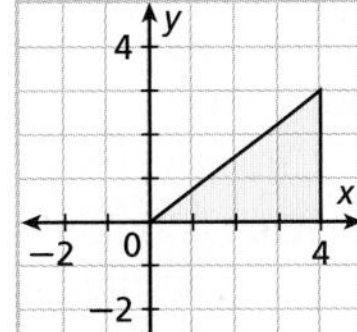
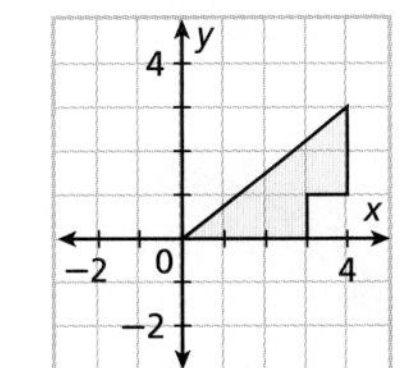

9-4 Exercises

Assignment Guide

Assign *Guided Practice* exercises as necessary.

If you finished Examples **1–2**
Basic 10–15, 19, 20
Average 10–15, 19, 20, 27
Advanced 10–15, 19, 20, 27–30

If you finished Examples **1–4**
Basic 10–20, 23–26, 32–37
Average 10–27, 32–37
Advanced 10–37

Homework Quick Check
Quickly check key concepts.
Exercises: 10, 12, 14, 16, 18, 20

Answers

3. isosceles triangle; $P = (6 + 6\sqrt{2})$ units; $A = 9$ units^2
4. isosceles triangle; $P = (8 + 4\sqrt{5})$ units; $A = 8$ units^2
5. rectangle; $P = 28$ units; $A = 40$ units^2
6. isosceles trapezoid; $P = (20 + 4\sqrt{5})$ units; $A = 40$ units^2

3–6. For graphs, see p. A25.

9. $A = 6$ units^2; $P = 12$ units; $A = 5$ units^2; $P = 12$ units

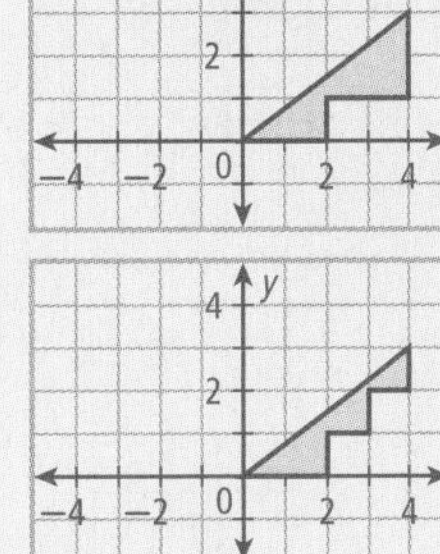

State Resources

Algebra In **Exercises 19** and **20,** students will be graphing lines. Remind students to find the coordinates of the intersections of the lines before finding the side lengths of the triangle.

Exercise 23 involves finding the area of a parallelogram in the coordinate plane. This exercise prepares students for the Multi-Step Test Prep on page 638.

Answers

12. right triangle; $P = 24$ units; $A = 24$ units^2
13. rhombus; $P = 4\sqrt{29}$ units; $A = 20$ units^2
14. scalene triangle; $P = (5 + 2\sqrt{2} + \sqrt{13})$ units; $A = 5$ units^2
15. isosceles trapezoid; $P = (8 + 2\sqrt{29})$ units; $A = 20$ units^2
18. B and C; in figure B, the rectangles have areas $4(1) = 4$, $1(1) = 1$, and $\sqrt{2}(2\sqrt{2}) = 4$, so the total area is 9 units^2. In figure C, the rectangles have areas $1(4) = 4$, $3(1) = 3$, and $\sqrt{2}(\sqrt{2}) = 2$, so the total area is 9 units^2.
19. $P(6 + 3\sqrt{2})$ units; $A = 4.5$ units^2
20. $P = 12 + 4\sqrt{5}$ units; $A = 16$ units^2
22. Possible answer: Draw polygon $ABCDE$. Draw a rectangle with base 6 and height 5 around the polygon. The rectangle has area 30 units^2, and the regions not included in $ABCDE$ have areas 6, 3, 1, and 3.5, so the area of $ABCDE$ is $30 - 6 - 3 - 1 - 3.5 = 16.5$ units^2.

12–15, 19, 20. For graphs, see pp. A25–26.

PRACTICE AND PROBLEM SOLVING

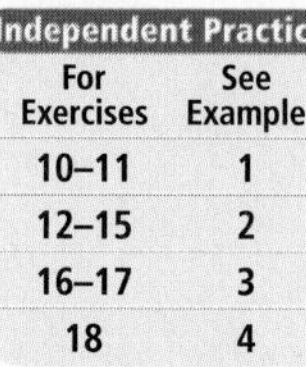

Independent Practice

For Exercises	See Example
10–11	1
12–15	2
16–17	3
18	4

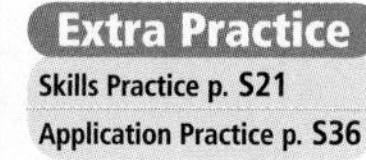

Extra Practice
Skills Practice p. S21
Application Practice p. S36

Estimate the area of each irregular shape.

10. 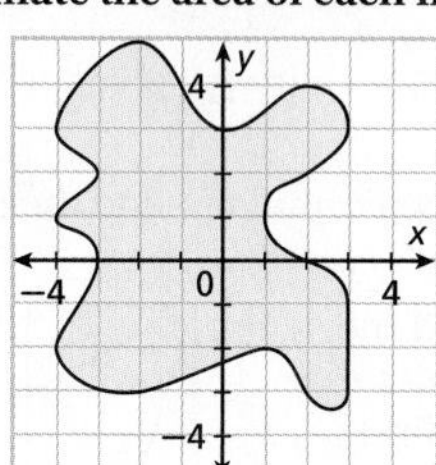

$A \approx 38.5$ units^2

11. 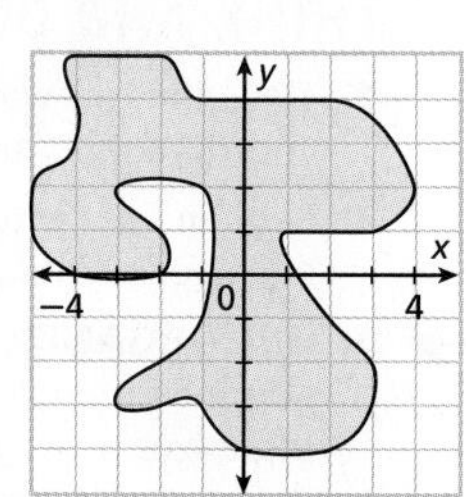

$A \approx 43.5$ units^2

Multi-Step **Draw and classify the polygon with the given vertices. Find the perimeter and area of the polygon.**

12. $H(-3, -3)$, $J(-3, 3)$, $K(5, 3)$
13. $L(7, 5)$, $M(5, 0)$, $N(3, 5)$, $P(5, 10)$
14. $X(2, 1)$, $Y(5, 3)$, $Z(7, 1)$
15. $A(-3, 5)$, $B(2, 7)$, $C(2, 1)$, $D(-3, 3)$

Find the area of each polygon with the given vertices.

16. $A(9, 9)$, $B(4, -4)$, $C(-4, 1)$ — **16.** $A = 64.5$ units^2
17. $T(-4, 4)$, $U(5, 3)$, $V(4, -5)$, $W(-5, 1)$ — **17.** $A = 53$ units^2
18. In which two figures do the rectangles cover the same area? Explain your reasoning.

A 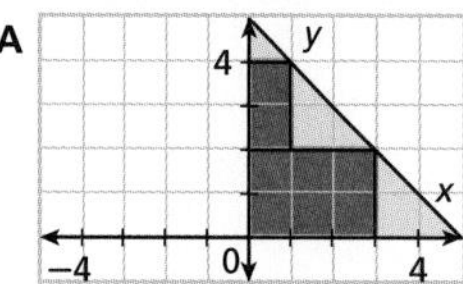

B 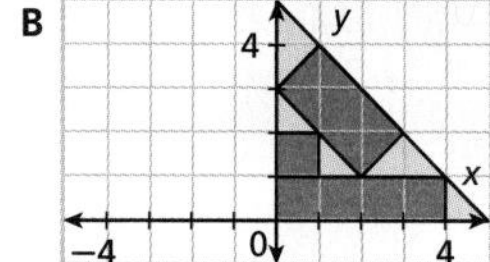

C 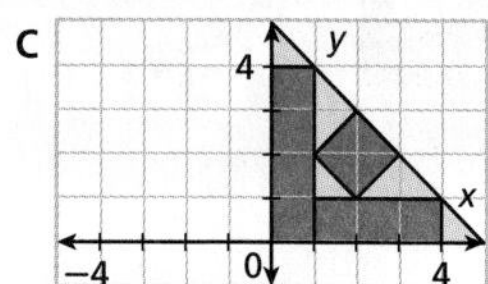

Algebra **Graph each set of lines to form a triangle. Find the area and perimeter.**

19. $y = 2$, $x = 5$, and $y = x$
20. $y = -5$, $x = 2$, and $y = -2x + 7$

21. **Transportation** The graph shows the speed of a boat versus time.
   a. If the base of each square on the graph represents 1 hour and the height represents 20 miles per hour, what is the area of one square on the graph? Include units in your answer.
   b. Estimate the shaded area in the graph.
   c. **Critical Thinking** Use your results from part **a** to interpret the meaning of the area you found in part **b**. (*Hint:* Look at the units.)

21a. $A = 20$ mi
21b. $A \approx 150$ mi^2
21c. The area represents the distance the boat traveled in 5 h.

22. **Write About It** Explain how to find the perimeter of the polygon with vertices $A(2, 3)$, $B(4, 0)$, $C(3, -2)$, $D(-1, -1)$, and $E(-2, 0)$.

MULTI-STEP TEST PREP

23. This problem will prepare you for the Multi-Step Test Prep on page 638. A carnival game uses a 10-by-10 board with three targets. Each player throws a dart at the board and wins a prize if it hits a target. $A = 6$ units^2
   a. One target is a parallelogram as shown. Find its area.
   b. What should the coordinates be for points C and H so that the triangular target $\triangle ABC$ and the kite-shaped target $EFGH$ have the same area as the parallelogram?

Possible answer: $C(2, 1)$ and $H(8, 2)$

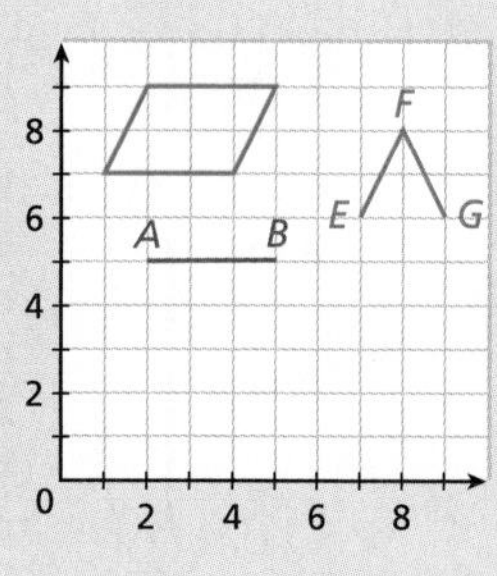

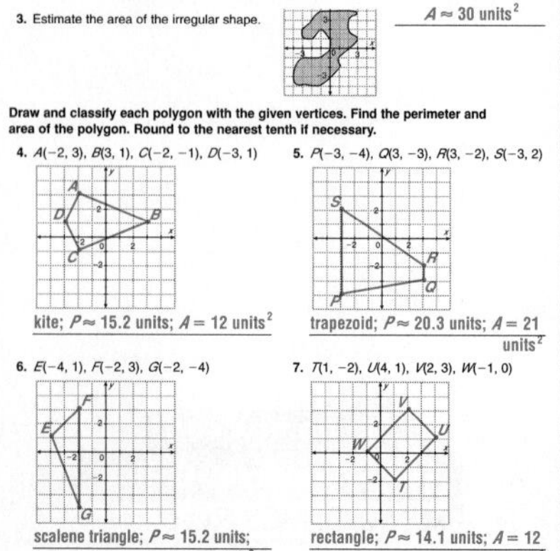

9-4 PRACTICE A
9-4 PRACTICE C
9-4 PRACTICE B

Lena and her older sister Margie love to play tetherball. They want to find how large the tetherball court is. They measure the court and find it has a 6-foot diameter.

1. Lena sketches the court in a coordinate plane in which each square represents 1 square foot. Estimate the size of the court from the figure. Possible answer: $A \approx 30$ ft^2
2. Margie has taken a geometry course, so she knows the formula for the area of a circle. Find the actual area of the court to the nearest tenth of a square foot. $A \approx 28.3$ ft^2
3. Estimate the area of the irregular shape. $A \approx 30$ units^2

Draw and classify each polygon with the given vertices. Find the perimeter and area of the polygon. Round to the nearest tenth if necessary.

4. $A(-2, 3)$, $B(3, 1)$, $C(-2, -1)$, $D(-3, 1)$ — kite; $P \approx 15.2$ units; $A = 12$ units^2
5. $P(-3, -4)$, $Q(3, -3)$, $R(3, -2)$, $S(-3, 2)$ — trapezoid; $P \approx 20.3$ units; $A = 21$ units^2
6. $E(-4, 1)$, $F(-2, 3)$, $G(-2, -4)$ — scalene triangle; $P \approx 15.2$ units; $A = 7$ units^2
7. $T(1, -2)$, $U(4, 1)$, $V(2, 3)$, $W(-1, 0)$ — rectangle; $P \approx 14.1$ units; $A = 12$ units^2

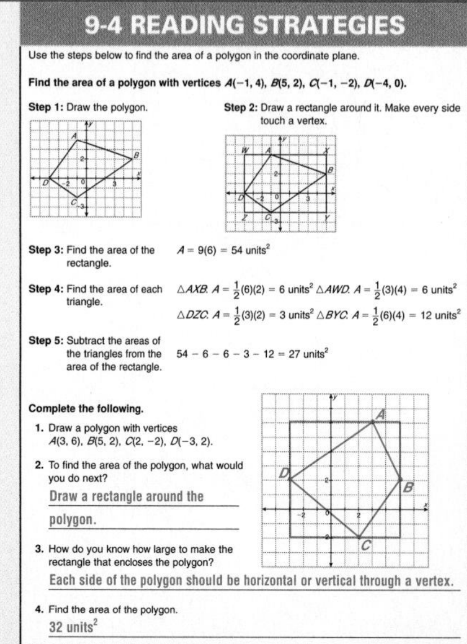

9-4 READING STRATEGIES

Use the steps below to find the area of a polygon in the coordinate plane.

Find the area of a polygon with vertices $A(-1, 4)$, $B(5, 2)$, $C(-1, -2)$, $D(-4, 0)$.

Step 1: Draw the polygon.

Step 2: Draw a rectangle around it. Make every side touch a vertex.

Step 3: Find the area of the rectangle. $A = 9(6) = 54$ units^2

Step 4: Find the area of each triangle. $\triangle AXB$: $A = \frac{1}{2}(6)(2) = 6$ units^2; $\triangle AWD$: $A = \frac{1}{2}(3)(4) = 6$ units^2; $\triangle DZC$: $A = \frac{1}{2}(3)(2) = 3$ units^2; $\triangle BYC$: $A = \frac{1}{2}(6)(4) = 12$ units^2

Step 5: Subtract the areas of the triangles from the area of the rectangle. $54 - 6 - 6 - 3 - 12 = 27$ units^2

Complete the following.

1. Draw a polygon with vertices $A(3, 6)$, $B(5, 2)$, $C(2, -2)$, $D(-3, 2)$.
2. To find the area of the polygon, what would you do next? Draw a rectangle around the polygon.
3. How do you know how large to make the rectangle that encloses the polygon? Each side of the polygon should be horizontal or vertical through a vertex.
4. Find the area of the polygon. 32 units^2

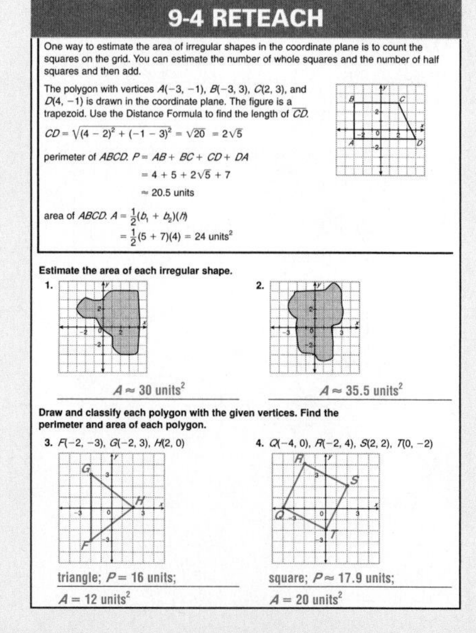

9-4 RETEACH

One way to estimate the area of irregular shapes in the coordinate plane is to count the squares on the grid. You can estimate the number of whole squares and the number of half squares and then add.

The polygon with vertices $A(-3, -1)$, $B(-3, 2)$, $C(2, 3)$, and $D(4, -1)$ is drawn in the coordinate plane. The figure is a trapezoid. Use the Distance Formula to find the length of $\overline{CD}$.

$CD = \sqrt{(4 - 2)^2 + (-1 - 3)^2} = \sqrt{20} = 2\sqrt{5}$

perimeter of $ABCD$: $P = AB + BC + CD + DA$
$= 4 + 5 + 2\sqrt{5} + 7$
≈ 20.5 units

area of $ABCD$: $A = \frac{1}{2}(b_1 + b_2)(h)$
$= \frac{1}{2}(5 + 7)(4) = 24$ units^2

Estimate the area of each irregular shape.

1. $A \approx 30$ units^2
2. $A \approx 35.5$ units^2

Draw and classify each polygon with the given vertices. Find the perimeter and area of each polygon.

3. $F(-2, -3)$, $G(-2, 3)$, $H(2, 0)$ — triangle; $P = 16$ units; $A = 12$ units^2
4. $Q(-4, 0)$, $R(-2, 4)$, $S(2, 2)$, $T(0, -2)$ — square; $P \approx 17.9$ units; $A = 20$ units^2

TEST PREP

24. A circle with center $(0, 0)$ passes through the point $(3, 4)$. What is the area of the circle to the nearest tenth of a square unit?

Ⓐ 15.7 Ⓑ 25.0 Ⓒ 31.4 **Ⓓ 78.5**

25. $\triangle ABC$ with vertices $A(1, 1)$ and $B(3, 5)$ has an area of 10 units^2. Which is NOT a possible location of the third vertex?

Ⓕ $C(-4, 1)$ Ⓖ $C(7, 3)$ Ⓗ $C(6, 1)$ **Ⓙ $C(3, -3)$**

26. **Extended Response** Mike estimated the area of the irregular figure to be 64 units^2.

a. Explain why his answer is not very accurate.

b. Explain how to use a composite figure to estimate the area.

c. Explain how to estimate the area by averaging the areas of two squares.

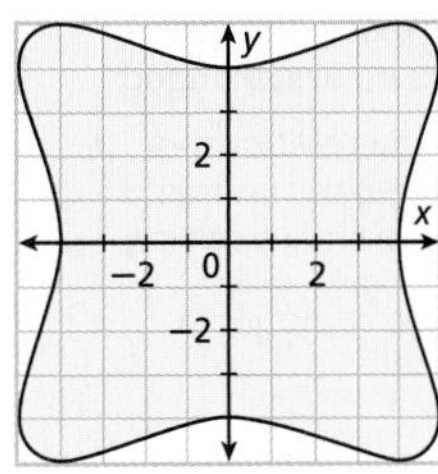

26a. Mike estimated the area by using a square with vertices at $(-4, 4)$, $(4, 4)$, $(4, -4)$, and $(-4, -4)$. This does not include the area in the corners of the graph.

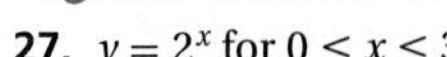

CHALLENGE AND EXTEND

Algebra Estimate the shaded area under each curve.

27. $y = 2^x$ for $0 \le x \le 3$

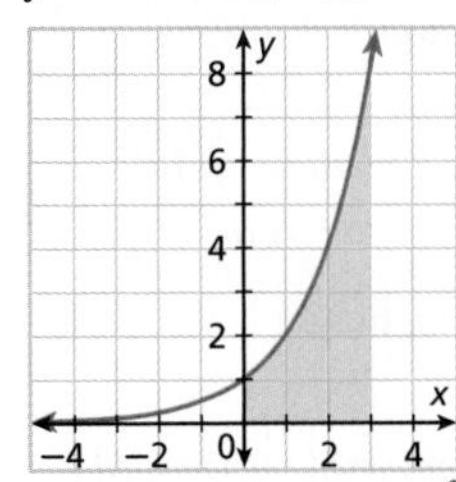

$A \approx 10.5$ units^2

28. $y = x^2$ for $0 \le x \le 3$

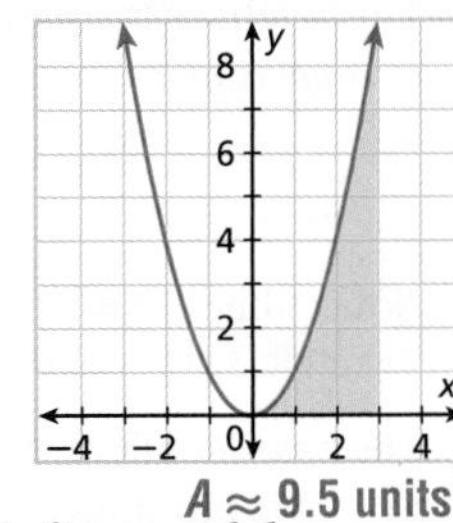

$A \approx 9.5$ units^2

29. $y = \sqrt{x}$ for $0 \le x \le 9$

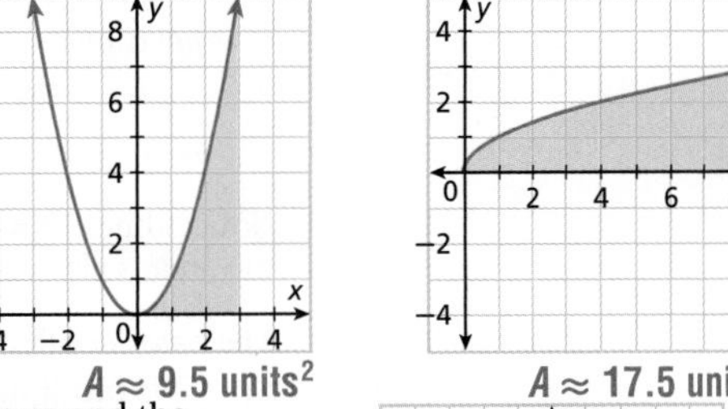

$A \approx 17.5$ units^2

30. **Estimation** Use a composite figure and the Distance Formula to estimate the perimeter of the irregular shape. $P \approx 28.7$ units

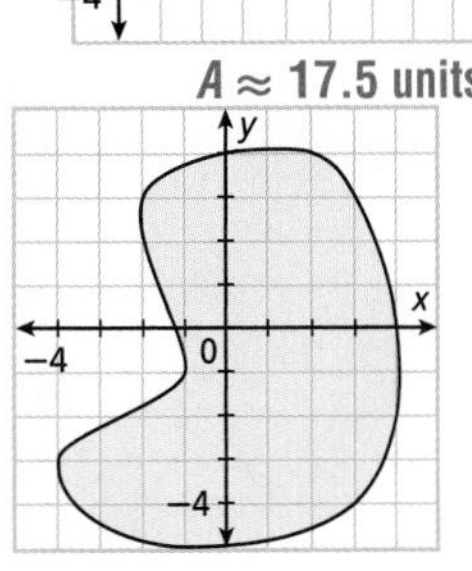

31. Graph a regular octagon on the coordinate plane with vertices on the x-and y-axes and on the lines $y = x$ and $y = -x$ so that the distance between opposite vertices is 2 units. Find the area and perimeter of the octagon. $P = 8\sqrt{2 - \sqrt{2}}$ units; $A = 2\sqrt{2}$ units^2

SPIRAL REVIEW

Solve and graph each compound inequality. *(Previous course)*

32. $-4 < x + 3 < 7$

33. $0 < 2a + 4 < 10$

34. $12 \le -2m + 10 \le 20$

35. **Given:** $\overline{DC} \cong \overline{BC}$, $\angle DCA \cong \angle ACB$
Prove: $\angle DAC \cong \angle BAC$ *(Lesson 4-6)*

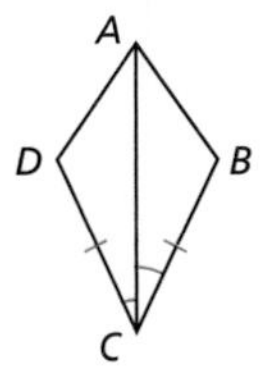

Find each measurement. *(Lesson 9-2)*

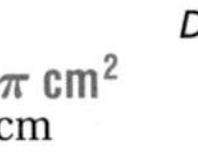

36. the area of $\odot C$ if the circumference is 16π cm $A = 64\pi$ cm^2

37. the diameter of $\odot H$ if the area is 121π ft^2 $d = 22$ ft

9-4 PROBLEM SOLVING

1. Find the perimeter and area of a polygon with vertices $A(-3, -2)$, $B(2, 4)$, $C(5, 2)$, and $D(0, -4)$. Round to the nearest tenth.

$P \approx 22.8$ units; $A = 28$ units^2

2. What are the perimeter and area of the triangle that is formed when the lines below are graphed in the coordinate plane? Round to the nearest tenth.

$y = 2x$, $y = 4$, and $y = x + 4$

$P \approx 12.1$ units; $A = 4$ units^2

3. Find the area of polygon $HJKL$ with vertices $H(-3, 3)$, $J(2, 1)$, $K(4, -4)$, and $L(-3, -3)$.

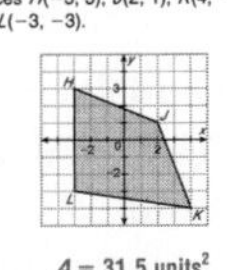

$A = 31.5$ units^2

4. The diagram represents train tracks in the children's area of a zoo. Estimate the area enclosed by the tracks. The side length of each square represents 1 meter.

Possible answer: $A \approx 36$ m^2

Choose the best answer.

5. A graph showing the top view of a circular fountain has its center at (4, 6). The circle representing the fountain passes through (2, 1). What is the area of the space covered by the fountain?

A $\sqrt{29}\pi$
B $2\sqrt{29}\pi$
Ⓒ 29π
D 58π

6. Trapezoid $QRST$ with vertices $Q(1, 5)$ and $R(9, 5)$ has an area of 12 square units. Which are possible locations for vertices S and T?

Ⓕ $S(6, 7)$ and $T(2, 7)$
G $S(4, 7)$ and $T(2, 7)$
H $S(6, 8)$ and $T(3, 8)$
J $S(6, 1)$ and $T(3, 1)$

7. Which is the best estimate for the area of the rock garden? The side length of each square represents 2 feet.

A 23 ft^2
B 46 ft^2
C 69 ft^2
Ⓓ 92 ft^2

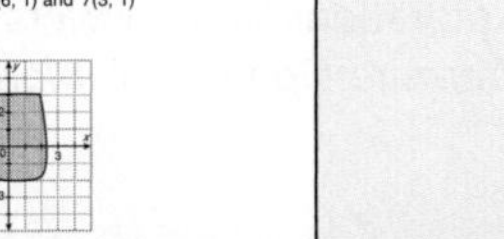

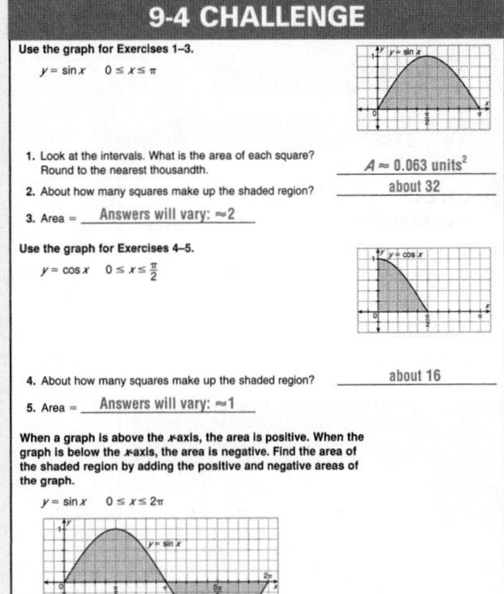

9-4 CHALLENGE

Use the graph for Exercises 1–3.

$y = \sin x \quad 0 \le x \le \pi$

1. Look at the intervals. What is the area of each square? Round to the nearest thousandth. $A \approx 0.063$ units^2

2. About how many squares make up the shaded region? about 32

3. Area = Answers will vary: ≈ 2

Use the graph for Exercises 4–5.

$y = \cos x \quad 0 \le x \le \frac{\pi}{2}$

4. About how many squares make up the shaded region? about 16

5. Area = Answers will vary: ≈ 1

When a graph is above the x-axis, the area is positive. When the graph is below the x-axis, the area is negative. Find the area of the shaded region by adding the positive and negative areas of the graph.

$y = \sin x \quad 0 \le x \le 2\pi$

6. Area = Answers will vary: ≈ 0

TEST PREP DOCTOR For **Exercise 24,** students can use the Distance Formula or the Pythagorean Theorem to find the radius of the circle.

For **Exercise 26,** remind students they can use the symmetry of the figure to estimate the area.

Answers

26b, 26c, 32–35. See p. A26.

31. For graph, see p. A26.

Journal

Have students draw a rectangle on a coordinate plane with a polygon in its interior. Have them explain how to use subtraction to find the area of the polygon.

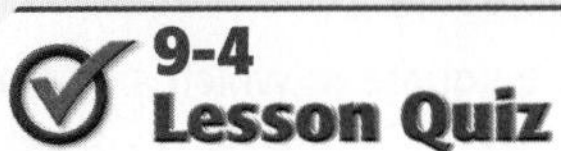

ALTERNATIVE ASSESSMENT

Have students draw a rectangle in a coordinate plane whose sides are not parallel to the x- or y-axis. Then have them show 3 methods of finding the area of the rectangle.

Power Presentations with PowerPoint®

9-4 Lesson Quiz

1. Estimate the area of the irregular shape.

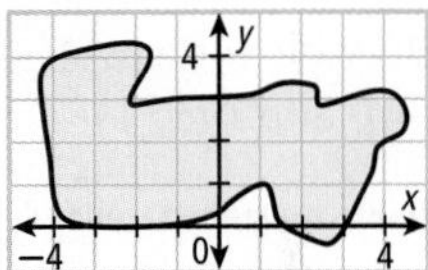

25.5 units^2

2. Draw and classify the polygon with vertices $L(-2, 1)$, $M(-2, 3)$, $N(0, 3)$, and $P(1, 0)$. Find the perimeter and area of the polygon.

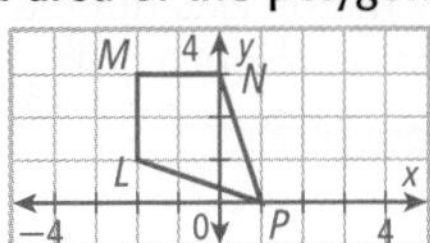

kite; $P = 4 + 2\sqrt{10}$ units; $A = 6$ units^2

3. Find the area of the polygon with vertices $S(-1, -1)$, $T(-2, 1)$, $V(3, 2)$, and $W(2, -2)$. $A = 12$ units^2

4. Show that the two composite figures cover the same area.

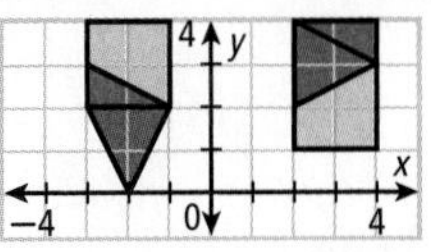

For both figures, $A = 3 + 1 + 2 = 6$ units^2.

Also available on transparency

9-5 Organizer

Pacing: Traditional 1 day
Block $\frac{1}{2}$ day

Objectives: Describe the effect on perimeter and area when one or more dimensions of a figure are changed.

Apply the relationship between perimeter and area in problem solving.

Technology Lab
In *Technology Lab Activities*

Online Edition
Tutorial Videos, Interactivity

Countdown Week 21

Power Presentations with PowerPoint®

Warm Up

Find the area of each figure. Give exact answers, using π if necessary.

1. a square in which $s = 4$ m
   16 m^2
2. a circle in which $r = 2$ ft
   $4\pi \text{ ft}^2$
3. $\triangle ABC$ with vertices $A(-3, 1)$, $B(2, 4)$, and $C(5, 1)$ 12 units^2

Also available on transparency

Math Humor

Q: A round pastry had radius 2. When the radius was doubled, what did the circumference do?

A: It ate pie (8π).

State Resources

go.hrw.com
State Resources Online
KEYWORD: MG7 Resources

9-5 Effects of Changing Dimensions Proportionally

Objectives
Describe the effect on perimeter and area when one or more dimensions of a figure are changed.

Apply the relationship between perimeter and area in problem solving.

Why learn this?
You can analyze a graph to determine whether it is misleading or to explain why it is misleading. (See Example 4.)

In the graph, the height of each DVD is used to represent the number of DVDs shipped per year. However as the height of each DVD increases, the width also increases, which can create a misleading effect.

EXAMPLE 1 Effects of Changing One Dimension

Describe the effect of each change on the area of the given figure.

A The height of the parallelogram is doubled.

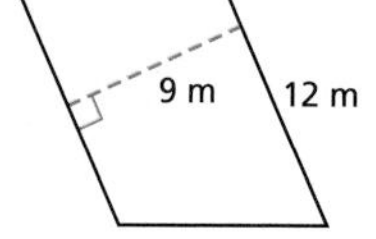

original dimensions:
$A = bh = 12(9)$
$= 108 \text{ cm}^2$

double the height:
$A = bh = 12(18)$
$= 216 \text{ cm}^2$

Notice that $216 = 2(108)$. If the height is doubled, the area is also doubled.

B The base length of the triangle with vertices $A(1, 1)$, $B(6, 1)$, and $C(3, 5)$ is multiplied by $\frac{1}{2}$.

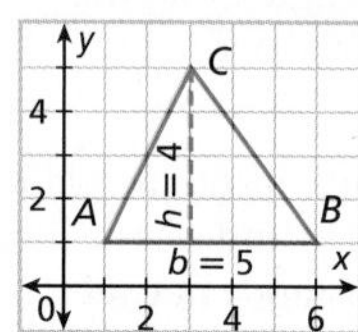

Draw the triangle in a coordinate plane and find the base and height.

original dimensions:

$$A = \frac{1}{2}bh = \frac{1}{2}(5)(4) = 10 \text{ units}^2$$

base multiplied by $\frac{1}{2}$:

$$A = \frac{1}{2}bh = \frac{1}{2}(2.5)(4) = 5 \text{ units}^2$$

Notice that $5 = \frac{1}{2}(10)$. If the base length is multiplied by $\frac{1}{2}$, the area is multiplied by $\frac{1}{2}$.

1. The height of the rectangle is tripled. Describe the effect on the area.
   The area is tripled.

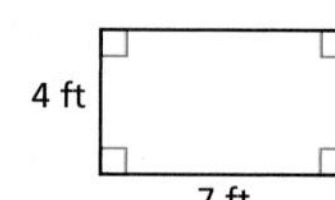

1 Introduce

EXPLORATION

9-5 Effects of Changing Dimensions Proportionally

Explore the effect on the perimeter and area of a figure when the dimensions of the figure are changed proportionally.

1. Find the perimeter (or circumference) and area of each figure. Record these on the left side of the table.

   5 in. | 3 in. | 2 cm | 1.7 m

	Original Figure		Dimensions Multiplied by 3	
	Perimeter	Area	Perimeter	Area
Rectangle				
Circle				
Hexagon				

2. Multiply the given dimensions of each figure by 3. Then find the perimeter and area of the new figures. Record these on the right side of the table.
3. For each figure, how is the perimeter of the new figure related to the perimeter of the original figure? How is the area of the new figure related to the area of the original figure?

THINK AND DISCUSS

Motivate

A decoration that is drawn on shrink plastic, cut out, and baked in the oven will shrink to a shape that is similar to the original. Explain that in this lesson, students will learn how the area of the decoration is affected if the height of the shrunken decoration is 40% of the original height.

Explorations and answers are provided in *Alternate Openers: Explorations Transparencies.*

EXAMPLE 2 Effects of Changing Dimensions Proportionally

Describe the effect of each change on the perimeter or circumference and the area of the given figure.

A **The base and height of a rectangle with base 8 m and height 3 m are both multiplied by 5.**

original dimensions:

$P = 2(8) + 2(3) = 22$ m — *$P = 2b + 2h$*

$A = 8 \cdot 3 = 24$ m^2 — *$A = bh$*

dimensions multiplied by 5:

$P = 2(40) + 2(15) = 110$ m — *$5(8) = 40$; $5(3) = 15$*

$A = 40(15) = 600$ m^2

The perimeter is multiplied by 5. — *$5(22) = 110$*

The area is multiplied by 5^2, or 25. — *$25(24) = 600$*

B **The radius of $\odot A$ is multiplied by $\frac{1}{3}$.**

original dimensions:

$C = 2\pi(9) = 18\pi$ in. — *$C = 2\pi r$*

$A = \pi(9)^2 = 81\pi$ in^2 — *$A = \pi r^2$*

dimensions multiplied by $\frac{1}{3}$:

$C = 2\pi(3) = 6\pi$ in. — *$\frac{1}{3}(9) = 3$*

$A = \pi(3)^2 = 9\pi$ in^2

The perimeter is multiplied by $\frac{1}{3}$. — *$\frac{1}{3}(18\pi) = 6\pi$*

The area is multiplied by $\left(\frac{1}{3}\right)^2$, or $\frac{1}{9}$. — *$\frac{1}{9}(81\pi) = 9\pi$*

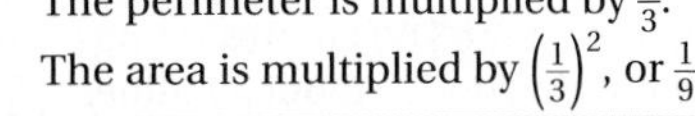

CHECK IT OUT! 2. The base and height of the triangle with vertices $P(2, 5)$, $Q(2, 1)$ and $R(7, 1)$ are tripled. Describe the effect on its area and perimeter. **The perimeter is tripled, and the area is multiplied by 9.**

Helpful Hint

If the radius of a circle or the side length of a square is changed, the size of the entire figure changes proportionally.

Know it! Note When all the dimensions of a figure are changed proportionally, the figure will be similar to the original figure.

Effects of Changing Dimensions Proportionally		
Change in Dimensions	**Perimeter or Circumference**	**Area**
All dimensions multiplied by a	Changes by a factor of a	Changes by a factor of a^2

EXAMPLE 3 Effects of Changing Area

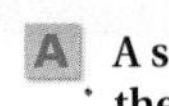

A **A square has side length 5 cm. If the area is tripled, what happens to the side length?**

The area of the original square is $A = s^2 = 5^2 = 25$ cm^2.

If the area is tripled, the new area is 75 cm^2.

$s^2 = 75$ — *Set the new area equal to s^2.*

$s = \sqrt{75} = 5\sqrt{3}$ — *Take the square root of both sides and simplify.*

Notice that $5\sqrt{3} = \sqrt{3}(5)$. The side length is multiplied by $\sqrt{3}$.

Power Presentations with PowerPoint®

Additional Examples

Example 1

Describe the effect of each change on the area of the given figure.

A. The height of the triangle is multiplied by 6.

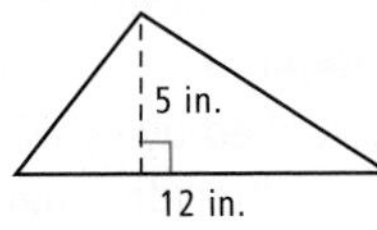

The area is multiplied by 6.

B. The diagonal $\overline{SU}$ of the kite with vertices $R(2, 2)$, $S(4, 0)$, $T(2, -2)$, and $U(-5, 0)$ is multiplied by $\frac{1}{3}$.

The area is multiplied by $\frac{1}{3}$.

Example 2

Describe the effect of each change on the perimeter or circumference and the area of the given figure.

A. The base and height of a rectangle with base 4 ft and height 5 ft are both doubled.

The perimeter is doubled. The area is multiplied by 2^2, or 4.

B. The radius of $\odot J$ is multiplied by $\frac{1}{5}$.

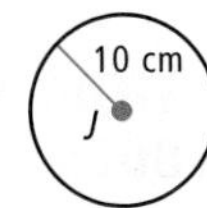

The circumference is multiplied by $\frac{1}{5}$. The area is multiplied by $\left(\frac{1}{5}\right)^2$, or $\frac{1}{25}$.

2 Teach

Guided Instruction

Review the perimeter and area formulas from Lessons 9-1 and 9-2. Discuss the effect of changing one dimension and of changing dimensions proportionally on the perimeter and area of a figure.

Teaching Tip **Critical Thinking** Remind students that a change in the radius of a circle or the side length of a square is equivalent to changing two dimensions because the figure stays similar.

Reaching All Learners

Through Communication

As you present each concept, ask students why they think each change in a dimension of a figure has a certain effect on its area. For instance, lead students to see that doubling the height of a rectangle doubles the rectangle's area because $b(2h) = 2(bh) = 2A$. Through discussion, help students see the reasoning behind the other dimension changes.

INTERVENTION

Questioning Strategies

EXAMPLE 1

- If one dimension of a figure is changed, how does the area change?

EXAMPLE 2

- If the dimensions of a figure are changed proportionally, how does the area change?

Power Presentations with PowerPoint®

Additional Examples

Example 3

A. A circle has a circumference of 32π in. If the area is multiplied by 4, what happens to the radius? It is doubled.

B. An equilateral triangle has a perimeter of 21 m. If the area is multiplied by $\frac{1}{2}$, what happens to the side length? It is multiplied by $\frac{\sqrt{2}}{2}$.

Example 4

Explain why the graph is misleading.

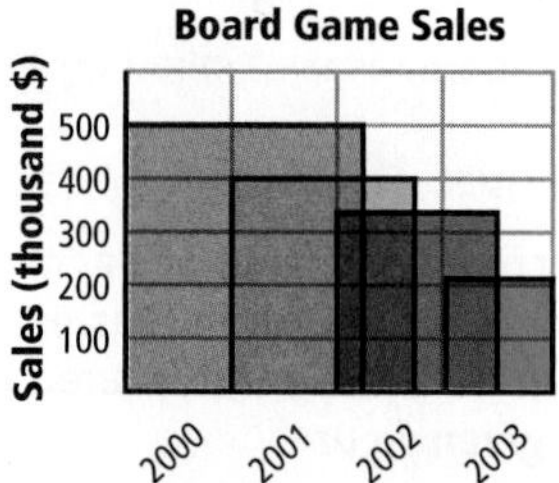

From 2000 to 2003, sales decreased by about 2.5 times, but they appear to have decreased by 6 times.

INTERVENTION

Questioning Strategies

EXAMPLE 3

- Does it make sense that the change in each dimension is smaller than the change in the figure's area? Explain.

EXAMPLE 4

- How can a graph that uses area be misleading?

B **A circle has a radius of 6 in. If the area is doubled, what happens to the circumference?**

The original area is $A = \pi r^2 = 36\pi \text{ in}^2$, and the circumference is $C = 2\pi r = 12\pi$ in. If the area is doubled, the new area is $72\pi \text{ in}^2$.

$\pi r^2 = 72\pi$ *Set the new area equal to πr^2.*

$r^2 = 72$ *Divide both sides by π.*

$r^2 = \sqrt{72} = 6\sqrt{2}$ *Take the square root of both sides and simplify.*

$C = 2\pi r = 2\pi(6\sqrt{2}) = 12\sqrt{2}\pi$ *Substitute $6\sqrt{2}$ for r and simplify.*

Notice that $12\sqrt{2}\pi = \sqrt{2}(12\pi)$. The circumference is multiplied by $\sqrt{2}$.

3. A square has a perimeter of 36 mm. If the area is multiplied by $\frac{1}{2}$, what happens to the side length?
The side length is multiplied by $\frac{1}{\sqrt{2}}$.

EXAMPLE 4 **Entertainment Application**

The graph shows that DVD shipments totaled about 182 million in 2000, 364 million in 2001, and 685 million in 2002. The height of each DVD is used to represent the number of DVDs shipped. Explain why the graph is misleading.

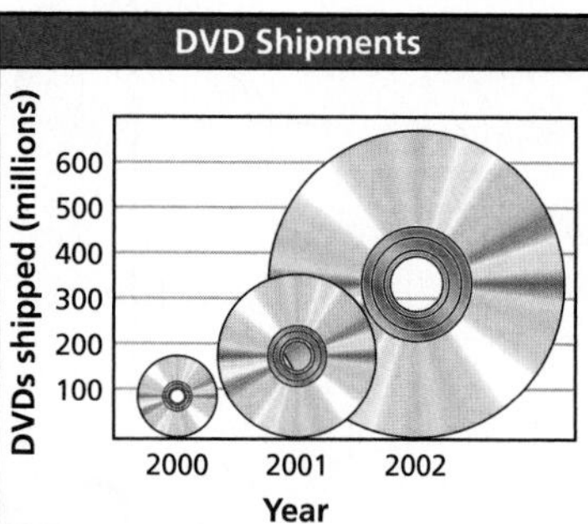

The height of the DVD representing shipments in 2002 is about 3.8 times the height of the DVD representing shipments in 2002.

This means that the area of the DVD is multiplied by about 3.8^2, or 14.4, so the area of the larger DVD is about 14.4 times the area of the smaller DVD.

The graph gives the misleading impression that the number of shipments in 2002 was more than 14 times the number in 2000, but it was actually closer to 4 times the number shipped in 2000.

4. Use the information above to create a version of the graph that is not misleading.

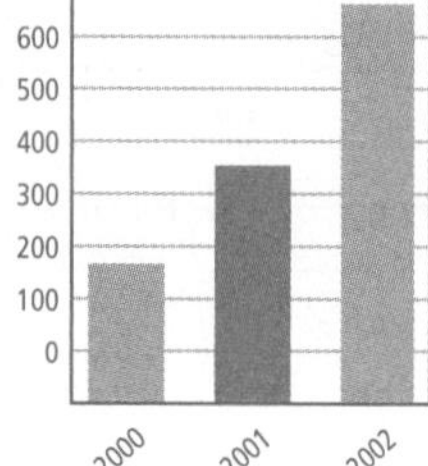

THINK AND DISCUSS

1. Discuss how changing both dimensions of a rectangle affects the area and perimeter.

Know it! Note

2. **GET ORGANIZED** Copy and complete the graphic organizer.

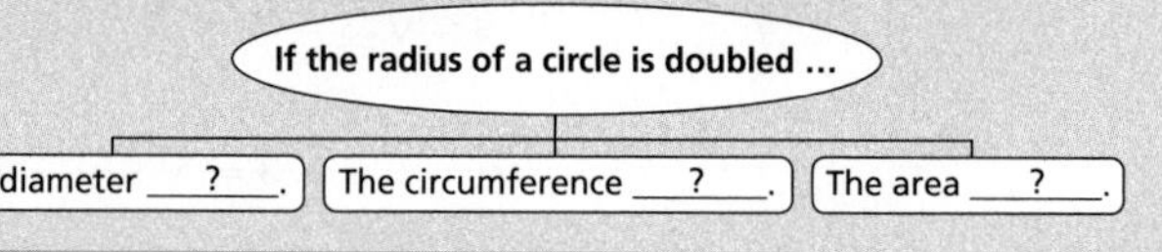

3 Close

Summarize

Discuss what happens to a figure's area when a dimension of the figure is changed. Then describe the effects on perimeter and area when both dimensions are changed. Ask students to describe 3 ways to double the area of a rectangle. Double the base, double the height, or multiply both the base and height by $\sqrt{2}$.

ONGOING ASSESSMENT and INTERVENTION

Diagnose **Before** the Lesson
9-5 Warm Up, TE p. 622

Monitor **During** the Lesson
Check It Out! Exercises, SE pp. 622–624
Questioning Strategies, TE pp. 623–624

Assess **After** the Lesson
9-5 Lesson Quiz, TE p. 627
Alternative Assessment, TE p. 627

Answers to *Think and Discuss*

1. If one dimension of a figure is multiplied by *a*, the area is also multiplied by *a*. If both dimensions of a rectangle are multiplied by *a*, the perimeter is also multiplied by *a*.
2. See p. A8.

go.hrw.com
Homework Help Online
KEYWORD: MG7 9-5
Parent Resources Online
KEYWORD: MG7 Parent

GUIDED PRACTICE

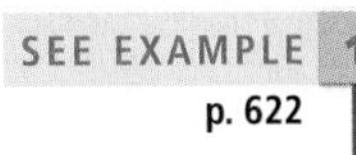

SEE EXAMPLE 1 p. 622

Describe the effect of each change on the area of the given figure.

1. The height of the triangle is doubled. The area is doubled.

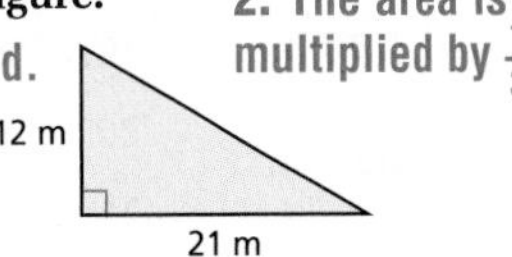

2. The height of a trapezoid with base lengths 12 cm and 18 cm and height 5 cm is multiplied by $\frac{1}{3}$.

2. The area is multiplied by $\frac{1}{3}$.

SEE EXAMPLE 2 p. 623

Describe the effect of each change on the perimeter or circumference and the area of the given figure. The perimeter is tripled. The area is multiplied by 9.

3. The base and height of a triangle with base 12 in. and height 6 in. are both tripled.
4. The base and height of the rectangle are both multiplied by $\frac{1}{2}$.

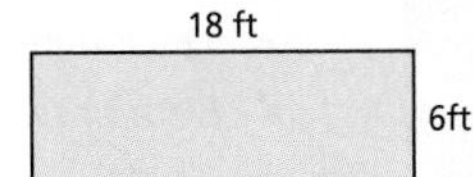

SEE EXAMPLE 3 p. 623

5. A square has an area of 36 m^2. If the area is doubled, what happens to the side length? The side length is multiplied by $\sqrt{2}$.
6. A circle has a diameter of 14 ft. If the area is tripled, what happens to the circumference? The circumference is multiplied by $\sqrt{3}$.

SEE EXAMPLE 4 p. 624

7. **Business** A restaurant has a weekly ad in a local newspaper that is 2 inches wide and 4 inches high and costs \$36.75 per week. The cost of each ad is based on its area. If the owner of the restaurant decides to double the width and height of the ad, how much will the new ad cost? \$147.00

PRACTICE AND PROBLEM SOLVING

Independent Practice

For Exercises	See Example
8–9	1
10–11	2
12–13	3
14	4

Extra Practice
Skills Practice p. S21
Application Practice p. S36

Describe the effect of each change on the area of the given figure.

8. The height of the triangle with vertices (1, 5), (2, 3), and (−1, −6) is multiplied by 4.
9. The base of the parallelogram is multiplied by $\frac{2}{3}$.

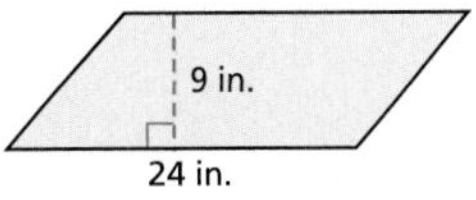

Describe the effect of each change on the perimeter or circumference and the area of the given figure.

10. The base and height of the triangle are both doubled. The perimeter is doubled. The area is multiplied by 4.

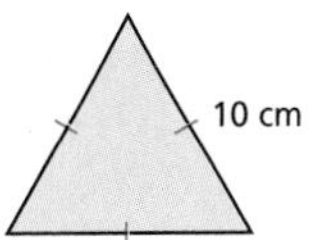

11. The radius of the circle with center (0, 0) that passes through (5, 0) is multiplied by $\frac{3}{5}$.

11. The circumference is multiplied by $\frac{3}{5}$. The area is multiplied by $\frac{9}{25}$.

12. A circle has a circumference of 16π mm. If you multiply the area by $\frac{1}{3}$, what happens to the radius? The radius is multiplied by $\frac{1}{\sqrt{3}}$.
13. A square has vertices (3, 2), (8, 2,) (8, 7), and (3, 7). If you triple the area, what happens to the side length? The side length is multiplied by $\sqrt{3}$.
14. **Entertainment** Two televisions have rectangular screens with the same ratio of base to height. One has a 32 in. diagonal, and the other has a 36 in. diagonal.
    a. What is the ratio of the height of the larger screen to that of the smaller screen? 9:8
    b. What is the ratio of the area of the larger screen to that of the smaller screen? 81:64

9-5 Exercises

Assignment Guide

Assign *Guided Practice* exercises as necessary.

If you finished Examples **1–2**
Basic 8–11, 15–22, 25, 26
Average 8–11, 15–22, 25–27
Advanced 8–11, 15–22, 25–27, 34–36

If you finished Examples **1–4**
Basic 8–23, 25–27, 29–33, 37–43
Average 8–21, 24–34, 37–43
Advanced 8–15, 16–20 even, 21–43

Homework Quick Check
Quickly check key concepts.
Exercises: 8, 10, 12, 14, 18, 26

Teaching Tip

Inclusion In **Exercise 7,** some students may make the mistake of squaring the cost. Suggest they set up a ratio of cost to area or find the cost of an ad per square inch before they find the cost of the new ad.

Answers

4. The perimeter is multiplied by $\frac{1}{2}$. The area is multiplied by $\frac{1}{4}$.
8. The area is multiplied by 4.
9. The area is multiplied by $\frac{2}{3}$.

State Resources

go.hrw.com
State Resources Online
KEYWORD: MG7 Resources

Critical Thinking For **Exercises 15–22,** suggest that students use reasoning strategies to predict the answer before attempting each exercise. For example, they could use the fact that circles and squares change proportionally to answer **Exercises 16** and **19.** They can extend this concept to regular polygons, such as the octagon in **Exercise 18** and the equilateral triangle in **Exercise 21.**

Exercise 29 involves applying the relationship between the diameter of a circle and its area to make it easier or harder to win at a carnival game. This exercise prepares students for the Multi-Step Test Prep on page 638.

Answers

25a. The area is multiplied by 3.
b. The area is multiplied by 3.
c. The area is multiplied by 9.

26a. The area is multiplied by 3.
b. The area is multiplied by 3.
c. The area is multiplied by 9.

27a. The area is multiplied by 3.
b. The area is multiplied by 3.
c. The area is multiplied by 9.

Describe the effect of each change on the area of the given figure.

15. The diagonals of a rhombus are both multiplied by 8. **The area is multiplied by 64.**
16. The circumference of a circle is multiplied by 2.4. **The area is multiplied by 5.76.**
17. The base of a rectangle is multiplied by 4, and the height is multiplied by 7.
18. The apothem of a regular octagon is tripled. **The area is multiplied by 9.**
19. The diagonal of a square is divided by 4. **The area is divided by 16.**
20. One diagonal of a kite is multiplied by $\frac{1}{7}$. **The area is multiplied by $\frac{1}{7}$.**
21. The perimeter of an equilateral triangle is doubled. **The area is multiplied by 4.**
22. Find the area of the trapezoid. Describe the effect of each change on the area. **b. The area is doubled.**
    a. The length of the top base is doubled.
    b. The length of both bases is doubled.
    c. The height is doubled. **The area is doubled.**
    d. Both bases and the height are doubled. **The area is multiplied by 4.**

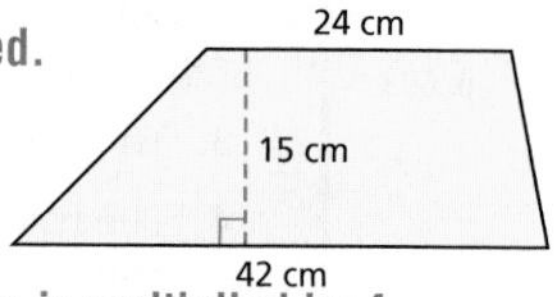

24 cm, 15 cm, 42 cm

17. The area is multiplied by 28.

22a. The area is multiplied by approximately 1.4.

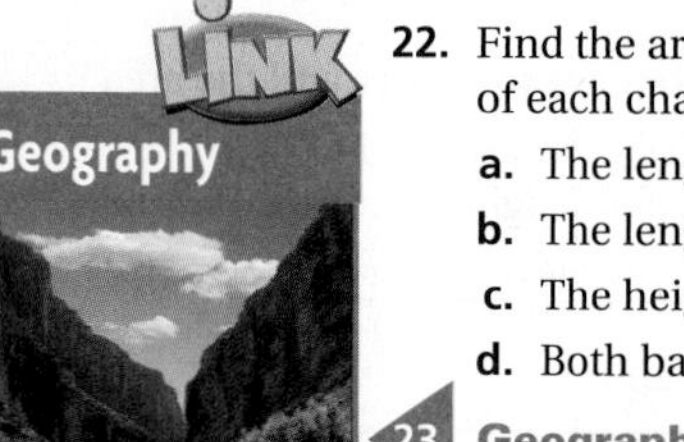

The altitude in Big Bend National Park ranges from approximately 1800 feet along the Rio Grande to 7800 feet in the Chisos Mountains.

23. **Geography** A map has the scale 1 inch = 10 miles. On the map, the area of Big Bend National Park in Texas is about 12.5 square inches. Estimate the actual area of the park in acres. (*Hint:* 1 square mile = 640 acres) **800,000 acres**
24. **Critical Thinking** If you want to multiply the dimensions of a figure so that the area is 50% of the original area, what is your scale factor? $\frac{1}{\sqrt{2}}$

Multi-Step For each figure in the coordinate plane, describe the effect on the area that results from each change.

a. Only the x-coordinates of the vertices are multiplied by 3.
b. Only the y-coordinates of the vertices are multiplied by 3.
c. Both the x- and y-coordinates of the vertices are multiplied by 3.

25.
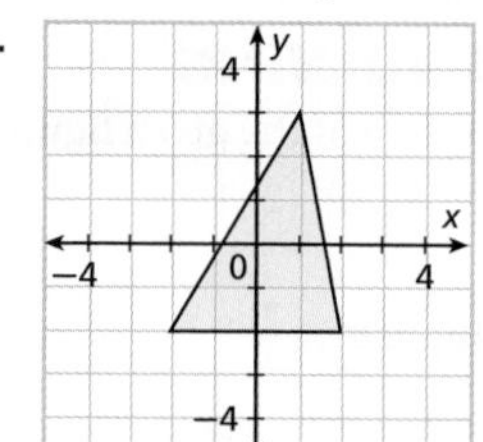

26.
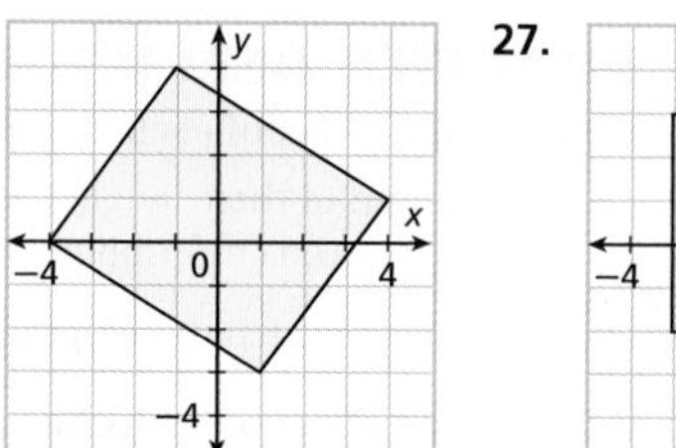

27.
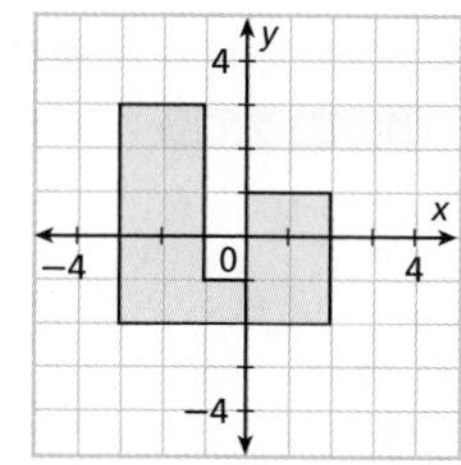

28. **Write About It** How could you change the dimensions of a parallelogram to increase the area by a factor of 5 if the parallelogram does not have to be similar to the original parallelogram? if the parallelogram does have to be similar to the original parallelogram? **Multiply the base or height by 5. Multiply the base and height by $\sqrt{5}$.**

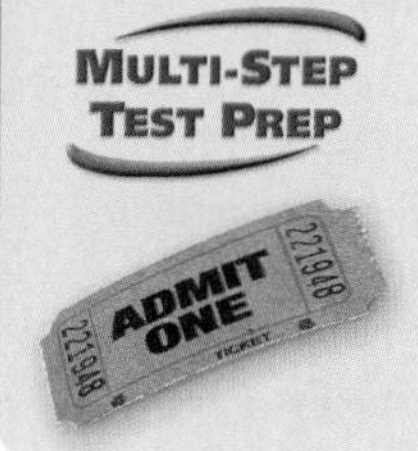

29. This problem will prepare you for the Multi-Step Test Prep on page 638.
To win a prize at a carnival, a player must toss a beanbag onto a circular disk with a diameter of 8 in.
    a. The organizer of the game wants players to win twice as often, so he changes the disk so that it has twice the area. What is the diameter of the new disk? **$8\sqrt{2}$ in.**
    b. Suppose the organizer wants players to win half as often. What should be the disk's diameter in this case? **$4\sqrt{2}$ in.**

9-5 PRACTICE A
9-5 PRACTICE C
9-5 PRACTICE B

Describe the effect of each change on the area of the given figure.

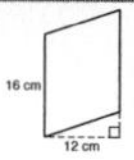

1. The base of the parallelogram is multiplied by $\frac{3}{4}$.
The area is multiplied by $\frac{3}{4}$.
2. The length of a rectangle with length 12 yd and width 11 yd is divided by 6.
The area is divided by 6.
3. The base of a triangle with vertices $A(2, 3)$, $B(5, 2)$, and $C(5, 4)$ is doubled.
The area is doubled.
4. The height of a trapezoid with base lengths 4 mm and 7 mm and height 9 mm is multiplied by $\frac{1}{3}$. 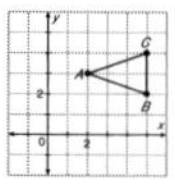
The area is multiplied by $\frac{1}{3}$.

16 cm, 12 cm

In Exercises 5–8, describe the effect of each change on the perimeter or circumference and the area of the given figure.

3 ft, 9 ft

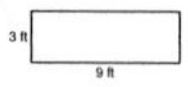

5. The length and width of the rectangle are multiplied by $\frac{4}{3}$.
The perimeter is multiplied by $\frac{4}{3}$. The area is multiplied by $\frac{16}{9}$.
6. The base and height of a triangle with base 1.5 m and height 6 m are both tripled.
The perimeter is tripled. The area is multiplied by 9.
7. The radius of a circle with center (2, 2) that passes through (0, 2) is divided by 2.
The perimeter is divided by 2.
The area is divided by 4. 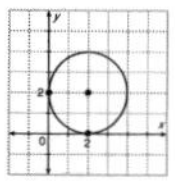
8. The bases and the height of a trapezoid with base lengths 4 in. and 8 in. and height 8 in. are all multiplied by $\frac{1}{8}$.
The perimeter is multiplied by $\frac{1}{8}$. The area is multiplied by $\frac{1}{64}$.
9. A rhombus has an area of 9 cm^2. The area is multiplied by 5. Describe the effects on the diagonals of the rhombus.
Both diagonals are multiplied by $\sqrt{5}$.
10. A circle has a circumference of 14π ft. The area is halved. Describe the effects on the circumference of the circle.
The circumference is divided by $\sqrt{2}$.

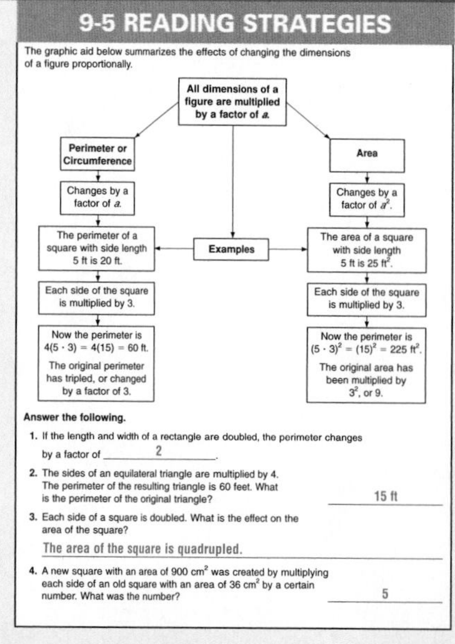

9-5 READING STRATEGIES

The graphic aid below summarizes the effects of changing the dimensions of a figure proportionally.

All dimensions of a figure are multiplied by a factor of a.

Perimeter or Circumference → Changes by a factor of a. → The perimeter of a square with side length 5 ft is 20 ft. → Each side of the square is multiplied by 3. → Now the perimeter is $4(5 \cdot 3) = 4(15) = 60$ ft. The original perimeter has tripled, or changed by a factor of 3.

Area → Changes by a factor of a^2. → The area of a square with side length 5 ft is 25 ft^2. → Each side of the square is multiplied by 3. → Now the perimeter is $(5 \cdot 3)^2 = (15)^2 = 225$ ft^2. The original area has been multiplied by 3^2, or 9.

Examples

Answer the following.

1. If the length and width of a rectangle are doubled, the perimeter changes by a factor of 2.
2. The sides of an equilateral triangle are multiplied by 4. The perimeter of the resulting triangle is 60 feet. What is the perimeter of the original triangle? 15 ft
3. Each side of a square is doubled. What is the effect on the area of the square?
The area of the square is quadrupled.
4. A new square with an area of 900 cm^2 was created by multiplying each side of an old square with an area of 36 cm^2 by a certain number. What was the number? 5

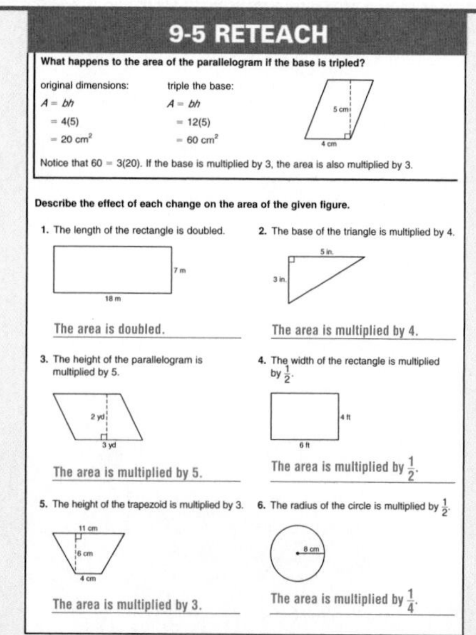

9-5 RETEACH

What happens to the area of the parallelogram if the base is tripled?

original dimensions:	triple the base:
$A = bh$	$A = bh$
$= 4(5)$	$= 12(5)$
$= 20$ cm^2	$= 60$ cm^2

5 cm, 4 cm

Notice that $60 = 3(20)$. If the base is multiplied by 3, the area is also multiplied by 3.

Describe the effect of each change on the area of the given figure.

1. The length of the rectangle is doubled. (7 m, 18 m)
The area is doubled.
2. The base of the triangle is multiplied by 4. (5 in., 3 in.)
The area is multiplied by 4.
3. The height of the parallelogram is multiplied by 5. (2 yd, 3 yd)
The area is multiplied by 5.
4. The width of the rectangle is multiplied by $\frac{1}{2}$. (4 ft, 6 ft)
The area is multiplied by $\frac{1}{2}$.
5. The height of the trapezoid is multiplied by 3. (11 cm, 6 cm, 4 cm)
The area is multiplied by 3.
6. The radius of the circle is multiplied by $\frac{1}{2}$. (8 cm)
The area is multiplied by $\frac{1}{4}$.

30. Which of the following describes the effect on the area of a square when the side length is doubled?
   - (A) The area remains constant.
   - (B) The area is reduced by a factor of $\frac{1}{2}$.
   - (C) The area is doubled.
   - **(D)** The area is increased by a factor of 4.

31. If the area of a circle is increased by a factor of 4, what is the change in the diameter of the circle?
   - (F) The diameter is $\frac{1}{2}$ of the original diameter.
   - **(G)** The diameter is 2 times the original diameter.
   - (H) The diameter is 4 times the original diameter.
   - (J) The diameter is 16 times the original diameter.

32. Tina and Kieu built rectangular play areas for their dogs. The play area for Tina's dog is 1.5 times as long and 1.5 times as wide as the play area for Kieu's dog. If the play area for Kieu's dog is 60 square feet, how big is the play area for Tina's dog?
   (A) 40 ft^2 (B) 90 ft^2 **(C)** 135 ft^2 (D) 240 ft^2

33. **Gridded Response** Suppose the dimensions of a triangle with a perimeter of 18 inches are doubled. Find the perimeter of the new triangle in inches. **36**

CHALLENGE AND EXTEND

34. **Algebra** A square has a side length of $(2x + 5)$ cm. If the side length is multiplied by 5, what is the area of the new square? $A = (100x^2 + 500x + 625)$ cm^2

35. **Algebra** A circle has a diameter of 6 in. If the circumference is multiplied by $(x + 3)$, what is the area of the new circle? $A = (9\pi x^2 + 54\pi x + 81\pi)$ in^2

36. **Write About It** How could you change the dimensions of the composite figure to double the area if the resulting figure does not have to be similar to the original figure? if the resulting figure does have to be similar to the original figure?
Multiply all the lengths of the horizontal segments by 2. Multiply all the side lengths by $\sqrt{2}$.

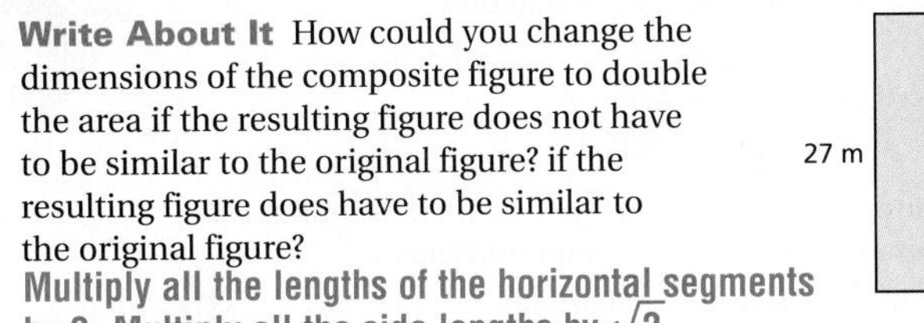

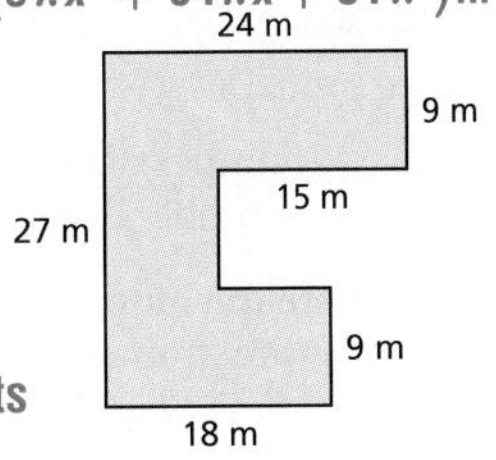

SPIRAL REVIEW

Write an equation that can be used to determine the value of the variable in each situation. *(Previous course)*

37. Steve can make 2 tortillas per minute. He makes t tortillas in 36 minutes. $\frac{t}{2} = 36$

38. A car gets 25 mi/gal. At the beginning of a trip of m miles, the car's gas tank contains 13 gal of gas. At the end of the trip, the car has 8 gal of gasoline left. $\frac{m}{25} = 13 - 8$

Find the measure of each interior and each exterior angle of each regular polygon. Round to the nearest tenth, if necessary. *(Lesson 6-1)*

39. heptagon **128.6°; 51.4°** 40. decagon **144°; 36°** 41. 14-gon **154.3°; 25.7°**

Find the area of each polygon with the given vertices. *(Lesson 9-4)*

42. $L(-1, 1)$, $M(5, 2)$, and $N(1, -5)$ $A = 19$ units^2

43. $A(-4, 2)$, $M(-2, 4)$, $C(4, 2)$ and $D(2, -4)$ $A = 32$ units^2

9-5 PROBLEM SOLVING

1. Mara has a photograph 5 inches by 7 inches. She wants to enlarge the photo so that the length and width are each tripled. Describe how the area of the photo will change.
   The area will be 9 times as great.
2. On a map, 1 inch = 2 miles. On the map, the area of a wildlife preserve is about 3 square inches. Estimate the actual area of the preserve in acres. (*Hint:* 1 square mile = 640 acres)
   7680 acres
3. A triangle has vertices $M(3, 5)$, $P(7, 2)$, and $Q(3, 1)$. Point P is moved to be twice as far from $\overline{NQ}$ as in the original triangle. Describe the effect on the area.
   The area is doubled.
4. The length of each base of a trapezoid is divided by 2. How does the area change?
   The area is divided by 2.

Use the information below for Exercises 5 and 6.

Steven's dog is on a chain 6 feet long with one end of the chain attached to the ground as shown in the diagram. Steven replaces the chain with one that is $1\frac{1}{2}$ times as long.

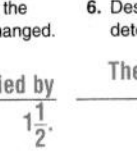

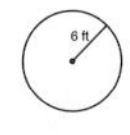

5. Describe how the circumference of the circle determined by the chain is changed.
   The circumference is multiplied by $1\frac{1}{2}$.
6. Describe how the area of the circle determined by the chain is changed.
   The area is multiplied by $\frac{9}{4}$.

Choose the best answer.

7. In kite $RSTU$, $RT = 2.5$ centimeters and $SU = 4.3$ centimeters. Both diagonals of the kite are doubled. What happens to the area of the kite?

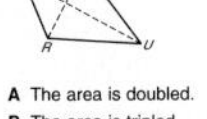

   - A The area is doubled.
   - B The area is tripled.
   - **(C)** The area is 4 times as great.
   - D The area is 8 times as great.

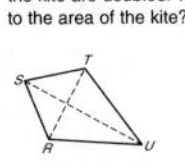

8. The side length of the regular hexagon is divided by 3. Which is a true statement?

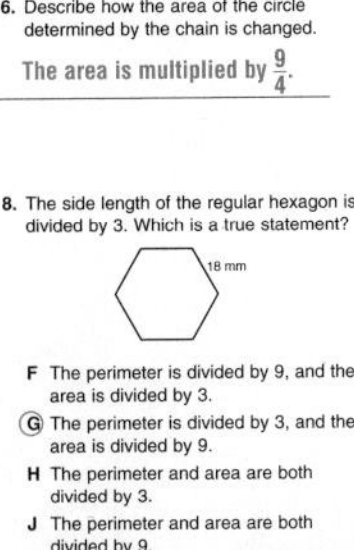

   - F The perimeter is divided by 9, and the area is divided by 3.
   - **(G)** The perimeter is divided by 3, and the area is divided by 9.
   - H The perimeter and area are both divided by 3.
   - J The perimeter and area are both divided by 9.

9-5 CHALLENGE

Many real-life situations involving area and volume require you to perform a familiar process "in reverse" to achieve a desired result.

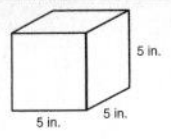

A manufacturer packages its product in a distinctive cubic package that has the dimensions shown at the right. The manufacturer wants to offer the product in a cubic package that has twice the volume.

(Cube: 5 in. × 5 in. × 5 in.)

1. a. What is the volume of the original package? 125 in^3
   b. What is the volume of the new package? 250 in^3
   c. Write the ratio $\frac{\text{volume of new package}}{\text{volume of original package}}$ in simplest form. $\frac{250}{125} = \frac{2}{1}$
2. a. What is the length of one edge of the original package? 5 in.
   b. What is the length of one edge of the new package? (*Hint:* When you multiply a number by itself three times, you are *cubing* the number. What is the inverse operation?) $\sqrt[3]{250}$ in. $= 5\sqrt[3]{2}$ in.
   c. Write the ratio $\frac{\text{length of edge of new package}}{\text{length of edge of original package}}$ in simplest form. $\frac{5\sqrt[3]{2}}{5} = \frac{\sqrt[3]{2}}{1}$
3. a. What is the surface area of the original package? 150 in^2
   b. What is the surface area of the new package? $150\sqrt[3]{4}$ in^2
   c. Write the ratio $\frac{\text{surface area of new package}}{\text{surface area of original package}}$ in simplest form. $\frac{150\sqrt[3]{4}}{150} = \frac{\sqrt[3]{4}}{1}$

Refer to the situation in Exercises 1–3. Suppose that the manufacturer wants to offer the product in a cubic package that has two-thirds the volume of the original. Write a ratio in simplest form to compare the given measure for the new package to the corresponding measure for the original package.

4. volume $\frac{2}{3}$ 5. length of an edge $\frac{\sqrt[3]{2}}{\sqrt[3]{3}}$ 6. surface area $\frac{\sqrt[3]{2^2}}{\sqrt[3]{3^2}} = \frac{\sqrt[3]{4}}{\sqrt[3]{9}}$
7. Complete this statement: Two cubes with volumes in the ratio $\frac{a}{b}$ have linear measures in the ratio $\frac{\sqrt[3]{a}}{\sqrt[3]{b}}$ and surface areas in the ratio $\frac{\sqrt[3]{a^2}}{\sqrt[3]{b^2}}$.
8. Refer to the statement in Exercise 7. Conduct an investigation to determine whether the statement is true when the word *cubes* is replaced by the phrase *similar solids*. Show your work on a separate sheet of paper. Investigations will vary. Students should arrive at the conclusion that the statement holds true for all similar solids.

In **Exercise 34,** students may square the side length and then multiply by 5. Remind them to multiply by 5 and square the result.

TEST PREP DOCTOR For **Exercises 30** and **31,** encourage students to draw a square with side x and a circle with diameter d and solve algebraically.

Students who answered **B** for **Exercise 32** multiplied only one dimension by 1.5.

Journal

Ask students what happens to the height of a rectangular picture if it is reduced proportionally by $\frac{1}{2}$ its area. How would the amount of framing material be affected?

ALTERNATIVE ASSESSMENT

Have students draw a rectangle, a triangle, and a trapezoid, each with an area of 9 cm^2, and then describe 2 ways of changing the dimensions of each figure to produce a figure with an area of 36 cm^2.

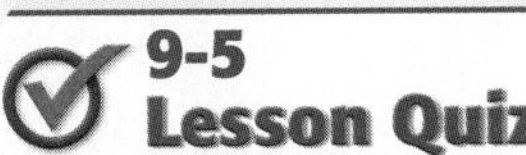

Power Presentations with PowerPoint®

9-5 Lesson Quiz

Describe the effect of each change on the area of the given figure.

1. The base length of the rectangle is multiplied by 8.
   (Rectangle: 1 mm by 3 mm)
   The area is multiplied by 8.
2. The radius of the circle is tripled.

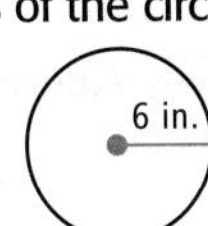

   The area is multiplied by 9.
3. A square has an area of 49 cm^2. If the area is quadrupled, what happens to the side length? The side length is doubled.
4. Rob had a 10 ft by 12 ft wall painted. For a wall twice as wide, the painter charged him twice as much. Is this reasonable? Explain. Yes; the second wall has twice the area of the first wall.

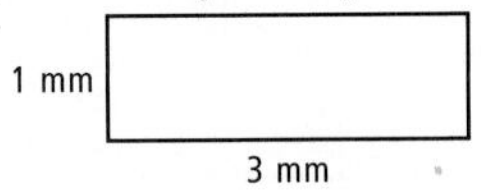

Also available on transparency

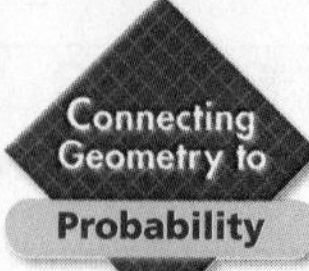

Organizer

Pacing:
Traditional $\frac{1}{2}$ day
Block $\frac{1}{4}$ day

Objective: Review basic probability concepts in preparation for geometric probability.

Online Edition

Countdown Week 21

Teach

Remember

Review probability concepts.

Visual Help students develop strategies for making organized lists, such as tree diagrams.

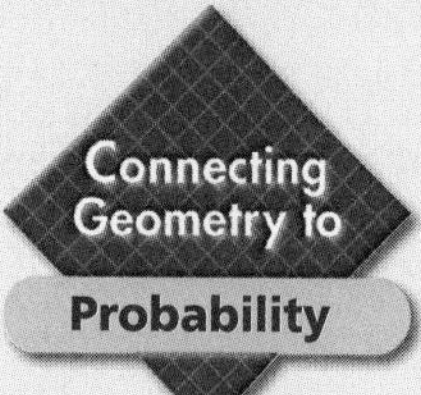

Probability

An *experiment* is an activity in which results are observed. Each result of an experiment is called an *outcome*. The *sample space* is the set of all outcomes of an experiment. An *event* is any set of outcomes.

The probability of an event is a number from 0 to 1 that tells you how likely the event is to happen. The closer the probability is to 0, the less likely the event is to happen. The closer it is to 1, the more likely the event is to happen.

An experiment is *fair* if all outcomes are equally likely. The *theoretical probability* of an event is the ratio of the number of outcomes in the event to the number of outcomes in the sample space.

$$P(E) = \frac{\text{number of outcomes in event } E}{\text{number of possible outcomes}}$$

Example 1

A fair number cube has six faces, numbered 1 through 6. An experiment consists of rolling the number cube.

A What is the sample space of the experiment?

The sample space has 6 possible outcomes.
The outcomes are 1, 2, 3, 4, 5, and 6.

B What is the probability of the event "rolling a 4"?

The event "rolling a 4" contains only 1 outcome.
The probability is

$$P(E) = \frac{\text{number of outcomes in event } E}{\text{number of possible outcomes}} = \frac{1}{6}.$$

C What are the outcomes in the event "rolling an odd number"? What is the probability of rolling an odd number?

The event "rolling an odd number" contains 3 outcomes.
The outcomes are 1, 3, and 5. The probability is

$$P(E) = \frac{\text{number of outcomes in event } E}{\text{number of possible outcomes}} = \frac{3}{6} = \frac{1}{2}.$$

If two events A and B have no outcomes in common, then the probability that A or B will happen is $P(A) + P(B)$.

The *complement of an event* is the set of outcomes that are *not* in the event. If the probability of an event is p, then the probability of the complement of the event is $1 - p$.

Example 2

The tiles shown below are placed in a bag. An experiment consists of drawing a tile at random from the bag.

A What is the sample space of the experiment?

The sample space has 9 possible outcomes. The outcomes are 1, 2, 3, 4, A, B, C, D, E, and F.

B What is the probability of choosing a 3 or a vowel?

The event "choosing a 3" contains only 1 outcome. The probability is

$P(A) = \frac{\text{number of outcomes in event } A}{\text{number of possible outcomes}} = \frac{1}{9}$.

The event "choosing a vowel" has 2 outcomes, A and E. The probability is

$P(B) = \frac{\text{number of outcomes in event } B}{\text{number of possible outcomes}} = \frac{2}{9}$.

The probability of choosing a 3 or a vowel is $\frac{1}{9} + \frac{2}{9} = \frac{3}{9} = \frac{1}{3}$.

C What is the probability of not choosing a letter?

The event "choosing a letter" contains 5 outcomes, A, B, C, D, and E. The probability is

$P(E) = \frac{\text{number of outcomes in event } E}{\text{number of possible outcomes}} = \frac{5}{9}$.

The event of not choosing a letter is the complement of the event of choosing a letter. The probability of not choosing a letter is $1 - \frac{5}{9} = \frac{4}{9}$.

Try This

An experiment consists of randomly choosing one of the given shapes.

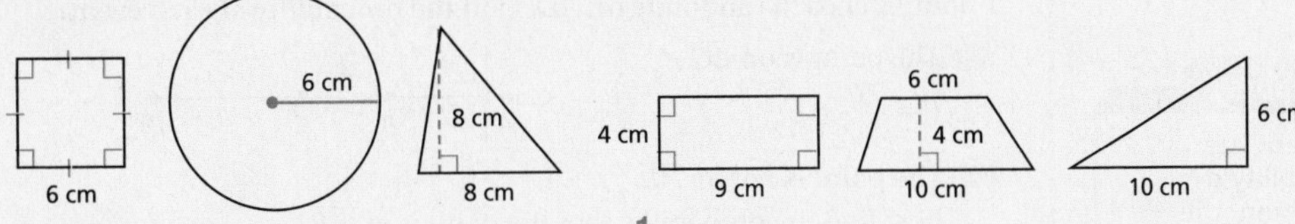

1. What is the probability of choosing a circle? $\frac{1}{6}$
2. What is the probability of choosing a shape whose area is 36 cm^2? $\frac{1}{3}$
3. What is the probability of choosing a quadrilateral or a triangle? $\frac{5}{6}$
4. What is the probability of not choosing a triangle? $\frac{2}{3}$

Close

Assess

Have students use algebra to verify that the sum of the probability of an event and the probability of its complement is always 1. If n is the probability, then $1 - n$ is the probability of the complement, and $n + 1 - n = 1$.

9-6 Organizer

Pacing: Traditional 1 day
Block $\frac{1}{2}$ day

Objectives: Calculate geometric probabilities.

Use geometric probability to predict results in real-world situations.

PREMIER Online Edition
Tutorial Videos

Countdown Week 21

Power Presentations with PowerPoint®

Warm Up

Find the area of each figure.

1. 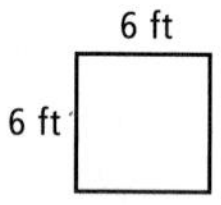

$A = 36 \text{ ft}^2$

2. 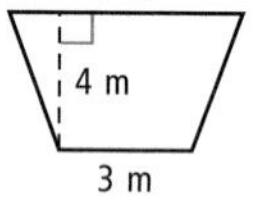

$A = 20 \text{ m}^2$

3. 3 points in the figure are chosen randomly. What is the probability that they are collinear?

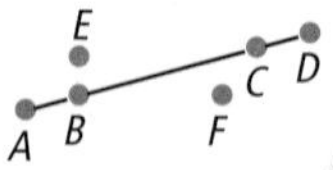

0.2

Also available on transparency

Math Humor

Q: 50% of the teacher's desk is covered with students' exams. What is the probability of spilling coffee on one?

A: Half-and-half.

9-6 Geometric Probability

Objectives
Calculate geometric probabilities.
Use geometric probability to predict results in real-world situations.

Vocabulary
geometric probability

Why learn this?
You can use geometric probability to estimate how long you may have to wait to cross a street. (See Example 2.)

Remember that in probability, the set of all possible outcomes of an experiment is called the *sample space.* Any set of outcomes is called an *event.*

If every outcome in the sample space is equally likely, the *theoretical probability* of an event is

$$P = \frac{\text{number of outcomes in the event}}{\text{number of outcomes in the sample space}}.$$

Geometric probability is used when an experiment has an infinite number of outcomes. In **geometric probability**, the probability of an event is based on a ratio of geometric measures such as length or area. The outcomes of an experiment may be points on a segment or in a plane figure. Three models for geometric probability are shown below.

Know it! Note

Geometric Probability

Model	Length	Angle Measure	Area
Example		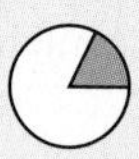	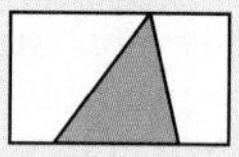
Sample space	All points on $\overline{AD}$	All points in the circle	All points in the rectangle
Event	All points on $\overline{BC}$	All points in the shaded region	All points in the triangle
Probability	$P = \frac{BC}{AD}$	$P = \frac{\text{measure of angle}}{360°}$	$P = \frac{\text{area of triangle}}{\text{area of rectangle}}$

EXAMPLE 1 Using Length to Find Geometric Probability

A point is chosen randomly on $\overline{AD}$. Find the probability of each event.

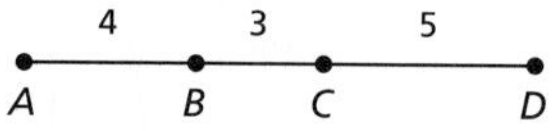

A **The point is on $\overline{AC}$.**

$P = \frac{AC}{AD} = \frac{7}{12}$

B **The point is not on $\overline{AB}$.**

First find the probability that the point is on $\overline{AB}$.

$P(\overline{AB}) = \frac{AB}{AD} = \frac{4}{12} = \frac{1}{3}$

Subtract from 1 to find the probability that the point is not on $\overline{AB}$.

$P(\text{not on } \overline{AB}) = 1 - \frac{1}{3} = \frac{2}{3}$

Remember!
If an event has a probability *p* of occurring, the probability of the event *not* occurring is $1 - p$.

State Resources

go.hrw.com
State Resources Online
KEYWORD: MG7 Resources

1 Introduce

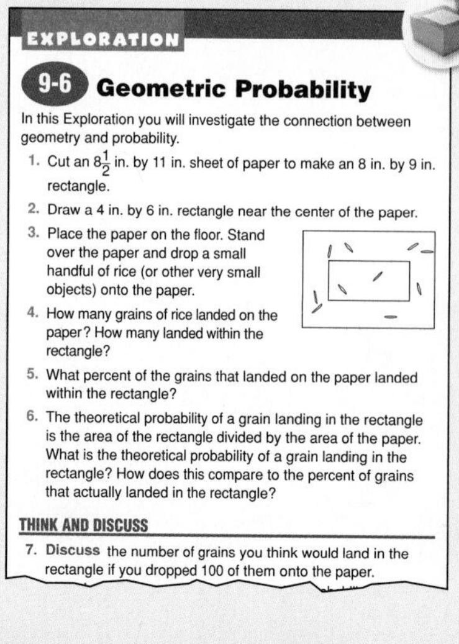
EXPLORATION

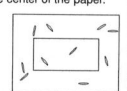

9-6 Geometric Probability

In this Exploration you will investigate the connection between geometry and probability.

1. Cut an $8\frac{1}{2}$ in. by 11 in. sheet of paper to make an 8 in. by 9 in. rectangle.
2. Draw a 4 in. by 6 in. rectangle near the center of the paper.
3. Place the paper on the floor. Stand over the paper and drop a small handful of rice (or other very small objects) onto the paper.
4. How many grains of rice landed on the paper? How many landed within the rectangle?
5. What percent of the grains that landed on the paper landed within the rectangle?
6. The theoretical probability of a grain landing in the rectangle is the area of the rectangle divided by the area of the paper. What is the theoretical probability of a grain landing in the rectangle? How does this compare to the percent of grains that actually landed in the rectangle?

THINK AND DISCUSS

7. Discuss the number of grains you think would land in the rectangle if you dropped 100 of them onto the paper.

Motivate

Have students draw this figure on a piece of paper and tape it to their desks. Have them toss a penny onto the paper. Tell them that finding how likely it is that the penny lands on the square requires using *geometric probability*.

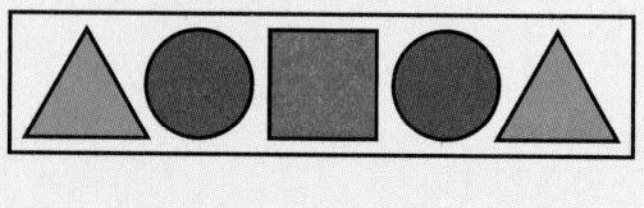

Explorations and answers are provided in *Alternate Openers: Explorations Transparencies.*

A point is chosen randomly on $\overline{AD}$. Find the probability of each event.

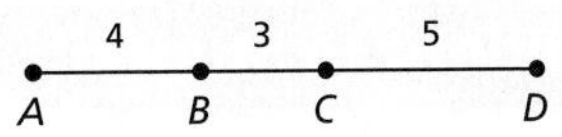

C The point is on $\overline{AB}$ or $\overline{CD}$.

$P(\overline{AB} \text{ or } \overline{CD}) = P(\overline{AB}) + P(\overline{CD}) = \frac{4}{12} + \frac{5}{12} = \frac{9}{12} = \frac{3}{4}$

1. Use the figure above to find the probability that the point is on $\overline{BD}$. $\frac{2}{3}$

EXAMPLE 2 ***Transportation Application***

A stoplight has the following cycle: green for 25 seconds, yellow for 5 seconds, and red for 30 seconds.

A What is the probability that the light will be yellow when you arrive?

To find the probability, draw a segment to represent the number of seconds that each color light is on.

Green Yellow Red
A 25 B C 5 30 D

$P = \frac{5}{60} = \frac{1}{12} \approx 0.08$ *The light is yellow for 5 out of every 60 seconds.*

B If you arrive at the light 50 times, predict about how many times you will have to stop and wait more than 10 seconds.

In the model, the event of stopping and waiting more than 10 seconds is represented by a segment that starts at C and ends 10 units from D. The probability of stopping and waiting more than 10 seconds is $P = \frac{20}{60} = \frac{1}{3}$.

If you arrive at the light 50 times, you will probably stop and wait more than 10 seconds about $\frac{1}{3}(50) \approx 17$ times.

2. Use the information above. What is the probability that the light will not be red when you arrive? $\frac{1}{2}$

EXAMPLE 3 **Using Angle Measures to Find Geometric Probability**

Use the spinner to find the probability of each event.

100° 80° 45° 75° 60°

A the pointer landing on red

$P = \frac{80}{360} = \frac{2}{9}$ *The angle measure in the red region is 80°.*

B the pointer landing on purple or blue

$P = \frac{75 + 60}{360} = \frac{135}{360} = \frac{3}{8}$ *The angle measure in the purple region is 75°. The angle measure in the blue region is 60°.*

C the pointer not landing on yellow

$P = \frac{360 - 100}{360}$ *The angle measure in the yellow region is 100°. Substract this angle measure from 360°.*

$= \frac{260}{360} = \frac{13}{18}$

Helpful Hint

In Example 3C, you can also find the probability of the pointer landing on yellow, and subtract from 1.

3. Use the spinner above to find the probability of the pointer landing on red or yellow. $\frac{1}{2}$

COMMON ERROR ALERT

Some students may think that the events in every experiment are equally likely. Point out that if a figure is divided into unequal parts, some events might be more likely than others.

Power Presentations with PowerPoint®

Additional Examples

Example 1

A point is chosen randomly on $\overline{PS}$. Find the probability of each event.

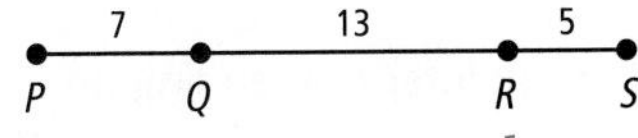

A. The point is on $\overline{RS}$. $\frac{1}{5}$

B. The point is not on $\overline{QR}$. $\frac{12}{25}$

C. The point is on $\overline{PQ}$ or $\overline{QR}$. $\frac{4}{5}$

Example 2

A pedestrian signal at a crosswalk has the following cycle: "WALK" for 45 seconds and "DON'T WALK" for 70 seconds.

A. What is the probability the signal will show "WALK" when you arrive? $\frac{9}{23}$, or 0.39

B. If you arrive at the signal 40 times, predict about how many times you will have to stop and wait more than 40 seconds. about 10 times

2 Teach

Guided Instruction

Review sample space and events. Remind students that the probability of an event is always a number from 0 to 1. Probability can be expressed as a fraction, a decimal, or a percent. Geometric probability is based on a ratio of geometric measures such as length, angle measures, or area. Discuss how to use each model to find the geometric probability of an event.

Reaching All Learners

Through Kinesthetic Experience

Have each student make a spinner like the one in **Example 3.** They will need a compass, protractor, ruler, paper, and colored pencils to color or label each area. They can cut out a pointer, attach it to a brad or paperclip, and then fasten it to the spinner. Have them each spin their spinner 20 times, and then combine the class results and compare them to the calculated probabilities.

INTERVENTION

Questioning Strategies

EXAMPLE 1

- Why do you add the probabilities when a point is selected on one segment *or* another segment?
- Can you think of more than one way to find the probability of selecting a point that is *not* on a segment?

EXAMPLE 2

- How is the probability of the signal showing "DON'T WALK" related to the number of times you will have to stop at the crosswalk?

Power Presentations with PowerPoint®

Additional Examples

Example 3

Use the spinner to find the probability of each event.

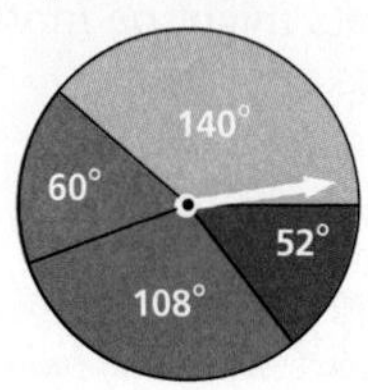

A. the pointer landing on yellow $\frac{7}{18}$

B. the pointer landing on blue or red $\frac{14}{45}$

C. the pointer not landing on green $\frac{7}{10}$

Example 4

Find the probability that a point chosen randomly inside the rectangle is in each shape. Round to the nearest hundredth.

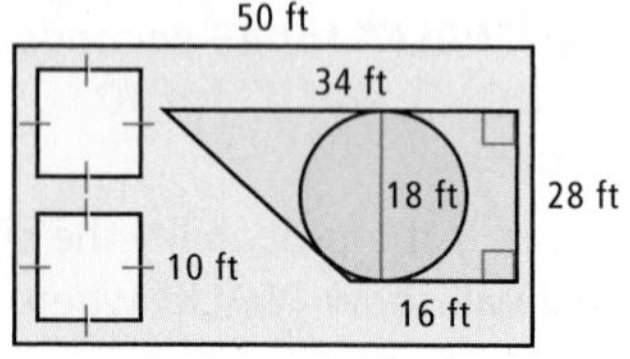

A. the circle 0.18

B. the trapezoid 0.32

C. one of the two squares 0.14

INTERVENTION
Questioning Strategies

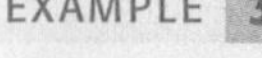

EXAMPLE 3

- Which color is most likely for the spinner to land on? Which is least likely? Explain.

EXAMPLE 4

- Which two shapes have the same probability? Explain.

Student to Student — Geometric Probability

Jeremy Denton
Memorial High School

I like to write a probability as a percent to see if my answer is reasonable.

The probability of the pointer landing on red is $\frac{80°}{360°} = \frac{2}{9} \approx 22\%$.

The angle measure is close to 90°, which is 25% of the circle, so the answer is reasonable.

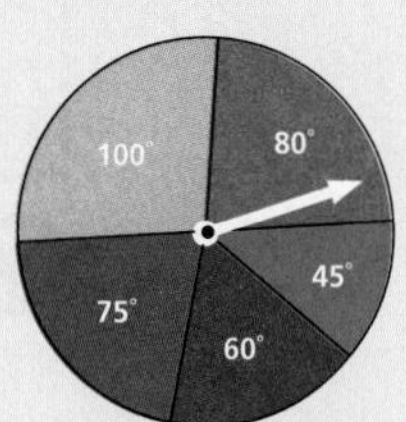

EXAMPLE 4 Using Area to Find Geometric Probability

Find the probability that a point chosen randomly inside the rectangle is in each given shape. Round to the nearest hundredth.

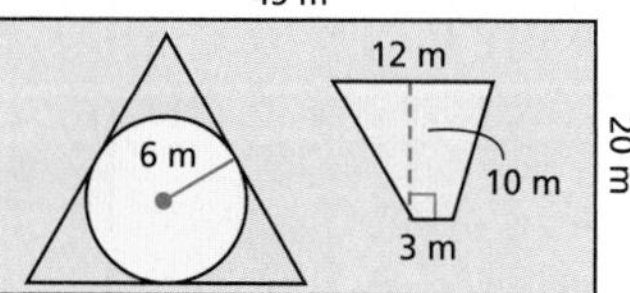

A the equilateral triangle

The area of the triangle is $A = \frac{1}{2}aP$

$= \frac{1}{2}(6)(36\sqrt{3}) \approx 187 \text{ m}^2.$

The area of the rectangle is $A = bh$

$= 45(20) = 900 \text{ m}^2.$

The probability is $P = \frac{187}{900} \approx 0.21.$

B the trapezoid

The area of the trapezoid is $A = \frac{1}{2}(b_1 + b_2)h$

$= \frac{1}{2}(3 + 12)(10) = 75 \text{ m}^2.$

The area of the rectangle is $A = bh$

$= 45(20) = 900 \text{ m}^2.$

The probability is $P = \frac{75}{900} \approx 0.08.$

C the circle

The area of the circle is $A = \pi r^2$

$= \pi(6^2) = 36\pi \approx 113.1 \text{ m}^2.$

The area of the rectangle is $A = bh$

$= 45(20) = 900 \text{ m}^2.$

The probability is $P = \frac{113.1}{900} \approx 0.13.$

4. Use the diagram above. Find the probability that a point chosen randomly inside the rectangle is not inside the triangle, circle, or trapezoid. Round to the nearest hundredth. 0.71

3 Close

Summarize

Discuss when geometric probability can be used and how it is different from theoretical probability. Draw a circle and use perpendicular diameters to divide it into four regions. Have students find the probability of a point being chosen in each region using angle measures and using areas, and compare the results.

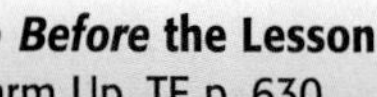

ONGOING ASSESSMENT and INTERVENTION

Diagnose **Before** the Lesson
9-6 Warm Up, TE p. 630

Monitor **During** the Lesson
Check It Out! Exercises, SE pp. 631–632
Questioning Strategies, TE pp. 631–632

Assess **After** the Lesson
9-6 Lesson Quiz, TE p. 636
Alternative Assessment, TE p. 636

THINK AND DISCUSS

1. Explain why the ratio used in theoretical probability cannot be used to find geometric probability.
2. A spinner is one-half red and one-third blue, and the rest is yellow. How would you find the probability of the pointer landing on yellow?

3. **GET ORGANIZED** Copy and complete the graphic organizer. In each box, give an example of the geometric probability model.

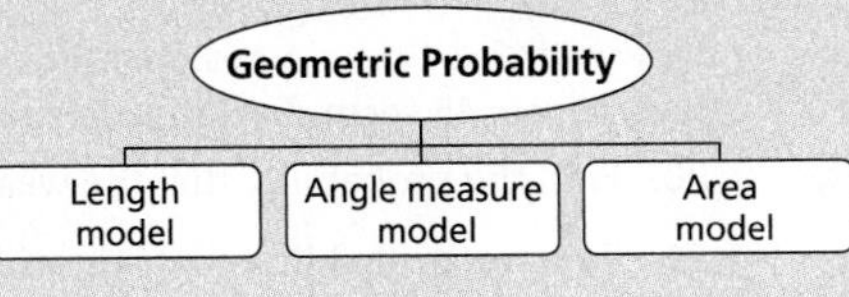

Answers to *Think and Discuss*

1. In a geometric model, there are infinitely many outcomes in each event.
2. Subtract $\frac{1}{2}$ and $\frac{1}{3}$ from 1 to find what part of the spinner is yellow.
3. See p. A8.

9-6 Exercises

go.hrw.com
Homework Help Online
KEYWORD: MG7 9-6
Parent Resources Online
KEYWORD: MG7 Parent

GUIDED PRACTICE

1. **Vocabulary** Give an example of a model used to find *geometric probability*. Possible answer: a spinner

SEE EXAMPLE 1 p. 630

A point is chosen randomly on $\overline{WZ}$. Find the probability of each event.

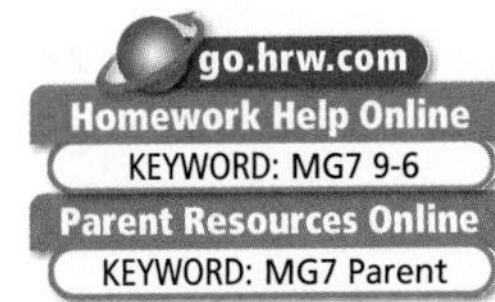

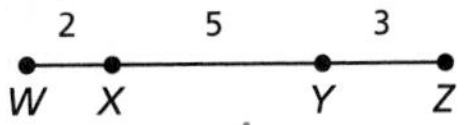

2. The point is on $\overline{XZ}$. $\frac{4}{5}$
3. The point is not on $\overline{XY}$. $\frac{1}{2}$
4. The point is on $\overline{WX}$ or $\overline{YZ}$. $\frac{1}{2}$
5. The point is on $\overline{WY}$. $\frac{7}{10}$

SEE EXAMPLE 2 p. 631

Transportation **A bus comes to a station once every 10 minutes and waits at the station for 1.5 minutes.**

6. Find the probability that the bus will be at the station when you arrive. 0.15
7. If you go to the station 20 times, predict about how many times you will have to wait less than 3 minutes. 9 times

SEE EXAMPLE 3 p. 631

Use the spinner to find the probability of each event.

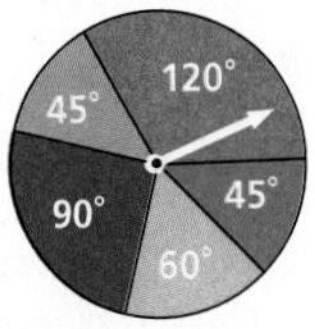

8. the pointer landing on green $\frac{1}{8}$
9. the pointer landing on orange or blue $\frac{3}{8}$
10. the pointer not landing on red $\frac{2}{3}$
11. the pointer landing on yellow or blue $\frac{5}{12}$

120° 45° 45° 90° 60°

SEE EXAMPLE 4 p. 632

Multi-Step **Find the probability that a point chosen randomly inside the rectangle is in each shape. Round to the nearest hundredth.**

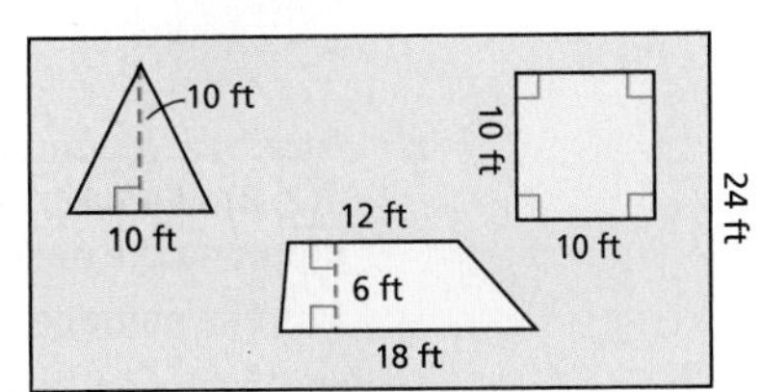

12. the triangle 0.04
13. the trapezoid 0.08
14. the square 0.09
15. the part of the rectangle that does not include the square, triangle, or trapezoid 0.79

9-6 Exercises

Assignment Guide

Assign *Guided Practice* exercises as necessary.

If you finished Examples 1–2
Basic 16–22
Average 16–22, 49
Advanced 16–22, 49

If you finished Examples 1–4
Basic 16–31, 33–37, 44–47, 52–57
Average 16–48, 52–57
Advanced 16–31, 33–57

Homework Quick Check
Quickly check key concepts.
Exercises: 16, 20, 24, 28, 30, 34

State Resources

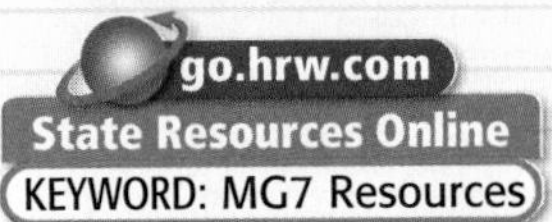

Teaching Tip **Kinesthetic** Have students work in pairs to model **Exercises 20–22.** Have one student use a stopwatch, and have the other student signal at a random time that they are turning the radio on. (Use shorter time intervals than those given in the problem.) Then have them compare their results to the calculated probabilities.

PRACTICE AND PROBLEM SOLVING

Independent Practice	
For Exercises	See Example
16–19	1
20–22	2
23–26	3
27–30	4

Extra Practice
Skills Practice p. S21
Application Practice p. S36

A point is chosen randomly on $\overline{HM}$. Find the probability of each event. Round to the nearest hundredth.

H —16.4— J —21.9— K —15.3— L —14.8— M

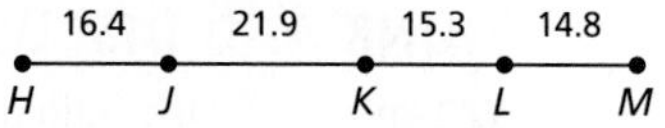

16. The point is on $\overline{JK}$. 0.32
17. The point is not on $\overline{LM}$. 0.78
18. The point is on $\overline{HJ}$ or $\overline{KL}$. 0.46
19. The point is not on $\overline{JK}$ or $\overline{LM}$. 0.46

Communications **A radio station gives a weather report every 15 minutes. Each report lasts 45 seconds. Suppose you turn on the radio at a random time.**

20. Find the probability that the weather report will be on when you turn on the radio. 0.05
21. Find the probability that you will have to wait more than 5 minutes to hear the weather report. 0.62
22. If you turn on the radio at 50 random times, predict about how many times you will have to wait less than 1 minute before the start of the next weather report. 3 times

Use the spinner to find the probability of each event.

23. the pointer landing on red $\frac{1}{2}$
24. the pointer landing on yellow or blue $\frac{1}{4}$
25. the pointer not landing on green $\frac{3}{4}$
26. the pointer landing on red or green $\frac{3}{4}$

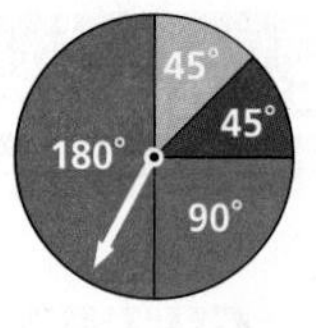

Multi-Step **Find the probability that a point chosen randomly inside the rectangle is in each shape. Round to the nearest hundredth, if necessary.**

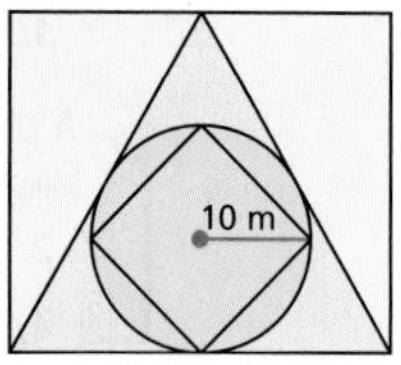

30 m
10 m

27. the equilateral triangle 0.5
28. the square 0.19
29. the part of the circle that does not include the square 0.11
30. the part of the rectangle that does not include the square, circle, or triangle 0.5

31. **ERROR ANALYSIS** In the spinner at right, the angle measure of the red region is 90°. The angle measure of the yellow region is 135°, and the angle measure of the blue region is 135°. Which value of the probability of the spinner landing on yellow is incorrect? Explain.

31. The value in A is incorrect because the sectors have different angle measures, so they are not equally likely outcomes.

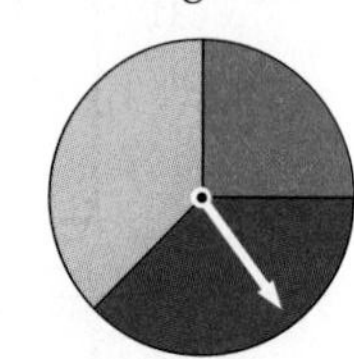

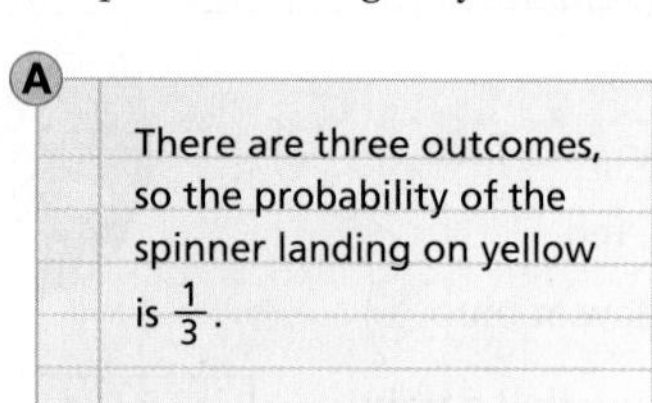

A
There are three outcomes, so the probability of the spinner landing on yellow is $\frac{1}{3}$.

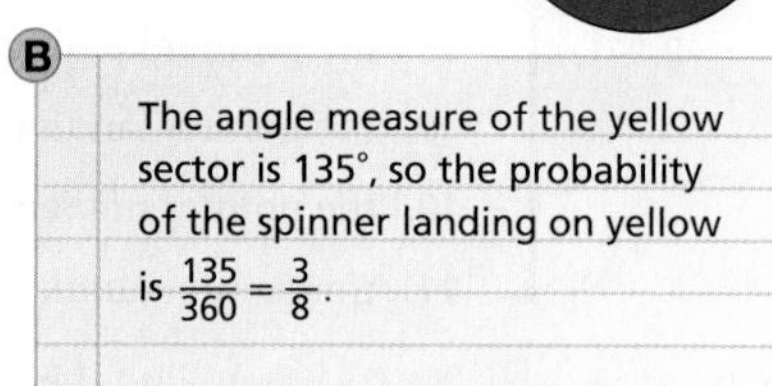

B
The angle measure of the yellow sector is 135°, so the probability of the spinner landing on yellow is $\frac{135}{360} = \frac{3}{8}$.

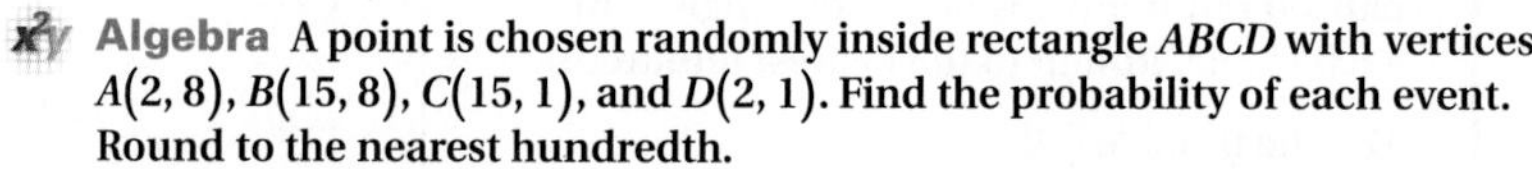

Algebra **A point is chosen randomly inside rectangle $ABCD$ with vertices $A(2, 8)$, $B(15, 8)$, $C(15, 1)$, and $D(2, 1)$. Find the probability of each event. Round to the nearest hundredth.**

32. The point lies in $\triangle KLM$ with vertices $K(4, 3)$, $L(5, 7)$, and $M(9, 5)$. 0.10
33. The point does not lie in $\odot P$ with center $P(2, 5)$ and radius 3. (*Hint:* draw the rectangle and circle.) 0.84

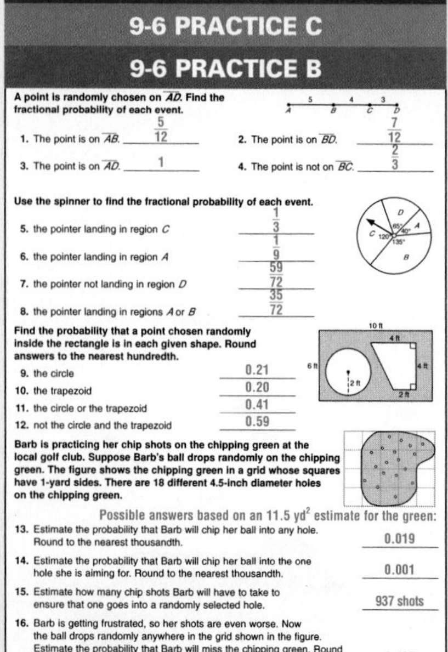

9-6 PRACTICE A
9-6 PRACTICE C
9-6 PRACTICE B

A point is randomly chosen on $\overline{AD}$. Find the fractional probability of each event.

A —5— B —4— C —3— D

1. The point is on $\overline{AB}$. $\frac{5}{12}$
2. The point is on $\overline{BD}$. $\frac{7}{12}$
3. The point is on $\overline{AD}$. 1
4. The point is not on $\overline{BC}$. $\frac{2}{3}$

Use the spinner to find the fractional probability of each event.

5. the pointer landing in region C $\frac{1}{3}$
6. the pointer landing in region A $\frac{1}{9}$
7. the pointer not landing in region D $\frac{59}{72}$
8. the pointer landing in regions A or B $\frac{35}{72}$

Find the probability that a point chosen randomly inside the rectangle is in each given shape. Round answers to the nearest hundredth.

9. the circle 0.21
10. the trapezoid 0.20
11. the circle or the trapezoid 0.41
12. not the circle and the trapezoid 0.59

Barb is practicing her chip shots on the chipping green at the local golf club. Suppose Barb's ball drops randomly on the chipping green. The figure shows the chipping green in a grid whose squares have 1-yard sides. There are 18 different 4.5-inch diameter holes on the chipping green.

Possible answers based on an 11.5 yd^2 estimate for the green:

13. Estimate the probability that Barb will chip her ball into any hole. Round to the nearest thousandth. 0.019
14. Estimate the probability that Barb will chip her ball into the one hole she is aiming for. Round to the nearest thousandth. 0.001
15. Estimate how many chip shots Barb will have to take to ensure that one goes into a randomly selected hole. 937 shots
16. Barb is getting frustrated, so her shots are even worse. Now the ball drops randomly anywhere in the grid shown in the figure. Estimate the probability that Barb will miss the chipping green. Round to the nearest thousandth. 0.425

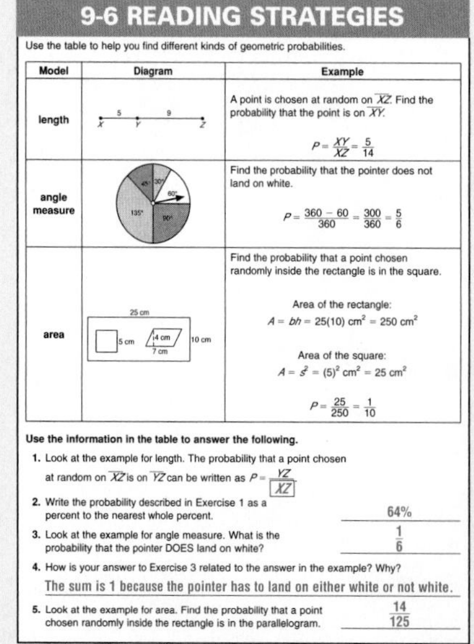

9-6 READING STRATEGIES

Use the table to help you find different kinds of geometric probabilities.

Model	Diagram	Example
length	X —5— Y —9— Z	A point is chosen at random on $\overline{XZ}$. Find the probability that the point is on $\overline{XY}$. $P = \frac{XY}{XZ} = \frac{5}{14}$
angle measure	(spinner: 45°, 30°, 60°, 90°, 135°)	Find the probability that the pointer does not land on white. $P = \frac{360 - 60}{360} = \frac{300}{360} = \frac{5}{6}$
area	(rectangle 25 cm by 10 cm; square 5 cm; parallelogram 4 cm, 7 cm)	Find the probability that a point chosen randomly inside the rectangle is in the square. Area of the rectangle: $A = bh = 25(10)\ cm^2 = 250\ cm^2$ Area of the square: $A = s^2 = (5)^2\ cm^2 = 25\ cm^2$ $P = \frac{25}{250} = \frac{1}{10}$

Use the information in the table to answer the following.

1. Look at the example for length. The probability that a point chosen at random on $\overline{XZ}$ is on $\overline{YZ}$ can be written as $P = \frac{YZ}{XZ}$.
2. Write the probability described in Exercise 1 as a percent to the nearest whole percent. 64%
3. Look at the example for angle measure. What is the probability that the pointer DOES land on white? $\frac{1}{6}$
4. How is your answer to Exercise 3 related to the answer in the example? Why? The sum is 1 because the pointer has to land on either white or not white.
5. Look at the example for area. Find the probability that a point chosen randomly inside the rectangle is in the parallelogram. $\frac{14}{125}$

9-6 RETEACH

The theoretical probability of an event occurring is $P = \frac{\text{number of outcomes in the event}}{\text{number of outcomes in the sample space}}$.

The **geometric probability** of an event occurring is found by determining a ratio of geometric measures such as length or area. Geometric probability is used when an experiment has an infinite number of outcomes.

Finding Geometric Probability	
Use Length	**Use Angle Measures**
A point is chosen randomly on $\overline{AD}$. Find the probability that the point is on $\overline{BD}$. A —2— B —4— C —6— D $P = \frac{\text{all points on } \overline{BD}}{\text{all points on } \overline{AD}} = \frac{BD}{AD} = \frac{10}{12} = \frac{5}{6}$	Use the spinner to find the probability of the pointer landing on the 160° space. (spinner: 80°, 160°, 120°) $P = \frac{\text{all points in 160° region}}{\text{all points in circle}} = \frac{160}{360} = \frac{4}{9}$

A point is chosen randomly on $\overline{EH}$. Find the probability of each event.

E —5— F —1— G —2— H

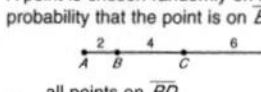

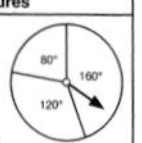

1. The point is on $\overline{FH}$. $\frac{3}{8}$
2. The point is not on $\overline{EF}$. $\frac{3}{8}$
3. The point is on $\overline{EF}$ or $\overline{GH}$. $\frac{7}{8}$
4. The point is on $\overline{EG}$. $\frac{3}{4}$

Use the spinner to find the probability of each event.

(spinner: 30°, 135°, 90°, 80°, 75°)

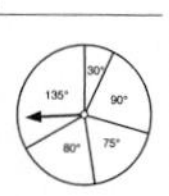

5. the pointer landing on 135° $\frac{3}{8}$
6. the pointer landing on 75° $\frac{5}{24}$
7. the pointer landing on 90° or 75° $\frac{11}{24}$
8. the pointer landing on 30° $\frac{1}{12}$

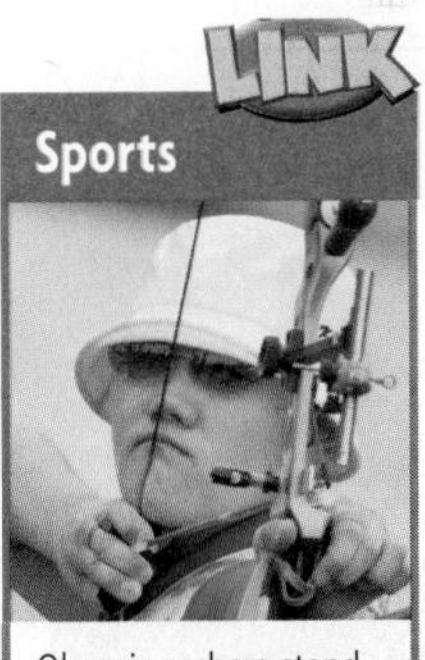

Sports

Olympic archers stand 70 m from their targets. From that distance, the target appears about the size of the head of a thumbtack held at arm's length.

Source: www.olympic.org

Algebra **LINK** A point is chosen at random in the coordinate plane such that $-5 \le x \le 5$ and $-5 \le y \le 5$. Find the probability of each event. Round to the nearest hundredth.

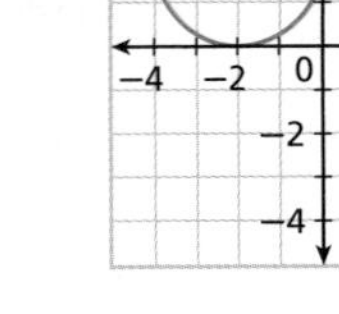

34. The point is inside the parallelogram. 0.06
35. The point is inside the circle. 0.13
36. The point is inside the triangle or the circle. 0.17
37. The point is not inside the triangle, the parallelogram, or the circle. 0.77
38. **Sports** The point value of each region of an Olympic archery target is shown in the diagram. The outer diameter of each ring is 12.2 cm greater than the inner diameter.
    a. What is the probability of hitting the center? 0.01
    b. What is the probability of hitting a blue or black ring? 0.48
    c. What is the probability of scoring higher than five points? 0.25
    d. **Write About It** In an actual event, why might the probabilities be different from those you calculated in parts **a**, **b**, and **c**?

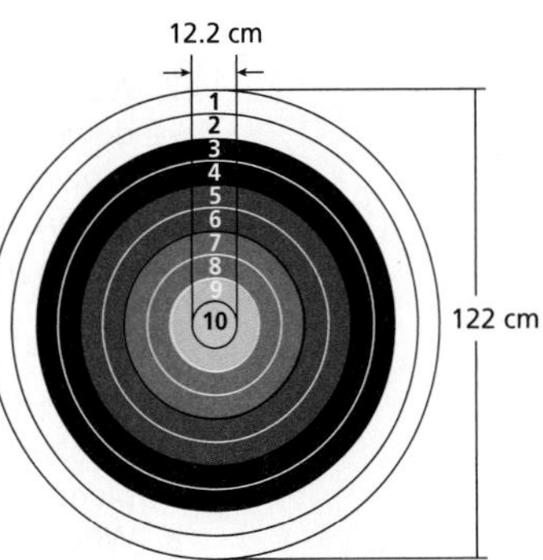

A point is chosen randomly in each figure. Describe an event with a probability of $\frac{1}{2}$.

39. 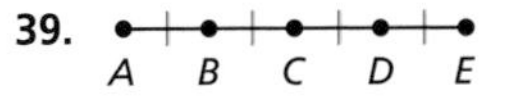

40. 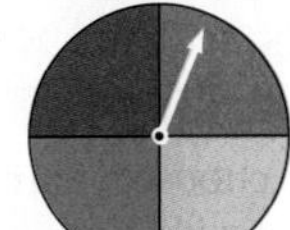

41. 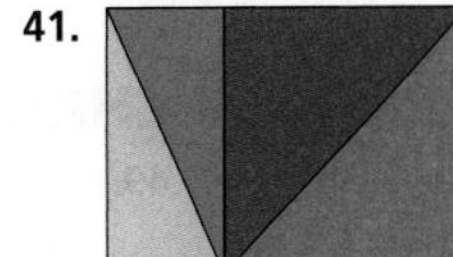

42. If a fly lands randomly on the tangram, what is the probability that it will land on each of the following pieces?
    a. the blue parallelogram $\frac{1}{8}$
    b. the medium purple triangle $\frac{1}{8}$
    c. the large yellow triangle $\frac{1}{4}$
    d. **Write About It** Do the probabilities change if you arrange the tangram pieces differently? Explain. no; because the areas are the same
43. **Critical Thinking** If a rectangle is divided into 8 congruent regions and 4 of them are shaded, what is the probability that you will randomly pick a point in the shaded area? Does it matter which four regions are shaded? Explain.

MULTI-STEP TEST PREP

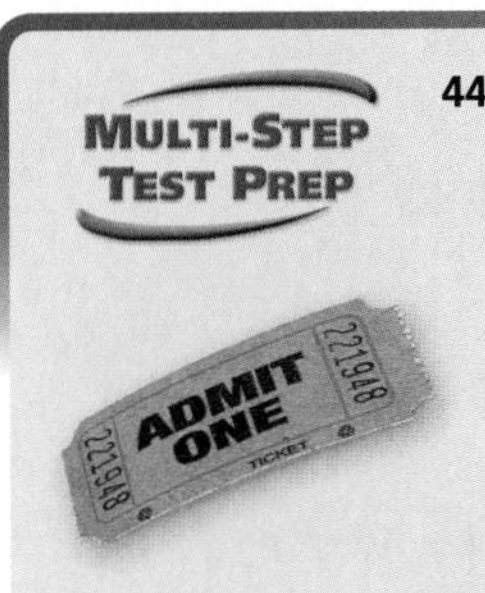

44. This problem will prepare you for the Multi-Step Test Prep on page 638.
    A carnival game board consists of balloons that are 3 inches in diameter and are attached to a rectangular board. A player who throws a dart at the board wins a prize if the dart pops a balloon.
    a. Find the probability of winning if there are 40 balloons on the board. 0.19
    b. How many balloons must be on the board for the probability of winning to be at least 0.25? 54 balloons

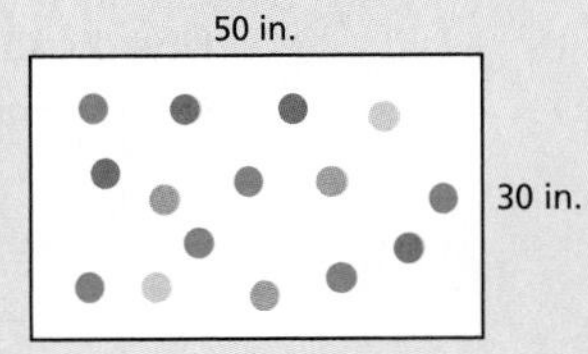

COMMON ERROR ALERT

In **Exercise 38,** some students may find the area of the entire circle instead of the area of only the given ring. Remind students to subtract the area of the inner circle to find the area of the ring.

Exercise 44 involves using area to find geometric probability. This exercise prepares students for the Multi-Step Test Prep on page 638.

Answers

38d. because an archer would be aiming for the center, not a random point

39–41. Possible answers given.

39. The point lies on $\overline{AC}$.

40. The point lies in the red region or in the yellow region.

41. The point lies in the blue triangle or the green triangle.

43. $\frac{1}{2}$; it does not matter which regions are shaded because they all have the same area.

9-6 PROBLEM SOLVING

Use the diagram of a spinner for Exercises 1 and 2.

1. Find the probability of the pointer landing on the 120° section. $\frac{1}{3}$
2. Find the probability of the pointer landing on the 100° section. $\frac{5}{18}$
3. Between 4:00 P.M. and 6:30 P.M., a radio station gives a traffic report every 20 minutes. This report lasts 15 seconds. Suppose you turn on the radio between 4:00 P.M. and 6:30 P.M. Find the probability that a traffic report will be on. 0.0117 or $\frac{7}{600}$
4. Find the probability that a point chosen randomly inside the rectangle is in the triangle. Round to the nearest hundredth. 0.09

Choose the best answer.

5. A point is chosen randomly on $\overline{JM}$. Find the probability that the point is on $\overline{JK}$ or $\overline{JL}$. Round to the nearest hundredth.
   A 0.41
   (B) 0.73
   C 0.81
   D 1.08
6. A train crosses at a railroad crossing 6 times a day—once every 4 hours. It takes an average of 5 minutes for the railroad gates to go down and then come up again. If you are approaching the railroad crossing, what is the probability that the gates are down?
   F $\frac{1}{360}$
   G $\frac{1}{120}$
   (H) $\frac{1}{48}$
   J $\frac{1}{30}$
7. On the dart board, the center circle has a diameter of 2 inches. What is the probability of hitting the shaded ring? Round to the nearest hundredth.
   A 0.01
   (B) 0.29
   C 0.30
   D 0.45
8. What is the probability that a coin randomly tossed into the rectangular fountain lands on one of the square "islands"? The "islands" are all the same size.
   F 0.03
   G 0.05
   (H) 0.15
   J 0.17

9-6 CHALLENGE

Suppose that two real numbers, x and y, are chosen at random so that $0 \le x \le 6$ and $0 \le y \le 6$. What is the probability that their sum is 8 or greater? Since there are infinitely many numbers involved, it many seem impossible to answer this question. However, you can solve the problem by graphing lines on a coordinate plane and calculating areas of figures that are formed by these lines.

1. a. Graph this system of inequalities on the coordinate plane at right. $\begin{cases} 0 \le x \le 6 \\ 0 \le y \le 6 \end{cases}$
   b. Find the area covered by the solution of the system. 36 square units
2. a. Graph the line with equation $x + y \ge 8$ on the coordinate plane.
   b. Find the area of the region where this graph overlaps the solution of the system in Exercise 1. 8 square units
3. a. What is the ratio of the area that you found in Exercise 2 to the area that you found in Exercise 1? $\frac{8}{36}$, or $\frac{2}{9}$
   b. What is the probability that two randomly chosen numbers x and y, with $0 \le x \le 6$ and $0 \le y \le 6$, have a sum that is 8 or greater? $\frac{2}{9}$

Two numbers, x and y, are chosen so that $0 \le x \le 6$ and $0 \le y \le 6$.

4. Find the probability that the sum of the numbers is within the given range.
   a. 10 or greater $\frac{1}{18}$
   b. 9 or less $\frac{7}{8}$
   c. 0 or greater 1, or 100%
   d. less than 0 0
5. Find the probability of each of the following.
   a. The difference $x - y$ is 3 or greater. $\frac{1}{8}$
   b. The difference $y - x$ is 3 or greater. $\frac{1}{8}$
   c. Either difference of the numbers is 3 or greater. $\frac{1}{4}$

In **Exercise 46,** students who answered **J** divided *AB* by *BC* to find the probability. Remind them to divide by the length of the entire segment.

Journal

Have students draw a segment divided into three or more parts and have them explain how to find the probability of randomly selecting a point on each part.

ALTERNATIVE ASSESSMENT

Have students make a rectangular target with three simple shapes on it. Ask them to find the probability of selecting a point in each shape. Have them toss a small handful of rice on the target, count the grains that land on each shape, and divide by the total. Ask them to compare their results to the calculated probabilities.

Power Presentations with PowerPoint®

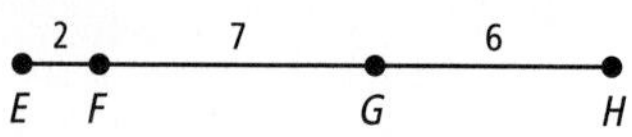

9-6 Lesson Quiz

A point is chosen randomly on $\overline{EH}$. Find the probability of each event.

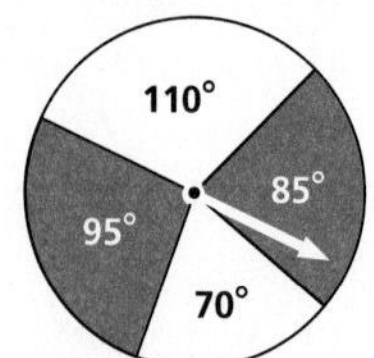

1. The point is on $\overline{EG}$. $\frac{3}{5}$
2. The point is not on $\overline{EF}$. $\frac{13}{15}$
3. An antivirus program has the following cycle: scan: 15 min, display results: 5 min, sleep: 40 min. Find the probability that the program will be scanning when you arrive at the computer. 0.25
4. Use the spinner to find the probability of the pointer landing on a shaded area. 0.5

5. Find the probability that a point chosen randomly inside the rectangle is in the triangle.

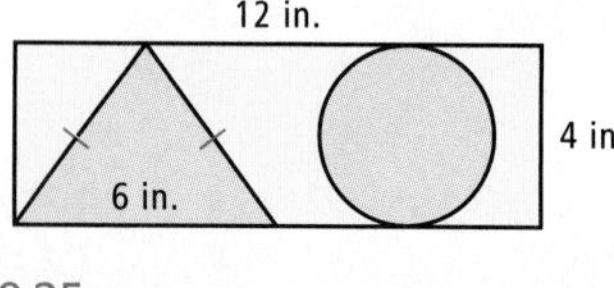

0.25

Also available on transparency

TEST PREP

45. What is the probability that a ball thrown randomly at the backboard of the basketball goal will hit the inside rectangle?

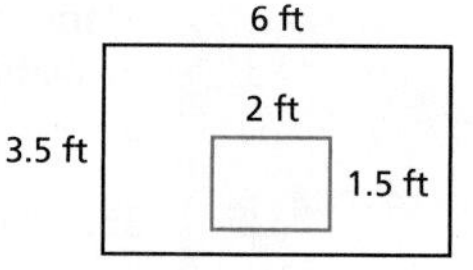

(A) 0.14 (B) 0.21 (C) 0.26 (D) 0.27

46. Point *B* is between *A* and *C*. If *AB* = 18 inches and *BC* = 24 inches, what is the probability that a point chosen at random is on $\overline{AB}$?

(F) 0.18 (G) 0.43 (H) 0.57 (J) 0.75

47. A skydiver jumps from an airplane and parachutes down to the 70-by-100-meter rectangular field shown. What is the probability that he will miss all three targets?

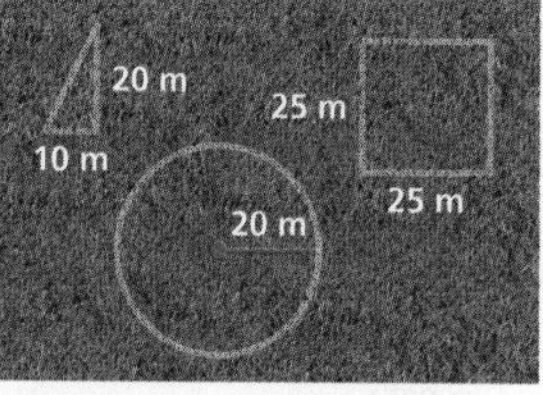

(A) 0.014 (B) 0.180 (C) 0.089 (D) 0.717

48. **Short Response** A spinner is divided into 12 congruent regions, colored red, blue, and green. Landing on red is twice as likely as landing on blue. Landing on blue and landing on green are equally likely.
   a. What is the probability of landing on green? Show your work or explain in words how you got your answer.
   b. How many regions of the spinner are colored green? Explain your reasoning. **3; the probability of landing on green is 0.25, so the number of green regions is 12(0.25) = 3**

CHALLENGE AND EXTEND

49. If you randomly choose a point on the grid, what is the probability that it will be in a red region? $\frac{4-\pi}{4} \approx 0.21$

50. You are designing a target that is a square inside an 18 ft by 24 ft rectangle. What size should the square be in order for the target to have a probability of $\frac{1}{3}$? to have a probability of $\frac{3}{4}$? **12 ft by 12 ft; 18 ft by 18 ft**

51. **Recreation** How would you design a spinner so that 1 point is earned for landing on yellow, 3 points for landing on blue and 6 points for landing on red? Explain.

SPIRAL REVIEW

Simplify each expression. *(Previous course)*

52. $(3x^2y)(4x^3y^2)$ $12x^5y^3$
53. $(2m^5)^2$ $4m^{10}$
54. $\frac{-8a^4b^6}{2ab^3}$ $-4a^3b^3$
55. **Given:** $A(0, 4)$, $B(4, 6)$, $C(4, 2)$, $D(8, 8)$, and $E(8, 0)$
Prove: $\triangle ABC \sim \triangle ADE$ *(Lesson 7-6)*

Find the shaded area. Round to the nearest tenth, if necessary. *(Lesson 9-3)*

56.

$A \approx 38.9 \text{ cm}^2$

57.

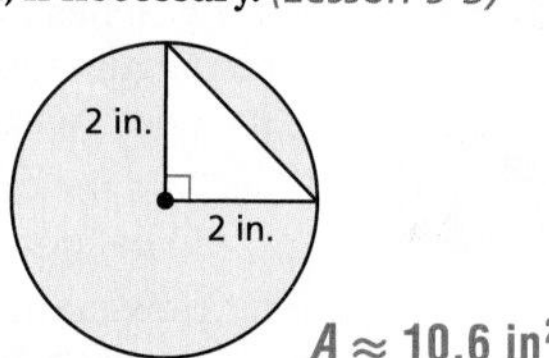

$A \approx 10.6 \text{ in}^2$

Answers

48a. 0.25; let *x* be the probability of landing on green. Blue and green are equally likely, so the probability of landing on blue is also *x*. Red is twice as likely as blue, so the probability of landing on red is 2*x*. The probabilities must add to 1, so $x + x + 2x = 1$. Solve to get $x = 0.25$.

51. Possible answer: The probabilities must add to 1, so $P(\text{yellow}) + P(\text{blue}) + P(\text{red}) = 1$. I would make the regions different sizes, and I would want each region to be worth more points the smaller it is. The point value for red is 6 times the point value for yellow, so I would make $6 \cdot P(\text{red}) = P(\text{yellow})$. The point value for blue is 3 times the point value for yellow, so I would make $3 \cdot P(\text{blue}) = P(\text{yellow})$. Then $P(\text{yellow}) + \frac{1}{3}P(\text{yellow}) + \frac{1}{6}P(\text{yellow}) = 1$. This means $P(\text{yellow}) = \frac{2}{3}$, $P(\text{blue}) = \frac{2}{9}$, and $P(\text{red}) = \frac{1}{9}$. The angle measure for the yellow region would be 240°, for the blue region would be 80°, and for the red region would be 40°.

55. By the Distance Formula, $AB = 2\sqrt{5}$, $AC = 2\sqrt{5}$, $BC = 4$, $AD = 4\sqrt{5}$, $AE = 4\sqrt{5}$, and $DE = 8$. $\frac{AB}{AD} = \frac{AC}{AE} = \frac{BC}{DE} = \frac{1}{2}$, so $\triangle ABC \sim \triangle ADE$ by SSS.

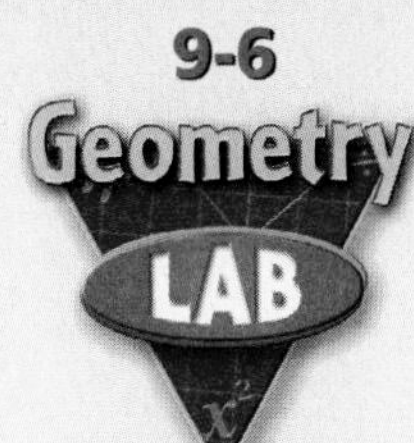

Use Geometric Probability to Estimate π

In this lab, you will use geometric probability to estimate π. The squares in the grid below are the same width as the diameter of a penny: 0.75 in., or 19.05 mm.

Use with Lesson 9-6

Activity

1. Toss a penny onto the grid 20 times. Let x represent the number of times the penny lands touching or covering an intersection of two grid lines.

Note: Grid is reduced in TE.

2. Estimate π using the formula $\pi \approx 4 \cdot \frac{x}{20}$.

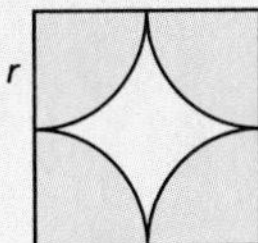

Try This

1. How close is your result to π? Average the results of the entire class to get a more accurate estimate. **Check students' work.**
2. In order for a penny to touch or cover an intersection, the center of the penny can land anywhere in the shaded area.
   a. Find the area of the shaded region. (*Hint:* Each corner part is one fourth of the circle. Put the four corner parts together to form a circle with radius r.) πr^2
   b. Find the area of the square. $4r^2$
   c. Write the expressions as a ratio and simplify to determine the probability of the center of the penny landing in the shaded area. $\frac{\pi r^2}{4r^2} = \frac{\pi}{4}$
3. Explain why the formula in the activity can be used to estimate π.
   The probability is $\frac{\pi}{4}$, so 4 times the probability is π.

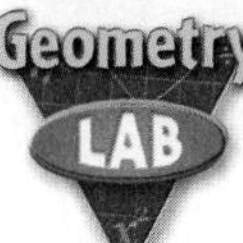

Organizer

Use with Lesson 9-6

Pacing:
Traditional $\frac{1}{2}$ day
Block $\frac{1}{4}$ day

Objective: Use geometric probability to estimate π.

Materials: penny

Online Edition

Countdown Week 21

Resources

Geometry Lab Activities
9-6 Lab Recording Sheet

Teach

Discuss

Ask students to identify the sample space of the experiment.

Alternative Approach

Photocopy the grid from the student text (do not enlarge or reduce) or use geometry software to create a grid with squares that are exactly 0.75 in. wide.

Close

Key Concept

You can use geometric probability to estimate π.

Assessment

Journal Have students explain why the experiment gives an estimate of π.

State Resources

go.hrw.com
State Resources Online
KEYWORD: MG7 Resources

Organizer

Objective: Assess students' ability to apply concepts and skills in Lessons 9-4 through 9-6 in a real-world format.

Online Edition

Resources

Geometry Assessments
www.mathtekstoolkit.org

Problem	Text Reference
1	Lesson 9-6
2	Lesson 9-5
3	Lesson 9-4
4	Lesson 9-6

State Resources

go.hrw.com
State Resources Online
KEYWORD: MG7 Resources

CHAPTER 9

MULTI-STEP TEST PREP

SECTION 9B

Applying Geometric Formulas

Step Right Up! A booster club organizes a carnival to raise money for sports uniforms. The carnival features several games that give visitors chances to win prizes.

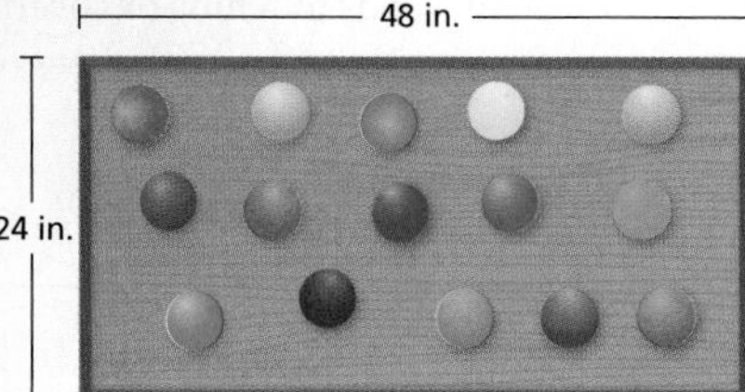

1. The balloon game consists of 15 balloons attached to a vertical rectangular board with the dimensions shown. Each balloon has a diameter of 4 in. Each player throws a dart at the board and wins a prize if the dart pops a balloon. Assuming that all darts hit the board at random, what is the probability of winning a prize? ≈ 0.16

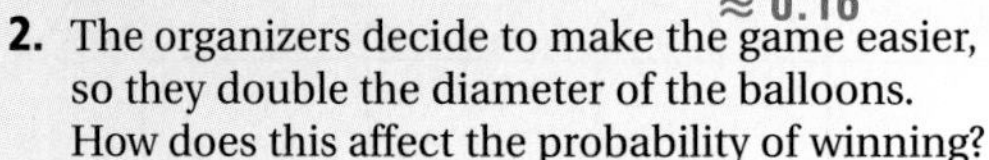

2. The organizers decide to make the game easier, so they double the diameter of the balloons. How does this affect the probability of winning? *2. The probability of winning is 4 times as great.*

3. The bean toss consists of a horizontal rectangular board that is divided into a grid. The board has coordinates $(0, 0)$, $(100, 0)$, $(100, 60)$, and $(0, 60)$. A quadrilateral on the board has coordinates $A(60,0)$, $B(100, 30)$, $C(40, 60)$, and $D(0, 40)$. Each player tosses a bean onto the board and wins a prize if the bean lands inside quadrilateral *ABCD*. Find the probability of winning a prize. ≈ 0.48

4. Of the three games described in Problems 1, 2, and 3, which one gives players the best chance of winning a prize? *4. the balloon game in Problem 2*

INTERVENTION

Scaffolding Questions

1. How can you find the area of the board? Multiply 24 in. by 48 in. How can you find the area of each balloon? Use the formula $A = \pi r^2$ with $r = 2$.
2. What happens to the area of a circle when the diameter doubles? The area is multiplied by 4. How will doubling the diameters of the balloons affect the probability in this problem? The probability is multiplied by 4.
3. Is *ABCD* a special quadrilateral? no What process can you use to find the area of *ABCD*? Find the area of the board and then subtract the areas of the four triangular regions in the exterior of *ABCD*.
4. What do you need to do in order to answer this question? Find the game in Problems **1**, **2**, and **3** with the greatest probability.

Extension

Suppose you want players to have a 0.5 probability of winning the balloon game. What should be the diameter of each balloon? about 7 in.

Quiz for Lessons 9-4 Through 9-6

9-4 Perimeter and Area in the Coordinate Plane

Draw and classify the polygon with the given vertices. Find the perimeter and area of the polygon.

1. $A(-2, 2), B(2, 4), C(2, -4), D(-2, -2)$ trapezoid; $P = (12 + 4\sqrt{5})$ units; $A = 24$ units^2
2. $E(-1, 5), F(3, 5), G(3, -3), H(-1, -3)$ rectangle; $P = 24$ units; $A = 32$ units^2

Find the area of each polygon with the given vertices.

3. $J(-3, 3), K(2, 2), L(-1, -3), M(-4, -1)$ $A = 21$ units^2
4. $N(-3, 1), P(3, 3), Q(5, 1), R(2, -4)$ $A = 28$ units^2

9-5 Effects of Changing Dimensions Proportionally

Describe the effect of each change on the perimeter and area of the given figure.

5. The side length of the square is tripled.
The perimeter is tripled.
The area is multiplied by 9.

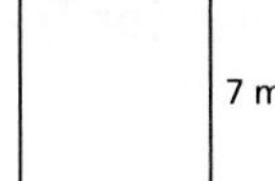

6. The diagonals of a rhombus in which $d_1 = 3$ ft and $d_2 = 9$ ft are both multiplied by $\frac{1}{3}$.
7. The base and height of the rectangle are both doubled.
The perimeter is doubled.
The area is multiplied by 4.

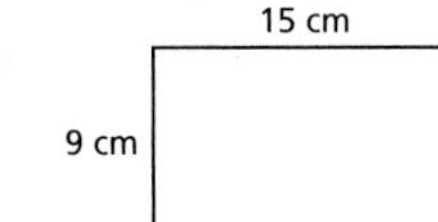

6. The perimeter is multiplied by $\frac{1}{3}$. The area is multiplied by $\frac{1}{9}$.

8. The base and height of a right triangle with base 15 in. and height 8 in. are multiplied by $\frac{1}{3}$. The perimeter is multiplied by $\frac{1}{3}$. The area is multiplied by $\frac{1}{9}$.
9. A square has vertices $(-1, 2)$, $(3, 2)$, $(3, -2)$, and $(-1, -2)$. If you quadruple the area, what happens to the side length? The side length is doubled.
10. A restaurant sells pancakes in two sizes, silver dollar and regular. The silver-dollar pancakes have a 4-inch diameter and require $\frac{1}{8}$ cup of batter per pancake. The diameter of a regular pancake is 2.5 times the diameter of a silver-dollar pancake. About how much batter is required to make a regular pancake? ≈ 0.78 cup

9-6 Geometric Probability

Use the spinner to find the probability of each event.

11. the pointer landing on red $\frac{1}{3}$
12. the pointer landing on red or yellow $\frac{11}{18}$
13. the pointer not landing on green $\frac{53}{72}$
14. the pointer landing on yellow or blue $\frac{29}{72}$
15. A radio station plays 12 commercials per hour. Each commercial is 1 minute long. If you turn on the radio at a random time, find the probability that a commercial will be playing. 0.2

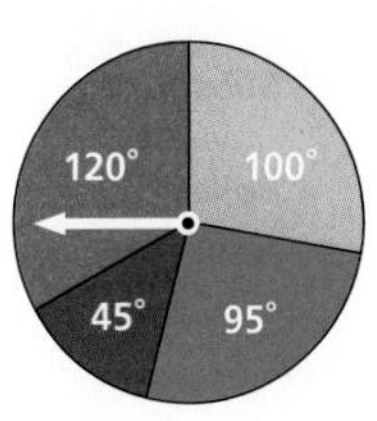

READY TO GO ON?

Organizer

Objective: Assess students' mastery of concepts and skills in Lessons 9-4 through 9-6.

Resources

 ***Assessment Resources***
Section 9B Quiz

Teacher One Stop™
Test & Practice Generator

INTERVENTION

Resources

 ***Ready to Go On? Intervention and Enrichment*** **Worksheets**

 ***Ready to Go On?*** **CD-ROM**

 ***Ready to Go On?*** **Online**

my.hrw.com

Answers

1–2. For graphs, see p. A26.

READY TO GO ON?
Diagnose and Prescribe

NO INTERVENE

Ready to Go On? Intervention	*Ready to Go On? Intervention,* Section 9B Worksheets	CD-ROM	Online
Lesson 9-4	9-4 Intervention	Activity 9-4	Diagnose and Prescribe Online
Lesson 9-5	9-5 Intervention	Activity 9-5	
Lesson 9-6	9-6 Intervention	Activity 9-6	

Organizer

Objective: Help students organize and review key concepts and skills presented in Chapter 9.

Online Edition
Multilingual Glossary

Countdown Week 21

Resources

Teacher One Stop™
PuzzleView
Test & Practice Generator

***Multilingual Glossary* Online**
go.hrw.com
KEYWORD: MG7 Glossary

Lesson Tutorial Videos
CD-ROM

Answers

1. apothem
2. center of a circle
3. geometric probability
4. $A = 81$ in^2
5. $P = 22$ cm
6. $h = 3x^2$ in.
7. $h = 8$ ft
8. $A = 252$ yd^2
9. $d_2 = 42xy^4$ in.
10. $A = 288$ m^2

Study Guide: Review

For a complete list of the postulates and theorems in this chapter, see p. PS12.

Vocabulary

Complete the sentences below with vocabulary words from the list above.

1. A(n) __?__ is the length of a segment perpendicular to a side of a regular polygon.
2. The point that is equidistant from every point on a circle is the __?__ .
3. __?__ is based on a ratio of geometric measures.

9-1 Developing Formulas for Triangles and Quadrilaterals *(pp. 589–597)*

EXAMPLES

Find each measurement.

- the perimeter of a square in which $A = 36$ in^2

$A = s^2 = 36$ in^2 *Use the Area Formula to find the side length.*
$S = \sqrt{36} = 6$ in.
$P = 4s = 4 \cdot 6 = 24$ in.

- the area of the triangle

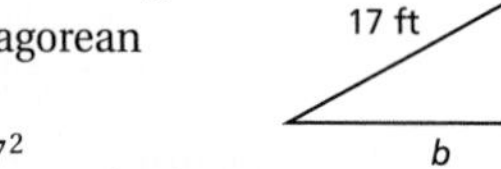

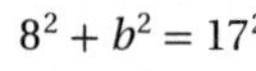

By the Pythagorean Theorem,
$8^2 + b^2 = 17^2$
$64 + b^2 = 289$
$b^2 = 225$, so $b = 15$ ft.
$A = \frac{1}{2}bh = \frac{1}{2}(15)(8) = 60$ ft^2

- the diagonal d_2 of a rhombus in which $A = 6x^3y^3$ m and $d_1 = 4x^2y$ m

$A = \frac{1}{2}d_1d_2$
$6x^3y^3 = \frac{1}{2}(4x^2y)d_2$ *Substitute the given values.*
$d_2 = 3xy^2$ *Solve for d_2.*

EXERCISES

Find each measurement.

4. the area of a square in which $P = 36$ in.
5. the perimeter of a rectangle in which $b = 4$ cm and $A = 28$ cm^2
6. the height of a triangle in which $A = 6x^3y$ in^2 and $b = 4xy$ in.
7. the height of the trapezoid, in which $A = 48xy$ ft^2

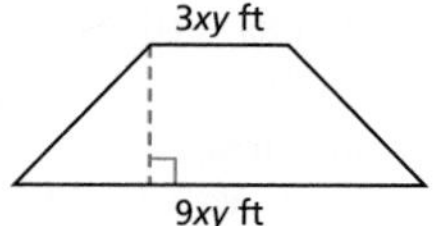

8. the area of a rhombus in which $d_1 = 21$ yd and $d_2 = 24$ yd
9. the diagonal d_2 of the rhombus, in which $A = 630x^3y^7$ in^2

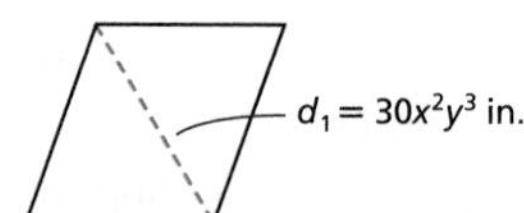

10. the area of a kite in which $d_1 = 32$ m and $d_2 = 18$ m

9-2 Developing Formulas for Circles and Regular Polygons *(pp. 600–605)*

EXAMPLES

Find each measurement.

- the circumference and area of $\odot B$ in terms of π

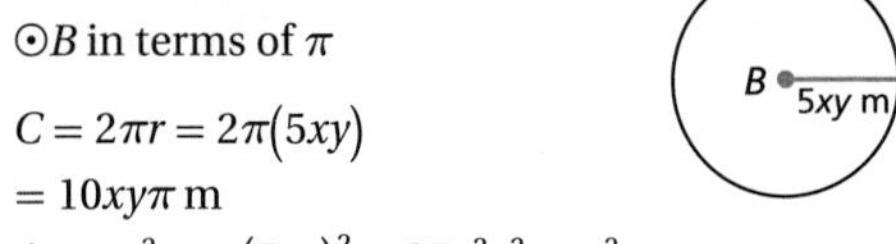

$C = 2\pi r = 2\pi(5xy)$
$= 10xy\pi$ m
$A = \pi r^2 = \pi(5xy)^2 = 25x^2y^2\pi$ m^2

- the area, to the nearest tenth, of a regular hexagon with apothem 9 yd

By the 30°-60°-90° Triangle Theorem, $x = \frac{9\sqrt{3}}{3} = 3\sqrt{3}$.
So $s = 2x = 6\sqrt{3}$, and
$P = 6(6\sqrt{3}) = 36\sqrt{3}$.
$A = \frac{1}{2}aP = \frac{1}{2}(9)(36\sqrt{3}) = 162\sqrt{3} \approx 280.6$ yd^2

EXERCISES

Find each measurement. Round to the nearest tenth, if necessary.

11. the circumference of $\odot G$

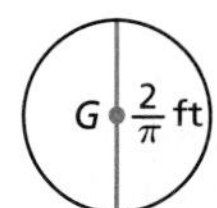

12. the area of $\odot J$ in which $C = 14\pi$ yd
13. the diameter of $\odot K$ in which $A = 64x^2\pi$ m^2
14. the area of a regular pentagon with side length 10 ft
15. the area of an equilateral triangle with side length 4 in.
16. the area of a regular octagon with side length 8 cm
17. the area of the square

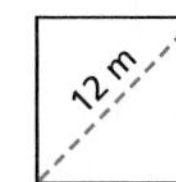

9-3 Composite Figures *(pp. 606–612)*

EXAMPLE

- **Find the shaded area. Round to the nearest tenth, if necessary.**

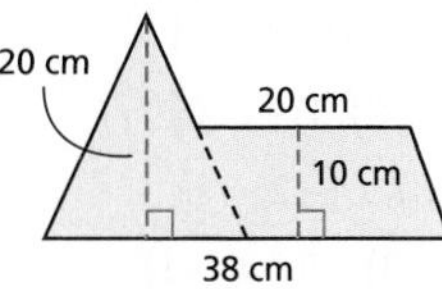

The area of the triangle is
$A = \frac{1}{2}(18)(20) = 180$ cm^2.
The area of the parallelogram is
$A = bh = 20(10) = 200$ cm^2.

The area of the figure is the sum of the two areas. $180 + 200 = 380$ cm^2

EXERCISES

Find the shaded area. Round to the nearest tenth, if necessary.

18. 19.

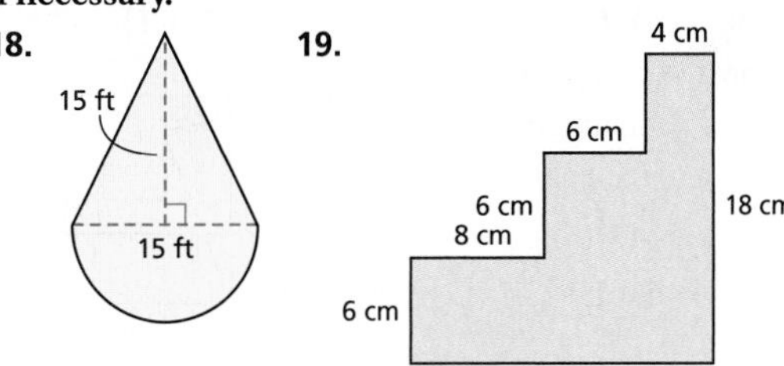

20.

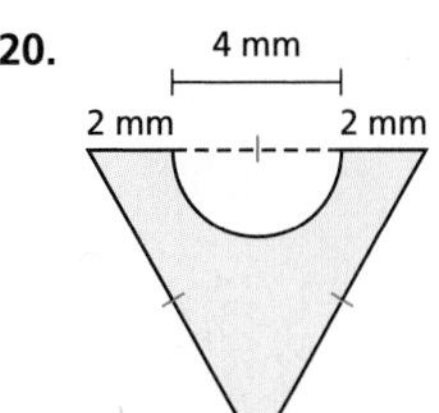

Answers

11. $C = 2$ ft
12. $A \approx 153.9$ yd^2
13. $d = 16x$ m
14. $A \approx 172.0$ ft^2
15. $A \approx 6.9$ in^2
16. $A \approx 309.0$ cm^2
17. $A = 72$ m^2
18. $A \approx 200.9$ ft^2
19. $A = 192$ cm^2
20. $A \approx 21.4$ mm^2

Answers

21. $A \approx 49.5$ units^2

22. $A \approx 44$ units^2

23. 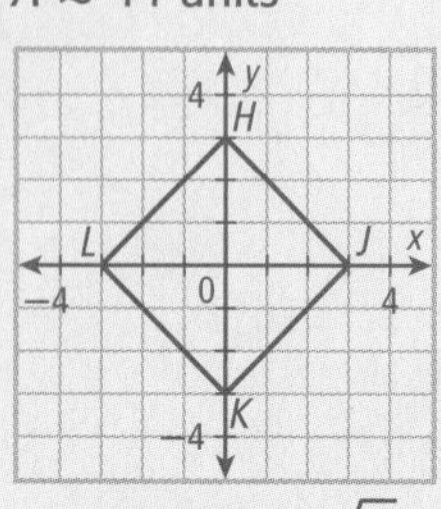

square; $P = 12\sqrt{2}$ units; $A = 18$ units^2

24. 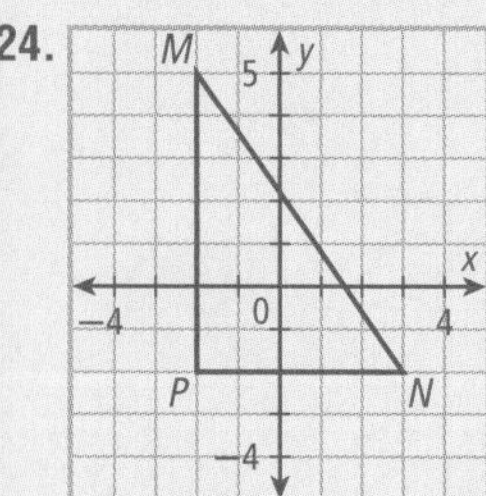

right triangle; $P = \left(12 + \sqrt{74}\right)$ units; $A = 17.5$ units^2

25. 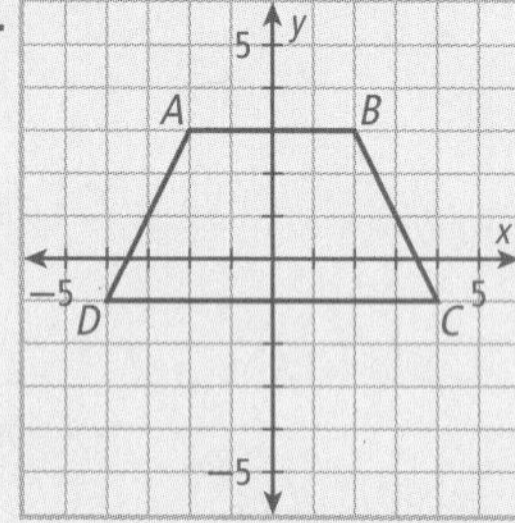

isosceles trapezoid; $P = \left(12 + 4\sqrt{5}\right)$ units; $A = 24$ units^2

26. 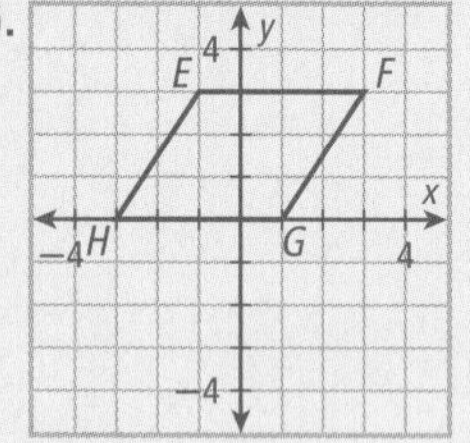

parallelogram; $P = \left(8 + 2\sqrt{13}\right)$ units; $A = 12$ units^2

27. $A = 30.5$ units^2

28. $A = 17.5$ units^2

29. $A = 12$ units^2

30. $A = 16$ units^2

9-4 Perimeter and Area in the Coordinate Plane *(pp. 616–621)*

EXAMPLES

■ **Estimate the area of the irregular shape.**

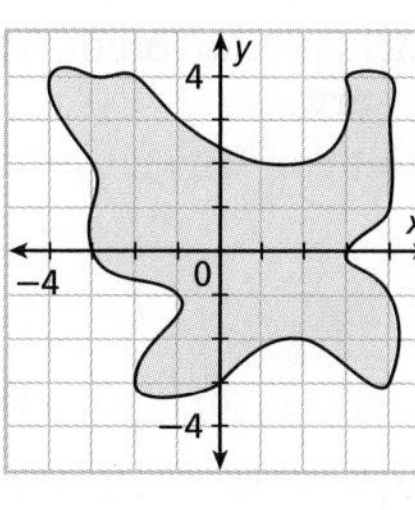

The shape has 28 approximately whole squares and 17 approximately half squares. The total area is approximately $28 + \frac{1}{2}(17) = 36.5$ units^2.

■ **Draw and classify the polygons with vertices $R(2, 4)$, $S(3, 1)$, $T(2, -2)$, and $U(1, 1)$. Find the perimeter and area of the polygon.**

RSTU appears to be a rhombus.

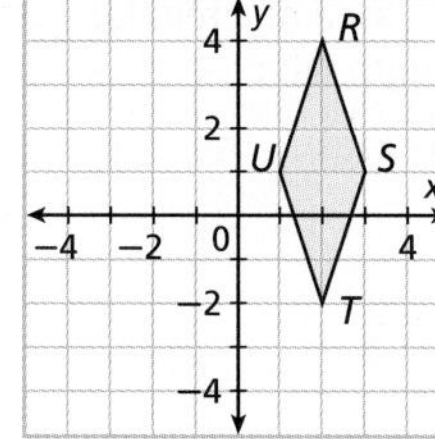

Verify this by showing that the four sides are congruent. By the Distance Formula, $UR = RS = ST = TU = \sqrt{10}$ units.

The perimeter is $4\sqrt{10}$ units.

The area is $A = \frac{1}{2}d_1d_2 = \frac{1}{2}US \cdot RT = \frac{1}{2}(2 \cdot 6) = 6$ units^2.

■ **Find the area of the polygon with vertices $A(-3, 4)$, $B(2, 3)$, $C(0, -2)$, and $D(-5, -1)$.**

area of rectangle:

$7(6) = 42$ units^2

area of triangles:

a: $A = \frac{1}{2}(2)(5)$
$= 5$ units^2

b: $A = \frac{1}{2}(5)(1)$
$= 2.5$ units^2

c: $A = \frac{1}{2}(2)(5) = 5$ units^2

d: $A = \frac{1}{2}(5)(1) = 2.5$ units^2

area of polygon: $A = 42 - 5 - 2.5 - 5 - 2.5$
$= 27$ units^2

EXERCISES

Estimate the area of each irregular shape.

21. 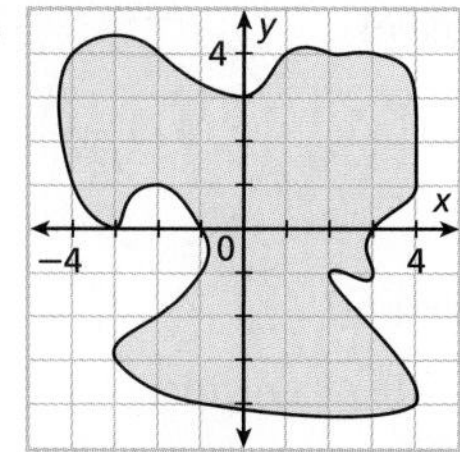

22. 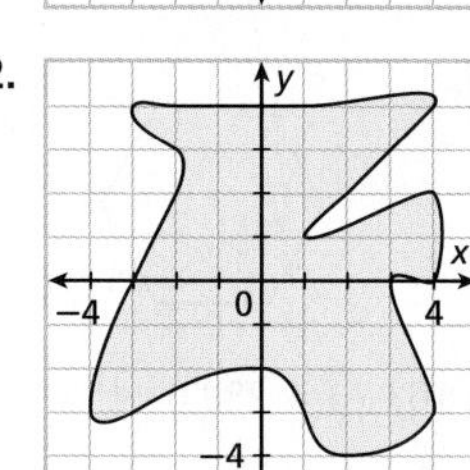

Draw and classify the polygon with the given vertices. Find the perimeter and area of the polygon.

23. $H(0, 3)$, $J(3, 0)$, $K(0, -3)$, $L(-3, 0)$

24. $M(-2, 5)$, $N(3, -2)$, $P(-2, -2)$

25. $A(-2, 3)$, $B(2, 3)$, $C(4, -1)$, $D(-4, -1)$

26. $E(-1, 3)$, $F(3, 3)$, $G(1, 0)$, $H(-3, 0)$

Find the area of the polygon with the given vertices.

27. $Q(1, 4)$, $R(4, 3)$, $S(2, -4)$, $T(-3, -2)$

28. $V(-2, 2)$, $W(4, 0)$, $X(2, -3)$, $Y(-3, 0)$

29. $A(1, 4)$, $B(2, 3)$, $C(0, -3)$, $D(-2, -1)$

30. $E(-1, 2)$, $F(2, 0)$, $G(1, -3)$, $H(-4, -1)$

9-5 Effects of Changing Dimensions Proportionally (pp. 622–627)

EXAMPLE

- **The base and height of a rectangle with base 10 cm and height 15 cm are both doubled. Describe the effect on the area and perimeter of the figure.**

  original: $P = 2b + 2h = 2(10) + 2(15) = 50$ cm

  $A = bh = 10(15) = 150$ cm^2

  doubled: $P = 2b + 2h = 2(20) + 2(30)$
  $= 100$ cm

  $A = bh = 20(30) = 600$ cm^2

  The perimeter increases by a factor of 2. The area increases by a factor of 4.

EXERCISES

Describe the effect of each change on the perimeter or circumference and area of the given figure.

31. The base and height of the triangle with vertices $X(-1, 3)$, $Y(-3, -2)$, and $Z(2, -2)$ are tripled.
32. The side length of the square with vertices $P(-1, 1)$, $Q(3, 1)$, $R(3, -3)$, and $S(-1, -3)$ is doubled.
33. The radius of $\odot A$ with radius 11 m is multiplied by $\frac{1}{2}$.
34. The base and height of a triangle with base 8 ft and height 20 ft are both multiplied by 4.

9-6 Geometric Probability (pp. 630–636)

EXAMPLES

A point is chosen randomly on $\overline{WZ}$. Find the probability of each event.

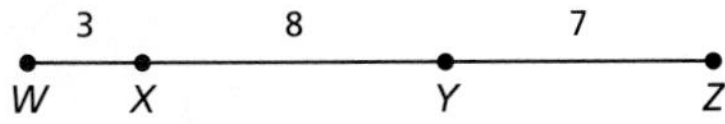

- The point is on $\overline{XZ}$.

  $P(\overline{XZ}) = \frac{XZ}{WZ} = \frac{15}{18} = \frac{5}{6}$

- The point is on $\overline{WX}$ or $\overline{YZ}$.

  $P(\overline{WX} \text{ or } \overline{YZ}) = P(\overline{WX}) + P(\overline{YZ}) = \frac{3}{18} + \frac{7}{18}$

  $= \frac{10}{18} = \frac{5}{9}$

- **Find the probability that a point chosen randomly inside the rectangle is inside the equilateral triangle.**

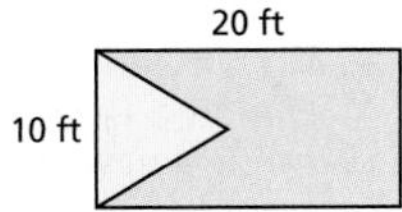

  area of rectangle

  $A = bh = 20(10) = 200$ ft^2

  area of triangle

  $A = \frac{1}{2}aP = \frac{1}{2}\left(\frac{5\sqrt{3}}{3}\right)(30) = 25\sqrt{3} \approx 43.3$ ft^2

  $P = \frac{43.3}{200} \approx 0.22$

EXERCISES

A point is chosen randomly on $\overline{AD}$. Find the probability of each event.

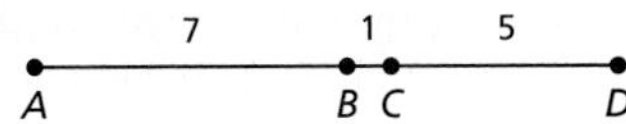

35. The point is on $\overline{AB}$.
36. The point is not on $\overline{CD}$.
37. The point is on $\overline{AB}$ or $\overline{CD}$.
38. The point is on $\overline{BC}$ or $\overline{CD}$.

Find the probability that a point chosen randomly inside the 40 m by 24 m rectangle is in each shape. Round to the nearest hundredth.

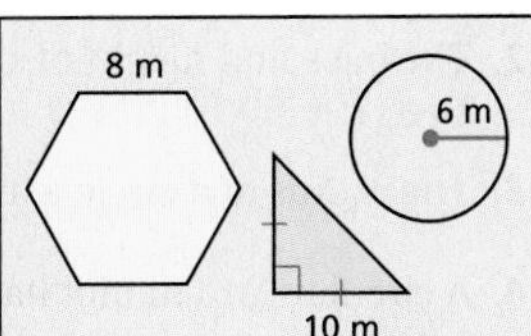

39. the regular hexagon
40. the triangle
41. the circle or the triangle
42. inside the rectangle but not inside the hexagon, triangle, or circle

Answers

31. The perimeter is multiplied by 3. The area is multiplied by 9.
32. The perimeter is doubled. The area is multiplied by 4.
33. The circumference is multiplied by $\frac{1}{2}$. The area is multiplied by $\frac{1}{4}$.
34. The perimeter is multiplied by 4. The area is multiplied by 16.
35. $\frac{7}{13}$
36. $\frac{8}{13}$
37. $\frac{12}{13}$
38. $\frac{6}{13}$
39. 0.17
40. 0.05
41. 0.17
42. 0.66

Organizer

Objective: Assess students' mastery of concepts and skills in Chapter 9.

 Online Edition

Resources

 ***Assessment Resources***

Chapter 9 Tests
- Free Response (Levels A, B, C)
- Multiple Choice (Levels A, B, C)
- Performance Assessment

Teacher One Stop™
Test & Practice Generator

State Resources

Find each measurement.

1. the height h of a triangle in which $A = 12x^2y$ ft^2 and $b = 3x$ ft $h = 8xy$ ft
2. the base b_1 of a trapezoid in which $A = 161.5$ cm^2, $h = 17$ cm, and $b_2 = 13$ cm $b_1 = 6$ cm
3. the area A of a kite in which $d_1 = 25$ in. and $d_2 = 12$ in. $A = 150$ in^2
4. Find the circumference and area of $\odot A$ with diameter 12 in. Give your answers in terms of π. $C = 12\pi$ in; $A = 36\pi$ in^2
5. Find the area of a regular hexagon with a side length of 14 m. Round to the nearest tenth. 509.2 m^2

Find the shaded area. Round to the nearest tenth, if necessary.

6. 
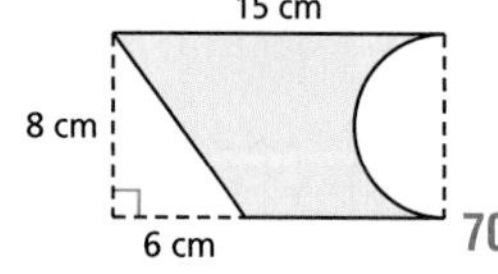

70.9 cm^2

7. 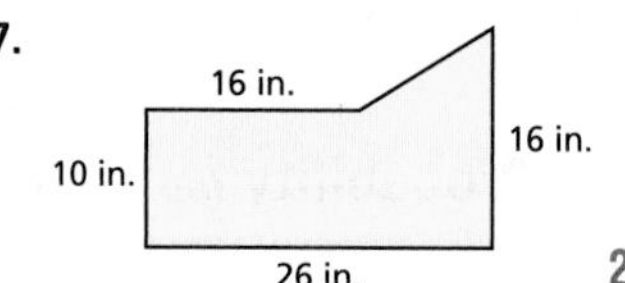

290 in^2

8. The diagram shows a plan for a pond. Use a composite figure to estimate the pond's area. The grid has squares with side lengths of 1 yd. 8 yd^2

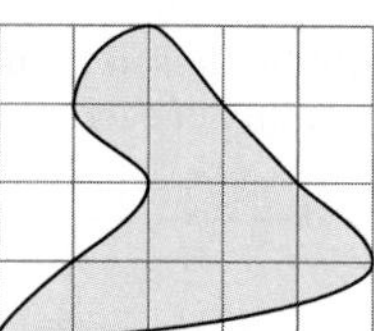

9. Draw and classify the polygon with vertices $A(1, 5)$, $B(2, 3)$, $C(-2, 1)$, and $D(-3, 3)$. Find the perimeter and area of the polygon.

Find the area of each polygon with the given vertices.

10. $E(-3, 4)$, $F(1, 1)$, $G(0, -4)$, $H(-4, 1)$ 20 units^2
11. $J(3, 4)$, $K(4, -1)$, $L(-2, -4)$, $M(-3, 3)$ 38 units^2

Describe the effect of each change on the perimeter or circumference and area of the given figure.

12. The base and height of a triangle with base 10 cm and height 12 cm are multiplied by 3. The perimeter is multiplied by 3. The area is multiplied by 9.
13. The radius of a circle with radius 12 m is multiplied by $\frac{1}{2}$. The circumference is multiplied by $\frac{1}{2}$. The area is multiplied by $\frac{1}{4}$.
14. A circular garden plot has a diameter of 21 ft. Janelle is planning a new circular plot with an area $\frac{1}{9}$ as large. How will the circumference of the new plot compare to the circumference of the old plot? The circumference will be $\frac{1}{3}$ as long.

A point is chosen randomly on $\overline{NS}$. Find the probability of each event.

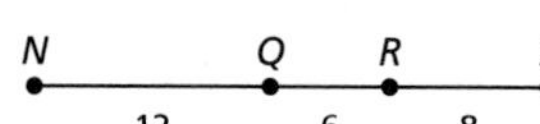

15. The point is on $\overline{NQ}$. $\frac{6}{13}$
16. The point is not on $\overline{QR}$. $\frac{10}{13}$
17. The point is on $\overline{NQ}$ or $\overline{RS}$. $\frac{10}{13}$
18. A shuttle bus for a festival stops at the parking lot every 18 minutes and stays at the lot for 2 minutes. If you go to the festival at a random time, what is the probability that the shuttle bus will be at the parking lot when you arrive? $\frac{1}{9}$

Answers

9. rectangle; $P = 6\sqrt{5}$ units; $A = 10$ units^2

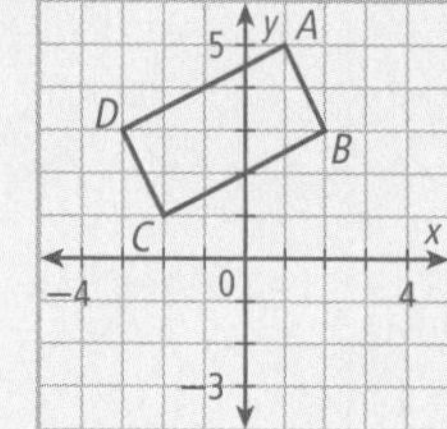

FOCUS ON SAT STUDENT-PRODUCED RESPONSES

There are two types of questions in the mathematics sections of the SAT: multiple-choice questions, where you select the correct answer from five choices, and student-produced response questions, for which you enter the correct answer in a special grid.

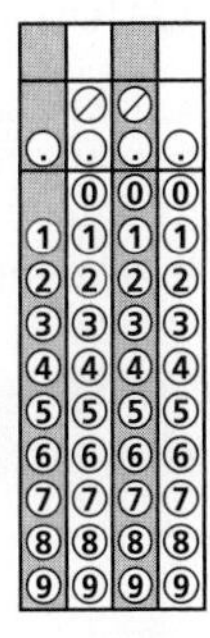

On the SAT, the student-produced response items do not have a penalty for incorrect answers. If you are uncertain of your answer and do not have time to rework the problem, you should still grid in the answer you have.

You may want to time yourself as you take this practice test. It should take you about 9 minutes to complete.

1. A triangle has two angles with a measure of 60° and one side with a length of 12. What is the perimeter of the triangle? **36**

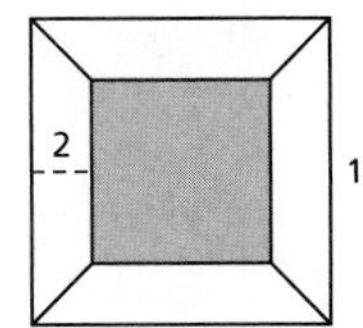

2. The figure above is composed of four congruent trapezoids arranged around a shaded square. What is the area of the shaded square? **36**

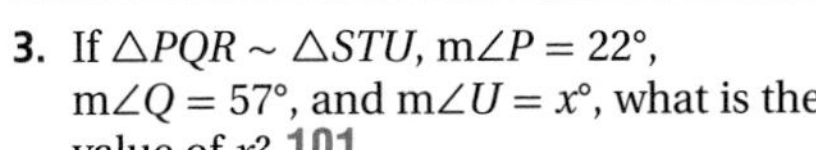

3. If $\triangle PQR \sim \triangle STU$, $m\angle P = 22°$, $m\angle Q = 57°$, and $m\angle U = x°$, what is the value of x? **101**

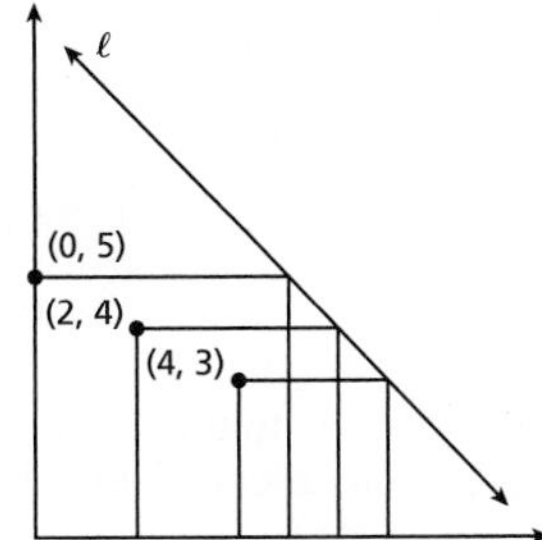

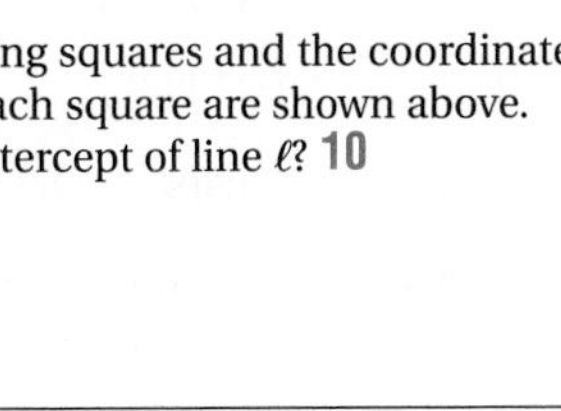

4. Three overlapping squares and the coordinates of a corner of each square are shown above. What is the y-intercept of line ℓ? **10**

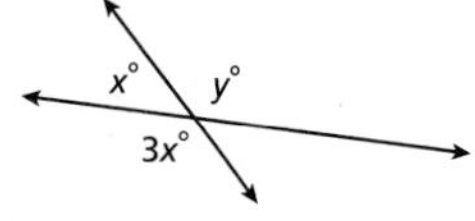

5. In the figure above, what is the value of y? **135**

6. The three angles of a triangle have measures $12x°$, $3x°$, and $7y°$, where $7y > 60$. If x and y are integers, what is the value of x? **5**

COLLEGE ENTRANCE EXAM PRACTICE

Organizer

Objective: Provide practice for college entrance exams such as the SAT.

Online Edition

Resources

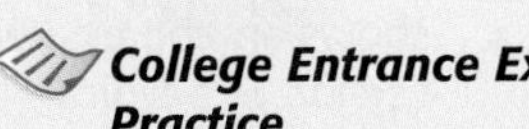

College Entrance Exam Practice

Questions on the SAT represent the following math strands:

Number and Operation, 20–25%

Algebra and Functions, 35–40%

Geometry and Measurement, 25–30%

Data Analysis, Statistics, and Probability, 10–15%

Items on this page focus on:

- Algebra and Functions
- Geometry and Measurement

Text References:

Item	1	2	3	4	5	6
Lesson	9-1	4-7	3-4	3-6	2-7	4-2

TEST PREP DOCTOR

1. Students may not know how to approach this test item. Remind students that a triangle with two 60° angles must be equiangular and therefore equilateral.
2. Students who answered 64 may have found the area of the four trapezoids instead of the shaded square. Remind students to read each question carefully.
3. Students who answered 22 or 57 may have matched up the corresponding angles incorrectly. Encourage them to draw a diagram and label the vertices of each triangle.
4. Students may not know how to approach this test item. Suggest that they find the coordinates of each vertex that lies on the line and then find the equation of the line.
5. Students who answered 45 may have found the value of x. Remind students to make sure they have answered the question completely.
6. Students may not know how to approach this test item. Remind them that the sum of the angle measures must be 180°. They can use the fact that $y > 60$ to write an inequality in terms of x and then find an integer value of x that satisfies the inequality.

Organizer

Objective: Provide opportunities to learn and practice common test-taking strategies.

Online Edition

This Test Tackler shows an abbreviated version of a typical formula sheet and explains how to use it to solve problems on a standardized test. Review with students what each variable represents and help them determine the appropriate formula to use for each problem.

TEST TACKLER

Standardized Test Strategies

Any Question Type: Use a Formula Sheet

When you take a standardized mathematics test, you may be given a formula sheet or a mathematics chart that accompanies the test. Although many common formulas are given on these sheets, you still need to know when the formulas are applicable, and what the variables in the formulas represent.

EXAMPLE 1

Mathematics Chart

Perimeter	rectangle	$P = 2\ell + 2w$ or $P = 2(\ell + w)$
Circumference	circle	$C = 2\pi r$ or $C = \pi d$
Area	rectangle	$A = \ell w$ or $A = bh$
	triangle	$A = \frac{1}{2}bh$ or $A = \frac{bh}{2}$
	trapezoid	$A = \frac{1}{2}(b_1 + b_2)h$ or $A = \frac{(b_1 + b_2)h}{2}$
	circle	$A = \pi r^2$

Multiple Choice **In the figure, a rectangle is inscribed in a circle. Which best represents the shaded area to the nearest tenth of a square meter?**

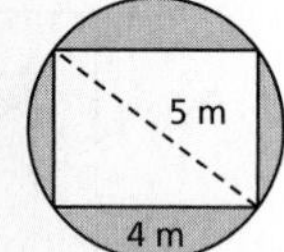

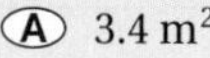

Ⓐ 3.4 m^2 Ⓒ 12.6 m^2

Ⓑ 7.6 m^2 Ⓓ 17.2 m^2

Which formula(s) do I need?

area of a circle, area of a rectangle

What do I substitute for each variable in the formulas?

To use the formula for the area of a circle, I need to know the radius. The diameter of the circle is 5 m, so the radius is 2.5 m. I should substitute 2.5 for r and 3.14 for π.

To use the formula for the area of a rectangle, I need to know its base and height. The base b is 4 m. To find the height, I can use the Pythagorean Theorem.

$4^2 + h^2 = 5^2$
$16 + h^2 = 25$
$h^2 = 9$
$h = 3$

What are the areas of the shapes?

circle: $A = \pi r^2 = \pi(2.5)^2 = 6.25\pi \text{ m}^2$
rectangle: $A = bh = 4(3) = 12 \text{ m}^2$

What do I do with the areas to find the answer?

shaded area = area of circle − area of rectangle
$= 6.25\pi - 12 \approx 7.6 \text{ m}^2$

Choice B is the correct answer.

Read each test problem and answer the questions that follow. Use the formula sheet below, if applicable.

Perimeter	
rectangle	$P = 2\ell + 2w$ or $P = 2(\ell + w)$
Circumference	
circle	$C = 2\pi r$ or $C = \pi d$
Area	
rectangle	$A = \ell w$ or $A = bh$
triangle	$A = \frac{1}{2}bh$ or $A = \frac{bh}{2}$
trapezoid	$A = \frac{1}{2}(b_1 + b_2)h$ or $A = \frac{(b_1 + b_2)h}{2}$
circle	$A = \pi r^2$
Pi	
π	$\pi \approx 3.14$ or $\pi \approx \frac{22}{7}$

Item A
The circumference of a circle is 48π meters. What is the radius in meters?

Ⓐ 6.9 meters
Ⓑ 24 meters
Ⓒ 12 meters
Ⓓ 36 meters

1. Which formula would you use to solve this problem?
2. After substituting the variables in the formula, what would you need to do to find the correct answer?

Item B
Gridded Response The area of a trapezoid is 171 square meters. The height is 9 meters, and one base length is 23 meters. What is the other base length of the trapezoid in meters?

3. What formula(s) would you use to solve this problem?
4. What would you substitute for each variable in the formula?

Before you begin a test, quickly review the formulas included on your formula sheet.

Item C
Gridded Response The area of the rectangle is 48 square miles. What is the perimeter in miles?

5. What formula(s) would you use to solve this problem?
6. What would you substitute for each variable in the formula?
7. After substituting the variables in the formula, what would you need to do to find the correct answer?

Item D
Short Response A point is chosen randomly inside the rectangle. Which is more likely: the point lies within the triangle, or the point does not lie inside the triangle or the trapezoid?

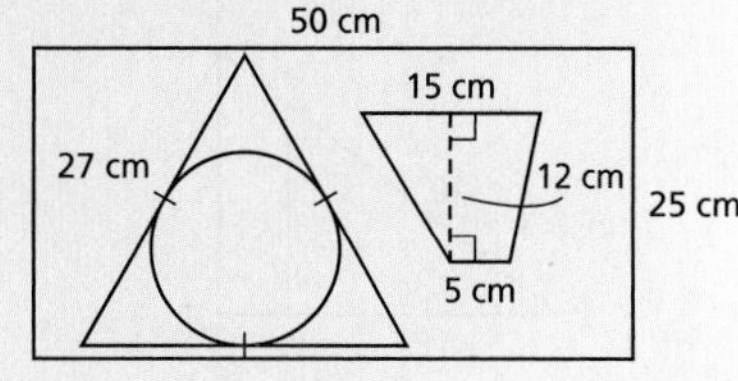

8. Which formulas would you use to solve this problem?
9. What would you substitute for each variable in the formula(s)?
10. After substituting the variables in the formula, what would you need to do to find the correct answer?

Answers

1. $C = 2\pi r$
2. Solve for r.
3. $A = \frac{1}{2}(b_1 + b_2)h$
4. I would substitute 171 for A, 9 for h, and 23 for b_1.
5. $A = \ell w$ and $P = 2\ell + 2w$
6. I would substitute 48 for A, 12 for ℓ, and 4 for w.
7. Solve the area formula for ℓ, and then substitute the value into the perimeter formula to find P.
8. $A = bh$, $A = \frac{1}{2}bh$, and $A = \frac{1}{2}(b_1 + b_2)h$
9. I would substitute 50 for b and 25 for h, 27 for b and $\frac{27\sqrt{3}}{2}$ for h, and 5 for b_1, 15 for b_2, and 12 for h, respectively.
10. Possible answer: Add the areas of the triangle and trapezoid, and divide the sum by the area of the rectangle. Subtract the result from 1.

Answers to Test Items

A. B
B. 15
C. 32
D. The point does not lie inside the triangle or trapezoid.

State Resources

go.hrw.com
State Resources Online
KEYWORD: MG7 Resources

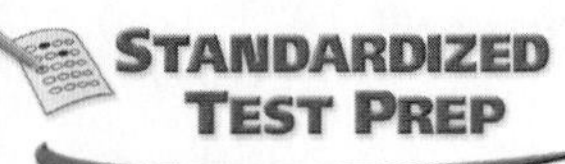

Organizer

Objective: Provide review and practice for Chapters 1–9 and standardized tests.

Online Edition

Resources

Assessment Resources

Chapter 9 Cumulative Test

go.hrw.com
KEYWORD: MG7 TestPrep

Answers

1. B
2. G
3. C
4. H
5. D
6. F
7. A
8. G
9. B
10. F
11. C
12. J
13. 5
14. 2
15. 80

State Resources

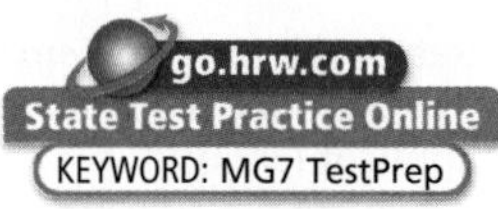

CUMULATIVE ASSESSMENT, CHAPTERS 1–9

Multiple Choice

1. The floor of a tent is a regular hexagon. If the side length of the tent floor is 5 feet, what is the area of the floor? Round to the nearest tenth.

Ⓐ 32.5 square feet

Ⓑ 65.0 square feet

Ⓒ 75.0 square feet

Ⓓ 129.9 square feet

2. If J is on the perpendicular bisector of $\overline{KL}$, what is the length of $\overline{KL}$?

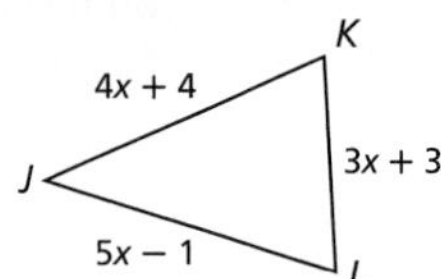

Ⓕ 12 Ⓗ 24

Ⓖ 18 Ⓙ 36

3. What is the length of $\overline{VY}$?

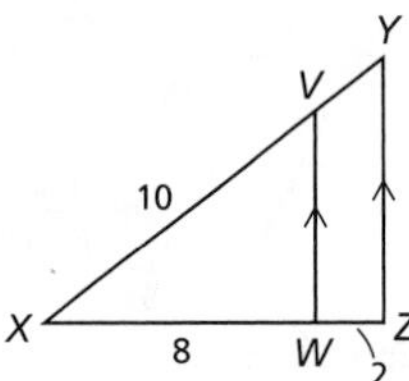

Ⓐ 1.6 Ⓒ 2.5

Ⓑ 2 Ⓓ 4

4. A sailor on a ship sights the light of a lighthouse at an angle of elevation of 15°. If the light in the lighthouse is 189 feet higher than the sailor's line of sight, what is the horizontal distance between the ship and the lighthouse? Round to the nearest foot.

Ⓕ 49 feet Ⓗ 705 feet

Ⓖ 51 feet Ⓙ 730 feet

5. If $ABCD$ is a rhombus in which $m\angle 1 = (x + 15)°$ and $m\angle 2 = (2x + 12)°$, what is the value of x?

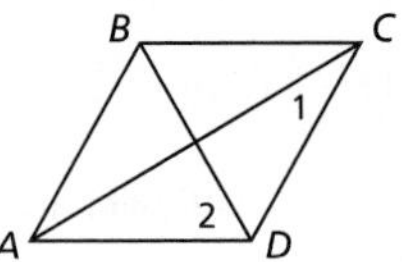

Ⓐ 3 Ⓒ 18

Ⓑ 9 Ⓓ 21

6. What is the area of the shaded portion of the rectangle?

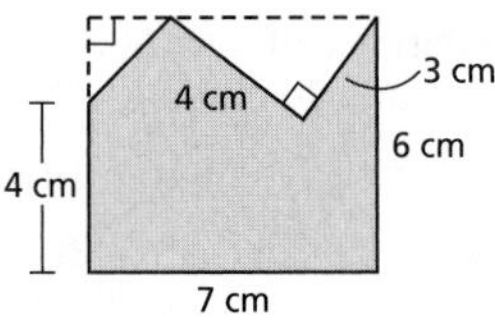

Ⓕ 34 square centimeters

Ⓖ 36 square centimeters

Ⓗ 38 square centimeters

Ⓙ 50 square centimeters

7. If $\triangle XYZ$ is isosceles and $m\angle Y > 100°$, which of the following must be true?

Ⓐ $m\angle X < 40°$ Ⓒ $\overline{XZ} \cong \overline{YZ}$

Ⓑ $m\angle X > 40°$ Ⓓ $\overline{XY} \cong \overline{XZ}$

8. The Eiffel Tower in Paris, France, is 300 meters tall. The first level of the tower has a height of 57 meters. A scale model of the Eiffel Tower in Shenzhen, China, is 108 meters tall. What is the height of the first level of the model? Round to the nearest tenth.

Ⓕ 15.8 meters Ⓗ 56.8 meters

Ⓖ 20.5 meters Ⓙ 61.6 meters

Answers

16.

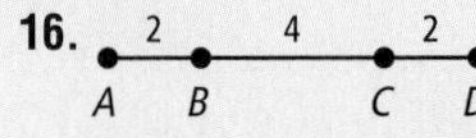

$\frac{1}{2}$; possible answer: let A represent one gas station and D represent the other. The probability that the car will be at least 2 mi from either gas station is the probability that a point chosen randomly on $\overline{AD}$ is on $\overline{BC}$.

$P(\overline{BC}) = \frac{BC}{AD} = \frac{4}{8} = \frac{1}{2}$

17a. 67°; possible answer: Use the Pythagorean Theorem to find CD.

$12^2 + CD^2 = 31.2^2$

$CD = 28.8$

BD is the geometric mean of AD and BC.

$AD\ (28.8) = 12^2$

$AD = 5$

Use the tangent ratio to find $m\angle A$.

$\tan A = \frac{12}{5}$

$m\angle A = \tan^{-1}\frac{12}{5} \approx 67°$

b. 33.8; Use the Segment Addition Postulate to find AC.

$AC = 5 + 28.8$

$= 33.8$

There is often more than one way to find a missing side length or angle measure in a figure. For example, you might be able to find a side length of a right triangle by using either the Pythagorean Theorem or a trigonometric ratio. Check your answer by using a different method than the one you originally used.

9. The lengths of both bases of a trapezoid are tripled. What is the effect of the change on the area of the trapezoid?

Ⓐ The area remains the same.

Ⓑ The area is tripled.

Ⓒ The area increases by a factor of 6.

Ⓓ The area increases by a factor of 9.

10. If $\angle 1$ and $\angle 2$ form a linear pair, which of the following must also be true about these angles?

Ⓕ They are adjacent.

Ⓖ They are complementary.

Ⓗ They are congruent.

Ⓙ They are vertical.

11. In $\triangle ABC$, $AB = 8$, $BC = 17$, and $AC = 2x + 1$. Which of the following is a possible value of x?

Ⓐ 3 Ⓒ 9

Ⓑ 4 Ⓓ 12

12. Which line is parallel to the line with the equation $y = -3x + 4$?

Ⓕ $y - 3x = 8$

Ⓖ $4y - 12x = 1$

Ⓗ $3y - x = 3$

Ⓙ $2y + 6x = 5$

Gridded Response

13. What is the radius of a circle in inches if the ratio of its area to its circumference is 2.5 square inches : 1 inch?

14. $\triangle JLM \sim \triangle RST$. If $JL = 5$, $LM = 4$, $RS = 3x - 1$, and $ST = x + 2$, what is the value of x?

15. If the two diagonals of a kite measure 16 centimeters and 10 centimeters, what is the area of the kite in square centimeters?

Short Response

16. Two gas stations on a straight highway are 8 miles apart. If a car runs out of gas at a random point between the two gas stations, what is the probability that the car will be at least 2 miles from either gas station? Draw a diagram or write and explanation to show how you determined your answer.

17. Use the figure below to find each measure. Show your work or explain in words how you found your answers. Round the angle measure to the nearest degree.

a. $m\angle A$

b. AC

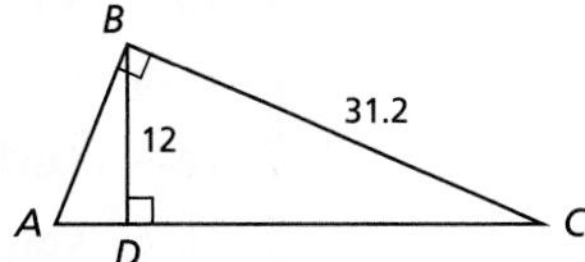

18. Given that $\overline{DE}$, $\overline{DF}$, and $\overline{EF}$ are midsegments of $\triangle ABC$, determine $m\angle C$ to the nearest degree. Show your work or explain in words how you determined your answer.

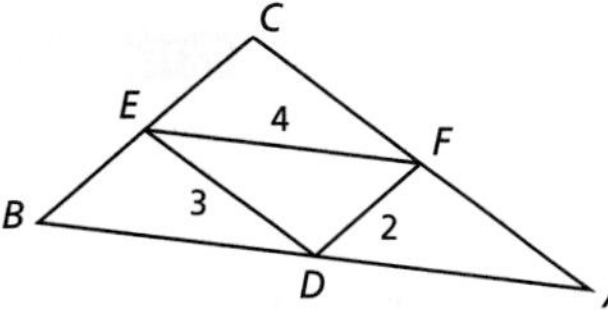

Extended Response

19. Quadrilateral $LMNP$ has vertices at $L(1, 4)$, $M(4, 4)$, $N(1, 0)$ and $P(-2, 0)$.

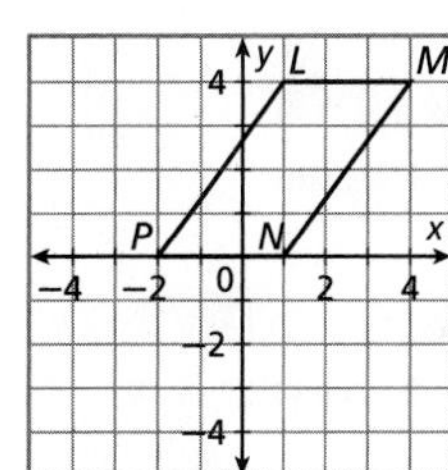

a. Write a coordinate proof showing that $LMNP$ is a parallelogram.

b. Draw a rectangle with the same area as figure $LMNP$. Explain how you know that the figures have the same area.

c. Does the rectangle you drew have the same perimeter as figure $LMNP$? Explain.

Short-Response Rubric

Items 16–18

2 Points = The student's answer is an accurate and complete execution of the task or tasks.

1 Point = The student's answer contains attributes of an appropriate response but is flawed.

0 Points = The student's answer contains no attributes of an appropriate response.

Extended-Response Rubric

Item 19

4 Points = The student's proof is correct, all work is shown, and explanations are complete. Work demonstrates a thorough understanding of concepts related to parallelograms as well as perimeter and area in the coordinate plane.

3 Points = The student's proof and answers are correct, but explanations may contain minor flaws. Work demonstrates an understanding of major concepts.

2 Points = The student's answers are correct but explanations are missing or incomplete, or the student answers only part of the problem. Work demonstrates a limited understanding of concepts related to perimeter and area in the coordinate plane.

1 Point = The student answers incorrectly but makes a reasonable attempt to show work.

0 Points = The student answers incorrectly and does not attempt all parts of the problem.

18. 104°; possible answer: by the $\triangle$ Midsegment Thm, $AB = 8$, $BC = 4$ and $AC = 6$. Use the Law of Cosines to find $m\angle C$.

$AB^2 = BC^2 + AC^2 - 2(BC)(AC)\cos C$

$8^2 = 4^2 + 6^2 - 2(4)(6)\cos C$

$12 = -48\cos C$

$-\frac{1}{4} = \cos C$

$m\angle C = \cos^{-1}\left(-\frac{1}{4}\right) \approx 104°$

19a. By the Dist. Formula, $LM = 3$ and $PN = 3$. Therefore $\overline{LM} \cong \overline{NP}$ by the def. of $\cong$ segments. By the Slope Formula, the slope of $\overline{LM}$ is 0 and the slope of $\overline{PN}$ is 0. Therefore $\overline{LM}$ and $\overline{PN}$ are par. by the Par. Lines Thm. Because $\overline{LM}$ and $\overline{PN}$ are par. and $\cong$, $LMNP$ is a parallelogram.

19b. Possible answer:

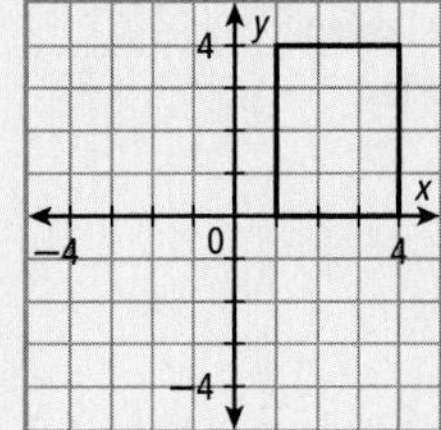

The area of $LMNP$ is $A = bh = (3)(4) = 12$ units^2. The area of the rectangle is $A = bh = (3)(4) = 12$ units^2.

c. No; $LM = 3$; $PN = 3$; $MN = \sqrt{(4-1)^2 + (4-0)^2} = 5$; $LP = 5$; The perimeter of $LMNP$ is $P = 2b + 2h = 2(3) + 2(5) = 16$ units. The perimeter of the rectangle is $P = 2b + 2h = 2(3) + 2(4) = 14$ units.

Spatial Reasoning

Section 10A

Three-Dimensional Figures

10-1 Solid Geometry
10-2 Representations of Three-Dimensional Figures
10-3 Geometry Lab Use Nets to Create Polyhedrons
10-3 Formulas in Three-Dimensions

Section 10B

Surface Area and Volume

10-4 Surface Area of Prisms and Cylinders
10-4 Geometry Lab Model Right and Oblique Cylinders
10-5 Surface Area of Pyramids and Cones
10-6 Volume of Prisms and Cylinders
10-7 Volume of Pyramids and Cones
Connecting Geometry to Algebra Cube Roots
10-8 Spheres
10-8 Technology Lab Compare Surface Areas and Volumes
EXTENSION Spherical Geometry

Pacing Guide for 45-Minute Classes

Teacher One Stop™
Calendar Planner®

Countdown Weeks 22, 23, 24

Chapter 10

DAY 1	DAY 2	DAY 3	DAY 4	DAY 5
10-1 Lesson	10-2 Lesson	10-3 Geometry Lab	10-3 Lesson	Multi-Step Test Prep Ready to Go On?
DAY 6	**DAY 7**	**DAY 8**	**DAY 9**	**DAY 10**
10-4 Lesson 10-4 Geometry Lab	10-5 Lesson	10-6 Lesson	10-7 Lesson	Connecting Geometry to Algebra
DAY 11	**DAY 12**	**DAY 13**	**DAY 14**	**DAY 15**
10-8 Lesson	EXTENSION	10-8 Technology Lab	Multi-Step Test Prep Ready to Go On?	Chapter 10 Review
DAY 16				
Chapter 10 Test				

Pacing Guide for 90-Minute Classes

Teacher One Stop™
Calendar Planner®

Chapter 10

DAY 1	DAY 2	DAY 3	DAY 4	DAY 5
10-1 Lesson 10-2 Lesson	10-3 Geometry Lab 10-3 Lesson	Multi-Step Test Prep Ready to Go On? 10-4 Lesson 10-4 Geometry Lab	10-5 Lesson 10-6 Lesson	10-7 Lesson Connecting Geometry to Algebra
DAY 6	**DAY 7**	**DAY 8**		
10-8 Lesson EXTENSION	10-8 Technology Lab Multi-Step Test Prep Ready to Go On?	Chapter 10 Review Chapter 10 Test		

ONGOING ASSESSMENT and INTERVENTION

	DIAGNOSE	PRESCRIBE
Assess Prior Knowledge	**Before Chapter 10**	
	Diagnose readiness for the chapter.	Prescribe intervention.
	Are You Ready? SE p. 651	***Are You Ready? Intervention***
Formative Assessment	**Before Every Lesson**	
	Diagnose readiness for the lesson.	Prescribe intervention.
	Warm Up TE	**Reteach** CRB
	During Every Lesson	
	Diagnose understanding of lesson concepts.	Prescribe intervention.
	Check It Out! SE	**Reading Strategies** CRB
	Questioning Strategies TE	***Success for Every Learner***
	Think and Discuss SE	***Lesson Tutorial Videos***
	Write About It SE	
	Journal TE	
	After Every Lesson	
	Diagnose mastery of lesson concepts.	Prescribe intervention.
	Lesson Quiz TE	**Reteach** CRB
	Test Prep SE	**Test Prep Doctor** TE
	Test and Practice Generator	***Homework Help* Online**
	Before Chapter 10 Testing	
	Diagnose mastery of concepts in chapter.	Prescribe intervention.
	Ready to Go On? SE pp. 679, 725	***Ready to Go On? Intervention***
	Multi-Step Test Prep SE pp. 678, 724	**Scaffolding Questions** TE pp. 678, 724
	Section Quizzes AR	**Reteach** CRB
	Test and Practice Generator	***Lesson Tutorial Videos***
	Before High Stakes Testing	
	Diagnose mastery of benchmark concepts.	Prescribe intervention.
	College Entrance Exam Practice SE p. 645	***College Entrance Exam Practice***
	Standardized Test Prep SE pp. 648–649	
Summative Assessment	**After Chapter 10**	
	Check mastery of chapter concepts.	Prescribe intervention.
	Multiple-Choice Tests (Forms A, B, C)	**Reteach** CRB
	Free-Response Tests (Forms A, B, C)	***Lesson Tutorial Videos***
	Performance Assessment AR	
	Cumulative Test AR	
	Test and Practice Generator	

KEY: **SE** = *Student Edition* **TE** = *Teacher's Edition* **CRB** = *Chapter Resource Book* **AR** = *Assessment Resources* Available online Available on CD- or DVD-ROM

Lesson Resources

Before the Lesson

Prepare ***Teacher One Stop***  
- Editable lesson plans
- Calendar Planner
- Easy access to all chapter resources

Lesson Transparencies
- Teacher Tools

Teach the Lesson

Introduce ***Alternate Openers: Explorations***

Lesson Transparencies
- Warm Up
- Problem of the Day

Teach ***Lesson Transparencies***
- Teaching Transparencies

Know-It Notebook™
- Vocabulary
- Key Concepts

Power Presentations

Lesson Tutorial Videos 

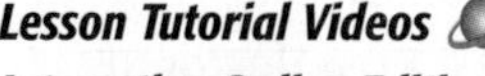

Interactive Online Edition
- Lesson Activities
- Lesson Tutorial Videos

Lab Activities

Lab Resources Online

Online Interactivities SPANISH

TechKeys

Practice the Lesson

Practice ***Chapter Resources***
- Practice A, B, C

Practice and Problem Solving Workbook

IDEA Works!® Modified Worksheets and Tests

ExamView Test and Practice Generator

Homework Help Online

Online Interactivities 

Interactive Online Edition
- Homework Help

Apply ***Chapter Resources***
- Problem Solving

Practice and Problem Solving Workbook

Interactive Online Edition
- Chapter Project

Project Teacher Support 

After the Lesson

Reteach ***Chapter Resources***
- Reteach
- Reading Strategies ELL

Success for Every Learner

Review ***Interactive Answers and Solutions***

Solutions Key

Know-It Notebook™
- Big Ideas
- Chapter Review

Extend ***Chapter Resources***
- Challenge

Technology Highlights for the Teacher

Power Presentations

Dynamic presentations to engage students. Complete PowerPoint® presentations for every lesson in Chapter 10.

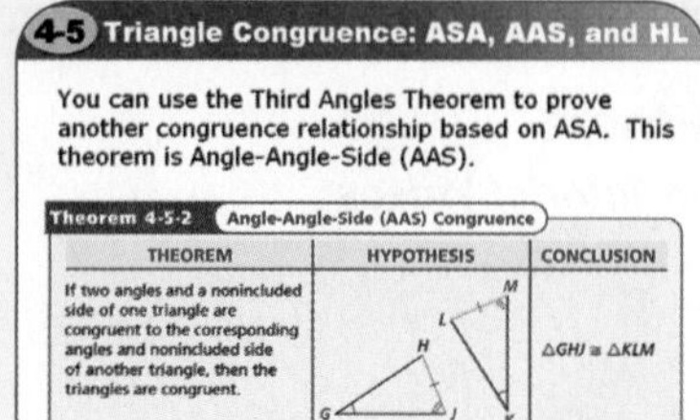

Teacher One Stop SPANISH

Easy access to Chapter 10 resources and assessments. Includes lesson planning, test generation, and puzzle creation software.

Premier Online Edition 

Chapter 10 includes Tutorial Videos, Lesson Activities, Lesson Quizzes, Homework Help, and Chapter Project.

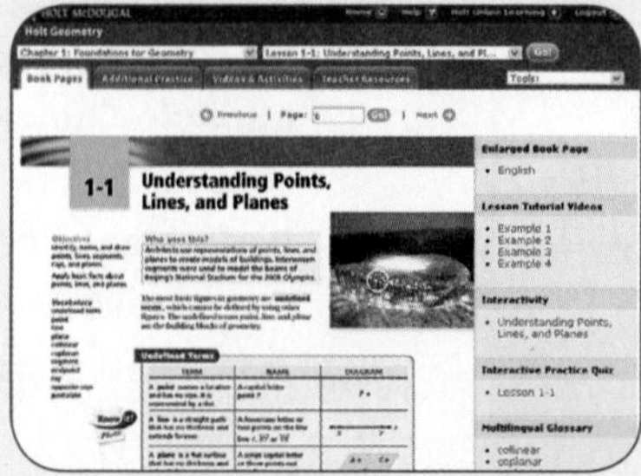

KEY: **SE** = *Student Edition* **TE** = *Teacher's Edition*  English Language Learners  Spanish version available 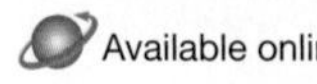 Available online  Available on CD- or DVD-ROM

Reaching All Learners

Teaching tips to help all learners appear throughout the chapter. A few that target specific students are included in the lists below.

All Learners

Lab Activities
Practice and Problem Solving Workbook
Know-It Notebook

Special Needs Students

Practice A .... CRB
Reteach .... CRB
Reading Strategies .... CRB
Are You Ready? .... SE p. 651
Inclusion .... TE pp. 665, 682, 713
IDEA Works!® Modified Worksheets and Tests
Ready to Go On? Intervention SPANISH
Know-It Notebook
Online Interactivities  SPANISH
Lesson Tutorial Videos  

Developing Learners

Practice A .... CRB
Reteach .... CRB
Reading Strategies .... CRB
Are You Ready? .... SE p. 651
Vocabulary Connections .... SE p. 652
Questioning Strategies .... TE
Ready to Go On? Intervention SPANISH
Know-It Notebook
Homework Help Online 
Online Interactivities  SPANISH
Lesson Tutorial Videos  

On-Level Learners

Practice B .... CRB
Problem Solving .... CRB
Vocabulary Connections .... SE p. 652
Questioning Strategies .... TE
Ready to Go On? Intervention SPANISH
Know-It Notebook
Homework Help Online
Online Interactivities  SPANISH

Advanced Learners

Practice C .... CRB
Challenge .... CRB
Challenge Exercises .... SE
Reading and Writing Math *Extend* .... TE p. 653
Critical Thinking .... TE p. 728
Are You Ready? Enrichment SPANISH
Ready To Go On? Enrichment 

English Language Learners

ENGLISH LANGUAGE LEARNERS

Reading Strategies .... CRB
Are You Ready? Vocabulary .... SE p. 651
Vocabulary Connections .... SE p. 652
Vocabulary Review .... SE p. 730
English Language Learners .... TE pp. 681, 699, 710, 740
Success for Every Learner
Know-It Notebook
Spanish Study Guide (Resumen y Repaso)
Multilingual Glossary
Lesson Tutorial Videos  

Technology Highlights for Reaching All Learners

 Lesson Tutorial Videos 

Starring Holt authors Ed Burger and Freddie Renfro! Live tutorials to support every lesson in Chapter 10.

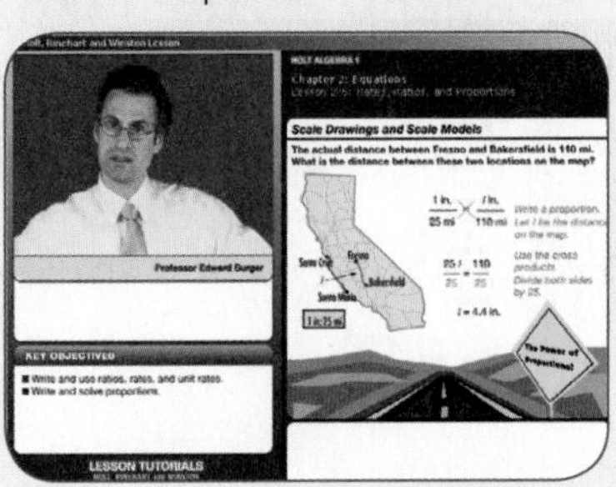

Multilingual Glossary

Searchable glossary includes definitions in English, Spanish, Vietnamese, Chinese, Hmong, Korean, and 4 other languages.

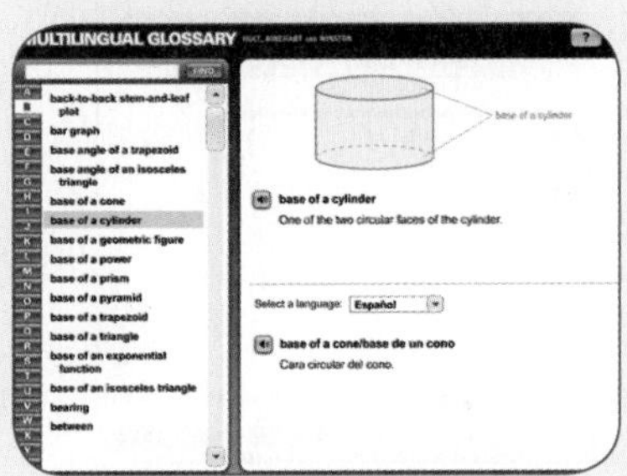

Online Interactivities

Interactive tutorials provide visually engaging alternative opportunities to learn concepts and master skills.

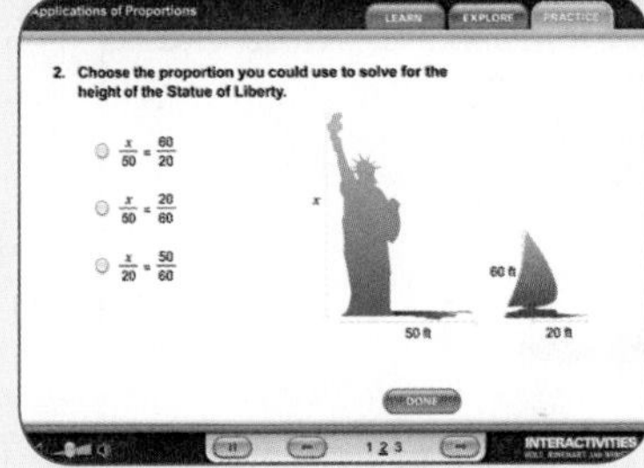

KEY: **SE** = *Student Edition* **TE** = *Teacher's Edition* **CRB** = *Chapter Resource Book*  Spanish version available  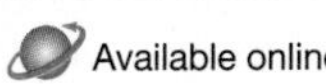 Available online  Available on CD- or DVD-ROM

Ongoing Assessment

Assessing Prior Knowledge

Determine whether students have the prerequisite concepts and skills for success in Chapter 10.

Are You Ready? SPANISH .... SE p. 651
Warm Up .... TE

Test Preparation

Provide review and practice for Chapter 10 and standardized tests.

Multi-Step Test Prep .... SE pp. 678, 724
Study Guide: Review .... SE pp. 730–733
Test Tackler .... SE pp. 736–737
Standardized Test Prep .... SE pp. 738–739
College Entrance Exam Practice .... SE p. 735
Countdown to Testing .... SE pp. C4-C27
IDEA Works!® Modified Worksheets and Tests

Alternative Assessment

Assess students' understanding of Chapter 10 concepts and combined problem-solving skills.

Chapter 10 Project .... SE p. 650
Alternative Assessment .... TE
Performance Assessment .... AR
Portfolio Assessment .... AR

Lesson Assessment

Provide formative assessment for each lesson of Chapter 10.

Questioning Strategies .... TE
Think and Discuss .... SE
Check It Out! Exercises .... SE
Write About It .... SE
Journal .... TE
Lesson Quiz .... TE
Alternative Assessment .... TE
IDEA Works!® Modified Worksheets and Tests

Weekly Assessment

Provide formative assessment for each section of Chapter 10.

Multi-Step Test Prep .... SE pp. 678, 724
Ready to Go On? SPANISH .... SE pp. 679, 725
Section Quizzes .... AR
Test and Practice Generator .... *Teacher One Stop*

Chapter Assessment

Provide summative assessment of Chapter 10 mastery.

Chapter 10 Test .... SE p. 734
Chapter Test (Levels A, B, C) .... AR
• Multiple Choice • Free Response
Cumulative Test .... AR
Test and Practice Generator .... *Teacher One Stop*
IDEA Works!® Modified Worksheets and Tests

Technology Highlights for Assessment

Are You Ready? SPANISH

Automatically assess readiness and prescribe intervention for Chapter 10 prerequisite skills.

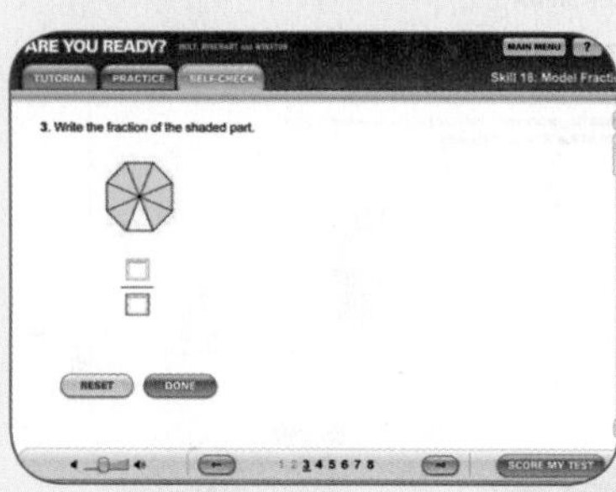

ARE YOU READY?
3. Write the fraction of the shaded part.

Ready to Go On?

Automatically assess understanding of and prescribe intervention for Sections 10A and 10B.

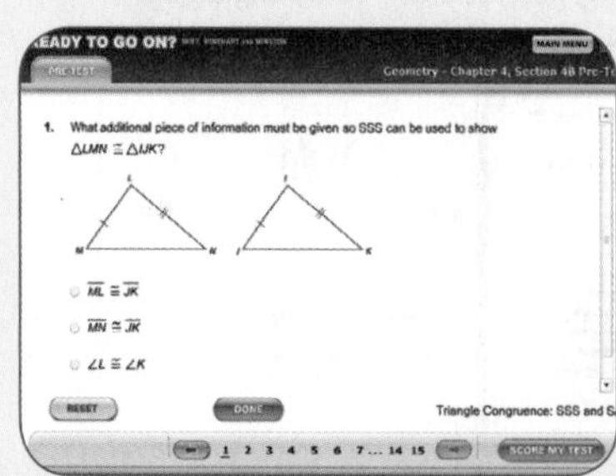

Test and Practice Generator

Use Chapter 10 problem banks to create assessments and worksheets to print out or deliver online. Includes dynamic problems.

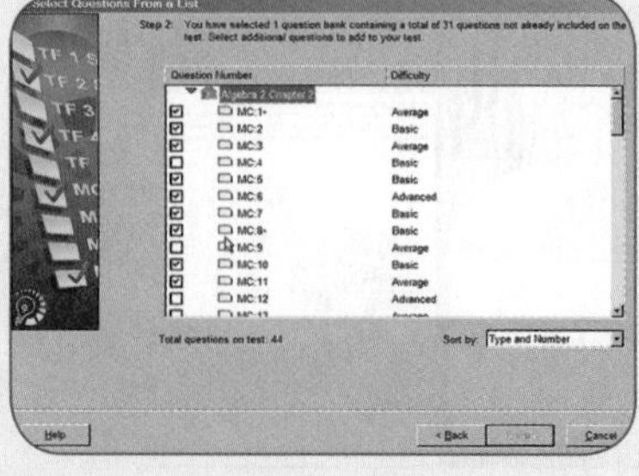

KEY: **SE** = *Student Edition* **TE** = *Teacher's Edition* **AR** = *Assessment Resources* SPANISH Spanish version available  Available online  Available on CD- or DVD-ROM

Formal Assessment

Three levels (A, B, C) of multiple-choice and free-response chapter tests, along with a performance assessment, are available in the *Assessment Resources.*

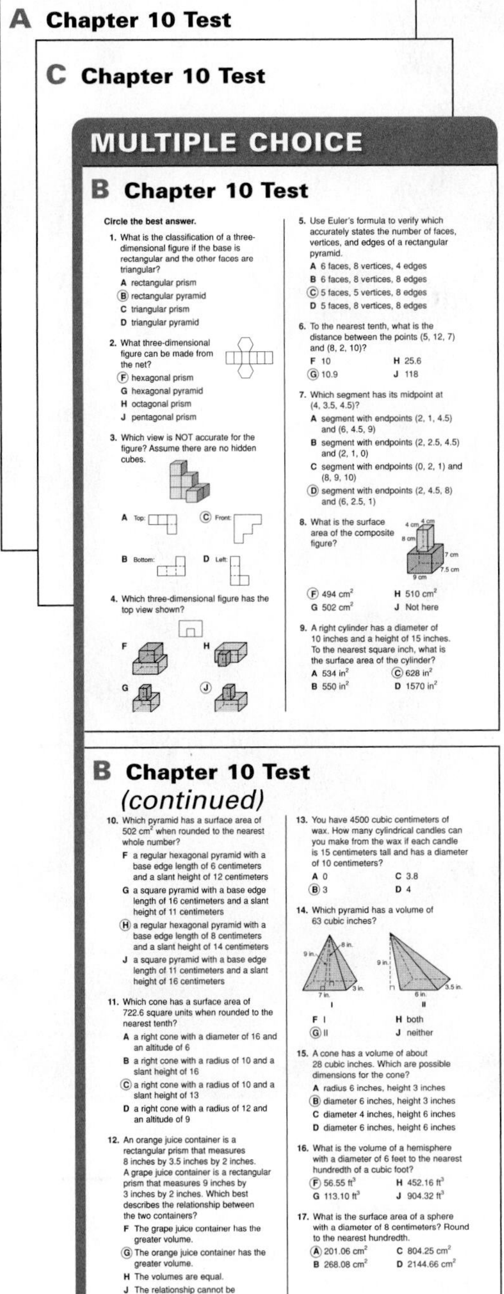

A Chapter 10 Test

C Chapter 10 Test

MULTIPLE CHOICE

B Chapter 10 Test

Circle the best answer.

1. What is the classification of a three-dimensional figure if the base is rectangular and the other faces are triangular?
   A rectangular prism
   (B) rectangular pyramid
   C triangular prism
   D triangular pyramid

2. What three-dimensional figure can be made from the net?
   (F) hexagonal prism
   G hexagonal pyramid
   H octagonal prism
   J pentagonal prism

3. Which view is NOT accurate for the figure? Assume there are no hidden cubes.
   A Top:
   (C) Front:
   B Bottom:
   D Left:

4. Which three-dimensional figure has the top view shown?
   F
   H
   G
   (J)

5. Use Euler's formula to verify which accurately states the number of faces, vertices, and edges of a rectangular pyramid.
   A 6 faces, 8 vertices, 4 edges
   B 6 faces, 8 vertices, 8 edges
   (C) 5 faces, 5 vertices, 8 edges
   D 5 faces, 8 vertices, 8 edges

6. To the nearest tenth, what is the distance between the points (5, 12, 7) and (8, 2, 10)?
   F 10　H 25.6
   (G) 10.9　J 118

7. Which segment has its midpoint at (4, 3.5, 4.5)?
   A segment with endpoints (2, 1, 4.5) and (6, 4.5, 9)
   B segment with endpoints (2, 2.5, 4.5) and (2, 1, 0)
   C segment with endpoints (0, 2, 1) and (8, 9, 10)
   (D) segment with endpoints (2, 4.5, 8) and (6, 2.5, 1)

8. What is the surface area of the composite figure?
   4 cm, 4 cm, 8 cm, 7 cm, 7.5 cm, 9 cm
   (F) 494 cm^2　H 510 cm^2
   G 502 cm^2　J Not here

9. A right cylinder has a diameter of 10 inches and a height of 15 inches. To the nearest square inch, what is the surface area of the cylinder?
   A 534 in^2　(C) 628 in^2
   B 550 in^2　D 1570 in^2

B Chapter 10 Test *(continued)*

10. Which pyramid has a surface area of 502 cm^2 when rounded to the nearest whole number?
    F a regular hexagonal pyramid with a base edge length of 6 centimeters and a slant height of 12 centimeters
    G a square pyramid with a base edge length of 16 centimeters and a slant height of 11 centimeters
    (H) a regular hexagonal pyramid with a base edge length of 8 centimeters and a slant height of 14 centimeters
    J a square pyramid with a base edge length of 11 centimeters and a slant height of 16 centimeters

11. Which cone has a surface area of 722.6 square units when rounded to the nearest tenth?
    A a right cone with a diameter of 16 and an altitude of 6
    B a right cone with a radius of 10 and a slant height of 16
    (C) a right cone with a radius of 10 and a slant height of 13
    D a right cone with a radius of 12 and an altitude of 9

12. An orange juice container is a rectangular prism that measures 8 inches by 3.5 inches by 2 inches. A grape juice container is a rectangular prism that measures 9 inches by 3 inches by 2 inches. Which best describes the relationship between the two containers?
    F The grape juice container has the greater volume.
    (G) The orange juice container has the greater volume.
    H The volumes are equal.
    J The relationship cannot be determined.

13. You have 4500 cubic centimeters of wax. How many cylindrical candles can you make from the wax if each candle is 15 centimeters tall and has a diameter of 10 centimeters?
    A 0　C 3.8
    (B) 3　D 4

14. Which pyramid has a volume of 63 cubic inches?
    I: 9 in., 8 in., 7 in., 3 in.　II: 9 in., 6 in., 3.5 in.
    F I　H both
    (G) II　J neither

15. A cone has a volume of about 28 cubic inches. Which are possible dimensions for the cone?
    A radius 6 inches, height 3 inches
    (B) diameter 6 inches, height 3 inches
    C diameter 4 inches, height 6 inches
    D diameter 6 inches, height 6 inches

16. What is the volume of a hemisphere with a diameter of 6 feet to the nearest hundredth of a cubic foot?
    (F) 56.55 ft^3　H 452.16 ft^3
    G 113.10 ft^3　J 904.32 ft^3

17. What is the surface area of a sphere with a diameter of 8 centimeters? Round to the nearest hundredth.
    (A) 201.06 cm^2　C 804.25 cm^2
    B 268.08 cm^2　D 2144.66 cm^2

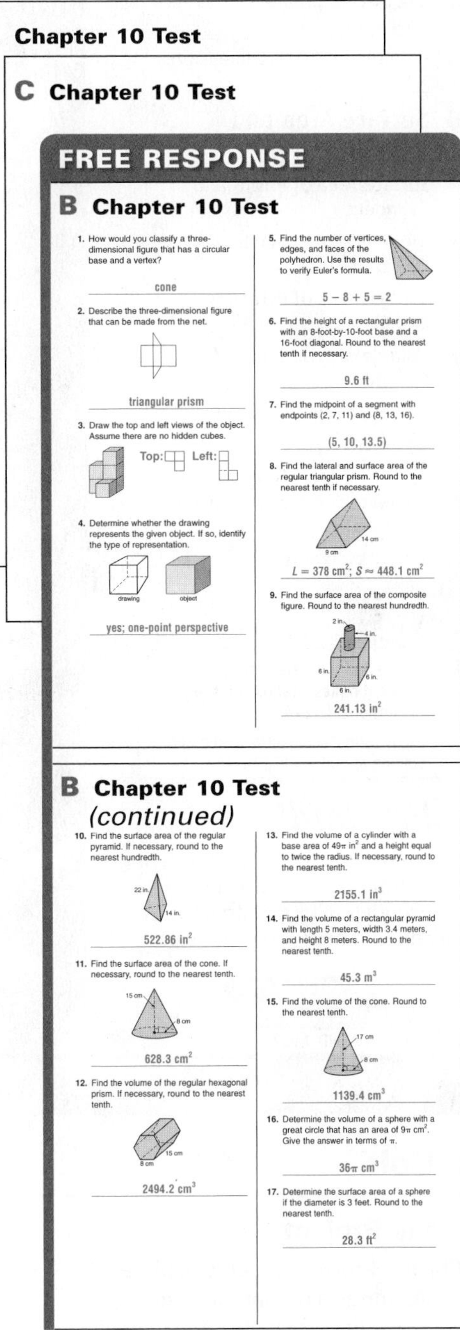

A Chapter 10 Test

C Chapter 10 Test

FREE RESPONSE

B Chapter 10 Test

1. How would you classify a three-dimensional figure that has a circular base and a vertex?
   cone

2. Describe the three-dimensional figure that can be made from the net.
   triangular prism

3. Draw the top and left views of the object. Assume there are no hidden cubes.
   Top: Left:

4. Determine whether the drawing represents the given object. If so, identify the type of representation.
   drawing　object
   yes; one-point perspective

5. Find the number of vertices, edges, and faces of the polyhedron. Use the results to verify Euler's formula.
   $5 - 8 + 5 = 2$

6. Find the height of a rectangular prism with an 8-foot-by-10-foot base and a 16-foot diagonal. Round to the nearest tenth if necessary.
   9.6 ft

7. Find the midpoint of a segment with endpoints (2, 7, 11) and (8, 13, 16).
   (5, 10, 13.5)

8. Find the lateral and surface area of the regular triangular prism. Round to the nearest tenth if necessary.
   14 cm, 9 cm
   $L = 378\text{ cm}^2$; $S \approx 448.1\text{ cm}^2$

9. Find the surface area of the composite figure. Round to the nearest hundredth.
   2 in., 4 in., 6 in., 6 in., 6 in.
   241.13 in^2

B Chapter 10 Test *(continued)*

10. Find the surface area of the regular pyramid. If necessary, round to the nearest hundredth.
    22 in., 14 in.
    522.86 in^2

11. Find the surface area of the cone. If necessary, round to the nearest tenth.
    15 cm, 8 cm
    628.3 cm^2

12. Find the volume of the regular hexagonal prism. If necessary, round to the nearest tenth.
    15 cm, 8 cm
    2494.2 cm^3

13. Find the volume of a cylinder with a base area of $49\pi\text{ in}^2$ and a height equal to twice the radius. If necessary, round to the nearest tenth.
    2155.1 in^3

14. Find the volume of a rectangular pyramid with length 5 meters, width 3.4 meters, and height 8 meters. Round to the nearest tenth.
    45.3 m^3

15. Find the volume of the cone. Round to the nearest tenth.
    17 cm, 8 cm
    1139.4 cm^3

16. Determine the volume of a sphere with a great circle that has an area of $9\pi\text{ cm}^2$. Give the answer in terms of π.
    $36\pi\text{ cm}^3$

17. Determine the surface area of a sphere if the diameter is 3 feet. Round to the nearest tenth.
    28.3 ft^2

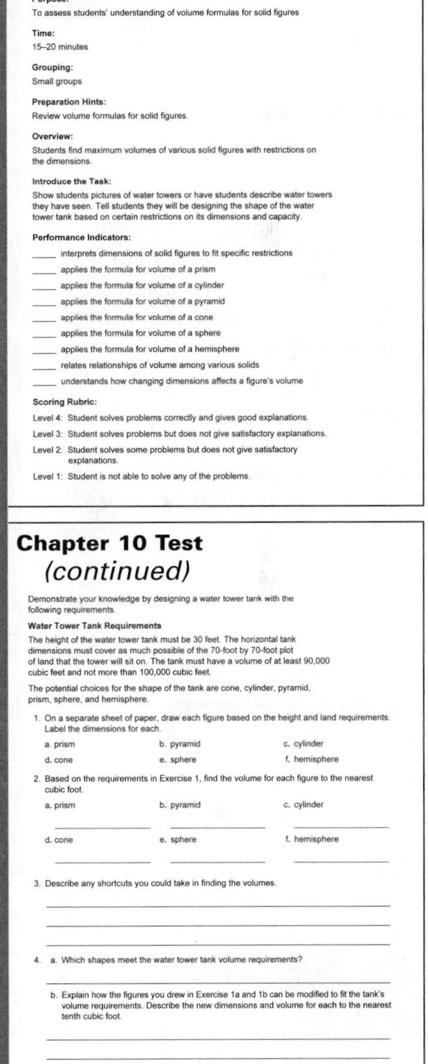

PERFORMANCE ASSESSMENT

Chapter 10 Test

Purpose:
To assess students' understanding of volume formulas for solid figures

Time:
15–20 minutes

Grouping:
Small groups

Preparation Hints:
Review volume formulas for solid figures.

Overview:
Students find maximum volumes of various solid figures with restrictions on the dimensions.

Introduce the Task:
Show students pictures of water towers or have students describe water towers they have seen. Tell students they will be designing the shape of the water tower tank based on certain restrictions on its dimensions and capacity.

Performance Indicators:
_____ interprets dimensions of solid figures to fit specific restrictions
_____ applies the formula for volume of a prism
_____ applies the formula for volume of a cylinder
_____ applies the formula for volume of a pyramid
_____ applies the formula for volume of a cone
_____ applies the formula for volume of a sphere
_____ applies the formula for volume of a hemisphere
_____ relates relationships of volume among various solids
_____ understands how changing dimensions affects a figure's volume

Scoring Rubric:
Level 4: Student solves problems correctly and gives good explanations.
Level 3: Student solves problems but does not give satisfactory explanations.
Level 2: Student solves some problems but does not give satisfactory explanations.
Level 1: Student is not able to solve any of the problems.

Chapter 10 Test *(continued)*

Demonstrate your knowledge by designing a water tower tank with the following requirements.

Water Tower Tank Requirements

The height of the water tower tank must be 30 feet. The horizontal tank dimensions must cover as much possible of the 70-foot by 70-foot plot of land that the tower will sit on. The tank must have a volume of at least 90,000 cubic feet and not more than 100,000 cubic feet.

The potential choices for the shape of the tank are cone, cylinder, pyramid, prism, sphere, and hemisphere.

1. On a separate sheet of paper, draw each figure based on the height and land requirements. Label the dimensions for each.
   a. prism　b. pyramid　c. cylinder
   d. cone　e. sphere　f. hemisphere

2. Based on the requirements in Exercise 1, find the volume for each figure to the nearest cubic foot.
   a. prism ______　b. pyramid ______　c. cylinder ______
   d. cone ______　e. sphere ______　f. hemisphere ______

3. Describe any shortcuts you could take in finding the volumes.
   ____

4. a. Which shapes meet the water tower tank volume requirements?
   ____
   b. Explain how the figures you drew in Exercise 1a and 1b can be modified to fit the tank's volume requirements. Describe the new dimensions and volume for each to the nearest tenth cubic foot.
   ____

Modified chapter tests that address special learning needs are available in *IDEA Works!® Modified Worksheets and Tests.*

Teacher One Stop™

Test & Practice Generator

Create and customize Chapter 10 Tests. Instantly generate multiple test versions, answer keys, and practice versions of test items.

CHAPTER 10

SECTION 10A
Three-Dimensional Figures

On page 678, students use representations of three-dimensional figures to model real-world camping situations.

Exercises designed to prepare students for success on the Multi-Step Test Prep can be found on pages 658, 666, and 675.

SECTION 10B
Surface Area and Volume

On page 724, students find surface area and volume to model a real-world manufacturing situation.

Exercises designed to prepare students for success on the Multi-Step Test Prep can be found on pages 686, 695, 703, 711, and 720.

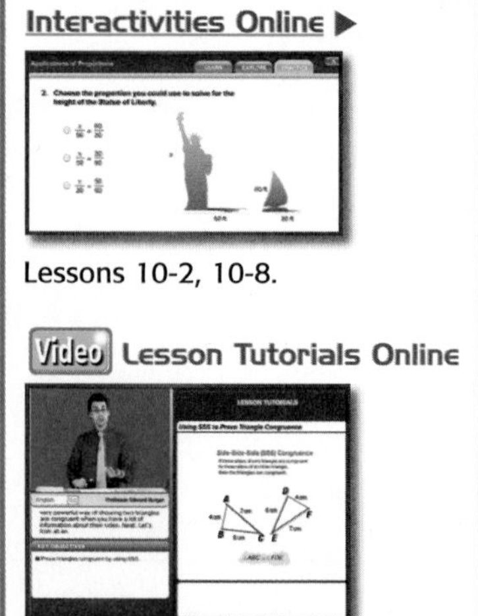

Interactivities Online ▶

Lessons 10-2, 10-8.

Video Lesson Tutorials Online

Lesson Tutorial Videos are available for EVERY example.

CHAPTER 10

Spatial Reasoning

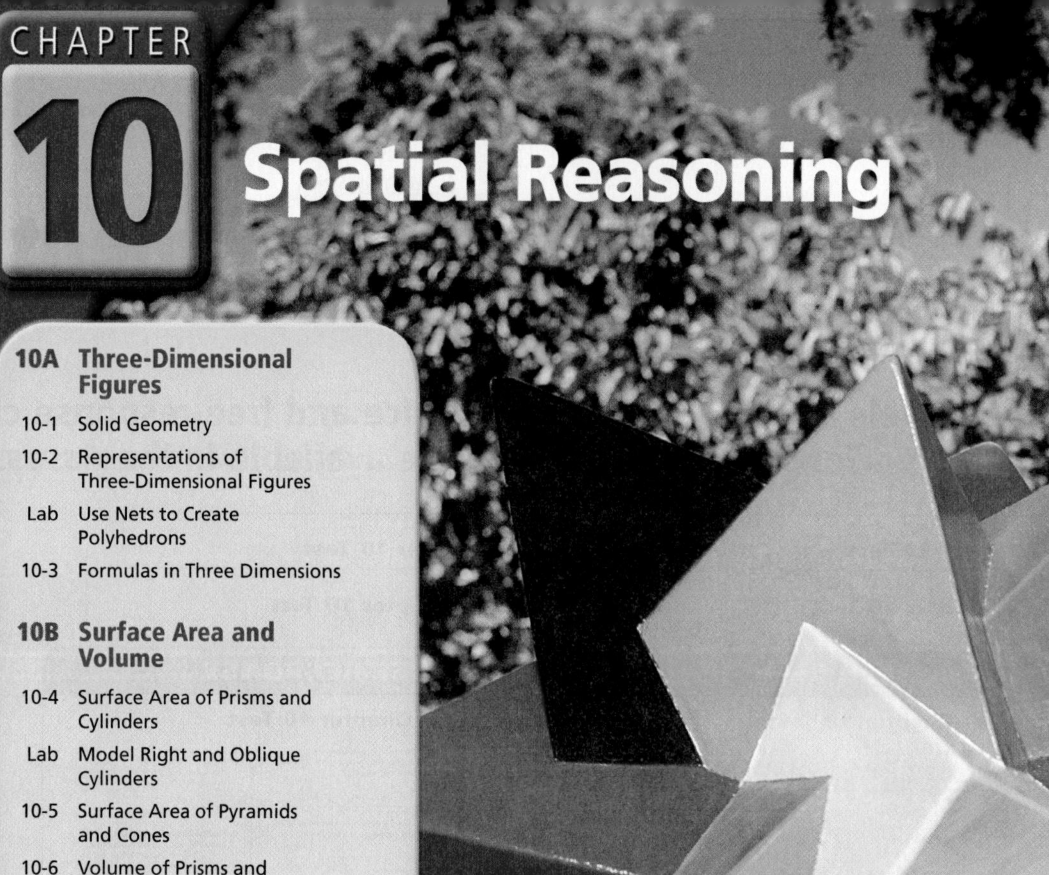

- Create and translate between different representations of three-dimensional figures.
- Apply formulas for surface area and volume to real-world problems.

Solid Gold!

This sculpture shows five intersecting tetrahedrons. You can use *nets* to create models of tetrahedrons and other three-dimensional figures.

Solid Gold

About the Project

In the Chapter Project, students explore nets to build models of Platonic and Archimedean solids. They also apply area and volume formulas to calculate the surface area and volume of one model.

Project Resources

All project resources for teachers and students are provided online.

Materials:

- heavy paper or card stock, scissors, rubber band, glue or tape, puffed rice cereal, cylinders or cans

Vocabulary

Match each term on the left with a definition on the right.

1. equilateral D
2. parallelogram C
3. apothem A
4. composite figure E

A. the distance from the center of a regular polygon to a side of the polygon
B. a quadrilateral with four right angles
C. a quadrilateral with two pairs of parallel sides
D. having all sides congruent
E. a figure made up of simple shapes, such as triangles, rectangles, trapezoids, and circles

Find Area in the Coordinate Plane

Find the area of each figure with the given vertices.

5. $\triangle ABC$ with $A(0, 3)$, $B(5, 3)$, and $C(2, -1)$ 10 units^2
6. rectangle $KLMN$ with $K(-2, 3)$, $L(-2, 7)$, $M(6, 7)$, and $N(6, 3)$ 32 units^2
7. $\odot P$ with center $P(2, 3)$ that passes through the point $Q(-6, 3)$ 64π units^2

Circumference and Area of Circles

Find the circumference and area of each circle. Give your answers in terms of π.

8. 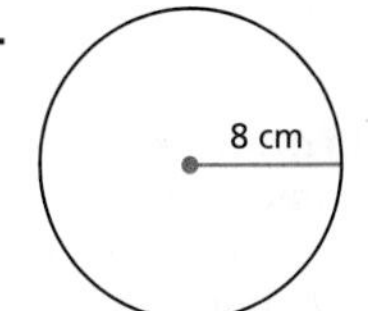

16π cm; 64π cm^2

9. 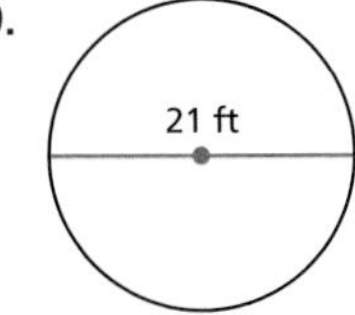

21π ft; 110.25π ft^2

10. 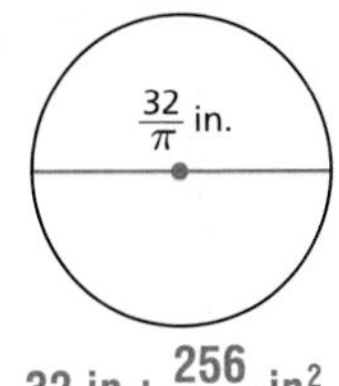

32 in.; $\frac{256}{\pi}$ in^2

Distance and Midpoint Formulas

Find the length and midpoint of the segment with the given endpoints.

11. $A(-3, 2)$ and $B(5, 6)$ 8.9 units; $(1, 4)$
12. $C(-4, -4)$ and $D(2, -3)$ 6.1 units; $(-1, -3.5)$
13. $E(0, 1)$ and $F(-3, 4)$ 4.2 units; $(-1.5, 2.5)$
14. $G(2, -5)$ and $H(-2, -2)$ 5 units; $(0, -3.5)$

Evaluate Expressions

Evaluate each expression for the given values of the variables.

15. $\sqrt{\frac{A}{\pi}}$ for $A = 121\pi$ cm^2 11 cm
16. $\frac{2A}{P}$ for $A = 128$ ft^2 and $P = 32$ ft 8 ft
17. $\sqrt{c^2 - a^2}$ for $a = 8$ m and $c = 17$ m 15 m
18. $\frac{2A}{h} - b_1$ for $A = 60$ in^2, $b_1 = 8$ in., and $h = 6$ in. 12 in.

CHAPTER 10

ARE YOU READY?

Organizer

Objective: Assess students' understanding of prerequisite skills.

Prerequisite Skills

Find Area in the Coordinate Plane
Circumference and Area of Circles
Distance and Midpoint Formulas
Evaluate Expressions

Assessing Prior Knowledge

Diagnose and Prescribe

Use this page to determine whether intervention is necessary or whether enrichment is appropriate.

Resources

 ***Are You Ready? Intervention and Enrichment*** **Worksheets**

 ***Are You Ready?* CD-ROM**

 ***Are You Ready?* Online**

my.hrw.com

ARE YOU READY? Diagnose and Prescribe

Prerequisite Skill	*Are You Ready? Intervention*, Chapter 10 Worksheets	CD-ROM	Online
Find Area in the Coordinate Plane	Skill 38	Activity 38	Diagnose and Prescribe Online
Circumference and Area of Circles	Skill 39	Activity 39	
Distance and Midpoint Formulas	Skill 73	Activity 73	
Evaluate Expressions	Skill 60	Activity 60	

***Are You Ready? Enrichment*, Chapter 10**

Worksheets
CD-ROM
Online

CHAPTER 10 **Study Guide: Preview**

Organizer

Objective: Help students organize the new concepts they will learn in Chapter 10.

Online Edition
Multilingual Glossary

Countdown Week 22

Resources

Teacher One Stop™
PuzzleView

***Multilingual Glossary* Online**

go.hrw.com
KEYWORD: MG7 Glossary

Answers to *Vocabulary Connections*

1. Polygon, polynomial; a polygon has many (3 or more) sides and a polynomial can have many terms.
2. A cone looks like the tip of a sharpened pencil.
3. the outside of something; the area of all the faces or surfaces on the outside of the figure
4. A net is a figure that can be folded to make a three-dimensional object.

CHAPTER 10

Study Guide: Preview

Where You've Been

Previously, you

- analyzed properties of figures in a plane.
- found the perimeters and areas of triangles, circles, polygons, and composite figures.
- studied the effects of changing dimensions of polygons proportionally.

In This Chapter

You will study

- properties of three-dimensional figures.
- the surface areas and volumes of three-dimensional figures.
- the effects of changing dimensions of three-dimensional figures proportionally.

Where You're Going

You can use the skills learned in this chapter

- in all your future math classes, including Precalculus.
- to study other fields such as chemistry, physics, and architecture.
- to solve problems concerning interior design, packaging, and construction.

Key Vocabulary/Vocabulario

cone	cono
cylinder	cilindro
net	plantilla
polyhedron	poliedro
prism	prisma
pyramid	pirámide
sphere	esfera
surface area	área total
volume	volumen

Vocabulary Connections

To become familiar with some of the vocabulary terms in the chapter, consider the following questions. You may refer to the chapter, the glossary, or a dictionary if you like.

1. The word **polyhedron** begins with the root *poly-*. List some other words that begin with *poly-*. What do all of these words have in common?
2. The word **cone** comes from the root *ko-*, which means "to sharpen." Think of sharpening a pencil. How do you think this relates to a cone?
3. What does the word *surface* mean? What do you think the **surface area** of a three-dimensional figure is?
4. The figure shown is a **net** for a cube. How do you think a net is related to a three-dimensional object?

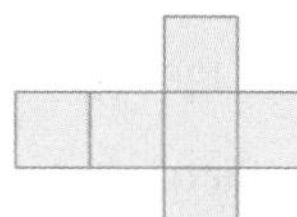

Writing Strategy: Draw Three-Dimensional Figures

When you encounter a three-dimensional figure such as a cylinder, cone, sphere, prism, or pyramid, it may help you to make a quick sketch so that you can visualize its shape.

Use these tips to help you draw quick sketches of three-dimensional figures.

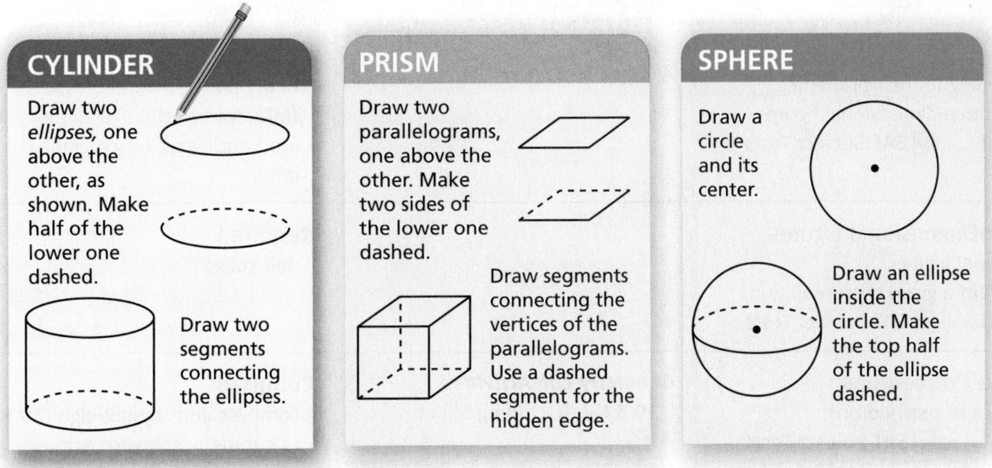

CYLINDER
Draw two *ellipses,* one above the other, as shown. Make half of the lower one dashed.
Draw two segments connecting the ellipses.
PRISM
Draw two parallelograms, one above the other. Make two sides of the lower one dashed.
Draw segments connecting the vertices of the parallelograms. Use a dashed segment for the hidden edge.
SPHERE
Draw a circle and its center.
Draw an ellipse inside the circle. Make the top half of the ellipse dashed.

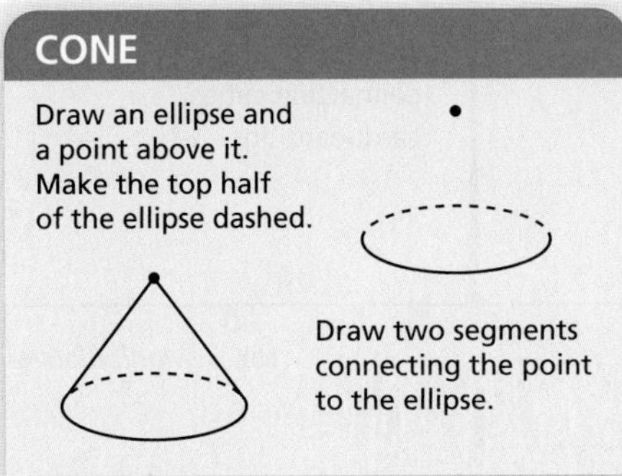

CONE
Draw an ellipse and a point above it. Make the top half of the ellipse dashed.
Draw two segments connecting the point to the ellipse.

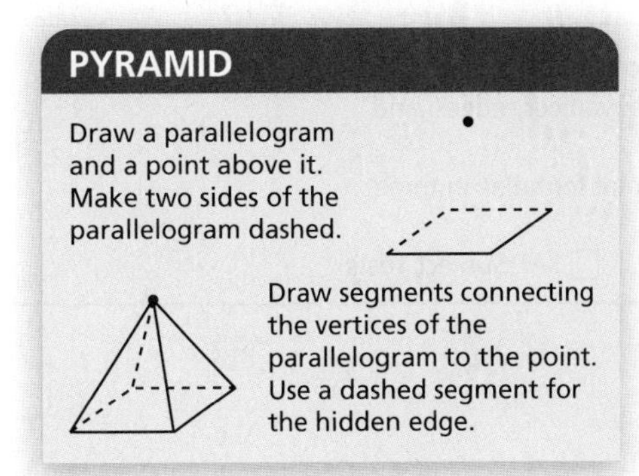

PYRAMID
Draw a parallelogram and a point above it. Make two sides of the parallelogram dashed.
Draw segments connecting the vertices of the parallelogram to the point. Use a dashed segment for the hidden edge.

Try This

1. Explain and show how to draw a *cube,* a prism with equal length, width, and height.
2. Draw a prism, starting with two hexagons. (*Hint:* Draw the hexagons as if you were viewing them at an angle.)

3. Draw a pyramid, starting with a triangle and a point above the triangle.

Reading and Writing Math CHAPTER 10

Organizer

Objective: Help students apply strategies to understand and retain key concepts.

Online Edition

Resources

Chapter 10 Resource Book
Reading Strategies

Study Strategy: Drawing Three-Dimensional Figures

Discuss Review the shapes cylinder, prism, sphere, cone, and pyramid. Discuss how a sketch of a three-dimensional figure can help solve problems.

Extend Once students are comfortable with the drawings on this page, ask them to draw the figures rotated so that the bases are vertical rather than horizontal.

Answers to *Try This*

1. Follow the same steps for drawing a prism, but make the sides of the parallelogram and the ht. of the prism the same length.
2. 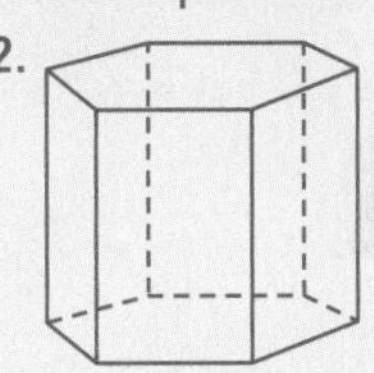
3. 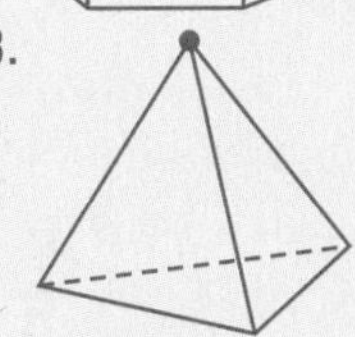

Reading Connection

The Platonic Solids Book
by Dan Radin

For 2500 years, the Platonic solids have exercised a hold on the human imagination that has been at once mathematical, aesthetic, and philosophical. This book explores all three aspects. Along the way, the author provides templates and detailed instructions for making each solid from paper.

Activity Challenge students to make the 20-sided icosahedron.

SECTION **10A**

Three-Dimensional Figures

One-Minute Section Planner

Lesson	Lab Resources	Materials
Lesson 10-1 Solid Geometry • Classify three-dimensional figures according to their properties. • Use nets and cross sections to analyze three-dimensional figures. ☐ SAT-10 ☑ NAEP ☑ ACT ☐ SAT ☑ SAT Subject Tests		**Optional** heavy paper, tape, 3-D models (MK), straws, chenille stems, food packages, 1-inch graph paper
Lesson 10-2 Representations of Three-Dimensional Figures • Draw representations of three-dimensional figures. • Recognize a three-dimensional figure from a given representation. ☐ SAT-10 ☑ NAEP ☑ ACT ☐ SAT ☑ SAT Subject Tests		**Required** unit cubes
10-3 Geometry Lab Use Nets to Create Polyhedrons • Use nets to create and explore properties of polyhedrons. ☐ SAT-10 ☐ NAEP ☐ ACT ☐ SAT ☐ SAT Subject Tests	***Geometry Lab Activities*** 10-3 Lab Recording Sheet	**Required** compass and straightedge (MK) or geometry software, scissors, tape
Lesson 10-3 Formulas in Three Dimensions • Apply Euler's formula to find the number of vertices, edges, and faces of a polyhedron. • Develop and apply the distance and midpoint formulas in three dimensions. ☐ SAT-10 ☐ NAEP ☐ ACT ☐ SAT ☐ SAT Subject Tests		**Optional** connecting cubes, cardboard box

MK = *Manipulatives Kit*

Math Background

REPRESENTATIONS OF THREE-DIMENSIONAL FIGURES

Lesson 10-2

Representing a three-dimensional object on a two-dimensional sheet of paper presents several challenges. Since ancient times, mathematicians, engineers, and artists have worked to develop drawing techniques to overcome these obstacles. However, each technique comes with its own set of advantages and disadvantages.

An *orthographic drawing* (or orthographic projection) shows multiple views of an object. Each orthographic view shows one side of the object (front, top, etc.) without distortion, so such drawings are especially useful for house plans and other diagrams that are used in construction.

The views of an orthographic drawing may be found by projecting the object onto the faces of a rectangular prism that surrounds the object. The figure illustrates how this projection technique is used to find three views of an object.

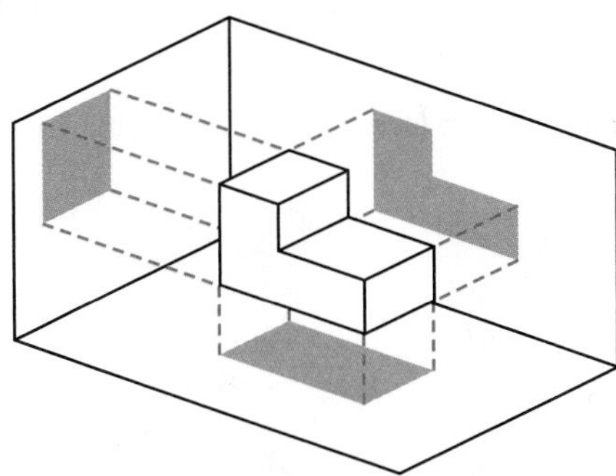

The disadvantage of an orthographic drawing is that imagining the overall appearance of the object based on the separate views may be difficult. This problem is solved by *pictorial drawings*, which show several sides of an object at the same time. An *isometric drawing* (or isometric projection) is an example of a pictorial drawing in which three sides are shown from a corner view.

In an isometric drawing, edges of the object that are parallel are rendered as parallel lines on the page. While this simplifies the drawing technique, it disregards the fact that objects appear to get smaller as they recede into the distance. Thus, gauging depth in complex isometric drawings can be difficult. The Dutch artist M.C. Escher used this limitation of isometric drawings to create some of his best known depictions of "impossible figures."

In contrast to isometric drawings, a *perspective drawing* is based on the idea that nonvertical parallel lines appear to converge in the distance. While this results in a more realistic representation of three-dimensional objects, it also results in *foreshortening*. For example, in a perspective drawing, a horizontal circle may appear to be an ellipse.

POLYHEDRONS

Lesson 10-3

A *polyhedron* is a three-dimensional figure formed by polygons that intersect only at their edges. Polyhedrons are the three-dimensional analogs of polygons and are usually named by the number of faces: tetrahedron (4 faces), pentahedron (5 faces), and so on.

In a *regular polyhedron*, the faces are congruent regular polygons and the same number of faces intersect at each vertex. Note that in this book, the study of polyhedrons is restricted to convex polyhedrons, so all regular polyhedrons are also assumed to be convex. It is possible to use Euler's Formula, which relates the number of vertices, edges, and faces of any convex polyhedron, to prove that there are exactly five convex regular polyhedrons. These polyhedrons, known since antiquity, are called the *Platonic solids* and are depicted on page 669.

Allowing non-convex polyhedrons results in four additional regular polyhedrons, as shown at right. These are known as the Kepler-Poinsot solids.

Great stellated dodecahedron

Great icosahedron

Small stellated dodecahedron

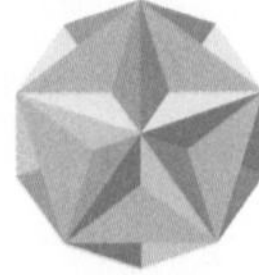

Great dodecahedron

10-1 Organizer

Pacing: Traditional 1 day
Block $\frac{1}{2}$ day

Objectives: Classify three-dimensional figures according to their properties.

Use nets and cross sections to analyze three-dimensional figures.

Online Edition
Tutorial Videos

Countdown Week 22

Power Presentations with PowerPoint®

Warm Up

Classify each polygon.

1. a polygon with three congruent sides equilateral triangle
2. a polygon with six congruent sides and six congruent angles regular hexagon
3. a polygon with four sides and with opposite sides parallel and congruent parallelogram

Also available on transparency

Math Humor

Q: What's the angriest part of a 3-D figure?

A: The cross section.

10-1 Solid Geometry

Objectives
Classify three-dimensional figures according to their properties.

Use nets and cross sections to analyze three-dimensional figures.

Vocabulary
face
edge
vertex
prism
cylinder
pyramid
cone
cube
net
cross section

Why learn this?

Some farmers in Japan grow cube-shaped watermelons to save space in small refrigerators. Each fruit costs about the equivalent of U.S. $80. (See Example 4.)

Three-dimensional figures, or *solids*, can be made up of flat or curved surfaces. Each flat surface is called a **face**. An **edge** is the segment that is the intersection of two faces. A **vertex** is the point that is the intersection of three or more faces.

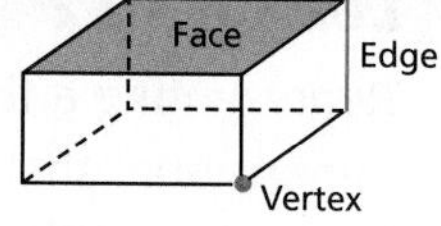

Know it! Note

Three-Dimensional Figures

TERM	EXAMPLE
A **prism** is formed by two parallel congruent polygonal faces called *bases* connected by faces that are parallelograms.	Bases
A **cylinder** is formed by two parallel congruent circular bases and a curved surface that connects the bases.	Bases
A **pyramid** is formed by a polygonal base and triangular faces that meet at a common vertex.	Vertex, Base
A **cone** is formed by a circular base and a curved surface that connects the base to a vertex.	Vertex, Base

A **cube** is a prism with six square faces. Other prisms and pyramids are named for the shape of their bases.

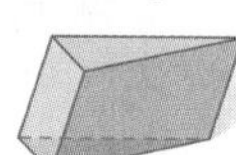
Triangular prism

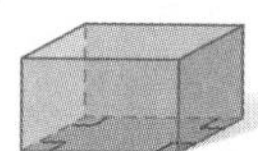
Rectangular prism

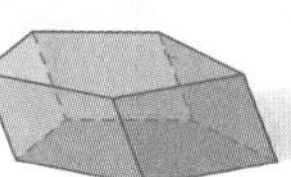
Pentagonal prism

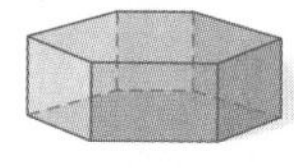
Hexagonal prism

Triangular pyramid

Rectangular pyramid

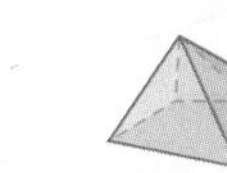
Pentagonal pyramid

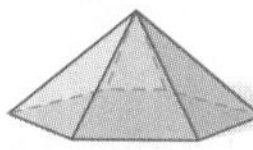
Hexagonal pyramid

State Resources

1 Introduce

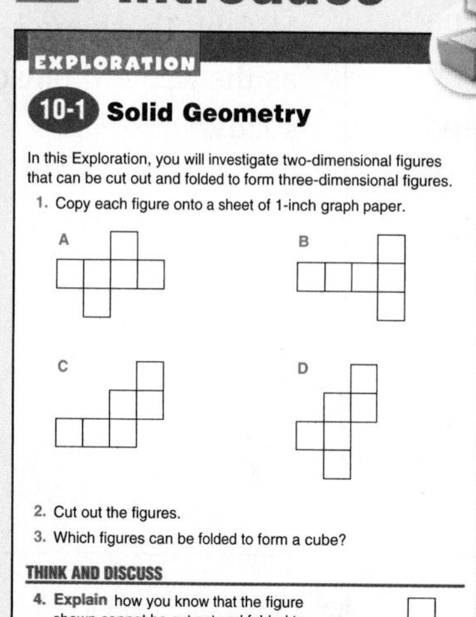

EXPLORATION
10-1 Solid Geometry
In this Exploration, you will investigate two-dimensional figures that can be cut out and folded to form three-dimensional figures.
1. Copy each figure onto a sheet of 1-inch graph paper.
A
B
C
D
2. Cut out the figures.
3. Which figures can be folded to form a cube?
THINK AND DISCUSS
4. Explain how you know that the figure shown cannot be cut out and folded to

Motivate

Cut six congruent squares out of heavy paper and arrange them on an overhead projector. Have students guess whether the arrangement of squares can be folded to make a cube. Then tape the squares together and test the conjecture. Try several arrangements, and have students try to state a rule for whether a given arrangement will work.

Explorations and answers are provided in *Alternate Openers: Explorations Transparencies.*

EXAMPLE 1 Classifying Three-Dimensional Figures

Classify each figure. Name the vertices, edges, and bases.

A

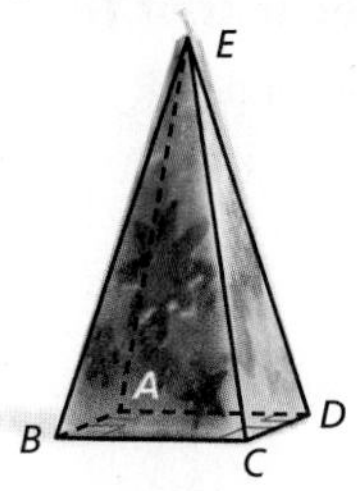

rectangular pyramid
vertices: A, B, C, D, E
edges: $\overline{AB}, \overline{BC}, \overline{CD}, \overline{AD}, \overline{AE}, \overline{BE}, \overline{CE}, \overline{DE}$
base: rectangle $ABCD$

B

cylinder
vertices: none
edges: none
bases: $\odot P$ and $\odot Q$

1a. cone; vertex: N; edges: none; base: $\odot M$

1b. triangular prism; vertices: T, U, V, W, X, Y; edges: $\overline{TU}, \overline{TV}, \overline{UV}, \overline{TW}, \overline{UX}, \overline{VY}, \overline{WX}, \overline{WY}, \overline{XY}$; bases: $\triangle TUV$, $\triangle WXY$

CHECK IT OUT! Classify each figure. Name the vertices, edges, and bases.

1a.

1b.

A **net** is a diagram of the surfaces of a three-dimensional figure that can be folded to form the three-dimensional figure. To identify a three-dimensional figure from a net, look at the number of faces and the shape of each face.

EXAMPLE 2 Identifying a Three-Dimensional Figure From a Net

Describe the three-dimensional figure that can be made from the given net.

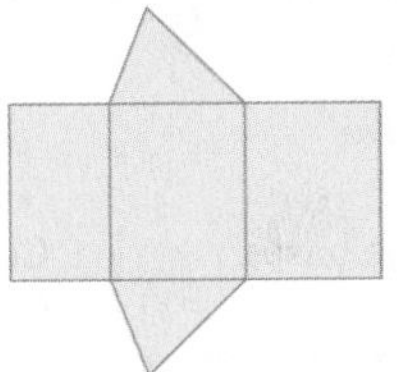

The net has two congruent triangular faces. The remaining faces are parallelograms, so the net forms a triangular prism.

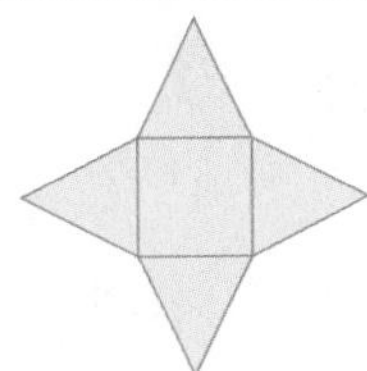

The net has one square face. The remaining faces are triangles, so the net forms a square pyramid.

CHECK IT OUT! Describe the three-dimensional figure that can be made from the given net.

2a.

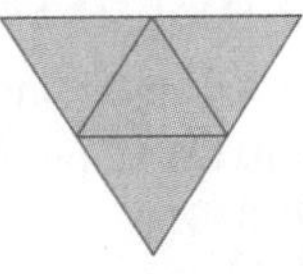

triangular pyramid

2b.

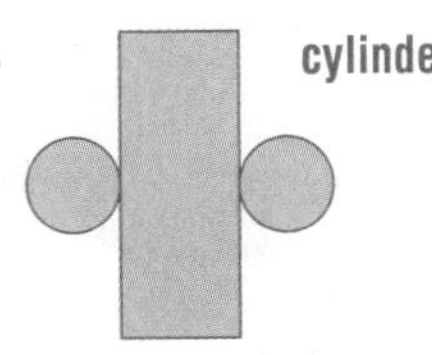

cylinder

COMMON ERROR ALERT

Students may confuse prisms and pyramids. Remind them of the shape of the Egyptian pyramids.

Power Presentations with PowerPoint®

Additional Examples

Example 1

Classify each figure. Name the vertices, edges, and bases.

A.

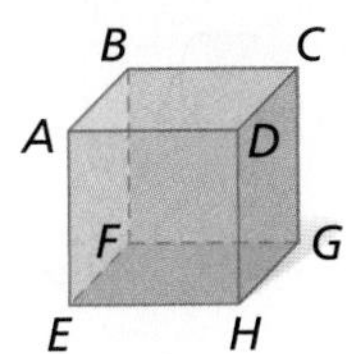

cube; vertices: A, B, C, D, E, F, G, H; edges: $\overline{AB}, \overline{BC}, \overline{CD}, \overline{DA}, \overline{EF}, \overline{FG}, \overline{GH}, \overline{HE}, \overline{AE}, \overline{BF}, \overline{CG}, \overline{DH}$; bases: possible answer: $ABCD$ and $EFGH$

B.

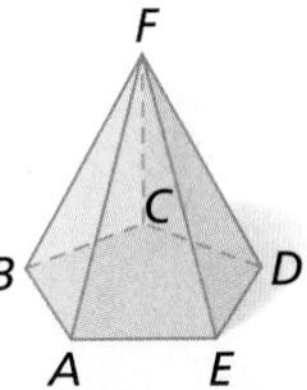

pentagonal pyramid; vertices: A, B, C, D, E, F; edges: $\overline{AB}, \overline{BC}, \overline{CD}, \overline{DE}, \overline{EA}, \overline{AF}, \overline{BF}, \overline{CF}, \overline{DF}, \overline{EF}$; base: $ABCDE$

Example 2

Describe the three-dimensional figure that can be made from the given net.

A.

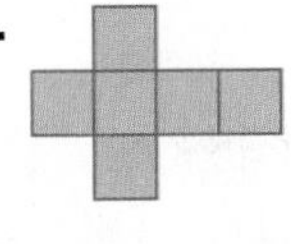

cube

B.

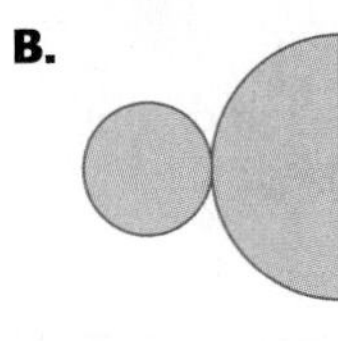

cone

2 Teach

Guided Instruction

Use a set of plastic or wooden models (MK) to demonstrate the meaning of *face, edge, vertex,* and *base*. Describe the characteristics of prisms, cylinders, pyramids, and cones. Discuss classifying figures and naming their vertices, edges, and bases.

Teaching Tip **Kinesthetic** Use paper or card-stock copies of nets to demonstrate how they can be folded to form three-dimensional figures.

Reaching All Learners

Through Concrete Manipulatives

Give students straws or chenille stems and have them build models of three-dimensional figures. Give students cereal boxes and other boxes to take apart and form nets. Illustrate cross sections using rubber bands around solid models.

Teaching Tip **Auditory** A way to remember an important fact about three-dimensional figures is the phrase "All bases are faces, but not all faces are bases."

INTERVENTION

Questioning Strategies

EXAMPLE 1

- In a pyramid, how is the number of faces related to the shape of its base? in a prism?

EXAMPLE 2

- How can you tell what three-dimensional figure can be made from a given net?

Power Presentations with PowerPoint®

Additional Examples

Example 3

Describe each cross section.

A.

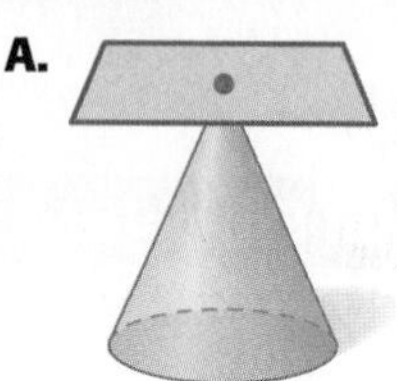

a point

B.

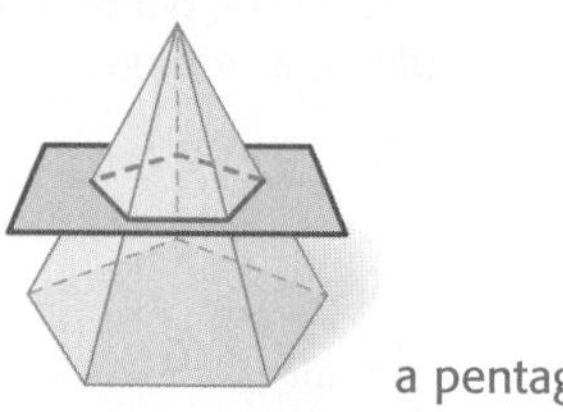

a pentagon

Example 4

A piece of cheese is a prism with equilateral triangular bases. How can you slice the cheese to make each shape?

A. an equilateral triangle Cut parallel to the bases.

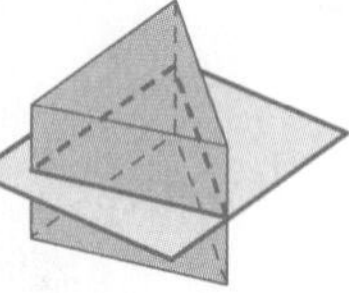

B. a rectangle Cut perpendicular to the bases.

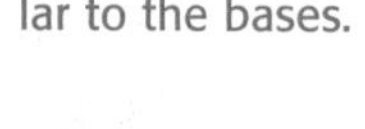

INTERVENTION
Questioning Strategies

EXAMPLES 3–4

- When is a cross section of a prism congruent to its bases?

A **cross section** is the intersection of a three-dimensional figure and a plane.

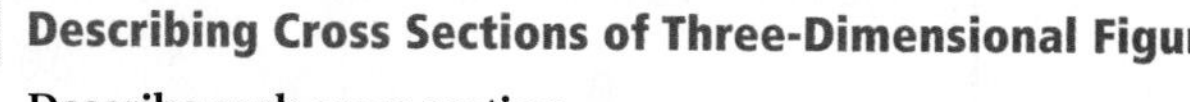

EXAMPLE 3 Describing Cross Sections of Three-Dimensional Figures

Describe each cross section.

A

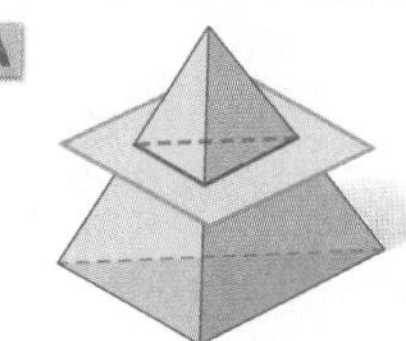

The cross section is a triangle.

B

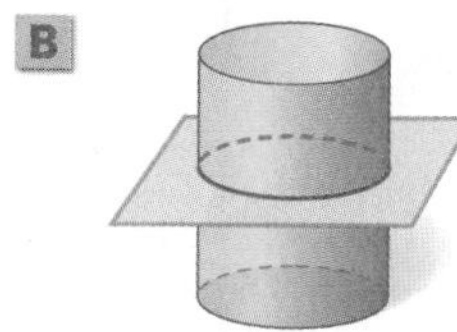

The cross section is a circle.

CHECK IT OUT! Describe each cross section.

3a.

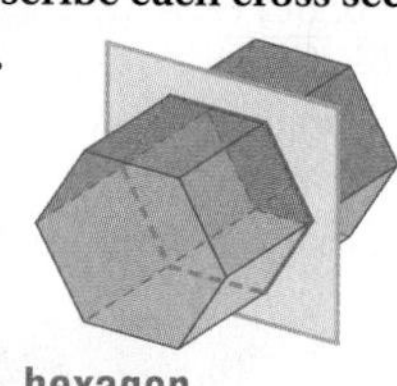

hexagon

3b.

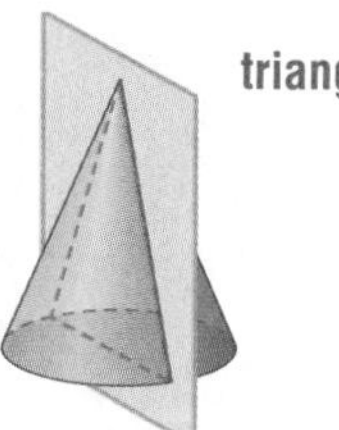

triangle

EXAMPLE 4 *Food Application*

A chef is slicing a cube-shaped watermelon for a buffet. How can the chef cut the watermelon to make a slice of each shape?

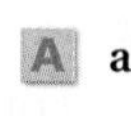

A a square

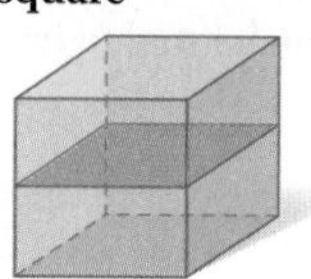

Cut parallel to the bases.

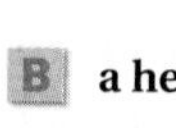

B a hexagon

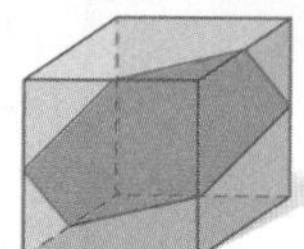

Cut through the midpoints of the edges.

4.

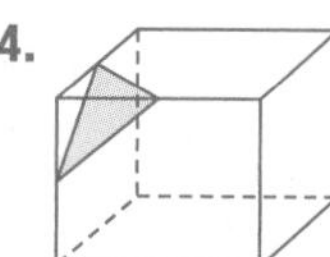

CHECK IT OUT!

4. How can a chef cut a cube-shaped watermelon to make slices with triangular faces? Cut through the midpoints of 3 edges that meet at 1 vertex.

THINK AND DISCUSS

Know it! Note

1. Compare prisms and cylinders.
2. **GET ORGANIZED** Copy and complete the graphic organizer.

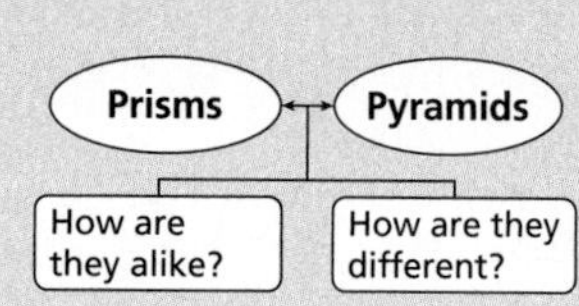

3 Close

Summarize

Review prisms, cylinders, pyramids, and cones and list the similarities and differences among them. 1) Prisms and cylinders both have two bases, while pyramids and cones both have only one base. 2) Prisms and pyramids have only flat surfaces, while cylinders and cones have curved surfaces. Review how a three-dimensional figure can be identified from a net by looking at the net's shape and number of faces.

ONGOING ASSESSMENT

and INTERVENTION

Diagnose ***Before*** **the Lesson**
10-1 Warm Up, TE p. 654

Monitor ***During*** **the Lesson**
Check It Out! Exercises, SE pp. 655–656
Questioning Strategies, TE pp. 655–656

Assess ***After*** **the Lesson**
10-1 Lesson Quiz, TE p. 660
Alternative Assessment, TE p. 660

Answers to *Think and Discuss*

1. Both prisms and cylinders have 2 congruent parallel bases. The bases of a prism are polygons, and the bases of a cylinder are circles. The bases of a prism are connected by parallelograms, and the bases of a cylinder are connected by a curved surface.
2. See p. A8.

10-1 Exercises

go.hrw.com
Homework Help Online
KEYWORD: MG7 10-1
Parent Resources Online
KEYWORD: MG7 Parent

GUIDED PRACTICE

1. **Vocabulary** A __?__ has two circular bases. (*prism, cylinder,* or *cone*) cylinder

SEE EXAMPLE 1 p. 655

Classify each figure. Name the vertices, edges, and bases.

2.

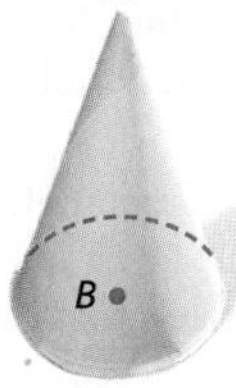

3.

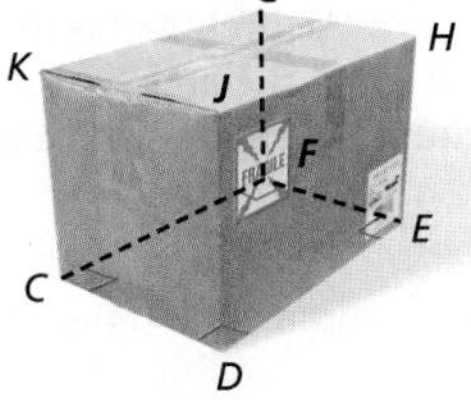

4.

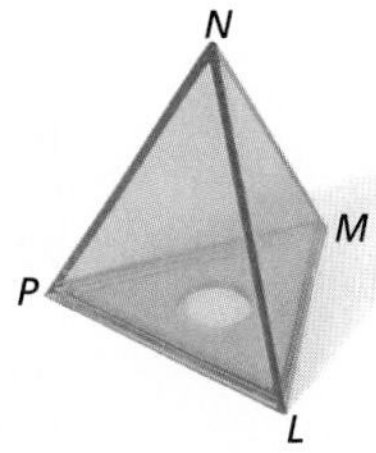

SEE EXAMPLE 2 p. 655

Describe the three-dimensional figure that can be made from the given net.

5. 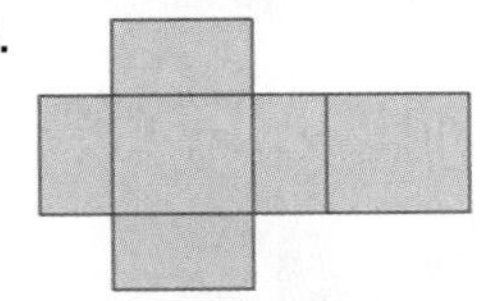
rectangular prism

6. 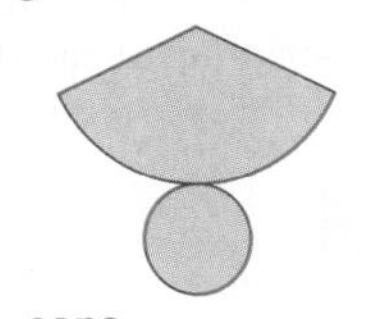
cone

7. 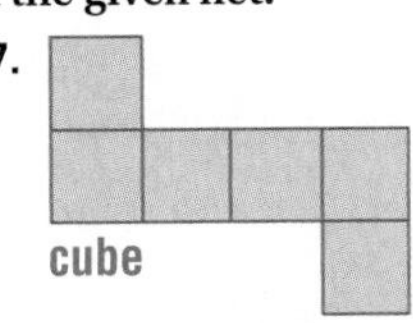
cube

SEE EXAMPLE 3 p. 656

Describe each cross section.

8. 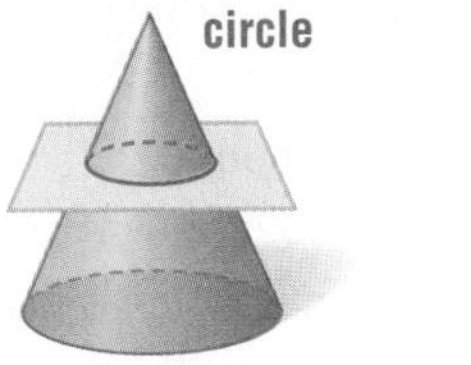 circle

9. 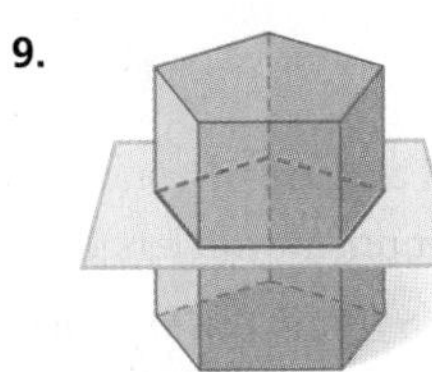
pentagon

10. 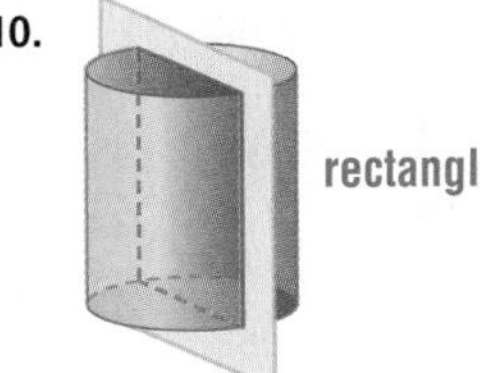
rectangle

SEE EXAMPLE 4 p. 656

Art A sculptor has a cylindrical piece of clay. How can the sculptor slice the clay to make a slice of each given shape?

11. a circle
Cut parallel to the bases.

12. a rectangle
Cut perpendicular to the bases.

PRACTICE AND PROBLEM SOLVING

Independent Practice

For Exercises	See Example
13–15	1
16–18	2
19–21	3
22–23	4

Extra Practice
Skills Practice p. S22
Application Practice p. S37

Classify each figure. Name the vertices, edges, and bases.

13. 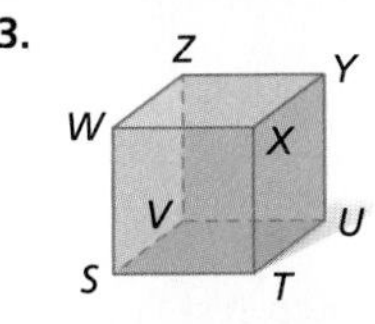

14. 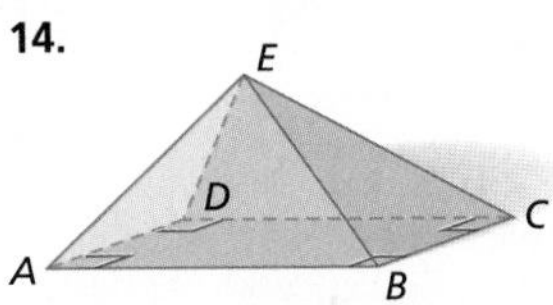

15. 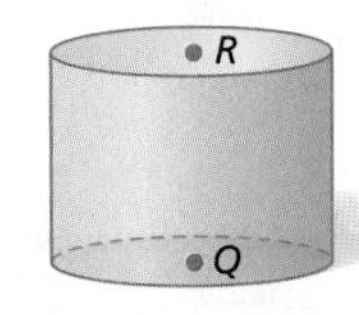

Describe the three-dimensional figure that can be made from the given net.

16. 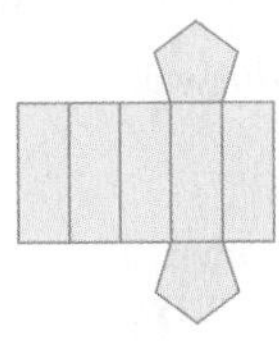

17. 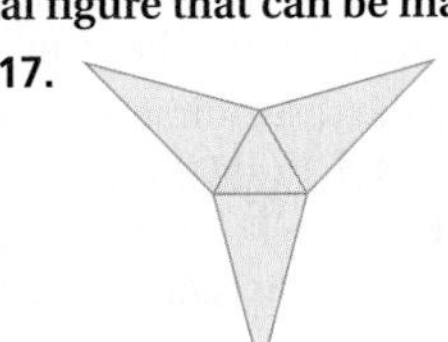

18. 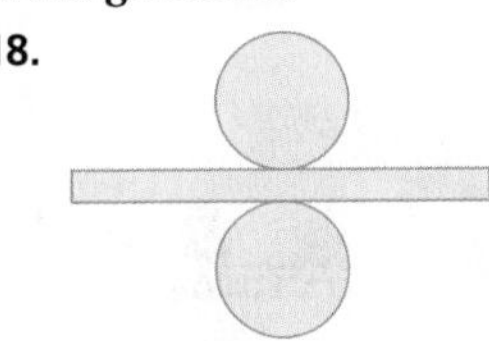

Answers

2. cone; vertex: A; edges: none; base: ⊙B
3. rectangular prism; vertices: C, D, E, F, G, H, J, K; edges: $\overline{GH}$, $\overline{GK}$, $\overline{HJ}$, $\overline{JK}$, $\overline{GF}$, $\overline{HE}$, $\overline{JD}$, $\overline{KC}$, $\overline{FC}$, $\overline{CD}$, $\overline{DE}$, $\overline{EF}$; bases: GHJK, CDEF
4. triangular pyramid; vertices: L, M, N, P; edges: $\overline{LM}$, $\overline{LN}$, $\overline{LP}$, $\overline{MN}$, $\overline{MP}$, $\overline{NP}$; base: △LMP
13. cube; vertices: S, T, U, V, W, X, Y, Z; edges: $\overline{ST}$, $\overline{TU}$, $\overline{UV}$, $\overline{VS}$, $\overline{SW}$, $\overline{TX}$, $\overline{UY}$, $\overline{VZ}$, $\overline{WX}$, $\overline{XY}$, $\overline{YZ}$, $\overline{ZW}$; bases: STUV, WXYZ
14. rectangular pyramid; vertices: A, B, C, D, E; edges: $\overline{AB}$, $\overline{BC}$, $\overline{CD}$, $\overline{AD}$, $\overline{AE}$, $\overline{BE}$, $\overline{CE}$, $\overline{DE}$; base: ABCD
15. cylinder; vertices: none; edges: none; bases: ⊙R, ⊙Q
16. pentagonal prism
17. triangular pyramid
18. cylinder

10-1 Exercises

Assignment Guide

Assign *Guided Practice* exercises as necessary.

If you finished Examples 1–2
Basic 13–18, 28–31
Average 13–18, 28–32
Advanced 13–18, 28–33

If you finished Examples 1–4
Basic 13–38, 41–44, 52–59
Average 13–25, 26–32 even, 33–46, 52–59
Advanced 13–23, 24–32 even, 33–37, 39–59

Homework Quick Check
Quickly check key concepts.
Exercises: 14, 16, 20, 22, 28

Teaching Tip

Kinesthetic For **Exercises 5–7** and **16–18,** students may have difficulty visualizing the three-dimensional figures. Suggest that they trace the nets onto a piece of paper and assemble the figures.

State Resources

go.hrw.com
State Resources Online
KEYWORD: MG7 Resources

Exercise 37 involves classifying a three-dimensional figure that represents a camping tent and drawing a net for this figure. This exercise prepares students for the Multi-Step Test Prep on page 678.

Answers

31. 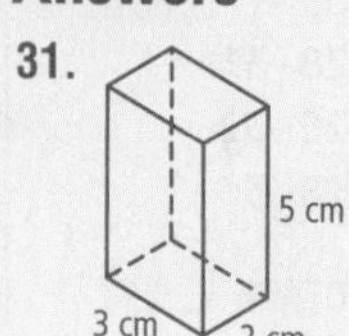

32. 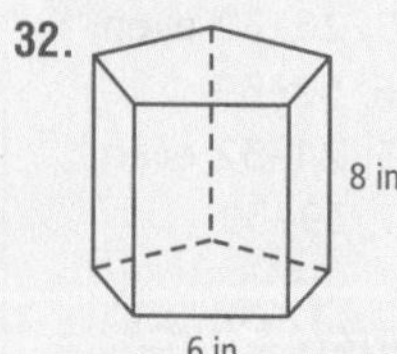

33. 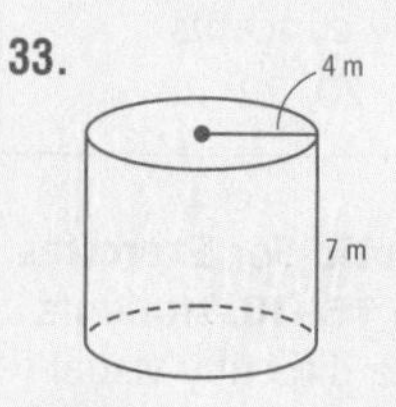

34. 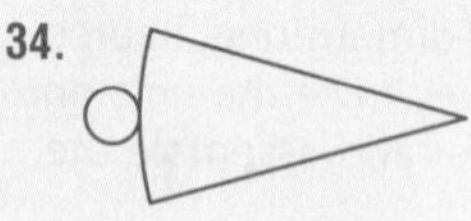

35. 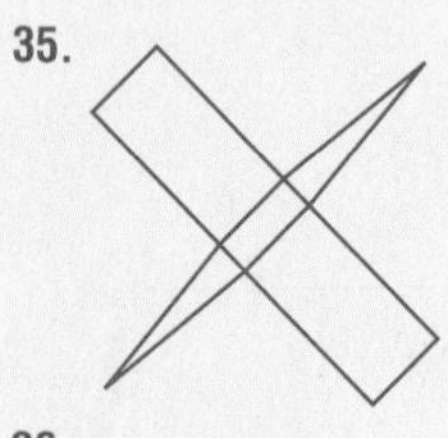

36. 

37c. See p. A26.

Describe each cross section.

19. 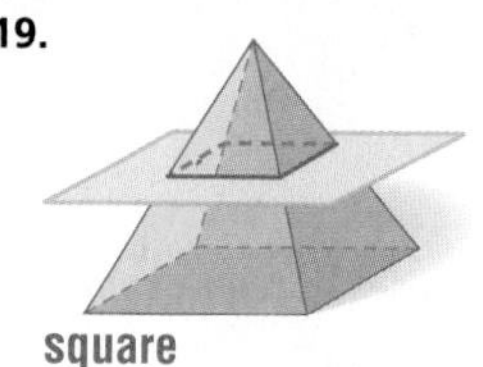

square

20. 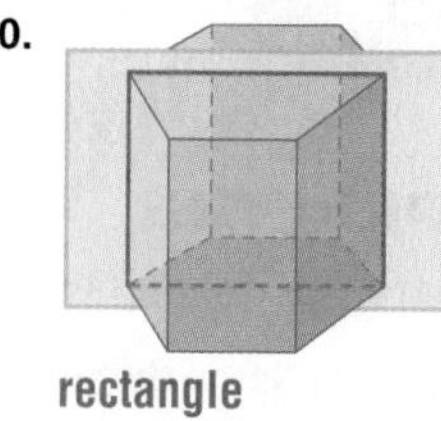

rectangle

21. 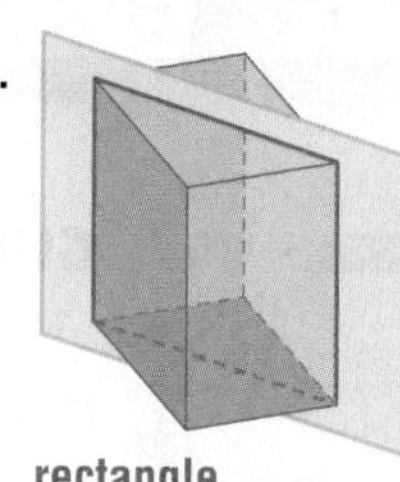

rectangle

Architecture An architect is drawing plans for a building that is a hexagonal prism. How could the architect draw a cutaway of the building that shows a cross section in the shape of each given figure?

22. a hexagon
Cut parallel to the ground.

23. a rectangle
Cut perpendicular to the ground.

Name a three-dimensional figure from which a cross section in the given shape can be made. 24–27. Possible answers:

24. square
cube

25. rectangle
rectangular prism

26. circle
cylinder

27. hexagon
hexagonal prism

Write a verbal description of each figure.

28. 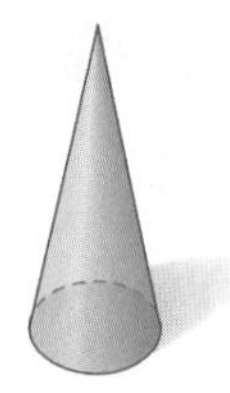

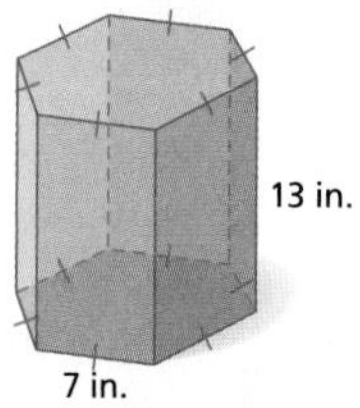

29. 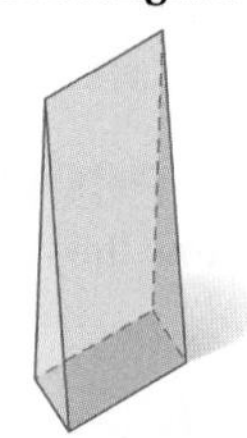

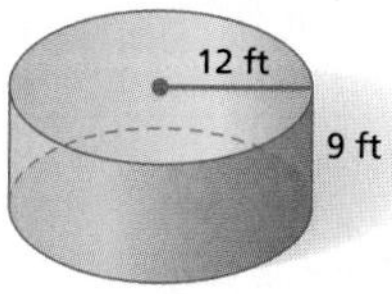

30. 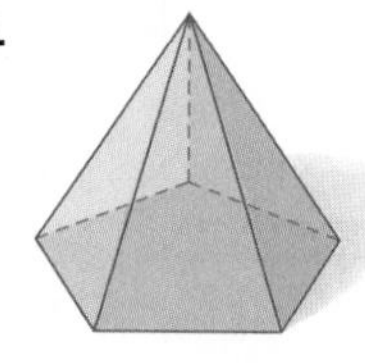

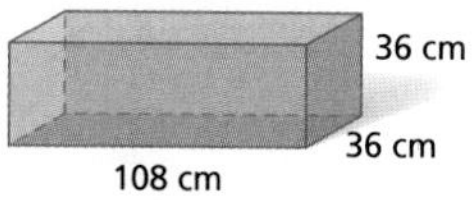

28–30. Possible answers:

28. The figure is a hexagonal prism whose bases are regular hexagons with 7 in. sides. The height of the prism is 13 in.

29. The figure is a cylinder whose bases each have a radius of 12 ft. The height of the cylinder is 9 ft.

30. The figure is a square prism with 36 cm by 36 cm bases and a height of 108 cm.

Draw and label a figure that meets each description.

31. rectangular prism with length 3 cm, width 2 cm, and height 5 cm

32. regular pentagonal prism with side length 6 in. and height 8 in.

33. cylinder with radius 4 m and height 7 m

Draw a net for each three-dimensional figure.

34. 35. 36.

MULTI-STEP TEST PREP

37. This problem will prepare you for the Multi-Step Test Prep on page 678.

A manufacturer of camping gear makes a wall tent in the shape shown in the diagram.

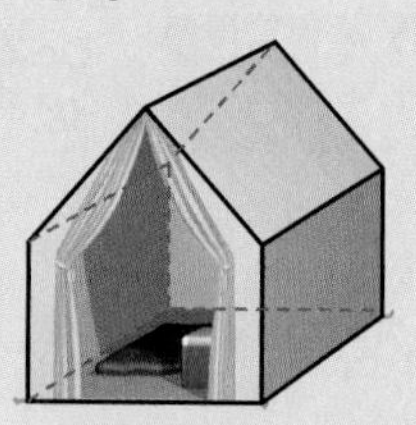

a. Classify the three-dimensional figure that the wall tent forms. pentagonal prism

b. What shapes make up the faces of the tent? How many of each shape are there? 2 pentagons and 5 rectangles

c. Draw a net for the wall tent.

10-1 PRACTICE A

10-1 PRACTICE C

10-1 PRACTICE B

Classify each figure. Name the vertices, edges, and bases.

1. hexagonal pyramid
vertices: *A*, *B*, *C*, *D*, *E*, *F*, and *G*
edges: $\overline{AB}$, $\overline{BC}$, $\overline{CD}$, $\overline{DE}$, $\overline{EF}$, $\overline{FA}$, $\overline{AG}$, $\overline{BG}$, $\overline{CG}$, $\overline{DG}$, $\overline{EG}$, $\overline{FG}$
base: hexagon *ABCDEF*

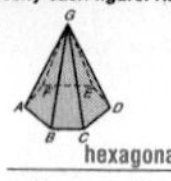

2. cone
vertices: *Y*
edges: none
base: $\odot Z$

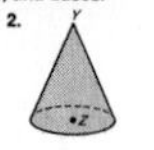

Name the type of solid each object is and sketch an example.

3. a shoe box 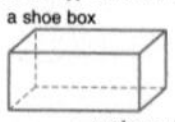
rectangular prism

4. a can of tuna 
cylinder

Describe the three-dimensional figure that can be made from the given net.

5. cylinder

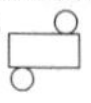

6. hexagonal prism

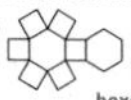

7. Two of the nets below make the same solid. Tell which one does not. III

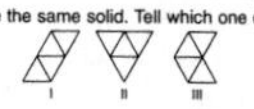

I II III

Describe each cross section.

8. circle

9. rectangle

10. After completing Exercises 8 and 9, Lloyd makes a conjecture about the shape of any cross section parallel to the base of a solid. Write your own conjecture.
Possible answer: If a cross section intersects a solid parallel to a base, then the cross section has the same shape as the base.

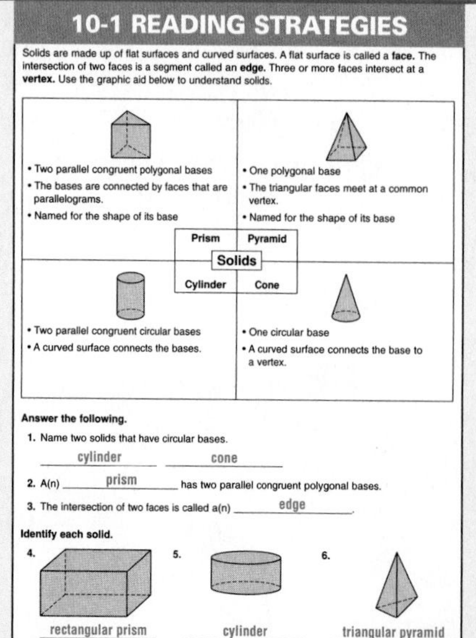

10-1 READING STRATEGIES

Solids are made up of flat surfaces and curved surfaces. A flat surface is called a **face.** The intersection of two faces is a segment called an **edge.** Three or more faces intersect at a **vertex.** Use the graphic aid below to understand solids.

Prism	Pyramid
• Two parallel congruent polygonal bases • The bases are connected by faces that are parallelograms. • Named for the shape of its base	• One polygonal base • The triangular faces meet at a common vertex. • Named for the shape of its base
Cylinder	**Cone**
• Two parallel congruent circular bases • A curved surface connects the bases.	• One circular base • A curved surface connects the base to a vertex.

Solids

Answer the following.

1. Name two solids that have circular bases.
cylinder cone

2. A(n) prism has two parallel congruent polygonal bases.

3. The intersection of two faces is called a(n) edge.

Identify each solid.

4. rectangular prism

5. cylinder

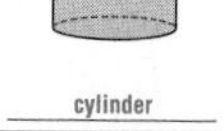

6. triangular pyramid

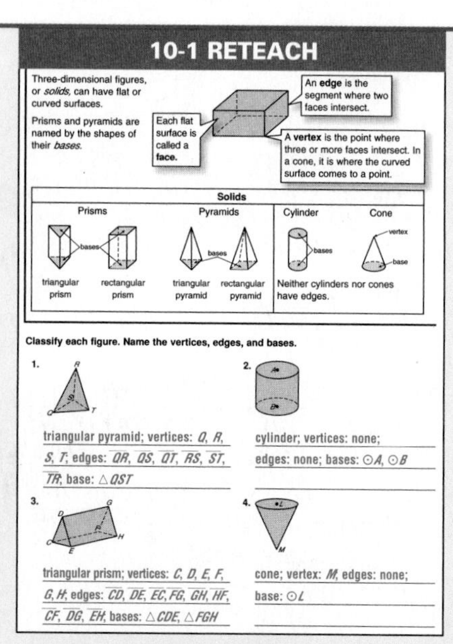

10-1 RETEACH

Three-dimensional figures, or *solids*, can have flat or curved surfaces.

Prisms and pyramids are named by the shapes of their *bases*.

Each flat surface is called a **face.**

An **edge** is the segment where two faces intersect.

A **vertex** is the point where three or more faces intersect. In a cone, it is where the curved surface comes to a point.

Solids

Prisms		Pyramids		Cylinder	Cone
triangular prism	rectangular prism	triangular pyramid	rectangular pyramid	Neither cylinders nor cones have edges.	

bases; bases; bases; vertex; base

Classify each figure. Name the vertices, edges, and bases.

1. triangular pyramid; vertices: *Q*, *R*, *S*, *T*; edges: $\overline{QR}$, $\overline{QS}$, $\overline{QT}$, $\overline{RS}$, $\overline{ST}$, $\overline{TR}$; base: $\triangle QST$

2. cylinder; vertices: none; edges: none; bases: $\odot A$, $\odot B$

3. triangular prism; vertices: *C*, *D*, *E*, *F*, *G*, *H*; edges: $\overline{CD}$, $\overline{DE}$, $\overline{EC}$, $\overline{FG}$, $\overline{GH}$, $\overline{HF}$, $\overline{CF}$, $\overline{DG}$, $\overline{EH}$; bases: $\triangle CDE$, $\triangle FGH$

4. cone; vertex: *M*; edges: none; base: $\odot L$

38. B; the bases are ≅ reg. hexagons, so the opposite sides of the cross section must be ≅.

39.

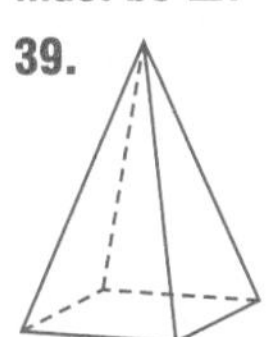

38. ///ERROR ANALYSIS/// A regular hexagonal prism is intersected by a plane as shown. Which cross section is incorrect? Explain.

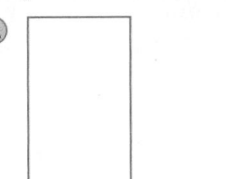

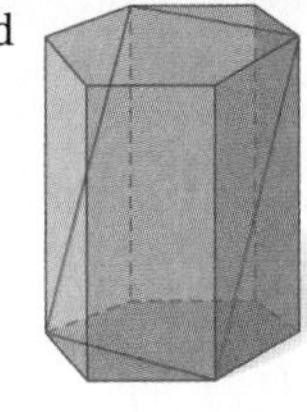

Ⓐ

Ⓑ

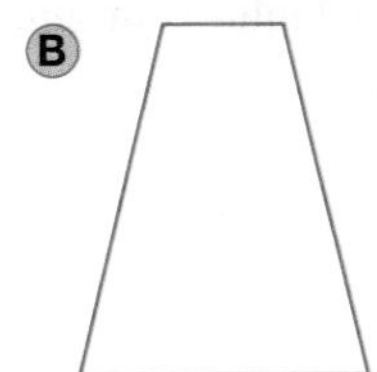

39. Critical Thinking A three-dimensional figure has 5 faces. One face is adjacent to every other face. Four of the faces are congruent. Draw a figure that meets these conditions.

40. Write About It Which of the following figures is not a net for a cube? Explain.

40. Figure B; when the figure is folded, the shaded faces will overlap.

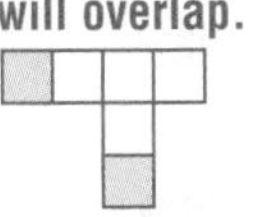

a. b.

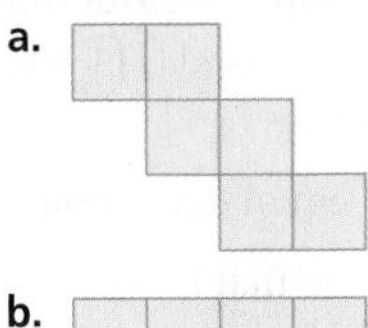

c.

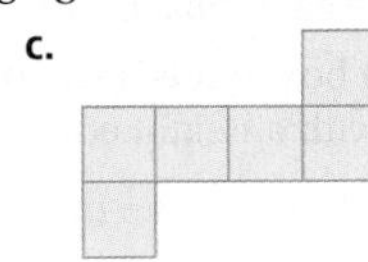

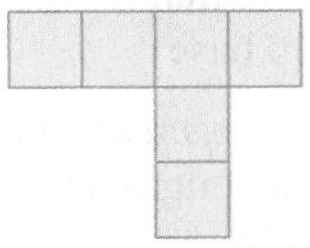

d.

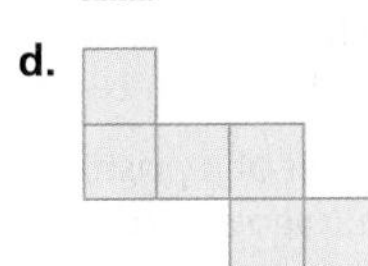

TEST PREP

41. Which three-dimensional figure does the net represent?

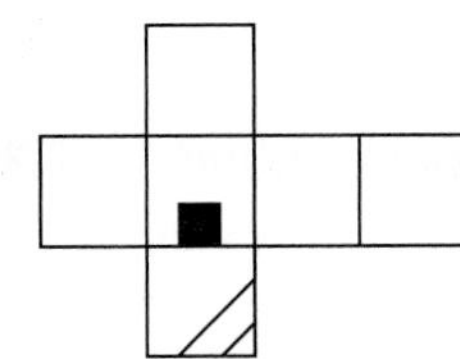

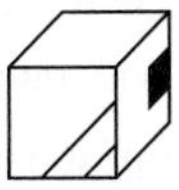

Ⓐ

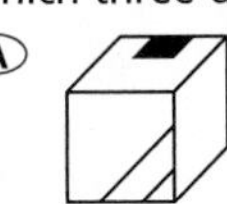

Ⓒ

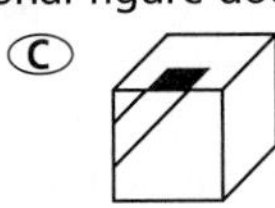

Ⓑ Ⓓ

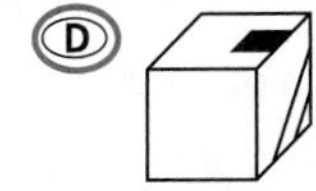

42. Which shape CANNOT be a face of a hexagonal prism?

Ⓕ triangle Ⓗ parallelogram

Ⓖ hexagon Ⓙ rectangle

43. What shape is the cross section formed by a cone and a plane that is perpendicular to the base and that passes through the vertex of the cone?

Ⓐ circle Ⓒ trapezoid

Ⓑ triangle Ⓓ rectangle

44. Which shape best represents a hexagonal prism viewed from the top?

Ⓕ

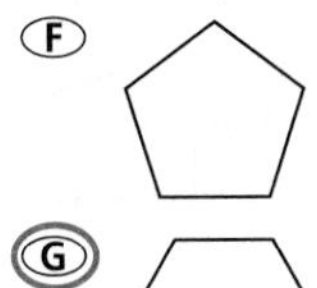

Ⓗ

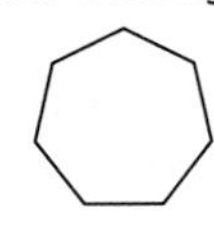

Ⓖ

Ⓙ

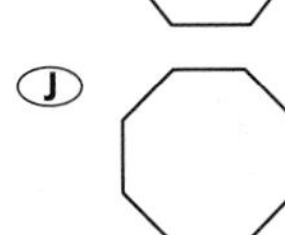

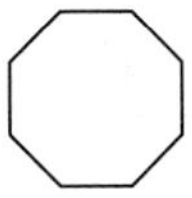

COMMON ERROR /// ALERT \\\

In **Exercise 32,** some students may think that all faces of the figure are supposed to be regular pentagons. Ask them to carefully read the definition of a prism on page 654 before they draw the figure. Remind them that a prism always has two congruent parallel bases and that all the other faces are parallelograms.

TEST PREP DOCTOR + In **Exercise 43,** students who choose **A** may be thinking of a plane *parallel* to the base rather than *perpendicular* to the base. It is not possible to form a cross section of a cone that is either a trapezoid or a rectangle, so this eliminates **C** and **D.**

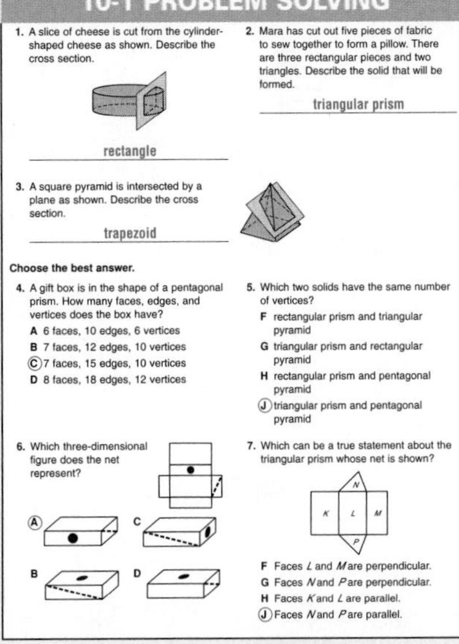

10-1 PROBLEM SOLVING

1. A slice of cheese is cut from the cylinder-shaped cheese as shown. Describe the cross section.
rectangle

2. Mara has cut out five pieces of fabric to sew together to form a pillow. There are three rectangular pieces and two triangles. Describe the solid that will be formed.
triangular prism

3. A square pyramid is intersected by a plane as shown. Describe the cross section.
trapezoid

Choose the best answer.

4. A gift box is in the shape of a pentagonal prism. How many faces, edges, and vertices does the box have?
A 6 faces, 10 edges, 6 vertices
B 7 faces, 12 edges, 10 vertices
Ⓒ 7 faces, 15 edges, 10 vertices
D 8 faces, 18 edges, 12 vertices

5. Which two solids have the same number of vertices?
F rectangular prism and triangular pyramid
G triangular prism and rectangular pyramid
H rectangular prism and pentagonal pyramid
Ⓙ triangular prism and pentagonal pyramid

6. Which three-dimensional figure does the net represent?
Ⓐ C B D

7. Which can be a true statement about the triangular prism whose net is shown?
F Faces *L* and *M* are perpendicular.
G Faces *N* and *P* are perpendicular.
H Faces *K* and *L* are parallel.
Ⓙ Faces *N* and *P* are parallel.

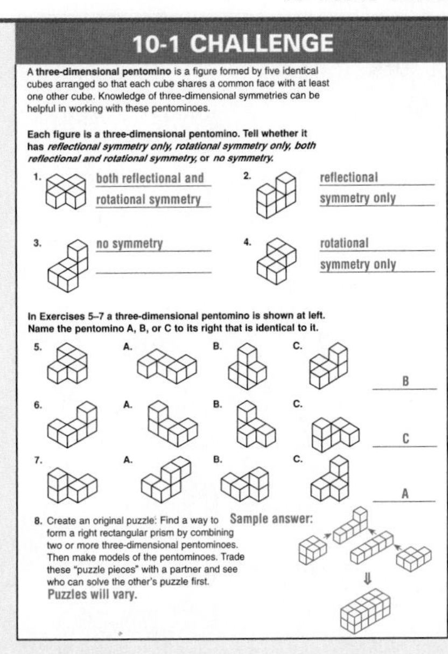

10-1 CHALLENGE

A **three-dimensional pentomino** is a figure formed by five identical cubes arranged so that each cube shares a common face with at least one other cube. Knowledge of three-dimensional symmetries can be helpful in working with these pentominoes.

Each figure is a three-dimensional pentomino. Tell whether it has *reflectional symmetry only, rotational symmetry only, both reflectional and rotational symmetry,* or *no symmetry.*

1. both reflectional and rotational symmetry
2. reflectional symmetry only
3. no symmetry
4. rotational symmetry only

In Exercises 5–7 a three-dimensional pentomino is shown at left. Name the pentomino A, B, or C to its right that is identical to it.

5. A. B. C. B
6. A. B. C. C
7. A. B. C. A

8. Create an original puzzle: Find a way to form a right rectangular prism by combining two or more three-dimensional pentominoes. Then make models of the pentominoes. Trade these "puzzle pieces" with a partner and see who can solve the other's puzzle first. Sample answer: Puzzles will vary.

Journal

Have students write a one-sentence definition for *prism, cylinder, pyramid,* and *cone,* and have them give a real-world example of each.

ALTERNATIVE ASSESSMENT

Have students work in pairs. Ask each student to list five solids, such as "hexagonal pyramid" or "square prism." Then have them trade papers and draw the five solids that their partners have listed. Also ask them to list the vertices, edges, faces, and bases of the solids they have drawn, and to label points as needed.

Power Presentations with PowerPoint®

10-1 Lesson Quiz

1. Classify the figure. Name the vertices, edges, and bases.

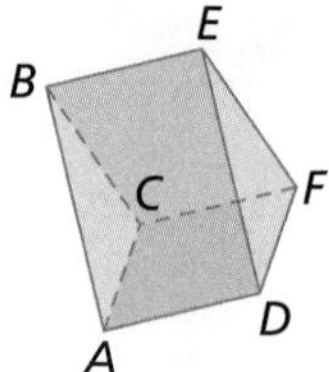

triangular prism; vertices: A, B, C, D, E, F; edges: $\overline{AB}, \overline{BC}, \overline{AC}, \overline{DE}, \overline{EF}, \overline{FD}, \overline{BE}, \overline{CF}, \overline{AD}$; bases: $\triangle ABC$ and $\triangle DEF$

2. Describe the three-dimensional figure that can be made from this net.

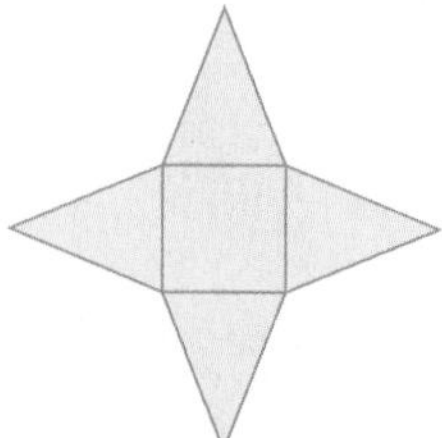

square pyramid

3. Describe the cross section.

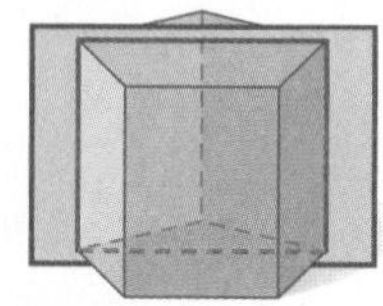

a rectangle

Also available on transparency

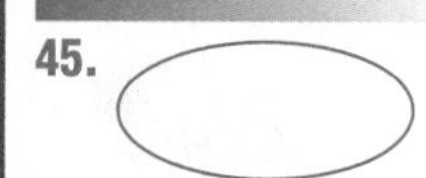

CHALLENGE AND EXTEND

A *double cone* is formed by two cones that share the same vertex. Sketch each cross section formed by a double cone and a plane.

45. 
46. 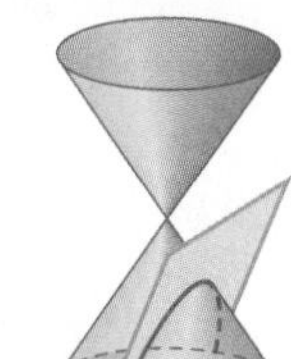
47. 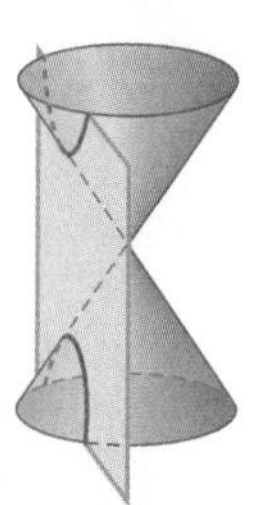

45. 
46.
47.

Crafts Elena is designing patterns for gift boxes. Draw a pattern that she can use to create each box. Be sure to include tabs for gluing the sides together.

48. a box that is a square pyramid where each triangular face is an isosceles triangle with a height equal to three times the width
49. a box that is a cylinder with the diameter equal to the height
50. a box that is a rectangular prism with a base that is twice as long as it is wide, and with a rectangular pyramid on the top base
51. A net of a prism is shown. The bases of the prism are regular hexagons, and the rectangular faces are all congruent.
    a. List all pairs of parallel faces in the prism.
    b. Draw a net of a prism with bases that are regular pentagons. How many pairs of parallel faces does the prism have?

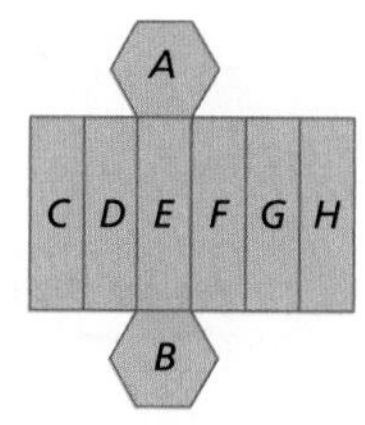

51a. *A* and *B*, *C* and *F*, *D* and *G*, *E* and *H*

SPIRAL REVIEW

Write the equation that fits the description. *(Previous course)*

52. the equation of the graph that is the reflection of the graph of $y = x^2$ over the x-axis $y = -x^2$
53. the equation of the graph of $y = x^2$ after a vertical translation of 6 units upward $y = x^2 + 6$
54. the quadratic equation of a graph that opens upward and is wider than $y = x^2$ Possible answer: $y = \frac{1}{2}x^2$

Name the largest and smallest angles of each triangle. *(Lesson 5-5)*

55. 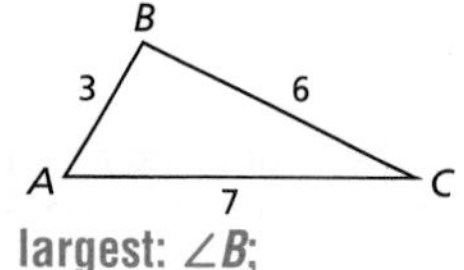

largest: $\angle B$; smallest: $\angle C$

56. 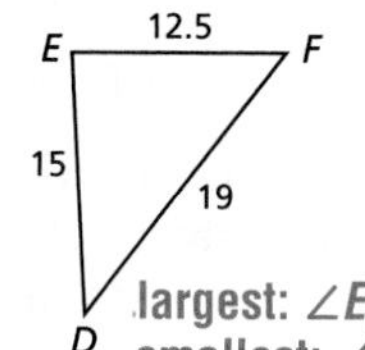

largest: $\angle E$; smallest: $\angle D$

57. 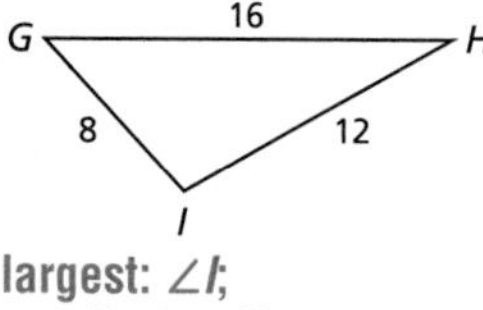

largest: $\angle I$; smallest: $\angle H$

Determine whether the two polygons are similar. If so, give the similarity ratio. *(Lesson 7-2)*

58. no

59. 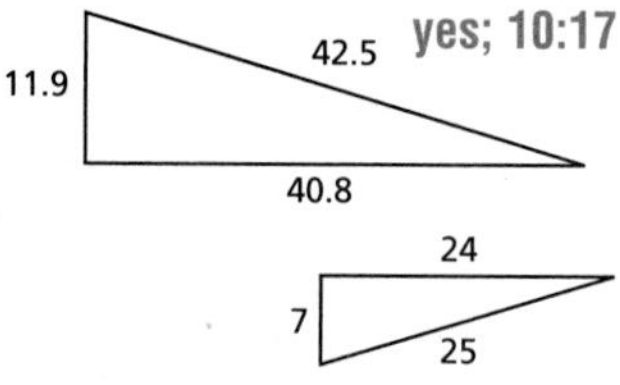

yes; 10:17

Answers

48. 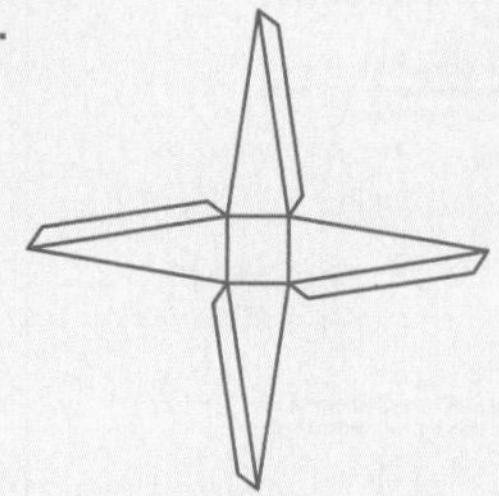

49. 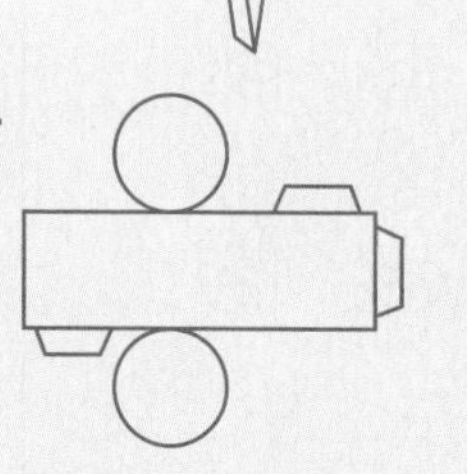

50. 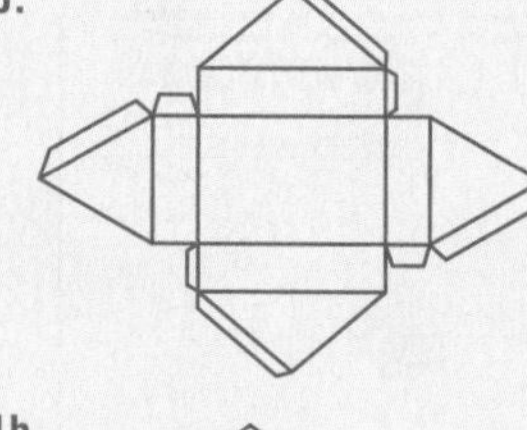

51b.  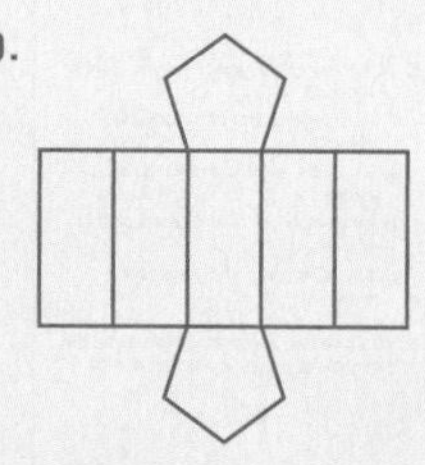

one

10-2 Representations of Three-Dimensional Figures

Objectives
Draw representations of three-dimensional figures.

Recognize a three-dimensional figure from a given representation.

Vocabulary
orthographic drawing
isometric drawing
perspective drawing
vanishing point
horizon

Who uses this?
Architects make many different kinds of drawings to represent three-dimensional figures. (See Exercise 34.)

There are many ways to represent a three-dimensional object. An **orthographic drawing** shows six different views of an object: top, bottom, front, back, left side, and right side.

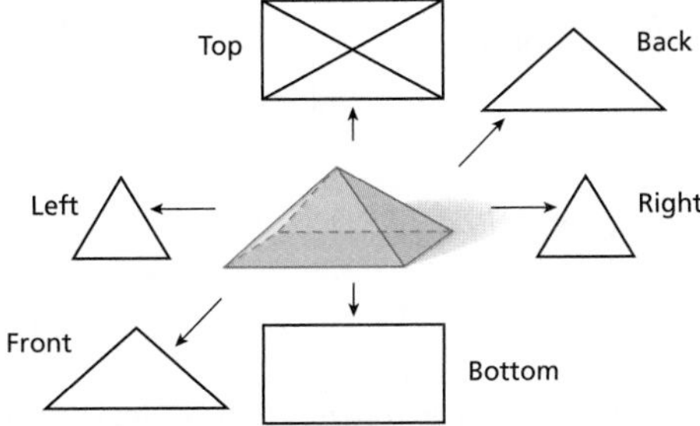

EXAMPLE 1 Drawing Orthographic Views of an Object

Draw all six orthographic views of the given object. Assume there are no hidden cubes.

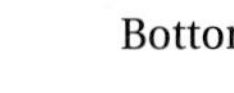

Top:

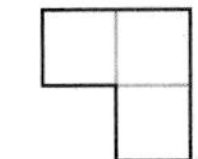

Bottom:

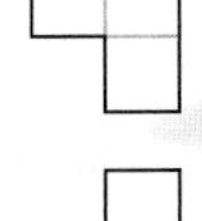

Front:

Back:

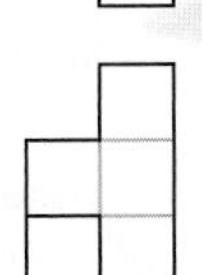

Left:

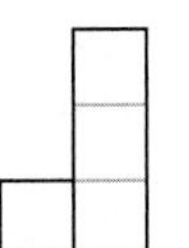

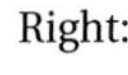

Right:

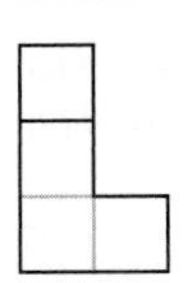

CHECK IT OUT! 1. Draw all six orthographic views of the given object. Assume there are no hidden cubes.

1. Front Back Left Right Top Bottom

10-2 Organizer

Pacing: Traditional 1 day
Block $\frac{1}{2}$ day

Objectives: Draw representations of three-dimensional figures.

Recognize a three-dimensional figure from a given representation.

Online Edition
Tutorial Videos, Interactivity, TechKeys

Countdown Week 22

Power Presentations with PowerPoint®

Warm Up

Write a description of each figure.

1. cube prism with 6 square faces
2. pentagonal prism prism with 2 pentagonal bases and 5 lateral faces that are parallelograms
3. cylinder figure with 2 circular bases connected by a curved surface

Also available on transparency

Math Humor

Q: How do you catch a 3-D figure?
A: With a net.

1 Introduce

EXPLORATION
10-2 Representations of Three-Dimensional Figures
Match each three-dimensional figure with its front view.
Front Views
THINK AND DISCUSS

Motivate

Have students write their names in block lettering. Then ask them to try to make the lettering look three-dimensional. Explain that one challenge of painting and drawing is to represent our three-dimensional world in two dimensions. In this lesson, they will learn about representations of three-dimensional figures.

Explorations and answers are provided in *Alternate Openers: Explorations Transparencies.*

State Resources

go.hrw.com
State Resources Online
KEYWORD: MG7 Resources

Power Presentations with PowerPoint®

Additional Examples

Example 1

Draw all six orthographic views of the given object. Assume there are no hidden cubes.

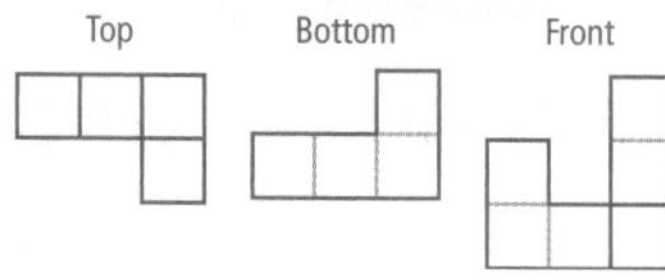

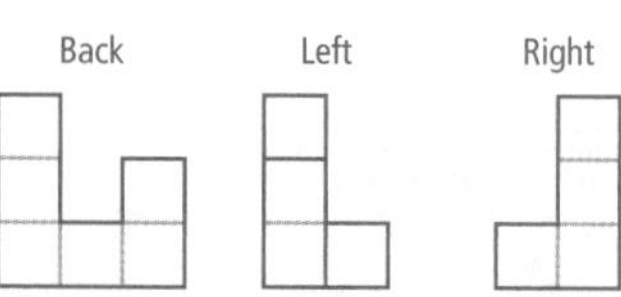

Example 2

Draw an isometric view of the given object. Assume there are no hidden cubes.

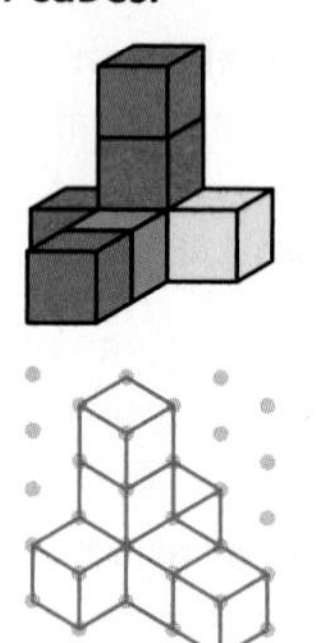

INTERVENTION
Questioning Strategies

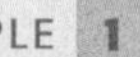

EXAMPLE 1

- How are the top and bottom orthographic views of an object related?

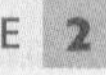

EXAMPLE 2

- How is an isometric view different from an orthographic view?

Isometric drawing is a way to show three sides of a figure from a corner view. You can use *isometric dot paper* to make an isometric drawing. This paper has diagonal rows of dots that are equally spaced in a repeating triangular pattern.

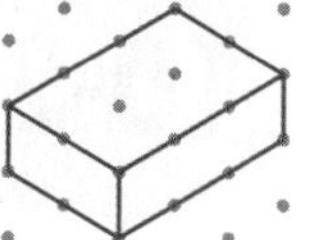

EXAMPLE 2 Drawing an Isometric View of an Object

Draw an isometric view of the given object. Assume there are no hidden cubes.

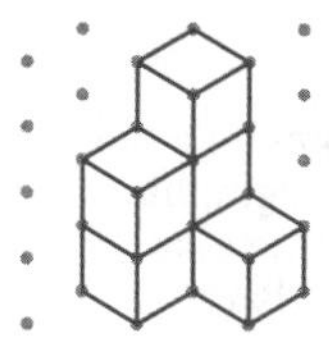

2. Draw an isometric view of the given object. Assume there are no hidden cubes.

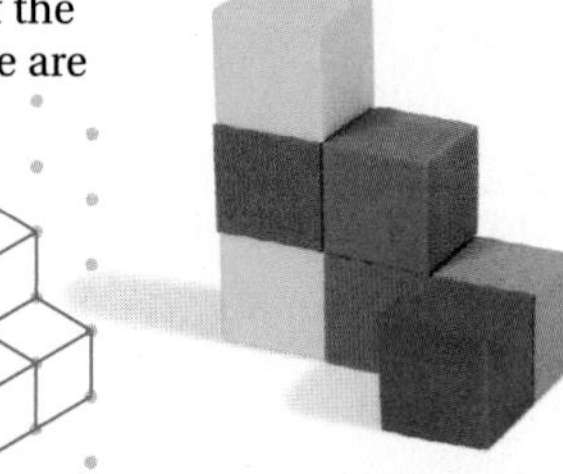

In a **perspective drawing**, nonvertical parallel lines are drawn so that they meet at a point called a **vanishing point**. Vanishing points are located on a horizontal line called the **horizon**. A one-point perspective drawing contains one vanishing point. A two-point perspective drawing contains two vanishing points.

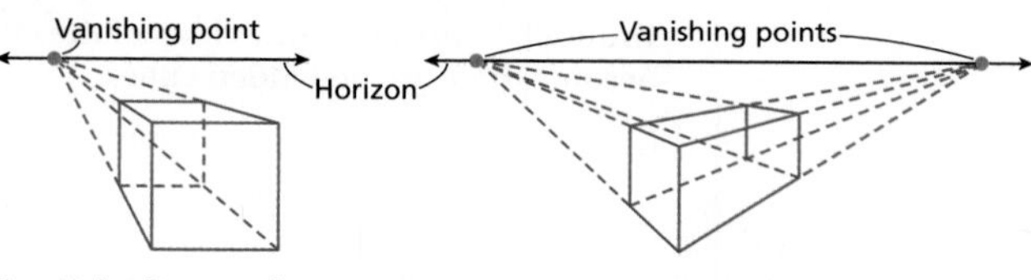

One-Point Perspective **Two-Point Perspective**

Student to Student
Perspective Drawing

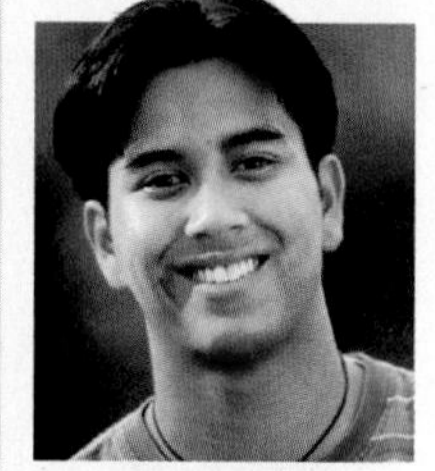

Jacob Martin
MacArthur High School

When making a perspective drawing, it helps me to remember that all vertical lines on the object will be vertical in the drawing.

Three-dimensional figure

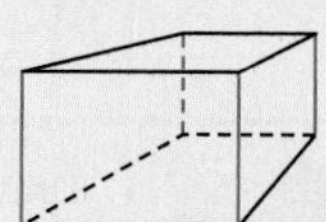

One-point perspective

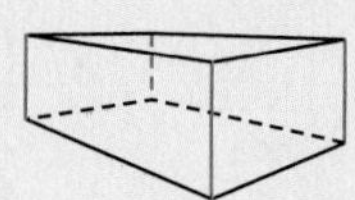

Two-point perspective

2 Teach

Guided Instruction

Compare the different representations of three-dimensional figures shown in the lesson: An orthographic view is a projection onto a flat surface. A one-point perspective drawing shows a figure with one side facing the viewer. A two-point perspective drawing shows a figure with one edge facing the viewer. An isometric drawing shows a figure with one corner facing the viewer.

Reaching All Learners
Through Kinesthetic Experience

Have students work in pairs. Give each pair a handful of unit cubes (MK) and ask them to arrange them to create a block figure. Have one student draw the top, front, and right views while the other draws the bottom, back, and left views. Then have the students compare their drawings and explain the relationships between the different views.

EXAMPLE 3 Drawing an Object in Perspective

A **Draw a cube in one-point perspective.**

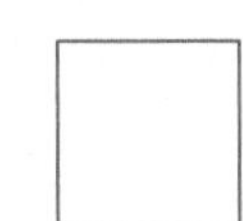

Draw a horizontal line to represent the horizon. Mark a vanishing point on the horizon. Then draw a square below the horizon. This is the front of the cube.

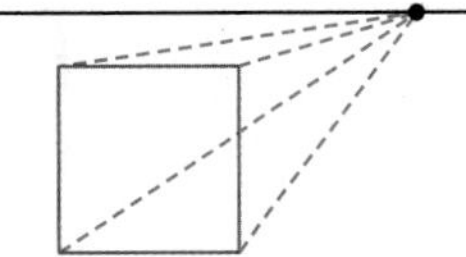

From each corner of the square, lightly draw dashed segments to the vanishing point.

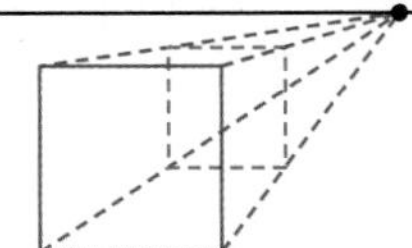

Lightly draw a smaller square with vertices on the dashed segments. This is the back of the cube.

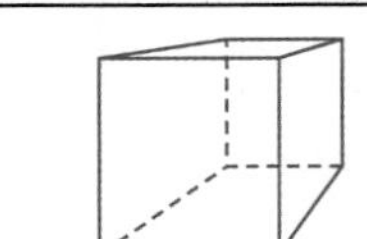

Draw the edges of the cube, using dashed segments for hidden edges. Erase any segments that are not part of the cube.

Helpful Hint

In a one-point perspective drawing of a cube, you are looking at a face. In a two-point perspective drawing, you are looking at a corner.

B **Draw a rectangular prism in two-point perspective.**

Draw a horizontal line to represent the horizon. Mark two vanishing points on the horizon. Then draw a vertical segment below the horizon and between the vanishing points. This is the front edge of the prism.

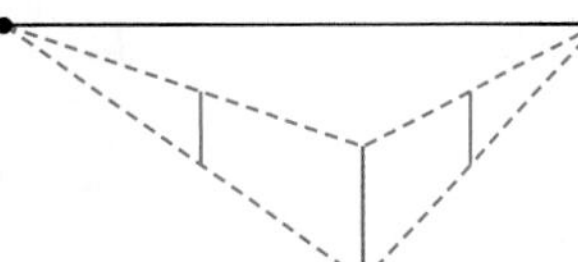

From each endpoint of the segment, lightly draw dashed segments to each vanishing point. Draw two vertical segments connecting the dashed lines. These are other vertical edges of the prism.

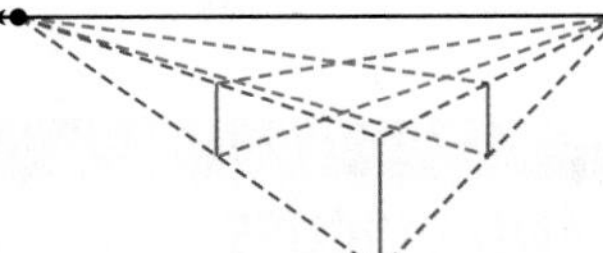

Lightly draw dashed segments from each endpoint of the two vertical segments to the vanishing points.

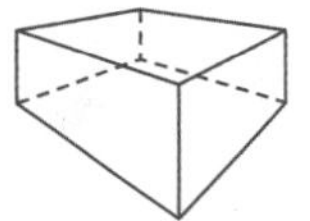

Draw the edges of the prism, using dashed lines for hidden edges. Erase any lines that are not part of the prism.

3a. Draw the block letter **L** in one-point perspective.

3b. Draw the block letter **L** in two-point perspective.

Answers to *Check It Out!*

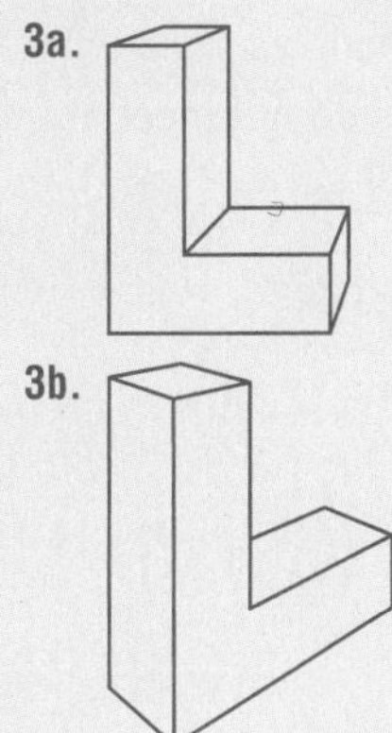

Some students may think that an isometric drawing is a type of perspective drawing. Point out that the parallel edges of a figure are always represented by parallel segments in an isometric drawing and do not converge to a vanishing point.

Power Presentations with PowerPoint®

Additional Examples

Example 3

A. Draw the block letter **U** in one-point perspective.

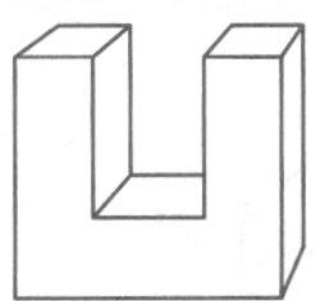

B. Draw the block letter **U** in two-point perspective.

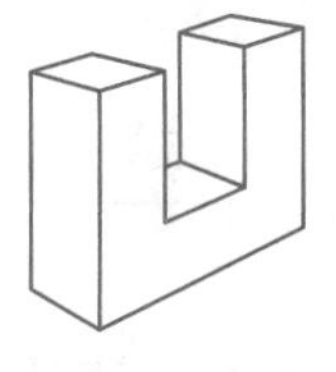

INTERVENTION
Questioning Strategies

EXAMPLE 3

- How do you know if you are looking at a one-point perspective drawing or a two-point perspective drawing?

Teaching Tip **Multiple Representations** Orthographic, isometric, and perspective drawings are ways to represent a three-dimensional object using two dimensions. However, each representation may distort some part of the figure. A net is a way to represent a three-dimensional figure in two dimensions without distorting any of the faces.

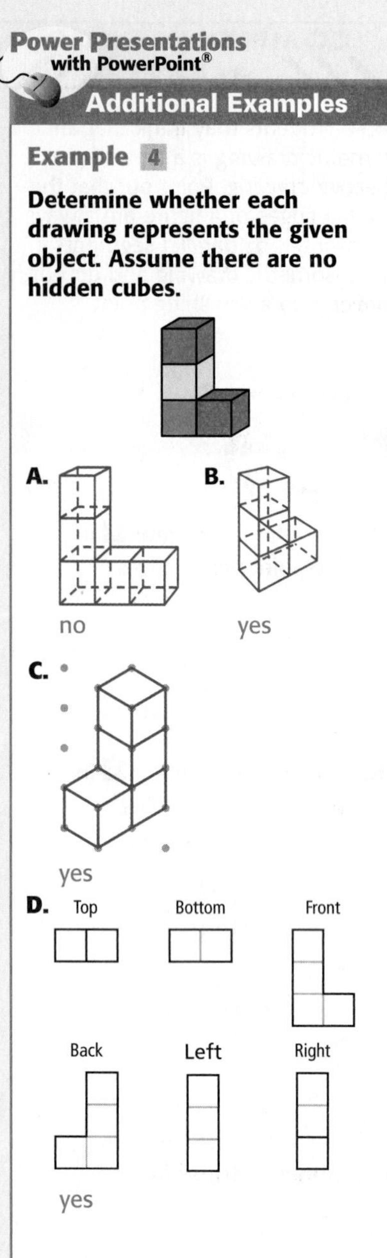

Power Presentations with PowerPoint®

Additional Examples

Example 4

Determine whether each drawing represents the given object. Assume there are no hidden cubes.

INTERVENTION

Questioning Strategies

EXAMPLE 4

- How can you tell if a drawing represents a given three-dimensional object?

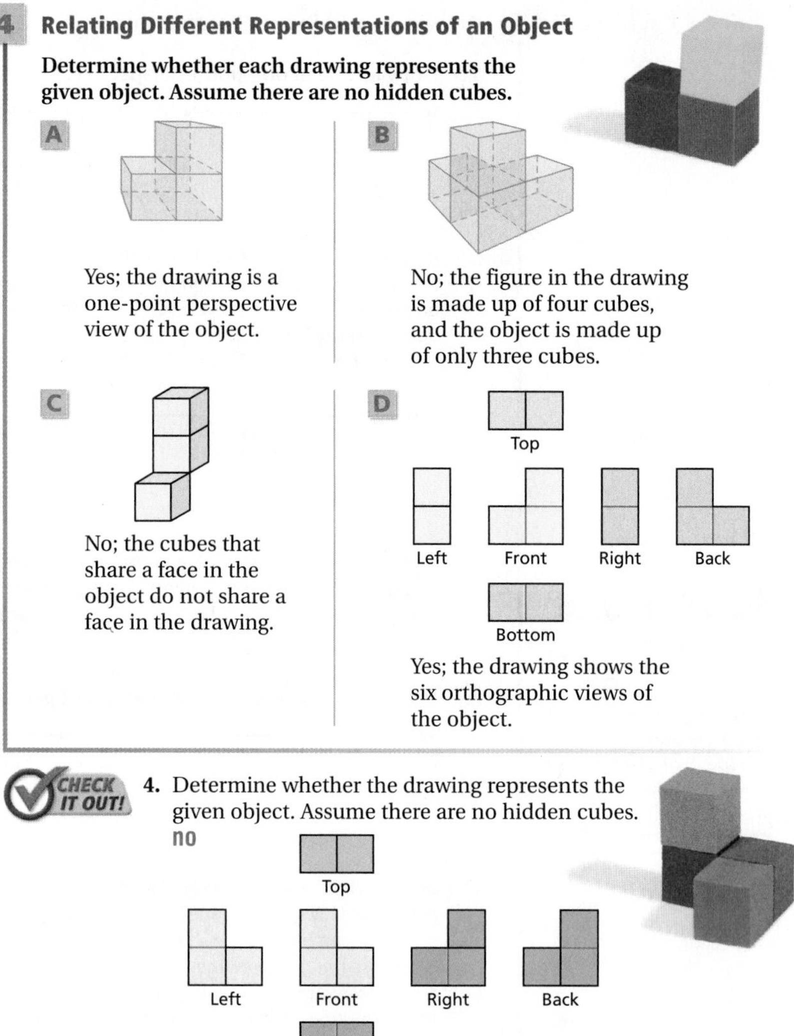

EXAMPLE 4 **Relating Different Representations of an Object**

Determine whether each drawing represents the given object. Assume there are no hidden cubes.

A

Yes; the drawing is a one-point perspective view of the object.

B

No; the figure in the drawing is made up of four cubes, and the object is made up of only three cubes.

C

No; the cubes that share a face in the object do not share a face in the drawing.

D

Yes; the drawing shows the six orthographic views of the object.

CHECK IT OUT! **4.** Determine whether the drawing represents the given object. Assume there are no hidden cubes. no

THINK AND DISCUSS

1. Describe the six orthographic views of a cube.

2. In a perspective drawing, are all parallel lines drawn so that they meet at a vanishing point? Why or why not?

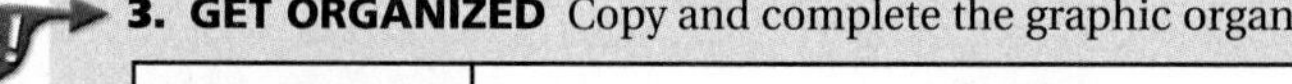

Know it! Note **3. GET ORGANIZED** Copy and complete the graphic organizer.

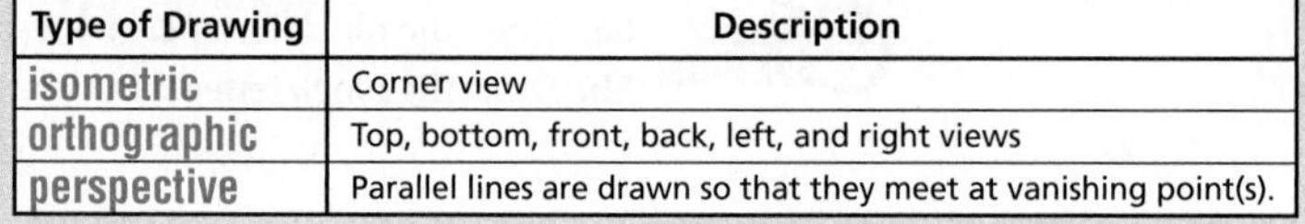

Type of Drawing	Description
isometric	Corner view
orthographic	Top, bottom, front, back, left, and right views
perspective	Parallel lines are drawn so that they meet at vanishing point(s).

3 Close

Summarize

Show students a cube and ask the following questions.

- Which type of drawing would show all six faces as squares? orthographic
- Which type of drawing would show only the front and back faces as squares? one-point perspective
- Which type of drawing would show the faces as parallelograms? isometric
- Which type of drawing would show only the vertical edges as parallel? two-point perspective

ONGOING ASSESSMENT and INTERVENTION

***Diagnose Before* the Lesson**
10-2 Warm Up, TE p. 661

***Monitor During* the Lesson**
Check It Out! Exercises, SE pp. 661–664
Questioning Strategies, TE pp. 662–664

***Assess After* the Lesson**
10-2 Lesson Quiz, TE p. 668
Alternative Assessment, TE p. 668

Answers to *Think and Discuss*

1. All 6 views are squares.
2. No; vertical lines do not meet at a vanishing point.

10-2 Exercises

go.hrw.com
Homework Help Online
KEYWORD: MG7 10-2
Parent Resources Online
KEYWORD: MG7 Parent

GUIDED PRACTICE

1. **Vocabulary** In a(n) __?__ drawing, the *vanishing points* are located on the *horizon*. (*orthographic, isometric,* or *perspective*) **perspective**

SEE EXAMPLE 1 p. 661

Draw all six orthographic views of each object. Assume there are no hidden cubes.

2.

3. 

4. 

SEE EXAMPLE 2 p. 662

Draw an isometric view of each object. Assume there are no hidden cubes.

5. 

6. 

7. 

SEE EXAMPLE 3 p. 663

Draw each object in one-point and two-point perspectives. Assume there are no hidden cubes.

8. rectangular prism
9. block letter C

SEE EXAMPLE 4 p. 664

Determine whether each drawing represents the given object. Assume there are no hidden cubes.

10. 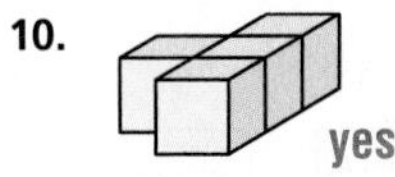
yes

11. 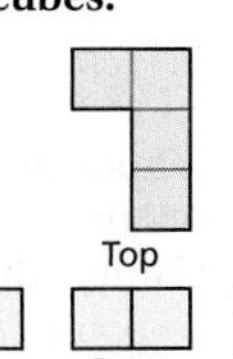

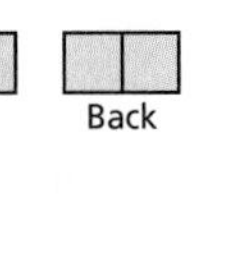
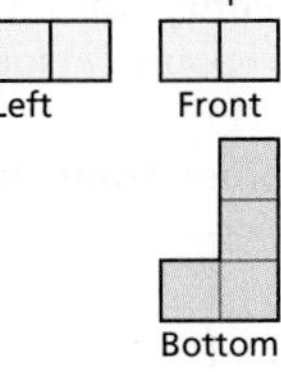

no

12. 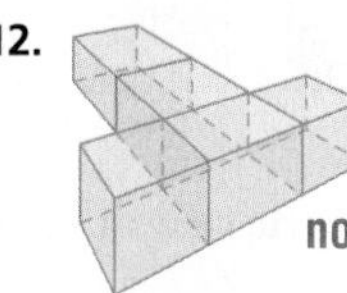
no

13. 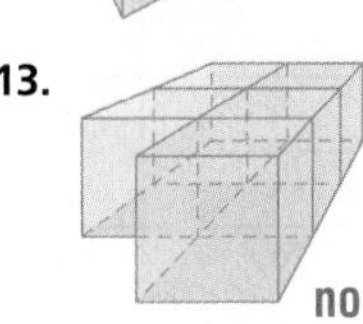
no

PRACTICE AND PROBLEM SOLVING

Draw all six orthographic views of each object. Assume there are no hidden cubes.

14. 

15. 

16. 

10-2 Exercises

Assignment Guide

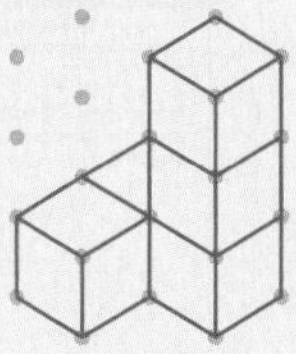

Assign *Guided Practice* exercises as necessary.

If you finished Examples **1–2**
Basic 14–19, 27, 28, 30, 31
Average 14–19, 27, 28, 30–32
Advanced 14–19, 27, 28, 30–32, 41

If you finished Examples **1–4**
Basic 14–32, 35–37, 43–51
Average 14–39, 43–51
Advanced 14–51

Homework Quick Check
Quickly check key concepts.
Exercises: 14, 18, 20, 22, 24, 28

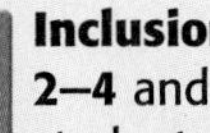

Inclusion For **Exercises 2–4** and **14–16,** encourage students who are having difficulty interpreting the three-dimensional figures to build the figures from unit cubes (MK). Then have them use their figures to draw the top, bottom, front, back, left, and right views.

Answers

2. 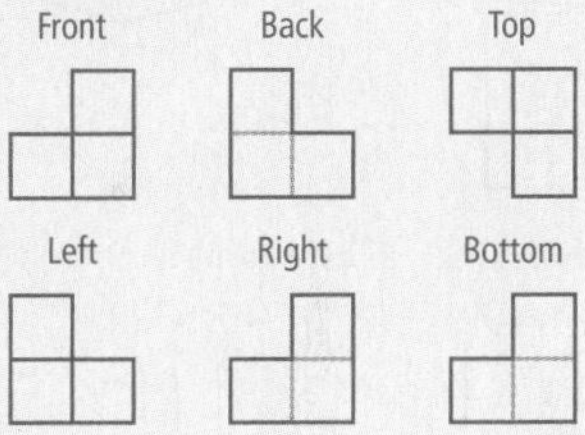 Front, Back, Top, Left, Right, Bottom

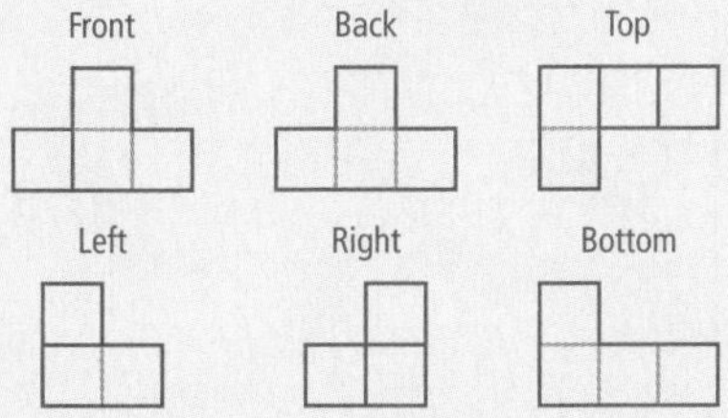

State Resources

go.hrw.com
State Resources Online
KEYWORD: MG7 Resources

Answers

3. 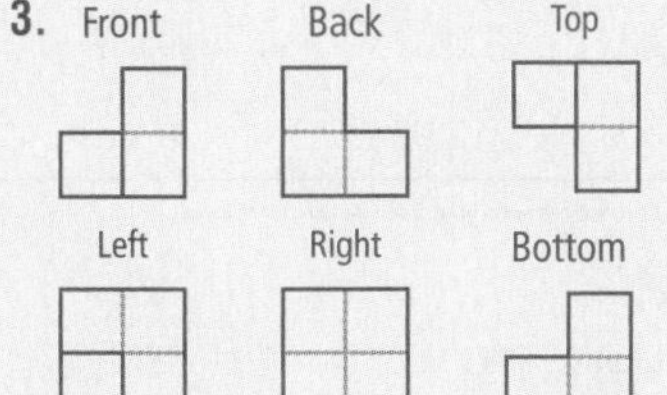

4. 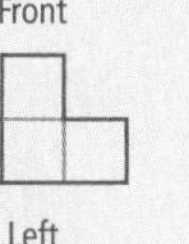
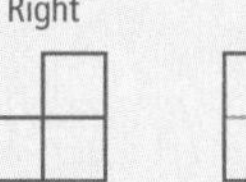

5. 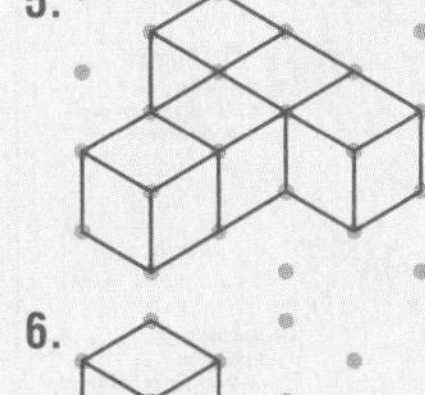

6. 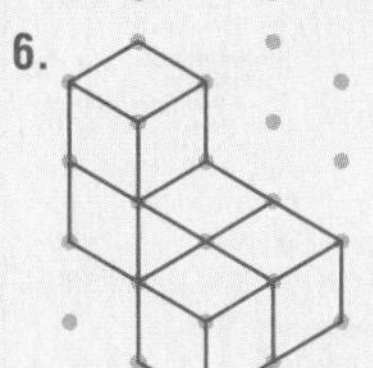

7.

8–9, 14–16. See p. A26.

Teaching Tip

Visual In **Exercises 18** and **23,** some students may forget to include the block at the back of the figure because it is almost hidden from view. Remind students to count the blocks carefully.

MULTI-STEP TEST PREP **Exercise 29** involves using orthographic views to sketch a camping tent. This exercise prepares students for the Multi-Step Test Prep on page 678.

Answers

17. 

18. 

19. 

20. 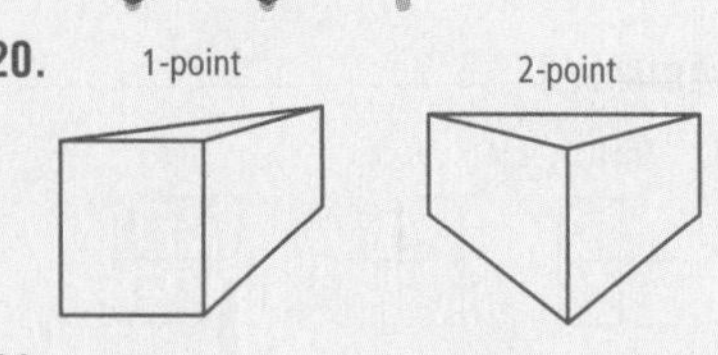

21. 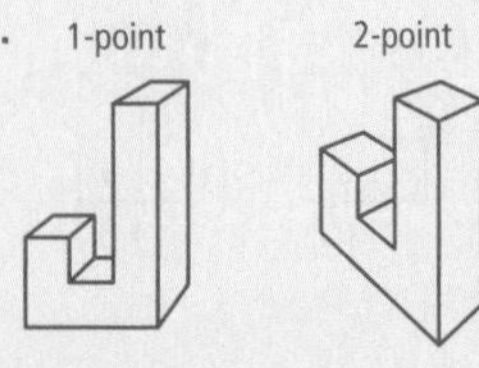

26. 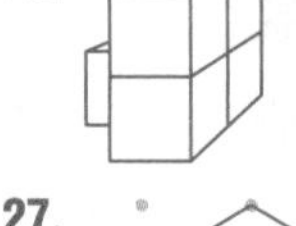

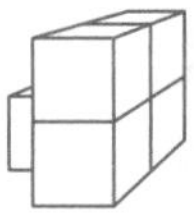

27.

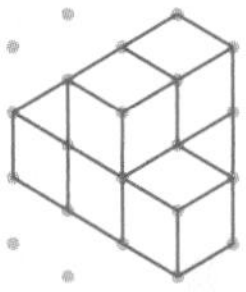

28.

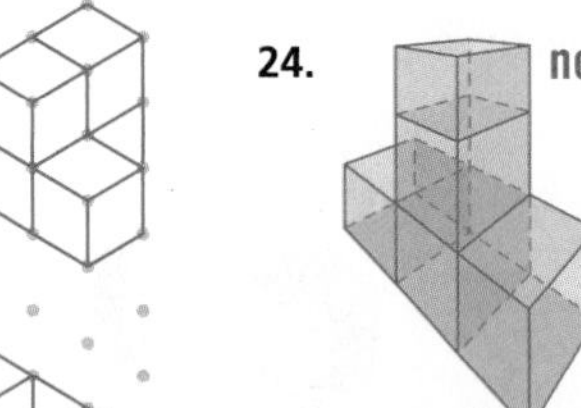

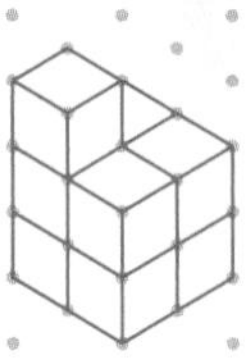

29a. Bottom

b.

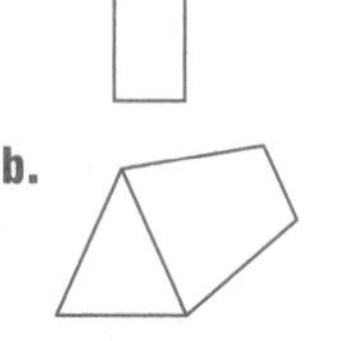

10-2 PRACTICE A

10-2 PRACTICE C

10-2 PRACTICE B

Draw all six orthographic views of each object. Assume there are no hidden cubes. In your answers, use a dashed line to show that the edges touch and a solid line to show that the edges do not touch.

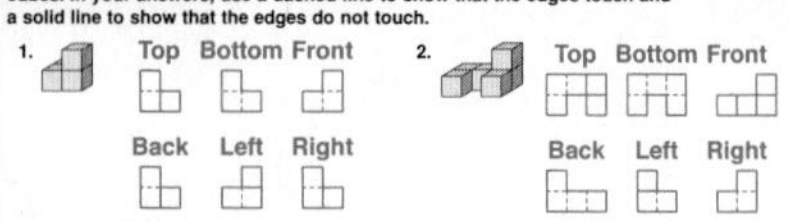

1. Top Bottom Front / Back Left Right

2. Top Bottom Front / Back Left Right

3. Draw an isometric view of the object in Exercise 1.

4. Draw an isometric view of the object in Exercise 2.

5. Draw a block letter T in one-point perspective. Possible answer:

6. Draw a block letter T in two-point perspective. (*Hint:* Draw the vertical line segment that will be closest to the viewer first.) Possible answer:

Determine whether each drawing represents the object at right. Assume there are no hidden cubes.

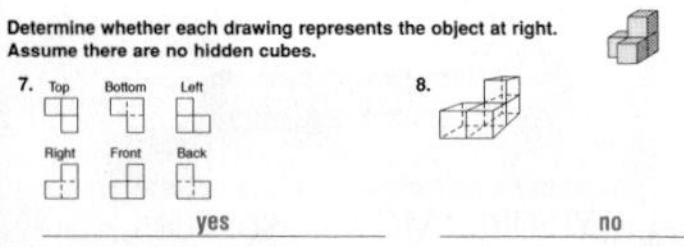

7. Top Bottom Left / Right Front Back — yes

8. no

Independent Practice	
For Exercises	See Example
14–16	1
17–19	2
20–21	3
22–25	4

Extra Practice
Skills Practice p. S22
Application Practice p. S37

Draw an isometric view of each object. Assume there are no hidden cubes.

17. 

18. 

19. 

Draw each object in one-point and two-point perspective. Assume there are no hidden cubes.

20. right triangular prism

21. block letter J

Determine whether each drawing represents the given object. Assume there are no hidden cubes.

22. yes

23. yes

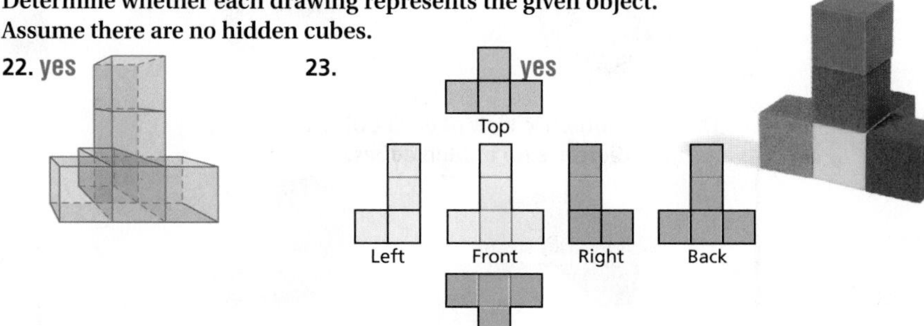

24. no

25. no

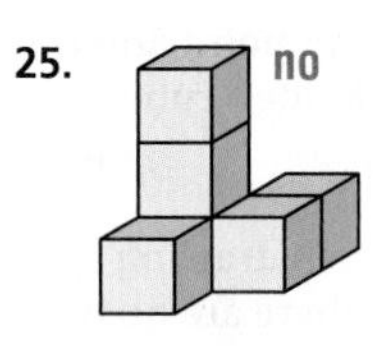

26. Use the top, front, side, and isometric views to build the three-dimensional figure out of unit cubes. Then draw the figure in one-point perspective.

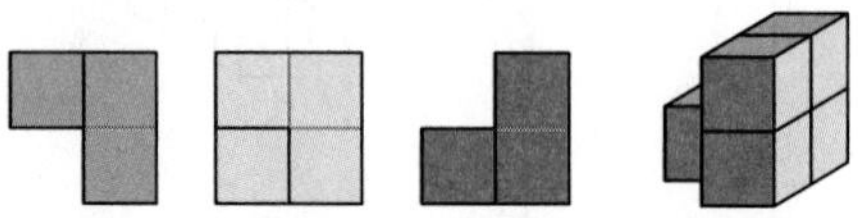

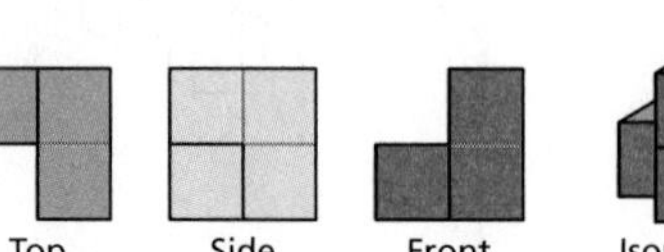

Use the top, side, and front views to draw an isometric view of each figure.

27. 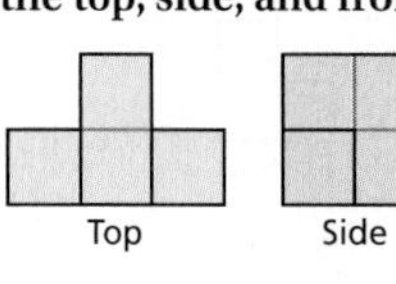 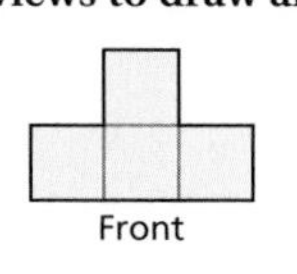

28. 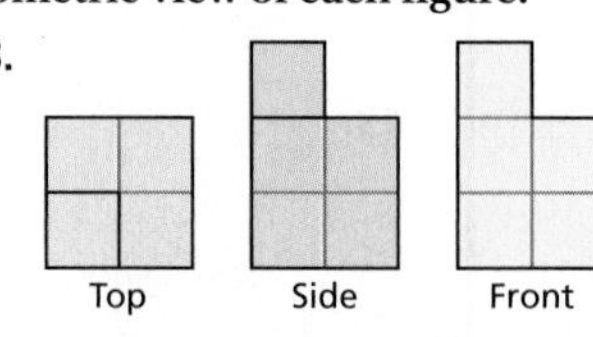

MULTI-STEP TEST PREP

29. This problem will prepare you for the Multi-Step Test Prep on page 678.

A camping gear catalog shows the three given views of a tent.

a. Draw a bottom view of the tent.

b. Make a sketch of the tent.

c. Each edge of the three-dimensional figure from part **b** represents one pole of the tent. How many poles does this tent have? 9

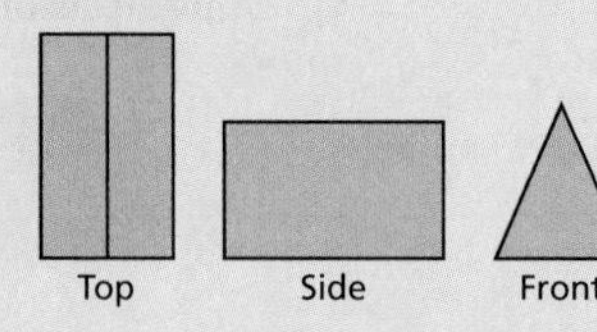

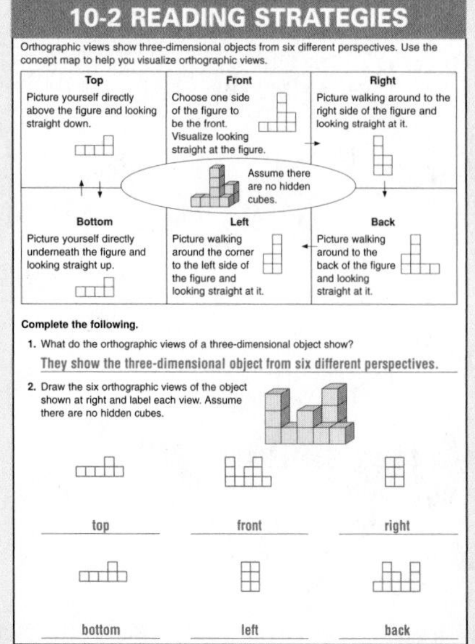

10-2 READING STRATEGIES

Orthographic views show three-dimensional objects from six different perspectives. Use the concept map to help you visualize orthographic views.

Top: Picture yourself directly above the figure and looking straight down.

Front: Choose one side of the figure to be the front. Visualize looking straight at the figure.

Right: Picture walking around to the right side of the figure and looking straight at it.

Assume there are no hidden cubes.

Bottom: Picture yourself directly underneath the figure and looking straight up.

Left: Picture walking around the corner to the left side of the figure and looking straight at it.

Back: Picture walking around to the back of the figure and looking straight at it.

Complete the following.

1. What do the orthographic views of a three-dimensional object show?
They show the three-dimensional object from six different perspectives.

2. Draw the six orthographic views of the object shown at right and label each view. Assume there are no hidden cubes.

top front right

bottom left back

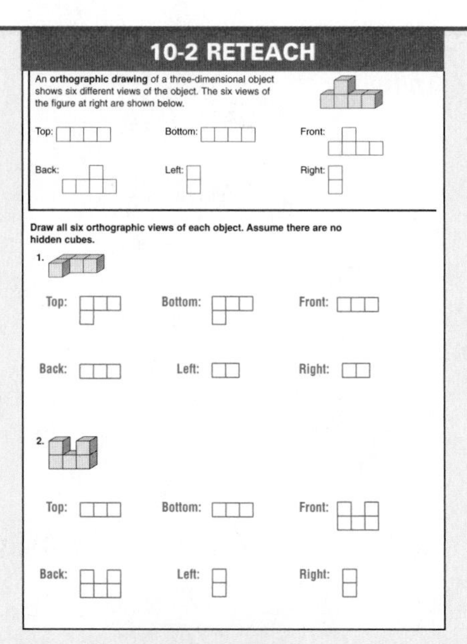

10-2 RETEACH

An **orthographic drawing** of a three-dimensional object shows six different views of the object. The six views of the figure at right are shown below.

Top: Bottom: Front:

Back: Left: Right:

Draw all six orthographic views of each object. Assume there are no hidden cubes.

1.

Top: Bottom: Front:

Back: Left: Right:

2.

Top: Bottom: Front:

Back: Left: Right:

Draw all six orthographic views of each object.

30.

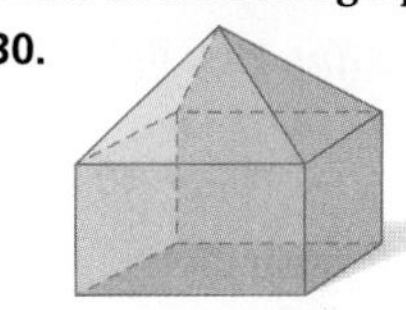

31.

32.

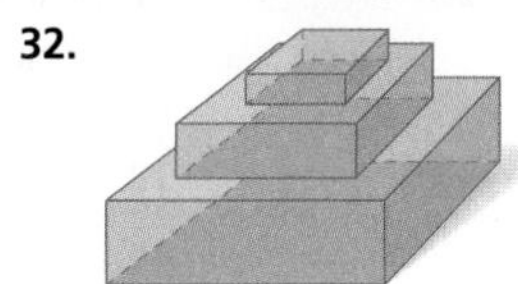

33. Critical Thinking Describe or draw two figures that have the same left, right, front, and back orthographic views but have different top and bottom views.

34a. 2-point perspective

b. Extend a pair of parallel lines to meet at each vanishing point.

34. Architecture Perspective drawings are used by architects to show what a finished room will look like.

a. Is the architect's sketch in one-point or two-point perspective?

b. **Write About It** How would you locate the vanishing point(s) in the architect's sketch?

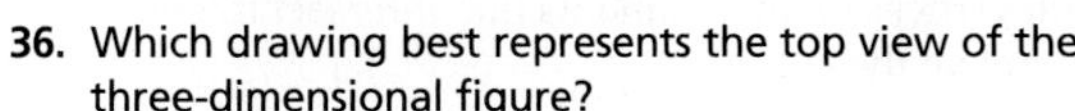

35. Which three-dimensional figure has these three views?

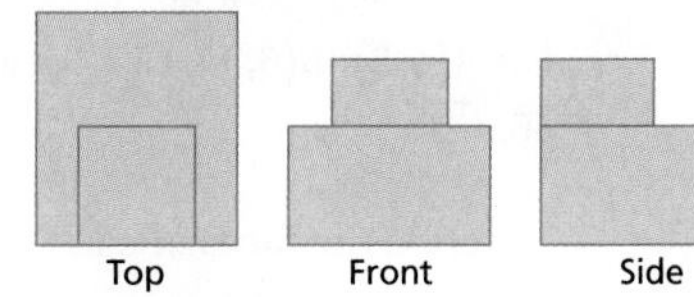

Ⓐ

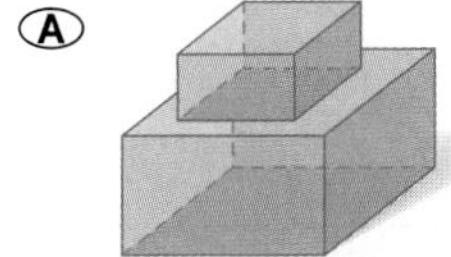

Ⓒ

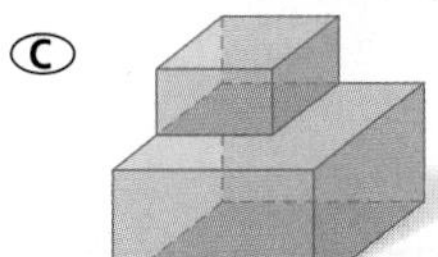

Ⓑ

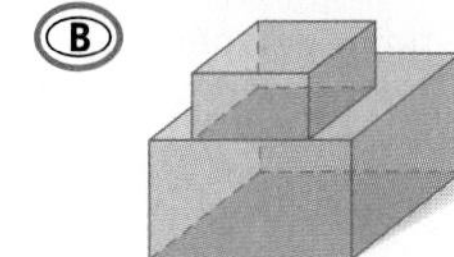

Ⓓ

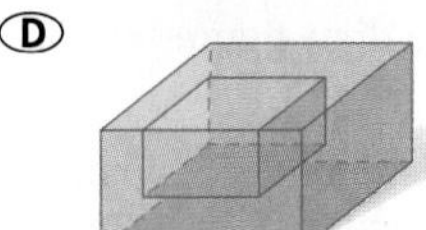

36. Which drawing best represents the top view of the three-dimensional figure?

Ⓕ

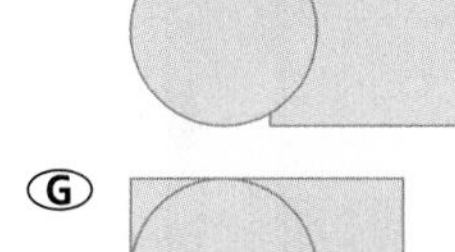

Ⓗ

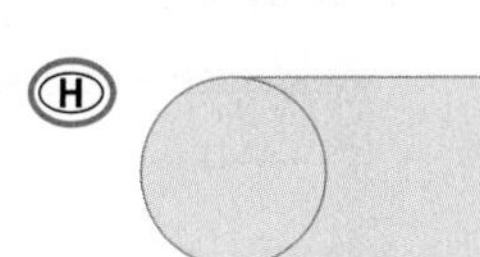

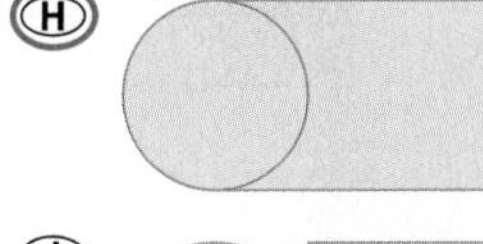

Ⓖ

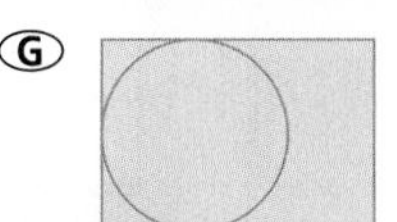

Ⓙ

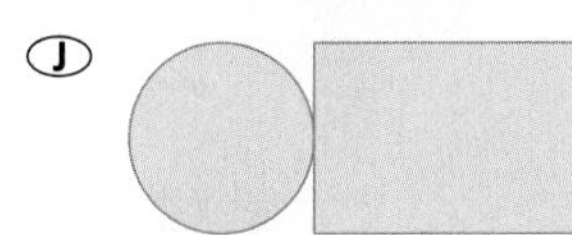

37. Short Response Draw a one-point perspective view and an isometric view of a triangular prism. Explain how the two drawings are different.

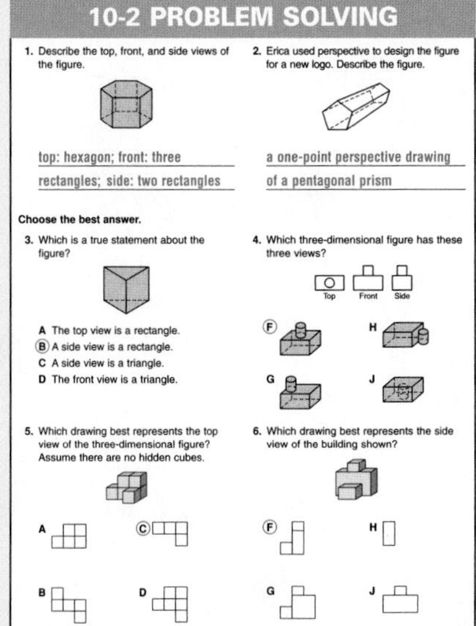

10-2 PROBLEM SOLVING

1. Describe the top, front, and side views of the figure.

top: hexagon; front: three rectangles; side: two rectangles

2. Erica used perspective to design the figure for a new logo. Describe the figure.

a one-point perspective drawing of a pentagonal prism

Choose the best answer.

3. Which is a true statement about the figure?

A The top view is a rectangle.
Ⓑ A side view is a rectangle.
C A side view is a triangle.
D The front view is a triangle.

4. Which three-dimensional figure has these three views?

Top Front Side

Ⓕ H G J

5. Which drawing best represents the top view of the three-dimensional figure? Assume there are no hidden cubes.

A Ⓒ B D

6. Which drawing best represents the side view of the building shown?

Ⓕ H G J

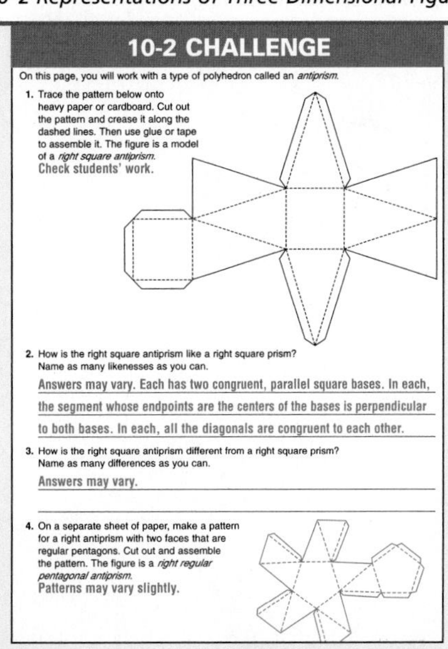

10-2 CHALLENGE

On this page, you will work with a type of polyhedron called an *antiprism*.

1. Trace the pattern below onto heavy paper or cardboard. Cut out the pattern and crease it along the dashed lines. Then use glue or tape to assemble it. The figure is a model of a *right square antiprism*.
Check students' work.

2. How is the right square antiprism like a right square prism? Name as many likenesses as you can.
Answers may vary. Each has two congruent, parallel square bases. In each, the segment whose endpoints are the centers of the bases is perpendicular to both bases. In each, all the diagonals are congruent to each other.

3. How is the right square antiprism different from a right square prism? Name as many differences as you can.
Answers may vary.

4. On a separate sheet of paper, make a pattern for a right antiprism with two faces that are regular pentagons. Cut out and assemble the pattern. The figure is a *right regular pentagonal antiprism*.
Patterns may vary slightly.

COMMON ERROR ALERT

In **Exercise 31,** students may try to include curved edges in every view. Encourage them to look at a real-world cylinder to see that the side views are rectangles.

TEST PREP DOCTOR Encourage students who answer **Exercise 35** incorrectly to look at the given views carefully. The smaller prism is on top of the larger one, eliminating choice **D.** The smaller prism is centered on the front edge of the larger one, eliminating choices **C** and **A.**

Answers

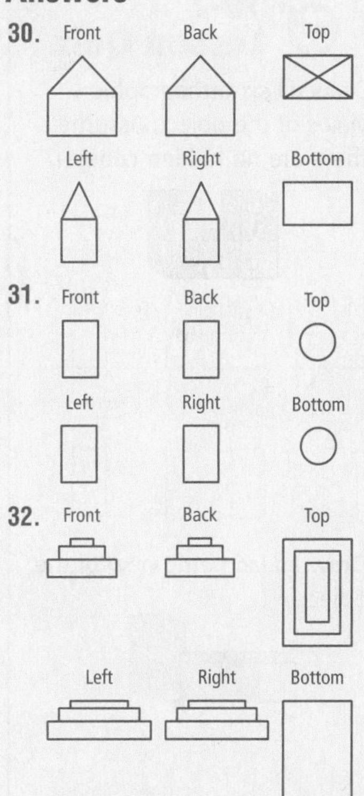

33. Possible answer: a right cylinder and a right square prism in which the diameter of the cylinder is equal to the side length of the square base of the prism and the heights are the same.

37. Possible answer:

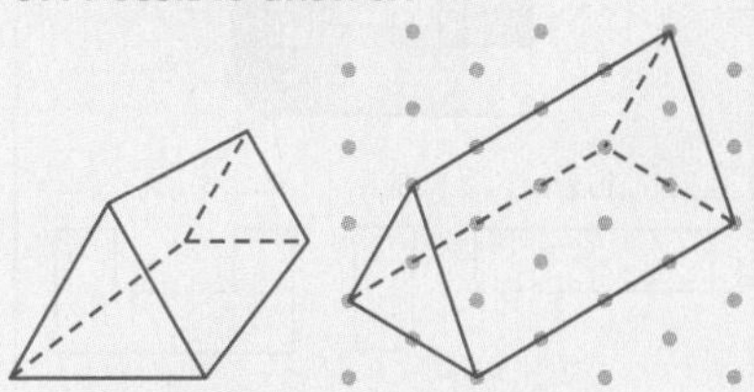

Some of the edges that are parallel on the 3-dimensional object are not parallel in the perspective drawing. If they were extended, they would meet at the vanishing point of the drawing. All the parallel edges of the prism are also parallel in the isometric drawing.

Have students describe how to draw a figure in two-point perspective, given an isometric drawing of the object.

Have students work in pairs. Give each student five unit cubes to build a block figure. Have them draw orthographic and isometric views of their block figures. Then have them exchange drawings, and have each build the figure created by the other student by using only the drawings.

Power Presentations with PowerPoint®

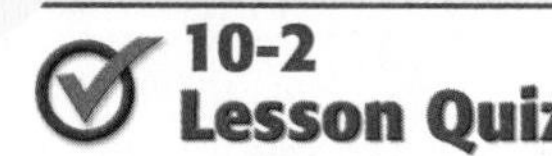

1. Draw all six orthographic views of the object. Assume there are no hidden cubes.

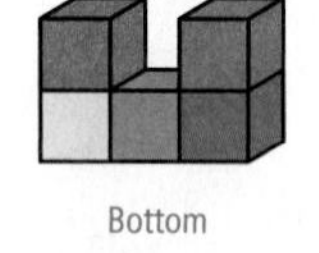

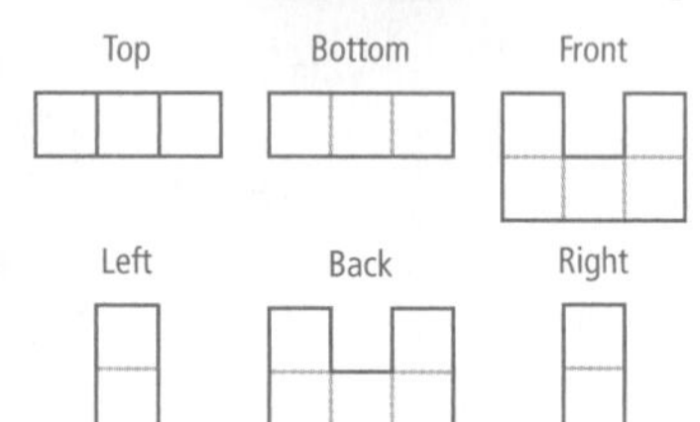

2. Draw an isometric view of the object.

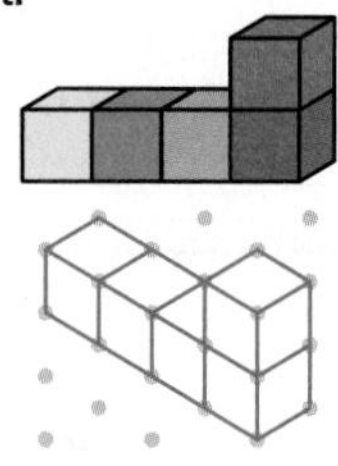

3. Determine whether each drawing represents the given object. Assume there are no hidden cubes.

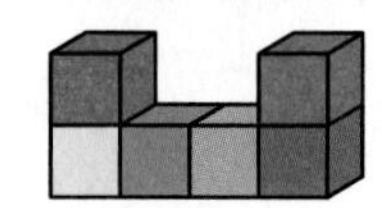

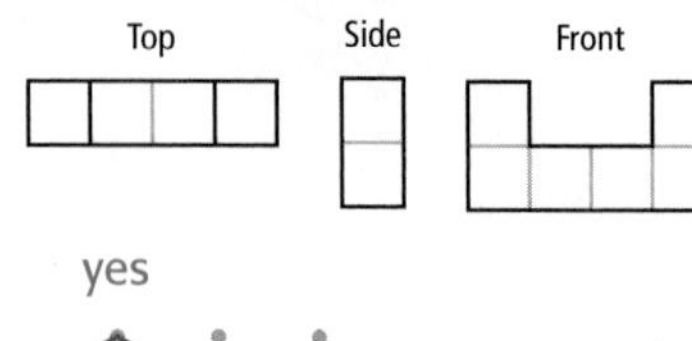

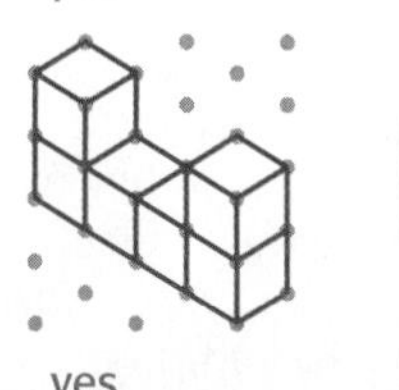

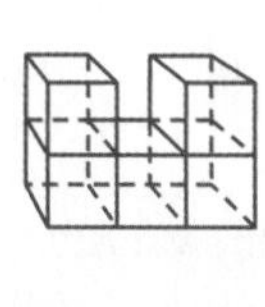

yes no

Also available on transparency

CHALLENGE AND EXTEND

Draw each figure using one-point perspective. (*Hint:* First lightly draw a rectangular prism. Enclose the figure in the prism.)

38. an octagonal prism
39. a cylinder
40. a cone

41. A *frustum* of a cone is a part of a cone with two parallel bases. Copy the diagram of the frustum of a cone.
   a. Draw the entire cone.
   b. Draw all six orthographic views of the frustum.
   c. Draw a net for the frustum.

42. **Art** Draw a one-point or two-point perspective drawing of the inside of a room. Include at least two pieces of furniture drawn in perspective.
Check students' drawings.

SPIRAL REVIEW

Find the two numbers. *(Previous course)*

43. The sum of two numbers is 30. The difference between 2 times the first number and 2 times the second number is 20.
The first number is 20, and the second number is 10.

44. The difference between the first number and the second number is 7. When the second number is added to 4 times the first number, the result is 38.
The first number is 9, and the second number is 2.

45. The second number is 5 more than the first number. Their sum is 5.
The first number is 0, and the second number is 5.

For $A(4, 2)$, $B(6, 1)$, $C(3, 0)$, and $D(2, 0)$, find the slope of each line. *(Lesson 3-5)*

46. $\overleftrightarrow{AB}$ $-\frac{1}{2}$
47. $\overleftrightarrow{AC}$ 2
48. $\overleftrightarrow{AD}$ 1

Describe the faces of each figure. *(Lesson 10-1)*

49. pentagonal prism
2 pentagons and 5 parallelograms

50. cube
6 squares

51. triangular pyramid
4 triangles

Using Technology

You can use geometry software to draw figures in one- and two-point perspectives.

1. a. Draw a horizontal line to represent the horizon. Create a vanishing point on the horizon. Draw a rectangle with two sides parallel to the horizon. Draw a segment from each vertex to the vanishing point. Check students' drawings.
   b. Draw a smaller rectangle with vertices on the segments that intersect the horizon. Hide these segments and complete the figure.
   c. Drag the vanishing point to different locations on the horizon. Describe what happens to the figure.

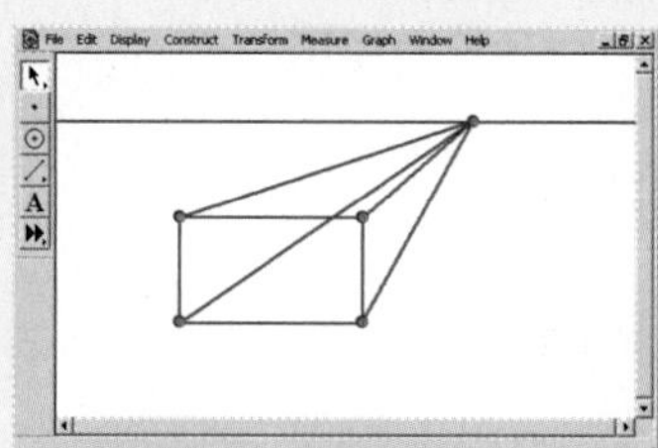

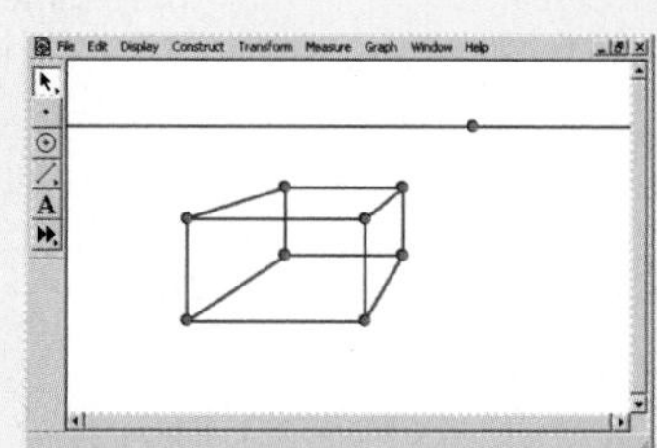

2. Describe how you would use geometry software to draw a figure in two-point perspective.

Answers

38.

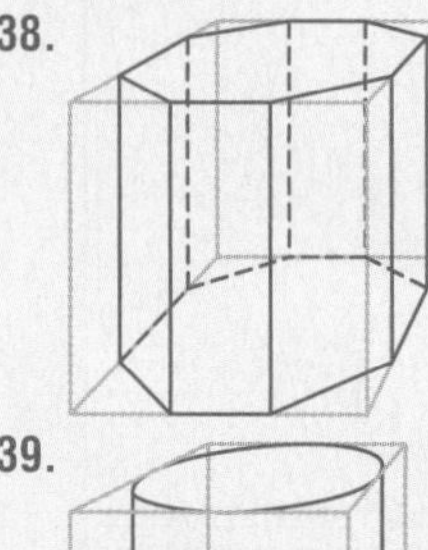

39.

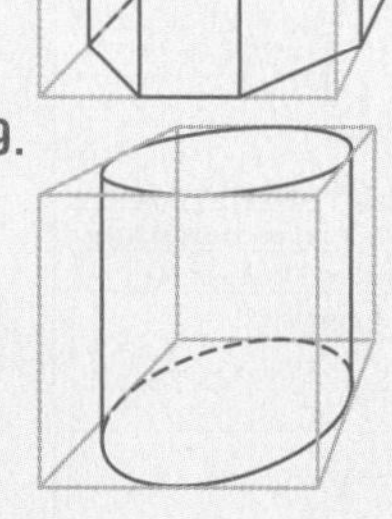

40.

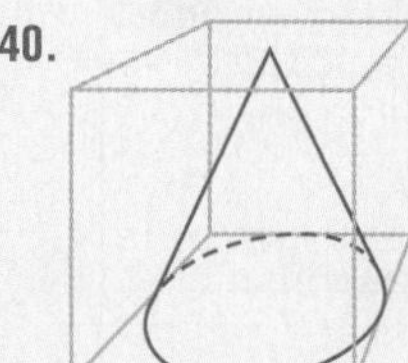

41a.

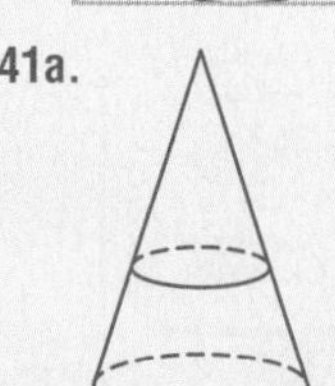

41b, c, Using Technology 2. See p. A26.

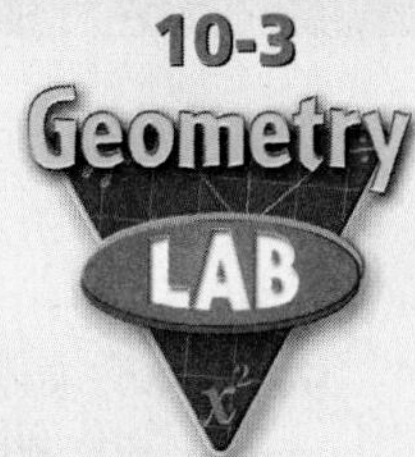

10-3 Geometry LAB

Use with Lesson 10-3

Use Nets to Create Polyhedrons

A *polyhedron* is formed by four or more polygons that intersect only at their edges. The faces of a *regular polyhedron* are all congruent regular polygons, and the same number of faces intersect at each vertex. Regular polyhedrons are also called *Platonic solids*. There are exactly five regular polyhedrons.

Activity

Use geometry software or a compass and straightedge to create a larger version of each net on heavy paper. Fold each net into a polyhedron.

REGULAR POLYHEDRONS			
NAME	FACES	EXAMPLE	NET
Tetrahedron	4 triangles		
Octahedron	8 triangles		
Icosahedron	20 triangles		
Cube	6 squares		
Dodecahedron	12 pentagons		

Try This

1. Complete the table for the number of vertices V, edges E, and faces F for each of the polyhedrons you made in Activity 1.
2. **Make a Conjecture** What do you think is true about the relationship between the number of vertices, edges, and faces of a polyhedron? **$V - E + F$ is always equal to 2.**

POLYHEDRON	V	E	F	$V - E + F$
Tetrahedron	4	6	4	2
Octahedron	6	12	8	2
Icosahedron	12	30	20	2
Cube	8	12	6	2
Dodecahedron	20	30	12	2

Teacher to Teacher

When introducing nets, I think it is helpful to show familiar objects such as a flattened cereal box. The designs on the box help students who have trouble visualizing three-dimensional objects see how the net fits together.

The more we can do to help students relate these objects to physical objects they are familiar with, the more helpful it will be to them.

Jamae Sellari
Jackson, MS

Organizer

Use with Lesson 10-3

Pacing:
Traditional 1 day
Block $\frac{1}{2}$ day

Objective: Use nets to create and explore properties of polyhedrons.

Materials: geometry software or compass and straightedge

Online Edition

Countdown Week 22

Resources

Geometry Lab Activities
10-3 Lab Recording Sheet

Teach

Discuss

Discuss the shapes of the faces of each regular polyhedron.

Close

Key Concept

For any polyhedron with V vertices, E edges, and F faces, $V - E + F = 2$.

Assessment

Journal Have students write out their conjectures in their own words.

Alternative Approach

You may wish to provide nets or have the students work in groups to complete the table.

State Resources

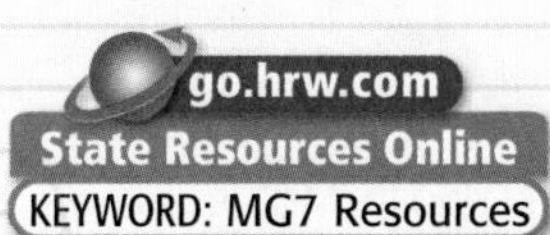

10-3 Organizer

Pacing: Traditional 1 day
Block $\frac{1}{2}$ day

Objectives: Apply Euler's formula to find the number of vertices, edges, and faces of a polyhedron.

Develop and apply the Distance and Midpoint Formulas in three dimensions.

Online Edition
Tutorial Videos

Countdown Week 22

Power Presentations with PowerPoint®

Warm Up

Find the unknown lengths.

1. the diagonal of a square with side length 5 cm $5\sqrt{2}$ cm
2. the base of a rectangle with diagonal 15 m and height 13 m 7.5 m
3. the height of a trapezoid with area 18 ft^2 and bases 3 ft and 9 ft 3 ft

Also available on transparency

Math Humor

Q: Who is the Tin Man's favorite mathematician?

A: Euler.

State Resources

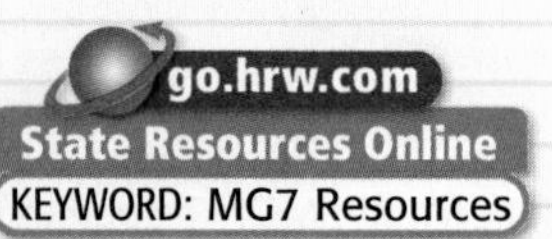

10-3 Formulas in Three Dimensions

Objectives
Apply Euler's formula to find the number of vertices, edges, and faces of a polyhedron.

Develop and apply the distance and midpoint formulas in three dimensions.

Vocabulary
polyhedron
space

Why learn this?
Divers can use a three-dimensional coordinate system to find distances between two points under water. (See Example 5.)

A **polyhedron** is formed by four or more polygons that intersect only at their edges. Prisms and pyramids are polyhedrons, but cylinders and cones are not.

Polyhedrons	Not polyhedrons
	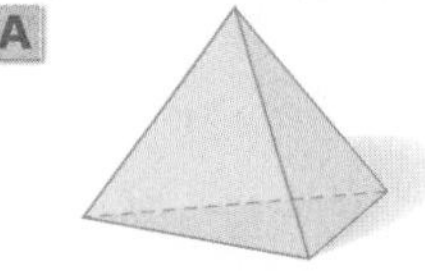

In the lab before this lesson, you made a conjecture about the relationship between the vertices, edges, and faces of a polyhedron. One way to state this relationship is given below.

Euler's Formula

For any polyhedron with V vertices, E edges, and F faces, $V - E + F = 2$.

EXAMPLE 1 Using Euler's Formula

Find the number of vertices, edges, and faces of each polyhedron. Use your results to verify Euler's formula.

A

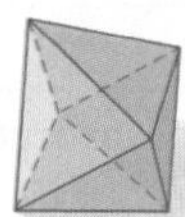

$V = 4, E = 6, F = 4$
$4 - 6 + 4 \stackrel{?}{=} 2$ *Use Euler's formula.*
$2 = 2$ *Simplify.*

B

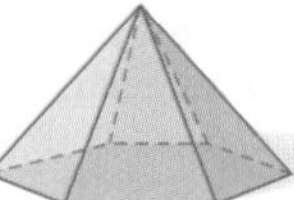

$V = 10, E = 15, F = 7$
$10 - 15 + 7 \stackrel{?}{=} 2$
$2 = 2$

Reading Math
Euler is pronounced "Oiler."

CHECK IT OUT! **Find the number of vertices, edges, and faces of the polyhedron. Use your results to verify Euler's formula.**

1a. **1b.**

1a. $V = 6$; $E = 12$; $F = 8$; $6 - 12 + 8 = 2$

1b. $V = 7$; $E = 12$; $F = 7$; $7 - 12 + 7 = 2$

1 Introduce

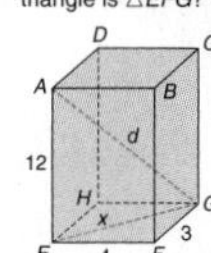

EXPLORATION
10-3 Formulas in Three Dimensions
In this Exploration, you will investigate how you can find the length of the diagonal of a right rectangular prism.
1. The figure shown is a right rectangular prism. What type of triangle is △EFG? Why?
2. Show how to find x.
3. What type of triangle is △AEG?
4. Show how to find d.
THINK AND DISCUSS
5. Explain which theorem you used to calculate both x and d.
6. Describe the steps you would use to find m in the right rectangular prism shown.

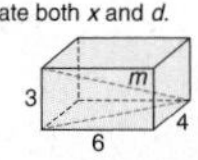

Motivate

Use a corner of the classroom to model the origin of a three-dimensional coordinate system. The intersection of two walls represents the z-axis, and the intersections of the walls and the floor represent the x- and y-axes. Have students use ordered triples to describe the location of several objects in the room.

Explorations and answers are provided in *Alternate Openers: Explorations Transparencies.*

A diagonal of a three-dimensional figure connects two vertices of two different faces. Diagonal d of a rectangular prism is shown in the diagram. By the Pythagorean Theorem, $\ell^2 + w^2 = x^2$, and $x^2 + h^2 = d^2$. Using substitution, $\ell^2 + w^2 + h^2 = d^2$.

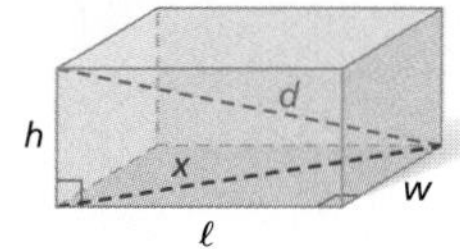

Diagonal of a Right Rectangular Prism

The length of a diagonal d of a right rectangular prism with length ℓ, width w, and height h is $d = \sqrt{\ell^2 + w^2 + h^2}$.

EXAMPLE 2 Using the Pythagorean Theorem in Three Dimensions

Find the unknown dimension in each figure.

A the length of the diagonal of a 3 in. by 4 in. by 5 in. rectangular prism

$d = \sqrt{3^2 + 4^2 + 5^2}$ *Substitute 3 for ℓ, 4 for w, and 5 for h.*

$= \sqrt{9 + 16 + 25}$ *Simplify.*

$= \sqrt{50} \approx 7.1$ in.

B the height of a rectangular prism with an 8 ft by 12 ft base and an 18 ft diagonal

$18 = \sqrt{8^2 + 12^2 + h^2}$ *Substitute 18 for d, 8 for ℓ, and 12 for w.*

$18^2 = \left(\sqrt{8^2 + 12^2 + h^2}\right)^2$ *Square both sides of the equation.*

$324 = 64 + 144 + h^2$ *Simplify.*

$h^2 = 116$ *Solve for h^2.*

$h = \sqrt{116} \approx 10.8$ ft *Take the square root of both sides.*

2. Find the length of the diagonal of a cube with edge length 5 cm.
$5\sqrt{3} \approx 8.7$ m

Space is the set of all points in three dimensions. Three coordinates are needed to locate a point in space. A three-dimensional coordinate system has 3 perpendicular axes: the x-axis, the y-axis, and the z-axis. An *ordered triple* (x, y, z) is used to locate a point. To locate the point $(3, 2, 4)$, start at $(0, 0, 0)$. From there move 3 units forward, 2 units right, and then 4 units up.

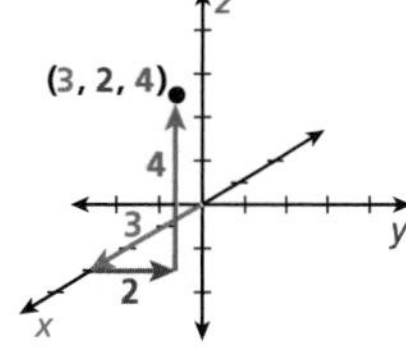

EXAMPLE 3 Graphing Figures in Three Dimensions

Graph each figure.

A a cube with edge length 4 units and one vertex at $(0, 0, 0)$

The cube has 8 vertices:
$(0, 0, 0)$, $(0, 4, 0)$, $(0, 0, 4)$, $(4, 0, 0)$, $(4, 4, 0)$, $(4, 0, 4)$, $(0, 4, 4)$, $(4, 4, 4)$.

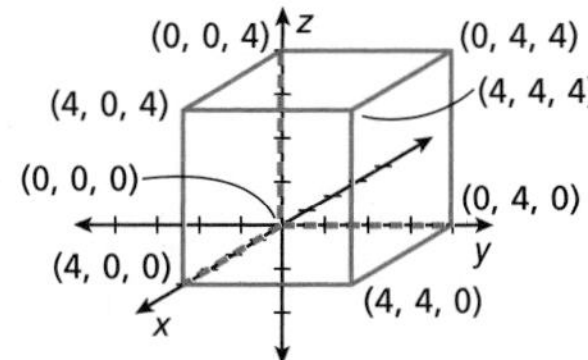

Power Presentations with PowerPoint®

Additional Examples

Example 1

Find the number of vertices, edges, and faces of each polyhedron. Use your results to verify Euler's formula.

A.

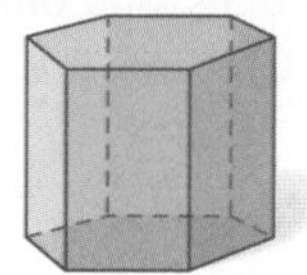

$V = 12$; $E = 18$; $F = 8$;
$12 - 18 + 8 = 2$

B.

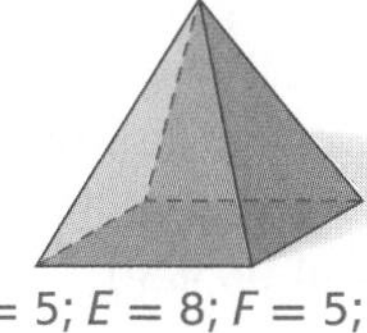

$V = 5$; $E = 8$; $F = 5$;
$5 - 8 + 5 = 2$

Example 2

Find the unknown dimension in each figure.

A. the length of the diagonal of a 6 cm by 8 cm by 10 cm rectangular prism $\sqrt{200} \approx 14.1$ cm

B. the height of a rectangular prism with a 12 in. by 7 in. base and a 15 in. diagonal $\sqrt{32} \approx 5.7$ in.

INTERVENTION
Questioning Strategies

EXAMPLE 1

- How is the number of vertices related to the number of sides of the base of a pyramid? of the base of a prism?

EXAMPLE 2

- How could you find the diagonal of a right rectangular prism by applying the Pythagorean Theorem twice?

2 Teach

Guided Instruction

Review the terms *vertices, edges,* and *faces*. Euler's formula gives the relationship between the number of vertices, edges, and faces of a polyhedron. Review plotting points and using the Distance and Midpoint Formulas in two dimensions and then explain how these ideas can be extended to three dimensions.

Reaching All Learners

Through Modeling

Have students use connecting cubes to create an x-, y-, and z-axis. To plot a point, they can locate the cube on the x-axis that represents the x-coordinate and attach a stack of cubes parallel to the y-axis. At the end of the stack, they would attach a stack of cubes parallel to the z-axis.

Graph each figure.

B **a cylinder with radius 3 units, height 5 units, and one base centered at (0, 0, 0)**

Graph the center of the bottom base at (0, 0, 0).

Since the height is 5, graph the center of the top base at (0, 0, 5).

The radius is 3, so the bottom base will cross the x-axis at (3, 0 ,0) and the y-axis at (0, 3, 0).

Draw the top base parallel to the bottom base and connect the bases.

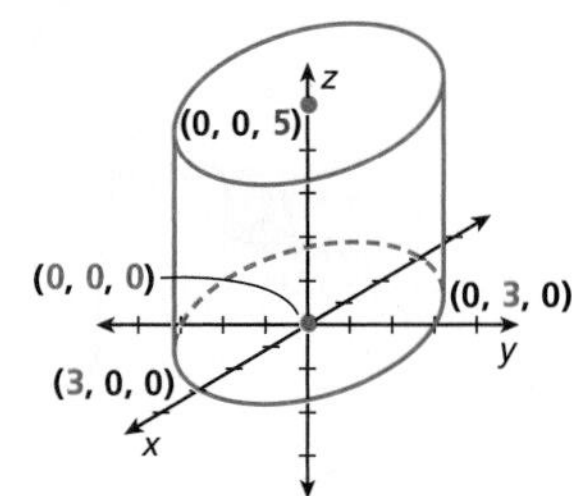

3. Graph a cone with radius 5 units, height 7 units, and the base centered at (0, 0, 0).

You can find the distance between the two points (x_1, y_1, z_1) and (x_2, y_2, z_2) by drawing a rectangular prism with the given points as endpoints of a diagonal. Then use the formula for the length of the diagonal. You can also use a formula related to the Distance Formula. (See Lesson 1-6.) The formula for the midpoint between (x_1, y_1, z_1) and (x_2, y_2, z_2) is related to the Midpoint Formula. (See Lesson 1-6.)

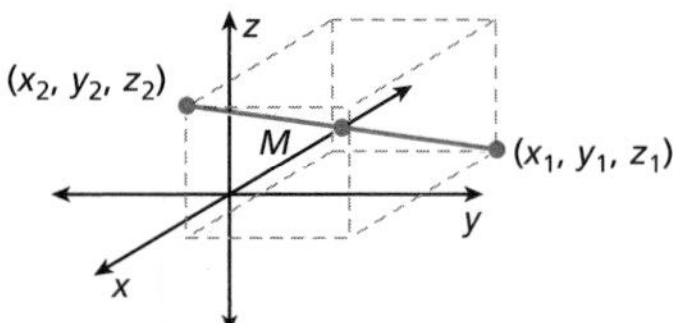

Know it! Note

Distance and Midpoint Formulas in Three Dimensions

The distance between the points (x_1, y_1, z_1) and (x_2, y_2, z_2) is

$$d = \sqrt{(x_2 - x_1)^2 + (y_2 - y_1)^2 + (z_2 - z_1)^2}.$$

The midpoint of the segment with endpoints (x_1, y_1, z_1) and (x_2, y_2, z_2) is

$$M\left(\frac{x_1 + x_2}{2}, \frac{y_1 + y_2}{2}, \frac{z_1 + z_2}{2}\right).$$

EXAMPLE 4 Finding Distances and Midpoints in Three Dimensions

Find the distance between the given points. Find the midpoint of the segment with the given endpoints. Round to the nearest tenth, if necessary.

A (0, 0, 0) and (3, 4, 12)

distance:

$$d = \sqrt{(x_2 - x_1)^2 + (y_2 - y_1)^2 + (z_2 - z_1)^2}$$
$$= \sqrt{(3 - 0)^2 + (4 - 0)^2 + (12 - 0)^2}$$
$$= \sqrt{9 + 16 + 144}$$
$$= \sqrt{169} = 13 \text{ units}$$

midpoint:

$$M\left(\frac{x_1 + x_2}{2}, \frac{y_1 + y_2}{2}, \frac{z_1 + z_2}{2}\right)$$
$$M\left(\frac{0 + 3}{2}, \frac{0 + 4}{2}, \frac{0 + 12}{2}\right)$$
$$M(1.5, 2, 6)$$

Power Presentations with PowerPoint®

Additional Examples

Example 3

Graph each figure.

A. a rectangular prism with length 5 units, width 3 units, height 4 units, and one vertex at (0, 0, 0)

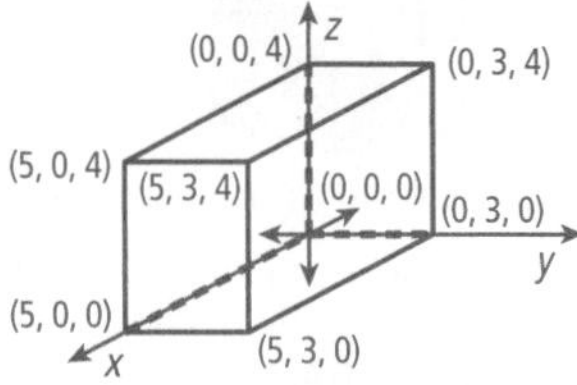

B. a cone with radius 3 units, height 5 units, and the base centered at (0, 0, 0)

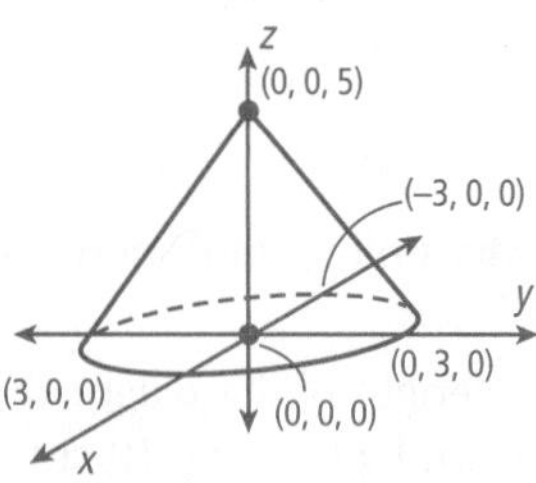

Example 4

Find the distance between the given points. Find the midpoint of the segment with the given endpoints. Round to the nearest tenth, if necessary.

A. (0, 0, 0) and (2, 8, 5)
$d \approx 9.6$ units; $M(1, 4, 2.5)$

B. (6, 11, 3) and (4, 6, 12)
$d \approx 10.5$ units; $M(5, 8.5, 7.5)$

INTERVENTION

Questioning Strategies

EXAMPLE 3

- How do you graph a figure in a three-dimensional coordinate system?

EXAMPLE 4

- How do you find the length and midpoint of a segment in a three-dimensional coordinate system?

Answers to *Check It Out!*

3.

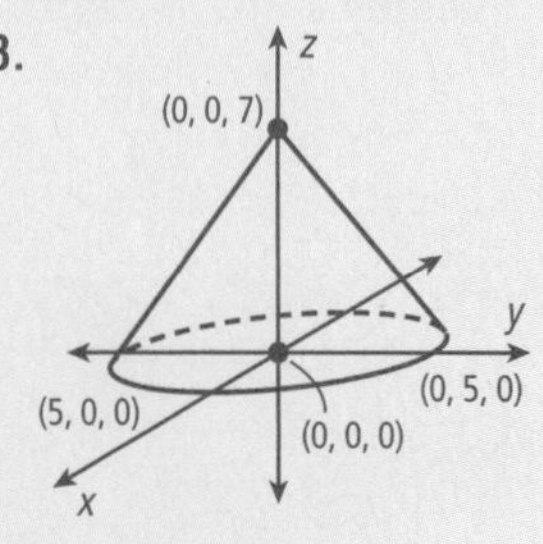

2 Teach *Continued*

Reaching All Learners

Through Critical Thinking

Starting with a simple polyhedron such as a cube, subdivide one of the faces by drawing a diagonal. Ask students to count the number of vertices, edges, and faces before and after the face is subdivided, and relate the result to Euler's formula. The number of vertices is the same, and the number of edges and faces each increase by 1. So $V - E + F$ is the same.

Math Background Leonhard Euler, pronounced "OIL-er," (1707–1783) was the most prolific mathematician of all time. He made important contributions in almost every area of mathematics.

Find the distance between the given points. Find the midpoint of the segment with the given endpoints. Round to the nearest tenth, if necessary.

B $(3, 8, 10)$ and $(7, 12, 15)$

distance:

$$d = \sqrt{(x_2 - x_1)^2 + (y_2 - y_1)^2 + (z_2 - z_1)^2}$$
$$= \sqrt{(7-3)^2 + (12-8)^2 + (15-10)^2}$$
$$= \sqrt{16 + 16 + 25}$$
$$= \sqrt{57} \approx 7.5 \text{ units}$$

midpoint:

$$M\left(\frac{x_1 + x_2}{2}, \frac{y_1 + y_2}{2}, \frac{z_1 + z_2}{2}\right)$$
$$M\left(\frac{3+7}{2}, \frac{8+12}{2}, \frac{10+15}{2}\right)$$
$$M(5, 10, 12.5)$$

Find the distance between the given points. Find the midpoint of the segment with the given endpoints. Round to the nearest tenth, if necessary.

4a. $(0, 9, 5)$ and $(6, 0, 12)$ $d \approx 12.9$ units; $M(3, 4.5, 8.5)$

4b. $(5, 8, 16)$ and $(12, 16, 20)$ $d \approx 11.4$ units; $M(8.5, 12, 18)$

EXAMPLE 5 ***Recreation Application***

Two divers swam from a boat to the locations shown in the diagram. How far apart are the divers?

The location of the boat can be represented by the ordered triple $(0, 0, 0)$, and the locations of the divers can be represented by the ordered triples $(18, 9, -8)$ and $(-15, -6, -12)$.

$$d = \sqrt{(x_2 - x_1)^2 + (y_2 - y_1)^2 + (z_2 - z_1)^2}$$ *Use the Distance Formula to find the distance between the divers.*
$$= \sqrt{(-15 - 18)^2 + (-6 - 9)^2 + (-12 + 8)^2}$$
$$= \sqrt{1330} \approx 36.5 \text{ ft}$$

5. What if...? If both divers swam straight up to the surface, how far apart would they be? 36.2 ft

THINK AND DISCUSS

1. Explain how to find the distance between two points in a three-dimensional coordinate system.

2. GET ORGANIZED Copy and complete the graphic organizer.

	Rectangular Prism	Rectangular Pyramid
Vertices V	8	5
Edges E	12	8
Faces F	6	5
$V - E + F$	2	2

COMMON ERROR ALERT

Students may confuse the diagonal of a right rectangular prism with the diagonal of the base of the figure. Remind them that a diagonal of a polyhedron connects vertices of two different faces of the polyhedron.

Power Presentations with PowerPoint®

Additional Examples

Example 5

Trevor drove 12 miles east and 25 miles south from a cabin while gaining 0.1 mile in elevation. Samira drove 8 miles west and 17 miles north from the cabin while gaining 0.15 mile in elevation. How far apart were the drivers? about 46.5 mi

INTERVENTION

Questioning Strategies

EXAMPLE 5

- How can a right rectangular prism be used to model a real-world problem in three dimensions?

Teaching Tip **Visual** To illustrate the diagonal of a right rectangular prism, show students an empty cardboard box with no lid. Use a stick or ruler to represent the diagonal.

3 Close

Summarize

Draw a cube with side length 5 that has one vertex at the origin and edges on the x-, y-, and z-axes. Ask students to find the coordinates of the remaining vertices and the length and the coordinates of the midpoint of a diagonal. $(0, 5, 5)$, $(5, 0, 5)$, $(5, 5, 0)$, and $(5, 5, 5)$; length of diagonal: $5\sqrt{3}$; midpoint of diagonal: $(2.5, 2.5, 2.5)$

ONGOING ASSESSMENT and INTERVENTION

***Diagnose Before* the Lesson**
10-3 Warm Up, TE p. 670

***Monitor During* the Lesson**
Check It Out! Exercises, SE pp. 670–673
Questioning Strategies, TE pp. 671–673

***Assess After* the Lesson**
10-3 Lesson Quiz, TE p. 677
Alternative Assessment, TE p. 677

Answers to *Think and Discuss*

1. Find the difference of the x-coordinates, the difference of the y-coordinates, and the difference of the z-coordinates. Square each result, and add. The distance is the square root of the sum.

10-3 Exercises

Assignment Guide

Assign *Guided Practice* exercises as necessary.

If you finished Examples **1–3**
- **Basic** 15–23, 28–33, 35–44, 52
- **Average** 15–23, 28–33, 35–44, 52, 53
- **Advanced** 15–23, 28–33, 35–44, 52, 53, 60

If you finished Examples **1–5**
- **Basic** 15–54, 57–59, 64–71
- **Average** 15–44, 46–50 even, 51–61, 64–71
- **Advanced** 15–44, 46–50 even, 51–71

Homework Quick Check
Quickly check key concepts.
Exercises: 16, 18, 22, 26, 27, 28, 32

Answers

2. $V = 6$; $E = 9$; $F = 5$; $6 - 9 + 5 = 2$
3. $V = 6$; $E = 10$; $F = 6$; $6 - 10 + 6 = 2$
4. $V = 10$; $E = 20$; $F = 12$; $10 - 20 + 12 = 2$
8.

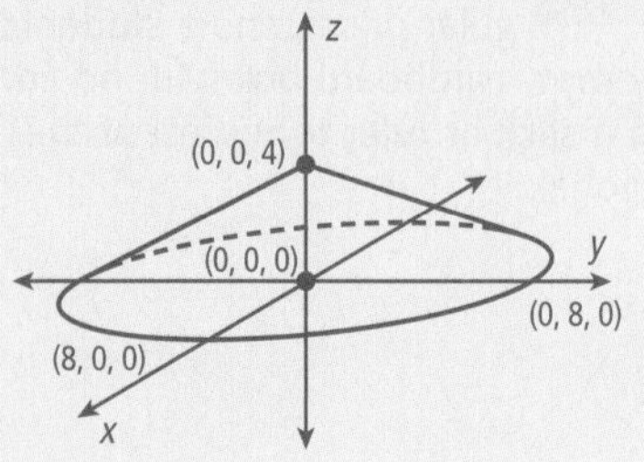

9.

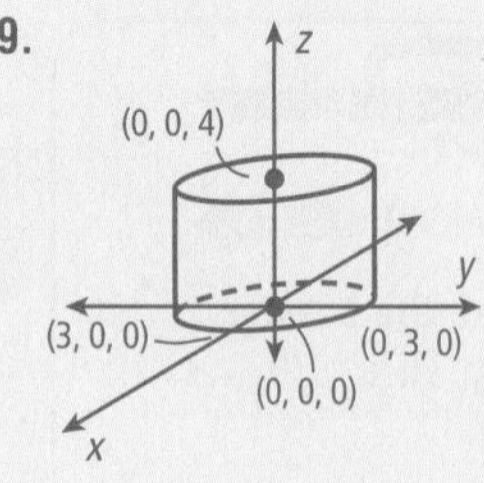

10.

11. $d \approx 14.4$ units; $M(2.5, 4.5, 5)$
12. $d \approx 9.7$ units; $M(3.5, 1.5, 11)$
13. $d \approx 9.3$ units; $M(6.5, 9, 12.5)$

State Resources

10-3 Exercises

go.hrw.com
Homework Help Online
KEYWORD: MG7 10-3
Parent Resources Online
KEYWORD: MG7 Parent

GUIDED PRACTICE

1. **Vocabulary** Explain why a cylinder is not a *polyhedron*. because the bases are circles, which are not polygons

SEE EXAMPLE 1 p. 670

Find the number of vertices, edges, and faces of each polyhedron. Use your results to verify Euler's formula.

2. 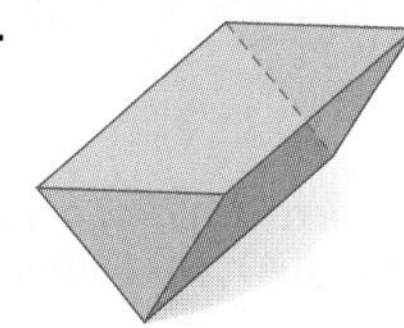
3. 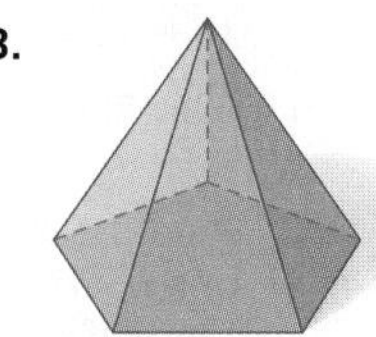
4. 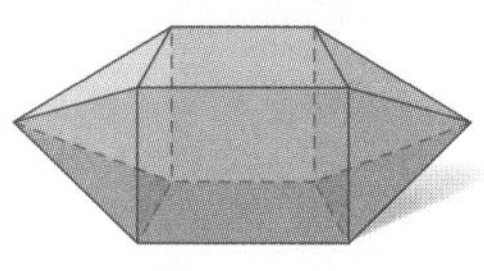

SEE EXAMPLE 2 p. 671

Find the unknown dimension in each figure. Round to the nearest tenth, if necessary.

5. the length of the diagonal of a 4 ft by 8 ft by 12 ft rectangular prism **15.0 ft**
6. the height of a rectangular prism with a 6 in. by 10 in. base and a 13 in. diagonal **5.7 in.**
7. the length of the diagonal of a square prism with a base edge length of 12 in. and a height of 1 in. **17 in.**

SEE EXAMPLE 3 p. 671

Graph each figure.

8. a cone with radius 8 units, height 4 units, and the base centered at $(0, 0, 0)$
9. a cylinder with radius 3 units, height 4 units, and one base centered at $(0, 0, 0)$
10. a cube with edge length 7 units and one vertex at $(0, 0, 0)$

SEE EXAMPLE 4 p. 672

Find the distance between the given points. Find the midpoint of the segment with the given endpoints. Round to the nearest tenth, if necessary.

11. $(0, 0, 0)$ and $(5, 9, 10)$
12. $(0, 3, 8)$ and $(7, 0, 14)$
13. $(4, 6, 10)$ and $(9, 12, 15)$

SEE EXAMPLE 5 p. 673

14. **Recreation** After a day hike, a group of hikers set up a camp 3 km east and 7 km north of the starting point. The elevation of the camp is 0.6 km higher than the starting point. What is the distance from the camp to the starting point? **7.6 km**

PRACTICE AND PROBLEM SOLVING

Independent Practice

For Exercises	See Example
15–17	1
18–20	2
21–23	3
24–26	4
27	5

Extra Practice
Skills Practice p. S22
Application Practice p. S37

Find the number of vertices, edges, and faces of each polyhedron. Use your results to verify Euler's formula.

15. 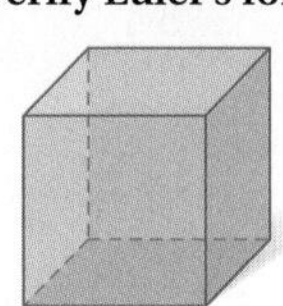
16. 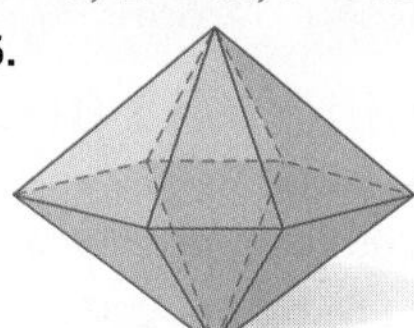
17. 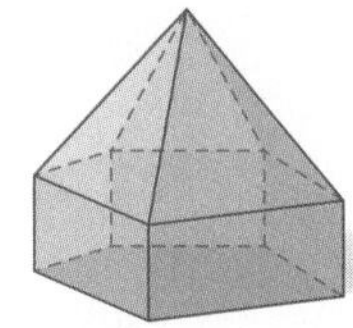

15. $V = 8$; $E = 12$; $F = 6$; $8 - 12 + 6 = 2$
16. $V = 8$; $E = 18$; $F = 12$; $8 - 18 + 12 = 2$
17. $V = 11$; $E = 20$; $F = 11$; $11 - 20 + 11 = 2$

Find the unknown dimension in each figure. Round to the nearest tenth, if necessary.

18. the length of the diagonal of a 7 yd by 8 yd by 16 yd rectangular prism $d \approx 19.2$ yd
19. the height of a rectangular prism with a 15 m by 6 m base and a 17 m diagonal $h \approx 5.3$ m
20. the edge length of a cube with an 8 cm diagonal $s \approx 4.6$ cm

Graph each figure.

21. a cylinder with radius 5 units, height 3 units, and one base centered at $(0, 0, 0)$

22. a cone with radius 2 units, height 4 units, and the base centered at $(0, 0, 0)$

23. a square prism with base edge length 5 units, height 3 units, and one vertex at $(0, 0, 0)$

LINK

Meteorology

A typical cumulus cloud weighs about 1.4 billion pounds, which is more than 100,000 elephants.

Source: usgs.gov

Find the distance between the given points. Find the midpoint of the segment with the given endpoints. Round to the nearest tenth, if necessary.

24. $(0, 0, 0)$ and $(4, 4, 4)$ 25. $(2, 3, 7)$ and $(9, 10, 10)$ 26. $(2, 5, 3)$ and $(8, 8, 10)$

27. **Meteorology** A cloud has an elevation of 6500 feet. A raindrop falling from the cloud was blown 700 feet south and 500 feet east before it hit the ground. How far did the raindrop travel from the cloud to the ground? **6557 ft**

28. **Multi-Step** Find the length of a diagonal of the rectangular prism at right. If the length, width, and height are doubled, what happens to the length of the diagonal? **13 ft; the diagonal is doubled.**

4 ft
3 ft
12 ft

For each three-dimensional figure, find the missing value and draw a figure with the correct number of vertices, edges, and faces.

	Vertices V	Edges E	Faces F	Diagram
	5	8	5	
29.	8	12	6	
30.	6	9	5	
31.	7	12	7	

24. $d \approx 6.9$ units; $M(2, 2, 2)$

25. $d \approx 10.3$ units; $M(5.5, 6.5, 8.5)$

26. $d \approx 9.7$ units; $M(5, 6.5, 6.5)$

32. **Algebra** Each base of a prism is a polygon with n sides. Write an expression for the number of vertices V, the number of edges E, and the number of faces F in terms of n. Use your results to show that Euler's formula is true for all prisms.

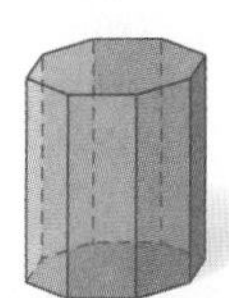

33. **Algebra** The base of a pyramid is a polygon with n sides. Write an expression for the number of vertices V, the number of edges E, and the number of faces F in terms of n. Use your results to show that Euler's formula is true for all pyramids.

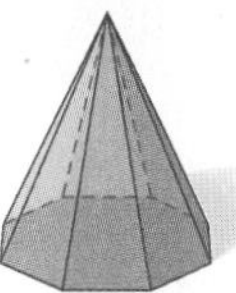

34a. $K(0, 2.5, 6)$; $L(0, 5, 0)$; $N(7, 2.5, 6)$; $P(7, 5, 0)$

MULTI-STEP TEST PREP

34. This problem will prepare you for the Multi-Step Test Prep on page 678.

The tent at right is a triangular prism where $\overline{NM} \cong \overline{NP}$ and $\overline{KJ} \cong \overline{KL}$ and has the given dimensions.

a. The tent manufacturer sets up the tent on a coordinate system so that J is at the origin and M has coordinates $(7, 0, 0)$. Find the coordinates of the other vertices.

b. The manufacturer wants to know the distance from K to P in order to make an extra support pole for the tent. Find KP to the nearest tenth. **9.6 ft**

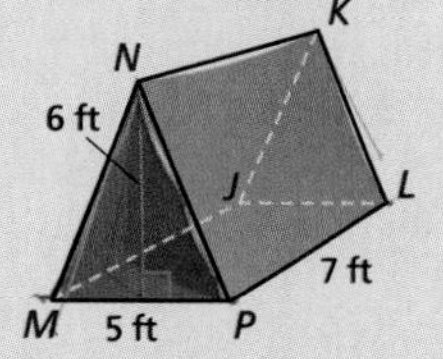

In **Exercises 29–31**, students may draw a prism when they should draw a pyramid, or vice versa. First make sure that they are applying Euler's formula correctly to find the missing value. Then, using models if necessary, help them see that $V = F$ in any pyramid, while $V > F$ in any prism.

MULTI-STEP TEST PREP **Exercise 34** involves placing a triangular prism that represents a tent in a three-dimensional coordinate system and using the Distance Formula in three dimensions to find the length of a diagonal. This exercise prepares students for the Multi-Step Test Prep on page 678.

Answers

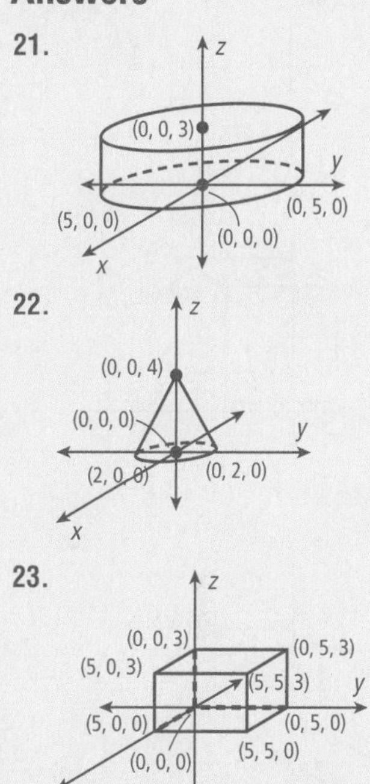

29–31. For diagrams, see p. A27.

32–33. See p. A27.

10-3 PRACTICE A

Match the letter of each formula to its name.

1. Euler's Formula ___b___
2. diagonal of a rectangular prism ___c___
3. distance in three dimensions ___d___
4. midpoint in three dimensions ___a___

a. $M\left(\frac{x_1 + x_2}{2}, \frac{y_1 + y_2}{2}, \frac{z_1 + z_2}{2}\right)$

b. $V - E + F = 2$

c. $d = \sqrt{\ell^2 + w^2 + h^2}$

d. $d = \sqrt{(x_2 - x_1)^2 + (y_2 - y_1)^2 + (z_2 - z_1)^2}$

Count the number of vertices, edges, and faces of each polyhedron. Use your results to verify Euler's Formula.

5. $V = 5$; $E = 8$; $F = 5$; $5 - 8 + 5 = 2$

6. $V = 8$; $E = 12$; $F = 6$; $8 - 12 + 6 = 2$

For Exercises 7–9, use the formula for the length of a diagonal to find the unknown dimension in each polyhedron. Round to the nearest tenth.

7. the length of a diagonal of a cube with edge length 3 in. ___5.2 in.___

8. the length of a diagonal of a 7-cm-by-10-cm-by-4-cm rectangular prism ___12.8 cm___

9. the height of a rectangular prism with a 6-m-by-6-m base and a 9 m diagonal ___3 m___

10. A rectangular prism with length 3, width 2, and height 4 has one vertex at (0, 0, 0). Three other vertices are at (3, 0, 0), (0, 2, 0), and (0, 0, 4). Find the four other vertices. Then graph the figure.

(0, 0, 4) (0, 2, 4) (3, 0, 4) (3, 2, 4) (0, 0, 0) (3, 0, 0) (0, 2, 0) (3, 2, 0)

___(3, 2, 0), (3, 2, 4), (3, 0, 4), (0, 2, 4)___

Use the formula for distance in three dimensions to find the distance between the given points. Use the midpoint formula in three dimensions to find the midpoint of the segment with the given endpoints. Round to the nearest tenth if necessary.

11. (0, 0, 0) and (2, 4, 6) ___7.5 units; (1, 2, 3)___

12. (1, 0, 5) and (0, 4, 0) ___6.5 units; (0.5, 2, 2.5)___

13. The world's largest ball of twine wound by a single individual weighs 17,400 pounds and has a 12-foot diameter. Roman climbs on top of the ball for a picture. To take the best picture, Lysandra moves 15 feet back and then 6 feet to her right. Find the distance from Lysandra to Roman. Round to the nearest tenth. ___24.9 feet___

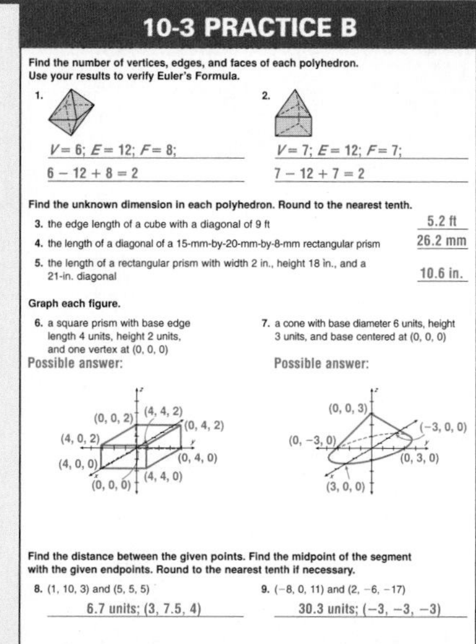

10-3 PRACTICE B

Find the number of vertices, edges, and faces of each polyhedron. Use your results to verify Euler's Formula.

1. $V = 6$; $E = 12$; $F = 8$; $6 - 12 + 8 = 2$

2. $V = 7$; $E = 12$; $F = 7$; $7 - 12 + 7 = 2$

Find the unknown dimension in each polyhedron. Round to the nearest tenth.

3. the edge length of a cube with a diagonal of 9 ft ___5.2 ft___

4. the length of a diagonal of a 15-mm-by-20-mm-by-8-mm rectangular prism ___26.2 mm___

5. the length of a rectangular prism with width 2 in., height 18 in., and a 21-in. diagonal ___10.6 in.___

Graph each figure.

6. a square prism with base edge length 4 units, height 2 units, and one vertex at (0, 0, 0)

Possible answer:

(0, 0, 2) (4, 4, 2) (0, 4, 2) (4, 0, 2) (4, 0, 0) (0, 4, 0) (0, 0, 0) (4, 4, 0)

7. a cone with base diameter 6 units, height 3 units, and base centered at (0, 0, 0)

Possible answer:

(0, 0, 3) (−3, 0, 0) (0, −3, 0) (0, 3, 0) (3, 0, 0)

Find the distance between the given points. Find the midpoint of the segment with the given endpoints. Round to the nearest tenth if necessary.

8. (1, 10, 3) and (5, 5, 5) ___6.7 units; (3, 7.5, 4)___

9. (−8, 0, 11) and (2, −6, −17) ___30.3 units; (−3, −3, −3)___

10-3 PRACTICE C

1. The distance from (0, 0, 0) to the surface of a solid is 4 units. Graph the solid.

2. Each edge of the solid shown in the figure measures 5 in. Find the length of $\overline{AB}$. Give an exact answer and an answer rounded to the nearest tenth. ___$5\sqrt{2}$ in.; 7.1 in.___

3. Find the length of $\overline{AB}$ if the bipyramid in Exercise 2 were based on a triangle rather than on a square. Round to the nearest tenth. ___8.2 in.___

4. Find the length of $\overline{AB}$ if the bipyramid in Exercise 2 were based on a pentagon rather than on a square. Round to the nearest tenth. ___5.3 in.___

5. If the bipyramid in Exercise 2 were based on a hexagon instead of a square, describe what sort of shape would result. Explain your answer.

The shape would be a flat hexagon; possible answer: The distance to the vertex of the bipyramid from the midpoint of a side (the slant height) would be $\frac{5\sqrt{3}}{2}$ in. The distance from the midpoint of a side to the center of the hexagon (the apothem) would also be $\frac{5\sqrt{3}}{2}$ in. Therefore, the height AB would be zero.

6. The distance from $A(-2, 7, 0)$ to $B(3, 2, b)$ and from A to $C(3, 2, c)$ is 10 units. D lies on $\overline{BC}$ so that AD is the shortest distance from A to $\overline{BC}$. Find the coordinates of D without calculating. Explain how you got the answer.

$D(3, 2, 0)$; possible answer: Because B and C have the same x- and y-coordinates, D must also have those x- and y-coordinates to lie on $\overline{BC}$. Any difference in length from A to $\overline{BC}$ is caused by changes in the z-coordinate, and the shortest distance occurs when D has the same z-coordinate as A.

7. A rectangular prism has vertices, in no particular order, at (−10, 8, 2), (−15, 8, 10), (−10, 5, 10), (−10, 5, 2), (−10, 8, 10), (−15, 5, 2), (−15, 5, 10), and (−15, 8, 2). Find the length of a diagonal of the prism. Round to the nearest tenth. ___$7\sqrt{2} \approx 9.9$ units___

8. Find the coordinates of a point that is equidistant from each of the eight vertices of the prism in Exercise 7. ___(−12.5, 6.5, 6)___

Tyrone has eight 1-in. cubes. He arranges all eight of them to make different rectangular prisms. Find the dimensions of the prisms based on the diagonal lengths given below.

9. $\sqrt{66}$ in. ___an 8-by-1-by-1 prism___

10. $\sqrt{21}$ in. ___a 4-by-2-by-1 prism___

11. $2\sqrt{3}$ in. ___a 2-by-2-by-2 prism___

Teaching Tip

Algebra In **Exercises 35–38,** remind students to apply the order of operations when evaluating the radicals used to calculate the diagonal of a right rectangular prism.

Answers

39.

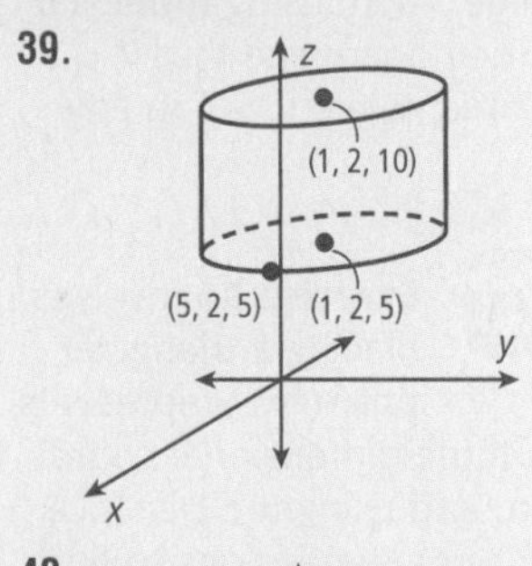

40.

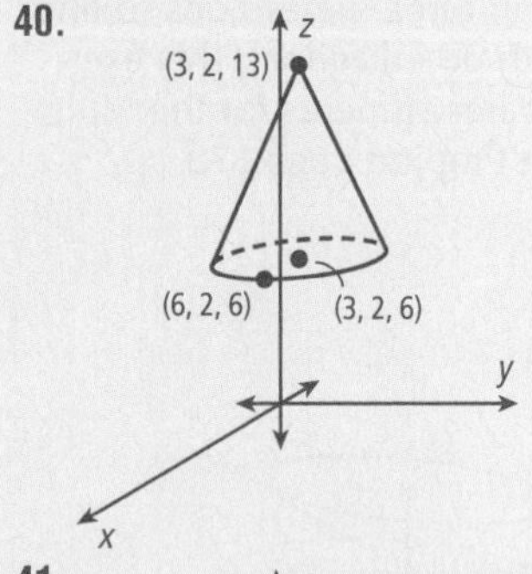

41.

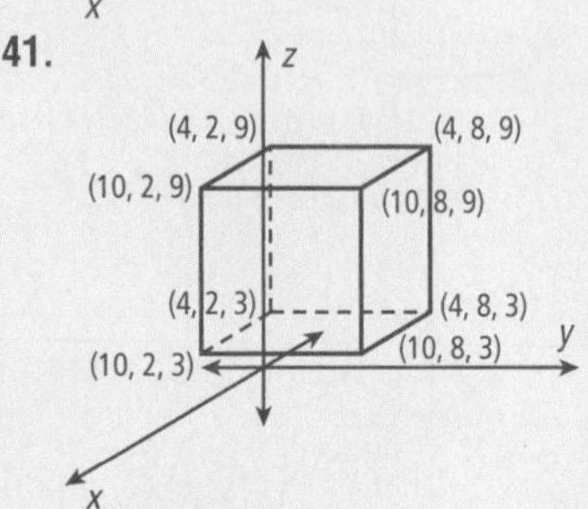

42.

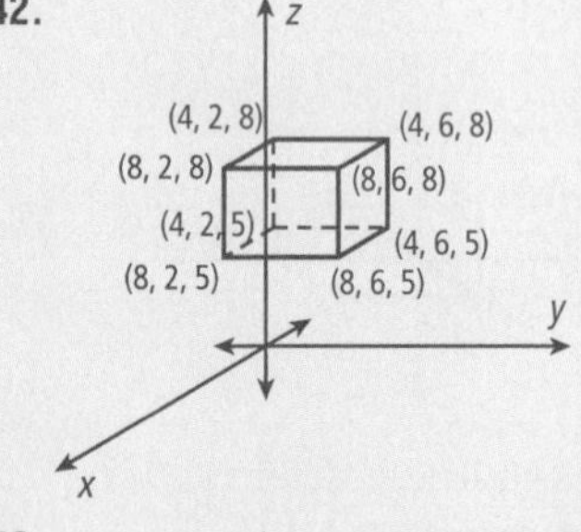

43.

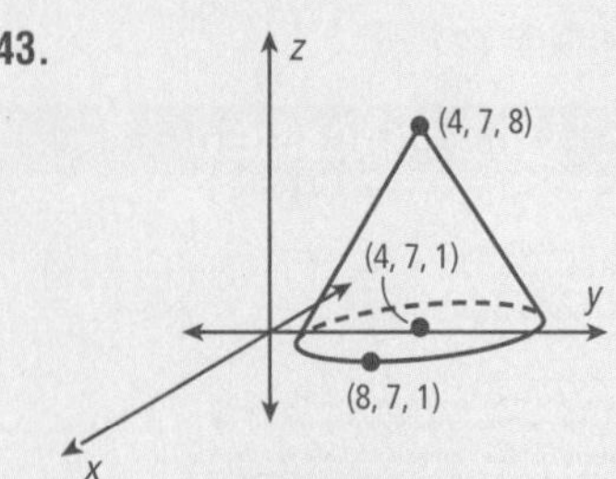

44.

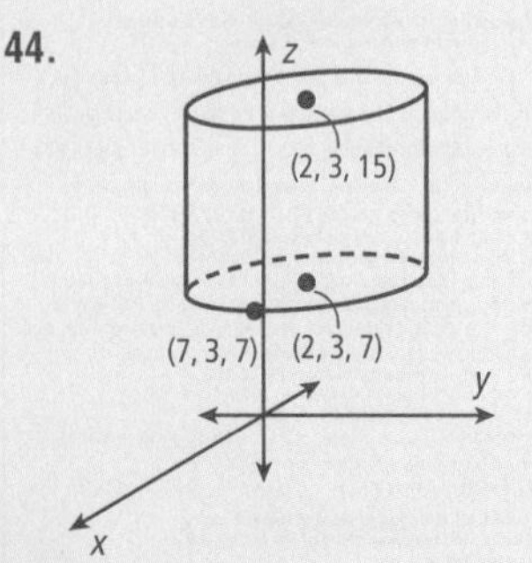

45–50. See p. A27.

Find the missing dimension of each rectangular prism. Give your answers in simplest radical form.

	Length ℓ	Width w	Height h	Diagonal d
35.	6 in.	6 in.	6 in.	$6\sqrt{3}$
36.	24	7	60	65
37.	12	18	$6\sqrt{3}$	24
38.	$\sqrt{3}$	2	3	4

Graph each figure.

39. a cylinder with radius 4 units, height 5 units, and one base centered at (1, 2, 5)

40. a cone with radius 3 units, height 7 units, and the base centered at (3, 2, 6)

41. a cube with edge length 6 units and one vertex at (4, 2, 3)

42. a rectangular prism with vertices at (4, 2, 5), (4, 6, 5), (4, 6, 8), (8, 6, 5), (8, 2, 5), (8, 6, 8), (4, 2, 8), and (8, 2, 8)

43. a cone with radius 4 units, the vertex at (4, 7, 8), and the base centered at (4, 7, 1)

44. a cylinder with a radius of 5 units and bases centered at (2, 3, 7) and (2, 3, 15)

Graph each segment with the given endpoints in a three-dimensional coordinate system. Find the length and midpoint of each segment.

45. (1, 2, 3) and (3, 2, 1) **46.** (4, 3, 3) and (7, 4, 4) **47.** (4, 7, 8) and (3, 1, 5)

48. (0, 0, 0) and (8, 3, 6) **49.** (6, 1, 8) and (2, 2, 6) **50.** (2, 8, 5) and (3, 6, 3)

51. Multi-Step Find z if the distance between $R(6, -1, -3)$ and $S(3, 3, z)$ is 13. **$z = 9$ or -15**

52. Draw a figure with 6 vertices and 6 faces.

53. Estimation Measure the net for a rectangular prism and estimate the length of a diagonal. **Possible answer: 1.8 in.**

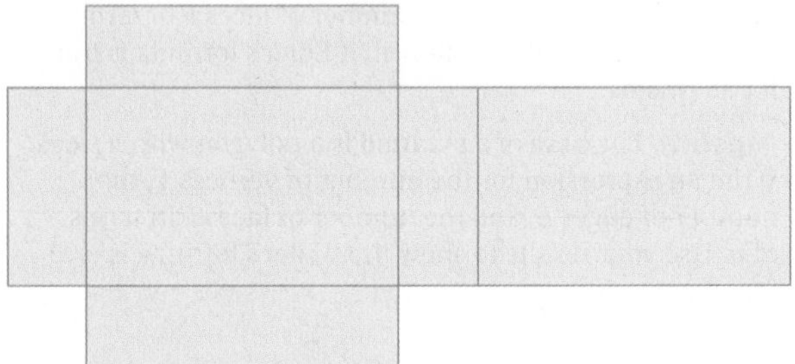

54. Make a Conjecture What do you think is the longest segment joining two points on a rectangular prism? Test your conjecture using at least three segments whose endpoints are on the prism with vertices $A(0, 0, 0)$, $B(1, 0, 0)$, $C(1, 2, 0)$, $D(0, 2, 0)$, $E(0, 0, 2)$, $F(1, 0, 2)$, $G(1, 2, 2)$, and $H(0, 2, 2)$.

55. Critical Thinking The points $A(3, 2, -3)$, $B(5, 8, 6)$, and $C(-3, -5, 3)$ form a triangle. Classify the triangle by sides and angles.

56. Write About It A cylinder has a radius of 4 cm and a height of 6 cm. What is the length of the longest segment with both endpoints on the cylinder? Describe the location of the endpoints and explain why it is the longest possible segment.

52. Possible answer:

54. Possible answer: a seg. that connects a vertex of 1 base to the opp. vertex of the other base; $AB = 1$ unit, $AC = \sqrt{5} \approx 2.2$ units, $AG = 3$ units

55. $AB = 11$, $AC = 11$, and $BC = 11\sqrt{2}$, so $\triangle ABC$ is an isosc. rt. $\triangle$.

56. 10 cm; the seg. is the hyp. of a rt. $\triangle$ in which 1 leg is a diam. of 1 base and the opp. vertex is on the other base; it is the longest seg. because a diam. is the longest possible seg. in a circle.

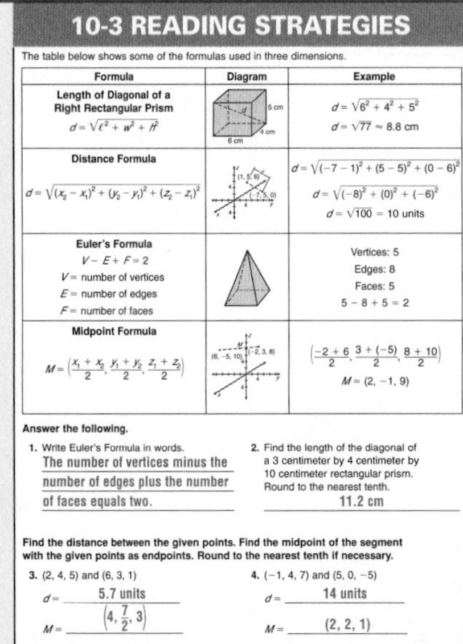

10-3 READING STRATEGIES

The table below shows some of the formulas used in three dimensions.

Formula	Diagram	Example
Length of Diagonal of a Right Rectangular Prism $d = \sqrt{\ell^2 + w^2 + h^2}$	5 cm, 4 cm, 6 cm, d	$d = \sqrt{6^2 + 4^2 + 5^2}$ $d = \sqrt{77} \approx 8.8$ cm
Distance Formula $d = \sqrt{(x_2 - x_1)^2 + (y_2 - y_1)^2 + (z_2 - z_1)^2}$	(1, 5, 6), (−7, 5, 0)	$d = \sqrt{(-7 - 1)^2 + (5 - 5)^2 + (0 - 6)^2}$ $d = \sqrt{(-8)^2 + (0)^2 + (-6)^2}$ $d = \sqrt{100} = 10$ units
Euler's Formula $V - E + F = 2$ V = number of vertices E = number of edges F = number of faces		Vertices: 5 Edges: 8 Faces: 5 $5 - 8 + 5 = 2$
Midpoint Formula $M = \left(\frac{x_1 + x_2}{2}, \frac{y_1 + y_2}{2}, \frac{z_1 + z_2}{2}\right)$	(6, −5, 10), (−2, 3, 8), M	$\left(\frac{-2 + 6}{2}, \frac{3 + (-5)}{2}, \frac{8 + 10}{2}\right)$ $M = (2, -1, 9)$

Answer the following.

1. Write Euler's Formula in words.
The number of vertices minus the number of edges plus the number of faces equals two.

2. Find the length of the diagonal of a 3 centimeter by 4 centimeter by 10 centimeter rectangular prism. Round to the nearest tenth.
11.2 cm

Find the distance between the given points. Find the midpoint of the segment with the given points as endpoints. Round to the nearest tenth if necessary.

3. (2, 4, 5) and (6, 3, 1)
$d =$ **5.7 units**
$M =$ **$\left(4, \frac{7}{2}, 3\right)$**

4. (−1, 4, 7) and (5, 0, −5)
$d =$ **14 units**
$M =$ **(2, 2, 1)**

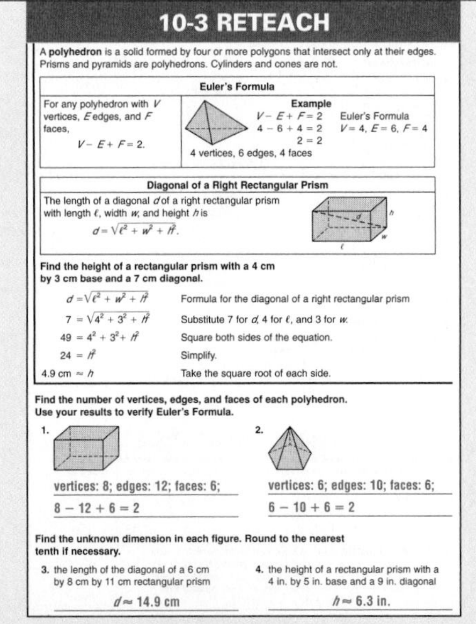

10-3 RETEACH

A **polyhedron** is a solid formed by four or more polygons that intersect only at their edges. Prisms and pyramids are polyhedrons. Cylinders and cones are not.

Euler's Formula	
For any polyhedron with V vertices, E edges, and F faces, $V - E + F = 2$.	**Example** $V - E + F = 2$ Euler's Formula $4 - 6 + 4 = 2$ $V = 4, E = 6, F = 4$ $2 = 2$ 4 vertices, 6 edges, 4 faces

Diagonal of a Right Rectangular Prism

The length of a diagonal d of a right rectangular prism with length ℓ, width w, and height h is

$$d = \sqrt{\ell^2 + w^2 + h^2}.$$

Find the height of a rectangular prism with a 4 cm by 3 cm base and a 7 cm diagonal.

$d = \sqrt{\ell^2 + w^2 + h^2}$	Formula for the diagonal of a right rectangular prism
$7 = \sqrt{4^2 + 3^2 + h^2}$	Substitute 7 for d, 4 for ℓ, and 3 for w.
$49 = 4^2 + 3^2 + h^2$	Square both sides of the equation.
$24 = h^2$	Simplify.
$4.9 \text{ cm} \approx h$	Take the square root of each side.

Find the number of vertices, edges, and faces of each polyhedron. Use your results to verify Euler's Formula.

1. **vertices: 8; edges: 12; faces: 6; $8 - 12 + 6 = 2$**

2. **vertices: 6; edges: 10; faces: 6; $6 - 10 + 6 = 2$**

Find the unknown dimension in each figure. Round to the nearest tenth if necessary.

3. the length of the diagonal of a 6 cm by 8 cm by 11 cm rectangular prism
$d \approx 14.9$ cm

4. the height of a rectangular prism with a 4 in. by 5 in. base and a 9 in. diagonal
$h \approx 6.3$ in.

TEST PREP

57. How many faces, edges, and vertices does a hexagonal pyramid have?

Ⓐ 6 faces, 10 edges, 6 vertices
Ⓒ 7 faces, 12 edges, 7 vertices
Ⓑ 7 faces, 10 edges, 7 vertices
Ⓓ 8 faces, 18 edges, 12 vertices

58. Which is closest to the length of the diagonal of the rectangular prism with length 12 m, width 8 m, and height 6 m?

Ⓕ 6.6 m Ⓖ 44 m Ⓗ 15.6 m Ⓙ 244.0 m

59. What is the distance between the points (7, 14, 8) and (9, 3, 12) to the nearest tenth?

Ⓐ 10.9 Ⓑ 11.9 Ⓒ 119.0 Ⓓ 141.0

CHALLENGE AND EXTEND

60. $d = \sqrt{4a^2 + h^2}$

61. $AB = BC = 2\sqrt{6}$, and $AC = 4\sqrt{6}$, so $AB + BC = AC$. The points are collinear.

60. **Multi-Step** The bases of the right hexagonal prism are regular hexagons with side length a, and the height of the prism is h. Find the length of the indicated diagonal in terms of a and h.

61. Determine if the points $A(-1, 2, 4)$, $B(1, -2, 6)$, and $C(3, -6, 8)$ are collinear.

62. **Algebra** Write a coordinate proof of the Midpoint Formula using the Distance Formula.

Given: points $A(x_1, y_1, z_1)$, $B(x_2, y_2, z_2)$, and $M\left(\frac{x_1 + x_2}{2}, \frac{y_1 + y_2}{2}, \frac{z_1 + z_2}{2}\right)$

Prove: A, B, and M are collinear, and $AM = MB$.

63. **Algebra** Write a coordinate proof that the diagonals of a rectangular prism are congruent and bisect each other.

Given: a rectangular prism with vertices $A(0, 0, 0)$, $B(a, 0, 0)$, $C(a, b, 0)$, $D(0, b, 0)$, $E(0, 0, c)$, $F(a, 0, c)$, $G(a, b, c)$, and $H(0, b, c)$

Prove: $\overline{AG}$ and $\overline{BH}$ are congruent and bisect each other.

SPIRAL REVIEW

The histogram shows the number of people by age group who attended a natural history museum opening. Find the following. *(Previous course)*

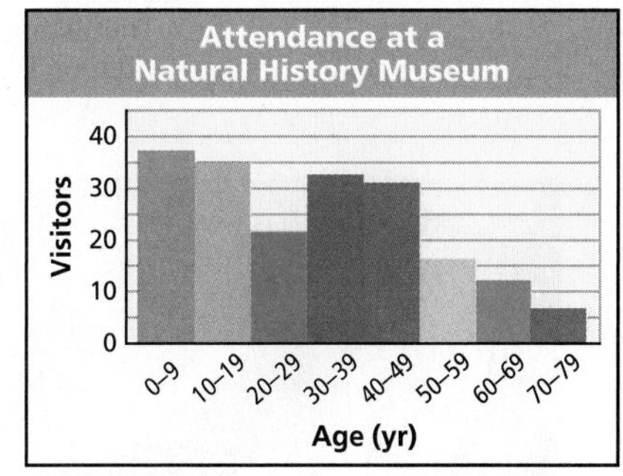

64. the number of people between 10 and 29 years of age that were in attendance **55**

65. the age group that had the greatest number of people in attendance **0–9 yr old**

Write a formula for the area of each figure after the given change. *(Lesson 9-5)*

66. A parallelogram with base b and height h has its height doubled. $A = 2bh$

67. A trapezoid with height h and bases b_1 and b_2 has its base b_1 multiplied by $\frac{1}{2}$. $A = \frac{1}{2}h\left(\frac{1}{2}b_1 + b_2\right)$

68. A circle with radius r has its radius tripled. $A = 9\pi r^2$

Use the diagram for Exercises 69–71. *(Lesson 10-1)*

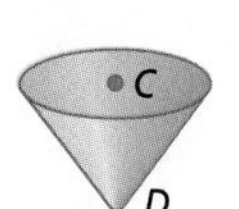

69. Classify the figure. **cone**
70. Name the edges. **none**
71. Name the base. **$\odot C$**

TEST PREP DOCTOR In Exercise **57**, students who chose **D** may have found the number of faces, edges, and vertices of a hexagonal prism instead of a pyramid. Remind students who chose **B** to check that $V - E + F = 2$.

Answers

62, 63. See p. A27.

Journal

Have students compare finding distances and midpoints in three dimensions with finding them in two dimensions.

ALTERNATIVE ASSESSMENT

Have students list all of the formulas they learned in this lesson. Then have them make up an example to show how each formula is used.

Power Presentations with PowerPoint®

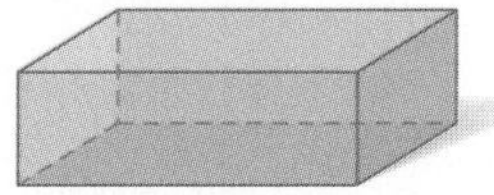

1. Find the number of vertices, edges, and faces of the polyhedron. Use your results to verify Euler's formula.

$V = 8$; $E = 12$; $F = 6$;
$8 - 12 + 6 = 2$

Find the unknown dimension in each figure. Round to the nearest tenth, if necessary.

2. the length of the diagonal of a cube with edge length 25 cm
43.3 cm

3. the height of a rectangular prism with a 20 cm by 12 cm base and a 30 cm diagonal
18.9 cm

4. Find the distance between the points (4, 5, 8) and (0, 14, 15). Find the midpoint of the segment with the given endpoints. Round to the nearest tenth, if necessary.
$d \approx 12.1$ units; $M(2, 9.5, 11.5)$

Also available on transparency

10-3 PROBLEM SOLVING

1. What is the height of the rectangular prism? Round to the nearest tenth if necessary.

22 cm
12 cm
17 cm

7.1 cm

2. After lunch, Justin leaves the cafeteria to go to class, which is 22 feet north and 15 feet west of where he ate. The classroom is on the second floor, so it is 10 feet above the cafeteria. What is the actual distance between where Justin ate lunch and the classroom? Round to the nearest tenth.

28.4 ft

3. Emily's hotel room is 18 feet south and 40 feet west of the pool. Her cousin Amber's hotel room is 22 feet north, 45 feet east, and 20 feet up on the third floor. How far apart are Emily's and Amber's rooms? Round to the nearest tenth.

45 ft
Amber's room
22 ft
18 ft
Emily's room
40 ft

96.0 ft

Choose the best answer.

4. How many faces, edges, and vertices does an octagonal pyramid have?
A 7 faces, 12 edges, 7 vertices
B 9 faces, 12 edges, 8 vertices
Ⓒ 9 faces, 16 edges, 9 vertices
D 10 faces, 24 edges, 16 vertices

5. Which does NOT describe a polyhedron?
F 8 vertices, 12 edges, 6 faces
Ⓖ 8 vertices, 10 edges, 6 faces
H 6 vertices, 9 edges, 5 faces
J 6 vertices, 10 edges, 6 faces

6. Point R has coordinates (8, 6, 1), and the midpoint of $\overline{RS}$ is $M(15, -2, 7)$. Which is the best estimate for the distance between point R and point S?
A 10.0 units C 21.0 units
B 12.2 units Ⓓ 24.4 units

7. A rectangular prism has the following vertices. What is the volume of the prism?
$A(0, 0, 4)$ $B(-4, 0, 0)$
$C(-4, 2, 0)$ $D(0, 2, 0)$
$E(0, 0, 0)$ $F(-4, 0, 4)$
$G(-4, 2, 4)$ $H(0, 2, 4)$
F 4 units³ Ⓗ 32 units³
G 16 units³ J 64 units³

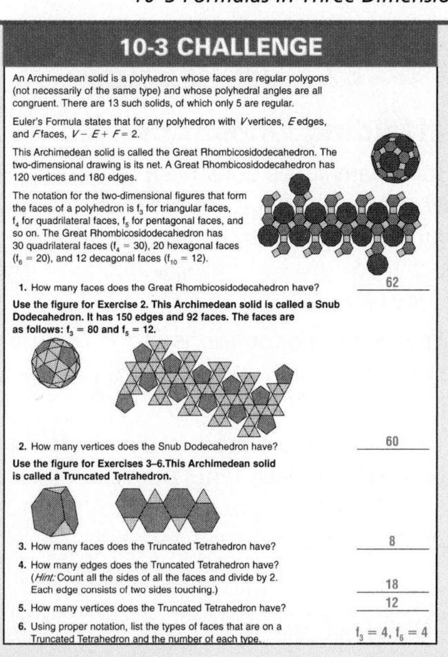

10-3 CHALLENGE

An Archimedean solid is a polyhedron whose faces are regular polygons (not necessarily of the same type) and whose polyhedral angles are all congruent. There are 13 such solids, of which only 5 are regular.

Euler's Formula states that for any polyhedron with V vertices, E edges, and F faces, $V - E + F = 2$.

This Archimedean solid is called the Great Rhombicosidodecahedron. The two-dimensional drawing is its net. A Great Rhombicosidodecahedron has 120 vertices and 180 edges.

The notation for the two-dimensional figures that form the faces of a polyhedron is f_3 for triangular faces, f_4 for quadrilateral faces, f_5 for pentagonal faces, and so on. The Great Rhombicosidodecahedron has 30 quadrilateral faces ($f_4 = 30$), 20 hexagonal faces ($f_6 = 20$), and 12 decagonal faces ($f_{10} = 12$).

1. How many faces does the Great Rhombicosidodecahedron have? **62**

Use the figure for Exercise 2. This Archimedean solid is called a Snub Dodecahedron. It has 150 edges and 92 faces. The faces are as follows: $f_3 = 80$ and $f_5 = 12$.

2. How many vertices does the Snub Dodecahedron have? **60**

Use the figure for Exercises 3–6. This Archimedean solid is called a Truncated Tetrahedron.

3. How many faces does the Truncated Tetrahedron have? **8**

4. How many edges does the Truncated Tetrahedron have? (*Hint:* Count all the sides of all the faces and divide by 2. Each edge consists of two sides touching.) **18**

5. How many vertices does the Truncated Tetrahedron have? **12**

6. Using proper notation, list the types of faces that are on a Truncated Tetrahedron and the number of each type. **$f_3 = 4$, $f_6 = 4$**

Organizer

Objective: Assess students' ability to apply concepts and skills in Lessons 10-1 through 10-3 in a real-world format.

Resources

 ***Geometry Assessments***
www.mathtekstoolkit.org

Problem	Text Reference
1	Lessons 10-1, 10-2
2	Lesson 10-3
3	Lesson 10-3
4	Lesson 10-3

Answers

1. See p. A28.

State Resources

SECTION 10A

Three-Dimensional Figures

Your Two Tents A manufacturer of camping gear offers two types of tents: an A-frame tent and a pyramid tent.

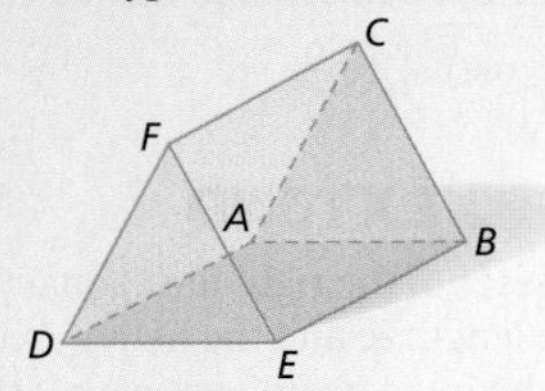

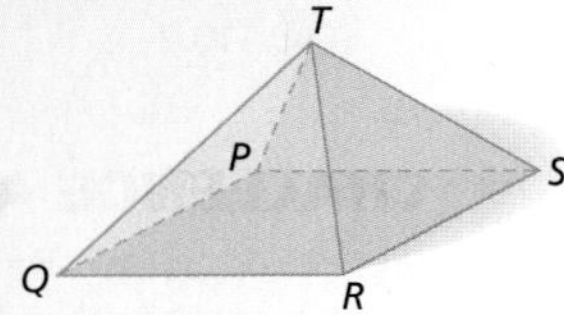

A-frame tent

Pyramid tent

1. The manufacturer's catalog shows the top, front, and side views of each tent. It shows a two-dimensional shape for each that can be folded to form the three-dimensional shape of the tent. Draw the catalog display for each tent.

The manufacturer uses a three-dimensional coordinate system to represent the vertices of each tent. Each unit of the coordinate system represents one foot.

2. Which tent offers a greater sleeping area? **the pyramid tent**
3. Compare the heights of the tents. Which tent offers more headroom?
4. A camper wants to purchase the tent that has shorter support poles so that she can fit the folded tent in her car more easily. Find the length of pole $\overline{EF}$ in the A-frame tent and the length of pole $\overline{TR}$ in the pyramid tent. Which tent should the camper buy?

3. A-frame tent: 7 ft; pyramid tent: 8 ft; the pyramid tent has more headroom.

4. $EF \approx 7.8$ ft; $TR \approx 9.8$ ft; the camper should buy the A-frame tent.

A-Frame Tent	
Vertex	Coordinates
A	(0, 0, 0)
B	(0, 7, 0)
C	(0, 3.5, 7)
D	(8, 0, 0)
E	(8, 7, 0)
F	(8, 3.5, 7)

Pyramid Tent	
Vertex	Coordinates
P	(0, 0, 0)
Q	(8, 0, 0)
R	(8, 8, 0)
S	(0, 8, 0)
T	(4, 4, 8)

INTERVENTION

Scaffolding Questions

1. How many faces does each tent have? What are the shapes of the faces? A-frame: 5 faces; 2 triangles and 3 rectangles; pyramid: 5 faces; 4 triangles and 1 square
2. What are the dimensions of the bottom of each tent? A-frame: 7 ft × 8 ft; pyramid: 8 ft × 8 ft
3. How can you use the coordinates to find the height of each tent? A-frame: use the *z*-coordinate of vertex *C* or *F*; pyramid: use the *z*-coordinate of vertex *T*.
4. How can you find the length of the segments in the tents? Use the Distance Formula.

Extension

A camper uses a special fishing rod that is 11 feet long. Will the rod fit in the A-frame tent? Why or why not? Yes; the distance from *D* to *C* is about 11.2 ft.

CHAPTER 10

SECTION 10A

Quiz for Lessons 10-1 Through 10-3

10-1 Solid Geometry

Classify each figure. Name the vertices, edges, and bases.

1. 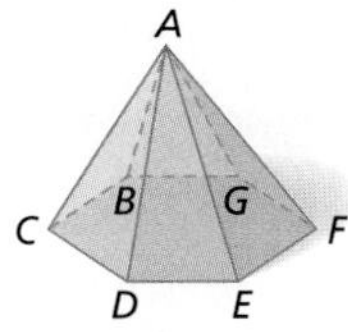

2. 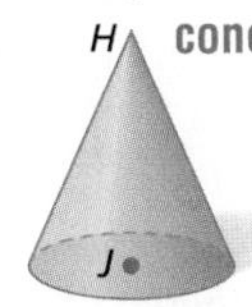 cone; H; none; $\odot J$

3.  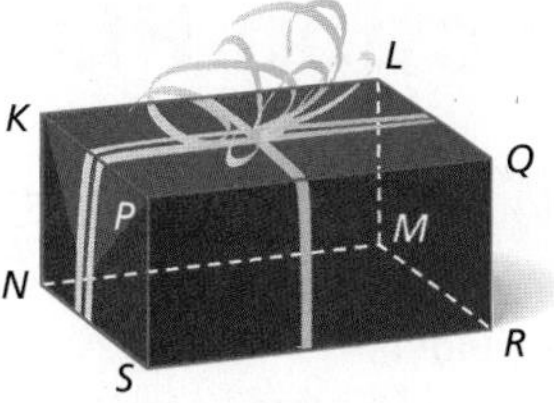

Describe the three-dimensional figure that can be made from the given net.

4. 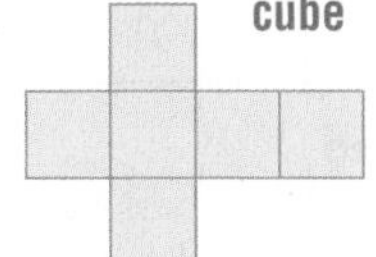 cube

5.  cone

6. 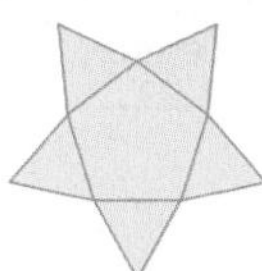 pentagonal pyramid

Describe each cross section.

7. 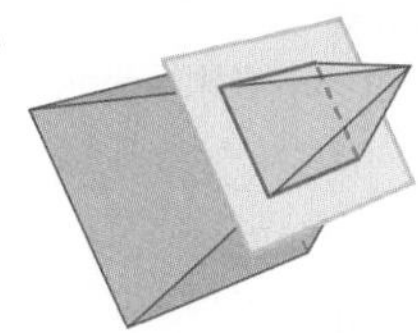 square

8. 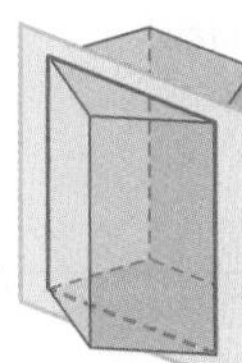 rectangle

9. 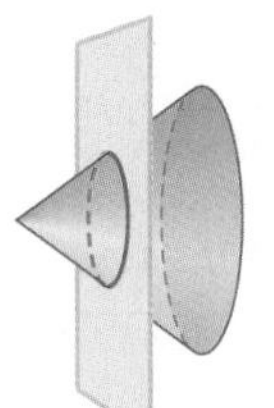 circle

10-2 Representations of Three-Dimensional Figures

Use the figure made of unit cubes for Problems 10 and 11. Assume there are no hidden cubes.

10. Draw all six orthographic views.
11. Draw an isometric view.
12. Draw the block letter **T** in one-point perspective.
13. Draw the block letter **T** in two-point perspective.

10-3 Formulas in Three Dimensions

Find the number of vertices, edges, and faces of each polyhedron. Use your results to verify Euler's formula.

14. a square prism
15. a hexagonal pyramid
16. a triangular pyramid
17. A bird flies from its nest to a point that is 6 feet north, 7 feet west, and 6 feet higher in the tree than the nest. How far is the bird from the nest? 11 ft

Find the distance between the given points. Find the midpoint of the segment with the given endpoints. Round to the nearest tenth, if necessary.

18. $(0, 0, 0)$ and $(4, 6, 12)$ 14 units; $(2, 3, 6)$
19. $(3, 1, -2)$ and $(5, -5, 7)$ 11 units; $(4, -2, 2.5)$
20. $(3, 5, 9)$ and $(7, 2, 0)$ 10.3 units; $(5, 3.5, 4.5)$

READY TO GO ON?

SECTION 10A

Organizer

Objective: Assess students' mastery of concepts and skills in Lessons 10-1 through 10-3.

Resources

 ***Assessment Resources***
Section 10A Quiz

Teacher One Stop™
Test & Practice Generator

INTERVENTION

Resources

 ***Ready to Go On? Intervention and Enrichment* Worksheets**

 ***Ready to Go On?* CD-ROM**

 ***Ready to Go On?* Online**

my.hrw.com

Answers

1. hexagonal pyramid; A, B, C, D, E, F, G; $\overline{AB}, \overline{AC}, \overline{AD}, \overline{AE}, \overline{AF}, \overline{AG}, \overline{BC}, \overline{CD}, \overline{DE}, \overline{EF}, \overline{FG}, \overline{BG}$; hexagon $BCDEFG$

3, 10–16. See p. A28.

READY TO GO ON? Diagnose and Prescribe

NO INTERVENE

YES ENRICH

Ready to Go On? Intervention	*Ready to Go On? Intervention,* Section 10A		
	Worksheets	CD-ROM	Online
Lesson 10-1	10-1 Intervention	Activity 10-1	Diagnose and Prescribe Online
Lesson 10-2	10-2 Intervention	Activity 10-2	
Lesson 10-3	10-3 Intervention	Activity 10-3	

***Ready to Go On? Enrichment,* Section 10A**

 Worksheets

 CD-ROM

 Online

SECTION 10B

Surface Area and Volume

One-Minute Section Planner

Lesson	Lab Resources	Materials
Lesson 10-4 Surface Area of Prisms and Cylinders • Learn and apply the formula for the surface area of a prism. • Learn and apply the formula for the surface area of a cylinder. ☑ SAT-10 ☑ NAEP ☐ ACT ☑ SAT ☑ SAT Subject Tests	***Technology Lab Activities*** 10-4 Technology Lab	**Optional** food packages, paper, scissors
10-4 Geometry Lab Model Right and Oblique Cylinders • Make models of right and oblique cylinders. ☐ SAT-10 ☑ NAEP ☐ ACT ☐ SAT ☐ SAT Subject Tests	***Geometry Lab Activities*** 10-4 Lab Recording Sheet	**Required** cardboard, compass (MK), scissors, paper clips, string or rubber bands, paper, tape
Lesson 10-5 Surface Area of Pyramids and Cones • Learn and apply the formula for the surface area of a pyramid. • Learn and apply the formula for the surface area of a cone. ☑ SAT-10 ☑ NAEP ☐ ACT ☐ SAT ☑ SAT Subject Tests	***Geometry Lab Activities*** 10-5 Geometry Lab	**Optional** 3-D models (MK), conical paper cups
Lesson 10-6 Volume of Prisms and Cylinders • Learn and apply the formula for the volume of a prism. • Learn and apply the formula for the volume of a cylinder. ☑ SAT-10 ☑ NAEP ☑ ACT ☑ SAT ☑ SAT Subject Tests		**Optional** 8.5 × 11 in. paper, popcorn or cereal, modeling clay, string
Lesson 10-7 Volume of Pyramids and Cones • Learn and apply the formula for the volume of a pyramid. • Learn and apply the formula for the volume of a cone. ☑ SAT-10 ☑ NAEP ☑ ACT ☑ SAT ☑ SAT Subject Tests		**Optional** 3-D models (MK), rice or cereal, scissors, paper or cardstock, tape
Lesson 10-8 Spheres • Learn and apply the formula for the volume of a sphere. • Learn and apply the formula for the surface area of a sphere. ☑ SAT-10 ☑ NAEP ☑ ACT ☐ SAT ☑ SAT Subject Tests		**Optional** orange, knife, plastic foam ball, globe, balls, string, scissors, rulers, paper, tape
10-8 Technology Lab Compare Surface Areas and Volumes • Use spreadsheet software to compare surface areas and volumes. ☑ SAT-10 ☑ NAEP ☑ ACT ☑ SAT ☑ SAT Subject Tests	***Technology Lab Activities*** 10-8 Lab Recording Sheet	**Required** spreadsheet software
Extension Spherical Geometry • Understand spherical geometry as an example of non-Euclidean geometry. ☐ SAT-10 ☐ NAEP ☐ ACT ☐ SAT ☑ SAT Subject Tests		

MK = *Manipulatives Kit*

Math Background

Professional Learning

SURFACE AREA AND LATERAL AREA

Lessons 10-4, 10-5

Surface area is the total area of all faces and curved surfaces of a three-dimensional figure. For the basic three-dimensional figures that are found in Lessons 10-4 and 10-5, the surface area of a figure may be found by determining the area of a net for the figure.

In general, the *lateral area* of a three-dimensional figure is the area of the figure's surfaces, not including the base or bases. Note that in the case of a rectangular prism, the lateral area is not well defined, since any pair of opposite faces may be considered to be bases. For most practical purposes, however, the faces of the prism that are meant to be bases will be clear from context.

VOLUME FORMULAS

Lessons 10-6 to 10-8

In Chapter 9, students saw that the formula for the area of a rectangle is the starting point for developing the area formulas for other polygons. In much the same way, the formula for the volume of a rectangular prism ($V = Bh$) is the starting point for developing the volume formulas for other three-dimensional figures. Another important ingredient in developing volume formulas is Cavalieri's Principle. This principle says that if two three-dimensional figures have the same height and the same cross-sectional area at every level, then they have the same volume.

To illustrate the use of Cavalieri's Principle, consider the following informal argument for the volume formula for a cylinder with height h and base area B. Construct a rectangular prism of height h so that each rectangular cross section has area B. As shown in the figure at the top of the next column, the prism and cylinder can be positioned so that the area of any cross section of the cylinder created by a plane parallel to the base has the same area as the corresponding cross section of the prism. By Cavalieri's Principle, the volume of the cylinder is equal to that of the prism. That is, $V = Bh$.

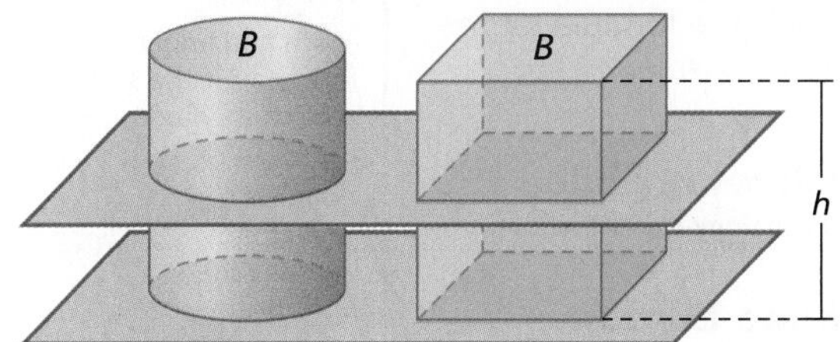

Note that the above argument works for all cylinders, oblique or right, and regardless of the shape of the base. In the case of a cylinder with a circular base, the volume formula may be written as $V = \pi r^2 h$.

For pyramids, cones, and spheres, the situation is somewhat more complex. Students can fill models of solids with sand or water to gain an intuitive sense of how the volumes of pyramids and cones are related to the volumes of prisms and cylinders, respectively. However, rigorous justifications of the volume formulas for pyramids, cones, and spheres all rely on clever applications of Cavalieri's Principle.

SPHERES

Lesson 10-8

A *sphere* is the locus of points in space that are a fixed distance from a given point. In three dimensions, a sphere may also be defined as the surface that is generated by rotating a circle in space about any line through the center of the circle.

When a sphere and a plane intersect, their intersection is either a single point (when the plane is tangent to the sphere) or a circle. If the plane passes through the center of the sphere, the circle that is formed has the same radius and same center as the sphere. Such a circle is called a *great circle*.

Great circles are the largest circles that lie on a sphere. Great circles also have another important property: Given two points on a sphere, the shortest path on the sphere between the points lies along the great circle that passes through the points. For this reason, ships and airplanes generally follow routes that are arcs of great circles.

10-4 Organizer

Pacing: Traditional $\frac{1}{2}$ day
Block $\frac{1}{4}$ day

Objectives: Learn and apply the formula for the surface area of a prism.

Learn and apply the formula for the surface area of a cylinder.

Technology Lab
In *Technology Lab Activities*

Online Edition
Tutorial Videos

Countdown Week 23

Power Presentations with PowerPoint®

Warm Up

Find the perimeter and area of each polygon.

1. a rectangle with base 14 cm and height 9 cm $P = 46$ cm; $A = 126$ cm^2
2. a right triangle with 9 cm and 12 cm legs $P = 36$ cm; $A = 54$ cm^2
3. an equilateral triangle with side length 6 cm $P = 18$ cm; $A = 9\sqrt{3}$ cm^2

Also available on transparency

Math Humor

Q: What happened to the 3-D figure who robbed a bank?

A: He got sent to prism.

10-4 Surface Area of Prisms and Cylinders

Objectives
Learn and apply the formula for the surface area of a prism.

Learn and apply the formula for the surface area of a cylinder.

Vocabulary
lateral face
lateral edge
right prism
oblique prism
altitude
surface area
lateral surface
axis of a cylinder
right cylinder
oblique cylinder

Why learn this?
The surface area of ice affects how fast it will melt. If the surface exposed to the air is increased, the ice will melt faster. (See Example 5.)

Prisms and cylinders have 2 congruent parallel bases. A **lateral face** is not a base. The edges of the base are called *base edges*. A **lateral edge** is not an edge of a base. The lateral faces of a **right prism** are all rectangles. An **oblique prism** has at least one nonrectangular lateral face.

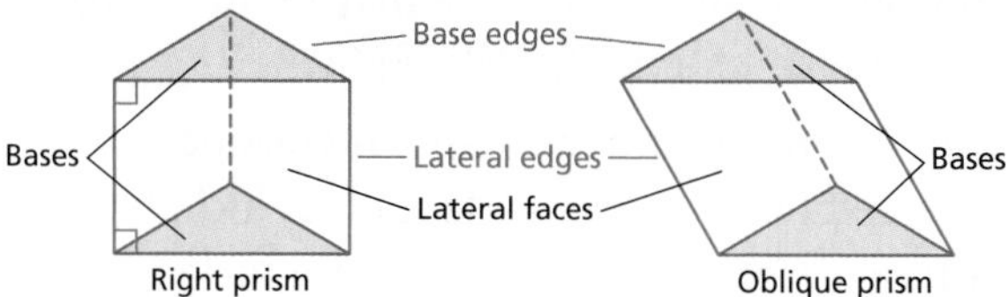

An **altitude** of a prism or cylinder is a perpendicular segment joining the planes of the bases. The *height* of a three-dimensional figure is the length of an altitude.

Altitude

Surface area is the total area of all faces and curved surfaces of a three-dimensional figure. The *lateral area* of a prism is the sum of the areas of the lateral faces.

The net of a right prism can be drawn so that the lateral faces form a rectangle with the same height as the prism. The base of the rectangle is equal to the perimeter of the base of the prism.

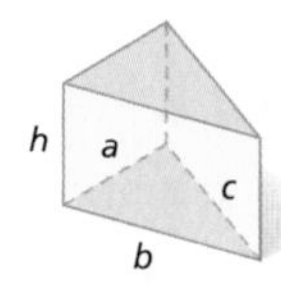

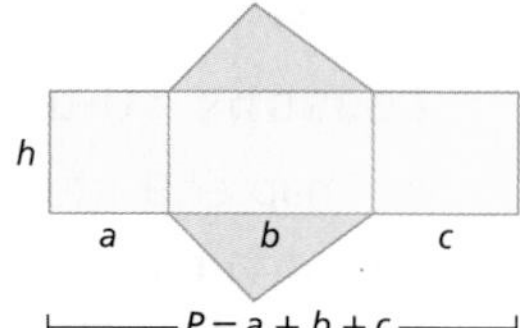

Know it! Note

Lateral Area and Surface Area of Right Prisms

The lateral area of a right prism with base perimeter P and height h is $L = Ph$.

The surface area of a right prism with lateral area L and base area B is $S = L + 2B$, or $S = Ph + 2B$.

The surface area of a cube with edge length s is $S = 6s^2$.

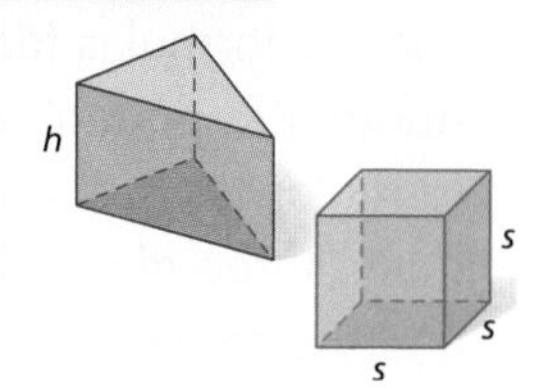

The surface area of a right rectangular prism with length ℓ, width w, and height h can be written as $S = 2\ell w + 2wh + 2\ell h$.

State Resources

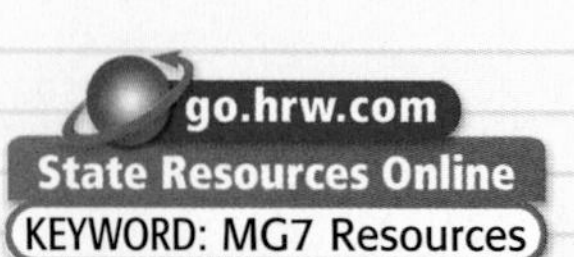

1 Introduce

EXPLORATION

10-4 Surface Area of Prisms and Cylinders

In this Exploration, you will relate the dimensions of a cylinder to the dimensions of a net for the cylinder.

1. What is the radius of the cylinder? What is the height of the cylinder?
2. The figure is a net for the cylinder. What is the height of the rectangle in the net?
3. What is the base of the rectangle in the net? (*Hint:* How is the base of the rectangle related to the distance around the cylinder?)
4. What is the radius of each circle in the net?

THINK AND DISCUSS

5. **Explain** how you can find the area of the rectangle in the net.
6. **Explain** how you can find the total area of the two circles in the net.

Motivate

Show students some food packages in the shape of prisms or cylinders, such as cereal boxes and oatmeal canisters. Take apart the packages to form nets. Show students that the sum of the areas of the faces and other surfaces of each net is the surface area of the original package.

Explorations and answers are provided in *Alternate Openers: Explorations Transparencies.*

EXAMPLE 1 Finding Lateral Areas and Surface Areas of Prisms

Find the lateral area and surface area of each right prism. Round to the nearest tenth, if necessary.

A **the rectangular prism**

$L = Ph$

$= (28)12 = 336 \text{ cm}^2$ *$P = 2(8) + 2(6) = 28$ cm*

$S = Ph + 2B$

$= 336 + 2(6)(8)$

$= 432 \text{ cm}^2$

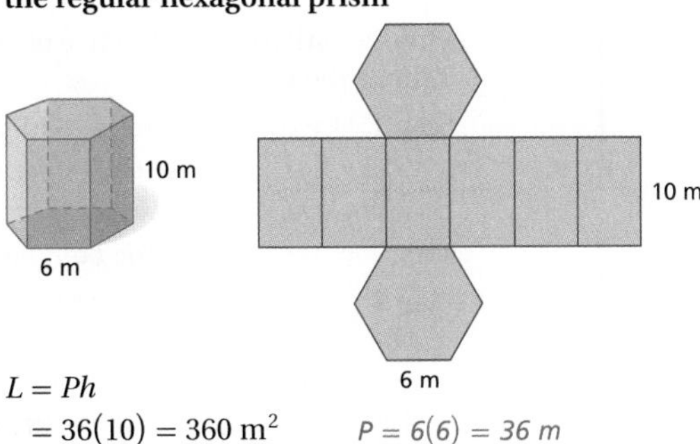

Caution!

The surface area formula is only true for right prisms. To find the surface area of an oblique prism, add the areas of the faces.

B **the regular hexagonal prism**

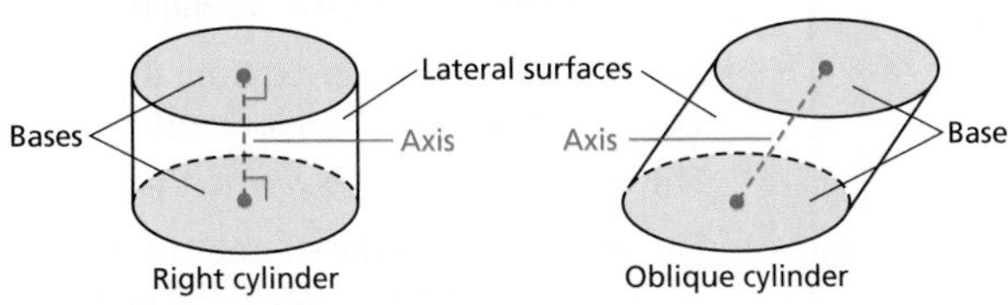

$L = Ph$

$= 36(10) = 360 \text{ m}^2$ *$P = 6(6) = 36$ m*

$S = Ph + 2B$

$= 360 + 2(54\sqrt{3})$ *The base area is $B = \frac{1}{2}aP = 54\sqrt{3}$ m.*

$\approx 547.1 \text{ m}^2$

CHECK IT OUT! **1.** Find the lateral area and surface area of a cube with edge length 8 cm. $L = 256 \text{ cm}^2$; $S = 384 \text{ cm}^2$

The **lateral surface** of a cylinder is the curved surface that connects the two bases. The **axis of a cylinder** is the segment with endpoints at the centers of the bases. The axis of a **right cylinder** is perpendicular to its bases. The axis of an **oblique cylinder** is not perpendicular to its bases. The altitude of a right cylinder is the same length as the axis.

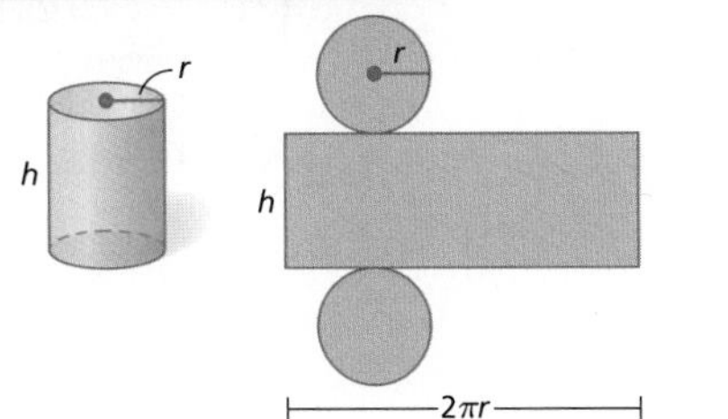

Right cylinder   Oblique cylinder

Know it! Note

Lateral Area and Surface Area of Right Cylinders

The lateral area of a right cylinder with radius r and height h is $L = 2\pi rh$.

The surface area of a right cylinder with lateral area L and base area B is $S = L + 2B$, or $S = 2\pi rh + 2\pi r^2$.

2 Teach

Guided Instruction

Review the perimeter and area of two-dimensional figures and extend these concepts to three-dimensional figures. Remind students that perimeter and circumference are measured in linear units, area and surface area are measured in square units, and volume is measured in cubic units.

Reaching All Learners

Through Multiple Representations

When finding the surface area of a three-dimensional figure, encourage students to sketch both the figure and a net. Suggest that they label the faces as left, right, top, bottom, front, and back. The net can be used to help students understand the formula and to check the results found by using a formula.

COMMON ERROR ALERT

When calculating the surface area of a right cylinder, students may leave out the 2 in $2\pi rh$ or $2\pi r^2$. Use a diagram or model to show them that the 2 in $2\pi rh$ comes from the formula for the circumference of a circle, $C = 2\pi r$, while the 2 in the term $2\pi r^2$ comes from the fact that there are two circular bases.

Teaching Tip **Reading Math** Remind students that the word *lateral* means "of or relating to the side." Think of the word *quadrilateral*, which means "four sides," or a *lateral* pass in football, which is thrown sideways. **English Language Learners**

Power Presentations with PowerPoint®

Additional Examples

Example 1

Find the lateral area and surface area of each right prism. Round to the nearest tenth, if necessary.

A.

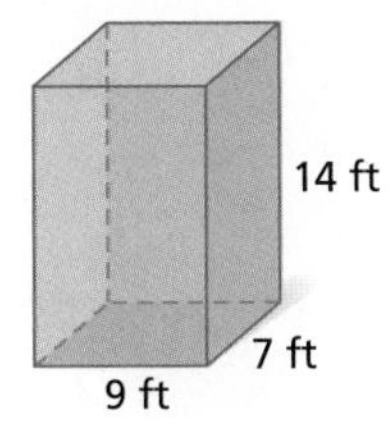

$L = 448 \text{ ft}^2$; $S = 574 \text{ ft}^2$

B. a right regular triangular prism with height 20 cm and base edges of length 10 cm
$L = 600 \text{ cm}^2$; $S = 686.6 \text{ cm}^2$

INTERVENTION

Questioning Strategies

EXAMPLE 1

- How would you use the formula $S = Ph + 2B$ to find the surface area of a cube with side length s?

Communicating Math Remind students that answers given in terms of π represent exact values and that answers rounded to a given place value are estimates.

Additional Examples

Example 2

Find the lateral area and surface area of each right cylinder. Give your answers in terms of π.

A.

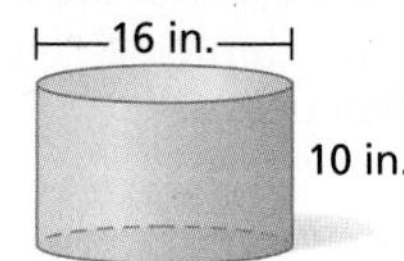

$L = 160\pi \text{ in}^2$; $S = 288\pi \text{ in}^2$

B. a cylinder with circumference 24π cm and a height equal to half the radius

$L = 144\pi \text{ cm}^2$; $S = 432\pi \text{ cm}^2$

Example 3

Find the surface area of the composite figure. 72 cm^2

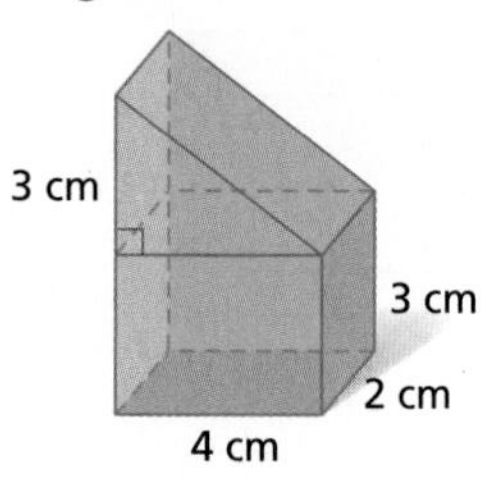

INTERVENTION

Questioning Strategies

EXAMPLE 2

- How would you find the surface area of a right cylinder, given the lateral area and the height?

EXAMPLE 3

- Does the surface area of a composite three-dimensional figure equal the sum of the surface areas of the shapes that it is composed of? Why or why not?

EXAMPLE 2 Finding Lateral Areas and Surface Areas of Right Cylinders

Find the lateral area and surface area of each right cylinder. Give your answers in terms of π.

A

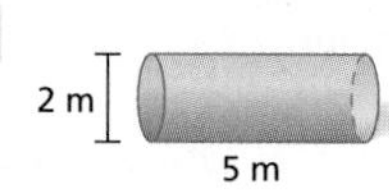

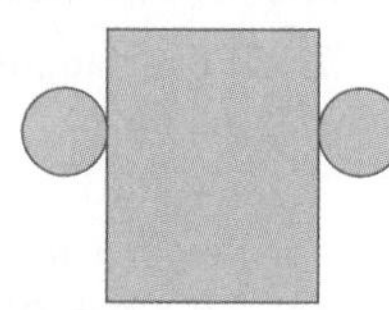

$L = 2\pi rh = 2\pi(1)(5) = 10\pi \text{ m}^2$ *The radius is half the diameter, or 1 m.*

$S = L + 2\pi r^2 = 10\pi + 2\pi(1)^2 = 12\pi \text{ m}^2$

B **a cylinder with a circumference of 10π cm and a height equal to 3 times the radius**

Step 1 Use the circumference to find the radius.

$C = 2\pi r$	*Circumference of a circle*
$10\pi = 2\pi r$	*Substitute 10π for C.*
$r = 5$	*Divide both sides by 2π.*

Step 2 Use the radius to find the lateral area and surface area. The height is 3 times the radius, or 15 cm.

$L = 2\pi rh = 2\pi(5)(15) = 150\pi \text{ cm}^2$ *Lateral area*

$S = 2\pi rh + 2\pi r^2 = 150\pi + 2\pi(5)^2 = 200\pi \text{ cm}^2$ *Surface area*

2. Find the lateral area and surface area of a cylinder with a base area of 49π and a height that is 2 times the radius. $L = 196\pi \text{ in}^2$; $S = 294\pi \text{ in}^2$

EXAMPLE 3 Finding Surface Areas of Composite Three-Dimensional Figures

Find the surface area of the composite figure. Round to the nearest tenth.

Remember!

Always round at the last step of the problem. Use the value of π given by the π key on your calculator.

The surface area of the right rectangular prism is

$S = Ph + 2B$

$= 80(20) + 2(24)(16) = 2368 \text{ ft}^2.$

A right cylinder is removed from the rectangular prism.

The lateral area is $L = 2\pi rh = 2\pi(4)(20) = 160\pi \text{ ft}^2$.

The area of each base is $B = \pi r^2 = \pi(4)^2 = 16\pi \text{ ft}^2$.

The surface area of the composite figure is the sum of the areas of all surfaces on the exterior of the figure.

$S = (\text{prism surface area}) + (\text{cylinder lateral area}) - (\text{cylinder base area})$

$= 2368 + 160\pi - 2(16\pi)$

$= 2368 + 128\pi \approx 2770.1 \text{ ft}^2$

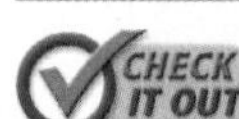

3. Find the surface area of the composite figure. Round to the nearest tenth. 239.7 cm^2

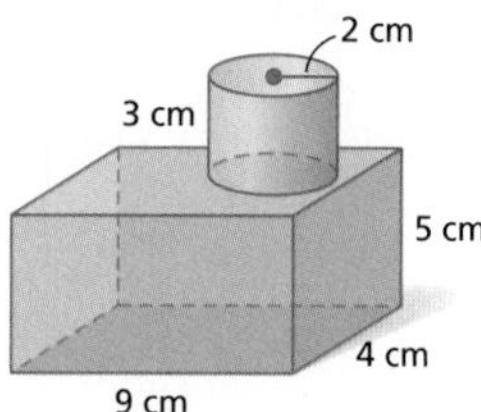

Inclusion Remind students that lateral area and surface area are measured in square units even though the figures are three-dimensional. Help them visualize this by showing them a three-dimensional figure and its net. The surface area of the figure is equal to the area of the net.

EXAMPLE 4 **Exploring Effects of Changing Dimensions**

The length, width, and height of the right rectangular prism are doubled. Describe the effect on the surface area.

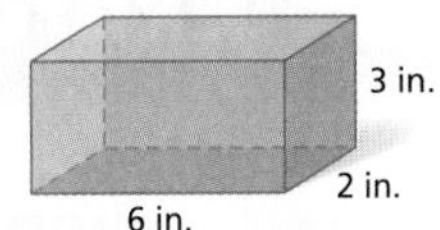

original dimensions:	length, width, and height doubled:
$S = Ph + 2B$	$S = Ph + 2B$
$= 16(3) + 2(6)(2)$	$= 32(6) + 2(12)(4)$
$= 72 \text{ in}^2$	$= 288 \text{ in}^2$

Notice that $288 = 4(72)$. If the length, width, and height are doubled, the surface area is multiplied by 2^2, or 4.

4. The height and diameter of the cylinder are multiplied by $\frac{1}{2}$. Describe the effect on the surface area.
The surface area is multiplied by $\frac{1}{4}$.

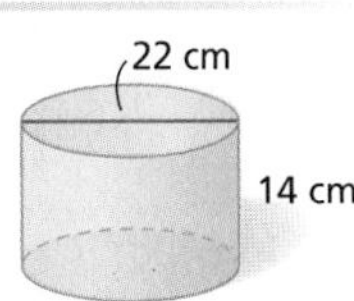

EXAMPLE 5 ***Chemistry Application***

If two pieces of ice have the same volume, the one with the greater surface area will melt faster because more of it is exposed to the air. One piece of ice shown is a rectangular prism, and the other is half a cylinder. Given that the volumes are approximately equal, which will melt faster?

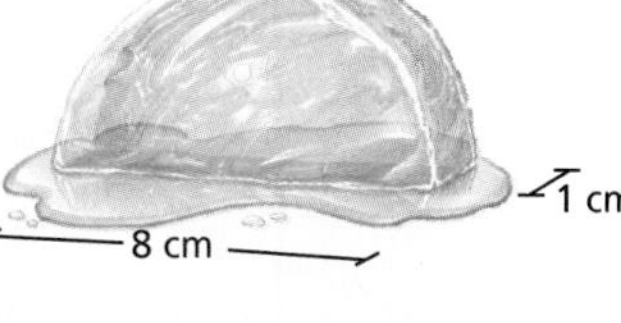

rectangular prism:
$S = Ph + 2B = 12(3) + 2(8) = 52 \text{ cm}^2$

half cylinder:
$S = \pi rh + \pi r^2 + 2rh = \pi(4)(1) + \pi(4)^2 + 8(1)$
$= 20\pi + 8 \approx 70.8 \text{ cm}^2$

3 cm, 4 cm, 2 cm

The half cylinder of ice will melt faster.

Use the information above to answer the following.

5. A piece of ice shaped like a 5 cm by 5 cm by 1 cm rectangular prism has approximately the same volume as the pieces above. Compare the surface areas. Which will melt faster?

5. The 5 cm by 5 cm by 1 cm prism has a surface area of 70 cm^2, which is greater than the 2 cm by 3 cm by 4 cm prism and about the same as the half cylinder. It will melt at about the same rate as the half cylinder.

THINK AND DISCUSS

1. Explain how to find the surface area of a cylinder if you know the lateral area and the radius of the base.
2. Describe the difference between an oblique prism and a right prism.
3. **GET ORGANIZED** Copy and complete the graphic organizer. Write the formulas in each box.

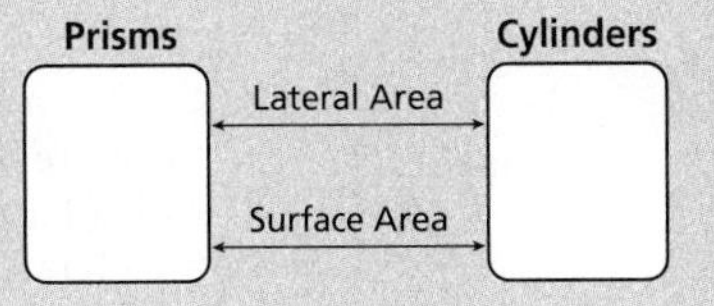

Power Presentations with PowerPoint®

Additional Examples

Example 4

The edge length of the cube is tripled. Describe the effect on the surface area. The surface area is multiplied by 9.

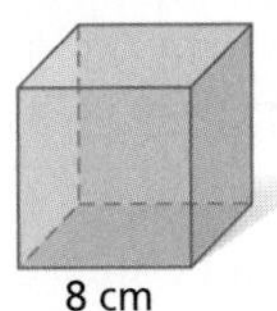

Example 5

A sporting goods company sells tents in two styles, shown below. The sides and floor of each tent are made of nylon.

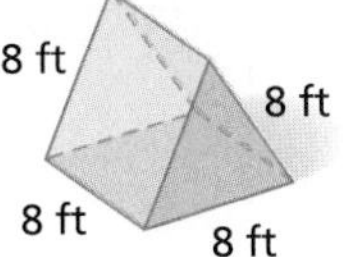

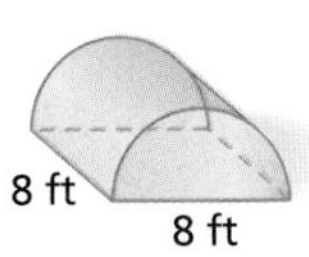

Which tent requires less nylon to manufacture? tunnel tent

INTERVENTION
Questioning Strategies

EXAMPLE 4

- How does the surface area of a prism change if the dimensions are multiplied by a positive number *n*?

EXAMPLE 5

- What is the difference between the surface area of a cylinder and that of a half-cylinder?

3 Close

Summarize

Review the relationship between the surface area of a right prism and that of a right cylinder: Both include the area of two bases and the lateral area. The lateral area is the distance around the base (perimeter or circumference) times the height of the figure.

ONGOING ASSESSMENT

and INTERVENTION

***Diagnose Before* the Lesson**
10-4 Warm Up, TE p. 680

***Monitor During* the Lesson**
Check It Out! Exercises, SE pp. 681–683
Questioning Strategies, TE pp. 681–683

***Assess After* the Lesson**
10-4 Lesson Quiz, TE p. 687
Alternative Assessment, TE p. 687

Answers to *Think and Discuss*

1. Use the radius of the base to find the base area, and then add twice the base area to the lateral area.
2. An oblique prism has at least 1 lateral face that is not a rectangle. All the lateral faces of a right prism are rectangles.
3. See p. A8.

10-4 Exercises

Assignment Guide

Assign *Guided Practice* exercises as necessary.

If you finished Examples **1–2**
- **Basic** 13–18, 23–31
- **Average** 13–18, 23–31, 41
- **Advanced** 13–18, 23–31, 41, 43

If you finished Examples **1–5**
- **Basic** 13–34, 37–40, 44–50
- **Average** 13–41, 44–50
- **Advanced** 13–50

Homework Quick Check
Quickly check key concepts.
Exercises: 14, 16, 20, 22, 23, 34

10-4 Exercises

GUIDED PRACTICE

1. **Vocabulary** How many *lateral faces* does a pentagonal prism have? **5**

SEE EXAMPLE 1 p. 681

Find the lateral area and surface area of each right prism.

2. 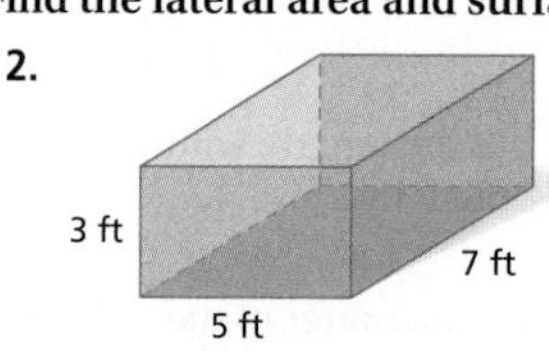

$L = 72 \text{ ft}^2$; $S = 142 \text{ ft}^2$

3. 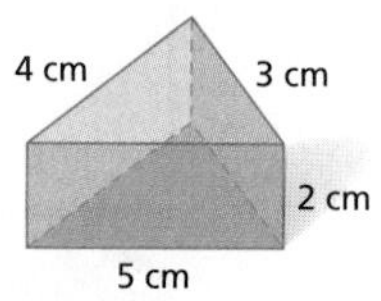 4 cm, 3 cm, 2 cm, 5 cm $L = 24 \text{ cm}^2$; $S = 36 \text{ cm}^2$

4. a cube with edge length 9 inches $L = 324 \text{ in}^2$; $S = 486 \text{ in}^2$

SEE EXAMPLE 2 p. 682

Find the lateral area and surface area of each right cylinder. Give your answers in terms of π.

5. 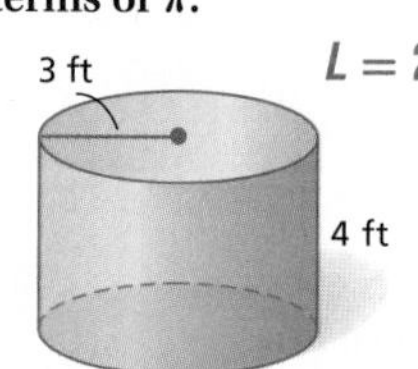

$L = 24\pi \text{ ft}^2$; $S = 42\pi \text{ ft}^2$

6. 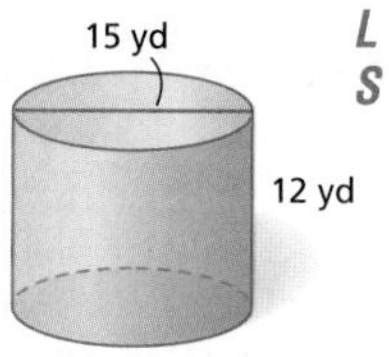 15 yd, 12 yd $L = 180\pi \text{ yd}^2$; $S = 292.5\pi \text{ yd}^2$

7. a cylinder with base area $64\pi \text{ m}^2$ and a height 3 meters less than the radius $L = 80\pi \text{ m}^2$; $S = 208\pi \text{ m}^2$

SEE EXAMPLE 3 p. 682

Multi-Step **Find the surface area of each composite figure. Round to the nearest tenth.**

8. 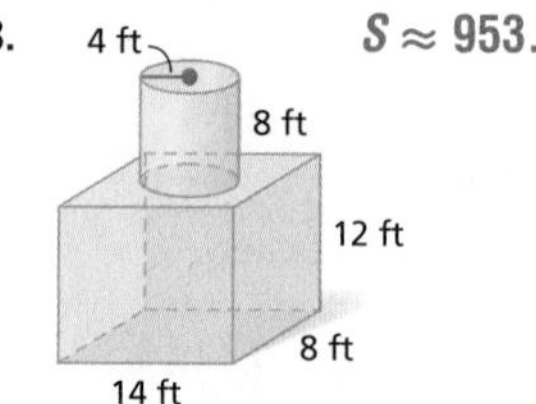

$S \approx 953.1 \text{ ft}^2$

9. 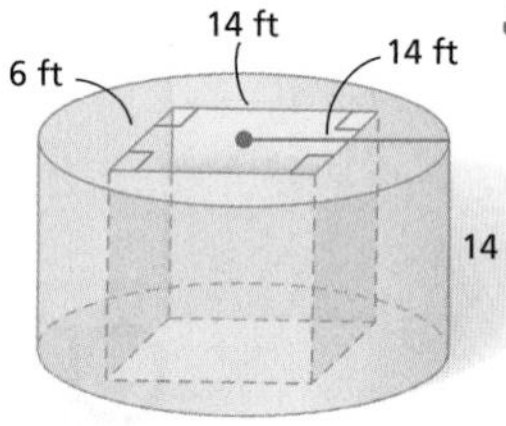 14 ft, 6 ft, 14 ft, 14 ft $S \approx 2855.0 \text{ ft}^2$

SEE EXAMPLE 4 p. 683

Describe the effect of each change on the surface area of the given figure.

10. The dimensions are cut in half. **The surface area is multiplied by $\frac{1}{4}$.**
8 yd, 4 yd

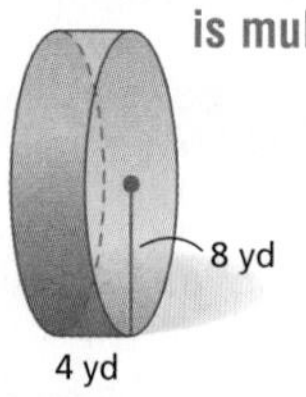

11. The dimensions are multiplied by $\frac{2}{3}$. **The surface area is multiplied by $\frac{4}{9}$.**
6 yd, 8 yd, 8 yd

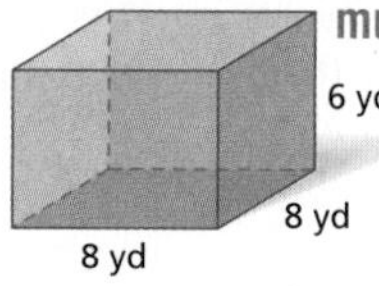

SEE EXAMPLE 5 p. 683

12. **Consumer Application** The greater the lateral area of a florescent light bulb, the more light the bulb produces. One cylindrical light bulb is 16 inches long with a 1-inch radius. Another cylindrical light bulb is 23 inches long with a $\frac{3}{4}$-inch radius. Which bulb will produce more light? **the 23 in. bulb**

State Resources

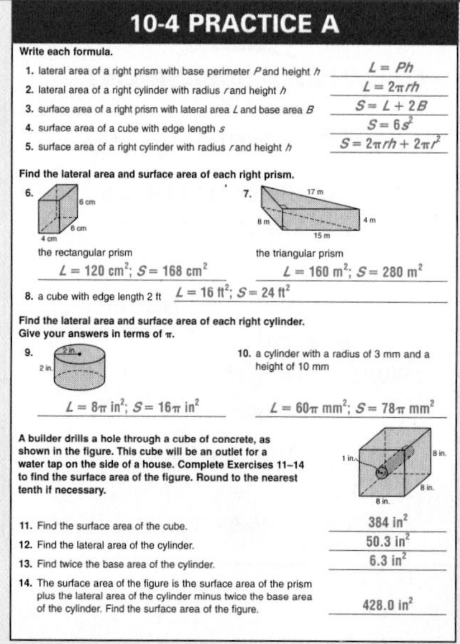

10-4 PRACTICE A

Write each formula.

1. lateral area of a right prism with base perimeter P and height h $L = Ph$
2. lateral area of a right cylinder with radius r and height h $L = 2\pi rh$
3. surface area of a right prism with lateral area L and base area B $S = L + 2B$
4. surface area of a cube with edge length s $S = 6s^2$
5. surface area of a right cylinder with radius r and height h $S = 2\pi rh + 2\pi r^2$

Find the lateral area and surface area of each right prism.

6. (6 cm, 6 cm, 4 cm) the rectangular prism $L = 120 \text{ cm}^2$; $S = 168 \text{ cm}^2$
7. (17 m, 8 m, 4 m, 15 m) the triangular prism $L = 160 \text{ m}^2$; $S = 280 \text{ m}^2$
8. a cube with edge length 2 ft $L = 16 \text{ ft}^2$; $S = 24 \text{ ft}^2$

Find the lateral area and surface area of each right cylinder. Give your answers in terms of π.

9. (2 in., 2 in.) $L = 8\pi \text{ in}^2$; $S = 16\pi \text{ in}^2$
10. a cylinder with a radius of 3 mm and a height of 10 mm $L = 60\pi \text{ mm}^2$; $S = 78\pi \text{ mm}^2$

A builder drills a hole through a cube of concrete, as shown in the figure. This cube will be an outlet for a water tap on the side of a house. Complete Exercises 11–14 to find the surface area of the figure. Round to the nearest tenth if necessary.

(1 in., 8 in., 8 in., 8 in.)

11. Find the surface area of the cube. 384 in^2
12. Find the lateral area of the cylinder. 50.3 in^2
13. Find twice the base area of the cylinder. 6.3 in^2
14. The surface area of the figure is the surface area of the prism plus the lateral area of the cylinder minus twice the base area of the cylinder. Find the surface area of the figure. 428.0 in^2

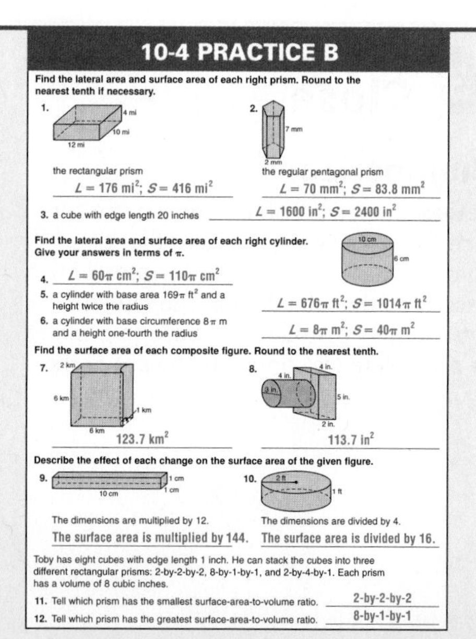

10-4 PRACTICE B

Find the lateral area and surface area of each right prism. Round to the nearest tenth if necessary.

1. (4 mi, 10 mi, 12 mi) the rectangular prism $L = 176 \text{ mi}^2$; $S = 416 \text{ mi}^2$
2. (7 mm, 2 mm) the regular pentagonal prism $L = 70 \text{ mm}^2$; $S = 83.8 \text{ mm}^2$
3. a cube with edge length 20 inches $L = 1600 \text{ in}^2$; $S = 2400 \text{ in}^2$

Find the lateral area and surface area of each right cylinder. Give your answers in terms of π.

(10 cm, 6 cm)

4. $L = 60\pi \text{ cm}^2$; $S = 110\pi \text{ cm}^2$
5. a cylinder with base area $169\pi \text{ ft}^2$ and a height twice the radius $L = 676\pi \text{ ft}^2$; $S = 1014\pi \text{ ft}^2$
6. a cylinder with base circumference 8π m and a height one-fourth the radius $L = 8\pi \text{ m}^2$; $S = 40\pi \text{ m}^2$

Find the surface area of each composite figure. Round to the nearest tenth.

7. (2 km, 6 km, 1 km, 6 km) 123.7 km^2
8. (4 in., 4 in., 3 in., 5 in., 2 in.) 113.7 in^2

Describe the effect of each change on the surface area of the given figure.

9. (1 cm, 1 cm, 10 cm) The dimensions are multiplied by 12. The surface area is multiplied by 144.
10. (2 ft, 1 ft) The dimensions are divided by 4. The surface area is divided by 16.

Toby has eight cubes with edge length 1 inch. He can stack the cubes into three different rectangular prisms: 2-by-2-by-2, 8-by-1-by-1, and 2-by-4-by-1. Each prism has a volume of 8 cubic inches.

11. Tell which prism has the smallest surface-area-to-volume ratio. 2-by-2-by-2
12. Tell which prism has the greatest surface-area-to-volume ratio. 8-by-1-by-1

PRACTICE AND PROBLEM SOLVING

Independent Practice	
For Exercises	See Example
13–15	1
16–18	2
19–20	3
21–22	4
23	5

Extra Practice
Skills Practice p. S22
Application Practice p. S37

Find the lateral area and surface area of each right prism. Round to the nearest tenth, if necessary.

13. 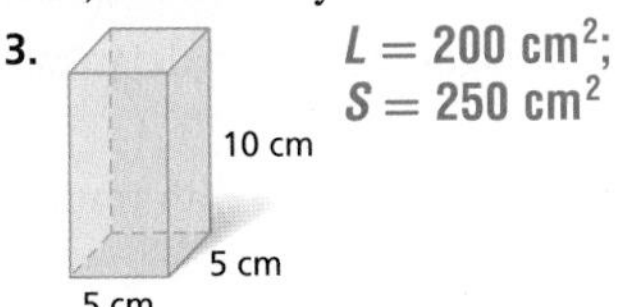

$L = 200 \text{ cm}^2$; $S = 250 \text{ cm}^2$

14. 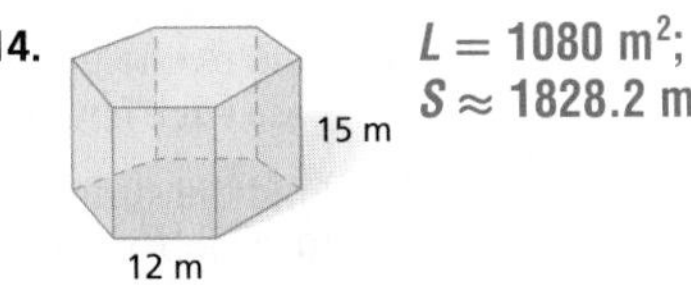

$L = 1080 \text{ m}^2$; $S \approx 1828.2 \text{ m}^2$

15. a right equilateral triangular prism with base edge length 8 ft and height 14 ft
$L = 336 \text{ ft}^2$; $S \approx 391.4 \text{ ft}^2$

Find the lateral area and surface area of each right cylinder. Give your answers in terms of π.

16. 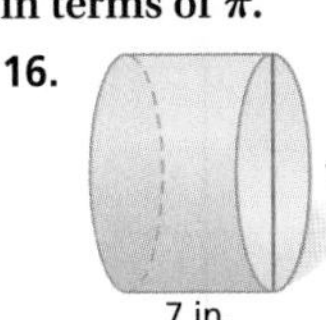

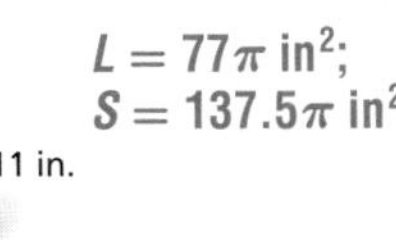
$L = 77\pi \text{ in}^2$; $S = 137.5\pi \text{ in}^2$

17. 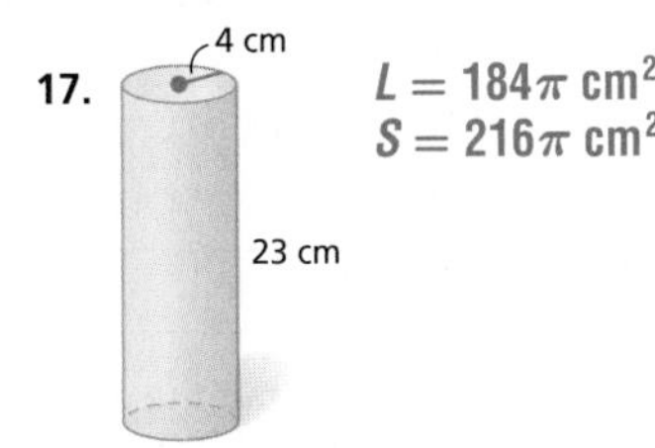

$L = 184\pi \text{ cm}^2$; $S = 216\pi \text{ cm}^2$

18. a cylinder with base circumference 16π yd and a height equal to 3 times the radius
$L = 384\pi \text{ yd}^2$; $S = 512\pi \text{ yd}^2$

Multi-Step **Find the surface area of each composite figure. Round to the nearest tenth.**

19. 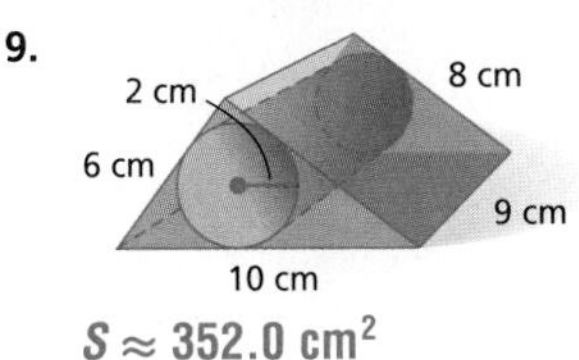

$S \approx 352.0 \text{ cm}^2$

20. 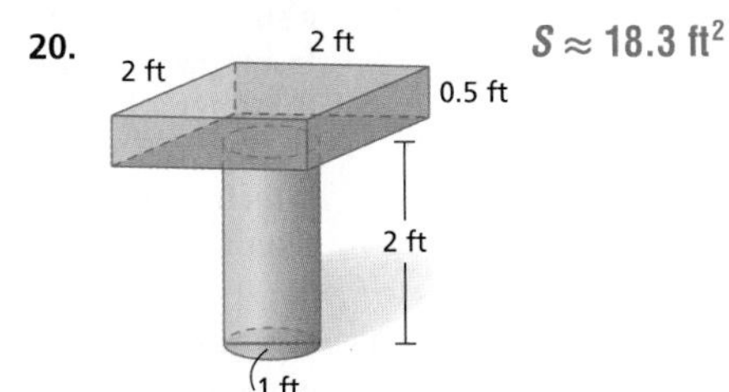

$S \approx 18.3 \text{ ft}^2$

Describe the effect of each change on the surface area of the given figure.

21. The dimensions are tripled.

The surface area is multiplied by 9.

22. The dimensions are doubled.
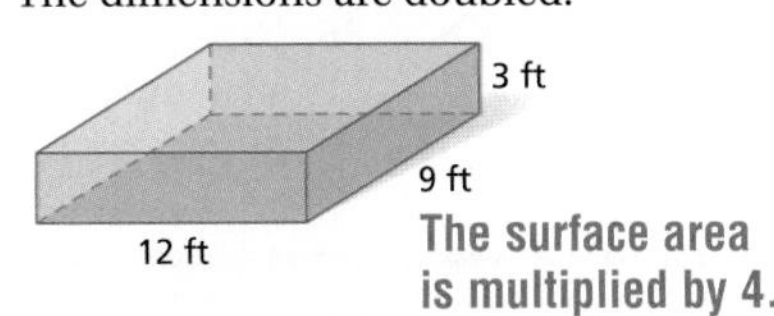

The surface area is multiplied by 4.

23. **Biology** Plant cells are shaped approximately like a right rectangular prism. Each cell absorbs oxygen and nutrients through its surface. Which cell can be expected to absorb at a greater rate? (*Hint:* 1 μm = 1 micrometer = 0.000001 meter)
the cell that measures 35 μm by 7 μm by 10 μm

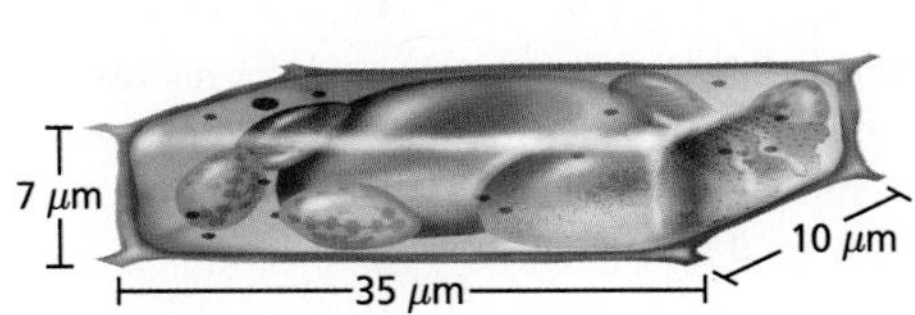

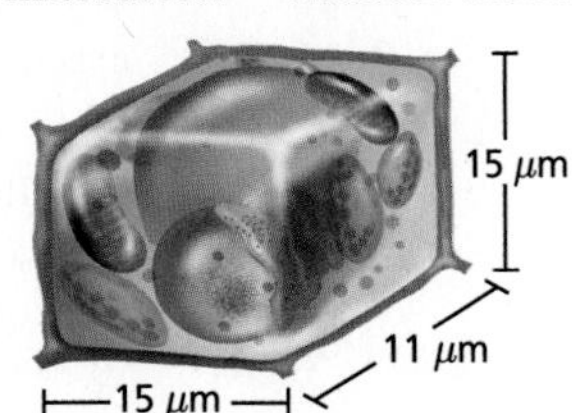

COMMON ERROR ALERT

In **Exercises 2–7** and **13–17,** some students may make errors because they are confusing the concepts of lateral area and surface area. The *lateral area* is the "side area," or the sum of the areas of all the side faces of a solid, excluding the bases. The *surface area* is the sum of the areas of all surfaces, including the bases.

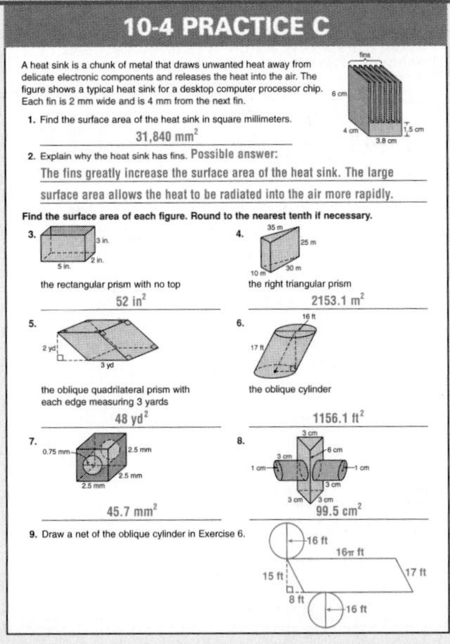

10-4 PRACTICE C

A heat sink is a chunk of metal that draws unwanted heat away from delicate electronic components and releases the heat into the air. The figure shows a typical heat sink for a desktop computer processor chip. Each fin is 2 mm wide and is 4 mm from the next fin.

1. Find the surface area of the heat sink in square millimeters. 31,840 mm²
2. Explain why the heat sink has fins. Possible answer: The fins greatly increase the surface area of the heat sink. The large surface area allows the heat to be radiated into the air more rapidly.

Find the surface area of each figure. Round to the nearest tenth if necessary.

3. the rectangular prism with no top — 52 in²
4. the right triangular prism — 2153.1 m²
5. the oblique quadrilateral prism with each edge measuring 3 yards — 48 yd²
6. the oblique cylinder — 1156.1 ft²
7. 45.7 mm²
8. 99.5 cm²
9. Draw a net of the oblique cylinder in Exercise 6.

MULTI-STEP TEST PREP **Exercise 37** involves finding the surface area of a juice box that is a rectangular prism. This exercise prepares students for the Multi-Step Test Prep on page 724.

24. Find the height of a right cylinder with surface area 160π ft^2 and radius 5 ft. $h = 11$ ft

25. Find the height of a right rectangular prism with surface area 286 m^2, length 10 m, and width 8 m. $h = 3.5$ m

26. Find the height of a right regular hexagonal prism with lateral area 1368 m^2 and base edge length 12 m. $h = 19$ m

27. Find the surface area of the right triangular prism with vertices at $(0, 0, 0)$, $(5, 0, 0)$, $(0, 2, 0)$, $(0, 0, 9)$, $(5, 0, 9)$, and $(0, 2, 9)$. $S \approx 121.5$ units^2

The dimensions of various coins are given in the table. Find the surface area of each coin. Round to the nearest hundredth.

	Coin	Diameter (mm)	Thickness (mm)	Surface Area (mm^2)
28.	Penny	19.05	1.55	662.81
29.	Nickel	21.21	1.95	836.58
30.	Dime	17.91	1.35	579.82
31.	Quarter	24.26	1.75	1057.86

32. How can the edge lengths of a rectangular prism be changed so that the surface area is multiplied by 9? Triple the edge lengths.

33. How can the radius and height of a cylinder be changed so that the surface area is multiplied by $\frac{1}{4}$? Multiply the radius and height by $\frac{1}{2}$.

34. Landscaping Ingrid is building a shelter to protect her plants from freezing. She is planning to stretch plastic sheeting over the top and the ends of a frame. Which of the frames shown will require more plastic? the triangular-prism-shaped frame

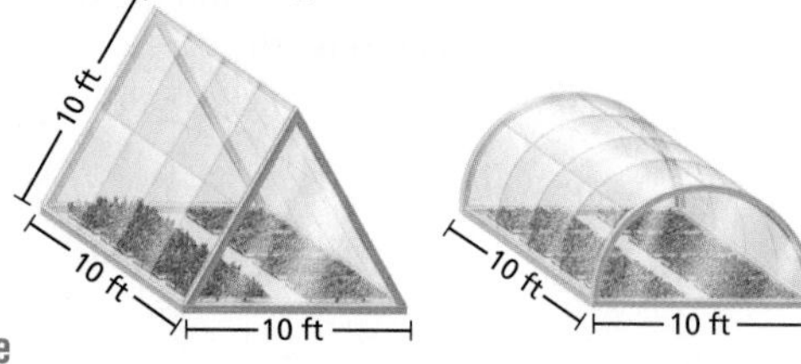

35. Critical Thinking If the length of the measurements of the net are correct to the nearest tenth of a centimeter, what is the maximum error in the surface area? 2.415 cm^2

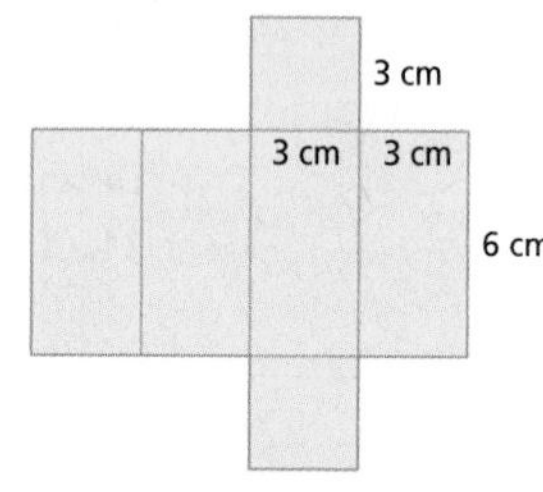

36. Write About It Explain how to use the net of a three-dimensional figure to find its surface area. Find the area of each part of the net, and add the areas.

MULTI-STEP TEST PREP

37. This problem will prepare you for the Multi-Step Test Prep on page 724.

A juice container is a square prism with base edge length 4 in. When an 8 in. straw is inserted into the container as shown, exactly 1 in. remains outside the container.

a. Find AB and BC. $AB = 7$ in.; $BC = 4\sqrt{2}$ in. ≈ 5.7 in.

b. What is the height AC of the container to the nearest tenth? 4.1 in.

c. Use your result from part **b** to find how much material is required to manufacture the container. Round to the nearest tenth. 97.6 in^2

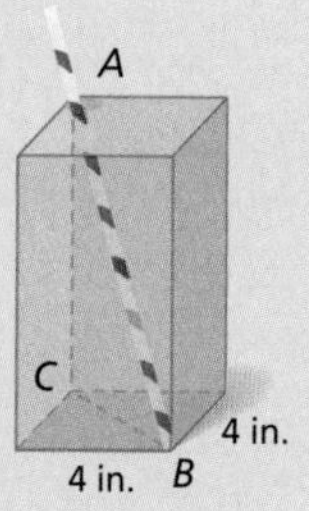

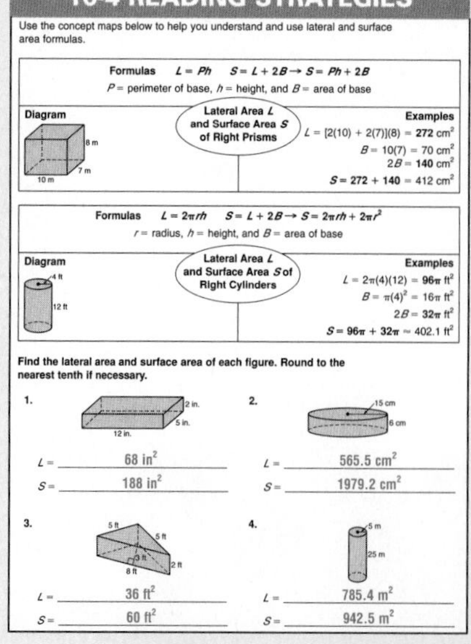

10-4 READING STRATEGIES

Use the concept maps below to help you understand and use lateral and surface area formulas.

Formulas $L = Ph$ $S = L + 2B \rightarrow S = Ph + 2B$

P = perimeter of base, h = height, and B = area of base

Lateral Area L and Surface Area S of Right Prisms

Diagram: 8 m, 7 m, 10 m

Examples
$L = [2(10) + 2(7)](8) = 272$ cm^2
$B = 10(7) = 70$ cm^2
$2B = 140$ cm^2
$S = 272 + 140 = 412$ cm^2

Formulas $L = 2\pi rh$ $S = L + 2B \rightarrow S = 2\pi rh + 2\pi r^2$

r = radius, h = height, and B = area of base

Lateral Area L and Surface Area S of Right Cylinders

Diagram: 4 ft, 12 ft

Examples
$L = 2\pi(4)(12) = 96\pi$ ft^2
$B = \pi(4)^2 = 16\pi$ ft^2
$2B = 32\pi$ ft^2
$S = 96\pi + 32\pi \approx 402.1$ ft^2

Find the lateral area and surface area of each figure. Round to the nearest tenth if necessary.

1. (2 in., 5 in., 12 in.) $L =$ 68 in^2 $S =$ 188 in^2

2. (15 cm, 6 cm) $L =$ 565.5 cm^2 $S =$ 1979.2 cm^2

3. (5 ft, 5 ft, 3 ft, 8 ft, 2 ft) $L =$ 36 ft^2 $S =$ 60 ft^2

4. (5 m, 25 m) $L =$ 785.4 m^2 $S =$ 942.5 m^2

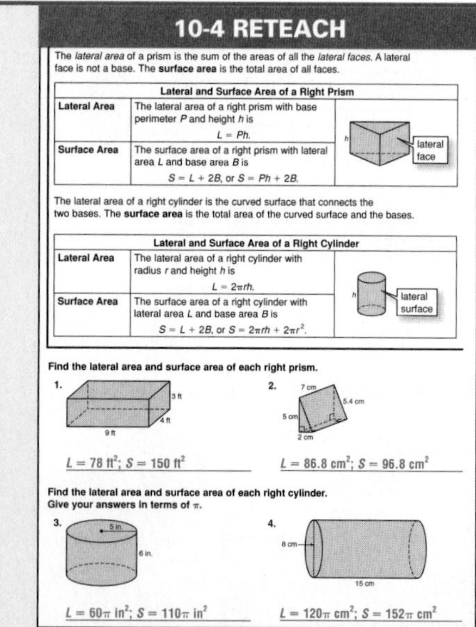

10-4 RETEACH

The *lateral area* of a prism is the sum of the areas of all the *lateral faces*. A lateral face is not a base. The **surface area** is the total area of all faces.

Lateral and Surface Area of a Right Prism		
Lateral Area	The lateral area of a right prism with base perimeter P and height h is $L = Ph$.	h, lateral face
Surface Area	The surface area of a right prism with lateral area L and base area B is $S = L + 2B$, or $S = Ph + 2B$.	

The lateral area of a right cylinder is the curved surface that connects the two bases. The **surface area** is the total area of the curved surface and the bases.

Lateral and Surface Area of a Right Cylinder		
Lateral Area	The lateral area of a right cylinder with radius r and height h is $L = 2\pi rh$.	h, lateral surface
Surface Area	The surface area of a right cylinder with lateral area L and base area B is $S = L + 2B$, or $S = 2\pi rh + 2\pi r^2$.	

Find the lateral area and surface area of each right prism.

1. (3 ft, 4 ft, 9 ft) $L = 78$ ft^2; $S = 150$ ft^2

2. (7 cm, 5.4 cm, 5 cm, 2 cm) $L = 86.8$ cm^2; $S = 96.8$ cm^2

Find the lateral area and surface area of each right cylinder. Give your answers in terms of π.

3. (5 in., 6 in.) $L = 60\pi$ in^2; $S = 110\pi$ in^2

4. (8 cm, 15 cm) $L = 120\pi$ cm^2; $S = 152\pi$ cm^2

TEST PREP

38. Measure the dimensions of the net of a cylinder to the nearest millimeter. Which is closest to the surface area of the cylinder?
    - (A) 35.8 cm² (circled)
    - (B) 18.8 cm²
    - (C) 16.0 cm²
    - (D) 13.2 cm²

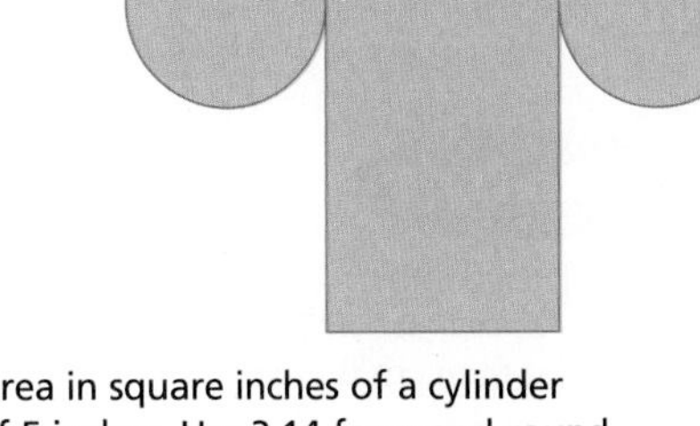

39. The base of a triangular prism is an equilateral triangle with a perimeter of 24 inches. If the height of the prism is 5 inches, find the lateral area.
    - (F) 120 in² (circled)
    - (G) 60 in²
    - (H) 40 in²
    - (J) 360 in²

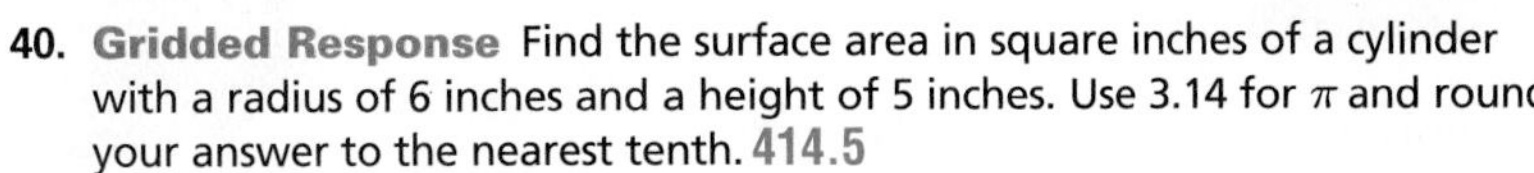

40. **Gridded Response** Find the surface area in square inches of a cylinder with a radius of 6 inches and a height of 5 inches. Use 3.14 for π and round your answer to the nearest tenth. **414.5**

CHALLENGE AND EXTEND

$h = 18$ cm 41. A cylinder has a radius of 8 cm and a height of 3 cm. Find the height of another cylinder that has a radius of 4 cm and the same surface area as the first cylinder.

4 gal; \$100 42. If one gallon of paint covers 250 square feet, how many gallons of paint will be needed to cover the shed, not including the roof? If a gallon of paint costs \$25, about how much will it cost to paint the walls of the shed?

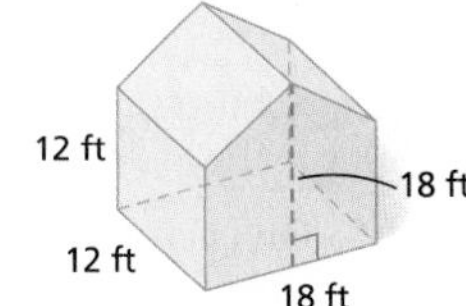

43. The lateral area of a right rectangular prism is 144 cm². Its length is three times its width, and its height is twice its width. Find its surface area. **198 cm²**

SPIRAL REVIEW

44. Rebecca's car can travel 250 miles on one tank of gas. Rebecca has traveled 154 miles. Write an inequality that models m, the number of miles farther Rebecca can travel on the tank of gas. *(Previous course)* $154 + m \le 250$

$70 \le s \le 110$ 45. Blood sugar is a measure of the number of milligrams of glucose in a deciliter of blood (mg/dL). Normal fasting blood sugar levels are above 70 mg/dL and below 110 mg/dL. Write an inequality that models s, the blood sugar level of a normal patient. *(Previous course)*

Find each measure. Round lengths to the nearest tenth and angle measures to the nearest degree. *(Lesson 8-5)*

46. BC **5.8**

47. $m\angle ABC$ **77°**

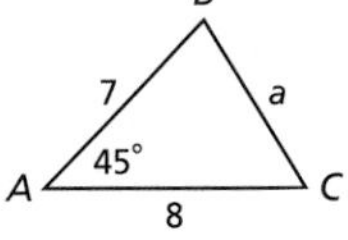

Draw the top, left, and right views of each object. Assume there are no hidden cubes. *(Lesson 10-2)*

48.

49.

50.

10-4 PROBLEM SOLVING

1. The lateral area of the regular pentagonal prism below is 220 mm². What is the surface area? Round to the nearest tenth if necessary.

   11 mm

   275.1 mm²

2. A sheet of metal 8 feet long and 6 feet wide is to be cut into cylindrical cans like the one shown. How many lateral surfaces for the cans can be cut from the metal with as little waste as possible?

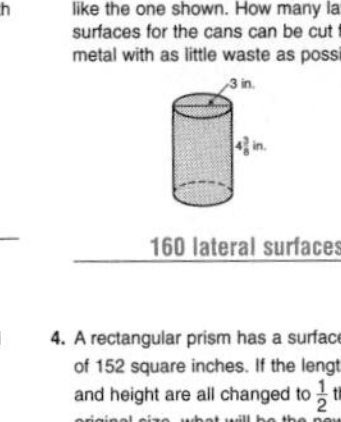

   160 lateral surfaces

Choose the best answer.

3. The surface area of a cube is increased so that it is 9 times its original surface area. How did the length of the cube change?
   - A The length was doubled.
   - (B) The length was tripled.
   - C The length was quadrupled.
   - D The length was multiplied by 9.

4. A rectangular prism has a surface area of 152 square inches. If the length, width, and height are all changed to $\frac{1}{2}$ their original size, what will be the new surface area of the prism?
   - F 19 in²
   - (G) 38 in²
   - H 76 in²
   - J 114 in²

5. Determine the surface area exposed to the air of the composite figure shown. Round to the nearest tenth.

   $1\frac{1}{2}$ in. 4 in. 6 in. 3 in.

   - A 98.1 in²
   - B 107.6 in²
   - (C) 108.7 in²
   - D 110.5 in²

6. Which of the two cylindrical cans has a greater surface area?

   x cm, $2x$ cm (pineapple juice); $2x$ cm, x cm (tuna)

   - F pineapple juice can
   - (G) tuna can
   - H The two cans have the same surface area.
   - J It is impossible to determine which can has a greater surface area.

Answers

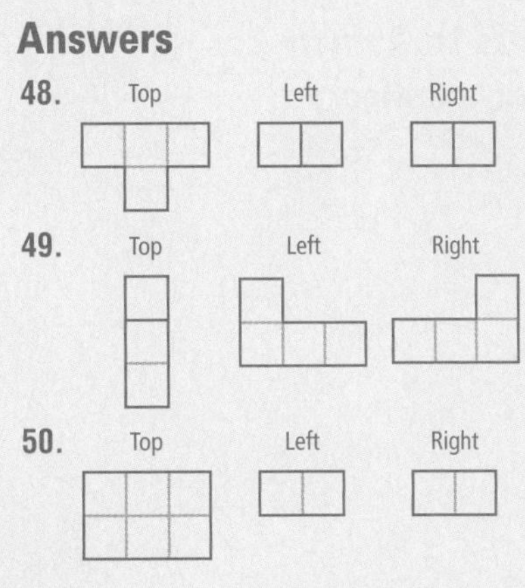

TEST PREP DOCTOR In **Exercise 38,** students who chose **A** used the diameter instead of the radius. Those who chose **C** included the area of only one of the bases. Students who chose **D** calculated only the lateral area instead of the entire surface area.

Journal

Have students describe how to find the surface area of a prism or cylinder without using the surface area formula.

ALTERNATIVE ASSESSMENT

Have students create nets for a right prism with a surface area of 72 in² and a right cylinder with a surface area of 24π in². Have them label all the dimensions of each net and make sure that each net folds correctly to form the given figure.

Power Presentations with PowerPoint®

10-4 Lesson Quiz

Find the lateral area and the surface area of each figure. Round to the nearest tenth, if necessary.

1. a cube with edge length 10 cm $L = 400$ cm²; $S = 600$ cm²
2. a regular hexagonal prism with height 15 in. and base edge length 8 in. $L = 720$ in²; $S \approx 1052.6$ in²
3. a right cylinder with base area 144π cm² and a height that is $\frac{1}{3}$ the radius $L \approx 301.6$ cm²; $S = 1206.4$ cm²
4. A cube has edge length 12 cm. If the edge length of the cube is doubled, what happens to the surface area? The surface area is multiplied by 4.
5. Find the surface area of the composite figure.

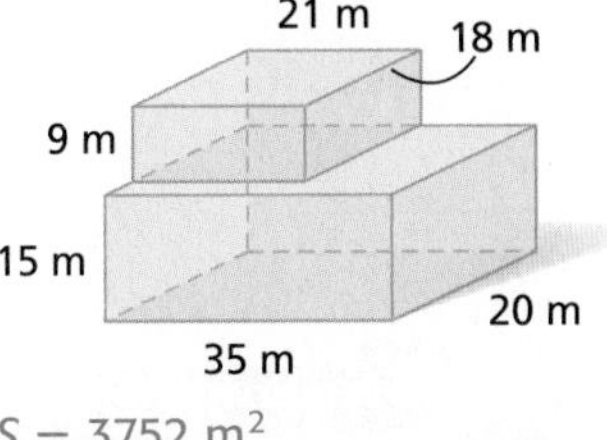

$S = 3752$ m²

Also available on transparency

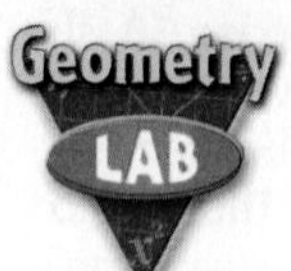

Organizer

Use with Lesson 10-4

Pacing:

Traditional $\frac{1}{2}$ day

Block $\frac{1}{4}$ day

Objective: Make models of right and oblique cylinders.

Materials: cardboard, compass, scissors, paper clips, string or rubber bands, paper, tape

Online Edition

Countdown Week 23

Resources

Geometry Lab Activities

10-4 Lab Recording Sheet

Teach

Discuss

The lateral area of an oblique cylinder cannot be found by using a formula.

Alternative Approach

Models can also be constructed using CDs by placing a large straw through their centers.

Close

Key Concept

The lateral surface of an oblique cylinder has a different shape than that of a right cylinder.

Assessment

Journal Have students explain how to estimate the lateral area of an oblique cylinder.

State Resources

go.hrw.com
State Resources Online
KEYWORD: MG7 Resources

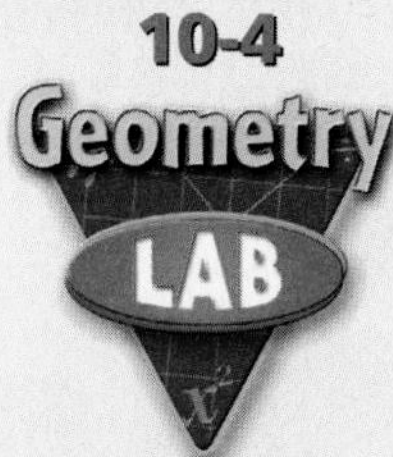

Use with Lesson 10-4

Model Right and Oblique Cylinders

In Lesson 10-4, you learned the difference between right and oblique cylinders. In this lab, you will make models of right and oblique cylinders.

Activity 1

1. Use a compass to draw at least 10 circles with a radius of 3 cm each on cardboard and then cut them out.
2. Poke a hole through the center of each circle.
3. Unbend a paper clip part way and push it through the center of each circle to model a cylinder. The stack of cardboard circles can be held straight to model a right cylinder or tilted to model an oblique cylinder.

Try This

1. On each cardboard model, use string or a rubber band to outline a cross section that is parallel to the base of the cylinder. What shape is each cross section? **circle**
2. Use string or a rubber band to outline a cross section of the cardboard model of the oblique cylinder that is perpendicular to the lateral surface. What shape is the cross section? **ellipse**

Activity 2

1. Roll a piece of paper to make a right cylinder. Tape the edges.
2. Cut along the bottom and top to approximate an oblique cylinder.
3. Untape the edge and unroll the paper. What does the net for an oblique cylinder look like?

Try This

3. Cut off the curved part of the net you created in Activity 2 and translate it to the opposite side to form a rectangle. How do the side lengths of the rectangle relate to the dimensions of the cylinder? Estimate the lateral area and surface area of the oblique cylinder.

Answers to *Activity 2*

3. Possible answer:

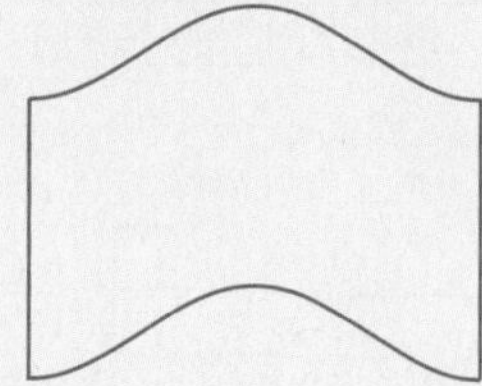

Answers to *Try This*

3. The base of the rectangle is the distance around the cylinder, the height of the rectangle is the slant height of the cylinder, and the area of the rectangle is the lateral area of the cylinder. Check students' estimates.

10-5 Surface Area of Pyramids and Cones

Objectives

Learn and apply the formula for the surface area of a pyramid.

Learn and apply the formula for the surface area of a cone.

Vocabulary

vertex of a pyramid
regular pyramid
slant height of a regular pyramid
altitude of a pyramid
vertex of a cone
axis of a cone
right cone
oblique cone
slant height of a right cone
altitude of a cone

Why learn this?

A speaker uses part of the lateral surface of a cone to produce sound. Speaker cones are usually made of paper, plastic, or metal. (See Example 5.)

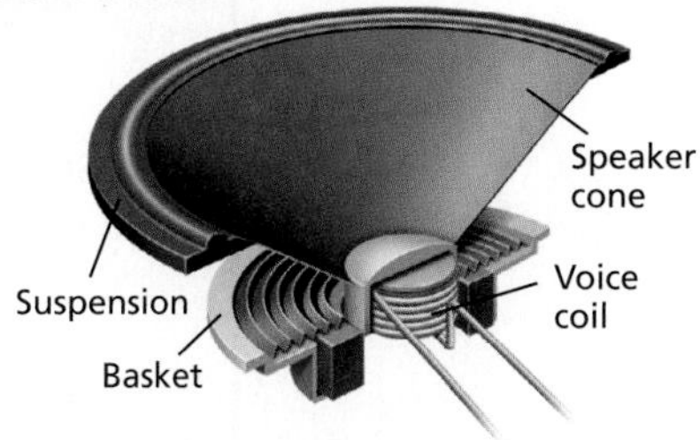

The **vertex of a pyramid** is the point opposite the base of the pyramid. The base of a **regular pyramid** is a regular polygon, and the lateral faces are congruent isosceles triangles. The **slant height of a regular pyramid** is the distance from the vertex to the midpoint of an edge of the base. The **altitude of a pyramid** is the perpendicular segment from the vertex to the plane of the base.

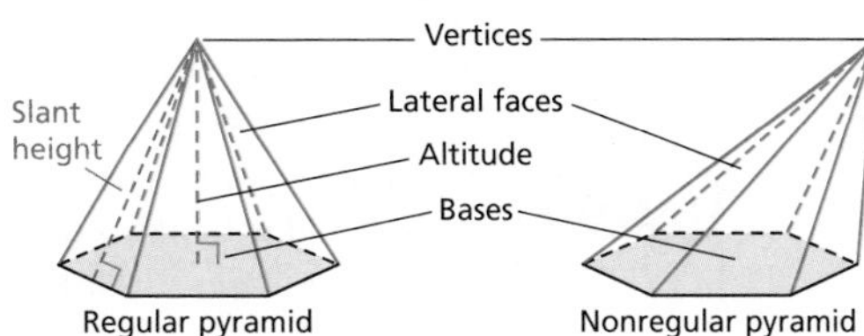

Regular pyramid Nonregular pyramid

The lateral faces of a regular pyramid can be arranged to cover half of a rectangle with a height equal to the slant height of the pyramid. The width of the rectangle is equal to the base perimeter of the pyramid.

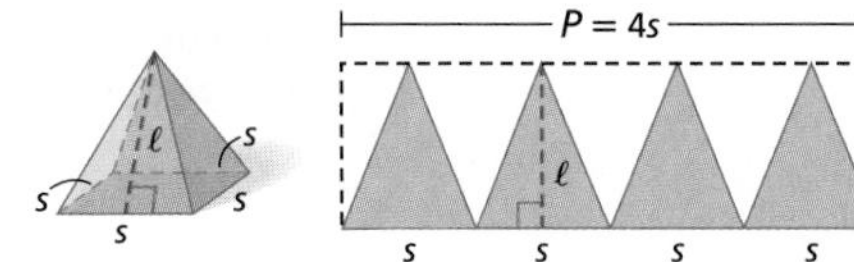

Lateral and Surface Area of a Regular Pyramid

The lateral area of a regular pyramid with perimeter P and slant height ℓ is $L = \frac{1}{2}P\ell$.

The surface area of a regular pyramid with lateral area L and base area B is $S = L + B$, or $S = \frac{1}{2}P\ell + B$.

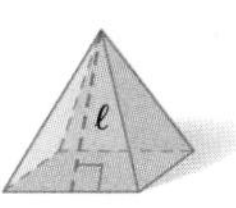

EXAMPLE 1 Finding Lateral Area and Surface Area of Pyramids

Find the lateral area and surface area of each pyramid.

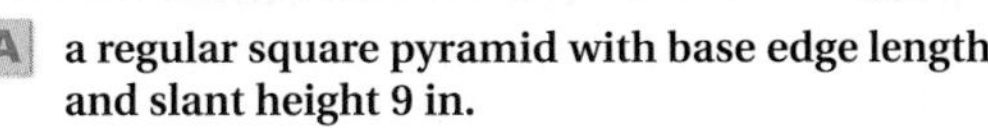

A **a regular square pyramid with base edge length 5 in. and slant height 9 in.**

$L = \frac{1}{2}P\ell$ *Lateral area of a regular pyramid*

$= \frac{1}{2}(20)(9) = 90 \text{ in}^2$ *$P = 4(5) = 20$ in.*

$S = \frac{1}{2}P\ell + B$ *Surface area of a regular pyramid*

$= 90 + 25 = 115 \text{ in}^2$ *$B = 5^2 = 25 \text{ in}^2$*

10-5 Organizer

Pacing: Traditional 1 day
Block $\frac{1}{2}$ day

Objectives: Learn and apply the formula for the surface area of a pyramid.

Learn and apply the formula for the surface area of a cone.

Geometry Lab
In Geometry Lab Activities

Online Edition
Tutorial Videos

Countdown Week 23

Warm Up

Find the missing side length of each right triangle with legs *a* and *b* and hypotenuse *c*.

1. $a = 7, b = 24$ $c = 25$

2. $c = 15, a = 9$ $b = 12$

3. $b = 40, c = 41$ $a = 9$

4. $a = 5, b = 5$ $c = 5\sqrt{2}$

5. $a = 4, c = 8$ $b = 4\sqrt{3}$

Also available on transparency

Q: What's refreshing and has triangular lateral faces?

A: A pyramint.

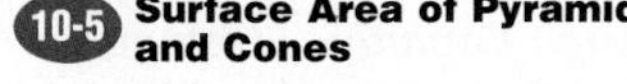

EXPLORATION

10-5 Surface Area of Pyramids and Cones

In this Exploration, you will relate the dimensions of a pyramid to the dimensions of a net for the pyramid.

1. The lateral faces of this pyramid are congruent isosceles triangles, each with height ℓ. The base is a regular hexagon with side length x. What is the perimeter of the base of the pyramid?
2. The figure is a net for the pyramid. What is the height of each triangle in the net?
3. What is the length of the base of each triangle in the net?
4. What is the total length of all the bases of the triangles in the net?

THINK AND DISCUSS

5. **Explain** how the total length of the bases of the triangles in the net is related to the perimeter of the base of the pyramid.
6. **Explain** how the area of the hexagon in the net is related to the area of the base of the pyramid.

Motivate

Show students a net for a cone and ask them to consider how the two pieces fit together. The curved edge of the lateral surface must have a length equal to the circumference of the circle. This will help them understand how the lateral area formula is derived.

Explorations and answers are provided in *Alternate Openers: Explorations Transparencies.*

Power Presentations with PowerPoint®

Additional Examples

Example 1

Find the lateral area and surface area of each regular pyramid. Round to the nearest tenth, if necessary.

A. a regular square pyramid with base edge length 14 cm and slant height 25 cm

$L = 700\text{ cm}^2$; $S = 896\text{ cm}^2$

B.

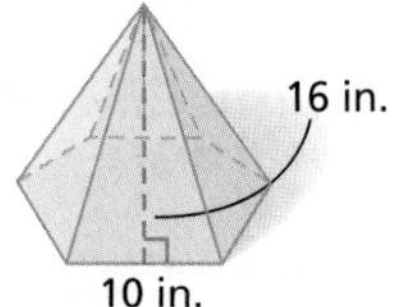

$L = 480\text{ in}^2$; $S \approx 739.8\text{ in}^2$

INTERVENTION 

Questioning Strategies

EXAMPLE 1

- How is the lateral area of a pyramid calculated differently than the lateral area of a prism?

Find the lateral area and surface area of each regular pyramid. Round to the nearest tenth.

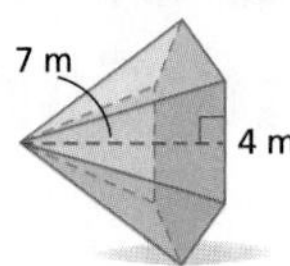

Step 1 Find the base perimeter and apothem.
The base perimeter is $6(4) = 24$ m.
The apothem is $2\sqrt{3}$ m, so the base area is $\frac{1}{2}aP = \frac{1}{2}(2\sqrt{3})(24) = 24\sqrt{3}\text{ m}^2$.

Step 2 Find the lateral area.

$L = \frac{1}{2}P\ell$ — *Lateral area of a regular pyramid*

$= \frac{1}{2}(24)(7) = 84\text{ m}^2$ — *Substitute 24 for P and 7 for ℓ.*

Step 3 Find the surface area.

$S = \frac{1}{2}P\ell + B$ — *Surface area of a regular pyramid*

$= 84 + 24\sqrt{3} \approx 125.6\text{ cm}^2$ — *Substitute $24\sqrt{3}$ for B.*

1. Find the lateral area and surface area of a regular triangular pyramid with base edge length 6 ft and slant height 10 ft.
$L = 90\text{ ft}^2$; $S \approx 105.6\text{ ft}^2$

The **vertex of a cone** is the point opposite the base. The **axis of a cone** is the segment with endpoints at the vertex and the center of the base. The axis of a **right cone** is perpendicular to the base. The axis of an **oblique cone** is *not* perpendicular to the base.

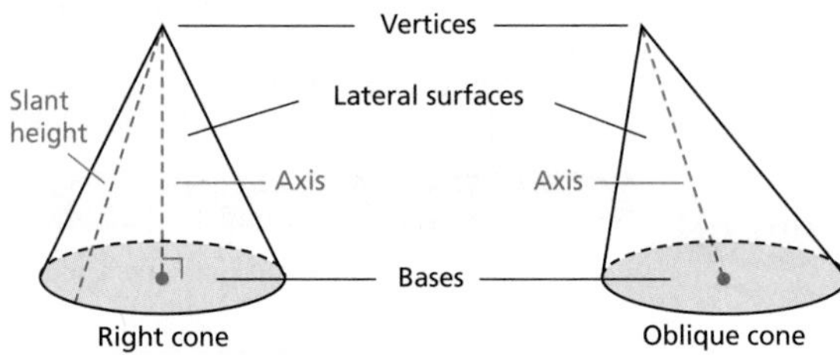

The **slant height of a right cone** is the distance from the vertex of a right cone to a point on the edge of the base. The **altitude of a cone** is a perpendicular segment from the vertex of the cone to the plane of the base.

Lateral and Surface Area of a Right Cone

The lateral area of a right cone with radius r and slant height ℓ is $L = \pi r\ell$.

The surface area of a right cone with lateral area L and base area B is $S = L + B$, or $S = \pi r\ell + \pi r^2$.

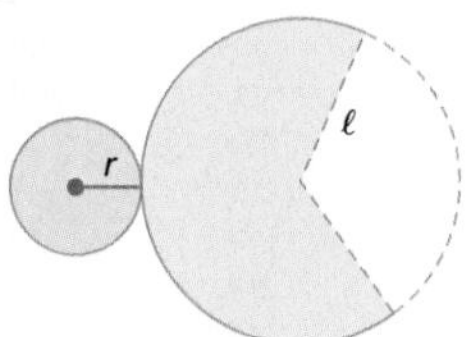

2 Teach

Guided Instruction

Show models of a pyramid and a cone (MK) and point out the vertex, slant height, and altitude of each. Show students that the slant height, height, and apothem or radius of a regular pyramid or a right cone form a right triangle, so the Pythagorean Theorem can be used to solve for an unknown measurement.

Reaching All Learners

Through Cognitive Strategies

Help students find relationships among the surface area formulas so that they are easier to remember.

Possible answers:
1) If the figure has a circular base, then the formula contains π.
2) Prisms and cylinders have 2 bases, so their surface area formulas contain $2B$.
3) Pyramids and cones have only 1 base, so their surface area formulas contain $1\,B$.

EXAMPLE 2 Finding Lateral Area and Surface Area of Right Cones

Find the lateral area and surface area of each cone. Give your answers in terms of π.

A **a right cone with radius 2 m and slant height 3 m**

$L = \pi r\ell$ — *Lateral area of a cone*

$= \pi(2)(3) = 6\pi \text{ m}^2$ — *Substitute 2 for r and 3 for ℓ.*

$S = \pi r\ell + \pi r^2$ — *Surface area of a cone*

$= 6\pi + \pi(2)^2 = 10\pi \text{ m}^2$ — *Substitute 2 for r and 3 for ℓ.*

B

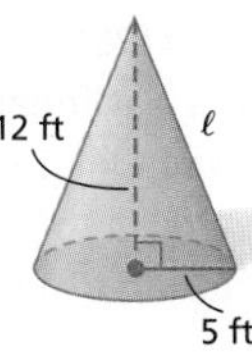

Step 1 Use the Pythagorean Theorem to find ℓ.

$\ell = \sqrt{5^2 + 12^2} = 13 \text{ ft}$

Step 2 Find the lateral area and surface area.

$L = \pi r\ell$ — *Lateral area of a right cone*

$= \pi(5)(13) = 65\pi \text{ ft}^2$ — *Substitute 5 for r and 13 for ℓ.*

$S = \pi r\ell + \pi r^2$ — *Surface area of a right cone*

$= 65\pi + \pi(5)^2 = 90\pi \text{ ft}^2$ — *Substitute 5 for r and 13 for ℓ.*

CHECK IT OUT! **2.** Find the lateral area and surface area of the right cone.
$L = 80\pi \text{ cm}^2$; $S \approx 144\pi \text{ cm}^2$

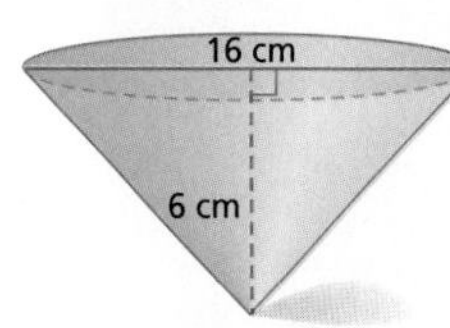

EXAMPLE 3 Exploring Effects of Changing Dimensions

The radius and slant height of the right cone are tripled. Describe the effect on the surface area.

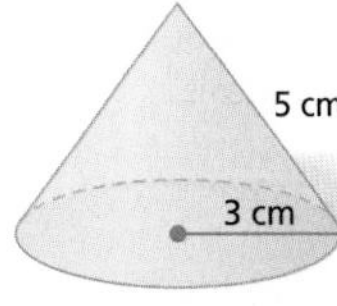

original dimensions:	radius and slant height tripled:
$S = \pi r\ell + \pi r^2$	$S = \pi r\ell + \pi r^2$
$= \pi(3)(5) + \pi(3)^2$	$= \pi(9)(15) + \pi(9)^2$
$= 24\pi \text{ cm}^2$	$= 216\pi \text{ cm}^2$

Notice that $216\pi = 9(24\pi)$. If the radius and slant height are tripled, the surface area is multiplied by 3^2, or 9.

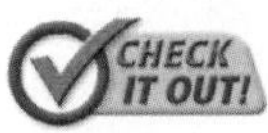

CHECK IT OUT! **3.** The base edge length and slant height of the regular square pyramid are both multiplied by $\frac{2}{3}$. Describe the effect on the surface area.
The surface area is multiplied by $\frac{4}{9}$.

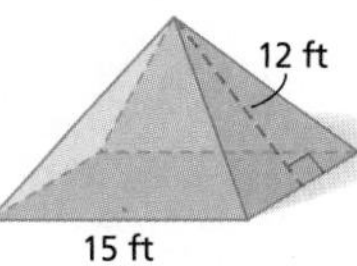

COMMON ERROR ALERT

Students may use the altitude to calculate surface area instead of the slant height. Remind them that, for regular pyramids and right cones, the altitude lies *inside* the figure and the slant height lies *on* it, so when they calculate the *surface* area, they should use the slant height.

Power Presentations with PowerPoint®

Additional Examples

Example 2

Find the lateral area and surface area of each cone.

A. a right cone with radius 9 cm and slant height 5 cm
$L = 45\pi \text{ cm}^2$; $S = 126\pi \text{ cm}^2$

B.

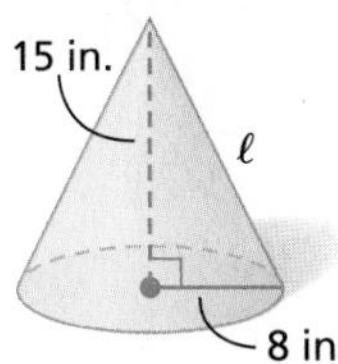

$L = 136\pi \text{ in}^2$; $S = 200\pi \text{ in}^2$

Example 3

The base edge length and slant height of the regular hexagonal pyramid are both divided by 5. Describe the effect on the surface area.

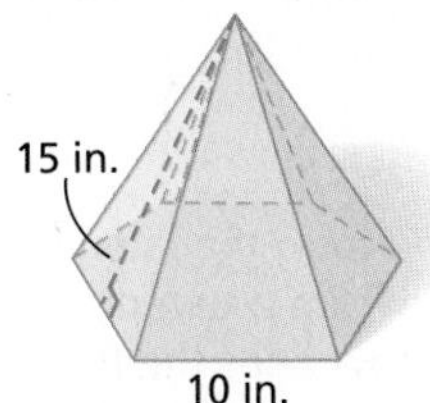

The surface area is divided by 25.

INTERVENTION
Questioning Strategies

EXAMPLE 2

- What is the difference between the slant height and the altitude of a right cone?

EXAMPLE 3

- How can you determine the effect of multiplying the dimensions of a pyramid or a cone by a scale factor without knowing the dimensions of the figure?

Reaching All Learners
Through Kinesthetic Experience

A conical paper cup can be used to represent the lateral surface of a cone. Have each student trace around the top of a cup and cut it out to make the base for the cone. Then have them cut their cups open, unroll them, and combine with the circular bases to form nets for their cones.

Power Presentations with PowerPoint®

Additional Examples

Example 4

Find the surface area of the composite figure.

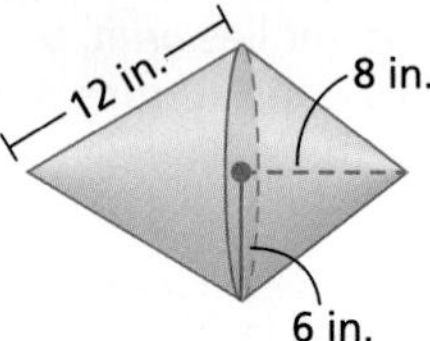

132π in^2

Example 5

If the pattern shown is used to make a paper cup, what is the diameter of the cup?

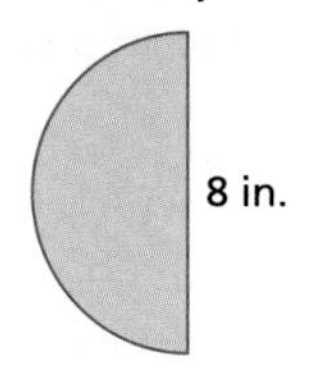

4 in.

INTERVENTION

Questioning Strategies

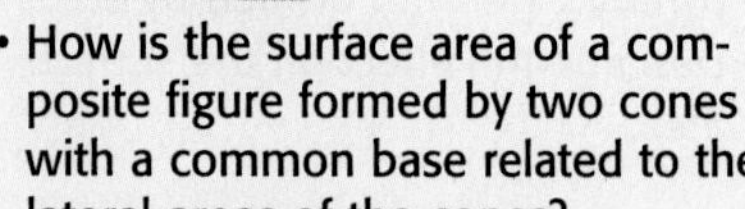

EXAMPLE 4

- How is the surface area of a composite figure formed by two cones with a common base related to the lateral areas of the cones?

EXAMPLE 5

- When you form the lateral surface of a cone from a two-dimensional pattern, how does the fraction of a circle that is used in the pattern affect the proportions of the cone?

EXAMPLE 4 Finding Surface Area of Composite Three-Dimensional Figures

Find the surface area of the composite figure.

The height of the cone is $90 - 45 = 45$ cm.
By the Pythagorean Theorem,
$\ell = \sqrt{28^2 + 45^2} = 53$ cm. The lateral area of the cone is

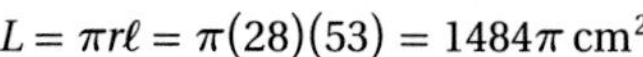

$L = \pi r \ell = \pi(28)(53) = 1484\pi \text{ cm}^2$.

28 cm, 90 cm, 45 cm

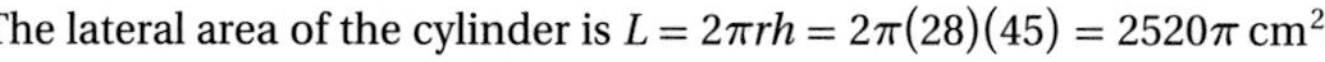

The lateral area of the cylinder is $L = 2\pi rh = 2\pi(28)(45) = 2520\pi \text{ cm}^2$.

The base area is $B = \pi r^2 = \pi(28)^2 = 784\pi \text{ cm}^2$.

$S = (\text{cone lateral area}) + (\text{cylinder lateral area}) + (\text{base area})$
$= 2520\pi + 784\pi + 1484\pi = 4788\pi \text{ cm}^2$

4. Find the surface area of the composite figure.
$S \approx 28.9$ yd^2

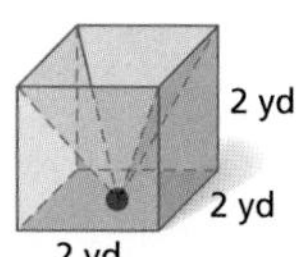

EXAMPLE 5 *Electronics Application*

LINK Electronics

The paper cones of antique speakers were both functional and decorative. Some had elaborate patterns or shapes.

Tim is replacing the paper cone of an antique speaker. He measured the existing cone and created the pattern for the lateral surface from a large circle. What is the diameter of the cone?

10 in.

The radius of the large circle used to create the pattern is the slant height of the cone.

The area of the pattern is the lateral area of the cone. The area of the pattern is also $\frac{3}{4}$ of the area of the large circle, so $\pi r\ell = \frac{3}{4}\pi r^2$.

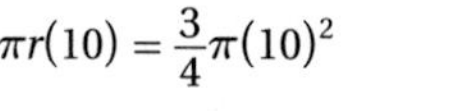

$\pi r(10) = \frac{3}{4}\pi(10)^2$ — *Substitute 10 for ℓ, the slant height of the cone and the radius of the large circle.*

$r = 7.5$ in. — *Solve for r.*

The diameter of the cone is $2(7.5) = 15$ in.

5. What if...? If the radius of the large circle were 12 in., what would be the radius of the cone? **9 in.**

THINK AND DISCUSS

1. Explain why the lateral area of a regular pyramid is $\frac{1}{2}$ the base perimeter times the slant height.

2. In a right cone, which is greater, the height or the slant height? Explain.

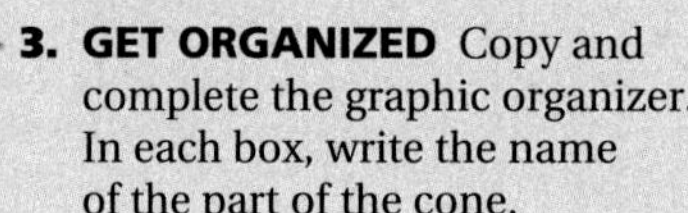

3. GET ORGANIZED Copy and complete the graphic organizer. In each box, write the name of the part of the cone.

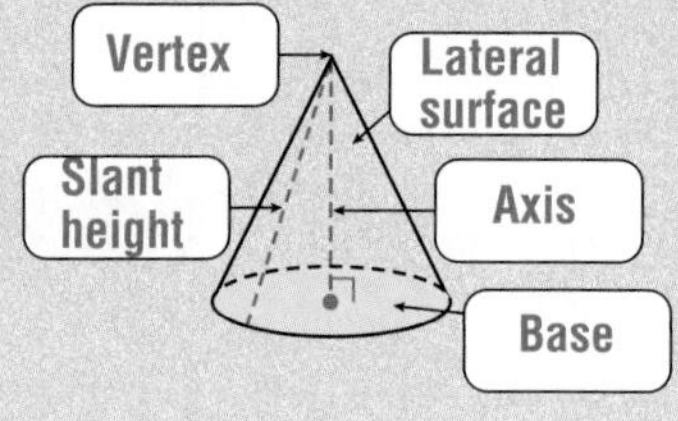

3 Close

Summarize

The surface area of a right prism is $Ph + 2B$, and the surface area of a regular pyramid is $\frac{1}{2}P\ell + B$. Substitute slant height for the height and divide by 2. The same relationship is true for right cylinders, $S = 2\pi rh + 2\pi r^2$, and right cones, $S = \pi r\ell + \pi r^2$.

ONGOING ASSESSMENT and INTERVENTION

Diagnose *Before* the Lesson
10-5 Warm Up, TE p. 689

Monitor *During* the Lesson
Check It Out! Exercises, SE pp. 690–692
Questioning Strategies, TE pp. 690–692

Assess *After* the Lesson
10-5 Lesson Quiz, TE p. 696
Alternative Assessment, TE p. 696

Answers to *Think and Discuss*

1. The lateral faces are all triangles with an area of $\frac{1}{2}$ the base edge length times the slant height ℓ. The perimeter P is the sum of the base edge lengths, so $L = \frac{1}{2}P\ell$.
2. A radius and the axis of a right cone form the legs of a right triangle. The length of the hypotenuse is the slant height of the cone. The hypotenuse of a right triangle is always the longest side, so the slant height is greater than the height.

go.hrw.com
Homework Help Online
KEYWORD: MG7 10-5
Parent Resources Online
KEYWORD: MG7 Parent

GUIDED PRACTICE

1. **Vocabulary** Describe the endpoints of an *axis of a cone*. **the vertex and the center of the base**

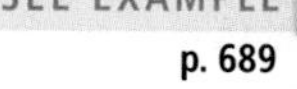

SEE EXAMPLE 1 p. 689

Find the lateral area and surface area of each regular pyramid.

2. 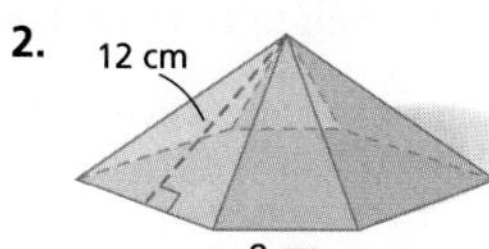

$L = 288\text{ cm}^2$; $S \approx 454.3\text{ cm}^2$

3. 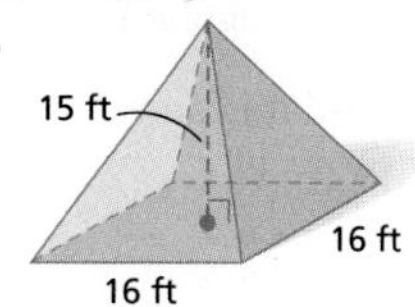

$L = 544\text{ ft}^2$; $S = 800\text{ ft}^2$

4. a regular triangular pyramid with base edge length 15 in. and slant height 20 in. $L = 450\text{ in}^2$; $S \approx 547.4\text{ in}^2$

SEE EXAMPLE 2 p. 691

Find the lateral area and surface area of each right cone. Give your answers in terms of π.

5. 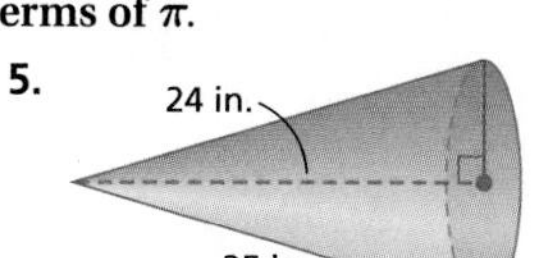

$L = 175\pi\text{ in}^2$; $S = 224\pi\text{ in}^2$

6. 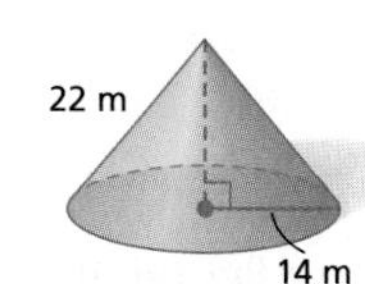

$L = 308\pi\text{ m}^2$; $S = 504\pi\text{ m}^2$

7. a cone with base area $36\pi\text{ ft}^2$ and slant height 8 ft $L = 48\pi\text{ ft}^2$; $S = 84\pi\text{ ft}^2$

SEE EXAMPLE 3 p. 691

Describe the effect of each change on the surface area of the given figure.

8. The dimensions are cut in half.
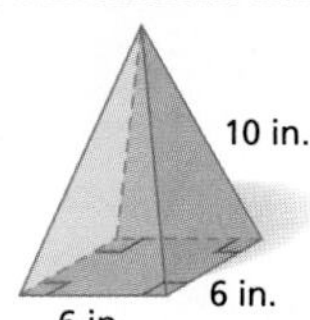

The surface area is multiplied by $\frac{1}{4}$.

9. The dimensions are tripled.
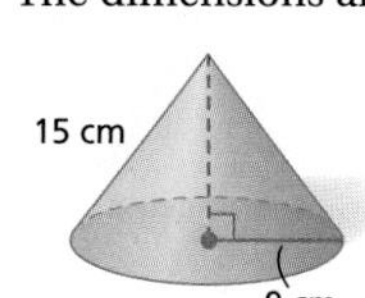

The surface area is multiplied by 9.

SEE EXAMPLE 4 p. 692

Find the surface area of each composite figure.

10. 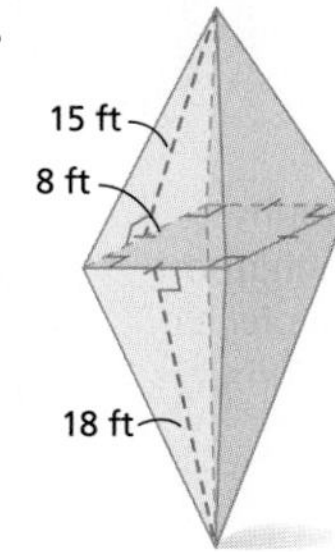

$S = 528\text{ ft}^2$

11. 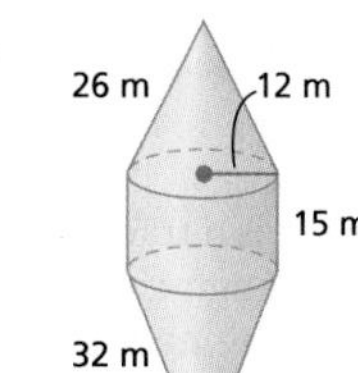

$S = 1056\pi\text{ m}^2$

SEE EXAMPLE 5 p. 692

12. **Crafts** Anna is making a birthday hat from a pattern that is $\frac{3}{4}$ of a circle of colored paper. If Anna's head is 7 inches in diameter, will the hat fit her? Explain.
No; the diameter of the hat will be 9 in., so the hat will be too large.

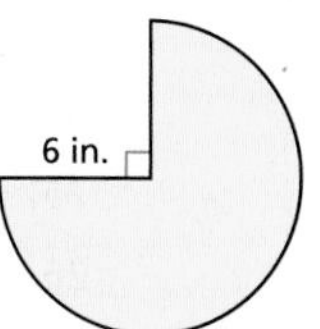

10-5 Exercises

Assignment Guide

Assign *Guided Practice* exercises as necessary.

If you finished Examples **1–3**
- **Basic** 13–20, 24–27
- **Average** 13–20, 24–27, 41
- **Advanced** 13–20, 24–27, 41, 42

If you finished Examples **1–5**
- **Basic** 13–35, 38–40, 44–52
- **Average** 13–41, 44–52
- **Advanced** 13–52

Homework Quick Check
Quickly check key concepts.
Exercises: 14, 16, 20, 22, 23, 34

State Resources

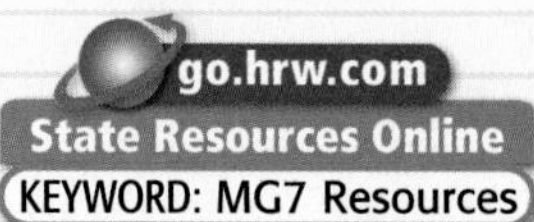
go.hrw.com
State Resources Online
KEYWORD: MG7 Resources

Teaching Tip

Kinesthetic In Exercise 23, some students may have difficulty seeing how the figure could form a cone. Draw an enlarged copy of this figure on a piece of paper or lightweight cardboard, cut it out, and fold it to form the cone. Remind students that the figure shown is a net for a cone without a base.

PRACTICE AND PROBLEM SOLVING

Independent Practice

For Exercises	See Example
13–15	1
16–18	2
19–20	3
21–22	4
23	5

Extra Practice

Skills Practice p. S23
Application Practice p. S37

Find the lateral area and surface area of each regular pyramid.

13. 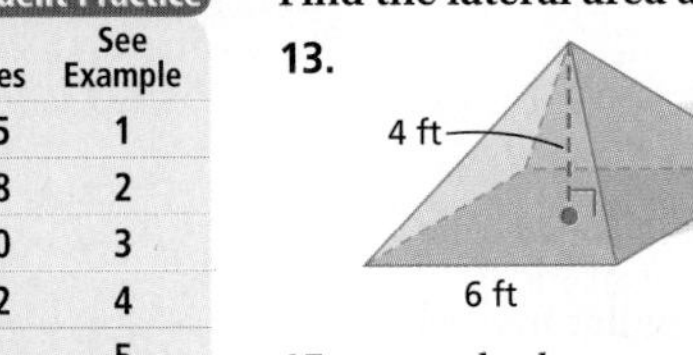

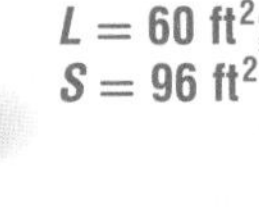
$L = 60\text{ ft}^2$; $S = 96\text{ ft}^2$

14. 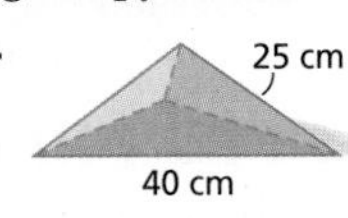

$L = 900\text{ cm}^2$; $S \approx 1592.8\text{ cm}^2$

15. a regular hexagonal pyramid with base edge length 7 ft and slant height 15 ft $L = 315\text{ ft}^2$; $S \approx 442.3\text{ ft}^2$

Find the lateral area and surface area of each right cone. Give your answers in terms of π.

16. 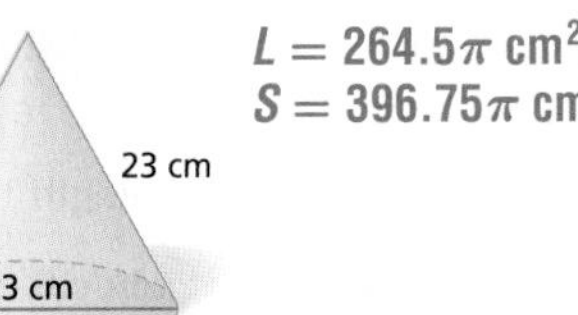

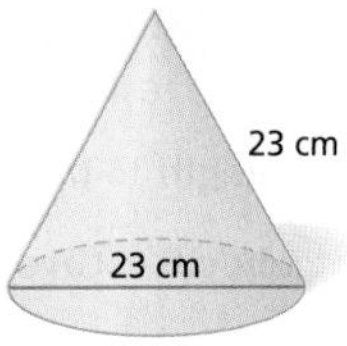

$L = 264.5\pi\text{ cm}^2$; $S = 396.75\pi\text{ cm}^2$

17. 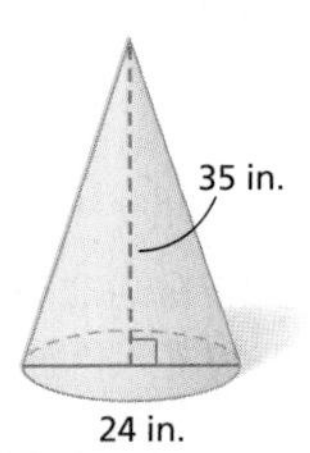

$L = 444\pi\text{ in}^2$; $S = 588\pi\text{ in}^2$

18. a cone with radius 8 m and height that is 1 m less than twice the radius $L = 136\pi\text{ m}^2$; $S = 200\pi\text{ m}^2$

Describe the effect of each change on the surface area of the given figure.

19. The dimensions are divided by 3. The surface area is divided by 9.

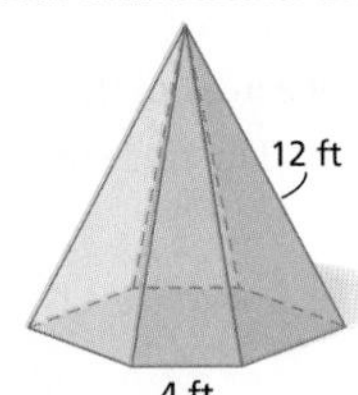

20. The dimensions are doubled. The surface area is multiplied by 4.

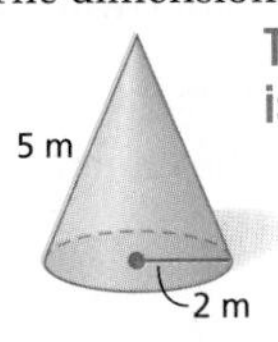

Find the surface area of each composite figure.

21. 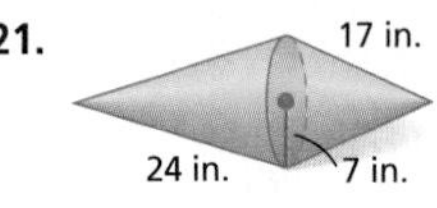

$S = 287\pi\text{ in}^2$

22. 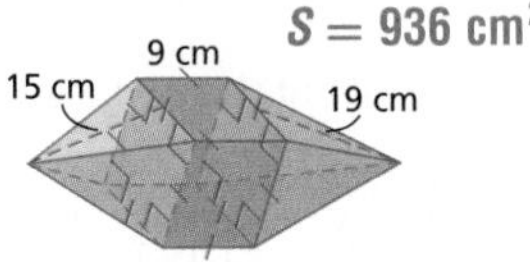

$S = 936\text{ cm}^2$

23. It is a tradition in England to celebrate May 1st by hanging cone-shaped baskets of flowers on neighbors' door handles. Addy is making a basket from a piece of paper that is a semicircle with diameter 12 in. What is the diameter of the basket? 6 in.

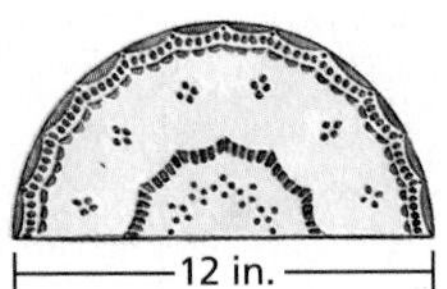

Find the surface area of each figure.

	Shape	Base Area	Slant Height	Surface Area
24.	Regular square pyramid	36 cm^2	5 cm	96 cm^2
25.	Regular triangular pyramid	$\sqrt{3}\text{ m}^2$	$\sqrt{3}$ m	$4\sqrt{3}\text{ m}^2$
26.	Right cone	$16\pi\text{ in}^2$	7 in.	$44\pi\text{ in}^2$
27.	Right cone	$\pi\text{ ft}^2$	2 ft	$3\pi\text{ ft}^2$

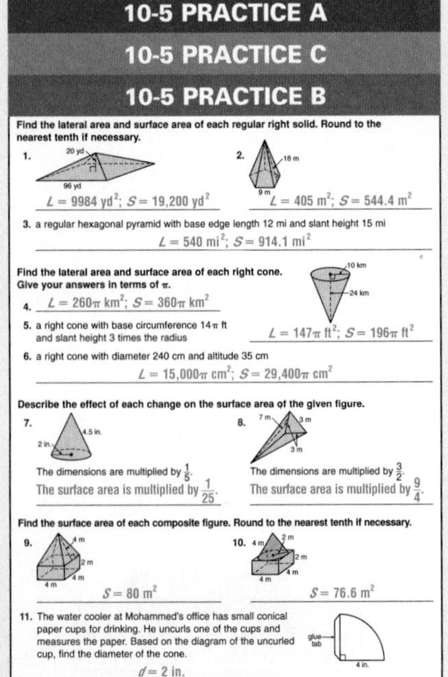

10-5 PRACTICE A
10-5 PRACTICE C
10-5 PRACTICE B

Find the lateral area and surface area of each regular right solid. Round to the nearest tenth if necessary.

1. (20 yd, 96 yd) $L = 9984\text{ yd}^2$; $S = 19{,}200\text{ yd}^2$
2. (18 m, 9 m) $L = 405\text{ m}^2$; $S = 544.4\text{ m}^2$
3. a regular hexagonal pyramid with base edge length 12 mi and slant height 15 mi $L = 540\text{ mi}^2$; $S = 914.1\text{ mi}^2$

Find the lateral area and surface area of each right cone. Give your answers in terms of π.

4. (10 km, 24 km) $L = 260\pi\text{ km}^2$; $S = 360\pi\text{ km}^2$
5. a right cone with base circumference 14π ft and slant height 3 times the radius $L = 147\pi\text{ ft}^2$; $S = 196\pi\text{ ft}^2$
6. a right cone with diameter 240 cm and altitude 35 cm $L = 15{,}000\pi\text{ cm}^2$; $S = 29{,}400\pi\text{ cm}^2$

Describe the effect of each change on the surface area of the given figure.

7. (4.5 in., 2 in.) The dimensions are multiplied by $\frac{1}{5}$. The surface area is multiplied by $\frac{1}{25}$.
8. (7 m, 3 m, 3 m) The dimensions are multiplied by $\frac{3}{2}$. The surface area is multiplied by $\frac{9}{4}$.

Find the surface area of each composite figure. Round to the nearest tenth if necessary.

9. (4 m, 2 m, 4 m, 4 m) $S = 80\text{ m}^2$
10. (4 m, 2 m, 2 m, 4 m, 4 m) $S = 76.6\text{ m}^2$
11. The water cooler at Mohammed's office has small conical paper cups for drinking. He uncurls one of the cups and measures the paper. Based on the diagram of the uncurled cup, find the diameter of the cone. (glue tab, 4 in.) $d = 2$ in.

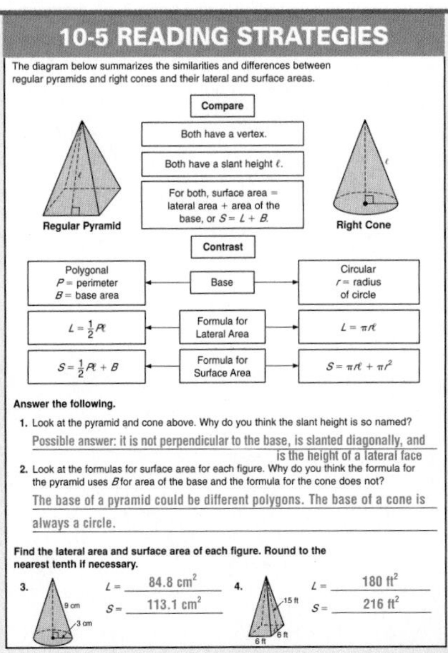

10-5 READING STRATEGIES

The diagram below summarizes the similarities and differences between regular pyramids and right cones and their lateral and surface areas.

Compare (Regular Pyramid / Right Cone)

- Both have a vertex.
- Both have a slant height ℓ.
- For both, surface area = lateral area + area of the base, or $S = L + B$.

Contrast

Regular Pyramid		Right Cone
Polygonal, P = perimeter, B = base area	Base	Circular, r = radius of circle
$L = \frac{1}{2}P\ell$	Formula for Lateral Area	$L = \pi r\ell$
$S = \frac{1}{2}P\ell + B$	Formula for Surface Area	$S = \pi r\ell + \pi r^2$

Answer the following.

1. Look at the pyramid and cone above. Why do you think the slant height is so named? Possible answer: it is not perpendicular to the base, is slanted diagonally, and is the height of a lateral face
2. Look at the formulas for surface area for each figure. Why do you think the formula for the pyramid uses B for area of the base and the formula for the cone does not? The base of a pyramid could be different polygons. The base of a cone is always a circle.

Find the lateral area and surface area of each figure. Round to the nearest tenth if necessary.

3. 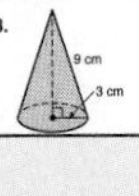 (9 cm, 3 cm) L = 84.8 cm^2 S = 113.1 cm^2
4. 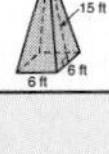 (15 ft, 6 ft, 6 ft) L = 180 ft^2 S = 216 ft^2

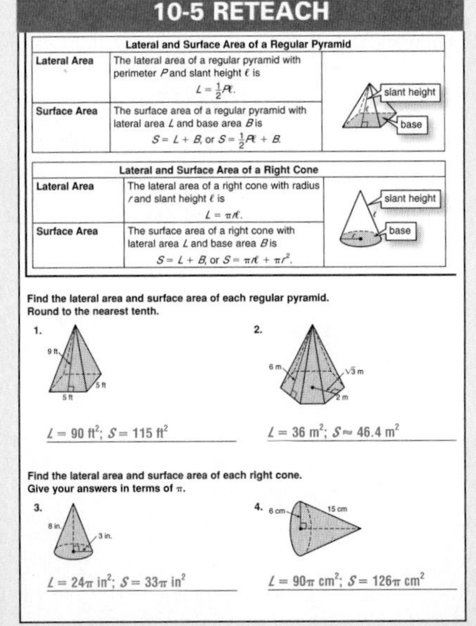

10-5 RETEACH

Lateral and Surface Area of a Regular Pyramid		
Lateral Area	The lateral area of a regular pyramid with perimeter P and slant height ℓ is $L = \frac{1}{2}P\ell$.	slant height, base
Surface Area	The surface area of a regular pyramid with lateral area L and base area B is $S = L + B$, or $S = \frac{1}{2}P\ell + B$.	

Lateral and Surface Area of a Right Cone		
Lateral Area	The lateral area of a right cone with radius r and slant height ℓ is $L = \pi r\ell$.	slant height, base
Surface Area	The surface area of a right cone with lateral area L and base area B is $S = L + B$, or $S = \pi r\ell + \pi r^2$.	

Find the lateral area and surface area of each regular pyramid. Round to the nearest tenth.

1. (9 ft, 5 ft, 5 ft) $L = 90\text{ ft}^2$; $S = 115\text{ ft}^2$
2. (6 m, $\sqrt{3}$ m, 2 m) $L = 36\text{ m}^2$; $S \approx 46.4\text{ m}^2$

Find the lateral area and surface area of each right cone. Give your answers in terms of π.

3. (8 in., 3 in.) $L = 24\pi\text{ in}^2$; $S = 33\pi\text{ in}^2$
4. (6 cm, 15 cm) $L = 90\pi\text{ cm}^2$; $S = 126\pi\text{ cm}^2$

MULTI-STEP TEST PREP

28. This problem will prepare you for the Multi-Step Test Prep on page 724. A juice container is a regular square pyramid with the dimensions shown.

a. Find the surface area of the container to the nearest tenth. **236.3 cm^2**

b. The manufacturer decides to make a container in the shape of a right cone that requires the same amount of material. The base diameter must be 9 cm. Find the slant height of the container to the nearest tenth. **12.2 cm**

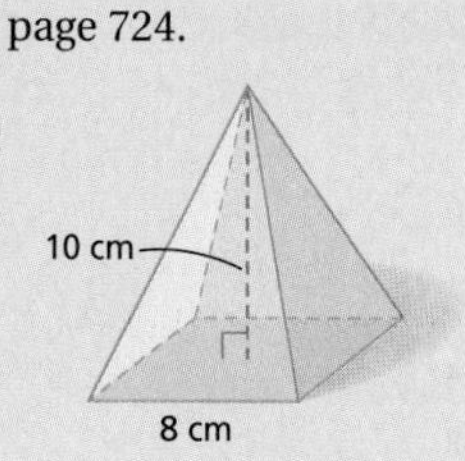

29. Find the radius of a right cone with slant height 21 m and surface area $232\pi \text{ m}^2$. **$r = 8$ m**

30. Find the slant height of a regular square pyramid with base perimeter 32 ft and surface area 256 ft^2. **$\ell = 12$ ft**

31. Find the base perimeter of a regular hexagonal pyramid with slant height 10 cm and lateral area 120 cm^2. **$P = 24$ cm**

32. Find the surface area of a right cone with a slant height of 25 units that has its base centered at $(0, 0, 0)$ and its vertex at $(0, 0, 7)$. **$S = 1176\pi \text{ units}^2$**

LINK

Architecture

The Pyramid Arena seats 21,000 people. The base of the pyramid is larger than six football fields.

Find the surface area of each composite figure.

33.

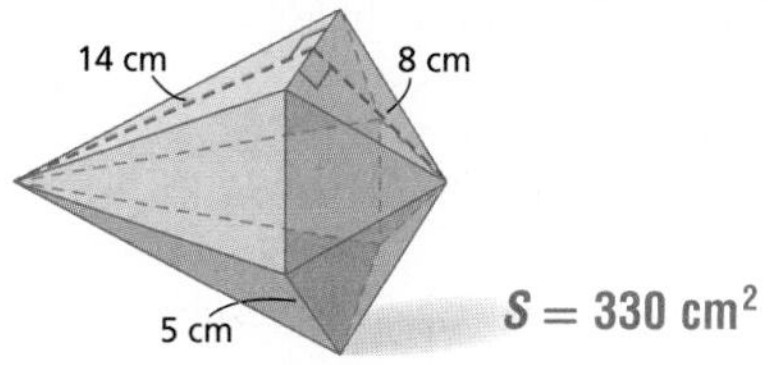

$S = 330 \text{ cm}^2$

34.

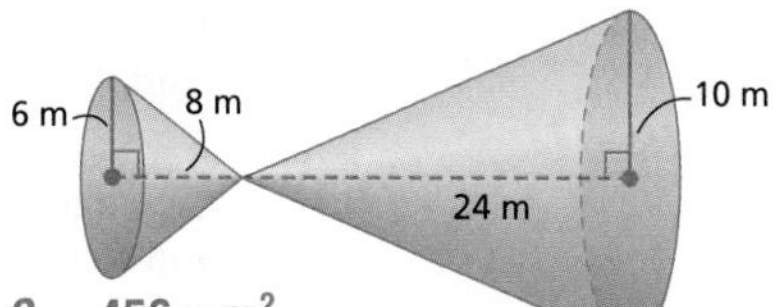

$S = 456\pi \text{ m}^2$

35. Architecture The Pyramid Arena in Memphis, Tennessee, is a square pyramid with base edge lengths of 200 yd and a height of 32 stories. Estimate the area of the glass on the sides of the pyramid. (*Hint:* 1 story $\approx$ 10 ft) **Possible answer: $526{,}000 \text{ ft}^2$**

36. Critical Thinking Explain why the slant height of a regular square pyramid must be greater than half the base edge length.

37. Write About It Explain why slant height is not defined for an oblique cone.

TEST PREP

38. Which expressions represent the surface area of the regular square pyramid?

I. $\frac{t^2}{16} + \frac{ts}{2}$ II. $\frac{t^2}{16} + \frac{t\ell}{2}$ III. $\frac{t}{2}\left(\frac{t}{8} + \ell\right)$

Ⓐ I only Ⓒ I and II

Ⓑ II only **Ⓓ II and III**

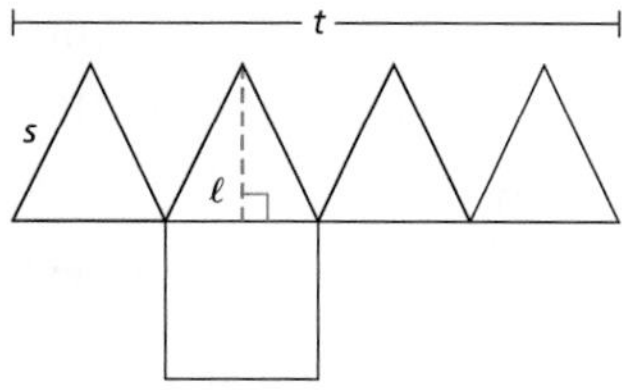

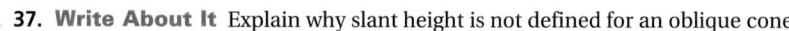

39. A regular square pyramid has a slant height of 18 cm and a lateral area of 216 cm^2. What is the surface area?

Ⓕ 252 cm^2 Ⓖ 234 cm^2 Ⓗ 225 cm^2 Ⓙ 240 cm^2

40. What is the lateral area of the cone?

Ⓐ $360\pi \text{ cm}^2$ Ⓒ $450\pi \text{ cm}^2$

Ⓑ $369\pi \text{ cm}^2$ Ⓓ $1640\pi \text{ cm}^2$

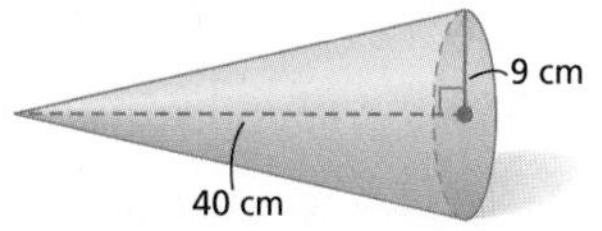

COMMON ERROR ALERT

In **Exercise 32,** some students may not recognize that the segment with endpoints $(0, 0, 0)$ and $(0, 0, 7)$ is the altitude of the cone. Remind students to sketch the figure and to include the right triangle formed by the radius, slant height, and altitude.

MULTI-STEP TEST PREP **Exercise 28** involves finding the slant height of a pyramid-shaped juice container. This exercise prepares students for the Multi-Step Test Prep on page 724.

TEST PREP DOCTOR In **Exercise 39,** students who chose **G** used the slant height of 18 cm instead of the base area of 36 cm^2. Those who chose **H** used 3 cm for the side of the base rather than 6 cm, and those who chose **J** used the perimeter of the base instead of the area of the base.

Answers

36. A triangle is formed with 2 vertices at the midpoints of opposite sides of the square base and the third vertex at the vertex of the pyramid. The side lengths of the triangle are ℓ, ℓ, and s, the edge length of the base. By the Triangle Inequality Theorem, $\ell + \ell > s$, so $2\ell > s$. Therefore $\ell > \frac{1}{2}s$.

37. In an oblique cone, the distance from a point on the edge of the base to the vertex is not the same for each point on the base.

10-5 PROBLEM SOLVING

1. Find the diameter of a right cone with slant height 18 centimeters and surface area 208π square centimeters. **16 cm**

2. Find the surface area of a regular pentagonal pyramid with base area 49 square meters and slant height 13 meters. Round to the nearest tenth. **222.4 mm^2**

3. A piece of paper in the shape shown is folded to form a cone. What is the diameter of the base of the cone that is formed? Round to the nearest tenth.

18.7 in.

4. The right cone has a surface area of 240π square millimeters. What is the radius of the cone?

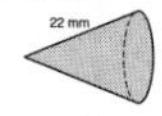

8 mm

Choose the best answer.

5. A square pyramid has a base with a side length of 9 centimeters and a slant height that is 4 centimeters more than $1\frac{1}{2}$ times the length of the base. Find the surface area of the pyramid.

A 162 cm^2 C 315 cm^2
B 243 cm^2 **Ⓓ 396 cm^2**

6. A cone has a surface area of 64π square inches. If the radius and height are each multiplied by $\frac{3}{4}$, what will be the new surface area of the cone?

Ⓕ $36\pi \text{ in}^2$ H $60\pi \text{ in}^2$
G $48\pi \text{ in}^2$ J $96\pi \text{ in}^2$

7. Find the surface area of the composite figure. Round to the nearest tenth.

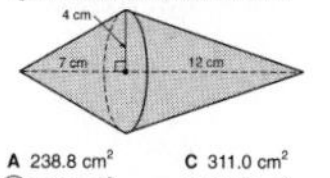

A 238.8 cm^2 C 311.0 cm^2
Ⓑ 260.3 cm^2 D 361.3 cm^2

8. A cone has a base diameter of 6 yards. What is the slant height of the cone if it has the same surface area as the square pyramid shown? Round to the nearest tenth.

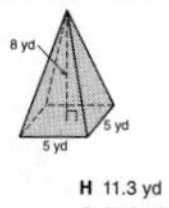

F 8.1 yd H 11.3 yd
Ⓖ 8.5 yd J 25.6 yd

10-5 CHALLENGE

Suppose that you need to make a model of a cone that has the dimensions given in the figure at right. You know that the net for the cone consists of a circular region for the base and a region bounded by a sector of a circle for the lateral surface. But how do you know the exact size of each piece?

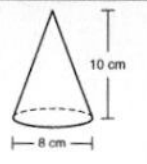

Give each measure for the right cone shown at right. When necessary, round to the nearest tenth of a centimeter.

1. radius **4 cm** 2. circumference **25.1 cm**

3. height **10 cm** 4. slant height **10.8 cm**

5. A sketch of a net for the cone shown above is given at right.

a. Label the sketch with as many of the measures from Exercises 1–4 as possible.

b. Suppose that you were to use the sketch to draw the net. Which important measure is still needed? **m∠ABC**

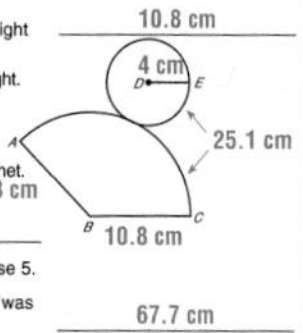

6. Refer to the net for the cone that you labeled in Exercise 5.

a. Suppose that the *entire* circle with center at point *B* was drawn. What would be its circumference? **67.7 cm**

b. What is the length of the arc that is drawn from *A* to *C*? **25.1 cm**

c. What percent of the entire circle is the arc from *A* to *C*? **$\frac{4}{10.77} \approx 37.1\%$**

d. Multiply 360° by your percent from part **c**. What is the measure of ∠*ABC*, rounded to the nearest whole degree? **134°**

7. Refer to your results from Exercises 5 and 6. Using a compass, ruler, and protractor, draw an accurate real-size net for the cone. Then assemble the net to make a model of the cone. **Check students' work.**

8. A sketch of a net for a right cone is given at right. In the blank space to its right, draw the cone, making the height and diameter of the cone in the drawing proportional to the actual height and diameter. Be sure to label the height and diameter.

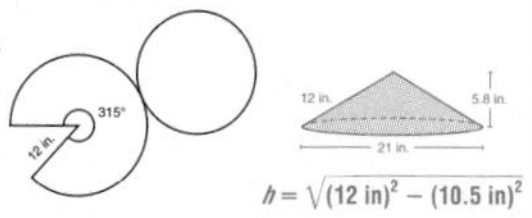

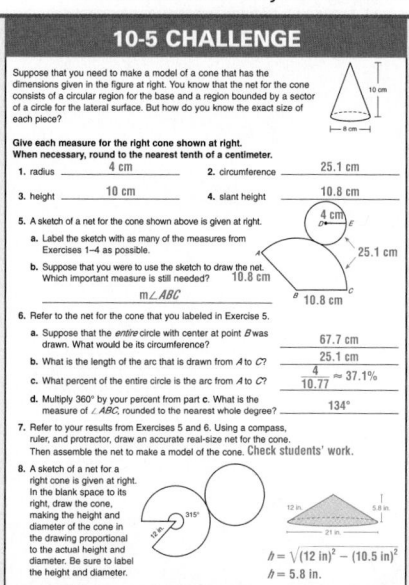

$h = \sqrt{(12 \text{ in})^2 - (10.5 \text{ in})^2}$
$h = 5.8$ in.

Journal

Have students describe how they would create a pattern for a cone-shaped party hat. Have them include how they would make sure the diameter of the hat is the correct size and how much material would be needed to make the hat.

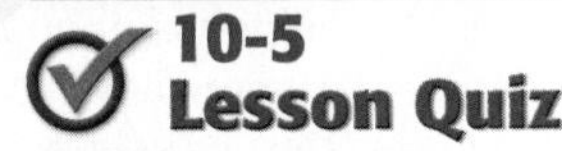

Alternative Assessment

Have students draw a net and find the surface area of a regular square pyramid with base edge length 4 cm and slant height 5 cm and a right cone with radius 4 cm and slant height 5 cm.

Power Presentations with PowerPoint®

10-5 Lesson Quiz

Find the lateral area and surface area of each figure. Round to the nearest tenth, if necessary.

1. a regular square pyramid with base edge length 9 ft and slant height 12 ft
   $L = 216$ ft^2; $S = 297$ ft^2
2. a regular triangular pyramid with base edge length 12 cm and slant height 10 cm
   $L = 180$ cm^2; $S \approx 242.4$ cm^2
3. a right cone with diameter 12 in. and slant height 11 in.
   $L \approx 207.3$ in^2; $S \approx 320.4$ in^2
4. A right cone has radius 3 and slant height 5. The radius and slant height are both multiplied by $\frac{3}{2}$. Describe the effect on the surface area. The surface area is multiplied by $\frac{9}{4}$.
5. Find the surface area of the composite figure. Give your answer in terms of π.

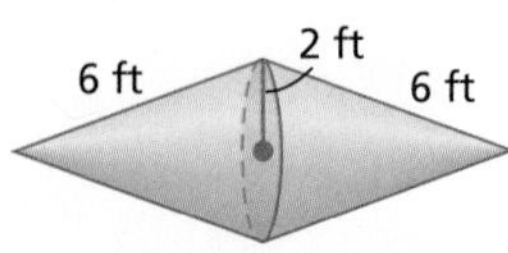

$S = 24\pi$ ft^2

Also available on transparency

CHALLENGE AND EXTEND

41d. $S = 500\pi - 100\pi + 25\pi = 425\pi$ cm^2

42. $A = 2(b_1 + b_2)\ell$

43a. $c = 2\pi r$
b. $C = 2\pi\ell$
c. $\frac{c}{C} = \frac{2\pi r}{2\pi\ell} = \frac{r}{\ell}$
d. The area of the larger circle is $A = \pi\ell^2$. The lateral surface area is $\frac{c}{C} = \frac{r}{\ell}$ times the area of the circle, so $L = \pi\ell^2\left(\frac{r}{\ell}\right) = \pi r\ell$.

41. A *frustum* of a cone is a part of the cone with two parallel bases. The height of the frustum of the cone is half the height of the original cone.
   a. Find the surface area of the original cone. $S = 500\pi$ cm^2
   b. Find the lateral area of the top of the cone. $L = 100\pi$ cm^2
   c. Find the area of the top base of the frustum. $B = 25\pi$ cm^2
   d. Use your results from parts **a**, **b**, and **c** to find the surface area of the frustum of the cone.

5 cm
20 cm
10 cm

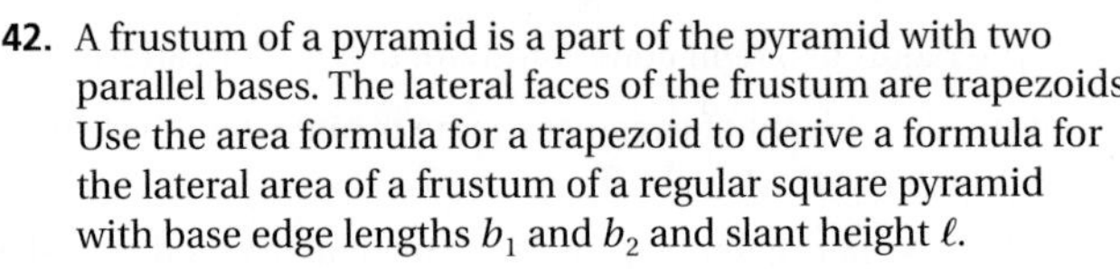

42. A frustum of a pyramid is a part of the pyramid with two parallel bases. The lateral faces of the frustum are trapezoids. Use the area formula for a trapezoid to derive a formula for the lateral area of a frustum of a regular square pyramid with base edge lengths b_1 and b_2 and slant height ℓ.

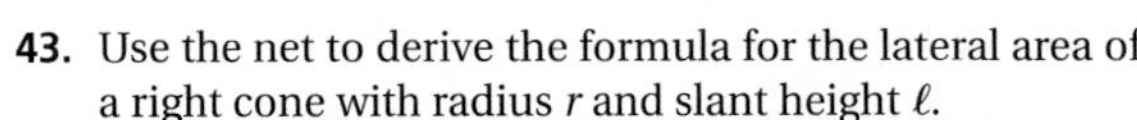

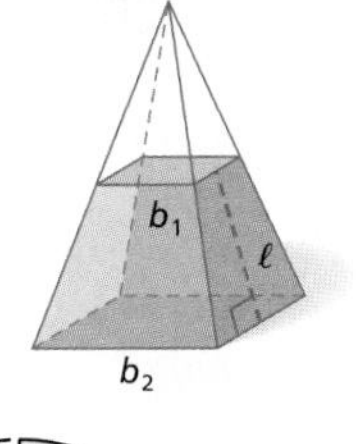

43. Use the net to derive the formula for the lateral area of a right cone with radius r and slant height ℓ.
   a. The length of the curved edge of the lateral surface must equal the circumference of the base. Find the circumference c of the base in terms of r.
   b. The lateral surface is part of a larger circle. Find the circumference C of the larger circle.
   c. The lateral surface area is $\frac{c}{C}$ times the area of the larger circle. Use your results from parts **a** and **b** to find $\frac{c}{C}$.
   d. Find the area of the larger circle. Use your result and the result from part **c** to find the lateral area L.

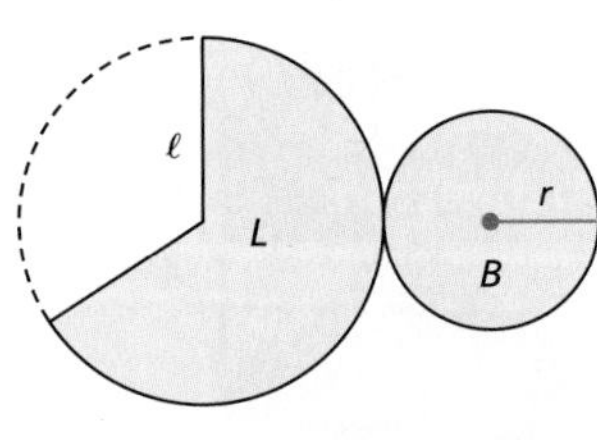

SPIRAL REVIEW

44. Since the area of a circle depends on the square of the circle's radius, the surface area of a cone cannot be described by a linear function.

45. Since perimeter is 1-dimensional, the perimeter of a rectangle can be described by a linear function.

46. Since the area of a circle depends on the square of the radius, it cannot be described by a linear function.

State whether the following can be described by a linear function. *(Previous course)*

44. the surface area of a right circular cone with height h and radius r
45. the perimeter of a rectangle with a height h that is twice as large as its width w
46. the area of a circle with radius r

A point is chosen randomly in *ACEF*. Find the probability of each event. Round to the nearest hundredth. *(Lesson 9-6)*

47. The point is in $\triangle BDG$. 0.25
48. The point is in $\odot H$. 0.79
49. The point is in the shaded region. 0.21

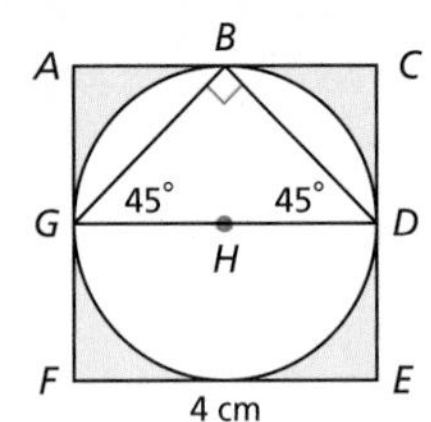

Find the surface area of each right prism or right cylinder. Round your answer to the nearest tenth. *(Lesson 10-4)*

50. 15 in. 17 in. 10 in.
$S = 520$ in^2

51. 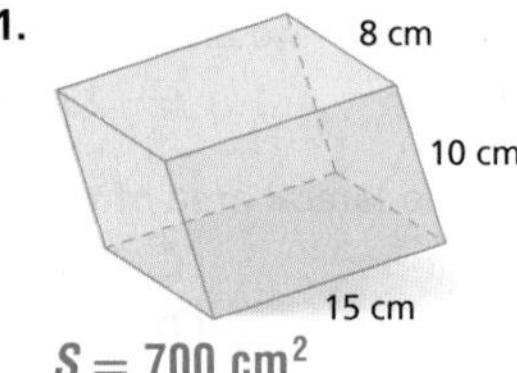

$S = 700$ cm^2

52. 2 cm 3 cm
$S \approx 62.8$ cm^2

10-6 Volume of Prisms and Cylinders

Objectives
Learn and apply the formula for the volume of a prism.

Learn and apply the formula for the volume of a cylinder.

Vocabulary
volume

Who uses this?
Marine biologists must ensure that aquariums are large enough to accommodate the number of fish inside them. (See Example 2.)

The **volume** of a three-dimensional figure is the number of nonoverlapping unit cubes of a given size that will exactly fill the interior.

A cube built out of 27 unit cubes has a volume of 27 cubic units.

Cavalieri's principle says that if two three-dimensional figures have the same height and have the same cross-sectional area at every level, they have the same volume.

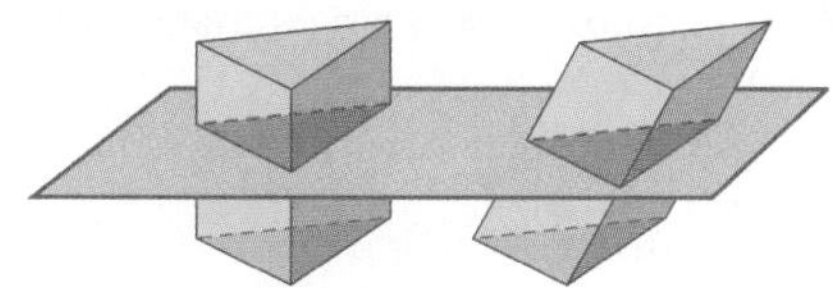

A right prism and an oblique prism with the same base and height have the same volume.

Volume of a Prism

The volume of a prism with base area B and height h is $V = Bh$.	The volume of a right rectangular prism with length ℓ, width w, and height h is $V = \ell wh$.	The volume of a cube with edge length s is $V = s^3$.
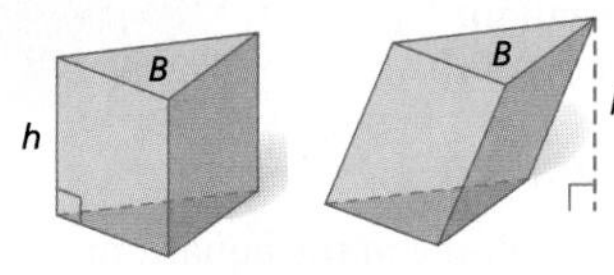	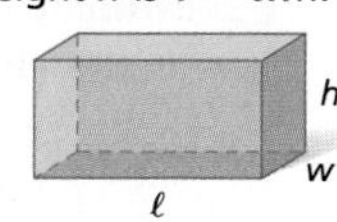	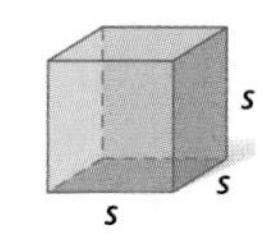

EXAMPLE 1 Finding Volumes of Prisms

Find the volume of each prism. Round to the nearest tenth, if necessary.

A

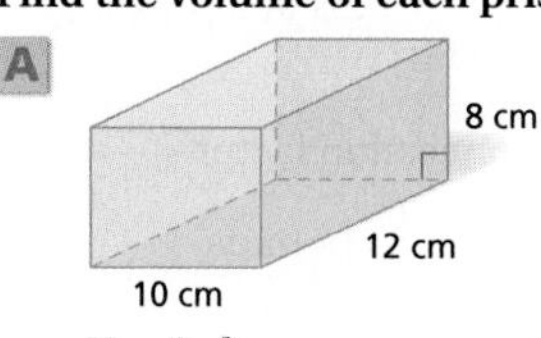

$V = \ell wh$ — *Volume of a right rectangular prism*

$= (10)(12)(8) = 960 \text{ cm}^3$ — *Substitute 10 for ℓ, 12 for w, and 8 for h.*

B a cube with edge length 10 cm

$V = s^3$ — *Volume of a cube*

$= 10^3 = 1000 \text{ cm}^3$ — *Substitute 10 for s.*

10-6 Organizer

Pacing: Traditional 1 day
Block $\frac{1}{2}$ day

Objectives: Learn and apply the formula for the volume of a prism.

Learn and apply the formula for the volume of a cylinder.

Online Edition
Tutorial Videos

Countdown Week 23

Power Presentations with PowerPoint®

Warm Up

Find the area of each figure. Round to the nearest tenth.

1. an equilateral triangle with edge length 20 cm
   173.2 cm²
2. a regular hexagon with edge length 14 m 509.2 m²
3. a circle with radius 6.8 in.
   145.3 in²
4. a circle with diameter 14 ft
   153.9 ft²

Also available on transparency

Math Humor

Q: What 3-D figure can cure strep throat?

A: A penicillinder.

1 Introduce

EXPLORATION

10-6 Volume of Prisms and Cylinders

The volume of a right rectangular prism with length ℓ, width w, and height h is given by the formula $V = \ell wh$. You can use this to derive the formula for the volume of a cylinder.

1. The figure shows a cylinder with radius r and height h. The cylinder is divided into eight congruent wedges, and the wedges are rearranged to form a geometric solid. What solid do the wedges approximate when they are arranged as shown?

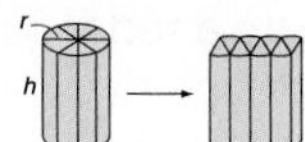

2. What is the height of the geometric solid?
3. What is the length of the solid in terms of r? (*Hint:* How is the length of the solid related to the distance around the cylinder?)
4. What is the width of the solid?
5. Express the volume of the solid in terms of h and r.

THINK AND DISCUSS

6. Explain how you can use your work to write a formula for the

Motivate

Use two sheets of 8.5 in. by 11 in. paper to create two different cylinders, one with height 8.5 in. and the other with height 11 in. Ask students to guess which cylinder will have a greater volume or whether they will have the same volume. Then fill the cylinders with popcorn or cereal to test their conjecture.

Explorations and answers are provided in *Alternate Openers: Explorations Transparencies.*

State Resources

go.hrw.com
State Resources Online
KEYWORD: MG7 Resources

Power Presentations with PowerPoint®

Additional Examples

Example 1

Find the volume of each prism. Round to the nearest tenth, if necessary.

A.

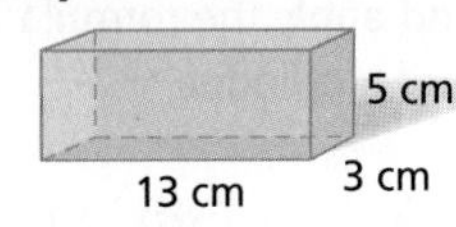

195 cm^3

B. a cube with edge length 15 in.

3375 in^3

C. the right regular hexagonal prism

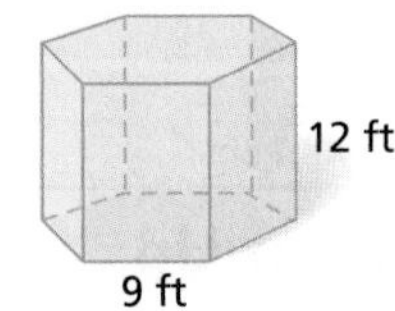

2525.3 ft^3

Example 2

A swimming pool is a rectangular prism. Estimate the volume of water in the pool in gallons when it is completely full (*Hint:* 1 gallon ≈ 0.134 ft^3). The density of water is about 8.33 pounds per gallon. Estimate the weight of the water in pounds.

volume ≈ 25,187 gallons; weight ≈ 209,804 pounds

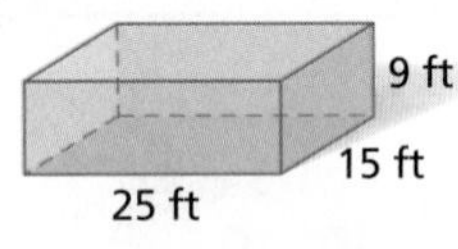

INTERVENTION

Questioning Strategies

EXAMPLE 1

- When is trigonometry needed to find the volume of a prism?

EXAMPLE 2

- What would the volume of water be if the aquarium were only $\frac{3}{4}$ full?

Remember!

To review the area of a regular polygon, see page 601. To review tangent ratios, see page 525.

Find the volume of each prism. Round to the nearest tenth, if necessary.

C **a right regular pentagonal prism with base edge length 5 m and height 7 m**

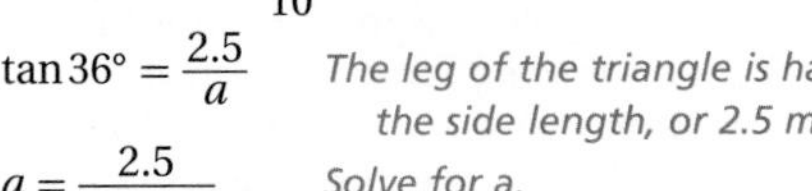

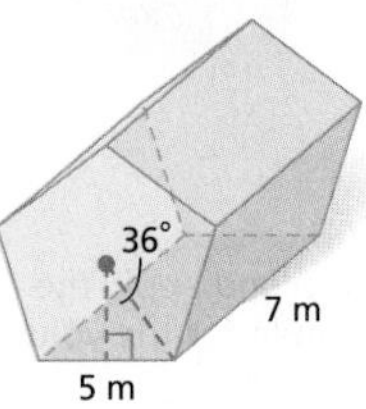

Step 1 Find the apothem a of the base. First draw a right triangle on one base as shown. The measure of the angle with its vertex at the center is $\frac{360°}{10} = 36°$.

$\tan 36° = \frac{2.5}{a}$ *The leg of the triangle is half the side length, or 2.5 m.*

$a = \frac{2.5}{\tan 36°}$ *Solve for a.*

Step 2 Use the value of a to find the base area.

$B = \frac{1}{2}aP = \frac{1}{2}\left(\frac{2.5}{\tan 36°}\right)(25) = \frac{31.25}{\tan 36°}$ *$P = 5(5) = 25$ m*

Step 3 Use the base area to find the volume.

$V = Bh = \frac{31.25}{\tan 36°} \cdot 7 \approx 301.1 \text{ m}^3$

CHECK IT OUT! 1. Find the volume of a triangular prism with a height of 9 yd whose base is a right triangle with legs 7 yd and 5 yd long.

$V = 157.5$ yd^3

EXAMPLE 2 ***Marine Biology Application***

The aquarium at the right is a rectangular prism. Estimate the volume of the water in the aquarium in gallons. The density of water is about 8.33 pounds per gallon. Estimate the weight of the water in pounds. (*Hint:* 1 gallon ≈ 0.134 ft^3)

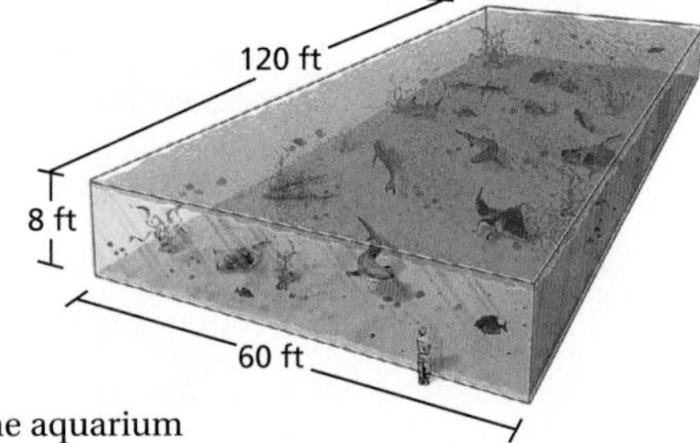

Step 1 Find the volume of the aquarium in cubic feet.

$V = \ell wh = (120)(60)(8) = 57{,}600 \text{ ft}^3$

Step 2 Use the conversion factor $\frac{1 \text{ gallon}}{0.134 \text{ ft}^3}$ to estimate the volume in gallons.

$57{,}600 \text{ ft}^3 \cdot \frac{1 \text{ gallon}}{0.134 \text{ ft}^3} \approx 429{,}851 \text{ gallons}$ *$\frac{1 \text{ gallon}}{0.134 \text{ ft}^3} = 1$*

Step 3 Use the conversion factor $\frac{8.33 \text{ pounds}}{1 \text{ gallon}}$ to estimate the weight of the water.

$429{,}851 \text{ gallons} \cdot \frac{8.33 \text{ pounds}}{1 \text{ gallon}} \approx 3{,}580{,}659 \text{ pounds}$ *$\frac{8.33 \text{ pounds}}{1 \text{ gallon}} = 1$*

The aquarium holds about 429,851 gallons. The water in the aquarium weighs about 3,580,659 pounds.

CHECK IT OUT! 2. **What if...?** Estimate the volume in gallons and the weight of the water in the aquarium above if the height were doubled.

859,702 gal; 7,161,318 lb

2 Teach

Guided Instruction

Before presenting **Example 1C,** you may need to review trigonometric ratios with the students. When discussing **Example 2,** review conversion factors. Show students that they need to remember only one formula for the volume of a prism or cylinder. The volume of *any* prism or cylinder is given by the formula $V = Bh$.

Reaching All Learners

Through Cooperative Learning

Have students work in groups to make cylinders out of modeling clay. Then have them use string to slice the cylinders into eight congruent sectors and arrange the sectors to approximate a rectangular prism. Have them use this shape to explain the volume formula for a cylinder.

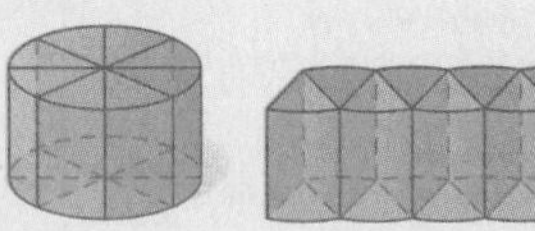

Cavalieri's principle also relates to cylinders. The two stacks have the same number of CDs, so they have the same volume.

Volume of a Cylinder

The volume of a cylinder with base area B, radius r, and height h is $V = Bh$, or $V = \pi r^2 h$.

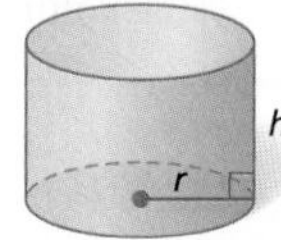

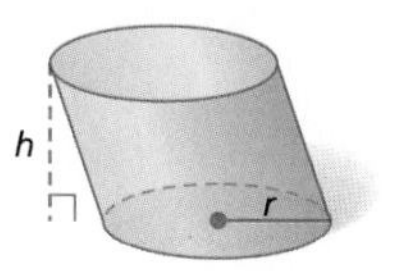

EXAMPLE 3 Finding Volumes of Cylinders

Find the volume of each cylinder. Give your answers both in terms of π and rounded to the nearest tenth.

A

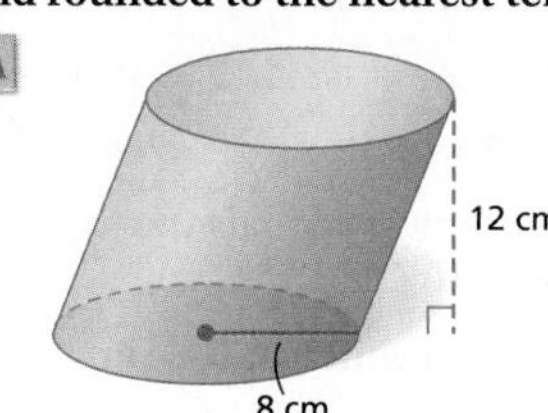

$V = \pi r^2 h$ *Volume of a cylinder*

$= \pi(8)^2(12)$ *Substitute 8 for r and 12 for h.*

$= 768\pi \text{ cm}^3 \approx 2412.7 \text{ cm}^3$

B **a cylinder with a base area of $36\pi \text{ in}^2$ and a height equal to twice the radius**

Step 1 Use the base area to find the radius.

$\pi r^2 = 36\pi$ *Substitute 36π for the base area.*

$r = 6$ *Solve for r.*

Step 2 Use the radius to find the height. The height is equal to twice the radius.

$h = 2r$

$= 2(6) = 12 \text{ cm}$

Step 3 Use the radius and height to find the volume.

$V = \pi r^2 h$ *Volume of a cylinder*

$= \pi(6)^2(12) = 432\pi \text{ in}^3$ *Substitute 6 for r and 12 for h.*

$\approx 1357.2 \text{ in}^3$

3. Find the volume of a cylinder with a diameter of 16 in. and a height of 17 in. Give your answer both in terms of π and rounded to the nearest tenth. **$V = 1088\pi \text{ in}^3 \approx 3418.1 \text{ in}^3$**

COMMON ERROR ALERT

Students may make careless errors if they do not read the problem carefully and use the given information correctly. For example, if the diameter of a cylinder is given, they must divide by 2 to find the radius before using the formula. Also, the slant height may be given instead of the height, or the base area instead of the radius.

Power Presentations with PowerPoint®

Additional Examples

Example 3

Find the volume of each cylinder. Give your answers in terms of π and rounded to the nearest tenth.

A.

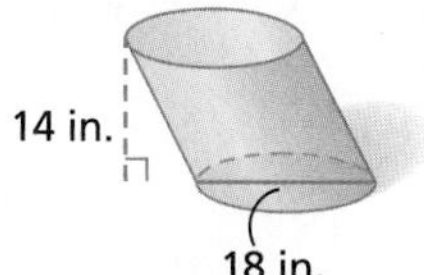

$1134\pi \text{ in}^3$; 3562.6 in^3

B. a cylinder with base area $121\pi \text{ cm}^2$ and a height equal to twice the radius

$2662\pi \text{ cm}^3$; 8362.9 cm^3

INTERVENTION

Questioning Strategies

EXAMPLE 3

- How would you find the volume of a cylinder with height 2 when given the diameter *d*? given the base area *B*?

Measurement To help students remember the appropriate units when working with three-dimensional figures, remind students that a cube can be filled with *unit cubes,* so volume is measured in *cubic units*. The faces of a cube are squares that can be covered with *unit squares,* so surface area is measured in *square units.*

ENGLISH LANGUAGE LEARNERS

Power Presentations with PowerPoint®

Additional Examples

Example 4

The radius and height of the cylinder are multiplied by $\frac{2}{3}$. Describe the effect on the volume.

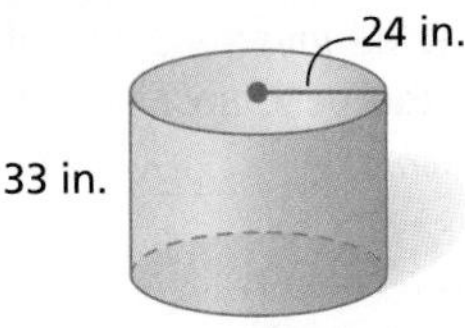

The volume is multiplied by $\frac{8}{27}$.

Example 5

Find the volume of the composite figure. Round to the nearest tenth. 270.9 cm^3

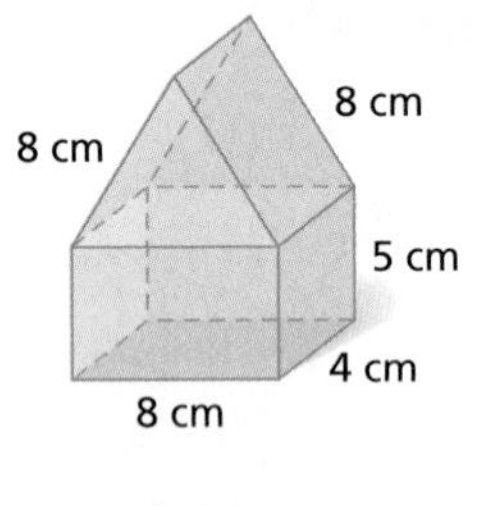

INTERVENTION
Questioning Strategies

EXAMPLE 4

- How is the ratio of the volumes of two similar prisms or cylinders related to the ratio of their dimensions?

EXAMPLE 5

- Is the volume of a composite three-dimensional figure the sum of the volumes of the individual figures? Explain.

EXAMPLE 4 Exploring Effects of Changing Dimensions

The radius and height of the cylinder are multiplied by $\frac{1}{2}$. Describe the effect on the volume.

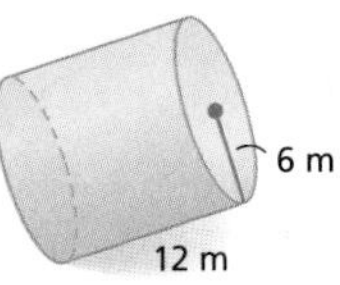

original dimensions:	radius and height multiplied by $\frac{1}{2}$:
$V = \pi r^2 h$	$V = \pi r^2 h$
$= \pi(6)^2(12)$	$= \pi(3)^2(6)$
$= 432\pi \text{ m}^3$	$= 54\pi \text{ m}^3$

Notice that $54\pi = \frac{1}{8}(432\pi)$. If the radius and height are multiplied by $\frac{1}{2}$, the volume is multiplied by $\left(\frac{1}{2}\right)^3$, or $\frac{1}{8}$.

4. The length, width, and height of the prism are doubled. Describe the effect on the volume.
The volume is multiplied by 8.

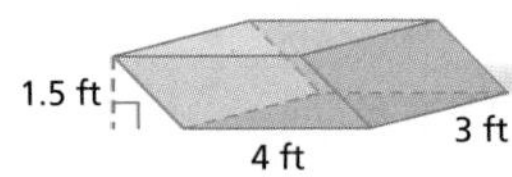

EXAMPLE 5 Finding Volumes of Composite Three-Dimensional Figures

Find the volume of the composite figure. Round to the nearest tenth.

The base area of the prism is $B = \frac{1}{2}(6)(8) = 24 \text{ m}^2$.
The volume of the prism is $V = Bh = 24(9) = 216 \text{ m}^3$.

The cylinder's diameter equals the hypotenuse of the prism's base, 10 m. So the radius is 5 m.

The volume of the cylinder is $V = \pi r^2 h = \pi(5)^2(5) = 125\pi \text{ m}^3$.

The total volume of the figure is the sum of the volumes.
$V = 216 + 125\pi \approx 608.7 \text{ m}^3$

5 m 9 m 6 m 8 m

5. Find the volume of the composite figure. Round to the nearest tenth.
$V \approx 51.4 \text{ cm}^3$

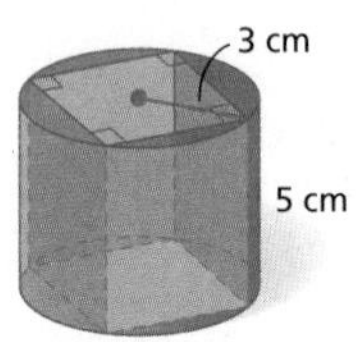

THINK AND DISCUSS

1. Compare the formula for the volume of a prism with the formula for the volume of a cylinder.
2. Explain how Cavalieri's principle relates to the formula for the volume of an oblique prism.

3. **GET ORGANIZED** Copy and complete the graphic organizer. In each box, write the formula for the volume.

Shape	Volume
Prism	$V = Bh$
Cube	$V = s^3$
Cylinder	$V = \pi r^2 h$

3 Close

Summarize

Have students imagine an arrangement of 3 rows of 4 unit cubes each. The cubes form a 3 × 4 × 1 rectangular prism with a volume of 12 cubic units. To find the volume of a 3 × 4 × 2 prism, imagine another layer of cubes stacked on top of the first one. To illustrate Cavalieri's Principle, imagine the layers rearranged into 2 rows of 6 cubes each.

ONGOING ASSESSMENT and INTERVENTION

Diagnose ***Before*** **the Lesson**
10-6 Warm Up, TE p. 697

Monitor ***During*** **the Lesson**
Check It Out! Exercises, SE pp. 698–700
Questioning Strategies, TE pp. 698–700

Assess ***After*** **the Lesson**
10-6 Lesson Quiz, TE p. 704
Alternative Assessment, TE p. 704

Answers to *Think and Discuss*

Possible answers:

1. In both formulas, the volume is equal to the base area times the height. The base area of a cylinder is given by πr^2, and the base area of a prism is given by the area formula for the type of polygon it is.
2. An oblique prism has the same cross-sectional area at every level as a right prism with the same base and height. By Cavalieri's Principle, the oblique prism and the right prism have the same volume.

10-6 Exercises

go.hrw.com
Homework Help Online
KEYWORD: MG7 10-6
Parent Resources Online
KEYWORD: MG7 Parent

GUIDED PRACTICE

1. **Vocabulary** In a right cylinder, the *altitude* is __?__ the axis. (*longer than, shorter than,* or *the same length as*) **the same length as**

SEE EXAMPLE 1 p. 697

Find the volume of each prism.

2. 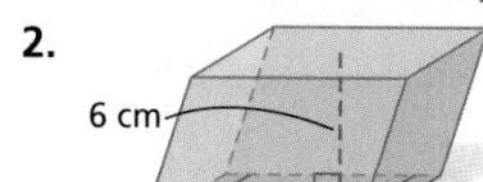

$V = 216$ cm^3

3. 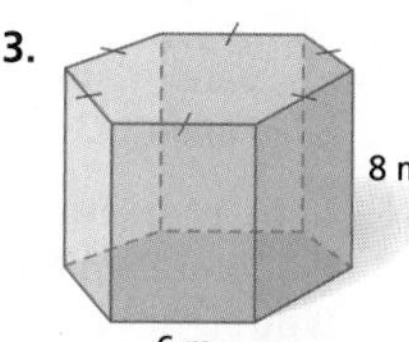

$V \approx 748.2$ m^3

4. a cube with edge length 8 ft $V = 512$ ft^3

SEE EXAMPLE 2 p. 698

5. **Food** The world's largest ice cream cake, built in New York City on May 25, 2004, was approximately a 19 ft by 9 ft by 2 ft rectangular prism. Estimate the volume of the ice cream cake in gallons. If the density of the ice cream was 4.73 pounds per gallon, estimate the weight of the cake. (*Hint:* 1 gallon $\approx$ 0.134 cubic feet) **2552 gal; 12,071 lb**

SEE EXAMPLE 3 p. 699

Find the volume of each cylinder. Give your answers both in terms of π and rounded to the nearest tenth.

6. 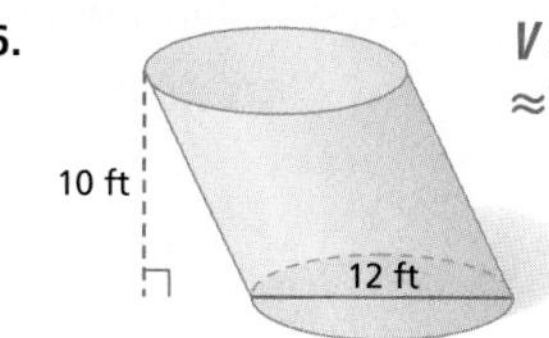

$V = 360\pi$ ft^3 ≈ 1131.0 ft^3

7. 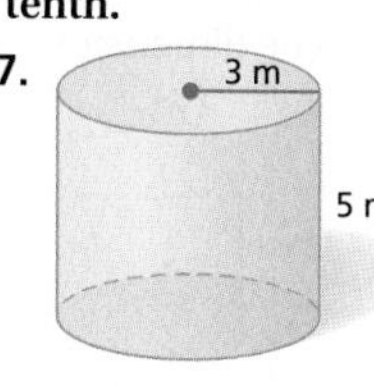

$V = 45\pi$ m^3 ≈ 141.4 m^3

8. a cylinder with base area 25π cm^2 and height 3 cm more than the radius $V = 200\pi$ cm$^3 \approx 628.3$ cm^3

SEE EXAMPLE 4 p. 700

Describe the effect of each change on the volume of the given figure.

9. The dimensions are multiplied by $\frac{1}{4}$.
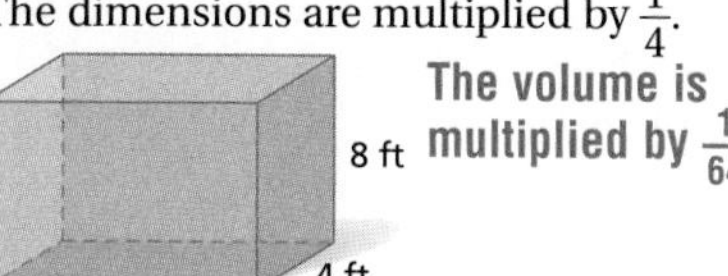

The volume is multiplied by $\frac{1}{64}$.

10. The dimensions are tripled.
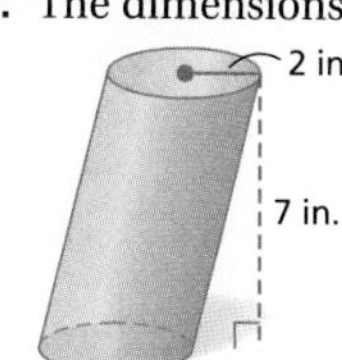

The volume is multiplied by 27.

SEE EXAMPLE 5 p. 700

Find the volume of each composite figure. Round to the nearest tenth.

11. 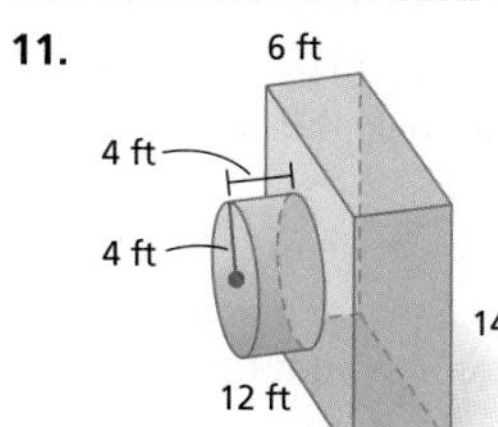

$V \approx 1209.1$ ft^3

12. 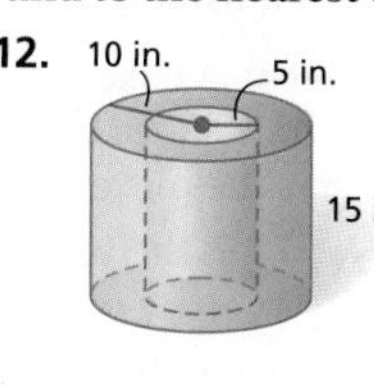

$V \approx 3534.3$ in^3

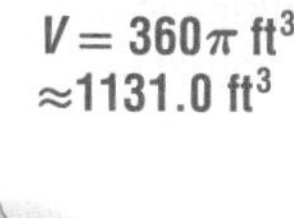

10-6 Exercises

Assignment Guide

Assign *Guided Practice* exercises as necessary.

If you finished Examples **1–3**
Basic 13–19, 24, 25, 27–34
Average 13–19, 24, 25, 27–34, 41
Advanced 13–19, 24, 25, 27–34, 41–43

If you finished Examples **1–5**
Basic 13–34, 37–40, 45–52
Average 13–41, 45–52
Advanced 13–52

Homework Quick Check
Quickly check key concepts.
Exercises: 14, 16, 18, 20, 22, 34

Teaching Tip

Science Link For **Exercise 5,** review the concept of *density*. This quantity is defined by the formula

$$\text{density} = \frac{\text{mass}}{\text{volume}}.$$

Some students may remember from science class that the density of water is 1, and they may wonder why the density of water is given as 8.33 lb/gal in **Exercise 30.** Explain that, in the metric system, the density of water is 1 g/mL.

State Resources

go.hrw.com
State Resources Online
KEYWORD: MG7 Resources

PRACTICE AND PROBLEM SOLVING

Independent Practice

For Exercises	See Example
13–15	1
16	2
17–19	3
20–21	4
22–23	5

Extra Practice

Skills Practice p. S23
Application Practice p. S37

Find the volume of each prism.

13. $V = 810 \text{ yd}^3$

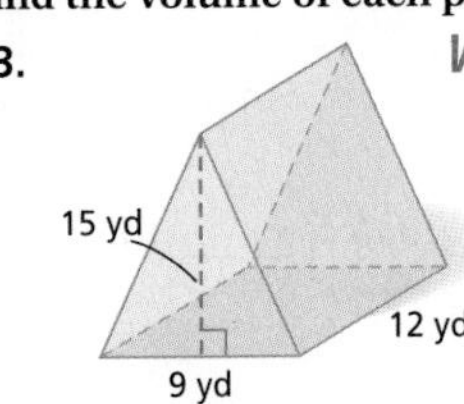

14. $V \approx 2580.7 \text{ m}^3$

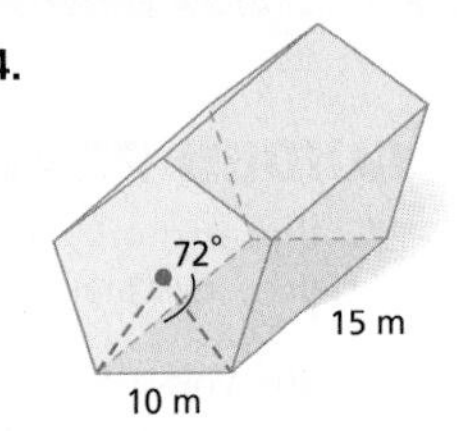

15. a square prism with a base area of 49 ft^2 and a height 2 ft less than the base edge length $V = 245 \text{ ft}^3$

16. Landscaping Colin is buying dirt to fill a garden bed that is a 9 ft by 16 ft rectangle. If he wants to fill it to a depth of 4 in., how many cubic yards of dirt does he need? If dirt costs \$25 per yd^3, how much will the project cost? (*Hint:* 1 yd^3 = 27 ft^3) 2 yd^3; \$50

Find the volume of each cylinder. Give your answers both in terms of π and rounded to the nearest tenth.

17. $V = 1764\pi \text{ cm}^3 \approx 5541.8 \text{ cm}^3$

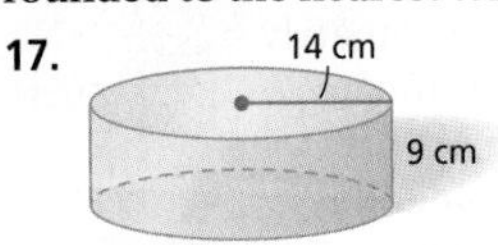

18. $V = 108\pi \text{ in}^3 \approx 339.3 \text{ in}^3$

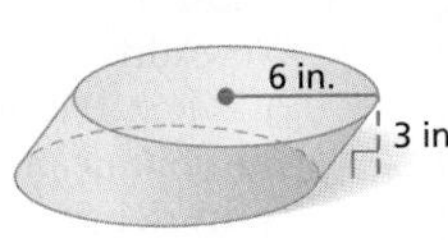

19. a cylinder with base area 24π cm^2 and height 16 cm $V = 384\pi \text{ cm}^3 \approx 1206.4 \text{ cm}^3$

Describe the effect of each change on the volume of the given figure.

20. The dimensions are multiplied by 5. The volume is multiplied by 125.

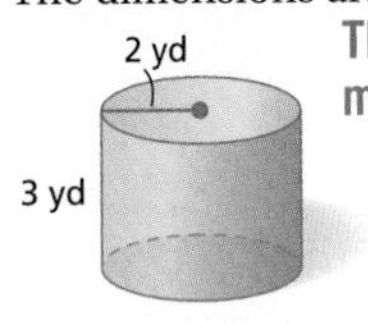

21. The dimensions are multiplied by $\frac{3}{5}$. The volume is multiplied by $\frac{27}{125}$.

Find the volume of each composite figure.

22. $V = 792 \text{ cm}^3$

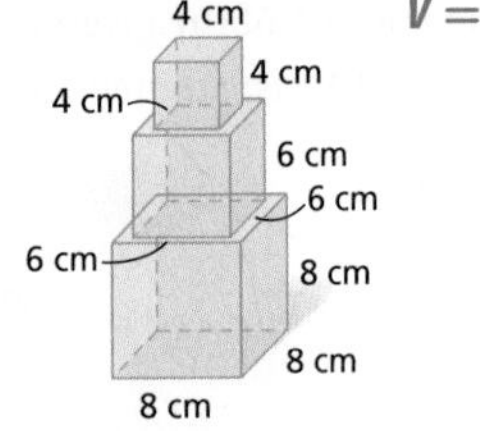

23. $V \approx 242.3 \text{ ft}^3$

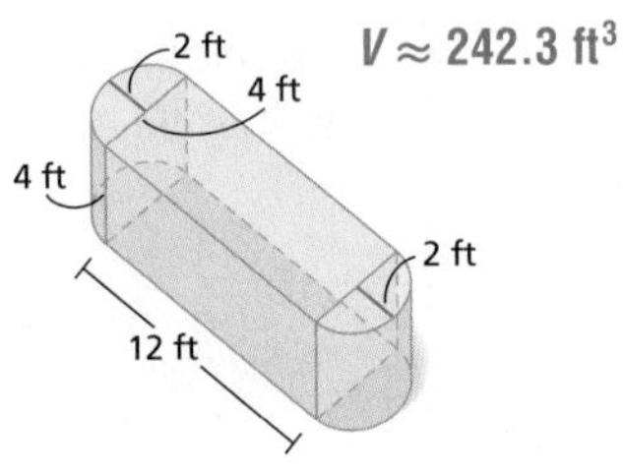

$h \approx 1.1489$ in.; $h \approx 2.0425$ in. **24.** One cup is equal to 14.4375 in^3. If a 1 c cylindrical measuring cup has a radius of 2 in., what is its height? If the radius is 1.5 in., what is its height?

25. Food A cake is a cylinder with a diameter of 10 in. and a height of 3 in. For a party, a coin has been mixed into the batter and baked inside the cake. The person who gets the piece with the coin wins a prize.

a. Find the volume of the cake. Round to the nearest tenth. 235.6 in^2

b. Probability Keka gets a piece of cake that is a right rectangular prism with a 3 in. by 1 in. base. What is the probability that the coin is in her piece? Round to the nearest hundredth. 0.04

10-6 PRACTICE A
10-6 PRACTICE C
10-6 PRACTICE B

Find the volume of each prism. Round to the nearest tenth if necessary.

1. the oblique rectangular prism $V = 42 \text{ mi}^3$
2. the regular octagonal prism $V \approx 7242.6 \text{ mm}^3$
3. a cube with edge length 0.75 m $V \approx 0.4 \text{ m}^3$

Find the volume of each cylinder. Give your answers both in terms of π and rounded to the nearest tenth.

4. $V = 32\pi \text{ yd}^3$; $V \approx 100.5 \text{ yd}^3$
5. $V = 13.5\pi \text{ km}^3$; $V \approx 42.4 \text{ km}^3$
6. a cylinder with base circumference 18π ft and height 10 ft $V = 810\pi \text{ ft}^3$; $V \approx 2544.7 \text{ ft}^3$
7. CDs have the dimensions shown in the figure. Each CD is 1 mm thick. Find the volume in cubic centimeters of a stack of 25 CDs. Round to the nearest tenth. $V \approx 278.3 \text{ cm}^3$

Describe the effect of each change on the volume of the given figure.

8. The dimensions are halved. The volume is divided by 8.
9. The dimensions are divided by 5. The volume is divided by 125.

Find the volume of each composite figure. Round to the nearest tenth.

10. $V \approx 109.9 \text{ ft}^3$
11. $V \approx 166.3 \text{ cm}^3$

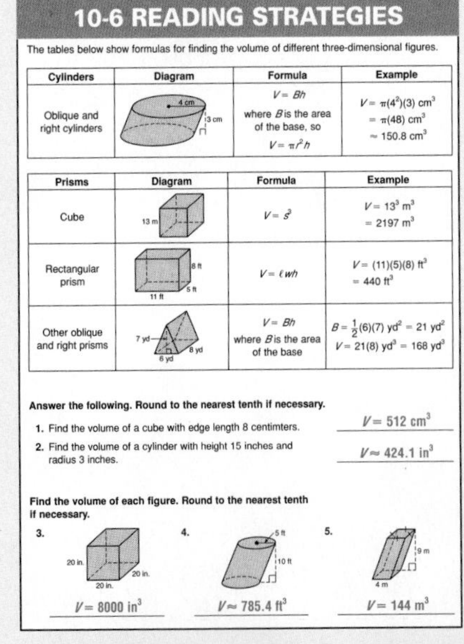

10-6 READING STRATEGIES

The tables below show formulas for finding the volume of different three-dimensional figures.

Cylinders	Diagram	Formula	Example
Oblique and right cylinders		$V = Bh$ where B is the area of the base, so $V = \pi r^2 h$	$V = \pi(4^2)(3) \text{ cm}^3 = \pi(48) \text{ cm}^3 \approx 150.8 \text{ cm}^3$

Prisms	Diagram	Formula	Example
Cube		$V = s^3$	$V = 13^3 \text{ m}^3 = 2197 \text{ m}^3$
Rectangular prism		$V = \ell wh$	$V = (11)(5)(8) \text{ ft}^3 = 440 \text{ ft}^3$
Other oblique and right prisms		$V = Bh$ where B is the area of the base	$B = \frac{1}{2}(6)(7) \text{ yd}^2 = 21 \text{ yd}^2$ $V = 21(8) \text{ yd}^3 = 168 \text{ yd}^3$

Answer the following. Round to the nearest tenth if necessary.

1. Find the volume of a cube with edge length 8 centimters. $V = 512 \text{ cm}^3$
2. Find the volume of a cylinder with height 15 inches and radius 3 inches. $V \approx 424.1 \text{ in}^3$

Find the volume of each figure. Round to the nearest tenth if necessary.

3. $V = 8000 \text{ in}^3$
4. $V \approx 785.4 \text{ ft}^3$
5. $V = 144 \text{ m}^3$

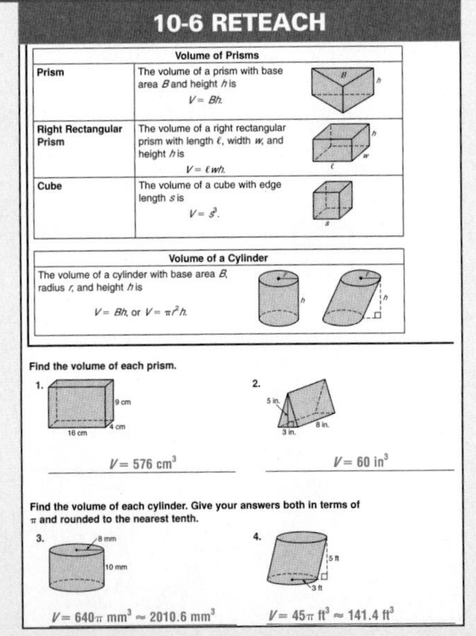

10-6 RETEACH

Volume of Prisms		
Prism	The volume of a prism with base area B and height h is $V = Bh$.	
Right Rectangular Prism	The volume of a right rectangular prism with length ℓ, width w, and height h is $V = \ell wh$.	
Cube	The volume of a cube with edge length s is $V = s^3$.	

Volume of a Cylinder	
The volume of a cylinder with base area B, radius r, and height h is $V = Bh$, or $V = \pi r^2 h$.	

Find the volume of each prism.

1. $V = 576 \text{ cm}^3$
2. $V = 60 \text{ in}^3$

Find the volume of each cylinder. Give your answers both in terms of π and rounded to the nearest tenth.

3. $V = 640\pi \text{ mm}^3 \approx 2010.6 \text{ mm}^3$
4. $V = 45\pi \text{ ft}^3 \approx 141.4 \text{ ft}^3$

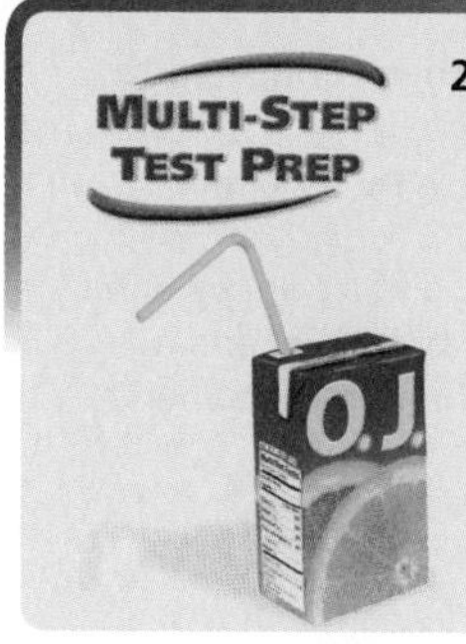

MULTI-STEP TEST PREP

26. This problem will prepare you for the Multi-Step Test Prep on page 724.

A cylindrical juice container with a 3 in. diameter has a hole for a straw that is 1 in. from the side. Up to 5 in. of a straw can be inserted. **24a. 4.6 in.**

a. Find the height h of the container to the nearest tenth.

b. Find the volume of the container to the nearest tenth.

c. How many ounces of juice does the container hold? (*Hint:* 1 in$^3 \approx 0.55$ oz) **b. 32.5 in^3; c. 17.9 oz**

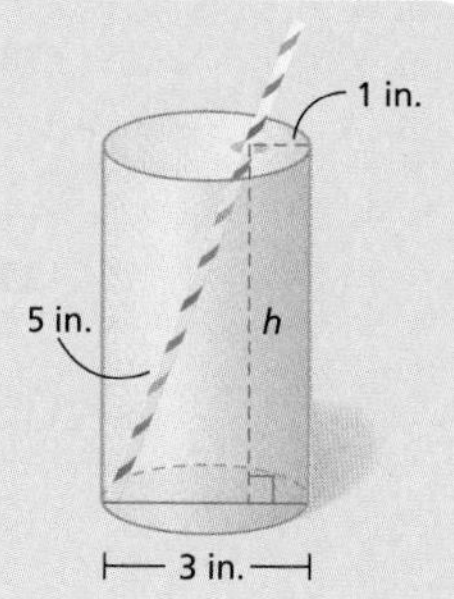

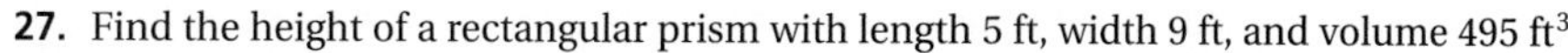

27. Find the height of a rectangular prism with length 5 ft, width 9 ft, and volume 495 ft^3.

28. Find the area of the base of a rectangular prism with volume 360 in^3 and height 9 in.

29. Find the volume of a cylinder with surface area 210π m^2 and height 8 m.

30. Find the volume of a rectangular prism with vertices $(0, 0, 0)$, $(0, 3, 0)$, $(7, 0, 0)$, $(7, 3, 0)$, $(0, 0, 6)$, $(0, 3, 6)$, $(7, 0, 6)$, and $(7, 3, 6)$.

31. You can use *displacement* to find the volume of an irregular object, such as a stone. Suppose the tank shown is filled with water to a depth of 8 in. A stone is placed in the tank so that it is completely covered, causing the water level to rise by 2 in. Find the volume of the stone. **576 in^3, or $\frac{1}{3}$ ft^3**

32. Food A 1 in. cube of cheese is one serving. How many servings are in a 4 in. by 4 in. by $\frac{1}{4}$ in. slice? **4 servings**

33. History In 1919, a cylindrical tank containing molasses burst and flooded the city of Boston, Massachusetts. The tank had a 90 ft diameter and a height of 52 ft. How many gallons of molasses were in the tank? (*Hint:* 1 gal $\approx$ 0.134 ft^3) **2,468,729 gal**

34. Meteorology If 3 in. of rain fall on the property shown, what is the volume in cubic feet? In gallons? The density of water is 8.33 pounds per gallon. What is the weight of the rain in pounds? (*Hint:* 1 gal $\approx$ 0.134 ft^3) **1250 ft^3; 9328 gal; 77,705 lb**

35. Critical Thinking The dimensions of a prism with volume V and surface area S are multiplied by a scale factor of k to form a similar prism. Make a conjecture about the ratio of the surface area of the new prism to its volume. Test your conjecture using a cube with an edge length of 1 and a scale factor of 2.

36. Write About It How can you change the edge length of a cube so that its volume is doubled? **Multiply the edge length by $\sqrt[3]{2}$.**

LINK

Math History

Archimedes (287–212 B.C.E.) used displacement to find the volume of a gold crown. He discovered that the goldsmith had cheated the king by substituting an equal weight of silver for part of the gold.

27. $h = 11$ ft
28. $B = 40$ in^2
29. $V = 392\pi$ m^3
30. $V = 126$ units^3

TEST PREP

37. Abigail has a cylindrical candle mold with the dimensions shown. If Abigail has a rectangular block of wax measuring 15 cm by 12 cm by 18 cm, about how many candles can she make after melting the block of wax?

(A) 14 (B) 31 (C) 35 (D) 76

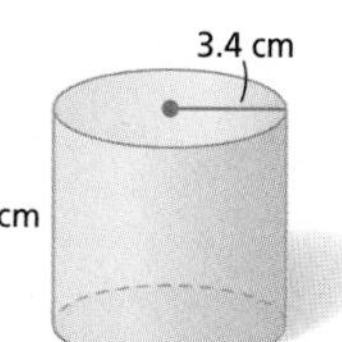

COMMON ERROR ALERT

In **Exercise 22,** some students may think they need to subtract the areas of the common surfaces that are shared by the touching cubes, as they would if they were finding the surface area of a composite figure. Using concrete models, show them that the volume of a composite made up of stacked blocks is the sum of the volumes of the individual blocks.

MULTI-STEP TEST PREP **Exercise 26** involves finding the volume of a cylindrical juice container. This exercise prepares students for the Multi-Step Test Prep on page 724.

Teaching Tip **Algebra** In **Exercise 29,** after substituting the given values in the formula $S = 2\pi rh + 2\pi r^2$, students should get the equation $210\pi = 16\pi r + 2\pi r^2$. Remind students that this is a quadratic equation and encourage them to review how to solve quadratic equations. Remind them that, in this context, a negative value for r is meaningless and must be rejected.

TEST PREP DOCTOR In **Exercise 37,** students who chose **B** forgot to square the radius in the volume formula. Students who chose **D** found the volume of the mold correctly, but did not divide the volume of the block of wax by the volume of the mold.

Answers

35. For a scale factor of k, the ratio of surface area to volume of the new prism is $\frac{1}{k}$ times the ratio of surface area to volume of the old prism. A cube with edge length 1 has a surface-area-to-volume ratio of 6:1. If each edge length is multiplied by 2, the surface-area-to-volume ratio is 24:8 = 3:1.

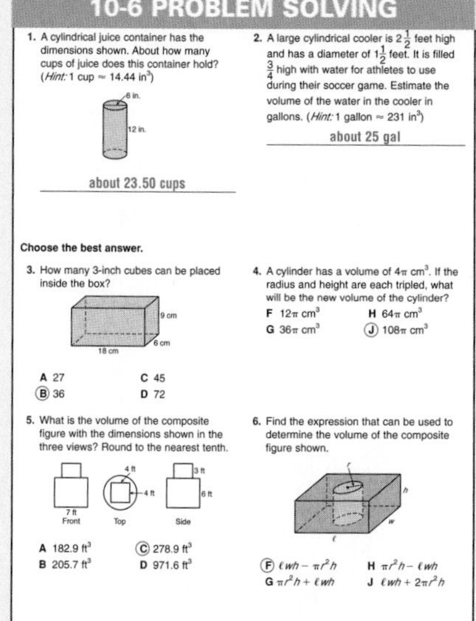

10-6 PROBLEM SOLVING

1. A cylindrical juice container has the dimensions shown. About how many cups of juice does this container hold? (*Hint:* 1 cup $\approx$ 14.44 in^3)

6 in.; 12 in.

about 23.50 cups

2. A large cylindrical cooler is $2\frac{1}{2}$ feet high and has a diameter of $1\frac{1}{2}$ feet. It is filled $\frac{3}{4}$ high with water for athletes to use during their soccer game. Estimate the volume of the water in the cooler in gallons. (*Hint:* 1 gallon $\approx$ 231 in^3)

about 25 gal

Choose the best answer.

3. How many 3-inch cubes can be placed inside the box?

9 cm; 6 cm; 18 cm

A 27 C 45
(B) 36 D 72

4. A cylinder has a volume of 4π cm^3. If the radius and height are each tripled, what will be the new volume of the cylinder?

F 12π cm^3 H 64π cm^3
G 36π cm^3 (J) 108π cm^3

5. What is the volume of the composite figure with the dimensions shown in the three views? Round to the nearest tenth.

4 ft; 4 ft; 3 ft; 6 ft; 7 ft; Front; Top; Side

A 182.9 ft^3 (C) 278.9 ft^3
B 205.7 ft^3 D 971.6 ft^3

6. Find the expression that can be used to determine the volume of the composite figure shown.

r; h; w; ℓ

(F) $\ell wh - \pi r^2 h$ H $\pi r^2 h - \ell wh$
G $\pi r^2 h + \ell wh$ J $\ell wh + 2\pi r^2 h$

10-6 CHALLENGE

Most baking recipes specify a certain size of baking pan. When that size of pan is not available, you may be able to adjust the recipe to a different size. Since many items are baked in the shape of a rectangular prism, this adjustment can be done by calculating volumes with the formula $V = \ell wh$. For example, the recipe at right requires a 13 × 9 × 2-inch pan. This type of pan is shaped like a rectangular prism that is 13 inches long, 9 inches wide, and 2 inches high, as shown below.

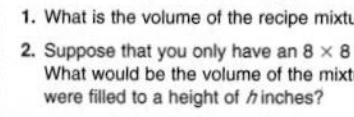

2 in.; 9 in.; 13 in.

Crackle Bars

3 tablespoons margarine
40 regular marshmallows, or
4 cups miniature marshmallows
6 cups toasted rice cereal

Melt the margarine in a large saucepan over low heat. Add the marshmallows and stir until they are completely melted. Remove from heat. Stir in the cereal until it is coated. Press the mixture into a greased 13 × 9 × 2-inch pan. Cut bars when cool.

Refer to the recipe for Crackle Bars that is given above. Assume that when you prepare the mixture according to the recipe, it fills the 13 × 9 × 2-inch pan to an unknown height of h inches.

1. What is the volume of the recipe mixture? **$117h$ in^3**

2. Suppose that you only have an 8 × 8 × 2-inch pan. What would be the volume of the mixture if the pan were filled to a height of h inches? **$64h$ in^3**

3. What percent of the recipe mixture would fill the 8 × 8 × 2-inch pan to a height of h inches? Round to the nearest whole percent. **55%**

4. Calculate the amount of each ingredient needed to make enough mixture to fill the 8 × 8 × 2-inch pan to a height of h inches with no extra mixture.

a. margarine (1 tablespoon equals 3 teaspoons) **$1\frac{2}{3}$ tablespoons**
b. regular marshmallows **22**
c. miniature marshmallows **$2\frac{1}{5}$ cups**
d. toasted rice cereal **$3\frac{1}{3}$ cups**

5. Use the method from Exercises 1–4. Adjust the amounts of ingredients in the Crackle Bar recipe so that the mixture fills a pan of the given dimensions to a height of h inches. When necessary, round to reasonable measures. Write your answers on a separate sheet of paper. **Check students' work.**

a. 9 in. × 9 in. × 2 in. b. 15 in. × 10 in. × $1\frac{1}{2}$ in. c. 25 cm × 35 cm × 4 cm

6. Explain how to adjust the Crackle Bar recipe so the mixture fills a pan that is a inches long, b inches wide, and c inches high to a height of $2h$ inches.

Multiply the amount of each ingredient by $\frac{2ab}{117}$. Round to reasonable measures. Make sure that c is less than or equal to $2h$.

Journal

Have students describe how to use the general volume formula $V = Bh$ to write a formula for the volume of a cube with side length s, a rectangular prism with base length ℓ and width w, and a cylinder with radius r.

ALTERNATIVE ASSESSMENT

Have students work in pairs. Each student should make up four application problems, two involving surface area and two involving volume. Then, they should exchange problems with their partners, and solve the problems that their partners have written.

Power Presentations with PowerPoint®

10-6 Lesson Quiz

Find the volume of each figure. Round to the nearest tenth, if necessary.

1. a right rectangular prism with length 14 cm, width 11 cm, and height 18 cm
   $V = 2772 \text{ cm}^3$
2. a cube with edge length 22 ft
   $V = 10{,}648 \text{ ft}^3$
3. a regular hexagonal prism with edge length 10 ft and height 10 ft $V \approx 2598.1 \text{ ft}^3$
4. a cylinder with diameter 16 in. and height 7 in.
   $V \approx 1407.4 \text{ in}^3$
5. a cylinder with base area $196\pi \text{ cm}^2$ and a height equal to the diameter
   $V \approx 17{,}241.1 \text{ cm}^3$
6. The edge length of the cube is tripled. Describe the effect on the volume.

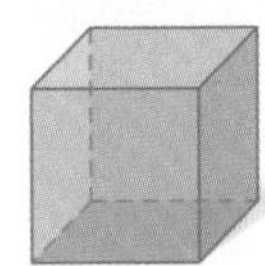

The volume is multiplied by 27.

7. Find the volume of the composite figure. Round to the nearest tenth.

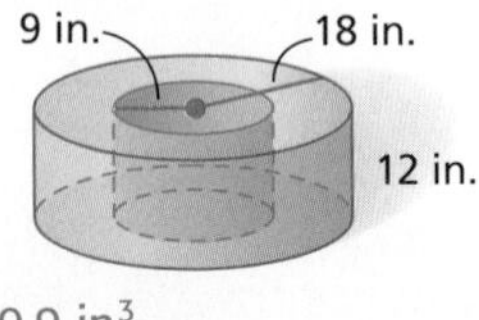

9160.9 in^3

Also available on transparency

38. A 96-inch piece of wire was cut into equal segments that were then connected to form the edges of a cube. What is the volume of the cube?
    (F) 512 in^3 (G) 576 in^3 (H) 729 in^3 (J) 1728 in^3

39. One juice container is a rectangular prism with a height of 9 in. and a 3 in. by 3 in. square base. Another juice container is a cylinder with a radius of 1.75 in. and a height of 9 in. Which best describes the relationship between the two containers?
    (A) The prism has the greater volume.
    (B) The cylinder has the greater volume.
    (C) The volumes are equivalent.
    (D) The volumes cannot be determined.

40. What is the volume of the three-dimensional object with the dimensions shown in the three views below?

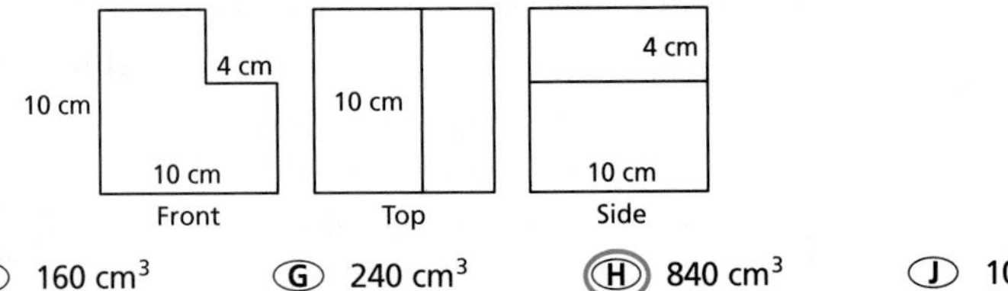

(F) 160 cm^3 (G) 240 cm^3 (H) 840 cm^3 (J) 1000 cm^3

CHALLENGE AND EXTEND

Algebra **Find the volume of each three-dimensional figure in terms of x.**

43. $V = \dfrac{x^3\sqrt{3} + x^2\sqrt{3}}{4}$

41. 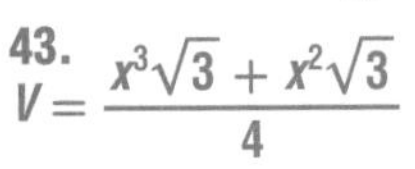

$V = x^3 + x^2 - 2x$

42. 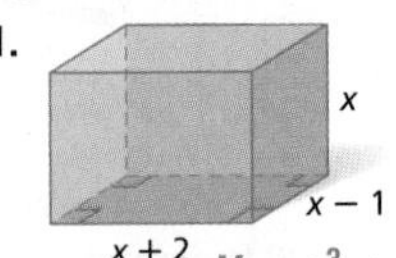

$V = \pi x^3 + 2\pi x^2 + \pi x$

43. 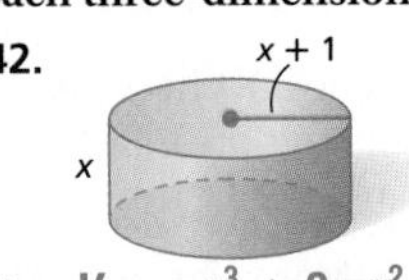

44. The volume in cubic units of a cylinder is equal to its surface area in square units. Prove that the radius and height must both be greater than 2.

SPIRAL REVIEW

45. Marcy, Rachel, and Tina went bowling. Marcy bowled 100 less than twice Rachel's score. Tina bowled 40 more than Rachel's score. Rachel bowled a higher score than Marcy. What is the greatest score that Tina could have bowled? *(Previous course)* **139**

46. Max can type 40 words per minute. He estimates that his term paper contains about 5000 words, and he takes a 15-minute break for every 45 minutes of typing. About how much time will it take Max to type his term paper? *(Previous course)* **155 min**

***ABCD* is a parallelogram. Find each measure.** *(Lesson 6-2)*

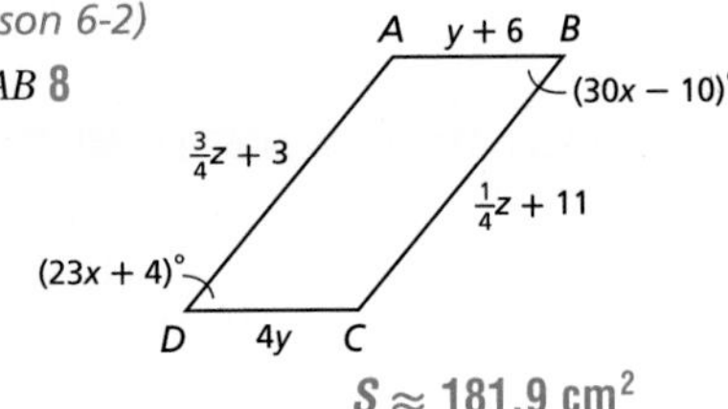

47. $m\angle ABC$ **50°**
48. BC **15**
49. AB **8**

Find the surface area of each figure. Round to the nearest tenth. *(Lesson 10-5)*

50. a square pyramid with slant height 10 in. and base edge length 8 in. $S = 224 \text{ in}^2$
51. a regular pentagonal pyramid with slant height 8 cm and base edge length 6 cm $S \approx 181.9 \text{ cm}^2$
52. a right cone with slant height 2 ft and a base with circumference of π ft $S \approx 3.9 \text{ ft}^2$

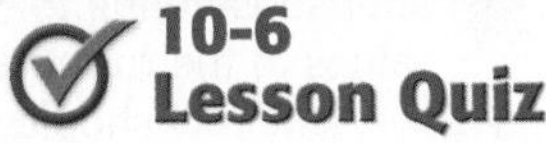

Answers

44. The volume is equal to the surface area, so $\pi r^2 h = 2\pi r^2 + 2\pi rh$. Solve for r to get $r = \frac{2h}{h-2}$. If $h < 2$, then $r < 0$, so h must be greater than 2. Similarly, if you solve for h, you get $h = \frac{2r}{r-2}$. If $r < 2$, then $h < 0$, so r must be greater than 2.

10-7 Volume of Pyramids and Cones

Objectives
Learn and apply the formula for the volume of a pyramid.
Learn and apply the formula for the volume of a cone.

Who uses this?
The builders of the Rainforest Pyramid in Galveston, Texas, needed to calculate the volume of the pyramid to plan the climate control system. (See Example 2.)

The volume of a pyramid is related to the volume of a prism with the same base and height. The relationship can be verified by dividing a cube into three congruent square pyramids, as shown.

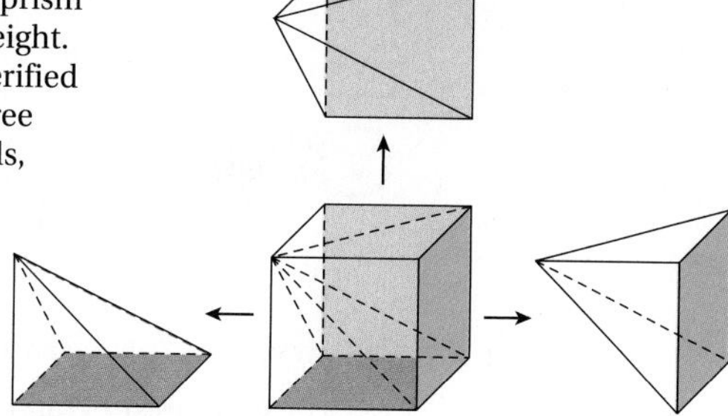

The square pyramids are congruent, so they have the same volume. The volume of each pyramid is one third the volume of the cube.

Volume of a Pyramid

The volume of a pyramid with base area B and height h is $V = \frac{1}{3}Bh$.

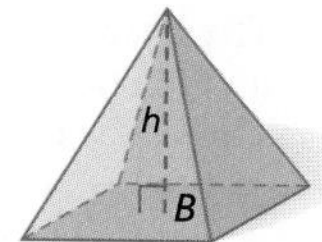

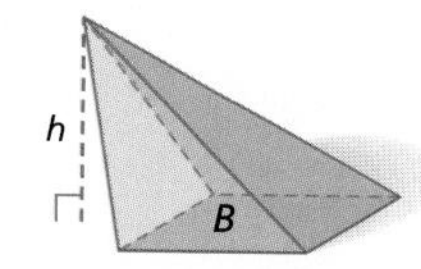

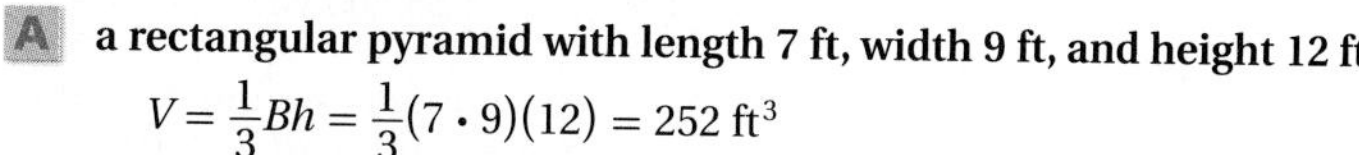

Finding Volumes of Pyramids

Find the volume of each pyramid.

A a rectangular pyramid with length 7 ft, width 9 ft, and height 12 ft

$$V = \frac{1}{3}Bh = \frac{1}{3}(7 \cdot 9)(12) = 252 \text{ ft}^3$$

B the square pyramid

The base is a square with a side length of 4 in., and the height is 6 in.

$$V = \frac{1}{3}Bh = \frac{1}{3}(4^2)(6) = 32 \text{ in}^3$$

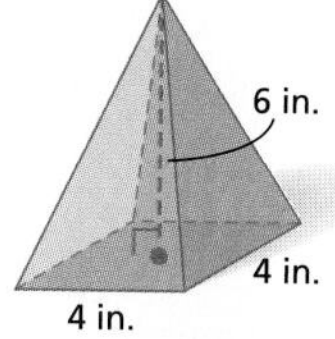

10-7 Organizer

Pacing: Traditional 1 day
Block $\frac{1}{2}$ day

Objectives: Learn and apply the formula for the volume of a pyramid.

Learn and apply the formula for the volume of a cone.

Online Edition
Tutorial Videos

Countdown Week 23

Power Presentations with PowerPoint®

Warm Up

Find the volume of each figure. Round to the nearest tenth, if necessary.

1. a square prism with base area 189 ft^2 and height 21 ft
3969 ft^3
2. a regular hexagonal prism with base edge length 24 m and height 10 m
14,964.9 m^3
3. a cylinder with diameter 16 in. and height 22 in. 4423.4 in^3

Also available on transparency

Math Humor

Q: What has a circular base and is surrounded by water?
A: Coney Island.

1 Introduce

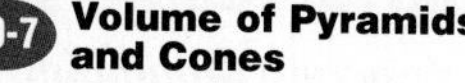

In this Exploration, you will use nets to investigate the volume of a pyramid.

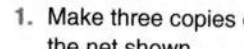

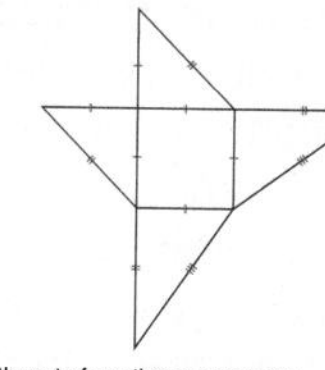

2. Cut out the nets and fold them to form three congruent pyramids.
3. Show how the three pyramids can be put together to form a cube.
4. How is the volume of each pyramid related to the volume of the cube?

THINK AND DISCUSS

5. Explain how you can use your conclusion to write a formula for the volume of a pyramid.

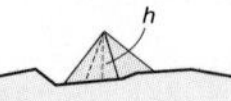

Motivate

Use models of a square prism and a square pyramid with the same base edge length and height. Fill the pyramid with rice or cereal, and pour it into the prism. Repeat two more times. Discuss how this shows that the volume of the prism is 3 times the volume of the pyramid.

Explorations and answers are provided in *Alternate Openers: Explorations Transparencies.*

State Resources

go.hrw.com
State Resources Online
KEYWORD: MG7 Resources

Find the volume of the pyramid.

C **the trapezoidal pyramid with base $ABCD$, where $\overline{AB} \parallel \overline{CD}$ and $\overline{AE} \perp$ plane ABC**

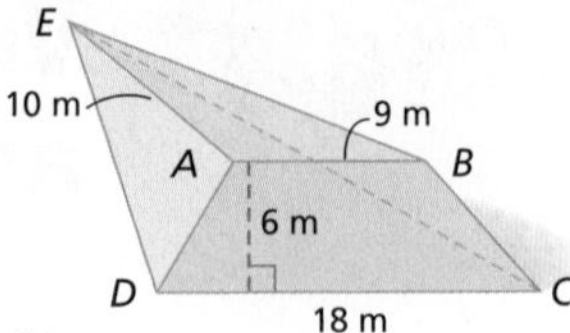

Step 1 Find the area of the base.

$B = \frac{1}{2}(b_1 + b_2)h$ *Area of a trapezoid*

$= \frac{1}{2}(9 + 18)6$ *Substitute 9 for b_1, 18 for b_2, and 6 for h.*

$= 81 \text{ m}^2$ *Simplify.*

Step 2 Use the base area and the height to find the volume. Because $\overline{AE} \perp$ plane ABC, $\overline{AE}$ is the altitude, so the height is equal to AE.

$V = \frac{1}{3}Bh$ *Volume of a pyramid*

$= \frac{1}{3}(81)(10)$ *Substitute 81 for B and 10 for h.*

$= 270 \text{ m}^3$

1. Find the volume of a regular hexagonal pyramid with a base edge length of 2 cm and a height equal to the area of the base.
$V = 36 \text{ cm}^3$

EXAMPLE 2 *Architecture Application*

The Rainforest Pyramid in Galveston, Texas, is a square pyramid with a base area of about 1 acre and a height of 10 stories. Estimate the volume in cubic yards and in cubic feet. (*Hint:* 1 acre = 4840 yd², 1 story ≈ 10 ft)

The base is a square with an area of about 4840 yd². The base edge length is $\sqrt{4840} \approx 70$ yd. The height is about $10(10) = 100$ ft, or about 33 yd.

First find the volume in cubic yards.

$V = \frac{1}{3}Bh$ *Volume of a regular pyramid*

$= \frac{1}{3}(70^2)(33) = 53{,}900 \text{ yd}^3$ *Substitute 70^2 for B and 33 for h.*

Then convert your answer to find the volume in cubic feet. The volume of one cubic yard is $(3 \text{ ft})(3 \text{ ft})(3 \text{ ft}) = 27 \text{ ft}^3$. Use the conversion factor $\frac{27 \text{ ft}^3}{1 \text{ yd}^3}$ to find the volume in cubic feet.

$$53{,}900 \text{ yd}^3 \cdot \frac{27 \text{ ft}^3}{1 \text{ yd}^3} \approx 1{,}455{,}300 \text{ ft}^3$$

2. **What if...?** What would be the volume of the Rainforest Pyramid if the height were doubled?
107,800 yd³ or 2,910,600 ft³

PowerPresentations with PowerPoint®

Additional Examples

Example 1

Find the volume of each pyramid.

A. a rectangular pyramid with length 11 m, width 18 m, and height 23 m 1518 m³

B. the square pyramid with base edge length 9 cm and height 14 cm 378 cm³

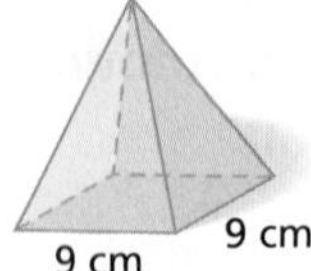

C. the regular hexagonal pyramid with height equal to the apothem of the base

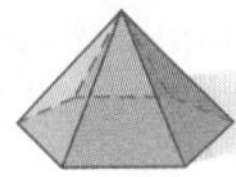

12 ft

1296 ft³

Example 2

An art gallery is a 6-story square pyramid with base area $\frac{1}{2}$ acre (1 acre = 4840 yd², 1 story ≈ 10 ft). Estimate the volume in cubic yards and cubic feet.
16,133 yd³ ≈ 16,100 yd³; 435,600 ft³ ≈ 436,000 ft³

INTERVENTION
Questioning Strategies

EXAMPLE 1

- What information do you need to find the volume of a regular pyramid?

EXAMPLE 2

- How do you find the base area of a pyramid in yards when given the area in acres?

2 Teach

Guided Instruction

Before presenting **Example 1C,** review how to find the area of a trapezoid. Explain that the volume of a pyramid or cone is one-third the volume of a prism or cylinder with the same base area and height.

Reaching All Learners
Through Concrete Manipulatives

Have students work in groups with models of pyramids, prisms, cylinders, and cones (MK). Have them measure the models and find the volumes of a pyramid and a prism with the same base edge length and height. Also have them find the volumes of a cylinder and a cone with the same radius and height.

Volume of Cones

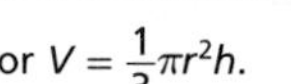

The volume of a cone with base area B, radius r, and height h is $V = \frac{1}{3}Bh$, or $V = \frac{1}{3}\pi r^2 h$.

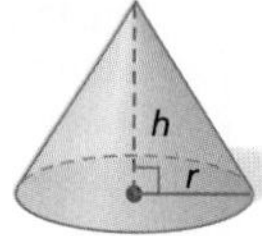

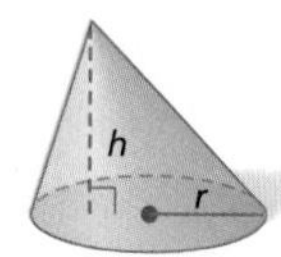

EXAMPLE 3 **Finding Volumes of Cones**

Find the volume of each cone. Give your answers both in terms of π and rounded to the nearest tenth.

A **a cone with radius 5 cm and height 12 cm**

$V = \frac{1}{3}\pi r^2 h$ *Volume of a cone*

$= \frac{1}{3}\pi(5)^2(12)$ *Substitute 5 for r and 12 for h.*

$= 100\pi \text{ cm}^3 \approx 314.2 \text{ cm}^3$ *Simplify.*

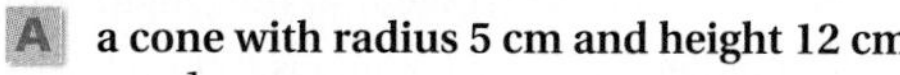

B **a cone with a base circumference of 21π cm and a height 3 cm less than twice the radius**

Step 1 Use the circumference to find the radius.

$2\pi r = 21\pi$ *Substitute 21π for C.*

$r = 10.5$ cm *Divide both sides by 2π.*

Step 2 Use the radius to find the height.

$2(10.5) - 3 = 18$ cm *The height is 3 cm less than twice the radius.*

Step 3 Use the radius and height to find the volume.

$V = \frac{1}{3}\pi r^2 h$ *Volume of a cone*

$= \frac{1}{3}\pi(10.5)^2(18)$ *Substitute 10.5 for r and 18 for h.*

$= 661.5\pi \text{ cm}^3 \approx 2078.2 \text{ cm}^3$ *Simplify.*

C

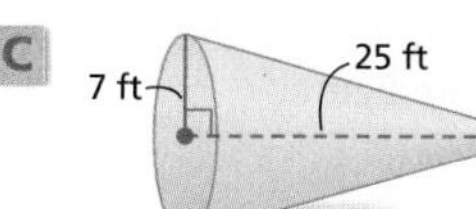

Step 1 Use the Pythagorean Theorem to find the height.

$7^2 + h^2 = 25^2$ *Pythagorean Theorem*

$h^2 = 576$ *Subtract 7^2 from both sides.*

$h = 24$ *Take the square root of both sides.*

Step 2 Use the radius and height to find the volume.

$V = \frac{1}{3}\pi r^2 h$ *Volume of a cone*

$= \frac{1}{3}\pi(7)^2(24)$ *Substitute 7 for r and 24 for h.*

$= 392\pi \text{ ft}^3 \approx 1231.5 \text{ ft}^3$ *Simplify.*

3. Find the volume of the cone.
$V = 216\pi \text{ m}^3 \approx 678.6 \text{ m}^3$

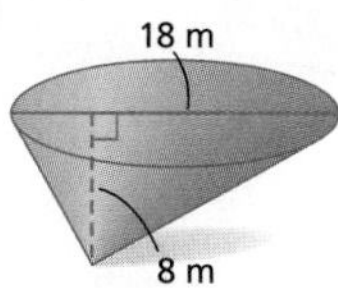

COMMON ERROR ALERT

When calculating volumes of pyramids and cones, some students may forget to multiply by $\frac{1}{3}$ (or divide by 3). Remind students that pyramids and cones need the factor of $\frac{1}{3}$ but prisms and cylinders do not.

Power Presentations with PowerPoint®

Additional Examples

Example 3

Find the volume of each cone. Give your answers both in terms of π and rounded to the nearest tenth.

A. a cone with radius 7 cm and height 15 cm $245\pi \text{ cm}^3 \approx 769.7 \text{ cm}^3$

B. a cone with base circumference 25π in. and a height 2 in. more than twice the radius $1406.3\pi \text{ in}^3 \approx 4417.9 \text{ in}^3$

C.

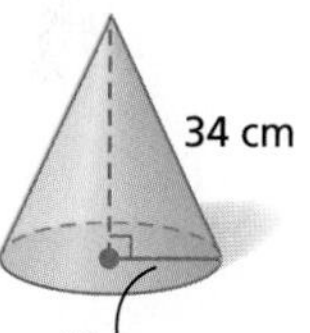

$2560\pi \text{ cm}^3 \approx 8042.5 \text{ cm}^3$

INTERVENTION
Questioning Strategies

EXAMPLE 3

- How do you find the volume of a right cone when given the diameter and the slant height of the cone?

Power Presentations with PowerPoint®

Additional Examples

Example 4

The diameter and height of the cone are divided by 3. Describe the effect on the volume.

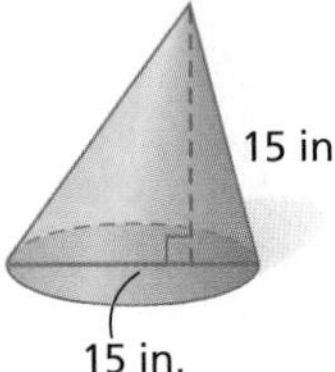

The volume is divided by 27.

Example 5

Find the volume of the composite figure. Round to the nearest tenth.

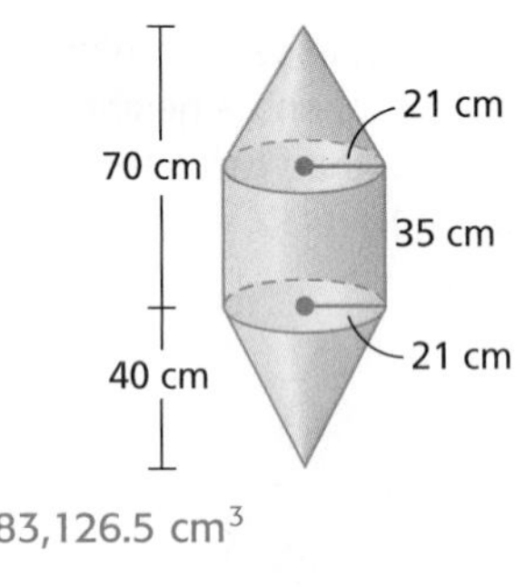

83,126.5 cm^3

INTERVENTION

Questioning Strategies

EXAMPLE 4

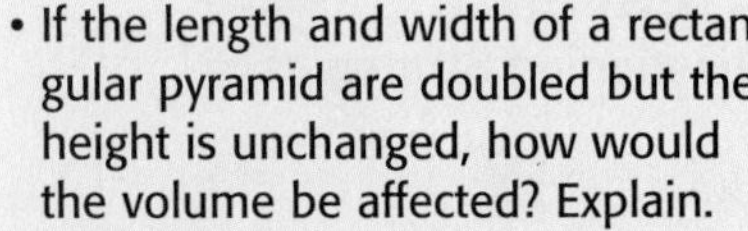

- If the length and width of a rectangular pyramid are doubled but the height is unchanged, how would the volume be affected? Explain.

EXAMPLE 5

- How do you know whether to add or subtract the volumes of the figures that form a composite figure?

EXAMPLE 4 Exploring Effects of Changing Dimensions

The length, width, and height of the rectangular pyramid are multiplied by $\frac{1}{4}$. Describe the effect on the volume.

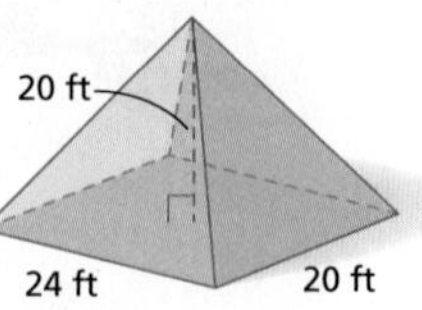

original dimensions:	length, width, and height multiplied by $\frac{1}{4}$:
$V = \frac{1}{3}Bh$	$V = \frac{1}{3}Bh$
$= \frac{1}{3}(24 \cdot 20)(20)$	$= \frac{1}{3}(6 \cdot 5)(5)$
$= 3200 \text{ ft}^3$	$= 50 \text{ ft}^3$

Notice that $50 = \frac{1}{64}(3200)$. If the length, width, and height are multiplied by $\frac{1}{4}$, the volume is multiplied by $\left(\frac{1}{4}\right)^3$, or $\frac{1}{64}$.

CHECK IT OUT! 4. The radius and height of the cone are doubled. Describe the effect on the volume.
The volume is multiplied by 8.

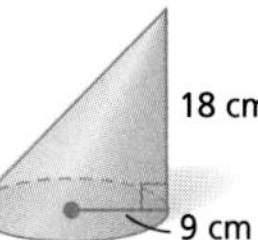

EXAMPLE 5 Finding Volumes of Composite Three-Dimensional Figures

Find the volume of the composite figure. Round to the nearest tenth.

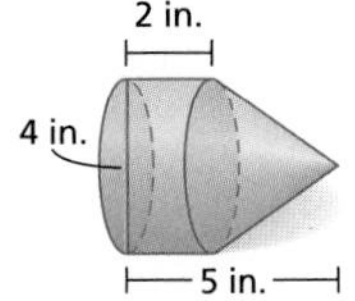

The volume of the cylinder is
$V = \pi r^2 h = \pi(2)^2(2) = 8\pi \text{ in}^3$.

The volume of the cone is
$V = \frac{1}{3}\pi r^2 h = \frac{1}{3}\pi(2)^2(3) = 4\pi \text{ in}^3$.

The volume of the composite figure is the sum of the volumes.
$V = 8\pi + 4\pi = 12\pi \text{ in}^3 \approx 37.7 \text{ in}^3$

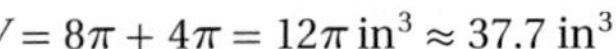

CHECK IT OUT! 5. Find the volume of the composite figure.
$V = 3000 \text{ ft}^3$

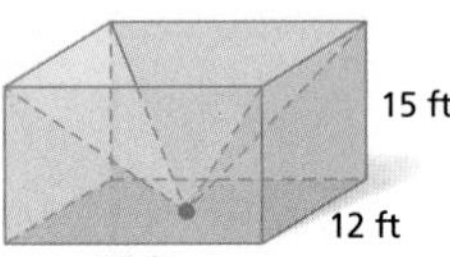

THINK AND DISCUSS

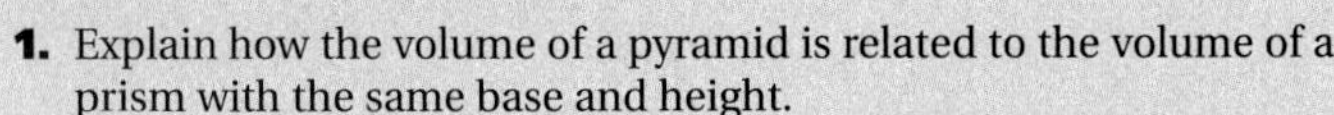

1. Explain how the volume of a pyramid is related to the volume of a prism with the same base and height.

2. **GET ORGANIZED** Copy and complete the graphic organizer.

Volumes of Three-Dimensional Figures		
Formula	$V = Bh$	$V = \frac{1}{3}Bh$
Shapes		
Examples		

3 Close

Summarize

Review with students how to find the volume of any prism or cylinder by applying the general formula $V = Bh$. Then review the general formula for the volume of a pyramid or cone, $V = \frac{1}{3}Bh$.

ONGOING ASSESSMENT and INTERVENTION

Diagnose ***Before*** **the Lesson**
10-7 Warm Up, TE p. 705

Monitor ***During*** **the Lesson**
Check It Out! Exercises, SE pp. 706–708
Questioning Strategies, TE pp. 706–708

Assess ***After*** **the Lesson**
10-7 Lesson Quiz, TE p. 712
Alternative Assessment, TE p. 712

Answers to *Think and Discuss*

1. The volume of a pyramid is $\frac{1}{3}$ the volume of a prism with the same base and height.
2. See p. A8.

go.hrw.com
Homework Help Online
KEYWORD: MG7 10-7
Parent Resources Online
KEYWORD: MG7 Parent

GUIDED PRACTICE

1. **Vocabulary** The *altitude* of a pyramid is ___?___ to the base. (*perpendicular, parallel,* or *oblique*) perpendicular

SEE EXAMPLE 1 p. 705

Find the volume of each pyramid. Round to the nearest tenth, if necessary.

2. $V = 136 \text{ in}^3$

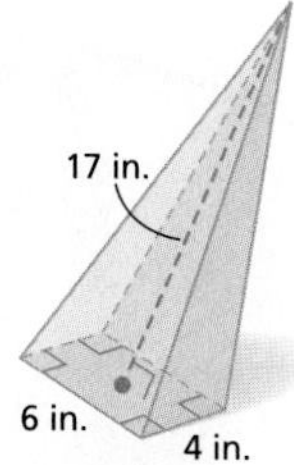
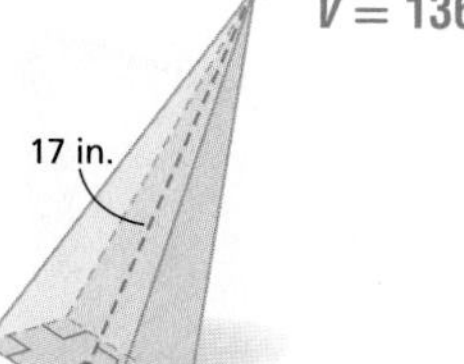

3. $V = 96 \text{ cm}^3$

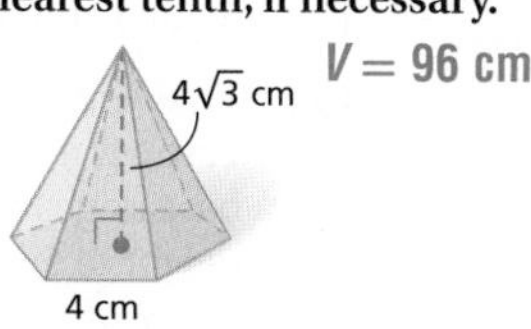

4. a hexagonal pyramid with a base area of 25 ft^2 and a height of 9 ft $V = 75 \text{ ft}^3$

SEE EXAMPLE 2 p. 706

5. **Geology** A crystal is cut into the shape formed by two square pyramids joined at the base. Each pyramid has a base edge length of 5.7 mm and a height of 3 mm. What is the volume to the nearest cubic millimeter of the crystal? $V \approx 65 \text{ mm}^3$

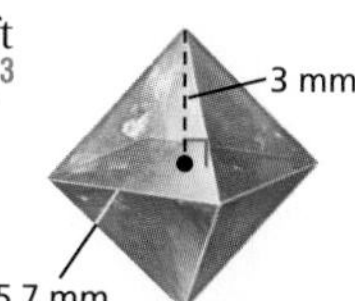

SEE EXAMPLE 3 p. 707

Find the volume of each cone. Give your answers both in terms of π and rounded to the nearest tenth.

6. $V = 378\pi \text{ cm}^3 \approx 1187.5 \text{ cm}^3$

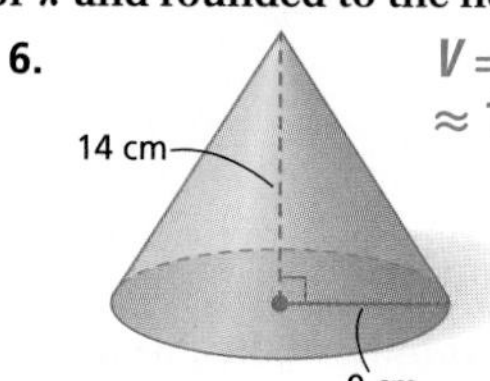

7. $V = 1440\pi \text{ in}^3 \approx 4523.9 \text{ in}^3$

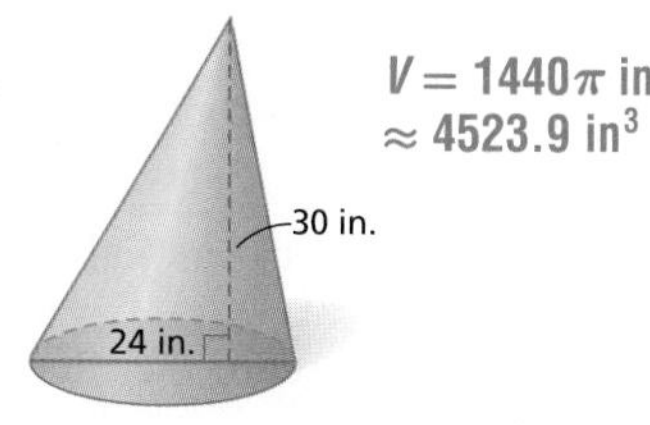

8. a cone with radius 12 m and height 20 m $V = 960\pi \text{ m}^3 \approx 3015.9 \text{ m}^3$

SEE EXAMPLE 4 p. 708

Describe the effect of each change on the volume of the given figure.

9. The dimensions are tripled. The volume is multiplied by 27.

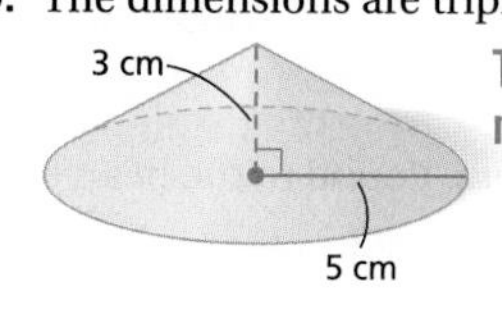

10. The dimensions are multiplied by $\frac{1}{2}$. The volume is multiplied by $\frac{1}{8}$.

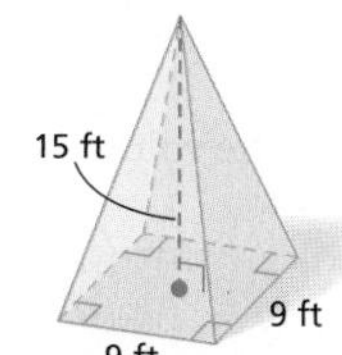

SEE EXAMPLE 5 p. 708

Find the volume of each composite figure. Round to the nearest tenth, if necessary.

11. $V = 2592 \text{ cm}^3$

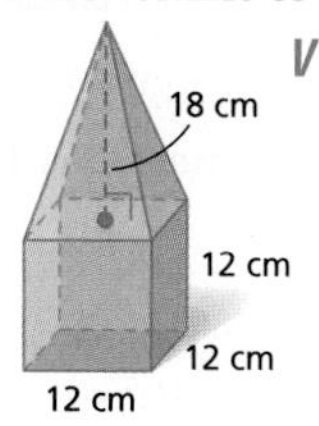

12. $V \approx 703.7 \text{ in}^3$

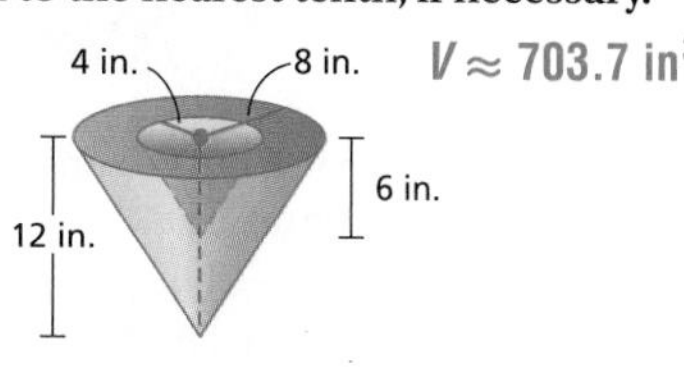

Assignment Guide

Assign *Guided Practice* exercises as necessary.

If you finished Examples 1–3
Basic 13–19, 24–37
Average 13–19, 24–37, 46
Advanced 13–19, 24–37, 46–50

If you finished Examples 1–5
Basic 13–38, 41–45, 51–59
Average 13–46, 51–59
Advanced 13–37, 39–59

Homework Quick Check
Quickly check key concepts.
Exercises: 14, 16, 18, 20, 22, 34

State Resources

go.hrw.com
State Resources Online
KEYWORD: MG7 Resources

Teaching Tip **Reading Math** For **Exercise 27,** ask questions to help students determine what information is required to use the volume formula. Sample questions: "What formula will you use?" $V = \frac{1}{3}\pi r^2 h$. "How can you find the radius?" Divide the diameter by 2. "How can you find the height?" Draw the right triangle formed by the radius, height, and slant height and then use the Pythagorean Theorem.

ENGLISH LANGUAGE LEARNERS

PRACTICE AND PROBLEM SOLVING

Independent Practice

For Exercises	See Example
13–15	1
16	2
17–19	3
20–21	4
22–23	5

Extra Practice

Skills Practice p. S23
Application Practice p. S37

Find the volume of each pyramid. Round to the nearest tenth, if necessary.

13. $V = 160$ ft^3

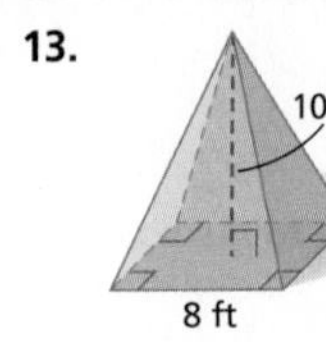

14. $V = 90$ m^3

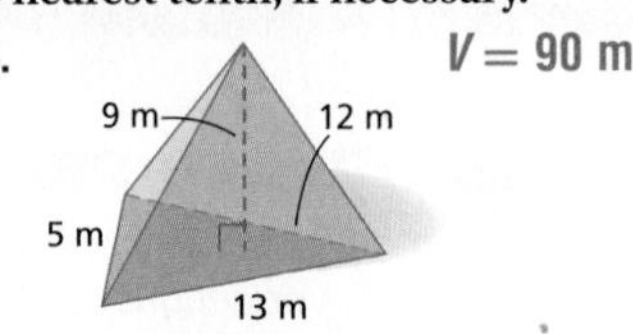

15. a regular square pyramid with base edge length 12 ft and slant height 10 ft $V = 384$ ft^3

16. Carpentry A roof that encloses an attic is a square pyramid with a base edge length of 45 feet and a height of 5 yards. What is the volume of the attic in cubic feet? In cubic yards?
$V = 10{,}125$ ft^3; $V = 375$ yd^3

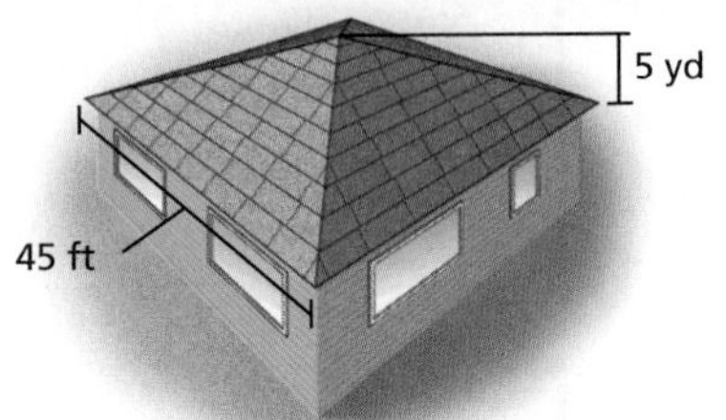

Find the volume of each cone. Give your answers both in terms of π and rounded to the nearest tenth.

17. $V = 1107\pi$ m^3 ≈ 3477.7 m^3

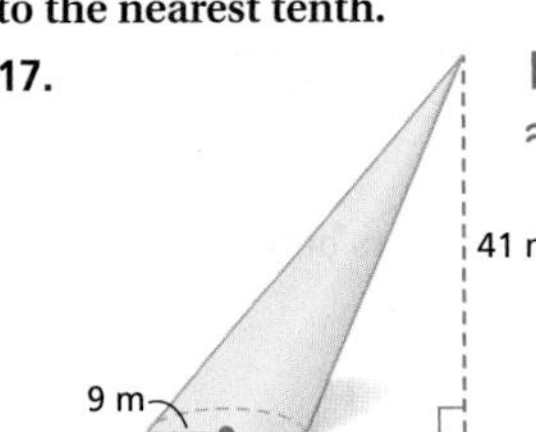

18. $V = \frac{16\pi}{3}$ in^3 ≈ 16.8 in^3

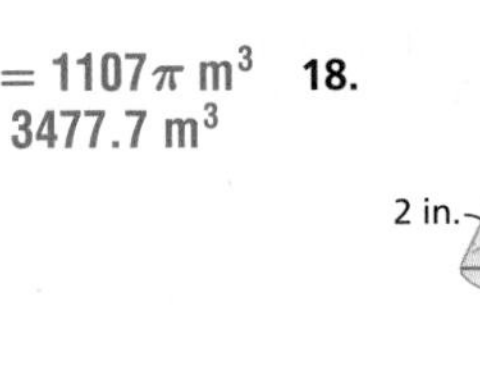

19. a cone with base area 36π ft^2 and a height equal to twice the radius
$V = 144\pi$ ft^3 ≈ 452.4 ft^3

Describe the effect of each change on the volume of the given figure.

20. The dimensions are multiplied by $\frac{1}{3}$.

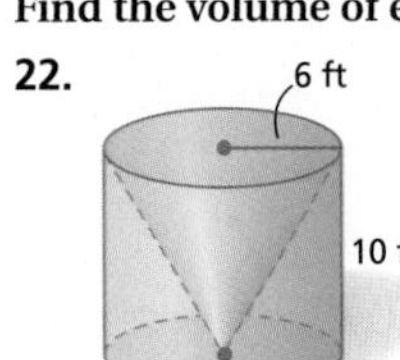

The volume is multiplied by $\frac{1}{27}$.

21. The dimensions are multiplied by 6.

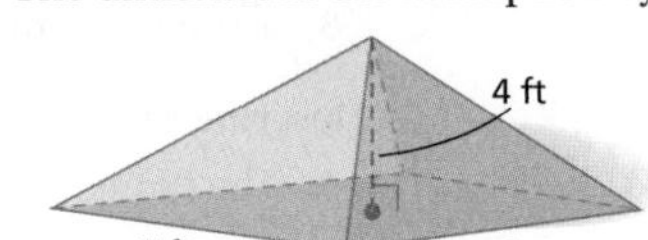

The volume is multiplied by 216.

Find the volume of each composite figure. Round to the nearest tenth, if necessary.

22. $V \approx 754.0$ ft^3

23.

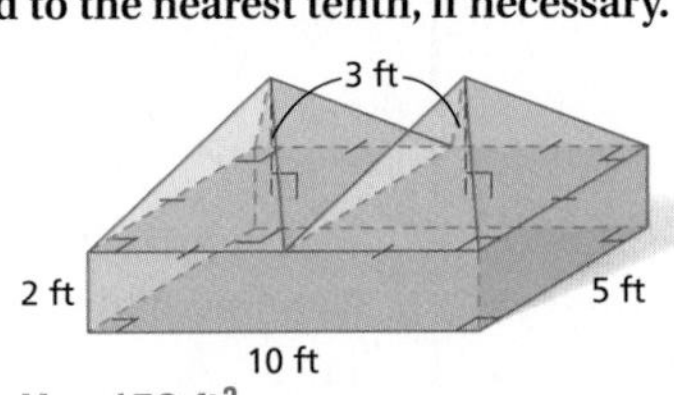

$V = 150$ ft^3

Find the volume of each right cone with the given dimensions. Give your answers in terms of π.

24. radius 3 in.
height 7 in.
$V = 21\pi$ in^3

25. diameter 5 m
height 2 m
$V = \frac{25\pi}{6}$ m^3

26. radius 28 ft
slant height 53 ft
$V = 11{,}760\pi$ ft^3

27. diameter 24 cm
slant height 13 cm
$V = 240\pi$ cm^3

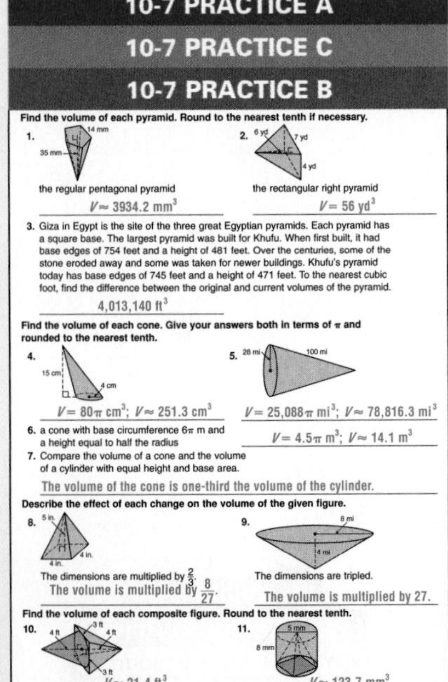

10-7 PRACTICE A
10-7 PRACTICE C
10-7 PRACTICE B

Find the volume of each pyramid. Round to the nearest tenth if necessary.

1. the regular pentagonal pyramid — $V \approx 3934.2$ mm^3
2. the rectangular right pyramid — $V = 56$ yd^3

3. Giza in Egypt is the site of the three great Egyptian pyramids. Each pyramid has a square base. The largest pyramid was built for Khufu. When first built, it had base edges of 754 feet and a height of 481 feet. Over the centuries, some of the stone eroded away and some was taken for newer buildings. Khufu's pyramid today has base edges of 745 feet and a height of 471 feet. To the nearest cubic foot, find the difference between the original and current volumes of the pyramid. 4,013,140 ft^3

Find the volume of each cone. Give your answers both in terms of π and rounded to the nearest tenth.

4. $V = 80\pi$ cm^3; $V \approx 251.3$ cm^3
5. $V = 25{,}088\pi$ mi^3; $V \approx 78{,}816.3$ mi^3

6. a cone with base circumference 6π m and a height equal to half the radius — $V = 4.5\pi$ m^3; $V \approx 14.1$ m^3

7. Compare the volume of a cone and the volume of a cylinder with equal height and base area. The volume of the cone is one-third the volume of the cylinder.

Describe the effect of each change on the volume of the given figure.

8. The dimensions are multiplied by $\frac{2}{3}$. The volume is multiplied by $\frac{8}{27}$.
9. The dimensions are tripled. The volume is multiplied by 27.

Find the volume of each composite figure. Round to the nearest tenth.

10. $V \approx 21.4$ ft^3
11. $V \approx 123.7$ mm^3

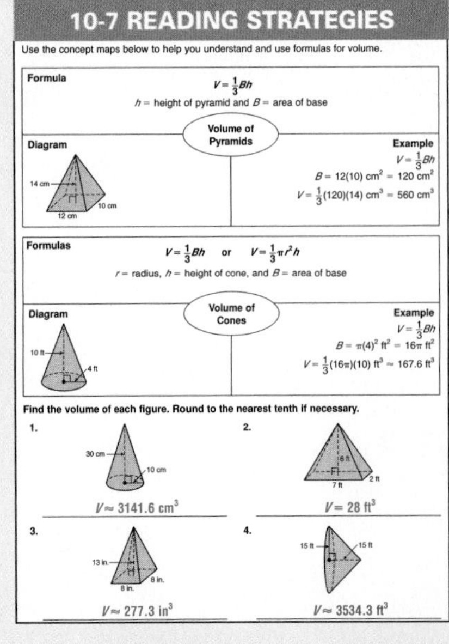

10-7 READING STRATEGIES

Use the concept maps below to help you understand and use formulas for volume.

Formula: $V = \frac{1}{3}Bh$
h = height of pyramid and B = area of base

Volume of Pyramids

Diagram — Example: $V = \frac{1}{3}Bh$; $B = 12(10)$ cm^2 = 120 cm^2; $V = \frac{1}{3}(120)(14)$ cm^3 = 560 cm^3

Formulas: $V = \frac{1}{3}Bh$ or $V = \frac{1}{3}\pi r^2 h$
r = radius, h = height of cone, and B = area of base

Volume of Cones

Diagram — Example: $V = \frac{1}{3}Bh$; $B = \pi(4)^2$ ft^2 = 16π ft^2; $V = \frac{1}{3}(16\pi)(10)$ ft^3 ≈ 167.6 ft^3

Find the volume of each figure. Round to the nearest tenth if necessary.

1. $V \approx 3141.6$ cm^3
2. $V = 28$ ft^3
3. $V \approx 277.3$ in^3
4. $V \approx 3534.3$ ft^3

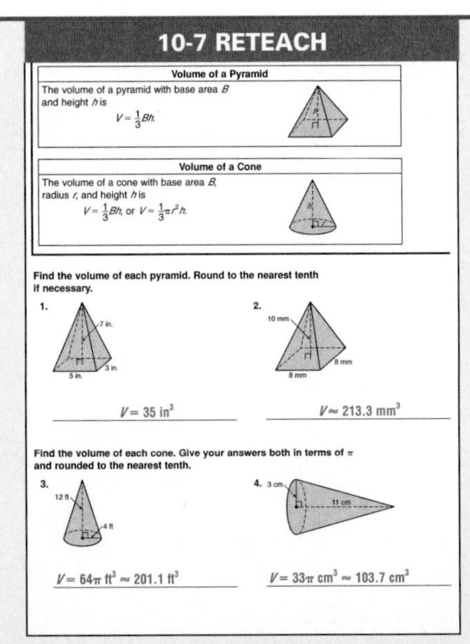

10-7 RETEACH

Volume of a Pyramid
The volume of a pyramid with base area B and height h is $V = \frac{1}{3}Bh$.

Volume of a Cone
The volume of a cone with base area B, radius r, and height h is $V = \frac{1}{3}Bh$, or $V = \frac{1}{3}\pi r^2 h$.

Find the volume of each pyramid. Round to the nearest tenth if necessary.

1. $V = 35$ in^3
2. $V \approx 213.3$ mm^3

Find the volume of each cone. Give your answers both in terms of π and rounded to the nearest tenth.

3. $V = 64\pi$ ft^3 ≈ 201.1 ft^3
4. $V = 33\pi$ cm^3 ≈ 103.7 cm^3

Find the volume of each regular pyramid with the given dimensions. Round to the nearest tenth, if necessary.

	Number of sides of base	Base edge length	Height	Volume
28.	3	10 ft	6 ft	86.6 ft^3
29.	4	15 m	18 m	1350 m^3
30.	5	9 in.	12 in.	557.4 in^3
31.	6	8 cm	3 cm	166.3 cm^3

32. Find the height of a rectangular pyramid with length 3 m, width 8 m, and volume 112 m^3. $h = 14$ m

$C = 10\pi\sqrt{3}$ cm 33. Find the base circumference of a cone with height 5 cm and volume 125π cm^3.

34. Find the volume of a cone with slant height 10 ft and height 8 ft. $V = 96\pi$ ft^3

$V = 1280$ in^3 35. Find the volume of a square pyramid with slant height 17 in. and surface area 800 in^2.

$S = 600\pi$ yd^2 36. Find the surface area of a cone with height 20 yd and volume 1500π yd^3.

37. Find the volume of a triangular pyramid with vertices (0, 0, 0), (5, 0, 0), (0, 3, 0), and (0, 0, 7). $V = 17.5$ $units^3$

38. **///ERROR ANALYSIS///** Which volume is incorrect? Explain the error.

38. The calculation shown in A is incorrect because it uses the slant height of the cone instead of the height.

A
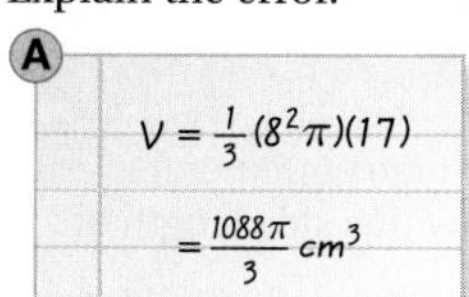

B
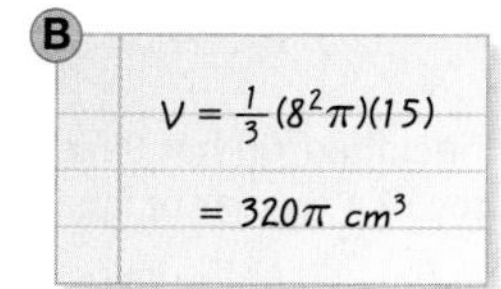

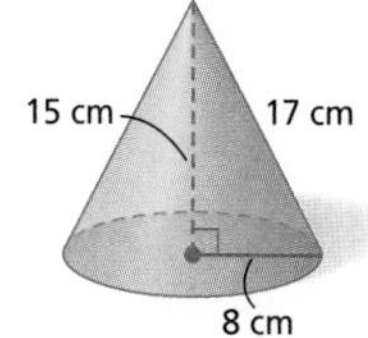

39. **Critical Thinking** Write a ratio comparing the volume of the prism to the volume of the composite figure. Explain your answer.

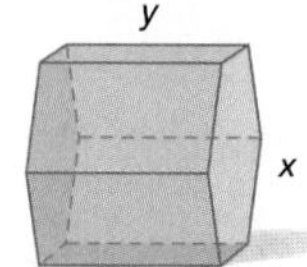

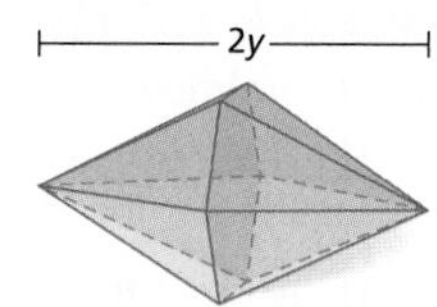

40. **Write About It** Explain how you would find the volume of a cone, given the radius and the surface area.

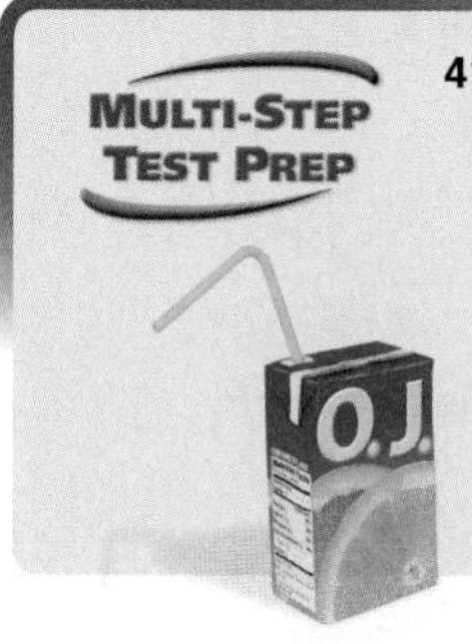

41. This problem will prepare you for the Multi-Step Test Prep on page 724.

A juice stand sells smoothies in cone-shaped cups that are 8 in. tall. The regular size has a 4 in. diameter. The jumbo size has an 8 in. diameter. a. 33.5 in^3; b. 134.0 in^3

a. Find the volume of the regular size to the nearest tenth.

b. Find the volume of the jumbo size to the nearest tenth.

c. The regular size costs \$1.25. What would be a reasonable price for the jumbo size? Explain your reasoning.

\$5; the large size holds 4 times as much.

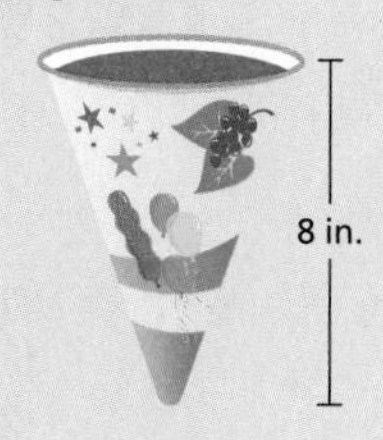

COMMON ERROR ALERT

In **Exercise 35,** students may try to divide the surface area by the slant height to find the base area. Encourage them to first use the surface area formula for a regular pyramid to write an expression in terms of the side length s and then to solve for s.

MULTI-STEP TEST PREP **Exercise 41** involves finding the volumes of cones of different sizes. This exercise prepares students for the Multi-Step Test Prep on page 724.

Answers

39. 3:2; the base areas are the same for both figures. The volume of the prism is By, and the volume of the figure formed by 2 pyramids is $\frac{1}{3}B(2y)$. The ratio of the volumes is $By : \frac{1}{3}B(2y)$, which is equivalent to 3:2.

40. Possible answer: I would substitute the given values for r and S into the surface area formula and solve for ℓ. Then I would use the Pythagorean Theorem and the values of r and ℓ to find h. Then I would substitute the values for r and h into the volume formula.

10-7 PROBLEM SOLVING

1. A regular square pyramid has a base area of 196 meters and a lateral area of 448 square meters. What is the volume of the pyramid? Round your answer to the nearest tenth.
   $V \approx 940.0$ m^3

2. A paper cone for serving roasted almonds has a volume of 406π cubic centimeters. A smaller cone has half the radius and half the height of the first cone. What is the volume of the smaller cone? Give your answer in terms of π.
   $V = 50.75\pi$ cm^3

3. The hexagonal base in the pyramid is a regular polygon. What is the volume of the pyramid if its height is 9 centimeters? Round to the nearest tenth.

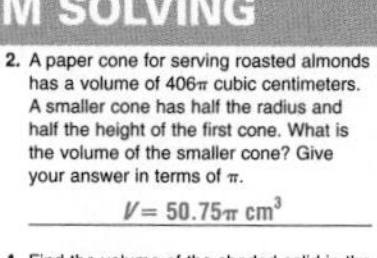

5.2 cm

   $V \approx 210.8$ cm^3

4. Find the volume of the shaded solid in the figure shown. Give your answer in terms of π.

9 in. 3 in. 6 in. 5 in.

   $V = 98\pi$ in^3

Choose the best answer.

5. The diameter of the cone equals the width of the cube, and the figures have the same height. Find the expression that can be used to determine the volume of the composite figure.
   (A) $4(4)(4) - \frac{1}{3}\pi(2^2)(4)$
   B $4(4)(4) + \frac{1}{3}\pi(2^2)(4)$
   C $4(4)(4) - \pi(2^2)(4)$
   D $4(4)(4) + \frac{1}{3}\pi(2^2)$

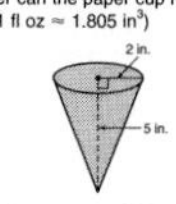

6. Approximately how many fluid ounces of water can the paper cup hold? (*Hint:* 1 fl oz ≈ 1.805 in^3)

2 in. 5 in.

   F 10.9 fl oz
   (G) 11.6 fl oz
   H 32.7 fl oz
   J 36.3 fl oz

7. The Step Pyramid of Djoser in Lower Egypt was the first pyramid in the history of architecture. Its original height was 204 feet, and it had a rectangular base measuring 411 feet by 358 feet. Which is the best estimate for the volume of the pyramid in cubic yards?
   (A) 370,570 yd^3
   B 1,111,709 yd^3
   C 3,335,128 yd^3
   D 10,005,384 yd^3

10-7 CHALLENGE

Draw a figure in a three-dimensional coordinate plane with vertices $A(0, 0, 0)$, $B(8, 0, 0)$, $C(0, 10, 0)$, $D(8, 10, 0)$, and $E(4, 4, 12)$. The height of the figure is EF. F is at (4, 4, 0).

1. Name the base of this figure and its shape. rectangle $ABDC$
2. What type of figure is $ABDCE$? rectangular pyramid
3. What is the formula for finding the volume of this figure? $V = \frac{1}{3}Bh$
4. Use the distance formula to find EF. 12 units
5. Find AB. 8 units
6. Find AC. 10 units
7. Find the volume of the figure. $V = 320$ $units^3$

Draw a figure in a three dimensional coordinate plane with vertices $P(0, 0, 0)$, $N(-10, 0, 0)$, $L(0, -10, 0)$, $M(-10, -10, 0)$, $K(-5, -5, -6)$, $J(-5, -5, 7)$.

8. Name the base of this figure and its shape. You might want to plot the base coordinates on an x-y plane. square $LMNP$
9. Find LP. 10 units
10. Find the area of the base in Exercise 8. 100 $units^2$
11. What type of figure is $JLMNPK$? octahedron
12. What is the formula for finding the volume of this figure? Explain.
    Consider the octahedron as two square pyramids with different altitudes, h_1 and h_2. $V = \frac{1}{3}B(h_1 + h_2)$ Note that altitude is always a positive number.
13. Find the volume of the three-dimensional shape named in Exercise 11. Round to the nearest tenth. $V \approx 433.3$ $units^3$

In Exercise 42, students who chose **C** found the height correctly, but did not multiply by $\frac{1}{3}$. Students who chose **B** used the slant height instead of finding the height.

Journal

Have students describe how to find the volume of a pyramid when given the surface area, slant height, and the base edge lengths.

ALTERNATIVE ASSESSMENT

Have students sketch 4 three-dimensional figures: 2 pyramids with different base shapes, a cone, and a composite shape. Remind students to label enough measurements on their sketches to determine the volume of each figure. Then have them calculate the volumes of their figures.

Power Presentations with PowerPoint®

10-7 Lesson Quiz

Find the volume of each figure. Round to the nearest tenth, if necessary.

1. a rectangular pyramid with length 25 cm, width 17 cm, and height 21 cm 2975 cm^3
2. a regular triangular pyramid with base edge length 12 in. and height 10 in. 207.8 in^3
3. a cone with diameter 22 cm and height 30 cm $V \approx 3801.3 \text{ cm}^3$
4. a cone with base circumference 8π m and a height 5 m more than $\frac{1}{2}$ the radius $V \approx 117.3 \text{ m}^2$
5. A cone has radius 2 in. and height 7 in. If the radius and height are multiplied by $\frac{1}{4}$, describe the effect on the volume. The volume is multiplied by $\frac{1}{64}$.
6. Find the volume of the composite figure. Give your answer in terms of π.

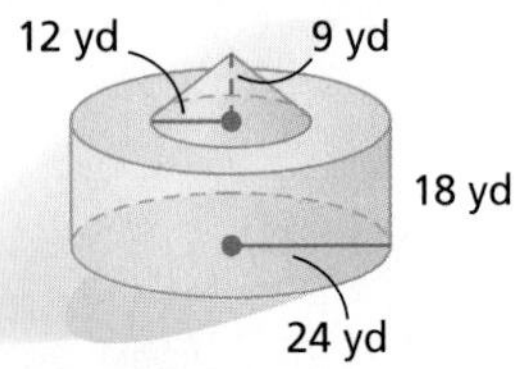

$10{,}800\pi \text{ yd}^3$

Also available on transparency

TEST PREP

42. Find the volume of the cone.
    Ⓐ $432\pi \text{ cm}^3$ Ⓒ $1296\pi \text{ cm}^3$
    Ⓑ $720\pi \text{ cm}^3$ Ⓓ $2160\pi \text{ cm}^3$

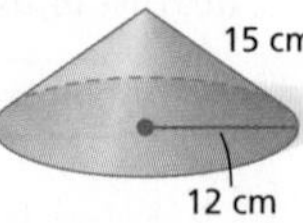

43. A square pyramid has a slant height of 25 m and a lateral area of 350 m^2. Which is closest to the volume?
    Ⓕ 392 m^3 Ⓖ 1176 m^3 Ⓗ 404 m^3 Ⓙ 1225 m^3

44. A cone has a volume of $18\pi \text{ in}^3$. Which are possible dimensions of the cone?
    Ⓐ Diameter 1 in., height 18 in. Ⓒ Diameter 3 in., height 6 in.
    Ⓑ Diameter 6 in., height 6 in. Ⓓ Diameter 6 in., height 3 in.

45. **Gridded Response** Find the height in centimeters of a square pyramid with a volume of 243 cm^3 and a base edge length equal to the height. 9

CHALLENGE AND EXTEND

Each cone is inscribed in a regular pyramid with a base edge length of 2 ft and a height of 2 ft. Find the volume of each cone.

46. 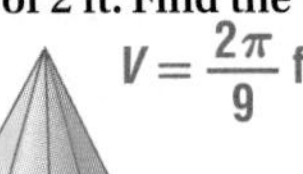 $V = \frac{2\pi}{9} \text{ ft}^3$

47. 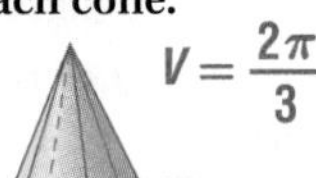 $V = \frac{2\pi}{3} \text{ ft}^3$

48. 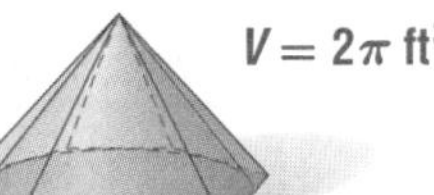 $V = 2\pi \text{ ft}^3$

49. A regular octahedron has 8 faces that are equilateral triangles. Find the volume of a regular octahedron with a side length of 10 cm. $V = \frac{1000\sqrt{2}}{3} \text{ cm}^3$

50. A cylinder has a radius of 5 in. and a height of 3 in. Without calculating the volumes, find the height of a cone with the same base and the same volume as the cylinder. Explain your reasoning.

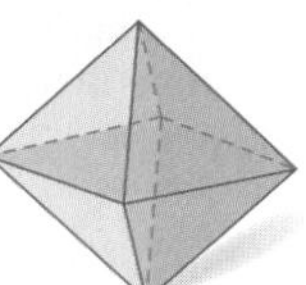

SPIRAL REVIEW

Find the unknown numbers. *(Previous course)*

51. The difference of two numbers is 24. The larger number is 4 less than 3 times the smaller number. 38 and 14
52. Three times the first number plus the second number is 88. The first number times 10 is equal to 4 times the second. 16 and 40
53. The sum of two numbers is 197. The first number is 20 more than $\frac{1}{2}$ of the second number. 79 and 118

Explain why the triangles are similar, then find each length. *(Lesson 7-3)*

54. AB SAS; $AB = 15$

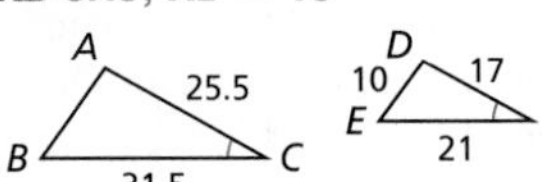

55. PQ AA; $PQ = 6$

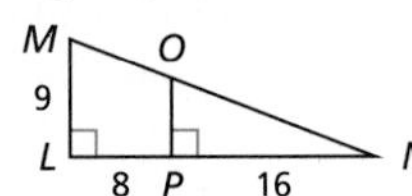

Find AB and the coordinates of the midpoint of $\overline{AB}$. Round to the nearest tenth, if necessary. *(Lesson 10-3)*

56. $A(1, 1, 2)$, $B(8, 9, 10)$ 13.3; $(4.5, 5, 6)$
57. $A(-4, -1, 0)$, $B(5, 1, -4)$ 10.0; $(0.5, 0, -2)$
58. $A(2, -2, 4)$, $B(-2, 2, -4)$ 9.8; $(0, 0, 0)$
59. $A(-3, -1, 2)$, $B(-1, 5, 5)$ 7; $(-2, 2, 3.5)$

Answers

50. $h = 9$ in.; the volume of a cone with the same base and height as the cylinder is $\frac{1}{3}$ the volume of the cylinder. For the cone to have the same volume as the cylinder, the height of the cone must be 3 times the height of the cylinder.

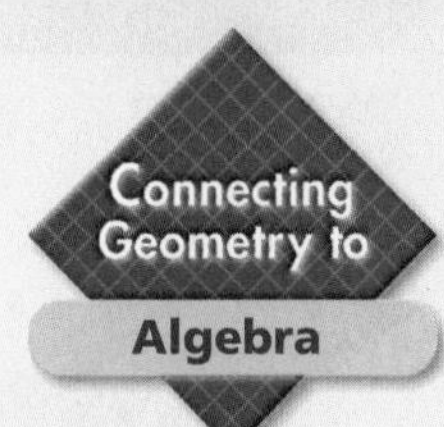

Cube Roots

If you know the area of a square, you can find the length of a side by taking the square root of the area. How can you find the length of a side of a cube if you know the volume?

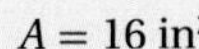

$A = 16 \text{ in}^2$ | $V = 27 \text{ in}^3$

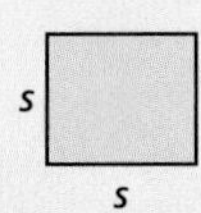

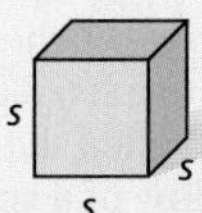

$s^2 = A$ | $s^3 = V$

$s^2 = 16$ | $s^3 = 27$

$s = \sqrt{16} = 4$ | $s = ?$

To find the side length, you need to find the *cube root* of 27. The cube root of 27 is 3 because $3^3 = 27$, so the side length of the cube above is 3 in. "The cube root of 27" can also be written as $\sqrt[3]{27}$.

Example

The volume of a cube is 64 m^3. Find the side length of the cube.

$s^3 = V$

$s^3 = 64$ — *Substitute 64 for V.*

$s = \sqrt[3]{64} = 4$ — *$4^3 = 64$, so the cube root of 64 is 4.*

The side length of the cube is 4 m.

Try This

Given the volume, find the side length of each cube.

1. $V = 8 \text{ cm}^3$ 2 cm
2. $V = 125 \text{ ft}^3$ 5 ft
3. $V = 216 \text{ in.}^3$ 6 in
4. $V = 1{,}000 \text{ yd}^3$ 10 yd
5. $V = 1 \text{ cm}^3$ 1 cm
6. $V = 0.064 \text{ m}^3$ 0.4 m
7. Carlos wants to buy an angelfish for a pet. The pet store recommends a fish tank that holds 2,197 in^3 of water. If the tank is in the shape of a cube, how long is each side? 13 in.

The *n*th root of *x* is the number *a* such that $a^n = x$. For example, the 4th root of 16 is 2 because $2^4 = 16$. "The *n*th root of x" can be written as $\sqrt[n]{x}$. In the example just given, $\sqrt[4]{16} = 2$. Simplify each expression.

8. $\sqrt[4]{81}$ 3
9. $\sqrt[5]{32}$ 2
10. $\sqrt[3]{729}$ 9
11. $\sqrt[5]{243}$ 3
12. $\sqrt[7]{1}$ 1
13. $\sqrt[4]{0.0016}$ 0.2

Organizer

Pacing:
Traditional 1 day
Block $\frac{1}{2}$ day

Objective: Calculate cube roots.

Online Edition

Countdown Week 24

Teach

Remember

Students review the concept of a square root and extend it to include cube roots and *n*th-roots.

Inclusion Some students may have difficulty making the transition from finding the cube roots of integers to finding the cube roots of decimals (Exercise 6). Suggest to students that they find the cube root of 64 first, and then change that number to a decimal that has the correct number of decimal places after it is cubed.

Close

Assess

Ask the students to explain how to find the volume of a cube given its side length, and then how to find the side length of a cube given its volume. cube the side length; take the cube root of the volume

State Resources

go.hrw.com
State Resources Online
KEYWORD: MG7 Resources

10-8 Organizer

Pacing: Traditional 1 day
Block $\frac{1}{2}$ day

Objectives: Learn and apply the formula for the volume of a sphere.

Learn and apply the formula for the surface area of a sphere.

Online Edition
Tutorial Videos, Interactivity

Countdown Week 24

Power Presentations with PowerPoint®

Warm Up

Find each measurement.

1. the radius of ⊙M if the diameter is 25 cm   12.5 cm
2. the circumference of ⊙X if the radius is 42.5 in. 85π in.
3. the area of ⊙T if the diameter is 26 ft 169π ft^2
4. the circumference of ⊙N if the area is 625π cm^2 50π cm

Also available on transparency

Math Humor

Q: What do you call the force on the surface of a balloon?

A: Sphere pressure.

10-8 Spheres

Objectives
Learn and apply the formula for the volume of a sphere.

Learn and apply the formula for the surface area of a sphere.

Vocabulary
sphere
center of a sphere
radius of a sphere
hemisphere
great circle

Who uses this?
Biologists study the eyes of deep-sea predators such as the giant squid to learn about their behavior. (See Example 2.)

A **sphere** is the locus of points in space that are a fixed distance from a given point called the **center of a sphere**. A **radius of a sphere** connects the center of the sphere to any point on the sphere. A **hemisphere** is half of a sphere. A **great circle** divides a sphere into two hemispheres.

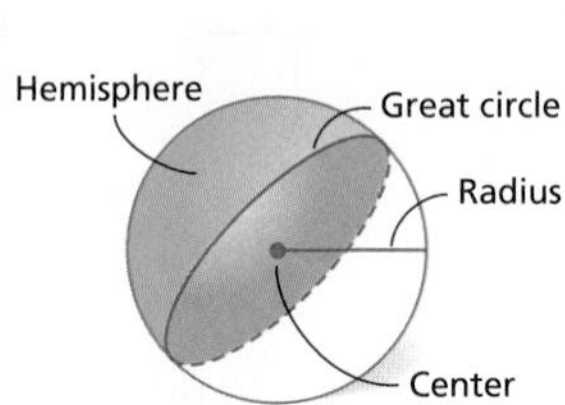

The figure shows a hemisphere and a cylinder with a cone removed from its interior. The cross sections have the same area at every level, so the volumes are equal by Cavalieri's Principle. You will prove that the cross sections have equal areas in Exercise 39.

$$V(\text{hemisphere}) = V(\text{cylinder}) - V(\text{cone})$$
$$= \pi r^2 h - \frac{1}{3}\pi r^2 h$$
$$= \frac{2}{3}\pi r^2 h$$
$$= \frac{2}{3}\pi r^2 (r) \quad \textit{The height of the hemisphere is equal to the radius.}$$
$$= \frac{2}{3}\pi r^3$$

The volume of a sphere with radius r is twice the volume of the hemisphere, or $V = \frac{4}{3}\pi r^3$.

Volume of a Sphere

The volume of a sphere with radius r is $V = \frac{4}{3}\pi r^3$.

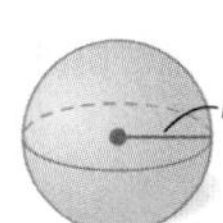

EXAMPLE 1 Finding Volumes of Spheres

Find each measurement. Give your answer in terms of π.

A the volume of the sphere

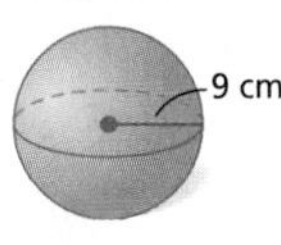

$V = \frac{4}{3}\pi r^3$

$V = \frac{4}{3}\pi (9)^3$ *Substitute 9 for r.*

$= 972\pi$ cm^3 *Simplify.*

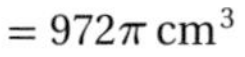

State Resources

go.hrw.com
State Resources Online
KEYWORD: MG7 Resources

1 Introduce

EXPLORATION

10-8 Spheres

In this Exploration, you will relate the radius of a sphere to its surface area. You will need a plastic foam sphere for this Exploration.

1. Carefully cut the sphere in half. Then trace around one half of the sphere to make two circles on a sheet of paper.
2. Cut out the circles. Then cut each circle into eight congruent pieces.
3. Rearrange the pieces and tape them together as shown.
4. Tape the pieces to one half of the sphere.
5. Approximately what fraction of the original sphere is covered by the pieces?

THINK AND DISCUSS

6. **Explain** how you can find the total area of the pieces if you know that the sphere has a radius of r.

Motivate

Cut an orange in half, and trace around the cut side 4 times. Then peel the orange and arrange the pieces of orange peel to cover the 4 circles. Explain to students that this demonstrates that the surface area is 4 times the area of a cross section, or $4\pi r^2$.

Explorations and answers are provided in *Alternate Openers: Explorations Transparencies.*

Find each measurement. Give your answer in terms of π.

B **the diameter of a sphere with volume 972π in^3**

$972\pi = \frac{4}{3}\pi r^3$ *Substitute 972π for V.*

$729 = r^3$ *Divide both sides by $\frac{4}{3}\pi$.*

$r = 9$ *Take the cube root of both sides.*

$d = 18$ in. *$d = 2r$*

C **the volume of the hemisphere**

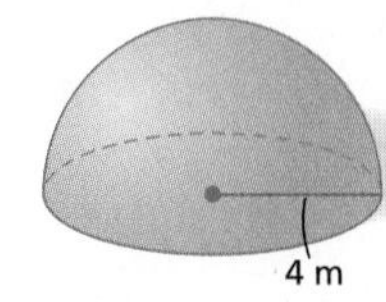

$V = \frac{2}{3}\pi r^3$ *Volume of a hemisphere*

$= \frac{2}{3}\pi(4)^3 = \frac{128\pi}{3}$ m^3 *Substitute 4 for r.*

1. Find the radius of a sphere with volume 2304π ft^3. $r = 12$ ft

EXAMPLE 2 ***Biology Application***

Giant squid need large eyes to see their prey in low light. The eyeball of a giant squid is approximately a sphere with a diameter of 25 cm, which is bigger than a soccer ball. A human eyeball is approximately a sphere with a diameter of 2.5 cm. How many times as great is the volume of a giant squid eyeball as the volume of a human eyeball?

human eyeball:

$V = \frac{4}{3}\pi r^3$

$= \frac{4}{3}\pi(1.25)^3 \approx 8.18$ cm^3

giant squid eyeball:

$V = \frac{4}{3}\pi r^3$

$= \frac{4}{3}\pi(12.5)^3 \approx 8181.23$ cm^3

A giant squid eyeball is about 1000 times as great in volume as a human eyeball.

2. A hummingbird eyeball has a diameter of approximately 0.6 cm. How many times as great is the volume of a human eyeball as the volume of a hummingbird eyeball? about 72.3 times

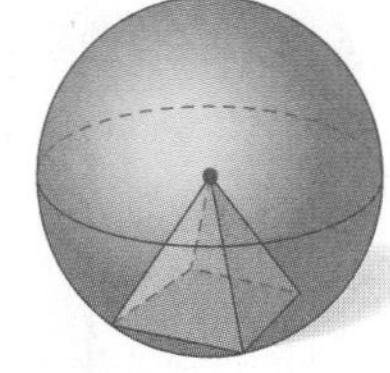

In the figure, the vertex of the pyramid is at the center of the sphere. The height of the pyramid is approximately the radius r of the sphere. Suppose the entire sphere is filled with n pyramids that each have base area B and height r.

$V(\text{sphere}) \approx \frac{1}{3}Br + \frac{1}{3}Br + \ldots + \frac{1}{3}Br$ *The sphere's volume is close to the sum of the volumes of the pyramids.*

$\frac{4}{3}\pi r^3 \approx n\left(\frac{1}{3}Br\right)$

$4\pi r^2 \approx nB$ *Divide both sides by $\frac{1}{3}\pi r$.*

If the pyramids fill the sphere, the total area of the bases is approximately equal to the surface area of the sphere S, so $4\pi r^2 \approx S$. As the number of pyramids increases, the approximation gets closer to the actual surface area.

Power Presentations with PowerPoint®

Additional Examples

Example 1

Find each measurement. Give your answers in terms of π.

A. the volume of the sphere

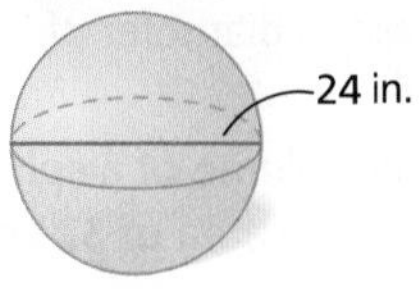

2304π in^3

B. the diameter of a sphere with volume $36{,}000\pi$ cm^3 60 cm

C. the volume of the hemisphere 2250π m^3

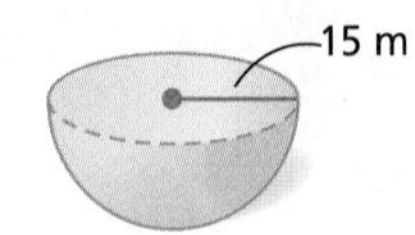

Example 2

A sporting goods store sells exercise balls in two sizes, standard (22 in. diameter) and jumbo (34 in. diameter). How many times as great is the volume of a jumbo ball as the volume of a standard ball? about 3.7 times

INTERVENTION

Questioning Strategies

EXAMPLE 1

- How would you find the volume of a hemisphere?

EXAMPLE 2

- Do the radii of two balls whose volumes have a 2 to 1 ratio also have a 2 to 1 ratio? How do you know?

2 Teach

Guided Instruction

Use a plastic-foam ball from a floral or craft store to discuss the vocabulary of spheres, cutting it in half to show a great circle, the radius, and the diameter. Explain that the surface area of the sphere is 4 times the area of a great circle.

Reaching All Learners

Through Curriculum Integration

Use a globe to demonstrate great circles (longitude lines and the equator) and hemispheres (Northern and Southern Hemispheres). Relate Earth's surface area to the amount of available land and Earth's volume to its mass.

Additional Examples

Example 3

Find each measurement. Give your answers in terms of π.

A. the surface area of a sphere with a diameter of 76 cm
$5776\pi \text{ cm}^2$

B. the volume of a sphere with a surface area of $324\pi \text{ in}^2$
$972\pi \text{ in}^3$

C. the surface area of a sphere with a great circle that has an area of $49\pi \text{ mi}^2$ $196\pi \text{ mi}^2$

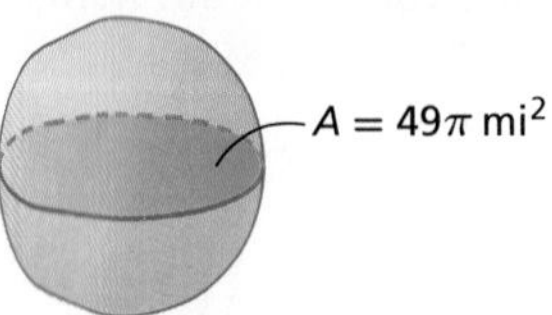

Example 4

The radius of the sphere is multiplied by $\frac{3}{4}$. Describe the effect on the volume.

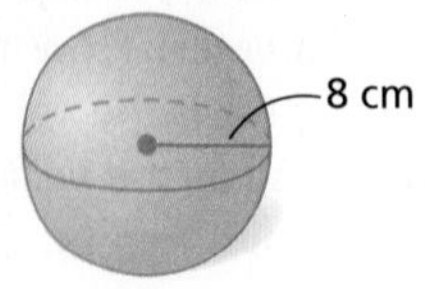

The volume is multiplied by $\frac{27}{64}$.

INTERVENTION

Questioning Strategies

EXAMPLE 3

- How can you find the volume of any sphere if you know its surface area?
- How can you find the surface area of any sphere if you know its volume?

EXAMPLE 4

- If you tripled the radius of a sphere, how would its surface area be affected?

Surface Area of a Sphere

The surface area of a sphere with radius r is $S = 4\pi r^2$.

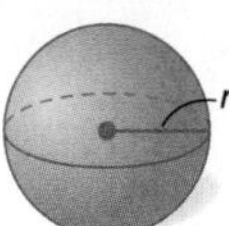

EXAMPLE 3 Finding Surface Area of Spheres

Find each measurement. Give your answers in terms of π.

A the surface area of a sphere with diameter 10 ft

$S = 4\pi r^2$

$S = 4\pi(5)^2 = 200\pi \text{ ft}^2$ *Substitute 5 for r.*

B the volume of a sphere with surface area $144\pi \text{ m}^2$

$S = 4\pi r^2$

$144\pi = 4\pi r^2$ *Substitute 144π for S.*

$6 = r$ *Solve for r.*

$V = \frac{4}{3}\pi r^3$

$= \frac{4}{3}\pi(6)^3 = 288\pi \text{ m}^3$ *Substitute 6 for r.*

The volume of the sphere is $288\pi \text{ m}^3$.

C the surface area of a sphere with a great circle that has an area of $4\pi \text{ in}^2$

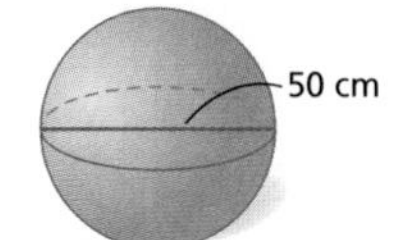

$\pi r^2 = 4\pi$ *Substitute 4π for A in the formula for the area of a circle.*

$r = 2$ *Solve for r.*

$S = 4\pi r^2$

$= 4\pi(2)^2 = 16\pi \text{ in}^2$ *Substitute 2 for r in the surface area formula.*

3. Find the surface area of the sphere.
$S = 2500\pi \text{ cm}^2$

50 cm

EXAMPLE 4 Exploring Effects of Changing Dimensions

The radius of the sphere is tripled. Describe the effect on the volume.

3 m

original dimensions:	radius tripled:
$V = \frac{4}{3}\pi r^3$	$V = \frac{4}{3}\pi r^3$
$= \frac{4}{3}\pi(3)^3$	$= \frac{4}{3}\pi(9)^3$
$= 36\pi \text{ m}^3$	$= 972\pi \text{ m}^3$

Notice that $972\pi = 27(36\pi)$. If the radius is tripled, the volume is multiplied by 27.

4. The radius of the sphere above is divided by 3. Describe the effect on the surface area. **The surface area is divided by 9.**

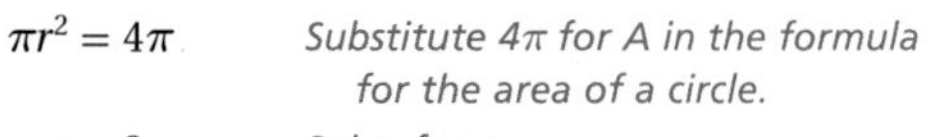

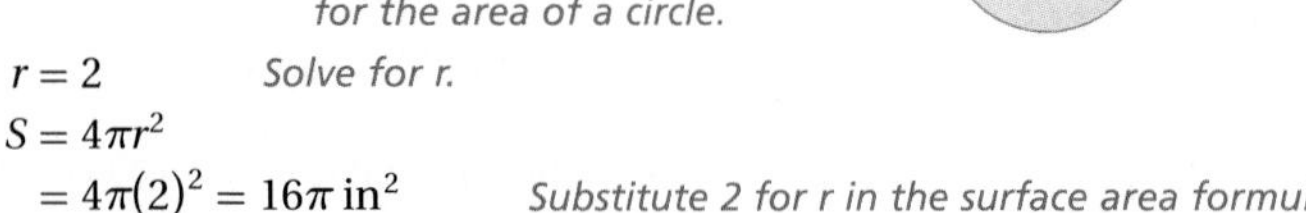

EXAMPLE 5 Finding Surface Areas and Volumes of Composite Figures

Find the surface area and volume of the composite figure. Give your answers in terms of π.

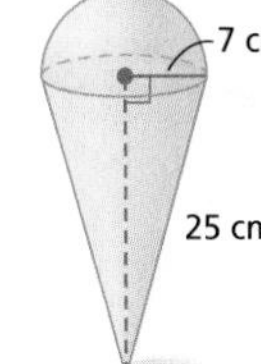

Step 1 Find the surface area of the composite figure.

The surface area of the composite figure is the sum of the surface area of the hemisphere and the lateral area of the cone.

$$S\text{ (hemisphere)} = \frac{1}{2}(4\pi r^2) = 2\pi(7)^2 = 98\pi \text{ cm}^2$$

$$L\text{ (cone)} = \pi r\ell = \pi(7)(25) = 175\pi \text{ cm}^2$$

The surface area of the composite figure is $98\pi + 175\pi = 273\pi$ cm^2.

Step 2 Find the volume of the composite figure.

First find the height of the cone.

$h = \sqrt{25^2 - 7^2}$ *Pythagorean Theorem*

$= \sqrt{576} = 24$ cm *Simplify.*

The volume of the composite figure is the sum of the volume of the hemisphere and the volume of the cone.

$$V\text{ (hemisphere)} = \frac{1}{2}\left(\frac{4}{3}\pi r^3\right) = \frac{2}{3}\pi(7)^3 = \frac{686\pi}{3} \text{ cm}^3$$

$$V\text{ (cone)} = \frac{1}{3}\pi r^2 h = \frac{1}{3}\pi(7)^2(24) = 392\pi \text{ cm}^3$$

The volume of the composite figure is $\frac{686\pi}{3} + 392\pi = \frac{1862\pi}{3}$ cm^3.

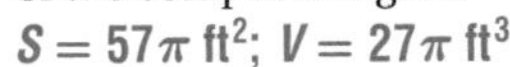

CHECK IT OUT! **5.** Find the surface area and volume of the composite figure.
$S = 57\pi$ ft^2; $V = 27\pi$ ft^3

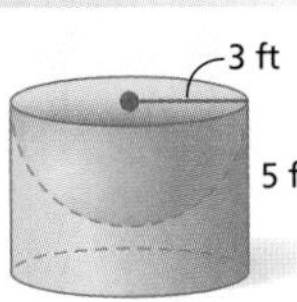

THINK AND DISCUSS

1. Explain how to find the surface area of a sphere when you know the area of a great circle.

2. Compare the volume of the sphere with the volume of the composite figure.

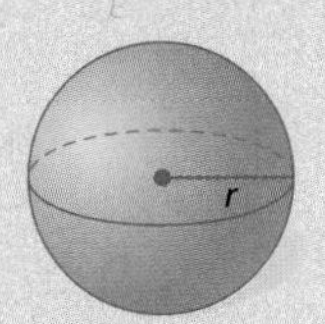

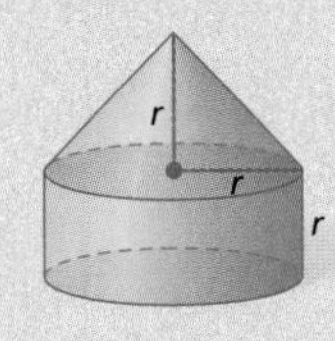

3. GET ORGANIZED Copy and complete the graphic organizer.

If the radius of a sphere is *r* ...

- The area of a great circle is ...
- The volume of the sphere is ...
- The surface area of the sphere is ...

COMMON ERROR ALERT

Some students may have difficulty remembering to use the correct units of measure in their answers. Encourage students to list the measurements of spheres that are given in linear, square, and cubic units. Linear units are used for a radius, a diameter, or a circumference; square units are used for surface area; and cubic units are used for volume.

Power Presentations with PowerPoint®

Additional Examples

Example 5

Find the surface area and volume of the composite figure. Give your answers in terms of π.

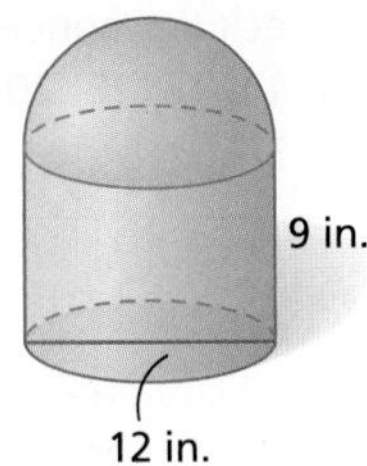

$S = 216\pi$ in^2; $V = 468\pi$ in^3

INTERVENTION
Questioning Strategies

EXAMPLE 5

- How do you calculate the surface area or volume of a composite three-dimensional figure?

3 Close

Summarize

Review the formulas for the volume and surface area of a sphere. The formula for volume includes r^3, and the volume is given in *cubic* units. The formula for surface area includes r^2, and the surface area is given in *square* units.

ONGOING ASSESSMENT and INTERVENTION

Diagnose ***Before*** **the Lesson**
10-8 Warm Up, TE p. 714

Monitor ***During*** **the Lesson**
Check It Out! Exercises, SE pp. 715–717
Questioning Strategies, TE pp. 715–717

Assess ***After*** **the Lesson**
10-8 Lesson Quiz, TE p. 721
Alternative Assessment, TE p. 721

Answers to *Think and Discuss*

1. The surface area is 4 times the area of the great circle.
2. Both the sphere and the composite figure have a volume of $\frac{4}{3}\pi r^3$.
3. See p. A8.

10-8 Exercises

Assignment Guide

Assign *Guided Practice* exercises as necessary.

If you finished Examples **1–3**
Basic 13–19, 24–27, 29–32, 34, 35–38
Average 13–19, 24–27, 29–32, 34, 35–38, 45
Advanced 13–19, 24–27, 29–32, 34, 35–38, 45–48

If you finished Examples **1–5**
Basic 13–38, 41–44, 49–54
Average 13–45, 49–54
Advanced 13–54

Homework Quick Check
Quickly check key concepts.
Exercises: 14, 16, 18, 20, 22, 30, 36

State Resources

go.hrw.com
State Resources Online
KEYWORD: MG7 Resources

10-8 Exercises

go.hrw.com
Homework Help Online
KEYWORD: MG7 10-8
Parent Resources Online
KEYWORD: MG7 Parent

GUIDED PRACTICE

1. **Vocabulary** Describe the endpoints of a *radius of a sphere*.
One endpoint is the center of the sphere, and the other is a point on the sphere.

SEE EXAMPLE 1 p. 714

Find each measurement. Give your answers in terms of π.

2. the volume of the hemisphere $V = \frac{2662\pi}{3}$ in^3

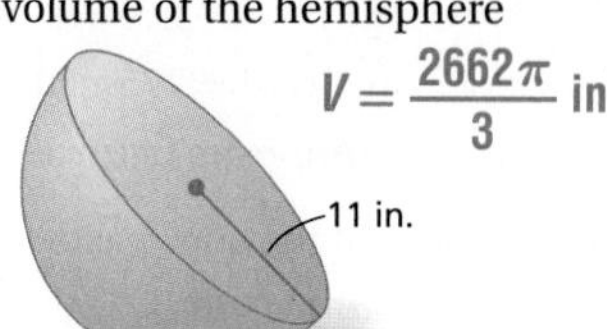

3. the volume of the sphere $V = \frac{4\pi}{3}$ m^3

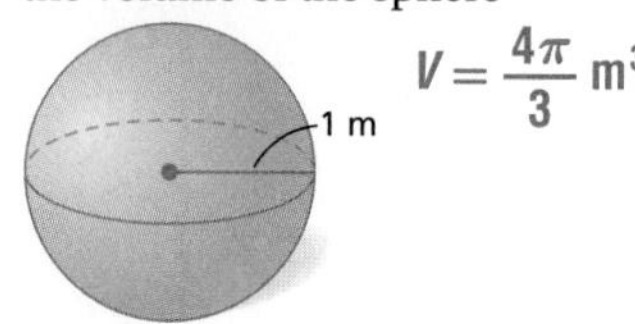

4. the radius of a sphere with volume 288π cm^3 $r = 6$ cm

SEE EXAMPLE 2 p. 715

5. **Food** Approximately how many times as great is the volume of the grapefruit as the volume of the lime? about 8 times as great

SEE EXAMPLE 3 p. 716

Find each measurement. Give your answers in terms of π.

6. the surface area of the sphere $S = 256\pi$ yd^2

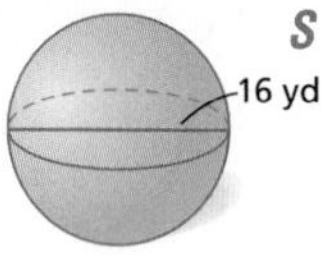

16 yd

7. the surface area of the sphere $S = 196\pi$ cm^2

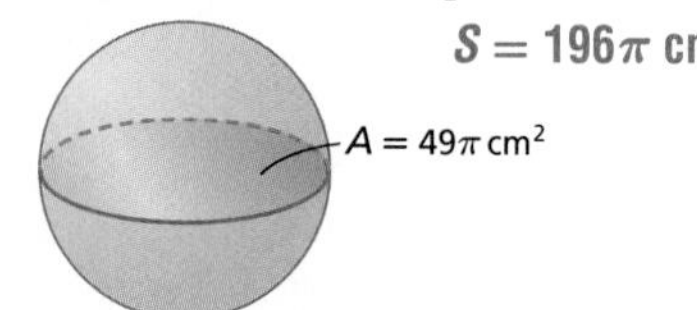

8. the volume of a sphere with surface area 6724π ft^2 $V = \frac{275{,}684\pi}{3}$ ft^3

SEE EXAMPLE 4 p. 716

Describe the effect of each change on the given measurement of the figure.

9. surface area
The dimensions are doubled.

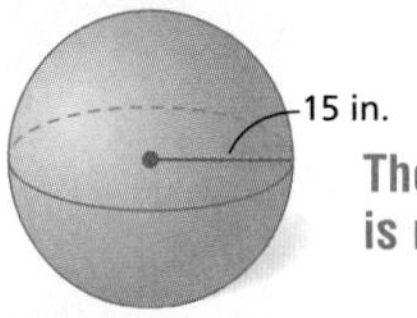

15 in.

The surface area is multiplied by 4.

10. volume
The dimensions are multiplied by $\frac{1}{4}$.

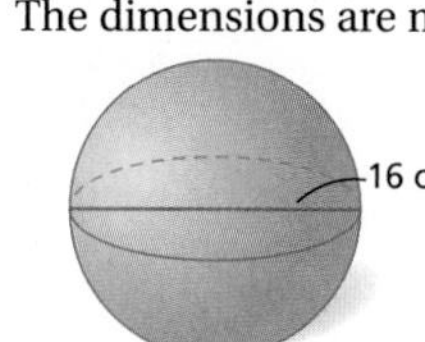

The volume is multiplied by $\frac{1}{64}$.

SEE EXAMPLE 5 p. 717

Find the surface area and volume of each composite figure.

11. $S = 36\pi$ ft^2; $V = \frac{92\pi}{3}$ ft^3

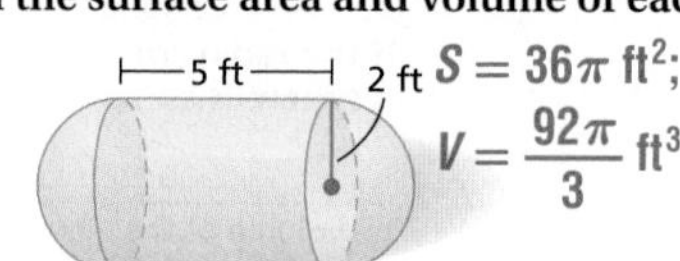

12. $S = 180\pi$ in^2; $V = \frac{560\pi}{3}$ in^3

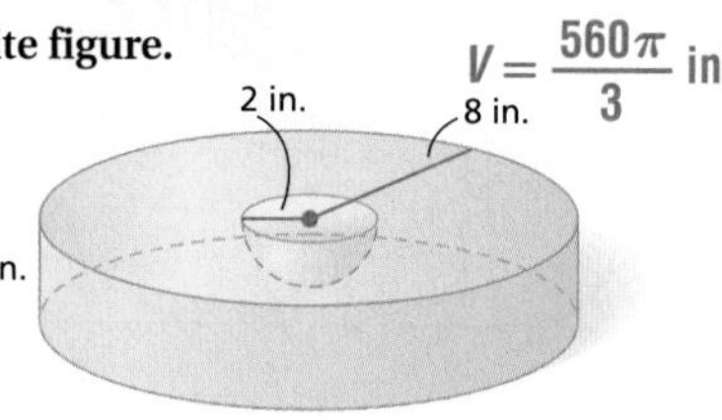

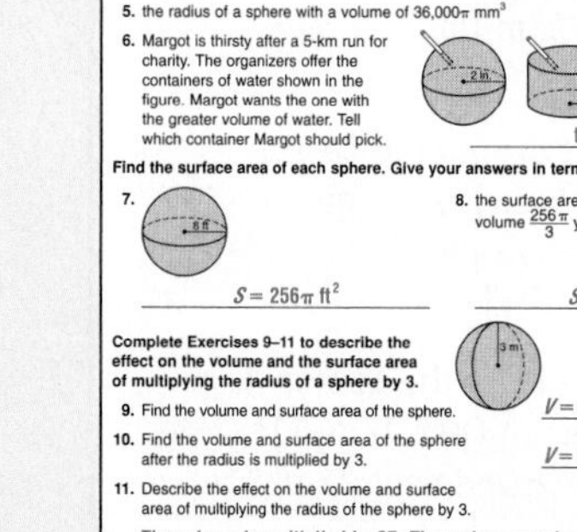

10-8 PRACTICE A

Write each formula.

1. volume of a sphere with radius r $V = \frac{4}{3}\pi r^3$
2. surface area of a sphere with radius r $S = 4\pi r^2$

Find each measurement. Give your answers in terms of π.

3. the volume of the sphere (8 cm) $V = 288\pi$ cm^3
4. the volume of the hemisphere (18 in.) $V = 486\pi$ in^3
5. the radius of a sphere with a volume of $36{,}000\pi$ mm^3 $r = 30$ mm
6. Margot is thirsty after a 5-km run for charity. The organizers offer the containers of water shown in the figure. Margot wants the one with the greater volume of water. Tell which container Margot should pick. (2 in.; 2 in., 2 in.) the sphere

Find the surface area of each sphere. Give your answers in terms of π.

7. (8 ft) $S = 256\pi$ ft^2
8. the surface area of a sphere with volume $\frac{256\pi}{3}$ yd^3 $S = 64\pi$ yd^2

Complete Exercises 9–11 to describe the effect on the volume and the surface area of multiplying the radius of a sphere by 3. (3 m)

9. Find the volume and surface area of the sphere. $V = 36\pi$ m^3; $S = 36\pi$ m^2
10. Find the volume and surface area of the sphere after the radius is multiplied by 3. $V = 972\pi$ m^3; $S = 324\pi$ m^2
11. Describe the effect on the volume and surface area of multiplying the radius of the sphere by 3.
The volume is multiplied by 27. The surface area is multiplied by 9.
12. Find the volume and surface area of the composite figure. Give your answers in terms of π. (7 mi; 3 mi)
$V = 81\pi$ mi^3; $S = 69\pi$ mi^2

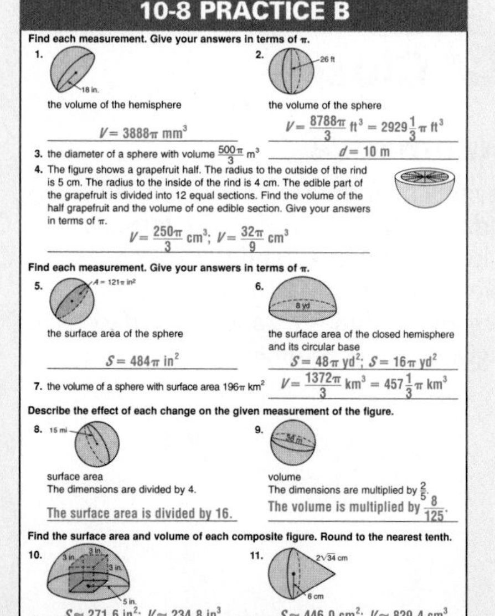

10-8 PRACTICE B

Find each measurement. Give your answers in terms of π.

1. (18 in.) the volume of the hemisphere $V = 3888\pi$ mm^3
2. (26 ft) the volume of the sphere $V = \frac{8788\pi}{3}$ ft^3 $= 2929\frac{1}{3}\pi$ ft^3
3. the diameter of a sphere with volume $\frac{500\pi}{3}$ m^3 $d = 10$ m
4. The figure shows a grapefruit half. The radius to the outside of the rind is 5 cm. The radius to the inside of the rind is 4 cm. The edible part of the grapefruit is divided into 12 equal sections. Find the volume of the half grapefruit and the volume of one edible section. Give your answers in terms of π.
$V = \frac{250\pi}{3}$ cm^3; $V = \frac{32\pi}{9}$ cm^3

Find each measurement. Give your answers in terms of π.

5. ($A = 121\pi$ in^2) the surface area of the sphere $S = 484\pi$ in^2
6. (8 yd) the surface area of the closed hemisphere and its circular base $S = 48\pi$ yd^2; $S = 16\pi$ yd^2
7. the volume of a sphere with surface area 196π km^2 $V = \frac{1372\pi}{3}$ km^3 $= 457\frac{1}{3}\pi$ km^3

Describe the effect of each change on the given measurement of the figure.

8. (15 mi) surface area
The dimensions are divided by 4.
The surface area is divided by 16.
9. (34 m) volume
The dimensions are multiplied by $\frac{2}{5}$.
The volume is multiplied by $\frac{8}{125}$.

Find the surface area and volume of each composite figure. Round to the nearest tenth.

10. (3 in., 3 in., 3 in., 5 in.) $S \approx 271.6$ in^2; $V \approx 234.8$ in^3
11. ($2\sqrt{34}$ cm, 6 cm) $S \approx 446.0$ cm^2; $V \approx 829.4$ cm^3

PRACTICE AND PROBLEM SOLVING

Independent Practice	
For Exercises	See Example
13–15	1
16	2
17–19	3
20–21	4
22–23	5

Extra Practice
Skills Practice p. S23
Application Practice p. S37

Find each measurement. Give your answers in terms of π.

13. the volume of the sphere $V = 972\pi \text{ cm}^3$

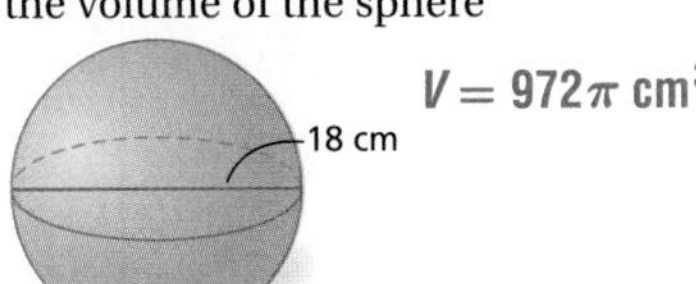

14. the volume of the hemisphere $V = \frac{686\pi}{3} \text{ ft}^3$

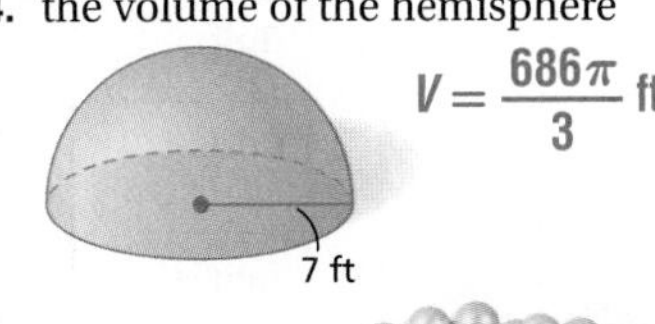

15. the diameter of a sphere with volume $7776\pi \text{ in}^3$ $d = 36 \text{ in.}$

16. **Jewelry** The size of a cultured pearl is typically indicated by its diameter in mm. How many times as great is the volume of the 9 mm pearl as the volume of the 6 mm pearl? **3.375 times as great**

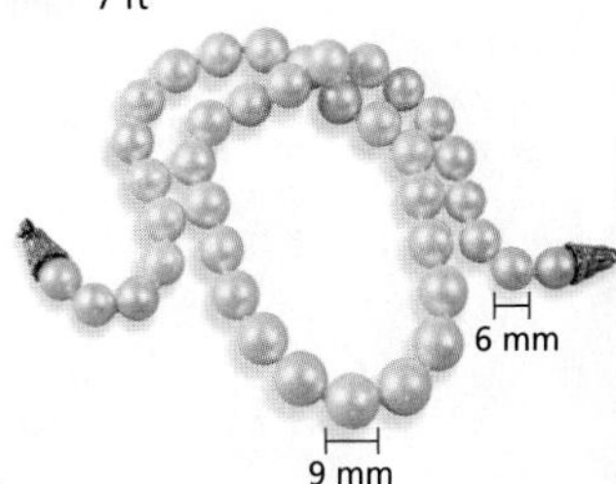

Find each measurement. Give your answers in terms of π.

17. the surface area of the sphere $S = 1764\pi \text{ in}^2$

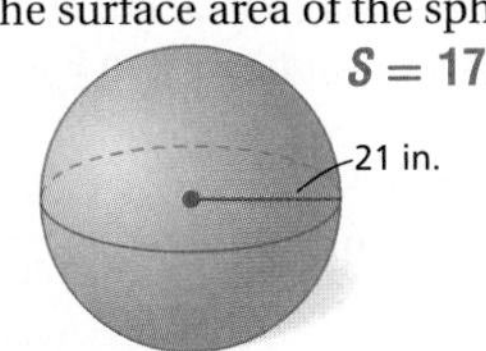

18. the surface area of the sphere $S = 324\pi \text{ in}^2$

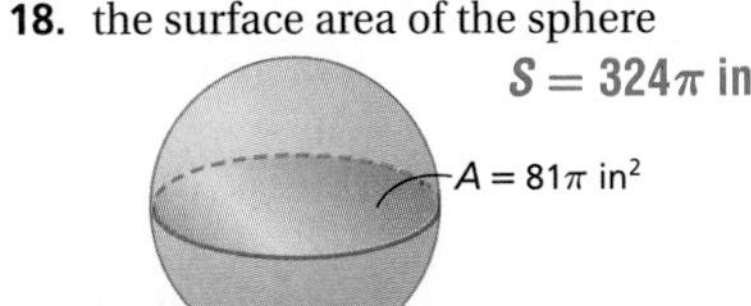

19. the volume of a sphere with surface area $625\pi \text{ m}^2$ $V = \frac{15{,}625\pi}{6} \text{ m}^3$

Describe the effect of each change on the given measurement of the figure.

20. surface area
The dimensions are multiplied by $\frac{1}{5}$.
1.2 ft
The surface area is multiplied by $\frac{1}{25}$.

21. volume
The dimensions are multiplied by 6.

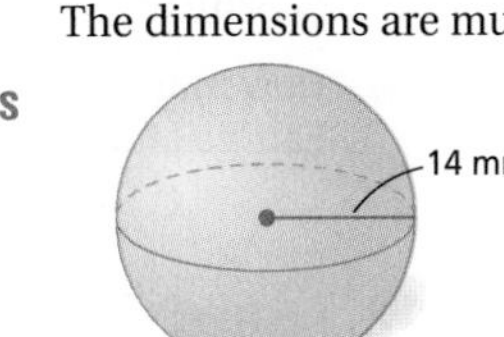

The volume is multiplied by 216.

Find the surface area and volume of each composite figure.

22.

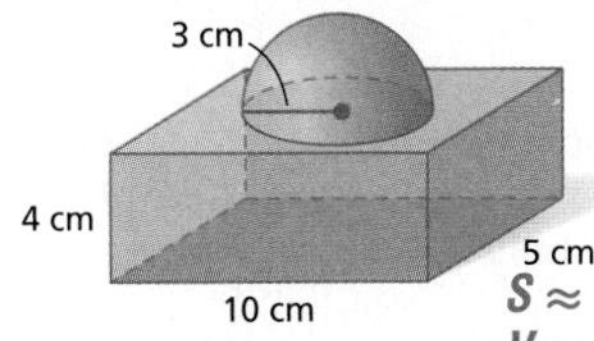

$S \approx 248.3 \text{ cm}^2$; $V \approx 256.5 \text{ cm}^3$

23.

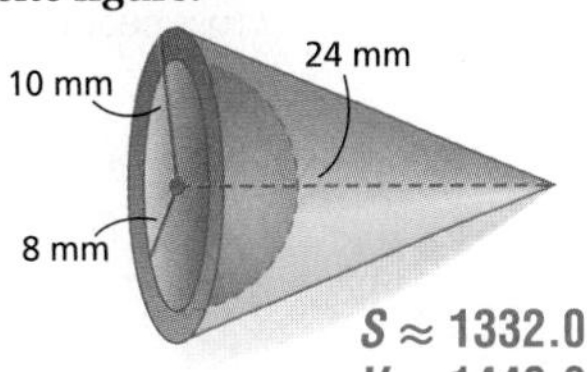

$S \approx 1332.0 \text{ mm}^2$; $V \approx 1440.9 \text{ mm}^3$

24. Find the radius of a hemisphere with a volume of $144\pi \text{ cm}^3$. $r = 6 \text{ cm}$

25. Find the circumference of a sphere with a surface area of $60\pi \text{ in}^2$. $C = 2\pi\sqrt{15} \text{ in.}$

26. Find the volume of a sphere with a circumference of 36π ft. $V = 7776\pi \text{ ft}^3$

27. Find the surface area and volume of a sphere centered at $(0, 0, 0)$ that passes through the point $(2, 3, 6)$. $S = 196\pi \text{ units}^2$; $V = \frac{1372\pi}{3} \text{ units}^3$

28. **Estimation** A bead is formed by drilling a cylindrical hole with a 2 mm diameter through a sphere with an 8 mm diameter. Estimate the surface area and volume of the bead.
Possible answer: $S \approx 245 \text{ mm}^2$; $V \approx 243 \text{ mm}^3$

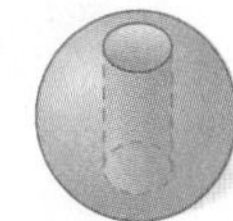

COMMON ERROR ALERT

In **Exercise 27,** some students may try to use only one of the coordinates of the point $(2, 3, 6)$ to find the radius. Remind them that the radius of a sphere is the distance between the center and any point on the sphere. This should help them realize that they need to use the Distance Formula in three dimensions to calculate the radius of the sphere.

10-8 PRACTICE C

1. A sphere has radius r. Draw a composite figure made up of a square prism (not a cube) and a square pyramid that has the same volume as the sphere.
Possible answer: r; πr; πr

2. Find the surface area of the composite figure you drew in Exercise 1.
Possible answer: $S = 4\pi r^2 + r^2 + r^2\sqrt{4\pi^2 + 1}$

3. Consider a composite figure made up of a cylinder and a cone that has the same volume as a sphere with radius r. Find the figure's surface area. $S = 3\pi r^2 + \pi r^2\sqrt{2}$

Use the figure for Exercises 4–6. The figure shows a hollow, sealed container with some water inside.

3 in.; 15 in.

4. There is just enough water in the container to exactly fill the hemisphere. The container is held so that the point of the cone is down and the altitude of the cone is exactly vertical. Find the height of the water in the cone. Round to the nearest tenth. $h \approx 11.1$ in.

5. Suppose the amount of water in the container is exactly enough to fill the cone. The container is held so that the hemisphere is down and the altitude of the cone is exactly vertical. Find the height of the water in the container. Round to the nearest tenth. $h \approx 6.9$ in.

6. Find the height of the cone with the same radius if the container were made so that the water would exactly fill either the hemisphere or the cone. $h = 6$ in.

7. A sphere has center (0, 0, 0). Its surface passes through the point (x, y, z). Find the sphere's surface area and volume.
$S = 4\pi(x^2 + y^2 + z^2)$; $V = \frac{4}{3}\pi(x^2 + y^2 + z^2)^{\frac{3}{2}}$

Use the figure for Exercises 8–10. The figure shows a can of three tennis balls. The can is just large enough so that the tennis balls will fit inside with the lid on. The diameter of each tennis ball is 2.5 in. Give exact fraction answers.

8. Find the total volume of the can. $V = \frac{375\pi}{32} \text{ in}^3$

9. Find the volume of empty space inside the can. $V = \frac{125\pi}{32} \text{ in}^3$

10. Tell what percent of the can is occupied by the tennis balls. $66\frac{2}{3}\%$

Teaching Tip **Social Studies Link** For **Exercise 34,** show students the longitude lines, or *meridians,* on a globe. The Prime Meridian passes through Greenwich, England, and is the 0° longitude line. It serves a role similar to zero on a number line or the origin on a coordinate plane.

Exercise 41 involves finding the volumes of a spherical juice container. This exercise prepares students for the Multi-Step Test Prep on page 724.

Sports Find the unknown dimensions of the ball for each sport.

	Sport	Ball	Diameter	Circumference	Surface Area	Volume
29.	Golf		1.68 in.	5.28 in.	8.87 in^2	2.48 in^3
30.	Cricket		2.86 in.	9 in.	25.78 in^2	12.31 in^3
31.	Tennis		2.5 in.	7.85 in.	19.63 in^2	8.18 in^3
32.	Petanque		74 mm	232.48 mm	17,203.36 mm^2	212,174.79 mm^3

LINK **Marine Biology**

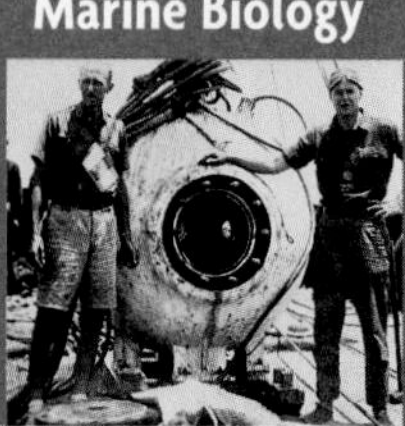

In 1934, the bathysphere reached a record depth of 3028 feet. The pressure on the hull was about half a ton per square inch.

33. **Marine Biology** The *bathysphere* was an early version of a submarine, invented in the 1930s. The inside diameter of the bathysphere was 54 inches, and the steel used to make the sphere was 1.5 inches thick. It had three 8-inch diameter windows. Estimate the volume of steel used to make the bathysphere. **Possible answer: 14,293 in^3**

34. **Geography** Earth's radius is approximately 4000 mi. About two-thirds of Earth's surface is covered by water. Estimate the land area on Earth. **67,000,000 mi^2**

Astronomy Use the table for Exercises 35–38.

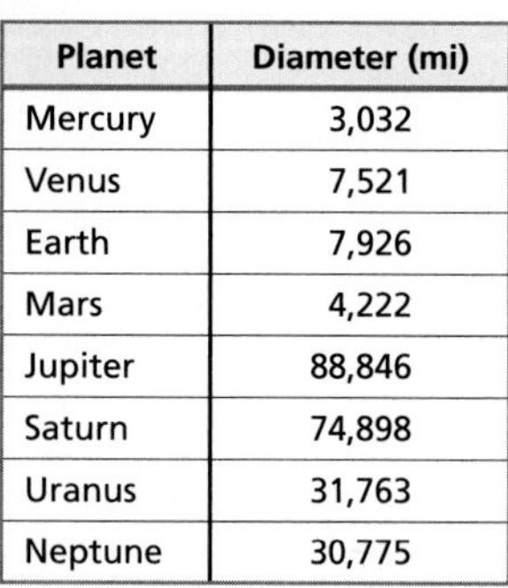

Planet	Diameter (mi)
Mercury	3,032
Venus	7,521
Earth	7,926
Mars	4,222
Jupiter	88,846
Saturn	74,898
Uranus	31,763
Neptune	30,775

35. How many times as great is the volume of Jupiter as the volume of Earth? **about 1408 times as great**

36. The sum of the volumes of Venus and Mars is about equal to the volume of which planet? **Earth**

37. Which is greater, the sum of the surface areas of Uranus and Neptune or the surface area of Saturn? **The surface area of Saturn is greater.**

38. How many times as great is the surface area of Earth as the surface area of Mars? **about 4 times as great**

39. **Critical Thinking** In the figure, the hemisphere and the cylinder both have radius and height r. Prove that the shaded cross sections have equal areas.

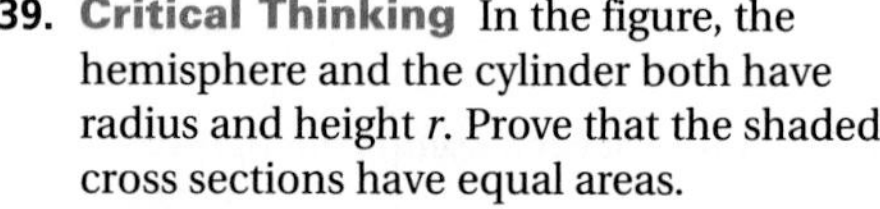

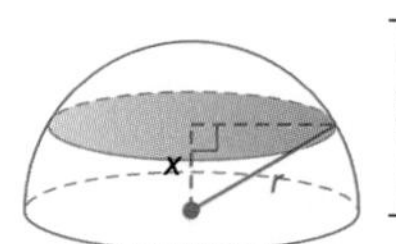

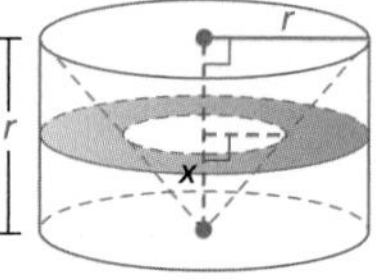

39. The cross section of the hemisphere is a circle with radius $\sqrt{r^2 - x^2}$, so its area is $A = \pi(r^2 - x^2)$. The cross section of the cylinder with the cone removed has an outer radius of r and an inner radius of x, so the area is $A = \pi r^2 - \pi x^2 = \pi(r^2 - x^2)$.

40. **Write About It** Suppose a sphere and a cube have equal surface areas. Using r for the radius of the sphere and s for the side of a cube, write an equation to show the relationship between r and s. $s = 2r \cdot \sqrt{\frac{\pi}{6}}$, or $s \approx 1.4r$

MULTI-STEP TEST PREP

41. This problem will prepare you for the Multi-Step Test Prep on page 724.

A company sells orange juice in spherical containers that look like oranges. Each container has a surface area of approximately 50.3 in^2.

a. What is the volume of the container? Round to the nearest tenth. **33.5 in^3**

b. The company decides to increase the radius of the container by 10%. What is the volume of the new container? **44.6 in^3**

720 Chapter 10 Spatial Reasoning

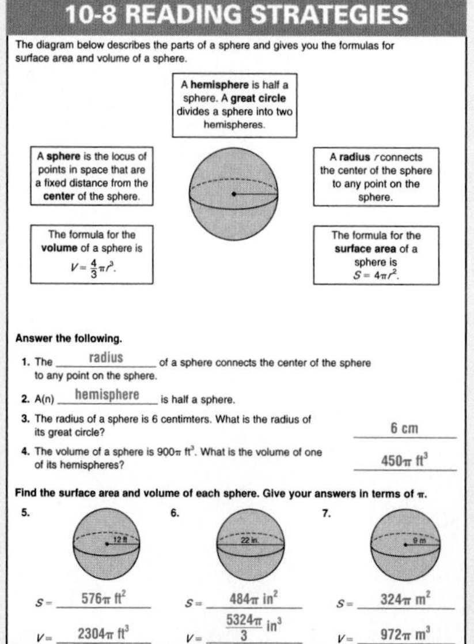

10-8 READING STRATEGIES

The diagram below describes the parts of a sphere and gives you the formulas for surface area and volume of a sphere.

A **hemisphere** is half a sphere. A **great circle** divides a sphere into two hemispheres.

A **sphere** is the locus of points in space that are a fixed distance from the **center** of the sphere.

A **radius** r connects the center of the sphere to any point on the sphere.

The formula for the **volume** of a sphere is $V = \frac{4}{3}\pi r^3$.

The formula for the **surface area** of a sphere is $S = 4\pi r^2$.

Answer the following.

1. The radius of a sphere connects the center of the sphere to any point on the sphere.
2. A(n) hemisphere is half a sphere.
3. The radius of a sphere is 6 centimters. What is the radius of its great circle? 6 cm
4. The volume of a sphere is 900π ft^3. What is the volume of one of its hemispheres? 450π ft^3

Find the surface area and volume of each sphere. Give your answers in terms of π.

5. (12 ft) $S =$ 576π ft^2; $V =$ 2304π ft^3
6. (22 in.) $S =$ 484π in^2; $V = \frac{5324\pi}{3}$ in^3
7. (9 m) $S =$ 324π m^2; $V =$ 972π m^3

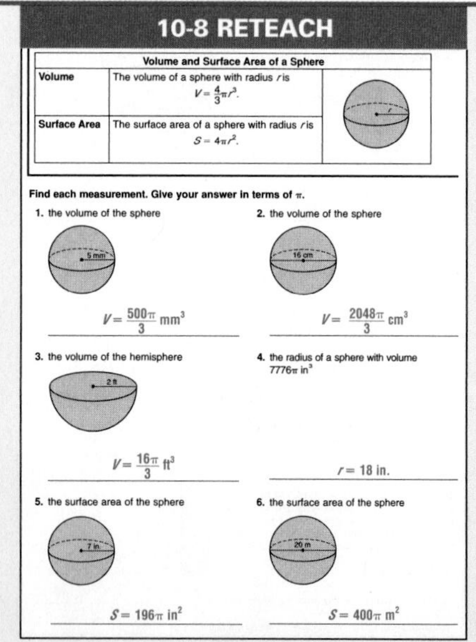

10-8 RETEACH

Volume and Surface Area of a Sphere		
Volume	The volume of a sphere with radius r is $V = \frac{4}{3}\pi r^3$.	
Surface Area	The surface area of a sphere with radius r is $S = 4\pi r^2$.	

Find each measurement. Give your answer in terms of π.

1. the volume of the sphere (5 mm) $V = \frac{500\pi}{3}$ mm^3
2. the volume of the sphere (16 cm) $V = \frac{2048\pi}{3}$ cm^3
3. the volume of the hemisphere (2 ft) $V = \frac{16\pi}{3}$ ft^3
4. the radius of a sphere with volume 7776π in^3 $r =$ 18 in.
5. the surface area of the sphere (7 in.) $S =$ 196π in^2
6. the surface area of the sphere (20 m) $S =$ 400π m^2

TEST PREP

42. A sphere with radius 8 cm is inscribed in a cube. Find the ratio of the volume of the cube to the volume of the sphere.
 (A) $2:\frac{1}{3}\pi$ (B) $2:3\pi$ (C) $1:\frac{4}{3}\pi$ (D) $1:\frac{2}{3}\pi$

43. What is the surface area of a sphere with volume $10\frac{2}{3}\pi$ in^3?
 (F) 8π in^2 (G) $10\frac{2}{3}\pi$ in^2 (H) 16π in^2 (J) 32π in^2

44. Which expression represents the volume of the composite figure formed by a hemisphere with radius r and a cube with side length $2r$?

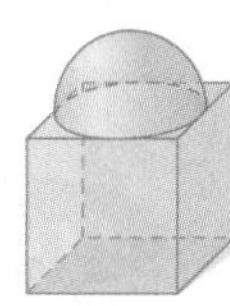

 (A) $r^3\left(\frac{2}{3}\pi + 8\right)$ (C) $2r^2(2\pi + 12)$
 (B) $\frac{4}{3}\pi r^3 + 2r^3$ (D) $\frac{4}{3}\pi r^3 + 8r^3$

CHALLENGE AND EXTEND

46a. $r = \sqrt{\frac{S}{4\pi}} = \frac{\sqrt{S\pi}}{2\pi}$
b. $V = \frac{S\sqrt{S\pi}}{6\pi}$
c. The shape of the graph is similar to half of a parabola.
47. The volume of the cylinder is 1.5 times the volume of the sphere.

45. **Food** The top of a gumball machine is an 18 in. sphere. The machine holds a maximum of 3300 gumballs, which leaves about 43% of the space in the machine empty. Estimate the diameter of each gumball. 1 in.

46. The surface area of a sphere can be used to determine its volume.
 a. Solve the surface area formula of a sphere to get an expression for r in terms of S.
 b. Substitute your result from part **a** into the volume formula to find the volume V of a sphere in terms of its surface area S.
 c. Graph the relationship between volume and surface area with S on the horizontal axis and V on the vertical axis. What shape is the graph?

Use the diagram of a sphere inscribed in a cylinder for Exercises 47 and 48.

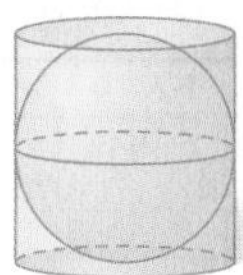

47. What is the relationship between the volume of the sphere and the volume of the cylinder?
48. What is the relationship between the surface area of the sphere and the lateral area of the cylinder?

SPIRAL REVIEW

48. The surface area of the sphere is equal to the lateral area of the cylinder.
53. The volume is multiplied by $\frac{27}{64}$.
54. The volume is multiplied by 25.

Write an equation that describes the functional relationship for each set of ordered pairs. *(Previous course)*

49. $\{(0, 1), (1, 2), (-1, 2), (2, 5), (-2, 5)\}$ $y = x^2 + 1$
50. $\{(-1, 9), (0, 10), (1, 11), (2, 12), (3, 13)\}$ $y = x + 10$

Find the shaded area. Round to the nearest tenth, if necessary. *(Lesson 9-3)*

51. 4 in. 4.6 in^2
52. 10 cm, 5 cm, 6 cm, 4 cm, 1 cm 48 cm^2

Describe the effect on the volume that results from the given change. *(Lesson 10-6)*

53. The side lengths of a cube are multiplied by $\frac{3}{4}$.
54. The height and the base area of a prism are multiplied by 5.

10-8 PROBLEM SOLVING

1. A globe has a volume of 288π in^3. What is the surface area of the globe? Give your answer in terms of π.
 144π in^2

2. Eight bocce balls are in a box 18 inches long, 9 inches wide, and 4.5 inches deep. If each ball has a diameter of 4.5 inches, what is the volume of the space around the balls? Round to the nearest tenth.
 4.5 in. 9 in. 18 in.
 347.3 in^3

Use the table for Exercises 3 and 4.

Ganymede, one of Jupiter's moons, is the largest moon in the solar system.

Moon	Diameter
Earth's moon	2160 mi
Ganymede	3280 mi

3. Approximately how many times as great as the volume of Earth's moon is the volume of Ganymede?
 about 3.5 times

4. Approximately how many times as great is the surface area of Ganymede than the surface area of Earth's moon?
 about 2.3 times

Choose the best answer.

5. What is the volume of a sphere with a great circle that has an area of 225π cm^2?
 A 300π cm^3 C 2500π cm^3
 B 900π cm^3 (D) 4500π cm^3

6. A hemisphere has a surface area of 972π cm^2. If the radius is multiplied by $\frac{1}{3}$, what will be the surface area of the new hemisphere?
 F 36π cm^2 H 162π cm^2
 (G) 108π cm^2 J 324π cm^2

7. Which expression represents the volume of the composite figure formed by the hemisphere and cone?
 6 mm 25 mm
 A 52π mm^3 C 276π mm^3
 (B) 156π mm^3 D 288π mm^3

8. Which best represents the surface area of the composite figure?
 3 in. 10 in. 6 in.
 F 129π in^2 (H) 201π in^2
 G 138π in^2 J 210π in^2

Answers

46c.

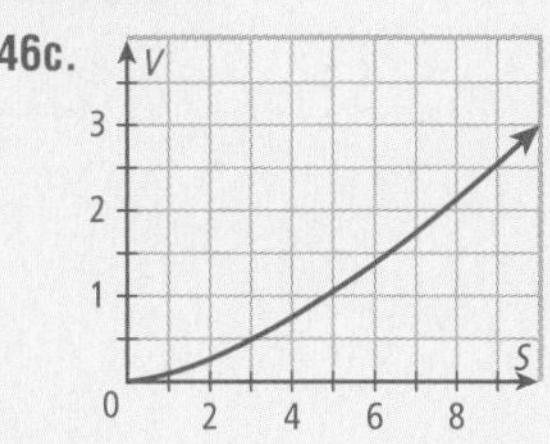

TEST PREP DOCTOR In **Exercise 42,** the cube must have a greater volume than the sphere because the sphere is inscribed in the cube. This eliminates all answer choices except **A.**

Journal

Have students explain how to find the volume of a hemisphere when given the surface area.

ALTERNATIVE ASSESSMENT

Supply the students with small balls or other spherical objects, string, scissors, and rulers. Have students measure the circumferences of their spheres. Then ask them to calculate the radius, diameter, surface area, and volume of each.

Power Presentations with PowerPoint®

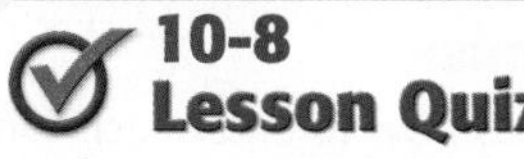

10-8 Lesson Quiz

Find each measurement. Give your answers in terms of π.

1. the volume and surface area of the sphere

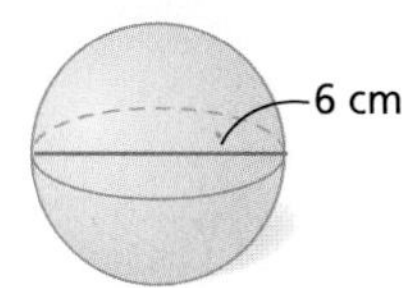

 $V = 36\pi$ cm^3; $S = 36\pi$ cm^2

2. the volume and surface area of a sphere with great circle area 36π in^2 $V = 288\pi$ in^3; $S = 144\pi$ in^2

3. the volume and surface area of the hemisphere

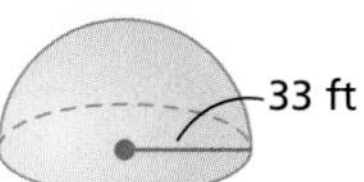

 $V = 23{,}958\pi$ ft^3; $S = 3267\pi$ ft^2

4. A sphere has radius 4. If the radius is multiplied by 5, describe what happens to the surface area. The surface area is multiplied by 25.

5. Find the volume and surface area of the composite figure. Give your answer in terms of π.

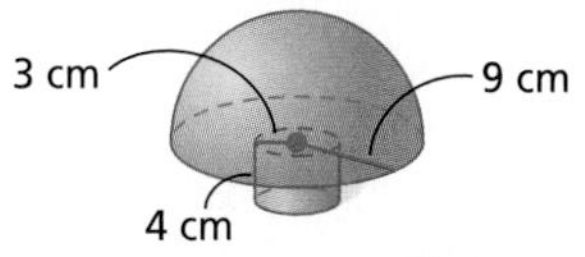

 $V = 522\pi$ ft^3; $S = 267\pi$ ft^2

Also available on transparency

Organizer

Use with Lesson 10-8

Pacing:
Traditional 1 day
Block $\frac{1}{2}$ day

Objective: Use spreadsheet software to compare surface areas and volumes.

Materials: spreadsheet software

Online Edition

Countdown Week 24

Resources

Technology Lab Activities
10-8 Lab Recording Sheet

Teach

Discuss

Discuss how to enter each formula into the spreadsheet. Also discuss any observations and conclusions students have made after they have completed each lab activity.

State Resources

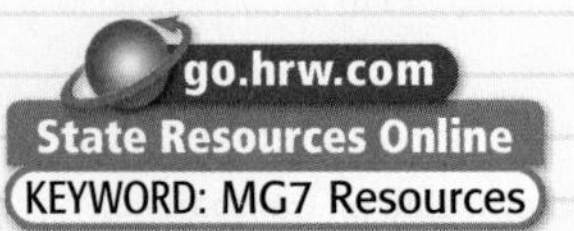

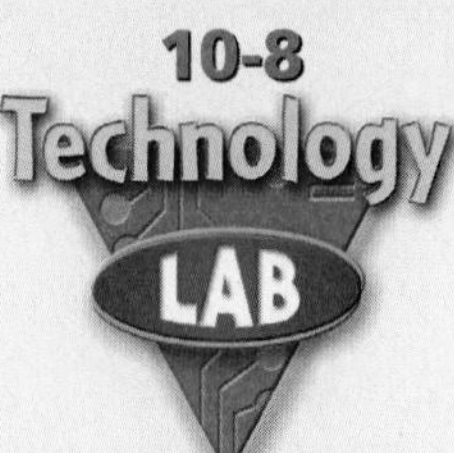

Use with Lesson 10-8

Compare Surface Areas and Volumes

In some situations you may need to find the minimum surface area for a given volume. In others you may need to find the maximum volume for a given surface area. Spreadsheet software can help you analyze these problems.

Activity 1

1. Create a spreadsheet to compare surface areas and volumes of rectangular prisms. Create columns for length L, width W, height H, surface area SA, volume V, and ratio of surface area to volume SA/V. In the column for SA, use the formula shown.

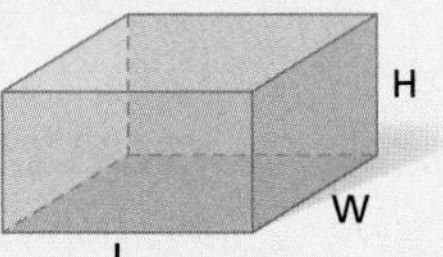

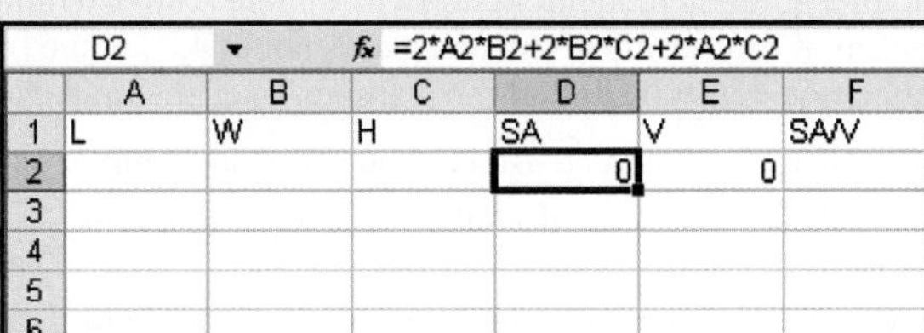

D2 ▾ fx =2*A2*B2+2*B2*C2+2*A2*C2

	A	B	C	D	E	F
1	L	W	H	SA	V	SA/V
2				0	0	
3						
4						
5						
6						

2. Create a formula for the V column and a formula for the SA/V column.

3. Fill in the measurements L = 8, W = 2, and H = 4 for the first rectangular prism.

F2 ▾ fx =D2/E2

	A	B	C	D	E	F
1	L	W	H	SA	V	SA/V
2	8	2	4	112	64	1.75
3						
4						
5						
6						

4. Choose several values for L, W, and H to create rectangular prisms that each have the same volume as the first one. Which has the least surface area? Sketch the prism and describe its shape in words. (Is it tall or short, skinny or wide, flat or cubical?) Make a conjecture about what type of shape has the minimum surface area for a given volume.
Check students' work. The rectangular prism with the minimum surface area for a given volume is a cube. Students may not have an exact cube in their spreadsheet, but their smallest surface area will be the surface area of the prism that is most cubical.

1. The cylinder with the minimum surface area will be the one in which the height and the diameter are closest to each other.

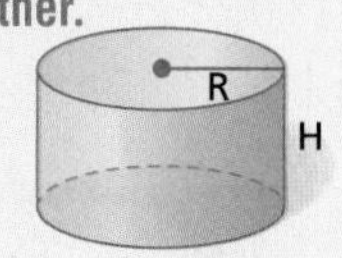

1. Repeat Activity 1 for cylinders. Create columns for radius R, height H, surface area SA, volume V, and ratio of surface area to volume SA/V. What shape cylinder has the minimum surface area for a given volume? (*Hint:* To use π in a formula, input "PI( )" into your spreadsheet.)
2. Investigate packages such as cereal boxes and soda cans. Do the manufacturers appear to be using shapes with the minimum surface areas for their volume? What other factors might influence a company's choice of packaging?
Possible answer: No; a package such as a cereal box might be designed to have a large surface area so that it stands out more on the shelf.

Activity 2

1 Create a new spreadsheet with the same column headings used in Activity 1. Fill in the measurements L = 8, W = 2, and H = 4 for the first rectangular prism. To create a new prism with the same surface area, choose new values for L and W, and use the formula shown to calculate H.

C3 | fx =(112/2-A3*B3)/(A3+B3)

	A	B	C	D	E	F
1	L	W	H	SA	V	SA/V
2	8	2	4	112	64	1.75
3	6	4	3.2	112		
4						
5						
6						

2 Choose several more values for L and W, and calculate H so that SA = 112. Examine the V and SA/V columns. Which prism has the greatest volume? Sketch the prism and describe it in words. Make a conjecture about what type of shape has the maximum volume for a given surface area.

2. The rectangular prism with the maximum volume for a given surface area is a cube. Students may not have an exact cube in their spreadsheet, but their greatest volume will be the volume of the prism that is most cubical.

Try This

3. Repeat Activity 2 for cylinders. Create columns for radius R, height H, surface area SA, volume V, and the ratio of surface area to volume SA/V. What shape cylinder has the maximum volume for a given surface area?
4. Solve the formula SA = 2LW + 2LH + 2WH for H. Use your result to explain the formula that was used to find H in Activity 2.
5. If a rectangular prism, a pyramid, a cylinder, a cone, and a sphere all had the same volume, which do you think would have the least surface area? Which would have the greatest surface area? Explain.
6. Use a spreadsheet to analyze what happens to the ratio of surface area to volume of a rectangular prism when the dimensions are doubled. Explain how you set up the spreadsheet and describe your results.

3. The cylinder with the maximum volume will have a height equal to its diameter.

Close

Key Concept

For many applications of three-dimensional figures, certain shapes will produce the minimum or maximum surface area for a given volume. Spreadsheet software is a useful tool for comparing the surface areas and volumes of solids.

Students should determine that a cube is the rectangular prism with the minimum surface area for a given volume, and with the maximum volume for a given surface area.

Assessment

Journal Have students explain what they have learned about the surface areas and volumes of various solids and what types of shapes should be used to increase or decrease the surface area for a given volume.

Answers

4. The formula SA = 2LW + 2LH + 2WH becomes $H = \frac{\left(\frac{SA}{2} - LW\right)}{L + W}$ when solved for H.
5. A sphere will have the minimum surface area and a pyramid will have the maximum surface area for a given volume.
6. If the dimensions of a rectangular prism are doubled, surface area is multiplied by 4 and the volume is multiplied by 8. So the ratio of surface area to volume is multiplied by $\frac{4}{8} = \frac{1}{2}$. Set up a spreadsheet as in Activity 1. Enter values for L, W, and H in one row, and enter the values 2L, 2W, and 2H in the next row. Repeat for several values of L, W, and H.

Organizer

Objective: Assess students' ability to apply concepts and skills in Lessons 10-4 through 10-8 in a real-world format.

Online Edition

Resources

Geometry Assessments
www.mathtekstoolkit.org

For additional assessment activities, see www.utdanacenter.org.

Problem	Text Reference
1	Lesson 10-4
2	Lesson 10-6
3	Lesson 10-4
4	Lesson 10-6
5	Lessons 10-4, 10-6

Answers

5. Possible answer: I would recommend the cylinder because the ratio of surface area to volume is about 3 in^2 per oz, and the ratio of surface area to volume of the prism is about 3.8 in^2 per oz. Thus the cylinder costs less to produce per oz of volume.

State Resources

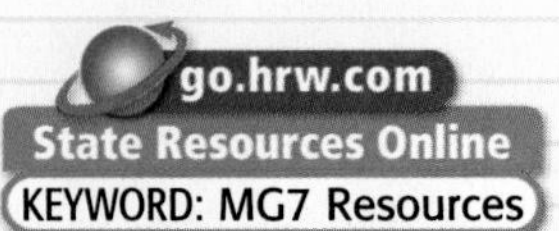

go.hrw.com
State Resources Online
KEYWORD: MG7 Resources

CHAPTER 10

MULTI-STEP TEST PREP

SECTION 10B

Surface Area and Volume

Juice for Fun You are in charge of designing containers for a new brand of juice. Your company wants you to compare several different container shapes. The container must be able to hold a 6-inch straw so that exactly 1 inch remains outside the container when the straw is inserted as far as possible.

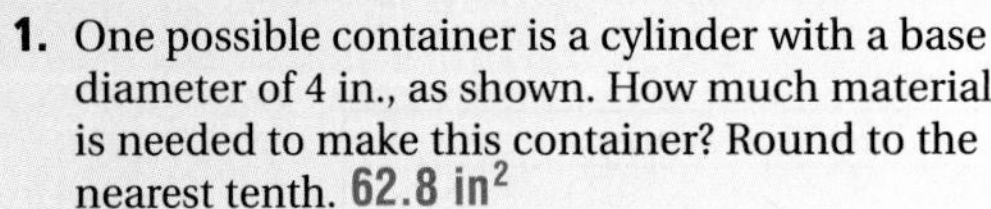

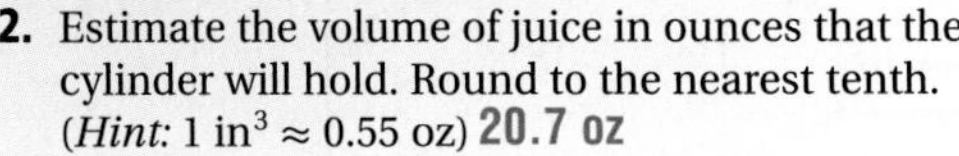

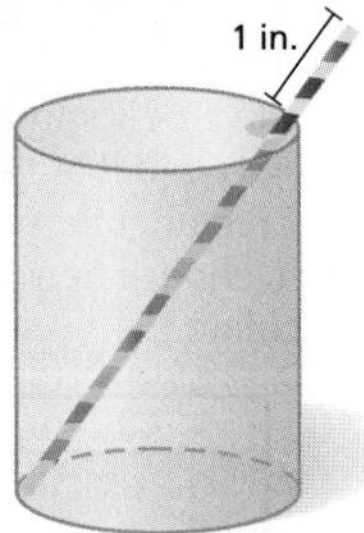

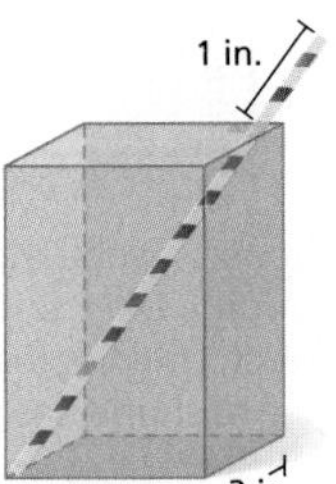

1. One possible container is a cylinder with a base diameter of 4 in., as shown. How much material is needed to make this container? Round to the nearest tenth. **62.8 in^2**
2. Estimate the volume of juice in ounces that the cylinder will hold. Round to the nearest tenth. (*Hint:* 1 in^3 ≈ 0.55 oz) **20.7 oz**
3. Another option is a square prism with a 3 in. by 3 in. base, as shown. How much material is needed to make this container? **49.7 in^2**
4. Estimate the volume of juice in ounces that the prism will hold. (*Hint:* 1 in^3 ≈ 0.55 oz) **13.1 oz**
5. Which container would you recommend to your company? Justify your answer.

INTERVENTION

Scaffolding Questions

1. How can you find the height of the cylinder? Pythag. Thm.
2. What formula can you use to find the volume of the container? $V = \pi r^2 h$
3. What is the length d of the diagonal of the base? $3\sqrt{2}$ in. How can you use d to find h? $d^2 + h^2 = 5^2$, so $h = \sqrt{7}$ in.
4. What formula can you use to find the volume of the container? $V = \ell wh$
5. Is the container that uses the least material necessarily the best choice? Explain. No; it holds less juice per square inch of packaging material.

Extension

Another container is a right cone with slant height 5 in. and base diameter 4 in. How much juice will the container hold? 19.2 in^3

READY TO GO ON?

CHAPTER 10

SECTION 10B

Quiz for Lessons 10-4 Through 10-8

10-4 Surface Area of Prisms and Cylinders

Find the surface area of each figure. Round to the nearest tenth, if necessary.

1. 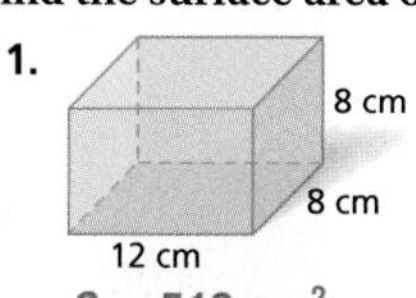

$S = 512\text{ cm}^2$

2. 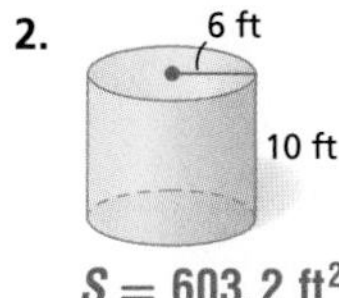

$S = 603.2\text{ ft}^2$

3. 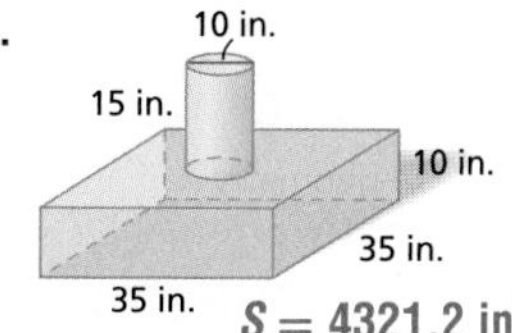

$S = 4321.2\text{ in}^2$

4. The dimensions of a 12 mm by 8 mm by 24 mm right rectangular prism are multiplied by $\frac{3}{4}$. Describe the effect on the surface area. The surface area is multiplied by $\frac{9}{16}$.

10-5 Surface Area of Pyramids and Cones

Find the surface area of each figure. Round to the nearest tenth, if necessary. 5. $S \approx 1457.4\text{ yd}^2$ 6. $S \approx 1508.0\text{ in}^2$ 7. $S \approx 1885.0\text{ ft}^2$

5. a regular pentagonal pyramid with base edge length 18 yd and slant height 20 yd
6. a right cone with diameter 30 in. and height 8 in.
7. the composite figure formed by two cones

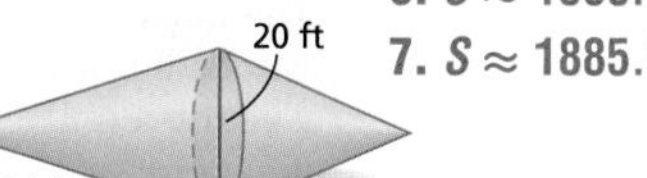

10-6 Volume of Prisms and Cylinders

Find the volume of each figure. Round to the nearest tenth, if necessary.

8. a regular hexagonal prism with base area 23 in^2 and height 9 in. $V = 207\text{ in}^3$
9. a cylinder with radius 8 yd and height 14 yd $V = 2814.9\text{ yd}^3$
10. A brick patio measures 10 ft by 12 ft by 4 in. Find the volume of the bricks. If the density of brick is 130 pounds per cubic foot, what is the weight of the patio in pounds? 40 ft^3; 5200 lb
11. The dimensions of a cylinder with diameter 2 ft and height 1 ft are doubled. Describe the effect on the volume. The volume is multiplied by 8.

10-7 Volume of Pyramids and Cones

Find the volume of each figure. Round to the nearest tenth, if necessary.

12.

$V = 2412.7\text{ ft}^3$

13. 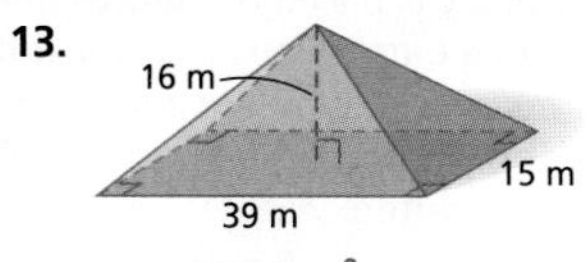

$V = 3120\text{ m}^3$

14. 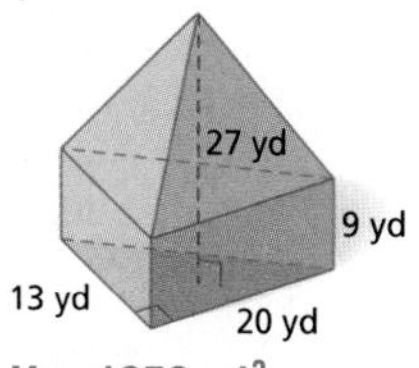

$V = 1950\text{ yd}^3$

10-8 Spheres

15. $S = 400\pi\text{ in}^2$; $V = \frac{4000}{3}\pi\text{ in}^3$

Find the surface area and volume of each figure.

15. a sphere with diameter 20 in.
16. a hemisphere with radius 12 in. $S = 432\pi\text{ in}^2$; $V = 1152\pi\text{ in}^3$
17. A baseball has a diameter of approximately 3 in., and a softball has a diameter of approximately 5 in. About how many times as great is the volume of a softball as the volume of a baseball? about 4.6 times as great

READY TO GO ON?

SECTION 10B

Organizer

Objective: Assess students' mastery of concepts and skills in Lessons 10-4 through 10-8.

Resources

 ***Assessment Resources***
Section 10B Quiz

Teacher One Stop™
Test & Practice Generator

INTERVENTION

Resources

 ***Ready to Go On? Intervention and Enrichment* Worksheets**

 ***Ready to Go On?* CD-ROM**

 ***Ready to Go On?* Online**

READY TO GO ON?

Diagnose and Prescribe

Ready to Go On? Intervention	*Ready to Go On? Intervention,* Section 10B		
	Worksheets	CD-ROM	Online
Lesson 10-4	10-4 Intervention	Activity 10-4	Diagnose and Prescribe Online
Lesson 10-5	10-5 Intervention	Activity 10-5	
Lesson 10-6	10-6 Intervention	Activity 10-6	
Lesson 10-7	10-7 Intervention	Activity 10-7	
Lesson 10-8	10-8 Intervention	Activity 10-8	

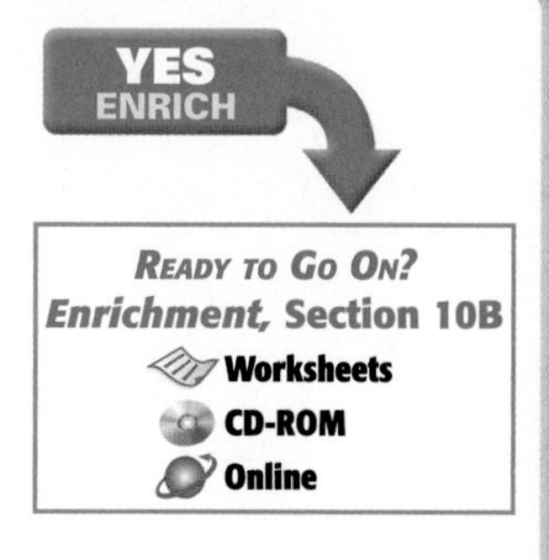

CHAPTER 10 Organizer

Pacing: Traditional 1 day
Block $\frac{1}{2}$ day

Objective: Understand spherical geometry as an example of non-Euclidean geometry.

Using the Extension

This topic extends the study of spheres in Lesson 10-8 and also ties in some topics from earlier in the course: the Parallel Postulate, the Triangle Sum Theorem, and the formula for the area of a triangle. This is a brief introduction to a non-Euclidean geometry that is based on figures in a sphere.

Multiple Representations Use a globe to help students understand that two points used to name a line cannot be exactly opposite each other on the sphere. Explain the Spherical Geometry Parallel Postulate to students and use various points on the globe to help them remember the postulate.

State Resources

EXTENSION Spherical Geometry

Objective
Understand spherical geometry as an example of non-Euclidean geometry.

Vocabulary
non-Euclidean geometry
spherical geometry

In Lesson 10-1, you learned that a cross section is the intersection of a three-dimensional object with a plane. When a plane intersects a sphere, the cross section is a circle. If the plane passes through the center of a sphere, the cross section is a great circle.

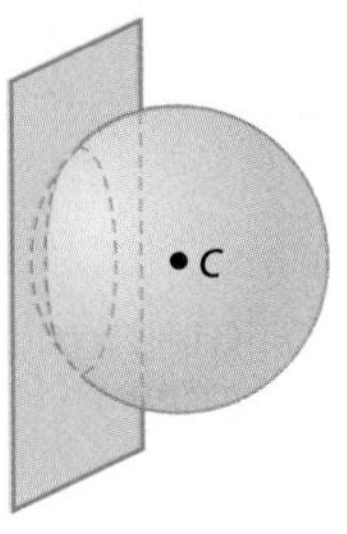

Plane intersects sphere in a circle.

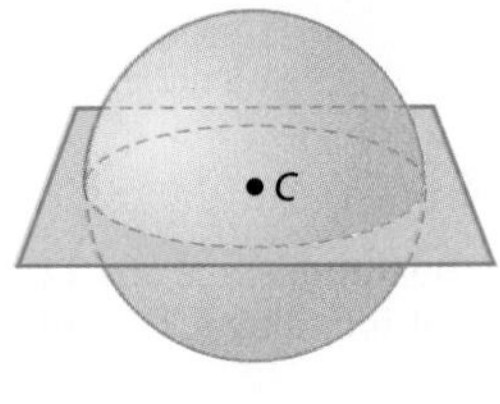

Plane passes through center of sphere, creating a great circle.

The Earth is a sphere, so what does it mean to walk a "straight line" on a sphere when all lines are curved? If you walk straight from point *A* to point *B*, you are walking along a great circle. Lines and line segments on a sphere all lie along great circles.

Caution!
The two points used to name a line cannot be exactly opposite each other on the sphere. In Example 1, $\overleftrightarrow{AB}$ could refer to more than one line.

EXAMPLE 1 Classifying Figures in Spherical Geometry

Name a line, a segment, and a triangle on the sphere.

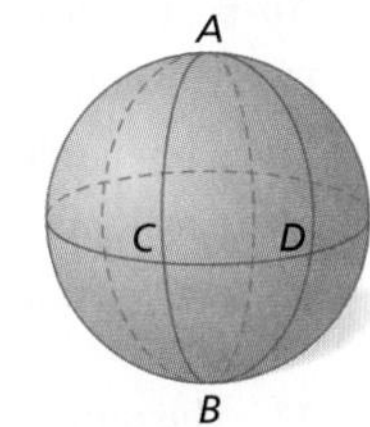

$\overleftrightarrow{AC}$ is a line.

$\overline{AC}$ is a segment.

$\triangle ACD$ is a triangle.

1. Name another line, segment, and triangle on the sphere above.
$\overleftrightarrow{AD}$; $\overline{AD}$; $\triangle BCD$

Euclidean geometry is based on figures in a plane. The figures you identified in Example 1 are on a curved surface. **Non-Euclidean geometry** describes figures on curved surfaces. In a non-Euclidean geometry system, the Parallel Postulate is not true. In spherical geometry, there are no parallel lines because all straight lines (great circles) intersect.

Know it! Note

Spherical Geometry Parallel Postulate

Through a point not on a line, there is no line parallel to a given line.

1 Introduce

Motivate

Use a plastic-foam ball and string to demonstrate that the shortest path between two points on a sphere is a part of a great circle, securing the ends of the string with pins. Scientists have found that some migrating birds fly in a very close approximation to a great circle and thus expend the least amount of energy.

2 Teach

Guided Instruction

Review the Parallel Postulate, the Triangle Sum Theorem, and the area formula for a triangle. Explain that the postulates and theorems they have learned so far are all in *Euclidean* geometry. Spherical geometry is a non-Euclidean geometry with different postulates and theorems. In the spherical triangle area formula, point out that $m\angle A + m\angle B + m\angle C - 180°$ is always positive because the sum of the angle measures of a spherical triangle is always greater than 180°.

In Lesson 4-2, you used the properties of parallel lines to prove that the sum of the interior angles of a triangle is 180°. Because the parallel postulate for spherical geometry is different, the sum of the angles of a triangle also follows a different rule.

In Example 1, the lines $\overleftrightarrow{AC}$ and $\overleftrightarrow{AD}$ are both perpendicular to $\overleftrightarrow{CD}$. This means that $\triangle ACD$ has two right angles. So the sum of its angle measures must be greater than 180°.

Imagine cutting an orange in half and then cutting each half in quarters using two perpendicular cuts. Each of the resulting triangles has three right angles.

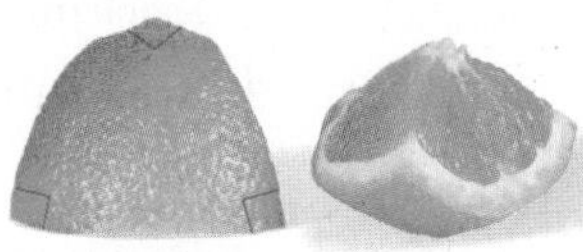

Spherical Triangle Sum Theorem

The sum of the angle measures of a spherical triangle is greater than 180°.

The area of a spherical triangle is part of the surface area of the sphere. For the piece of orange on page 726, the area is $\frac{1}{8}$ of the surface area of the orange, or $\frac{1}{8}(4\pi r^2) = \frac{\pi r^2}{2}$. If you know the radius of a sphere and the measure of each angle, you can find the area of the triangle.

Area of a Spherical Triangle

The area of spherical $\triangle ABC$ on a sphere with radius r is

$A = \frac{\pi r^2}{180°}(m\angle A + m\angle B + m\angle C - 180°)$.

EXAMPLE 2 Finding the Area of Spherical Triangles

Find the area of each spherical triangle. Round to the nearest tenth, if necessary.

A $\triangle ABC$

$$A = \frac{\pi r^2}{180°}(m\angle A + m\angle B + m\angle C - 180°)$$

$$A = \frac{\pi(14)^2}{180°}(100 + 106 + 114 - 180) \approx 152.4 \text{ cm}^2$$

B **$\triangle DEF$ on Earth's surface with $m\angle D = 75°$, $m\angle E = 80°$, and $m\angle F = 30°$. (*Hint:* average radius of Earth = 3959 miles)**

$$A = \frac{\pi r^2}{180°}(m\angle D + m\angle E + m\angle F - 180°)$$

$$= \frac{\pi(3959)^2}{180°}(75 + 80 + 30 - 180) \approx 1{,}367{,}786.7 \text{ mi}^2$$

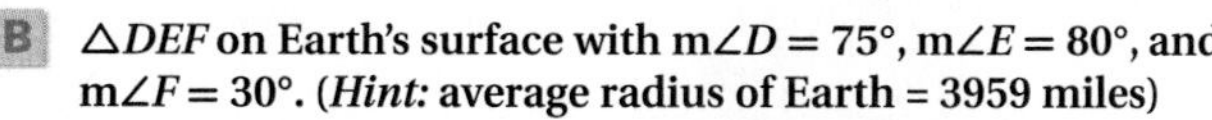

CHECK IT OUT! **2.** Find the area of $\triangle KLM$ on a sphere with diameter 20 ft, where $m\angle K = 90°$, $m\angle L = 90°$, and $m\angle M = 30°$. Round to the nearest tenth. $A \approx 52.4 \text{ ft}^2$

Additional Examples

Example 1

Name a line, a segment, and a triangle on the sphere.

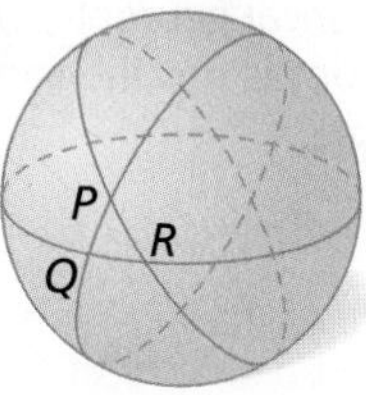

$\overleftrightarrow{PQ}$ is a line; $\overline{PQ}$ is a segment; $\triangle PQR$ is a triangle.

Example 2

Find the area of each spherical triangle. Round to the nearest tenth, if necessary.

A. $\triangle MNP$

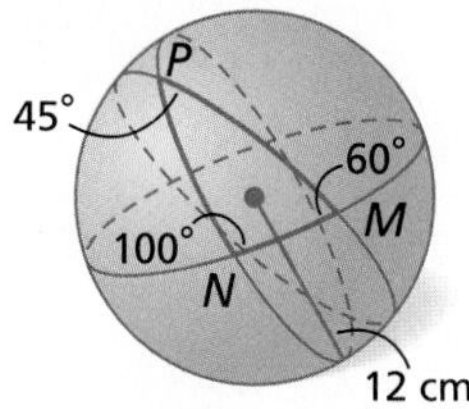

62.8 cm²

B. $\triangle QRS$ on Earth with $m\angle Q = 78°$, $m\angle R = 92°$, and $m\angle S = 45°$. 9,574,506.9 mi²

INTERVENTION
Questioning Strategies

EXAMPLE 1

- How is a great circle on a sphere like a circumference of a circle?

EXAMPLE 2

- If two spherical triangles have the same angle measures, do they always have the same area? Explain.

3 Close

Summarize

Relate spherical geometry to Euclidean geometry. Compare the Spherical Geometry Parallel Postulate, the Spherical Triangle Sum Theorem, and the spherical triangle area formula to the Euclidean Parallel Postulate, Triangle Sum Theorem, and triangle area formula.

Critical Thinking In Euclidean geometry, if you know the measures of two angles of a triangle, you can determine the measure of the third angle. Remind students that this is not the case in spherical geometry because the angle sum is not the same for every triangle.

7a. $\sqrt{R^2 - d^2}$

b. Circles formed by planes that intersect a sphere at the same distance from the center will have equal radii.

c. No; the cross section will be a single point.

EXTENSION

Exercises

Use the figure for Exercises 1–3.

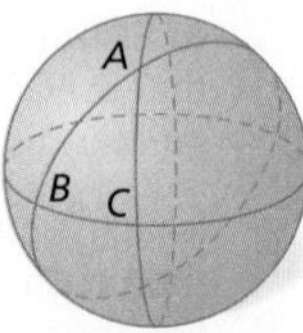

1. Name all lines on the sphere. $\overleftrightarrow{AB}$, $\overleftrightarrow{AC}$, and $\overleftrightarrow{BC}$
2. Name three segments on the sphere. $\overline{AB}$, $\overline{AC}$, and $\overline{BC}$
3. Name a triangle on the sphere. $\triangle ABC$

Determine whether each figure is a line in spherical geometry.

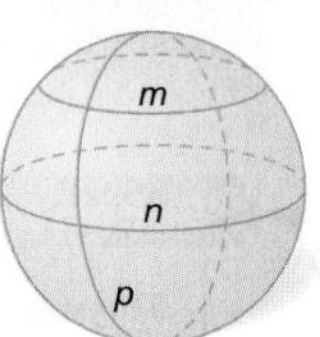

4. m **no**
5. n **yes**
6. p **yes**

7. A plane intersects a sphere with a radius of R. The plane is a distance d from the center C of the sphere.
   a. Use the Pythagorean theorem to find the radius of the circle.
   b. If two planes intersect the sphere at the same distance from the center, what will be true of the radii of the two circles formed?
   c. What happens if $d = R$? Will the cross section still be a circle?

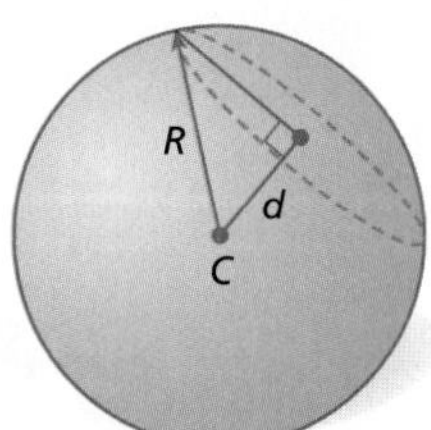

Find the area of each spherical triangle.

8. $A \approx 301.6 \text{ in}^2$

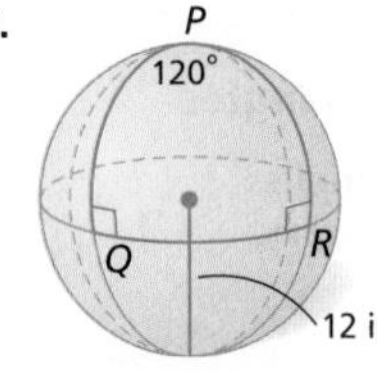

9. $A \approx 84.7 \text{ m}^2$

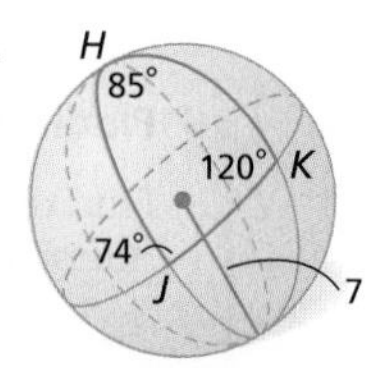

10. $A \approx 145.7 \text{ ft}^2$

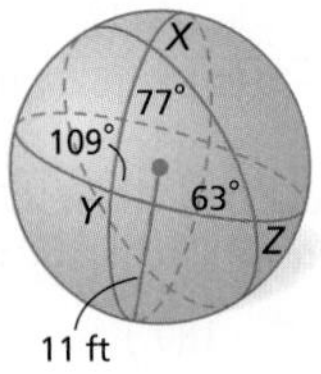

11. $A \approx 52.4 \text{ cm}^2$

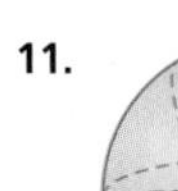

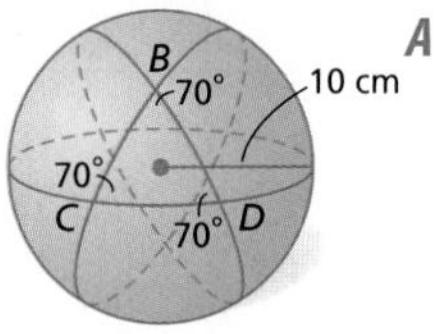

12. $\triangle ABC$ on the Moon's surface with $m\angle A = 35°$, $m\angle B = 48°$, and $m\angle C = 100°$ (*Hint:* average radius of the Moon $\approx$ 1079 miles) $A \approx 60{,}959.5 \text{ mi}^2$

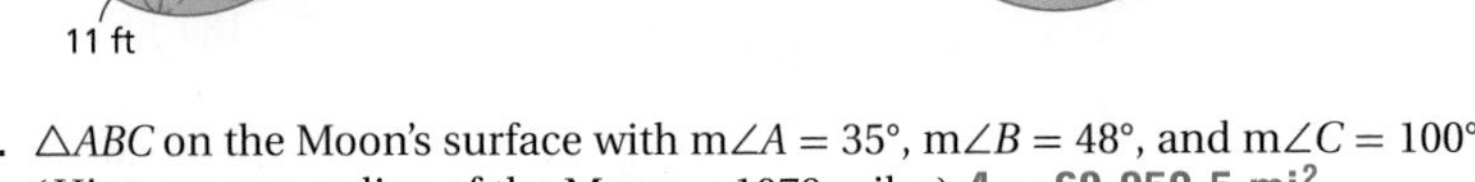

13. $\triangle RST$ on a scale model of Earth with radius 6 m, $m\angle R = 80°$, $m\angle S = 130°$, and $m\angle T = 150°$ $A \approx 113.1 \text{ m}^2$

14a. $m\angle A + m\angle B + m\angle C < 270°$

b. area $< \frac{\pi r^2}{2}$

c. The area of an acute spherical triangle is less than $\frac{1}{8}$ of the surface area of the sphere.

16. $\frac{1}{2}$ the length of a great circle

17. $\frac{1}{4}$ the length of a great circle

14. $\triangle ABC$ is an acute triangle.

a. Write an inequality for the sum of the angle measures of $\triangle ABC$, based on the fact that $\triangle ABC$ is acute.

b. Use your result from part **a** to write an inequality for the area of $\triangle ABC$.

c. Use your result from part **b** to compare the area of an acute spherical triangle to the total surface area of the sphere.

15. Draw a quadrilateral on a sphere. Include one diagonal in your drawing. Use the sum of the angle measures of the quadrilateral to write an inequality. $m\angle A + m\angle B + m\angle C + m\angle D > 360°$

Geography **Compare each length to the length of a great circle on Earth.**

16. the distance between the North Pole and the South Pole

17. the distance between the North Pole and any point on the equator

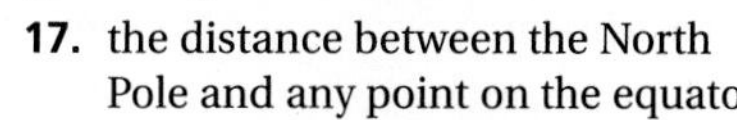

18. **Geography** If the area of a triangle on Earth's surface is 100,000 mi^2, what is the sum of its angle measures? (*Hint:* average radius of Earth ≈ 3959 miles) **180.4°**

19. **Sports** Describe the curves on the basketball that are lines in spherical geometry.

20. **Navigation** Pilots navigating long distances often travel along the lines of spherical geometry. Using a globe and string, determine the shortest route for a plane traveling from Washington, D.C., to London, England. What do you notice?

21. **Write About It** Can a spherical triangle be right and obtuse at the same time? Explain.

22. **Write About It** A 2-gon is a polygon with two edges. Draw two lines on a sphere. How many 2-gons are formed? What can you say about the positions of the vertices of the 2-gons on the sphere?

23. **Challenge** Another type of non-Euclidean geometry, called *hyperbolic geometry*, is defined on a surface that is curved like the bell of a trumpet. What do you think is true about the sum of the angle measures of the triangle shown at right? Compare the sum of the angle measures of a triangle in Euclidean, spherical, and hyperbolic geometry.

In **Exercise 4,** students may identify *m* as a line because in geography, lines of latitude are called "lines" even though they are not lines in spherical geometry. Point out to students that lines in spherical geometry are defined as great circles because they represent the shortest path between two points. The only "line" of latitude that is also a great circle is the equator.

Answers

15. Possible drawing:

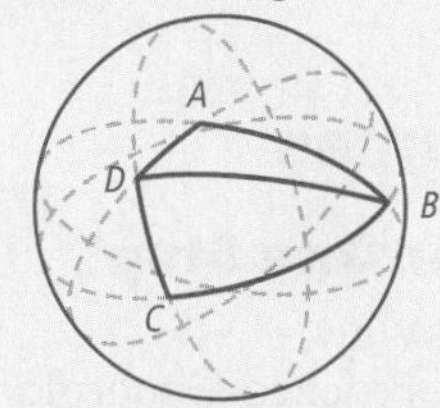

19. Possible answer: 2 curves are circles that go around the middle of the ball, and the other curve is a shape that intersects each of these circles in 2 places. The circles are lines in spherical geometry, and the other curve is not.

20. Possible answer: The route goes farther north than London, and then back south again.

21. Possible answer: Yes; a spherical triangle can have the angle measures 90°, 90°, and 100°. It is a right triangle because it contains a right angle, and it is also an obtuse triangle because it contains an obtuse angle.

22. Possible answer: The vertices of a 2-gon are exactly opposite each other on the sphere.

23. 42-gons are formed; possible answer: The sum of the angle measures is less than 180°. In Euclidean geometry, the sum of the angle measures is always equal to 180°, in spherical geometry it is always greater, and in hyperbolic geometry it is always less.

Organizer

Objective: Help students organize and review key concepts and skills in Chapter 10.

Online Edition
Multilingual Glossary

Countdown Week 24

Resources

Teacher One Stop™
PuzzleView
Test & Practice Generator

***Multilingual Glossary* Online**
go.hrw.com
KEYWORD: MG7 Glossary

Lesson Tutorial Videos
CD-ROM

Answers

1. oblique prism
2. cross section
3. cone; vertex: *M*; edges: none; base: ⊙*L*
4. rectangular pyramid; vertices: *N, P, Q, R, S*; edges: $\overline{NP}$, $\overline{NQ}$, $\overline{NR}$, $\overline{NS}$, $\overline{PQ}$, $\overline{QR}$, $\overline{RS}$, $\overline{SP}$; base: *PQRS*
5. cylinder
6. square pyramid

CHAPTER 10 Study Guide: Review

For a complete list of the postulates and theorems in this chapter, see p. PS12.

Vocabulary

- **altitude** 680
- **altitude of a cone** 690
- **altitude of a pyramid** 689
- **axis of a cone** 690
- **axis of a cylinder** 681
- **center of a sphere** 714
- **cone** 654
- **cross section** 656
- **cube** 654
- **cylinder** 654
- **edge** 654
- **face** 654
- **great circle** 714
- **hemisphere** 714
- **horizon** 662
- **isometric drawing** 662
- **lateral edge** 680
- **lateral face** 680
- **lateral surface** 681
- **net** 655
- **oblique cone** 690
- **oblique cylinder** 681
- **oblique prism** 680
- **orthographic drawing** 661
- **perspective drawing** 662
- **polyhedron** 670
- **prism** 654
- **pyramid** 654
- **radius of a sphere** 714
- **regular pyramid** 689
- **right cone** 690
- **right cylinder** 681
- **right prism** 680
- **slant height of a regular pyramid** 689
- **slant height of a right cone** 690
- **space** 671
- **sphere** 714
- **surface area** 680
- **vanishing point** 662
- **vertex** 654
- **vertex of a cone** 690
- **vertex of a pyramid** 689
- **volume** 697

Complete the sentences below with vocabulary words from the list above.

1. A(n) __?__ has at least one nonrectangular lateral face.
2. A name given to the intersection of a three-dimensional figure and a plane is __?__ .

10-1 Solid Geometry *(pp. 654–660)*

EXAMPLES

- **Classify the figure. Name the vertices, edges, and bases.**

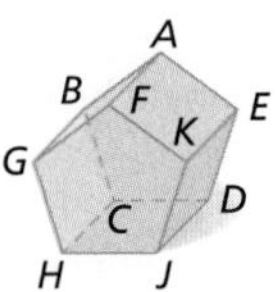

pentagonal prism

vertices: *A, B, C, D, E, F, G, H, J, K*

edges: $\overline{AB}$, $\overline{BC}$, $\overline{CD}$, $\overline{DE}$, $\overline{AE}$, $\overline{FG}$, $\overline{GH}$, $\overline{HJ}$, $\overline{JK}$, $\overline{KF}$, $\overline{AF}$, $\overline{EK}$, $\overline{DJ}$, $\overline{CH}$, $\overline{BG}$

bases: *ABCDE, FGHJK*

- **Describe the three-dimensional figure that can be made from the given net.**

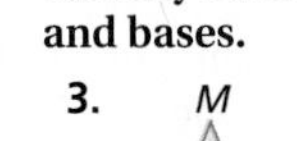

The net forms a rectangular prism.

EXERCISES

Classify each figure. Name the vertices, edges, and bases.

3. M, L

4.

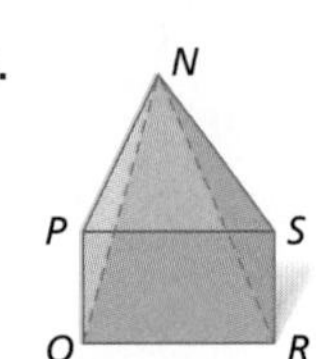

Describe the three-dimensional figure that can be made from the given net.

5.

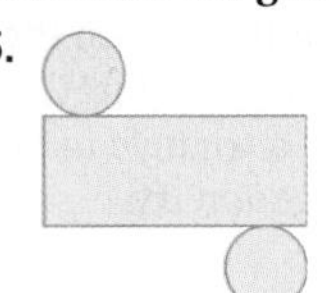

6.

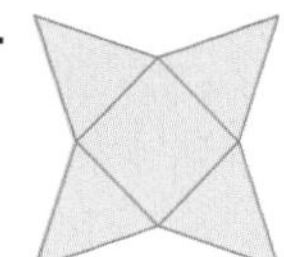

10-2 Representations of Three-Dimensional Figures *(pp. 661–668)*

EXAMPLES

■ **Draw all six orthographic views of the given object. Assume there are no hidden cubes.**

Top: Bottom:

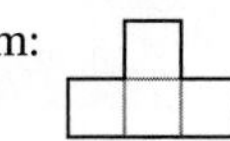

Front: Back:

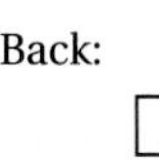

Left: Right:

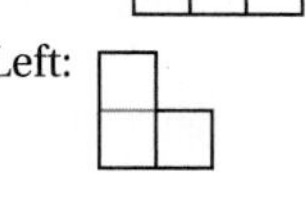

■ **Draw an isometric view of the given object. Assume there are no hidden cubes.**

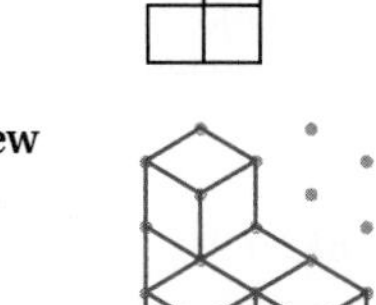

EXERCISES

Use the figure made of unit cubes for Exercises 7–10. Assume there are no hidden cubes.

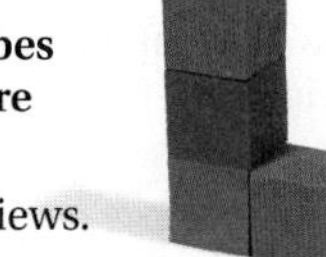

7. Draw all six orthographic views.

8. Draw an isometric view.

9. Draw the object in one-point perspective.

10. Draw the object in two-point perspective.

Determine whether each drawing represents the given object. Assume there are no hidden cubes.

11.

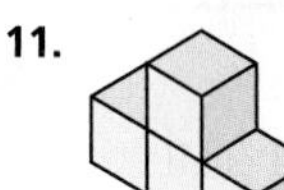

12.

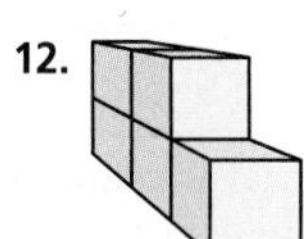

10-3 Formulas in Three Dimensions *(pp. 670–677)*

EXAMPLES

■ **Find the number of vertices, edges, and faces of the given polyhedron. Use your results to verify Euler's formula.**

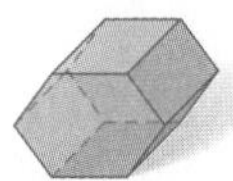

$V = 12, E = 18, F = 8$

$12 - 18 + 8 = 2$

■ **Find the distance between the points $(6, 3, 4)$ and $(2, 7, 9)$. Find the midpoint of the segment with the given endpoints. Round to the nearest tenth, if necessary.**

distance:

$$d = \sqrt{(2-6)^2 + (7-3)^2 + (9-4)^2}$$

$$= \sqrt{57} \approx 7.5$$

midpoint:

$$M\left(\frac{6+2}{2}, \frac{3+7}{2}, \frac{4+9}{2}\right)$$

$$M(4, 5, 6.5)$$

EXERCISES

Find the number of vertices, edges, and faces of each polyhedron. Use your results to verify Euler's formula.

13.

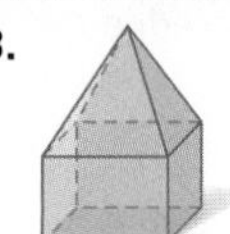

14.

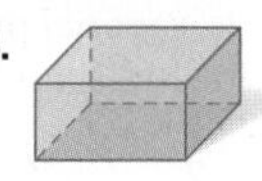

Find the distance between the given points. Find the midpoint of the segment with the given endpoints. Round to the nearest tenth, if necessary.

15. $(2, 6, 4)$ and $(7, 1, 1)$

16. $(0, 3, 0)$ and $(5, 7, 8)$

17. $(7, 2, 6)$ and $(9, 1, 5)$

18. $(6, 2, 8)$ and $(2, 7, 4)$

Answers

7.

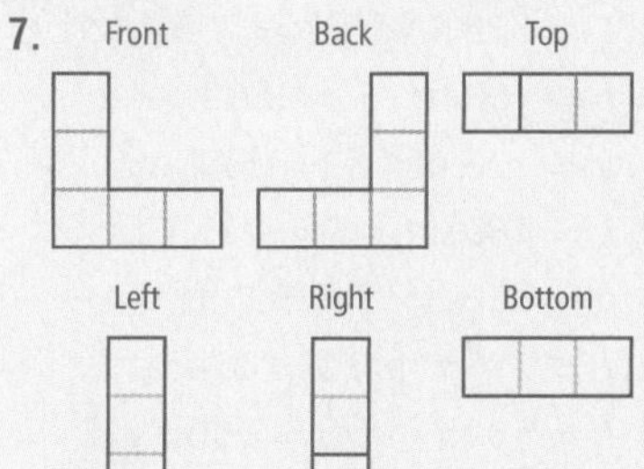

8.

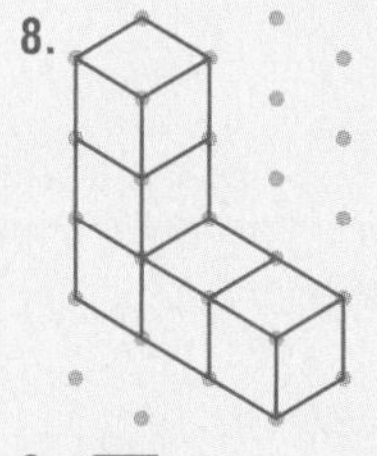

9.

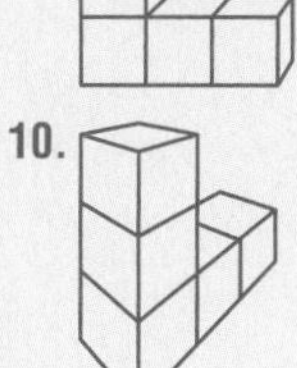

10.

11. yes

12. no

13. $V = 9$; $E = 16$; $F = 9$; $9 - 16 + 9 = 2$

14. $V = 8$; $E = 12$; $F = 6$; $8 - 12 + 6 = 2$

15. $d \approx 7.7$; $M(4.5, 3.5, 2.5)$

16. $d \approx 10.2$; $M(2.5, 5, 4)$

17. $d \approx 2.4$; $M(8, 1.5, 5.5)$

18. $d \approx 7.5$; $M(4, 4.5, 6)$

Study Guide: Review **731**

Answers

19. $L \approx 628.3\text{ yd}^2$; $S \approx 785.4\text{ yd}^2$
20. $L = 100\text{ ft}^2$; $S = 150\text{ ft}^2$
21. $L = 126\text{ m}^2$; $S \approx 157.2\text{ m}^2$
22. $L = 160\text{ cm}^2$; $S \approx 215.1\text{ cm}^2$
23. $L = 630\text{ ft}^2$; $S = 855\text{ ft}^2$
24. $L = 175\pi\text{ m}^2$; $S = 224\pi\text{ m}^2$
25. $L = 150\pi\text{ in}^2$; $S = 250\pi\text{ in}^2$
26. $S = 800\text{ ft}^2$
27. $S = 448\pi\text{ m}^2$
28. $V = 1080\text{ ft}^3$
29. $V \approx 1651.7\text{ cm}^3$

10-4 Surface Area of Prisms and Cylinders *(pp. 680–687)*

EXAMPLES

Find the lateral area and surface area of each right prism or cylinder.

- 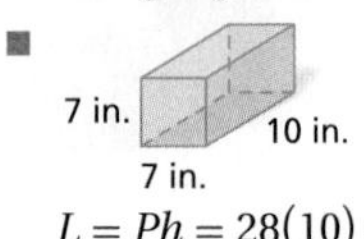

  $L = Ph = 28(10) = 280\text{ in}^2$

  $S = Ph + 2B = 280 + 2(49) = 378\text{ in}^2$

- a cylinder with radius 8 m and height 12 m

  $L = 2\pi rh = 2\pi(8)(12) = 192\pi \approx 603.2\text{ m}^2$

  $S = L + 2B = 192\pi + 2\pi(8)^2 = 320\pi$
  $\approx 1005.3\text{ m}^2$

EXERCISES

Find the lateral area and surface area of each right prism or cylinder. Round to the nearest tenth, if necessary.

19. 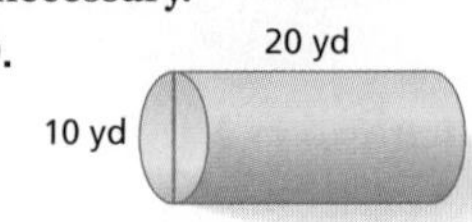

20. a cube with side length 5 ft
21. an equilateral triangular prism with height 7 m and base edge lengths 6 m
22. a regular pentagonal prism with height 8 cm and base edge length 4 cm

10-5 Surface Area of Pyramids and Cones *(pp. 689–696)*

EXAMPLES

Find the lateral area and surface area of each right pyramid or cone.

- 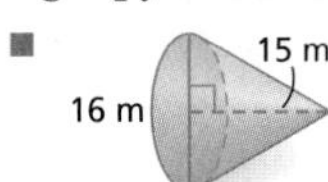

  The radius is 8 m, so the slant height is $\sqrt{8^2 + 15^2} = 17\text{ m}$.

  $L = \pi r\ell = \pi(8)(17) = 136\pi\text{ m}^2$

  $S = \pi r\ell + \pi r^2 = 136\pi + (8)^2\pi = 200\pi\text{ m}^2$

- a regular hexagonal pyramid with base edge length 8 in. and slant height 20 in.

  $L = \frac{1}{2}P\ell = \frac{1}{2}(48)(20) = 480\text{ in}^2$

  $S = L + B = 480 + \frac{1}{2}(4\sqrt{3})(48) \approx 646.3\text{ in}^2$

EXERCISES

Find the lateral area and surface area of each right pyramid or cone.

23. a square pyramid with side length 15 ft and slant height 21 ft
24. a cone with radius 7 m and height 24 m
25. a cone with diameter 20 in. and slant height 15 in.

Find the surface area of each composite figure.

26. 27.

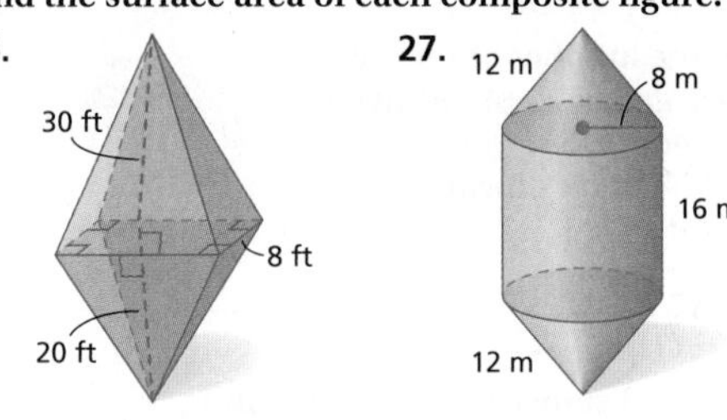

10-6 Volume of Prisms and Cylinders *(pp. 697–704)*

EXAMPLES

- **Find the volume of the prism.**

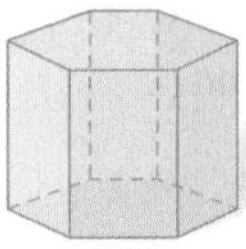

  12 cm

  8 cm

  $V = Bh = \left(\frac{1}{2}aP\right)h$

  $= \frac{1}{2}(4\sqrt{3})(48)(12)$

  $= 1152\sqrt{3} \approx 1995.3\text{ cm}^3$

EXERCISES

Find the volume of each prism.

28.

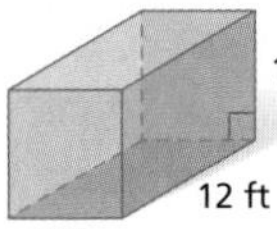

10 ft

12 ft

9 ft

29.

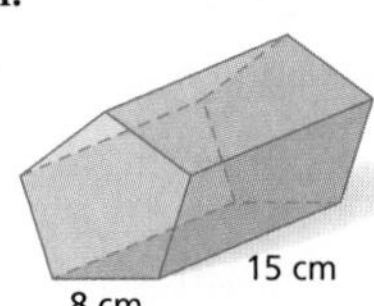

- **Find the volume of the cylinder.**

$V = \pi r^2 h = \pi(6)^2(14)$

$= 504\pi \approx 1583.4 \text{ ft}^3$

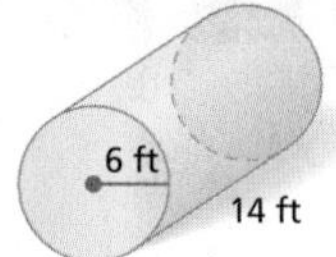

Find the volume of each cylinder.

30. **31.**

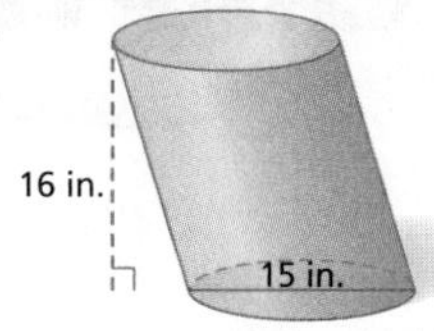

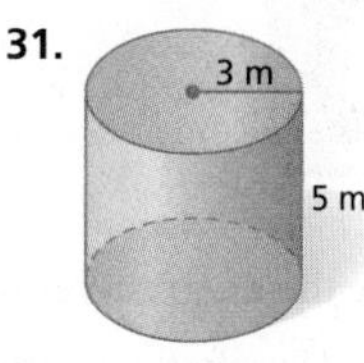

10-7 Volume of Pyramids and Cones *(pp. 705–712)*

EXAMPLES

- **Find the volume of the pyramid.**

$V = \frac{1}{3}Bh = \frac{1}{3}(8 \cdot 3)(14)$

$= 112 \text{ in}^3$

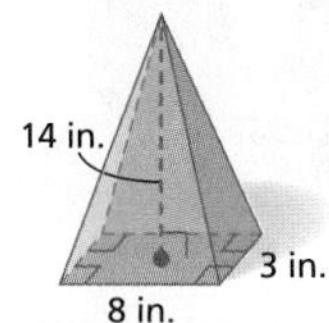

- **Find the volume of the cone.**

$V = \frac{1}{3}\pi r^2 h = \frac{1}{3}\pi(9)^2(16)$

$= 432\pi \text{ ft}^3 \approx 1357.2 \text{ ft}^3$

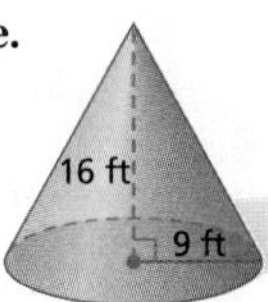

EXERCISES

Find the volume of each pyramid or cone.

32. a hexagonal pyramid with base area 42 m^2 and height 8 m

33. an equilateral triangular pyramid with base edge 3 cm and height 8 cm

34. a cone with diameter 12 cm and height 10 cm

35. a cone with base area $16\pi \text{ ft}^2$ and height 9 ft

Find the volume of each composite figure.

36.

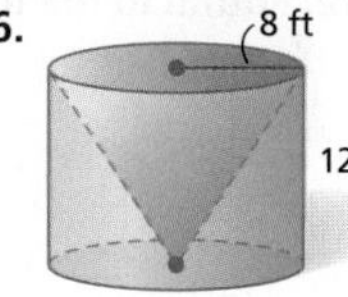

37.

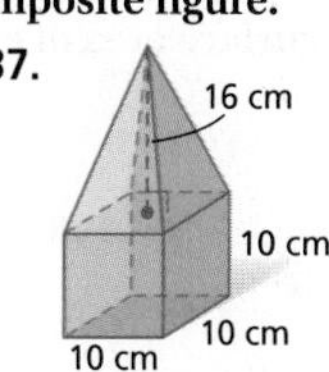

10-8 Spheres *(pp. 714–721)*

EXAMPLE

- **Find the volume and surface area of the sphere. Give your answers in terms of π.**

$V = \frac{4}{3}\pi r^3 = \frac{4}{3}\pi(9)^3 = 972\pi \text{ m}^2$

$S = 4\pi r^2 = 4\pi(9)^2 = 324\pi \text{ m}^2$

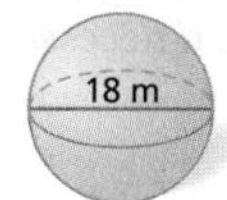

EXERCISES

Find each measurement. Give your answers in terms of π.

38. the volume of a sphere with surface area $100\pi \text{ m}^2$

39. the surface area of a sphere with volume $288\pi \text{ in}^3$

40. the diameter of a sphere with surface area $256\pi \text{ ft}^2$

Find the surface area and volume of each composite figure.

41.

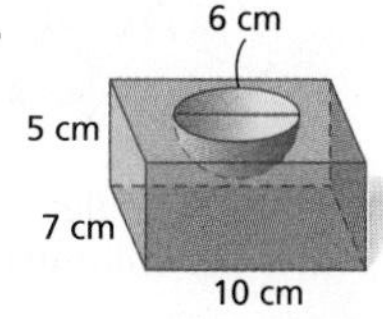

42.

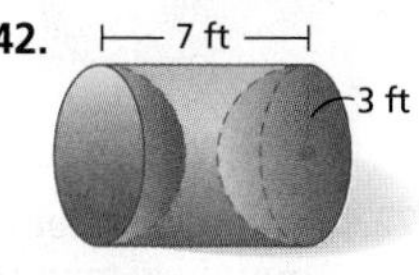

Answers

30. $V = 900\pi \text{ in}^3$
31. $V = 45\pi \text{ m}^3$
32. $V = 112 \text{ m}^3$
33. $V \approx 10.4 \text{ cm}^3$
34. $V = 120\pi \text{ cm}^3$
35. $V = 48\pi \text{ ft}^3$
36. $V = 512\pi \text{ ft}^3$
37. $V \approx 1533.3 \text{ cm}^3$
38. $V = \frac{500\pi}{3} \text{ m}^3$
39. $S = 144\pi \text{ in}^2$
40. $d = 16 \text{ ft}$
41. $S \approx 338.3 \text{ cm}^2$; $V \approx 293.5 \text{ cm}^3$
42. $S \approx 245.0 \text{ ft}^2$; $\approx 84.8 \text{ ft}^3$

Organizer

Objective: Assess students' mastery of concepts and skills in Chapter 10.

Online Edition

Resources

Assessment Resources

Chapter 10 Tests
- Free Response (Levels A, B, C)
- Multiple Choice (Levels A, B, C)
- Performance Assessment

Teacher One Stop™
Test & Practice Generator

State Resources

Use the diagram for Items 1–3.

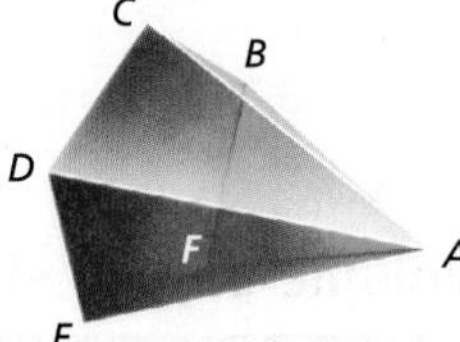

1. Classify the figure. Name the vertices, edges, and bases.
2. Describe a cross section made by a plane parallel to the base. **pentagon**
3. Find the number of vertices, edges, and faces of the polyhedron. Use your results to verify Euler's formula. $V = 6$; $E = 10$; $F = 6$; $6 - 10 + 6 = 2$

Use the figure made of unit cubes for Items 4–6. Assume there are no hidden cubes.

4. Draw all six orthographic views.
5. Draw an isometric view.
6. Draw the object in one-point perspective.

Find the distance between the given points. Find the midpoint of the segment with the given endpoints. Round to the nearest tenth, if necessary.

7. $(0, 0, 0)$ and $(5, 5, 5)$ $d \approx 8.7$ units; $M(2.5, 2.5, 2.5)$
8. $(6, 0, 9)$ and $(7, 1, 4)$ $d \approx 5.2$ units; $M(6.5, 0.5, 6.5)$
9. $(-1, 4, 3)$ and $(2, -5, 7)$ $d \approx 10.3$ units; $M(0.5, -0.5, 5)$

Find the surface area of each figure. Round to the nearest tenth, if necessary.

10. 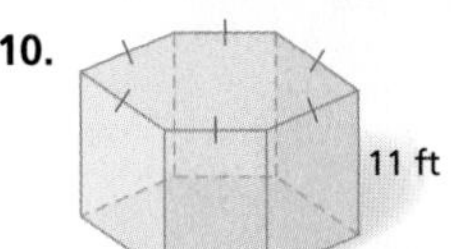

$S \approx 860.6\text{ ft}^2$

11. 
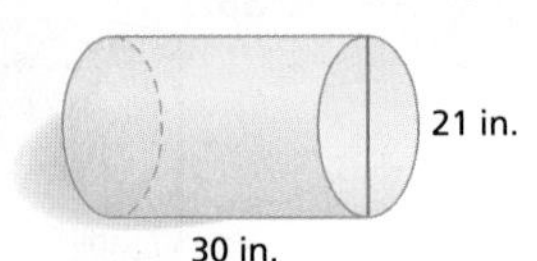

$S \approx 2671.9\text{ in}^2$

12. 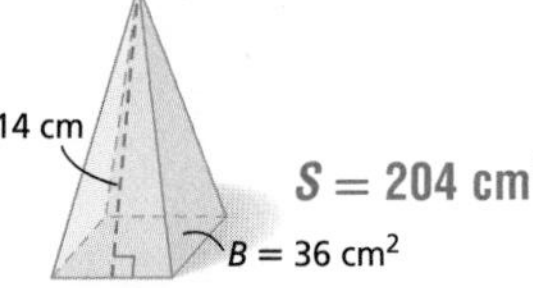

$S = 204\text{ cm}^2$

13. 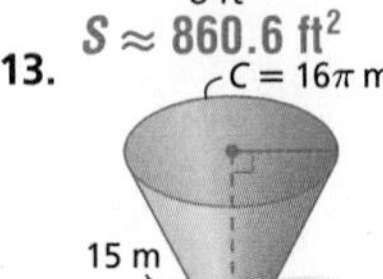

$S \approx 628.3\text{ m}^2$

14. 
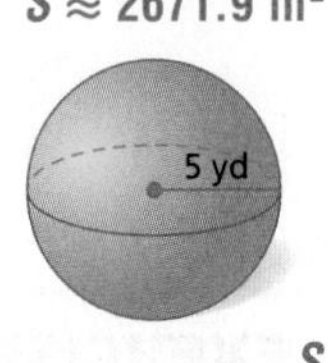

$S \approx 314.2\text{ yd}^2$

15. 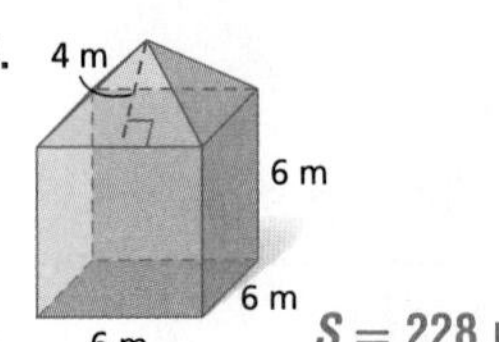

$S = 228\text{ m}^2$

Find the volume of each figure. Round to the nearest tenth, if necessary.

16. 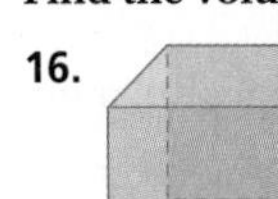

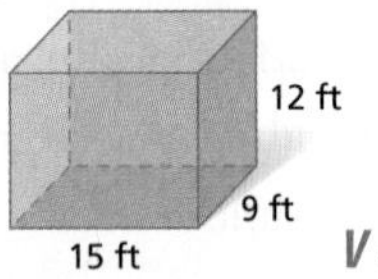

$V = 1620\text{ ft}^3$

17. 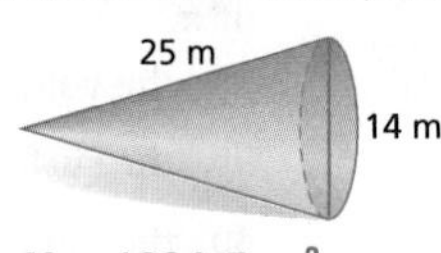

$V \approx 1231.5\text{ m}^3$

18. 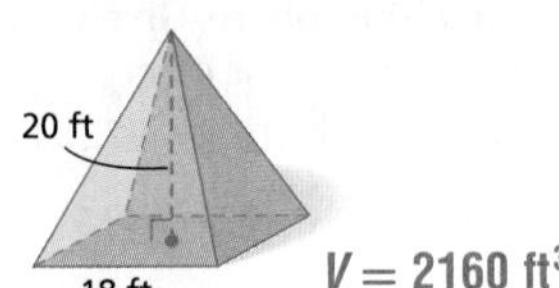

$V = 2160\text{ ft}^3$

19. 6 in.; 2 in.
$V \approx 56.5\text{ in}^3$

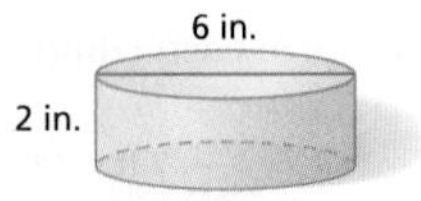

20. 7 cm; 4 cm; 5 cm
$V \approx 268.1\text{ cm}^3$

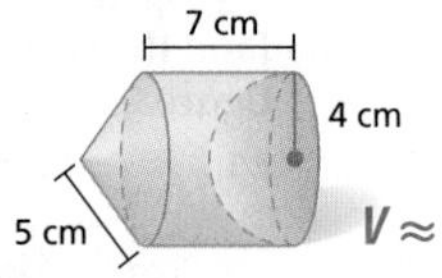

21. 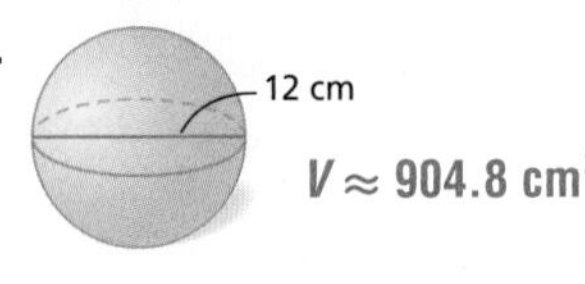

$V \approx 904.8\text{ cm}^3$

22. Earth's diameter is approximately 7930 miles. The Moon's diameter is approximately 2160 miles. About how many times as great is the volume of Earth as the volume of the Moon? **about 49.5 times as great**

Answers

1. pentagonal pyramid; vertices: *A*, *B*, *C*, *D*, *E*, *F*; edges: $\overline{AB}$, $\overline{AC}$, $\overline{AD}$, $\overline{AE}$, $\overline{AF}$, $\overline{BC}$, $\overline{CD}$, $\overline{DE}$, $\overline{EF}$, $\overline{FB}$; faces: $\triangle ABC$, $\triangle ACD$, $\triangle ADE$, $\triangle AEF$, $\triangle AFB$, pentagon *BCDEF*

4. 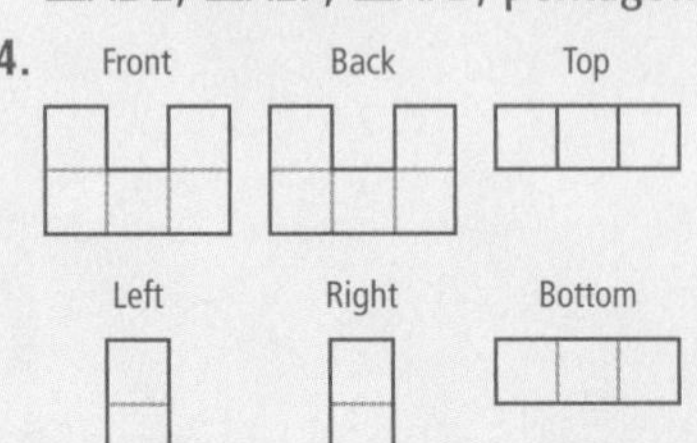

5. 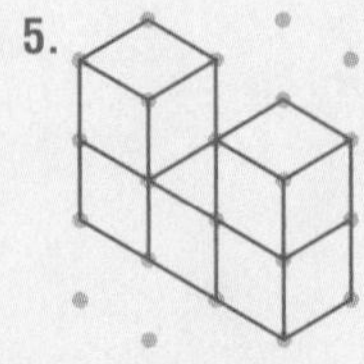

6. 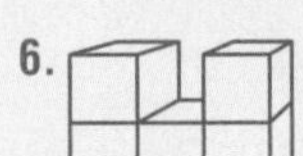

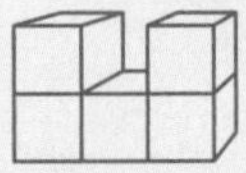

COLLEGE ENTRANCE EXAM PRACTICE

FOCUS ON SAT MATHEMATICS SUBJECT TEST

SAT Mathematics Subject Test results include scaled scores and percentiles. Your scaled score is a number from 200 to 800, calculated using a formula that varies from year to year. The percentile indicates the percentage of people who took the same test and scored lower than you did.

You may want to time yourself as you take this practice test. It should take you about 6 minutes to complete.

The questions are written so that you should not need to do any lengthy calculations. If you find yourself getting involved in a long calculation, think again about all of the information in the problem to see if you might have missed something helpful.

1. A line intersects a cube at two points, A and B. If each edge of the cube is 4 cm, what is the greatest possible distance between A and B?

(A) $2\sqrt{3}$ cm

(B) 4 cm

(C) $4\sqrt{2}$ cm

(D) $4\sqrt{3}$ cm (circled)

(E) $16\sqrt{3}$ cm

2. The lateral area of a right cylinder is 3 times the area of its base. What is the height h of the cylinder in terms of its radius r?

(A) $\frac{1}{2}r$

(B) $\frac{2}{3}r$

(C) $\frac{3}{2}r$ (circled)

(D) $3r$

(E) $3r^2$

3. What is the lateral area of a right cone with radius 6 ft and height 8 ft?

(A) 30π ft²

(B) 48π ft²

(C) 60π ft² (circled)

(D) 180π ft²

(E) 360π ft²

4. If triangle ABC is rotated about the x-axis, what is the volume of the resulting cone?

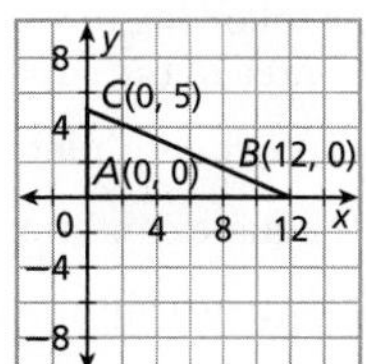

(A) 100π cubic units (circled)

(B) 144π cubic units

(C) 240π cubic units

(D) 300π cubic units

(E) 720π cubic units

5. An oxygen tank is the shape of a cylinder with a hemisphere at each end. If the radius of the tank is 5 inches and the overall length is 32 inches, what is the volume of the tank?

(A) $\frac{500}{3\pi}$ in³

(B) $\frac{2275}{12}\pi$ in³

(C) $\frac{1900}{3}\pi$ in³

(D) $\frac{2150}{3}\pi$ in³ (circled)

(E) $\frac{2900}{3}\pi$ in³

COLLEGE ENTRANCE EXAM PRACTICE

CHAPTER 10

Organizer

Objective: Provide practice for college entrance exams such as the SAT Mathematics Subject Tests.

PREMIER **Online Edition**

Resources

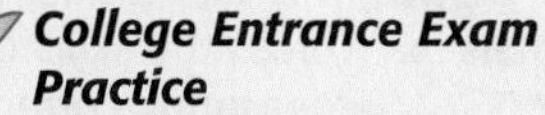

College Entrance Exam Practice

Questions on the SAT Mathematics Subject Tests Levels 1 and 2 represent the following math content areas:

	Levels	
	1	2
Number and Operations	10-14%	10-14%
Algebra and Functions	38-42%	48-52%
Geometry and Measurement	38-42%	28-32%
Plane Euclidean	18-22%	0%
Coordinate	8-12%	10-14%
Three-Dimensional	4-6%	4-6%
Trigonometry	6-8%	12-16%
Data Analysis and Statistics	6-10%	6-10%

Items on this page focus on:

- Three-dimensional Geometry

Text References:

Item	1	2	3	4	5
Lesson	10-3	10-4	10-5	10-7	10-6, 10-8

TEST PREP DOCTOR

1. Students who chose **C** found the length of the diagonal of one face, which is not the greatest possible distance between A and B. Students who chose **E** did not simplify $\sqrt{48}$ correctly.

2. Students who chose **A** did not use the given information that the lateral area of the cylinder is three times the area of the base.

3. Students who chose **B** used the height of the cone instead of the slant height of the cone. Students who chose **A** recognized that the radius and height formed a right triangle similar to a 3-4-5 triangle but did not double the slant height.

4. Students who chose **C** rotated the figure about the y-axis instead of the x-axis. Students who chose **D** did not multiply the product of the base area and the height of the cone by $\frac{1}{3}$.

5. Students who chose **E** did not subtract twice the radius from the overall length of the tank to find the height of the cylinder. Students who chose **C** found the volume of the cylinder with a hemisphere at only one end.

College Entrance Exam Practice 735

Organizer

Objective: Provide opportunities to learn and practice common test-taking strategies.

Online Edition

TEST PREP DOCTOR

This Test Tackler reinforces the skills of measuring correctly and using measurements to calculate surface areas and volumes of solids. Review metric and customary measure and rounding rules. Students may be provided a printed ruler when taking a standardized test that requires measurement.

As you read through each test item, show students some of the common mistakes that they might make when they measure lengths of different dimensions of solids. Remind students to round properly and to use the π key on their calculators when applicable.

Any Question Type: Measure to Solve Problems

On some tests, you may have to measure a figure in order to answer a question. Pay close attention to the units of measure asked for in the question. Some questions ask you to measure to the nearest centimeter, and some ask you to measure to the nearest inch.

EXAMPLE 1

Multiple Choice: The net of a square pyramid is shown below. Use a ruler to measure the dimensions of the pyramid to the nearest centimeter.

Which of the following best represents the total surface area of the square pyramid?

Ⓐ 9 square centimeters

Ⓑ 21 square centimeters

Ⓒ 33 square centimeters

Ⓓ 36 square centimeters

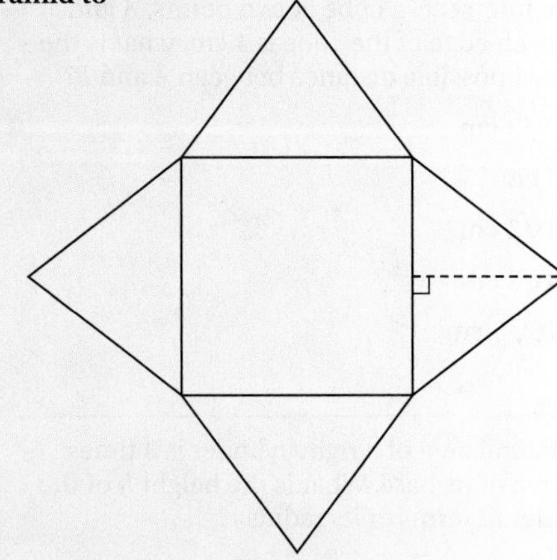

Use a centimeter ruler to measure one side of the square base. The measurement to the nearest centimeter is 3 cm. The base is a square, so all four side lengths are 3 cm.

Measure the altitude of a triangular face, which is the slant height of the pyramid. The altitude is 2 cm. Label the drawing with the measurements.

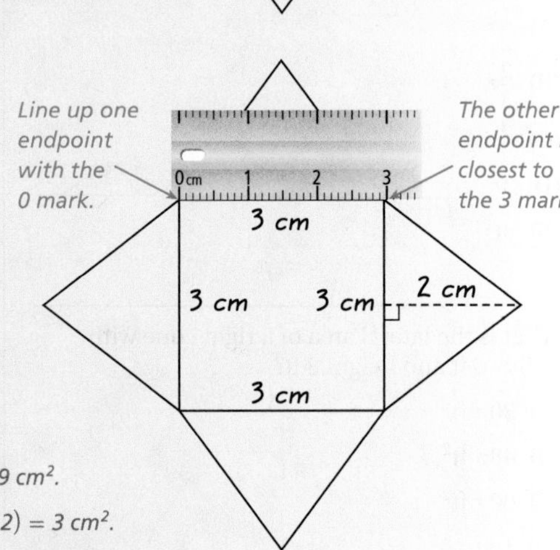

To find the total surface area of the pyramid, find the base area and the lateral area.

The base of the pyramid is a square. The base area of the pyramid is $A = s^2 = (3)^2 = 9\ cm^2$.

The area of one triangular face is $A = \frac{1}{2}bh = \frac{1}{2}(3)(2) = 3\ cm^2$.

The pyramid has 4 faces, so the lateral area is $4(3) = 12\ cm^2$.

The total surface area is $9 + 12 = 21\ cm^2$. The correct answer choice is B.

Read each test item and answer the questions that follow.

Measure carefully and make sure you are using the correct units to measure the figure.

Item A

The net of a cube is shown below. Use a ruler to measure the dimensions of the cube to the nearest $\frac{1}{4}$ inch.

Which best represents the volume of the cube to the nearest cubic inch?

(A) 1 cubic inch

(B) 2 cubic inches

(C) 5 cubic inches

(D) 9 cubic inches

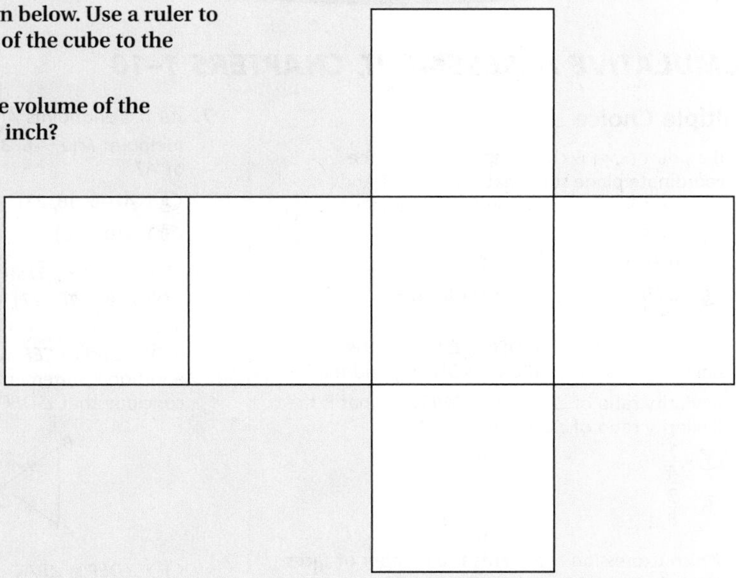

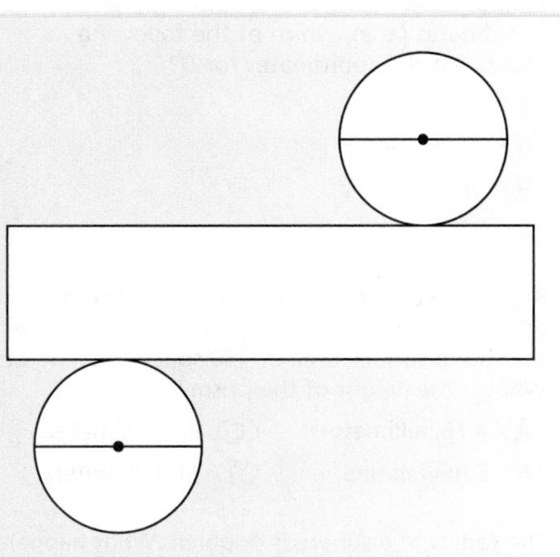

1. Measure one edge of the net for the cube. What is the length to the nearest $\frac{1}{4}$ inch?
2. How would you use the measurement to find the volume of the cube?

Item B

The net of a cylinder is shown below. Use a ruler to measure the dimensions of the cylinder to the nearest tenth of a centimeter.

Which best represents the total surface area of the cylinder to the nearest square centimeter?

(F) 6 square centimeters

(G) 16 square centimeters

(H) 19 square centimeters

(J) 42 square centimeters

3. Which part of the net do you need to measure in order to find the height of the cylinder? Find the height of the cylinder to the nearest tenth of a centimeter.
4. What other measurement(s) do you need in order to find the surface area of the cylinder? Find the measurement(s) to the nearest tenth of a centimeter.
5. How would you use the measurements to find the surface area of the cylinder?

Answers

1. $1\frac{1}{4}$ in.
2. I would use the formula $V = s^3$, where s is the length of each edge of the cube.
3. the height of the rectangle; 1.7 cm
4. the radius of one of the circles; 1.1 cm
5. I would use the formula $S = 2\pi r^2 + \pi rh$, where r is the radius of the circle and h is the height of the rectangle.

Answers to Test Items

A. B

B. H

State Resources

go.hrw.com
State Resources Online
KEYWORD: MG7 Resources

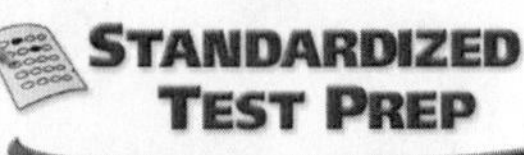

Organizer

Objective: Provide review and practice for Chapters 1–10 and standardized tests.

Resources

 ***Assessment Resources***

Chapter 10 Cumulative Test

go.hrw.com
KEYWORD: MG7 TestPrep

Answers

1. A
2. G
3. B
4. H
5. C
6. G
7. D
8. J
9. D
10. F
11. B
12. H
13. 3.6
14. 18
15. 5
16. 160

State Resources

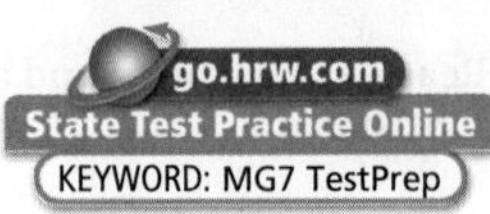

CUMULATIVE ASSESSMENT, CHAPTERS 1–10

Multiple Choice

1. If a point (x, y) is chosen at random in the coordinate plane such that $-1 \le x \le 1$ and $-5 \le y \le 3$, what is the probability that $x \ge 0$ and $y \ge 0$?

Ⓐ 0.1875 Ⓑ 0.25 Ⓒ 0.375 Ⓓ 0.8125

2. $\triangle ABC \sim \triangle DEF$, and $\triangle DEF \sim \triangle GHI$. If the similarity ratio of $\triangle ABC$ to $\triangle DEF$ is $\frac{1}{2}$ and the similarity ratio of $\triangle DEF$ to $\triangle GHI$ is $\frac{3}{4}$, what is the similarity ratio of $\triangle ABC$ to $\triangle GHI$?

Ⓕ $\frac{1}{4}$ Ⓖ $\frac{3}{8}$ Ⓗ $\frac{2}{3}$ Ⓙ $\frac{3}{2}$

3. Which expression represents the number of faces of a prism with bases that are n-gons?

Ⓐ $n + 1$ Ⓑ $n + 2$ Ⓒ $2n$ Ⓓ $3n$

4. Parallelogram $ABCD$ has a diagonal $\overline{AC}$ with endpoints $A(-1, 3)$ and $C(-3, -3)$. If B has coordinates (x, y), which of the following represents the coordinates for D?

Ⓕ $D(-3x, -y)$
Ⓖ $D(-x, -y)$
Ⓗ $D(-x - 4, -y)$
Ⓙ $D(x - 2, y)$

5. Right $\triangle ABC$ with legs $AB = 9$ millimeters and $BC = 12$ millimeters is the base of a right prism that has a surface area of 450 square millimeters. What is the height of the prism?

Ⓐ 4.75 millimeters Ⓑ 6 millimeters Ⓒ 9.5 millimeters Ⓓ 11 millimeters

6. The radius of a sphere is doubled. What happens to the ratio of the volume of the sphere to the surface area of the sphere?

Ⓕ It remains the same.
Ⓖ It is doubled.
Ⓗ It is increased by a factor of 4.
Ⓙ It is increased by a factor of 8.

7. $\overline{AB}$ has endpoints $A(x, y, z)$ and $B(-2, 6, 13)$ and midpoint $M(2, -6, 3))$ What are the coordinates of A?

Ⓐ $A(-6, 18, 23)$
Ⓑ $A(0, 0, 8)$
Ⓒ $A(2, -6, 19)$
Ⓓ $A(6, -18, -7)$

8. If $\overline{DE}$ bisects $\angle CEF$, which of the following additional statements would allow you to conclude that $\triangle DEF \cong \triangle ABC$?

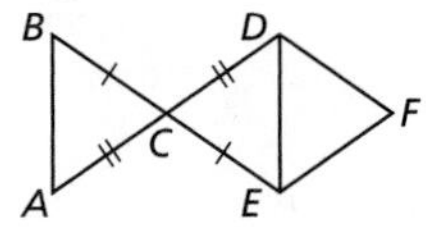

Ⓕ $\angle DEF \cong \angle BAC$
Ⓖ $\angle DEF \cong \angle CDE$
Ⓗ $\overline{EF} \cong \overline{CD}$
Ⓙ $\overline{EF} \cong \overline{EC}$

9. To the nearest tenth of a cubic centimeter, what is the volume of a right regular octagonal prism with base edge length 4 centimeters and height 7 centimeters?

Ⓐ 180.3 cubic centimeters
Ⓑ 224.0 cubic centimeters
Ⓒ 270.4 cubic centimeters
Ⓓ 540.8 cubic centimeters

10. Which of the following must be true about a conditional statement?

Ⓕ If the inverse is false, then the converse is false.
Ⓖ If the conditional is true, then the contrapositive is false.
Ⓗ If the conditional is true, then the converse is false.
Ⓙ If the hypothesis of the conditional is true, then the conditional is true.

Answers

17a. 9 cm

Use the formula for the area of a trapezoid, $A = \frac{1}{2}(b_1 + b_2)h$, and solve for h.

$$103.5 \text{ cm}^2 = \tfrac{1}{2}(7 \text{ cm} + 16 \text{ cm})h$$
$$2(103.5 \text{ cm}^2) = (23 \text{ cm})h$$
$$\frac{2(103.5 \text{ cm}^2)}{23 \text{ cm}} = h$$
$$9 \text{ cm} = h$$

b. 50.0°

Use the sine ratio to find $m\angle J$.

$$\sin J = \frac{h}{11.75} = \frac{9}{11.75}$$
$$m\angle J = \sin^{-1}\left(\frac{9}{11.75}\right) \approx 50.0°$$

18.

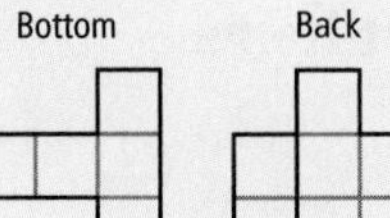

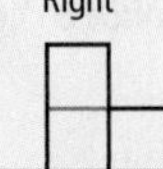

19a.

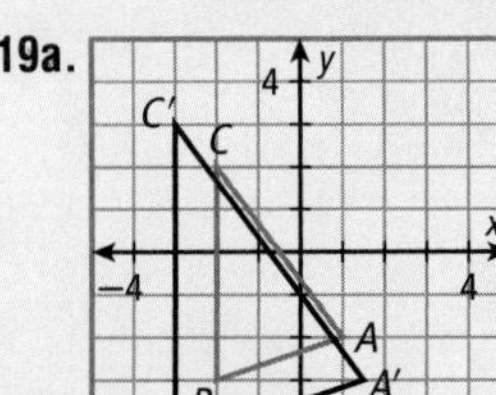

It may be helpful to include units in your calculations of measures of geometric figures. If your answer includes the proper units, you are less likely to have made an error.

11. A right cylinder has a height of 10 inches. The area of the base is 63.6 square inches. To the nearest tenth of a square inch, what is the lateral area for this cylinder?

Ⓐ 53.6 square inches

Ⓑ 282.7 square inches

Ⓒ 409.9 square inches

Ⓓ 634.6 square inches

12. The volume of the smaller sphere is 288 cubic centimeters. Find the volume of the larger sphere.

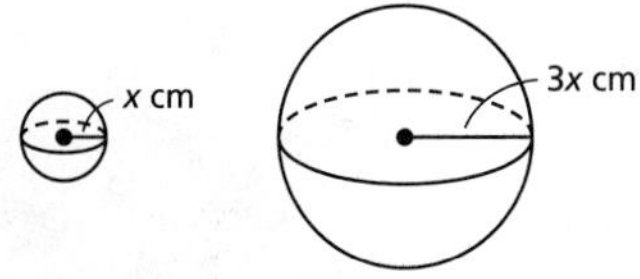

Ⓕ 864 cubic centimeters

Ⓖ 2,592 cubic centimeters

Ⓗ 7,776 cubic centimeters

Ⓙ 23,328 cubic centimeters

Gridded Response

13. $\vec{u} = \langle 3, -7 \rangle$, and $\vec{v} = \langle -6, 5 \rangle$. What is the magnitude of the resultant vector to the nearest tenth?

14. If a polyhedron has 12 vertices and 8 faces, how many edges does the polyhedron have?

15. If Y is the circumcenter of $\triangle PQR$, what is the value of x?

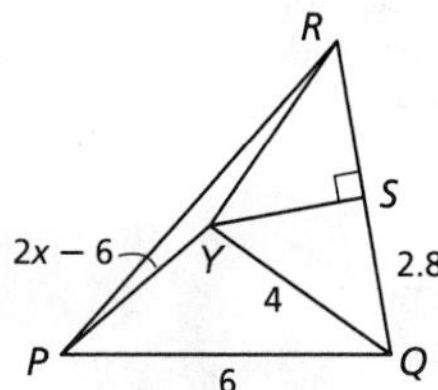

16. How many cubes with edge length 3 centimeters will fit in a box that is a rectangular prism with length 12 centimeters, width 15 centimeters, and height 24 centimeters?

Short Response

17. The area of trapezoid $GHIJ$ is 103.5 square centimeters. Find each of the following. Round answers to the nearest tenth. Show your work or explain in words how you found your answers.

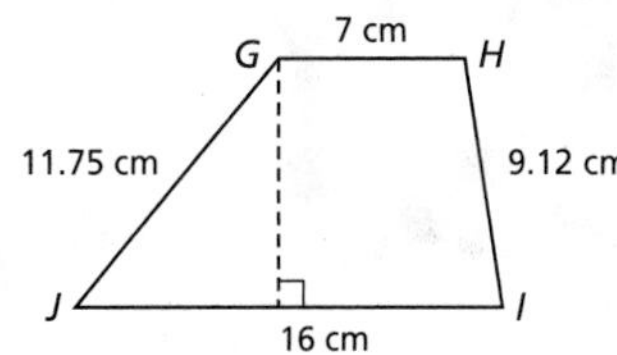

a. the height of trapezoid $GHIJ$

b. $m\angle J$

18. The figure shows the top view of a stack of cubes. The number on each cube represents the number of stacked cubes. Draw the bottom, back, and right views of the object.

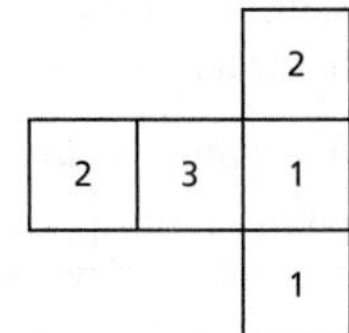

19. $\triangle ABC$ has vertices $A(1, -2)$, $B(-2, -3)$, and $C(-2, 2)$.

a. Graph $\triangle A'B'C'$, the image of $\triangle ABC$, after a dilation with a scale factor of $\frac{3}{2}$.

b. Show that $\overleftrightarrow{AB} \parallel \overleftrightarrow{A'B'}$, $\overleftrightarrow{BC} \parallel \overleftrightarrow{B'C'}$, and $\overleftrightarrow{CA} \parallel \overleftrightarrow{C'A'}$. Use slope to justify your answer.

Extended Response

20. A right cone has a lateral area of 30π square inches and a slant height of 6 inches.

a. Find the height of the cone. Show your work or explain in words how you determined your answer. Round your answer to the nearest tenth.

b. Find the volume of this cone. Round your answer to the nearest tenth.

c. Given a right cone with a lateral area of L and a slant height of ℓ, find an equation for the volume in terms of L and ℓ. Show your work.

Short-Response Rubric

Items 17–19

2 Points = The student's answer is an accurate and complete execution of the task or tasks.

1 Point = The student's answer contains attributes of an appropriate response but is flawed.

0 Points = The student's answer contains no attributes of an appropriate response.

Extended-Response Rubric

Item 20

4 Points = The student correctly calculates the height and the volume of the cone and finds the correct formula for the volume of the cone. Work demonstrates a thorough understanding of concepts related to the surface area and volume of a right cone.

3 Points = The student answers correctly, but explanations may contain minor flaws. Work demonstrates a basic understanding of major concepts.

2 Points = The student answers correctly, but explanations are missing or incomplete. Work demonstrates a limited understanding of concepts.

1 Point = The student answers incorrectly but makes a reasonable attempt to show work.

0 Points = The student answers incorrectly and does not attempt all parts of the problem.

b. The slope of $\overleftrightarrow{AB}$ is $\frac{-3+2}{-2-1} = \frac{1}{3}$. The slope of $\overleftrightarrow{A'B'}$ is $\frac{-4.5+3}{-3-1.5} = \frac{1}{3}$. The slope of $\overleftrightarrow{BC}$ is undef. because $\frac{2+3}{-2+2} = \frac{5}{0}$. The slope of $\overleftrightarrow{B'C'}$ is undef. because $\frac{3+4.5}{-3+3} = \frac{7.5}{0}$. So both $\overleftrightarrow{BC}$ and $\overleftrightarrow{B'C'}$ are vert. lines. The slope of $\overleftrightarrow{CA}$ is $\frac{2+2}{-2-1} = \frac{4}{-3}$. The slope of $\overleftrightarrow{C'A'}$ is $\frac{3+3}{-3-1.5} = \frac{6}{-4.5} = \frac{4}{-3}$. So by the Par. Lines Thm, $\overleftrightarrow{AB} \parallel \overleftrightarrow{A'B'}$, $\overleftrightarrow{BC} \parallel \overleftrightarrow{B'C'}$, and $\overleftrightarrow{CA} \parallel \overleftrightarrow{C'A'}$.

20a. 3.3 in; use the formula for lat. area of a rt. cone.

$30\pi \text{ in}^2 = \pi r(6 \text{ in.})$

$\frac{30\pi \text{ in}^2}{\pi 6 \text{ in.}} = r$

$5 \text{ in.} = r$

Since this is a rt. cone, the radius, slant ht., and ht. form a rt. Δ. Use the Pythagorean Thm to find the ht.

$5^2 + h^2 = 6^2$

$25 + h^2 = 36$

$h^2 = 11$

$h \approx 3.3$ in.

b. 86.4 in³ use the formula for vol. of a cone.

$V = \frac{1}{3}\pi(5)^2(3.3) \approx 86.4 \text{ in}^3$

c. $V = \frac{1}{3}\pi\left(\frac{L}{\pi\ell}\right)^2\left(\sqrt{\ell^2 - \left(\frac{L}{\pi\ell}\right)^2}\right)$

$= \frac{1}{3\pi}\left(\frac{L}{\ell}\right)^2\left(\sqrt{\ell^2 - \left(\frac{L}{\pi\ell}\right)^2}\right)$

Use the lat. area formula for a rt. cone to find r: $L = \pi r \ell$; $r = \frac{L}{\pi\ell}$

Since this is a rt. cone, the radius, slant ht., and ht. form a rt. Δ. Use the Pythagorean Thm to find the ht: $r^2 + h^2 = \ell^2$. Substitute $r = \frac{L}{\pi\ell}$: $\left(\frac{L}{\pi\ell}\right)^2 + h^2 = \ell^2$. Solve for h:

$h = \sqrt{\ell^2 - \left(\frac{L}{\pi\ell}\right)^2}$.

Now substitute the values of r and h in the eqn. for vol. of a cone.

$V = \frac{1}{3}\pi\left(\frac{L}{\pi\ell}\right)^2\left(\sqrt{\ell^2 - \left(\frac{L}{\pi\ell}\right)^2}\right)$

$= \frac{1}{3\pi}\left(\frac{L}{\ell}\right)^2\left(\sqrt{\ell^2 - \left(\frac{L}{\pi\ell}\right)^2}\right)$

Real-World CONNECTIONS

Organizer

Objective: Choose appropriate problem-solving strategies and use them with skills from Chapters 9 and 10 to solve real-world problems.

The Mellon Arena

Reading Strategies

ENGLISH LANGUAGE LEARNERS

Make sure that students understand what *retract* means. Spanish-speaking ELL students may recognize its similarity to the Spanish word *retractarse*.

Using Data Students will need to use the data in the table to solve **Problems 2** and **3.** They will need to decide whether to use the data about the perimeter, the area, or both.

Discuss with students their methods for solving **Problems 2** and **3.** Ask students to share as many different strategies and approaches as possible.

State Resources

The Mellon Arena

When Pittsburgh's Mellon Arena opened in 1961, it was the world's first auditorium with a retractable roof. The arena became the home of the Penguins in 1967. In 2008, ground was broken for a new arena.

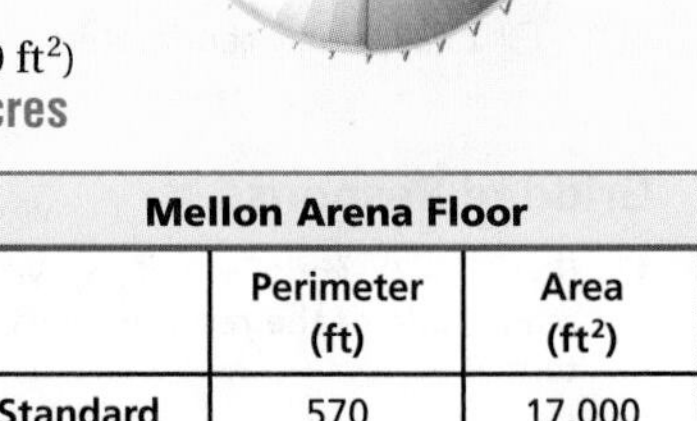

Choose one or more strategies to solve each problem.

1. The Mellon Arena appears to be a perfect circle. However it actually consists of two semi-circles that are connected by a narrow rectangle, as shown in the figure. Approximately how many acres of land does the arena cover? (*Hint:* 1 acre = 43,560 ft²) **3 acres**

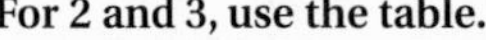

For 2 and 3, use the table.

2. For hockey games, the arena's standard rectangular floor is used. The ratio of the floor's length to its width is 40 : 17. What are the dimensions of the standard arena floor? **200 ft × 85 ft**
3. For special events, some of the seating can be removed to create an expanded rectangular floor. In this case, the length is 130 ft greater than the width. What are the dimensions of the expanded arena floor? **250 ft × 120 ft**

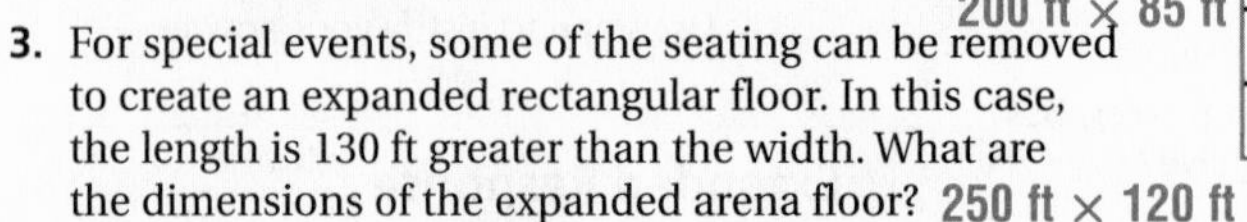

Mellon Arena Floor

	Perimeter (ft)	Area (ft²)
Standard	570	17,000
Expanded	740	30,000

4. The arena's roof is a stainless steel dome. It consists of eight congruent wedge-shaped sections. When the roof is retracted, six of the sections rotate and come to rest under the two sections that remain fixed. Suppose you choose a seat in the arena at random. When the roof is retracted, what is the probability that you are sitting under one of the fixed sections? What is the probability that you are sitting under the open sky? $\frac{1}{4}$; $\frac{3}{4}$

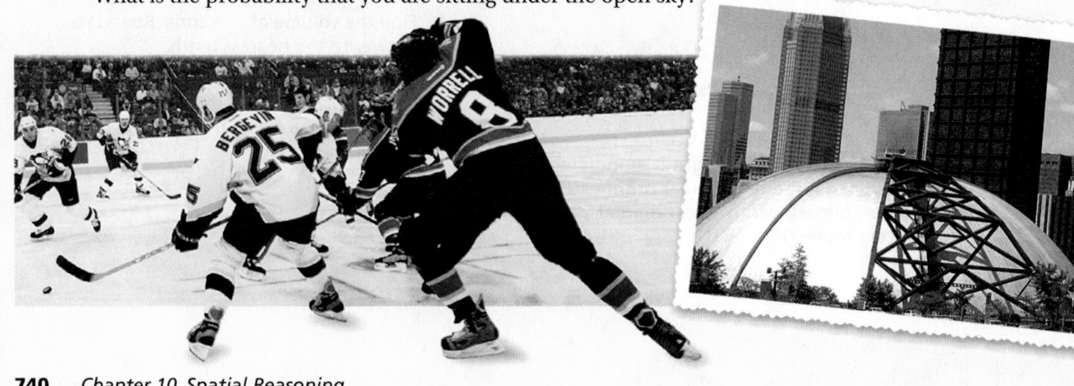

Problem-Solving Focus

For **Problems 2** and **3,** focus on the final step of the problem-solving process: **(4) Look Back.** Once students have found the floor's dimensions, ask them how they can use the data in the table to check their answers. Calculate the perimeter and area that correspond to the dimensions. Check to see if these match the perimeter and area given in the table.

The U.S. Mint

Chances are good that you have a souvenir of Philadelphia in your pocket. Since 1792, the U.S. mint has had a facility in Philadelphia, and over the years it has produced trillions of coins. In 2004 alone, the Philadelphia mint turned out approximately 3 billion pennies.

Choose one or more strategies to solve each problem. For 1–4, use the table.

1. Coins are stamped out of a rectangular metal strip that is 13 in. wide by 1,500 ft long. Given that the diameter of a quarter is just under an inch (0.955 in.), what is the minimum number of strips that would be needed to stamp out 700,000 quarters? 3
2. A penny contains a small amount of copper, but most of the metal in a penny is zinc. The volume of copper in a penny is about 11 mm^3. What percentage of the penny is copper? 2.5%
3. Nickels are made from a metal that is a mixture of nickel and copper. About how many nickels can be made if a 1 m^3 block of this metal is melted down? 1.45 million
4. Rolls of 50 dimes are packaged in clear plastic sleeves. How much plastic is needed to enclose one roll of dimes? 4302 mm^2

Coin Specifications

	Diameter (mm)	Thickness (mm)
Penny	19.05	1.55
Nickel	21.21	1.95
Dime	17.91	1.35
Quarter	24.26	1.75

The U.S. Mint

Reading Strategies

Have students read **Problem 1.** Then ask them to list the essential information that is presented in the problem. Ask students if they have everything they need to solve the problem or if additional data is required.

Using Data Students will need to work with large numbers to solve these problems. As a warm up, ask students to explain the relationship between one thousand, one million, and one billion. One million is a thousand thousands; one billion is a thousand millions. In discussing **Problem 3,** ask students how many cubic millimeters are in one cubic meter. If students have difficulty with this, sketch a 1 m^3 cube and point out that there are 1000 mm along its length, 1000 mm along its width, and 1000 mm along its height. So the total number of 1 mm^3 cubes is 1000 × 1000 × 1000, or 1,000,000,000 (one billion).

Problem-Solving Focus

Ask students what strategy (or combination of strategies) they would use to solve **Problem 1.** Possible answer: Students may want to use the strategy Solve a Simpler Problem. In this case they might first calculate the number of quarters that can be stamped out of a single strip. Students may also wish to use the strategy Draw a Diagram to help them visualize how the coins can be stamped out in rows.

Circles

Section 11A	Section 11B
Lines and Arcs in Circles	**Angles and Segments in Circles**
11-1 Lines That Intersect Circles	**11-4 Inscribed Angles**
Connecting Geometry to Data Analysis Circle Graphs	**11-5 Technology Lab** Explore Angle Relationships in Circles
11-2 Arcs and Chords	**11-5 Angle Relationships in Circles**
11-3 Sector Area and Arc Length	**11-6 Technology Lab** Explore Segment Relationships in Circles
	11-6 Segment Relationships in Circles
	11-7 Circles in the Coordinate Plane
	EXTENSION Polar Coordinates

Pacing Guide for 45-Minute Classes

Teacher One Stop™
Calendar Planner®

Chapter 11

DAY 1	DAY 2	DAY 3	DAY 4	DAY 5
11-1 Lesson	Connecting Geometry to Data Analysis 11-2 Lesson	11-2 Lesson	11-3 Lesson	11-3 Lesson
DAY 6	**DAY 7**	**DAY 8**	**DAY 9**	**DAY 10**
Multi-Step Test Prep Ready to Go On?	11-4 Lesson	11-5 Technology Lab	11-5 Lesson	11-6 Technology Lab
DAY 11	**DAY 12**	**DAY 13**	**DAY 14**	**DAY 15**
11-6 Lesson	11-7 Lesson	Extension	Multi-Step Test Prep Ready to Go On?	Chapter 11 Review
DAY 16				
Chapter 11 Test				

Pacing Guide for 90-Minute Classes

Teacher One Stop™
Calendar Planner®

Chapter 11

DAY 1	DAY 2	DAY 3	DAY 4	DAY 5
11-1 Lesson Connecting Geometry to Data Analysis 11-2 Lesson	11-2 Lesson 11-3 Lesson	11-3 Lesson Multi-Step Test Prep Ready to Go On?	11-4 Lesson 11-5 Technology Lab	11-5 Lesson 11-6 Technology Lab
DAY 6	**DAY 7**	**DAY 8**		
11-6 Lesson 11-7 Lesson	Extension Multi-Step Test Prep Ready to Go On?	Chapter 11 Review Chapter 11 Test		

ONGOING ASSESSMENT and INTERVENTION

	DIAGNOSE	PRESCRIBE
Assess Prior Knowledge	**Before Chapter 11**	
	Diagnose readiness for the chapter.	Prescribe intervention.
	 **Are You Ready?** SE p. 743	 ***Are You Ready? Intervention***
Formative Assessment	**Before Every Lesson**	
	Diagnose readiness for the lesson.	Prescribe intervention.
	Warm Up TE	**Reteach** CRB
	During Every Lesson	
	Diagnose understanding of lesson concepts.	Prescribe intervention.
	Check It Out! SE	**Reading Strategies** CRB
	Questioning Strategies TE	***Success for Every Learner***
	Think and Discuss SE	***Lesson Tutorial Videos***
	Write About It SE	
	Journal TE	
	After Every Lesson	
	Diagnose mastery of lesson concepts.	Prescribe intervention.
	Lesson Quiz TE	**Reteach** CRB
	Test Prep SE	**Test Prep Doctor** TE
	Test and Practice Generator	**Homework Help Online**
	Before Chapter 11 Testing	
	Diagnose mastery of concepts in chapter.	Prescribe intervention.
	Ready to Go On? SE pp. 771, 807	***Ready to Go On? Intervention***
	Multi-Step Test Prep SE pp. 770, 806	**Scaffolding Questions** TE pp. 770, 806
	Section Quizzes AR	**Reteach** CRB
	Test and Practice Generator	***Lesson Tutorial Videos***
	Before High Stakes Testing	
	Diagnose mastery of benchmark concepts.	Prescribe intervention.
	College Entrance Exam Practice SE p. 815	***College Entrance Exam Practice***
	Standardized Test Prep SE pp. 818–819	
Summative Assessment	**After Chapter 11**	
	Check mastery of chapter concepts.	Prescribe intervention.
	Multiple-Choice Tests (Forms A, B, C)	**Reteach** CRB
	Free-Response Tests (Forms A, B, C)	 ***Lesson Tutorial Videos***
	Performance Assessment AR	
	Cumulative Test AR	
	Test and Practice Generator	

KEY: **SE** = *Student Edition* **TE** = *Teacher's Edition* **CRB** = *Chapter Resource Book* **AR** = *Assessment Resources* Available online 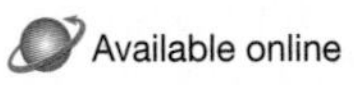 Available on CD- or DVD-ROM

Lesson Resources

Before the Lesson

Prepare *Teacher One Stop* SPANISH
- Editable lesson plans
- Calendar Planner
- Easy access to all chapter resources

Lesson Transparencies
- Teacher Tools

Teach the Lesson

Introduce *Alternate Openers: Explorations*

Lesson Transparencies
- Warm Up
- Problem of the Day

Teach *Lesson Transparencies*
- Teaching Transparencies

Know-It Notebook™
- Vocabulary
- Key Concepts

Power Presentations

Lesson Tutorial Videos 

Interactive Online Edition
- Lesson Activities
- Lesson Tutorial Videos

Lab Activities

Lab Resources Online

Online Interactivities 

TechKeys

Practice the Lesson

Practice *Chapter Resources*
- Practice A, B, C

Practice and Problem Solving Workbook

IDEA Works!® Modified Worksheets and Tests

ExamView Test and Practice Generator

Homework Help Online

Online Interactivities 

Interactive Online Edition
- Homework Help

Apply *Chapter Resources*
- Problem Solving

Practice and Problem Solving Workbook

Interactive Online Edition
- Chapter Project

Project Teacher Support

After the Lesson

Reteach *Chapter Resources*
- Reteach
- Reading Strategies ELL

Success for Every Learner

Review *Interactive Answers and Solutions*

Solutions Key

Know-It Notebook™
- Big Ideas
- Chapter Review

Extend *Chapter Resources*
- Challenge

Technology Highlights for the Teacher

 Power Presentations

Dynamic presentations to engage students. Complete PowerPoint® presentations for every lesson in Chapter 11.

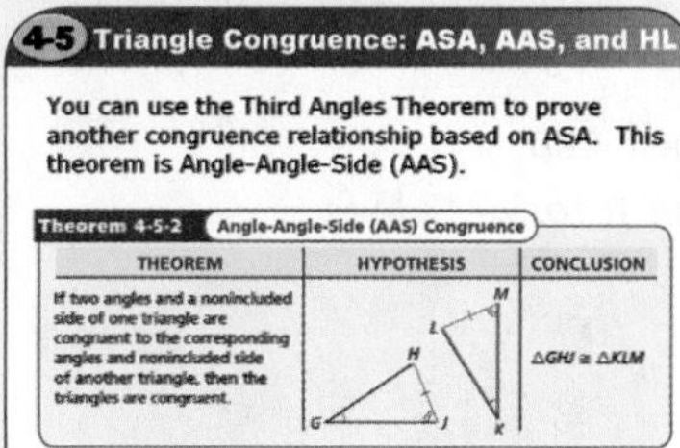

Teacher One Stop 

Easy access to Chapter 11 resources and assessments. Includes lesson planning, test generation, and puzzle creation software.

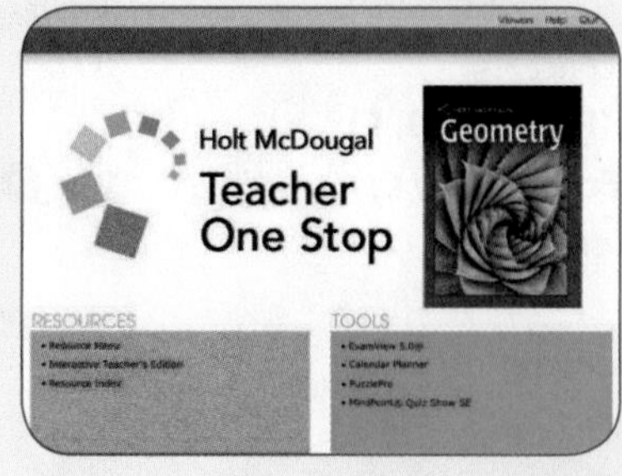

Premier Online Edition SPANISH

Chapter 11 includes Tutorial Videos, Lesson Activities, Lesson Quizzes, Homework Help, and Chapter Project.

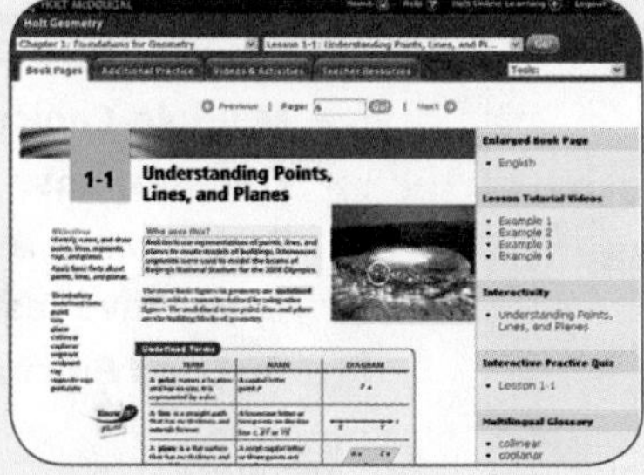

KEY: **SE** = *Student Edition* **TE** = *Teacher's Edition*  English Language Learners  Spanish version available  Available online  Available on CD- or DVD-ROM

Reaching All Learners

Teaching tips to help all learners appear throughout the chapter. A few that target specific students are included in the lists below.

All Learners

Lab Activities
Practice and Problem Solving Workbook
Know-It Notebook

Special Needs Students

Practice A .... CRB
Reteach .... CRB
Reading Strategies .... CRB
Are You Ready? .... SE p. 743
Inclusion .... TE pp. 761, 762, 808
IDEA Works!® Modified Worksheets and Tests
Ready to Go On? Intervention SPANISH
Know-It Notebook
Online Interactivities 
Lesson Tutorial Videos 

Developing Learners

Practice A .... CRB
Reteach .... CRB
Reading Strategies .... CRB
Are You Ready? .... SE p. 743
Vocabulary Connections .... SE p. 744
Questioning Strategies .... TE
Ready to Go On? Intervention SPANISH
Know-It Notebook
Homework Help Online
Online Interactivities  
Lesson Tutorial Videos 

On-Level Learners

Practice B .... CRB
Problem Solving .... CRB
Vocabulary Connections .... SE p. 744
Questioning Strategies .... TE
Ready to Go On? Intervention SPANISH
Know-It Notebook
Homework Help Online
Online Interactivities SPANISH

Advanced Learners

Practice C .... CRB
Challenge .... CRB
Challenge Exercises .... SE
Reading and Writing Math *Extend* .... TE p. 745
Critical Thinking .... TE pp. 748, 774, 775, 777, 803
Are You Ready? Enrichment SPANISH
Ready To Go On? Enrichment SPANISH

English Language Learners

ENGLISH LANGUAGE LEARNERS

Reading Strategies .... CRB
Are You Ready? Vocabulary .... SE p. 743
Vocabulary Connections .... SE p. 744
Vocabulary Review .... SE p. 810
English Language Learners .... TE pp. 745, 752, 767
Success for Every Learner
Know-It Notebook
Spanish Study Guide (Resumen y Repaso)
Multilingual Glossary
Lesson Tutorial Videos  

Technology Highlights for Reaching All Learners

Lesson Tutorial Videos SPANISH

Starring Holt authors Ed Burger and Freddie Renfro! Live tutorials to support every lesson in Chapter 11.

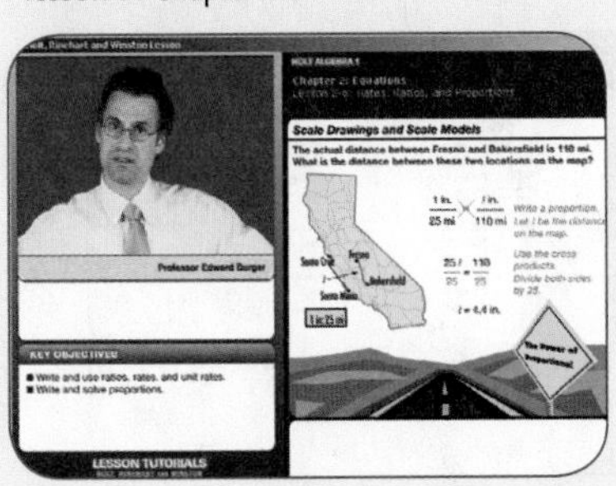

Multilingual Glossary

Searchable glossary includes definitions in English, Spanish, Vietnamese, Chinese, Hmong, Korean, and 4 other languages.

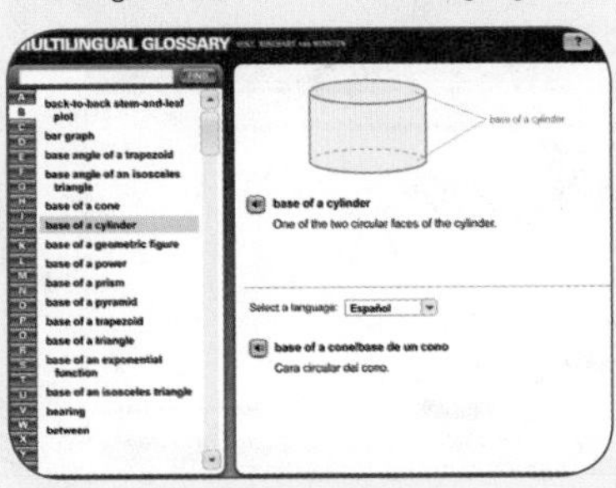

Online Interactivities

Interactive tutorials provide visually engaging alternative opportunities to learn concepts and master skills.

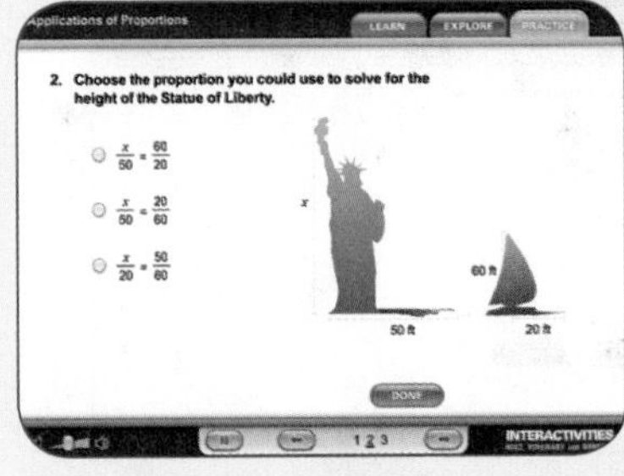

KEY: **SE** = *Student Edition* **TE** = *Teacher's Edition* **CRB** = *Chapter Resource Book* SPANISH Spanish version available  Available online Available on CD- or DVD-ROM

Ongoing Assessment

Assessing Prior Knowledge

Determine whether students have the prerequisite concepts and skills for success in Chapter 11.

Are You Ready? SPANISH .... SE p.743
Warm Up .... TE

Test Preparation

Provide review and practice for Chapter 11 and standardized tests.

Multi-Step Test Prep .... SE pp. 770, 806
Study Guide: Review .... SE pp. 810–813
Test Tackler .... SE pp. 816–817
Standardized Test Prep .... SE pp. 818–819
College Entrance Exam Practice .... SE p. 815
Countdown to Testing .... SE pp. C4-C27
IDEA Works!® Modified Worksheets and Tests

Alternative Assessment

Assess students' understanding of Chapter 11 concepts and combined problem-solving skills.

Chapter 11 Project .... SE p. 742
Alternative Assessment .... TE
Performance Assessment .... AR
Portfolio Assessment .... AR

Lesson Assessment

Provide formative assessment for each lesson of Chapter 11.

Questioning Strategies .... TE
Think and Discuss .... SE
Check It Out! Exercises .... SE
Write About It .... SE
Journal .... TE
Lesson Quiz .... TE
Alternative Assessment .... TE
IDEA Works!® Modified Worksheets and Tests

Weekly Assessment

Provide formative assessment for each section of Chapter 11.

Multi-Step Test Prep .... SE pp. 770, 806
Ready to Go On? SPANISH .... SE pp. 771, 807
Section Quizzes .... AR
Test and Practice Generator .... *Teacher One Stop*

Chapter Assessment

Provide summative assessment of Chapter 11 mastery.

Chapter 11 Test .... SE p. 814
Chapter Test (Levels A, B, C) .... AR
• Multiple Choice • Free Response
Cumulative Test .... AR
Test and Practice Generator .... *Teacher One Stop*
IDEA Works!® Modified Worksheets and Tests

Technology Highlights for Assessment

 **Are You Ready?** 

Automatically assess readiness and prescribe intervention for Chapter 11 prerequisite skills.

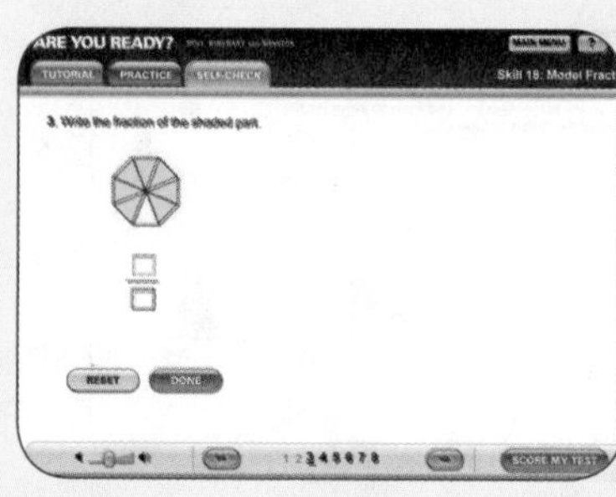

Ready to Go On?

Automatically assess understanding of and prescribe intervention for Sections 11A and 11B.

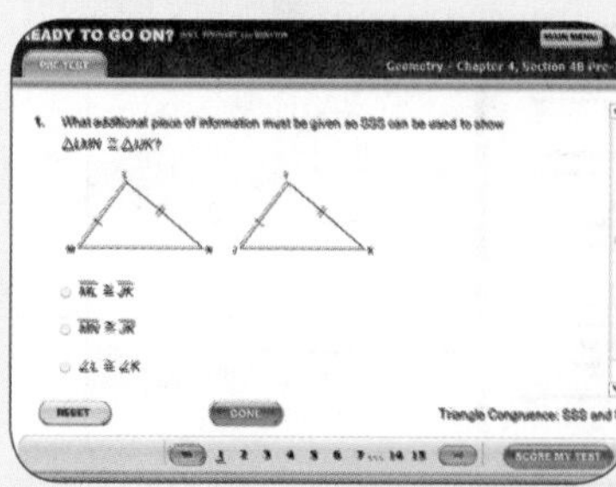

 **Test and Practice Generator**

Use Chapter 11 problem banks to create assessments and worksheets to print out or deliver online. Includes dynamic problems.

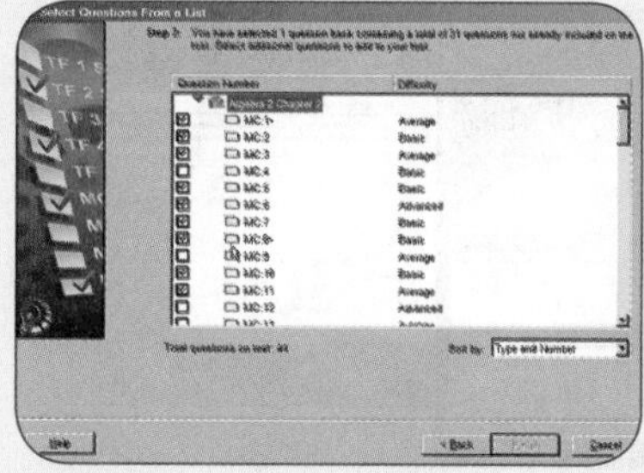

KEY: **SE** = *Student Edition* **TE** = *Teacher's Edition* **AR** = *Assessment Resources*  Spanish version available Available online  Available on CD- or DVD-ROM

Formal Assessment

Three levels (A, B, C) of multiple-choice and free-response chapter tests, along with a performance assessment, are available in the *Assessment Resources.*

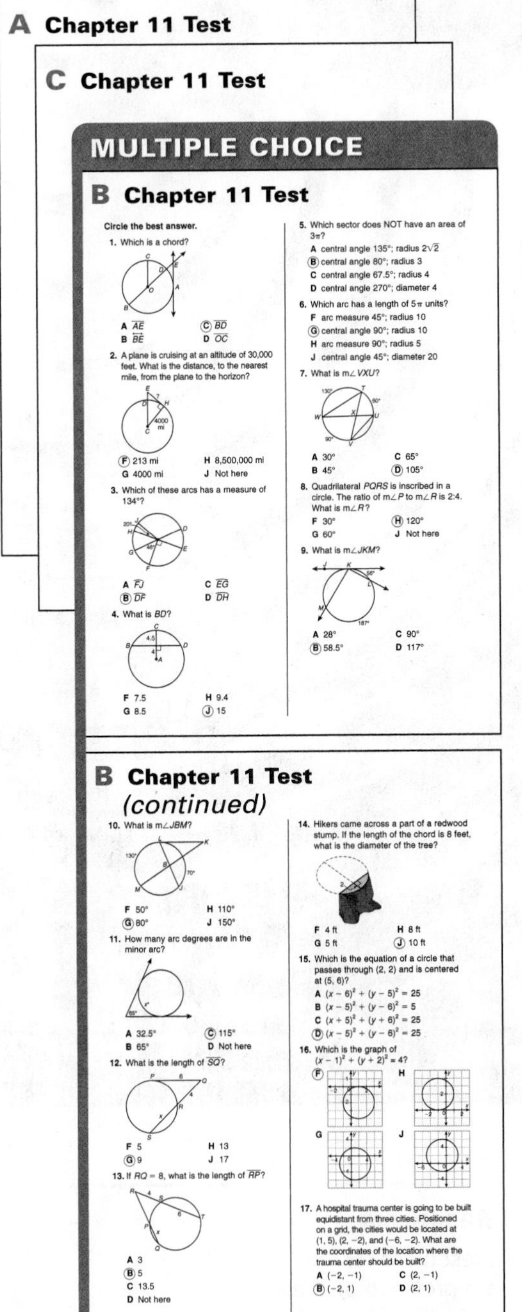

A Chapter 11 Test

C Chapter 11 Test

MULTIPLE CHOICE

B Chapter 11 Test

Circle the best answer.

1. Which is a chord?
   A $\overline{AE}$ B $\overleftrightarrow{BE}$ (C) $\overline{BD}$ D $\overline{OC}$
2. A plane is cruising at an altitude of 30,000 feet. What is the distance, to the nearest mile, from the plane to the horizon?
   (F) 213 mi G 4000 mi H 8,500,000 mi J Not here
3. Which of these arcs has a measure of 134°?
   A $\overset{\frown}{FJ}$ (B) $\overset{\frown}{DF}$ C $\overset{\frown}{EG}$ D $\overset{\frown}{DH}$
4. What is BD?
   F 7.5 G 8.5 H 9.4 (J) 15
5. Which sector does NOT have an area of 3π?
   A central angle 135°; radius $2\sqrt{2}$
   (B) central angle 80°; radius 3
   C central angle 67.5°; radius 4
   D central angle 270°; diameter 4
6. Which arc has a length of 5π units?
   F arc measure 45°; radius 10
   (G) central angle 90°; radius 10
   H arc measure 90°; radius 5
   J central angle 45°; diameter 20
7. What is $m\angle VXU$?
   A 30° B 45° C 65° (D) 105°
8. Quadrilateral $PQRS$ is inscribed in a circle. The ratio of $m\angle P$ to $m\angle R$ is 2:4. What is $m\angle R$?
   F 30° G 60° (H) 120° J Not here
9. What is $m\angle JKM$?
   A 28° (B) 58.5° C 90° D 117°

B Chapter 11 Test (continued)

10. What is $m\angle JBM$?
    F 50° (G) 80° H 110° J 150°
11. How many arc degrees are in the minor arc?
    A 32.5° B 65° (C) 115° D Not here
12. What is the length of $\overline{SQ}$?
    F 5 (G) 9 H 13 J 17
13. If $RQ = 8$, what is the length of $\overline{RP}$?
    A 3 (B) 5 C 13.5 D Not here
14. Hikers came across a part of a redwood stump. If the length of the chord is 8 feet, what is the diameter of the tree?
    F 4 ft G 5 ft H 8 ft (J) 10 ft
15. Which is the equation of a circle that passes through (2, 2) and is centered at (5, 6)?
    A $(x-6)^2+(y-5)^2=25$
    B $(x-5)^2+(y-6)^2=5$
    C $(x+5)^2+(y+6)^2=25$
    (D) $(x-5)^2+(y-6)^2=25$
16. Which is the graph of $(x-1)^2+(y+2)^2=4$?
    (F) G H J
17. A hospital trauma center is going to be built equidistant from three cities. Positioned on a grid, the cities would be located at (1, 5), (2, −2), and (−6, −2). What are the coordinates of the location where the trauma center should be built?
    A (−2, −1) (B) (−2, 1) C (2, −1) D (2, 1)

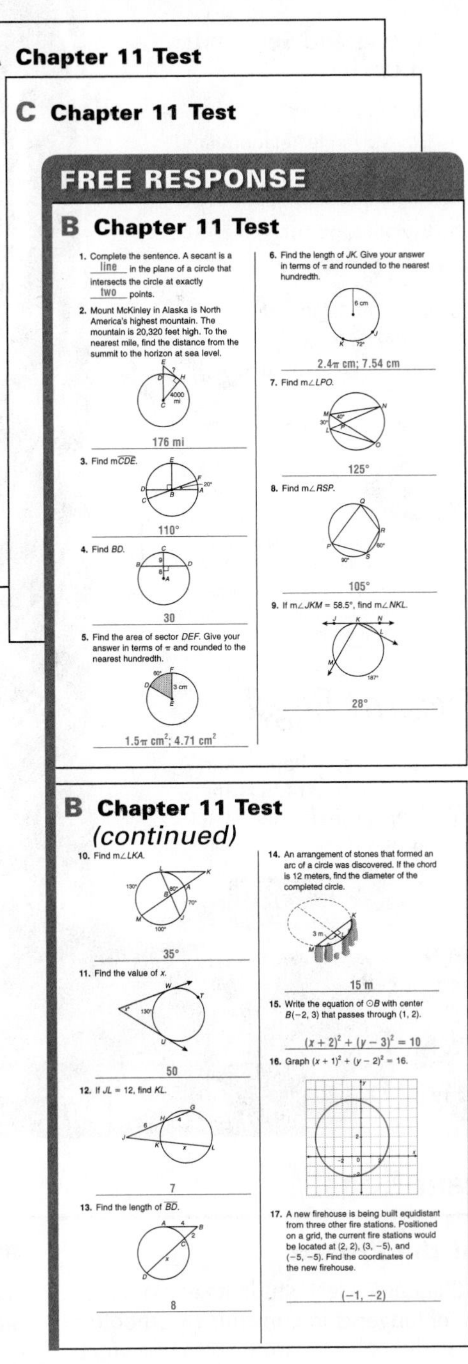

A Chapter 11 Test

C Chapter 11 Test

FREE RESPONSE

B Chapter 11 Test

1. Complete the sentence. A secant is a __line__ in the plane of a circle that intersects the circle at exactly __two__ points.
2. Mount McKinley in Alaska is North America's highest mountain. The mountain is 20,320 feet high. To the nearest mile, find the distance from the summit to the horizon at sea level.
   176 mi
3. Find $m\overset{\frown}{CDE}$.
   110°
4. Find BD.
   30
5. Find the area of sector DEF. Give your answer in terms of π and rounded to the nearest hundredth.
   1.5π cm²; 4.71 cm²
6. Find the length of JK. Give your answer in terms of π and rounded to the nearest hundredth.
   2.4π cm; 7.54 cm
7. Find $m\angle LPO$.
   125°
8. Find $m\angle RSP$.
   105°
9. If $m\angle JKM = 58.5°$, find $m\angle NKL$.
   28°

B Chapter 11 Test (continued)

10. Find $m\angle LKA$.
    35°
11. Find the value of x.
    50
12. If $JL = 12$, find KL.
    7
13. Find the length of $\overline{BD}$.
    8
14. An arrangement of stones that formed an arc of a circle was discovered. If the chord is 12 meters, find the diameter of the completed circle.
    15 m
15. Write the equation of $\odot B$ with center $B(-2, 3)$ that passes through (1, 2).
    $(x+2)^2+(y-3)^2=10$
16. Graph $(x+1)^2+(y-2)^2=16$.
17. A new firehouse is being built equidistant from three other fire stations. Positioned on a grid, the current fire stations would be located at (2, 2), (3, −5), and (−5, −5). Find the coordinates of the new firehouse.
    (−1, −2)

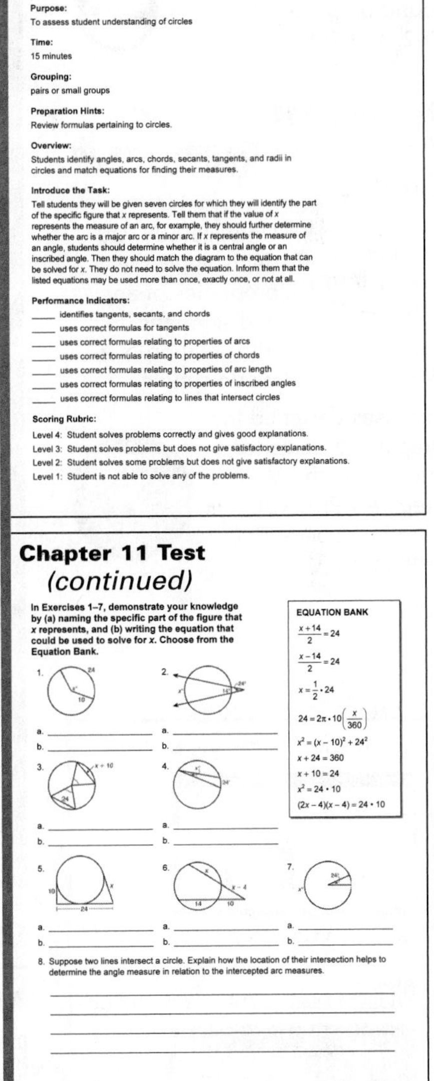

PERFORMANCE ASSESSMENT

Chapter 11 Test

Purpose:
To assess student understanding of circles

Time:
15 minutes

Grouping:
pairs or small groups

Preparation Hints:
Review formulas pertaining to circles.

Overview:
Students identify angles, arcs, chords, secants, tangents, and radii in circles and match equations for finding their measures.

Introduce the Task:
Tell students they will be given seven circles for which they will identify the part of the specific figure that x represents. Tell them that if the value of x represents the measure of an arc, for example, they should further determine whether the arc is a major arc or a minor arc. If x represents the measure of an angle, students should determine whether it is a central angle or an inscribed angle. Then they should match the diagram to the equation that can be solved for x. They do not need to solve the equation. Inform them that the listed equations may be used more than once, exactly once, or not at all.

Performance Indicators:
_____ identifies tangents, secants, and chords
_____ uses correct formulas for tangents
_____ uses correct formulas relating to properties of arcs
_____ uses correct formulas relating to properties of chords
_____ uses correct formulas relating to properties of arc length
_____ uses correct formulas relating to properties of inscribed angles
_____ uses correct formulas relating to lines that intersect circles

Scoring Rubric:
Level 4: Student solves problems correctly and gives good explanations.
Level 3: Student solves problems but does not give satisfactory explanations.
Level 2: Student solves some problems but does not give satisfactory explanations.
Level 1: Student is not able to solve any of the problems.

Chapter 11 Test (continued)

In Exercises 1–7, demonstrate your knowledge by (a) naming the specific part of the figure that x represents, and (b) writing the equation that could be used to solve for x. Choose from the Equation Bank.

EQUATION BANK
$\frac{x+14}{2}=24$
$\frac{x-14}{2}=24$
$x=\frac{1}{2}\cdot 24$
$24=2\pi\cdot 10\left(\frac{x}{360}\right)$
$x^2=(x-10)^2+24^2$
$x+24=360$
$x+10=24$
$x^2=24\cdot 10$
$(2x-4)(x-4)=24\cdot 10$

1. a. ______ b. ______
2. a. ______ b. ______
3. a. ______ b. ______
4. a. ______ b. ______
5. a. ______ b. ______
6. a. ______ b. ______
7. a. ______ b. ______
8. Suppose two lines intersect a circle. Explain how the location of their intersection helps to determine the angle measure in relation to the intercepted arc measures.

Modified chapter tests that address special learning needs are available in *IDEA Works!*® *Modified Worksheets and Tests.*

Teacher One Stop™
Test & Practice Generator

Create and customize Chapter 11 Tests. Instantly generate multiple test versions, answer keys, and practice versions of test items.

CHAPTER 11

SECTION 11A
Lines and Arcs in Circles

On page 770, students use the properties of lines that intersect circles to model real-world situations involving bicycles.

Exercises designed to prepare students for success on the Multi-Step Test Prep can be found on pages 753, 762, and 768.

SECTION 11B
Angles and Segments in Circles

On page 806, students apply the properties of angles and segments in circles to model the creation of a design in a real-world setting.

Exercises designed to prepare students for success on the Multi-Step Test Prep can be found on pages 777, 788, and 797.

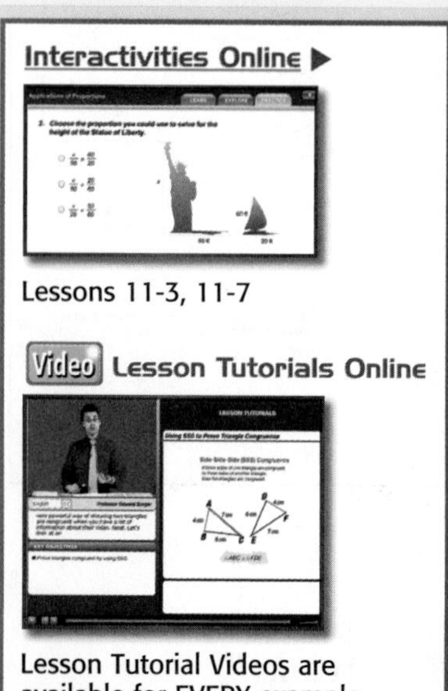

Interactivities Online
Lessons 11-3, 11-7
Video Lesson Tutorials Online
Lesson Tutorial Videos are available for EVERY example.

CHAPTER 11 Circles

Chapter Focus

- Develop and apply the properties of lines and angles that intersect circles.
- Analyze the properties of circles in the coordinate plane and use them to solve real-world problems.

Elegant Eggs!

Constructing egg shapes from curves of different radii is an ancient art form that goes back to prehistoric times.

go.hrw.com
Chapter Project Online
KEYWORD: MG7 ChProj

742 Chapter 11

Elegant Eggs!

About the Project

In this Chapter Project, students explore the role of tangents in constructing smooth curves. Students also learn how to construct elegant egg shapes from curves of different radii. Finally students use reverse curves to create their own designs.

Project Resources

All project resources for teachers and students are provided online.

Materials:

- compass and straightedge
- geometry software

ARE YOU READY?

Vocabulary

Match each term on the left with a definition on the right.

1. radius C
2. pi E
3. circle B
4. circumference A

A. the distance around a circle
B. the locus of points in a plane that are a fixed distance from a given point
C. a segment with one endpoint on a circle and one endpoint at the center of the circle
D. the point at the center of a circle
E. the ratio of a circle's circumference to its diameter

Tables and Charts

The table shows the number of students in each grade level at Middletown High School. Find each of the following.

Year	Number of Students
Freshman	192
Sophomore	208
Junior	216
Senior	184

5. the percentage of students who are freshman 24%
6. the percentage of students who are juniors 27%
7. the percentage of students who are sophomores or juniors 53%

Circle Graphs

The circle graph shows the age distribution of residents of Mesa, Arizona, according to the 2000 census. The population of the city is 400,000.

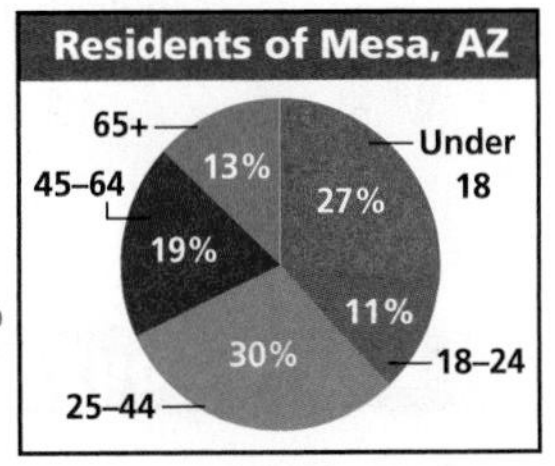

8. How many residents are between the ages of 18 and 24? 44,000
9. How many residents are under the age of 18? 108,000
10. What percentage of the residents are over the age of 45? 32%
11. How many residents are over the age of 45? 128,000

Solve Equations with Variables on Both Sides

Solve each equation.

12. $11y - 8 = 8y + 1$ 3
13. $12x + 32 = 10 + x$ -2
14. $z + 30 = 10z - 15$ 5
15. $4y + 18 = 10y + 15$ $\frac{1}{2}$
16. $-2x - 16 = x + 6$ $-\frac{22}{3}$
17. $-2x - 11 = -3x - 1$ 10

Solve Quadratic Equations

Solve each equation.

18. $17 = x^2 - 32$ ± 7
19. $2 + y^2 = 18$ ± 4
20. $4x^2 + 12 = 7x^2$ ± 2
21. $188 - 6x^2 = 38$ ± 5

CHAPTER 11

ARE YOU READY?

Organizer

Objective: Assess students' understanding of prerequisite skills.

Prerequisite Skills

Tables and Charts
Circle Graphs
Solve Equations with Variables on Both Sides
Solve Quadratic Equations

Assessing Prior Knowledge

INTERVENTION 

Diagnose and Prescribe

Use this page to determine whether intervention is necessary or whether enrichment is appropriate.

Resources

 ***Are You Ready? Intervention and Enrichment* Worksheets**

 ***Are You Ready?* CD-ROM**

 ***Are You Ready?* Online**

my.hrw.com

ARE YOU READY?

Prerequisite Skill	*Are You Ready? Intervention*, Chapter 11 — Worksheets	CD-ROM	Online
Tables and Charts	Skill 83	Activity 83	Diagnose and Prescribe Online
Circles Graphs	Skill 85	Activity 85	
Solve Equations with Variables on Both Sides	Skill 70	Activity 70	
Solve Quadratic Equations	Skill 81	Activity 81	

CHAPTER 11 Study Guide: Preview

Organizer

Objective: Help students organize the new concepts they will learn in Chapter 11.

Online Edition
Multilingual Glossary

Resources

Teacher One Stop™
PuzzleView

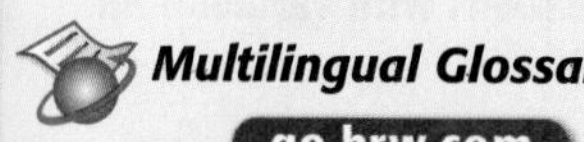

***Multilingual Glossary* Online**
go.hrw.com
KEYWORD: MG7 Glossary

Answers to *Vocabulary Connections*

1. Possible answers: semiannual, semiweekly, semifinal; all the words refer to halves or parts of a whole.
2. A central ∠ has its vertex at the center of a ⊙.
3. The line touches the ⊙. (For example, it intersects the ⊙ at 1 pt.)
4. The line cuts the ⊙. (For example, it intersects the ⊙ at 2 pts.)

CHAPTER 11 Study Guide: Preview

Where You've Been

Previously, you

- used the fundamental vocabulary of circles.
- developed and applied formulas for the area and circumference of circles.
- used circles to solve problems.

In This Chapter

You will study

- solving problems involving circles.
- finding lengths, angle measures, and areas associated with circles.
- applying circle theorems to solve a wide range of problems.

Where You're Going

You can use the skills learned in this chapter

- in Algebra 2 and Precalculus.
- in other classes, such as in Biology when you explore cells, in Physics when you study the laws of motion and kinematic principles, and in Art when you create images.
- to calculate distances, interpret information in newspaper and magazine charts, and make designs.

Key Vocabulary/Vocabulario

arc	arco
arc length	longitud de arco
central angle	ángulo central
chord	cuerda
secant	secante
sector of a circle	sector de un círculo
segment of a circle	segmento de un círculo
semicircle	semicírculo
tangent of a circle	tangente de un círculo

Vocabulary Connections

To become familiar with some of the vocabulary terms in the chapter, answer the following questions. You may refer to the chapter, the glossary, or a dictionary if you like.

1. The word **semicircle** begins with the prefix *semi-*. List some other words that begin with *semi-*. What do all of these words have in common?
2. The word *central* means "located at the center." How can you use this definition to understand the term **central angle** of a circle?
3. The word **tangent** comes from the Latin word *tangere*, which means "to touch." What does this tell you about a line that is a tangent to a circle?
4. The word **secant** comes from the Latin word *secare*, which means "to cut." What does this tell you about a line that is a secant to a circle?

Reading Strategy: Read to Solve Problems

A word problem may be overwhelming at first. Once you identify the important parts of the problem and translate the words into math language, you will find that the problem is similar to others you have solved.

Reading Tips:

- ✔ Read each phrase slowly. Write down what the words mean as you read them.
- ✔ Draw a diagram. Label the diagram so it makes sense to you.
- ✔ Read the problem again before finding your solution.
- ✔ Translate the words or phrases into math language.
- ✔ Highlight what is being asked.

From Lesson 10-3: Use the **Reading Tips** to help you understand this problem.

14. After a day hike, a group of hikers set up a camp 3 km east and 7 km north of the starting point. The elevation of the camp is 0.6 km higher than the starting point. What is the distance from the camp to the starting point?

Identify Key Words	Translate Words into Math	Draw a Diagram
After a day hike, a group of hikers set up a camp *3 km east* and *7 km north* of the *starting point*. The *elevation* of the camp is *0.6 km higher than the starting point*. What is the *distance* from the *camp* to the *starting point*?	The *starting point* can be represented by the ordered triple $(0, 0, 0)$. The *camp* can be represented by the ordered triple $(3, 7, 0.6)$. *Distance* can be found using the *Distance Formula*.	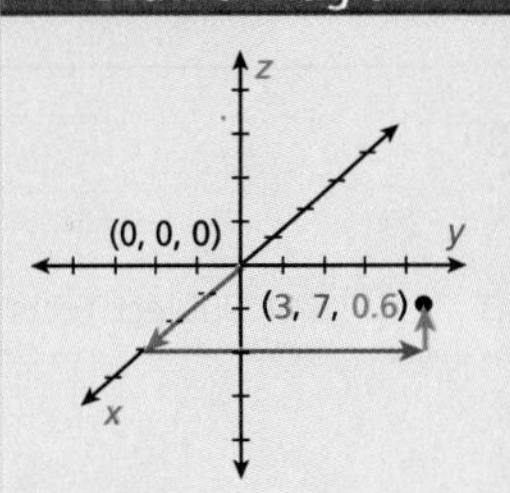

Use the Distance Formula to find the distance between the camp and the starting point.

$$d = \sqrt{(x_2 - x_1)^2 + (y_2 - y_1)^2 + (z_2 - z_1)^2}$$
$$= \sqrt{(3-0)^2 + (7-0)^2 + (0.6-0)^2} \approx 7.6 \text{ km}$$

Try This

For the following problem, apply the following reading tips. Do not solve.

- Identify key words.
- Translate each phrase into math language.
- Draw a diagram to represent the problem.

1. The height of a cylinder is 4 ft, and the diameter is 9 ft. What effect does doubling each measure have on the volume?

Reading and Writing Math CHAPTER 11

Organizer

Objective: Help students apply strategies to understand and retain key concepts.

Resources

 ***Chapter 11 Resource Book***
Reading Strategies

ENGLISH LANGUAGE LEARNERS

Reading Strategy: Read to Solve Problems

Discuss Students benefit from identifying important parts of a word problem and translating the words into math language.

Extend As students work through Chapter 11, have them identify and discuss the key parts of the word problems in the exercises.

Answers

1. cylinder, height is 4 ft, diam. is 9 ft, doubling each measure, effect on volume; original cylinder: $h = 4, d = 9$; new cylinder: $h = 8, d = 18$

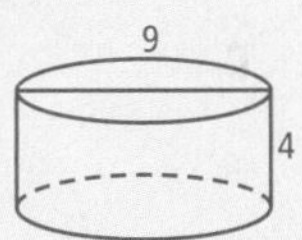

Reading Connection

Circumferences
by Nicholas Nicastro

The story of Eratosthenes's amazingly accurate estimate of the Earth's circumference is the centerpiece of this fascinating book. But the author goes far beyond that tale to portray the full story of the man and his times.

Activity Have students describe Eratosthenes's method for measuring the Earth's circumference, which is based on arcs and proportions, and then try their hand at duplicating his experiment.

SECTION

11A Lines and Arcs in Circles

One-Minute Section Planner

Lesson	Lab Resources	Materials
Lesson 11-1 Lines That Intersect Circles • Identify tangents, secants, and chords. • Use properties of tangents to solve problems. ☐ SAT-10 ☑ NAEP ☑ ACT ☑ SAT ☐ SAT Subject Tests		**Required** compass (MK), straightedge **Optional** coin, photo of bicycle, hula hoop, photos of Native American dream catchers or medicine wheels, protractor (MK)
Lesson 11-2 Arcs and Chords • Apply properties of arcs. • Apply properties of chords. ☐ SAT-10 ☑ NAEP ☐ ACT ☐ SAT ☐ SAT Subject Tests	***Technology Lab Activities*** 11-2 Technology Lab	**Required** compass (MK), protractor (MK), straightedge **Optional** colored pens, circular paper, patty paper
Lesson 11-3 Sector Area and Arc Length • Find the area of sectors. • Find arc lengths. ☐ SAT-10 ☑ NAEP ☐ ACT ☐ SAT ☐ SAT Subject Tests	***Geometry Lab Activities*** 11-3 Geometry Lab	**Required** compass (MK), straightedge, calculator **Optional** long piece of string, compass (MK), protractor (MK), straightedge, ruler (MK)

MK = *Manipulatives Kit*

Math Background

Professional Learning

TANGENTS

Lesson 11-1

Most theorems related to circles that appear in Chapter 11 were known to the mathematicians of antiquity. In fact, Euclid devoted Book III of his *Elements* to definitions and propositions about circles. One of the first definitions in *Elements* states that a straight line *touches* a circle if the line meets the circle but does not cut it. In modern terms, such a line is called a *tangent* to the circle, with the word *tangent* originating from the Latin *tangere*, which means "to touch."

The essential idea is that a circle and a tangent to the circle have exactly one point in common. This common point is called the *point of tangency*. Given a point on a circle, Theorem 11-1-2 provides a technique for constructing the tangent at this point, because it states that the tangent is the line that is perpendicular to the radius of the circle at the given point. Theorem 11-1-1 ensures that this is the *only* tangent line because, according to the contrapositive of this theorem, if a line is not perpendicular to the radius at the point of tangency, then the line is not tangent to the circle.

ARCS

Lesson 11-2

In the most general terms, an *arc* is any smooth curve that joins two points. In the context of circles, an arc is a continuous portion of a circle. An arc of a circle is closely related to the central angle that is defined by the endpoints of the arc and the center of the circle. Students should be aware that most of the theorems about arcs have proofs that depend on working back and forth between properties of arcs and properties of angles.

The Arc Addition Postulate states that the measure of an arc formed by two adjacent arcs is the sum of the measures of the two adjacent arcs. This postulate is analogous to the Angle Addition Postulate. In fact, the Arc Addition Postulate can be stated as a theorem, with its proof drawing on the Angle Addition Postulate. However, a rigorous proof is somewhat tedious in that it requires several cases to account for various combinations of major arcs, minor arcs, and semicircles. For this reason, the principle is simply presented as a postulate in this text.

CHORDS

Lesson 11-2

Theorem 11-2-4 states that in a circle, the perpendicular bisector of any chord is a diameter. This theorem has several important and practical consequences. First, it guarantees that the perpendicular bisector of a chord passes through the center of the circle. This fact can be used to locate the center of a given circle. As shown in the figure, you can draw any two chords of the given circle and construct their perpendicular bisectors. The intersection of the perpendicular bisectors must be the center of the circle, since the center lies on both of these lines.

Theorem 11-2-4 also guarantees that no three points on a circle are collinear. If three points A, B, and C on a circle were collinear, then the perpendicular bisectors of $\overline{AB}$ and $\overline{BC}$ would be parallel. However, this situation is impossible because the perpendicular bisectors of the chords both pass through the center of the circle and must therefore intersect.

SECTOR AREA AND ARC LENGTH

Lesson 11-3

The underlying idea of Lesson 11-3 is proportionality. Students should realize that they can use proportional reasoning to find areas of sectors and arc lengths. They can also use proportionality to derive the relevant formulas if they forget them. For example, to derive the formula for the area of a sector of a circle, set up a proportion as shown.

$$\frac{\text{Area of sector}}{\text{Area of circle}} = \frac{\text{Measure of central angle}}{360^\circ}$$

$$\frac{A}{\pi r^2} = \frac{m^\circ}{360^\circ}$$

Solving the proportion for A gives $A = \pi r^2\left(\frac{m^\circ}{360^\circ}\right)$. Similar reasoning yields the formula for the length of an arc.

11-1 Organizer

Pacing: Traditional 1 day
Block $\frac{1}{2}$ day

Objectives: Identify tangents, secants, and chords.

Use properties of tangents to solve problems.

Power Presentations with PowerPoint®

Warm Up

Write the equation of each line.

1. $\overleftrightarrow{FG}$ $x = -2$ **2.** $\overleftrightarrow{EH}$ $y = 3$

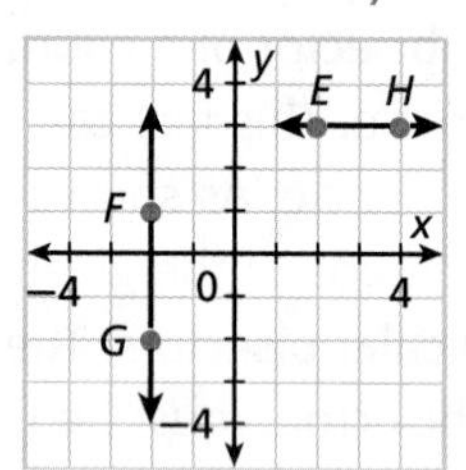

Solve for *x*.

3. $2(25 - x) = x + 2$ $x = 16$

4. $3x + 8 = 4x$ $x = 8$

Also available on transparency

Math Humor

Q: What is the hidden math term?

A: Tangent

State Resources

11-1 Lines That Intersect Circles

Objectives
Identify tangents, secants, and chords.

Use properties of tangents to solve problems.

Vocabulary
interior of a circle
exterior of a circle
chord
secant
tangent of a circle
point of tangency
congruent circles
concentric circles
tangent circles
common tangent

Why learn this?
You can use circle theorems to solve problems about Earth. (See Example 3.)

This photograph was taken 216 miles above Earth. From this altitude, it is easy to see the curvature of the horizon. Facts about circles can help us understand details about Earth.

Recall that a circle is the set of all points in a plane that are equidistant from a given point, called the center of the circle. A circle with center *C* is called circle *C*, or $\odot C$.

The **interior of a circle** is the set of all points inside the circle. The **exterior of a circle** is the set of all points outside the circle.

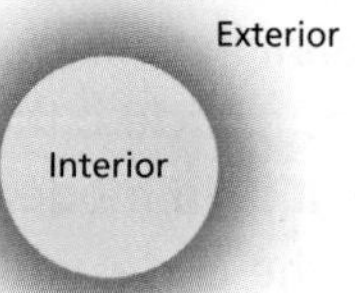

Lines and Segments That Intersect Circles

TERM	DIAGRAM
A **chord** is a segment whose endpoints lie on a circle.	Chord; A; B
A **secant** is a line that intersects a circle at two points.	Secant; ℓ
A **tangent** is a line in the same plane as a circle that intersects it at exactly one point.	Tangent; m
The point where the tangent and a circle intersect is called the **point of tangency**.	C; Point of tangency

EXAMPLE 1 **Identifying Lines and Segments That Intersect Circles**

Identify each line or segment that intersects $\odot A$.

chords: $\overline{EF}$ and $\overline{BC}$

tangent: ℓ

radii: $\overline{AC}$ and $\overline{AB}$

secant: $\overleftrightarrow{EF}$

diameter: $\overline{BC}$

1 Introduce

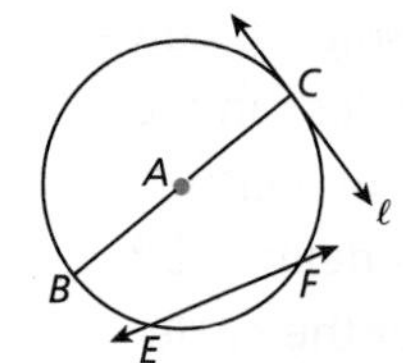

EXPLORATION
11-1 Lines That Intersect Circles

A *tangent* to a circle is a line that is in the same plane as the circle and that intersects it at exactly one point.

1. Construct a circle.
2. Use a straightedge to draw a tangent to the circle.
3. Draw a radius to the point where the tangent intersects the circle.
4. Use a protractor to measure the angle formed by the tangent and the radius. What is the angle measure?
5. Draw three more circles of different sizes and repeat Steps 1–4. Draw the tangent to each circle in a different position.

THINK AND DISCUSS

6. **Describe** what you observed about all of the angles that you measured.
7. **Explain** how you can use your observations to make a conjecture about a tangent to a circle and the radius ...

Motivate

Use the overhead to display a coin standing so that its edge is resting on a line drawn on a transparency. Explain to the students that if the coin represents a circle, then the line represents a tangent, a special line that intersects the circle. You can show students a photo of a bicycle. Explain that the spokes on the wheels represent radii and that the road beneath the bike is tangent to the wheels.

Explorations and answers are provided in *Alternate Openers: Explorations Transparencies.*

1. Identify each line or segment that intersects $\odot P$.

chords: $\overline{QR}$, $\overline{ST}$; secant: $\overleftrightarrow{ST}$; tangent: $\overleftrightarrow{UV}$; diam.: $\overline{ST}$; radii: $\overline{PQ}$, $\overline{PT}$, $\overline{PS}$

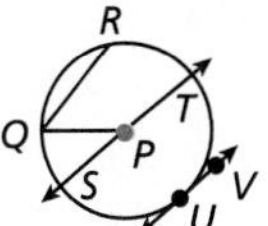

Remember that the terms *radius* and *diameter* may refer to line segments, or to the lengths of segments.

Pairs of Circles

TERM	DIAGRAM
Two circles are **congruent circles** if and only if they have congruent radii.	$\odot A \cong \odot B$ if $\overline{AC} \cong \overline{BD}$. $\overline{AC} \cong \overline{BD}$ if $\odot A \cong \odot B$.
Concentric circles are coplanar circles with the same center.	
Two coplanar circles that intersect at exactly one point are called **tangent circles**.	Internally tangent circles; Externally tangent circles

EXAMPLE 2 Identifying Tangents of Circles

Find the length of each radius. Identify the point of tangency and write the equation of the tangent line at this point.

radius of $\odot A$: 4 — *Center is $(-1, 0)$. Pt. on $\odot$ is $(3, 0)$. Dist. between the 2 pts. is 4.*

radius of $\odot B$: 2 — *Center is $(1, 0)$. Pt. on $\odot$ is $(3, 0)$. Dist. between the 2 pts. is 2.*

point of tangency: $(3, 0)$ — *Pt. where the $\odot$s and tangent line intersect*

equation of tangent line: $x = 3$ — *Vert. line through $(3, 0)$*

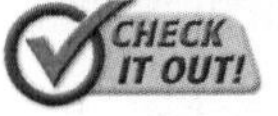

2. Find the length of each radius. Identify the point of tangency and write the equation of the tangent line at this point.

radius of $\odot C$: 1; radius of $\odot D$: 3; pt. of tangency: $(2, -1)$; eqn. of tangent line: $y = -1$

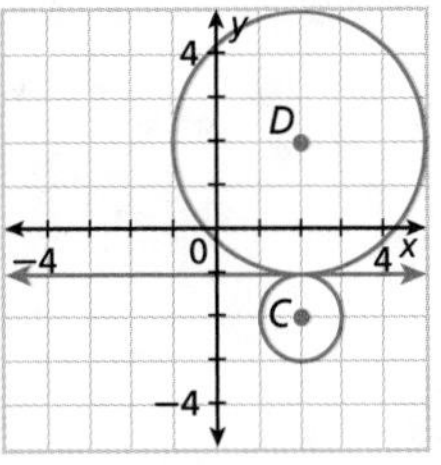

Power Presentations with PowerPoint®

Additional Examples

Example 1

Identify each line or segment that intersects $\odot L$. chords: $\overline{JM}$ and $\overline{KM}$; secant: $\overleftrightarrow{JM}$; tangent: m; diam.: $\overline{KM}$; radii: $\overline{LK}$, $\overline{LJ}$ and $\overline{LM}$

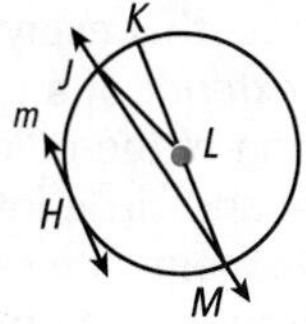

Example 2

Find the length of each radius. Identify the point of tangency and write the equation of the tangent line at this point.

radius of $\odot R$: 2; radius of $\odot S$: 1.5; pt. of tangency: $(-2, 0)$; eqn. of tangent line: $y = 0$

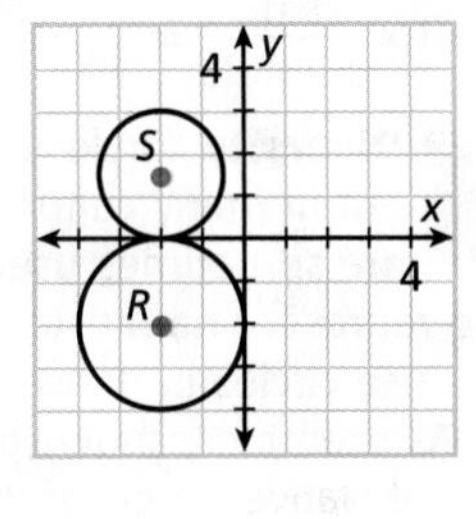

INTERVENTION

Questioning Strategies

EXAMPLE 1

- Explain the relationship between a chord and a diameter. How are they alike? How are they different?
- How many radii are in a circle?

EXAMPLE 2

- How do you know if the equation of a tangent line that is an axis should be written as "$x =$" or "$y =$"?

2 Teach

Guided Instruction

Discuss with students the definitions of chord, secant, and tangent. Place a small hula hoop on a bulletin board and use it to illustrate each vocabulary term. For example, use moveable tangent lines to show examples of external and internal tangents. Discuss pairs of circles and the definitions of congruent, concentric, and tangent circles. Demonstrate for students the construction of a tangent to a circle at a point. Explain how they will use properties of tangents to find segment lengths.

Reaching All Learners

Through Cooperative Learning

Divide students into groups. Instruct each group to draw circles with the following:

1. two common internal and two common external tangents.
2. one common internal and two common external tangents.
3. no common internal and two common external tangents.
4. only one common tangent.
5. no common tangents.

Encourage groups to share their drawings with the class and to identify the properties of the tangents they have drawn.

Construction

Remind students to extend $\overline{PQ}$ far enough to make it easy to draw the arcs with a compass. Compasses can be found in the Manipulatives Kit (MK).

Teaching Tip **Critical Thinking** When you are discussing common tangents with the class, reiterate that every tangent line lies in the *exterior* of a circle, with the exception of the point where the tangent and circle intersect. Common tangents are called *external* or *internal* based on whether the lines themselves intersect *between* the circles. In the diagram, the common external tangents to circles *A* and *B* will intersect if they are extended.

Multiple Representations Students can also use a conversion ratio to change feet to miles in **Example 3**.

$$29{,}000 \text{ ft } x \frac{1 \text{ mi}}{5280 \text{ ft}} = ?$$

Diversity Circles are present in many cultures. They are sometimes used in art work to represent narratives. Some cultures use circles in dances and rituals. As examples, show students pictures of Native American dream catchers and medicine wheels or aboriginal paintings that often use concentric circles.

A **common tangent** is a line that is tangent to two circles.

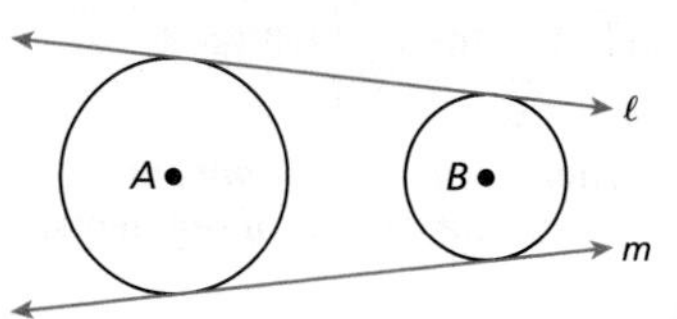

Lines ℓ and m are common external tangents to $\odot A$ and $\odot B$.

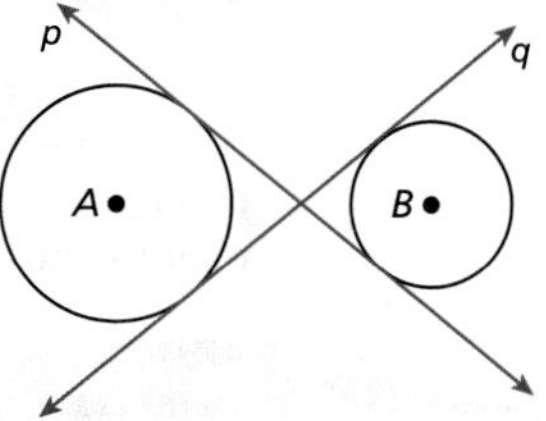

Lines p and q are common internal tangents to $\odot A$ and $\odot B$.

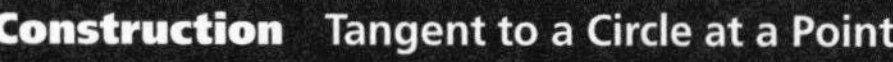

Construction Tangent to a Circle at a Point

1

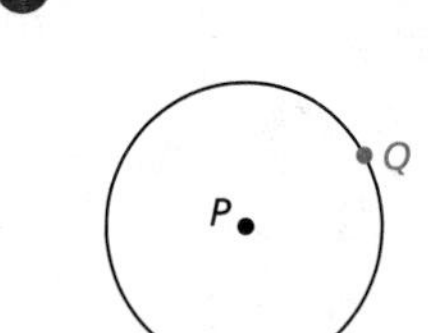

Draw $\odot P$. Locate a point on the circle and label it Q.

2

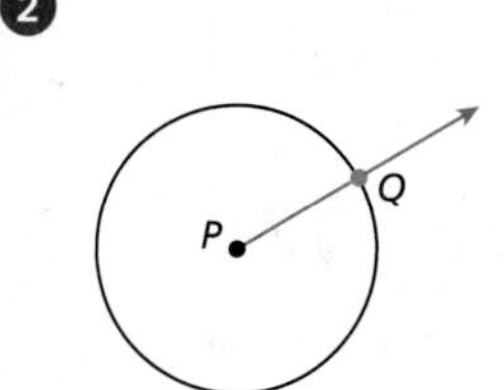

Draw $\overrightarrow{PQ}$.

3

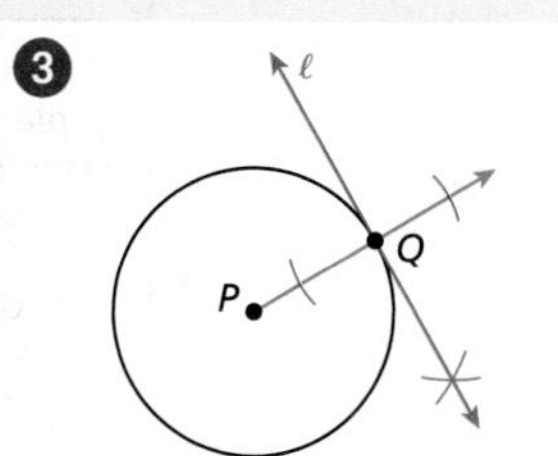

Construct the perpendicular ℓ to $\overrightarrow{PQ}$ at Q. This line is tangent to $\odot P$ at Q.

Notice that in the construction, the tangent line is perpendicular to the radius at the point of tangency. This fact is the basis for the following theorems.

Reading Math

Theorem 11-1-2 is the converse of Theorem 11-1-1.

Theorems

THEOREM		HYPOTHESIS	CONCLUSION
11-1-1	If a line is tangent to a circle, then it is perpendicular to the radius drawn to the point of tangency. (line tangent to $\odot$ → line $\perp$ to radius)	ℓ is tangent to $\odot A$	$\ell \perp \overline{AB}$
11-1-2	If a line is perpendicular to a radius of a circle at a point on the circle, then the line is tangent to the circle. (line $\perp$ to radius → line tangent to $\odot$)	m is $\perp$ to $\overline{CD}$ at D	m is tangent to $\odot C$.

You will prove Theorems 11-1-1 and 11-1-2 in Exercises 28 and 29.

EXAMPLE 3 Problem Solving Application

 Algebra

The summit of Mount Everest is approximately 29,000 ft above sea level. What is the distance from the summit to the horizon to the nearest mile?

1 Understand the Problem

The **answer** will be the length of an imaginary segment from the summit of Mount Everest to Earth's horizon.

2 Make a Plan

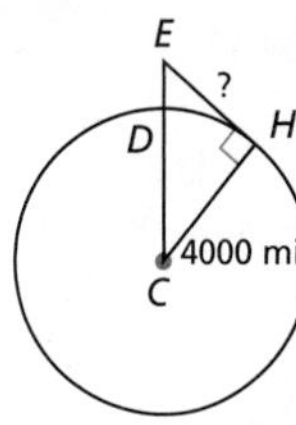

Draw a sketch. Let C be the center of Earth, E be the summit of Mount Everest, and H be a point on the horizon. You need to find the length of $\overline{EH}$, which is tangent to $\odot C$ at H. By Theorem 11-1-1, $\overline{EH} \perp \overline{CH}$. So $\triangle CHE$ is a right triangle.

Helpful Hint

5280 ft = 1 mi
Earth's radius ≈ 4000 mi

 **3 Solve**

$ED = 29{,}000$ ft	*Given*
$= \frac{29{,}000}{5280} \approx 5.49$ mi	*Change ft to mi.*
$EC = CD + ED$	*Seg. Add. Post.*
$= 4000 + 5.49 = 4005.49$ mi	*Substitute 4000 for CD and 5.49 for ED.*
$EC^2 = EH^2 + CH^2$	*Pyth. Thm.*
$4005.49^2 = EH^2 + 4000^2$	*Substitute the given values.*
$43{,}950.14 \approx EH^2$	*Subtract 4000^2 from both sides.*
$210 \text{ mi} \approx EH$	*Take the square root of both sides.*

4 Look Back

The problem asks for the distance to the nearest mile. Check if your answer is reasonable by using the Pythagorean Theorem. Is $210^2 + 4000^2 \approx 4005^2$? Yes, $16{,}044{,}100 \approx 16{,}040{,}025$.

CHECK IT OUT! 3. Kilimanjaro, the tallest mountain in Africa, is 19,340 ft tall. What is the distance from the summit of Kilimanjaro to the horizon to the nearest mile? **171 mi**

Know it! Note — **Theorem 11-1-3**

THEOREM	HYPOTHESIS	CONCLUSION
If two segments are tangent to a circle from the same external point, then the segments are congruent. (2 segs. tangent to ⊙ from same ext. pt. → segs. ≅)	$\overline{AB}$ and $\overline{AC}$ are tangent to $\odot P$.	$\overline{AB} \cong \overline{AC}$

You will prove Theorem 11-1-3 in Exercise 30.

COMMON ERROR ALERT

Some students may assume a segment is tangent to a circle based on the segment's appearance only. Reinforce the fact that a segment is tangent to a circle if and only if it intersects the circle at a point where it is perpendicular to the radius of the circle. Present the example below.

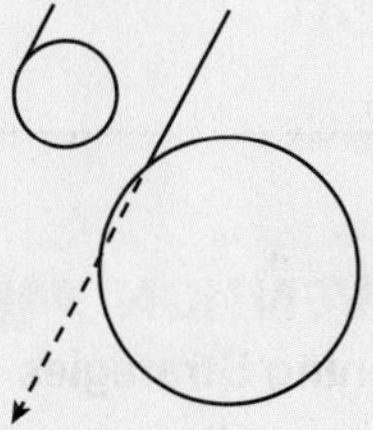

Power Presentations with PowerPoint®

Additional Examples

Example 3

Early in its flight, the Apollo 11 spacecraft orbited Earth at an altitude of 120 miles. What was the distance from the spacecraft to Earth's horizon rounded to the nearest mile? ≈ 987 mi

INTERVENTION

Questioning Strategies

EXAMPLE 3

- Suppose you were trying to find the distance from the center of Earth to the horizon. If Earth is represented by a circle, what angle is formed by a segment from the center of Earth and the tangent at the horizon?

Teaching Tip **Visual** In **Example 3,** explain that since it is given that H is a point on the horizon, then the entire circle represents Earth's horizon. Explain that H could be anywhere on the circle and the solution method would be the same.

Power Presentations with PowerPoint®

Additional Examples

Example 4

$\overline{HK}$ and $\overline{HG}$ are tangent to ⊙F. Find HG. 28

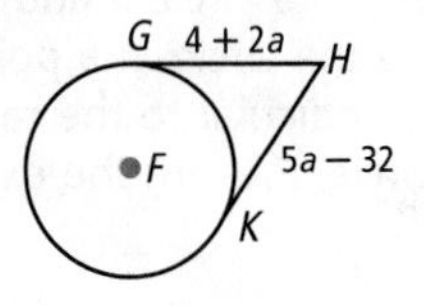

INTERVENTION

Questioning Strategies

EXAMPLE 4

- If two segments are tangent to a circle from two different external points, can you conclude that the segments are congruent? Explain.

You can use Theorem 11-1-3 to find the length of segments drawn tangent to a circle from an exterior point.

EXAMPLE 4 Using Properties of Tangents

$\overline{DE}$ and $\overline{DF}$ are tangent to ⊙C. Find DF.

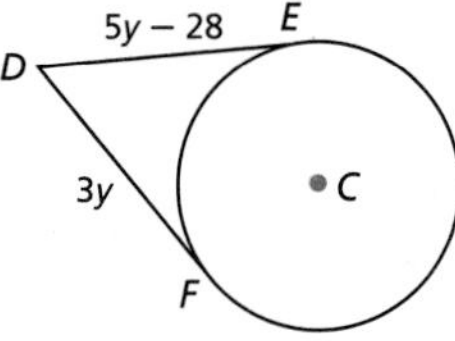

$DE = DF$	*2 segs. tangent to ⊙ from same ext. pt. → segs. ≅.*
$5y - 28 = 3y$	*Substitute 5y – 28 for DE and 3y for DF.*
$2y - 28 = 0$	*Subtract 3y from both sides.*
$2y = 28$	*Add 28 to both sides.*
$y = 14$	*Divide both sides by 2.*
$DF = 3(14)$	*Substitute 14 for y.*
$= 42$	*Simplify.*

CHECK IT OUT! $\overline{RS}$ and $\overline{RT}$ are tangent to ⊙Q. Find RS.

4a.

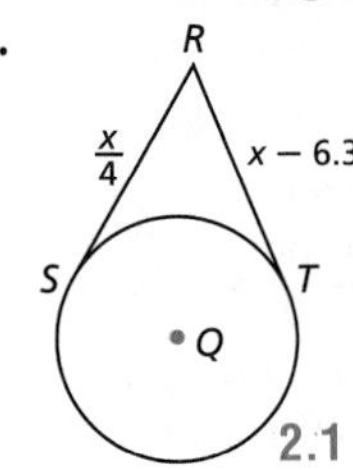

2.1

4b.

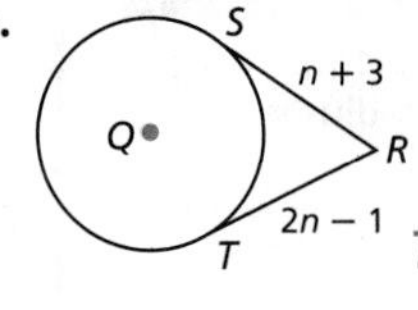

7

THINK AND DISCUSS

1. Consider ⊙A and ⊙B. How many different lines are common tangents to both circles? Copy the circles and sketch the common external and common internal tangent lines.

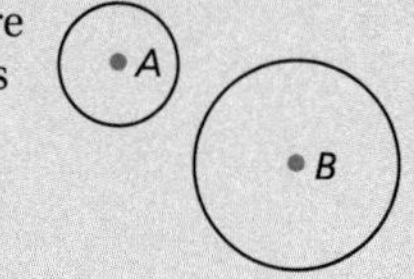

2. Is it possible for a line to be tangent to two concentric circles? Explain your answer.
3. Given ⊙P, is the center P a part of the circle? Explain your answer.
4. In the figure, $\overline{RQ}$ is tangent to ⊙P at Q. Explain how you can find m∠PRQ.

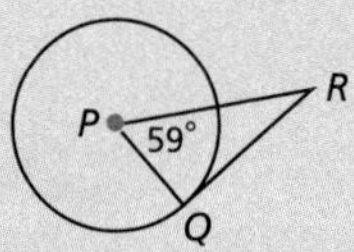

5. **GET ORGANIZED** Copy and complete the graphic organizer below. In each box, write a definition and draw a sketch.

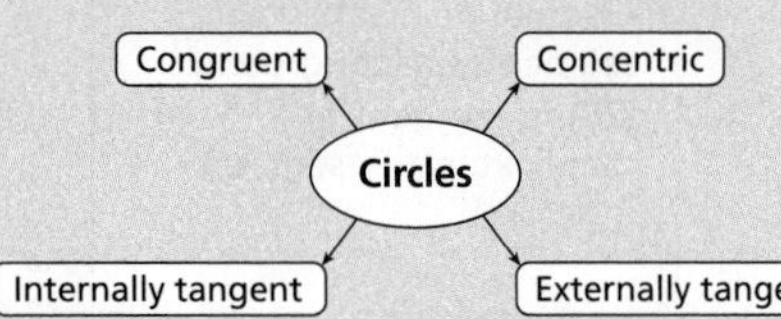

3 Close

Summarize

Have students sketch on the board or overhead examples of each type of line and segment that intersects a circle. Explain the differences between congruent circles, concentric circles, and tangent circles. Review common internal and common external tangents. Remind students that the distance from the center of a circle is measured perpendicularly to a tangent to the circle.

ONGOING ASSESSMENT and INTERVENTION

***Diagnose Before* the Lesson**
11-1 Warm Up, TE p. 746

***Monitor During* the Lesson**
Check It Out! Exercises, SE pp. 747–750
Questioning Strategies, TE pp. 747–750

***Assess After* the Lesson**
11-1 Lesson Quiz, TE p. 754
Alternative Assessment, TE p. 754

Answers to *Think and Discuss*

Possible answers:

1. 4 lines; for sketch, see p. A28.
2. No; if the line is tangent to the ⊙ with the larger radius, it will not intersect the ⊙ with the smaller radius. If the line is tangent to the ⊙ with the smaller radius, it will intersect the ⊙ with the larger radius at 2 pts.
3. No; a ⊙ consists only of those pts. which are a given dist. from the center.
4. By Thm. 11-1-1, m∠PQR = 90°, so by the △ Sum Thm., m∠PRQ = 31°.
5. See p. A8.

11-1 Exercises

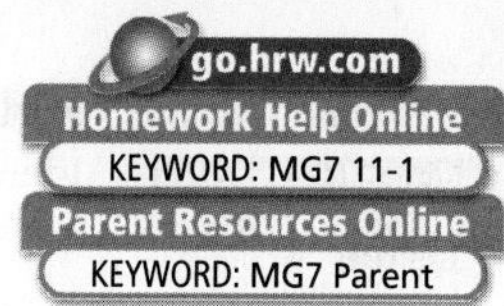

GUIDED PRACTICE

Vocabulary Apply the vocabulary from this lesson to answer each question.

1. A __?__ is a line in the plane of a circle that intersects the circle at two points. **secant**
(*secant* or *tangent*)

2. Coplanar circles that have the same center are called __?__. **concentric**
(*concentric* or *congruent*)

3. $\odot Q$ and $\odot R$ both have a radius of 3 cm. Therefore the circles are __?__. **congruent**
(*concentric* or *congruent*)

SEE EXAMPLE 1
p. 746

Identify each line or segment that intersects each circle.

4. 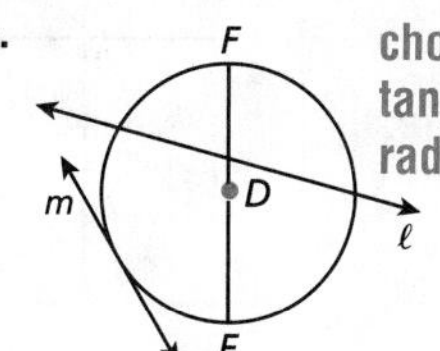

chord: $\overline{EF}$; secant: ℓ; tangent: m; diam.: $\overline{EF}$; radii: $\overline{DE}$, $\overline{DF}$

5. 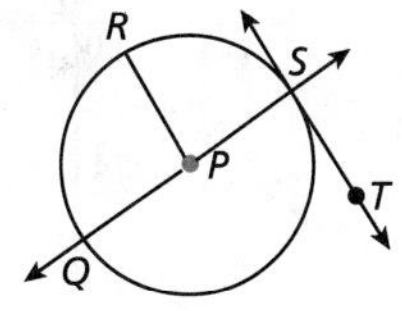

chord: $\overline{QS}$; secant: $\overleftrightarrow{QS}$; tangent: $\overleftrightarrow{ST}$; diam.: $\overline{QS}$; radii: $\overline{PR}$, $\overline{PQ}$, $\overline{PS}$

SEE EXAMPLE 2
p. 747

Multi-Step Find the length of each radius. Identify the point of tangency and write the equation of the tangent line at this point.

6. 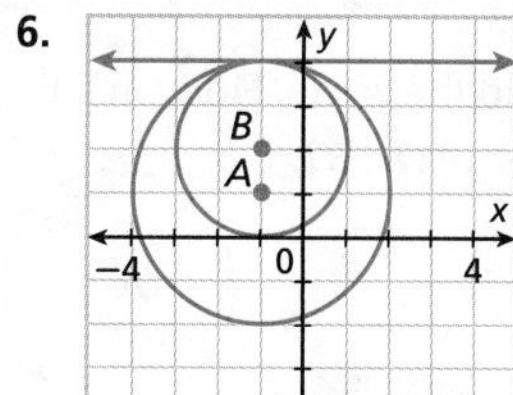

radius of $\odot A$: 3; radius of $\odot B$: 2; pt. of tangency: $(-1, 4)$; eqn. of tangent line: $y = 4$

7. 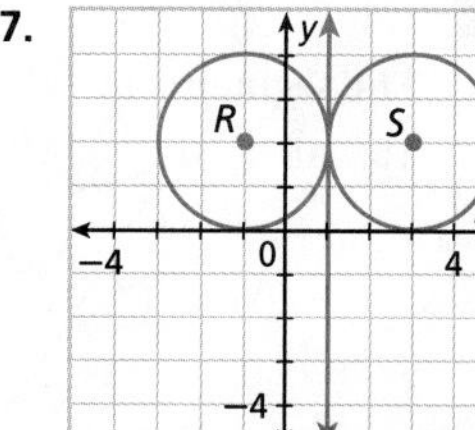

radius of $\odot R$: 2; radius of $\odot S$: 2; pt. of tangency: $(1, 2)$; eqn. of tangent line: $x = 1$

SEE EXAMPLE 3
p. 749

8. **Space Exploration** The International Space Station orbits Earth at an altitude of 240 mi. What is the distance from the space station to Earth's horizon to the nearest mile? **1406 mi**

SEE EXAMPLE 4
p. 750

The segments in each figure are tangent to the circle. Find each length.

9. JK

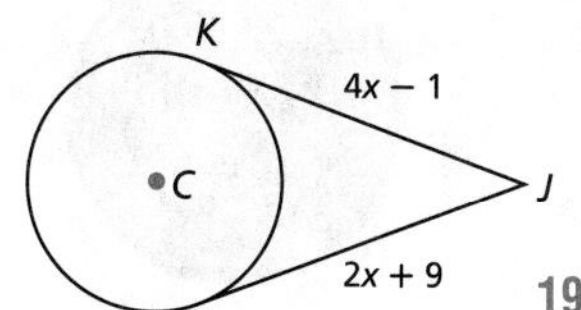

19

10. ST

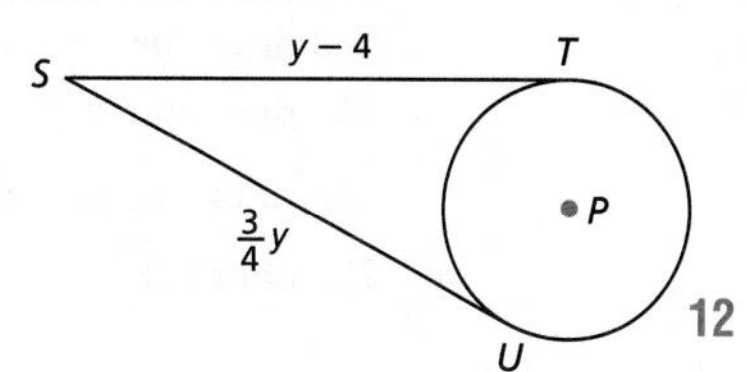

12

11-1 Exercises

Assignment Guide

Assign *Guided Practice* exercises as necessary.

If you finished Examples **1–2**
Basic 11–14, 18, 19, 22–24
Average 11–14, 18, 19, 22–25
Advanced 11–14, 18, 19, 22–25, 41

If you finished Examples **1–4**
Basic 11–28, 31–35, 38–40, 44–48
Average 11–41, 44–48
Advanced 11–48

Homework Quick Check
Quickly check key concepts.
Exercises: 12, 14, 15, 16, 20, 26

State Resources

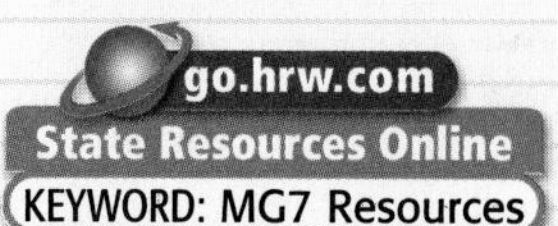

Teaching Tip **Reading Math** **Exercises 18–22** provide an opportunity for students to practice the Reading and Writing Math study strategy they learned on page 745. Advise students to carefully translate the words of these exercises into diagrams and math language before finding their solutions. ENGLISH LANGUAGE LEARNERS

PRACTICE AND PROBLEM SOLVING

Independent Practice	
For Exercises	See Example
11–12	1
13–14	2
15	3
16–17	4

Extra Practice
Skills Practice p. S24
Application Practice p. S38

Identify each line or segment that intersects each circle.

11. 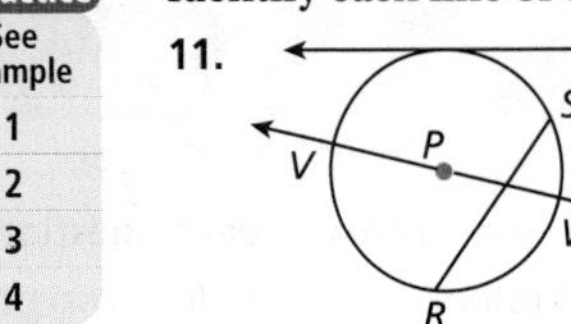

chords: $\overline{RS}$, $\overline{VW}$; secant: $\overleftrightarrow{VW}$; tangent: ℓ; diam.: $\overline{VW}$; radii: $\overline{PV}$, $\overline{PW}$

12. 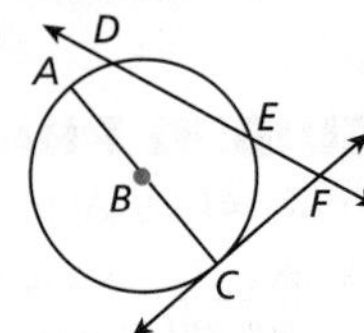

chords: $\overline{DE}$, $\overline{AC}$; secant: $\overleftrightarrow{DE}$; tangent: $\overleftrightarrow{CF}$; diam.: $\overline{AC}$; radii: $\overline{BA}$, $\overline{BC}$

Multi-Step **Find the length of each radius. Identify the point of tangency and write the equation of the tangent line at this point.**

13. 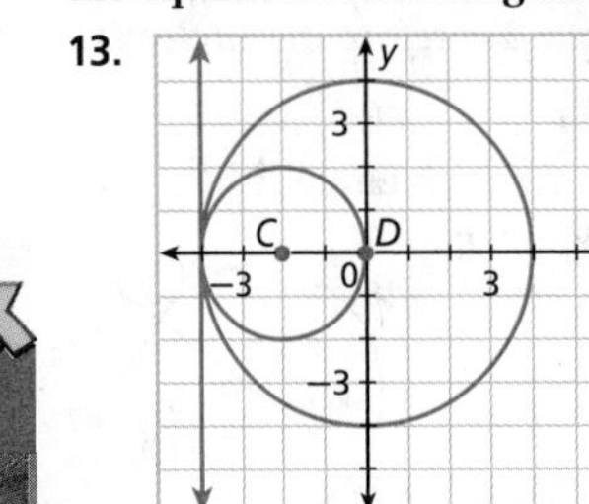

radius of ⊙C: 2; radius of ⊙D: 4; pt. of tangency: (–4, 0); eqn. of tangent line: $x = -4$

14. 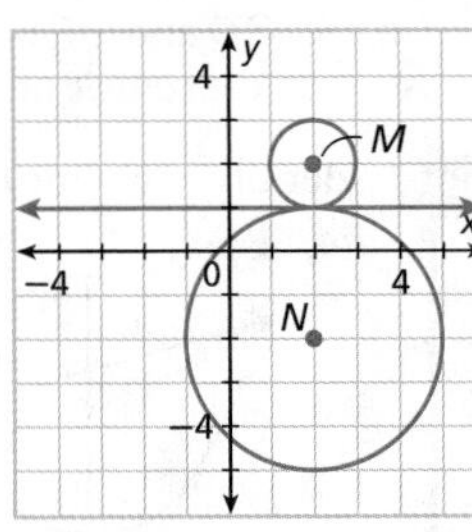

radius of ⊙M: 1; radius of ⊙N: 3; pt. of tangency: (2, 1); eqn. of tangent line: $y = 1$

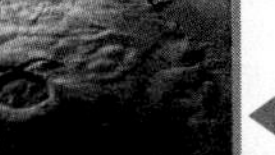

Astronomy

Olympus Mons, located on Mars, is the tallest known volcano in the solar system.

15. **Astronomy** Olympus Mons's peak rises 25 km above the surface of the planet Mars. The diameter of Mars is approximately 6794 km. What is the distance from the peak of Olympus Mons to the horizon to the nearest kilometer? **413 km**

The segments in each figure are tangent to the circle. Find each length.

16. AB 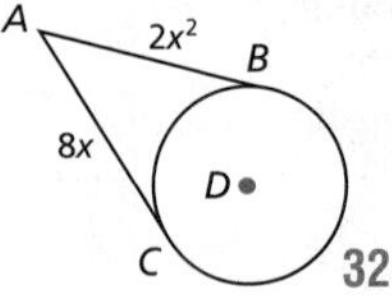

32

17. RT 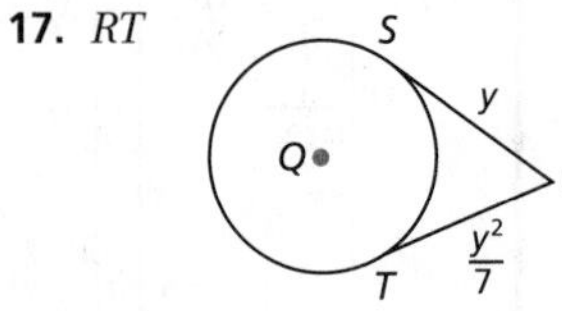

7

Tell whether each statement is sometimes, always, or never true.

18. Two circles with the same center are congruent. **S**

19. A tangent to a circle intersects the circle at two points. **N**

20. Tangent circles have the same center. **N**

21. A tangent to a circle will form a right angle with a radius that is drawn to the point of tangency. **A**

22. A chord of a circle is a diameter. **S**

Graphic Design **Use the following diagram for Exercises 23–25.**

The peace symbol was designed in 1958 by Gerald Holtom, a professional artist and designer. Identify the following.

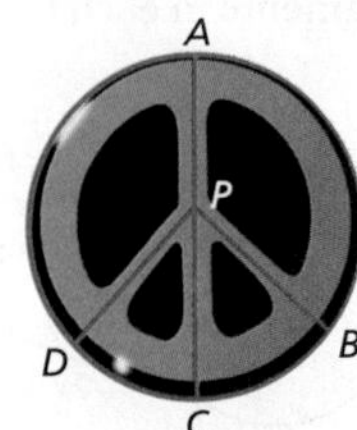

23. diameter $\overline{AC}$

24. radii $\overline{PA}$, $\overline{PB}$, $\overline{PC}$, $\overline{PD}$

25. chord $\overline{AC}$

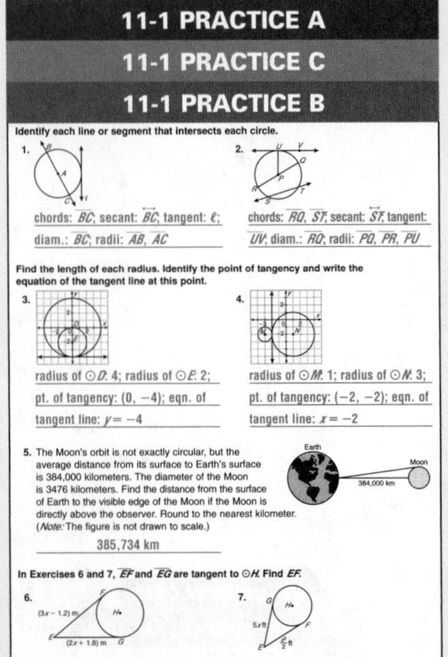
11-1 PRACTICE A
11-1 PRACTICE C
11-1 PRACTICE B

Identify each line or segment that intersects each circle.

1. chords: $\overline{BC}$; secant: $\overleftrightarrow{BC}$; tangent: ℓ; diam.: $\overline{BC}$; radii: $\overline{AB}$, $\overline{AC}$

2. chords: $\overline{RQ}$, $\overline{ST}$; secant: $\overleftrightarrow{ST}$; tangent: $\overleftrightarrow{UV}$; diam.: $\overline{RQ}$; radii: $\overline{PQ}$, $\overline{PR}$, $\overline{PU}$

Find the length of each radius. Identify the point of tangency and write the equation of the tangent line at this point.

3. radius of ⊙D: 4; radius of ⊙E: 2; pt. of tangency: (0, –4); eqn. of tangent line: $y = -4$

4. radius of ⊙M: 1; radius of ⊙N: 3; pt. of tangency: (–2, –2); eqn. of tangent line: $x = -2$

5. The Moon's orbit is not exactly circular, but the average distance from its surface to Earth's surface is 384,000 kilometers. The diameter of the Moon is 3476 kilometers. Find the distance from the surface of Earth to the visible edge of the Moon if the Moon is directly above the observer. Round to the nearest kilometer. (*Note:* The figure is not drawn to scale.)
385,734 km

In Exercises 6 and 7, $\overline{EF}$ and $\overline{EG}$ are tangent to ⊙H. Find EF.

6. 7.8 m

7. 50 ft

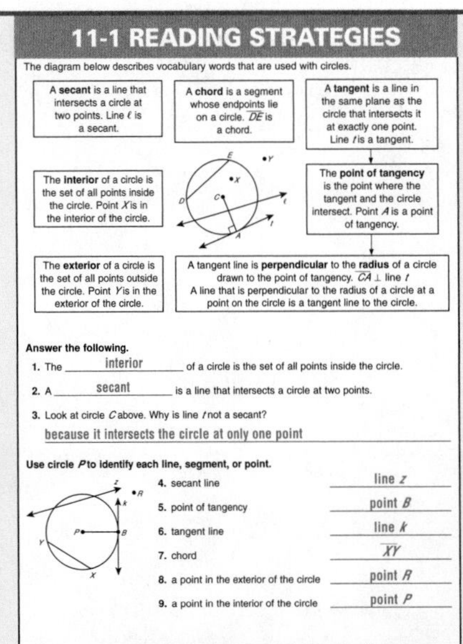
11-1 READING STRATEGIES

The diagram below describes vocabulary words that are used with circles.

A **secant** is a line that intersects a circle at two points. Line ℓ is a secant.

A **chord** is a segment whose endpoints lie on a circle. $\overline{DE}$ is a chord.

A **tangent** is a line in the same plane as the circle that intersects it at exactly one point. Line *t* is a tangent.

The **interior** of a circle is the set of all points inside the circle. Point *X* is in the interior of the circle.

The **point of tangency** is the point where the tangent and the circle intersect. Point *A* is a point of tangency.

The **exterior** of a circle is the set of all points outside the circle. Point *Y* is in the exterior of the circle.

A tangent line is **perpendicular** to the **radius** of a circle drawn to the point of tangency. $\overline{CA}$ ⊥ line *t*. A line that is perpendicular to the radius of a circle at a point on the circle is a tangent line to the circle.

Answer the following.

1. The interior of a circle is the set of all points inside the circle.
2. A secant is a line that intersects a circle at two points.
3. Look at circle *C* above. Why is line *t* not a secant? because it intersects the circle at only one point

Use circle *P* to identify each line, segment, or point.

4. secant line — line *z*
5. point of tangency — point *B*
6. tangent line — line *k*
7. chord — $\overline{XY}$
8. a point in the exterior of the circle — point *R*
9. a point in the interior of the circle — point *P*

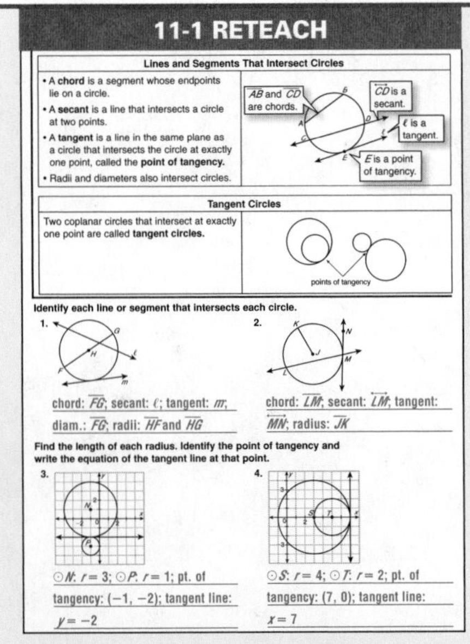
11-1 RETEACH

Lines and Segments That Intersect Circles

- A **chord** is a segment whose endpoints lie on a circle.
- A **secant** is a line that intersects a circle at two points.
- A **tangent** is a line in the same plane as a circle that intersects the circle at exactly one point, called the **point of tangency**.
- Radii and diameters also intersect circles.

$\overline{AB}$ and $\overline{CD}$ are chords. $\overleftrightarrow{CD}$ is a secant. ℓ is a tangent. *E* is a point of tangency.

Tangent Circles

Two coplanar circles that intersect at exactly one point are called **tangent circles**.

points of tangency

Identify each line or segment that intersects each circle.

1. chord: $\overline{FG}$; secant: ℓ; tangent: *m*; diam.: $\overline{FG}$; radii: $\overline{HF}$ and $\overline{HG}$

2. chord: $\overline{LM}$; secant: $\overleftrightarrow{LM}$; tangent: $\overleftrightarrow{MN}$; radius: $\overline{JK}$

Find the length of each radius. Identify the point of tangency and write the equation of the tangent line at that point.

3. ⊙N: r = 3; ⊙P: r = 1; pt. of tangency: (–1, –2); tangent line: $y = -2$

4. ⊙S: r = 4; ⊙T: r = 2; pt. of tangency: (7, 0); tangent line: $x = 7$

In each diagram, $\overline{PR}$ and $\overline{PS}$ are tangent to $\odot Q$. Find each angle measure.

26. $m\angle Q$ **138°**

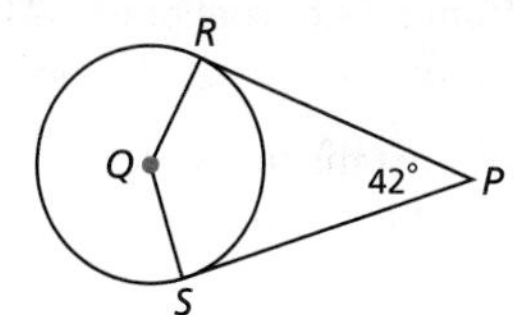

27. $m\angle P$ **45°**

28a. The ⊥ seg. from a pt. to a line is the shortest seg. from the pt. to the line.
b. *B*
c. radius
d. line $\ell \perp \overline{AB}$

28. Complete this indirect proof of Theorem 11-1-1.
Given: ℓ is tangent to $\odot A$ at point *B*.
Prove: $\ell \perp \overline{AB}$

Proof: Assume that ℓ is not $\perp \overline{AB}$. Then it is possible to draw $\overline{AC}$ such that $\overline{AC} \perp \ell$. If this is true, then $\triangle ACB$ is a right triangle. $AC < AB$ because **a.** __?__ . Since ℓ is a tangent line, it can only intersect $\odot A$ at **b.** __?__ , and *C* must be in the exterior of $\odot A$. That means that $AC > AB$ since $\overline{AB}$ is a **c.** __?__ . This contradicts the fact that $AC < AB$. Thus the assumption is false, and **d.** __?__ .

29. Prove Theorem 11-1-2.
Given: $m \perp \overline{CD}$
Prove: *m* is tangent to $\odot C$.
(*Hint:* Choose a point on *m*. Then use the Pythagorean Theorem to prove that if the point is not *D*, then it is not on the circle.)

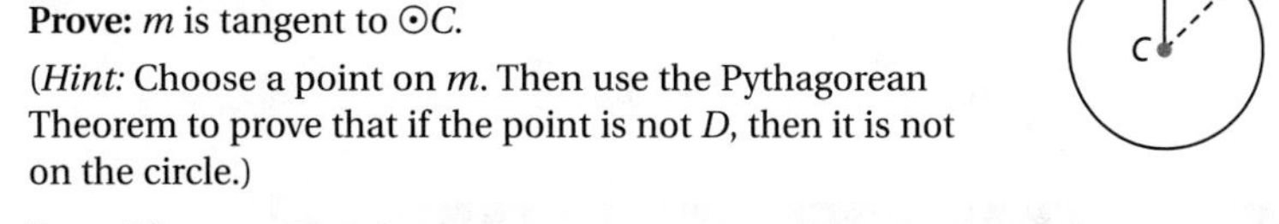

30. Prove Theorem 11-1-3.
Given: $\overline{AB}$ and $\overline{AC}$ are tangent to $\odot P$.
Prove: $\overline{AB} \cong \overline{AC}$
Plan: Draw auxiliary segments $\overline{PA}$, $\overline{PB}$, and $\overline{PC}$. Show that the triangles formed are congruent. Then use CPCTC.

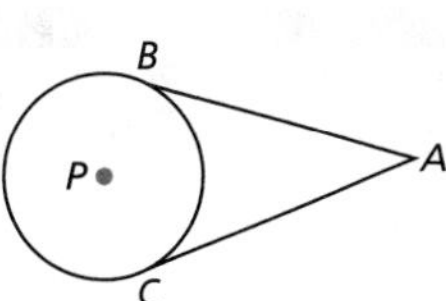

Algebra Assume the segments that appear to be tangent are tangent. Find each length.

31. *ST* **8**

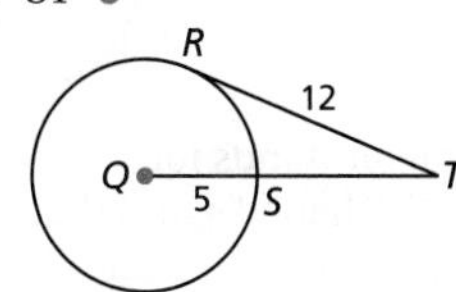

32. *DE* **18**

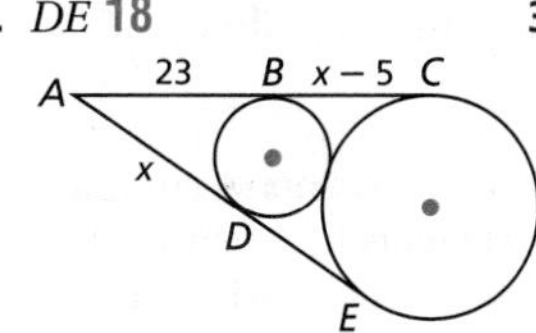

33. *JL* **22**

34. $\odot M$ has center $M(2, 2)$ and radius 3. $\odot N$ has center $N(-3, 2)$ and is tangent to $\odot M$. Find the coordinates of the possible points of tangency of the two circles. **(−1, 2); (5, 2)**

MULTI-STEP TEST PREP

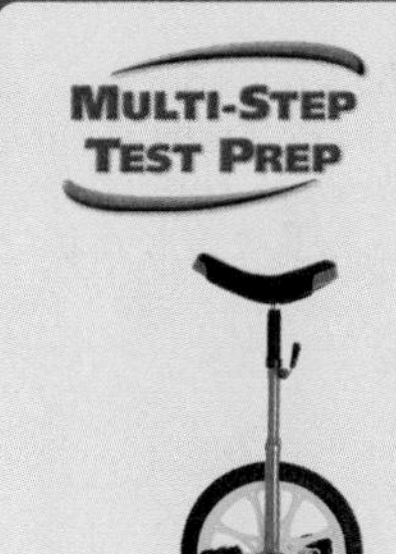

35. This problem will prepare you for the Multi-Step Test Prep on page 770.
The diagram shows the gears of a bicycle. $AD = 5$ in., and $BC = 3$ in. *CD*, the length of the chain between the gears, is 17 in.

a. What type of quadrilateral is *BCDE*? Why?
b. Find *BE* and *AE*. **17 in.; 2 in.**
c. What is *AB* to the nearest tenth of an inch? **17.1 in.**

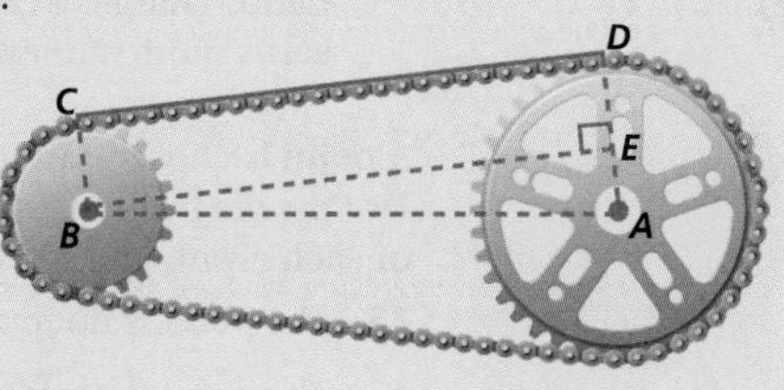

COMMON ERROR ALERT

In **Exercise 15,** some students may try to convert kilometers to miles, as they did with other application problems in the lesson. Caution students to pay close attention to units so that they do not try to perform unnecessary conversions.

MULTI-STEP TEST PREP **Exercise 35** involves using the properties of tangents to find the distance between the centers of two circles, or two wheels of a bicycle. This exercise prepares students for the Multi-Step Test Prep on page 770.

Answers

29. Let *E* be any pt. on line *m* other than *D*. It is given that line $m \perp \overline{CD}$, so $\triangle CDE$ is a rt. △ with hyp. $\overline{CE}$. Therefore $CE > CD$. Since $\overline{CD}$ is a radius, *E* must lie in the ext. of $\odot C$. Thus *D* is the only pt. on line *m* that is also on the ⊙. This means line *m* is tangent to the ⊙.

30. Since 2 pts. determine a line, draw auxiliary line segs. $\overline{PA}$, $\overline{PB}$, and $\overline{PC}$. Since $\overline{AB}$ and $\overline{AC}$ are tangents to $\odot P$, $\overline{AB} \perp \overline{PB}$ and $\overline{AC} \perp \overline{PC}$, so $\triangle ABP$ and $\triangle ACP$ are rt. △s. $\overline{PB} \cong \overline{PC}$ since they are both radii of $\odot P$, and $\overline{PA} \cong \overline{PA}$ by the Reflex. Prop. of ≅. Therefore $\triangle ABP \cong \triangle ACP$ by the HL ≅ Thm., and $\overline{AB} \cong \overline{AC}$ by CPCTC.

35a. rect.; $\angle BCD$ and $\angle EDC$ are rt. ∠s because a line tangent to a ⊙ is ⊥ to a radius. It is given that $\angle DEB$ is a rt. ∠. $\angle CBE$ must also be a rt. ∠ because the sum of the ∠s of a quad. is 360°. Thus *BCDE* has 4 rt. ∠s and is a rect.

11-1 PROBLEM SOLVING

1. The cruising altitude of a commercial airplane is about 9000 meters. Use the diagram to find *AB*, the distance from an airplane at cruising altitude to Earth's horizon. Round to the nearest kilometer.
339 km

2. In the figure, segments that appear to be tangent are tangent. Find *QS*.
27

3. The area of $\odot H$ is 100π, and $HF = 26$ centimeters. What is the perimeter of quadrilateral *EFGH*?
68 cm

4. $\overrightarrow{IH}$, $\overline{IK}$, and $\overrightarrow{KL}$ are tangent to $\odot A$. What is *IK*?
47

Choose the best answer.

5. A teardrop-shaped roller coaster loop is a section of a spiral in which the radius is constantly changing. The radius at the bottom of the loop is much larger than the radius at the top of the loop, as shown in the figure. Which is a true statement?
A $\odot K$ and $\odot M$ have two points of tangency.
B $\odot K$, $\odot L$, and $\odot M$ have one point of tangency.
(C) $\odot L$ is internally tangent to $\odot K$ and $\odot M$.
D $\odot L$ is externally tangent to $\odot K$ and $\odot M$.

6. $\odot G$ has center (2, 5) and radius 3. $\odot H$ has center (2, 0). If the circles are tangent, which line could be tangent to both circles?
F $x = 2$
G $x = 0$
(H) $y = 2$
J $y = 5$

7. The Hubble Space Telescope orbits 353 miles above Earth, and Earth's radius is about 3960 miles. Which is closest to the distance from the telescope to Earth's horizon?
A 1634 mi
(B) 1709 mi
C 3976 mi
D 5855 mi

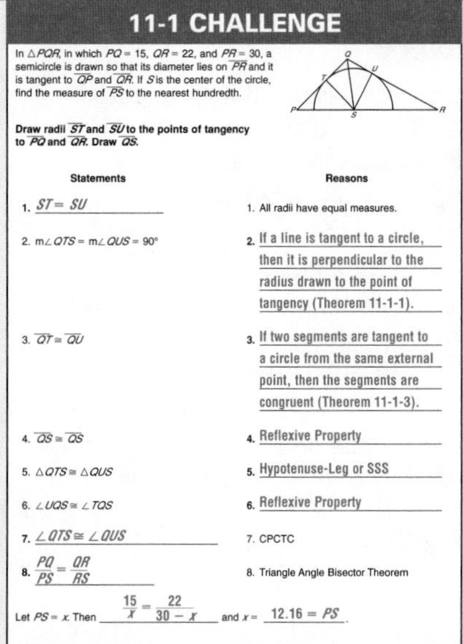

11-1 CHALLENGE

In $\triangle PQR$, in which $PQ = 15$, $QR = 22$, and $PR = 30$, a semicircle is drawn so that its diameter lies on $\overline{PR}$ and it is tangent to $\overline{QP}$ and $\overline{QR}$. If *S* is the center of the circle, find the measure of $\overline{PS}$ to the nearest hundredth.

Draw radii $\overline{ST}$ and $\overline{SU}$ to the points of tangency to $\overline{PQ}$ and $\overline{QR}$. Draw $\overline{QS}$.

Statements	Reasons
1. $ST = SU$	1. All radii have equal measures.
2. $m\angle QTS = m\angle QUS = 90°$	2. If a line is tangent to a circle, then it is perpendicular to the radius drawn to the point of tangency (Theorem 11-1-1).
3. $\overline{QT} \cong \overline{QU}$	3. If two segments are tangent to a circle from the same external point, then the segments are congruent (Theorem 11-1-3).
4. $\overline{QS} \cong \overline{QS}$	4. Reflexive Property
5. $\triangle QTS \cong \triangle QUS$	5. Hypotenuse-Leg or SSS
6. $\angle UQS \cong \angle TQS$	6. Reflexive Property
7. $\angle QTS \cong \angle QUS$	7. CPCTC
8. $\frac{PQ}{PS} = \frac{QR}{RS}$	8. Triangle Angle Bisector Theorem

Let $PS = x$. Then $\frac{15}{x} = \frac{22}{30 - x}$ and $x = 12.16 = PS$.

TEST PREP DOCTOR Students who chose choice **F** for **Exercise 39** are not remembering that the equation for the *x*-aaxis is $y = 0$. Have them subtract 2 from each solution to see if the values they obtained match either the *x*- or *y*-coordinate of the center.

Journal

Have students explain why distance from the center of a circle is determined by a radius drawn perpendicularly to a tangent at the point of tangency. Have them support their explanations with sketches.

ALTERNATIVE ASSESSMENT

Have each student draw a circle and construct two intersecting tangents at two different points on the circle. Then have them measure each tangent and the angle that a radius makes with a tangent. Have them describe which theorems have been demonstrated in their constructions.

Power Presentations with PowerPoint®

11-1 Lesson Quiz

1. Identify each line or segment that intersects $\odot Q$. chords $\overline{VT}$ and $\overline{WR}$; secant: $\overleftrightarrow{VT}$; tangent: *s*; diam.: $\overline{WR}$; radii: $\overline{QW}$ and $\overline{QR}$

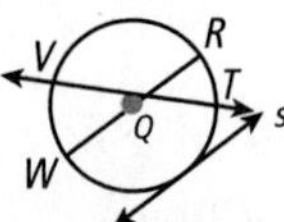

2. Find the length of each radius. Identify the point of tangency and write the equation of the tangent line at this point. radius of $\odot C$: 3; radius of $\odot D$: 2; pt. of tangency: (3, 2); eqn. of tangent line: $x = 3$

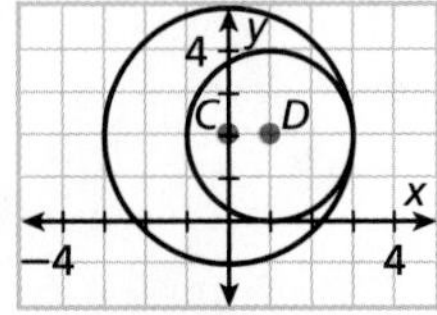

3. Mount Mitchell peaks at 6,684 feet. What is the distance from this peak to the horizon, rounded to the nearest mile? ≈101 mi

4. $\overline{FE}$ and $\overline{FG}$ are tangent to $\odot J$. Find *FG*. 90

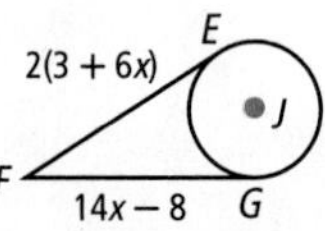

Also available on transparency

36. **Critical Thinking** Given a circle with diameter $\overline{BC}$, is it possible to draw tangents to *B* and *C* from an external point *X*? If so, make a sketch. If not, explain why it is not possible.

37. **Write About It** $\overline{PR}$ and $\overline{PS}$ are tangent to $\odot Q$. Explain why $\angle P$ and $\angle Q$ are supplementary.

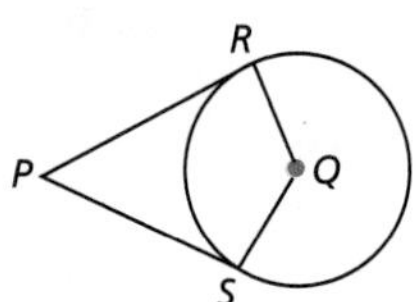

TEST PREP

38. $\overline{AB}$ and $\overline{AC}$ are tangent to $\odot D$. Which of these is closest to *AD*?

    Ⓐ 9.5 cm Ⓒ 10.4 cm Ⓑ 10 cm Ⓓ 13 cm

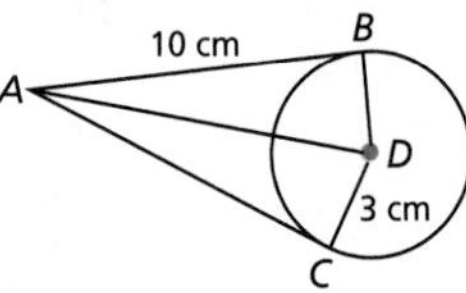

39. $\odot P$ has center *P*(3, −2) and radius 2. Which of these lines is tangent to $\odot P$?

    Ⓕ $x = 0$ Ⓖ $y = -4$ Ⓗ $y = -2$ Ⓙ $x = 4$

40. $\odot A$ has radius 5. $\odot B$ has radius 6. What is the ratio of the area of $\odot A$ to that of $\odot B$?

    Ⓐ $\frac{125}{216}$ Ⓑ $\frac{25}{36}$ Ⓒ $\frac{5}{6}$ Ⓓ $\frac{36}{25}$

CHALLENGE AND EXTEND

41. **Given:** $\odot G$ with $\overline{GH} \perp \overline{JK}$
    Prove: $\overline{JH} \cong \overline{KH}$

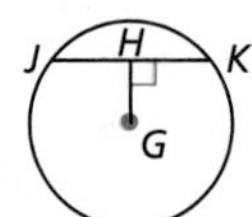

42. **Multi-Step** $\odot A$ has radius 5, $\odot B$ has radius 2, and $\overline{CD}$ is a common tangent. What is *AB*? (*Hint:* Draw a perpendicular segment from *B* to *E*, a point on $\overline{AC}$.) $3\sqrt{17}$

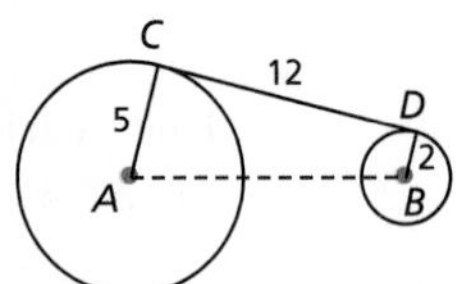

43. **Manufacturing** A company builds metal stands for bicycle wheels. A new design calls for a V-shaped stand that will hold wheels with a 13 in. radius. The sides of the stand form a 70° angle. To the nearest tenth of an inch, what should be the length *XY* of a side so that it is tangent to the wheel? **18.6 in.**

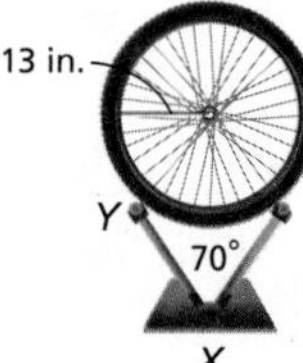

SPIRAL REVIEW

44. Andrea and Carlos both mow lawns. Andrea charges $14.00 plus $6.25 per hour. Carlos charges $12.50 plus $6.50 per hour. If they both mow *h* hours and Andrea earns more money than Carlos, what is the range of values of *h*? *(Previous course)* $0 < h < 6$

A point is chosen randomly on $\overline{LR}$. Use the diagram to find the probability of each event. *(Lesson 9-6)*

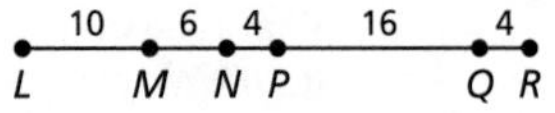

L —10— M —6— N —4— P —16— Q —4— R

45. The point is not on $\overline{MP}$. $\frac{3}{4}$

46. The point is on $\overline{LP}$. $\frac{1}{2}$

47. The point is on $\overline{MN}$ or $\overline{PR}$. $\frac{13}{20}$

48. The point is on $\overline{QR}$. $\frac{1}{10}$

Answers

36. It is not possible. If it were possible, △XBC would contain 2 rt. ∡, which contradicts the △ Sum Thm.

37. The sum of the ∠ measures in quad. *PRQS* is 360°. Since a line tangent to a ⊙ is ⊥ to a radius, ∠*R* and ∠*S* are rt. ∡. By subst., m∠*P* + m∠*R* + m∠*Q* + m∠*S* = m∠*P* + 90° + m∠*Q* + 90° = 360°. By subtr., m∠*P* + m∠*Q* = 180°. Thus by def., ∠*P* and ∠*Q* are supp. ∡.

41. Since 2 pts. determine a line, draw auxiliary segs. $\overline{GJ}$ and $\overline{GK}$. It is given that $\overline{GH} \perp \overline{JK}$, so ∠*GHJ* and ∠*GHK* are rt. ∡. Therefore △*GHJ* and △*GHK* are rt. ∡. $\overline{GH} \cong \overline{GH}$ by the Reflex. Prop. of ≅, and $\overline{GJ} \cong \overline{GK}$ because they are radii of $\odot G$. Thus △*GHJ* ≅ △*GHK* by the HL ≅ Thm., and $\overline{JH} \cong \overline{KH}$ by CPCTC.

Circle Graphs

A circle graph compares data that are parts of a whole unit. When you make a circle graph, you find the measure of each *central angle*. A *central angle* is an angle whose vertex is the center of the circle.

Example

Make a circle graph to represent the following data.

Books in the Bookmobile	
Fiction	110
Nonfiction	40
Children's	300
Audio books	150

Step 1 Add all the amounts. *110 + 40 + 300 + 150 = 600*

Step 2 Write each part as a fraction of the whole.

fiction: $\frac{110}{600}$; nonfiction: $\frac{40}{600}$; children's: $\frac{300}{600}$; audio books: $\frac{150}{600}$

Step 3 Multiply each fraction by 360° to calculate the central angle measure.

$\frac{110}{600}(360°) = 66°$; $\frac{40}{600}(360°) = 24°$; $\frac{300}{600}(360°) = 180°$; $\frac{150}{600}(360°) = 90°$

Step 4 Make a circle graph. Then color each section of the circle to match the data.

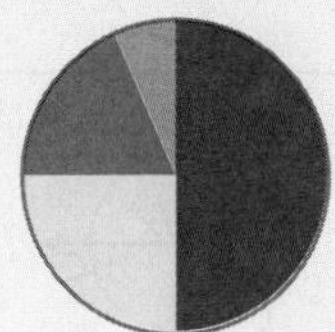

The section with a central angle of 66° is green, 24° is orange, 180° is purple, and 90° is yellow.

Try This

Choose the circle graph that best represents the data. Show each step.

A
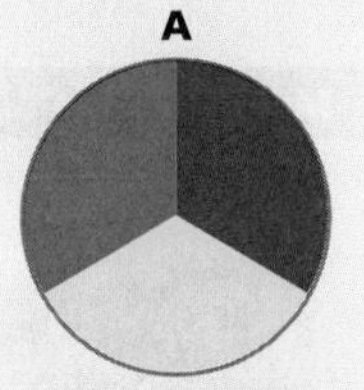

B
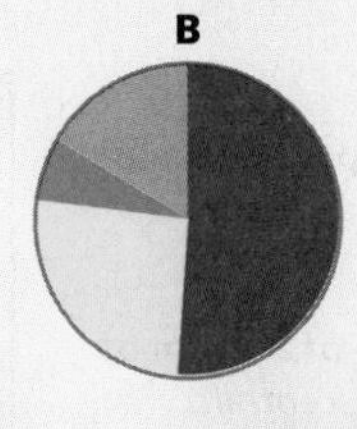

C
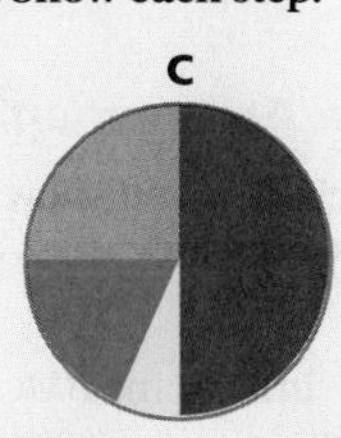

D
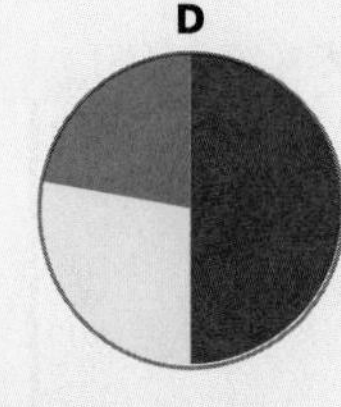

1.

Books in Linda's Library	
Novels	18
Reference	10
Textbooks	8

D

2.

Vacation Expenses ($)	
Travel	450
Meals	120
Lodging	900
Other	330

C

3.

Puppy Expenses ($)	
Food	190
Health	375
Training	120
Other	50

B

Organizer

Pacing:
Traditional $\frac{1}{2}$ day
Block $\frac{1}{4}$ day

Objective: Students identify circle graphs that represent given data.

Online Edition

Teach

Remember

Students review measuring angles and estimating angle measures.

Kinesthetic Have students use a corner of a piece of paper to estimate if an angle is greater than 90° or less than 90°.

Close

Assess

Have students explain how they know which color and label to use for the 90° angle in the example.

State Resources

11-2 Organizer

Pacing: Traditional $1\frac{1}{2}$ day
Block $\frac{3}{4}$ day

Objectives: Apply properties of arcs.

Apply properties of chords.

Technology Lab
In *Technology Lab Activities*

Online Edition
Tutorial Videos

Power Presentations with PowerPoint®

Warm Up

1. What percent of 60 is 18? 30
2. What number is 44% of 6? 2.64
3. Find m∠*WVX*. 104.4°

Payment Methods

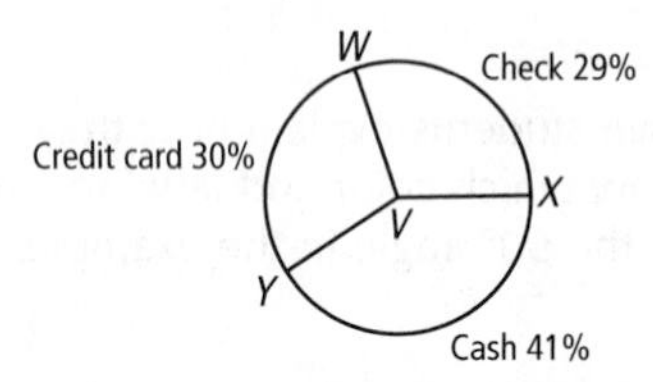

Also available on transparency

Q: What is the hidden math term?

A: Circle graph.

11-2 Arcs and Chords

Objectives
Apply properties of arcs.

Apply properties of chords.

Vocabulary
central angle
arc
minor arc
major arc
semicircle
adjacent arcs
congruent arcs

Who uses this?
Market analysts use circle graphs to compare sales of different products.

A **central angle** is an angle whose vertex is the center of a circle. An **arc** is an unbroken part of a circle consisting of two points called the endpoints and all the points on the circle between them.

Writing Math
Minor arcs may be named by two points. Major arcs and semicircles must be named by three points.

Arcs and Their Measure

ARC	MEASURE	DIAGRAM
A **minor arc** is an arc whose points are on or in the interior of a central angle.	The measure of a minor arc is equal to the measure of its central angle. $m\overset{\frown}{AC} = m\angle ABC = x°$	A, B, C, x°
A **major arc** is an arc whose points are on or in the exterior of a central angle.	The measure of a major arc is equal to 360° minus the measure of its central angle. $m\overset{\frown}{ADC} = 360° - m\angle ABC = 360° - x°$	A, B, C, D, x°
If the endpoints of an arc lie on a diameter, the arc is a **semicircle**.	The measure of a semicircle is equal to 180°. $m\overset{\frown}{EFG} = 180°$	F, E, G

EXAMPLE 1 ***Data Application***

The circle graph shows the types of music sold during one week at a music store. Find m$\overset{\frown}{BC}$.

$m\overset{\frown}{BC} = m\angle BMC$ *m of arc = m of central ∠.*

$m\angle BMC = 0.13(360°) = 46.8°$ *Central ∠ is 13% of the ⊙.*

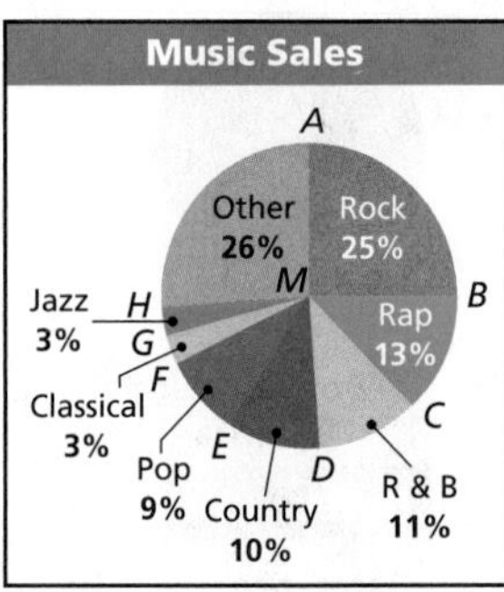

Use the graph to find each of the following.

1a. m∠*FMC* **108°** **1b.** m$\overset{\frown}{AHB}$ **270°** **1c.** m∠*EMD* **36°**

State Resources

1 Introduce

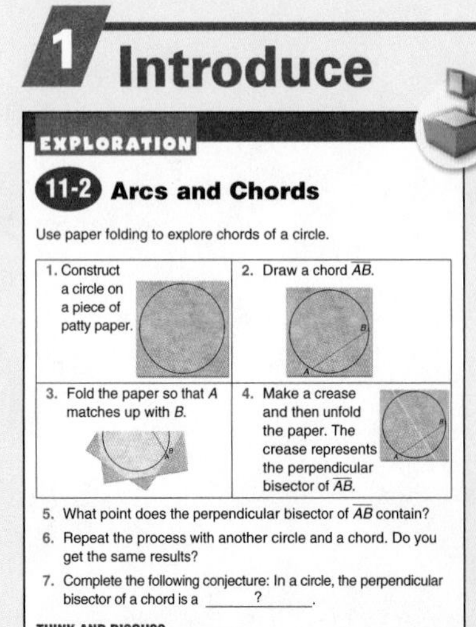
EXPLORATION

11-2 Arcs and Chords

Use paper folding to explore chords of a circle.

1. Construct a circle on a piece of patty paper.
2. Draw a chord $\overline{AB}$.
3. Fold the paper so that A matches up with B.
4. Make a crease and then unfold the paper. The crease represents the perpendicular bisector of $\overline{AB}$.
5. What point does the perpendicular bisector of $\overline{AB}$ contain?
6. Repeat the process with another circle and a chord. Do you get the same results?
7. Complete the following conjecture: In a circle, the perpendicular bisector of a chord is a ___?___.

THINK AND DISCUSS

8. **Explain** how you can use your conjecture to draw a diameter of a circle.

Motivate

Have students inscribe a hexagon in a circle. For help with this activity refer to page 380. Remind students that six congruent equilateral triangles are formed when you draw the radii of the circle. Tell students that in this lesson they will learn that an angle such as ∠*BPC* is called a central angle. Since ∠*BPC* is equilateral, m ∠*BPC* = 60°. Similarly, the circle is divided into six equal parts, so each arc will measure 60°.

Explorations and answers are provided in *Alternate Openers: Explorations Transparencies.*

Adjacent arcs are arcs of the same circle that intersect at exactly one point. $\widehat{RS}$ and $\widehat{ST}$ are adjacent arcs.

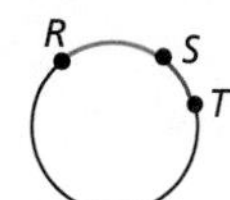

Postulate 11-2-1 Arc Addition Postulate

The measure of an arc formed by two adjacent arcs is the sum of the measures of the two arcs.

$m\widehat{ABC} = m\widehat{AB} + m\widehat{BC}$

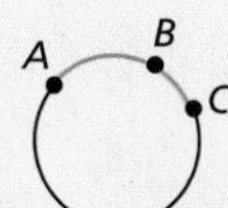

EXAMPLE 2 Using the Arc Addition Postulate

Find $m\widehat{CDE}$

$m\widehat{CD} = 90°$	*m∠CFD = 90°*
$m\angle DFE = 18°$	*Vert. ∠s Thm.*
$m\widehat{DE} = 18°$	*m∠DFE = 18°*
$m\widehat{CE} = m\widehat{CD} + m\widehat{DE}$	*Arc Add. Post.*
$= 90° + 18° = 108°$	*Substitute and simplify.*

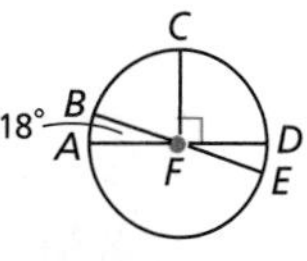

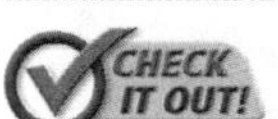

Find each measure.

2a. $m\widehat{JKL}$ **140°** **2b.** $m\widehat{LJN}$ **295°**

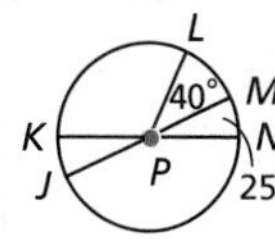

Within a circle or congruent circles, **congruent arcs** are two arcs that have the same measure. In the figure, $\widehat{ST} \cong \widehat{UV}$.

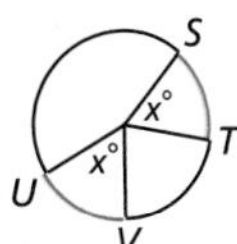

Theorem 11-2-2

THEOREM	HYPOTHESIS	CONCLUSION
In a circle or congruent circles:		
(1) Congruent central angles have congruent chords.	∠EAD ≅ ∠BAC	$\overline{DE} \cong \overline{BC}$
(2) Congruent chords have congruent arcs.	$\overline{ED} \cong \overline{BC}$	$\widehat{DE} \cong \widehat{BC}$
(3) Congruent arcs have congruent central angles.	$\widehat{ED} \cong \widehat{BC}$	∠DAE ≅ ∠BAC

You will prove parts 2 and 3 of Theorem 11-2-2 in Exercises 40 and 41.

2 Teach

Guided Instruction

Review with students segment and angle addition and adjacent and vertical angles. Explain that in this lesson they will learn similar ways to use arc addition and adjacent arcs. Use one circle to compare minor and major arcs and then sketch a semicircle. Remind students that the shortest distance between a point and a line is the length of a perpendicular segment from the point to the line. Then discuss Theorems 11-2-3 and 11-2-4.

Reaching All Learners

Through Cognitive Strategies

Draw a circle with diameter $\overline{AB}$ and radius $\overline{AC}$. Use colored pens to emphasize the minor and major arcs on the circle. Explain that a semicircle equals 180°. Since a minor arc is shorter than a semicircle, it must have a measure that is less than 180°. A major arc is longer than a semicircle, so it must have a measure that is more than 180°.

Power Presentations with PowerPoint®

Additional Examples

Example 1

The circle graph shows the types of grass planted in the yards of one neighborhood. Find $m\widehat{KLF}$.

234°

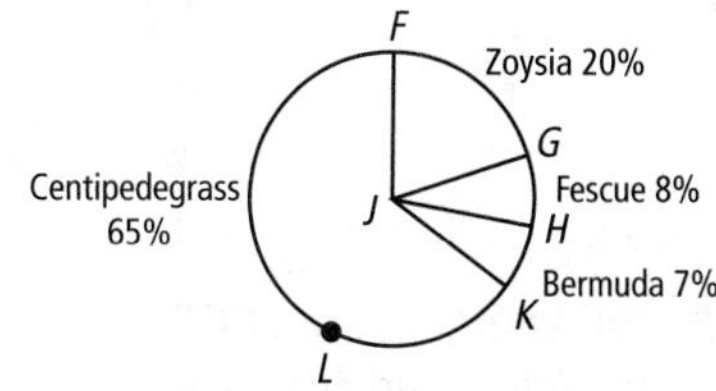

Example 2

Find $m\widehat{BD}$. 128°

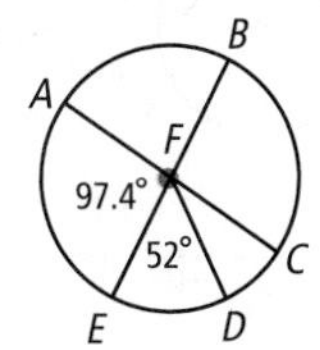

INTERVENTION

Questioning Strategies

EXAMPLE 1

- What two segments form a central angle?

EXAMPLE 2

- How would you verify that the corresponding arcs of vertical central angles are congruent?

Alegbra Students can also use the proportion $\frac{\text{angle measure}}{360} = \frac{\text{percentage}}{100}$ to find the central angle measure in a circle graph. For **Example 1,** the proportion would be $\frac{m\angle BMC}{360} = \frac{13}{100}$.

Power Presentations with PowerPoint®

Additional Examples

Example 3

Find each measure.

A. $\overline{TV} \cong \overline{WS}$. Find m$\widehat{WS}$ 88°

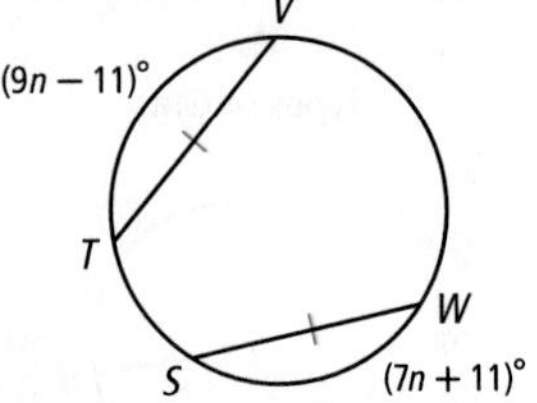

B. ⊙C ≅ ⊙J, and m∠GCD ≅ m∠NJM. Find NM. 16

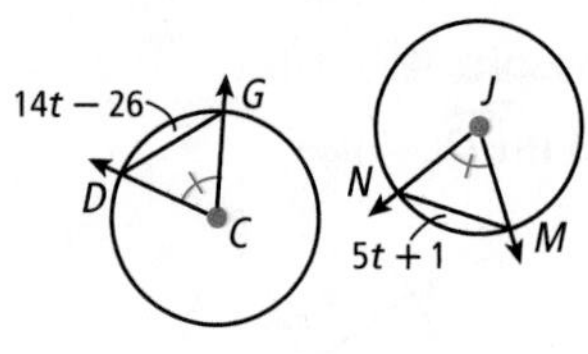

INTERVENTION

Questioning Strategies

EXAMPLE 3

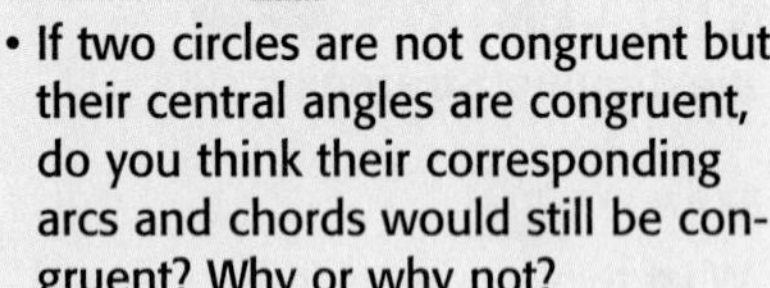

- If two circles are not congruent but their central angles are congruent, do you think their corresponding arcs and chords would still be congruent? Why or why not?

The converses of the parts of Theorem 11-2-2 are also true. For example, with part 1, congruent chords have congruent central angles.

PROOF

Theorem 11-2-2 (Part 1)

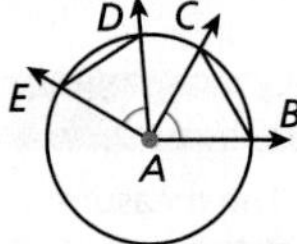

Given: ∠BAC ≅ ∠DAE
Prove: $\overline{BC} \cong \overline{DE}$

Proof:

Statements	Reasons
1. ∠BAC ≅ ∠DAE	1. Given
2. $\overline{AB} \cong \overline{AD}$, $\overline{AC} \cong \overline{AE}$	2. All radii of a ⊙ are ≅.
3. △BAC ≅ △DAE	3. SAS *Steps 2, 1*
4. $\overline{BC} \cong \overline{DE}$	4. CPCTC

EXAMPLE 3 **Applying Congruent Angles, Arcs, and Chords**

Find each measure.

Algebra

A $\overline{RS} \cong \overline{TU}$. **Find m$\widehat{RS}$.**

$\widehat{RS} \cong \widehat{TU}$	*≅ chords have ≅ arcs.*
$m\widehat{RS} = m\widehat{TU}$	*Def. of ≅ arcs*
$3x = 2x + 27$	*Substitute the given measures.*
$x = 27$	*Subtract 2x from both sides.*
$m\widehat{RS} = 3(27)$	*Substitute 27 for x.*
$= 81°$	*Simplify.*

R 3x° S T U (2x + 27)°

B ⊙B ≅ ⊙E, and $\widehat{AC} \cong \widehat{DF}$. **Find m∠DEF.**

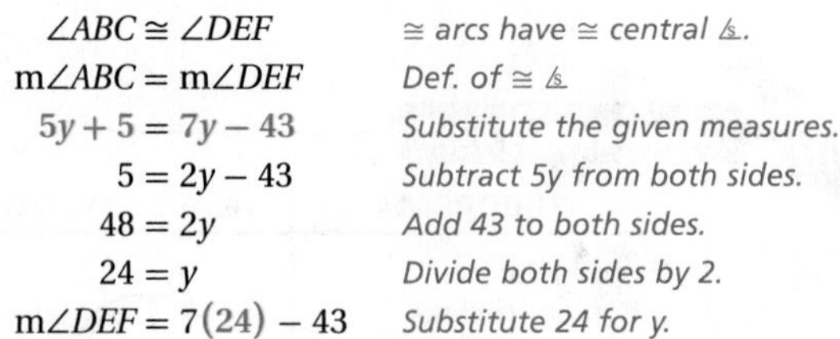

∠ABC ≅ ∠DEF	*≅ arcs have ≅ central ∠s.*
m∠ABC = m∠DEF	*Def. of ≅ ∠s*
$5y + 5 = 7y - 43$	*Substitute the given measures.*
$5 = 2y - 43$	*Subtract 5y from both sides.*
$48 = 2y$	*Add 43 to both sides.*
$24 = y$	*Divide both sides by 2.*
m∠DEF = 7(24) − 43	*Substitute 24 for y.*
= 125°	*Simplify.*

(5y + 5)° A B C E F D (7y − 43)°

CHECK IT OUT! **Find each measure.**

3a. $\overrightarrow{PT}$ bisects ∠RPS. Find RT. **12**

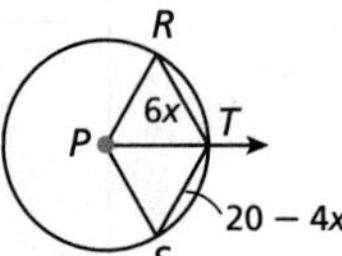

3b. ⊙A ≅ ⊙B, and $\overline{CD} \cong \overline{EF}$. Find m$\widehat{CD}$. **100°**

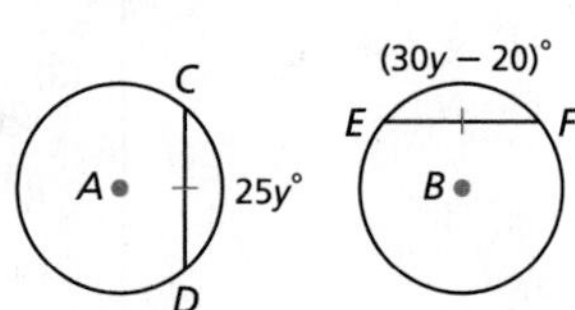

Theorems

THEOREM	HYPOTHESIS	CONCLUSION
11-2-3 In a circle, if a radius (or diameter) is perpendicular to a chord, then it bisects the chord and its arc.	$\overline{CD} \perp \overline{EF}$	$\overline{CD}$ bisects $\overline{EF}$ and $\widehat{EF}$.
11-2-4 In a circle, the perpendicular bisector of a chord is a radius (or diameter).	$\overline{JK}$ is $\perp$ bisector of $\overline{GH}$.	$\overline{JK}$ is a diameter of $\odot A$.

You will prove Theorems 11-2-3 and 11-2-4 in Exercises 42 and 43.

EXAMPLE 4 **Using Radii and Chords**

Algebra

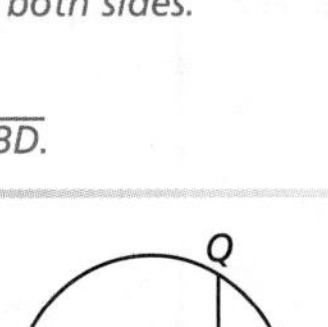

Find BD.

Step 1 Draw radius $\overline{AD}$.

$AD = 5$ — *Radii of a ⊙ are ≅.*

Step 2 Use the Pythagorean Theorem.

$CD^2 + AC^2 = AD^2$

$CD^2 + 3^2 = 5^2$ — *Substitute 3 for AC and 5 for AD.*

$CD^2 = 16$ — *Subtract 3^2 from both sides.*

$CD = 4$ — *Take the square root of both sides.*

Step 3 Find BD.

$BD = 2(4) = 8$ — *$\overline{AE} \perp \overline{BD}$, so $\overline{AE}$ bisects $\overline{BD}$.*

4. Find QR to the nearest tenth. **34.6**

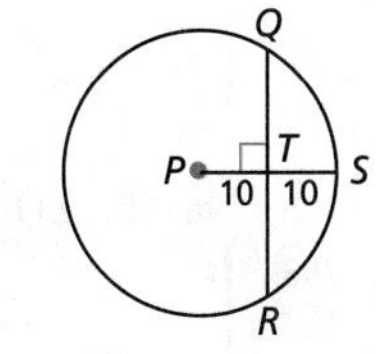

THINK AND DISCUSS

1. What is true about the measure of an arc whose central angle is obtuse?
2. Under what conditions are two arcs the same measure but not congruent?

3. **GET ORGANIZED** Copy and complete the graphic organizer. In each box, write a definition and draw a sketch.

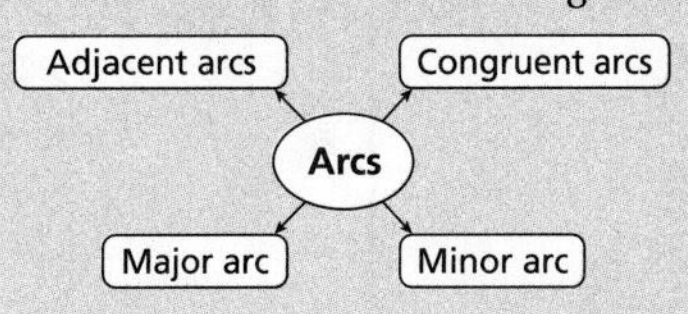

COMMON ERROR ALERT

Some students may confuse arc length with linear length. Emphasize that arc length is measured in degrees and linear length is measured in units such as inches or centimeters. Point out that they cannot convert one to the other. They should use degrees to measure angles and arcs and use inches and centimeters to measure length and distance.

Power Presentations with PowerPoint®

Additional Examples

Example 4

Find NP. 30

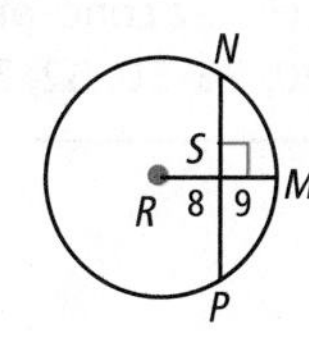

INTERVENTION

Questioning Strategies

EXAMPLE 4

- Why does it help to draw a radius from the center to the endpoint of the chord?

3 Close

Summarize

Draw a circle containing two radii and two chords. Highlight a minor and a major arc. Then illustrate congruent central angles, congruent chords, and congruent arcs. Draw another chord that is perpendicular to one of the radii and show that it is bisected by the radius.

ONGOING ASSESSMENT and INTERVENTION

***Diagnose Before* the Lesson**
11-2 Warm Up, TE p. 756

***Monitor During* the Lesson**
Check It Out! Exercises, SE pp. 756–759
Questioning Strategies, TE pp. 757–759

***Assess After* the Lesson**
11-2 Lesson Quiz, TE p. 763
Alternative Assessment, TE p. 763

Answers to *Think and Discuss*

1. The arc measures between 90° and 180°.
2. if the arcs are on 2 different ⊙s with different radii
3. See p. A8.

Assignment Guide

Assign *Guided Practice* exercises as necessary.

If you finished Examples **1–2**
Basic 19–28, 33, 36
Average 19–28, 33, 34, 36
Advanced 19–28, 33, 34, 36, 54

If you finished Examples **1–4**
Basic 19–40, 45, 47–50, 55–61
Average 19–51, 55–61
Advanced 19–44, 46–61

Homework Quick Check
Quickly check key concepts.
Exercises: 20, 26, 30, 32, 38, 40

11-2 Exercises

go.hrw.com
Homework Help Online
KEYWORD: MG7 11-2
Parent Resources Online
KEYWORD: MG7 Parent

GUIDED PRACTICE

Vocabulary **Apply the vocabulary from this lesson to answer each question.**

1. An arc that joins the endpoints of a diameter is called a __?__. (*semicircle* or *major arc*) **semicircle**
2. How do you recognize a *central angle* of a circle? **Vertex is the center of the ⊙.**
3. In ⊙P m$\widehat{ABC}$ = 205°. Therefore $\widehat{ABC}$ is a __?__. (*major arc* or *minor arc*) **major arc**
4. In a circle, an arc that is less than a semicircle is a __?__. (*major arc* or *minor arc*) **minor arc**

SEE EXAMPLE 1 p. 756

Consumer Application **Use the following information for Exercises 5–10.**

The circle graph shows how a typical household spends money on energy. Find each of the following.

5. m∠PAQ **162°**
6. m∠VAU **25.2°**
7. m∠SAQ **61.2°**
8. m$\widehat{UT}$ **36°**
9. m$\widehat{RQ}$ **39.6°**
10. m$\widehat{UPT}$ **324°**

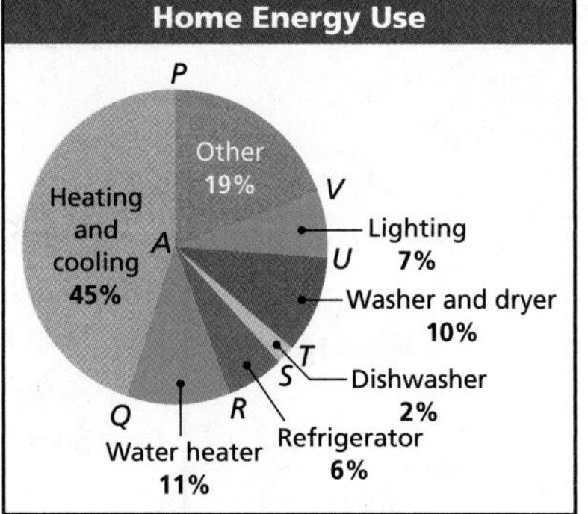

SEE EXAMPLE 2 p. 757

Find each measure.

11. m$\widehat{DF}$ **129°**
12. m$\widehat{DEB}$ **270°**

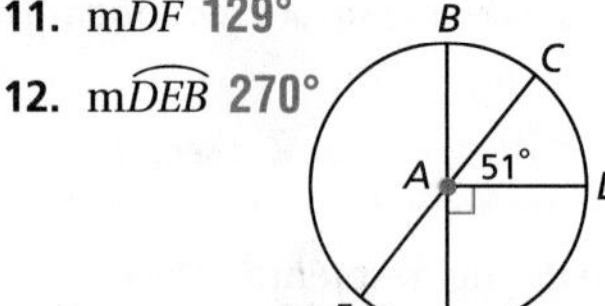

13. m$\widehat{JL}$ **108°**
14. m$\widehat{HLK}$ **210°**

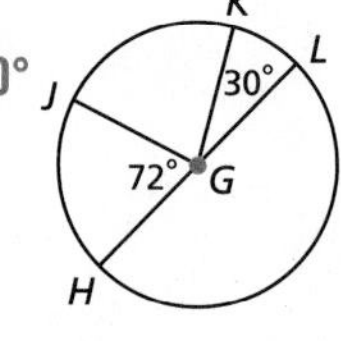

SEE EXAMPLE 3 p. 758

15. ∠QPR ≅ ∠RPS. Find QR. **24**

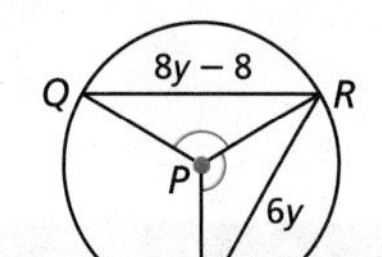

16. ⊙A ≅ ⊙B, and $\widehat{CD}$ ≅ $\widehat{EF}$. Find m∠EBF. **135°**

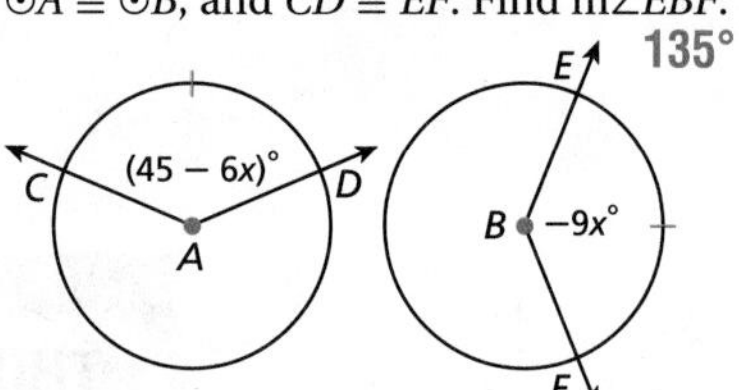

SEE EXAMPLE 4 p. 759

Multi-Step **Find each length to the nearest tenth.**

17. RS

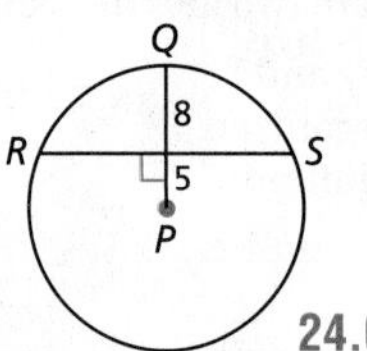

24.0

18. EF

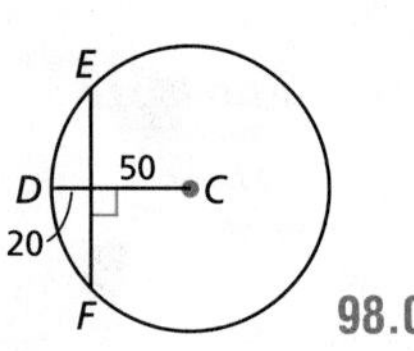

98.0

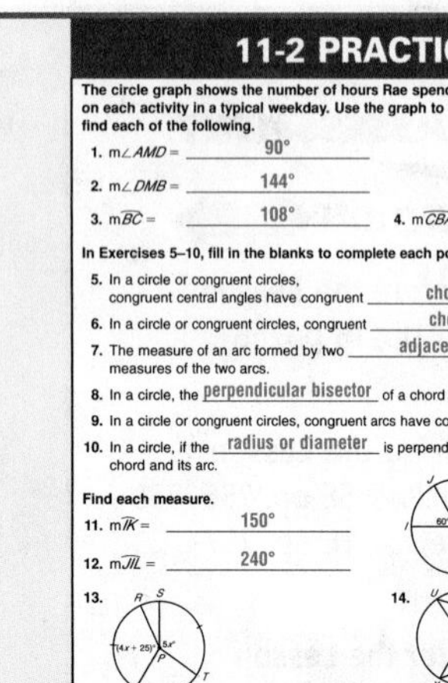

11-2 PRACTICE A

The circle graph shows the number of hours Rae spends on each activity in a typical weekday. Use the graph to find each of the following.

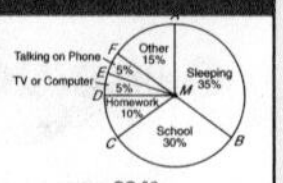

1. m∠AMD = **90°**
2. m∠DMB = **144°**
3. m$\widehat{BC}$ = **108°**
4. m$\widehat{CBA}$ = **234°**

In Exercises 5–10, fill in the blanks to complete each postulate or theorem.

5. In a circle or congruent circles, congruent central angles have congruent **chords**.
6. In a circle or congruent circles, congruent **chords** have congruent arcs.
7. The measure of an arc formed by two **adjacent** arcs is the sum of the measures of the two arcs.
8. In a circle, the **perpendicular bisector** of a chord is a radius (or diameter).
9. In a circle or congruent circles, congruent arcs have congruent **central angles**.
10. In a circle, if the **radius or diameter** is perpendicular to a chord, then it bisects the chord and its arc.

Find each measure.

11. m$\widehat{IK}$ = **150°**
12. m$\widehat{JIL}$ = **240°** 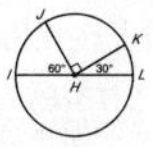
13. 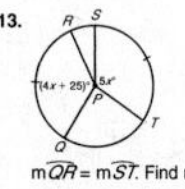 m$\widehat{QR}$ = m$\widehat{ST}$. Find m∠QPR. **125°**
14. ∠UTV ≅ ∠XTW. Find WX. **11 cm**

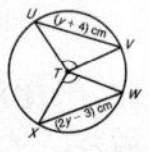

Find the length of each chord. (*Hint:* Use the Pythagorean Theorem to find half the chord length, and then double that to get the answer.)

15. CE = **30 in.**
16. LN = **96 m**

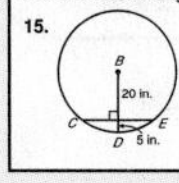

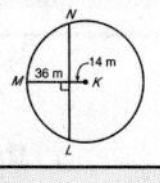

11-2 PRACTICE B

The circle graph shows data collected by the U.S. Census Bureau in 2004 on the highest completed educational level for people 25 and older. Use the graph to find each of the following. Round to the nearest tenth if necessary.

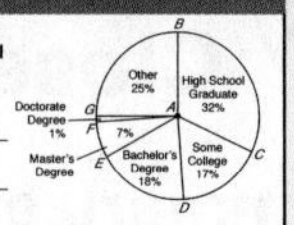

1. m∠CAB **115.2°**
2. m∠DAG **93.6°**
3. m∠EAC **126°**
4. m$\widehat{BG}$ **90°**
5. m$\widehat{GF}$ **3.6°**
6. m$\widehat{BDE}$ **241.2°**

Find each measure.

7. m$\widehat{QS}$ **125°**
m$\widehat{RQT}$ **227°**

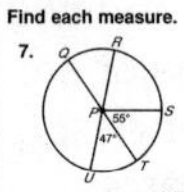

8. m$\widehat{HG}$ **67°**
m$\widehat{FEH}$ **203°**

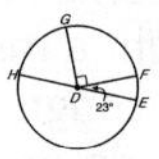

9. $\widehat{UW}$ ≅ $\widehat{VX}$
Find m∠UTW. **98°**

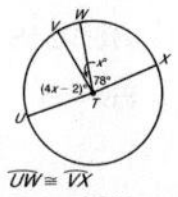

10. ⊙B ≅ ⊙E, and ∠CBD ≅ ∠FEG.
Find FG. **49 cm**

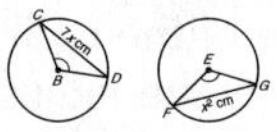

Find each length. Round to the nearest tenth.

11. ZY **76.3 mi**
12. EG **4.9 km**

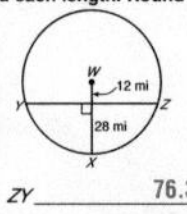

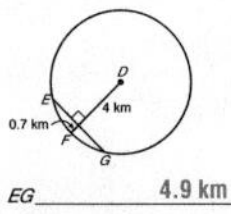

State Resources

go.hrw.com
State Resources Online
KEYWORD: MG7 Resources

PRACTICE AND PROBLEM SOLVING

Independent Practice

For Exercises	See Example
19–24	1
25–28	2
29–30	3
31–32	4

Extra Practice

Skills Practice p. S24

Application Practice p. S38

Sports Use the following information for Exercises 19–24. The key shows the number of medals won by U.S. athletes at the 2004 Olympics in Athens. Find each of the following to the nearest tenth.

Medals	
Gold	35
Silver	39
Bronze	29

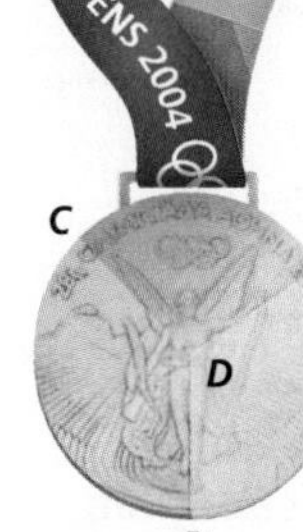

19. m∠ADB 122.3° 20. m∠ADC 101.4°
21. m$\widehat{AB}$ 122.3° 22. m$\widehat{BC}$ 136.3°
23. m$\widehat{ACB}$ 237.7° 24. m$\widehat{CAB}$ 223.7°

Find each measure.

25. m$\widehat{MP}$ 152°
26. m$\widehat{QNL}$ 208°

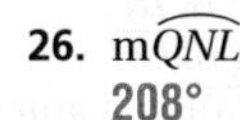

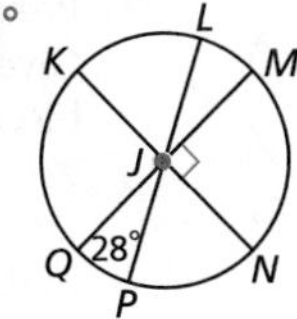

27. m$\widehat{WT}$ 155°
28. m$\widehat{WTV}$ 235°

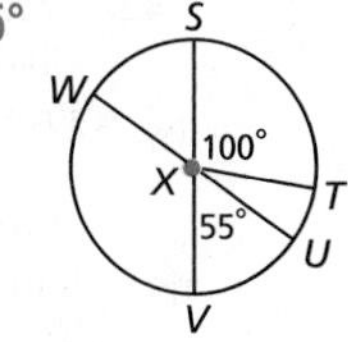

29. ⊙A ≅ ⊙B, and $\widehat{CD} \cong \widehat{EF}$. Find m∠$CAD$. 147°

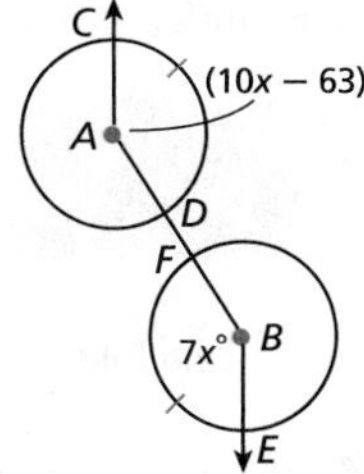

30. $\overline{JK} \cong \overline{LM}$. Find m$\widehat{JK}$. 85°

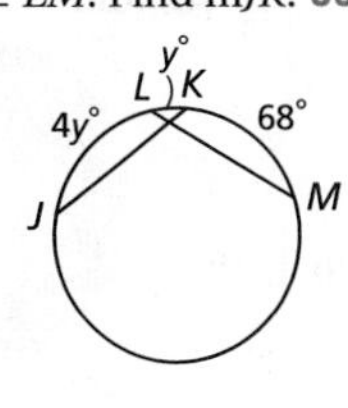

Multi-Step Find each length to the nearest tenth.

31. CD 6.6

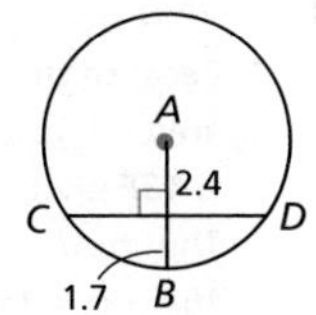

32. RS 10.4

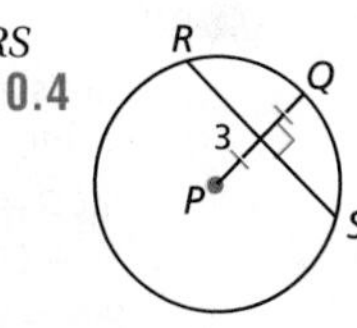

Determine whether each statement is true or false. If false, explain why.

33. The central angle of a minor arc is an acute angle. F
34. Any two points on a circle determine a minor arc and a major arc. F
35. In a circle, the perpendicular bisector of a chord must pass through the center of the circle. T
36. **Data Collection** Use a graphing calculator, a pH probe, and a data-collection device to collect information about the pH levels of ten different liquids. Then create a circle graph with the following sectors: strong basic $(9 < \text{pH} < 14)$, weak basic $(7 < \text{pH} < 9)$, neutral $(\text{pH} = 7)$, weak acidic $(5 < \text{pH} < 7)$, and strong acidic $(0 < \text{pH} < 5)$.
37. In ⊙E, the measures of ∠AEB, ∠BEC, and ∠CED are in the ratio 3 : 4 : 5. Find m$\widehat{AB}$, m$\widehat{BC}$, and m$\widehat{CD}$.
45°; 60°; 75°

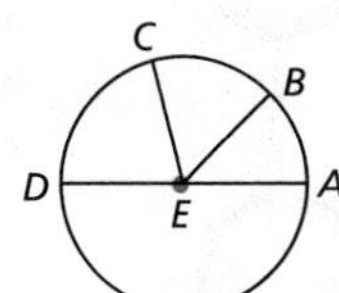

33. A minor arc is always less than 180°, so its central ∠ may be obtuse.

34. If the 2 pts. are the endpts. of a diam., they determine 2 semicircles.

36. Check students' graphs.

COMMON ERROR ALERT

Some students may confuse the number of medals won in **Exercises 19–24** with the angle measures or percentages in the circle graph. Remind students that they have to first find the sum of the gold, silver, and bronze medals. Then they find each percentage and calculate the central angle measures before working the exercises.

Data Collection For help with **Exercise 36,** see *Technology Lab Activities*. Some suggestions for liquids are muriatic acid, household lye and ammonia, cola, white soda, diluted and concentrated lemon juice, distilled water, salt water, orange juice, household bleach, baking soda dissolved in water, antacid, vinegar, and shampoo.

Teaching Tip

Inclusion Point out to students that, in **Exercise 37,** ∠DEA is a straight angle and its measure is 180°.

11-2 PRACTICE C

Write proofs for Exercises 1 and 2.

1. **Given:** $\overline{AC} \cong \overline{EC}$, $\overline{AE} \perp \overline{FG}$
   Prove: ⊙A ≅ ⊙E

Possible answer: Draw $\overline{AF}$ and $\overline{EF}$. It is given that $\overline{AE}$ is perpendicular to $\overline{FG}$. Therefore ∠ACF and ∠ECF are right angles and are congruent. It is also given that $\overline{AC} \cong \overline{EC}$. $\overline{FC} \cong \overline{FC}$ by the Reflexive Property of Congruence. So △AFC ≅ △EFC by SAS. By CPCTC, $\overline{AF} \cong \overline{EF}$. $\overline{AF}$ and $\overline{EF}$ are radii of ⊙A and ⊙E, and circles with congruent radii are congruent circles, so ⊙A ≅ ⊙E.

2. **Given:** $\widehat{RSU} \cong \widehat{RTU}$
   Prove: ⊙P ≅ ⊙Q

Possible answer: Draw $\overline{RU}$, $\overline{PR}$, $\overline{PU}$, $\overline{QR}$, and $\overline{QU}$. Because $\overline{PR}$ and $\overline{PU}$ are radii of ⊙P, they are congruent and △PRU is isosceles. Similar reasoning shows that △QRU is also isosceles. By the Base Angles Theorem, ∠PUR ≅ ∠PRU and ∠QRU ≅ ∠QUR. So m∠PUR and m∠PRU are each equal to $\frac{1}{2}$(180 − m∠RPU). Also, m∠QRU and m∠QUR are each equal to $\frac{1}{2}$(180 − m∠RQU). It is given that $\widehat{RSU} \cong \widehat{RTU}$, so m$\widehat{RSU}$ = m$\widehat{RTU}$. The measure of an arc is equal to the measure of its central angle, so m∠RPU = m∠RQU. Substitution shows that m∠PUR = m∠PRU = m∠QRU = m∠QUR. $\overline{RU} \cong \overline{RU}$ by the Reflexive Property of Congruence. So △PRU ≅ △QRU by SAS. By CPCTC, $\overline{PR} \cong \overline{QR}$ and circles with congruent radii are congruent circles, so ⊙P ≅ ⊙Q.

Give the degree measure of the arc intercepted by the chord described in Exercises 3–8. The figure is given for reference. Round to the nearest tenth if necessary.

3. a chord congruent to the radius 60°
4. a chord one-third the length of the radius 19.2°
5. a chord congruent to the segment from the center to the chord 53.1°
6. a chord twice the length of the segment from the center to the chord 90°
7. a chord one-fourth the length of the circumference 103.5°
8. a chord $\frac{1}{\pi}$ multiplied by the length of the circumference 180°

Find the length of a chord that intercepts an arc of each given measure. Give your answer in terms of the radius r. Round to the nearest tenth.

9. 10° 0.2r 10. 45° 0.8r 11. 136° 1.9r

Inclusion Remind students that a diagonal divides a circle into two 180° arcs.

Kinesthetic If students have difficulty with **Exercise 44,** provide them with circular paper to fold so that they can check their reasoning. They can also use their folded circle as a model to draw a circle graph using estimation.

Exercise 47 involves using Theorems 11-2-3 and 11-2-4 to find the length of the top of a bike stand. This exercise prepares students for the Multi-Step Test Prep on page 770.

Answers

40.1. $\overline{BC} \cong \overline{DE}$ (Given)
2. $\overline{AB} \cong \overline{AD}$ and $\overline{AC} \cong \overline{AE}$ (All radii of a ⊙ are ≅.)
3. $\triangle BAC \cong \triangle DAE$ (SSS)
4. $\angle BAC \cong \angle DAE$ (CPCTC)
5. $m\angle BAC = m\angle DAE$ (Def. of ≅ ∠s)
6. $m\overset{\frown}{BC} = m\overset{\frown}{DE}$ (Def. of arc measures)
7. $\overset{\frown}{BC} \cong \overset{\frown}{DE}$ (Def. of ≅ arcs)

42.1. $\overline{CD} \perp \overline{EF}$ (Given)
2. Draw radii $\overline{CE}$ and $\overline{CF}$. (2 pts. determine a line.)
3. $\overline{CE} \cong \overline{CF}$ (All radii of a ⊙ are ≅.)
4. $\overline{CM} \cong \overline{CM}$ (Reflex. Prop. of ≅)
5. $\angle CMF$ and $\angle CME$ are rt. ∠s. (Def. of ⊥)
6. $\triangle CMF$ and $\triangle CME$ are rt. △s (Def. of rt. △)
7. $\triangle CMF \cong \triangle CME$ (HL Steps 3, 4)
8. $\overline{FM} \cong \overline{EM}$ (CPCTC)
9. $\overline{CD}$ bisects $\overline{EF}$. (Def. of bisect)
10. $\angle FCD \cong \angle ECD$ (CPCTC)
11. $m\angle FCD = m\angle ECD$ (Def. of ≅ ∠s)
12. $m\overset{\frown}{FD} = m\overset{\frown}{ED}$ (Def. of arc measure)
13. $\overset{\frown}{FD} \cong \overset{\frown}{ED}$ (Def. of ≅ arcs)
14. $\overline{CD}$ bisects $\overset{\frown}{EF}$. (Def. of bisect)

Algebra Find the indicated measure.

38. $m\overset{\frown}{JL}$ 136°

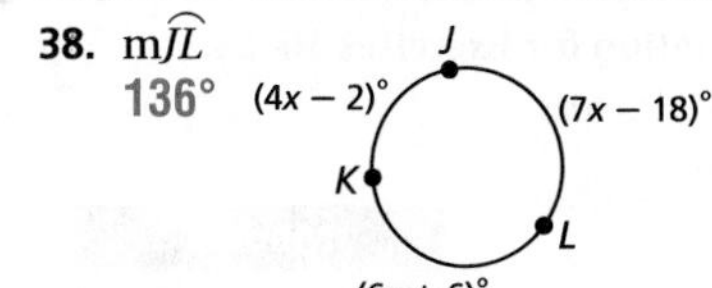

39. $m\angle SPT$ 108°

40. Prove ≅ chords have ≅ arcs.
Given: ⊙A, $\overline{BC} \cong \overline{DE}$
Prove: $\overset{\frown}{BC} \cong \overset{\frown}{DE}$

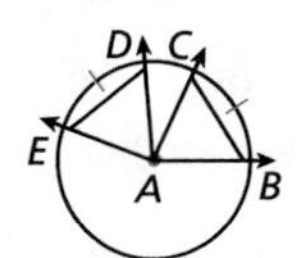

41. Prove ≅ arcs have ≅ central ∠s.
Given: ⊙A, $\overset{\frown}{BC} \cong \overset{\frown}{DE}$
Prove: $\angle BAC \cong \angle DAE$

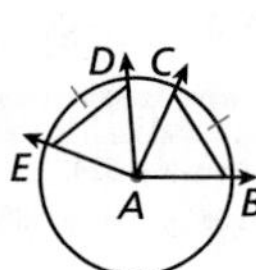

41.
1. $\overset{\frown}{BC} \cong \overset{\frown}{DE}$ (Given)
2. $m\overset{\frown}{BC} = m\overset{\frown}{DE}$ (Def. of ≅ arcs)
3. $m\angle BAC = m\angle DAE$ (Def. of arc measures)
4. $\angle BAC \cong \angle DAE$ (Def. of ≅ ∠s)

42. Prove Theorem 11-2-3.
Given: ⊙C, $\overline{CD} \perp \overline{EF}$
Prove: $\overline{CD}$ bisects $\overline{EF}$ and $\overset{\frown}{EF}$.
(*Hint:* Draw $\overline{CE}$ and $\overline{CF}$ and use the HL Theorem.)

43. Prove Theorem 11-2-4.
Given: ⊙A, $\overline{JK} \perp$ bisector of $\overline{GH}$
Prove: $\overline{JK}$ is a diameter
(*Hint:* Use the Converse of the ⊥ Bisector Theorem.)

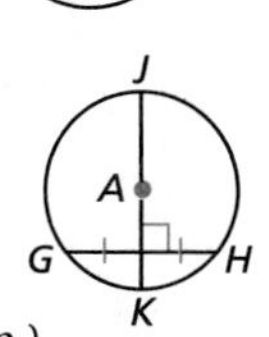

43.
1. $\overline{JK}$ is the ⊥ bisector of $\overline{GH}$. (Given)
2. *A* is equidistant from *G* and *H*. (Def. of center of ⊙)
3. *A* lies on the ⊥ bisector of $\overline{GH}$. (⊥ Bisector Thm.)
4. $\overline{JK}$ is a diam. of ⊙A. (Def. of diam.)

44. Critical Thinking Roberto folds a circular piece of paper as shown. When he unfolds the paper, how many different-sized central angles will be formed? 3

One fold

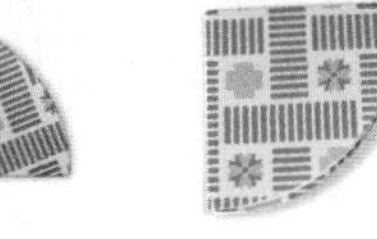
Two folds

Three folds

45. ERROR ANALYSIS Below are two solutions to find the value of *x*. Which solution is incorrect? Explain the error.

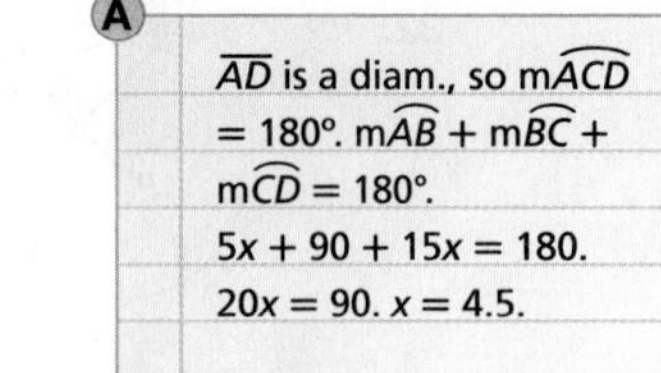

A
$\overline{AD}$ is a diam., so $m\overset{\frown}{ACD}$
= 180°. $m\overset{\frown}{AB} + m\overset{\frown}{BC} +$
$m\overset{\frown}{CD} = 180°$.
$5x + 90 + 15x = 180$.
$20x = 90$. $x = 4.5$.

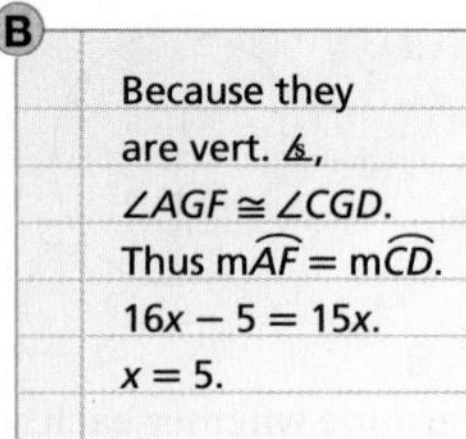

B
Because they
are vert. ∠s,
$\angle AGF \cong \angle CGD$.
Thus $m\overset{\frown}{AF} = m\overset{\frown}{CD}$.
$16x - 5 = 15x$.
$x = 5$.

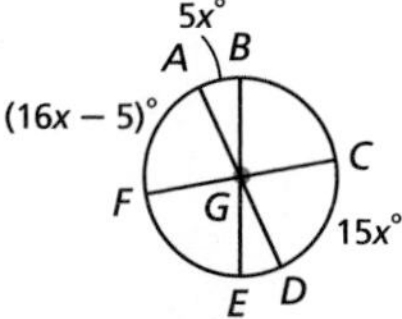

Solution A is incorrect because it assumes that ∠BGC is a rt. ∠.

46. Write About It According to a school survey, 40% of the students take a bus to school, 35% are driven to school, 15% ride a bike, and the remainder walk. Explain how to use central angles to create a circle graph from this data.

46. To make the circle graph, draw a ⊙ and then draw central ∠s that measure 144°, 126°, 54°, and 36°.

47. This problem will prepare you for the Multi-Step Test Prep on page 770.
Chantal's bike has wheels with a 27 in. diameter.
a. What are *AC* and *AD* if *DB* is 7 in.? 13.5 in.; 6.5 in.
b. What is *CD* to the nearest tenth of an inch? 11.8 in.
c. What is *CE*, the length of the top of the bike stand? 23.7 in.

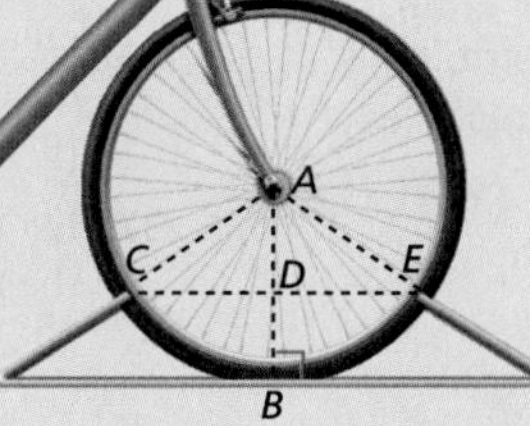

762 *Chapter 11 Circles*

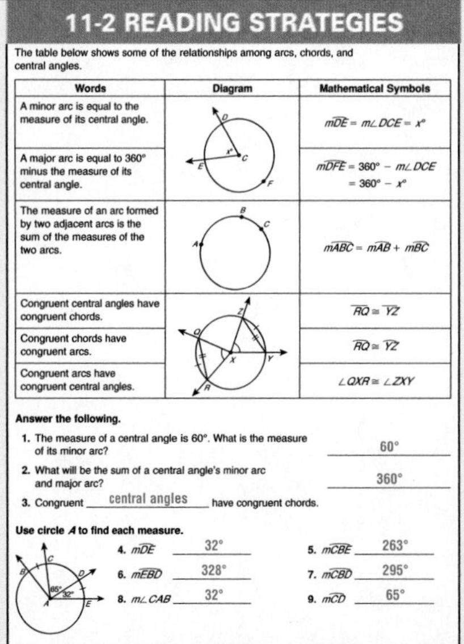

11-2 READING STRATEGIES

The table below shows some of the relationships among arcs, chords, and central angles.

Words	Diagram	Mathematical Symbols
A minor arc is equal to the measure of its central angle.		$m\overset{\frown}{DE} = m\angle DCE = x°$
A major arc is equal to 360° minus the measure of its central angle.		$m\overset{\frown}{DFE} = 360° - m\angle DCE = 360° - x°$
The measure of an arc formed by two adjacent arcs is the sum of the measures of the two arcs.		$m\overset{\frown}{ABC} = m\overset{\frown}{AB} + m\overset{\frown}{BC}$
Congruent central angles have congruent chords.		$\overline{RQ} \cong \overline{YZ}$
Congruent chords have congruent arcs.		$\overset{\frown}{RQ} \cong \overset{\frown}{YZ}$
Congruent arcs have congruent central angles.		$\angle QXR \cong \angle ZXY$

Answer the following.

1. The measure of a central angle is 60°. What is the measure of its minor arc? 60°
2. What will be the sum of a central angle's minor arc and major arc? 360°
3. Congruent central angles have congruent chords.

Use circle *A* to find each measure.

4. $m\overset{\frown}{DE}$ 32°
5. $m\overset{\frown}{CBE}$ 263°
6. $m\overset{\frown}{EBD}$ 328°
7. $m\overset{\frown}{CBD}$ 295°
8. $m\angle CAB$ 32°
9. $m\overset{\frown}{CD}$ 65°

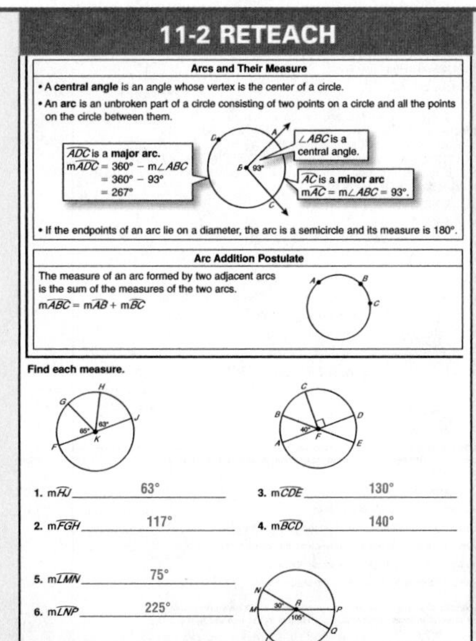

11-2 RETEACH

Arcs and Their Measure

- A **central angle** is an angle whose vertex is the center of a circle.
- An **arc** is an unbroken part of a circle consisting of two points on a circle and all the points on the circle between them.

$\overset{\frown}{ADC}$ is a **major arc.** $m\overset{\frown}{ADC} = 360° - m\angle ABC = 360° - 93° = 267°$

$\angle ABC$ is a central angle.

$\overset{\frown}{AC}$ is a **minor arc** $m\overset{\frown}{AC} = m\angle ABC = 93°$.

- If the endpoints of an arc lie on a diameter, the arc is a semicircle and its measure is 180°.

Arc Addition Postulate

The measure of an arc formed by two adjacent arcs is the sum of the measures of the two arcs.
$m\overset{\frown}{ABC} = m\overset{\frown}{AB} + m\overset{\frown}{BC}$

Find each measure.

1. $m\overset{\frown}{HJ}$ 63°
2. $m\overset{\frown}{FGH}$ 117°
3. $m\overset{\frown}{CDE}$ 130°
4. $m\overset{\frown}{BCD}$ 140°
5. $m\overset{\frown}{LMN}$ 75°
6. $m\overset{\frown}{LNP}$ 225°

TEST PREP

48. Which of these arcs of $\odot Q$ has the greatest measure?

Ⓐ $\widehat{WT}$ Ⓒ $\widehat{VR}$

Ⓑ $\widehat{UW}$ Ⓓ $\widehat{TV}$

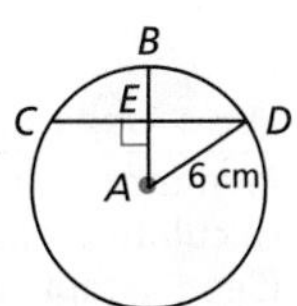

49. In $\odot A$, $CD = 10$. Which of these is closest to the length of $\overline{AE}$?

Ⓕ 3.3 cm Ⓗ 5 cm

Ⓖ 4 cm Ⓙ 7.8 cm

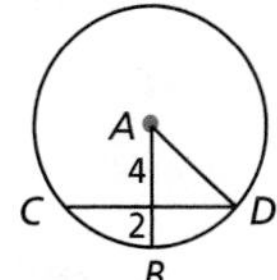

50. **Gridded Response** $\odot P$ has center $P(2, 1)$ and radius 3. What is the measure, in degrees, of the minor arc with endpoints $A(-1, 1)$ and $B(2, -2)$? **90**

CHALLENGE AND EXTEND

51. In the figure, $\overline{AB} \perp \overline{CD}$. Find $m\widehat{BD}$ to the nearest tenth of a degree. **48.2°**

A, 4, C, 2, D, B

52. Two points on a circle determine two distinct arcs. How many arcs are determined by n points on a circle? (*Hint:* Make a table and look for a pattern.) $n(n-1)$

53. An angle measure other than degrees is *radian* measure. 360° converts to 2π radians, or 180°converts to π radians.
 a. Convert the following radian angle measures to degrees: $\frac{\pi}{2}, \frac{\pi}{3}, \frac{\pi}{4}$. **90°; 60°; 45°**
 b. Convert the following angle measures to radians: 135°, 270°. $\frac{3}{4}\pi$; $\frac{3}{2}\pi$

SPIRAL REVIEW

Simplify each expression. *(Previous course)*

54. $(3x)^3(2y^2)(3^{-2}y^2)$ $6x^3y^4$

55. $a^4b^3(-2a)^{-4}$ $\frac{b^3}{16}$

56. $(-2t^3s^2)(3ts^2)^2$ $-18t^5s^6$

Find the next term in each pattern. *(Lesson 2-1)*

57. 1, 3, 7, 13, 21, ... **31**

58. C, E, G, I, K, ... **M**

59. 1, 6, 15, ... **28**

In the figure, $\overline{QP}$ and $\overline{QM}$ are tangent to $\odot N$. Find each measure. *(Lesson 11-1)*

60. $m\angle NMQ$ **90°**

61. MQ **9**

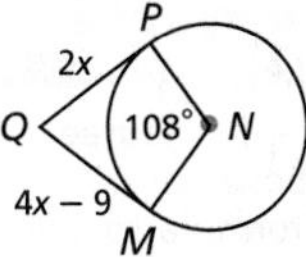

Construction Circle Through Three Noncollinear Points

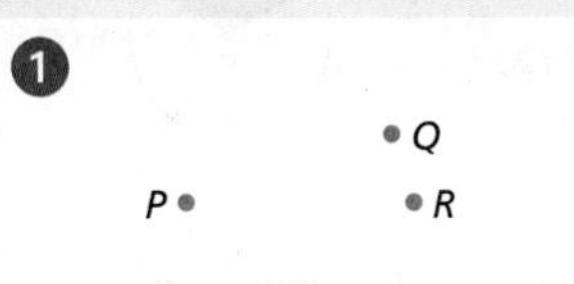

Draw three noncollinear points.

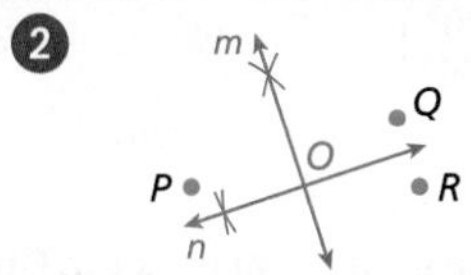

Construct m and n, the ⊥ bisectors of $\overline{PQ}$ and $\overline{QR}$. Label the intersection O.

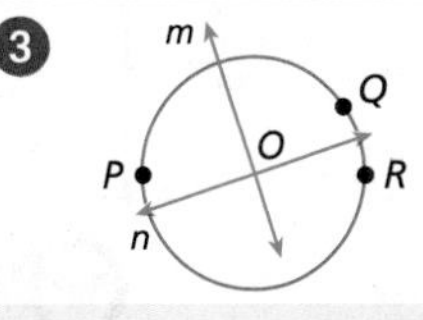

Center the compass at O. Draw a circle through P.

1. Explain why $\odot O$ with radius $\overline{OP}$ also contains Q and R.

TEST PREP DOCTOR Point out to students that they can use Pythagorean triples to eliminate the whole number answer choices in **Exercise 49.**

Journal

Instruct students to make a table with two columns and five rows. Write "Arc Length," "Arc Addition," "Congruent Circles," "Congruent Angles, Arcs, and Chords," and "Radii and Chords" in the first column." In the second column, ask students to draw labeled diagrams.

ALTERNATIVE ASSESSMENT

Have students use a compass to draw two large circles on a sheet of paper. Tell them not to mark the centers. Then ask them to exchange papers with other students and use Theorems 11-2-3 and 11-2-4 to find the center of the two circles. (Students should draw chords and construct the perpendicular bisectors.)

11-2 PROBLEM SOLVING

1. Circle D has center $(-2, -7)$ and radius 7. What is the measure, in degrees, of the major arc that passes through points $H(-2, 0)$, $J(5, -7)$, and $K(-9, -7)$? **270°**

2. A circle graph is composed of sectors with central angles that measure $3x°$, $3x°$, $4x°$, and $5x°$. What is the measure, in degrees, of the smallest minor arcs? **72°**

Use the following information for Exercises 3 and 4.

The circle graph shows the results of a survey in which teens were asked what says the most about them at school. Find each of the following.

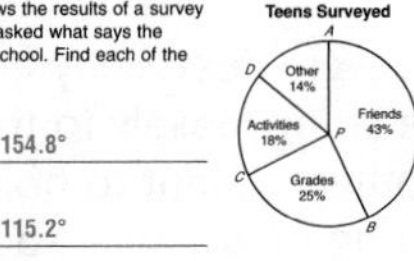

3. $m\widehat{AB}$ **154.8°**

4. $m\angle APC$ **115.2°**

Choose the best answer.

5. Students were asked to name their favorite cafeteria food. The results of the survey are shown in the table. In a circle graph showing these results, which is closest to the measure of the central angle for the section representing chicken tenders?
 A 21° Ⓒ 83°
 B 75° D 270°

Favorite Lunch	Number of Students
Pizza	108
Chicken tenders	75
Taco salad	90
Other	54

6. The diameter of $\odot R$ is 15 units, and $HJ = 12$ units. What is the length of $\overline{ST}$?

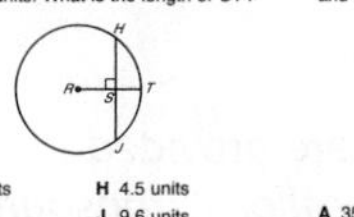

 F 2.1 units H 4.5 units
 Ⓖ 3 units J 9.6 units

7. In the stained glass window, $\overline{AB} \cong \overline{CD}$ and $\overline{AB} \parallel \overline{CD}$. What is $m\widehat{CBD}$?

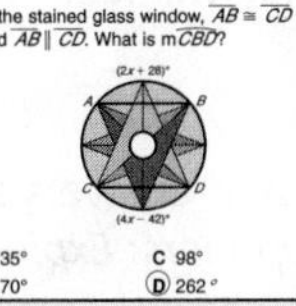

 A 35° C 98°
 B 70° Ⓓ 262°

Answers to *Construction*

1. O is on the ⊥ bisector of $\overline{PQ}$, so by the Conv. of the ⊥ Bisector Thm., $OP = OQ$. Similarly, O is on the ⊥ bisector of $\overline{QR}$, so $OQ = OR$. Thus $\overline{OP}$, $\overline{OQ}$, and $\overline{OR}$ are radii of the ⊙, and $\odot O$ contains Q and R.

Power Presentations with PowerPoint®

11-2 Lesson Quiz

1. The circle graph shows the types of cuisine available in a city. Find $m\widehat{TRQ}$. 158.4°

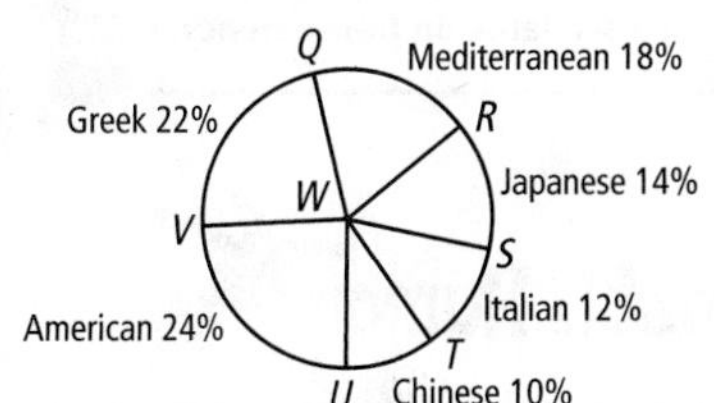

Find each measure.

2. $\widehat{NGH}$ 139° 3. HL 21

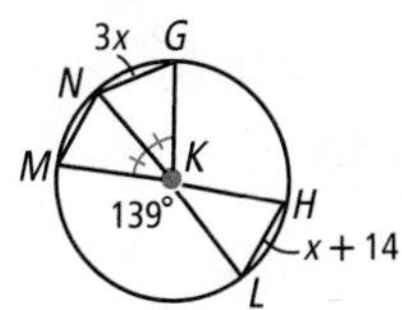

4. $\odot T \cong \odot U$, and $AC = 47.2$. Find PL to the nearest tenth. ≈12.9

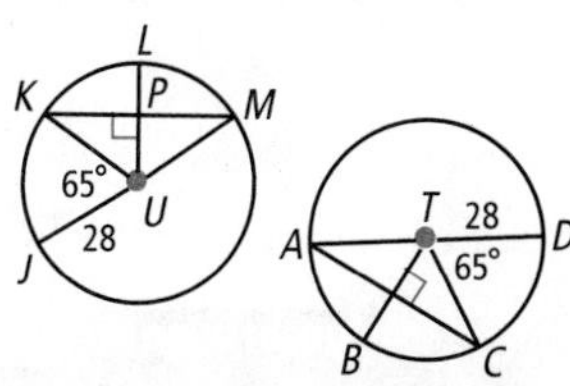

Also available on transparency

11-3 Organizer

Pacing: Traditional 2 days
Block 1 day

Objectives: Find the area of sectors.

Find arc lengths.

Geometry Lab
In *Geometry Lab Activities*

Online Edition
Tutorial Videos, Interactivity

Power Presentations with PowerPoint®

Warm Up

1. Find *w*, *y*, and *z*. Give the answers in simplest radical form.
$w = 20\sqrt{3}$; $y = \frac{40\sqrt{3}}{3}$; $z = \frac{20\sqrt{3}}{3}$

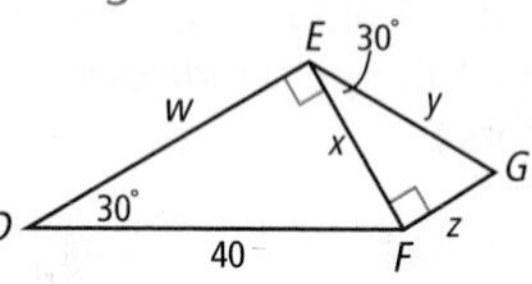

Find each measure.

2. $\widehat{RT}$ 54° 3. *UQ* $4\sqrt{2}$ ft

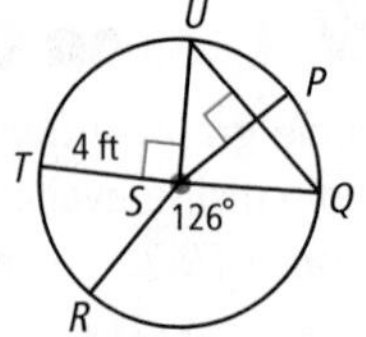

Also available on transparency

Math Humor

Q: What's the difference between the diameter and the radius?

A: The radius!

State Resources

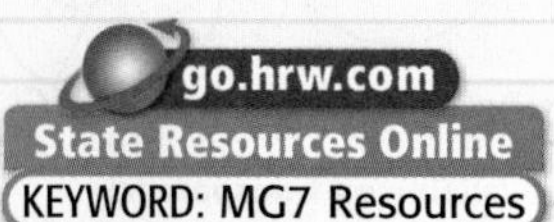

11-3 Sector Area and Arc Length

Objectives
Find the area of sectors.
Find arc lengths.

Vocabulary
sector of a circle
segment of a circle
arc length

Who uses this?
Farmers use irrigation radii to calculate areas of sectors. (See Example 2.)

The area of a sector is a fraction of the circle containing the sector. To find the area of a sector whose central angle measures $m°$, multiply the area of the circle by $\frac{m°}{360°}$.

Know it! Note — Sector of a Circle

TERM	NAME	DIAGRAM	AREA
A **sector of a circle** is a region bounded by two radii of the circle and their intercepted arc.	sector *ACB*		$A = \pi r^2\left(\frac{m°}{360°}\right)$

EXAMPLE 1 Finding the Area of a Sector

Find the area of each sector. Give your answer in terms of π and rounded to the nearest hundredth.

A sector *MPN*

$A = \pi r^2\left(\frac{m°}{360°}\right)$ *Use formula for area of a sector.*

$= \pi(3)^2\left(\frac{80°}{360°}\right)$ *Substitute 3 for r and 80 for m.*

$= 2\pi \text{ in}^2 \approx 6.28 \text{ in}^2$ *Simplify.*

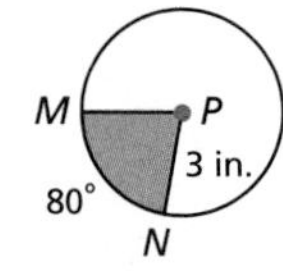

B sector *EFG*

$A = \pi r^2\left(\frac{m°}{360°}\right)$ *Use formula for area of a sector.*

$= \pi(6)^2\left(\frac{120°}{360°}\right)$ *Substitute 6 for r and 120 for m.*

$= 12\pi \approx 37.70 \text{ cm}^2$ *Simplify.*

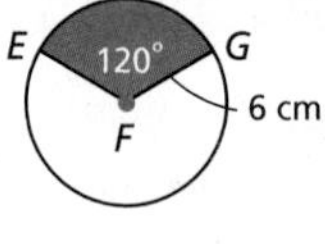

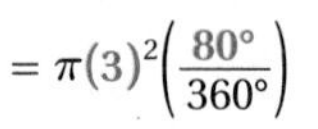
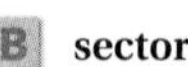

Helpful Hint
Write the degree symbol after *m* in the formula to help you remember to use degree measure not arc length.

CHECK IT OUT! Find the area of each sector. Give your answer in terms of π and rounded to the nearest hundredth.

1a. sector *ACB* $\frac{\pi}{4}$ m²; 0.79 m²

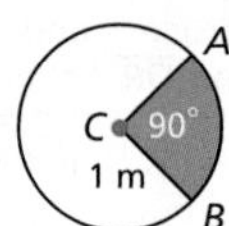

1b. sector *JKL* 25.6π in²; 80.42 in²

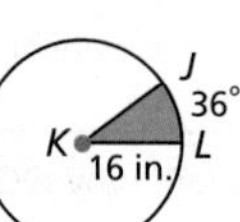

1 Introduce

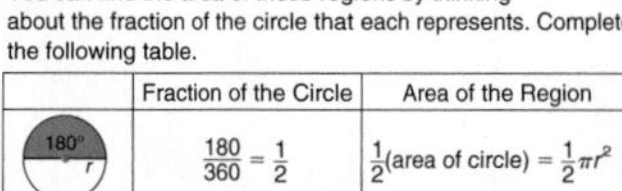

EXPLORATION
11-3 Sector Area and Arc Length

In this Exploration, you will investigate the areas of regions bounded by two radii of a circle and their intercepted arc.

1. You can find the area of these regions by thinking about the fraction of the circle that each represents. Complete the following table.

	Fraction of the Circle	Area of the Region
180°	$\frac{180}{360} = \frac{1}{2}$	$\frac{1}{2}$(area of circle) $= \frac{1}{2}\pi r^2$
90°		
50°		
37°		

2. Look for a pattern and write a general formula for the area of the region shown.

Motivate

Have a student stand several feet away from a classroom wall. Tie a string loosely to the student's arm. Ask another student to hold the opposite end of the string on the wall so that it is taut. Explain that the string represents the radius of a circle. Direct the first student to walk in an arc toward the wall. Ask the class how they might measure the distance traveled by the student. Explain that they will learn how to find arc lengths in this lesson.

Explorations and answers are provided in *Alternative Openers: Explorations Transparencies*.

EXAMPLE 2 Agriculture Application

A circular plot with a 720 ft diameter is watered by a spray irrigation system. To the nearest square foot, what is the area that is watered as the sprinkler rotates through an angle of 50°?

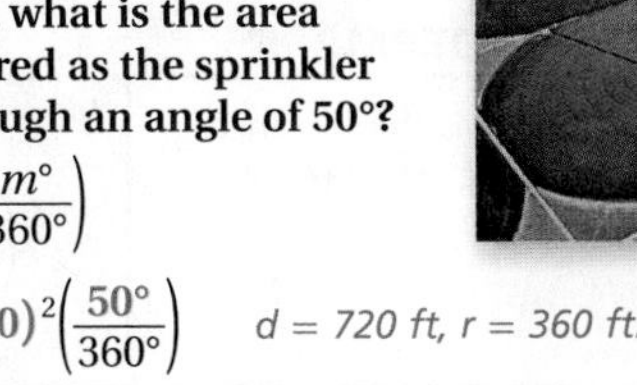

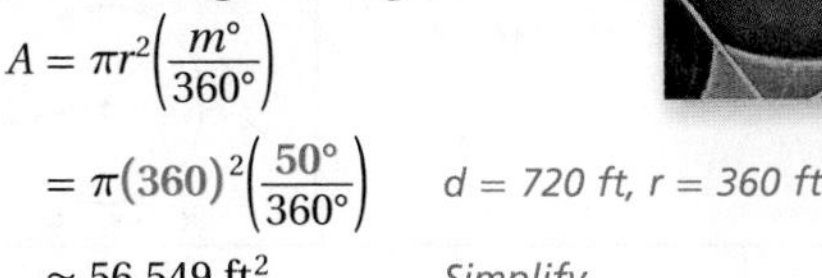

$$A = \pi r^2\left(\frac{m°}{360°}\right)$$

$$= \pi(360)^2\left(\frac{50°}{360°}\right) \quad \textit{d = 720 ft, r = 360 ft.}$$

$$\approx 56{,}549 \text{ ft}^2 \quad \textit{Simplify.}$$

CHECK IT OUT! **2.** To the nearest square foot, what is the area watered in Example 2 as the sprinkler rotates through a semicircle? **203,575 ft²**

A **segment of a circle** is a region bounded by an arc and its chord. The shaded region in the figure is a segment.

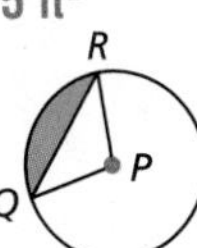

Know it! Note — Area of a Segment

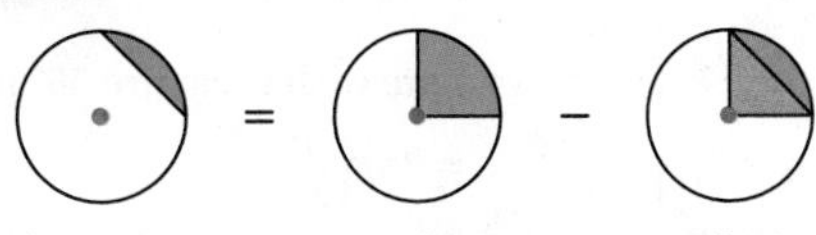

area of segment = area of sector – area of triangle

EXAMPLE 3 Finding the Area of a Segment

Find the area of segment ACB to the nearest hundredth.

Step 1 Find the area of sector ACB.

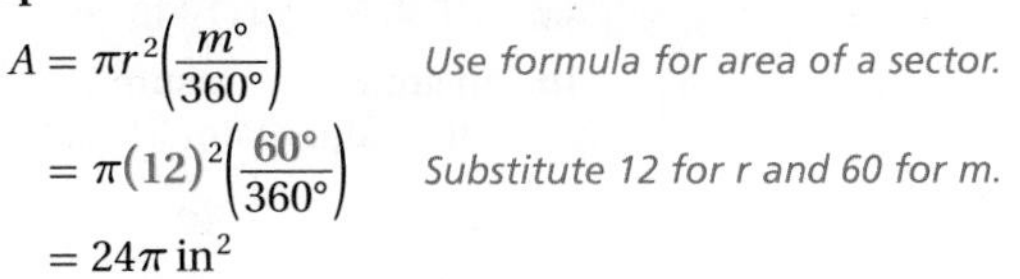

$$A = \pi r^2\left(\frac{m°}{360°}\right) \quad \textit{Use formula for area of a sector.}$$

$$= \pi(12)^2\left(\frac{60°}{360°}\right) \quad \textit{Substitute 12 for r and 60 for m.}$$

$$= 24\pi \text{ in}^2$$

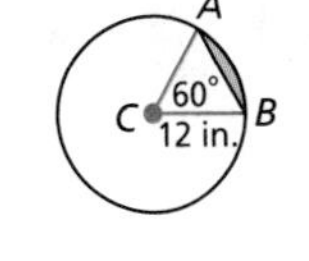

Step 2 Find the area of $\triangle ACB$.

Draw altitude $\overline{AD}$.

$$A = \frac{1}{2}bh = \frac{1}{2}(12)(6\sqrt{3}) \quad \textit{CD = 6 in., and } h = 6\sqrt{3} \textit{ in.}$$

$$= 36\sqrt{3} \text{ in}^2 \quad \textit{Simplify.}$$

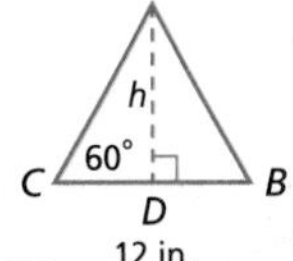

Step 3 area of segment = area of sector ACB – area of $\triangle ACB$

$$= 24\pi - 36\sqrt{3}$$

$$\approx 13.04 \text{ in}^2$$

Remember!

In a 30°-60°-90° triangle, the length of the leg opposite the 60° angle is $\sqrt{3}$ times the length of the shorter leg.

CHECK IT OUT! **3.** Find the area of segment RST to the nearest hundredth. **4.57 m²**

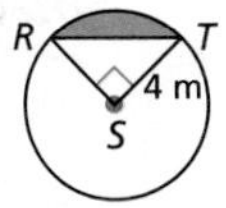

COMMON ERROR ALERT

Students may not understand why the segment of a circle is named by three letters. Explain that the "end" letters represent the endpoints of the chord and that the middle letter is the center of the circle.

Power Presentations with PowerPoint®

Additional Examples

Example 1

Find the area of each sector. Give answers in terms of π and rounded to the nearest hundredth.

A. sector HGJ
52.4π m²
≈ 164.62 m²

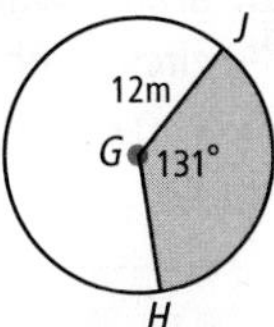

B. sector ABC
≈ 1.74π ft²
≈ 5.45 ft²

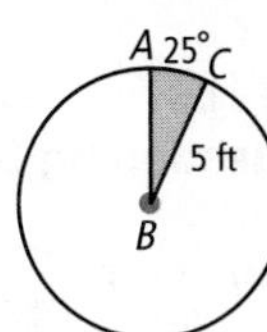

Example 2

A windshield wiper blade is 18 inches long. To the nearest square inch, what is the area covered by the blade as it rotates through an angle of 122°?
≈ 345 in²

Example 3

Find the area of segment LNM to the nearest hundredth.
≈ 49.75 cm²

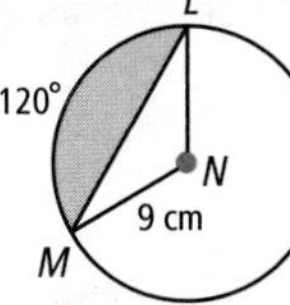

INTERVENTION

Questioning Strategies

EXAMPLE 1

- How could you calculate the area of a sector by using the area of the circle and the percentage shaded by the sector?

EXAMPLE 2

- Is the actual covered area more or less than the calculated answer?

EXAMPLE 3

- Is the area of a segment more accurate when answers are left in terms of π? Explain.

2 Teach

Guided Instruction

Have students fold a piece of paper in half. Then separate each half into two columns. On the top half, have students write the terms *sector* and *segment*. On the bottom half, have them draw a model of each term, write each term's definition, and give the method for finding the area of each shape. Then define and explain the formula for *arc length*.

Teaching Tip **Algebra** Point out that the m in the formula for area of a sector represents the arc measure, not the central angle measure.

Reaching All Learners

Through Critical Thinking

Explain to students that when they divide the measure of an arc by 360°, they are actually finding the percentage of the circumference of the circle covered by the arc. Show how an arc that measures 180° covers 0.5, or 50%, of the circumference of a circle. Lead them to see that they find the *area of a sector* when they multiply this percentage by the *area formula*, and they find the *arc length* when they multiply it by the *circumference formula*.

Power Presentations with PowerPoint®

Additional Examples

Example 4

Find each arc length. Give answers in terms of π and rounded to the nearest hundredth.

A. $\widehat{FG}$ $\approx 5.96\pi$ cm ≈ 18.71 cm

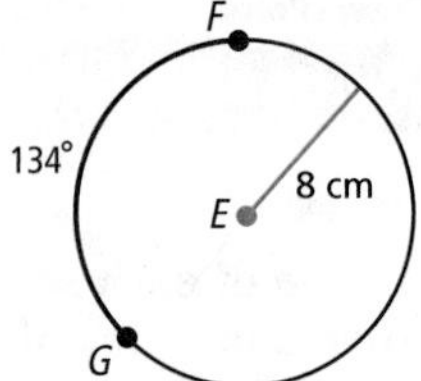

B. an arc with measure 62° in a circle with radius 2 m
$\approx 0.69\pi$ m ≈ 2.16 m

INTERVENTION

Questioning Strategies

EXAMPLE 4

- Why is the answer for arc length in units and not in square units?

Visual Students have long associated the word *segment* with a line segment. Now they must visualize a *segment of a circle* as the area between a chord and an arc. Point out that line segments are one-dimensional and circle segments are two-dimensional.

In the same way that the area of a sector is a fraction of the area of the circle, the length of an arc is a fraction of the circumference of the circle.

Arc Length

TERM	DIAGRAM	LENGTH
Arc length is the distance along an arc measured in linear units.	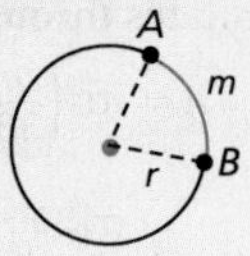 (circle with A, B, m, r)	$L = 2\pi r\left(\frac{m°}{360°}\right)$

EXAMPLE 4 Finding Arc Length

Find each arc length. Give your answer in terms of π and rounded to the nearest hundredth.

A $\widehat{CD}$

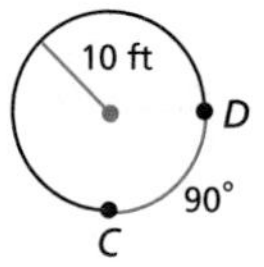

$L = 2\pi r\left(\frac{m°}{360°}\right)$ *Use formula for arc length.*

$= 2\pi(10)\left(\frac{90°}{360°}\right)$ *Substitute 10 for r and 90 for m.*

$= 5\pi \text{ ft} \approx 15.71 \text{ ft}$ *Simplify.*

B **an arc with measure 35° in a circle with radius 3 in.**

$L = 2\pi r\left(\frac{m°}{360°}\right)$ *Use formula for arc length.*

$= 2\pi(3)\left(\frac{35°}{360°}\right)$ *Substitute 3 for r and 35 for m.*

$= \frac{7}{12} \text{ in.} \approx 1.83 \text{ in.}$ *Simplify.*

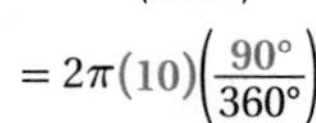

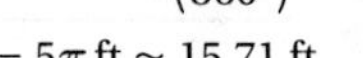

Find each arc length. Give your answer in terms of π and rounded to the nearest hundredth.

4a. $\widehat{GH}$ $\frac{4}{3}\pi$ **m; 4.19 m**

4b. an arc with measure 135° in a circle with radius 4 cm 3π **cm; 9.42 cm**

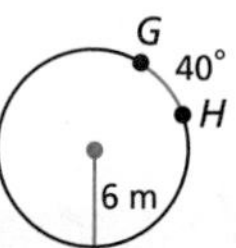

THINK AND DISCUSS

1. What is the difference between arc measure and arc length?
2. A slice of pizza is a sector of a circle. Explain what measurements you would need to make in order to calculate the area of the slice.
3. **GET ORGANIZED** Copy and complete the graphic organizer.

	Formula	Diagram
Area of a Sector		
Area of a Segment		
Arc Length		

3 Close

Summarize

Remind students of the definitions of a sector of a circle and a segment of a circle by drawing a picture of each one. Review the formulas for finding the area of a sector and the length of an arc. Tell students that arc length is expressed as a part of the circle's circumference and the area of a sector is expressed as a part of the circle's area. Emphasize that the method for finding the area of a segment involves finding the area of a sector and then subtracting the area of the triangle.

ONGOING ASSESSMENT and INTERVENTION

Diagnose ***Before*** **the Lesson**
11-3 Warm Up, TE p. 764

Monitor ***During*** **the Lesson**
Check It Out! Exercises, SE pp. 764–766
Questioning Strategies, TE pp. 765–766

Assess ***After*** **the Lesson**
11-3 Lesson Quiz, TE p. 769
Alternative Assessment, TE p. 769

Answers to *Think and Discuss*

1. Arc measure is measured in degrees. Arc length is measured in linear units.
2. the radius of the sector and its central ∠
3. See p. A8.

11-3 Exercises

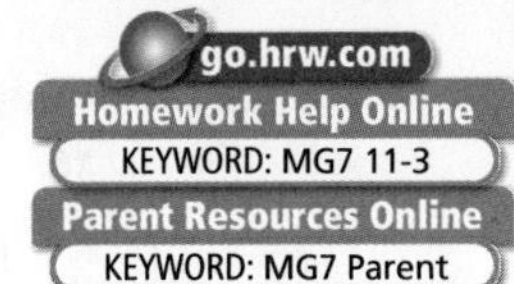

GUIDED PRACTICE

1. **Vocabulary** In a circle, the region bounded by a chord and an arc is called a ___?___ . (*sector* or *segment*) seg.

SEE EXAMPLE 1 p. 764

Find the area of each sector. Give your answer in terms of π and rounded to the nearest hundredth.

2. sector PQR 9π m^2; 28.27 m^2

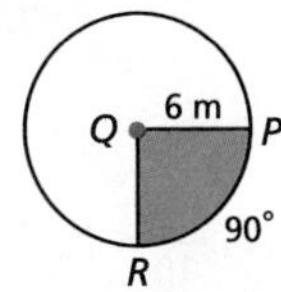

3. sector JKL 24π cm^2; 75.40 cm^2

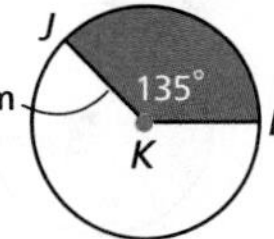

4. sector ABC $\frac{2}{9}\pi$ ft^2; 0.70 ft^2

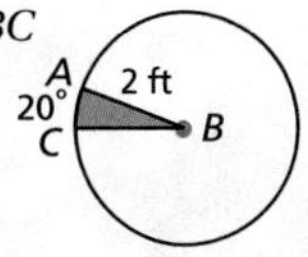

SEE EXAMPLE 2 p. 765

5. **Navigation** The beam from a lighthouse is visible for a distance of 3 mi. To the nearest square mile, what is the area covered by the beam as it sweeps in an arc of 150°? 12 mi^2

SEE EXAMPLE 3 p. 765

Multi-Step **Find the area of each segment to the nearest hundredth.**

6.

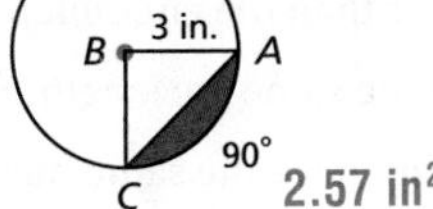

2.57 in^2

7.

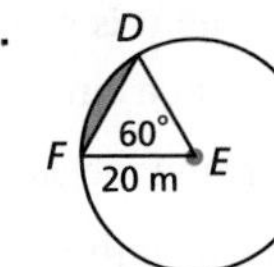

36.23 m^2

8.

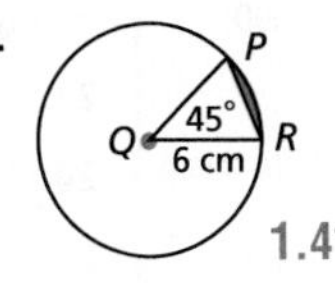

1.41 cm^2

SEE EXAMPLE 4 p. 766

Find each arc length. Give your answer in terms of π and rounded to the nearest hundredth.

9. $\widehat{EF}$

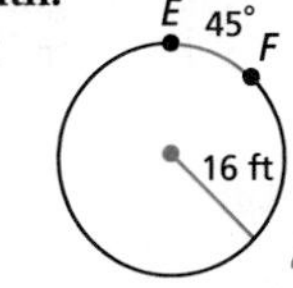

4π ft; 12.57 ft

10. $\widehat{PQ}$

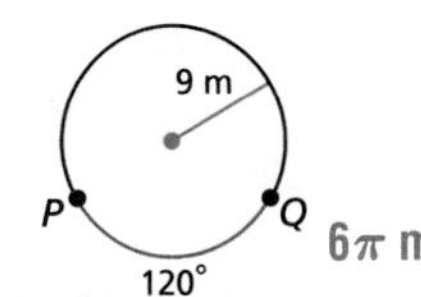

6π m; 18.85 m

11. an arc with measure 20° in a circle with radius 6 in. $\frac{2}{3}\pi$ in; 2.09 in.

PRACTICE AND PROBLEM SOLVING

Independent Practice	
For Exercises	See Example
12–14	1
15	2
16–18	3
19–21	4

Extra Practice
Skills Practice p. S24
Application Practice p. S38

Find the area of each sector. Give your answer in terms of π and rounded to the nearest hundredth.

12. sector DEF $\frac{500}{3}\pi$ m^2; 523.60 m^2

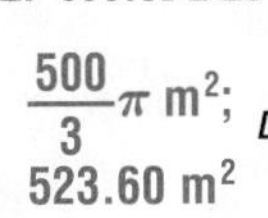

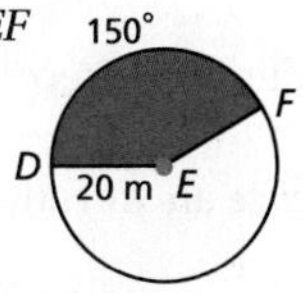

13. sector GHJ $\frac{45}{2}\pi$ in^2; 70.69 in^2

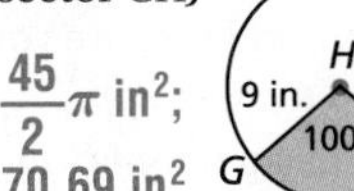

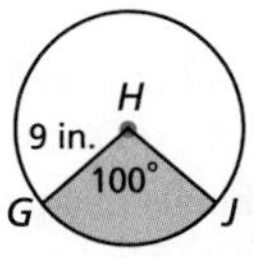

14. sector RST $\frac{47}{90}\pi$ ft^2; 1.64 ft^2

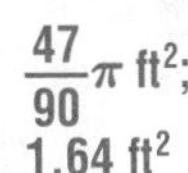
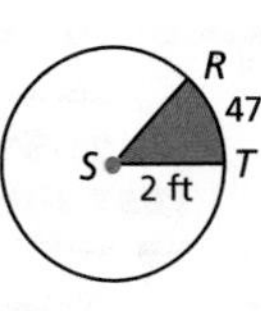

15. **Architecture** A *lunette* is a semicircular window that is sometimes placed above a doorway or above a rectangular window. To the nearest square inch, what is the area of the lunette? 628 in^2

11-3 Exercises

Assignment Guide

Assign *Guided Practice* exercises as necessary.

If you finished Examples 1–2
Basic 12–15, 26
Average 12–15, 26, 35
Advanced 12–15, 26, 35, 37

If you finished Examples 1–4
Basic 12–34, 38–45
Average 12–35, 38–45
Advanced 12–45

Homework Quick Check
Quickly check key concepts.
Exercises: 12, 15, 18, 20, 21, 24

Teaching Tip **Visual** Point out the difference between arc *measure* and arc *length* to students. If an exercise asks for the *measure* of an arc, the notation will be $m\widehat{AB}$. **Exercise 9** asks for $\widehat{EF}$, which is the notation for arc *length*.

Teaching Tip **Reading Math** Explain that the word *lunette* In **Exercise 15** comes from the Latin word *luna*, which means "moon." The lunette window looks like a crescent moon. ENGLISH LANGUAGE LEARNERS

State Resources

go.hrw.com
State Resources Online
KEYWORD: MG7 Resources

Exercise 29 involves using the formula for arc length to find the distance traveled by a bike and to find the angle through which the pedals must turn to move the bike a certain distance. This exercise prepares students for the Multi-Step Test Prep on page 770.

Algebra As students work through **Exercise 29b**, encourage them to use variables to solve for the angle and then to substitute a distance of 4.5 ft in the formula.

Multi-Step Find the area of each segment to the nearest hundredth.

16. 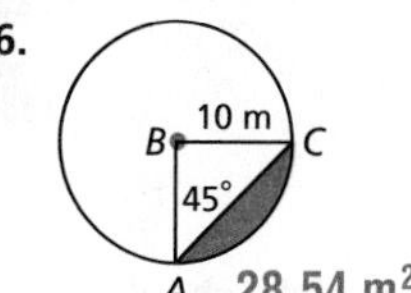

28.54 m^2

17. 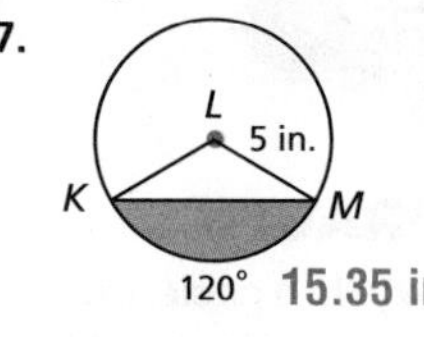

15.35 in^2

18. 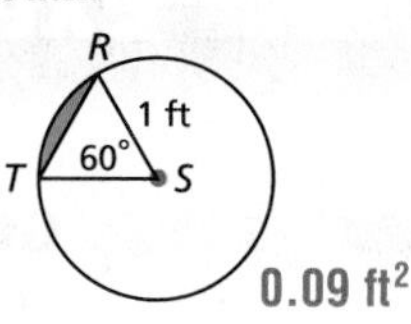

0.09 ft^2

Find each arc length. Give your answer in terms of π and rounded to the nearest hundredth.

19. $\widehat{UV}$ (50°, 5 mm) $\frac{25}{18}\pi$ mm; 4.36 mm

20. $\widehat{AB}$ (1.5 m, 160°) $\frac{4}{3}\pi$ m; 4.19 m

21. an arc with measure 9° in a circle with diameter 4 ft $\frac{1}{10}\pi$ ft; 0.31 ft

22. **Math History** Greek mathematicians studied the *salinon*, a figure bounded by four semicircles. What is the perimeter of this salinon to the nearest tenth of an inch? (1 in., 1 in.) 18.8 in.

LINK Math History

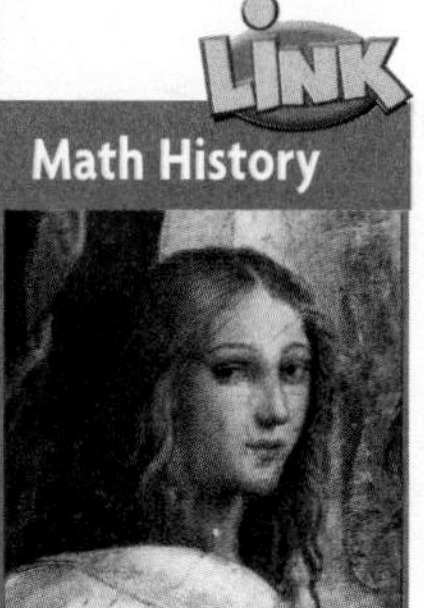

Hypatia lived 1600 years ago. She is considered one of history's most important mathematicians. She is credited with contributions to both geometry and astronomy.

Tell whether each statement is sometimes, always, or never true.

23. The length of an arc of a circle is greater than the circumference of the circle. N

24. Two arcs with the same measure have the same arc length. S

25. In a circle, two arcs with the same length have the same measure. A

Find the radius of each circle.

26. area of sector $ABC = 9\pi$ 6

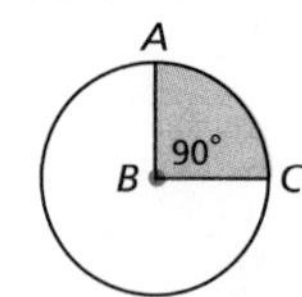

27. arc length of $\widehat{EF} = 8\pi$ 12

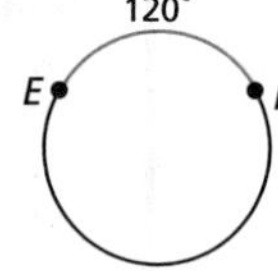

28. **Estimation** The fraction $\frac{22}{7}$ is an approximation for π. (X, 90°, 7 in., Y)
  a. Use this value to estimate the arc length of $\widehat{XY}$. 11 in.
  b. Use the π key on your calculator to find the length of $\widehat{XY}$ to 8 decimal places. 10.99557429 in.
  c. Was your estimate in part **a** an overestimate or an underestimate? overestimate

MULTI-STEP TEST PREP

29. This problem will prepare you for the Multi-Step Test Prep on page 770.

The pedals of a penny-farthing bicycle are directly connected to the front wheel.

  a. Suppose a penny-farthing bicycle has a front wheel with a diameter of 5 ft. To the nearest tenth of a foot, how far does the bike move when you turn the pedals through an angle of 90°? 3.9 ft
  b. Through what angle should you turn the pedals in order to move forward by a distance of 4.5 ft? Round to the nearest degree. 103°

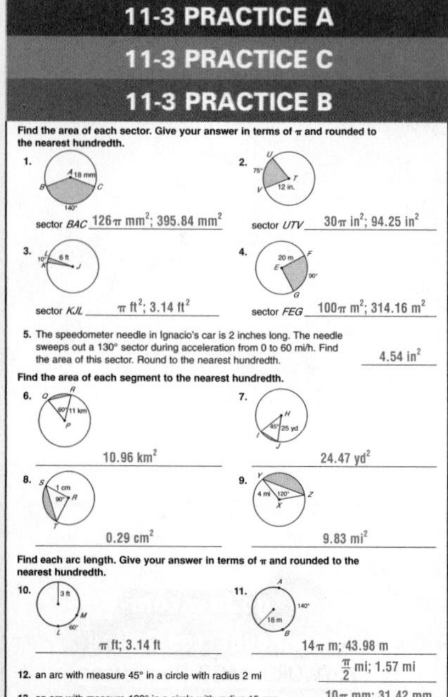

11-3 PRACTICE A
11-3 PRACTICE C
11-3 PRACTICE B

Find the area of each sector. Give your answer in terms of π and rounded to the nearest hundredth.

1. sector *BAC* $126\pi \text{ mm}^2$; 395.84 mm^2
2. sector *UTV* $30\pi \text{ in}^2$; 94.25 in^2
3. sector *KJL* $\pi \text{ ft}^2$; 3.14 ft^2
4. sector *FEG* $100\pi \text{ m}^2$; 314.16 m^2
5. The speedometer needle in Ignacio's car is 2 inches long. The needle sweeps out a 130° sector during acceleration from 0 to 60 mi/h. Find the area of this sector. Round to the nearest hundredth. 4.54 in^2

Find the area of each segment to the nearest hundredth.

6. 10.96 km^2
7. 24.47 yd^2
8. 0.29 cm^2
9. 9.83 mi^2

Find each arc length. Give your answer in terms of π and rounded to the nearest hundredth.

10. π ft; 3.14 ft
11. 14π m; 43.98 m
12. an arc with measure 45° in a circle with radius 2 mi $\frac{\pi}{2}$ mi; 1.57 mi
13. an arc with measure 120° in a circle with radius 15 mm 10π mm; 31.42 mm

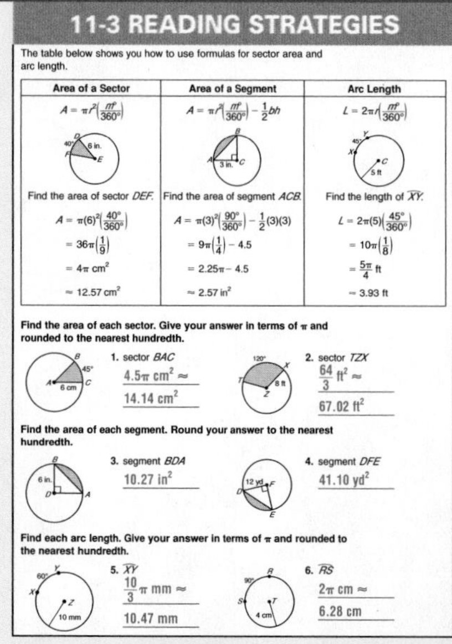

11-3 READING STRATEGIES

The table below shows you how to use formulas for sector area and arc length.

Area of a Sector	Area of a Segment	Arc Length
$A = \pi r^2\left(\frac{m°}{360°}\right)$	$A = \pi r^2\left(\frac{m°}{360°}\right) - \frac{1}{2}bh$	$L = 2\pi r\left(\frac{m°}{360°}\right)$
Find the area of sector *DEF*.	Find the area of segment *ACB*.	Find the length of $\widehat{XY}$.
$A = \pi(6)^2\left(\frac{40°}{360°}\right) = 36\pi\left(\frac{1}{9}\right) = 4\pi \text{ cm}^2 \approx 12.57 \text{ cm}^2$	$A = \pi(3)^2\left(\frac{90°}{360°}\right) - \frac{1}{2}(3)(3) = 9\pi\left(\frac{1}{4}\right) - 4.5 = 2.25\pi - 4.5 \approx 2.57 \text{ in}^2$	$L = 2\pi(5)\left(\frac{45°}{360°}\right) = 10\pi\left(\frac{1}{8}\right) = \frac{5\pi}{4} \text{ ft} \approx 3.93 \text{ ft}$

Find the area of each sector. Give your answer in terms of π and rounded to the nearest hundredth.

1. sector *BAC* $4.5\pi \text{ cm}^2 \approx 14.14 \text{ cm}^2$
2. sector *TZX* $\frac{64}{3} \text{ ft}^2 \approx 67.02 \text{ ft}^2$

Find the area of each segment. Round your answer to the nearest hundredth.

3. segment *BDA* 10.27 in^2
4. segment *DFE* 41.10 yd^2

Find each arc length. Give your answer in terms of π and rounded to the nearest hundredth.

5. $\widehat{XY}$ $\frac{10}{3}\pi \text{ mm} \approx 10.47$ mm
6. $\widehat{RS}$ $2\pi \text{ cm} \approx 6.28$ cm

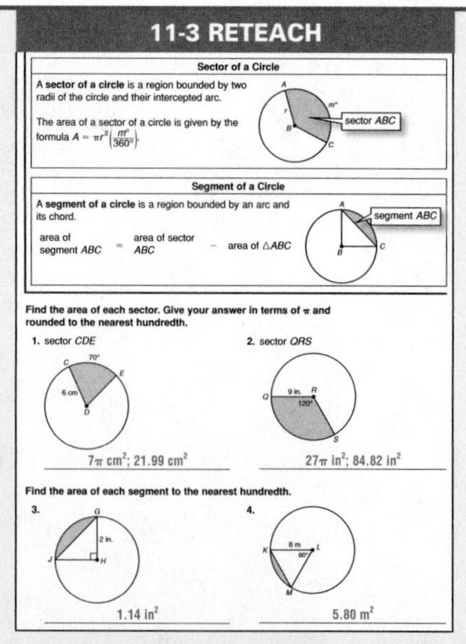

11-3 RETEACH

Sector of a Circle

A **sector of a circle** is a region bounded by two radii of the circle and their intercepted arc.

The area of a sector of a circle is given by the formula $A = \pi r^2\left(\frac{m°}{360°}\right)$.

Segment of a Circle

A **segment of a circle** is a region bounded by an arc and its chord.

area of segment *ABC* = area of sector *ABC* − area of $\triangle ABC$

Find the area of each sector. Give your answer in terms of π and rounded to the nearest hundredth.

1. sector *CDE* $7\pi \text{ cm}^2$; 21.99 cm^2
2. sector *QRS* $27\pi \text{ in}^2$; 84.82 in^2

Find the area of each segment to the nearest hundredth.

3. 1.14 in^2
4. 5.80 m^2

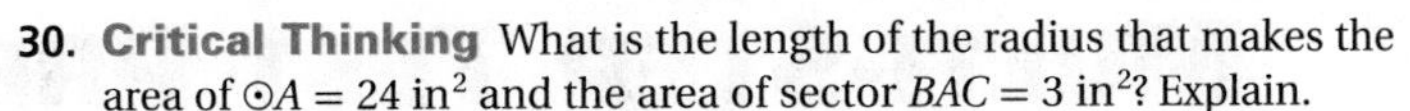

30. **Critical Thinking** What is the length of the radius that makes the area of $\odot A = 24\text{ in}^2$ and the area of sector $BAC = 3\text{ in}^2$? Explain.

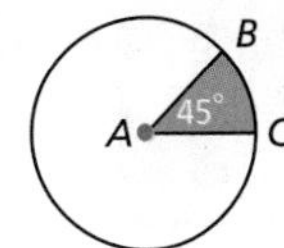

31. **Write About It** Given the length of an arc of a circle and the measure of the arc, explain how to find the radius of the circle.

32. What is the area of sector AOB?

Ⓐ 4π Ⓑ 16π Ⓒ 32π Ⓓ 64π

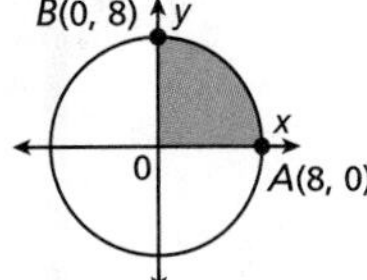

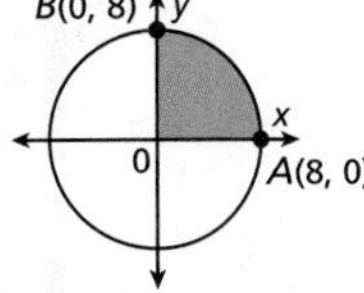

33. What is the length of $\overset{\frown}{AB}$?

Ⓕ 2π Ⓖ 4π Ⓗ 8π Ⓙ 16π

34. **Gridded Response** To the nearest hundredth, what is the area of the sector determined by an arc with measure 35° in a circle with radius 12? **43.98**

CHALLENGE AND EXTEND

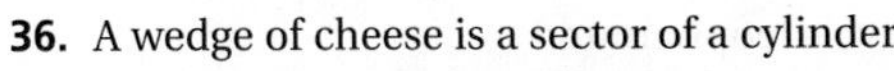

35. In the diagram, the larger of the two concentric circles has radius 5, and the smaller circle has radius 2. What is the area of the shaded region in terms of π? $\frac{7}{3}\pi$

36. A wedge of cheese is a sector of a cylinder.
    a. To the nearest tenth, what is the volume of the wedge with the dimensions shown? **12.6 in^3**
    b. What is the surface area of the wedge of cheese to the nearest tenth? **38.7 in^2**

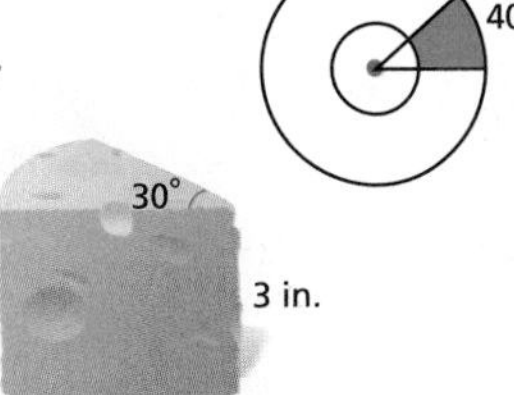

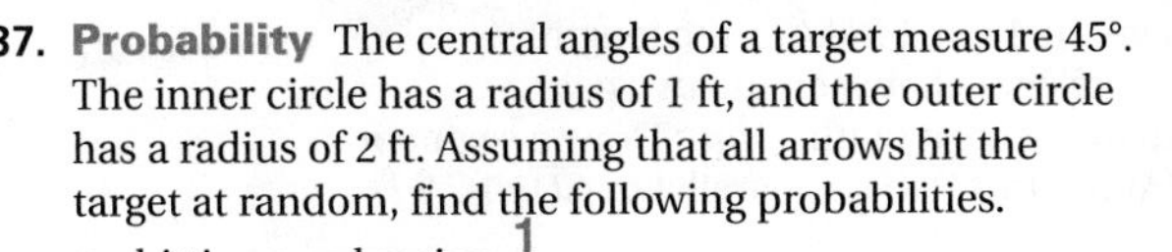

37. **Probability** The central angles of a target measure 45°. The inner circle has a radius of 1 ft, and the outer circle has a radius of 2 ft. Assuming that all arrows hit the target at random, find the following probabilities.
    a. hitting a red region $\frac{1}{8}$
    b. hitting a blue region $\frac{3}{8}$
    c. hitting a red or blue region $\frac{1}{2}$

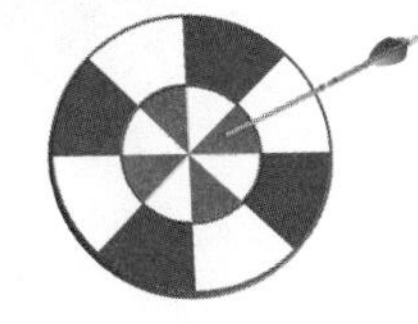

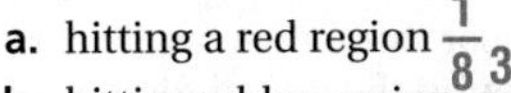

SPIRAL REVIEW

Determine whether each line is parallel to $y = 4x - 5$, perpendicular to $y = 4x - 5$, or neither. *(Previous course)*

38. $8x - 2y = 6$ $\parallel$

39. line passing through the points $\left(\frac{1}{2}, 0\right)$ and $\left(1\frac{1}{2}, 2\right)$ **neither**

40. line with x-intercept 4 and y-intercept 1 $\perp$

Find each measurement. Give your answer in terms of π. *(Lesson 10-8)*

41. volume of a sphere with radius 3 cm **36π cm^3**

42. circumference of a great circle of a sphere whose surface area is $4\pi\text{ cm}^2$ **2π cm**

Find the indicated measure. *(Lesson 11-2)*

43. $m\angle KLJ$ **122°**

44. $m\overset{\frown}{KJ}$ **122°**

45. $m\overset{\frown}{JFH}$ **302°**

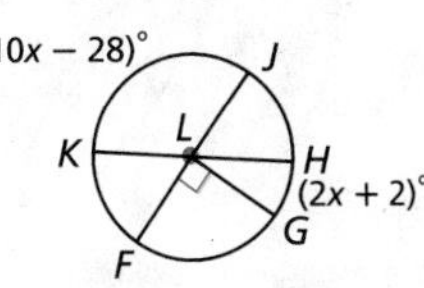

11-3 PROBLEM SOLVING

1. A circle with a radius of 20 centimeters has a sector that has an arc measure of 105°. What is the area of the sector? Round to the nearest tenth.
366.5 cm^2

2. A sector whose central angle measures 72° has an area of 16.2π square feet. What is the radius of the circle?
9 ft

3. The archway below is to be painted. What is the area of the archway to the nearest tenth?
5.7 ft; 90°; 1.5 ft; 4 ft
4.0 ft^2

4. Circle N has a circumference of 16π millimeters. What is the area of the shaded region to the nearest tenth?
B; 120°; 120°; N; A; C
78.6 mm^2

Choose the best answer.

5. The circular shelves in diagram are each 28 inches in diameter. The "cut-out" portion of each shelf is 90°. Approximately how much shelf paper is needed to cover both shelves?
A 154 in^2
B 308 in^2
C 462 in^2
Ⓓ 924 in^2

6. Find the area of the shaded region. Round to the nearest tenth.
G; 5 in.; J; H
F 8.2 in^2 Ⓗ 71.4 in^2
G 19.6 in^2 J 78.5 in^2

7. A semicircular garden with a diameter of 6 feet is to have 2 inches of mulch spread over it. To the nearest tenth, what is the volume of mulch that is needed?
Ⓐ 2.4 ft^3 C 14.1 ft^3
B 4.8 ft^3 D 28.3 ft^3

8. A round cheesecake 12 inches in diameter and 3 inches high is cut into 8 equal-sized pieces. If eight pieces have been taken, what is the approximate volume of the cheesecake that remains?
F 42.4 in^3 Ⓗ 127.2 in^3
G 70.7 in^3 J 212.1 in^3

Answers

30. $\approx$ 2.76 in.; Since the area of the $\odot$ is 8 times the area of the sector, the radius of each are the same.

31. If the length of the arc is L and the degree measure of the arc is m, then $L = 2\pi r\left(\frac{m°}{360°}\right)$. Solving for r gives $r = \frac{180L}{m\pi}$.

COMMON ERROR ALERT

Some students may mistakenly use the radius instead of the diameter in **Exercise 21.** Remind students to read all the problems carefully as they work through them.

TEST PREP DOCTOR In **Exercise 32**, students can quickly divide the area of the circle by 4 to find the answer.

Journal

Have students draw a picture that describes each new term in this lesson.

ALTERNATIVE ASSESSMENT

Have each student construct two circles of different sizes, both with two radii drawn. Ask them to shade a sector in the first circle and a segment in the second. Have students use protractors (MK) and rulers (MK) to find the areas of the sectors and the arc lengths of their circles. Then have them find the area of the segment in the second circle.

Power Presentations with PowerPoint®

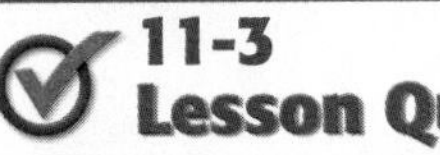

11-3 Lesson Quiz

Find each measure. Give answers in terms of π and rounded to the nearest hundredth.

1. area of sector LQM $7.5\pi\text{ in}^2 \approx 23.56\text{ in}^2$

2. length of $\overset{\frown}{NP}$ 2.5π in. $\approx$ 7.85 in.

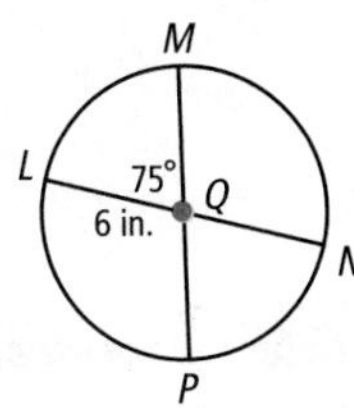

3. The gear of a grandfather clock has a radius of 3 in. To the nearest tenth of an inch, what distance does the gear cover when it rotates through an angle of 88°? $\approx$ 4.6 in.

4. Find the area of segment GHJ to the nearest hundredth.
$\approx$ 55.94 m^2

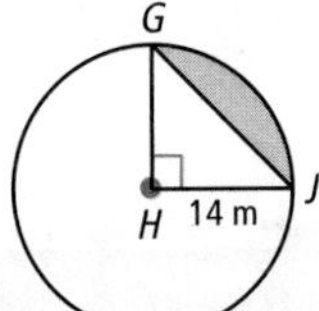

Also available on transparency

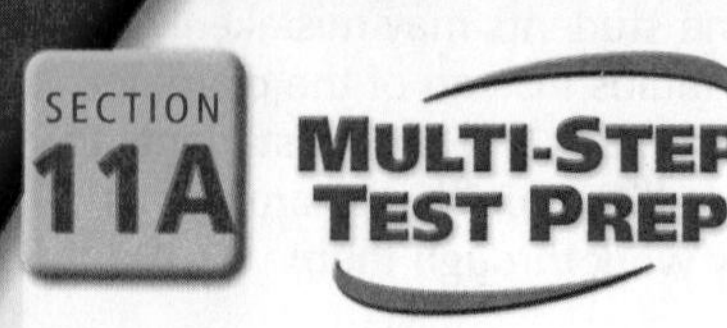

Organizer

Objective: Assess students' ability to apply concepts and skills in Lessons 11-1 through 11-3 in a real-world format.

Online Edition

Resources

Problem	Text Reference
1	Lesson 11-1
2	Lesson 11-2
3	Lesson 11-3

State Resources

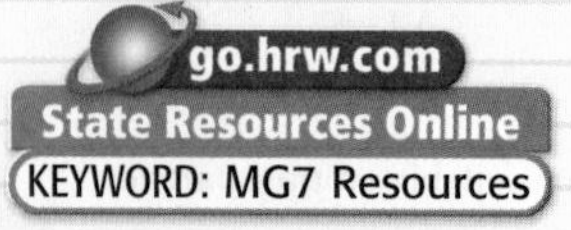

CHAPTER 11

SECTION 11A

MULTI-STEP TEST PREP

Lines and Arcs in Circles

As the Wheels Turn The bicycle was invented in the 1790s. The first models didn't even have pedals—riders moved forward by pushing their feet along the ground! Today the bicycle is a high-tech machine that can include hydraulic brakes and electronic gear changers.

1. A road race bicycle wheel is 28 inches in diameter. A manufacturer makes metal bicycle stands that are 10 in. tall. How long should a stand be to the nearest tenth in order to support a 28 in. wheel? (*Hint:* Consider the triangle formed by the radii and the top of the stand.) **26.8 in.**

2. The chain of a bicycle loops around a large gear connected to the bike's pedals and a small gear attached to the rear wheel. In the diagram, the distance AB between the centers of the gears the nearest tenth is 15 in. Find CD, the length of the chain between the two gears to the nearest tenth. (*Hint:* Draw a segment from B to $\overline{AD}$ that is parallel to $\overline{CD}$.) **14.9 in.**

3. By pedaling, you turn the large gear through an angle of 60°. How far does the chain move around the circumference of the gear to the nearest tenth? **4.2 in.**

4. As the chain moves, it turns the small gear. If you use the distance you calculated in Problem 3, through what angle does the small gear turn to the nearest degree? **120°**

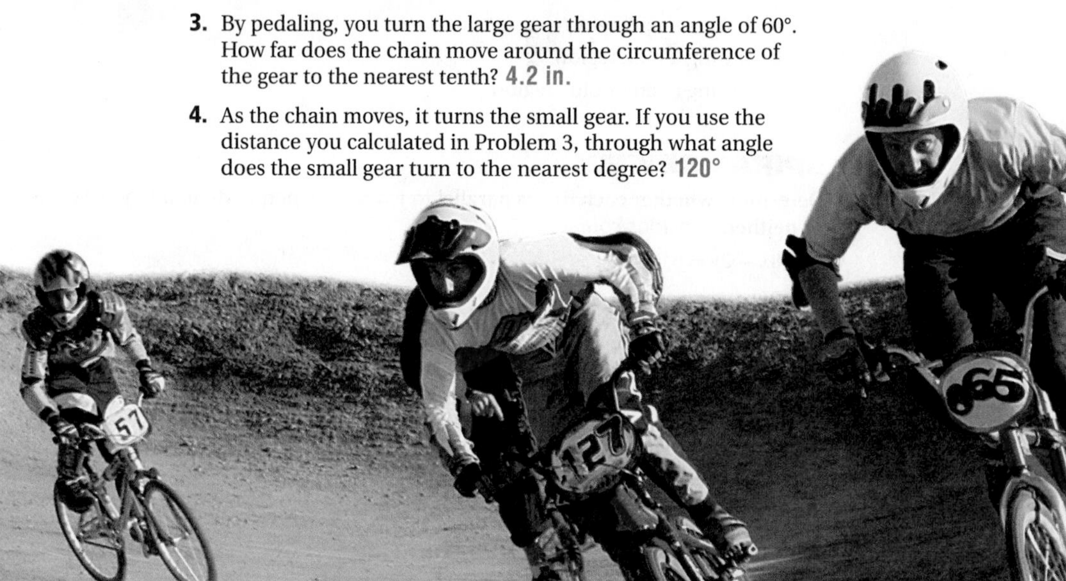

Scaffolding Questions

1. What is the radius of the wheel? 14 in. What type of triangle is formed in the figure? rt. △
2. What do you know about $\angle BCD$ and $\angle ADC$? They are rt. ∠s. When you draw a segment from B to $\overline{AD}$ that is parallel to $\overline{CD}$, what type of quadrilateral is formed? rect. Do you know any side lengths of the right triangle? Hyp. is 15 in., and one leg is 2 in. How can you find the other side length? Pyth. Thm.
3. What formula can you use to find the length of an arc that measures 60° ? $L = 2\pi r\left(\frac{m°}{360°}\right)$ What is the radius r in this case? 4 in.
4. What information is known in this problem? radius and arc length What do you need to calculate? degree measure of the arc

Extension

While you were pedaling, the small gear made one complete revolution. By what angle did you turn the large gear? 180°

CHAPTER 11

SECTION 11A

Quiz for Lessons 11-1 Through 11-3

11-1 Lines That Intersect Circles

Identify each line or segment that intersects each circle.

1. 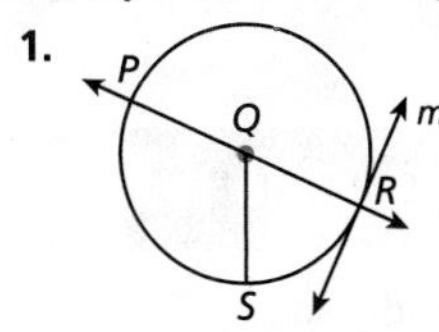

chord: $\overline{PR}$; tangent: m; radii: $\overline{QP}$, $\overline{QR}$, $\overline{QS}$; secant: $\overleftrightarrow{PR}$; diam.: $\overline{PR}$

2. 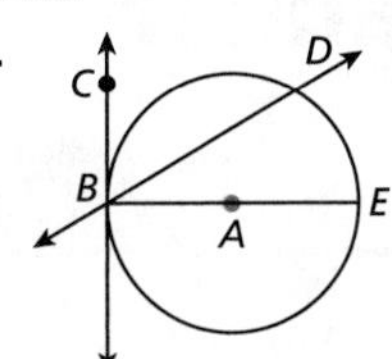

chords: $\overline{BD}$, $\overline{BE}$; tangent: $\overleftrightarrow{BC}$; radii: $\overline{AB}$, $\overline{AE}$; secant: $\overleftrightarrow{BD}$; diam.: $\overline{BE}$

3. The tallest building in Africa is the Carlton Centre in Johannesburg, South Africa. What is the distance from the top of this 732 ft building to the horizon to the nearest mile? (*Hint:* 5280 ft = 1 mi; radius of Earth = 4000 mi) 33 mi

11-2 Arcs and Chords

Find each measure.

4. $\widehat{BC}$ 41°
5. $\widehat{BED}$ 270°

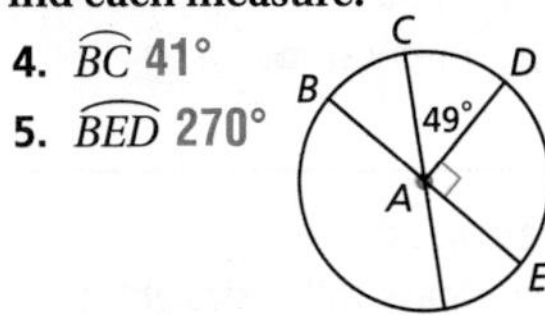

6. $\widehat{SR}$ 109°
7. $\widehat{SQU}$ 249°

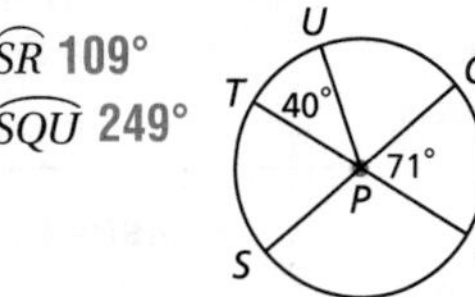

Find each length to the nearest tenth.

8. JK 11.5

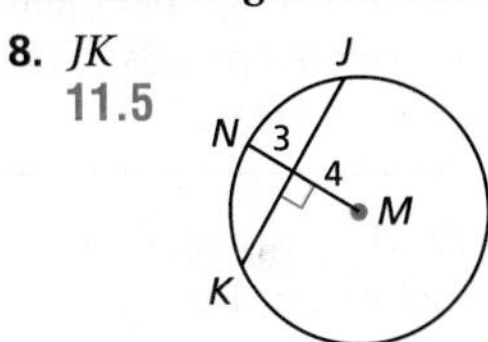

9. XY 13.9

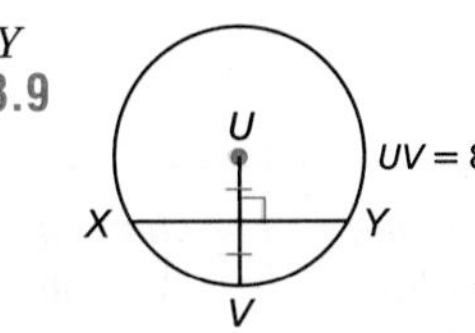

11-3 Sector Area and Arc Length

10. As part of an art project, Peter buys a circular piece of fabric and then cuts out the sector shown. What is the area of the sector to the nearest square centimeter? 338 cm²

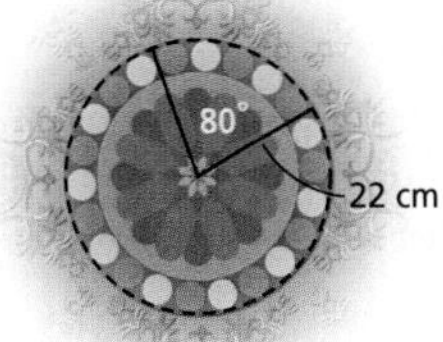

Find each arc length. Give your answer in terms of π and rounded to the nearest hundredth.

11. $\widehat{AB}$

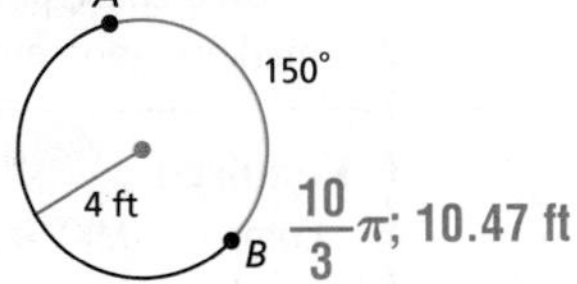

$\frac{10}{3}\pi$; 10.47 ft

12. $\widehat{EF}$

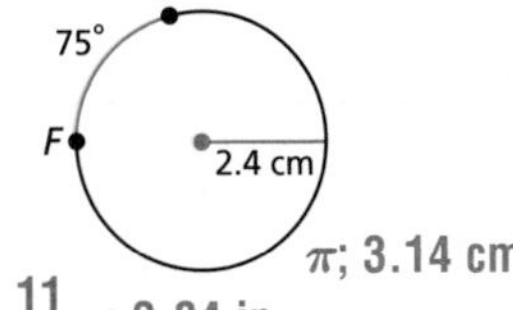

π; 3.14 cm

13. an arc with measure 44° in a circle with diameter 10 in. $\frac{11}{9}\pi$; 3.84 in.
14. a semicircle in a circle with diameter 92 m 46π; 144.51 m

READY TO GO ON? SECTION 11A

Organizer

Objective: Assess students' mastery of concepts and skills in Lessons 11-1 through 11-3.

Resources

 ***Assessment Resources***

Section 11A Quiz

Teacher One Stop™

Test & Practice Generator

INTERVENTION

Resources

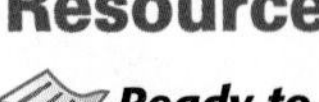
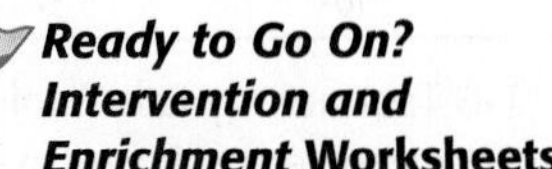
Ready to Go On? Intervention and Enrichment Worksheets

 ***Ready to Go On?*** **CD-ROM**

 ***Ready to Go On?*** **Online**

my.hrw.com

READY TO GO ON? Diagnose and Prescribe

NO INTERVENE

Ready to Go On? Intervention	Worksheets	CD-ROM	Online
	Ready to Go On? Intervention, Section 11A		
Lesson 11-1	11-1 Intervention	Activity 11-1	Diagnose and Prescribe Online
Lesson 11-2	11-2 Intervention	Activity 11-2	
Lesson 11-3	11-3 Intervention	Activity 11-3	

YES ENRICH

Ready to Go On? Enrichment, Section 11A

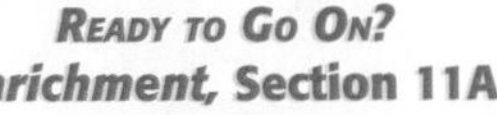
Worksheets

CD-ROM

Online

SECTION

11B Angles and Segments in Circles

One-Minute Section Planner

Lesson	Lab Resources	Materials
Lesson 11-4 Inscribed Angles • Find the measure of an inscribed angle. • Use inscribed angles and their properties to solve problems. ☐ SAT-10 ☑ NAEP ☐ ACT ☐ SAT ☐ SAT Subject Tests		**Required** compass (MK), straightedge **Optional** camera, paper tubes, geoboards, colored rubber bands (MK), geometry software
11-5 Technology Lab Explore Angle Relationships in Circles • Use geometry software to explore angle relationships in circles. ☑ SAT-10 ☑ NAEP ☑ ACT ☐ SAT ☐ SAT Subject Tests	***Technology Lab Activities*** 11-5 Lab Recording Sheet	**Required** geometry software
Lesson 11-5 Angle Relationships in Circles • Find the measures of angles formed by lines that intersect circles. • Use angle measures to solve problems. ☑ SAT-10 ☑ NAEP ☑ ACT ☐ SAT ☑ SAT Subject Tests	***Geometry Lab Activities*** 11-5 Geometry Lab	**Required** compass (MK), straightedge **Optional** literature or songs that mention circles, colored pencils, geometry software
11-6 Technology Lab Explore Segment Relationships in Circles • Use geometry software to explore segment relationships in circles. ☐ SAT-10 ☑ NAEP ☑ ACT ☑ SAT ☑ SAT Subject Tests	***Technology Lab Activities*** 11-6 Lab Recording Sheet	**Required** geometry software
Lesson 11-6 Segment Relationships in Circles • Find the lengths of segments formed by lines that intersect circles. • Use the lengths of segments in circles to solve problems. ☑ SAT-10 ☑ NAEP ☑ ACT ☑ SAT ☑ SAT Subject Tests	***Geometry Lab Activities*** 11-6 Geometry Lab	**Required** compass (MK), straightedge **Optional** textiles, rugs, furniture, or pottery designs with lines that intersect circles, family crests, colored chalk, pencils, or markers, geometry software
Lesson 11-7 Circles in the Coordinate Plane • Write equations and graph circles in the coordinate plane. • Use the equation and graph of a circle to solve problems. ☑ SAT-10 ☑ NAEP ☑ ACT ☑ SAT ☑ SAT Subject Tests		**Required** compass (MK), straightedge, graph paper **Optional** circle magnets, geometry software, graphing calculator, transparent paper
Extension Polar Coordinates • Convert between polar and rectangular coordinates. • Plot points using polar coordinates. ☑ SAT-10 ☐ NAEP ☑ ACT ☑ SAT ☑ SAT Subject Tests		**Required** graphing calculator

MK = *Manipulatives Kit*

Math Background

INSCRIBED ANGLES

Lesson 11-4

The Inscribed Angle Theorem states that the measure of an inscribed angle is half the measure of its intercepted arc. The theorem has several interesting corollaries, including the fact that an inscribed angle subtends a semicircle if and only if the angle is a right angle.

This corollary points to an enlightening way to define a circle. Draw a segment $\overline{AB}$ and consider all the lines through point *A*. For each of these lines, identify the intersection of the perpendicular from *B* to the line (this is called the *foot* of the perpendicular from *B* to the line). The locus of all such points, shown below in red, is a circle that has $\overline{AB}$ as a diameter.

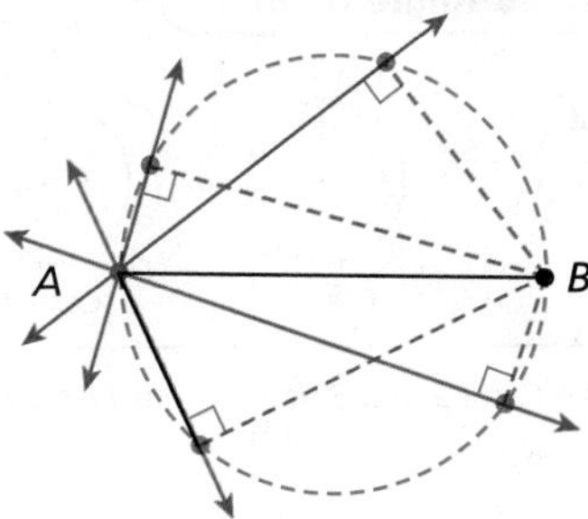

The Inscribed Angle Theorem is also connected to the theory of cyclic quadrilaterals. A *cyclic quadrilateral* is a quadrilateral that can be inscribed in a circle. That is, it is a quadrilateral whose four vertices all lie on a single circle. Theorem 11-4-4 asserts that opposite angles of a cyclic quadrilateral are supplementary. Euclid stated this theorem in Book III of his *Elements*. The converse of the theorem is also true. In other words, if the opposite angles of a quadrilateral are supplementary, then the quadrilateral is cyclic.

SEGMENT RELATIONSHIPS

Lesson 11-6

The theorems that are presented in Lesson 11-6 are sometimes known as *power theorems*. In particular, the Chord-Chord Product Theorem, the Secant-Secant Product Theorem, and the Secant-Tangent Product Theorem may be stated in an all-inclusive general form called the Power of a Point Theorem.

THE POWER OF A POINT THEOREM

Given a circle, a point *P* not on the circle, and two lines through *P* that intersect the circle at points *A* and *B* and at points *C* and *D*, respectively, $AP \cdot BP = CP \cdot DP$.

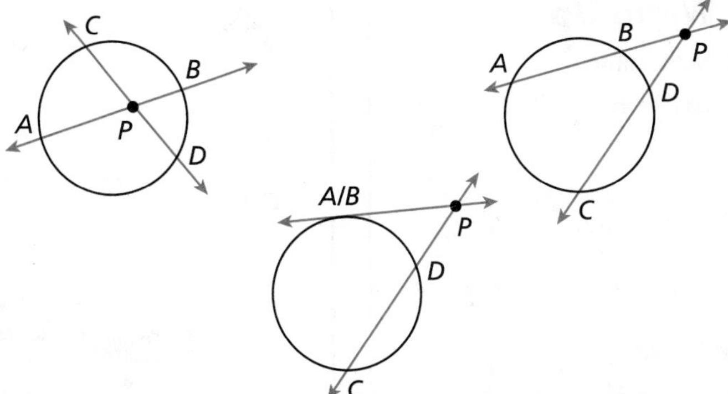

As shown in the figures, *P* may lie in the interior or exterior of the circle. In the case where a line through *P* is tangent to the circle, the two points of intersection coincide and the theorem reduces to the Secant-Tangent Product Theorem.

A COORDINATE APPROACH

Lesson 11-7

The equation of a circle with center (h, k) and radius *r* is $(x - h)^2 + (y - k)^2 = r^2$. This equation follows immediately from the Distance Formula. In addition, squaring and simplifying shows that every circle is the graph of an equation of the form $x^2 + y^2 + Ax + By + C = 0$. Given an equation in this form, the center and radius of the circle may be found by completing the square.

The equation of a circle easily generalizes to three dimensions to give the equation of a sphere. In particular, the equation of a sphere with center (h, j, k) and radius *r* is $(x - h)^2 + (y - j)^2 + (z - k)^2 = r^2$. This equation may be derived directly from the Distance Formula in three dimensions, which was introduced in Lesson 10-3.

11-4 Organizer

Pacing: Traditional 1 day
Block $\frac{1}{2}$ day

Objectives: Find the measure of an inscribed angle.

Use inscribed angles and their properties to solve problems.

Power Presentations with PowerPoint®

Warm Up

Find each value.

1. $m\angle BCA$ 63.5° **2.** t 116.5°

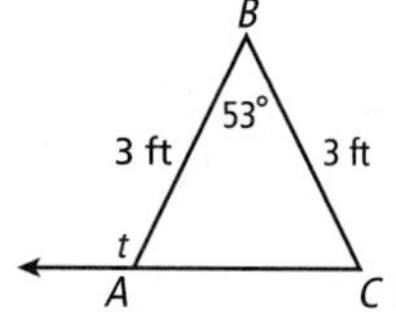

Solve for *x*.

3. $58 - x = 4(x + 7)$ 6

4. $2(x - 8) = 8$ 12

Also available on transparency

Q: I love my new bracelet, but why does it have the word *angle* written on it?

A: It's your very own *inscribed* angle!

11-4 Inscribed Angles

Objectives
Find the measure of an inscribed angle.

Use inscribed angles and their properties to solve problems.

Vocabulary
inscribed angle
intercepted arc
subtend

Why learn this?
You can use inscribed angles to find measures of angles in string art. (See Example 2.)

String art often begins with pins or nails that are placed around the circumference of a circle. A long piece of string is then wound from one nail to another. The resulting pattern may include hundreds of *inscribed angles.*

An **inscribed angle** is an angle whose vertex is on a circle and whose sides contain chords of the circle. An **intercepted arc** consists of endpoints that lie on the sides of an inscribed angle and all the points of the circle between them. A chord or arc **subtends** an angle if its endpoints lie on the sides of the angle.

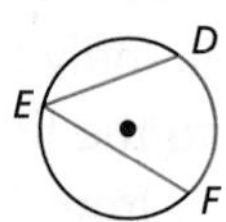

$\angle DEF$ is an inscribed angle.

$\widehat{DF}$ is the intercepted arc.

$\widehat{DF}$ subtends $\angle DEF$.

Theorem 11-4-1 **Inscribed Angle Theorem**

The measure of an inscribed angle is half the measure of its intercepted arc.

$$m\angle ABC = \frac{1}{2}m\widehat{AC}$$

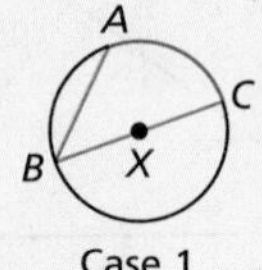

Case 1

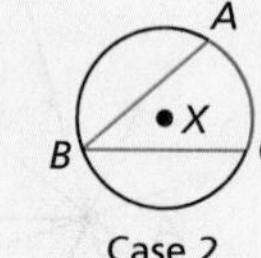

Case 2

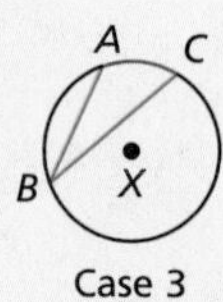

Case 3

You will prove Cases 2 and 3 of Theorem 11-4-1 in Exercises 30 and 31.

PROOF

Inscribed Angle Theorem

Given: $\angle ABC$ is inscribed in $\odot X$.
Prove: $m\angle ABC = \frac{1}{2}m\widehat{AC}$

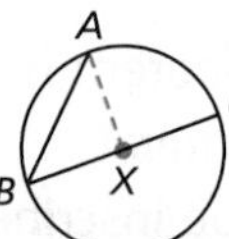

Proof Case 1:

$\angle ABC$ is inscribed in $\odot X$ with X on $\overline{BC}$. Draw $\overline{XA}$. $m\widehat{AC} = m\angle AXC$. By the Exterior Angle Theorem $m\angle AXC = m\angle ABX + m\angle BAX$. Since $\overline{XA}$ and $\overline{XB}$ are radii of the circle, $\overline{XA} \cong \overline{XB}$. Then by definition $\triangle AXB$ is isosceles. Thus $m\angle ABX = m\angle BAX$.

By the Substitution Property, $m\widehat{AC} = 2m\angle ABX$ or $2m\angle ABC$. Thus $\frac{1}{2}m\widehat{AC} = m\angle ABC$.

State Resources

1 Introduce

EXPLORATION

11-4 Inscribed Angles

An *inscribed angle* is an angle whose vertex is on a circle and whose sides contain chords of the circle. $\angle XYZ$ is an inscribed angle.

1. Use geometry software to construct a circle.
2. Plot and label points *A*, *B*, and *C* on the circle.
3. Draw $\overline{BA}$ and $\overline{BC}$ to make inscribed $\angle ABC$.
4. Use the Measure menu to find $m\angle ABC$ and $m\widehat{AC}$.

$m\angle ABC = 46.57°$
$m\widehat{AC} = 93.14°$

5. How are $m\angle ABC$ and $m\widehat{AC}$ related?
6. Drag the vertices of $\angle ABC$ and change the size of the circle. Is the relationship between $m\angle ABC$ and $m\widehat{AC}$ always the same?

THINK AND DISCUSS

Motivate

Help students understand inscribed angles by explaining a camera angle. You can use the edges of a board to form the inscribed angles or you can go outside the school building. As students step away from the building, have different students move until they can view the edges of the building exactly, no more and no less. Students can look through an actual camera or a paper tube. Point out to the students that they form the vertices of the inscribed angles.

Explorations and answers are provided in *Alternate Openers: Explorations Transparencies.*

EXAMPLE 1 Finding Measures of Arcs and Inscribed Angles

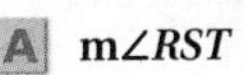

Find each measure.

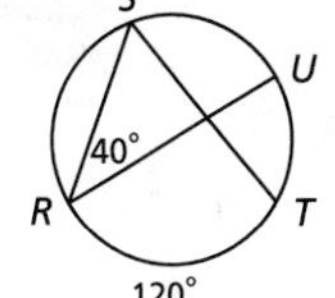

A m∠*RST*

$m\angle RST = \frac{1}{2}m\overset{\frown}{RT}$ *Inscribed ∠ Thm.*

$= \frac{1}{2}(120°) = 60°$ *Substitute 120 for* $m\overset{\frown}{RT}$.

B $m\overset{\frown}{SU}$

$m\angle SRU = \frac{1}{2}m\overset{\frown}{SU}$ *Inscribed ∠ Thm.*

$40° = \frac{1}{2}m\overset{\frown}{SU}$ *Substitute 40 for m∠SRU.*

$m\overset{\frown}{SU} = 80°$ *Mult. both sides by 2.*

CHECK IT OUT! Find each measure.

1a. $m\overset{\frown}{ADC}$ **270°**

1b. m∠*DAE* **38°**

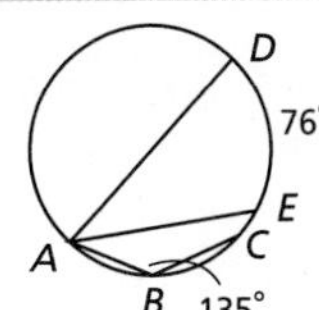

Corollary 11-4-2

COROLLARY	HYPOTHESIS	CONCLUSION
If inscribed angles of a circle intercept the same arc or are subtended by the same chord or arc, then the angles are congruent.	∠*ACB*, ∠*ADB*, and ∠*AEB* intercept $\overset{\frown}{AB}$.	∠*ACB* ≅ ∠*ADB* ≅ ∠*AEB* (and ∠*CAE* ≅ ∠*CBE*)

You will prove Corollary 11-4-2 in Exercise 32.

EXAMPLE 2 *Hobby Application*

Find m∠*DEC*, if $m\overset{\frown}{AD} = 86°$.

∠*BAC* ≅ ∠*BDC* *∠BAC and ∠BDC intercept* $\overset{\frown}{BC}$.

m∠*BAC* = m∠*BDC* *Def. of ≅*

m∠*BDC* = 60° *Substitute 60 for m∠BDC.*

$m\angle ACD = \frac{1}{2}m\overset{\frown}{AD}$ *Inscribed ∠ Thm.*

$= \frac{1}{2}(86°)$ *Substitute 86 for* $m\overset{\frown}{AD}$.

= 43° *Simplify.*

m∠*DEC* + 60 + 43 = 180 *△ Sum Theorem*

m∠*DEC* = 77° *Simplify.*

CHECK IT OUT! **2.** Find m∠*ABD* and $m\overset{\frown}{BC}$ in the string art. **43°; 120°**

2 Teach

Guided Instruction

Provide visual examples of the terms *inscribed angle* and *inscribed triangle*, *intercepted arc*, and *subtend*. You can fold paper, use a compass and straightedge, or geometry software. Ask students to devise various ways of finding the center of a circle. Then show them how to use perpendicular chords to construct the center of a circle. Have students find the angle measures in an inscribed quadrilateral and show that the opposite angles are supplementary.

Reaching All Learners
Through Modeling

Ask each student to draw a circle of any size with a compass. Have students select two points on their circles and ask each to label a minor arc. Have each student use a straightedge to draw three different inscribed angles that intercept the arc. Explain that an intercepted arc is the piece of the circumference that is "cut off" by the sides of the inscribed angle. Ask the class to use protractors to find and compare the measures of the inscribed angles.

Power Presentations with PowerPoint®

Additional Examples

Example 1

Find each measure.

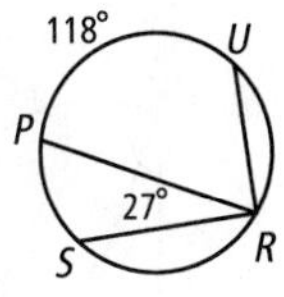

A. m∠*PRU* 59°

B. $m\overset{\frown}{SP}$ 54°

Example 2

An art student turns in an abstract design for his art project. Find m∠*DFA*. 115°

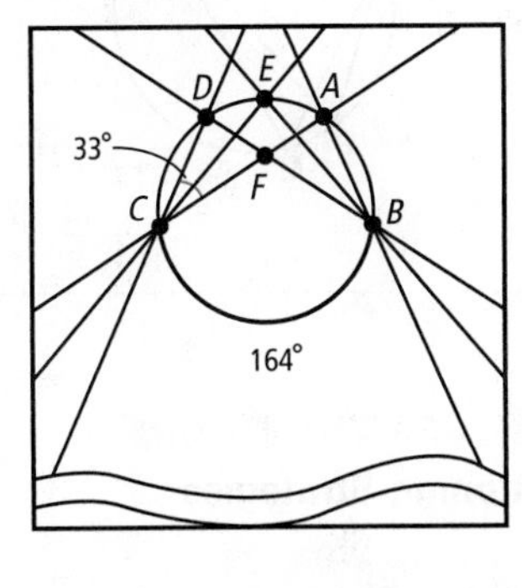

INTERVENTION
Questioning Strategies

EXAMPLE 1

- Does the angle measure change if one side of an inscribed angle passes through the center of the circle? Why or why not?

EXAMPLE 2

- Do you think Corollary 11-4-2 applies to angles that are not inscribed in a circle? Explain.

Teaching Tip **Kinesthetic** Students can benefit from creating the figures in this lesson on geoboards (MK). The experience of creating the figures with colored rubber bands (MK) will help students understand the relationships between various angles and the other parts of the circle.

Additional Examples

Example 3

Find each value.

A. a 14

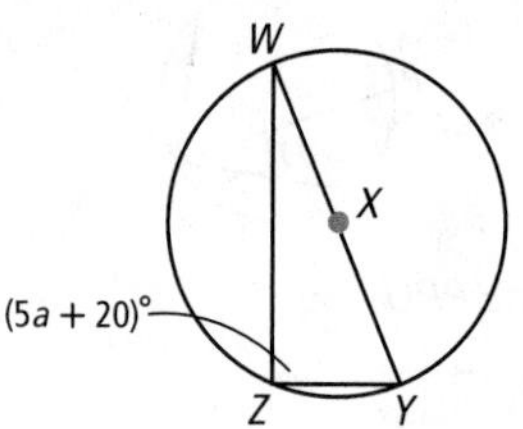

B. m∠LJM 10.5°

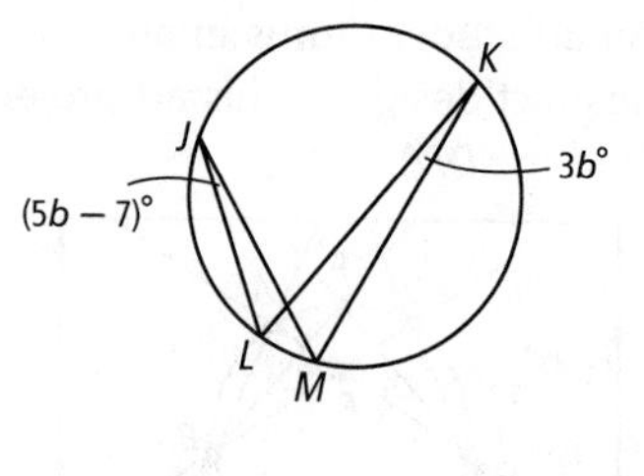

INTERVENTION

Questioning Strategies

EXAMPLE 3

- When given a diagram of a circle with an inscribed angle, how do you know if the inscribed angle subtends a semicircle?

Construction

Advise students to draw chords $\overline{AB}$ and $\overline{DE}$ far enough from the edge of the circle so they can see the chords' corresponding segments but not so far that the chords come close to passing through the middle of the circle. This will make it easier to construct perpendicular lines to the chords.

Teaching Tip **Critical Thinking** Point out that Theorem 11-4-3 is a biconditional statement. Ask students to select a point on the circle and to draw two segments from the point to each endpoint of a circle with a given diameter. Students should recognize that if the angle subtends a semicircle, then the subtended chord is the diameter of the circle.

Theorem 11-4-3

An inscribed angle subtends a semicircle if and only if the angle is a right angle.

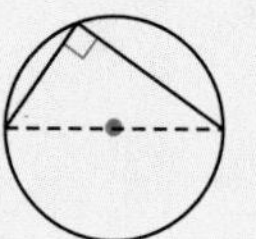

You will prove Theorem 11-4-3 in Exercise 43.

EXAMPLE 3 Finding Angle Measures in Inscribed Triangles

Algebra

Find each value.

A x

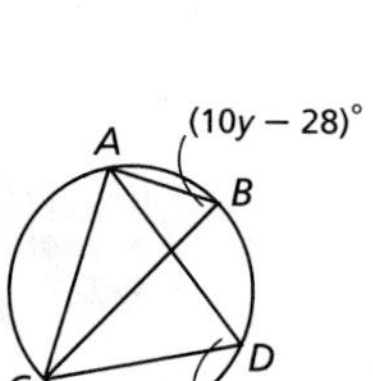

∠RQT is a right angle	*∠RQT is inscribed in a semicircle.*
$m\angle RQT = 90°$	*Def. of rt. ∠*
$4x + 6 = 90$	*Substitute 4x + 6 for m∠RQT.*
$4x = 84$	*Subtract 6 from both sides.*
$x = 21$	*Divide both sides by 4.*

B m∠ADC

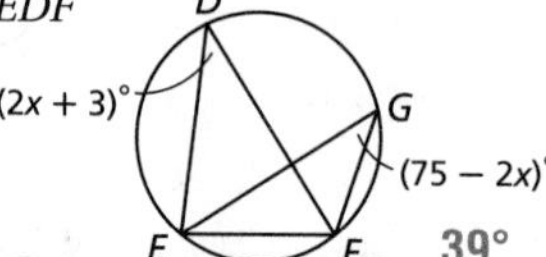

$m\angle ABC = m\angle ADC$	*∠ABC and ∠ADC both intercept $\widehat{AC}$.*
$10y - 28 = 7y - 1$	*Substitute the given values.*
$3y - 28 = -1$	*Subtract 7y from both sides.*
$3y = 27$	*Add 28 to both sides.*
$y = 9$	*Divide both sides by 3.*
$m\angle ADC = 7(9) - 1 = 62°$	*Substitute 9 for y.*

CHECK IT OUT! Find each value.

3a. z

3b. m∠EDF

12 39°

Construction Center of a Circle

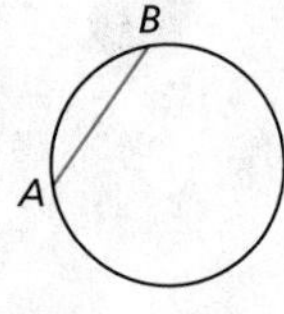

1. Draw a circle and chord $\overline{AB}$.

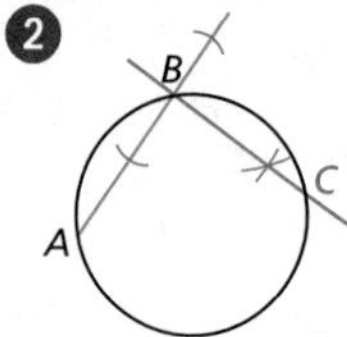

2. Construct a line perpendicular to $\overline{AB}$ at B. Where the line and the circle intersect, label the point C.

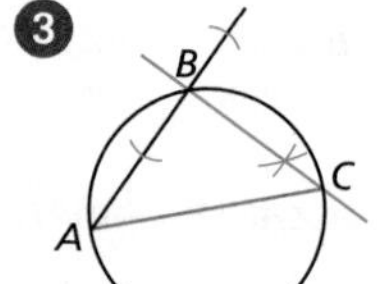

3. Draw chord $\overline{AC}$.

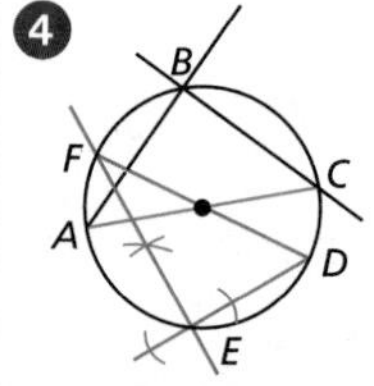

4. Repeat steps to draw chords $\overline{DE}$ and $\overline{DF}$. The intersection of $\overline{AC}$ and $\overline{DF}$ is the center of the circle.

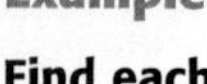
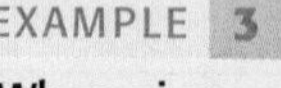

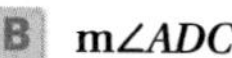

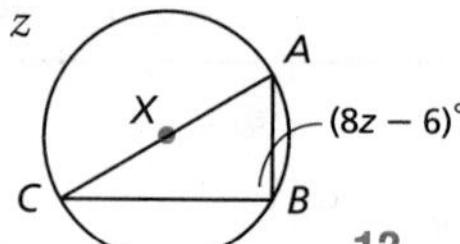

Theorem 11-4-4

THEOREM	HYPOTHESIS	CONCLUSION
If a quadrilateral is inscribed in a circle, then its opposite angles are supplementary.	 *ABCD* is inscribed in ⊙*E*.	∠*A* and ∠*C* are supplementary. ∠*B* and ∠*D* are supplementary.

You will prove Theorem 11-4-4 in Exercise 44.

EXAMPLE 4 **Finding Angle Measures in Inscribed Quadrilaterals**

Algebra

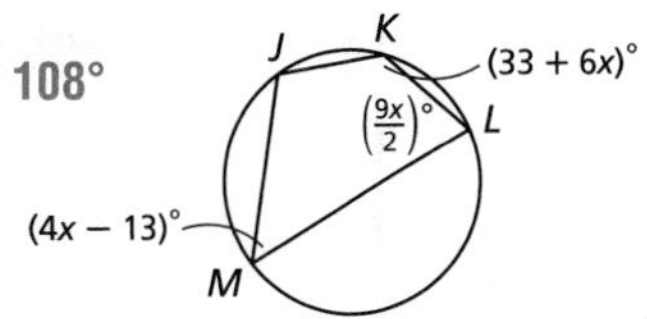

Find the angle measures of *PQRS*.

Step 1 Find the value of *y*.

$m\angle P + m\angle R = 180°$ — *PQRS is inscribed in a ⊙.*

$6y + 1 + 10y + 19 = 180$ — *Substitute the given values.*

$16y + 20 = 180$ — *Simplify.*

$16y = 160$ — *Subtract 20 from both sides.*

$y = 10$ — *Divide both sides by 16.*

Step 2 Find the measure of each angle.

$m\angle P = 6(10) + 1 = 61°$ — *Substitute 10 for y in each expression.*

$m\angle R = 10(10) + 19 = 119°$

$m\angle Q = 10^2 + 48 = 148°$

$m\angle Q + m\angle S = 180°$ — *∠Q and ∠S are supp.*

$148° + m\angle S = 180°$ — *Substitute 148 for m∠Q.*

$m\angle S = 32°$ — *Subtract 148 from both sides.*

CHECK IT OUT! **4.** Find the angle measures of *JKLM*. **51°; 129°; 72°; 108°**

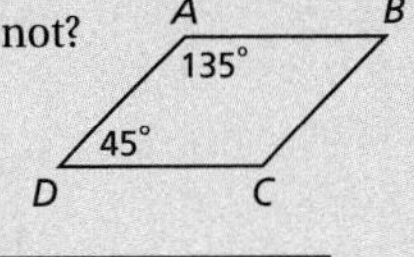

THINK AND DISCUSS

1. Can ▱*ABCD* be inscribed in a circle? Why or why not?

2. An inscribed angle intercepts an arc that is $\frac{1}{4}$ of the circle. Explain how to find the measure of the inscribed angle.

3. GET ORGANIZED Copy and complete the graphic organizer. In each box write a definition, properties, an example, and a nonexample.

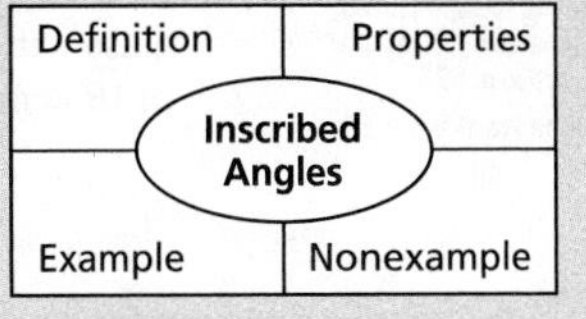

Definition	Properties
Inscribed Angles	
Example	Nonexample

COMMON ERROR ALERT

Remind students that if the center point of a circle is not labeled or if a segment is not given as a diameter of the circle, they cannot assume that a chord is a diameter of the circle. In **Example 3A**, $\overline{RT}$ passes through the center of the circle, so students know it is a diameter. However in **Example 3B**, it looks like $\overline{BC}$ is a diameter, but there is no indication that it is one.

Critical Thinking Help students recognize that the converse of Theorem 11-4-4 is also true.

Power Presentations with PowerPoint®

Additional Examples

Example 4

Find the angle measures of *GHJK*.

m∠*G* = 70°; m∠*H* = 99°; m∠*J* = 110°; m∠*K* = 81°

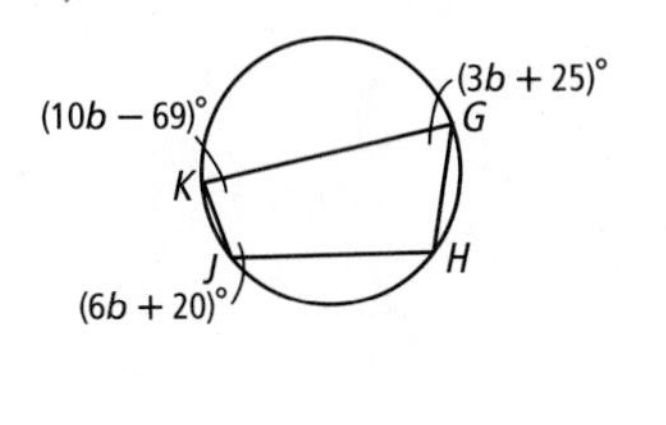

INTERVENTION

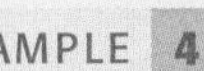

Questioning Strategies

EXAMPLE 4

- Can you assume any relationship between the adjacent angles of an inscribed quadrilateral? Why or why not?
- How can you check if the four angle measurements are reasonable answers?

3 Close

Summarize

Review the terms *inscribed angle*, *intercepted arc*, and *subtend*. Discuss the relationship between all four theorems presented in the lesson. Help students recognize that all inscribed angles with the same intercepted arc are congruent and the measure of each is half the measure of the central angle with the same intercepted arc. Remind students that if a quadrilateral is inscribed in a circle, then the opposite angles are supplementary.

ONGOING ASSESSMENT and INTERVENTION

Diagnose ***Before*** **the Lesson**
11-4 Warm Up, TE p. 772

Monitor ***During*** **the Lesson**
Check It Out! Exercises, SE pp. 773–775
Questioning Strategies, TE pp. 773–775

Assess ***After*** **the Lesson**
11-4 Lesson Quiz, TE p. 779
Alternative Assessment, TE p. 779

Answers to *Think and Discuss*

Possible answers:

1. No; a quad. can be inscribed in a ⊙ if and only if its opp. ∠s are supp.
2. An arc that is $\frac{1}{4}$ of a ⊙ measures 90°. If the arc measures 90°, then the measure of the inscribed ∠ is half of this, or 45°.
3. See p. A9.

11-4 Exercises

Assignment Guide

Assign *Guided Practice* exercises as necessary.

If you finished Examples **1–2**
Basic 12–16, 19, 23, 26–32
Average 12–16, 19, 23, 26–32, 46
Advanced 12–16, 19, 23, 26–32, 46, 47

If you finished Examples **1–4**
Basic 12–30, 33, 35, 36, 39–42, 48–53
Average 12–44, 48–53
Advanced 12–53

Homework Quick Check
Quickly check key concepts.
Exercises: 13, 16, 18, 22, 26

State Resources

11-4 Exercises

go.hrw.com
Homework Help Online
KEYWORD: MG7 11-4
Parent Resources Online
KEYWORD: MG7 Parent

GUIDED PRACTICE

1. **Vocabulary** *A*, *B*, and *C* lie on ⊙*P*. ∠*ABC* is an example of an ___?___ angle. (*intercepted* or *inscribed*) **inscribed**

SEE EXAMPLE 1 p. 773

Find each measure.

2. m∠*DEF* **39°**
3. m$\overset{\frown}{EG}$ **58°**

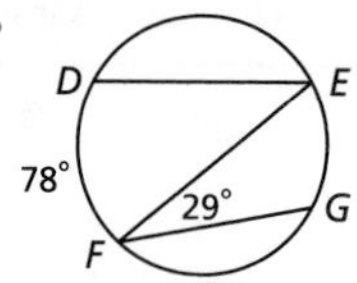

4. m$\overset{\frown}{JKL}$ **204°**
5. m∠*LKM* **26°**

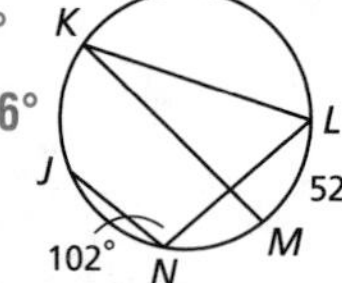

SEE EXAMPLE 2 p. 773

6. **Crafts** A circular loom can be used for knitting. What is the m∠*QTR* in the knitting loom? **110°**

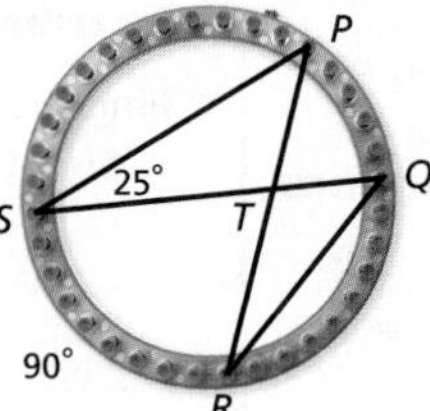

SEE EXAMPLE 3 p. 774

Find each value.

7. *x* **112.5**

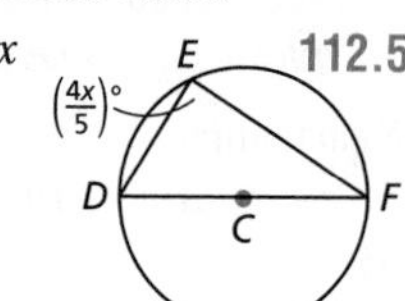

8. *y* **13**

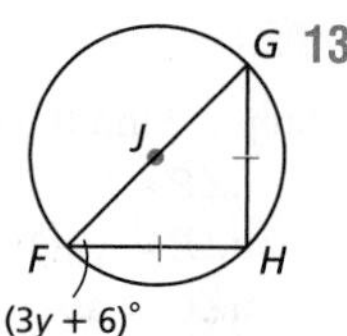

9. m∠*XYZ* **46°**

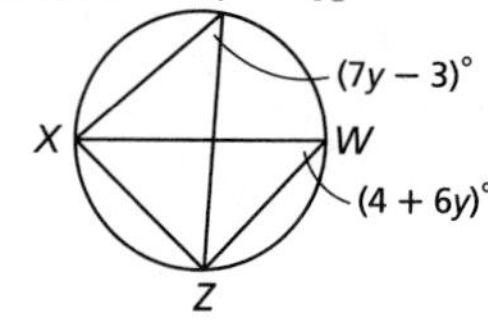

SEE EXAMPLE 4 p. 775

Multi-Step Find the angle measures of each quadrilateral.

10. *PQRS*

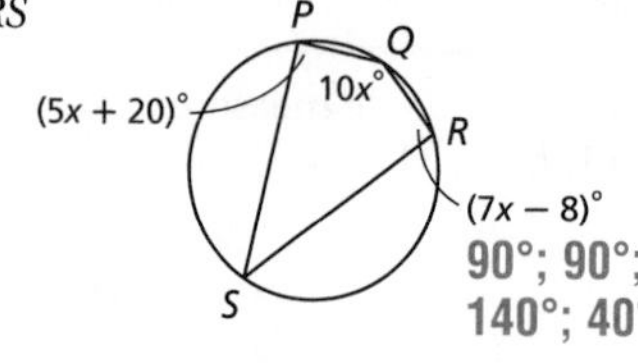

90°; 90°; 140°; 40°

11. *ABCD*

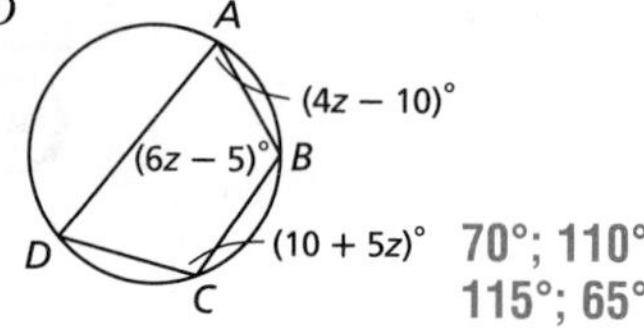

70°; 110°; 115°; 65°

PRACTICE AND PROBLEM SOLVING

Independent Practice	
For Exercises	See Example
12–15	1
16	2
17–20	3
21–22	4

Extra Practice
Skills Practice p. S25
Application Practice p. S38

Find each measure.

12. m$\overset{\frown}{ML}$ **86°**
13. m∠*KMN* **47.5°**

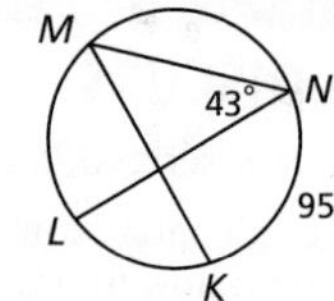

14. m$\overset{\frown}{EGH}$ **278°**
15. m∠*GFH* **47.6°**

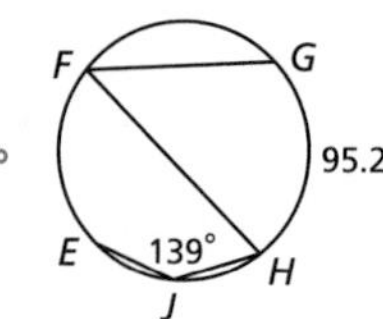

16. **Crafts** An artist created a stained glass window. If m∠*BEC* = 40° and m$\overset{\frown}{AB}$ = 44°, what is m∠*ADC*? **62°**

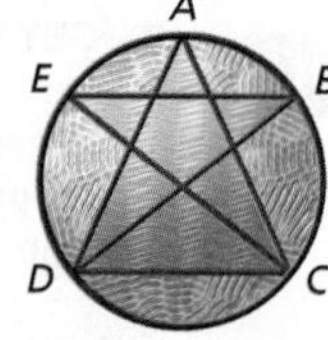

11-4 PRACTICE A

In Exercises 1–4, fill in the blanks to complete each theorem.

1. If a quadrilateral is inscribed in a circle, then its opposite angles are ___supplementary___.
2. If inscribed angles of a circle intercept the same arc or are subtended by the same chord or arc, then the angles are ___congruent___.
3. The measure of an inscribed angle is ___half___ the measure of its intercepted arc.
4. An inscribed angle subtends a semicircle if and only if the angle is a ___right angle___.

Find each measure.

5. m∠*BAC* = ___3°___ m$\overset{\frown}{FE}$ = ___140°___
6. m∠*IHJ* = ___45°___ m$\overset{\frown}{GH}$ = ___40°___

Find each value.

7. *x* = ___15___
8. *z* = ___25___
9. m∠*VUS* = ___42°___
10. m∠*ZWY* = ___71°___

Find the angle measures of each inscribed quadrilateral.

11. m∠*B* = ___120°___ m∠*C* = ___90°___ m∠*D* = ___60°___ m∠*E* = ___90°___
12. m∠*F* = ___130°___ m∠*G* = ___100°___ m∠*H* = ___50°___ m∠*I* = ___80°___

13. Iyla has not learned how to stop on ice skates yet, so she just skates straight across the circular rink until she hits a wall. She starts at *P*, turns 75° at *Q*, and turns 100° at *R*. Find how many degrees Iyla will turn at *S* to get back to her starting point.

___105°___

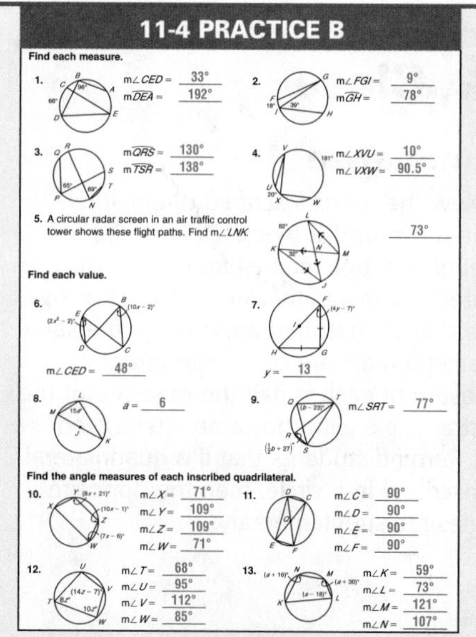

11-4 PRACTICE B

Find each measure.

1. m∠*CED* = ___33°___ m$\overset{\frown}{DEA}$ = ___192°___
2. m∠*FGI* = ___9°___ m$\overset{\frown}{GH}$ = ___78°___
3. m$\overset{\frown}{QRS}$ = ___130°___ m$\overset{\frown}{TSR}$ = ___138°___
4. m∠*XVU* = ___10°___ m∠*VXW* = ___90.5°___
5. A circular radar screen in an air traffic control tower shows these flight paths. Find m∠*LNK*. ___73°___

Find each value.

6. m∠*CED* = ___48°___
7. *y* = ___13___
8. *a* = ___6___
9. m∠*SRT* = ___77°___

Find the angle measures of each inscribed quadrilateral.

10. m∠*X* = ___71°___ m∠*Y* = ___109°___ m∠*Z* = ___109°___ m∠*W* = ___71°___
11. m∠*C* = ___90°___ m∠*D* = ___90°___ m∠*E* = ___90°___ m∠*F* = ___90°___
12. m∠*T* = ___68°___ m∠*U* = ___95°___ m∠*V* = ___112°___ m∠*W* = ___85°___
13. m∠*K* = ___59°___ m∠*L* = ___73°___ m∠*M* = ___121°___ m∠*N* = ___107°___

Algebra Find each value.

17. y ± 6

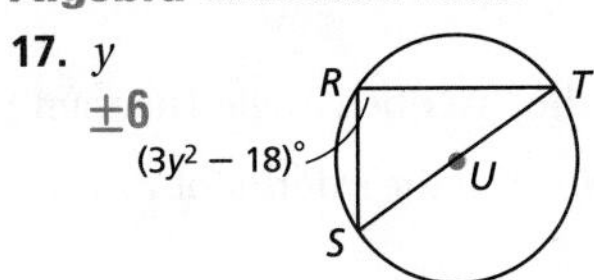

18. z $10\frac{2}{3}$

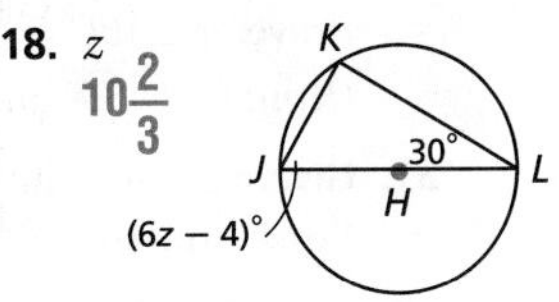

19. $m\overset{\frown}{AB}$ 100°

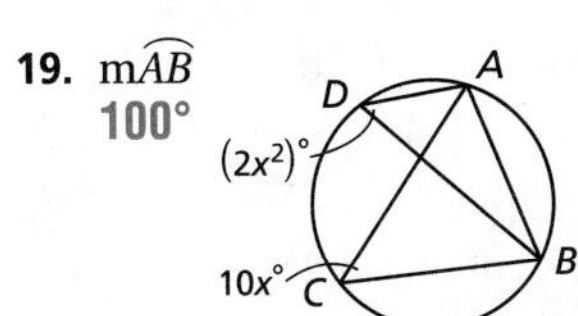

20. $m\angle MPN$ 55°

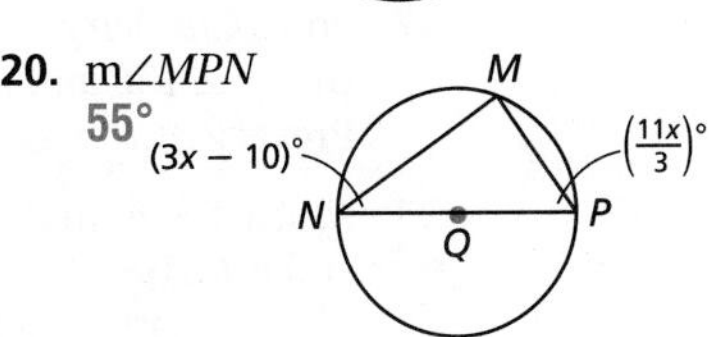

Multi-Step Find the angle measures of each quadrilateral.

21. $BCDE$

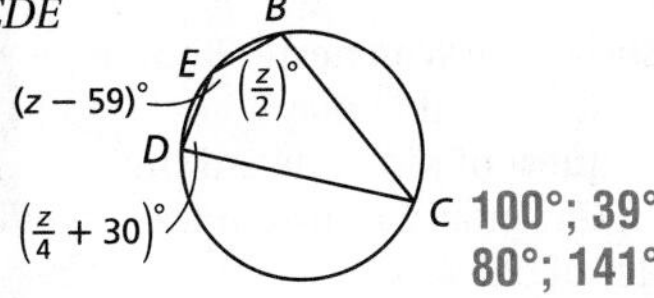

100°; 39°, 80°; 141°

22. $TUVW$

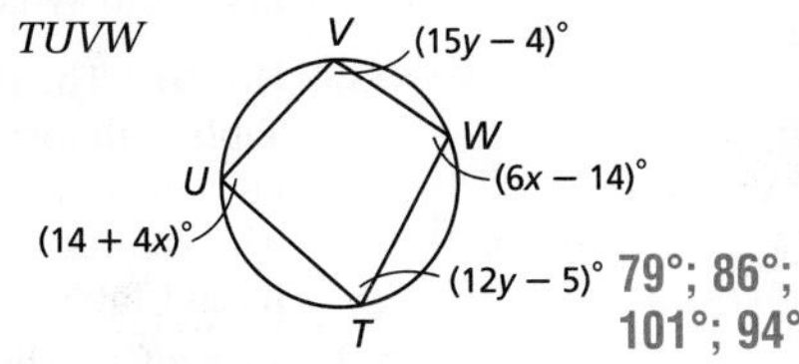

79°; 86°; 101°; 94°

Tell whether each statement is sometimes, always, or never true.

23. Two inscribed angles that intercept the same arc of a circle are congruent. A

24. When a right triangle is inscribed in a circle, one of the legs of the triangle is a diameter of the circle. N

25. A trapezoid can be inscribed in a circle. S

Multi-Step Find each angle measure.

26. $m\angle ABC$ if $m\angle ADC = 112°$ 56°

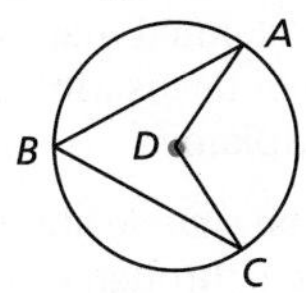

27. $m\angle PQR$ if $m\overset{\frown}{PQR} = 130°$ 115°

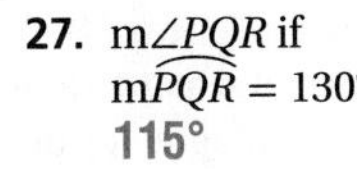

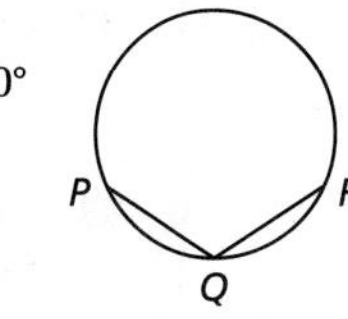

29c. Rt.; $\angle FBC$ is inscribed in a semicircle, so it must be a rt. $\angle$; therefore $\triangle FBC$ is a rt. $\triangle$.

28. Prove that the measure of a central angle subtended by a chord is twice the measure of the inscribed angle subtended by the chord.
Given: In $\odot H$ $\overline{JK}$ subtends $\angle JHK$ and $\angle JLK$.
Prove: $m\angle JHK = 2m\angle JLK$

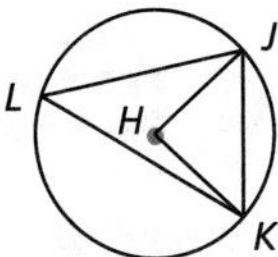

MULTI-STEP TEST PREP

29. This problem will prepare you for the Multi-Step Test Prep on page 806.

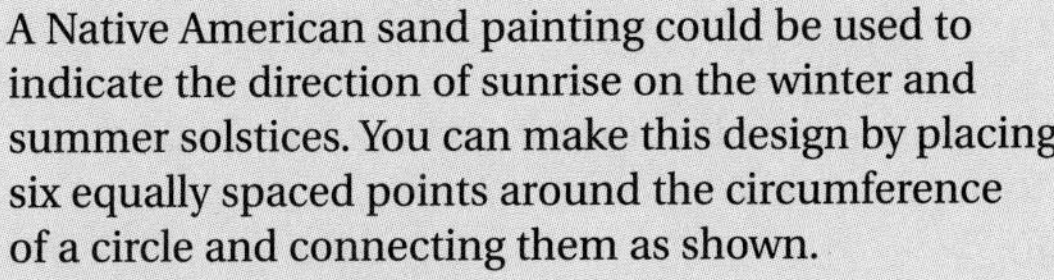

A Native American sand painting could be used to indicate the direction of sunrise on the winter and summer solstices. You can make this design by placing six equally spaced points around the circumference of a circle and connecting them as shown.

a. Find $m\angle BAC$. 30°

b. Find $m\angle CDE$. 120°

c. What type of triangle is $\triangle FBC$? Why?

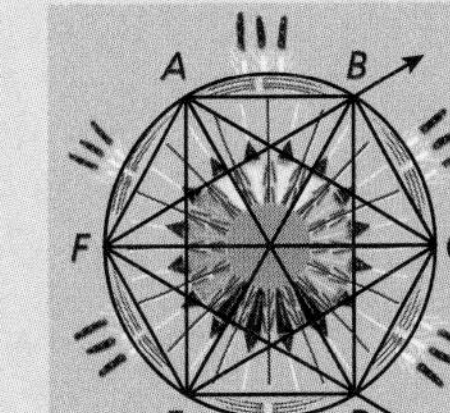

For **Exercises 23–25**, advise students to read the words carefully. They may find it helpful to draw diagrams as they read the exercises. Some students may overlook the word *legs* in **Exercise 24**. Ask these students to consider what part of the right triangle is the diameter of the circle.

Teaching Tip

Critical Thinking In **Exercise 29**, students are not given any angle or arc measures. Encourage them to use their prior knowledge of circles and the given information of "six equally spaced points" to first find arc measures.

Exercise 29 involves using the Inscribed Angle Theorem to find the measures of inscribed angles. This exercise prepares students for the Multi-Step Test Prep on page 806.

Answers

28. By the def. of arc measure, $m\overset{\frown}{JK} = m\angle JHK$. Also, the measure of an $\angle$ inscribed in a $\odot$ is half the measure of the intercepted arc, so $m\angle JLK = \frac{1}{2}m\angle \overset{\frown}{JK}$. Multiplying both sides of the eqn. by 2 gives $2m\angle JLK = m\overset{\frown}{JK}$. Thus by subst., $m\angle JHK = 2m\angle JLK$.

11-4 PRACTICE C

Write paragraph proofs for Exercises 1 and 2.

1. Given: $\overline{AC} \cong \overline{AD}$
Prove: $\angle ABC \cong \angle AED$

Possible answer: It is given that $\overline{AC} \cong \overline{AD}$. In a circle, congruent chords intercept congruent arcs, so $\overset{\frown}{ABC} \cong \overset{\frown}{AED}$. $\overset{\frown}{DC}$ is congruent to itself by the Reflexive Property of Congruence. By the Arc Addition Postulate and the Addition Property of Congruence, $\overset{\frown}{ACD} \cong \overset{\frown}{ADC}$. $\angle ABC$ intercepts $\overset{\frown}{ADC}$, so $m\angle ABC = \frac{1}{2}m\angle\overset{\frown}{ADC}$. $\angle AED$ intercepts $\overset{\frown}{ACD}$, so $m\angle AED = \frac{1}{2}m\overset{\frown}{ACD}$. By substitution, $m\angle ABC = m\angle AED$. Therefore $\angle ABC \cong \angle AED$.

2. Given: $\overset{\frown}{PQ} \cong \overset{\frown}{RS}$
Prove: $\overline{QR} \parallel \overline{PS}$

Possible answer: It is given that $\overset{\frown}{PQ} \cong \overset{\frown}{RS}$. By the definition of congruent arcs, $m\overset{\frown}{PQ} = m\overset{\frown}{RS}$. $\angle PSQ$ intercepts $\overset{\frown}{PQ}$, and $\angle RQS$ intercepts $\overset{\frown}{RS}$. So $m\angle PSQ$ must equal $m\angle RQS$. Therefore $\angle PSQ \cong \angle RQS$. $\angle PSQ$ and $\angle RQS$ are congruent alternate interior angles of $\overline{QR}$ and $\overline{PS}$. So $\overline{QR} \parallel \overline{PS}$.

For each quadrilateral described, tell whether it can be inscribed in a circle. If so, describe a method for doing so using a compass and straightedge, and draw an example.

3. a parallelogram that is not a rectangle or a square
cannot be inscribed in a circle

4. a kite
Can be inscribed in a circle; possible answer: The two congruent angles of the kite are opposite, so they must be right angles. Draw a diameter. Draw segments from opposite ends of the diameter to any point on the circle. Use the compass to copy one of the segments across the diameter. Draw the fourth side.

5. a trapezoid

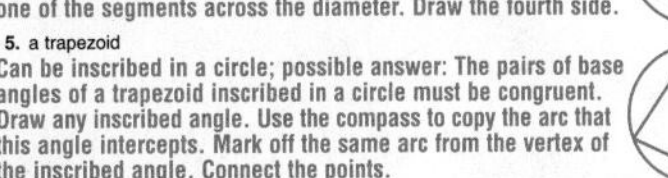

Can be inscribed in a circle; possible answer: The pairs of base angles of a trapezoid inscribed in a circle must be congruent. Draw any inscribed angle. Use the compass to copy the arc that this angle intercepts. Mark off the same arc from the vertex of the inscribed angle. Connect the points.

6. a rhombus that is not a square
cannot be inscribed in a circle

TEST PREP DOCTOR Students who selected choice **G** for **Exercise 40** forgot to double the inscribed angle. Encourage them to find $m\widehat{XZ}$ before dividing the measure by two. Encourage students to mark the answer choices in **Exercise 42** on the diagram so they can better see the choices and solve the problem more quickly. Point out that a good strategy to use might be to locate all the vertices of the angles. In this case, the vertices are T, P, S, and Q. Then make a visual guess before calculating the exact angle measurements.

Answers

30.

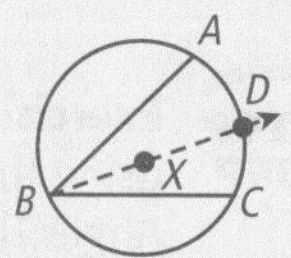

Since any 2 pts. determine a line, draw $\overrightarrow{BX}$. Let D be the pt. on $\widehat{AC}$ where $\overrightarrow{BX}$ intersects $\widehat{AC}$. By Case 1 of the Inscribed ∠ Thm., $m\angle ABD = \frac{1}{2}m\widehat{AD}$ and $m\angle DBC = \frac{1}{2}m\widehat{DC}$. By the Add. Prop. of =, $m\angle ABD + m\angle DBC = \frac{1}{2}m\widehat{AD} + \frac{1}{2}m\widehat{DC}$. By the Distrib. Prop. of =, $\frac{1}{2}m\widehat{AD} + \frac{1}{2}m\widehat{DC} = \frac{1}{2}(m\widehat{AD} + m\widehat{DC})$. $m\angle ABD + m\angle DBC = \frac{1}{2}(m\widehat{AD} + m\widehat{DC})$ by the Trans. Prop. of =. Thus by the ∠ Add. Post. and the Arc Add. Post., $m\angle ABC = \frac{1}{2}m\widehat{AC}$.

31.

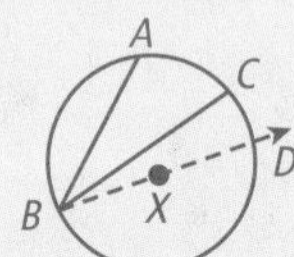

Since any 2 pts. determine a line, draw $\overrightarrow{BX}$. Let D be the pt. on $\widehat{ACB}$ where $\overrightarrow{BX}$ intersects $\widehat{ACB}$. By Case 1 of the Inscribed ∠ Thm., $m\angle ABD = \frac{1}{2}m\widehat{AD}$ and $m\angle CBD = \frac{1}{2}m\widehat{CD}$. By the Subt. Prop. of =, $m\angle ABD - m\angle CBD = \frac{1}{2}m\widehat{AD} - \frac{1}{2}m\widehat{CD}$. By the Distrib. Prop. of =, $\frac{1}{2}m\widehat{AD} - \frac{1}{2}m\widehat{CD} = \frac{1}{2}(m\widehat{AD} - m\widehat{CD})$. $m\angle ABD - m\angle DBC = \frac{1}{2}(m\widehat{AD} - m\widehat{CD})$ by the Trans. Prop. of =. By the ∠ Add. Post. and the Arc Add. Post., $m\angle ABC = \frac{1}{2}m\widehat{AC}$.

32, 34, 35a, 36–37. See p. A28.

---

30. **Given:** $\angle ABC$ is inscribed in $\odot X$ with X in the interior of $\angle ABC$.
Prove: $m\angle ABC = \frac{1}{2}m\widehat{AC}$
(*Hint:* Draw $\overrightarrow{BX}$ and use Case 1 of the Inscribed Angle Theorem.)

31. **Given:** $\angle ABC$ is inscribed in $\odot X$ with X in the exterior of $\angle ABC$.
Prove: $m\angle ABC = \frac{1}{2}m\widehat{AC}$

32. Prove Corollary 11-4-2.
Given: $\angle ACB$ and $\angle ADB$ intercept $\widehat{AB}$.
Prove: $\angle ACB \cong \angle ADB$

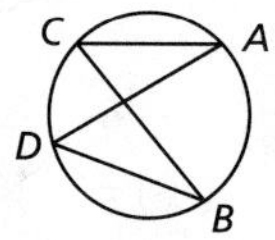

33. Multi-Step In the diagram, $m\widehat{JKL} = 198°$, and $m\widehat{KLM} = 216°$. Find the measures of the angles of quadrilateral $JKLM$. **72°; 99°; 108°; 81°**

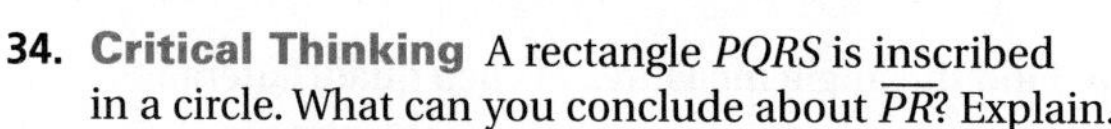

34. Critical Thinking A rectangle $PQRS$ is inscribed in a circle. What can you conclude about $\overline{PR}$? Explain.

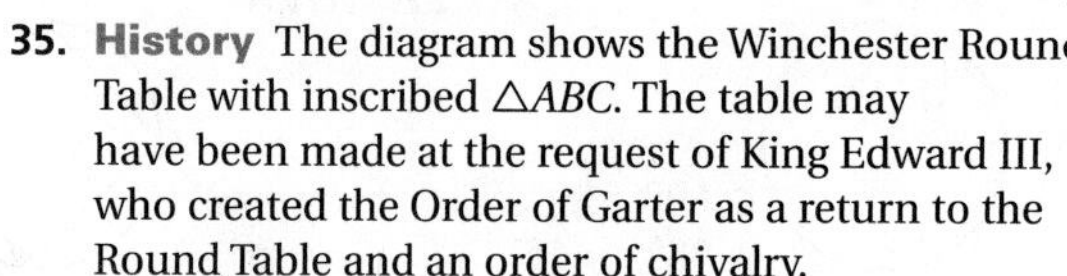

35. History The diagram shows the Winchester Round Table with inscribed $\triangle ABC$. The table may have been made at the request of King Edward III, who created the Order of Garter as a return to the Round Table and an order of chivalry.

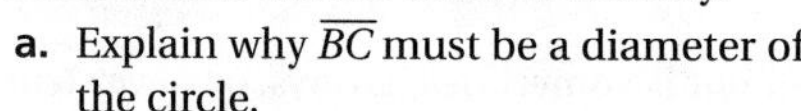

a. Explain why $\overline{BC}$ must be a diameter of the circle.

b. Find $m\widehat{AC}$. **≈ 102°**

36. To inscribe an equilateral triangle in a circle, draw a diameter $\overline{BC}$. Open the compass to the radius of the circle. Place the point of the compass at C and make arcs on the circle at D and E, as shown. Draw $\overline{BD}$, $\overline{BE}$, and $\overline{DE}$. Explain why $\triangle BDE$ is an equilateral triangle.

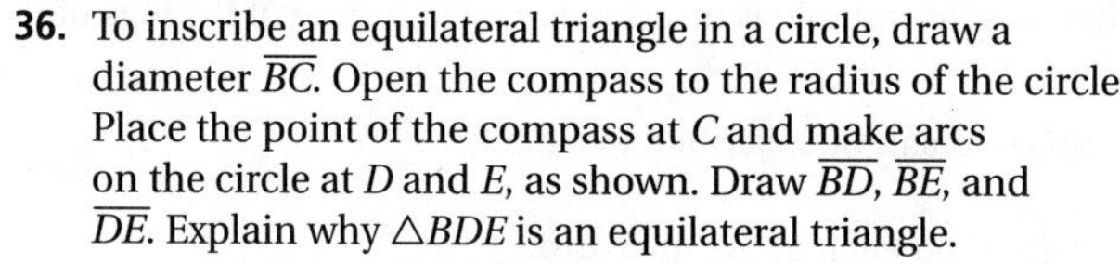

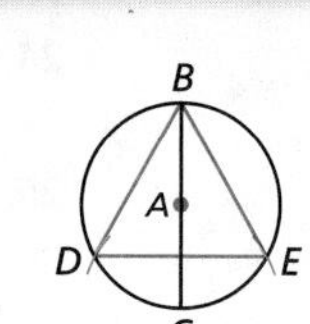

37. Write About It A student claimed that if a parallelogram contains a 30° angle, it cannot be inscribed in a circle. Do you agree or disagree? Explain.

38. Construction Circumscribe a circle about a triangle. (*Hint:* Follow the steps for the construction of a circle through three given noncollinear points.)
Check students' constructions.

39. What is $m\angle BAC$?

Ⓐ 38° Ⓑ 43° Ⓒ 66° **Ⓓ 81°**

40. Equilateral $\triangle XCZ$ is inscribed in a circle. If $\overline{CY}$ bisects $\angle C$, what is $m\widehat{XY}$?

Ⓕ 15° Ⓖ 30° **Ⓗ 60°** Ⓙ 120°

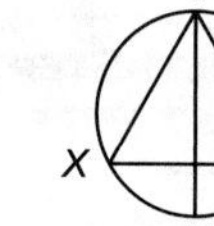

41. Quadrilateral $ABCD$ is inscribed in a circle. The ratio of $m\angle A$ to $m\angle C$ is 4:5. What is $m\angle A$?

Ⓐ 20° Ⓑ 40° **Ⓒ 80°** Ⓓ 100°

42. Which of these angles has the greatest measure?

Ⓕ ∠STR Ⓖ ∠QPR Ⓗ ∠QSR Ⓙ ∠PQS

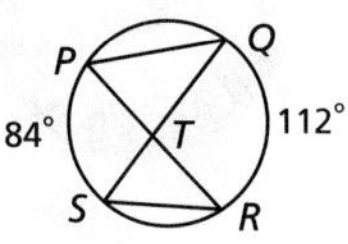

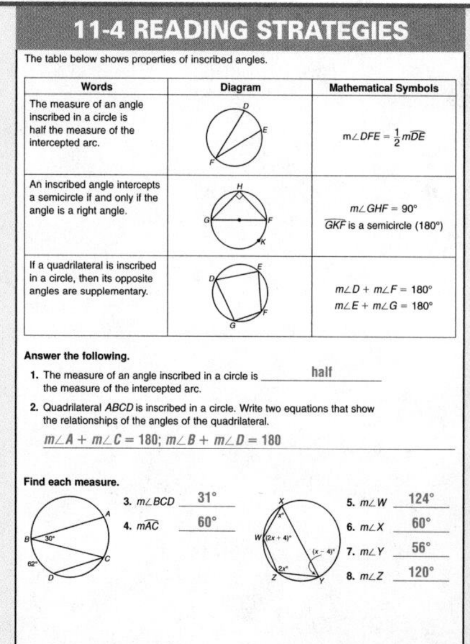

11-4 READING STRATEGIES

The table below shows properties of inscribed angles.

Words	Diagram	Mathematical Symbols
The measure of an angle inscribed in a circle is half the measure of the intercepted arc.		$m\angle DFE = \frac{1}{2}m\widehat{DE}$
An inscribed angle intercepts a semicircle if and only if the angle is a right angle.		$m\angle GHF = 90°$; $\widehat{GKF}$ is a semicircle (180°)
If a quadrilateral is inscribed in a circle, then its opposite angles are supplementary.		$m\angle D + m\angle F = 180°$; $m\angle E + m\angle G = 180°$

Answer the following.

1. The measure of an angle inscribed in a circle is **half** the measure of the intercepted arc.
2. Quadrilateral $ABCD$ is inscribed in a circle. Write two equations that show the relationships of the angles of the quadrilateral.
$m\angle A + m\angle C = 180$; $m\angle B + m\angle D = 180$

Find each measure.

3. $m\angle BCD$ **31°**
4. $m\widehat{AC}$ **60°**
5. $m\angle W$ **124°**
6. $m\angle X$ **60°**
7. $m\angle Y$ **56°**
8. $m\angle Z$ **120°**

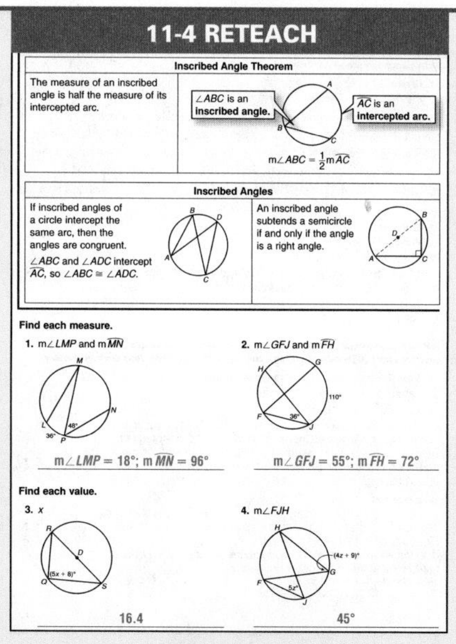

11-4 RETEACH

Inscribed Angle Theorem

The measure of an inscribed angle is half the measure of its intercepted arc.

$\angle ABC$ is an **inscribed angle.** $\widehat{AC}$ is an **intercepted arc.**

$m\angle ABC = \frac{1}{2}m\widehat{AC}$

Inscribed Angles

If inscribed angles of a circle intercept the same arc, then the angles are congruent.
$\angle ABC$ and $\angle ADC$ intercept $\widehat{AC}$, so $\angle ABC \cong \angle ADC$.

An inscribed angle subtends a semicircle if and only if the angle is a right angle.

Find each measure.

1. $m\angle LMP$ and $m\widehat{MN}$
$m\angle LMP = 18°$; $m\widehat{MN} = 96°$
2. $m\angle GFJ$ and $m\widehat{FH}$
$m\angle GFJ = 55°$; $m\widehat{FH} = 72°$

Find each value.

3. x
16.4
4. $m\angle FJH$
45°

CHALLENGE AND EXTEND

43. Prove that an inscribed angle subtends a semicircle if and only if the angle is a right angle. (*Hint:* There are two parts.)

44. Prove that if a quadrilateral is inscribed in a circle, then its opposite angles are supplementary. (*Hint:* There are two parts.)

45. Find $m\widehat{PQ}$ to the nearest degree. **134°**

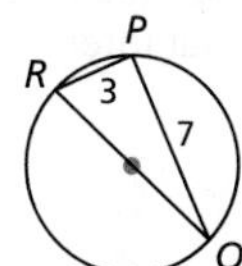

46. Find $m\angle ABD$. **55°**

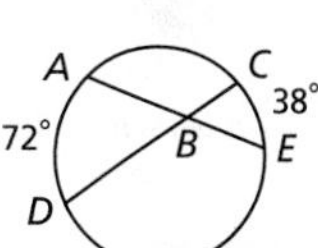

47. Construction To circumscribe an equilateral triangle about a circle, construct $\overline{AB}$ parallel to the horizontal diameter of the circle and tangent to the circle. Then use a 30°-60°-90° triangle to draw $\overline{AC}$ and $\overline{BC}$ so that they form 60° angles with $\overline{AB}$ and are tangent to the circle.
Check students' constructions.

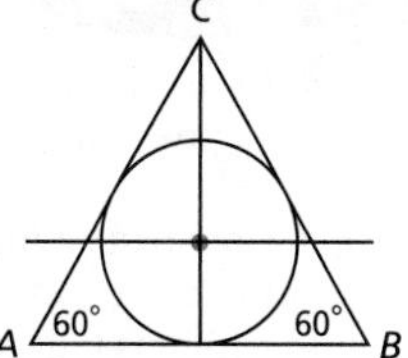

SPIRAL REVIEW

48. Tickets for a play cost \$15.00 for section C, \$22.50 for section B, and \$30.00 for section A. Amy spent a total of \$255.00 for 12 tickets. If she spent the same amount on section C tickets as section A tickets, how many tickets for section B did she purchase? *(Previous course)* **6**

Write a ratio expressing the slope of the line through each pair of points. *(Lesson 7-1)*

49. $\left(4\frac{1}{2}, -6\right)$ and $\left(8, \frac{1}{2}\right)$ $\frac{13}{7}$ **50.** $(-9, -8)$ and $(0, -2)$ $\frac{2}{3}$ **51.** $(3, -14)$ and $(11, 6)$ $\frac{5}{2}$

Find each of the following. *(Lesson 11-2)*

52. $m\widehat{ST}$ **116°**

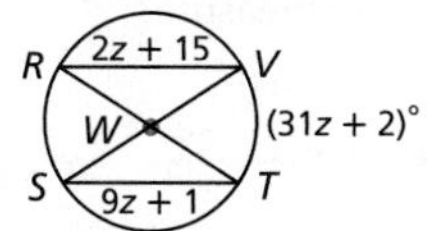

53. area of $\triangle ABD$ **3 m²**

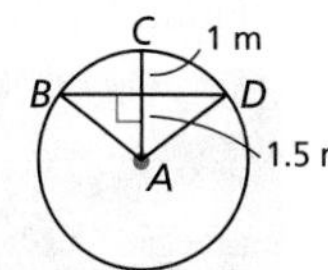

Construction Tangent to a Circle From an Exterior Point

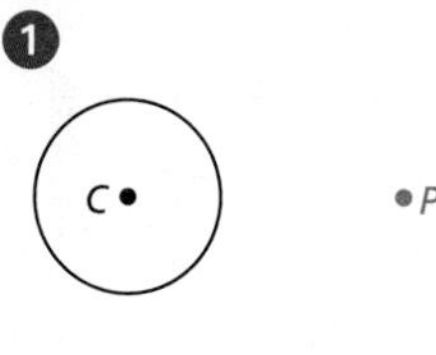

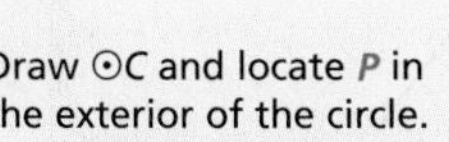

Draw ⊙C and locate P in the exterior of the circle.

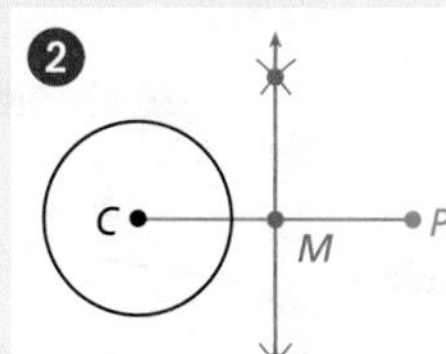

Draw $\overline{CP}$. Construct M, the midpoint of $\overline{CP}$.

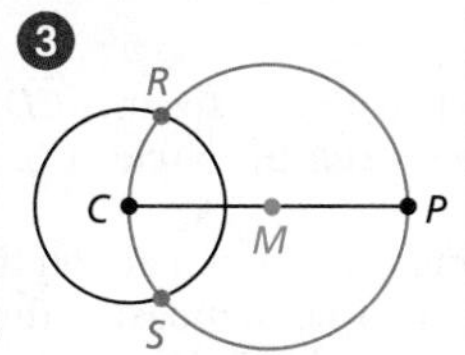

Center the compass at M. Draw a circle through C and P. It will intersect ⊙C at R and S.

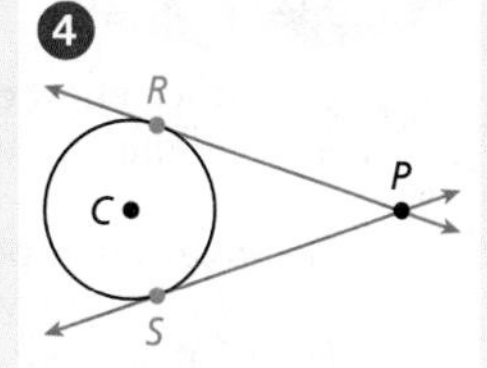

R and S are the tangent points. Draw $\overleftrightarrow{PR}$ and $\overleftrightarrow{PS}$ tangent to ⊙C.

1. Can you draw $\overline{CR} \perp \overleftrightarrow{RP}$? Explain. **Yes; $\overline{CR}$ is a radius of ⊙C. If a line is tangent to a ⊙, then it is ⊥ to the radius.**

Answers

43–44. See pp. A28–29.

Construction

Make sure students place P at a distance from the circle that is greater than the length of the radius of the circle.

Journal

Have students inscribe an isosceles triangle in a circle and then draw a diameter so that it bisects the vertex angle. Ask them to explain if they think the diameter also bisects the arc that subtends this angle.

ALTERNATIVE ASSESSMENT

Have students draw two circles. Have them draw an inscribed triangle in one circle and have them draw an inscribed quadrilateral in the second. Then have them use a protractor to measure the inscribed angles and indicate which theorem or corollary applies to their inscribed angles.

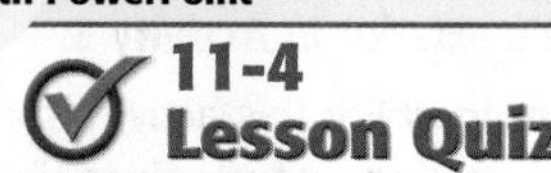

11-4 Lesson Quiz

Find each measure.

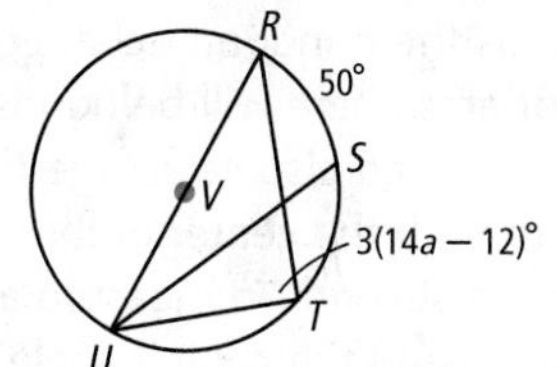

1. ∠RUS 25° **2.** a 3

3. A manfacturer designs a circular ornament with lines of glitter as shown. Find m∠KJN. 130°

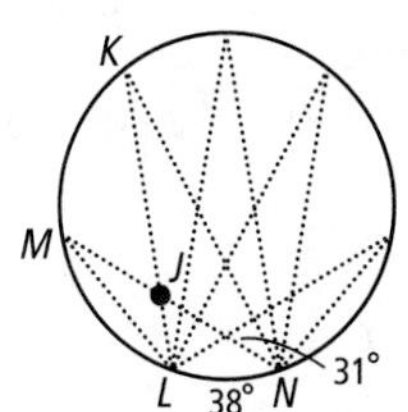

4. Find the angle measures of ABCD. m∠A = 95°; m∠B = 85°; m∠C = 85°; m∠D = 95°

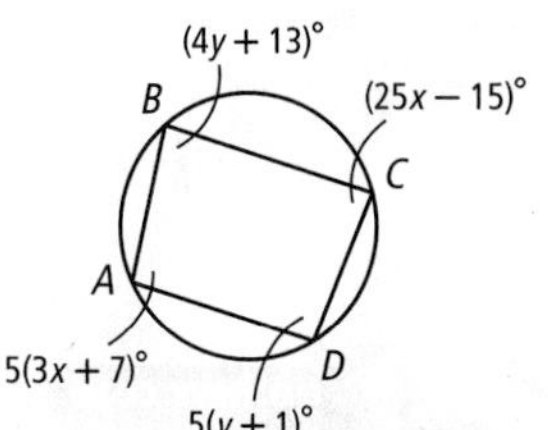

Also available on transparency

11-4 PROBLEM SOLVING

1. Find $m\widehat{AB}$. **160°**
2. Find the angle measures of RSTU. **112°; 52°; 68°; 128°**

Choose the best answer.

Use the diagram of a floor tile for Exercises 3 and 4. Points Q, R, S, T, U, V, W, and X are equally spaced around ⊙L.

3. Find m∠RQT.
   A 15° (C) 45°
   B 30° D 60°
4. Find m∠QRS.
   F 67.5° H 180°
   (G) 135° J 270°
5. If m∠KLM = 20° and $m\widehat{MP}$ = 30°, what is m∠KNP?
   A 25° C 50°
   (B) 35° D 70°
6. In ⊙M, m∠AMB = 74°. What is m∠CDB?
   (F) 37° H 74°
   G 53° J 106°

11-4 CHALLENGE

Line designs are sets of segments arranged in a pattern that creates the illusion of a curve. Different figures can be used as the basis of a line design. For instance, the simple line design at right is formed by connecting equally spaced *anchor points* on the sides of a right angle. On this page, you will investigate line designs that are based on circles.

In the design at right, 32 anchor points are equally spaced on a circle. Segments connect each anchor point to the two anchor points that are exactly 12 spaces away from it. There is an illusion of a circle within the circle.

1. Fill in the blanks to make a true statement:
   Each segment that joins two anchor points is a(n) **chord** of the circle. Two segments that share a common anchor point form a(n) **inscribed** angle of the circle.
2. Let x represent the degree measure of each angle formed by two segments with a common endpoint.
   a. What is the value of x in the figure above? **45°**
   b. Suppose that the segments connected each anchor point to the two anchor points exactly 10 spaces away from it. What is value of x? **67.5°**
   c. Let n represent the number of spaces between two anchor points that are connected by a segment. Write an expression for x. (*Hint:* Be sure to account for values of n that are greater than 16.) $|180 - 11.25n|$
   d. What restrictions must be placed on the value of n in part c? $0 < |n - 16| < 16$
   e. Let p represent the number of equally spaced anchor points, and let n represent the number of spaces between two anchor points connected by a segment. Write an expression for x. State any restrictions on n.
   $\left|180 - \frac{360n}{p}\right|$, or $\left|180\left(1 - \frac{2n}{p}\right)\right|$, where $0 < n - \left|n - \frac{p}{2}\right| < \frac{p}{2}$
   f. Find values of n and p, $p \neq 32$, for which $x = 30$.
   Answers will vary. Students may choose any values of n and p for which $\frac{n}{p} = \frac{5}{12}$. Sample answer: n = 15, p = 36
3. The type of line design that you investigated on this page is just one of countless types of line designs based on circles. Using the library or the Internet as a resource, find a different type of circle line design and re-create it on a separate paper, using only a compass and straightedge. **Results of research will vary.**

Organizer

Use with Lesson 11-5

Pacing:
Traditional 1 day
Block $\frac{1}{2}$ day

Objective: Use geometry software to explore angle relationships in circles.

Materials: geometry software

Online Edition

Resources

Technology Lab Activities
11-5 Lab Recording Sheet

Teach

Discuss

As you work through the activities, ask students to think about the types of lines they are constructing and where the lines intersect. Explain that they are using a tangent and a secant that intersect on the circle in **Activity 1**, two secants that intersect in the circle's interior in **Activity 2**, and two secants that intersect in the circle's exterior in **Activity 3**.

Technology For this activity, measure arcs with *three points* since you will be dragging points around the circle. Then as the minor arcs change to major arcs, there will be no loss of data. You can also select the *three points*, with the center of the circle selected second. To measure a major arc, measure the central angle associated with the minor arc, then subtract this result from 360°.

State Resources

go.hrw.com
State Resources Online
KEYWORD: MG7 Resources

11-5 Technology LAB

Explore Angle Relationships in Circles

Use with Lesson 11-5

In Lesson 11-4, you learned that the measure of an angle inscribed in a circle is half the measure of its intercepted arc. Now you will explore other angles formed by pairs of lines that intersect circles.

Activity 1

1. Create a circle with center *A*. Label the point on the circle as *B*. Create a radius segment from *A* to a new point *C* on the circle.

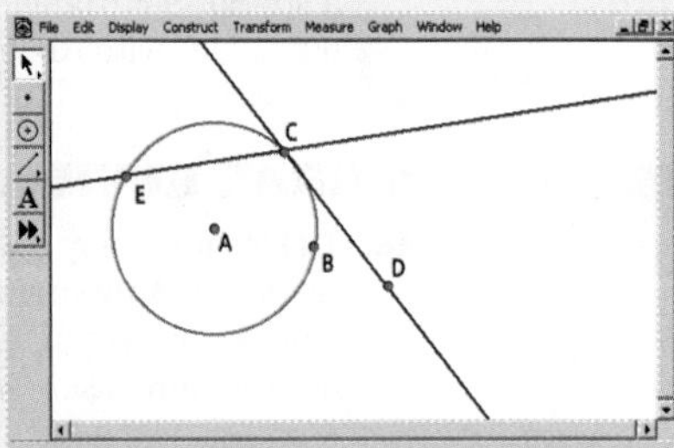

2. Construct a line through *C* perpendicular to radius $\overline{AC}$. Create a new point *D* on this line, which is tangent to circle *A* at *C*. Hide radius $\overline{AC}$.

3. Create a new point *E* on the circle and then construct secant $\overleftrightarrow{CE}$.

4. Measure $\angle DCE$ and measure $\widehat{CBE}$. (*Hint:* To measure an arc in degrees, select the three points and the circle and then choose Arc Angle from the Measure menu.)

5. Drag *E* around the circle and examine the changes in the measures. Fill in the angle and arc measures in a chart like the one below. Try to create acute, right, and obtuse angles. Can you make a conjecture about the relationship between the angle measure and the arc measure?

$m\angle DCE$					
$m\widehat{CBE}$					
Angle Type					

Check students' tables. The measure of an ∠ formed by a tangent and a secant intersecting at the pt. of tangency will be half the measure of the intercepted arc.

Activity 2

1. Construct a new circle with two secants $\overleftrightarrow{CD}$ and $\overleftrightarrow{EF}$ that intersect *inside* the circle at *G*.

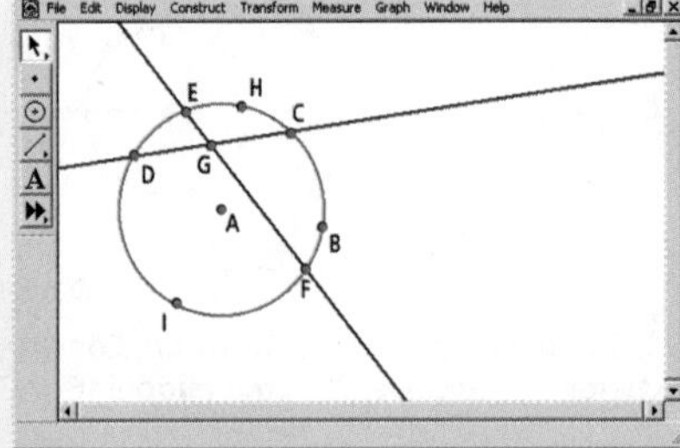

2. Create two new points *H* and *I* that are on the circle as shown. These will be used to measure the arcs. Hide *B* if desired. (It controls the circle's size.)

3. Measure $\angle DGF$ formed by the secant lines and measure $\widehat{CHE}$ and $\widehat{DIF}$.

4. Drag *F* around the circle and examine the changes in measures. Be sure to keep *H* between *C* and *E* and *I* between *D* and *F* for accurate arc measurement. Move them if needed.

5. Fill in the angle and arc measures in a chart like the one below. Try to create acute, right, and obtuse angles. Can you make a conjecture about the relationship between the angle measure and the two arc measures?

m∠DGF					
m$\overset{\frown}{CHE}$					
m$\overset{\frown}{DIF}$					
Sum of Arcs					

Check students' tables. The measure of an ∠ formed by 2 secants (or chords) intersecting inside the ⊙ will be half the sum of the measures of the intercepted arcs.

Activity 3

1. Use the same figure from Activity 2. Drag points around the circle so that the intersection *G* is now *outside* the circle. Move *H* so it is between *E* and *D* and *I* is between *C* and *F*, as shown.

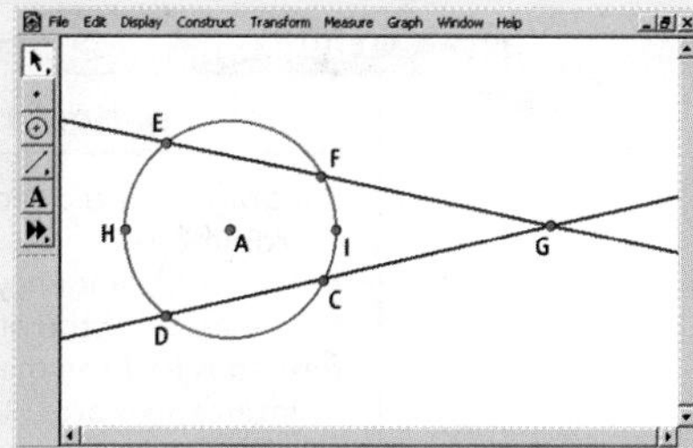

2. Measure ∠*FGC* formed by the secant lines and measure $\overset{\frown}{CIF}$ and $\overset{\frown}{DHE}$.

3. Drag points around the circle and examine the changes in measures. Fill in the angle and arc measures in a chart like the one below. Can you make a conjecture about the relationship between the angle measure and the two arc measures?

m∠FGC					
m$\overset{\frown}{CIF}$					
m$\overset{\frown}{DHE}$					
Number of Arcs					

Check students' tables. The measure of an ∠ formed by 2 secants intersecting outside the ⊙ will be half the difference of the measures of the intercepted arcs.

Try This

1. How does the relationship you observed in Activity 1 compare to the relationship between an inscribed angle and its intercepted arc?
2. Why do you think the radius $\overline{AC}$ is needed in Activity 1 for the construction of the tangent line? What theorem explains this?
3. In Activity 3, try dragging points so that the secants become tangents. What conclusion can you make about the angle and arc measures?
4. Examine the conjectures and theorems about the relationships between angles and arcs in a circle. What is true of an angle with a vertex *on* the circle? What is true of an angle with a vertex *inside* the circle? What is true of an angle with a vertex *outside* the circle? Summarize your findings.
5. Does using geometry software to compare angle and arc measures constitute a formal proof of the relationship observed?

Close

Key Concept

In this lab, students should have observed the following relationships: An angle formed by a tangent and a secant is half the measure of its intercepted arc. If the vertex of the angle formed by two secants is inside the circle, the measure of each angle will be half the sum of the measures of its intercepted arcs. If it is outside the circle, the measure of the angle will be half the difference of the measures of its intercepted arcs. If it is on the circle, the measure of the angle will be equal to half the measure of its intercepted arc.

Assessment

Journal Have students summarize the observations they made about angle relationships in circles.

Answers to *Try This*

1. The relationship is the same. Both types of ∠s have a measure = to half the measure of the arc.
2. A tangent line must be ⊥ to the radius at the pt. of tangency. If the construction is done without this ⊥ relationship, then the tangent line created is not guaranteed to intersect the ⊙ at only 1 pt. If a line is ⊥ to a radius of a ⊙ at a pt. on the ⊙, then the line is tangent to the ⊙.
3. The relationship remains the same. The measure of the ∠ is half the difference of the intercepted arcs.
4. An ∠ whose vertex is *on* the ⊙ (inscribed ∠s and ∠s created by a tangent and a secant intersecting at the pt. of tangency) will have a measure = to half its intercepted arc.

   An ∠ whose vertex is *inside* the ⊙ (∠s created by intersecting secants or chords) will have a measure = to half the sum of its intercepted arcs.

   An ∠ whose vertex is *outside* the ⊙ (∠s created by secants and/or tangents that intersect outside the ⊙) will have a measure = to half the difference of its intercepted arcs.
5. No; it is a means to discover relationships and make conjectures.

11-5 Organizer

Pacing: Traditional 1 day
Block $\frac{1}{2}$ day

Objectives: Find the measures of angles formed by lines that intersect circles.

Use angle measures to solve problems.

Geometry Lab
In Geometry Lab Activities

Online Edition
Tutorial Videos

Power Presentations with PowerPoint®

Warm Up

1. Identify each line or segment that intersects ⊙*F*. chords: $\overline{AE}$, $\overline{CD}$; secant: $\overleftrightarrow{AE}$; tangent: $\overrightarrow{AB}$

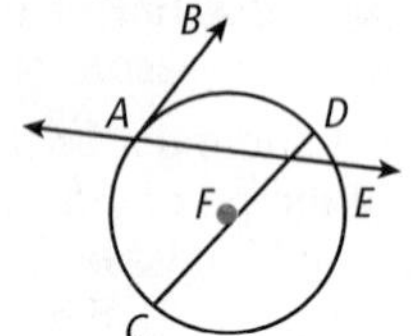

Find each measure.

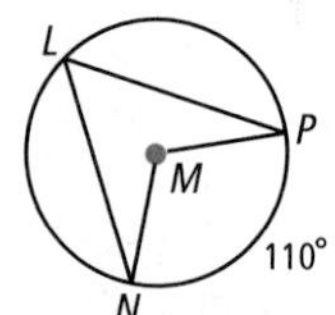

2. m∠*NMP* 110° **3.** m∠*NLP* 55°

Also available on transparency

Q: Why was the chord upset with the tangent after their race?

A: They came in secant!

State Resources

State Resources Online
KEYWORD: MG7 Resources

11-5 Angle Relationships in Circles

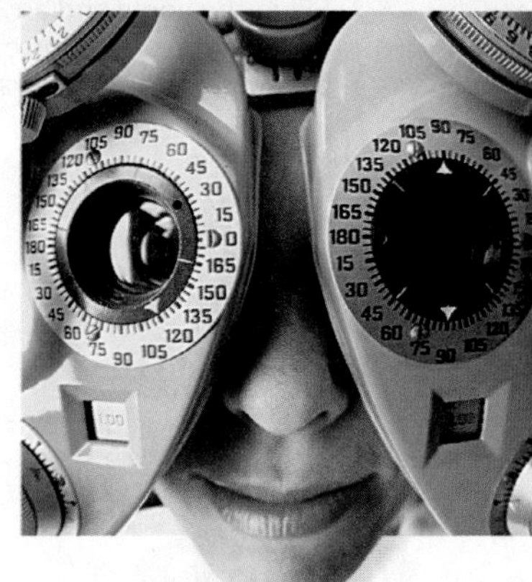

Objectives
Find the measures of angles formed by lines that intersect circles.

Use angle measures to solve problems.

Who uses this?
Circles and angles help optometrists correct vision problems. (See Example 4.)

Theorem 11-5-1 connects arc measures and the measures of tangent-secant angles with tangent-chord angles.

Know it! Note

Theorem 11-5-1

THEOREM	HYPOTHESIS	CONCLUSION
If a tangent and a secant (or chord) intersect on a circle at the point of tangency, then the measure of the angle formed is half the measure of its intercepted arc.	Tangent $\overrightarrow{BC}$ and secant $\overrightarrow{BA}$ intersect at *B*.	$m\angle ABC = \frac{1}{2}m\overset{\frown}{AB}$

You will prove Theorem 11-5-1 in Exercise 45.

EXAMPLE 1 Using Tangent-Secant and Tangent-Chord Angles

Find each measure.

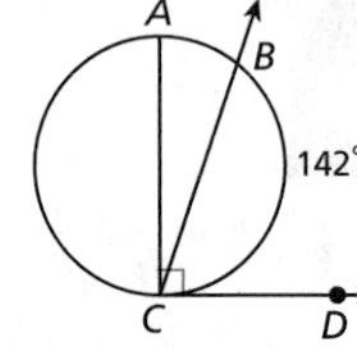

A m∠*BCD*

$$m\angle BCD = \frac{1}{2}m\overset{\frown}{BC}$$

$$m\angle BCD = \frac{1}{2}(142°)$$

$$= 71°$$

B $m\overset{\frown}{ABC}$

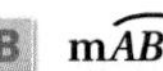

$$m\angle ACD = \frac{1}{2}m\overset{\frown}{ABC}$$

$$90° = \frac{1}{2}m\overset{\frown}{ABC}$$

$$180° = m\overset{\frown}{ABC}$$

Find each measure.

1a. m∠*STU* **83°**

1b. $m\overset{\frown}{SR}$ **142°**

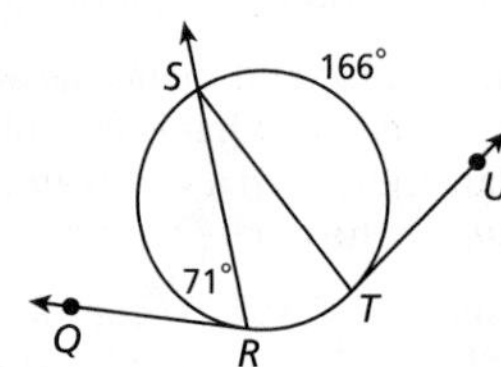

1 Introduce

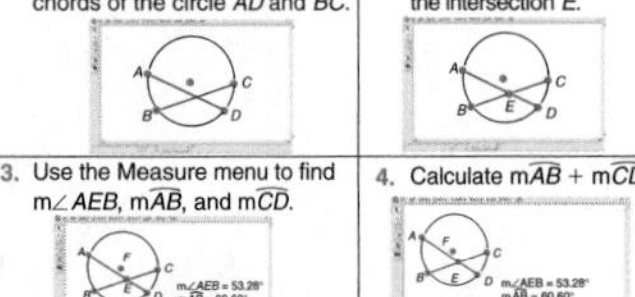

EXPLORATION

11-5 Angle Relationships in Circles

Use geometry software to explore the angle formed by two intersecting chords of a circle.

1. Construct a circle. Then construct two intersecting chords of the circle $\overline{AD}$ and $\overline{BC}$.
2. Construct the intersection of the chords. Label the intersection *E*.
3. Use the Measure menu to find m∠*AEB*, $m\overset{\frown}{AB}$, and $m\overset{\frown}{CD}$.
4. Calculate $m\overset{\frown}{AB} + m\overset{\frown}{CD}$.
5. How is m∠*AEB* related to $m\overset{\frown}{AB} + m\overset{\frown}{CD}$?
6. Drag the endpoints of the chords and change the size of the circle. Is the relationship between m∠*AEB* and $m\overset{\frown}{AB} + m\overset{\frown}{CD}$ always the same?

THINK AND DISCUSS

7. Explain how you can use your findings to state a conjecture about the measure of the angle formed by two intersecting

Motivate

Give students instances in literature or in song lyrics that mention circles. Have them write their own examples or captions that contain the word *circle*. Ask students to provide an illustration or cartoon to display on the bulletin board for each example they write. If there were no circles, could you ride through town on a square-type bike?

Explorations and answers are provided in *Alternate Openers: Explorations Transparencies.*

Theorem 11-5-2

THEOREM	HYPOTHESIS	CONCLUSION
If two secants or chords intersect in the interior of a circle, then the measure of each angle formed is half the sum of the measures of its intercepted arcs.	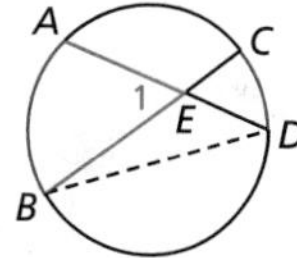 Chords $\overline{AD}$ and $\overline{BC}$ intersect at E.	$m\angle 1 = \frac{1}{2}(m\widehat{AB} + m\widehat{CD})$

PROOF **Theorem 11-5-2**

Given: $\overline{AD}$ and $\overline{BC}$ intersect at E.

Prove: $m\angle 1 = \frac{1}{2}(m\widehat{AB} + m\widehat{CD})$

Proof:

Statements	Reasons
1. $\overline{AD}$ and $\overline{BC}$ intersect at E.	1. Given
2. Draw $\overline{BD}$.	2. Two pts. determine a line.
3. $m\angle 1 = m\angle EDB + m\angle EBD$	3. Ext. $\angle$ Thm.
4. $m\angle EDB = \frac{1}{2}m\widehat{AB}$, $m\angle EBD = \frac{1}{2}m\widehat{CD}$	4. Inscribed $\angle$ Thm.
5. $m\angle 1 = \frac{1}{2}m\widehat{AB} + \frac{1}{2}m\widehat{CD}$	5. Subst.
6. $m\angle 1 = \frac{1}{2}(m\widehat{AB} + m\widehat{CD})$	6. Distrib. Prop.

EXAMPLE 2 **Finding Angle Measures Inside a Circle**

Find each angle measure.

m∠SQR

$$m\angle SQR = \frac{1}{2}(m\widehat{PT} + m\widehat{SR})$$
$$= \frac{1}{2}(32^\circ + 100^\circ)$$
$$= \frac{1}{2}(132^\circ)$$
$$= 66^\circ$$

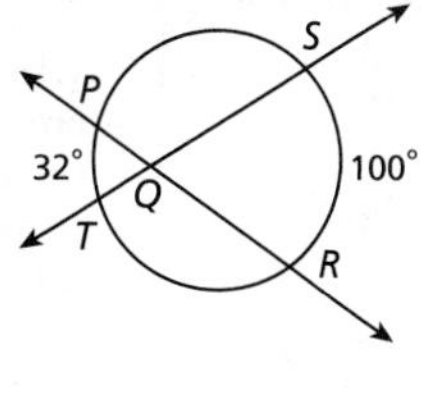

Find each angle measure.

2a. $m\angle ABD$ 51°

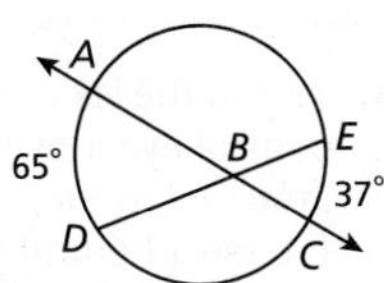

2b. $m\angle RNM$ 22°

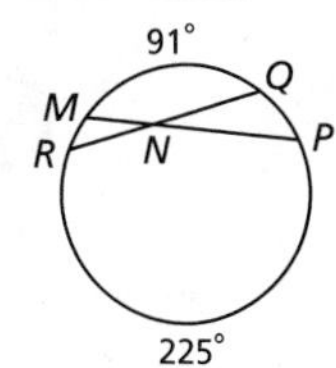

2 Teach

Guided Instruction

Use geometry software or a compass, straightedge, and protractor to show students how to find the measures of angles formed by pairs of lines that intersect circles. Explain that the angles are identified by the lines that form them. Examine three configurations of the tangent-secant or tangent-chord angle: right, acute, and obtuse. Next show students how to measure the angles formed when lines intersect in the interior or exterior of a circle. Show students how they could use a spreadsheet to record their data.

Reaching All Learners

Through Multiple Representations

Have students work in pairs to draw figures similar to the ones given in each of the theorems in the lesson. They can use different colored pencils to indicate the different angles formed. Have students exchange papers and measure each angle. Then they should identify each angle by the lines that form it.

Power Presentations with PowerPoint®

Additional Examples

Example 1

Find each measure.

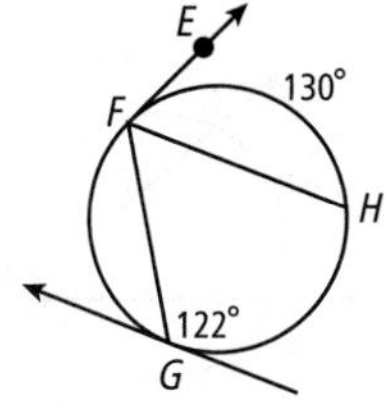

A. $m\angle EFH$ 65°

B. $m\widehat{GF}$ 116°

Example 2

Find $m\angle AEB$. 126°

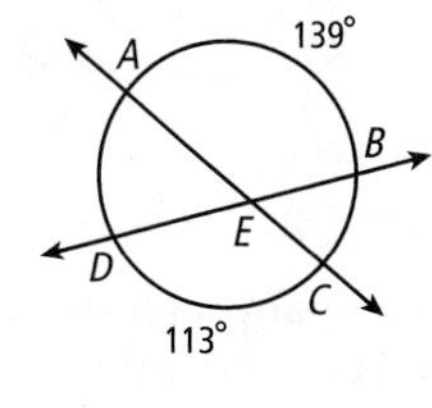

INTERVENTION

Questioning Strategies

EXAMPLE 1

- How are these problems with tangent-secant angles similar to those with inscribed angles?

EXAMPLE 2

- What happens if the chords intersect at the center of the circle? Can you still find the measure of the angle using the same method?

Power Presentations with PowerPoint®

Additional Examples

Example 3

Find the value of x.

A. 40°

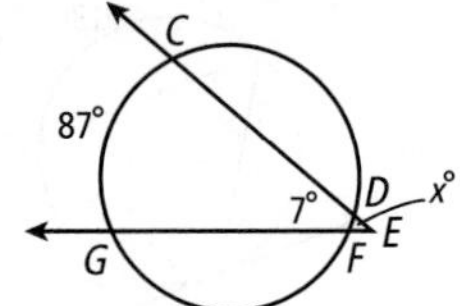

B. 63°

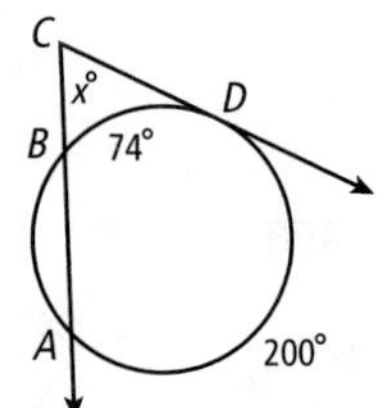

Example 4

In the company logo shown, $m\widehat{FH} = 108°$, and $m\widehat{LJ} = 12°$. What is $m\angle FKH$? 48°

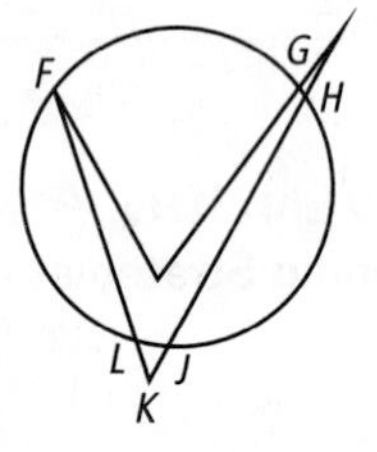

INTERVENTION 

Questioning Strategies

EXAMPLE  3

- How is finding an angle measure in the exterior of a circle different from finding an angle measure in the interior of a circle?

EXAMPLE  4

- The measure of a tangent-tangent angle with its vertex outside the circle is the measure of the major arc minus what degree measure?

Know it! Note

Theorem 11-5-3

If a tangent and a secant, two tangents, or two secants intersect in the exterior of a circle, then the measure of the angle formed is half the difference of the measures of its intercepted arcs.

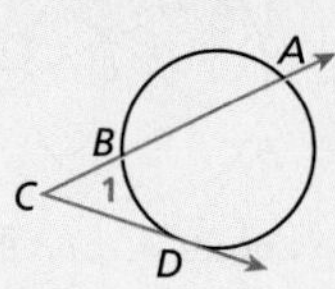

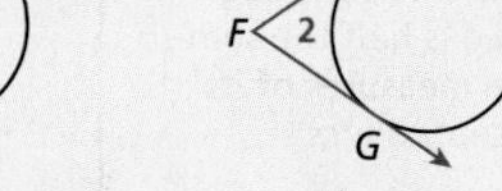

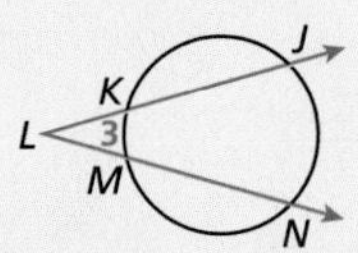

$m\angle 1 = \frac{1}{2}(m\widehat{AD} - m\widehat{BD})$ $m\angle 2 = \frac{1}{2}(m\widehat{EHG} - m\widehat{EG})$ $m\angle 3 = \frac{1}{2}(m\widehat{JN} - m\widehat{KM})$

You will prove Theorem 11-5-3 in Exercises 34–36.

EXAMPLE 3 Finding Measures Using Tangents and Secants

Find the value of x.

A

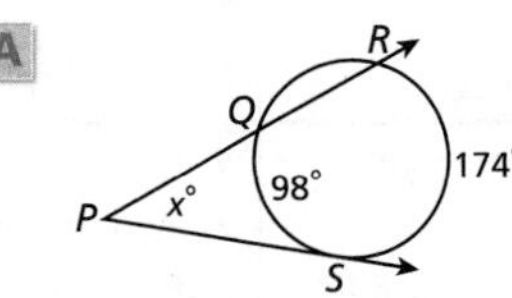

$x = \frac{1}{2}(m\widehat{RS} - m\widehat{QS})$

$= \frac{1}{2}(174° - 98°)$

$= 38°$

B

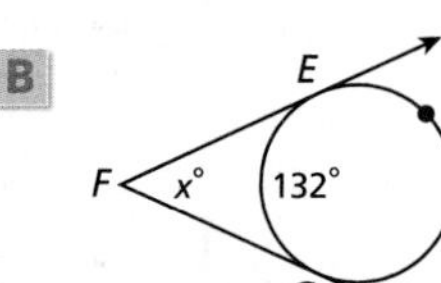

$x = \frac{1}{2}(m\widehat{EHG} - m\widehat{EG})$

$= \frac{1}{2}(228° - 132°)$

$= 48°$

Helpful Hint

$\widehat{EHG}$ and $\widehat{EG}$ joined together make a whole circle. So $m\widehat{EHG} = 360° - 132° = 228°$

 **CHECK IT OUT!** **3.** Find the value of x. 33

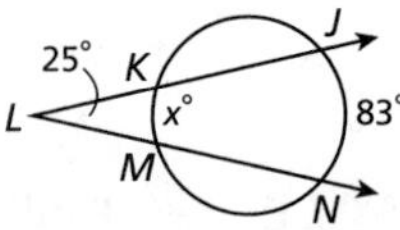

EXAMPLE 4 *Biology Application*

When a person is farsighted, light rays enter the eye and are focused behind the retina. In the eye shown, light rays converge at R. If $m\widehat{PS} = 60°$ and $m\widehat{QT} = 14°$, what is $m\angle PRS$?

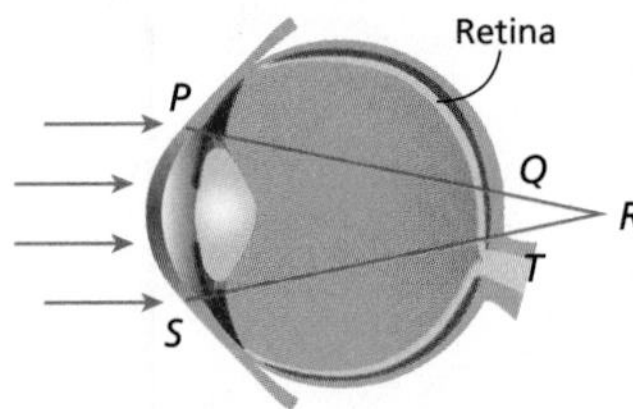

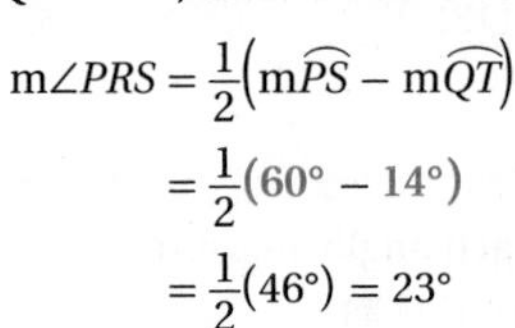

$m\angle PRS = \frac{1}{2}(m\widehat{PS} - m\widehat{QT})$

$= \frac{1}{2}(60° - 14°)$

$= \frac{1}{2}(46°) = 23°$

 **CHECK IT OUT!** **4.** Two of the six muscles that control eye movement are attached to the eyeball and intersect behind the eye. If $m\widehat{AEB} = 225°$, what is $m\angle ACB$? 45°

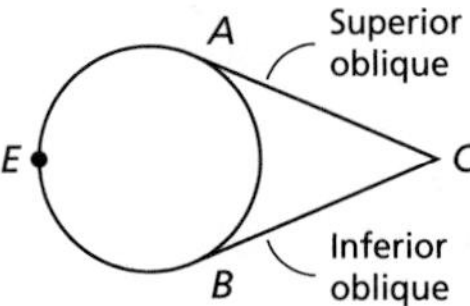

Teacher to Teacher

Have students research hyperopia (farsightedness) and myopia (nearsightedness) and report on how various treatments such as glasses, contacts, and LASIK eye surgery work to correct these problems. Post reports and diagrams in the classroom or make a class poster of students' findings.

Most students find this topic very interesting and relevant. This is also a good activity for the end of the course because students are likely to encounter various geometric concepts while researching this topic.

Greg Davis
Lodi, WI

Angle Relationships in Circles

VERTEX OF THE ANGLE	MEASURE OF ANGLE	DIAGRAMS	
On a circle	Half the measure of its intercepted arc	$m\angle 1 = 60°$	$m\angle 2 = 100°$
Inside a circle	Half the sum of the measures of its intercepted arcs		$m\angle 1 = \frac{1}{2}(44° + 86°)$ $= 65°$
Outside a circle	Half the difference of the measures of its intercepted arcs	$m\angle 1 = \frac{1}{2}(202° - 78°)$ $= 62°$	$m\angle 2 = \frac{1}{2}(125° - 45°)$ $= 40°$

EXAMPLE 5 **Finding Arc Measures**

Find $m\widehat{AF}$.

Step 1 Find $m\widehat{ADB}$.

$m\angle ABC = \frac{1}{2}m\widehat{ADB}$ *If a tangent and secant intersect on a ⊙ at the pt. of tangency, then the measure of the ∠ formed is half the measure of its intercepted arc.*

$110° = \frac{1}{2}m\widehat{ADB}$ *Substitute 110 for m∠ABC.*

$m\widehat{ADB} = 220°$ *Mult. both sides by 2.*

Step 2 Find $m\widehat{AD}$.

$m\widehat{ADB} = m\widehat{AD} + m\widehat{DB}$ *Arc Add. Post.*

$220° = m\widehat{AD} + 160°$ *Substitute.*

$m\widehat{AD} = 60°$ *Subtract 160 from both sides.*

Step 3 Find $m\widehat{AF}$.

$m\widehat{AF} = 360° - (m\widehat{AD} + m\widehat{DB} + m\widehat{BF})$ *Def. of a ⊙*

$= 360° - (60° + 160° + 48°)$ *Substitute.*

$= 92°$ *Simplify.*

5. Find $m\widehat{LP}$. 72°

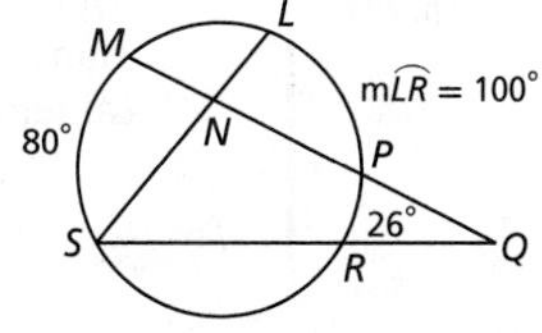

3 Close

Summarize

To review the theorems in this lesson, have students make a study guide by folding a sheet of paper in fourths. They should write "Angle Relationships in Circles" on one section of their guide. On the other sections, students should write the process for finding the measure of an angle whose vertex is on a circle, inside a circle, and outside a circle. They should include a diagram of each, using colored pencils to draw the angles.

ONGOING ASSESSMENT and INTERVENTION

***Diagnose Before* the Lesson**
11-5 Warm Up, TE p. 782

***Monitor During* the Lesson**
Check It Out! Exercises, SE pp. 782–785
Questioning Strategies, TE pp. 783–785

***Assess After* the Lesson**
11-5 Lesson Quiz, TE p. 789
Alternative Assessment, TE p. 789

COMMON ERROR ALERT

Students may forget whether they need to find the sum or the difference of the measures of the intercepted arcs. Draw several examples on the board, with lines intersecting inside the circle and outside the circle. Have students name the lines and say whether they would add or subtract arc measures to find the angle measures.

Power Presentations with PowerPoint®

Additional Examples

Example 5

Find $m\widehat{YZ}$. 164°

INTERVENTION

Questioning Strategies

EXAMPLE 5

- Do you think there is more than one way to work problems with multiple angle relationships in circles? Explain.

Auditory Ask students to note the key words that will help them determine the method of solving a problem involving angle relationships in circles. Have one student recite each of the three relationships in this lesson. Then have the student's partner draw a diagram of what the first student has said. Each student should then measure the angles in the diagram as a check.

1. Vertex ***on*** a circle means you take ***half the measure*** of *one* arc.
2. Vertex ***inside*** a circle means you take ***half the sum*** of *two* arcs.
3. Vertex ***outside*** a circle means you take ***half the difference*** of *two* arcs.

Answers to *Think and Discuss*

Possible answers:

1. For both chords and secants that intersect in the interior of a ⊙, the measure of the ∠ formed is half the sum of the measures of their intercepted arcs.
2. See p. A9.

THINK AND DISCUSS

1. Explain how the measure of an angle formed by two chords of a circle is related to the measure of the angle formed by two secants.

2. **GET ORGANIZED** Copy and complete the graphic organizer. In each box write a theorem and draw a diagram according to where the angle's vertex is in relationship to the circle.

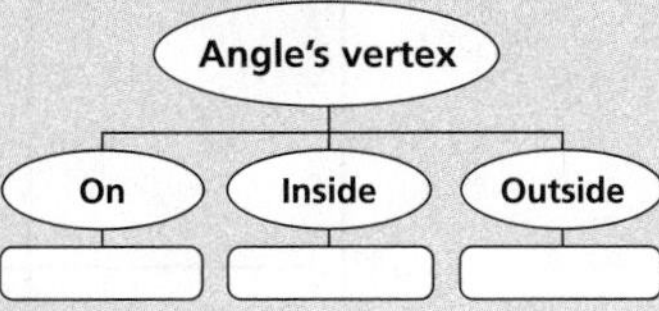

11-5 Exercises

Assignment Guide

Assign *Guided Practice* exercises as necessary.

If you finished Examples **1–3**

Basic 16–25, 32, 34–36, 39, 40

Average 16–25, 32, 34–36, 39, 40, 45

Advanced 16–25, 32, 34–36, 39, 40, 45, 46

If you finished Examples **1–5**

Basic 16–34, 39–44, 49–57

Average 16–45, 49–57

Advanced 16–57

Homework Quick Check

Quickly check key concepts.

Exercises: 16, 20, 24, 26, 28, 30

State Resources

go.hrw.com

State Resources Online

KEYWORD: MG7 Resources

11-5 Exercises

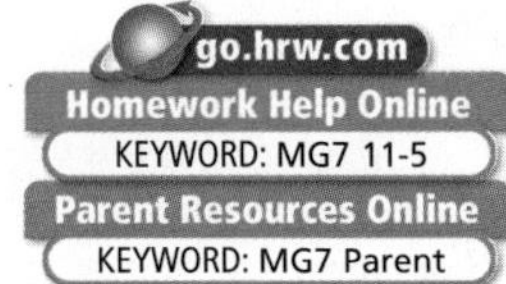

GUIDED PRACTICE

SEE EXAMPLE 1 p. 782

Find each measure.

1. m∠*DAB* **70°**
2. m$\widehat{AC}$ **54°**

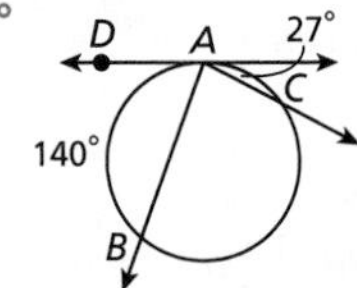

3. m$\widehat{PN}$ **122°**
4. m∠*MNP* **119°**

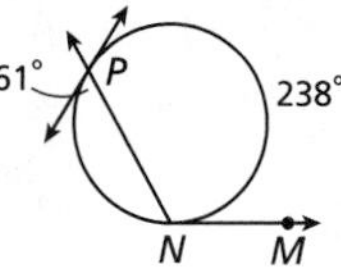

SEE EXAMPLE 2 p. 783

5. m∠*STU* **67°**

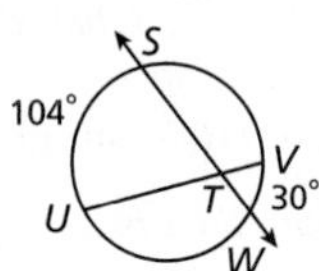

6. m∠*HFG* **41°**

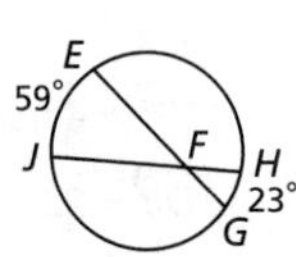

7. m∠*NPK* **94°**

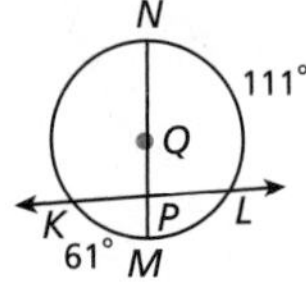

SEE EXAMPLE 3 p. 784

Find the value of *x*.

8. **47**

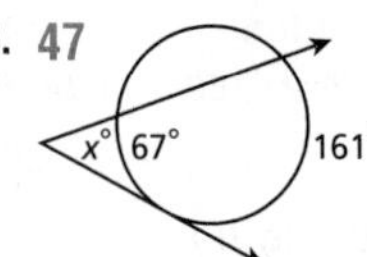

9. **58**

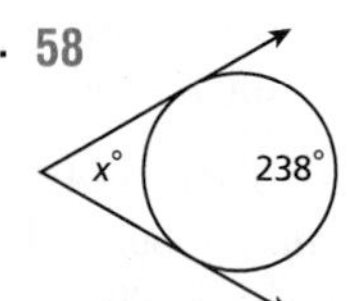

10. **94**

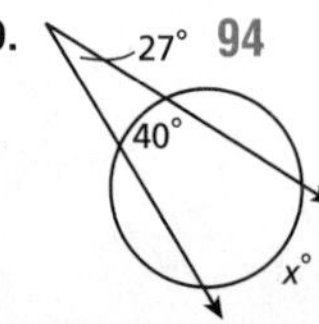

SEE EXAMPLE 4 p. 784

11. **Science** A satellite orbits Mars. When it reaches *S* it is about 12,000 km above the planet. How many arc degrees of the planet are visible to a camera in the satellite? **142°**

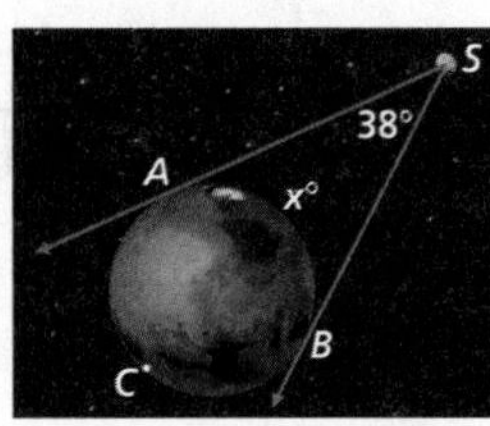

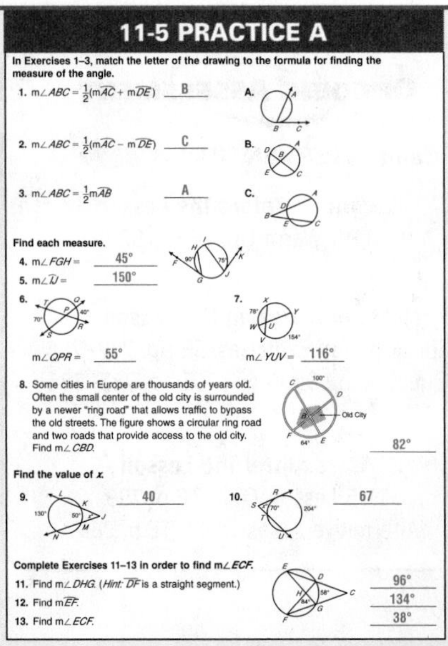

11-5 PRACTICE A

In Exercises 1–3, match the letter of the drawing to the formula for finding the measure of the angle.

1. $m\angle ABC = \frac{1}{2}(m\widehat{AC} + m\widehat{DE})$ **B**
2. $m\angle ABC = \frac{1}{2}(m\widehat{AC} - m\widehat{DE})$ **C**
3. $m\angle ABC = \frac{1}{2}m\widehat{AB}$ **A**

A. B. C.

Find each measure.

4. m∠*FGH* = **45°**
5. m$\widehat{IJ}$ = **150°**
6. m∠*QPR* = **55°**
7. m∠*YUV* = **116°**
8. Some cities in Europe are thousands of years old. Often the small center of the old city is surrounded by a newer "ring road" that allows traffic to bypass the old streets. The figure shows a circular ring road and two roads that provide access to the old city. Find m∠*CBD*. **82°**

Old City

Find the value of *x*.

9. **40**
10. **67**

Complete Exercises 11–13 in order to find m∠*ECF*.

11. Find m∠*DHG*. (*Hint:* $\overline{DF}$ is a straight segment.) **96°**
12. Find m$\widehat{EF}$. **134°**
13. Find m∠*ECF*. **38°**

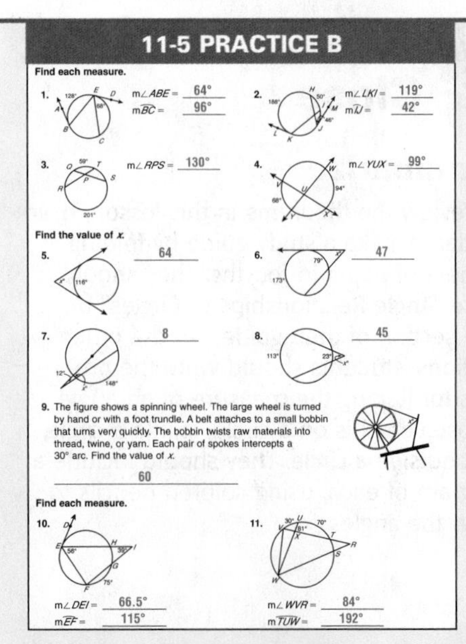

11-5 PRACTICE B

Find each measure.

1. m∠*ABE* = **64°** m$\widehat{BC}$ = **96°**
2. m∠*LKI* = **119°** m$\widehat{IJ}$ = **42°**
3. m∠*RPS* = **130°**
4. m∠*YUX* = **99°**

Find the value of *x*.

5. **64**
6. **47**
7. **8**
8. **45**
9. The figure shows a spinning wheel. The large wheel is turned by hand or with a foot trundle. A belt attaches to a small bobbin that turns very quickly. The bobbin twists raw materials into thread, twine, or yarn. Each pair of spokes intercepts a 30° arc. Find the value of *x*. **60**

Find each measure.

10. m∠*DEI* = **66.5°** m$\widehat{EF}$ = **115°**
11. m∠*WVR* = **84°** m$\widehat{TUW}$ = **192°**

SEE EXAMPLE 5 p. 785

Multi-Step Find each measure.

12. $m\widehat{DF}$ **50°**
13. $m\widehat{CD}$ **96°**
14. $m\widehat{PN}$ **110°**
15. $m\widehat{KN}$ **116°**

PRACTICE AND PROBLEM SOLVING

Independent Practice	
For Exercises	See Example
16–19	1
20–22	2
23–25	3
26	4
27–30	5

Extra Practice

Skills Practice p. S25

Application Practice p. S38

Find each measure.

16. $m\angle BCD$ **56°**
17. $m\angle ABC$ **124°**

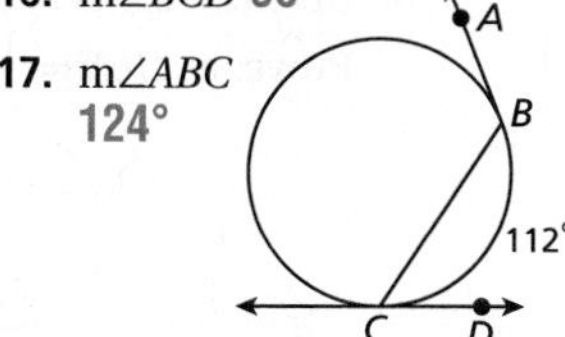

18. $m\angle XZW$ **90°**
19. $m\widehat{XZV}$ **260°**

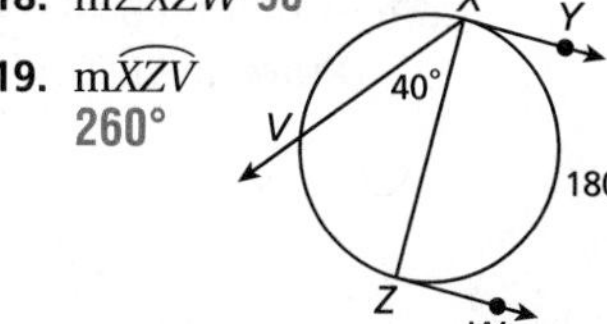

20. $m\angle QPR$ **64.5°**

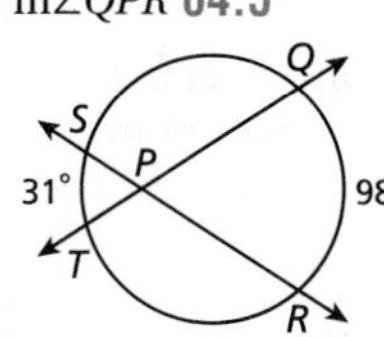

21. $m\angle ABC$ **107.5°**

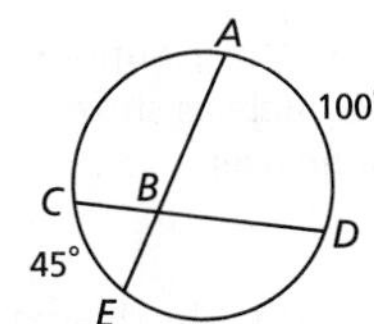

22. $m\angle MKJ$ **135°**

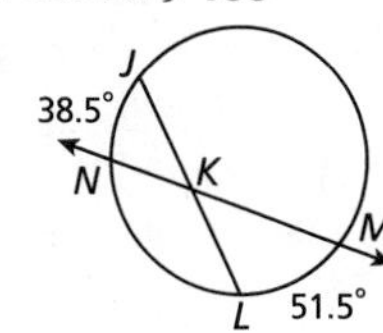

Find the value of x.

23. **57.5**

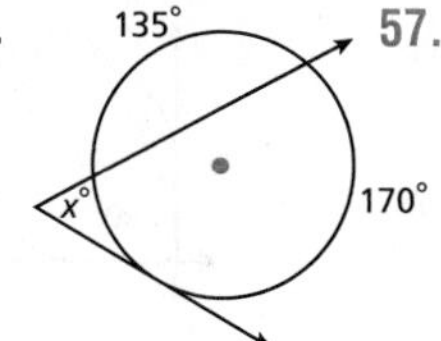

24. **40**

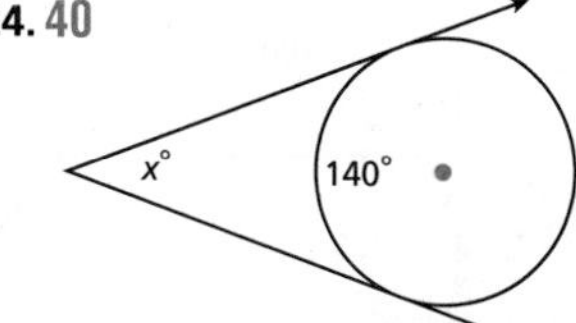

25. **18**

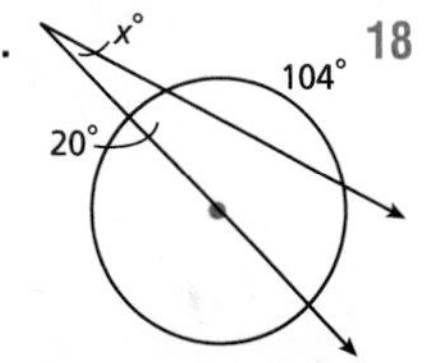

26. **Archaeology** Stonehenge is a circular arrangement of massive stones near Salisbury, England. A viewer at V observes the monument from a point where two of the stones A and B are aligned with stones at the endpoints of a diameter of the circular shape. Given that $m\widehat{AB} = 48°$, what is $m\angle AVB$? **66°**

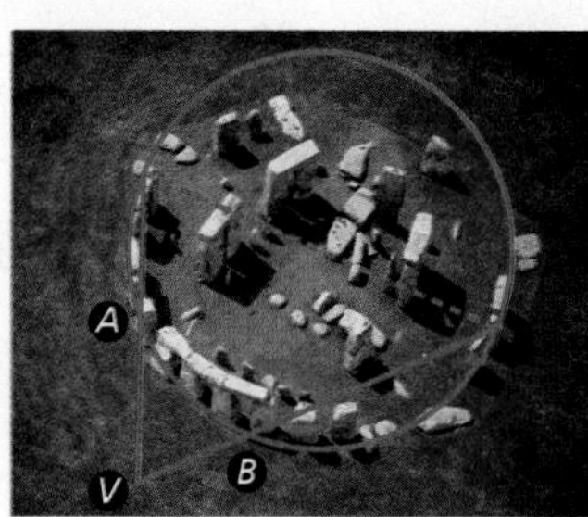

Multi-Step Find each measure.

27. $m\widehat{EG}$ **45°**
28. $m\widehat{DE}$ **117°**

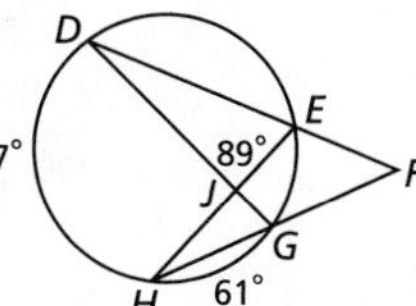

29. $m\widehat{PR}$ **90°**
30. $m\widehat{LP}$ **100°**

COMMON ERROR ALERT

Some students may have difficulty with problems that have more than one angle relationship, as is the case in **Exercises 27–30**. To help students keep their information organized, suggest that they each write a brief plan before performing any calculations. For example, in **Exercises 29,** they could write the following:

1. Find $m\angle MPN$ by taking *half* of $m\widehat{LR}$.
2. Use supp. ∠s and subtract to find $m\angle NPQ$.
3. Double $m\angle NPQ$ to find $m\widehat{PR}$.

11-5 PRACTICE C

Write paragraph proofs for Exercises 1–3.

1. **Given:** $\overline{AB} \cong \overline{EB}$
   Prove: $m\widehat{DE} = 2m\widehat{BC}$

Possible answer: It is given that $\overline{AB} \cong \overline{EB}$. So $\triangle ABE$ is an isosceles triangle, and $\angle BAC \cong \angle BEA$. $\angle BEA$ is an inscribed angle, so $m\angle BEA = \frac{1}{2}m\widehat{BC}$. By substitution, $m\angle BAC = \frac{1}{2}m\widehat{BC}$. $\overline{AD}$ and $\overline{AE}$ are secants that intersect in the exterior of the circle. So $m\angle BAC = \frac{1}{2}(m\widehat{DE} - m\widehat{BC})$. Substitution leads to $\frac{1}{2}m\widehat{BC} = \frac{1}{2}(m\widehat{DE} - m\widehat{BC})$. This simplifies to $m\widehat{DE} = 2m\widehat{BC}$.

2. **Given:** $\widehat{RS} \cong \widehat{TU}$, $\widehat{RU} \cong \widehat{ST}$
   Prove: Q is the center of the circle.
   (*Hint:* Show that Q is equidistant from three points on the circle.)

Possible answer: Draw chords $\overline{RU}$ and $\overline{ST}$. It is given that $\widehat{RU} \cong \widehat{ST}$. Because congruent arcs have congruent chords, $\overline{RU} \cong \overline{ST}$. It is given that $\widehat{RS} \cong \widehat{TU}$. $\angle RUS$, $\angle URT$, $\angle TSU$, and $\angle STR$ are all inscribed angles that intercept either $\widehat{RS}$ or $\widehat{TU}$. Therefore all four angles have the same measure and are congruent. By SAS, $\triangle QRU$ and $\triangle QST$ are congruent triangles. Furthermore, the base angles are all the same, so they are isosceles triangles. So $\overline{RQ}$, $\overline{UQ}$, and $\overline{SQ}$ (and $\overline{TQ}$) are congruent by CPCTC and the Isosceles Triangle Theorem. Congruent segments have equal lengths, so Q is equidistant from points R, U, and S (and T) that lie on the circle. Therefore Q is the center of the circle.

3. **Given:** $\overrightarrow{JK}$ and $\overrightarrow{JM}$ are tangent to the circle.
   Prove: $m\widehat{KM} < 180°$ (*Hint:* Use an indirect proof and consider two cases.)

Possible answer: Draw chord $\overline{KM}$. Assume that $m\widehat{KM} = 180°$. Because a circle contains 360°, $m\widehat{KLM}$ would also equal 180°. $\overrightarrow{JK}$ and $\overrightarrow{JM}$ intersect outside the circle, thus $m\angle KJM = \frac{1}{2}(m\widehat{KLM} - m\widehat{KM}) = 0°$. A triangle cannot contain a 0° angle, so $\triangle JKM$ does not exist, and $m\widehat{KM} = 180°$ cannot be true. Assume that $m\widehat{KM} > 180°$. Tangent $\overrightarrow{JM}$ and chord $\overline{KM}$ intersect at the point of tangency, M. So $m\angle JMK = \frac{1}{2}m\widehat{KM}$, which means $m\angle JMK > 90°$. Similar reasoning shows that $m\angle JKM$ is also greater than 90°. A triangle cannot contain two obtuse angles, so $\triangle JKM$ does not exist, and $m\widehat{KM} > 180°$ cannot be true. Therefore $m\widehat{KM} < 180°$.

Find the measure of the minor arc intercepted by the two tangents.

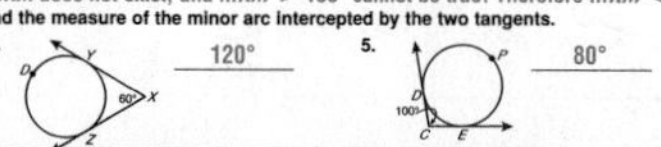

Communicating Math If students are having difficulty with **Exercises 34–36,** point out to them that even though the diagrams are different, the proofs for all three exercises are the same. The students must first form a triangle, and then the measure of the angle outside the circle is the difference between the measures of an external angle and an internal angle of the triangle.

Exercise 41 involves using angle relationships in circles to find the measures of angles. This exercise prepares students for the Multi-Step Test Prep on page 806.

Answers

34.

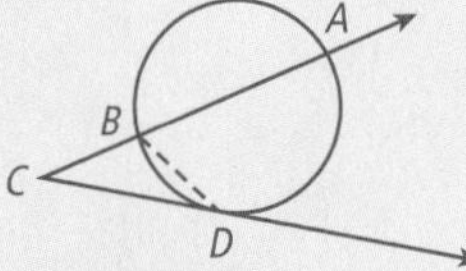

Since 2 pts. determine a line, draw $\overline{BD}$. By the Ext. ∠ Thm., $m\angle ABD = m\angle ACD + m\angle BDC$, so $m\angle ACD = m\angle ABD - m\angle BDC$. $m\angle ABD = \frac{1}{2}m\widehat{AD}$ by the Inscribed ∠ Thm., and $m\angle BDC = \frac{1}{2}m\widehat{BD}$ by Thm. 11-5-1. By subst., $m\angle ACD = \frac{1}{2}m\widehat{AD} - \frac{1}{2}m\widehat{BD}$. Thus by the Distrib. Prop. of =, $m\angle ACD = \frac{1}{2}(m\widehat{AD} - m\widehat{BD})$.

35.

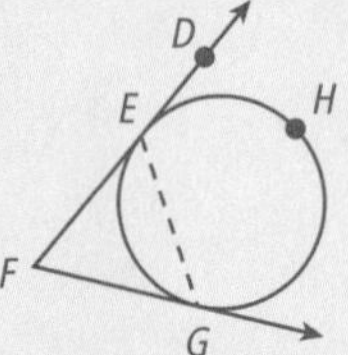

Since 2 pts. determine a line, draw $\overline{EG}$. By the Ext. ∠ Thm., $m\angle DEG = m\angle EFG + m\angle EGF$, so $m\angle EFG = m\angle DEG - m\angle EGF$. $m\angle DEG = \frac{1}{2}m\widehat{EHG}$, and $m\angle EGF = \frac{1}{2}m\widehat{EG}$ by Thm. 11-5-1. By subst., $m\angle EFG = \frac{1}{2}m\widehat{EHG} - \frac{1}{2}m\widehat{EG}$. Thus by the Distrib. Prop. of =, $m\angle EFG = \frac{1}{2}(m\widehat{EHG} - m\widehat{EG})$.

36, 38. See p. A29.

In the diagram, $m\angle ABC = x°$. Write an expression in terms of x for each of the following.

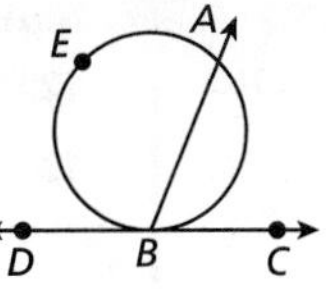

31. $m\widehat{AB}$ $2x°$ **32.** $m\angle ABD$ $(180 - x)°$ **33.** $m\widehat{AEB}$ $(360 - 2x)°$

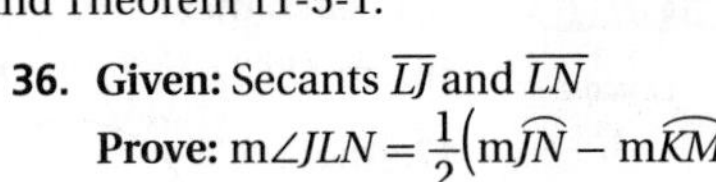

34. Given: Tangent $\overrightarrow{CD}$ and secant $\overrightarrow{CA}$
Prove: $m\angle ACD = \frac{1}{2}(m\widehat{AD} - m\widehat{BD})$
Plan: Draw auxiliary line segment $\overline{BD}$. Use the Exterior Angle Theorem to show that $m\angle ACD = m\angle ABD - m\angle BDC$. Then use the Inscribed Angle Theorem and Theorem 11-5-1.

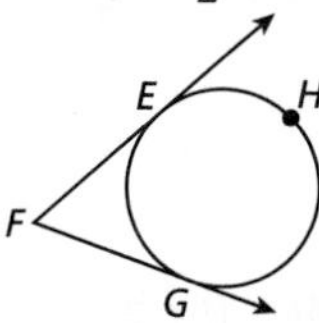

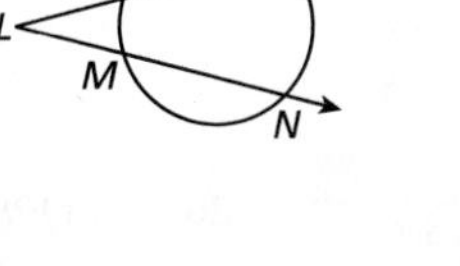

35. Given: Tangents $\overrightarrow{FE}$ and $\overrightarrow{FG}$
Prove: $m\angle EFG = \frac{1}{2}(m\widehat{EHG} - m\widehat{EG})$

36. Given: Secants $\overrightarrow{LJ}$ and $\overrightarrow{LN}$
Prove: $m\angle JLN = \frac{1}{2}(m\widehat{JN} - m\widehat{KM})$

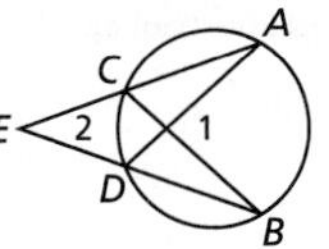

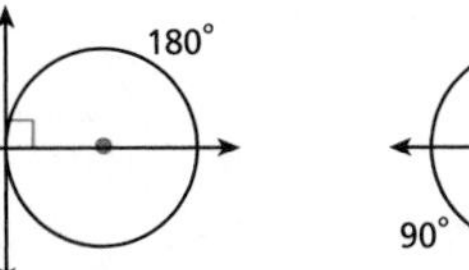

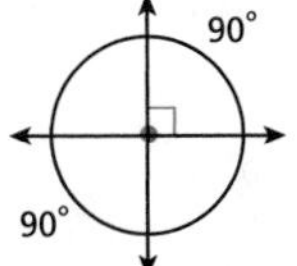

37. $m\angle 1 > m\angle 2$ because $m\angle 1 = \frac{1}{2}(m\widehat{AB} + m\widehat{CD})$ and $m\angle 2 = \frac{1}{2}(m\widehat{AB} - m\widehat{CD})$. Since $m\widehat{CD} > 0$, the expression for $m\angle 1$ is greater.

37. Critical Thinking Suppose two secants intersect in the exterior of a circle as shown. What is greater, $m\angle 1$ or $m\angle 2$? Justify your answer.

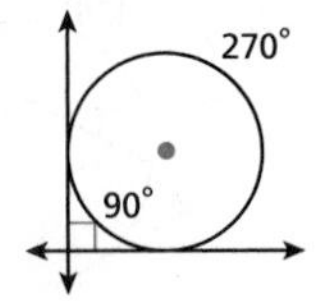

38. Write About It The diagrams show the intersection of perpendicular lines on a circle, inside a circle, and outside a circle. Explain how you can use these to help you remember how to calculate the measures of the angles formed.

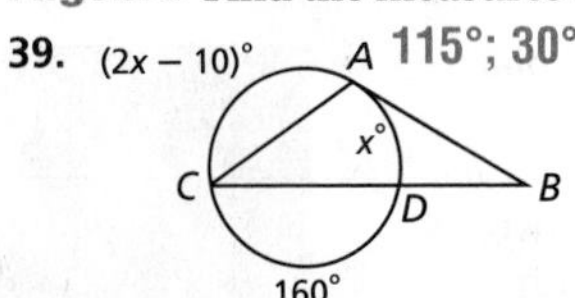

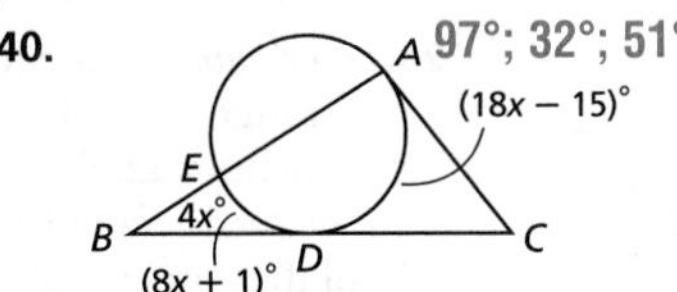

Algebra Find the measures of the three angles of $\triangle ABC$.

39. 115°; 30°; 35°

40. 97°; 32°; 51°

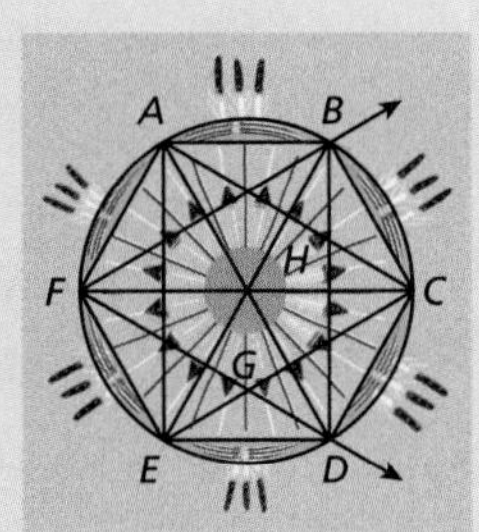

MULTI-STEP TEST PREP

41. This problem will prepare you for the Multi-Step Test Prep on page 806.
The design was made by placing six equally-spaced points on a circle and connecting them.
a. Find $m\angle BHC$. 60°
b. Find $m\angle EGD$. 120°
c. Classify $\triangle EGD$ by its angle measures and by its side lengths. obtuse isosceles

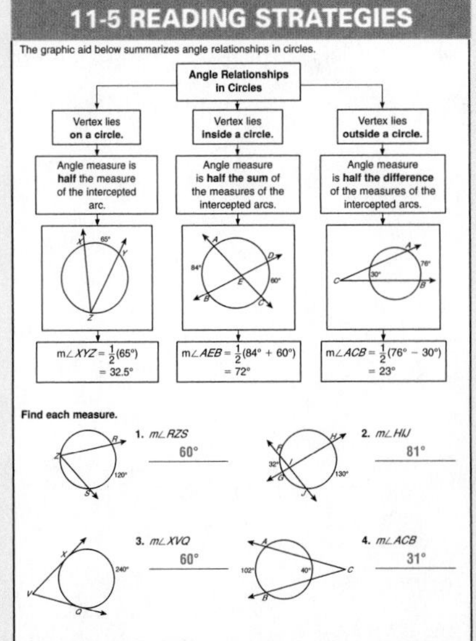

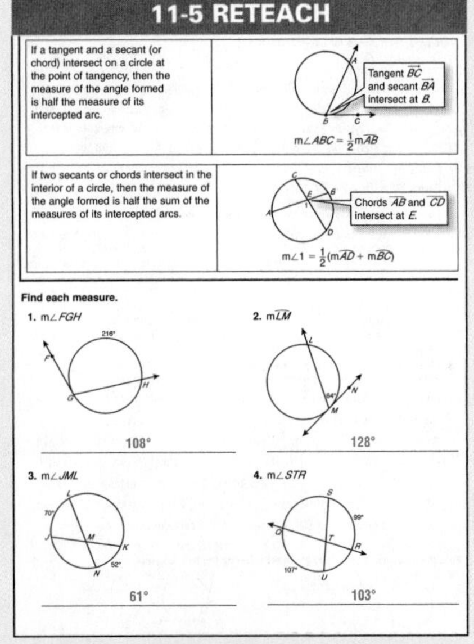

42. What is m∠DCE?

Ⓐ 19° Ⓑ 21° Ⓒ 79° Ⓓ 101°

43. Which expression can be used to calculate m∠ABC?

Ⓕ $\frac{1}{2}(m\widehat{AD} + m\widehat{AF})$

Ⓖ $\frac{1}{2}(m\widehat{DE} + m\widehat{AF})$

Ⓗ $\frac{1}{2}(m\widehat{DE} - m\widehat{AF})$

Ⓙ $\frac{1}{2}(m\widehat{AD} - m\widehat{AF})$

44. **Gridded Response** In ⊙Q, $m\widehat{MN} = 146°$ and m∠JLK = 45°. Find the degree measure of $\widehat{JK}$. 56

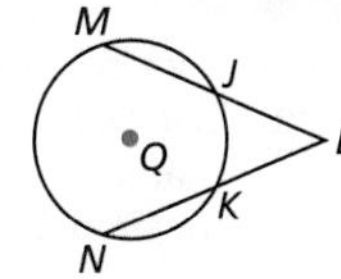

CHALLENGE AND EXTEND

45. Prove Theorem 11-5-1.
Given: Tangent $\overrightarrow{BC}$ and secant $\overline{BA}$
Prove: $m\angle ABC = \frac{1}{2}m\widehat{AB}$
(*Hint:* Consider two cases, one where $\overline{AB}$ is a diameter and one where $\overline{AB}$ is not a diameter.)

46. **Given:** $\overline{YZ}$ and $\overline{WZ}$ are tangent to ⊙X. $m\widehat{WY} = 90°$
Prove: WXYZ is a square.

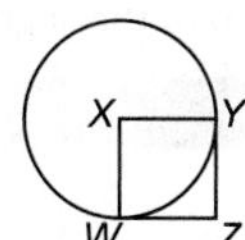

47. Find x. 95°

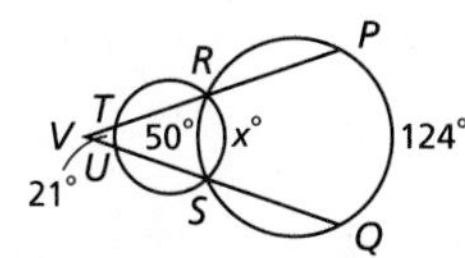

48. Find $m\widehat{GH}$. 79°

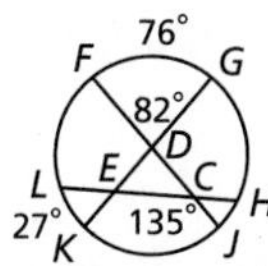

SPIRAL REVIEW

Determine whether the ordered pair (7, −8) is a solution of the following functions. *(Previous course)*

49. $g(x) = 2x^2 - 15x - 1$ yes
50. $f(x) = 29 - 3x$ no
51. $y = -\frac{7}{8}x$ no

Find the volume of each pyramid or cone. Round to the nearest tenth. *(Lesson 10-7)*

52. regular hexagonal pyramid with a base edge of 4 m and a height of 7 m $56\sqrt{3}\ m^3 \approx 97.0\ m^3$
53. right cone with a diameter of 12 cm and lateral area of $60\pi\ cm^2$ $96\pi\ cm^3 \approx 301.6\ cm^3$
54. regular square pyramid with a base edge of 24 in. and a surface area of 1200 in^2 960 in^3

In ⊙P, find each angle measure. *(Lesson 11-4)*

55. m∠BCA 37°
56. m∠DBC 23°
57. m∠ADC 53°

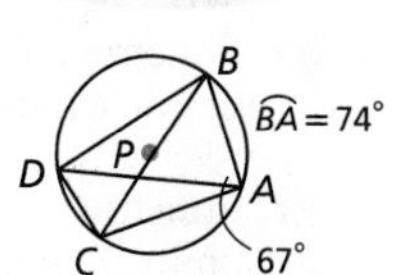

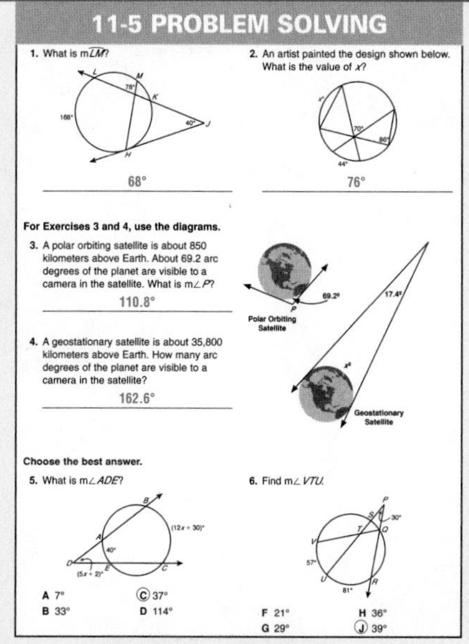

11-5 PROBLEM SOLVING

1. What is $m\widehat{LM}$? 68°
2. An artist painted the design shown below. What is the value of x? 76°

For Exercises 3 and 4, use the diagrams.

3. A polar orbiting satellite is about 850 kilometers above Earth. About 69.2 arc degrees of the planet are visible to a camera in the satellite. What is m∠P? 110.8°
4. A geostationary satellite is about 35,800 kilometers above Earth. How many arc degrees of the planet are visible to a camera in the satellite? 162.6°

Choose the best answer.

5. What is m∠ADE?
A 7° B 33° Ⓒ 37° D 114°

6. Find m∠VTU.
F 21° G 29° H 36° Ⓙ 39°

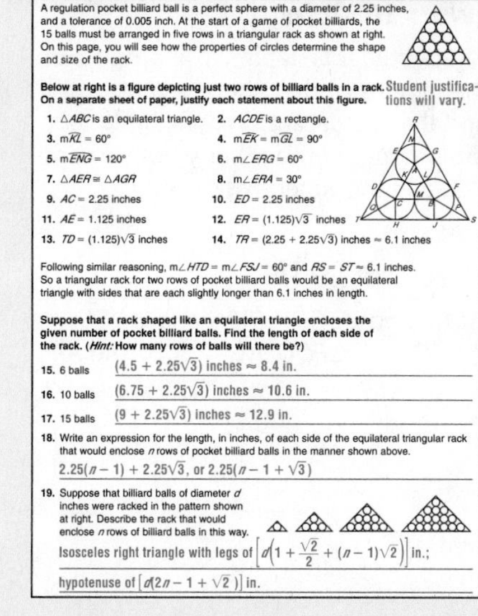

11-5 CHALLENGE

A regulation pocket billiard ball is a perfect sphere with a diameter of 2.25 inches, and a tolerance of 0.005 inch. At the start of a game of pocket billiards, the 15 balls must be arranged in five rows in a triangular rack as shown at right. On this page, you will see how the properties of circles determine the shape and size of the rack.

Below at right is a figure depicting just two rows of billiard balls in a rack. On a separate sheet of paper, justify each statement about this figure. Student justifications will vary.

1. △ABC is an equilateral triangle.
2. ACDE is a rectangle.
3. $m\widehat{KL} = 60°$
4. $m\widehat{EK} = m\widehat{GL} = 90°$
5. $m\widehat{ENG} = 120°$
6. m∠ERG = 60°
7. △AER ≅ △AGR
8. m∠ERA = 30°
9. AC = 2.25 inches
10. ED = 2.25 inches
11. AE = 1.125 inches
12. $ER = (1.125)\sqrt{3}$ inches
13. $TD = (1.125)\sqrt{3}$ inches
14. $TR = (2.25 + 2.25\sqrt{3})$ inches ≈ 6.1 inches

Following similar reasoning, m∠HTD = m∠FSJ = 60° and RS = ST ≈ 6.1 inches. So a triangular rack for two rows of pocket billiard balls would be an equilateral triangle with sides that are each slightly longer than 6.1 inches in length.

Suppose that a rack shaped like an equilateral triangle encloses the given number of pocket billiard balls. Find the length of each side of the rack. (*Hint:* How many rows of balls will there be?)

15. 6 balls $(4.5 + 2.25\sqrt{3})$ inches ≈ 8.4 in.
16. 10 balls $(6.75 + 2.25\sqrt{3})$ inches ≈ 10.6 in.
17. 15 balls $(9 + 2.25\sqrt{3})$ inches ≈ 12.9 in.
18. Write an expression for the length, in inches, of each side of the equilateral triangular rack that would enclose n rows of pocket billiard balls in the manner shown above.
$2.25(n - 1) + 2.25\sqrt{3}$, or $2.25(n - 1 + \sqrt{3})$
19. Suppose that billiard balls of diameter d inches were racked in the pattern shown at right. Describe the rack that would enclose n rows of billiard balls in this way.
Isosceles right triangle with legs of $\left[d\left(1 + \frac{\sqrt{2}}{2} + (n-1)\sqrt{2}\right)\right]$ in.; hypotenuse of $\left[d(2n - 1 + \sqrt{2})\right]$ in.

Answers

45–46. See p. A29.

TEST PREP DOCTOR If students know they will need to use the difference in **Exercise 43**, they can immediately eliminate the choices with the sum of two arc measures.

Journal

Ask students to explain in their own words how the *Angle Relationships in Circles* table will help them remember the angle relationships determined by the location of the vertex of the angle.

ALTERNATIVE ASSESSMENT

Have students draw and label an example to represent each of the three angle relationships from this lesson. Ask students to find the angle measures of their diagrams. They should indicate which theorem was applied to find each angle measure and write its measure in a table similar to the summary box on page 785.

Power Presentations with PowerPoint®

11-5 Lesson Quiz

Find each measure.

1. m∠FGJ 41.5°
2. m∠HJK 65°

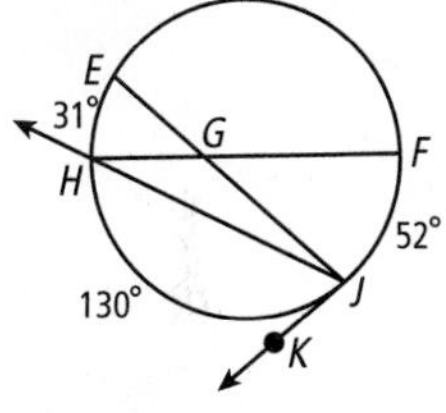

3. An oberver watches people riding a Ferris wheel that has 12 equally spaced cars. Find x. 30°

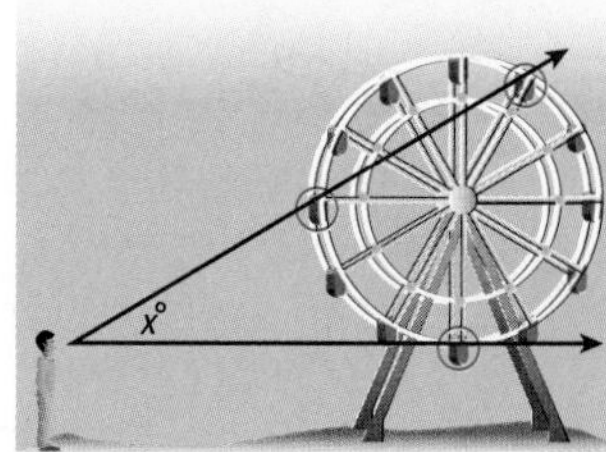

4. Find $m\widehat{CE}$. 12°

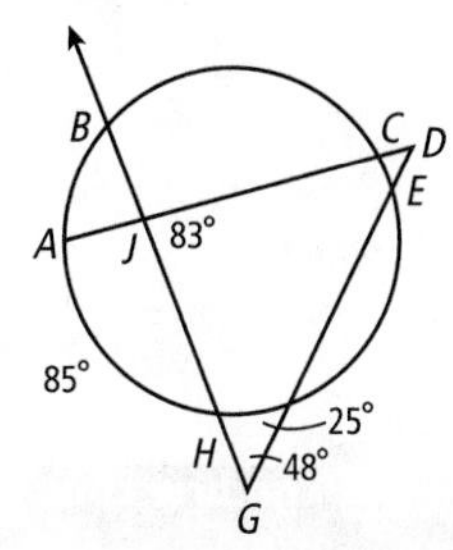

Also available on transparency

Organizer

Use with Lesson 11-6

Pacing:
Traditional 1 day
Block $\frac{1}{2}$ day

Objective: Use geometry software to explore segment relationships in circles.

Materials: Geometry software

Online Edition
TechKeys

Resources

Technology Lab Activities
11-6 Lab Recording Sheet

Teach

Discuss

As students follow the instructions of each activity, have them note whether they are constructing chords, secants, or tangents. Based on whether the segments intersect inside or outside the circle discuss with students the different ways they are relating the segment lengths to one another.

State Resources

Use with Lesson 11-6

Explore Segment Relationships in Circles

When secants, chords, or tangents of circles intersect, they create several segments. You will measure these segments and investigate their relationships.

go.hrw.com
Lab Resources Online
KEYWORD: MG7 Lab11

Activity 1

1. Construct a circle with center *A*. Label the point on the circle as *B*. Construct two secants $\overleftrightarrow{CD}$ and $\overleftrightarrow{EF}$ that intersect *outside* the circle at *G*. Hide *B* if desired. (It controls the circle's size.)

2. Measure $\overline{GC}$, $\overline{GD}$, $\overline{GE}$, and $\overline{GF}$. Drag points around the circle and examine the changes in the measurements.

3. Fill in the segment lengths in a chart like the one below. Find the products of the lengths of segments on the *same* secant. Can you make a conjecture about the relationship of the segments formed by intersecting secants of a circle?

GC	GD	GC · GD	GE	GF	GE · GF

Try This

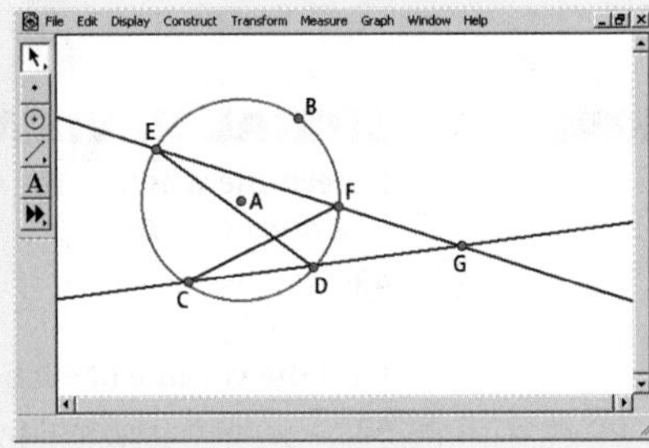

1. Make a sketch of the diagram from Activity 1, and create $\overline{CF}$ and $\overline{DE}$ to create $\triangle CFG$ and $\triangle EDG$ as shown.
2. Name pairs of congruent angles in the diagram. How are $\triangle CFG$ and $\triangle EDG$ related? Explain your reasoning.
3. Write a proportion involving sides of the triangles. Cross-multiply and state the result. What do you notice? $\frac{GC}{GF} = \frac{GE}{GD}$; $GC \cdot GD = GE \cdot GF$

Activity 2

1. Construct a new circle with center *A*. Label the point on the circle as *B*. Create a radius segment from *A* to a new point *C* on the circle.

2. Construct a line through *C* perpendicular to radius $\overline{AC}$. Create a new point *D* on this line, which is tangent to circle *A* at *C*. Hide radius $\overline{AC}$.

Answers to *Activity 1*

3. Check students' tables. The product of the lengths of the whole secant seg. and the ext. secant seg. will be = to the product of the other whole secant seg. and the other ext. secant seg.

Answers to *Try This*

2. $\angle CGF$ and $\angle EGD$; $\angle FCG$ and $\angle DEG$; $\triangle CFG$ and $\triangle EDG$ are ~ ⚠s by the AA ~ Post.

3. Create a secant line through D that intersects the circle at two new points E and F, as shown.

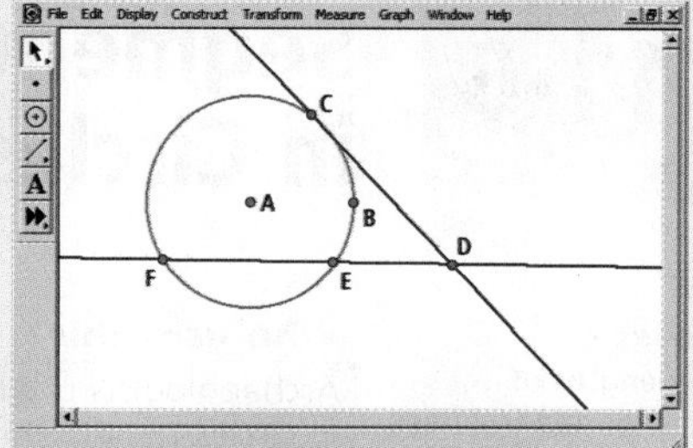

4. Measure $\overline{DC}$, $\overline{DE}$, and $\overline{DF}$. Drag points around the circle and examine the changes in the measurements. Fill in the measurements in a chart like the one below. Can you make a conjecture about the relationship between the segments of a tangent and a secant of a circle?

DE	DF	DE•DF	DC	?

Try This

4. How are the products for a tangent and a secant similar to the products for secant segments?
5. Try dragging E and F so they overlap (to make the secant segment look like a tangent segment). What do you notice about the segment lengths you measured in Activity 2? Can you state a relationship about two tangent segments from the same exterior point?
6. **Challenge** Write a formal proof of the relationship you found in Problem 2.

5. Two tangent segs. from the same ext. pt. will have = lengths, so the segs. are ≅.

Activity 3

1. Construct a new circle with two chords $\overline{CD}$ and $\overline{EF}$ that intersect inside the circle at G.
2. Measure $\overline{GC}$, $\overline{GD}$, $\overline{GE}$, and $\overline{GF}$. Drag points around the circle and examine the changes in the measurements.
3. Fill in the segment lengths in a chart like the ones used in Activities 1 and 2. Find the products of the lengths of segments on the same chord. Can you make a conjecture about the relationship of the segments formed by intersecting chords of a circle?

Check students' tables. The product of the lengths of the segs. on 1 chord will = the product of the lengths of the segs. on the other chord when 2 chords intersect inside a ⊙.

Try This

7. Connect the endpoints of the chords to form two triangles. Name pairs of congruent angles. How are the two triangles that are formed related? Explain your reasoning.
8. Examine the conclusions you made in all three activities about segments formed by secants, chords, and tangents in a circle. Summarize your findings.

7. ∠DGE and ∠FGC; ∠GDE and ∠GFC; ∠GED and ∠GCF; △DGE and △FGC are ~ ▲ by the AA ~ Post.

Close

Key Concept

There is a proportional relationship between segment lengths formed by the intersection of chords, secants, and tangents. The type of proportion used depends on the location of the intersection point.

Assessment

Journal Have students summarize the observations they made about segment relationships in circles.

Answers to *Activity 2*

4. Check students' tables. The product of the lengths of segs. on a secant will be = to the square of the length of the tangent seg. from the same ext. pt.

Answers to *Try This*

4. The products of seg. lengths for a tangent and a secant are ~ to the products of seg. lengths for 2 secants because for a tangent there is only 1 seg. Thus the "whole segment" multiplied by the "ext. seg." becomes the square of the tangent seg.
6. In the diagram, ⊙A is given with tangents $\overline{DC}$ and $\overline{DE}$ from D. Since 2 pts. determine a line, draw radii $\overline{AC}$, $\overline{AE}$, and $\overline{AD}$. $\overline{AC} \cong \overline{AE}$ because all radii are ≅. $\overline{AD} \cong \overline{AD}$ by the Reflex Prop of ≅. ∠ACD and ∠AED are rt ∠s because they are each formed by a radius and a tangent intersecting at the pt. of tangency. Thus △ACD and △AED are rt. ▲. △ACD ≅ △AED by the HL ≅ Thm. Therefore $\overline{DC} \cong \overline{DE}$ by CPCTC.
8. When 2 secants or 2 chords of a ⊙ intersect, 4 segs. will be formed, each with the pt. of intersection as 1 endpt. The product of the lengths of the segs. on 1 secant/chord will = the product of the lengths of the segs. on the other secant/chord.

   If a secant and a tangent of a ⊙ intersect at an ext. pt., 3 segs. will be formed, each with the ext. pt. as an endpt. The product of the lengths of the secant segments will = the square of the length of the tangent seg.

11-6 Organizer

Pacing: Traditional 1 day
Block $\frac{1}{2}$ day

Objectives: Find the lengths of segments formed by lines that intersect circles.

Use the lengths of segments in circles to solve problems.

Geometry Lab
In Geometry Lab Activities

Online Edition
Tutorial Videos

Power Presentations with PowerPoint®

Warm Up

Solve for *x*.

1. $\frac{x}{5} = \frac{28}{35}$ 4 **2.** $3x = 12^2$ 48

3. $\overline{BC}$ and $\overline{DC}$ are tangent to ⊙*A*. Find BC. 14

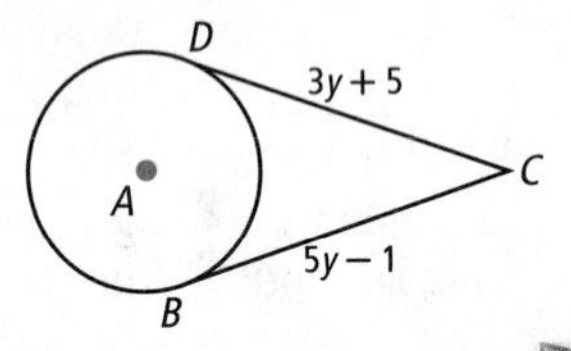

Also available on transparency

Q: How many mathematicians does it take to tie up a package?

A: None. You just need a chord.

11-6 Segment Relationships in Circles

Objectives
Find the lengths of segments formed by lines that intersect circles.

Use the lengths of segments in circles to solve problems.

Vocabulary
secant segment
external secant segment
tangent segment

Who uses this?
Archaeologists use facts about segments in circles to help them understand ancient objects. (See Example 2.)

In 1901, divers near the Greek island of Antikythera discovered several fragments of ancient items. Using the mathematics of circles, scientists were able to calculate the diameters of the complete disks.

The following theorem describes the relationship among the four segments that are formed when two chords intersect in the interior of a circle.

Know it! Note

Theorem 11-6-1 Chord-Chord Product Theorem

THEOREM	HYPOTHESIS	CONCLUSION
If two chords intersect in the interior of a circle, then the products of the lengths of the segments of the chords are equal.	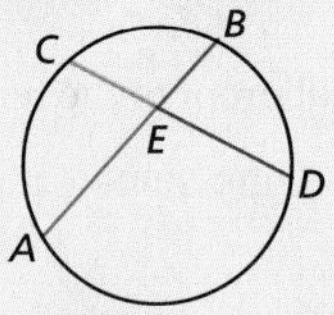 [circle with chords AB and CD intersecting at E] Chords $\overline{AB}$ and $\overline{CD}$ intersect at *E*.	$AE \cdot EB = CE \cdot ED$

You will prove Theorem 11-6-1 in Exercise 28.

EXAMPLE 1 Applying the Chord-Chord Product Theorem

Algebra

Find the value of *x* and the length of each chord.

$$PQ \cdot QR = SQ \cdot QT$$
$$6(4) = x(8)$$
$$24 = 8x$$
$$3 = x$$
$$PR = 6 + 4 = 10$$
$$ST = 3 + 8 = 11$$

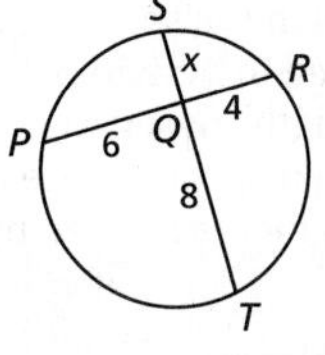

1. Find the value of *x* and the length of each chord.
3.75; $AB = 11$; $CD = 11.75$

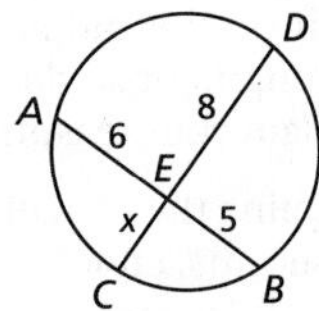

State Resources

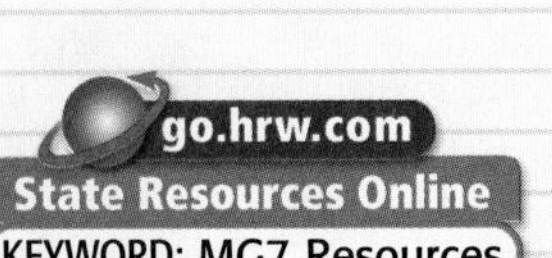

go.hrw.com
State Resources Online
KEYWORD: MG7 Resources

1 Introduce

EXPLORATION

11-6 Segment Relationships in Circles

Use geometry software to explore the segments formed by two intersecting chords of a circle.

1. Construct a circle. Then construct two intersecting chords of the circle $\overline{AB}$ and $\overline{CD}$. 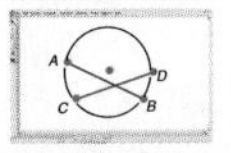
2. Construct the intersection of the chords. Label the intersection *E*. 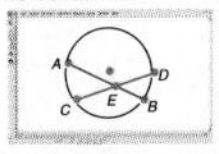
3. Measure *AE*, *EB*, *CE*, and *ED*. 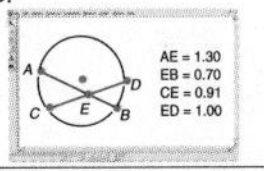
4. Calculate $AE \cdot EB$ and $CE \cdot ED$. 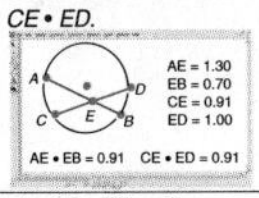
5. What do you notice about the products $AE \cdot EB$ and $CE \cdot ED$?
6. Drag the endpoints of the chords and change the size of the circle. Is the relationship between the products of the segments the same?

THINK AND DISCUSS

Motivate

Explain to students that designers and artists often make designs with lines that intersect circles. Show designs found in textile and rug patterns, furniture, and pottery. Tell students that designers not only need to know the angle measures of the intersecting lines. They also need to know the lengths of the segments. Have students collect samples of other designs such as family crests or symbols of their culture for display on the bulletin board.

Explorations and answers are provided in *Alternate Openers: Explorations Transparencies.*

EXAMPLE 2 Archaeology Application

x^2_y Algebra

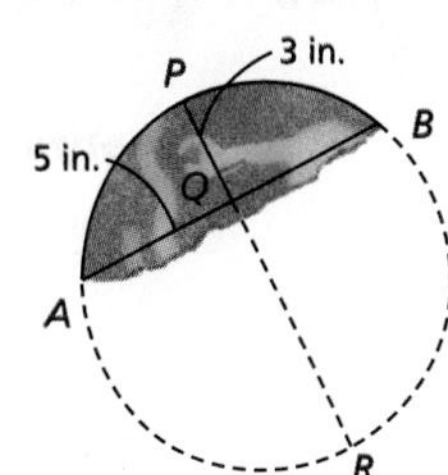

Archaeologists discovered a fragment of an ancient disk. To calculate its original diameter, they drew a chord $\overline{AB}$ and its perpendicular bisector $\overline{PQ}$. Find the disk's diameter.

Since $\overline{PQ}$ is the perpendicular bisector of a chord, $\overline{PR}$ is a diameter of the disk.

$$AQ \cdot QB = PQ \cdot QR$$
$$5(5) = 3(QR)$$
$$25 = 3QR$$
$$8\frac{1}{3}\text{ in.} = QR$$
$$PR = 3 + 8\frac{1}{3} = 11\frac{1}{3}\text{ in.}$$

2. What if...? Suppose the length of chord $\overline{AB}$ that the archaeologists drew was 12 in. In this case how much longer is the disk's diameter compared to the disk in Example 2? $3\frac{2}{3}$ in.

A **secant segment** is a segment of a secant with at least one endpoint on the circle. An **external secant segment** is a secant segment that lies in the exterior of the circle with one endpoint on the circle.

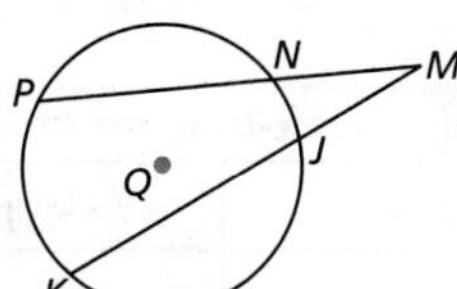

$\overline{PM}$, $\overline{NM}$, $\overline{KM}$, and $\overline{JM}$ are secant segments of $\odot Q$. $\overline{NM}$ and $\overline{JM}$ are external secant segments.

Theorem 11-6-2 Secant-Secant Product Theorem

THEOREM	HYPOTHESIS	CONCLUSION
If two secants intersect in the exterior of a circle, then the product of the lengths of one secant segment and its external segment equals the product of the lengths of the other secant segment and its external segment. (whole • outside = whole • outside)	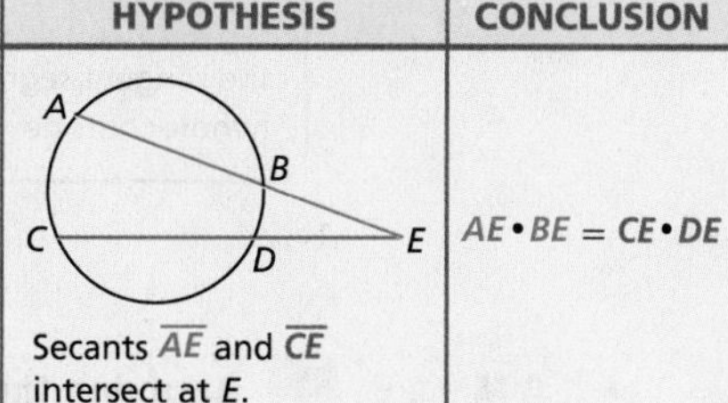 Secants $\overline{AE}$ and $\overline{CE}$ intersect at E.	$AE \cdot BE = CE \cdot DE$

Secant-Secant Product Theorem

Given: Secant segments $\overline{AE}$ and $\overline{CE}$
Prove: $AE \cdot BE = CE \cdot DE$

Proof: Draw auxiliary line segments $\overline{AD}$ and $\overline{CB}$. $\angle EAD$ and $\angle ECB$ both intercept $\widehat{BD}$, so $\angle EAD \cong \angle ECB$. $\angle E \cong \angle E$ by the Reflexive Property of $\cong$. Thus $\triangle EAD \sim \triangle ECB$ by AA Similarity. Therefore corresponding sides are proportional, and $\frac{AE}{CE} = \frac{DE}{BE}$. By the Cross Products Property, $AE \cdot BE = CE \cdot DE$.

2 Teach

Guided Instruction

Review with students ratio and proportion. Illustrate the terms *secant segment, external secant segment*, and *tangent segment*, using a different color for each in a diagram. Then use copies of the diagrams from the three theorems in the lesson. Have students practice naming chords, secant segments, external secant segments, and tangent segments before introducing the calculations to find the lengths of the segments.

Reaching All Learners

Through Visual Cues

As you discuss each theorem with the class, use colored chalk or markers to highlight the segments that are proportional to one another. Use the same colors to write the parts of the proportion so students can better see and understand the relationships. Encourage students to use colored pencils in their notes.

Some students might multiply the wrong segments for the Chord-Chord Product Theorem. Show them that $\triangle AEC \sim \triangle DEB$. Thus $\frac{AE}{ED} = \frac{CE}{EB}$, or $AE \cdot EB = CE \cdot ED$.

Power Presentations with PowerPoint®

Additional Examples

Example 1

Find the value of x and the length of each chord. $x = 5$; $FE = 17$; $GH = 19$

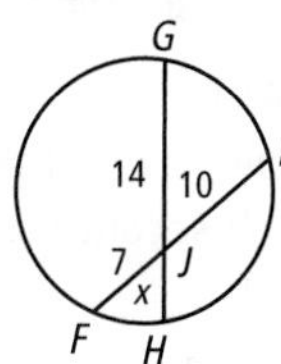

Example 2

The art department is contracted to construct a wooden moon for a play. One of the artists creates a sketch of what it needs to look like by drawing a chord and its perpendicular bisector. Find the diameter of the circle used to draw the outer edge of the moon. $18\frac{1}{8}$ in

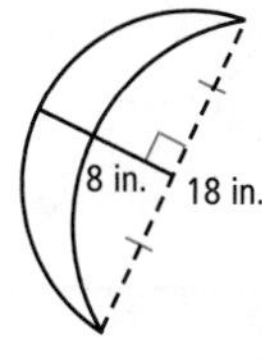

INTERVENTION

Questioning Strategies

EXAMPLE 1

- Do intersecting chords have to be equal in length to use the Chord-Chord Product Theorem?

EXAMPLE 2

- How do you know your strategy will give you the answer for the diameter of the circle?

Teaching Tip **Kinesthetic** Have students model each theorem using a cutout circles taped to their desks, lengths of different colored string for chords, secants, and tangents, and rulers to find and compare segment measures.

Teaching Tip **Math Background** Point out to students that in Theorem 11-6-3 the tangent is the mean proportional between the secant and its external segment.

Power Presentations with PowerPoint®

Additional Examples

Example 3

Find the value of x and the length of each secant segment.

$x = 6$; $ED = 16$; $EG = 14$

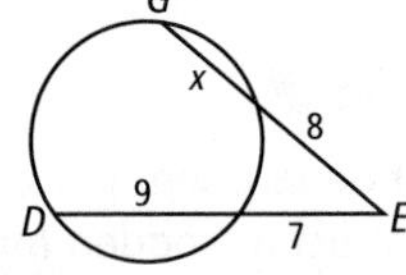

Example 4

Find the value of x. 10

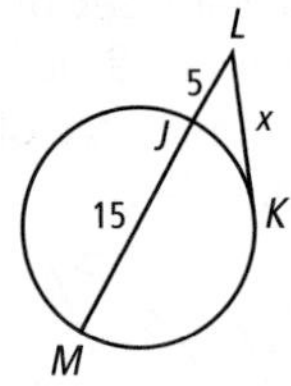

INTERVENTION

Questioning Strategies

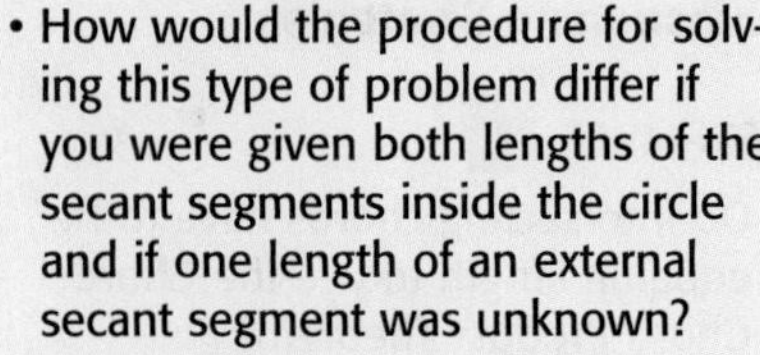

EXAMPLE 3

- How would the procedure for solving this type of problem differ if you were given both lengths of the secant segments inside the circle and if one length of an external secant segment was unknown?

EXAMPLE 4

- How do you know when to use the Secant-Secant Product Theorem or the Secant-Tangent Product Theorem?

EXAMPLE 3 Applying the Secant-Secant Product Theorem

Algebra

Find the value of x and the length of each secant segment.

$RT \cdot RS = RQ \cdot RP$

$10(4) = (x + 5)5$

$40 = 5x + 25$

$15 = 5x$

$3 = x$

$RT = 4 + 6 = 10$

$RQ = 5 + 3 = 8$

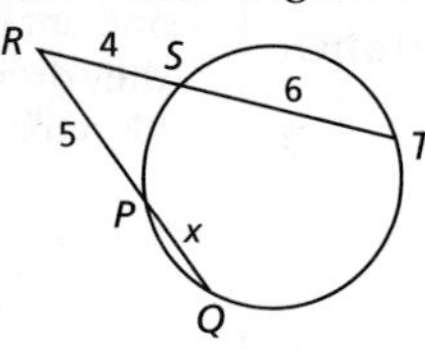

CHECK IT OUT! **3.** Find the value of z and the length of each secant segment.

$z = 14$; $JG = 27$; $LG = 39$

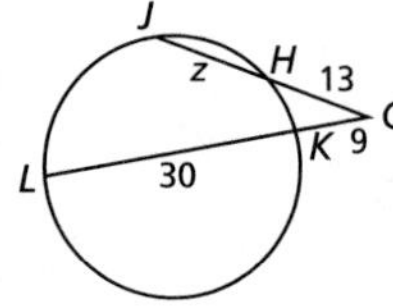

A **tangent segment** is a segment of a tangent with one endpoint on the circle. $\overline{AB}$ and $\overline{AC}$ are tangent segments.

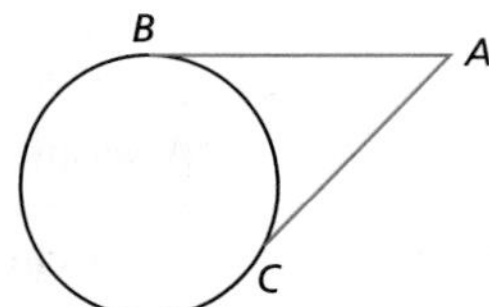

Know it! Note

Theorem 11-6-3 **Secant-Tangent Product Theorem**

THEOREM	HYPOTHESIS	CONCLUSION
If a secant and a tangent intersect in the exterior of a circle, then the product of the lengths of the secant segment and its external segment equals the length of the tangent segment squared. (whole • outside = tangent²)	Secant $\overline{AC}$ and tangent $\overline{DC}$ intersect at *C*.	$AC \cdot BC = DC^2$

You will prove Theorem 11-6-3 in Exercise 29.

EXAMPLE 4 Applying the Secant-Tangent Product Theorem

Algebra

Find the value of x.

$SQ \cdot RQ = PQ^2$

$9(4) = x^2$

$36 = x^2$

$\pm 6 = x$

The value of x must be 6 since it represents a length.

CHECK IT OUT! **4.** Find the value of y. $7\frac{2}{7}$

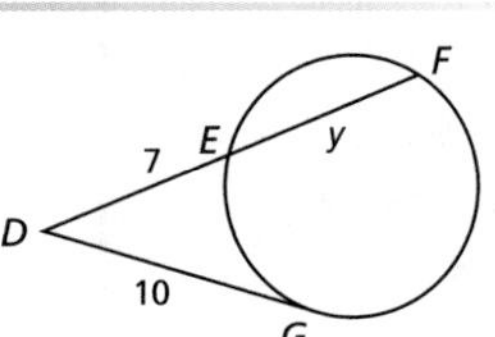

3 Close

Summarize

Summarize the segment relationships in circles by presenting the theorems in a table. Draw a diagram in the first column. In the second write the location of the vertex. In the third column name the types of segments. Then write the conclusion in the last column. Remind students that Theorem 11-6-1 applies to two chords that intersect in the interior of a circle and that Theorems 11-6-2 and 11-6-3 apply to segments that intersect in the exterior of a circle.

ONGOING ASSESSMENT and INTERVENTION

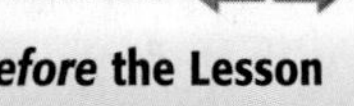

***Diagnose Before* the Lesson**
11-6 Warm Up, TE p. 792

***Monitor During* the Lesson**
Check It Out! Exercises, SE pp. 792–794
Questioning Strategies, TE pp. 793–794

***Assess After* the Lesson**
11-6 Lesson Quiz, TE p. 798
Alternative Assessment, TE p. 798

THINK AND DISCUSS

1. Does the Chord-Chord Product Theorem apply when both chords are diameters? If so, what does the theorem tell you in this case?
2. Given A in the exterior of a circle, how many different tangent segments can you draw with A as an endpoint?

3. **GET ORGANIZED** Copy and complete the graphic organizer.

	Theorem	Diagram	Example
Chord–Chord			
Secant–Secant			
Secant–Tangent			

Answers to *Think and Discuss*

Possible answers:

1. Yes; in this case, the chords intersect at the center of the ⊙. So the segs. of the chords are all radii, and the thm. simplifies to $r^2 = r^2$.
2. 2
3. See p. A9.

11-6 Exercises

go.hrw.com
Homework Help Online
KEYWORD: MG7 11-6
Parent Resources Online
KEYWORD: MG7 Parent

GUIDED PRACTICE

1. **Vocabulary** $\overleftrightarrow{AB}$ intersects $\odot P$ at exactly one point. Point A is in the exterior of $\odot P$, and point B lies on $\odot P$. $\overline{AB}$ is a(n) ___?___. (*tangent segment* or *external secant segment*) tangent seg.

SEE EXAMPLE 1 p. 792

Find the value of the variable and the length of each chord.

2. 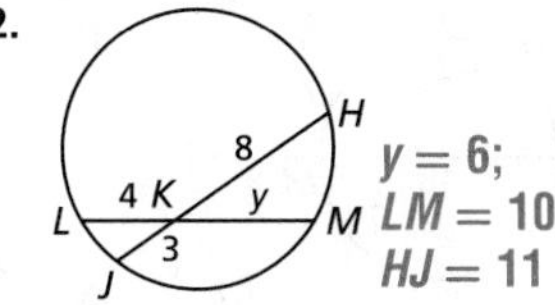

$y = 6$; $LM = 10$; $HJ = 11$

3. 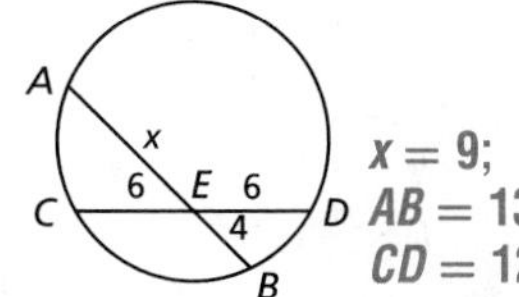

$x = 9$; $AB = 13$; $CD = 12$

4. 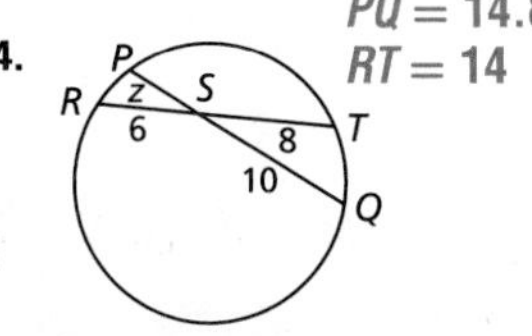

$z = 4.8$; $PQ = 14.8$; $RT = 14$

SEE EXAMPLE 2 p. 793

5. **Engineering** A section of an aqueduct is based on an arc of a circle as shown. $\overline{EF}$ is the perpendicular bisector of $\overline{GH}$. $GH = 50$ ft, and $EF = 20$ ft. What is the diameter of the circle? $51\frac{1}{4}$ ft

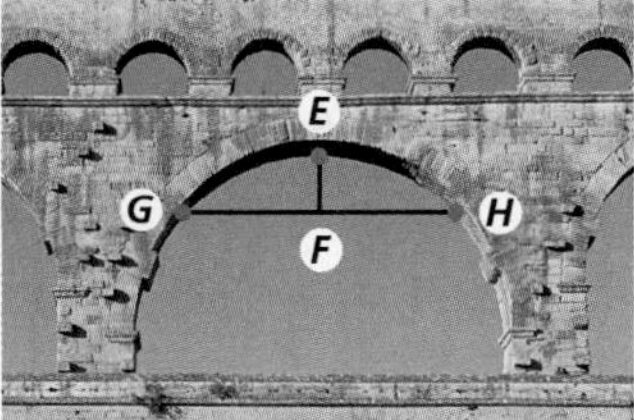

SEE EXAMPLE 3 p. 794

Find the value of the variable and the length of each secant segment.

6. 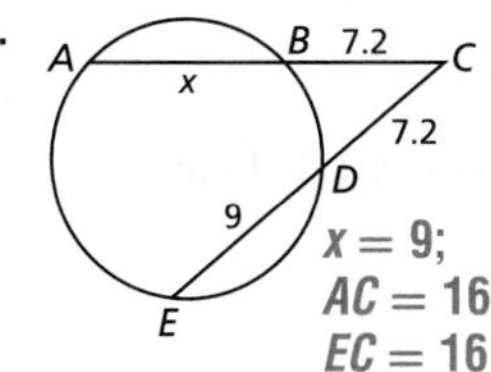

$x = 9$; $AC = 16.2$; $EC = 16.2$

7. 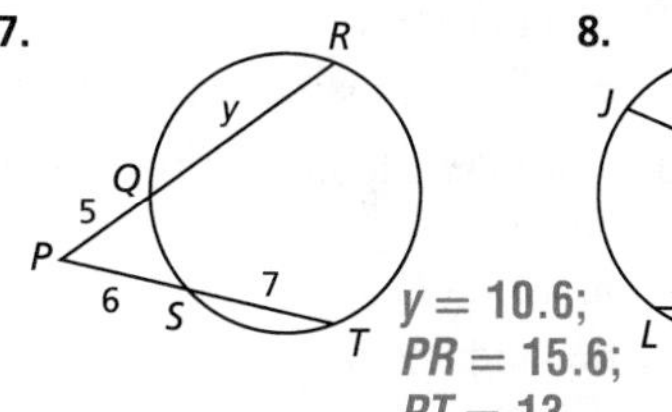

$y = 10.6$; $PR = 15.6$; $PT = 13$

8. 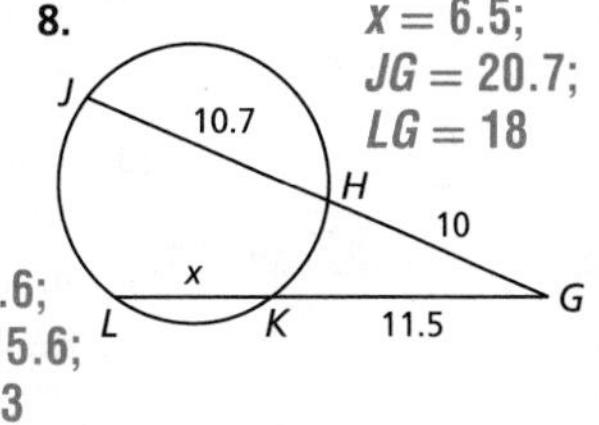

$x = 6.5$; $JG = 20.7$; $LG = 18$

11-6 Exercises

Assignment Guide

Assign *Guided Practice* exercises as necessary.

If you finished Examples **1–2**
Basic 12–15, 22, 23
Average 12–15, 22, 23, 28
Advanced 12–15, 22, 23, 28, 38

If you finished Examples **1–4**
Basic 12–28, 32–35, 40–47,
Average 12–36, 40–47
Advanced 12–26, 28–47

Homework Quick Check
Quickly check key concepts.
Exercises: 12, 14, 15, 16, 20, 22

State Resources

go.hrw.com
State Resources Online
KEYWORD: MG7 Resources

Algebra In **Exercises 16–21**, point out that students can set up and solve proportions to find segment lengths.

SEE EXAMPLE 4 p. 794

Find the value of the variable.

9. 4

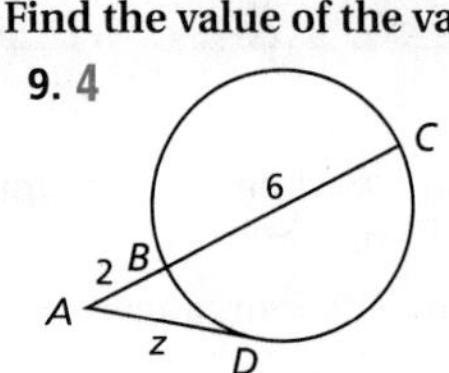

10. $2\frac{1}{3}$

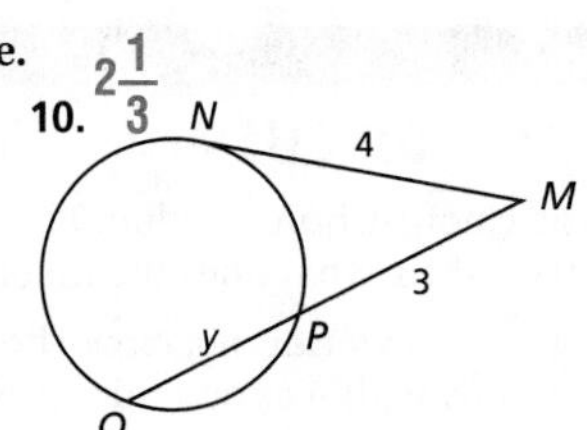

11. $\sqrt{33}$

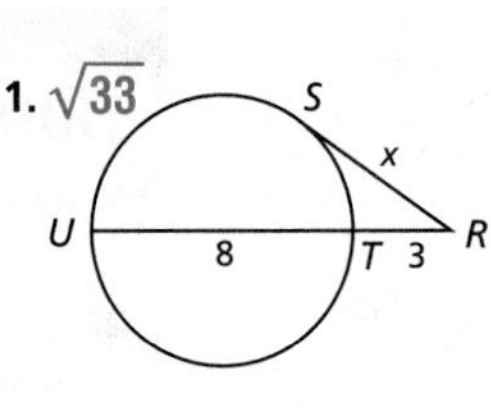

PRACTICE AND PROBLEM SOLVING

Independent Practice	
For Exercises	See Example
12–14	1
15	2
16–18	3
19–21	4

Extra Practice

Skills Practice p. S25
Application Practice p. S38

Find the value of the variable and the length of each chord.

12. $y = 6$; $DE = 7$; $FG = 8$

13.

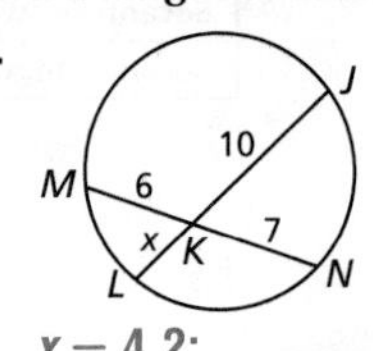

$x = 4.2$; $JL = 14.2$; $MN = 13$

14. $x = 3\frac{7}{11}$; $UV = 13$; $WZ = 14\frac{7}{11}$

15. **Geology** Molokini is a small, crescent-shaped island $2\frac{1}{2}$ miles from the Maui coast. It is all that remains of an extinct volcano. To approximate the diameter of the mouth of the volcano, a geologist can use a diagram like the one shown. What is the approximate diameter of the volcano's mouth to the nearest foot? 1770 ft

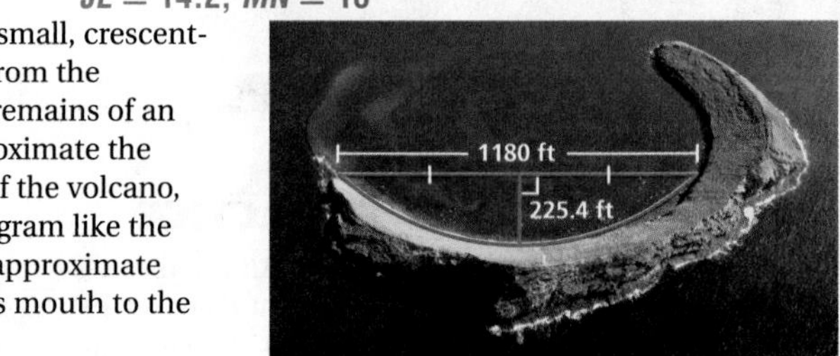

Find the value of the variable and the length of each secant segment.

16.

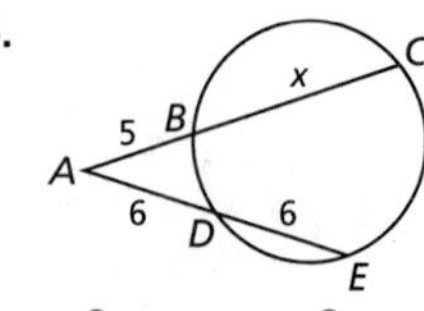

$x = 9\frac{2}{5}$; $AC = 14\frac{2}{5}$; $AE = 12$

17. $y = 14.3$; $HL = 24.3$; $NL = 27$

18. $x = 11.5$; $PT = 13.5$; $PR = 9$

Find the value of the variable.

19.

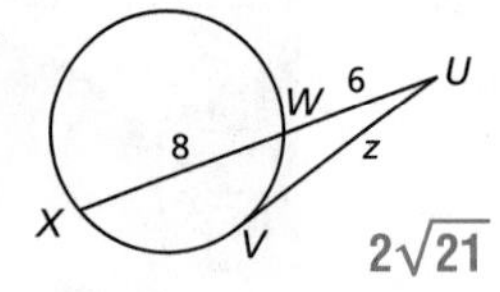

$2\sqrt{21}$

20.

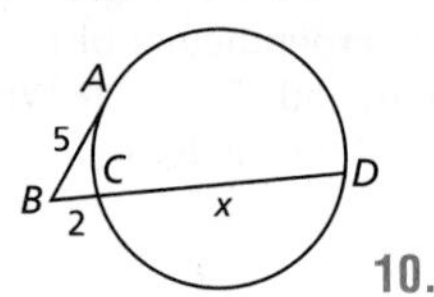

10.5

21. $4\sqrt{10}$

Use the diagram for Exercises 22 and 23.

22. M is the midpoint of $\overline{PQ}$. $RM = 10$ cm, and $PQ = 24$ cm.
   a. Find MS. 14.4 cm
   b. Find the diameter of $\odot O$. 24.4 cm

23. M is the midpoint of $\overline{PQ}$. The diameter of $\odot O$ is 13 in., and $RM = 4$ in.
   a. Find PM. 6 in.
   b. Find PQ. 12 in.

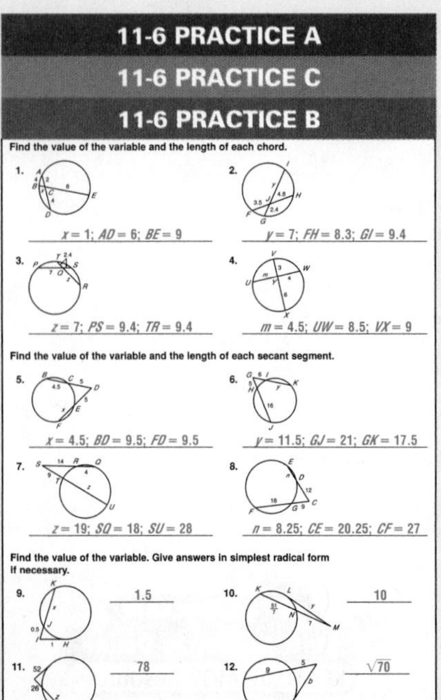

11-6 PRACTICE A

11-6 PRACTICE C

11-6 PRACTICE B

Find the value of the variable and the length of each chord.

1. $x = 1$; $AD = 6$; $BE = 9$
2. $y = 7$; $FH = 8.3$; $GI = 9.4$
3. $z = 7$; $PS = 9.4$; $TR = 9.4$
4. $m = 4.5$; $UW = 8.5$; $VX = 9$

Find the value of the variable and the length of each secant segment.

5. $x = 4.5$; $BD = 9.5$; $FD = 9.5$
6. $y = 11.5$; $GJ = 21$; $GK = 17.5$
7. $z = 19$; $SQ = 18$; $SU = 28$
8. $n = 8.25$; $CE = 20.25$; $CF = 27$

Find the value of the variable. Give answers in simplest radical form if necessary.

9. 1.5
10. 10
11. 78
12. $\sqrt{70}$

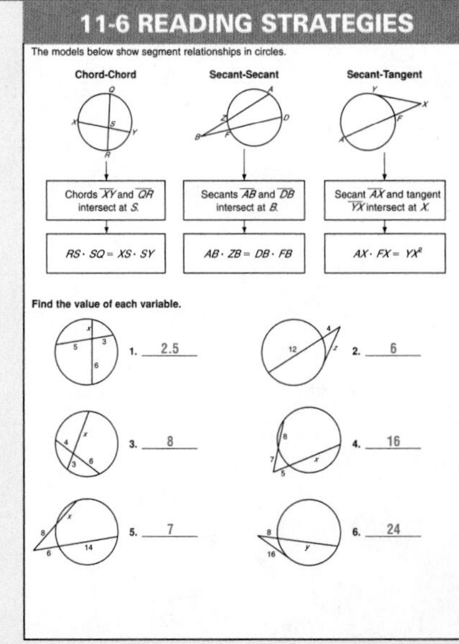

11-6 READING STRATEGIES

The models below show segment relationships in circles.

Chord-Chord	Secant-Secant	Secant-Tangent
Chords $\overline{XY}$ and $\overline{QR}$ intersect at S.	Secants $\overline{AB}$ and $\overline{DB}$ intersect at B.	Secant $\overline{AX}$ and tangent $\overline{YX}$ intersect at X.
$RS \cdot SQ = XS \cdot SY$	$AB \cdot ZB = DB \cdot FB$	$AX \cdot FX = YX^2$

Find the value of each variable.

1. 2.5
2. 6
3. 8
4. 16
5. 7
6. 24

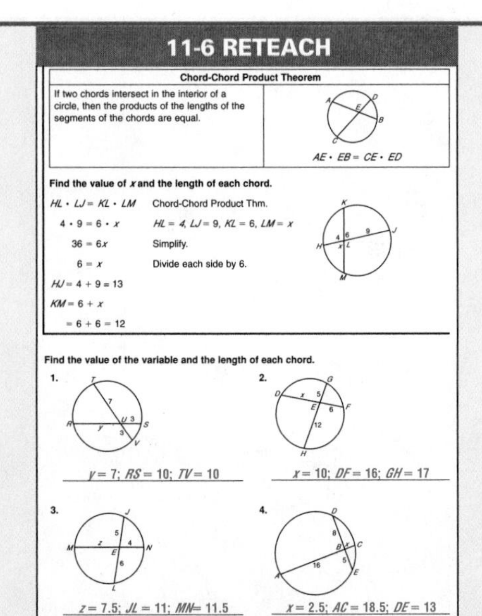

11-6 RETEACH

Chord-Chord Product Theorem

If two chords intersect in the interior of a circle, then the products of the lengths of the segments of the chords are equal.

$AE \cdot EB = CE \cdot ED$

Find the value of x and the length of each chord.

$HL \cdot LJ = KL \cdot LM$ Chord-Chord Product Thm.

$4 \cdot 9 = 6 \cdot x$ $HL = 4$, $LJ = 9$, $KL = 6$, $LM = x$

$36 = 6x$ Simplify.

$6 = x$ Divide each side by 6.

$HJ = 4 + 9 = 13$

$KM = 6 + x$

$= 6 + 6 = 12$

Find the value of the variable and the length of each chord.

1. $y = 7$; $RS = 10$; $TV = 10$
2. $x = 10$; $DF = 16$; $GH = 17$
3. $z = 7.5$; $JL = 11$; $MN = 11.5$
4. $x = 2.5$; $AC = 18.5$; $DE = 13$

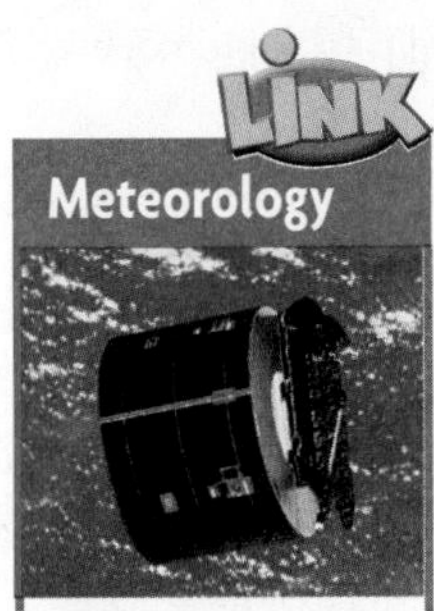

Meteorology

Satellites are launched to an area above the atmosphere where there is no friction. The idea is to position them so that when they fall back toward Earth, they fall at the same rate as Earth's surface falls away from them.

Multi-Step Find the value of both variables in each figure.

24. 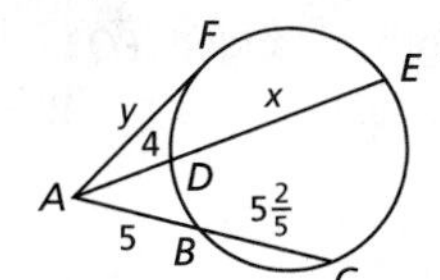

$x = 9$; $y = 2\sqrt{13}$

25. 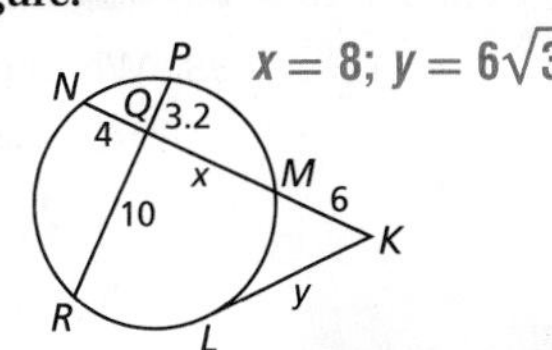

$x = 8$; $y = 6\sqrt{3}$

26. **Meteorology** A weather satellite S orbits Earth at a distance SE of 6000 mi. Given that the diameter of the earth is approximately 8000 mi, what is the distance from the satellite to P? Round to the nearest mile. **9165 mi**

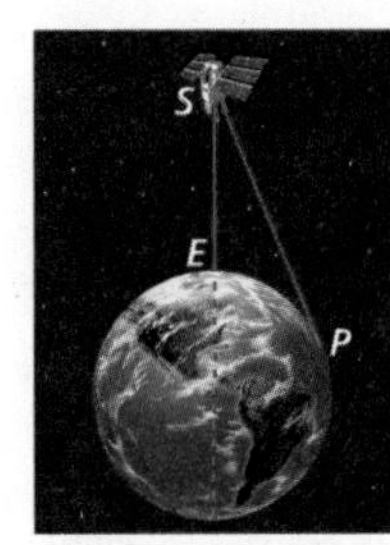

27. **ERROR ANALYSIS** The two solutions show how to find the value of x. Which solution is incorrect? Explain the error.

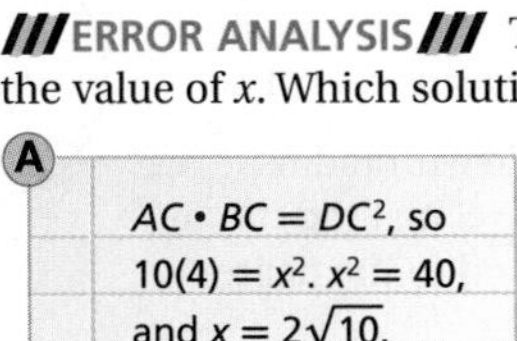

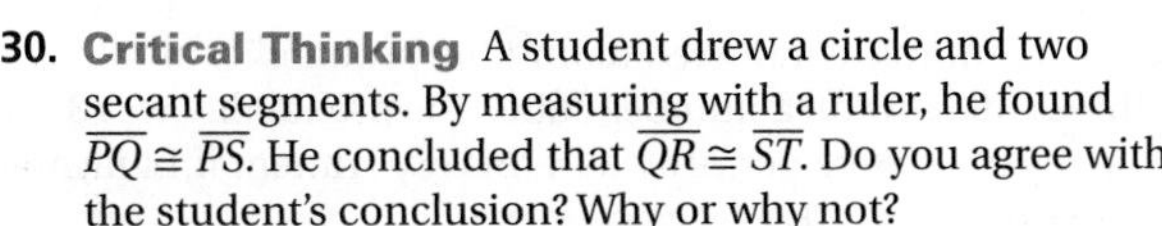

A
$AC \cdot BC = DC^2$, so
$10(4) = x^2$. $x^2 = 40$,
and $x = 2\sqrt{10}$.

B
$AB \cdot BC = DC^2$, so
$6(4) = x^2$. $x^2 = 24$,
and $x = 2\sqrt{6}$.

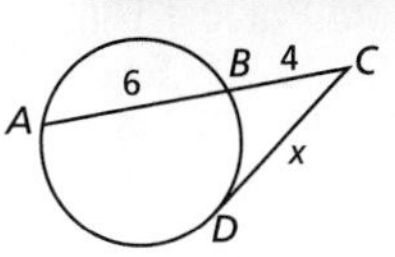

27. Solution B is incorrect. The first step should be $AC \cdot BC = DC^2$, not $AB \cdot BC = DC^2$.

28. Prove Theorem 11-6-1.
Given: Chords $\overline{AB}$ and $\overline{CD}$ intersect at point E.
Prove: $AE \cdot EB = CE \cdot ED$
Plan: Draw auxiliary line segments $\overline{AC}$ and $\overline{BD}$. Show that $\triangle ECA \sim \triangle EBD$. Then write a proportion comparing the lengths of corresponding sides.

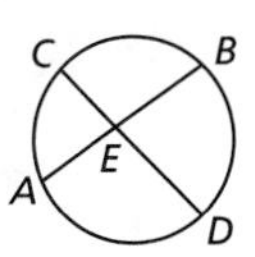

29. Prove Theorem 11-6-3.
Given: Secant segment $\overline{AC}$, tangent segment $\overline{DC}$
Prove: $AC \cdot BC = DC^2$

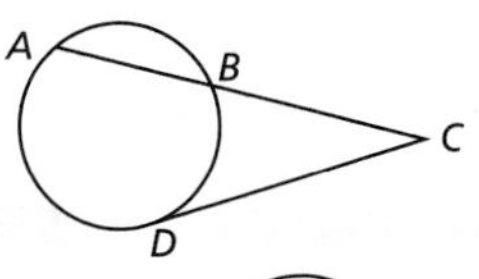

30. **Critical Thinking** A student drew a circle and two secant segments. By measuring with a ruler, he found $\overline{PQ} \cong \overline{PS}$. He concluded that $\overline{QR} \cong \overline{ST}$. Do you agree with the student's conclusion? Why or why not?

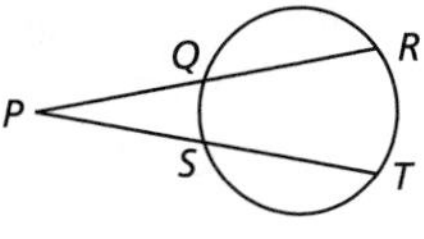

30. Yes; $PR \cdot PQ = PT \cdot PS$, and it is given that $PQ = PS$, so $PR = PT$. Subtracting the $\cong$ segs. from each of these shows that $\overline{QR} \cong \overline{ST}$.

31. **Write About It** The radius of $\odot A$ is 4. $CD = 4$, and $\overline{CB}$ is a tangent segment. Describe two different methods you can use to find BC.

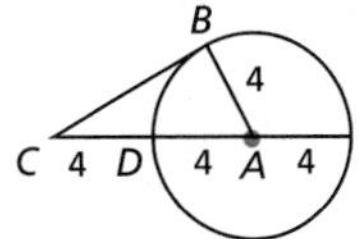

MULTI-STEP TEST PREP

32. This problem will prepare you for the Multi-Step Test Prep on page 806.
Some Native American designs are based on eight points that are placed around the circumference of a circle. In $\odot O$, $BE = 3$ cm. $AE = 5.2$ cm, and $EC = 4$ cm.
a. Find DE to the nearest tenth. **6.9 cm**
b. What is the diameter of the circle to the nearest tenth? **9.9 cm**
c. What is the length of $\overline{OE}$ to the nearest hundredth? **1.97 cm**

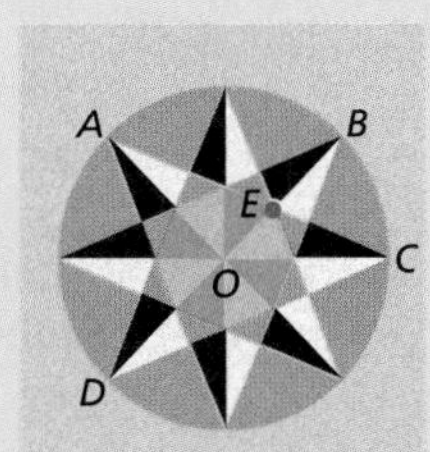

COMMON ERROR ALERT

Students might assume the diagram in **Exercises 22–23** is drawn to scale. Remind students not to assume that a diagram is drawn to scale based on its appearance. If they are confused by the absence of a right angle symbol, remind them that a line that bisects a chord and passes through the center of a circle is perpendicular to the chord.

Teaching Tip **Science Link** In **Exercises 5, 15,** and **26** show examples of how constructing a perpendicular bisector to a chord of a partial circle can be useful in engineering, geology, and meteorology. It may also be applied in other areas such as chemistry and physics.

MULTI-STEP TEST PREP **Exercise 32** involves using segment relationships in circles to find the measures of segments on lines that intersect circles. This exercise prepares students for the Multi-Step Test Prep on page 806.

Answers

28. 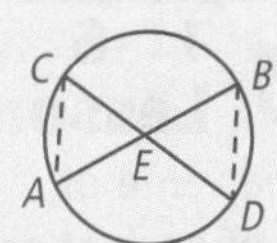

Since 2 pts. determine a line, draw $\overline{AC}$ and $\overline{BD}$. $\angle ACD \cong \angle DBA$ because they intercept the same arc. $\angle CEA \cong \angle BED$ by the Vert. ∠s Thm. Therefore $\triangle ECA \sim \triangle EBD$ by the AA ~ Post. Corr. sides are proportional, so $\frac{AE}{ED} = \frac{CE}{EB}$. By the Cross Products Prop. $AE \cdot EB = CE \cdot ED$.

29. 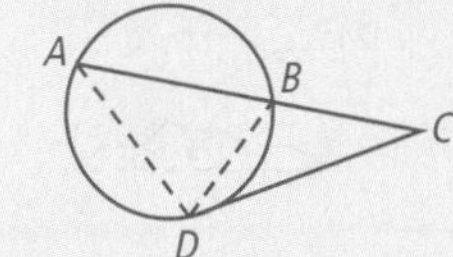

Since 2 pts. determine a line, draw $\overline{AD}$ and $\overline{BD}$. $m\angle CAD = \frac{1}{2}m\overset{\frown}{BD}$ by the Inscribed ∠ Thm. $m\angle BDC = \frac{1}{2}m\overset{\frown}{BD}$ by Thm. 11-5-1. Thus $\angle CAD \cong \angle BDC$. Also $\angle C \cong \angle C$ by the Reflex. Prop. of $\cong$. Therefore $\triangle CAD \sim \triangle CDB$ by the AA ~ Post. Corr. sides are proportional, so $\frac{AC}{DC} = \frac{DC}{BC}$. By the Cross Products Prop. $AC \cdot BC = DC^2$.

31. See p. A29.

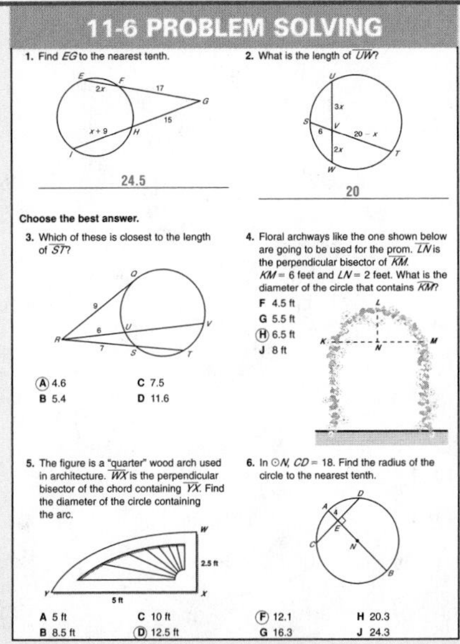

11-6 PROBLEM SOLVING

1. Find EG to the nearest tenth. **24.5**
2. What is the length of $\overline{UW}$? **20**

Choose the best answer.

3. Which of these is closest to the length of $\overline{ST}$?
(A) 4.6 C 7.5
B 5.4 D 11.6

4. Floral archways like the one shown below are going to be used for the prom. $\overline{LN}$ is the perpendicular bisector of $\overline{KM}$. $KM = 6$ feet and $LN = 2$ feet. What is the diameter of the circle that contains $\overset{\frown}{KM}$?
F 4.5 ft
G 5.5 ft
(H) 6.5 ft
J 8 ft

5. The figure is a "quarter" wood arch used in architecture. $\overline{WX}$ is the perpendicular bisector of the chord containing $\overline{YX}$. Find the diameter of the circle containing the arc.
A 5 ft C 10 ft
B 8.5 ft (D) 12.5 ft

6. In $\odot N$, $CD = 18$. Find the radius of the circle to the nearest tenth.
(F) 12.1 H 20.3
G 16.3 J 24.3

11-6 CHALLENGE

For an observer at a point O above Earth, the horizon is the place where Earth appears to "meet the sky." The higher above Earth's surface the observer is, the farther away the horizon appears to be. It may surprise you to learn that you can calculate this distance to the horizon by applying your knowledge of tangents and secants.

Refer to the diagram of Earth at right.

1. Name the segment that represents each measure.
a. the diameter of Earth **$\overline{RS}$**
b. the observer's altitude above Earth's surface **$\overline{OS}$**
c. the distance the observer can see to the horizon **$\overline{OH}$**

2. Justify the following equation: $(OH)^2 = OR \cdot OS$
$\overline{OH}$ is a tangent segment of circle C, $\overline{OR}$ is a secant segment, and $\overline{OS}$ is its external secant segment. So $(OH)^2 = OR \cdot OS$.

When the observer's altitude above Earth's surface is small relative to the diameter of Earth, you can replace OR with RS in the equation from Exercise 2. Then, since the diameter of Earth is approximately 7920 miles, you obtain the formula for OH shown at right. In this formula, the unit for both OH and OS is miles.

$$(OH)^2 = OR \cdot OS$$
$$(OH)^2 \approx RS \cdot OS$$
$$(OH)^2 \approx 7920 \cdot OS$$
$$OH \approx \sqrt{7920 \cdot OS}$$

Use the formula above to find the distance to the horizon for each altitude. Assume that it is a clear day and that the view is not obstructed. Round answers to the nearest tenth of a mile.

3. 2.5 miles **140.7 mi**
4. 30,000 feet **212.1 mi**

5. Rewrite the formula above so that you can input OS as a number of feet and find the distance to the horizon in *miles*.
$\left(\textit{Hint: } OH \text{ miles} = \sqrt{7920 \text{ miles} \cdot \frac{1 \text{ mile}}{? \text{ feet}} \cdot OS \text{ feet}}\right)$ **$OH \approx \sqrt{1.5 \cdot OS}$**

Use your formula from Exercise 5 to find the distance to the horizon for each altitude. Assume that it is a clear day and that the view is not obstructed. Round answers to the nearest tenth of a mile.

6. 10 feet **3.9 mi**
7. 200 feet **17.3 mi**

Find the altitude above Earth's surface that an observer must attain in order to see the given distance to the horizon. Round answers to the nearest tenth.

8. 1 mile **0.7 ft, or about 8 in.**
9. 300 miles **11.4 mi**

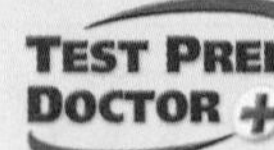

TEST PREP DOCTOR Students who answered **A** for **Exercise 33** used the product of the exterior secant segment and the chord $\overline{SR}$ instead of the segment $\overline{SP}$. Remind them that it may be helpful to write down the length of the entire secant segment and to lightly mark over the chord length.

Journal

Have students describe and use colored pencils to make sketches that will help them remember when each theorem should be used.

ALTERNATIVE ASSESSMENT

Have students draw an example of each theorem in the lesson. Then have them measure each segment length and verify their answers using the Chord-Chord, Secant-Secant, or Secant-Tangent Product Theorems.

Power Presentations with PowerPoint®

11-6 Lesson Quiz

1. Find the value of d and the length of each chord. $d = 9$; $ZV = 17$; $WY = 18$

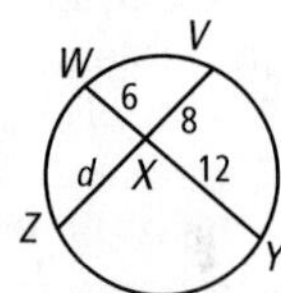

2. Find the diagonal of the plate. $8\frac{1}{8}$ in.

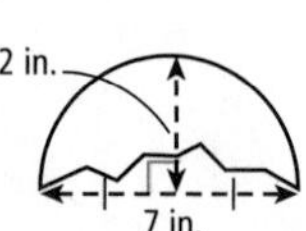

3. Find the value of x and the length of each secant segment. $x = 10$; $QP = 8$; $QR = 12$

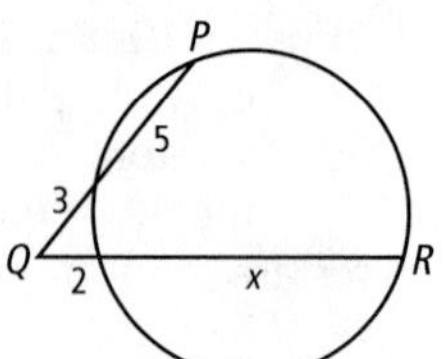

4. Find the value of a. 8

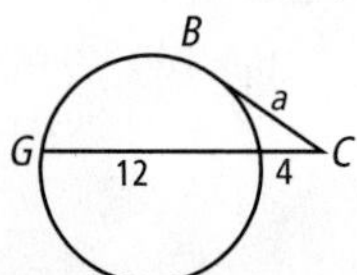

Also available on transparency

TEST PREP

33. Which of these is closest to the length of tangent $\overline{PQ}$?
Ⓐ 6.9 Ⓑ 9.2 Ⓒ 9.9 Ⓓ 10.6

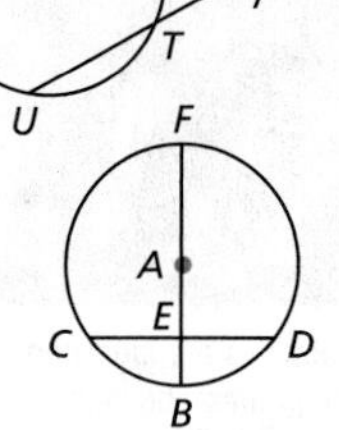

34. What is the length of $\overline{UT}$?
Ⓕ 5 Ⓖ 7 Ⓗ 12 Ⓙ 14

35. **Short Response** In ⊙A, $\overline{AB}$ is the perpendicular bisector of $\overline{CD}$. $CD = 12$, and $EB = 3$. Find the radius of ⊙A. Explain your steps.

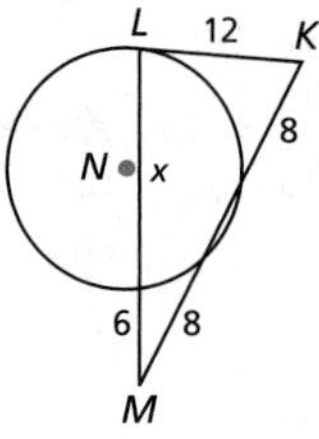

35. $CE = ED = 6$ and by the Chord-Chord Product Thm., $6 \cdot 6 = 3 \cdot EF$. So $EF = 12$, $FB = 15$, and the radius AB must be 7.5.

CHALLENGE AND EXTEND

36. **Algebra** $\overline{KL}$ is a tangent segment of ⊙N.
a. Find the value of x. 18
b. Classify $\triangle KLM$ by its angle measures. Explain. acute

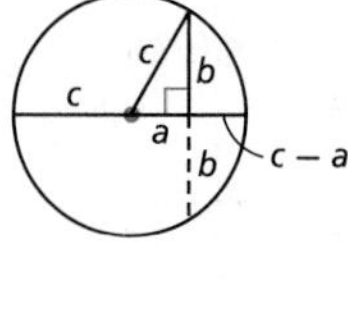

37. $\overline{PQ}$ is a tangent segment of a circle with radius 4 in. Q lies on the circle, and $PQ = 6$ in. Find the distance from P to the circle. Round to the nearest tenth of an inch. 3.2 in.

38. The circle in the diagram has radius c. Use this diagram and the Chord-Chord Product Theorem to prove the Pythagorean Theorem.

38. By the Chord-Chord Product Thm., $(c + a)(c - a) = b \cdot b$, so $c^2 - a^2 = b^2$ or $a^2 + b^2 = c^2$.

39. Find the value of y to the nearest hundredth. 7.44

SPIRAL REVIEW

40. An experiment was conducted to find the probability of rolling two threes in a row on a number cube. The probability was 3.5%. How many trials were performed in this experiment if 14 favorable outcomes occurred? *(Previous course)* 400

41. Two coins were flipped together 50 times. In 36 of the flips, at least one coin landed heads up. Based on this experiment, what is the experimental probability that at least one coin will land heads up when two coins are flipped? *(Previous course)* 72%

Name each of the following. *(Lesson 1-1)*

42. two rays that do not intersect $\overrightarrow{BA}$ and $\overrightarrow{CD}$
43. the intersection of $\overrightarrow{AC}$ and $\overrightarrow{CD}$ $\overrightarrow{CD}$
44. the intersection of $\overrightarrow{CA}$ and $\overrightarrow{BD}$ $\overline{BC}$

Find each measure. Give your answer in terms of π and rounded to the nearest hundredth. *(Lesson 11-3)*

45. area of the sector XZW
46. arc length of $\widehat{XW}$
47. $m\angle YZX$ if the area of the sector YZW is 40π ft² 45°

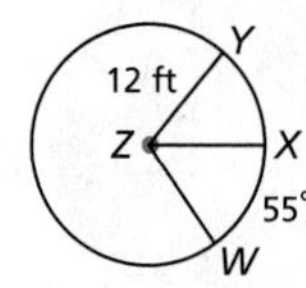

45. 22π ft²; 69.12 ft²

46. $3\frac{2}{3}\pi$ ft; 11.52 ft

11-7 Circles in the Coordinate Plane

Objectives
Write equations and graph circles in the coordinate plane.

Use the equation and graph of a circle to solve problems.

Who uses this?
Meteorologists use circles and coordinates to plan the location of weather stations. (See Example 3.)

CHANGING WEATHER PATTERNS

The equation of a circle is based on the Distance Formula and the fact that all points on a circle are equidistant from the center.

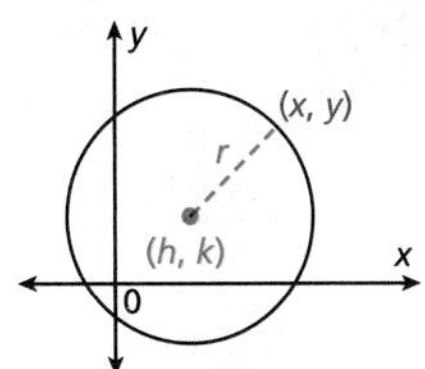

$d = \sqrt{(x_2 - x_1)^2 + (y_2 - y_1)^2}$ *Distance Formula*

$r = \sqrt{(x - h)^2 + (y - k)^2}$ *Substitute the given values.*

$r^2 = (x - h)^2 + (y - k)^2$ *Square both sides.*

Theorem 11-7-1 Equation of a Circle

The equation of a circle with center (h, k) and radius r is $(x - h)^2 + (y - k)^2 = r^2$.

EXAMPLE 1 Writing the Equation of a Circle

Write the equation of each circle.

A $\odot A$ with center $A(4, -2)$ and radius 3

$(x - h)^2 + (y - k)^2 = r^2$ *Equation of a circle*

$(x - 4)^2 + (y - (-2))^2 = 3^2$ *Substitute 4 for h, −2 for k, and 3 for r.*

$(x - 4)^2 + (y + 2)^2 = 9$ *Simplify.*

B $\odot B$ that passes through $(-2, 6)$ and has center $B(-6, 3)$

$r = \sqrt{(-2 - (-6))^2 + (6 - 3)^2}$ *Distance Formula*

$= \sqrt{25} = 5$ *Simplify.*

$(x - (-6))^2 + (y - 3)^2 = 5^2$ *Substitute −6 for h, 3 for k, and 5 for r.*

$(x + 6)^2 + (y - 3)^2 = 25$ *Simplify.*

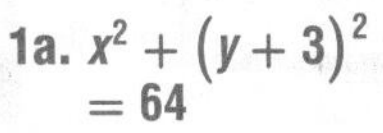

CHECK IT OUT! Write the equation of each circle.

1a. $\odot P$ with center $P(0, -3)$ and radius 8

1b. $\odot Q$ that passes through $(2, 3)$ and has center $Q(2, -1)$

1a. $x^2 + (y + 3)^2 = 64$

1b. $(x - 2)^2 + (y + 1)^2 = 16$

11-7 Organizer

Pacing: Traditional 1 day
Block $\frac{1}{2}$ day

Objectives: Write equations and graph circles in the coordinate plane.

Use the equation and graph of a circle to solve problems.

Online Edition
Tutorial Videos, Interactivity, TechKeys

Power Presentations with PowerPoint®

Warm Up

Use the Distance Formula to find the distance, to the nearest tenth, between each pair of points.

1. $A(6, 2)$ and $D(-3, -2)$ 9.8
2. $C(4, 5)$ and $D(0, 2)$ 5
3. $V(8, 1)$ and $W(3, 6)$ 7.1
4. Fill in the table of values for the equation $y = x - 14$.

x	−1	0	1	2
y	−15	−14	−13	−12

Also available on transparency

Q: What is a polar bear?

A: A rectangular bear after a coordinate conversion!

1 Introduce

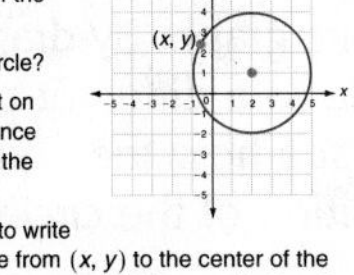

EXPLORATION

11-7 Circles in the Coordinate Plane

Recall that all the points on a circle are equidistant from the center of the circle. You can use this fact to develop the equation of a circle.

1. What are the coordinates of the center of the circle?
2. What is the radius of the circle?
3. Suppose (x, y) is any point on the circle. What is the distance from (x, y) to the center of the circle?
4. Use the Distance Formula to write an equation for the distance from (x, y) to the center of the circle. Replace the first two squares with the coordinates of the center of the circle and the last square with the radius of the circle.
$\sqrt{(x - \blacksquare)^2 + (y - \blacksquare)^2} = \blacksquare$
5. Square both sides of the equation in Step 4 to write an equation for the circle.

THINK AND DISCUSS

6. Explain how you could use Steps 1–4 to write an equation for ⊙P.

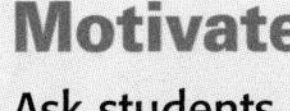

Motivate

Ask students if they are familiar with circle magnets. Bring one to class, show it to students, and trace around the magnet to draw the circle on a piece of grid paper. Tell students that designers and printers can use this technique for spacing and aligning items to be printed on circle magnets. Explain that they will learn how to use circles in the coordinate plane in this lesson.

Explorations and answers are provided in *Alternate Openers: Explorations Transparencies.*

State Resources

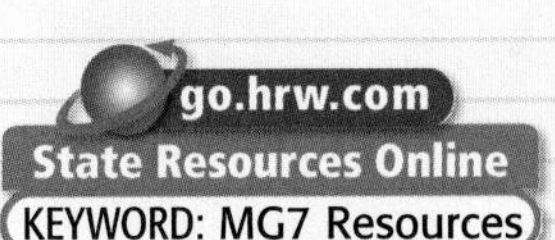

If you are given the equation of a circle, you can graph the circle by making a table or by identifying its center and radius.

EXAMPLE 2 Graphing a Circle

Algebra

Graph each equation.

A $x^2 + y^2 = 25$

Step 1 Make a table of values.

Since the radius is $\sqrt{25}$, or 5, use ± 5 and the values between for x-values.

x	−5	−4	−3	0	3	4	5
y	0	±3	±4	±5	±4	±3	0

Step 2 Plot the points and connect them to form a circle.

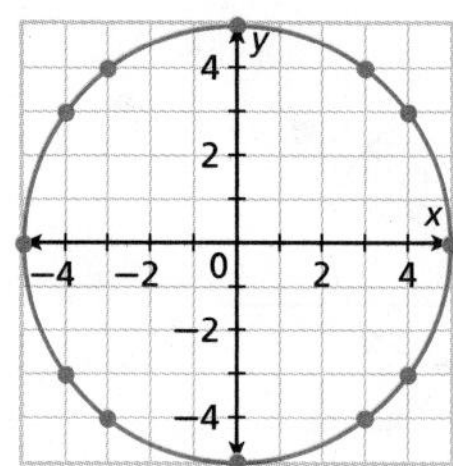

Helpful Hint

Always compare the equation to the form $(x - h)^2 + (y - k)^2 = r^2$.

B $(x + 1)^2 + (y - 2)^2 = 9$

The equation of the given circle can be written as $(x - (-1))^2 + (y - 2)^2 = 3^2$.

So $h = -1$, $k = 2$, and $r = 3$.

The center is $(-1, 2)$, and the radius is 3. Plot the point $(-1, 2)$. Then graph a circle having this center and radius 3.

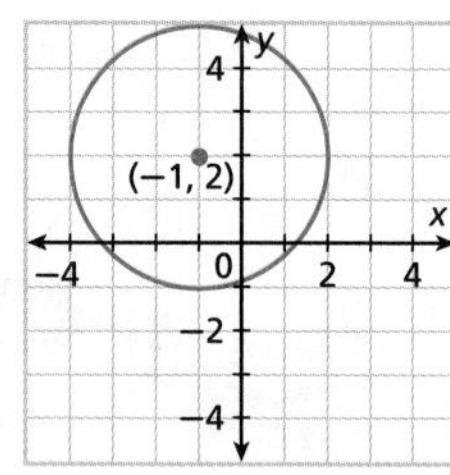

Graph each equation.

2a. $x^2 + y^2 = 9$

2b. $(x - 3)^2 + (y + 2)^2 = 4$

Student to Student

Graphing Circles

Christina Avila
Crockett High School

I found a way to use my calculator to graph circles. You first need to write the circle's equation in y = form.

For example, to graph $x^2 + y^2 = 16$, first solve for y.

$$y^2 = 16 - x^2$$

$$y = \pm\sqrt{16 - x^2}$$

Now enter and graph the two equations

$$y_1 = \sqrt{16 - x^2} \text{ and } y_2 = -\sqrt{16 - x^2}.$$

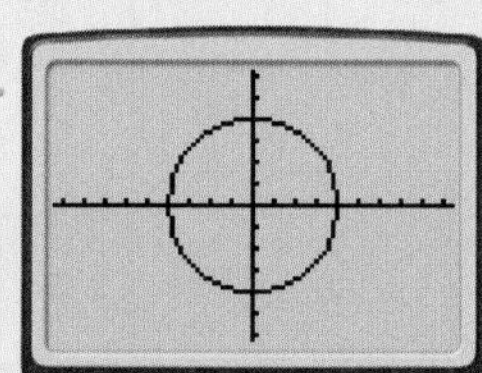

Power Presentations with PowerPoint®

Additional Examples

Example 1

Write the equation of each circle.

A. ⊙J with center $J(2, 2)$ and radius 4

$(x - 2)^2 + (y - 2)^2 = 16$

B. ⊙K that passes through $J(6, 4)$ and has center $K(1, -8)$

$(x - 1)^2 + (y + 8)^2 = 169$

Example 2

A. $x^2 + y^2 = 16$

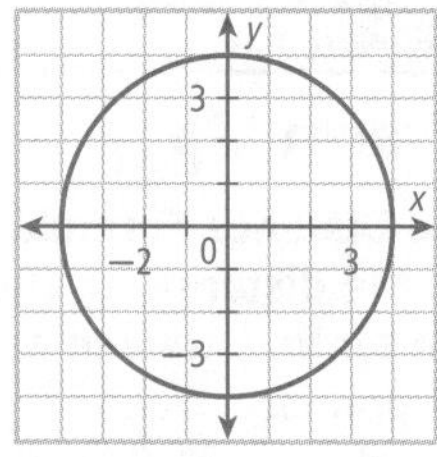

B. $(x - 3)^2 + (y + 4)^2 = 9$

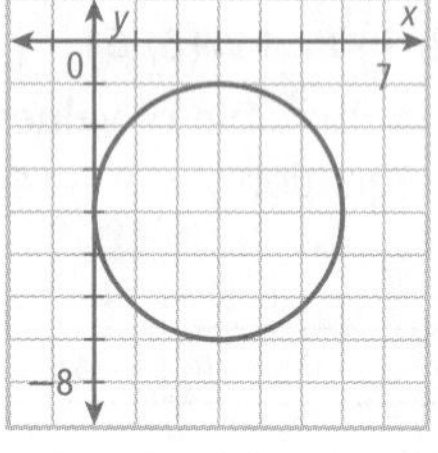

INTERVENTION

Questioning Strategies

EXAMPLE 1

- Can you write the equation for a circle if the given point does not lie on the circle? Explain.

EXAMPLE 2

- How do the different values of h, k, and r change the graphs of the circles?

Answers

2a–2b. See p. A29.

2 Teach

Guided Instruction

Review with students the coordinate plane, the Distance Formula, and graphing points. Discuss the equation of a circle, emphasizing the meaning of h, k, and r. Show students how to graph circles by plotting points and by using the equation of a circle.

Technology Point out to students that the graph of a circle on a graphing calculator will look like an ellipse if the window setting is not a square window.

Reaching All Learners

Through Multiple Representations

Use geometry software to show students the relationship between the equation of a circle and its graph. By dragging the center of the circle to a different position, students can see how the equation changes as the position of the circle changes.

EXAMPLE 3 Meteorology Application

Meteorologists are planning the location of a new weather station to cover Osceola, Waco, and Ireland, Texas. To optimize radar coverage, the station must be equidistant from the three cities which are located on a coordinate plane at $A(2, 5)$, $B(3, -2)$, and $C(-5, -2)$.

a. What are the coordinates where the station should be built?

b. If each unit of the coordinate plane represents 8.5 miles, what is the diameter of the region covered by the radar?

Step 1 Plot the three given points.

Step 2 Connect A, B, and C to form a triangle.

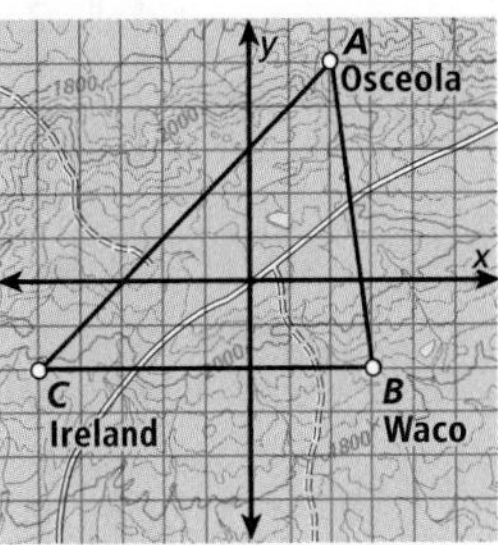

Step 3 Find a point that is equidistant from the three points by constructing the perpendicular bisectors of two of the sides of $\triangle ABC$.

The perpendicular bisectors of the sides of $\triangle ABC$ intersect at a point that is equidistant from A, B, and C.

The intersection of the perpendicular bisectors is $P(-1, 1)$. P is the center of the circle that passes through A, B, and C.

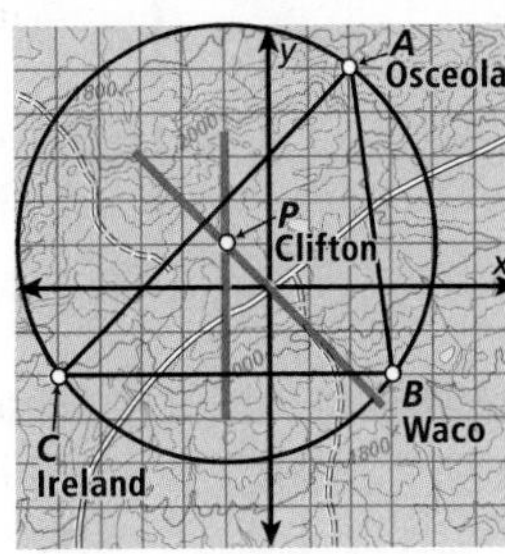

The weather station should be built at $P(-1, 1)$, Clifton, Texas.

There are approximately 10 units across the circle. So the diameter of the region covered by the radar is approximately 85 miles.

Remember!

The perpendicular bisectors of a triangle are concurrent at a point equidistant from each vertex.

CHECK IT OUT! 3. **What if...?** Suppose the coordinates of the three cities in Example 3 are $D(6, 2)$, $E(5, -5)$, and $F(-2, -4)$. What would be the location of the weather station? $(2, -1)$

THINK AND DISCUSS

1. What is the equation of a circle with radius r whose center is at the origin?
2. A circle has a diameter with endpoints $(1, 4)$ and $(-3, 4)$. Explain how you can find the equation of the circle.
3. Can a circle have a radius of -6? Justify your answer.

4. **GET ORGANIZED** Copy and complete the graphic organizer. First select values for a center and radius. Then use the center and radius you wrote to fill in the other circles. Write the corresponding equation and draw the corresponding graph.

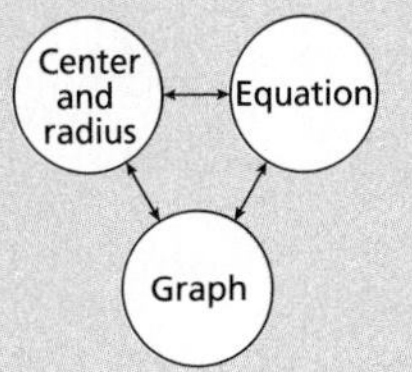

COMMON ERROR ALERT

When students are writing the equation of a circle or when given the equation of a circle, they often write the incorrect signs for h and k. Point out that the standard equation of a circle includes subtraction and that this may mean taking the opposite of one of the values of h and k. For example, if $(x - 7)^2 + (y + 3)^2 = 36$, $h = 7$, and $k = -3$. Have students practice writing equations with centers located in each of the four quadrants.

Power Presentations with PowerPoint®

Additional Examples

Example 3

An amateur radio operator wants to build a radio antenna near his home without using his house as a bracing point. He uses three poles to brace the antenna. The poles are to be inserted in the ground at three points equidistant from the antenna located at $J(4, 4)$, $K(-3, -1)$, and $L(2, -8)$. What are the coordinates of the base of the antenna? $(3, -2)$

INTERVENTION

Questioning Strategies

EXAMPLE 3

- How could you use the Distance Formula to make sure that the center of the circle is equidistant from the three points?

3 Close

Summarize

Review with students the equation of a circle with center (h, k) and radius r. Show them how to graph a circle from its equation. Then practice changing an equation of a circle into the form $y_1 = \sqrt{\ }$ and $y_2 = \sqrt{\ }$. Demonstrate for students how to find the coordinates of the center of a circle when they are given three points on the circle.

ONGOING ASSESSMENT and INTERVENTION

***Diagnose* Before the Lesson**
11-7 Warm Up, TE p. 799

***Monitor* During the Lesson**
Check It Out! Exercises, SE pp. 799–801
Questioning Strategies, TE pp. 800–801

***Assess* After the Lesson**
11-7 Lesson Quiz, TE p. 805
Alternative Assessment, TE p. 805

Answers to *Think and Discuss*

Possible answers:

1. $x^2 + y^2 = r^2$
2. First find the center by finding the mdpt. of the diam. By the Mdpt. Formula, the center of the ⊙ is $(-1, 4)$. The radius is half the length of the diam., so $r = 2$. The eqn. is $(x + 1)^2 + (y - 4)^2 = 4$.
3. No; a radius represents length, and length cannot be neg.
4. See p. A9.

Assignment Guide

Assign *Guided Practice* exercises as necessary.

If you finished Examples 1–3
Basic 10–35, 37–40, 42–44, 48–54
Average 10–45, 48–54
Advanced 10–54

Homework Quick Check

Quickly check key concepts.
Exercises: 11, 15, 18, 20, 24

Answers

5.
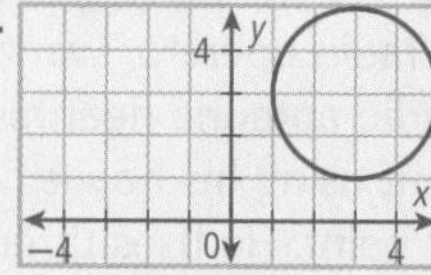

6.
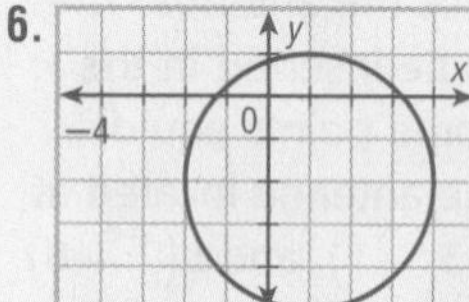

7.
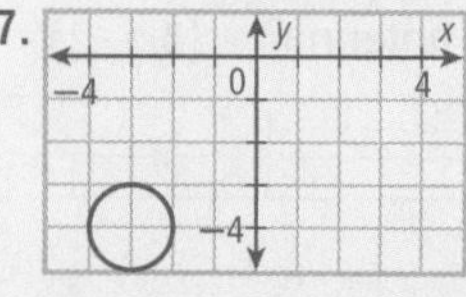

8.
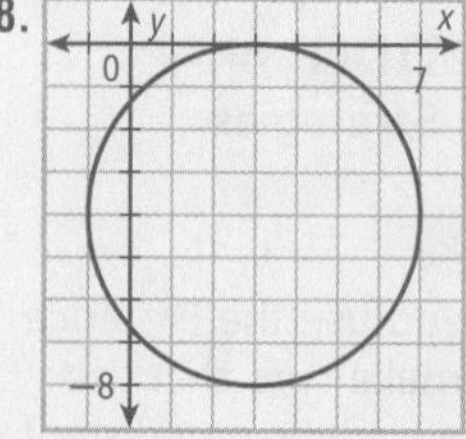

State Resources

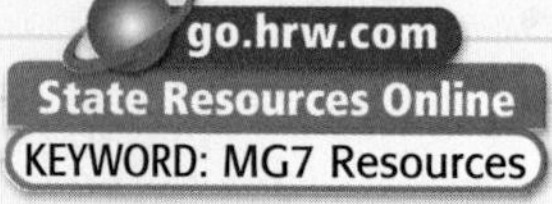

11-7 Exercises

go.hrw.com
Homework Help Online
KEYWORD: MG7 11-7
Parent Resources Online
KEYWORD: MG7 Parent

GUIDED PRACTICE

SEE EXAMPLE 1 p. 799

Write the equation of each circle.

1. $\odot A$ with center $A(3, -5)$ and radius 12 $(x - 3)^2 + (y + 5)^2 = 144$
2. $\odot B$ with center $B(-4, 0)$ and radius 7 $(x + 4)^2 + y^2 = 49$
3. $\odot M$ that passes through $(2, 0)$ and that has center $M(4, 0)$ $(x - 4)^2 + y^2 = 4$
4. $\odot N$ that passes through $(2, -2)$ and that has center $N(-1, 2)$ $(x + 1)^2 + (y - 2)^2 = 25$

SEE EXAMPLE 2 p. 800

Multi-Step Graph each equation.

5. $(x - 3)^2 + (y - 3)^2 = 4$
6. $(x - 1)^2 + (y + 2)^2 = 9$
7. $(x + 3)^2 + (y + 4)^2 = 1$
8. $(x - 3)^2 + (y + 4)^2 = 16$

SEE EXAMPLE 3 p. 801

9. **Communications** A radio antenna tower is kept perpendicular to the ground by three wires of equal length. The wires touch the ground at three points on a circle whose center is at the base of the tower. The wires touch the ground at $A(2, 6)$, $B(-2, -2)$, and $C(-5, 7)$.
   a. What are the coordinates of the base of the tower? $(-2, 3)$
   b. Each unit of the coordinate plane represents 1 ft. What is the diameter of the circle? 10 ft

PRACTICE AND PROBLEM SOLVING

Independent Practice	
For Exercises	See Example
10–13	1
14–17	2
18	3

Extra Practice
Skills Practice p. S25
Application Practice p. S38

Write the equation of each circle.

10. $\odot R$ with center $R(-12, -10)$ and radius 8 $(x + 12)^2 + (y + 10)^2 = 64$
11. $\odot S$ with center $S(1.5, -2.5)$ and radius $\sqrt{3}$ $(x - 1.5)^2 + (y + 2.5)^2 = 3$
12. $\odot C$ that passes through $(2, 2)$ and that has center $C(1, 1)$ $(x - 1)^2 + (y - 1)^2 = 2$
13. $\odot D$ that passes through $(-5, 1)$ and that has center $D(1, -2)$ $(x - 1)^2 + (y + 2)^2 = 45$

Multi-Step Graph each equation.

14. $x^2 + (y - 2)^2 = 9$
15. $(x + 1)^2 - y^2 = 16$
16. $x^2 + y^2 = 100$
17. $x^2 + (y + 2)^2 = 4$

18. **Anthropology** Hundreds of stone circles can be found along the Gambia River in western Africa. The stones are believed to be over 1000 years old. In one of the circles at Ker Batch, three stones have approximate coordinates of $A(3, 1)$, $B(4, -2)$, and $C(-6, -2)$. $(-1, -2)$
   a. What are the coordinates of the center of the stone circle?
   b. Each unit of the coordinate plane represents 1 ft. What is the diameter of the stone circle? 10 ft

11-7 PRACTICE A

1. Write the equation of a circle with center (h, k) and radius r. $(x - h)^2 + (y - k)^2 = r^2$

Write the equation of each circle.

2. $\odot A$ centered at the origin with radius 6 $x^2 + y^2 = 36$
3. $\odot D$ with center $D(3, 3)$ and radius 2 $(x - 3)^2 + (y - 3)^2 = 4$
4. $\odot L$ with center $L(-3, -3)$ and radius 1 $(x + 3)^2 + (y + 3)^2 = 1$
5. $\odot M$ with center $M(0, -2)$ and radius 9 $x^2 + (y + 2)^2 = 81$
6. $\odot Q$ with center $Q(7, 0)$ and radius 3 $(x - 7)^2 + y^2 = 9$

Complete Exercises 7 and 8 to write the equation of $\odot F$ with center $F(2, -1)$ that passes through (10, 5).

7. Use the distance formula with the two given points to find the radius of $\odot F$. 10
8. Write the equation of $\odot F$. $(x - 2)^2 + (y + 1)^2 = 100$

Graph each equation. First locate the center point, and use the radius to plot four points around the center that lie on the circle. Then draw a circle through the four points.

9. $x^2 + y^2 = 16$ (0, 0)
10. $x^2 + y^2 = 4$ (0, 0)

A county planning department is meeting to choose the location of a rural fire station. The fire station needs to be the same distance from each of the three towns it will serve. The towns are located at $A(-3, 2)$, $B(-3, -4)$, and $C(1, -4)$. Complete Exercises 11–13 in order to find the best location for the fire station.

11. Plot A, B, and C. Draw $\triangle ABC$.
12. Draw the perpendicular bisectors of $\overline{AB}$ and $\overline{BC}$.
13. The intersection point of the perpendicular bisectors is the same distance from the three points. So it is the center of a circle that intersects A, B, and C. Find the coordinates where the fire station should be built. $(-1, -1)$

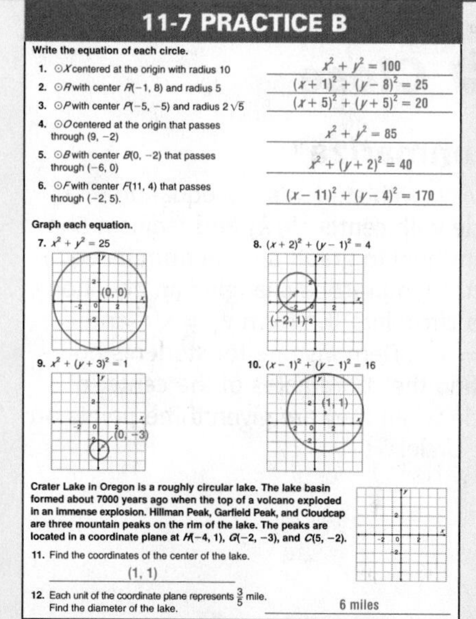

11-7 PRACTICE B

Write the equation of each circle.

1. $\odot X$ centered at the origin with radius 10 $x^2 + y^2 = 100$
2. $\odot R$ with center $R(-1, 8)$ and radius 5 $(x + 1)^2 + (y - 8)^2 = 25$
3. $\odot P$ with center $P(-5, -5)$ and radius $2\sqrt{5}$ $(x + 5)^2 + (y + 5)^2 = 20$
4. $\odot O$ centered at the origin that passes through $(9, -2)$ $x^2 + y^2 = 85$
5. $\odot B$ with center $B(0, -2)$ that passes through $(-6, 0)$ $x^2 + (y + 2)^2 = 40$
6. $\odot F$ with center $F(11, 4)$ that passes through $(-2, 5)$. $(x - 11)^2 + (y - 4)^2 = 170$

Graph each equation.

7. $x^2 + y^2 = 25$ (0, 0)
8. $(x + 2)^2 + (y - 1)^2 = 4$ (−2, 1)
9. $x^2 + (y + 3)^2 = 1$ (0, −3)
10. $(x - 1)^2 + (y - 1)^2 = 16$ (1, 1)

Crater Lake in Oregon is a roughly circular lake. The lake basin formed about 7000 years ago when the top of a volcano exploded in an immense explosion. Hillman Peak, Garfield Peak, and Cloudcap are three mountain peaks on the rim of the lake. The peaks are located in a coordinate plane at $H(-4, 1)$, $G(-2, -3)$, and $C(5, -2)$.

11. Find the coordinates of the center of the lake. (1, 1)
12. Each unit of the coordinate plane represents $\frac{3}{5}$ mile. Find the diameter of the lake. 6 miles

Algebra Write the equation of each circle.

19. 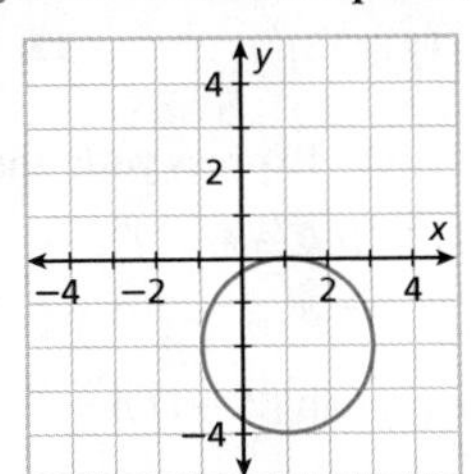 $(x-1)^2 + (y+2)^2 = 4$

20. 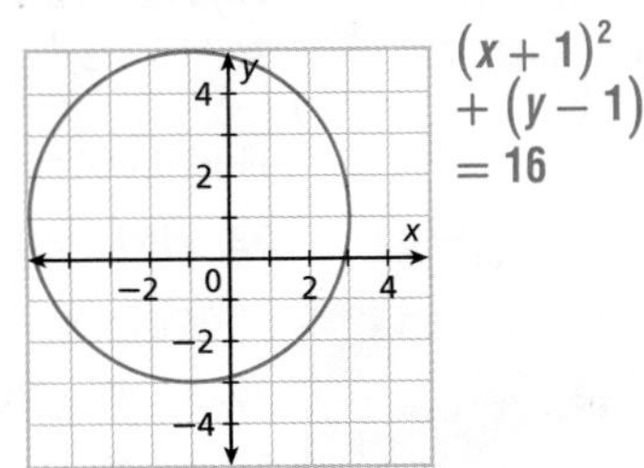 $(x+1)^2 + (y-1)^2 = 16$

21. **Entertainment** In 2004, the world's largest carousel was located at the House on the Rock, in Spring Green, Wisconsin. Suppose that the center of the carousel is at the origin and that one of the animals on the circumference of the carousel has coordinates $(24, 32)$.
   a. If one unit of the coordinate plane equals 1 ft, what is the diameter of the carousel? **80 ft**
   b. As the carousel turns, the animals follow a circular path. Write the equation of this circle. $x^2 + y^2 = 1600$

Determine whether each statement is true or false. If false, explain why.

22. The circle $x^2 + y^2 = 7$ has radius 7. **F; the radius is $\sqrt{7}$.**
23. The circle $(x-2)^2 + (y+3)^2 = 9$ passes through the point $(-1, -3)$. **T**
24. The center of the circle $(x-6)^2 + (y+4)^2 = 1$ lies in the second quadrant.
25. The circle $(x+1)^2 + (y-4)^2 = 4$ intersects the y-axis. **T**
26. The equation of the circle centered at the origin with diameter 6 is $x^2 + y^2 = 36$.

24. F; the center is $(6, -4)$, which is in the fourth quadrant.

26. F; the eqn. is $x^2 + y^2 = 9$.

27a. Possible answer: 28 square units
b. $r = 3$; 28.3

27. **Estimation** You can use the graph of a circle to estimate its area.
   a. Estimate the area of the circle by counting the number of squares of the coordinate plane contained in its interior. Be sure to count partial squares.
   b. Find the radius of the circle. Then use the area formula to calculate the circle's area to the nearest tenth.
   c. Was your estimate in part **a** an overestimate or an underestimate? **Check students' work.**

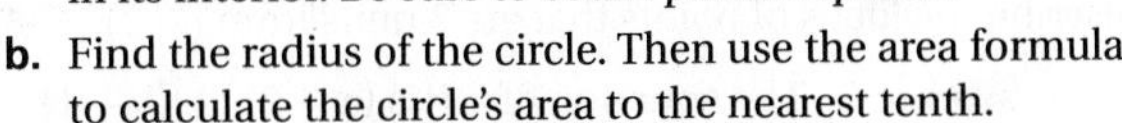

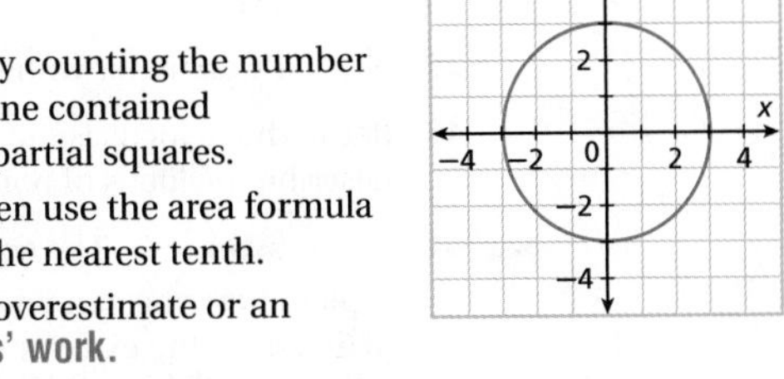

28. Consider the circle whose equation is $(x-4)^2 + (y+6)^2 = 25$. Write, in point-slope form, the equation of the line tangent to the circle at $(1, -10)$. $y + 10 = -\frac{3}{4}(x-1)$

MULTI-STEP TEST PREP

29. This problem will prepare you for the Multi-Step Test Prep on page 806.
A *hogan* is a traditional Navajo home. An artist is using a coordinate plane to draw the symbol for a hogan. The symbol is based on eight equally spaced points placed around the circumference of a circle.

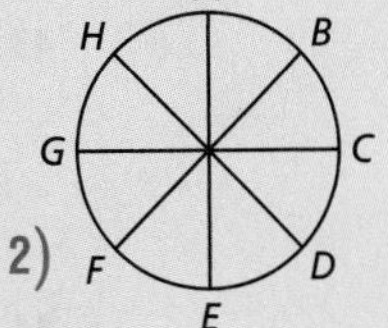

   a. She positions the symbol at $A(-3, 5)$ and $C(0, 2)$. What are the coordinates of E and G? **$E(-3, -1)$; $G(-6, 2)$**
   b. What is the length of a diameter of the symbol? **6**
   c. Use your answer from part **b** to write an equation of the circle. $(x+3)^2 + (y-2)^2 = 9$

COMMON ERROR ALERT

Students may forget to consider 0 as either h or k for the equation of a circle. In **Exercise 14**, remind students that x^2 is the same as $(x - 0)^2$.

Teaching Tip **Critical Thinking** Remind students that they used a similar method as the one stated in **Exercise 27** when they estimated the area of irregular shapes in Chapter 9.

MULTI-STEP TEST PREP **Exercise 29** involves using the coordinate plane to find coordinates of a circle and to write its equation. This exercise prepares students for the Multi-Step Test Prep on page 806.

Answers

14. 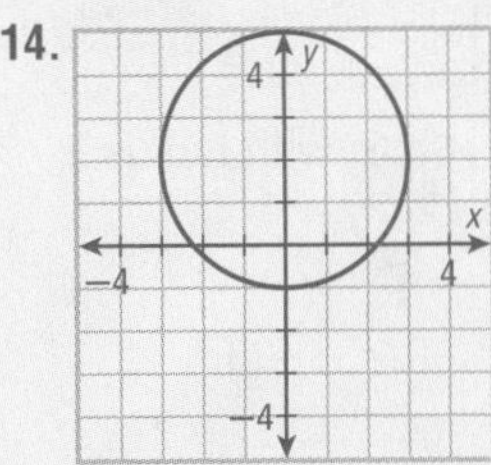

15. 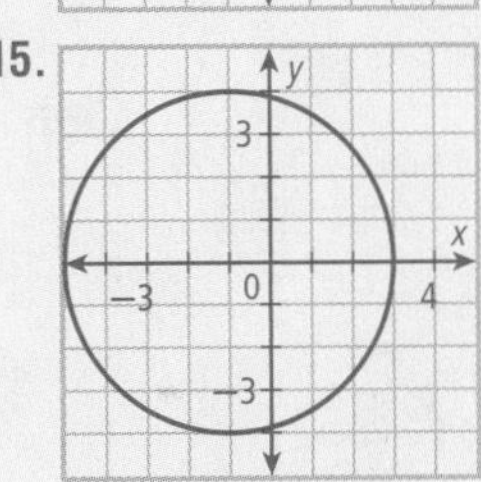

16. 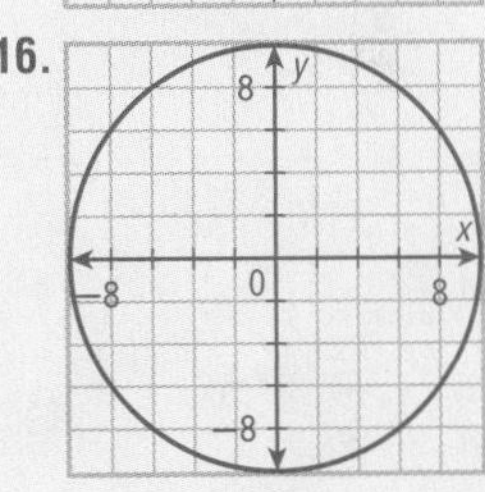

17. 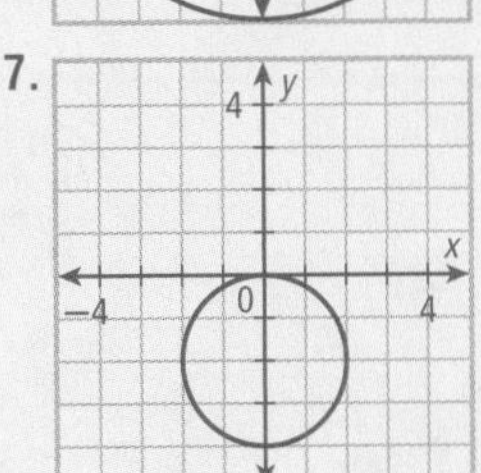

11-7 PRACTICE C

1. Points A, B, and C lie on the circumference of a circle. AB is twice the radius of the circle. Find $m\angle ACB$.
   90°
2. Points A, B, and C lie on the circumference of a circle. The center of the circle lies in the exterior of $\triangle ABC$. Classify $\triangle ABC$ by its angles.
   obtuse

Give answers in simplest radical form if necessary.

3. The points $X(3, 4)$ and $Y(9, 1)$ lie on the circumference of a circle. There is exactly 60° of arc between X and Y. Find the radius of the circle.
   $3\sqrt{5}$
4. Find the coordinates of all possible centers of the circle in Exercise 3.
   $(3.4, -2.7)$; $(8.6, 7.8)$
5. Find the intersection point(s) of the circle $(x+2)^2 + y^2 = 25$ and the line $2x + y = 3$.
   $\left(\frac{4+2\sqrt{19}}{5}, \frac{7-4\sqrt{19}}{5}\right), \left(\frac{4-2\sqrt{19}}{5}, \frac{7+4\sqrt{19}}{5}\right)$
6. Find the intersection point(s) of the circle $(x+2)^2 + y^2 = 25$ and the line $y = \frac{4}{3}x - \frac{17}{3}$.
   $(2, -3)$
7. Describe the relationship between the circle and the line in Exercise 6.
   The line is tangent to the circle at the point $(2, -3)$.
8. Find the intersection point(s) of the circle $(x+2)^2 + y^2 = 25$ and the circle $x^2 + y^2 = 9$.
   $(3, 0)$
9. Describe the relationship between the two circles in Exercise 8.
   The circles are internally tangent at the point $(3, 0)$.

TEST PREP DOCTOR If students have difficulty finding the radius of each equation in **Exercise 42**, suggest that they take the square root of the radius and then compare the value to k in the $(y - k)$ part of the circle equation. Point out to students that in order for the circle to intersect the x-axis, k must be greater than or equal to r. This will eliminate choices **A**, **B**, and **D**.

In **Exercise 43**, students who answered **F** forgot to square the radius. Students who answered **J** forgot to subtract h and k in the equation.

Answers

40.

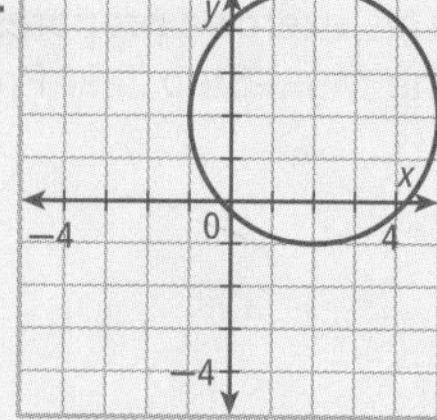

The locus is a ⊙ with radius 3 centred at (2, 2).

---

36. The graph is a single pt., (0, 0).

LINK Geology

The New Madrid earthquake of 1811 was one of the largest earthquakes known in American history. Large areas sank into the earth, new lakes were formed, forests were destroyed, and the course of the Mississippi River was changed.

The Granger Collection, New York

39. $(x - 1)^2 + (y + 2)^2 = 16$

Find the center and radius of each circle.

30. $(x - 2)^2 + (y + 3)^2 = 81$ **(2, −3); 9**
31. $x^2 + (y + 15)^2 = 25$ **(0, −15); 5**
32. $(x + 1)^2 + y^2 = 7$ **$(-1, 0); \sqrt{7}$**

Find the area and circumference of each circle. Express your answer in terms of π.

33. circle with equation $(x + 2)^2 + (y - 7)^2 = 9$ $A = 9\pi$; $C = 6\pi$

34. circle with equation $(x - 8)^2 + (y + 5)^2 = 7$ $A = 7\pi$; $C = 2\sqrt{7}\pi$

35. circle with center $(-1, 3)$ that passes through $(2, -1)$ $A = 25\pi$; $C = 10\pi$

36. Critical Thinking Describe the graph of the equation $x^2 + y^2 = r^2$ when $r = 0$.

37. Geology A seismograph measures ground motion during an earthquake. To find the epicenter of an earthquake, scientists take readings in three different locations. Then they draw a circle centered at each location. The radius of each circle is the distance the earthquake is from the seismograph. The intersection of the circles is the epicenter. Use the data below to find the epicenter of the New Madrid earthquake. **(−200, −100)**

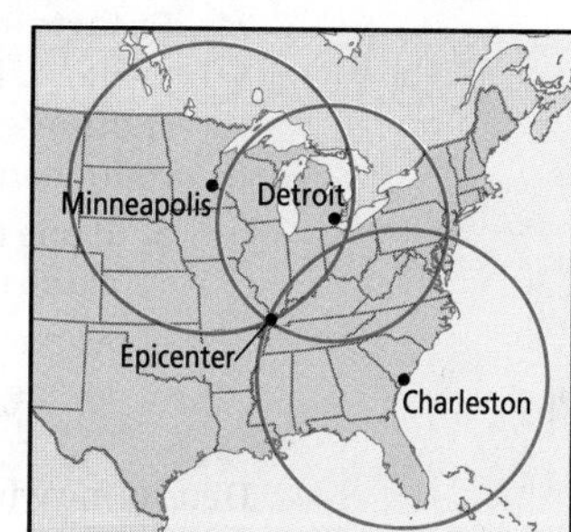

Seismograph	Location	Distance to Earthquake
A	(−200, 200)	300 mi
B	(400, −100)	600 mi
C	(100, −500)	500 mi

38. For what value(s) of the constant k is the circle $x^2 + (y - k)^2 = 25$ tangent to the x-axis? ± 5

39. ⊙A has a diameter with endpoints $(-3, -2)$ and $(5, -2)$. Write the equation of ⊙A.

40. Recall that a locus is the set of points that satisfy a given condition. Draw and describe the locus of points that are 3 units from (2, 2).

41. Write About It The equation of ⊙P is $(x - 2)^2 + (y - 1)^2 = 9$. Without graphing, explain how you can determine whether the point $(3, -1)$ lies on ⊙P, in the interior of ⊙P, or in the exterior of ⊙P.
The pt. does not lie on the ⊙ because it is not a solution to the eqn. $(x - 2)^2 + (y - 1)^2 = 9$. Since $(3 - 2)^2 + (-1 - 1)^2 < 9$, the pt. lies in the int. of the ⊙.

TEST PREP

42. Which of these circles intersects the x-axis?

Ⓐ $(x - 3)^2 + (y + 3)^2 = 4$
Ⓑ $(x + 1)^2 + (y - 4)^2 = 9$
Ⓒ $(x + 2)^2 + (y + 1)^2 = 1$
Ⓓ $(x + 1)^2 + (y + 4)^2 = 9$

43. What is the equation of a circle with center $(-3, 5)$ that passes through the point $(1, 5)$?

Ⓕ $(x + 3)^2 + (y - 5)^2 = 4$
Ⓖ $(x - 3)^2 + (y + 5)^2 = 4$
Ⓗ $(x + 3)^2 + (y - 5)^2 = 16$
Ⓙ $(x - 3)^2 + (y + 5)^2 = 16$

44. On a map of a park, statues are located at $(4, -2)$, $(-1, 3)$, and $(-5, -5)$. A circular path connects the three statues, and the circle has a fountain at its center. Find the coordinates of the fountain.

Ⓐ $(-1, -2)$ Ⓑ $(2, 1)$ Ⓒ $(-2, 1)$ Ⓓ $(1, -2)$

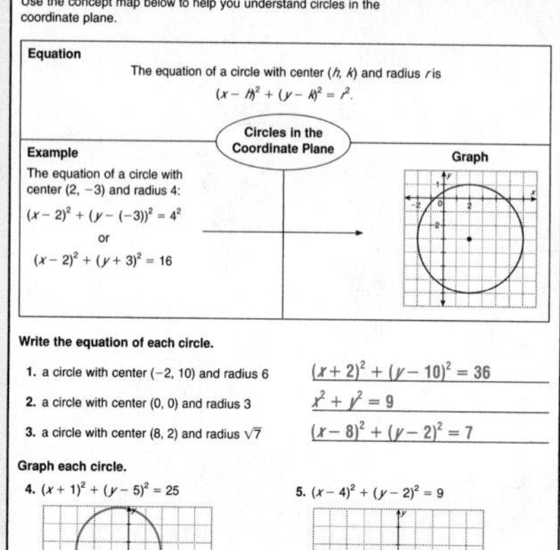

11-7 READING STRATEGIES

Use the concept map below to help you understand circles in the coordinate plane.

Equation
The equation of a circle with center (h, k) and radius r is $(x - h)^2 + (y - k)^2 = r^2$.

Circles in the Coordinate Plane

Example
The equation of a circle with center $(2, -3)$ and radius 4:
$(x - 2)^2 + (y - (-3))^2 = 4^2$
or
$(x - 2)^2 + (y + 3)^2 = 16$

Graph

Write the equation of each circle.

1. a circle with center $(-2, 10)$ and radius 6 $(x + 2)^2 + (y - 10)^2 = 36$
2. a circle with center $(0, 0)$ and radius 3 $x^2 + y^2 = 9$
3. a circle with center $(8, 2)$ and radius $\sqrt{7}$ $(x - 8)^2 + (y - 2)^2 = 7$

Graph each circle.

4. $(x + 1)^2 + (y - 5)^2 = 25$
5. $(x - 4)^2 + (y - 2)^2 = 9$

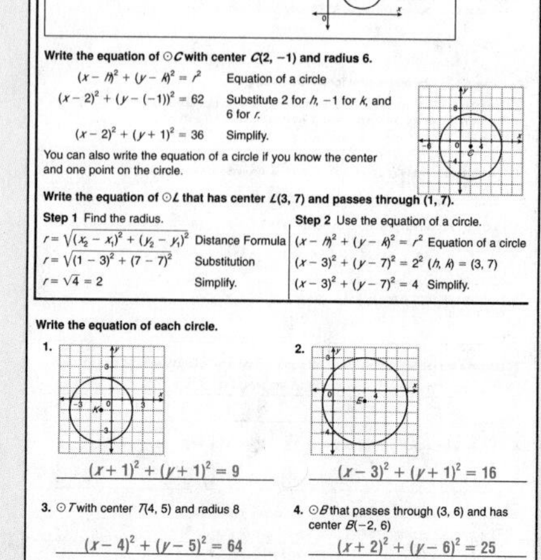

11-7 RETEACH

Equation of a Circle
The equation of a circle with center (h, k) and radius r is $(x - h)^2 + (y - k)^2 = r^2$.

Write the equation of ⊙C with center $C(2, -1)$ and radius 6.

$(x - h)^2 + (y - k)^2 = r^2$ Equation of a circle
$(x - 2)^2 + (y - (-1))^2 = 6^2$ Substitute 2 for h, −1 for k, and 6 for r.
$(x - 2)^2 + (y + 1)^2 = 36$ Simplify.

You can also write the equation of a circle if you know the center and one point on the circle.

Write the equation of ⊙L that has center $L(3, 7)$ and passes through $(1, 7)$.

Step 1 Find the radius.
$r = \sqrt{(x_2 - x_1)^2 + (y_2 - y_1)^2}$ Distance Formula
$r = \sqrt{(1 - 3)^2 + (7 - 7)^2}$ Substitution
$r = \sqrt{4} = 2$ Simplify.

Step 2 Use the equation of a circle.
$(x - h)^2 + (y - k)^2 = r^2$ Equation of a circle
$(x - 3)^2 + (y - 7)^2 = 2^2$ $(h, k) = (3, 7)$
$(x - 3)^2 + (y - 7)^2 = 4$ Simplify.

Write the equation of each circle.

1. $(x + 1)^2 + (y + 1)^2 = 9$
2. $(x - 3)^2 + (y + 1)^2 = 16$
3. ⊙T with center $T(4, 5)$ and radius 8 $(x - 4)^2 + (y - 5)^2 = 64$
4. ⊙B that passes through $(3, 6)$ and has center $B(-2, 6)$ $(x + 2)^2 + (y - 6)^2 = 25$

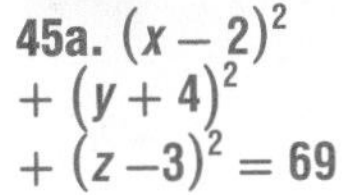

CHALLENGE AND EXTEND

45a. $(x-2)^2 + (y+4)^2 + (z-3)^2 = 69$

b. 15; if 2 segs. are tangent to a ⊙ or sphere from the same ext. pt., then the segs. are ≅.

45. In three dimensions, the equation of a sphere is similar to that of a circle. The equation of a sphere with center (h, j, k) and radius r is $(x-h)^2 + (y-j)^2 + (z-k)^2 = r^2$.

a. Write the equation of a sphere with center $(2, -4, 3)$ that contains the point $(1, -2, -5)$.

b. $\overleftrightarrow{AC}$ and $\overleftrightarrow{BC}$ are tangents from the same exterior point. If $AC = 15$ m, what is BC? Explain.

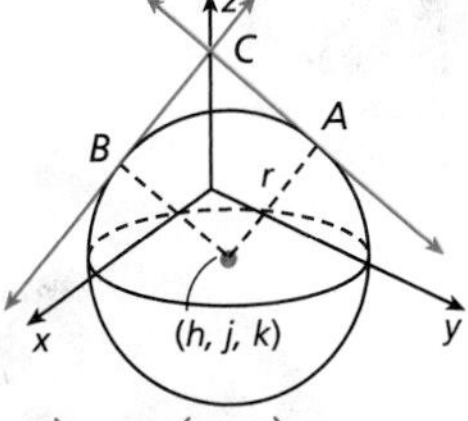

46. Algebra Find the point(s) of intersection of the line $x + y = 5$ and the circle $x^2 + y^2 = 25$ by solving the system of equations. Check your result by graphing the line and the circle. **(0, 5) and (5, 0); check students' graphs.**

47. Find the equation of the circle with center $(3, 4)$ that is tangent to the line whose equation is $y = 2x + 3$. (*Hint:* First find the point of tangency.) $(x-3)^2 + (y-4)^2 = 5$

SPIRAL REVIEW

Simplify each expression. *(Previous course)*

48. $\dfrac{2x^2 - 2(4x^2 + 1)}{2}$ $-3x^2 - 1$ **49.** $\dfrac{18a + 4(9a + 3)}{6}$ $9a + 2$ **50.** $3(x + 3y) - 4(3x + 2y) - (x - 2y)$ $-10x + 3y$

In isosceles $\triangle DEF$, $\overline{DE} \cong \overline{EF}$. m∠E = 60°, and m∠D = $(7x + 4)°$. $DE = 2y + 10$, and $EF = 4y - 1$. Find the value of each variable. *(Lesson 4-8)*

51. x **8** **52.** y **5.5**

Find each measure. *(Lesson 11-5)*

53. m$\widehat{LNQ}$ **196°** **54.** m∠NMP **57°**

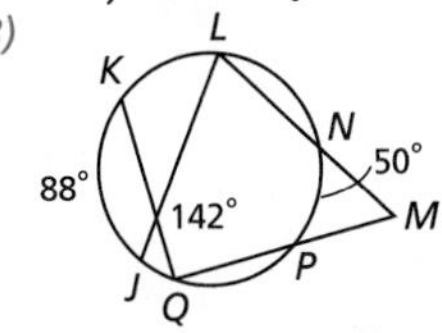

Career Path

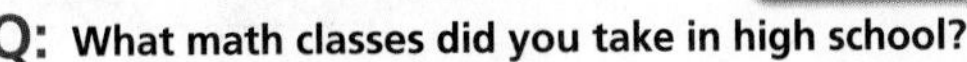

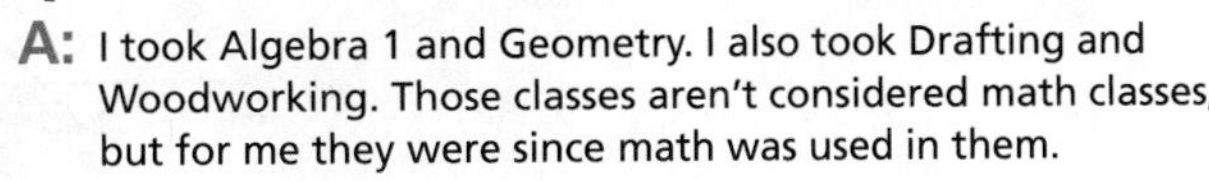

go.hrw.com
Career Resources Online
KEYWORD: MG7 Career

Bryan Moreno
Furniture Maker

Q: What math classes did you take in high school?

A: I took Algebra 1 and Geometry. I also took Drafting and Woodworking. Those classes aren't considered math classes, but for me they were since math was used in them.

Q: What type of furniture do you make?

A: I mainly design and make household furniture, such as end tables, bedroom furniture, and entertainment centers.

Q: How do you use math?

A: Taking appropriate and precise measurements is very important. If wood is not measured correctly, the end result doesn't turn out as expected. Understanding angle measures is also important. Some of the furniture I build has 30° or 40° angles at the edges.

Q: What are your future plans?

A: Someday I would love to design all the furniture in my own home. It would be incredibly satisfying to know that all my furniture was made with quality and attention to detail.

Journal

Ask students to explain how to write an equation for a circle with center $C(2, 3)$ and radius 9 and how they would graph the circle. Then have them actually graph the circle.

Alternative Assessment

Give students graph paper and four circles cut out of transparent paper. The diameters of the circles should match the units of the grid and be whole numbers. Have students place their transparent circles on their grids, one in each of the four quadrants. Have students find the radius, center, and equation of each circle.

Power Presentations with PowerPoint®

11-7 Lesson Quiz

Write the equation of each circle.

1. ⊙L with center $L(-5, -6)$ and radius 9 $(x+5)^2 + (y+6)^2 = 81$

2. ⊙D that passes through $(-2, -1)$ and has center $D(2, -4)$ $(x-2)^2 + (y+4)^2 = 25$

Graph the equation.

3. $x^2 + y^2 = 4$

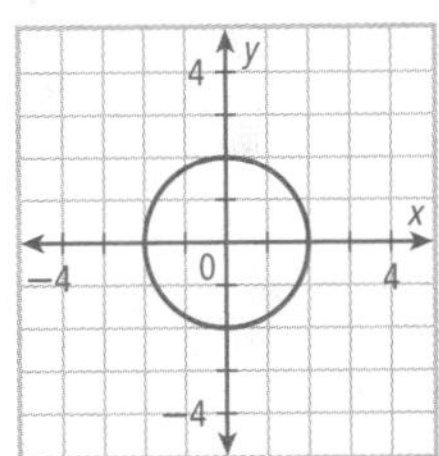

4. $(x-2)^2 + (y+4)^2 = 16$

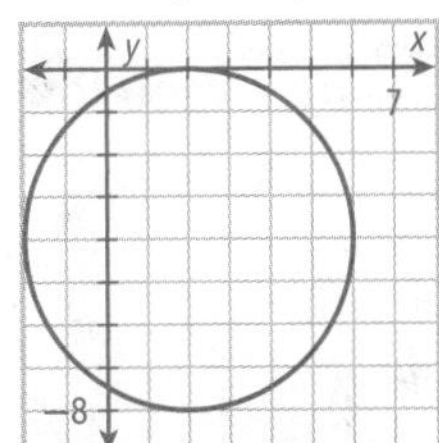

5. A carpenter is planning to build a circular gazebo that requires the center of the structure to be equidistant from three support columns located at $E(-2, -4)$, $F(-2, 6)$, and $G(10, 2)$. What are the coordinates for the location of the center of the gazebo? $(3, 1)$

Also available on transparency

11-7 PROBLEM SOLVING

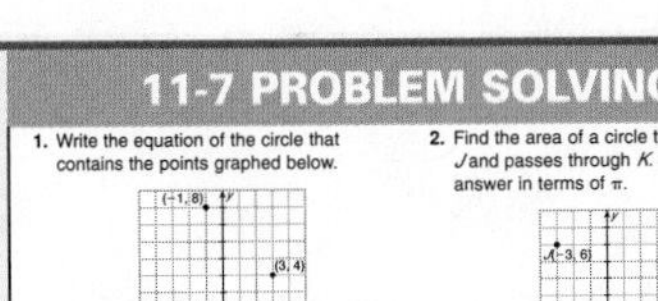

1. Write the equation of the circle that contains the points graphed below. $(x+1)^2 + (y-4)^2 = 16$

2. Find the area of a circle that has center J and passes through K. Express your answer in terms of π. $A = 74\pi$

Choose the best answer.

3. An English knot garden has hedges planted to form geometric shapes. A blueprint of a knot garden contains three circular hedges as described in the table. Flowers are to be planted in the space that is within all three circles. Which is a point that could be planted with flowers?

Circular Hedge	Center	Radius
A	(3, 2)	3 ft
B	(7, 2)	4 ft
C	(5, −1)	3 ft

A (7, 1) C (0, 5)
Ⓑ (5, 1) D (0, 0)

4. Which of these circles intersects the circle that has center (0, 6) and radius 1?

F $(x-5)^2 + (y+3)^2 = 4$
G $(x-4)^2 + (y-3)^2 = 9$
H $(x+5)^2 + (y+1)^2 = 16$
Ⓙ $(x+1)^2 + (y-4)^2 = 4$

5. The center of ⊙S is (9, 2), and the radius of the circle is 5 units. Which is a point on the circle?

Ⓐ (4, 2) C (9, 4)
B (14, 0) D (9, −5)

6. Which is an equation for a circle that has the same center as ⊙P but has a circumference that is four times as great?

F $(x-4)^2 + y^2 = 36$
Ⓖ $(x-4)^2 + y^2 = 144$
H $x^2 + (y-4)^2 = 36$
J $x^2 + (y-4)^2 = 144$

7. The Maxair amusement park ride consists of a circular ring that holds 50 riders. Suppose that the center of the ride is at the origin and that one of the riders on the circular ring is at (16, 15.1). If one unit on the coordinate plane equals 1 foot, which is a close approximation of the circumference of the ride?

A 22 ft Ⓒ 138 ft
B 44 ft D 1521 ft

11-7 CHALLENGE

Find the area of the intersection of two circles. The equation for circle A is $(x-2)^2 + (y-3)^2 = 16$. The equation for circle B is $(x+5)^2 + (y-5)^2 = 36$.

1. Graph each circle in the coordinate grid. Shade the area of intersection of the two circles.
2. Draw $\overline{AB}$.
3. Find AB to the nearest whole number. $AB \approx 7.28 \approx 7$
4. Label the points of intersection of the two circles C and D.
5. a. Solve each equation for y. $y = 3 \pm \sqrt{16 - (x-2)^2}$; $y = 5 \pm \sqrt{36 - (x+5)^2}$
   b. Graph the positive square root equation for each curve on a graphing calculator and find the point of intersection, C. Round coordinates to the nearest hundredth. (0.73, 6.79)
   c. Graph the negative square root equation for each curve on a graphing calculator and find the point of intersection, D. Round coordinates to the nearest hundredth. (−1.08, 0.45)
6. Draw radii $\overline{BC}$, $\overline{AC}$, $\overline{BD}$, and $\overline{AD}$.
7. Find AC and BC. $AC = 4$, $BC = 6$
8. Find m∠CBA. Round to the nearest whole degree. (*Hint:* Use the Law of Cosines.) 33°
9. Find m∠CBD. Round to the nearest whole degree. 66°
10. Find m∠CAB. Round to the nearest whole degree. 55°
11. Find m∠CAD. Round to the nearest whole degree. 110°
12. Draw chord $\overline{CD}$.

For Exercises 13–19, round to the nearest hundredth.

13. Find the area of sector BCD. 20.73 square units
14. Find the area of $\triangle BCD$. (*Hint:* Assume $\overline{BD}$ is the base of $\triangle BCD$. Find the height of the triangle first. You know that $\overline{BC}$ and $\overline{BD}$ are both radii of circle B.) 16.44 square units
15. Subtract the area of $\triangle BCD$ from the area of sector BCD. 4.29 square units
16. Find the area of sector ACD. 15.36 square units
17. Find the area of $\triangle ACD$. (*Hint:* Assume $\overline{AD}$ is the base of $\triangle ACD$. $\overline{AD}$ and $\overline{AC}$ are both radii of circle A.) 7.52 square units
18. Subtract the area of $\triangle ACD$ from the area of sector ACD. 7.84 square units
19. Find the sum of your answers to Exercises 15 and 18. This is the area of the intersection of the two circles. 12.11 square units

Organizer

Objective: Assess students' ability to apply concepts and skills in Lessons 11-4 through 11-7 in a real-world format.

Online Edition

Resources

Geometry Assessments
www.mathtekstoolkit.org

Problem	Text Reference
1	Lesson 11-4
2	Lesson 11-5
3	Lesson 11-6
4	Lesson 11-7

State Resources

go.hrw.com
State Resources Online
KEYWORD: MG7 Resources

CHAPTER 11

MULTI-STEP TEST PREP

SECTION 11B

Angles and Segments in Circles

Native American Design
The members of a Native American cultural center are painting a circle of colors on their gallery floor. They start by laying out the circle and chords shown. Before they apply their paint to the design, they measure angles and lengths to check for accuracy.

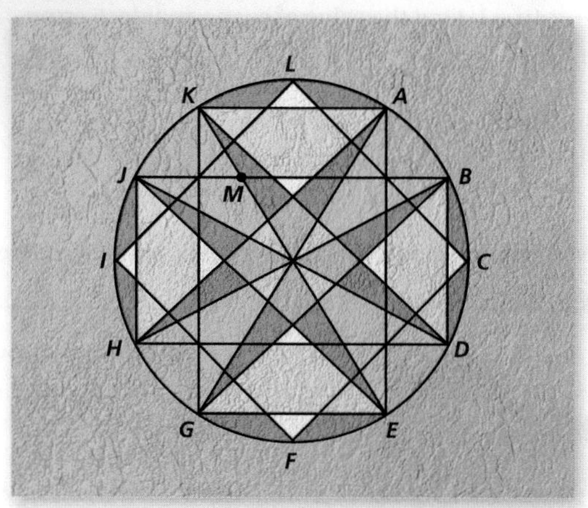

1. The circle design is based on twelve equally spaced points placed around the circumference of the circle. As the group lays out the design, what should be $m\angle AGB$? **15°**
2. What should be $m\angle KAE$? Why? **90°; the ∠ is inscribed in a semicircle, so it is a rt. ∠.**
3. What should be $m\angle KMJ$? Why? **60°; $m\widehat{KJ} = 30°$, and $m\widehat{BE} = 90°$, so $m\angle KMJ = \frac{1}{2}(30° + 90°)$**
4. The diameter of the circle is 22 ft. $KM \approx 4.8$ ft, and $JM \approx 6.4$ ft. What should be the length of $\overline{MB}$? **≈12.9 ft**
5. The group members use a coordinate plane to help them position the design. Each square of a grid represents one square foot, and the center of the circle is at (20, 14). What is the equation of the circle? **$(x - 20)^2 + (y - 14)^2 = 121$**
6. What are the coordinates of points L, C, F, and I? **L(20, 25); C(31, 14); F(20, 3); I(9, 14)**

INTERVENTION

Scaffolding Questions

1. What can you say about the measure of each of the arcs, such as $m\widehat{AB}$, $m\widehat{BC}$, and $m\widehat{CD}$? The arc measures are =, so they are all 30°. How is $m\angle AGB$ related to $m\widehat{AB}$? $m\angle AGB = \frac{1}{2} m\widehat{AB}$
2. What do you notice about the arc that is intercepted by ∠KAE? The arc is a semicircle. What does this tell you about ∠KAE? ∠KAE must be a rt. ∠.
3. How can you calculate $m\angle KMJ$? Take the average of the measures of $\widehat{JK}$ and $\widehat{BE}$.
4. What can you say about the length of $\overline{ME}$? $ME = 17.2$ ft What is the relationship among JM, MB, KM and ME? $JM \cdot MB = KM \cdot ME$
5. What is the general equation for a circle with center (h, k) and radius r? $(x - h)^2 + (y - h)^2 + (y - k)^2 = r^2$ What is the radius of the circle in the design? $r = 11$
6. How far from the center of the circle are points L, C, F, and I? 11 ft

Extension

What are the coordinates of point A to the nearest tenth? A(25.5, 23.5)

CHAPTER 11

SECTION 11B

Quiz for Lessons 11-4 Through 11-7

11-4 Inscribed Angles

Find each measure.

1. $m\angle BAC$ 51°
2. $m\widehat{CD}$ 76°

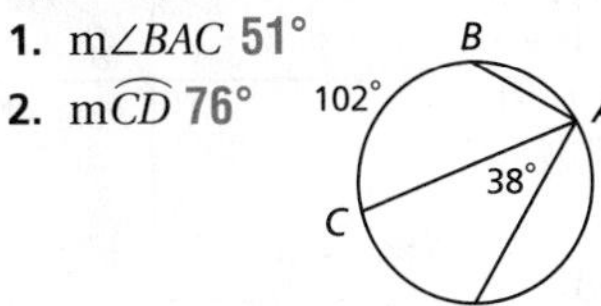

3. $m\angle FGH$ 90°
4. $m\widehat{JGF}$ 310°

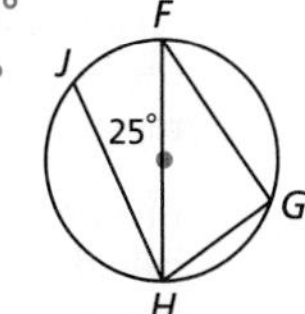

11-5 Angle Relationships in Circles

Find each measure.

5. $m\angle RST$ 133°

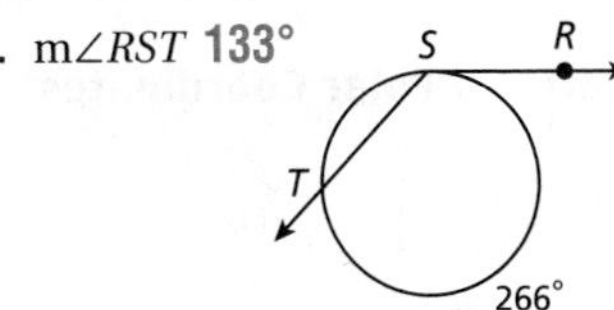

6. $m\angle AEC$ 76°

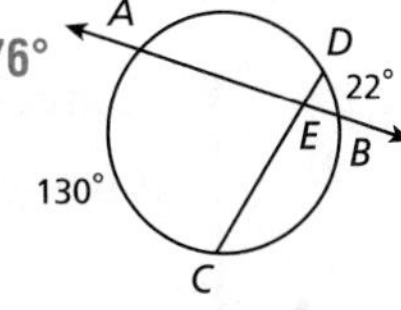

7. A manufacturing company is creating a plastic stand for DVDs. They want to make the stand with $m\widehat{MN} = 102°$. What should be the measure of $\angle MPN$? 78°

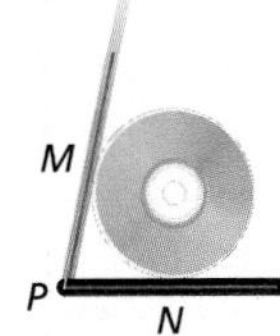

11-6 Segment Relationships in Circles

Find the value of the variable and the length of each chord or secant segment.

8. 4; $AB = 8$; $CD = 7$

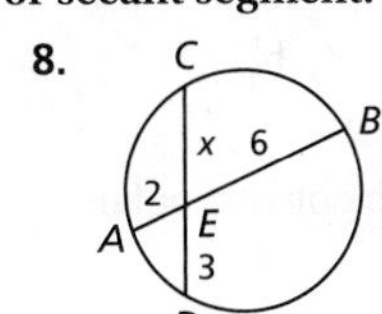

9. $6\frac{1}{3}$; $FH = 9\frac{1}{3}$; $KH = 7$

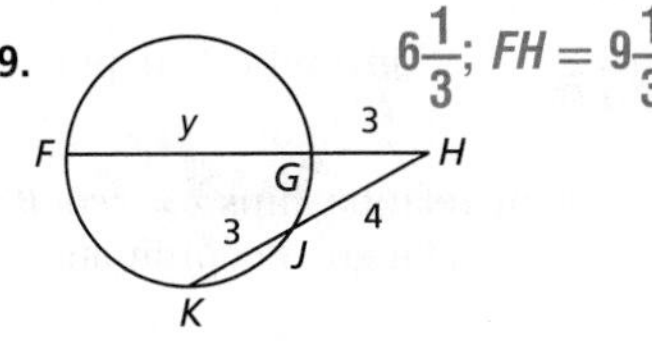

10. An archaeologist discovers a portion of a circular stone wall, shown by $\widehat{ST}$ in the figure. $ST = 12.2$ m, and $UR = 3.9$ m. What was the diameter of the original circular wall? Round to the nearest hundredth. 13.44 m

11-7 Circles in the Coordinate Plane

Write the equation of each circle.

11. $\odot A$ with center $A(-2, -3)$ and radius 3 $(x + 2)^2 + (y + 3)^2 = 9$
12. $\odot B$ that passes through $(1, 1)$ and that has center $B(4, 5)$ $(x - 4)^2 + (y - 5)^2 = 25$
13. A television station serves residents of three cities located at $J(5, 2)$, $K(-7, 2)$, and $L(-5, -8)$. The station wants to build a new broadcast facility that is equidistant from the three cities. What are the coordinates of the location where the facility should be built? $(-1, -2)$

READY TO GO ON? SECTION 11B

Organizer

Objective: Assess students' mastery of concepts and skills in Lessons 11-4 through 11-7.

Resources

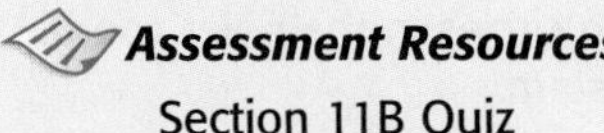

Assessment Resources

Section 11B Quiz

Teacher One Stop™

Test & Practice Generator

INTERVENTION

Resources

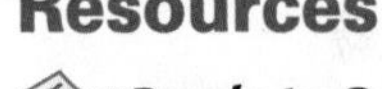

Ready to Go On? Intervention and Enrichment **Worksheets**

Ready to Go On? **CD-ROM**

Ready to Go On? **Online**

my.hrw.com

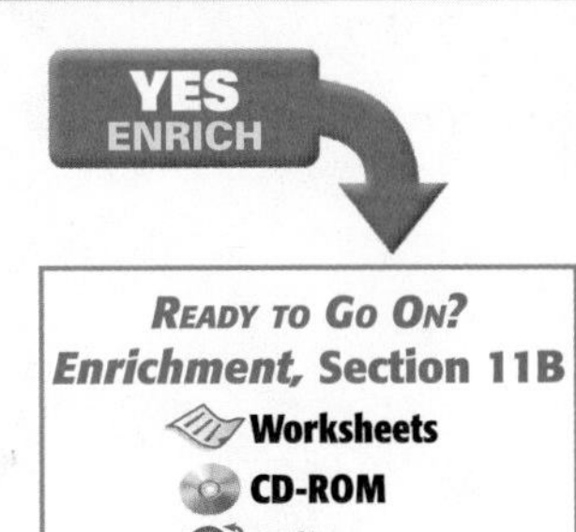

READY TO GO ON? Diagnose and Prescribe

NO INTERVENE

Ready to Go On? Intervention	Worksheets	CD-ROM	Online
	Ready to Go On? Intervention, Section 11B		
Lesson 11-4	11-4 Intervention	Activity 11-4	Diagnose and Prescribe Online
Lesson 11-5	11-5 Intervention	Activity 11-5	
Lesson 11-6	11-6 Intervention	Activity 11-6	
Lesson 11-7	11-7 Intervention	Activity 11-7	

YES ENRICH

Ready to Go On? Enrichment, Section 11B

Worksheets

CD-ROM

Online

CHAPTER
11 Organizer

Pacing: Traditional 1 day
Block $\frac{1}{2}$ day

Objectives: Convert between polar and rectangular coordinates.

Plot points using polar coordinates

Using the Extension

In **Lesson 11-7**, students use the equation of a circle to graph circles in the Cartesian coordinate system. In this extension, students learn how to graph circles in the polar coordinate system.

Additional Examples

Example 1

Convert (2, 5) to polar coordinates. (5.4, 68°)

INTERVENTION

Questioning Strategies

EXAMPLE 1

- How does the location of a point with rectangular coordinates compare to the location of its corresponding polar coordinates?

Inclusion Show students both the graph of the location of a point in a rectangular coordinate plane and a graph of its corresponding polar coordinates in the polar coordinate system.

State Resources

EXTENSION Polar Coordinates

Objectives
Convert between polar and rectangular coordinates.
Plot points using polar coordinates.

Vocabulary
polar coordinate system
pole
polar axis

In a Cartesian coordinate system, a point is represented by the two coordinates x and y. In a **polar coordinate system**, a point A is represented by its distance from the origin r, and an angle θ. θ is measured counterclockwise from the horizontal axis to $\overrightarrow{OA}$. The ordered pair (r, θ) represents the polar coordinates of point A.

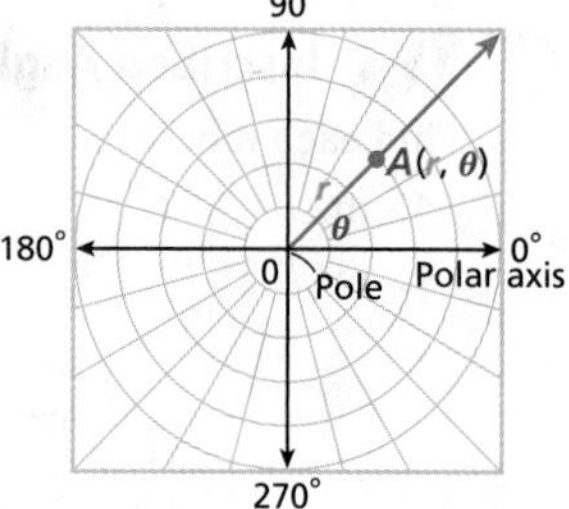

In a polar coordinate system, the origin is called the **pole**. The horizontal axis is called the **polar axis**.

You can use the equation of a circle $r^2 = x^2 + y^2$ and the tangent ratio $\theta = \frac{y}{x}$ to convert rectangular coordinates to polar coordinates.

EXAMPLE 1 **Converting Rectangular Coordinates to Polar Coordinates**

Convert (3, 4) to polar coordinates.

$r^2 = x^2 + y^2$

$r^2 = 3^2 + 4^2$

$r^2 = 25$

$r = 5$

$\tan\theta = \frac{4}{3}$

$\theta = \tan^{-1}\left(\frac{4}{3}\right) \approx 53°$

The polar coordinates are (5, 53°).

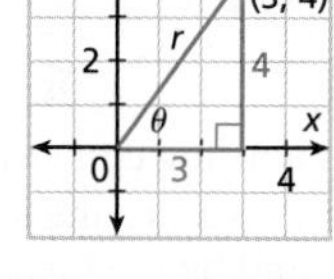

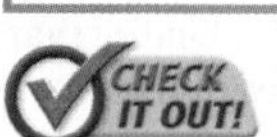

1. Convert (4, 1) to polar coordinates. (4.12, 14°)

You can use the relationships $x = r\cos\theta$ and $y = r\sin\theta$ to convert polar coordinates to rectangular coordinates.

EXAMPLE 2 **Converting Polar Coordinates to Rectangular Coordinates**

Convert (2, 130°) to rectangular coordinates.

$x = r\cos\theta$ $y = r\sin\theta$

$x = 2\cos 130°$ $y = 2\sin 130°$

≈ -1.29 ≈ 1.53

The rectangular coordinates are (−1.29, 1.53).

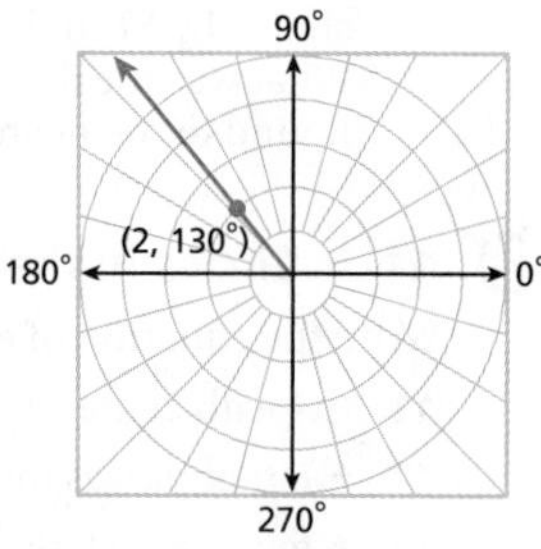

CHECK IT OUT!

2. Convert (4, 60°) to rectangular coordinates. (2, 3.46)

1 Introduce

Motivate

Discuss with students some areas where polar coordinates might be useful, such as aviation, navigation, astronomy, and cartography. Explain that in chemistry, molecular modeling uses polar coordinates to describe the position and orientation of chemical bonds between atoms and molecules. Tell students that they will learn about the polar coordinate system, which uses the equation of a circle and an angle measure.

2 Teach

Guided Instruction

Use a diagram to introduce the terms *polar coordinate system*, *pole*, and *polar axis*. Review the trigonometric functions that are used to convert between rectangular and polar coordinates. Explain how ordered pairs are represented on the graph. Discuss conversions between rectangular and polar coordinates.

EXAMPLE 3 **Plotting Polar Coordinates**

Plot the point $(4, 225°)$.

Step 1 Measure 225° counterclockwise from the polar axis.

Step 2 Locate the point on the ray that is 4 units from the pole.

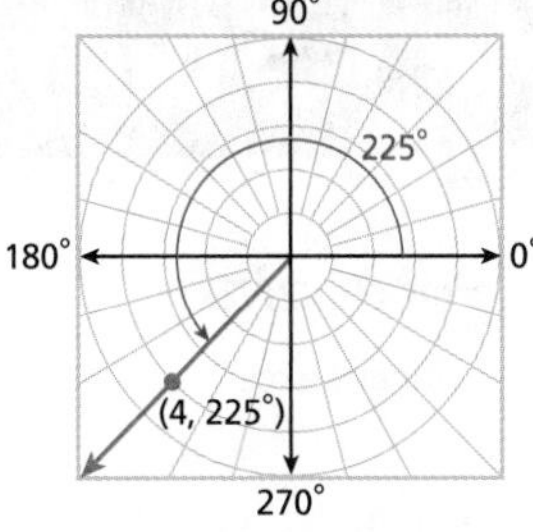

3. Plot the point $(4, 300°)$.

EXAMPLE 4 **Graphing Polar Equations**

Graph $r = 4$.

Make a table of values and plot the points.

θ	0°	45°	135°	270°	300°
r	4	4	4	4	4

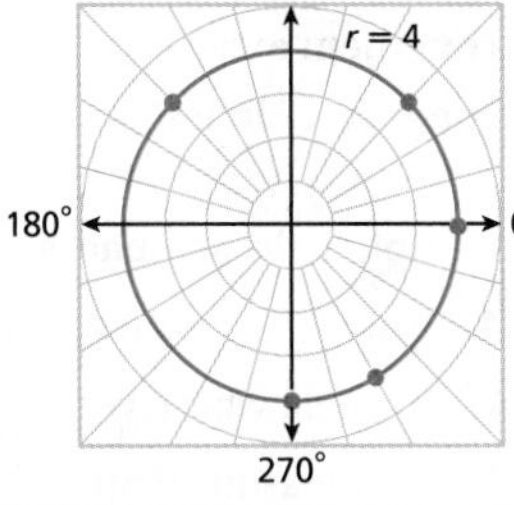

4. Graph $r = 2$.

EXTENSION Exercises

Convert to polar coordinates.

1. $(2, 2)$ (2.83, 45°) **2.** $(1, 0)$ (1, 0°) **3.** $(3, 7)$ (7.62, 67°) **4.** $(0, 15)$ (15, 90°)

Convert to rectangular coordinates.

5. $(3, 150°)$ (−2.60, 1.5) **6.** $(5, 214°)$ (−4.15, −2.80) **7.** $(4, 303°)$ (2.18, −3.35) **8.** $(4.5, 90°)$ (0, 4.5)

Plot each point.

9. $(4, 45°)$ **10.** $(3, 165°)$ **11.** $(1, 240°)$ **12.** $(3.5, 315°)$

13. Critical Thinking Graph the equation $r = 5$. What can you say about the graph of an equation of the form $r = a$, where a is a positive real number?

13. The graph of $r = a$ is a ⊙ centered at the pole with a radius of a units.

Technology Graph each equation.

14. $r = -5\sin\theta$ **15.** $r = 3\sin 4\theta$ **16.** $r = -4\cos\theta$

17. $r = 5\cos 3\theta$ **18.** $r = 3\cos 2\theta$ **19.** $r = 2 + 4\sin\theta$

3 Close

Summarize

Review with students how to convert between rectangular and polar coordinates. Give an example of how to plot polar coordinates and how to graph polar equations.

Answers to *Check It Out!*

3. 90° 180° 0° 270°

4. See p. A29.

Answers

9–12. See p. A29.

13. See p. A29 for graph.

14–19. See pp. A29–30.

COMMON ERROR ALERT

If students are using graphing calculators to graph polar equations and are not getting the same graph as is in the example, they are probably using the wrong mode. Have students choose MODE and change from rectangular to polar. Tell students that polar equations may be graphed in either radians or degrees. If they press the Y=, they should see *r* instead of *y*.

Power Presentations with PowerPoint®

Additional Examples

Example 2

Convert, $(6, 78°)$ to rectangular coordinates. (1.25, 5.87)

Example 3

Plot the point (2, 50°).

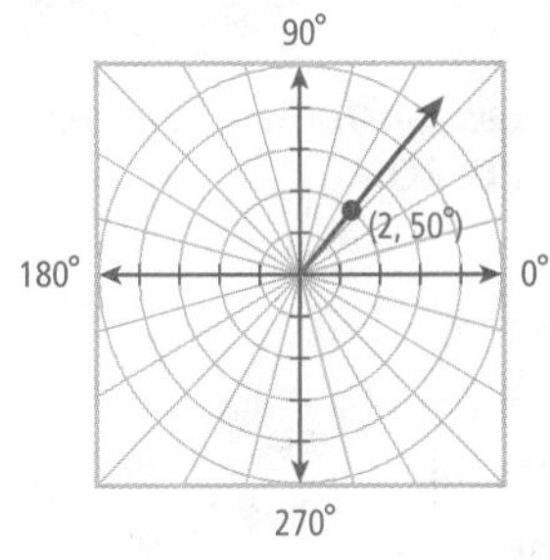

Example 4

Graph $r = 3$.

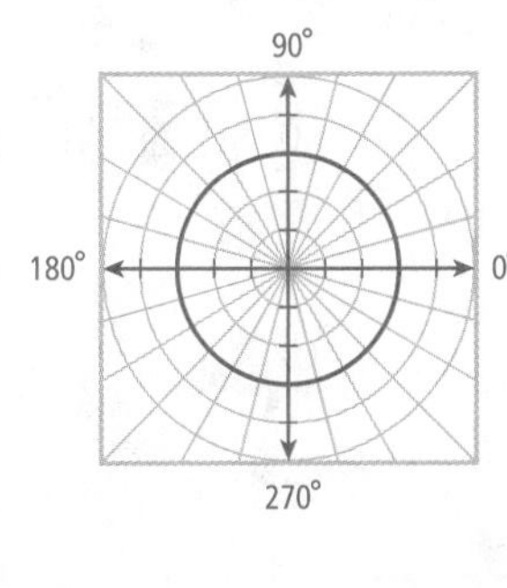

INTERVENTION

Questioning Strategies

EXAMPLE 2

- How are trigonometric functions used to find *x* and *y*? Explain.

EXAMPLE 3

- Can a point have more than one pair of polar coordinates? Explain.

EXAMPLE 4

- If *r* is the distance between a point and the origin, is it the same as the radius of a circle? Why or why not?

Organizer

Objective: Help students organize and review key concepts and skills presented in Chapter 11.

Online Edition Multilingual Glossary

Resources

Teacher One Stop™

PuzzleView
Test & Practice Generator

***Multilingual Glossary* Online**

go.hrw.com
KEYWORD: MG7 Glossary

***Lesson Tutorial Videos* CD-ROM**

Answers

1. segment of a circle
2. central angle
3. major arc
4. concentric circles
5. chords $\overline{QS}$, $\overline{UV}$; tangent: ℓ; radii: $\overline{PQ}$, $\overline{PS}$, secant: $\overleftrightarrow{UV}$; diam.: $\overline{QS}$
6. chords: $\overline{KH}$, $\overline{MN}$; tangent: $\overleftrightarrow{KL}$; radii: $\overline{JH}$, $\overline{JK}$, $\overline{JM}$, $\overline{JN}$; secant: $\overleftrightarrow{MN}$; diams.: $\overline{KH}$, $\overline{MN}$
7. 25
8. 12
9. 7
10. 1.8

CHAPTER 11

Study Guide: Review

For a complete list of the postulates and theorems in this chapter, see p. PS12.

Vocabulary

Complete the sentences below with vocabulary words from the list above.

1. A(n) __?__ is a region bounded by an arc and a chord.
2. An angle whose vertex is at the center of a circle is called a(n) __?__ .
3. The measure of a(n) __?__ is 360° minus the measure of its central angle.
4. __?__ are coplanar circles with the same center.

11-1 Lines That Intersect Circles *(pp. 746–754)*

EXAMPLES

■ **Identify each line or segment that intersects $\odot A$.**

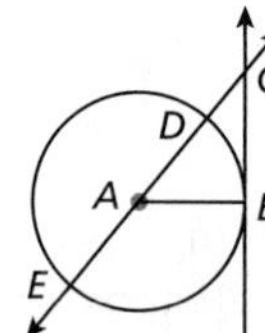

chord: $\overline{DE}$
tangent: $\overleftrightarrow{BC}$
radii: $\overline{AE}$, $\overline{AD}$, and $\overline{AB}$
secant: $\overleftrightarrow{DE}$
diameter: $\overline{DE}$

■ **$\overline{RS}$ and $\overline{RW}$ are tangent to $\odot T$. $RS = x + 5$ and $RW = 3x - 7$. Find RS.**

$RS = RW$	*2 segs. tangent to ⊙ from same ext. pt. → segs. ≅.*
$x + 5 = 3x - 7$	*Substitute the given values.*
$-2x + 5 = -7$	*Subtract 3x from both sides.*
$-2x = -12$	*Subtract 5 from both sides.*
$x = 6$	*Divide both sides by −2.*
$RS = 6 + 5$	*Substitute 6 for y.*
$= 11$	*Simplify.*

EXERCISES

Identify each line or segment that intersects each circle.

5. 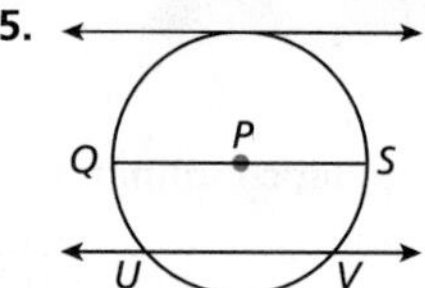

6. 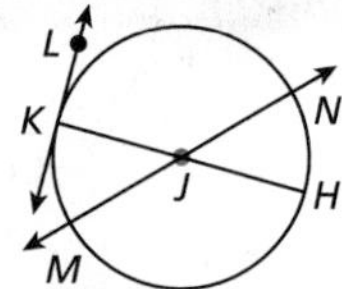

Given the measures of the following segments that are tangent to a circle, find each length.

7. $AB = 9x - 2$ and $BC = 7x + 4$. Find AB.
8. $EF = 5y + 32$ and $EG = 8 - y$. Find EG.
9. $JK = 8m - 5$ and $JL = 2m + 4$. Find JK.
10. $WX = 0.8x + 1.2$ and $WY = 2.4x$. Find WY.

11-2 Arcs and Chords *(pp. 756–763)*

EXAMPLES

Find each measure.

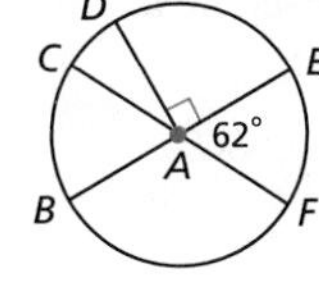

- $m\widehat{BF}$

  $\angle BAF$ and $\angle FAE$ are supplementary, so $m\angle BAF = 180° - 62° = 118°$. $m\widehat{BF} = m\angle BAF = 118°$

- $m\widehat{DF}$

  Since $m\angle DAE = 90°$, $m\widehat{DE} = 90°$. $m\angle EAF = 62°$, so $m\widehat{EF} = 62°$. By the Arc Addition Postulate, $m\widehat{DF} = m\widehat{DE} + m\widehat{EF} = 90° + 62° = 152°$.

EXERCISES

Find each measure.

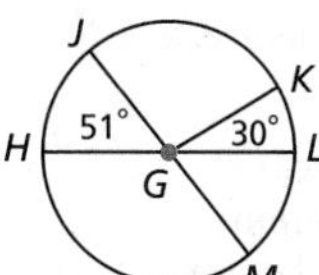

11. $m\widehat{KM}$
12. $m\widehat{HMK}$
13. $m\widehat{JK}$
14. $m\widehat{MJK}$

Find each length to the nearest tenth.

15. ST

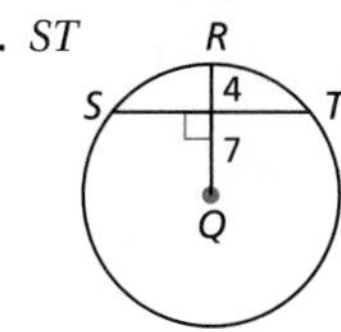

16. CD

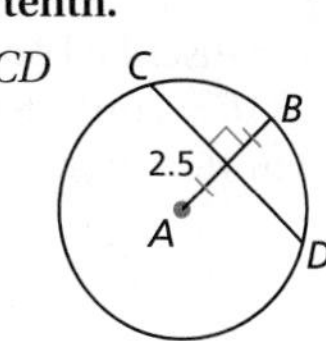

11-3 Sector Area and Arc Length *(pp. 764–769)*

EXAMPLES

- **Find the area of sector *PQR*. Give your answer in terms of π and rounded to the nearest hundredth.**

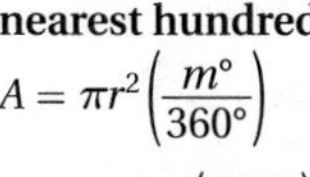

$$A = \pi r^2\left(\frac{m°}{360°}\right)$$
$$= \pi(4)^2\left(\frac{135°}{360}\right)$$
$$= 16\pi\left(\frac{3}{8}\right)$$
$$= 6\pi \text{ m}^2$$
$$\approx 18.85 \text{ m}^2$$

- **Find the length of $\widehat{AB}$. Give your answer in terms of π and rounded to the nearest hundredth.**

$$L = 2\pi r\left(\frac{m°}{360°}\right)$$
$$= 2\pi(9)\left(\frac{80°}{360°}\right)$$
$$= 18\pi\left(\frac{4}{9}\right)$$
$$= 8\pi \text{ ft}$$
$$\approx 25.13 \text{ ft}$$

EXERCISES

Find the area of each sector. Give your answer in terms of π and rounded to the nearest hundredth.

17. sector DEF

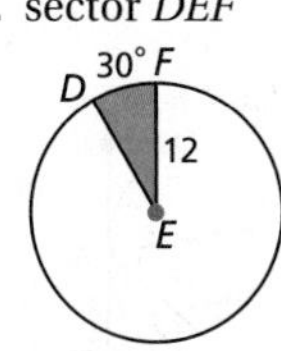

18. sector JKL

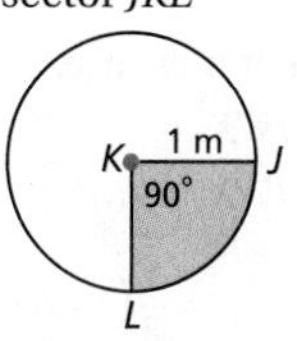

Find each arc length. Give your answer in terms of π and rounded to the nearest hundredth.

19. $\widehat{GH}$

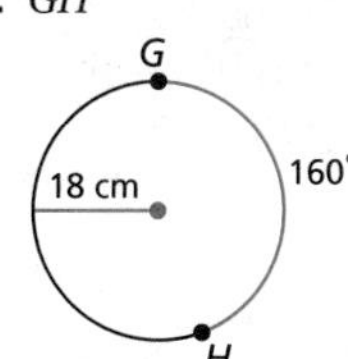

20. $\widehat{MNP}$

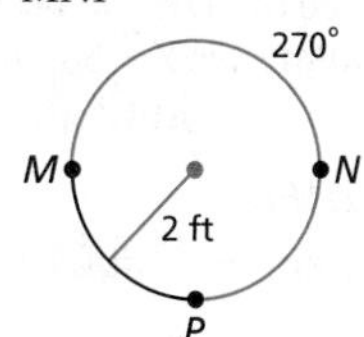

Answers

11. 81°
12. 210°
13. 99°
14. 279°
15. 17.0
16. 8.7
17. 12π in^2; 37.70 in^2
18. $\frac{\pi}{4}$ m^2; 0.79 m^2
19. 16π cm; 50.27 cm
20. 3π ft; 9.42 ft

Study Guide: Review **811**

Answers

21. 164°
22. 32°
23. 26
24. 39°
25. 82°
26. 79°
27. 67°
28. 90°

11-4 Inscribed Angles *(pp. 772–779)*

EXAMPLES

Find each measure.

- $m\angle ABD$

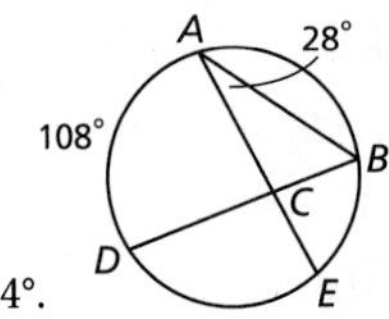

By the Inscribed Angle Theorem, $m\angle ABD = \frac{1}{2}m\widehat{AD}$, so $m\angle ABD = \frac{1}{2}(108°) = 54°$.

- $m\widehat{BE}$

By the Inscribed Angle Theorem, $m\angle BAE = \frac{1}{2}m\widehat{BE}$. So $28° = \frac{1}{2}m\widehat{BE}$, and $m\widehat{BE} = 2(28°) = 56°$.

EXERCISES

Find each measure.

21. $m\widehat{JL}$
22. $m\angle MKL$

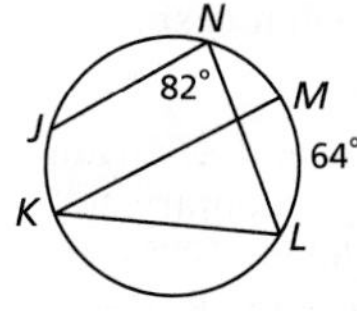

Find each value.

23. x

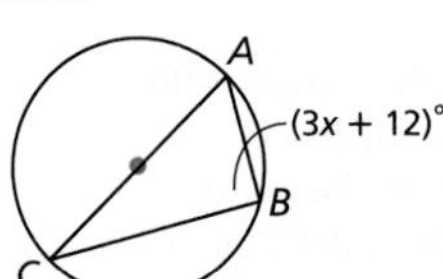

24. $m\angle RSP$

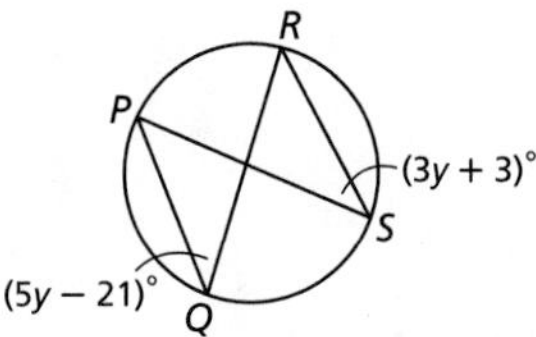

11-5 Angle Relationships in Circles *(pp. 782–789)*

EXAMPLES

Find each measure.

- $m\angle UWX$

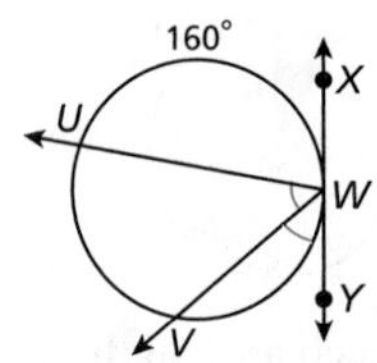

$$m\angle UWX = \frac{1}{2}m\widehat{UW}$$
$$= \frac{1}{2}(160°)$$
$$= 80°$$

- $m\widehat{VW}$

Since $m\angle UWX = 80°$, $m\angle UWY = 100°$ and $m\angle VWY = 50°$. $m\angle VWY = \frac{1}{2}m\widehat{VW}$. So $50° = \frac{1}{2}m\widehat{VW}$, and $m\widehat{VW} = 2(50°) = 100°$.

- $m\angle AED$

$$m\angle AED = \frac{1}{2}(m\widehat{AD} + m\widehat{BC})$$
$$= \frac{1}{2}(31° + 87°)$$
$$= \frac{1}{2}(118°)$$
$$= 59°$$

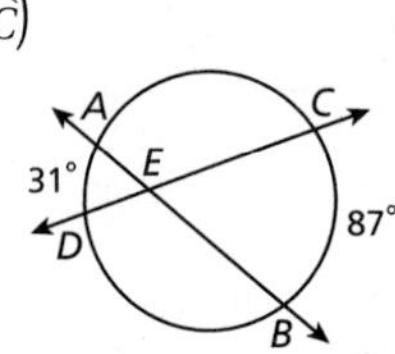

EXERCISES

Find each measure.

25. $m\widehat{MR}$
26. $m\angle QMR$

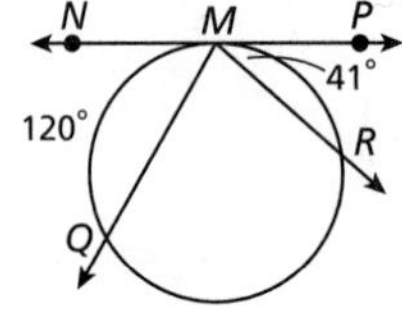

27. $m\angle GKH$

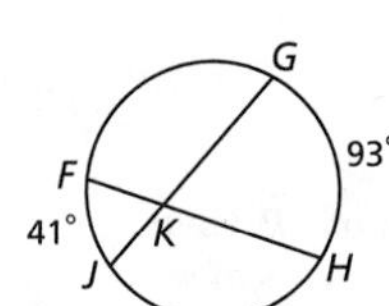

28. A piece of string art is made by placing 16 evenly spaced nails around the circumference of a circle. A piece of string is wound from A to B to C to D. What is $m\angle BXC$?

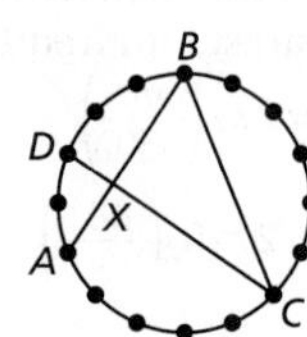

11-6 Segment Relationships in Circles *(pp. 792–798)*

EXAMPLES

- **Find the value of x and the length of each chord.**

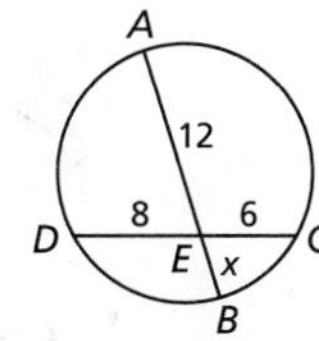
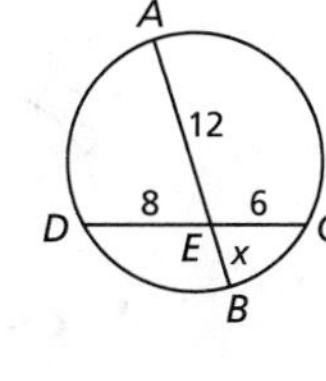

$AE \cdot EB = DE \cdot EC$

$12x = 8(6)$

$12x = 48$

$x = 4$

$AB = 12 + 4 = 16$

$DC = 8 + 6 = 14$

- **Find the value of x and the length of each secant segment.**

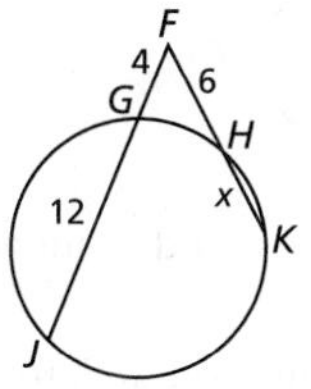

$FJ \cdot FG = FK \cdot FH$

$16(4) = (6 + x)6$

$64 = 36 + 6x$

$28 = 6x$

$x = 4\frac{2}{3}$

$FJ = 12 + 4 = 16$

$FK = 4\frac{2}{3} + 6 = 10\frac{2}{3}$

EXERCISES

Find the value of the variable and the length of each chord.

29.

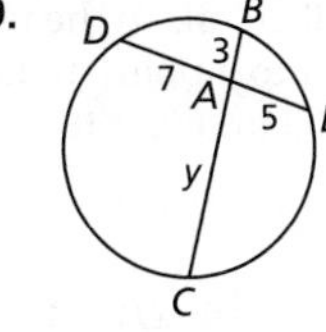

30.

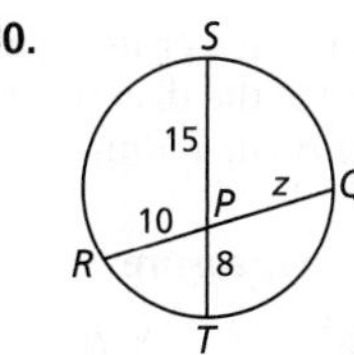

Find the value of the variable and the length of each secant segment.

31.

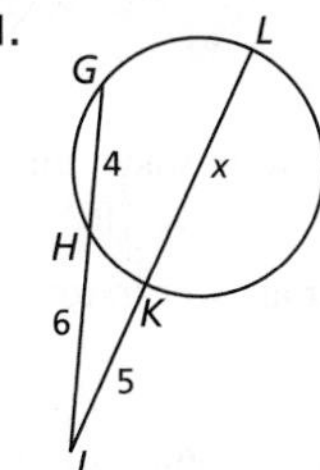

32.

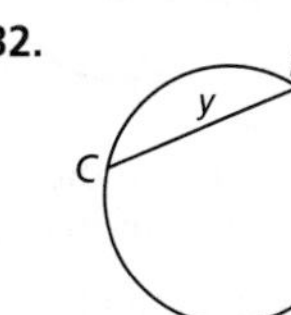

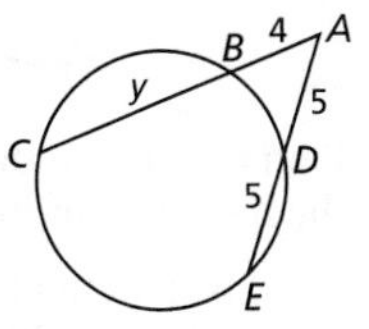

11-7 Circles in the Coordinate Plane *(pp. 799–805)*

EXAMPLES

- **Write the equation of $\odot A$ that passes through $(-1, 1)$ and that has center $A(2, 3)$.**

The equation of a circle with center (h, k) and radius r is $(x - h)^2 + (y - k)^2 = r^2$.

$r = \sqrt{(2 - (-1))^2 + (3 - 1)^2} = \sqrt{3^2 + 2^2} = \sqrt{13}$

The equation of $\odot A$ is $(x - 2)^2 + (y - 3)^2 = 13$.

- **Graph $(x - 2)^2 + (y + 1)^2 = 4$.**

The center of the circle is $(2, -1)$, and the radius is $\sqrt{4} = 2$.

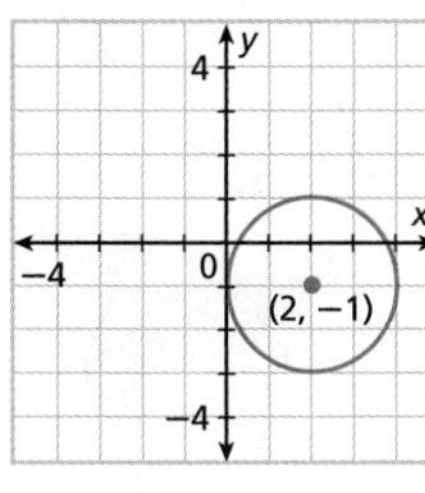

EXERCISES

Write the equation of each circle.

33. $\odot A$ with center $(-4, -3)$ and radius 3

34. $\odot B$ that passes through $(-2, -2)$ and that has center $B(-2, 0)$

35. $\odot C$

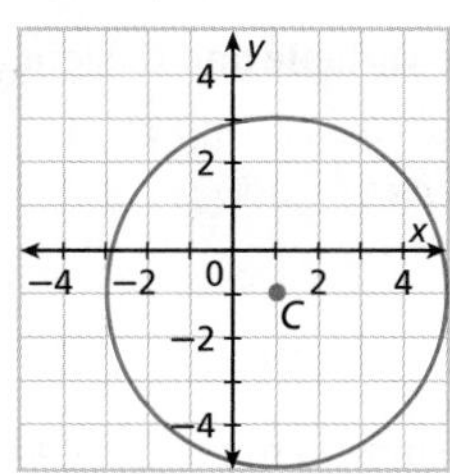

36. Graph $(x + 2)^2 + (y - 2)^2 = 1$.

Answers

29. $11\frac{2}{3}$; $DE = 12$; $BC = 14\frac{2}{3}$
30. 12; $RQ = 22$; $ST = 23$
31. 7; $JG = 10$; $JL = 12$
32. $8\frac{1}{2}$; $AC = 12\frac{1}{2}$; $AE = 10$
33. $(x + 4)^2 + (y + 3)^2 = 9$
34. $(x + 2)^2 + y^2 = 4$
35. $(x - 1)^2 + (y + 1)^2 = 16$
36.

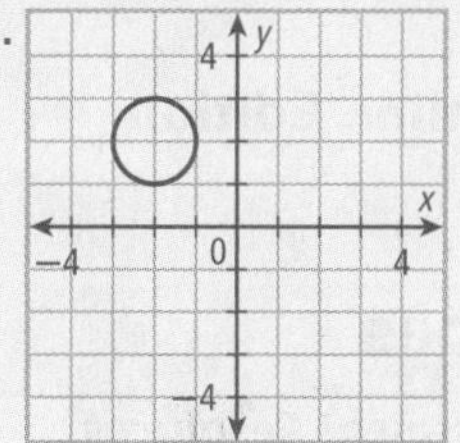

Study Guide: Review **813**

Organizer

Objective: Assess students' mastery of concepts and skills in Chapter 11.

Online Edition

Resources

Assessment Resources

Chapter 11 Tests
- Free Response (Levels A, B, C)
- Multiple Choice (Levels A, B, C)
- Performance Assessment

Teacher One Stop™

Test & Practice Generator

State Resources

go.hrw.com
State Resources Online
KEYWORD: MG7 Resources

CHAPTER 11 CHAPTER TEST

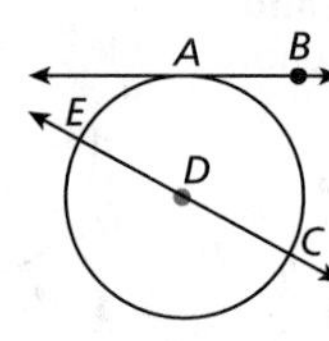

1. Identify each line or segment that intersects the circle.
2. A jet is at a cruising altitude of 6.25 mi. To the nearest mile, what is the distance from the jet to a point on Earth's horizon? (*Hint:* The radius of Earth is 4000 mi.) **224 mi**

1. chord: $\overline{EC}$; tangent: $\overleftrightarrow{AB}$; radii: $\overline{DE}$, $\overline{DC}$; secant: $\overleftrightarrow{EC}$; diam.: $\overline{EC}$

Find each measure.

3. $m\widehat{JK}$ **19°**

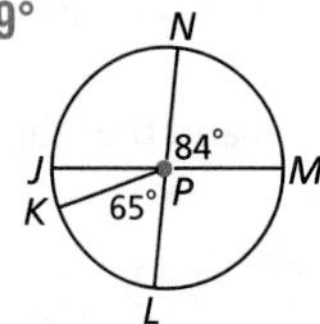

4. UV **24**

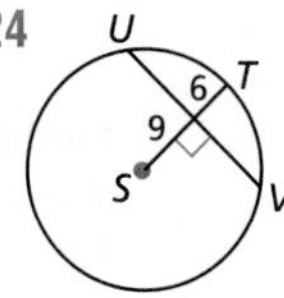

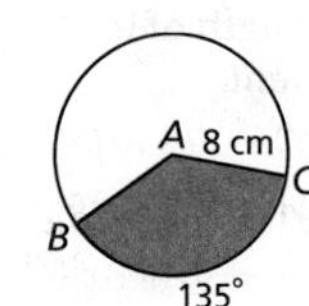

5. Find the area of the sector. Give your answer in terms of π and rounded to the nearest hundredth. **24π cm²; 75.40 cm²**
6. Find the length of $\widehat{BC}$. Give your answer in terms of π and rounded to the nearest hundredth. **6π cm; 18.85 cm**

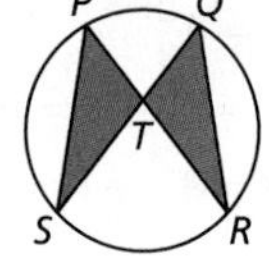

7. If $m\angle SPR = 47°$ in the diagram of a logo, find $m\widehat{SR}$. **94°**
8. A printer is making a large version of the logo for a banner. According to the specifications, $m\widehat{PQ} = 58°$. What should the measure of $\angle QTR$ be? **104°**

Find each measure.

9. $m\angle ABC$ **116°**

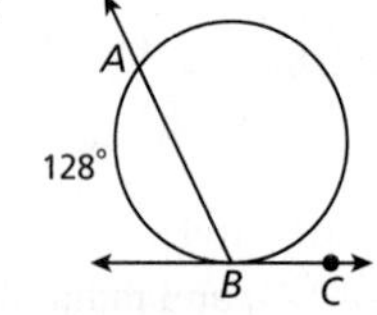

10. $m\angle NKL$ **92°**

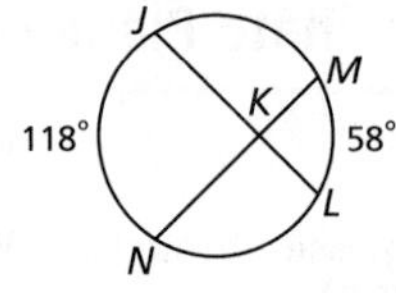

11. A surveyor S is studying the positions of four columns A, B, C, and D that lie on a circle. He finds that $m\angle CSD = 42°$ and $m\widehat{CD} = 124°$. What is $m\widehat{AB}$? **40°**

Find the value of the variable and the length of each chord or secant segment.

12. **12; $HG = 10$; $EF = 14$**

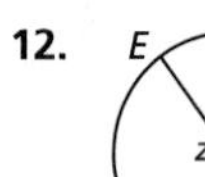
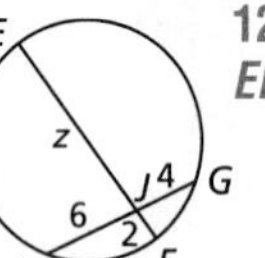

13. **10; $PT = 16$; $PR = 12$**

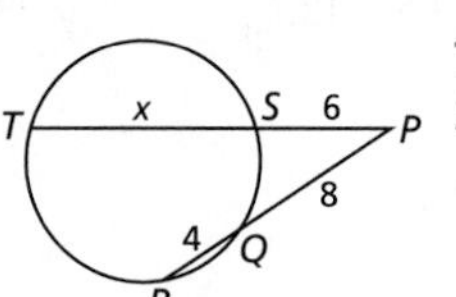
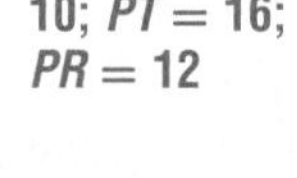

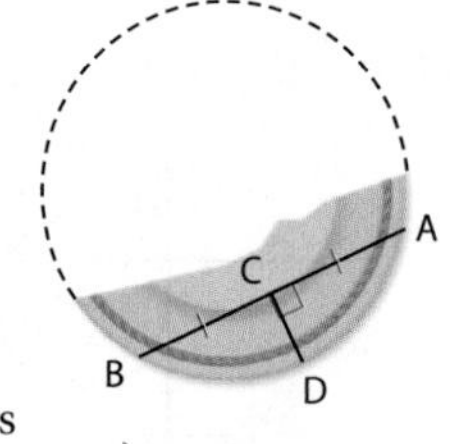

14. The illustration shows a fragment of a circular plate. $AB = 8$ in., and $CD = 2$ in. What is the diameter of the plate? **10 in.**
15. Write the equation of the circle that passes through $(-2, 4)$ and that has center $(1, -2)$. $(x-1)^2 + (y+2)^2 = 45$
16. An artist uses a coordinate plane to plan a mural. The mural will include portraits of civic leaders at $X(2, 4)$, $Y(-6, 0)$, and $Z(2, -8)$ and a circle that passes through all three portraits. What are the coordinates of the center of the circle? **(0, −2)**

COLLEGE ENTRANCE EXAM PRACTICE

CHAPTER 11

FOCUS ON SAT MATHEMATICS SUBJECT TESTS

The topics covered on the SAT Mathematics Subject Tests vary only slightly each time the test is administered. You can find out the general distribution of questions across topics, then determine which areas need more of your attention when you are studying for the test.

HOT TIP! To prepare for the SAT Mathematics Subject Tests, start reviewing course material a couple of months before your test date. Take sample tests to find the areas you might need to focus on more. Remember that you are not expected to have studied all topics on the test.

You may want to time yourself as you take this practice test. It should take you about 6 minutes to complete.

1. $\overline{AC}$ and $\overline{BD}$ intersect at the center of the circle shown. If $m\angle BDC = 30°$, what is the measure of minor $\widehat{AB}$?

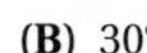

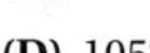

(A) 15°
(B) 30°
(C) 60°
(D) 105°
(E) 120°

Note: Figure not drawn to scale.

2. Which of these is the equation of a circle that is tangent to the lines $x = 1$ and $y = 3$ and has radius 2?

(A) $(x+1)^2 + (y-1)^2 = 4$
(B) $(x-1)^2 + (y+1)^2 = 4$
(C) $x^2 + (y-1)^2 = 4$
(D) $(x-1)^2 + y^2 = 4$
(E) $x^2 + y^2 = 4$

3. If $LK = 6$, $LN = 10$, and $PK = 3$, what is PM?

(A) 7
(B) 8
(C) 9
(D) 10
(E) 11

4. Circle D has radius 6, and $m\angle ABC = 25°$. What is the length of minor $\widehat{AC}$?

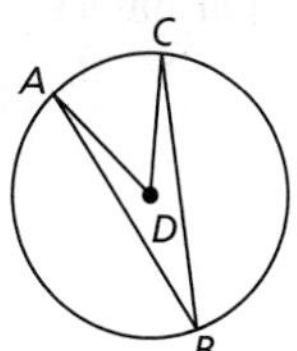

Note: Figure not drawn to scale.

(A) $\frac{5\pi}{6}$
(B) $\frac{5\pi}{4}$
(C) $\frac{5\pi}{3}$
(D) 3π
(E) 5π

5. A square is inscribed in a circle as shown. If the radius of the circle is 9, what is the area of the shaded region, rounded to the nearest hundredth?

(A) 11.56
(B) 23.12
(C) 57.84
(D) 104.12
(E) 156.23

COLLEGE ENTRANCE EXAM PRACTICE CHAPTER 11

Organizer

Objective: Provide practice for college entrance exams such as the SAT Mathematics Subject Tests.

Online Edition

Resources

College Entrance Exam Practice

Questions on the SAT Mathematics Subject Tests Levels 1 and 2 represent the following math content areas:

	Levels 1	Levels 2
Number and Operations	10-14%	10-14%
Algebra and Functions	38-42%	48-52%
Geometry and Measurement	38-42%	28-32%
Plane Euclidean	18-22%	0%
Coordinate	8-12%	10-14%
Three-Dimensional	4-6%	4-6%
Trigonometry	6-8%	12-16%
Data Analysis and Statistics	6-10%	6-10%

Items on this page focus on:
- **Algebra**
- **Plane Euclidean Geometry**

Text References:

Item	1	2	3	4	5
Lesson	11-4	11-1, 11-7	11-6	11-3	11-3

TEST PREP DOCTOR

1. Students who chose **C** may not have read the problem carefully and found the measure of minor $\widehat{BC}$. Or students who chose **C** may think that the measure of a central angle is half the measure of the intercepted arc.
2. Students who chose **B** may have correctly found the coordinates of the center but made an error in applying the equation of a circle. Students who chose **E** did not account for the coordinates of the center of the circle.
3. Students who chose **B** may have found *KM* instead of *PM*. Students who chose **D** may have used addition instead of multiplication in the Chord-Chord Product Theorem.
4. Students who chose **A** used the measure of the inscribed angle instead of the measure of the central angle to calculate arc length. Students who chose **E** used the formula for the area of a sector rather than the arc length formula.
5. Students who chose **A** may not have correctly applied the properties of a 45-45-90 triangle. Students who chose **D** found the area of the triangle formed by the side of the square and the radii to that side and added the area of the corresponding sector instead of subtracting.

Organizer

Objective: Provide opportunities to learn and practice common test-taking strategies.

TEST PREP DOCTOR This test tackler focuses on choosing the best answer when there are multiple correct answers or combinations of answers. Remind students to read the problem statement and answer choices thoroughly. Make sure students know to investigate each possible combination of given answers before moving on to the next test item.

Standardized Test Strategies

Multiple Choice: Choose Combinations of Answers

Given a multiple-choice test item where you are asked to choose from a combination of statements, the correct response is the most complete answer choice available. A strategy to use when solving these types of test items is to compare each given statement with the question and determine if it is true or false. If you determine that more than one of the statements is correct, then you can choose the combination that contains each correct statement.

EXAMPLE 1

Given that $\ell \parallel m$ and n is a transversal, which statement(s) are correct?

I. $\angle 1 \cong \angle 3$ II. $\angle 2 \cong \angle 5$ III. $\angle 2 \cong \angle 8$

Ⓐ I only Ⓒ II only

Ⓑ I and II Ⓓ I and III

Look at each statement separately and determine if it is true or false. As you consider each statement, write true or false beside the statement.

Consider statement I: Because $\angle 1$ and $\angle 3$ are vertical angles and vertical angles are congruent, then this statement is TRUE. So the answer could be choice A, B, or D.

Consider statement II: $\angle 2 \cong \angle 4$ because they are vertical angles. $\angle 4$ and $\angle 5$ are supplementary angles because they are same-side interior angles. So $\angle 2$ and $\angle 5$ must be supplementary, not congruent. This statement is FALSE. The answer is NOT choice B or C.

Consider statement III: Because $\angle 2$ and $\angle 8$ are alternate exterior angles and alternate exterior angles are congruent, this statement is TRUE.

Since statements I and III are both true, choice D is correct.

You can also keep track of your statements in a table.

Statement	True/False
I	TRUE
II	FALSE
III	TRUE

Only I and III are TRUE statements.

Make a table or write *T* or *F* beside each statement to keep track of whether it is true or false.

Read each test item and answer the questions that follow.

Item A
Which are chords of circle *W*?

I. $\overleftrightarrow{AB}$
II. $\overline{WG}$
III. $\overline{EC}$
IV. $\overline{FD}$

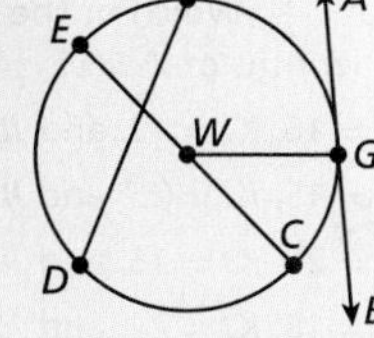

Ⓐ I only
Ⓑ III only
Ⓒ I and II
Ⓓ III and IV

1. What is the definition of a chord?
2. Determine if statements I, II, III, and IV are true or false. Explain your reasoning for each.
3. Kristin realized that statement III was true and selected choice B as her response. Do you agree? Why or why not?

Item B
Classify △*DEF*.

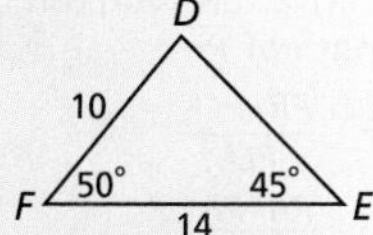

Ⓕ acute
Ⓖ acute scalene
Ⓗ obtuse
Ⓙ right equilateral

4. How can you use the Triangle Sum Theorem to find all of the angle measures of △*DEF*?
5. Consider the angle measures of △*DEF*. Is the triangle acute, right, or obtuse?
6. Explain how you can use your answer to Problem 5 to eliminate two answer choices.
7. Can a triangle be classified in any other way than by its angles? Explain.
8. Which choice gives the most complete response?

Item C
Which describes the arc length of $\widehat{AB}$?

I. $\frac{17}{72}(24\pi)$
II. $\frac{17\pi}{3}$
III. $\frac{17}{36}(24\pi)$

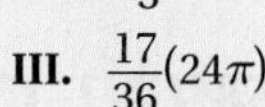

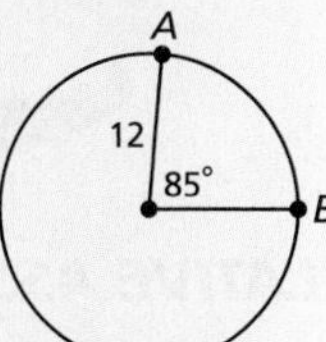

Ⓐ I only
Ⓑ II only
Ⓒ I and II
Ⓓ I, II, and III

9. What is the formula to find arc length?
10. Is statement I true or false? Explain.
11. Decide if statement II is true or false. Should you select the answer choice yet? Why or why not?
12. Can any answer choice be eliminated? Explain.
13. Describe how you know which combination of statements is correct.

Item D
A rectangular prism has a length of 5 m, a height of 10 m, and a width of 4 m. Describe the change if the height and width of the prism are multiplied by $\frac{1}{2}$.

I. The new volume is one fourth of the original volume.
II. The new height is 20 m, and the new width is 2 m.
III. The new surface area is less than half of the original surface area.

Ⓕ I only
Ⓖ II and III
Ⓗ I, II, and II
Ⓙ I and III

14. Create a table and determine if each statement is true or false.
15. Using your table, which choice is the most accurate?

As students practice this strategy, remind them to choose the best, most complete answer, not just the first correct answer they discover. Use **Questions 4–8** to show students how to arrive at the most specific answer. Review the elimination strategy and guide students to use logic to eliminate any obviously incorrect answer choice. If students are struggling with organization, show them how a table can be used to organize their processes.

Answers

Possible answers:

1. A chord is a seg. whose endpts. lie on a ⊙.
2. Statement I is false because $\overleftrightarrow{AB}$ is a tangent line, which touches the ⊙ at 1 pt. Statement II is false because $\overline{WG}$ is a radius. It is a seg. from the center of the ⊙ to a pt. on the ⊙. Statement III is true because $\overline{EC}$ is a diam., which is a chord that passes through the center of the ⊙. Statement IV is true because $\overline{FD}$ is a seg. whose endpts. lie on a ⊙.
3. No; check if statement IV is true before selecting an answer choice.
4. Subtract the sum of 50 and 45 from 180.
5. △*DEF* is acute because the measures of all the ∡ of the △ are less than 90°.
6. answer choices H and J because they do not describe the △ as acute
7. yes; by its side lengths
8. Choice **G** correctly classifies the △ by both its ∡ and its sides.

State Resources

go.hrw.com
State Resources Online
KEYWORD: MG7 Resources

Answers to Test Items

A. D
B. G
C. C
D. J

Answers

Possible answers:

9. $L = \frac{M}{360}(2\pi r)$, where *M* is the degree measure of an arc and *r* is the radius of the ⊙.

10. True; $M = 85°$ and $r = 12$. So
$$L = \frac{M}{360}(2\pi r) = \frac{85}{360}(2\pi)(12)$$
$$= \frac{5(17)}{5(72)}(24\pi) = \frac{17}{72}(24\pi)$$
Choice B can be eliminated because it does not include statement I as an option.

11. True; $M = 85°$ and $r = 12$. So
$$L = \frac{M}{360}(2\pi r) = \frac{85}{360}(2\pi)(12)$$
$$= \frac{5(17)}{5(72)}(24\pi) = \frac{17}{72}(24\pi)$$
$$= \frac{17}{3(24)}(1)(24)(\pi) = \frac{17}{3}(\pi)$$
$$= \frac{17\pi}{3}$$
The answer choice should not be selected yet because you still have to see if statement III is true or false.

12–15. See p. A30.

Organizer

Objective: Provide review and practice for Chapters 1–11 and standardized tests.

 Online Edition

Resources

Chapter 11 Cumulative Test

go.hrw.com
KEYWORD: MG7 TestPrep

Answers

1. C	11. D
2. G	12. H
3. B	13. C
4. G	14. 9
5. C	15. 8
6. J	16. 2
7. B	17. 10.4
8. F	18. 15.71
9. C	19. 452.39
10. G	20. 3

State Resources

CUMULATIVE ASSESSMENT, CHAPTERS 1–11

Multiple Choice

1. The composite figure is a right prism that shares a base with the regular pentagonal pyramid on top. If the lateral area of this figure is 328 square feet, what is the slant height of the pyramid?

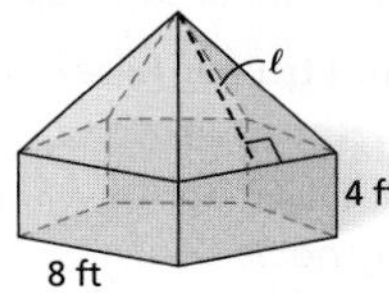

Ⓐ 2.5 feet Ⓑ 5.0 feet Ⓒ 8.4 feet Ⓓ 9.0 feet

2. What is the area of the polygon with vertices $A(2, 3)$, $B(12, 3)$, $C(6, 0)$, and $D(2, 0)$?

Ⓕ 12 square units Ⓖ 21 square units Ⓗ 30 square units Ⓙ 42 square units

Use the diagram for Items 3–5.

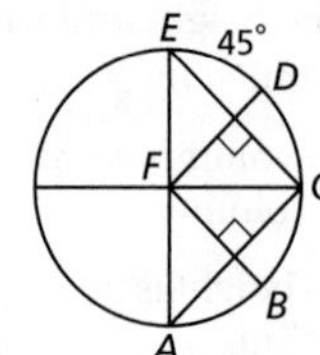

3. What is $m\widehat{BC}$?

Ⓐ 36° Ⓑ 45° Ⓒ 54° Ⓓ 72°

4. If the length of $\widehat{ED}$ is 6π centimeters, what is the area of sector EFD?

Ⓕ 20π square centimeters
Ⓖ 72π square centimeters
Ⓗ 120π square centimeters
Ⓙ 240π square centimeters

5. Which of these line segments is NOT a chord of $\odot F$?

Ⓐ $\overline{EC}$ Ⓑ $\overline{CA}$ Ⓒ $\overline{AF}$ Ⓓ $\overline{AE}$

6. $\triangle JKL$ is a right triangle where $m\angle K = 90°$ and $\tan J = \frac{3}{4}$. Which of the following could be the side lengths of $\triangle JKL$?

Ⓕ $KL = 16$, $KJ = 12$, and $JL = 20$
Ⓖ $KL = 15$, $KJ = 25$, and $JL = 20$
Ⓗ $KL = 20$, $KJ = 16$, and $JL = 12$
Ⓙ $KL = 18$, $KJ = 24$, and $JL = 30$

Use the diagram for Items 7 and 8.

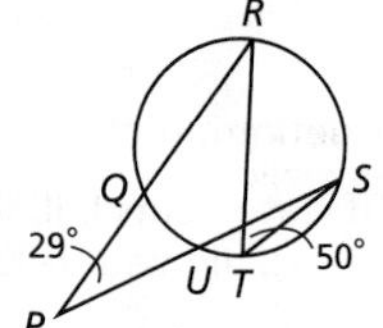

7. What is $m\widehat{QU}$?

Ⓐ 25° Ⓑ 42° Ⓒ 58° Ⓓ 71°

8. Which expression can be used to calculate the length of $\overline{PS}$?

Ⓕ $\frac{PR \cdot PQ}{PU}$ Ⓖ $\frac{PR \cdot PR}{PU}$ Ⓗ $\frac{PQ \cdot QR}{PU}$ Ⓙ $\frac{PQ \cdot PR}{PS}$

9. $\triangle ABC$ has vertices $A(0, 0)$, $B(-1, 3)$, and $C(2, 4)$. If $\triangle ABC \sim \triangle DEF$ and $\triangle DEF$ has vertices $D(5, -3)$, $E(4, -2)$, and $F(3, y)$, what is the value of y?

Ⓐ −7 Ⓑ −5 Ⓒ −3 Ⓓ −1

10. What is the equation of the circle with diameter $\overline{MN}$ that has endpoints $M(-1, 1)$ and $N(3, -5)$?

Ⓕ $(x + 1)^2 + (y - 2)^2 = 13$
Ⓖ $(x - 1)^2 + (y + 2)^2 = 13$
Ⓗ $(x + 1)^2 + (y - 2)^2 = 26$
Ⓙ $(x - 1)^2 + (y + 2)^2 = 52$

Answers

21. 14; possible answer:
$180 - 7x = \frac{1}{2}(4x + 10 + 6x + 14)$
$180 - 7x = \frac{1}{2}(10x + 24)$
$180 - 7x = 5x + 12$
$-12x = -168$ or $x = 14$

22a. The first storage unit; the first storage unit has a volume of 10 ft × 5 ft × 9 ft = 450 ft³, and the second has a volume of 11 ft × 4 ft × 8 ft = 352 ft³. So the first storage unit costs $\frac{\$85}{450 \text{ ft}^3} \approx \frac{\$0.19}{\text{ft}^3}$, and the second storage unit costs $\frac{\$70}{352 \text{ ft}^3} \approx \frac{\$0.20}{\text{ft}^3}$. The first storage unit has a lower price per cubic foot.

22b. Possible answer: length = 10 ft, width = 5 ft, and height = 8 ft. To find the total volume of the storage unit, use the proportion $\frac{\$100}{V} = \frac{\$0.25}{1 \text{ ft}^3}$. So $V = \frac{\$100 \cdot 1 \text{ ft}^3}{\$0.25} = 400 \text{ ft}^3$.

23a.

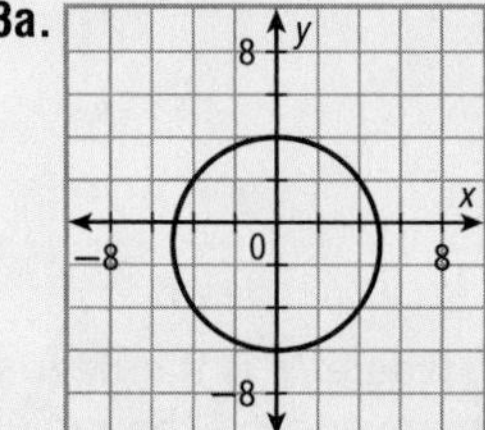

b. $y = -\frac{3}{4}x + 5\frac{1}{4}$; first use the slope formula to find the slope of the line passing through the center of $\odot C$, $(0, -1)$, and the pt. of tangency,

Remember that an important part of writing a proof is giving a justification for each step in the proof. Justifications may include theorems, postulates, definitions, properties, or the information that is given to you.

11. Kite *PQRS* has diagonals $\overline{PR}$ and $\overline{QS}$ that intersect at *T*. Which of the following is the shortest segment from *Q* to $\overline{PR}$?

Ⓐ $\overline{PT}$ Ⓒ $\overline{RQ}$

Ⓑ $\overline{QP}$ Ⓓ $\overline{TQ}$

12. If the perimeter of an equilateral triangle is reduced by a factor of $\frac{1}{2}$, what is the effect on the area of the triangle?

Ⓕ The area remains constant.

Ⓖ The area is reduced by a factor of $\frac{1}{2}$.

Ⓗ The area is reduced by a factor of $\frac{1}{4}$.

Ⓙ The area is reduced by a factor of $\frac{1}{6}$.

13. The area of a right isosceles triangle is 36 m^2. What is the length of the hypotenuse of the triangle?

Ⓐ 6 meters Ⓒ 12 meters

Ⓑ $6\sqrt{2}$ meters Ⓓ $12\sqrt{2}$ meters

Gridded Response

14. The ratio of the side lengths of a triangle is 4:5:8. If the perimeter is 38.25 centimeters, what is the length in centimeters of the shortest side?

15. What is the geometric mean of 4 and 16?

16. For $\triangle HGJ$ and $\triangle LMK$ suppose that $\angle H \cong \angle L$, $HG = 4x + 5$, $KL = 9$, $HJ = 5x - 1$, and $LM = 13$. What must be the value of *x* to prove that $\triangle HGJ$ and $\triangle LMK$ are congruent by SAS?

17. If the length of a side of a regular hexagon is 2, what is the area of the hexagon to the nearest tenth?

18. What is the arc length of a semicircle in a circle with radius 5 millimeters? Round to the nearest hundredth.

19. What is the surface area of a sphere whose volume is 288π cubic centimeters? Round to the nearest hundredth.

20. Convert (6, 60°) to rectangular coordinates. What is the value of the *x*-coordinate?

Short Response

21. Use the diagram to find the value of *x*. Show your work or explain in words how you determined your answer.

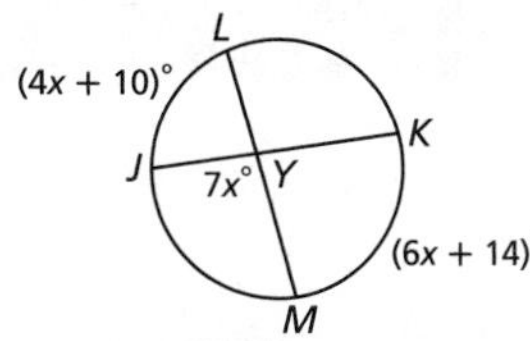

22. Paul needs to rent a storage unit. He finds one that has a length of 10 feet, a width of 5 feet, and a height of 9 feet. He finds a second storage unit that has a length of 11 feet, a width of 4 feet, and a height of 8 feet. Suppose that the first storage unit costs \$85.00 per month and that the second storage unit costs \$70.00 per month.

a. Which storage unit has a lower price per cubic foot? Show your work or explain in words how you determined your answer.

b. Paul finds a third storage unit that charges \$0.25 per cubic foot per month. What are possible dimensions of the storage unit if the charge is \$100.00 per month?

23. The equation of $\odot C$ is $x^2 + (y + 1)^2 = 25$.

a. Graph $\odot C$.

b. Write the equation of the line that is tangent to $\odot C$ at (3, 3). Show your work or explain in words how you determined your answer.

24. A tangent and a secant intersect on a circle at the point of tangency and form an acute angle. Explain how you would find the range of possible measures for the intercepted arc.

Extended Response

25. Let *ABCD* be a quadrilateral inscribed in a circle such that $\overline{AB} \parallel \overline{DC}$.

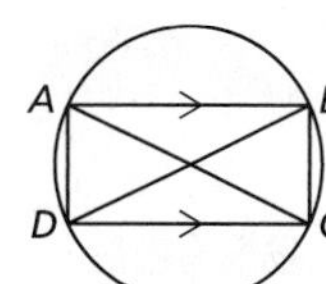

a. Prove that $m\widehat{AD} = m\widehat{BC}$.

b. Suppose *ABCD* is a trapezoid. Show that *ABCD* must be isosceles. Justify your answer.

c. If *ABCD* is not a trapezoid, explain why *ABCD* must be a rectangle.

Short-Response Rubric

Items 21–24

2 Points = The student's answer is an accurate and complete execution of the task or tasks.

1 Point = The student's answer contains attributes of an appropriate response but is flawed.

0 Points = The student's answer contains no attributes of an appropriate response.

Extended-Response Rubric

Item 25

4 Points = The student's proof and explanations are correct and complete. Work demonstrates a thorough understanding of all concepts related to inscribed angles and quadrilaterals in circles.

3 Points = The student's proof and explanations are correct but may contain minor flaws. Work demonstrates an understanding of major concepts.

2 Points = The student's proof is missing steps, or explanations are incomplete. Work demonstrates a limited understanding of concepts.

1 Point = The student answers incorrectly but makes a reasonable attempt to show work.

0 Points = The student does not answer correctly and does not attempt all parts of the problem.

(3, 3). This slope is $\frac{3-(-1)}{3-0} = \frac{4}{3}$. If a line is $\perp$ to the radius of a $\odot$ at a pt. on the $\odot$, then the line is tangent to the $\odot$. So find the eqn. of the line that passes through (3, 3) and is $\perp$ to the line through (0, −1) and (3, 3). By the $\perp$ Lines Thm., the slope of this line is $-\frac{3}{4}$. Now find the eqn. of the line with slope $-\frac{3}{4}$ passing through (3, 3).

24. greater than 0° and less than 180°

25a. Possible answer:

1. $\overline{AB} \parallel \overline{DC}$ (Given)

2. $\angle BDC \cong \angle ABD$ (Alt. Int. ∠s Thm.)

3. $m\angle BDC = m\angle ABD$ (Def. of ≅ ∠s)

4. $m\angle ACD = \frac{1}{2}m\widehat{AD}$, $m\angle BDC = \frac{1}{2}m\widehat{BC}$ (Inscribed ∠ Thm.)

5. $\frac{1}{2}m\widehat{BC} = \frac{1}{2}m\widehat{AD}$ (Subst. Prop.)

6. $m\widehat{BC} = m\widehat{AD}$ (Mult. Prop. of =)

b. Possible answer: Since $\overline{AB} \parallel \overline{DC}$, I know from part **a** that $m\widehat{AD} = m\widehat{BC}$. Also, by the Inscribed ∠ Thm., $m\angle ADC = \frac{1}{2}m\widehat{AC}$, and $m\angle BCD = \frac{1}{2}m\widehat{BD}$. Use the Arc Add. Post. to get $m\angle ADC = \frac{1}{2}(m\widehat{AB} + m\widehat{BC})$ and $m\angle BCD = \frac{1}{2}(m\widehat{AB} + m\widehat{AD})$. Substitute $m\widehat{BC}$ for $m\widehat{AD}$: $m\angle BCD = \frac{1}{2}(m\widehat{AB} + m\widehat{BC}) = m\angle ADC$. Since *ABCD* has 1 pair of ≅ base ∠s, *ABCD* is isosc.

b. Possible answer: Since $\overline{AB} \parallel \overline{DC}$, and *ABCD* is not a trap., $\overline{AD} \parallel \overline{BC}$. So *ABCD* is a ▱ which means $\angle ADC \cong \angle ABC$. So by def. of ≅, $m\angle ADC = m\angle ABC$. Also, since *ABCD* can be inscribed in a $\odot$, $\angle ADC$ and $\angle ABC$ are supp. so $m\angle ADC + m\angle ABC = 180°$. Substitute and solve for $m\angle ABC$: $m\angle ABC + m\angle ABC = 180°$; $2m\angle ABC = 180°$; $m\angle ABC = 90°$, so $\angle ABC$ is a rt. ∠. Since *ABCD* is a ▱, every ∠ is a rt. ∠. So *ABCD* is a rect.

Extending Transformational Geometry

Section 12A: Congruence Transformations	Section 12B: Patterns
12-1 Reflections	12-5 Symmetry
12-2 Translations	EXTENSION Solids of Revolution
Connecting Geometry to Algebra Transformations of Functions	12-6 Tessellations
12-3 Rotations	12-7 Dilations
12-3 Technology Lab Explore Transformations with Matrices	EXTENSION Using Patterns to Generate Fractals
12-4 Compositions of Transformations	

Pacing Guide for 45-Minute Classes

Teacher One Stop™
Calendar Planner®

Chapter 12

DAY 1	DAY 2	DAY 3	DAY 4	DAY 5
12-1 Lesson	12-2 Lesson	Connecting Geometry to Algebra	12-3 Lesson	12-3 Technology Lab
DAY 6	**DAY 7**	**DAY 8**	**DAY 9**	**DAY 10**
12-4 Lesson	Ready to Go On? Multi-Step Test Prep	12-5 Lesson	EXTENSION	12-6 Lesson
DAY 11	**DAY 12**	**DAY 13**	**DAY 14**	**DAY 15**
12-7 Lesson	EXTENSION	Multi-Step Test Prep Ready to Go On?	Chapter 12 Review	Chapter 12 Test

Pacing Guide for 90-Minute Classes

Teacher One Stop™
Calendar Planner®

Chapter 12

DAY 1	DAY 2	DAY 3	DAY 4	DAY 5
12-1 Lesson 12-2 Lesson	Connecting Geometry to Algebra 12-3 Lesson	12-3 Technology Lab 12-4 Lesson	Ready to Go On? Multi-Step Test Prep 12-5 Lesson	EXTENSION 12-6 Lesson
DAY 6	**DAY 7**	**DAY 8**		
12-7 Lesson EXTENSION	Multi-Step Test Prep Ready to Go On? Chapter 12 Review	Chapter 12 Test		

ONGOING ASSESSMENT and INTERVENTION

	DIAGNOSE	PRESCRIBE
Assess Prior Knowledge	**Before Chapter 12**	
	Diagnose readiness for the chapter.	Prescribe intervention.
	Are You Ready? SE p. 821	***Are You Ready? Intervention***
Formative Assessment	**Before Every Lesson**	
	Diagnose readiness for the lesson.	Prescribe intervention.
	Warm Up TE	**Reteach** CRB
	During Every Lesson	
	Diagnose understanding of lesson concepts.	Prescribe intervention.
	Check It Out! SE	**Reading Strategies** CRB
	Questioning Strategies TE	***Success for Every Learner***
	Think and Discuss SE	***Lesson Tutorial Videos***
	Write About It SE	
	Journal TE	
	After Every Lesson	
	Diagnose mastery of lesson concepts.	Prescribe intervention.
	Lesson Quiz TE	**Reteach** CRB
	Test Prep SE	**Test Prep Doctor** TE
	Test and Practice Generator	**Homework Help Online**
	Before Chapter 12 Testing	
	Diagnose mastery of concepts in chapter.	Prescribe intervention.
	Ready to Go On? SE pp. 855, 881	***Ready to Go On? Intervention***
	Multi-Step Test Prep SE pp. 854, 880	**Scaffolding Questions** TE pp. 854, 880
	Section Quizzes AR	**Reteach** CRB
	Test and Practice Generator	***Lesson Tutorial Videos***
	Before High Stakes Testing	
	Diagnose mastery of benchmark concepts.	Prescribe intervention.
	College Entrance Exam Practice SE p. 889	***College Entrance Exam Practice***
	Standardized Test Prep SE pp. 892–893	
Summative Assessment	**After Chapter 12**	
	Check mastery of chapter concepts.	Prescribe intervention.
	Multiple-Choice Tests (Forms A, B, C)	**Reteach** CRB
	Free-Response Tests (Forms A, B, C)	***Lesson Tutorial Videos***
	Performance Assessment AR	
	Cumulative Test AR	
	Test and Practice Generator	

KEY: **SE** = *Student Edition* **TE** = *Teacher's Edition* **CRB** = *Chapter Resource Book* **AR** = *Assessment Resources* 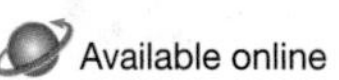 Available online Available on CD- or DVD-ROM

Lesson Resources

Before the Lesson

Prepare
Teacher One Stop SPANISH
- Editable lesson plans
- Calendar Planner
- Easy access to all chapter resources

Lesson Transparencies
- Teacher Tools

Teach the Lesson

Introduce
Alternate Openers: Explorations
Lesson Transparencies
- Warm Up
- Problem of the Day

Teach
Lesson Transparencies
- Teaching Transparencies

Know-It Notebook™
- Vocabulary
- Key Concepts

Power Presentations
Lesson Tutorial Videos  SPANISH
Interactive Online Edition 
- Lesson Activities
- Lesson Tutorial Videos

Lab Activities
Lab Resources Online 
Online Interactivities  SPANISH
TechKeys

Practice the Lesson

Practice
Chapter Resources
- Practice A, B, C

Practice and Problem Solving Workbook
IDEA Works!® Modified Worksheets and Tests
ExamView Test and Practice Generator
Homework Help Online
Online Interactivities SPANISH
Interactive Online Edition
- Homework Help

Apply
Chapter Resources
- Problem Solving

Practice and Problem Solving Workbook
Interactive Online Edition
- Chapter Project

Project Teacher Support

After the Lesson

Reteach
Chapter Resources
- Reteach
- Reading Strategies  ELL

Success for Every Learner

Review
Interactive Answers and Solutions
Solutions Key
Know-It Notebook™
- Big Ideas
- Chapter Review

Extend
Chapter Resources
- Challenge

Technology Highlights for the Teacher

Power Presentations

Dynamic presentations to engage students. Complete PowerPoint® presentations for every lesson in Chapter 12.

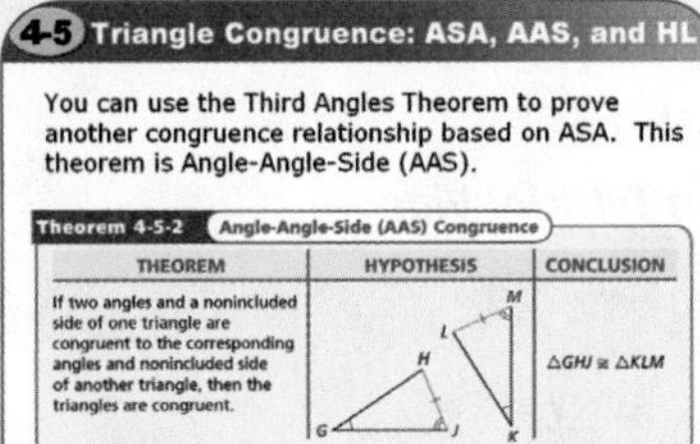

Teacher One Stop SPANISH

Easy access to Chapter 12 resources and assessments. Includes lesson planning, test generation, and puzzle creation software.

Premier Online Edition SPANISH

Chapter 12 includes Tutorial Videos, Lesson Activities, Lesson Quizzes, Homework Help, and Chapter Project.

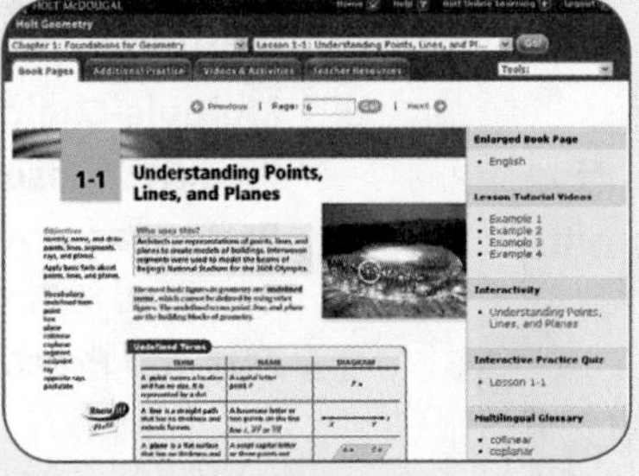

KEY: **SE** = *Student Edition* **TE** = *Teacher's Edition*  ELL English Language Learners SPANISH Spanish version available Available online  Available on CD- or DVD-ROM

Reaching All Learners

Teaching tips to help all learners appear throughout the chapter. A few that target specific students are included in the lists below.

All Learners

Lab Activities
Practice and Problem Solving Workbook
Know-It Notebook

Special Needs Students

Practice A .... CRB
Reteach .... CRB
Reading Strategies .... CRB
Are You Ready? .... SE p. 821
Inclusion .... TE pp. 838, 840, 875
IDEA Works!® Modified Worksheets and Tests
Ready to Go On? Intervention SPANISH
Know-It Notebook
Online Interactivities SPANISH
Lesson Tutorial Videos SPANISH

Developing Learners

Practice A .... CRB
Reteach .... CRB
Reading Strategies .... CRB
Are You Ready? .... SE p. 821
Vocabulary Connections .... SE p. 822
Questioning Strategies .... TE
Ready to Go On? Intervention SPANISH
Know-It Notebook
Homework Help Online
Online Interactivities SPANISH

Lesson Tutorial Videos SPANISH

On-Level Learners

Practice B .... CRB
Problem Solving .... CRB
Vocabulary Connections .... SE p. 822
Questioning Strategies .... TE
Ready to Go On? Intervention SPANISH
Know-It Notebook
Homework Help Online
Online Interactivities SPANISH

Advanced Learners

Practice C .... CRB
Challenge .... CRB
Challenge Exercises .... SE
Reading and Writing Math *Extend* .... TE p. 823
Critical Thinking .... TE pp. 862, 873
Are You Ready? Enrichment SPANISH
Ready To Go On? Enrichment SPANISH

English Language Learners

ENGLISH LANGUAGE LEARNERS

Reading Strategies .... CRB
Are You Ready? Vocabulary .... SE p. 821
Vocabulary Connections .... SE p. 822
Vocabulary Review .... SE p. 810
English Language Learners .... TE pp. 840, 849, 882, 895
Success for Every Learner
Know-It Notebook
Spanish Study Guide (Resumen y Repaso)
Multilingual Glossary
Lesson Tutorial Videos SPANISH

Technology Highlights for Reaching All Learners

Lesson Tutorial Videos SPANISH

Starring Holt authors Ed Burger and Freddie Renfro! Live tutorials to support every lesson in Chapter 12.

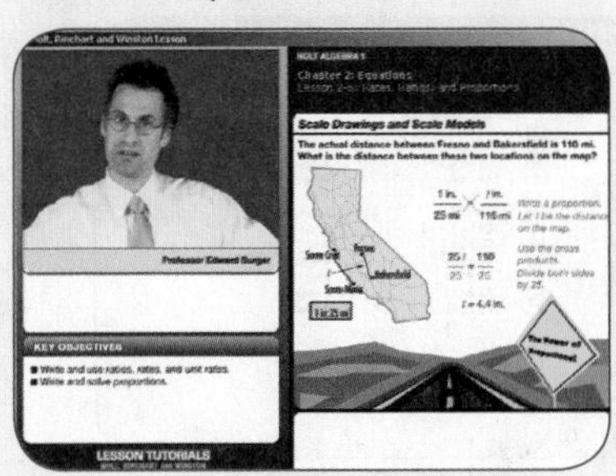

Multilingual Glossary

Searchable glossary includes definitions in English, Spanish, Vietnamese, Chinese, Hmong, Korean, and 4 other languages.

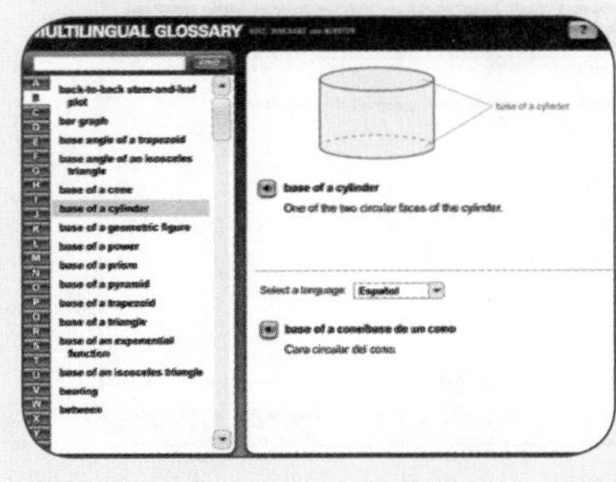

Online Interactivities

Interactive tutorials provide visually engaging alternative opportunities to learn concepts and master skills.

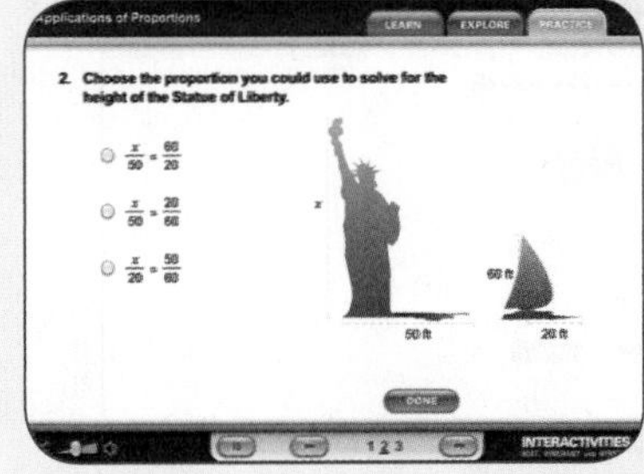

KEY: **SE** = *Student Edition* **TE** = *Teacher's Edition* **CRB** = *Chapter Resource Book* SPANISH Spanish version available; Available online; Available on CD- or DVD-ROM

Ongoing Assessment

Assessing Prior Knowledge

Determine whether students have the prerequisite concepts and skills for success in Chapter 12.

Are You Ready? SPANISH .... SE p. 821
Warm Up .... TE

Test Preparation

Provide review and practice for Chapter 12 and standardized tests.

Multi-Step Test Prep .... SE pp. 854, 880
Study Guide: Review .... SE pp. 884–887
Test Tackler .... SE pp. 890–891
Standardized Test Prep .... SE pp. 892–893
College Entrance Exam Practice .... SE p. 889
Countdown to Testing .... SE pp. C4-C27
IDEA Works!® Modified Worksheets and Tests

Alternative Assessment

Assess students' understanding of Chapter 12 concepts and combined problem-solving skills.

Chapter 12 Project .... SE p. 820
Alternative Assessment .... TE
Performance Assessment .... AR
Portfolio Assessment .... AR

Lesson Assessment

Provide formative assessment for each lesson of Chapter 12.

Questioning Strategies .... TE
Think and Discuss .... SE
Check It Out! Exercises .... SE
Write About It .... SE
Journal .... TE
Lesson Quiz .... TE
Alternative Assessment .... TE
IDEA Works!® Modified Worksheets and Tests

Weekly Assessment

Provide formative assessment for each section of Chapter 12.

Multi-Step Test Prep .... SE pp. 854, 880
Ready to Go On? SPANISH .... SE pp. 855, 881
Section Quizzes .... AR
Test and Practice Generator .... *Teacher One Stop*

Chapter Assessment

Provide summative assessment of Chapter 12 mastery.

Chapter 12 Test .... SE p. 888
Chapter Test (Levels A, B, C) .... AR
- Multiple Choice • Free Response

Cumulative Test .... AR
Test and Practice Generator .... *Teacher One Stop*
IDEA Works!® Modified Worksheets and Tests

Technology Highlights for Assessment

Are You Ready? SPANISH

Automatically assess readiness and prescribe intervention for Chapter 12 prerequisite skills.

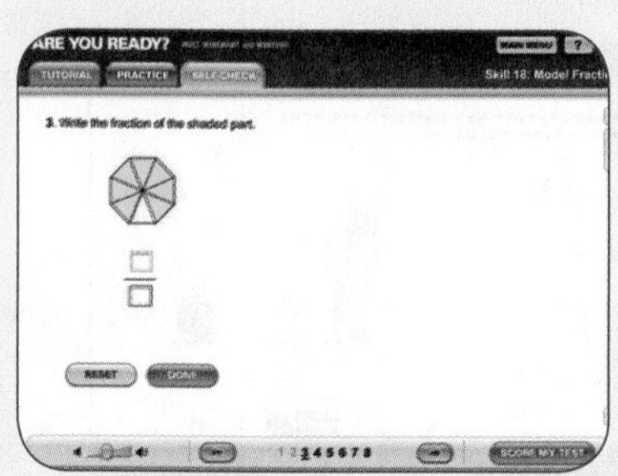

Ready to Go On?

Automatically assess understanding of and prescribe intervention for Sections 12A and 12B.

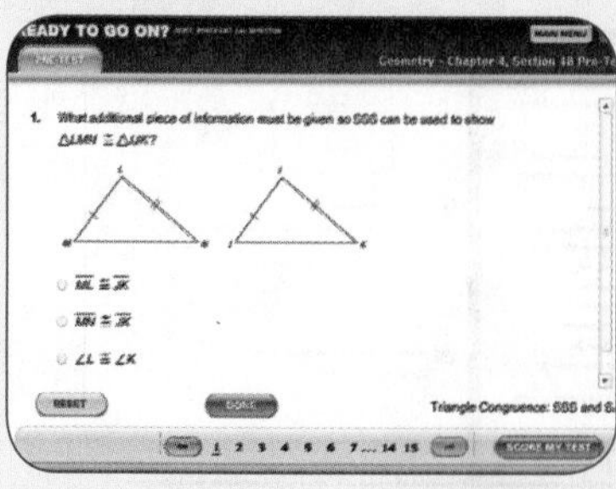

Test and Practice Generator

Use Chapter 12 problem banks to create assessments and worksheets to print out or deliver online. Includes dynamic problems.

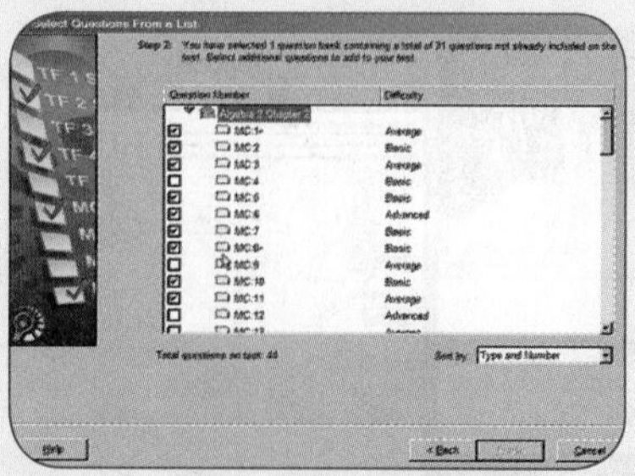

KEY: **SE** = *Student Edition* **TE** = *Teacher's Edition* **AR** = *Assessment Resources* SPANISH Spanish version available  Available online  Available on CD- or DVD-ROM

Formal Assessment

Three levels (A, B, C) of multiple-choice and free-response chapter tests, along with a performance assessment, are available in the *Assessment Resources.*

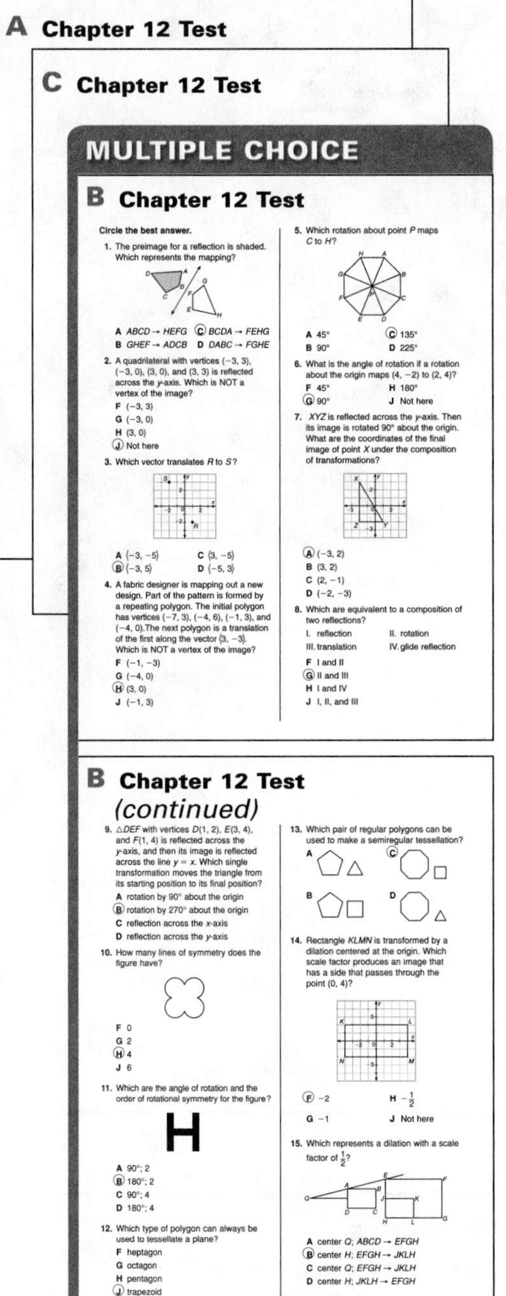

A Chapter 12 Test

C Chapter 12 Test

MULTIPLE CHOICE

B Chapter 12 Test

Circle the best answer.

1. The preimage for a reflection is shaded. Which represents the mapping?
   A $ABCD \to HEFG$ Ⓒ $BCDA \to FEHG$
   B $GHEF \to ADCB$ D $DABC \to FGHE$
2. A quadrilateral with vertices (−3, 3), (−3, 0), (3, 0), and (3, 3) is reflected across the *y*-axis. Which is NOT a vertex of the image?
   F (−3, 3)
   G (−3, 0)
   H (3, 0)
   Ⓙ Not here
3. Which vector translates *R* to *S*?
   A ⟨−3, −5⟩ C ⟨3, −5⟩
   Ⓑ ⟨−3, 5⟩ D ⟨−5, 3⟩
4. A fabric designer is mapping out a new design. Part of the pattern is formed by a repeating polygon. The initial polygon has vertices (−7, 3), (−4, 6), (−1, 3), and (−4, 0). The next polygon is a translation of the first along the vector ⟨3, −3⟩. Which is NOT a vertex of the image?
   F (−1, −3)
   G (−4, 0)
   Ⓗ (3, 0)
   J (−1, 3)
5. Which rotation about point *P* maps *C* to *H*?
   A 45° Ⓒ 135°
   B 90° D 225°
6. What is the angle of rotation if a rotation about the origin maps (4, −2) to (2, 4)?
   F 45° H 180°
   Ⓖ 90° J Not here
7. *XYZ* is reflected across the *y*-axis. Then its image is rotated 90° about the origin. What are the coordinates of the final image of point *X* under the composition of transformations?
   Ⓐ (−3, 2)
   B (3, 2)
   C (2, −1)
   D (−2, −3)
8. Which are equivalent to a composition of two reflections?
   I. reflection II. rotation
   III. translation IV. glide reflection
   F I and II
   Ⓖ II and III
   H I and IV
   J I, II, and III

B Chapter 12 Test (continued)

9. △*DEF* with vertices *D*(1, 2), *E*(3, 4), and *F*(1, 4) is reflected across the *y*-axis, and then its image is reflected across the line $y = x$. Which single transformation moves the triangle from its starting position to its final position?
   A rotation by 90° about the origin
   Ⓑ rotation by 270° about the origin
   C reflection across the *x*-axis
   D reflection across the *y*-axis
10. How many lines of symmetry does the figure have?
   F 0
   G 2
   Ⓗ 4
   J 6
11. Which are the angle of rotation and the order of rotational symmetry for the figure?
   A 90°; 2
   Ⓑ 180°; 2
   C 90°; 4
   D 180°; 4
12. Which type of polygon can always be used to tessellate a plane?
   F heptagon
   G octagon
   H pentagon
   Ⓙ trapezoid
13. Which pair of regular polygons can be used to make a semiregular tessellation?
14. Rectangle *KLMN* is transformed by a dilation centered at the origin. Which scale factor produces an image that has a side that passes through the point (0, 4)?
   Ⓕ −2 H $-\frac{1}{2}$
   G −1 J Not here
15. Which represents a dilation with a scale factor of $\frac{1}{2}$?
   A center *Q*; $ABCD \to EFGH$
   Ⓑ center *H*; $EFGH \to JKLH$
   C center *Q*; $EFGH \to JKLH$
   D center *H*; $JKLH \to EFGH$

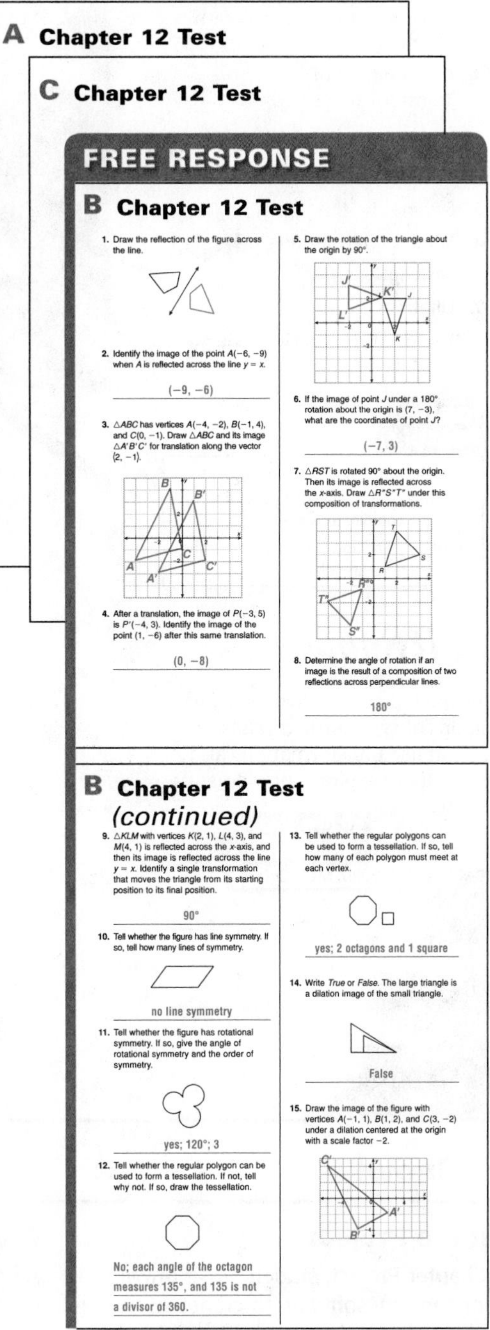

A Chapter 12 Test

C Chapter 12 Test

FREE RESPONSE

B Chapter 12 Test

1. Draw the reflection of the figure across the line.
2. Identify the image of the point *A*(−6, −9) when *A* is reflected across the line $y = x$.
   (−9, −6)
3. △*ABC* has vertices *A*(−4, −2), *B*(−1, 4), and *C*(0, −1). Draw △*ABC* and its image △*A′B′C′* for translation along the vector ⟨2, −1⟩.
4. After a translation, the image of *P*(−3, 5) is *P′*(−4, 3). Identify the image of the point (1, −6) after this same translation.
   (0, −8)
5. Draw the rotation of the triangle about the origin by 90°.
6. If the image of point *J* under a 180° rotation about the origin is (7, −3), what are the coordinates of point *J*?
   (−7, 3)
7. △*RST* is rotated 90° about the origin. Then its image is reflected across the *x*-axis. Draw △*R″S″T″* under this composition of transformations.
8. Determine the angle of rotation if an image is the result of a composition of two reflections across perpendicular lines.
   180°

B Chapter 12 Test (continued)

9. △*KLM* with vertices *K*(2, 1), *L*(4, 3), and *M*(4, 1) is reflected across the *x*-axis, and then its image is reflected across the line $y = x$. Identify a single transformation that moves the triangle from its starting position to its final position.
   90°
10. Tell whether the figure has line symmetry. If so, tell how many lines of symmetry.
   no line symmetry
11. Tell whether the figure has rotational symmetry. If so, give the angle of rotational symmetry and the order of symmetry.
   yes; 120°; 3
12. Tell whether the regular polygon can be used to form a tessellation. If not, tell why not. If so, draw the tessellation.
   No; each angle of the octagon measures 135°, and 135 is not a divisor of 360.
13. Tell whether the regular polygons can be used to form a tessellation. If so, tell how many of each polygon must meet at each vertex.
   yes; 2 octagons and 1 square
14. Write *True* or *False*. The large triangle is a dilation image of the small triangle.
   False
15. Draw the image of the figure with vertices *A*(−1, 1), *B*(1, 2), and *C*(3, −2) under a dilation centered at the origin with a scale factor −2.

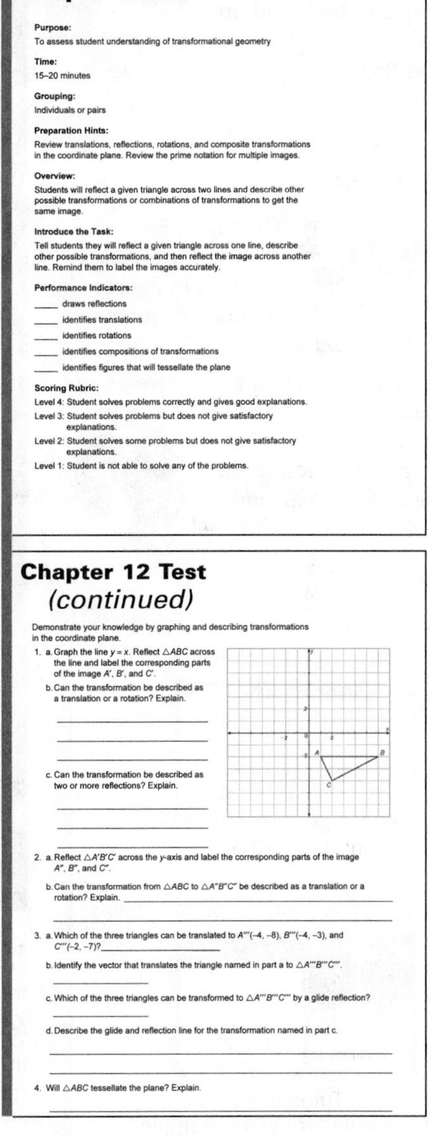

PERFORMANCE ASSESSMENT

Chapter 12 Test

Purpose:
To assess student understanding of transformational geometry

Time:
15–20 minutes

Grouping:
Individuals or pairs

Preparation Hints:
Review translations, reflections, rotations, and composite transformations in the coordinate plane. Review the prime notation for multiple images.

Overview:
Students will reflect a given triangle across two lines and describe other possible transformations or combinations of transformations to get the same image.

Introduce the Task:
Tell students they will reflect a given triangle across one line, describe other possible transformations, and then reflect the image across another line. Remind them to label the images accurately.

Performance Indicators:
____ draws reflections
____ identifies translations
____ identifies rotations
____ identifies compositions of transformations
____ identifies figures that will tessellate the plane

Scoring Rubric:
Level 4: Student solves problems correctly and gives good explanations.
Level 3: Student solves problems but does not give satisfactory explanations.
Level 2: Student solves some problems but does not give satisfactory explanations.
Level 1: Student is not able to solve any of the problems.

Chapter 12 Test (continued)

Demonstrate your knowledge by graphing and describing transformations in the coordinate plane.

1. a. Graph the line $y = x$. Reflect △*ABC* across the line and label the corresponding parts of the image *A′*, *B′*, and *C′*.
   b. Can the transformation be described as a translation or a rotation? Explain.
   c. Can the transformation be described as two or more reflections? Explain.
2. a. Reflect △*A′B′C′* across the *y*-axis and label the corresponding parts of the image *A″*, *B″*, and *C″*.
   b. Can the transformation from △*ABC* to △*A″B″C″* be described as a translation or a rotation? Explain.
3. a. Which of the three triangles can be translated to *A‴*(−4, −8), *B‴*(−4, −3), and *C‴*(−2, −7)?
   b. Identify the vector that translates the triangle named in part a to △*A‴B‴C‴*.
   c. Which of the three triangles can be transformed to △*A‴B‴C‴* by a glide reflection?
   d. Describe the glide and reflection line for the transformation named in part c.
4. Will △*ABC* tessellate the plane? Explain.

Modified chapter tests that address special learning needs are available in *IDEA Works!*® *Modified Worksheets and Tests.*

Teacher One Stop™

Test & Practice Generator

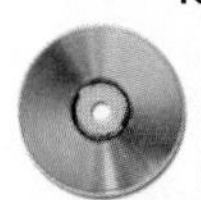

Create and customize Chapter 12 Tests. Instantly generate multiple test versions, answer keys, and practice versions of test items.

CHAPTER 12

SECTION 12A

Congruence Tranformations

On page 854, students use transformations to model a miniature golf course.

Exercises designed to prepare students for success on the Multi-Step Test Prep can be found on pages 829, 835, 843, and 853.

SECTION 12B

Patterns

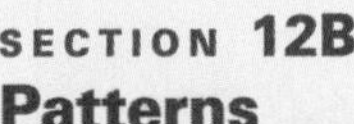

On page 880, students use patterns in figures to analyze works by M. C. Escher.

Exercises designed to prepare students for success on the Multi-Step Test Prep can be found on pages 861, 868, and 876.

Interactivities Online ▶

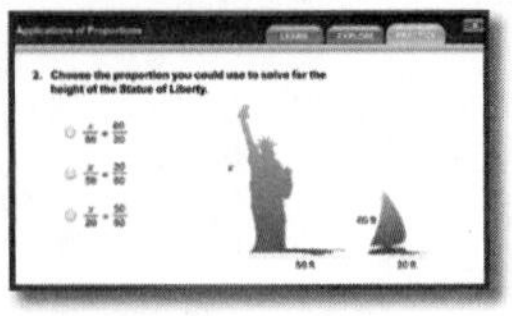

Lessons 12-1, 12-6.

Video Lesson Tutorials Online

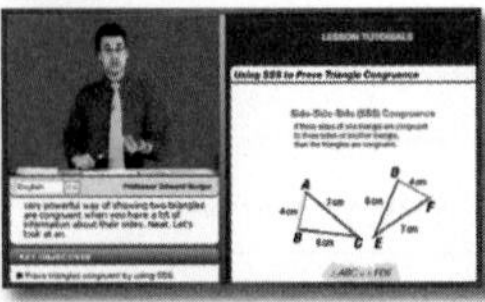

Lesson Tutorial Videos are available for EVERY example.

CHAPTER 12

Extending Transformational Geometry

Chapter Focus

- Apply reflections, translations, and rotations to simple geometric figures in the coordinate plane.
- Understand how symmetry and transformations are related.

Let it Snow!

A blanket of snow is formed by trillions of symmetric crystals. You can use transformations and symmetry to explore snow crystals.

go.hrw.com Chapter Project Online KEYWORD: MG7 ChProj

820 Chapter 12

Let it Snow!

About the Project

In the Chapter Project, students use drawing tools or geometry software to create snow crystals based on reflections and rotations. Then they use paper folding to explore the symmetry of snow crystals.

Project Resources

All project resources for teachers and students are provided online.

Materials:

- patty paper
- geometry software

go.hrw.com Project Teacher Support KEYWORD: MG7 ProjectTS

ARE YOU READY?

Vocabulary

Match each term on the left with a definition on the right.

1. image **E**
2. preimage **C**
3. transformation **A**
4. vector **D**

A. a mapping of a figure from its original position to a new position
B. a ray that divides an angle into two congruent angles
C. a shape that undergoes a transformation
D. a quantity that has both a size and a direction
E. the shape that results from a transformation of a figure

Ordered Pairs

Graph each ordered pair.

5. $(0, 4)$
6. $(-3, 2)$
7. $(4, 3)$
8. $(3, -1)$
9. $(-1, -3)$
10. $(-2, 0)$

Congruent Figures

Can you conclude that the given triangles are congruent? If so, explain why.

11. $\triangle PQS$ and $\triangle PRS$ **no**

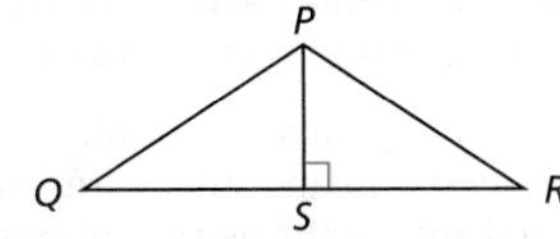

12. $\triangle DEG$ and $\triangle FGE$

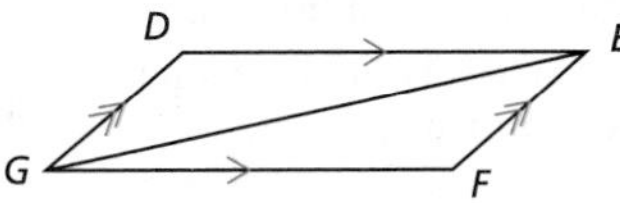

Identify Similar Figures

Can you conclude that the given figures are similar? If so, explain why.

13. $\triangle JKL$ and $\triangle JMN$

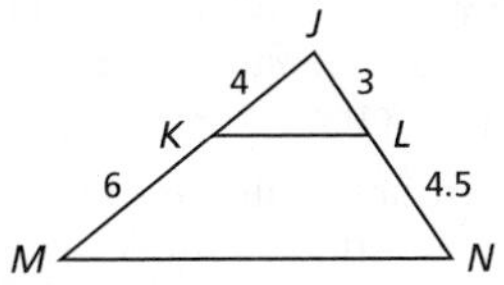

14. rectangle $PQRS$ and rectangle $UVWX$

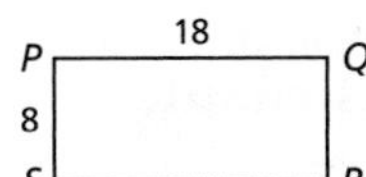

Angles in Polygons

15. Find the measure of each interior angle of a regular octagon. **135°**
16. Find the sum of the interior angle measures of a convex pentagon. **540°**
17. Find the measure of each exterior angle of a regular hexagon. **60°**
18. Find the value of x in hexagon $ABCDEF$. **$x = 126$**

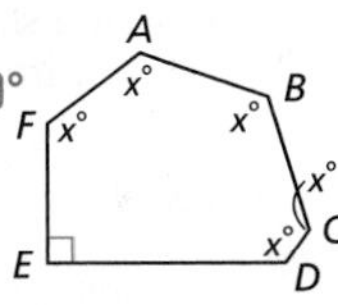

CHAPTER 12

ARE YOU READY?

Organizer

Objective: Assess students' understanding of prerequisite skills.

Prerequisite Skills

Ordered Pairs
Congruent Figures
Identify Similar Figures
Angles in Polygons

Assessing Prior Knowledge

INTERVENTION

Diagnose and Prescribe

Use this page to determine whether intervention is necessary or whether enrichment is appropriate.

Resources

***Are You Ready? Intervention and Enrichment* Worksheets**

***Are You Ready?* CD-ROM**

***Are You Ready?* Online**

my.hrw.com

Answers

5–10, 12–14. See p. A30.

ARE YOU READY? Diagnose and Prescribe

Prerequisite Skill	*Are You Ready? Intervention,* Chapter 12 — Worksheets	CD-ROM	Online
Ordered Pairs	Skill 79	Activity 79	Diagnose and Prescribe Online
Congruent Figures	Skill 33	Activity 33	
Identify Similar Figures	Skill 34	Activity 34	
Angles in Polygons	Skill 28	Activity 28	

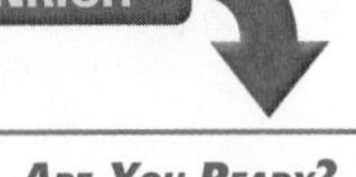

***Are You Ready? Enrichment,* Chapter 12**

Worksheets
CD-ROM
Online

CHAPTER 12 Study Guide: Preview

Organizer

Objective: Help students organize the new concepts they will learn in Chapter 12.

Resources

Teacher One Stop™
PuzzleView

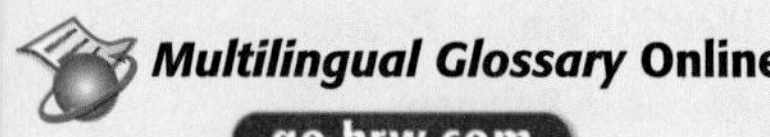

go.hrw.com
KEYWORD: MG7 Glossary

Answers to *Vocabulary Connections*

1. A composition is 2 or more transformations performed in a certain order on the same figure.
2. The preimage and image have = measures (side lengths, areas, etc.)
3. A geometric figure has symmetry if there is a transformation of the figure such that the image coincides with the preimage.
4. A mosaic covers a surface with tiles, and a tessellation covers a plane with a pattern of shapes.

CHAPTER 12 Study Guide: Preview

Where You've Been

Previously, you

- graphed figures on a coordinate plane.
- studied congruent figures, similar figures, parallel lines, and perpendicular lines.
- used transformations to explore properties of figures.

In This Chapter

You will study

- rules for transformations in the coordinate plane.
- transformations that preserve congruence of figures.
- properties of figures such as symmetry.

Where You're Going

You can use the skills learned in this chapter

- in all your future math classes, including Algebra 2.
- in other classes, such as Art, Chemistry, Biology, and Physics.
- to find shortest paths, build furniture, and create artwork.

Key Vocabulary/Vocabulario

composition of transformations	composición de transformaciones
glide reflection	deslizamiento con inversión
isometry	isometría
symmetry	simetría
tessellation	teselado

Vocabulary Connections

To become familiar with some of the vocabulary terms in the chapter, consider the following. You may refer to the chapter, the glossary, or a dictionary if you like.

1. A *composition* is something that has been put together. How can you use this idea to understand what is meant by a **composition of transformations**?
2. The prefix *iso-* means "equal." The suffix *-metry* means "measure." What do you think might be true about the preimage and image of a figure under a transformation that is an **isometry**?
3. Give some examples of how the words *symmetry* and *symmetric* are used in everyday speech. What do you think it means for a geometric figure to have **symmetry**?
4. *Tessera* are small tiles used to create a mosaic. How do you think this relates to the meaning of the word **tessellation**?

Study Strategy: Prepare for Your Final Exam

Math is a cumulative subject, so your final exam will probably cover all of the material you have learned since the beginning of the course. Preparation is essential for you to be successful on your final exam. It may help you to make a study timeline like the one below.

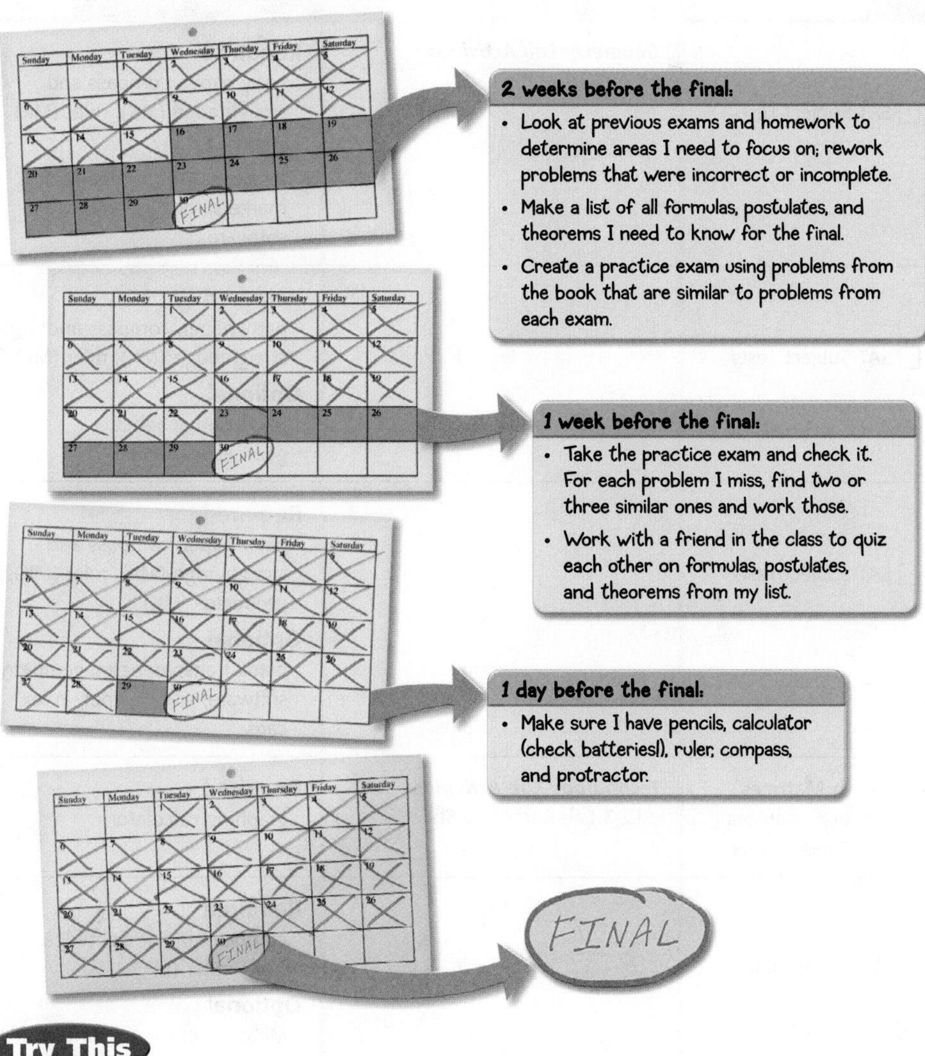

2 weeks before the final:
• Look at previous exams and homework to determine areas I need to focus on; rework problems that were incorrect or incomplete.
• Make a list of all formulas, postulates, and theorems I need to know for the final.
• Create a practice exam using problems from the book that are similar to problems from each exam.
1 week before the final:
• Take the practice exam and check it. For each problem I miss, find two or three similar ones and work those.
• Work with a friend in the class to quiz each other on formulas, postulates, and theorems from my list.
1 day before the final:
• Make sure I have pencils, calculator (check batteries!), ruler, compass, and protractor.
FINAL

Try This

1. Create a timeline that you will use to study for your final exam.

Reading and Writing Math CHAPTER 12

Organizer

Objective: Help students apply strategies to understand and retain key concepts.

Study Strategy: Preparing for Your Final Exam

Discuss In their timelines, students may include only the topics that they had difficulty with. Remind them that even though some topics may not have caused them difficulty when first introduced, they should be careful to include all major topics in their lists of items for review.

Extend Ask students to relate each topic they study in Chapter 12 to an item in their list of formulas, postulates, and theorems.

Have students add each new topic from Chapter 12 to their study list as the lessons in this chapter are introduced.

Answers to *Try This*

1. Check students' timelines.

Reading Connection

***Origami Tessellations* by Eric Gjerde**

Origami tessellations are different from conventional origami figures. The object is to crease lines on paper to make flat and extremely complex weaves, pleats, twists, and mosaic-like patterns. The author provides step-by-step instructions for 25 tessellation projects, accompanying each with beautiful and useful illustrations.

Activity Challenge students to complete one of the ten beginner projects. They can present their designs to the class, explaining why each is a tessellation.

SECTION 12A Congruence Transformations

One-Minute Section Planner

Lesson	Lab Resources	Materials
Lesson 12-1 Reflections • Identify and draw reflections. ☐ SAT-10 ☑ NAEP ☐ ACT ☐ SAT ☐ SAT Subject Tests	***Geometry Lab Activities*** 12-1 Geometry Lab	**Required** patty paper, compass and straightedge (MK), ruler (MK) **Optional** rubber stamp, whiteboard markers, Mira, geometry software
Lesson 12-2 Translations • Identify and draw translations. ☐ SAT-10 ☑ NAEP ☑ ACT ☐ SAT ☐ SAT Subject Tests		**Required** patty paper, compass and straightedge (MK), ruler (MK) **Optional** uncooked spaghetti, geometry software
Lesson 12-3 Rotations • Identify and draw rotations. ☐ SAT-10 ☑ NAEP ☑ ACT ☐ SAT ☐ SAT Subject Tests		**Required** patty paper, compass and straightedge (MK), ruler (MK), protractor (MK) **Optional** blank transparencies, geometry software, graph paper, index card
12-3 Technology Lab Explore Transformations with Matrices • Use a graphing calculator to explore transformations with matrices ☐ SAT-10 ☐ NAEP ☑ ACT ☑ SAT ☑ SAT Subject Tests	***Technology Lab Activities*** 12-3 Lab Recording Sheet	**Required** graphing calculator
Lesson 12-4 Compostions of Tranformations • Apply theorems about isometries. • Identify and draw compositions of transformations, such as glide reflections. ☐ SAT-10 ☑ NAEP ☐ ACT ☑ SAT ☑ SAT Subject Tests		**Required** compass and straightedge (MK), ruler (MK) **Optional** Miras or mirrors, geometry software, pattern blocks (MK)

MK = *Manipulatives Kit*

Math Background

ISOMETRIES

Lessons 12-1 to 12-4

An *isometry* is a transformation that preserves distance. This means that under an isometry, the distance between any two points of the pre-image is the same as the distance between the corresponding points of the image. So, an isometry does not change the size or shape of a figure.

Isometries are also called *congruence mappings*. In fact, congruence may be defined in terms of isometries as follows: Two figures are congruent if and only if there is an isometry that maps one figure to the other.

In the plane, there are four types of isometries: *reflections*, *translations*, *rotations*, and *glide reflections*. The *identity transformation*, which maps every point to itself, may be considered a separate isometry or it may be considered a special case of a translation or rotation.

It is natural to ask whether there are other isometries. For example, it seems intuitively obvious that a composition of isometries (one isometry followed by another) is also an isometry. Therefore, it makes sense to ask whether the composition of a translation and a rotation is a new type of isometry or whether the resulting transformation is equivalent to one of the four basic isometries. The somewhat surprising answer is that every isometry is indeed a reflection, translation, rotation, or glide reflection.

REFLECTIONS

Lesson 12-1

Reflections have two properties that distinguish them from translations and rotations. First, reflections reverse the orientation of a figure. To understand what is meant by this, consider the reflection of $\triangle ABC$ across line m.

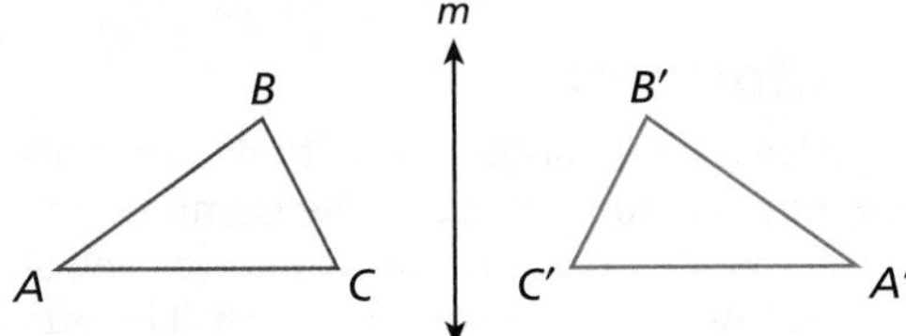

When you move from vertex A to vertex B to vertex C in $\triangle ABC$, you move clockwise around the triangle. When you trace the images of the vertices in the same order in $\triangle A'B'C'$, you move counterclockwise around the triangle. Mirrors offer a familiar example of reflections and their property of reversing orientation. When you look in a mirror and move your hand from left to right, the person you see in the mirror appears to move his or her hand from right to left.

Reflections are also distinguished by the fact that they have more than one fixed point. For example, all of the points of line m remain fixed under the reflection shown above. By contrast, (non-identity) translations have no fixed points and (non-identity) rotations have exactly one fixed point (the center of the rotation).

COMPOSITIONS

Lesson 12-4

As discussed above, every isometry is a reflection, translation, rotation, or glide reflection. Thus, the composition of any two of these isometries must be equivalent to one of the four basic isometries. The following table summarizes the results of all possible compositions.

Compositions of Isometries

	Refl.	Trans.	Rot.	Glide
Refl.	Trans. or Rot.	Glide	Glide	Trans. or Rot.
Trans.	Glide	Trans.	Rot.	Refl. or Glide
Rot.	Glide	Rot.	Trans. or Rot.	Glide
Glide	Trans. or Rot.	Refl. or Glide	Glide	Trans. or Rot.

It is also interesting to consider "decomposing" transformations. According to Theorem 12-4-3, any translation or rotation is equivalent to a composition of two reflections. A glide reflection, which is a composition of a reflection and a translation, is therefore equivalent to three reflections. Thus, every isometry is equivalent to at most three reflections.

12-1 Organizer

Pacing: Traditional 1 day
Block $\frac{1}{2}$ day

Objective: Identify and draw reflections.

Geometry Lab
In *Geometry Lab Activities*

Online Edition
Tutorial Videos, Interactivity

Power Presentations with PowerPoint®

Warm Up

Given that $\triangle ABC \cong \triangle DEF$, identify a segment or angle congruent to each of the following.

1. $\angle B$ $\angle E$ **2.** $\overline{DE}$ $\overline{AB}$
3. $\overline{AC}$ $\overline{DF}$ **4.** $\angle F$ $\angle C$
5. $\angle A$ $\angle D$ **6.** $\overline{BC}$ $\overline{EF}$

Also available on transparency

Math Humor

Q: What did the carpenter say as he cut down his oak?

A: Isometry! (I saw my tree!)

12-1 Reflections

Objective
Identify and draw reflections.

Vocabulary
isometry

Who uses this?
Trail designers use reflections to find shortest paths. (See Example 3.)

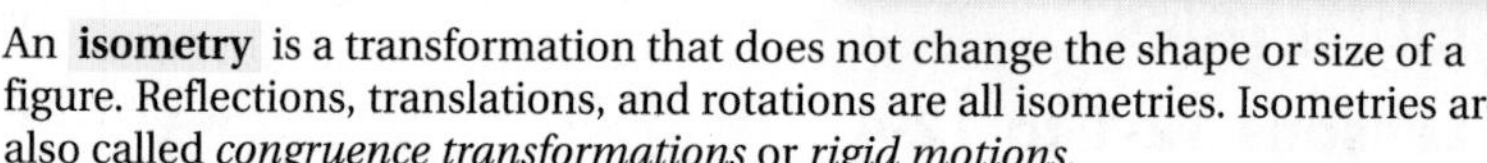

An **isometry** is a transformation that does not change the shape or size of a figure. Reflections, translations, and rotations are all isometries. Isometries are also called *congruence transformations* or *rigid motions.*

Recall that a reflection is a transformation that moves a figure (the preimage) by flipping it across a line. The reflected figure is called the image. A reflection is an isometry, so the image is always congruent to the preimage.

Remember!
To review basic transformations, see Lesson 1-7, pages 50–55.

EXAMPLE 1 Identifying Reflections

Tell whether each transformation appears to be a reflection. Explain.

A

Yes; the image appears to be flipped across a line.

B

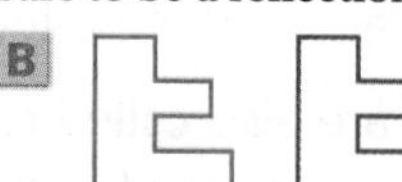

No; the figure does not appear to be flipped.

CHECK IT OUT! **Tell whether each transformation appears to be a reflection.**

1a.

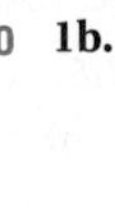

no

1b.

yes

Construction Reflect a Figure Using Patty Paper

1

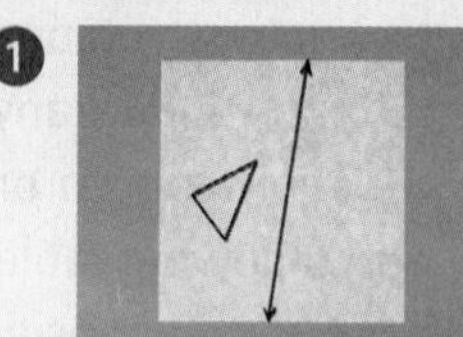

Draw a triangle and a line of reflection on a piece of patty paper.

2

Fold the patty paper back along the line of reflection.

3

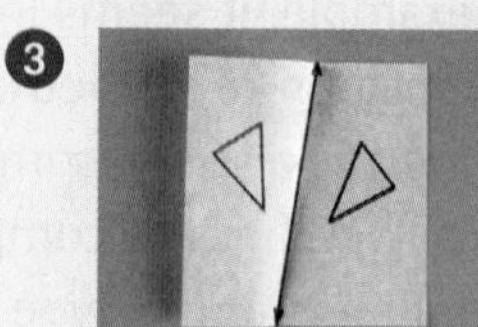

Trace the triangle. Then unfold the paper.

Draw a segment from each vertex of the preimage to the corresponding vertex of the image. Your construction should show that the line of reflection is the perpendicular bisector of every segment connecting a point and its image.

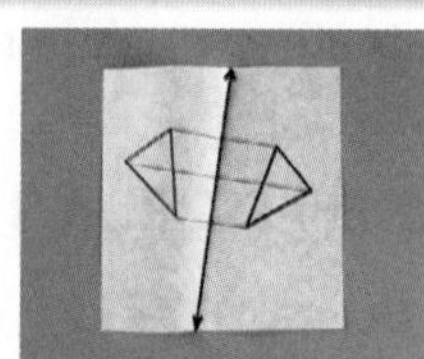

State Resources

go.hrw.com
State Resources Online
KEYWORD: MG7 Resources

1 Introduce

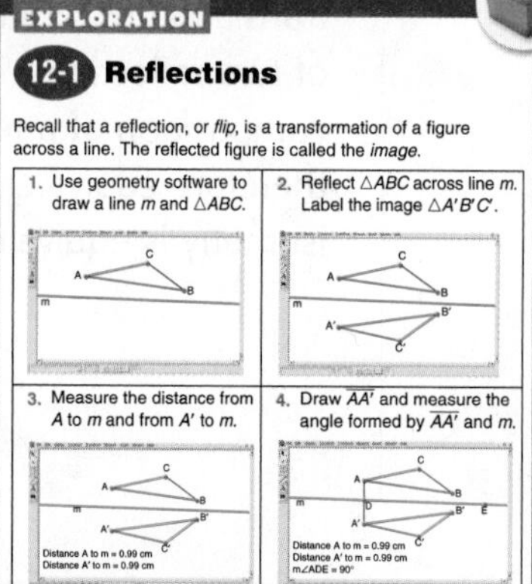

EXPLORATION

12-1 Reflections

Recall that a reflection, or *flip*, is a transformation of a figure across a line. The reflected figure is called the *image*.

1. Use geometry software to draw a line *m* and $\triangle ABC$.
2. Reflect $\triangle ABC$ across line *m*. Label the image $\triangle A'B'C'$.
3. Measure the distance from *A* to *m* and from *A'* to *m*.
4. Draw $\overline{AA'}$ and measure the angle formed by $\overline{AA'}$ and *m*.
5. How is line *m* related to $\overline{AA'}$? Does this relationship always hold as you drag points and lines in your figure?

Motivate

Use a large rubber stamp to demonstrate a reflection for students. Color the stamp using markers for white boards or transparencies and stamp the surface immediately. For chalkboards, press a clean stamp into a wet sponge and press it onto the board. Compare the image to the stamp. The stamp and its image are congruent, but the image is reversed.

Explorations and answers are provided in *Alternate Openers: Explorations Transparencies.*

Reflections

A reflection is a transformation across a line, called the line of reflection, so that the line of reflection is the perpendicular bisector of each segment joining each point and its image.

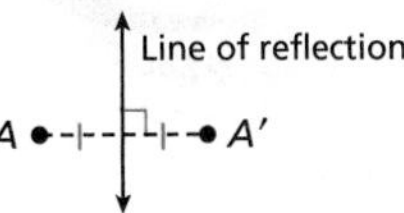

EXAMPLE 2 **Drawing Reflections**

Copy the quadrilateral and the line of reflection. Draw the reflection of the quadrilateral across the line.

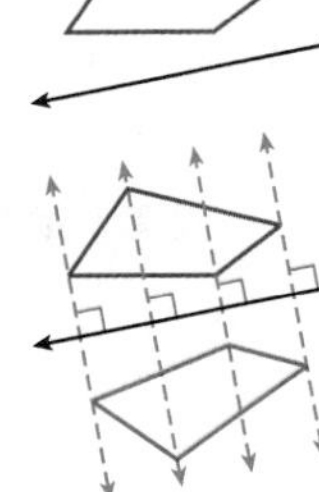

Step 1 Through each vertex draw a line perpendicular to the line of reflection.

Step 2 Measure the distance from each vertex to the line of reflection. Locate the image of each vertex on the opposite side of the line of reflection and the same distance from it.

Step 3 Connect the images of the vertices.

2. Copy the quadrilateral and the line of reflection. Draw the reflection of the quadrilateral across the line.

EXAMPLE 3 ***Problem-Solving Application***

A trail designer is planning two trails that connect campsites A and B to a point on the river. He wants the total length of the trails to be as short as possible. Where should the trail meet the river?

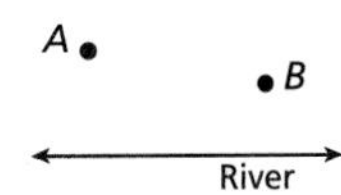

 **Understand the Problem**

The problem asks you to locate point X on the river so that $AX + XB$ has the least value possible.

 **Make a Plan**

Let B' be the reflection of point B across the river. For any point X on the river, $\overline{XB'} \cong \overline{XB}$, so $AX + XB = AX + XB'$. $AX + XB'$ is least when A, X, and B' are collinear.

 **Solve**

Reflect B across the river to locate B'. Draw $\overline{AB'}$ and locate X at the intersection of $\overline{AB'}$ and the river.

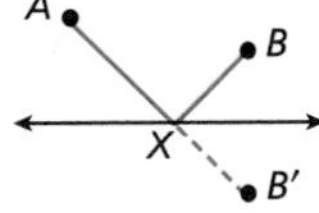

 **Look Back**

To verify your answer, choose several possible locations for X and measure the total length of the trails for each location.

3. **What if...?** If A and B were the same distance from the river, what would be true about $\overline{AX}$ and $\overline{BX}$?
$\overline{AX}$ and $\overline{BX}$ would be congruent.

Construction

To help students see the relationship between the triangles, have them label the vertices of the preimage A, B, and C and the corresponding vertices of the image A', B', and C'.

Power Presentations with PowerPoint®

Additional Examples

Example 1

Tell whether each transformation appears to be a reflection.

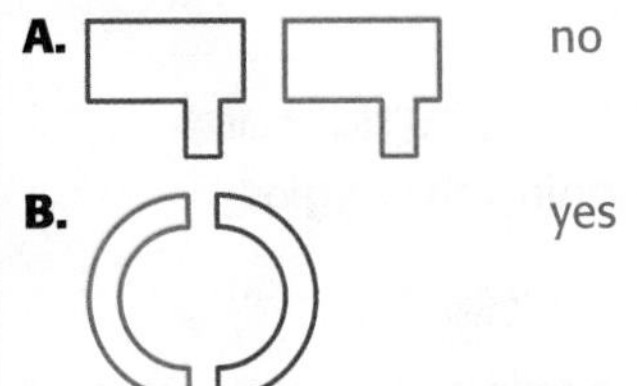

A. no

B. yes

Example 2

Copy the triangle and the line of reflection. Draw the reflection of the triangle across the line.

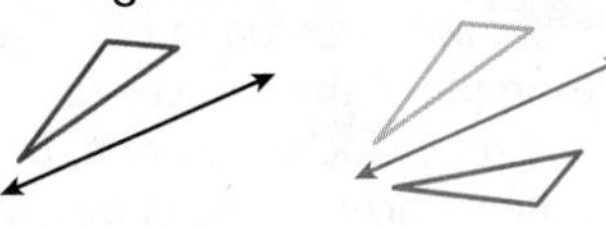

Example 3

Two buildings located at A and B are to be connected to the same point on the water line. Where should they connect so that the least amount of pipe will be used?

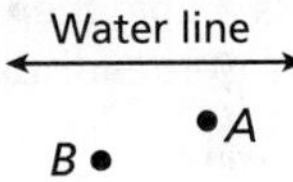

Reflect A across the water line. The connection should be where $\overline{A'B}$ intersects the water line.

2 Teach

Guided Instruction

Show students that the line of reflection is the perpendicular bisector of each segment joining a point and its image. Emphasize that the image of a reflection is congruent to the preimage, so the corresponding vertices should be written in the same order.

Visual Use blank transparencies on a whiteboard to perform transformations. They will stick to the board, allowing you to trace the figures.

Reaching All Learners

Through Auditory Cues

A reflection maps a figure onto its image. Arrow notation describes the mapping. For example, we write $\triangle GHI \rightarrow \triangle G'H'I'$ and say that $\triangle GHI$ "maps onto" $\triangle G'H'I'$. Have students draw a triangle and its reflected image, describe the relationship using arrow notation, and read the mapping relationship aloud, including the mapping relationships between each pair of corresponding sides and vertices.

INTERVENTION

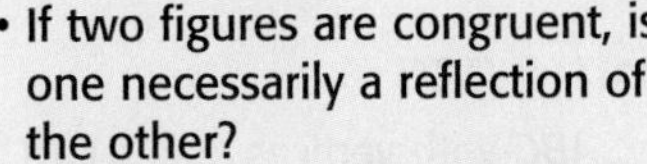

Questioning Strategies

EXAMPLE 1

- If two figures are congruent, is one necessarily a reflection of the other?
- How do you know when a transformation is a reflection?

EXAMPLE 2

- When given the preimage and the image, how could you locate the line of reflection?

EXAMPLE 3

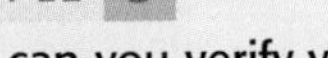

- How can you verify your answer?

Power Presentations with PowerPoint®

Additional Examples

Example 4

Reflect the figure with the given vertices across the given line.

A. $X(2, -1)$, $Y(-4, -3)$, $Z(3, 2)$; x-axis $X'(2, 1)$, $Y'(-4, 3)$, $Z'(3, -2)$

B. $R(-2, 2)$, $S(5, 0)$, $T(3, -1)$; $y = x$ $R'(2, -2)$, $S'(0, 5)$, $T'(-1, 3)$

INTERVENTION

Questioning Strategies

EXAMPLE 4

- How is reflecting a figure across the x-axis different from reflecting a figure across the y-axis?

Math Background A reflection is said to *reverse the orientation* of a figure. For example, if the vertices of a triangle read clockwise are A, B, C, then the vertices of the image will occur counterclockwise in the order A', B', C'.

Technology Geometry software can help students explore properties of reflections. Have students reflect a point A across a line, then verify that the line is the perpendicular bisector of $\overline{AA'}$.

Reflections in the Coordinate Plane

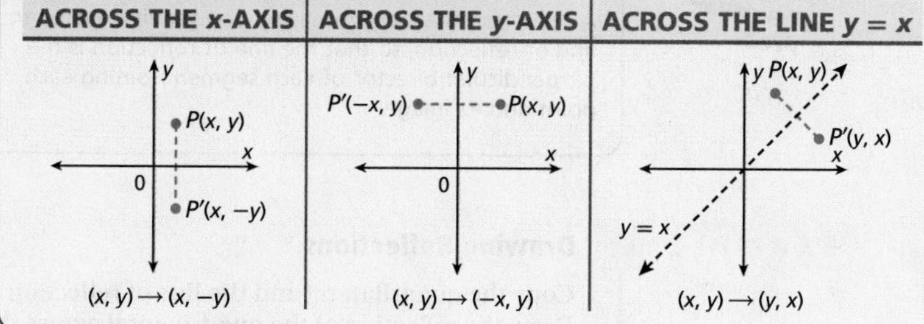

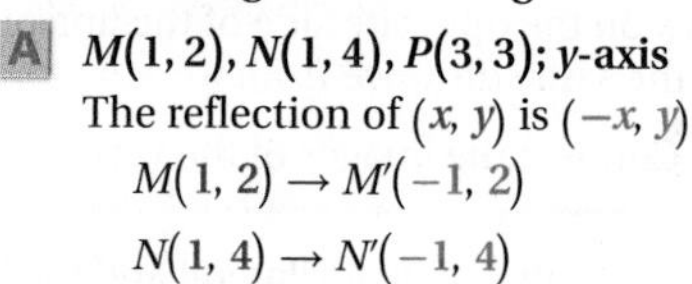

EXAMPLE 4 Drawing Reflections in the Coordinate Plane

Reflect the figure with the given vertices across the given line.

A $M(1, 2)$, $N(1, 4)$, $P(3, 3)$; y-axis

The reflection of (x, y) is $(-x, y)$.

$M(1, 2) \rightarrow M'(-1, 2)$

$N(1, 4) \rightarrow N'(-1, 4)$

$P(3, 3) \rightarrow P'(-3, 3)$

Graph the preimage and image.

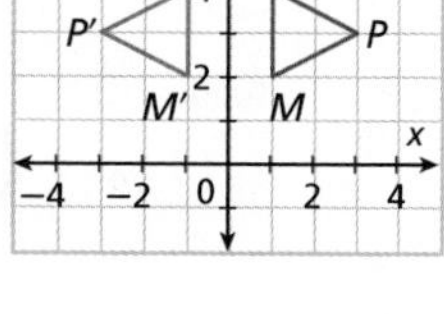

B $D(2, 0)$, $E(2, 2)$, $F(5, 2)$, $G(5, 1)$; $y = x$

The reflection of (x, y) is (y, x).

$D(2, 0) \rightarrow D'(0, 2)$

$E(2, 2) \rightarrow E'(2, 2)$

$F(5, 2) \rightarrow F'(2, 5)$

$G(5, 1) \rightarrow G'(1, 5)$

Graph the preimage and image.

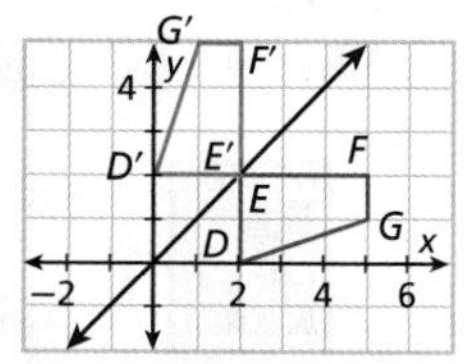

4. 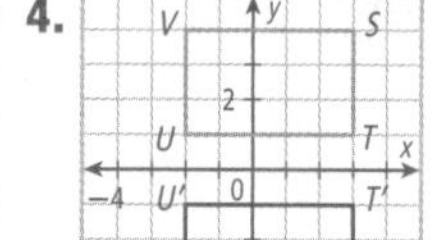

4. Reflect the rectangle with vertices $S(3, 4)$, $T(3, 1)$, $U(-2, 1)$, and $V(-2, 4)$ across the x-axis.

THINK AND DISCUSS

1. Acute scalene $\triangle ABC$ is reflected across $\overline{BC}$. Classify quadrilateral $ABA'C$. Explain your reasoning.
2. Point A' is a *reflection* of point A across line ℓ. What is the relationship of ℓ to $\overline{AA'}$?

3. **GET ORGANIZED** Copy and complete the graphic organizer.

Line of Reflection	Image of (a, b)	Example
x-axis		
y-axis		
$y = x$		

3 Close

Summarize

Draw $\triangle ABC$ with vertices $A(2, 4)$, $B(2, 1)$, and $C(6, 1)$. Reflect $\triangle ABC$ across the x-axis, the y-axis, and the line $y = x$ and compare the results. For each transformation, connect a vertex with its image and show that the line of reflection is the perpendicular bisector of the segment that is formed.

ONGOING ASSESSMENT

and INTERVENTION

***Diagnose Before* the Lesson**
12-1 Warm Up, TE p. 824

***Monitor During* the Lesson**
Check It Out! Exercises, SE pp. 824–826
Questioning Strategies, TE pp. 825–826

***Assess After* the Lesson**
12-1 Lesson Quiz, TE p. 830
Alternative Assessment, TE p. 830

Answers to *Think and Discuss*

Possible answers:

1. $ABA'C$ is a kite, because $\overline{AB} \cong \overline{A'B}$ and $\overline{AC} \cong \overline{A'C}$, so there are exactly 2 pairs of $\cong$ adj. sides.
2. ℓ is the $\perp$ bisector of $\overline{AA'}$.
3. See p. A9.

12-1 Exercises

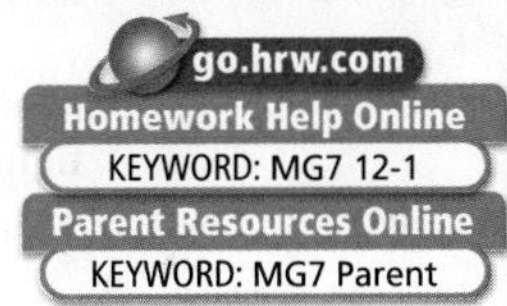

GUIDED PRACTICE

1. **Vocabulary** If a transformation is an *isometry*, how would you describe the relationship between the preimage and the image? **They are congruent.**

SEE EXAMPLE 1 p. 824

Tell whether each transformation appears to be a reflection.

2. 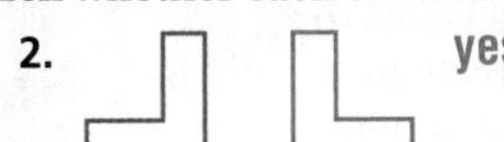 yes

3.  no

4. 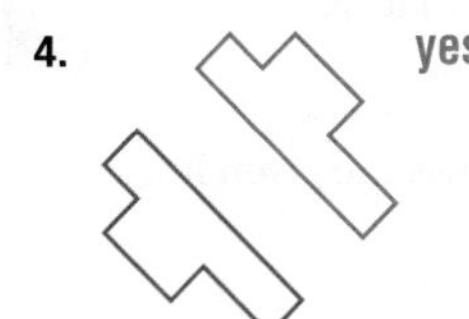 yes

5. 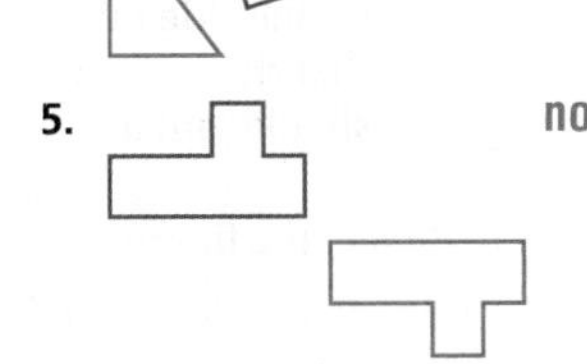 no

SEE EXAMPLE 2 p. 825

Multi-Step **Copy each figure and the line of reflection. Draw the reflection of the figure across the line.**

6. 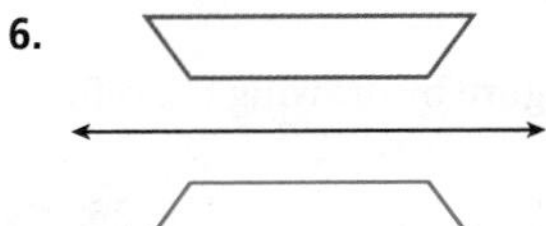

7. 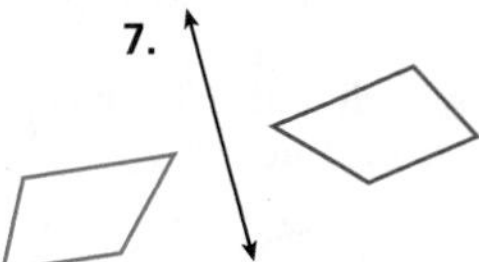

SEE EXAMPLE 3 p. 825

8. **City Planning** The towns of San Pablo and Tanner are located on the same side of Highway 105. Two access roads are planned that connect the towns to a point P on the highway. Draw a diagram that shows where point P should be located in order to make the total length of the access roads as short as possible.

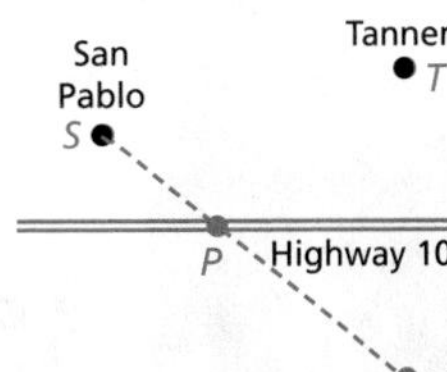

SEE EXAMPLE 4 p. 826

Reflect the figure with the given vertices across the given line.

9. $A(-2, 1)$, $B(2, 3)$, $C(5, 2)$; x-axis
10. $R(0, -1)$, $S(2, 2)$, $T(3, 0)$; y-axis
11. $M(2, 1)$, $N(3, 1)$, $P(2, -1)$, $Q(1, -1)$; $y = x$
12. $A(-2, 2)$, $B(-1, 3)$, $C(1, 2)$, $D(-2, -2)$; $y = x$

PRACTICE AND PROBLEM SOLVING

Independent Practice

For Exercises	See Example
13–16	1
17–18	2
19	3
20–23	4

Extra Practice
Skills Practice p. S26
Application Practice p. S39

Tell whether each transformation appears to be a reflection.

13. 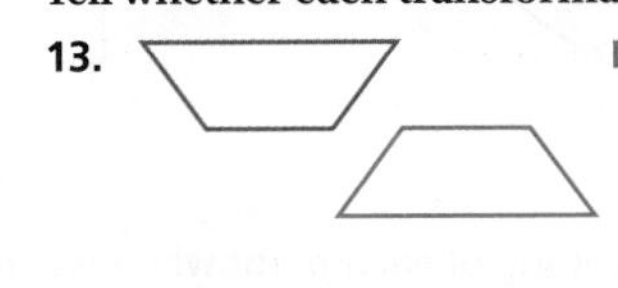 no

14. 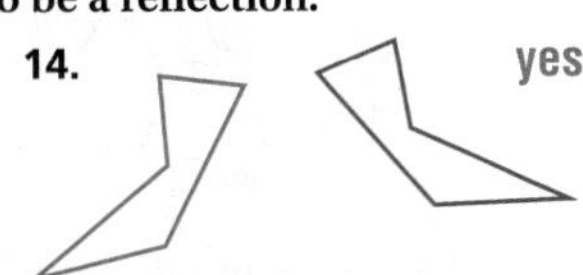 yes

15.  yes

16. 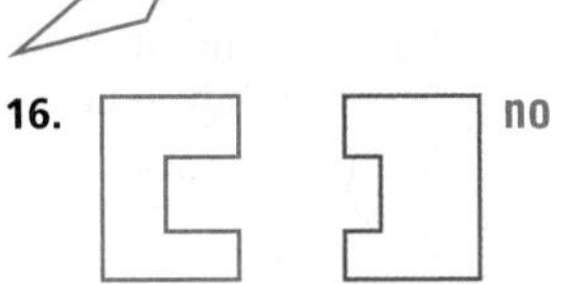 no

Answers

9. and 10.

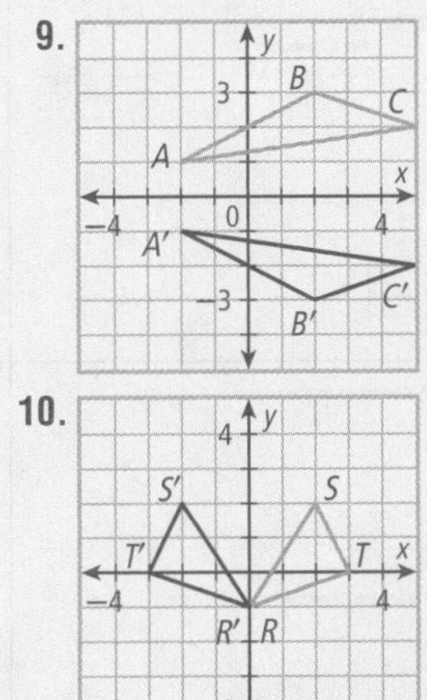

11. and 12.

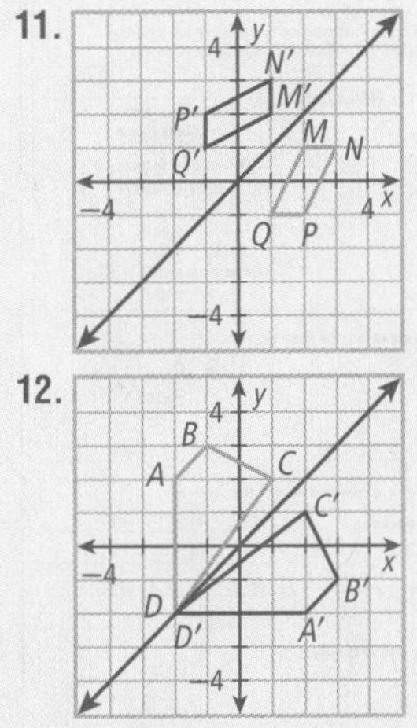

12-1 Exercises

Assignment Guide

Assign *Guided Practice* exercises as necessary.

If you finished Examples 1–2
Basic 13–18, 24–26, 28–30
Average 13–18, 24–26, 28–30, 43–45, 52
Advanced 13–18, 24–26, 28–30, 43–45, 52–57

If you finished Examples 1–4
Basic 13–37, 40, 41, 46–48, 58–66
Average 13–23, 24–36 even, 37–51, 58–66
Advanced 13–23, 24–36 even, 37–66

Homework Quick Check
Quickly check key concepts.
Exercises: 14, 18, 19, 20, 24

Kinesthetic Suggest that students copy the figures in **Exercises 2–5** and use paper folding or Miras to identify their reflection images.

State Resources

go.hrw.com
State Resources Online
KEYWORD: MG7 Resources

Science A chiral molecule is one that cannot be superimposed on its mirror image. The word *chiral* means "hand-like." The mirror image of your left hand can be superimposed on your right hand, but not on your left hand. In contrast to the chiral molecule shown in **Exercise 27,** an *achiral* molecule, such as 2-propanol, is a molecule whose top half is a mirror image of its bottom half and whose mirror images can be superimposed on one another.

Answers

19. See p. A30.

20. 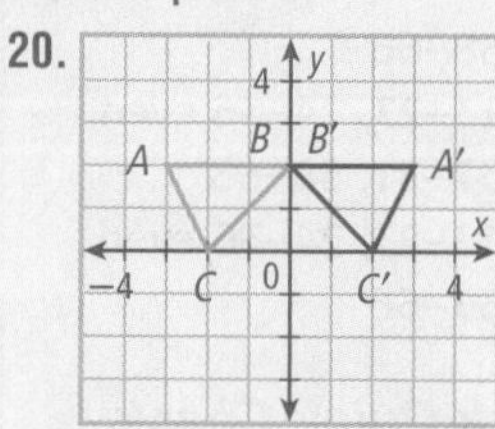

21. 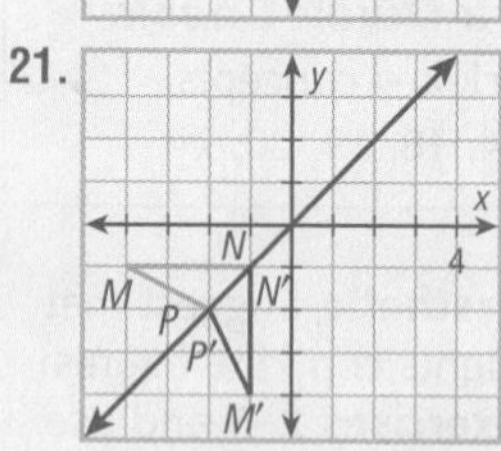

22. 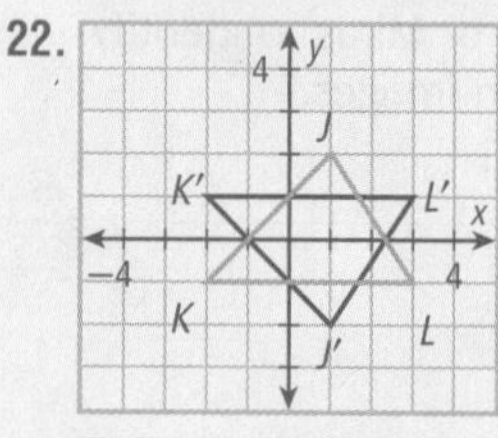

23. 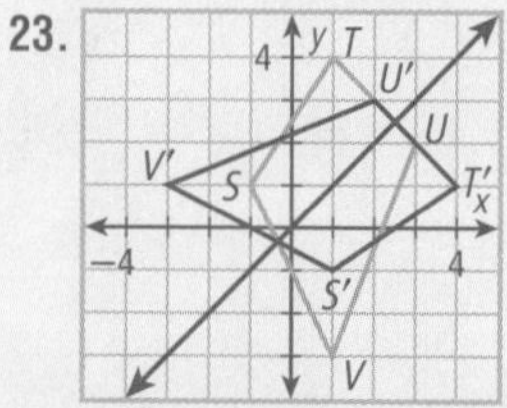

31. (5, 2) → (5, −2)

32. (−3, −7) → (3, −7)

33. (0, 12) → (0, −12)

34. (−3, −6) → (−6, −3)

35. (0, −5) → (−5, 0)

36. (4, 4) → (4, 4)

Multi-Step Copy each figure and the line of reflection. Draw the reflection of the figure across the line.

17.  

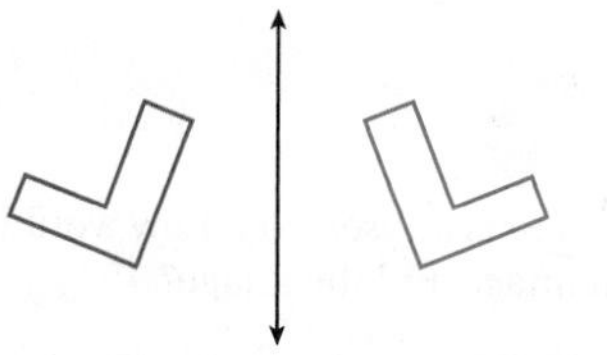

18. 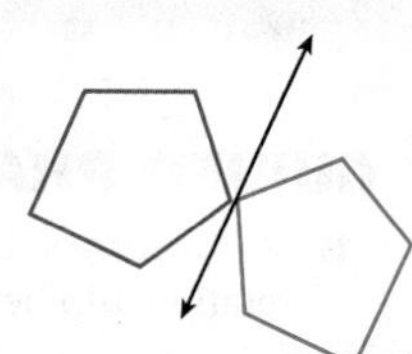

19. **Recreation** Cara is playing pool. She wants to hit the ball at point *A* without hitting the ball at point *B*. She has to bounce the cue ball, located at point *C*, off the side rail and into her ball. Draw a diagram that shows the exact point along the rail that Cara should aim for.

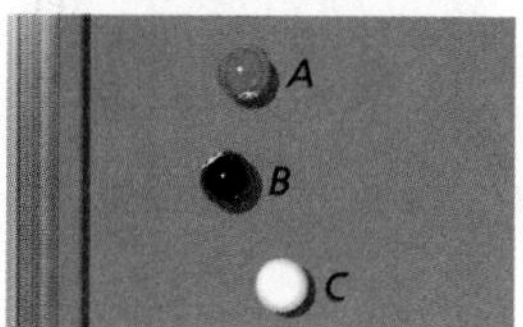

Reflect the figure with the given vertices across the given line.

20. $A(-3, 2)$, $B(0, 2)$, $C(-2, 0)$; y-axis
21. $M(-4, -1)$, $N(-1, -1)$, $P(-2, -2)$; $y = x$
22. $J(1, 2)$, $K(-2, -1)$, $L(3, -1)$; x-axis
23. $S(-1, 1)$, $T(1, 4)$, $U(3, 2)$, $V(1, -3)$; $y = x$

Copy each figure. Then complete the figure by drawing the reflection image across the line.

24. 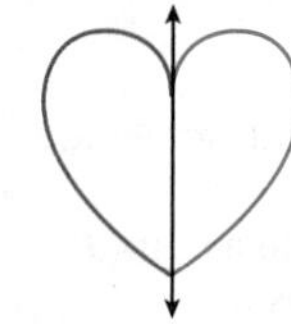

25. M A T H

26. 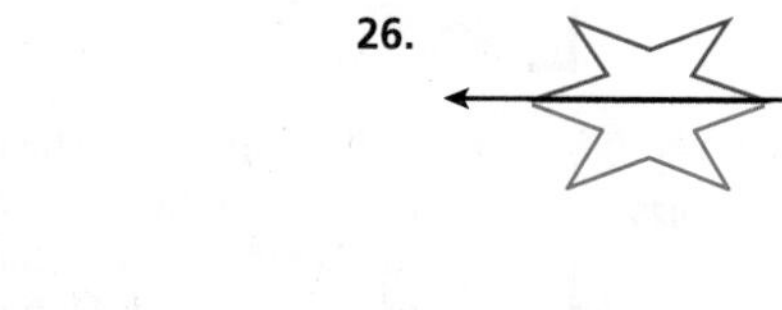

Chemistry

Louis Pasteur (1822–1895) is best known for the pasteurization process, which kills germs in milk. He discovered chemical chirality when he observed that two salt crystals were mirror images of each other.

27. **Chemistry** In chemistry, *chiral* molecules are mirror images of each other. Although they have similar structures, chiral molecules can have very different properties. For example, the compound R-(+)-limonene smells like oranges, while its mirror image, S-(−)-limonene, smells like lemons. Use the figure and the given line of reflection to draw S-(−)-limonene.

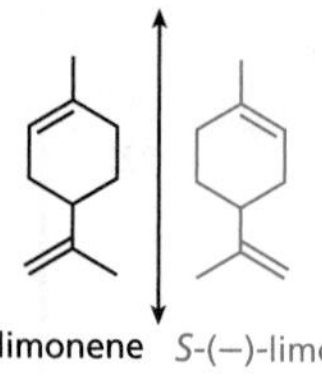

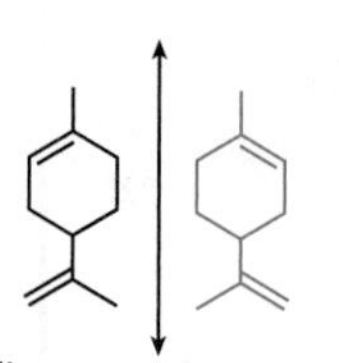

Each figure shows a preimage and image under a reflection. Copy the figure and draw the line of reflection.

28. 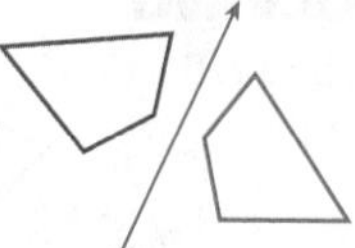

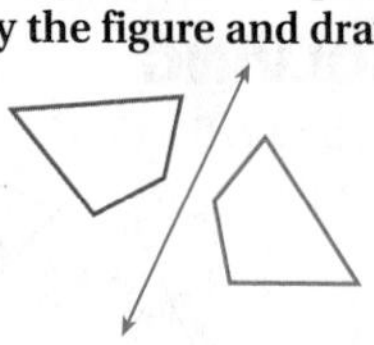

29. 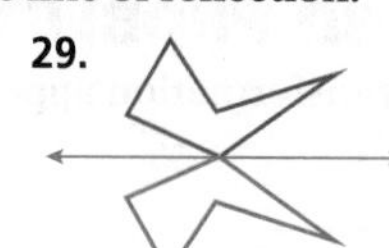

30. 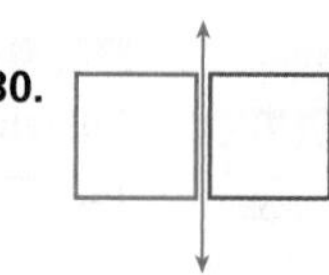

Use arrow notation to describe the mapping of each point when it is reflected across the given line.

31. (5, 2); x-axis
32. (−3, −7); y-axis
33. (0, 12); x-axis
34. (−3, −6); $y = x$
35. (0, −5); $y = x$
36. (4, 4); $y = x$

12-1 PRACTICE A
12-1 PRACTICE C
12-1 PRACTICE B

Tell whether each transformation appears to be a reflection.

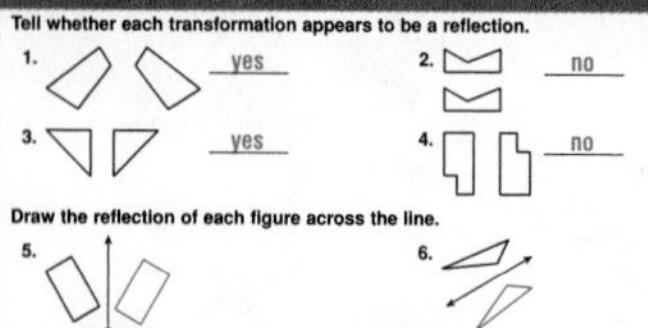

1. yes
2. no
3. yes
4. no

Draw the reflection of each figure across the line.

5.
6.

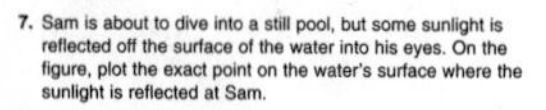

7. Sam is about to dive into a still pool, but some sunlight is reflected off the surface of the water into his eyes. On the figure, plot the exact point on the water's surface where the sunlight is reflected at Sam.

Reflect the figure with the given vertices across the given line.

8. $A(4, 4)$, $B(3, -1)$, $C(1, -2)$; y-axis
9. $D(-4, -1)$, $E(-2, 3)$, $F(-1, 1)$; $y = x$

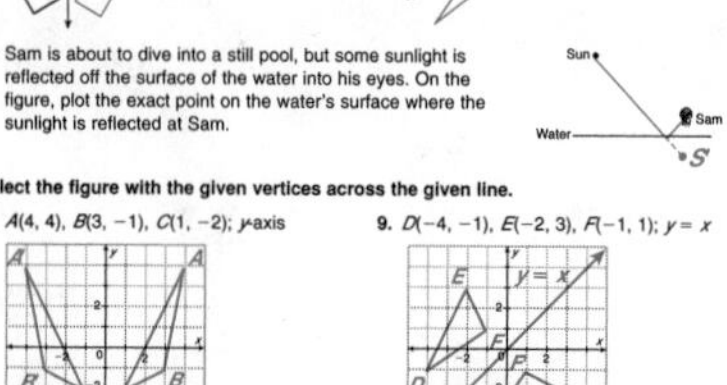

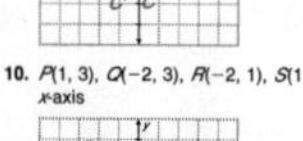

10. $P(1, 3)$, $Q(-2, 3)$, $R(-2, 1)$, $S(1, 0)$; x-axis
11. $J(3, -4)$, $K(1, -1)$, $L(-1, -1)$, $M(-2, -4)$; $y = x$

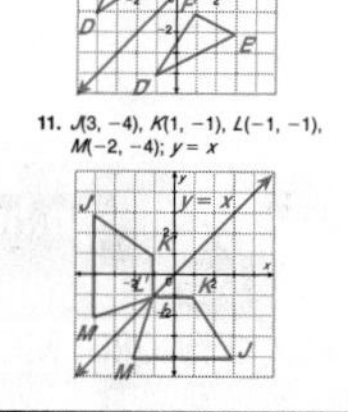

12-1 READING STRATEGIES

Use the concept map below to help you understand reflections.

Definition

A **reflection** is a transformation that moves a figure, called the preimage, by flipping it across a line. The reflected figure is called the image.

Reflections

Examples

Reflections in the Coordinate Plane

Reflections can be made
- across the x-axis $(x, y) \rightarrow (x, -y)$
- across the y-axis $(x, y) \rightarrow (-x, y)$
- across the line $y = x$ $(x, y) \rightarrow (y, x)$

Tell whether each transformation appears to be a reflection.

1. no
2. yes
3. yes

Give the vertices of the image after it is reflected across the given line.

4. $A(2, 1)$, $B(6, 1)$, $C(4, 3)$ across the x-axis — $A'(2, -1)$, $B'(6, -1)$, $C'(4, -3)$
5. $M(1, 2)$, $P(3, 5)$, $Q(3, 7)$, $R(1, 6)$ across the line $y = x$ — $M'(2, 1)$, $P'(5, 3)$, $Q'(7, 3)$, $R'(6, 1)$

Draw the reflection of each figure across the line.

6.
7.
8.

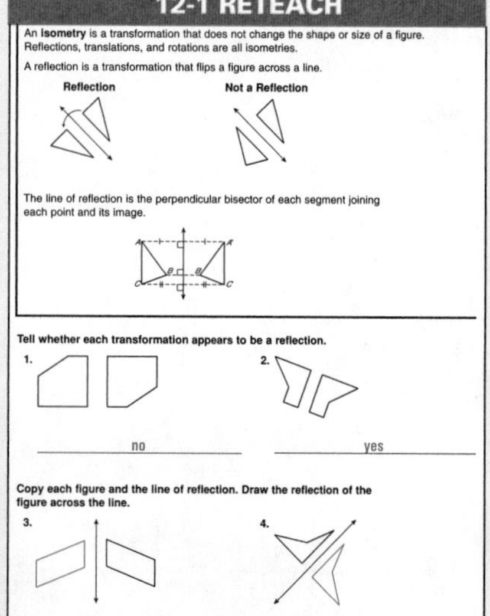

12-1 RETEACH

An **isometry** is a transformation that does not change the shape or size of a figure. Reflections, translations, and rotations are all isometries.

A reflection is a transformation that flips a figure across a line.

Reflection **Not a Reflection**

The line of reflection is the perpendicular bisector of each segment joining each point and its image.

Tell whether each transformation appears to be a reflection.

1. no
2. yes

Copy each figure and the line of reflection. Draw the reflection of the figure across the line.

3.
4.

37. This problem will prepare you for the Multi-Step Test Prep on page 854.

The figure shows one hole of a miniature golf course.

a. Is it possible to hit the ball in a straight line from the tee T to the hole H? **no**

b. Find the coordinates of H', the reflection of H across $\overline{BC}$. **(7, 4)**

c. The point at which a player should aim in order to make a hole in one is the intersection of $\overline{TH'}$ and $\overline{BC}$. What are the coordinates of this point? **(6, 3.5)**

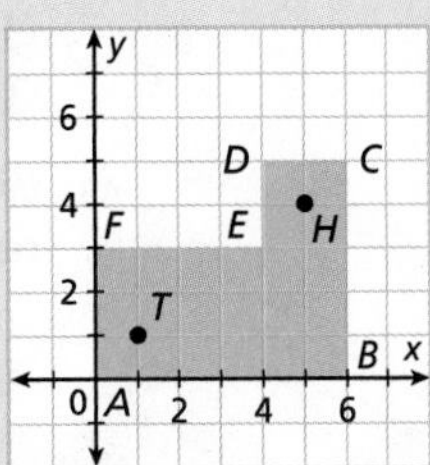

38. Critical Thinking Sketch the next figure in the sequence below.

39. Critical Thinking Under a reflection in the coordinate plane, the point (3, 5) is mapped to the point (5, 3). What is the line of reflection? Is this the only possible line of reflection? Explain.

39. The line of reflection is the line $y = x$. It is the only possible line of reflection because the line of reflection is the perpendicular bisector of the segment connecting the points; there is only one such perpendicular bisector.

Draw the reflection of the graph of each function across the given line.

40. x-axis

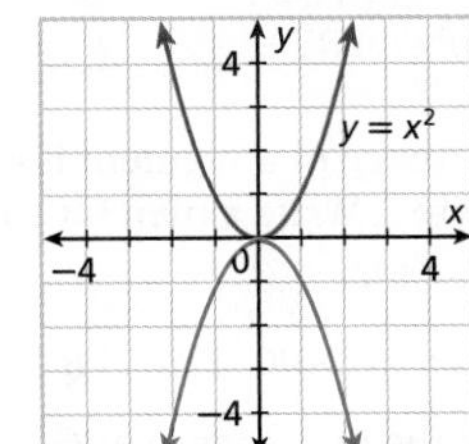

41. y-axis

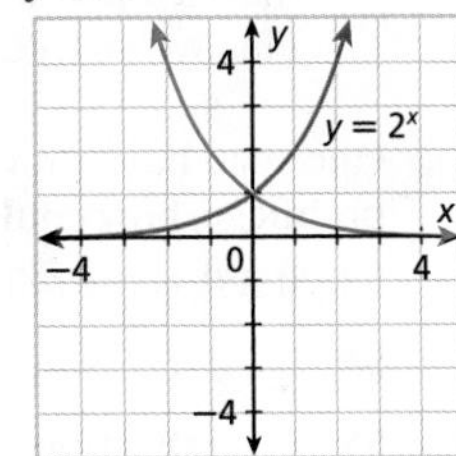

42. Write About It Imagine reflecting all the points in a plane across line ℓ. Which points remain fixed under this transformation? That is, for which points is the image the same as the preimage? Explain.

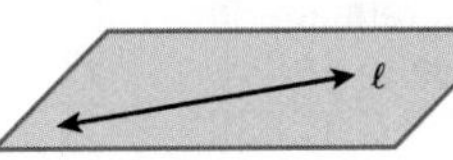

Construction **Use the construction of a line perpendicular to a given line through a given point (see page 179) and the construction of a segment congruent to a given segment (see page 14) to construct the reflection of each figure across a line.**

43. a point **44.** a segment **45.** a triangle

43–45. Check students' constructions.

46. Daryl is using a coordinate plane to plan a garden. He draws a flower bed with vertices (3, 1), (3, 4), (−2, 4), and (−2, 1). Then he creates a second flower bed by reflecting the first one across the x-axis. Which of these is a vertex of the second flower bed?

Ⓐ (−2, −4) (circled)
Ⓑ (−3, 1)
Ⓒ (2, 1)
Ⓓ (−3, −4)

COMMON ERROR ALERT

Students may draw the graph of $x = y^2$ in **Exercise 40,** assuming incorrectly that the graph must be symmetrical to the x-axis. Remind them to check their tables of values for both graphs to verify that (x, y) in the preimage maps to $(x, -y)$ in the image.

MULTI-STEP TEST PREP **Exercise 37** involves finding a reflection of a point across a line. This exercise prepares students for the Multi-Step Test Prep on page 854.

If students chose **B** or **C** in **Exercise 46,** they reflected across the y-axis. Remind them that only the y-coordinate changes in a reflection across the x-axis.

Remind students that an isometry does not change the shape or size of a figure. Therefore the image in **Exercise 47** is congruent to the preimage, so the vertices should be listed in corresponding order.

Answers

42. The points on line ℓ remain fixed. Each of these points is its own image under a reflection across line ℓ.

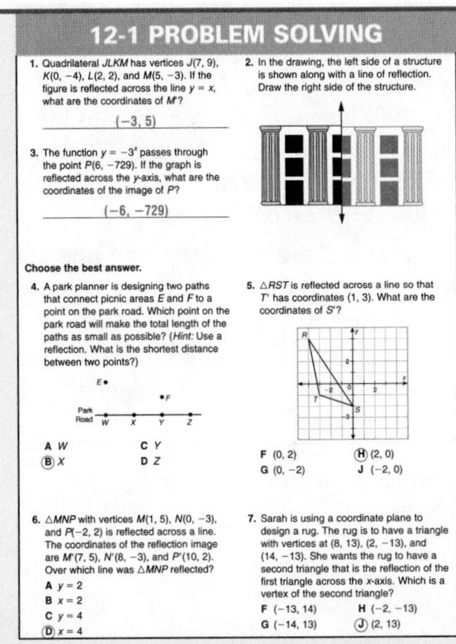

12-1 PROBLEM SOLVING

1. Quadrilateral $JLKM$ has vertices $J(7, 9)$, $K(0, -4)$, $L(2, 2)$, and $M(5, -3)$. If the figure is reflected across the line $y = x$, what are the coordinates of M'?
   (−3, 5)

2. In the drawing, the left side of a structure is shown along with a line of reflection. Draw the right side of the structure.

3. The function $y = -3^x$ passes through the point $P(6, -729)$. If the graph is reflected across the y-axis, what are the coordinates of the image of P?
   (−6, −729)

Choose the best answer.

4. A park planner is designing two paths that connect picnic areas E and F to a point on the park road. Which point on the park road will make the total length of the paths as small as possible? (*Hint:* Use a reflection. What is the shortest distance between two points?)

   Park Road: W X Y Z

   A W
   Ⓑ X
   C Y
   D Z

5. $\triangle RST$ is reflected across a line so that T' has coordinates (1, 3). What are the coordinates of S'?

   F (0, 2)
   G (0, −2)
   Ⓗ (2, 0)
   J (−2, 0)

6. $\triangle MNP$ with vertices $M(1, 5)$, $N(0, -3)$, and $P(-2, 2)$ is reflected across a line. The coordinates of the reflection image are $M'(7, 5)$, $N'(8, -3)$, and $P'(10, 2)$. Over which line was $\triangle MNP$ reflected?

   A $y = 2$
   B $x = 2$
   C $y = 4$
   Ⓓ $x = 4$

7. Sarah is using a coordinate plane to design a rug. The rug is to have a triangle with vertices at (8, 13), (2, −13), and (14, −13). She wants the rug to have a second triangle that is the reflection of the first triangle across the x-axis. Which is a vertex of the second triangle?

   F (−13, 14)
   G (−14, 13)
   H (−2, −13)
   Ⓙ (2, 13)

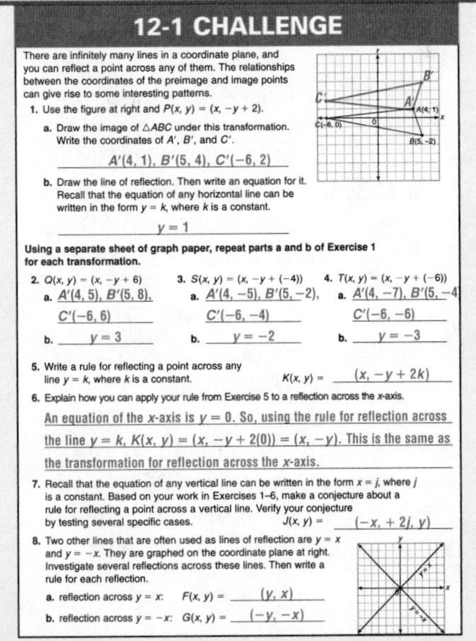

12-1 CHALLENGE

There are infinitely many lines in a coordinate plane, and you can reflect a point across any of them. The relationships between the coordinates of the preimage and image points can give rise to some interesting patterns.

1. Use the figure at right and $P(x, y) = (x, -y + 2)$.
   a. Draw the image of $\triangle ABC$ under this transformation. Write the coordinates of A', B', and C'.
   $A'(4, 1)$, $B'(5, 4)$, $C'(-6, 2)$
   b. Draw the line of reflection. Then write an equation for it. Recall that the equation of any horizontal line can be written in the form $y = k$, where k is a constant.
   $y = 1$

Using a separate sheet of graph paper, repeat parts a and b of Exercise 1 for each transformation.

2. $Q(x, y) = (x, -y + 6)$
   a. $A'(4, 5)$, $B'(5, 8)$, $C'(-6, 6)$
   b. $y = 3$
3. $S(x, y) = (x, -y + (-4))$
   a. $A'(4, -5)$, $B'(5, -2)$, $C'(-6, -4)$
   b. $y = -2$
4. $T(x, y) = (x, -y + (-6))$
   a. $A'(4, -7)$, $B'(5, -4$ $C'(-6, -6)$
   b. $y = -3$
5. Write a rule for reflecting a point across any line $y = k$, where k is a constant. $K(x, y) =$ $(x, -y + 2k)$
6. Explain how you can apply your rule from Exercise 5 to a reflection across the x-axis.
   An equation of the x-axis is $y = 0$. So, using the rule for reflection across the line $y = k$, $K(x, y) = (x, -y + 2(0)) = (x, -y)$. This is the same as the transformation for reflection across the x-axis.
7. Recall that the equation of any vertical line can be written in the form $x = j$, where j is a constant. Based on your work in Exercises 1–6, make a conjecture about a rule for reflecting a point across a vertical line. Verify your conjecture by testing several specific cases. $J(x, y) =$ $(-x, + 2j, y)$
8. Two other lines that are often used as lines of reflection are $y = x$ and $y = -x$. They are graphed on the coordinate plane at right. Investigate several reflections across these lines. Then write a rule for each reflection.
   a. reflection across $y = x$: $F(x, y) =$ (y, x)
   b. reflection across $y = -x$: $G(x, y) =$ $(-y, -x)$

Math Background
Exercise 52 demonstrates a proof of only one case of the statement $\overline{AB} \cong \overline{A'B'}$. The statement can also be proved when A and B are on opposite sides of ℓ, when A or B lies on ℓ and $\overline{AB} \perp \ell$, and when A or B lies on ℓ and $\overline{AB} \perp \ell$.

Journal

For a transformation that appears to be a reflection, have students explain how they would use a compass and straightedge or a ruler and a right angle to verify that it is a reflection.

ALTERNATIVE ASSESSMENT

Have students write a rule for reflecting the point (x, y) across each of the lines $y = 3$, $x = 2$, and $y = -x$. Have them test their rules by reflecting a triangle across each line.

Power Presentations with PowerPoint®

12-1 Lesson Quiz

1. Tell whether the transformation appears to be a reflection.

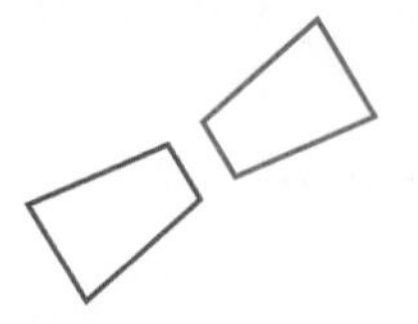

yes

2. Copy the figure and the line of reflection. Draw the reflection of the figure across the line.

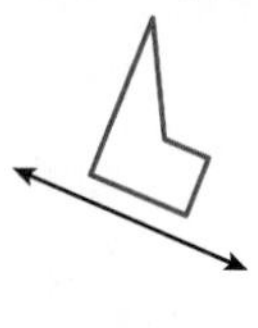

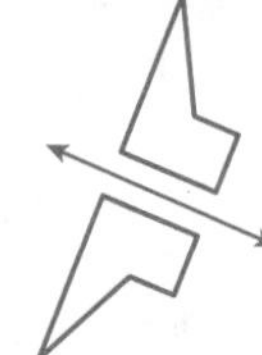

Reflect the figure with the given vertices across the given line.

3. $A(2, 3)$, $B(-1, 5)$, $C(4, -1)$; $y = x$
$A'(3, 2)$, $B'(5, -1)$, $C(-1, 4)$
4. $U(-8, 2)$, $V(-3, -1)$, $W(3, 3)$; y-axis
$U'(8, 2)$, $V'(3, -1)$, $W'(-3, 3)$
5. $E(-3, -2)$, $F(6, -4)$, $G(-2, 1)$; x-axis
$E'(-3, 2)$, $F'(6, 4)$, $G(-2, -1)$

Also available on transparency

47. In the reflection shown, the shaded figure is the preimage. Which of these represents the mapping?
Ⓕ $MJNP \rightarrow DSWG$　Ⓗ $JMPN \rightarrow GWSD$
Ⓖ $DGWS \rightarrow MJNP$　Ⓙ $PMJN \rightarrow SDGW$

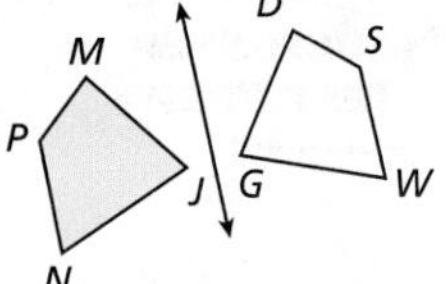

48. What is the image of the point $(-3, 4)$ when it is reflected across the y-axis?
Ⓐ $(4, -3)$　Ⓒ $(3, 4)$
Ⓑ $(-3, -4)$　Ⓓ $(-4, -3)$

CHALLENGE AND EXTEND

Find the coordinates of the image when each point is reflected across the given line.

49. $(4, 2)$; $y = 3$ $(4, 4)$
50. $(-3, 2)$; $x = 1$ $(5, 2)$
51. $(3, 1)$; $y = x + 2$ $(-1, 5)$

52. Prove that the reflection image of a segment is congruent to the preimage.
Given: $\overline{A'B'}$ is the reflection image of $\overline{AB}$ across line ℓ.
Prove: $\overline{AB} \cong \overline{A'B'}$
Plan: Draw auxiliary lines $\overline{AA'}$ and $\overline{BB'}$ as shown. First prove that $\triangle ACD \cong \triangle A'CD$. Then use CPCTC to conclude that $\angle CDA \cong \angle CDA'$. Therefore $\angle ADB \cong \angle A'DB'$, which makes it possible to prove that $\triangle ADB \cong \triangle A'DB'$. Finally use CPCTC to conclude that $\overline{AB} \cong \overline{A'B'}$.

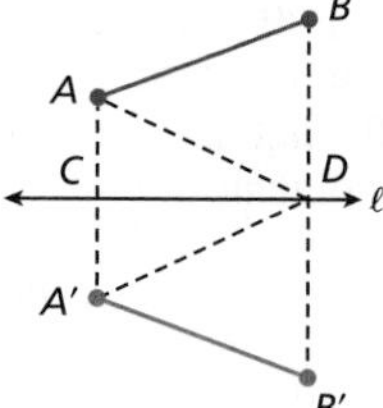

Once you have proved that the reflection image of a segment is congruent to the preimage, how could you prove the following? Write a plan for each proof.

53. If $\overline{A'B'}$ is the reflection of $\overline{AB}$, then $AB = A'B'$.
54. If $\angle A'B'C'$ is the reflection of $\angle ABC$, then $m\angle ABC = m\angle A'B'C'$.
55. The reflection $\triangle A'B'C'$ is congruent to the preimage $\triangle ABC$.
56. If point C is between points A and B, then the reflection C' is between A' and B'.
57. If points A, B, and C are collinear, then the reflections A', B', and C' are collinear.

53. Use the fact that the reflection of a seg. is ≅ to the preimage and the def. of ≅ segs.

55. Use the fact that the reflection of a seg. is ≅ to the preimage to prove $\triangle ABC \cong \triangle A'B'C'$ by SSS.

56. If C is between A and B, then $AC + BC = AB$. Use the fact that the reflection of a seg. is ≅ to the preimage to prove $A'C' + B'C' = A'B'$. Then use the def. of betweenness to prove C' is between A' and B'.

SPIRAL REVIEW

A jar contains 2 red marbles, 6 yellow marbles, and 4 green marbles. One marble is drawn and replaced, and then a second marble is drawn. Find the probability of each outcome. *(Previous course)*

58. Both marbles are green. $\frac{1}{9}$
59. Neither marble is red. $\frac{25}{36}$
60. The first marble is yellow, and the second is green. $\frac{1}{6}$

The width of a rectangular field is 60 m, and the length is 105 m. Use each of the following scales to find the perimeter of a scale drawing of the field. *(Lesson 7-5)*

61. 1 cm : 30 m 11 cm
62. 1.5 cm : 15 m 33 cm
63. 1 cm : 25 m 13.2 cm

Find each unknown measure. Round side lengths to the nearest hundredth and angle measures to the nearest degree. *(Lesson 8-3)*

64. BC 1.73
65. $m\angle A$ 41°
66. $m\angle C$ 49°

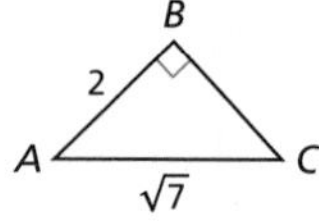

Answers

52. Draw auxiliary lines $\overline{AA'}$ and $\overline{BB'}$ and let C be the pt. where $\overline{AA'}$ intersects ℓ and let D be the pt. where $\overline{BB'}$ intersects ℓ. By the def. of reflection, line ℓ is the ⊥ bisector of $\overline{AA'}$ and $\overline{BB'}$. Therefore, $\angle ACD$ and $\angle A'CD$ are rt. ∠s, and so $\angle ACD \cong \angle A'CD$. Also $\overline{AC} \cong \overline{A'C}$ by the def. of bisector, and $\overline{CD} \cong \overline{CD}$ by the Refl. Prop. of ≅. Thus, $\triangle ACD \cong \triangle A'CD$ by SAS. By CPCTC, $\angle CDA \cong \angle CDA'$. $\angle ADB$ is comp. to $\angle CDA$, and $\angle A'DB'$ is comp. to $\angle CDA'$. So $\angle ADB \cong \angle A'DB'$. $\overline{AD} \cong \overline{A'D}$ by CPCTC, and $\overline{BD} \cong \overline{B'D}$ by the def. of bisector. Therefore, $\triangle ADB \cong \triangle A'DB'$ by SAS. By CPCTC, $\overline{AB} \cong \overline{A'B'}$.

54. Draw auxiliary segs. $\overline{AC}$ and $\overline{A'C'}$ to form $\triangle ABC$ and $\triangle A'B'C'$. Use the fact that the reflection of a seg. is ≅ to the preimage to prove $\triangle ABC \cong \triangle A'B'C'$ by SSS. By CPCTC, $\angle ABC \cong \angle A'B'C'$, so $m\angle ABC = m\angle A'B'C'$ by def. of ≅ ∠s.

57. If A, B, and C are collinear, then one point is between the other two. Case 1: If C is between A and B, then $AC + BC = AB$. Use the fact that the reflection of a seg. is ≅ to the preimage to prove $A'C' + B'C' = A'B'$. Then C' is between A' and B', so A', B', and C' are collinear. Prove the other two cases similarly.

12-2 Translations

Objective
Identify and draw translations.

Who uses this?
Marching band directors use translations to plan their bands' field shows. (See Example 4.)

A translation is a transformation where all the points of a figure are moved the same distance in the same direction. A translation is an isometry, so the image of a translated figure is congruent to the preimage.

EXAMPLE 1 Identifying Translations

Tell whether each transformation appears to be a translation. Explain.

A

No; not all of the points have moved the same distance.

B

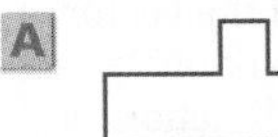

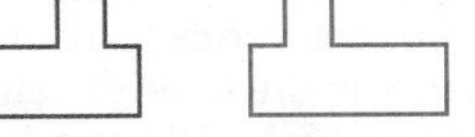

Yes; all of the points have moved the same distance in the same direction.

CHECK IT OUT! Tell whether each transformation appears to be a translation.

1a. yes

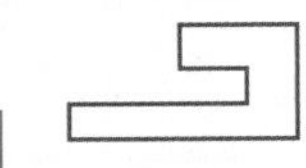

1b. no

Construction Translate a Figure Using Patty Paper

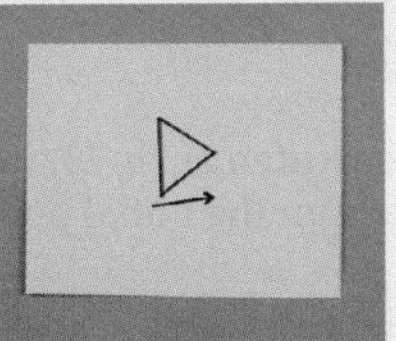

1. Draw a triangle and a translation vector on a sheet of paper.

2. Place a sheet of patty paper on top of the diagram. Trace the triangle and vector.

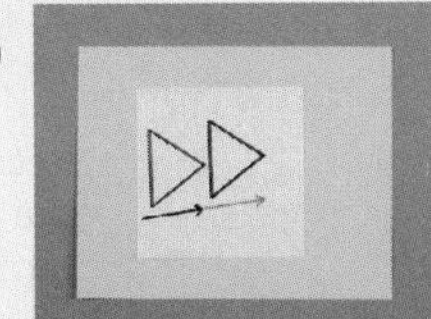

3. Slide the bottom paper in the direction of the vector until the head of the top vector aligns with the tail of the bottom vector. Trace the triangle.

Remember!
To review vectors, see Lesson 8-6, pages 559–567.

Draw a segment from each vertex of the preimage to the corresponding vertex of the image. Your construction should show that every segment connecting a point and its image is the same length as the translation vector. These segments are also parallel to the translation vector.

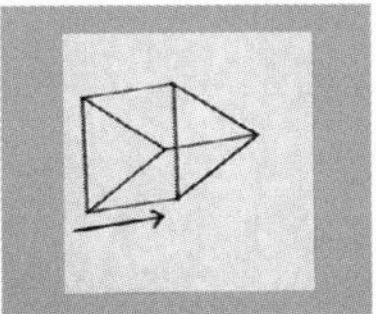

12-2 Organizer

Pacing: Traditional 1 day
Block $\frac{1}{2}$ day

Objective: Identify and draw translations.

Online Edition
Tutorial Videos

Power Presentations with PowerPoint®

Warm Up

Find the coordinates of the image of $\triangle ABC$ with vertices $A(3, 4)$, $B(-1, 4)$, and $C(5, -2)$, after each reflection.

1. across the x-axis
$A'(3, -4), B'(-1, -4), C'(5, 2)$
2. across the y-axis
$A'(-3, 4), B'(1, 4), C'(-5, -2)$
3. across the line $y = x$
$A'(4, 3), B'(4, -1), C'(-2, 5)$

Also available on transparency

Math Humor

French Woman: How did you get lost? Didn't I tell you my office was one floor up and three doors down?

American Woman: I didn't understand your translation!

1 Introduce

EXPLORATION

12-2 Translations

Recall that a translation, or *slide*, is a transformation of a figure such that all the points move in the same direction by the same distance.

1. Use geometry software to draw $\triangle ABC$ and $\overline{DE}$.
2. Translate $\triangle ABC$ along the vector from D to E. Label the image $\triangle A'B'C'$.

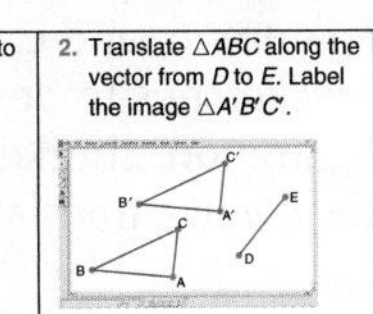

3. Drag points D and E to different locations. What is true about $\triangle ABC$ and its image?
4. Is it possible to create a translation image of $\triangle ABC$ that is NOT congruent to $\triangle ABC$? If so, how?

THINK AND DISCUSS

5. Explain why a translation is an isometry.
6. Discuss whether $\triangle PQR$ appears to be the image of $\triangle JKL$ under a translation.

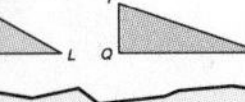

Motivate

Compare a translation of a figure to a waiter carrying a tray full of glasses. The tray must not tilt or flip, or the glasses will fall off. When a figure is translated, all the points move the same distance in the same direction, so the figure does not turn or flip.

Explorations and answers are provided in *Alternate Openers: Explorations Transparencies.*

State Resources

go.hrw.com
State Resources Online
KEYWORD: MG7 Resources

Power Presentations with PowerPoint®

Additional Examples

Example 1

Tell whether each transformation appears to be a translation.

A. no

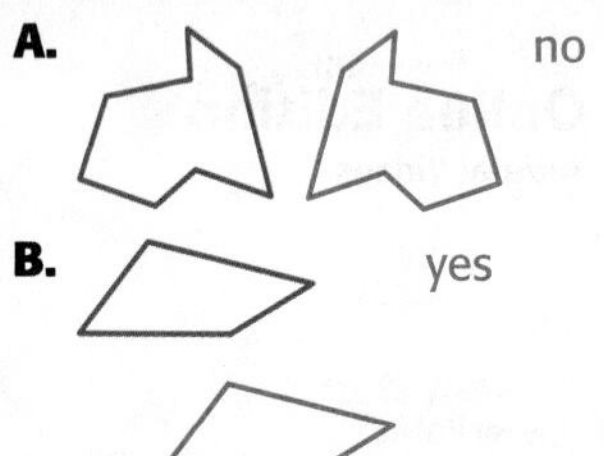

B. yes

Example 2

Copy the quadrilateral and the translation vector. Draw the translation along $\vec{v}$

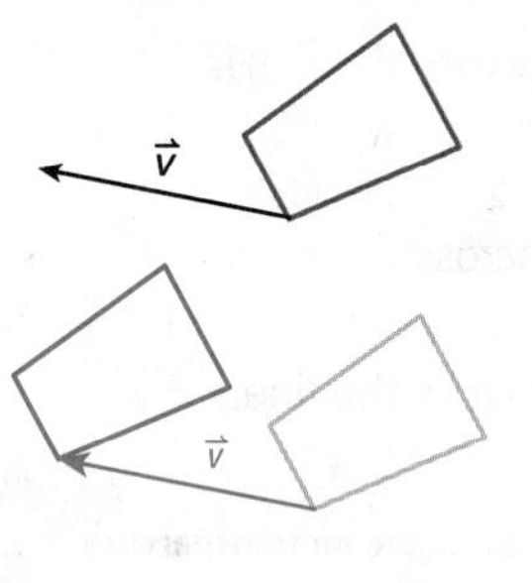

INTERVENTION

Questioning Strategies

EXAMPLE 1

- What is the difference between a translation and a reflection?

EXAMPLE 2

- How do you know that the distance between each point and its image is the same for each pair of corresponding points?
- How do you know that the direction each point has moved is the same for each pair of corresponding points?

Technology Have students use geometry software to create a triangle and label the vertices *A*, *B*, and *C*. Have them translate the triangle along a vector and measure to verify that $AA' = BB' = CC'$.

Translations

A translation is a transformation along a vector such that each segment joining a point and its image has the same length as the vector and is parallel to the vector.

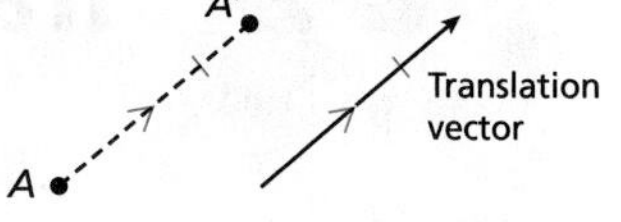

EXAMPLE 2 **Drawing Translations**

Copy the triangle and the translation vector. Draw the translation of the triangle along $\vec{v}$.

Step 1 Draw a line parallel to the vector through each vertex of the triangle.

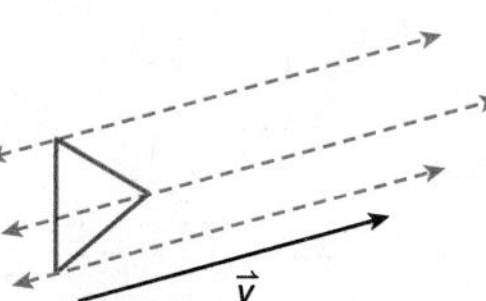

Step 2 Measure the length of the vector. Then, from each vertex mark off this distance in the same direction as the vector, on each of the parallel lines.

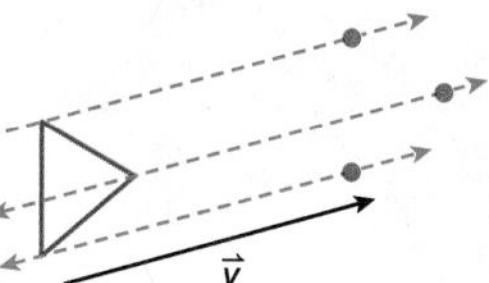

Step 3 Connect the images of the vertices.

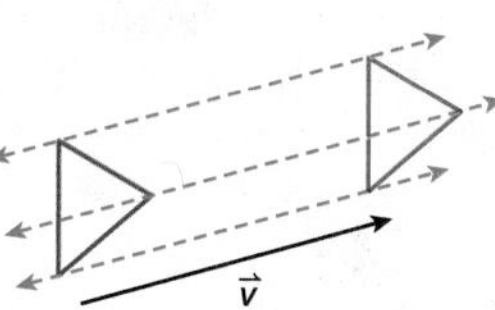

2. Copy the quadrilateral and the translation vector. Draw the translation of the quadrilateral along $\vec{w}$.

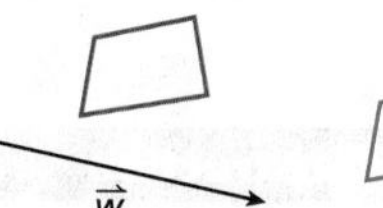

Recall that a vector in the coordinate plane can be written as $\langle a, b\rangle$, where a is the horizontal change and b is the vertical change from the initial point to the terminal point.

Translations in the Coordinate Plane

HORIZONTAL TRANSLATION ALONG VECTOR $\langle a, 0\rangle$	VERTICAL TRANSLATION ALONG VECTOR $\langle 0, b\rangle$	GENERAL TRANSLATION ALONG VECTOR $\langle a, b\rangle$
$P(x, y)$ $P'(x + a, y)$	$P'(x, y + b)$ $P(x, y)$	$P(x, y)$ $P'(x + a, y + b)$
$(x, y) \rightarrow (x + a, y)$	$(x, y) \rightarrow (x, y + b)$	$(x, y) \rightarrow (x + a, y + b)$

2 Teach

Guided Instruction

Review vector notation. Under a translation, all points move the same distance in the same direction, so each segment in the preimage is parallel to the corresponding segment in the image.

Kinesthetic Have students trace the blue triangle in **Example 2** and then use a piece of uncooked spaghetti the same length as the vector to locate the vertices of the image.

Reaching All Learners

Through Home Connection

Bring to class some board games such as chess, backgammon, and checkers. Have students use sketches to describe how chess, backgammon, checkers, and other board games involve translations of game pieces.

EXAMPLE 3 **Drawing Translations in the Coordinate Plane**

Translate the triangle with vertices $A(-2, -4)$, $B(-1, -2)$, and $C(-3, 0)$ along the vector $\langle 2, 4 \rangle$.

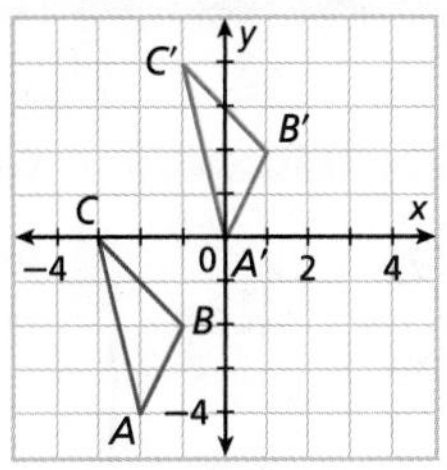

The image of (x, y) is $(x + 2, y + 4)$.

$A(-2, -4) \to A'(-2 + 2, -4 + 4) = A'(0, 0)$

$B(-1, -2) \to B'(-1 + 2, -2 + 4) = B'(1, 2)$

$C(-3, 0) \to C'(-3 + 2, 0 + 4) = C'(-1, 4)$

Graph the preimage and image.

3. 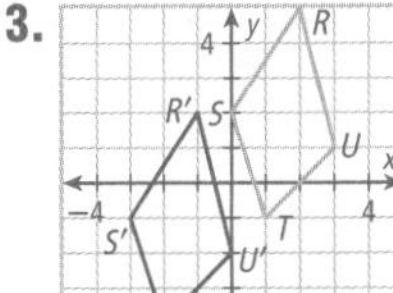

3. Translate the quadrilateral with vertices $R(2, 5)$, $S(0, 2)$, $T(1, -1)$, and $U(3, 1)$ along the vector $\langle -3, -3 \rangle$.

EXAMPLE 4 ***Entertainment Application***

In a marching drill, it takes 8 steps to march 5 yards. A drummer starts 8 steps to the left and 8 steps up from the center of the field. She marches 16 steps to the right to her second position. Then she marches 24 steps down the field to her final position. What is the drummer's final position? What single translation vector moves her from the starting position to her final position?

The drummer's starting coordinates are $(-8, 8)$.

Her second position is $(-8 + 16, 8) = (8, 8)$.

Her final position is $(8, 8 - 24) = (8, -16)$.

The vector that moves her directly from her starting position to her final position is $\langle 16, 0 \rangle + \langle 0, -24 \rangle = \langle 16, -24 \rangle$.

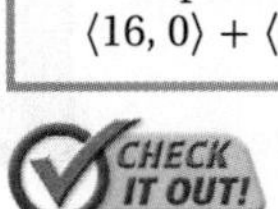

4. **What if...?** Suppose another drummer started at the center of the field and marched along the same vectors as above. What would this drummer's final position be? (16, −24)

THINK AND DISCUSS

1. Point A' is a *translation* of point A along $\vec{v}$. What is the relationship of $\vec{v}$ to $\overline{AA'}$?
2. $\overline{AB}$ is translated to form $\overline{A'B'}$. Classify quadrilateral $AA'B'B$. Explain your reasoning.
3. **GET ORGANIZED** Copy and complete the graphic organizer.

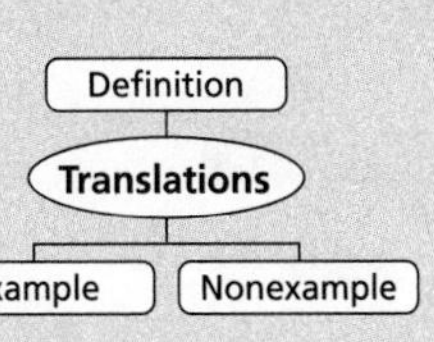

Power Presentations with PowerPoint®

Additional Examples

Example 3

Translate the triangle with vertices $D(-3, -1)$, $E(5, -3)$, and $F(-2, -2)$ along the vector $\langle 3, -1 \rangle$.

$D'(0, -2)$, $E'(8, -4)$, $F'(1, -3)$

Example 4

A sailboat has coordinates 100° west and 5° south. The boat sails 50° due west. Then the boat sails 10° due south. What is the boat's final position? What single translation vector moves it from its first position to its final position?

150° west, 15° south; $\langle -50, -10 \rangle$.

INTERVENTION 

Questioning Strategies

EXAMPLE 3

- How is the translation vector related to $\overline{DD'}$?

EXAMPLE 4

- How do you find the vector that moves an object directly from its starting position to its final position?

Kinesthetic For **Example 4** and **Check It Out Exercise 4,** suggest that students draw a grid and move pennies on the grid to model the positions of the drummer.

3 Close

Summarize

Draw a figure on lined paper and draw a translation vector along one of the paper's lines. Draw the translation and show that the translation vectors and the segments joining the corresponding vertices are parallel.

ONGOING ASSESSMENT and INTERVENTION

***Diagnose Before* the Lesson**
12-2 Warm Up, TE p. 831

***Monitor During* the Leson**
Check It Out! Exercises, SE pp. 831–833
Questioning Strategies, TE pp. 832–833

***Assess After* the Lesson**
12-2 Lesson Quiz, TE p. 837
Alternative Assessment, TE p. 837

Answers to *Think and Discuss*

Possible answers:

1. $\vec{v} \parallel \overline{AA'}$ and $|\vec{v}| = AA'$
2. $\overline{AA'}$ and $\overline{BB'}$ are both ⊥ to the translation vector, so they are ∥ to each other. They are ≅ because a translation is an isometry. So $AA'B'B$ is a ▱, because opp. sides $\overline{AA'}$ and $\overline{BB'}$ are ∥ and ≅.
3. See p. A9.

12-2 Exercises

Assignment Guide

Assign *Guided Practice* exercises as necessary.

If you finished Examples **1–2**
- **Basic** 12–17, 24, 25
- **Average** 12–17, 25, 26, 36–38, 44
- **Advanced** 12–17, 25, 26, 36–38, 44–49

If you finished Examples **1–4**
- **Basic** 12–27, 29–35, 40–42, 50–57
- **Average** 12–43, 50–57
- **Advanced** 12–57

Homework Quick Check
Quickly check key concepts.
Exercises: 12, 16, 18, 20, 22, 24

Kinesthetic Have students draw segments between the corresponding vertices of the figures in **Exercises 11–14.** Then have them decide if the segments appear to be parallel and congruent. If not, the transformation is not a translation.

Answers

5.

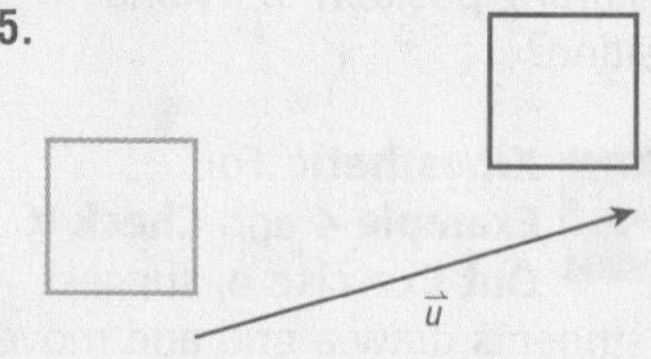

6–9. See p. A30.

State Resources

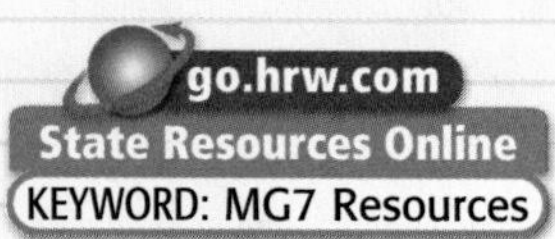

12-2 Exercises

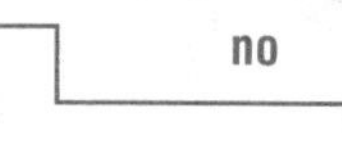

GUIDED PRACTICE

SEE EXAMPLE 1 p. 831

Tell whether each transformation appears to be a translation.

1. no

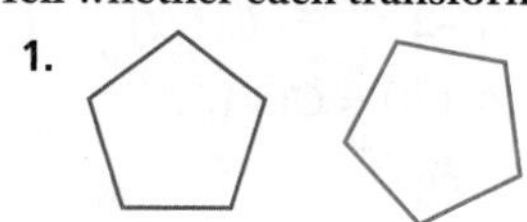

2. no

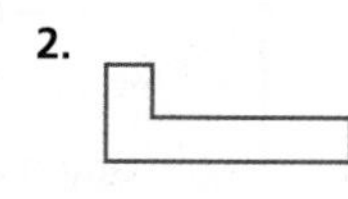

3. yes

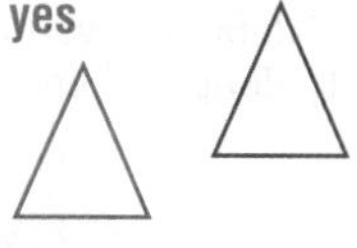

4. no

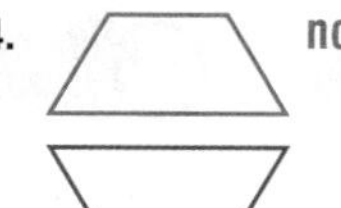

SEE EXAMPLE 2 p. 832

Multi-Step Copy each figure and the translation vector. Draw the translation of the figure along the given vector.

5.

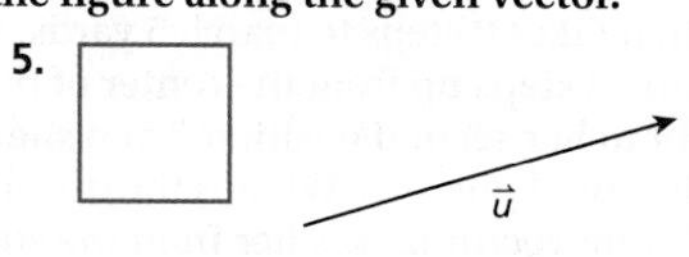

6.

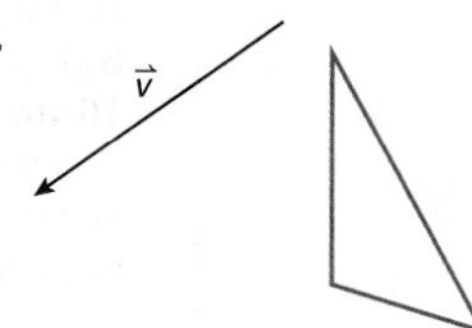

SEE EXAMPLE 3 p. 833

Translate the figure with the given vertices along the given vector.

7. $A(-4, -4)$, $B(-2, -3)$, $C(-1, 3)$; $\langle 5, 0\rangle$
8. $R(-3, 1)$, $S(-2, 3)$, $T(2, 3)$, $U(3, 1)$; $\langle 0, -4\rangle$
9. $J(-2, 2)$, $K(-1, 2)$, $L(-1, -2)$, $M(-3, -1)$; $\langle 3, 2\rangle$

SEE EXAMPLE 4 p. 833

10. **Art** The Zulu people of southern Africa are known for their beadwork. To create a typical Zulu pattern, translate the polygon with vertices $(1, 5)$, $(2, 3)$, $(1, 1)$, and $(0, 3)$ along the vector $\langle 0, -4\rangle$. Translate the image along the same vector. Repeat to generate a pattern. What are the vertices of the fourth polygon in the pattern?

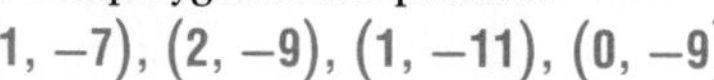
$(1, -7)$, $(2, -9)$, $(1, -11)$, $(0, -9)$

PRACTICE AND PROBLEM SOLVING

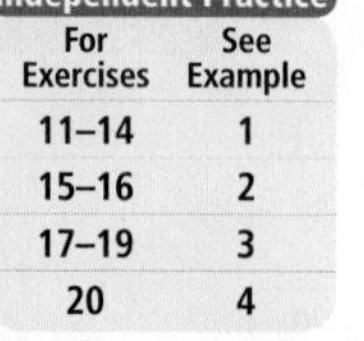

Independent Practice	
For Exercises	See Example
11–14	1
15–16	2
17–19	3
20	4

Extra Practice
Skills Practice p. S26
Application Practice p. S39

Tell whether each transformation appears to be a translation.

11. yes

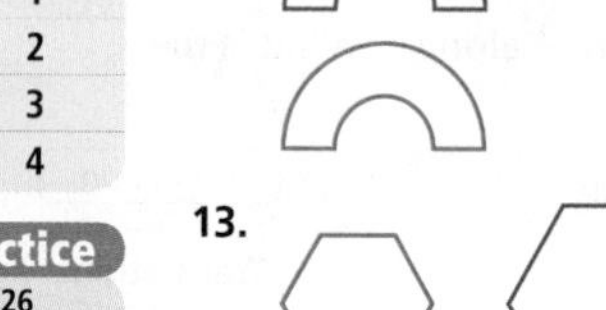

12. no

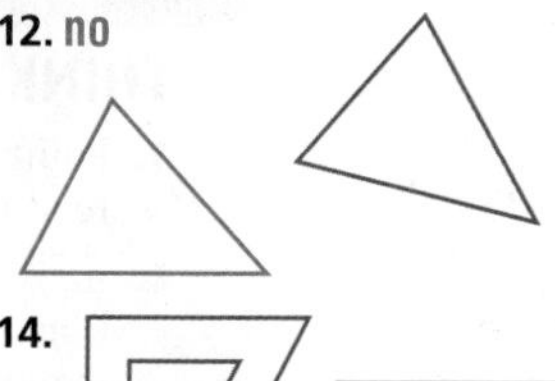

13. no

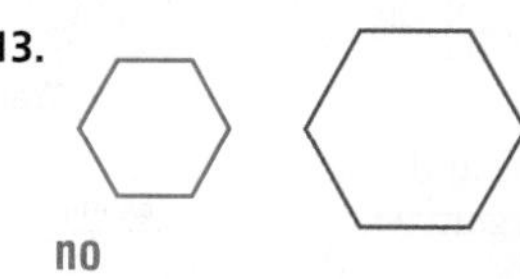

14. yes

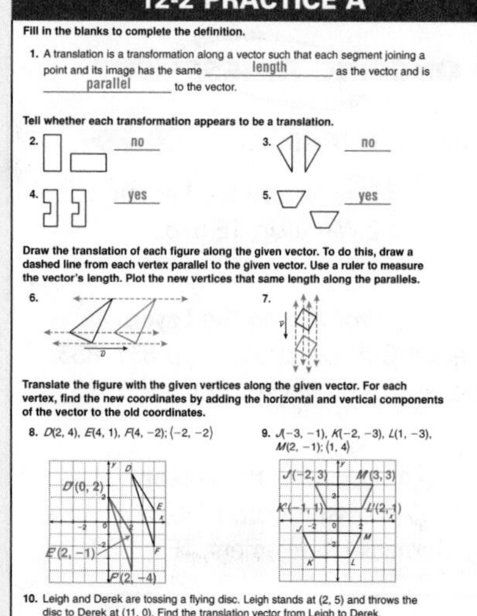

12-2 PRACTICE A

Fill in the blanks to complete the definition.

1. A translation is a transformation along a vector such that each segment joining a point and its image has the same ___length___ as the vector and is ___parallel___ to the vector.

Tell whether each transformation appears to be a translation.

2. no
3. no
4. yes
5. yes

Draw the translation of each figure along the given vector. To do this, draw a dashed line from each vertex parallel to the given vector. Use a ruler to measure the vector's length. Plot the new vertices that same length along the parallels.

6.
7.

Translate the figure with the given vertices along the given vector. For each vertex, find the new coordinates by adding the horizontal and vertical components of the vector to the old coordinates.

8. $D(2, 4)$, $E(4, 1)$, $F(4, -2)$; $\langle -2, -2\rangle$
$D'(0, 2)$, $E'(2, -1)$, $F'(2, -4)$
9. $J(-3, -1)$, $K(-2, -3)$, $L(1, -3)$, $M(2, -1)$; $\langle 1, 4\rangle$
$J'(-2, 3)$, $M'(3, 3)$, $K'(-1, 1)$, $L'(2, 1)$
10. Leigh and Derek are tossing a flying disc. Leigh stands at (2, 5) and throws the disc to Derek at (11, 0). Find the translation vector from Leigh to Derek.
___$\langle 9, -5\rangle$___

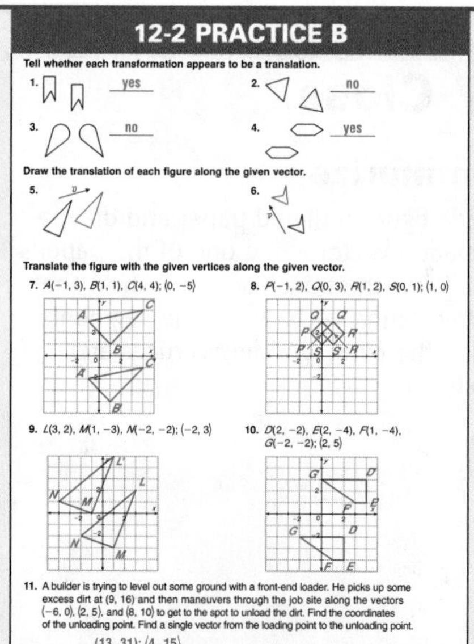

12-2 PRACTICE B

Tell whether each transformation appears to be a translation.

1. yes
2. no
3. no
4. yes

Draw the translation of each figure along the given vector.

5.
6.

Translate the figure with the given vertices along the given vector.

7. $A(-1, 3)$, $B(1, 1)$, $C(4, 4)$; $\langle 0, -5\rangle$
8. $P(-1, 2)$, $Q(0, 3)$, $R(1, 2)$, $S(0, 1)$; $\langle 1, 0\rangle$
9. $L(3, 2)$, $M(1, -3)$, $N(-2, -2)$; $\langle -2, 3\rangle$
10. $D(2, -2)$, $E(2, -4)$, $F(1, -4)$, $G(-2, -2)$; $\langle 2, 5\rangle$
11. A builder is trying to level out some ground with a front-end loader. He picks up some excess dirt at (9, 16) and then maneuvers through the job site along the vectors $\langle -6, 0\rangle$, $\langle 2, 5\rangle$, and $\langle 8, 10\rangle$ to get to the spot to unload the dirt. Find the coordinates of the unloading point. Find a single vector from the loading point to the unloading point.
___$(13, 31)$; $\langle 4, 15\rangle$___

Multi-Step Copy each figure and the translation vector. Draw the translation of the figure along the given vector.

15. 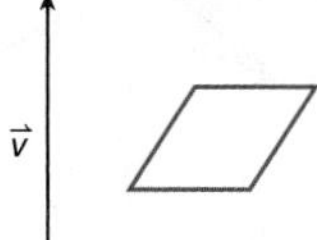

16. 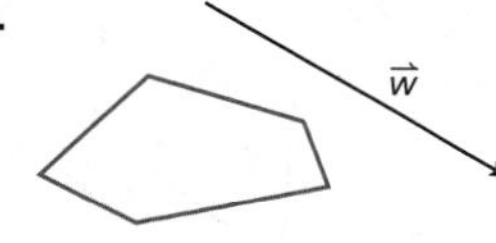

LINK

Animation

Each frame of a computer-animated feature represents $\frac{1}{24}$ of a second of film.

Source: www.pixar.com

Translate the figure with the given vertices along the given vector.

17. $P(-1, 2)$, $Q(1, -1)$, $R(3, 1)$, $S(2, 3)$; $\langle -3, 0\rangle$

18. $A(1, 3)$, $B(-1, 2)$, $C(2, 1)$, $D(4, 2)$; $\langle -3, -3\rangle$

19. $D(0, 15)$, $E(-10, 5)$, $F(10, -5)$; $\langle 5, -20\rangle$

20. **Animation** An animator draws the ladybug shown and then translates it along the vector $\langle 1, 1\rangle$, followed by a translation of the new image along the vector $\langle 2, 2\rangle$, followed by a translation of the second image along the vector $\langle 3, 3\rangle$.

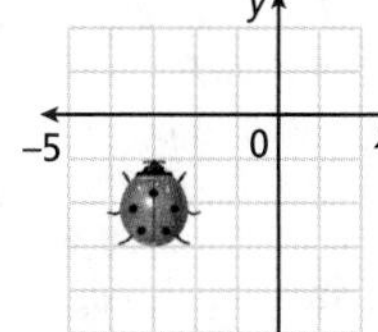

a. Sketch the ladybug's final position.

b. What single vector moves the ladybug from its starting position to its final position? $\langle 6, 6\rangle$

Draw the translation of the graph of each function along the given vector.

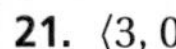

21. $\langle 3, 0\rangle$

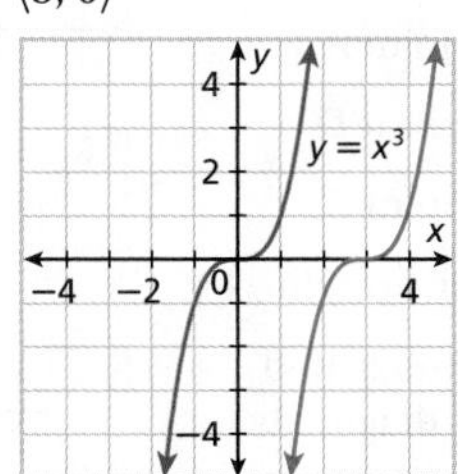

22. $\langle -1, -1\rangle$

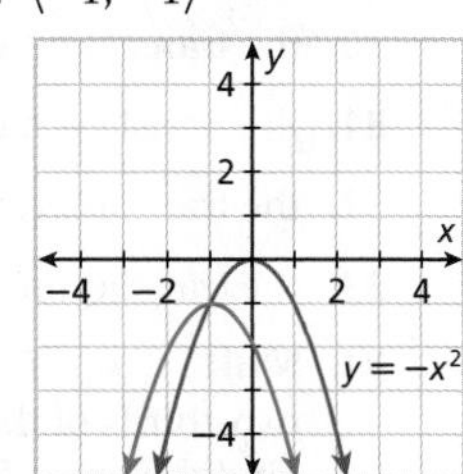

23. **Probability** The point $P(3, 2)$ is translated along one of the following four vectors chosen at random: $\langle -3, 0\rangle$, $\langle -1, -4\rangle$, $\langle 3, -2\rangle$, and $\langle 2, 3\rangle$. Find the probability of each of the following.

a. The image of P is in the fourth quadrant. $\frac{1}{4}$

b. The image of P is on an axis. $\frac{1}{2}$

c. The image of P is at the origin. 0

24c. $\langle 2, 1\rangle + \langle 4, -2\rangle = \langle 6, -1\rangle$

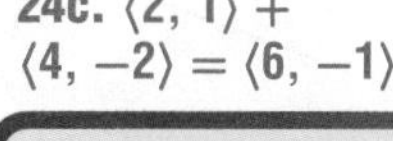

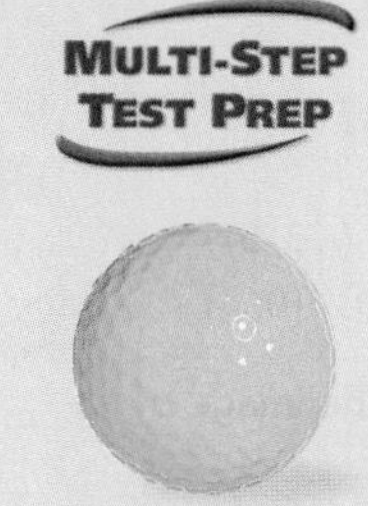

24. This problem will prepare you for the Multi-Step Test Prep on page 854.

The figure shows one hole of a miniature golf course and the path of a ball from the tee T to the hole H.

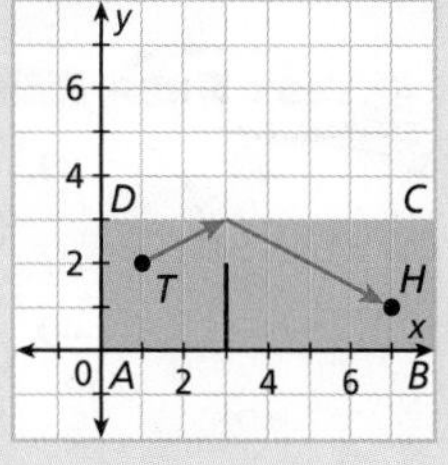

a. What translation vector represents the path of the ball from T to $\overline{DC}$? $\langle 2, 1\rangle$

b. What translation vector represents the path of the ball from $\overline{DC}$ to H? $\langle 4, -2\rangle$

c. Show that the sum of these vectors is equal to the vector that represents the straight path from T to H.

COMMON ERROR ALERT

For exercises involving a given vector, such as **Exercise 20,** some students may confuse the given vectors with the coordinates of points in the plane. Remind them that $\langle a, b\rangle$ is the component form of a vector with a horizontal component of length a and a vertical component of length b.

Teaching Tip

Algebra For **Exercises 21 and 22,** encourage students to use the equations to find the coordinates of several points on the graph. Then they can translate each point to help locate the image of the graph of the function.

Teaching Tip

Probability Students are asked to determine theoretical probabilities in **Exercise 23.** Remind them that the probability of each event is the number of outcomes in the event divided by the number of outcomes in the sample space. Because P can be randomly translated by one of 4 vectors, the sample space is made up of the 4 possible images. So the probability of any event can be 0, $\frac{1}{4}$, $\frac{1}{2}$, $\frac{3}{4}$, or 1.

Exercise 24 involves finding translation vectors. This exercise prepares students for the Multi-Step Test Prep on page 854.

Answers

15.

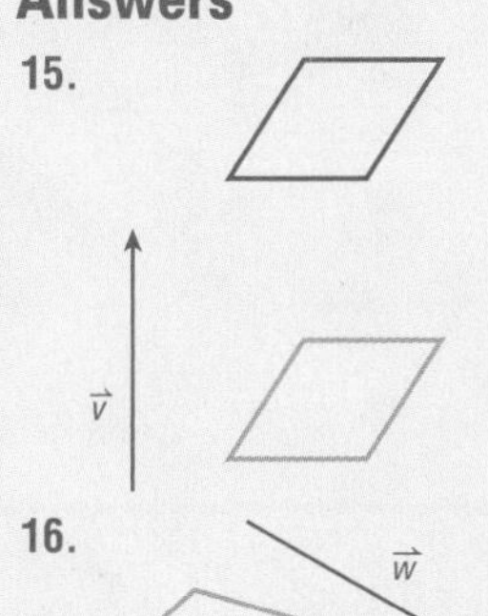

16.

$\vec{w}$

12-2 PRACTICE C

Reflect each figure across ℓ_1. Then reflect that image across ℓ_2. Describe the relation of the second image to the original preimage.

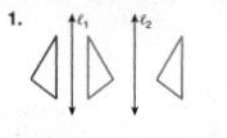

1. The second image is a translation of the original preimage.

2. The second image is a rotation of the original preimage.

3. A translation can be interpreted as successive reflections across two lines. Tell what relationship the lines must have for this to be true.

The lines must be parallel.

4. Measure the distance between the lines in Exercise 1. Measure the distance from one vertex of the original triangle to the same vertex in the final image in your answer. Compare the two measures. Explain why the answer you find is true.

The distance of the translation is twice the distance between the two lines. Possible answer: Call the distance from ℓ_1 to a vertex of the first image x and the distance from ℓ_2 to that same vertex y. A reflected point will be the same distance from the reflection line as the original point was. The distance of the reflection across ℓ_1 is $2x$, and the distance of the reflection across ℓ_2 is $2y$. The distance between the lines is $x + y$. So the distance of the translation is $2(x + y)$ or twice the distance between the two lines.

A vector in the form $\langle a, b\rangle$ is called a *component vector.* Vectors can also be written as *polar vectors* in the form $\langle r, d^\circ\rangle$ where r is the magnitude of the vector and d is the measure of the angle the vector makes with the positive x-axis. Angles are measured from 0° to 360° in a counterclockwise direction. Rewrite each component vector as a polar vector. Round to the nearest tenth if necessary.

5. $\langle 5, 9\rangle$ — $\langle 10.3, 60.9^\circ\rangle$

6. $\langle -6, -1\rangle$ — $\langle 6.1, 189.5^\circ\rangle$

7. $\langle 0, -2\rangle$ — $\langle 2, 270^\circ\rangle$

Find the x- and y-coordinates of each given point after a translation along the given polar vector. Round to the nearest tenth if necessary.

8. $(12, -8)$; $\langle 7, 115^\circ\rangle$ — $(9.0, -1.7)$

9. $(-3, -11)$; $\langle 8, 90^\circ\rangle$ — $(-3, -3)$

10. $(4, 0)$; $\langle 2.5, 230^\circ\rangle$ — $(2.4, -1.9)$

17.

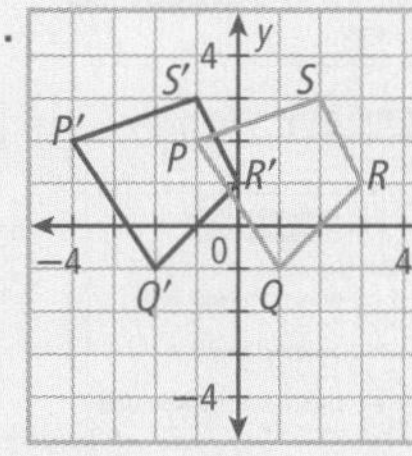

19.

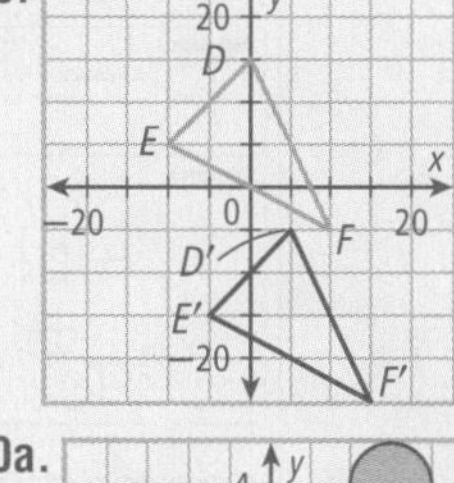

18.

20a.

TEST PREP DOCTOR If students have difficulty with **Exercise 40,** remind them that the slope of the line between $(3, -1)$ and its image should be the same as the slope of $\overline{AB}$.

In **Exercise 41,** students who chose **C** or **D** moved in the opposite horizontal or vertical direction. Encourage students to draw the horizontal and vertical vectors from Q to P, and to make sure that they include the arrows on both vectors.

Answers

28. First use the adjustable parallels to draw a line through the given point that is parallel to the given vector. Then use a ruler to measure a distance along this line that is equal to the magnitude of the vector. The only additional tool needed to do this construction is the ruler.

35. The distance between P and its image is equal to the magnitude of the translation vector, $\langle a, b\rangle$. By the Distance Formula, the magnitude of this vector is $\sqrt{a^2 + b^2}$.

Each figure shows a preimage (blue) and its image (red) under a translation. Copy the figure and draw the vector along which the polygon is translated.

25.

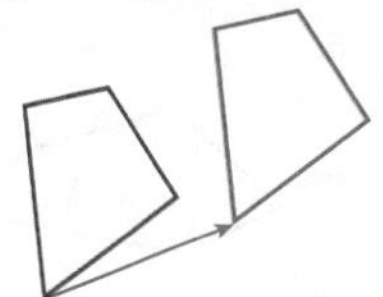

26.

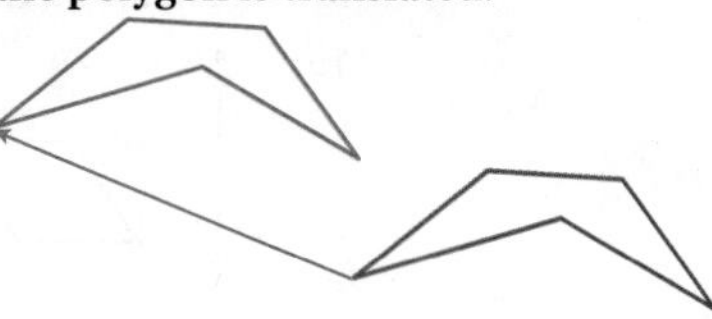

27. **Critical Thinking** The points of a plane are translated along the given vector $\overrightarrow{AB}$. Do any points remain fixed under this transformation? That is, are there any points for which the image coincides with the preimage? Explain.

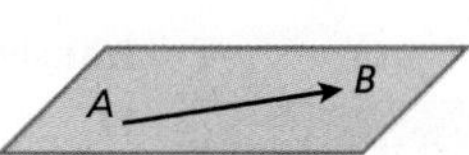

27. No; there are no fixed points because, by definition of a translation, every point must move by the same distance.

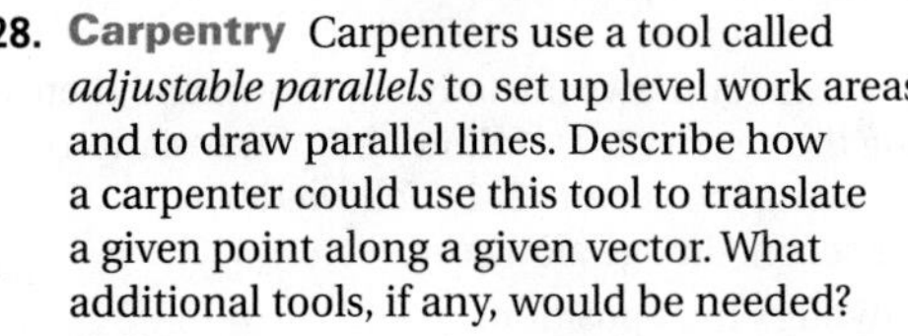

28. **Carpentry** Carpenters use a tool called *adjustable parallels* to set up level work areas and to draw parallel lines. Describe how a carpenter could use this tool to translate a given point along a given vector. What additional tools, if any, would be needed?

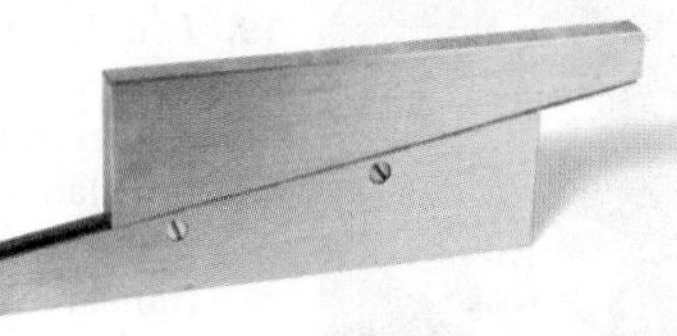

Find the vector associated with each translation. Then use arrow notation to describe the mapping of the preimage to the image.

29. the translation that maps point A to point B $\langle 4, 0\rangle$, $(-3, 2) \rightarrow (1, 2)$

30. the translation that maps point B to point A $\langle -4, 0\rangle$, $(1, 2) \rightarrow (-3, 2)$

31. the translation that maps point C to point D $\langle -3, -2\rangle$, $(3, -1) \rightarrow (0, -3)$

32. the translation that maps point E to point B $\langle 5, 5\rangle$, $(-4, -3) \rightarrow (1, 2)$

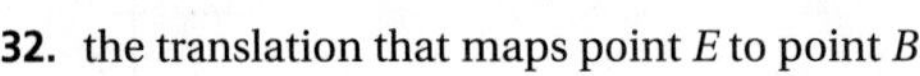

33. the translation that maps point C to the origin $\langle -3, 1\rangle$, $(3, -1) \rightarrow (0, 0)$

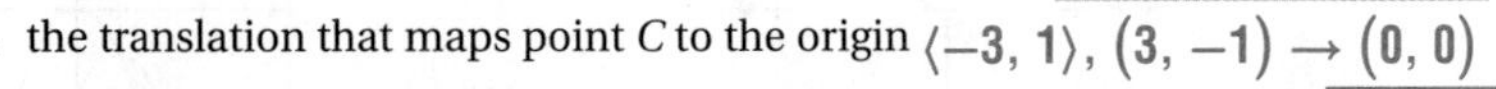

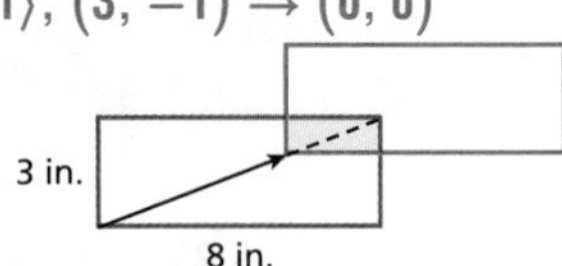

34. **Multi-Step** The rectangle shown is translated two-thirds of the way along one of its diagonals. Find the area of the region where the rectangle and its image overlap. $2\frac{2}{3}$ in^2

35. **Write About It** Point P is translated along the vector $\langle a, b\rangle$. Explain how to find the distance between point P and its image.

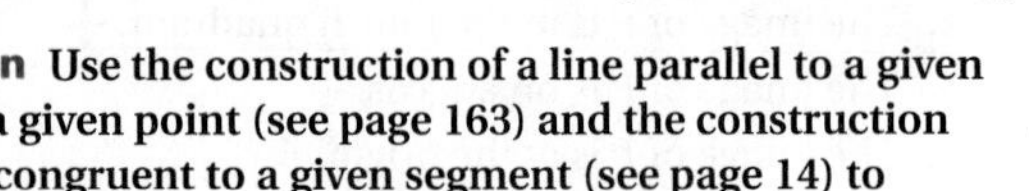

Construction **Use the construction of a line parallel to a given line through a given point (see page 163) and the construction of a segment congruent to a given segment (see page 14) to construct the translation of each figure along a vector.**

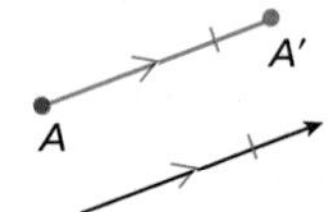

36. a point
37. a segment
38. a triangle

36–38. Check students' constructions.

TEST PREP

39. What is the image of $P(1, 3)$ when it is translated along the vector $\langle -3, 5\rangle$?
- **A** $(-2, 8)$
- B $(0, 6)$
- C $(1, 3)$
- D $(0, 4)$

40. After a translation, the image of $A(-6, -2)$ is $B(-4, -4)$. What is the image of the point $(3, -1)$ after this translation?
- F $(-5, 1)$
- **G** $(5, -3)$
- H $(5, 1)$
- J $(-5, -3)$

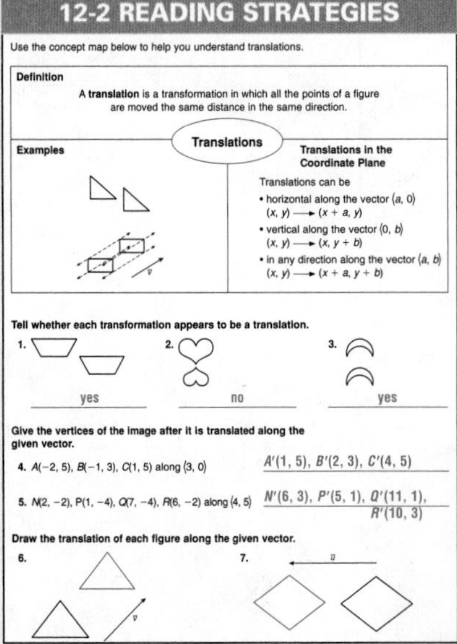

12-2 READING STRATEGIES

Use the concept map below to help you understand translations.

Definition

A **translation** is a transformation in which all the points of a figure are moved the same distance in the same direction.

Translations

Examples

Translations in the Coordinate Plane

Translations can be
- horizontal along the vector ⟨a, 0⟩ (x, y) → (x + a, y)
- vertical along the vector ⟨0, b⟩ (x, y) → (x, y + b)
- in any direction along the vector ⟨a, b⟩ (x, y) → (x + a, y + b)

Tell whether each transformation appears to be a translation.

1. yes 2. no 3. yes

Give the vertices of the image after it is translated along the given vector.

4. A(−2, 5), B(−1, 3), C(1, 5) along ⟨3, 0⟩ A′(1, 5), B′(2, 3), C′(4, 5)

5. N(2, −2), P(1, −4), Q(7, −4), R(6, −2) along ⟨4, 5⟩ N′(6, 3), P′(5, 1), Q′(11, 1), R′(10, 3)

Draw the translation of each figure along the given vector.

6. 7.

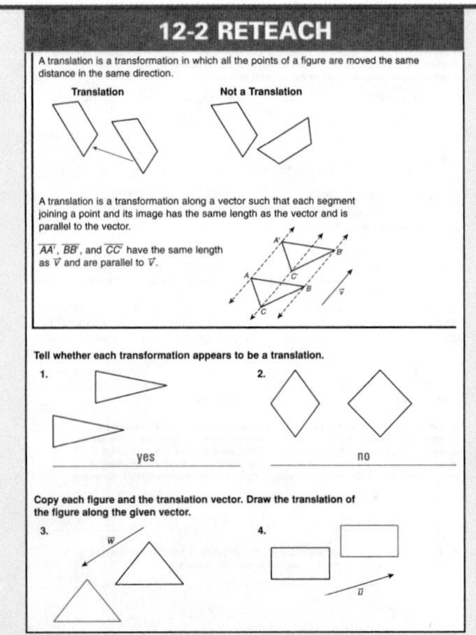

12-2 RETEACH

A translation is a transformation in which all the points of a figure are moved the same distance in the same direction.

Translation **Not a Translation**

A translation is a transformation along a vector such that each segment joining a point and its image has the same length as the vector and is parallel to the vector.

$\overline{AA'}$, $\overline{BB'}$, and $\overline{CC'}$ have the same length as $\vec{v}$ and are parallel to $\vec{v}$.

Tell whether each transformation appears to be a translation.

1. yes 2. no

Copy each figure and the translation vector. Draw the translation of the figure along the given vector.

3. 4.

41. Which vector translates point Q to point P?

Ⓐ $\langle -2, -4\rangle$ Ⓒ $\langle -2, 4\rangle$

Ⓑ $\langle 4, -2\rangle$ Ⓓ $\langle 2, -4\rangle$

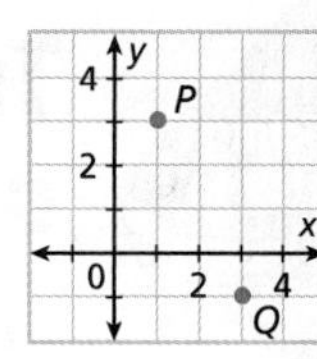

CHALLENGE AND EXTEND

42. The point $M(1, 2)$ is translated along a vector that is parallel to the line $y = 2x + 4$. The translation vector has magnitude $\sqrt{5}$. What are the possible images of point M? (0, 0) and (2, 4)

43. A cube has edges of length 2 cm. Point P is translated along $\vec{u}$, $\vec{v}$, and $\vec{w}$ as shown.

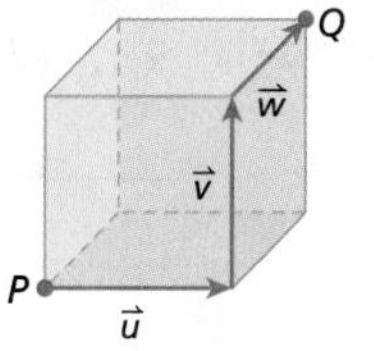

a. Describe a single translation vector that maps point P to point Q. the vector $\overrightarrow{PQ}$

b. Find the magnitude of this vector to the nearest hundredth. 3.46 cm

44. Prove that the translation image of a segment is congruent to the preimage.
Given: $\overline{A'B'}$ is the translation image of $\overline{AB}$.
Prove: $\overline{AB} \cong \overline{A'B'}$
(*Hint:* Draw auxiliary lines $\overline{AA'}$ and $\overline{BB'}$. What can you conclude about $\overline{AA'}$ and $\overline{BB'}$?)

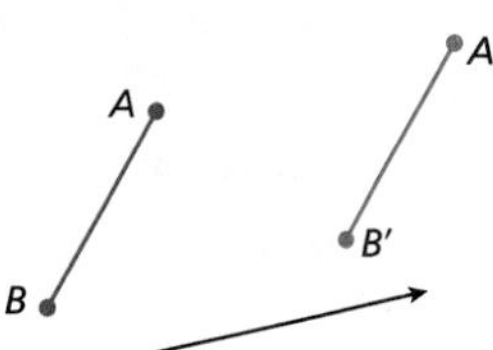

44. Draw auxiliary lines $\overline{AA'}$ and $\overline{BB'}$. By the def. of translation, $\overline{AA'} \cong \overline{BB'}$ and $\overline{AA'} \parallel \overline{BB'}$. Opposite sides $\overline{AA'}$ and $\overline{BB'}$ and are ≅ and ∥, so $AA'B'B$ is a parallelogram. Opposite sides of a parallelogram are congruent, so $\overline{AB} \cong \overline{A'B'}$.

Once you have proved that the translation image of a segment is congruent to the preimage, how could you prove the following? Write a plan for each proof.

45. If $\overline{A'B'}$ is a translation of $\overline{AB}$, then $AB = A'B'$.

46. If $\angle A'B'C'$ is a translation of $\angle ABC$, then $m\angle ABC = m\angle A'B'C'$.

47. The translation $\triangle A'B'C'$ is congruent to the preimage $\triangle ABC$.

48. If point C is between points A and B, then the translation C' is between A' and B'.

49. If points A, B, and C are collinear, then the translations A', B', and C' are collinear.

45. Use the fact that the translation of a seg. is ≅ to the preimage and the def. of ≅ segs.

47. Use the fact that the translation of a seg. is ≅ to the preimage to prove $\triangle ABC \cong \triangle A'B'C'$ by SSS.

SPIRAL REVIEW

Solve each system of equations and check your solution. *(Previous course)*

50. $\begin{cases} -5x - 2y = 17 \\ 6x - 2y = -5 \end{cases}$

51. $\begin{cases} 2x - 3y = -7 \\ 6x + 5y = 49 \end{cases}$ (4, 5)

52. $\begin{cases} 4x + 4y = -1 \\ 12x - 8y = -8 \end{cases}$ $\left(-\frac{1}{2}, \frac{1}{4}\right)$

Solve to find x and y in each diagram. *(Lesson 3-4)*

53. $x = 15$, $y = 5$

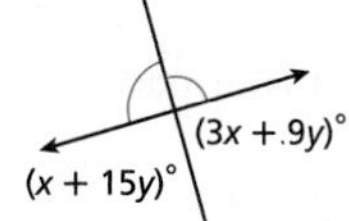

54. $x = 22.5$, $y = 45$

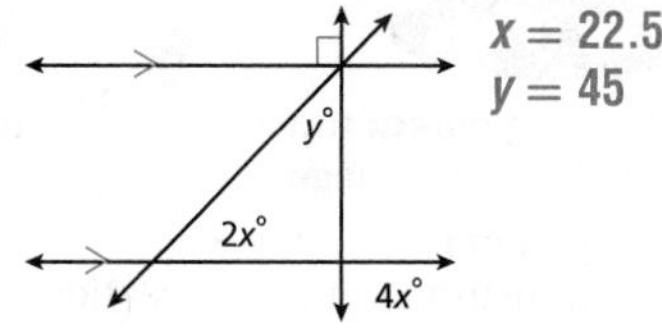

48. If C is between A and B, then $AC + BC = AB$. Use the fact that the translation of a seg. is ≅ to the preimage to prove $A'C' + B'C' = A'B'$. Then use the def. of betweenness to prove C' is between A' and B'.

$\triangle MNP$ has vertices $M(-2, 0)$, $N(-3, 2)$, and $P(0, 4)$. Find the coordinates of the vertices of $\triangle M'N'P'$ after a reflection across the given line. *(Lesson 12-1)*

55. x-axis

56. y-axis

57. $y = x$

Journal

For a transformation that appears to be a translation, have students explain how they would use a compass and a straightedge or a ruler and a protractor to verify that it is a translation.

Answers

46, 49–50, 55–57. See p. A30.

ALTERNATIVE ASSESSMENT

Have students look for a design that includes a translation of a geometric figure. Ask them to trace the design, connect the corresponding vertices of the figure and its image, and draw the translation vector. Then have the students copy the design onto a coordinate plane and write the translation vector in coordinate form.

Power Presentations with PowerPoint®

12-2 Lesson Quiz

1. Tell whether the transformation appears to be a translation.

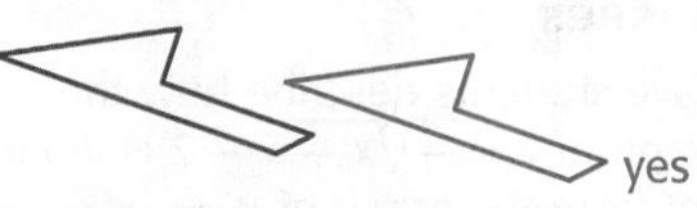

yes

2. Copy the triangle and the translation vector. Draw the translation of the triangle along $\vec{v}$.

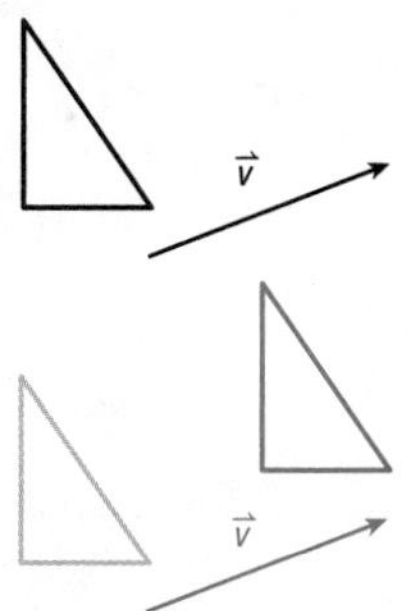

Translate the figure with the given vertices along the given vector.

3. $G(8, 2)$, $H(-4, 5)$, $I(3, -1)$; $\langle -2, 0\rangle$ $G'(6, 2)$, $H'(-6, 5)$, $I'(1, -1)$

4. $S(0, -7)$, $T(-4, 4)$, $U(-5, 2)$, $V(8, 1)$; $\langle -4, 5\rangle$ $S'(-4, -2)$, $T'(-8, 9)$, $U'(-9, 7)$, $V'(4, 6)$

5. A rook on a chessboard has coordinates (3, 4). The rook is moved up two spaces. Then it is moved three spaces to the left. What is the rook's final position? What single vector moves the rook from its starting position to its final position? (0, 6); $\langle -3, 2\rangle$

Also available on transparency

12-2 PROBLEM SOLVING

1. A checker player's piece begins at K and, through a series of moves, lands on L. What translation vector represents the path from K to L?
$\langle -4, 6\rangle$

2. The preimage of M' has coordinates $(-6, 5)$. What is the vector that translates $\triangle MNP$ to $\triangle M'N'P'$?
$\langle 3, -9\rangle$

3. In a quilt pattern, a polygon with vertices $(3, -2)$, $(7, -1)$, $(9, -5)$, and $(5, -6)$ is translated repeatedly along the vector $\langle 4, 5\rangle$. What are the coordinates of the third polygon in the pattern?
(11, 8), (15, 9), (17, 5), (13, 4)

4. A group of hikers walks 2 miles east and then 1 mile north. After taking a break, they then hike 4 miles east and set up camp. What vector describes their hike from their starting position to their camp? Let 1 unit represent 1 mile.
$\langle 6, 1\rangle$

Choose the best answer.

5. In a video game, a character at (8, 3) moves three times, as described by the translations shown at right. What is the final position of the character after the three moves?

Move 1: $\langle 2, 7\rangle$
Move 2: $\langle -10, -4\rangle$
Move 3: $\langle 1, -5\rangle$

A $(-8, 3)$ Ⓒ $(1, 1)$
B $(-7, -2)$ D $(9, 2)$

6. The logo is translated along the vector $\langle 8, 15\rangle$. What are the coordinates of R'?

Ⓕ $(4, 17)$ H $(15, 18)$
G $(12, 17)$ J $(11, 19)$

7. $\triangle DEF$ is translated so that the image of E has coordinates $(0, 3)$. What is the image of F after this translation?

A $(1, -1)$ Ⓒ $(-2, -2)$
B $(4, -2)$ D $(-2, 6)$

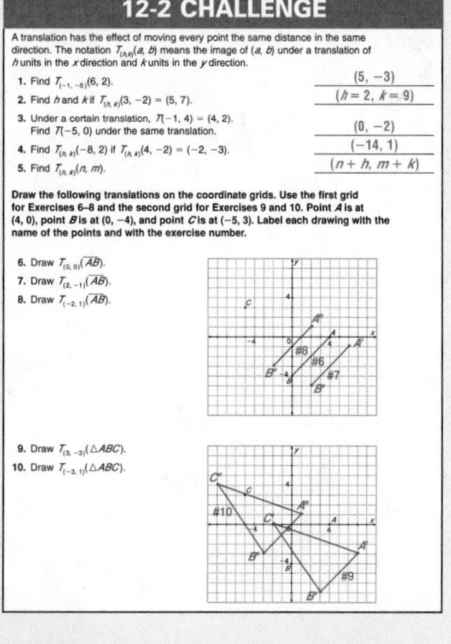

12-2 CHALLENGE

A translation has the effect of moving every point the same distance in the same direction. The notation $T_{(h,k)}(a, b)$ means the image of (a, b) under a translation of h units in the x direction and k units in the y direction.

1. Find $T_{(-1,-5)}(6, 2)$. (5, −3)
2. Find h and k if $T_{(h,k)}(3, -2) = (5, 7)$. ($h = 2$, $k = 9$)
3. Under a certain translation, $T(-1, 4) = (4, 2)$. Find $T(-5, 0)$ under the same translation. (0, −2)
4. Find $T_{(h,k)}(-8, 2)$ if $T_{(h,k)}(4, -2) = (-2, -3)$. (−14, 1)
5. Find $T_{(h,k)}(n, m)$. $(n + h, m + k)$

Draw the following translations on the coordinate grids. Use the first grid for Exercises 6–8 and the second grid for Exercises 9 and 10. Point A is at (4, 0), point B is at (0, −4), and point C is at (−5, 3). Label each drawing with the name of the points and with the exercise number.

6. Draw $T_{(0,0)}(\overline{AB})$.
7. Draw $T_{(2,-1)}(\overline{AB})$.
8. Draw $T_{(-2,1)}(\overline{AB})$.
9. Draw $T_{(3,-3)}(\triangle ABC)$.
10. Draw $T_{(-3,1)}(\triangle ABC)$.

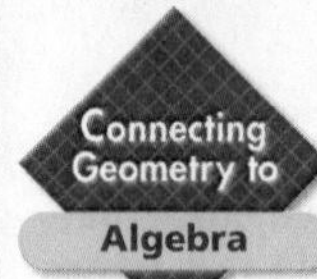

Organizer

Pacing:
Traditional 1 day
Block $\frac{1}{2}$ day

Objective: Reflect and translate functions in the coordinate plane and write a rule for the transformation.

Online Edition

Teach

Remember

Students review transformations in the coordinate plane.

Inclusion Remind students that the y-values change as they cross the x-axis and that the x-values change as they cross the y-axis.

Close

Assess

Have students describe how the graph of $y = -\sqrt{x+5} - 2$ is different from the graph of $y = -\sqrt{x}$.

go.hrw.com
State Resources Online
KEYWORD: MG7 Resources

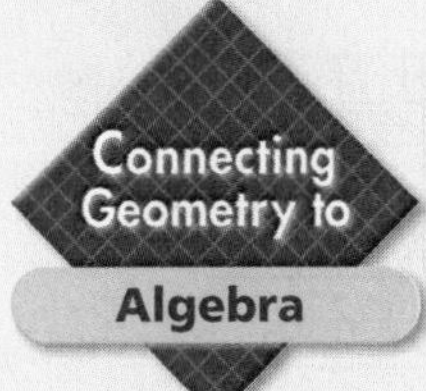

Transformations of Functions

Transformations can be used to graph complicated functions by using the graphs of simpler functions called *parent functions*. The following are examples of parent functions and their graphs.

$y = |x|$

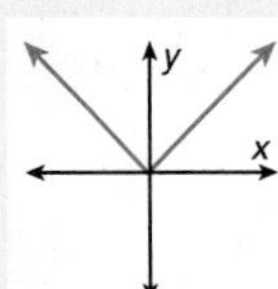

$y = \sqrt{x}$

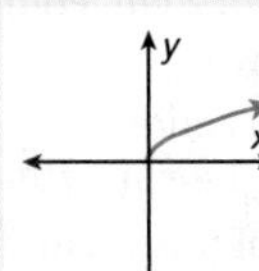

$y = x^2$

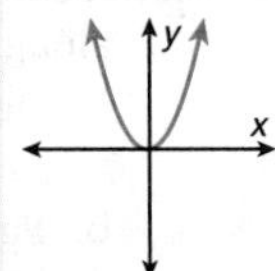

Transformation of Parent Function $y = f(x)$		
Reflection	**Vertical Translation**	**Horizontal Translation**
Across x-axis: $y = -f(x)$ Across y-axis: $y = f(-x)$	$y = f(x) + k$ Up k units if $k > 0$ Down k units if $k < 0$	$y = f(x - h)$ Right h units if $h > 0$ Left h units if $h < 0$

Example

For the parent function $y = x^2$, write a function rule for the given transformation and graph the preimage and image.

A **a reflection across the x-axis**
function rule: $y = -x^2$
graph:

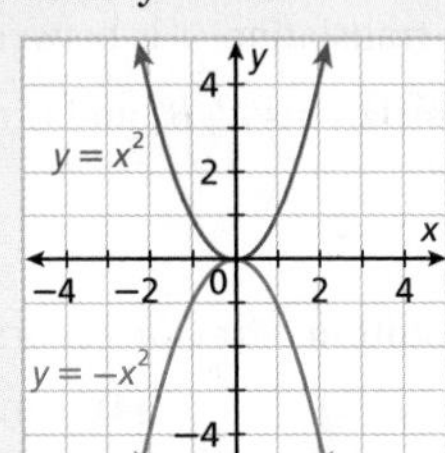

B **a translation up 2 units and right 3 units**
function rule: $y = (x - 3)^2 + 2$
graph:

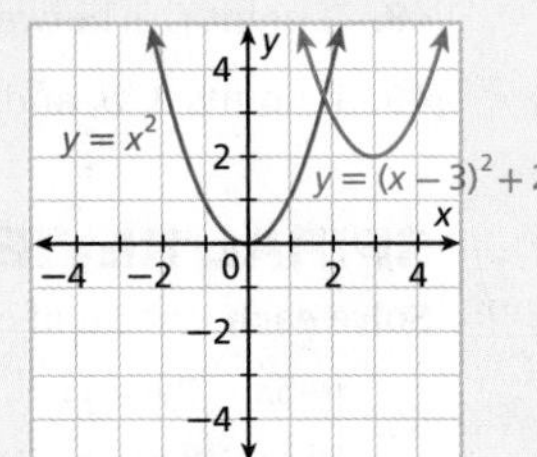

Try This

For each parent function, write a function rule for the given transformation and graph the preimage and image.

1. parent function: $y = x^2$
   transformation: a translation down 1 unit and right 4 units $y = (x - 4)^2 - 1$
2. parent function: $y = \sqrt{x}$
   transformation: a reflection across the x-axis $y = -\sqrt{x}$
3. parent function: $y = |x|$
   transformation: a translation up 2 units and left 1 unit $y = |x + 1| + 2$

Answers

1.
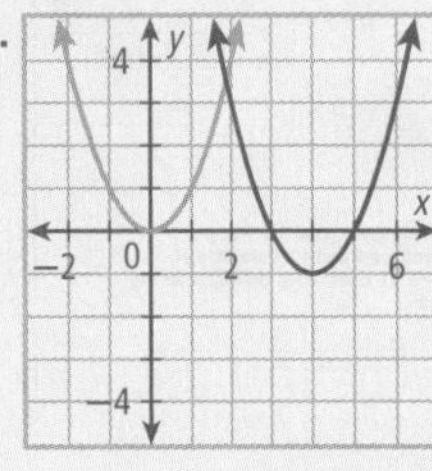

2.
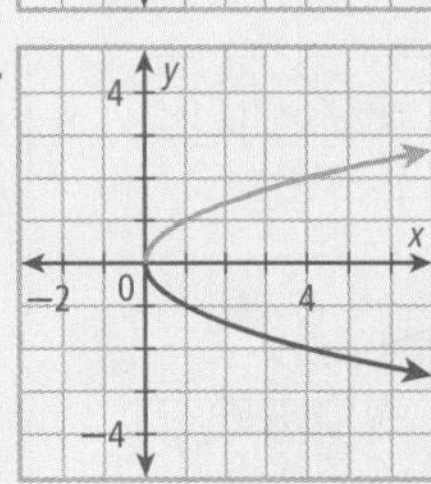

3.

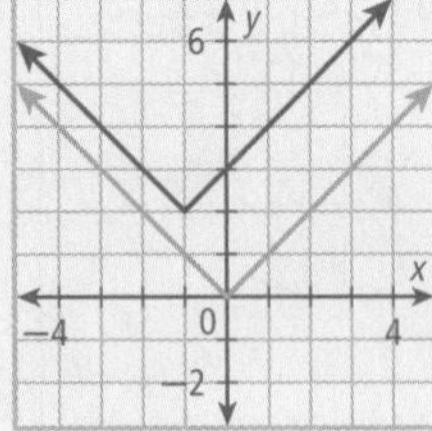

12-3 Rotations

Objective
Identify and draw rotations.

Who uses this?
Astronomers can use properties of rotations to analyze photos of star trails. (See Exercise 35.)

Remember that a rotation is a transformation that turns a figure around a fixed point, called the center of rotation. A rotation is an isometry, so the image of a rotated figure is congruent to the preimage.

EXAMPLE 1 Identifying Rotations

Tell whether each transformation appears to be a rotation. Explain.

A

Yes; the figure appears to be turned around a point.

B

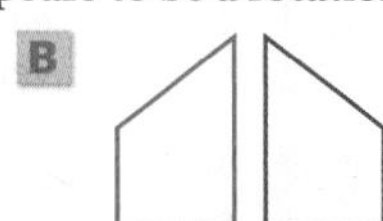

No; the figure appears to be flipped, not turned.

Tell whether each transformation appears to be a rotation.

1a. 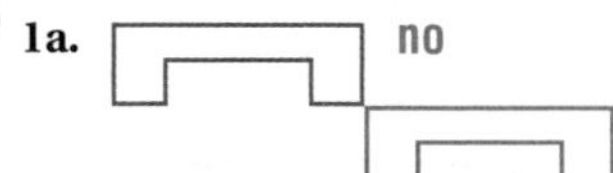 no

1b.  yes

Construction Rotate a Figure Using Patty Paper

1. On a sheet of paper, draw a triangle and a point. The point will be the center of rotation.

2. Place a sheet of patty paper on top of the diagram. Trace the triangle and the point.

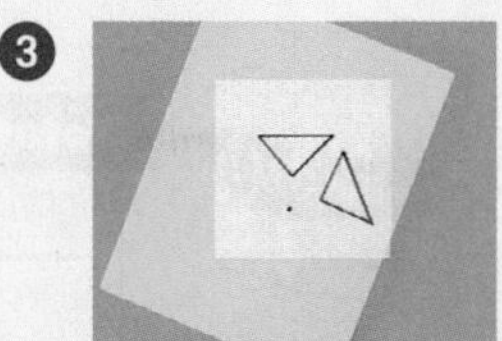

3. Hold your pencil down on the point and rotate the bottom paper counterclockwise. Trace the triangle.

Draw a segment from each vertex to the center of rotation. Your construction should show that a point's distance to the center of rotation is equal to its image's distance to the center of rotation. The angle formed by a point, the center of rotation, and the point's image is the angle by which the figure was rotated.

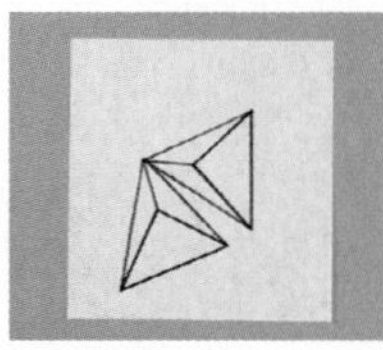

12-3 Organizer

Pacing: Traditional 1 day
Block $\frac{1}{2}$ day

Objective: Identify and draw rotations.

Online Edition
Tutorial Videos

Power Presentations with PowerPoint®

Warm Up

1. The translation image of $P(-3, -1)$ is $P'(1, 3)$. Find the translation image of $Q(2, -4)$. $Q'(6, 0)$

Solve for x. Round to the nearest tenth.

2. $\cos 30° = \frac{x}{50}$ $x \approx 43.3$
3. $\sin 30° = \frac{x}{50}$ $x = 25$

Also available on transparency

Math Humor

Doctor: Where did you get that sprain?

Patient: The ankle of rotation.

Construction

Have students measure the angle of rotation and the distance from a point and from its image to the center of rotation to verify the properties of rotations on page 840.

1 Introduce

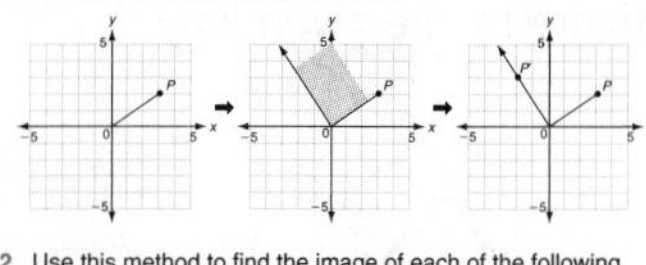

EXPLORATION

12-3 Rotations

Recall that a rotation, or *turn*, is a transformation of a figure about a fixed point, called the *center of rotation*. Use graph paper to explore rotations in the coordinate plane.

1. Find the image of point *P* under a 90° rotation about the origin as follows. Draw a segment from *P* to the origin. Use an index card to draw a ray at a 90° angle as shown. Then find point *P'* on the ray that is the same distance from the origin as *P*. Use the Distance Formula to check.
2. Use this method to find the image of each of the following points under a 90° rotation about the origin.

Point	(1, 4)	(3, 0)	(−2, 3)	(−1, −2)
Image				

3. Look for a pattern. What do you notice?

THINK AND DISCUSS

Motivate

Copy the following figure onto a transparency. Discuss with students how to form a flower with 5 petals by using consecutive rotations of 72°. Ask students how they would form flowers with 6 and 8 petals. Use rotations of 60° and 45°.

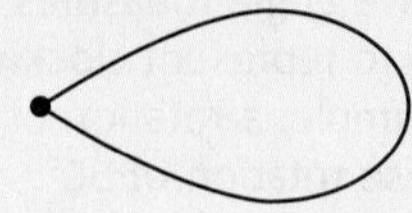

Explorations and answers are provided in *Alternate Openers: Explorations Transparencies.*

State Resources

go.hrw.com
State Resources Online
KEYWORD: MG7 Resources

Power Presentations with PowerPoint®

Additional Examples

Example 1

Tell whether each transformation appears to be a rotation.

A. no

B. yes

Example 2

Copy the figure and the angle of rotation. Draw the rotation of the triangle about point Q by $\angle A$.

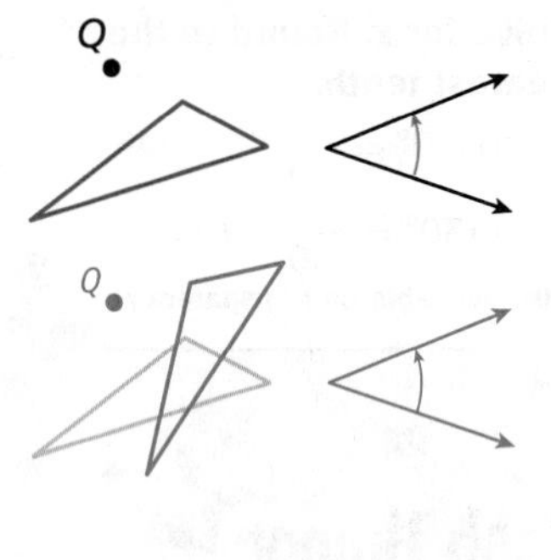

INTERVENTION

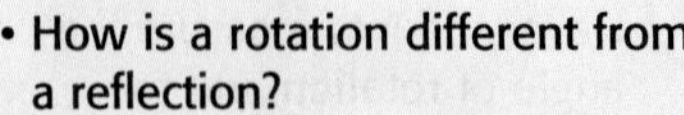

Questioning Strategies

EXAMPLE 1

- How is a rotation different from a reflection?

EXAMPLE 2

- How can you verify your answer?

Teaching Tip

Inclusion Remind students that *counterclockwise* means "in the direction opposite to the course of the hands of a clock."

ENGLISH LANGUAGE LEARNERS

Know it! Note

Rotations

A rotation is a transformation about a point P, called the center of rotation, such that each point and its image are the same distance from P, and such that all angles with vertex P formed by a point and its image are congruent. In the figure, $\angle APA'$ is the angle of rotation.

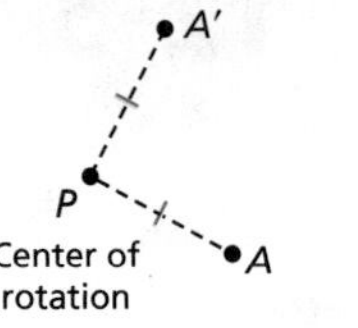

EXAMPLE 2 Drawing Rotations

Copy the figure and the angle of rotation. Draw the rotation of the triangle about point P by $m\angle A$.

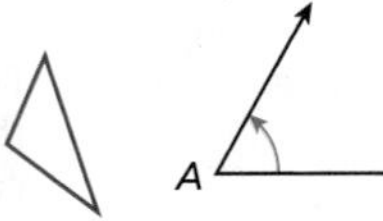

Step 1 Draw a segment from each vertex to point P.

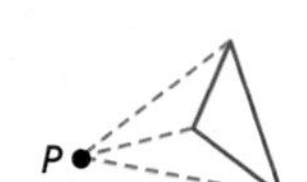

Helpful Hint

Unless otherwise stated, all rotations in this book are counterclockwise.

Step 2 Construct an angle congruent to $\angle A$ onto each segment. Measure the distance from each vertex to point P and mark off this distance on the corresponding ray to locate the image of each vertex.

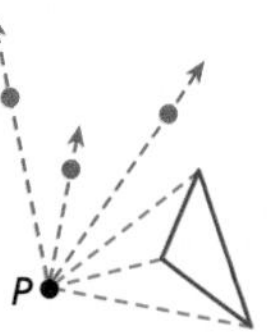

Step 3 Connect the images of the vertices.

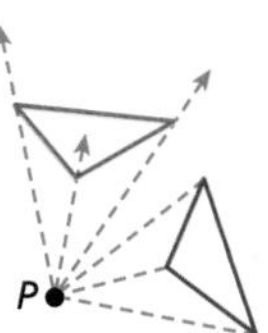

2. Copy the figure and the angle of rotation. Draw the rotation of the segment about point Q by $m\angle X$.

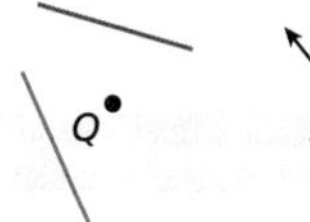
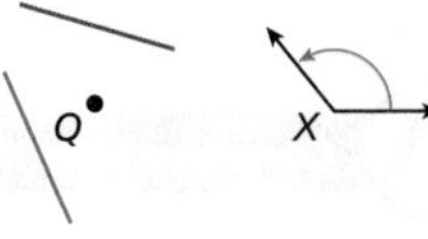

Know it! Note

Rotations in the Coordinate Plane

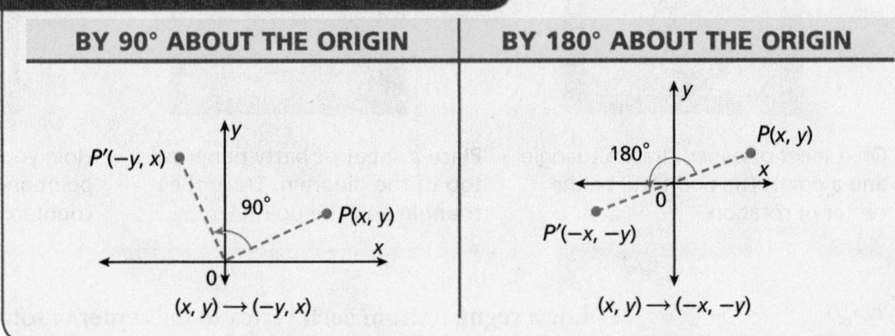

If the angle of a rotation in the coordinate plane is not a multiple of 90°, you can use sine and cosine ratios to find the coordinates of the image.

840 Chapter 12 Extending Transformational Geometry

2 Teach

Guided Instruction

Explain that the center of rotation is called a *fixed* point because it does not move when a figure is rotated about that point. The center of rotation can be inside, on, or outside the preimage. Point out to students that negative angle measures are sometimes used to represent clockwise rotations. For example, a rotation of –50° means a clockwise rotation of 50°.

Reaching All Learners

Through Concrete Manipulatives

Have students create a "rotation ruler" by cutting an angle out of a piece of paper and using a ruler and compass to mark it at regular intervals. They can use this ruler to rotate a figure by the given angle.

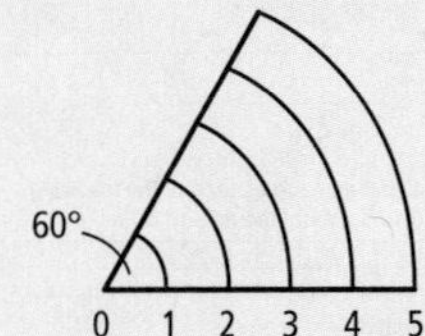

EXAMPLE 3 Drawing Rotations in the Coordinate Plane

Rotate $\triangle ABC$ with vertices $A(2, -1)$, $B(4, 1)$, and $C(3, 3)$ by 90° about the origin.

The rotation of (x, y) is $(-y, x)$.

$A(2, -1) \rightarrow A'(1, 2)$

$B(4, 1) \rightarrow B'(-1, 4)$

$C(3, 3) \rightarrow C'(-3, 3)$

Graph the preimage and image.

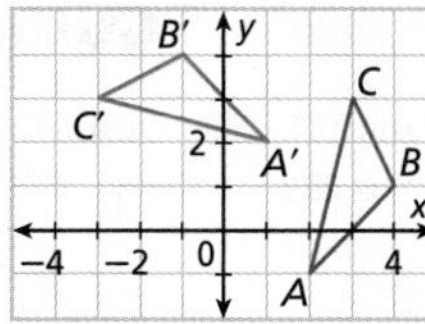

3. 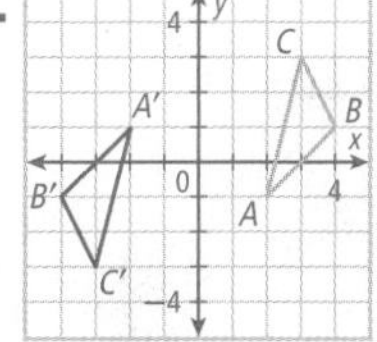

CHECK IT OUT! 3. Rotate $\triangle ABC$ by 180° about the origin.

EXAMPLE 4 *Engineering Application*

The London Eye observation wheel has a radius of 67.5 m and takes 30 minutes to make a complete rotation. A car starts at position (67.5, 0). What are the coordinates of the car's location after 5 minutes?

Step 1 Find the angle of rotation. Five minutes is $\frac{5}{30} = \frac{1}{6}$ of a complete rotation, or $\frac{1}{6}(360°) = 60°$.

Step 2 Draw a right triangle to represent the car's location (x, y) after a rotation of 60° about the origin.

(x, y)
67.5
60°
0
67.5
(67.5, 0)
Starting position

Step 3 Use the cosine ratio to find the x-coordinate.

$\cos 60° = \frac{x}{67.5}$ *$\cos = \frac{adj.}{hyp.}$*

$x = 67.5 \cos 60° \approx 33.8$ *Solve for x.*

Step 4 Use the sine ratio to find the y-coordinate.

$\sin 60° = \frac{y}{67.5}$ *$\sin = \frac{opp.}{hyp.}$*

$y = 67.5 \sin 60° \approx 58.5$ *Solve for y.*

The car's location after 5 minutes is approximately (33.8, 58.5).

Remember!

To review the sine and cosine ratios, see Lesson 8-2, pages 525–532.

4. Find the coordinates of the observation car after 6 minutes. Round to the nearest tenth. (20.9, 64.2)

THINK AND DISCUSS

1. Describe the image of a rotation of a figure by an angle of 360°.
2. Point A' is a rotation of point A about point P. What is the relationship of $\overline{AP}$ to $\overline{A'P}$?
3. **GET ORGANIZED** Copy and complete the graphic organizer.

	Reflection	Translation	Rotation
Definition			
Example			

Power Presentations with PowerPoint®

Additional Examples

Example 3

Rotate $\triangle JKL$ with vertices $J(2, 2)$, $K(4, -5)$, and $L(-1, 6)$ by 180° about the origin.

$J'(-2, -2)$, $K'(-4, 5)$, $L'(1, -6)$

Example 4

A Ferris wheel has a 100 ft diameter and takes 8 min to make a complete rotation. A chair starts at (50, 0). After 1 min, what are the coordinates of its location to the nearest tenth?

(35.4, 35.4)

INTERVENTION

Questioning Strategies

EXAMPLE 3

- If all three vertices of a triangle are in Quadrant II and the triangle is rotated 90° about the origin, in which quadrant will the vertices of the rotated triangle lie?

EXAMPLE 4

- Why do we use the cosine ratio to find the x-coordinate and the sine ratio to find the y-coordinate?

Technology Encourage students to use geometry software to explore the rotation of a figure. Have them draw $\triangle ABC$ and rotate it about point P, then measure to verify that $m\angle APA' = m\angle BPB' = m\angle CPC'$.

3 Close

Summarize

Remind students that a rotation is an isometry, so the image of a rotated figure is congruent to the preimage. Compare a rotation in the coordinate plane by 180° about the origin with a reflection across the x-axis followed by a reflection across the y-axis.

ONGOING ASSESSMENT and INTERVENTION

***Diagnose Before* the Lesson**
12-3 Warm Up, TE p. 839

***Monitor During* the Lesson**
Check It Out! Exercises, SE pp. 839–841
Questioning Strategies, TE pp. 840–841

***Assess After* the Lesson**
12-3 Lesson Quiz, TE p. 845
Alternative Assessment, TE p. 845

Answers to *Think and Discuss*

1. The image is in the same position as the preimage.
2. $\overline{AP} \cong \overline{A'P}$
3. See p. A9.

12-3 Exercises

Assignment Guide

Assign *Guided Practice* exercises as necessary.

If you finished Examples **1–2**

Basic 13–18, 24–30, 32–34

Average 13–18, 24–30, 32–34, 42, 46

Advanced 13–18, 24–31, 33–35, 42, 46–51

If you finished Examples **1–4**

Basic 13–36, 41, 42–44, 52–59

Average 13–31, 35, 37–46, 52–59

Advanced 13–31, 35, 37–59

Homework Quick Check

Quickly check key concepts.

Exercises: 14, 16, 18, 20, 22, 28

Visual For **Exercise 11,** suggest that students first plot the car's initial position in the coordinate plane, connect the point to the origin with a line segment, and then sketch a 30° angle using that line segment as one of the rays of the angle.

Answers

7.

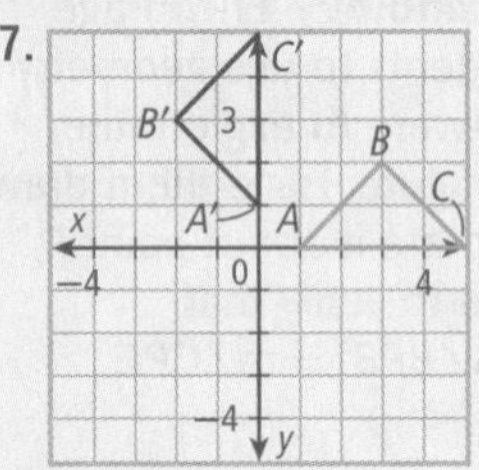

8–10. See p. A30.

State Resources

12-3 Exercises

go.hrw.com
Homework Help Online
KEYWORD: MG7 12-3
Parent Resources Online
KEYWORD: MG7 Parent

GUIDED PRACTICE

SEE EXAMPLE 1 p. 839

Tell whether each transformation appears to be a rotation.

1. yes

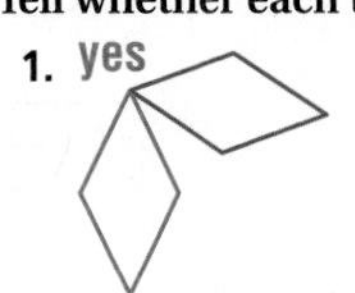

2. no

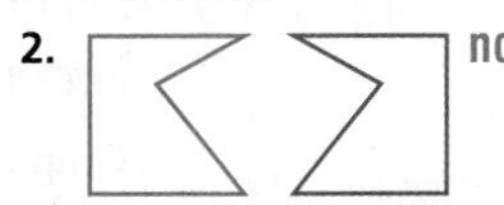

3. no

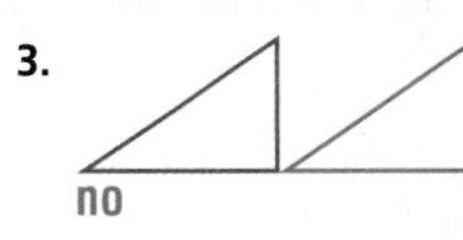

4. yes

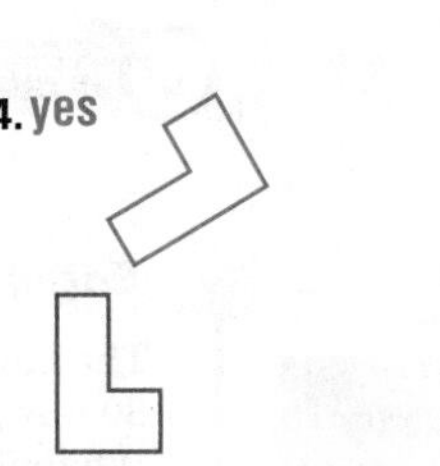

SEE EXAMPLE 2 p. 840

Copy each figure and the angle of rotation. Draw the rotation of the figure about point P by $m\angle A$.

5.

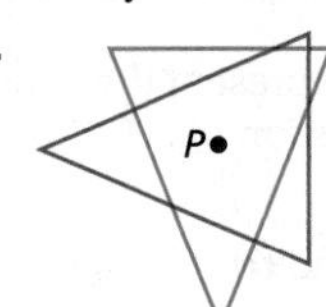

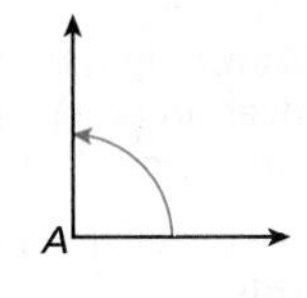

6.

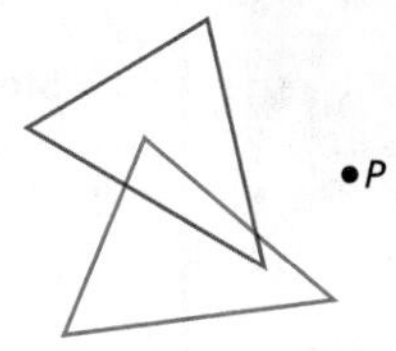

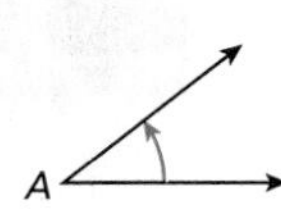

SEE EXAMPLE 3 p. 841

Rotate the figure with the given vertices about the origin using the given angle of rotation.

7. $A(1, 0), B(3, 2), C(5, 0)$; 90°
8. $J(2, 1), K(4, 3), L(2, 4), M(-1, 2)$; 90°
9. $D(2, 3), E(-1, 2), F(2, 1)$; 180°
10. $P(-1, -1), Q(-4, -2), R(0, -2)$; 180°

SEE EXAMPLE 4 p. 841

11. **Animation** An artist uses a coordinate plane to plan the motion of an animated car. To simulate the car driving around a curve, the artist places the car at the point (10, 0) and then rotates it about the origin by 30°. Give the car's final position, rounding the coordinates to the nearest tenth. (8.7, 5)

PRACTICE AND PROBLEM SOLVING

For Exercises	See Example
12–15	1
16–17	2
18–21	3
22	4

Independent Practice

Extra Practice
Skills Practice p. S26
Application Practice p. S39

Tell whether each transformation appears to be a rotation.

12. no

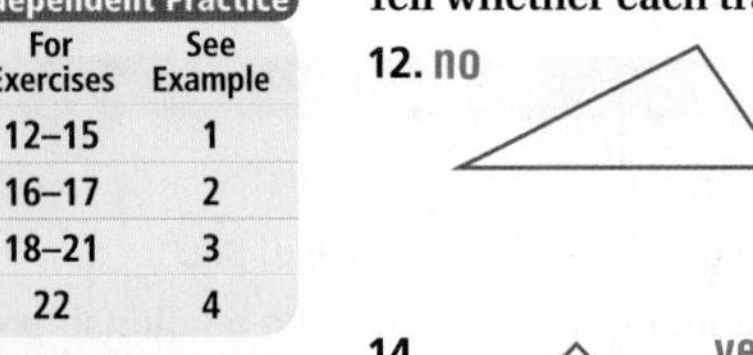

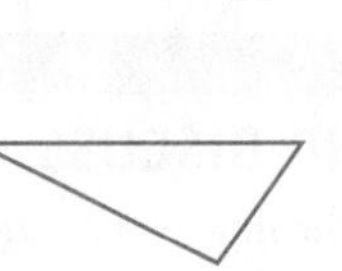

13. yes

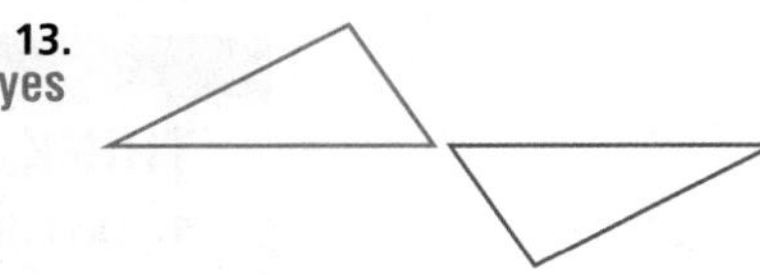

14. yes

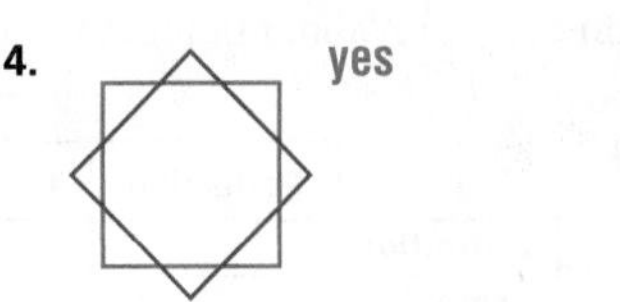

15. no

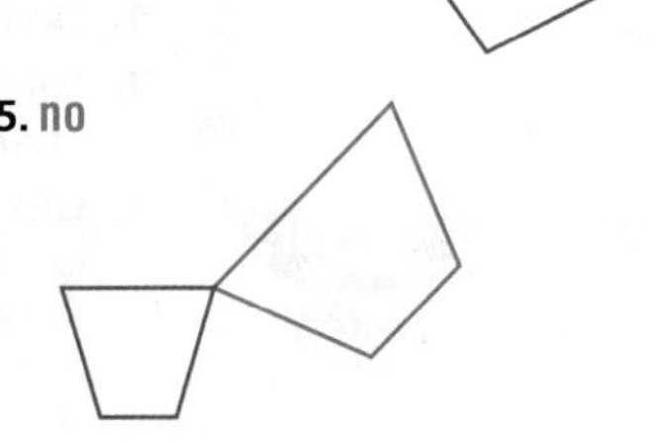

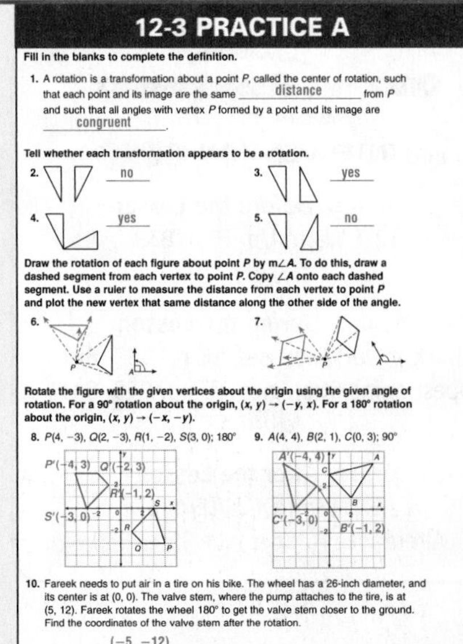

12-3 PRACTICE A

Fill in the blanks to complete the definition.

1. A rotation is a transformation about a point P, called the center of rotation, such that each point and its image are the same ___distance___ from P and such that all angles with vertex P formed by a point and its image are ___congruent___.

Tell whether each transformation appears to be a rotation.

2. no
3. yes
4. yes
5. no

Draw the rotation of each figure about point P by $m\angle A$. To do this, draw a dashed segment from each vertex to point P. Copy $\angle A$ onto each dashed segment. Use a ruler to measure the distance from each vertex to point P and plot the new vertex that same distance along the other side of the angle.

6.
7.

Rotate the figure with the given vertices about the origin using the given angle of rotation. For a 90° rotation about the origin, $(x, y) \to (-y, x)$. For a 180° rotation about the origin, $(x, y) \to (-x, -y)$.

8. $P(4, -3), Q(2, -3), R(1, -2), S(3, 0)$; 180°
9. $A(4, 4), B(2, 1), C(0, 3)$; 90°

10. Fareek needs to put air in a tire on his bike. The wheel has a 26-inch diameter, and its center is at (0, 0). The valve stem, where the pump attaches to the tire, is at (5, 12). Fareek rotates the wheel 180° to get the valve stem closer to the ground. Find the coordinates of the valve stem after the rotation.

___(−5, −12)___

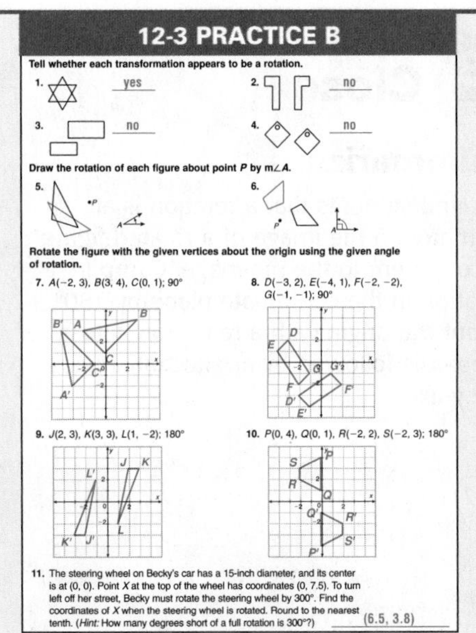

12-3 PRACTICE B

Tell whether each transformation appears to be a rotation.

1. yes
2. no
3. no
4. no

Draw the rotation of each figure about point P by $m\angle A$.

5.
6.

Rotate the figure with the given vertices about the origin using the given angle of rotation.

7. $A(-2, 3), B(3, 4), C(0, 1)$; 90°
8. $D(-3, 2), E(-4, 1), F(-2, -2), G(-1, -1)$; 90°
9. $J(2, 3), K(3, 3), L(1, -2)$; 180°
10. $P(0, 4), Q(0, 1), R(-2, 2), S(-2, 3)$; 180°

11. The steering wheel on Becky's car has a 15-inch diameter, and its center is at (0, 0). Point X at the top of the wheel has coordinates (0, 7.5). To turn left off her street, Becky must rotate the steering wheel by 300°. Find the coordinates of X when the steering wheel is rotated. Round to the nearest tenth. (*Hint:* How many degrees short of a full rotation is 300°?) ___(6.5, 3.8)___

Copy each figure and the angle of rotation. Draw the rotation of the figure about point P by $m\angle A$.

16\.

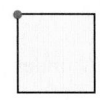

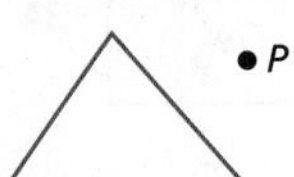

17\.

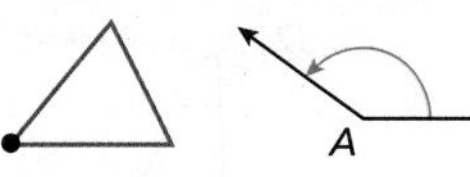

Rotate the figure with the given vertices about the origin using the given angle of rotation.

18\. $E(-1, 2)$, $F(3, 1)$, $G(2, 3)$; 90°

19\. $A(-1, 0)$, $B(-1, -3)$, $C(1, -3)$, $D(1, 0)$; 90°

20\. $P(0, -2)$, $Q(2, 0)$, $R(3, -3)$; 180°

21\. $L(2, 0)$, $M(-1, -2)$, $N(2, -2)$; 180°

22\. **Architecture** The CN Tower in Toronto, Canada, features a revolving restaurant that takes 72 minutes to complete a full rotation. A table that is 50 feet from the center of the restaurant starts at position $(50, 0)$. What are the coordinates of the table after 6 minutes? Round coordinates to the nearest tenth. **(43.3, 25)**

Copy each figure. Then draw the rotation of the figure about the red point using the given angle measure.

23\. 90°

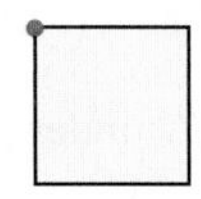

24\. 180°

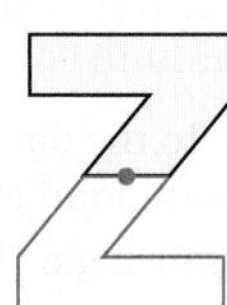

25\. 180°

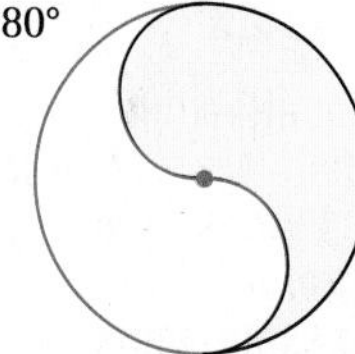

26\. Point Q has coordinates $(2, 3)$. After a rotation about the origin, the image of point Q lies on the y-axis.

a. Find the angle of rotation to the nearest degree. **34°**

b. Find the coordinates of the image of point Q. Round to the nearest tenth. **(0, 3.6)**

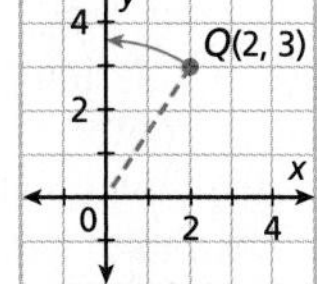

Rectangle $RSTU$ is the image of rectangle $LMNP$ under a 180° rotation about point A. Name each of the following.

27\. the image of point N **T**

28\. the preimage of point S **M**

29\. the image of $\overline{MN}$ **$\overline{ST}$**

30\. the preimage of $\overline{TU}$ **$\overline{NP}$**

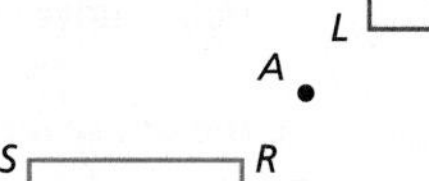

MULTI-STEP TEST PREP

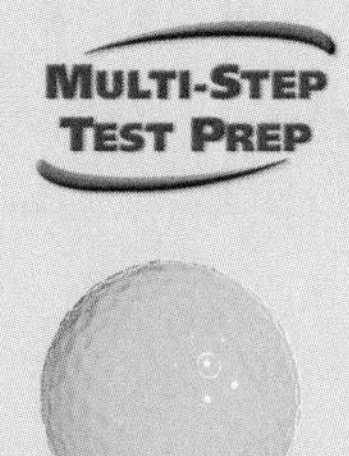

31\. This problem will prepare you for the Multi-Step Test Prep on page 854.

A miniature golf course includes a hole with a windmill. Players must hit the ball through the opening at the base of the windmill while the blades rotate.

a. The blades take 20 seconds to make a complete rotation. Through what angle do the blades rotate in 4 seconds? **72°**

b. Find the coordinates of point A after 4 seconds. (*Hint:* $(4, 3)$ is the center of rotation.) **(4.9, 5.9)**

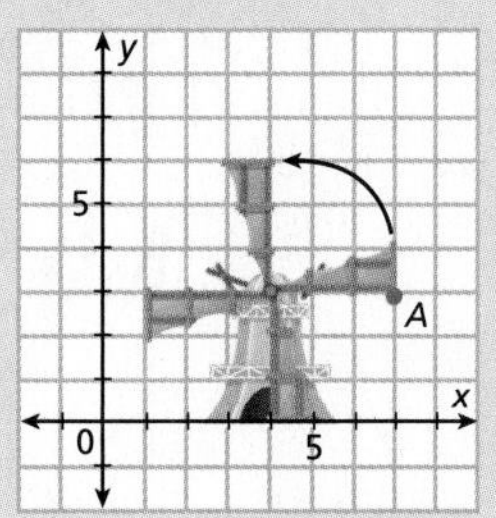

COMMON ERROR ALERT

In **Exercises 16** and **17,** students may rotate the figure by the wrong angle measure or in the wrong direction. Remind them to measure the angle of rotation and to rotate in the direction indicated by the arrow.

MULTI-STEP TEST PREP **Exercise 31** involves rotating a figure in the coordinate plane. This exercise prepares students for the Multi-Step Test Prep on page 854.

Answers

16\.

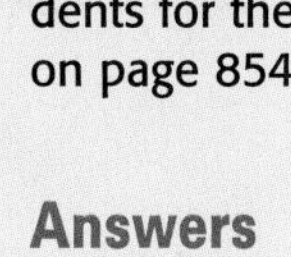

17\.

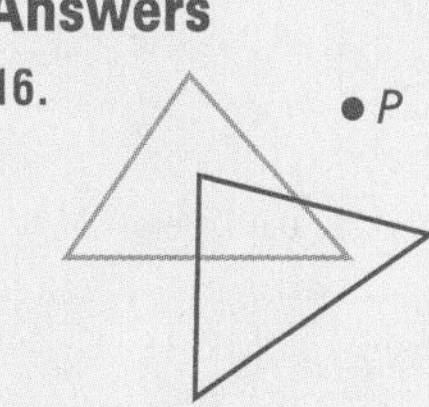

18\.

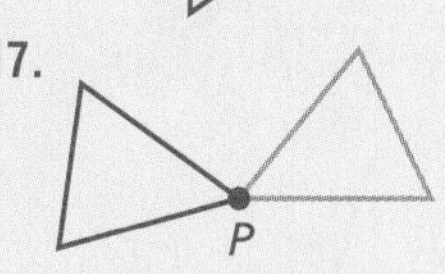

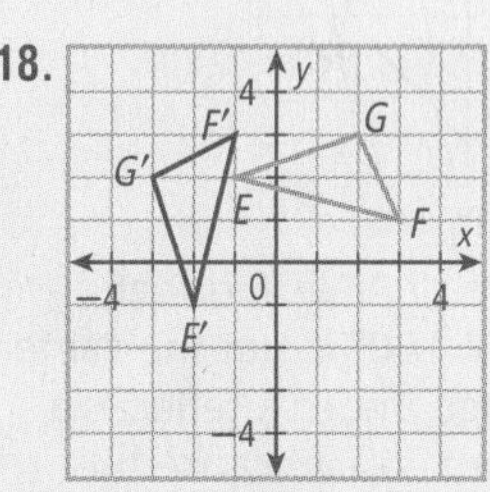

19\.

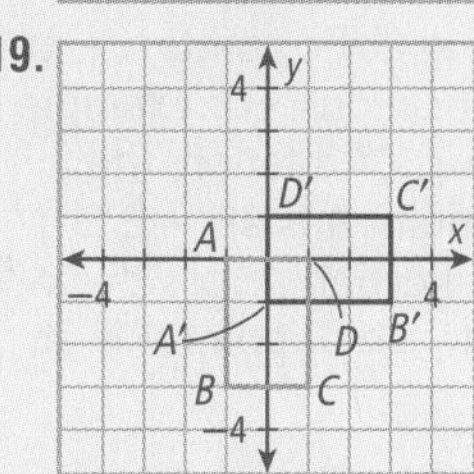

20\.

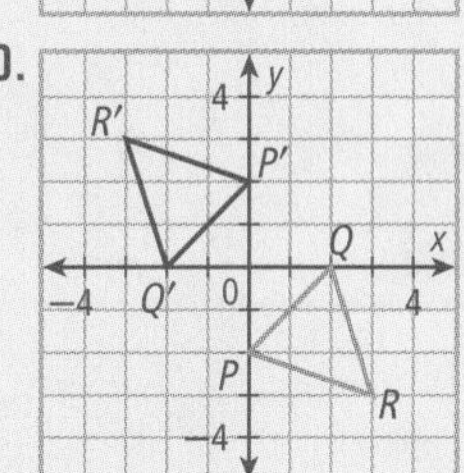

21\.

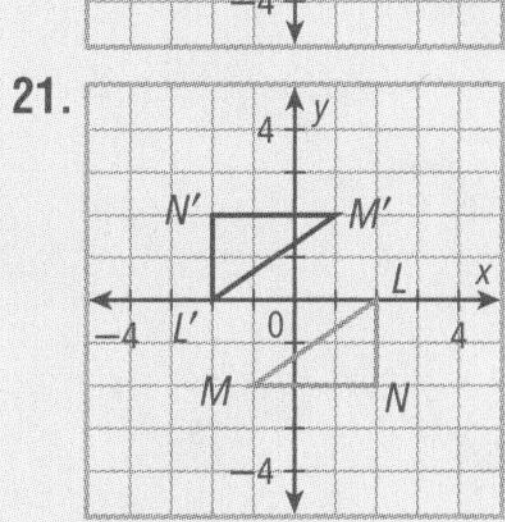

23\.

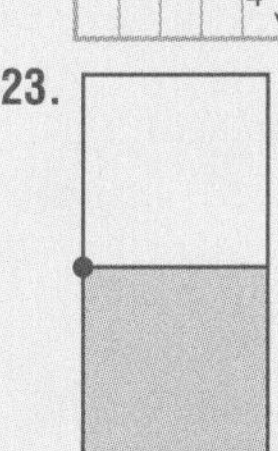

12-3 PRACTICE C

Find the measure of the angle of rotation for each point and its image given below. Round to the nearest degree. Assume each rotation is around the origin.

1\. $A(19.3, 5.2)$, $A'(-11.5, 16.4)$ **110°**

2\. $B(5, 0)$, $B'(-4.4, -2.3)$ **208°**

3\. $C(3.5, -6.1)$, $C'(6.1, 3.5)$ **90°**

4\. $D(-2.6, 3.1)$, $D'(-3.5, 2)$ **20°**

5\. $E(0.4, -2.1)$, $E'(-2.1, -0.4)$ **270°**

6\. $F(-10.8, -1.9)$, $F'(0, -11)$ **80°**

Find the coordinates of the image of each point after a rotation about the origin through the given angle. Round to the nearest tenth.

7\. $G(0, 3.2)$; 67° **(−2.9, 1.3)**

8\. $H(12.3, 8.6)$; 270° **(8.6, −12.3)**

9\. $I(-0.8, 3.9)$, 102° **(−3.7, −1.6)**

10\. $J(0.1, 0.9)$; 180° **(−0.1, −0.9)**

11\. $K(-10, 0)$; 307° **(−6.0, 8.0)**

12\. $L(-8, -13.9)$; 4° **(−7.0, −14.4)**

13\. A point has a negative x-coordinate and a positive y-coordinate. After a rotation around the origin, the image of the point has a positive x-coordinate and a negative y-coordinate. Find the range of possible values for A, the measure of the angle of rotation. Remember that zero is considered neither positive nor negative.

$90° < A < 270°$

14\. A rotation through an angle that measures 520° will be indistinguishable from a rotation through an angle less than 360° that measures how many degrees? **160°**

15\. Reflect the triangle across ℓ_1. Then reflect that image across ℓ_2. Describe the relation of the second image to the original preimage.

The second image is a rotation of the original preimage.

16\. A rotation can be interpreted as successive reflections across two intersecting lines. Tell which point is the center of rotation.

The center of rotation is the point where the lines intersect.

17\. On your answer to Exercise 15, draw a line from one vertex of the preimage to the center of rotation. Draw another line from the corresponding vertex in the final image to the center of rotation. The measure of this angle is the magnitude of the rotation. Compare this angle measure to the angle measure between the intersecting lines.

The magnitude of the rotation is twice the angle measure between the intersecting lines.

Teaching Tip

Visual To estimate the angle of rotation in **Exercise 36,** it may be helpful to lightly draw circles (or arcs) through each point and its image, centered at the center of rotation.

Answers

34.

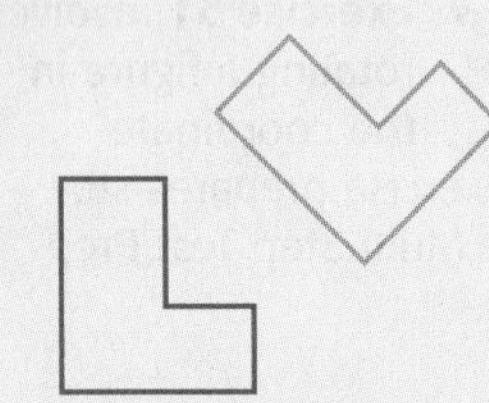

38.

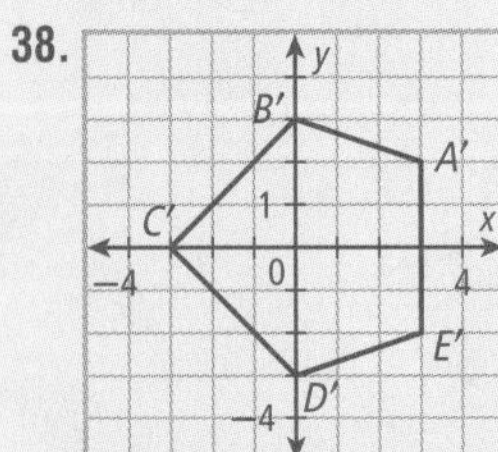

39.

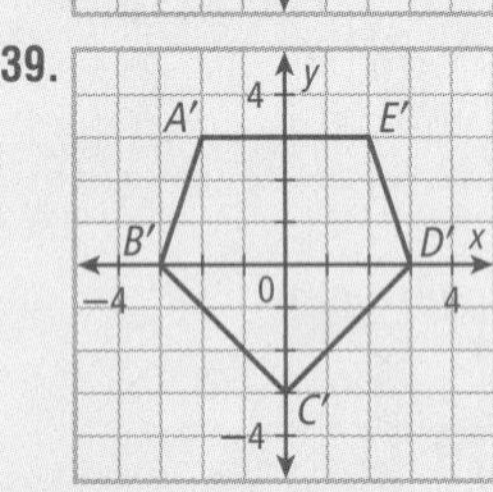

40. The image of *ABCDE* under a rotation of 180° is not the same as its image under a reflection across the *x*-axis because the images of specific points are in different locations. For example, under the 180° rotation, the image of point *A* is at $(-2, 3)$; under a reflection across the *x*-axis, the image of point *A* is at $(2, 3)$.

Each figure shows a preimage and its image under a rotation. Copy the figure and locate the center of rotation.

32.

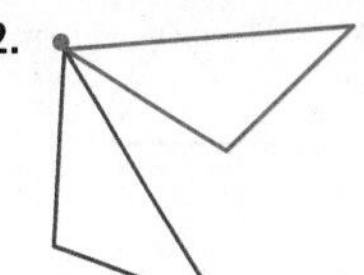

33.

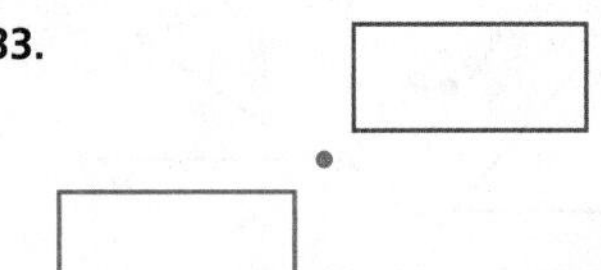

34.

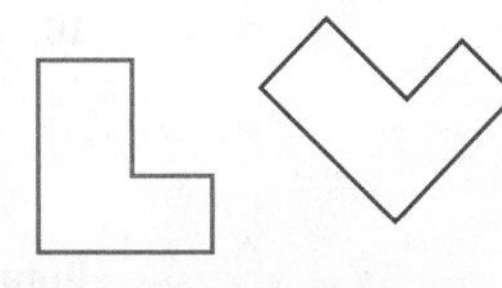

35. Astronomy The photograph was made by placing a camera on a tripod and keeping the camera's shutter open for a long time. Because of Earth's rotation, the stars appear to rotate around Polaris, also known as the North Star.

a. **Estimation** Estimate the angle of rotation of the stars in the photo. **90°**

b. **Estimation** Use your result from part **a** to estimate the length of time that the camera's shutter was open. (*Hint:* If the shutter was open for 24 hours, the stars would appear to make one complete rotation around Polaris.) **6 hours**

36. Estimation In the diagram, $\triangle ABC \rightarrow \triangle A'B'C'$ under a rotation about point *P*.

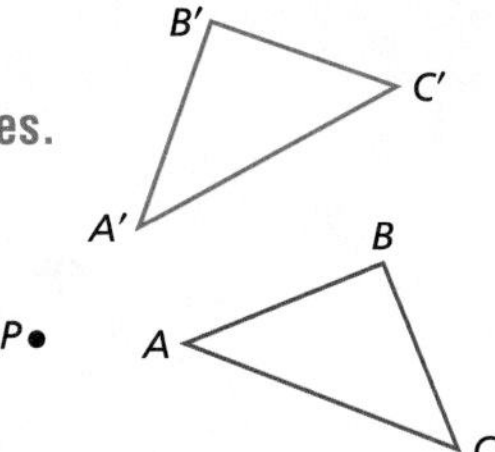

a. Estimate the angle of rotation. **Check students' estimates.**

b. Explain how you can draw two segments and can then use a protractor to measure the angle of rotation.

c. Copy the figure. Use the method from part **b** to find the angle of rotation. How does your result compare to your estimate? **50°**

37. Critical Thinking A student wrote the following in his math journal. "Under a rotation, every point moves around the center of rotation by the same angle measure. This means that every point moves the same distance." Do you agree? Explain.

36b. Draw $\overline{AP}$ and $\overline{A'P}$ and use the protractor to measure $\angle A'PA$.

37. No; although all points are rotated around the center of rotation by the same angle, points that are farther from the center of rotation move a greater distance than points that are closer to the center of rotation.

38. $A'(3, 2)$, $B'(0, 3)$, $C'(-3, 0)$, $D'(0, -3)$, $E'(3, -2)$

39. $A'(-2, 3)$, $B'(-3, 0)$, $C'(0, -3)$, $D'(3, 0)$, $E'(2, 3)$

Use the figure for Exercises 38–40.

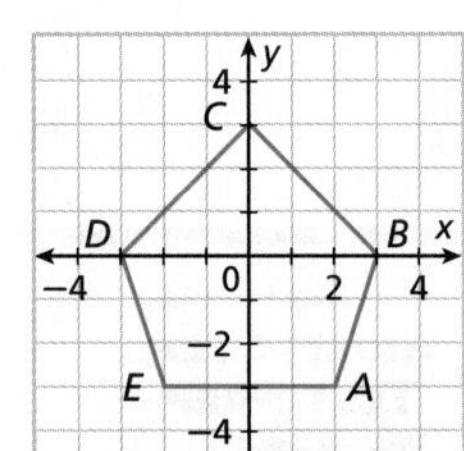

38. Sketch the image of pentagon *ABCDE* under a rotation of 90° about the origin. Give the vertices of the image.

39. Sketch the image of pentagon *ABCDE* under a rotation of 180° about the origin. Give the vertices of the image.

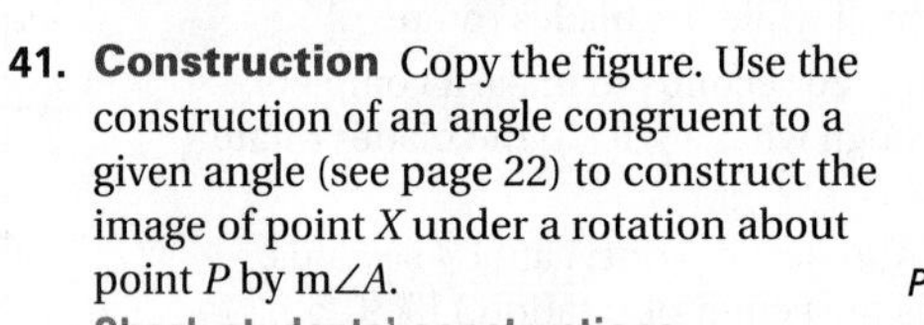

40. Write About It Is the image of *ABCDE* under a rotation of 180° about the origin the same as its image under a reflection across the *x*-axis? Explain your reasoning.

41. Construction Copy the figure. Use the construction of an angle congruent to a given angle (see page 22) to construct the image of point *X* under a rotation about point *P* by $m\angle A$.
Check students' constructions.

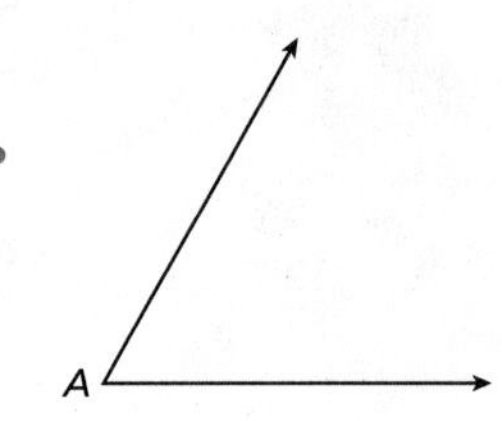

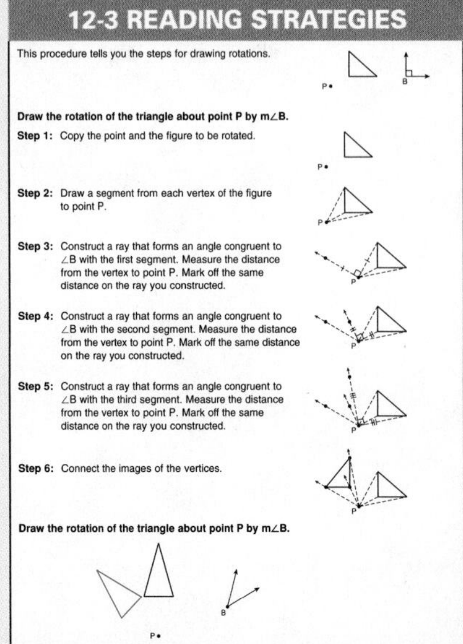

12-3 READING STRATEGIES

This procedure tells you the steps for drawing rotations.

Draw the rotation of the triangle about point P by m∠B.

Step 1: Copy the point and the figure to be rotated.

Step 2: Draw a segment from each vertex of the figure to point P.

Step 3: Construct a ray that forms an angle congruent to ∠B with the first segment. Measure the distance from the vertex to point P. Mark off the same distance on the ray you constructed.

Step 4: Construct a ray that forms an angle congruent to ∠B with the second segment. Measure the distance from the vertex to point P. Mark off the same distance on the ray you constructed.

Step 5: Construct a ray that forms an angle congruent to ∠B with the third segment. Measure the distance from the vertex to point P. Mark off the same distance on the ray you constructed.

Step 6: Connect the images of the vertices.

Draw the rotation of the triangle about point P by m∠B.

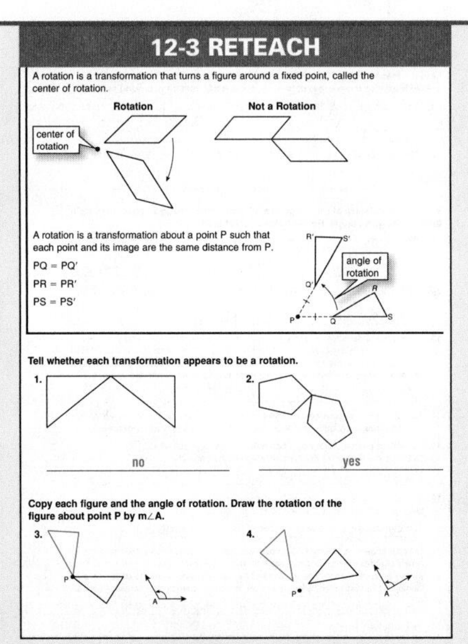

12-3 RETEACH

A rotation is a transformation that turns a figure around a fixed point, called the center of rotation.

Rotation — center of rotation

Not a Rotation

A rotation is a transformation about a point P such that each point and its image are the same distance from P.

PQ = PQ′
PR = PR′
PS = PS′

angle of rotation

Tell whether each transformation appears to be a rotation.

1. no

2. yes

Copy each figure and the angle of rotation. Draw the rotation of the figure about point P by m∠A.

3.

4.

TEST PREP

42. What is the image of the point $(-2, 5)$ when it is rotated about the origin by 90°?
Ⓐ $(-5, 2)$ Ⓑ $(5, -2)$ Ⓒ $(-5, -2)$ (circled) Ⓓ $(2, -5)$

43. The six cars of a Ferris wheel are located at the vertices of a regular hexagon. Which rotation about point P maps car A to car C?
Ⓕ 60° Ⓖ 90° Ⓗ 120° (circled) Ⓙ 135°

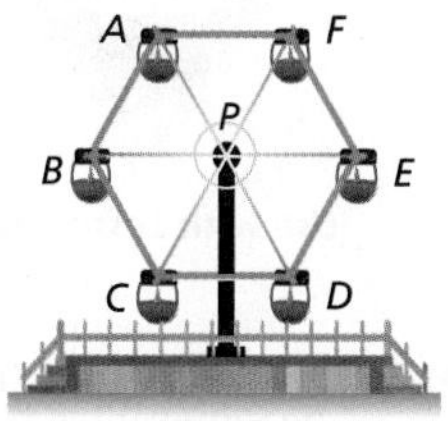

44. **Gridded Response** Under a rotation about the origin, the point $(-3, 4)$ is mapped to the point $(3, -4)$. What is the measure of the angle of rotation? **180**

CHALLENGE AND EXTEND

45. **Engineering** Gears are used to change the speed and direction of rotating parts in pieces of machinery. In the diagram, suppose gear B makes one complete rotation in the counterclockwise direction. Give the angle of rotation and direction for the rotation of gear A. Explain how you got your answer.

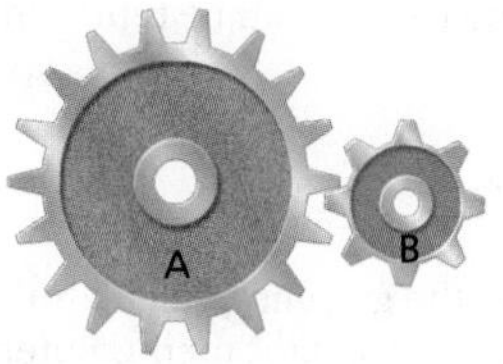

45. 160°; clockwise; gear B has 8 teeth, so one complete rotation of gear B in the counterclockwise direction will move gear A by 8 teeth in the clockwise direction. Gear A has 18 teeth, so 8 teeth is $\frac{4}{9}$ of a complete rotation, or $\frac{4}{9}(360°) = 160°$.

46. **Given:** $\overline{A'B'}$ is the rotation image of $\overline{AB}$ about point P.
Prove: $\overline{AB} \cong \overline{A'B'}$
(*Hint:* Draw auxiliary lines $\overline{AP}$, $\overline{BP}$, $\overline{A'P}$, and $\overline{B'P}$ and show that $\triangle APB \cong \triangle A'PB'$.)

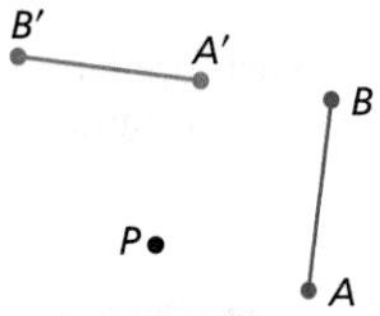

Once you have proved that the rotation image of a segment is congruent to the preimage, how could you prove the following? Write a plan for each proof.

47. If $\overline{A'B'}$ is a rotation of $\overline{AB}$, then $AB = A'B'$.

47. Use the fact that the rotation of a seg. is ≅ to the preimage and the def. of ≅ segs.

48. If $\angle A'B'C'$ is a rotation of $\angle ABC$, then $m\angle ABC = m\angle A'B'C'$.
49. The rotation $\triangle A'B'C'$ is congruent to the preimage $\triangle ABC$.
50. If point C is between points A and B, then the rotation C' is between A' and B'.
51. If points A, B, and C are collinear, then the rotations A', B', and C' are collinear.

49. Use the fact that the rotation of a seg. is ≅ to the preimage to prove $\triangle ABC \cong \triangle A'B'C'$ by SSS.

SPIRAL REVIEW

Find the value(s) of x when y is 3. *(Previous course)*

52. $y = x^2 - 4x + 7$ **2**
53. $y = 2x^2 - 5x - 9$ $-\frac{3}{2}$, **4**
54. $y = x^2 - 2$ $-\sqrt{5}$, $\sqrt{5}$

Find each measure. *(Lesson 6-6)*

55. $m\angle XYR$ **94°**
56. QR **4.4**

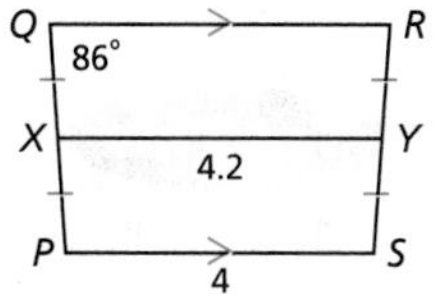

Given the points $A(1, 3)$, $B(5, 0)$, $C(-3, -2)$, and $D(5, -6)$, find the vector associated with each translation. *(Lesson 12-2)*

57. the translation that maps point A to point D $\langle 4, -9 \rangle$
58. the translation that maps point D to point B $\langle 0, 6 \rangle$
59. the translation that maps point C to the origin $\langle 3, 2 \rangle$

TEST PREP DOCTOR If students have difficulty with **Exercise 42,** have them consider which pair of points forms a 90° angle with the origin.

If students have difficulty with **Exercise 43,** have them consider how they can determine the measure of a central angle of a hexagon.

Answers

46, 48, 50, 51. See p. A31.

Journal

For a transformation that appears to be a rotation, have students explain how they would use a compass and a straightedge or a ruler and a protractor to verify that it is a rotation.

ALTERNATIVE ASSESSMENT

Have students draw a triangle in a coordinate plane and state the coordinates of the vertices. Ask them to draw a 90° rotation of the triangle about the origin, a 180° rotation about the origin, and a rotation about C by $m\angle C$.

Power Presentations with PowerPoint®

12-3 Lesson Quiz

1. Tell whether the transformation appears to be a rotation.

yes

2. Copy the figure and the angle of rotation. Draw the rotation of the triangle about P by $\angle A$.

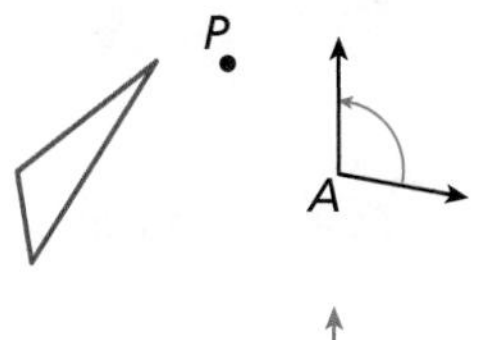

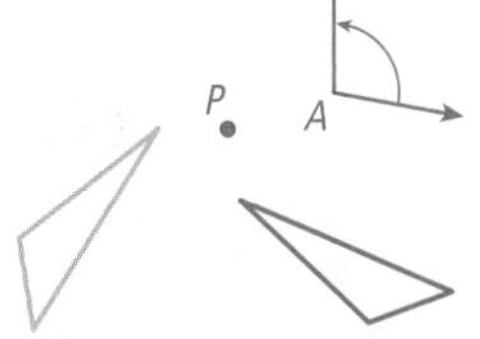

Rotate $\triangle RST$ with vertices $R(-1, 4)$, $S(2, 1)$, and $T(3, -3)$ about the origin by the given angle.

3. 90° $R'(-4, -1)$, $S'(-1, 2)$, $T'(3, 3)$
4. 180° $R'(1, -4)$, $S'(-2, -1)$, $T'(-3, 3)$

Also available on transparency

12-3 PROBLEM SOLVING

1. $\triangle ABC$ is rotated about the origin so that A' has coordinates $(-1, -5)$. What are the coordinates of B'?

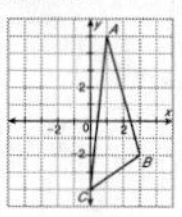

$(-3, 2)$

2. A spinning ride at an amusement park is a wheel that has a radius of 21.5 feet and rotates counterclockwise 12 times per minute. A car on the ride starts at position (21.5, 0). What are the coordinates of the car's location after 6 seconds? Round coordinates to the nearest tenth.

(6.6, 20.4)

3. To make a design, Trent rotates the figure 120° about point P, and then rotates that image 120° about point P. Draw the final design.

Choose the best answer.

4. Point K has coordinates (6, 8). After a rotation about the origin, the image of point K lies on the y-axis. What are the coordinates of K'?
A (0, 5) C (0, 8)
B (0, 6) Ⓓ (0, 10)

5. $\triangle NPQ$ has vertices $M(-6, -4)$, $P(-3, 4)$, and $Q(1, 1)$. If the triangle is rotated 90° about the origin, what are the coordinates of P'?
Ⓕ (−4, −3) H (3, 4)
G (−4, 3) J (3, −4)

6. The Top of the World Restaurant in Las Vegas, Nevada, revolves 360° in 1 hour and 20 minutes. A piano that is 38 feet from the center of the restaurant starts at position (38, 0). What are the coordinates of the piano after 15 minutes? Round coordinates to the nearest tenth if necessary.
A (0, 38)
B (−38, 0)
Ⓒ (14.5, 35.1)
D (35.1, 14.5)

7. The five blades of a ceiling fan form a regular pentagon. Which clockwise rotation about point P maps point B to point D?

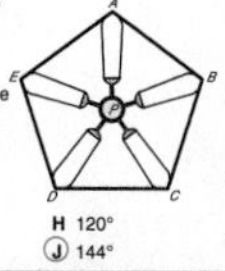

F 60° H 120°
G 72° Ⓙ 144°

12-3 CHALLENGE

As the minute hand of a clock moves, its tip traces a circular path. The radius of the path is the length of the minute hand. How far does the tip travel in one hour? Clearly, the distance depends on the length of the hand. For example:

- If the length is 4 inches, then the distance traveled is $2\pi(4)$ inches, or about 25.1 inches.
- If the length is 3 feet, then the distance traveled is $2\pi(3)$ feet, or about 18.8 feet.

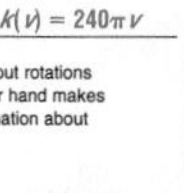

Apply the formula for the circumference of a circle with radius r: $C = 2\pi r$.

The distance the tip travels is a function of the length of the minute hand. If this function is named f, a rule for the function is $f(x) = 2\pi x$, where x is the length of the minute hand.

Write a rule for each specified function.

1. The function g relates the distance that the tip of the minute hand travels in one minute to the length of the minute hand, x. $g(x) = \frac{\pi}{30}x$
2. The function h relates the distance that the tip of the hour hand travels in one hour to the length of the hour hand, y. $h(y) = \frac{\pi}{6}y$
3. The function j relates the distance that the tip of a 3-inch hour hand travels to the number of hours, z. $j(z) = \frac{\pi}{2}z$
4. The function k relates the distance that the tip of a 5-inch minute hand travels to the number of days, v. $k(v) = 240\pi v$

In writing rules for the above functions, you used common knowledge about rotations on a clock: The minute hand makes one rotation every hour, and the hour hand makes one rotation every 12 hours. In other situations, you must be given information about rotations before you can write a function rule.

5. A Ferris wheel with a radius of 4 yards is rotating at a constant speed. It takes 90 seconds to make one complete rotation. Write a rule for the function, f, that relates the number of feet that a rider travels to the number of minutes, t, that the wheel has been rotating. $f(t) = 16\pi t$
6. The diameter of each wheel of a bicycle is 26 inches, and the wheel rotates 5 times every 2 seconds. Write a rule for the function, m, that relates the number of minutes that the bicycle travels to the number of miles traveled, d. $m(d) = \frac{1056}{65\pi}d$
7. Describe an original rotation situation that can be specified by the function rule $f(x) = 18\pi x$.
Situations will vary.

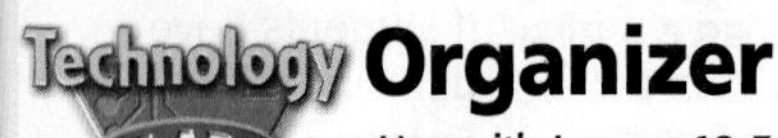

Organizer

Use with Lesson 12-3

Pacing:
Traditional 1 day
Block $\frac{1}{2}$ day

Objective: Use a graphing calculator to explore transformations with matrices.

Materials: graphing calculator

Online Edition
TechKeys

Resources

Technology Lab Activities
12-3 Lab Recording Sheet

Teach

Discuss

Be sure students understand how to use a point matrix to represent the vertices of a polygon. Review how to enter matrices and to perform matrix operations on a graphing calculator.

As students graph the image of each transformation, encourage them to write a rule for the transformation and to analyze how each element of the matrix affects the position of the image.

State Resources

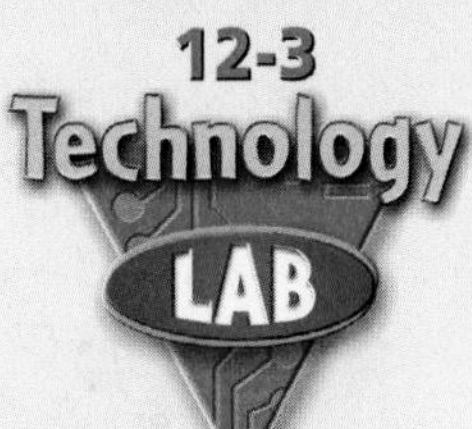

Explore Transformations with Matrices

Use with Lesson 12-3

The vertices of a polygon in the coordinate plane can be represented by a *point matrix* in which row 1 contains the *x*-values and row 2 contains the *y*-values. For example, the triangle with vertices $(1, 2)$, $(-2, 0)$, and $(3, -4)$ can be represented by $\begin{bmatrix} 1 & -2 & 3 \\ 2 & 0 & -4 \end{bmatrix}$.

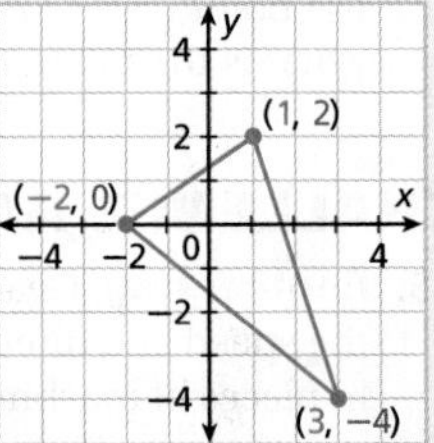

On the graphing calculator, enter a matrix using the **Matrix Edit** menu. Enter the number of rows and columns and then enter the values.

Matrix operations can be used to perform transformations.

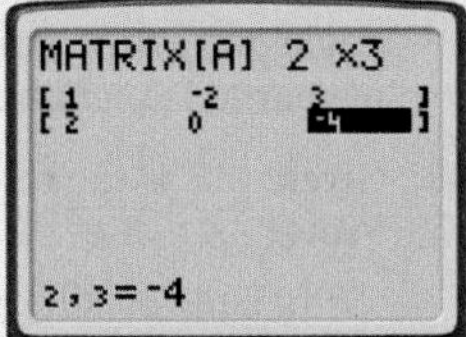

Activity 1

1. Graph the triangle with vertices (1, 0), (2, 4), and (5, 3) on graph paper. Enter the point matrix that represents the vertices into matrix **[B]** on your calculator. $[B] = \begin{bmatrix} 1 & 2 & 5 \\ 0 & 4 & 3 \end{bmatrix}$

2. Enter the matrix $\begin{bmatrix} 1 & 0 \\ 0 & -1 \end{bmatrix}$ into matrix **[A]** on your calculator. Multiply **[A]** $*$ **[B]** and use the resulting matrix to graph the image of the triangle. Describe the transformation. **a reflection across the *x*-axis**

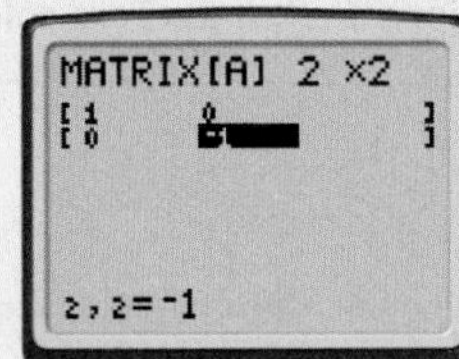

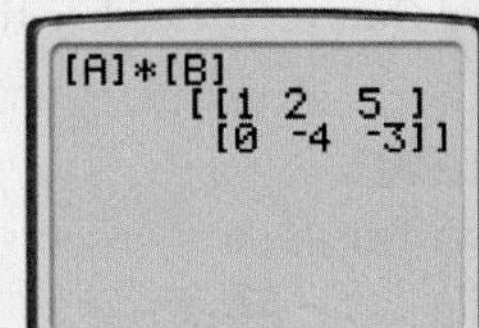

Try This

1. Enter the matrix $\begin{bmatrix} -1 & 0 \\ 0 & 1 \end{bmatrix}$ into matrix **[A]**. Multiply **[A]** $*$ **[B]** and use the resulting matrix to graph the image of the triangle. Describe the transformation.
a reflection across the *y*-axis

2. Enter the matrix $\begin{bmatrix} 0 & 1 \\ 1 & 0 \end{bmatrix}$ into matrix **[A]**. Multiply **[A]** $*$ **[B]** and use the resulting matrix to graph the image of the triangle. Describe the transformation.
a reflection across the line $y = x$

Answers to *Activity 1*

1.
2.

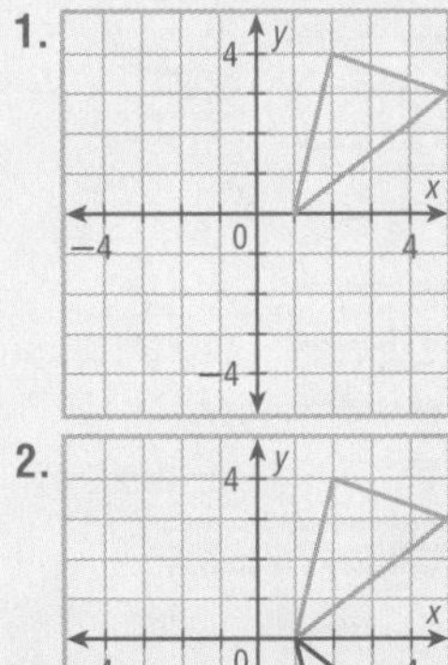

Answers to *Try This*

1. $[A]\,[B] = \begin{bmatrix} -1 & -2 & -5 \\ 0 & 4 & 3 \end{bmatrix}$

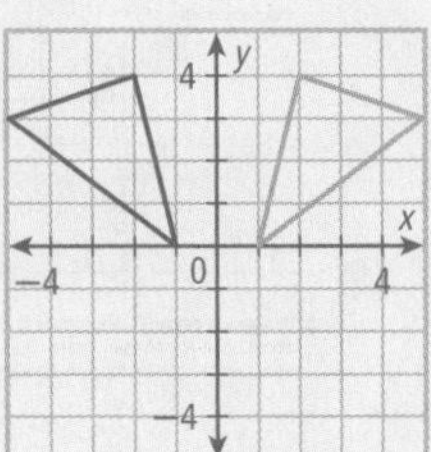

2. $[A]\,[B] = \begin{bmatrix} 0 & 4 & 3 \\ 1 & 2 & 5 \end{bmatrix}$

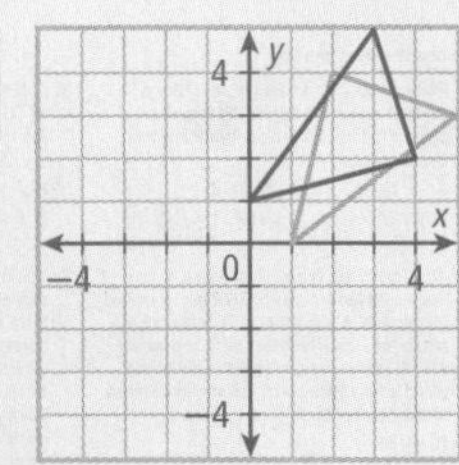

Activity 2

1 Graph the triangle with vertices (0, 0), (3, 1), and (2, 4) on graph paper. Enter the point matrix that represents the vertices into matrix **[B]** on your calculator. **[B] = $\begin{bmatrix} 0 & 3 & 2 \\ 0 & 1 & 4 \end{bmatrix}$**

2 Enter the matrix $\begin{bmatrix} 0 & 0 & 0 \\ 2 & 2 & 2 \end{bmatrix}$ into matrix **[A]**. Add **[A] + [B]** and use the resulting matrix to graph the image of the triangle. Describe the transformation. **a translation 2 units up**

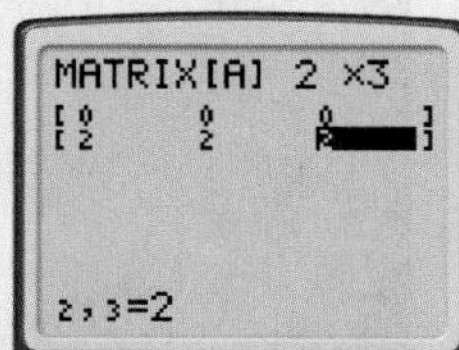

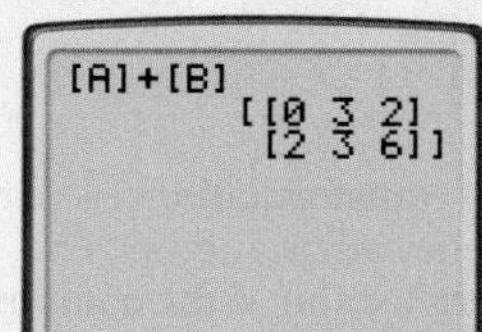

Try This

3. Enter the matrix $\begin{bmatrix} -1 & -1 & -1 \\ 4 & 4 & 4 \end{bmatrix}$ into matrix **[A]**. Add **[A] + [B]** and use the resulting matrix to graph the image of the triangle. Describe the transformation.
3. [A] + [B] = $\begin{bmatrix} -1 & 2 & 1 \\ 4 & 5 & 8 \end{bmatrix}$
a translation 1 unit left and 4 units up

4. **Make a Conjecture** How do you think you could use matrices to translate a triangle by the vector $\langle a, b \rangle$? Choose several values for a and b and test your conjecture.
Let [A] = $\begin{bmatrix} a & a & a \\ b & b & b \end{bmatrix}$. Add [A] + [B] and use the solution matrix to graph the image of the triangle.

Activity 3

1 Graph the triangle with vertices (1, 1), (4, 1), and (1, 2) on graph paper. Enter the point matrix that represents the vertices into matrix **[B]** on your calculator. **[B] = $\begin{bmatrix} 1 & 4 & 1 \\ 1 & 1 & 2 \end{bmatrix}$**

2 Enter the matrix $\begin{bmatrix} 0 & -1 \\ 1 & 0 \end{bmatrix}$ into matrix **[A]**. Multiply **[A] * [B]** and use the resulting matrix to graph the image of the triangle. Describe the transformation.
[A] * [B] = $\begin{bmatrix} -1 & -1 & -2 \\ 1 & 4 & 1 \end{bmatrix}$
a 90° rotation about the origin

Try This

5. Enter the values $\begin{bmatrix} -1 & 0 \\ 0 & -1 \end{bmatrix}$ into matrix **[A]**. Multiply **[A] * [B]** and use the resulting matrix to graph the image of the triangle. Describe the transformation. **a 180° rotation about the origin**

6. Enter the values $\begin{bmatrix} 0 & 1 \\ -1 & 0 \end{bmatrix}$ into matrix **[A]**. Multiply **[A] * [B]** and use the resulting matrix to graph the image of the triangle. Describe the transformation.
[A] * [B] = $\begin{bmatrix} 1 & 1 & 2 \\ -1 & -4 & -1 \end{bmatrix}$
a 270° rotation about the origin

Answers to *Activity 2*

1.

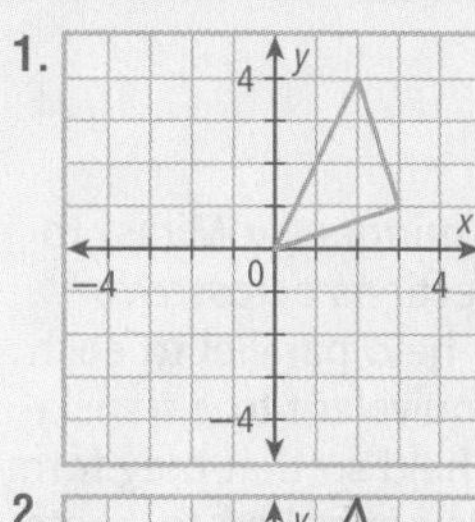

2.

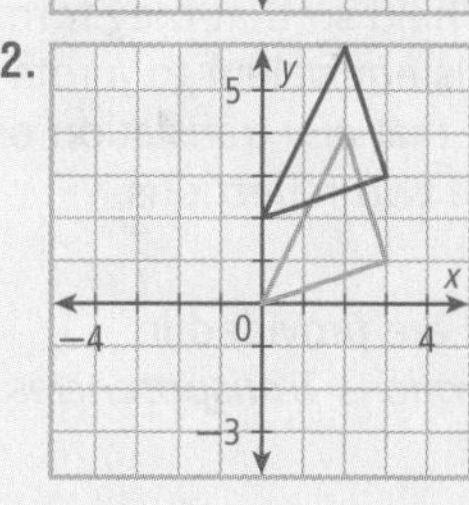

Answers to *Activity 3*

1.

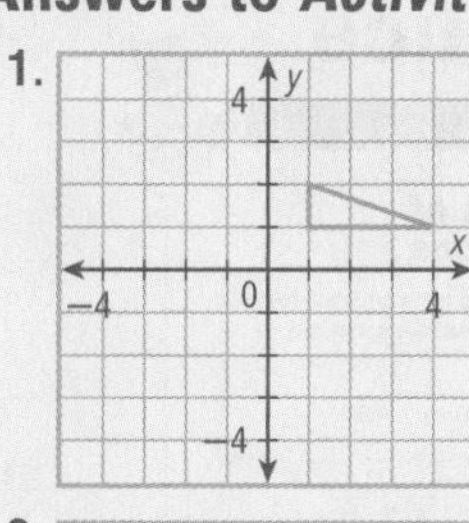

2.

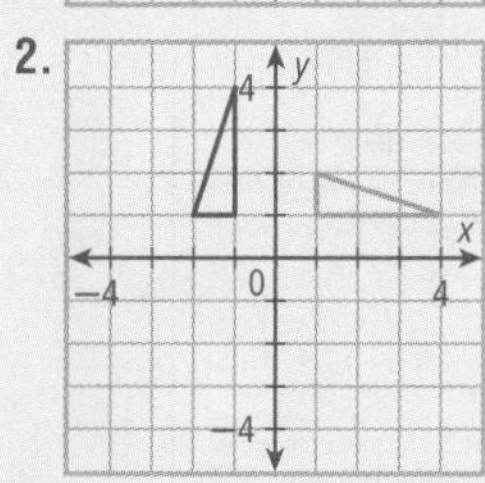

Close

Key Concept

Reflection matrices:

$\begin{bmatrix} 1 & 0 \\ 0 & -1 \end{bmatrix}$ across the x-axis

$\begin{bmatrix} -1 & 0 \\ 0 & 1 \end{bmatrix}$ across the y-axis

$\begin{bmatrix} 0 & 1 \\ 1 & 0 \end{bmatrix}$ across the line $y = x$

Translation matrices:

$\begin{bmatrix} a & a & a \\ b & b & b \end{bmatrix}$ by the vector $\langle a, b \rangle$

Rotation matrices:

$\begin{bmatrix} 0 & -1 \\ 1 & 0 \end{bmatrix}$ 90°

$\begin{bmatrix} -1 & 0 \\ 0 & 1 \end{bmatrix}$ 180°

$\begin{bmatrix} 0 & 1 \\ -1 & 0 \end{bmatrix}$ 270°

Assessment

Journal Have students explain how to use a graphing calculator to find the image of a triangle when it is reflected over the x-axis, translated by the vector $\langle 2, 3 \rangle$, or rotated by 180° about the origin.

Answers to *Try This*

3.

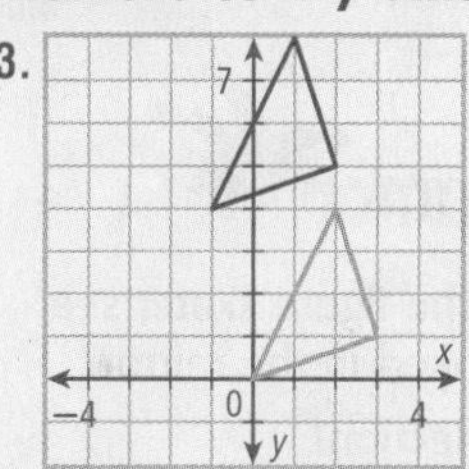

5. $[A][B] = \begin{bmatrix} -1 & -4 & -1 \\ -1 & -1 & -2 \end{bmatrix}$

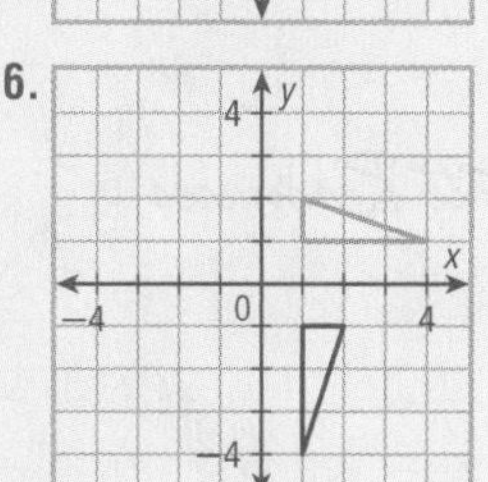

6.

12-4 Organizer

Pacing: Traditional 1 day
Block $\frac{1}{2}$ day

Objective: Apply theorems about isometries.

Identify and draw compositions of transformations, such as glide reflections.

Online Edition
Tutorial Videos

Power Presentations with PowerPoint®

Warm Up

Determine the coordinates of the image of $P(4, -7)$ under each transformation.

1. a translation 3 units left and 1 unit up $(1, -6)$
2. a rotation of 90° about the origin $(7, 4)$
3. a reflection across the y-axis $(-4, -7)$

Also available on transparency

Math Humor

Q: What did the figure skater see when she looked in the mirror?

A: A glide reflection!

12-4 Compositions of Transformations

Objectives

Apply theorems about isometries.

Identify and draw compositions of transformations, such as glide reflections.

Vocabulary

composition of transformations
glide reflection

Why learn this?

Compositions of transformations can be used to describe chess moves. (See Exercise 11.)

A **composition of transformations** is one transformation followed by another. For example, a **glide reflection** is the composition of a translation and a reflection across a line parallel to the translation vector.

The glide reflection that maps $\triangle JKL$ to $\triangle J'K'L'$ is the composition of a translation along $\vec{v}$ followed by a reflection across line ℓ.

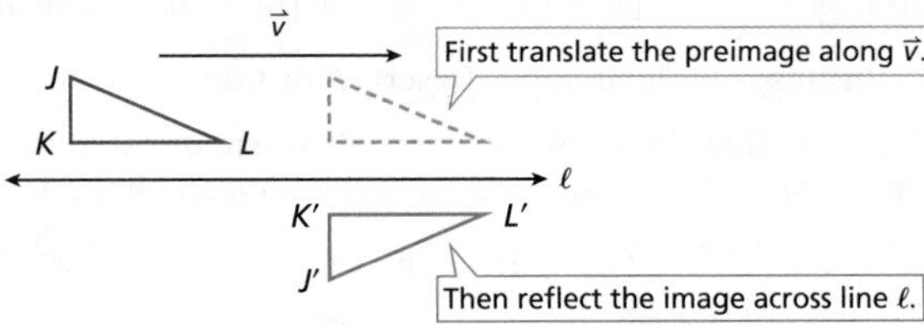

The image after each transformation is congruent to the previous image. By the Transitive Property of Congruence, the final image is congruent to the preimage. This leads to the following theorem.

Know it! Note

Theorem 12-4-1

A composition of two isometries is an isometry.

EXAMPLE 1 Drawing Compositions of Isometries

Draw the result of the composition of isometries.

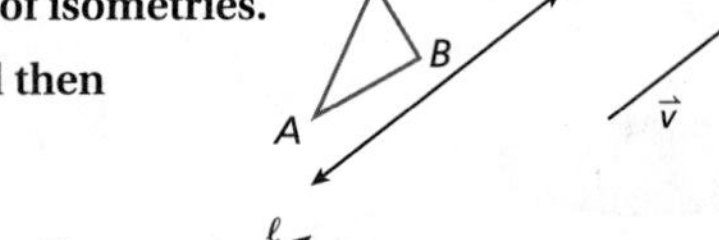

A **Reflect $\triangle ABC$ across line ℓ and then translate it along $\vec{v}$.**

Step 1 Draw $\triangle A'B'C'$, the reflection image of $\triangle ABC$.

Step 2 Translate $\triangle A'B'C'$ along $\vec{v}$ to find the final image, $\triangle A''B''C''$.

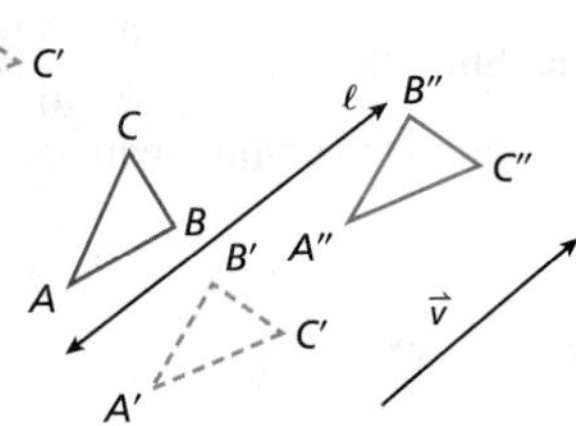

State Resources

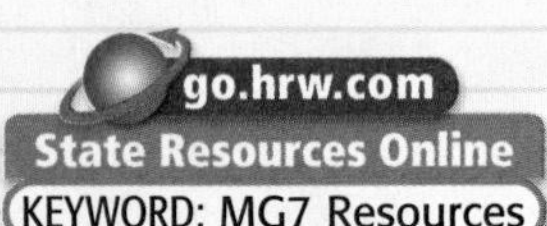

State Resources Online
KEYWORD: MG7 Resources

1 Introduce

EXPLORATION

12-4 Compositions of Transformations

A composition of transformations is one transformation followed by another. Use geometry software to explore compositions of reflections.

1. Construct parallel lines *m* and *n*.	2. Draw $\triangle ABC$.
3. Reflect $\triangle ABC$ across line *m*.	4. Reflect the image of $\triangle ABC$ across line *n*.

5. How does the final image of the triangle appear to be related to $\triangle ABC$? Is there a single transformation that maps $\triangle ABC$ to the final image?

Motivate

Draw a figure and use two mirrors (or Miras) to show a composition of reflections across two lines. When the mirrors are held parallel to each other, the composition is equivalent to a translation. When the mirrors are held so that they form an angle, the composition is equivalent to a rotation. Discuss with students that any translation or rotation is a composition of two reflections.

Explorations and answers are provided in *Alternate Openers: Explorations Transparencies.*

B $\triangle RST$ has vertices $R(1, 2)$, $S(1, 4)$, and $T(-3, 4)$. Rotate $\triangle RST$ 90° about the origin and then reflect it across the y-axis.

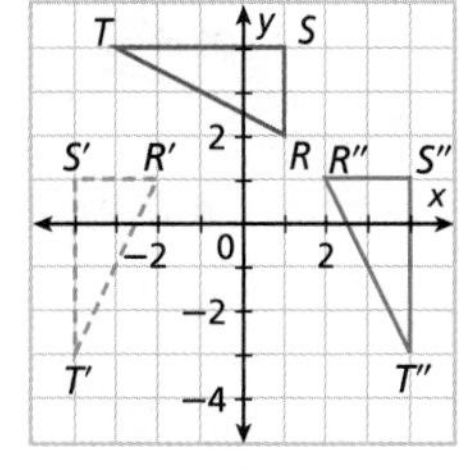

Step 1 The rotation image of (x, y) is $(-y, x)$.
$R(1, 2) \rightarrow R'(-2, 1)$, $S(1, 4) \rightarrow S'(-4, 1)$, and $T(-3, 4) \rightarrow T'(-4, -3)$.

Step 2 The reflection image of (x, y) is $(-x, y)$.
$R'(-2, 1) \rightarrow R''(2, 1)$, $S'(-4, 1) \rightarrow S''(4, 1)$, and $T'(-4, -3) \rightarrow T''(4, -3)$.

Step 3 Graph the preimage and images.

1. 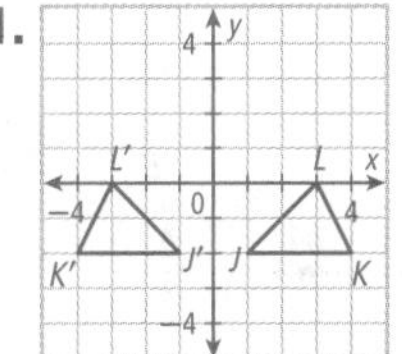

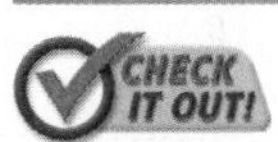

1. $\triangle JKL$ has vertices $J(1, -2)$, $K(4, -2)$, and $L(3, 0)$. Reflect $\triangle JKL$ across the x-axis and then rotate it 180° about the origin.

Theorem 12-4-2

The composition of two reflections across two parallel lines is equivalent to a translation.

- The translation vector is perpendicular to the lines.
- The length of the translation vector is twice the distance between the lines.

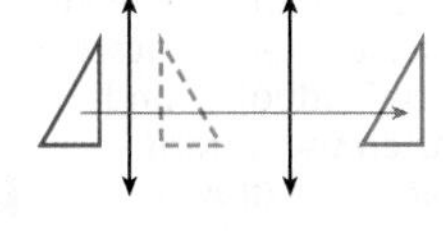

The composition of two reflections across two intersecting lines is equivalent to a rotation.

- The center of rotation is the intersection of the lines.
- The angle of rotation is twice the measure of the angle formed by the lines.

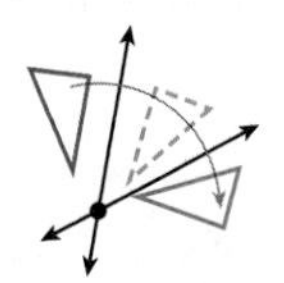

EXAMPLE 2 ***Art Application***

Tabitha is creating a design for an art project. She reflects a figure across line ℓ and then reflects the image across line m. Describe a single transformation that moves the figure from its starting position to its final position.

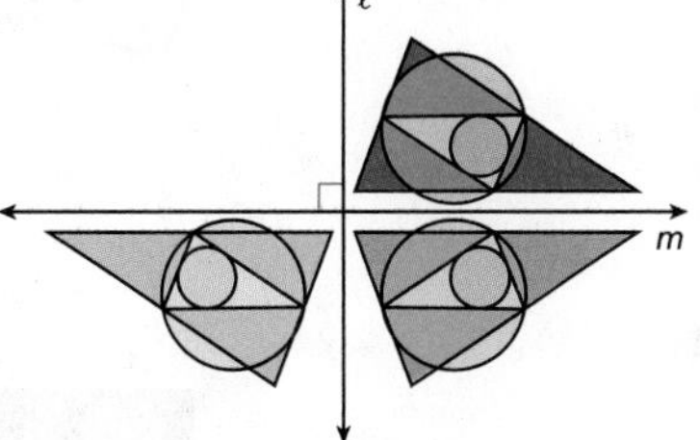

By Theorem 12-4-2, the composition of two reflections across intersecting lines is equivalent to a rotation about the point of intersection. Since the lines are perpendicular, they form a 90° angle. By Theorem 12-4-2, the angle of rotation is $2 \cdot 90° = 180°$.

2. **What if...?** Suppose Tabitha reflects the figure across line n and then the image across line p. Describe a single transformation that is equivalent to the two reflections.

a translation in direction ⊥ to n and p, by distance of 6 in.

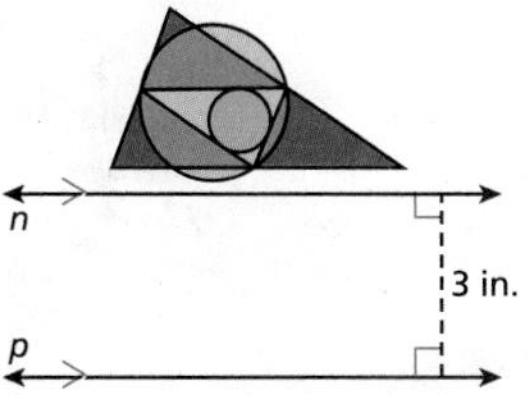

Reading Math The notation $A' \rightarrow A''$ is read "A prime is mapped to A double prime."

ENGLISH LANGUAGE LEARNERS

Power Presentations with PowerPoint®

Additional Examples

Example 1

Draw the result of the composition of isometries.

A. Reflect $PQRS$ across line m and then translate it along $\vec{v}$.

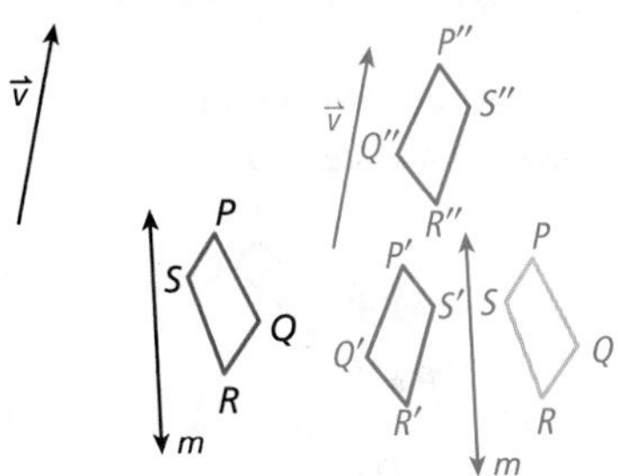

B. $\triangle KLM$ has vertices $K(4, -1)$, $L(5, -2)$, and $M(1, -4)$. Rotate $\triangle KLM$ 180° about the origin and then reflect it across the y-axis.

$K(4, -1) \rightarrow K'(-4, 1) \rightarrow K''(4, 1)$;
$L(5, -2) \rightarrow L'(-5, 2) \rightarrow L''(5, 2)$;
$M(1, -4) \rightarrow M'(-1, 4) \rightarrow M''(1, 4)$

Example 2

Sean reflects a design across line p and then reflects the image across line q. Describe a single transformation that moves the design from the original position to the final position.

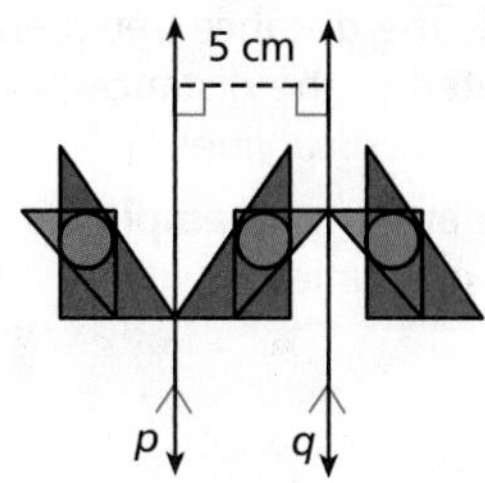

a translation 10 cm to the rt.

2 Teach

Guided Instruction

Review the properties of an isometry. Explain that a rotation or a translation is a composition of two reflections, so any transformation can be defined using only reflections.

Math Background The quadrants in the coordinate plane are numbered in a counterclockwise direction. In trigonometry, angles of rotation in the coordinate plane are measured counterclockwise from the positive x-axis.

Reaching All Learners

Through Modeling

Have students use geometry software to reflect a figure across a line and then to reflect this image across another line. Have them drag the points on the figure and drag the lines to see how the composition image is affected. Then have them try to rotate or translate the figure so that the image coincides with the image of the composition of reflections.

INTERVENTION

Questioning Strategies

EXAMPLE 1

- How is the orientation of an image related to its preimage after a glide reflection?

EXAMPLE 2

- Is the answer the same if the order of transformations is reversed?

Power Presentations with PowerPoint®

Additional Examples

Example 3

Copy each figure and draw two lines of reflection that produce an equivalent transformation.

A. translation: $\triangle XYZ \rightarrow \triangle X'Y'Z'$

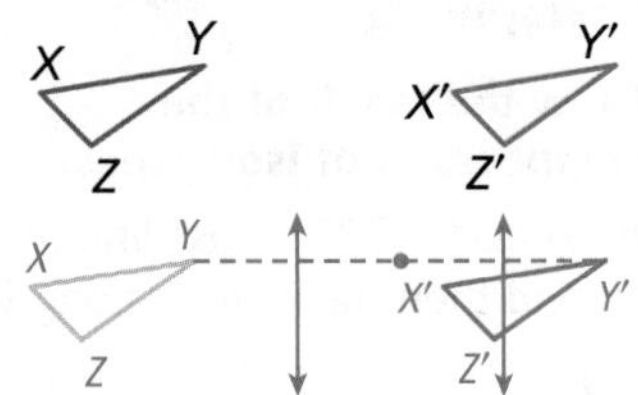

B. rotation with center P; $ABCD \rightarrow A'B'C'D'$

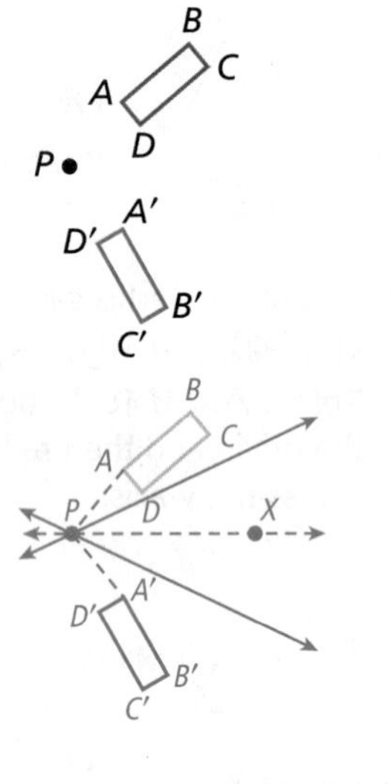

INTERVENTION

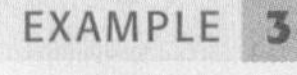

Questioning Strategies

EXAMPLE 3

- How is the distance between X and X' related to the distance between the two vertical lines?
- Which angle in **Example 3B** is the angle of rotation?

Theorem 12-4-3

Any translation or rotation is equivalent to a composition of two reflections.

EXAMPLE 3 Describing Transformations in Terms of Reflections

Copy each figure and draw two lines of reflection that produce an equivalent transformation.

A translation: $\triangle ABC \rightarrow \triangle A'B'C'$

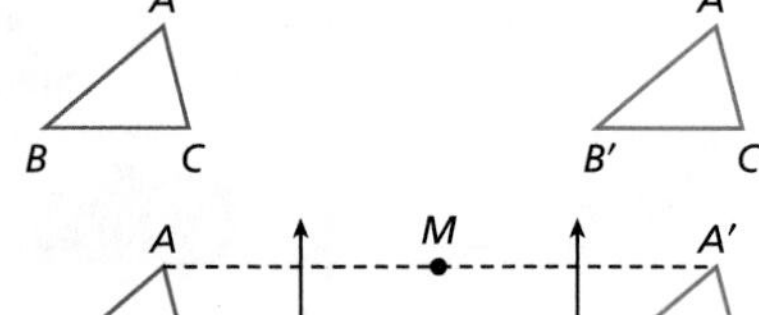

Step 1 Draw $\overline{AA'}$ and locate the midpoint M of $\overline{AA'}$.

Step 2 Draw the perpendicular bisectors of $\overline{AM}$ and $\overline{A'M}$.

Remember!

To draw the perpendicular bisector of a segment, use a ruler to locate the midpoint, and then use a right angle to draw a perpendicular line.

B rotation with center P: $\triangle DEF \rightarrow \triangle D'E'F'$

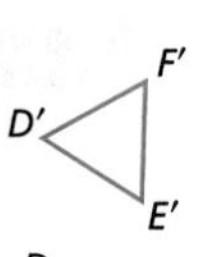

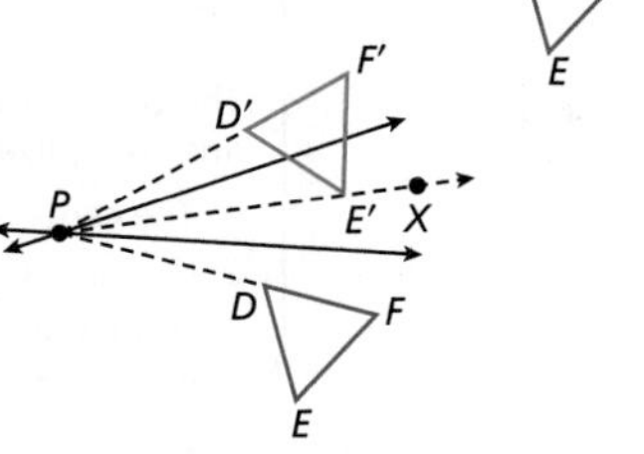

Step 1 Draw $\angle DPD'$. Draw the angle bisector $\overrightarrow{PX}$.

Step 2 Draw the bisectors of $\angle DPX$ and $\angle D'PX$.

3. Copy the figure showing the translation that maps $LMNP \rightarrow L'M'N'P'$. Draw the lines of reflection that produce an equivalent transformation.

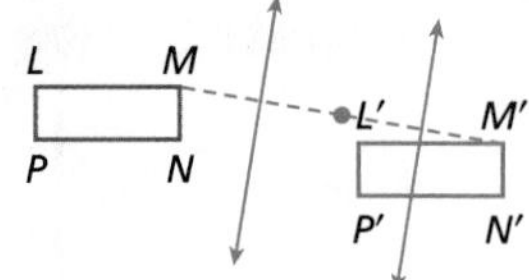

THINK AND DISCUSS

1. Which theorem explains why the image of a rectangle that is translated and then rotated is congruent to the preimage?
2. Point A' is a glide reflection of point A along $\vec{v}$ and across line ℓ. What is the relationship between $\vec{v}$ and ℓ? Explain the steps you would use to draw a glide reflection.
3. **GET ORGANIZED** Copy and complete the graphic organizer. In each box, describe an equivalent transformation and sketch an example.

Composition of Two Reflections
- Across parallel lines
- Across intersecting lines

3 Close

Summarize

Draw a figure in a coordinate plane and have students describe two or more transformations. Perform the composition of these transformations and then have students determine a transformation or a composition of transformations that will map the image back onto the original figure.

ONGOING ASSESSMENT and INTERVENTION

Diagnose ***Before*** **the Lesson**
12-4 Warm Up, TE p. 848

Monitor ***During*** **the Lesson**
Check It Out! Exercises, SE pp. 849–850
Questioning Strategies, TE pp. 849–850

Assess ***After*** **the Lesson**
12-4 Lesson Quiz, TE p. 853
Alternative Assessment, TE p. 853

Answers to *Think and Discuss*

Possible answers:

1. Theorem 12-4-1; a composition of two isometries is an isometry.
2. $\vec{v} \parallel \ell$; possible answer: Translate the preimage along the vector then reflect the image across the line.
3. See p. A10.

12-4 Exercises

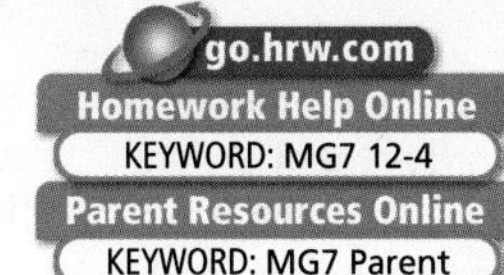

GUIDED PRACTICE

1. **Vocabulary** Explain the steps you would use to draw a *glide reflection*.
Draw a figure and translate it along a vector. Then reflect the image across a line.

SEE EXAMPLE 1 p. 848

Draw the result of each composition of isometries.

2. Translate $\triangle DEF$ along $\vec{u}$ and then reflect it across line ℓ.

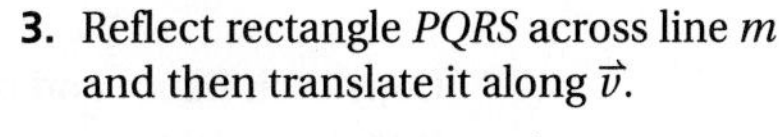

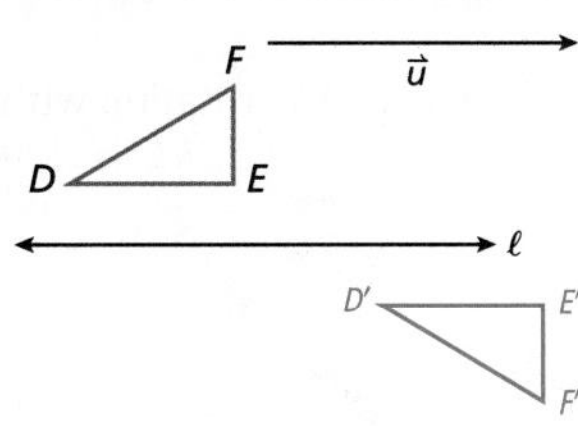

3. Reflect rectangle $PQRS$ across line m and then translate it along $\vec{v}$.

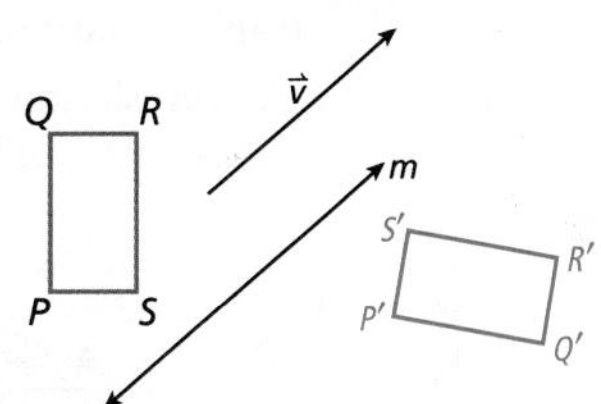

4. $\triangle ABC$ has vertices $A(1, -1)$, $B(4, -1)$, and $C(3, 2)$. Reflect $\triangle ABC$ across the y-axis and then translate it along the vector $\langle 0, -2 \rangle$.

SEE EXAMPLE 2 p. 849

5. **Sports** To create the opening graphics for a televised football game, an animator reflects a picture of a football helmet across line ℓ. She then reflects its image across line m, which intersects line ℓ at a 50° angle. Describe a single transformation that moves the helmet from its starting position to its final position.
a rotation of 100° about the point of intersection of the lines

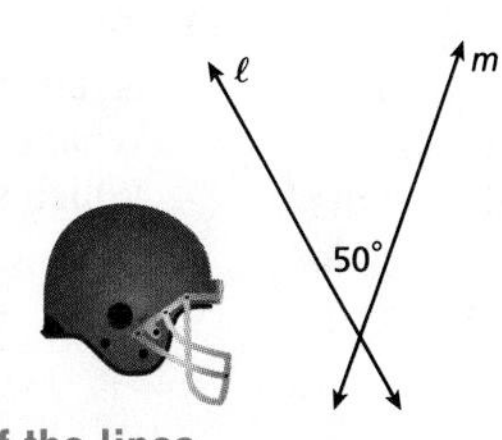

SEE EXAMPLE 3 p. 850

Copy each figure and draw two lines of reflection that produce an equivalent transformation.

6. translation: $\triangle EFG \rightarrow \triangle E'F'G'$

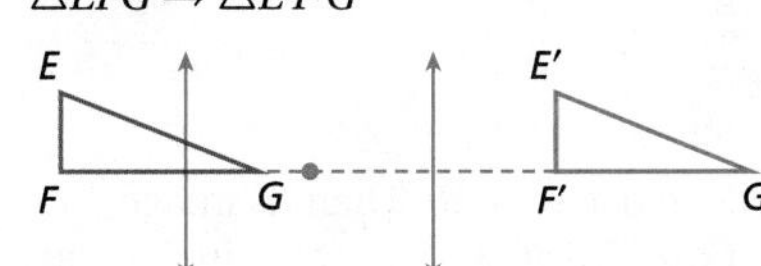

7. rotation with center P: $\triangle ABC \rightarrow \triangle A'B'C'$

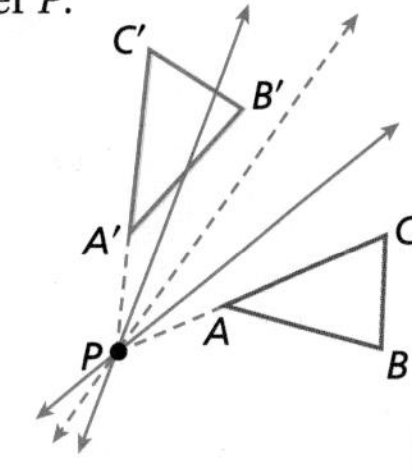

PRACTICE AND PROBLEM SOLVING

Independent Practice	
For Exercises	See Example
8–10	1
11	2
12–13	3

Extra Practice
Skills Practice p. S26
Application Practice p. S39

Draw the result of each composition of isometries.

8. Translate $\triangle RST$ along $\vec{u}$ and then translate it along $\vec{v}$.

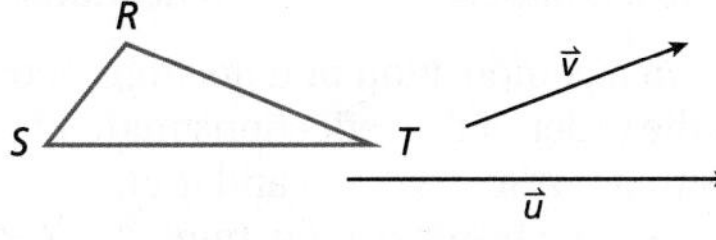

9. Rotate $\triangle ABC$ 90° about point P and then reflect it across line ℓ.

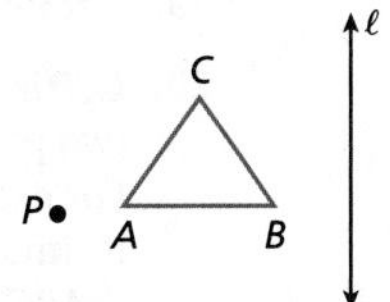

10. $\triangle GHJ$ has vertices $G(1, -1)$, $H(3, 1)$, and $J(3, -2)$. Reflect $\triangle GHJ$ across the line $y = x$ and then reflect it across the x-axis.

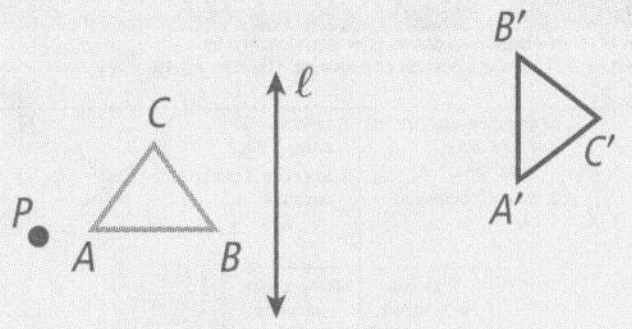

In **Exercise 8,** some students may reverse the order of transformations. Have them first translate $\triangle RST$, and then reflect it. Then ask them to first reflect $\triangle RST$, then translate it, and compare their results.

12-4 Exercises

Assignment Guide

Assign *Guided Practice* exercises as necessary.

If you finished Examples **1–3**
Basic 8–19, 22–25, 29–36
Average 8–25, 29–36
Advanced 8–13, 15–36

Homework Quick Check
Quickly check key concepts.
Exercises: 8, 10–12, 16, 18

Teaching Tip

Kinesthetic For **Exercises 2–3** and **8–9,** encourage students to cut the shapes out of paper and perform the transformations using the paper cutouts. Have them trace the resulting shapes after each transformation.

Answers

4.

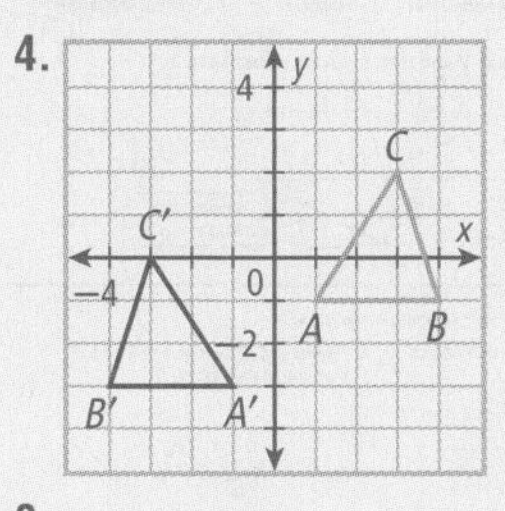

8.

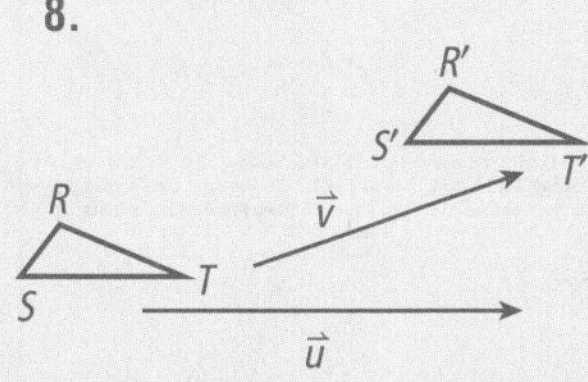

9.

B′
C′
A′
C
ℓ
P
A
B

10.

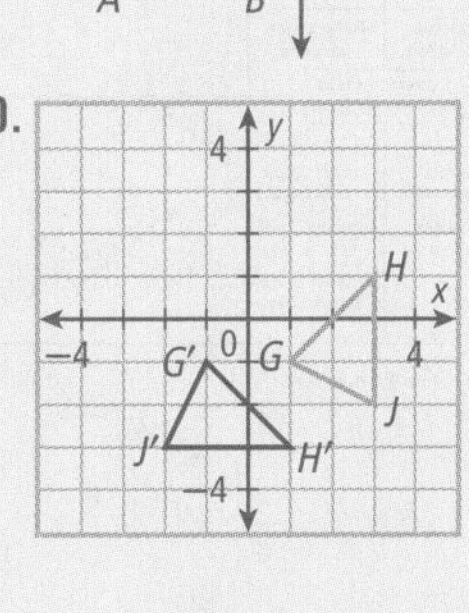

State Resources

Teaching Tip **Math Background** Point out that translations and rotations preserve the orientation of a figure, but reflections and glide reflections reverse the orientation. If a figure is reflected twice, the figure is returned to its original orientation.

Teaching Tip **Kinesthetic** For **Exercise 15,** give students triangles from a set of pattern blocks (MK). Have them trace the triangles and label the vertices, perform the transformations by moving the triangle, and then trace the triangle again to locate the image.

Answers

11b.

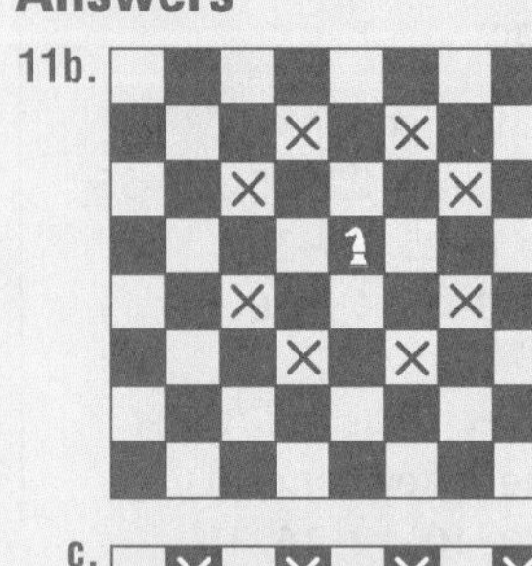

c.

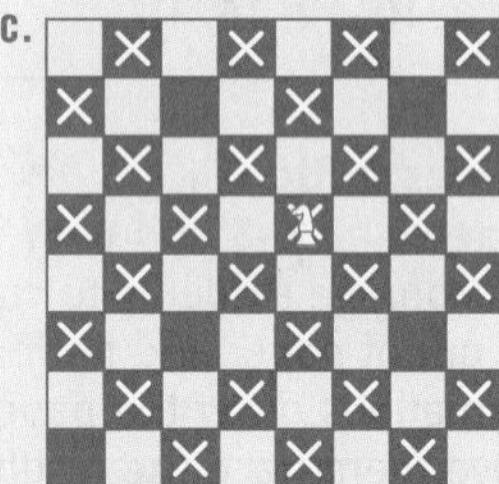

15.

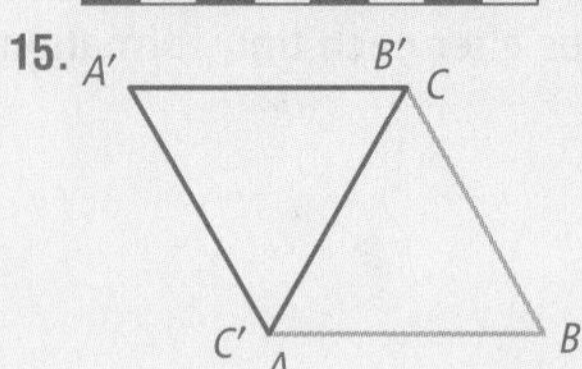

20. For explanation, see p. A31.

11a. The move is a horizontal or vertical translation by 2 spaces followed by a vertical or horizontal translation by 1 space.

11. **Games** In chess, a knight moves in the shape of the letter L. The piece moves two spaces horizontally or vertically. Then it turns 90° in either direction and moves one more space.
   a. Describe a knight's move as a composition of transformations.
   b. Copy the chessboard with the knight. Label all the positions the knight can reach in one move.
   c. Label all the positions the knight can reach in two moves.

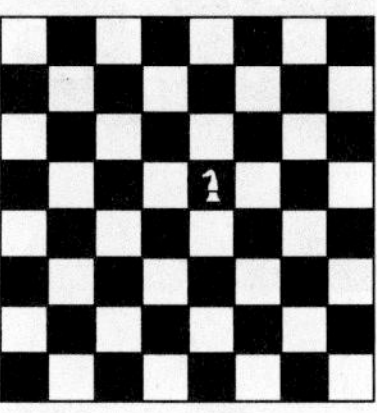

Copy each figure and draw two lines of reflection that produce an equivalent transformation.

12. translation: $ABCD \rightarrow A'B'C'D'$

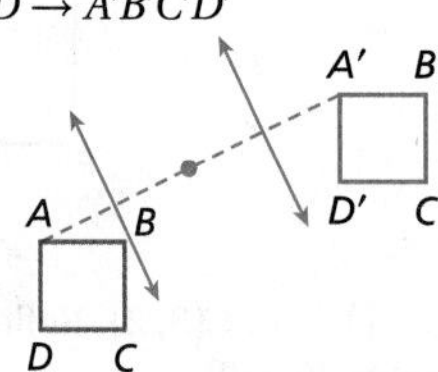

13. rotation with center Q: $\triangle JKL \rightarrow \triangle J'K'L'$

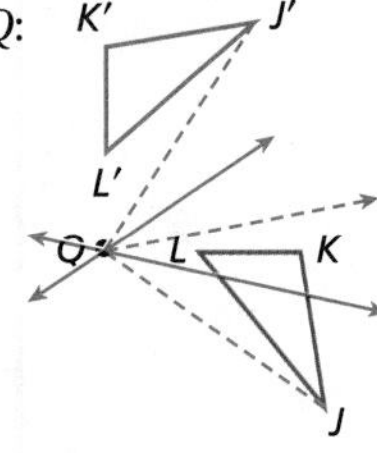

14. Solution A is incorrect because the endpoints are not written in the same order as they are written for the preimage.

14. **/// ERROR ANALYSIS ///** The segment with endpoints $A(4, 2)$ and $B(2, 1)$ is reflected across the y-axis. The image is reflected across the x-axis. What transformation is equivalent to the composition of these two reflections? Which solution is incorrect? Explain the error.

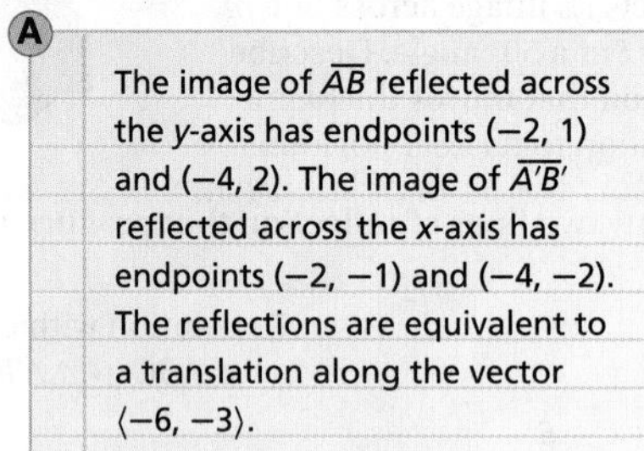

A

The image of $\overline{AB}$ reflected across the y-axis has endpoints $(-2, 1)$ and $(-4, 2)$. The image of $\overline{A'B'}$ reflected across the x-axis has endpoints $(-2, -1)$ and $(-4, -2)$. The reflections are equivalent to a translation along the vector $\langle -6, -3 \rangle$.

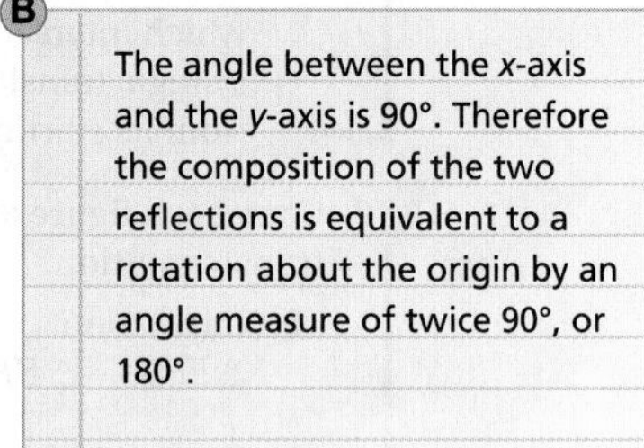

B

The angle between the x-axis and the y-axis is 90°. Therefore the composition of the two reflections is equivalent to a rotation about the origin by an angle measure of twice 90°, or 180°.

15. Equilateral $\triangle ABC$ is reflected across $\overline{AB}$. Then its image is translated along $\overrightarrow{BC}$. Copy $\triangle ABC$ and draw its final image.

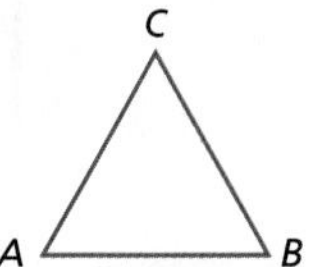

Tell whether each statement is sometimes, always, or never true.

16. The composition of two reflections is equivalent to a rotation. sometimes
17. An isometry changes the size of a figure. never
18. The composition of two isometries is an isometry. always
19. A rotation is equivalent to a composition of two reflections. always
20. **Critical Thinking** Given a composition of reflections across two parallel lines, does the order of the reflections matter? For example, does reflecting $\triangle ABC$ across m and then its image across n give the same result as reflecting $\triangle ABC$ across n and then its image across m? Explain. yes

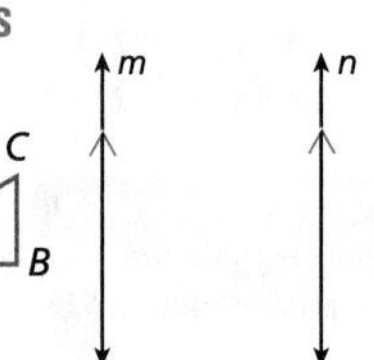

21. The line of reflection is the x-axis, and the translation vector is $\langle 5, 0 \rangle$.

21. **Write About It** Under a glide reflection, $\triangle RST \rightarrow \triangle R'S'T'$. The vertices of $\triangle RST$ are $R(-3, -2)$, $S(-1, -2)$, and $T(-1, 0)$. The vertices of $\triangle R'S'T'$ are $R'(2, 2)$, $S'(4, 2)$, and $T'(4, 0)$. Describe the reflection and translation that make up the glide reflection.

852 *Chapter 12 Extending Transformational Geometry*

12-4 PRACTICE A

12-4 PRACTICE C

12-4 PRACTICE B

Draw the result of each composition of isometries.

1. Rotate $\triangle XYZ$ 90° about point P and then translate it along $\vec{v}$.
2. Reflect $\triangle LMN$ across line q and then translate it along $\vec{u}$.
3. $ABCD$ has vertices $A(-3, 1)$, $B(-1, 1)$, $C(-1, -1)$, and $D(-3, -1)$. Rotate $ABCD$ 180° about the origin and then translate it along the vector $\langle 1, -3 \rangle$.
4. $\triangle PQR$ has vertices $P(1, -1)$, $Q(4, -1)$, and $R(3, 1)$. Reflect $\triangle PQR$ across the x-axis and then reflect it across $y = x$.
5. Ray draws equilateral $\triangle EFG$. He draws two lines that make a 60° angle through the triangle's center. Ray wants to reflect $\triangle EFG$ across both lines. Describe what will be the same and what will be different about the image of $\triangle E''F''G''$ compared to $\triangle EFG$.
The sides of the image will lie on the sides of the preimage, but the position of the vertices will be different. E'' will coincide with F, F'' with G, and G'' with E.

Draw two lines of reflection that produce an equivalent transformation for each figure.

6. translation: $STUV \rightarrow S'T'U'V'$
7. rotation with center P: $STUV \rightarrow S'T'U'V'$

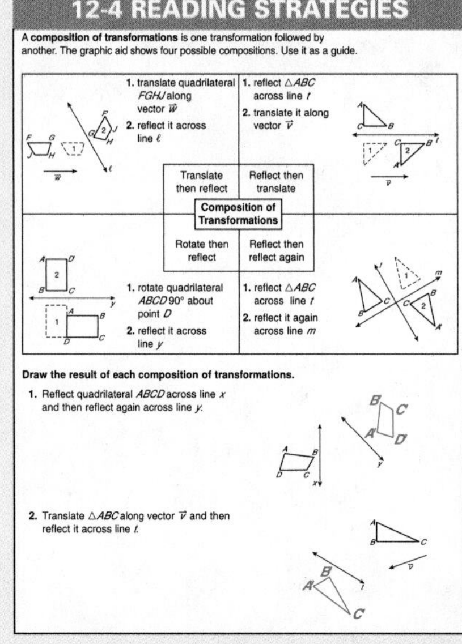

12-4 READING STRATEGIES

A **composition of transformations** is one transformation followed by another. The graphic aid shows four possible compositions. Use it as a guide.

Composition of Transformations: Translate then reflect — 1. translate quadrilateral $FGHJ$ along vector $\vec{w}$ 2. reflect it across line ℓ; Reflect then translate — 1. reflect $\triangle ABC$ across line r 2. translate it along vector $\vec{v}$; Rotate then reflect — 1. rotate quadrilateral $ABCD$ 90° about point D 2. reflect it across line y; Reflect then reflect again — 1. reflect $\triangle ABC$ across line r 2. reflect it again across line m

Draw the result of each composition of transformations.

1. Reflect quadrilateral $ABCD$ across line x and then reflect again across line y.
2. Translate $\triangle ABC$ along vector $\vec{v}$ and then reflect it across line ℓ.

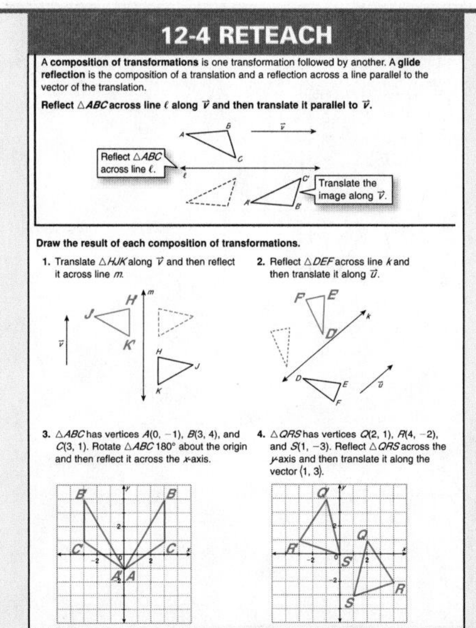

12-4 RETEACH

A **composition of transformations** is one transformation followed by another. A **glide reflection** is the composition of a translation and a reflection across a line parallel to the vector of the translation.

Reflect $\triangle ABC$ across line ℓ along $\vec{v}$ and then translate it parallel to $\vec{v}$.

Reflect $\triangle ABC$ across line ℓ. Translate the image along $\vec{v}$.

Draw the result of each composition of transformations.

1. Translate $\triangle HJK$ along $\vec{v}$ and then reflect it across line m.
2. Reflect $\triangle DEF$ across line k and then translate it along $\vec{u}$.
3. $\triangle ABC$ has vertices $A(0, -1)$, $B(3, 4)$, and $C(3, 1)$. Rotate $\triangle ABC$ 180° about the origin and then reflect it across the x-axis.
4. $\triangle QRS$ has vertices $Q(2, 1)$, $R(4, -2)$, and $S(1, -3)$. Reflect $\triangle QRS$ across the y-axis and then translate it along the vector $\langle 1, 3 \rangle$.

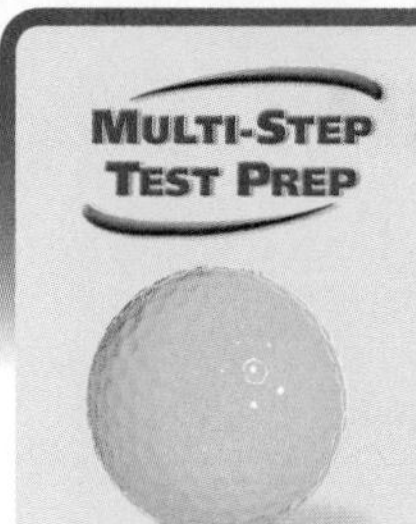

22. This problem will prepare you for the Multi-Step Test Prep on page 854.

The figure shows one hole of a miniature golf course where T is the tee and H is the hole.

a. Yuriko makes a hole in one as shown by the red arrows. Write the ball's path as a composition of translations. $\langle 1, 3\rangle + \langle 3, 1\rangle$

b. Find a different way to make a hole in one, and write the ball's path as a composition of translations. Possible answer: $\langle 3, -3\rangle + \langle 4, 4\rangle + \langle -3, 3\rangle$

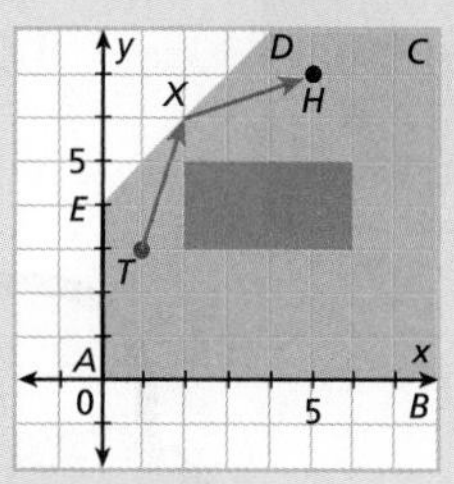

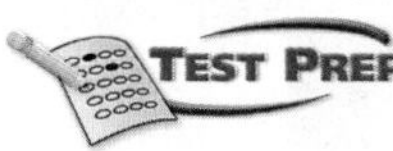

23. $\triangle ABC$ is reflected across the y-axis. Then its image is rotated 90° about the origin. What are the coordinates of the final image of point A under this composition of transformations?

(A) $(-1, -2)$ (B) $(-2, 1)$ (C) $(1, 2)$ (D) $(-2, -1)$

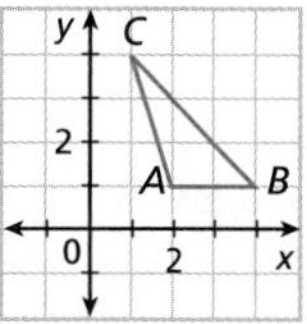

24. Which composition of transformations maps $\triangle ABC$ into the fourth quadrant?

(F) Reflect across the x-axis and then reflect across the y-axis.
(G) Rotate about the origin by 180° and then reflect across the y-axis.
(H) Translate along the vector $\langle -5, 0\rangle$ and then rotate about the origin by 90°.
(J) Rotate about the origin by 90° and then translate along the vector $\langle 1, -2\rangle$.

25. Which is equivalent to the composition of two translations?

(A) Reflection (B) Rotation (C) Translation (D) Glide reflection

CHALLENGE AND EXTEND

26. The point $A(3, 1)$ is rotated 90° about the point $P(-1, 2)$ and then reflected across the line $y = 5$. Find the coordinates of the image A'. $(0, 4)$

27. For any two congruent figures in a plane, one can be transformed to the other by a composition of no more than three reflections. Copy the figure. Show how to find a composition of three reflections that maps $\triangle MNP$ to $\triangle M'N'P'$.

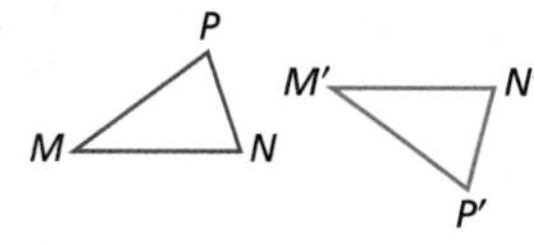

28. A figure in the coordinate plane is reflected across the line $y = x + 1$ and then across the line $y = x + 3$. Find a translation vector that is equivalent to the composition of the reflections. Write the vector in component form. $\langle -2, 2\rangle$

SPIRAL REVIEW

Determine whether the set of ordered pairs represents a function. *(Previous course)*

29. $\{(-6, -5), (-1, 0), (0, -5), (1, 0)\}$ yes
30. $\{(-3, -1), (1, 2), (-3, 1), (5, 10)\}$ no

Find the length of each segment. *(Lesson 11-6)*

31. $\overline{EJ}$ 6.4
32. $\overline{CD}$ 7.8
33. $\overline{FH}$ 8

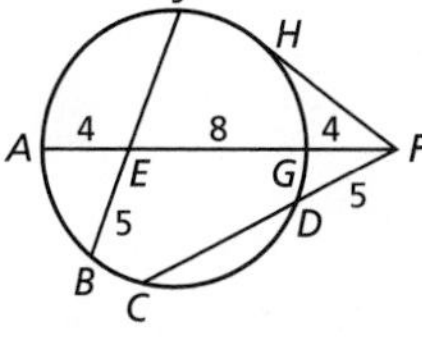

Determine the coordinates of each point after a rotation about the origin by the given angle of rotation. *(Lesson 12-3)*

34. $F(2, 3)$; 90° $F'(-3, 2)$
35. $N(-1, -3)$; 180° $N'(1, 3)$
36. $Q(-2, 0)$; 90° $Q'(0, -2)$

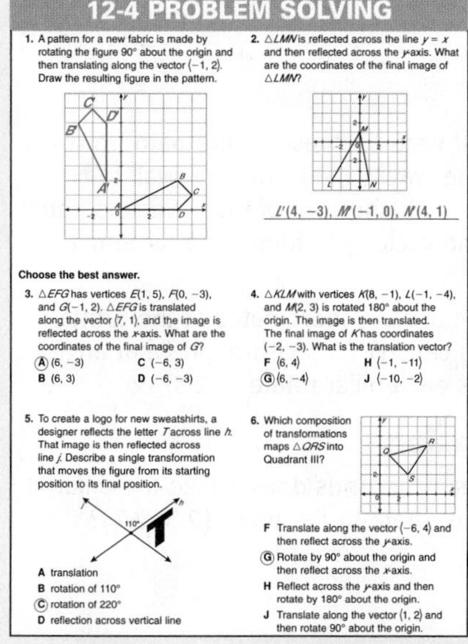

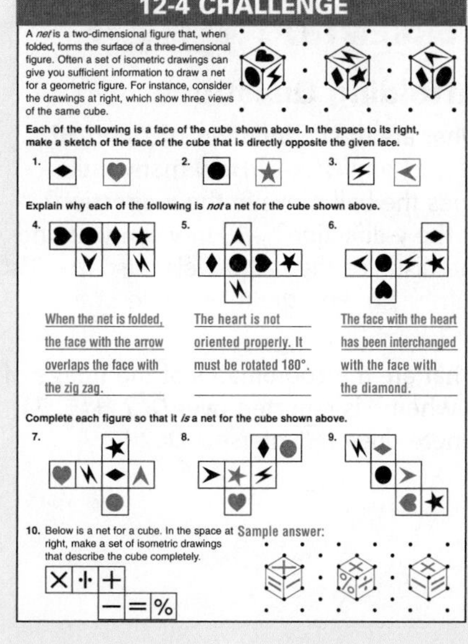

Exercise 22 involves identifying a composition of translations. This exercise prepares students for the Multi-Step Test Prep on page 854.

In **Exercise 24,** ask students who choose **J** whether the horizontal component of the translation vector is large enough to map $\triangle ABC$ to the fourth quadrant.

Answers

27. See p. A31.

Journal

Have students explain how to find the two lines of reflection that produce a transformation equivalent to a rotation or a translation.

ALTERNATIVE ASSESSMENT

Give students a diagram with two congruent figures and have them describe a composition of transformations that will map one to the other.

Power Presentations with PowerPoint®

12-4 Lesson Quiz

PQR has vertices P(5, −2), Q(1, −4), and P(−3, 3).

1. Translate $\triangle PQR$ along the vector $\langle -2, 1\rangle$ and then reflect it across the x-axis. $P''(3, 1), Q''(-1, 3), R''(-5, -4)$
2. Reflect $\triangle PQR$ across the line $y = x$ and then rotate it 90° about the origin. $P''(-5, -2), Q''(-1, 4), R''(3, 3)$
3. Copy the figure and draw two lines of reflection that produce an equivalent transformation of the translation $\triangle FGH \to \triangle F'G'H'$.

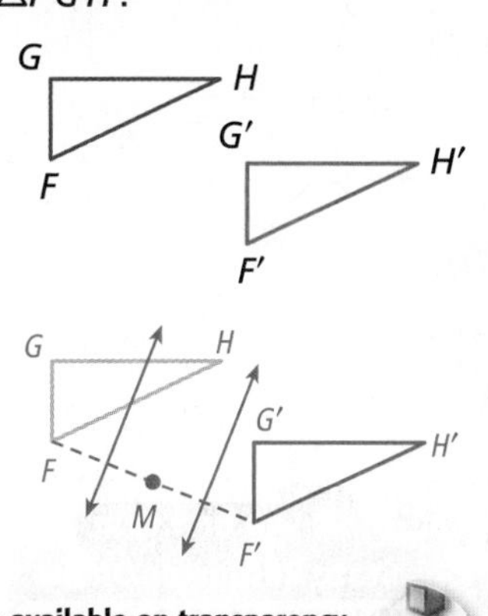

Also available on transparency

Organizer

Objective: Assess students' ability to apply concepts and skills in Lessons 12-1 through 12-4 in a real-world format.

Online Edition

Resources

Geometry Assessments
www.mathtekstoolkit.org

Problem	Text Reference
1	Lesson 12-2
2	Lesson 12-1
3	Lesson 12-4
4	Lesson 12-3

State Resources

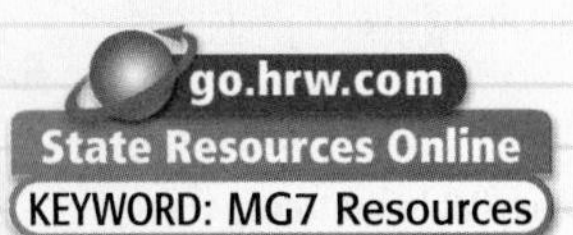

CHAPTER 12

SECTION 12A

Congruence Transformations

A Hole in One The figure shows a plan for one hole of a miniature golf course. The tee is at point T and the hole is at point H. Each unit of the coordinate plane represents one meter.

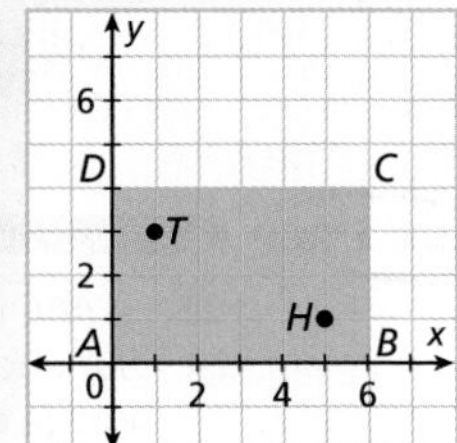

1. When a player hits the ball in a straight line from T to H, the path of the ball can be represented by a translation. What is the translation vector? How far does the ball travel? Round to the nearest tenth. $\langle 4, -2 \rangle$; 4.5 m
2. The designer of the golf course decides to make the hole more difficult by placing a barrier between the tee and the hole, as shown. To make a hole in one, a player must hit the ball so that it bounces off wall $\overline{DC}$. What point along the wall should a player aim for? Explain.

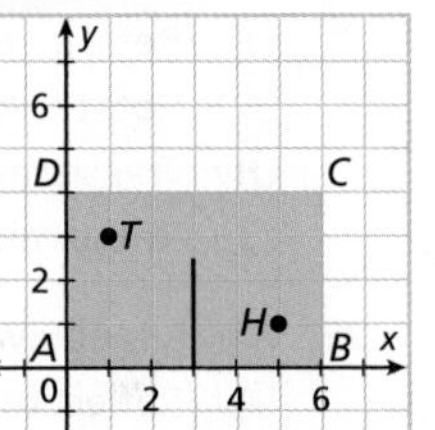

2. (2, 4); to find this point, first reflect H across $\overline{DC}$. The image is $H'(5, 7)$. Then draw the segment connecting T and H' and find this segment's intersection with $\overline{DC}$.

3. Write the path of the ball in Problem 2 as a composition of two translations. What is the total distance that the ball travels in this case? Round to the nearest tenth. $\langle 1, 1 \rangle + \langle 3, -3 \rangle$; 5.7 m
4. The designer decides to remove the barrier and put a revolving obstacle between the tee and the hole. The obstacle consists of a turntable with four equally spaced pillars, as shown. The designer wants the turntable to make one complete rotation in 16 seconds. What should be the coordinates of the pillar at (4, 2) after 2 seconds? (3.7, 2.7)

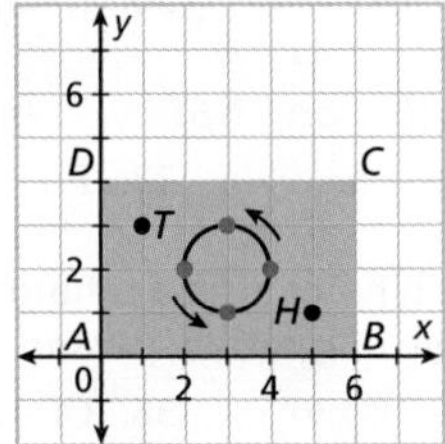

INTERVENTION

Scaffolding Questions

1. What are the coordinates of T and H? $T(1, 3)$ and $H(5, 1)$ How many units does the ball move in the x-direction? 4 in the y-direction? −2 How can you find the distance the ball travels? Use the Dist. Formula or find the magnitude of the vector.
2. What are the coordinates of the image of H when it is reflected over $\overline{DC}$? $H'(5, 7)$ Where does $\overline{TH'}$ intersect $\overline{DC}$? (2, 4)
3. What vector represents the path from T to the wall? $\langle 1, 1 \rangle$ from the wall to H? $\langle 3, -3 \rangle$ Is the sum of these vectors equal to the vector you found in **Problem 1**? yes
4. What are the coordinates of the turntable's center? (3, 2) Through what angle does each pillar rotate in 2 s? 45°

Extension

How many seconds does it take the pillar at (4, 2) to rotate to the point (2.3, 2.7)? 6 s

Quiz for Lessons 12-1 Through 12-4

12-1 Reflections

Tell whether each transformation appears to be a reflection.

1. yes

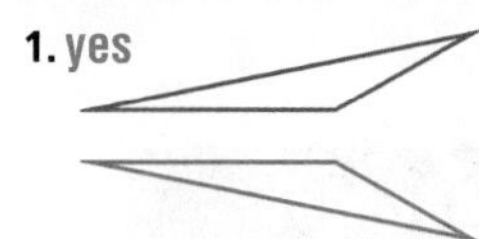

2. no

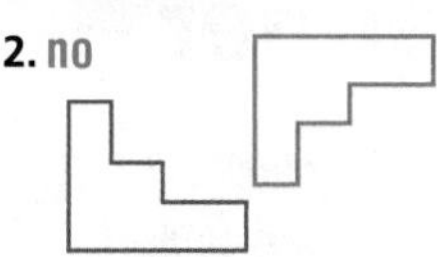

Copy each figure and the line of reflection. Draw the reflection of the figure across the line.

3.

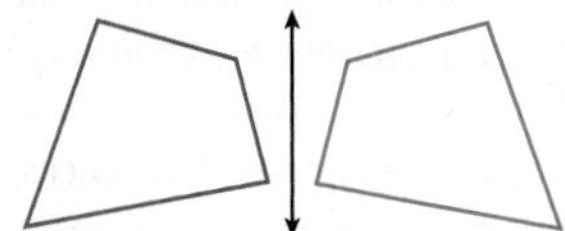

4.

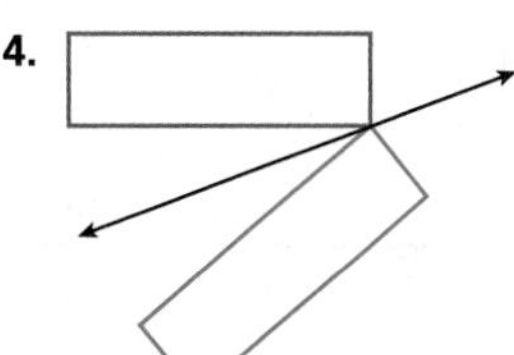

12-2 Translations

Tell whether each transformation appears to be a translation.

5. no

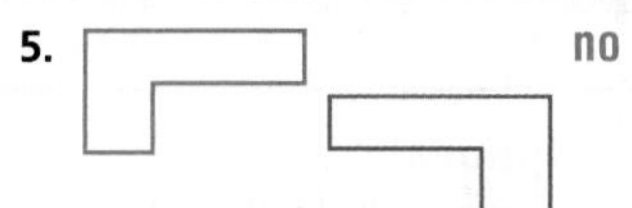

6. yes

7. A landscape architect represents a flower bed by a polygon with vertices $(1, 0)$, $(4, 0)$, $(4, 2)$, and $(1, 2)$. She decides to move the flower bed to a new location by translating it along the vector $\langle -4, -3 \rangle$. Draw the flower bed in its final position.

12-3 Rotations

Tell whether each transformation appears to be a rotation.

8. yes

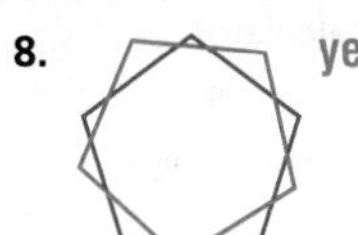

9. yes

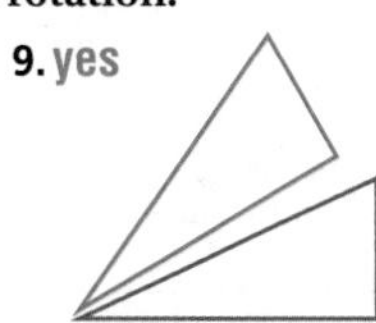

Rotate the figure with the given vertices about the origin using the given angle of rotation.

10. $A(1, 0)$, $B(4, 1)$, $C(3, 2)$; 180°

11. $R(-2, 0)$, $S(-2, 4)$, $T(-3, 4)$, $U(-3, 0)$; 90°

12-4 Compositions of Transformations

12. Draw the result of the following composition of transformations. Translate *GHJK* along $\vec{v}$ and then reflect it across line *m*.

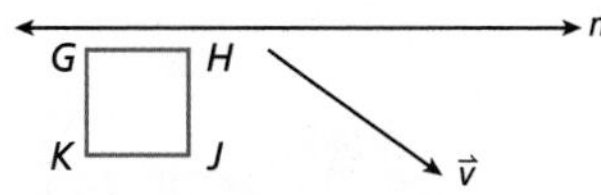

13. $\triangle ABC$ with vertices $A(1, 0)$, $B(1, 3)$, and $C(2, 3)$ is reflected across the *y*-axis, and then its image is reflected across the *x*-axis. Describe a single transformation that moves the triangle from its starting position to its final position.
rotation by 180° about the origin

READY TO GO ON? SECTION 12A

Organizer

Objective: Assess students' mastery of concepts and skills in Lessons 12-1 through 12-4.

Resources

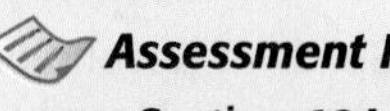

Assessment Resources
Section 12A Quiz

Teacher One Stop™
Test & Practice Generator

INTERVENTION

Resources

***Ready to Go On? Intervention and Enrichment* Worksheets**

***Ready to Go On?* CD-ROM**

***Ready to Go On?* Online**

my.hrw.com

Answers

7, 10–12. See p. A31.

READY TO GO ON? Diagnose and Prescribe

NO INTERVENE

Ready to Go On? Intervention	*Ready to Go On? Intervention,* Section 12A: Worksheets	CD-ROM	Online
Lesson 12-1	12-1 Intervention	Activity 12-1	Diagnose and Prescribe Online
Lesson 12-2	12-2 Intervention	Activity 12-2	
Lesson 12-3	12-3 Intervention	Activity 12-3	
Lesson 12-4	12-4 Intervention	Activity 12-4	

YES ENRICH

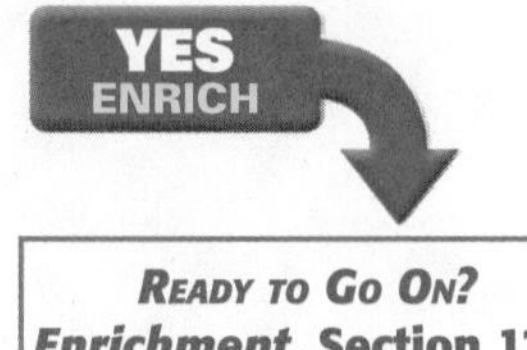

***Ready to Go On? Enrichment,* Section 12A**
Worksheets

CD-ROM

Online

Patterns

One-Minute Section Planner

Lesson	Lab Resources	Materials
Lesson 12-5 Symmetry • Identify and describe symmetry in geometric figures. ☐ SAT-10 ☑ NAEP ☑ ACT ☑ SAT ☑ SAT Subject Tests		**Optional** overhead projector, blank transparencies, geometry software, Mira, patty paper, modeling clay, toothpicks, string
Extension Solids of Revolution • Understand how solids can be produced by rotating a two-dimensional figure through space. ☐ SAT-10 ☐ NAEP ☐ ACT ☐ SAT ☐ SAT Subject Tests		**Optional** construction paper, tape
Lesson 12-6 Tessellations • Use transformations to draw tessellations. • Identify regular and semiregular tessellations and figures that will tessellate. ☐ SAT-10 ☐ NAEP ☐ ACT ☐ SAT ☑ SAT Subject Tests	***Technology Lab Activities*** 12-6 Technology Lab	**Optional** pattern blocks (MK), tracing paper
Lesson 12-7 Dilations • Identify and draw dilations. ☐ SAT-10 ☑ NAEP ☐ ACT ☐ SAT ☐ SAT Subject Tests		**Required** compass and straightedge (MK), graphing calculator **Optional** overhead projector, geometry software
Extension Using Patterns to Generate Fractals • Describe iterative patterns that generate fractals. ☐ SAT-10 ☐ NAEP ☐ ACT ☐ SAT ☐ SAT Subject Tests		**Optional** satellite photos

MK = *Manipulatives Kit*

SYMMETRY, WALLPAPER PATTERNS, AND TESSELLATIONS

Lessons 12-5, 12-6

In general terms, an object, figure, or pattern has *symmetry* if a transformation can be performed on the object, figure, or pattern so that its image looks exactly like its preimage. If the relevant transformation is a reflection, the figure has *line symmetry* (or reflection symmetry). If the transformation is a rotation, the figure has *rotational symmetry*. It is also possible for a figure to have translation symmetry or glide-reflection symmetry, but these terms apply only to patterns that continue indefinitely, such as the frieze patterns and tessellations that are introduced in Lesson 12-6.

A *wallpaper pattern* is a planar repeating pattern. A tessellation is a special type of wallpaper pattern in which repeating figures cover the plane with no gaps or overlaps. The figures below show some simple examples of wallpaper patterns. Only the pattern on the right is a tessellation.

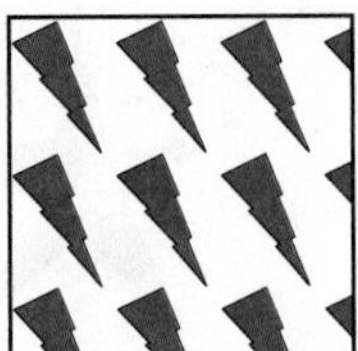

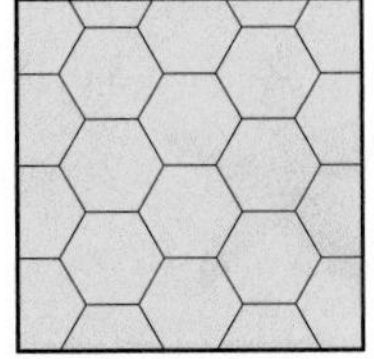

Mathematicians classify wallpaper patterns based on the symmetries they exhibit. In the above examples, the pattern on the left has only translation symmetry. The pattern in the center has translation and reflection symmetry. The pattern on the right has these symmetries plus 60° rotational symmetry.

Every wallpaper pattern can be classified by identifying its symmetries. Surprisingly, there are precisely 17 different classifications. That is, any repeating pattern that covers a plane can be reduced to one of 17 basic types. This unusual mathematical fact has had far-reaching applications in a number of fields, including chemistry and crystallography.

DILATIONS

Lesson 12-7

A *dilation* is a transformation that changes the size of a figure, but not its shape. As such, a dilation is an example of a transformation that is not an isometry (unless the scale factor of the dilation is 1). Every dilation has exactly one fixed point, which is the center of the dilation.

Although dilations do not preserve distance, they do preserve other properties of a figure. For example, dilations preserve angle measure. In other words, under a dilation, an angle in the preimage is congruent to the corresponding angle in the image. Dilations also preserve parallel lines. That is, two lines that are parallel in the preimage are mapped to two parallel lines in the image.

As discussed in the Math Background notes for Section 12A, if two figures are congruent, then there is an isometry that maps one figure onto the other. If two figures are similar, one may be mapped onto the other through a composition of a dilation and an isometry. For example, the equilateral triangles $\triangle ABC$ and $\triangle A'B'C'$ shown below are similar, and $\triangle ABC$ may be mapped onto $\triangle A'B'C'$ by a dilation with scale factor 2 and center B followed by a 180° rotation about point P.

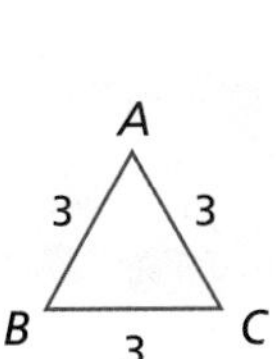

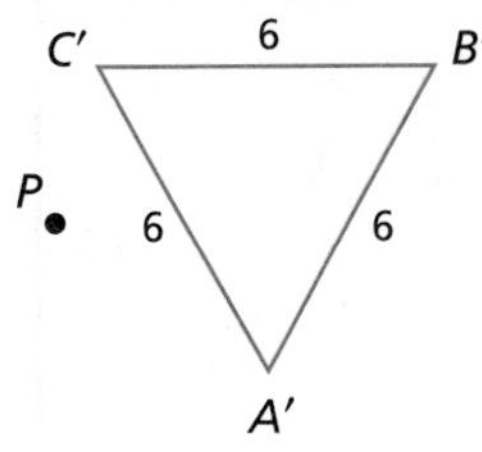

A dilation with a scale factor greater than 1 is an enlargement. A dilation with a scale factor greater than 0 but less than 1 is a reduction. It is also possible to extend the definition of a dilation to allow a scale factor of 0 (in this case, the entire preimage is collapsed to a single point, the center of dilation) and negative scale factors. A dilation with a scale factor of $-k$, where $k > 0$, is equivalent to the dilation with scale factor k followed by a rotation of 180° about the center of dilation.

12-5 Organizer

Pacing: Traditional 1 day
Block $\frac{1}{2}$ day

Objective: Identify and describe symmetry in geometric figures.

Online Edition
Tutorial Videos

Power Presentations with PowerPoint®

Warm Up

Identify each transformation.

1. 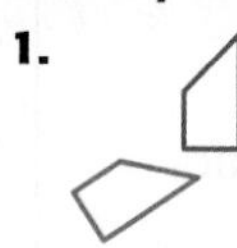 rotation

2. reflection

Rotate $\triangle ABC$ with the given vertices by the given angle.

3. $A(3, -4)$, $B(5, 1)$, $C(-4, 0)$; $180°$ $A'(-3, 4)$, $B'(-5, -1)$, $C'(4, 0)$

4. $A(1, -5)$, $B(7, -1)$, $C(3, 6)$; $90°$ $A'(5, 1)$, $B'(1, 7)$, $C'(-6, 3)$

Also available on transparency

Math Humor

Q: Why do figures with rotational symmetry get bored?

A: No matter which way they turn, it's always the same.

12-5 Symmetry

Objective
Identify and describe symmetry in geometric figures.

Vocabulary
symmetry
line symmetry
line of symmetry
rotational symmetry

Who uses this?
Marine biologists use symmetry to classify diatoms.

Diatoms are microscopic algae that are found in aquatic environments. Scientists use a system that was developed in the 1970s to classify diatoms based on their *symmetry*.

A figure has **symmetry** if there is a transformation of the figure such that the image coincides with the preimage.

Know it! Note

Line Symmetry

A figure has **line symmetry** (or reflection symmetry) if it can be reflected across a line so that the image coincides with the preimage. The **line of symmetry** (also called the axis of symmetry) divides the figure into two congruent halves.

EXAMPLE 1 Identifying Line Symmetry

Tell whether each figure has line symmetry. If so, copy the shape and draw all lines of symmetry.

A 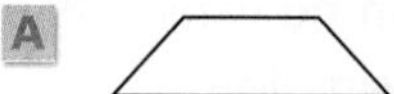 yes; one line of symmetry 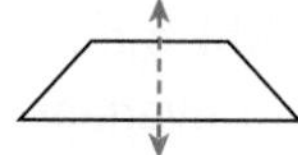

B 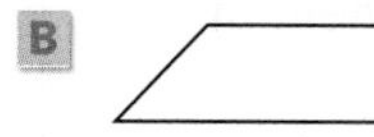 no line symmetry

C  yes; five lines of symmetry 

CHECK IT OUT! **Tell whether each figure has line symmetry. If so, copy the shape and draw all lines of symmetry.**

1a.  **1b.** B **1c.** 

1a. yes; two lines of symmetry

1b. yes; one line of symmetry

1c. yes; one line of symmetry

State Resources

go.hrw.com
State Resources Online
KEYWORD: MG7 Resources

1 Introduce

EXPLORATION

12-5 Symmetry

A figure has *line symmetry* if it can be reflected across a line so that the image coincides with the preimage. The *line of symmetry* divides the figure into two congruent halves.

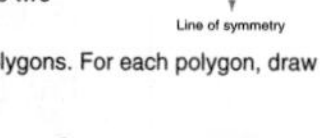
Line of symmetry

1. Copy the following regular polygons. For each polygon, draw all the lines of symmetry.

2. Look for a pattern. How many lines of symmetry does a regular n-gon have?
3. Sketch a regular polygon that has exactly eight lines of symmetry.

THINK AND DISCUSS

4. **Discuss** whether it is possible for a regular polygon to have exactly two lines of symmetry.
5. **Explain** how you could use paper folding to find all the lines of symmetry of regular pentagon *ABCDE*.

Motivate

Human faces appear to have symmetry, but most people's faces aren't perfectly symmetric. Photocopy a picture of a face onto two transparencies and cut each one down the center of the face. Flip the pieces of one transparency over and put the two left sides together and the two right sides together to create two different faces with perfect symmetry. Discuss with students how to tell if a figure has symmetry.

Explorations and answers are provided in *Alternate Openers: Explorations Transparencies.*

Rotational Symmetry

A figure has **rotational symmetry** (or *radial symmetry*) if it can be rotated about a point by an angle greater than 0° and less than 360° so that the image coincides with the preimage.

The *angle of rotational symmetry* is the smallest angle through which a figure can be rotated to coincide with itself. The number of times the figure coincides with itself as it rotates through 360° is called the *order* of the rotational symmetry.

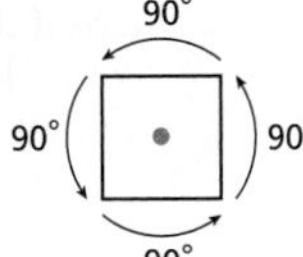

Angle of rotational symmetry: 90°
Order: 4

EXAMPLE 2 Identifying Rotational Symmetry

Tell whether each figure has rotational symmetry. If so, give the angle of rotational symmetry and the order of the symmetry.

A 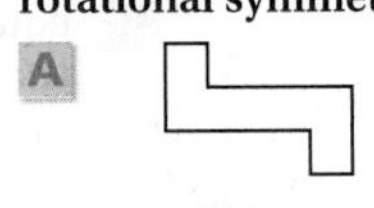
yes; 180°; order: 2

B 
no rotational symmetry

C 
yes; 60°; order: 6

CHECK IT OUT! Tell whether each figure has rotational symmetry. If so, give the angle of rotational symmetry and the order of the symmetry.

2a. 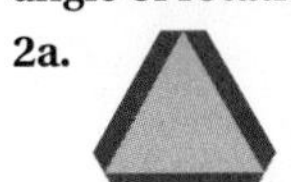
yes; 120°; order: 3

2b. 
yes; 180°; order: 2

2c. 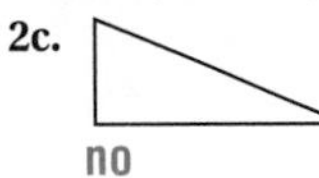
no

EXAMPLE 3 *Biology Application*

Describe the symmetry of each diatom. Copy the shape and draw any lines of symmetry. If there is rotational symmetry, give the angle and order.

A 
line symmetry and rotational symmetry; angle of rotational symmetry: 180°; order: 2

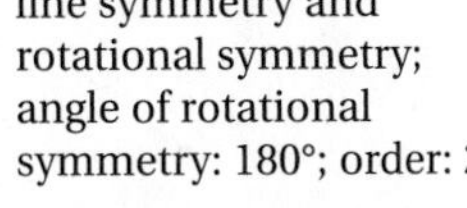

B 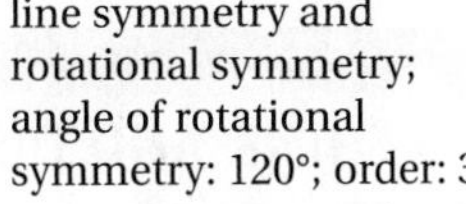
line symmetry and rotational symmetry; angle of rotational symmetry: 120°; order: 3

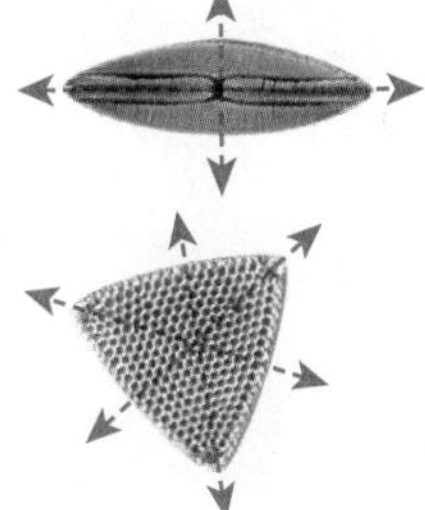

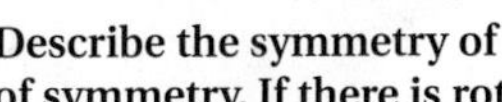

CHECK IT OUT! Describe the symmetry of each diatom. Copy the shape and draw any lines of symmetry. If there is rotational symmetry, give the angle and order.

3a. 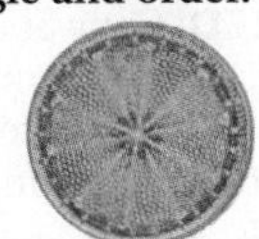

3b. 

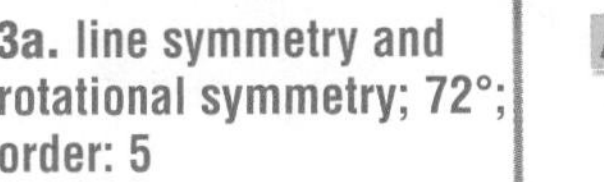

3a. line symmetry and rotational symmetry; 72°; order: 5

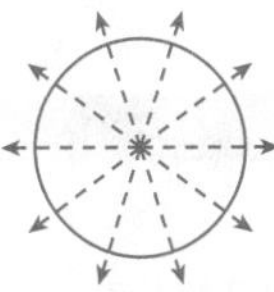

3b. line symmetry and rotational symmetry; 51.4°; order: 7

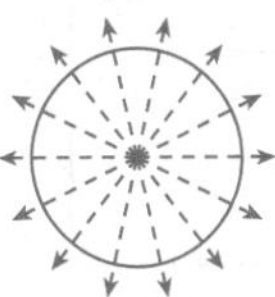

2 Teach

Guided Instruction

Review reflections and rotations. Discuss how line symmetry is related to a reflection of a figure and how rotational symmetry is related to a rotation. Use three-dimensional objects such as prisms and cylinders to demonstrate plane symmetry and symmetry about an axis.

Reaching All Learners

Through Modeling

Have students use geometry software or cut out figures to examine the symmetry of regular polygons. Then have them use inductive reasoning to make conjectures about the number of lines of symmetry and the order of rotational symmetry of a regular *n*-gon. *n* lines of symmetry, order *n*

Power Presentations with PowerPoint®

Additional Examples

Example 1

Tell whether each figure has line symmetry. If so, copy the shape and draw all lines of symmetry.

A. 
yes

B. 
no

C. 
yes

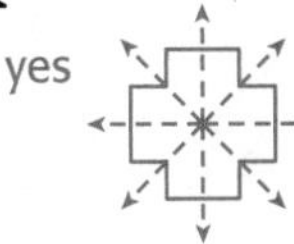

Example 2

Tell whether each figure has rotational symmetry. If so, give the angle of rotational symmetry and the order.

A. 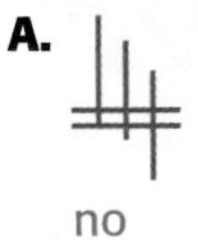
no

B. 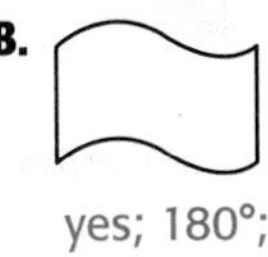
yes; 180°; order: 2

C. 
yes; 90°; order: 4

Example 3

Describe the symmetry of each icon. Copy each shape and draw any lines of symmetry. If there is rotational symmetry, give the angle and the order.

A. 
rotational symmetry; 180°; order 2

B. 

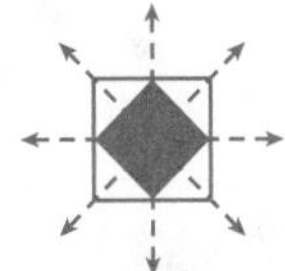

line symmetry and rotational symmetry; 90°; order 4

INTERVENTION

Questioning Strategies

EXAMPLE 1

- How do you locate a figure's line of symmetry?

EXAMPLES 2–3

- How do you determine a figure's angle of rotational symmetry?

Power Presentations with PowerPoint®

Additional Examples

Example 4

Tell whether each figure has plane symmetry, symmetry about an axis, or neither.

A. square pyramid

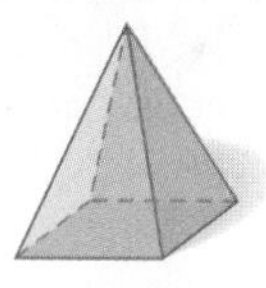
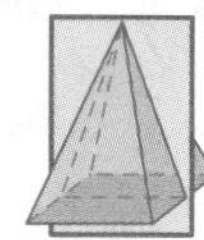
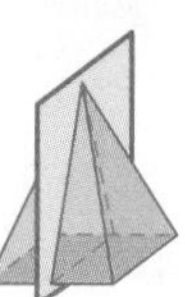
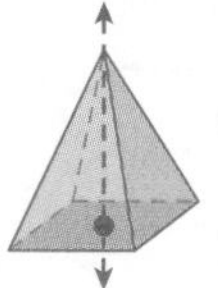

plane symmetry and symmetry about an axis

B.

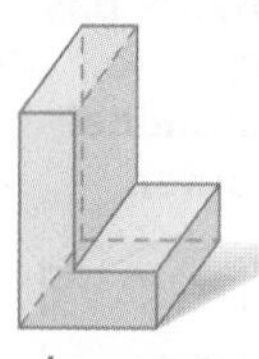
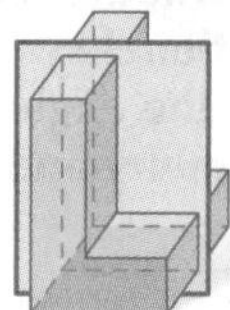

plane symmetry

INTERVENTION
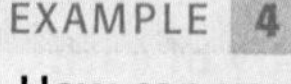
Questioning Strategies

EXAMPLE 4

- How can you tell if a three-dimensional figure has plane symmetry?

A three-dimensional figure has *plane symmetry* if a plane can divide the figure into two congruent reflected halves.

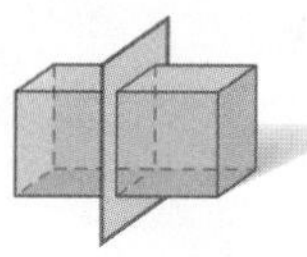
Plane symmetry

A three-dimensional figure has *symmetry about an axis* if there is a line about which the figure can be rotated (by an angle greater than 0° and less than 360°) so that the image coincides with the preimage.

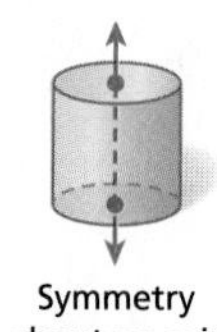
Symmetry about an axis

EXAMPLE 4 Identifying Symmetry in Three Dimensions

Tell whether each figure has plane symmetry, symmetry about an axis, or neither.

A **trapezoidal prism**

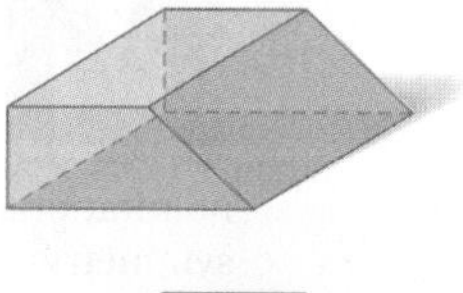
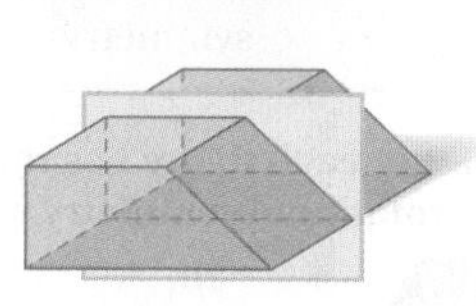

plane symmetry

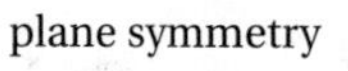

B **equilateral triangular prism**

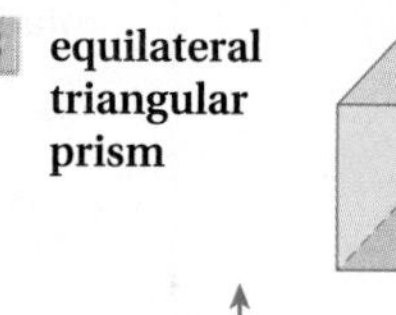
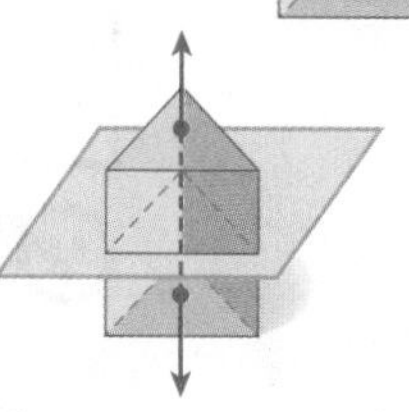

plane symmetry and symmetry about an axis

CHECK IT OUT! **Tell whether each figure has plane symmetry, symmetry about an axis, or no symmetry.**

4a. cone both

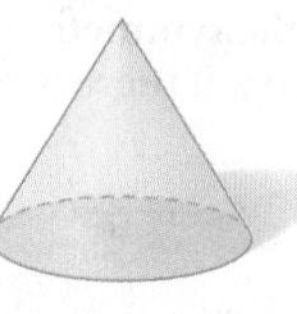

4b. pyramid neither

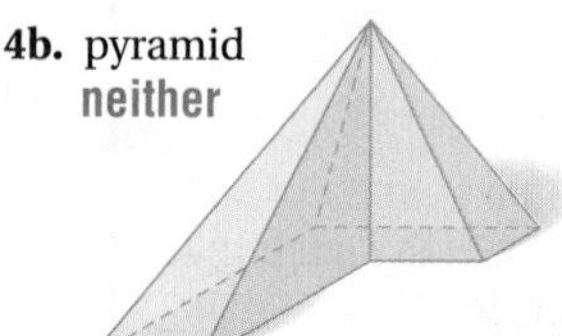

THINK AND DISCUSS

1. Explain how you could use scissors and paper to cut out a shape that has line symmetry.

2. Describe how you can find the angle of rotational symmetry for a regular polygon with n sides.

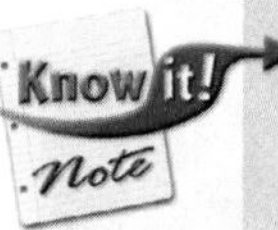

3. GET ORGANIZED Copy and complete the graphic organizer. In each region, draw a figure with the given type of symmetry.

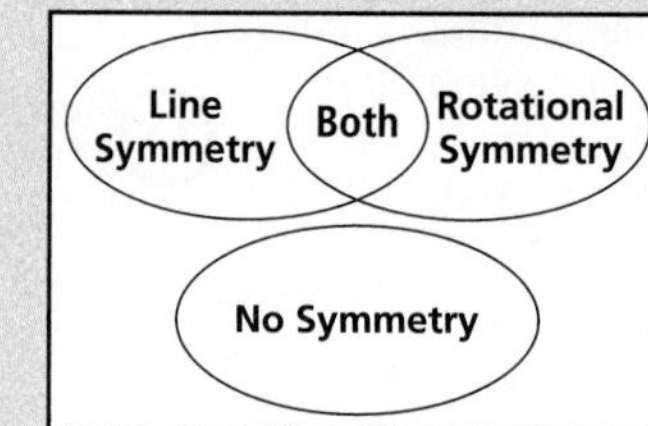

3 Close

Summarize

Have students name a letter of the alphabet with each type of symmetry:
- a horizontal line of symmetry B C D E
- a vertical line of symmetry A I M T U V W Y
- two lines of symmetry H O X
- rotational symmetry but not line symmetry N S Z
- no symmetry F G J K L P Q R

ONGOING ASSESSMENT and INTERVENTION

***Diagnose Before* the Lesson**
12-5 Warm Up, TE p. 856

***Monitor During* the Lesson**
Check It Out! Exercises, SE pp. 856–858
Questioning Strategies, TE pp. 857–858

***Assess After* the Lesson**
12-5 Lesson Quiz, TE p. 862
Alternative Assessment, TE p. 862

Answers to *Think and Discuss*

1. First, fold the paper in half. Cut out a design that goes up to the fold, then unfold the paper.
2. The ∠ of rotational symmetry is $\frac{360°}{n}$.
3. See p. A10.

12-5 Exercises

go.hrw.com
Homework Help Online
KEYWORD: MG7 12-5
Parent Resources Online
KEYWORD: MG7 Parent

GUIDED PRACTICE

Vocabulary Apply the vocabulary from this lesson to answer each question.

1. Describe the *line of symmetry* of an isosceles triangle.
The line of symmetry is the perpendicular bisector of the base.
2. The capital letter T has __?__ . (*line symmetry* or *rotational symmetry*)
line symmetry

SEE EXAMPLE 1 p. 856

Tell whether each figure has line symmetry. If so, copy the shape and draw all lines of symmetry.

3. 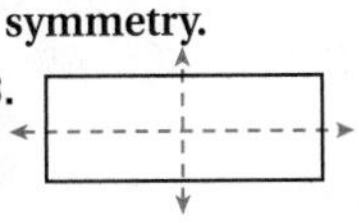 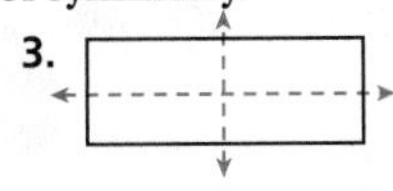
yes; two lines of symmetry

4. 
yes; one line of symmetry

5. 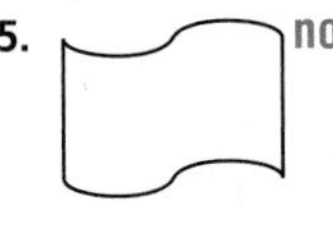 no

SEE EXAMPLE 2 p. 857

Tell whether each figure has rotational symmetry. If so, give the angle of rotational symmetry and the order of the symmetry.

6.  S yes; 180°; order: 2
7. 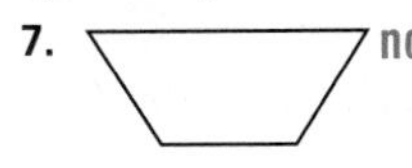 no
8.  yes; 120°; order: 3

SEE EXAMPLE 3 p. 857

9. **Architecture** The Pentagon in Alexandria, Virginia, is the world's largest office building. Copy the shape of the building and draw all lines of symmetry. Give the angle and order of rotational symmetry. 72°; order: 5

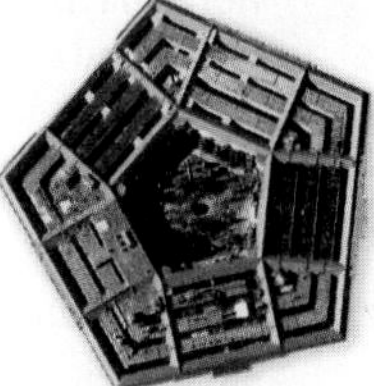

SEE EXAMPLE 4 p. 858

Tell whether each figure has plane symmetry, symmetry about an axis, or neither.

10. prism
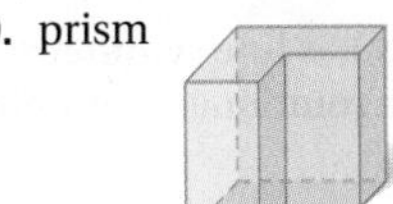
plane symmetry

11. cylinder

both

12. rectangular prism
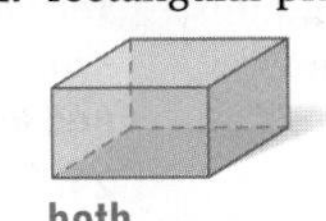
both

PRACTICE AND PROBLEM SOLVING

Independent Practice

For Exercises	See Example
13–15	1
16–18	2
19	3
20–22	4

Extra Practice
Skills Practice p. S27
Application Practice p. S39

Tell whether each figure has line symmetry. If so, copy the shape and draw all lines of symmetry.

13. 
yes; one line of symmetry

14. 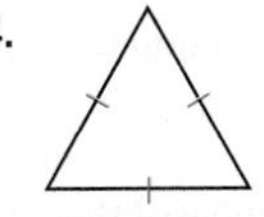
yes; three lines of symmetry

15. 

no

Tell whether each figure has rotational symmetry. If so, give the angle of rotational symmetry and the order of the symmetry.

16. 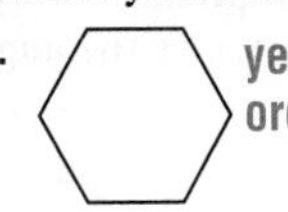 yes; 60°; order: 6
17.  yes; 72°; order: 5
18.  yes; 72°; order 5

Answers

9.
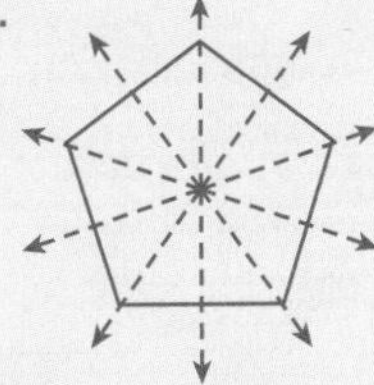

13.
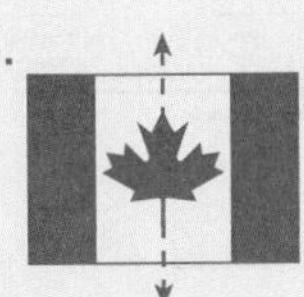

14.
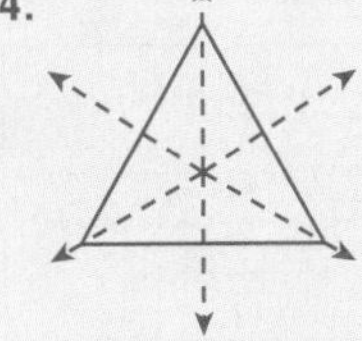

12-5 Exercises

Assignment Guide

Assign *Guided Practice* exercises as necessary.

If you finished Examples **1–2**
Basic 13–18, 23–32, 34–36, 38–42, 47–49
Average 13–18, 23–32, 34–36, 38–42, 47–49, 55
Advanced 13–18, 23–32, 34–36, 38–42, 47–49, 55–59

If you finished Examples **1–4**
Basic 13–43, 45, 47–49, 51–54, 63–69
Average 13–28, 30–55, 63–69
Advanced 13–28, 30–36 even, 37–69

Homework Quick Check
Quickly check key concepts.
Exercises: 14, 16, 19, 20, 24, 30

Visual To help students visualize a line of symmetry in **Exercise 14,** encourage them to copy the figure and use paper folding or a Mira to see if half of the image coincides with the other half.

State Resources

go.hrw.com
State Resources Online
KEYWORD: MG7 Resources

Kinesthetic Give students modeling clay to make the figures in **Exercises 20–22.** Have them use toothpicks to locate any axes of symmetry, and then slice the figures with string to verify plane symmetry.

Diversity Sand drawings like the one in **Exercise 33** are used as memory aids by the Chokwe people. The storyteller uses the drawing to help remember the story. The number of rows and columns in the sand drawing depends on the story it represents.

Answers

29–32. For graphs, see p. A31.

34. line symmetry; $x = 0$

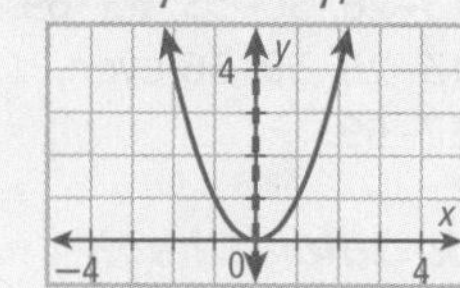

35. line symmetry; $x = 2$

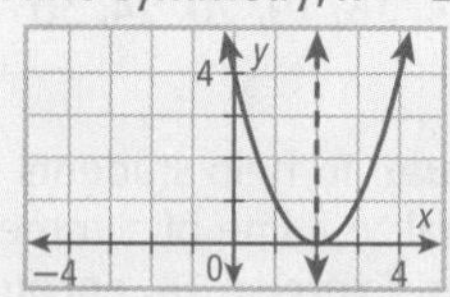

36. rotational symmetry; 180°; order: 2

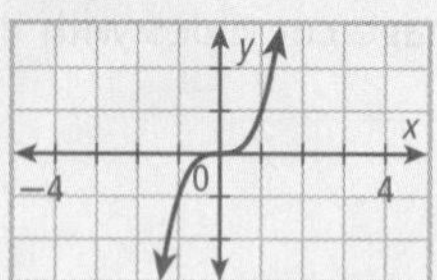

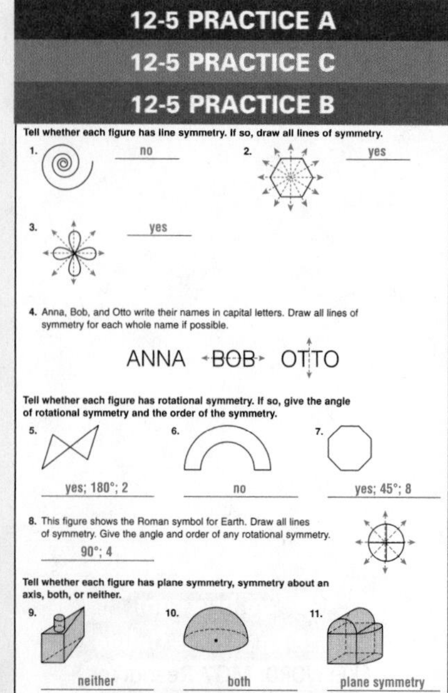

12-5 PRACTICE A

12-5 PRACTICE C

12-5 PRACTICE B

Tell whether each figure has line symmetry. If so, draw all lines of symmetry.

1. no
2. yes
3. yes

4. Anna, Bob, and Otto write their names in capital letters. Draw all lines of symmetry for each whole name if possible.

ANNA BOB OTTO

Tell whether each figure has rotational symmetry. If so, give the angle of rotational symmetry and the order of the symmetry.

5. yes; 180°; 2
6. no
7. yes; 45°; 8

8. This figure shows the Roman symbol for Earth. Draw all lines of symmetry. Give the angle and order of any rotational symmetry. 90°; 4

Tell whether each figure has plane symmetry, symmetry about an axis, both, or neither.

9. neither
10. both
11. plane symmetry

19\.

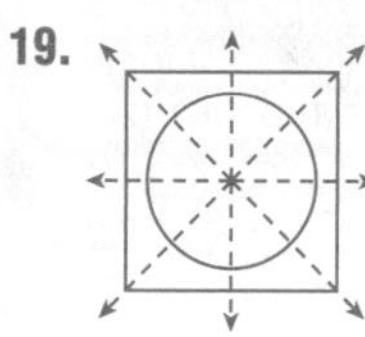

19. **Art** *Op art* is a style of art that uses optical effects to create an impression of movement in a painting or sculpture. The painting at right, *Vega-Tek*, by Victor Vasarely, is an example of op art. Sketch the shape in the painting and draw any lines of symmetry. If there is rotational symmetry, give the angle and order. **90°; order: 4**

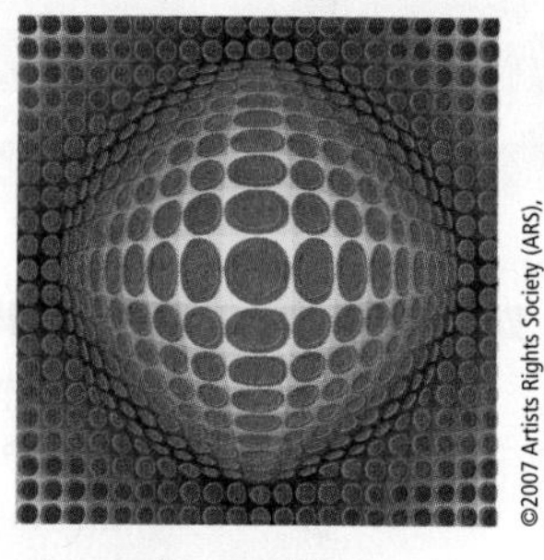

Tell whether each figure has plane symmetry, symmetry about an axis, or neither.

20. sphere **both**
21. triangular pyramid **neither**
22. torus **both**

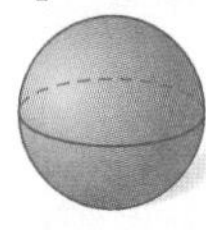 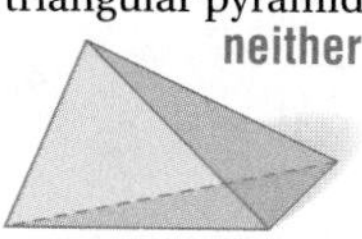 

Draw a triangle with the following number of lines of symmetry. Then classify the triangle.

23. exactly one line of symmetry
24. three lines of symmetry
25. no lines of symmetry

23. isosceles

24. equilateral

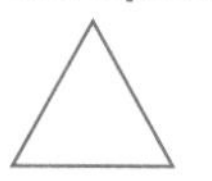

25. scalene

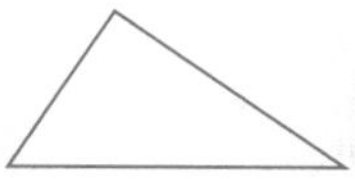

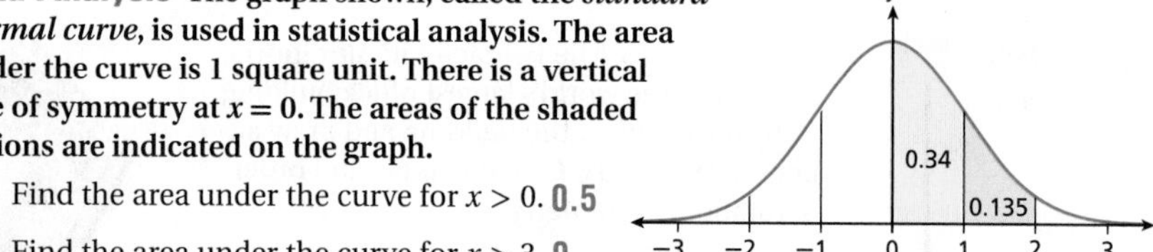

Data Analysis **The graph shown, called the *standard normal curve*, is used in statistical analysis. The area under the curve is 1 square unit. There is a vertical line of symmetry at $x = 0$. The areas of the shaded regions are indicated on the graph.**

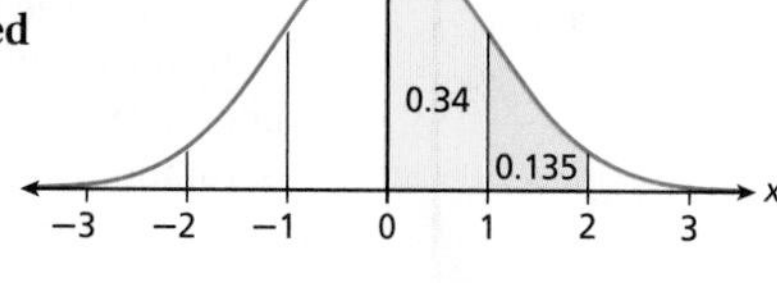

26. Find the area under the curve for $x > 0$. **0.5**
27. Find the area under the curve for $x > 3$. **0**
28. If a point under the curve is selected at random, what is the probability that the x-value of the point will be between -1 and 1? **0.68**

Tell whether the figure with the given vertices has line symmetry and/or rotational symmetry. Give the angle and order if there is rotational symmetry. Draw the figure and any lines of symmetry.

29. $A(-2, 2)$, $B(2, 2)$, $C(1, -2)$, $D(-1, -2)$ **line symmetry**
30. $R(-3, 3)$, $S(3, 3)$, $T(3, -3)$, $U(-3, -3)$
31. $J(4, 4)$, $K(-2, 2)$, $L(2, -2)$ **line symmetry**
32. $A(3, 1)$, $B(0, 2)$, $C(-3, 1)$, $D(-3, -1)$, $E(0, -2)$, $F(3, -1)$

30. line symmetry and rotational symmetry; 90°; order: 4

32. line symmetry and rotational symmetry; 180°; order: 2

33. **Art** The Chokwe people of Angola are known for their traditional sand designs. These complex drawings are traced out to illustrate stories that are told at evening gatherings. Classify the symmetry of the Chokwe design shown. **rotational symmetry of order 4**

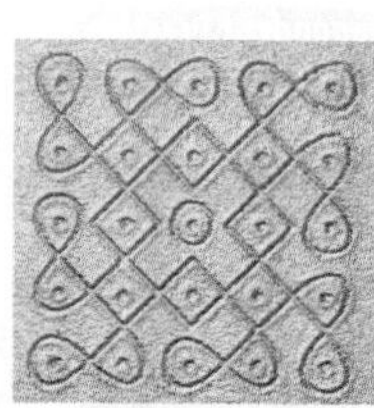

Algebra **Graph each function. Tell whether the graph has line symmetry and/or rotational symmetry. If there is rotational symmetry, give the angle and order. Write the equations of any lines of symmetry.**

34. $y = x^2$
35. $y = (x - 2)^2$
36. $y = x^3$

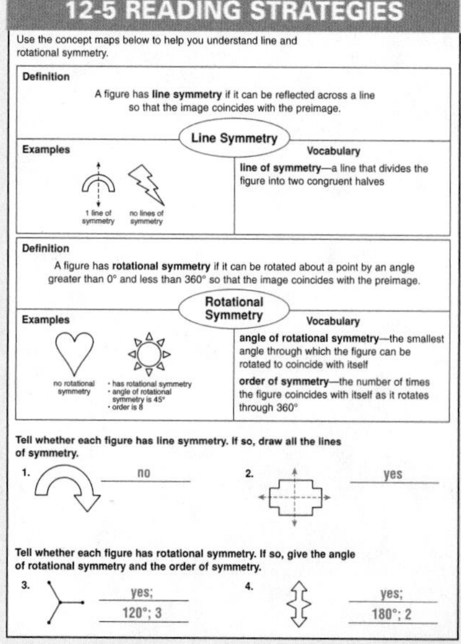

12-5 READING STRATEGIES

Use the concept maps below to help you understand line and rotational symmetry.

Definition: A figure has **line symmetry** if it can be reflected across a line so that the image coincides with the preimage.

Line Symmetry

Examples: 1 line of symmetry; no lines of symmetry

Vocabulary: **line of symmetry**—a line that divides the figure into two congruent halves

Definition: A figure has **rotational symmetry** if it can be rotated about a point by an angle greater than 0° and less than 360° so that the image coincides with the preimage.

Rotational Symmetry

Examples: no rotational symmetry; • has rotational symmetry • angle of rotational symmetry is 45° • order is 8

Vocabulary: **angle of rotational symmetry**—the smallest angle through which the figure can be rotated to coincide with itself; **order of symmetry**—the number of times the figure coincides with itself as it rotates through 360°

Tell whether each figure has line symmetry. If so, draw all the lines of symmetry.

1. no
2. yes

Tell whether each figure has rotational symmetry. If so, give the angle of rotational symmetry and the order of symmetry.

3. yes; 120°; 3
4. yes; 180°; 2

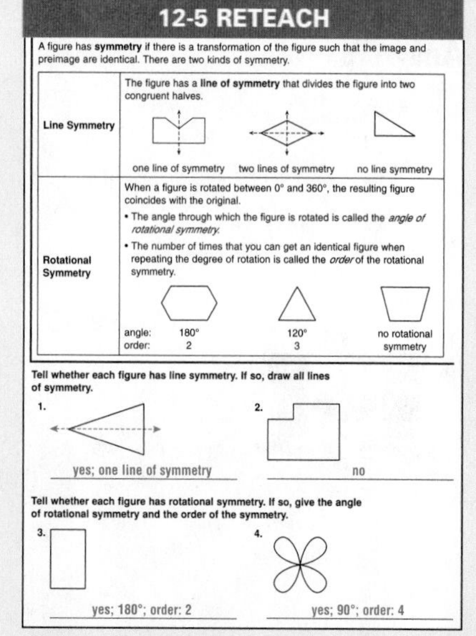

12-5 RETEACH

A figure has **symmetry** if there is a transformation of the figure such that the image and preimage are identical. There are two kinds of symmetry.

Line Symmetry: The figure has a **line of symmetry** that divides the figure into two congruent halves. one line of symmetry; two lines of symmetry; no line symmetry

Rotational Symmetry: When a figure is rotated between 0° and 360°, the resulting figure coincides with the original.
- The angle through which the figure is rotated is called the *angle of rotational symmetry*.
- The number of times that you can get an identical figure when repeating the degree of rotation is called the *order* of the rotational symmetry.

angle: 180°, order: 2; angle: 120°, order: 3; no rotational symmetry

Tell whether each figure has line symmetry. If so, draw all lines of symmetry.

1. yes; one line of symmetry
2. no

Tell whether each figure has rotational symmetry. If so, give the angle of rotational symmetry and the order of the symmetry.

3. yes; 180°; order: 2
4. yes; 90°; order: 4

37. This problem will prepare you for the Multi-Step Test Prep on page 880.

This woodcut on the right, entitled *Circle Limit III,* was made by Dutch artist M. C. Escher.

a. Does the woodcut have line symmetry? If so, describe the lines of symmetry. If not, explain why not.

b. Does the woodcut have rotational symmetry? If so, give the angle and order of the symmetry. If not, explain why not. **yes; 180°; 2**

c. Does your answer to part **b** change if color is not taken into account? Explain.

37a. No; there is no line that divides the woodcut into two identical reflected halves.
c. Yes; if color is not taken into account the angle of rotational symmetry is 90°.

45. It has rotational symmetry of order 3, with an angle of rotational symmetry of 120°.

46. The figures all have rotational symmetry of order 2.

50. If the angle of rotational symmetry is $x°$, then the order of the rotational symmetry is $\frac{360}{x}$. If the order of the rotational symmetry is x, then the angle of rotational symmetry is $\left(\frac{360}{x}\right)°$.

Classify the quadrilateral that meets the given conditions. First make a conjecture and then verify your conjecture by drawing a figure.

38. two lines of symmetry perpendicular to the sides and order-2 rotational symmetry **rectangle**

39. no line symmetry and order-2 rotational symmetry **parallelogram**

40. two lines of symmetry through opposite vertices and order-2 rotational symmetry **rhombus**

41. four lines of symmetry and order-4 rotational symmetry **square**

42. one line of symmetry through a pair of opposite vertices and no rotational symmetry **kite**

43. **Physics** High-speed photography makes it possible to analyze the physics behind a water splash. When a drop lands in a bowl of liquid, the splash forms a crown of evenly spaced points. What is the angle of rotational symmetry for a crown with 24 points? **15°**

44. **Critical Thinking** What can you conclude about a rectangle that has four lines of symmetry? Explain.

45. **Geography** The Isle of Man is an island in the Irish Sea. The island's symbol is a *triskelion* that consists of three running legs radiating from the center. Describe the symmetry of the triskelion.

46. **Critical Thinking** Draw several examples of figures that have two perpendicular lines of symmetry. What other type of symmetry do these figures have? Make a conjecture based on your observation.

Each figure shows part of a shape with a center of rotation and a given rotational symmetry. Copy and complete each figure.

47. order 4

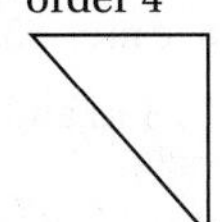

48. order 6

49. order 2

50. **Write About It** Explain the connection between the angle of rotational symmetry and the order of the rotational symmetry. That is, if you know one of these, explain how you can find the other.

In **Exercises 47–49,** students may attempt to reflect the figures over a line. Remind them that the center of rotation will map to itself and that all other points in the figure will be mapped to another position.

Exercise 37 involves identifying lines of symmetry and rotational symmetry as well as angles of rotational symmetry. This exercise prepares students for the Multi-Step Test Prep on page 880.

Answers

38.–42.

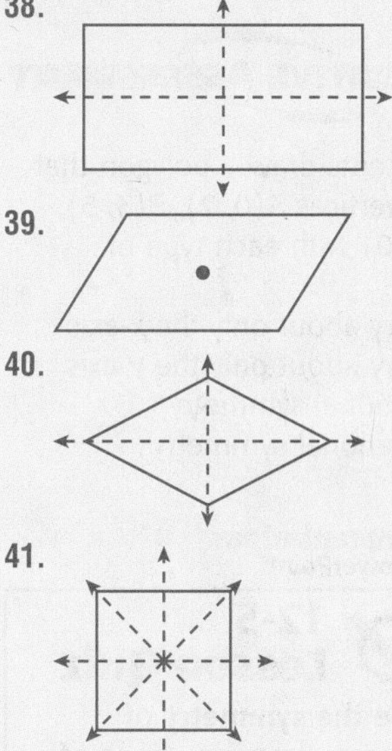

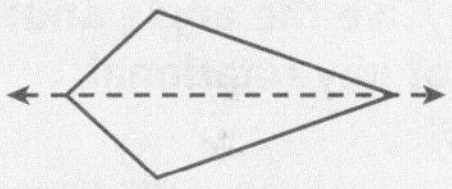

44. All rectangles have 2 lines of symmetry, 1 through the midpoints of each pair of opposite sides. The only other possible lines of symmetry are through opposite vertices, which means that the adjacent sides are congruent. Therefore, the rectangle must be a square.

47.–49.

12-5 PROBLEM SOLVING

1. Tell whether the window has line symmetry. If so, draw all the lines of symmetry. **yes**

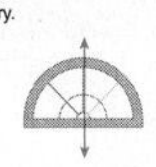

2. Tell whether the quilt block design has rotational symmetry. If so, give the angle of rotational symmetry and the order of the symmetry. **yes; 180°; order: 2**

3. Tell whether the hemisphere has plane symmetry, symmetry about an axis, both, or neither. **both**

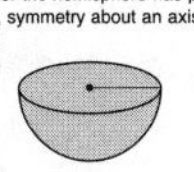

4. The figure is a net of an octahedron. Describe the symmetry of the net. **rotational symmetry of order 2**

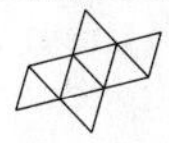

Choose the best answer.

5. Which is a true statement about the figure with vertices $Q(-2, -4)$, $R(0, 1)$, $S(8, 1)$, and $T(5, -4)$?
   A *QRST* has line symmetry only.
   B *QRST* has rotational symmetry only.
   C *QRST* has both line symmetry and rotational symmetry.
   (D) *QRST* has neither line symmetry nor rotational symmetry.

6. What is the order of rotational symmetry for the figure shown? 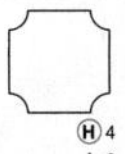
   F 2
   G 3
   (H) 4
   J 6

7. Which of these figures has exactly three lines of symmetry?
   A
   B
   C
   (D)

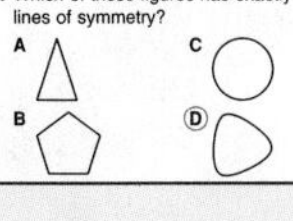

8. Consider the graphs of the following equations. Which graph has the line $x = 3$ as a line of symmetry?
   F $y = x^2 + 3$
   G $y = (x + 3)^2$
   (H) $y = (x - 3)^2$
   J $y = x^3$

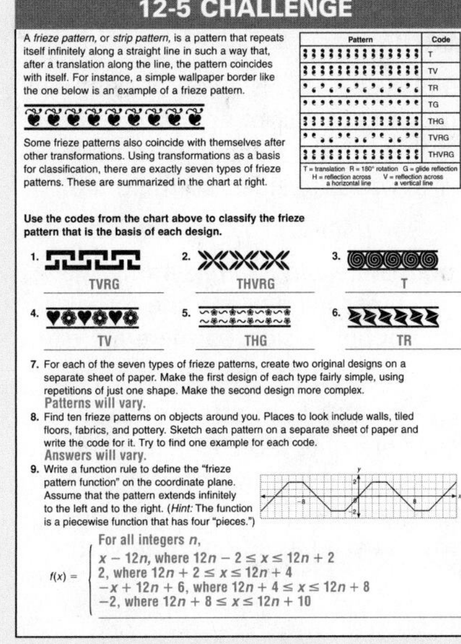

12-5 CHALLENGE

A *frieze pattern,* or *strip pattern,* is a pattern that repeats itself infinitely along a straight line in such a way that, after a translation along the line, the pattern coincides with itself. For instance, a simple wallpaper border like the one below is an example of a frieze pattern.

Some frieze patterns also coincide with themselves after other transformations. Using transformations as a basis for classification, there are exactly seven types of frieze patterns. These are summarized in the chart at right.

Pattern	Code
	T
	TV
	TR
	TG
	THG
	TVRG
	THVRG

T = translation R = 180° rotation G = glide reflection H = reflection across a horizontal line V = reflection across a vertical line

Use the codes from the chart above to classify the frieze pattern that is the basis of each design.

1. **TVRG**
2. **THVRG**
3. **T**
4. **TV**
5. **THG**
6. **TR**

7. For each of the seven types of frieze patterns, create two original designs on a separate sheet of paper. Make the first design of each type fairly simple, using repetitions of just one shape. Make the second design more complex. **Patterns will vary.**

8. Find ten frieze patterns on objects around you. Places to look include walls, tiled floors, fabrics, and pottery. Sketch each pattern on a separate sheet of paper and write the code for it. Try to find one example for each code. **Answers will vary.**

9. Write a function rule to define the "frieze pattern function" on the coordinate plane. Assume that the pattern extends infinitely to the left and to the right. (*Hint:* The function is a piecewise function that has four "pieces.")

For all integers n,

$$f(x) = \begin{cases} x - 12n, \text{ where } 12n - 2 \le x \le 12n + 2 \\ 2, \text{ where } 12n + 2 \le x \le 12n + 4 \\ -x + 12n + 6, \text{ where } 12n + 4 \le x \le 12n + 8 \\ -2, \text{ where } 12n + 8 \le x \le 12n + 10 \end{cases}$$

If students have difficulty with **Exercise 53,** remind them that when the y-axis is a line of symmetry, every point (x, y) has a mirror image $(-x, y)$ on the graph.

Critical Thinking For **Exercise 55,** encourage students to use inductive reasoning to write a formula for the angle of rotational symmetry.

Journal

Have students cut out pictures with symmetry from magazines or a newspaper. Have them tape the pictures to paper in their journal and describe the symmetry of each.

ALTERNATIVE ASSESSMENT

Have students draw a polygon that includes vertices $A(0, 2)$, $B(3, 5)$, and $C(1, 0)$ with each type of symmetry.

- symmetry about only the x-axis
- symmetry about only the y-axis
- 90° rotational symmetry
- 180° rotational symmetry

Power Presentations with PowerPoint®

12-5 Lesson Quiz

Describe the symmetry of each figure. Draw any lines of symmetry. Give the angle and the order of any rotational symmetry.

1.

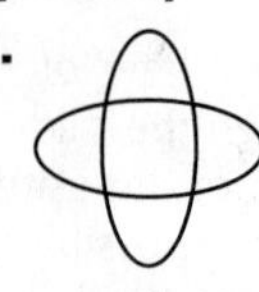

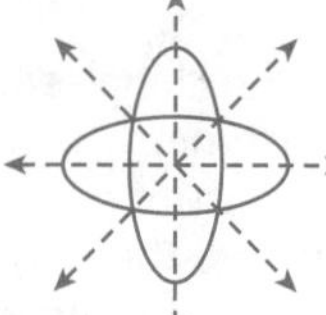

line symmetry and rotational symmetry; 90°; order: 4

2.

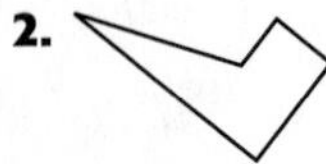

no symmetry

Tell whether each figure has plane symmetry, symmetry about an axis, or neither.

3.

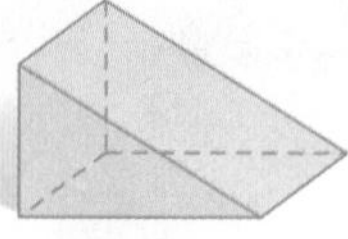

plane symmetry

4.

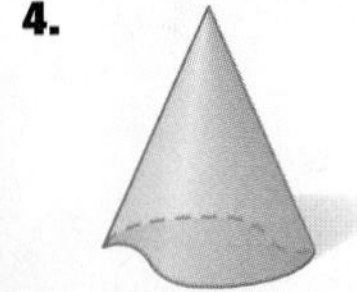

symmetry about an axis

Also available on transparency

TEST PREP

51. What is the order of rotational symmetry for the hexagon shown?

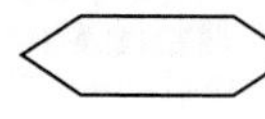

Ⓐ 2 Ⓑ 3 Ⓒ 4 Ⓓ 6

52. Which of these figures has exactly four lines of symmetry?

Ⓕ Regular octagon Ⓗ Isosceles triangle
Ⓖ Equilateral triangle Ⓙ Square

53. Consider the graphs of the following equations. Which graph has the y-axis as a line of symmetry?

Ⓐ $y = (x - 3)^2$ Ⓑ $y = x^3$ Ⓒ $y = x^2 - 3$ Ⓓ $y = |x + 3|$

54. Donnell designed a garden plot that has rotational symmetry, but not line symmetry. Which of these could be the shape of the plot?

Ⓕ  Ⓖ  Ⓗ  Ⓙ  

CHALLENGE AND EXTEND

55. A regular polygon has an angle of rotational symmetry of 5°. How many sides does the polygon have? 72

56. How many lines of symmetry does a regular n-gon have if n is even? if n is odd? Explain your reasoning. n; n

Find the equation of the line of symmetry for the graph of each function.

57. $y = (x + 4)^2$ $x = -4$ **58.** $y = |x - 2|$ $x = 2$ **59.** $y = 3x^2 + 5$ $x = 0$

Give the number of axes of symmetry for each regular polyhedron. Describe all axes of symmetry.

60. cube 13

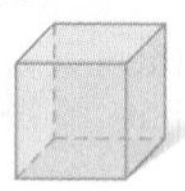

61. tetrahedron 8

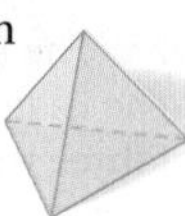

62. octahedron 13

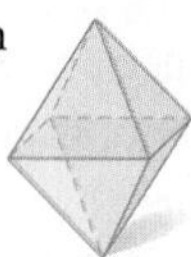

SPIRAL REVIEW

63. Shari worked 16 hours last week and earned \$197.12. The amount she earns in one week is directly proportional to the number of hours she works in that week. If Shari works 20 hours one week, how much does she earn? *(Previous course)* \$246.40

Find the slant height of each figure. *(Lesson 10-5)*

64. a right cone with radius 5 in. and surface area 61π in^2 7.2 in.

65. a square pyramid with lateral area 45 cm^2 and surface area 65.25 cm^2 5 cm

66. a regular triangular pyramid with base perimeter $24\sqrt{3}$ m and surface area $120\sqrt{3}$ m^2 6 m

Determine the coordinates of the final image of the point $P(-1, 4)$ under each composition of isometries. *(Lesson 12-4)*

$P'(6, -5)$ **67.** Reflect point P across the line $y = x$ and then translate it along the vector $\langle 2, -4\rangle$.

$P'(4, -1)$ **68.** Rotate point P by 90° about the origin and then reflect it across the y-axis.

$P'(0, -4)$ **69.** Translate point P along the vector $\langle 1, 0\rangle$ and then rotate it 180° about the origin.

Answers

56. If n is even, there is a line of symmetry through each pair of opposite vertices and through the midpoints of each pair of opposite sides, so there are $\frac{n}{2} + \frac{n}{2} = n$ lines of symmetry. If n is odd, there is a line of symmetry through each vertex and the midpoint of the opposite side, so there are n lines of symmetry.

60. a line through the centers of each pair of opposite faces (3 lines), a line through the midpoints of each pair of opposite edges (6 lines), and a line through each pair of opposite vertices (4 lines)

61. a line through each vertex and the center of the opposite face (4 lines) and a line through the midpoints of each pair of opposite edges (4 lines)

62. a line through the centers of each pair of opposite faces (4 lines), a line through the midpoints of each pair of opposite edges (6 lines), and a line through each pair of opposite vertices (3 lines)

EXTENSION

Solids of Revolution

Objectives
Understand how solids can be produced by rotating a two-dimensional figure through space.

Vocabulary
solid of revolution

If you rotate a rectangle around one of its sides, the path it makes through space is a cylinder. A **solid of revolution** is a three-dimensional figure that is formed by rotating a two-dimensional shape around an axis.

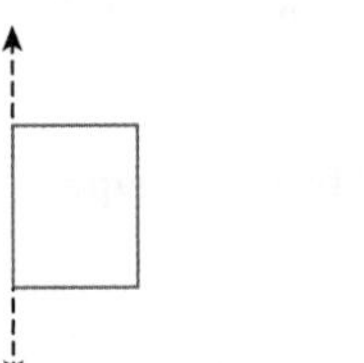
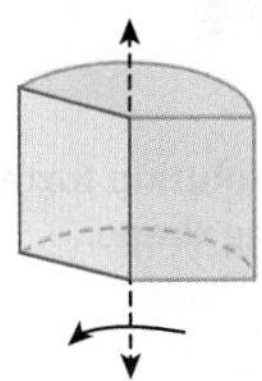
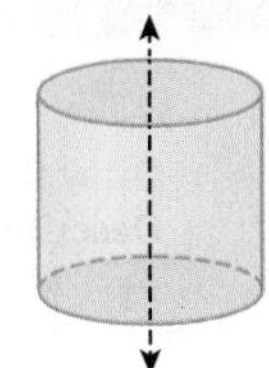

EXAMPLE 1 Sketching a Solid of Revolution

Draw the solid of revolution formed by the shape rotated around the axis given. Describe the resulting shape.

A right triangle rotated around an axis that passes through one of the legs forms a cone.

1. A donut shape, also called a torus.

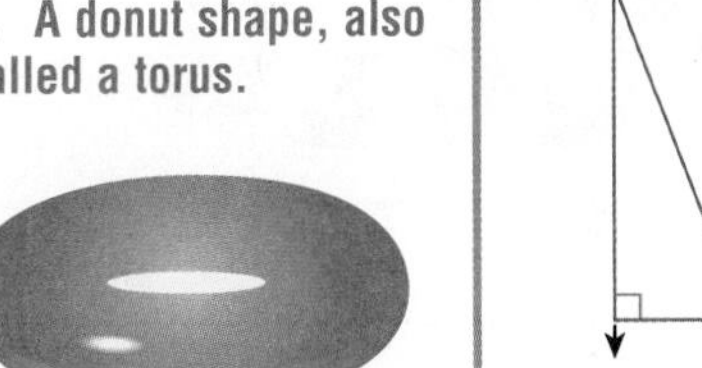

CHECK IT OUT!

1. Draw the solid of revolution formed by the given shape rotated around the axis given. Describe the resulting shape.

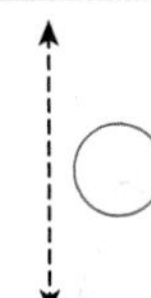

EXAMPLE 2 Recreation Application

A chess pawn is a solid of revolution. Draw a two-dimensional shape and an axis of rotation that could form the pawn.

The two-dimensional shape should match the outline of one side of the pawn.

CHAPTER 12 Organizer

Pacing: Traditional 1 day
Block $\frac{1}{2}$ day

Objectives: Draw and analyze figures that can be formed by rotating a two-dimensional shape around an axis.

Using the Extension

In Chapter 10, students learned about the properties of three-dimensional shapes, and in Lesson 12-5, they learned about rotational symmetry. In this extension, students will combine the two concepts to learn about solids of revolution.

Power Presentations with PowerPoint®

Additional Examples

Example 1

Draw the solid of revolution formed by the shape rotated around the axis given. Describe the resulting shape.

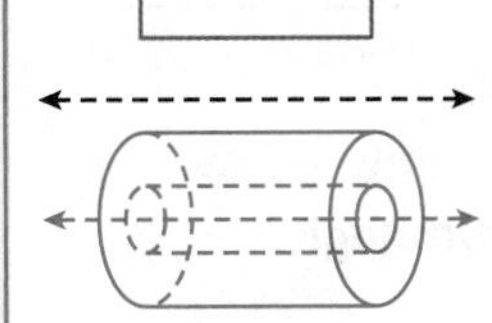

a cylinder with the center removed

INTERVENTION 
Questioning Strategies

EXAMPLE 1

- How would the solid be different if the axis of rotation were horizontal?

1 Introduce

Motivate

To help students visualize the cylinder in the lesson opener, use a pencil or straw as an axis. Tape a cardboard rectangle to the pencil and turn the shape in your hands to demonstrate the shape that the rectangle traces out.

2 Teach

Guided Instruction

Review the definition of a rotation in the plane. Explain to students that they can think of a circle as a point rotated about another fixed point in the plane. In a similar way, a two-dimensional shape rotated through space will form a solid.

State Resources

go.hrw.com
State Resources Online
KEYWORD: MG7 Resources

For Exercises 5 and 6, students may be confused about how to find the height and radii of the solids of revolution. Remind them that they need to find the distance between the points given in the graphs and the origin (0, 0, 0).

Power Presentations with PowerPoint®

Additional Examples

Example 2

Draw a two-dimensional shape and axis of rotation that could form each figure.

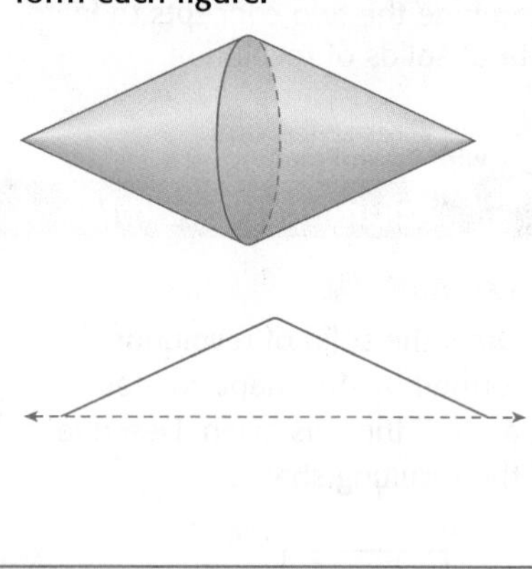

INTERVENTION

Questioning Strategies

EXAMPLE 2

- How could you use tracing paper to draw the two-dimensional shape?

Answers

2.

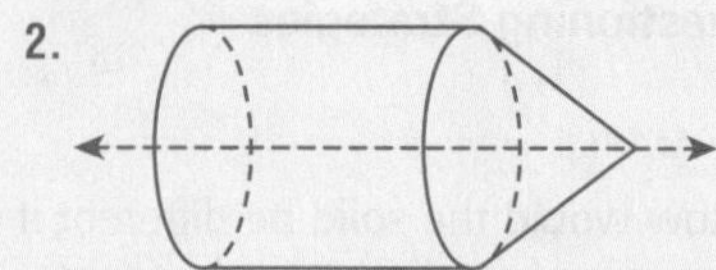

2. Draw a two-dimensional shape and axis of rotation that could form the sports drink bottle.

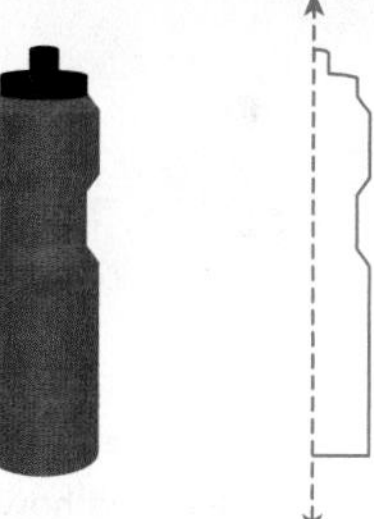

EXTENSION

Exercises

Draw the solid of revolution formed by each shape rotated around the axis given. Describe the resulting shape.

1.

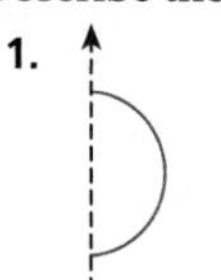

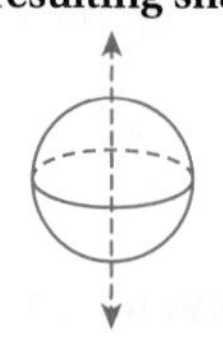

2.

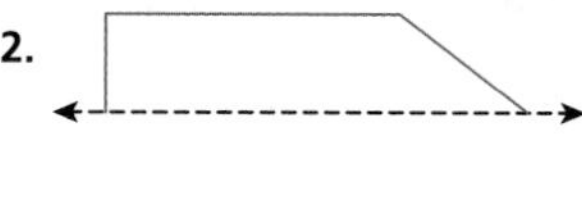

Draw a two-dimensional shape and axis of rotation that could form each figure.

3.

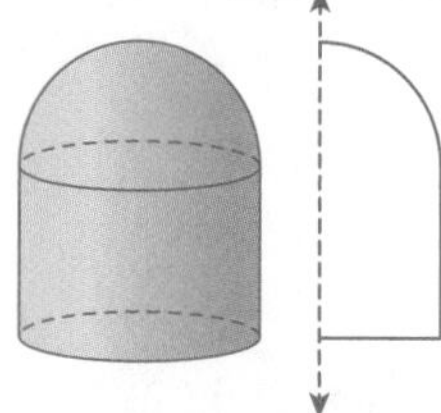

4.

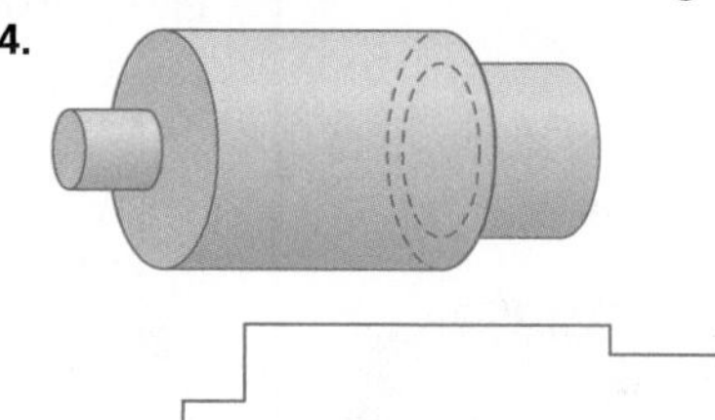

Draw the solid of revolution formed by each shape rotated around the z-axis. Then find the volume of the solid to the nearest tenth of a unit.

5. 62.8 units^3

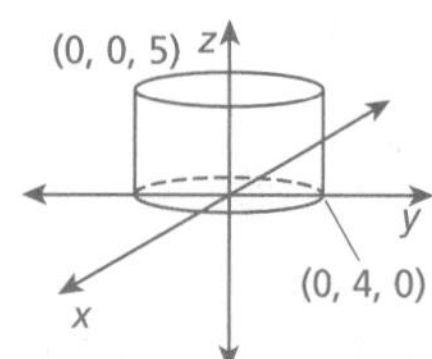

5.

z
(0, 0, 5)
(0, 4, 0) y
x

6. 18.8 units^3

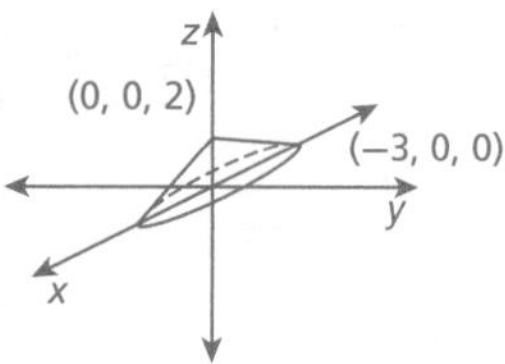

6.

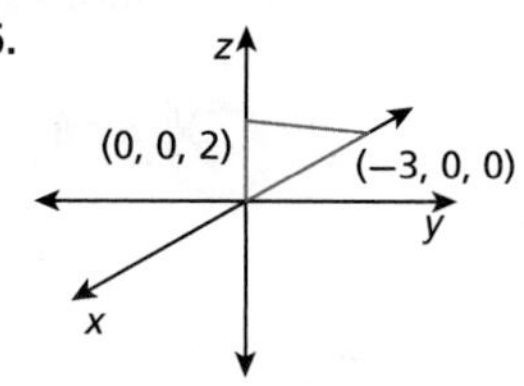

7. **Critical Thinking** If you find the cross section of a solid of revolution in a plane that's perpendicular to the axis of rotation, you will always get the same shape. What is it? Use drawings to support your answer.
Circle. Check students' drawings

8. **Write About It** Will rotation of the blue figure about either axis shown in the figure produce a sphere? Explain why or why not.
Only rotation about the vertical axis will produce a sphere. Rotation about the horizontal axis will form a hemisphere.

9. **Challenge** Is an oblique cylinder a solid of revolution? Explain your reasoning.
No. Students explanations may vary. Sample: An oblique cylinder does not have rotational symmetry, so you cannot draw a shape and an axis of rotation that could form the cylinder.

3 Close

Summarize

Review the definition of solid of revolution and discuss what two-dimensional figures can be used to create a cone, cylinder, and sphere.

12-6 Tessellations

Objectives
Use transformations to draw tessellations.

Identify regular and semiregular tessellations and figures that will tessellate.

Vocabulary
translation symmetry
frieze pattern
glide reflection symmetry
tessellation
regular tessellation
semiregular tessellation

Who uses this?
Repeating patterns play an important role in traditional Native American art.

A pattern has **translation symmetry** if it can be translated along a vector so that the image coincides with the preimage. A **frieze pattern** is a pattern that has translation symmetry along a line.

Both of the frieze patterns shown below have translation symmetry. The pattern on the right also has *glide reflection symmetry*. A pattern with **glide reflection symmetry** coincides with its image after a glide reflection.

EXAMPLE 1 ***Art Application***

Identify the symmetry in each frieze pattern.

A

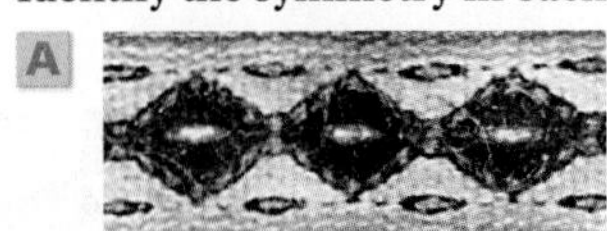

translation symmetry and glide reflection symmetry

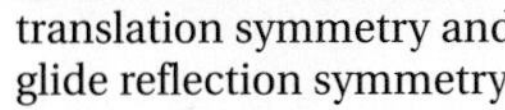

B

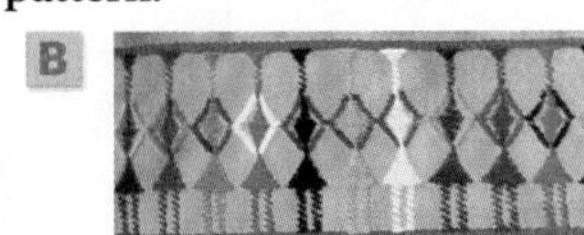

translation symmetry

Helpful Hint

When you are given a frieze pattern, you may assume that the pattern continues forever in both directions.

CHECK IT OUT! **Identify the symmetry in each frieze pattern.**

1a.

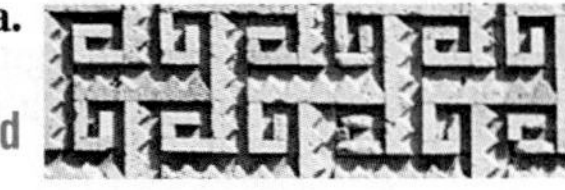

1b.

1a. translation symmetry
1b. translation symmetry and glide reflection symmetry

A **tessellation**, or *tiling*, is a repeating pattern that completely covers a plane with no gaps or overlaps. The measures of the angles that meet at each vertex must add up to 360°.

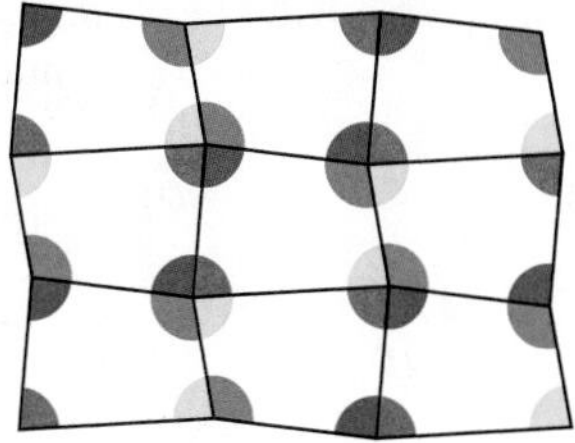

In the tessellation shown, each angle of the quadrilateral occurs once at each vertex. Because the angle measures of any quadrilateral add to 360°, any quadrilateral can be used to tessellate the plane. Four copies of the quadrilateral meet at each vertex.

12-6 Organizer

Pacing: Traditional 1 day
Block $\frac{1}{2}$ day

Objectives: Use transformations to draw tessellations.

Identify regular and semiregular tessellations and figures that will tessellate.

Technology Lab
In Technology Lab Activities

PREMIER **Online Edition**
Tutorial Videos, Interactivity

Power Presentations with PowerPoint®

Warm Up

Find the sum of the interior angle measures of each polygon.

1. quadrilateral 360°
2. octagon 1080°

Find the interior angle measure of each regular polygon.

3. square 90°
4. pentagon 108°
5. hexagon 120°
6. octagon 135°

Also available on transparency

Math Humor

Q: Why did the mathematician put the figure in the icebox?

A: She wanted to make a frieze pattern!

1 Introduce

EXPLORATION

12-6 Tessellations

A *tessellation* is a repeating pattern that completely covers a plane with no gaps or overlaps.

1. Fold a sheet of paper in half three times, as shown.

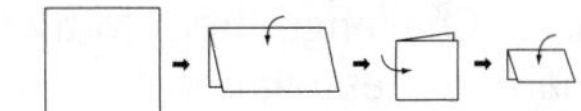

2. Draw a triangle on the folded paper and then cut it out. This will produce eight congruent triangles.
3. Arrange the triangles to form a pattern that you could continue indefinitely to cover a plane. Sketch the pattern.
4. Repeat the process by drawing a different triangle on the folded paper. Can you use this triangle to make a tessellation?
5. Do you think it is possible to use *any* triangle to make a tessellation?

THINK AND DISCUSS

6. **Discuss** how you can use this figure and the Triangle Sum Theorem to explain why any

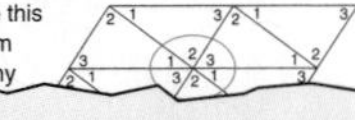

Motivate

Accordion-fold a strip of paper and then fold it in half again. Cut out half of a paper doll on the fold. Then unfold the paper and show the students the chain of dolls. Have students fold a piece of paper and cut out their own chains of objects. If a chain continued infinitely in both directions, it would form a frieze pattern with translation symmetry. Have students draw a translation vector from any point on one doll to the corresponding point on the adjacent doll.

Explorations and answers are provided in *Alternate Openers: Explorations Transparencies.*

State Resources

go.hrw.com
State Resources Online
KEYWORD: MG7 Resources

Example 1

Identify the symmetry in each wallpaper border pattern.

A. 

translation symmetry

B. translation symmetry and glide reflection symmetry

Example 2

Copy the given figure and use it to create a tessellation.

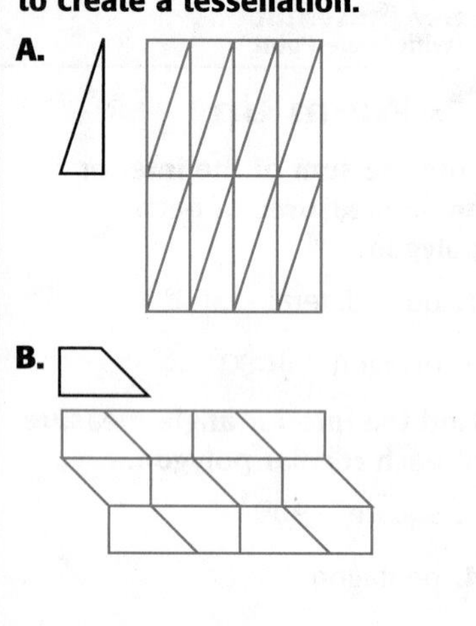

A.

B.

INTERVENTION

Questioning Strategies

EXAMPLE 1

- How can you tell if a pattern has translation symmetry or glide reflection symmetry?

EXAMPLE 2

- Do you have to first rotate the figures to create tessellations? Explain.

Kinesthetic For **Example 2,** suggest that students trace and cut out the figures and use them to follow the steps to create the tessellations.

The angle measures of any triangle add up to 180°. This means that any triangle can be used to tessellate a plane. Six copies of the triangle meet at each vertex, as shown.

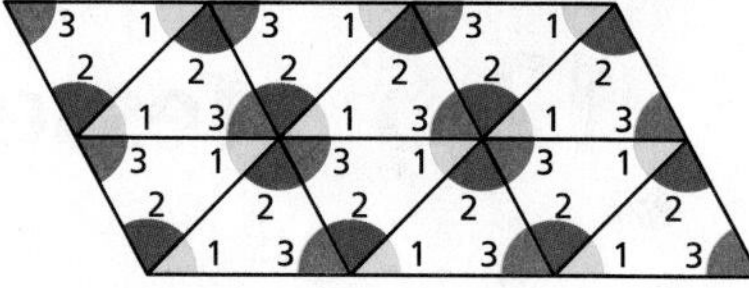

$$m\angle 1 + m\angle 2 + m\angle 3 = 180°$$
$$m\angle 1 + m\angle 2 + m\angle 3 + m\angle 1 + m\angle 2 + m\angle 3 = 360°$$

EXAMPLE 2 Using Transformations to Create Tessellations

Copy the given figure and use it to create a tessellation.

A 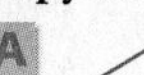

Step 1 Rotate the triangle 180° about the midpoint of one side.

Step 2 Translate the resulting pair of triangles to make a row of triangles.

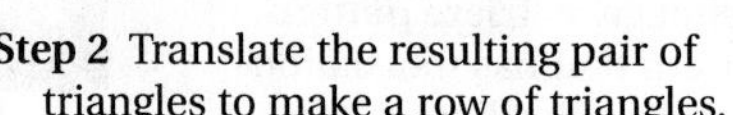

Step 3 Translate the row of triangles to make a tessellation.

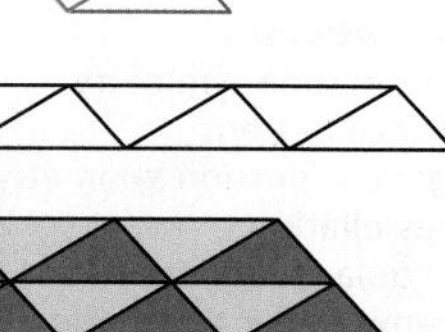

B 

Step 1 Rotate the quadrilateral 180° about the midpoint of one side.

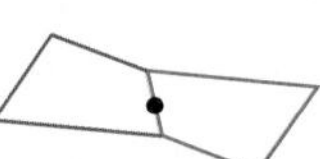

Step 2 Translate the resulting pair of quadrilaterals to make a row of quadrilaterals.

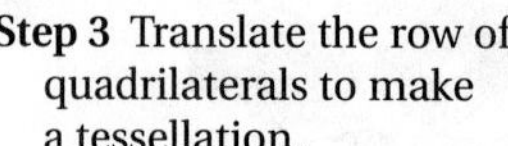

Step 3 Translate the row of quadrilaterals to make a tessellation.

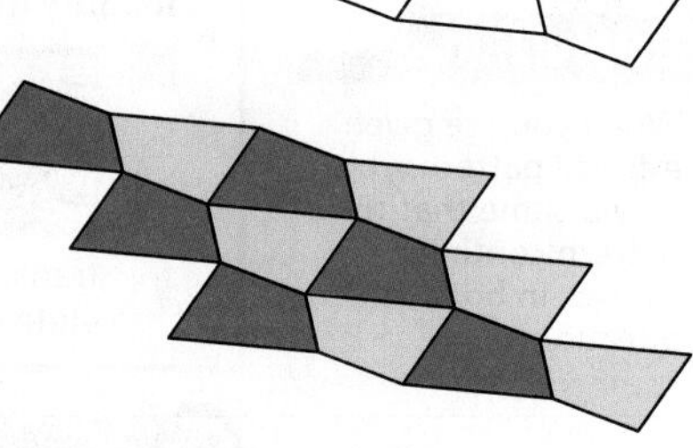

2. 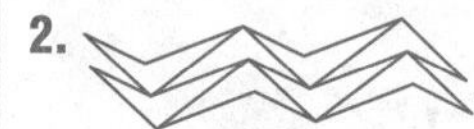

CHECK IT OUT! 2. Copy the given figure and use it to create a tessellation.

A **regular tessellation** is formed by congruent regular polygons. A **semiregular tessellation** is formed by two or more different regular polygons, with the same number of each polygon occurring in the same order at every vertex.

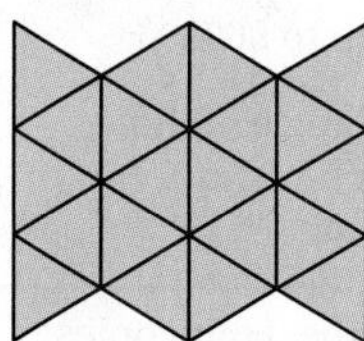

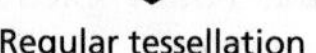

Regular tessellation

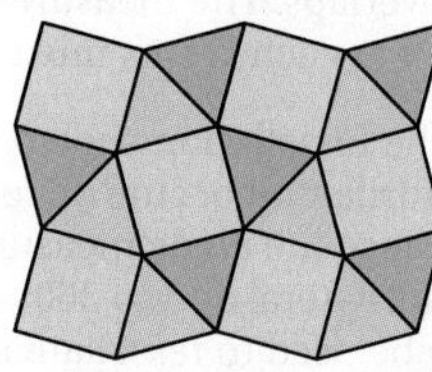

Semiregular tessellation

Every vertex has two squares and three triangles in this order: square, triangle, square, triangle, triangle.

2 Teach

Guided Instruction

Review line and rotational symmetry. If a pattern has translation symmetry, it must continue infinitely, both in the direction of the translation vector and in the opposite direction. Tessellations can have translation symmetry along more than one vector and can also have line and rotational symmetry.

Reaching All Learners

Through Multiple Representations

Have students use geometry software to create the tessellations in the examples and the exercises. Challenge them to try to create more than one tessellation from the same figure or figures.

Student to Student

Tessellations

Ryan Gray
Sunset High School

When I need to decide if given figures can be used to tessellate a plane, I look at angle measures. To form a regular tessellation, the angle measures of a regular polygon must be a divisor of 360°. To form a semiregular tessellation, the angle measures around a vertex must add up to 360°.

For example, regular octagons and equilateral triangles cannot be used to make a semiregular tessellation because no combination of 135° and 60° adds up to exactly 360°.

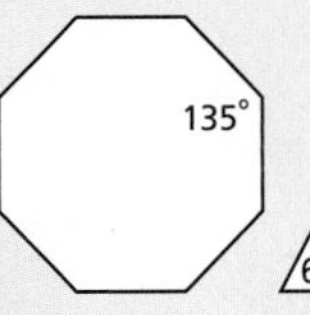

EXAMPLE 3 **Classifying Tessellations**

Classify each tessellation as regular, semiregular, or neither.

A

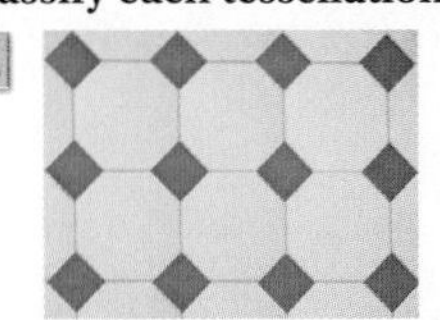

Two regular octagons and one square meet at each vertex. The tessellation is semiregular.

B

Only squares are used. The tessellation is regular.

C

Irregular hexagons are used in the tessellation. It is neither regular nor semiregular.

CHECK IT OUT! **Classify each tessellation as regular, semiregular, or neither.**

3a.

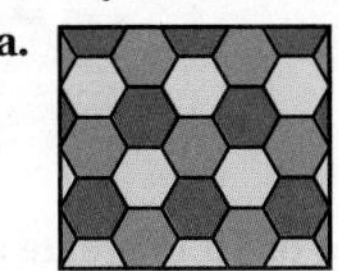

regular

3b.

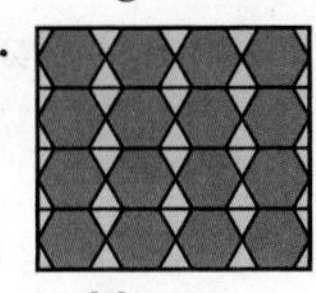

neither

3c.

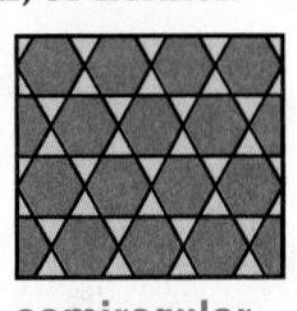

semiregular

EXAMPLE 4 **Determining Whether Polygons Will Tessellate**

Determine whether the given regular polygon(s) can be used to form a tessellation. If so, draw the tessellation.

A

No; each angle of the pentagon measures 108°, and 108 is not a divisor of 360.

B

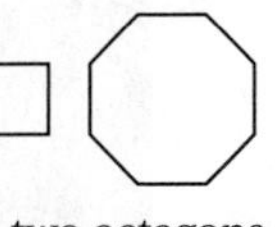

Yes; two octagons and one square meet at each vertex.
$135° + 135° + 90° = 360°$

4a.

CHECK IT OUT! **Determine whether the given regular polygon(s) can be used to form a tessellation. If so, draw the tessellation.**

4a.

yes

4b.

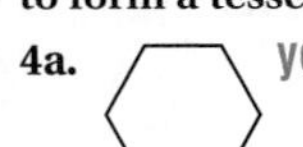

no

3 Close

Summarize

Draw a triangle and show students how to translate it repeatedly to create a frieze pattern. Then show how to translate the entire row of triangles to create a tessellation.

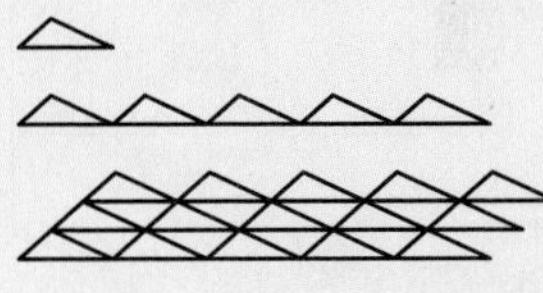

ONGOING ASSESSMENT and INTERVENTION

*Diagnose **Before** the Lesson*
12-6 Warm Up, TE p. 863

*Monitor **During** the Lesson*
Check It Out! Exercises, SE pp. 863–865
Questioning Strategies, TE pp. 864–865

*Assess **After** the Lesson*
12-6 Lesson Quiz, TE p. 869
Alternative Assessment, TE p. 869

Power Presentations with PowerPoint®

Additional Examples

Example 3

Classify each tessellation as regular, semiregular, or neither.

A.

neither

B.

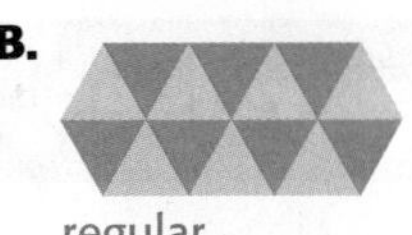

regular

C.

semiregular

Example 4

Determine whether the given regular polygon(s) can be used to form a tessellation. If so, draw the tessellation.

A.

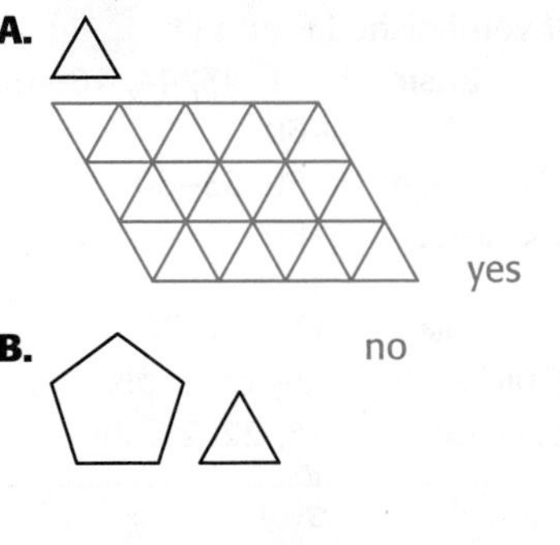

yes

B. no

INTERVENTION
Questioning Strategies

EXAMPLE 3

- What is the difference between a regular tessellation and a semiregular tessellation?

EXAMPLE 4

- What is the sum of the measures of all the angles that meet at each vertex of a tessellation?

Answers to *Think and Discuss*

Possible answers:

1. In a pattern that has glide reflection symmetry, you go from 1 figure to the next by a composition of a translation and a reflection.
2. It is not possible. No matter how the ⊙s are arranged to cover the plane, there will always be overlaps or gaps between them.
3. See p. A10.

THINK AND DISCUSS

1. Explain how you can identify a frieze pattern that has glide reflection symmetry.
2. Is it possible to tessellate a plane using circles? Why or why not?
3. **GET ORGANIZED** Copy and complete the graphic organizer.

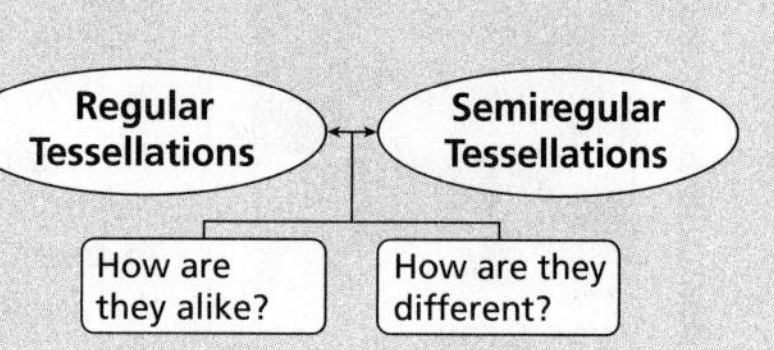

Know it! Note

12-6 Exercises

12-6 Exercises

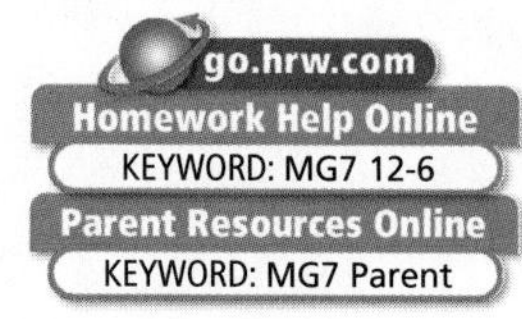

Assignment Guide

Assign *Guided Practice* exercises as necessary.

If you finished Examples **1–2**
- **Basic** 15–20, 28–33, 37–41
- **Average** 15–20, 28–33, 37–41 43, 44
- **Advanced** 15–20, 28–33, 37–41 43, 44, 49

If you finished Examples **1–4**
- **Basic** 15–41, 43, 44, 46–48, 53–60
- **Average** 15–50, 53–60
- **Advanced** 15–60

Homework Quick Check

Quickly check key concepts.
Exercises: 16, 18, 22, 24, 28

Answers

3–8. See p. A31.
13. For tessellation, see p. A31.

State Resources

go.hrw.com
State Resources Online
KEYWORD: MG7 Resources

GUIDED PRACTICE

Vocabulary Apply the vocabulary from this lesson to answer each question.

1. Sketch a pattern that has *glide reflection symmetry.*

1. Possible answer:

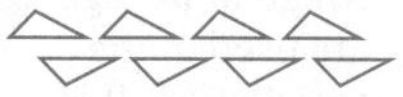

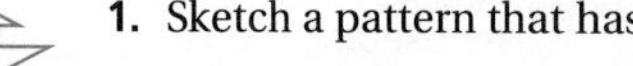

2. Describe a real-world example of a *regular tessellation.*

Possible answers: checkerboard, hexagonal floor tiles, honeycomb

SEE EXAMPLE 1 p. 865

Transportation The tread of a tire is the part that makes contact with the ground. Various tread patterns help improve traction and increase durability. Identify the symmetry in each tread pattern.

3. 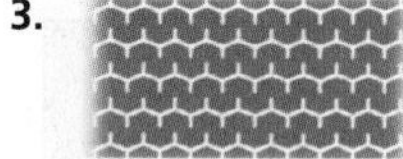
4. 
5. 

SEE EXAMPLE 2 p. 866

Copy the given figure and use it to create a tessellation.

6. 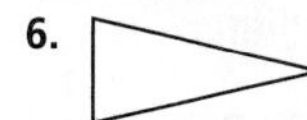
7. 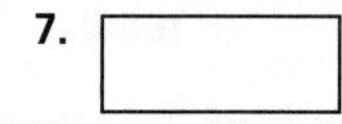
8. 

SEE EXAMPLE 3 p. 867

Classify each tessellation as regular, semiregular, or neither.

9. 
regular

10.  neither

11. 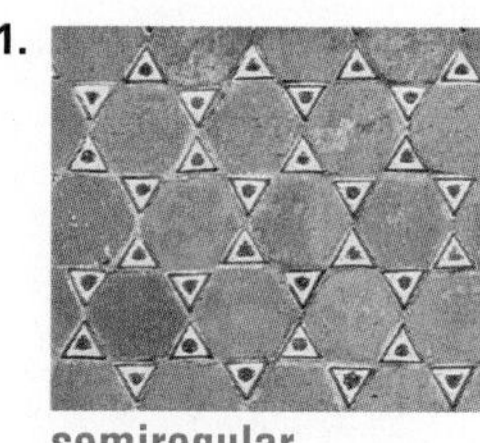
semiregular

SEE EXAMPLE 4 p. 867

Determine whether the given regular polygon(s) can be used to form a tessellation. If so, draw the tessellation.

12. 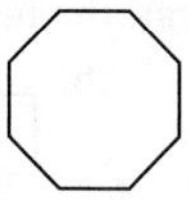 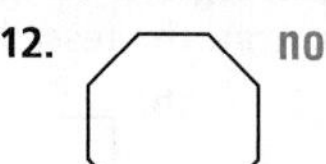 no
13. 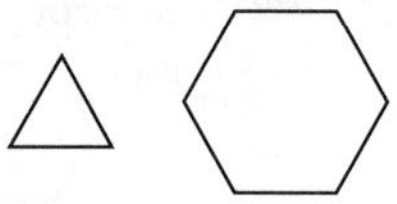 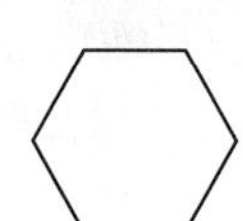 yes
14. 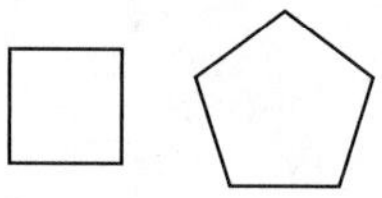 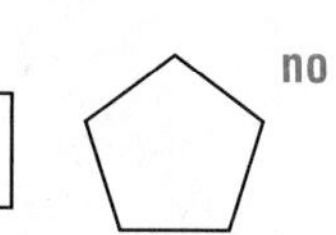 no

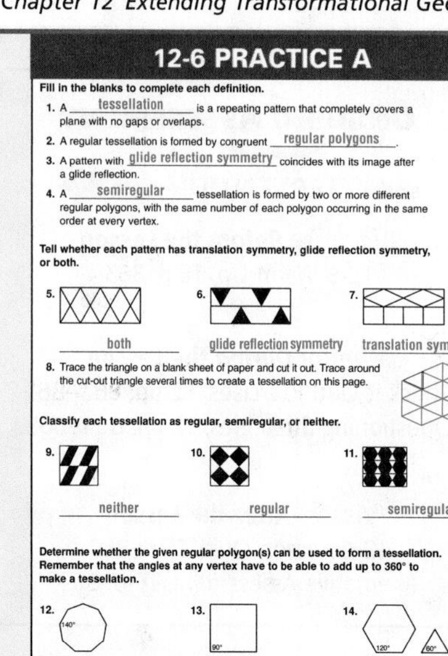

12-6 PRACTICE A

Fill in the blanks to complete each definition.

1. A tessellation is a repeating pattern that completely covers a plane with no gaps or overlaps.
2. A regular tessellation is formed by congruent regular polygons.
3. A pattern with glide reflection symmetry coincides with its image after a glide reflection.
4. A semiregular tessellation is formed by two or more different regular polygons, with the same number of each polygon occurring in the same order at every vertex.

Tell whether each pattern has translation symmetry, glide reflection symmetry, or both.

5. both
6. glide reflection symmetry
7. translation symmetry

8. Trace the triangle on a blank sheet of paper and cut it out. Trace around the cut-out triangle several times to create a tessellation on this page.

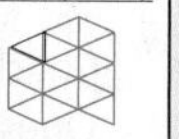

Classify each tessellation as regular, semiregular, or neither.

9. neither
10. regular
11. semiregular

Determine whether the given regular polygon(s) can be used to form a tessellation. Remember that the angles at any vertex have to be able to add up to 360° to make a tessellation.

12. 140° no
13. 90° yes
14. 120° 60° yes

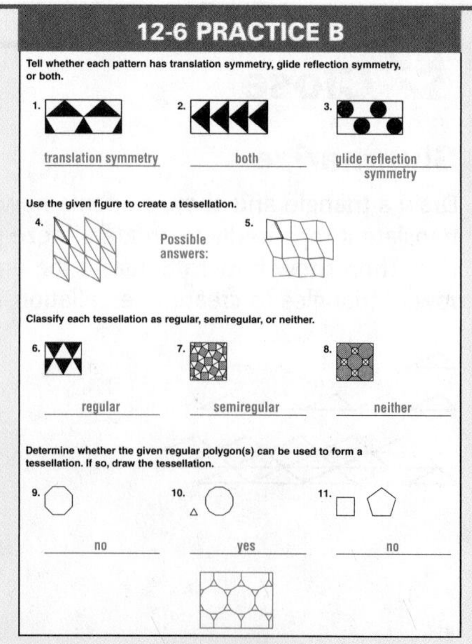

12-6 PRACTICE B

Tell whether each pattern has translation symmetry, glide reflection symmetry, or both.

1. translation symmetry
2. both
3. glide reflection symmetry

Use the given figure to create a tessellation.

4. 5. Possible answers:

Classify each tessellation as regular, semiregular, or neither.

6. regular
7. semiregular
8. neither

Determine whether the given regular polygon(s) can be used to form a tessellation. If so, draw the tessellation.

9. no
10. yes
11. no

PRACTICE AND PROBLEM SOLVING

Independent Practice

For Exercises	See Example
15–17	1
18–20	2
21–23	3
24–26	4

Extra Practice
Skills Practice p. S27
Application Practice p. S39

Interior Decorating Identify the symmetry in each wallpaper border.

15.  translation symmetry

16. 16. translation symmetry and glide reflection symmetry

17.  translation symmetry

Copy the given figure and use it to create a tessellation.

18. 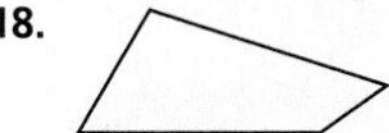

19. 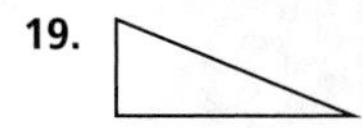

20. 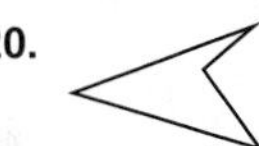

Classify each tessellation as regular, semiregular, or neither.

21. 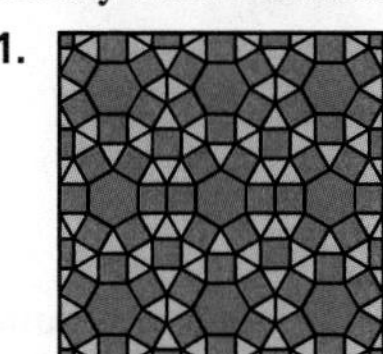 neither

22.  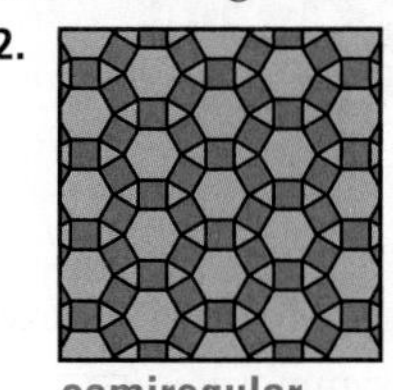 semiregular

23. 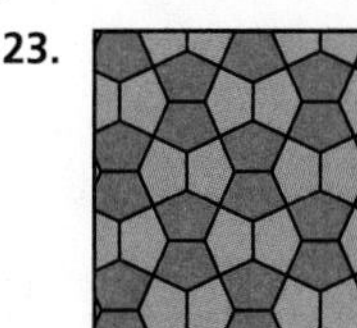 neither

Determine whether the given regular polygon(s) can be used to form a tessellation. If so, draw the tessellation.

24. no

25.  no

26. yes 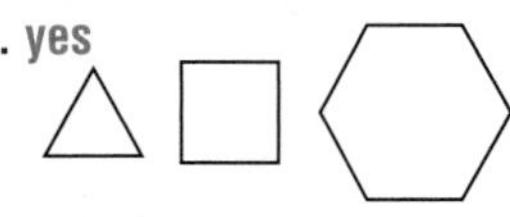

26.  

27. **Physics** A truck moving down a road creates whirling pockets of air called a *vortex train*. Use the figure to classify the symmetry of a vortex train.

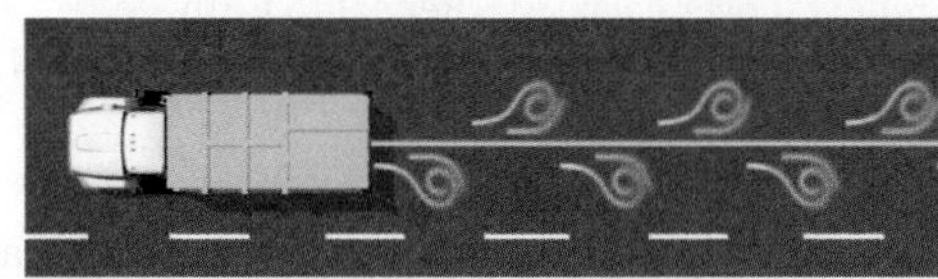

translation symmetry and glide reflection symmetry

Identify all of the types of symmetry (translation, glide reflection, and/or rotation) in each tessellation.

28. 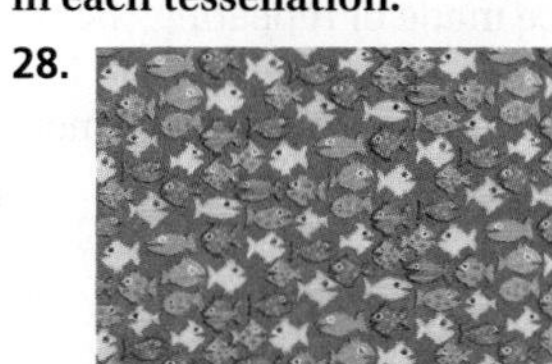 translation

29. 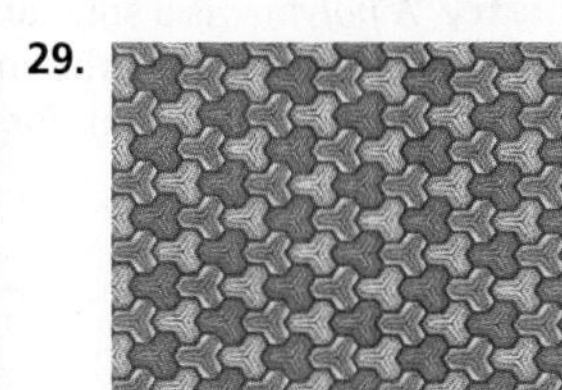 translation, glide reflection, rotation

30. 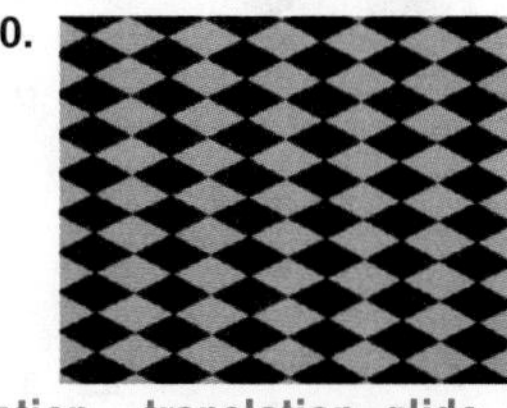 translation, glide reflection, rotation

Tell whether each statement is sometimes, always, or never true.

31. A triangle can be used to tessellate a plane. always
32. A frieze pattern has glide reflection symmetry. sometimes
33. The angles at a vertex of a tessellation add up to 360°. always
34. It is possible to use a regular pentagon to make a regular tessellation. never
35. A semiregular tessellation includes scalene triangles. never

COMMON ERROR ALERT

Students may answer *semiregular* to **Exercise 21** because all of the polygons in the tessellation are regular. Remind them that the same number of each polygon must occur in the same order at every vertex of a semiregular tessellation.

Teaching Tip **Kinesthetic** For **Exercises 24–26,** have students use pattern blocks (MK) to explore tessellations that use the given polygons.

Answers

18.–20. 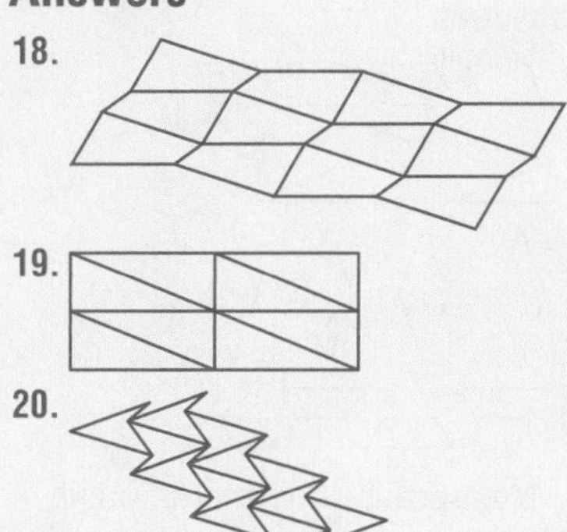

12-6 PRACTICE C

1. A tiling can be made using these three regular polygons: a decagon, a triangle, and one other polygon. Find the other polygon. 15-gon
2. Describe a regular or semiregular tiling that uses a nonagon. Explain how you know this is the only possible tiling using a nonagon.
The tiling uses a nonagon, a triangle, and an 18-gon; possible answer: Each angle in a regular nonagon measures 140°, which does not divide evenly into 360°. So the nonagon cannot be used in a regular tessellation. If two nonagons are used in a semiregular tessellation, then the measures of the angles of the polygons that are not nonagons must be 360° − 280° = 80°. There is no polygon or combination of polygons with angles that measure 80°. If one nonagon is used in a semiregular tessellation, then the measures of the angles of the polygon or combination of polygons that are not nonagons must be 360° − 140° = 220°. No polygon can have an angle measure greater than 180°, so a combination of polygons must make up 220°. A triangle has 60° angles, so that leaves 160°. The formula for interior angle measure of a regular polygon shows that an 18-gon has 160° angles. This tiling works, but there could be more. A square would leave 130°, a pentagon would leave 112°, a hexagon would leave 100°, and an octagon would leave 85°. No polygon or combination of polygons makes up any of those angle measures. So there is only one possible tiling using a nonagon.
3. There are 12 theoretically possible regular or semiregular tessellations using the regular polygons having between 3 and 12 vertices. Describe each tessellation by giving the number and types of the polygons that meet at each vertex.
six triangles; four triangles and one hexagon; three triangles and two squares; two triangles and two hexagons; two triangles, one square, and one dodecagon; one triangle and two dodecagons; one triangle, two squares, and one hexagon; four squares; one square and two octagons; one square, one hexagon, and one dodecagon; two pentagons and one decagon; three hexagons
4. Draw the tessellation you listed in Exercise 3 that includes a pentagon.
5. Tell what is remarkable about the drawing. Although the angles at each vertex add to 360°, the polygons do not tessellate. They overlap.
6. Choose which of these two figures will tessellate. Draw the tessellation.

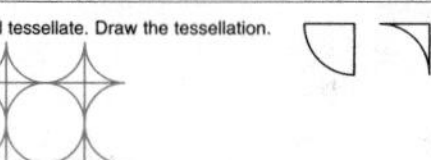

Exercise 36 involves identifying the figures in a tessellation. This exercise prepares students for the Multi-Step Test Prep on page 880.

Science Link The arrangement of carbon and hydrogen atoms in the polymer in **Exercise 43** makes up the *backbone* of the polymer. The attached chain, CH_3, is called a *pendant group*. Polymer compounds are in DNA, foods such as milk and potatoes, acrylic paints, car tires, plastic containers, and rubber trees.

Answers

37.–40.

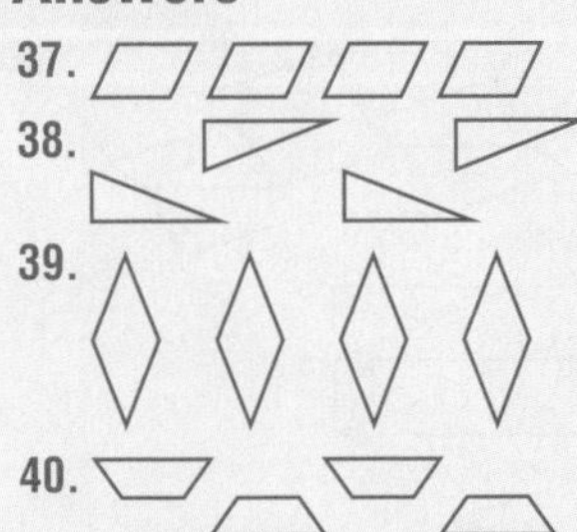

42. No, because the interior angle measures of a regular hexagon and a regular pentagon are 120° and 108°, and there is no possible arrangement of both these angle measures that adds to 360°.

43.

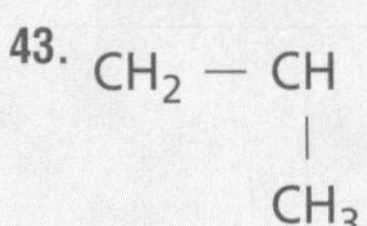

$$\begin{array}{l} CH_2 - CH \\ \quad\quad\quad | \\ \quad\quad\; CH_3 \end{array}$$

44.

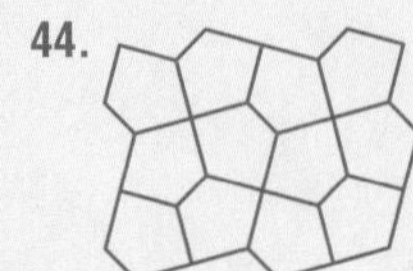

MULTI-STEP TEST PREP

36. This problem will prepare you for the Multi-Step Test Prep on page 880.

Many of the patterns in M. C. Escher's works are based on simple tessellations. For example, the pattern at right is based on a tessellation of equilateral triangles. Identify the figure upon which each pattern is based.

a.

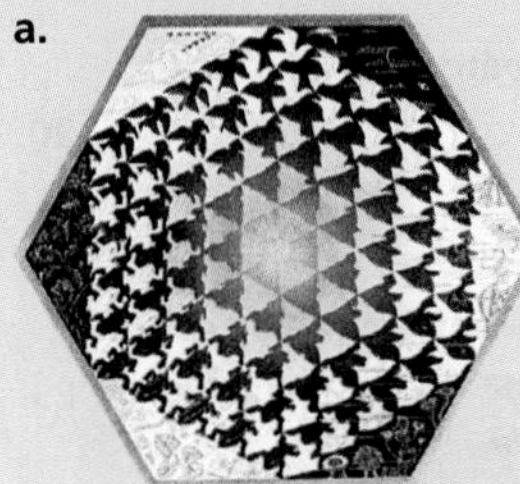

equilateral triangle

b.

parallelogram

Use the given figure to draw a frieze pattern with the given symmetry.

37. translation symmetry

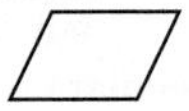

38. glide reflection symmetry

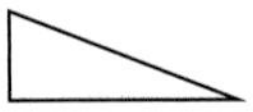

39. translation symmetry

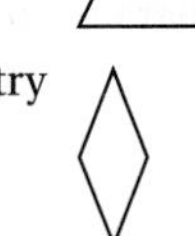

40. glide reflection symmetry

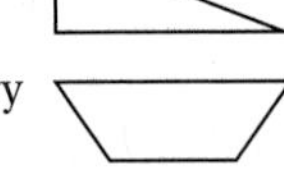

41. **Optics** A kaleidoscope is formed by three mirrors joined to form the lateral surface of a triangular prism. Copy the triangular faces and reflect it over each side. Repeat to form a tessellation. Describe the symmetry of the tessellation.

41. The tessellation has translation symmetry, reflection symmetry, and order 3 rotation symmetry.

42. **Critical Thinking** The pattern on a soccer ball is a tessellation of a sphere using regular hexagons and regular pentagons. Can these two shapes be used to tessellate a plane? Explain your reasoning.

43. **Chemistry** A *polymer* is a substance made of repeating chemical units or molecules. The *repeat unit* is the smallest structure that can be repeated to create the chain. Draw the repeat unit for polypropylene, the polymer shown below.

$$\begin{array}{cccccccccccccccc} - & CH_2 & - & CH & - & CH_2 & - & CH & - & CH_2 & - & CH & - & CH_2 & - & CH \; - \\ & & & | & & & & | & & & & | & & & & | \\ & & & CH_3 & & & & CH_3 & & & & CH_3 & & & & CH_3 \end{array}$$

44. The *dual* of a tessellation is formed by connecting the centers of adjacent polygons with segments. Copy or trace the semiregular tessellation shown and draw its dual. What type of polygon makes up the dual tessellation? pentagon

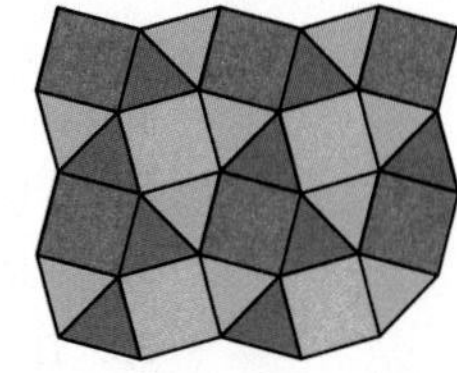

45. Equilateral triangles, squares, and regular hexagons are the only regular polygons with interior angle measures that divide evenly into 360°.

45. **Write About It** You can make a regular tessellation from an equilateral triangle, a square, or a regular hexagon. Explain why these are the only three regular tessellations that are possible.

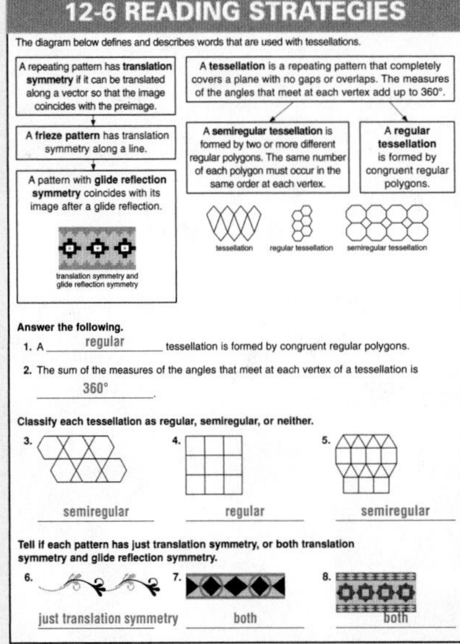

12-6 READING STRATEGIES

The diagram below defines and describes words that are used with tessellations.

A repeating pattern has **translation symmetry** if it can be translated along a vector so that the image coincides with the preimage.

A **frieze pattern** has translation symmetry along a line.

A pattern with **glide reflection symmetry** coincides with its image after a glide reflection.

translation symmetry and glide reflection symmetry

A **tessellation** is a repeating pattern that completely covers a plane with no gaps or overlaps. The measures of the angles that meet at each vertex add up to 360°.

A **semiregular tessellation** is formed by two or more different regular polygons. The same number of each polygon must occur in the same order at each vertex.

A **regular tessellation** is formed by congruent regular polygons.

tessellation regular tessellation semiregular tessellation

Answer the following.

1. A regular tessellation is formed by congruent regular polygons.

2. The sum of the measures of the angles that meet at each vertex of a tessellation is 360°.

Classify each tessellation as regular, semiregular, or neither.

3. semiregular 4. regular 5. semiregular

Tell if each pattern has just translation symmetry, or both translation symmetry and glide reflection symmetry.

6. just translation symmetry 7. both 8. both

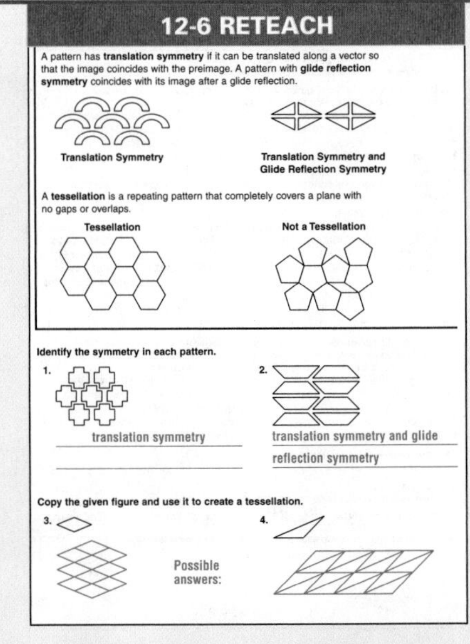

12-6 RETEACH

A pattern has **translation symmetry** if it can be translated along a vector so that the image coincides with the preimage. A pattern with **glide reflection symmetry** coincides with its image after a glide reflection.

Translation Symmetry

Translation Symmetry and Glide Reflection Symmetry

A **tessellation** is a repeating pattern that completely covers a plane with no gaps or overlaps.

Tessellation

Not a Tessellation

Identify the symmetry in each pattern.

1. translation symmetry

2. translation symmetry and glide reflection symmetry

Copy the given figure and use it to create a tessellation.

3. 4.

Possible answers:

TEST PREP

46. Which frieze pattern has glide reflection symmetry?

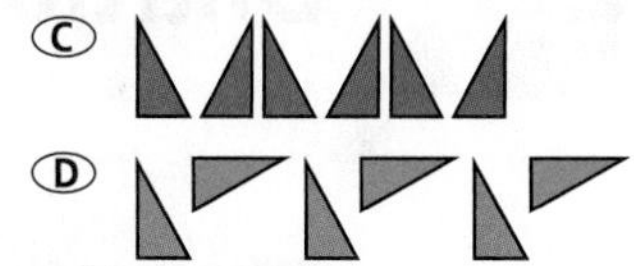

Ⓐ Ⓑ (circled) Ⓒ Ⓓ

47. Which shape CANNOT be used to make a regular tessellation?

Ⓕ Equilateral triangle Ⓗ Regular pentagon (circled)
Ⓖ Square Ⓙ Regular hexagon

48. Which pair of regular polygons can be used to make a semiregular tessellation?

Ⓐ 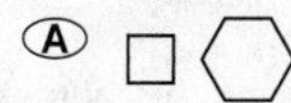 Ⓑ 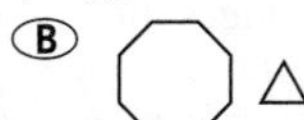 Ⓒ 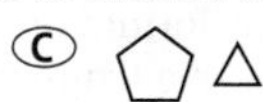 Ⓓ (circled) 

CHALLENGE AND EXTEND

49. Possible answer:

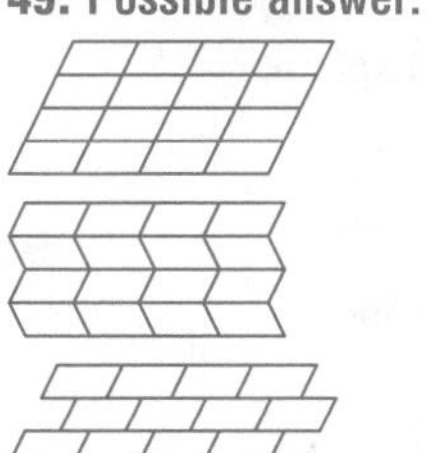

49. Some shapes can be used to tessellate a plane in more than one way. Three tessellations that use the same rectangle are shown. Draw a parallelogram and draw at least three tessellations using that parallelogram.

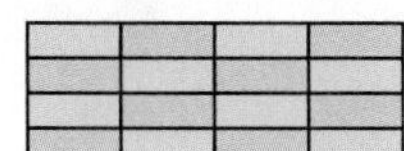

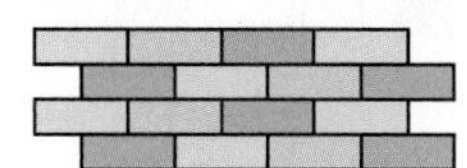

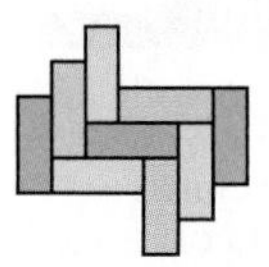

Determine whether each figure can be used to tessellate three-dimensional space.

50.  **no**

51. 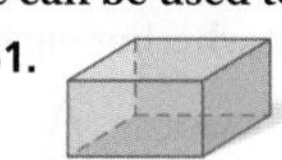 **yes**

52.  **yes**

SPIRAL REVIEW

53. A book is on sale for 15% off the regular price of $8.00. If Harold pays with a $10 bill and receives $2.69 in change, what is the sales tax rate on the book? *(Previous course)* **7.5%**

54. Louis lives 5 miles from school and jogs at a rate of 6 mph. Andrea lives 3.9 miles from school and jogs at a rate of 6.5 mph. Andrea leaves her house at 7:00 A.M. When should Louis leave his house to arrive at school at the same time as Andrea? *(Previous course)* **6:46 A.M.**

Write the equation of each circle. *(Lesson 11-7)*

55. ⊙P with center $(-2, 3)$ and radius $\sqrt{5}$ $(x+2)^2 + (y-3)^2 = 5$

56. ⊙Q that passes through $(3, 4)$ and has center $(0, 0)$ $x^2 + y^2 = 25$

57. ⊙T that passes through $(1, -1)$ and has center $(5, -3)$ $(x-5)^2 + (y+3)^2 = 20$

Tell whether each figure has rotational symmetry. If so, give the angle of rotational symmetry and the order of the symmetry. *(Lesson 12-5)*

58. 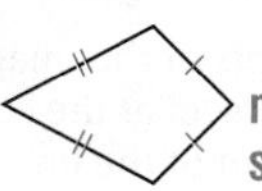 **no rotational symmetry**

59. 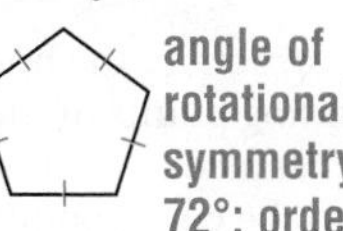 **angle of rotational symmetry: 72°; order: 5**

60. 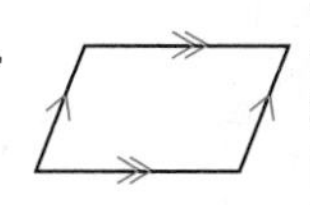 **angle of rotational symmetry: 180°; order: 2**

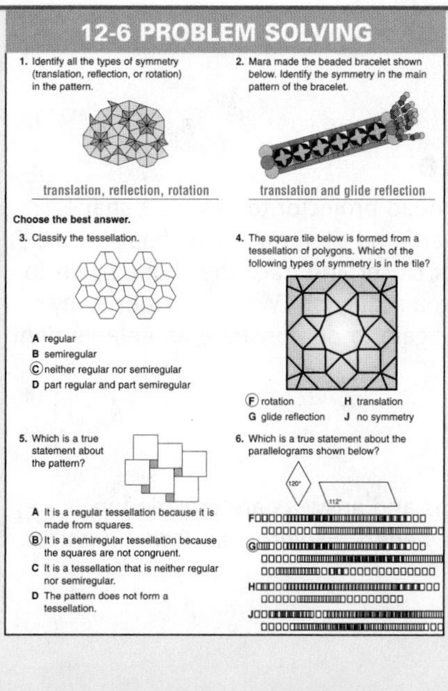

12-6 PROBLEM SOLVING

1. Identify all the types of symmetry (translation, reflection, or rotation) in the pattern.

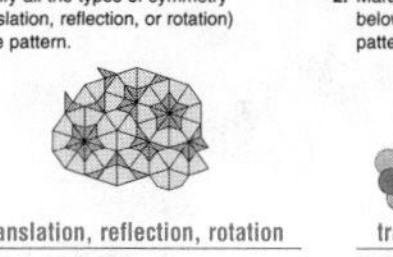

translation, reflection, rotation

2. Mara made the beaded bracelet shown below. Identify the symmetry in the main pattern of the bracelet.

translation and glide reflection

Choose the best answer.

3. Classify the tessellation.

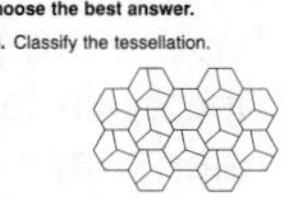

A regular
B semiregular
Ⓒ neither regular nor semiregular
D part regular and part semiregular

4. The square tile below is formed from a tessellation of polygons. Which of the following types of symmetry is in the tile?

Ⓕ rotation H translation
G glide reflection J no symmetry

5. Which is a true statement about the pattern?

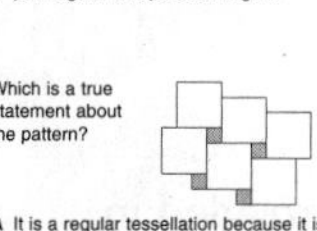

A It is a regular tessellation because it is made from squares.
Ⓑ It is a semiregular tessellation because the squares are not congruent.
C It is a tessellation that is neither regular nor semiregular.
D The pattern does not form a tessellation.

6. Which is a true statement about the parallelograms shown below?

120° 112°

F [illegible]
Ⓖ [illegible]
H [illegible]
J [illegible]

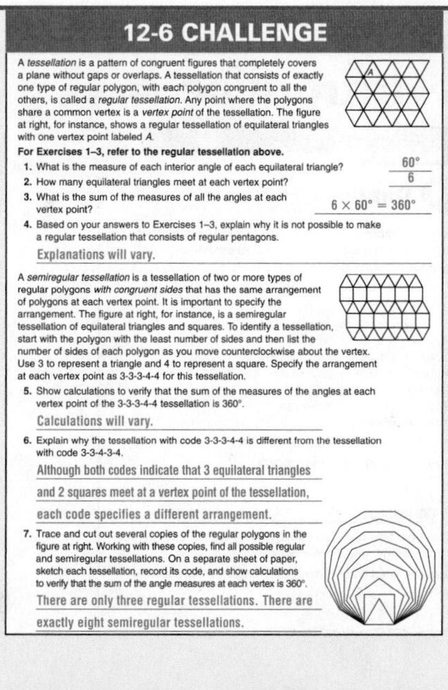

12-6 CHALLENGE

A *tessellation* is a pattern of congruent figures that completely covers a plane without gaps or overlaps. A tessellation that consists of exactly one type of regular polygon, with each polygon congruent to all the others, is called a *regular tessellation*. Any point where the polygons share a common vertex is a *vertex point* of the tessellation. The figure at right, for instance, shows a regular tessellation of equilateral triangles with one vertex point labeled *A*.

For Exercises 1–3, refer to the regular tessellation above.

1. What is the measure of each interior angle of each equilateral triangle? **60°**
2. How many equilateral triangles meet at each vertex point? **6**
3. What is the sum of the measures of all the angles at each vertex point? **$6 \times 60° = 360°$**
4. Based on your answers to Exercises 1–3, explain why it is not possible to make a regular tessellation that consists of regular pentagons.

Explanations will vary.

A *semiregular tessellation* is a tessellation of two or more types of regular polygons *with congruent sides* that has the same arrangement of polygons at each vertex point. It is important to specify the arrangement. The figure at right, for instance, is a semiregular tessellation of equilateral triangles and squares. To identify a tessellation, start with the polygon with the least number of sides and then list the number of sides of each polygon as you move counterclockwise about the vertex. Use 3 to represent a triangle and 4 to represent a square. Specify the arrangement at each vertex point as 3-3-3-4-4 for this tessellation.

5. Show calculations to verify that the sum of the measures of the angles at each vertex point of the 3-3-3-4-4 tessellation is 360°.

Calculations will vary.

6. Explain why the tessellation with code 3-3-3-4-4 is different from the tessellation with code 3-3-4-3-4.

Although both codes indicate that 3 equilateral triangles and 2 squares meet at a vertex point of the tessellation, each code specifies a different arrangement.

7. Trace and cut out several copies of the regular polygons in the figure at right. Working with these copies, find all possible regular and semiregular tessellations. On a separate sheet of paper, sketch each tessellation, record its code, and show calculations to verify that the sum of the angle measures at each vertex is 360°.

There are only three regular tessellations. There are exactly eight semiregular tessellations.

TEST PREP DOCTOR If students have difficulty with **Exercise 48,** have them list possible arrangements of the polygons around a vertex, and see if the angle measures add to 360°.

Journal

Have students explain how they would determine the number of possible semiregular tessellations.

ALTERNATIVE ASSESSMENT

Have students use the figure shown to create one frieze pattern with only translation symmetry, one frieze pattern with translation and glide reflection symmetry, and two different tessellations.

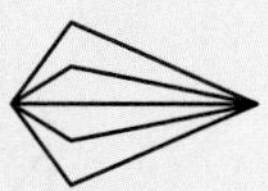

Power Presentations with PowerPoint®

12-6 Lesson Quiz

1. Identify the symmetry in the frieze pattern.

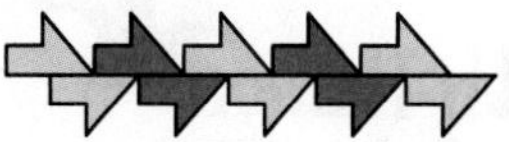

translation symmetry and glide reflection symmetry

2. Copy the given figure and use it to create a tessellation.

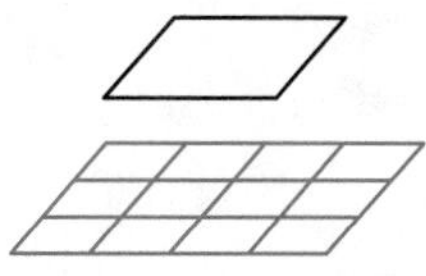

3. Classify the tessellation as regular, semiregular, or neither.

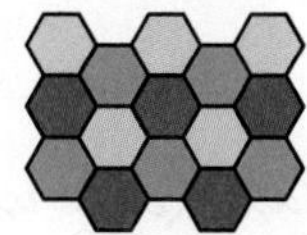

regular

4. Determine whether the given regular polygons can be used to form a tessellation. If so, draw the tessellation.

Also available on transparency

12-7 Organizer

Pacing: Traditional 1 day
Block $\frac{1}{2}$ day

Objective: Identify and draw dilations.

Online Edition
Tutorial Videos, TechKeys

Power Presentations with PowerPoint®

Warm Up

1. Translate the triangle with vertices $A(2, -1)$, $B(4, 3)$, and $C(-5, 4)$ along the vector $\langle 2, 2 \rangle$. $A'(4, 1)$, $B'(6, 5)$, $C'(-3, 6)$
2. $\triangle ABC \sim \triangle JKL$. Find the value of JK. $5\frac{1}{3}$

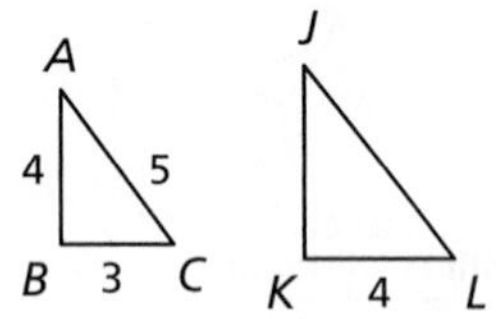

Also available on transparency

Q: Why don't scale factors die early?
A: Because they dilate!

12-7 Dilations

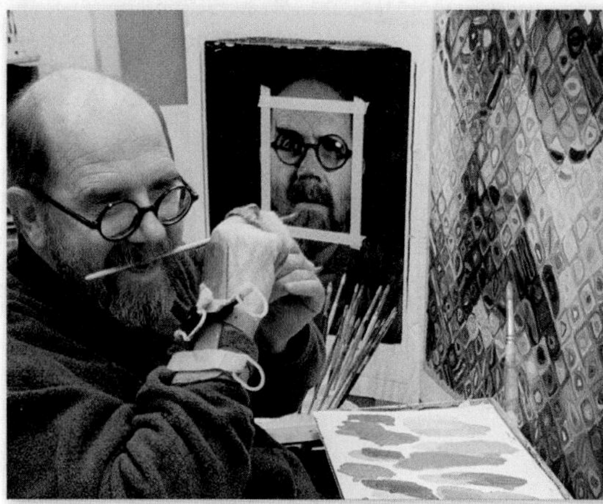

Objective
Identify and draw dilations.

Vocabulary
center of dilation
enlargement
reduction

Who uses this?
Artists use dilations to turn sketches into large-scale paintings. (See Example 3.)

Recall that a dilation is a transformation that changes the size of a figure but not the shape. The image and the preimage of a figure under a dilation are similar.

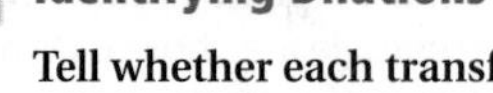

EXAMPLE 1 Identifying Dilations

Tell whether each transformation appears to be a dilation. Explain.

A Yes; the figures are similar, and the image is not turned or flipped.

B No; the figures are not similar.

Helpful Hint

For a dilation with scale factor k, if $k > 0$, the figure is not turned or flipped. If $k < 0$, the figure is rotated by 180°.

CHECK IT OUT! Tell whether each transformation appears to be a dilation.

1a. no

1b. yes

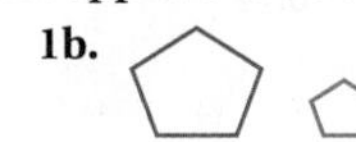

Construction Dilate a Figure by a Scale Factor of 2

1. Draw a triangle and a point outside the triangle. The point is the *center of dilation*.

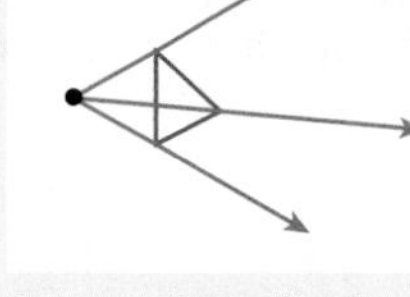

2. Use a straightedge to draw a line through the center of dilation and each vertex of the triangle.

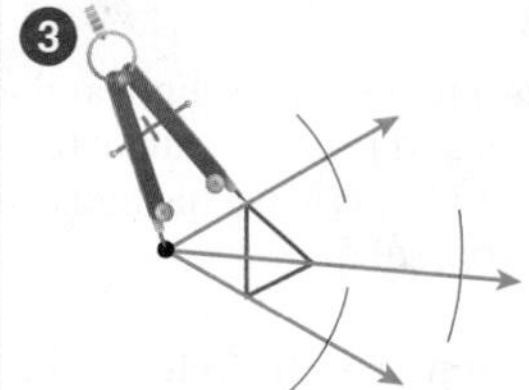

3. Set the compass to the distance from the center of dilation to a vertex. Mark this distance along the line for each vertex as shown.

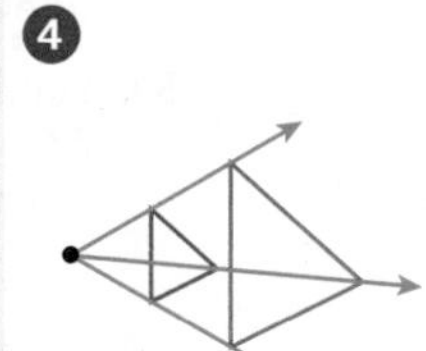

4. Connect the vertices of the image.

In the construction, the lines connecting points of the image with the corresponding points of the preimage all intersect at the center of dilation. Also, the distance from the center to each point of the image is twice the distance to the corresponding point of the preimage.

State Resources

go.hrw.com
State Resources Online
KEYWORD: MG7 Resources

1 Introduce

EXPLORATION

12-7 Dilations

A *dilation* is a transformation that changes the size of a figure, but not its shape. In this Exploration you will investigate dilations where the scale factor is negative.

1. Write the coordinates of P, Q, and R.
2. P', Q', and R' are the images of P, Q, and R under a dilation centered at the origin with a scale factor of -2. Multiply each of the x- and y-coordinates of P, Q, and R by -2 to find the coordinates of P', Q', and R'.
3. Plot P', Q', and R'. Then draw $\triangle P'Q'R'$.
4. How is $\triangle P'Q'R'$ related to $\triangle PQR$?

THINK AND DISCUSS

5. **Describe** how a dilation with a scale factor of -2 is different from a dilation with a scale factor of 2.
6. **Discuss** what it would mean for a dilation to have a scale factor of -1.

Motivate

Use an overhead projector to project a shape onto the board and then trace the shape. Move the projector closer and trace the shape again to demonstrate a reduction. Move it farther away and trace it again to demonstrate an enlargement.

Explorations and answers are provided in *Alternate Openers: Explorations Transparencies.*

Dilations

A dilation, or *similarity transformation*, is a transformation in which the lines connecting every point P with its image P' all intersect at a point C, called the **center of dilation**. $\frac{CP'}{CP}$ is the same for every point P.

The scale factor k of a dilation is the ratio of a linear measurement of the image to a corresponding measurement of the preimage. In the figure, $k = \frac{P'Q'}{PQ}$.

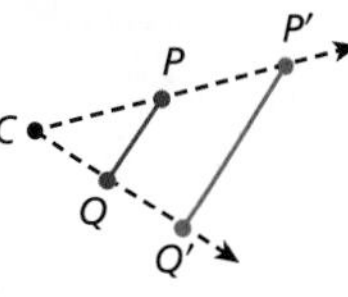

A dilation enlarges or reduces all dimensions proportionally. A dilation with a scale factor greater than 1 is an **enlargement**, or *expansion*. A dilation with a scale factor greater than 0 but less than 1 is a **reduction**, or *contraction*.

EXAMPLE  **Drawing Dilations**

Copy the triangle and the center of dilation P. Draw the image of $\triangle ABC$ under a dilation with a scale factor of $\frac{1}{2}$.

Step 1 Draw a line through P and each vertex.

Step 2 On each line, mark half the distance from P to the vertex.

Step 3 Connect the vertices of the image.

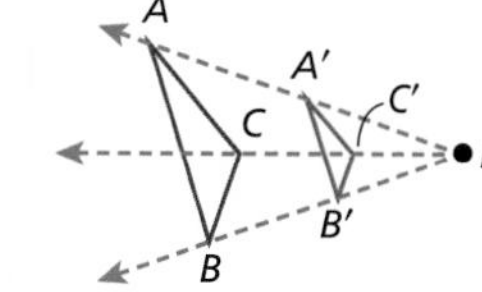

 **2.** Copy the figure and the center of dilation. Draw the dilation of $RSTU$ using center Q and a scale factor of 3.

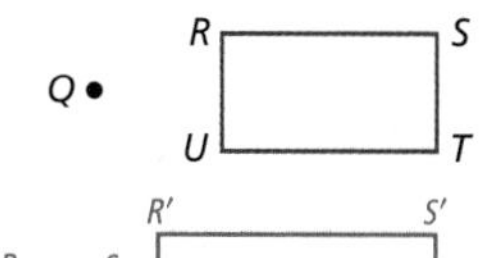

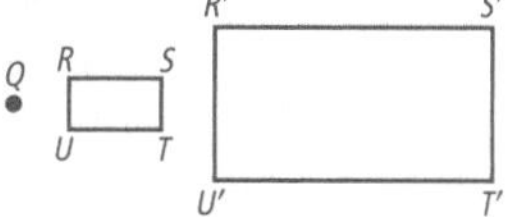

EXAMPLE  ***Art Application***

An artist is creating a large painting from a photograph by dividing the photograph into squares and dilating each square by a scale factor of 4. If the photograph is 20 cm by 25 cm, what is the perimeter of the painting?

The scale factor of the dilation is 4, so a 1 cm by 1 cm square on the photograph represents a 4 cm by 4 cm square on the painting.

Find the dimensions of the painting.

$b = 4(25) = 100$ cm   *Multiply each dimension by the scale factor, 4.*

$h = 4(20) = 80$ cm

Find the perimeter of the painting.

$P = 2(100 + 80) = 360$ cm $P = 2(b + h)$

 **3. What if...?** In Example 3, suppose the photograph is a square with sides of length 10 in. Find the area of the painting. **1600 in^2**

Teach

Guided Instruction

Review similar polygons and the similarity theorems in Chapter 7. Explain that the image of a dilation is generally not congruent to the preimage, so a dilation is not an isometry. An exception is a dilation with a scale factor of −1, which is equivalent to a 180° rotation about the center of dilation.

Reaching All Learners

Through Critical Thinking

Have students use the Distance Formula to prove that the triangles in **Example 4** are similar. Students can work in groups of two or three and then share their results with the class.

Power Presentations with PowerPoint®

Additional Examples

Example 1

Tell whether each transformation appears to be a dilation.

A.

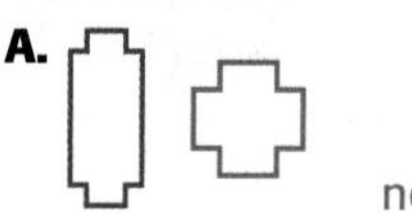

no

B.

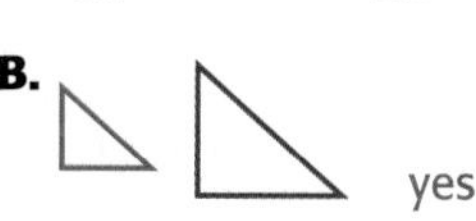

yes

Example 2

Copy the figure and the center of dilation P. Draw the image of $\triangle RST$ under a dilation with a scale factor of 2.

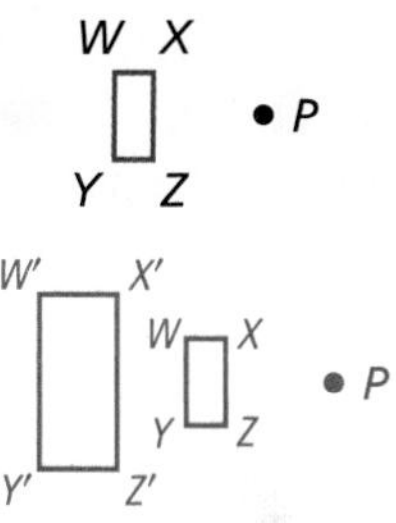

Example 3

On a sketch of a flower, 4 in. represent 1 in. on the actual flower. If the flower has a 3 in. diameter in the sketch, find the diameter of the actual flower. 0.75 in.

INTERVENTION 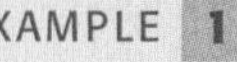

Questioning Strategies

EXAMPLE 1

- How do you know when a transformation is a dilation?

EXAMPLE 2

- In a drawing of a dilation, where is the image in relation to the preimage and the center of dilation if $0 < k < 1$?

EXAMPLE 3

- If 1 in. on an enlargement represents x in. on the preimage, what is the scale factor of the enlargement? $k = \frac{1}{x}$

Power Presentations with PowerPoint®

Additional Examples

Example 4

Draw the image of the triangle with vertices $P(-4, 4)$, $Q(-2, -2)$, and $R(4, 0)$ under a dilation with a scale factor of $-\frac{1}{2}$ centered at the origin.

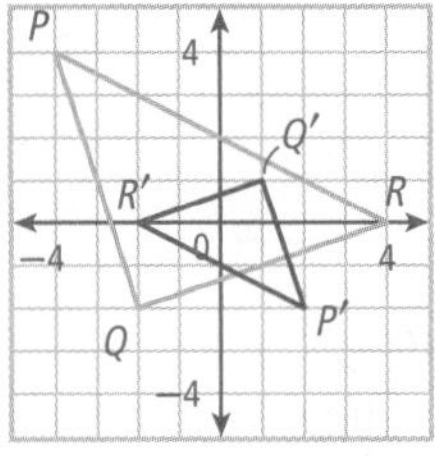

INTERVENTION 

Questioning Strategies

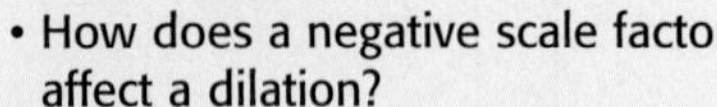

EXAMPLE 4

- How does a negative scale factor affect a dilation?

Algebra The scalar multiplication

$$-2\begin{bmatrix} -1 & -2 & -1 \\ 1 & -1 & -2 \end{bmatrix} = \begin{bmatrix} 2 & 4 & 2 \\ -2 & 2 & 4 \end{bmatrix}$$

can be used to find the coordinates of the vertices of the dilation in **Example 4.**

Dilations in the Coordinate Plane

If $P(x, y)$ is the preimage of a point under a dilation centered at the origin with scale factor k, then the image of the point is $P'(kx, ky)$.

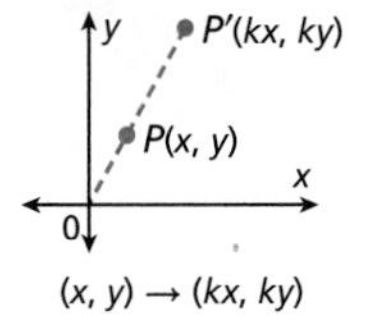

If the scale factor of a dilation is negative, the preimage is rotated by 180°. For $k > 0$, a dilation with a scale factor of $-k$ is equivalent to the composition of a dilation with a scale factor of k that is rotated 180° about the center of dilation.

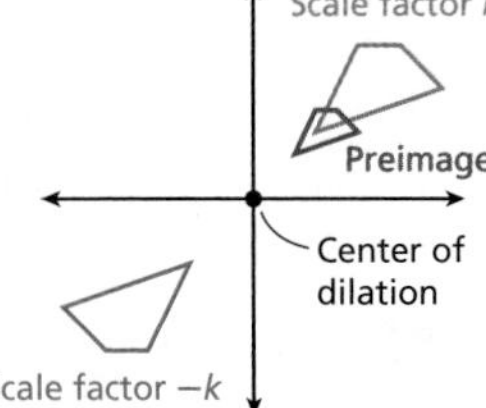

EXAMPLE 4 Drawing Dilations in the Coordinate Plane

Draw the image of a triangle with vertices $A(-1, 1)$, $B(-2, -1)$, and $C(-1, -2)$ under a dilation with a scale factor of -2 centered at the origin.

The dilation of (x, y) is $(-2x, -2y)$.

$A(-1, 1) \rightarrow A'(-2(-1), -2(1)) = A'(2, -2)$

$B(-2, -1) \rightarrow B'(-2(-2), -2(-1)) = B'(4, 2)$

$C(-1, -2) \rightarrow C'(-2(-1), -2(-2)) = C'(2, 4)$

Graph the preimage and image.

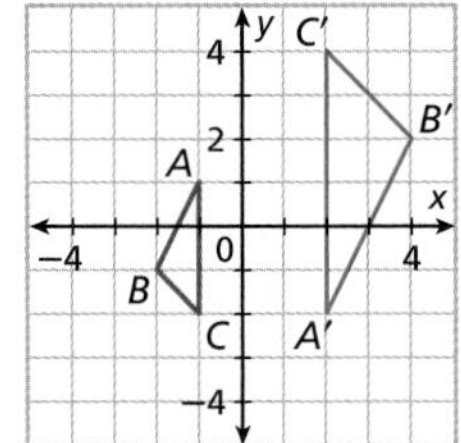

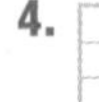

4.

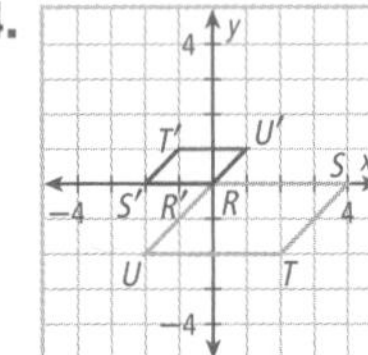

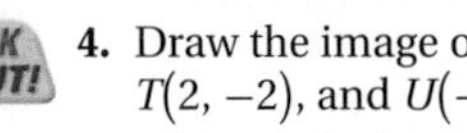

4. Draw the image of a parallelogram with vertices $R(0, 0)$, $S(4, 0)$, $T(2, -2)$, and $U(-2, -2)$ under a dilation centered at the origin with a scale factor of $-\frac{1}{2}$.

THINK AND DISCUSS

1. Given a triangle and its image under a dilation, explain how you could use a ruler to find the scale factor of the dilation.
2. A figure is dilated by a scale factor of k, and then the image is rotated 180° about the center of dilation. What single transformation would produce the same image?

3. **GET ORGANIZED** Copy and complete the graphic organizer. In each box, describe the dilation with the given scale factor.

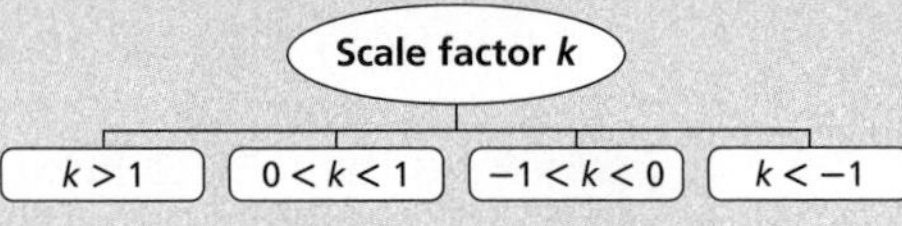

3 Close

Summarize

Draw $\triangle ABC$ with midsegment $\overline{DE}$. Have students complete the following statements:

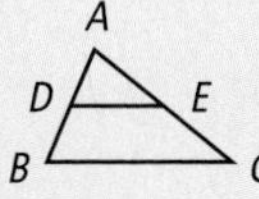

$\triangle ABC$ is a dilation of ___ centered at ___ with scale factor ___. *$\triangle ADE$; A, 2*

$\triangle ADE$ is a dilation of ___ centered at ___ with scale factor ___. *$\triangle ABC$; A, $\frac{1}{2}$*

ONGOING ASSESSMENT and INTERVENTION

***Diagnose Before* the Lesson**
12-7 Warm Up, TE p. 872

***Monitor During* the Lesson**
Check It Out! Exercises, SE pp. 872–874
Questioning Strategies, TE pp. 873–874

***Assess After* the Lesson**
12-7 Lesson Quiz, TE p. 879
Alternative Assessment, TE p. 879

Answers to *Think and Discuss*

1. Measure the length of 1 side of the image and the length of the corr. side of the preimage. Form the ratio of these 2 lengths to find the scale factor.
2. a dilation by a scale factor of $-k$
3. See p. A10.

12-7 Exercises

go.hrw.com
Homework Help Online
KEYWORD: MG7 12-7
Parent Resources Online
KEYWORD: MG7 Parent

GUIDED PRACTICE

1. **Vocabulary** What are the *center of dilation* and scale factor for the transformation $(x, y) \rightarrow (3x, 3y)$? The center is the origin; the scale factor is 3.

SEE EXAMPLE 1 p. 872

Tell whether each transformation appears to be a dilation.

2. 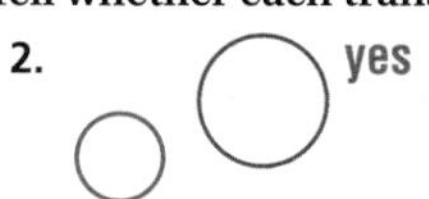 yes

3. 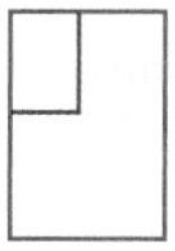 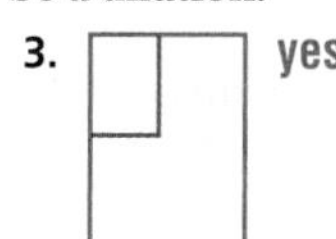 yes

4.  no

5.  yes

SEE EXAMPLE 2 p. 873

Copy each triangle and center of dilation *P*. Draw the image of the triangle under a dilation with the given scale factor.

6. Scale factor: 2

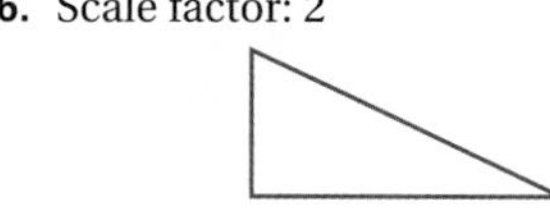

7. Scale factor: $\frac{1}{2}$

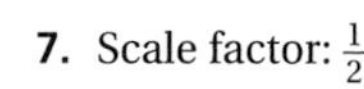

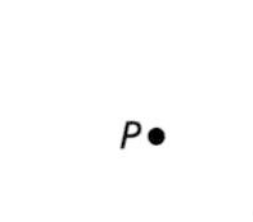

SEE EXAMPLE 3 p. 873

8. **Architecture** A blueprint shows a reduction of a room using a scale factor of $\frac{1}{50}$. In the blueprint, the room's length is 8 in., and its width is 6 in. Find the perimeter of the room. 1400 in. (or 116 ft 8 in.)

SEE EXAMPLE 4 p. 874

Draw the image of the figure with the given vertices under a dilation with the given scale factor centered at the origin.

9. $A(1, 0)$, $B(2, 2)$, $C(4, 0)$; scale factor: 2
10. $J(-2, 2)$, $K(4, 2)$, $L(4, -2)$, $M(-2, -2)$; scale factor: $\frac{1}{2}$
11. $D(-3, 3)$, $E(3, 6)$, $F(3, 0)$; scale factor: $-\frac{1}{3}$
12. $P(-2, 0)$, $Q(-1, 0)$, $R(0, -1)$, $S(-3, -1)$; scale factor: -2

PRACTICE AND PROBLEM SOLVING

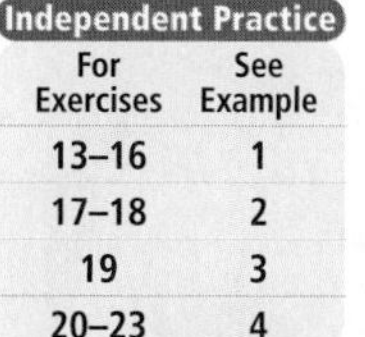

Independent Practice

For Exercises	See Example
13–16	1
17–18	2
19	3
20–23	4

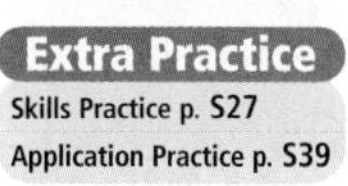

Extra Practice
Skills Practice p. S27
Application Practice p. S39

Tell whether each transformation appears to be a dilation.

13. 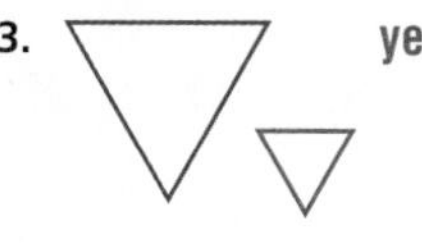 yes

14. 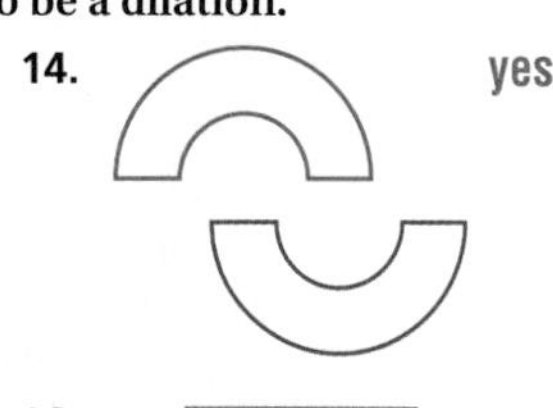 yes

15.  no

16. 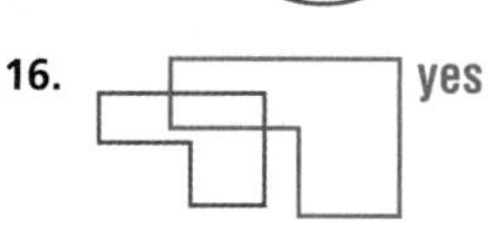 yes

Teacher to Teacher

I have developed an activity using geometry software in which students do multiple dilations to emphasize the relationship between reciprocals and the effect that negative signs have on objects in the coordinate plane. I often use this in the Algebra 1 classroom, too. Students do a dilation by a fixed ratio on the preimage and then on the resulting image by using reciprocals $\left(\text{e.g., } \frac{3}{2} \text{ and } \frac{2}{3}, -\frac{3}{2} \text{ and } -\frac{2}{3}\right)$. They can see that the second dilation coincides with the preimage.

E. Robin Staudenmeier
Standford, IL

12-7 Exercises

Assignment Guide

Assign *Guided Practice* exercises as necessary.

If you finished Examples **1–2**
Basic 13–18, 24–29, 33
Average 13–18, 24–29, 42–45
Advanced 13–18, 24–29, 33, 42–45

If you finished Examples **1–4**
Basic 13–41, 46–49, 52–56
Average 13–49, 51–56
Advanced 13–30, 32–56

Homework Quick Check
Quickly check key concepts.
Exercises: 14, 18, 19, 20, 24

Teaching Tip

Inclusion Because the two figures in **Exercise 14** are congruent, some students may assume the transformation is not a dilation. Remind students that the image under a dilation with a scale factor of −1 is congruent to the preimage and is rotated 180°.

Answers

6. 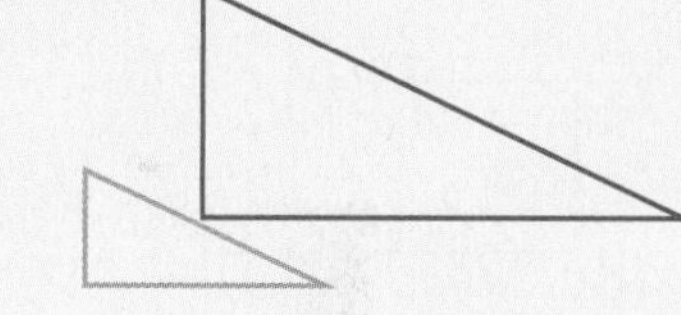

9–12. See p. A31.

State Resources

go.hrw.com
State Resources Online
KEYWORD: MG7 Resources

Math Background In **Exercise 26,** a rectangular prism is enlarged by a dilation with a scale factor of 4. When a solid is enlarged by a factor of *k*, its surface area increases by a factor of k^2, and its volume increases by a factor of k^3. Encourage students to use examples to verify this.

Exercise 30 involves determining the scale factor of a dilation. This exercise prepares students for the Multi-Step Test Prep on page 880.

Answers

17.

20.

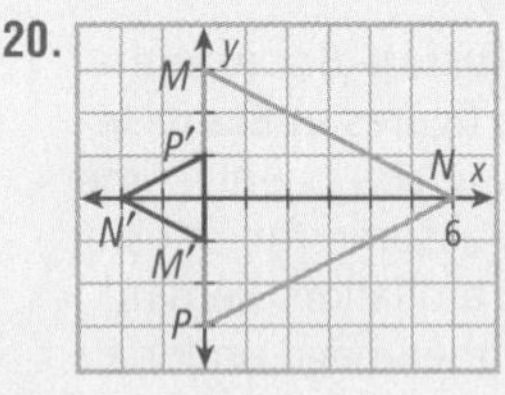

21.

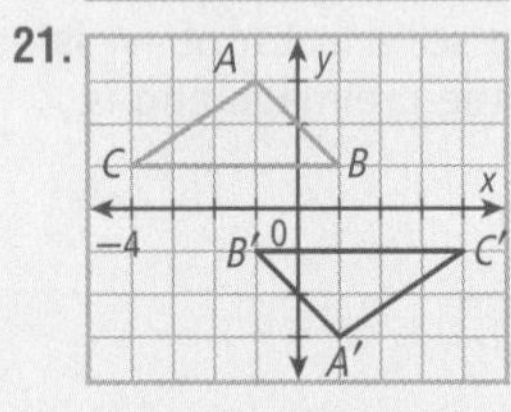

22.

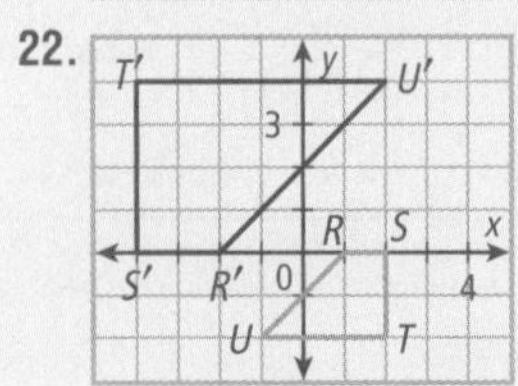

23, 27–29. See p. A32.

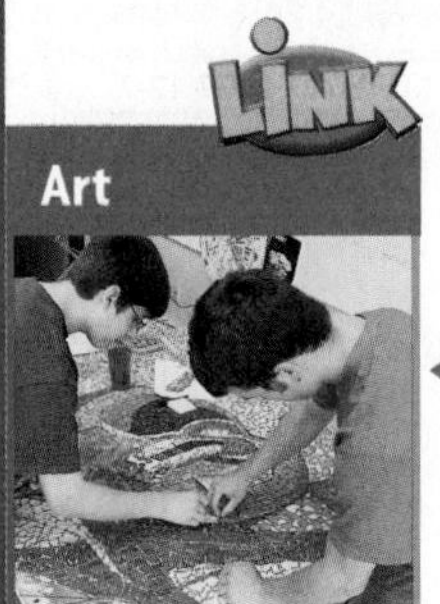

LINK Art

Mosaic is an ancient art form that is over 4000 years old and is still popular today. Creators of early mosaics used pebbles and other objects, but mosaic titles, or *tesserae,* have been in use since at least 200 B.C.E.

Copy each rectangle and the center of dilation *P*. Draw the image of the rectangle under a dilation with the given scale factor.

17. scale factor: 3

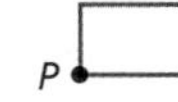

18. scale factor: $\frac{1}{2}$

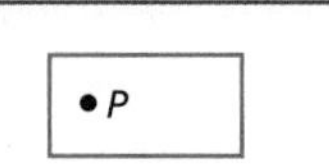

19. **Art** Jeff is making a mosaic by gluing 1 cm square tiles onto a photograph. He starts with a 6 cm by 8 cm rectangular photo and enlarges it by a scale factor of 1.5. How many tiles will Jeff need in order to cover the enlarged photo? **108**

Draw the image of the figure with the given vertices under a dilation with the given scale factor centered at the origin.

20. $M(0, 3)$, $N(6, 0)$, $P(0, -3)$; scale factor: $-\frac{1}{3}$
21. $A(-1, 3)$, $B(1, 1)$, $C(-4, 1)$; scale factor: -1
22. $R(1, 0)$, $S(2, 0)$, $T(2, -2)$, $U(-1, -2)$; scale factor: -2
23. $D(4, 0)$, $E(2, -4)$, $F(-2, -4)$, $G(-4, 0)$, $H(-2, 4)$, $J(2, 4)$; scale factor: $-\frac{1}{2}$

Each figure shows the preimage (blue) and image (red) under a dilation. Write a similarity statement based on the figure.

24. **$\triangle FGH \sim \triangle KLM$**

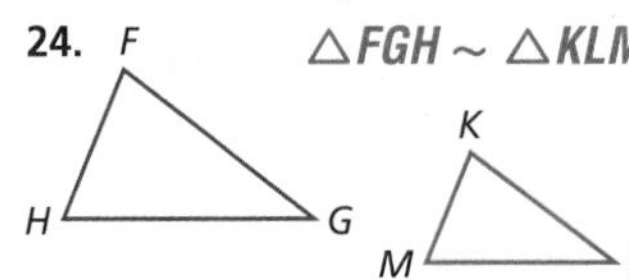

25. **$ABCDE \sim MNPQR$**

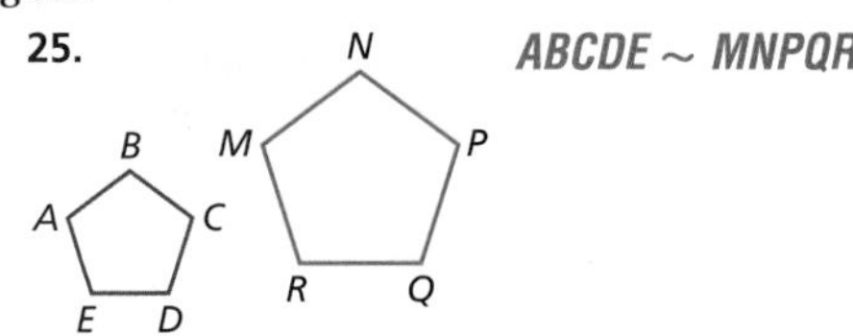

26. The rectangular prism shown is enlarged by a dilation with scale factor 4. Find the surface area and volume of the image.
$S = 992 \text{ cm}^2$; $V = 1920 \text{ cm}^3$

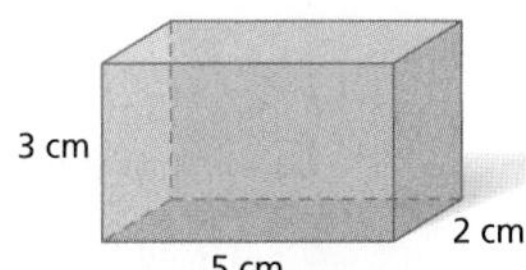

Copy each figure and locate the center of dilation.

27.

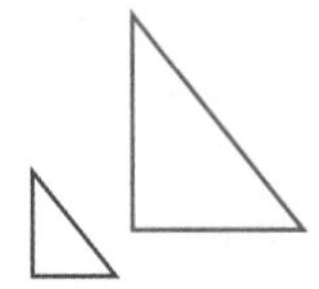

28.

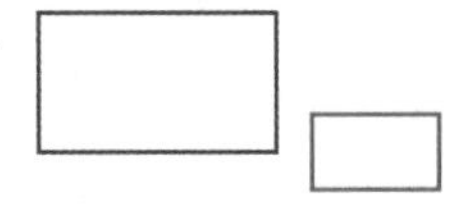

29.

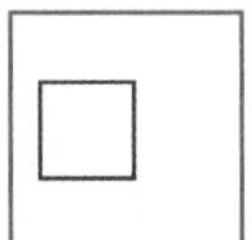

MULTI-STEP TEST PREP

30. This problem will prepare you for the Multi-Step Test Prep on page 880.

This lithograph, *Drawing Hands,* was made by M. C. Escher in 1948.

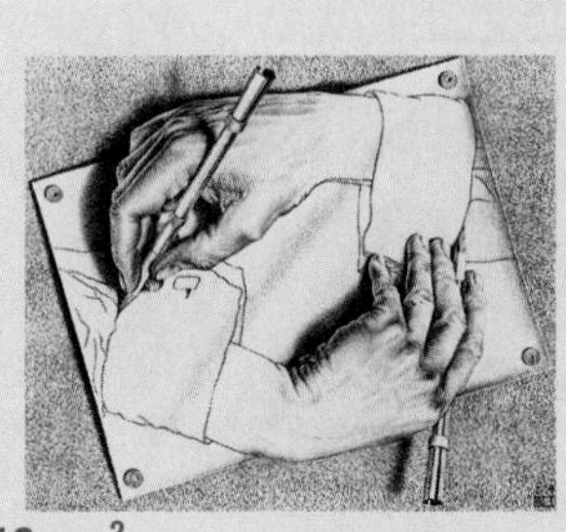

a. In the original drawing, the rectangular piece of paper from which the hands emerge measures 27.6 cm by 19.9 cm. On a poster of the drawing, the paper is 82.8 cm long. What is the scale factor of the dilation that was used to make the poster? **3**

b. What is the area of the paper on the poster? **4943.16 cm²**

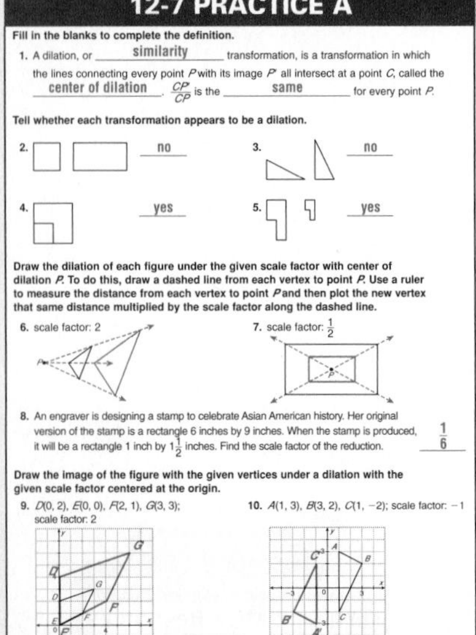

12-7 PRACTICE A

Fill in the blanks to complete the definition.

1. A dilation, or **similarity** transformation, is a transformation in which the lines connecting every point *P* with its image *P'* all intersect at a point *C*, called the **center of dilation**. $\frac{CP'}{CP}$ is the **same** for every point *P*.

Tell whether each transformation appears to be a dilation.

2. **no**
3. **no**
4. **yes**
5. **yes**

Draw the dilation of each figure under the given scale factor with center of dilation *P*. To do this, draw a dashed line from each vertex to point *P*. Use a ruler to measure the distance from each vertex to point *P* and then plot the new vertex that same distance multiplied by the scale factor along the dashed line.

6. scale factor: 2
7. scale factor: $\frac{1}{2}$

8. An engraver is designing a stamp to celebrate Asian American history. Her original version of the stamp is a rectangle 6 inches by 9 inches. When the stamp is produced, it will be a rectangle 1 inch by $1\frac{1}{2}$ inches. Find the scale factor of the reduction. **$\frac{1}{6}$**

Draw the image of the figure with the given vertices under a dilation with the given scale factor centered at the origin.

9. $D(0, 2)$, $E(0, 0)$, $F(2, 1)$, $G(3, 3)$; scale factor: 2
10. $A(1, 3)$, $B(3, 2)$, $C(1, -2)$; scale factor: -1

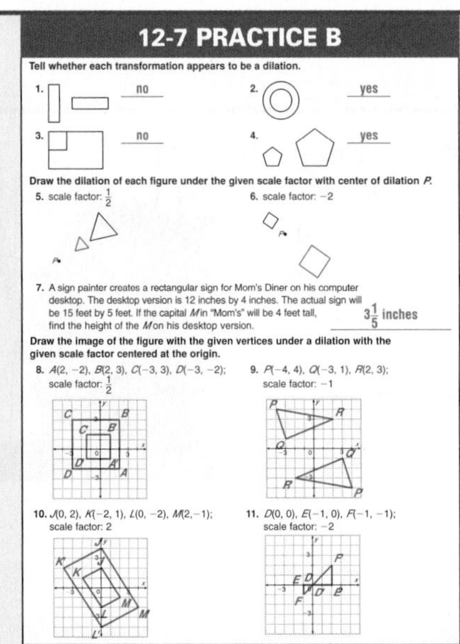

12-7 PRACTICE B

Tell whether each transformation appears to be a dilation.

1. **no**
2. **yes**
3. **no**
4. **yes**

Draw the dilation of each figure under the given scale factor with center of dilation *P*.

5. scale factor: $\frac{1}{2}$
6. scale factor: -2

7. A sign painter creates a rectangular sign for Mom's Diner on his computer desktop. The desktop version is 12 inches by 4 inches. The actual sign will be 15 feet by 5 feet. If the capital *M* in "Mom's" will be 4 feet tall, find the height of the *M* on his desktop version. **$3\frac{1}{5}$ inches**

Draw the image of the figure with the given vertices under a dilation with the given scale factor centered at the origin.

8. $A(2, -2)$, $B(2, 3)$, $C(-3, 3)$, $D(-3, -2)$; scale factor: $\frac{1}{2}$
9. $P(-4, 4)$, $Q(-3, 1)$, $R(2, 3)$; scale factor: -1
10. $J(0, 2)$, $K(-2, 1)$, $L(0, -2)$, $M(2, -1)$; scale factor: 2
11. $D(0, 0)$, $E(-1, 0)$, $F(-1, -1)$; scale factor: -2

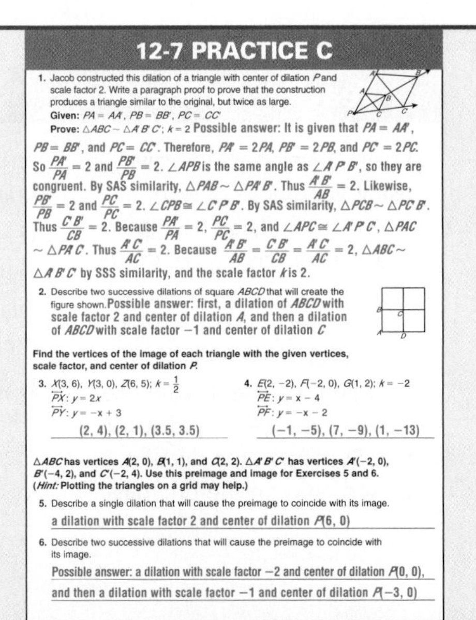

12-7 PRACTICE C

1. Jacob constructed this dilation of a triangle with center of dilation *P* and scale factor 2. Write a paragraph proof to prove that the construction produces a triangle similar to the original, but twice as large.
Given: $PA = AA'$, $PB = BB'$, $PC = CC'$
Prove: $\triangle ABC \sim \triangle A'B'C'$; $k = 2$ **Possible answer: It is given that $PA = AA'$, $PB = BB'$, and $PC = CC'$. Therefore, $PA' = 2PA$, $PB' = 2PB$, and $PC' = 2PC$. So $\frac{PA'}{PA} = 2$ and $\frac{PB'}{PB} = 2$. $\angle APB$ is the same angle as $\angle A'PB'$, so they are congruent. By SAS similarity, $\triangle PAB \sim \triangle PA'B'$. Thus $\frac{A'B'}{AB} = 2$. Likewise, $\frac{PB'}{PB} = 2$ and $\frac{PC'}{PC} = 2$. $\angle CPB \cong \angle C'PB'$. By SAS similarity, $\triangle PCB \sim \triangle PC'B'$. Thus $\frac{C'B'}{CB} = 2$. Because $\frac{PA'}{PA} = 2$, $\frac{PC'}{PC} = 2$, and $\angle APC \cong \angle A'PC'$, $\triangle PAC \sim \triangle PA'C'$. Thus $\frac{A'C'}{AC} = 2$. Because $\frac{A'B'}{AB} = \frac{C'B'}{CB} = \frac{A'C'}{AC} = 2$, $\triangle ABC \sim \triangle A'B'C'$ by SSS similarity, and the scale factor *k* is 2.**

2. Describe two successive dilations of square *ABCD* that will create the figure shown. **Possible answer: first, a dilation of *ABCD* with scale factor 2 and center of dilation *A*, and then a dilation of *ABCD* with scale factor −1 and center of dilation *C***

Find the vertices of the image of each triangle with the given vertices, scale factor, and center of dilation *P*.

3. $X(3, 6)$, $Y(3, 0)$, $Z(6, 5)$; $k = \frac{1}{2}$
$\overleftrightarrow{PX}: y = 2x$
$\overleftrightarrow{PY}: y = -x + 3$
(2, 4), (2, 1), (3.5, 3.5)

4. $E(2, -2)$, $F(-2, 0)$, $G(1, 2)$; $k = -2$
$\overleftrightarrow{PE}: y = x - 4$
$\overleftrightarrow{PF}: y = -x - 2$
(−1, −5), (7, −9), (1, −13)

$\triangle ABC$ has vertices $A(2, 0)$, $B(1, 1)$, and $C(2, 2)$. $\triangle A'B'C'$ has vertices $A'(-2, 0)$, $B'(-4, 2)$, and $C'(-2, 4)$. Use this preimage and image for Exercises 5 and 6. (*Hint:* Plotting the triangles on a grid may help.)

5. Describe a single dilation that will cause the preimage to coincide with its image.
a dilation with scale factor 2 and center of dilation $P(6, 0)$

6. Describe two successive dilations that will cause the preimage to coincide with its image.
Possible answer: a dilation with scale factor −2 and center of dilation $P(0, 0)$, and then a dilation with scale factor −1 and center of dilation $P(-3, 0)$

31. Solution B is incorrect. The area of rectangle $A'B'C'D'$ is $(2.5)^2 \times 6 = 37.5$.

31. ///ERROR ANALYSIS/// Rectangle $A'B'C'D'$ is the image of rectangle $ABCD$ under a dilation. Which calculation of the area of rectangle $A'B'C'D'$ is incorrect? Explain the error.

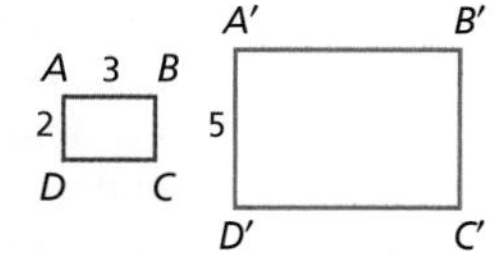

A The scale factor of the dilation is $\frac{5}{2}$, or 2.5, so the length of $\overline{A'B'}$ must be $2.5 \times 3 = 7.5$. Then the area of rectangle $A'B'C'D'$ is $5 \times 7.5 = 37.5$.

B The area of rectangle $ABCD$ is $2 \times 3 = 6$, and the scale factor of the dilation is $\frac{5}{2}$, or 2.5. Therefore the area of rectangle $A'B'C'D'$ is $2.5 \times 6 = 15$.

32. **Optometry** The pupil is the circular opening that allows light into the eye.

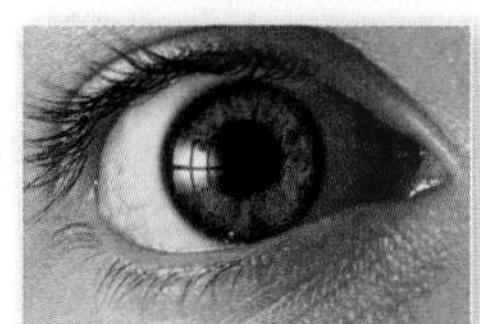

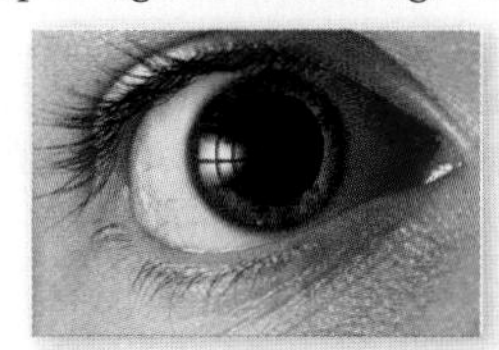

$1\frac{1}{3}$ a. An optometrist dilates a patient's pupil from 6 mm to 8 mm. What is the scale factor for this dilation?

b. To the nearest tenth, find the area of the pupil before and after the dilation. $28.3\ \text{mm}^2$; $50.3\ \text{mm}^2$

78% c. As a percentage, how much more light is admitted to the eye after the dilation?

33a. Check student's estimates.
b. Measure $\overline{A'B'}$ and $\overline{AB}$, then calculate $\frac{A'B'}{AB}$.
c. 2.5

33. **Estimation** In the diagram, $\triangle ABC \rightarrow \triangle A'B'C'$ under a dilation with center P.

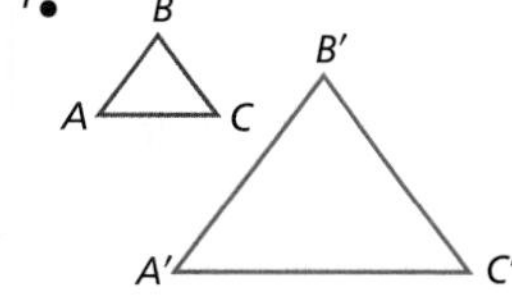

a. Estimate the scale factor of the dilation.

b. Explain how you can use a ruler to make measurements and to calculate the scale factor.

c. Use the method from part **b** to calculate the scale factor. How does your result compare to your estimate?

34b. Same graph as part a.
c. The images are the same. The order of the transformations does not matter.

34. $\triangle ABC$ has vertices $A(-1, 1)$, $B(2, 1)$, and $C(2, 2)$.

a. Draw the image of $\triangle ABC$ under a dilation centered at the origin with scale factor 2 followed by a reflection across the x-axis.

b. Draw the image of $\triangle ABC$ under a reflection across the x-axis followed by a dilation centered at the origin with scale factor 2.

c. Compare the results of parts **a** and **b.** Does the order of the transformations matter?

35. **Astronomy** The image of the sun projected through the hole of a pinhole camera (the center of dilation) has a diameter of $\frac{1}{4}$ in. The diameter of the sun is 870,000 mi. What is the scale factor of the dilation? -4.5×10^{-12}

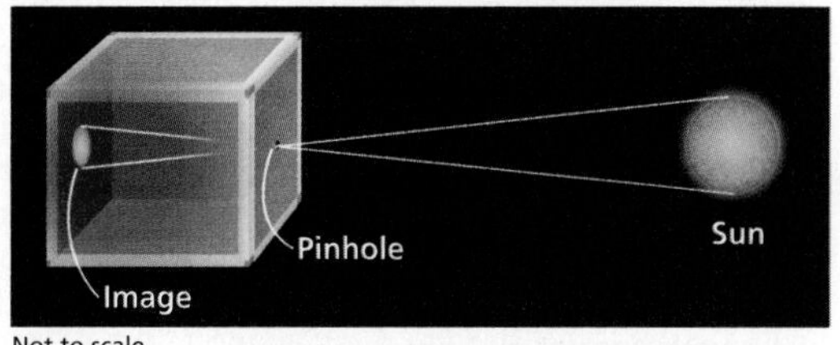

Not to scale

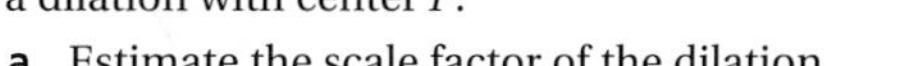

Answers

34a.

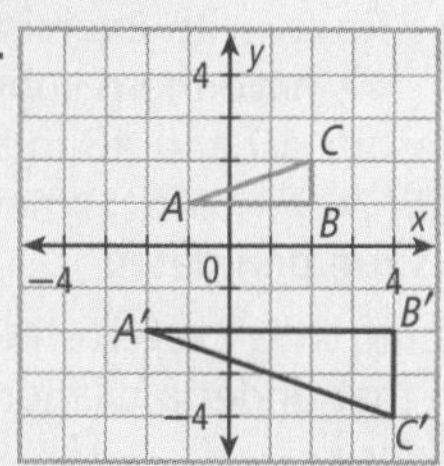

TEST PREP DOCTOR If students have difficulty with **Exercise 47,** have them substitute the values for AD and AB in the expression $2.5(2AD + 2AB)$, where $2AD + 2AB$ is the perimeter.

To help students with **Exercise 48,** remind them that under a dilation with scale factor k, $(x, y) \to (kx, ky)$.

Answers

36. 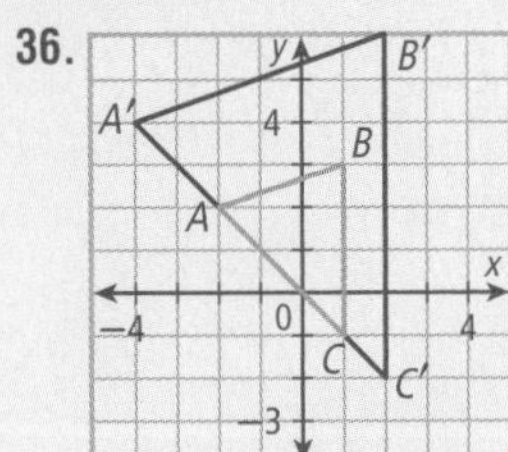

37. 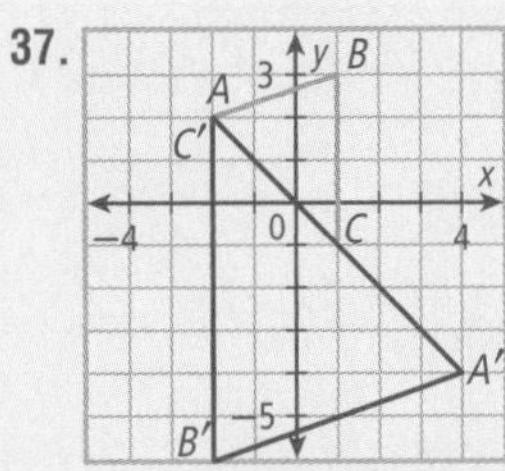

38. 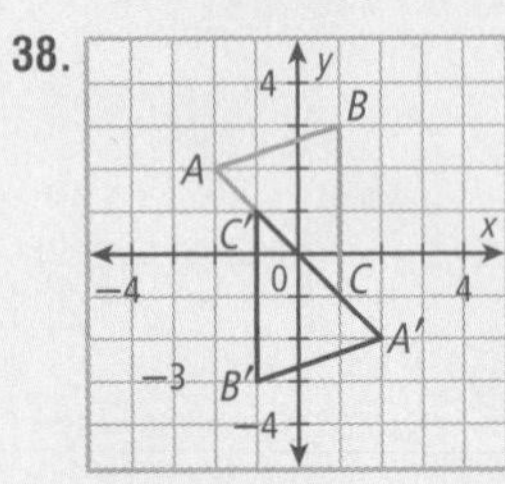

40. A dilation is equivalent to a rotation by 180° when the scale factor is -1. In this case, the image has the same size as the preimage, so the only effect of the transformation is the rotation by 180°.

41. Yes; the first dilation multiplies all the linear measures of the preimage by m. The second dilation multiplies all the linear measures of the image by n. The overall effect is to multiply all the linear dimensions by mn, which is equivalent to a single dilation with scale factor mn.

36. $k = 2$; $B'(2, 6)$, $C'(2, -2)$

37. $k = -2$; $A'(4, -4)$, $B'(-2, -6)$

38. $k = -1$; $A'(2, -2)$, $C'(-1, 1)$

39. $k = 1$ and $k = -1$; for $k = 1$, the image and preimage are the same. For $k = -1$, the dilation is equivalent to a 180° rotation. A rotation is an isometry, so the image is congruent to the preimage.

Multi-Step $\triangle ABC$ with vertices $A(-2, 2)$, $B(1, 3)$, and $C(1, -1)$ is transformed by a dilation centered at the origin. For each given image point, find the scale factor of the dilation and the coordinates of the remaining image points. Graph the preimage and image on a coordinate plane.

36. $A'(-4, 4)$ 37. $C'(-2, 2)$ 38. $B'(-1, -3)$

39. **Critical Thinking** For what values of the scale factor is the image of a dilation congruent to the preimage? Explain.

40. **Write About It** When is a dilation equivalent to a rotation by 180°? Why?

41. **Write About It** Is the composition of a dilation with scale factor m followed by a dilation with scale factor n equivalent to a single dilation with scale factor mn? Explain your reasoning.

Construction Copy each figure. Then use a compass and straightedge to construct the dilation of the figure with the given scale factor and point P as the center of dilation. **42–45. Check students' constructions.**

42. scale factor: $\frac{1}{2}$

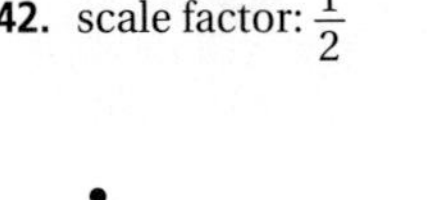
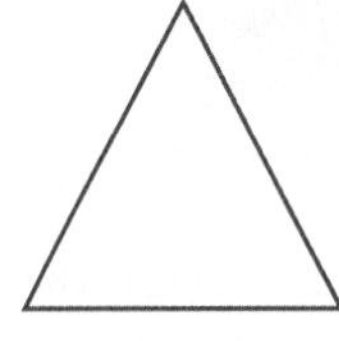

43. scale factor: 2

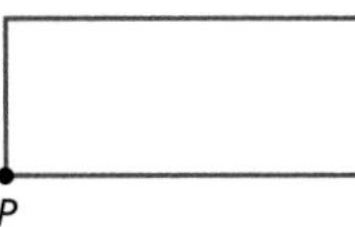

44. scale factor: -1

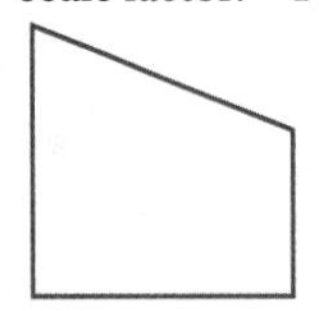

45. scale factor: -2

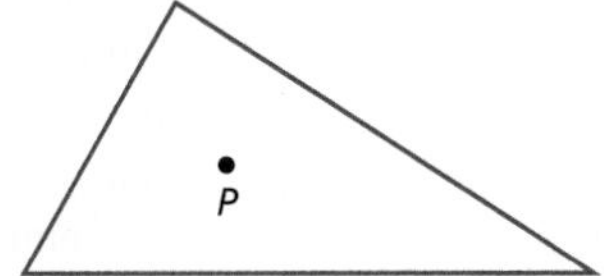

TEST PREP

46. Rectangle $ABCD$ is transformed by a dilation centered at the origin. Which scale factor produces an image that has a vertex at $(0, -2)$?

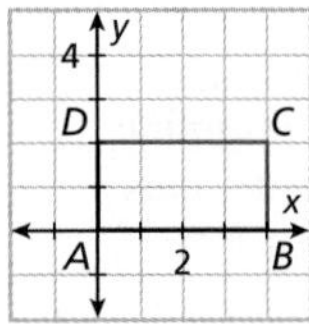

Ⓐ $-\frac{1}{2}$ Ⓒ -2
Ⓑ -1 Ⓓ -4

47. Rectangle $ABCD$ is enlarged under a dilation centered at the origin with scale factor 2.5. What is the perimeter of the image?

Ⓕ 15 Ⓖ 24 Ⓗ 30 Ⓙ 50

48. **Gridded Response** What is the scale factor of a dilation centered at the origin that maps the point $(-2, 3)$ to the point $(-8.4, 12.6)$? **4.2**

49. **Short Response** The rules for a photo contest state that entries must have an area no greater than 100 cm². Amber has a 6 cm by 8 cm digital photo, and she uses software to enlarge it by a scale factor of 1.5. Does the enlargement meet the requirements of the contest? Show the steps you used to decide your answer. **No; the dimensions of the enlargement are $1.5 \times 6 = 9$ cm by $1.5 \times 8 = 12$ cm. The area of the enlargement is $9 \times 12 = 108$ cm².**

878 *Chapter 12 Extending Transformational Geometry*

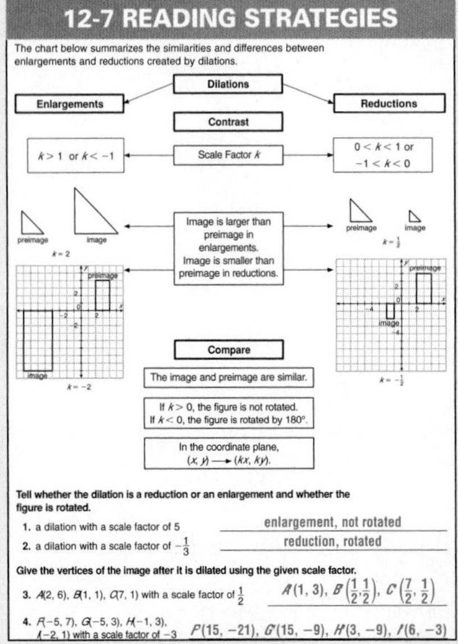

12-7 READING STRATEGIES

The chart below summarizes the similarities and differences between enlargements and reductions created by dilations.

Dilations — Enlargements / Reductions

Contrast: Scale Factor k: $k > 1$ or $k < -1$ (enlargements); $0 < k < 1$ or $-1 < k < 0$ (reductions)

Image is larger than preimage in enlargements. Image is smaller than preimage in reductions.

Compare: The image and preimage are similar. If $k > 0$, the figure is not rotated. If $k < 0$, the figure is rotated by 180°. In the coordinate plane, $(x, y) \to (kx, ky)$.

Tell whether the dilation is a reduction or an enlargement and whether the figure is rotated.

1. a dilation with a scale factor of 5 — enlargement, not rotated
2. a dilation with a scale factor of $-\frac{1}{3}$ — reduction, rotated

Give the vertices of the image after it is dilated using the given scale factor.

3. $A(2, 6)$, $B(1, 1)$, $C(7, 1)$ with a scale factor of $\frac{1}{2}$ — $A'(1, 3)$, $B'\left(\frac{1}{2}, \frac{1}{2}\right)$, $C'\left(\frac{7}{2}, \frac{1}{2}\right)$
4. $F(-5, 7)$, $G(-5, 3)$, $H(-1, 3)$, $J(-2, 1)$ with a scale factor of -3 — $F'(15, -21)$, $G'(15, -9)$, $H'(3, -9)$, $J'(6, -3)$

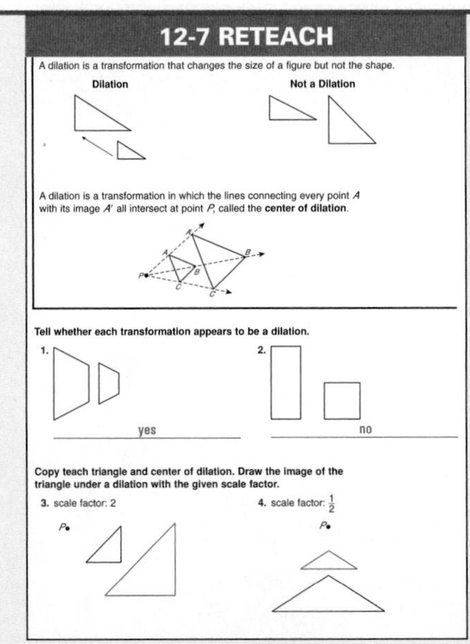

12-7 RETEACH

A dilation is a transformation that changes the size of a figure but not the shape.

Dilation / Not a Dilation

A dilation is a transformation in which the lines connecting every point A with its image A' all intersect at point P, called the **center of dilation**.

Tell whether each transformation appears to be a dilation.

1. yes
2. no

Copy each triangle and center of dilation. Draw the image of the triangle under a dilation with the given scale factor.

3. scale factor: 2
4. scale factor: $\frac{1}{2}$

CHALLENGE AND EXTEND

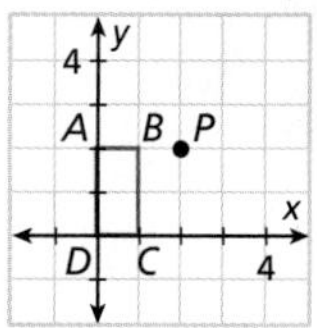

50. Rectangle $ABCD$ has vertices $A(0, 2)$, $B(1, 2)$, $C(1, 0)$, and $D(0, 0)$.
   a. Draw the image of $ABCD$ under a dilation centered at point P with scale factor 2.
   b. Describe the dilation in part **a** as a composition of a dilation centered at the origin followed by a translation.
   c. Explain how a dilation with scale factor k and center of dilation (a, b) can be written as a composition of a dilation centered at the origin and a translation.

51. The equation of line ℓ is $y = -x + 2$. Find the equation of the image of line ℓ after a dilation centered at the origin with scale factor 3. $y = -x + 6$

SPIRAL REVIEW

52. Jerry has a part-time job waiting tables. He kept records comparing the number of customers served to his total amount of tips for the day. If this trend continues, how many customers would he need to serve in order to make $68.00 in tips for the day? *(Previous course)* **45**

Customers per Day	15	20	25	30
Tips per Day ($)	20	28	36	44

Find the perimeter and area of each polygon with the given vertices. *(Lesson 9-4)*

53. $J(-3, -2)$, $K(0, 2)$, $L(7, 2)$, and $M(4, -2)$ $P = 24$ units, $A = 28$ units^2

54. $D(-3, 0)$, $E(1, 2)$, and $F(-1, -4)$ $\left(4\sqrt{5} + 2\sqrt{10}\right)$units, 10 units^2

Determine whether the polygons can be used to tessellate a plane. *(Lesson 12-6)*

55. a right triangle and a square **yes**

56. a regular nonagon and an equilateral triangle **no**

Using Technology

Use a graphing calculator to complete the following.

1. $\triangle ABC$ with vertices $A(3, 4)$, $B(5, 2)$, and $C(1, 1)$ can be represented by the point matrix $\begin{bmatrix} 3 & 5 & 1 \\ 4 & 2 & 1 \end{bmatrix}$. Enter these values into matrix **[B]** on your calculator. (See page 846.)

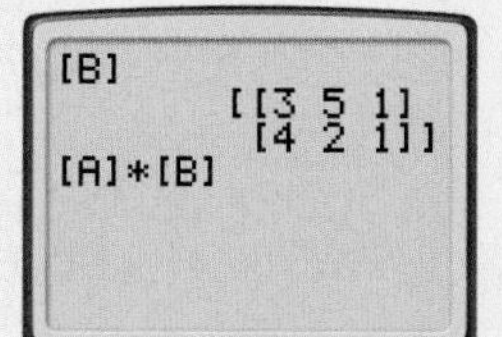

2. The matrix $\begin{bmatrix} 2 & 0 \\ 0 & 2 \end{bmatrix}$ can be used to perform a dilation with scale factor 2. Enter these values into matrix **[A]** on your calculator and find **[A] * [B]**. Graph the triangle represented by the resulting point matrix.
3. Make a conjecture about the matrix that could be used to perform a dilation with scale factor $-\frac{1}{2}$. Enter the values into matrix **[A]** on your calculator.
4. Test your conjecture by finding **[A] * [B]** and graphing the triangle represented by the resulting point matrix.

Journal

For a transformation that appears to be a dilation, have students explain how they would use a ruler to verify that it is a dilation.

ALTERNATIVE ASSESSMENT

Have each student write a rule for dilating the point (x, y) with a scale factor of k centered at the point $(4, 3)$. Have students test their rules by dilating a triangle using a scale factor of 2 and a scale factor of -2.

Answers

50a–c. See p. A32.

Answers to Using Technology

2–4. See p. A32.

Power Presentations with PowerPoint®

12-7 Lesson Quiz

1. Tell whether the transformation appears to be a dilation.

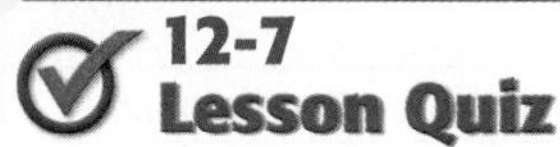

yes

2. Copy $\triangle RST$ and the center of dilation. Draw the image of $\triangle RST$ under a dilation with a scale factor of $\frac{1}{3}$.

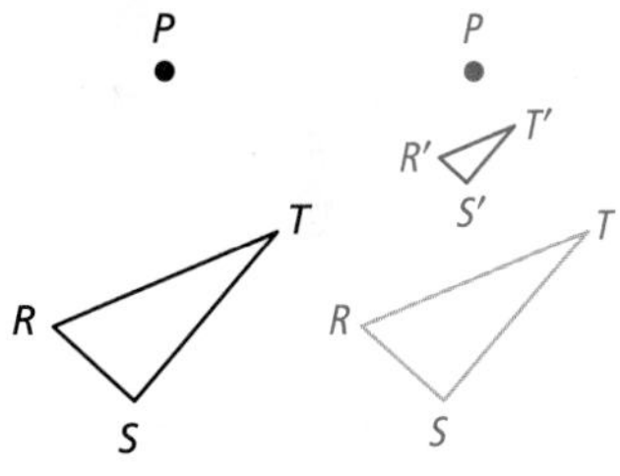

3. A rectangle on a transparency has length 6 cm and width 4 cm. On the transparency 1 cm represents 12 cm on the projection. Find the perimeter of the rectangle in the projection. 240 cm

4. Draw the image of the triangle with vertices $E(2, 1)$, $F(1, 2)$, and $G(-2, 2)$ under a dilation with a scale factor of -2 centered at the origin.

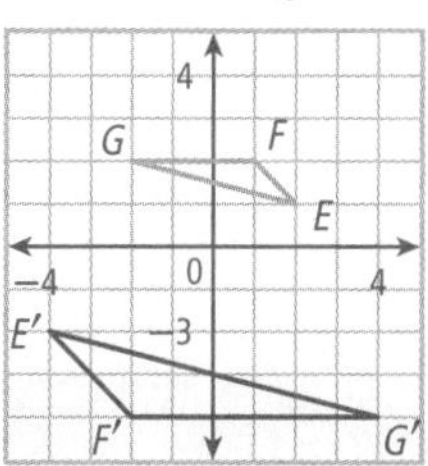

Also available on transparency

12-7 PROBLEM SOLVING

1. An artist is designing wallpaper by dilating triangles such that $\triangle KLM \rightarrow \triangle K'L'M'$. Use a ruler to make measurements and estimate the scale factor that the artist is using.
   Possible answer: 3.5 (Accept answers reasonably close to 3.5.)
2. $\triangle DEF$ is transformed by a dilation centered at the origin. What scale factor produces an image that has a vertex at $(-1, -1)$? Find the coordinates of the other two vertices after the dilation.
   $-\frac{1}{2}$; $E'(-3, -3.5)$, $F'(-2, 0)$

Choose the best answer.

3. $\triangle STU$ is dilated with a scale factor centered at the origin so that T' has coordinates $(-9, 6)$. What are the coordinates of S'?
   Ⓐ (12, −3) C (−12, 8) B (−12, 3) D (12, −5)
4. A blueprint for a horse stable shows a reduction of the stable using a scale factor of $\frac{1}{24}$. In the blueprint, a horse stall is shown by the diagram below. What is the actual area of the stall?
   F 144 ft² H 576 ft² Ⓖ 196 ft² J 1176 ft²
5. Steven is enlarging a photograph by a scale factor of 2.5 and then placing 2-inch matting around the perimeter of the enlarged photograph. If the photograph is 3 inches by 5 inches, what will be the area of the matting?
   A 37.5 in² Ⓒ 96 in² B 93.75 in² D 189.75 in²
6. What is the scale factor of a dilation centered at the origin that maps $A(5, -6)$ to $A'(-15.5, 18.6)$?
   F 2 G 3 H −2.1 Ⓙ −3.1

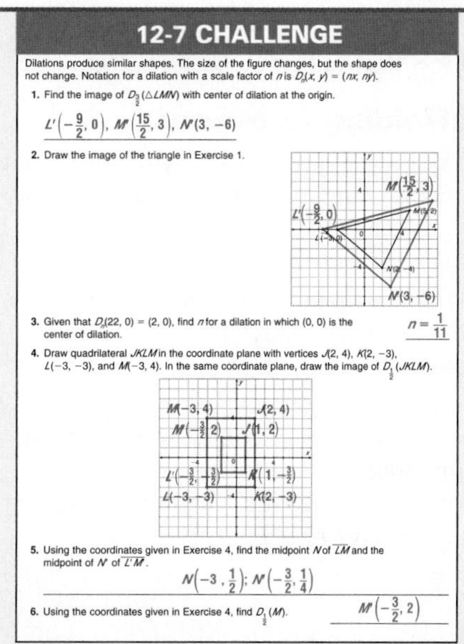

12-7 CHALLENGE

Dilations produce similar shapes. The size of the figure changes, but the shape does not change. Notation for a dilation with a scale factor of n is $D_n(x, y) = (nx, ny)$.

1. Find the image of $D_{\frac{3}{2}}(\triangle LMN)$ with center of dilation at the origin.
   $L'\left(-\frac{9}{2}, 0\right)$, $M'\left(\frac{15}{2}, 3\right)$, $N'(3, -6)$
2. Draw the image of the triangle in Exercise 1.
3. Given that $D_n(22, 0) = (2, 0)$, find n for a dilation in which (0, 0) is the center of dilation. $n = \frac{1}{11}$
4. Draw quadrilateral $JKLM$ in the coordinate plane with vertices $J(2, 4)$, $K(2, -3)$, $L(-3, -3)$, and $M(-3, 4)$. In the same coordinate plane, draw the image of $D_{\frac{1}{2}}(JKLM)$.
5. Using the coordinates given in Exercise 4, find the midpoint N of $\overline{LM}$ and the midpoint of N' of $\overline{L'M'}$.
   $N\left(-3, \frac{1}{2}\right)$; $N'\left(-\frac{3}{2}, \frac{1}{4}\right)$
6. Using the coordinates given in Exercise 4, find $D_{\frac{1}{2}}(M)$. $M'\left(-\frac{3}{2}, 2\right)$

SECTION 12B **MULTI-STEP TEST PREP**

Organizer

Objective: Assess students' ability to apply concepts and skills in Lessons 12-5 through 12-7 in a real-world format.

 **Online Edition**

Resources

 ***Geometry Assessments***
www.mathtekstoolkit.org

Problem	Text Reference
1	Lesson 12-5
2	Lesson 12-5
3	Lesson 12-6
4	Lesson 12-7

State Resources

CHAPTER 12

MULTI-STEP TEST PREP

SECTION 12B

Patterns

Tessellation Fascination A museum is planning an exhibition of works by the Dutch artist M. C. Escher (1898–1972). The exhibit will include the five drawings shown here.

1. Tell whether each drawing has parallel lines of symmetry, intersecting lines of symmetry, or no lines of symmetry.
2. Tell whether each drawing has rotational symmetry. If so, give the angle of rotational symmetry and the order of the symmetry.
3. Tell whether each drawing is a tessellation. If so, identify the basic figure upon which the tessellation is based.

1. A: none; B: parallel; C: none; D: intersecting; E: none

2. A: no; B: no; C: yes, 60°, order: 6; D: yes, 120°, order: 3; E: no

3. A: yes, parallelogram; B: yes, parallelogram; C: no; D: yes, equilateral triangle; E: no

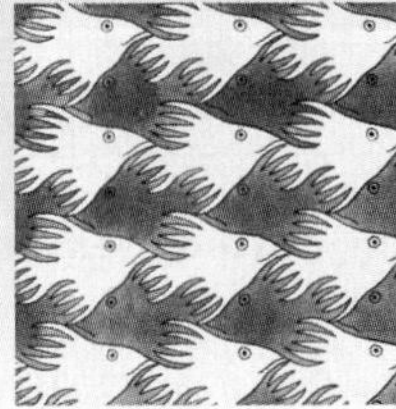
Drawing A

Drawing B

Drawing C

Drawing D

4. The entrance to the exhibit will include a large mural based on drawing E. In the original drawing, the cover of the book measures 13.2 cm by 11.1 cm. In the mural, the book cover will have an area of 21,098.88 cm^2. What is the scale factor of the dilation that will be used to make the mural? **12**

Drawing E

INTERVENTION

Scaffolding Questions

1. If a drawing has a line of symmetry, what must be true about the parts of the drawing on either side of the line? They are mirror images of each other.
2. What must be true of a drawing that has rotational symmetry? You can rotate it by less than 360° so that it will coincide with itself.
3. In which drawings could the pattern be continued to cover a plane? A, B, D, E Which could be created by repeating one basic figure? A, B, E
4. If the scale factor is k, what are the book cover's dimensions in the mural? $13.2k$ cm by $11.1k$ cm What is the book cover's area in the mural? $146.52k^2$ cm^2 What equation can you use to solve this problem? $146.52k^2 = 21{,}098.88$

Extension

For the tessellations you identified in **Problem 3,** name the geometric shape upon which the repeated figure is based. A: ▱; B: rect.; E: hexagon

READY TO GO ON?

Quiz for Lessons 12-5 Through 12-7

12-5 Symmetry

Explain whether each figure has line symmetry. If so, copy the figure and draw all lines of symmetry.

1.  yes
2. 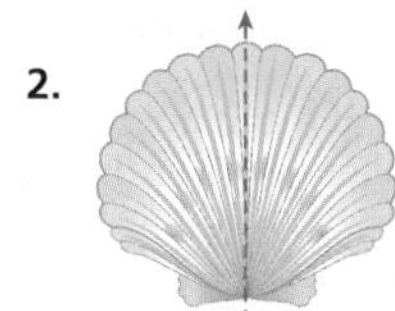 yes
3. 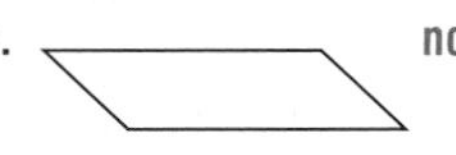 no

Explain whether each figure has rotational symmetry. If so, give the angle of rotational symmetry and the order of the symmetry.

4.  yes; 180°; 2
5.  yes; 30°; 12
6.  yes; 72°; 5

12-6 Tessellations

Copy the given figure and use it to create a tessellation.

7. 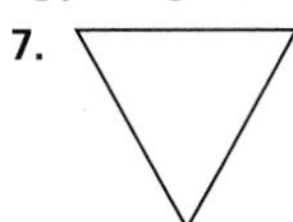
8. 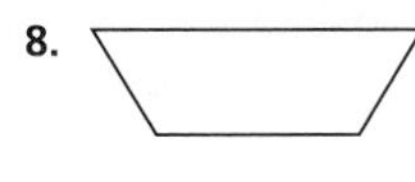

9. 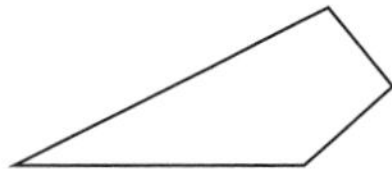

Classify each tessellation as regular, semiregular, or neither.

10. 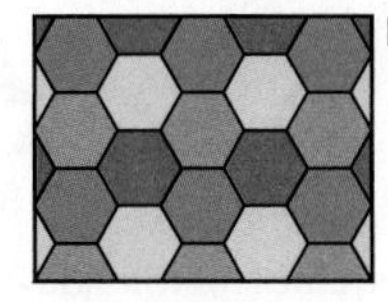 regular
11. 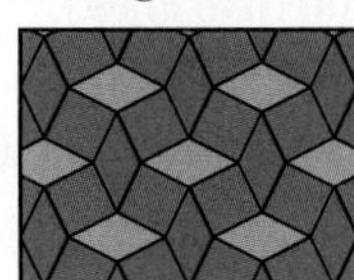 neither
12.  semiregular

13. Determine whether it is possible to tessellate a plane with regular octagons. If so, draw the tessellation. If not, explain why.
No; each interior angle of a regular octagon measures 135°, which is not a divisor of 360°.

12-7 Dilations

Tell whether each transformation appears to be a dilation.

14. 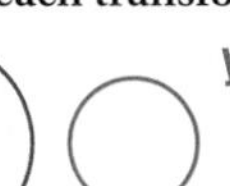 yes
15.  no
16. yes 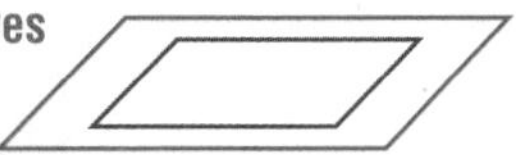

Draw the image of the figure with the given vertices under a dilation with the given scale factor centered at the origin.

17. $A(0, 2)$, $B(-1, 0)$, $C(0, -1)$, $D(1, 0)$; scale factor: 2
18. $P(-4, -2)$, $Q(0, -2)$, $R(0, 0)$, $S(-4, 0)$; scale factor: $-\frac{1}{2}$

READY TO GO ON? SECTION 12B

Organizer

Objective: Assess students' mastery of concepts and skills in Lessons 12-5 through 12-7.

Resources

 ***Assessment Resources***
Section 12B Quiz

Teacher One Stop™
Test & Practice Generator

INTERVENTION

Resources

 ***Ready to Go On? Intervention and Enrichment* Worksheets**

 ***Ready to Go On?* CD-ROM**

***Ready to Go On?* Online**

my.hrw.com

Answers

7–9, 17, 18. See p. A32.

READY TO GO ON?

Diagnose and Prescribe

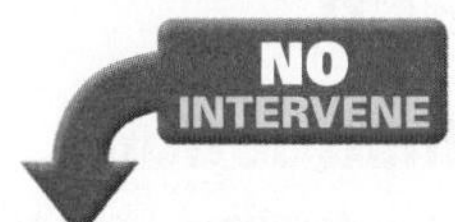

Ready to Go On? Intervention	*Ready to Go On? Intervention*, Section 12B: Worksheets	CD-ROM	Online
Lesson 12-5	12-5 Intervention	Activity 12-5	Diagnose and Prescribe Online
Lesson 12-6	12-6 Intervention	Activity 12-6	
Lesson 12-7	12-7 Intervention	Activity 12-7	

***Ready to Go On? Enrichment*, Section 12B**

Worksheets
CD-ROM
Online

CHAPTER 12 **Organizer**

Pacing: Traditional 1 day
Block $\frac{1}{2}$ day

Objective: Describe iterative patterns that generate fractals.

Using the Extension

In **Chapter 12,** students learn to use transformations, symmetry, and tessellations to create similar figures. In this extension, students use iterations to draw self-similar figures, or fractals.

Reading Math Relate the word *iteration* to the word *reiterate,* which means "to repeat something."

ENGLISH LANGUAGE LEARNERS

Teaching Tip **Math Background** A Koch snowflake has a finite area because it can be enclosed in a circle with a finite area. However, the perimeter of each stage is $\frac{4}{3}$ the perimeter of the previous stage, so at the limit, the figure has an infinite perimeter.

State Resources

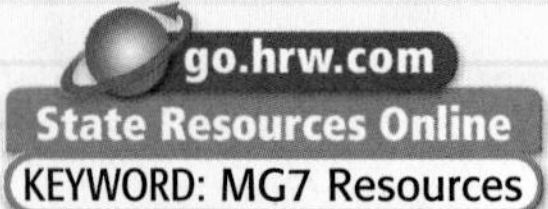

EXTENSION

Using Patterns to Generate Fractals

Objective
Describe iterative patterns that generate fractals.

Vocabulary
self-similar
iteration
fractal

Look closely at one of the large spirals in the Romanesco broccoli. You will notice that it is composed of many smaller spirals, each of which has the same shape as the large one. This is an example of *self-similarity.*

A figure is **self-similar** if it can be divided into parts that are similar to the entire figure. You can draw self-similar figures by **iteration**, the repeated application of a rule.

To create a self-similar tree, start with the figure shown in stage 0. Replace each of its branches with the original figure to get the figure in stage 1. Again replace the branches with the original figure to get the figure in stage 2. Continue the pattern to generate the tree.

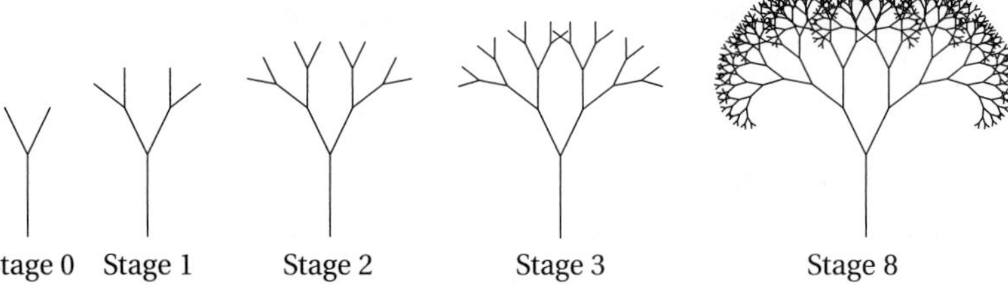

Stage 0 Stage 1 Stage 2 Stage 3 Stage 8

A figure that is generated by iteration is called a **fractal**.

EXAMPLE 1 Creating Fractals

Continue the pattern to draw stages 3 and 4 of this fractal, which is called the Sierpinski triangle.

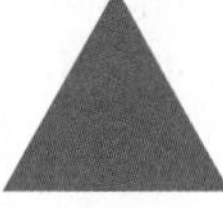
Stage 0

Stage 1

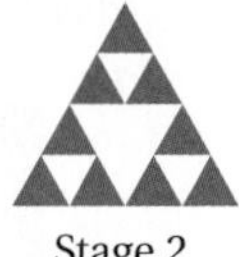
Stage 2

To go from one stage to the next, remove an equilateral triangle from each remaining blue triangle.

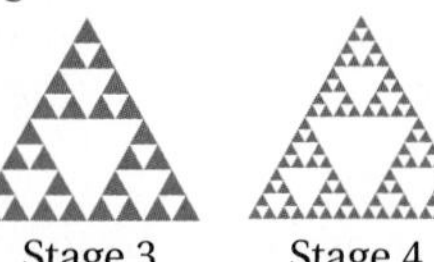
Stage 3 Stage 4

1. Explain how to go from one stage to the next to create the Koch snowflake fractal.

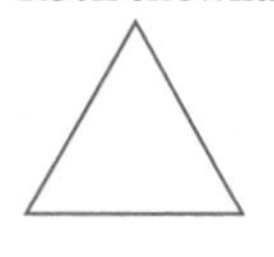
Stage 0

Stage 1

Stage 2

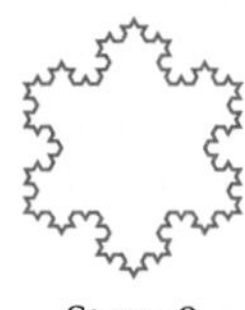
Stage 3

1. Replace each segment with the figure shown.

1 Introduce

Motivate

Self-similarity is a property of fractals. Have students research on the Internet for examples of this property. One example they might find is in satellite photos of a coastline at several different magnifications. Certain coastlines that appear rugged when viewed from a low magnification will still appear rugged when a small portion is examined at a higher magnification.

2 Teach

Guided Instruction

As you show the iterations used to create a fractal, emphasize how each part of a stage of the fractal is similar to the original figure. Discuss the concept of a *limit:* as the iteration is performed infinitely many times, the figure approaches the fractal. In the tree fractal, the number of branches increases exponentially by a power of 2 from one stage to the next.

EXTENSION

Exercises

Explain how to go from one stage to the next to generate each fractal.

1. Replace each segment with the figure shown.

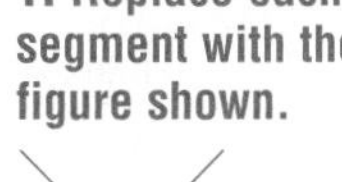

Figure alternates orientation with each replacement.

1. Stage 0 Stage 1 Stage 2 Stage 3

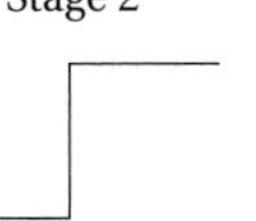

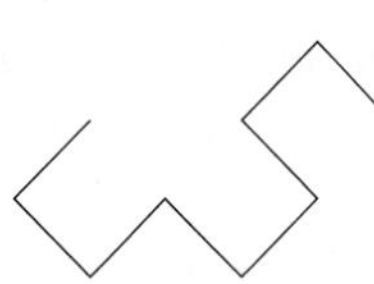

Stage 4 Stage 10

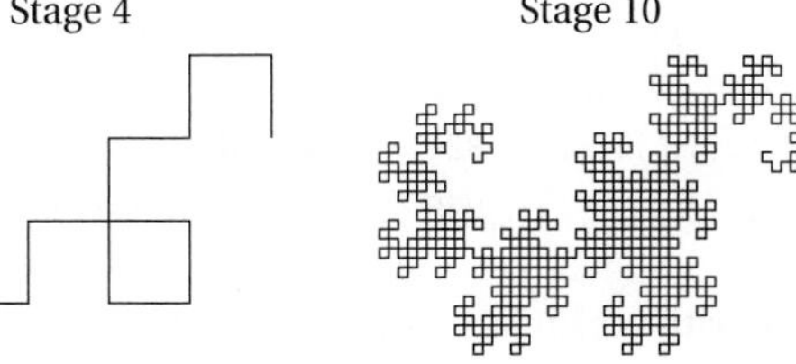

2. Replace each segment with the figure shown.

Figure alternates orientation with each replacement.

2. Stage 0 Stage 1 Stage 2 Stage 3

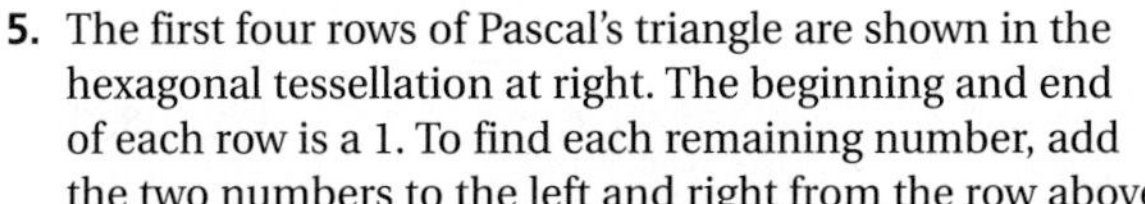

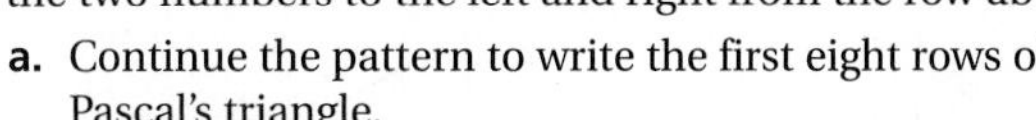

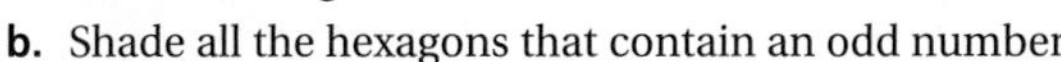

3. Stage 0 Stage 1 Stage 2

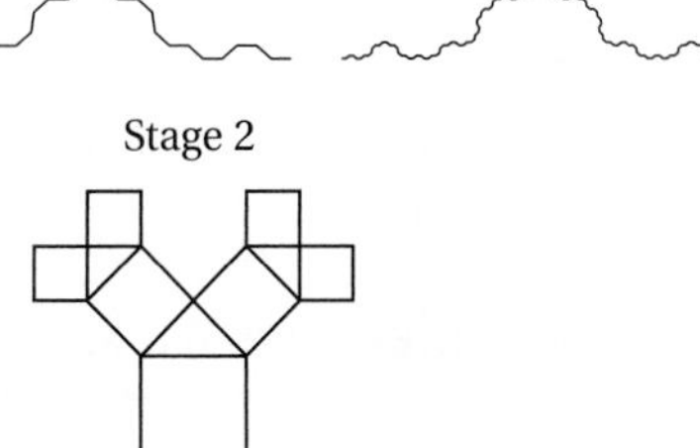

3. At each stage, add two smaller squares at the top of each existing square, forming an isosceles triangle between the three.

4. A fractal is generated according to the following rules.

Stage 0 is a segment.

To go from one stage to the next, replace each segment with the figure at right.

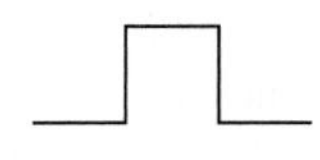

Draw Stage 2 of this fractal.

4.

5. The first four rows of Pascal's triangle are shown in the hexagonal tessellation at right. The beginning and end of each row is a 1. To find each remaining number, add the two numbers to the left and right from the row above.

a. Continue the pattern to write the first eight rows of Pascal's triangle.

b. Shade all the hexagons that contain an odd number.

c. What fractal does the resulting pattern resemble? Sierpinski triangle

6. Write About It Explain why the fern leaf at right is an example of self-similarity. The fern leaf has self-similarity because each of its smaller leaves has the same shape as the whole leaf.

In **Exercise 1,** students may replace only the segments in the middle of Stage 1 with the given figure. Remind them to replace all the segments at every stage. It may help to use tracing paper on top of the previous stage.

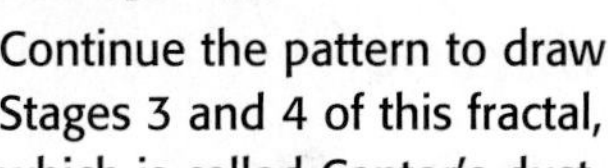

Power Presentations with PowerPoint®

Additional Examples

Example 1

Continue the pattern to draw Stages 3 and 4 of this fractal, which is called Cantor's dust.

Stage 0

Stage 1

Stage 2

Stage 3

Stage 4

INTERVENTION

Questioning Strategies

EXAMPLE 1

- How do iterations produce a self-similar figure?

Science Link Point out that the growth of each fractal is exponential and that computers are necessary to create fractal models with large numbers of iterations.

Answers

5a.

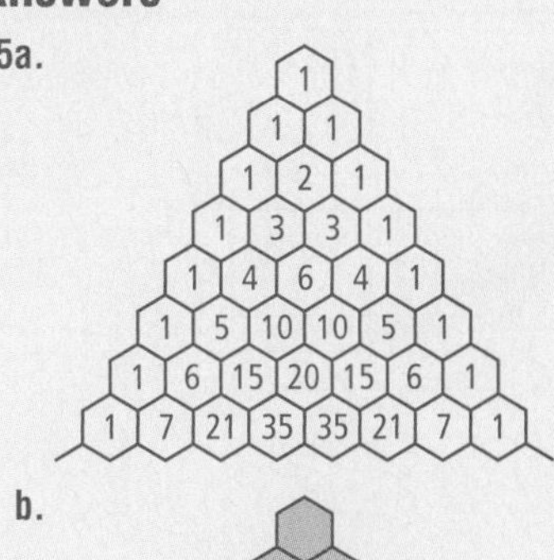

b.

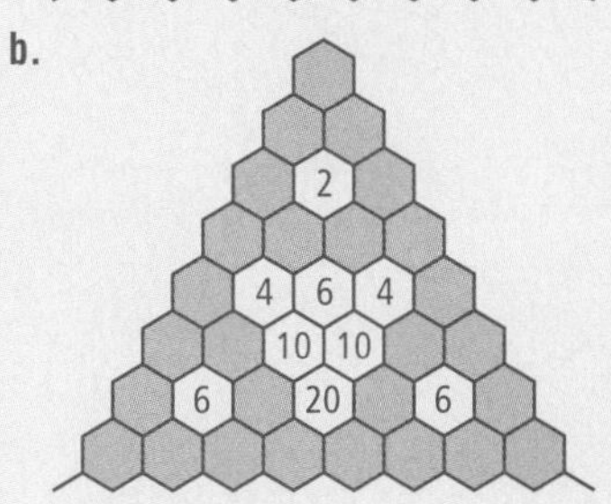

3 Close

Summarize

Review the definitions of self-similar figures and iterations, and discuss how to create fractals using iterations.

Organizer

Objective: Help students organize and review key concepts and skills in Chapter 12.

Resources

Teacher One Stop™

PuzzleView
Test & Practice Generator

***Multilingual Glossary* Online**

go.hrw.com
KEYWORD: MG7 Glossary

Tutorial Videos
CD-ROM

Answers

1. regular tessellation
2. frieze pattern
3. isometry
4. composition of transformations
5. yes
6. no
7. no
8. yes
9. 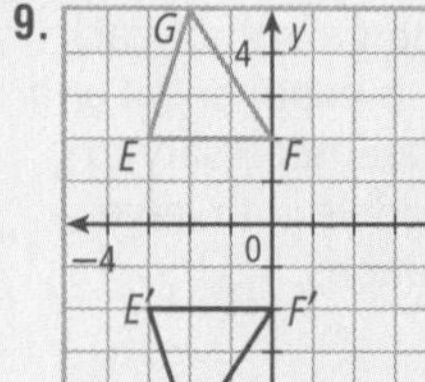
10.

11. 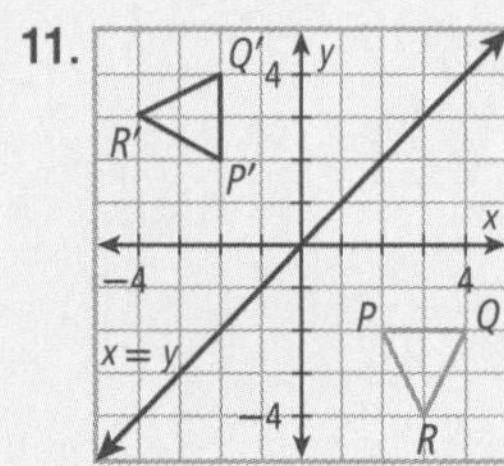

12. 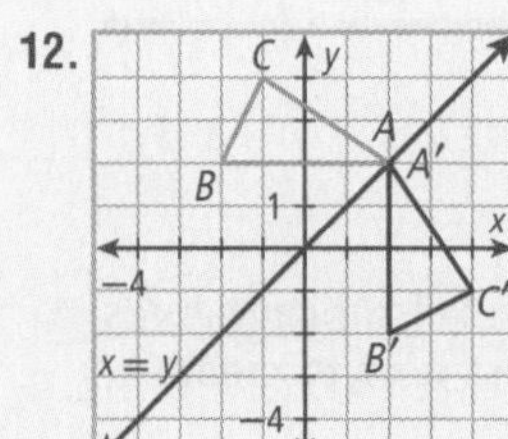

Study Guide: Review

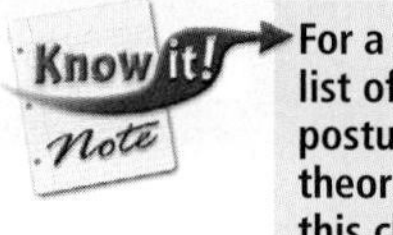

For a complete list of the postulates and theorems in this chapter, see p. PS12.

Vocabulary

Complete the sentences below with vocabulary words from the list above.

1. A(n) __?__ is a pattern formed by congruent regular polygons.
2. A pattern that has translation symmetry along a line is called a(n) __?__ .
3. A transformation that does not change the size or shape of a figure is a(n) __?__ .
4. One transformation followed by another is called a(n) __?__ .

12-1 Reflections *(pp. 824–830)*

EXAMPLE

■ **Reflect the figure with the given vertices across the given line.**

$A(1, -2), B(4, -3), C(3, 0); y = x$

To reflect across the line $y = x$, interchange the x- and y-coordinates of each point. The images of the vertices are $A'(-2, 1)$, $B'(-3, 4)$, and $C'(0, 3)$.

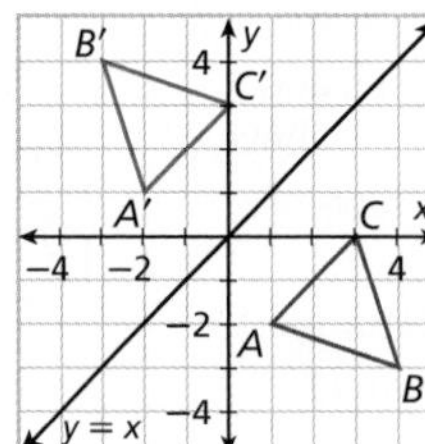

EXERCISES

Tell whether each transformation appears to be a reflection.

5. 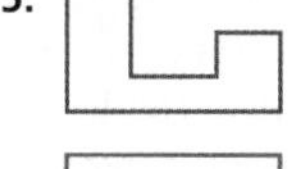 

6. 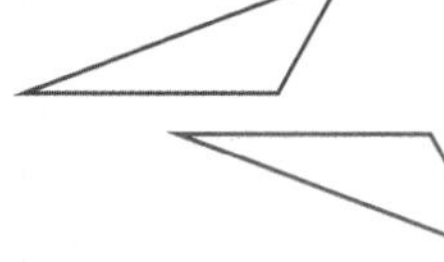

7. 

8. 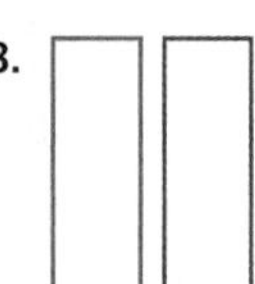

Reflect the figure with the given vertices across the given line.

9. $E(-3, 2), F(0, 2), G(-2, 5)$; x-axis
10. $J(2, -1), K(4, -2), L(4, -3), M(2, -3)$; y-axis
11. $P(2, -2), Q(4, -2), R(3, -4)$; $y = x$
12. $A(2, 2), B(-2, 2), C(-1, 4)$; $y = x$

12-2 Translations *(pp. 831–837)*

EXAMPLE

- **Translate the figure with the given vertices along the given vector.**

  $D(-4, 4), E(-4, 2), F(-1, 1), G(-2, 3); \langle 5, -5 \rangle$

  To translate along $\langle 5, -5 \rangle$, add 5 to the x-coordinate of each point and add -5 to the y-coordinate of each point. The vertices of the image are $D'(1, -1)$, $E'(1, -3)$, $F'(4, -4)$, and $G'(3, -2)$.

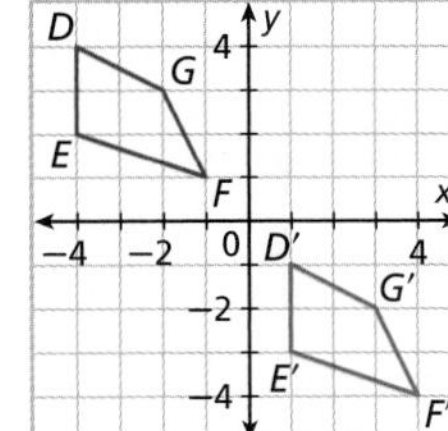

EXERCISES

Tell whether each transformation appears to be a translation.

13.
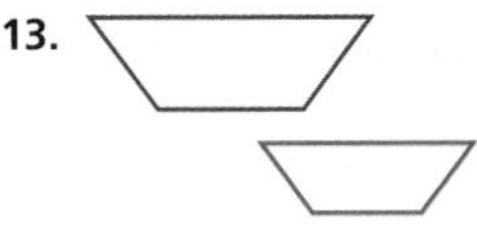

14.
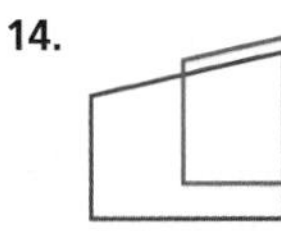

15.
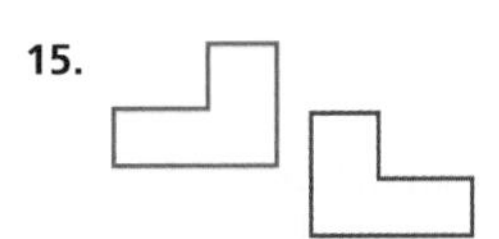

16.

Translate the figure with the given vertices along the given vector.

17. $R(1, -1), S(1, -3), T(4, -3), U(4, -1); \langle -5, 2 \rangle$
18. $A(-4, -1), B(-3, 2), C(-1, -2); \langle 6, 0 \rangle$
19. $M(1, 4), N(4, 4), P(3, 1); \langle -3, -3 \rangle$
20. $D(3, 1), E(2, -2), F(3, -4), G(4, -2); \langle -6, 2 \rangle$

12-3 Rotations *(pp. 839–845)*

EXAMPLE

- **Rotate the figure with the given vertices about the origin using the given angle of rotation.**

  $A(-2, 0), B(-1, 3), C(-4, 3); 180°$

  To rotate by 180°, find the opposite of the x- and y-coordinate of each point. The vertices of the image are $A'(2, 0)$, $B'(1, -3)$, and $C'(4, -3)$.

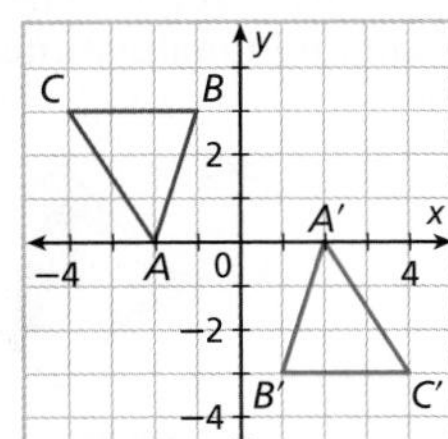

EXERCISES

Tell whether each transformation appears to be a rotation.

21.
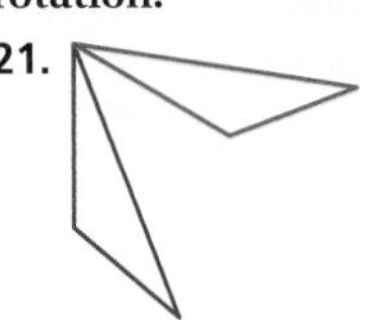

22.

23.
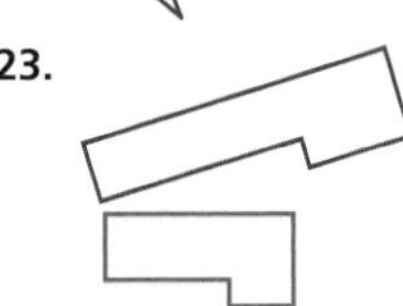

24.
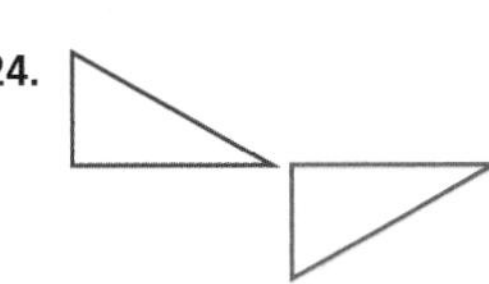

Rotate the figure with the given vertices about the origin using the given angle of rotation.

25. $A(1, 3), B(4, 1), C(4, 4); 90°$
26. $A(1, 3), B(4, 1), C(4, 4); 180°$
27. $M(2, 2), N(5, 2), P(3, -2), Q(0, -2); 90°$
28. $G(-2, 1), H(-3, -2), J(-1, -4); 180°$

Answers

13. no
14. yes
15. no
16. no
17.
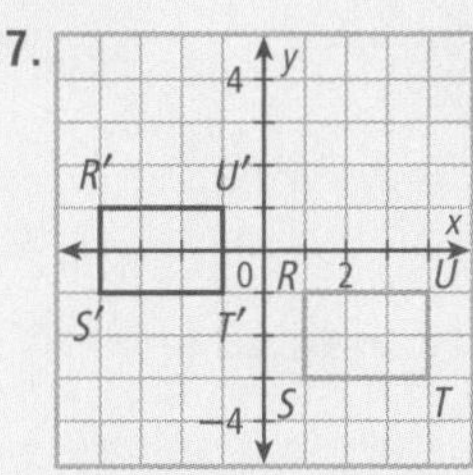
18.
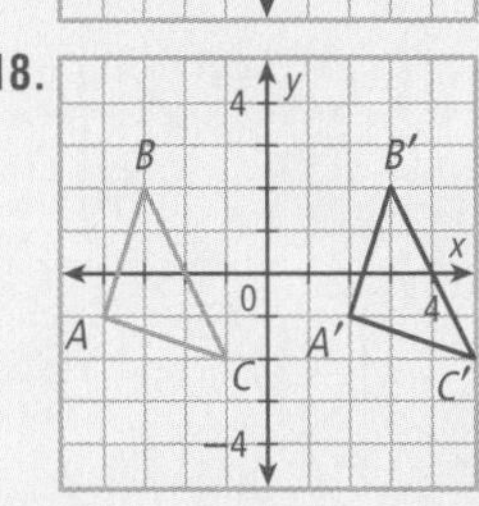
19.
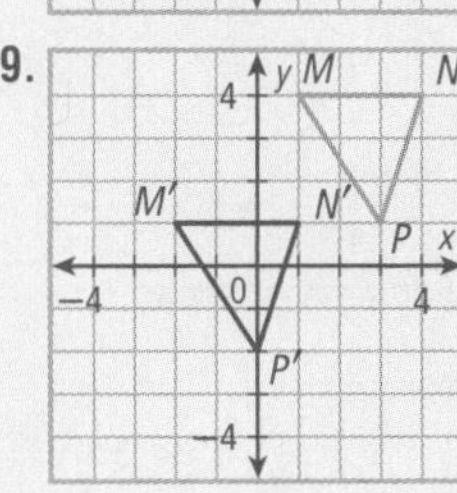
20.
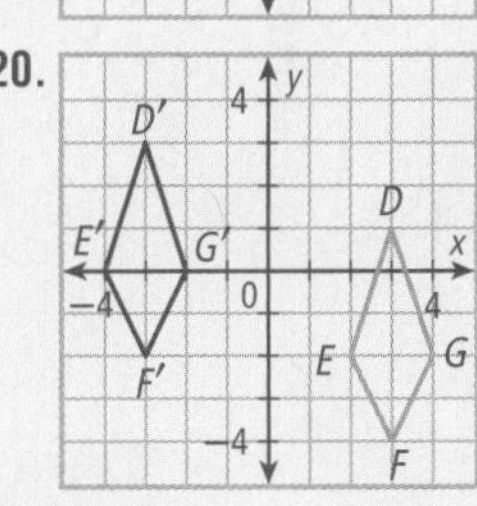
21. yes
22. yes
23. no
24. no

25.

26.
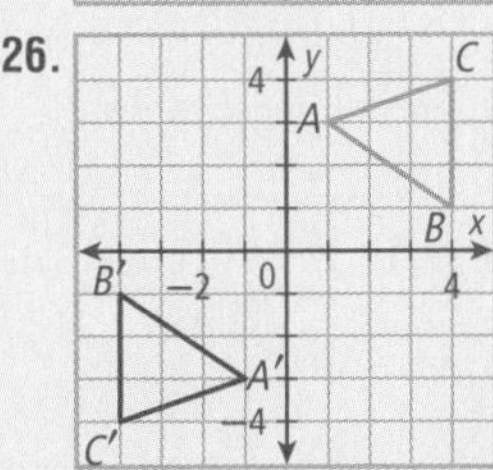

27.
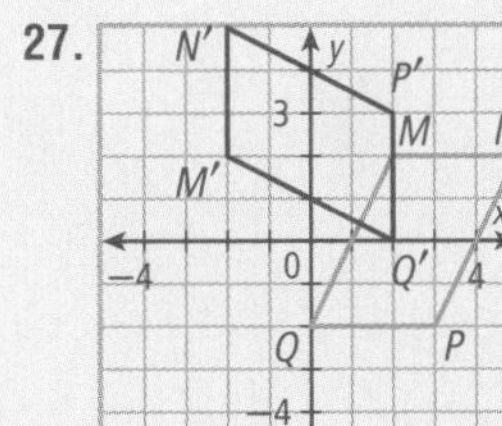

28.
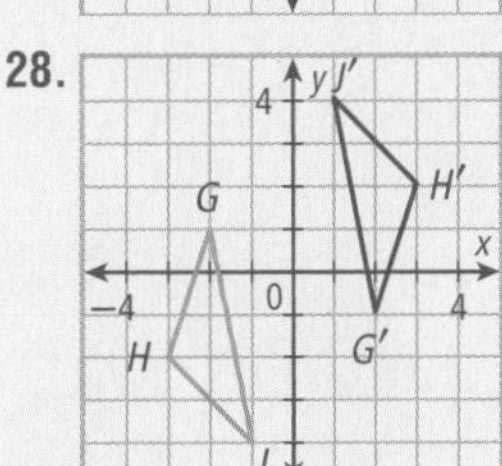

Study Guide: Review 885

12-4 Compositions of Transformations *(pp. 848–853)*

EXAMPLE

- **Draw the result of the composition of isometries.**

Translate △*MNP* along $\vec{v}$ and then reflect it across line ℓ.

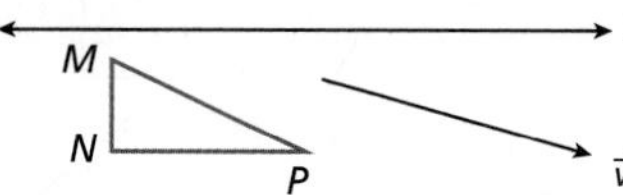

First draw △*M′N′P′*, the translation image of △*MNP*. Then reflect △*M′N′P′* across line ℓ to find the final image, △*M″N″P″*.

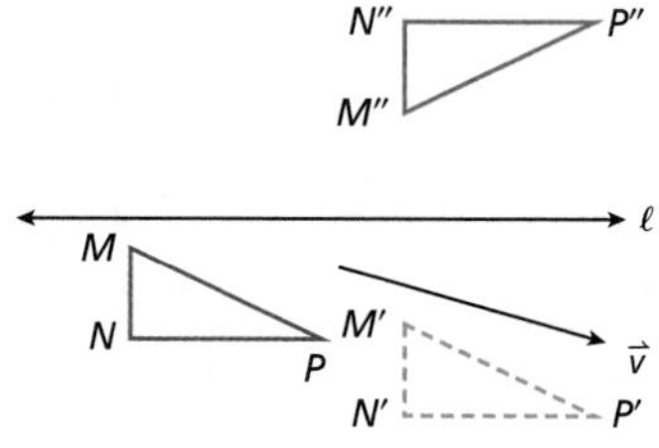

EXERCISES

Draw the result of the composition of isometries.

29. Translate *ABCD* along $\vec{v}$ and then reflect it across line *m*.

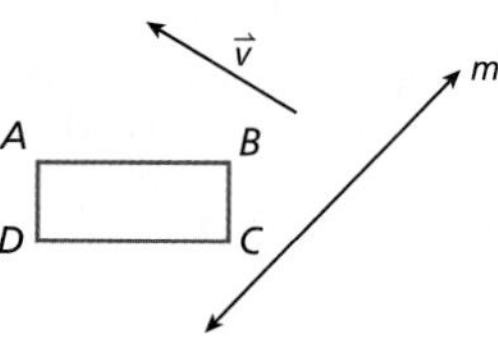

30. Reflect △*JKL* across line *m* and then rotate it 90° about point *P*.

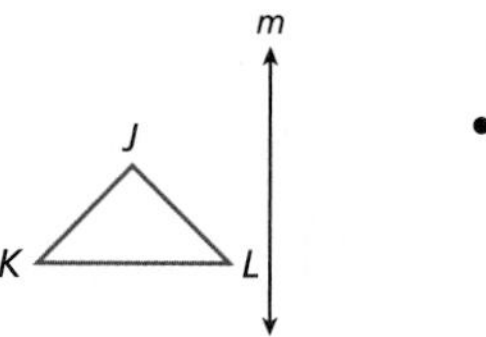

12-5 Symmetry *(pp. 856–862)*

EXAMPLES

Tell whether each figure has rotational symmetry. If so, give the angle of rotational symmetry and the order of the symmetry.

- 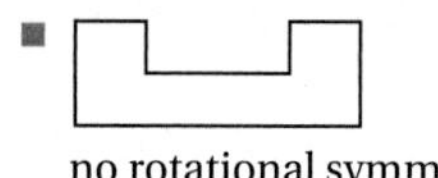

no rotational symmetry

- 

The figure coincides with itself when it is rotated by 90°. Therefore the angle of rotational symmetry is 90°. The order of symmetry is 4.

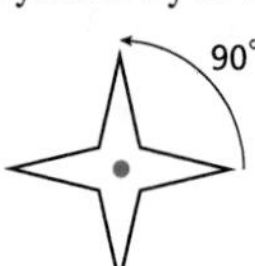

EXERCISES

Tell whether each figure has line symmetry. If so, copy the figure and draw all lines of symmetry.

31. 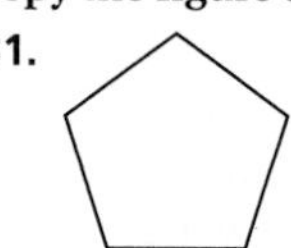

32. 

Tell whether each figure has rotational symmetry. If so, give the angle of rotational symmetry and the order of symmetry.

33. 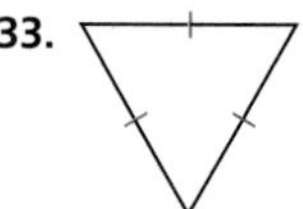

34. 

35. 

36. 

Answers

29. 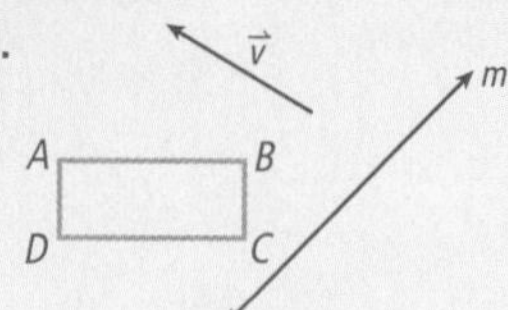

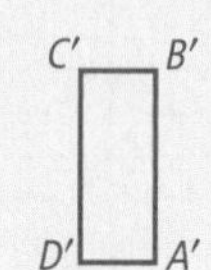

30. 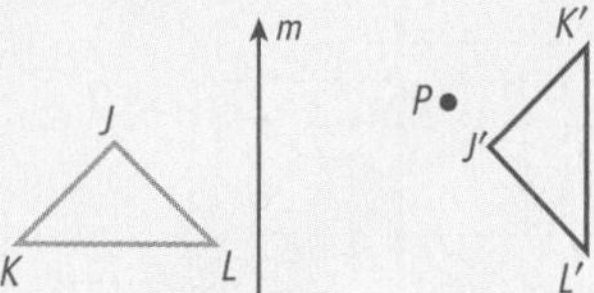

31. yes 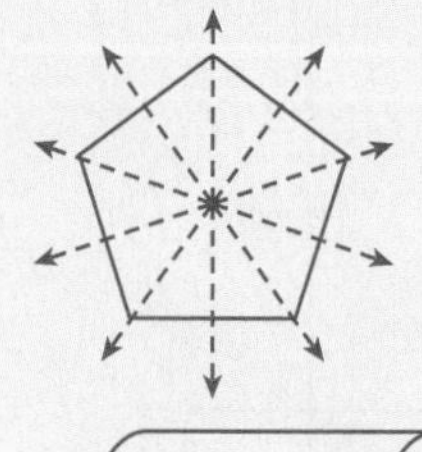

32. yes

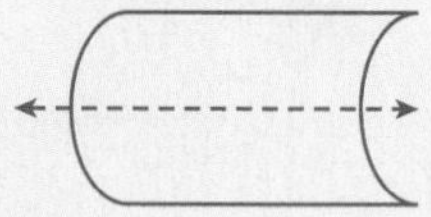

33. yes; 120°; 3

34. no

35. yes; 120°; 3

36. yes; 180°; 2

12-6 Tessellations (pp. 865–871)

EXAMPLES

■ **Copy the given figure and use it to create a tessellation.**

Rotate the quadrilateral 180° about the midpoint of one side.

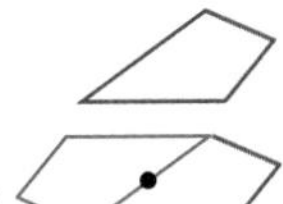

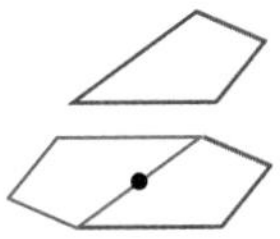

Translate the resulting pair of quadrilaterals to make a row.

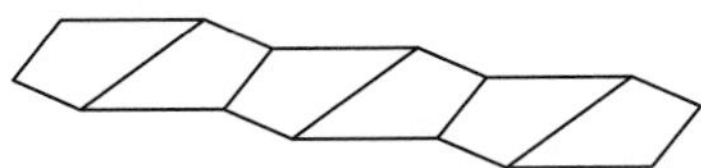

Translate the row to make a tessellation.

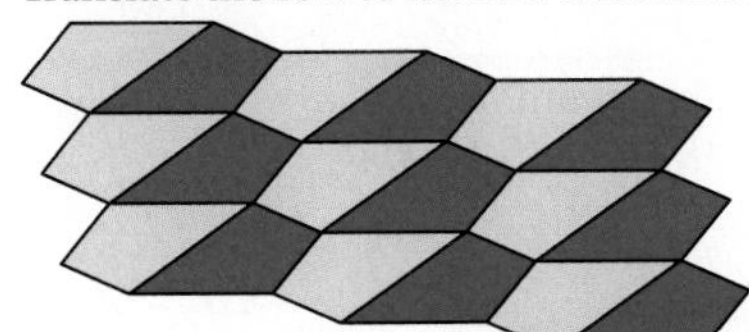

■ **Classify the tessellation as regular, semiregular, or neither.**

The tessellation is made of two different regular polygons, and each vertex has the same polygons in the same order. Therefore the tessellation is semiregular.

EXERCISES

Copy the given figure and use it to create a tessellation.

37. 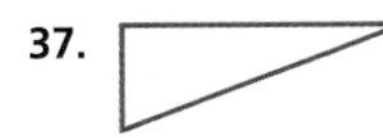

38. 

39. 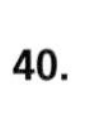

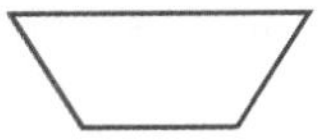

40. 

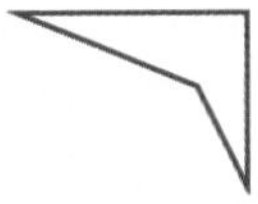

Classify each tessellation as regular, semiregular, or neither.

41. 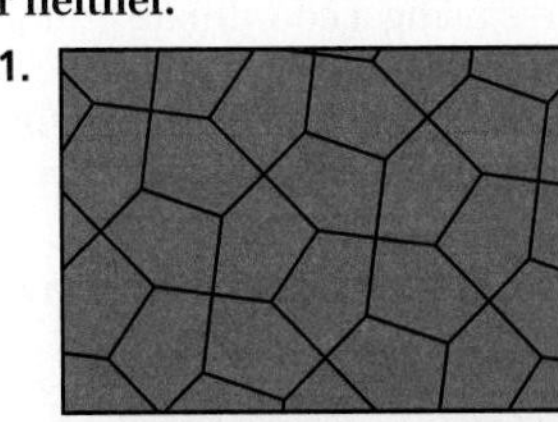

42. 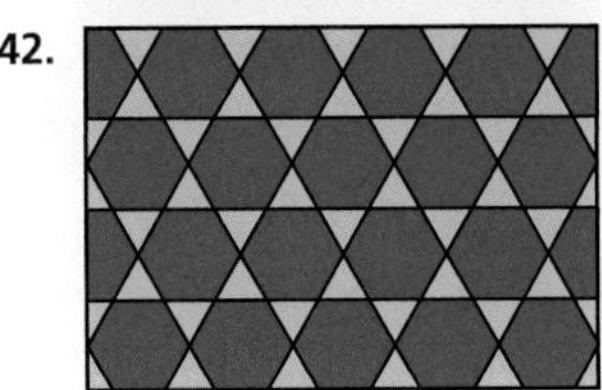

12-7 Dilations (pp. 872–879)

EXAMPLE

■ **Draw the image of the figure with the given vertices under a dilation centered at the origin using the given scale factor.**
$A(0, -2), B(2, -2), C(2, 0)$; scale factor: 2

Multiply the x- and y-coordinates of each point by 2. The vertices of the image are $A'(0, -4)$, $B'(4, -4)$, and $C'(4, 0)$.

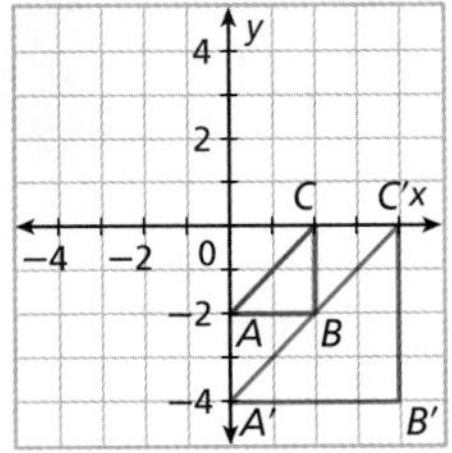

EXERCISES

Tell whether each transformation appears to be a dilation.

43. 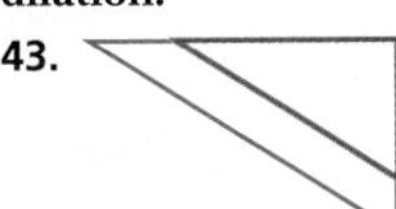

44.

Draw the image of the figure with the given vertices under a dilation centered at the origin using the given scale factor.

45. $R(0, 0), S(4, 4), T(4, -4)$; scale factor: $-\frac{1}{2}$

46. $D(0, 2), E(-2, 2), F(-2, 0)$; scale factor: -2

Answers

37. 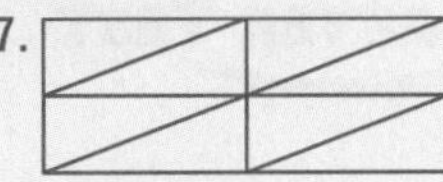

38. 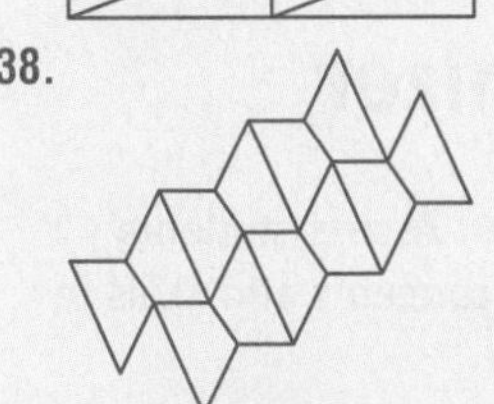

39. 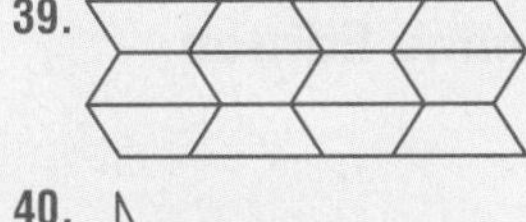

40. 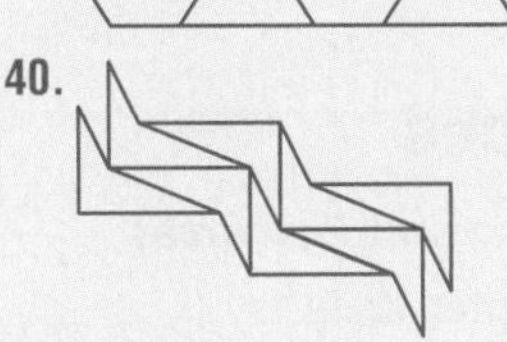

41. neither
42. semiregular
43. yes
44. yes

45. 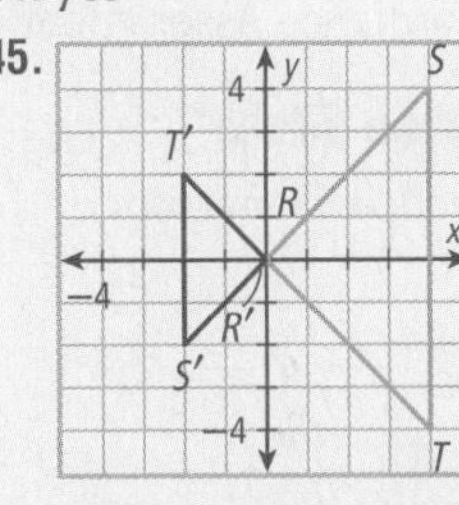

46. 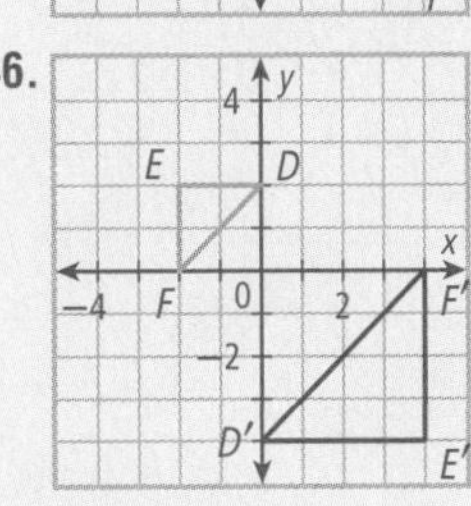

Organizer

Objective: Assess students' mastery of concepts and skills in Chapter 12.

Online Edition

Resources

Assessment Resources

Chapter 12 Tests
- Free Response (Levels A, B, C)
- Multiple Choice (Levels A, B, C)
- Performance Assessment

Teacher One Stop™

Test & Practice Generator

Answers

5.

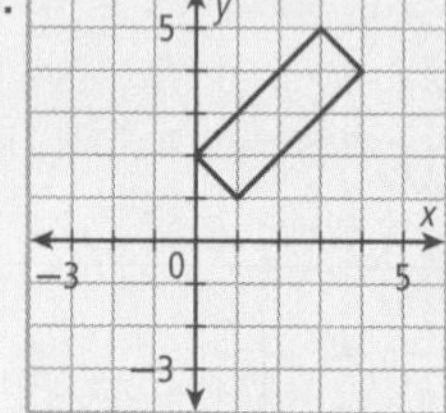

State Resources

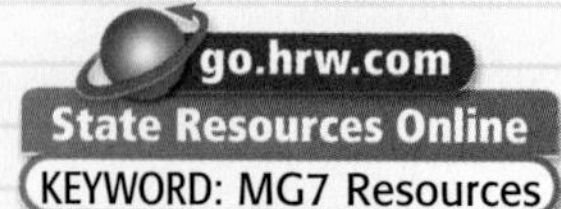

Tell whether each transformation appears to be a reflection.

1. no

2. yes

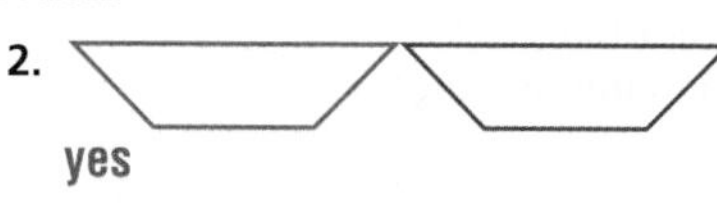

Tell whether each transformation appears to be a translation.

3. no

4. yes

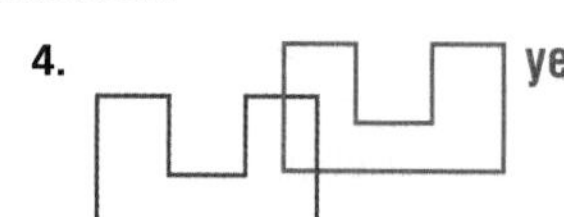

5. An interior designer is using a coordinate grid to place furniture in a room. The position of a sofa is represented by a rectangle with vertices $(1, 3)$, $(2, 2)$, $(5, 5)$, and $(4, 6)$. He decides to move the sofa by translating it along the vector $\langle -1, -1\rangle$. Draw the sofa in its final position.

Tell whether each transformation appears to be a rotation.

6. yes

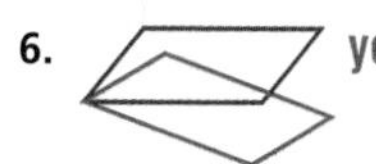

7. yes

8. Rotate rectangle $DEFG$ with vertices $D(1, -1)$, $E(4, -1)$, $F(4, -3)$, and $G(1, -3)$ about the origin by 180°.

9. Rectangle $ABCD$ with vertices $A(3, -1)$, $B(3, -2)$, $C(1, -2)$, and $D(1, -1)$ is reflected across the y-axis, and then its image is reflected across the x-axis. Describe a single transformation that moves the rectangle from its starting position to its final position. **rotation by 180° about the origin**

10. Tell whether the "no entry" sign has line symmetry. If so, copy the sign and draw all lines of symmetry. **yes**

11. Tell whether the "no entry" sign has rotational symmetry. If so, give the angle of rotational symmetry and the order of the symmetry. **yes; 180°; order: 2**

Copy the given figure and use it to create a tessellation.

12.

13.

14.

15. Classify the tessellation shown as regular, semiregular, or neither. **semiregular**

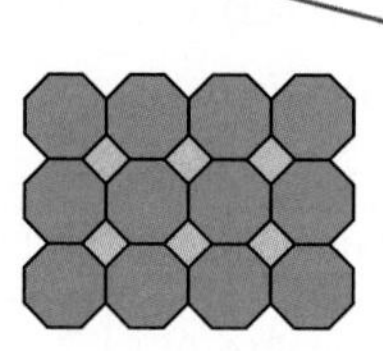

Tell whether each transformation appears to be a dilation.

16. yes

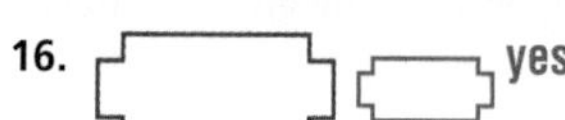

17. no

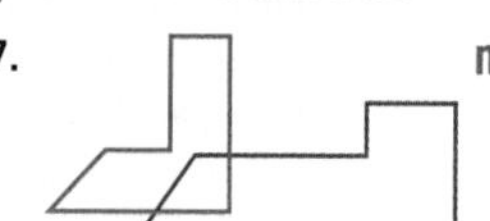

18. Draw the image of $\triangle ABC$ with vertices $A(2, -1)$, $B(1, -4)$, and $C(4, -4)$ under a dilation centered at the origin with scale factor $-\frac{1}{2}$.

8.

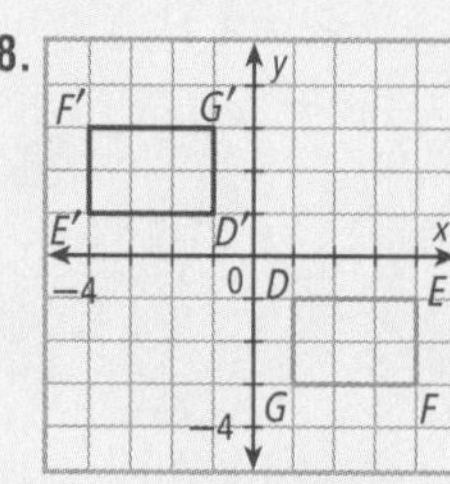

10.

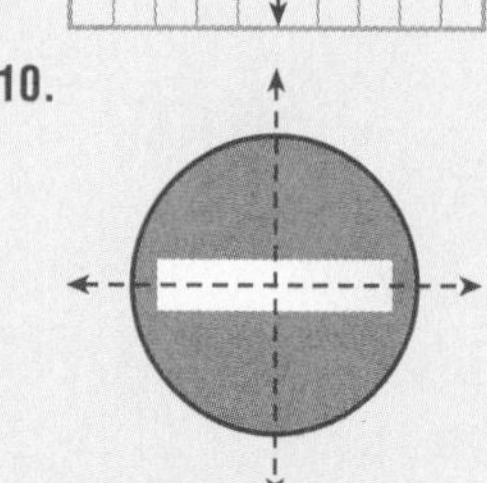

12.

13.

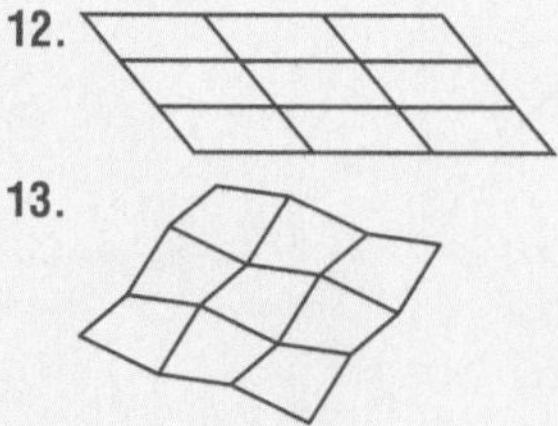

14.

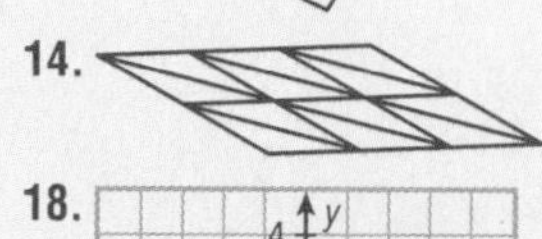

18.

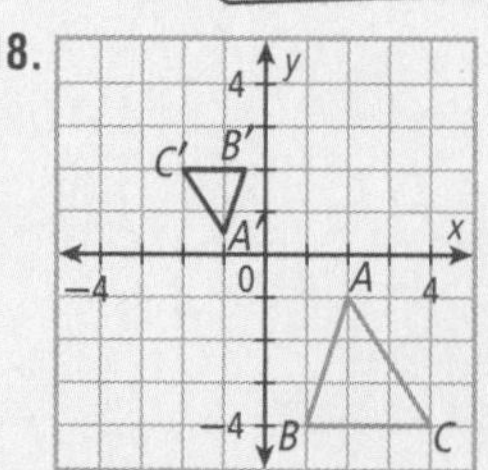

College Entrance Exam Practice

FOCUS ON ACT

No question on the ACT Mathematics Test requires the use of a calculator, but you may bring certain types of calculators to the test. Check www.actstudent.org for a descriptive list of calculators that are prohibited or allowed with slight modifications.

If you are not sure how to solve a problem, looking through the answer choices may provide you with a clue to the solution method. It may take longer to work backward from the answers provided, so make sure you are monitoring your time.

You may want to time yourself as you take this practice test. It should take you about 5 minutes to complete.

1. Which of the following functions has a graph that is symmetric with respect to the y-axis?

(A) $f(x) = x^4 - 2$

(B) $f(x) = (x + 2)^4$

(C) $f(x) = 2x - 4$

(D) $f(x) = x^2 + 4x$

(E) $f(x) = (x - 4)^2$

2. What is the image of the point $(-4, 5)$ after the translation that maps the point $(1, -3)$ to the point $(-1, -7)$?

(F) $(4, 1)$

(G) $(-6, 1)$

(H) $(-8, 3)$

(J) $(-2, 9)$

(K) $(0, 7)$

3. When the point $(-2, -5)$ is reflected across the x-axis, what is the resulting image?

(A) $(-5, -2)$

(B) $(2, 5)$

(C) $(2, -5)$

(D) $(-2, 5)$

(E) $(5, 2)$

4. After a composition of transformations, the line segment from $A(1, 4)$ to $B(4, 2)$ maps to the line segment from $C(-1, -2)$ to $D(-4, -4)$. Which of the following describes the composition that is applied to $\overline{AB}$ to obtain $\overline{CD}$?

(F) Translate 5 units to the left and then reflect across the y-axis.

(G) Reflect across the y-axis and then reflect across the x-axis.

(H) Reflect across the y-axis and then translate 6 units down.

(J) Reflect across the x-axis and then reflect across the y-axis.

(K) Translate 6 units down and then reflect across the x-axis.

5. What is the image of the following figure after rotating it counterclockwise by 270°?

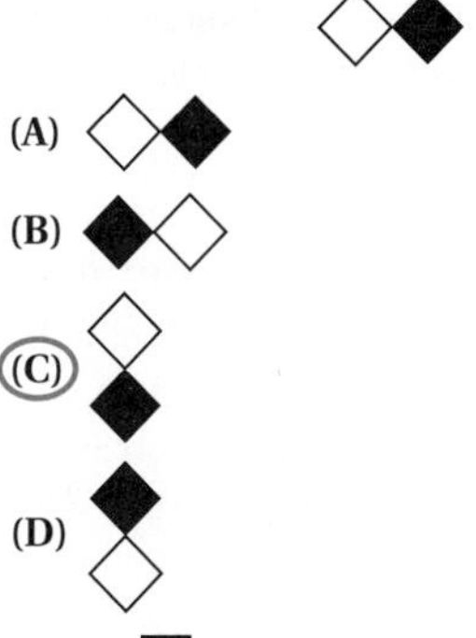

(A)

(B)

(C)

(D)

(E)

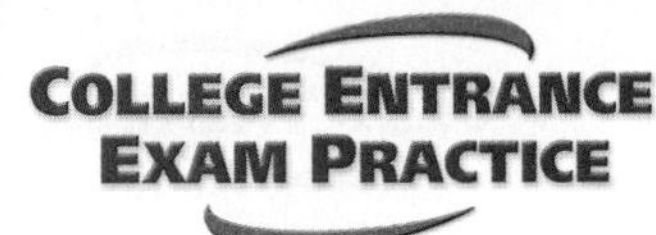

Organizer

Objective: Provide practice for college entrance exams such as the ACT.

PREMIER **Online Edition**

Resources

College Entrance Exam Practice

Questions on the ACT represent the following content areas:

Pre-Algebra, 23%

Elementary Algebra, 17%

Intermediate Algebra, 15%

Coordinate Geometry, 15%

Plane Geometry, 23%

Trigonometry, 7%

Items on this page focus on:

- Coordinate Geometry
- Plane Geometry

Text References:

Item	1	2	3	4	5
Lesson	12-2	12-2	12-1	12-4	12-3

TEST PREP DOCTOR

1. Students may choose answer **B** or **E** because they mistook a horizontal translation of the parent function for a vertical translation.

2. Students may choose answer **F** because they think the transformation applied is a reflection across the y-axis. Students may choose answer **H** because they reversed the translations in x and y.

3. Students may choose answer **C** because they reflected across the y-axis instead of the x-axis. Students may choose answer **B** because they reflected across both the x- and y-axes, or the origin.

4. Students may choose answer **G** because the segment could have been reflected across the y-axis first but the segment would not have been reflected across the x-axis to obtain segment CD. Students may choose answer **G** because this composition results in the correct x-coordinates but not the correct y-coordinates.

5. Students may choose answer **D** because it is the result of rotating 270° clockwise.

College Entrance Exam Practice **889**

Organizer

Objective: Provide opportunities to learn and practice common test-taking strategies.

TEST PREP DOCTOR + This Test Tackler demonstrates how to identify the main idea of a word problem and how to determine the important information given in the problem. Show students how to use the process shown in the example problems to highlight the main idea of a word problem. Inform them that this process can be used on any type of test item.

Standardized Test Strategies

Any Question Type: Highlight Main Ideas

Before answering a test item, identify the important information given in the problem and make sure you clearly identify the question being asked. Outlining the question or breaking a problem into parts can help you to understand the main idea.

A common error in answering multi-step questions is to complete only the first step. In multiple-choice questions, partial answers are often used as the incorrect answer choices. If you start by outlining all steps needed to solve the problem, you are less likely to choose one of these incorrect answers.

EXAMPLE 1

Gridded Response

A blueprint shows a rectangular building's layout reduced using a scale factor of $\frac{1}{30}$. On the blueprint, the building's width is 15 in. and its length is 6 in. Find the area of the actual building in square feet.

What are you asked to find?

the area of the actual building in square feet

List the given information you need to solve the problem.

The scale factor is $\frac{1}{30}$.

On the blueprint, the width is 15 in. and the length is 6 in.

EXAMPLE 2

Short Response

An animator uses a coordinate plane to show the motion of a flying bird. The bird begins at the point $(12, 0)$ and is then rotated about the origin by 15° every 0.005 second. Give the bird's position after 0.015 second. Round the coordinates to the nearest tenth. Explain the steps you used to get your answer.

What are you asked to find?

the coordinates of the bird's position after 0.015 seconds, to the nearest tenth

What information are you given?

the initial position of the bird and the angle of rotation for every 0.005 second

Sometimes important information is given in a diagram.

Read each test item and answer the questions that follow.

Item A
Multiple Choice Jonas is using a coordinate plane to plan an archaeological dig. He outlines a rectangle with vertices at $(5, 2)$, $(5, 9)$, $(10, 9)$, and $(10, 2)$. Then he outlines a second rectangle by reflecting the first area across the x-axis and then across the y-axis. Which is a vertex of the second outlined rectangle?

Ⓐ $(-5, 2)$ Ⓒ $(-2, -10)$
Ⓑ $(-5, -9)$ Ⓓ $(10, -9)$

1. Identify the sentence that gives the information regarding the coordinates of the initial rectangle.
2. What are you being asked to do?
3. How many transformations does Jonas perform before he sketches the second rectangle? Which sentence leads you to this answer?
4. A student incorrectly marked choice A as her response. What part of the test item did she fail to complete?

Item B
Short Response A picture frame can hold a picture that is no greater than 320 in^2. Gabby has a digital photo with dimensions 3.5 in. by 5 in., and she uses software to enlarge it by a scale factor of 5. Does the enlargement fit the frame? Show the steps you used to decide your answer.

5. Make a list stating the information given and what you are being asked to do.
6. Are there any intermediate steps you have to make to obtain a solution for the problem? If so, describe the steps.

Item C
Short Response Rectangle $A'B'C'D'$ is the image of rectangle $ABCD$ under a dilation. Identify the scale factor and determine the area of rectangle $A'B'C'D'$.

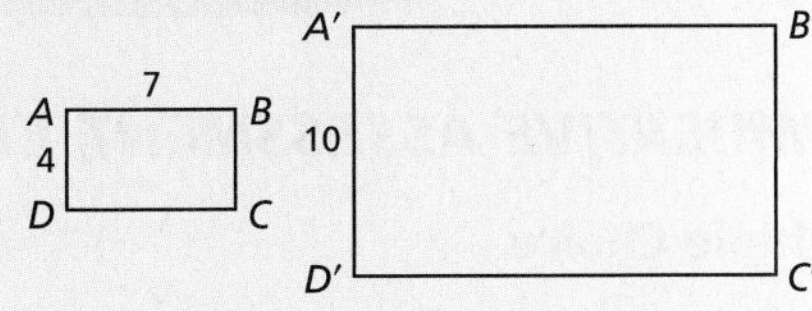

7. How many parts are there to this item? Make a list of what needs to be included in your response.
8. Where in the test item can you find the important information (data) needed to solve the problem? Make a list of this information.

Item D
Multiple Choice $\triangle ABC$ is reflected across the x-axis. Then its image is rotated 180° about the origin. What are the coordinates of the image of point B after the reflection?

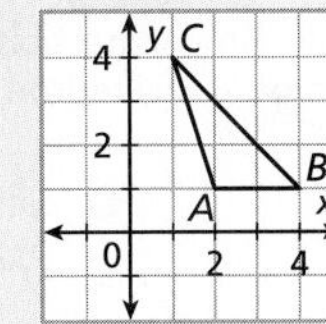

Ⓐ $(-4, -1)$ Ⓒ $(1, -4)$
Ⓑ $(-1, 4)$ Ⓓ $(4, -1)$

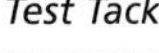

9. Identify the transformations described in the problem statement.
10. What are you being asked to do?
11. Identify any part of the problem statement that you will not use to answer the question.
12. There are only two pieces of information given in this test item that are important to answering this question. What are they?

As you read through each test item, show students some of the common mistakes that may be made if they read a question too quickly. For example, **Item D** is asking for the image of point B after only the reflection. If students also rotate point B, they will choose an incorrect answer.

Use **Items C** and **D** to show students that a diagram provided with a word problem may contain information needed to answer the question.

Answers to Test Items

A. B

B. No; the dimensions of the enlargement are 17.5 in. by 25 in. The area of the enlargement is $17.5(25) = 437.5$ in^2, which is greater than 320 in^2.

C. The scale factor is $\frac{10}{4} = 2.5$. The dimensions of $A'B'C'D'$ are 10 units by 17.5 units, so the area of $A'B'C'D'$ is 175 square units.

D. D

Answers

1. He outlines a rectangle with vertices at $(5, 2)$, $(5, 9)$, $(10, 9)$ and $(10, 2)$.
2. Find the vertices of the image.
3. 2; then he outlines a second rectangle by reflecting the first area across the x-axis, and then across the y-axis.
4. She reflected the rectangle across the y-axis, but not across the x-axis.
5. The area must be less than or equal to 320 in^2. The original photo is 3.5 in. by 5 in. The scale factor is 5. I am being asked to find whether the area of the enlarged photo is less than or equal to 320 in^2.
6. Yes; I need to multiply each dimension of the original by 5, then multiply to find the area of the enlarged photo.
7. 2; the scale factor and the area of $A'B'C'D'$
8. in the diagram; $AD = 4$, $AB = 7$, $A'D' = 10$
9. a reflection across the x-axis and a 180° rotation about the origin
10. Find the coordinates of the image of point B after the reflection.
11. The image is rotated 180° about the origin.
12. the coordinates of B, and the fact that point B is reflected across the x-axis

State Resources

go.hrw.com
State Resources Online
KEYWORD: MG7 Resources

Organizer

Objective: Provide review and practice for Chapters 1–12 and standardized tests.

 **Online Edition**

Resources

Assessment Resources

Chapter 12 Cumulative Test

go.hrw.com
KEYWORD: MG7 TestPrep

Answers

1. C	**10.** F
2. H	**11.** D
3. C	**12.** G
4. H	**13.** D
5. B	**14.** 28.9
6. G	**15.** 29.25
7. D	**16.** 6
8. H	**17.** 12
9. D	

State Resources

CUMULATIVE ASSESSMENT, CHAPTER 1–12

Multiple Choice

1. Which of the following best represents the area of the shaded figure if each square in the grid has a side length of 1 centimeter?

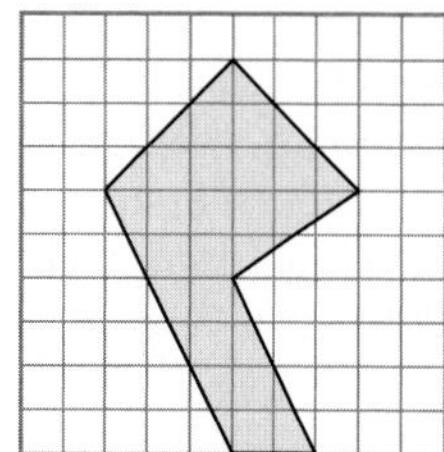

Ⓐ 17 square centimeters
Ⓑ 21 square centimeters
Ⓒ 25 square centimeters
Ⓓ 29 square centimeters

2. Which of the following expressions represents the number of edges of a polyhedron with n vertices and n faces?

Ⓕ $n - 2$ Ⓗ $2(n - 1)$
Ⓖ $2n - 1$ Ⓙ $2(n + 1)$

3. The image of point A under a 90° rotation about the origin is $A'(10, -4)$. What are the coordinates of point A?

Ⓐ $(-10, -4)$ Ⓒ $(-4, -10)$
Ⓑ $(-10, 4)$ Ⓓ $(4, 10)$

4. A cylinder has a volume of 24 cubic centimeters. The height of a cone with the same radius is two times the height of the cylinder. What is the volume of the cone?

Ⓕ 8 cubic centimeters
Ⓖ 12 cubic centimeters
Ⓗ 16 cubic centimeters
Ⓙ 48 cubic centimeters

5. Marty conjectures that the sum of any two prime numbers is even. Which of the following is a counterexample that shows Marty's conjecture is false?

Ⓐ $2 + 2 = 4$ Ⓒ $2 + 9 = 11$
Ⓑ $2 + 7 = 9$ Ⓓ $3 + 5 = 8$

Use the graph for Items 6–8.

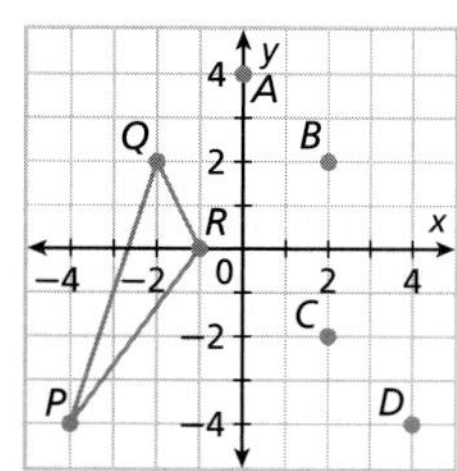

6. What are the coordinates of the image of point C under the same translation that maps point D to point B?

Ⓕ $(4, 4)$ Ⓗ $(0, 8)$
Ⓖ $(0, 4)$ Ⓙ $(4, -8)$

7. $\triangle PQR$ is the image of a triangle under a dilation centered at the origin with scale factor $-\frac{1}{2}$. Which point is a vertex of the preimage of $\triangle PQR$ under this dilation?

Ⓐ A Ⓒ C
Ⓑ B Ⓓ D

8. What is the measure of $\angle PRQ$? Round to the nearest degree.

Ⓕ 63° Ⓗ 117°
Ⓖ 127° Ⓙ 45°

9. Which mapping represents a rotation of 270° about the origin?

Ⓐ $(x, y) \rightarrow (-x, -y)$
Ⓑ $(x, y) \rightarrow (x, -y)$
Ⓒ $(x, y) \rightarrow (-y, -x)$
Ⓓ $(x, y) \rightarrow (y, -x)$

Answers

18. Possible answer: The slope of $\overleftrightarrow{AB}$ is $-\frac{1}{2}$, and the slope of $\overleftrightarrow{BC}$ is 2. So, by the Perpendicular Lines Theorem, $\overleftrightarrow{AB} \perp \overleftrightarrow{BC}$. Thus, $\angle B$ is a right angle. Since $ABCD$ is a rhombus, it is also a parallelogram. Since $ABCD$ is a parallelogram, $\angle D$ is also a right angle. Since $\overleftrightarrow{AB} \perp \overleftrightarrow{BC}$ and $\overleftrightarrow{CD} \parallel \overleftrightarrow{AB}$, then $\overleftrightarrow{CD} \perp \overleftrightarrow{BC}$, and $\angle C$ is a right angle. Since $ABCD$ is a parallelogram, then $\angle A$ is also a right angle. So, $ABCD$ is a rectangle. Since $ABCD$ is both a rhombus and a rectangle, $ABCD$ is a square.

19a. $\odot P$ has center $(2, 2)$ and radius 2.

b. A reflection of $ABCD$ over the x-axis, followed by a dilation with scale factor 2 centered at $(2, 2)$; $\odot P$ is inscribed in the image of $ABCD$.

20. 13; possible answer: Since $\triangle ABC \cong \triangle BDC$, then $\overline{AC} \cong \overline{BC}$ by CPCTC. Also, since $\overline{BC} \cong \overline{AB}$, we have $\overline{AC} \cong \overline{BC} \cong \overline{AB}$. So, $\triangle ABC$ is an equilateral triangle. Since $\triangle ABC$ is an equilateral triangle, $\triangle ABC$ is equiangular, and $m\angle A = (3x + 21)° = 60°$. Solve for x.

$$3x + 21 = 60$$
$$3x = 39$$
$$x = 13$$

When problems involve geometric figures in the coordinate plane, it may be useful to describe properties of the figures algebraically. For example, you can use slope to verify that sides of a figure are parallel or perpendicular, or you can use the Distance Formula to find side lengths of the figure.

10. What are the coordinates of the center of the circle $(x + 1)^2 + (y + 4)^2 = 4$?

Ⓕ $(-1, -4)$ Ⓗ $(1, 2)$
Ⓖ $(-1, -2)$ Ⓙ $(1, 4)$

11. Which regular polygon can be used with an equilateral triangle to tessellate a plane?

Ⓐ Heptagon
Ⓑ Octagon
Ⓒ Nonagon
Ⓓ Dodecagon

12. What is the measure of $\angle TSV$ in $\odot P$?

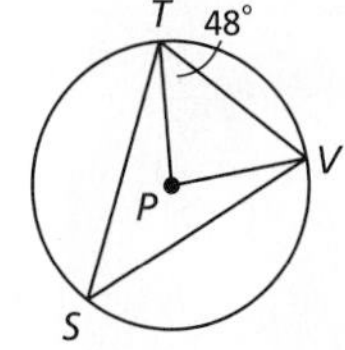

Ⓕ 24° Ⓗ 45°
Ⓖ 42° Ⓙ 48°

13. Given the points $B(-1, 2)$, $C(-7, y)$, $D(1, -3)$, and $E(-3, -2)$, what is the value of y if $\overline{BD} \parallel \overline{CE}$?

Ⓐ −12 Ⓒ 3.5
Ⓑ −8 Ⓓ 8

Gridded Response

14. $\triangle ABC$ is a right triangle such that $m\angle B = 90°$. If $AC = 12$ and $BC = 9$, what is the perimeter of $\triangle ABC$? Round to the nearest tenth.

15. A blueprint for an office space uses a scale of 3 inches: 20 feet. What is the area in square inches of the office space on the blueprint if the actual office space has area 1300 square feet?

16. How many lines of symmetry does a regular hexagon have?

17. What is the x-coordinate of the image of the point $A(12, -7)$ if A is reflected across the x-axis?

Short Response

18. $A(-4, -2)$, $B(-2, -3)$, and $C(-3, -5)$ are three of the vertices of rhombus $ABCD$. Show that $ABCD$ is a square. Justify your answer.

19. $ABCD$ is a square with vertices $A(3, -1)$, $B(3, -3)$, $C(1, -3)$, and $D(1, -1)$. $\odot P$ is a circle with equation $(x - 2)^2 + (y - 2)^2 = 4$.
   a. What is the center and radius of $\odot P$?
   b. Describe a reflection and dilation of $ABCD$ so that $\odot P$ is inscribed in the image of $ABCD$. Justify your answer.

20. Determine the value of x if $\triangle ABC \cong \triangle BDC$. Justify your answer.

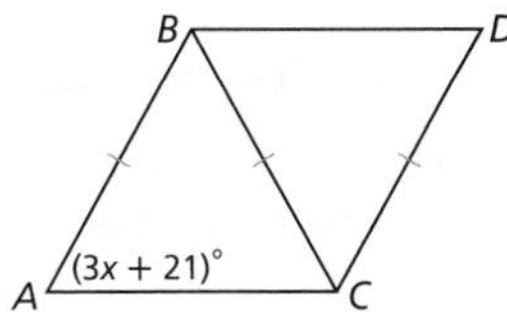

21. $\triangle ABC$ is reflected across line m.
   a. What observations can be made about $\triangle ABC$ and its reflected image $\triangle A'B'C'$ regarding the following properties: collinearity, betweenness, angle measure, triangle congruence, and orientation?
   b. Explain.

22. Given the coordinates of points A, B, and C, explain how you could demonstrate that the three points are collinear.

23. Proving that the diagonals of rectangle $KLMN$ are equal using a coordinate proof involves placement of the rectangle and selection of coordinates.
   a. Is it possible to always position rectangle $KLMN$ so that one vertex coincides with the origin?
   b. Why is it convenient to place rectangle $KLMN$ so that one vertex is at the origin?

Extended Response

24. $\overline{AB}$ has endpoints $A(0, 3)$ and $B(2, 5)$.
   a. Draw $\overline{AB}$ and its image, $\overline{A'B'}$, under the translation $\langle 0, -8 \rangle$.
   b. Find the equations of two lines such that the composition of the two reflections across the lines will also map $\overline{AB}$ to $\overline{A'B'}$. Show your work or explain in words how you found your answer.
   c. Show that any glide reflection is equivalent to a composition of three reflections.

Short-Response Rubric

Items 18–23

2 Points = The student's answer is an accurate and complete execution of the task or tasks.

1 Point = The student's answer contains attributes of an appropriate response but is flawed.

0 Points = The student's answer contains no attributes of an appropriate response.

Extended-Response Rubric

Item 24

4 Points = The student correctly graphs $\overline{AB}$ and $\overline{A'B'}$ and finds correct equations of the two lines of reflection. Explanations are complete, and work demonstrates a thorough understanding of all concepts related to compositions of reflections.

3 Points = The student's explanations are correct but may contain minor flaws. Work demonstrates an understanding of major concepts.

2 Points = The student answers correctly, but explanations are missing or incomplete. Work demonstrates a limited understanding of concepts.

1 Point = The student answers incorrectly but makes a reasonable attempt to show work or offer an explanation.

0 Points = The student does not answer correctly and does not attempt all parts of the problem.

21a. These properties are preserved.
b. Line reflection is an isometry.
22. Possible answer: Show that the slope of $\overleftrightarrow{AB}$ = the slope of $\overleftrightarrow{AC}$.
23a. Yes; the axes are ⊥ and form one of the rt. ∡ of the rect.
b. It is easier to use the Dist. Formula.
24a.

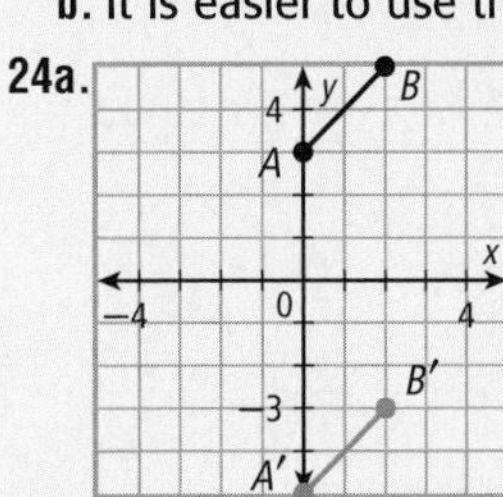

b. Possible answer: $y = 1$ and $y = -3$; the midpt. M of $\overline{AA'}$ is $\left(0, \frac{3-5}{2}\right) = (0, -1)$. The composition of two reflections across two ∥ lines is equivalent to a translation of twice the distance between the lines in a direction ⊥ to the lines. So the lines of reflection are the ⊥ bisectors of $\overline{AM}$ and $\overline{A'M}$.
The midpt. of $\overline{AM}$ is $\left(0, \frac{3-1}{2}\right) = (0, 1)$, and the midpt. of $\overline{A'M}$ is $\left(0, \frac{-5-1}{2}\right) = (0, -3)$. Since $\overleftrightarrow{AM}$ and $\overleftrightarrow{AM'}$ are vertical lines, the ⊥ bisectors of $\overline{AM}$ and $\overline{A'M}$ are horiz. lines passing through $(0, 1)$ and $(0, -3)$. The equations of the lines of reflection are $y = 1$ and $y = -3$.
c. A glide reflection is the composition of a translation and reflection.
Because the translation is equivalent to a composition of two reflections, the glide reflection is equivalent to the composition of two reflections followed by another reflection. So any glide reflection is equivalent to the composition of three reflections.

Organizer

Objective: Choose appropriate problem-solving strategies and use them with skills from Chapters 11 and 12 to solve real-world problems.

Sandy Hook Lighthouse

Reading Strategies

ENGLISH LANGUAGE LEARNERS

For **Problem 3,** have students reread the problem and then ask them what they need to know in order to identify the order of the lighthouse's lens.

Using Data Discuss with students what information the table gives. the diameter of each order of Fresnel lens Have students use the information in the table to estimate the order of the lens in the picture.

State Resources

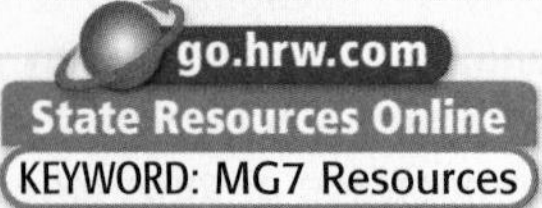

go.hrw.com
State Resources Online
KEYWORD: MG7 Resources

Sandy Hook Lighthouse

Sandy Hook Lighthouse in northern New Jersey has been guiding ships into New York Harbor for nearly 250 years. Built in 1764, the 85-foot tower is the oldest working lighthouse in the country.

Choose one or more strategies to solve each problem.

1. The beam from the lighthouse is visible for up to 19 miles at sea. To the nearest square mile, what is the area of water covered by the beam as it rotates through an angle of 60°? 189 mi^2
2. Given that Earth's radius is approximately 4000 miles, find the distance from the top of the tower to the horizon. 11.3 mi
3. Most lighthouses use *Fresnel lenses,* named after their inventor, Augustine Fresnel. The chart shows the sizes, or *orders,* of the circular lenses. Use the diagram of the lens to determine the order of the Fresnel lens at the Sandy Hook Lighthouse. third

Fresnel Lenses	
Order	Diameter
First	6 ft 1 in.
Second	4 ft 7 in.
Third	3 ft 3 in.
Fourth	1 ft 8 in.
Fifth	1 ft 3 in.
Sixth	1 ft 0 in.

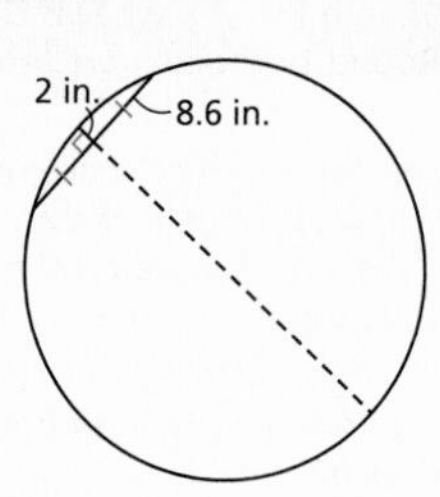

Problem-Solving Focus

Discuss with students the strategies they used to solve each problem. Have students share with the class any diagrams they may have drawn.

Moveable Bridges

New Jersey is home to more than two dozen moveable bridges. A moveable bridge has a section that can be lifted, tilted, or swung out of the way so that tall boats can pass.

1. The Cape May Canal Bridge is a *swing bridge.* Part of the roadbed can pivot horizontally to let boats pass. What transformation describes the motion of the bridge? The pivoting section moves through an angle of 90°. How far does a point 10 ft from the pivot travel as the bridge opens? **rotation; 14.1 ft**

A *lift bridge* contains a section that can be translated vertically. For 2–4, use the table.

Lift Bridges		
Name	Vertical Clearance (Lowered Position)	Vertical Clearance (Raised Position)
Burlington-Bristol Bridge	35 ft	138 ft
Delair Lift Bridge	49 ft	135 ft

2. It takes 2 min to completely lift the roadbed of the Burlington-Bristol Bridge. At what speed in feet per minute does the lifting mechanism translate the roadbed? **51.5 ft/min**
3. To the nearest second, how long does it take the Burlington-Bristol Bridge's lifting mechanism to translate the roadbed 10 ft? **12 s**
4. Suppose the Delair Lift Bridge can be raised at the same speed as the Burlington-Bristol Bridge. To the nearest second, how long would it take to completely lift its roadbed? **100 s**
5. The HX Drawbridge in Secaucus is a *bascule bridge.* Weights are used to raise part of its deck at an angle. The moveable section of the HX Drawbridge is 151 ft long. Find the height of the deck above the roadway after it has been rotated by an angle of 20°. **51.6 ft**

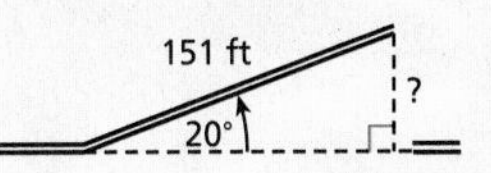

Moveable Bridges

Reading Strategies

English Language Learners

For **Problem 5,** tell students that the term bascule comes from the French word for seesaw. Then ask students how they think a bascule bridge might operate.

Using Data Discuss with students what information the table gives. information about the heights of bridges in their raised and lowered positions Have students use the information in the table to determine whether the bridge in the picture is raised or lowered.

Problem-Solving Focus

For **Problem 3,** focus on the second step of the problem-solving process: **(2) Make a Plan.**

Discuss with students what they already know about the bridge from their solution to **Problem 2.** Remind students that the speed in ft/min gives the distance the roadbed moves in 1 min. Encourage students to use proportional reasoning. Ask them to rewrite the problem in the following form: "If the roadbed takes 60 s to move 51.5 ft, then it takes x s to move 10 ft." This may help students set up an appropriate proportion.

Ask students what strategies they used to solve each problem. Have them compare the different strategies they each used to solve **Problem 5.** One student might have created an accurate scale drawing and used a compass and straightedge to construct the rotation. Another might have used trigonometry to find the height of the deck.

Additional Topics in Geometry

ADDITIONAL TOPIC

A-1 Organizer

Objectives: Solve locus problems and apply loci to real-world applications.

Warm Up

Use the figure to name each of the following.

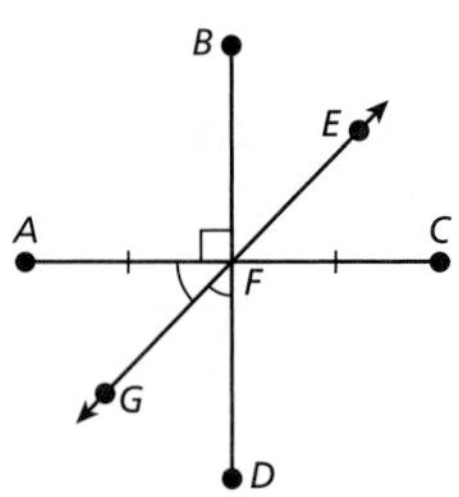

1. perpendicular bisector of $\overline{AC}$ $\overline{BD}$
2. angle bisector of ∠BFC $\overleftrightarrow{GE}$
3. two points equidistant from $\overline{BD}$ A and C

Additional Examples

Example 1

Draw the locus of points that are equidistant from the endpoints of a 3-cm line segment

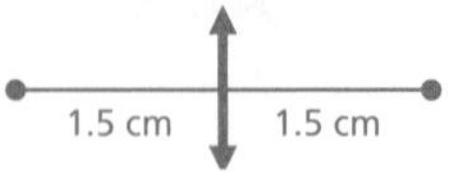

State Resources

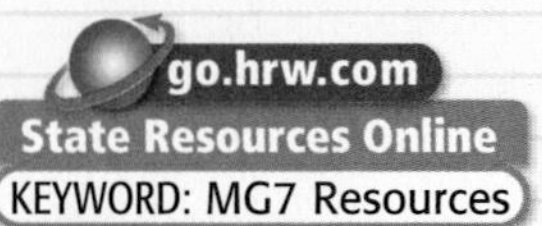

ADDITIONAL TOPIC

A-1 Loci

Objectives

Solve locus problems and apply loci to real-world applications.

Vocabulary

compound locus

In Chapter 5, you learned that a locus is a set of points that satisfies a given condition. For example, a perpendicular bisector of a segment is the locus of points that are equidistant from the endpoints of the segment.

The table summarizes some of the basic loci you've already learned about.

Locus	Object
All points a fixed distance from a point in the plane	Circle
All points equidistant from the endpoints of a segment	Perpendicular bisector
All points equidistant from two rays of an angle	Angle bisector

EXAMPLE 1 Drawing a Locus

Draw the locus of points that are 1 cm from a line in a plane.

First draw a line. Then draw several points that are 1 cm from the line to see if there is a pattern.

If you connect the points you've drawn, you get a line 1 cm above the line and another 1 cm below the line. The locus consists of two parallel lines above and below the original line.

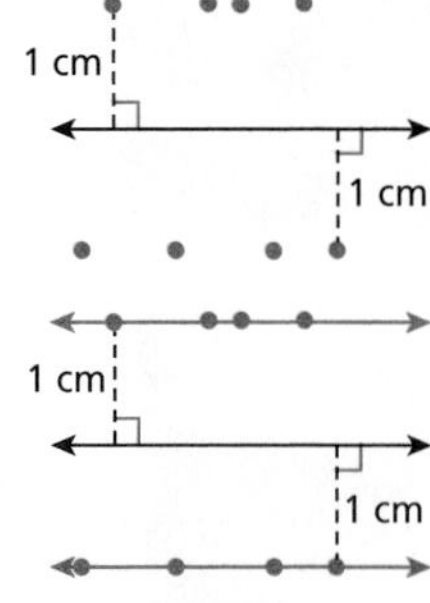

Remember!

The distance from a point to a line is the length of the perpendicular segment from the point to the line.

1. Note: In this lesson, the locus in each answer is represented by thick lines or shading.

CHECK IT OUT! **1.** Draw the locus of points that are equidistant from the sides of a right angle.

You can extend the concept of a locus to three-dimensional space. For example, a sphere is the locus of points a fixed distance from a point in space.

EXAMPLE 2 Drawing a Locus in Space

Draw the locus of points that are 1 cm from a line in space.

As in Example 1, the points that satisfy this locus lie on lines, but now the lines aren't limited to just above and below. The lines lie along circles of radius 1 cm centered on the original line.

The locus is a cylinder that is centered on the line and extends without end in both directions.

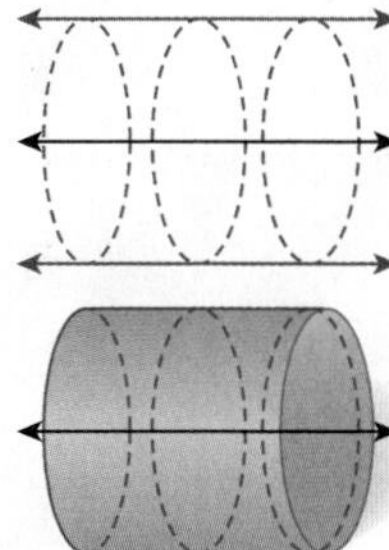

1 Introduce

Motivate

Show students a map of the local area. Choose an intersection of two roads and explain that a new business is going to open a store, and the location should be on one of the two roads and less than 0.5 mile from the intersection. Ask students to find possible locations given those conditions. Explain that loci problems involve finding points that satisfy one or more given conditions.

2 Teach

Guided Instruction

Have students use a compass and a customary and metric ruler to construct the loci in the examples one step at a time. You may want to encourage them to use these tools for all of the exercises because they may make fewer mistakes in identifying loci if their drawings are accurate.

2.

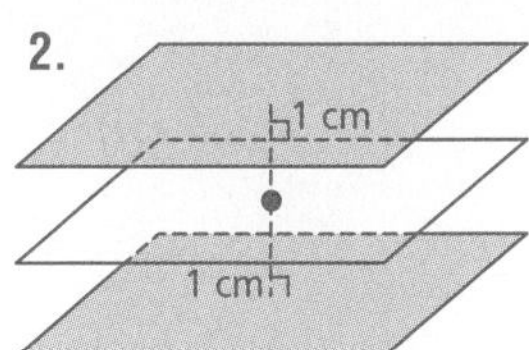

2. Draw the locus of points that are 1 cm from a plane in space.

Loci can involve several conditions. A **compound locus** is a set of points that satisfies two or more conditions. To draw a compound locus, find the locus of each condition and then find where the loci intersect.

EXAMPLE 3 Drawing a Compound Locus

Draw the locus of points that are 1 cm from a line and 2 cm from a point on that line in a plane.

First draw a line and a point P on that line. The points that satisfy the first condition of the locus are two parallel lines above and below the original line.

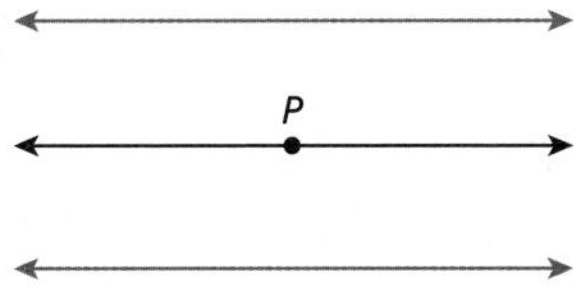

Next, draw the points that satisfy the second condition of the locus. Points that are 2 cm from P lie on a circle with radius 2 cm centered on P.

The intersections of the two conditions are the locus. Points A, B, C, and D are the locus of points that are 1 cm from the line and 2 cm from point P.

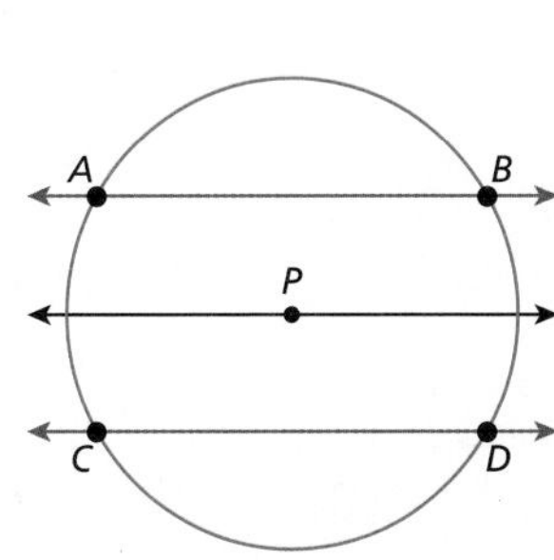

3.

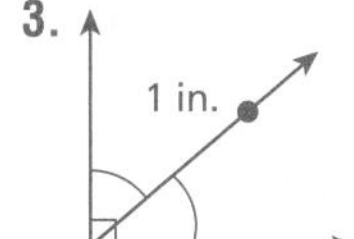

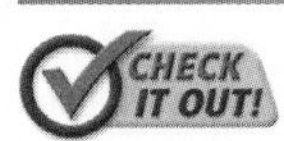

3. Draw the locus of points that are equidistant from the sides of a right angle and are 1 in from the vertex of the angle in a plane.

EXAMPLE 4 City Planning Application

A new bus station must be built on Main Street or Pine Street. Main is represented by the y-axis, and Pine is represented by the x-axis. The bus station must also be 2 miles from the intersection of Main and Pine. One unit on the coordinate grid represents 1 mile. Where are the possible locations for the new station?

The intersection of Main and Pine is at the origin. The locus of points 2 miles from the origin is a circle of radius 2.

The intersection of the circle with Main and Pine are (0, 2), (2, 0), (0, −2), and (−2, 0). These are the four possible locations for the new bus station.

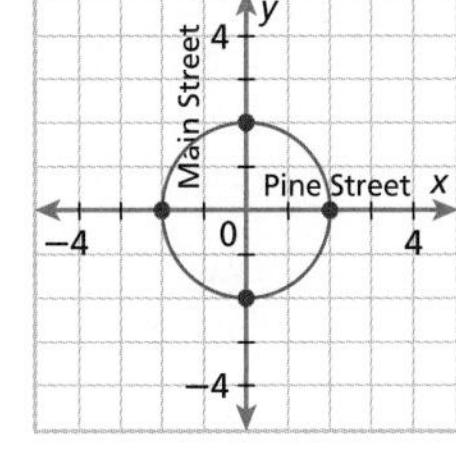

4. Suppose Main Street is represented by the line $x = 1$. If the rest of the conditions are the same, where are the possible locations for the new bus station? (1, 2), (3, 0), (−1, 0), (1, −2)

Additional Examples

Example 2

Draw the locus of points 2 cm from a point in space.

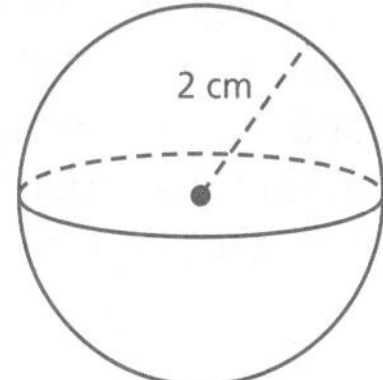

Example 3

Draw the locus of points equidistant from the endpoints of a 1-in. segment and 0.25 in. from the segment itself.

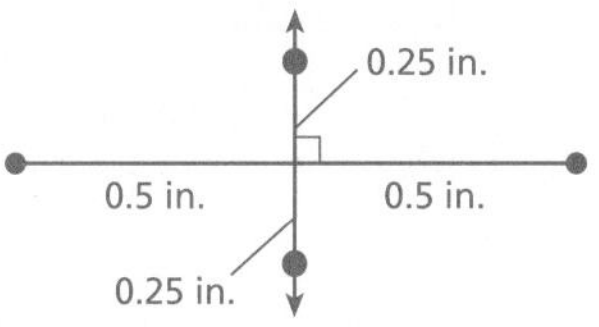

Example 4

The plan for the new bus station described in Example 4 has changed. The station must be 3 miles *or less* from the intersection, but it must be located on Pine St. Where are the possible locations of the station?

Any point on the segment with endpoints (−3, 0), (3, 0), including those endpoints.

INTERVENTION
Questioning Strategies

EXAMPLE 1

- If you draw a line segment from the original line to another point, what two properties must that line segment have in order for the point to be part of the locus?

EXAMPLE 2

- Could the locus be a rectangular prism centered on the given line? Why or why not?

EXAMPLE 3

- Do any other points on $\overleftrightarrow{AB}$ or $\overleftrightarrow{CD}$ satisfy both conditions? Why or why not?

EXAMPLE 4

- How do you graph a circle centered at the origin with a radius of 2?

In **Exercise 12,** students may have difficulty determining which point on the line $y = x$ satisfies the conditions of the locus. Explain that the towns of Kensington and Briar Falls are endpoints of a line segment, and they need to find the locus of points that are equidistant from those two points.

Answers

13a.

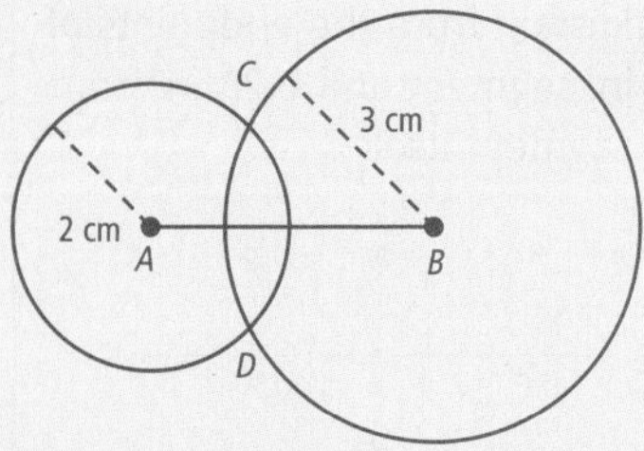

13b. Check students' drawings. *AB* must be greater than 5 cm.

13c. Check students' drawings. *AB* must be exactly 5 cm.

14.

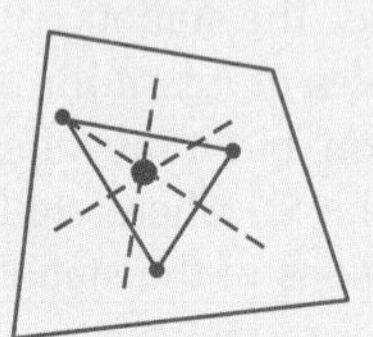

16.

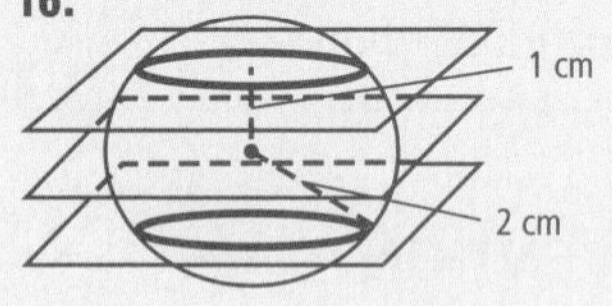

A-1 Exercises

1.

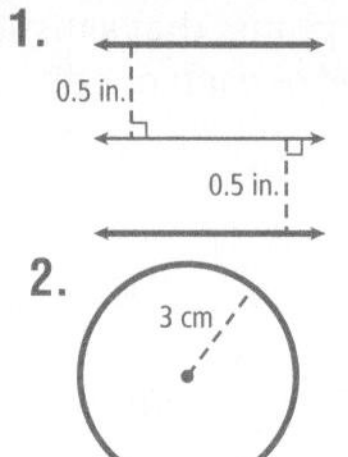

2. 3 cm

3. 1 in. 1 in.

4.

5. P 1 in.

6. 3 cm 3 cm

7. 25 mm

8.

9. 3.5 cm

10. 1 cm 2 cm 2 cm 1 cm

11. 1.5 in. 1.5 in. 1.5 in. 1.5 in.

Draw each locus in a plane.

1. the locus of points 0.5 in. from a line
2. the locus of points 3 cm from a point
3. the locus of points equidistant from the endpoints of a 2-in. line segment
4. the locus of points equidistant from two parallel lines

Draw each locus in space.

5. the locus of points 1 in. from a point
6. the locus of points 3 cm from a plane
7. the locus of points 25 mm from a line
8. the locus of points equidistant from two parallel planes

Draw each compound locus in a plane.

9. the locus of points equidistant from the sides of a 60° angle and 3.5 cm from the vertex of the angle
10. the locus of points equidistant from the endpoints of a 4-cm line segment and 1 cm from the segment itself
11. the locus of points equidistant from two perpendicular lines and 1.5 in. from the intersection of the lines

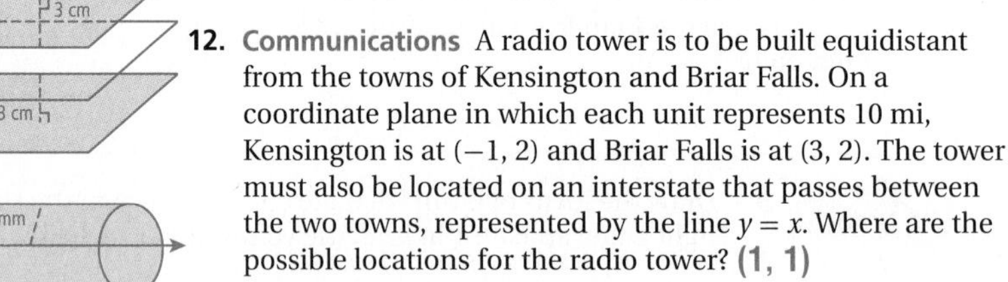

12. **Communications** A radio tower is to be built equidistant from the towns of Kensington and Briar Falls. On a coordinate plane in which each unit represents 10 mi, Kensington is at $(-1, 2)$ and Briar Falls is at $(3, 2)$. The tower must also be located on an interstate that passes between the two towns, represented by the line $y = x$. Where are the possible locations for the radio tower? **(1, 1)**

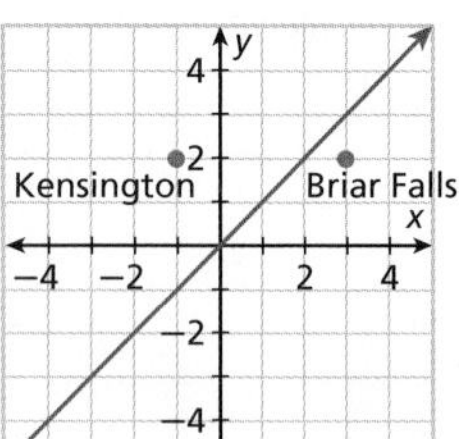

13. Line segment $\overline{AB}$ is 4 cm long.
    a. Draw the locus of points 2 cm from point *A* and 3 cm from point *B* in a plane.
    b. Give a length for $\overline{AB}$ that would have no points in the locus described in part **a.** Sketch the locus.
    c. Give a length for $\overline{AB}$ that would have only one point in the locus from part **a.** Sketch the locus.
14. **Recreation** The city's park department wants to install a barbeque grill in a spot that is equidistant from three picnic tables. Copy the map given and draw the locus of points equidistant from the picnic tables. Describe how you determined the locus. (*Hint:* The three picnic tables form a triangle. Find the point or points that are equidistant from the triangle's vertices.)

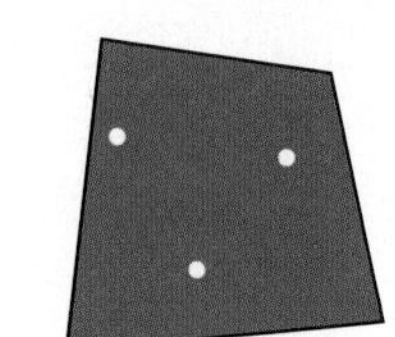

15. Write a locus question to which point *A* could be the answer. **What is the locus of points that are equidistant from the sides of the triangle?**

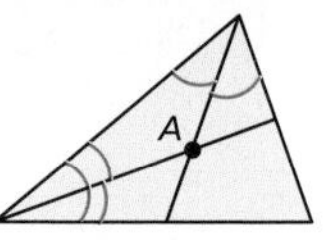

16. **Challenge** Draw the locus of points in space that are 1 cm from a plane and 2 cm from a point *P* in that plane.

3 Close

Summarize

Have students explain in words the locus that satisfies each condition.

1. the set of points equidistant from point *A* in a plane a circle with center *A*
2. the set of points 1 inch from a plane *R* in space two parallel planes, 1 in. on either side of plane *R*
3. the set of points equidistant from the sides of ∠*ABC* the angle bisector of ∠*ABC*

Trisect Line Segments

In Lesson 3-4, you learned to construct the perpendicular bisector of a segment. What if you want to trisect a segment, dividing it into 3 equal segments? You can use a construction based on parallel lines and similarity.

Activity

Trisect $\overline{AB}$.

1. Use the straightedge to draw the ray $\overrightarrow{AC}$. The measure of the angle isn't important, but you should make it 30° or more to give yourself room to work.
2. Place the compass point on A and draw an arc through $\overrightarrow{AC}$. Label the intersection D. Using the same compass setting, place the point on D and draw a second arc and label the intersection E. Repeat this a third time at point E and label the intersection F.

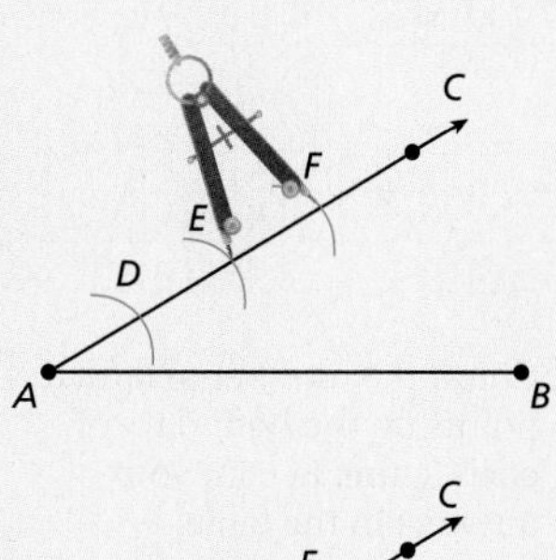

3. Connect points B and F.
4. Construct an angle congruent to $\angle AFB$ with E as its vertex. Label the intersection of the angle with $\overline{AB}$ as point G.
5. Repeat Step 4 with D as the vertex. Label the intersection as point H.

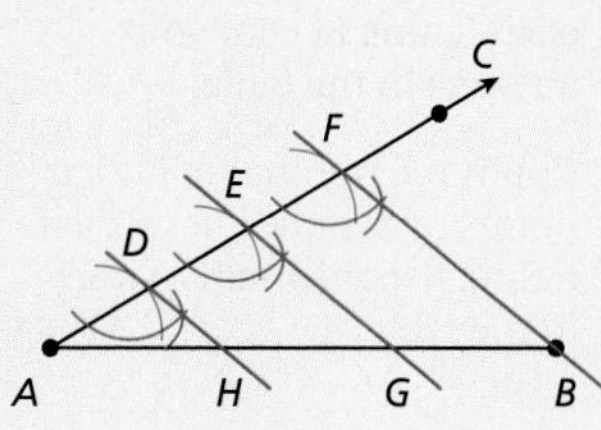

In the final figure, $AH = HG = GB = \frac{1}{3}AB$.

Try This

1. Explain why $\overline{DH} \parallel \overline{EG} \parallel \overline{FB}$. **$\angle AFB \cong \angle AEG \cong \angle ADH$ by construction. By the Converse of the Corresponding Angles Postulate, $\overline{DH} \parallel \overline{EG} \parallel \overline{FB}$.**
2. Why does the fact that $\overline{DH} \parallel \overline{EG} \parallel \overline{FB}$ guarantee that $AH = HG = GB$? (*Hint:* Start with the fact that $AD = DE = EF$ and use a theorem about parallel lines intersected by two transversals.)
3. Draw a segment $\overline{XY}$ that is approximately 5 to 6 in long.
   a. Use the construction in the activity, but modify it so you can divide $\overline{XY}$ into 4 congruent segments. **Check students' work.**
   b. Is there another way to divide $\overline{XY}$ into 4 congruent segments using compass and straightedge? Explain. **Yes; you can construct the perpendicular bisector of $\overline{XY}$, and then construct the perpendicular bisectors of those two segments. The result will be four congruent segments.**

Answer

2. $AD = DE = EF$ and $\overline{DH} \parallel \overline{EG} \parallel \overline{FB}$ by construction. By the Two-Transversal Proportionality Corollary, $\frac{AD}{DE} = \frac{AH}{HG}$ and $\frac{DE}{EF} = \frac{HG}{GB}$. Because $AD = DE$ and $DE = EF$, their ratios are 1:1, and so are the ratios of AH to HG and HG to GB. Therefore $AH = HG = GB$.

Organizer

Objectives: Use a compass and a straightedge to trisect a line segment.

Materials: compass, straightedge

Teach

Discuss

Explain to students that *trisect* means to divide something into three congruent parts. To trisect a line segment, they will use a special property of parallel lines and transversals to construct the three congruent segments.

Close

Key Concept

You can use a construction based on the Two-Transversal Proportionality Theorem from Lesson 7-4 to divide a segment into three congruent segments.

Assessment

Journal Have students perform the construction and, next to each step, list all sets of congruent segments and parallel lines.

State Resources

Organizer

Objective: Use patterns to develop Pick's Theorem for the area of a lattice polygon.

Materials: graph paper, pencil

Teach

Discuss

The shapes are ordered to help students see a pattern. Encourage students who have trouble finding the formula to draw more shapes.

Alternative Approach

To find the areas of the polygons, assign one group figures *A–F,* another group figures *G–L,* and a third group figures *M–R.*

Close

Key Concept

Pick's Theorem can be used to find the area of a lattice polygon.

Assessment

Journal Have students explain how to use Pick's Theorem to find the area of a lattice polygon.

State Resources

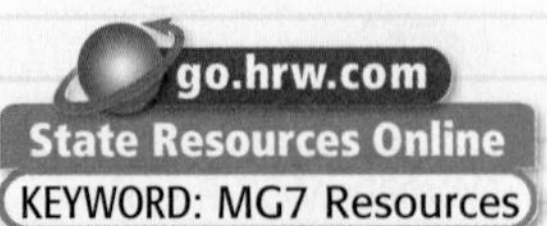

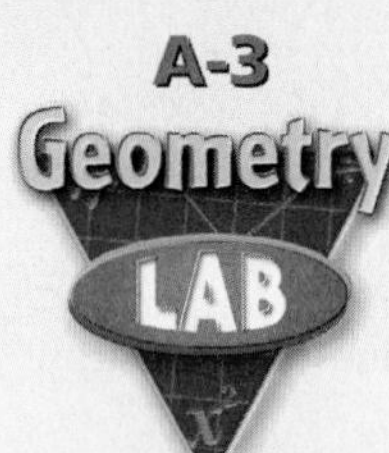

Develop Pick's Theorem for Area of Lattice Polygons

A *lattice polygon* is a polygon drawn on graph paper so that all its vertices are on intersections of grid lines, called *lattice points.* The lattice points of the grid at right are shown in red.

In this lab, you will discover a formula called Pick's Theorem, which is used to find the area of lattice polygons.

Activity 1

1. Find the area of each figure. Create a table like the one below with a row for each shape to record your answers. The first one is done for you.

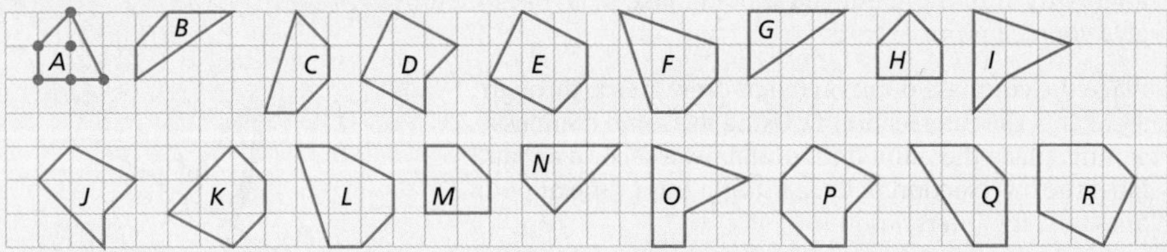

2. Count the number of lattice points on the boundary of each figure. Record your answers in the table.

3. Count the number of lattice points in the interior of each figure. Record your answers in the table.

Figure	Area	Number of Lattice Points	
		On Boundary	In Interior
A	2.5	5	1
B			
C			
D			
E			
F			

Try This

Possible answer: $A = \frac{1}{2}B + I - 1$

1. **Make a Conjecture** What do you think is true about the relationship between the area of a figure and the number of lattice points on the boundary and in the interior of the figure? Write your conjecture as a formula in terms of the number of lattice points on the boundary *B* and the number of lattice points in the interior *I.*
2. Test your conjecture by drawing at least three different figures on graph paper and by finding their areas. **Check students' work.**
3. Estimate the area of the curved figure by using a lattice polygon.
4. Find the shaded area in the figure by subtracting. Test your formula on this figure. Does your formula work for figures with holes in them? **6.5 units^2; no**

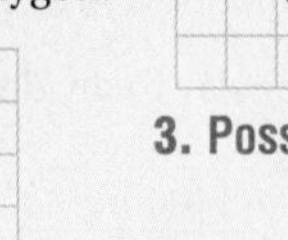

3. Possible answer: 5 units^2

Activity 1-3.

Figure	Area	Number of Lattice Points	
		On Boundary	In Interior
A	2.5	5	1
B	2.5	5	1
C	3.5	5	2
D	4.5	5	3
E	5.5	5	4
F	5.5	5	4
G	3	6	1
H	3	6	1
I	4	6	2
J	4	6	2
K	5	6	3
L	6	6	4
M	3.5	7	1
N	3.5	7	1
O	4.5	7	2
P	5.5	7	3
Q	5.5	7	3
R	6.5	7	4

ADDITIONAL TOPIC

A-4 Introduction to Graph Theory

Objectives
Explore and apply properties of vertex-edge graphs.

Vocabulary
graph
vertex
edge
path
connected graph
degree
Euler path
circuit
Euler circuit
coloring

In the branch of mathematics known as graph theory, a **graph** is a network of points and line segments or arcs that connect the points. A point of a graph is called a **vertex**. A line segment or arc that connects vertices is called an **edge**.

Graph theory has many real-world applications. For example, the graph at right shows the flights offered by a regional airline. The cities served by the airline are represented by vertices. Flights that connect cities are represented by edges.

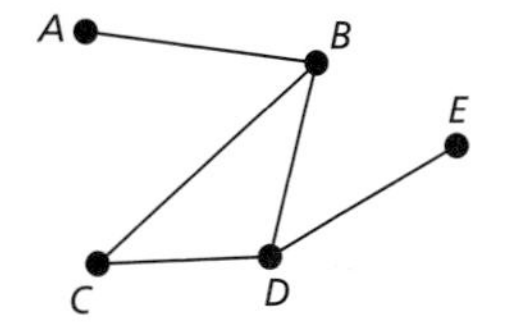

A **path** is a way to get from one vertex to another along one or more edges. A graph is a **connected graph** if there is at least one path connecting every pair of vertices. The **degree** of a vertex is the number of edges touching the vertex.

EXAMPLE 1 **Analyzing a Graph**

Use the graph at right for each problem.

A **Find the degree of each vertex.**

Vertex	Degree
A	1
B	3
C	2
D	3
E	1
F	0

B **Describe two different paths from vertex *A* to vertex *E*.**
Vertex *A* to vertex *B* to vertex *D* to vertex *E*
Vertex *A* to vertex *B* to vertex *C* to vertex *D* to vertex *E*

C **Determine whether the graph is connected. Explain.**
The graph is not connected. There is no path between vertex *F* and another vertex.

1a. Nashville: 2; Cincinnati: 3; Raleigh: 2; Knoxville: 3; Atlanta: 2

1b. Atlanta - Knoxville - Raleigh; Atlanta - Nashville - Cincinnati - Raleigh

1c. Yes; there is a path between every pair of vertices.

Reading Math

Euler paths are named after the mathematician Leonard Euler (1707–1783), (pronounced *oiler*).

CHECK IT OUT! **Use the airline graph above Example 1 for each problem.**

1a. Find the degree of each vertex.
1b. Describe two different paths from Atlanta to Raleigh.
1c. Determine whether the graph is connected. Explain.

An **Euler path** is a path that goes through every edge of a connected graph exactly once. A **circuit** is a path that ends at the same vertex at which it began and that does not go through any edge more than once. An **Euler circuit** is a circuit that goes through every edge of a connected graph exactly once.

1 Introduce

Motivate

Ask students if they have ever used a tree diagram to solve a problem. If so, have them describe the problem and ask them to explain how they used the tree diagram. Then tell students that a tree diagram is a type of graph. Point out that the definition of the word *graph* in this lesson is different from the definition that students are most familiar with.

2 Teach

Guided Instruction

Draw a set of points on the board and connect them with arcs or segments. Explain that this network is known as a graph. Introduce the vocabulary associated with graphs and give students a chance to find paths and circuits through simple graphs that you provide. Emphasize that graphs may be used to model real-world situations and then use **Example 2** to demonstrate how a map can be represented, and simplified, by a graph

ADDITIONAL TOPIC

A-4 Organizer

Objectives: Explore and apply properties of vertex-edge graphs.

Warm Up

Fill in each blank.

1. A __?__ is perfectly straight and extends forever in both directions. line
2. A __?__ is the part of a line between two points. line segment
3. A __?__ names a location. point

Additional Examples

Example 1

Use the graph below.

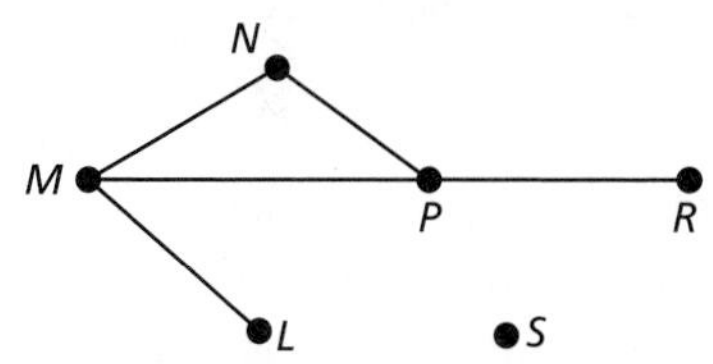

A. Find the degree of each vertex. *L: 1; M: 3; N: 2; P: 3; R: 1; S: 0*

B. Describe two different paths from vertex *M* to vertex *R*. *M - P - R; M - N - P - R*

C. Determine whether the graph is connected. Explain. No; there is no path between vertex *S* and another vertex.

State Resources

Additional Examples

Example 2

Determine whether an Euler circuit exists for the graph shown below. If not, explain why not. If so, describe an Euler circuit of the graph.

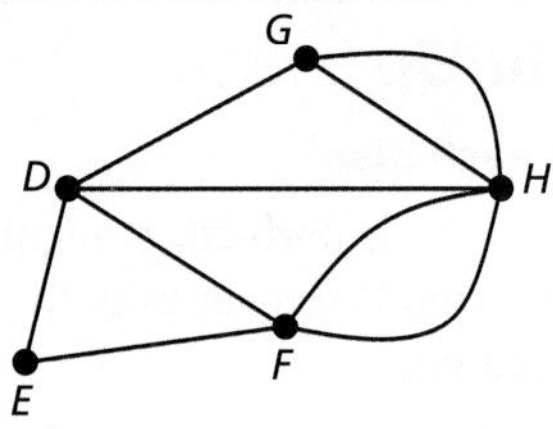

No; two of the vertices (*G* and *H*) have an odd degree, so there is no Euler circuit for the graph

INTERVENTION 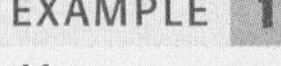
Questioning Strategies

EXAMPLE 1

- How can you find the degree of a vertex in a graph?

EXAMPLE 2

- What is an Euler circuit?
- What do you need to check in order to determine if an Euler circuit exists?

In an Euler circuit, every vertex must have an even degree. To see why this is true, suppose a vertex of a graph has an odd degree. In an Euler circuit, two edges are required each time a path enters and exits the vertex. A vertex with an odd degree would have an edge that would be traveled twice or not at all.

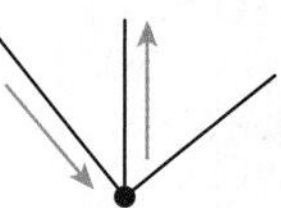

The Königsberg bridge problem is one of the most famous problems in graph theory. The goal is to find a path that crosses every bridge only once and returns to the starting point. Solving the Königsberg bridge problem is equivalent to finding an Euler circuit in a graph.

EXAMPLE 2 *Social Studies Application*

Determine whether the Königsberg bridges, shown in the map below, can be traversed in an Euler circuit.

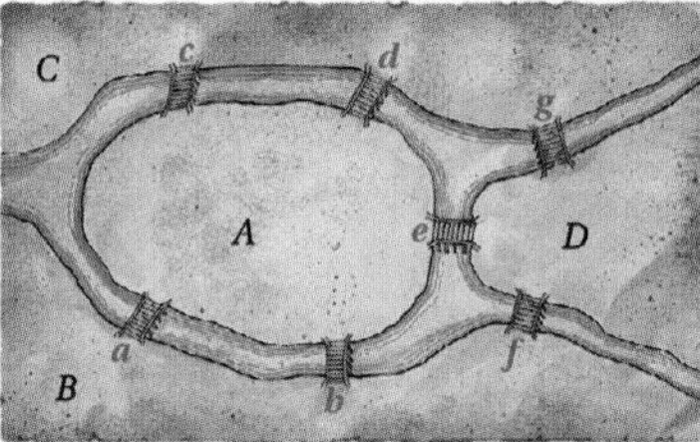

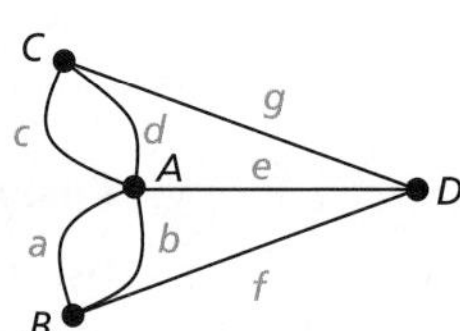

Create a graph to represent the landmasses and bridges, as shown above. In the graph, the vertices represent land and edges represent bridges.

The bridges cannot be traversed through an Euler circuit because there is a vertex in the graph with an odd degree. (In fact, all of the vertices have an odd degree.)

2. Determine whether an Euler circuit exists for the graph shown here. If not, explain why not. If so, describe an Euler circuit of the graph.
Yes; possible answer:
M - P - N - Q - R - S - N - M

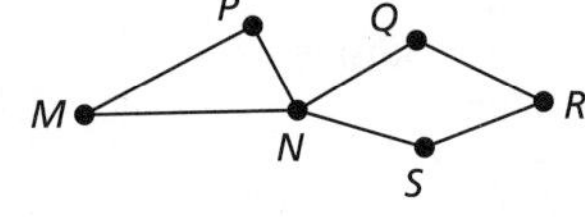

Some problems in graph theory can be solved using graph coloring. A **coloring** of a graph assigns a color to each vertex of the graph so that no two adjacent vertices have the same color.

The figures show colorings of several graphs. In each case, the minimum number of different colors is used to color the graph.

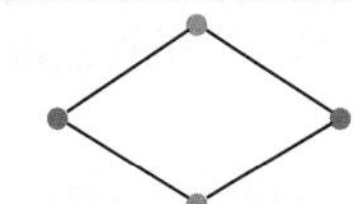

This graph can be colored with 2 colors.

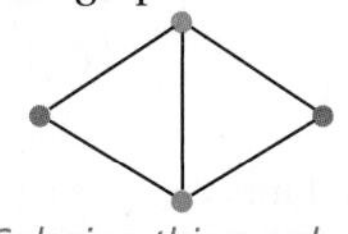

Coloring this graph requires 3 colors.

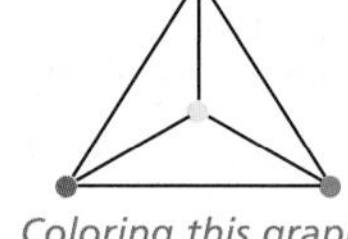

Coloring this graph requires 4 colors.

3 Close

Summarize

Ask students to draw an example of a connected graph. Have them give the degree of each vertex and have them explain whether an Euler circuit exists for the graph.

Teaching Tip

Kinesthetic Use chalk to draw a simple graph on the floor of the classroom. Have students walk from vertex to vertex along the graph's edges. As they do so, ask them to determine whether an Euler circuit exists for the graph.

Graph coloring can be used to solve many problems about avoiding conflicts, such as scheduling problems or problems about shared resources.

EXAMPLE 3 Solving a Scheduling Problem

A college offers five art courses: Art A, B, C, D, and E. An employee of the college must schedule final exams for the courses in either morning or afternoon time slots from Monday to Friday. However, some students are enrolled in more than one art course. In the table, an X means there is at least one student enrolled in both of the courses corresponding to that cell of the table. Show how the employee can schedule the exams using the fewest number of time slots.

	A	B	C	D	E
A		X	X		
B	X		X	X	
C	X	X		X	
D		X	X		X
E				X	

Step 1 Represent the courses as the vertices of a graph.

B A C D E

Step 2 Draw an edge between any two vertices that represent courses that have students in common.

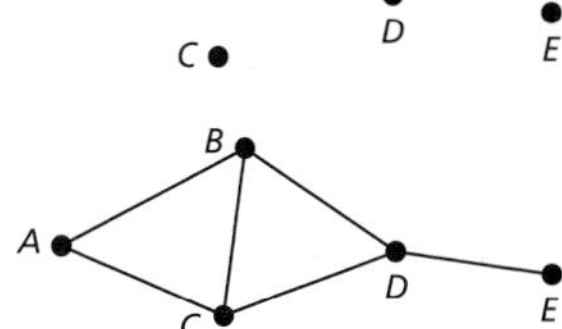

Step 3 Color the graph using the minimum number of colors. Each color represents a different exam time. Remember that no two adjacent vertices can have the same color.

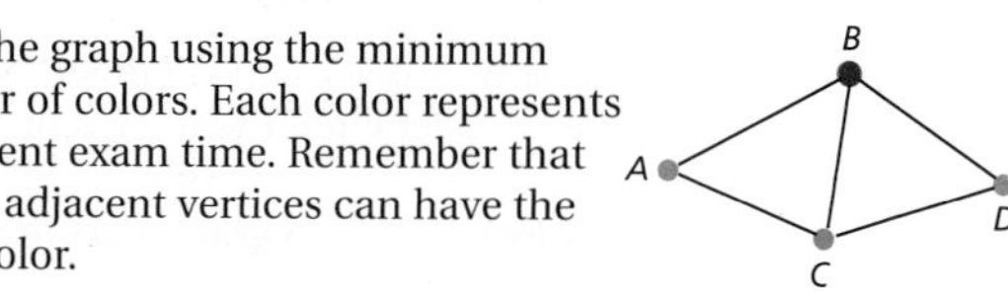

Step 4 Interpret the coloring of the graph.

The employee can schedule the exams using a minimum of three time slots. For example, the exams could be scheduled as follows.

Monday morning (red vertices): Art A, Art D

Monday afternoon (blue vertices): Art B, Art E

Tuesday morning (green vertex): Art C

3. Time slot 1: Budget, Music, Clean Up; Time slot 2: Safety, Food, Publicity

3. A parade organizer wants to schedule one-hour meetings for six different committees. The table shows the names of the committees, and an X indicates committees that share one or more members. Show how the organizer can schedule the meetings using the least number of one-hour time slots.

	Budget	Safety	Food	Music	Publicity	Clean Up
Budget		X	X			
Safety	X			X		
Food	X			X		
Music		X	X		X	
Publicity				X		X
Clean Up					X	

In **Example 3,** students may notice that there are 12 Xs in the table and try to draw 12 edges in their graph. Point out to students that pairs of courses that have students in common are each represented by two Xs in the table. Therefore, there are 6 conflicting pairs of courses and these are represented with 6 edges.

Additional Examples

Example 3

A high school has five clubs: soccer *(S)*, French *(F)*, drama *(D)*, chess *(C)*, and literature *(L)*. A teacher wants to schedule one-hour meetings of the clubs. In the table, an X means there is at least one student who is a member of both of the clubs corresponding to that cell of the table. Show how the teacher can schedule the meetings in the least number of time slots.

	S	F	D	C	L
S			X		
F					X
D	X			X	X
C			X		X
L		X	X	X	

Time slot 1: soccer, French, chess

Time slot 2: drama

Time slot 3: literature

INTERVENTION
Questioning Strategies

- How can you make a graph that represents the data in the table?
- What does each vertex of your graph represent?
- What does each edge of your graph represent?

Answers

9. Possible answer: *A*: red; *B, C, D, E, F,* and *G*: blue
10. Possible answer: *J, L, M,* and *P*: red; *K* and *N*: blue
11. Possible answer:

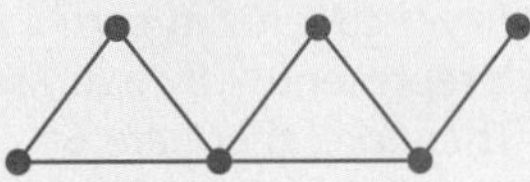

12. Possible answer:

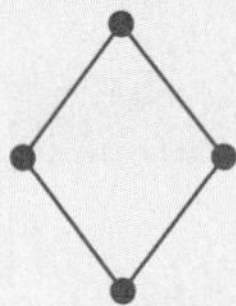

13. Possible answer:

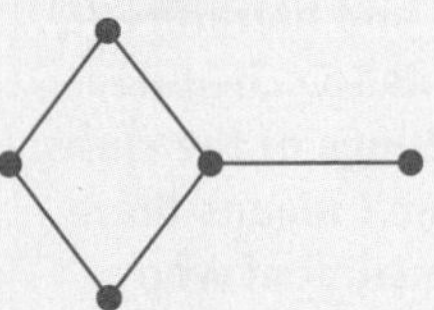

14. Possible answer:

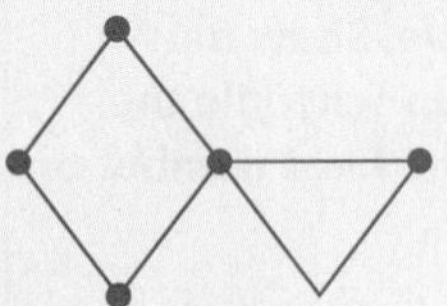

15b. Possible answer:

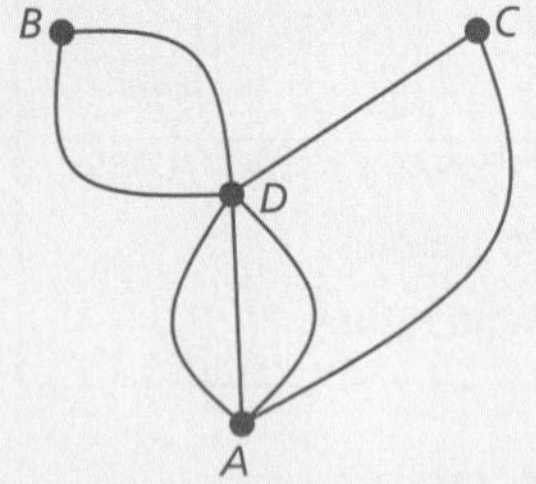

State Resources

A-4 Exercises

1. *M*: 2; *N*: 4; *P*: 2; *Q*: 2; *R*: 4; *S*: 2

2. Possible answers: *M - N - R - P*; *M - N - S - R - P*

3. Yes; there is a path between every pair of vertices.

4. Yes; possible answer: *M - N - R - Q - P - R - S - N - M*

5. *A*: 2; *B*: 4; *C*: 4; *D*: 2; *E*: 2; *F*: 2

6. Possible answer: *A - B - E - F - C - D*

7. Possible answer: *A* and *D*: red; *C* and *E*: blue; *B* and *F*: green

8. Yes; possible answer: *A - B - E - F - C - D - B - C - A*

15c. Yes; there is a path between every pair of vertices.

Use the graph at right for Exercises 1–4.

1. Find the degree of each vertex.
2. Describe two different paths from vertex *M* to vertex *P*.
3. Determine whether the graph is connected. Explain.
4. Determine whether an Euler circuit exists for the graph. If not, explain why not. If so, describe an Euler circuit of the graph.

Use the graph at right for Exercises 5–8.

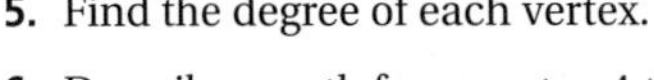

5. Find the degree of each vertex.
6. Describe a path from vertex *A* to vertex *D* that passes through every vertex of the graph.

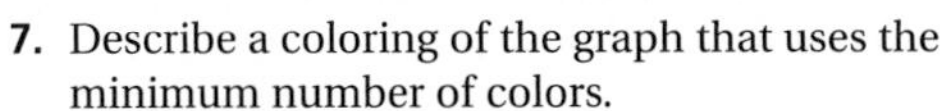

7. Describe a coloring of the graph that uses the minimum number of colors.
8. Determine whether an Euler circuit exists for the graph. If not, explain why not. If so, describe an Euler circuit of the graph.

Describe a coloring of each graph that uses the minimum number of different colors.

9.

10.

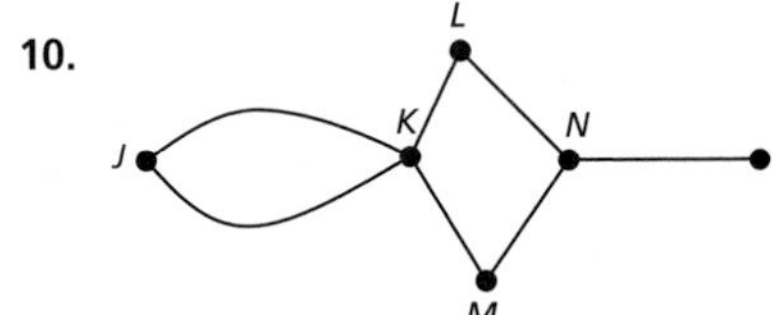

Draw a graph with the given characteristics.

11. a graph with 6 vertices and 7 edges
12. a graph with 4 vertices, all of degree 2
13. a connected graph for which there is no Euler circuit
14. a graph with 6 vertices that can be colored with 3 colors
15. The map shows the coastline of a city *A* and three islands *B, C,* and *D*. The landmasses are connected by bridges as shown.

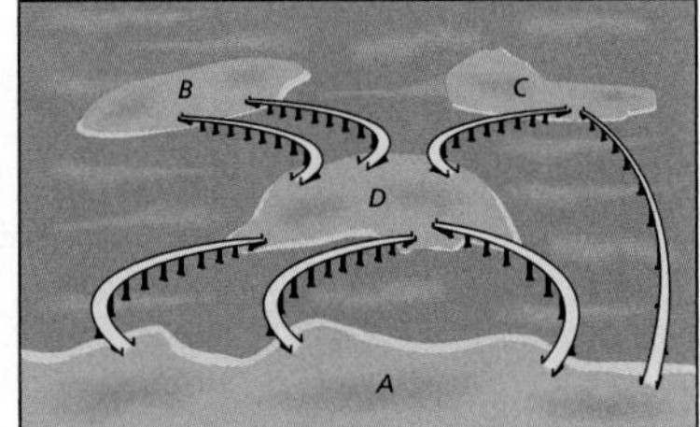

a. If the information in the map is represented by a graph, what do the vertices represent? What do the edges represent? **landmasses; bridges**

b. Draw and label a graph to represent the information in the map.

c. Is the graph connected? Why or why not? **Yes; every vertex has an even degree.**

d. Is it possible to traverse the bridges in an Euler circuit? Explain.

16. No; vertices *B* and *D* have an odd degree, so there is no Euler circuit.

16. The graph shows the homes on Chloe's paper route. The vertices represent the homes that receive a paper and the edges represent streets. Chloe would like to find a route that begins and ends at her house C. She would also like to go down each street exactly once. Is such a route possible? Explain.

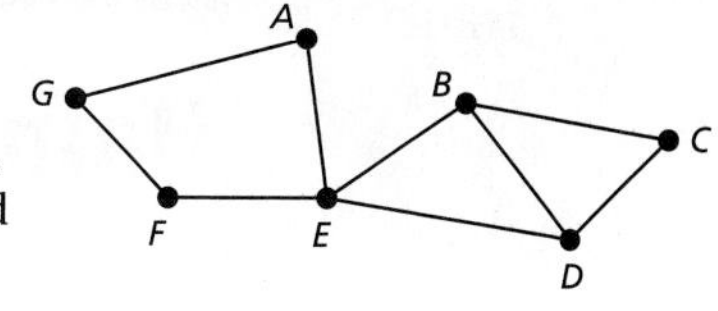

17. A human-resources manager wants to schedule interviews for five job applicants, named Alex (A), Brenda (B), Chan (C), Diego (D), and Erika (E). Multiple applicants can be interviewed at the same time, as long as they have not applied for the same job. In the table, an X means that the two candidates corresponding to that cell of the table have applied for the same job.

	A	B	C	D	E
A		X	X	X	X
B	X			X	
C	X				
D	X	X			X
E	X			X	

a. Draw a graph to represent the situation.

b. Explain how the manager can schedule the interviews using the least number of time slots.

17b. Time slot 1: A; Time slot 2: B, C, and E; Time slot 3: D

18. Viet is scheduling status meetings for six projects, known as Projects J, K, L, M, N, and P. Some team members work on more than one project at the same time. In the table, an X means that the two projects corresponding to that cell of the table share a team member. What is the least number of time slots Viet needs in order to schedule the meetings? **3**

	J	K	L	M	N	P
J		X		X	X	
K	X		X			
L		X		X		X
M	X		X		X	
N	X			X		
P			X			

A graph is said to be *k*-colorable if there is a coloring of the graph that uses *k* colors. The minimum value of *k* for which a coloring of the graph exists is called the *chromatic number* of the graph. Find the chromatic number of each graph.

19.

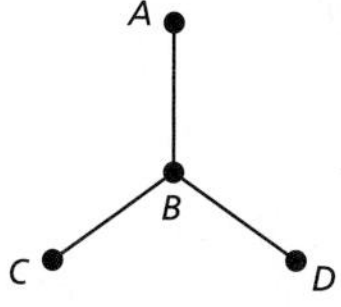

20.

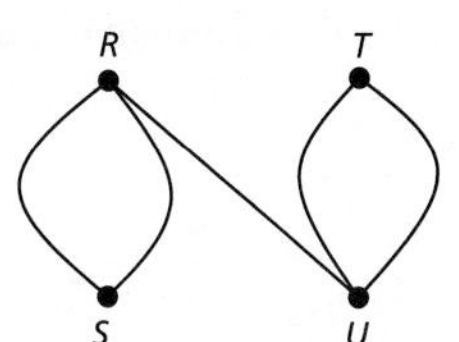

21.

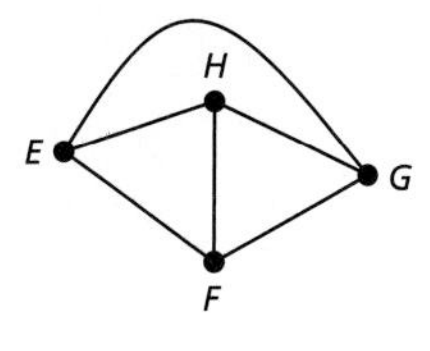

22. A *Hamiltonian circuit* is a path that ends at the beginning vertex and passes through each of the other vertices in the graph exactly once. A Hamiltonian circuit need not go through every edge. Describe a Hamiltonian circuit for the graph at right that begins and ends at vertex *A*. ***A* to *D* to *E* to *C* to *F* to *G* to *B* to *A***

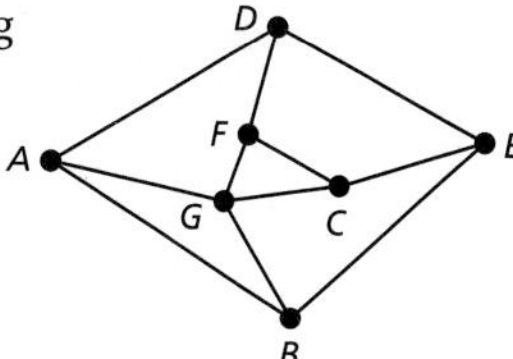

23. **Critical Thinking** Is it possible for an Euler path that is not a circuit to end at a vertex with an even degree? If so, draw an example. If not, explain why not.

23. No; the degree of the ending vertex must be odd because each pair of entrances and exits at the vertex requires 2 edges and there must be 1 additional edge for the final entrance at the vertex.

Answers

17a.

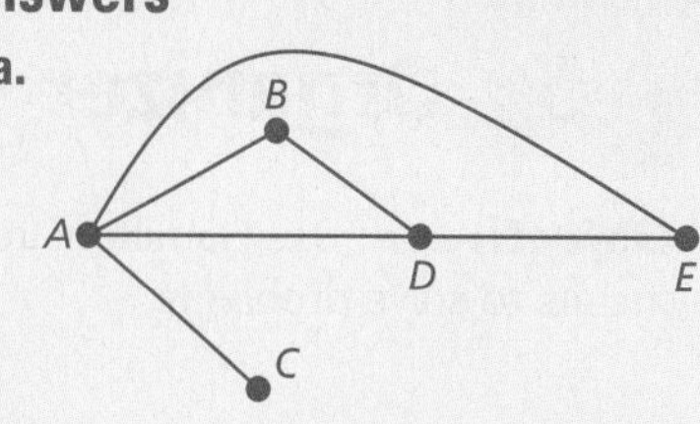

19. 2

20. 2

21. 4

A-4 Introduction to Graph Theory **AT11**

ADDITIONAL TOPIC
A-5 Organizer

Objectives: : Use Hamiltonian circuits to solve problems.

Warm Up

1. Name four line segments in the figure below. Any 4 of $\overline{AB}$, $\overline{AC}$, $\overline{BC}$, $\overline{AD}$, $\overline{CD}$, $\overline{BD}$

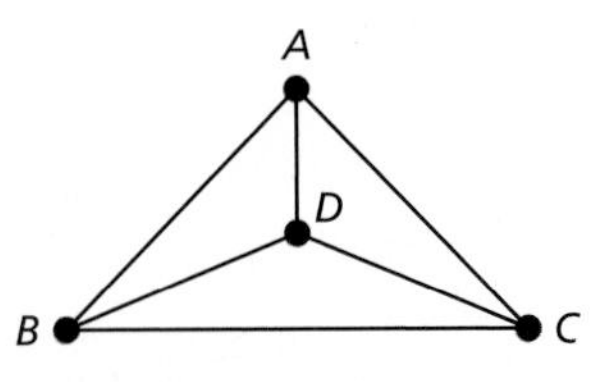

Additional Examples

Example 1

Find a Hamiltonian circuit in the graph.

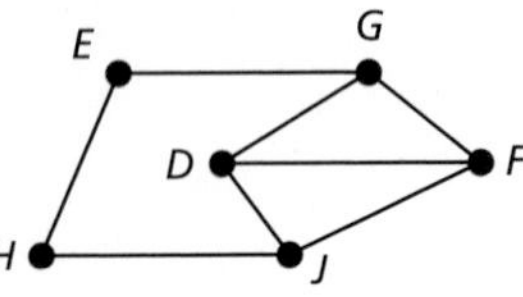

Possible answer: *E* to *G* to *F* to *D* to *J* to *H* to *E*

INTERVENTION
Questioning Strategies

EXAMPLE 1

- What is a circuit of a graph?
- What makes a Hamiltonian circuit different from other circuits?
- What should you do to check that your circuit is a Hamiltonian circuit?

State Resources

ADDITIONAL TOPIC
A-5 Hamiltonian Circuits

Objective
Use Hamiltonian circuits to solve problems.

Vocabulary
circuit
Hamiltonian circuit

Recall that in graph theory, a graph is a network of points and line segments or arcs that connect the points. A point of a graph is called a vertex. A line segment or arc that connects vertices is called an edge.

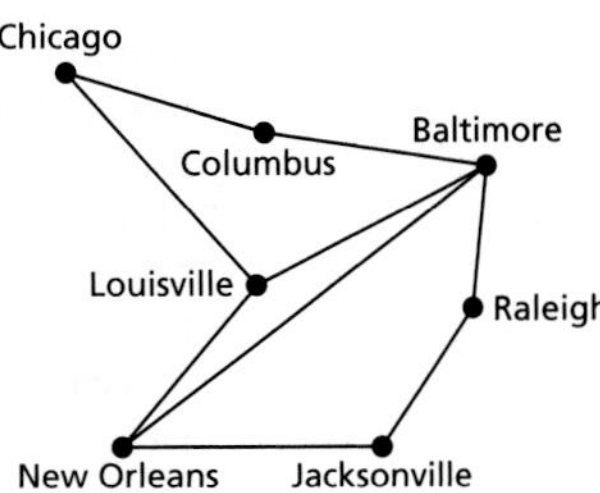

Graph theory has many practical applications. For example, consider a sales representative who visits clients in seven cities. The cities may be shown as the vertices of a graph. The edges of the graph represent flights that connect the cities.

A path is a way to get from one vertex to another along one or more edges. A **circuit** is a path that ends at the same vertex at which it began and that does not go through any edge more than once. If the sales representative lives in Raleigh, she might use the circuit shown here to visit all of the cities and return home at the end of the trip.

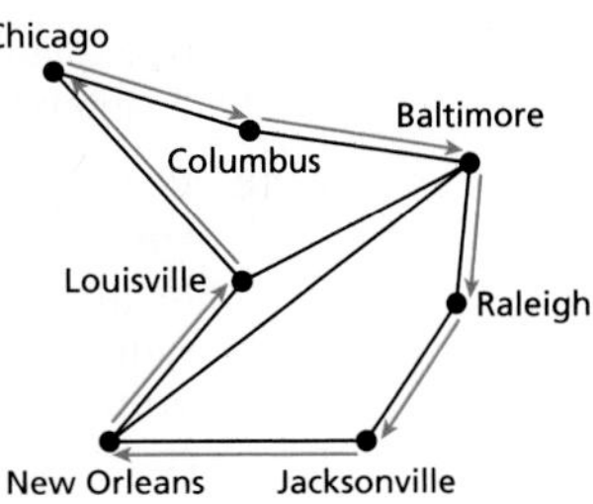

A **Hamiltonian circuit** is a path that ends at the beginning vertex and that passes through each of the other vertices of the graph exactly once. Note that a Hamiltonian circuit need not traverse every edge. The sales representative's path shown above is a Hamiltonian circuit.

EXAMPLE 1 **Finding Hamiltonian Circuits**

Find a Hamiltonian circuit in the graph.

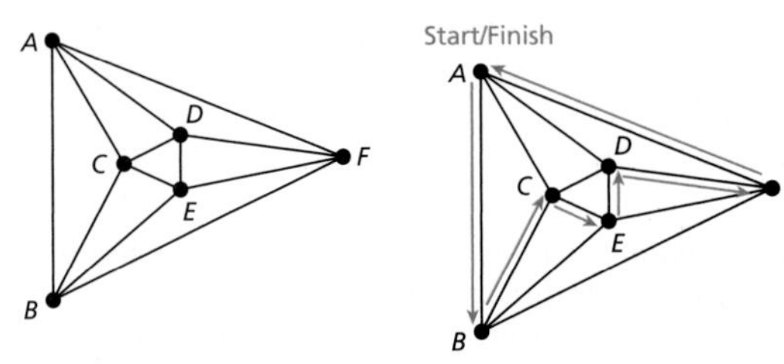

Choose a starting vertex. Visit each vertex once, but do not necessarily traverse each edge.

A Hamiltonian circuit is ***A*** to ***B*** to ***C*** to ***E*** to ***D*** to ***F*** to ***A***.

1. Find a Hamiltonian circuit in the graph.

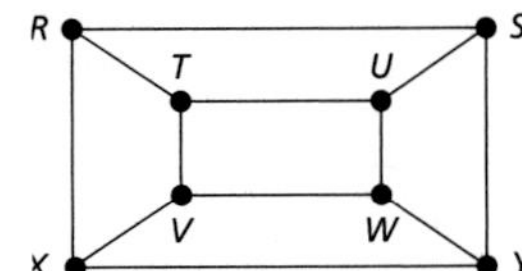

Possible answer: *R* to *S* to *U* to *T* to *V* to *W* to *Y* to *X* to *R*

1 Introduce

Motivate

Draw several points on the board and label them with the names of common locations, such as *library, theater, bank,* and so on. Label one point as home. Ask students how they can start at home, visit all the locations, and end back at home. Trace students' suggested paths on the board. Then tell the class that mathematicians study these types of paths and explain they are called circuits.

2 Teach

Guided Instruction

Introduce circuits and Hamiltonian circuits. Emphasize that a graph may have many different Hamiltonian circuits, and encourage students to look for multiple correct answers when asked to find a Hamiltonian circuit. Point out that when the edges of a graph have numerical values associated with them, as in Example 2, one of the graph's Hamiltonian circuits may represent an optimum solution, such as a shortest overall distance or a least cost.

Hamiltonian circuits may be used to solve optimization problems. For example, when a distance is associated with each edge of a graph, finding the Hamiltonian circuit with the least total distance provides the shortest (optimum) route through all the vertices.

EXAMPLE 2 **Travel Application**

Kendra lives in Charlotte and is planning a road trip to visit friends in Durham, Savannah, and Atlanta. The graph shows the driving distances between the cities. Find the shortest path Kendra can take.

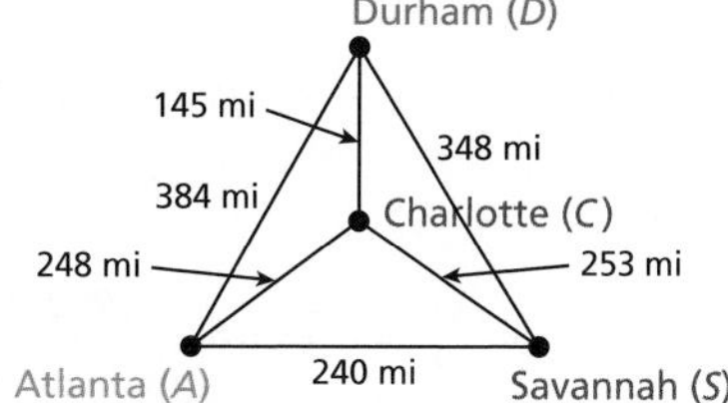

Find all the Hamiltonian circuits that begin and end in Charlotte. For each circuit, find the total length of the path.

$C \xrightarrow{253 \text{ mi}} S \xrightarrow{240 \text{ mi}} A \xrightarrow{384 \text{ mi}} D \xrightarrow{145 \text{ mi}} C$ 1022 mi

$C \xrightarrow{253 \text{ mi}} S \xrightarrow{348 \text{ mi}} D \xrightarrow{384 \text{ mi}} A \xrightarrow{248 \text{ mi}} C$ 1233 mi

$C \xrightarrow{248 \text{ mi}} A \xrightarrow{240 \text{ mi}} S \xrightarrow{384 \text{ mi}} D \xrightarrow{145 \text{ mi}} C$ 1017 mi

There are three additional Hamiltonian circuits, which are the above paths in reverse.

To minimize her driving distance, Kendra should take the path $C \to A \to S \to D \to C$ or the reverse path, $C \to D \to S \to A \to C$.

2. An office has five computers, indicated by vertices on the graph. The edges show distances between the computers. Jack wants to connect the computers in a circuit that begins and ends at Computer *A*. Find the circuit that requires the least amount of cable.

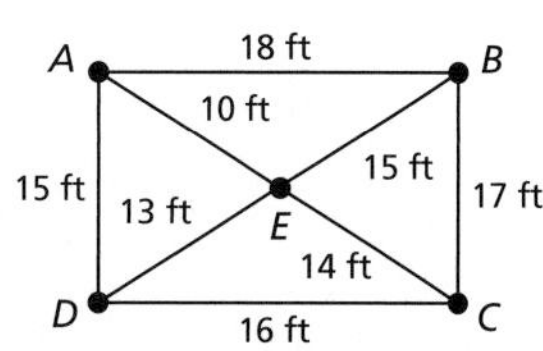

A to E to B to C to D to A

A-5 Exercises

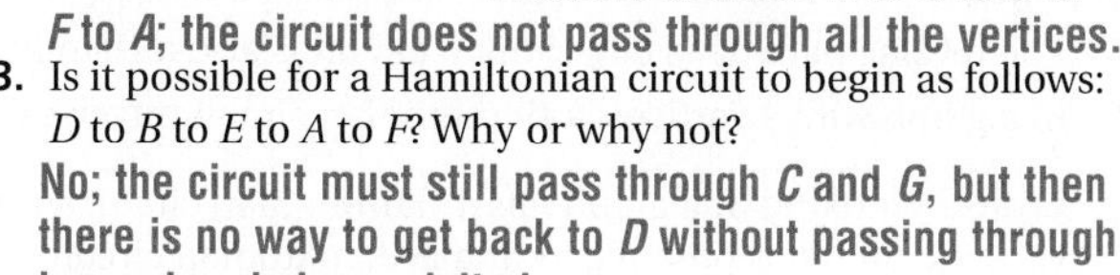

Use the graph at right for Exercises 1–3.

1. Describe a Hamiltonian circuit starting at vertex *E*.
Possible answer: *E* to *A* to *G* to *C* to *F* to *D* to *B* to *E*
2. Describe a circuit starting at vertex *A* that is *not* a Hamiltonian circuit. Explain why the circuit is not a Hamiltonian circuit. **Possible answer: *A* to *G* to *C* to *F* to *A*; the circuit does not pass through all the vertices.**
3. Is it possible for a Hamiltonian circuit to begin as follows: *D* to *B* to *E* to *A* to *F*? Why or why not?
No; the circuit must still pass through *C* and *G*, but then there is no way to get back to *D* without passing through vertices that have already been visited.

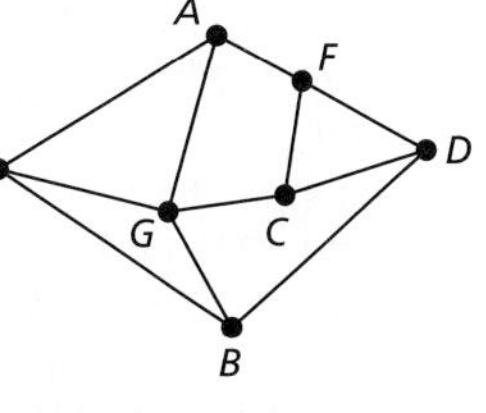

Additional Examples

Example 2

A florist must deliver flowers to three houses that are represented by the vertices *R*, *Q*, and *T* in the graph below. The florist's store is at vertex *F*. The graph shows driving distances. Assuming the delivery route starts and ends at *F*, find the shortest path the florist can take.

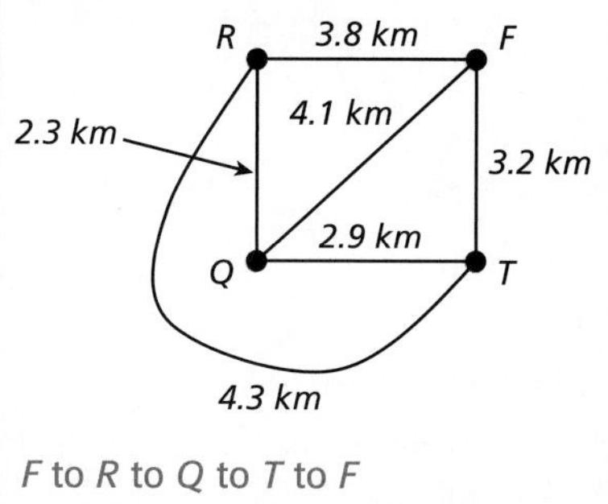

F to *R* to *Q* to *T* to *F*

INTERVENTION
Questioning Strategies

EXAMPLE 2

- What must be true of every circuit that you find as part of your solution process?
- Do you need to find every Hamiltonian circuit for the graph? Why or why not?
- How do you determine the total driving distance for a given circuit?

3 Close

Summarize

Ask students to draw an example of a graph that has a Hamiltonian circuit and an example of a graph that does not have a Hamiltonian circuit.

Teaching Tip **Visual** As students work on the examples and exercises in this lesson, encourage them to redraw the graphs in their notebooks and use a highlighter to mark Hamiltonian circuits. Students can use a second color to highlight the vertex that is the starting and ending point of each circuit.

COMMON ERROR ALERT

In **Example 2,** students might be tempted to consider a path that passes through one of the vertices more than once, such as *C* to *D* to *S* to *A* to *D* to *C*. Tell students that they should restrict their work to Hamiltonian circuits and remind them that in a Hamiltonian circuit the path begins and ends at the same point and passes through each of the other vertices exactly once.

10. Possible answer:

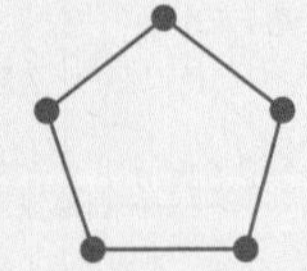

11. Possible answer:

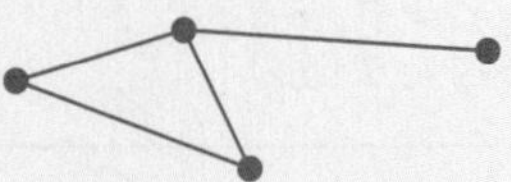

12. Possible answer:

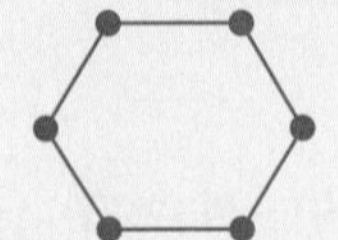

13. Any circuit that passed through vertex *J* would have to pass through vertex *H* twice, and the definition of a Hamiltonian circuit does not permit this.

17. Possible answer: The given Hamiltonian circuit must pass through all the vertices. To start at another vertex, find the vertex in the given Hamiltonian circuit and follow the same sequence of vertices until you complete the circuit.

Find a Hamiltonian circuit in each graph.

4.

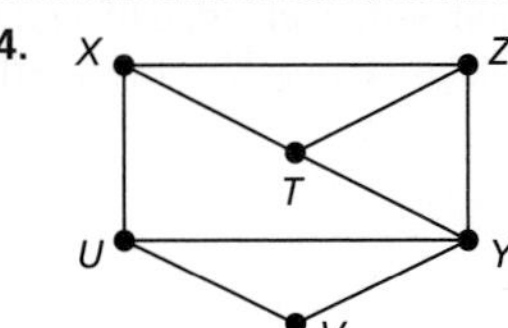

Possible answer: *X to Z to T to Y to V to U to X*

5.

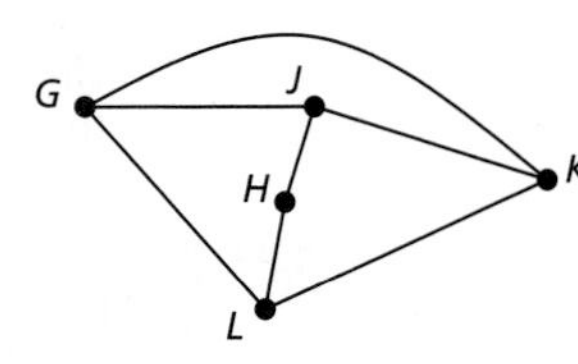

Possible answer: *G to K to J to H to L to G*

6.

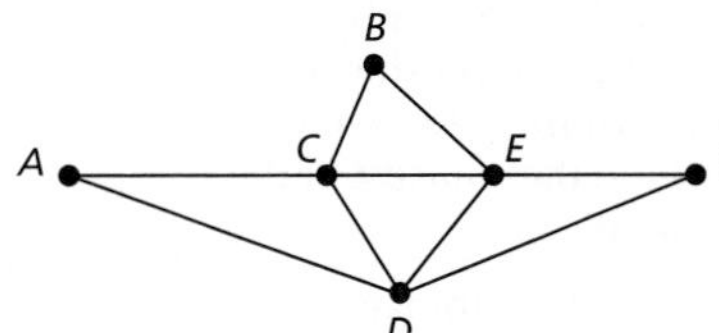

Possible answer: *A* to *C* to *B* to *E* to *F* to *D* to *A*

7.

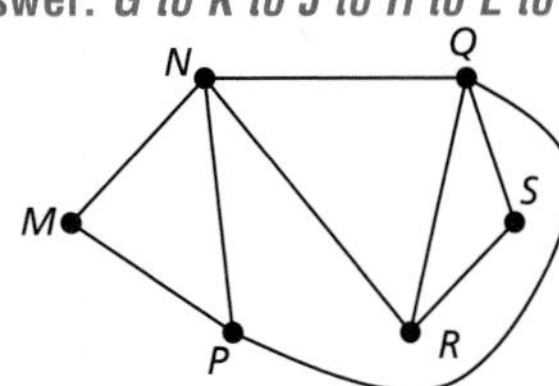

Possible answer: *M* to *N* to *R* to *S* to *Q* to *P* to *M*

8. The graph shows the roads between five cities, which are represented by the graph's vertices.

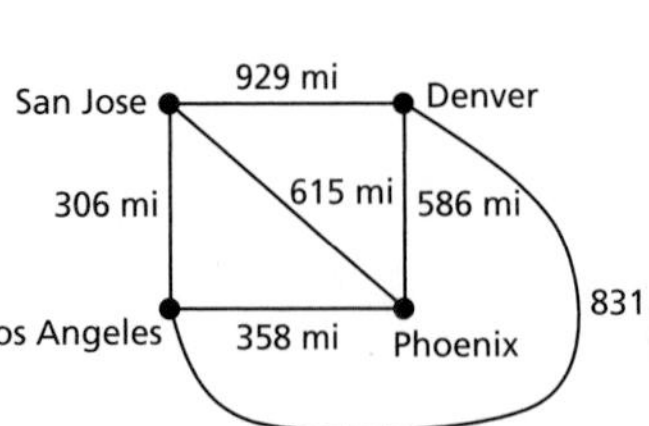

a. Find the shortest Hamiltonian circuit that begins at *V*. What is the length of the circuit? *V* to *W* to *X* to *Y* to *T* to *V*; 51 km

b. Find the longest Hamiltonian circuit that begins at *V*. What is the length of the circuit? *V* to *Y* to *X* to *W* to *T* to *V*; 55 km

c. How much distance do you save by traveling the shortest Hamiltonian circuit among the cities rather than the longest? 4 km

9. Alberto earns frequent-flier points for each mile that he flies. From his home in San Jose, he wants to visit Los Angeles, Phoenix, and Denver, and then return home. The graph shows the distances between the cities. What circuit should Alberto use in order to earn the greatest number of frequent-flier miles? How many miles will he fly?

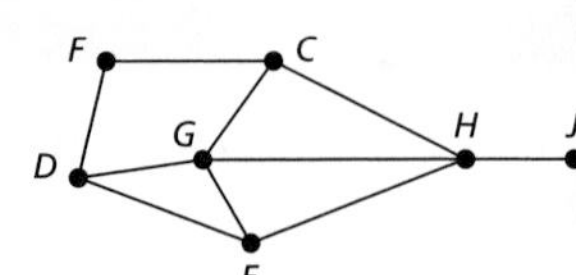

San Jose to Denver to Los Angeles to Phoenix to San Jose; 2733 mi

In Exercises 10–12, draw a graph with the given characteristics.

10. a graph with 5 vertices for which there is a Hamiltonian circuit

11. a graph with 4 vertices for which there is no Hamiltonian circuit

12. a graph whose Hamiltonian circuit consists of 6 edges

13. Some students were asked to find a Hamiltonian circuit for the graph at right. Without trying any paths, one student immediately replied that there is no Hamiltonian circuit for the graph. How did the student know?

F C G H J D E

Determine whether each statement is *always, sometimes,* or *never* true.

14. A graph with 3 vertices has a Hamiltonian circuit. sometimes

15. The reverse path of a Hamiltonian circuit is also a Hamiltonian circuit. always

16. In a graph with 4 vertices, a Hamiltonian circuit traverses 5 edges. never

17. Critical Thinking If a graph has a Hamiltonian circuit starting at one of its vertices, then it is possible to find a Hamiltonian circuit starting at any of the graph's vertices. Explain why this is so.

ADDITIONAL TOPIC

A-6 Weighted Graphs

Objectives
Use minimum spanning trees and critical-path analysis to solve problems involving weighted graphs.

Vocabulary
weighted graph
weight of a path
tree
spanning tree
minimum spanning tree
directed graph
critical path

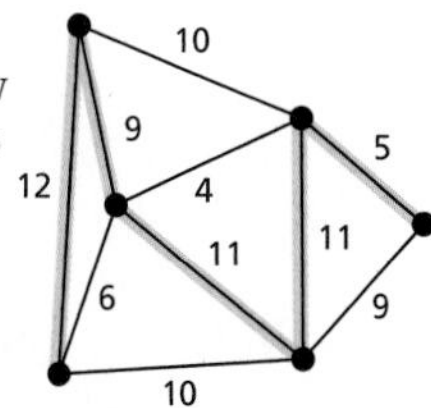

A **weighted graph** is a graph in which a numerical value is associated with every edge of the graph. You saw weighted graphs in the previous lesson, where the edges of some graphs were labeled with distances.

In a weighted graph, the **weight of a path** is the sum of the weights of the path's edges. In the graph at right, the highlighted path has weight $12 + 9 + 11 + 11 + 5 = 48$.

A **tree** is a subset of a graph in which each pair of vertices is connected by exactly one path. A **spanning tree** includes all the vertices of a graph. The highlighted path shown above is a spanning tree. In many applications, it is useful to find a **minimum spanning tree**, which is a tree whose weight is less than or equal to that of every other spanning tree.

EXAMPLE  1

Finding Minimum Spanning Trees

An electric company is laying new cable in a neighborhood. In the graph, vertices represent houses and the weights represent the cost, in thousands of dollars, of laying the cable. Determine how the company can connect all the houses at minimum cost. Then find the cost.

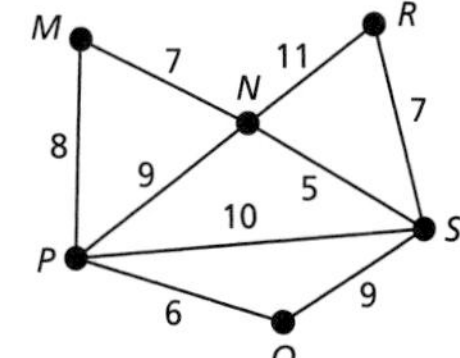

Step 1 Choose any vertex as the starting point. For example, choose vertex M.

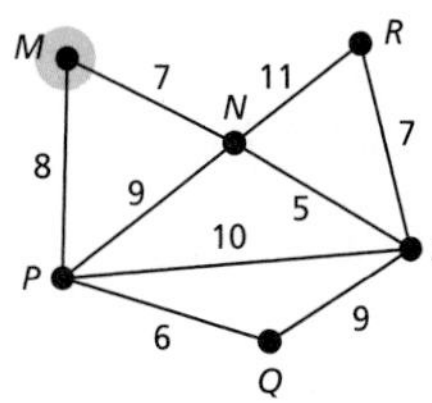

Step 2 Among all the vertices connected to M, choose the one that is connected by an edge with the least value. Vertices N and P are connected to M, and the edge connecting M and N has the least value. Highlight this edge and vertex N.

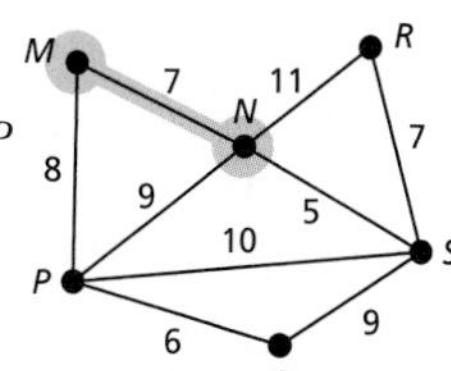

Step 3 Among all the vertices connected to M or N, choose the one that is connected by an edge with the least value. Vertices P, S, and R are connected to M or N, and the edge connecting N and S has the least value. Highlight this edge and vertex S.

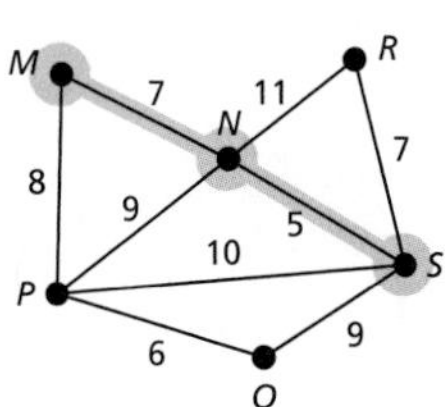

1 Introduce

Motivate

Ask students if they have ever seen a diagram that shows the driving distances between major U.S. cities. If possible, share such a diagram with the class. Explain that the diagram is a type of graph and that the cities are represented by the graph's vertices. The graph's edges are labeled with distances. Point out that this makes the graph a special type of graph, known as a weighted graph, which will be explored in this lesson.

2 Teach

Guided Instruction

Draw a simple weighted graph on the board and use it to introduce the vocabulary of the lesson. Use the graph to give an example of a tree, a spanning tree, and a minimum spanning tree. In each case, show students how to calculate the weight of the tree. Then present Example 1. Next introduce directed graphs by comparing them to flowcharts. Ask students to identify similarities and differences between directed graphs and flowcharts.

ADDITIONAL TOPIC

A-6 Organizer

Objectives: Use minimum spanning trees and critical-path analysis to solve problems involving weighted graphs.

Warm Up

For each set, find the sum of the three smallest numbers.

1. 3, 5, 7, 9, 10 15

2. 11, 3, 6, 9 18

3. 45 10, 6, 3 19

4. 5, 2, 3, 4, 7, 8 9

Additional Examples

Example 1

A technician is connecting the phones in a new office. In the graph, vertices represent phones and the weights represent the length, in meters, of the required wiring. Determine how the technician can connect all the phones using the minimum amount of wire, then find the amount of wire needed.

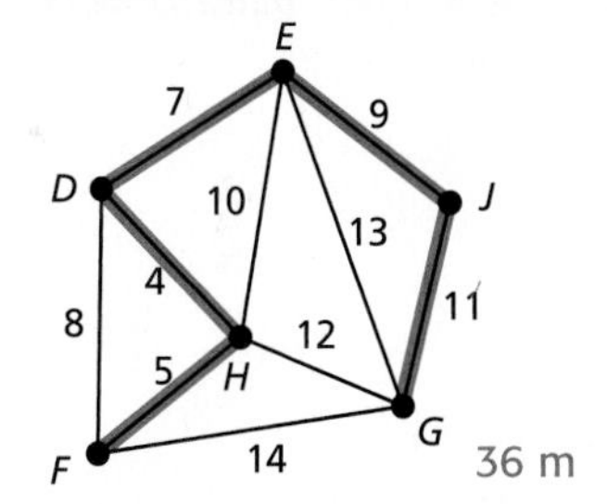

36 m

State Resources

Additional Examples

Example 2

The graph shows the workflow for replacing the tiles on a roof. Find the critical path and determine the shortest time possible to replace the tiles.

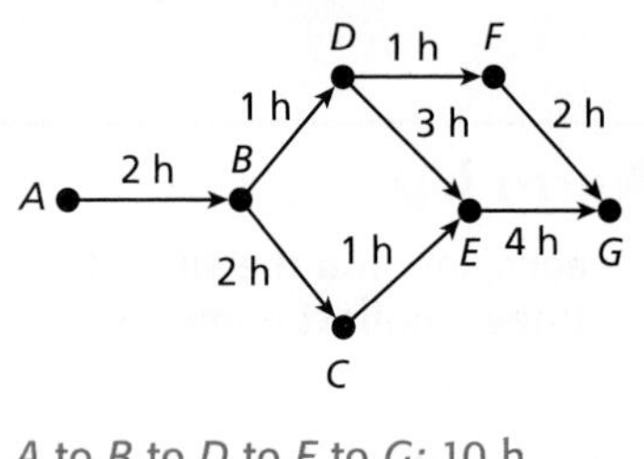

A to B to D to E to G; 10 h

INTERVENTION
Questioning Strategies

EXAMPLE 1

- What type of tree do you need to find in order to solve this problem?
- What is the first step in finding a minimum spanning tree for the given graph?

EXAMPLE 2

- What do the times in the graph represent?
- What do the arrows in the graph represent?
- What is a critical path? How do you find it?

Step 4 Continue in this way until all vertices have been highlighted. The figure shows the minimum spanning tree for the given graph.

The cost of laying the cable is $6 + 8 + 7 + 5 + 7 = 33$, or \$33,000.

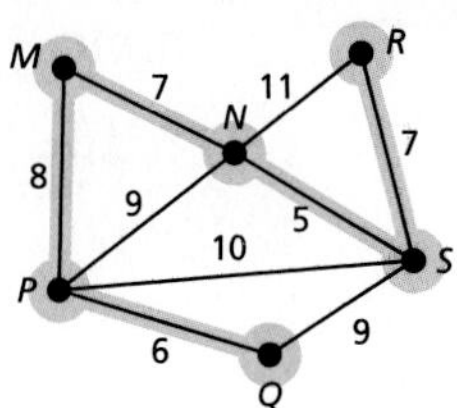

91 ft

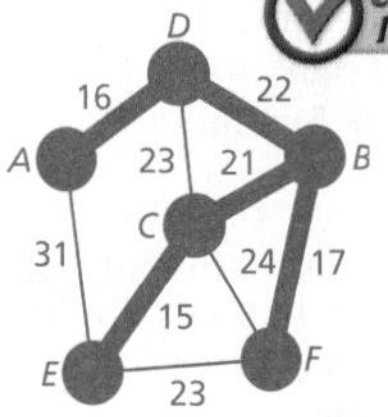

CHECK IT OUT! **1.** In the graph, vertices represent computers and the weights represent the length, in feet, of cable required to connect the computers. Determine how Marion can connect all the computers using the minimum length of cable. Then find the length.

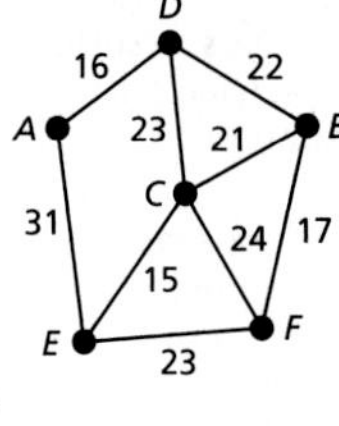

A **directed graph** is a graph in which each edge has a direction indicated by an arrow. Directed graphs are useful in managing projects. For example, the directed graph at right shows the workflow for remodeling a kitchen. The edge weights give the duration of various activities. Notice that the graph also shows which activities must be completed before others can begin.

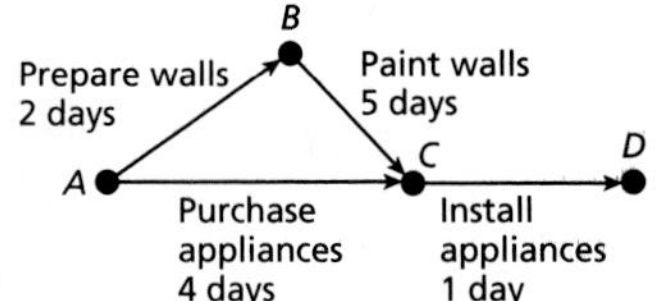

When a directed graph represents the workflow of a project, the **critical path** is the path from the starting vertex to the ending vertex that has the greatest total duration. The total duration of the critical path is the shortest time possible to complete the project.

EXAMPLE 2 **Business Application**

The graph shows the workflow for developing a web site. Find the critical path and determine the shortest time possible to develop the web site.

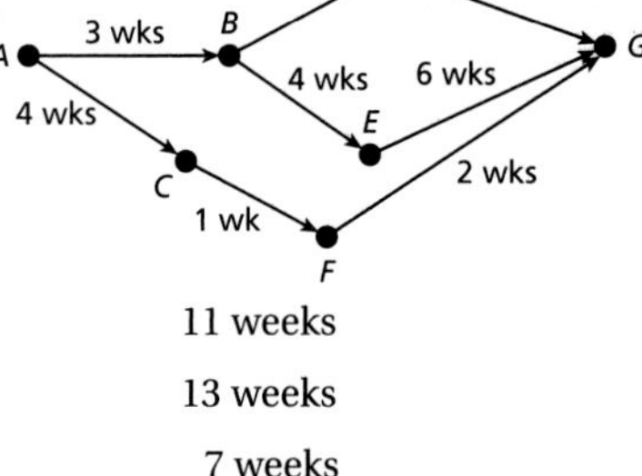

Find the total duration of all paths from *A* to *G*.

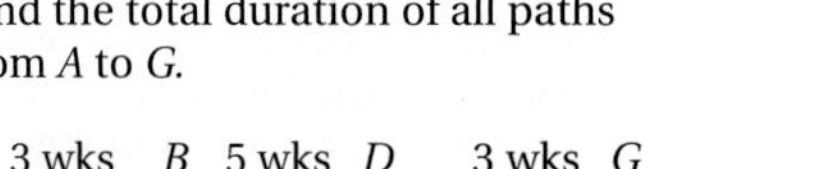

Path	Total
$A \xrightarrow{3\text{ wks}} B \xrightarrow{5\text{ wks}} D \xrightarrow{3\text{ wks}} G$	11 weeks
$A \xrightarrow{3\text{ wks}} B \xrightarrow{4\text{ wks}} E \xrightarrow{6\text{ wks}} G$	13 weeks
$A \xrightarrow{4\text{ wks}} C \xrightarrow{1\text{ wk}} F \xrightarrow{2\text{ wks}} G$	7 weeks

The path with the greatest total duration is the critical path. The critical path is *A* to *B* to *E* to *G*.

To shortest possible time to develop the web site is 13 weeks.

3 Close

Summarize

Review key definitions from the lesson.

Weighted graph: a graph in which a numerical value is associated with every edge

Tree: a subset of a graph in which any two vertices are connected by exactly one path

Spanning tree: a tree that includes all the vertices of a graph

Directed graph: a graph in which each edge has a direction

Teaching Tip

Math Background The algorithm that is used to find a minimum spanning tree in Example 1 is known as Prim's algorithm. It was developed by computer scientist Robert Prim in 1957. Although the algorithm works well for graphs with relatively few vertices, a computer is required if the algorithm is to be applied to larger graphs. Finding the fastest possible algorithm for minimum spanning trees remains an open problem in computer science.

2. The graph shows the workflow for replacing the water main under a street. Find the critical path and determine the shortest time possible to replace the water main.
A to C to B to E to F; 8 days

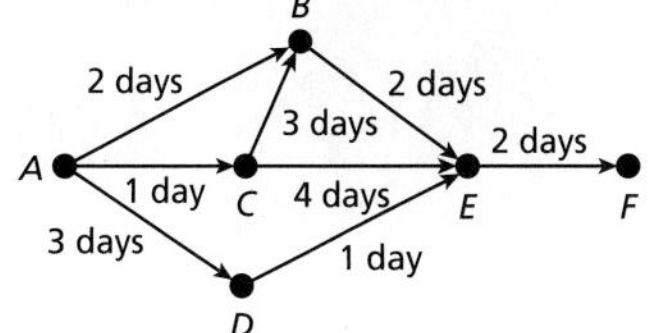

In **Example 2,** students are asked to find the shortest time possible to develop the web site. For this reason, students might choose the path *A* to *C* to *F* to *G* as the critical path because it has the shortest total duration. Remind students that the critical path is the path with the greatest total duration.

A-6 Exercises

Copy each graph and highlight its minimum spanning tree. Give the weight of the minimum spanning tree.

1. 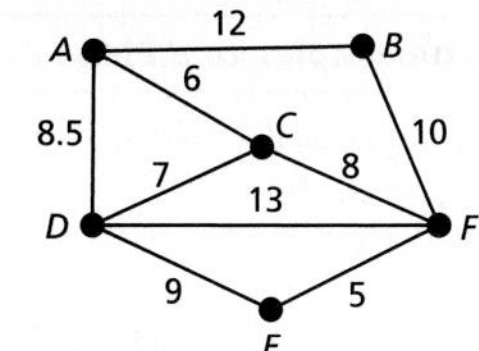

2. 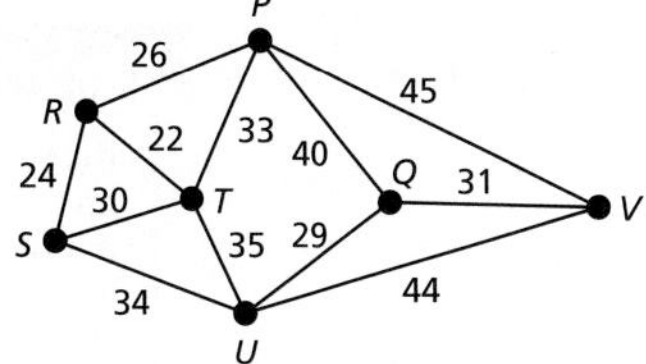

3. A company has offices in several locations. The company's office manager wants to have special phone lines installed to connect the offices. In the graph, vertices represent office locations and the weights represent the cost, in thousands of dollars, of connecting the offices. Determine how the company can connect all the offices at minimum cost. Then find the cost. **$30,000**

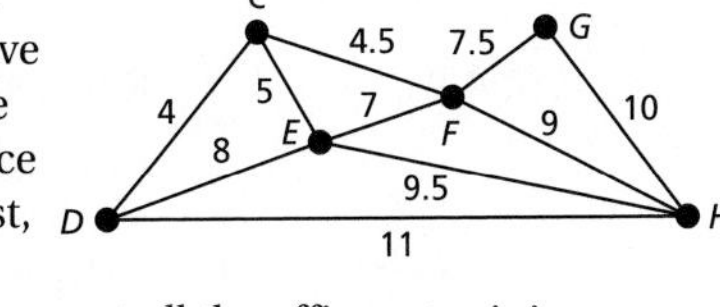

4. The graph shows the workflow for landscaping the area around a building. Find the critical path and determine the shortest time possible to landscape the area.
A to C to E to G; 10 weeks

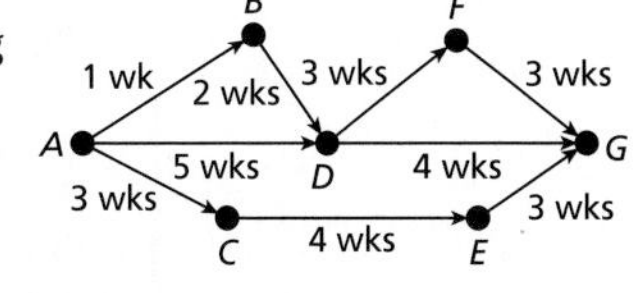

5. The graph shows the workflow for producing a magazine article.
   a. What is the shortest time possible to produce the article? **12 days**
   b. Name an activity that could take one day longer than scheduled without increasing the total amount of time needed to produce the article. **Possible answer: take photos**
   c. Name an activity that will increase the amount of time needed to produce the article if the activity takes longer than scheduled.
   Possible answer: write article

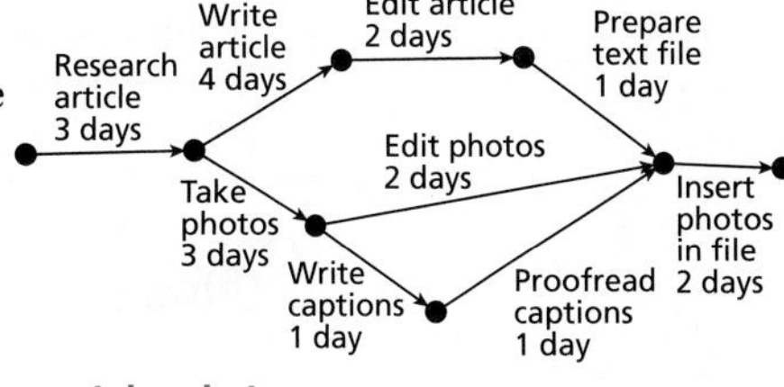

In Exercises 6–8, draw a weighted graph with the given characteristics.

6. The minimum spanning tree includes all but one edge.
7. The minimum spanning tree has a weight of 12.
8. There are two different minimum spanning trees.

1. 36

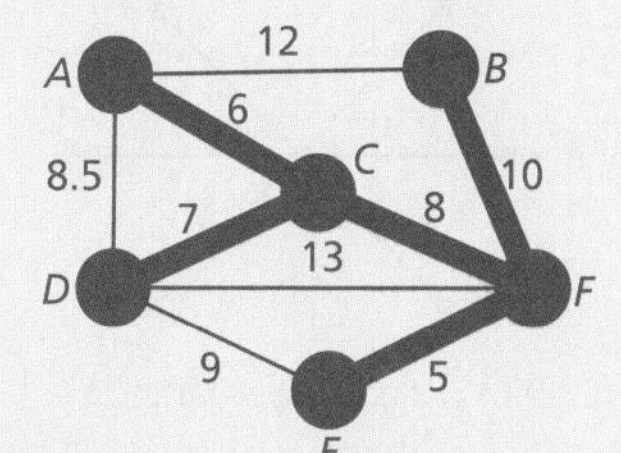

2. 166

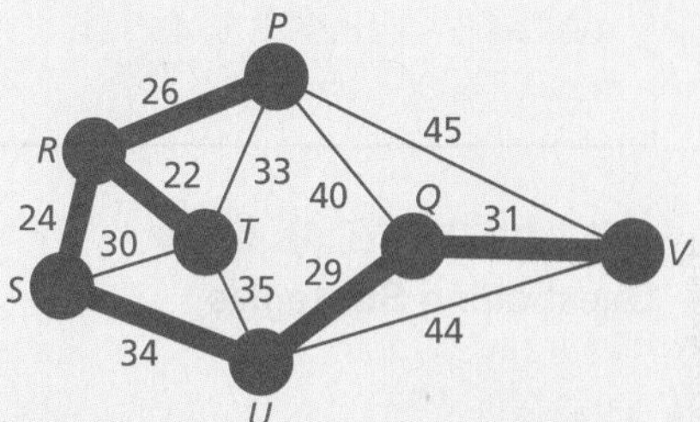

6. Possible answer:

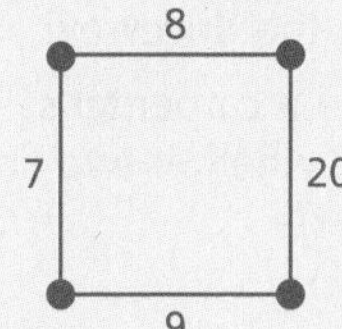

7. Possible answer:

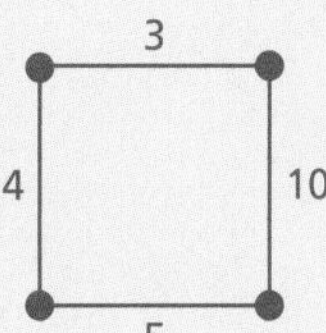

8. Possible answer:

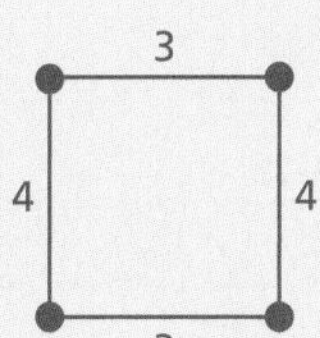

A-6 Weighted Graphs **AT17**

ADDITIONAL TOPIC

A-7 Organizer

Objectives: Prove and apply theorems about lines perpendicular to planes.

Warm Up

1. Explain why $\overline{SV} \perp \overline{TW}$.

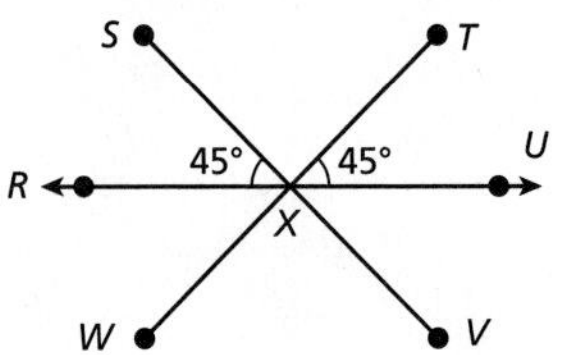

$m\angle RXU = m\angle RXS + m\angle SXT + m\angle TXU$. Substituting $m\angle RXS = m\angle TXU = 45°$ and $m\angle RXU = 180°$ into the equation gives $180° = 45° + m\angle SXT + 45°$. So $m\angle SXT = 90°$, and $\overline{SV} \perp \overline{TW}$.

INTERVENTION
Questioning Strategies

EXAMPLE 1

- What do you need to show in order to conclude that the pole is perpendicular to the driveway?
- How can use you a carpenter's triangle to check whether two lines are perpendicular?

State Resources

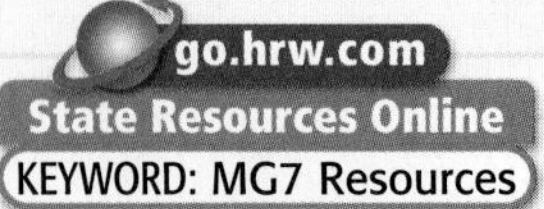

ADDITIONAL TOPIC

A-7 Lines Perpendicular to Planes

Objectives
Prove and apply theorems about lines perpendicular to planes.

If you want to put up a basketball hoop in your driveway, how can you tell that the pole is straight? To answer this question, you need to know what it means for a line to be perpendicular to a plane.

A line ℓ is defined as perpendicular to a plane P if ℓ is perpendicular to every line in P that intersects ℓ. To prove that a line is perpendicular to a plane, you do not have to show that the line is perpendicular to every line in the plane. You can use the postulate given below as a shortcut.

Postulate A-1-1 **Line Perpendicular to a Plane Postulate**

If line ℓ intersects lines a and b in plane P and is perpendicular to both a and b, then ℓ is perpendicular to plane P at the point of intersection of a and b.

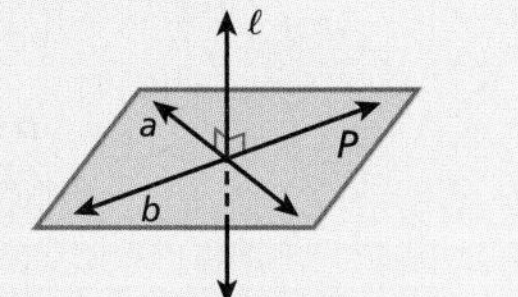

EXAMPLE 1 **Recreation Application**

Doug is putting up a basketball hoop in his driveway. How can he use a carpenter's triangle (shown) to make sure the pole of the basketball hoop is perpendicular to the driveway?

Doug can apply Postulate A-1-1 by using the carpenter's triangle to measure the angle the pole makes to any two lines in the driveway. If the pole is perpendicular to lines m and n, for example, then the pole is perpendicular to the plane of the driveway.

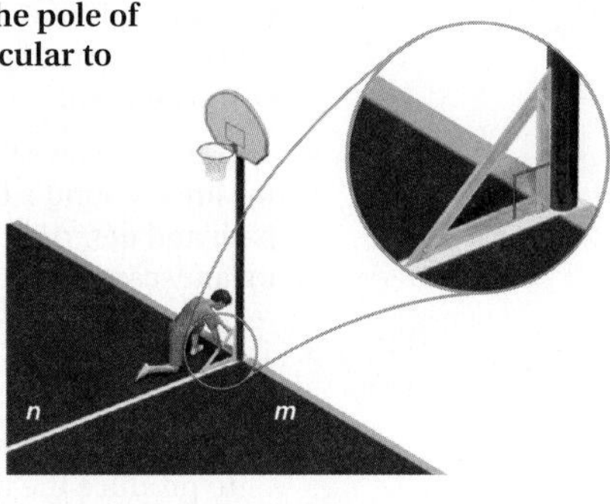

CHECK IT OUT!

1. The diagrams show the view of a stop sign from the front and from the side. Use the pictures to explain why you must check that a line is perpendicular to at least two lines in a plane before you can conclude the line is perpendicular to the plane.

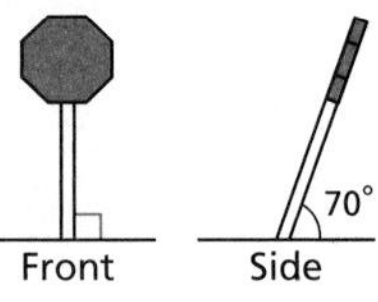

1. The sign is perpendicular to the ground along one direction, but not the other. You can only guarantee the sign is perpendicular to the ground if it is perpendicular to two different lines along the ground.

The theorems on the next page show that there is only one line perpendicular to a point in a plane, and only one plane perpendicular to a line at a point on the line.

1 Introduce

Motivate

Remind students that two lines are perpendicular if they intersect to form right angles. Ask students what they think it would mean for a line and a plane to be perpendicular. If students suggest that the line and plane must intersect to form right angles, ask them how they would measure the angles formed by a line and a plane. This discussion can motivate the definition of perpendicularity that is presented in the opening paragraphs of the lesson.

2 Teach

Guided Instruction

As you present the theorems that are introduced in this lesson, draw a sketch on the board to illustrate each theorem's hypothesis and conclusion. Before discussing the proof of Theorem A-1-2, remind students of the steps in an indirect proof: (1) identify the conjecture to be proven; (2) assume opposite of the conclusion is true; (3) use direct reasoning to show that the assumption leads to a contradiction; (4) conclude that the original conjecture must be true.

Helpful Hint

If a line is perpendicular to a plane at point A, you can also say that the plane is perpendicular to the line at point A.

Theorems

	THEOREM	HYPOTHESIS	CONCLUSION
A-1-2	Given a point on a plane, there is one and only one line perpendicular to the plane through that point.	Line ℓ is $\perp$ to plane P at point A.	Line ℓ is the only line $\perp$ to plane P at point A.
A-1-3	Given a point on a line, there is one and only one plane perpendicular to the line through that point.	Plane R is $\perp$ to line m at point B.	Plane R is the only plane $\perp$ to line m at point B.

PROOF

Theorem A-1-2

Given: ℓ is $\perp$ to plane P at point A.
Prove: Line ℓ is the only line $\perp$ to plane P at point A.

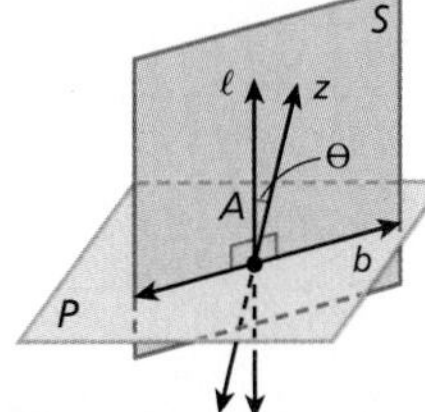

Indirect proof:

Assume that there is another line, z, that is also perpendicular to plane P at point A. Lines ℓ and z lie in a plane S that intersects plane P in a straight line b. The intersection of lines ℓ and z form an angle θ in plane S. By definition of a line perpendicular to a plane, ℓ is perpendicular to every line in plane P, so it is also perpendicular to line b. The same is true for line z. However, lines ℓ and z cannot both be perpendicular to line b because $\theta + 90° + 90° > 180°$. Therefore, there can only be one line perpendicular to plane P at point A.

EXAMPLE 2 Applying Theorems About Lines Perpendicular to Planes

Identify each statement as true or false and justify your answers. In the diagram, planes A and B intersect at line k, and line h is perpendicular to plane A.

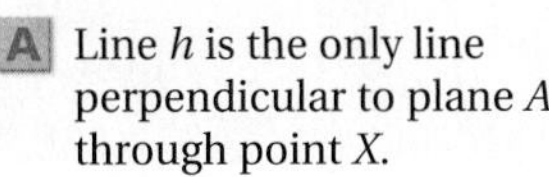

A Line h is the only line perpendicular to plane A through point X.

True. Theorem A-1-2 says that there is only one line perpendicular to a plane through any given point.

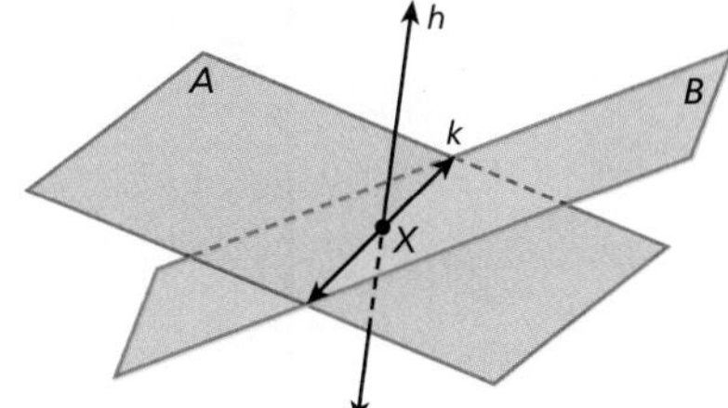

B Plane B is perpendicular to line h at point X.

False. Theorem A-1-3 states that there is only one plane perpendicular to line h at point X. Plane A is perpendicular to line h, so plane B cannot also be perpendicular to line h.

Teaching Tip

Kinesthetic Students may have difficultly visualizing intersecting lines and planes based on two-dimensional figures. Encourage students to recreate the figures in three dimensions by using pencils to represent lines and sheets of paper or pieces of cardboard to represent planes.

Additional Examples

Example 1

A radio tower, $\overline{PQ}$, is supported by guy wires $\overline{PA}$ and $\overline{PB}$ as shown. A technician checks the angles of the guy wires and finds that $m\angle PAQ = m\angle PBQ = 60°$ and $m\angle APQ = m\angle BPQ = 30°$. Can the technician conclude that the tower is perpendicular to the ground? Explain.

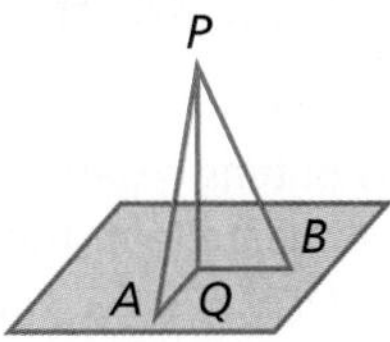

By the Triangle Sum Theorem, $m\angle PQA = m\angle PQB = 90°$. Thus, the tower is perpendicular to $\overline{QA}$ and $\overline{QB}$, so by Postulate A-1-1, the tower is perpendicular to the ground.

Example 2

Identify each statement as true or false and justify your answers. In the diagram, line *m* is perpendicular to plane *R* at point *A* and lines *m* and *n* intersect at point *A*.

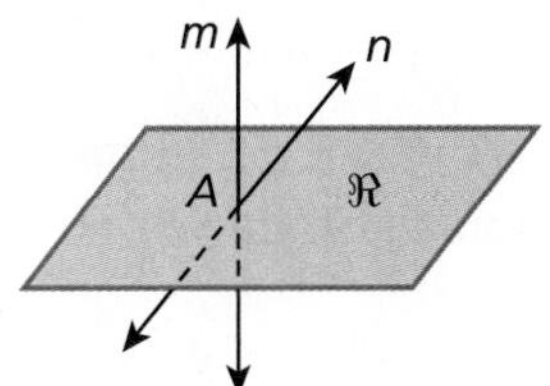

A. Plane R is the only plane perpendicular to line m at point A. True. Theorem A-1-3 says that there is only one plane perpendicular to a line through a point on the line.

B. Line n is perpendicular to plane R. False. Theorem A-1-2 says that there is only one line perpendicular to a plane through any given point in the plane. Since line m is perpendicular to plane R at point A, line n cannot also be perpendicular to plane R at this point.

INTERVENTION
Questioning Strategies

EXAMPLE 2

- How can you use Theorems A-1-2 and A-1-3 to draw conclusions about the lines and planes in the figure?

Remind students that they cannot assume that a line is perpendicular to a plane simply because it appears to be perpendicular in a diagram. The line must be marked as perpendicular with a right-angle mark or it must be said to be perpendicular in the statement of the problem.

Additional Examples

Example 3

A crew is putting together the frame for a large tent. The legs of the tent, $\overline{AE}$, $\overline{BF}$, $\overline{CG}$, and $\overline{DH}$, are all perpendicular to plane *ABC*. How can the crew be sure that a pole with a light fixture, $\overline{DX}$, is in plane *ABC*?

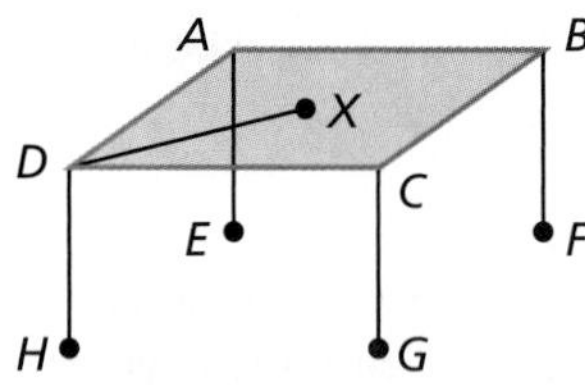

The crew should check that $\overline{DX}$ is perpendicular to $\overline{DH}$. Then by Theorem A-1-5, $\overline{DX}$ is contained in plane *ABC*.

INTERVENTION

Questioning Strategies

EXAMPLE 3

- What does the problem ask you to show?
- Which of the theorems in this lesson can you apply to the situation in the problem?
- How can you apply the theorem?

2. True or false: Line *h* is perpendicular to line *k*. Explain. **True. Line *h* is perp. to plane *A* through point *X*, so by def., line *h* is perp. to all lines in plane *A* that pass through *X*.**

There are two additional theorems that describe the relationship between lines perpendicular to a given plane.

Theorems

	THEOREM	HYPOTHESIS	CONCLUSION
A-1-4	Two lines perpendicular to the same plane are coplanar.	Lines *m* and *n* are both ⊥ to plane *P*.	Lines *m* and *n* are coplanar.
A-1-5	If a line is perpendicular to a plane, any line perpendicular to that line at the point of intersection of the line and the plane is contained in the plane.	Line *a* is ⊥ to plane *R* through point *Y* and line *b* is ⊥ to line *a* at point *Y*.	Line *b* is contained in plane *R*.

EXAMPLE 3 **Construction Application**

The Empire State Carousel was built by over 1,000 volunteers from New York State. The construction began in 1984 and was completed in 2003. The center beam *c* is perpendicular to plane *L*. If another row of lights is added (*r*), how can the builder be sure that *r* is in plane *L*?

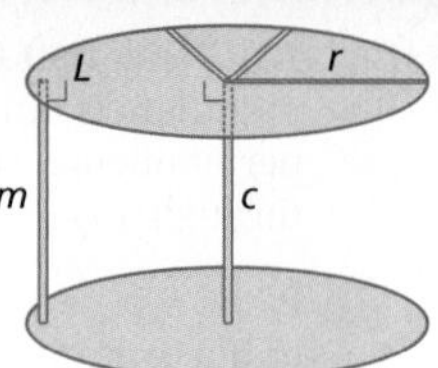

The builder can apply Theorem A-1-5. If the new row of lights *r* is perpendicular to *c*, then by Theorem A-1-5, *r* is in plane *L*.

3. If the beam labeled *m* is also perpendicular to plane *L*, what does Theorem A-1-4 let you conclude about lines *c* and *m*? **Lines *c* and *m* are coplanar.**

3 Close

Summarize

Have students tell whether each statement is true or false and give a postulate or theorem to justify their answer.

1. Two goal posts that are perpendicular to a playing field both lie in the same plane. True; Theorem A-1-4
2. Lines *p* and *q* can both intersect plane *A* at point *X* and can both be perpendicular to plane *A*. False; Theorem A-1-2
3. If lines *m* and *n* lie in plane *R* and intersect at point *P*, then any line perpendicular to *m* and *n* at point *P* is perpendicular to plane *R*. True; Postulate A-1-1

A-7 Exercises

Use the diagram at right for Exercises 1 and 2. Identify each statement as true or false and justify your answers. Lines *g* and *h* are contained in plane *S*.

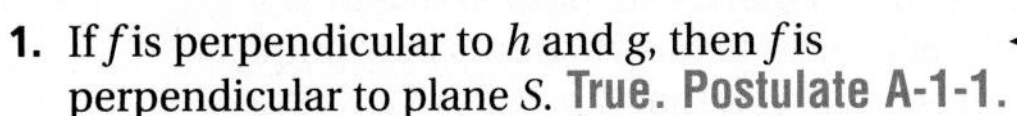

1. If *f* is perpendicular to *h* and *g*, then *f* is perpendicular to plane *S*. **True. Postulate A-1-1.**

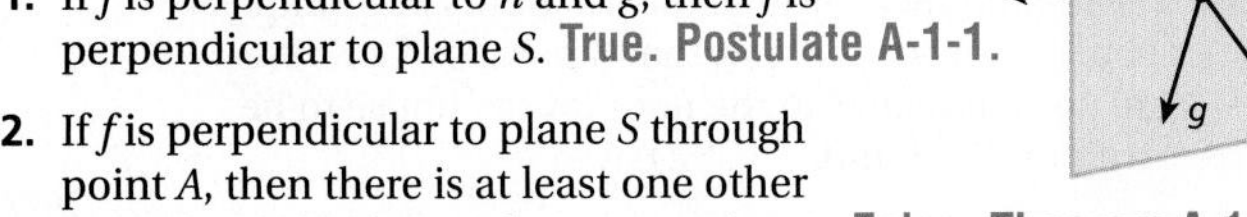

2. If *f* is perpendicular to plane *S* through point *A*, then there is at least one other line perpendicular to plane *S* at point *A*. **False. Theorem A-1-2.**

3a. Use the triangle to make sure $\overline{HE}$ is perpendicular to $\overline{AD}$ and $\overline{EF}$. Postulate A-1-1.

3. Sports Miguel and Shawna are setting up the net for a tennis court. Explain how they can use a carpenter's triangle to verify each situation below. Use a postulate or theorem to justify your answers.

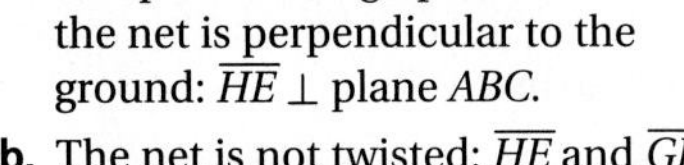

a. The pole holding up one end of the net is perpendicular to the ground: $\overline{HE} \perp$ plane *ABC*.

b. The net is not twisted: $\overline{HE}$ and $\overline{GF}$ are coplanar.
Use the triangle to make sure $\overline{HE}$ and $\overline{GF}$ are both perpendicular to *ABC*. Theorem A-1-4.

Use the diagram of the triangular prism at right for Exercises 4–7. Classify each statement as *never*, *sometimes*, or *always* true.

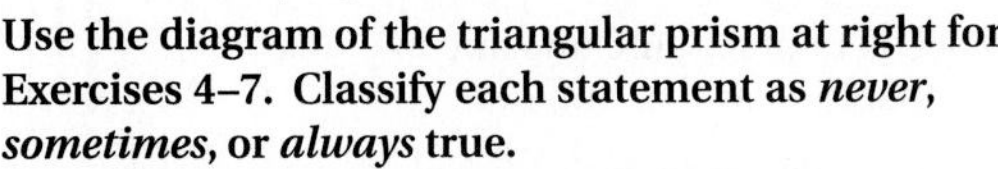

4. If $\overline{NR} \perp$ plane *QRS*, then $\overline{XR} \perp$ plane *QRS*. **never**

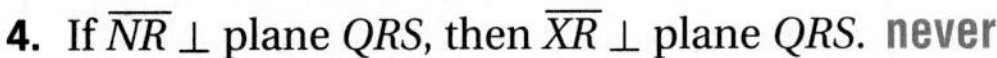

5. If $\overline{NR} \perp$ plane *QRS* at point *R*, there is at least one other plane that is perpendicular to $\overline{NR}$ at point R. **never**

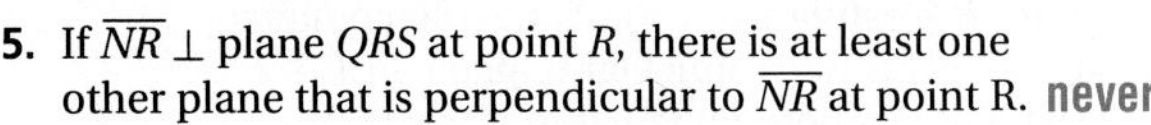

6. If $\overline{NR} \perp$ plane *MNP*, then $\overline{NZ}$ is contained in plane *MNP*. **sometimes**

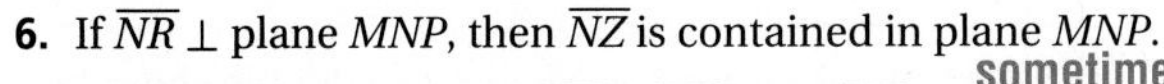

7. If $\overline{NR} \perp$ plane *MNP* and $\overline{NZ} \perp \overline{NR}$, then $\overline{NZ}$ is contained in plane *MNP*. **always**

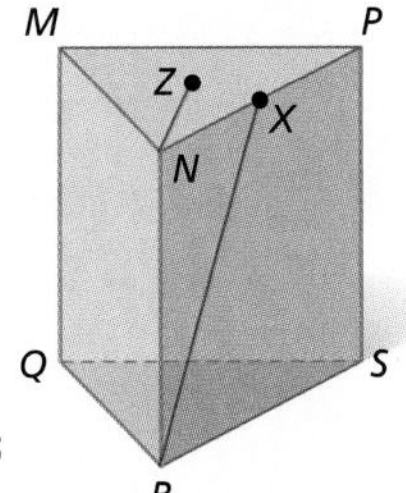

8a. $\overleftrightarrow{BD}$
8b. *R*
8c. perpendicular
8d. 90°
8e. angle addition postulate
8f. 90°
8g. m∠*DBC*
8h. *P*

8. Challenge Complete the paragraph proof for Theorem A-1-5.

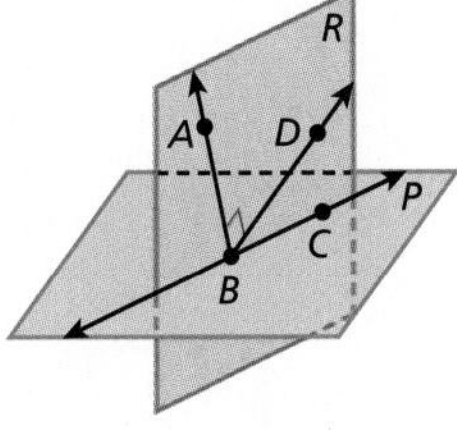

Given: $\overleftrightarrow{AB}$ is ⊥ to plane *P* at point *B*, $\overleftrightarrow{BD} \perp \overleftrightarrow{AB}$

Prove: $\overleftrightarrow{BD}$ is in plane *P*.

Indirect proof: Assume that **a.** _____ is not in plane *P*. $\overleftrightarrow{AB}$ and $\overleftrightarrow{BD}$ are contained in plane **b.** _____, and planes *P* and *R* intersect at $\overleftrightarrow{BC}$. $\overleftrightarrow{AB}$ is **c.** _____ to $\overleftrightarrow{BC}$ by the definition of a line perpendicular to a plane, so m∠*ABC* = **d.** _____. m∠*ABC* = m∠*ABD* + m∠*DBC* by the **e.** _____. But $\overleftrightarrow{BD} \perp \overleftrightarrow{AB}$ is given, so m∠*ABD* = **f.** _____. Substituting into the equation, we get 90° = 90° + m∠*DBC*, which is only true if **g.** _____ = 0°. Therefore, the assumption is false and $\overleftrightarrow{BD}$ is in plane **h.** _____.

A-7 Lines Perpendicular to Planes **AT21**

ADDITIONAL TOPIC

A-8 Organizer

Objectives: Apply properties of perpendicular planes.

Warm Up

Tell whether each statement is *sometimes, always,* or *never* true.

1. When two planes intersect, their intersection is a single point. never
2. When two planes intersect, their intersection is a straight line. always
3. If line a is in plane A and line b is in plane B and plane A intersects plane B, then lines a and b also intersect. sometimes

INTERVENTION

Questioning Strategies

EXAMPLE 1

- What does it mean for two planes to be perpendicular?
- What does it mean for a line to be perpendicular to a plane?
- Which postulate or theorem can you use to help you solve the problem?

State Resources

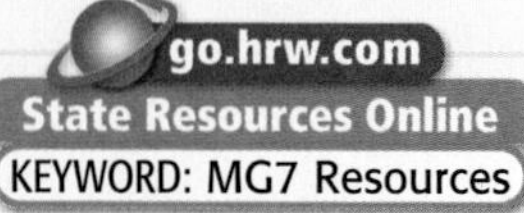

ADDITIONAL TOPIC

A-8 Perpendicular Planes

Objective
Apply properties of perpendicular planes.

Knowing when two planes are perpendicular is key to architecture and construction. For example, a builder needs to know that the walls of a house are perpendicular to the floor for the house to be structurally sound.

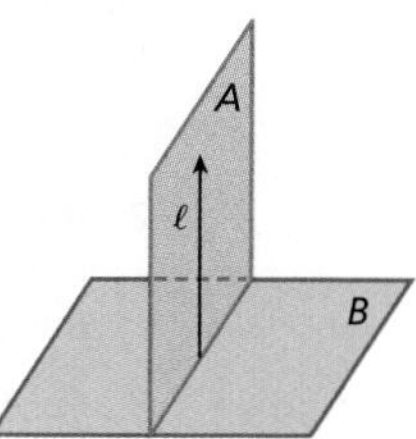

Two planes are defined as perpendicular if one plane contains a line that is perpendicular to the other plane. Plane A is perpendicular to plane B if there is a line ℓ in A that is perpendicular to plane B.

EXAMPLE 1 Construction Application

Sharon is overseeing the construction of a house. How can she check to see that the wall (plane *ABC*) is perpendicular to the floor (plane *BCF*)?

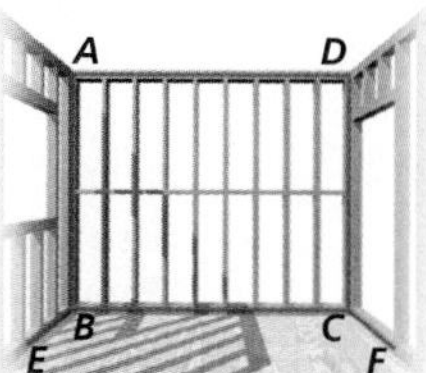

Sharon needs to make sure one line in plane ABC is perpendicular to plane BCF.

If $\overline{AB}$ is perpendicular to both $\overline{BC}$ and $\overline{BE}$, then $\overline{AB}$ is perpendicular to plane BCF at point B (Postulate A-1-1). Plane ABC contains a line that is perpendicular to plane BCF, so plane ABC is perpendicular to plane BCF.

1. Explain how Sharon can double check her work by using a different line. **She can check that $\overline{DC}$ is perpendicular to $\overline{BC}$ and $\overline{CF}$.**

If a line is perpendicular to a plane, every plane that contains that line is perpendicular to the plane. Imagine rotating plane A around line ℓ, which is perpendicular to plane P. Every rotational image of plane A contains ℓ, so plane B is also perpendicular to P.

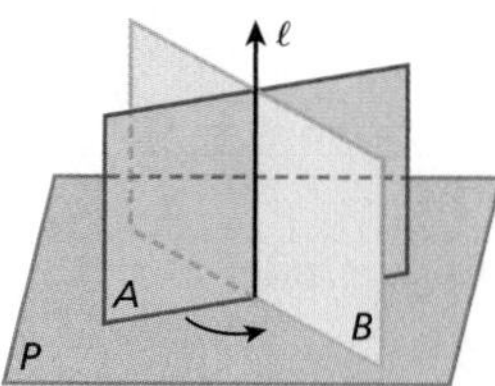

Theorem A-2-1

THEOREM	HYPOTHESIS	CONCLUSION
If a line is perpendicular to a plane, then all planes containing that line are perpendicular to the plane.	Line ℓ is $\perp$ to plane P.	Any plane that contains line ℓ is $\perp$ to plane P.

1 Introduce

Motivate

Ask students to give an example of two planes in the classroom that are parallel. Possible answer: the floor and ceiling Then ask students to name two planes in the classroom that are perpendicular. Possible answer: a wall and the floor Have students explain what they think it means for these planes to be perpendicular. Use this discussion to motivate the definition of perpendicular planes that is presented in this lesson.

2 Teach

Guided Instruction

Remind students that they learned the definition of perpendicular lines in Chapter 3 and they learned what it means for a line and a plane to be perpendicular in Lesson A-7. Tell students they will now extend the definition of perpendicularity to two planes. After presenting this definition, discuss the examples with the class, using objects such as a book cover and a desktop to help represent the three-dimensional relationships.

EXAMPLE 2 **Architecture Application**

The figure below shows a set of revolving doors. $\overline{ST}$ is the axis around which the doors turn, and $\overline{ST}$ is perpendicular to plane *RTU* (the floor). As the doors rotate, do the planes of the doors, *STU* and *QRT*, remain perpendicular to plane *RTU*? Explain.

Planes *STU* and *QRT* remain perpendicular to plane *RTU* at all times. Because planes *STU* and *QRT* always contain the axis of rotation, $\overline{ST}$, Theorem A-2-1 allows you to conclude that planes *STU* and *QRT* are always perpendicular to plane *RTU*.

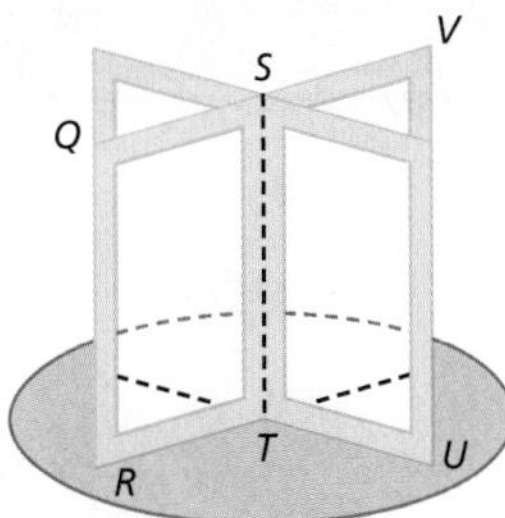

2. In the figure above, the planes of the two doors, *STU* and *QRT*, are also perpendicular to each other. How can the builder use $\overline{RT}$ to make sure that plane *QRT* is perpendicular to plane *STU*?
The builder needs to check that $\overline{RT}$ is perpendicular to both $\overline{TU}$ and $\overline{ST}$.

A-8 Exercises

1. **Construction** Mr. Spinoza is putting up a divider in his classroom so that students can be tutored privately. He uses a chalk line to mark $\overline{DF}$ on the room divider and $\overline{FH}$ on the floor.

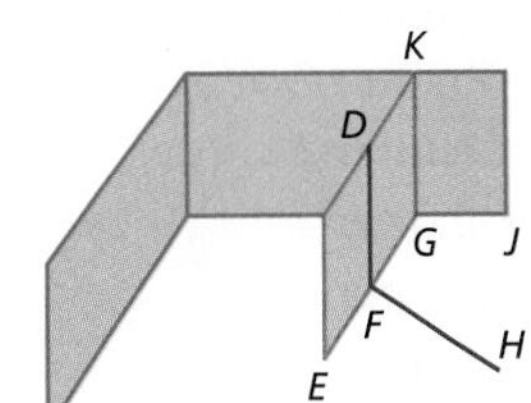

   a. How can he use these two lines and a carpenter's triangle to make sure the divider (plane *DFE*) is perpendicular to the floor (plane *EFH*)?

   1a. Use the triangle to make sure $\overline{DF}$ is perpendicular to $\overline{EG}$ and $\overline{FH}$. $\overline{DF}$ is then perpendicular to plane *EFH*. Since plane *DFE* contains $\overline{DF}$, plane *DFE* is perpendicular to plane *EFH*.

   b. How can he check that the divider is perpendicular to the existing wall (plane *JGK*)? **Check that $\overline{EG}$ is perpendicular to $\overline{GK}$ and $\overline{GJ}$.**

Use the diagram at right for Exercises 2 and 3.

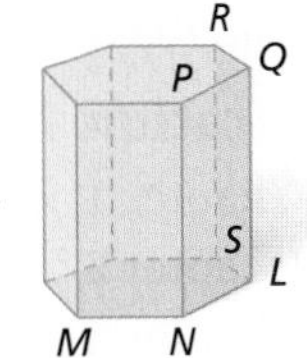

2. If $\overline{PN}$ is perpendicular to plane *MNL*, what planes can you conclude are perpendicular to plane *MNL*? **planes *PMN* and *PNL***
3. What line must be perpendicular to plane *MNL* for you to conclude that planes *RSL* and *PNL* are both perpendicular to plane *MNL*? **$\overline{QL}$**
4. **Write About It** Find an example of perpendicular planes in your home or school. Draw a sketch of them and explain how you could verify that the two planes are perpendicular. **Check students' work.**

Additional Examples

Example 1

Mineralogists use three-dimensional geometry to identify and classify crystals. In the crystal shown below, how can a mineralogist check that the top face of the crystal (plane *ABC*) is perpendicular to the side face (plane *DCE*)?

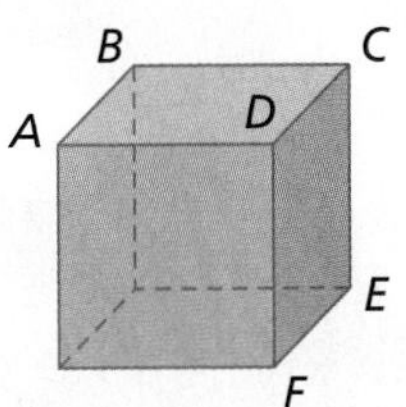

Check that $\overline{AD}$ is perpendicular to both $\overline{DC}$ and $\overline{DF}$. Then $\overline{AD}$ is perpendicular to plane *DCE* by Postulate A-1-1. Plane *ABC* contains a line that is perpendicular to plane *DCE*, so plane *ABC* is perpendicular to plane *DCE*.

Example 2

A box kite is usually made up of a box-shaped frame. Parts of the frame are covered with fabric, which allows the kite to catch the wind. In the kite below, $\overline{CE}$ is perpendicular to plane *ABC*. Can you conclude that planes *BCE* and *FCE* are perpendicular to plane *ABC*? Explain.

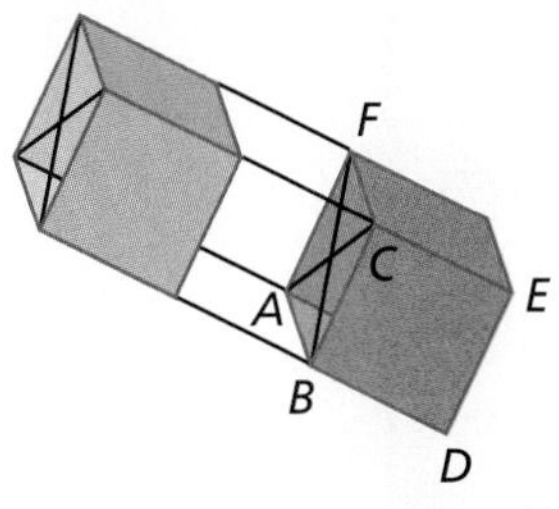

Planes *BCE* and *FCE* both contain $\overline{CE}$. By Theorem A-2-1, both planes are perpendicular to plane *ABC*.

Teaching Tip **Math Background** In higher mathematics, objects that are perpendicular to each other are said to be *orthogonal*. In future math courses, students will learn how to extend the idea of orthogonality to vectors, matrices, and functions.

3 Close

Summarize

Have students state the definition of perpendicular planes in their own words and have them illustrate the definition using lines and planes that are found in the classroom. Ask students to use a similar process to restate Theorem A-2-1.

INTERVENTION
Questioning Strategies

EXAMPLE 2

- What information about the lines and planes are you given?
- Can you apply Theorem A-2-1 to this problem? If so, how?

Student Handbook

Student Handbook

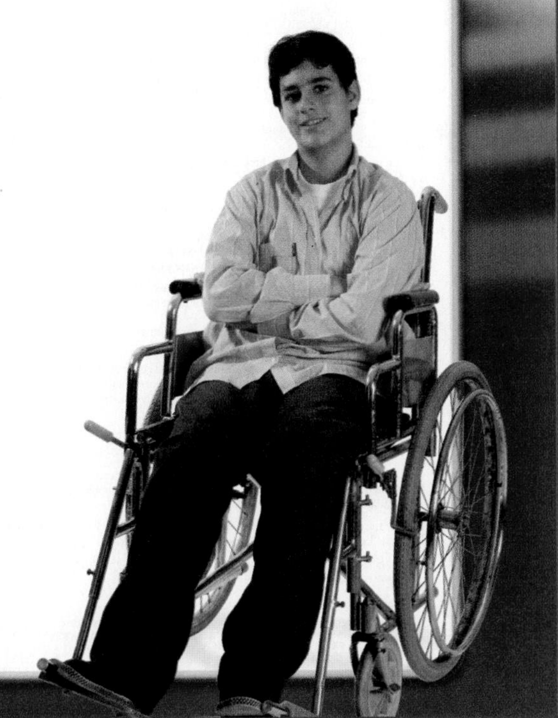

Extra Practice

Extra Practice

Chapter 1 ■ Skills Practice

Lesson 1-1

Name each of the following. 1–6. Possible answers:

1. two points H, I 2. two lines $\overleftrightarrow{JK}$, $\overleftrightarrow{IH}$
3. two planes $\mathcal{P}$, $\mathcal{V}$ 4. a point on $\overleftrightarrow{IH}$ H
5. a line that contains L and J $\overleftrightarrow{LJ}$
6. a plane that contains L, K, and H $\mathcal{P}$

Draw and label each of the following.

7. a ray with endpoint A that passes through B
8. a line $\overleftrightarrow{PQ}$ that intersects plane $\mathcal{D}$ 7–8. See p. A32.

Lesson 1-2

Find each length.

9. MN 8 10. MO 14

11. Segments that have the same length are ___?___. ≅
12. Construct a segment congruent to AB. Then construct the midpoint M.

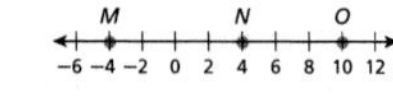

Check students' constructions.

13. M is the midpoint of $\overline{PR}$, $PM = 2x + 5$, and $MR = 4x - 7$. Solve for x and find PR. $x = 6$, $PR = 34$

Lesson 1-3

Z is in the interior of $\angle WXY$. Find each of the following.

14. $m\angle WXY$ if $\angle WXZ = 23°$ and $m\angle ZXY = 51°$ 74°
15. $m\angle WXZ$ if $m\angle WXY = 44°$ and $m\angle ZXY = 20°$ 24°

$\overrightarrow{EH}$ bisects $\angle DEF$. Find each of the following.

16. $m\angle DEH$ if $m\angle DEH = (10z - 2)°$ and $m\angle HEF = (6z + 10)°$ 28°
17. $m\angle DEF$ if $m\angle DEH = (9x + 3)°$ and $m\angle HEF = (5x + 11)°$ 42°
18. A ___?___ is formed by two opposite rays and measures ___?___°. straight ∠; 180
19. There are ___?___° in a circle. 360

Lesson 1-4

Tell whether the angles are only adjacent, adjacent and form a linear pair, or not adjacent.

20. $\angle AOB$ and $\angle DOE$ 21. $\angle AOE$ and $\angle DOE$
22. $\angle COE$ and $\angle EOA$ 23. $\angle AOB$ and $\angle BOD$
24. Name a pair of vertical angles. Possible answers: $\angle AOE$ and $\angle BOC$

20. not adj.
21. only adj.
22. adj. and a lin. pair
23. only adj.

Given $m\angle A = 41.7°$ and $m\angle B = (24.2 - x)°$, find the measure of each of the following.

25. complement of $\angle A$ 48.3° 26. supplement of $\angle A$ 138.3° 27. supplement of $\angle B$ 27. $(155.8 + x)°$

Lesson 1-5

Find the perimeter and area of each figure. 28–33. See p. A32.

28.

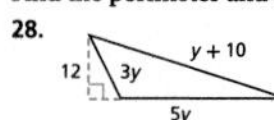

29. 1.45 cm

30.

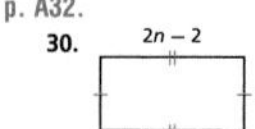

Find the circumference and area of each circle. Give your answer to the nearest hundredth.

31. 2.6 ft 32. 4 m 33.

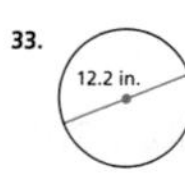

Lesson 1-6

34. The formula to find the midpoint M of $\overline{AB}$ with endpoints $A(x_1, y_1)$ and $B(x_2, y_2)$ is ___?___. See p. A32.

Find the coordinates of the midpoint of each segment.

35. $\overline{WX}$ with endpoints $W(-4, 1)$ and $X(2, 9)$ $(-1, 5)$
36. $\overline{YZ}$ with midpoints $Y(4, 8)$ and $Z(-1, -4)$ 36. $\left(1\frac{1}{2}, 2\right)$
37. M is the midpoint of $\overline{RS}$. R has coordinates $(-7, -3)$, and M has coordinates $(1, 1)$. Find the coordinates of S. $(9, 5)$

Find the length of the given segments and determine if they are congruent.

38. $\overline{VW}$ and $\overline{PQ}$
39. $\overline{RS}$ and $\overline{TU}$

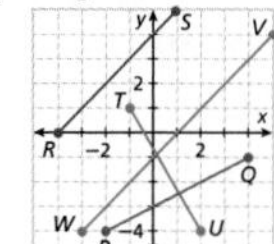

38. $\overline{VW} = 8\sqrt{2}$; $\overline{PQ} = 3\sqrt{5}$; no
39. $\overline{RS} = \overline{TU} = \sqrt{34}$; yes

Lesson 1-7

Identify each transformation. Then use arrow notation to describe the transformation.

40.

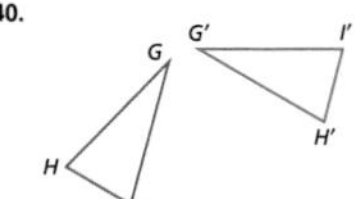

rotation; $\triangle GHI \rightarrow \triangle G'H'I'$

41. 41–44. See p. A32.

42. A figure has vertices at $(1, 1)$, $(2, 4)$, and $(5, 3)$. After a transformation, the image of the figure has vertices at $(-3, -2)$, $(-2, 1)$, and $(1, 0)$. Draw the preimage and image. Then describe the transformation.
43. A figure has vertices at $(5, 5)$, $(2, 6)$, $(1, 5)$, and $(2, 4)$. After a transformation, the image of the figure has vertices at $(5, 5)$, $(6, 8)$, $(5, 9)$, and $(4, 8)$. Draw the preimage and image. Then describe the transformation.
44. The coordinates of the vertices of quadrilateral $DEFG$ are $(3, 0)$, $(2, 3)$, $(-3, 2)$, and $(-2, -1)$. Find the coordinates for the image of rectangle $DEFG$ after the translation $(x, y) \rightarrow (x, -y)$. Draw the preimage and image. Then describe the transformation.

Chapter 2 ■ Skills Practice

Lesson 2-1

Find the next item in each pattern.

1. 3, 7, 11, 15, … 19 2. −3, 6, −12, 24, … −48
3. Complete the conjecture "The product of two negative numbers is ___?___." positive
4. Show that the conjecture "The quotient of two integers is an integer" is false by finding a counterexample. $3 \div 2 = 1.5$

Lesson 2-2

Identify the hypothesis and conclusion of each conditional.

5. A number is divisible by 10 if it ends in zero. H: A number ends in a zero. C: A number is divisible by 10.
6. If the temperature reaches 100° F, it will rain. H: The temperature reaches 100° F. C: It will rain.

Write a conditional statement from each of the following.

7. Perpendicular lines intersect to form 90° angles. If 2 lines are ⊥, then they intersect to form 90° ∡.
8.

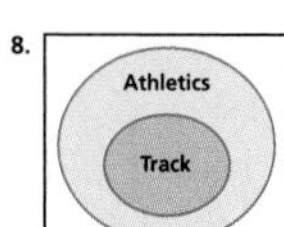

If a student is on the track team, then the student is in athletics.

9. The sum of two supplementary angles is 180°. If 2 ∡ are supp., then their sum is 180°.

Lesson 2-3

Determine if each conditional is true. If false, give a counterexample.

10. If a figure has four sides, then it is a square. F; a parallelogram has 4 sides but is not a square.
11. If $x = 3$, then $5x = 15$. T
12. Does the conclusion use inductive or deductive reasoning?
To rent a boat, you must take a boating safety course. Jason rented a boat, so Jessica concludes that he has taken a boating safety course. deductive
13. Determine if the conjecture is valid by the Law of Detachment.
Given: If a student is in tenth grade, then the student may participate in student council. Eric is a tenth-grader.
Conjecture: Eric may participate in student council. valid
14. Determine if the conjecture is valid by the Law of Syllogism.
Given: If a triangle is isosceles, then it has two congruent sides. If a triangle has two congruent angles, then it has two congruent sides.
Conjecture: If a triangle is isosceles, then it has two congruent angles. invalid
15. Draw a conclusion from the given information.
Given: If the sum of the angles of a polygon is 360°, then it is a quadrilateral. If a polygon is a quadrilateral, then it has four sides. The sum of the angles of polygon R is 360°. Polygon R has 4 sides.

Lesson 2-4

16. Write the conditional statement and converse within the biconditional "A triangle is equilateral if and only if it has three congruent sides."
17. For the conditional "If a triangle is scalene, then its sides have different lengths," write the converse and a biconditional statement. 16–17. See p. A33.
18. Determine if the biconditional "$n + 3 = -1 \leftrightarrow n = -4$" is true. If false, give a counterexample. T

Write each definition as a biconditional.

19. A parallelogram is a quadrilateral with two pairs of parallel sides. A quad. is a parallelogram if and only if it has 2 pairs of parallel sides.
20. Congruent angles have equal measures. 2 ∡ are ≅ if and only if they have = measures.

Lesson 2-5

Solve each equation. Write a justification for each step.

21. $2x + 3 = 9$ See p. A33.
22. $\frac{x+2}{5} = 3$ $\frac{x+2}{5} = 3$ (Given); $x + 2 = 15$ (Mult. Prop. of =); $x = 13$ (Subtr. Prop. of =)

Write a justification for each step.

23. $AC = AB + BC$
$9x - 5 = (3x + 6) + (5x + 2)$
$9x - 5 = 8x + 8$
$x - 5 = 8$
$x = 13$

Seg. Add. Post.; Subst.; Simplify; Subtr. Prop. of =; Add. Prop. of =

Lesson 2-6

24. Fill in the blanks to complete the two-column proof.

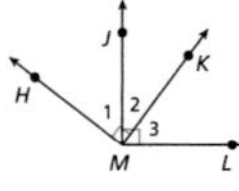

Given: $\angle HMK$ and $\angle JML$ are right angles.
Prove: $\angle 1 \cong \angle 3$
Proof:

Statements	Reasons
1. a. ___?___	1. Given
2. b. ___?___ c. ___?___	2. Adjacent angles that form a right angle are complementary.
3. $\angle 1 \cong \angle 3$	3. d. ___?___ ≅ Comps. Thm.

24a. $\angle HMK$ and $\angle JML$ are rt. ∡.
b. $\angle 1$ and $\angle 2$ are comp.
c. $\angle 2$ and $\angle 3$ are comp.

25. Use the given plan to write a two-column proof of the Transitive Property of Congruence.
Given: $\overline{AB} \cong \overline{CD}$, $\overline{CD} \cong \overline{EF}$
Prove: $\overline{AB} \cong \overline{EF}$
Plan: Use the definition of congruent segments to write the given congruence statements as statements of equality. Then use the Transitive Property of Equality to show that $AB = EF$. So $\overline{AB} \cong \overline{EF}$ by the definition of congruent segments.

Lesson 2-7

26. Use the given two-column proof to write a flowchart proof.
Given: $\angle 2 \cong \angle 3$
Prove: $m\angle 1 = m\angle 4$
Proof:

Statements	Reasons
1. $\angle 2 \cong \angle 3$	1. Given
2. $\angle 1$ and $\angle 2$ are supplementary. $\angle 3$ and $\angle 4$ are supplementary.	2. Lin. Pair Thm.
3. $\angle 1 \cong \angle 4$	3. ≅ Supps. Thm.
4. $m\angle 1 = m\angle 4$	4. Def. of ≅ ∡

25–26. See p. A33.

27. Use the given two-column proof to write a paragraph proof.
Given: $\angle 1 \cong \angle 3$
Prove: $\angle 4 \cong \angle 5$
Proof:

Statements	Reasons
1. $\angle 1 \cong \angle 3$	1. Given
2. $\angle 1 \cong \angle 4$, $\angle 3 \cong \angle 5$	2. Vert. ∡ Thm.
3. $\angle 1 \cong \angle 5$	3. Trans. Prop. of ≅
4. $\angle 4 \cong \angle 5$	4. Trans. Prop. of ≅

It is given that $\angle 1 \cong \angle 3$. By the Vert. ∡ Thm., $\angle 1 \cong \angle 4$ and $\angle 3 \cong \angle 5$. By the Trans. Prop. of ≅, $\angle 1 \cong \angle 5$. Similarly, $\angle 4 \cong \angle 5$.

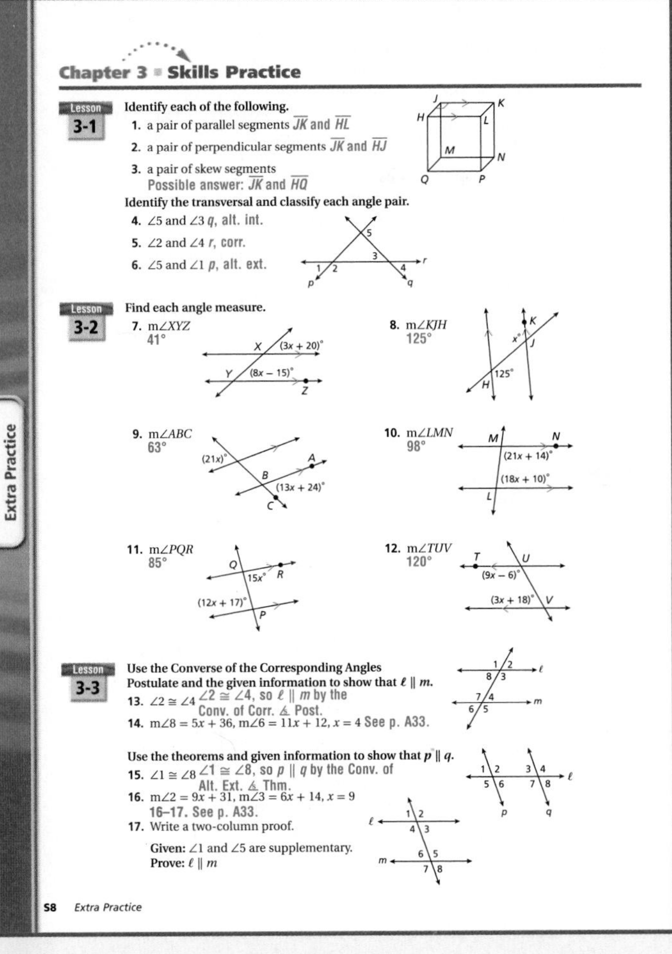

Chapter 3 ■ Skills Practice

Lesson 3-1 Identify each of the following.

1. a pair of parallel segments $\overline{JK}$ and $\overline{HL}$
2. a pair of perpendicular segments $\overline{JK}$ and $\overline{HJ}$
3. a pair of skew segments Possible answer: $\overline{JK}$ and $\overline{HQ}$

Identify the transversal and classify each angle pair.

4. $\angle 5$ and $\angle 3$ q, alt. int.
5. $\angle 2$ and $\angle 4$ r, corr.
6. $\angle 5$ and $\angle 1$ p, alt. ext.

Lesson 3-2 Find each angle measure.

7. $m\angle XYZ$ 41°
8. $m\angle KJH$ 125°
9. $m\angle ABC$ 63°
10. $m\angle LMN$ 98°
11. $m\angle PQR$ 85°
12. $m\angle TUV$ 120°

Lesson 3-3 Use the Converse of the Corresponding Angles Postulate and the given information to show that $\ell \parallel m$.

13. $\angle 2 \cong \angle 4$ $\angle 2 \cong \angle 4$, so $\ell \parallel m$ by the Conv. of Corr. ∠s Post.
14. $m\angle 8 = 5x + 36$, $m\angle 6 = 11x + 12$, $x = 4$ See p. A33.

Use the theorems and given information to show that $p \parallel q$.

15. $\angle 1 \cong \angle 8$ $\angle 1 \cong \angle 8$, so $p \parallel q$ by the Conv. of Alt. Ext. ∠s Thm.
16. $m\angle 2 = 9x + 31$, $m\angle 3 = 6x + 14$, $x = 9$ 16–17. See p. A33.
17. Write a two-column proof.
    Given: $\angle 1$ and $\angle 5$ are supplementary.
    Prove: $\ell \parallel m$

S8 Extra Practice

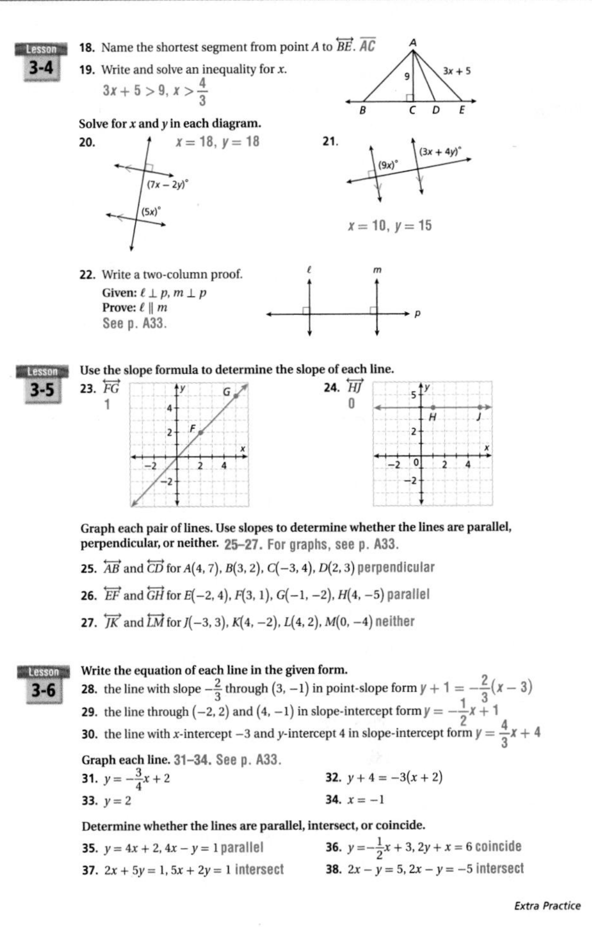

Lesson 3-4

18. Name the shortest segment from point A to $\overleftrightarrow{BE}$. $\overline{AC}$
19. Write and solve an inequality for x. $3x + 5 > 9$, $x > \frac{4}{3}$

Solve for x and y in each diagram.

20. $x = 18$, $y = 18$
21. $x = 10$, $y = 15$
22. Write a two-column proof.
    Given: $\ell \perp p$, $m \perp p$
    Prove: $\ell \parallel m$
    See p. A33.

Lesson 3-5 Use the slope formula to determine the slope of each line.

23. $\overleftrightarrow{FG}$ 1
24. $\overleftrightarrow{HJ}$ 0

Graph each pair of lines. Use slopes to determine whether the lines are parallel, perpendicular, or neither. 25–27. For graphs, see p. A33.

25. $\overleftrightarrow{AB}$ and $\overleftrightarrow{CD}$ for $A(4, 7)$, $B(3, 2)$, $C(-3, 4)$, $D(2, 3)$ perpendicular
26. $\overleftrightarrow{EF}$ and $\overleftrightarrow{GH}$ for $E(-2, 4)$, $F(3, 1)$, $G(-1, -2)$, $H(4, -5)$ parallel
27. $\overleftrightarrow{JK}$ and $\overleftrightarrow{LM}$ for $J(-3, 3)$, $K(4, -2)$, $L(4, 2)$, $M(0, -4)$ neither

Lesson 3-6 Write the equation of each line in the given form.

28. the line with slope $-\frac{2}{3}$ through $(3, -1)$ in point-slope form $y + 1 = -\frac{2}{3}(x - 3)$
29. the line through $(-2, 2)$ and $(4, -1)$ in slope-intercept form $y = -\frac{1}{2}x + 1$
30. the line with x-intercept -3 and y-intercept 4 in slope-intercept form $y = \frac{4}{3}x + 4$

Graph each line. 31–34. See p. A33.

31. $y = -\frac{3}{4}x + 2$
32. $y + 4 = -3(x + 2)$
33. $y = 2$
34. $x = -1$

Determine whether the lines are parallel, intersect, or coincide.

35. $y = 4x + 2$, $4x - y = 1$ parallel
36. $y = -\frac{1}{2}x + 3$, $2y + x = 6$ coincide
37. $2x + 5y = 1$, $5x + 2y = 1$ intersect
38. $2x - y = 5$, $2x - y = -5$ intersect

Extra Practice S9

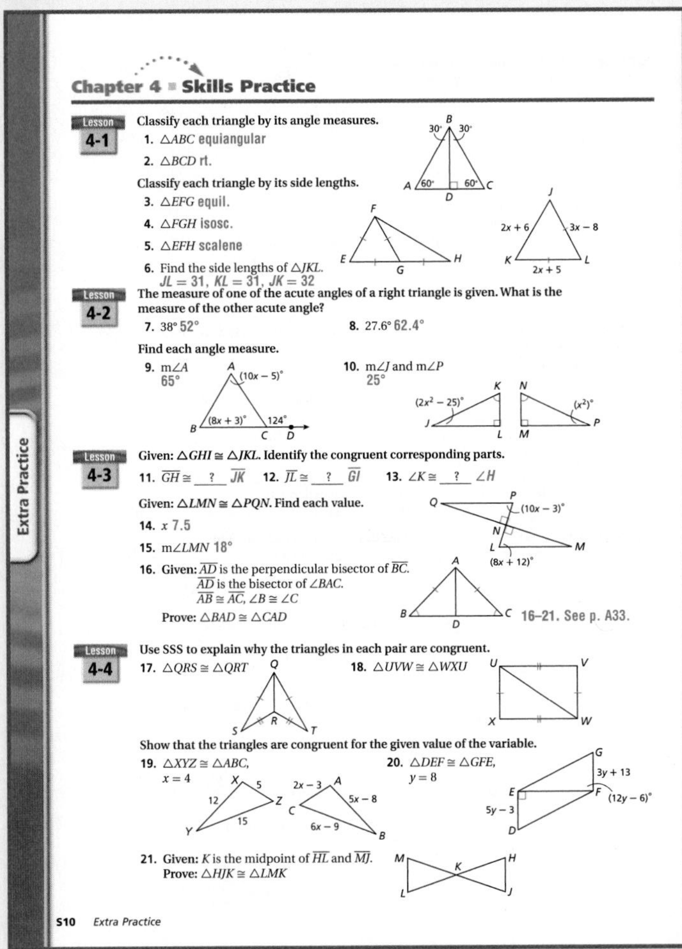

Chapter 4 ■ Skills Practice

Lesson 4-1 Classify each triangle by its angle measures.

1. $\triangle ABC$ equiangular
2. $\triangle BCD$ rt.

Classify each triangle by its side lengths.

3. $\triangle EFG$ equil.
4. $\triangle FGH$ isosc.
5. $\triangle EFH$ scalene
6. Find the side lengths of $\triangle JKL$. $JL = 31$, $KL = 31$, $JK = 32$

Lesson 4-2 The measure of one of the acute angles of a right triangle is given. What is the measure of the other acute angle?

7. 38° 52°
8. 27.6° 62.4°

Find each angle measure.

9. $m\angle A$ 65°
10. $m\angle J$ and $m\angle P$ 25°

Lesson 4-3 Given: $\triangle GHI \cong \triangle JKL$. Identify the congruent corresponding parts.

11. $\overline{GH} \cong$? $\overline{JK}$
12. $\overline{JL} \cong$? $\overline{GI}$
13. $\angle K \cong$? $\angle H$

Given: $\triangle LMN \cong \triangle PQN$. Find each value.

14. x 7.5
15. $m\angle LMN$ 18°
16. Given: $\overline{AD}$ is the perpendicular bisector of $\overline{BC}$. $\overline{AD}$ is the bisector of $\angle BAC$. $\overline{AB} \cong \overline{AC}$, $\angle B \cong \angle C$
    Prove: $\triangle BAD \cong \triangle CAD$ 16–21. See p. A33.

Lesson 4-4 Use SSS to explain why the triangles in each pair are congruent.

17. $\triangle QRS \cong \triangle QRT$
18. $\triangle UVW \cong \triangle WXU$

Show that the triangles are congruent for the given value of the variable.

19. $\triangle XYZ \cong \triangle ABC$, $x = 4$
20. $\triangle DEF \cong \triangle GFE$, $y = 8$
21. Given: K is the midpoint of $\overline{HL}$ and $\overline{MJ}$.
    Prove: $\triangle HJK \cong \triangle LMK$

S10 Extra Practice

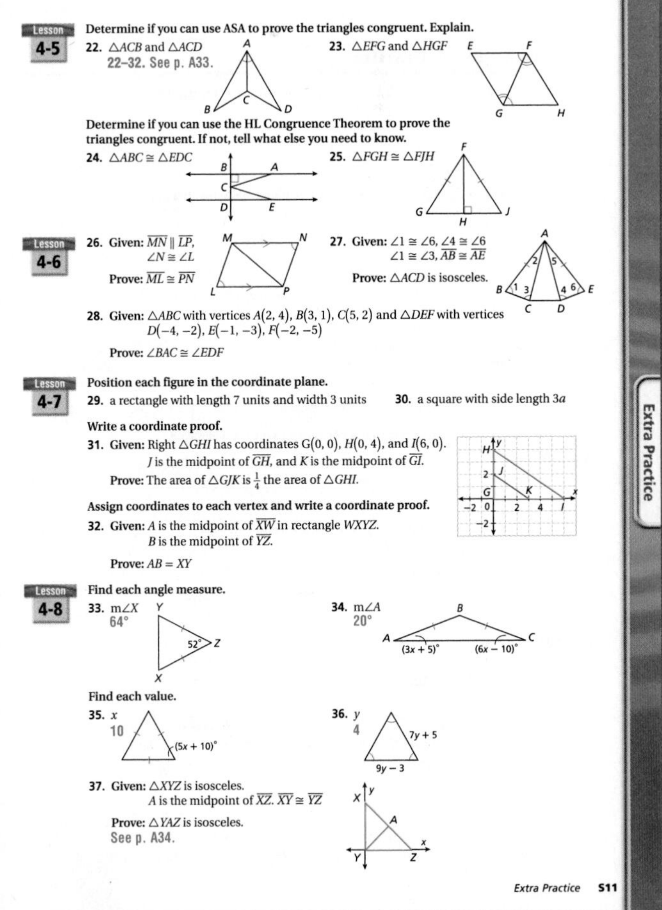

Lesson 4-5 Determine if you can use ASA to prove the triangles congruent. Explain.

22. $\triangle ACB$ and $\triangle ACD$ 22–32. See p. A33.
23. $\triangle EFG$ and $\triangle HGF$

Determine if you can use the HL Congruence Theorem to prove the triangles congruent. If not, tell what else you need to know.

24. $\triangle ABC \cong \triangle EDC$
25. $\triangle FGH \cong \triangle FJH$

Lesson 4-6

26. Given: $\overline{MN} \parallel \overline{LP}$, $\angle N \cong \angle L$
    Prove: $\overline{ML} \cong \overline{PN}$
27. Given: $\angle 1 \cong \angle 6$, $\angle 4 \cong \angle 6$, $\angle 1 \cong \angle 3$, $\overline{AB} \cong \overline{AE}$
    Prove: $\triangle ACD$ is isosceles.
28. Given: $\triangle ABC$ with vertices $A(2, 4)$, $B(3, 1)$, $C(5, 2)$ and $\triangle DEF$ with vertices $D(-4, -2)$, $E(-1, -3)$, $F(-2, -5)$
    Prove: $\angle BAC \cong \angle EDF$

Lesson 4-7 Position each figure in the coordinate plane.

29. a rectangle with length 7 units and width 3 units
30. a square with side length $3a$

Write a coordinate proof.

31. Given: Right $\triangle GHI$ has coordinates $G(0, 0)$, $H(0, 4)$, and $I(6, 0)$. J is the midpoint of $\overline{GH}$, and K is the midpoint of $\overline{GI}$.
    Prove: The area of $\triangle GJK$ is $\frac{1}{4}$ the area of $\triangle GHI$.

Assign coordinates to each vertex and write a coordinate proof.

32. Given: A is the midpoint of $\overline{XW}$ in rectangle $WXYZ$. B is the midpoint of $\overline{YZ}$.
    Prove: $AB = XY$

Lesson 4-8 Find each angle measure.

33. $m\angle X$ 64°
34. $m\angle A$ 20°

Find each value.

35. x 10
36. y 4
37. Given: $\triangle XYZ$ is isosceles. A is the midpoint of $\overline{XZ}$. $\overline{XY} \cong \overline{YZ}$
    Prove: $\triangle YAZ$ is isosceles.
    See p. A34.

Extra Practice S11

Extra Practice

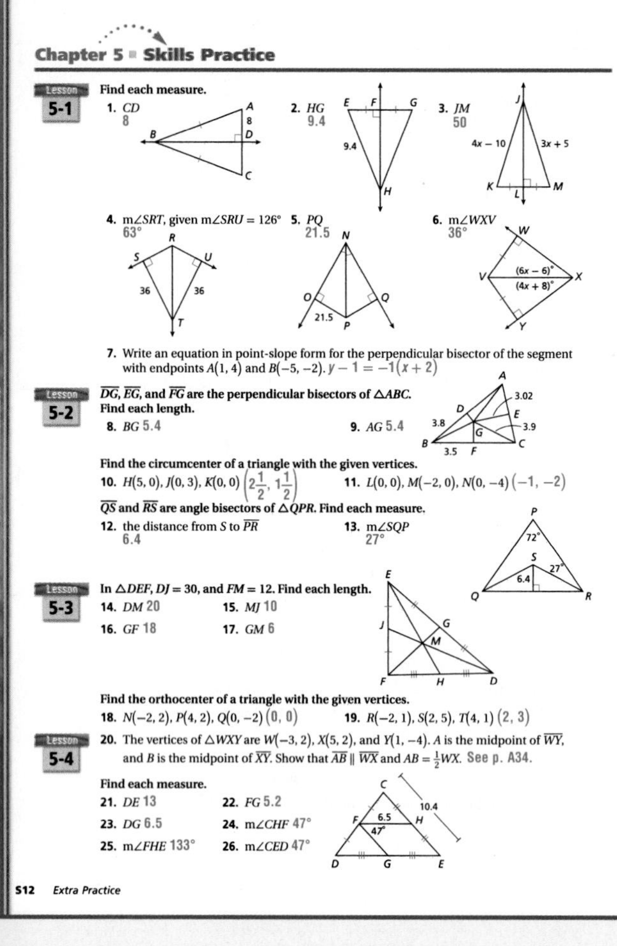

Chapter 5 ■ Skills Practice

Lesson 5-1 Find each measure.

1. CD 8
2. HG 9.4
3. JM 50
4. $m\angle SRT$, given $m\angle SRU = 126°$ 63°
5. PQ 21.5
6. $m\angle WXV$ 36°
7. Write an equation in point-slope form for the perpendicular bisector of the segment with endpoints $A(1, 4)$ and $B(-5, -2)$. $y - 1 = -1(x + 2)$

Lesson 5-2 $\overline{DG}$, $\overline{EG}$, and $\overline{FG}$ are the perpendicular bisectors of $\triangle ABC$. Find each length.

8. BG 5.4
9. AG 5.4

Find the circumcenter of a triangle with the given vertices.

10. $H(5, 0), J(0, 3), K(0, 0)$ $\left(2\frac{1}{2}, 1\frac{1}{2}\right)$
11. $L(0, 0), M(-2, 0), N(0, -4)$ $(-1, -2)$

$\overline{QS}$ and $\overline{RS}$ are angle bisectors of $\triangle QPR$. Find each measure.

12. the distance from S to $\overline{PR}$ 6.4
13. $m\angle SQP$ 27°

Lesson 5-3 In $\triangle DEF$, $DJ = 30$, and $FM = 12$. Find each length.

14. DM 20
15. MJ 10
16. GF 18
17. GM 6

Find the orthocenter of a triangle with the given vertices.

18. $N(-2, 2), P(4, 2), Q(0, -2)$ $(0, 0)$
19. $R(-2, 1), S(2, 5), T(4, 1)$ $(2, 3)$

Lesson 5-4

20. The vertices of $\triangle WXY$ are $W(-3, 2)$, $X(5, 2)$, and $Y(1, -4)$. A is the midpoint of $\overline{WY}$, and B is the midpoint of $\overline{XY}$. Show that $\overline{AB} \parallel \overline{WX}$ and $AB = \frac{1}{2}WX$. See p. A34.

Find each measure.

21. DE 13
22. FG 5.2
23. DG 6.5
24. $m\angle CHF$ 47°
25. $m\angle FHE$ 133°
26. $m\angle CED$ 47°

S12 Extra Practice

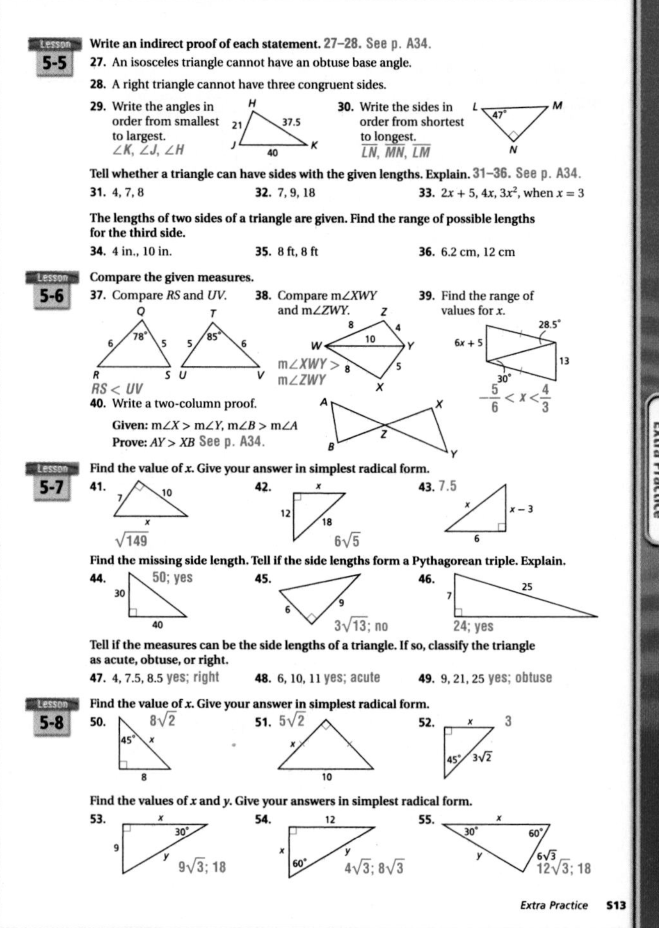

Lesson 5-5 Write an indirect proof of each statement. 27–28. See p. A34.

27. An isosceles triangle cannot have an obtuse base angle.
28. A right triangle cannot have three congruent sides.
29. Write the angles in order from smallest to largest. $\angle K, \angle J, \angle H$
30. Write the sides in order from shortest to longest. $\overline{LN}, \overline{MN}, \overline{LM}$

Tell whether a triangle can have sides with the given lengths. Explain. 31–36. See p. A34.

31. 4, 7, 8
32. 7, 9, 18
33. $2x + 5, 4x, 3x^2$, when $x = 3$

The lengths of two sides of a triangle are given. Find the range of possible lengths for the third side.

34. 4 in., 10 in.
35. 8 ft, 8 ft
36. 6.2 cm, 12 cm

Lesson 5-6 Compare the given measures.

37. Compare RS and UV. $RS < UV$
38. Compare $m\angle XWY$ and $m\angle ZWY$. $m\angle XWY > m\angle ZWY$
39. Find the range of values for x. $-\frac{5}{6} < x < \frac{4}{3}$
40. Write a two-column proof.
Given: $m\angle X > m\angle Y$, $m\angle B > m\angle A$
Prove: $AY > XB$ See p. A34.

Lesson 5-7 Find the value of x. Give your answer in simplest radical form.

41. $\sqrt{149}$
42. $6\sqrt{5}$
43. 7.5

Find the missing side length. Tell if the side lengths form a Pythagorean triple. Explain.

44. 50; yes
45. $3\sqrt{13}$; no
46. 24; yes

Tell if the measures can be the side lengths of a triangle. If so, classify the triangle as acute, obtuse, or right.

47. 4, 7.5, 8.5 yes; right
48. 6, 10, 11 yes; acute
49. 9, 21, 25 yes; obtuse

Lesson 5-8 Find the value of x. Give your answer in simplest radical form.

50. $8\sqrt{2}$
51. $5\sqrt{2}$
52. 3

Find the values of x and y. Give your answers in simplest radical form.

53. $9\sqrt{3}$; 18
54. $4\sqrt{3}$; $8\sqrt{3}$
55. $12\sqrt{3}$; 18

Extra Practice S13

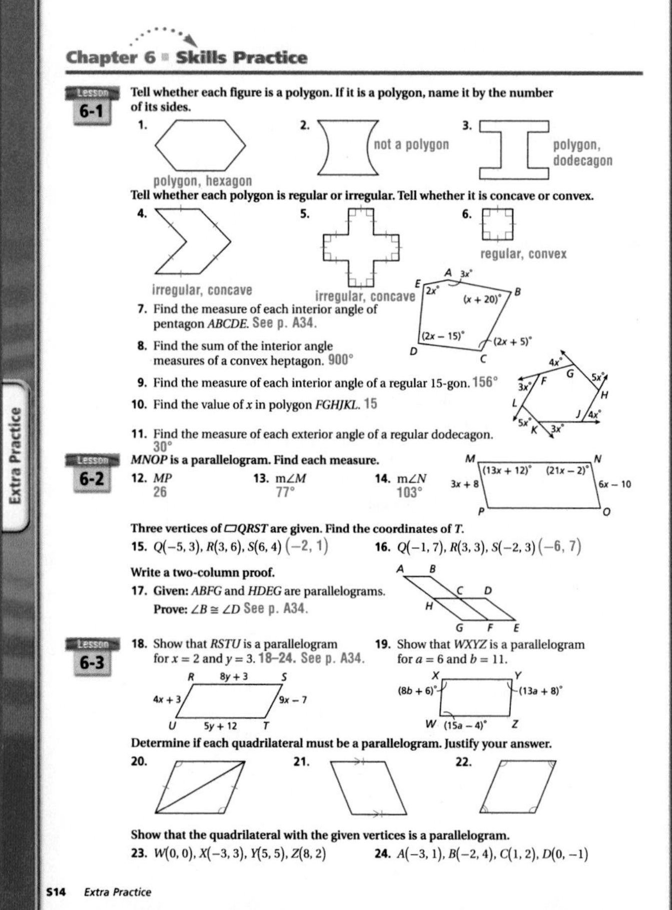

Chapter 6 ■ Skills Practice

Lesson 6-1 Tell whether each figure is a polygon. If it is a polygon, name it by the number of its sides.

1. polygon, hexagon
2. not a polygon
3. polygon, dodecagon

Tell whether each polygon is regular or irregular. Tell whether it is concave or convex.

4. irregular, concave
5. irregular, concave
6. regular, convex
7. Find the measure of each interior angle of pentagon $ABCDE$. See p. A34.
8. Find the sum of the interior angle measures of a convex heptagon. 900°
9. Find the measure of each interior angle of a regular 15-gon. 156°
10. Find the value of x in polygon $FGHJKL$. 15
11. Find the measure of each exterior angle of a regular dodecagon. 30°

Lesson 6-2 $MNOP$ is a parallelogram. Find each measure.

12. MP 26
13. $m\angle M$ 77°
14. $m\angle N$ 103°

Three vertices of $\square QRST$ are given. Find the coordinates of T.

15. $Q(-5, 3), R(3, 6), S(6, 4)$ $(-2, 1)$
16. $Q(-1, 7), R(3, 3), S(-2, 3)$ $(-6, 7)$

Write a two-column proof.

17. Given: $ABFG$ and $HDEG$ are parallelograms.
Prove: $\angle B \cong \angle D$ See p. A34.

Lesson 6-3

18. Show that $RSTU$ is a parallelogram for $x = 2$ and $y = 3$. 18–24. See p. A34.
19. Show that $WXYZ$ is a parallelogram for $a = 6$ and $b = 11$.

Determine if each quadrilateral must be a parallelogram. Justify your answer.

20.
21.
22.

Show that the quadrilateral with the given vertices is a parallelogram.

23. $W(0, 0), X(-3, 3), Y(5, 5), Z(8, 2)$
24. $A(-3, 1), B(-2, 4), C(1, 2), D(0, -1)$

S14 Extra Practice

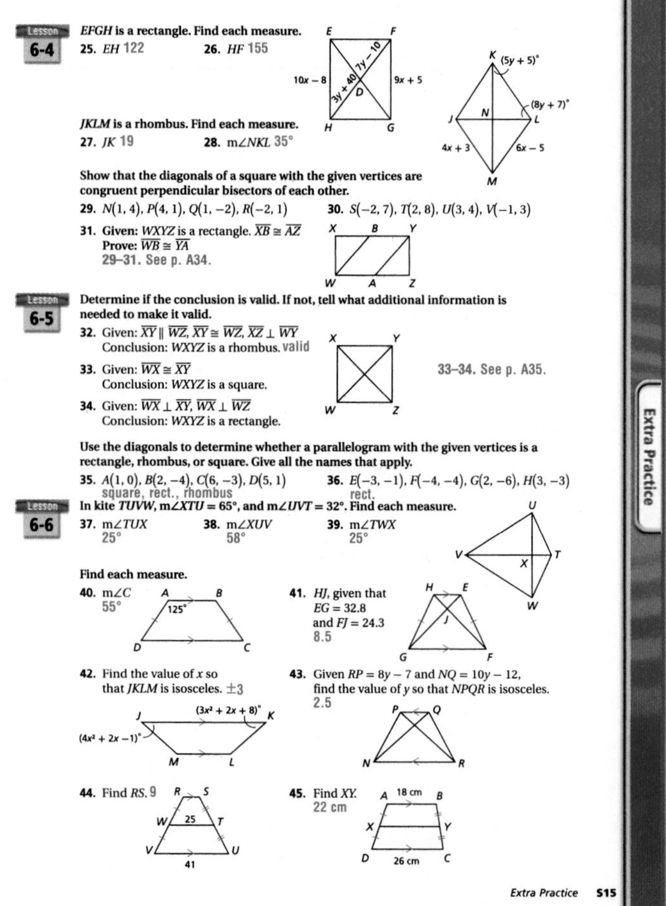

Lesson 6-4 $EFGH$ is a rectangle. Find each measure.

25. EH 122
26. HF 155

$JKLM$ is a rhombus. Find each measure.

27. JK 19
28. $m\angle NKL$ 35°

Show that the diagonals of a square with the given vertices are congruent perpendicular bisectors of each other.

29. $N(1, 4), P(4, 1), Q(1, -2), R(-2, 1)$
30. $S(-2, 7), T(2, 8), U(3, 4), V(-1, 3)$
31. Given: $WXYZ$ is a rectangle. $\overline{XB} \cong \overline{AZ}$
Prove: $\overline{WB} \cong \overline{YA}$
29–31. See p. A34.

Lesson 6-5 Determine if the conclusion is valid. If not, tell what additional information is needed to make it valid.

32. Given: $\overline{XY} \parallel \overline{WZ}$, $\overline{XY} \cong \overline{WZ}$, $\overline{XZ} \perp \overline{WY}$
Conclusion: $WXYZ$ is a rhombus. valid
33. Given: $\overline{WX} \cong \overline{XY}$
Conclusion: $WXYZ$ is a square.
34. Given: $\overline{WX} \perp \overline{XY}$, $\overline{WX} \perp \overline{WZ}$
Conclusion: $WXYZ$ is a rectangle.

33–34. See p. A35.

Use the diagonals to determine whether a parallelogram with the given vertices is a rectangle, rhombus, or square. Give all the names that apply.

35. $A(1, 0), B(2, -4), C(6, -3), D(5, 1)$ square, rect., rhombus
36. $E(-3, -1), F(-4, -4), G(2, -6), H(3, -3)$ rect.

Lesson 6-6 In kite $TUVW$, $m\angle XTU = 65°$, and $m\angle UVT = 32°$. Find each measure.

37. $m\angle TUX$ 25°
38. $m\angle XUV$ 58°
39. $m\angle TWX$ 25°

Find each measure.

40. $m\angle C$ 55°
41. HJ, given that $EG = 32.8$ and $FJ = 24.3$ 8.5
42. Find the value of x so that $JKLM$ is isosceles. ± 3
43. Given $RP = 8y - 7$ and $NQ = 10y - 12$, find the value of y so that $NPQR$ is isosceles. 2.5
44. Find RS. 9
45. Find XY. 22 cm

Extra Practice S15

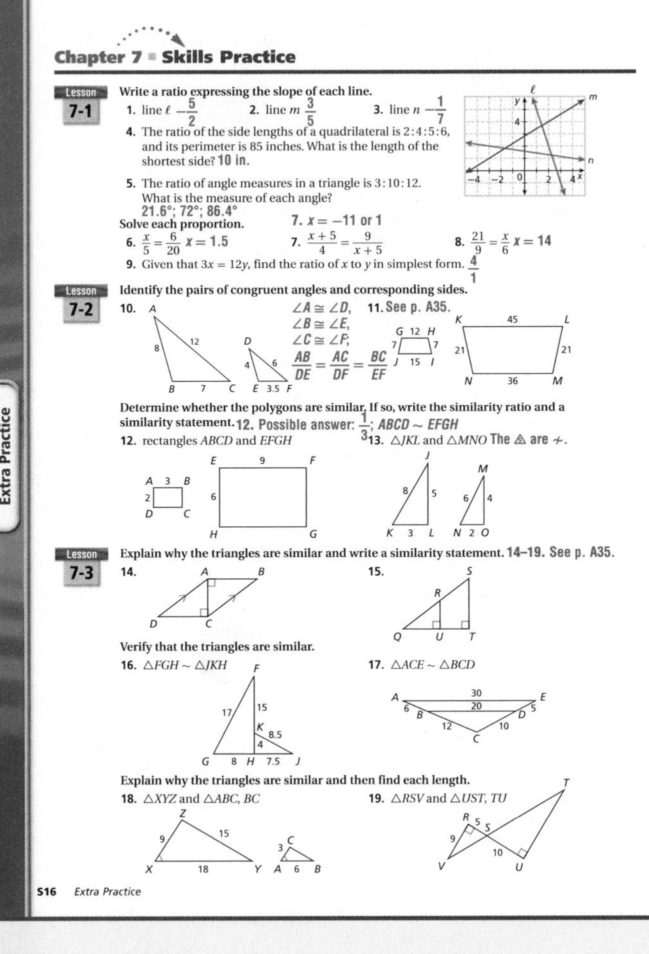

Chapter 7 ■ Skills Practice

Lesson 7-1 Write a ratio expressing the slope of each line.

1. line ℓ $-\frac{5}{2}$ 2. line m $\frac{3}{5}$ 3. line n $-\frac{1}{7}$
4. The ratio of the side lengths of a quadrilateral is 2:4:5:6, and its perimeter is 85 inches. What is the length of the shortest side? **10 in.**
5. The ratio of angle measures in a triangle is 3:10:12. What is the measure of each angle? **21.6°; 72°; 86.4°**

Solve each proportion.

6. $\frac{x}{5}=\frac{6}{20}$ **$x = 1.5$** 7. $\frac{x+5}{4}=\frac{9}{x+5}$ **$x = -11$ or 1** 8. $\frac{21}{9}=\frac{x}{6}$ **$x = 14$**
9. Given that $3x = 12y$, find the ratio of x to y in simplest form. **$\frac{4}{1}$**

Lesson 7-2 Identify the pairs of congruent angles and corresponding sides.

10. **$\angle A \cong \angle D$, $\angle B \cong \angle E$, $\angle C \cong \angle F$, $\frac{AB}{DE}=\frac{AC}{DF}=\frac{BC}{EF}$** 11. **See p. A35.**

Determine whether the polygons are similar. If so, write the similarity ratio and a similarity statement. **12. Possible answer: $\frac{1}{3}$; $ABCD \sim EFGH$**

12. rectangles $ABCD$ and $EFGH$ 13. $\triangle JKL$ and $\triangle MNO$ **The △s are not ~.**

Lesson 7-3 Explain why the triangles are similar and write a similarity statement. **14–19. See p. A35.**

14. 15.

Verify that the triangles are similar.

16. $\triangle FGH \sim \triangle JKH$ 17. $\triangle ACE \sim \triangle BCD$

Explain why the triangles are similar and then find each length.

18. $\triangle XYZ$ and $\triangle ABC$, BC 19. $\triangle RSV$ and $\triangle UST$, TU

S16 Extra Practice

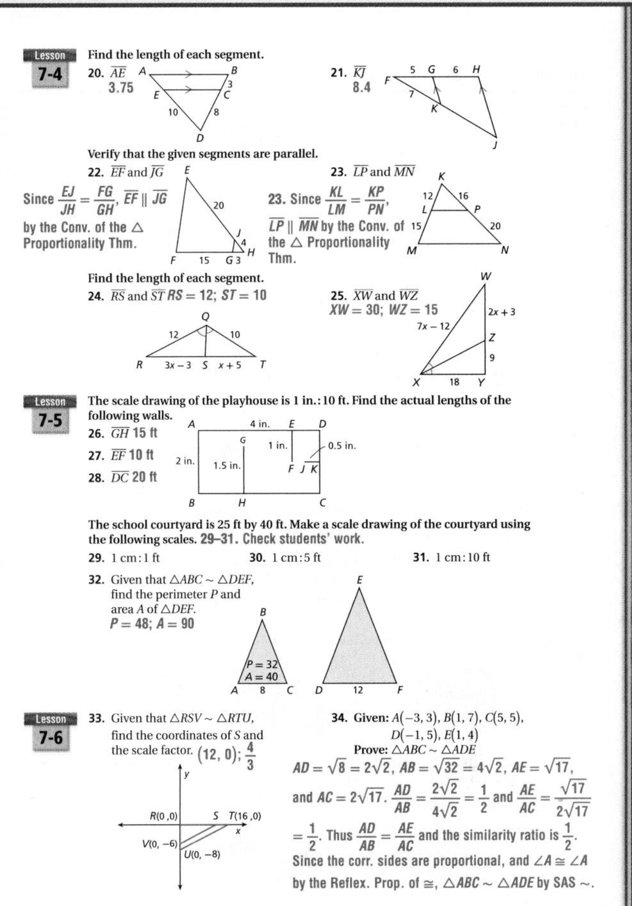

Lesson 7-4 Find the length of each segment.

20. $\overline{AE}$ **3.75** 21. $\overline{KJ}$ **8.4**

Verify that the given segments are parallel.

22. $\overline{EF}$ and $\overline{JG}$ **Since $\frac{EJ}{JH}=\frac{FG}{GH}$, $\overline{EF} \parallel \overline{JG}$ by the Conv. of the △ Proportionality Thm.**
23. $\overline{LP}$ and $\overline{MN}$ **23. Since $\frac{KL}{LM}=\frac{KP}{PN}$, $\overline{LP} \parallel \overline{MN}$ by the Conv. of the △ Proportionality Thm.**

Find the length of each segment.

24. $\overline{RS}$ and $\overline{ST}$ **$RS = 12$; $ST = 10$** 25. $\overline{XW}$ and $\overline{WZ}$ **$XW = 30$; $WZ = 15$**

Lesson 7-5 The scale drawing of the playhouse is 1 in.:10 ft. Find the actual lengths of the following walls.

26. $\overline{GH}$ **15 ft** 27. $\overline{EF}$ **10 ft** 28. $\overline{DC}$ **20 ft**

The school courtyard is 25 ft by 40 ft. Make a scale drawing of the courtyard using the following scales. **29–31. Check students' work.**

29. 1 cm:1 ft 30. 1 cm:5 ft 31. 1 cm:10 ft
32. Given that $\triangle ABC \sim \triangle DEF$, find the perimeter P and area A of $\triangle DEF$. **$P = 48$; $A = 90$**

Lesson 7-6

33. Given that $\triangle RSV \sim \triangle RTU$, find the coordinates of S and the scale factor. **$(12, 0)$; $\frac{4}{3}$**
34. **Given:** $A(-3, 3)$, $B(1, 7)$, $C(5, 5)$, $D(-1, 5)$, $E(1, 4)$ **Prove:** $\triangle ABC \sim \triangle ADE$
$AD = \sqrt{8} = 2\sqrt{2}$, $AB = \sqrt{32} = 4\sqrt{2}$, $AE = \sqrt{17}$, and $AC = 2\sqrt{17}$. $\frac{AD}{AB} = \frac{2\sqrt{2}}{4\sqrt{2}} = \frac{1}{2}$ and $\frac{AE}{AC} = \frac{\sqrt{17}}{2\sqrt{17}} = \frac{1}{2}$. Thus $\frac{AD}{AB} = \frac{AE}{AC}$ and the similarity ratio is $\frac{1}{2}$. Since the corr. sides are proportional, and $\angle A \cong \angle A$ by the Reflex. Prop. of ≅, $\triangle ABC \sim \triangle ADE$ by SAS ~.

Extra Practice S17

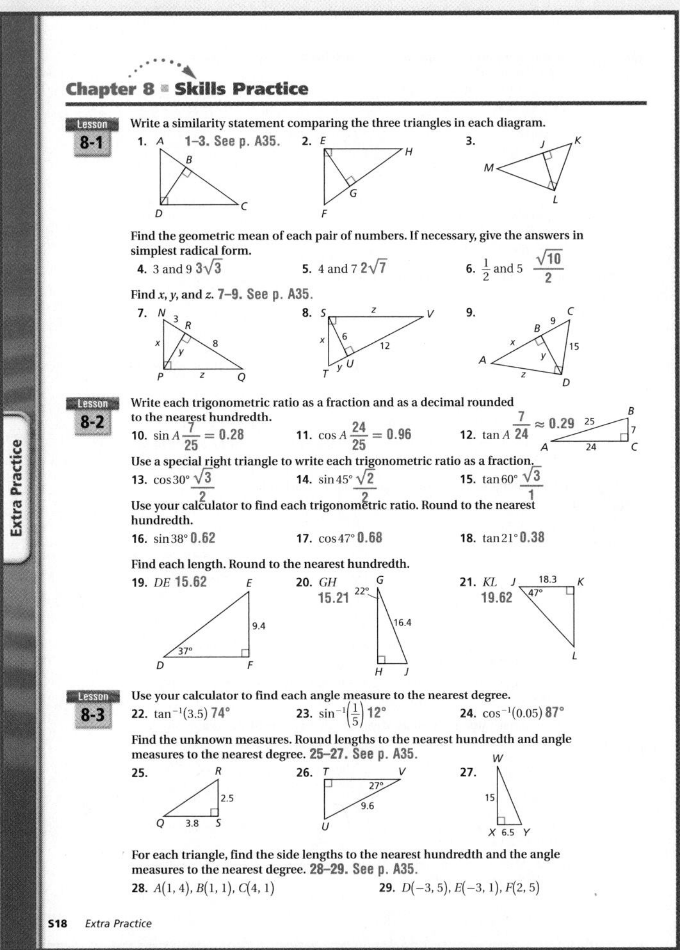

Chapter 8 ■ Skills Practice

Lesson 8-1 Write a similarity statement comparing the three triangles in each diagram.

1. **1–3. See p. A35.** 2. 3.

Find the geometric mean of each pair of numbers. If necessary, give the answers in simplest radical form.

4. 3 and 9 **$3\sqrt{3}$** 5. 4 and 7 **$2\sqrt{7}$** 6. $\frac{1}{2}$ and 5 **$\frac{\sqrt{10}}{2}$**

Find x, y, and z. **7–9. See p. A35.**

7. 8. 9.

Lesson 8-2 Write each trigonometric ratio as a fraction and as a decimal rounded to the nearest hundredth.

10. $\sin A$ **$\frac{7}{25} = 0.28$** 11. $\cos A$ **$\frac{24}{25} = 0.96$** 12. $\tan A$ **$\frac{7}{24} \approx 0.29$**

Use a special right triangle to write each trigonometric ratio as a fraction.

13. $\cos 30°$ **$\frac{\sqrt{3}}{2}$** 14. $\sin 45°$ **$\frac{\sqrt{2}}{2}$** 15. $\tan 60°$ **$\frac{\sqrt{3}}{1}$**

Use your calculator to find each trigonometric ratio. Round to the nearest hundredth.

16. $\sin 38°$ **0.62** 17. $\cos 47°$ **0.68** 18. $\tan 21°$ **0.38**

Find each length. Round to the nearest hundredth.

19. DE **15.62** 20. GH **15.21** 21. KL **19.62**

Lesson 8-3 Use your calculator to find each angle measure to the nearest degree.

22. $\tan^{-1}(3.5)$ **74°** 23. $\sin^{-1}\left(\frac{1}{5}\right)$ **12°** 24. $\cos^{-1}(0.05)$ **87°**

Find the unknown measures. Round lengths to the nearest hundredth and angle measures to the nearest degree. **25–27. See p. A35.**

25. 26. 27.

For each triangle, find the side lengths to the nearest hundredth and the angle measures to the nearest degree. **28–29. See p. A35.**

28. $A(1, 4)$, $B(1, 1)$, $C(4, 1)$ 29. $D(-3, 5)$, $E(-3, 1)$, $F(2, 5)$

S18 Extra Practice

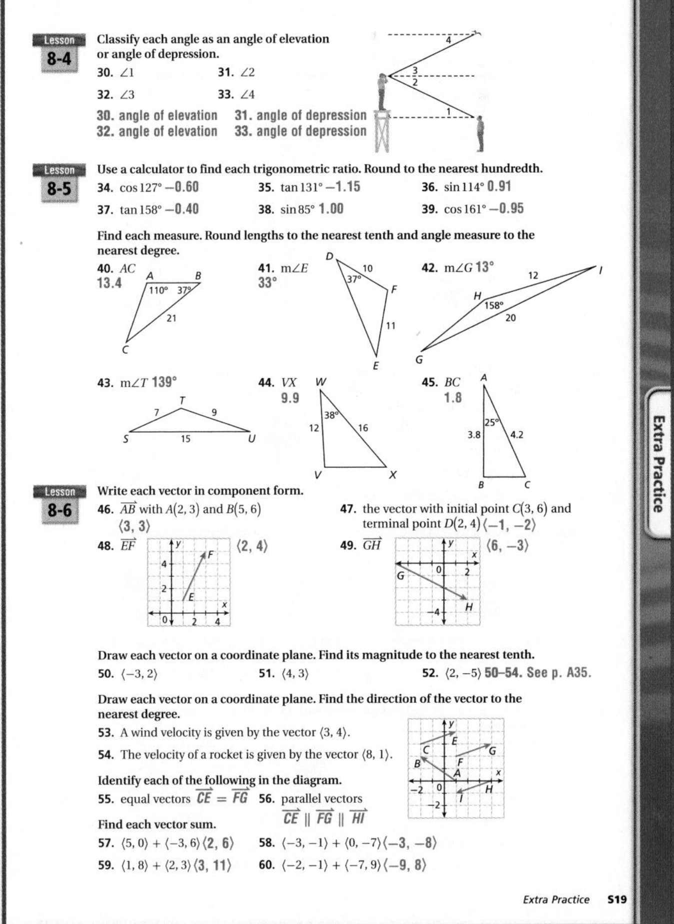

Lesson 8-4 Classify each angle as an angle of elevation or angle of depression.

30. ∠1 31. ∠2
32. ∠3 33. ∠4

30. angle of elevation 31. angle of depression
32. angle of elevation 33. angle of depression

Lesson 8-5 Use a calculator to find each trigonometric ratio. Round to the nearest hundredth.

34. $\cos 127°$ **−0.60** 35. $\tan 131°$ **−1.15** 36. $\sin 114°$ **0.91**
37. $\tan 158°$ **−0.40** 38. $\sin 85°$ **1.00** 39. $\cos 161°$ **−0.95**

Find each measure. Round lengths to the nearest tenth and angle measure to the nearest degree.

40. AC **13.4** 41. $m\angle E$ **33°** 42. $m\angle G$ **13°**
43. $m\angle T$ **139°** 44. VX **9.9** 45. BC **1.8**

Lesson 8-6 Write each vector in component form.

46. $\overrightarrow{AB}$ with $A(2, 3)$ and $B(5, 6)$ **⟨3, 3⟩** 47. the vector with initial point $C(3, 6)$ and terminal point $D(2, 4)$ **⟨−1, −2⟩**
48. $\overrightarrow{EF}$ **⟨2, 4⟩** 49. $\overrightarrow{GH}$ **⟨6, −3⟩**

Draw each vector on a coordinate plane. Find its magnitude to the nearest tenth.

50. ⟨−3, 2⟩ 51. ⟨4, 3⟩ 52. ⟨2, −5⟩ **50–54. See p. A35.**

Draw each vector on a coordinate plane. Find the direction of the vector to the nearest degree.

53. A wind velocity is given by the vector ⟨3, 4⟩.
54. The velocity of a rocket is given by the vector ⟨8, 1⟩.

Identify each of the following in the diagram.

55. equal vectors **$\overrightarrow{CE} = \overrightarrow{FG}$** 56. parallel vectors **$\overrightarrow{CE} \parallel \overrightarrow{FG} \parallel \overrightarrow{HI}$**

Find each vector sum.

57. ⟨5, 0⟩ + ⟨−3, 6⟩ **⟨2, 6⟩** 58. ⟨−3, −1⟩ + ⟨0, −7⟩ **⟨−3, −8⟩**
59. ⟨1, 8⟩ + ⟨2, 3⟩ **⟨3, 11⟩** 60. ⟨−2, −1⟩ + ⟨−7, 9⟩ **⟨−9, 8⟩**

Extra Practice S19

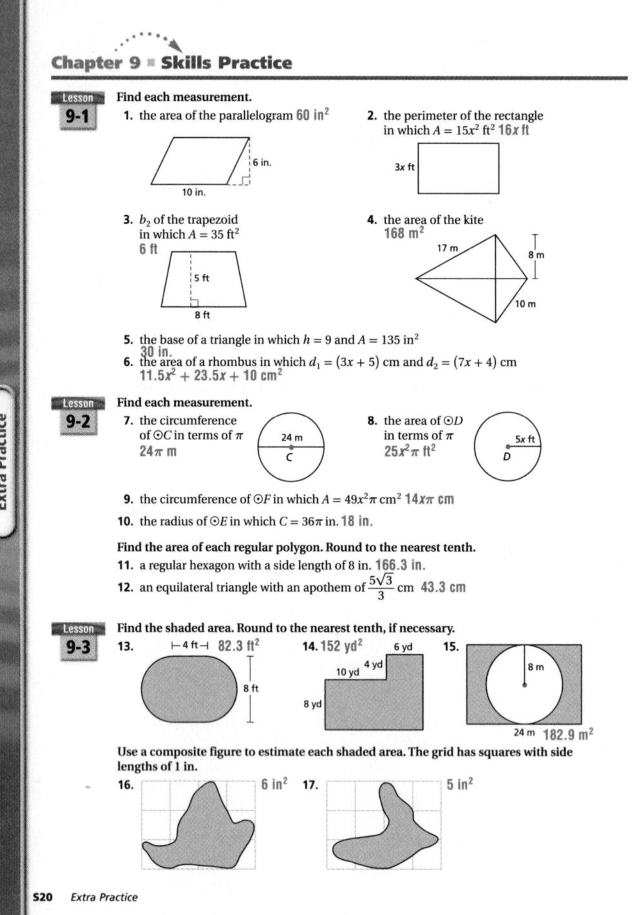

Chapter 9 ■ Skills Practice

Lesson 9-1 Find each measurement.

1. the area of the parallelogram 60 in²
2. the perimeter of the rectangle in which $A = 15x^2$ ft² 16x ft
3. b_2 of the trapezoid in which $A = 35$ ft² 6 ft
4. the area of the kite 168 m²
5. the base of a triangle in which $h = 9$ and $A = 135$ in² 30 in.
6. the area of a rhombus in which $d_1 = (3x + 5)$ cm and $d_2 = (7x + 4)$ cm $11.5x^2 + 23.5x + 10$ cm²

Lesson 9-2 Find each measurement.

7. the circumference of ⊙C in terms of π 24π m
8. the area of ⊙D in terms of π $25x^2\pi$ ft²
9. the circumference of ⊙F in which $A = 49x^2\pi$ cm² 14xπ cm
10. the radius of ⊙E in which $C = 36\pi$ in. 18 in.

Find the area of each regular polygon. Round to the nearest tenth.

11. a regular hexagon with a side length of 8 in. 166.3 in.
12. an equilateral triangle with an apothem of $\frac{5\sqrt{3}}{3}$ cm 43.3 cm

Lesson 9-3 Find the shaded area. Round to the nearest tenth, if necessary.

13. 82.3 ft²
14. 152 yd²
15. 182.9 m²

Use a composite figure to estimate each shaded area. The grid has squares with side lengths of 1 in.

16. 6 in²
17. 5 in²

S20 *Extra Practice*

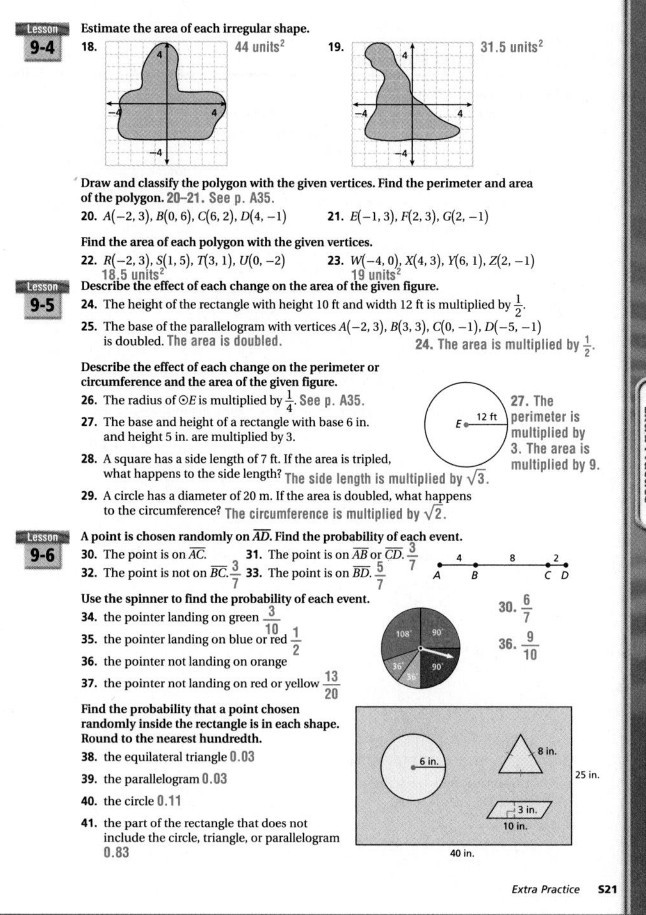

Lesson 9-4 Estimate the area of each irregular shape.

18. 44 units²
19. 31.5 units²

Draw and classify the polygon with the given vertices. Find the perimeter and area of the polygon. 20–21. See p. A35.

20. $A(-2, 3), B(0, 6), C(6, 2), D(4, -1)$
21. $E(-1, 3), F(2, 3), G(2, -1)$

Find the area of each polygon with the given vertices.

22. $R(-2, 3), S(1, 5), T(3, 1), U(0, -2)$ 18.5 units²
23. $W(-4, 0), X(4, 3), Y(6, 1), Z(2, -1)$ 19 units²

Lesson 9-5 Describe the effect of each change on the area of the given figure.

24. The height of the rectangle with height 10 ft and width 12 ft is multiplied by $\frac{1}{2}$.
25. The base of the parallelogram with vertices $A(-2, 3), B(3, 3), C(0, -1), D(-5, -1)$ is doubled. The area is doubled.

24. The area is multiplied by $\frac{1}{2}$.

Describe the effect of each change on the perimeter or circumference and the area of the given figure.

26. The radius of ⊙E is multiplied by $\frac{1}{4}$. See p. A35.
27. The base and height of a rectangle with base 6 in. and height 5 in. are multiplied by 3.
28. A square has a side length of 7 ft. If the area is tripled, what happens to the side length? The side length is multiplied by $\sqrt{3}$.
29. A circle has a diameter of 20 m. If the area is doubled, what happens to the circumference? The circumference is multiplied by $\sqrt{2}$.

27. The perimeter is multiplied by 3. The area is multiplied by 9.

Lesson 9-6 A point is chosen randomly on $\overline{AD}$. Find the probability of each event.

30. The point is on $\overline{AC}$.
31. The point is on $\overline{AB}$ or $\overline{CD}$. $\frac{3}{7}$
32. The point is not on $\overline{BC}$. $\frac{3}{7}$
33. The point is on $\overline{BD}$. $\frac{5}{7}$

Use the spinner to find the probability of each event.

34. the pointer landing on green $\frac{3}{10}$
35. the pointer landing on blue or red $\frac{1}{2}$
36. the pointer not landing on orange
37. the pointer not landing on red or yellow $\frac{13}{20}$

30. $\frac{6}{7}$
36. $\frac{9}{10}$

Find the probability that a point chosen randomly inside the rectangle is in each shape. Round to the nearest hundredth.

38. the equilateral triangle 0.03
39. the parallelogram 0.03
40. the circle 0.11
41. the part of the rectangle that does not include the circle, triangle, or parallelogram 0.83

Extra Practice S21

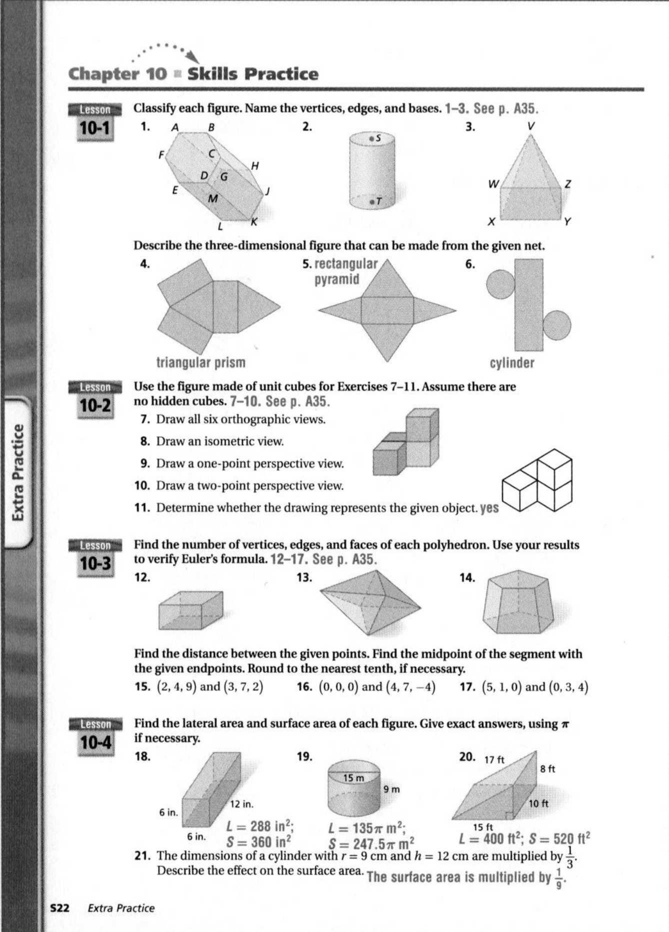

Chapter 10 ■ Skills Practice

Lesson 10-1 Classify each figure. Name the vertices, edges, and bases. 1–3. See p. A35.

1. 2. 3.

Describe the three-dimensional figure that can be made from the given net.

4. triangular prism
5. rectangular pyramid
6. cylinder

Lesson 10-2 Use the figure made of unit cubes for Exercises 7–11. Assume there are no hidden cubes. 7–10. See p. A35.

7. Draw all six orthographic views.
8. Draw an isometric view.
9. Draw a one-point perspective view.
10. Draw a two-point perspective view.
11. Determine whether the drawing represents the given object. yes

Lesson 10-3 Find the number of vertices, edges, and faces of each polyhedron. Use your results to verify Euler's formula. 12–17. See p. A35.

12. 13. 14.

Find the distance between the given points. Find the midpoint of the segment with the given endpoints. Round to the nearest tenth, if necessary.

15. (2, 4, 9) and (3, 7, 2)
16. (0, 0, 0) and (4, 7, −4)
17. (5, 1, 0) and (0, 3, 4)

Lesson 10-4 Find the lateral area and surface area of each figure. Give exact answers, using π if necessary.

18. $L = 288$ in²; $S = 360$ in²
19. $L = 135\pi$ m²; $S = 247.5\pi$ m²
20. $L = 400$ ft²; $S = 520$ ft²
21. The dimensions of a cylinder with $r = 9$ cm and $h = 12$ cm are multiplied by $\frac{1}{3}$. Describe the effect on the surface area. The surface area is multiplied by $\frac{1}{9}$.

S22 *Extra Practice*

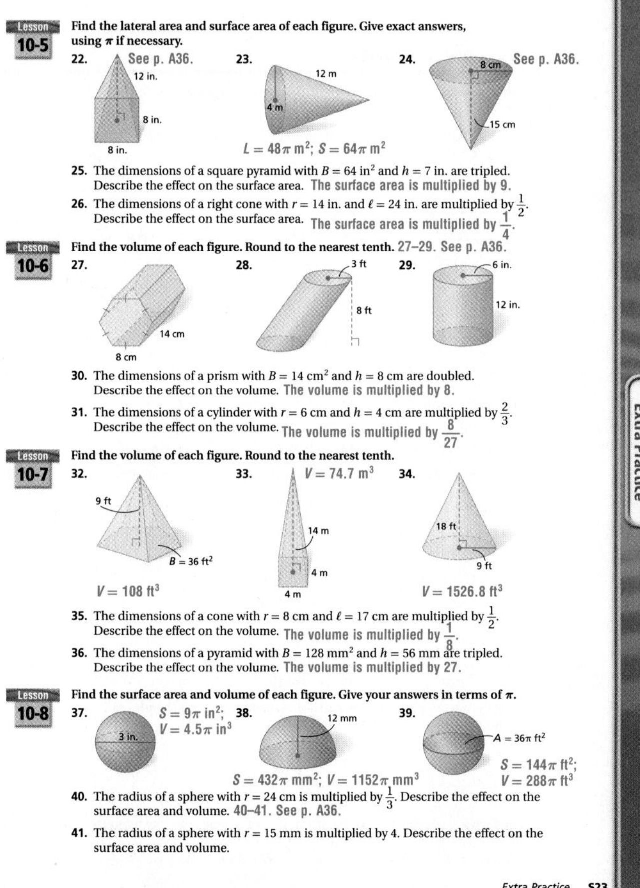

Lesson 10-5 Find the lateral area and surface area of each figure. Give exact answers, using π if necessary.

22. See p. A36.
23. $L = 48\pi$ m²; $S = 64\pi$ m²
24. See p. A36.
25. The dimensions of a square pyramid with $B = 64$ in² and $h = 7$ in. are tripled. Describe the effect on the surface area. The surface area is multiplied by 9.
26. The dimensions of a right cone with $r = 14$ in. and $\ell = 24$ in. are multiplied by $\frac{1}{2}$. Describe the effect on the surface area. The surface area is multiplied by $\frac{1}{4}$.

Lesson 10-6 Find the volume of each figure. Round to the nearest tenth. 27–29. See p. A36.

27. 28. 29.

30. The dimensions of a prism with $B = 14$ cm² and $h = 8$ cm are doubled. Describe the effect on the volume. The volume is multiplied by 8.
31. The dimensions of a cylinder with $r = 6$ cm and $h = 4$ cm are multiplied by $\frac{2}{3}$. Describe the effect on the volume. The volume is multiplied by $\frac{8}{27}$.

Lesson 10-7 Find the volume of each figure. Round to the nearest tenth.

32. $V = 108$ ft³
33. $V = 74.7$ m³
34. $V = 1526.8$ ft³
35. The dimensions of a cone with $r = 8$ cm and $\ell = 17$ cm are multiplied by $\frac{1}{2}$. Describe the effect on the volume. The volume is multiplied by $\frac{1}{8}$.
36. The dimensions of a pyramid with $B = 128$ mm² and $h = 56$ mm are tripled. Describe the effect on the volume. The volume is multiplied by 27.

Lesson 10-8 Find the surface area and volume of each figure. Give your answers in terms of π.

37. $S = 9\pi$ in²; $V = 4.5\pi$ in³
38. $S = 432\pi$ mm²; $V = 1152\pi$ mm³
39. $S = 144\pi$ ft²; $V = 288\pi$ ft³
40. The radius of a sphere with $r = 24$ cm is multiplied by $\frac{1}{3}$. Describe the effect on the surface area and volume. 40–41. See p. A36.
41. The radius of a sphere with $r = 15$ mm is multiplied by 4. Describe the effect on the surface area and volume.

Extra Practice S23

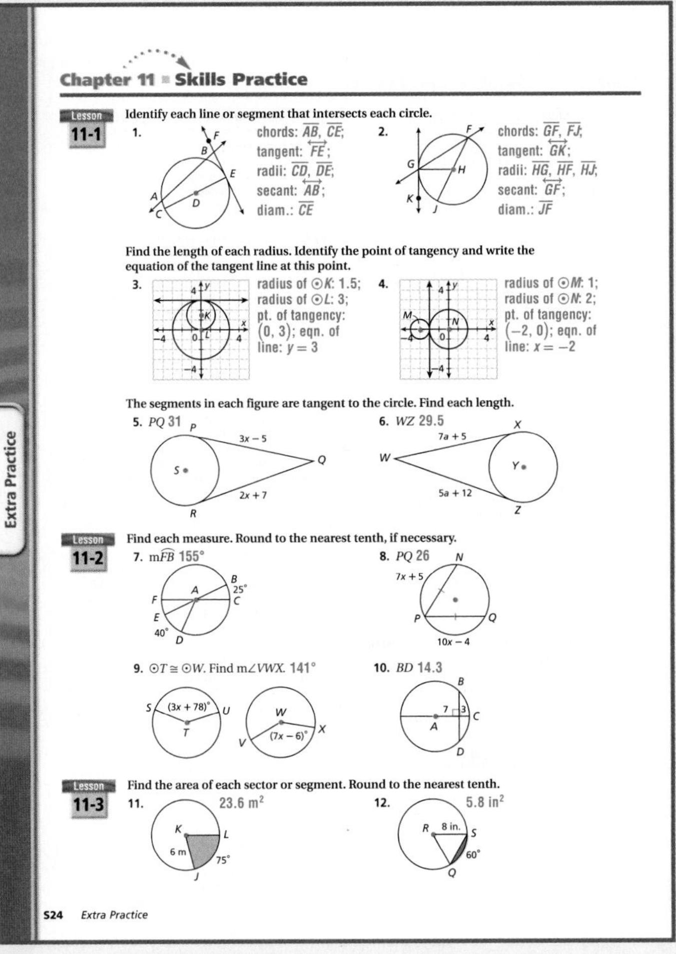

Chapter 11 ■ Skills Practice

Lesson 11-1 Identify each line or segment that intersects each circle.

1. chords: $\overline{AB}$, $\overline{CE}$; tangent: $\overleftrightarrow{FE}$; radii: $\overline{CD}$, $\overline{DE}$; secant: $\overleftrightarrow{AB}$; diam.: $\overline{CE}$
2. chords: $\overline{GF}$, $\overline{FJ}$; tangent: $\overleftrightarrow{GK}$; radii: $\overline{HG}$, $\overline{HF}$, $\overline{HJ}$; secant: $\overleftrightarrow{GF}$; diam.: $\overline{JF}$

Find the length of each radius. Identify the point of tangency and write the equation of the tangent line at this point.

3. radius of ⊙K: 1.5; radius of ⊙L: 3; pt. of tangency: (0, 3); eqn. of line: $y = 3$
4. radius of ⊙M: 1; radius of ⊙N: 2; pt. of tangency: (−2, 0); eqn. of line: $x = -2$

The segments in each figure are tangent to the circle. Find each length.

5. PQ 31
6. WZ 29.5

Lesson 11-2 Find each measure. Round to the nearest tenth, if necessary.

7. $m\widehat{FB}$ 155°
8. PQ 26
9. ⊙T ≅ ⊙W. Find m∠VWX. 141°
10. BD 14.3

Lesson 11-3 Find the area of each sector or segment. Round to the nearest tenth.

11. 23.6 m²
12. 5.8 in²

S24 Extra Practice

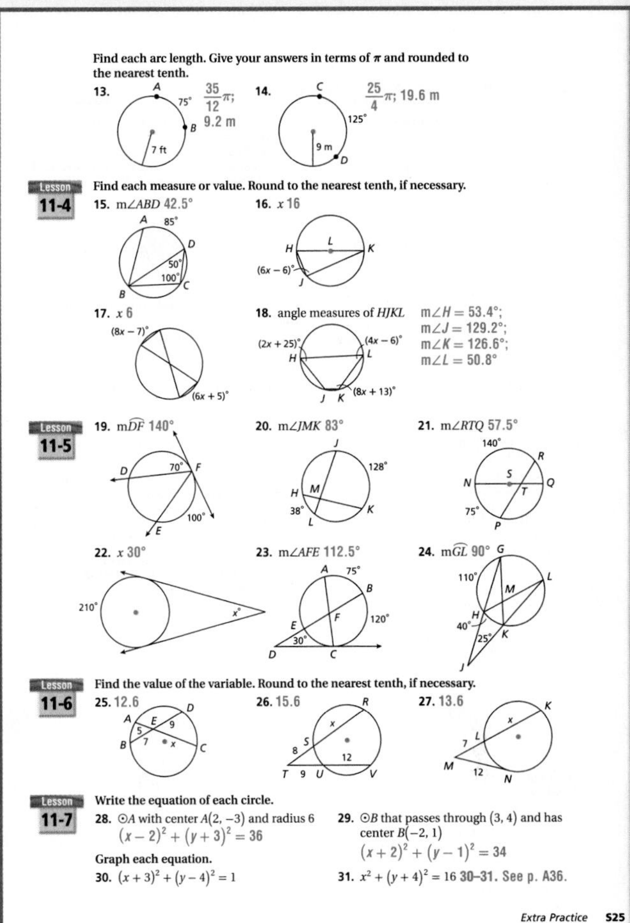

Find each arc length. Give your answers in terms of π and rounded to the nearest tenth.

13. $\frac{35}{12}\pi$; 9.2 m
14. $\frac{25}{4}\pi$; 19.6 m

Lesson 11-4 Find each measure or value. Round to the nearest tenth, if necessary.

15. m∠ABD 42.5°
16. x 16
17. x 6
18. angle measures of $HJKL$: m∠H = 53.4°; m∠J = 129.2°; m∠K = 126.6°; m∠L = 50.8°

Lesson 11-5

19. $m\widehat{DF}$ 140°
20. m∠JMK 83°
21. m∠RTQ 57.5°
22. x 30°
23. m∠AFE 112.5°
24. $m\widehat{GL}$ 90°

Lesson 11-6 Find the value of the variable. Round to the nearest tenth, if necessary.

25. 12.6
26. 15.6
27. 13.6

Lesson 11-7 Write the equation of each circle.

28. ⊙A with center A(2, −3) and radius 6: $(x-2)^2 + (y+3)^2 = 36$
29. ⊙B that passes through (3, 4) and has center B(−2, 1): $(x+2)^2 + (y-1)^2 = 34$

Graph each equation.

30. $(x+3)^2 + (y-4)^2 = 1$
31. $x^2 + (y+4)^2 = 16$

30–31. See p. A36.

Extra Practice S25

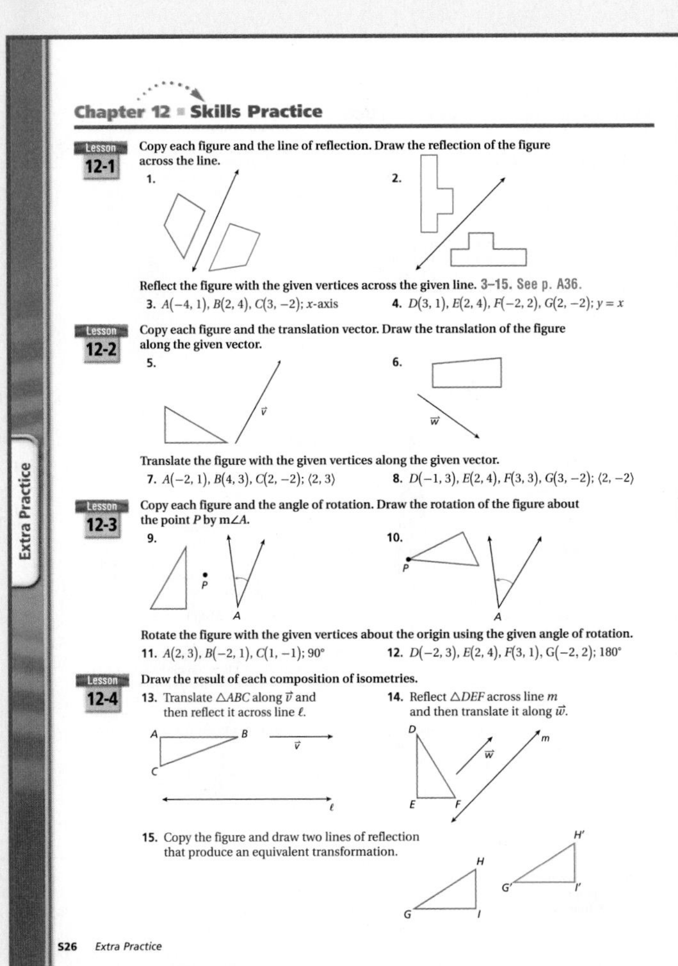

Chapter 12 ■ Skills Practice

Lesson 12-1 Copy each figure and the line of reflection. Draw the reflection of the figure across the line.

1.
2.

Reflect the figure with the given vertices across the given line. 3–15. See p. A36.

3. $A(-4, 1)$, $B(2, 4)$, $C(3, -2)$; x-axis
4. $D(3, 1)$, $E(2, 4)$, $F(-2, 2)$, $G(2, -2)$; $y = x$

Lesson 12-2 Copy each figure and the translation vector. Draw the translation of the figure along the given vector.

5.
6.

Translate the figure with the given vertices along the given vector.

7. $A(-2, 1)$, $B(4, 3)$, $C(2, -2)$; $\langle 2, 3\rangle$
8. $D(-1, 3)$, $E(2, 4)$, $F(3, 3)$, $G(3, -2)$; $\langle 2, -2\rangle$

Lesson 12-3 Copy each figure and the angle of rotation. Draw the rotation of the figure about the point P by m∠A.

9.
10.

Rotate the figure with the given vertices about the origin using the given angle of rotation.

11. $A(2, 3)$, $B(-2, 1)$, $C(1, -1)$; 90°
12. $D(-2, 3)$, $E(2, 4)$, $F(3, 1)$, $G(-2, 2)$; 180°

Lesson 12-4 Draw the result of each composition of isometries.

13. Translate △ABC along $\vec{v}$ and then reflect it across line ℓ.
14. Reflect △DEF across line m and then translate it along $\vec{w}$.
15. Copy the figure and draw two lines of reflection that produce an equivalent transformation.

S26 Extra Practice

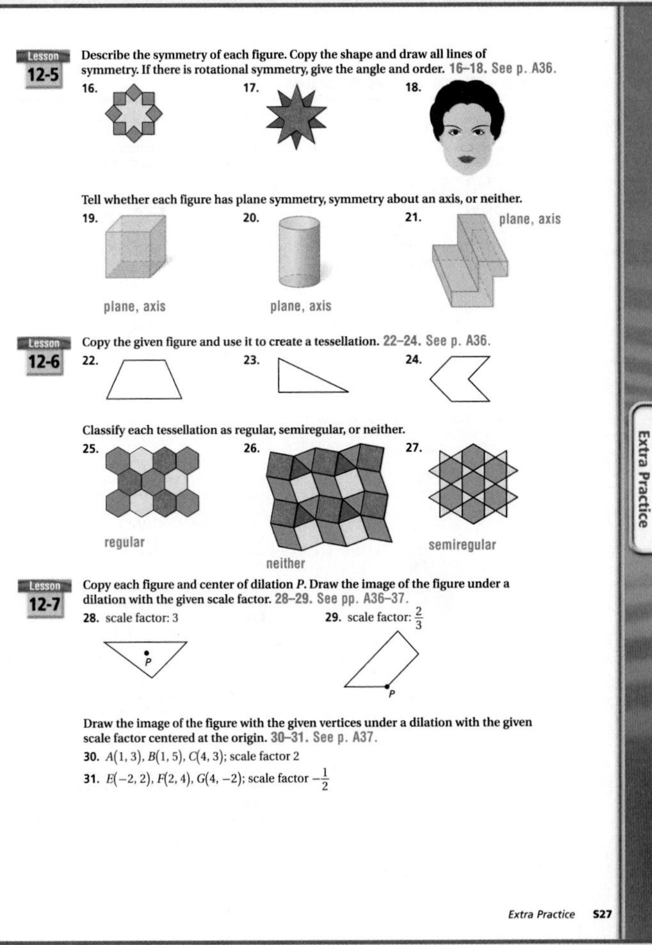

Lesson 12-5 Describe the symmetry of each figure. Copy the shape and draw all lines of symmetry. If there is rotational symmetry, give the angle and order. 16–18. See p. A36.

16.
17.
18.

Tell whether each figure has plane symmetry, symmetry about an axis, or neither.

19. plane, axis
20. plane, axis
21. plane, axis

Lesson 12-6 Copy the given figure and use it to create a tessellation. 22–24. See p. A36.

22.
23.
24.

Classify each tessellation as regular, semiregular, or neither.

25. regular
26. neither
27. semiregular

Lesson 12-7 Copy each figure and center of dilation P. Draw the image of the figure under a dilation with the given scale factor. 28–29. See pp. A36–37.

28. scale factor: 3
29. scale factor: $\frac{2}{3}$

Draw the image of the figure with the given vertices under a dilation with the given scale factor centered at the origin. 30–31. See p. A37.

30. $A(1, 3)$, $B(1, 5)$, $C(4, 3)$; scale factor 2
31. $E(-2, 2)$, $F(2, 4)$, $G(4, -2)$; scale factor $-\frac{1}{2}$

Extra Practice S27

Chapter 1 ■ Applications Practice

Athletics **Use the following information for Exercises 1–3.**

During gym class, a teacher notices the following. Decide if each resembles a point, segment, ray, or line. *(Lesson 1-1)*

1. Kyle starts running in a straight line. Suppose he does not stop running. ray
2. Agnes runs a quarter-mile in a straight line. seg.
3. Jimmy stands perfectly still. pt.

Travel **Use the following information for Exercises 4–6.**

The Perez family is driving from Austin, Texas, to Dallas, Texas. The city of Waco is the approximate midpoint between these two cities. It is 102 miles from Austin to Waco. *(Lesson 1-2)*

4. What is the total distance from Austin to Dallas? 204 mi
5. The approximate midpoint from Waco to Dallas is Milford. What is the distance from Austin to Milford? 153 mi
6. The Perez family averages 64 miles per hour. About how long will the entire drive take? approximately 3 h 11 min

Probability **Use the following information for Exercises 7 and 8.** See p. A37.

In a carnival game, each contestant spins the wheel and wins the prize indicated by the color. *(Lesson 1-3)*

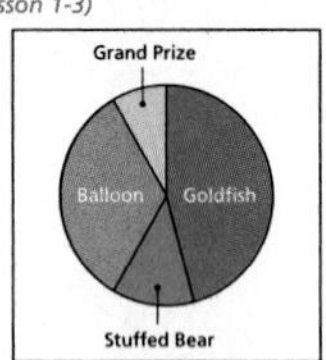

7. Using a protractor, measure each angle on the wheel.
8. Since there are 360° in a circle, the probability of the wheel landing on a given color is the number of degrees in the angle divided by 360°. Find the probability of the wheel landing on each prize. Express your answer as a fraction in lowest terms.

9. **Entomology** Because the insect is symmetrical, $\angle 1 \cong \angle 4$ and $\angle 2 \cong \angle 3$. Also, $\angle 1$ and $\angle 2$ are complementary, and $\angle 3$ and $\angle 4$ are complementary. If $m\angle 1 = 48.5°$, find $m\angle 2$, $m\angle 3$, and $m\angle 4$. *(Lesson 1-4)*

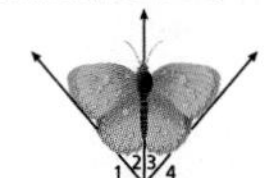

$m\angle 2 = m\angle 3 = 41.5°$; $m\angle 4 = 48.5°$

Architecture **Use the following information for Exercises 10 and 11.**

The bricks used to make a building are one-fourth as tall as they are wide, and the bricks are 2.25 inches tall. *(Lesson 1-5)*

10. What is the area of the largest face of each brick? $20.25\ \text{in}^2$
11. A certain exterior wall is 33 bricks long and 20 bricks tall. What is the area of the wall in square inches? $13{,}365\ \text{in}^2$
12. **Sports** A football coach has his team run sprints diagonally across a football field. If the field is 120 yards long and 160 feet wide, what is the distance they run? Write your answer to the nearest hundredth of a foot. *(Lesson 1-6)* 393.95 ft
13. **Crafts** The picture below shows half of a stenciled design. The full design should resemble a sun. Name two transformations that can be performed on the image so that the image and its preimage form a complete picture. Be as specific as possible, referring to *L* and *P*. *(Lesson 1-7)*

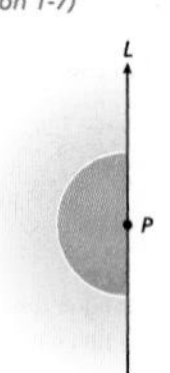

reflection across *L*, rotation of 180° about *P*

Chapter 2 ■ Applications Practice

1. **Health** Mike collected the following data about the heights of twelve students in his tenth-grade class. Use the table to make a conjecture about the heights of boys and girls in the tenth grade. *(Lesson 2-1)* See p. A37.

Height (in.) of Tenth-Grade Students						
Boys	70	71	68	67	70	67
Girls	67	64	64	65	68	66

2. **Government** Presidential elections are held every four years. Elections for senators are held every two years. So in years not divisible by 4, only Senate seats are up for election. The table shows voter turnout for a small town during recent election years. Make a conjecture based on the data. *(Lesson 2-1)* See p. A37.

Voter Turnout	
Year	Voters
1996	12,530
1998	8,750
2000	15,210
2002	7,370
2004	14,380

3. **Biology** Write the converse, inverse, and contrapositive of the conditional statement "If an animal is a fish, then it swims in salt water." Find the truth value of each. *(Lesson 2-2)* See p. A37.
4. **Gardening** Write the converse, inverse, and contrapositive of the conditional statement "If a plant is watered, then it will grow." Find the truth value of each. *(Lesson 2-2)* See p. A37.
5. **Sports** Determine if the conjecture is valid by the Law of Detachment. *(Lesson 2-3)* invalid
   Given: If you participate in a triathlon, then you run, swim, and bike. Margie runs, swims, and bikes.
   Conjecture: Margie participates in a triathlon.
6. **Health** Students are required to have certain immunizations before attending school to prevent the spread of disease. Write the conditional statement and converse within the biconditional "Students can attend public school if and only if they have the required immunizations." *(Lesson 2-4)* See p. A37.
7. **Weather** Hurricanes are assigned category numbers to describe the amount of flooding and wind damage they are likely to cause. Write the statement "If a hurricane has sustained winds of more than 155 miles per hour, then it is Category 5" as a biconditional statement. *(Lesson 2-4)* See p. A37.
8. **Athletics** The equation $c = 5w + 25$ relates the number of workouts w to the cost c of a weight training group. If Matthew plans to spend \$200 on weight training, how many workouts can he participate in? Solve the equation for w and justify each step. *(Lesson 2-5)* See p. A37.
9. **Nutrition** Rick has allotted himself 200 Calories for his evening snack, which consists of a glass of milk and crackers. A glass of milk has 110 Calories, and each cracker has 15 Calories. The equation $s = 110 + 15c$ relates the number of crackers c to the total number of Calories s in Rick's evening snack. How many crackers can Rick have? Solve the equation for c and justify each step. *(Lesson 2-5)* See p. A37.
10. **Travel** On a city map, the library, post office, and police station are collinear points in that order. The distance from the library to the post office is 2.3 miles. The distance from the post office to the police station is 5.1 miles. Which theorem can you use to conclude that the distance from the library to the police station is 7.4 miles? *(Lesson 2-6)* Seg. Add. Post.
11. **Recreation** Kyle is making a kite from the pattern below by cutting four triangles from different pieces of material. Write a paragraph proof to show that $m\angle 3 = 90°$. *(Lesson 2-7)*

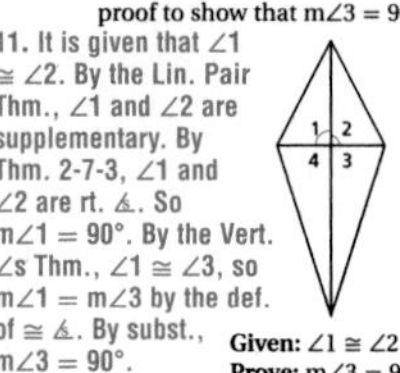

Given: $\angle 1 \cong \angle 2$
Prove: $m\angle 3 = 90°$

11. It is given that $\angle 1 \cong \angle 2$. By the Lin. Pair Thm., $\angle 1$ and $\angle 2$ are supplementary. By Thm. 2-7-3, $\angle 1$ and $\angle 2$ are rt. ⦣. So $m\angle 1 = 90°$. By the Vert. ∠s Thm., $\angle 1 \cong \angle 3$, so $m\angle 1 = m\angle 3$ by the def. of ≅ ⦣. By subst., $m\angle 3 = 90°$.

Chapter 3 ■ Applications Practice

1. **Recreation** A scuba diver leaves a flag on the surface of the water to alert boaters of his location. Describe two parallel lines and a transversal in the flag. *(Lesson 3-1)*

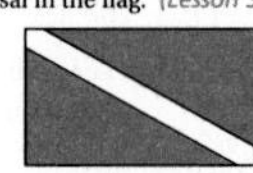

Possible answer: The top and the bottom of the flag are ∥. The white stripe is a transv.

2. **Carpentry** In the stairs shown, the horizontal treads and the vertical risers are all parallel. $m\angle 1 = (14x + 6)°$ and $m\angle 2 = (19x - 24)°$. Find x. *(Lesson 3-2)* $x = 6$

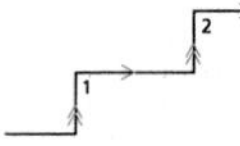

3. **Transportation** The train tracks shown cross the street lanes. The lanes of the street are parallel. Find x in the diagram. *(Lesson 3-3)* $x = 10$

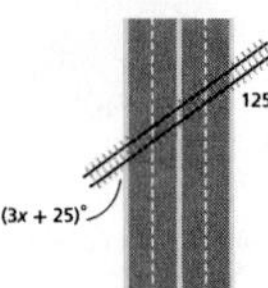

4. **Sports** At a track meet, the starting blocks are placed along a line that is a transversal to the lanes. $m\angle 1 = 12x - 8$, $m\angle 2 = 8x + 12$, and $x = 5$. Show that the lines between the lanes are parallel. *(Lesson 3-3)* See p. A37.

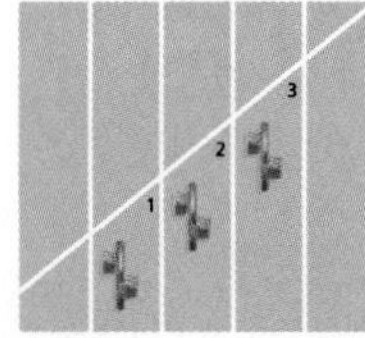

5. **Transportation** The railroad ties in the diagram are all parallel. $m\angle 1 = 19x - 5$ and $m\angle 2 = 4x + 5y$. Find x and y so that the ties are all perpendicular to the tracks. *(Lesson 3-4)* $x = 5$, $y = 14$

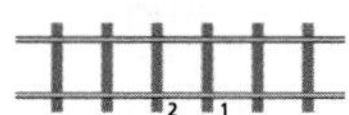

6. **Art** The sides of a picture frame are cut so that the opposite sides of the frame are parallel and the consecutive sides are perpendicular. Find the values of x and y in the diagram. *(Lesson 3-4)* $x = 5$, $y = 25$

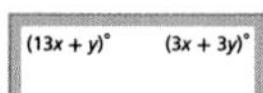

7. **Recreation** At 1:00 P.M., a boat on a river passes a point that is 3 miles from a lodge. At 5:30 P.M., the boat passes a point that is 8 miles from the lodge. Graph the line that represents the boat's distance from the lodge. Find and interpret the slope of the line. *(Lesson 3-5)* See p. A37.
8. **Sports** A marathon runner runs 10 miles by 3:00 P.M. and 25 miles by 4:30 P.M. Graph the line that represents her distance run. Find and interpret the slope of the line. *(Lesson 3-5)* See p. A37.
9. **Business** A cab company charges \$8 per ride plus \$0.25 per mile. Another cab company charges \$5 per ride plus \$0.35 per mile. For how many miles will two cab rides cost the same amount? *(Lesson 3-6)* 30 miles
10. **Food** A pizza parlor is catering a school event. Pete's Pizza charges \$85 for the first 20 students and \$5 for each additional student. Polly's Pizza charges \$125 for the first 20 students and \$3 for each additional student. For how many students will the pizza parlors cost the same? *(Lesson 3-6)* 40 students

Chapter 4 ■ Applications Practice

1. **Camping** Three poles are used to create the frame for a tent. The front of the tent is an isosceles triangle with $\overline{AB} \cong \overline{BC}$. The length of the base is 1.5 times the length of the sides. The perimeter of the triangle is 21 ft. Find each side length. *(Lesson 4-1)* $AB = 6$, $BC = 6$, $AC = 9$
2. **Geography** The universities in Durham, Chapel Hill, and Raleigh, North Carolina form what is known as the Research Triangle. Use the map to find the measure of the angle whose vertex is at Durham. *(Lesson 4-2)* 88°

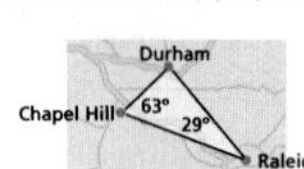

3. **Business** Oil derricks are used as supports for oil drilling equipment. Use the diagram to prove the following. *(Lesson 4-3)*

Given: $\overline{AB} \cong \overline{HG}$, $\overline{HB} \cong \overline{AG}$, $\angle GAB \cong \angle BHG$, $\angle AGB \cong \angle HBG$

Prove: $\triangle AGB \cong \triangle HBG$

See p. A37.

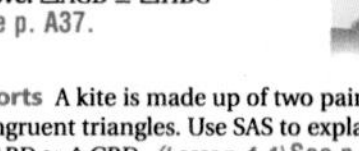

4. **Sports** A kite is made up of two pairs of congruent triangles. Use SAS to explain why $\triangle ABD \cong \triangle CBD$. *(Lesson 4-4)* See p. A37.

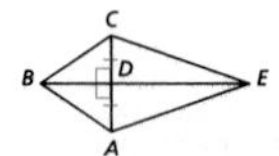

5. **Recreation** A student is estimating the height of a water slide. From a certain distance, the angle from where he is standing to a point on the highest part of the slide is 35°. From a distance 200 m closer, the same angle is 45°.
   a. Draw a triangle with the point at the top of the slide as one vertex, and the points where the measurements were taken as the other vertices. See p. A37.
   b. Which postulate or theorem can be used to show that this triangle is uniquely determined? *(Lesson 4-5)* AAS or ASA
6. **Surveying** To find the distance *AB* across a lake, first locate point *C*. Then measure the distance from *C* to *B*. Locate point *D* the same distance from *C* as *B*, but in the opposite direction. Then measure the distance from *C* to *A* and locate point *E* in a similar manner. What is the distance *AB* across the lake? *(Lesson 4-6)* 135 yd

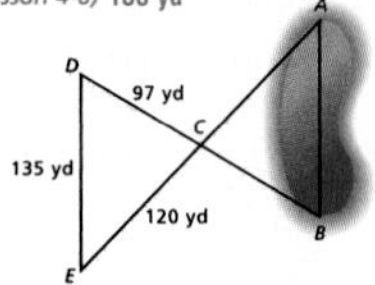

7. The first step in creating a Sierpinski triangle is to connect the midpoints of the sides of a triangle as shown. *(Lesson 4-7)* See p. A37.

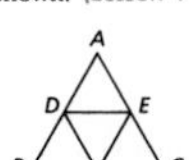

Given: Equilateral $\triangle ABC$, *D* is the midpoint of $\overline{AB}$, *E* is the midpoint of $\overline{AC}$, and *F* is the midpoint of $\overline{BC}$.

Prove: The area of $\triangle DEF$ is $\frac{1}{4}$ the area of $\triangle ABC$.

8. **Recreation** A boat is sailing parallel to the coastline along $\overleftrightarrow{XY}$. When the boat is at *X*, the measure of the angle from the lighthouse *W* to the boat is 30°. After the boat has traveled 5 miles to *Y*, the angle from the lighthouse to the boat is 60°. How can you find *WY*? *(Lesson 4-8)*

8. Since the boat is parallel to the coastline, $\overline{WZ} \parallel \overline{YX}$. So $\angle ZWX \cong \angle WXY$. Since $m\angle YWZ = 60°$ and $m\angle XWZ = 30°$, by subtr., $m\angle YWX = 30°$. Therefore $\triangle WYX$ is isosc. and $\overline{WY} \cong \overline{YX}$. Thus $WY = 5$.

Chapter 5 ■ Applications Practice

1. **Building** The guy wires $\overline{AB}$ and $\overline{CB}$ supporting a cell phone tower are congruent and are equally spaced from the base of the tower. How do these wires ensure that the cell phone tower is perpendicular to the ground? *(Lesson 5-1)* See p. A37.

2. **Safety** City planners want to relocate their town's firehouse so that it is the same distance from the three main streets of the town. Draw a sketch to show where the firehouse should be positioned. Justify your sketch. *(Lesson 5-2)* See p. A37.

3. **Safety** A lifeguard needs to watch three areas of a water park. Draw a sketch to show where she should stand to be the same distance from all the swimmers. Justify your sketch. *(Lesson 5-2)* See p. A38.

4. **Art** An artist is designing a sculpture composed of a pedestal with a triangular top. The vertices of the top are $A(-4, 2)$, $B(2, 4)$, and $C(4, -3)$. Where should the artist attach the pedestal so that the triangle is balanced? *(Lesson 5-3)* See p. A38.

5. **Measurement** City engineers plan to build a bridge across the pond shown. What will be the length of the bridge, GH? *(Lesson 5-4)* 25 m

Engineering **Use the following information for Exercises 6 and 7.** See p. A38.

Playground engineers are planning a sidewalk that will connect the swings, seesaw, and slide. *(Lesson 5-5)*

6. If the angle at the swings is the largest, which portion of the sidewalk will be the longest?

7. The distance from the swings to the slide is 37 ft. Can the lengths of the other sides be 40 ft and 50 ft? Explain.

8. **Geography** The cities of Allenville, Baytown, College City, and Dean Park are shown on the map. Baytown and Dean Park are each 30 miles from College City. Which city is closer to Allenville: Baytown or Dean Park? *(Lesson 5-6)* Baytown

9. Mark is late for school. He usually goes around the park so he can walk along the water. Today he decides to cut through the park. About how many feet does he save by going through the park? *(Lesson 5-7)* about 178 ft

10. **Sports** A baseball diamond is a square with a side length of 90 ft. What is the distance from first base to third base? *(Lesson 5-8)* See p. A38.

11. **Recreation** Haley, who is 5 ft tall, is flying a kite on 100 ft of string. How high is the kite? *(Lesson 5-8)* $5 + 50\sqrt{3}$ ft, or about 91.6 ft

Chapter 6 ■ Applications Practice

1. **Safety** A stop sign is in the shape of a regular octagon. What is the value of x? *(Lesson 6-1)* 45°

2. **Hobbies** Nancy is planting a garden shaped like a regular pentagon. She bought metal edging to surround the garden and prevent weeds. What angle should the edging form at the vertices of the garden? *(Lesson 6-1)* 108°

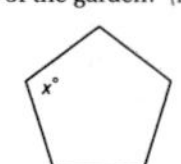

Fishing **Use the following information for Exercises 3–5.**

The hinges for the trays in a tackle box form parallelograms to ensure that the trays stay parallel to the base of the box. In ▱$ABCD$, $AB = 21$ in., $AE = 9$ in., and $m\angle BCD = 125°$. Find each measure. *(Lesson 6-2)*

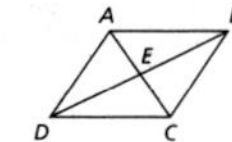

3. DC 21 in.

4. EC 9 in.

5. $m\angle ADC$ 55°

6. **Design** A glide rocker uses hinged parallelograms to move the chair back and forth. In ▱$ABCD$, $AB = DC$, and $AD = BC$. The sides of the parallelogram, $\overline{AD}$ and $\overline{BC}$, rotate together to move the chair. Why is $ABCD$ always a parallelogram? *(Lesson 6-3)* See p. A38.

Design **Use the following information for Exercises 7–9.**

When extended, the legs of a folding table must form a rectangle so the tabletop is parallel to the ground. Given that $JK = 48$ in. and $KN = 36$ in., find each length. *(Lesson 6-4)*

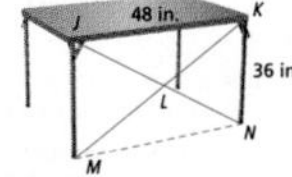

7. JM 36 in.

8. JN 60 in.

9. NM 48 in.

10. **Hobbies** Elise is creating a decorative page for her scrapbook. She has a piece of ribbon that is 12 inches long. She wants to outline a rhombus with the ribbon. How can Elise cut the ribbon to ensure that the final shape is a rhombus? *(Lesson 6-5)* See p. A38.

11. **Carpentry** Luke is cutting a rectangular window frame. The dimensions of the window are to be 3 feet by 4 feet. What should the diagonal of the frame measure so that the window is rectangular? *(Lesson 6-5)* 5 ft

12. **Hobbies** Addie is making a kite with diagonals of 32 inches and 18 inches. She wants to put a ribbon around the edge of the kite. She will add an 8-foot tail to the kite, made of the same ribbon. If ribbon can be purchased in packages of 3 yards, how many packages should she buy for the entire project? *(Lesson 6-6)* 2 packages

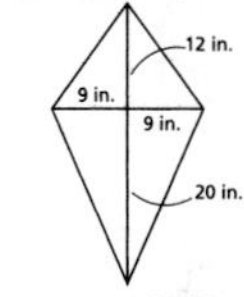

13. **Carpentry** Aaron is building a shadow box for his baseball memorabilia. The shadow box will be in the shape of a trapezoid, as shown below. The wood for the box costs \$1.59 per foot. Estimate the cost of the lumber. *(Lesson 6-6)* about \$9.28

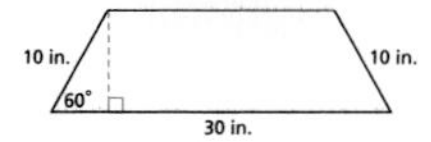

Chapter 7 ■ Applications Practice

Hobbies **Use the following information for Exercises 1–4.**

Jason and Matthew share 210 CDs. The ratio between Matthew's CDs and Jason's CDs is 4:3. *(Lesson 7-1)*

1. Write a proportion that can be used to find the number of CDs each one has. See p. A38.

2. How many CDs does Jason have? 90

3. The number of Matthew's CDs is what fraction of the total number of CDs? $\frac{4}{7}$

4. Jason wants to have the most CDs. What is the least number of CDs he would have to purchase to have more than Matthew? 31

5. **Carpentry** Ava's dollhouse is a scale model of a castle. The great room of the castle has a width of 40 ft and a length of 50 ft. The width of the great room of the dollhouse is 8 in. What is the length of the great room of the dollhouse? *(Lesson 7-1)* 10 in.

6. **Travel** A map is a scale model of a real city. The scale on the map is 1 in.:30 mi. Two cities are 165 mi apart. How far apart will the cities be on the map? *(Lesson 7-2)* 5.5 in.

7. **Recreation** The sails on the sailboat below have the given dimensions. Use similar triangles to prove $\triangle ABC \sim \triangle DEF$. *(Lesson 7-3)* See p. A38.

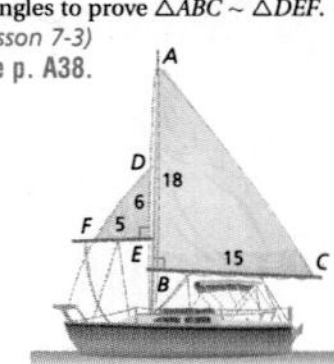

8. **Graphics** A photograph shows a smaller version of the real item. The height of the Washington Monument is approximately 555 ft. The monument in a photo is 5 in. tall. What is the scale factor of the actual monument to the monument in the photo? *(Lesson 7-3)* 111 ft:1 in.

9. **Geography** Riverside Park has campsites available for rent. Lot A has 50 ft of street frontage and 80 ft of river frontage. Find the river frontage for lots B, C, and D. *(Lesson 7-4)* $B = 51.2$ ft; $C = 64$ ft; $D = 120$ ft

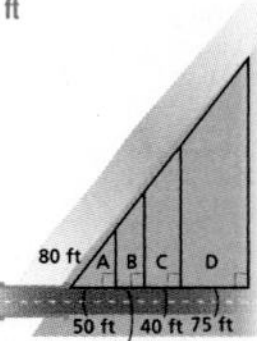

10. **Architecture** An amphitheater is being built according to the design shown. If the total footage on the right of the rows of seats is 232.5 ft, find the length of each section. *(Lesson 7-4)* See p. A38.

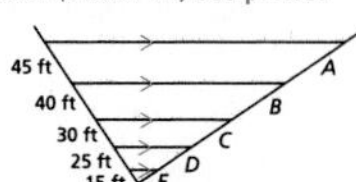

11. Jake wants to know the height of the oak tree in his front yard. He measured his height as 68 inches and his shadow as 34 inches. At the same time, the tree has a shadow of 5.5 feet. How tall is the tree? *(Lesson 7-5)* 11 ft

12. **Recreation** The kiddie pool and the lap pool at Centerville Park are similar rectangles. The lap pool measures 25 ft wide by 48 ft long. The kiddie pool is 8 ft long. How wide is the kiddie pool to the nearest tenth? *(Lesson 7-5)* 4.2 ft

13. Melissa is enlarging her 4-by-6 photo by 150%. Find the coordinates of the enlarged photo. *(Lesson 7-6)* (0, 0), (0, 9), (6, 0), (6, 9)

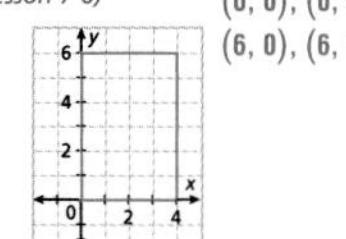

Chapter 8 ■ Applications Practice

1. **Diving** To estimate the height of a diving platform, a spectator stands so that his lines of sight to the top and bottom of the platform form a right angle as shown. The spectator's eyes are 5 ft above the ground. He is standing 15 ft from the diving platform. How high is the platform? *(Lesson 8-1)* 50 ft

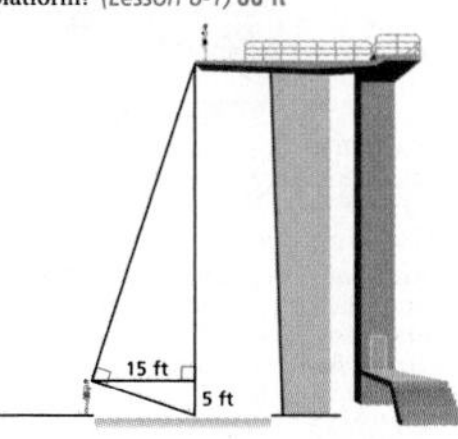

2. **Recreation** A neighborhood park has a 15-foot-long space available to install a playground slide. If the maximum height of the slide is 6 ft, what are the lengths of the slide x and ladder y that should be installed? Round to the nearest tenth of a foot. *(Lesson 8-1)* 13.4 ft; 6.7 ft

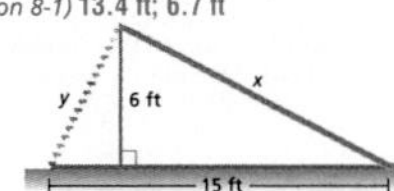

3. **Building** The escalator at the mall forms a 35° angle with the floor. The vertical distance from the bottom of the escalator to the top is 25 ft. How long is the escalator? Round to the nearest foot. *(Lesson 8-2)* 44 ft

4. **Sports** A 3-foot-long skateboard ramp forms a 40° angle with the ground. How far above the ground is the end of the ramp? Round to the nearest foot. *(Lesson 8-2)* 2 ft

5. **Running** A race includes a 0.25-mile hill on which runners travel from 510 ft of elevation to 570 ft of elevation. What angle does the hill form? Round to the nearest degree. *(Lesson 8-3)* 3°

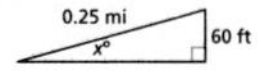

6. **Safety** A lifeguard sees a swimmer struggling in the water at an angle of depression of 15°. The stand is 10 feet tall. What is the horizontal distance from the stand to the swimmer? Round to the nearest foot. *(Lesson 8-4)* 37 ft

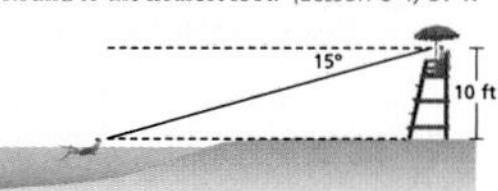

7. **Aviation** A helicopter pilot flying at an altitude of 1200 ft sees two landing pads directly in front of him. The angle of depression to the first landing pad is 40°. The angle of depression to the second pad is 28°. What is the distance between the two pads? Round to the nearest foot. *(Lesson 8-4)* 827 ft

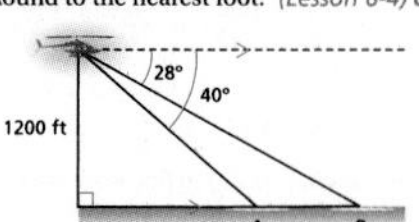

8. **Carpentry** Sean is creating a triangular frame from three wooden dowels, which are 18 in., 12 in., and 15 in. long. What are the measures of each angle of the triangle? Round to the nearest degree. *(Lesson 8-5)* 41°, 56°, 83°

9. **Sports** To estimate the width of the sand trap on a golf course, Matthew locates three points and measures the distances shown. What is the width, XZ, of the sand trap to the nearest foot? *(Lesson 8-5)* 107 ft

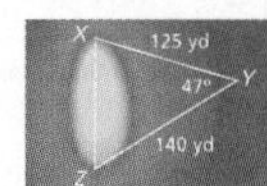

10. **Recreation** Jill swims due east across a river at 2 mi/h. The river is flowing north at 1.5 mi/h. What are Jill's actual speed and direction? Round the speed to the nearest tenth and the direction to the nearest degree. *(Lesson 8-6)* 2.5 mi/h; 37°, or N 53° E

Chapter 9 ■ Applications Practice

1. **Recreation** Kathy is making a kite with diagonals of lengths 30 inches and 20 inches. How many square inches of fabric will she need? *(Lesson 9-1)* **300 in²**

Agriculture Use the following information for Exercises 2 and 3. An acre is 43,560 square feet. *(Lesson 9-1)*

2. If a one-acre piece of land is a rectangle with a base of 100 ft, what is its height? **435.6 ft**
3. If a one-acre piece of land is a square, what is the length of each side? Round to the nearest tenth. **208.7 ft**
4. The garden shown is a regular hexagon with a circular fountain at the center. What is the area of the garden? Round to the nearest square foot. *(Lesson 9-2)* **1631 ft²**

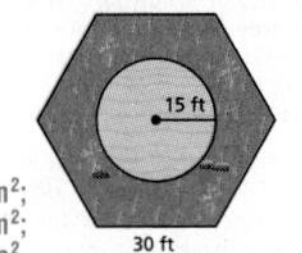

5. 254 cm²; 380 cm²; 531 cm²

5. **Food** A bakery has cheesecake pans with three diameters: 18 cm, 22 cm, and 26 cm. Find the area of the bottom of each pan. Round to the nearest square centimeter. *(Lesson 9-2)*
6. **Recreation** A track for a toy car is a 2 ft by 2 ft square with a semicircle at each end. What is the distance around the track? Round to the nearest foot. *(Lesson 9-3)* **10 ft**
7. **Art** Jonas is painting the shape shown on his ceiling. If a quart of paint covers 75 square feet, will one quart be enough to paint the entire shape? Explain. *(Lesson 9-3)*

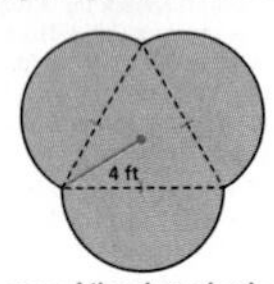

No, the area of the shape is about 77.3 ft².

Transportation Use the following information for Exercises 8 and 9. The graph shows the speed of a car versus time. The base of each square on the graph represents 10 minutes, and the height represents 10 miles per hour. *(Lesson 9-4)*

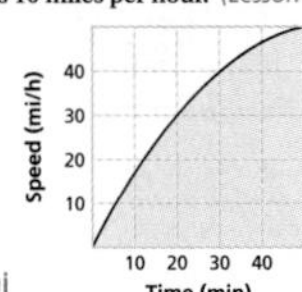

8. $1\frac{2}{3}$ mi

8. What is the area of one square on the graph?
9. Estimate the shaded area of the graph. **$\approx 26\frac{2}{3}$ mi**
10. **Art** Rasha is cutting a mat for a poster with an area of 480 in². To find the dimensions of the mat, she multiplies the dimensions of the poster by 1.2. To find the dimensions of the opening, she multiplies the dimensions of the poster by 0.9. What is the area of the remaining part of the mat? *(Lesson 9-5)* **302.4 in²**
11. **Food** A restaurant sells two sizes of pizzas. The smaller pizza has a 12-inch diameter. If the area of the larger pizza is twice the area of the smaller pizza, what is the diameter of the larger pizza? Round to the nearest inch. *(Lesson 9-5)* **17 in.**
12. **Transportation** A commuter train stops at a station every 3 minutes and stays at the station for 20 seconds. If you arrive at the station at a random time, what is the probability that you will have to wait more than one minute for a train? Round to the nearest hundredth. *(Lesson 9-6)* **0.56**
13. **Sports** A skydiver is delivering the game ball for a baseball game. Suppose he lands at a random point on the field. What is the probability that he will not land on the pitcher's mound? Round to the nearest hundredth. *(Lesson 9-6)* **0.97**

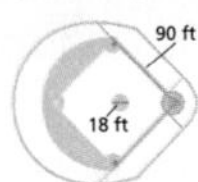

Chapter 10 ■ Applications Practice

1. **Food** Cookie dough is rolled in the shape of a cylinder. How can the dough be sliced to make circular cookies? *(Lesson 10-1)* **Slice parallel to the bases.**
2. **Recreation** The tent shown is in the shape of a pentagonal prism. If a wall is used to divide the tent into two rooms, what shapes could the wall be? *(Lesson 10-1)* **rectangles or pentagons**

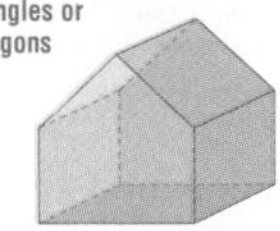

3. **Business** Eli is creating a logo for his business by drawing his name in block capital letters using one-point perspective. Draw Eli's logo. *(Lesson 10-2)* **See p. A38.**
4. **Recreation** Two hot air balloons were launched from the same location. The first balloon is 5 miles north, 9 miles east, and 0.5 mile above the launching point. The second balloon is 9 miles north, 5 miles east, and 0.8 mile above the launching point. How far apart are the two balloons? Round to the nearest tenth. *(Lesson 10-3)* **5.7 m**
5. **Manufacturing** The two packages shown hold the same amount of food. Which requires a greater amount of material to produce? *(Lesson 10-4)* **package B**

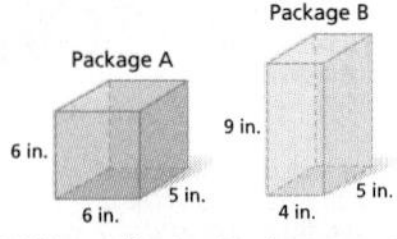

6. **Hobbies** Ashley is using the pattern shown to make cones to protect her plants from freezing. How tall can the plants be to fit in the cone? Round to the nearest tenth. *(Lesson 10-5)* **5.3 in.**

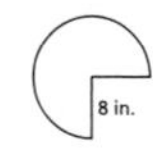

7. **Camping** The tent structure shown is in the shape of a square pyramid. How many square inches of canvas are required to cover the tent? Round to the nearest square inch. *(Lesson 10-5)* **189 in²**

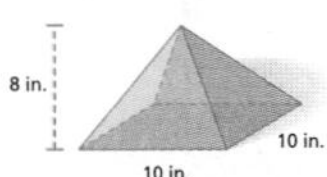

Recreation Use the following information for Exercises 8 and 9.

A cylindrical pool has a 10 ft diameter. *(Lesson 10-6)*

8. How many gallons of water are needed to fill the pool to a depth of 4 feet? Round to the nearest gallon. (*Hint:* 1 gallon ≈ 0.134 cubic feet.) **2344 gal**
9. If the pool is filled to a depth of 4 feet, how much will the water weigh? Round to the nearest pound. (*Hint:* 1 gallon weighs about 8.34 pounds.) **19,553 lb**
10. **Hobbies** The greenhouse shown is in the shape of a cube with a square pyramid on top. What is the volume of the greenhouse? *(Lesson 10-7)* **5120 ft³**

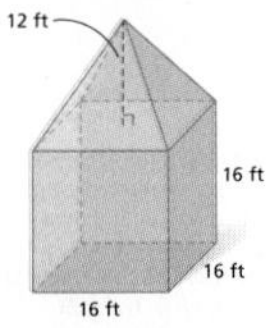

11. **Food** A snow-cone cup has a 3-inch diameter and is 4 inches tall. Another snow-cone cup has a 4-inch diameter and is 3 inches tall. Which cup will hold more? *(Lesson 10-7)* **the 4 in. diameter cup**
12. **Sports** The circumference of a size 3 soccer ball is 24 in. The circumference of a size 5 soccer ball is 28 in. How many times as great is the volume of a size 5 ball as the volume of a size 3 ball? *(Lesson 10-8)* **about 1.6 times as great**

Chapter 11 ■ Applications Practice

1. **Measurement** There is a water tower near Peter's house in the shape of a cylinder. He wants to find the diameter of the tank. Peter stands 25 feet from the tower. The distance from Peter to a point of tangency on the tower is 80 feet. What is the diameter of the tank? *(Lesson 11-1)* **231 ft**
2. **Travel** Pikes Peak is 14,110 feet above sea level. What is the distance from the summit to the horizon, to the nearest mile? (*Hint:* Earth's radius ≈ 4000 mi) *(Lesson 11-1)* **146 mi**

Hobbies Use the circle graph to find each measure for Exercises 3–6 to the nearest degree.

Eric collects baseball cards. He has 85 cards from the 1970s, 95 cards from the 1980s, and 125 cards from the 1990s. *(Lesson 11-2)*

Baseball Card Collection

A, 1990s, 1970s, D, C, 1980s, B

3. $\widehat{AB}$ **148°** 4. $\widehat{AC}$ **100°**

5. $\angle CDB$ **112°** 6. $\angle ADC$ **100°**

Data Use the circle graph to find each measure for Exercises 7–10 to the nearest degree.

The circle graph shows the color of cars in a parking lot at the mall. *(Lesson 11-2)*

7. $\widehat{HG}$
8. $\widehat{CD}$
9. $\angle AJH$
10. $\angle FJE$

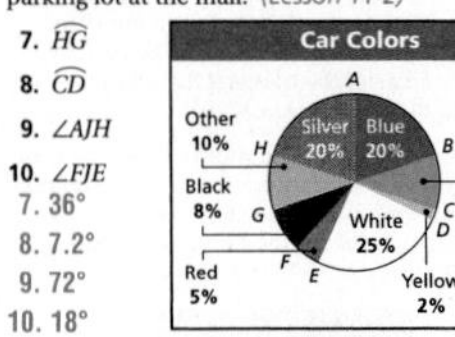

7. 36°
8. 7.2°
9. 72°
10. 18°

Hobbies Use the following information to find each area to the nearest tenth for Exercises 11 and 12.

A sprinkler system has three types of sprinkler heads: a quarter circle, a semicircle, and a full circle. The sprinkler will spray a distance of 15 feet from the sprinkler head. *(Lesson 11-3)*

11. What is the area of the sector that will be watered by the quarter circle sprinkler head? **176.7 ft²**
12. What is the area of the sector that will be watered by the semicircle sprinkler head? **353.4 ft²**

Art Use the diagram to find each value for Exercises 13–15.

The diagram represents an engraving on a stained glass window. *(Lesson 11-4)*

13. x
14. y
15. $m\widehat{FE}$

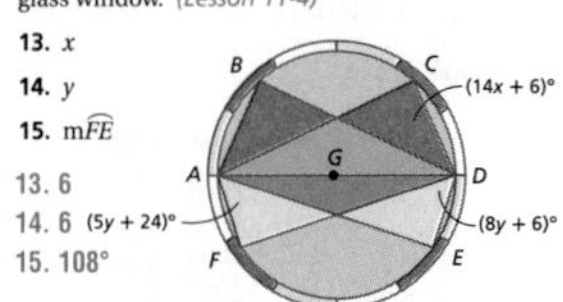

13. 6
14. 6
15. 108°

16. **Astronomy** Two satellites are orbiting Earth. Satellite A is 10,000 km above Earth, and satellite B is 13,000 km above Earth. How many arc degrees of Earth does each satellite see? *(Lesson 11-5)* **A: 136°; B: 148°**

17. **Entertainment** A group of friends ate most of a pepperoni pizza. All that was left was a piece of crust. What was the diameter of the original pizza? *(Lesson 11-6)* **6.5 in.**

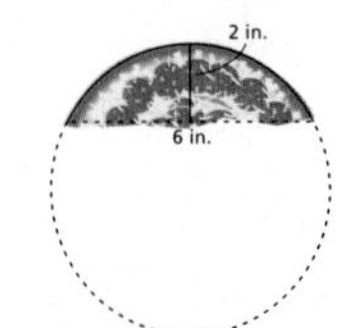

18. **Safety** Three small towns have agreed to share a new fire station. To make sure each town has equal response time, the station should be the same distance from each town. The three towns are located on a coordinate plane at (0, 0), (6, 0), and (0, 8). At which coordinates should the station be built? *(Lesson 11-7)* **(3, 4)**

Chapter 12 ■ Applications Practice

1. **Transportation** Two towns are located on the same side of a river. Two roads are being built to meet at the same point P on the river. Draw a diagram that shows where P should be located in order to make the total length of the roads as short as possible. *(Lesson 12-1)* **See p. A38.**

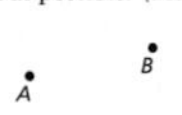

2. **Fashion** A piece of fabric used for a scarf has a repeating pattern of trapezoids. To create the pattern, translate the trapezoid with vertices (−1, 3), (3, 3), (4, 1), (−2, 1) along the vector ⟨0, −2⟩. Repeat to generate a pattern. What are the vertices of the third trapezoid in the pattern? *(Lesson 12-2)*
3. **Computers** A screen saver moves an icon around a screen. The icon starts at (20, 0), and then it is rotated about the origin by 50°. Give the icon's next position. Round each coordinate to the nearest tenth. *(Lesson 12-3)*
4. **Recreation** A hole at a miniature golf course has a barrier between the tee T and the hole H. Copy the figure and draw a diagram that shows how to make a hole in one. *(Lesson 12-3)* **See p. A38.**

5. **Sports** A team's Web site shows a baseball moving across the screen. The ball is reflected over line ℓ and is then reflected over line m. Describe a single transformation that moves the ball from its starting point to its final position. *(Lesson 12-4)* **a 90° rotation**

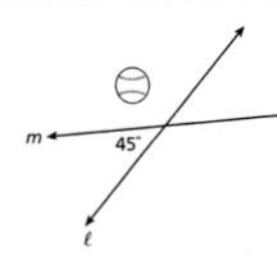

Agriculture Use the following information for Exercises 6–8.

Cattle ranchers brand their cattle to show ownership. Three different brands are shown. *(Lesson 12-5)*

6. Which brands have rotational symmetry? **Bar O Bar**
7. Which brands have line symmetry? **Double A, Bar O Bar**
8. Which capital letters could be used to create a brand with rotational symmetry? **H, I, N, O, S, X, Z**

Interior Design Use the following information for Exercises 9–11.

Three kitchen backsplash tile patterns are shown. Identify the symmetry in each pattern. *(Lesson 12-6)*

9. 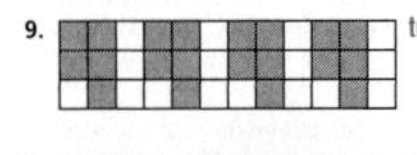 **translation**
10. **translation and glide reflection**
11. 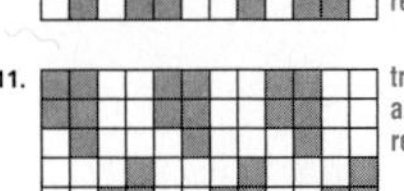 **translation and glide reflection**

12. **Hobbies** Reid has a baseball card that is 2.5-by-3.5 inches. He wants to enlarge it to poster size using a scale factor of 8. What size poster frame should he buy? *(Lesson 12-7)*
13. **Hobbies** A 40 in. by 30 in. piece of art is being made into a 1 in. by $\frac{3}{4}$ in. postage stamp. What scale factor should be used to reduce the art? *(Lesson 12-7)* **$\frac{1}{40}$**

2. (−1, −1), (3, −1), (4, −3), (−2, −3)
3. (12.9, 15.3)
12. 20 in. by 28 in.

Problem-Solving Handbook

Problem-Solving Handbook

Draw a Diagram

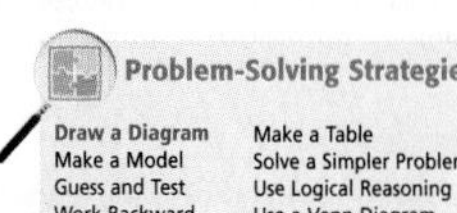

Problem-Solving Strategies

Draw a Diagram	Make a Table
Make a Model	Solve a Simpler Problem
Guess and Test	Use Logical Reasoning
Work Backward	Use a Venn Diagram
Find a Pattern	Make an Organized List

When a problem involves objects, distances, or places, drawing a diagram can make the problem clearer. You can draw a diagram to help understand and solve the problem.

EXAMPLE

During a team-building activity, five people stand in a circle. Pieces of ribbon will be used to connect each person to each of the other four people in the circle. How many pieces of ribbon are needed to connect all five people in this way?

1 Understand the Problem

List the important information.

- There are five people standing in a circle.
- Each person should be connected to each of the other four people with a piece of ribbon.

The answer is the number of pieces of ribbon needed to connect all five people.

2 Make a Plan

Draw a diagram to represent the information in the problem.

3 Solve

Draw a circle. Add five points to the circle to represent the five people in the problem. Then draw segments to connect each point to each of the other four points.

Count the number of segments in the final diagram. The total number of segments is the answer to the problem. It takes 10 pieces of ribbon to connect each person to each of the other four people.

4 Look Back

Check that the diagram is drawn correctly and that you counted the number of line segments accurately.

PRACTICE

1. A delivery truck driver travels 15 miles south to deliver his first package. He then goes 9 miles east and 6 miles north to deliver his next package. From there, the driver travels 12 miles east to make his last delivery. How far is the driver from his starting point? Round to the nearest tenth of a mile. 22.8 mi

Make a Model

Problem-Solving Strategies

Draw a Diagram	Make a Table
Make a Model	Solve a Simpler Problem
Guess and Test	Use Logical Reasoning
Work Backward	Use a Venn Diagram
Find a Pattern	Make an Organized List

When a problem involves manipulating objects, you can use those or similar objects to make a model. This can help you to understand the problem and find the solution.

EXAMPLE

During a geometry class, Zach cuts out a parallelogram with base 12 cm and height 6 cm. Catherine cuts out a rectangle with the same base and height. Show that the two shapes have the same area.

1 Understand the Problem

List the important information.

- There are two geometric shapes, a parallelogram and a rectangle.
- The base and the height of the two shapes are the same.

To solve the problem, you need to show that the areas of the two shapes are equal.

2 Make a Plan

You can make a model of the figures by cutting them out of paper or cardboard. Then compare the areas by placing one on top of the other.

3 Solve

If the shaded area of the parallelogram is cut and moved to the opposite side, the figure becomes a rectangle.

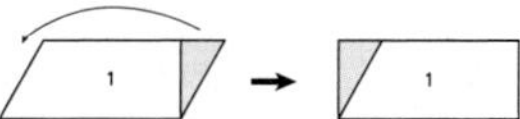

Place the two shapes on top of each other to compare the area.

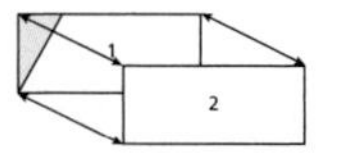

The shapes have the same base and height, so these shapes have the same area.

4 Look Back

Check that your models have the correct dimensions. Use the formulas for the area of a rectangle and a parallelogram to confirm that the shapes have the same area.

PRACTICE

1. Find the dimensions of a rectangular prism made up of 16 1-inch cubes. Possible answer: 2 in. × 2 in. × 4 in.
2. Two triangles are formed by cutting a rectangle along its diagonal. What possible shapes can be formed by arranging these triangles? isosceles triangle, rectangle, kite, or parallelogram

Guess and Test

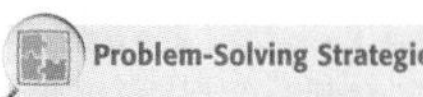

Problem-Solving Strategies

Draw a Diagram	Make a Table
Make a Model	Solve a Simpler Problem
Guess and Test	Use Logical Reasoning
Work Backward	Use a Venn Diagram
Find a Pattern	Make an Organized List

For complex problems, you can use clues to make guesses and narrow your choices for the solution. Test whether your guess solves the problem, and then continue guessing until you find the solution.

EXAMPLE

Edgar is designing a party invitation in the shape of a right triangle. If all three side measures are to be whole numbers of inches, what is the smallest possible perimeter for the birthday card?

1 Understand the Problem

List the important information.

- The invitation is to be a right triangle.
- The legs and hypotenuse must be whole numbers.

To solve the problem, you need to find the smallest possible perimeter for the right triangle.

2 Make a Plan

You can guess and test, starting with the smallest possible whole numbers.

3 Solve

Let a and b be the legs of the right triangle, and let c be the hypotenuse. So the relationship $a^2 + b^2 = c^2$ must hold. Start by using $(1, 1)$ for (a, b) and solve for c^2. Since c must be a whole number, continue to guess and test until c^2 is a perfect square.

Guess	Test
(1, 1)	$1^2 + 1^2 = 2$ ✗
(1, 2)	$1^2 + 2^2 = 5$ ✗
(1, 3)	$1^2 + 3^2 = 10$ ✗
(1, 4)	$1^2 + 4^2 = 17$ ✗
(1, 5)	$1^2 + 5^2 = 26$ ✗

Guess	Test
(2, 2)	$2^2 + 2^2 = 8$ ✗
(2, 3)	$2^2 + 3^2 = 13$ ✗
(2, 4)	$2^2 + 4^2 = 20$ ✗
(2, 5)	$2^2 + 5^2 = 29$ ✗

Guess	Test
(3, 3)	$3^2 + 3^2 = 18$ ✗
(3, 4)	$3^2 + 4^2 = 25$ ✓

Based on the tables, 5 is the smallest possible whole number for c, 3 for a, and 4 for b. So the smallest possible perimeter for the card is 3 in. + 4 in. + 5 in. = 12 in.

4 Look Back

Since $3^2 + 4^2 = 5^2$, these are reasonable dimensions for the card. The problem asks for the perimeter, which is 12 inches.

PRACTICE

1. The sum of Cary's age and his brother's age is 34. The difference between their ages is 4. How old are Cary and his brother? 15 and 19
2. Adult tickets for a theater performance cost \$8 and children's tickets cost \$3. A group with twice as many adults as children attends the performance and spends \$133 on tickets. How many people are in the group? 21

Work Backward

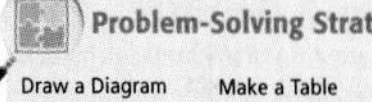

Problem-Solving Strategies

Draw a Diagram	Make a Table
Make a Model	Solve a Simpler Problem
Guess and Test	Use Logical Reasoning
Work Backward	Use a Venn Diagram
Find a Pattern	Make an Organized List

Some problems involve a series of events, giving you information about the last event, and then ask you to solve something related to the initial situation. You can work backward to solve these problems.

EXAMPLE

Sandy is creating a pattern made from isosceles right triangles as shown below. If the hypotenuse of the fifth triangle is 4 in., what are the dimensions of the smallest triangle?

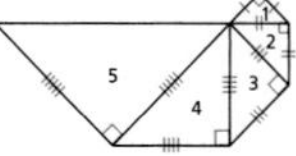

1 Understand the Problem

List the important information.

- Each triangle is an isosceles right triangle, so each triangle's legs are congruent.
- The hypotenuse of one triangle is equal to the leg length of the next triangle.
- The fifth triangle's hypotenuse is 4 in.

You must work backward to find the dimensions of the first triangle.

2 Make a Plan

Let h be the hypotenuse and s be the leg length of each triangle. Start with a hypotenuse length of 4 and work backward using the Pythagorean Theorem, which states that $h^2 = s^2 + s^2 = 2s^2$.

3 Solve

Triangle 5: $h = 4$; $s = \sqrt{8}$ — *$4^2 = 2s^2$, so $s = \sqrt{8}$*

Triangle 4: $h = \sqrt{8}$; $s = 2$ — *The hypotenuse of Triangle 4 equals the leg length of Triangle 5. $(\sqrt{8})^2 = 2s^2$, so $s = 2$.*

Triangle 3: $h = 2$; $s = \sqrt{2}$ — *$2^2 = 2s^2$, so $s = \sqrt{2}$.*

Triangle 2: $h = \sqrt{2}$; $s = 1$ — *$(\sqrt{2})^2 = 2s^2$, so $s = 1$.*

Triangle 1: $h = 1$; $s = \sqrt{0.5}$ — *$1^2 = 2s^2$, so $s = \sqrt{0.5}$.*

The first triangle should have a leg length of $\sqrt{0.5}$ and a hypotenuse of 1.

4 Look Back

Recreate the diagram starting with the dimensions you found for the first triangle, and confirm that the fifth triangle has a hypotenuse of 4 inches.

PRACTICE

1. In a trivia game, each question is worth twice as many points as the one before it. Chelsea answers 5 questions and earns 1550 points. How many points was her first question worth? 50 points
2. Sheryl has 4 siblings. She is 4 years younger than her sister Meagan. Meagan is twice as old as Tina. Jack is 3 years older than Tina, and Tina is 1 year older than Bryan, who is 9. How old is Sheryl? 16

Find a Pattern

In some problems, there is a relationship between different pieces of information. You can find a pattern to help solve these problems.

Problem-Solving Strategies

Draw a Diagram	Make a Table
Make a Model	Solve a Simpler Problem
Guess and Test	Use Logical Reasoning
Work Backward	Use a Venn Diagram
Find a Pattern	Make an Organized List

EXAMPLE

Frank plants turnips in rows and columns. Each year, he increases the size of his turnip patch by adding one row and one column, as shown in the diagram. How many turnip plants will Frank have after year 5?

Year 1 Year 2 Year 3

1 Understand the Problem

List the important information.

- In year 1, Frank has 3 turnip plants.
- In year 2, he has 8 turnip plants.
- In year 3, he has 15 turnip plants.

The answer will be the number of turnip plants in year 5.

2 Make a Plan

Find the pattern based on the diagram.

3 Solve

Make a table of the given information and find a pattern.

	Number of Turnip Plants	Possible Pattern
Year 1	3	0 + 3
Year 2	8	3 + 5
Year 3	15	8 + 7

The pattern seems to be the number of turnip plants in the previous year plus the next odd number. So in year 4, Frank will have $15 + 9 = 24$ turnip plants, and in year 5, he will have $24 + 11 = 35$ turnip plants.

4 Look Back

By thinking of the number of plants as the product of the number of rows and columns, you might notice another pattern, $n(n + 2)$, where n is the year number. Use this to confirm your answer.

Year 4: $4(4 + 2) = 24$ turnip plants

Year 5: $5(5 + 2) = 35$ turnip plants

PRACTICE

1. Use the key GDB = DAY to decode the sentence DQ DSSOH D GDB NHHSV WKH GRFWRU DZDB. **An apple a day keeps the doctor away.**
2. Describe the pattern 15, 22, 29, 36, 43, ... and find the next two numbers. **Add seven to each term; 50; 57**

Make a Table

To solve a problem that involves a relationship between two sets of numbers, you can make a table to organize and analyze the data.

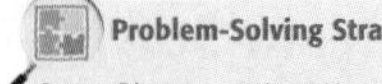

Draw a Diagram	**Make a Table**
Make a Model	Solve a Simpler Problem
Guess and Test	Use Logical Reasoning
Work Backward	Use a Venn Diagram
Find a Pattern	Make an Organized List

EXAMPLE

Roy's Geometry class is playing a game to practice identifying shapes. There are eight shapes in the game: an acute triangle, a right triangle, a square, a rectangle, a rhombus, a parallelogram, a kite, and an isosceles trapezoid. On Roy's turn, the teacher reads the following clues: The shape is a quadrilateral with four right angles in which all sides are not congruent. Which shape should Roy select?

1 Understand the Problem

List the important information.

- The possible shapes are an acute triangle, a right triangle, a square, a rectangle, a rhombus, a parallelogram, a kite, and an isosceles trapezoid.
- Roy's shape is a quadrilateral with four right angles.
- Roy's shape does not have four congruent sides.

The answer will be the shape that matches Roy's clues.

2 Make a Plan

Make a table and use the given information to identify Roy's shape.

3 Solve

Use the given clues to complete a table and identify Roy's shape.

Shape	Quadrilateral?	4 Right Angles?	Sides Not Congruent?
Acute triangle	N	N	N
Right triangle	N	N	N
Square	Y	Y	N
Rectangle	Y	Y	Y
Rhombus	Y	N	N
Parallelogram	Y	N	N
Kite	Y	N	Y
Isosceles trapezoid	Y	N	Y

The rectangle is the only shape that satisfies the given clues.

4 Look Back

Make sure that your answer satisfies the given clues.

PRACTICE

1. Katie gets the following clues: The shape has at least one right angle, has no parallel sides, and is not the kite. Which shape should Katie select? **right triangle**
2. Mary gets the following clues: The shape has no congruent sides. How many possible shapes might Mary select? **2 (acute triangle or right triangle)**

Solve a Simpler Problem

A problem with many steps or involving very large numbers can be overwhelming. Sometimes it helps to solve a simpler problem first, or to break the complex problem into multiple simpler ones.

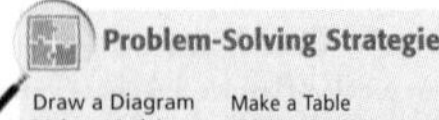

Draw a Diagram	Make a Table
Make a Model	**Solve a Simpler Problem**
Guess and Test	Use Logical Reasoning
Work Backward	Use a Venn Diagram
Find a Pattern	Make an Organized List

EXAMPLE

Tom plans to repaint his patio, which has the measurements shown below. What is the total area that Tom needs to paint?

1 Understand the Problem

List the important information.

- $AH = FG = 4$ ft
- $DE = 3$ ft
- $CD = 20$ ft
- $GH = EF = 5$ ft

The answer will be the total area of the patio.

2 Make a Plan

To simplify the problem, divide the patio into basic geometric shapes and add their areas together.

3 Solve

Find the area of the patio as if it were a complete rectangle, and then subtract the area of the smaller rectangle that is not part of the patio.

Step 1: Find the area of each rectangle.

	Larger rectangle	Smaller rectangle
Length	$CD = 20$ ft	$GH = 5$ ft
Width	$AH + FG + DE = 11$ ft	$FG = 4$ ft
Area	$\ell w = (20)(11) = 220$ ft^2	$\ell w = (5)(4) = 20$ ft^2

Step 2: Subtract the areas to find the area of the patio.

Area of patio $= 220 - 20 = 200$ ft^2

Tom needs to paint 200 square feet.

4 Look Back

Divide the patio into a different arrangement of smaller shapes to check your answer. For example, by dividing the patio into three rectangles stacked on top of each other, you find that $(4)(20) + (4)(15) + (3)(20) = 200$ ft^2, which confirms the first answer.

PRACTICE

1. How much paint does Rose need to repaint her patio? **335 ft^2**
2. Rose plans to add a decorative railing around the outer edges of her patio. The railing will cover every edge except the 30-foot side of the patio that joins her house. About how many feet of railing does Rose need? Round to the nearest foot. **56 ft**

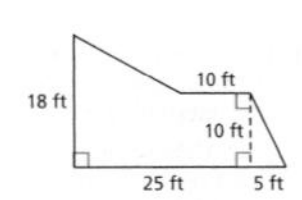

Use Logical Reasoning

Some problems provide clues and facts that you must use to find the solution. To use logical reasoning, identify these facts and draw conclusions from them.

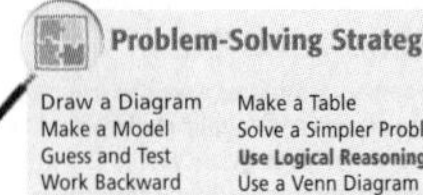

Draw a Diagram	Make a Table
Make a Model	Solve a Simpler Problem
Guess and Test	**Use Logical Reasoning**
Work Backward	Use a Venn Diagram
Find a Pattern	Make an Organized List

EXAMPLE

Dawn, Chloe, and Tyra finish first through third in a cross-country race. The girls wear the numbers 7, 8, and 12. Dawn does not wear an even number. The one who wears number 8 comes in first. Chloe comes in third. Who wears which number, and in what place did each runner finish?

1 Understand the Problem

List the important information.

- Dawn wears an odd number.
- The girl who wears number 8 comes in first place.
- Chloe comes in third place.

The answer will be a list of who wears which number and each girl's finishing position.

2 Make a Plan

Start with the clues given in the problem. Use logical reasoning to determine each girl's number and finishing position.

3 Solve

Make a table. Read the clues one at a time, and mark the table appropriately.

- **Dawn wears an odd number, so she must wear number 7. No other girl can wear number 7.**
- **The girl who wears number 8 comes in first place. No other number is the first-place winner. Also, since Dawn wears number 7, she didn't come in first.**
- **Chloe comes in third. By process of elimination, Dawn must have come in second, and Tyra came in first. So Tyra wears number 8, and thus Chloe wears number 12.**

	7	8	12	1st	2nd	3rd
Dawn	✓	✗	✗	✗	✓	✗
Chloe	✗	✗	✓	✗	✗	✓
Tyra	✗	✓	✗	✓	✗	✗
1st	✗	✓	✗			
2nd	✓	✗	✗			
3rd	✗	✗	✓			

4 Look Back

Compare your answer to the facts given in the problem. Make sure none of your conclusions conflict with the given clues.

PRACTICE

1. Mike, Jack, and Ann each wear a different type of top in three different colors. The tops are a button-down shirt, a pullover, and a sweater. The colors are blue, yellow, and red. Mike wears a blue shirt, and Jack wears a button-down. The yellow top is a pullover. Who wears the sweater and who wears the red top? **Mike; Jack**
2. The Warriors, Jaguars, and Cougars each have a different-colored shape on their team shirt. The colors are green, purple, and red, and the shapes are a triangle, a rectangle, and a hexagon. The Warriors' shape has the most sides, the color of the Jaguars' shape is green, and the rectangle is purple. Which team has which shape and in which color? **Warriors: red hexagon; Jaguars: green triangle; Cougars: purple rectangle**

Use a Venn Diagram

A Venn diagram can be useful when you solve a problem involving relationships among sets or groups.

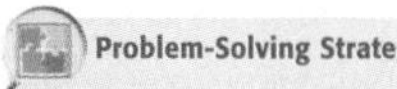

Draw a Diagram
Make a Model
Guess and Test
Work Backward
Find a Pattern
Make a Table
Solve a Simpler Problem
Use Logical Reasoning
Use a Venn Diagram
Make an Organized List

EXAMPLE

In a class of 15 students, ten play on at least one of the school sports teams—the basketball team or the baseball team. Five of them are on the basketball team. Three students are on both the basketball team and the baseball team. How many of the students play on the baseball team?

1 Understand the Problem

List the important information.

- 5 students play on the basketball team.
- 3 students play on both teams.

The answer is the number of students who play on the baseball team.

2 Make a Plan

Organize the information by drawing a Venn diagram.

3 Solve

Draw and label the Venn diagram.

- 3 people will be in the overlapping area.
- Since 5 people play on the basketball team, and 3 of them are also on the baseball team, only 2 people play on only the basketball team.

There are 10 student players in all, and five are already accounted for. Therefore, the remaining five play only baseball.

Adding the three students who also play basketball, a total of eight students in the class play on the baseball team.

Student Players in Class

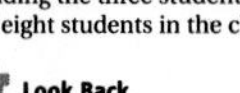

4 Look Back

Check your Venn diagram to make sure it is an accurate representation of the information given in the problem. Confirm that the numbers in each of the labeled sections add up to the total number of students in the problem.

PRACTICE

1. At Lucy's Home-Style Restaurant, four of the meals include a side salad, six include only soup as a side, and two meals come with both salad and soup as sides. If all meals come with at least one side, how many different meals are on Lucy's menu? 10
2. A cupboard contains 12 cups, and each cup has a lid, a handle, or both. There are seven cups with handles, and three cups with both a lid and a handle. How many cups have only a lid? 5

Make an Organized List

If a problem involves multiple outcomes, it may be useful to make an organized list to record the data and count the different outcomes.

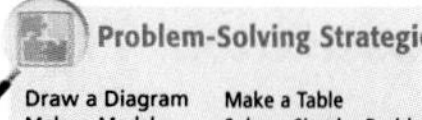

Draw a Diagram
Make a Model
Guess and Test
Work Backward
Find a Pattern
Make a Table
Solve a Simpler Problem
Use Logical Reasoning
Use a Venn Diagram
Make an Organized List

EXAMPLE

Sally randomly selects two shapes from a bag that contains five different cut-outs: a triangle, a square, a rectangle, a pentagon, and a hexagon. The sum of the number of sides of the two shapes is eight. What combinations of shapes might Sally have selected?

1 Understand the Problem

List the important information.

- The possible shapes are a triangle, a square, a rectangle, a pentagon, and a hexagon.
- The sum of the number of the sides is 9.

The answer will be the two shapes Sally selected.

2 Make a Plan

Make an organized list of the possible combinations of shapes. Then list the number of sides and the sum of the sides.

3 Solve

List the possible combinations of shapes, and find the sum of the shapes' sides.

Triangle (3)	x	x	x	x						
Square (4)	x				x	x	x			
Rectangle (4)		x			x			x	x	
Pentagon (5)			x			x		x		x
Hexagon (6)				x			x		x	x
Total number of sides	7	7	8	9	8	9	10	9	10	11

There are two combinations of shapes that have a total number of eight sides: the triangle and pentagon and the square and rectangle.

4 Look Back

Make sure all possible combinations are shown in the table. Check that the total number of sides for both combinations (triangle and pentagon, and square and rectangle) is 8.

PRACTICE

1. How many ways can you make $0.30 by using quarters, dimes, nickels, and pennies? 18 ways
2. Pete's Pizza Palace has 5 choices of meat, 4 choices of vegetables, and 2 choices of cheese. You want to order a pizza with one of each. How many combinations can you order? 40 combinations

Postulates, Theorems, and Corollaries

Chapter 1

Post. 1-1-1 Through any two points there is exactly one line. (p. 7)

Post. 1-1-2 Through any three noncollinear points there is exactly one plane containing them. (p. 7)

Post. 1-1-3 If two points lie in a plane, then the line containing those points lies in the plane. (p. 7)

Thm. 1-1-4 If two lines intersect, then they intersect in exactly one point. (p. 8)

Post. 1-1-5 If two planes intersect, then they intersect in exactly one line. (p. 8)

Post. 1-2-1 Ruler Postulate The points on a line can be put into a one-to-one correspondence with the real numbers. (Ruler Post.; p. 13)

Post. 1-2-2 Segment Addition Postulate If B is between A and C, then $AB + BC = AC$. (Seg. Add. Post.; p. 14)

Post. 1-3-1 Protractor Postulate Given $\overleftrightarrow{AB}$ and a point O on $\overleftrightarrow{AB}$, all rays that can be drawn from O can be put into a one-to-one correspondence with the real numbers from 0 to 180. (Protractor Post.; p. 20)

Post. 1-3-2 Angle Addition Postulate If S is in the interior of $\angle PQR$, then $m\angle PQS + m\angle SQR = m\angle PQR$. ($\angle$ Add. Post.; p. 22)

Thm. 1-6-1 Pythagorean Theorem In a right triangle, the sum of the squares of the lengths of the legs is equal to the square of the length of the hypotenuse. (Pyth. Thm.; p. 45)

Chapter 2

Thm. 2-6-1 Linear Pair Theorem If two angles form a linear pair, then they are supplementary. (Lin. Pair Thm.; p. 110)

Thm. 2-6-2 Congruent Supplements Theorem If two angles are supplementary to the same angle (or to two congruent angles), then the two angles are congruent. ($\cong$ Supps. Thm.; p. 111)

Thm. 2-6-3 Right Angle Congruence Theorem All right angles are congruent. (Rt. $\angle \cong$ Thm.; p. 112)

Thm. 2-6-4 Congruent Complements Theorem If two angles are complementary to the same angle (or to two congruent angles), then the two angles are congruent. ($\cong$ Comps. Thm.; p. 112)

Thm. 2-7-1 Common Segments Theorem Given collinear points A, B, C, and D arranged as shown, if $\overline{AB} \cong \overline{CD}$, then $\overline{AC} \cong \overline{BD}$. (Common Segs. Thm.; p. 118)

A B C D

Thm. 2-7-2 Vertical Angles Theorem Vertical angles are congruent. (Vert. $\angle$s Thm.; p. 120)

Thm. 2-7-3 If two congruent angles are supplementary, then each angle is a right angle. ($\cong$ $\angle$s supp. $\rightarrow$ rt. $\angle$s; p. 120)

Chapter 3

Post. 3-2-1 Corresponding Angles Postulate If two parallel lines are cut by a transversal, then the pairs of corresponding angles are congruent. (Corr. $\angle$s Post.; p. 155)

Thm. 3-2-2 Alternate Interior Angles Theorem If two parallel lines are cut by a transversal, then the pairs of alternate interior angles are congruent. (Alt. Int. $\angle$s Thm.; p. 156)

Thm. 3-2-3 Alternate Exterior Angles Theorem If two parallel lines are cut by a transversal, then the two pairs of alternate exterior angles are congruent. (Alt. Ext. $\angle$s Thm.; p. 156)

Thm. 3-2-4 Same-Side Interior Angles Theorem If two parallel lines are cut by a transversal, then the two pairs of same-side interior angles are supplementary. (Same-Side Int. $\angle$s Thm.; p. 156)

Post. 3-3-1 Converse of the Corresponding Angles Postulate If two coplanar lines are cut by a transversal so that a pair of corresponding angles are congruent, then the two lines are parallel. (Conv. of Corr. $\angle$s Post.; p. 162)

Post. 3-3-2 Parallel Postulate Through a point P not on line ℓ, there is exactly one line parallel to ℓ. (Parallel Post.; p. 163)

Thm. 3-3-3 Converse of the Alternate Interior Angles Theorem If two coplanar lines are cut by a transversal so that a pair of alternate interior angles are congruent, then the two lines are parallel. (Conv. of Alt. Int. $\angle$s Thm.; p. 163)

Thm. 3-3-4 Converse of the Alternate Exterior Angles Theorem If two coplanar lines are cut by a transversal so that a pair of alternate exterior angles are congruent, then the two lines are parallel. (Conv. of Alt. Ext. $\angle$s Thm.; p. 163)

Thm. 3-3-5 Converse of the Same-Side Interior Angles Theorem If two coplanar lines are cut by a transversal so that a pair of same-side interior angles are supplementary, then the two lines are parallel. (Conv. of Same-Side Int. $\angle$s Thm.; p. 163)

Thm. 3-4-1 If two intersecting lines form a linear pair of congruent angles, then the lines are perpendicular. (2 intersecting lines form lin. pair of $\cong$ $\angle$s $\rightarrow$ lines $\perp$; p. 173)

Thm. 3-4-2 Perpendicular Transversal Theorem In a plane, if a transversal is perpendicular to one of two parallel lines, then it is perpendicular to the other line. ($\perp$ Transv. Thm.; p. 173)

Thm. 3-4-3 If two coplanar lines are perpendicular to the same line, then the two lines are parallel to each other. (2 lines $\perp$ to same line $\rightarrow$ 2 lines $\parallel$; p. 173)

Thm. 3-5-1 Parallel Lines Theorem In a coordinate plane, two nonvertical lines are parallel if and only if they have the same slope. Any two vertical lines are parallel. ($\parallel$ Lines Thm.; p. 184)

Thm. 3-5-2 Perpendicular Lines Theorem In a coordinate plane, two nonvertical lines are perpendicular if and only if the product of their slopes is -1. Vertical and horizontal lines are perpendicular. ($\perp$ Lines Thm.; p. 184)

Chapter 4

Thm. 4-2-1 Triangle Sum Theorem The sum of the angle measures of a triangle is 180°. ($\triangle$ Sum Thm.; p. 223)

Cor. 4-2-2 The acute angles of a right triangle are complementary. (Acute $\angle$s of rt. $\triangle$ are comp.; p. 224)

Cor. 4-2-3 The measure of each angle of an equiangular triangle is 60°. (p. 224)

Thm. 4-2-4 Exterior Angle Theorem The measure of an exterior angle of a triangle is equal to the sum of the measures of its remote interior angles. (Ext. $\angle$ Thm.; p. 225)

Thm. 4-2-5 Third Angles Theorem If two angles of one triangle are congruent to two angles of another triangle, then the third pair of angles are congruent. (Third $\angle$s Thm.; p. 226)

Post. 4-4-1 Side-Side-Side (SSS) Congruence Postulate If three sides of one triangle are congruent to three sides of another triangle, then the triangles are congruent. (SSS; p. 242)

Post. 4-4-2 Side-Angle-Side (SAS) Congruence Postulate If two sides and the included angle of one triangle are congruent to two sides and the included angle of another triangle, then the triangles are congruent. (SAS; p. 243)

Post. 4-5-1 Angle-Side-Angle (ASA) Congruence Postulate If two angles and the included side of one triangle are congruent to two angles and the included side of another triangle, then the triangles are congruent. (ASA; p. 252)

Thm. 4-5-2 Angle-Angle-Side (AAS) Congruence Theorem If two angles and a nonincluded side of one triangle are congruent to the corresponding angles and nonincluded side of another triangle, then the triangles are congruent. (AAS; p. 254)

Thm. 4-5-3 Hypotenuse-Leg (HL) Congruence Theorem If the hypotenuse and a leg of a right triangle are congruent to the hypotenuse and a leg of another right triangle, then the triangles are congruent. (HL; p. 255)

Thm. 4-8-1 Isosceles Triangle Theorem If two sides of a triangle are congruent, then the angles opposite the sides are congruent. (Isosc. $\triangle$ Thm.; p. 273)

Thm. 4-8-2 Converse of the Isosceles Triangle Theorem If two angles of a triangle are congruent, then the sides opposite those angles are congruent. (Conv. of Isosc. $\triangle$ Thm.; p. 273)

Cor. 4-8-3 If a triangle is equilateral, then it is equiangular. (equilateral $\triangle \rightarrow$ equiangular; p. 274)

Cor. 4-8-4 If a triangle is equiangular, then it is equilateral. (equiangular $\triangle \rightarrow$ equilateral; p. 275)

Chapter 5

Thm. 5-1-1 Perpendicular Bisector Theorem If a point is on the perpendicular bisector of a segment, then it is equidistant from the endpoints of the segment. ($\perp$ Bisector Thm.; p. 300)

Thm. 5-1-2 Converse of the Perpendicular Bisector Theorem If a point is equidistant from the endpoints of a segment, then it is on the perpendicular bisector of the segment. (Conv. of $\perp$ Bisector Thm.; p. 300)

Thm. 5-1-3 Angle Bisector Theorem If a point is on the bisector of an angle, then it is equidistant from the sides of the angle. ($\angle$ Bisector Thm.; p. 301)

Thm. 5-1-4 Converse of the Angle Bisector Theorem If a point in the interior of an angle is equidistant from the sides of the angle, then it is on the bisector of the angle. (Conv. of $\angle$ Bisector Thm.; p. 301)

Thm. 5-2-1 Circumcenter Theorem The circumcenter of a triangle is equidistant from the vertices of the triangle. (Circumcenter Thm.; p. 307)

Thm. 5-2-2 Incenter Theorem The incenter of a triangle is equidistant from the sides of the triangle. (Incenter Thm.; p. 309)

Thm. 5-3-1 Centroid Theorem The centroid of a triangle is located $\frac{2}{3}$ of the distance from each vertex to the midpoint of the opposite side. (Centroid Thm.; p. 314)

Thm. 5-4-1 Triangle Midsegment Theorem A midsegment of a triangle is parallel to a side of a triangle, and its length is half the length of that side. ($\triangle$ Midsegment Thm.; p. 323)

Thm. 5-5-1 If two sides of a triangle are not congruent, then the larger angle is opposite the longer side. (In $\triangle$, larger $\angle$ is opp. longer side; p. 333)

Thm. 5-5-2 If two angles of a triangle are not congruent, then the longer side is opposite the larger angle. (In $\triangle$, longer side is opp. larger $\angle$; p. 333)

Thm. 5-5-3 Triangle Inequality Theorem The sum of any two side lengths of a triangle is greater than the third side length. ($\triangle$ Inequal. Thm.; p. 334)

Thm. 5-6-1 Hinge Theorem If two sides of one triangle are congruent to two sides of another triangle and the included angles are not congruent, then the longer third side is across from the larger included angle. (Hinge Thm.; p. 340)

Thm. 5-6-2 Converse of the Hinge Theorem If two sides of one triangle are congruent to two sides of another triangle and the third sides are not congruent, then the larger included angle is across from the longer third side. (Conv. of Hinge Thm.; p. 340)

Thm. 5-7-1 Converse of the Pythagorean Theorem If the sum of the squares of the lengths of two sides of a triangle is equal to the square of the length of the third side, then the triangle is a right triangle. (Conv. of Pyth. Thm.; p. 350)

Thm. 5-7-2 Pythagorean Inequalities Theorem In $\triangle ABC$, c is the length of the longest side. If $c^2 > a^2 + b^2$, then $\triangle ABC$ is an obtuse triangle. If $c^2 < a^2 + b^2$, then $\triangle ABC$ is an acute triangle. (Pyth. Inequal. Thm.; p. 351)

Thm. 5-8-1 45°-45°-90° Triangle Theorem In a 45°-45°-90° triangle, both legs are congruent, and the length of the hypotenuse is the length of a leg times $\sqrt{2}$. (45°-45°-90° $\triangle$ Thm.; p. 356)

Thm. 5-8-2 30°-60°-90° Triangle Theorem In a 30°-60°-90° triangle, the length of the hypotenuse is 2 times the length of the shorter leg, and the length of the longer leg is the length of the shorter leg times $\sqrt{3}$. (30°-60°-90° $\triangle$ Thm.; p. 358)

Chapter 6

Thm. 6-1-1 Polygon Angle Sum Theorem The sum of the interior angle measures of a convex polygon with n sides is $(n - 2)180°$. (Polygon $\angle$ Sum Thm.; p. 383)

Thm. 6-1-2 Polygon Exterior Angle Sum Theorem The sum of the exterior angle measures, one angle at each vertex, of a convex polygon is 360°. (Polygon Ext. $\angle$ Sum Thm.; p. 384)

Thm. 6-2-1 If a quadrilateral is a parallelogram, then its opposite sides are congruent. ($\square \rightarrow$ opp. sides $\cong$; p. 391)

Thm. 6-2-2 If a quadrilateral is a parallelogram, then its opposite angles are congruent. ($\square \rightarrow$ opp. $\angle$s $\cong$; p. 392)

Thm. 6-2-3 If a quadrilateral is a parallelogram, then its consecutive angles are supplementary. ($\square \rightarrow$ cons. $\angle$s supp.; p. 392)

Thm. 6-2-4 If a quadrilateral is a parallelogram, then its diagonals bisect each other. ($\square \rightarrow$ diags. bisect each other; p. 392)

Thm. 6-3-1 If one pair of opposite sides of a quadrilateral are parallel and congruent, then the quadrilateral is a parallelogram. (quad. with pair of opp. sides $\parallel$ and $\cong \rightarrow \square$; p. 398)

Thm. 6-3-2 If both pairs of opposite sides of a quadrilateral are congruent, then the quadrilateral is a parallelogram. (quad. with opp. sides $\cong \rightarrow \square$; p. 398)

Thm. 6-3-3 If both pairs of opposite angles of a quadrilateral are congruent, then the quadrilateral is a parallelogram. (quad. with opp. $\angle$s $\cong \rightarrow \square$; p. 398)

Thm. 6-3-4 If an angle of a quadrilateral is supplementary to both of its consecutive angles, then the quadrilateral is a parallelogram. (quad. with $\angle$ supp. to cons. $\angle$s $\rightarrow \square$; p. 399)

Thm. 6-3-5 If the diagonals of a quadrilateral bisect each other, then the quadrilateral is a parallelogram. (quad. with diags. bisecting each other $\rightarrow \square$; p. 399)

Thm. 6-4-1 If a quadrilateral is a rectangle, then it is a parallelogram. (rect. $\rightarrow \square$; p. 408)

Thm. 6-4-2 If a parallelogram is a rectangle, then its diagonals are congruent. (rect. $\rightarrow$ diags. $\cong$; p. 408)

Thm. 6-4-3 If a quadrilateral is a rhombus, then it is a parallelogram. (rhombus $\rightarrow \square$; p. 409)

Thm. 6-4-4 If a parallelogram is a rhombus, then its diagonals are perpendicular. (rhombus $\rightarrow$ diags. $\perp$; p. 409)

Thm. 6-4-5 If a parallelogram is a rhombus, then each diagonal bisects a pair of opposite angles. (rhombus $\rightarrow$ each diag. bisects opp. $\angle$s; p. 409)

Thm. 6-5-1 If one angle of a parallelogram is a right angle, then the parallelogram is a rectangle. ($\square$ with one rt. $\angle \rightarrow$ rect.; p. 418)

Thm. 6-5-2 If the diagonals of a parallelogram are congruent, then the parallelogram is a rectangle. ($\square$ with diags. $\cong \rightarrow$ rect.; p. 418)

Thm. 6-5-3 If one pair of consecutive sides of a parallelogram are congruent, then the parallelogram is a rhombus. ($\square$ with one pair cons. sides $\cong \rightarrow$ rhombus; p. 419)

Thm. 6-5-4 If the diagonals of a parallelogram are perpendicular, then the parallelogram is a rhombus. ($\square$ with diags. $\perp \rightarrow$ rhombus; p. 419)

Thm. 6-5-5 If one diagonal of a parallelogram bisects a pair of opposite angles, then the parallelogram is a rhombus. ($\square$ with diags. bisecting opp. $\angle$s $\rightarrow$ rhombus; p. 419)

Thm. 6-6-1 If a quadrilateral is a kite, then its diagonals are perpendicular. (kite $\rightarrow$ diags. $\perp$; p. 427)

Thm. 6-6-2 If a quadrilateral is a kite, then exactly one pair of opposite angles are congruent. (kite $\rightarrow$ one pair opp. $\angle$s $\cong$; p. 427)

Thm. 6-6-3 If a quadrilateral is an isosceles trapezoid, then each pair of base angles are congruent. (isosc. trap. $\rightarrow$ base $\angle$s $\cong$; p. 429)

Thm. 6-6-4 If a trapezoid has one pair of congruent base angles, then the trapezoid is isosceles. (trap. with pair base $\angle$s $\cong \rightarrow$ isosc. trap.; p. 429)

Thm. 6-6-5 A trapezoid is isosceles if and only if its diagonals are congruent. (isosc. trap $\leftrightarrow$ diags. $\cong$; p. 429)

Thm. 6-6-6 Trapezoid Midsegment Theorem The midsegment of a trapezoid is parallel to each base, and its length is one half the sum of the lengths of the bases. (Trap. Midsegment Thm.; p. 431)

Chapter 7

Post. 7-3-1 Angle-Angle (AA) Similarity Postulate If two angles of one triangle are congruent to two angles of another triangle, then the triangles are similar. (AA ~ Post.; p. 470)

Thm. 7-3-2 Side-Side-Side (SSS) Similarity Theorem If the three sides of one triangle are proportional to the three corresponding sides of another triangle, then the triangles are similar. (SSS ~ Thm.; p. 470)

Thm. 7-3-3 Side-Angle-Side (SAS) Similarity Theorem If two sides of one triangle are proportional to two sides of another triangle and their included angles are congruent, then the triangles are similar. (SAS ~ Thm.; p. 471)

Thm. 7-4-1 Triangle Proportionality Theorem If a line parallel to a side of a triangle intersects the other two sides, then it divides those sides proportionally. ($\triangle$ Proportionality Thm.; p. 481)

Thm. 7-4-2 Converse of the Triangle Proportionality Theorem If a line divides two sides of a triangle proportionally, then it is parallel to the third side. (Conv. of $\triangle$ Proportionality Thm.; p. 482)

Cor. 7-4-3 Two-Transversal Proportionality Corollary If three or more parallel lines intersect two transversals, then they divide the transversals proportionally. (2-Transv. Proportionality Cor.; p. 482)

Thm. 7-4-4 Triangle Angle Bisector Theorem An angle bisector of a triangle divides the opposite side into two segments whose lengths are proportional to the lengths of the other two sides. ($\triangle$ $\angle$ Bisector Thm.; p. 483)

Thm. 7-5-1 Proportional Perimeters and Areas Theorem If the similarity ratio of two similar figures is $\frac{a}{b}$, then the ratio of their perimeters is $\frac{a}{b}$, and the ratio of their areas is $\frac{a^2}{b^2}$ or $\left(\frac{a}{b}\right)^2$. (p. 490)

Chapter 8

Thm. 8-1-1 The altitude to the hypotenuse of a right triangle forms two triangles that are similar to each other and to the original triangle. (p. 518)

Cor. 8-1-2 **Geometric Means Corollary** The length of the altitude to the hypotenuse of a right triangle is the geometric mean of the lengths of the two segments of the hypotenuse. (p. 519)

Cor. 8-1-3 **Geometric Means Corollary** The length of a leg of a right triangle is the geometric mean of the lengths of the hypotenuse and the segment of the hypotenuse adjacent to that leg. (p. 519)

Thm. 8-5-1 **The Law of Sines** For any $\triangle ABC$ with side lengths a, b, and c, $\frac{\sin A}{a} = \frac{\sin B}{b} = \frac{\sin C}{c}$. (p. 552)

Thm. 8-5-2 **The Law of Cosines** For any $\triangle ABC$ with sides a, b, and c, $a^2 = b^2 + c^2 - 2bc\cos A$, $b^2 = a^2 + c^2 - 2ac\cos B$, and $c^2 = a^2 + b^2 - 2ab\cos C$. (p. 553)

Chapter 9

Post. 9-1-1 **Area Addition Postulate** The area of a region is equal to the sum of the areas of its nonoverlapping parts. (Area Add. Post.; p. 589)

Chapter 11

Thm. 11-1-1 If a line is tangent to a circle, then it is perpendicular to the radius drawn to the point of tangency. (line tangent to ⊙ → line ⊥ to radius; p. 748)

Thm. 11-1-2 If a line is perpendicular to a radius of a circle at a point on the circle, then the line is tangent to the circle. (line ⊥ to radius → line tangent to ⊙; p. 748)

Thm. 11-1-3 If two segments are tangent to a circle from the same external point, then the segments are congruent. (2 segs. tangent to ⊙ from same ext. pt. → segs. ≅; p. 749)

Post. 11-2-1 **Arc Addition Postulate** The measure of an arc formed by two adjacent arcs is the sum of the measures of the two arcs. (Arc Add. Post.; p. 757)

Thm. 11-2-2 In a circle or congruent circles: (1) congruent central angles have congruent chords, (2) congruent chords have congruent arcs, and (3) congruent arcs have congruent central angles. (≅ arcs have ≅ central ∠s have ≅ chords; p. 757)

Thm. 11-2-3 In a circle, if a radius (or diameter) is perpendicular to a chord, then it bisects the chord and its arc. (Diam. ⊥ chord → diam. bisects chord and arc; p. 759)

Thm. 11-2-4 In a circle, the perpendicular bisector of a chord is a radius (or diameter). (⊥ bisector of chord is diam.; p. 759)

Thm. 11-4-1 **Inscribed Angle Theorem** The measure of an inscribed angle is half the measure of its intercepted arc. (Inscribed ∠ Thm.; p. 772)

Cor. 11-4-2 If inscribed angles of a circle intercept the same arc or are subtended by the same chord or arc, then the angles are congruent. (p. 773)

Thm. 11-4-3 An inscribed angle subtends a semicircle if and only if the angle is a right angle. (p. 774)

Thm. 11-4-4 If a quadrilateral is inscribed in a circle, then its opposite angles are supplementary. (Quad. inscribed in circle → opp. ∠s supp.; p. 775)

Thm. 11-5-1 If a tangent and a secant (or chord) intersect on a circle at the point of tangency, then the measure of the angle formed is half the measure of its intercepted arc. (p. 782)

Thm. 11-5-2 If two secants or chords intersect in the interior of a circle, then the measure of each angle formed is half the sum of the measures of its intercepted arcs. (p. 783)

Thm. 11-5-3 If a tangent and a secant, two tangents, or two secants intersect in the exterior of a circle, then the measure of the angle formed is half the difference of the measures of its intercepted arcs. (p. 784)

Thm. 11-6-1 **Chord-Chord Product Theorem** If two chords intersect in the interior of a circle, then the products of the lengths of the segments of the chords are equal. (p. 792)

Thm. 11-6-2 **Secant-Secant Product Theorem** If two secants intersect in the exterior of a circle, then the product of the lengths of one secant segment and its external segment equals the product of the lengths of the other secant segment and its external segment. (whole • outside = whole • outside; p. 793)

Thm. 11-6-3 **Secant-Tangent Product Theorem** If a secant and a tangent intersect in the exterior of a circle, then the product of the lengths of the secant segment and its external segment equals the length of the tangent segment squared. (whole • outside = tangent^2; p. 794)

Thm. 11-7-1 **Equation of a Circle** The equation of a circle with center (h, k) and radius r is $(x - h)^2 + (y - k)^2 = r^2$. (p. 799)

Chapter 12

Thm. 12-4-1 A composition of two isometries is an isometry. (p. 848)

Thm. 12-4-2 The composition of two reflections across two parallel lines is equivalent to a translation. The translation vector is perpendicular to the lines. The length of the translation vector is twice the distance between the lines. The composition of two reflections across two intersecting lines is equivalent to a rotation. The center of rotation is the intersection of the lines. The angle of rotation is twice the measure of the angle formed by the lines. (p. 849)

Thm. 12-4-3 Any translation or rotation is equivalent to a composition of two reflections. (p. 850)

Constructions

Selected Answers

Selected Answers

Chapter 1

1-1

Check It Out! 1. Possible answer: plane ℛ and plane ABC **2.** (figure: M, N) **3.** Possible answer: plane GHF **4.** (figure)

Exercises 3. A, B, C, D, E **5.** Possible answer: planes ABC and 𝒩 **7.** (figure: M, N) **9.** Possible answer: $\overleftrightarrow{AB}$ **11.** (figure) **13.** B, E, A **15.** Possible answer: ABC **17.** (figure: R) **19.** Possible answer: planes 𝒯 and 𝒮 **21.** (figure) **23.** (figure: M, ℋ) **25.** U **27.** U **29.** If 2 lines intersect, then they intersect in exactly 1 pt. **31.** A **33.** A **35.** Post. 1-1-3 **37.** Post. 1-1-2 **39.** C **41.** D **43.** 6 **45.** $\frac{n(n-1)}{2}$ **47.** Mother is 36; twins are 11. **49.** no **51.** mean: 0.442; median: 0.44; mode: 0.44

1-2

Check It Out! 1a. $3\frac{1}{2}$ **1b.** $4\frac{1}{2}$ **3a.** $1\frac{2}{3}$ **3b.** 24 **4.** 591.25 m **5.** RS = 4; ST = 4; RT = 8

Exercises 1. $\overline{XM}$ and $\overline{MY}$ **3.** 3.5 **7.** 29 **9.** x = 4; KL = 7; JL = 14 **11.** $5\frac{11}{12}$ **15.** 5 **17.** DE = EF = 14; DF = 28 **19a.** C is the mdpt. of $\overline{AE}$. **b.** 16 **21.** 7.1 **23.** 4 **25.** S **27.** Statement A **29.** 6.5; −1.5 **31.** 3.375 **33.** 9 **37.** J **39.** H **41.** (figure: X, A, D, N)

43. 14.02 m **45.** 12 **47.** −23 **49.** −8x + 6 **51.** $\overline{AD}, \overline{BD}$ **53.** $\overrightarrow{CB}$

1-3

Check It Out! 1. ∠RTQ, ∠T, ∠STR, ∠1, ∠2 **2a.** 40°; acute **2b.** 125°; obtuse **2c.** 105°; obtuse **3.** 62° **4a.** 34° **4b.** 46°

Exercises 1. ∠A, ∠R, ∠O **3.** ∠AOB, ∠BOA, or ∠1; ∠BOC, ∠COB, or ∠2; ∠AOC or ∠COA **5.** 105°; obtuse **7.** 70° **9.** 28° **11.** ∠1 or ∠JMK; ∠2 or ∠LMK; ∠M or ∠JML **13.** 93°; obtuse **15.** 66.6° **17.** 20° **19.** acute **21.** acute **27.** 67.5°; 22.5° **29.** $16\frac{1}{3}$ **31.** 9 **33a.** 9 **b.** 12 **c.** 0 < x < 15.6 **35.** m∠COD = 72°; m∠BOC = 90° **37.** No; an obtuse ∠ measures greater than 90°, so it cannot be ≅ to an acute ∠ (less than 90°). **41.** D **43.** C **45.** The ∡ are acute. An obtuse ∠ measures between 90° and 180°. Since $\frac{1}{2}$ of 180 is 90, the resulting ∡ must measure less than 90°. **47.** 36° or 4° **49.** 8100 **51.** 22.4 **53.** (figure: A, B, C) **55.**

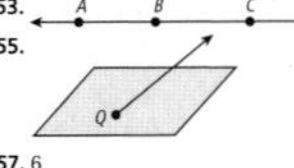

57. 6

1-4

Check It Out! 1a. adj.; lin. pair **1b.** not adj. **1c.** not adj. **2a.** $(102 - 7x)°$ **2b.** $63\frac{1}{2}°$ **3.** 68° **4.** m∠1 = m∠2 = 62.4°; m∠4 = 27.6° **5.** Possible answer: ∠EDG and ∠FDH; m∠EDG ≈ m∠FDH ≈ 45°

Exercises 1. $(90 - x)°$; $(180 - x)°$ **3.** adj.; lin. pair **5.** not adj. **7.** 98.8° **9.** $(185 - 6x)°$ **11.** 69° **13.** ∠ABE, ∠CBD; ∠ABC, ∠EBD **15.** adj.; lin. pair **17.** not adj. **19.** 33.6° **21.** $(94 - 2x)°$ **23.** m∠2 = 22.3°; m∠3 = m∠4 = 67.7° **25.** $\frac{1}{3}$ **27.** 72°; 108° **29.** 61°; 29° **31.** 10°; 80° **33a.** m∠JAH = 64°; m∠KAH = 26° **b.** m∠JAH = 131.5°; m∠KAH = 48.5° **c.** m∠JAH = m∠KAH = 7°

35. F **37.** T **39.** C **41.** C **43.** 12 **45.** 30° **47.** x = 8 **49.** y = 3 **51.** 17 **53.** 32 **55.** 52°

1-5

Check It Out! 1. P = 14 in.; A = 12.25 in² **2.** 65 in² **3.** C ≈ 88.0 m; A ≈ 615.8 m²

Exercises 1. Both terms refer to the dist. around a figure. **3.** P = 30 mm; A = 44 mm² **5.** P = (x + 21) m; A = (2x + 6) m² **7.** C ≈ 13.2 m; A ≈ 13.9 m² **9.** C ≈ 50.3 cm; A ≈ 201.1 cm² **11.** P = 4x + 12; A = $x^2 + 6x$ **13.** 72 in² **15.** C ≈ 39.3 ft; A ≈ 122.7 ft² **17.** 82.81 yd² **19.** 6.1875 in² **21.** 17.1 cm **23.** Statement A **25.** $9y^2\pi$ **27.** For a square, the length and width are both s, so P = 2l + 2w = 2s + 2s = 4s and A = lw = s(s) = s^2. **29.** b = 41 in.; h = 38 in. **31a.** ac + ad + bc + bd **b.** (a + 1)(c + 1); ac + a + c + 1 **c.** $(a + 1)^2$; $a^2 + 2a + 1$ **33.** 28 ft **35.** 26.46 ft² **37.** $25\frac{2}{3}$ yd² or 231 ft² **39.** 10 ft **41.** $\frac{15}{8}$ **43.** 50 **45.** Measure any side as the base. Then measure the height of the △ at a rt. ∠ to the base. **47.** B **49.** A **51.** 83.7 in² **53.** 5; 8; 9 **55.** width = 16 in.; length = 20 in. **57.** D: {4, −2, 16}; R: {−2, 8, 0} **59.** line or segment **61.** 3

1-6

Check It Out! 1. $\left(\frac{3}{2}, 0\right)$ **2.** (4, 3) **3.** EF = 5; GH = 5; $\overline{EF} \cong \overline{GH}$ **4a.** 6.7 **4b.** 8.5 **5.** 60.5 ft

Exercises 1. hypotenuse **3.** $\left(1\frac{1}{2}, -4\right)$ **5.** (0, −2) **7.** $\sqrt{29}$; $3\sqrt{5}$; no **9.** 15.0 **11.** 27.2 ft **13.** $\left(3\frac{1}{2}, -4\frac{1}{2}\right)$ **15.** (8, 4) **17.** $2\sqrt{5}$; $\sqrt{29}$; no **19.** 8.9 **21.** 18 in. **23.** 4.47 **25.** Divide each coord. by 2. **27.** 2.5 mi **31.** 1 **33.** Let M be the mdpt. of $\overline{AC}$; AM = MC = 5.0 ft; MB = MD ≈ 6.4 ft. **35.** G **37.** J **39.** ±2 **41.** $AB = \sqrt{x^2 + y^2}$ **43.** yes **45.** 90°; rt. **47.** 135°; obtuse **49.** 4 ft²

1-7

Check It Out! 1a. translation; MNOP → M′N′O′P′ **1b.** rotation; △XYZ → △X′Y′Z′ **2.** rotation; 90° **3.** J′(−1, −5); K′(1, 5); L′(1, 0); M′(−1, 0) **4.** (x, y) → (x − 4, y − 4)

Exercises 1. Preimage is △XYZ; image is △X′Y′Z′. **3.** reflection; △ABC → △A′B′C′ **5.** reflection across the y-axis **7.** (x, y) → (x + 4, y + 4) **9.** reflection; WXYZ → W′X′Y′Z′ **11.** A′(−1, −1), B′(4, −1), C(4, −4), D(−1, −4) **13.** reflection **15.** reflection **17.**

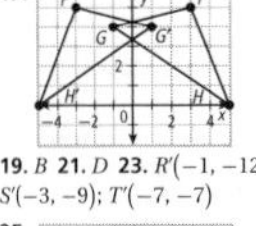

19. B **21.** D **23.** R′(−1, −12); S′(−3, −9); T′(−7, −7) **25.**

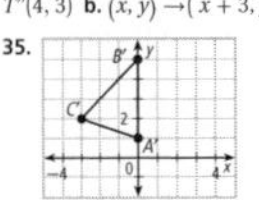

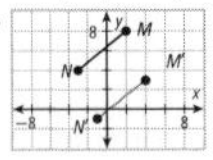

29. A **31.** A **33a.** R″(1, 0); S″(0, 3); T″(4, 3) **b.** (x, y) → (x + 3, y + 2) **35.**

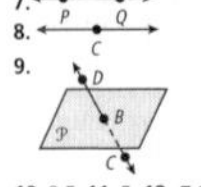

37. (−x, y) **39.** x = −6 or x = 3 **41.** x = 1 or x = 2 **43.** 13.9° **45.** 4.1 **47.** 6.3

Study Guide: Review

1. angle bisector **2.** complementary angles **3.** hypotenuse **4.** A, F, E, G or C, G, D, B **5.** Possible answer: $\overrightarrow{GC}$ **6.** Possible answer: plane AEG **7.** (figure: P, Q) **8.** (figure: C) **9.** (figure) **10.** 3.5 **11.** 5 **12.** 7.6 **13.** 22 **14.** 13; 13; 26 **15.** 18; 18; 36 **16.** ∠VYX: rt.; ∠VYZ: obtuse; ∠XYZ: acute; ∠XYW: rt.; ∠ZYW: acute; ∠VYW: straight **17.** 59° **18.** 96° **19.** only adj. **20.** adj. and a lin. pair **21.** not adj. **22.** 15.4°; 105.4° **23.** $(94 - 2x)°$; $(184 - 2x)°$ **24.** 73° **25.** 14x − 2; $12x^2 - 3x$ **26.** 4x + 16; $x^2 + 8x + 16$ **27.** x + 15; 4x − 20 **28.** 10x + 54; 100x + 140 **29.** A ≈ 1385.4 m²; C ≈ 131.9 m **30.** A ≈ 153.9 ft²; C ≈ 44.0 ft **31.** 12 m **32.** Y(1, 3) **33.** B(−9, 6) **34.** A(0, 2) **35.** 8.5 **36.** 7.3 **37.** 8.1 **38.** 90° rotation; DEFG → D′E′F′G′ **39.** translation; PQRS → P′Q′R′S′ **40.** X′(−1, 1); Y′(1, 4); Z′(2, 3)

Chapter 2

2-1

Check It Out! 1. 0.0004 **2.** odd **3.** Female whales are longer than male whales. **4a.** Possible answer: x = $\frac{1}{2}$ **4b.** Possible answer: (figure) **4c.** Jupiter or Saturn

Exercises 3. $\frac{4}{6}$ **5.** even **7.** The number of bacteria doubles every 20 minutes. **9.** The 3 pts. are collinear. **11.** 5 P.M. **13.** (hexagon) **15.** n − 1 **17.** Possible answer: y = −1 **19.** m∠1 = m∠2 = 90° **21.** Possible answer: each term is the previous term multiplied by $\frac{1}{2}$; $\frac{1}{16}$; $\frac{1}{32}$. **23.** 2n + 1 **25.** F **27.** T **29.** $\frac{1}{11} = 0.\overline{09}$, $\frac{2}{11} = 0.\overline{18}$, $\frac{3}{11} = 0.\overline{27}$,...; the fraction pattern is multiples of $\frac{1}{11}$, and the decimal pattern is repeating multiples of 0.09. **31.** 34, 55, 89; each term is the sum of the 2 previous terms. **33.** odd **37.** C **39.** D **41.** 12 years **43.** m∠CAB = m∠CBA; AC = CB **45.** yes **47.** no **49.** 10x − 6 **51.** 6πx **53.** (3, −2), (4, 0), (8, −1)

2-2

Check It Out! 1. Hypothesis: A number is divisible by 6. Conclusion: A number is divisible by 3. **2.** If 2 ∡ are comp., then they are acute. **3.** F; possible answer: 7 **4.** Converse: If an animal has 4 paws, then it is a cat; F. Inverse: If an animal is not a cat, then it does not have 4 paws; F. Contrapositive: If an animal does not have 4 paws, then it is not a cat; T.

Exercises 1. converse **3.** Hypothesis: A person is at least 16 years old. Conclusion: A person can drive a car. **5.** Hypothesis: a − b < a. Conclusion: b is a positive number. **7.** If 0 < a < b, then $\left(\frac{a}{b}\right)^2 < \frac{a}{b}$. **9.** T **11.** F **13.** Hypothesis: An animal is a tabby. Conclusion: An animal is a cat. **15.** Hypothesis: 8 ounces of cereal cost $2.99. Conclusion: 16 ounces of cereal cost $5.98. **17.** If the batter makes 3 strikes, then the batter is out. **19.** T **21.** T **25.** T **27.** F **29.** F **35.** If a person is a Texan, then the person is an American. **37a.** H: Only you can find it. C: Everything's got a moral. **b.** If only you can find it, then everything's got a moral. **43.** If a mineral has a hardness less than 5, then it is not apatite; T. **45.** If a mineral is not apatite, then it is calcite; F. **47.** If a mineral is calcite, then it has a hardness less than 5; T. **51.** H **53.** J **55.** Some students are adults. Some adults are students. **57.** 3 **59.** y = 2x + 1 **61.** T **63.** T **65.** $\frac{2}{81}$

2-3

Check It Out! 1. deductive reasoning **2.** valid **3.** valid **4.** Polygon P is not a quad.

Exercises 3. deductive reasoning **5.** valid **7.** invalid **9.** deductive reasoning **11.** invalid **13.** Dakota gets better grades in Social Studies. **15.** valid **17.** valid **19.** yes; no; because the first conditional is false **23.** D **25.** 196 **27a.** If you live in San Diego, then you live in the United States. **b.** If you do not live in California, then you do not live in San Diego. If you do not live in the United States, then you do not live in California. **c.** If you do not live in the United States, then you do not live in San Diego. **d.** They are contrapositives of each other. **29.** 2x + 10 **31.** −7c + 14 **33.** (−1.5, 3.5)

2-4

Check It Out! 1a. Conditional: If an ∠ is acute, then its measure is greater than 0° and less than 90°. Converse: If an ∠'s measure is greater than 0° and less than 90°, then the ∠ is acute. **1b.** Conditional: If Cho is a member, then he has paid the $5 dues. Converse: If Cho has paid the $5 dues, then he is a member. **2a.** Converse: If it is Independence Day, then the date is July 4th. Biconditional: It is July 4th if and only if it is Independence Day. **2b.** Converse: If pts. are collinear, then they lie on the same line. Biconditional: Pts. lie on the same line if and only if they are collinear. **3a.** T **3b.** F; y = 5 **4a.** A figure is a quad. if and only if it is a 4-sided polygon. **4b.** An ∠ is a straight ∠ if and only if its measure is 180°.

Exercises 3. Conditional: If your medicine will be ready by 5 P.M., then you dropped your prescription off by 8 A.M. Converse: If you drop your prescription off by 8 A.M., then your medicine will be ready by 5 P.M. **5.** Converse: If 2 segs. are ≅, then they have the same length. Biconditional: 2 segs. have the same length if and only if they are ≅. **7.** F **9.** An animal is a hummingbird if and only if it is a tiny, brightly colored bird with narrow wings, a slender bill, and a long tongue. **11.** Conditional: If a ▭ is a rect., then it has 4 rt. ∡. Converse: If a ▭ has 4 rt. ∡, then it is a rect. **13.** Converse: If it is the weekend, then today is Saturday or Sunday. Biconditional: Today is Saturday or Sunday if and only if it is the weekend. **15.** Converse: If a △ is a rt. △, then it contains a rt. ∠. Biconditional: A △ contains a rt. ∠ if and only if it is a rt. △. **17.** T **19.** A player is a catcher if and only if the player is positioned behind home plate and catches throws from the pitcher. **21.** yes **23.** no **25.** A square is a quad. with 4 ≅ sides and 4 rt. ∡. **31.** no **33.** 5 **37a.** If I say it, then I mean it. If I mean it, then I say it. **39.** G **43a.** If an ∠ does not measure 105°, then the ∠ is not obtuse. **b.** If an ∠ is not obtuse, then it does not measure 105°. **c.** It is the contrapositive of the original. **d.** F; the inverse is false, and its converse is true. **47.** The graph is reflected across the x-axis and shifted 1 unit down and is narrower than the graph of the parent function. **49.** T **51.** S **53.** F

2-5

Check It Out! 1. $\frac{1}{2}t = -7$ (Given); $2\left(\frac{1}{2}t\right) = 2(-7)$ (Mult. Prop. of =); t = −14 (Simplify.) **2.** $C = \frac{5}{9}(F - 32)$ (Given); $C = \frac{5}{9}(86 - 32)$ (Subst.); $C = \frac{5}{9}(54)$ (Simplify.); C = 30 (Simplify.) **3.** ∠ Add. Post.; Subst.; Simplify.; Subtr. Prop. of =; Mult. Prop. of = **4a.** Sym. Prop. of = **4b.** Reflex. Prop. of = **4c.** Trans. Prop. of = **4d.** Sym. Prop. of ≅

Exercises 3. t − 3.2 = −8.3 (Given); t = −5.1 (Add. Prop. of =) **5.** $\frac{x+3}{-2} = 8$ (Given); x + 3 = −16 (Mult. Prop. of =); x = −19 (Subtr. Prop. of =) **7.** 0 = 2(r − 3) + 4 (Given); 0 = 2r − 6 + 4 (Distrib. Prop.); 0 = 2r − 2 (Simplify.); 2 = 2r (Add. Prop. of =); 1 = r (Div. Prop. of =) **9.** C = $5.75 + $0.89m (Given); $11.98 = $5.75 + $0.89m (Subst.); $6.23 = $0.89m (Subtr. Prop. of =); m = 7 (Div. Prop. of =) **11.** Seg. Add. Post.; Subst.; Subtr. Prop. of =; Add. Prop. of =; Div. Prop. of = **13.** Trans. Prop. of = **15.** Trans. Prop. of ≅ **17.** 1.6 = 3.2n (Given); 0.5 = n (Div. Prop. of =) **19.** −(h + 3) = 72 (Given); −h − 3 = 72 (Distrib. Prop.); −h = 75 (Add. Prop. of =); h = −75 (Mult. Prop. of =) **21.** $\frac{1}{2}(p - 16) = 13$ (Given); $\frac{1}{2}p - 8 = 13$ (Distrib. Prop.); $\frac{1}{2}p = 21$ (Add. Prop. of =); p = 42 (Mult. Prop. of =) **23.** ∠ Add. Post.; Subst.; Simplify.; Subtr. Prop. of =; Add. Prop. of =; Div. Prop. of =

25. Sym. Prop. of ≅ **27.** Trans. Prop. of = **29.** x = 16; 2(3.1x − 0.87) = 94.36 (Given); 6.2x − 1.74 = 94.36 (Distrib. Prop.); 6.2x = 96.1 (Add. Prop. of =); x = 15.5 (Div. Prop. of =); possible answer: the exact solution rounds to the estimate. **31.** ∠A ≅ ∠T **33.** $\frac{x+1}{2} = 3$ (Mdpt. Formula); x + 1 = 6 (Mult. Prop. of =); x = 5 (Subtr. Prop. of =); $\frac{1+y}{2} = 5$ (Mdpt. Formula); 1 + y = 10 (Mult. Prop. of =); y = 9 (Subtr. Prop. of =) **35a.** 1733.65 = 92.50 + 79.96 + 983 + 10,820x (Given); 1733.65 = 1155.46 + 10,820x (Simplify.); 578.19 = 10,820x (Subtr. Prop. of =); 0.05 ≈ x (Div. Prop. of =) **b.** $1.71 **37a.** x + 15 ≤ 63 (Given); x ≤ 48 (Subtr. Prop. of Inequal.) **b.** −2x > 36 (Given); x < −18 (Div. Prop. of Inequal.) **39.** B **41.** D **43.** PR = PA + RA (Seg. Add. Post.); PA = QB, QB = RA (Given); PA = RA (Trans. Prop. of =); PR = PA + PA (Subst.); PR = 18(Given); PR = 18 + 18 (Subst.); PR = 36 in. (Simplify.) **45.** 7 − 3x > 19 (Given); −3x > 12 (Subtr. Prop. of Inequal.); x < −4 (Div. Prop. of Inequal.) **49.** deductive reasoning

2-6

Check It Out!

1. 1. Given
2. Def. of mdpt.
3. Given
4. Trans. Prop. of ≅

2a. ∠1 and ∠2 are supp., and ∠2 and ∠3 are supp. **2b.** m∠1 + m∠2 = m∠2 + m∠3 **2c.** Subtr. Prop. of = **2d.** ∠1 ≅ ∠3

3. 1. ∠1 and ∠2 are comp. ∠2 and ∠3 are comp. (Given)
2. m∠1 + m∠2 = 90°, m∠2 + m∠3 = 90° (Def. of comp. ∡)
3. m∠1 + m∠2 = m∠2 + m∠3 (Subst.)
4. m∠2 = m∠2 (Reflex. Prop. of =)
5. m∠1 = m∠3 (Subtr. Prop. of =)
6. ∠1 ≅ ∠3 (Def. of ≅ ∡)

Exercises 1. statements; reasons **3.** 1. Given
2. Subst.
3. Simplify.
4. Add. Prop. of =
5. Simplify.
6. Def. of supp. ∡

5. 1. X is the mdpt. of $\overline{AY}$. Y is the mdpt. of $\overline{XB}$. (Given)
2. $\overline{AX} \cong \overline{XY}$, $\overline{XY} \cong \overline{YB}$ (Def. of mdpt.)
3. $\overline{AX} \cong \overline{YB}$ (Trans. Prop. of ≅)

7a. m∠1 + m∠2 = 180°, m∠3 + m∠4 = 180° **b.** Subst. **c.** m∠1 = m∠4 **d.** Def. of ≅ ∡

9. 1. $\overline{BE} \cong \overline{CE}$, $\overline{DE} \cong \overline{AE}$ (Given)
2. BE = CE, DE = AE (Def. of ≅ segs.)
3. AE + BE = AB, CE + DE = CD (Seg. Add. Post.)
4. DE + CE = AB (Subst.)
5. AB = CD (Subst.)
6. $\overline{AB} \cong \overline{CD}$ (Def. of ≅ segs.)

11. 132° **13.** 59° **17.** S **19.** N **21.** x = 16 **25.** C **27.** D **29.** a = 17; 37.5°, 52.5°, and 37.5° **31.** 24% **35.** Sym. Prop. of ≅

2-7

Check It Out!

1. 1. RS = UV, ST = TU (Given)
2. RS + ST = TU + UV (Add. Prop. of =)
3. RS + ST = RT, TU + UV = TV (Seg. Add. Post.)
4. RT = TV (Subst.)
5. $\overline{RT} \cong \overline{TV}$ (Def. of ≅ segs.)

2.

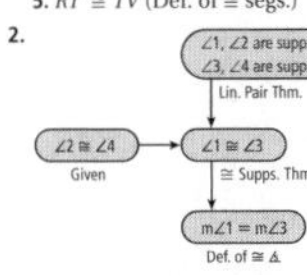

3. 1. ∠WXY is a rt. ∠. (Given)
2. m∠WXY = 90° (Def. of rt. ∠)
3. m∠2 + m∠3 = m∠WXY (∠ Add. Post.)
4. m∠2 + m∠3 = 90° (Subst.)
5. ∠1 ≅ ∠3 (Given)
6. m∠1 = m∠3 (Def. of ≅ ∡)
7. m∠2 + m∠1 = 90° (Subst.)
8. ∠1 and ∠2 are comp. (Def. of comp. ∡)

4. It is given that ∠1 ≅ ∠4. By the Vert. ∡ Thm., ∠1 ≅ ∠2 and ∠3 ≅ ∠4. By the Trans. Prop. of ≅, ∠2 ≅ ∠4. Similarly, ∠2 ≅ ∠3.

Exercises 1. flowchart

3. 1. ∠1 ≅ ∠2 (Given)
2. ∠1 and ∠2 are supp. (Lin. Pair Thm.)
3. ∠1 and ∠2 are rt. ∡. (≅ ∡ supp. → rt. ∡)

5. 1. ∠2 ≅ ∠4 (Given)
2. ∠1 ≅ ∠2, ∠3 ≅ ∠4 (Vert. ∡ Thm.)
3. ∠1 ≅ ∠4 (Trans. Prop. of ≅)
4. ∠1 ≅ ∠3 (Trans. Prop. of ≅)

7. 1. B is the mdpt. of $\overline{AC}$. (Given)
2. $\overline{AB} \cong \overline{BC}$ (Def. of mdpt.)
3. AB = BC (Def. of ≅ segs.)
4. AD + DB = AB, BE + EC = BC (Seg. Add. Post.)
5. AD + DB = BE + EC (Subst.)
6. AD = EC (Given)
7. DB = BE (Subtr. Prop. of =)

9. 1. ∠1 ≅ ∠4 (Given)
2. ∠1 ≅ ∠2 (Vert. ∡ Thm.)
3. ∠4 ≅ ∠2 (Trans. Prop. of ≅)
4. m∠4 = m∠2 (Def. of ≅ ∡)
5. ∠3 and ∠4 are supp. (Lin. Pair Thm.)
6. m∠3 + m∠4 = 180° (Def. of supp. ∡)
7. m∠3 + m∠2 = 180° (Subst.)
8. ∠2 and ∠3 are supp. (Def. of supp. ∡)

11. 13 cm; conv. of the Common Segs. Thm. **13.** 37°, Vert. ∡ Thm. **15.** y = 11 **17.** A **21.** C **23.** D

25. 1. ∠AOC ≅ ∠BOD (Given)
2. m∠AOC = m∠BOD (Def. of ≅ ∡)
3. m∠AOB + m∠BOC = m∠AOC, m∠BOC + m∠COD = m∠BOD (∠ Add. Post.)
4. m∠AOB + m∠BOC = m∠BOC + m∠COD (Subst.)
5. m∠BOC = m∠BOC (Reflex. Prop. of =)
6. m∠AOB = m∠COD (Subtr. Prop. of =)
7. ∠AOB ≅ ∠COD (Def. of ≅ ∡)

27. x = 31 and y = 11.5; 86°, 94°, 86°, and 94° **29.** (−4, 5)

Study Guide: Review

1. theorem **2.** deductive reasoning **3.** counterexample **4.** conjecture **5.** The rightmost △ is duplicated, rotated 180°, and shifted to the right. The next 2 items are (figure) and (figure). **6.** Each item is $\frac{1}{6}$ greater than the previous one. The next 2 items are $\frac{5}{6}$ and 1. **7.** The white section is halved. If the white section is a rect. but not a square, it is halved horiz. and the upper portion is colored yellow. If the white section is a square, it is halved vert. and the left portion is colored yellow. The next 2 items are

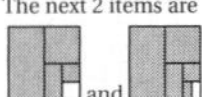

8. odd **9.** positive **10.** F; 0 **11.** T **12.** T **13.** F; during a leap year, there are 29 days in February. **14.** Check students' constructions. Possible answer: The 3 ∠ bisectors of a △ intersect in the int. of the △. **15.** If it is Monday, then it is a weekday. **16.** If something is a lichen, then it is a fungus. **17.** T **18.** F; possible answer: $\sqrt{2}$ and $\sqrt{2}$ **19.** Converse: If m∠X = 90°, then ∠X is a rt. ∠; T. Inverse: If ∠X is not a rt. ∠, then m∠X ≠ 90°; T. Contrapositive: If m∠X ≠ 90°, then ∠X is not a rt. ∠; T. **20.** Converse: If x = 2, then x is a whole number; T. Inverse: If x is not a whole number, then x ≠ 2; T. Contrapositive: If x ≠ 2, then x is not a whole number; F. **21.** F **22.** T **23.** F **24.** Sara's call lasted 7 min. **25.** The cost of Paulo's long-distance call is $2.78. **26.** No conclusion; the number and length of calls are unknown. **27.** yes **28.** no; possible answer: x = 2 **29.** no; possible answer: a seg. with endpoints (3, 7) and (−5, −1) **30.** yes **31.** comp. **32.** positive **33.** greater than 50 mi/h **34.** 4s **35.** $\frac{m}{-5} + 3 = -4.5$ (Given); $\frac{m}{-5} = -7.5$ (Subtr. Prop. of =); m = 37.5 (Mult. Prop. of =) **36.** −47 = 3x − 59 (Given); 12 = 3x (Add. Prop. of =); 4 = x (Div. Prop. of =) **37.** Reflex. Prop. of = **38.** Sym. Prop. of ≅ **39.** Trans. Prop. of = **40.** figure ABCD **41.** m∠5 = m∠2 **42.** $\overline{CD} \cong \overline{EF}$ **43.** I = Prt (Given); 4200 = P(0.06)(4) (Subst.); 4200 = P(0.24) (Simplify.);

17,500 = P (Div. Prop. of =)
44. 1. Given
2. Def. of comp. ∡
3. Given
4. Def. of ≅ ∡
5. Subst.
6. Def. of comp. ∡
45a. Given **b.** $TU = UV$
c. $SU + UV = SV$ **d.** Subst.
46. $z = 22.5$ **47.** $x = 17$
48.

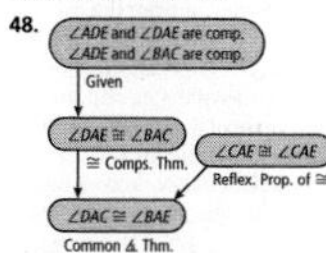

49. It is given that ∠ADE and ∠DAE are comp. and ∠ADE and ∠BAC are comp. By the ≅ Comps. Thm., ∠DAE ≅ ∠BAC. By the Reflex. Prop. of ≅, ∠CAE ≅ ∠CAE. By the Common ∡ Thm., ∠DAC ≅ ∠BAE. **50.** $w = 45$; Vert. ∡ Thm. **51.** $x = 45$; ≅ ∡ supp. → rt. ∡

Chapter 3

3-1

Check It Out! 1–2. Possible answers given. **1a.** $\overline{BF} \parallel \overline{EJ}$ **1b.** $\overline{BF}$ and $\overline{DE}$ are skew. **1c.** $\overline{BF} \perp \overline{FJ}$ **1d.** plane FJH ∥ plane BCD **2a.** ∠1 and ∠3 **2b.** ∠2 and ∠7 **2c.** ∠1 and ∠8 **2d.** ∠2 and ∠3 **3.** transv. n; same-side int. ∡

Exercises 1. alternate interior angles **3–9.** Possible answers given. **3.** $\overline{AB}$ and $\overline{DH}$ are skew. **5.** plane ABC ∥ plane EFG **7.** ∠6 and ∠8 **9.** ∠2 and ∠3 **11.** transv. m; alt. ext. ∡ **13.** transv. p, same-side int. ∡ **15–21.** Possible answers given. **15.** $\overline{AB}$ and $\overline{CF}$ are skew. **17.** plane ABC ∥ plane DEF **19.** ∠1 and ∠8 **21.** ∠2 and ∠5 **23.** transv. q; alt. int. ∡ **25.** transv. p; same-side int. ∡ **27.** corr.∡ **29.** same-side int. ∡ **31.** Possible answer: $\overline{CD}$ and $\overline{FG}$ **33a.** plane MNR ∥ plane KLP; plane LMQ ∥ plane KNP; plane PQR ∥ plane KLM

b. same-side int. ∡ **35–39.** Possible answers given. **35.** ∠5 and ∠8 **37.** ∠1 and ∠5 **39.** transv. n; alt. int. ∡ **41.** The lines are skew. **45.** G **47.** F **49.** transv. m: ∠1 and ∠3, ∠2 and ∠4, ∠5 and ∠7, ∠6 and ∠8; transv. n: ∠9 and ∠11, ∠10 and ∠12, ∠13 and ∠15, ∠14 and ∠16; transv. p: ∠1 and ∠9, ∠2 and ∠10, ∠5 and ∠13, ∠6 and ∠14; transv. q: ∠3 and ∠11, ∠4 and ∠12, ∠7 and ∠15, ∠8 and ∠16 **51.** transv. m: ∠1 and ∠8, ∠4 and ∠5; transv. n: ∠9 and ∠16, ∠12 and ∠13; transv. p: ∠1 and ∠14, ∠2 and ∠13; transv. q: ∠3 and ∠16, ∠4 and ∠15 **53.** corr. ∡ **55.** −3; −7; −3; 9; 29 **57.** −8; −9; −8; −5; 0 **59.** $C = 11.9$ m; $A = 11.3$ m² **61.** Lin. Pair Thm.

3-2

Check It Out! 1. m∠QRS = 62° **2.** m∠ABD = 60° **3.** 55° and 60°

Exercises 1. m∠JKL = 127° **3.** m∠1 = 90° **5.** $x = 8$; $y = 9$ **7.** m∠VYX = 100° **9.** m∠EFG = 102° **11.** m∠STU = 90° **13.** 120°; Corr. ∡ Post. **15.** 60°; Same-Side Int. ∡ Thm. **17.** 60°; Lin. Pair Thm. **19.** 120°; Vert. ∡ Thm. **21.** $x = 4$; Same-Side Int. ∡ Thm.; m∠3 = 103°; m∠4 = 77° **23.** $x = 3$; Corr. ∡ Post.; m∠1 = m∠4 = 42° **25a.** ∠1 ≅ ∠3 **b.** Corr. ∡ Post. **c.** ∠1 ≅ ∠2 **d.** Trans. Prop. of ≅ **29a.** same-side int. ∡ **b.** By the Same-Side Int. ∡ Thm., m∠QRT + m∠STR = 180°. m∠QRT = 25° + 90° = 115°, so m∠STR = 65°. **31.** A **35.** J **37.** m∠1 = 75° **39.** $x = 4$; $y = 12$ **41.** increase **43.** m∠1 + m∠2 = 180° **45–47.** Possible answers given. **45.** ∠3 and ∠6 **47.** ∠3 and ∠5

3-3

Check It Out! 1a. ∠1 ≅ ∠3, so ℓ ∥ m by the Conv. of Corr. ∡ Post. **1b.** m∠7 = 77° and m∠5 = 77°, so ∠7 ≅ ∠5. ℓ ∥ m by the Conv. of Corr. ∡ Post. **2a.** ∠4 ≅ ∠8, so r ∥ s by the Conv. of Alt. Int. ∡ Thm. **2b.** m∠3 = 100° and m∠7 = 100°, so ∠3 ≅ ∠7. r ∥ s by the Conv. of Alt. Int. ∡ Thm.
3. 1. ∠1 ≅ ∠4 (Given)
2. m∠1 = m∠4 (Def. ≅ ∡)
3. ∠3 and ∠4 are supp. (Given)
4. m∠3 + m∠4 = 180° (Def. supp. ∡)
5. m∠3 + m∠1 = 180° (Subst.)
6. m∠2 = m∠3 (Vert. ∡ Thm.)
7. m∠2 + m∠1 = 180° (Subst.)
8. ℓ ∥ m (Conv. of Same-Side Int. ∡ Thm.)
4. $4y - 2 = 4(8) - 2 = 30°$; $3y + 6 = 3(8) + 6 = 30°$; The ∡ are ≅, so the oars are ∥ by the Conv. of Corr. ∡ Post.

Exercises 1. ∠4 ≅ ∠5, so p ∥ q by the Conv. of Corr. ∡ Post. **3.** m∠4 = 47°, and m∠5 = 47°, so ∠4 ≅ ∠5. p ∥ q by the Conv. of Corr. ∡ Post. **5.** ∠3 and ∠4 are supp., so r ∥ s by the Conv. of Same-Side Int. ∡ Thm. **7.** m∠4 = 61°, and m∠8 = 61°, so ∠4 ≅ ∠8. r ∥ s by the Conv. of Alt. Int. ∡ Thm. **9.** m∠2 = 132°, and m∠6 = 132°, so ∠2 ≅ ∠6. r ∥ s by the Conv. of Alt. Ext. ∡ Thm. **11.** m∠1 = 60°, and m∠2 = 60°, so ∠1 ≅ ∠2. By the Conv. of Alt. Int. ∡ Thm., the landings are ∥. **13.** m∠4 = 54°, and m∠8 = 54°, so ∠4 ≅ ∠8. ℓ ∥ m by the Conv. of Corr. ∡ Post. **15.** m∠1 = 55°, and m∠5 = 55°, so ∠1 ≅ ∠5. ℓ ∥ m by the Conv. of Corr. ∡ Post. **17.** ∠2 ≅ ∠7, so n ∥ p by the Conv. of Alt. Ext. ∡ Thm. **19.** m∠1 = 105°, and m∠8 = 105°, so ∠1 ≅ ∠8. n ∥ p by the Conv. of Alt. Ext. ∡ Thm. **21.** m∠3 = 75°, and m∠5 = 105°. 75° + 105° = 180°, so ∠3 and ∠5 are supp. n ∥ p by the Conv. of Same-Side Int. ∡ Thm. **23.** If $x = 6$, then m∠1 = 20° and m∠2 = 20°. So $\overline{DJ} \parallel \overline{EK}$ by the Conv. of Corr. ∡ Post. **25.** Conv. of Alt. Ext. ∡ Thm. **27.** Conv. of Corr. ∡ Post. **29.** Conv. of Same-Side Int. ∡ Thm. **31.** m ∥ n; Conv. of Same-Side Int. ∡ Thm. **33.** m ∥ n; Conv. of Alt. Ext. ∡ Thm. **35.** ℓ ∥ n; Conv. of Same-Side Int. ∡ Thm. **37a.** ∠URT; m∠URT = m∠URS + m∠SRT by the ∠ Add. Post. It is given that m∠SRT = 25° and m∠URS = 90°, so m∠URT = 25° + 90° = 115°. **b.** It is given that m∠SUR = 65°. From part **a**, m∠URT = 115°. 65° + 115° = 180°, so $\overline{SU} \parallel \overline{RT}$ by the Conv. of Same-Side Int. ∡ Thm. **39.** It is given that ∠1 and ∠2 are supp., so m∠1 + m∠2 = 180°. By the Lin. Pair Thm., m∠2 + m∠3 = 180°. By the Trans. Prop. of =, m∠1 + m∠2 = m∠2 + m∠3. By the Subtr. Prop. of =, m∠1 = m∠3. By the Conv. of Corr. ∡ Post., ℓ ∥ m. **41.** The Reflex. Prop. is not true for ∥ lines, because a line is not ∥ to itself. The Sym. Prop. is true, because if ℓ ∥ m, then ℓ and m are coplanar and do not intersect. So m ∥ ℓ. The Trans. Prop. is not true for ∥ lines, because if ℓ ∥ m and m ∥ n, then ℓ and n could be the same line. So they would not be ∥. **43.** C **45.** 15 **47.** No lines can be proven ∥. **49.** q ∥ r by the Conv. of Alt. Int. ∡ Thm. **51.** s ∥ t by the Conv. of Alt. Ext. ∡ Thm. **53.** No lines can be proven ∥. **55.** By the Vert. ∡ Thm., ∠6 ≅ ∠3, so m∠6 = m∠3. It is given that m∠2 + m∠3 = 180°. By subst., m∠2 + m∠6 = 180°. By the Conv. of Same-Side Int. ∡ Thm., ℓ ∥ m. **57.** $a = b - c$ **59.** $y = -\frac{3}{5}x + 3$ **63.** $\overline{AD} \parallel \overline{BC}$ **65.** $\overline{AB} \perp \overline{AD}$

3-4

Check It Out! 1a. $\overline{AB}$ **1b.** $x < 17$
2. 1. ∠EHF ≅ ∠HFG (Given)
2. $\overleftrightarrow{EH} \parallel \overleftrightarrow{FG}$ (Conv. of Alt. Int. ∡ Thm.)
3. $\overleftrightarrow{FG} \perp \overleftrightarrow{GH}$ (Given)
4. $\overleftrightarrow{EH} \perp \overleftrightarrow{GH}$ (⊥ Transv. Thm.)
3. The shoreline and the path of the swimmer should both be ⊥ to the current, so they should be ∥ to each other.

Exercises 1. $\overline{AB}$ and $\overline{CD}$ are ⊥. $\overline{AC}$ and $\overline{BC}$ are ≅. **3.** $x > -5$ **5.** The service lines are coplanar lines that are ⊥ to the same line (the center line), so they must be ∥ to each other. **7.** $x < 11$ **9.** Both the frets are lines that are ⊥ to the same line (the string), so the frets must be ∥ to each other. **11.** $x > \frac{8}{3}$ **13.** $x = 6$, $y = 15$ **15.** $x = 60$, $y = 60$ **17.** no **19.** no **21.** yes **23a.** It is given that $\overline{QR} \perp \overline{PQ}$ and $\overline{PQ} \parallel \overline{RS}$, so $\overline{QR} \perp \overline{RS}$ by the ⊥ Transv. Thm. It is given that $\overline{PS} \parallel \overline{QR}$. Since $\overline{QR} \perp \overline{RS}$, $\overline{PS} \perp \overline{RS}$ by the ⊥ Transv. Thm. **b.** It is given that $\overline{PS} \parallel \overline{QR}$ and $\overline{QR} \perp \overline{PQ}$. So $\overline{PQ} \perp \overline{PS}$ by the ⊥ Transv. Thm. **25.** Possible answer: 1.6 cm **31.** C **33.** D **35a.** n ⊥ p **b.** AB; AB; the shortest distance from a point to a line is measured along a perpendicular segment. **c.** The distance between two parallel lines is the length of a segment that is perpendicular to both lines and has one endpoint on each line. **39.** 30 games **41.** 25° **43.** Conv. of Alt. Ext. ∠ Thm. **45.** Conv. of Same-Side Int. ∠ Thm.

3-5

Check It Out! 1. $m = 2$ **2.** 390 m **3a.** ⊥ **3b.** neither **3c.** ∥

Exercises 1. rise; run **3.** $m = -\frac{5}{9}$ **5.** $m = \frac{5}{2}$ **7.** ∥ **9.** neither **11.** $m = 0$ **13.** $m = -\frac{7}{3}$ **15.** ∥ **17.** ⊥ **19.** $m = \frac{1}{10}$ **21.** $m = \frac{1}{2}$ **23.** $m < -1$ **25a.** 66 ft/s **b.** 45 mi/h **27.** F **29.** $\overline{JK}$ is a vert. line. **33.** Possible answer: $x = 1$, $y = -6$ **35.** x-int.: 0.25; y-int.: 1
37. 1. ∠1 is supp. to ∠3. (Given)
2. ∠1 and ∠2 are supp. (Lin. Pair Thm.)
3. ∠2 ≅ ∠3 (≅ Supps. Thm.)
39. T: Corr. ∡ Post.

3-6

Check It Out! 1a. $y = 6$ **1b.** $y - 2 = 0$
2a. **2b.** **2c.** **3.** parallel **4.** The lines would be ∥.

Exercises 1. The slope-intercept form of an equation is solved for y. The x term is first, and the constant term is second. **3.** $y - 2 = \frac{3}{4}(x + 4)$
5. **7.**
9. intersect **11.** ∥ **13.** $y + 2 = 2x$ **15.** $y + 4 = \frac{2}{3}(x - 6)$

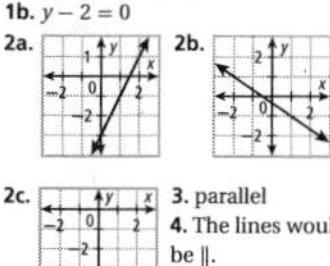

17.

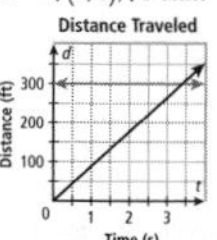

19. intersect **21.** coincide **23.** $1000 per week **33.** no **35.** yes **37.** ∥ line: $y = 3x - 3$; ⊥ line: $y = -\frac{1}{3}x + \frac{11}{3}$ **39.** ∥ line: $y = -\frac{4}{3}x + \frac{10}{3}$; ⊥ line: $y = \frac{3}{4}x - 5$ **41.** yes; ∠B **43.** no **45.** For 4 toppings, both pizzas will cost $14. **47.** $y = -\frac{1}{2}x + \frac{17}{2}$ **49.** $y = 2x + \frac{7}{2}$ **51.** $y = 2x - 1$; (2, 3); $\sqrt{5}$ units
53a–b.

Distance Traveled

b. the time when the car has traveled 300 ft **c.** Possible answer: 3.5 s **59.** I **61.** J **63.** Possible answer: $y = -\frac{8}{15}x + 8$ **65.** no **67.** 6 **69.** (1, 0) **71.** $m = \frac{2}{5}$ **73.** $m = -\frac{4}{3}$

Study Guide: Review

1. alternate interior angles **2.** skew lines **3.** transversal **4.** point-slope form **5.** rise; run **6.** Possible answer: $\overline{DE}$ and $\overline{BC}$ are skew. **7.** $\overline{AB} \parallel \overline{DE}$ **8.** $\overline{AD} \perp \overline{DE}$ **9.** plane ABC ∥ plane DEF **10.** ℓ; alt. int. ∡ **11.** n; corr. ∡ **12.** ℓ; same-side int. ∡ **13.** m; alt. ext. ∡ **14.** m∠WYZ = 90° **15.** m∠KLM = 100° **16.** m∠DEF = 79° **17.** m∠QRS = 76° **18.** ∠4 ≅ ∠6, so c ∥ d by the Conv. of Alt. Int. ∡ Thm. **19.** m∠1 = 107° and m∠5 = 107°, so ∠1 ≅ ∠5. c ∥ d by the Conv. of Corr. ∡ Post. **20.** m∠6 = 66°, m∠3 = 114°, and 66° + 114° ≠ 180°, so ∠6 and ∠3 are supp. c ∥ d by the Conv. of Same-Side Int. ∡ Thm. **21.** m∠1 ≠ 99°, and m∠7 = 99°, so ∠1 ≅ ∠7. c ∥ d by the Conv. of Alt. Ext. ∡ Thm. **22.** $\overline{KM}$ **23.** $x < 13$
24. 1. $\overline{AD} \parallel \overline{BC}$, $\overline{AD} \perp \overline{AB}$, $\overline{DC} \perp \overline{BC}$ (Given);
2. $\overline{AB} \perp \overline{BC}$ (⊥ Transv. Thm.);
3. $\overline{AB} \parallel \overline{CD}$ (2 lines ⊥ to same line → 2 lines ∥)
25. $m = -\frac{1}{2}$ **26.** $m = \frac{5}{3}$ **27.** neither **28.** ∥ **29.** ⊥ **30.** $y = -\frac{4}{9}x + \frac{11}{3}$ **31.** $y = \frac{3}{5}x - 2$

32. $y - 0 = 2(x - 1)$ **33.** ∥ **34.** intersect **35.** coincide

Chapter 4

4-1

Check It Out! 1. equiangular **2.** scalene **3.** 17; 17; 17 **4a.** 4 **4b.** 3

Exercises 1. An equilateral △ has 3 ≅ sides. **3.** rt. **5.** obtuse **7.** scalene **9.** 36; 36; 36 **11.** 6 **13.** obtuse **15.** equil. **17.** scalene **19.** 8.6; 8.6 **21.** 18 ft; 18 ft; 24 ft
23.
25.

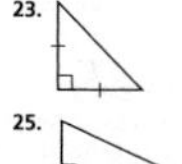

27. not possible **29.** 35 in. **31.** isosc. rt. **33a.** 173 ft; 87 ft **b.** scalene **35.** S **37.** A **41.** D **43.** D **45.** It is an isosc. △ since 2 sides of the △ have length a. It is a rt. △ since 2 sides of the △ lie on the coord. axes and form a rt. ∠. **47.** $y = -3$ **49.** $y = x^2$ **51.** $y = x^2$ **53.** T **55.** ∥ **57.** coincides

4-2

Check It Out! 1. 32° **2a.** 26.3° **2b.** $(90 - x)°$ **2c.** $41\frac{3}{5}°$ **3.** 141° **4.** 32°; 32°

Exercises 3. auxiliary lines **5.** 36°; 80°; 64° **7.** $(90 - y)°$ **9.** 28° **11.** 52°; 63° **13.** 89°; 89° **15.** 84° **17.** $(90 - 2x)°$ **19.** 162° **21.** 48°; 48° **23.** 15°; 60°; 105° **29.** 36° **31.** 48° **33.** 120°; 360° **35.** 18° **37.** The ext. ∡ at the same vertex of a △ are vert. ∡. Since vert. ∡ are ≅, the 2 ext. ∡ have the same measure. **41.** C **43.** D **45.** $y = 7$ or $y = -7$ **47.** Since an ext. ∠ is = to a sum of 2 remote int. ∡, it must be greater than either ∠. Therefore it cannot be ≅ to a remote int. ∠. **49.** 38°
51.

x	−2	0	1	4
f(x)	5	1	2	17

53. 6 in.; Seg. Add. Post.

55. scalene **57.** △ACD is equil.

4-3

Check It Out! 1. ∠L ≅ ∠E, ∠M ≅ ∠F, ∠N ≅ ∠G, ∠P ≅ ∠H, $\overline{LM} \cong \overline{EF}$, $\overline{MN} \cong \overline{FG}$, $\overline{NP} \cong \overline{GH}$, $\overline{LP} \cong \overline{EH}$ **2a.** 4 **2b.** 37°
3. 1. ∠A ≅ ∠D (Given)
2. ∠BCA ≅ ∠ECD (Vert. ∡ are ≅.)
3. ∠ABC ≅ ∠DEC (Third ∡ Thm.)
4. $\overline{AB} \cong \overline{DE}$ (Given)
5. $\overline{AD}$ bisects $\overline{BE}$, and $\overline{BE}$ bisects $\overline{AD}$. (Given)
6. $\overline{BC} \cong \overline{EC}$, $\overline{AC} \cong \overline{DC}$ (Def. of bisector)
7. △ABC ≅ △DEC (Def. of ≅ ∡)
4. 1. $\overline{JK} \parallel \overline{ML}$ (Given)
2. ∠KJN ≅ ∠MLN, ∠JKN ≅ ∠LMN (Alt. Int. ∡ Thm.)
3. ∠JNK ≅ ∠LNM (Vert. ∡ Thm.)
4. $\overline{JK} \cong \overline{ML}$ (Given)
5. $\overline{MK}$ bisects $\overline{JL}$, and $\overline{JL}$ bisects $\overline{MK}$. (Given)
6. $\overline{JN} \cong \overline{LN}$, $\overline{MN} \cong \overline{KN}$ (Def. of bisector)
7. △JKN ≅ △MLN (Def. of ≅ ∡)

Exercises 1. You find the ∡ and sides that are in the same, or matching, places in the 2 ∡. **3.** $\overline{LM}$ **5.** ∠M **7.** ∠R **9.** KL = 9 **11a.** Given **b.** Alt. Int. ∡ Thm. **c.** Given **d.** Given **e.** $\overline{AE} \cong \overline{CE}$, $\overline{DE} \cong \overline{BE}$; **f.** Vert. ∡ Thm. **g.** Def. of ≅ ∡ **13.** $\overline{LM}$ **15.** ∠N **17.** m∠C = 31° **19a.** Given **b.** Given **c.** ∠NMP ≅ ∠RMP **d.** ∠NPM ≅ ∠RPM **e.** Given **f.** $\overline{PN} \cong \overline{PR}$ **g.** Given **h.** Reflex. Prop. of ≅ **21.** △GSR ≅ △KPH; △SRG ≅ △PHK; △RGS ≅ △HKP **23.** $x = 30$; $AB = 50$ **25.** $x = 2$; $BC = 17$ **29.** solution A **31.** B **33.** D **35.** $x = 5.5$; yes; $UV = WV = 41.5$, and $UT = WT = 33$. $TV = TV$ by the Reflex. Prop. of =. It is given that ∠VWT ≅ ∠VUT and ∠WTV ≅ ∠UTV. ∠WVT ≅ ∠UVT by the Third ∡ Thm. Thus △TUV ≅ △TWV by the def. of ≅ ∡. **39.** $\frac{1}{5}$ **41.** rt. **43.** 72° **45.** 146°

4-4

Check It Out! 1. It is given that $\overline{AB} \cong \overline{CD}$ and $\overline{BC} \cong \overline{DA}$. By the Reflex. Prop. of ≅, $\overline{AC} \cong \overline{CA}$. So △ABC ≅ △CDA by SSS. **2.** It is given that $\overline{BA} \cong \overline{BD}$ and ∠ABC ≅ ∠DBC. By the Reflex. Prop. of ≅, $\overline{BC} \cong \overline{BC}$. So △ABC ≅ △DBC by SAS. **3.** $DA = DC = 13$, so $\overline{DA} \cong \overline{DC}$ by def. of ≅. m∠ADB = m∠CDB = 32°, so ∠ADB ≅ ∠CDB by def. of ≅. $\overline{DB} \cong \overline{DB}$ by the Reflex. Prop. of ≅. Therefore △ADB ≅ △CDB by SAS.
4. 1. $\overline{QR} \cong \overline{QS}$ (Given)
2. $\overline{QP}$ bisects ∠RQS. (Given)
3. ∠RQP ≅ ∠SQP (Def. of bisector)
4. $\overline{QP} \cong \overline{QP}$ (Reflex. Prop. of ≅)
5. △RQP ≅ △SQP (SAS Steps 1, 3, 4)

Exercises 1. ∠T **3.** It is given that $\overline{MN} \cong \overline{MQ}$ and $\overline{NP} \cong \overline{QP}$. $\overline{MP} \cong \overline{MP}$ by the Reflex. Prop. of ≅. Thus △MNP ≅ △MQP by SSS. **5.** When $x = 4$, $HI = GH = 3$, and $IJ = GJ = 5$. $\overline{HJ} \cong \overline{HJ}$ by the Reflex. Prop. of ≅. Therefore △GHJ ≅ △IHJ by SSS. **7a.** Given **b.** ∠JKL ≅ ∠MLK **c.** Reflex. Prop. of ≅ **d.** SAS Steps 1, 2, 3 **9.** It is given that $\overline{KJ} \cong \overline{LJ}$ and $\overline{GK} \cong \overline{GL}$. $\overline{GJ} \cong \overline{GJ}$ by the Reflex. Prop. of ≅. So △GJK ≅ △GJL by SSS. **11.** When $y = 3$, $NQ = NM = 3$, and $QP = MP = 4$. So by the def. of ≅, $\overline{NQ} \cong \overline{NM}$ and $\overline{QP} \cong \overline{MP}$. m∠M = m∠Q = 90°, so ∠M ≅ ∠Q by the def. of ≅. Thus △MNP ≅ △QNP by SAS. **13a.** Given **b.** $\overline{CB} \cong \overline{AB}$ ⊥ $\overline{DC}$ **d.** Def. of ⊥ **e.** Rt. ∠ ≅ Thm. **f.** $\overline{AB} \cong \overline{AB}$ **g.** SAS Steps 2, 5, 6 **15.** SAS **17.** neither **19.** $QS = TV = \sqrt{5}$, $SR = VU = 4$, $QR = TU = \sqrt{13}$. The ∡ are ≅ by SSS. **21a.** Given **b.** Def. of ≅ **c.** m∠WVY = m∠ZYV **d.** Def. of ≅ **e.** Given **f.** $\overline{VY} \cong \overline{YV}$ **g.** SAS Steps 6, 5, 7 **25.** Measure the lengths of the logs. If the lengths of the logs in 1 wing deflector match the lengths of the logs in the other wing deflector, the ∡ will be ≅ by SAS or SSS. **27.** Yes; if each side is ≅ to the corr. side of the second △, they can be in any order. **29.** G **31.** J **35.** $x = 27$; $FK = FH = 171$, so $\overline{FK} \cong \overline{FH}$ by the def. of ≅. ∠KFJ ≅ ∠HFJ by the def. of ∠ bisector. $\overline{FJ} \cong \overline{FJ}$ by the Reflex. Prop. of ≅. So △FJK ≅ △FJH by SAS. **37.** $a < 4$

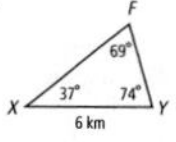

43. 34°

4-5

Check It Out! 1. Yes; the △ is uniquely determined by AAS. **2.** By the Alt. Int. ∡ Thm., ∠KLN ≅ ∠MNL. $\overline{LN} \cong \overline{LN}$ by the Reflex. Prop. of ≅. No other congruence relationships can be determined, so ASA cannot be applied. **3.** Given: $\overline{JL}$ bisects ∠KLM, and ∠K ≅ ∠M.
Prove: △JKL ≅ △JML

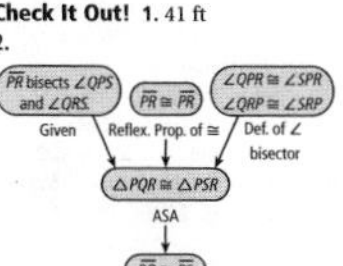

4. Yes; it is given that $\overline{AC} \cong \overline{DB}$. $\overline{CB} \cong \overline{CB}$ by the Reflex. Prop. of ≅. Since ∠ABC and ∠DCB are rt. ∡, △ABC and △DCB are rt. ∡. △ABC ≅ △DCB by HL.

Exercises 1. The included side $\overline{BC}$ is enclosed between ∠ABC and ∠ACB. **3.** Yes, the △ is determined by AAS. **5.** No; you need to know that a pair of corr. sides are ≅. **7.** Yes; it is given that ∠D and ∠B are rt. ∡ and $\overline{AD} \cong \overline{BC}$. △ABC and △CDA are rt. ∡ by def. $\overline{AC} \cong \overline{CA}$ by the Reflex. Prop. of ≅. So △ABC ≅ △CDA by HL.
9.

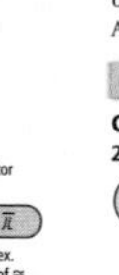

11. No; you need to know that ∠MKJ ≅ ∠MKL. **13a.** ∠A ≅ ∠D **b.** Given **c.** ∠C ≅ ∠F **d.** AAS **15.** Yes; E is a mdpt. So by def., $\overline{BE} \cong \overline{CE}$, and $\overline{AE} \cong \overline{DE}$. ∠A and ∠D are ≅ by the Rt. ∠ ≅ Thm. By def. △ABE and △DCE are rt. ∡. So △ABE ≅ △DCE by HL. **17.** △FEG ≅ △QSR; rotation **19a.** No; there is not enough information given to use any of the congruence theorems. **b.** HL **21.** It is given that △ABC and △DEF are rt.∡. $\overline{AC} \cong \overline{DF}$, $\overline{BC} \cong \overline{EF}$, and ∠C and ∠F are rt. ∡. ∠C ≅ ∠F by the Rt. ∠ ≅ Thm. Thus △ABC ≅ △DEF by SAS. **27.** J **29.** G **31.** Yes; the sum of the ∠ measures in each △ must be 180°, which makes it possible to solve for x and y. The value of x is 15, and the value of y is 12. Each △ has ∡ measuring 82°, 68°, and 30°. $\overline{VU} \cong \overline{VU}$ by the Reflex. Prop. of ≅. So △VSU ≅ △VTU by ASA or AAS. **35.** 2; −6 **37.** 1; 5 **39.** 36.9°

4-6

Check It Out! 1. 41 ft
2.

3. 1. J is the mdpt. of $\overline{KM}$ and $\overline{NL}$. (Given)
2. $\overline{KJ} \cong \overline{MJ}$, $\overline{NJ} \cong \overline{LJ}$ (Def. of mdpt.)
3. ∠KJL ≅ ∠MJN (Vert. ∡ Thm.)
4. △KJL ≅ △MJN (SAS Steps 2, 3)
5. ∠LKJ ≅ ∠NMJ (CPCTC)
6. $\overline{KL} \parallel \overline{MN}$ (Conv. of Alt. Int. ∡ Thm.)
4. $RJ = JL = \sqrt{5}$, $RS = JK = \sqrt{10}$, and $ST = KL = \sqrt{17}$. So △JKL ≅ △RST by SSS. ∠JKL ≅ ∠RST by CPCTC.

Exercises 1. corr. ∡ and corr. sides. **3a.** Def. of ⊥ **b.** Rt. ∠ ≅ Thm. **c.** Reflex. Prop. of ≅ **d.** Def. of mdpt. **e.** △RXS ≅ △RXT **f.** CPCTC **5.** $EF = JK = 2$ and $EG = FG = JL = KL = \sqrt{10}$. So △EFG ≅ △JKL by SSS. ∠EFG ≅ ∠JKL by CPCTC. **7.** 420 ft
9. 1. $\overline{WX} \cong \overline{XY} \cong \overline{YZ} \cong \overline{ZW}$ (Given)
2. $\overline{ZX} \cong \overline{ZX}$ (Reflex. Prop. of ≅)
3. △WXZ ≅ △YZX (SSS)
4. ∠W ≅ ∠Y (CPCTC)
11. 1. $\overline{LM}$ bisects ∠JLK. (Given)
2. ∠JLM ≅ ∠KLM (Def. of ∠ bisector)
3. $\overline{JL} \cong \overline{KL}$ (Given)
4. $\overline{LM} \cong \overline{LM}$ (Reflex. Prop. of ≅)
5. △JLM ≅ △KLM (SAS Steps 3, 2, 4)
6. $\overline{JM} \cong \overline{KM}$ (CPCTC)
7. M is the mdpt. of $\overline{JK}$. (Def. of mdpt.)
13. $AB = DE = \sqrt{13}$, $BC = EF = 5$, and $AC = DF = \sqrt{18} = 3\sqrt{2}$. So △ABC ≅ △DEF by SSS. ∠BAC ≅ ∠EDF by CPCTC.
15. 1. E is the mdpt. of $\overline{AC}$ and $\overline{BD}$. (Given)
2. $\overline{AE} \cong \overline{CE}$; $\overline{BE} \cong \overline{DE}$ (Def. of mdpt.)
3. ∠AEB ≅ ∠CED (Vert. ∡ Thm.)
4. △AEB ≅ △CED (SAS Steps 2, 3)
5. ∠A ≅ ∠C (CPCTC)
6. $\overline{AB} \parallel \overline{DC}$ (Conv. of Alt. Int. ∡ Thm.)
17. 14 **25.** G **27.** G **29.** Any diag. on any face of the cube is the hyp. of a rt. △ whose legs are edges of the cube. Any 2 of these ∡ are ≅ by SAS. Therefore any 2 diags. are ≅ by CPCTC. **33.** 94 **35.** reflection across the x-axis **37.** Yes; it is given that ∠B ≅ ∠D and $\overline{BC} \cong \overline{DC}$. By the Vert. ∠ Thm., ∠BCA ≅ ∠DCE. Therefore △ABC ≅ △EDC by ASA.

4-7

Check It Out!
1. Possible answer:

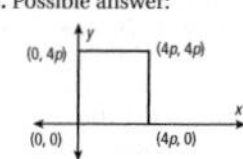

2. △ABC is a rt. △ with height AB and base BC. The area of △ABC is $\frac{1}{2}(4)(6) = 12$ square units. By the Mdpt. Formula, the coords. of D are $\left(\frac{0+4}{2}, \frac{6+0}{2}\right) = (2, 3)$. With $\overline{AB}$ as the base of △ADB, the x-coord. of D gives the height of △ADB. The area of $△ADB = \frac{1}{2}bh = \frac{1}{2}(6)(2) = 6$ square units. Since $6 = \frac{1}{2}(12)$, the area of △ADB is the area of △ABC.
3. Possible answer:

4. $\triangle ABC$ is a rt. $\triangle$ with height $2j$ and base $2n$. The area of $\triangle ABC = \frac{1}{2}bh = \frac{1}{2}(2n)(2j) = 2nj$ square units. By the Mdpt. Formula, the coords. of D are (n, j). The base of $\triangle ABD$ is $2j$ units and the height is n units. So the area of $\triangle ADB = \frac{1}{2}bh = \frac{1}{2}(2j)(n) = nj$ square units. Since $nj = \frac{1}{2}(2nj)$, the area of $\triangle ADB$ is $\frac{1}{2}$ the area of $\triangle ABC$.

Exercises

7. By the Mdpt. Formula, the coords. of A are $(0, a)$ and the coords. of B are $(b, 0)$. By the Dist. Formula, $PQ = \sqrt{(0-2b)^2 + (2a)^2} = \sqrt{(-2b)^2 + (2a)^2} = \sqrt{4b^2 + 4a^2} = 2\sqrt{b^2 + a^2}$ units. $AB = \sqrt{(0-b)^2 + (a-0)^2} = \sqrt{(-b)^2 + a^2} = \sqrt{b^2 + a^2}$ units. So $AB = \frac{1}{2}PQ$.

13. By the Mdpt. Formula, the coords. of E are $(0, a)$ and the coords. of F are $(2c, a)$. By the Dist. Formula, $AD = \sqrt{(2c-0)^2 + (2a-2a)^2} = \sqrt{(2c)^2} = 2c$ units. Similarly, $EF = \sqrt{(2c-0)^2 + (a-a)^2} = \sqrt{(2c)^2} = 2c$ units. So $EF = AD$.

15a.

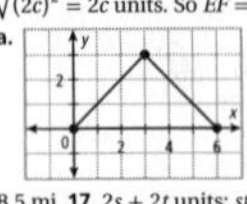

b. 8.5 mi **17.** $2s + 2t$ units; st square units **19.** $(p, 0)$ **21.** $AB \approx$ 128 nautical miles; $AP = BP \approx 64$ nautical miles; so P is the mdpt. of $\overline{AB}$. **23.** By the Dist. Formula, $AB = \sqrt{(x_2 - x_1)^2 + (y_2 - y_1)^2}$ and $AM = \sqrt{\left(\frac{x_1 + x_2}{2} - x_1\right)^2 + \left(\frac{y_1 + y_2}{2} - y_1\right)^2} = \sqrt{\left(\frac{x_1 + x_2}{2} - \frac{2x_1}{2}\right)^2 + \left(\frac{y_1 + y_2}{2} - \frac{2y_1}{2}\right)^2} = \sqrt{\frac{1}{4}(x_2 - x_1)^2 + \frac{1}{4}(y_2 - y_1)^2} = \frac{1}{2}\sqrt{(x_2 - x_1)^2 + (y_2 - y_1)^2}$. So $AM = \frac{1}{2}AB$. **27.** B **29.** D **31.** $(a + c, b)$ **35.** $x = -2.5$ or $x = 0.25$ **37.** $x = 2$ or $x = -1.67$ **39.** 22

4-8

Check It Out! **1.** 4.2×10^{13}; since it is 6 months between September and March, the $\angle$ measures will be the same between Earth and the star. By the Conv. of the Isosc. $\triangle$ Thm., the $\triangle$s created are isosc. and the dist. is the same. **2a.** 66° **2b.** 48° **3.** 10 **4.** By the Mdpt. Formula, the coords. of X are $(-a, b)$, the coords. of Y are (a, b), and the coords. of Z are $(0, 0)$. By the Dist. Formula, $XZ = YZ = \sqrt{a^2 + b^2}$. So $\overline{XZ} \cong \overline{YZ}$ and $\triangle XYZ$ is isosc.

Exercises **1.** legs: $\overline{KJ}$ and $\overline{KL}$; base: $\overline{JL}$; base $\angle$s: $\angle J$ and $\angle L$ **3.** 118° **5.** 27° **7.** $y = 5$ **9.** 20 **11.** It is given that $\triangle ABC$ is rt. isosc., $\overline{AB} \cong \overline{BC}$, and X is the mdpt. of $\overline{AC}$. By the Mdpt. Formula, the coords. of X are (a, a). By the Dist. Formula, $AX = BX = a\sqrt{2}$. So $\triangle AXB$ is isosc. by def. of an isosc. $\triangle$. **13.** 69° **15.** 130° or 172° **17.** $z = 92$ **19.** 26 **21.** It is given that $\triangle ABC$ is isosc., $\overline{AB} \cong \overline{AC}$, P is the mdpt. of $\overline{AB}$, and Q is the mdpt. of $\overline{AC}$. By the Mdpt. Formula, the coords. of P are (a, b) and the coords. of Q are $(3a, b)$. By the Dist. Formula, $PC = QB = \sqrt{9a^2 + b^2}$, so $\overline{PC} \cong \overline{QB}$ by the def of $\cong$ segs. **23.** S **25.** N **27a.** 38° **b.** $m\angle PQR = m\angle PRQ = 53°$ **29.** $m\angle 1 = 127°$; $m\angle 2 = 26.5°$; $m\angle 3 = 53°$ **33.** 20
39. **1.** $\triangle ABC \cong \triangle CBA$ (Given)
2. $\overline{AB} \cong \overline{CB}$ (CPCTC)
3. $\triangle ABC$ is isosceles (Def. of Isosc)
43. H **47.** $(2a, 0)$, $(0, 2b)$, or any pt. on the $\perp$ bisector of $\overline{AB}$ **49.** $x = 3$ or $x = 1$ **51.** $m = -3$ **53.** $m = \frac{2}{3}$

Study Guide: Review

1. isosceles triangle
2. corresponding angles
3. included side **4.** equiangular; equil. **5.** obtuse; scalene **6.** 60° **7.** 66.5° **8.** $\overline{XZ}$ **9.** $\angle Q$ **10.** 25 **11.** 7
12. **1.** $\overline{AB} \cong \overline{DE}$, $\overline{DB} \cong \overline{AE}$ (Given)
2. $\overline{DA} \cong \overline{DA}$ (Reflex. Prop. of $\cong$)
3. $\triangle ADB \cong \triangle DAE$ (SSS *Steps 1, 2*)
13. **1.** $\overline{GJ}$ bisects $\overline{FH}$, and $\overline{FH}$ bisects $\overline{GJ}$. (Given)
2. $\overline{GK} \cong \overline{JK}$, $\overline{FK} \cong \overline{HK}$ (Def. of seg. Bisect)
3. $\angle GKF \cong \angle JKH$ (Vert. $\angle$s Thm.)
4. $\triangle FGK \cong \triangle HJK$ (SAS *Steps 2, 3*)
14. $BC = (-6)^2 + 36 = 72$; $YZ = 2(-6)^2 = 72$; $\overline{BC} \cong \overline{YZ}$; $\angle C \cong \angle Z$; $\overline{AC} \cong \overline{XZ}$; so $\triangle ABC \cong \triangle XYZ$ by SAS. **15.** $PQ = 25 - 1 = 24$; $QR = 25$; $PR = 25^2 - (25-1)^2 - 42 = 7$; $\overline{LM} \cong \overline{PQ}$; $\overline{MN} \cong \overline{QR}$; $\overline{LN} \cong \overline{PR}$; so $\triangle LMN \cong \triangle PQR$ by SSS.
16. **1.** C is the mdpt. of $\overline{AG}$. (Given)
2. $\overline{GC} \cong \overline{AC}$ (Def. of mdpt.)
3. $\overline{HA} \parallel \overline{GB}$ (Given)
4. $\angle HAC \cong \angle BGC$ (Alt. Int. $\angle$s Thm.)
5. $\angle HCA \cong \angle BCG$ (Vert. $\angle$s Thm.)
6. $\triangle HAC \cong \triangle BGC$ (ASA *Steps 4, 2, 5*)
17. **1.** $\overline{WX} \perp \overline{XZ}$, $\overline{YZ} \perp \overline{ZX}$ (Given)
2. $\angle WXZ$ and $\angle YZX$ are rt. $\angle$s. (Def. of $\perp$)
3. $\triangle WZX$ and $\triangle YXZ$ are rt. $\triangle$s. (Def. of rt. $\triangle$)
4. $\overline{XZ} \cong \overline{XZ}$ (Reflex. Prop. of $\cong$)
5. $\overline{WZ} \cong \overline{YX}$ (Given)
6. $\triangle WZX \cong \triangle YXZ$ (HL *Steps 5, 4*)
18. **1.** $\angle S$ and $\angle V$ are rt. $\angle$s. (Given)
2. $\angle S \cong \angle V$ (Rt. $\angle \cong$ Thm.)
3. $RT = UW$ (Given)
4. $\overline{RT} \cong \overline{UW}$ (Def. of $\cong$)
5. $m\angle T = m\angle W$ (Given)
6. $\angle T \cong \angle W$ (Def. of $\cong$)
7. $\triangle RST \cong \triangle UVW$ (AAS *Steps 2, 6, 4*)
19. **1.** M is the mdpt. of $\overline{BD}$. (Given)
2. $\overline{MB} \cong \overline{DM}$ (Def. of mdpt.)
3. $\overline{BC} \cong \overline{DC}$ (Given)
4. $\overline{CM} \cong \overline{CM}$ (Reflex. Prop. of $\cong$)
5. $\triangle CBM \cong \triangle CDM$ (SSS *Steps 2, 3, 4*)
6. $\angle 1 \cong \angle 2$ (CPCTC)

20. **1.** $\overline{PQ} \cong \overline{RQ}$ (Given)
2. $\overline{PS} \cong \overline{RS}$ (Given)
3. $\overline{QS} \cong \overline{QS}$ (Reflex. Prop. of $\cong$)
4. $\triangle PQS \cong \triangle RQS$ (SSS *Steps 1, 2, 3*)
5. $\angle PQS \cong \angle RQS$ (CPCTC)
6. $\overline{QS}$ bisects $\angle PQR$. (Def. of bisect)
21. **1.** H is mdpt. of line $\overline{GJ}$, and L is mdpt. of $\overline{MK}$. (Given)
2. $GH = JH$, $ML = KL$ (Def. of mdpt.)
3. $\overline{GH} \cong \overline{JH}$, $\overline{ML} \cong \overline{KL}$ (Def. of $\cong$)
4. $\overline{GJ} \cong \overline{KM}$ (Given)
5. $\overline{GH} \cong \overline{KL}$ (Div. Prop. of $\cong$)
6. $\overline{GM} \cong \overline{KJ}$, $\angle G \cong \angle K$ (Given)
7. $\triangle GMH \cong \triangle KJL$ (SAS *Steps 5, 6*)
8. $\angle GMH \cong \angle KJL$ (CPCTC)
22. $(0, 0)$, $(r, 0)$, $(0, s)$ **23.** $(0, 0)$, $(2p, 0)$, $(2p, p)$, $(0, p)$ **24.** $(0, 0)$, $(8m, 0)$, $(8m, 8m)$, $(0, 8m)$ **25.** Use coords. $A(0, 0)$, $B(2a, 0)$, $C(2a, 2b)$, and $D(0, 2b)$. Then, by the Mdpt. Formula, $E(a, 0)$, $F(2a, b)$, $G(a, 2b)$, and $H(0, b)$. By the Dist. Formula, $EF = \sqrt{(2a-a)^2 + (b-0)^2} = \sqrt{a^2 + b^2}$, and $GH = \sqrt{(0-a)^2 + (b-2b)^2} = \sqrt{a^2 + b^2}$. So $\overline{EF} \cong \overline{GH}$ by the def. of $\cong$.
26. Use coords. $P(0, 2b)$, $Q(0, 0)$, and $R(2a, 0)$. Then, by the Mdpt. Formula, $M(a, b)$. By the Dist. Formula, $QM = \sqrt{(a-0)^2 + (b-0)^2} = \sqrt{a^2 + b^2}$, $PM = \sqrt{(a-0)^2 + (b-2b)^2} = \sqrt{a^2 + b^2}$, and $RM = \sqrt{(2a-a)^2 + (0-b)^2} = \sqrt{a^2 + b^2}$. So $QM = PM = RM$. By def. M is equidistant from the vertices of $\triangle PQR$ **27.** To be a rt. $\triangle$, the side lengths must have lengths such that $a^2 + b^2 = c^2$. $\sqrt{(3-3)^2 + (5-2)^2} = 3$, $\sqrt{(3-2)^2 + (2-5)^2} = \sqrt{10}$, and $\sqrt{(2-3)^2 + (5-5)^2} = 1$. Since $3^2 + 1^2 = \left(\sqrt{10^2}\right)$, or $9 + 1 = 10$, the triangle is a rt. $\triangle$. **28.** $x = -5$ **29.** $RS = 13.5$ **30.** 70 units

Chapter 5

5-1

Check It Out! **1a.** 14.6 **1b.** 10.4 **2a.** 3.05 **2b.** 126° **3.** $\overrightarrow{QS}$ bisects $\angle PQR$. **4.** $y + 1 = -\frac{2}{3}(x - 3)$

Exercises **1.** perpendicular bisector **3.** 25.9 **5.** 21.9 **7.** 38° **9.** $y - 1 = x + 2$ **11.** $y - 2 = \frac{4}{3}(x + 3)$ **13.** 26.5 **15.** 1.3 **17.** 54° **19.** $y + 3 = -\frac{1}{2}(x + 2)$ **21.** $y + 3 = \frac{5}{2}(x - 2)$ **23.** 38 **25.** 38 **27.** 24 **29.** Possible answer: $C(3, 2)$
31. **1.** $\overrightarrow{PS}$ bisects $\angle QPR$. $\overline{SQ} \perp \overrightarrow{PQ}$, $\overline{SR} \perp \overrightarrow{PR}$ (Given)
2. $\angle QPS \cong \angle RPS$ (Def. of $\angle$ bisector)
3. $\angle SQP$ and $\angle SRP$ are rt. $\angle$s. (Def. of $\perp$)
4. $\angle SQP \cong \angle SRP$ (Rt. $\angle \cong$ Thm.)
5. $\overline{PS} \cong \overline{PS}$ (Reflex. Prop. of $\cong$)
6. $\triangle PQS \cong \triangle PRS$ (AAS)
7. $\overline{SQ} \cong \overline{SR}$ (CPCTC)
8. $SQ = SR$ (Def. of $\cong$ segs.)
33a. $y = -\frac{3}{4}x + 2$ **b.** 2 **c.** 6.4 mi **35.** D **39.** the lines $y = x$ and $y = -x$ **43.** parallel **45.** perpendicular **47.** $y = -\frac{1}{2}x - 10$

5-2

Check It Out! **1a.** 14.5 **1b.** 18.6 **1c.** 19.9 **2.** $(4, -4.5)$ **3a.** 19.2 **3b.** 52°

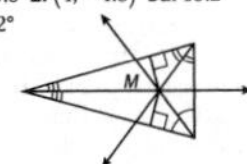

4. By the Incenter Thm., the incenter of a $\triangle$ is equidistant from the sides of the $\triangle$. Draw the $\triangle$ formed by the streets and draw the $\angle$ bisectors to find the incenter, point M. The city should place the monument at point M.

Exercises **1.** They do not intersect at a single point. **3.** 5.64 **5.** 3.95 **7.** $(2, 6)$ **9.** 42.1 **11.** The largest possible ⊙ in the int. of the $\triangle$ is its inscribed ⊙, and the center of the inscribed ⊙ is the incenter. Draw the $\triangle$ and its $\angle$ bisectors. Center the ⊙ at E, the pt. of concurrency of the $\angle$ bisectors. **13.** 63.9 **15.** 63.9 **17.** $(-1.5, 9.5)$ **19.** 55°

23. perpendicular bisector **25.** angle bisector **27.** neither **29.** S **31.** N **33.** $(4, 3)$ **35a.** $\angle$ Bisector Thm. **b.** the bisector of $\angle B$ **c.** $PX = PZ$ **37a.** $\left(4, -\frac{7}{6}\right)$ **b.** outside **c.** 4.2 mi **41.** F **45.** $t = 4$ **47.** $y = 120$ **49.** 35° **51.** yes **53.** no

5-3

Check It Out! **1a.** 21 **1b.** 5.4 **2.** 3; 4; possible answer: the x-coordinate of the centroid is the average of the x-coordinates of the vertices of the $\triangle$, and the y-coordinate of the centroid is the average of the y-coordinates of the vertices of the $\triangle$. **3.** Possible answer: An equation of the altitude to $\overline{JK}$ is $y = -\frac{1}{2}x + 3$. It is true that $4 = -\frac{1}{2}(-2) + 3$, so $(-2, 4)$ is a solution of this equation. Therefore this altitude passes through the orthocenter.

Exercises **1.** centroid **3.** 136 **5.** 156 **7.** $(4, 2)$ **9.** $(2, -3)$ **11.** $(-1, 2)$ **13.** 7.2 **15.** 5.8 **17.** $(0, -2)$ **19.** $(-2, 9)$ **21.** 12 **23.** 5 **25.** 36 units **27.** $(10, -2)$ **29.** 54 **31.** 48 **33.** Possible answer: $\perp$ bisector of the base; bisector of the vertex $\angle$; median to the base; altitude to the base **35.** A **37.** A **41.** D **43.** D **45a.** slope of $\overline{RS} = \frac{c}{b}$; slope of $\overline{ST} = \frac{c}{b-a}$; slope of $\overline{RT} = 0$
b. Since $\ell \perp \overline{RS}$, slope of $\ell = -\frac{b}{c}$. Since $m \perp \overline{ST}$, slope of $m = -\frac{b-a}{c} = \frac{a-b}{c}$. Since $n \perp \overline{RT}$, n is a vertical line, and its slope is undefined.
c. An equation of ℓ is $y - 0 = -\frac{b}{c}(x - a)$, or $y = -\frac{b}{c}x + \frac{ab}{c}$. An equation of m is $y - 0 = \frac{a-b}{c}(x - 0)$, or $y = \frac{a-b}{c}x$. An equation of n is $x = b$.
d. $\left(b, \frac{ab - b^2}{c}\right)$ **e.** Since the equation of line n is $x = b$ and the x-coordinate of P is b, P lies on n.
f. Lines ℓ, m, and n are concurrent at P. **47.** F **49.** 14.0 **51.** 108°

Check It Out! **1.** $M(1, 1)$; $N(3, 4)$; slope of $\overline{MN} = \frac{3}{2}$; slope of $\overline{RS} = \frac{3}{2}$; since the slopes are the same, $\overline{MN} \parallel \overline{RS}$. $MN = \sqrt{13}$; $RS = \sqrt{52} = 2\sqrt{13}$; the length of $\overline{MN}$ is half the length of $\overline{RS}$. **2a.** 72 **2b.** 48.5

2c. 102° **3.** 775 m

Exercises **1.** midpoints **3.** 5.1 **5.** 5.6 **7.** 29° **9.** less than 5 yd **11.** 38 **13.** 19 **15.** 55° **17.** yes **19.** 17 **21.** $n = 36$ **23.** $n = 8$ **25.** $n = 4$ **27.** B **29.** Possible answer: about 18 parking spaces **31.** 11 **33.** 57° **35.** 123° **37a.** 2.25 mi **b.** 28.5 mi **39.** D **41.** D **43.** equilateral and equiangular **45.** 7 **47a.** 32; 16; 8; 4 **b.** $\frac{1}{4}$ **c.** $64\left(\frac{1}{2}\right)^n = 2^{6-n}$ **49.** 2.25% **51.** $(4, -2)$, $(8, -1)$, $(5, -4)$ **53.** 6 **55.** 9

Check It Out!
1. Possible answer:
Given: $\triangle RST$
Prove: $\triangle RST$ cannot have 2 rt. $\angle$s.
Proof: Assume that $\triangle RST$ has 2 rt. $\angle$s. Let $\angle R$ and $\angle S$ be the rt. $\angle$s. By the def. of rt. $\angle$, $m\angle R = 90°$ and $m\angle S = 90°$. By the $\triangle$ Sum Thm., $m\angle R + m\angle S + m\angle T = 180°$. But then $90° + 90° + m\angle T = 180°$ by subst., so $m\angle T = 0°$. However, a $\triangle$ cannot have an $\angle$ with a measure of 0°. So there is no $\triangle RST$, which contradicts the given information. This means the assumption is false, and $\triangle RST$ cannot have 2 rt. $\angle$s.
2a. $\angle B$, $\angle A$, $\angle C$ **2b.** $\overline{EF}$, $\overline{DF}$, $\overline{DE}$ **3a.** No; $8 + 13 = 21$, which is not greater than the third side length. **3b.** Yes; the sum of each pair of 2 lengths is greater than the third length. **3c.** Yes; when $t = 4$, the value of $t - 2$ is 2, the value of $4t$ is 16, and the value of $t^2 + 1$ is 17. The sum of each pair of 2 lengths is greater than the third length.
4. greater than 5 in. and less than 39 in. **5.** 28 mi $< d <$ 72 mi

Exercises
3. Possible answer:
Given: $\triangle PQR$ is an isosc. $\triangle$ with base $\overline{PR}$.
Prove: $\triangle PQR$ cannot have a base $\angle$ that is a rt. $\angle$.
Proof: Assume that $\triangle PQR$ has a base $\angle$ that is a rt. $\angle$. Let $\angle P$ be the rt $\angle$. By the Isosc. $\triangle$ Thm., $\angle R \cong \angle P$, so $\angle R$ is also a rt. $\angle$. By the def. of rt. $\angle$, $m\angle P = 90°$ and $m\angle R = 90°$. By the $\triangle$ Sum Thm., $m\angle P + m\angle Q + m\angle R = 180°$. By subst., $90° + m\angle Q + 90° = 180°$, so $m\angle Q = 0°$. However, a $\triangle$ cannot have an $\angle$ with a measure of 0°. So there is no $\triangle PQR$, which contradicts the given information. This means the assumption is false, and therefore $\triangle PQR$ cannot have a base $\angle$ that is rt.
5. $\overline{YZ}$, $\overline{XZ}$, $\overline{XY}$ **7.** no **9.** no **11.** yes **13.** greater than 0 ft and less than 32 ft **15a.** the path from the refrigerator to the stove **b.** no **19.** $\overline{RS}$, $\overline{ST}$, $\overline{RT}$ **21.** no **23.** yes **25.** no **27.** greater than 5 km and less than 51 km **29.** greater than 1.18 m and less than 4.96 m **31.** greater than $2\frac{2}{3}$ ft and less than $10\frac{1}{3}$ ft **33.** $a > 7.5$, where a is the length of a leg. **35.** $\overline{EF}$, $\overline{DE}$, $\overline{DF}$ **37.** $m\angle Y < 90°$, and $\angle Y$ is an obtuse angle. **39.** $\overline{AB} \perp \overline{BC}$, and $\overline{AB} \parallel \overline{BC}$. **41.** x is a multiple of 4, and x is prime. **43.** < **45.** = **47.** > **49.** > **51.** < **53.** = **55.** $\angle L$, $\angle K$, $\angle J$ **57.** $\angle J$, $\angle L$, $\angle K$ **59a.** 0.4 h $< t <$ 2 h **b.** no **61.** $1 < n < 6$ **63.** $n > 0$ **65.** $n > 0.5$ **67a.** def. of $\cong$ segs. **b.** Isosc. $\triangle$ Thm. **c.** def. of $\cong$ $\angle$s **d.** $m\angle 1 + m\angle 3$ **e.** subst. **f.** $m\angle S$ **g.** Trans. Prop. of Inequal. **71.** H **73.** $\frac{3}{10}$, or 30% **77.** $-2x + y = 6$ **79.** $BC = 10$, $EF = 11$, and $m\angle ABC = 102°$, so $\triangle ABC \cong \triangle EFD$ by SAS. **81.** $(0, 0)$

5-6

Check It Out! **1a.** $m\angle EGF > m\angle EGH$ **1b.** $BC > AB$ **2.** The $\angle$ of the swing at full speed is greater than the $\angle$ at low speed.
3a. **1.** C is the mdpt. of $\overline{BD}$. $m\angle 1 = m\angle 2$, $m\angle 3 > m\angle 4$ (Given)
2. $\overline{BC} \cong \overline{DC}$ (Def. of mdpt.)
3. $\angle 1 \cong \angle 2$ (Def. of $\cong$ $\angle$s)
4. $\overline{AC} \cong \overline{EC}$ (Conv. of Isosc. $\triangle$ Thm.)
5. $AB > ED$ (Hinge Thm.)
3b. **1.** $\angle SRT \cong \angle STR$, $TU > RU$ (Given)
2. $\overline{ST} \cong \overline{SR}$ (Conv. of Isosc. $\triangle$ Thm.)
3. $\overline{SU} \cong \overline{SU}$ (Reflex. Prop. of $\cong$)
4. $m\angle TSU > m\angle RSU$ (Conv. of Hinge Thm.)

Exercises **1.** $AC < XZ$ **3.** $KL > KN$ **5.** $1.2 < x < 3$ **7.** the second position **9.** $m\angle DCA > m\angle BCA$ **11.** $TU > SV$ **13.** $-3.5 < z < 32.5$ **15.** the second position **17.** $BC = YZ$ **19.** > **21.** = **23.** < **25.** $m\angle RSV < m\angle TSV$ **27.** $m\angle YMX > m\angle ZMX$ **31.** D **33.** Group A is closer to the camp. **37.** 14; none **39.** $m\angle 2 = m\angle 6 = 36°$; $m \parallel n$ by the Conv. of the Corr. $\angle$s Post. **41.** 2.5 **43.** 85°

5-7

Check It Out! **1a.** $x = 4\sqrt{5}$ **1b.** $x = 16$ **2.** 29 ft 1 in. **3a.** $2\sqrt{41}$; no; $2\sqrt{41}$ is not a whole number. **3b.** 10; yes; the 3 side lengths are nonzero whole numbers that satisfy the equation $a^2 + b^2 = c^2$. **3c.** 2.6; no; 2.4 and 2.6 are not whole numbers. **3d.** 34; yes; the 3 side lengths are nonzero whole numbers that satisfy the equation $a^2 + b^2 = c^2$. **4a.** yes; obtuse **4b.** no **4c.** yes, acute

Exercises **1.** no **3.** $x = 6\sqrt{2}$ **5.** width: 14.8 in.; height: 11.9 in. **7.** 16; yes **9.** triangle; acute **11.** triangle; right **13.** triangle; acute **15.** $x = 10$ **17.** $x = 24$ **19.** 6; no **21.** $3\sqrt{5}$; no **23.** not a triangle **25.** triangle; right **27.** triangle; acute **29.** B **31.** $x = 8 + \sqrt{13}$ **33.** $x = 4\sqrt{6}$ **35.** $x = 6\sqrt{13}$ **39.** perimeter: $16 + 4\sqrt{7}$ units; area: $12\sqrt{7}$ square units **41.** perimeter: $14 + 2\sqrt{13}$ units; area: 18 square units **43.** perimeter: 22 units; area: 26 square units **47a.** King City **b.** $m\angle SRM > 90°$ **49.** B **51a.** $PA = \sqrt{2}$; $PB = \sqrt{3}$; $PC = 2$; $PD = \sqrt{5}$; $PE = \sqrt{6}$; $PF = \sqrt{7}$ **55a.** no **b.** yes. **c.** no **d.** no **57.** $x = -5$ **61.** $-\frac{1}{3} < x < 2$

Check It Out! **1a.** $x = 20$ **1b.** $x = 8\sqrt{2}$ **2.** 43 cm **3a.** $x = 9\sqrt{3}$; $y = 27$ **3b.** $x = 5\sqrt{3}$; $y = 10$ **3c.** $x = 12$; $y = 12\sqrt{3}$ **3d.** $x = 6\sqrt{3}$; $y = 3\sqrt{3}$ **4.** 34.6 cm

Exercises **1.** $x = 14\sqrt{2}$ **3.** $x = 9$ **5.** $x = 3$; $y = 3\sqrt{3}$ **7.** $x = 21$; $y = 14\sqrt{3}$ **9.** $x = \frac{15\sqrt{2}}{2}$ **11.** $x = 18$ **13.** $x = 48$; $y = 24\sqrt{3}$ **15.** $x = \frac{2\sqrt{3}}{3}$; $y = \frac{4\sqrt{3}}{3}$ **17.** perimeter: $\left(12 + 12\sqrt{2}\right)$ in.; area: 36 in² **19.** perimeter: $36\sqrt{2}$ m; area: 162 m² **21.** perimeter: $60\sqrt{3}$ yd; area: $300\sqrt{3}$ yd² **23.** no **25.** $(10, 3)$ **27.** $\left(5, 10 - 12\sqrt{3}\right)$ **29a.** 640 mi **b.** 453 mi **c.** 234 mi **31.** F **33.** 443.4 **35.** $x = \frac{32}{9}$ **39.** $y = (x - 5)^2 - 27$; $x = 5$ **41.** obtuse **43.** right **45.** 132°

Study Guide: Review

1. equidistant **2.** midsegment **3.** incenter **4.** locus **5.** 7.4 **6.** 13.4 **7.** 5.8 **8.** 52° **9.** $y = x - 1$ **10.** $y - 6 = -0.25(x - 4)$ **11.** No; to apply the Conv. of the $\angle$ Bisector Thm., you need to know that $\overline{AP} \perp \overline{AB}$ and $\overline{CP} \perp \overline{CB}$. **12.** Yes; because $\overline{AP} \perp \overline{AB}$, $\overline{CP} \perp \overline{CB}$, and $\overline{AP} \cong \overline{CP}$, P is on the bisector of $\angle ABC$ by the Conv. of the $\angle$ Bisector Thm. **13.** 42.2 **14.** 46 **15.** 57.6 **16.** 46 **17.** 18 **18.** 37° **19.** $(4, 3)$ **20.** $(-6, -3.5)$ **21.** 16.4 **22.** 8.2 **23.** 5.8 **24.** 17.4 **25.** $(-6, 0)$ **26.** $(1, 2)$ **27.** $(7, 4)$ **28.** $(3, 0)$ **29.** $(3, 4)$ **30.** 35.1 **31.** 64.8 **32.** 32.4 **33.** 42° **34.** 138° **35.** 42° **36.** $V(-1, -1)$; $W(6, 1)$; slope of $\overline{VW} = \frac{2}{7}$; slope of $\overline{GJ} = \frac{2}{7}$; since the slopes are the same, $\overline{VW} \parallel \overline{GJ}$. $VW = \sqrt{53}$; $GJ = 2\sqrt{53}$; since $\sqrt{53} = \frac{1}{2}\left(2\sqrt{53}\right)$, $VW = \frac{1}{2}GJ$. **37.** $\overline{BC}$, $\overline{AC}$, $\overline{AB}$ **38.** $\angle F$, $\angle H$, $\angle G$ **39.** greater than 9 cm and less than 18 cm **40.** Yes; possible answer: the sum of each pair of 2 lengths is greater than the third length. **41.** No; possible answer: when $z = 5$, the value of $3z$ is 15. So the 3 lengths are 5, 5, and 15. The sum of 5 and 5 is 10, which is not greater than 15. By the $\triangle$ Inequality Thm., a $\triangle$ cannot have these side lengths. **43.** $PS < RS$ **44.** $m\angle BCA < m\angle DCA$ **45.** $-1.4 < n < 3$ **46.** $2.75 < n < 12.5$ **47.** $x = 2\sqrt{10}$ **48.** $x = 2\sqrt{33}$ **49.** 6; the lengths do not form a Pythagorean triple because 4.5 and 7.5 are not whole numbers. **50.** 40; the lengths do form a Pythagorean triple because they are nonzero whole numbers that satisfy the equation $a^2 + b^2 = c^2$. **51.** triangle; obtuse **52.** not a triangle **53.** triangle; right **54.** triangle; acute **55.** $x = 26\sqrt{2}$ **56.** $x = 6\sqrt{2}$ **57.** $x = 32$ **58.** $x = 24$; $y = 24\sqrt{3}$ **59.** $x = 6\sqrt{3}$; $y = 12$ **60.** $x = \frac{14\sqrt{3}}{3}$; $y = \frac{28\sqrt{3}}{3}$ **61.** 21 ft 3 in. **62.** 15 ft 7 in.

Chapter 6

Check It Out! **1a.** not a polygon **1b.** polygon, nonagon **1c.** not a polygon **2a.** regular, convex **2b.** irregular, concave **3a.** 2340° **3b.** 144° **4a.** 30° **4b.** $r = 15$ **5.** 45°

Exercises **3.** not a polygon **5.** not a polygon **7.** irregular, concave **9.** $m\angle A = m\angle D = 81°$; $m\angle B = 108°$; $m\angle C = m\angle E = 135°$ **11.** 3240° **13.** 72° **15.** $m\angle Q = m\angle S = 135°$ **17.** not a polygon **19.** irregular, concave **21.** irregular, convex **23.** 160° **25.** 40° **27.** 120° **29.** 61.5 **31.** 72 **33.** 10 **35.** pentagon **37.** dodecagon **39.** 3; 60° **41.** 10; 144° **43.** A **45a.** heptagon **b.** 900° **c.** 140° **53.** A **55.** D **57.** $x = 36$; $y = 36$; $z = 72$ **59.** Yes, if you allow for $\angle$ measures greater than 180° **61.** $x = -3$ or $x = 4$ **63.** $0 < x < 8$ **65.** $4 < x < 10$ **67.** $5\sqrt{3}$

Check It Out! **1a.** 28 in. **1b.** 74° **1c.** 13 in. **2a.** 12 **2b.** 18 **3.** $(7, 6)$
4. **1.** $GHJN$ and $JKLM$ are ▱s. (Given)
2. $\angle N$ and $\angle HJN$ are supp. $\angle K$ and $\angle MJK$ are supp. (▱ → cons. $\angle$s supp.)
3. $\angle HJN \cong \angle MJK$ (Vert. $\angle$s Thm.)
4. $\angle N \cong \angle K$ ($\cong$ Supps. Thm.)

Exercises **3.** 36 **5.** 18 **7.** 70° **9.** 24.5 **11.** 51° **13.** $(-6, -1)$ **15.** 82.9 **17.** 82.9 **19.** 130° **21.** 10 **23.** 28 **25.** $(-1, 3)$ **27.** $PQ = QR = RS = SP = 21$ **29.** $PQ = RS = 17.5$; $QR = SP = 24.5$ **31a.** $\angle 3 \cong \angle 1$ (Corr. $\angle$s Post.); $\angle 6 \cong \angle 1$ (▱ → opp. $\angle$s $\cong$); $\angle 8 \cong \angle 1$ (▱ → opp. $\angle$s $\cong$) **b.** $\angle 2$ is supp. to $\angle 1$ (▱ → cons. $\angle$s supp.); $\angle 4$ is supp. to $\angle 1$ (▱ → cons. $\angle$s supp.); $\angle 5$ is supp. to $\angle 1$ (▱ → cons. $\angle$s supp.); $\angle 7$ is supp. to $\angle 1$ (Subst.) **33.** $\angle KMP$ (▱ → opp. $\angle$s $\cong$) **35.** $\overline{KM}$ (▱ → opp. sides $\cong$) **37.** $\overline{RP}$ (Def. of ▱) **39.** $\angle RTP$ (Vert. $\angle$s Thm.) **41.** $x = 119$; $y = 61$; $z = 119$ **43.** $x = 24$; $y = 50$; $z = 50$ **47.** $x = 5$; $y = 8$ **49a.** no **b.** no **51.** A **53.** 26.4 **55.** $(2, 4)$, $(4, -6)$, $(-6, -2)$ **59.** no correlation **61.** alt. ext. $\angle$s **63.** corr. $\angle$s **65.** 8 sides; 45°

6-3

Check It Out! **1.** $PQ = RS = 16.8$, so $\overline{PQ} \cong \overline{RS}$. $m\angle Q = 74°$, and $m\angle R = 106°$, so $\angle Q$ and $\angle R$ are supp., which means that $\overline{PQ} \parallel \overline{RS}$. So 1 pair of opp. sides of $PQRS$ are $\parallel$ and $\cong$. By Thm. 6-3-1, $PQRS$ is a ▱. **2a.** Yes; possible answer: the diag. of the quad. forms 2 $\triangle$s. 2 $\angle$s of 1 $\triangle$ are $\cong$ to 2 $\angle$s of the other, so the third pair of $\angle$s are $\cong$ by the Third $\angle$s Thm. So both pairs of opp. $\angle$s of the quad. are $\cong$. By Thm. 6-3-3, the quad. is a ▱. **2b.** No; 2 pairs of cons. sides are $\cong$. None of the sets of conditions for a ▱ are met. **3.** Possible answer: slope of $\overline{KL}$ = slope of $\overline{MN} = -\frac{7}{2}$; slope of $\overline{LM}$ = slope of $\overline{NK} = -\frac{1}{4}$; both pairs of opp. sides have the same slope, so $\overline{KL} \parallel \overline{MN}$ and $\overline{LM} \parallel \overline{NK}$; by def., $KLMN$ is a ▱. **4.** Possible answer: Since $ABRS$ is a ▱, it is always true that $\overline{AB} \parallel \overline{RS}$. Since $\overline{AB}$ stays vert., $\overline{RS}$ also remains vert. no matter how the frame is adjusted. Therefore the viewing $\angle$ never changes.

Exercises **1.** $FJ = HJ = 10$, so $\overline{FJ} \cong \overline{HJ}$. Thus $\overline{EG}$ bisects $\overline{FH}$. $EJ = GJ = 18$, so $\overline{EJ} \cong \overline{GJ}$. Thus $\overline{FH}$ bisects $\overline{EG}$. So the diags. of $EFGH$ bisect each other. By Thm. 6-3-5, $EFGH$ is a ▱. **3.** yes **5.** yes **7.** Possible answer: slope of $\overline{ST}$ = slope of $\overline{UR} = 0$; $\overline{ST}$ and $\overline{UR}$ have the same slope, so $\overline{ST} \parallel \overline{UR}$; $ST = UR = 6$; 1 pair of opp. sides are $\parallel$ and $\cong$; by Thm. 6-3-1, $RSTU$ is a ▱. **9.** $BC = GH = 16.6$, so $\overline{BC} \cong \overline{GH}$. $CG = HB = 28$, so $\overline{CG} \cong \overline{HB}$. Since both pairs of opp. sides of $BCGH$ are $\cong$, $BCGH$ is a ▱ by Thm. 6-3-2. **11.** yes **13.** no **15.** Possible answer: slope of $\overline{PQ}$ = slope of $\overline{RS} = \frac{5}{3}$; $\overline{PQ}$ and $\overline{RS}$ have the same slope, so $\overline{PQ}$

$\parallel \overline{RS}$; $PQ = RS = \sqrt{34}$; 1 pair of opp. sides are $\parallel$ and $\cong$; by Thm. 6-3-1, $PQRS$ is a $\square$. **17.** no **19.** yes
21. $a = 16.5$; $b = 23.2$
23. $a = 8.4$; $b = 20$ **27a.** $\angle Q$
b. $\angle S$. **c.** $\overline{SP}$ **d.** $\overline{RS}$ **e.** $\square$
35 B **37.** no **39.** $(3, 1)$; $(-6, -3.5)$

41.

x	-5	-2	0	0.5
y	-38	-17	-3	0.5

43.

x	-5	-2	0	0.5
y	77	14	2	2.75

47. 12 **49.** 12

6-4

Check It Out! **1a.** 48 in. **1b.** 61.6 in. **2a.** 42.5 **2b.** 17° **3.** $SV = TW = \sqrt{122}$, so $\overline{SV} \cong \overline{TW}$. Slope of $\overline{SV} = \frac{1}{11}$, and slope of $\overline{TW} = -11$, so $\overline{SV} \perp \overline{TW}$. The coordinates of the mdpt. of $\overline{SV}$ and $\overline{TW}$ are $\left(\frac{1}{2}, -\frac{7}{2}\right)$, so $\overline{SV}$ and $\overline{TW}$ bisect each other. So the diags. of $STVW$ are $\cong \perp$ bisectors of each other.
4. Possible answer:
1. $PQTS$ is a rhombus. (Given)
2. $\overline{PT}$ bisects $\angle QPS$. (Rhombus → each diag. bisects opp. ∡)
3. $\angle QPR \cong \angle SPR$ (Def. of ∠ bisector)
4. $\overline{PQ} \cong \overline{PS}$ (Def. of rhombus)
5. $\overline{PR} \cong \overline{PR}$ (Reflex. Prop. of ≅)
6. $\triangle QPR \cong \triangle SPR$ (SAS)
7. $\overline{RQ} \cong \overline{RS}$ (CPCTC)

Exercises **1.** rhombus; rectangle; square **3.** 160 ft **5.** 380 ft **7.** 122°
9. Possible answer:
1. $RECT$ is a rect. $\overline{RX} \cong \overline{TY}$ (Given)
2. $\overline{XY} \cong \overline{XY}$ (Reflex. Prop. of ≅)
3. $RX = TY$, $XY = XY$ (Def. of ≅ segs.)
4. $RX + XY = TY + XY$ (Add. Prop. of =)
5. $RX + XY = RY$, $TY + XY = TX$ (Seg. Add. Post.)
6. $RY = TX$ (Subst.)
7. $\overline{RY} \cong \overline{TX}$ (Def. of ≅ segs.)
8. $\angle R$ and $\angle T$ are rt. ∡. (Def. of rect.)
9. $\angle R \cong \angle T$ (Rt. ∠ ≅ Thm.)
10. $RECT$ is a $\square$. (Rect. → $\square$)
11. $\overline{RE} \cong \overline{TC}$ ($\square$ → opp. sides ≅)
12. $\triangle REY \cong \triangle TCX$ (SAS)

11. 25 **13.** $14\frac{1}{2}$ **15.** $m\angle VWX = 132°$; $m\angle WYX = 66°$
17. Possible answer:
1. $RHMB$ is a rhombus. $\overline{HB}$ is a diag. of $RHMB$. (Given)
2. $\overline{MH} \cong \overline{RH}$ (Def. of rhombus)
3. $\overline{HB}$ bisects $\angle RHM$. (Rhombus → each diag. bisects opp. ∡)
4. $\angle MHX \cong \angle RHX$ (Def. of ∠ bisector)
5. $\overline{HX} \cong \overline{HX}$ (Reflex. Prop. of ≅)
6. $\triangle MHX \cong \triangle RHX$ (SAS)
7. $\angle HMX \cong \angle HRX$ (CPCTC)

19. $m\angle 1 = 54°$; $m\angle 2 = 36°$; $m\angle 3 = 54°$; $m\angle 4 = 108°$; $m\angle 5 = 72°$ **21.** $m\angle 1 = 126°$; $m\angle 2 = 27°$; $m\angle 3 = 27°$; $m\angle 4 = 126°$; $m\angle 5 = 27°$ **23.** $m\angle 1 = 64°$; $m\angle 2 = 64°$; $m\angle 3 = 26°$; $m\angle 4 = 90°$; $m\angle 5 = 64°$ **25.** S **27.** S **29.** A **31.** S **35a.** Rect. → $\square$ **b.** $\overline{HG}$ **c.** Reflex. Prop. of ≅ **d.** Def. of rect. **e.** $\angle GHE$ **f.** SAS **g.** CPCTC **41.** $28\sqrt{2}$ in. ≈ 39.60 in.; 98 in² **45.** D **47.** H **51.** 45 **53.** T **55.** no

6-5

Check It Out! **1.** Both pairs of opp. sides of $WXYZ$ are ≅, so $WXYZ$ is a $\square$. The contractor can use the carpenter's square to see if 1 ∠ of $WXYZ$ is a rt. ∠. If 1 ∠ is a rt. ∠, then by Thm. 6-5-1 the frame is a rect. **2.** Not valid; by Thm. 6-5-1, if 1 ∠ of a $\square$ is a rt. ∠, then the $\square$ is a rect. To apply this thm., you need to know that $ABCD$ is a $\square$. **3a.** rect., rhombus, square **3b.** rhombus

Exercises **3.** valid **5.** rhombus **7.** valid **9.** square, rect., rhombus **11.** $\square$, rect. **13.** $\square$, rect., rhombus, square **15.** $\square$, rect., rhombus, square **17.** B **19.** $\overline{PR} \cong \overline{QS}$ **21.** $(2, 6)$ **23.** $(-2, -2)$ **25.** $x = 3$ **27.** rhombus **29a.** slope of $\overline{AB}$ = slope of $\overline{CD} = -\frac{1}{3}$; slope of $\overline{AD}$ = slope of $\overline{CB} = -3$ **b.** Slope of $\overline{AC} = -1$; slope of $\overline{BD} = 1$; the slopes are negative reciprocals of each other, so $\overline{AC} \perp \overline{BD}$. **c.** $ABCD$ is a rhombus, since it is a $\square$ and its diags. are ⊥ (Thm. 6-5-4.) **33b.** $\square$ **c.** square **39.** A **41a.** $15x = 13x + 12$; $x = 6$ **b.** yes **c.** no **d.** yes **43b.** no **c.** no **45.** linear **47.** linear **49.** $31 + \sqrt{61} \approx 38.8$ **51.** $y = 4$

6-6

Check It Out! **1.** about 191.3 in.; 3 packages **2a.** 51° **2b.** 110° **2c.** 62° **3a.** 131° **3b.** 25.4 **4.** $x = 4$ or $x = -4$ **5.** 8

Exercises **1.** bases: $\overline{RS}$ and $\overline{PV}$; legs: $\overline{PR}$ and $\overline{VS}$; midsegment: $\overline{QT}$ **3.** about 20.1 in.; 3 sun catchers **5.** 63° **7.** 106° **9.** $z = 2$ or $z = -2$ **11.** 14 **13.** about 56.6 in.; about 418.3 in. **15.** 122° **17.** 62° **19.** $\pm 4\sqrt{5}$ **21.** 3.6 **23.** S **25.** N **27.** $m\angle 1 = 82°$; $m\angle 2 = 128°$ **29.** $m\angle 1 = 51°$; $m\angle 2 = 16°$ **31.** $m\angle 1 = 120°$ **33a.** $EF = FG = \sqrt{17}$, and $GH = HE = \sqrt{29}$, so $\overline{EF} \cong \overline{FG}$, and $\overline{GH} \cong \overline{HE}$. Thus $EFGH$ is a kite, since it has exactly 2 pairs of ≅ cons. sides. **b.** $m\angle E = m\angle G = 126°$ **35.** 13 **37.** $m\angle PAQ = 108°$; $m\angle OAQ = 130°$; $m\angle OBP = 22°$ **41.** kite **43.** isosc. trap. **47.** B **49.** 18 **51.** $AD = 7.08$ in.; $AB = CD = 5.08$ in.; $BC = 10.16$ in. **53.** $2x < x + 6$; $x < 6$ **55.** rect., rhombus, square

Study Guide: Review

1. vertex of a polygon **2.** convex **3.** rhombus **4.** base of a trapezoid **5.** not a polygon **6.** polygon; △ **7.** polygon; dodecagon **8.** irregular; concave **9.** irregular; convex **10.** reg.; convex **11.** 1800° **12.** 162° **13.** 90° **14.** $m\angle A = m\angle D = 144°$; $m\angle B = m\angle E = 126°$; $m\angle C = m\angle F = 90°$ **15.** 37.5 **16.** 62.4 **17.** 37.5 **18.** 79° **19.** 101° **20.** 101° **21.** 9.5 **22.** 9.5 **23.** 54° **24.** 126° **25.** 54° **26.** 126° **27.** $T(6, -5)$
28.
1. $GHLM$ is a $\square$. $\angle L \cong \angle JMG$ (Given)
2. $\angle G \cong \angle L$ ($\square$ → opp. ∡ ≅)
3. $\angle G \cong \angle JMG$ (Trans. Prop. of ≅)
4. $\overline{GJ} \cong \overline{MJ}$ (Conv. of Isosc. △ Thm.)
5. $\triangle GJM$ is isosc. (Def. of isosc. △)

29. $m\angle A = m\angle E = 63°$; $m\angle G = 117°$; since $117° + 63° = 180°$, $\angle G$ is supp. to $\angle A$ and to $\angle E$. So 1 ∠ of $ACEG$ is supp. to both of its cons. ∡. By Thm. 6-3-4, $ACEG$ is a $\square$. **30.** $RS = QT = 25$, so $\overline{RS} \cong \overline{QT}$. $m\angle R = 76°$, $m\angle Q = 104°$, and $m\angle R + m\angle Q = 180°$, so $\angle R$ is supp. to

$\angle Q$. Since $\angle R$ and $\angle Q$ are a pair of same-side int. ∡, and they are supp., $\overline{RS} \parallel \overline{QT}$. So 1 pair of opp. sides of $QRST$ are ∥ and ≅. By Thm. 6-3-1, $QRST$ is a $\square$.
31. Yes; the diags. of the quad. bisect each other. By Thm. 6-3-5, the quad. is a $\square$. **32.** No; a pair of alt. int. ∡ are ≅, so 1 pair of opp. sides are ∥. A different pair of opp. sides are ≅. None of the conditions for a $\square$ are met. **33.** slope of $\overline{BD}$ = slope of $\overline{FH} = \frac{1}{5}$; slope of $\overline{BH}$ = slope of $\overline{DF} = -6$; both pairs of opp. sides have the same slope, so $\overline{BD} \parallel \overline{FH}$ and $\overline{BH} \parallel \overline{DF}$; by def., $BDFH$ is a $\square$. **34.** 18 **35.** 39.6 **36.** 39.6 **37.** 19.8 **38.** 25.5 **39.** 10.5 **40.** 25.5 **41.** 21 **42.** 41° **43.** 49° **44.** 82° **45.** 98° **46.** $m\angle 1 = 57°$; $m\angle 2 = 66°$; $m\angle 3 = 33°$; $m\angle 4 = 114°$; $m\angle 5 = 57°$ **47.** $m\angle 1 = 37°$; $m\angle 2 = 53°$; $m\angle 3 = 90°$; $m\angle 4 = 37°$; $m\angle 5 = 53°$ **48.** $RT = SU = 2\sqrt{10}$, so $\overline{RT} \cong \overline{SU}$. Slope of $\overline{RT} = -3$, and slope of $\overline{SU} = \frac{1}{3}$, so $\overline{RT} \perp \overline{SU}$. The coordinates of the mdpt. of $\overline{RT}$ and $\overline{SU}$ are $(-4, -3)$, so $\overline{RT}$ and $\overline{SU}$ bisect each other. So the diags. of $RSTU$ are $\cong \perp$ bisectors of each other. **49.** $EG = FH = 3\sqrt{2}$, so $\overline{EG} \cong \overline{FH}$. Slope of $\overline{EG} = -1$, and slope of $\overline{FH} = 1$, so $\overline{EG} \perp \overline{FH}$. The coordinates of the mdpt. of $\overline{EG}$ and $\overline{FH}$ are $\left(\frac{7}{2}, -\frac{1}{2}\right)$, so $\overline{EG}$ and $\overline{FH}$ bisect each other. So the diags. of $EFGH$ are $\cong \perp$ bisectors of each other. **50.** Not valid; by Thm. 6-5-2, if the diags. of a $\square$ are ≅, then the $\square$ is a rect. By Thm. 6-5-4, if the diags. of a $\square$ are ⊥, then the $\square$ is a rhombus. If a $\square$ is both a rect. and a rhombus, then the $\square$ is a square. To apply this chain of reasoning, you must first know that $EFRS$ is a $\square$. **51.** valid **52.** valid **53.** rhombus **54.** rect. **55.** rect., rhombus, square **56.** 64° **57.** 25° **58.** 65° **59.** 123° **60.** $m\angle R = 126°$; $m\angle S = 54°$ **61.** 51.6 **62.** 48.5 **63.** 3.5 **64.** $n = 3$ or $n = -3$ **65.** kite **66.** trap. **67.** isosc. trap.

Chapter 7

7-1

Check It Out! **1.** $\frac{1}{4}$ **2.** 9°; 54°; 117° **3a.** $x = 21$ **3b.** $y = \pm 3$ **3c.** $d = 9$ **3d.** $x = 3$ or -9 **4.** 4:5 **5.** 1527.2 m

Exercises **1.** means: 3 and 2; extremes: 1 and 6 **3.** $\frac{1}{2}$ **5.** $-\frac{2}{3}$ **7.** 95° **9.** $y = 9$ **11.** $y = \pm 9$ **13.** $x = 0$ or $x = 3$ **15.** 2:9 **17.** $\frac{3}{1}$ **19.** $\frac{3}{2}$ **21.** 72°; 108°; 72°; 108° **23.** $x = 20$ **25.** $m = 2$ or $m = -4$ **27.** $x = \pm 8$ **29.** 3:5 **31.** $5b$ **33.** $\frac{b}{7}$ **35.** $\frac{1}{3}$ **37.** -3 **39a.** $\frac{1.25 \text{ in.}}{15 \text{ in.}} = \frac{x \text{ in.}}{9600 \text{ in.}}$ **b.** 800 in., or 66 ft 8 in. **41.** $\frac{4}{9}$ **45.** H **47.** First, cross multiply: $36x = 15(72)$, or $36x = 1080$. Then divide both sides by 36: $\frac{36x}{36} = \frac{1080}{36}$. Finally, simplify: $x = 30$. You must assume that $x \neq 0$. **49.** Given $\frac{a}{b} = \frac{c}{d}$, add 1 to both sides of the eqn. as shown: $\frac{a}{b} + \frac{b}{b} = \frac{c}{d} + \frac{d}{d}$. Adding the fractions on both sides of the eqn. gives $\frac{a+b}{b} = \frac{c+d}{d}$. **51.** $\frac{x+3}{x-6}$, where $x \neq \pm 6$ **53.** 1 **55.** 96° **57.** acute **59.** right

7-2

Check It Out! **1.** $\angle A \cong \angle J$; $\angle B \cong \angle G$; $\angle C \cong \angle H$; $\frac{AB}{JG} = \frac{BC}{GH} = \frac{AC}{JH} = 2$ **2.** yes; $\frac{5}{2}$; $\triangle LMJ \sim \triangle PNS$ **3.** 5 in.

Exercises **3.** $\angle A \cong \angle H$; $\angle B \cong \angle J$; $\angle C \cong \angle K$; $\angle D \cong \angle L$; $\frac{AB}{HJ} = \frac{BC}{JK} = \frac{CD}{KL} = \frac{DA}{LH} = \frac{2}{3}$ **5.** yes; $\frac{2}{3}$; $\triangle RMP \sim \triangle XWU$ **7.** $\angle J \cong \angle S$; $\angle K \cong \angle T$; $\angle L \cong \angle U$; $\angle M \cong \angle V$; $\frac{JK}{ST} = \frac{KL}{TU} = \frac{LM}{UV} = \frac{MJ}{VS} = \frac{5}{6}$ **9.** yes; $\frac{7}{8}$; $\triangle RSQ \sim \triangle UZX$ **11.** 14 ft **13.** S **15.** N **17.** S **19.** 5 **23.** $\angle O$; $\angle Q$ **27.** C **29.** The ratios of the sides are not the same; $\frac{12}{3.5} = \frac{24}{7}$; $\frac{10}{2.5} = 4$; $\frac{6}{1.5} = 4$. **33a.** rect. $ABCD \sim$ rect. $BCFE$ **b.** $\frac{\ell}{1} = \frac{1}{\ell - 1}$ **c.** $\ell = \frac{1+\sqrt{5}}{2}$ **d.** $\ell \approx 1.6$ **35.** 90° **37.** 70° **39.** $\frac{4}{x}$

7-3

Check It Out! **1.** By the △ Sum Thm., $m\angle C = 47°$, so $\angle C \cong \angle F$. $\angle B \cong \angle E$ by the Rt. ∠ ≅ Thm. Therefore $\triangle ABC \sim \triangle DEF$ by AA ~. **2.** $\angle TXU \cong \angle VXW$ by the Vert. ∡ Thm. $\frac{TX}{VX} = \frac{12}{16} = \frac{3}{4}$, and $\frac{XU}{XW} = \frac{15}{20} = \frac{3}{4}$. Therefore $\triangle TXU \sim \triangle VXW$ by SAS ~. **3.** It is given that $\angle RSV \cong \angle T$. By the Reflex. Prop. of ≅, $\angle R \cong \angle R$. Therefore $\triangle RSV \sim \triangle RTU$ by AA ~. $RT = 15$.
4.
1. M is the mdpt. of $\overline{JK}$, N is the mdpt. of $\overline{KL}$, and P is the mdpt. of $\overline{JL}$. (Given)
2. $MP = \frac{1}{2}KL$, $MN = \frac{1}{2}JL$, $NP = \frac{1}{2}KJ$ (△Midsegs. Thm.)
3. $\frac{MP}{KL} = \frac{MN}{JL} = \frac{NP}{KJ} = \frac{1}{2}$ (Div. Prop. of =)
4. $\triangle JKL \sim \triangle NPM$ (SSS ~ *Step 3*)

5. 5

Exercises **1.** By the △ Sum Thm., $m\angle A = 47°$. So by the def. of ≅, $\angle A \cong \angle F$, and $\angle C \cong \angle H$. Therefore $\triangle ABC \sim \triangle FGH$ by AA ~. **3.** $\frac{DF}{JL} = \frac{DE}{JK} = \frac{EF}{KL} = \frac{1}{2}$, so $\triangle DEF \sim \triangle JKL$ by SSS ~. **5.** It is given that $\angle AED \cong \angle ACB$. $\angle A \cong \angle A$ by the Reflex. Prop. of ≅. Therefore $\triangle AED \sim \triangle ACB$ by AA ~. $AB = 10$
7.
1. $\overline{MN} \parallel \overline{KL}$ (Given)
2. $\angle JMN \cong \angle JKL$, $\angle JNM \cong \angle JLK$ (Corr. ∡ Post.)
3. $\triangle JMN \sim \triangle JKL$ (AA ~ *Step 2*)

9. SAS or SSS ~ Thm. **11.** It is given that $\angle GLH \cong \angle K$. $\angle G \cong \angle G$ by the Reflex. Prop. of ≅. Therefore $\triangle HLG \sim \triangle JKG$ by AA ~. **13.** $\angle K \cong \angle K$ by the Reflex. Prop. of ≅. $\frac{KL}{KN} = \frac{KM}{KL} = \frac{3}{2}$. Therefore $\triangle KLM \sim \triangle KNL$ by SAS ~. **15.** It is given that $\angle ABD \cong \angle C$. $\angle A \cong \angle A$ by the Reflex. Prop. of ≅. Therefore $\triangle ABD \sim \triangle ACB$ by AA ~. $AB = 8$
17.
1. $CD = 3AC$, $CE = 3BC$ (Given)
2. $\frac{CD}{AC} = 3$, $\frac{CE}{BC} = 3$ (Div. Prop. of =)
3. $\angle ACB \cong \angle DCE$ (Vert. ∡ Thm.)
4. $\triangle ABC \sim \triangle DEC$ (SAS ~ *Steps 2, 3*)

19. 1.5 ft **21.** yes; SSS ~ **23.** $x = 3$ **25a.** Pyramids A and C are ~ because the ratios of their corr. side lengths are =. **b.** $\frac{5}{4}$ **27.** 2 ft; 4 ft **31a.** The ∡ are ~ by AA ~ if you assume that the camera is ∥ to the hurricane (that is, $\overline{YX} \parallel \overline{AB}$). **b.** $\triangle YWZ \sim \triangle BCZ$, and $\triangle XWZ \sim \triangle ACZ$, also by AA ~. **c.** 105 mi **35.** J **37.** 30 **41.** 94 **43.** Possible answer: $(0, k)$, $(2k, k)$, $(2k, 0)$, $(0, 0)$ **45.** $y = \pm 15$

7-4

Check It Out! **1.** 7.5 **2.** $AD = 16$, and $BE = 12$, so $\frac{DC}{AD} = \frac{20}{16} = \frac{5}{4}$, and $\frac{EC}{BE} = \frac{15}{12} = \frac{5}{4}$. Since $\frac{DC}{AD} = \frac{EC}{BE}$, $\overline{DE} \parallel \overline{AB}$ by the Conv. of the △ Proportionality Thm. **3.** $LM \approx 1.5$ cm; $MN \approx 2.4$ cm **4.** $AC = 16$; $DC = 9$

Exercises **1.** 30 **3.** $\frac{EC}{AC} = 1$, and $\frac{ED}{DB} = 1$. Since $\frac{EC}{AC} = \frac{ED}{DB}$, $\overline{AB} \parallel \overline{CD}$ by the Conv. of the △ Proportionality Thm. **5.** 286 ft **7.** $CD = 4$; $AD = 6$ **9.** 20 **11.** $\frac{PM}{MQ} = \frac{6.3}{2.7} = 2\frac{1}{3}$, and $\frac{PN}{NR} = \frac{7}{3} = 2\frac{1}{3}$. Since $\frac{PM}{MQ} = \frac{PN}{NR}$, $\overline{MN} \parallel \overline{QR}$ by the Conv. of the △ Proportionality Thm. **13.** $BC = 6$; $CD = 5$ **15.** CE **17.** BD **19.** DF **21.** 15 in. or $26\frac{2}{3}$ in.
23.
1. $\frac{AE}{EB} = \frac{AF}{FC}$ (Given)
2. $\angle A \cong \angle A$ (Reflex. Prop. of □)
3. $\triangle AEF \sim \triangle ABC$ (SAS ~ *Steps 1, 2*)
4. $\angle AEF \cong \angle ABC$ (Def. of ~ △)
5. $\overleftrightarrow{EF} \parallel \overline{BC}$ (Conv. of Corr. ∡ Post.)

25a. $PR = 6$; $RT = 8$; $QS = 3$; $SU = 4$ **b.** $\frac{PR}{RT} = \frac{QS}{SU}$, or $\frac{6}{8} = \frac{3}{4}$ **27.** 15 **33.** J **39.** Check students' work. **41.** $3n$ **43.** $(5, -18)$ **45.** $\angle KLJ \cong \angle NLM$ by the Vert. ∡ Thm. By the △ Sum Thm., $m\angle MNL = 68°$. So $\angle JKL \cong \angle MNL$. Therefore $\triangle JKL \sim \triangle MLN$ by AA ~.

7-5

Check It Out! **1.** 15 ft 7 in. **2.** 900 m, or 0.9 km **3.** Check students' work. The drawing should be 3.7 in. by 3 in. **4.** $P = 14$ mm; $A = 10\frac{2}{3}$ mm²

Exercises **1.** indirect measurement **3.** 12 ft **5.** 60 ft **11.** 27 cm² **13.** ≈ 57 km **19.** 864 m² **21.** ≈ 25 ft **23.** ≈ 39 ft **25.** $\frac{4}{5}$ **27.** 0.3 ft by 1.2 ft **29.** 20 in.; 12 in. **31a.** $\frac{1}{24}$ **b.** $\frac{1}{576}$ **c.** 24 ft² **33.** $\frac{1}{9}$ cm **35.** 1 cm:5 m; since each centimeter will equal 5 m, this drawing will be $\frac{1}{5}$ the size of the drawing with a scale of 1 cm:1 m. **39.** D **41.** C **43a.** 150 m **b.** 1.28 cm **47.** $x = -4$ or $x = 10$ **49.** $x \approx 0.65$ or $x \approx -4.65$ **51.** The slopes of $\overline{JK}$ and $\overline{LM} = 1$. The slopes of $\overline{KL}$ and $\overline{JM} = -1$. Since both pairs of opp. sides have the same slope, $\overline{JK} \parallel \overline{LM}$, and $\overline{KL} \parallel \overline{JM}$. By def., $JKLM$ is a $\square$.

7-6

Check It Out! **1.** The photo should have vertices $A'(0, 0)$, $B'(0, 2)$, $C'(1.5, 2)$, and $D'(1.5, 0)$. **2.** $N(0, -20)$; $\frac{2}{3}$ **3.** $RS = \sqrt{2}$, $RU = 3\sqrt{2}$, $RT = \sqrt{5}$, and $RV = 3\sqrt{5}$, so $\frac{RS}{RU} = \frac{RT}{RV} = \frac{1}{3}$. $\angle R \cong \angle R$ by the Reflex. Prop. of ≅. So $\triangle RST \sim \triangle RUV$ by SAS ~. **4.** Check students' work. The image of $\triangle MNP$ has vertices $M'(-6, 3)$, $N'(6, 6)$, and $P'(-3, -3)$. $MP = \sqrt{5}$, $MN = \sqrt{17}$, and $PN = 3\sqrt{2}$. $M'P' = 3\sqrt{5}$, $M'N' = 3\sqrt{17}$, and $P'N' = 9\sqrt{2}$. $\frac{M'P'}{MP} = \frac{M'N'}{MN} = \frac{P'N'}{PN} = 3$. So $\triangle M'N'P' \sim \triangle MNP$ by SSS ~.

Exercises **1.** dilation **5.** $S(0, -8)$; $\frac{5}{2}$ **7.** $JK = 2\sqrt{5}$, $JM = 3\sqrt{5}$, $JL = 2\sqrt{5}$, and $JN = 3\sqrt{5}$, so $\frac{JK}{JM} = \frac{JL}{JN} = \frac{2}{3}$. $\angle J \cong \angle J$ by the Reflex. Prop. of ≅. So $\triangle JKL \sim \triangle JMN$ by SAS ~. **9.** The image of $\triangle RST$ has vertices $R'(-3, 3)$, $S'(3, 6)$, and $T'(0, -3)$. $RS = 2\sqrt{5}$, $RT = 2\sqrt{5}$, and $ST = 2\sqrt{10}$. $R'S' = 3\sqrt{5}$, $R'T' = 3\sqrt{5}$, and $S'T' = 3\sqrt{10}$. $\frac{R'S'}{RS} = \frac{R'T'}{RT} = \frac{S'T'}{ST} = \frac{3}{2}$. So $\triangle RST \sim \triangle R'S'T'$ by SSS ~. **11.** $X(-24, 0)$; $\frac{8}{3}$ **13.** $DE = 2\sqrt{5}$, $DG = 3\sqrt{5}$, $DF = 4\sqrt{2}$, and $DH = 6\sqrt{2}$, so $\frac{DE}{DG} = \frac{DF}{DH} = \frac{2}{3}$. $\angle D \cong \angle D$ by the Reflex. Prop. of ≅. So $\triangle DEF \sim \triangle DGH$ by SAS ~. **15.** The image of $\triangle JKL$ has vertices $J'(-6, 0)$, $K'(-3, -3)$, and $L'(-9, -6)$. $JK = \sqrt{2}$, $JL = \sqrt{5}$, and $LK = \sqrt{5}$. $J'K' = 3\sqrt{2}$, $J'L' = 3\sqrt{5}$, and $L'K' = 3\sqrt{5}$. $\frac{J'K'}{JK} = \frac{J'L'}{JL} = \frac{L'K'}{LK} = 3$. So $\triangle JKL \sim \triangle J'K'L'$ by SSS ~. **17.** It is not a dilation; because it changes the shape of the figure. **21.** A **23.** A **25.** 12 **31.** 5 **33.** 12 **35.** 6

Study Guide: Review

1. proportion **2.** dilation **3.** means **4.** ratio **5.** $\frac{1}{5}$ **6.** $-\frac{1}{2}$ **7.** $\frac{3}{2}$ **8.** 54 **9.** 17.5; 30; 17.5; 30 **10.** $y = 21$ **11.** $s = 10$ **12.** $x = \pm 6$ **13.** $z = 13$ or $z = -11$ **14.** $x = \pm 8$ **15.** $y = 3$ or $y = -5$ **16.** yes; $\frac{5}{3}$; $JKLM \sim PQRS$ **17.** yes; 2; $\triangle TUV \sim \triangle WXY$
18.
1. $JL = \frac{1}{3}JN$, $JK = \frac{1}{3}JM$ (Given)
2. $\frac{JL}{JN} = \frac{1}{3}$, $\frac{JK}{JM} = \frac{1}{3}$ (Div. Prop. of =)
3. $\frac{JL}{JN} = \frac{JK}{JM}$ (Trans. Prop. of =)
4. $\angle J \cong \angle J$ (Reflex. Prop. of ≅)
5. $\triangle JKL \sim \triangle JMN$ (SAS ~ *Steps 3, 4*)

19.
1. $\overline{QR} \parallel \overline{ST}$ (Given)
2. $\angle RQP \cong \angle STP$ (Alt. Int. ∠ Thm.)
3. $\angle RPQ \cong \angle SPT$ (Vert. ∡ Thm.)
4. $\triangle PQR \sim \triangle PTS$ (AA ~ *Steps 2, 3*)

20.
1. $\overline{BC} \parallel \overline{CE}$ (Given)
2. $\angle ABD \cong \angle C$ (Corr. ∠ Post.)
3. $\angle ADB \cong \angle E$ (Corr. ∠ Post.)
4. $\triangle ABD \sim \triangle ACE$ (AA ~ *Steps 2, 3*)
5. $\frac{AB}{AC} = \frac{BD}{CE}$ (Def. of ~ polygons)
6. $AB(CE) = AC(BD)$ (Cross Products Prop.)

21. 10 **22.** $3\frac{1}{3}$ **23.** $\frac{JK}{JM} = \frac{JL}{JN} = \frac{1}{2}$. Since $\frac{JK}{JM} = \frac{JL}{JN}$, $\overline{KL} \parallel \overline{MN}$ by the Conv. of the △ Proportionality Thm. **24.** $\frac{EC}{EA} = \frac{ED}{EB} = \frac{3}{7}$. Since $\frac{EC}{EA} = \frac{ED}{EB}$, $\overline{AB} \parallel \overline{CD}$ by the Conv. of the △ Proportionality Thm. **25.** $SU = 4$; $SV = 6$ **26.** 18 **27.** $4x + 8$ **28.** 25 ft 4 in. **29.** 3 ft **30.** By the Dist. Formula, $RS = 2\sqrt{2}$, $RU = 4\sqrt{2}$, $RT = \sqrt{10}$, and $RV = 2\sqrt{10}$. $\frac{RS}{RU} = \frac{RT}{RV} = \frac{1}{2}$. $\angle R \cong \angle R$ by the Reflex. Prop. of ≅. So $\triangle RST \sim \triangle RUV$ by SAS ~. **31.** By the Dist. Formula, $JK = \sqrt{5}$, $JM = 4\sqrt{5}$, $JL = 2$, and $JN = 8$. $\frac{JK}{JM} = \frac{JL}{JN} = \frac{1}{4}$. $\angle J \cong \angle J$ by the Reflex. Prop. of ≅. So $\triangle JKL \sim \triangle JMN$ by SAS ~. **32.** $(0, -6)$; $\frac{2}{3}$ **33.** The image of $\triangle KLM$ has vertices $K'(0, 9)$, $L'(0, 0)$, and $M'(12, 0)$. By the Dist. Formula, $KL = 3$, $LM = 4$, $KM = 5$, $K'L' = 9$, $L'M' = 12$; and $K'M' = 15$. $\frac{K'L'}{KL} = \frac{L'M'}{LM} = \frac{K'M'}{KM} = \frac{3}{1}$. Therefore $\triangle KLM \sim \triangle K'L'M'$ by SSS ~.

Chapter 8

8-1

Check It Out! **1.** $\triangle LJK \sim \triangle JMK \sim \triangle LMJ$ **2a.** 4 **2b.** $10\sqrt{3}$ **2c.** $6\sqrt{2}$ **3.** 27; $3\sqrt{10}$; $9\sqrt{10}$ **4.** 148 ft

Exercises **1.** 8 is the geometric mean of 2 and 32. **3.** $\triangle BED \sim \triangle ECD \sim \triangle BCE$ **5.** 10 **7.** 2 **9.** 20 **11.** $2\sqrt{15}$; $2\sqrt{6}$; $2\sqrt{10}$ **13.** 12; $4\sqrt{13}$; 8 **15.** $\triangle MPN \sim \triangle PQN \sim \triangle MQP$ **17.** $\triangle RSU \sim \triangle RTS \sim \triangle STU$ **19.** $3\sqrt{5}$ **21.** $2\sqrt{5}$ **23.** $\frac{3\sqrt{5}}{10}$ **25.** $20\sqrt{3}$; $10\sqrt{21}$; $20\sqrt{7}$ **27.** 1670 ft **29.** $\frac{10}{3}$, or $3\frac{1}{3}$ **31.** $x + y$ **33.** z **35.** x **37.** $4\sqrt{5}$ **39.** $\frac{\sqrt{10}}{2}$ **41.** B **43.** By Corollary 8-1-3, $a^2 = x(x + y)$, and $b^2 = y(x + y)$. So $a^2 + b^2 = x(x + y) + y(x + y)$. By the Distrib. Prop., this expression simplifies to $(x + y)(x + y) = (x + y)^2 = c^2$. So $a^2 + b^2 = c^2$. **47.** D **49.** A **51.** 7; $\sqrt{35}$; $2\sqrt{15}$ **53.** $AC \approx 15.26$ cm; $AB \approx 8.53$ cm **55.** -4; 2 **57.** 6 **59.** 4 **61.** 39°

8-2

Check It Out! **1a.** $\frac{24}{25} = 0.96$ **1b.** $\frac{24}{7} \approx 3.43$ **1c.** $\frac{24}{25} = 0.96$ **2.** $\frac{s}{s} = 1$ **3a.** 0.19 **3b.** 0.88 **3c.** 0.87 **4a.** 21.87 m **4b.** 7.06 in. **4c.** 36.93 ft **4d.** 6.17 cm **5.** 14.34 ft

Exercises **1.** $\frac{LK}{JL}$ **3.** $\frac{4}{5} = 0.80$ **5.** $\frac{4}{5} = 0.80$ **7.** $\frac{4}{3} \approx 1.33$ **9.** $\frac{1}{2}$ **11.** $\frac{\sqrt{2}}{2}$ **13.** 0.39 **15.** 0.03 **17.** 0.16 **19.** 9.65 m **21.** 7 ft 6 in. **23.** $\frac{15}{8} \approx 1.88$ **25.** $\frac{15}{17} \approx 0.88$ **27.** $\frac{15}{17} \approx 0.88$ **29.** $\frac{1}{2}$ **31.** 1.23 **33.** 0.22 **35.** 0.82 **37.** 3.58 cm **39.** 19.67 ft **41.** 5.27 ft **43.** 6.10 m **45.** sine; cosine **47.** 60° **49.** 1.2 ft **53.** 0.6 **55.** 753 ft **59.** $\left(\frac{1}{2}\right)^2 + \left(\frac{\sqrt{3}}{2}\right)^2 = \frac{1}{4} + \frac{3}{4} = 1$ **61a.** $\sin A = \frac{a}{c}$; $\cos A = \frac{b}{c}$ **b.** $(\sin A)^2 + (\cos A)^2 = \left(\frac{a}{c}\right)^2 + \left(\frac{b}{c}\right)^2 = \frac{a^2}{c^2} + \frac{b^2}{c^2} = \frac{a^2 + b^2}{c^2} = \frac{c^2}{c^2} = 1$ **63.** 18.64 cm; 16.00 cm² **65.** 22.60 in.; 14.69 in² **69.** H **71.** $x \approx 5$; $AB \approx 20$; $BC \approx 18$; $AC \approx 27$ **75.** 1.25 **77.** 0.75 **79.** Possible answers: $(-2, 11)$; $(0, 10)$; $(2, 9)$ **81.** Trans. Prop. of ≅ **83.** Sym. Prop. of ≅ **85.** 12

8-3

Check It Out! **1a.** $\angle 2$ **1b.** $\angle 1$ **2a.** 37° **2b.** 87° **2c.** 42° **3.** $DF \approx 16.51$; $EF \approx 8.75$; $m\angle D = 32°$ **4.** $RS = ST = 7$; $RT \approx 9.90$; $m\angle S = 90°$; $m\angle R = m\angle T = 45°$ **5.** 21°

Exercises **1.** $\angle 1$ **3.** $\angle 1$ **5.** $\angle 2$ **7.** 65° **9.** 34° **11.** 38° **13.** $RP \approx 9.42$; $m\angle P \approx 19°$; $m\angle R \approx 71°$ **15.** $YZ \approx 13.96$; $m\angle Y \approx 38°$; $m\angle Z \approx 52°$ **17.** $RS = 5$; $ST = 6$; $RT \approx 7.81$; $m\angle S = 90°$; $m\angle R \approx 50°$; $m\angle T \approx 40°$ **19.** $AB = 2$; $BC = 4$; $AC \approx 4.47$; $m\angle B = 90°$; $m\angle A \approx 63°$; $m\angle C \approx 27°$ **21.** $\angle 2$ **23.** $\angle 1$ **25.** $\angle 2$ **27.** 18° **29.** 37° **31.** 57° **33.** $JK \approx 2.88$; $LK \approx 1.40$; $m\angle L = 64°$ **35.** $QR \approx 4.90$; $m\angle P \approx 36°$; $m\angle R \approx 54°$ **37.** $MN = NP = 4$; $MP \approx 5.66$; $m\angle N = 90°$; $m\angle M = m\angle P = 45°$ **39.** 74° **41.** cos **43.** 0.93 **47a.** 5° **b.** 85° **c.** 31 ft 1 in. **49.** 23°; 67° **51.** The acute ∠ measure changes from about 58° to about 73°, an increase by a factor of 1.26. **53a.** $AB = 5\sqrt{2}$; $BC = 2\sqrt{10}$; $AC = \sqrt{10}$ **b.** $AC^2 + BC^2 = AB^2$, so $\triangle ABC$ is a rt. △, and $\angle C$ is the rt. ∠. **c.** $m\angle A = 63°$; $m\angle B = 27°$ **55.** 35° **57.** 62° **59.** 72° **61.** 39° **65.** D **67.** A **69.** 58° **71.** 34° **73.** x **77.** F **79.** F **81.** -1 **83.** 0.89 **85.** 2.05

8-4

Check It Out! **1a.** angle of depression **1b.** angle of elevation **2.** 6314 ft **3.** 1717 ft **4.** 32,300 ft

Exercises **1.** elevation **3.** angle of elevation **5.** angle of elevation **7.** 18 ft **9.** 64.6 m **11.** angle of elevation **13.** angle of depression **15.** 1962 ft **17.** T **19.** F **21.** $\angle 1$ and $\angle 3$ **25a.** 424 ft **b.** 276 ft **27a.** 2080 ft **b.** 14 s **29.** J **31.** 98 m **33.** 1318 ft **35.** 6 min **37.** rhombus and square **39.** rectangle, rhombus, and square **41.** 4 **43.** $\frac{16}{3}$

8-5

Check It Out! **1a.** -0.09 **1b.** -0.03 **1c.** 0.34 **2a.** 34.9 **2b.** 29° **2c.** 26° **2d.** 17.7 **3a.** 6.5 **3b.** 30° **3c.** 7.0 **3d.** 65° **4.** 68.6 m; 54°

Exercises **1.** 0.98 **3.** -28.64 **5.** -0.68 **7.** 0.54 **9.** -0.91 **11.** 43° **13.** 44° **15.** 17.3 **17.** -0.09 **19.** -1.88 **21.** 0.99 **23.** -0.87 **25.** 0.79 **27.** 20.6 **29.** 10.4 **31.** 65° **33.** 33° **35.** 8.4 **37.** 21° **39.** 8.2 cm **41.** 50° **43.** no **45.** 63° **47.** 41.2 ft **49.** 42°; 138° **51.** Law of Sines **53.** Law of Sines **55.** $BC \approx 10.73$; $AB \approx 10.34$; $m\angle ABC \approx 50°$ **57a.** $y^2 + h^2$ **b.** b^2 **c.** $a^2 = c^2 - 2cx + x^2 + h^2$ **d.** $a^2 = c^2 + b^2 - 2cx$ **e.** $b \cos A$ **f.** Subst. **59.** A **61.** C **63.** 31° **65.** $3n$ **67.** $2n + 2$ **69.** Alt. Int. ∡ Thm. **71.** Alt. Ext. ∡ Thm. **73.** $\angle 1$

8-6

Check It Out! **1a.** $\langle -3, -4 \rangle$ **1b.** $\langle 7, 1 \rangle$
2. 3.2 **3.** 23°
4a. $\overrightarrow{PQ} = \overrightarrow{RS}$ **4b.** $\overrightarrow{PQ} \parallel \overrightarrow{RS}$; $\overrightarrow{XY} \parallel \overrightarrow{MN}$ **5.** 4.4 mi/h; 58°, or N 32° E

Exercises **1.** equal **3.** magnitude **5.** $\langle 8, -8 \rangle$ **7.** 4.1 **9.** 5.8 **11.** 11° **13.** $\overrightarrow{CD} = \overrightarrow{EF}$ **15.** $\overrightarrow{RS} = \overrightarrow{XY}$ **17.** 4.6 mi; 20°, or N 70° E **19.** $\langle -3.5, 5.5 \rangle$ **21.** 2.0 **23.** 4.3 **25.** 36° **27.** $\overrightarrow{DE} = \overrightarrow{LM}$ **29.** $\overrightarrow{RS} = \overrightarrow{UV}$ **31.** 190.1 km/h; 54°, or N 36° E **33.** $\langle 2, 2 \rangle$ **35.** $\langle 6, 2 \rangle$ **37a.** 98° **b.** 68.9 mi/h **c.** 36° **d.** N 81° E **39.** $\langle 7.1, 1.1 \rangle$ **41.** $\langle 2.2, 5.4 \rangle$ **43a.** $\frac{1}{12}$ **b.** $\frac{1}{6}$ **45.** 4; 0° **47.** 3.6; 56° **49.** $\langle 0, 10 \rangle$, $\langle 10, 0 \rangle$; $\langle 10, 10 \rangle$; the magnitude of the resultant is $10\sqrt{2}$, and the direction of the resultant is $\tan^{-1}\left(\frac{10}{10}\right) = 45°$. **53.** $\langle 3.5, 1 \rangle$; 3.6; 16° **55.** $\langle 4, 4 \rangle$; 5.7; 45° **57a.** $\langle 1, 3 \rangle$; $\langle 2, 6 \rangle$ **b.** $\sqrt{10}$; $2\sqrt{10}$; the magnitude of $2\vec{v}$ is twice the magnitude of $\vec{v}$. **c.** 72°; 72°; the direction of $2\vec{v}$ is the same as the direction of $\vec{v}$. **d.** Multiply each component by k. **e.** $-\vec{v} = -1\vec{v} = -1\langle x, y \rangle = \langle -x, -y \rangle$ **61.** G **63.** 8.2 **65.** 180° **67.** 6.4 mi/h at a bearing of N 58° E **69.** $(2, 7)$ **71.** $(6, -1)$ **73.** 54 cm² **75.** 73°

Study Guide: Review

1. component form **2.** equal vectors **3.** geometric mean **4.** angle of elevation **5.** trigonometric ratio **6.** $\triangle PRQ \sim \triangle RSQ \sim \triangle PSR$ **7.** 5 **8.** $\sqrt{51}$ **9.** $x = \sqrt{35}$; $y = 2\sqrt{15}$; $z = 2\sqrt{21}$ **10.** $x = 3$; $y = 3\sqrt{5}$; $z = 6\sqrt{5}$ **11.** $x = 5$; $y = \sqrt{5}$; $z = \sqrt{30}$ **12.** 11.17 m **13.** 6.30 m **14.** 10.32 cm **15.** 1.31 cm **16.** $m\angle C = 68°$; $AB \approx 4.82$; $AC \approx 1.95$ **17.** $m\angle H \approx 53°$; $m\angle G \approx 37°$; $HG \approx 5.86$ **18.** $m\angle S = 40°$; $RS \approx 42.43$; $RT \approx 27.27$ **19.** $m\angle Q \approx 41°$; $m\angle N \approx 49°$; $QN \approx 13.11$

20. angle of depression **21.** angle of elevation **22.** 36 ft **23.** 458 m **24.** 22° **25.** 31.4 **26.** 20.1 **27.** 56° **28.** $\langle -7, 2\rangle$ **29.** $\langle 1, -6\rangle$ **30.** $\langle -2, -5\rangle$

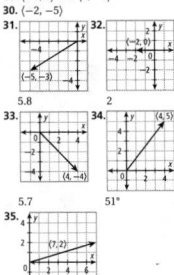

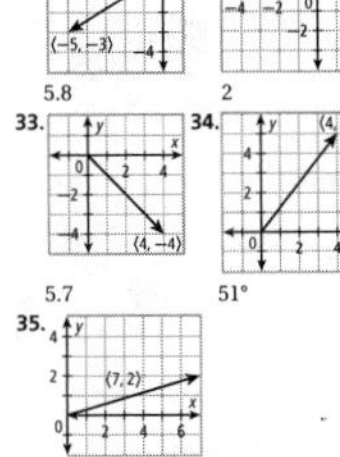

31. 5.8 **32.** 2 **33.** 5.7 **34.** 51° **35.** 16°

36. 641.6 mi/h; 32°, or N 58° E

Chapter 9

9-1

Check It Out! 1. $b = 0.5$ yd **2.** $A = 96\text{ m}^2$ **3.** $d_2 = 8y$ m **4.** $P = (4 + 4\sqrt{2})$ cm; $A = 4\text{ cm}^2$

Exercises 1. $A = 120\text{ cm}^2$ **3.** $P = 52$ cm **5.** $b = 13$ in. **7.** $A = 336\text{ in}^2$ **9.** $d_2 = 8xy^2$ cm **11.** $h = 1.25$ m **13.** $A = (21x^2 + 32x - 5)\text{ ft}^2$ **15.** $h = 20$ cm **17.** $A = 196\sqrt{3}\text{ in}^2$ **19.** $A = (12x^2 + 34x + 20)$ ft **21.** $A = 4.5\text{ in}^2$ **23.** $A = 30\sqrt{3}\text{ cm}^2$ **25.** $A = 300\text{ in}^2$ **27.** $A = \frac{x^2\sqrt{3}}{2}$ **29a.** $h = 31.2$ in. **b.** $A = 561.2\text{ in}^2$ **c.** 734.8 in^2 **31.** 8; 50 **33.** 9; 24 **35.** $h = 5$ cm **37.** 9 **39.** 100 **41.** $A = 108\text{ ft}^2$ **43a.** $A = \frac{1}{2}(a+b)^2$ **b.** $\frac{1}{2}ab$; $\frac{1}{2}ab$; $\frac{1}{2}c^2$ **c.** $\frac{1}{2}(a+b)^2 = \frac{1}{2}ab + \frac{1}{2}ab + \frac{1}{2}c^2$; $a^2 + b^2 = c^2$ **47a.** Possible answers: *A*: 4.2 cm²; *B*: 3.8 cm²; *C*: 4.3 cm² **b.** *C* has the greatest area. **49.** 23 cases **53.** H **55.** H **57.** $h = 4$ in. **59.** $b = (7x + 5)$ cm; $h = (6x + 3)$ cm **61a.** $A = x(12 - x)$ **b.** D: $0 < x < 12$; R: $0 < y \le 36$ **c.** 6 ft by 6 ft **d.** Solve the area formula for *y* and substitute the expression into the perimeter formula. Graph, and find the minimum value. **63.** $-2 \le y \le 2$ **65.** $P = 2x + 8$; $A = \frac{7x}{2}$ **67.** (6, 8)

9-2

Check It Out! 1. $A = (4x^2 - 12x + 9)\pi\text{ m}^2$ **2.** $C \approx 31.4$ in.; $C \approx 37.7$ in.; $C \approx 44.0$ in. **3.** $A \approx 77.3\text{ cm}^2$

Exercises 1. Draw a segment perpendicular to a side with one endpoint at the center. The apothem is $\frac{1}{2}s$. **3.** $A = 9x^2\pi\text{ in}^2$ **5.** $A \approx 50.3\text{ in}^2$; $A \approx 78.5\text{ in}^2$; $A \approx 113.1\text{ in}^2$ **7.** $A \approx 32.7\text{ cm}^2$ **9.** $A \approx 279.9\text{ m}^2$ **11.** $C = 5\pi$ m **13.** $A \approx 962.1\text{ ft}^2$; $A \approx 1963.5\text{ ft}^2$; $A \approx 3421.2\text{ ft}^2$ **15.** $A \approx 13.3\text{ ft}^2$ **17.** $A \approx 14.5\text{ ft}^2$ **19.** 90° **21.** 60° **23.** 45° **25.** 36° **27.** $A \approx 84.3\text{ cm}^2$ **29.** $A \approx 46.8\text{ m}^2$ **31.** $A \approx 90.8\text{ ft}^2$ **35.** $20\frac{\sqrt{\pi}}{\pi}$; $10\frac{\sqrt{\pi}}{\pi}$; $20\sqrt{\pi}$ **37.** 36; 18; 324π **39a.** $A \approx 745.6\text{ in}^2$ **b.** $A \approx 1073.6\text{ in}^2$ **c.** 44% **43.** B **45.** B **47.** $A = \frac{C^2}{4\pi}$ **49.** $y = 3x - 13$ **51.** $m\angle B = 124°$ **53.** $d_2 = 1.4$ cm

9-3

Check It Out! 1. $A = 1781.3\text{ m}^2$ **2.** $A \approx 10.3\text{ in}^2$ **3.** 23,296.5 gal **4.** $A \approx 12\text{ ft}^2$

Exercises 3. $A \approx 16.3\text{ ft}^2$ **5.** $A = 17.5\text{ m}^2$ **7.** $A \approx 4.5\text{ in}^2$ **9.** $A = 49.5\text{ mm}^2$ **11.** $A \approx 2.3\text{ m}^2$ **13.** 7 qt **15.** $A \approx 9\text{ m}^2$ **17.** $A = 540\text{ in}^2$ **19.** $A = \left(25\sqrt{3} + \frac{75\pi}{2}\right)\text{ in}^2$ **21.** Possible answer: 35,000 mi² **23a.** $A = 675\text{ in}^2$ **b.**

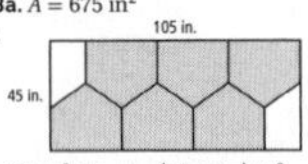

c. 675 in^2 **25.** $A = (26 + 2\pi)\text{ in}^2$ **27.** $A = 2$ **29.** Possible answer: $A \approx 10\text{ cm}^2$ **31.** A **33.** C **37.** 15.96 **39.** 1.4 **41.** $A \approx 3.9\text{ cm}^2$

9-4

Check It Out! 1. $A \approx 38\text{ units}^2$ **2.** parallelogram; $P \approx 20.8\text{ units}^2$; $A = 25\text{ units}^2$ **3.** $A = 48\text{ units}^2$

Exercises 1. $A \approx 40.5\text{ units}^2$ **3.** isosceles triangle; $P = (6 + 6\sqrt{2})$ units; $A = 9\text{ units}^2$ **5.** rectangle; $P = 28$ units; $A = 40\text{ units}^2$ **7.** $A = 20\text{ units}^2$ **9.** $A = 6\text{ units}^2$; $P = 12$ units; $A = 5\text{ units}^2$; $P = 12$ units

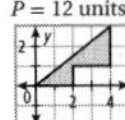
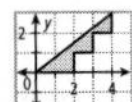

11. $A \approx 43.5\text{ units}^2$ **13.** rhombus; $P = 4\sqrt{29}$ units; $A = 20\text{ units}^2$ **15.** isosceles trapezoid; $P = (8 + 2\sqrt{29})$ units; $A = 20\text{ units}^2$ **17.** $A = 53\text{ units}^2$ **19.** $P = (6 + 3\sqrt{2})$ units; $A = 4.5\text{ units}^2$ **21a.** $A = 20$ mi **b.** $A \approx 150\text{ mi}^2$. The area represents the distance the boat traveled in 5 h. **23a.** $A = 6\text{ units}^2$ **b.** Possible answer: $C(2, 1)$ and $H(8, 2)$ **25.** J **27.** $A \approx 10.5\text{ units}^2$ **29.** $A \approx 17.5\text{ units}^2$ **31.** $P = 8\sqrt{2 - \sqrt{2}}$ units; $A = 2\sqrt{2}\text{ units}^2$ **33.** $-2 < a < 3$ **37.** $d = 22$ ft

9-5

Check It Out! 1. The area is tripled. **2.** The perimeter is tripled, and the area is multiplied by 9. **3.** The side length is multiplied by $\frac{1}{\sqrt{2}}$. **4.** Possible answer:

DVD Shipments (millions)

Exercises 1. The area is doubled. **3.** The perimeter is tripled. The area is multiplied by 9. **5.** The side length is multiplied by $\sqrt{2}$. **7.** $147.00 **9.** The area is multiplied by $\frac{2}{3}$. **11.** The circumference is multiplied by $\frac{3}{5}$. The area is multiplied by $\frac{9}{25}$. **13.** The side length is multiplied by $\sqrt{3}$. **15.** The area is multiplied by 64. **17.** The area is multiplied by 28. **19.** The area is divided by 16. **21.** The area is multiplied by 4. **23.** 800,000 acres **25a.** The area is multiplied by 3. **b.** The area is multiplied by 3 **c.** The area is multiplied by 9. **27a.** The area is multiplied by 3. **b.** The area is multiplied by 3. **c.** The area is multiplied by 9. **29a.** $8\sqrt{2}$ in. **b.** $4\sqrt{2}$ in. **31.** G **33.** 36 **35.** $A = (9\pi x^2 + 54\pi x + 81\pi)\text{ in}^2$ **37.** $\frac{t}{2} = 36$ **39.** 128.6°; 51.4° **41.** 154.3°; 25.7° **43.** $A = 32\text{ units}^2$

9-6

Check It Out! 1. $\frac{2}{3}$ **2.** $\frac{1}{2}$ **3.** $\frac{1}{2}$ **4.** 0.71

Exercises 3. $\frac{1}{2}$ **5.** $\frac{7}{10}$ **7.** 9 times **9.** $\frac{3}{8}$ **11.** $\frac{5}{12}$ **13.** 0.08 **15.** 0.79 **17.** 0.78 **19.** 0.46 **21.** 0.62 **23.** $\frac{1}{2}$ **25.** $\frac{3}{4}$ **27.** 0.5 **29.** 0.11 **31.** A **33.** 0.84 **35.** 0.13 **37.** 0.77 **39–41.** Possible answers given. **39.** The point lies on AC. **41.** The point lies in the blue triangle or the green triangle. **43.** $\frac{1}{2}$; it does not matter which regions are shaded because they all have the same area. **45.** A **47.** D **49.** $\frac{4-\pi}{4} \approx 0.21$ **53.** $4m^{10}$ **55.** By the Distance Formula, $AB = 2\sqrt{5}$, $AC = 2\sqrt{5}$, $BC = 4$, $AD = 4\sqrt{5}$, $AE = 4\sqrt{5}$, and $DE = 8$. $\frac{AB}{AD} = \frac{AC}{AE} = \frac{BC}{DE} = \frac{1}{2}$, so $\triangle ABC \sim \triangle ADE$ by SSS. **57.** $A \approx 10.6\text{ in}^2$

Study Guide: Review

1. apothem **2.** center of a circle **3.** geometric probability **4.** $A = 81\text{ in}^2$ **5.** $P = 22$ cm **6.** $h = 3x^2$ in. **7.** $h = 8$ ft **8.** $A = 252\text{ yd}^2$ **9.** $d_2 = 42xy^4$ in. **10.** $A = 288\text{ m}^2$ **11.** $C = 2$ ft **12.** $A \approx 153.9\text{ yd}^2$ **13.** $d = 16x$ m **14.** $A \approx 172.0\text{ ft}^2$ **15.** $A \approx 6.9\text{ in}^2$ **16.** $A \approx 309.0\text{ cm}^2$ **17.** $A = 72\text{ m}^2$ **18.** $A \approx 200.9\text{ ft}^2$ **19.** $A = 192\text{ cm}^2$ **20.** $A \approx 21.4\text{ mm}^2$ **21.** $A \approx 49.5\text{ units}^2$ **22.** $A \approx 44\text{ units}^2$ **23.** square; $P = 12\sqrt{2}$ units; $A = 18\text{ units}^2$ **24.** right triangle; $P = (12 + \sqrt{74})$ units; $A = 17.5\text{ units}^2$ **25.** isosceles trapezoid; $P = (12 + 4\sqrt{5})$ units; $A = 24\text{ units}^2$ **26.** parallelogram; $P = (8 + 2\sqrt{13})$ units; $A = 12\text{ units}^2$ **27.** $A = 30.5\text{ units}^2$ **28.** $A = 17.5\text{ units}^2$ **29.** $A = 12\text{ units}^2$ **30.** $A = 16\text{ units}^2$ **31.** The perimeter is multiplied by 3. The area is multiplied by 9. **32.** The perimeter is doubled. The area is multiplied by 4. **33.** The circumference is multiplied by $\frac{1}{2}$. The area is multiplied by $\frac{1}{4}$. **34.** The perimeter is multiplied by 4. The area is multiplied by 16. **35.** $\frac{7}{13}$ **36.** $\frac{8}{13}$ **37.** $\frac{12}{13}$ **38.** $\frac{6}{13}$ **39.** 0.17 **40.** 0.05 **41.** 0.17 **42.** 0.66

Chapter 10

10-1

Check It Out! 1a. cone; vertex: *N*; edges: none; base: $\odot M$ **1b.** triangular prism; vertices: *T*, *U*, *V*, *W*, *X*, *Y*; edges: $\overline{TU}$, $\overline{TV}$, $\overline{UV}$, $\overline{TW}$, $\overline{UX}$, $\overline{VY}$, $\overline{WX}$, $\overline{WY}$, $\overline{XY}$; bases: $\triangle TUV$, $\triangle WXY$ **2a.** triangular pyramid **2b.** cylinder **3a.** hexagon **3b.** triangle **4.** Cut through the midpoints of 3 edges that meet at 1 vertex.

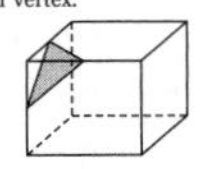

Exercises 1. cylinder **3.** rectangular prism; vertices: *C*, *D*, *E*, *F*, *G*, *H*, *J*, *K*; edges: $\overline{GH}$, $\overline{GK}$, $\overline{HJ}$, $\overline{JK}$, $\overline{GF}$, $\overline{HE}$, $\overline{JD}$, $\overline{KC}$, $\overline{FC}$, $\overline{CD}$, $\overline{DE}$, $\overline{EF}$; bases: *GHJK*, *CDEF* **5.** rectangular prism **7.** cube **9.** pentagon **11.** Cut parallel to the bases. **13.** cube; vertices: *S*, *T*, *U*, *V*, *W*, *X*, *Y*, *Z*; edges: $\overline{ST}$, $\overline{TU}$, $\overline{UV}$, $\overline{VS}$, $\overline{SW}$, $\overline{TX}$, $\overline{UY}$, $\overline{VZ}$, $\overline{WX}$, $\overline{XY}$, $\overline{YZ}$, $\overline{ZW}$; bases: *STUV*, *WXYZ* **15.** cylinder; vertices: none; edges: none; bases: $\odot R$, $\odot Q$ **17.** triangular pyramid **19.** square **21.** rectangle **23.** Cut perpendicular to the ground. **25.** rectangular prism **27.** hexagonal prism **29.** The figure is a cylinder whose bases each have a radius of 12 ft. The height of the cylinder is 9 ft. **31.**

33.

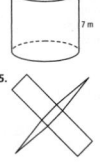

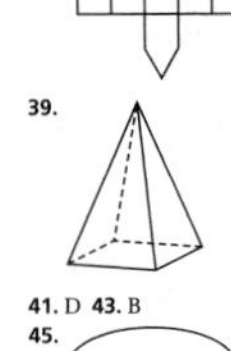

35.

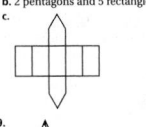

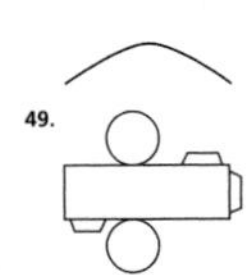

37a. pentagonal prism **b.** 2 pentagons and 5 rectangles **c.**

39.

41. D **43.** B **45.**

47.

49.

51a. *A* and *B*, *C* and *F*, *D* and *G*, *E* and *H* **b.** one **53.** $y = x^2 + 6$ **55.** largest: $\angle B$; smallest: $\angle C$ **57.** largest: $\angle I$; smallest: $\angle H$ **59.** yes; 10:17

10-2

Check It Out!

1.

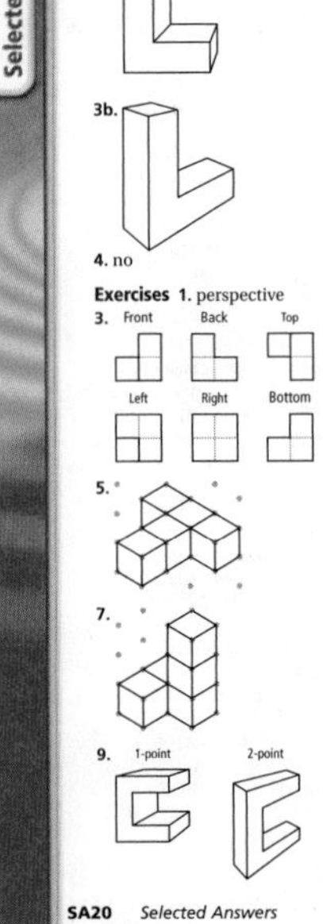

3b.

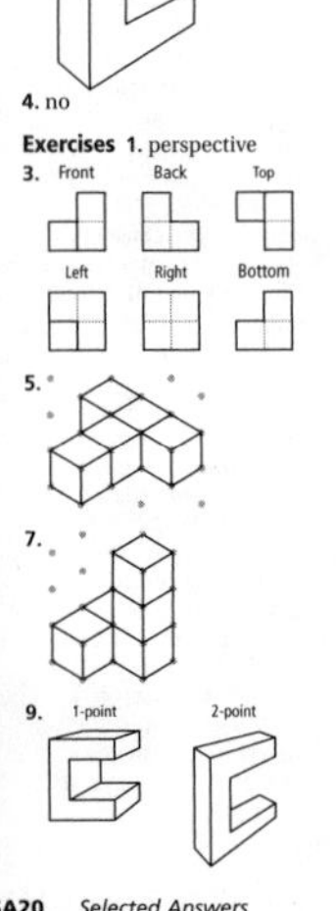

4. no

Exercises 1. perspective **3.**

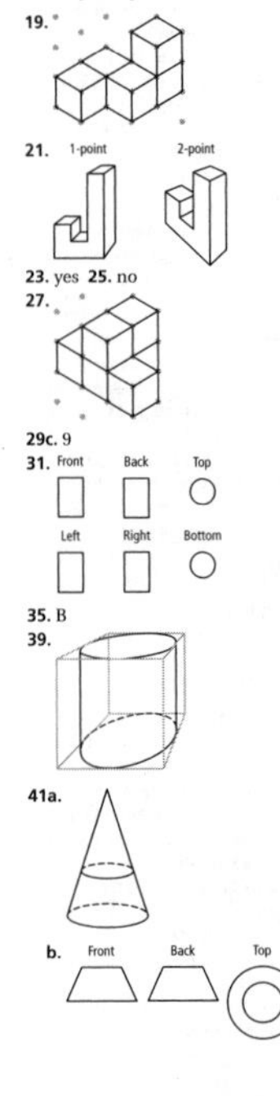

11. no **13.** no **15.**

23. yes **25.** no **27.**

29c. 9 **31.**

35. B **39.**

41a.

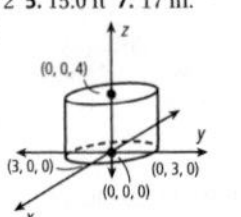

b.

c.

43. The first number is 20, and the second number is 10. **45.** The first number is 0, and the second number is 5. **47.** 2 **49.** 2 pentagons and 5 parallelograms **51.** 4 triangles

10-3

Check It Out! 1a. $V = 6$; $E = 12$; $F = 8$; $6 - 12 + 8 = 2$ **1b.** $V = 7$; $E = 12$; $F = 7$; $7 - 12 + 7 = 2$ **2.** $5\sqrt{3} \approx 8.7$ m **3.**

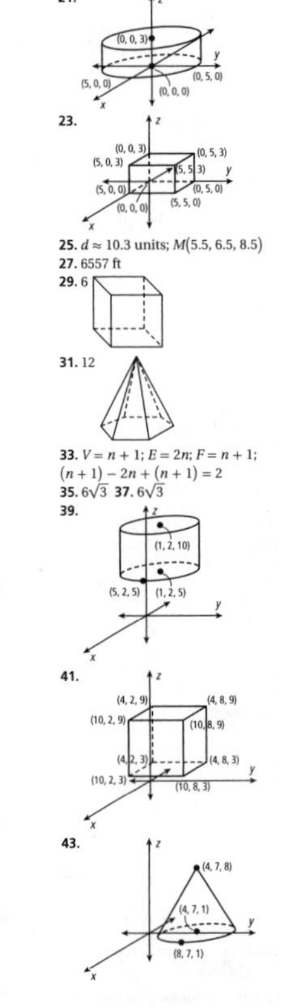

4a. $d \approx 12.9$ units; $M(3, 4.5, 8.5)$ **4b.** $d \approx 11.4$ units; $M(8.5, 12, 18)$ **5.** 36.2 ft

Exercises 1. because the bases are circles, which are not polygons **3.** $V = 6$; $E = 10$; $F = 6$; $6 - 10 + 6 = 2$ **5.** 15.0 ft **7.** 17 in. **9.**

11. $d \approx 14.4$ units; $M(2.5, 4.5, 5)$ **13.** $d \approx 9.3$ units; $M(6.5, 9, 12.5)$ **15.** $V = 8$; $E = 12$; $F = 6$; $8 - 12 + 6 = 2$ **17.** $V = 11$; $E = 20$; $F = 11$; $11 - 20 + 11 = 2$ **19.** $h \approx 5.3$ m

21.

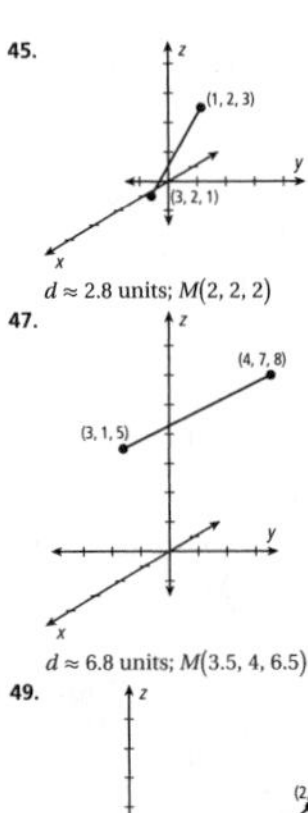

25. $d \approx 10.3$ units; $M(5.5, 6.5, 8.5)$ **27.** 6557 ft **29.** 6

31. 12

33. $V = n + 1$; $E = 2n$; $F = n + 1$; $(n + 1) - 2n + (n + 1) = 2$ **35.** $6\sqrt{3}$ **37.** $6\sqrt{3}$ **39.**

45.

$d \approx 2.8$ units; $M(2, 2, 2)$

47.

$d \approx 6.8$ units; $M(3.5, 4, 6.5)$

49.

$d \approx 4.6$ units; $M(4, 1.5, 7)$

51. $z = 9$ or $z = -15$ **53.** Possible answer: 1.8 in. **55.** $AB = 11$, $AC = 11$, and $BC = 11\sqrt{2}$, so $\triangle ABC$ is an isosc. rt. △. **57.** C **59.** B **61.** $AB = BC = 2\sqrt{6}$, and $AC = 4\sqrt{6}$, so $AB + BC = AC$. The points are collinear. **65.** 0–9 yr old **67.** $A = \frac{1}{2}h\left(\frac{1}{2}b_1 + b_2\right)$ **69.** cone **71.** $\odot C$

10-4

Check It Out! 1. $L = 256\text{ cm}^2$; $S = 384\text{ cm}^2$ **2.** $L = 196\pi\text{ in}^2$; $S = 294\pi\text{ in}^2$ **3.** 239.7 cm^2 **4.** The surface area is multiplied by $\frac{1}{4}$. **5.** It will melt at about the same rate as the half cylinder.

Exercises 1. 5 **3.** $L = 24\text{ cm}^2$; $S = 36\text{ cm}^2$ **5.** $L = 24\pi\text{ ft}^2$; $S = 42\pi\text{ ft}^2$ **7.** $L = 80\pi\text{ m}^2$; $S = 208\pi\text{ m}^2$ **9.** $S \approx 2855.0\text{ ft}^2$ **11.** The surface area is multiplied by $\frac{4}{9}$. **13.** $L = 200\text{ cm}^2$; $S = 250\text{ cm}^2$ **15.** $L = 336\text{ ft}^2$; $S \approx 391.4\text{ ft}^2$ **17.** $L = 184\pi\text{ cm}^2$; $S = 216\pi\text{ cm}^2$ **19.** $S \approx 352.0\text{ cm}^2$ **21.** The surface area is multiplied by 9. **23.** the cell that measures 35 μm by 7 μm by 10 μm **25.** $h = 3.5$ m **27.** $S \approx 121.5\text{ units}^2$ **29.** 836.58 **31.** 1057.86 **33.** Multiply the radius and height by $\frac{1}{2}$. **35.** 2.415 cm^2 **37a.** $AB = 7$ in.; $BC = 4\sqrt{2}$ in. ≈ 5.7 in. **b.** 4.1 in. **c.** 97.6 in^2 **39.** F **41.** $h = 18$ cm **43.** 198 cm^2 **45.** $70 \le s \le 110$ **47.** 77° **49.**

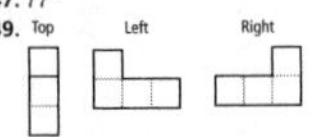

10-5

Check It Out! 1. $L = 90\text{ ft}^2$; $S \approx 105.6\text{ ft}^2$ **2.** $L = 80\pi\text{ cm}^2$; $S \approx 144\pi\text{ cm}^2$ **3.** The surface area is multiplied by $\frac{4}{9}$. **4.** $S \approx 28.9\text{ yd}^2$ **5.** 9 in.

Exercises 1. the vertex and the center of the base **3.** $L = 544\text{ ft}^2$; $S = 800\text{ ft}^2$ **5.** $L = 175\pi\text{ in}^2$; $S = 224\pi\text{ in}^2$ **7.** $L = 48\pi\text{ ft}^2$; $S = 84\pi\text{ ft}^2$ **9.** The surface area is multiplied by 9. **11.** $S = 1056\pi\text{ m}^2$ **13.** $L = 60\text{ ft}^2$; $S = 96\text{ ft}^2$ **15.** $L = 315\text{ ft}^2$; $S \approx 442.3\text{ ft}^2$ **17.** $L = 444\pi\text{ in}^2$; $S = 588\pi\text{ in}^2$ **19.** The surface area is divided by 9. **21.** $S = 287\pi\text{ in}^2$ **23.** 6 in. **25.** $4\sqrt{3}\text{ m}^2$ **27.** $3\pi\text{ ft}^2$ **29.** $r = 8$ m **31.** $P = 24$ cm **33.** $S = 330\text{ cm}^2$ **35.** Possible answer: 526,000 ft² **39.** F **41a.** $S = 500\pi\text{ cm}^2$ **b.** $L = 100\pi\text{ cm}^2$ **c.** $B = 25\pi\text{ cm}^2$ **d.** $S = 500\pi - 100\pi + 25\pi = 425\pi\text{ cm}^2$ **43a.** $c = 2\pi r$ **b.** $C = 2\pi\ell$ **c.** $\frac{c}{C} = \frac{2\pi r}{2\pi\ell} = \frac{r}{\ell}$ **d.** The area of the larger circle is $A = \pi\ell^2$. The lateral surface area is $\frac{c}{C} = \frac{r}{\ell}$ times the area of the circle, so $L = \pi\ell^2\left(\frac{r}{\ell}\right) = \pi r\ell$ **45.** yes **47.** 0.25 **49.** 0.21 **51.** $S = 700\text{ cm}^2$

10-6

Check It Out! 1. $V = 157.5\text{ yd}^3$ **2.** 859,702 gal; 7,161,318 lb **3.** $V = 1088\pi\text{ in}^3 \approx 3418.1\text{ in}^3$ **4.** The volume is multiplied by 8. **5.** $V \approx 51.4\text{ cm}^3$

Exercises **1.** the same length as **3.** $V \approx 748.2 \text{ m}^3$ **5.** 2552 gal; 12,071 lb **7.** $V = 45\pi \text{ m}^3 \approx 141.4 \text{ m}^3$ **9.** The volume is multiplied by $\frac{1}{64}$. **11.** $V \approx 1209.1 \text{ ft}^3$ **13.** $V = 810 \text{ yd}^3$ **15.** $V = 245 \text{ ft}^3$ **17.** $V = 1764\pi \text{ cm}^3 \approx 5541.8 \text{ cm}^3$ **19.** $V = 384\pi \text{ cm}^3 \approx 1206.4 \text{ cm}^3$ **21.** The volume is multiplied by $\frac{27}{125}$. **23.** $V \approx 242.3 \text{ ft}^3$ **25a.** 235.6 in^2 **25b.** 0.04 **27.** $h = 11$ ft **29.** $V = 392\pi \text{ m}^3$ **31.** 576 in^3, or $\frac{1}{3} \text{ ft}^3$ **33.** 2,468,729 gal **37.** A **39.** B **41.** $V = x^3 + x^2 - 2x$ **43.** $V = \frac{x^3\sqrt{3} + x^2\sqrt{3}}{4}$ **45.** 139 **47.** 50° **49.** 8 **51.** $S \approx 181.9 \text{ cm}^2$

10-7

Check It Out! **1.** $V = 36 \text{ cm}^3$ **2.** $107{,}800 \text{ yd}^3$ or $2{,}910{,}600 \text{ ft}^3$ **3.** $V = 216\pi \text{ m}^3 \approx 678.6 \text{ m}^3$ **4.** The volume is multiplied by 8. **5.** $V = 3000 \text{ ft}^3$

Exercises **1.** perpendicular **3.** $V = 96 \text{ cm}^3$ **5.** $V \approx 65 \text{ mm}^3$ **7.** $V = 1440\pi \text{ in}^3 \approx 4523.9 \text{ in}^3$ **9.** The volume is multiplied by 27. **11.** $V = 2592 \text{ cm}^3$ **13.** $V = 160 \text{ ft}^3$ **15.** $V = 384 \text{ ft}^3$ **17.** $V = 1107\pi \text{ m}^3 \approx 3477.7 \text{ m}^3$ **19.** $V = 144\pi \text{ ft}^3 \approx 452.4 \text{ ft}^3$ **21.** The volume is multiplied by 216. **23.** $V = 150 \text{ ft}^3$ **25.** $V = \frac{25\pi}{6} \text{ m}^3$ **27.** $V = 240\pi \text{ cm}^3$ **29.** 1350 m^3 **31.** 166.3 cm^3 **33.** $C = 10\pi\sqrt{3}$ cm **35.** $V = 1280 \text{ in}^3$ **37.** $V = 17.5 \text{ units}^3$ **39.** 3:2 **41a.** 33.5 in^3 **b.** 134.0 in^3 **c.** \$5; the large size holds 4 times as much. **43.** H **45.** 9 **47.** $V = \frac{2\pi}{3} \text{ ft}^3$ **49.** $V = \frac{1000\sqrt{2}}{3} \text{ cm}^3$ **51.** 38 and 14 **53.** 79 and 118 **55.** AA; $PQ = 6$ **57.** 10.0; $(0.5, 0, -2)$ **59.** 7; $(-2, 2, 3.5)$

10-8

Check It Out! **1.** $r = 12$ ft **2.** about 72.3 times as great **3.** $S = 2500\pi \text{ cm}^2$ **4.** The surface area is divided by 9. **5.** $S = 57\pi \text{ ft}^2$; $V = 27\pi \text{ ft}^3$

Exercises **1.** One endpoint is the center of the sphere, and the other is a point on the sphere. **3.** $V = \frac{4\pi}{3} \text{ m}^3$ **5.** about 8 times as great **7.** $S = 196\pi \text{ cm}^2$ **9.** The surface area is multiplied by 4.

11. $S = 36\pi \text{ ft}^2$; $V = \frac{92\pi}{3} \text{ ft}^3$ **13.** $V = 972\pi \text{ cm}^3$ **15.** $d = 36$ in. **17.** $S = 1764\pi \text{ in}^2$ **19.** $V = \frac{15{,}625\pi}{6} \text{ m}^3$ **21.** The volume is multiplied by 216. **23.** $S \approx 1332.0 \text{ mm}^2$; $V \approx 1440.9 \text{ mm}^3$ **25.** $C = 2\pi\sqrt{15}$ in. **27.** $S = 196\pi \text{ units}^2$; $V = \frac{1372\pi}{3} \text{ units}^3$ **29.** 5.28 in.; 8.87 in^2; 2.48 in^3 **31.** 7.85 in.; 19.63 in^2; 8.18 in^3 **33.** Possible answer: $14{,}293 \text{ in}^3$ **35.** about 1408 times as great **37.** The surface area of Saturn is greater. **39.** The cross section of the hemisphere is a circle with radius $\sqrt{r^2 - x^2}$, so its area is $A = \pi(r^2 - x^2)$. The cross section of the cylinder with the cone removed has an outer radius of r and an inner radius of x, so the area is $A = \pi r^2 - \pi x^2 = \pi(r^2 - x^2)$. **41a.** 33.5 in^3 **b.** 44.6 in^3 **43.** H **45.** 1 in. **47.** The volume of the cylinder is 1.5 times the volume of the sphere. **49.** $y = x^2 + 1$ **51.** 4.6 in^2 **53.** The volume is multiplied by $\frac{27}{64}$.

Study Guide: Review

1. oblique prism **2.** cross section **3.** cone; vertex: M; edges: none; base: $\odot L$ **4.** rectangular pyramid; vertices: N, P, Q, R, S; edges: $\overline{NP}$, $\overline{NQ}, \overline{NR}, \overline{NS}, \overline{PQ}, \overline{QR}, \overline{RS}, \overline{SP}$; base: $PQRS$ **5.** cylinder **6.** square pyramid

7. Front Back Top Left Right Bottom

8.

9. **10.**

11. yes **12.** no **13.** $V = 9$; $E = 16$; $F = 9$; $9 - 16 + 9 = 2$ **14.** $V = 8$; $E = 12$; $F = 6$; $8 - 12 + 6 = 2$ **15.** $d \approx 7.7$; $M(4.5, 3.5, 2.5)$ **16.** $d \approx 10.2$; $M(2.5, 5, 4)$ **17.** $d \approx 2.4$; $M(8, 1.5, 5.5)$ **18.** $d \approx 7.5$; $M(4, 4.5, 6)$ **19.** $L \approx 628.3 \text{ yd}^2$; $S \approx 785.4 \text{ yd}^2$ **20.** $L = 100 \text{ ft}^2$; $S = 150 \text{ ft}^2$ **21.** $L = 126 \text{ m}^2$; $S \approx 157.2 \text{ m}^2$ **22.** $L = 160 \text{ cm}^2$; $S \approx 215.1 \text{ cm}^2$ **23.** $L = 630 \text{ ft}^2$; $S = 855 \text{ ft}^2$ **24.** $L = 175\pi \text{ m}^2$; $S = 224\pi \text{ m}^2$ **25.** $L = 150\pi \text{ in}^2$; $S = 250\pi \text{ in}^2$ **26.** $S = 800 \text{ ft}^2$ **27.** $S = 448\pi \text{ m}^2$ **28.** $V = 1080 \text{ ft}^3$ **29.** $V \approx 1651.7 \text{ cm}^3$ **30.** $V = 900\pi \text{ in}^3$ **31.** $V = 45\pi \text{ m}^3$ **32.** $V = 112 \text{ m}^3$ **33.** $V \approx 10.4 \text{ cm}^3$ **34.** $V = 120\pi \text{ cm}^3$ **35.** $V = 48\pi \text{ ft}^3$ **36.** $V = 512\pi \text{ ft}^3$ **37.** $V \approx 1533.3 \text{ cm}^3$ **38.** $V = \frac{500\pi}{3} \text{ m}^3$ **39.** $S = 144\pi \text{ in}^2$ **40.** $d = 16$ ft **41.** $S \approx 338.3 \text{ cm}^2$; $V \approx 293.5 \text{ cm}^3$ **42.** $S \approx 245.0 \text{ ft}^2$; $V \approx 84.8 \text{ ft}^3$

Chapter 11

11-1

Check It Out! **1.** chords: $\overline{QR}, \overline{ST}$; secant: $\overleftrightarrow{ST}$; tangent: $\overleftrightarrow{UV}$; diam.: $\overline{ST}$; radii: $\overline{PQ}, \overline{PT}, \overline{PS}$ **2.** radius of $\odot C$: 1; radius of $\odot D$: 3; pt. of tangency: $(2, -1)$; eqn. of tangent line: $y = -1$ **3.** 171 mi **4a.** 2.1 **4b.** 7

Exercises **1.** secant **3.** congruent **5.** chord: $\overline{QS}$; secant: $\overleftrightarrow{QS}$; tangent: $\overleftrightarrow{ST}$; diam.: $\overline{QS}$; radii: $\overline{PR}, \overline{PQ}, \overline{PS}$ **7.** radius of $\odot R$: 2; radius of $\odot S$: 2; pt. of tangency: $(1, 2)$; eqn. of tangent line: $x = 1$ **9.** 19 **11.** chords: $\overline{RS}, \overline{VW}$; secant: $\overleftrightarrow{VW}$; tangent: ℓ; diam.: $\overline{VW}$; radii: $\overline{PV}, \overline{PW}$ **13.** radius of $\odot C$: 2; radius of $\odot D$: 4; pt. of tangency: $(-4, 0)$; eqn. of tangent line: $x = -4$ **15.** 413 km **17.** 7 **19.** N **21.** A **23.** $\overline{AC}$ **25.** $\overline{AC}$ **27.** 45° **31.** 8 **33.** 22 **35a.** rect.; $\angle BCD$ and $\angle EDC$ are rt. ∠s because a line tangent to a $\odot$ is $\perp$ to a radius. It is given that $\angle DEB$ is a rt. ∠. $\angle CBE$ must also be a rt. ∠ because the sum of the ∠s of a quad. is 360°. Thus $BCDE$ has 4 rt. ∠s and is a rect. **b.** 17 in.; 2 in. **c.** 17.1 in. **39.** G **43.** 18.6 in. **45.** $\frac{3}{4}$ **47.** $\frac{13}{20}$

11-2

Check It Out! **1a.** 108° **1b.** 270° **1c.** 36° **2a.** 140° **2b.** 295° **3a.** 12 **3b.** 100° **4.** 34.6

Exercises **1.** semicircle **3.** major arc **5.** 162° **7.** 61.2° **9.** 39.6° **11.** 129° **13.** 108° **15.** 24 **17.** 24.0 **19.** 122.3° **21.** 122.3° **23.** 237.7° **25.** 152° **27.** 155° **29.** 147° **31.** 6.6 **33.** F **35.** T **37.** 45°; 60°; 75° **39.** 108°

41. 1. $\widehat{BC} \cong \widehat{DE}$ (Given)
2. $m\widehat{BC} = m\widehat{DE}$ (Def. of ≅ arcs)
3. $m\angle BAC = m\angle DAE$ (Def. of arc measures)
4. $\angle BAC \cong \angle DAE$ (Def. of ≅ ∠s)

43. 1. $\overline{JK}$ is the ⊥ bisector of $\overline{GH}$. (Given)
2. A is equidistant from G and H. (Def. of center of $\odot$)
3. A lies on the ⊥ bisector of $\overline{GH}$. (⊥ Bisector Thm.)
4. $\overline{JK}$ is a diam. of $\odot A$. (Def. of diam.)

45. Solution A **47a.** 13.5 in.; 6.5 in. **b.** 11.8 in. **c.** 23.7 in. **49.** F **51.** 48.2° **53a.** 90°; 60°; 45° **b.** $\frac{3}{4}\pi$; $\frac{3}{2}\pi$ **55.** $\frac{b^3}{16}$ **57.** 31 **59.** 28 **61.** 9

11-3

Check It Out! **1a.** $\frac{\pi}{4} \text{ m}^2$; 0.79 m^2 **1b.** $25.6\pi \text{ in}^2$; 80.42 in^2 **2.** $203{,}575 \text{ ft}^2$ **3.** 4.57 m^2 **4a.** $\frac{4}{3}\pi$ m; 4.19 m **4b.** 3π cm; 9.42 cm

Exercises **1.** seg. **3.** $24\pi \text{ cm}^2$; 75.40 cm^2 **5.** 12 mi^2 **7.** 36.23 m^2 **9.** 4π ft; 12.57 ft **11.** $\frac{2}{3}\pi$ in; 2.09 in. **13.** $\frac{45}{2}\pi \text{ in}^2$; 70.69 in^2 **15.** 628 in^2 **17.** 15.35 in^2 **19.** $\frac{25}{18}\pi$ mm; 4.36 mm **21.** $\frac{1}{10}\pi$ ft; 0.31 ft **23.** N **25.** A **27.** 12 **29a.** 3.9 ft **b.** 103° **33.** G **35.** $\frac{7}{3}\pi$ **37a.** $\frac{1}{8}$ **b.** $\frac{3}{8}$ **c.** $\frac{1}{2}$ **39.** neither **41.** $36\pi \text{ cm}^3$ **43.** 122° **45.** 302°

11-4

Check It Out! **1a.** 270° **1b.** 38° **2.** 43°; 120° **3a.** 12 **3b.** 39° **4.** 51°; 129°; 72°; 108°

Exercises **1.** inscribed **3.** 58° **5.** 26° **7.** 112.5 **9.** 46° **11.** 70°; 110°; 115°; 65° **13.** 47.5° **15.** 47.6° **17.** ±6 **19.** 100° **21.** 100°; 39°, 80°; 141° **23.** A **25.** S **27.** 115° **29a.** 30° **b.** 120° **c.** Rt.; $\angle FBC$ is inscribed in a semicircle, so it must be a rt. ∠; therefore $\triangle FBC$ is a rt. △. **33.** 72°; 99°; 108°; 81° **35a.** $AB^2 + AC^2 = BC^2$, so by the Conv. of the Pyth. Thm., $\triangle ABC$ is a rt. △ with rt. $\angle A$. Since $\angle A$ is an inscribed rt. ∠, it intercepts a semicircle. This means that $\overline{BC}$ is a diam. **b.** 102° **39.** D **41.** C **45.** 134° **49.** $\frac{13}{7}$ **51.** $\frac{5}{2}$ **53.** 3 m^2

11-5

Check It Out! **1a.** 83° **1b.** 142° **2a.** 51° **2b.** 22° **3.** 33 **4.** 45° **5.** 72°

Exercises **1.** 70° **3.** 122° **5.** 67° **7.** 94° **9.** 58 **11.** 142° **13.** 96° **15.** 116° **17.** 124° **19.** 260° **21.** 107.5° **23.** 57.5 **25.** 18 **27.** 45° **29.** 90° **31.** $2x°$ **33.** $(360 - 2x)°$ **39.** 115°; 30°; 35° **41a.** 60° **b.** 120° **c.** obtuse isosceles **43.** J **45.** Case 1: Assume $\overline{AB}$ is a diam. of the circle. Then $m\widehat{AB} = 180°$, and $\angle ABC$ is a rt. ∠. Thus $m\angle ABC = \frac{1}{2}m\widehat{AB}$. Case 2: Assume $\overline{AB}$ is not a diam. of the $\odot$. Let X be the center of the $\odot$ and draw radii $\overline{XA}$ and $\overline{XB}$. Since they are radii, $\overline{XA} \cong \overline{XB}$, so $\triangle AXB$ is isosceles. Thus $\angle XAB \cong \angle XBA$ and $2m\angle XBA + m\angle AXB = 180$. This means that $m\angle XBA = 90 - \frac{1}{2}m\angle AXB$. By Thm. 11-1-1, $\angle XBC$ is a rt. ∠, so $m\angle XBA + m\angle ABC = 90$ or $m\angle ABC = 90 - m\angle XBA$. By subst., $m\angle ABC = 90 - \left(90 - \frac{1}{2}m\angle AXB\right)$. Simplifying gives $m\angle ABC = \frac{1}{2}m\angle AXB$. $m\angle AXB = m\widehat{AB}$ because $\angle AXB$ is a central ∠. Thus $m\angle ABC = \frac{1}{2}\widehat{AB}$. **47.** 95° **49.** yes **51.** no **53.** $96\pi \text{ cm}^3 \approx 301.6 \text{ cm}^3$ **55.** 37° **57.** 53°

11-6

Check It Out! **1.** 3.75; $AB = 11$; $CD = 11.75$ **2.** $3\frac{2}{3}$ in. **3.** $z = 14$; $JG = 27$; $LG = 39$ **4.** $7\frac{2}{7}$

Exercises **1.** tangent seg. **3.** $x = 9$; $AB = 13$; $CD = 12$ **5.** $51\frac{1}{4}$ ft **7.** $y = 10.6$; $PR = 15.6$; $PT = 13$ **9.** 4 **11.** $\sqrt{33}$ **13.** $x = 4.2$; $JL = 14.2$; $MN = 13$ **15.** ≈ 1770 ft **17.** $y = 14.3$; $HL = 24.3$; $NL = 27$ **19.** $2\sqrt{21}$ **21.** $4\sqrt{10}$ **23a.** 6 in. **b.** 12 in. **25.** $x = 8$; $y = 6\sqrt{3}$ **27.** Solution B **33.** B **35.** $CE = ED = 6$ and by the Chord-Chord Product Thm., $6 \cdot 6 = 3 \cdot EF$. So $EF = 12$, $FB = 15$, and the radius AB must be 7.5. **37.** 3.2 in. **39.** 7.44 **41.** 72% **43.** $\overrightarrow{CD}$ **45.** $22\pi \text{ ft}^2$; 69.12 ft^2 **47.** 45°

11-7

Check It Out! **1a.** $x^2 + (y + 3)^2 = 64$ **1b.** $(x - 2)^2 + (y + 1)^2 = 16$

2a. **2b.**

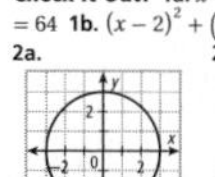

3. $(2, -1)$

Exercises **1.** $(x - 3)^2 + (y + 5)^2 = 144$ **3.** $(x - 4)^2 + y^2 = 4$

5. **7.**

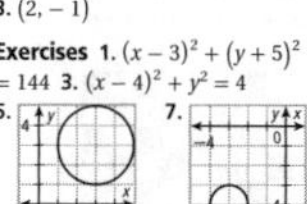

9a. $(-2, 3)$ **b.** 10 ft **11.** $(x - 1.5)^2 + (y + 2.5)^2 = 3$ **13.** $(x - 1)^2 + (y + 2)^2 = 45$

15.

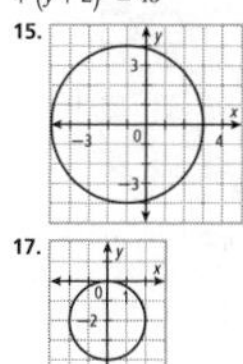

17.

19. $(x - 1)^2 + (y + 2)^2 = 4$ **21a.** 80 ft **b.** $x^2 + y^2 = 1600$ **23.** T **25.** T **29a.** $E(-3, -1)$; $G(-6, 2)$ **b.** 6 **c.** $(x + 3)^2 + (y - 2)^2 = 9$ **31.** $(0, -15)$; 5 **33.** $A = 9\pi$; $C = 6\pi$ **35.** $A = 25\pi$; $C = 10\pi$ **37.** $(-200, -100)$ **39.** $(x - 1)^2 + (y + 2)^2 = 16$ **43.** H **45a.** $(x - 2)^2 + (y + 4)^2 + (z - 3)^2 = 69$ **b.** 15; if 2 segs. are tangent to a $\odot$ or sphere from the same ext. pt., then the segs. are ≅. **47.** $(x - 3)^2 + (y - 4)^2 = 5$ **49.** $9a + 2$ **51.** 8 **53.** 196°

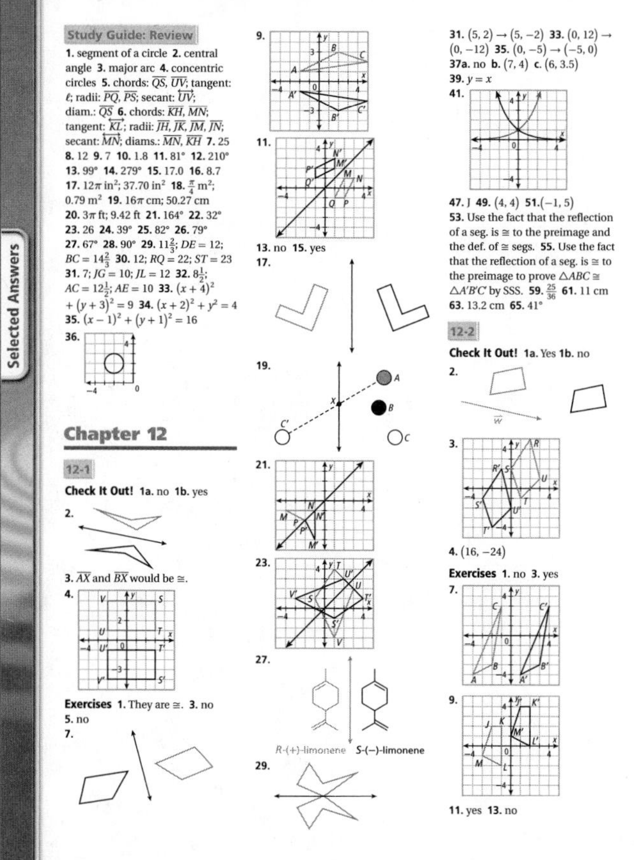

Study Guide: Review

1. segment of a circle **2.** central angle **3.** major arc **4.** concentric circles **5.** chords: $\overline{QS}, \overline{UV}$; tangent: ℓ; radii: $\overline{PQ}, \overline{PS}$; secant: $\overleftrightarrow{UV}$; diam.: $\overline{QS}$ **6.** chords: $\overline{KH}, \overline{MN}$; tangent: $\overleftrightarrow{KL}$; radii: $\overline{JH}, \overline{JK}, \overline{JM}, \overline{JN}$; secant: $\overleftrightarrow{MN}$; diams.: $\overline{MN}, \overline{KH}$ **7.** 25 **8.** 12 **9.** 7 **10.** 1.8 **11.** 81° **12.** 210° **13.** 99° **14.** 279° **15.** 17.0 **16.** 8.7 **17.** $12\pi \text{ in}^2$; 37.70 in^2 **18.** $\frac{\pi}{4} \text{ m}^2$; 0.79 m^2 **19.** 16π cm; 50.27 cm **20.** 3π ft; 9.42 ft **21.** 164° **22.** 32° **23.** 26 **24.** 39° **25.** 82° **26.** 79° **27.** 67° **28.** 90° **29.** $11\frac{2}{3}$; $DE = 12$; $BC = 14\frac{2}{3}$ **30.** 12; $RQ = 22$; $ST = 23$ **31.** 7; $JG = 10$; $JL = 12$ **32.** $8\frac{1}{2}$; $AC = 12\frac{1}{2}$; $AE = 10$ **33.** $(x + 4)^2 + (y + 3)^2 = 9$ **34.** $(x + 2)^2 + y^2 = 4$ **35.** $(x - 1)^2 + (y + 1)^2 = 16$ **36.**

Chapter 12

12-1

Check It Out! **1a.** no **1b.** yes **2.** **3.** $\overline{AX}$ and $\overline{BX}$ would be ≅. **4.**

Exercises **1.** They are ≅. **3.** no **5.** no **7.** **9.** **11.** **13.** no **15.** yes **17.** **19.** **21.** **23.** **27.** R-(+)-limonene S-(–)-limonene **29.**

31. $(5, 2) \to (5, -2)$ **33.** $(0, 12) \to (0, -12)$ **35.** $(0, -5) \to (-5, 0)$ **37a.** no **b.** $(7, 4)$ **c.** $(6, 3.5)$ **39.** $y = x$ **41.** **47.** J **49.** $(4, 4)$ **51.** $(-1, 5)$ **53.** Use the fact that the reflection of a seg. is ≅ to the preimage and the def. of ≅ segs. **55.** Use the fact that the reflection of a seg. is ≅ to the preimage to prove $\triangle ABC \cong \triangle A'B'C'$ by SSS. **59.** $\frac{25}{36}$ **61.** 11 cm **63.** 13.2 cm **65.** 41°

12-2

Check It Out! **1a.** Yes **1b.** no **2.** **3.** **4.** $(16, -24)$

Exercises **1.** no **3.** yes **7.** **9.** **11.** yes **13.** no

SA24 Selected Answers

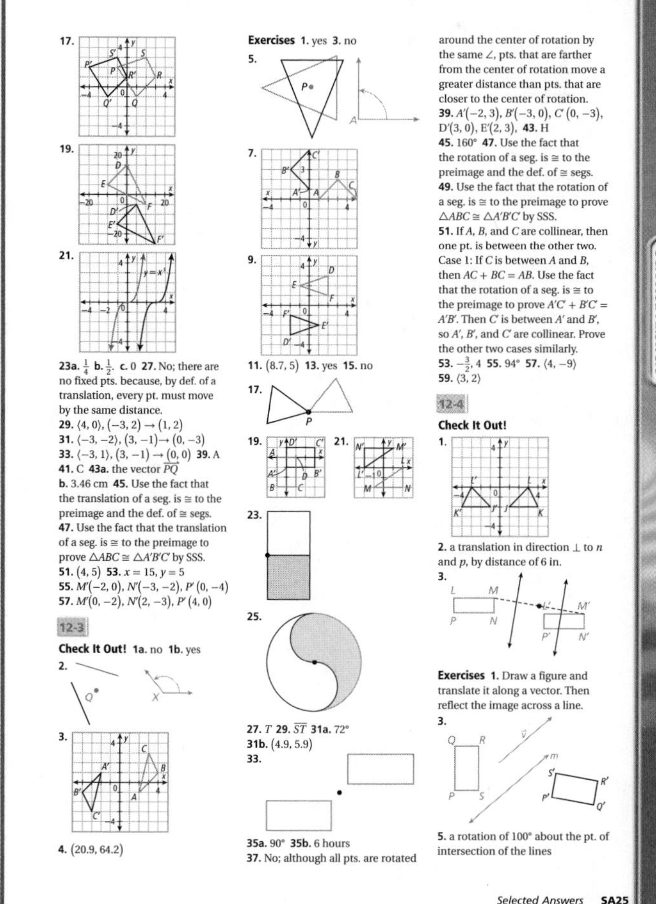

17. **19.** **21.**

23a. $\frac{1}{4}$ **b.** $\frac{1}{2}$ **c.** 0 **27.** No; there are no fixed pts. because, by def. of a translation, every pt. must move by the same distance. **29.** $\langle 4, 0\rangle$, $(-3, 2) \to (1, 2)$ **31.** $(-3, -2)$, $\langle 3, -1\rangle \to (0, -3)$ **33.** $(-3, 1)$, $\langle 3, -1\rangle \to (0, 0)$ **39.** A **41.** C **43a.** the vector $\overrightarrow{PQ}$ **b.** 3.46 cm **45.** Use the fact that the translation of a seg. is ≅ to the preimage and the def. of ≅ segs. **47.** Use the fact that the translation of a seg. is ≅ to the preimage to prove $\triangle ABC \cong \triangle A'B'C'$ by SSS. **51.** $\langle 4, 5\rangle$ **53.** $x = 15$, $y = 5$ **55.** $M'(-2, 0)$, $N'(-3, -2)$, $P'(0, -4)$ **57.** $M'(0, -2)$, $N'(2, -3)$, $P'(4, 0)$

12-3

Check It Out! **1a.** no **1b.** yes **2.** **3.** **4.** $(20.9, 64.2)$

Exercises **1.** yes **3.** no **5.** **7.** **9.** **11.** $(8.7, 5)$ **13.** yes **15.** no **17.** **19.** **21.** **23.** **25.** **27.** T **29.** $\overline{ST}$ **31a.** 72° **31b.** $(4.9, 5.9)$ **33.** **35a.** 90° **35b.** 6 hours **37.** No; although all pts. are rotated around the center of rotation by the same ∠, pts. that are farther from the center of rotation move a greater distance than pts. that are closer to the center of rotation. **39.** $A'(-2, 3)$, $B'(-3, 0)$, $C'(0, -3)$, $D'(3, 0)$, $E'(2, 3)$, **43.** H **45.** 160° **47.** Use the fact that the rotation of a seg. is ≅ to the preimage and the def. of ≅ segs. **49.** Use the fact that the rotation of a seg. is ≅ to the preimage to prove $\triangle ABC \cong \triangle A'B'C'$ by SSS. **51.** If A, B, and C are collinear, then one pt. is between the other two. Case 1: If C is between A and B, then $AC + BC = AB$. Use the fact that the rotation of a seg. is ≅ to the preimage to prove $A'C' + B'C' = A'B'$. Then C' is between A' and B', so A', B', and C' are collinear. Prove the other two cases similarly. **53.** $-\frac{3}{2}$, 4 **55.** 94° **57.** $\langle 4, -9\rangle$ **59.** $\langle 3, 2\rangle$

12-4

Check It Out! **1.** **2.** a translation in direction ⊥ to n and p, by distance of 6 in. **3.**

Exercises **1.** Draw a figure and translate it along a vector. Then reflect the image across a line. **3.** **5.** a rotation of 100° about the pt. of intersection of the lines

Selected Answers SA25

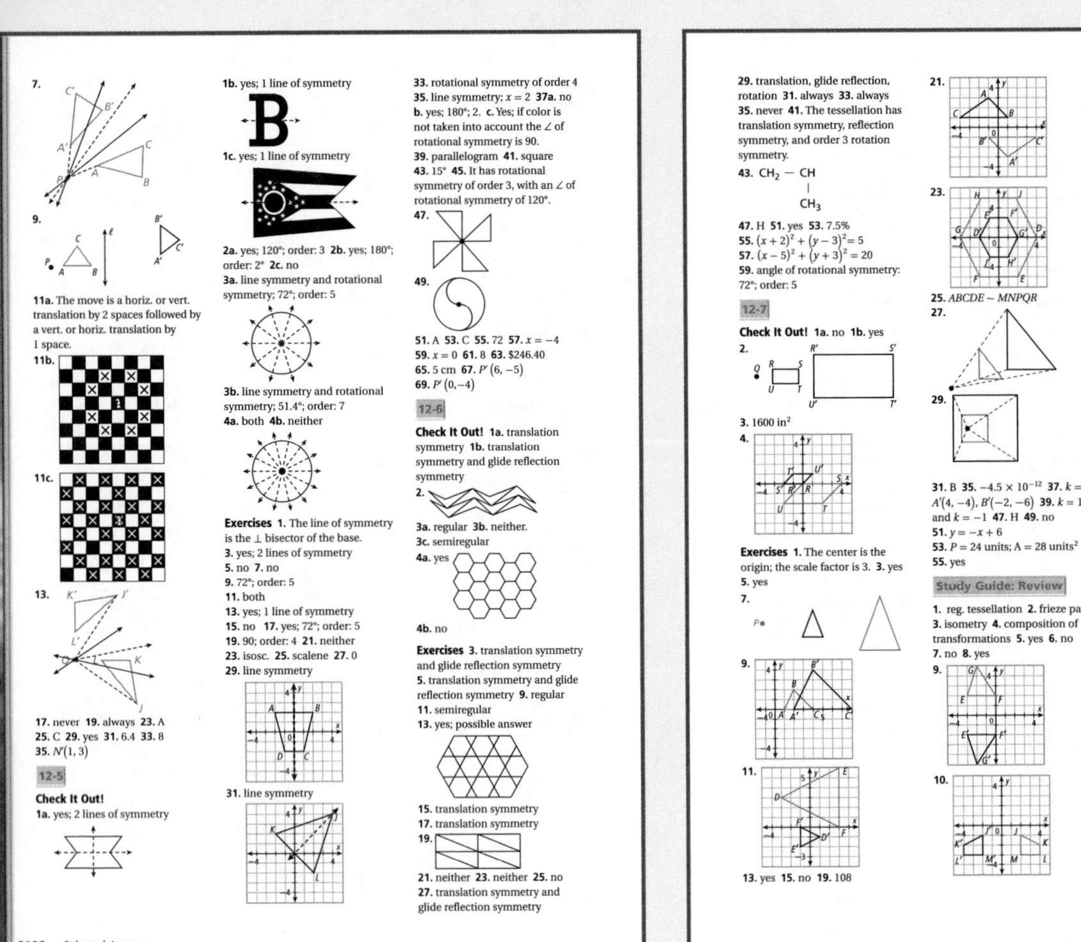

7.

9.

11a. The move is a horiz. or vert. translation by 2 spaces followed by a vert. or horiz. translation by 1 space.

11b.

11c.

13.

17. never 19. always 23. A 25. C 29. yes 31. 6.4 33. 8 35. $N'(1, 3)$

12-5

Check It Out!
1a. yes; 2 lines of symmetry

1b. yes; 1 line of symmetry

1c. yes; 1 line of symmetry

2a. yes; 120°; order: 3 2b. yes; 180°; order: 2° 2c. no
3a. line symmetry and rotational symmetry; 72°; order: 5

3b. line symmetry and rotational symmetry; 51.4°; order: 7
4a. both 4b. neither

Exercises 1. The line of symmetry is the ⊥ bisector of the base.
3. yes; 2 lines of symmetry
5. no 7. no
9. 72°; order: 5
11. both
13. yes; 1 line of symmetry
15. no 17. yes; 72°; order: 5
19. 90; order: 4 21. neither
23. isosc. 25. scalene 27. 0
29. line symmetry

31. line symmetry

33. rotational symmetry of order 4
35. line symmetry; $x = 2$ 37a. no
b. yes; 180°; 2. c. Yes; if color is not taken into account the ∠ of rotational symmetry is 90.
39. parallelogram 41. square
43. 15° 45. It has rotational symmetry of order 3, with an ∠ of rotational symmetry of 120°.
47.

49.

51. A 53. C 55. 72 57. $x = -4$
59. $x = 0$ 61. 8 63. $246.40
65. 5 cm 67. $P'(6, -5)$
69. $P'(0, -4)$

12-6

Check It Out! 1a. translation symmetry 1b. translation symmetry and glide reflection symmetry
2.

3a. regular 3b. neither.
3c. semiregular
4a. yes

4b. no

Exercises 3. translation symmetry and glide reflection symmetry
5. translation symmetry and glide reflection symmetry 9. regular
11. semiregular
13. yes; possible answer

15. translation symmetry
17. translation symmetry
19.

21. neither 23. neither 25. no
27. translation symmetry and glide reflection symmetry

SA26 Selected Answers

29. translation, glide reflection, rotation 31. always 33. always
35. never 41. The tessellation has translation symmetry, reflection symmetry, and order 3 rotation symmetry.
43. $CH_2 - CH$ with CH_3 bonded below the CH

47. H 51. yes 53. 7.5%
55. $(x + 2)^2 + (y - 3)^2 = 5$
57. $(x - 5)^2 + (y + 3)^2 = 20$
59. angle of rotational symmetry: 72°; order: 5

12-7

Check It Out! 1a. no 1b. yes
2.

3. 1600 in^2
4.

Exercises 1. The center is the origin; the scale factor is 3. 3. yes
5. yes
7.

9.

11.

13. yes 15. no 19. 108

21.

23.

25. $ABCDE \sim MNPQR$
27.

29.

31. B 35. -4.5×10^{-12} 37. $k = -2$; $A'(4, -4)$, $B'(-2, -6)$ 39. $k = 1$ and $k = -1$ 47. H 49. no
51. $y = -x + 6$
53. $P = 24$ units; $A = 28$ $units^2$
55. yes

Study Guide: Review

1. reg. tessellation 2. frieze pattern
3. isometry 4. composition of transformations 5. yes 6. no
7. no 8. yes
9.

10.

11.

12.

13. no 14. yes 15. no 16. no
17.

18.

19.

20.

21. yes 22. yes 23. no
24. no
25.

Selected Answers SA27

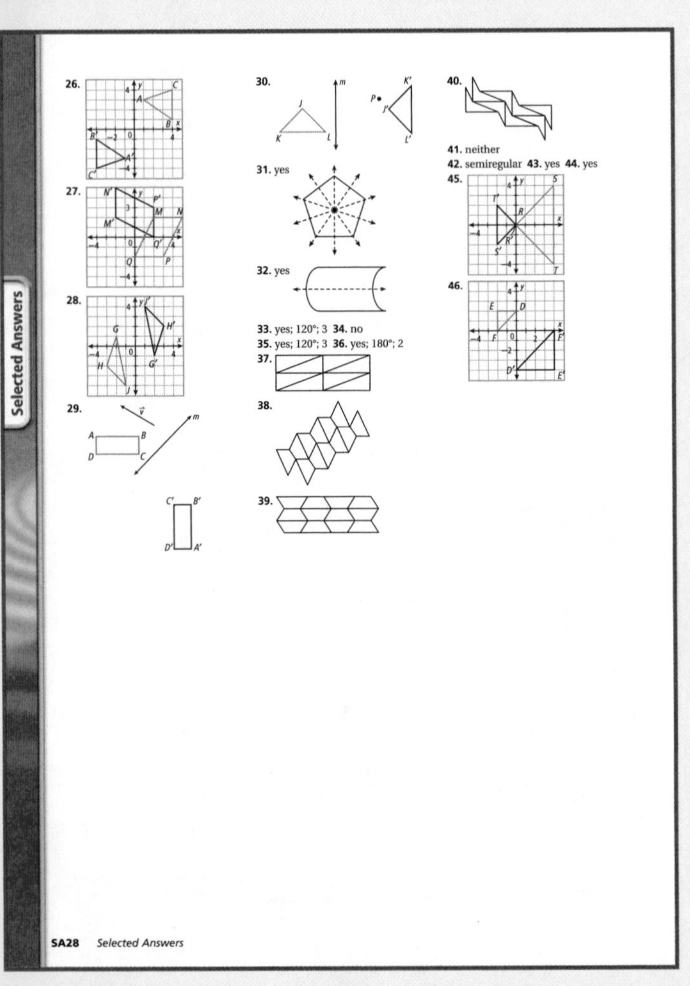

26.

27.

28.

29.

30.

31. yes

32. yes

33. yes; 120°; 3 34. no
35. yes; 120°; 3 36. yes; 180°; 2
37.

38.

39.

40.

41. neither
42. semiregular 43. yes 44. yes
45.

46.

SA28 Selected Answers

Notes

Graphic Organizer Answers

Possible answers given.

Chapter 1

Lesson 1-1

5.

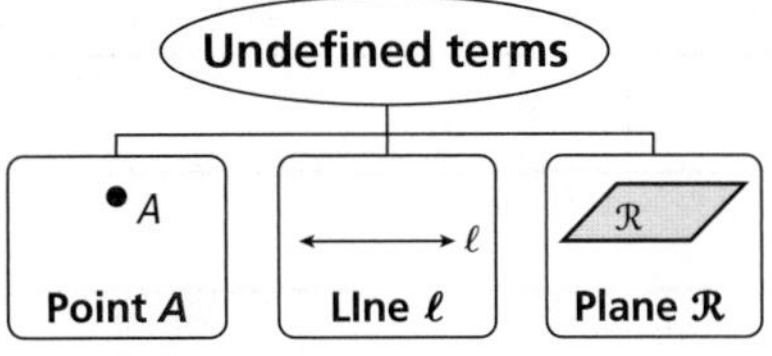

Lesson 1-2

2.

B is between A and C.	B is the mdpt. of $\overline{AC}$.
A B C (points on a segment) $AB + BC = AC$	A B C (points on a segment) $AC = 2BC = 2AB$ $AB = BC$

Lesson 1-3

3.

Angle	Measure	Diagram	Name
Acute	Greater than 0° and less than 90°	A	$\angle A$
Right	90°	B	$\angle B$
Obtuse	Greater than 90° and less than 180°	C	$\angle C$
Straight	180°	A B C	$\angle ABC$

Lesson 1-4

3.

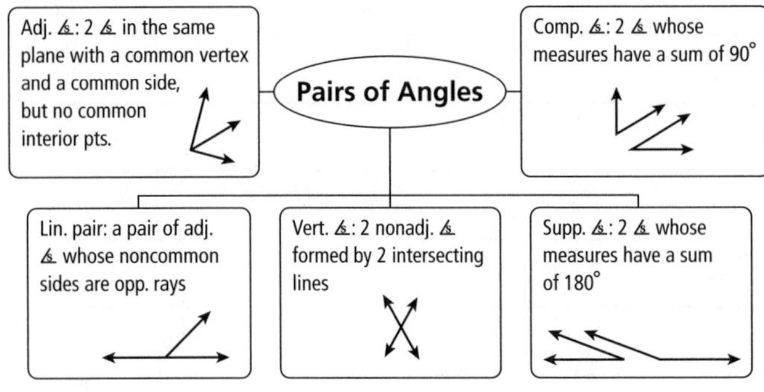

Pairs of Angles
Adj. ∡: 2 ∡ in the same plane with a common vertex and a common side, but no common interior pts.
Comp. ∡: 2 ∡ whose measures have a sum of 90°
Lin. pair: a pair of adj. ∡ whose noncommon sides are opp. rays
Vert. ∡: 2 nonadj. ∡ formed by 2 intersecting lines
Supp. ∡: 2 ∡ whose measures have a sum of 180°

Lesson 1-5

2.

Formulas

- **Rectangle** $P = 2\ell + 2w$, $A = \ell w$
- **Square** $P = 4s$, $A = s^2$
- **Circle** $C = 2\pi r$, $A = \pi r^2$
- **Triangle** $A = \frac{1}{2}bh$

Lesson 1-6

5.

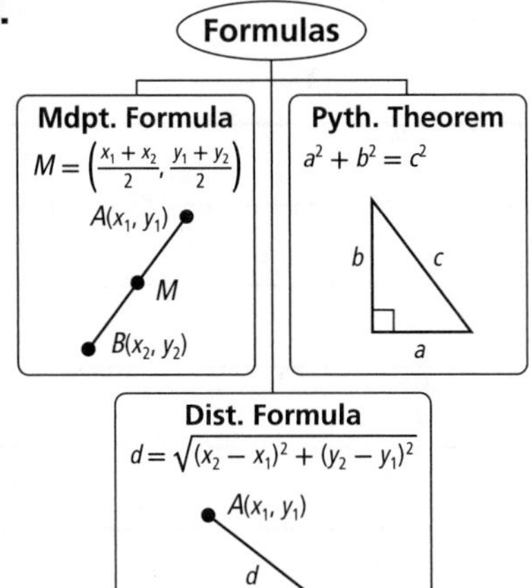

Lesson 1-7

2.

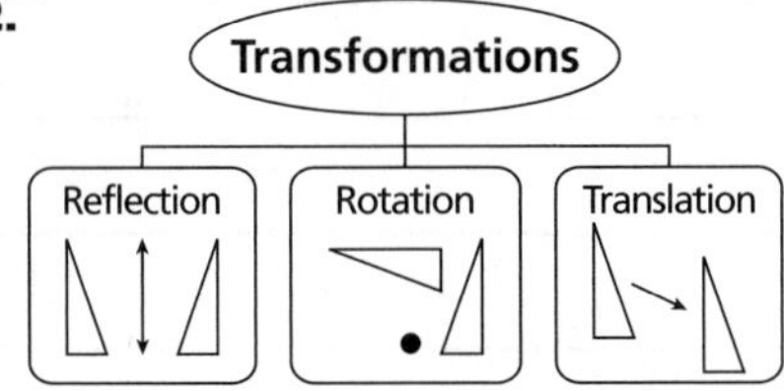

Chapter 2

Lesson 2-1

2.

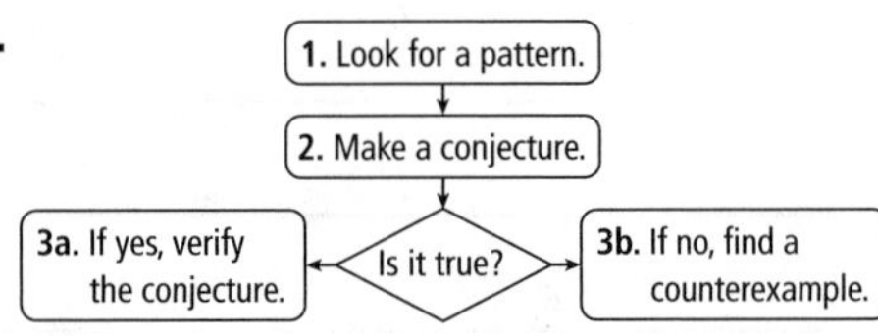

Lesson 2-2

4.

Conditional statement: a statement that can be written in the form "if p, then q;" if $x = 2$, then $y = 3$.

- Converse: the statement formed by switching the hypothesis and conclusion; if $y = 3$, then $x = 2$.
- Inverse: the statement formed by negating the hypothesis and conclusion; if $x \neq 2$, then $y \neq 3$.
- Contrapositive: the statement formed by negating and switching the hypothesis and conclusion; if $y \neq 3$, then $x \neq 2$.

Lesson 2-3

3.

- Law of Detachment: If a conditional statement is true and the hypothesis is true, then the conclusion is true. If $a \rightarrow b$ is true and a is true, then b is true.
- Law of Syllogism: If two conditionals are true and the conclusion of the first is the hypothesis of the second, then you can create a true conditional from the hypothesis of the first and the conclusion of the second. If $a \rightarrow b$ and $b \rightarrow c$ are true, then $a \rightarrow c$ is true.

Lesson 2-4

3.

Biconditional: A figure is a polygon iff it is a closed plane figure formed by 3 or more segments where each segment intersects exactly 2 other segments only at their endpoints, and no two segments with a common endpoint are collinear.

Conditional: If a figure is a polygon, then it is a closed plane figure formed by 3 or more segments where each segment intersects exactly 2 other segments only at their endpoints, and no two segments with a common endpoint are collinear.

Converse: If a figure is a closed plane figure formed by 3 or more segments where each segment intersects exactly 2 other segments only at their endpoints, and no two segments with a common endpoint are collinear, then the figure is a polygon.

Lesson 2-5

3.

Property	Equality	Congruence
Reflexive	$1 = 1$	$\overline{AB} \cong \overline{AB}$
Symmetric	If $x = y$, then $y = x$.	If $\overline{AB} \cong \overline{BC}$, then $\overline{BC} \cong \overline{AB}$.
Transitive	If $x = 0$ and $0 = y$, then $x = y$.	If $\overline{AB} \cong \overline{BC}$ and $\overline{BC} \cong \overline{CD}$, then $\overline{AB} \cong \overline{CD}$.

Lesson 2-6

4.

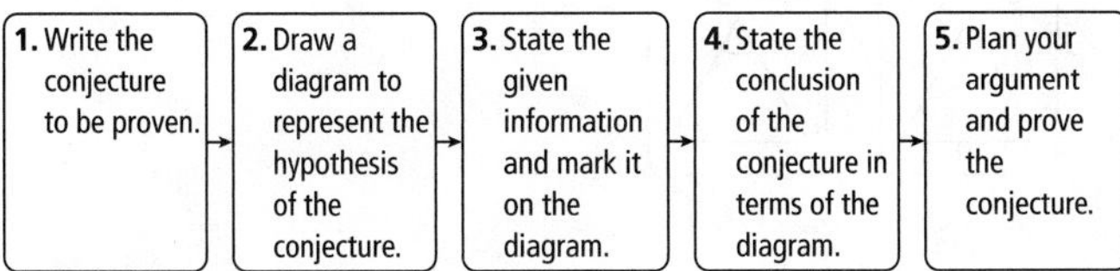

1. Write the conjecture to be proven.
2. Draw a diagram to represent the hypothesis of the conjecture.
3. State the given information and mark it on the diagram.
4. State the conclusion of the conjecture in terms of the diagram.
5. Plan your argument and prove the conjecture.

Lesson 2-7

3.

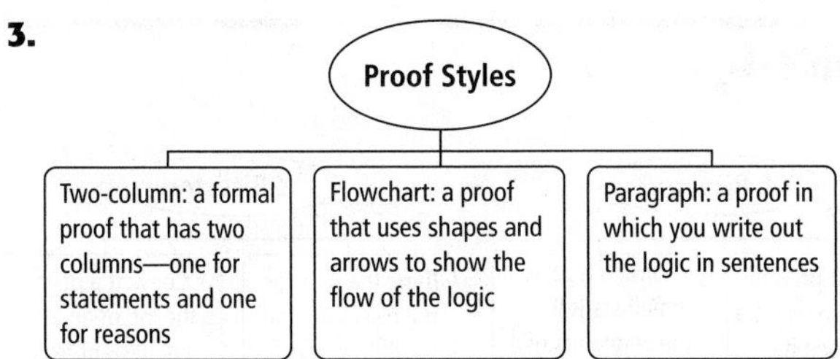

Proof Styles
Two-column: a formal proof that has two columns—one for statements and one for reasons
Flowchart: a proof that uses shapes and arrows to show the flow of the logic
Paragraph: a proof in which you write out the logic in sentences

Chapter 3

Lesson 3-1

3.

Pairs of Angles

- Corresponding: ∠1 and ∠3; ∠2 and ∠4; ∠5 and ∠7; ∠6 and ∠8
- Alternate interior: ∠2 and ∠7; ∠3 and ∠6
- Alternate exterior: ∠1 and ∠8; ∠4 and ∠5
- Same-side interior: ∠2 and ∠3; ∠6 and ∠7

Lesson 3-2

2.

Corr. ∠s Post.

Alt. Int. ∠s Thm.: ∠1 and ∠3 are vert. ∠s, so ∠1 ≅ ∠3. ∠1 and ∠2 are corr. ∠s, so ∠1 ≅ ∠2. ∠2 ≅ ∠3 by Trans. Prop. of ≅

Same-Side Int. ∠s Thm.: ∠1 and ∠5 form a lin. pair, so m∠1 + m∠5 = 180°. ∠1 and ∠2 are corr. ∠s, so m∠1 = m∠2. m∠2 + m∠5 = 180° by subst. m∠2 and m∠5 are supp. ∠s by def. of supp. ∠s

Alt. Ext. ∠s Thm.: ∠2 and ∠4 are vert. ∠s, so ∠2 ≅ ∠4. ∠1 and ∠2 are corr. ∠s, so ∠1 ≅ ∠2. ∠1 ≅ ∠4 by Trans. Prop. of ≅

Lesson 3-3

3.

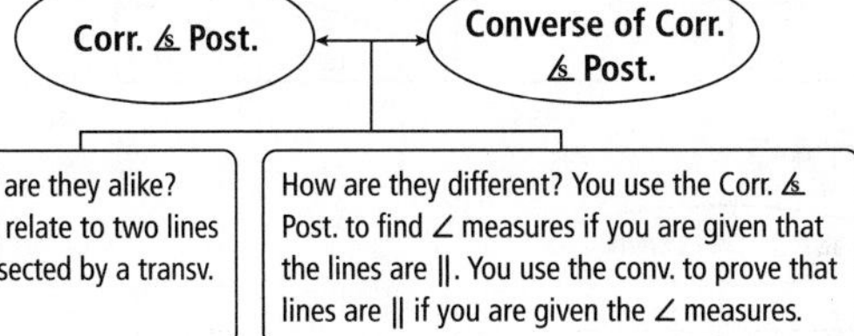

Corr. ∠s Post.
Converse of Corr. ∠s Post.
How are they alike? Both relate to two lines intersected by a transv.
How are they different? You use the Corr. ∠s Post. to find ∠ measures if you are given that the lines are ||. You use the conv. to prove that lines are || if you are given the ∠ measures.

Lesson 3-5

3.

Pairs of Lines		
Type	**Slopes**	**Example**
Parallel	same	$y = 2x + 5$ $y = 2x - 3$
Perpendicular	opposite reciprocals	$y = 2x + 5$ $y = -\frac{1}{2}x - 3$

Lesson 3-6

3.

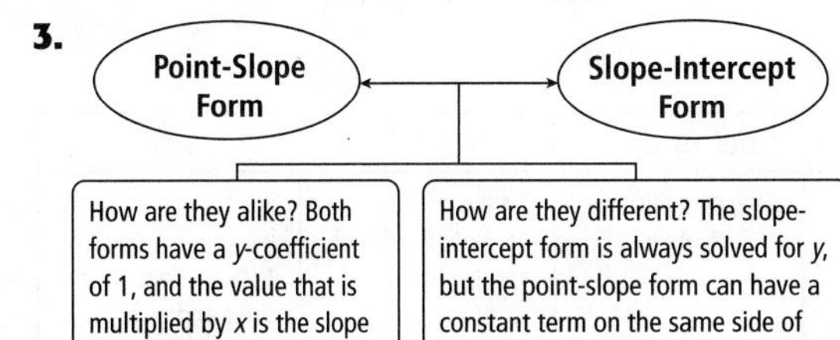

Point-Slope Form
Slope-Intercept Form
How are they alike? Both forms have a y-coefficient of 1, and the value that is multiplied by x is the slope in both forms.
How are they different? The slope-intercept form is always solved for y, but the point-slope form can have a constant term on the same side of the equation as the y.

Chapter 4

Lesson 4-1

5.

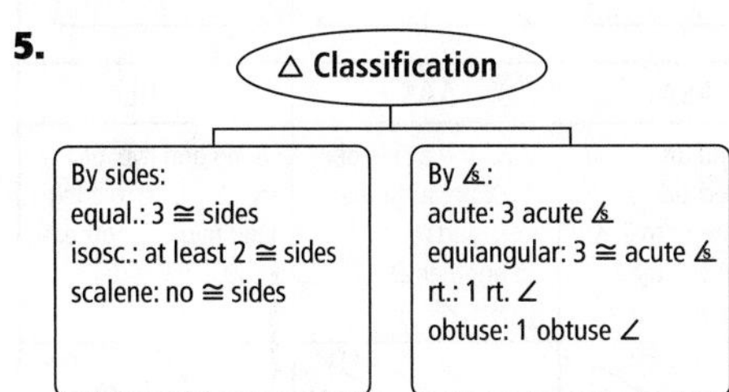

△ Classification
By sides:
equal.: 3 ≅ sides
isosc.: at least 2 ≅ sides
scalene: no ≅ sides
By ∠s:
acute: 3 acute ∠s
equiangular: 3 ≅ acute ∠s
rt.: 1 rt. ∠
obtuse: 1 obtuse ∠

Lesson 4-2

3.

Theorem	Words	Diagram
△ Sum Thm.	The sum of the measures of the int. ∡ of a △ is 180°.	$m\angle 1 + m\angle 2 + m\angle 3 = 180°$
Ext. ∠ Thm.	The measure of an ext. ∠ of a △ is = to the sum of the measures of its remote int. ∡.	$m\angle 4 = m\angle 1 + m\angle 2$
Third ∡ Thm.	If 2 ∡ of 1 △ are ≅ to 2 ∡ of another △, then the third pair of ∡ are ≅.	$\angle 1 \cong \angle 2$

Lesson 4-3

2.

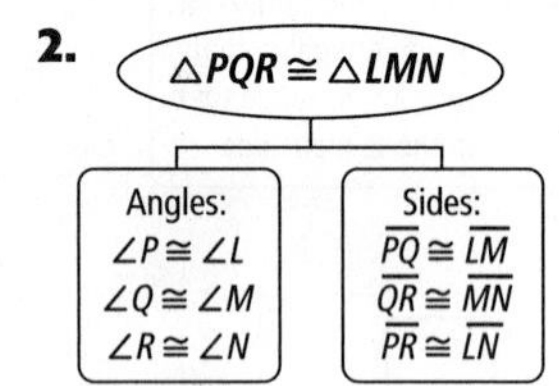

Lesson 4-4

3.

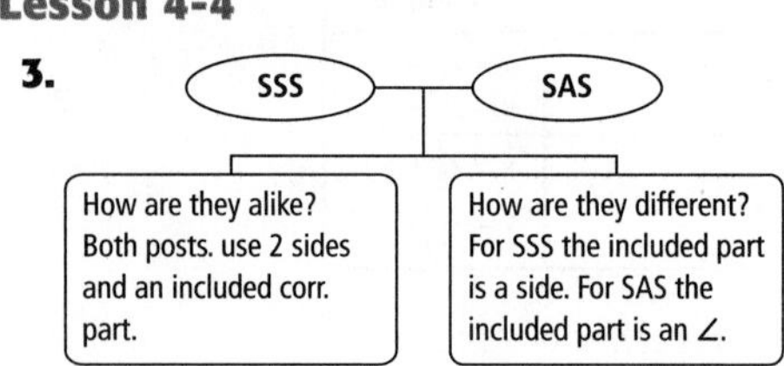

Lesson 4-5

3.

	Def. of △ ≅	SSS	SAS
Words	All 6 corr. parts of 2 ⚠ are ≅.	3 sides of 1 △ are ≅ to 3 sides of another △.	2 sides and an included ∠ of 1 △ are ≅ to 2 sides and an included ∠ in another △.
Pictures			
	ASA	**AAS**	**HL**
Words	2 ∡ and an included side of 1 △ are ≅ to 2 ∡ and an included side in another △.	2 ∡ and a side of 1 △ are ≅ to their corr. parts in another △.	A leg and hyp. of 1 rt. △ are ≅ to a leg and hyp. in another rt △.
Pictures			

Lesson 4-6

2.

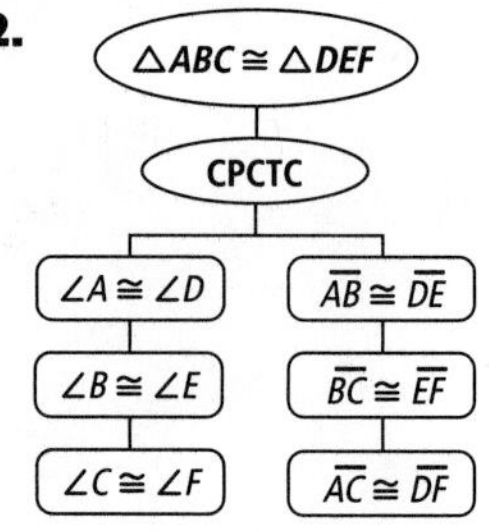

Lesson 4-7

4. Possible answer:

Use origin as a vertex.

Center figure at origin.

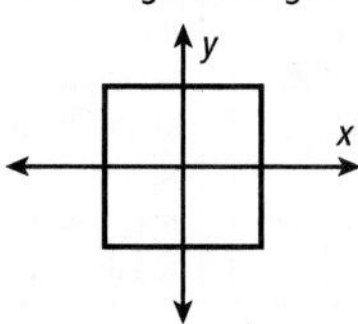

Center side of figure at origin.

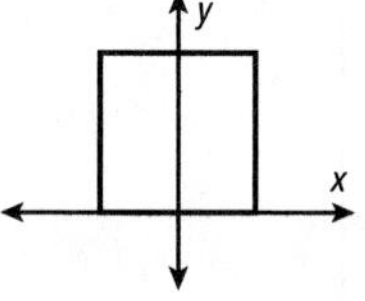

Use axes as sides of figure.

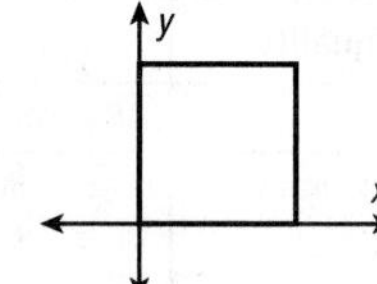

Lesson 4-8

2.

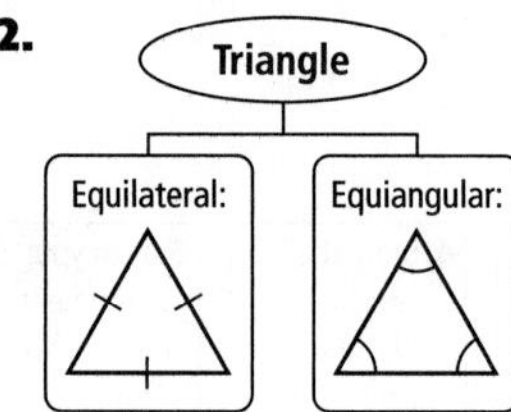

Chapter 5

Lesson 5-1

3.

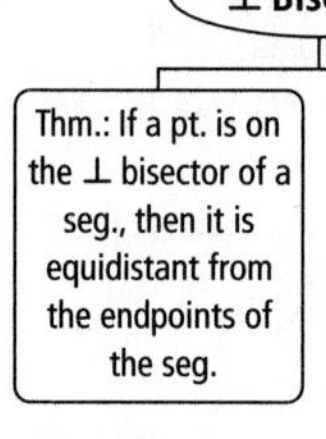

⊥ Bisector
Thm.: If a pt. is on the ⊥ bisector of a seg., then it is equidistant from the endpoints of the seg.
Conv.: If a pt. is equidistant from the endpoints of a seg., then the pt. is on the ⊥ bisector of a seg.
∠ Bisector
Thm.: If a pt. is on the bisector of an ∠, then it is equidistant from the sides of the ∠.
Conv.: If a pt. in the int. of an ∠ is equidistant from the sides of the ∠, then the pt. is on the bisector of the ∠.

Lesson 5-2

3.

	Circumcenter	Incenter
Definition	The pt. of concurrency of the ⊥ bisectors	The pt. of concurrency of the ∠ bisectors
Distance	Equidistant from the vertices of the △	Equidistant from the sides of the △
Location (Inside, Outside, or On)	Can be inside, outside, or on the △	Inside the △

Lesson 5-3

4.

	Centroid	Orthocenter
Definition	The pt. of concurrency of the medians	The pt. of concurrency of the altitudes
Location (Inside, Outside, or On)	Inside the △	Can be inside, outside, or on the △

Lesson 5-4

2.

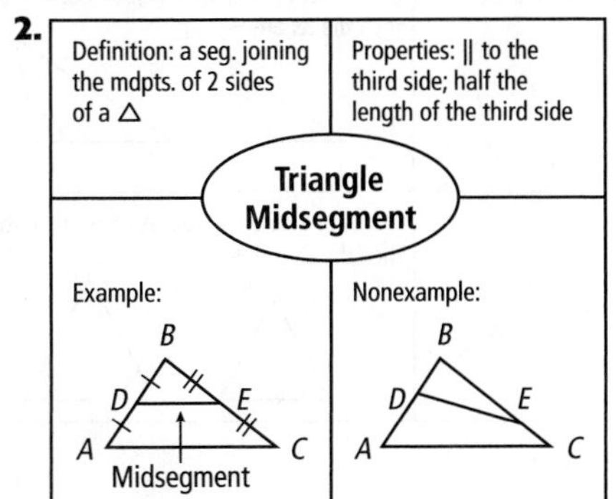

Definition: a seg. joining the mdpts. of 2 sides of a △
Properties: ∥ to the third side; half the length of the third side
Triangle Midsegment
Example:
B
D
E
A
C
Midsegment
Nonexample:
B
D
E
A
C

Lesson 5-5

3.

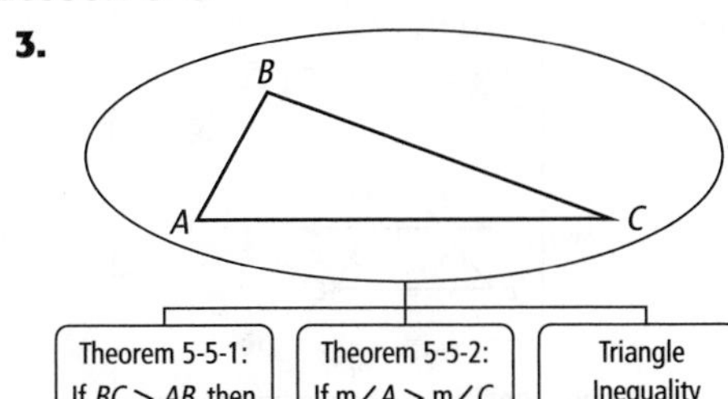

Theorem 5-5-1:	Theorem 5-5-2:	Triangle Inequality Theorem:
If $BC > AB$, then $m\angle A > m\angle C$. If $BC > AC$, then $m\angle A > m\angle B$. If $AC > BC$, then $m\angle B > m\angle A$. If $AC > AB$, then $m\angle B > m\angle C$. If $AB > BC$, then $m\angle C > m\angle A$. If $AB > AC$, then $m\angle C > m\angle B$.	If $m\angle A > m\angle C$, then $BC > AB$. If $m\angle A > m\angle B$, then $BC > AC$. If $m\angle B > m\angle A$, then $AC > BC$. If $m\angle B > m\angle C$, then $AC > AB$. If $m\angle C > m\angle A$, then $AB > BC$. If $m\angle C > m\angle B$, then $AB > AC$.	$AB + BC > AC$ $BC + AC > AB$ $AB + AC > BC$

Lesson 5-6

3.

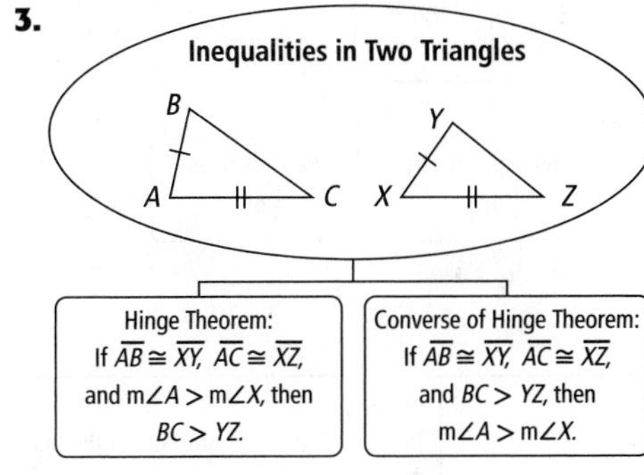

Inequalities in Two Triangles
B
A
C
Y
X
Z
Hinge Theorem: If $\overline{AB} \cong \overline{XY}$, $\overline{AC} \cong \overline{XZ}$, and $m\angle A > m\angle X$, then $BC > YZ$.
Converse of Hinge Theorem: If $\overline{AB} \cong \overline{XY}$, $\overline{AC} \cong \overline{XZ}$, and $BC > YZ$, then $m\angle A > m\angle X$.

Lesson 5-7

4.

Pythagorean Relationships

- Pyth. Thm.: In a rt.△, the sum of the squares of the leg lengths equals the square of the hypotenuse.
- Conv. of the Pyth. Thm.: If the sum of the squares of 2 side lengths of a △ equals the square of the third side length, then the △ is a rt. △.
- Pyth. Inequal. Thm.: In a △ with c as the length of the longest side, if $c^2 > a^2 + b^2$, the △ is obtuse, but if $c^2 < a^2 + b^2$, the △ is acute.

Lesson 5-8

3.

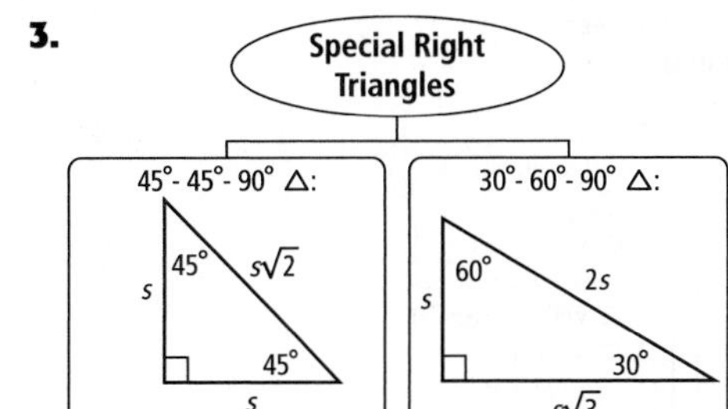

Chapter 6

Lesson 6-1

3.

	Interior Angles	Exterior Angles
Sum of Angle Measures	$(n-2)180°$	$360°$
One Angle Measure	$\frac{(n-2)180°}{n}$	$\frac{360°}{n}$

Lesson 6-2

3.

Properties of Parallelograms				
Opp. sides ∥:	Opp. sides ≅:	Opp. ∠s ≅:	Cons. ∠s supp.: $(180-x)°$ $x°$ $x°$ $(180-x)°$	Diags. bisect each other:

Lesson 6-3

3.

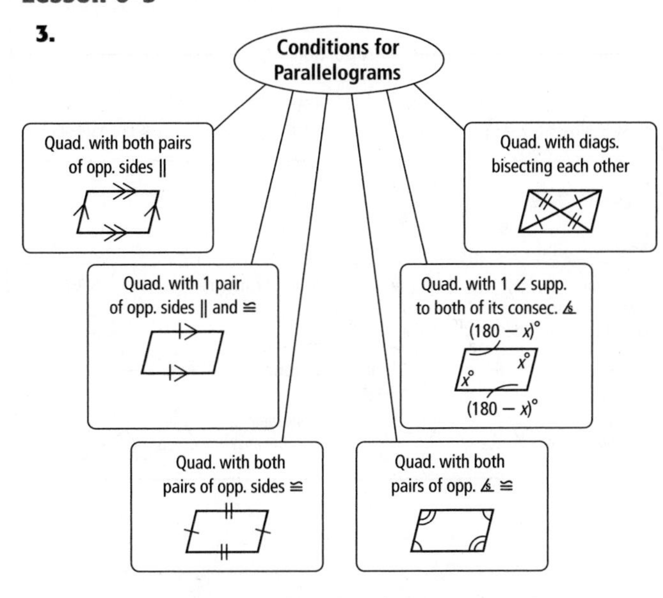

Lesson 6-4

3.

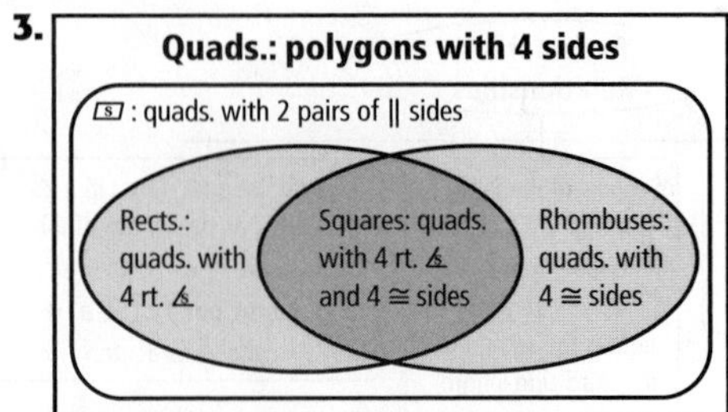

Lesson 6-5

4.

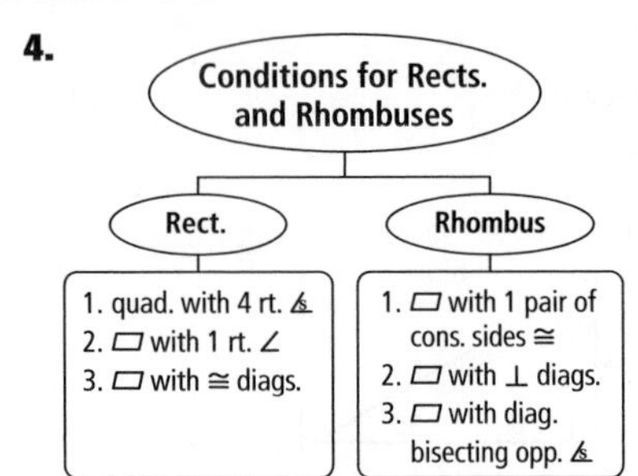

Conditions for Rects. and Rhombuses
Rect.
Rhombus
1. quad. with 4 rt. ∠s
2. ▱ with 1 rt. ∠
3. ▱ with ≅ diags.
1. ▱ with 1 pair of cons. sides ≅
2. ▱ with ⊥ diags.
3. ▱ with diag. bisecting opp. ∠s

Lesson 6-6

3.

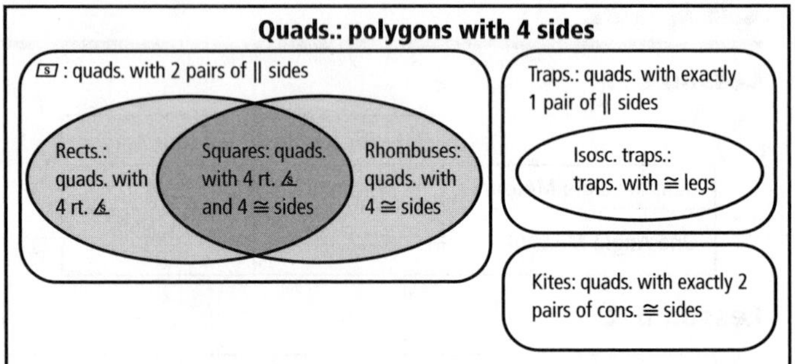

Chapter 7

Lesson 7-1

3.

Definition: A proportion is an eqn. stating that 2 ratios are =.	Properties: If $\frac{a}{b}=\frac{c}{d}$, then $ad=bc$, $\frac{b}{a}=\frac{d}{c}$, and, $\frac{a}{c}=\frac{b}{d}$
Proportion	
Example: Possible answer: $\frac{1}{3}=\frac{4}{12}$ is a proportion.	Nonexample: Possible answer: $\frac{1}{3}=\frac{4}{13}$ is not a proportion.

Lesson 7-2

4.

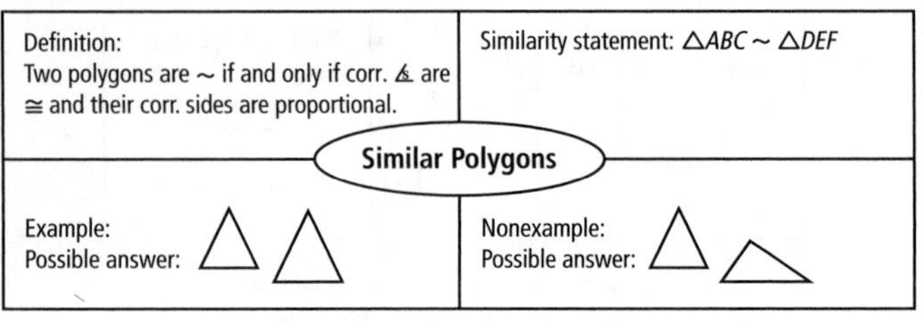

Definition:
Two polygons are ~ if and only if corr. ∠s are ≅ and their corr. sides are proportional.
Similarity statement: △ABC ~ △DEF
Similar Polygons
Example:
Possible answer:
Nonexample:
Possible answer:

Lesson 7-3

4.

	Congruence	Similarity
SSS	If 3 sides of 1 △ are respectively ≅ to 3 sides of another △, then the △s are ≅.	If 3 sides of 1 △ are proportional to the 3 corr. sides of another △, then the △s are ~.
SAS	If 2 sides and the included ∠ of 1 △ are ≅ to 2 sides and the included ∠ of another △, then the △s are ≅.	If 2 sides of 1 △ are proportional to 2 sides of another △ and their included ∠s are ≅, then the △s are ~.
AA		If 2 ∠s of 1 △ are ≅ to 2 ∠s of another △, then the △s are ~.

Lesson 7-4

2. Possible answer:

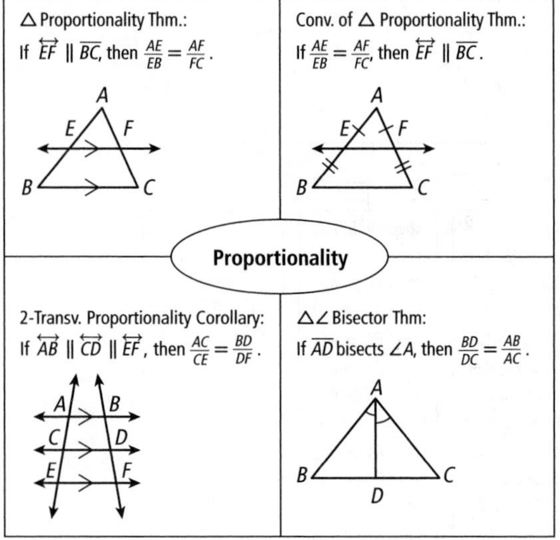

△ Proportionality Thm.:
If $\overleftrightarrow{EF} \parallel \overline{BC}$, then $\frac{AE}{EB}=\frac{AF}{FC}$.
Conv. of △ Proportionality Thm.:
If $\frac{AE}{EB}=\frac{AF}{FC}$, then $\overleftrightarrow{EF} \parallel \overline{BC}$.
Proportionality
2-Transv. Proportionality Corollary:
If $\overleftrightarrow{AB} \parallel \overleftrightarrow{CD} \parallel \overleftrightarrow{EF}$, then $\frac{AC}{CE}=\frac{BD}{DF}$.
△∠ Bisector Thm:
If $\overline{AD}$ bisects ∠A, then $\frac{BD}{DC}=\frac{AB}{AC}$.

Lesson 7-5

2.

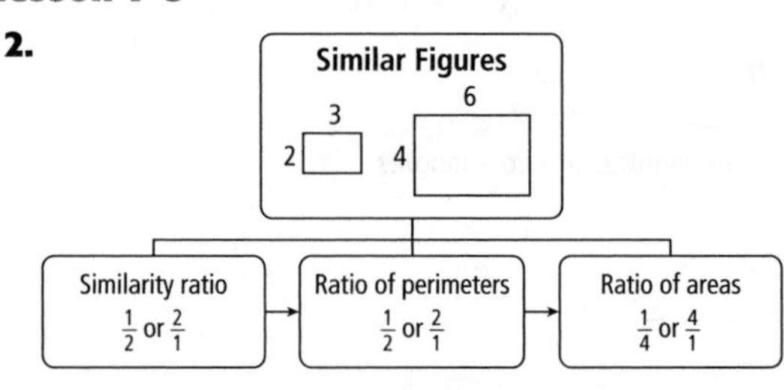

Lesson 7-6

2.

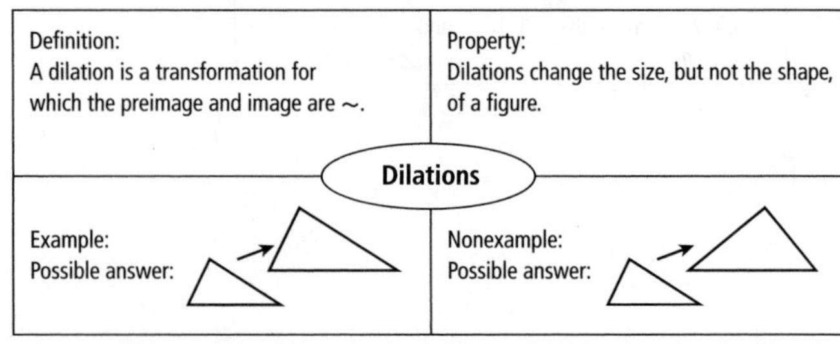

Definition:
A dilation is a transformation for which the preimage and image are ~.
Property:
Dilations change the size, but not the shape, of a figure.
Dilations
Example:
Possible answer:
Nonexample:
Possible answer:

Chapter 8

Lesson 8-1

2.

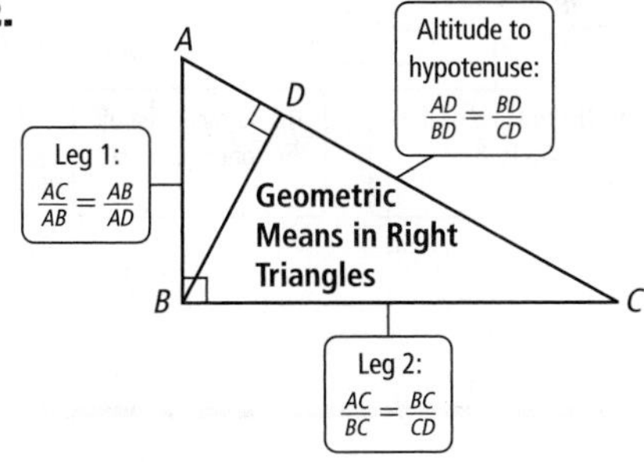

Lesson 8-2

3.

Abbreviation	Words	Diagram
$\sin = \frac{\text{opp. leg}}{\text{hyp.}}$	The sine of an ∠ is the ratio of the length of the opp. leg to the length of the hyp.	Hypotenuse, Opposite, A
$\cos = \frac{\text{adj. leg}}{\text{hyp.}}$	The cosine of an ∠ is the ratio of the length of the adj. leg to the length of the hyp.	Hypotenuse, Adjacent, A
$\tan = \frac{\text{opp. leg}}{\text{adj. leg}}$	The tangent of an ∠ is the ratio of the length of the opp. leg to the length of the adj. leg.	Opposite, Adjacent, A

Lesson 8-3

3.

	Trigonometric Ratio	Inverse Trigonometric Function
Sine	$\sin A = \frac{3}{5}$	$\sin^{-1}\left(\frac{3}{5}\right) = m\angle A$
Cosine	$\cos A = \frac{4}{5}$	$\cos^{-1}\left(\frac{4}{5}\right) = m\angle A$
Tangent	$\tan A = \frac{3}{4}$	$\tan^{-1}\left(\frac{3}{4}\right) = m\angle A$

Lesson 8-4

2.

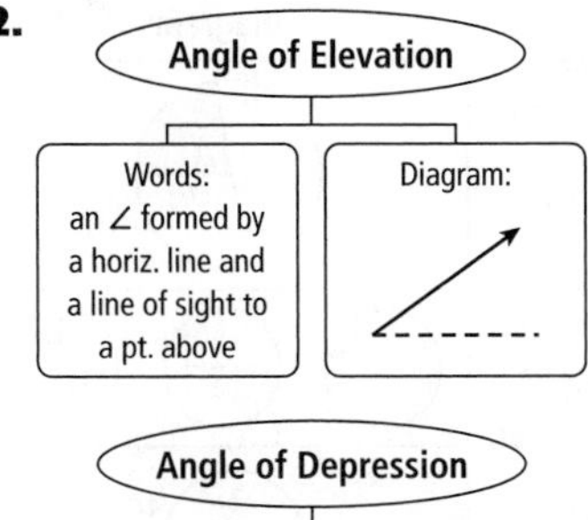

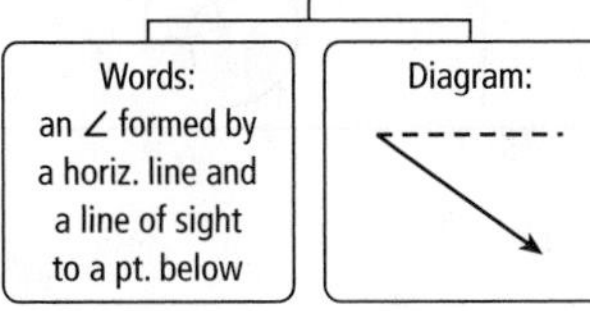

Words: an ∠ formed by a horiz. line and a line of sight to a pt. below
Diagram:

Lesson 8-5

2.

Given Information	Method	Example
Two angle measures and any side length	Law of Sines	12, 20°, 70°
Two side lengths and a nonincluded angle measure	Law of Sines	12, 8, 20°
Two side lengths and the included angle measure	Law of Cosines	12, 20°, 15
Three side lengths	Law of Cosines	12, 8, 15

Lesson 8-6

4.

Definition: a quantity with magnitude and direction	Names: $\vec{v}$, $\overrightarrow{AB}$, or $\langle x, y\rangle$
Vector	
Examples: the velocity of a ship, the force applied to an object	Nonexamples: a line segment, speed

Chapter 9

Lesson 9-1

3.

Area Formula	Shape(s)	Example(s)
$A = bh$	rectangle, paralleogram	
$A = \frac{1}{2}bh$	triangle	
$A = \frac{1}{2}(b_1 + b_2)h$	trapezoid	
$A = \frac{1}{2}d_1d_2$	kite, rhombus	

Lesson 9-2

3.

Regular Polygons (side length = 1)					
Polygon	**Number of Sides**	**Perimeter**	**Central Angle**	**Apothem**	**Area**
Triangle	3	3	120°	$\frac{\sqrt{3}}{6}$	$\frac{\sqrt{3}}{4}$
Square	4	4	90°	$\frac{1}{2}$	1
Hexagon	6	6	60°	$\frac{\sqrt{3}}{2}$	$\frac{3\sqrt{3}}{2}$

Lesson 9-3

3.

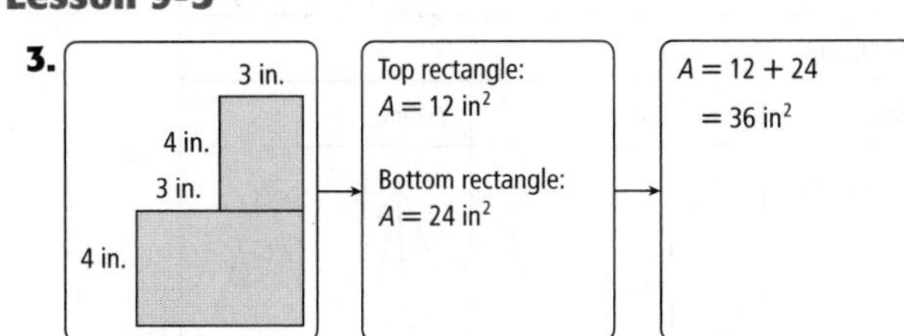

Lesson 9-4

3.

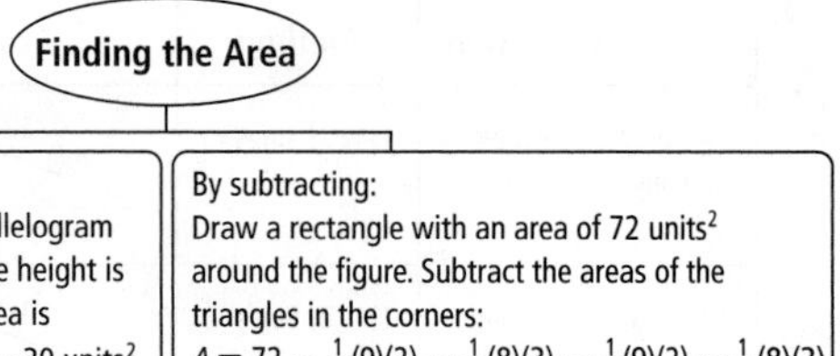

Finding the Area
Using the formula: The base of the parallelogram is $3\sqrt{5}$ units, and the height is $2\sqrt{5}$ units, so the area is $A = (3\sqrt{5})(2\sqrt{5}) = 30$ units^2.
By subtracting: Draw a rectangle with an area of 72 units^2 around the figure. Subtract the areas of the triangles in the corners:
$A = 72 - \frac{1}{2}(9)(2) - \frac{1}{2}(8)(3) - \frac{1}{2}(9)(2) - \frac{1}{2}(8)(3)$
$= 30$ units^2.

Lesson 9-5

2.

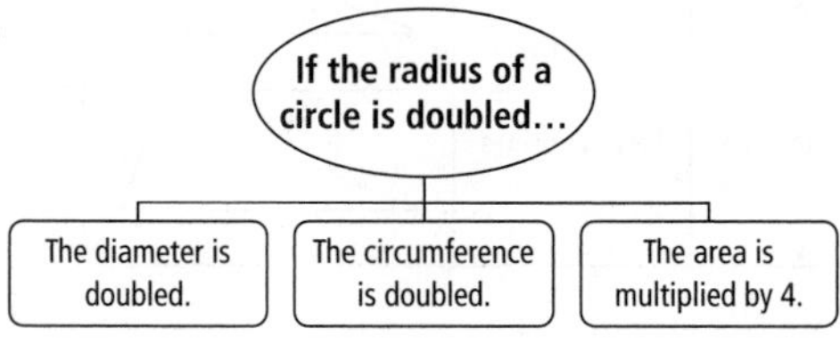

Lesson 9-6

3.

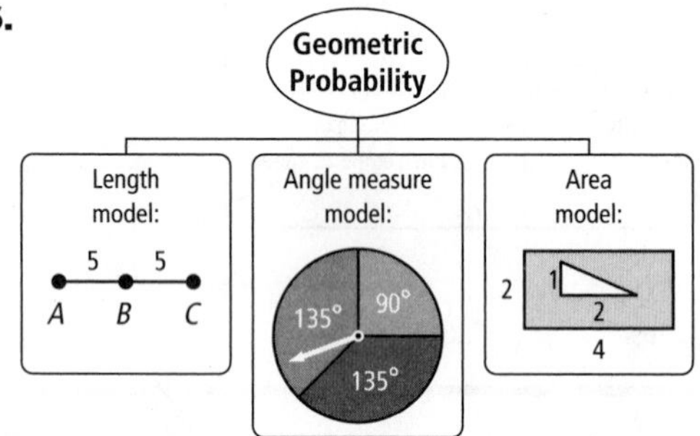

Chapter 10

Lesson 10-1

3.

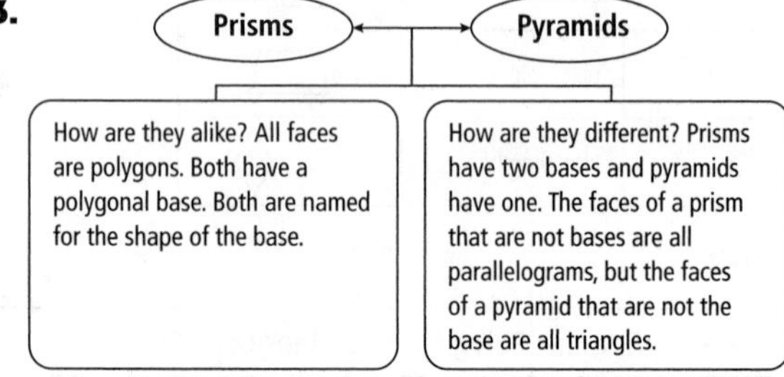

Prisms
Pyramids
How are they alike? All faces are polygons. Both have a polygonal base. Both are named for the shape of the base.
How are they different? Prisms have two bases and pyramids have one. The faces of a prism that are not bases are all parallelograms, but the faces of a pyramid that are not the base are all triangles.

Lesson 10-4

3.

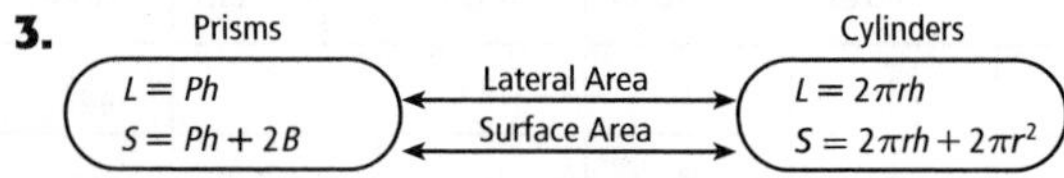

Prisms
$L = Ph$
$S = Ph + 2B$
Lateral Area
Surface Area
Cylinders
$L = 2\pi rh$
$S = 2\pi rh + 2\pi r^2$

Lesson 10-7

2.

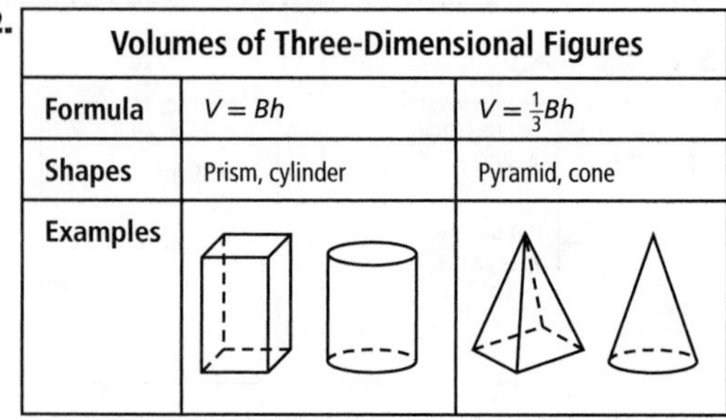

Volumes of Three-Dimensional Figures		
Formula	$V = Bh$	$V = \frac{1}{3}Bh$
Shapes	Prism, cylinder	Pyramid, cone
Examples		

Lesson 10-8

3.

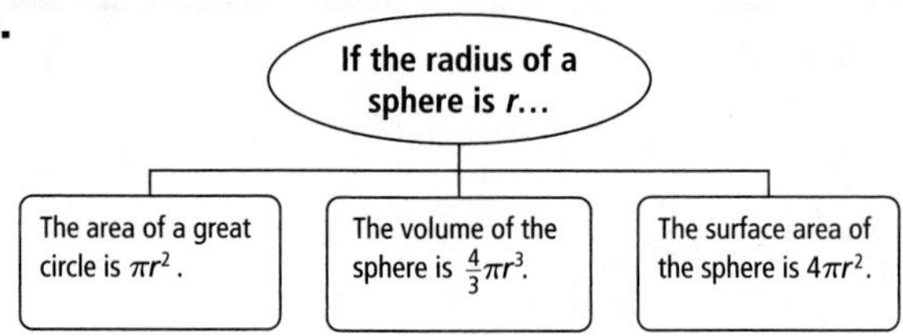

If the radius of a sphere is *r*...
The area of a great circle is πr^2.
The volume of the sphere is $\frac{4}{3}\pi r^3$.
The surface area of the sphere is $4\pi r^2$.

Chapter 11

Lesson 11-1

5.

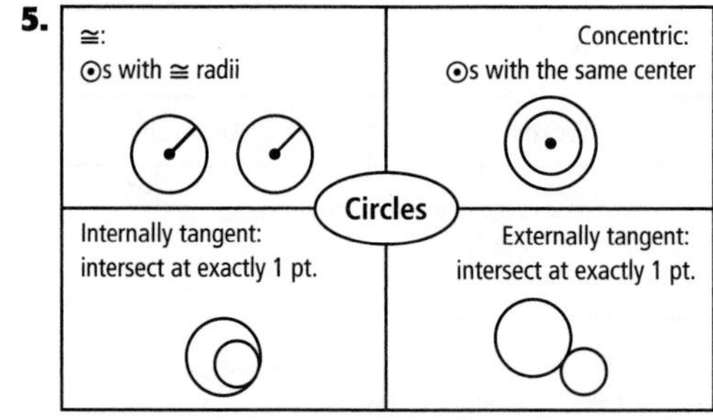

Lesson 11-2

3.

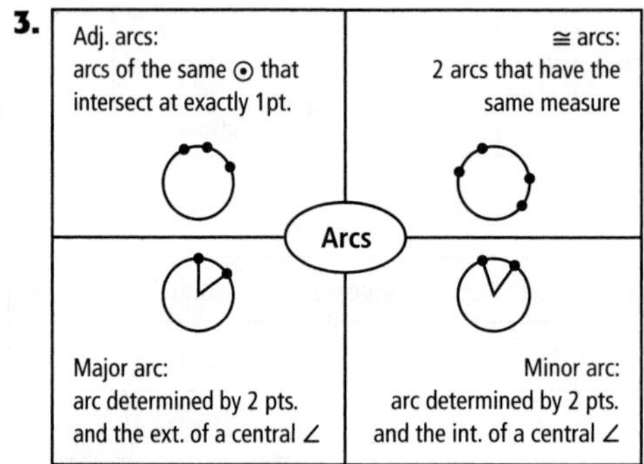

Adj. arcs: arcs of the same ⊙ that intersect at exactly 1pt.
≅ arcs: 2 arcs that have the same measure
Arcs
Major arc: arc determined by 2 pts. and the ext. of a central ∠
Minor arc: arc determined by 2 pts. and the int. of a central ∠

Lesson 11-3

3.

	Formula	Diagram
Area of a Sector	$A = \pi r^2\left(\frac{m°}{360°}\right)$	
Area of a Segment	Area of seg. = area of sector − area of △	
Arc Length	$L = 2\pi r\left(\frac{m°}{360°}\right)$	

Lesson 11-4

3.

Def.: an ∠ whose vertex is on the ⊙ and whose sides contain chords of the ⊙	Prop.: The measure of an inscribed ∠ is half the measure of its intercepted arc. If inscribed ∠s intercept the same arc, they are ≅. An inscribed ∠ that intercepts a semicircle is a rt. ∠.
Inscribed Angles	
Example:	Nonexamples:

Lesson 11-5

2.

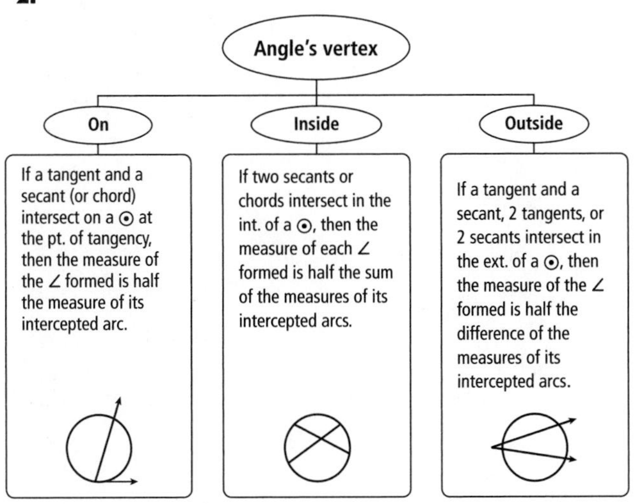

Angle's vertex
On
Inside
Outside
If a tangent and a secant (or chord) intersect on a ⊙ at the pt. of tangency, then the measure of the ∠ formed is half the measure of its intercepted arc.
If two secants or chords intersect in the int. of a ⊙, then the measure of each ∠ formed is half the sum of the measures of its intercepted arcs.
If a tangent and a secant, 2 tangents, or 2 secants intersect in the ext. of a ⊙, then the measure of the ∠ formed is half the difference of the measures of its intercepted arcs.

Lesson 11-6

3.

	Theorem	Diagram	Example
Chord-Chord	If 2 chords intersect in the int. of a ⊙, then the products of the lengths of the segs. of the chords are =.	C, B, 3, 4, E, 8, 6, D, A	$3 \cdot 8 = 4 \cdot 6$
Secant-Secant	If 2 secants intersect in the ext. of a ⊙, then the product of the lengths of 1 secant seg. and its external seg. = the product of the lengths of the other secant seg. and its external seg.	A, B, 2, 6, C, 8, D, 4, E	$8 \cdot 6 = 12 \cdot 4$
Secant-Tangent	If a secant and a tangent intersect in the ext. of a ⊙, then the product of the lengths of the secant seg. and its ext. seg. = the length of the tangent seg. squared.	A, 5, B, 4, C, D, 6	$9 \cdot 4 = 6^2$

Lesson 11-7

4.

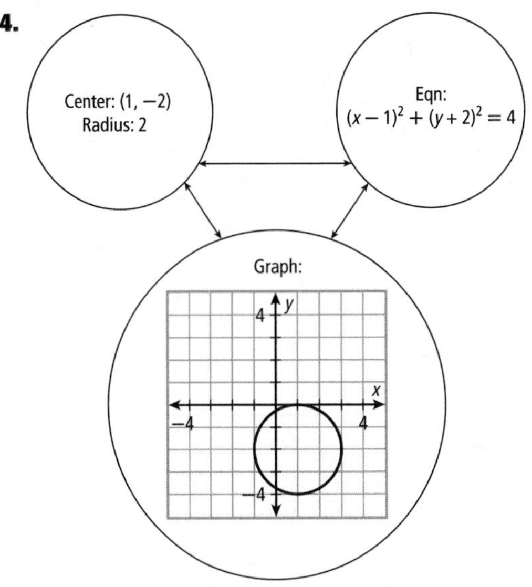

Chapter 12

Lesson 12-1

3.

Line of Reflection	Image of (*a*, *b*)	Example
x-axis	(*a*, −*b*)	(1, 2) → (1, −2)
y-axis	(−*a*, *b*)	(1, 2) → (−1, 2)
y = *x*	(*b*, *a*)	(1, 2) → (2, 1)

Lesson 12-2

3.

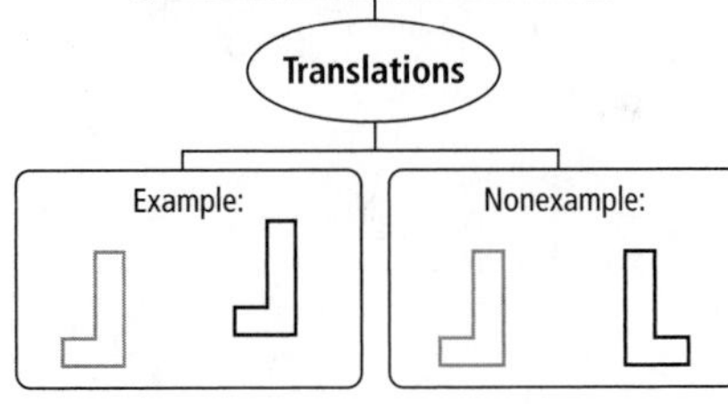

Lesson 12-3

3.

	Reflection	Translation	Rotation
Definition	A transformation across a line (the line of reflection) such that the line of reflection is the ⊥ bisector of each seg. joining a point and its image	A transformation along a vector such that each seg. joining a point and its image has the same length as the vector and is ∥ to it	A transformation about a pt. *P* such that each pt. and its image are the same dist. from *P* and all of the ∠s with vertex *P* formed by a pt. and its image are ≅
Example			

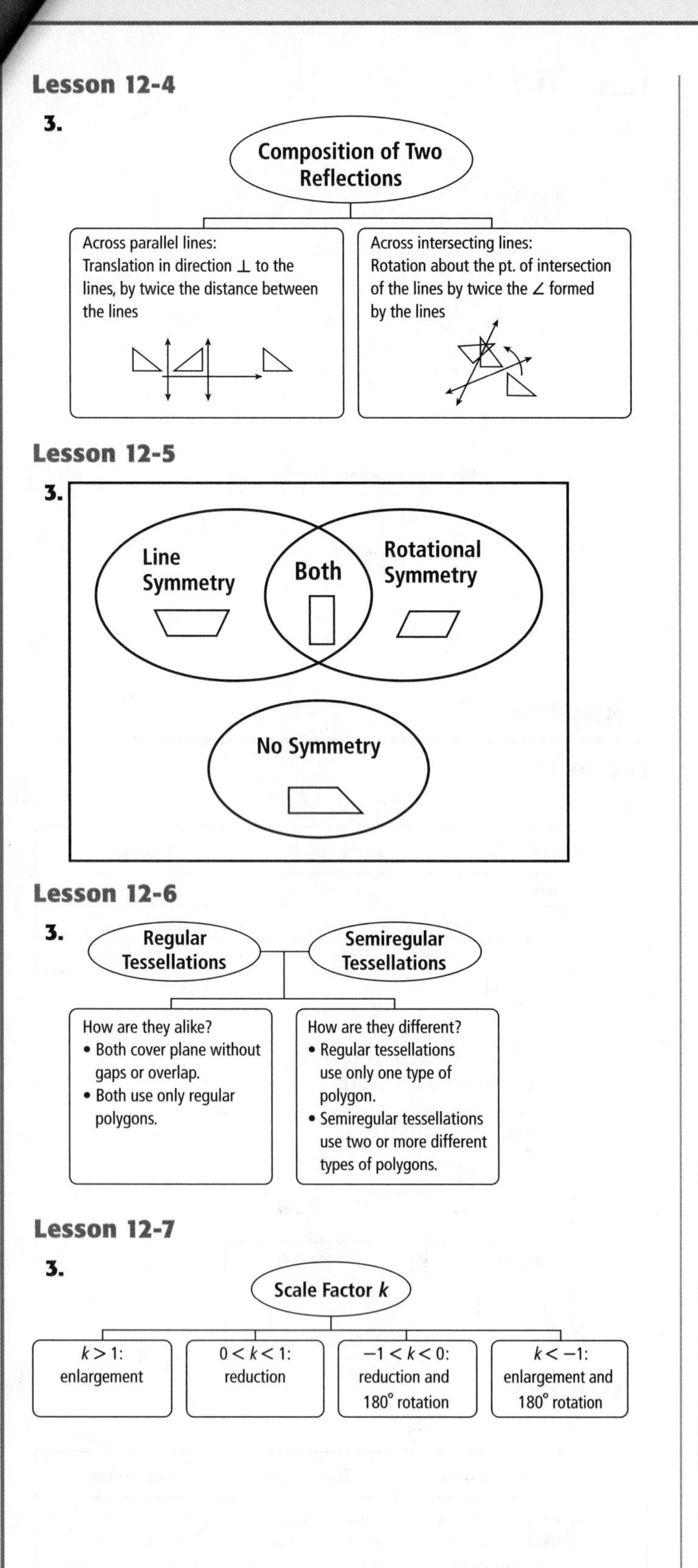
Lesson 12-4
3.
Composition of Two Reflections
Across parallel lines: Translation in direction ⊥ to the lines, by twice the distance between the lines
Across intersecting lines: Rotation about the pt. of intersection of the lines by twice the ∠ formed by the lines
Lesson 12-5
3.
Line Symmetry
Both
Rotational Symmetry
No Symmetry
Lesson 12-6
3.
Regular Tessellations
Semiregular Tessellations
How are they alike?
• Both cover plane without gaps or overlap.
• Both use only regular polygons.
How are they different?
• Regular tessellations use only one type of polygon.
• Semiregular tessellations use two or more different types of polygons.
Lesson 12-7
3.
Scale Factor k
k > 1: enlargement
0 < k < 1: reduction
−1 < k < 0: reduction and 180° rotation
k < −1: enlargement and 180° rotation

Additional Answers

Chapter 1

1B *Ready to Go On?*

12. $H'(-1, 3)$; $J'(2, 3)$; $K'(2, 0)$; $L(-1, 0)$

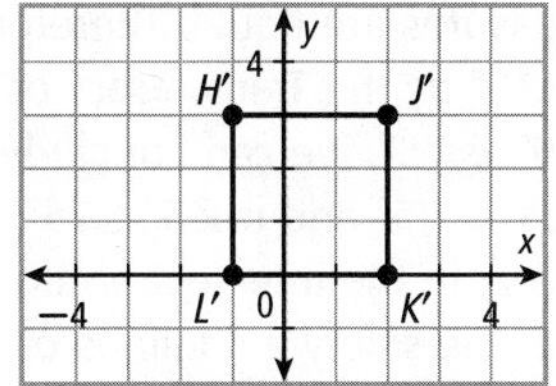

13.

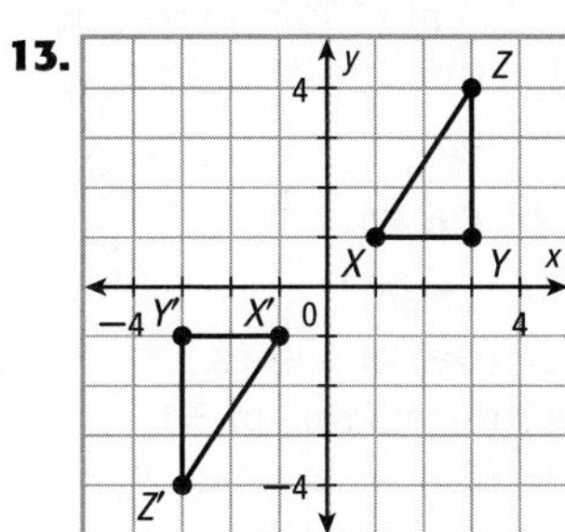

rotation of 180°

1-7 *Exercises*

24. Both translations move figures in the same direction. However the second trans. moves figures twice as far horiz. and vert. as the first trans..

25.

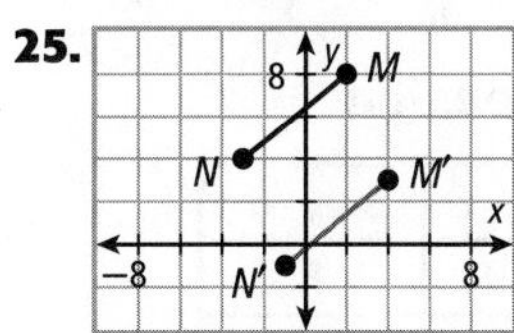

26.

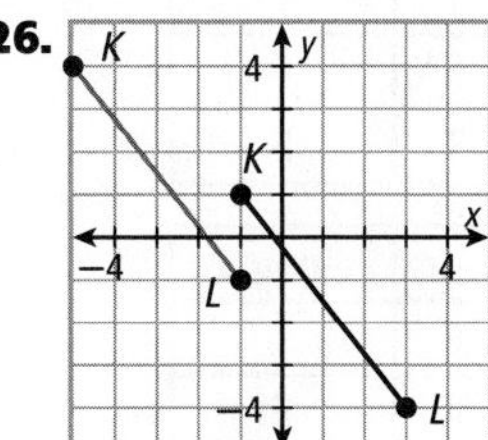

27. Find the coords. of the vertices of the given $\triangle$. Add 1 to the x-coord. and to the y-coord. Plot the new set of pts. and connect them using a straightedge.

Chapter 2

Reading and Writing Math

1. Can assume: W, A, and Y are col. X, A, and Z are col. All pts. are coplanar. A is between W and Y and between X and Z. $\overleftrightarrow{XZ}$ and $\overleftrightarrow{WY}$ are lines. $\angle XAW$ and $\angle WAZ$, $\angle WAZ$ and $\angle ZAY$, and $\angle ZAY$ and $\angle YAX$ are adj. $\angle$s. $\angle XAW$ and $\angle WAZ$, $\angle WAZ$ and $\angle ZAY$, $\angle ZAY$ and $\angle YAX$, and $\angle YAX$ and $\angle XAW$ form lin. pairs. $\angle XAW$ and $\angle ZAY$ and $\angle WAZ$ and $\angle YAX$ are vert. $\angle$s. Cannot assume: anything about measures of $\angle$s and segs; whether $\angle XAW \cong \angle WAZ$ or $\overline{YA} \cong \overline{AZ}$.

2. Can assume: P and S, S and R, R and Q, and Q and P are col. All pts. are coplanar. $\overleftrightarrow{PS}$, $\overleftrightarrow{SR}$, $\overleftrightarrow{RQ}$, and $\overleftrightarrow{QP}$ are lines. Cannot assume: $\angle P$, $\angle Q$, $\angle R$, or $\angle S$ are rt. $\angle$s; whether $\angle P \cong \angle R$, $\angle P \cong \angle Q$, $\overline{PQ} \cong \overline{SR}$, or $\overline{PQ} \cong \overline{PS}$.

2-1 *Exercises*

40.

x	$x^2 + x + 11$
1	13
2	17
3	23
4	31
5	41
6	53
7	67
8	83

Possible answer: prime; $x = 10$

42a.

Week	Sit-ups
1	15
2	35
3	55
4	75
5	95
6	115
7	135
8	155
9	175
10	195

b. week 8

c. $20(n - 1) + 15$, or $20n - 5$

43.

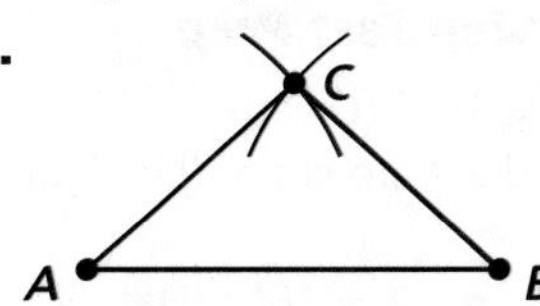

$m\angle CAB = m\angle CBA$; $AC = CB$; possible answer: if a pt. is equidistant from the endpts. of a seg., then the 2 $\angle$s formed by connecting the pt. to the endpts. of the seg. are $\cong$.

2-4 *Exercises*

14. Conv.: If Greg wins the race, then he has the fastest time.
Bicond.: Greg has the fastest time iff he wins the race.

15. Conv.: If a $\triangle$ is a rt. $\triangle$, then it contains a rt. $\angle$. Bicond.: A $\triangle$ contains a rt. $\angle$ iff it is a rt. $\triangle$.

18. A fig. is a $\bigcirc$ iff it is the set of all pts. that are a fixed dist. from a given pt.

19. A player is a catcher iff the player is positioned behind home plate and catches throws from the pitcher.

35. A statement is a bicond. iff it can be written in the form "*p* iff *q*." Cond.: If a statement is a bicond., then it can be written in the form "*p* iff *q*." Conv.: If a statement can be written in the form "*p* iff *q*," then it is a bicond.. Since the cond. and its conv. are true, the def. is true.

36. Possible answer: If you write the def. as a bicond., "A ray is an $\angle$ bisector iff it divides the $\angle$ into 2 $\cong$ $\angle$s," you can use it forward or backward. If you know the ray is an $\angle$ bisector, you can conclude that the 2 $\angle$s formed are $\cong$. If you know 2 adj. $\angle$s formed by a ray are $\cong$, then you know the ray is an $\angle$ bisector.

37a. If I say it, then I mean it. If I mean it, then I say it.

b. Possible answer: Alice implies "I say it iff I mean it." This bicond. is not true. People often mean things without saying them or say things they don't mean.

41. Cond.: If you get a traffic ticket, then you are speeding. Conv.: If you are speeding, then you will get a traffic ticket. The bicond. is false because both statements are false. You can get a ticket while not speeding. Also, you can speed without getting a ticket.

42. The two ovals will exactly overlap. If one condition is met, then the other is necessarily met, which is true of the conditions in a good def.

44. T; it is given that the cond. is true. The conv. "If D is in the int. of $\angle ABC$, then $m\angle ABD + m\angle DBC = m\angle ABC$" is true by the $\angle$ Add. Post. Since the cond. and its conv. are true, the bicond. is true.

47. The graph is reflected across the x-axis and shifted 1 unit down and is narrower than the graph of the parent function.

2A *Ready to Go On?*

5. Possible answer: A male lion weighs about 412.4 lb.

14. Converse: If a number is divisible by 4, then the number is even; T. Inverse: If a number is not even, then the number is not divisible by 4; T. Contrapositive: If a number is not divisible by 4, then the number is not even; F.

17. Converse: If the sum of the measures of 2 ∠s is 180°, then the ∠s are supp. Biconditional: 2 ∠s are supp. if and only if the sum of their measures is 180°.

2-5 *Exercises*

29. $x = 16$; $(23.1x - 0.87) = 94.36$ (Given); $6.2x - 1.74 = 94.36$ (Distrib. Prop.); $6.2x = 96.1$ (Add. Prop. of =); $x = 15.5$ (Div. Prop. of =); possible answer: the exact solution rounds to the estimate.

33. $\frac{x+1}{2} = 3$ (Mdpt. Formula);
$x + 1 = 6$ (Mult. Prop. of =);
$x = 5$ (Subtr. Prop. of =);
$\frac{1+y}{2} = 5$ (Mdpt. Formula);
$1 + y = 10$ (Mult. Prop. of =);
$y = 9$ (Subtr. Prop. of =)

34. $169.50 = 35 + 21(3) + 1.10x$ (Given); $169.50 = 98 + 1.10x$ (Simplify.); $71.50 = 1.10x$ (Subtr. Prop. of =); $65 = x$ (Div. Prop. of =); $x = 65$ (Sym. Prop. of =)

35a. $1733.65 = 92.50 + 79.96 + 983 + 10{,}820x$ (Given); $1733.65 = 1155.46 + 10{,}820x$ (Simplify.); $578.19 = 10{,}820x$ (Subtr. Prop. of =); $0.05 \approx x$ (Div. Prop. of =)

36. Given $\overline{PR}$, you know from the Reflex. Prop. of = that $PR = PR$. By the def. of ≅ segs., $\overline{PR} \cong \overline{PR}$. Given that $\overline{PR} \cong \overline{ST}$, you know from the def. of ≅ segs. that $PR = ST$. By the Sym. Prop. of =, $ST = PR$. By the def. of ≅ segs., $\overline{ST} \cong \overline{PR}$. Given that $\overline{AB} \cong \overline{CD}$ and $\overline{CD} \cong \overline{EF}$, you know from the def. of ≅ segs. that $AB = CD$ and $CD = EF$. By the Trans. Prop. of =, $AB = EF$. Therefore $\overline{AB} \cong \overline{EF}$ by the def. of ≅ segs.

37a. $x + 15 \leq 63$ (Given); $x \leq 48$ (Subtr. Prop. of Inequal.)
b. $-2x > 36$ (Given); $x < -18$ (Div. Prop. of Inequal.)

38. Possible answer: The conclusion of a deductive proof has been proven true in all cases, but a conjecture is based on observation and is not proven to be true.

43. $PR = PA + RA$ (Seg. Add. Post.); $PA = QB$, $QB = RA$ (Given); $PA = RA$ (Trans. Prop. of =); $PR = PA + PA$ (Subst.); $PA = 18$ (Given); $PR = 18 + 18$ (Subst.); $PR = 36$ in. (Simplify.)

45. $7 - 3x > 19$ (Given); $-3x > 12$ (Subtr. Prop. of Inequal.); $x < -4$ (Div. Prop. of Inequal.)

2-6 *Geometry Lab*

2. Plan: Use the def. of ∠ bis. to show that $m\angle 1 = m\angle 2$. Then use the ∠ Add. Post. and subst. to show that $2m\angle 1 = m\angle ABC$.
Two-column proof:
1. $\overrightarrow{BD}$ bisects $\angle ABC$. (Given)
2. $\angle 1 \cong \angle 2$ (Def. of ∠ bis.)
3. $m\angle 1 = m\angle 2$ (Def. of ≅ ∠s)
4. $m\angle 1 + m\angle 2 = m\angle ABC$ (∠ Add. Post.)
5. $m\angle 1 + m\angle 1 = m\angle ABC$ (Subst.)
6. $2m\angle 1 = m\angle ABC$ (Simplify.)

3. Plan: Since $\angle LXN$ is a right angle, its measure is 90°. By the ∠ Add. Post., $m\angle 1 + m\angle 2 = m\angle LXN$. So by subst., $m\angle 1 + m\angle 2 = 90°$, which means that ∠1 and ∠2 are comp.
Two-column proof:
1. $\angle LXN$ is a rt. ∠. (Given)
2. $m\angle LXN = 90°$ (Def of rt. ∠)
3. $m\angle 1 + m\angle 2 = m\angle LXN$ (∠ Add. Post.)
4. $m\angle 1 + m\angle 2 = 90°$ (Subst.)
5. ∠1 and ∠2 are comp. (Def. of comp. ∠s)

2B *Multi-Step Test Prep*

3. 1. $m\angle 2 = 145°$ (Given)
2. ∠1 and ∠2 are supp. (Lin. Pair Thm.)
3. $m\angle 1 + m\angle 2 = 180°$ (Def. of supp. ∠s)
4. $m\angle 1 + 145° = 180°$ (Subst.)
5. $m\angle 1 = 35°$ (Subtr. Prop. of =)
6. $\angle 1 \cong \angle 3$ (Vert. ∠s Thm.
7. $m\angle 1 = m\angle 3$ (Def. of ≅ ∠s)
8. $m\angle 3 = 35°$ (Trans. Prop. of =)
9. $m\angle 1 < 75°$ and $m\angle 3 < 75°$ (Def. of Inequal.)

4. A surveyor found that $m\angle 2 = 145°$. Since ∠1 and ∠2 are supp. by the Lin. Pair Thm., $m\angle 1 + m\angle 2 = 180°$ by the def. of supp. ∠s. By using subst. and the Subtr. Prop. of =, we can conclude that $m\angle 1 = 35°$. By the Vert. ∠s Thm., $\angle 1 \cong \angle 3$, so their measures are equal. Therefore, $m\angle 3 = 35°$ by the Trans. Prop. of =. Since $35° < 75°$, we can conclude that $m\angle 1 < 75°$ and $m\angle 3 < 75°$. Thus the ∠s in the intersection do not meet the safety guidelines of the U.S. Department of Transportation, and the intersection should be reconstructed.

2B *Ready to Go On?*

9. 1. $\overline{AB} \cong \overline{EF}$ (Given)
2. $AB = EF$ (Def. of ≅ segs.)
3. $EF = AB$ (Sym. Prop. of =)
4. $\overline{EF} \cong \overline{AB}$ (Def. of ≅ segs.)

10.

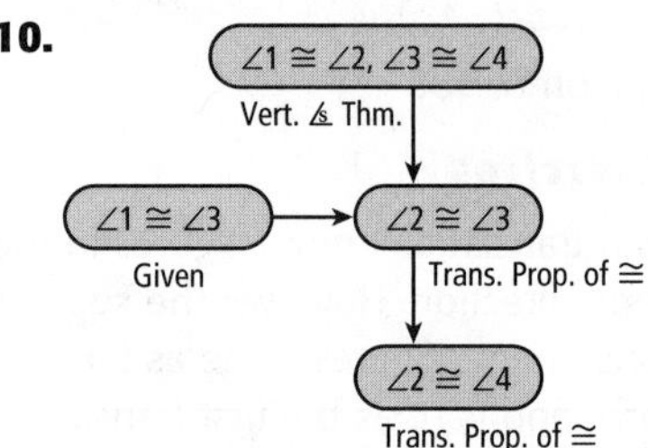

Chapter 2 Extension

7.

s	t	$\sim t$	$s \wedge \sim t$
T	T	F	F
T	F	T	T
F	T	F	F
F	F	T	F

8.

u	t	$\sim u$	$\sim u \vee t$
T	T	F	T
T	F	F	F
F	T	T	T
F	F	T	T

9.

u	s	t	$\sim u$	$(s \wedge t)$	$\sim u \vee (s \wedge t)$
T	T	T	F	T	T
T	T	F	F	F	F
T	F	T	F	F	F
T	F	F	F	F	F
F	T	T	T	T	T
F	T	F	T	F	T
F	F	T	T	F	T
F	F	F	T	F	T

10.

p	q	$\sim p$	$\sim q$	$p \to q$	$\sim q \to \sim p$
T	T	F	F	T	T
T	F	F	T	F	F
F	T	T	F	T	T
F	F	T	T	T	T

11.

q	p	$\sim q$	$\sim p$	$q \to p$	$\sim p \to \sim q$
T	T	F	F	T	T
F	T	T	F	T	T
T	F	F	T	F	F
F	F	T	T	T	T

12.

p	q	$p \to q$	$q \to p$	$(p \to q) \wedge (q \to p)$
T	T	T	T	T
T	F	F	T	F
F	T	T	F	F
F	F	T	T	T

13a.

p	T	T	F	F
q	T	F	T	F
$\sim p$	F	F	T	T
$\sim q$	F	T	F	T
$p \wedge q$	T	F	F	F
$\sim(p \wedge q)$	F	T	T	T
$\sim p \vee \sim q$	F	T	T	T

p	T	T	F	F
q	T	F	T	F
$\sim p$	F	F	T	T
$\sim q$	F	T	F	T
$p \vee q$	T	T	T	F
$\sim(p \vee q)$	F	F	F	T
$\sim p \wedge \sim q$	F	F	F	T

Chapter 2 Test

23. 1. $\angle AFB \cong \angle EFD$ (Given)

2. $\angle EFD \cong \angle BFC$ (Vert. ∡ Thm.)

3. $\angle AFB \cong \angle BFC$ (Trans. Prop. of $\cong$)

4. $\overrightarrow{FB}$ bisects $\angle AFC$. (Def. of $\angle$ bisector)

24. It is given that $\angle AFB \cong \angle EFD$. By the Vert. ∡ Thm., $\angle EFD \cong \angle BFC$. Therefore, $\angle AFB \cong \angle BFC$ by the Trans. Prop. of $\cong$. So $\overrightarrow{FB}$ bisects $\angle AFC$ by the def. of $\angle$ bisector.

25.

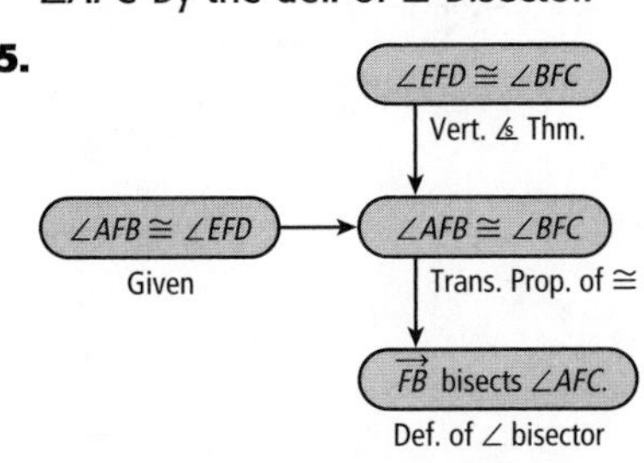

Chapter 3

3-1 *Exercises*

49. transv. m: $\angle 1$ and $\angle 3$, $\angle 2$ and $\angle 4$, $\angle 5$ and $\angle 7$, $\angle 6$ and $\angle 8$; transv. n: $\angle 9$ and $\angle 11$, $\angle 10$ and $\angle 12$, $\angle 13$ and $\angle 15$, $\angle 14$ and $\angle 16$; transv. p: $\angle 1$ and $\angle 9$, $\angle 2$ and $\angle 10$, $\angle 5$ and $\angle 13$, $\angle 6$ and $\angle 14$; transv. q: $\angle 3$ and $\angle 11$, $\angle 4$ and $\angle 12$, $\angle 7$ and $\angle 15$, $\angle 8$ and $\angle 16$

50. transv. m: $\angle 2$ and $\angle 7$, $\angle 3$ and $\angle 6$; transv. n: $\angle 10$ and $\angle 15$, $\angle 11$ and $\angle 14$; transv. p: $\angle 5$ and $\angle 10$, $\angle 6$ and $\angle 9$; transversal q: $\angle 7$ and $\angle 12$, $\angle 8$ and $\angle 11$

51. transv. m: $\angle 1$ and $\angle 8$, $\angle 4$ and $\angle 5$; transv. n: $\angle 9$ and $\angle 16$, $\angle 12$ and $\angle 13$; transv. p: $\angle 1$ and $\angle 14$, $\angle 2$ and $\angle 13$; transv. q: $\angle 3$ and $\angle 16$, $\angle 4$ and $\angle 15$

52. transv. m: $\angle 2$ and $\angle 3$, $\angle 6$ and $\angle 7$; transv. n: $\angle 10$ and $\angle 11$, $\angle 14$ and $\angle 15$; transv. p: $\angle 5$ and $\angle 9$, $\angle 6$ and $\angle 10$; transv. q: $\angle 7$ and $\angle 11$, $\angle 8$ and $\angle 12$

53. corr. ∡

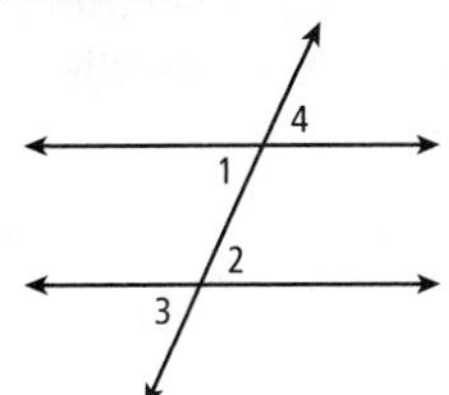

3-3 *Exercises*

55. By the Vert. ∡ Thm., $\angle 6 \cong \angle 3$, so $m\angle 6 = m\angle 3$. It is given that $m\angle 2 + m\angle 3 = 180°$. By subst., $m\angle 2 + m\angle 6 = 180°$. By the Conv. of the Same-Side Int. ∡ Thm., $\ell \parallel m$.

56. It is given that $m\angle 2 + m\angle 5 = 180°$. By the Lin. Pair Thm., $m\angle 4 + m\angle 5 = 180°$. By the Trans. Prop. of =, $m\angle 2 + m\angle 5 = m\angle 4 + m\angle 5$. By the Subtr. Prop. of =, $m\angle 2 = m\angle 4$. By the Conv. of the Corr. ∡ Post., $\ell \parallel n$.

60. Converse: If an animal has wings, then it is a bat; F; Inverse: If an animal is not a bat, then it does not have wings; F; Contrapositive: If an animal does not have wings, then it is not a bat; T.

61. Converse: If a polygon has exactly 3 sides, then it is a triangle; T; Inverse: If a polygon is not a triangle, then it does not have exactly 3 sides; T; Contrapositive: If a polygon does not have exactly 3 sides, then it is not a triangle; T.

62. Converse: If a whole number is even, then the digit in the ones place is 2; F; Inverse: If a whole number does not have a 2 in the ones place, then the number is not even; F; Contrapositive: If a whole number is not even, then it does not have a 2 in the ones place; T.

3A *Multi-Step Test Prep*

1. The table top is parallel to the floor and ceiling of the room and perpendicular to the walls.

2. The table top is parallel to the floor, which forms a 25° angle with the ground. Thus the table top also forms a 25° angle relative to the ground. If a ball were placed on the table, it would roll down the table top. To a person in the room, the table would appear to be level and the ball would appear to roll of its own power.

3. $\overline{RS}$ forms a transversal to the board and the ground. The board is parallel to the ground by the Converse of the Alternate Interior Angles Theorem. From the point of view of a person inside the room, the person on one end of the board would appear higher than the person on the other end of the board.

4. The lamp is hanging straight down, so it would form a 25° angle with the walls. To a person inside the room, the walls would appear straight, so the lamp would appear to be hanging at a 25° tilt.

3A *Ready to Go On?*

12. $m\angle 8 = 59°$ and $m\angle 6 = 59°$, so $\angle 8 \cong \angle 6$. $a \parallel b$ by the Conv. of Corr. ∡ Post.

13. $a \parallel b$ by the Conv. of Alt. Ext. ∡ Thm.

14. $\angle 8$ and $\angle 7$ are supp., so $a \parallel b$ by the Conv. of Same-Side Int. ∡ Thm.

15. $\angle 8 \cong \angle 4$, so $a \parallel b$ by the Conv. of Alt. Int. ∡ Thm.

3-5 *Exercises*

15. ∥

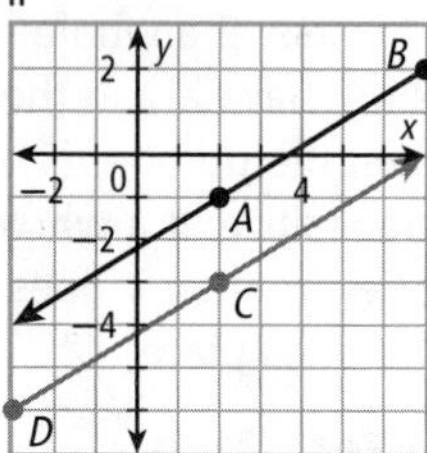

16. neither

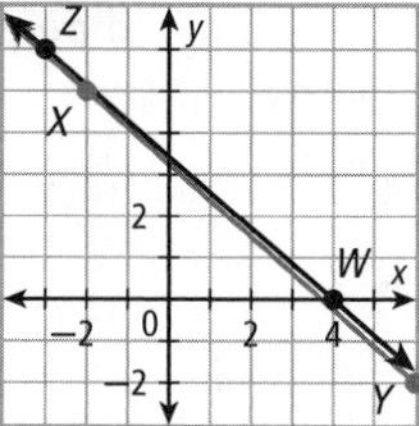

17. ⊥

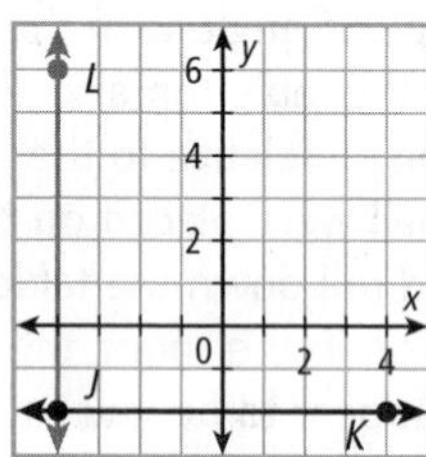

31. Slope of $\overline{AB}$: 1
Slope of $\overline{BC}$: −1
Slope of $\overline{CD}$: 1
Slope of $\overline{DA}$: −1

a. The opp. sides $\overline{AB}$ and $\overline{CD}$ both have slope 1, so they are ∥. The opp. sides $\overline{BC}$ and $\overline{DA}$ both have slope −1, so they are ∥.

b. The slopes of any 2 consecutive sides are opp. reciprocals, so the consecutive sides are ⊥.

c. By the Dist. Formula,

$AB = \sqrt{(6-0)^2 + (4+2)^2}$
$= 6\sqrt{2}$

$BC = \sqrt{(0-6)^2 + (10-4)^2}$
$= 6\sqrt{2}$

$CD = \sqrt{(-6-0)^2 + (4-10)^2}$
$= 6\sqrt{2}$

$DA = \sqrt{(0+6)^2 + (-2-4)^2}$
$= 6\sqrt{2}$

All 4 sides have the same length, so they are ≅.

3-6 *Exercises*

1. The slope-intercept form of an equation is solved for *y*. The *x*-term is first, and the constant term is second.

5.

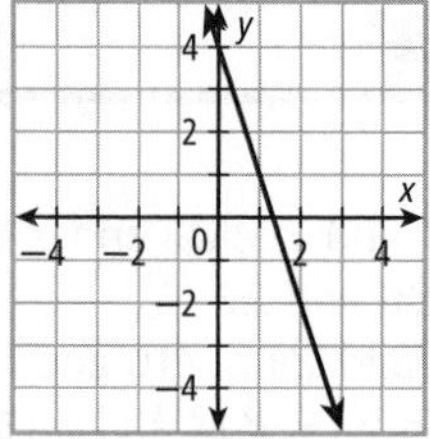

6.

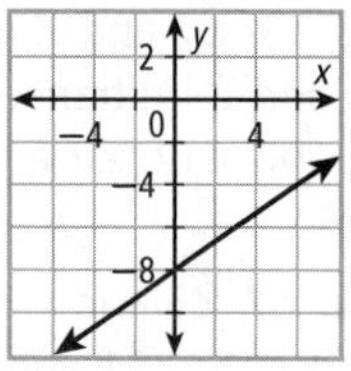

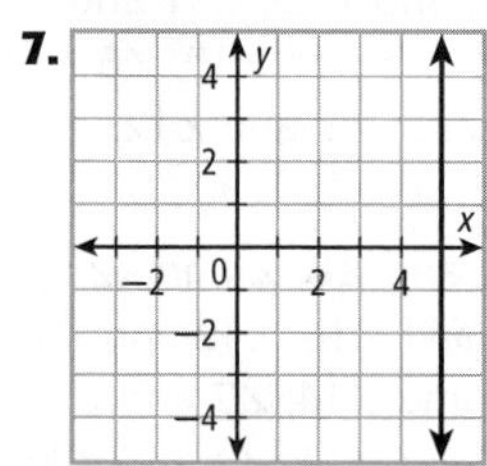

7.

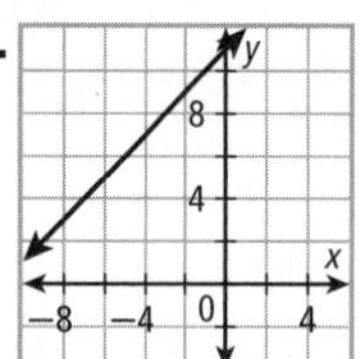

12. For 72 mi/h, the tickets will cost approximately the same. A ticket in Conroe would be $122, and a ticket in Lakeville would be $120. Because the speeds are measured to the nearest mile per hour, the cost of the tickets will never be exactly equal.

16.

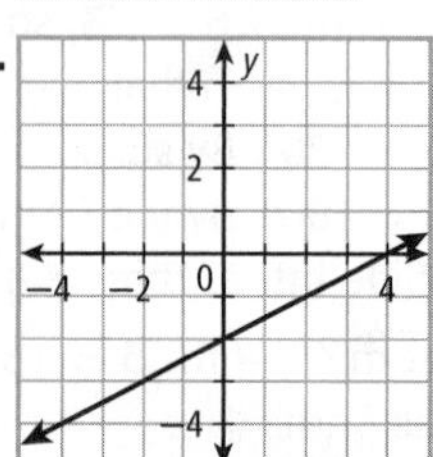

17.

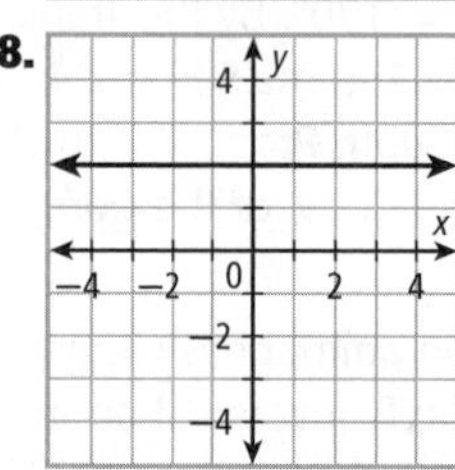

18.

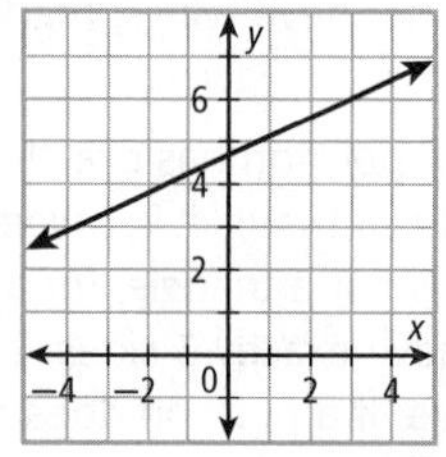

24. $y = \frac{4}{9}x + \frac{14}{13}$

25. $y = 3$

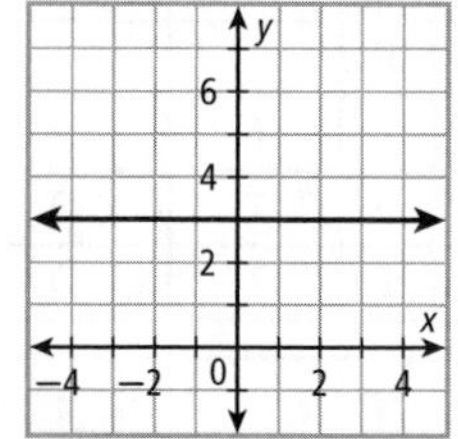

26. $y = \frac{2}{3}x - \frac{16}{3}$

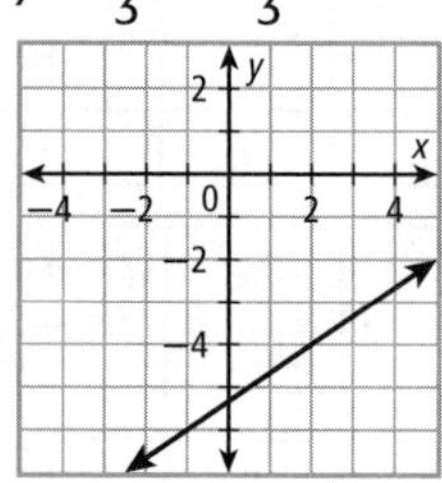

27. $y = \frac{3}{4}x - 3$

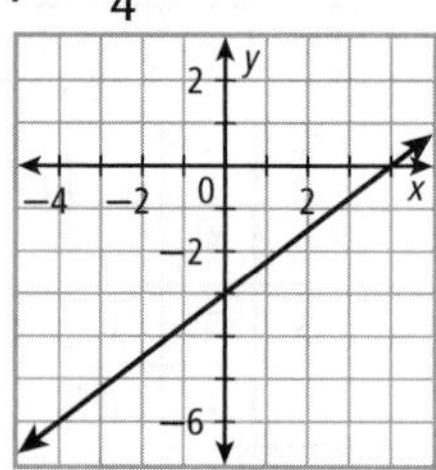

28. $y - 2 = -\frac{1}{2}x$

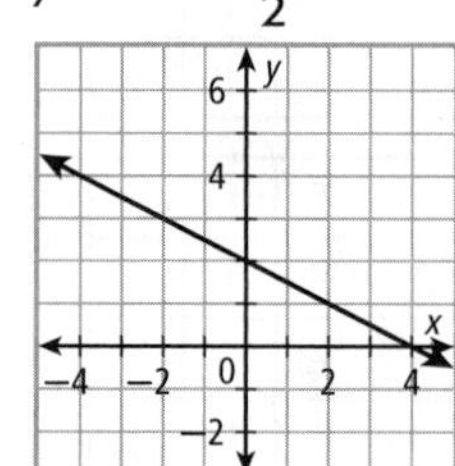

29. $y = \frac{3}{4}(x + 2)$

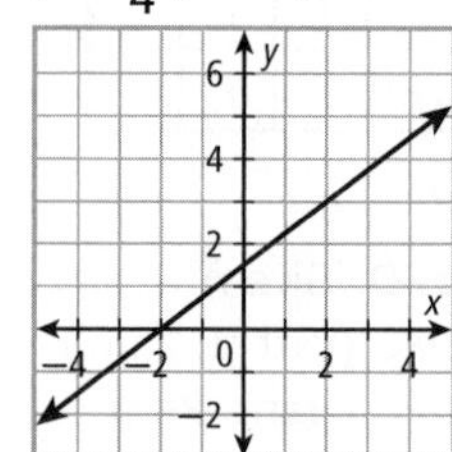

30. $y + 1 = -(x - 5)$

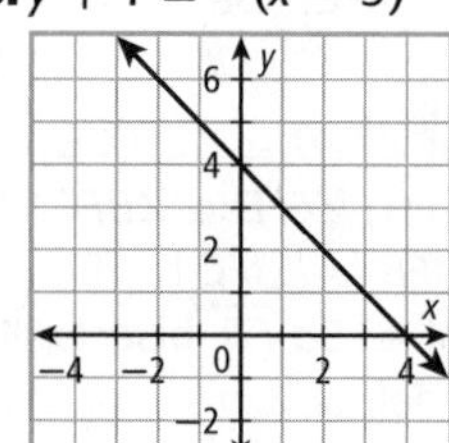

31. $y - 6 = \frac{11}{6}(x - 4)$

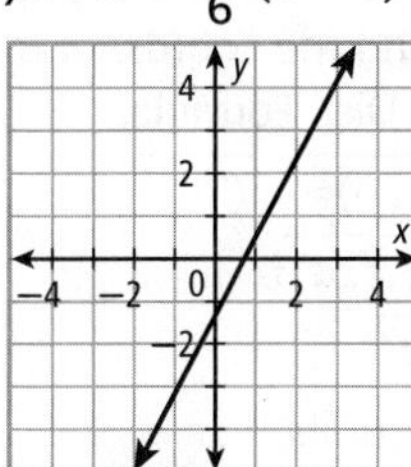

66b. Possible answer: The graph of the equation $y = 2x^2 - 8x + 10$ is a parabola with vertex (2, 2), which means that the minimum of the square of the distance is 2, so the minimum distance is $\sqrt{2}$. The perpendicular line $y = -x + 5$ intersects $y = x + 1$ at (2, 3). The distance from (3, 2) to (2, 3) is $\sqrt{(3-2)^2 + (2-3)^2} = \sqrt{2}$.

3B *Ready to Go On?*

10. ||

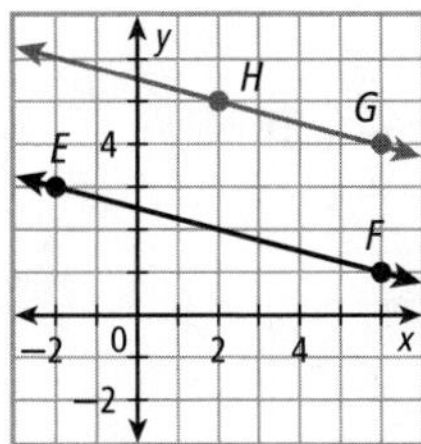

11. neither

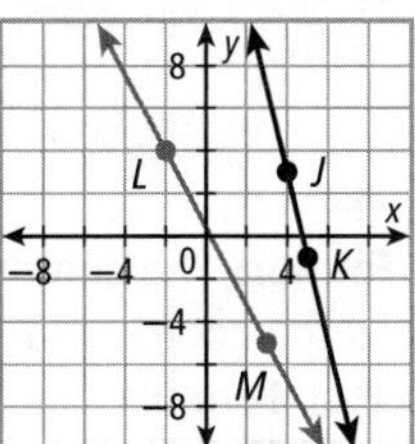

12. ⊥

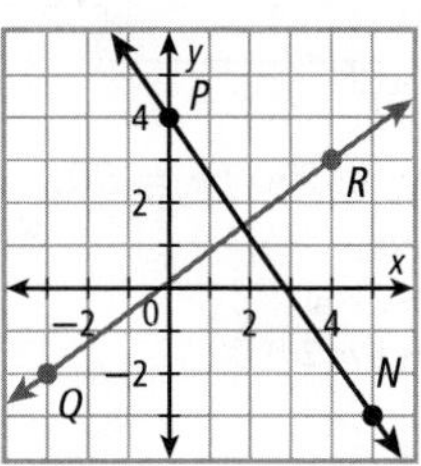

13. ⊥

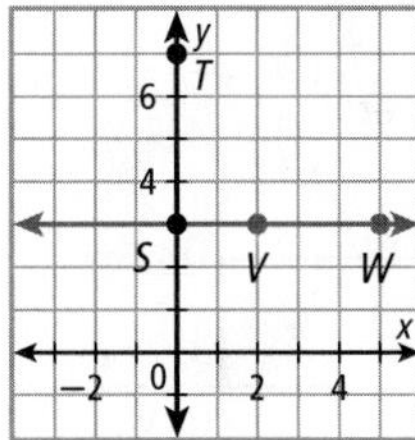

17.

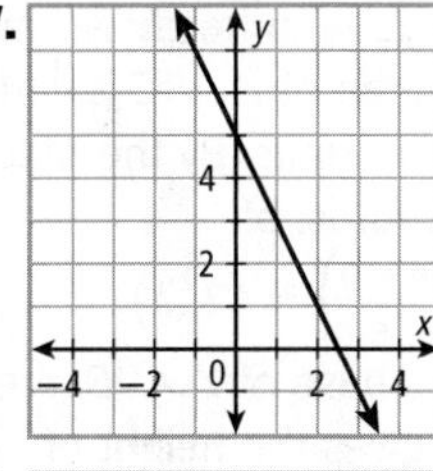

18.

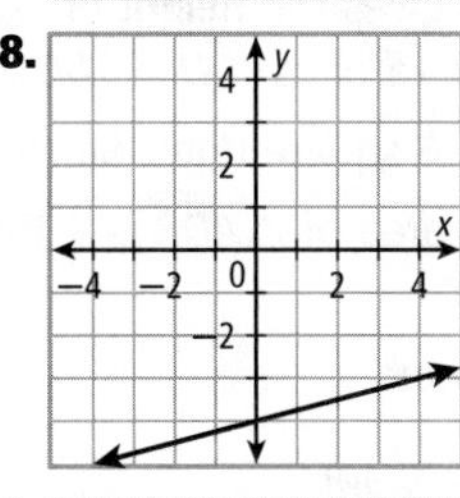

19.

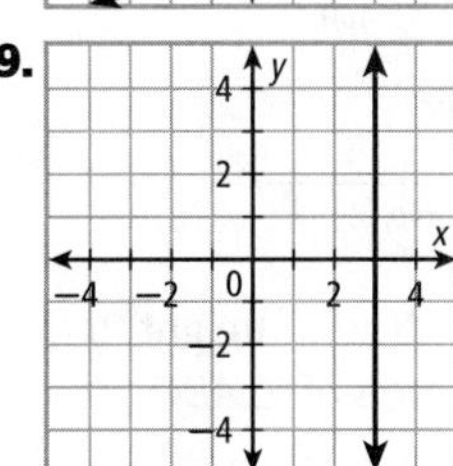

Chapter 4

4-2 *Exercises*

50.

x	−2	0	1	4
$f(x)$	−10	−4	−1	8

51.

x	−2	0	1	4
$f(x)$	5	1	2	17

52.

x	−2	0	1	4
$f(x)$	30	14	9	6

4-3 *Check It Out!*

3. 1. $\angle A \cong \angle D$ (Given)
2. $\angle BCA \cong \angle ECD$ (Vert. ∠s are ≅.)
3. $\angle ABC \cong \angle DEC$ (Third ∠s Thm.)
4. $\overline{AB} \cong \overline{DE}$ (Given)
5. $\overline{AD}$ bisects $\overline{BE}$, and $\overline{BE}$ bisects $\overline{AD}$. (Given)
6. $\overline{BC} \cong \overline{EC}$, $\overline{AC} \cong \overline{DC}$ (Def. of bisector)
7. $\triangle ABC \cong \triangle DEC$ (Def. of ≅ △s)

4. 1. $\overline{JK} \parallel \overline{ML}$ (Given)
2. $\angle KJN \cong \angle MLN$, $\angle JKN \cong \angle LMN$ (Alt. Int. ∠s Thm.)
3. $\angle JNK \cong \angle LNM$ (Vert. ∠s Thm.)
4. $\overline{JK} \cong \overline{ML}$ (Given)
5. $\overline{MK}$ bisects $\overline{JL}$, and $\overline{JL}$ bisects $\overline{MK}$. (Given)
6. $\overline{JN} \cong \overline{LN}$, $\overline{MN} \cong \overline{KN}$ (Def. of bisector)
7. $\triangle JKN \cong \triangle MLN$ (Def. of ≅ △s)

4-4 *Exercises*

39.
$4x - 7 = 21$ (Given)
$4x - 7 + 7 = 21 + 7$ (Add. Prop. of =)
$4x = 28$ (Simplify.)
$\frac{4x}{4} = \frac{28}{4}$ (Div. Prop. of =)
$x = 7$ (Simplify.)

40.
$\frac{a}{4} + 5 = -8$ (Given)
$\frac{a}{4} + 5 - 5 = -8 - 5$ (Subtr. Prop. of =)
$\frac{a}{4} = -13$ (Simplify.)
$4\left(\frac{a}{4}\right) = 4(-13)$ (Mult. Prop. of =)
$a = -52$ (Simplify.)

41.
$6r = 4r + 10$ (Given)
$6r - 4r = 4r - 4r + 10$ (Subtr. Prop. of =)
$2r = 10$ (Simplify.)
$\frac{2r}{2} = \frac{10}{2}$ (Div. Prop. of =)
$r = 5$ (Simplify.)

4-5 *Exercises*

33.

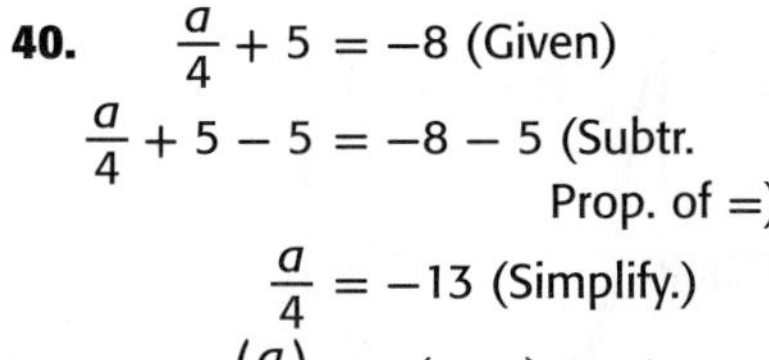

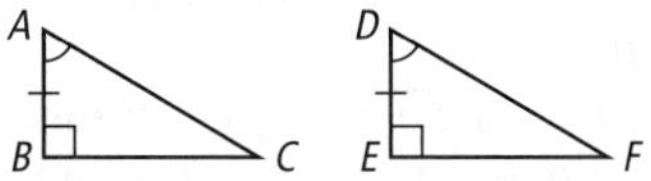

Case 1: Given rt. $\triangle ABC$ and rt. $\triangle DEF$ with $\angle A \cong \angle D$ and $\overline{AB} \cong \overline{DE}$
1. $\angle A \cong \angle D$ (Given)
2. $\overline{AB} \cong \overline{DE}$ (Given)
3. $\angle B \cong \angle E$ (Rt. ∠ ≅ Thm.)
4. $\triangle ABC \cong \triangle DEF$ (ASA *Steps 1, 2, 3*)

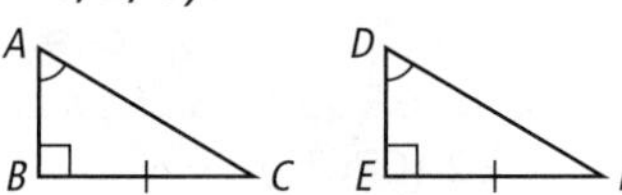

Case 2: Given rt. $\triangle ABC$ and rt. $\triangle DEF$ with $\angle A \cong \angle D$ and $\overline{BC} \cong \overline{EF}$
1. $\angle A \cong \angle D$ (Given)
2. $\overline{BC} \cong \overline{EF}$ (Given)
3. $\angle B \cong \angle E$ (Rt. ∠ ≅ Thm.)
4. $\triangle ABC \cong \triangle DEF$ (AAS *Steps 1, 3, 2*)

35.

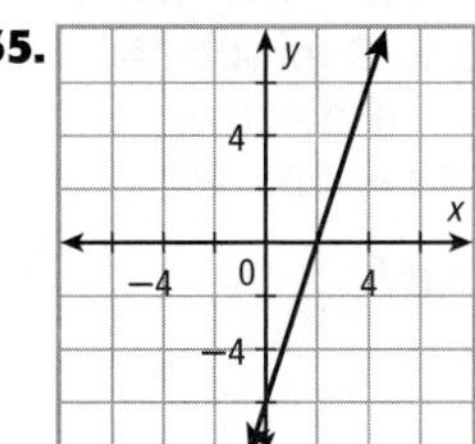

36.

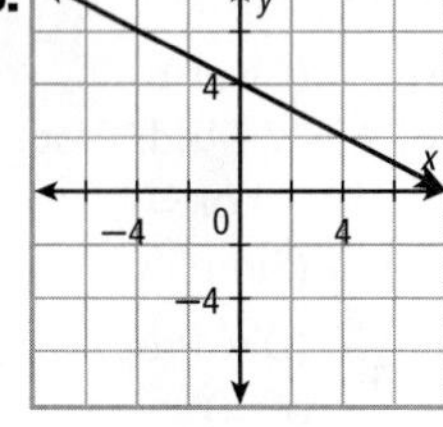

37.

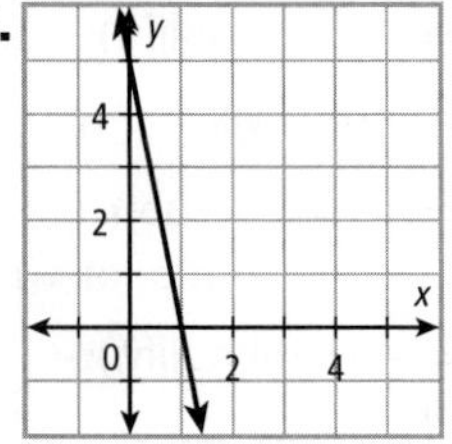

4-6 *Check It Out!*

2.

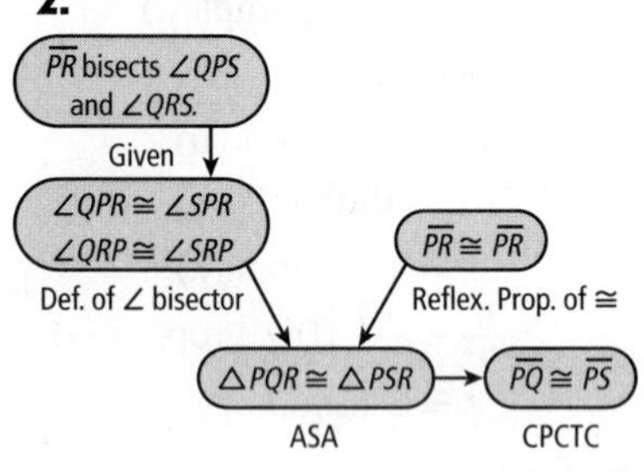

3. **1.** J is the mdpt. of $\overline{KM}$ and $\overline{NL}$. (Given)
2. $\overline{KJ} \cong \overline{MJ}$, $\overline{NJ} \cong \overline{LJ}$ (Def. of mdpt.)
3. $\angle KJL \cong \angle MJN$ (Vert. ∡ Thm.)
4. $\triangle KJL \cong \triangle MJN$ (SAS *Steps 2, 3*)
5. $\angle LKJ \cong \angle NMJ$ (CPCTC)
6. $\overline{KL} \parallel \overline{MN}$ (Conv. of Alt. Int. ∡ Thm.)

4-6 *Exercises*

21. **1.** $PS = RQ$, $PQ = RS$ (Given)
2. $\overline{PS} \cong \overline{RQ}$, $\overline{PQ} \cong \overline{RS}$ (Def. of ≅)
3. $\overline{SQ} \cong \overline{QS}$ (Reflex. Prop. of ≅)
4. $\triangle PSQ \cong \triangle RQS$ (SSS *Steps 2, 3*)
5. $\angle 3 \cong \angle 2$ (CPCTC)
6. $\overline{PQ} \parallel \overline{RS}$ (Conv. of Alt. Int. ∡ Thm.)

23.

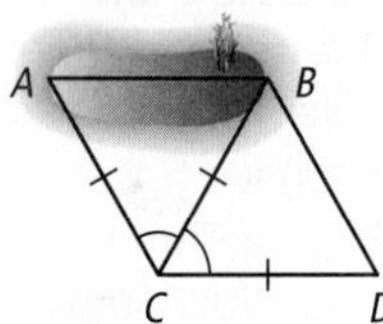

The distance from C to A, from C to B, and from C to D must be ≅. $\angle ACB \cong \angle DCB$. If $\triangle ACB \cong \triangle DCB$ by SAS, then $AB = DB$.

4-7 *Check It Out!*

1. Possible answer:

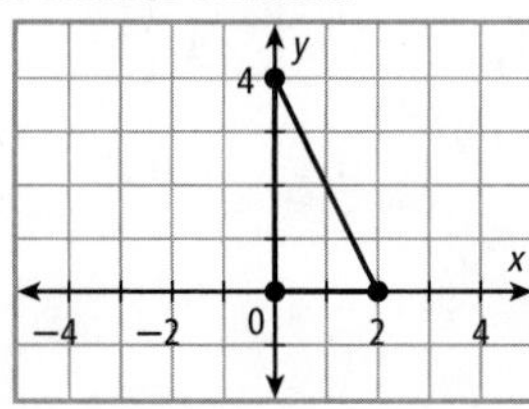

2. $\triangle ABC$ is a rt. △ with height AB and base BC. The area of $\triangle ABC$ is $\frac{1}{2}(4)(6) = 12$ square units. By the Mdpt. Formula the coords. of D are $\left(\frac{0+4}{2}, \frac{6+0}{2}\right) = (2, 3)$.
With $\overline{AB}$ as the base of $\triangle ADB$, the x-coord. of D gives the height of $\triangle ADB$. The area of $\triangle ADB = \frac{1}{2}bh$ $= \frac{1}{2}(6)(2) = 6$ square units. Since $6 = \frac{1}{2}(12)$, the area of $\triangle ADB$ is $\frac{1}{2}$ the area of $\triangle ABC$.

3. Possible answer:

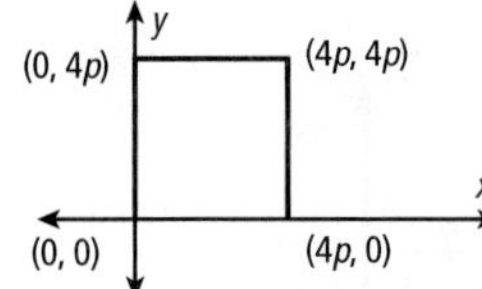

4. $\triangle ABC$ is a rt. △ with height $2j$ and base $2n$. The area of $\triangle ABC$ $= \frac{1}{2}bh = \frac{1}{2}(2n)(2j) = 2nj$ square units. By the Mdpt. Formula, the coords. of D are (n, j). The base of $\triangle ABD$ is $2j$ units and the height is n units. So the area of $\triangle ADB = \frac{1}{2}bh$ $= \frac{1}{2}(2j)(n) = nj$ square units. Since $nj = \frac{1}{2}(2nj)$, the area of $\triangle ADB$ is $\frac{1}{2}$ the area of $\triangle ABC$.

4-7 *Exercises*

4. By the Mdpt. Formula, the coords. of A are $(0, 3)$ and the coords. of B are $(4, 0)$. By the Dist. Formula,

$PQ = \sqrt{(0-8)^2 + (6-0)^2}$
$= \sqrt{(-8)^2 + 6^2} = \sqrt{64 + 36}$
$= \sqrt{100} = 10$ units.
$AB = \sqrt{(0-4)^2 + (3-0)^2}$
$= \sqrt{(-4)^2 + 3^2} = \sqrt{16 + 9}$
$= \sqrt{25} = 5$ units.
So $AB = \frac{1}{2}PQ$.

6. Possible answer:

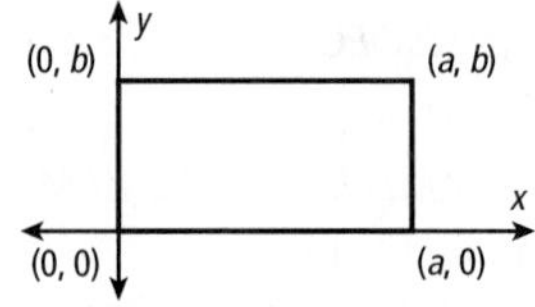

7.

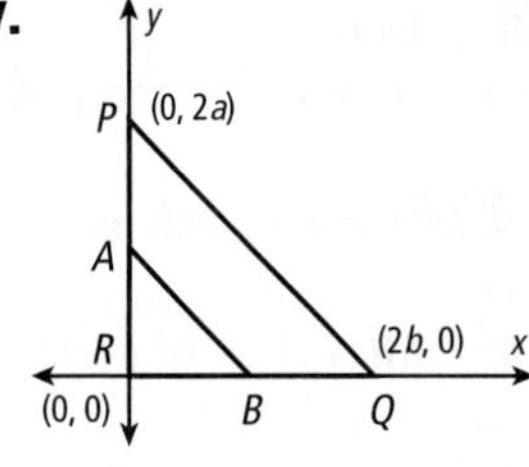

By the Mdpt. Formula, the coords. of A are $(0, a)$ and the coords. of B are $(b, 0)$. By the Dist. Formula,

$PQ = \sqrt{(0-2b)^2 + (2a)^2}$
$= \sqrt{(-2b)^2 + (2a)^2}$
$= \sqrt{4b^2 + 4a^2}$
$= 2\sqrt{b^2 + a^2}$ units.
$AB = \sqrt{(0-b)^2 + (a-0)^2}$
$= \sqrt{(-b)^2 + a^2}$
$= \sqrt{b^2 + a^2}$ units.
So $AB = \frac{1}{2}PQ$.

8. Possible answer:

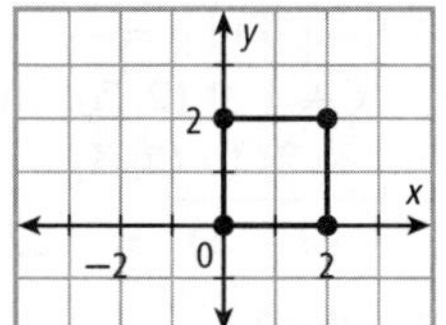

9. Possible answer:

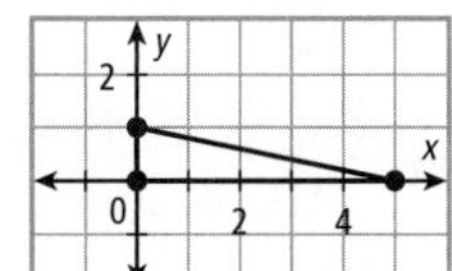

10.

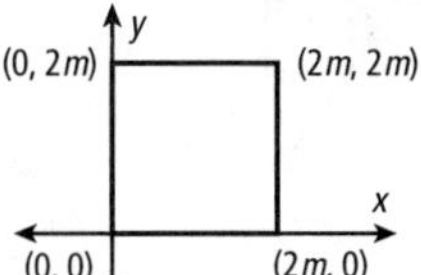

By the Mdpt. Formula, the coords. of E are $(0, 5)$ and the coords. of F are $(6, 5)$. By the Dist. Formula,

$BC = \sqrt{(6-0)^2 + (10-10)^2}$
$= \sqrt{36} = 6$ units.
$EF = \sqrt{(6-0)^2 + (5-5)^2}$
$= \sqrt{36} = 6$ units. So $EF = BC$.

11. Possible answer:

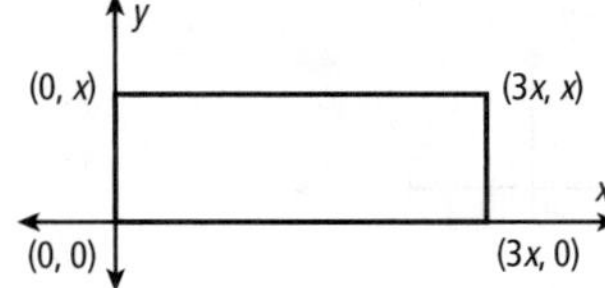

12. Possible answer:

13.

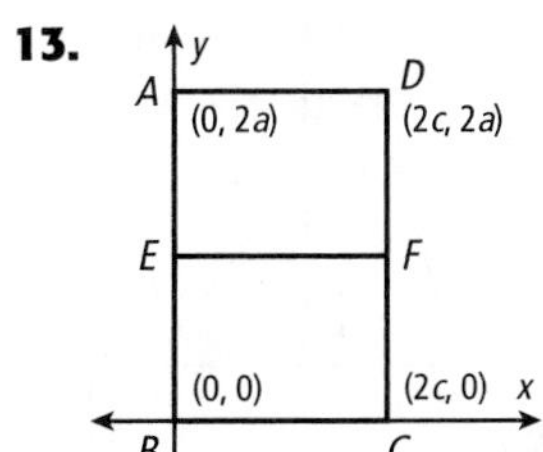

By the Mdpt. Formula, the coords. of E are $(0, a)$, and the coords. of F are $(2c, a)$. By the Dist. Formula,
$AD = \sqrt{(2c-0)^2 + (2a-2a)^2}$
$= \sqrt{(2c)^2} = 2c$ units. Similarly,
$EF = \sqrt{(2c-0)^2 + (a-a)^2}$
$= \sqrt{(2c)^2} = 2c$ units. So $EF = AD$.

23. By the Dist. Formula,
$AB = \sqrt{(x_2 - x_1)^2 + (y_2 - y_1)^2}$ and
$AM =$
$\sqrt{\left(\frac{x_1 + x_2}{2} - x_1\right)^2 + \left(\frac{y_1 + y_2}{2} - y_1\right)^2} =$
$\sqrt{\left(\frac{x_1 + x_2}{2} - \frac{2x_1}{2}\right)^2 + \left(\frac{y_1 + y_2}{2} - \frac{2y_1}{2}\right)^2}$
$= \sqrt{\frac{1}{4}(x_2 - x_1)^2 + \frac{1}{4}(y_2 - y_1)^2}$
$= \frac{1}{2}\sqrt{(x_2 - x_1)^2 + (y_2 - y_1)^2}$.
So $AM = \frac{1}{2}AB$.

24.

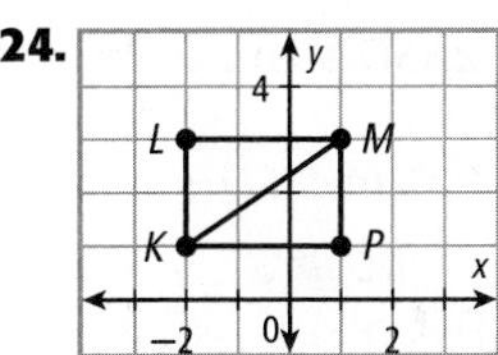

By the Dist. Formula,
$KL = \sqrt{(-2+2)^2 + (1-3)^2}$
$= \sqrt{0+4} = 2$,
$MP = \sqrt{(1-1)^2 + (3-1)^2}$
$= \sqrt{0+4} = 2$,
$LM = \sqrt{(-2-1)^2 + (3-3)^2}$
$= \sqrt{9+0} = 3$, and
$PK = \sqrt{(1+2)^2 + (1-1)^2}$
$= \sqrt{9+0} = 3$.
Thus $KL = MP$ and $LM = PK$ by the Trans. Prop. of ≅. $\overline{KL} \cong \overline{MP}$ and $\overline{LM} \cong \overline{PK}$ by the def. of ≅, and $\overline{KM} \cong \overline{MK}$ by the Reflex. Prop. of ≅. Thus △KLM ≅ △MPK by SSS.

4-8 *Exercises*

41. **1.** △ABC and △DEF (Given)
2. Draw $\overrightarrow{EF}$ so that $FG = CB$. (Through any 2 pts. there is exactly 1 line.)
3. $\overline{FG} \cong \overline{CB}$ (Def. of ≅ segs.)
4. $\overline{AC} \cong \overline{DF}$ (Given)
5. ∠C and ∠F are rt. ∠s. (Given)
6. $\overline{DF} \perp \overline{EG}$ (Def. of ⊥ lines)
7. ∠DFG is a rt. ∠. (Def. of rt. ∠)
8. ∠DFG ≅ ∠C (Rt. ∠ ≅ Thm.)
9. △ABC ≅ △DGF (SAS *Steps 3, 8, 4*)
10. $\overline{DG} \cong \overline{AB}$ (CPCTC)
11. $\overline{AB} \cong \overline{DE}$ (Given)
12. $\overline{DG} \cong \overline{DE}$ (Trans. Prop. of ≅)
13. ∠G ≅ ∠E (Isosc. △ Thm.)
14. ∠DFG ≅ ∠DFE (Rt. ∠ ≅ Thm.)
15. △DGF ≅ △DEF (AAS *Steps 13, 14, 12*)
16. △ABC ≅ △DEF (Trans. Prop. of ≅)

4B *Ready to Go On?*

1. It is given that $\overline{AC} \cong \overline{BC}$. $\overline{DC} \cong \overline{DC}$ by the Reflex. Prop. of ≅. By the Rt. ∠ ≅ Thm., ∠ACD ≅ ∠BCD. Therefore △ACD ≅ △BCD by SAS.

2. **1.** $\overline{JK}$ bisects ∠MJN. (Given)
2. ∠MJK ≅ ∠NJK (Def. of bisect)
3. $\overline{MJ} \cong \overline{NJ}$ (Given)
4. $\overline{JK} \cong \overline{JK}$ (Reflex. Prop. of ≅)
5. △MJK ≅ △NJK (SAS *Steps 3, 2, 4*)

7. **1.** $\overline{CD} \parallel \overline{BE}$ and $\overline{DE} \parallel \overline{CB}$ (Given)
2. ∠DEC ≅ ∠BCE and ∠DCE ≅ ∠BEC (Alt. Int. ∠s Thm.)
3. $\overline{EC} \cong \overline{CE}$ (Reflex. Prop. of ≅)
4. △DEC ≅ △BCE (ASA *Steps 2, 3*)
5. ∠D ≅ ∠B (CPCTC)

9. It is given that ABCD is a rect. M is the mdpt. of $\overline{AB}$, and N is the mdpt. of $\overline{AD}$. Use the coords. $A(0, 0)$, $B(2a, 0)$, $C(2a, 2b)$, and $D(0, 2b)$. By the Mdpt. Formula, the coords. of M are $\left(\frac{0+2a}{2}, \frac{0+0}{2}\right) = (a, 0)$, and the coords. of N are $\left(\frac{0+0}{2}, \frac{0+2b}{2}\right) = (0, b)$. The area of rect. ABCD is the length of $\overline{AB}$ times the length of $\overline{BC}$, or $2a(2b) = 4ab$. The area of △AMN is $\frac{1}{2}$ the length of $\overline{AM}$ times the length of $\overline{AN}$, or $\frac{1}{2}ab$, which is $\frac{1}{8}$ the area of rect. ABCD.

12. It is given that isosc. △JKL has coords. $J(0, 0)$, $K(2a, 2b)$, and $L(4a, 0)$. M is the mdpt. of $\overline{JK}$, and N is the mdpt. of $\overline{KL}$. By the Mdpt. Formula, the coords. of M are $\left(\frac{2a+0}{2}, \frac{2b+0}{2}\right) = (a, b)$ and the coords. of N are $\left(\frac{2a+4a}{2}, \frac{2b+0}{2}\right) = (3a, b)$. By the Dist. Formula,
$MK = \sqrt{(2a-a)^2 + (2b-b)^2}$
$= \sqrt{a^2 + b^2}$, and
$NK = \sqrt{(3a-2a)^2 + (b-2b)^2}$
$= \sqrt{a^2 + b^2}$. Thus $\overline{MK} \cong \overline{NK}$. So △KMN is isosc. by the def. of an isosc. △.

Chapter 4 Extension

2. Draw $\overline{PA}$, $\overline{PB}$, $\overline{AQ}$, and $\overline{BQ}$ (through any 2 pts. there is exactly 1 line). Since the same compass setting was used, $\overline{PA} \cong \overline{PB}$, and $\overline{AQ} \cong \overline{BQ}$. Also, $\overline{PQ} \cong \overline{PQ}$ by the Reflex. Prop. of ≅. △APQ ≅ △BPQ by SSS, and ∠APQ ≅ ∠BPQ by CPCTC. Label the pt. where $\overleftrightarrow{PQ}$ intersects $\overleftrightarrow{AB}$ as M. $\overline{PM} \cong \overline{PM}$ by the Reflex. Prop. of ≅, and △APM ≅ △BPM by SAS. ∠PMA ≅ ∠PMB by CPCTC, so ∠PMA and ∠PMB are rt. ∠s (≅ ∠s that form a lin. pair are rt. ∠s). $\overleftrightarrow{PQ} \perp \overleftrightarrow{AB}$ by the def. of ⊥.

3. Since the same compass setting was used, $\overline{AB} \cong \overline{DE}$, and $\overline{AC} \cong \overline{DF}$. ∠BAC ≅ ∠EDF by the construction of ≅ ∠s. Therefore △BAC ≅ △EDF by SAS.

4. Since the same compass setting was used, $\overline{AC} \cong \overline{DF}$. By the construction of ≅ ∠s, ∠BAC ≅ ∠EDF, and ∠ACB ≅ ∠DFE. Therefore △BAC ≅ △EDF by ASA.

Chapter 4 Test

15. Use coords. $A(0, 0)$, $B(a, 0)$, $C(a, a)$, and $D(0, a)$. By the Dist. Formula,
$AC = \sqrt{(a-0)^2 + (a-0)^2}$
$= a\sqrt{2}$ and
$BD = \sqrt{(a-0)^2 + (0-a)^2}$
$= a\sqrt{2}$. Since $AC = BD$, $\overline{AC} \cong \overline{BD}$ by the def. of ≅.

18. It is given that △ABC is isosc. with coordinates $A(2a, 0)$, $B(0, 2b)$, and $C(-2a, 0)$. D is the mdpt. of $\overline{AC}$, and E is the mdpt. of $\overline{AB}$. By the Mdpt. Formula, the coords. of D are $\left(\frac{-2a+2a}{2}, 0\right) = (0, 0)$, and the coords. of E are $\left(\frac{2a+0}{2}\right), \left(\frac{0+2b}{2}\right) = (a, b)$. By the Dist. Formula,
$DE = \sqrt{(a-0)^2 + (b-0)^2}$
$= \sqrt{a^2 + b^2}$, and AE
$= \sqrt{(2a-a)^2 + (0-b)^2}$
$= \sqrt{a^2 + b^2}$. Therefore $\overline{DE} \cong \overline{AE}$ and △AED is isosc.

Chapter 5

Are You Ready?

18. 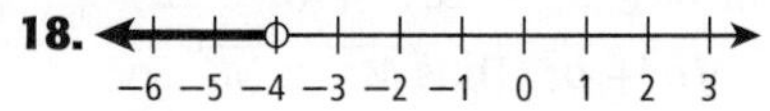

19. −3 −2 −1 0 1 2 3 4 5 6

20. −6 −5 −4 −3 −2 −1 0 1 2 3

21. −60 −40 −20 0 20 40 60

5-1 *Exercises*

30. Draw line $\ell \perp$ to $\overline{AB}$ through X. So $m\angle AYX = 90°$ and $m\angle BYX = 90°$ by the def. of $\perp$. It is given that $AX = BX$. So $\overline{AX} \cong \overline{BX}$ by the def. of $\cong$ segs. By the Reflex. Prop. of $\cong$, $\overline{XY} \cong \overline{XY}$. So $\triangle AYX \cong \triangle BYX$ by HL. Then $\overline{AY} \cong \overline{BY}$ by CPCTC. By the def. of mdpt., Y is the mdpt. of $\overline{AB}$. Since ℓ is $\perp$ to $\overline{AB}$ at its mdpt., ℓ is the $\perp$ bisector of $\overline{AB}$. Therefore X is on the $\perp$ bisector of $\overline{AB}$.

31. **1.** $\overrightarrow{PS}$ bisects $\angle QPR$. $\overline{SQ} \perp \overrightarrow{PQ}$, $\overline{SR} \perp \overrightarrow{PR}$ (Given)
2. $\angle QPS \cong \angle RPS$ (Def. of $\angle$ bisector)
3. $\angle SQP$ and $\angle SRP$ are rt. ⦣. (Def. of $\perp$)
4. $\angle SQP \cong \angle SRP$ (Rt. $\angle \cong$ Thm.)
5. $\overline{PS} \cong \overline{PS}$ (Reflex. Prop. of $\cong$)
6. $\triangle PQS \cong \triangle PRS$ (AAS)
7. $\overline{SQ} \cong \overline{SR}$ (CPCTC)
8. $SQ = SR$ (Def. of $\cong$ segs.)

32. Possible answer: By stating that the pt. must be in the int. of the $\angle$, the thm. implies that it must be in the same plane as the $\angle$. It is possible for a pt. to be equidistant from the sides of an $\angle$ but to lie in a different plane. In the diagram, $\angle ABC$ is in plane Z, and P is equidistant from the sides of $\angle ABC$, but P does not lie in plane Z. Thus P cannot be on the bisector of the $\angle$, because the bisector must lie in the same plane as the $\angle$.

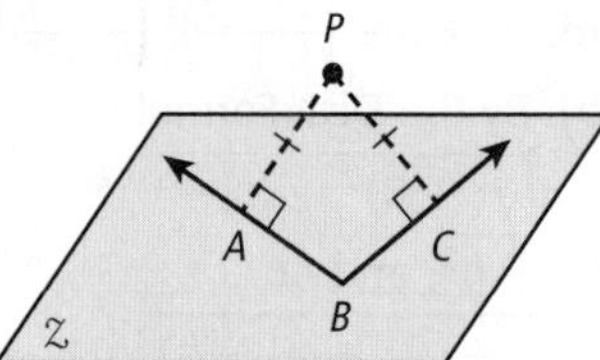

40. **1.** $\overline{VX} \perp \overrightarrow{YX}$, $\overline{VZ} \perp \overrightarrow{YZ}$, $VX = VZ$ (Given)
2. $\angle VXY$ and $\angle VZY$ are rt. ⦣. (Def. of $\perp$)
3. $\overline{YV} \cong \overline{YV}$ (Reflex. Prop. of $\cong$)
4. $\triangle YXV \cong \triangle YZV$ (HL)
5. $\angle XYV \cong \angle ZYV$ (CPCTC)
6. $\overrightarrow{YV}$ bisects $\angle XYZ$. (Def. of $\angle$ bisector)

41. It is given that $\overline{KN}$ is the $\perp$ bisector of $\overline{JL}$ and $\overline{LN}$ is the $\perp$ bisector of $\overline{KM}$. By the $\perp$ Bisector Thm., $JK = KL$ and $KL = ML$. Thus $JK = ML$ by the Trans. Prop. of =. By the def. of $\cong$ segs., $\overline{JK} \cong \overline{ML}$. By the Seg. Add. Post., $JR + RL = JL$ and $MT + TK = MK$. By the def. of $\perp$ bisector, R is the mdpt. of $\overline{JL}$ and T is the mdpt. of $\overline{MK}$. Thus $\overline{JR} \cong \overline{RL}$ and $\overline{MT} \cong \overline{TK}$ by the def. of mdpt. By the def. of $\cong$ segs., $JR = RL$ and $MT = TK$. By Subst., $JR + JR = JL$ and $MT + MT = MK$. It is given that $\overline{JR} \cong \overline{MT}$. So $JR = MT$ by the def. of $\cong$ segs. By Subst., $JR + JR = MK$. By the Trans. Prop. of =, $JL = MK$, so $\overline{JL} \cong \overline{MK}$ by the def. of $\cong$ segs. By the Reflex. Prop. of $\cong$, $\overline{JM} \cong \overline{JM}$. Therefore $\triangle JKM \cong \triangle MLJ$ by SSS, and $\angle JKM \cong \angle MLJ$ by CPCTC.

5-2 *Exercises*

21.

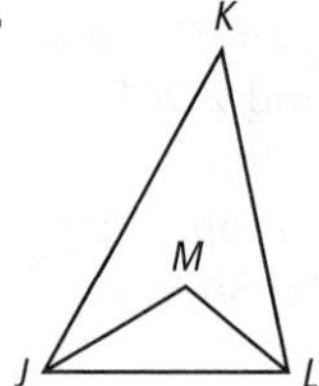

Possible answer: If $\angle JML$ is a rt. $\angle$, then $m\angle MJL + m\angle MLJ = 90°$ because the acute ⦣ of a rt. $\triangle$ are comp. Since M is the incenter of $\triangle JKL$, $\overrightarrow{JM}$ and $\overrightarrow{LM}$ are $\angle$ bisectors of $\triangle JKL$. So by the def. of $\angle$ bisector, $m\angle KJL = 2m\angle MJL$ and $m\angle KLJ = 2m\angle MLJ$. By subst., $m\angle KJL + m\angle KLJ = 2(m\angle MJL + m\angle MLJ) = 2(90°) = 180°$. But by the $\triangle$ Sum Thm., $m\angle K = 180° - (m\angle KJL + m\angle KLJ) = 180° - 180° = 0°$. This would mean that $\triangle JKL$ is not a $\triangle$. Therefore $\angle JML$ cannot be a rt. $\angle$.

29.

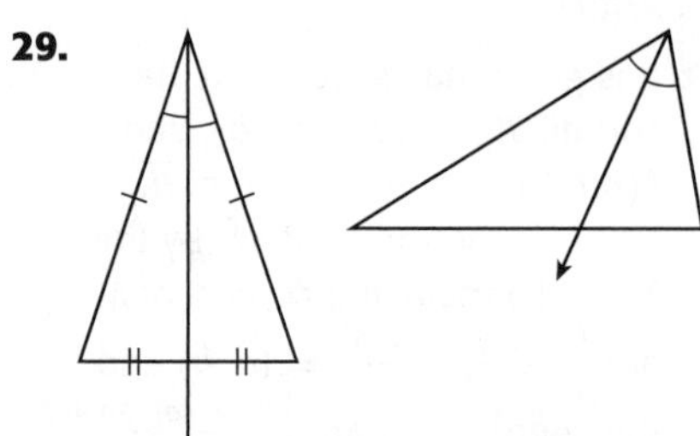

30.

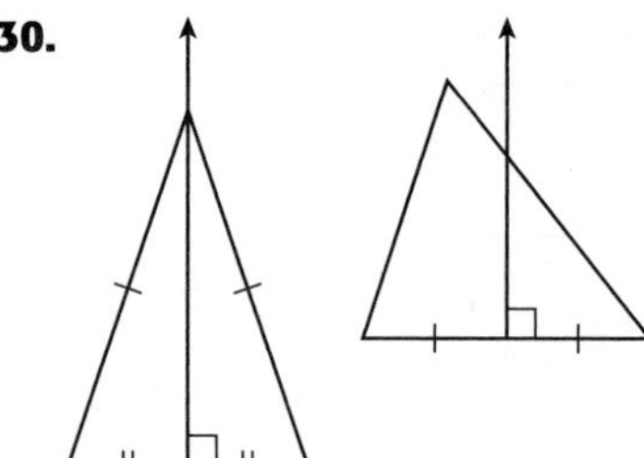

32.

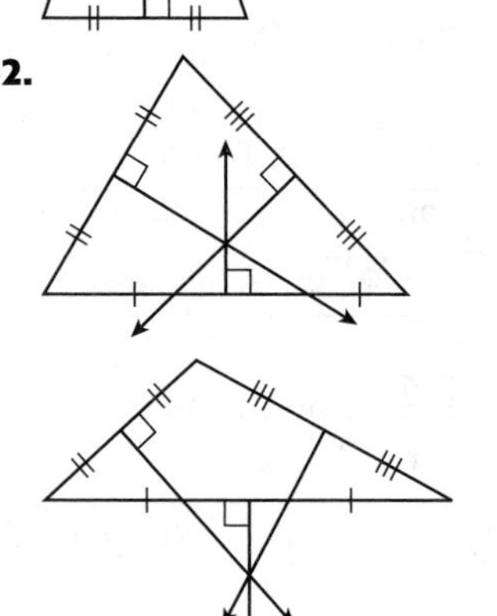

36. **1.** $\overleftrightarrow{QS}$ bisects $\angle PQR$. $\overline{PQ} \cong \overline{RQ}$ (Given)
2. $\angle PQS \cong \angle RQS$ (Def. of $\angle$ bisector)
3. $\overline{QS} \cong \overline{QS}$ (Reflex. Prop. of $\cong$)
4. $\triangle PQS \cong \triangle RQS$ (SAS)
5. $\angle PSQ \cong \angle RSQ$ (CPCTC)
6. $\angle PSQ$ and $\angle RSQ$ are supp. (Lin. Pair Thm.)
7. $\angle PSQ$ and $\angle RSQ$ are rt. ⦣. ($\cong$ ⦣ supp. $\rightarrow$ rt. ⦣)
8. $m\angle PSQ = 90°$, $m\angle RSQ = 90°$ (Def. of rt. $\angle$)
9. $\overleftrightarrow{QS} \perp \overline{PR}$ (Def. of $\perp$)
10. $\overline{PS} \cong \overline{RS}$ (CPCTC)
11. S is the mdpt. of $\overline{PR}$. (Def. of mdpt.)
12. $\overleftrightarrow{QS}$ is the $\perp$ bisector of $\overline{PR}$. (Def. of $\perp$ bisector)

38. Possible answers: Similarities: Both are circles. Both intersect the triangle in exactly 3 points.
Differences: The inscribed circle is smaller than the circumscribed circle. Except for the points of intersection, the inscribed circle lies inside the triangle, while the circumscribed circle lies outside. The center of the inscribed circle is always inside the triangle, while the center of the circumscribed circle may be inside, outside, or on the triangle. The center of the inscribed circle is the point of concurrency of the angle bisectors, while the center of the circumscribed circle is the point of concurrency of the perpendicular bisectors.

43a. Possible answer:
Given: M is the mdpt. of $\overline{QR}$.
Prove: $PM = QM = RM$
Proof: The coordinates of M are
$\left(\frac{0 + 2a}{2}, \frac{2b + 0}{2}\right) = (a, b)$.
By the Distance Formula,
$PM = \sqrt{(a - 0)^2 + (b - 0)^2}$
$= \sqrt{a^2 + b^2}$,
$QM = \sqrt{(a - 0)^2 + (b - 2b)^2}$
$= \sqrt{a^2 + (-b)^2} = \sqrt{a^2 + b^2}$,
and $RM = \sqrt{(a - 2a)^2 + (b - 0)^2}$
$= \sqrt{(-a)^2 + b^2} = \sqrt{a^2 + b^2}$.
Therefore $PM = QM = RM$.

b. Possible answer: The circumcenter of a rt. △ is the mdpt. of the hyp.

5-3 *Exercises*

39. Check students' work. Possible answer: The centroid of a triangle is also called its center of gravity because the weight of the triangular shape is evenly distributed in every direction from this point. This means the triangular shape will rest in a horizontal position when it is supported at this point.

44c. Possible answer: The ⊥ bisectors of a △ are concurrent at the circumcenter, and the ∠ bisectors are concurrent at the incenter. The medians of a △ are concurrent at the centroid, and the altitudes of a △ are concurrent at the orthocenter. But in an equil. △, the ⊥ bisector through a given vertex also contains the ∠ bisector, the median, and the altitude through that vertex. So the pts. of concurrency must all be the same pt. That is, the circumcenter, the incenter, the centroid, and the orthocenter in an equil. △ are the same pt.

45a. slope of $\overline{RS} = \frac{c}{b}$; slope of $\overline{ST} = \frac{c}{b - a}$; slope of $\overline{RT} = 0$

b. Since $\ell \perp \overline{RS}$, slope of $\ell = -\frac{b}{c}$. Since $m \perp \overline{ST}$, slope of $m = -\frac{b - a}{c} = \frac{a - b}{c}$. Since $n \perp \overline{RT}$, n is a vertical line, and its slope is undefined.

c. An equation of ℓ is $y - 0 = -\frac{b}{c}(x - a)$, or $y = -\frac{b}{c}x + \frac{ab}{c}$. An equation of m is $y - 0 = \frac{a - b}{c}(x - 0)$, or $y = \frac{a - b}{c}x$. An equation of n is $x = b$.

d. $\left(b, \frac{ab - b^2}{c}\right)$

e. Since the equation of line n is $x = b$ and the x-coordinate of P is b, P lies on n.

f. Lines ℓ, m, and n are concurrent at P.

5-5 *Geometry Lab*

2. Possible answer: The longest side is opp. the largest ∠, and the shortest side is opp. the smallest ∠.

5. Possible answer: If the sum of any 2 lengths is greater than the third length, then the set of stems can form a △. If the sum of any 2 lengths is equal to or less than the third length, then the set of stems cannot form a △.

5-5 *Check It Out!*

1. Possible answer:
Given: △RST
Prove: △RST cannot have 2 rt. ∠s.
Proof: Assume that △RST has 2 rt. ∠s. Let ∠R and ∠S be the rt. ∠s. By the def. of rt. ∠, m∠R = 90° and m∠S = 90°. By the △ Sum Thm., m∠R + m∠S + m∠T = 180°. But then 90° + 90° + m∠T = 180° by subst., so m∠T = 0°. However, a △ cannot have an ∠ with a measure of 0°. So there is no △RST, which contradicts the given information. This means the assumption is false, and △RST cannot have 2 rt. ∠s.

5-5 *Exercises*

1. Possible answer: To prove something indirectly, you assume the opposite of what you are trying to prove. Then you use logic to lead to a contradiction of given information, a definition, a postulate, or a previously proven theorem. You can then conclude that the assumption was false and the original statement is true.

2. Possible answer:
Given: △ABC is a scalene triangle.
Prove: △ABC cannot have 2 ≅ ∠s.
Proof: Assume that △ABC does have 2 ≅ ∠s. Let ∠A and ∠C be the ≅ ∠s. Then $\overline{AB} \cong \overline{CB}$ by the Conv. of the Isosc. △ Thm. However, a scalene triangle by def. has no ≅ sides. So △ABC is not scalene, which contradicts the given information. This means the assumption is false, and therefore △ABC cannot have 2 ≅ ∠s.

3. Possible answer:
Given: △PQR is an isosc. △ with base $\overline{PR}$.
Prove: △PQR cannot have a base ∠ that is a rt. ∠.
Proof: Assume that △PQR has a base ∠ that is a rt. ∠. Let ∠P be the rt ∠. By the Isosc. △ Thm., ∠R ≅ ∠P, so ∠R is also a rt. ∠. By the def. of rt. ∠, m∠P = 90° and m∠R = 90°. By the △ Sum Thm., m∠P + m∠Q + m∠R = 180°. By subst., 90° + m∠Q + 90° = 180°, so m∠Q = 0°. However, a △ cannot have an ∠ with a measure of 0°. So there is no △PQR, which contradicts the given information. This means the assumption is false, and therefore △PQR cannot have a base ∠ that is rt.

10. No; when $x = 5$, the value of $3x$ is 15, the value of $2x - 1$ is 9, and the value of x^2 is 25. 15 + 9 = 24, which is not greater than the third side length.

11. Yes; when $c = 2$, the value of $7c + 6$ is 20, the value of $10c - 7$ is 13, and the value of $3c^2$ is 12. The sum of each pair of 2 lengths is greater than the third length.

12. greater than 4 mm and less than 20 mm

13. greater than 0 ft and less than 32 ft

14. greater than 0.6 cm and less than 23.4 cm

15a. the path from the refrigerator to the stove

b. No; the sum of 4 and 5 is 9, which is not greater than 9. By the △ Inequal. Thm., a △ cannot have these side lengths.

16.

Possible answer:
Given: △ABC is scalene. $\overline{XZ}$ and $\overline{YZ}$ are midsegments of △ABC.
Prove: △ABC cannot have 2 ≅ midsegments.
Proof: Assume that △ABC does have 2 ≅ midsegments. Let $\overline{XZ}$ and $\overline{YZ}$ be the ≅ midsegments. By the def. of ≅ segs., $XZ = YZ$. By the △ Midsegment Thm., $XZ = \frac{1}{2}BC$ and $YZ = \frac{1}{2}BA$. So $\frac{1}{2}BC = \frac{1}{2}BA$ by subst.

Additional Answers

But then $BC = BA$, and by the def. of ≅ segs., $\overline{BC} \cong \overline{BA}$. However, a scalene △ by def. has no ≅ sides. So △ABC is not scalene, which contradicts the given information. This means the assumption is false, and therefore a scalene △ cannot have 2 ≅ midsegments.

17. Possible answer:
Given: ∠J and ∠K are supp.
Prove: ∠J and ∠K cannot both be obtuse.
Proof: Assume that ∠J and ∠K are both obtuse. Then m∠J > 90° and m∠K > 90° by the def. of obtuse. If the 2 inequalities are added, m∠J + m∠K > 180°. However, by the def. of supp. ∠s, m∠J + m∠K = 180°. So m∠J + m∠K > 180° contradicts the given information. This means the assumption is false, and therefore ∠J and ∠K cannot both be obtuse.

69. Possible answer: A rt. △ has a rt. ∠ and 2 acute ∠s. By def., the rt. ∠ has the greatest measure. Since the hyp. is the side opposite the rt. ∠, by Thm. 5-5-2, the hyp. is the longest side. Similarly, the diag. of a square forms 2 rt. △s, with the diag. being the hyp. of each. Since the diag. is longer than the leg lengths in both △s, the diag. is longer than the side length of the square.

75. **1.** $\overline{PX} \perp \ell$. Y is any pt. on ℓ other than X. (Given)
2. m∠1 = 90° (Def. of ⊥)
3. ∠1 is a rt. ∠. (Def. of rt. ∠)
4. △XPY is a rt. △. (Def. of rt. △)
5. ∠2 and ∠P are comp. (Acute ∠s of rt. △ are comp.)
6. 90° = m∠2 + m∠P (Def. of comp. ∠s)
7. 90° > m∠2 (Comparison Prop. of Inequal.)
8. m∠1 > m∠2 (Subst.)
9. $PY > PX$ (In △, longer side is opp. larger ∠.)

5-6 *Exercises*

28. Possible answer: As the angle made by a door hinge gets larger, the width of the door opening increases. As the angle made by the hinge gets smaller, the width of the door opening decreases. This is like the side opposite an angle in a triangle getting larger as the measure of the angle increases or getting smaller as the angle decreases.

29. Possible answer:
Similarities: Both the SAS Congruence Postulate and the Hinge Theorem concern the relationship between 2 triangles. Both involve 2 sides and the included angle of each triangle.
Differences: To apply the SAS Congruence Postulate, you must know that 2 sides and the included angle of 1 triangle are congruent to 2 sides and the included angle of the second triangle. To apply the Hinge Theorem, you must know that 2 sides of 1 triangle are congruent to 2 sides of the second triangle but the included angles are unequal in measure. The SAS Congruence Postulate allows you to conclude that the 2 triangles are congruent; then you can show by CPCTC that the sides opposite the congruent angles are congruent. The Hinge Theorem involves 2 triangles that are not congruent; in this case, the sides opposite the included angles are unequal in length, and the exact relationship between the lengths is determined by the sizes of the included angles.

33. Group A is closer to the camp. Possible answer: the 6.5 mi and 4 mi paths together with the distance lines back to the camp form 2 △s. 2 sides of 1 △ are ≅ to 2 sides of the other △. In the △ for Group A, the measure of the included ∠ is 90° + 35°, or 125°. In the △ for Group B, the measure of the included ∠ is 90° + 45°, or 135°. By the Hinge Thm., the side opposite the 125° ∠ is shorter than the side opposite the 135° ∠. So Group A is closer to the camp.

35a. Locate point P outside △ABC so that ∠ABP ≅ ∠DEF and $\overline{BP} \cong \overline{EF}$. It is given that $\overline{AB} \cong \overline{DE}$, so △$ABP$ ≅ △DEF by SAS. Thus $\overline{AP} \cong \overline{DF}$ by CPCTC.

b. Locate point Q on $\overline{AC}$ so that $\overline{BQ}$ bisects ∠PBC. By the def. of ∠ bisector, ∠QBC ≅ ∠QBP. It is given that $\overline{BC} \cong \overline{EF}$. Since $\overline{BP} \cong \overline{EF}$ from part **a,** it follows that $\overline{BC} \cong \overline{BP}$ by the Trans. Prop. of ≅. By the Reflex. Prop. of ≅, $\overline{BQ} \cong \overline{BQ}$. So △$BQP$ ≅ △BQC by SAS, and $\overline{QP} \cong \overline{QC}$ by CPCTC.

c. $AQ + QP > AP$ by applying the △ Inequal. Thm. in △AQP. $AQ + QC = AC$ by the Seg. Add. Post. From part **b,** $\overline{QP} \cong \overline{QC}$, so $QP = QC$ by the def. of ≅ segs. Thus $AQ + QC > AP$ by subst. So $AC > AP$ by subst. From part **a,** $\overline{AP} \cong \overline{DF}$. So by the def. of ≅ segs., $AP = DF$. Therefore $AC > DF$ by subst.

5-7 *Exercises*

51a. $PA = \sqrt{2}$; $PB = \sqrt{3}$; $PC = 2$; $PD = \sqrt{5}$; $PE = \sqrt{6}$; $PF = \sqrt{7}$

b. $\sqrt{10}$; possible answer: for each △ added to the pattern, the number under the radical symbol increases by 1. So the length of the hyp. of the seventh △ would be $\sqrt{8}$, the length of the hyp. of the eighth △ would be $\sqrt{9}$, and the length of the hyp. of the ninth △ would be $\sqrt{10}$.

c. $\sqrt{n+1}$; possible answer: the length of the hyp. is the square root of the whole number 1 greater than the number of the △.

53.

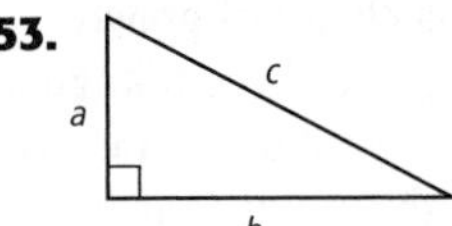

By the △ Inequal. Thm., $a + b > c$. By the Pyth. Thm., $c = \sqrt{a^2 + b^2}$. So by subst., $a + b > \sqrt{a^2 + b^2}$.

55a. No; possible answer: let $a = 3$, $b = 4$, and $c = 5$. So $a + 1 = 4$, $b + 1 = 5$, and $c + 1 = 6$. 3, 4, and 5 form a Pyth. triple, but 4, 5, and 6 do not because $4^2 + 5^2 \neq 6^2$.

b. Yes; possible answer: if a, b, and c form a Pyth. triple, $a^2 + b^2 = c^2$ is true. Multiply both sides by 4 to get the equation $4a^2 + 4b^2 = 4c^2$. This is equivalent to $(2a)^2 + (2b)^2 = (2c)^2$. So by def., $2a$, $2b$, and $2c$ also form a Pyth. triple.

c. No; possible answer: let $a = 3$, $b = 4$, and $c = 5$. So $a^2 = 9$, $b^2 = 16$, and $c^2 = 25$. 3, 4, and 5 form a Pyth. triple, but 9, 16, and 25 do not because $9^2 + 16^2 \neq 25^2$.

d. No; possible answer: let $a = 3$, $b = 4$, and $c = 5$. So $\sqrt{a} = \sqrt{3}$, $\sqrt{b} = 2$, and $\sqrt{c} = \sqrt{5}$. 3, 4, and 5 form a Pyth. triple, but $\sqrt{3}$, 2, and $\sqrt{5}$ do not because $\left(\sqrt{3}\right)^2 + 2^2 \neq \left(\sqrt{5}\right)^2$.

59. By the Mdpt. Formula, the coordinates of M are (a, b). By the Distance Formula,
$AM = \sqrt{(a-0)^2 + (b-0)^2}$
$= \sqrt{a^2 + b^2}$ and

Additional Answers

$MB = \sqrt{(0 - a)^2 + (2b - b)^2}$
$= \sqrt{a^2 + b^2}$. So by subst. $AM = MB$.

5B *Multi-Step Test Prep*

1. H is the intersection of $\overline{AC}$ and $\overline{BD}$. Assume that a different point X, not on $\overline{AC}$ and not on $\overline{BD}$, results in the least combined distance to the cities. Then $AX + CX > AC$ by the △ Inequal. Thm., so $AX + CX > AH + CH$. Similarly, $BX + DX > BH + DH$. If the inequalities are added, $AX + BX + CX + DX > AH + BH + CH + DH$. This contradicts the assumption that X results in the least combined distance. So H must result in the least combined distance.
4. The longest route is the one between Dumas and Colfax. $DC \approx 346.4$ mi, $DB = 400$ mi, $AB = 200$ mi, $BC = 200$ mi, and $AC \approx 282.8$ mi. So $DC > AB$, $DC > BC$, and $DC > AC$. Since $AC > AH$ and $AC > CH$, it follows that $DC > AH$ and $DC > CH$. In △BCH, m∠$BHC = 75°$ and m∠$BCH = 45°$, so $BC > BH$. Since $DC > BC$, it follows that $DC > BH$. Similarly in △DCH, m∠$DHC = 105°$ and m∠$DCH = 45°$, so $DC > DH$. Also $\overline{AB} \cong \overline{BC}$, $\overline{DB} \cong \overline{DB}$, and m∠$ABD = 30° <$ m∠$DBC = 60°$. So by the Hinge Thm., $DC > AD$. Thus $\overline{DC}$ is the longest route.

5B *Ready to Go On?*

1. Possible answer:
Given: ∠A and ∠B are supplementary. ∠A is an acute angle.
Prove: ∠B cannot be an acute angle.
Proof: Assume that ∠B is an acute angle. By the def. of acute, m∠$A < 90°$ and m∠$B < 90°$. When the 2 inequalities are added, m∠A + m∠$B < 180°$. However, by the def. of supp. ∠s, m∠A + m∠$B = 180°$. So m∠A + m∠$B < 180°$ contradicts the given information, and the assumption that ∠B is an acute ∠ is false. Therefore ∠B cannot be acute.
4. No; possible answer: the sum of 8.3 and 10.5 is 18.8, which is not greater than 18.8. By the △ Inequality Thm., a △ cannot have these side lengths.
5. Yes; possible answer: when $s = 4$, the value of $4s$ is 16, the value of $s + 10$ is 14, and the value of s^2 is 16. The sum of each pair of 2 lengths is greater than the third length. So a △ can have sides with these lengths.
11. $2\sqrt{10}$; the side lengths do not form a Pythagorean triple, because $2\sqrt{10}$ is not a whole number.

Chapter 6

Are You Ready?

10. m∠1 = 124°; m∠2 = 56°; m∠3 = 124°; m∠4 = 56°
11. m∠1 = 79°; m∠2 = 101°; m∠3 = 90°; m∠4 = 90°
12. m∠1 = 72°; m∠2 = 108°

6-1 *Geometry Lab*

6. Check students' work. Possible answer: Bisect ∠EPF, ∠FPG, ∠GPH, ∠HPJ, and ∠JPE. Connect the 5 pts. where the ∠ bisectors intersect the circle to pts. E, F, G, H, and J in order around the circle.

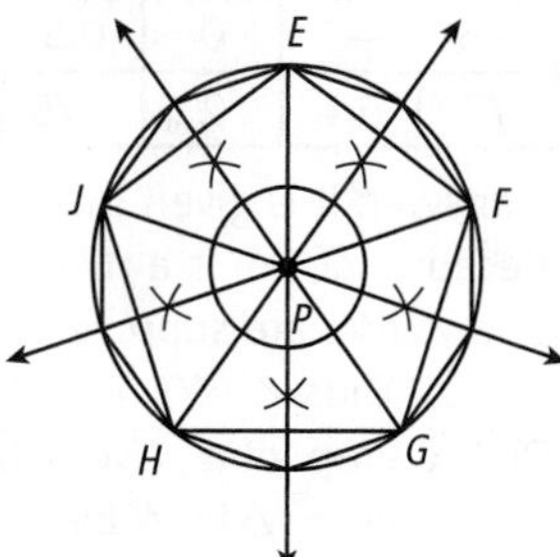

6-2 *Exercises*

49. Possible answers:

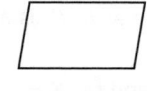

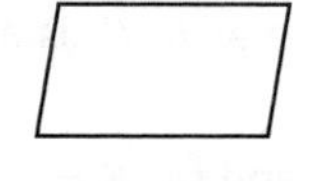

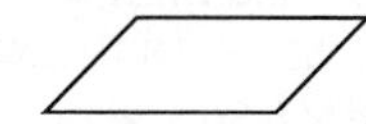

a. Possible answer: the drawings show a counterexample.
b. Possible answer: for any given set of side lengths, a ▱ could have many different shapes.

50. Possible answer: A quad. is a polygon with 4 sides. Since every ▱ has 4 sides, every ▱ is a quad. A ▱ has 2 pairs of ∥ sides. Since the sides of a quad. are not necessarily ∥, a quad. is not necessarily a ▱.

56. 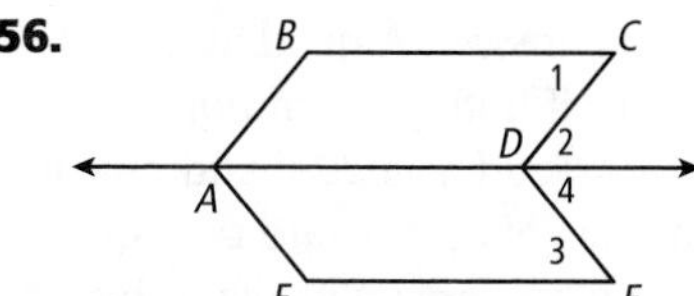

Let ∠1 = x° and ∠CDE = y°.
Draw $\overleftrightarrow{AD}$. $ABCD$ and $AFED$ are ▱s, so $\overline{BC} \parallel \overline{AD}$ and $\overline{FE} \parallel \overline{AD}$ by def. So ∠1 ≅ ∠2 and ∠3 ≅ ∠4 by the Alt. Int. ∠s Thm. Thus m∠1 = m∠2 and m∠3 = m∠4. Then m∠1 + m∠3 = m∠2 + m∠4 by the Add. Prop. of =. By the ∠ Add. Post., m∠2 + m∠4 = m∠CDE. So m∠1 + m∠3 = m∠CDE. Since $ABCD$ and $AFED$ are ≅, with ∠1 corr. to ∠3, m∠1 = m∠3. So m∠1 + m∠1 = m∠CDE by subst. So 2m∠1 = m∠CDE, or $y = 2x$.

57. 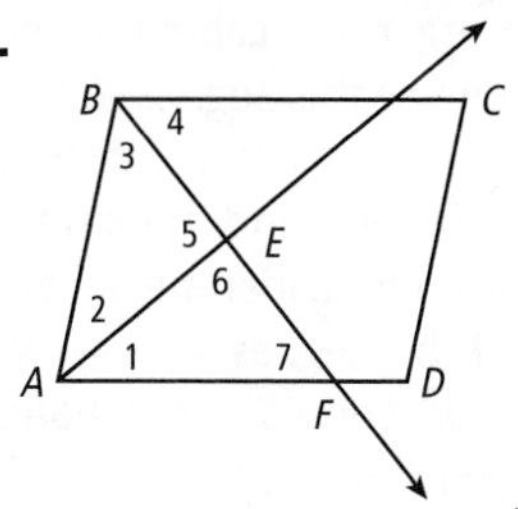

Given: $ABCD$ is a ▱. $\overrightarrow{AE}$ bisects ∠DAB. $\overrightarrow{BE}$ bisects ∠CBA.
Prove: $\overrightarrow{AE} \perp \overrightarrow{BE}$

1. $ABCD$ is a ▱. $\overrightarrow{AE}$ bisects ∠DAB. $\overrightarrow{BE}$ bisects ∠CBA. (Given)
2. ∠1 ≅ ∠2, ∠3 ≅ ∠4 (Def. of ∠ bisector)
3. $\overline{BC} \parallel \overline{AD}$ (Def. of ▱)
4. ∠4 ≅ ∠7 (Alt. Int. ∠s Thm.)
5. ∠3 ≅ ∠7 (Trans. Prop. of ≅)
6. $\overline{AE} \cong \overline{AE}$ (Reflex. Prop. of ≅)
7. △ABE ≅ △AFE (AAS)
8. ∠5 ≅ ∠6 (CPCTC)
9. ∠5 and ∠6 are supp. (Lin. Pair Thm.)
10. ∠5 and ∠6 are rt. ∠s. (≅ ∠s supp. → rt. ∠s)
11. $\overrightarrow{AE} \perp \overrightarrow{BE}$ (Def. of ⊥)

6-3 *Exercises*

31. Possible answer:

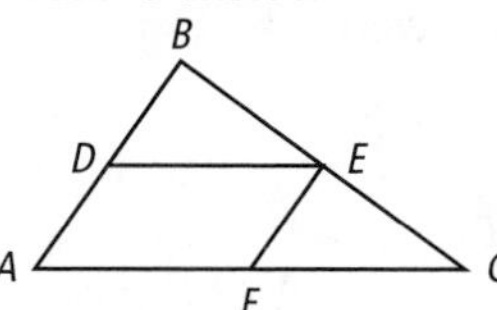

Given: $\overline{DE}$ and $\overline{EF}$ are midsegments of △ABC.

Additional Answers

Prove: $ADEF$ is a ▱.

1. $\overline{DE}$ and $\overline{EF}$ are midsegments of $\triangle ABC$. (Given)

2. $\overline{DE} \parallel \overline{FA}$, $\overline{AD} \parallel \overline{EF}$ ($\triangle$ Midsegment Thm.)

3. $ADEF$ is a ▱. (Def. of ▱)

32. Possible answer: A quad. is a ▱ if and only if both pairs of opp. sides are ≅. A quad. is a ▱ if and only if both pairs of opp. ∡ are ≅. A quad. is a ▱ if and only if its diags. bisect each other.

33. Possible answer:

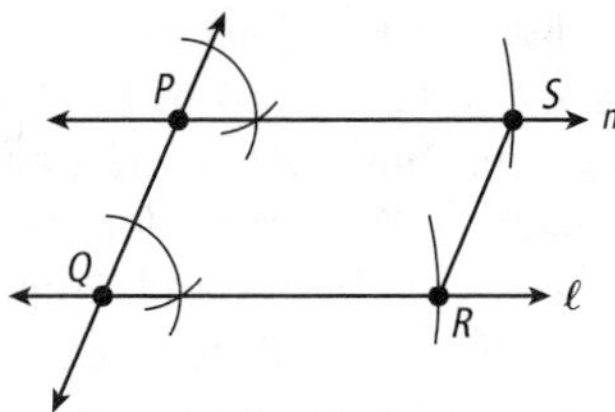

Draw line ℓ. Draw P that is not on ℓ. Draw a line through P that intersects ℓ at Q. Construct $m \parallel$ to ℓ through P. Place the compass point at Q and mark off a seg. on ℓ. Label the second endpoint of this seg. as R. Using the same compass setting, place the compass point at P and mark off a ≅ segment on m. Label the second endpoint of this seg. as S. Draw $\overline{RS}$. Since $\overline{PS} \parallel \overline{QR}$ and $\overline{PS} \cong \overline{QR}$, $PSRQ$ is a ▱ by Thm. 6-3-1.

37. Possible answer: slope of $\overline{RS} = \frac{3}{4}$, slope of $\overline{TV} = 1$; $\overline{RS}$ and $\overline{TV}$ do not have the same slope, so $\overline{RS} \nparallel \overline{TV}$; $\overline{RS}$ and $\overline{TV}$ are opp. sides of $RSTV$; by def., both pairs of opp. sides of a ▱ are ∥, so $RSTV$ is not a ▱.

38. The top and bottom of each step form a small ▱ with the back of the stairs and the base of the railing. The vertices of each ▱ have joints that allow the pieces to move. But the lengths of the sides of the ▱s stay the same. Since they start out as ▱s with opp. sides that are ≅ and the lengths do not change, they remain ▱s. Therefore the top and bottom of each step, and thus the upper platform as well, remain ∥ to the ground regardless of the position of the staircase.

40. Possible answer:

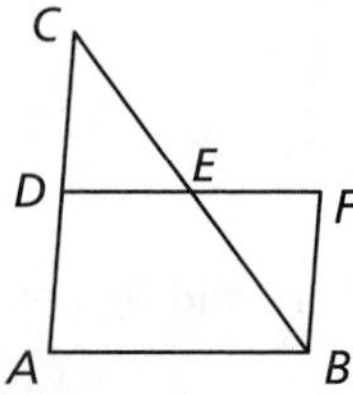

Draw F collinear with D and E such that $\overline{DE} \cong \overline{EF}$. Since E is the mdpt. of $\overline{BC}$, $\overline{CE} \cong \overline{EB}$. By the Vert. ∡ Thm., $\angle CED \cong \angle BEF$. Thus $\triangle CED \cong \triangle BEF$ by SAS. By CPCTC, $\overline{CD} \cong \overline{FB}$. Since D is the mdpt. of $\overline{AC}$, $\overline{CD} \cong \overline{AD}$. So by the Trans. Prop. of ≅, $\overline{AD} \cong \overline{FB}$. Also by CPCTC, $\angle CDE \cong \angle BFE$. By the Conv. of the Alt. Int. ∡ Thm., $\overline{AC} \parallel \overline{FB}$. Thus $DFBA$ is a ▱ since 1 pair of opp. sides are ≅ and ∥. Since $DFBA$ is a ▱, $\overline{DE} \parallel \overline{AB}$ by def. Since opp. sides of a ▱ are ≅, $\overline{AB} \cong \overline{DF}$ and $AB = DF$ by the def. of ≅ segs. Since $\overline{DE} \cong \overline{EF}$, E is the mdpt. of $\overline{DF}$, and $DE = \frac{1}{2}DF$. By subst., $DE = \frac{1}{2}AB$.

41.

x	-5	-2	0	0.5
y	-38	-17	-3	0.5

42.

x	-5	-2	0	0.5
y	-1.5	0	1	1.25

43.

x	-5	-2	0	0.5
y	77	14	2	2.75

45. Possible answer: It is given that $\overline{TW} \cong \overline{VW}$. Because $\angle UWV$ is a rt. ∠ and $\angle UWV$ and $\angle UWT$ are supp., $\angle UWT$ is also a rt. ∠. Thus $\angle UWT \cong \angle UWV$. By the Reflex. Prop. of ≅, $\overline{UW} \cong \overline{UW}$. Therefore $\triangle TUW \cong \triangle VUW$ by SAS.

6A *Ready to Go On?*

20. $RS = TV = 48$, so $\overline{RS} \cong \overline{TV}$. $RV = TS = 28$, so $\overline{RV} \cong \overline{TS}$. Thus both pairs of opp. sides of $RSTV$ are ≅. $RSTV$ is a ▱ by Thm. 6-3-2.

21. $m\angle G = m\angle J = 55°$, and $m\angle K = 125°$. Since $125° + 55° = 180°$, $\angle K$ is supp. to $\angle G$ and $\angle J$. So 1 ∠ of $GHJK$ is supp. to both of its cons. ∡. $GHJK$ is a ▱ by Thm. 6-3-4.

22. Both pairs of opp. sides of the quad. are ∥. By def., the quad. is a ▱.

23. 1 pair of opp. ∡ of the quad. are ≅. None of the conditions for a ▱ are met.

24. The diags. are divided into 2 segs. at their point of intersection, and each seg. of 1 diag. is ≅ to a seg. of the other diag. None of the conditions for a ▱ are met.

25. Slope of $\overline{CD}$ = slope of $\overline{EF} = \frac{4}{5}$; slope of $\overline{DE}$ = slope of $\overline{FC} = -\frac{1}{3}$; both pairs of opp. sides have the same slope, so $\overline{CD} \parallel \overline{EF}$ and $\overline{DE} \parallel \overline{FC}$; $CDEF$ is a ▱ by def.

6-4 *Exercises*

32. No; possible answer: a rhombus with int. ∡ that measure 70°, 110°, 70°, and 110° is equilateral, but it is not equiangular. A rect. with sides that measure 5, 7, 5, and 7 is equiangular, but it is not equilateral.

43a. By def., a square is a quad. with 4 ≅ sides. So it is true that both pairs of opp. sides are ≅. Therefore, a square is a ▱ by Thm. 6-3-2.

b. By def., a square is a quad. with 4 rt. ∡ and 4 ≅ sides. So a square is a rect., because by def., a rect. is a quad. with 4 rt. ∡.

c. By def., a square is a quad. with 4 rt. ∡ and 4 ≅ sides. So a square is a rhombus, because by def., a rhombus is a quad. with 4 ≅ sides.

44. (1) Both pairs of opp. sides are ∥. Both pairs of opp. sides are ≅. Both pairs of opp. ∡ are ≅. All pairs of cons. ∡ are supp. Its diags. bisect each other.

(2) Its diags. are ≅.

(3) Its diags. are ⊥. Each diag. bisects a pair of opp. ∡.

46. The perimeter of $\triangle RST$ is 7.2 cm. Possible answer: Opp. sides of a rect. are ≅, so $RS = QT = 2.4$ and $ST = QR = 1.8$. The diags. of a rect. bisect each other, so $QS = 2QP = 2(1.5) = 3$. The diags. of a rect. are ≅, so $TR = QS = 3$. Therefore the perimeter of $\triangle RST$ is $2.4 + 1.8 + 3 = 7.2$.

49. Possible answer:

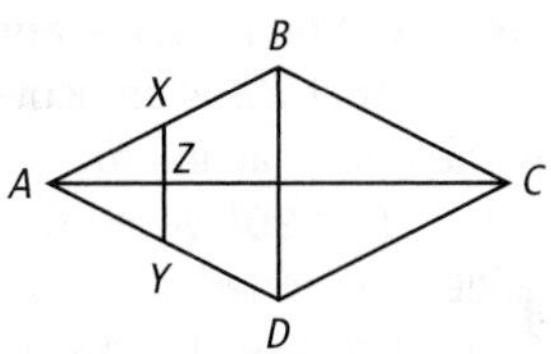

Given: $ABCD$ is a rhombus.
X is the mdpt. of $\overline{AB}$.
Y is the mdpt. of $\overline{AD}$.

Prove: $\overline{XY} \parallel \overline{BD}$; $\overline{XY} \perp \overline{AC}$

Since X is the mdpt. of $\overline{AB}$ and Y is the mdpt. of $\overline{AD}$, $\overline{XY}$ is a midsegment of $\triangle ABD$ by def. By the $\triangle$ Midsegment Thm., $\overline{XY} \parallel \overline{BD}$. It is given that $ABCD$ is a rhombus. By Thm. 6-4-4, if a ▱ is a rhombus, then its diags. are ⊥. So $\overline{AC} \perp \overline{BD}$. Since $\overline{AC} \perp \overline{BD}$ and $\overline{BD} \parallel \overline{XY}$, it follows by the ⊥ Transv. Thm. that $\overline{AC} \perp \overline{XY}$.

50. Possible answer: The midsegment of a rect. is a seg. whose endpoints are mdpts. of opp. sides of the rect.

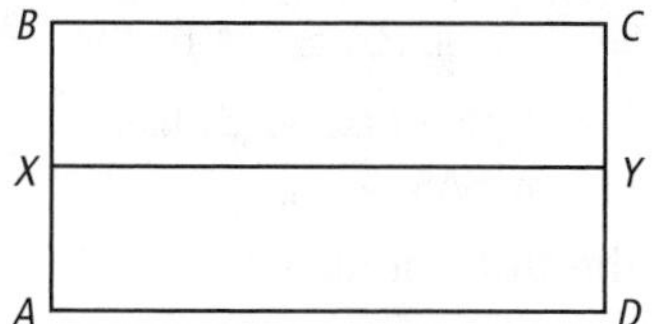

Given: $ABCD$ is a rect.
X is the mdpt. of $\overline{AB}$.
Y is the mdpt. of $\overline{CD}$.
Prove: $AXYD \cong BXYC$
A rect. is a ▱, so $ABCD$ is a ▱. Since opp. sides of a ▱ are $\cong$, $\overline{AB} \cong \overline{CD}$, and $\overline{AD} \cong \overline{BC}$. Since X is the mdpt. of $\overline{AB}$, $\overline{AX} \cong \overline{XB}$. Since Y is the mdpt. of $\overline{CD}$, $\overline{DY} \cong \overline{YC}$. But because $\overline{AB} \cong \overline{CD}$, you can conclude that $\overline{AX} \cong \overline{XB} \cong \overline{DY} \cong \overline{YC}$. Opp. sides of a ▱ are $\parallel$ by def., so $\overline{AX} \parallel \overline{DY}$. Since $\overline{AX} \cong \overline{DY}$ and $\overline{AX} \parallel \overline{DY}$, a pair of opp. sides are $\cong$ and $\parallel$, so $AXDY$ is a ▱. But since $ABCD$ is a rect., $\angle A$ is a rt. $\angle$. So ▱$AXDY$ contains a rt. $\angle$ and is therefore a rect. By similar reasoning, you can conclude that $BXYC$ is a rect. $\overline{XY} \cong \overline{XY}$ by the Reflex. Prop. of $\cong$. It has been shown that all corr. sides are $\cong$. Also, all rt. $\angle$s are $\cong$, so all corr. $\angle$s are $\cong$. Therefore, $AXYD \cong BXYC$ by the def. of $\cong$.

54. Possible answer: Suppose a ⊙ has a diam. of 4 cm and an area of 4π cm^2. If the diam. is doubled to 8 cm, the area of the ⊙ changes to 16π cm^2. The new area is 4 times as large as the original area.

6-5 *Exercises*

46.

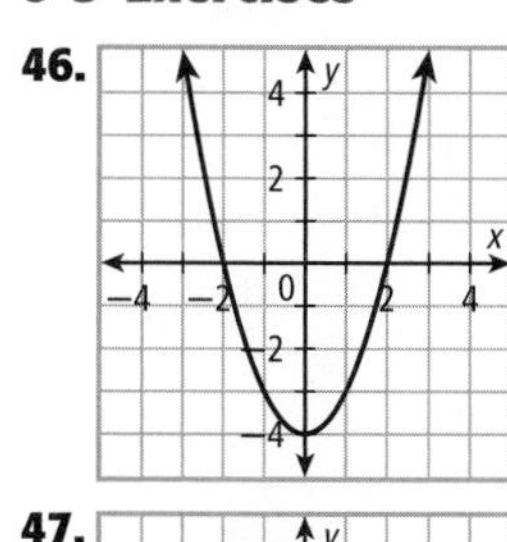

47.

6-6 *Exercises*

39. Possible answer:

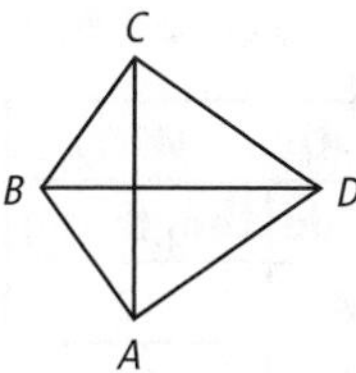

Given: $ABCD$ is a kite with $\overline{AB} \cong \overline{CB}$ and $\overline{AD} \cong \overline{CD}$.
Prove: $\overline{BD} \perp \overline{AC}$
It is given that $\overline{AB} \cong \overline{CB}$ and $\overline{AD} \cong \overline{CD}$. This means that B and D are both equidistant from A and C. By the Conv. of the $\perp$ Bisector Thm., if a pt. is equidistant from the endpoints of a seg., then it is on the $\perp$ bisector of the seg. Through any 2 pts. there is exactly 1 line, so the line that contains B and D must be the $\perp$ bisector of $\overline{AC}$. Therefore $\overline{BD} \perp \overline{AC}$.

50. Possible answer:

1. $WXYZ$ is a trap. with $\overline{XZ} \cong \overline{YW}$. (Given)
2. Draw $\overline{XU}$ through X so that $\overline{XU} \perp \overline{WZ}$. Draw $\overline{YV}$ through Y so that $\overline{YV} \perp \overline{WZ}$. (There is exactly 1 line through a pt. not on a line that is $\perp$ to that line.)
3. $m\angle XUZ = 90°$, $m\angle YVW = 90°$ (Def. of $\perp$ lines)
4. $\angle XUZ$ and $\angle YVW$ are right $\angle$s. (Def. of rt. $\angle$)
5. $\triangle XUZ$ and $\triangle YVW$ are right $\triangle$s. (Def. of rt. $\triangle$)
6. $\overline{XU} \parallel \overline{YV}$ (2 lines $\perp$ to 3rd line $\to$ 2 lines $\parallel$)
7. $\overline{XY} \parallel \overline{WZ}$ (Def. of trap.)
8. $XYVU$ is a ▱. (Def. of ▱)
9. $\overline{XU} \cong \overline{YV}$ (▱ $\to$ opp. sides $\cong$)
10. $\triangle XUZ \cong \triangle YVW$ (HL)
11. $\angle XZW \cong \angle YWZ$ (CPCTC)
12. $\overline{WZ} \cong \overline{WZ}$ (Reflex. Prop. of $\cong$)
13. $\triangle XZW \cong \triangle YWZ$ (SAS)
14. $\overline{XW} \cong \overline{YZ}$ (CPCTC)
15. $WXYZ$ is an isosc. trap. (Def. of isosc. trap.)

6-6 *Construction*

1. Choose B and D both above or both below $\overline{AC}$.

6B *Multi-Step Test Prep*

3. By the Distance Formula, $PR = SQ = 4\sqrt{5}$, so the diags. of $PQRS$ are $\cong$. By Thm. 6-5-2, $PQRS$ is a rect.

6B *Ready to Go On?*

7. 1. $QSTV$ is a rhombus. $\overline{PT} \cong \overline{RT}$ (Given)
2. $\overline{QT}$ bisects $\angle PTR$. (Rhombus $\to$ each diag. bisects opp. $\angle$s)
3. $\angle QTP \cong \angle QTR$ (Def. of $\angle$ bisector)
4. $\overline{QT} \cong \overline{QT}$ (Reflex. Prop. of $\cong$)
5. $\triangle PQT \cong \triangle RQT$ (SAS)
6. $\overline{PQ} \cong \overline{RQ}$ (CPCTC)

8. By Thm. 6-5-4, if the diags. of a ▱ are $\perp$, then the ▱ is a rhombus. But you need to know that $ABCD$ is a ▱.

12. Possible answer: Since $\overline{VX}$ is a midsegment of $\triangle TWY$, $\overline{VX} \parallel \overline{TZ}$ by the $\triangle$ Midsegment Thm. Similarly, $\overline{XZ} \parallel \overline{TV}$. So $TVXZ$ is a ▱ by def. Since $\overline{VX}$ is a midsegment of $\triangle TWY$, V is the mdpt. of $\overline{TW}$. Thus $TV = \frac{1}{2}TW$ by the def. of mdpt. Similarly, $TZ = \frac{1}{2}TY$ since $\overline{ZX}$ is a midsegment of $\triangle TWY$. It is given that $\overline{TW} \cong \overline{TY}$, so $TW = TY$ by the def. of $\cong$ segs. By subst., $TZ = \frac{1}{2}TW$, and thus $TZ = TV$. By the def. of $\cong$ segs., $\overline{TZ} \cong \overline{TV}$. Since $TVXZ$ is a ▱ with 1 pair of cons. sides $\cong$, $TVXZ$ is a rhombus.

Chapter 7

7-3 *Exercises*

6. Since $\overline{UV} \parallel \overline{XY}$, $\angle U \cong \angle Y$, and $\angle V \cong \angle X$ by the Alt. Int. $\angle$s Thm. Therefore $\triangle UWV \sim \triangle YWX$ by AA $\sim$. $WY = 11.25$

7. 1. $\overline{MN} \parallel \overline{KL}$ (Given)
2. $\angle JMN \cong \angle JKL$, $\angle JNM \cong \angle JLK$ (Corr. $\angle$s Post.)
3. $\triangle JMN \sim \triangle JKL$ (AA $\sim$ Step 2)

8. 1. $SQ = 2QP$, $TR = 2RP$ (Given)
2. $SP = SQ + QP$, $TP = TR + RP$ (Seg. Add. Post.)
3. $SP = 2QP + QP$, $TP = 2RP + RP$ (Subst.)
4. $SP = 3QP$, $TP = 3RP$ (Seg. Add. Post.)
5. $\frac{SP}{QP} = 3$, $\frac{TP}{RP} = 3$ (Div. Prop. of =)
6. $\angle P \cong \angle P$ (Reflex. Prop. of $\cong$)
7. $\triangle PQR \sim \triangle PST$ (SAS $\sim$ Steps 5, 6)

39. Assume that $AB < DE$ and choose X on $\overline{DE}$ so that $\overline{XE} \cong \overline{AB}$. Then choose Y on $\overline{EF}$ so that $\overline{XY} \parallel \overline{DF}$. $\angle EXY \cong \angle EDF$ by the Corr. $\angle$s Post. $\angle E \cong \angle E$ by the Reflex. Prop. of $\cong$. So $\triangle XEY \sim \triangle DEF$ by AA $\sim$. By the def. of $\sim$ $\triangle$s, $\frac{XE}{DE} = \frac{EY}{EF}$. It is given that $\frac{AB}{DE} = \frac{BC}{EF}$. By the def. of $\cong$, $XE = AB$, so $\frac{XE}{DE} = \frac{BC}{EF}$. Thus by the def. of $\cong$, $BC = EY$, and $\overline{BC} \cong \overline{EY}$. It is also given that $\angle B \cong \angle E$, so $\triangle ABC \cong \triangle XEY$ by SAS $\cong$ Thm. It follows that $\triangle ABC \sim \triangle XEY$. Then by the Trans. Prop. of $\sim$, $\triangle ABC \sim \triangle DEF$.

7A *Ready to Go On?*

13. **1.** $ABCD$ is a ▱. (Given)
2. $\overline{AD} \parallel \overline{BC}$ (Def. of ▱)
3. $\angle EDG \cong \angle FBG$ (Alt. Int. ∠s Thm.)
4. $\angle EGD \cong \angle FGB$ (Vert. ∠s Thm.)
5. $\triangle EDG \sim \triangle FBG$ (AA $\sim$ *Steps 3, 4*)

14. **1.** $MQ = \frac{1}{3}MN$, $MR = \frac{1}{3}MP$ (Given)
2. $\frac{MQ}{MN} = \frac{1}{3}$, $\frac{MR}{MP} = \frac{1}{3}$ (Div. Prop. of =)
3. $\frac{MQ}{MN} = \frac{MR}{MP}$ (Trans. Prop. of =)
4. $\angle M \cong \angle M$ (Reflex. Prop. of $\cong$)
5. $\triangle MQR \sim \triangle MNP$ (SAS $\sim$ *Steps 3, 4*)

7-4 *Exercises*

37. Given: $\triangle ABC \sim \triangle XYZ$, $\overline{AD}$ bisects $\angle BAC$, and $\overline{XW}$ bisects $\angle YXZ$.

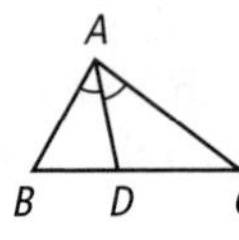

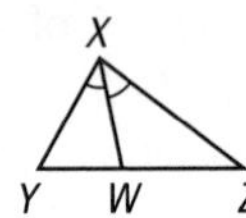

Prove: $\frac{AD}{XW} = \frac{AB}{XY}$

1. $\triangle ABC \sim \triangle XYZ$ (Given)
2. $\angle B \cong \angle Y$ (Def. of $\sim$ polygons)
3. $m\angle BAC = m\angle YXZ$ (Def. of $\sim$ polygons)
4. $\overline{AD}$ bisects $\angle BAC$, and $\overline{XW}$ bisects $\angle YXZ$. (Given)
5. $m\angle BAC = 2m\angle BAD$, $m\angle YXZ = 2m\angle YXW$ (Def. of ∠ bisector)
6. $2m\angle BAD = 2m\angle YXW$ (Trans. Prop. of =)
7. $m\angle BAD = m\angle YXW$ (Div. Prop. of =)
8. $\triangle ABD \sim \triangle XYW$ (AA $\sim$ *Steps 2, 7*)
9. $\frac{AD}{XW} = \frac{AB}{XY}$ (△ Proportionality Thm.)

38. **1.** In $\triangle ABC$, $\overline{AD}$ bisects $\angle A$. (Given)
2. Draw $\overline{BX} \parallel \overline{AD}$ and extend $\overline{AC}$ to X. (∥ Post.)
3. $\frac{BD}{DC} = \frac{AX}{AC}$ (△ Proportionality Thm.)
4. $\angle CAD \cong \angle AXB$ (Corr. ∠s Post.)
5. $\angle CAD \cong \angle DAB$ (Def. of ∠ bisector)
6. $\angle DAB \cong \angle ABX$ (Alt. Int. ∠s Thm.)
7. $\angle DAB \cong \angle AXB$ (Trans. Prop. of $\cong$)
8. $\angle ABX \cong \angle AXB$ (Trans. Prop. of $\cong$)
9. $\overline{AX} \cong \overline{AB}$ (Conv. of Isosc. △ Thm.)
10. $AX = AB$ (Def. of $\cong$)

11. $\frac{BD}{DC} = \frac{AB}{AC}$ (Subst.)

7-5 *Exercises*

46b.

Quad. *PQRS*		Quad. *WXYZ*	
Side	**Length (m)**	**Side**	**Length (m)**
PQ	6	*WX*	12
QR	7	*XY*	14
RS	10	*YZ*	20
PS	12	*WZ*	24

c.

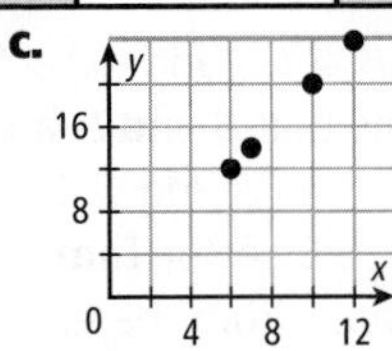

50. The slopes of $\overline{AB}$ and $\overline{CD} = \frac{2}{3}$. The slopes of $\overline{BC}$ and $\overline{AD} = 0$. Since opp. sides in each pair have the same slope, $\overline{AB} \parallel \overline{CD}$, and $\overline{BC} \parallel \overline{AC}$. By def., $ABCD$ is a ▱.

51. The slopes of $\overline{JK}$ and $\overline{LM} = 1$. The slopes of $\overline{KL}$ and $\overline{JM} = -1$. Since opp. sides in each pair have the same slope, $\overline{JK} \parallel \overline{LM}$, and $\overline{KL} \parallel \overline{JM}$. By def., $JKLM$ is a ▱.

7-6 *Exercises*

8. Check students' work. The image of $\triangle ABC$ has vertices $A'(2, 8)$, $B'(2, 2)$, and $C'(6, 2)$. $AB = 3$, $BC = 2$, and $AC = \sqrt{13}$. $A'B' = 6$, $B'C' = 4$, and $A'C' = 2\sqrt{13}$. $\frac{A'B'}{AB} = \frac{B'C'}{BC} = \frac{A'C'}{AC} = 2$. So $\triangle ABC \sim \triangle A'B'C'$ by SSS $\sim$.

9. Check students' work. The image of $\triangle RST$ has vertices $R'(-3, 3)$, $S'(3, 6)$, and $T'(0, -3)$. $RS = 2\sqrt{5}$, $RT = 2\sqrt{5}$, and $ST = 2\sqrt{10}$. $R'S' = 3\sqrt{5}$, $R'T' = 3\sqrt{5}$, and $S'T' = 3\sqrt{10}$. $\frac{R'S'}{RS} = \frac{R'T'}{RT} = \frac{S'T'}{ST} = \frac{3}{2}$. So $\triangle RST \sim \triangle R'S'T'$ by SSS $\sim$.

16. Check students' work. The image of $\triangle MNP$ has vertices $M'(0, 2)$, $N'(2, 1)$, and $P'(1, -1)$. $MN = 2\sqrt{5}$, $MP = 2\sqrt{10}$, and $PN = 2\sqrt{5}$. $M'N' = \sqrt{5}$, $M'P' = \sqrt{10}$, and $P'N' = \sqrt{5}$. $\frac{M'N'}{MN} = \frac{M'P'}{MP} = \frac{P'N'}{PN} = \frac{1}{2}$. So $\triangle MNP \sim \triangle M'N'P'$ by SSS $\sim$.

20a. He should use the origin as the vertex of the rt. ∠; $J(0, 1)$; $K(0, 0)$; $L(3, 0)$.

b.

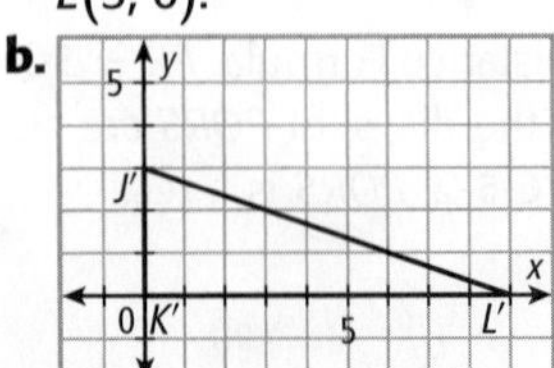

7B *Ready to Go On?*

9. By the Dist. Formula, $AD = \sqrt{5}$, $AB = 2\sqrt{5}$, $AE = \sqrt{5}$, and $AC = 2\sqrt{5}$. $\frac{AD}{AB} = \frac{AE}{AC} = \frac{1}{2}$. $\angle A \cong \angle A$ by the Reflex. Prop. of $\cong$. So $\triangle ADE \sim \triangle ABC$ by SAS $\sim$.

10. By the Dist. Formula, $RS = \sqrt{5}$, $RT = 3$, $RU = 2\sqrt{5}$, and $RV = 6$. $\frac{RS}{RU} = \frac{RT}{RV} = \frac{1}{2}$. $\angle SRT \cong \angle URV$ by the Vert. ∠s Thm. So $\triangle RST \sim \triangle RUV$ by SAS $\sim$.

11.

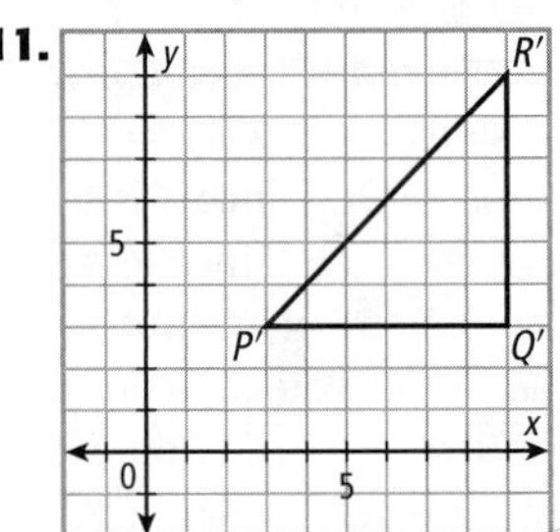

By the Dist. Formula, $PQ = QR = 2$, $PR = 2\sqrt{2}$, $P'Q' = Q'R' = 6$, and $P'R' = 6\sqrt{2}$. $\frac{PQ}{P'Q'} = \frac{QR}{Q'R'} = \frac{PR}{P'R'} = \frac{1}{3}$. So $\triangle PQR \sim \triangle R'Q'R'$ by SSS $\sim$.

12.

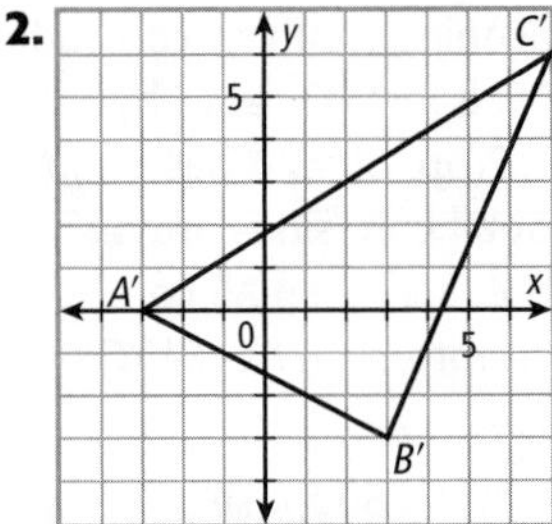

By the Dist. Formula, $AB = 2\sqrt{5}$, $BC = 2\sqrt{10}$, $AC = 2\sqrt{13}$, $A'B' = 3\sqrt{5}$, $B'C' = 3\sqrt{10}$, and $A'C' = 3\sqrt{13}$. $\frac{AB}{A'B'} = \frac{BC}{B'C'} = \frac{AC}{A'C'} = \frac{2}{3}$. So $\triangle ABC \sim \triangle A'B'C'$ by SSS $\sim$.

Chapter 8

8-4 *Geometry Lab*

1. The ∠ reading from the clinometer is the comp. of the ∠ of elevation.
3. Check students' work. The results should be similar.
4. Possible answers: measuring the distance between the observer and the object, measuring the height of the eyes of the observer, and reading the ∠ measure from the clinometer
5. It can be used to measure the height of tall objects that cannot be measured directly.

8B *Ready to Go On?*

9.

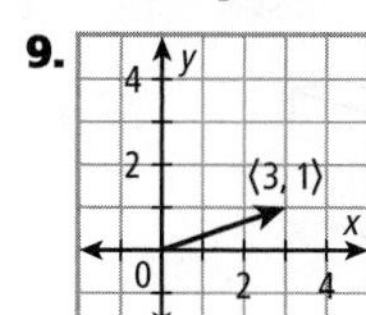

10.

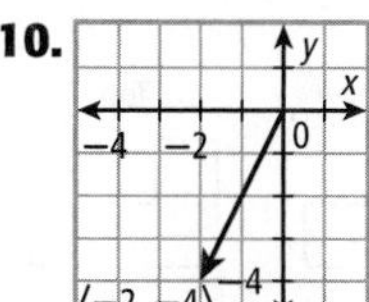

11.

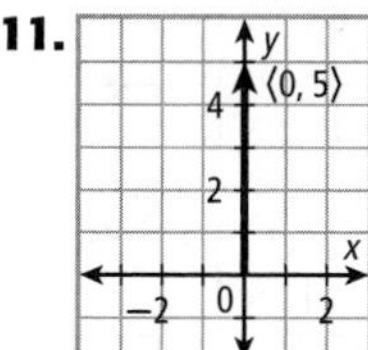

12.

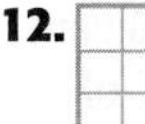

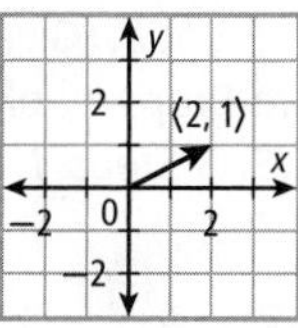

13.

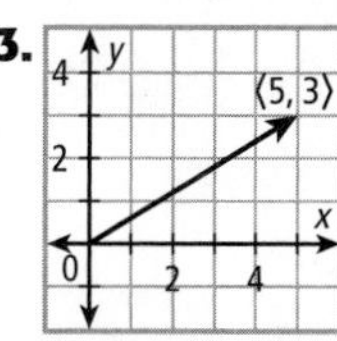

14.

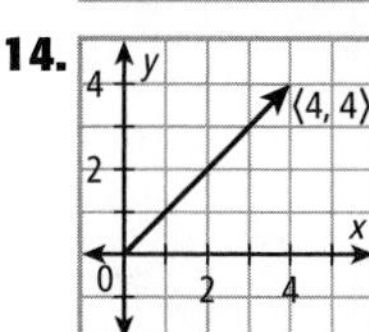

Chapter 8 Extension

1.

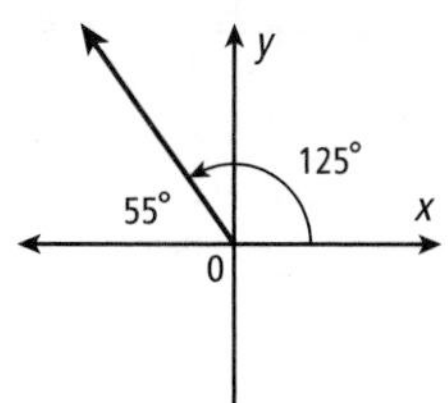

2.

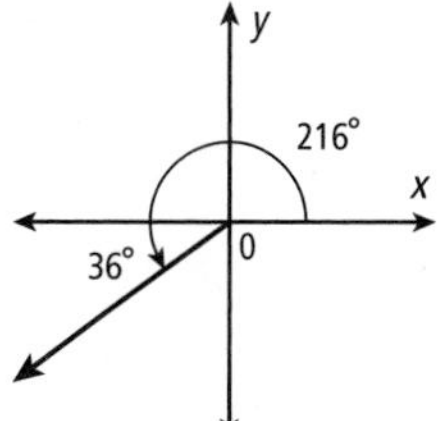

3.

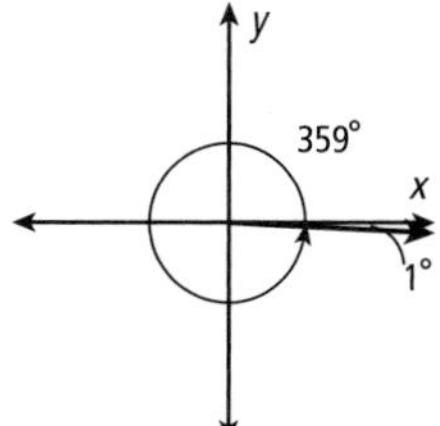

Chapter 9

9-4 *Exercises*

3.

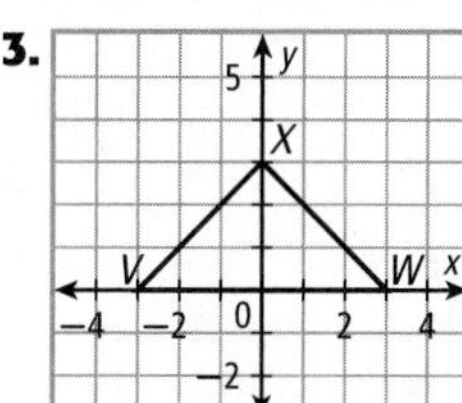

4.

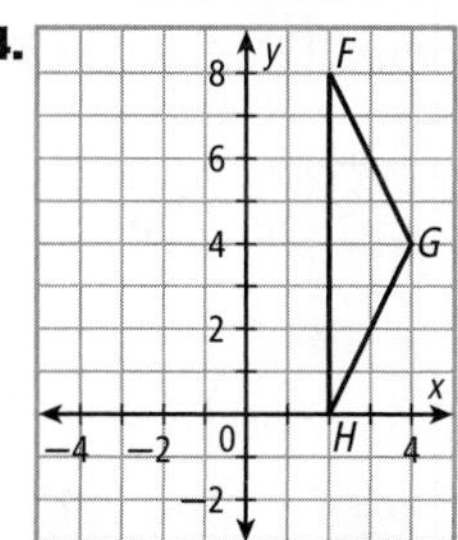

5.

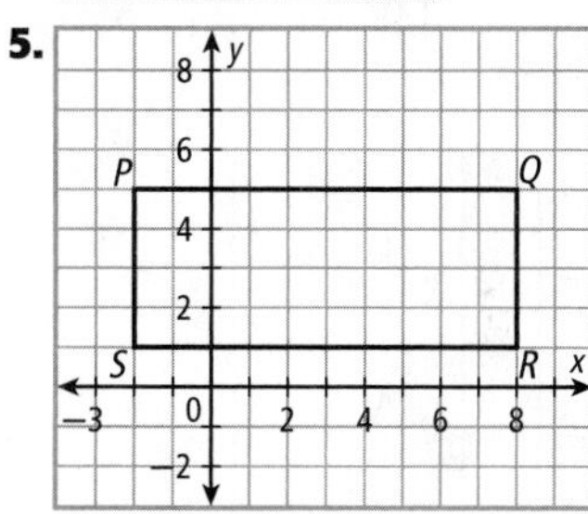

6.

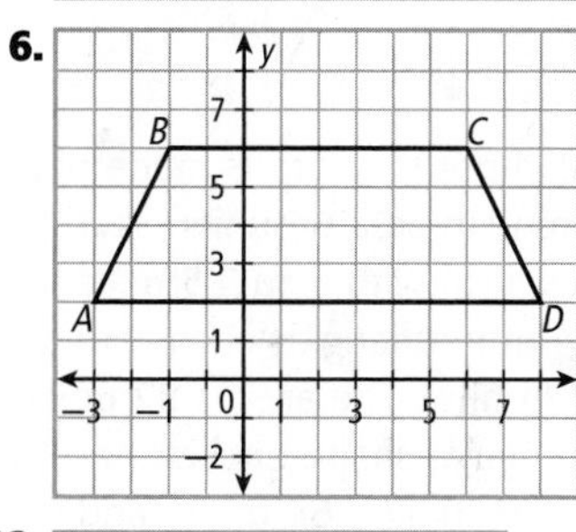

12.

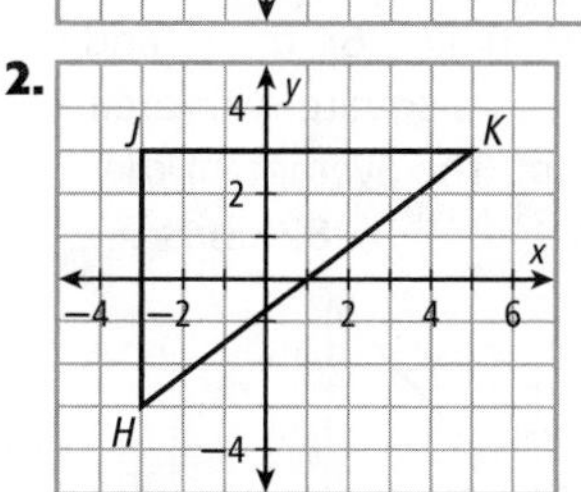

13.

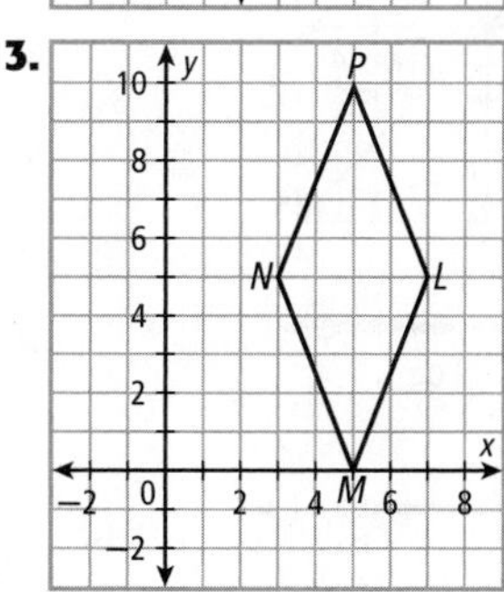

Additional Answers

14.

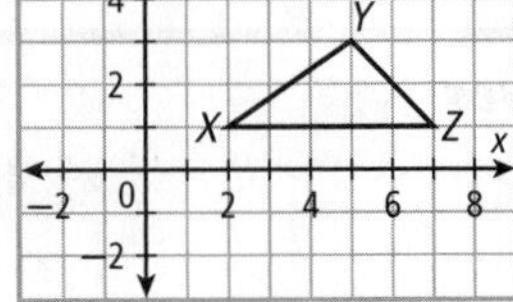

15.

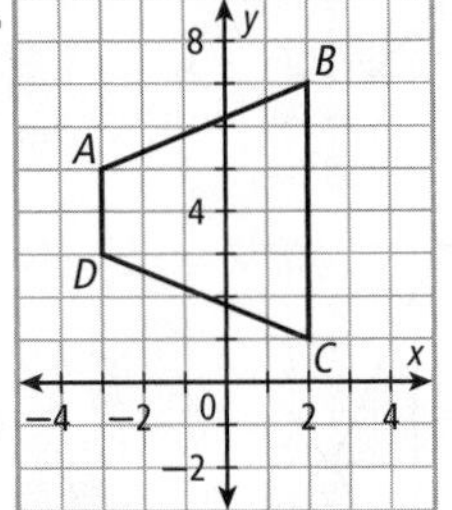

19.

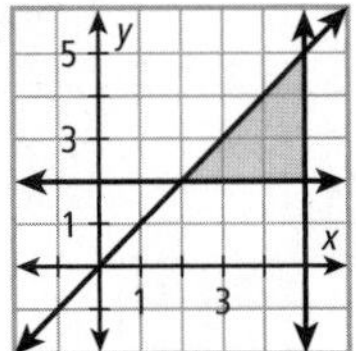

20.

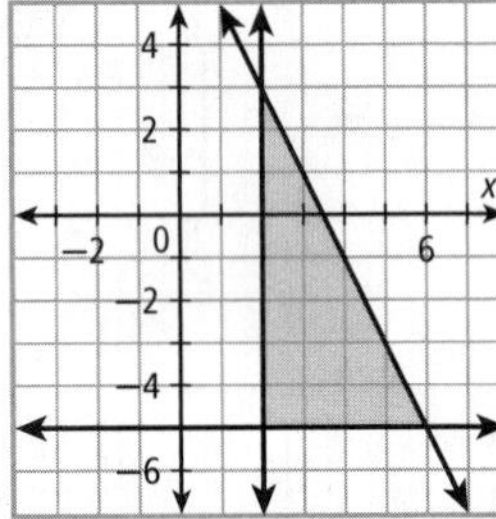

26b. The composite figure is made of a square with area 64 units^2, 4 triangles each with area 2.5 units^2, and 4 other triangles each with area 2 units^2. The area is 82 units^2.

c. The irregular shape encloses a square with area 64 units^2 and is enclosed in a square with area 100 units^2. The average of the areas is $\frac{64 + 100}{2} = 82$ units^2.

31.

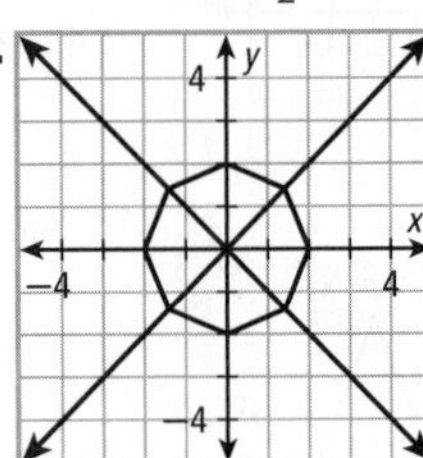

32. $-7 < x < 4$

−7 0 4

33. $-2 < a < 3$

−2 0 3

34. $-5 \le m \le -1$

−5 −1 0

35. **1.** $\overline{DC} \cong \overline{BC}$, $\angle DCA \cong \angle ACB$ (Given)
2. $\overline{AC} \cong \overline{AC}$ (Reflexive Property of $\cong$)
3. $\triangle DCA \cong \triangle BCA$ (SAS *Steps 1, 2*)
4. $\angle DAC \cong \angle BAC$ (CPCTC)

9B *Ready to Go On?*

1.

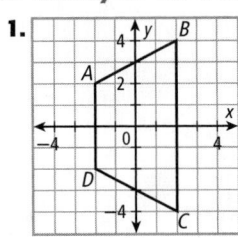

2.

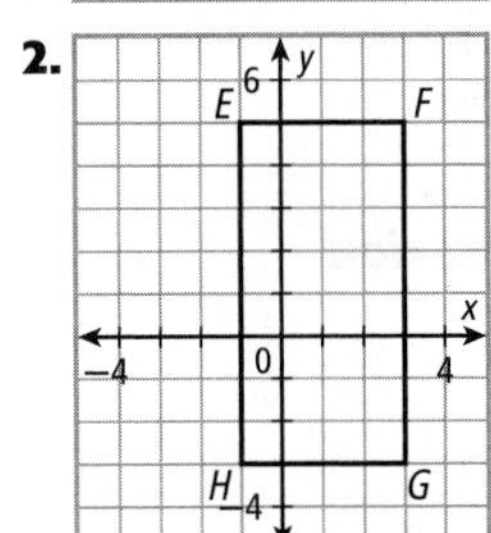

Chapter 10

10-1 *Exercises*

37c.

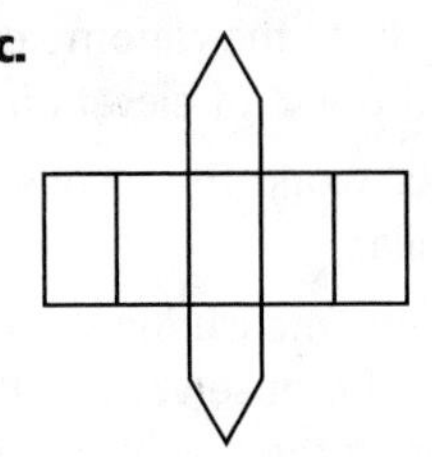

10-2 *Exercises*

8. 1-point 2-point

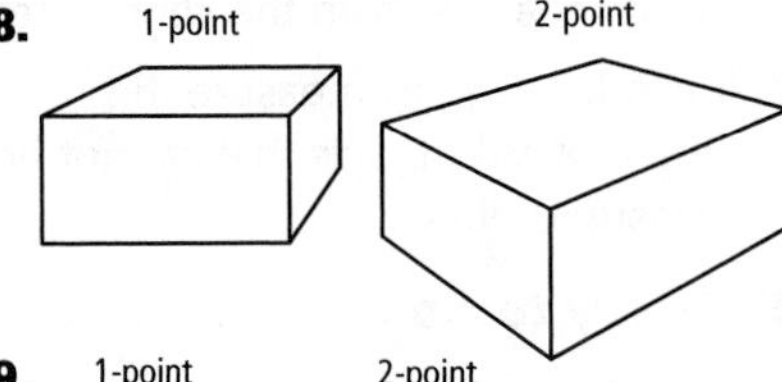

9. 1-point 2-point

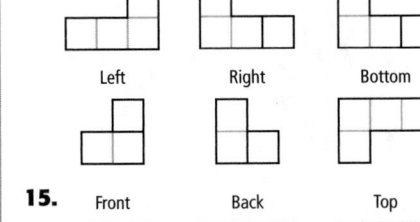

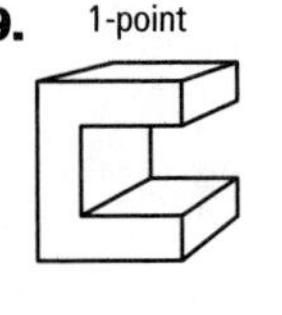

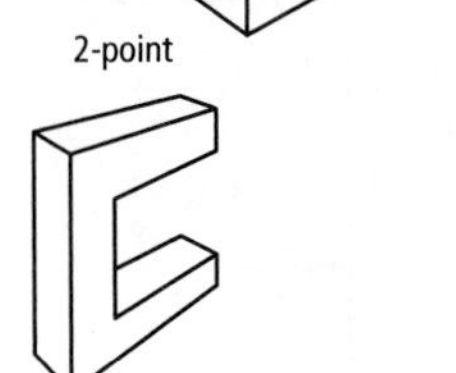

14. Front Back Top

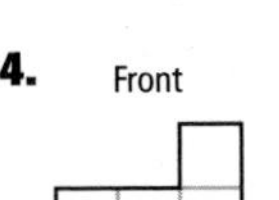

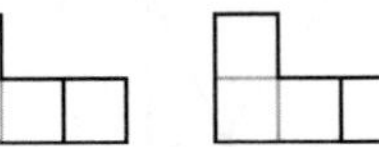

Left Right Bottom

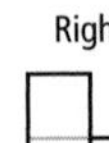

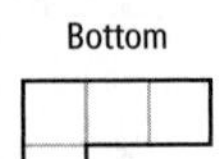

15. Front Back Top

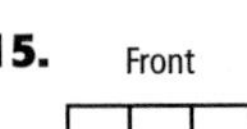

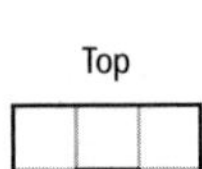

Left Right Bottom

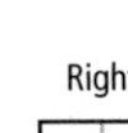

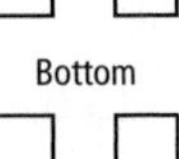

16. Front Back Top

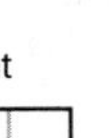

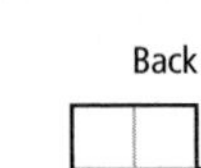

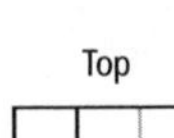

Left Right Bottom

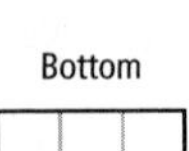

41b.

Front Back Top

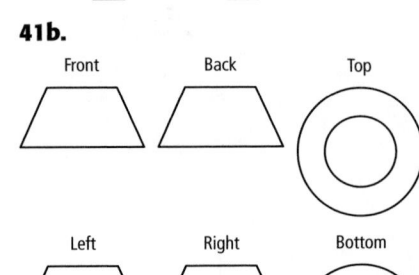

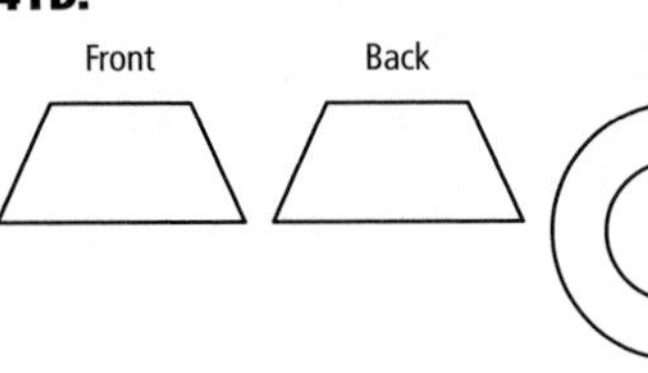

Left Right Bottom

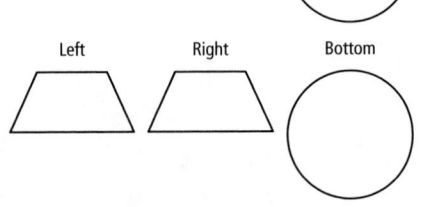

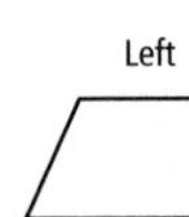

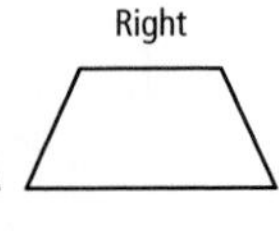

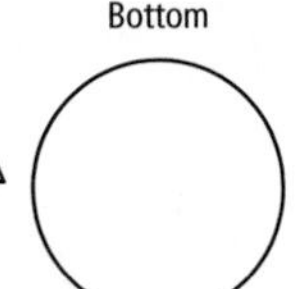

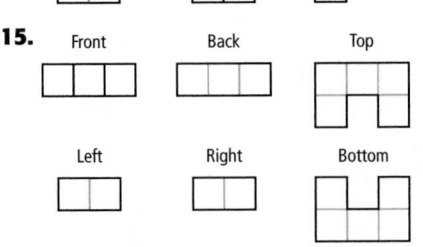

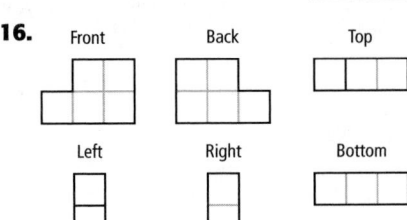

c.

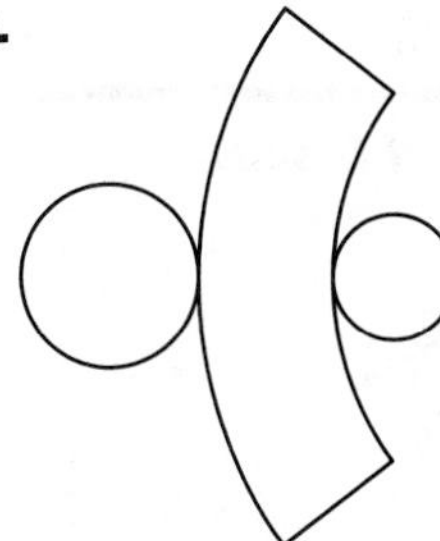

10-2 *Using Techonology*

2. Possible answer: First I would draw a horizontal line to represent the horizon and locate 2 vanishing points A and B on the line. Then I would draw a vertical segment $\overline{CD}$ and draw segments $\overline{CA}$, $\overline{CB}$, $\overline{DA}$, and $\overline{DB}$. I would draw 2 more vertical segments, 1 with endpoints on $\overline{CA}$ and $\overline{DA}$ and the other with endpoints on $\overline{CB}$ and $\overline{DB}$. I would then connect each endpoint of these segments to both vanishing points to form a rectangular prism.

10-3 *Exercises*

29.

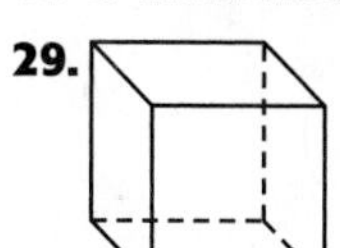

30.

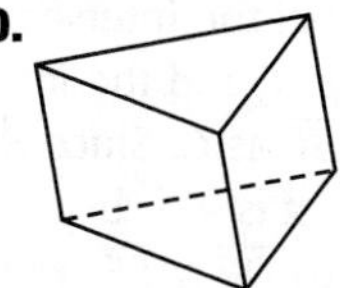

31.

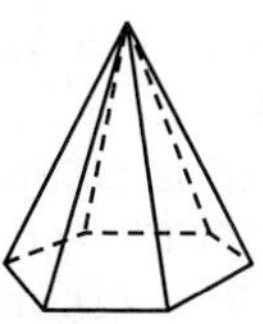

32. vertices: $2n$; edges: $3n$; faces: $n + 2$; $2n - 3n + (n + 2) = 2$

33. vertices: $n + 1$; edges: $2n$; faces: $n + 1$; $(n + 1) - 2n + (n + 1) = 2$

45.

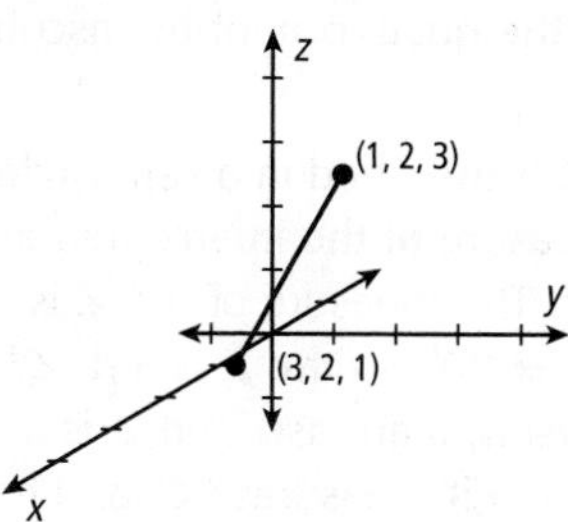

$d \approx 2.8$ units; $M(2, 2, 2)$

46.

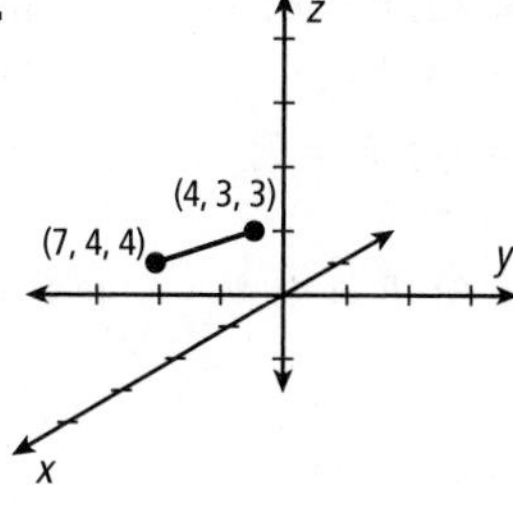

$d \approx 3.3$ units; $M(5.5, 3.5, 3.5)$

47.

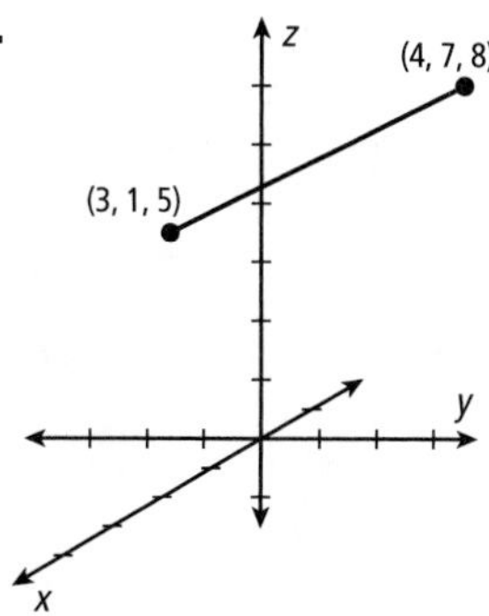

$d \approx 6.8$ units; $M(3.5, 4, 6.5)$

48.

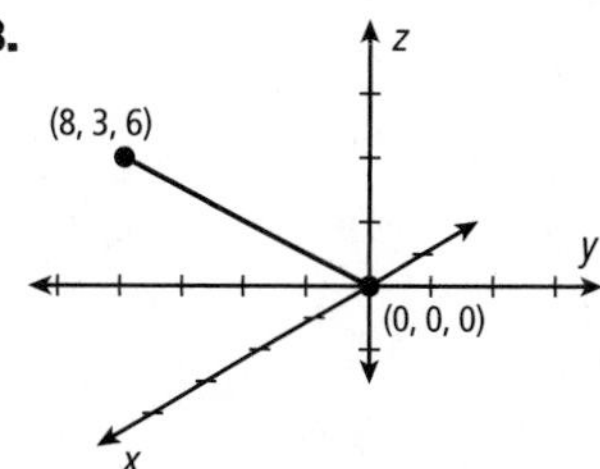

$d \approx 10.4$ units; $M(4, 1.5, 3)$

49.

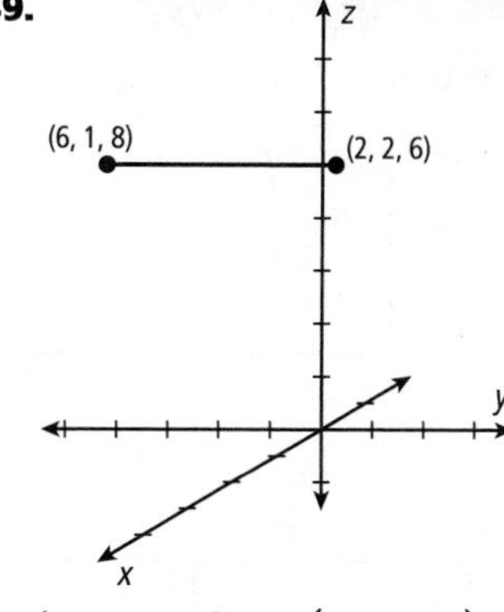

$d \approx 4.6$ units; $M(4, 1.5, 7)$

50.

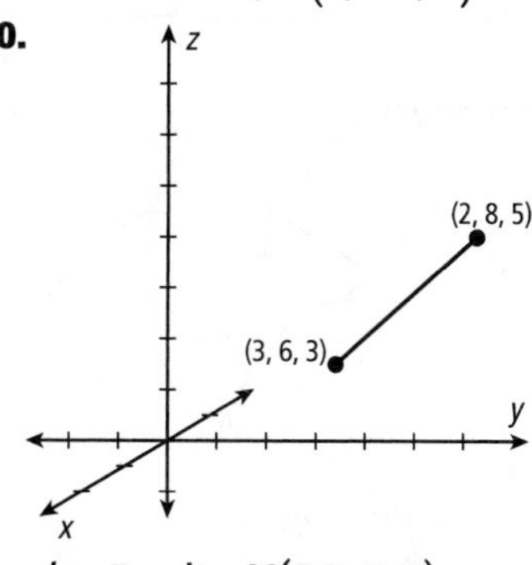

$d = 3$ units; $M(2.5, 7, 4)$

62. $AB = \sqrt{(x_2 - x_1)^2 + (y_2 - y_1)^2 + (z_2 - z_1)^2}$,

$$AM = \sqrt{\left(\frac{x_1 + x_2}{2} - x_1\right)^2 + \left(\frac{y_1 + y_2}{2} - y_1\right)^2 + \left(\frac{z_1 + z_2}{2} - z_1\right)^2}$$

$$= \sqrt{\left(\frac{x_2}{2} - \frac{x_1}{2}\right)^2 + \left(\frac{y_2}{2} - \frac{y_1}{2}\right)^2 + \left(\frac{z_2}{2} - \frac{z_1}{2}\right)^2}, \text{ and}$$

$$MB = \sqrt{\left(x_2 - \frac{x_1 + x_2}{2}\right)^2 + \left(y_2 - \frac{y_1 + y_2}{2}\right)^2 + \left(z_2 - \frac{z_1 + z_2}{2}\right)^2}$$

$$= \sqrt{\left(\frac{x_2}{2} - \frac{x_1}{2}\right)^2 + \left(\frac{y_2}{2} - \frac{y_1}{2}\right)^2 + \left(\frac{z_2}{2} - \frac{z_1}{2}\right)^2}.$$

So $AM = MB$. Also, $AM + MB = 2\sqrt{\left(\frac{x_2}{2} - \frac{x_1}{2}\right)^2 + \left(\frac{y_2}{2} - \frac{y_1}{2}\right)^2 + \left(\frac{z_2}{2} - \frac{z_1}{2}\right)^2}$

$= 2\sqrt{\frac{1}{4}(x_2 - x_1)^2 + \frac{1}{4}(y_2 - y_1)^2 + \frac{1}{4}(z_2 - z_1)^2}$

$= \sqrt{(x_2 - x_1)^2 + (y_2 - y_1)^2 + (z_2 - z_1)^2} = AB$, so A, M, and B are collinear. Since M is on $\overline{AB}$ and $AM = MB$, M is the midpoint of $\overline{AB}$ by def. of midpt.

63. $AG = \sqrt{(a - 0)^2 + (b - 0)^2 + (c - 0)^2} = \sqrt{a^2 + b^2 + c^2}$, and $BH = \sqrt{(0 - a)^2 + (b - 0)^2 + (c - 0)^2} = \sqrt{a^2 + b^2 + c^2}$. $AG = BH$, so $\overline{AG} \cong \overline{BH}$ by def. of $\cong$ segs. The midpt. of $\overline{AG}$ is $M\left(\frac{0 + a}{2}, \frac{0 + b}{2}, \frac{0 + c}{2}\right)$, or $M\left(\frac{a}{2}, \frac{b}{2}, \frac{c}{2}\right)$, and the midpt of $\overline{BH}$ is $M\left(\frac{a + 0}{2}, \frac{0 + b}{2}, \frac{0 + c}{2}\right)$, or $M\left(\frac{a}{2}, \frac{b}{2}, \frac{c}{2}\right)$. The segs. have the same midpt., so they bisect each other.

10A *Multi-Step Test Prep*

1. A-frame tent:

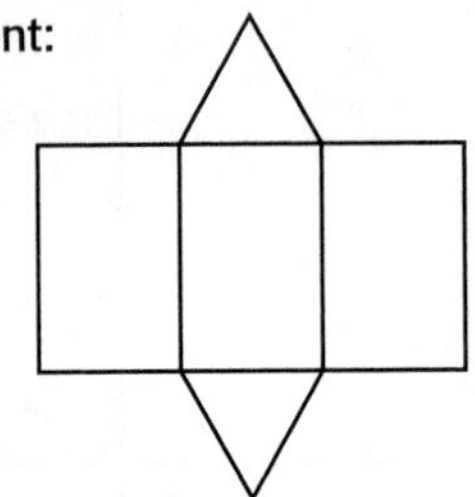

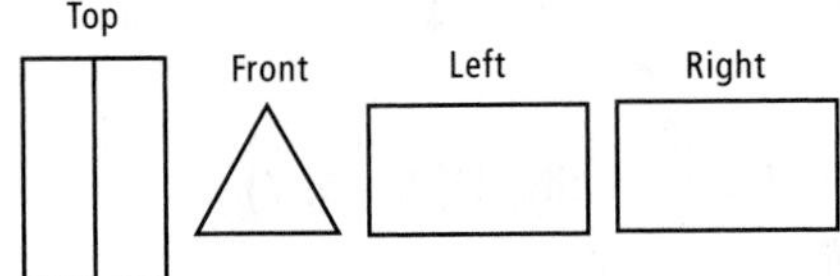

pyramid-tent:

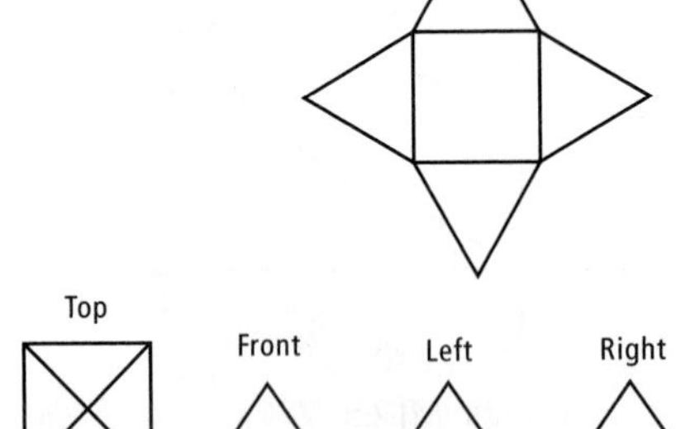

Top Front Left Right

10A *Ready to Go On?*

3. rectangular prism; K, L, M, N, P, Q, R, S; $\overline{KL}, \overline{LM}, \overline{MN}, \overline{NK}, \overline{PQ}, \overline{QR}, \overline{RS}, \overline{PS}, \overline{KP}, \overline{LQ}, \overline{MR}, \overline{NS}$; $KLMN$, $PQRS$

10.

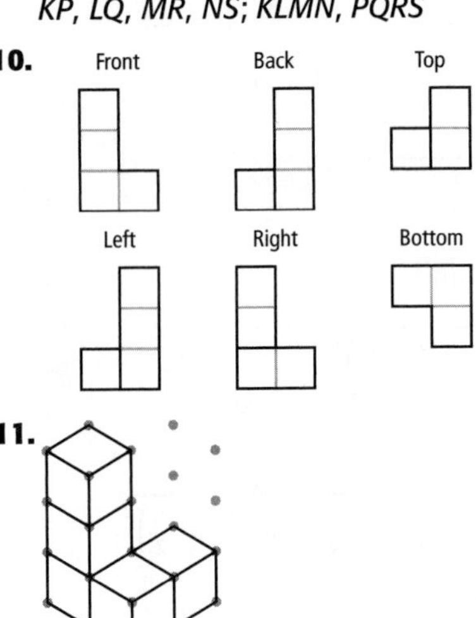

11.

12.

13.

14. $V = 8$; $E = 12$; $F = 6$; $8 - 12 + 6 = 2$

15. $V = 7$; $E = 12$; $F = 7$; $7 - 12 + 7 = 2$

16. $V = 4$; $E = 6$; $F = 4$; $4 - 6 + 4 = 2$

Chapter 11

11-1 *Think and Discuss*

1.

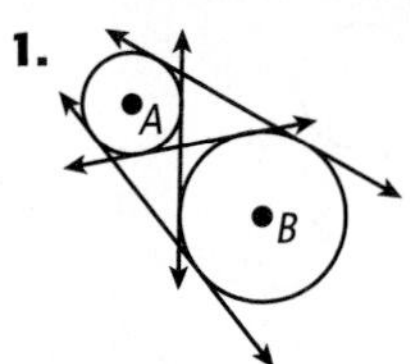

11-4 *Exercises*

32. By the Inscribed ∠ Thm., $m\angle ACD = \frac{1}{2}m\widehat{AB}$ and $m\angle ADB = \frac{1}{2}m\widehat{AB}$. By substitution, $m\angle ACB = m\angle ADB$, and therefore $\angle ACB \cong \angle ADB$.

34. $\overline{PR}$ is a diag. of the $PQRS$. $\angle Q$ is an inscribed rt. ∠, so its intercepted arc is a semicircle. Thus $\overline{PR}$ is a diam. of the ⊙.

35a. $AB^2 + AC^2 = BC^2$, so by the Converse of the Pyth. Thm., $\triangle ABC$ is a rt. △ with rt. $\angle A$. Since $\angle A$ is an inscribed rt. ∠, it intercepts a semicircle. This means that $\overline{BC}$ is a diam.

36.

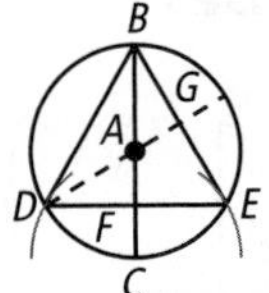

Draw diam. $\overline{DG}$. Label the intersection of $\overline{BC}$ and $\overline{DE}$ as F and the intersection of $\overline{DG}$ and $\overline{BE}$ as G. Since $\overline{BC}$ is a diam. of the ⊙, it is a ⊥ bisector of chord $\overline{DE}$. Thus $\overline{DF} \cong \overline{EF}$, and $\angle BFD$ and $\angle BFE$ are ≅ rt. ∠s. $\overline{BF} \cong \overline{BF}$ by the Reflex. Prop. of ≅. Thus $\triangle BFD \cong \triangle BFE$ by SAS. $\overline{BD} \cong \overline{BE}$ by CPCTC. Similarly, $\triangle DEG \cong \triangle DBG$ by SAS. $\overline{BD} \cong \overline{ED}$ by CPCTC. By the Transitive Prop. of ≅, $\overline{BE} \cong \overline{ED}$. Thus by def., $\triangle DBE$ is equil.

37. Agree; opp. ∠s of a ▱ are ≅, so the ∠ opp. the 30° ∠ also measures 30°. Since this pair of opp. ∠s are not supp., the quad. cannot be inscribed in a ⊙.

43. If an ∠ is inscribed in a semicircle, the measure of the intercepted arc is 180°. The measure of the ∠ is $\frac{1}{2}(180°) = 90°$, so the ∠ is a rt. ∠. Conversely, if an inscribed ∠ is a rt. ∠, then it measures 90° and its intercepted arc measures $2(90°) = 180°$. An arc that measures 180° is a semicircle.

44. Suppose quad. $ABCD$ is inscribed in a ⊙. Then $m\angle A = \frac{1}{2}m\widehat{BCD}$, and $m\angle C = \frac{1}{2}m\widehat{DAB}$. By the Add. Prop.

of =, $m\angle A + m\angle C = \frac{1}{2}m\widehat{BCD} + \frac{1}{2}m\widehat{DAB}$. By the Distrib. Prop. of =, $\frac{1}{2}m\widehat{BCD} + \frac{1}{2}m\widehat{DAB} = \frac{1}{2}(m\widehat{BCD} + m\widehat{DAB})$. By the Trans. Prop. of =, $m\angle A + m\angle C = \frac{1}{2}(m\widehat{BCD} + m\widehat{DAB})$. $m\widehat{BCD} + m\widehat{DAB} = 360°$. By subst., $m\angle A + m\angle C = \frac{1}{2}(360°) = 180°$. Thus $\angle A$ and $\angle C$ are supp. A similar proof shows that $\angle B$ and $\angle D$ are supp.

11-5 *Exercises*

36.

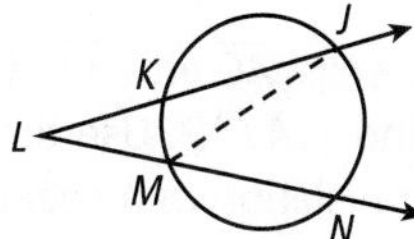

Since 2 pts. determine a line, draw $\overline{JM}$. By the Ext. $\angle$ Thm., $m\angle JMN = m\angle JLN + m\angle KJM$, so $m\angle JLN = m\angle JMN - m\angle KJM$. $m\angle JMN = \frac{1}{2}m\widehat{JN}$ and $m\angle KJM = \frac{1}{2}m\widehat{KM}$ by the Inscribed $\angle$ Thm. By subst., $m\angle JLN = \frac{1}{2}m\widehat{JN} - \frac{1}{2}m\widehat{KM}$. Thus by the Distrib. Prop., $m\angle JLN = \frac{1}{2}(m\widehat{JN} - m\widehat{KM})$.

38. The diagram shows that when a tangent and secant intersect on the ⊙, the measure of the $\angle$ formed is half the measure of the intercepted arc. When 2 secants intersect in the int. of the ⊙, the measure of each $\angle$ formed is half the sum of its intercepted arcs, or $\frac{1}{2}(90° + 90°)$. When 2 secants intersect in the ext. of the ⊙, the measure of the $\angle$ formed is half the difference of its intercepted arcs, or $\frac{1}{2}(270° - 90°)$.

45. Case 1: Assume $\overline{AB}$ is a diam. of the circle. Then $m\widehat{AB} = 180°$, and $\angle ABC$ is a rt. $\angle$. Thus $m\angle ABC = \frac{1}{2}m\widehat{AB}$. Case 2: Assume $\overline{AB}$ is not a diam. of the ⊙. Let X be the center of the ⊙ and draw radii $\overline{XA}$ and $\overline{XB}$. Since they are radii, $\overline{XA} \cong \overline{XB}$, so $\triangle AXB$ is isosceles. Thus $\angle XAB \cong \angle XBA$, and $2m\angle XBA + m\angle AXB = 180$. This means that $m\angle XBA = 90 - \frac{1}{2}m\angle AXB$. By Thm. 11-1-1, $\angle XBC$ is a rt. $\angle$, so $m\angle XBA + m\angle ABC = 90$ or $m\angle ABC = 90 - m\angle XBA$. By subst., $m\angle ABC = 90 - (90 - \frac{1}{2}m\angle AXB)$. Simplifying gives $m\angle ABC = \frac{1}{2}m\angle AXB$. $m\angle AXB = m\widehat{AB}$ because $\angle AXB$ is a central $\angle$. Thus $m\angle ABC = \frac{1}{2}m\widehat{AB}$.

46. Since $m\widehat{WY} = 90°$, $m\angle YXW = 90°$ because it is a central $\angle$. By Thm 11-1-1, $\angle XYZ$ and $\angle XWZ$ are rt. ∠s. The sum of the measures of the ∠s of a quad. is 360°, so $m\angle WZY = 90°$. Thus all 4 ∠s of $WXYZ$ are rt. ∠s, so $WXYZ$ is a rect. $\overline{XY} \cong \overline{XW}$ because they are radii. By Thm 6-5-3, $WXYZ$ is a rhombus. Since $WXYZ$ is both a rect. and a rhombus, it must also be a square by Thm. 6-5-6.

11-6 *Exercises*

31. Method 1: By the Secant-Tangent Product Thm., $BC^2 = 12 \cdot 4$ and so $BC = \sqrt{48} = 4\sqrt{3}$. Method 2: By Thm. 11-1-1, $\angle ABC$ is a rt. $\angle$. By the Pyth. Thm., $BC^2 + 4^2 = 8^2$. Thus $BC^2 = 64 - 16 = 48$ and $BC = 4\sqrt{3}$.

11-7 *Check It Out!*

2a.

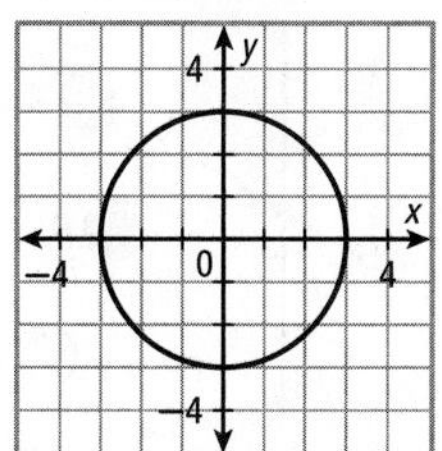

2b.

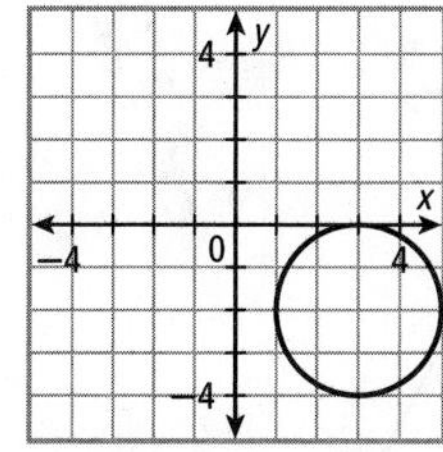

Chapter 11 Extension Check It Out!

4.

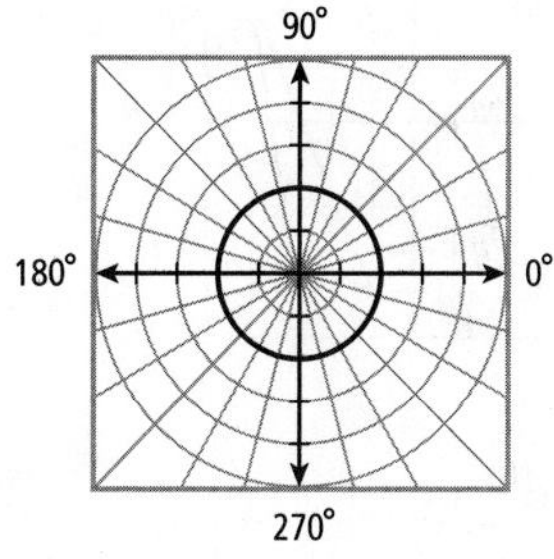

Chapter 11 Extension Exercises

9–12.

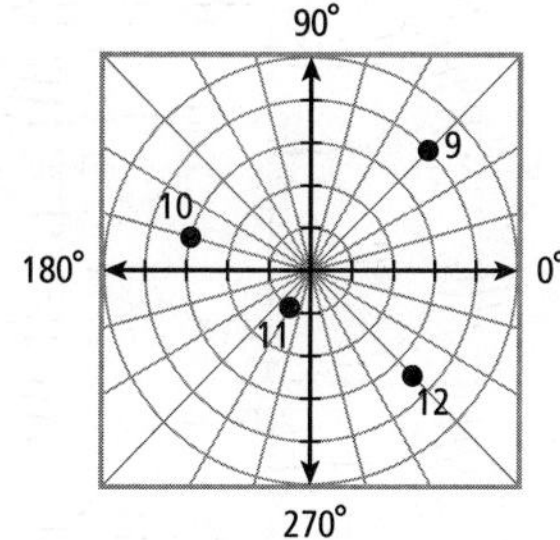

13.

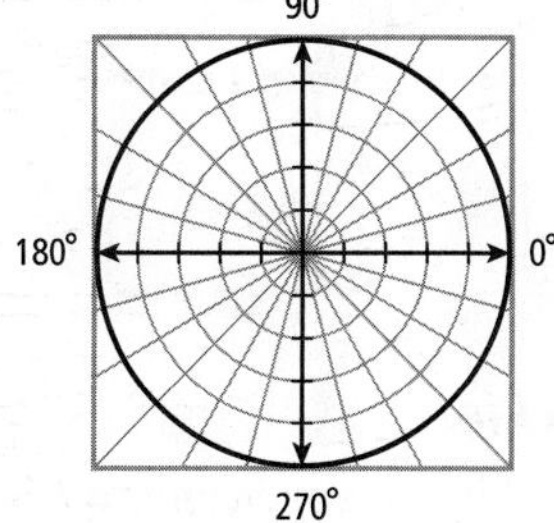

14.

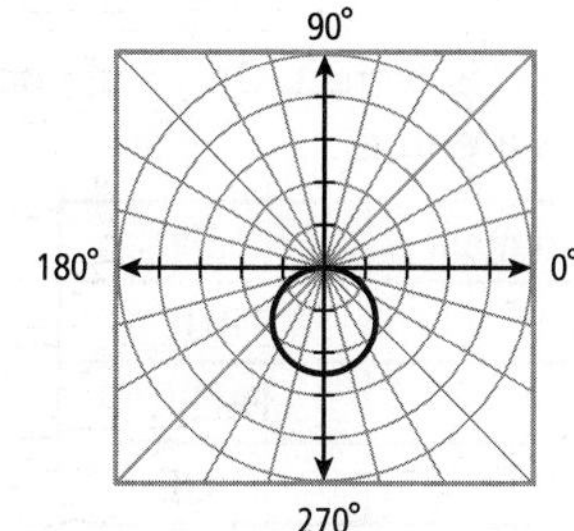

15.

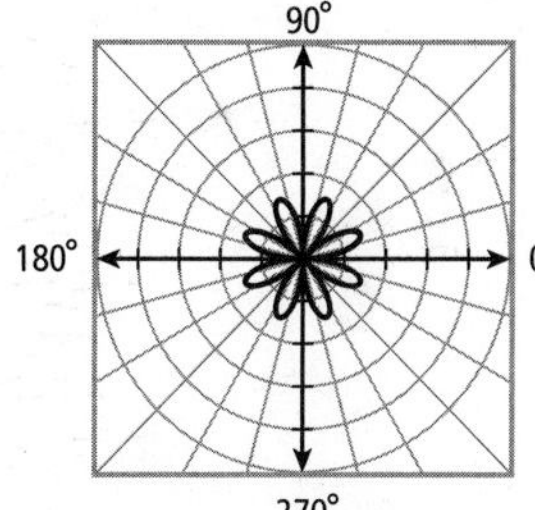

16.

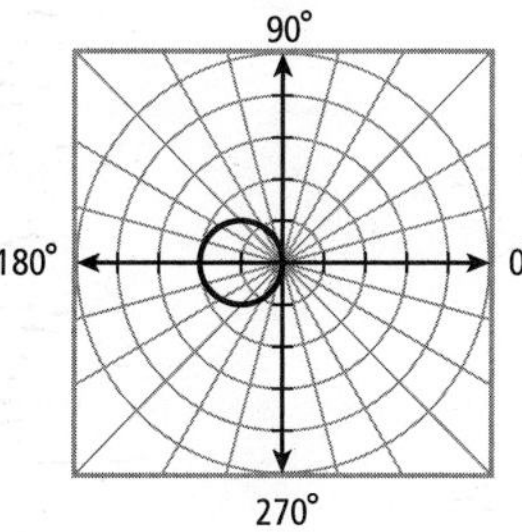

17.

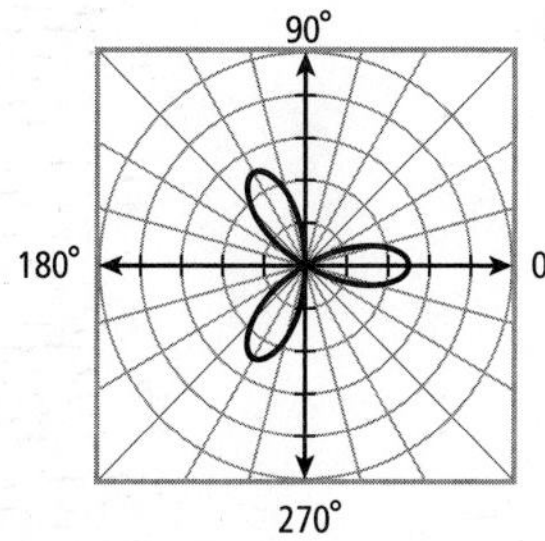

Additional Answers

18.

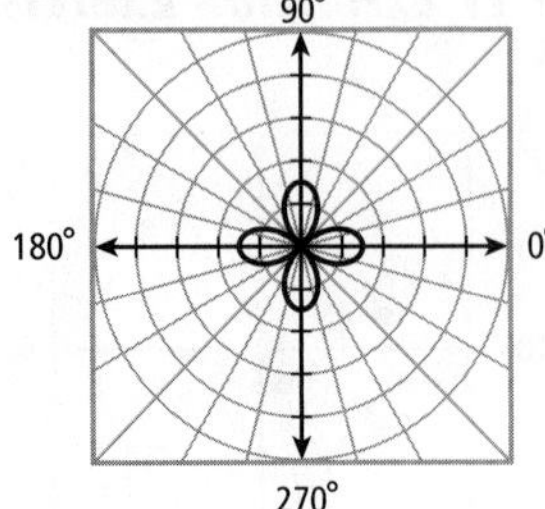

19.

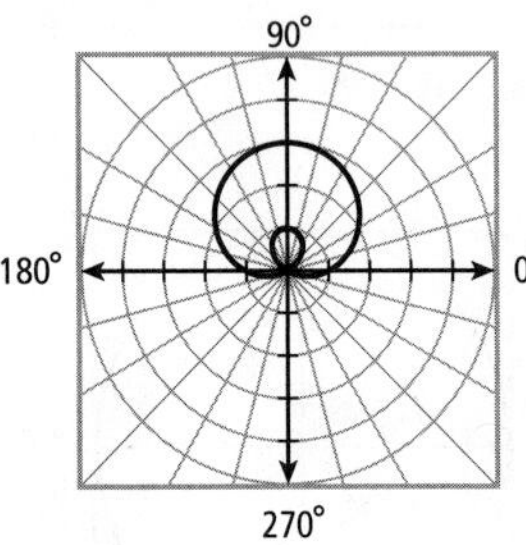

Test Tackler

12. False; it is not equivalent to $L = \frac{M}{360}(2\pi r)$ when $M = 85°$ and $r = 12$.

13. Choice C is correct. Only statements I and II are true.

14.

Statement	True/False
I	TRUE
II	FALSE
III	TRUE

15. J

Chapter 12

Are You Ready?

5–10.

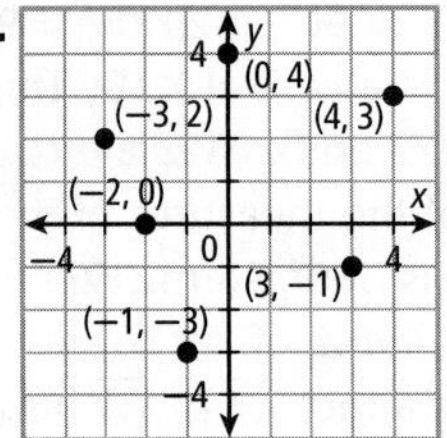

12. Yes; $\angle DEG \cong \angle FGE$ and $\angle DGE \cong \angle FEG$ By the Alt. Int. $\angle$s Thm. Also, $\overline{GE} \cong \overline{GE}$ by the Reflex. Prop. of $\cong$. So the $\triangle$s are $\cong$ by ASA.

13. Yes; $\frac{JK}{JM} = \frac{JL}{JN}$ and $\angle J \cong \angle J$, so the $\triangle$s are similar by the SAS Similarity Thm.

14. Yes; corr. $\angle$s are $\cong$ (all $\angle$s of rectangles are rt. $\angle$s), and corr. sides are proportional $\left(\frac{PQ}{UV} = \frac{QR}{VW} = \frac{RS}{WX} = \frac{SP}{XU} = 2\right)$.

12-1 *Exercises*

19.

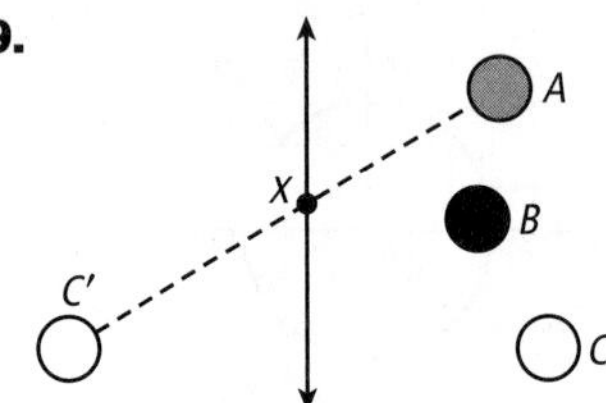

12-2 *Exercises*

6.

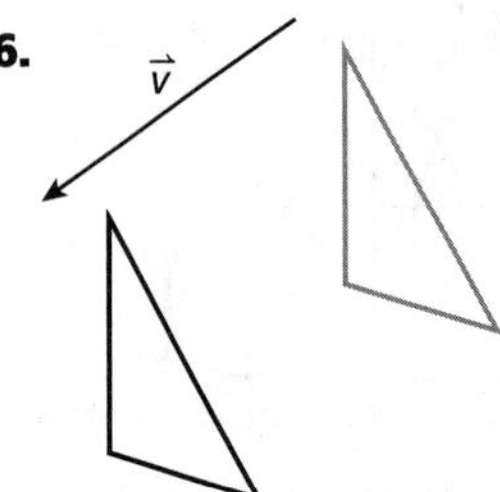

7.

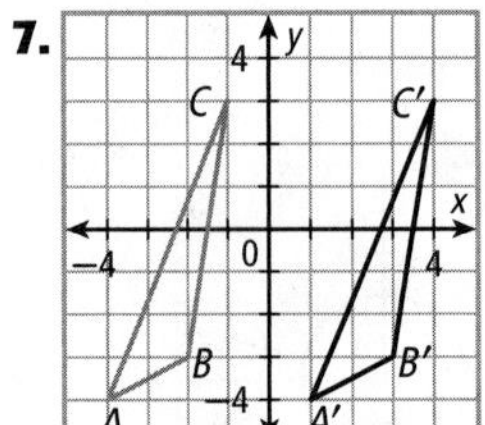

8.

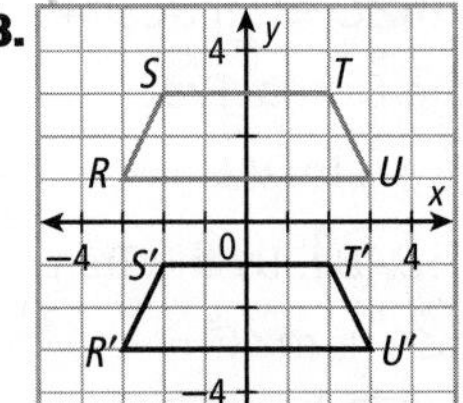

9.

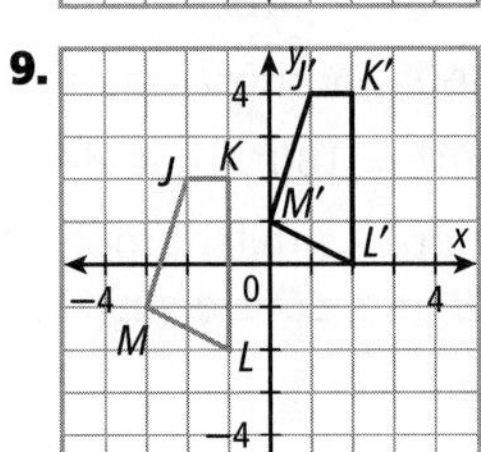

46. Draw auxiliary segs. $\overline{AC}$ and $\overline{A'C'}$ to form $\triangle ABC$ and $\triangle A'B'C'$. Use the fact that the translation of a seg. is $\cong$ to the preimage to prove $\triangle ABC \cong \triangle A'B'C'$ by SSS. By CPCTC, $\angle ABC \cong \angle A'B'C'$, so $m\angle ABC = m\angle A'B'C'$ by def. of $\cong$ $\angle$s.

49. If A, B, and C are collinear, then one point is between the other two. Case 1: If C is between A and B, then $AC + BC = AB$. Use the fact that the translation of a seg. is $\cong$ to the preimage to prove $A'C' + B'C' = A'B'$. Then C' is between A' and B', so A', B', and C' are collinear. Prove the other two cases similarly.

50. $\left(-2, -\frac{7}{2}\right)$

55. $M'(-2, 0)$, $N'(-3, -2)$, $P'(0, -4)$

56. $M'(2, 0)$, $N'(3, 2)$, $P'(0, 4)$

57. $M'(0, -2)$, $N'(2, -3)$, $P'(4, 0)$

12-3 *Exercises*

8.

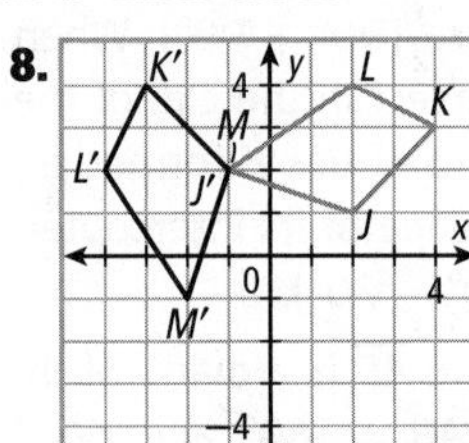

9.

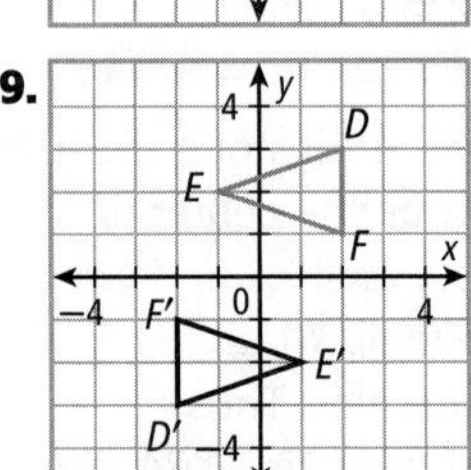

10.

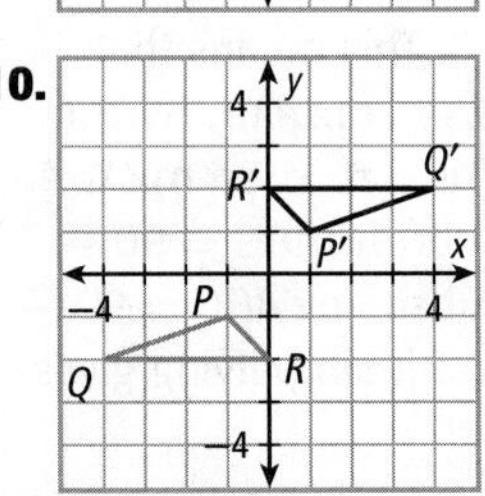

46. Draw auxiliary segs. $\overline{AP}$, $\overline{BP}$, $\overline{A'P}$, and $\overline{B'P}$. By the definition of rotation, $\overline{AP} \cong \overline{A'P}$ and $\overline{BP} \cong \overline{B'P}$. Also by the definition of rotation, $\angle A'PA \cong \angle B'PB$. By the Common Angle Theorem, $\angle B'PA' \cong \angle BPA$. Thus, $\triangle B'PA' \cong \triangle BPA$ by SAS, and $\overline{AB} \cong \overline{A'B'}$ by CPCTC.

48. Draw auxiliary segs. $\overline{AC}$ and $\overline{A'C'}$ to form $\triangle ABC$ and $\triangle A'B'C'$. Use the fact that the rotation of a seg. is ≅ to the preimage to prove $\triangle ABC \cong \triangle A'B'C'$ by SSS. By CPCTC, $\angle ABC \cong \angle A'B'C'$, so $m\angle ABC = m\angle A'B'C'$ by def. of ≅ ⦞.

50. If C is between A and B, then $AC + BC = AB$. Use the fact that the rotation of a seg. is ≅ to the preimage to prove $A'C' + B'C' = A'B'$. Then use the def. of betweenness to prove C' is between A' and B'.

51. If A, B, and C are collinear, then one point is between the other two. Case 1: If C is between A and B, then $AC + BC = AB$. Use the fact that the rotation of a seg. is ≅ to the preimage to prove $A'C' + B'C' = A'B'$. Then C' is between A' and B', so A', B', and C' are collinear. Prove the other two cases similarly.

12-4 *Exercises*

20. The order matters, as shown in the figures.

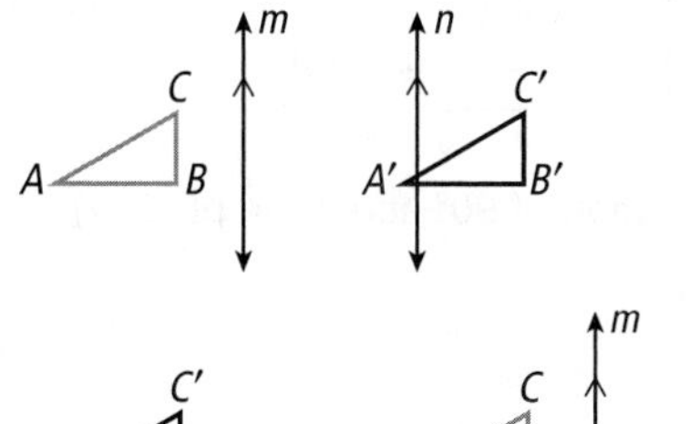

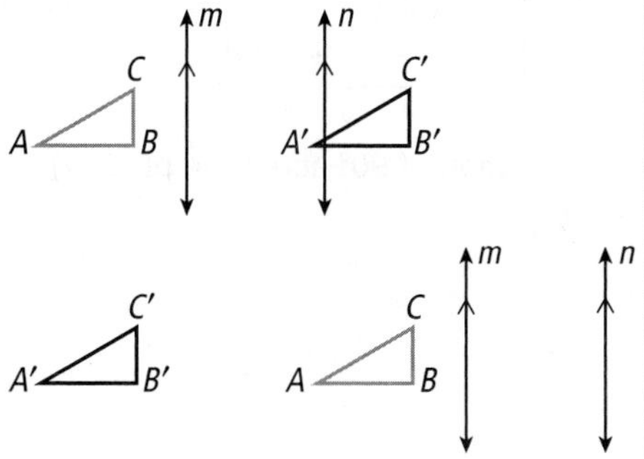

27. Possible answer: Reflect $\triangle MNP$ across a horizontal line ℓ. $\triangle M'N'P'$ is a translation of this image. This means there are two parallel lines such that the composition of the reflections across the lines is equivalent to the translation. Those lines can be found as shown in the figure.

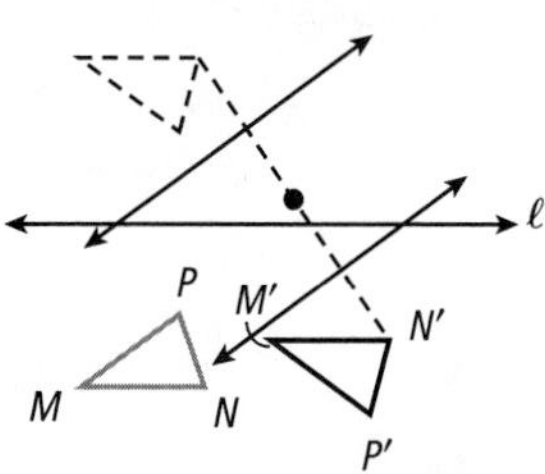

12A *Ready To Go On?*

7.

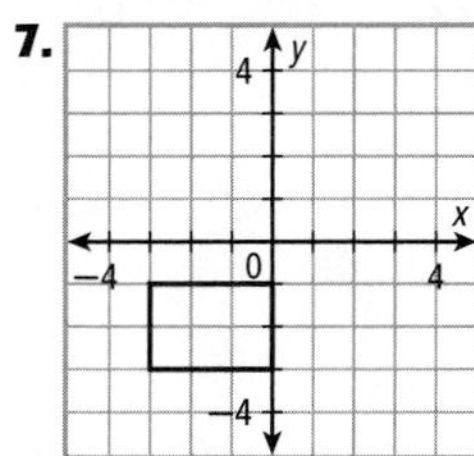

10.

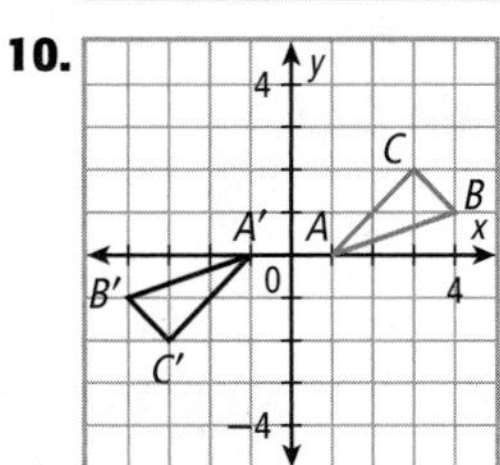

11.

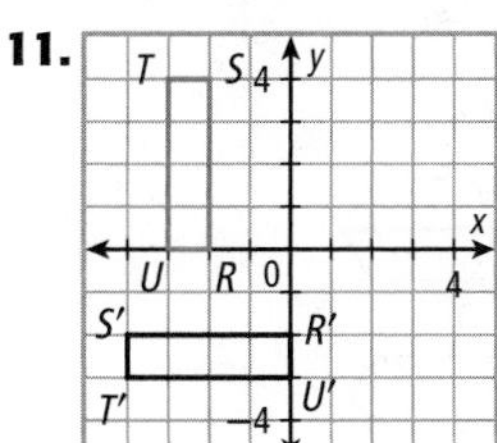

12.

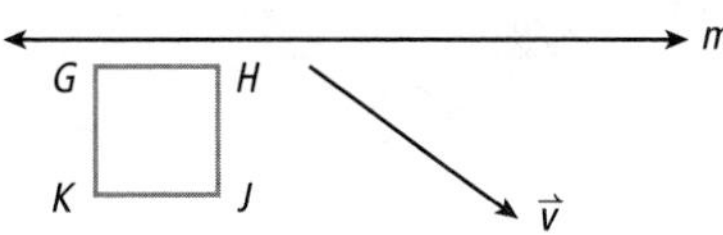

12-5 *Exercises*

29.

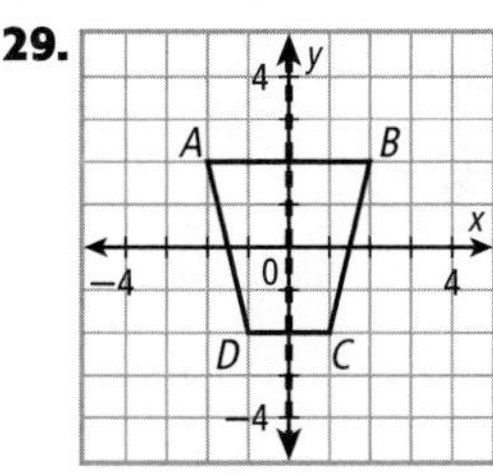

30.

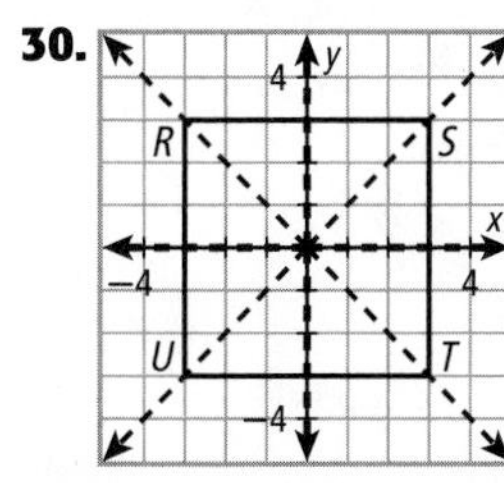

31.

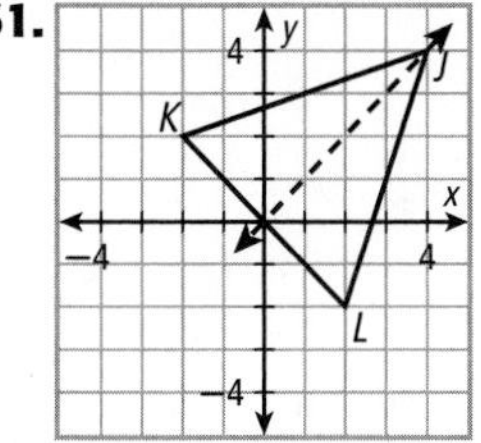

32.

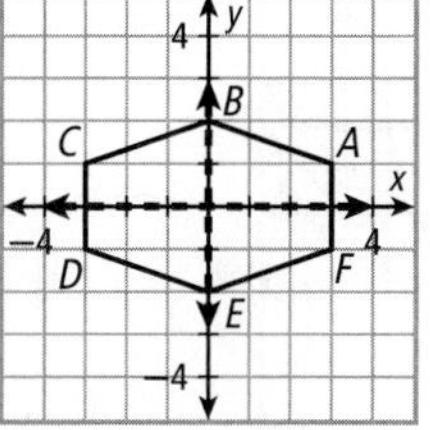

12-6 *Exercises*

3. translation symmetry and glide reflection symmetry

4. translation symmetry and glide reflection symmetry

5. translation symmetry and glide reflection symmetry

6.

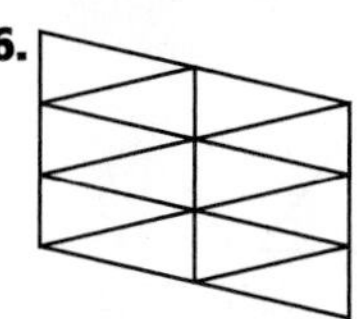

7.

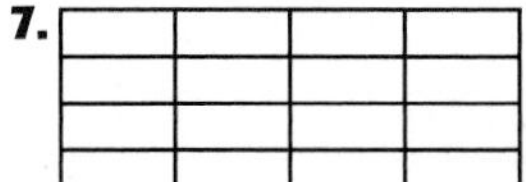

8.

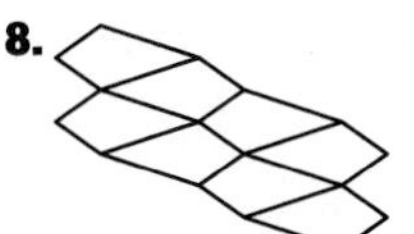

13. Possible answer:

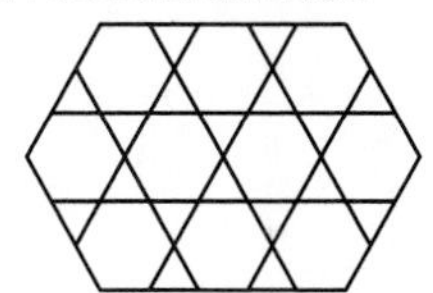

12-7 *Exercises*

9.

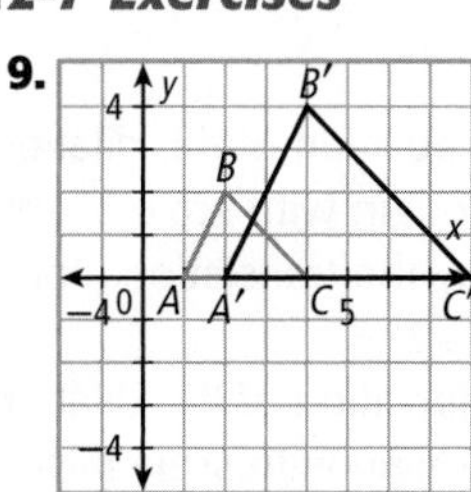

10.

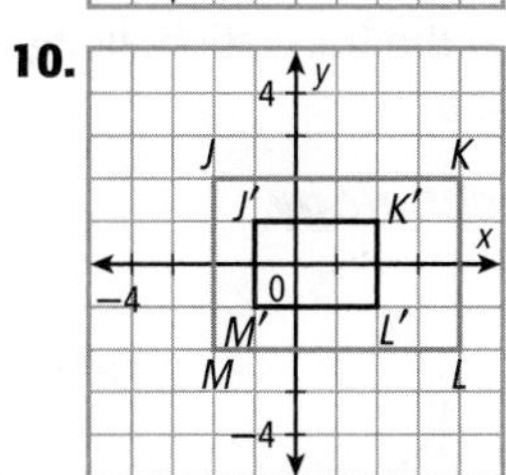

11.

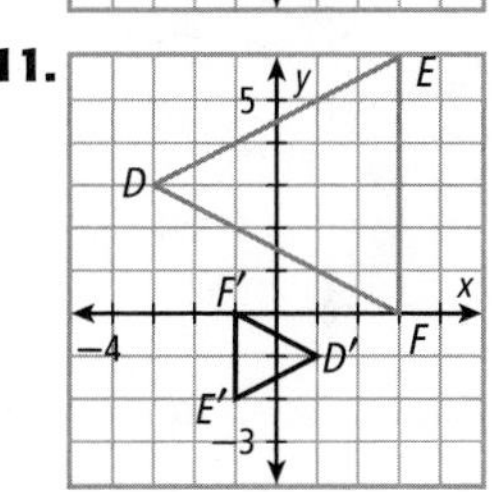

Additional Answers

12.
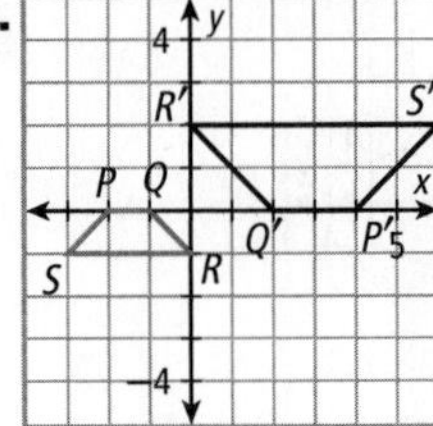

23.
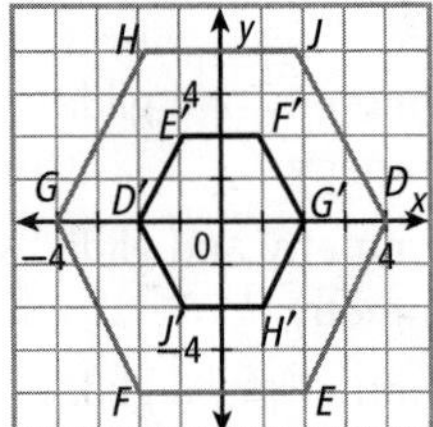

27.
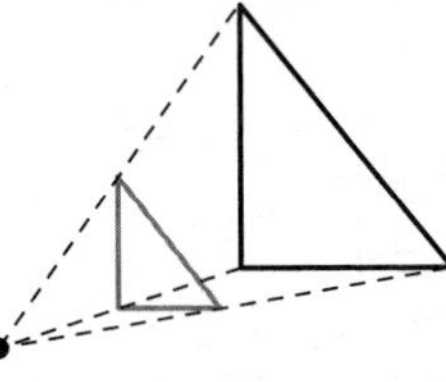

28.
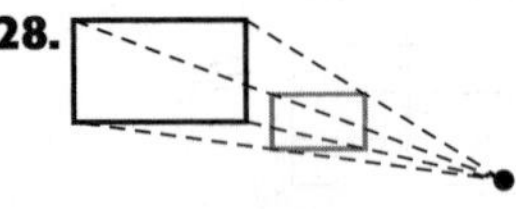

29.
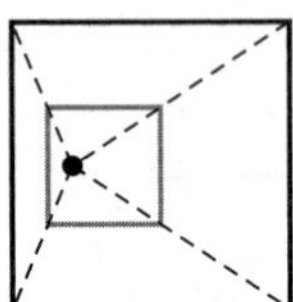

50a.
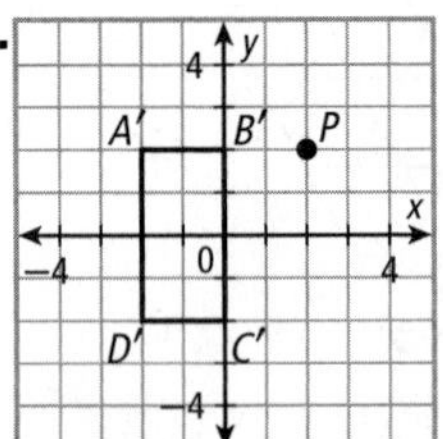

b. It is the composition of the dilation centered at origin with scale factor 2 followed by the translation along vector $\langle -2, -2 \rangle$.

c. It is the composition of the dilation centered at origin with scale factor k followed by the translation along vector $\langle -a, -b \rangle$.

12-7 *Using Technology*

2. $\begin{bmatrix} 6 & 10 & 2 \\ 8 & 4 & 2 \end{bmatrix}$

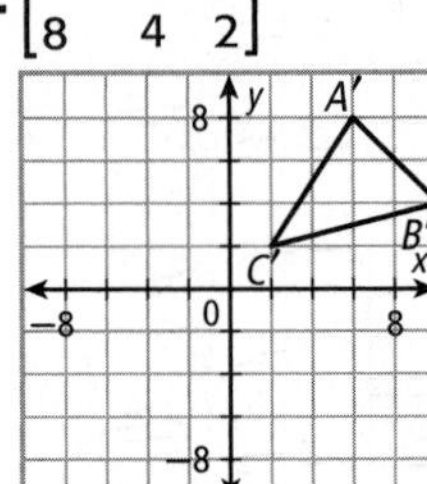

3. $\begin{bmatrix} -\frac{1}{2} & 0 \\ 0 & -\frac{1}{2} \end{bmatrix}$

4. $[A]*[B] = \begin{bmatrix} -1.5 & -2.5 & -0.5 \\ -2 & -1 & -0.5 \end{bmatrix}$

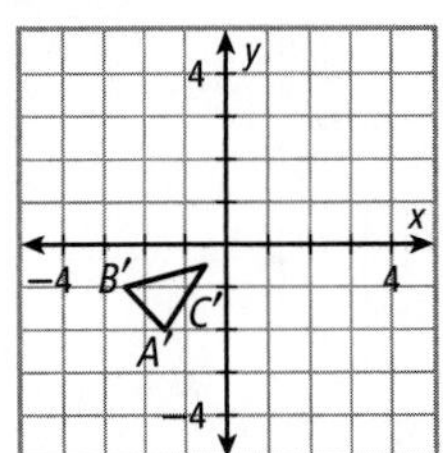

12B *Ready To Go On?*

7.

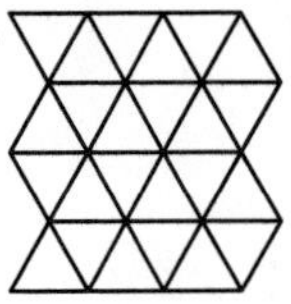

8.
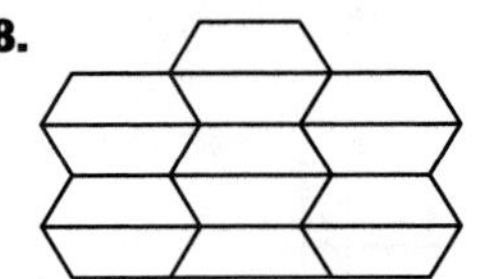

9.
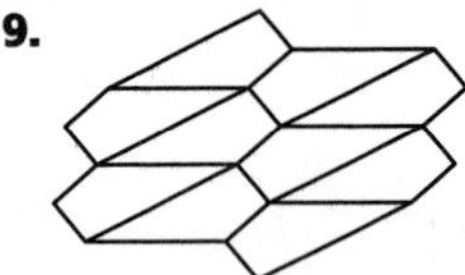

17.
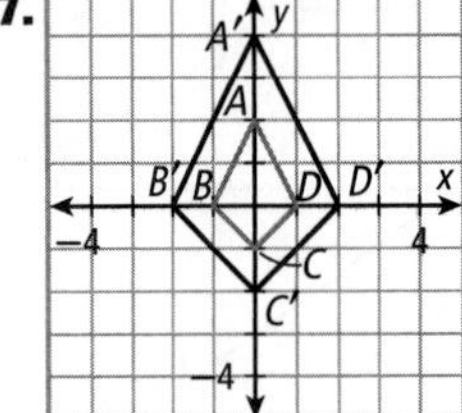

18.
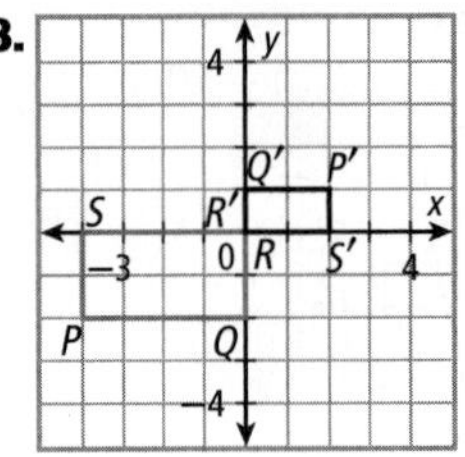

Extra Practice

Chapter 1 Skills

7. A B

8.
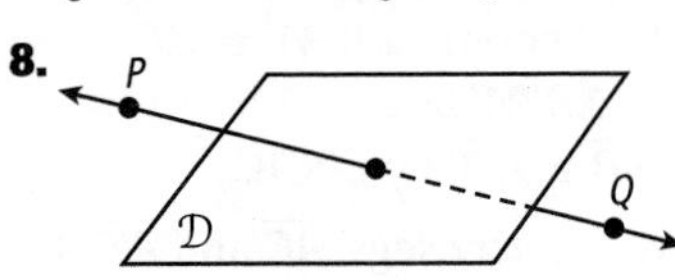

28. $P = 9y + 10$; $A = 30y$

29. $P = 5.8$ cm; $A = 2.1025$ cm^2

30. $P = 4n + 2$; $A = 6n - 6$

31. $C = 8.17$ ft; $A = 5.31$ ft^2

32. $C = 25.13$ m; $A = 50.27$ m^2

33. $C = 38.33$ in.; $A = 116.90$ in.^{2}

34. $M\left(\frac{x_1 + x_2}{2}, \frac{y_1 + y_2}{2}\right)$

41. translation; pentagon $ABCDE \rightarrow$ pentagon $A'B'C'D'E'$

42.
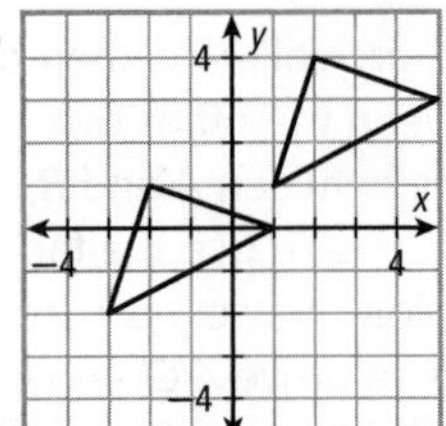

translation to the left 4 and down 3

43.
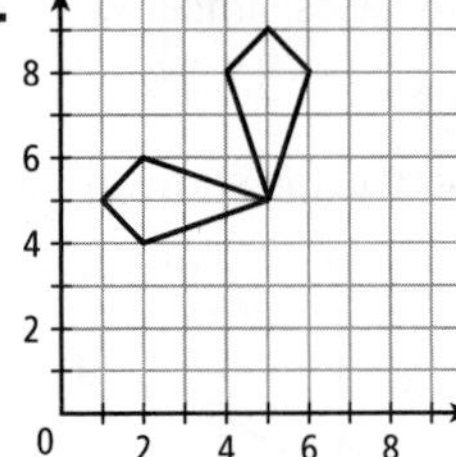

rotation of 90° about the pt.(5, 5)

44.

(3, 0), (2, −3), (−3, −2), and (−2, 1); reflection across the *x*-axis

Chapter 2 Skills

16. Cond.: If a triangle is equil., then it has 3 ≅ sides. Conv.: If a triangle has 3 ≅ sides, then it is equil.

17. Conv.: If a triangle's sides have different lengths, then it is scalene. Bicond.: A triangle is scalene if and only if its sides have different lengths.

21. $2x + 3 = 9$ (Given); $2x = 6$ (Subtr. Prop. of =); $x = 3$ (Div. Prop. of =)

25. **1.** $\overline{AB} \cong \overline{CD}$, $\overline{CD} \cong \overline{EF}$ (Given)
2. $AB = CD$, $CD = EF$ (Def. of ≅ segs.)
3. $AB = EF$ (Trans. Prop. of =)
4. $\overline{AB} = \overline{EF}$ (Def. of ≅ segs.)

26.

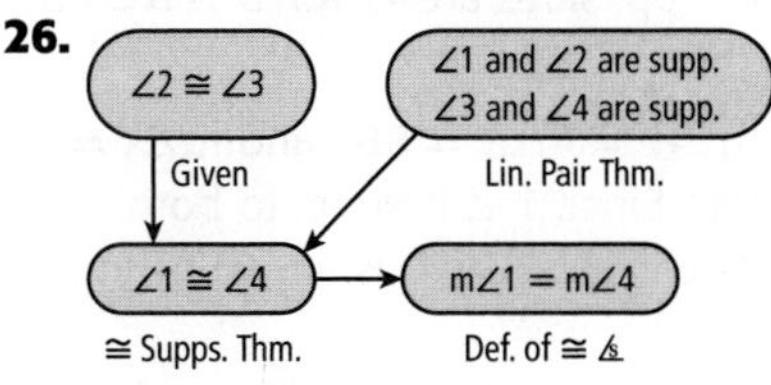

Chapter 3 Skills

14. $m\angle 8 = 5(4) + 36 = 56°$ and $m\angle 6 = 11(4) + 12 = 56°$, so $\ell \parallel m$ by Conv. of Corr. ∠s Post.

16. $m\angle 2 = 9(9) + 31 = 112°$, $m\angle 3 = 6(9) + 14 = 68°$, and $m\angle 2 + m\angle 3 = 112 + 68 = 180°$, so $p \parallel q$ by the Conv. of Same-Side Int. ∠s Thm.

17. **1.** ∠1 and ∠5 are supp. (Given)
2. $m\angle 1 + m\angle 5 = 180°$ (Def. of supp. ∠s)
3. $\angle 1 \cong \angle 3$ (Vert. ∠s Thm.)
4. $m\angle 1 = m\angle 3$ (Def. ≅ ∠s)
5. $m\angle 3 + m\angle 5 = 180°$ (Subst. Prop. of =)
6. $\ell \parallel m$ (Conv. of Same-Side Int. ∠s Thm.)

22. **1.** $\ell \perp p$ (Given)
2. $m \perp p$ (Given)
3. $\ell \parallel m$ (⊥ Trans. Thm.)

25.

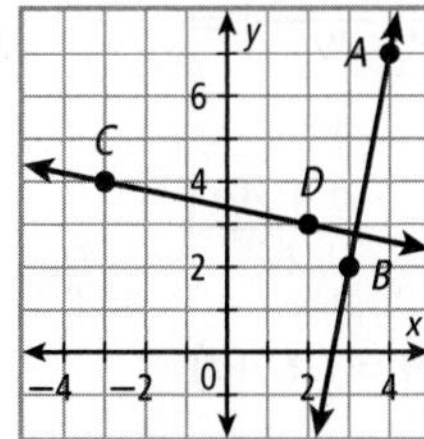

26.

27.

31.

32.

33.

34.

Chapter 4 Skills

16. **1.** $\overline{AD}$ is the ⊥ bisector of $\overline{BC}$. (Given)
2. ∠BDA and ∠CDA are rt. ∠s. (Def. of ⊥)
3. $\angle BDA \cong \angle CDA$ (Rt. ∠s are ≅.)
4. $\overline{BD} \cong \overline{CD}$ (Def. of bisector)
5. $\overline{AD}$ is the bisector of ∠BAC. (Given)
6. $\angle BAD \cong \angle CAD$ (Def. of bisector)
7. $\overline{AB} \cong \overline{AC}$ (Given)
8. $\angle B \cong \angle C$ (Given)
9. $\overline{AD} \cong \overline{AD}$ (Reflex. Prop. of ≅)
10. $\triangle BAD \cong \triangle CAD$ (Def. of ≅ △s)

17. It is given that $\overline{SQ} \cong \overline{TQ}$ and $\overline{SR} \cong \overline{TR}$. By the Reflex. Prop. of ≅, $\overline{QR} \cong \overline{QR}$. Therefore $\triangle QRS \cong \triangle QRT$ by SSS.

18. It is given that $\overline{UV} \cong \overline{WX}$ and $\overline{UX} \cong \overline{WV}$. By the Reflex. Prop. of ≅, $\overline{UW} \cong \overline{UW}$. Therefore $\triangle UVW \cong \triangle WXU$ by SSS.

19. $AC = 2x - 3 = 2(4) - 3 = 5$, $AB = 5x - 8 = 5(4) - 8 = 12$, $CB = 6x - 9 = 6(4) - 9 = 15$, $\overline{AC} \cong \overline{XZ}$, $\overline{AB} \cong \overline{XY}$, $\overline{CB} \cong \overline{ZY}$. So $\triangle XYZ \cong \triangle ABC$ by SSS.

20. $m\angle EFG = 12y - 6 = 12(8) - 6 = 90$, $DE = 5y - 3 = 5(8) - 3 = 37$, $GF = 3y + 13 = 3(8) + 13 = 37$, $\overline{DE} \cong \overline{GF}$, $\angle EFG \cong \angle FED$ and $\overline{EF} \cong \overline{FE}$ by the Reflex. Prop. of ≅. So $\triangle DEF \cong \triangle GFE$ by SAS.

21. **1.** K is the mdpt. of $\overline{HL}$ and $\overline{MJ}$. (Given)
2. $\overline{HK} \cong \overline{LK}$ (Def. of mdpt.)
3. $\overline{JK} \cong \overline{MK}$ (Def. of mdpt.)
4. $\angle HKJ \cong \angle LKM$ (Vert. ∠s are ≅.)
5. $\triangle HJK \cong \triangle LMK$ (SAS *Steps 2, 4, and 3*)

22. No; you need to show $\angle ACB \cong \angle ACD$ in order to use ASA.

23. Yes; $\angle EFG \cong \angle HGF$, $\overline{FG} \cong \overline{FG}$, and $\angle EGF \cong \angle HFG$.

24. No; neither a leg nor the hyp. can be shown ≅.

25. Yes; it is given that $\overline{FG} \cong \overline{FJ}$. From the diagram △FGH and △FJH are rt. △s. $\overline{FH} \cong \overline{FH}$ by the Reflex. Prop. of ≅. Therefore $\triangle FGH \cong \triangle FJH$ by HL.

26. **1.** $\overline{MN} \parallel \overline{LP}$ (Given)
2. $\angle N \cong \angle L$ (Given)
3. $\angle NMP \cong \angle LPM$ (Alt. Int. ∠s Thm.)
4. $\overline{MP} \cong \overline{PM}$ (Reflex. Prop. of ≅)
5. $\triangle MLP \cong \triangle PNM$ (AAS *Steps 2, 3, and 4*)
6. $\overline{ML} \cong \overline{PN}$ (CPCTC)

27. 1. $\angle 1 \cong \angle 6$ (Given)
2. $\angle 4 \cong \angle 6$ (Given)
3. $\angle 1 \cong \angle 3$ (Given)
4. $\overline{AB} \cong \overline{AE}$ (Given)
5. $\overline{AB} \cong \overline{AC}$ (Isosc. △ Thm.)
6. $\overline{AE} \cong \overline{AC}$ (Trans. Prop of ≅)
7. $\overline{AE} \cong \overline{AD}$ (Isosc. △ Thm.)
8. $\overline{AD} \cong \overline{AC}$ (Trans. Prop of ≅)
9. $\triangle ACD$ is isosc. (Def. of isos. △)

28. $AB = \sqrt{(3-2)^2 + (1-4)^2}$
$= \sqrt{1+9} = \sqrt{10},$
$BC = \sqrt{(5-3)^2 + (2-1)^2}$
$= \sqrt{4+1} = \sqrt{5}$
$AC = \sqrt{(5-2)^2 + (2-4)^2}$
$= \sqrt{9+4} = \sqrt{13}$
$DE = \sqrt{(-1-(-4))^2 + (-3-(-2))^2}$
$= \sqrt{9+1} = \sqrt{10}$
$EF = \sqrt{(-2-(-1))^2 + (-5-(-3))^2}$
$= \sqrt{1+4} = \sqrt{5}$
$DF = \sqrt{(-2-(-4))^2 + (-5-(-2))^2}$
$= \sqrt{4+9} = \sqrt{13}$
So $\overline{AB} \cong \overline{DE}$, $\overline{BC} \cong \overline{EF}$, and $\overline{AC} \cong \overline{DF}$. Therefore $\triangle ABC \cong \triangle DEF$ by SSS, and $\angle BAC \cong \angle EDF$ by CPCTC.

29.

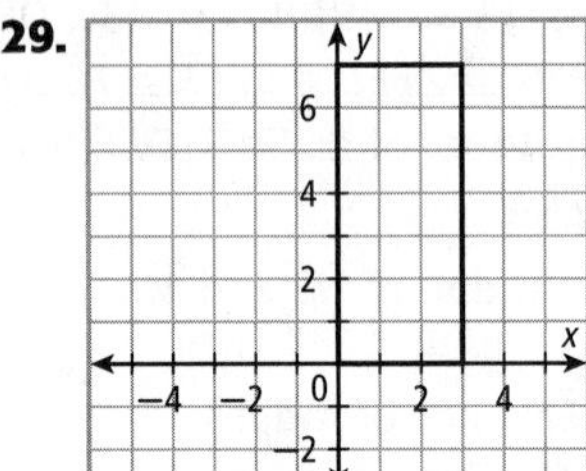

30.

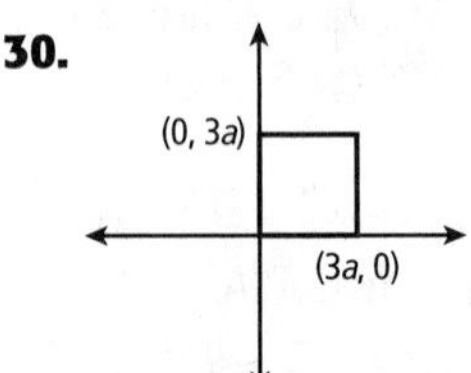

31. $\triangle GHI$ is a rt. △ with height HG and base GI. J is the mdpt. of $\overline{GH}$ with coords. $(0, 2)$. K is the mdpt. of $\overline{GI}$ with coords. $(3, 0)$. The area of $\triangle GHI = \frac{1}{2}(6)(4) = 12$. The area of $\triangle GJK = \frac{1}{2}(3)(2) = 3$. Since $3 = \frac{1}{4}(12)$, the are a of $\triangle GJK$ is $\frac{1}{4}$ the area of $\triangle GHI$.

32. The coords. are $W(0, 0)$, $X(2a, 0)$, $Z(0, 4a)$, $Y(2a, 4a)$. Using the Mdpt. Formula,
$A = \left(\frac{0+2a}{2}, \frac{0+0}{2}\right) = \left(\frac{2a}{2}, 0\right)$
$= (a, 0),$
$B = \left(\frac{0+2a}{2}, \frac{4a+4a}{2}\right)$
$= \left(\frac{2a}{2}, \frac{8a}{2}\right) = (a, 4a)$
Using the Dist. Formula,
$AB = \sqrt{(a-a)^2 + (0-4a)^2}$
$= \sqrt{0 + 16a^2} = \sqrt{16a^2} = 4a,$
$XY = \sqrt{(2a-2a)^2 + (0-4a)^2}$
$= \sqrt{0 + 16a^2} = \sqrt{16a^2} = 4a.$
Therefore $AB = XY$.

37. Assign coordinates $Y(0, 0)$, $X(0, 4a)$, and $Z(4a, 0)$. By the Mdpt. Formula, $A = \left(\frac{4a+0}{2}, \frac{0+4a}{2}\right) = (2a, 2a)$.
By the Dist. Formula,
$YA = \sqrt{(0-2a)^2 + (0-2a)^2}$
$= \sqrt{4a^2 + 4a^2} = \sqrt{8a^2},$
$AZ = \sqrt{(4a-2a)^2 + (0-2a)^2}$
$= \sqrt{4a^2 + 4a^2} = \sqrt{8a^2}$. Since $YA = AZ$, $\overline{YA} \cong \overline{AZ}$ by def. So $\triangle YAZ$ is isosc.

Chapter 5 Skills

20. The slope of $\overline{WX} = 0$, and the slope of $\overline{AB} = 0$, so $\overline{AB} \parallel \overline{WX}$. $WX = 8$ and $AB = 4$, so $AB = \frac{1}{2}WX$.

27. Given: $\triangle ABC$ is isosc. with $\overline{AB} \cong \overline{BC}$.
Prove: $\angle A$ is not obtuse.
Proof: Assume that $\angle A$ is obtuse, so $m\angle A > 90°$. Since the base ∠s of an isosc. △ are ≅, $m\angle C > 90°$. Adding these expressions, it follows that $m\angle A + m\angle C > 180°$. But this contradicts the fact that $m\angle A + m\angle B + m\angle C = 180°$ by the △ Sum Thm. So $\angle A$ is not obtuse.

28. Given: $\triangle ABC$ is a rt. △ with $\angle B$ a rt.∠.
Prove: $\triangle ABC$ does not have 3 ≅ sides.
Proof: Assume all 3 sides of $\triangle ABC$ are ≅. Then by def., $\triangle ABC$ is equil. It follows that $\triangle ABC$ is equiangular. But this means that $m\angle B = 60°$, which contradicts the given information that $\angle B$ is a rt.∠. Therefore a rt. △ cannot have 3 ≅ sides.

31. Yes; the sum of each pair of lengths is greater than the third length.

32. No; $7 + 9 = 16$, which is not greater than the third length.

33. No; when $x = 3$, the 3 lengths are 11, 12, and 27. But $11 + 12 = 23$, and $23 < 27$.

34. between 6 in. and 14 in.

35. between 0 ft and 16 ft

36. between 5.8 cm and 18.2 cm

40. 1. $m\angle X > m\angle Y$, $m\angle B > m\angle A$ (Given)
2. $AZ > ZB$, $ZY > XZ$ (In △, longer side is opp. larger ∠.)
3. $AZ + ZY > ZB + XZ$ (If $a > b$ and $c > d$, then $a + c > b + d$.)
4. $AZ + ZY = AY$, $ZB + XZ = XB$ (Seg. Add. Post.)
5. $AY > XB$ (Subst.)

Chapter 6 Skills

7. $m\angle A = 159°$; $m\angle B = 73°$; $m\angle C = 111°$; $m\angle D = 91°$; $m\angle E = 106°$

17. $ABFG$ and $HDEG$ are ▱s. (Given); $\angle B \cong \angle G$ (▱ → opp. ∠s ≅); $\angle G \cong \angle D$ (▱ → opp. ∠s ≅); $\angle B \cong \angle D$ (Trans. Prop. of ≅)

18. $RS = UT = 27$, so $\overline{RS} \cong \overline{UT}$. $UR = TS = 11$, so $\overline{UR} \cong \overline{TS}$. Since both pairs of opp. sides are ≅, $RSTU$ is a ▱ by Thm. 6-3-2.

19. $m\angle W = m\angle Y = 86°$, and $m\angle X = 94°$. Since 1 ∠ is supp. to both of its cons. ∠s, $WXYZ$ is a ▱ by Thm. 6-3-4.

20. No; 1 pair of opp. sides and 1 pair of opp. ∠s are ≅. None of the sets of conditions for a ▱ are met.

21. Yes; possible answer: 1 pair of opp. sides is ∥ and ≅, so the quad. is a ▱ by Thm. 6-3-1.

22. Yes; possible answer: both pairs of opp. ∠s are ≅, so the quad. is a ▱ by Thm. 6-3-2.

23. Possible answer: slope of $\overline{WX}$ = slope of $\overline{YZ} = -1$; slope of $\overline{WZ}$ = slope of $\overline{XY} = \frac{1}{4}$. Both pairs of opp. sides have the same slope, so $\overline{WX} \parallel \overline{YZ}$ and $\overline{WZ} \parallel \overline{XY}$; by def., $WXYZ$ is a ▱.

24. Possible answer: slope of $\overline{AB}$ = slope of $\overline{CD} = 3$; $\overline{AB}$ and $\overline{CD}$ have the same slope, so $\overline{AB} \parallel \overline{CD}$; $AB = CD = \sqrt{10}$; 1 pair of opp. sides are ∥ and ≅; by Thm. 6-3-1, $PQRS$ is a ▱.

29. $NQ = PR = 6$, so $\overline{NQ} \cong \overline{PR}$. Slope of $\overline{NQ} = \frac{-6}{0}$, and slope of $\overline{PR} = 0$.

Since $\overline{NQ}$ is vertical and $\overline{PR}$ is horizontal, $\overline{NQ} \perp \overline{PR}$. The coordinates of the mdpt. of $\overline{NQ}$ and $\overline{PR}$ are $(1, 1)$, so $\overline{NQ}$ and $\overline{PR}$ bisect each other. So the diags. of $NPQR$ are $\cong$ $\perp$ bisectors of each other.

30. $SU = TV = \sqrt{34}$, so $\overline{SU} \cong \overline{TV}$. Slope of $\overline{SU} = -\frac{3}{5}$, and slope of $TV = \frac{5}{3}$, so $\overline{SU} \perp \overline{TV}$. The coordinates of the mdpt. of $\overline{SU}$ and $\overline{TV}$ are $\left(\frac{1}{2}, 5\frac{1}{2}\right)$, so $\overline{SU}$ and $\overline{TV}$ bisect each other. So the diags. of $STUV$ are $\cong$ $\perp$ bisectors of each other.

31. $WXYZ$ is a rect. (Given); $WXYZ$ is a ▱. (Rect. → ▱); $\overline{WX} \cong \overline{YZ}$ (▱ → opp. sides $\cong$); $\angle X$ and $\angle Z$ are rt. ∠s. (Def. of rect.); $\angle X \cong \angle Z$ (Rt. $\angle \cong$ Thm.); $\overline{XB} \cong \overline{AZ}$ (Given); $\triangle WXB \cong \triangle YZA$ (SAS); $\overline{WB} \cong \overline{YA}$ (CPCTC)

33. Not valid; it cannot be shown that $WXYZ$ is a ▱, so it cannot be shown that $WXYZ$ is a square.

34. Not valid; by Thm. 6-5-1, a ▱ with 1 rt. ∠ is a rect., but to apply this thm., you must first know that $WXYZ$ is a ▱.

Chapter 7 Skills

11. $\angle J \cong \angle L$, $\angle G \cong \angle M$, $\angle H \cong \angle N$, $\angle I \cong \angle K$; $\frac{JG}{LM} = \frac{GH}{MN} = \frac{HI}{NK} = \frac{JI}{LK}$

14. Since $\overline{AC} \perp \overline{DC}$, $\angle C$ is a rt. ∠. Since $\overline{CA} \perp \overline{BA}$, $\angle A$ is a rt. ∠. By the Rt. $\angle \cong$ Thm., $\angle C \cong \angle A$. Since $\overline{DA} \parallel \overline{CB}$, $\angle DAC \cong \angle BCA$ by the Alt. Int. ∠s Thm. Therefore $\triangle ADC \sim \triangle CBA$ by the AA ~ Post.

15. Since $\overline{RU} \perp \overline{QU}$, $\angle U$ is a rt. ∠. Since $\overline{ST} \perp \overline{QT}$, $\angle T$ is a rt. ∠. By the Rt. $\angle \cong$ Thm., $\angle U \cong \angle T$. The △s share $\angle Q$. Therefore $\triangle QRU \sim \triangle QST$ by the AA ~ Postulate.

16. $\frac{FG}{JK} = \frac{17}{8.5} = \frac{2}{1}$, $\frac{GH}{KH} = \frac{8}{4} = \frac{2}{1}$, and $\frac{FH}{JH} = \frac{15}{7.5} = \frac{2}{1}$. Therefore $\triangle FGH \sim \triangle JKH$ by SSS ~.

17. $\frac{AC}{BC} = \frac{18}{12} = \frac{3}{2}$, $\frac{AE}{BD} = \frac{30}{20} = \frac{3}{2}$, and $\frac{CE}{CD} = \frac{15}{10} = \frac{3}{2}$. Therefore $\triangle ACE \sim \triangle BCD$ by SSS ~.

18. Since $\frac{XZ}{AC} = \frac{XY}{AB} = \frac{3}{1}$ and $\angle X \cong \angle A$, $\triangle XYZ \sim \triangle ABC$ by SAS ~. $BC = 5$

19. Since $\angle R$ and $\angle U$ are rt. ∠s, $\angle R \cong \angle U$ by the Rt. ∠s $\cong$ Thm. $\angle RSV \cong \angle UST$ because vert. ∠s are $\cong$. So $\triangle RSV \sim \triangle UST$ by AA ~. $TU = 18$

Chapter 8 Skills

1. $\triangle ADC \sim \triangle DBC \sim \triangle ABD$

2. $\triangle EFH \sim \triangle GFE \sim \triangle GEH$

3. $\triangle MKL \sim \triangle MLJ \sim \triangle LKJ$

7. $x = \sqrt{33}$; $y = 2\sqrt{6}$; $z = 2\sqrt{22}$

8. $x = 3\sqrt{5}$; $y = 3$; $z = 6\sqrt{5}$

9. $x = 16$; $y = 12$; $z = 20$

25. $QR = 4.55$; $m\angle Q \approx 33°$; $m\angle R \approx 57°$

26. $TU \approx 4.36$; $TV \approx 8.55$; $m\angle U = 63°$

27. $WY \approx 16.35$; $m\angle W \approx 23°$; $m\angle Y \approx 67°$

28. $AB = 3$; $BC = 3$; $AC \approx 4.24$; $m\angle A = 45°$; $m\angle B = 90°$; $m\angle C = 45°$

29. $DE = 4$; $EF \approx 6.40$; $DF = 5$; $m\angle D = 90°$; $m\angle E \approx 51°$; $m\angle F \approx 39°$

50. 3.6

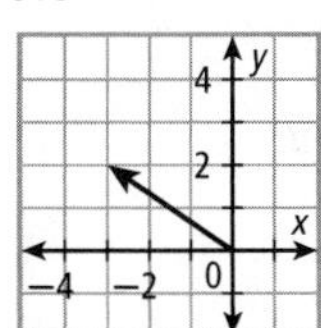

51. 5

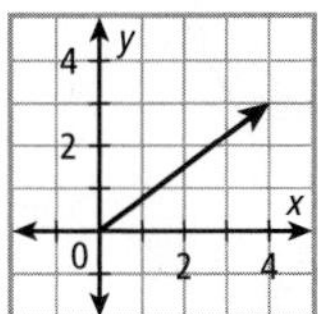

52. 5.4

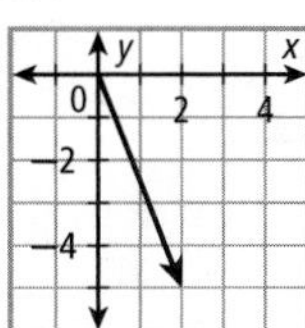

53. 53°

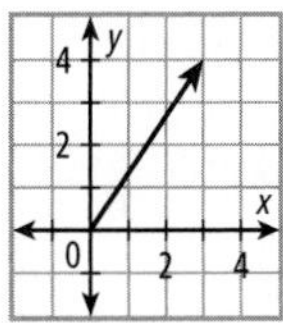

54. 7°

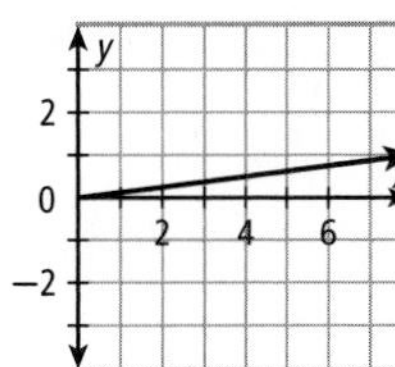

Chapter 9 Skills

20.

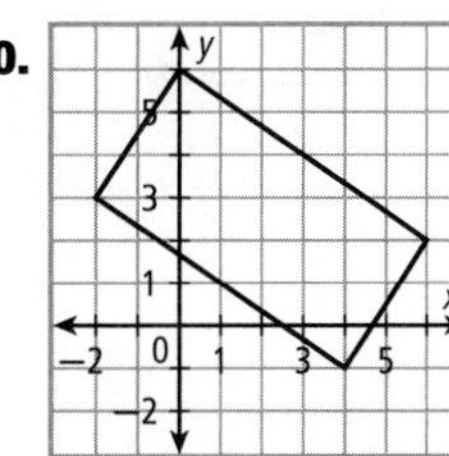

rectangle, $P = 6\sqrt{13}$ units, $A = 26$ units^2

21.

right triangle, $P = 12$ units, $A = 6$ units^2

26. The circumference is multiplied by $\frac{1}{4}$. The area is multiplied by $\frac{1}{16}$.

Chapter 10 Skills

1. hexagonal prism; vertices: $A, B, C, D, E, F, G, H, J, K, L, M$; edges: $\overline{AB}, \overline{BC}, \overline{CD}, \overline{DE}, \overline{EF}, \overline{AF}, \overline{AG}, \overline{BH}, \overline{CJ}, \overline{DK}, \overline{EL}, \overline{FM}, \overline{GH}, \overline{HJ}, \overline{JK}, \overline{KL}, \overline{LM}, \overline{MG}$; bases: $ABCDEF$, $GHJKLM$

2. cylinder; vertices: none; edges: none; bases: ⊙S, ⊙T

3. rectangular pyramid; vertices: V, W, X, Y, Z; edges: $\overline{WV}, \overline{XV}, \overline{YV}, \overline{ZV}, \overline{WZ}, \overline{ZY}, \overline{YX}, \overline{WX}$; base: $WXYZ$

7. top

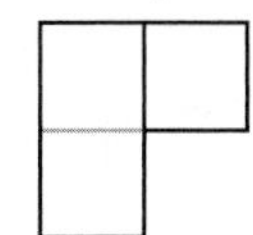

bottom

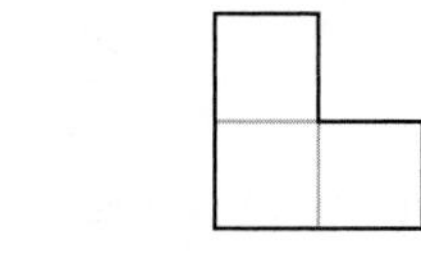

front

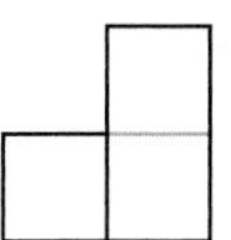

back

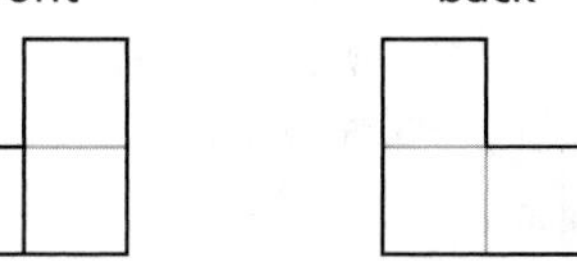

left

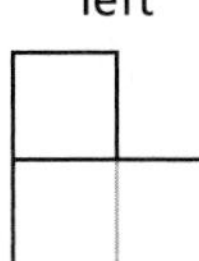

right

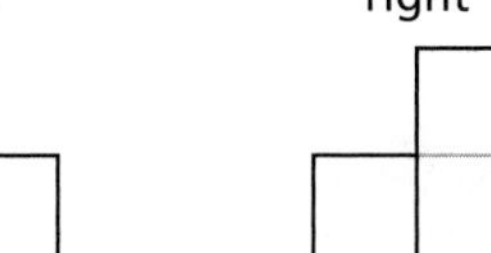

8.

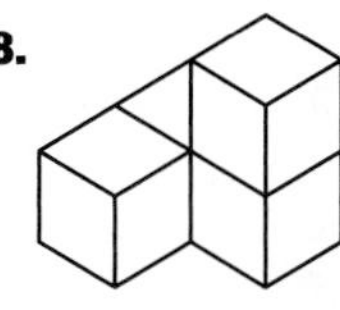

9.

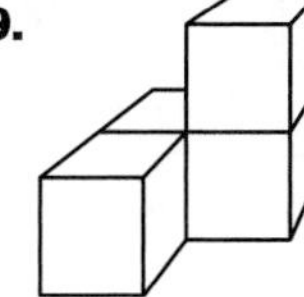

10.

12. $V = 8$, $E = 12$, $F = 6$, $8 - 12 + 6 = 2$

13. $V = 6$, $E = 12$, $F = 8$, $6 - 12 + 8 = 2$

14. $V = 10$, $E = 15$, $F = 7$, $10 - 15 + 7 = 2$

Additional Answers

15. 7.7, (2.5, 5.5, 5.5)

16. 9, (2, 3.5, −2)

17. 6.7, (2.5, 2, 2)

22. $L = 64\sqrt{10}$ in^2, $S = 64\sqrt{10} + 64$ in^2

24. $L = 136\pi$ cm^2; $S = 200\pi$ cm^2

27. $V = 2327.9$ cm^3

28. $V = 5654.9$ ft^3

29. $V = 1357.2$ in^2

40. The surface area is multiplied by $\frac{1}{9}$. The volume is multiplied by $\frac{1}{27}$.

41. The surface area is multiplied by 16. The volume is multiplied by 64.

Chapter 11 Skills

30.

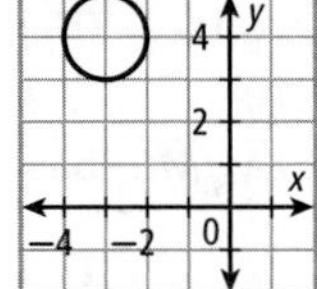

31.

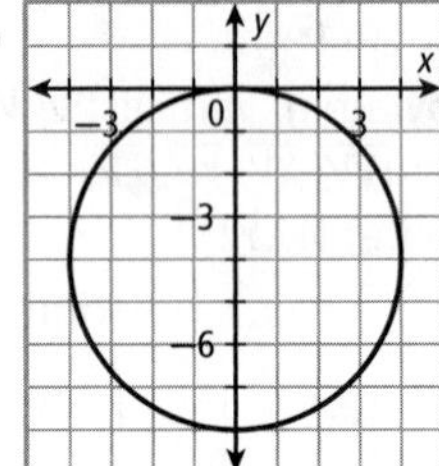

Chapter 12 Skills

3.

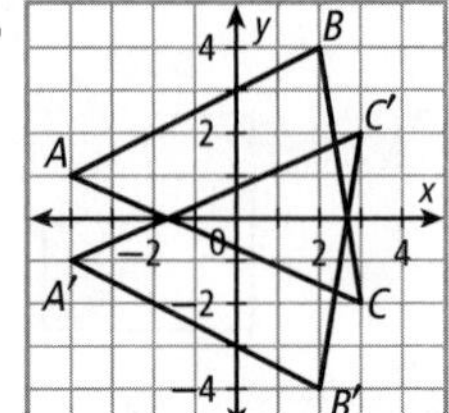

4.

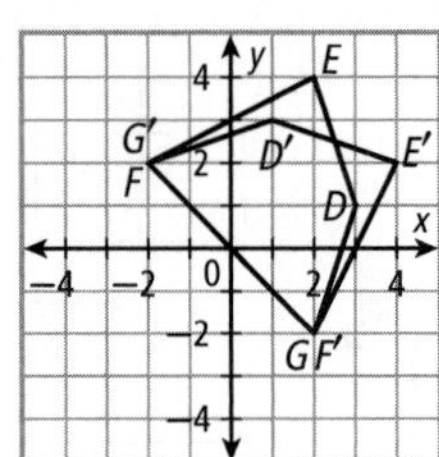

5.

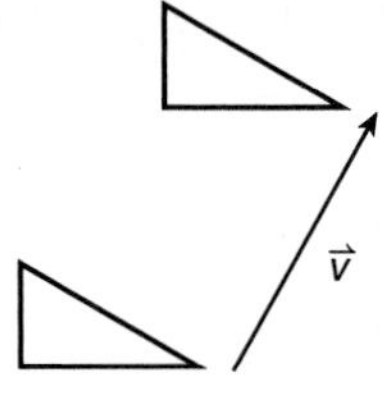

6.

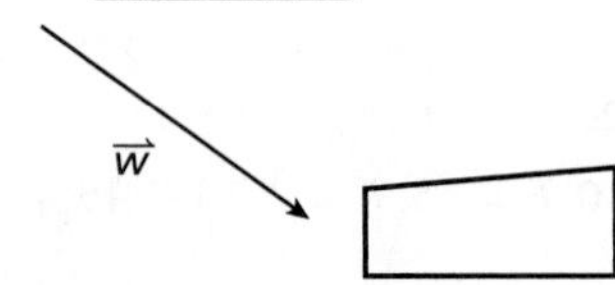

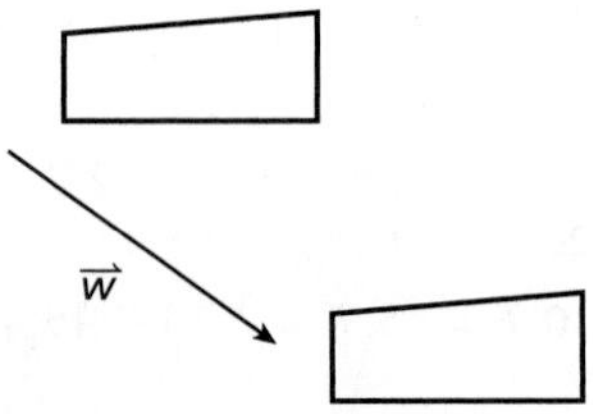

7.

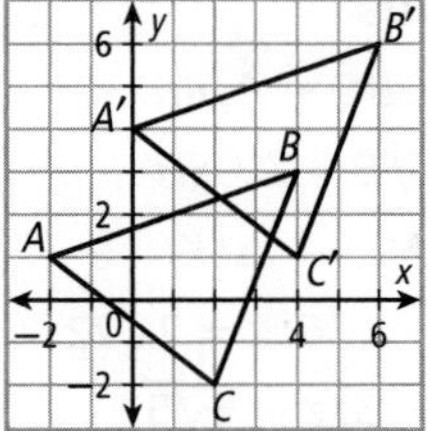

8.

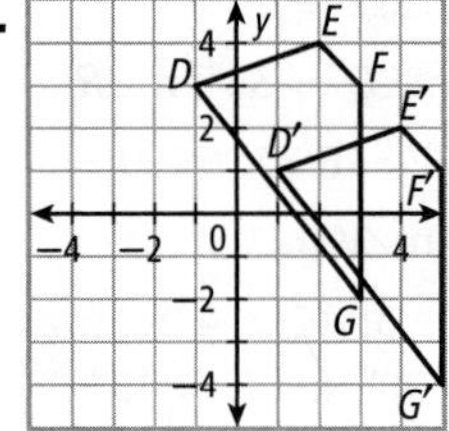

9.

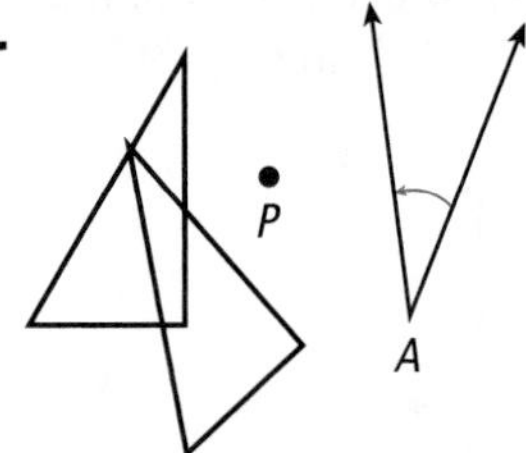

10.

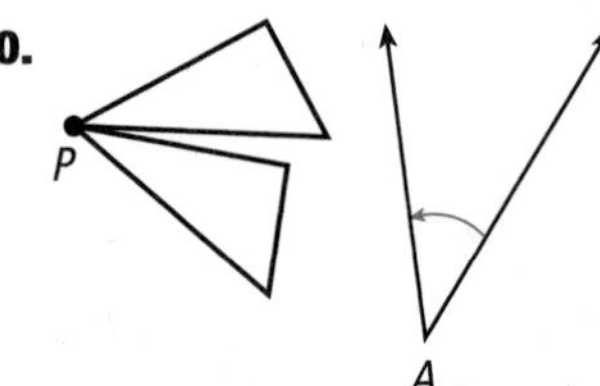

11.

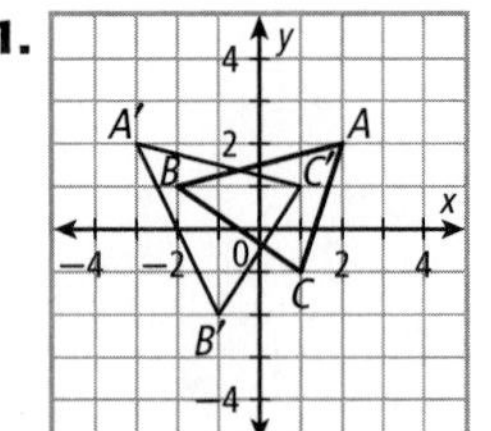

12.

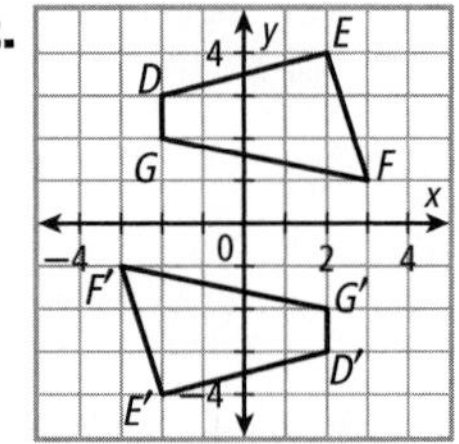

13.

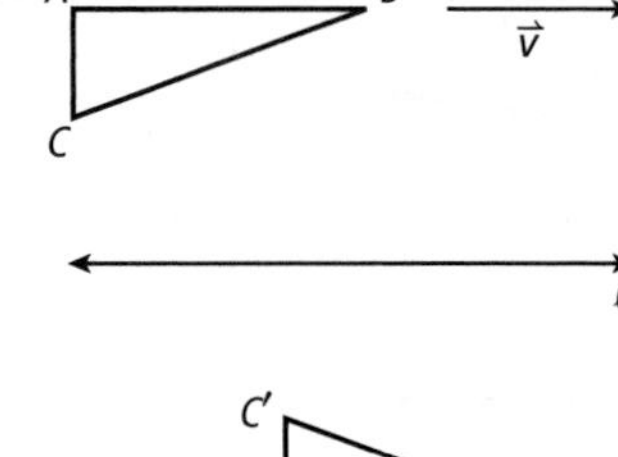

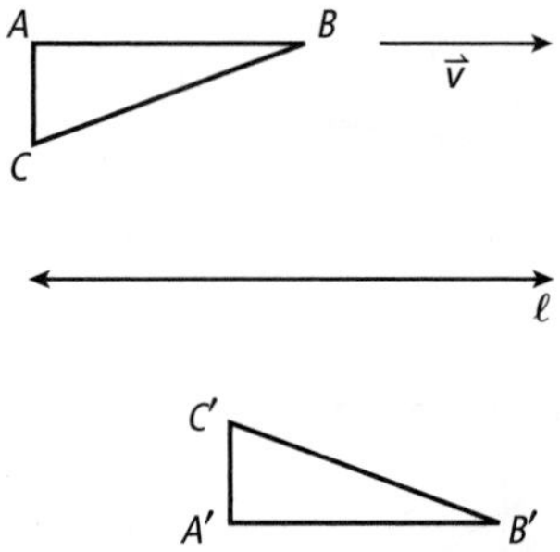

14.

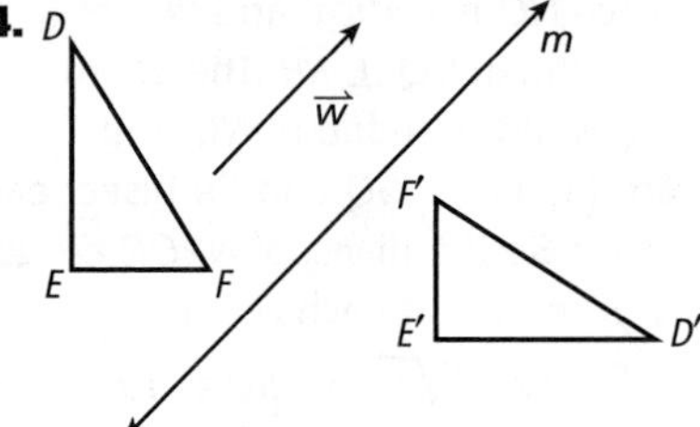

15.

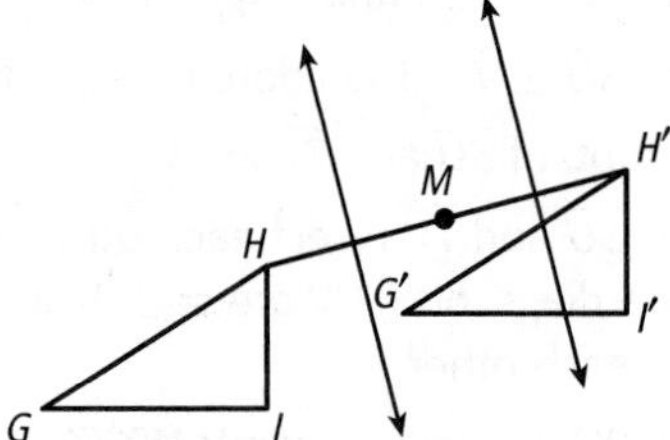

16. line symmetry and rotational symmetry; ; 45°, 8

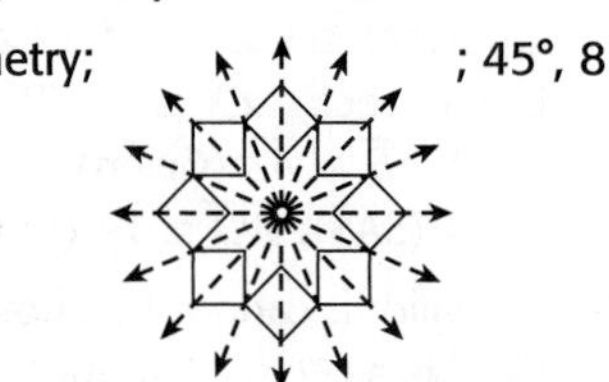

17. line symmetry and rotational symmetry; ; 72°, 5

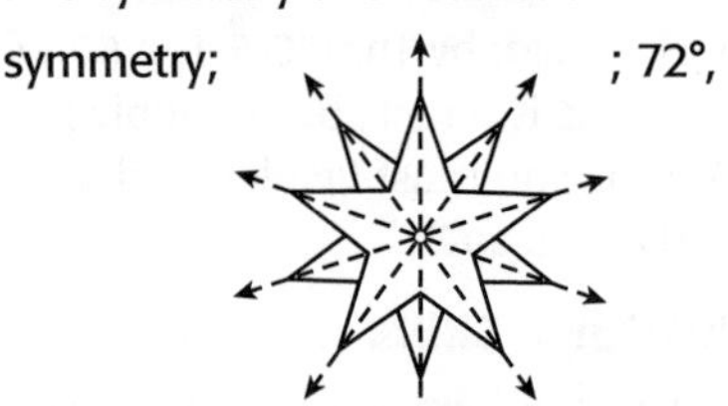

18. line symmetry;

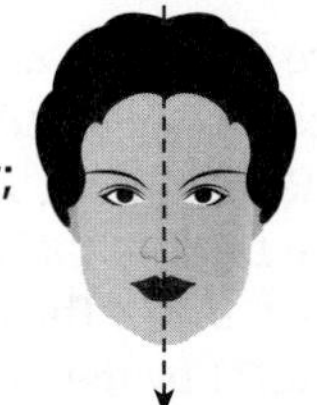

22.

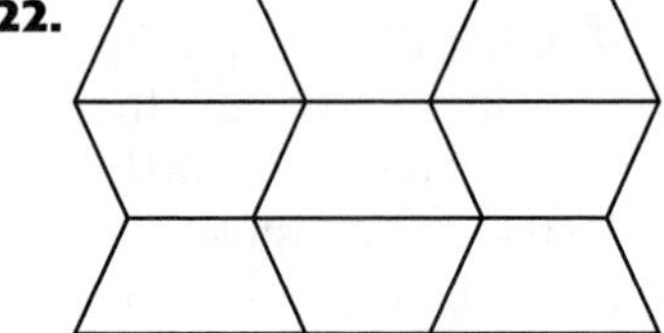

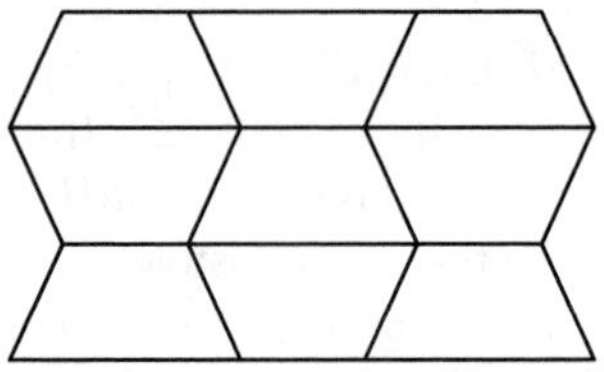

23.

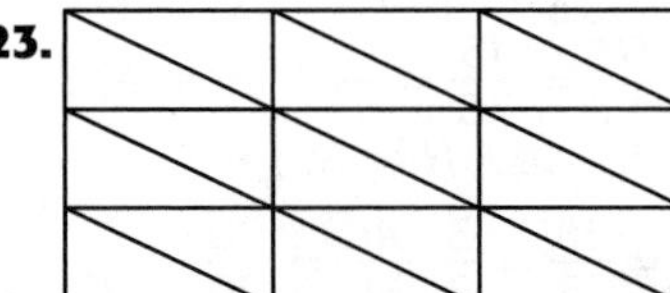

24.

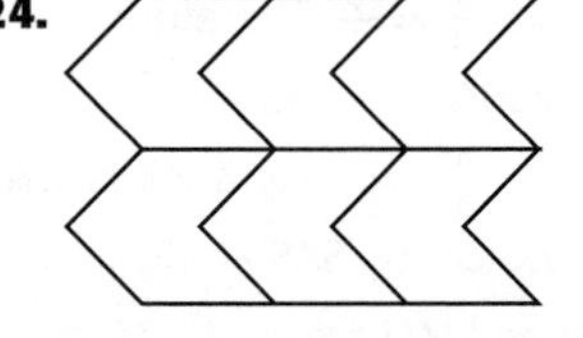

28.

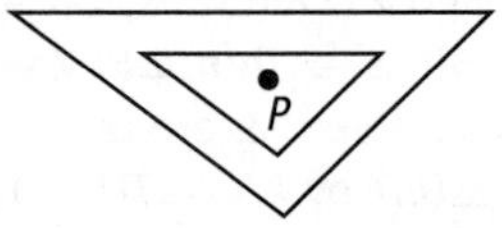

P

Additional Answers

29.

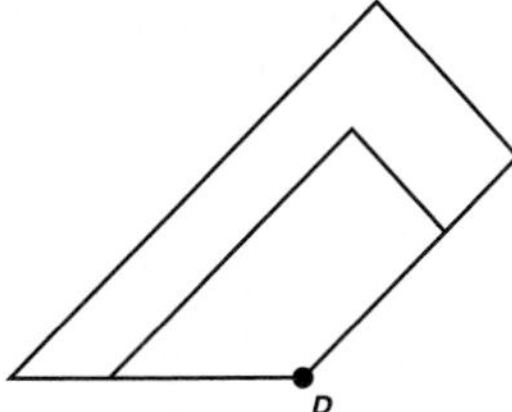

30.

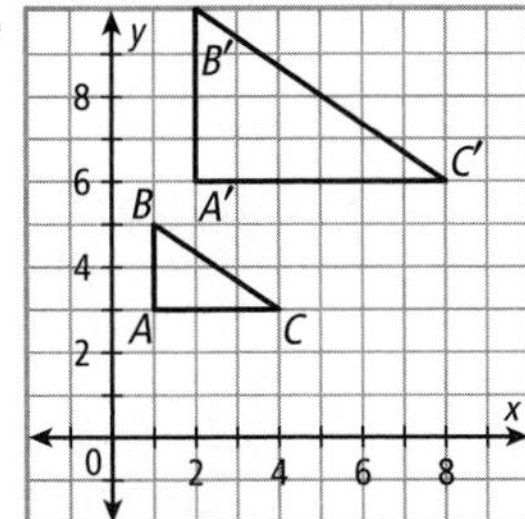

31.

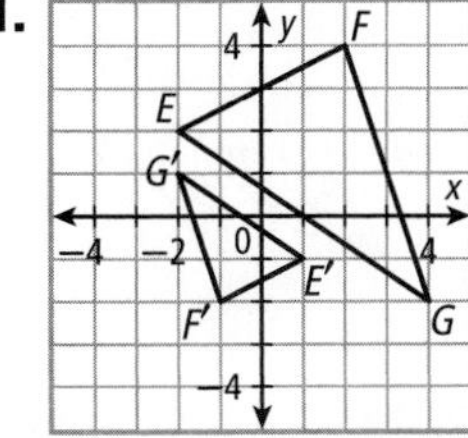

Chapter 1 Applications

7. Possible answers: blue: 165°; red: 120°; green: 45°; yellow: 30°

8. goldfish: $\frac{11}{24}$, balloon: $\frac{1}{3}$, stuffed bear: $\frac{1}{8}$, grand prize: $\frac{1}{12}$

Chapter 2 Applications

1. Possible answer: Tenth-grade boys are taller than tenth-grade girls.

2. Possible answer: More people vote during presidential election years.

3. Conv.: If an animal swims in salt water, then it is a fish; F.
Inv.: If an animal is not a fish, then it does not swim in salt water; F.
Contra.: If an animal does not swim in salt water, then it is not a fish; F.

4. Conv.: If a plant grows, then it was watered; T.
Inv.: If a plant is not watered, then it will not grow; T.
Contra.: If a plant does not grow, then it was not watered; F.

6. Cond.: If you can attend public school, then you have the required immunizations.
Conv.: If you have the required immunizations, then you can attend public school.

7. A hurricane is Category 5 iff it has sustained winds of more than 155 miles per hour.

8. $c = 5w + 25$ (Given); $200 = 5w + 25$ (Subst.); $175 = 5w$ (Subtr. Prop. of =); $35 = w$ (Div. Prop. of =)

9. $s = 110 + 15c$ (Given); $200 = 110 + 15c$ (Subst.); $90 = 15c$ (Subtr. Prop. of =); $6 = c$ (Div. Prop. of =)

Chapter 3 Applications

4. $m\angle 1 = 12(5) - 8 = 52°$ and $m\angle 2 = 8(5) + 12 = 52°$, so the lines are ∥ by the Conv. of the Corr. ∠s Post.

7.

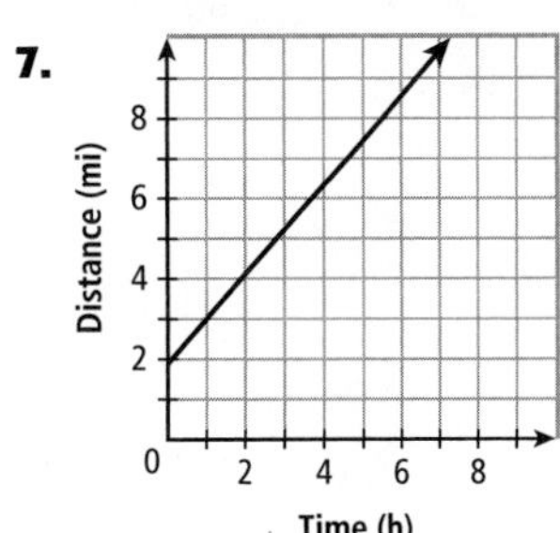

The slope is $\frac{10}{9}$, which means that the boat is traveling at an average speed of $\frac{10}{9}$ mi/h.

8.

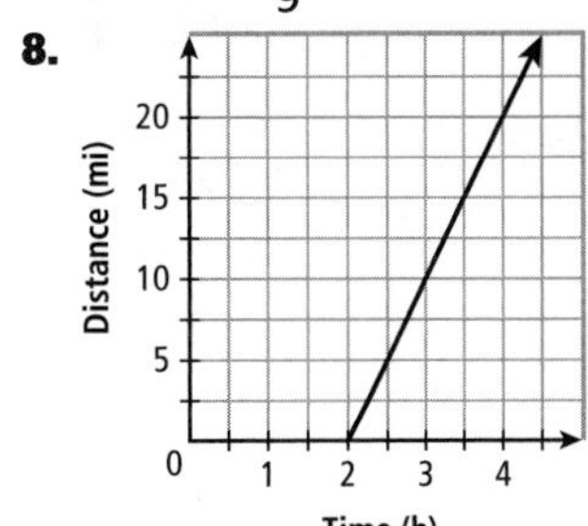

The slope is 10, which means that the runner is running at an average speed of 10 mi/h.

Chapter 4 Applications

3.
1. $\overline{AB} \cong \overline{HG}$, $\overline{HB} \cong \overline{AG}$, $\angle GAB \cong \angle BHG$, $\angle AGB \cong \angle HBG$ (Given)
2. $\overline{BG} \cong \overline{GB}$ (Reflex. Prop. of ≅)
3. $m\angle GAB = m\angle BHG$; $m\angle AGB = m\angle HBG$; (Def. of ≅ ∠s)
4. $m\angle GAB + m\angle ABG + m\angle AGB = 180°$ (△ Sum Thm.)
5. $m\angle BHG + m\angle HBG + m\angle HGB = 180°$ (△ Sum Thm.)
6. $m\angle GAB + m\angle ABG + m\angle AGB = m\angle BHG + m\angle HBG + m\angle HGB$ (Trans. Prop. of =)
7. $m\angle BHG + m\angle AGB + m\angle ABG = m\angle BHG + m\angle HBG + m\angle HGB$ (Subst. Prop. of =)
8. $m\angle AGB + m\angle ABG = m\angle HBG + m\angle HGB$ (Subtr.)
9. $m\angle HBG + m\angle ABG = m\angle HBG + m\angle HGB$ (Subst. Prop. of =)
10. $m\angle ABG = m\angle HGB$ (Subtr.)
11. $\triangle AGB \cong \triangle HBG$ (Def. of ≅ △s)

4. It is given that $\overline{AD} \cong \overline{CD}$ and $\angle ADB$ and $\angle CDB$ are rt. ∠s. Therefore $\angle ADB \cong \angle CDB$ because all rt. ∠s are ≅. $\overline{BD} \cong \overline{BD}$ by the Reflex. Prop. of ≅. Therefore $\triangle ABD \cong \triangle CBD$ by SAS.

5a.

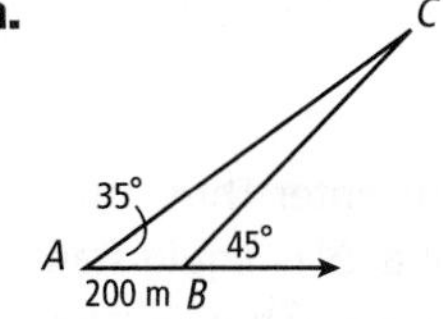

7. Assign the coordinates $A(0, 3.5a)$, $B(-2a, 0)$, $C(2a, 0)$. Using the Mdpt. Formula $D = \left(\frac{-2a + 0}{2}, \frac{0 + 3.5a}{2}\right) = (-a, 1.75a)$, $E = \left(\frac{2a + 0}{2}, \frac{0 + 3.5a}{2}\right) = (a, 1.75a)$, and $F = \left(\frac{-2a + 2a}{2}, \frac{0 + 0}{2}\right) = (0, 0)$. Use the Mdpt. Formula to find the mdpt. G of $\overline{DE}$. $G = \left(\frac{-a + a}{2}, \frac{1.75a + 1.75a}{2}\right) = (0, 1.75a)$. By the Dist. Formula, $GF = 1.75a$ and $DE = 2a$. Therefore the area of $\triangle DEF = \frac{1}{2}(2a)(1.75a) = 1.75a^2$. By the Dist. Formula, $BC = 4a$ and $AF = 3.5a$. Therefore the area of $\triangle ABC = \frac{1}{2}(4a)(3.5a) = 7a^2$. Since $1.75a^2$ is $\frac{1}{4}$ of $7a^2$, the area of $\triangle DEF$ is $\frac{1}{4}$ the area of $\triangle ABC$.

Chapter 5 Applications

1. It is given that $\overline{AB} \cong \overline{BC}$. So B is on the ⊥ bisector of $\overline{AC}$ by the Conv. of the ⊥ Bisector Thm. Since the wires are equally spaced from the base of the tower, D is the mdpt. of $\overline{AC}$. So $\overline{BD}$ is the ⊥ bisector of $\overline{AC}$ and the tower is ⊥ to the ground.

2.

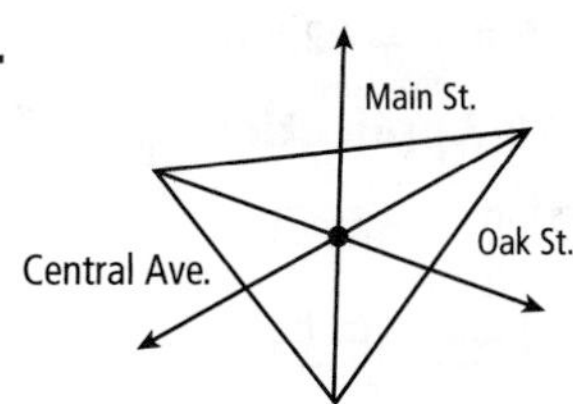

By the Incenter Thm., the incenter of a △ is equidistant from the sides of the △. Draw the △ formed by the streets and draw the ∠ bisectors to find the incenter, point X. The city should position the firehouse at X.

Additional Answers

3.

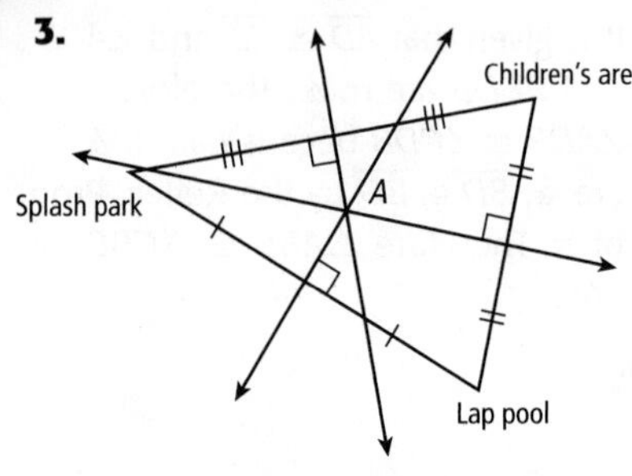

By the Circumcenter Thm., the circumcenter of a △ is equidistant from the vertices of the △. Draw the △ formed by the 3 locations and draw the ⊥ bisectors of each side to find the circumcenter, point *A*. The lifeguard should position herself at *A*.

4. $\left(\frac{2}{3}, 1\right)$

6. the sidewalk from the seesaw to the slide

7. Yes; the sum of each pair of 2 lengths is greater than the third length.

10. $90\sqrt{2}$ ft, or about 127.3 ft

Chapter 6 Applications

6. When the rocker moves, the ∠ measures change but *AB*, *BC*, *CD*, and *AD* stay the same. So it is always true that $\overline{AB} \cong \overline{DC}$ and $\overline{AD} \cong \overline{BC}$. Since both pairs of opp. sides of the quad. are ≅, *ABCD* is always a ▱.

10. Elise should cut 4 pieces of ribbon that are the same length. This ensures that the shape is a rhombus by def.

Chapter 7 Applications

1. Jason: $\frac{3}{7} = \frac{x}{210}$; Matthew: $\frac{4}{7} = \frac{x}{210}$

7. $\frac{AB}{DE} = \frac{18}{6} = 3$ *and* $\frac{BC}{EF} = \frac{15}{5} = 3$. Since $\frac{AB}{DE} = \frac{BC}{EF}$ and $\angle E \cong \angle B$ by the Rt. ∠ ≅ Thm., $\triangle ABC \sim \triangle DEF$ by the SAS ~.

10. $A = 67.5$ ft; $B = 60$ ft; $C = 45$ ft; $D = 37.5$ ft; $E = 22.5$ ft

Chapter 10 Applications

3.

Chapter 12 Applications

1.

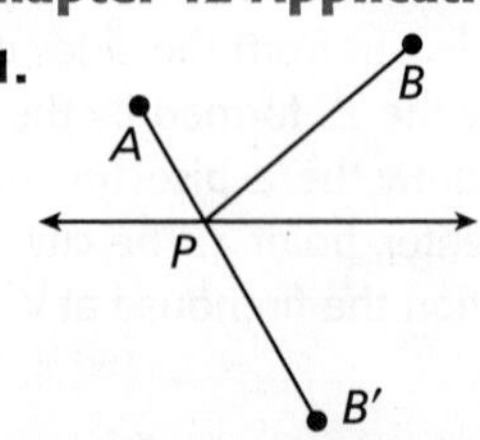

4. Aim for point *X* in the figure. *H′* is the reflection of point *H* across the edge.

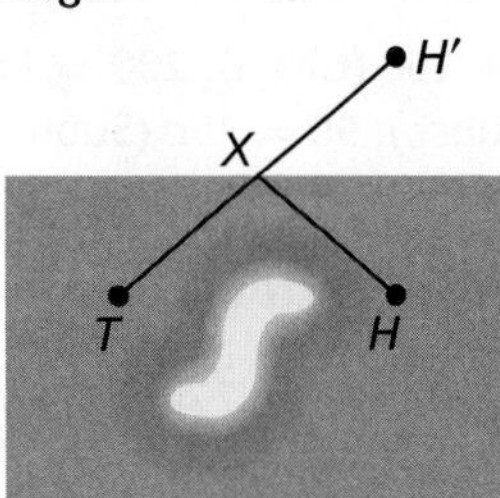

Glossary/Glosario

go.hrw.com
Multilingual Glossary Online
KEYWORD: MG7 Glossary

A

ENGLISH	SPANISH	EXAMPLES
acute angle (p. 21) An angle that measures greater than 0° and less than 90°.	**ángulo agudo** Ángulo que mide más de 0° y menos de 90°.	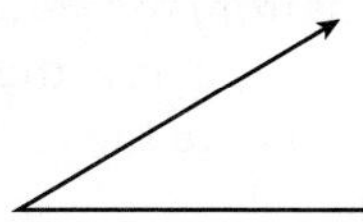
acute triangle (p. 216) A triangle with three acute angles.	**triángulo acutángulo** Triángulo con tres ángulos agudos.	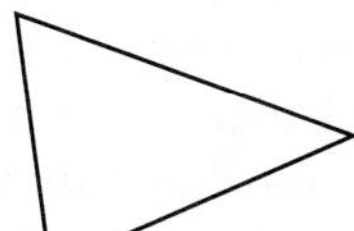
adjacent angles (p. 28) Two angles in the same plane with a common vertex and a common side, but no common interior points.	**ángulos adyacentes** Dos ángulos en el mismo plano que tienen un vértice y un lado común pero no comparten puntos internos.	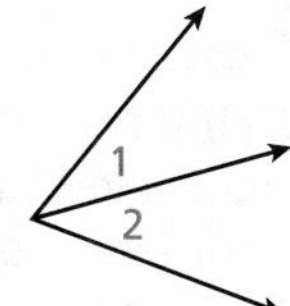 ∠1 and ∠2 are adjacent angles.
adjacent arcs (p. 757) Two arcs of the same circle that intersect at exactly one point.	**arcos adyacentes** Dos arcos del mismo círculo que se cruzan en un punto exacto.	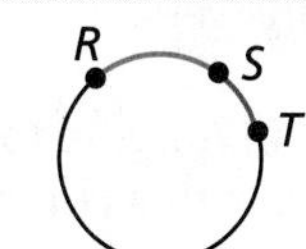 $\overset{\frown}{RS}$ and $\overset{\frown}{ST}$ are adjacent arcs.
alternate exterior angles (p. 147) For two lines intersected by a transversal, a pair of angles that lie on opposite sides of the transversal and outside the other two lines.	**ángulos alternos externos** Dadas dos líneas cortadas por una transversal, par de ángulos no adyacentes ubicados en los lados opuestos de la transversal y fuera de las otras dos líneas.	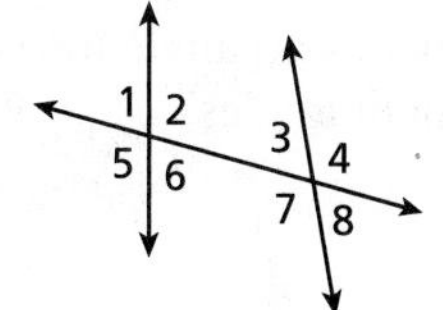 ∠4 and ∠5 are alternate exterior angles.
alternate interior angles (p. 147) For two lines intersected by a transversal, a pair of nonadjacent angles that lie on opposite sides of the transversal and between the other two lines.	**ángulos alternos internos** Dadas dos líneas cortadas por una transversal, par de ángulos no adyacentes ubicados en los lados opuestos de la transversal y entre las otras dos líneas.	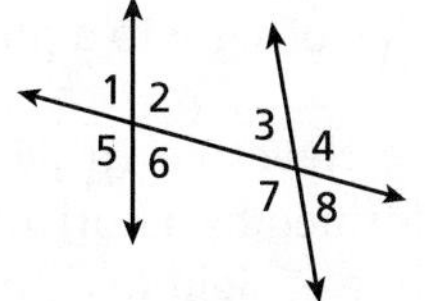 ∠3 and ∠6 are alternate interior angles.
altitude of a cone (p. 690) A segment from the vertex to the plane of the base that is perpendicular to the plane of the base.	**altura de un cono** Segmento que se extiende desde el vértice hasta el plano de la base y es perpendicular al plano de la base.	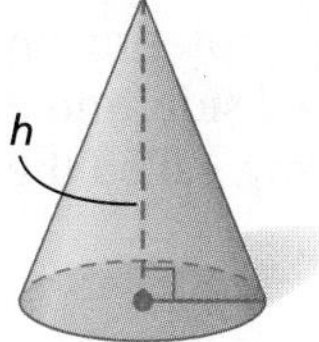
altitude of a cylinder (p. 680) A segment with its endpoints on the planes of the bases that is perpendicular to the planes of the bases.	**altura de un cilindro** Segmento con sus extremos en los planos de las bases que es perpendicular a los planos de las bases.	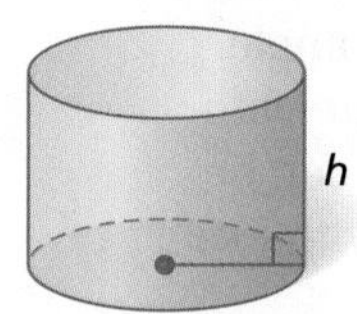 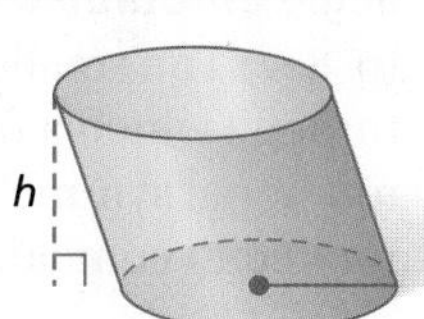

Glossary/Glosario G1

ENGLISH	SPANISH	EXAMPLES
altitude of a prism (p. 680) A segment with its endpoints on the planes of the bases that is perpendicular to the planes of the bases.	**altura de un prisma** Segmento con sus extremos en los planos de las bases que es perpendicular a los planos de las bases.	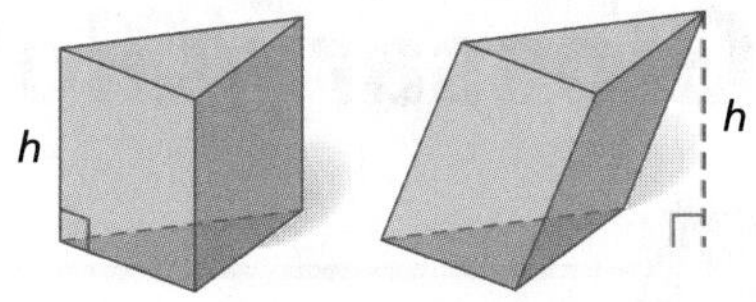 h h
altitude of a pyramid (p. 689) A segment from the vertex to the plane of the base that is perpendicular to the plane of the base.	**altura de una pirámide** Segmento que se extiende desde el vértice hasta el plano de la base y es perpendicular al plano de la base.	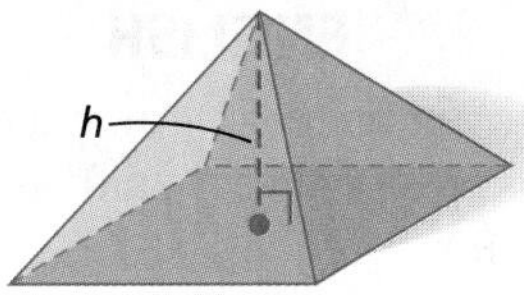 h
altitude of a triangle (p. 316) A perpendicular segment from a vertex to the line containing the opposite side.	**altura de un triángulo** Segmento perpendicular que se extiende desde un vértice hasta la línea que forma el lado opuesto.	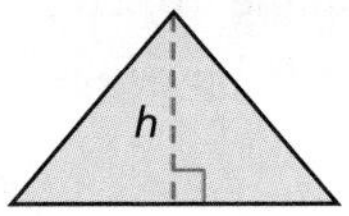 h
ambiguous case of the Law of Sines (p. 556) If two sides and a nonincluded angle of a triangle are given in order to solve the triangle using the Law of Sines, it is possible to have two different answers.	**caso ambiguo de la ley de los senos** Si se conocen dos lados y un ángulo no incluido de un triángulo y se quiere resolver el triángulo aplicando la ley de los senos, es posible obtener dos respuestas diferentes.	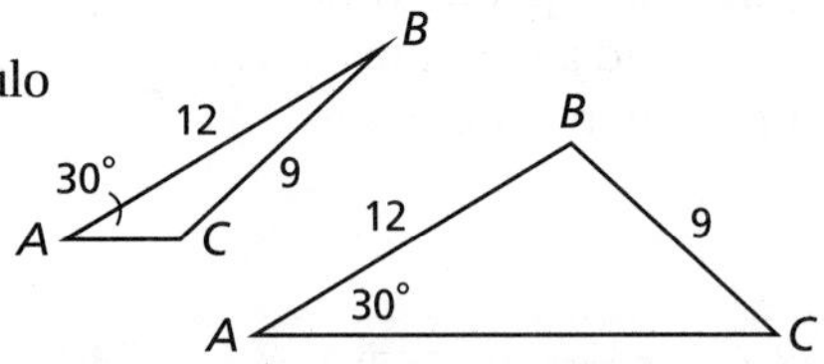 B 12 30° 9 A C; B 12 9 30° A C
angle (p. 20) A figure formed by two rays with a common endpoint.	**ángulo** Figura formada por dos rayos con un extremo común.	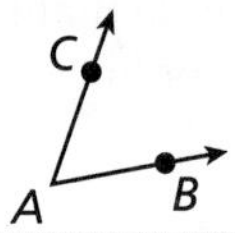 C A B
angle bisector (p. 23) A ray that divides an angle into two congruent angles.	**bisectriz de un ángulo** Rayo que divide un ángulo en dos ángulos congruentes.	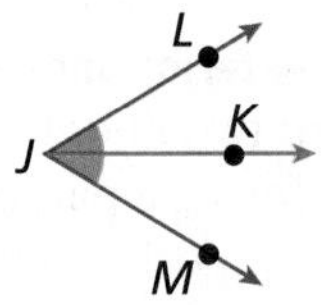 L K J M $\overrightarrow{JK}$ is an angle bisector of $\angle LJM$.
angle of depression (p. 544) The angle formed by a horizontal line and a line of sight to a point below.	**ángulo de depresión** Ángulo formado por una línea horizontal y una línea visual a un punto inferior.	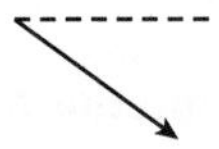
angle of elevation (p. 544) The angle formed by a horizontal line and a line of sight to a point above.	**ángulo de elevación** Ángulo formado por una línea horizontal y una línea visual a un punto superior.	
angle of rotation (p. 840) An angle formed by a rotating ray, called the terminal side, and a stationary reference ray, called the initial side.	**ángulo de rotación** Ángulo formado por un rayo rotativo, denominado lado terminal, y un rayo de referencia estático, denominado lado inicial.	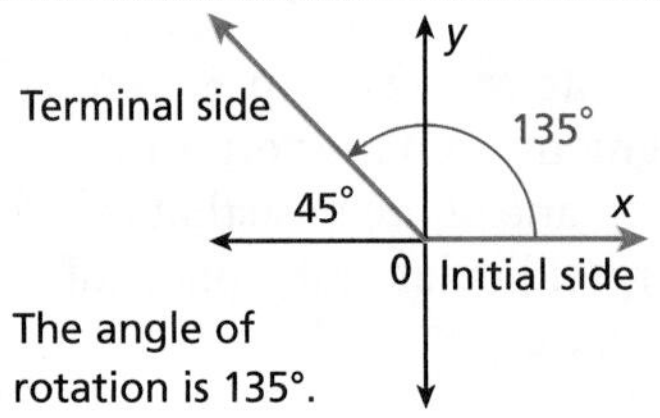 Terminal side y 135° 45° x 0 Initial side The angle of rotation is 135°.
angle of rotational symmetry (p. 857) The smallest angle through which a figure with rotational symmetry can be rotated to coincide with itself.	**ángulo de simetría de rotación** El ángulo más pequeño alrededor del cual se puede rotar una figura con simetría de rotación para que coincida consigo misma.	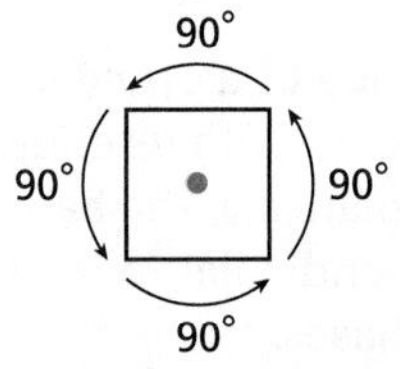 90° 90° 90° 90°

G2 Glossary/Glosario

ENGLISH	SPANISH	EXAMPLES
annulus (p. 612) The region between two concentric circles.	**corona circular** Región comprendida entre dos círculos concéntricos.	
apothem (p. 601) The perpendicular distance from the center of a regular polygon to a side of the polygon.	**apotema** Distancia perpendicular desde el centro de un polígono regular hasta un lado del polígono.	a
arc (p. 756) An unbroken part of a circle consisting of two points on the circle, called the endpoints, and all the points on the circle between them.	**arco** Parte continua de una circunferencia formada por dos puntos de la circunferencia denominados extremos y todos los puntos de la circunferencia comprendidos entre éstos.	R S
arc length (p. 766) The distance along an arc measured in linear units.	**longitud de arco** Distancia a lo largo de un arco medida en unidades lineales.	10 ft, D, 90°, C; $m\widehat{CD} = 5\pi$ ft
arc marks (p. 22) Marks used on a figure to indicate congruent angles.	**marcas de arco** Marcas utilizadas en una figura para indicar ángulos congruentes.	D, C, Arc marks, F, E, A, B
area (p. 36) The number of nonoverlapping unit squares of a given size that will exactly cover the interior of a plane figure.	**área** Cantidad de cuadrados unitarios de un determinado tamaño no superpuestos que cubren exactamente el interior de una figura plana.	5, 2; The area is 10 square units.
arrow notation (p. 50) A symbol used to describe a transformation.	**notación de flecha** Símbolo utilizado para describir una transformación.	B, Preimage, A, C, B′, Image, A′, C′; $\triangle ABC \rightarrow \triangle A'B'C'$
auxiliary line (p. 223) A line drawn in a figure to aid in a proof.	**línea auxiliar** Línea dibujada en una figura como ayuda en una demostración.	Auxiliary line, B, ?, 4, 2, 5, 1, 3, A, C
axiom (p. 7) *See* postulate.	**axioma** *Ver* postulado.	
axis of a cone (p. 690) The segment with endpoints at the vertex and the center of the base.	**eje de un cono** Segmento cuyos extremos se encuentran en el vértice y en el centro de la base.	Axis

Glossary/Glosario

Glossary/Glosario G3

ENGLISH	SPANISH	EXAMPLES
axis of a cylinder (p. 681) The segment with endpoints at the centers of the two bases.	**eje de un cilindro** Segmentos cuyos extremos se encuentran en los centros de las dos bases.	Axis
axis of symmetry (p. 856) A line that divides a plane figure or a graph into two congruent reflected halves.	**eje de simetría** Línea que divide una figura plana o una gráfica en dos mitades reflejadas congruentes.	Axis of symmetry

B

base angle of a trapezoid (p. 429) One of a pair of consecutive angles whose common side is a base of the trapezoid.	**ángulo base de un trapecio** Uno de los dos ángulos consecutivos cuyo lado en común es la base del trapecio.	Base angles B C A D Base angles
base angle of an isosceles triangle (p. 273) One of the two angles that have the base of the triangle as a side.	**ángulo base de un triángulo isósceles** Uno de los dos ángulos que tienen como lado la base del triángulo.	A Base angle Base angle B C
base of a cone (p. 654) The circular face of the cone.	**base de un cono** Cara circular del cono.	Base
base of a cylinder (p. 654) One of the two circular faces of the cylinder.	**base de un cilindro** Una de las dos caras circulares del cilindro.	Bases
base of a geometric figure (p. 36, p. 654) A side of a polygon; a face of a three-dimensional figure by which the figure is measured or classified.	**base de una figura geométrica** Lado de un polígono; cara de una figura tridimensional por la cual se mide o clasifica la figura.	h b Bases
base of a prism (p. 654) One of the two congruent parallel faces of the prism.	**base de un prisma** Una de las dos caras paralelas y congruentes del prisma.	Bases
base of a pyramid (p. 654) The face of the pyramid that is opposite the vertex.	**base de una pirámide** Cara de la pirámide opuesta al vértice.	Base
base of a trapezoid (p. 429) One of the two parallel sides of the trapezoid.	**base de un trapecio** Uno de los dos lados paralelos del trapecio.	b_1 b_2
base of a triangle (p. 36) Any side of a triangle.	**base de un triángulo** Cualquier lado de un triángulo.	c a b

G4 Glossary/Glosario

ENGLISH	SPANISH	EXAMPLES
base of an isosceles triangle (p. 273) The side opposite the vertex angle.	**base de un triángulo isósceles** Lado opuesto al ángulo del vértice.	A, B, C, Base
bearing (p. 252) Indicates direction. The number of degrees in the angle whose initial side is a line due north and whose terminal side is determined by a clockwise rotation.	**rumbo** Indica dirección. La cantidad de grados en el ángulo cuyo lado inicial es una línea recta en dirección norte y cuyo lado terminal se determina por una rotación en el sentido de las agujas del reloj.	N, B, 30°, W, A, E, S
between (p. 14) Given three points *A*, *B*, and *C*, *B* is between *A* and *C* if and only if all three of the points lie on the same line, and $AB + BC = AC$.	**entre** Dados tres puntos *A*, *B* y *C*, *B* está entre *A* y *C* si y sólo si los tres puntos se encuentran en la misma línea y $AB + BC = AC$.	A, B, C
biconditional statement (p. 96) A statement that can be written in the form "*p* if and only if *q*."	**enunciado bicondicional** Enunciado que puede expresarse en la forma "*p* si y sólo si *q*".	A figure is a triangle if and only if it is a three-sided polygon.
bisect (p. 15) To divide into two congruent parts.	**trazar una bisectriz** Dividir en dos partes congruentes.	L, K, J, M $\overrightarrow{JK}$ bisects $\angle LJM$.

C

ENGLISH	SPANISH	EXAMPLES
Cartesian coordinate system (p. 808) *See* coordinate plane.	**sistema de coordenadas cartesianas** *Ver* plano cartesiano.	
center of a circle (p. 600) The point inside a circle that is the same distance from every point on the circle.	**centro de un círculo** Punto dentro de un círculo que se encuentra a la misma distancia de todos los puntos del círculo.	A
center of a regular polygon (p. 601) The point that is equidistant from all vertices of the regular polygon.	**centro de un polígono regular** Punto equidistante de todos los vértices del polígono regular.	
center of a sphere (p. 714) The point inside a sphere that is the same distance from every point on the sphere.	**centro de una esfera** Punto dentro de una esfera que está a la misma distancia de cualquier punto de la esfera.	center
center of dilation (p. 873) The intersection of the lines that connect each point of the image with the corresponding point of the preimage.	**centro de dilatación** Intersección de las líneas que conectan cada punto de la imagen con el punto correspondiente de la imagen original.	center

Glossary/Glosario

Glossary/Glosario G5

ENGLISH	SPANISH	EXAMPLES
center of rotation (p. 840) The point around which a figure is rotated.	**centro de rotación** Punto alrededor del cual rota una figura.	90° 90° Center 90° 90°
central angle of a circle (p. 756) An angle whose vertex is the center of a circle.	**ángulo central de un círculo** Ángulo cuyo vértice es el centro de un círculo.	
central angle of a regular polygon (p. 601) An angle whose vertex is the center of the regular polygon and whose sides pass through consecutive vertices.	**ángulo central de un polígono regular** Ángulo cuyo vértice es el centro del polígono regular y cuyos lados pasan por vértices consecutivos.	Central angle
centroid of a triangle (p. 314) The point of concurrency of the three medians of a triangle. Also known as the *center of gravity*.	**centroide de un triángulo** Punto donde se encuentran las tres medianas de un triángulo. También conocido como *centro de gravedad*.	B X P Y A Z C The centroid is *P*.
chord (p. 746) A segment whose endpoints lie on a circle.	**cuerda** Segmento cuyos extremos se encuentran en un círculo.	A Chord B
circle (p. 600) The set of points in a plane that are a fixed distance from a given point called the center of the circle.	**círculo** Conjunto de puntos en un plano que se encuentran a una distancia fija de un punto determinado denominado centro del círculo.	
circle graph (p. 755) A way to display data by using a circle divided into non-overlapping sectors.	**gráfica circular** Forma de mostrar datos mediante un círculo dividido en sectores no superpuestos.	**Residents of Mesa, AZ** 65+ 13%; 45–64 19%; 25–44 30%; 18–24 11%; Under 18 27%
circumcenter of a triangle (p. 307) The point of concurrency of the three perpendicular bisectors of a triangle.	**circuncentro de un triángulo** Punto donde se cortan las tres mediatrices de un triángulo.	B P A C The circumcenter is *P*.
circumference (p. 37) The distance around the circle.	**circunferencia** Distancia alrededor del círculo.	Circumference

G6 Glossary/Glosario

ENGLISH	SPANISH	EXAMPLES
circumscribed circle (p. 308) Every vertex of the polygon lies on the circle.	**círculo circunscrito** Todos los vértices del polígono se encuentran sobre el círculo.	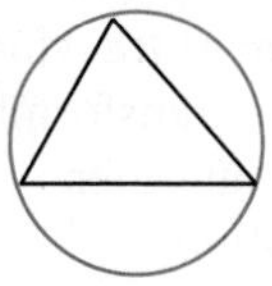
circumscribed polygon (p. 599) Each side of the polygon is tangent to the circle.	**polígono circunscrito** Todos los lados del polígono son tangentes al círculo.	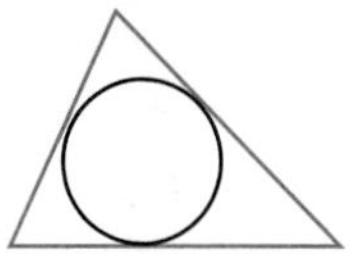
coincide (p. 221) To correspond exactly; to be identical.	**coincidir** Corresponder exactamente, ser idéntico.	
collinear (p. 6) Points that lie on the same line.	**colineal** Puntos que se encuentran sobre la misma línea.	 *K*, *L*, and *M* are collinear points.
common tangent (p. 748) A line that is tangent to two circles.	**tangente común** Línea que es tangente a dos círculos.	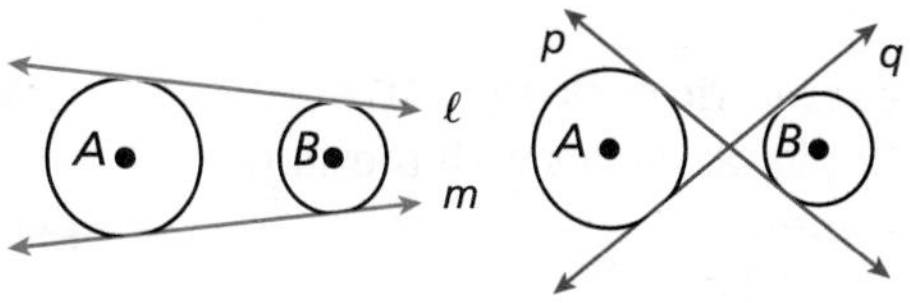
complement of an angle (p. 29) The sum of the measures of an angle and its complement is 90°.	**complemento de un ángulo** La suma de las medidas de un ángulo y su complemento es 90°.	The complement of a 53° angle is a 37° angle.
complement of an event (p. 628) All outcomes in the sample space that are not in an event *E*, denoted $\overline{E}$.	**complemento de un suceso** Todos los resultados en el espacio muestral que no están en el suceso *E* y se expresan $\overline{E}$.	In the experiment of rolling a number cube, the complement of rolling a 3 is rolling a 1, 2, 4, 5, or 6.
complementary angles (p. 29) Two angles whose measures have a sum of 90°.	**ángulos complementarios** Dos ángulos cuyas medidas suman 90°.	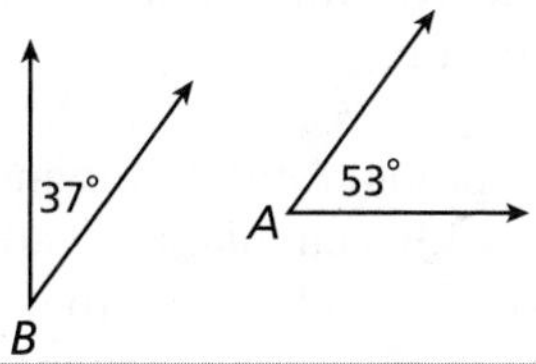
component form (p. 559) The form of a vector that lists the vertical and horizontal change from the initial point to the terminal point.	**forma de componente** Forma de un vector que muestra el cambio horizontal y vertical desde el punto inicial hasta el punto terminal.	The component form of $\overrightarrow{CD}$ is $\langle 2, 3 \rangle$.
composite figure (p. 600) A plane figure made up of triangles, rectangles, trapezoids, circles, and other simple shapes, or a three-dimensional figure made up of prisms, cones, pyramids, cylinders, and other simple three-dimensional figures.	**figura compuesta** Figura plana compuesta por triángulos, rectángulos, trapecios, círculos y otras figuras simples, o figura tridimensional compuesta por prismas, conos, pirámides, cilindros y otras figuras tridimensionales simples.	

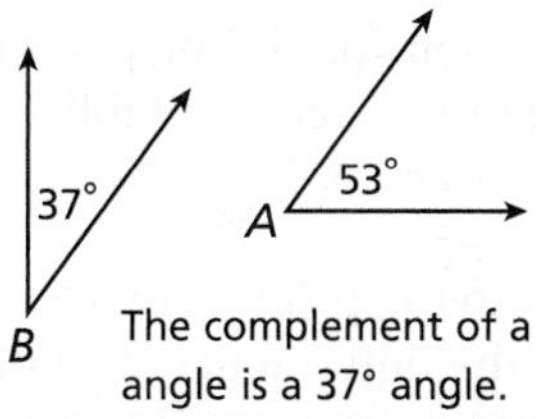

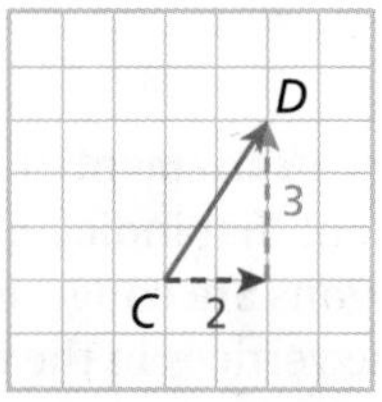

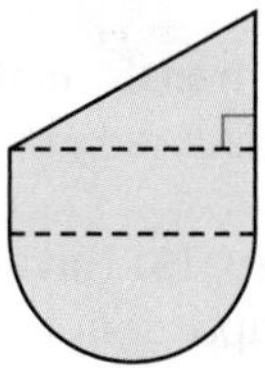

Glossary/Glosario G7

ENGLISH	SPANISH	EXAMPLES
composition of transformations (p. 848) One transformation followed by another transformation.	**composición de transformaciones** Una transformación seguida de otra transformación.	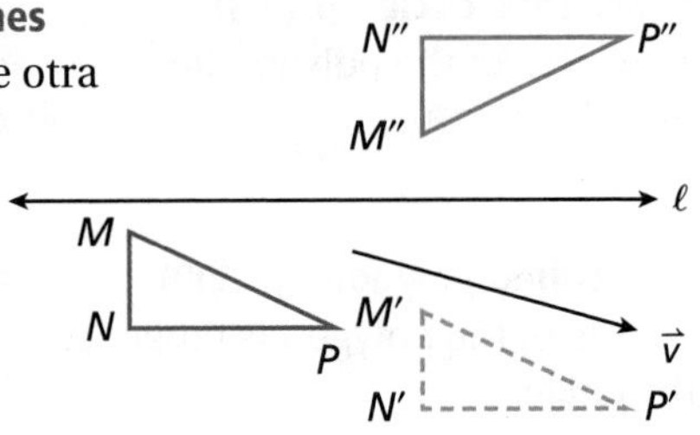 N″ P″ M″ ℓ M N P M′ N′ P′ $\vec{v}$
compound statement (p. 128) Two statements that are connected by the word *and* or *or*.	**enunciado compuesto** Dos enunciados unidos por la palabra *y* u *o*.	The sky is blue and the grass is green. I will drive to school or I will take the bus.
concave polygon (p. 383) A polygon in which a diagonal can be drawn such that part of the diagonal contains points in the exterior of the polygon.	**polígono cóncavo** Polígono en el cual se puede trazar una diagonal tal que parte de la diagonal contiene puntos ubicados fuera del polígono.	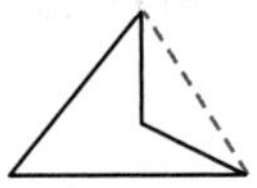 Concave quadrilateral
concentric circles (p. 747) Coplanar circles with the same center.	**círculos concéntricos** Círculos coplanares que comparten el mismo centro.	 center
conclusion (p. 81) The part of a conditional statement following the word *then*.	**conclusión** Parte de un enunciado condicional que sigue a la palabra *entonces*.	If $x + 1 = 5$, then $\underbrace{x = 4}_{\text{Conclusion}}$.
concurrent (p. 307) Three or more lines that intersect at one point.	**concurrente** Tres o más líneas que se cortan en un punto.	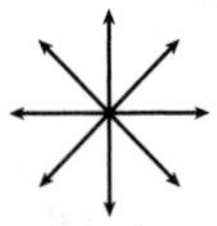
conditional statement (p. 81) A statement that can be written in the form "if *p*, then *q*," where *p* is the hypothesis and *q* is the conclusion.	**enunciado condicional** Enunciado que se puede expresar como "si *p*, entonces *q*", donde *p* es la hipótesis y *q* es la conclusión.	If $\underbrace{x + 1 = 5}_{\text{Hypothesis}}$, then $\underbrace{x = 4}_{\text{Conclusion}}$.
cone (p. 654) A three-dimensional figure with a circular base and a curved lateral surface that connects the base to a point called the vertex.	**cono** Figura tridimensional con una base circular y una superficie lateral curva que conecta la base con un punto denominado vértice.	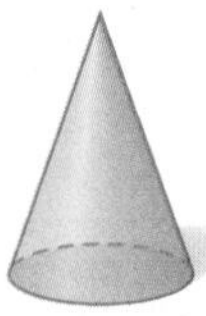
congruence statement (p. 231) A statement that indicates that two polygons are congruent by listing the vertices in the order of correspondence.	**enunciado de congruencia** Enunciado que indica que dos polígonos son congruentes enumerando los vértices en orden de correspondencia.	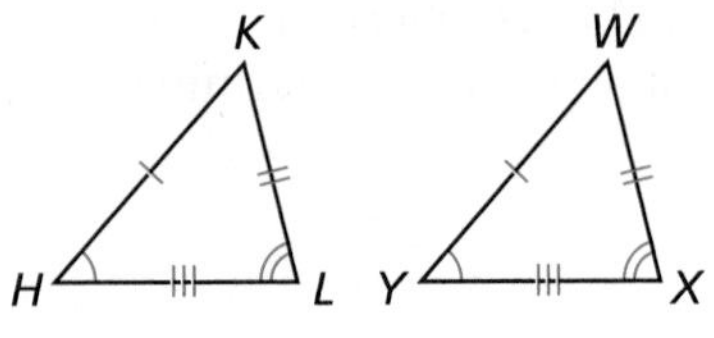 K W H L Y X $\triangle HKL \cong \triangle YWX$
congruence transformation (p. 824) *See* isometry.	**transformación de congruencia** *Ver* isometría.	
congruent (p. 13) Having the same size and shape, denoted by ≅.	**congruente** Que tiene el mismo tamaño y la misma forma, expresado por ≅.	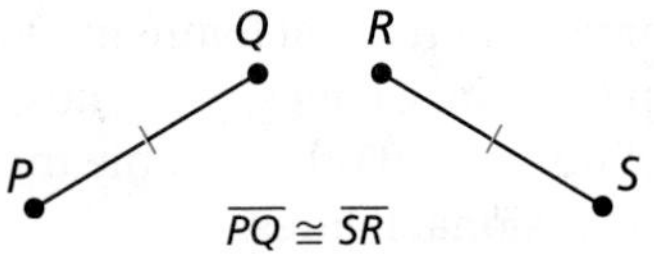 Q R P S $\overline{PQ} \cong \overline{SR}$

G8 *Glossary/Glosario*

ENGLISH	SPANISH	EXAMPLES
congruent angles (p. 22) Angles that have the same measure.	**ángulos congruentes** Ángulos que tienen la misma medida.	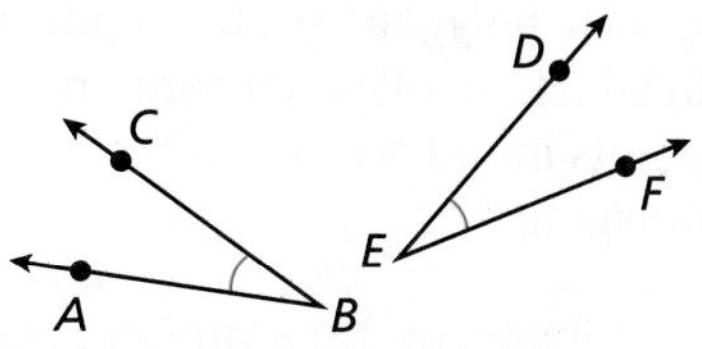 $\angle ABC \cong \angle DEF$
congruent arcs (p. 757) Two arcs that are in the same or congruent circles and have the same measure.	**arcos congruentes** Dos arcos que se encuentran en el mismo círculo o en círculos congruentes y que tienen la misma medida.	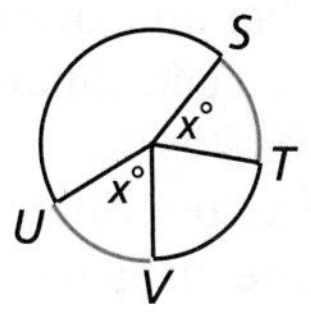
congruent circles (p. 747) Two circles that have congruent radii.	**círculos congruentes** Dos círculos que tienen radios congruentes.	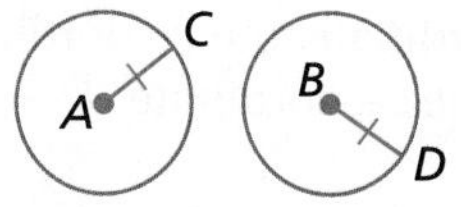
congruent polygons (p. 231) Two polygons whose corresponding sides and angles are congruent.	**polígonos congruentes** Dos polígonos cuyos lados y ángulos correspondientes son congruentes.	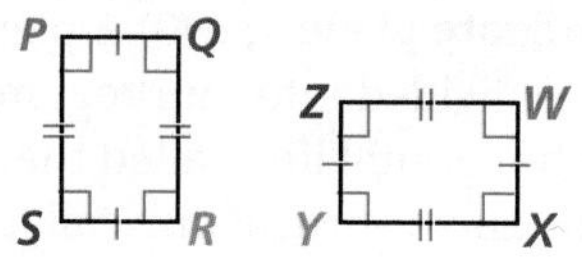
congruent segments (p. 13) Two segments that have the same length.	**segmentos congruentes** Dos segmentos que tienen la misma longitud.	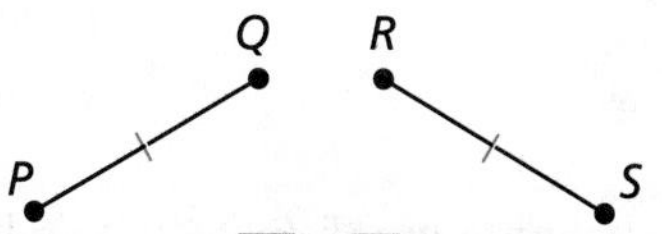 $\overline{PQ} \cong \overline{SR}$
conjecture (p. 74) A statement that is believed to be true.	**conjetura** Enunciado que se supone verdadero.	A sequence begins with the terms 2, 4, 6, 8, 10. A reasonable conjecture is that the next term in the sequence is 12.
conjunction (p. 128) A compound statement that uses the word *and.*	**conjunción** Enunciado compuesto que contiene la palabra *y.*	3 is less than 5 AND greater than 0.
consecutive interior angles (p. 147) *See* same-side interior angles.	**ángulos internos consecutivos** *Ver* ángulos internos del mismo lado.	
construction (p. 14) A method of creating a figure that is considered to be mathematically precise. Figures may be constructed by using a compass and straightedge, geometry software, or paper folding.	**construcción** Método para crear una figura que es considerado matemáticamente preciso. Se pueden construir figuras utilizando un compás y una regla, un programa de computación de geometría o plegando papeles.	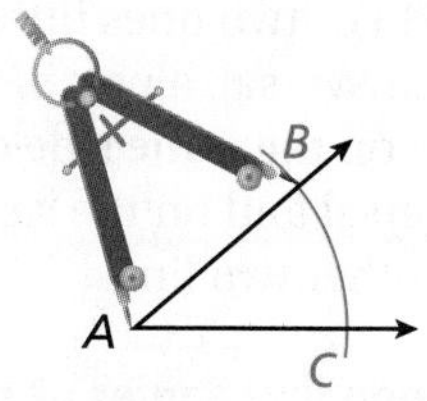
contraction (p. 873) *See* reduction.	**contracción** *Ver* reducción.	
contrapositive (p. 83) The statement formed by both exchanging and negating the hypothesis and conclusion of a conditional statement.	**contrarrecíproco** Enunciado que se forma al intercambiar y negar la hipótesis y la conclusión de un enunciado condicional.	Statement: If $n + 1 = 3$, then $n = 2$ Contrapositive: If $n \neq 2$, then $n + 1 \neq 3$
converse (p. 83) The statement formed by exchanging the hypothesis and conclusion of a conditional statement.	**recíproco** Enunciado que se forma intercambiando la hipótesis y la conclusión de un enunciado condicional.	Statement: If $n + 1 = 3$, then $n = 2$ Converse: If $n = 2$, then $n + 1 = 3$

Glossary/Glosario G9

ENGLISH	SPANISH	EXAMPLES
convex polygon (p. 383) A polygon in which no diagonal contains points in the exterior of the polygon.	**polígono convexo** Polígono en el cual ninguna diagonal contiene puntos fuera del polígono.	 Convex quadrilateral
coordinate (p. 13) A number used to identify the location of a point. On a number line, one coordinate is used. On a coordinate plane, two coordinates are used, called the *x*-coordinate and the *y*-coordinate. In space, three coordinates are used, called the *x*-coordinate, the *y*-coordinate, and the *z*-coordinate.	**coordenada** Número utilizado para identificar la ubicación de un punto. En una recta numérica se utiliza una coordenada. En un plano cartesiano se utilizan dos coordenadas, denominadas coordenada *x* y coordenada *y*. En el espacio se utilizan tres coordenadas, denominadas coordenada *x*, coordenada *y* y coordenada *z*.	A; −1 0 1 2 3 4 5 The coordinate of point *A* is 3. 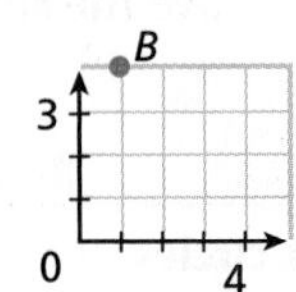 The coordinates of point *B* are (1, 4).
coordinate plane (p. 43) A plane that is divided into four regions by a horizontal line called the *x*-axis and a vertical line called the *y*-axis.	**plano cartesiano** Plano dividido en cuatro regiones por una línea horizontal denominada eje *x* y una línea vertical denominada eje *y*.	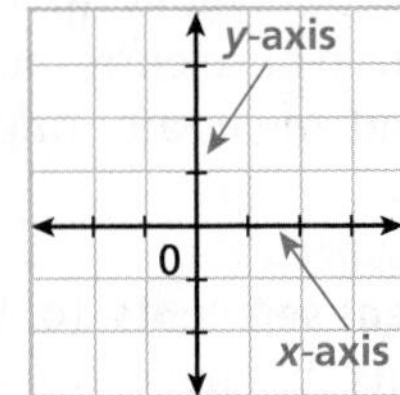
coordinate proof (p. 267) A style of proof that uses coordinate geometry and algebra.	**prueba de coordenadas** Tipo de demostración que utiliza geometría de coordenadas y álgebra.	
coplanar (p. 6) Points that lie in the same plane.	**coplanar** Puntos que se encuentran en el mismo plano.	
corollary (p. 224) A theorem whose proof follows directly from another theorem.	**corolario** Teorema cuya demostración proviene directamente de otro teorema.	
corresponding angles of lines intersected by a transversal (p. 147) For two lines intersected by a transversal, a pair of angles that lie on the same side of the transversal and on the same sides of the other two lines.	**ángulos correspondientes de líneas cortadas por una transversal** Dadas dos líneas cortadas por una transversal, el par de ángulos ubicados en el mismo lado de la transversal y en los mismos lados de las otras dos líneas.	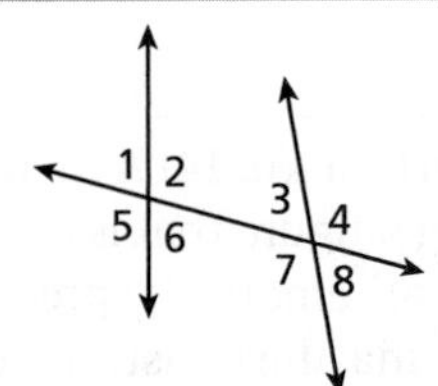 ∠1 and ∠3 are corresponding.
corresponding angles of polygons (p. 231) Angles in the same position in two different polygons that have the same number of angles.	**ángulos correspondientes de los polígonos** Ángulos que tienen la misma posición en dos polígonos diferentes que tienen el mismo número de ángulos.	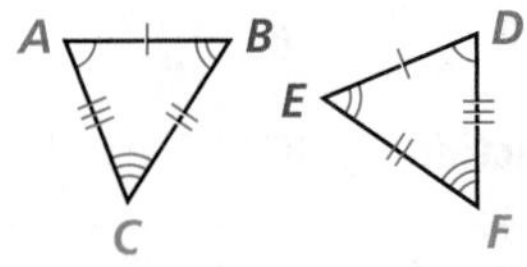 ∠*A* and ∠*D* are corresponding angles.
corresponding sides of polygons (p. 231) Sides in the same position in two different polygons that have the same number of sides.	**lados correspondientes de los polígonos** Lados que tienen la misma posición en dos polígonos diferentes que tienen el mismo número de lados.	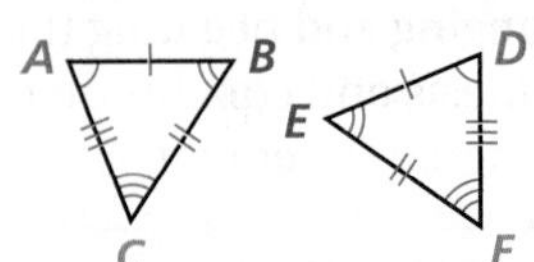 $\overline{AB}$ and $\overline{DE}$ are corresponding sides.

G10 *Glossary/Glosario*

ENGLISH / SPANISH / EXAMPLES

cosecant (p. 532) In a right triangle, the cosecant of angle A is the ratio of the length of the hypotenuse to the length of the side opposite A. It is the reciprocal of the sine function.

cosecante En un triángulo rectángulo, la cosecante del ángulo A es la razón entre la longitud de la hipotenusa y la longitud del cateto opuesto a A. Es la inversa de la función seno.

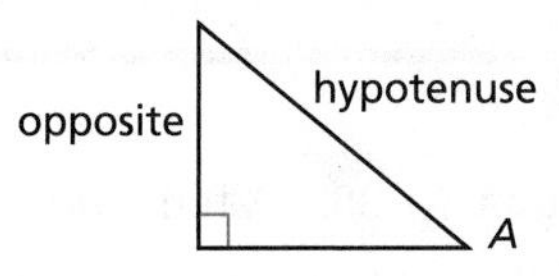

$$\csc A = \frac{\text{hypotenuse}}{\text{opposite}} = \frac{1}{\sin A}$$

---

cosine (p. 525) In a right triangle, the cosine of angle A is the ratio of the length of the leg adjacent to angle A to the length of the hypotenuse. It is the reciprocal of the secant function.

coseno En un triángulo rectángulo, el coseno del ángulo A es la razón entre la longitud del cateto adyacente al ángulo A y la longitud de la hipotenusa. Es la inversa de la función secante.

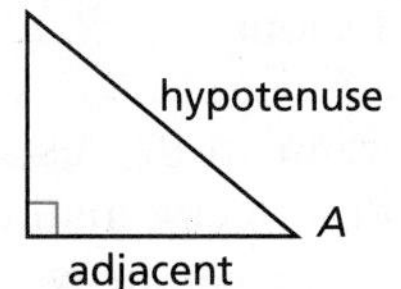

$$\cos A = \frac{\text{adjacent}}{\text{hypotenuse}} = \frac{1}{\sec A}$$

---

cotangent (p. 532) In a right triangle, the cotangent of angle A is the ratio of the length of the side adjacent to A to the length of the side opposite A. It is the reciprocal of the tangent function.

cotangente En un triángulo rectángulo, la cotangente del ángulo A es la razón entre la longitud del cateto adyacente a A y la longitud del cateto opuesto a A. Es la inversa de la función tangente.

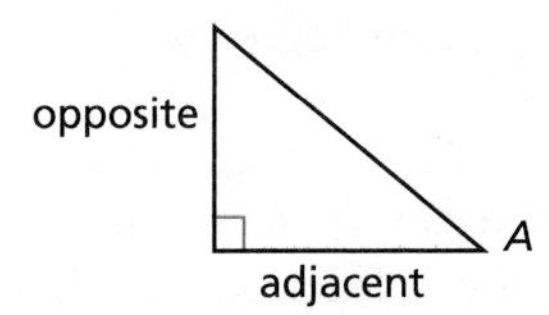

$$\cot A = \frac{\text{adjacent}}{\text{opposite}} = \frac{1}{\tan A}$$

---

counterexample (p. 75) An example that proves that a conjecture or statement is false.

contraejemplo Ejemplo que demuestra que una conjetura o enunciado es falso.

CPCTC (p. 260) An abbreviation for "Corresponding Parts of Congruent Triangles are Congruent," which can be used as a justification in a proof after two triangles are proven congruent.

PCTCC Abreviatura que significa "Las partes correspondientes de los triángulos congruentes son congruentes", que se puede utilizar para justificar una demostración después de demostrar que dos triángulos son congruentes (CPCTC, por sus siglas en inglés).

---

cross products (p. 455) In the statement $\frac{a}{b} = \frac{c}{d}$, bc and ad are the cross products.

productos cruzados En el enunciado $\frac{a}{b} = \frac{c}{d}$, bc y ad son los productos cruzados.

$$\frac{1}{2} = \frac{3}{6}$$

Product of means: $2 \cdot 3 = 6$

Product of extremes: $1 \cdot 6 = 6$

---

cross section (p. 656) The intersection of a three-dimensional figure and a plane.

sección transversal Intersección de una figura tridimensional y un plano.

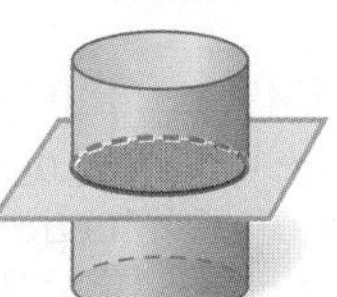

---

cube (p. 654) A prism with six square faces.

cubo Prisma con seis caras cuadradas.

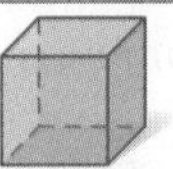

---

cylinder (p. 654) A three-dimensional figure with two parallel congruent circular bases and a curved lateral surface that connects the bases.

cilindro Figura tridimensional con dos bases circulares congruentes y paralelas y una superficie lateral curva que conecta las bases.

Glossary/Glosario G11

ENGLISH	SPANISH	EXAMPLES
D		
decagon (p. 382) A ten-sided polygon.	**decágono** Polígono de diez lados.	
deductive reasoning (p. 88) The process of using logic to draw conclusions.	**razonamiento deductivo** Proceso en el que se utiliza la lógica para sacar conclusiones.	
definition (p. 97) A statement that describes a mathematical object and can be written as a true biconditional statement.	**definición** Enunciado que describe un objeto matemático y se puede expresar como un enunciado bicondicional verdadero.	
degree (p. 20) A unit of angle measure; one degree is $\frac{1}{360}$ of a circle.	**grado** Unidad de medida de los ángulos; un grado es $\frac{1}{360}$ de un círculo.	
denominator (p. 451) The bottom number of a fraction, which tells how many equal parts are in the whole.	**denominador** El número inferior de una fracción, que indica la cantidad de partes iguales que hay en un entero.	The denominator of $\frac{3}{7}$ is 7.
diagonal of a polygon (p. 382) A segment connecting two nonconsecutive vertices of a polygon.	**diagonal de un polígono** Segmento que conecta dos vértices no consecutivos de un polígono.	A B C D E Diagonal
diagonal of a polyhedron (p. 671) A segment whose endpoints are vertices of two different faces of a polyhedron.	**diagonal de un poliedro** Segmento cuyos extremos son vértices de dos caras diferentes de un poliedro.	*d*
diameter (p. 37) A segment that has endpoints on the circle and that passes through the center of the circle; also the length of that segment.	**diámetro** Segmento que atraviesa el centro de un círculo y cuyos extremos están sobre la circunferencia; longitud de dicho segmento.	
dilation (p. 495) A transformation in which the lines connecting every point P with its preimage P' all intersect at a point C known as the center of dilation, and $\frac{CP'}{CP}$ is the same for every point P; a transformation that changes the size of a figure but not its shape.	**dilatación** Transformación en la cual las líneas que conectan cada punto P con su imagen original P' se cruzan en un punto C conocido como centro de dilatación, y $\frac{CP'}{CP}$ es igual para cada punto P; transformación que cambia el tamaño de una figura pero no su forma.	C D E F D′ E′ F′
direct reasoning (p. 332) The process of reasoning that begins with a true hypothesis and builds a logical argument to show that a conclusion is true.	**razonamiento directo** Proceso de razonamiento que comienza con una hipótesis verdadera y elabora un argumento lógico para demostrar que una conclusión es verdadera.	

G12 Glossary/Glosario

ENGLISH	SPANISH	EXAMPLES
direct variation (p. 501) A linear relationship between two variables, x and y, that can be written in the form $y = kx$, where k is a nonzero constant.	**variación directa** Relación lineal entre dos variables, x e y, que puede expresarse en la forma $y = kx$, donde k es una constante distinta de cero.	3, $y = 4x$, 0, 4
direction of a vector (p. 560) The orientation of a vector, which is determined by the angle the vector makes with a horizontal line.	**dirección de un vector** Orientación de un vector, determinada por el ángulo que forma el vector con una línea horizontal.	B, 60°, A
disjunction (p. 128) A compound statement that uses the word *or*.	**disyunción** Enunciado compuesto que contiene la palabra *o*.	John will walk to work or he will stay home.
distance between two points (p. 13) The absolute value of the difference of the coordinates of the points.	**distancia entre dos puntos** Valor absoluto de la diferencia entre las coordenadas de los puntos.	A, B, a, b $AB = \|a - b\| = \|b - a\|$
distance from a point to a line (p. 172) The length of the perpendicular segment from the point to the line.	**distancia desde un punto hasta una línea** Longitud del segmento perpendicular desde el punto hasta la línea.	P, A, C The distance from P to $\overleftrightarrow{AC}$ is 5 units.
dodecagon (p. 382) A 12-sided polygon.	**dodecágono** Polígono de 12 lados.	
dodecahedron (p. 669) A polyhedron with 12 faces. The faces of a regular dodecahedron are regular pentagons, with three faces meeting at each vertex.	**dodecaedro** Poliedro con 12 caras. Las caras de un dodecaedro regular son pentágonos regulares, con tres caras que concurren en cada vértice.	

E

ENGLISH	SPANISH	EXAMPLES
edge of a graph (p. 95) A curve or segment that joins two vertices of the graph.	**arista de una gráfica** Curva o segmento que une dos vértices de la gráfica.	(0, 0), Edge, (1, 0), $\left(0, \frac{3}{4}\right)$
edge of a three-dimensional figure (p. 654) A segment that is the intersection of two faces of the figure.	**arista de una figura tridimensional** Segmento que constituye la intersección de dos caras de la figura.	Edge
endpoint (p. 7) A point at an end of a segment or the starting point of a ray.	**extremo** Punto en el final de un segmento o punto de inicio de un rayo.	A, B, D
enlargement (p. 873) A dilation with a scale factor greater than 1. In an enlargement, the image is larger than the preimage.	**agrandamiento** Dilatación con un factor de escala mayor que 1. En un agrandamiento, la imagen es más grande que la imagen original.	

Glossary/Glosario

Glossary/Glosario G13

ENGLISH	SPANISH	EXAMPLES
equal vectors (p. 561) Two vectors that have the same magnitude and the same direction.	**vectores iguales** Dos vectores de la misma magnitud y con la misma dirección.	$\lvert\vec{u}\rvert = \lvert\vec{v}\rvert = 2\sqrt{5}$
equiangular polygon (p. 382) A polygon in which all angles are congruent.	**polígono equiangular** Polígono cuyos ángulos son todos congruentes.	
equiangular triangle (p. 216) A triangle with three congruent angles.	**triángulo equiangular** Triángulo con tres ángulos congruentes.	
equidistant (p. 300) The same distance from two or more objects.	**equidistante** Igual distancia de dos o más objetos.	*X* is equidistant from *A* and *B*.
equilateral polygon (p. 382) A polygon in which all sides are congruent.	**polígono equilátero** Polígono cuyos lados son todos congruentes.	
equilateral triangle (p. 217) A triangle with three congruent sides.	**triángulo equilátero** Triángulo con tres lados congruentes.	
Euclidean geometry (p. 726) The system of geometry described by Euclid. In particular, the system of Euclidean geometry satisfies the Parallel Postulate, which states that there is exactly one line through a given point parallel to a given line.	**geometría euclidiana** Sistema geométrico desarrollado por Euclides. Específicamente, el sistema de la geometría euclidiana cumple con el postulado de las paralelas, que establece que por un punto dado se puede trazar una única línea paralela a una línea dada.	
Euler line (p. 321) The line containing the circumcenter (*U*), centroid (*C*), and orthocenter (*O*) of a triangle.	**recta de Euler** Recta que contiene el circuncentro (*U*), el centroide (*C*) y el ortocentro (*O*) de un triángulo.	
event (p. 628) An outcome or set of outcomes in a probability experiment.	**suceso** Resultado o conjunto de resultados en un experimento de probabilidad.	In the experiement of rolling a number cube, the event "an odd number" consists of the outcomes 1, 3, 5.
expansion (p. 873) *See* enlargement.	**expansión** *Ver* agrandamiento.	
experiment (p. 628) An operation, process, or activity in which outcomes can be used to estimate probability.	**experimento** Una operación, proceso o actividad en la que se usan los resultados para estimar una probabilidad.	Tossing a coin 10 times and noting the number of heads.

G14 Glossary/Glosario

ENGLISH	SPANISH	EXAMPLES
exterior of a circle (p. 746) The set of all points outside a circle.	**exterior de un círculo** Conjunto de todos los puntos que se encuentran fuera de un círculo.	Exterior
exterior of an angle (p. 20) The set of all points outside an angle.	**exterior de un ángulo** Conjunto de todos los puntos que se encuentran fuera de un ángulo.	Exterior
exterior of a polygon (p. 225) The set of all points outside a polygon.	**exterior de un polígono** Conjunto de todos los puntos que se encuentran fuera de un polígono.	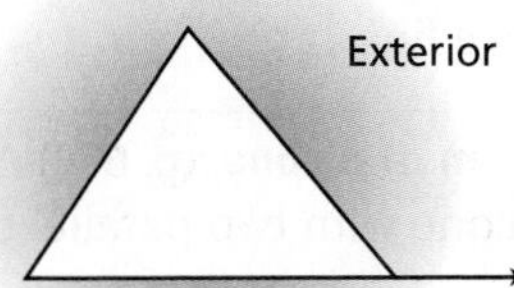
exterior angle of a polygon (p. 225) An angle formed by one side of a polygon and the extension of an adjacent side.	**ángulo externo de un polígono** Ángulo formado por un lado de un polígono y la prolongación del lado adyacente.	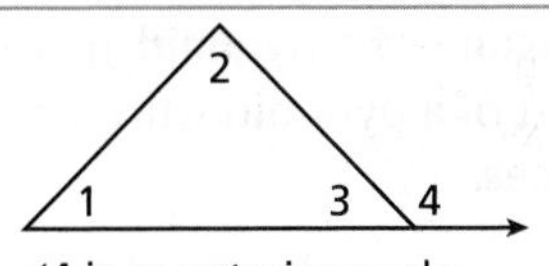 $\angle 4$ is an exterior angle.
external secant segment (p. 793) A segment of a secant that lies in the exterior of the circle with one endpoint on the circle.	**segmento secante externo** Segmento de una secante que se encuentra en el exterior del círculo y tiene un extremo sobre el círculo.	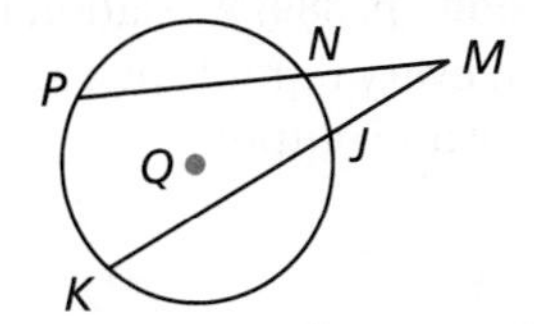 $\overline{NM}$ is an external secant segment.
extremes of a proportion (p. 455) In the proportion $\frac{a}{b} = \frac{c}{d}$, a and d are the extremes. If the proportion is written as $a{:}b = c{:}d$, the extremes are in the first and last positions.	**valores extremos de una proporción** En la proporción $\frac{a}{b} = \frac{c}{d}$, a y d son los valores extremos. Si la proporción se expresa como $a{:}b = c{:}d$, los extremos están en la primera y última posición.	

ENGLISH	SPANISH	EXAMPLES
face of a polyhedron (p. 654) A flat surface of the polyhedron.	**cara de un poliedro** Superficie plana de un poliedro.	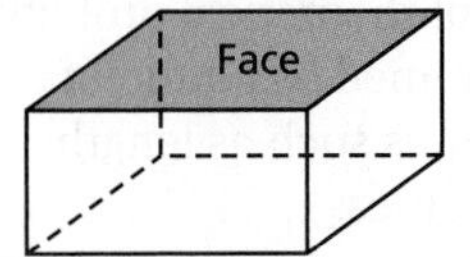
fair (p. 628) When all outcomes of an experiment are equally likely.	**justo** Cuando todos los resultados de un experimento son igualmente probables.	When tossing a fair coin, heads and tails are equally likely. Each has a probability of $\frac{1}{2}$.
Fibonacci sequence (p. 78) The infinite sequence of numbers beginning with 1, 1, … such that each term is the sum of the two previous terms.	**sucesión de Fibonacci** Sucesión infinita de números que comienza con 1, 1, … de forma tal que cada término es la suma de los dos términos anteriores.	1, 1, 2, 3, 5, 8, 13, 21, …

Glossary/Glosario G15

Glossary/Glosario

ENGLISH	SPANISH	EXAMPLES
flip (p. 50) *See* reflection.	**inversión** *Ver* reflexión.	
flowchart proof (p. 118) A style of proof that uses boxes and arrows to show the structure of the proof.	**demostración con diagrama de flujo** Tipo de demostración que se vale de cuadros y flechas para mostrar la estructura de la prueba.	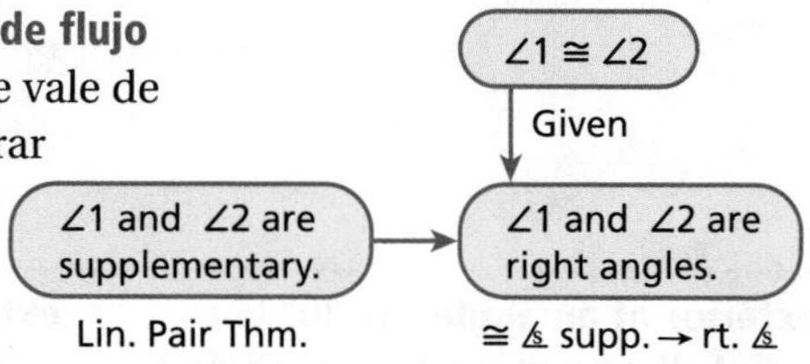 $\angle 1 \cong \angle 2$ → Given → $\angle 1$ and $\angle 2$ are right angles. ← $\angle 1$ and $\angle 2$ are supplementary. (Lin. Pair Thm.) ($\cong$ ∡ supp. → rt. ∡)
fractal (p. 882) A figure that is generated by iteration.	**fractal** Figura generada por iteración.	
frieze pattern (p. 865) A pattern that has translation symmetry along a line.	**patrón de friso** Patrón con simetría de traslación a lo largo de una línea.	
frustum of a cone (p. 668) A part of a cone with two parallel bases.	**tronco de cono** Parte de un cono con dos bases paralelas.	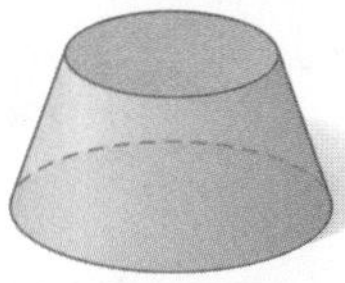
frustum of a pyramid (p. 696) A part of a pyramid with two parallel bases.	**tronco de pirámide** Parte de una pirámide con dos bases paralelas.	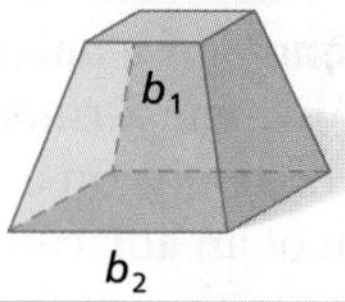 b_1, b_2
function (p. 389) A relation in which every input is paired with exactly one output.	**función** Una relación en la que cada entrada corresponde exactamente a una salida.	Function: {(0, 5), (1, 3),(2, 1), (3, 3)} Not a Function: {(0, 1), (0, 3), (2, 1), (2, 3)}

G

ENGLISH	SPANISH	EXAMPLES
geometric mean (p. 519) For positive numbers a and b, the positive number x such that $\frac{a}{x} = \frac{x}{b}$. In a geometric sequence, a term that comes between two given nonconsecutive terms of the sequence.	**media geométrica** Dados los números positivos a y b, el número positivo x tal que $\frac{a}{x} = \frac{x}{b}$. En una sucesión geométrica, un término que está entre dos términos no consecutivos dados de la sucesión.	$\frac{a}{x} = \frac{x}{b}$ $x^2 = ab$ $x = \sqrt{ab}$
geometric probability (p. 630) A form of theoretical probability determined by a ratio of geometric measures such as lengths, areas, or volumes.	**probabilidad geométrica** Una forma de la probabilidad teórica determinada por una razón de medidas geométricas, como longitud, área o volumen.	 100°, 80°, 45°, 60°, 75° The probability of the pointer landing on red is $\frac{2}{9}$.
glide reflection (p. 848) A composition of a translation and a reflection across a line parallel to the translation vector.	**deslizamiento con inversión** Composición de una traslación y una reflexión sobre una línea paralela al vector de traslación.	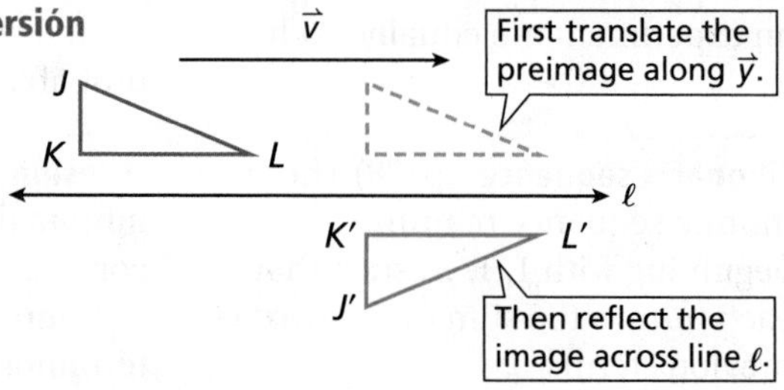 $\vec{v}$ First translate the preimage along $\vec{v}$. J, K, L, ℓ, K', L', J' Then reflect the image across line ℓ.

G16 Glossary/Glosario

ENGLISH	SPANISH	EXAMPLES
glide reflection symmetry (p. 865) A pattern has glide reflection symmetry if it coincides with its image after a glide reflection.	**simetría de deslizamiento con inversión** Un patrón tiene simetría de deslizamiento con inversión si coincide con su imagen después de un deslizamiento con inversión.	
golden ratio (p. 460) If a segment is divided into two parts so that the ratio of the lengths of the whole segment to the longer part equals the ratio of the lengths of the longer part to the shorter part, then that ratio is called the golden ratio. The golden ratio is equal to $\frac{1+\sqrt{5}}{2} \approx 1.618$.	**razón áurea** Si se divide un segmento en dos partes de forma tal que la razón entre la longitud de todo el segmento y la de la parte más larga sea igual a la razón entre la longitud de la parte más larga y la de la parte más corta, entonces dicha razón se denomina razón áurea. La razón áurea es igual a $\frac{1+\sqrt{5}}{2} \approx 1.618$.	Golden ratio $= \frac{AC}{AB} = \frac{AB}{BC}$ Create segment such that $\frac{AC}{AB} \approx 1.62$ and $\frac{AB}{BC} \approx 1.62$ 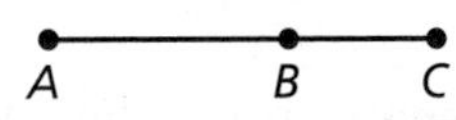
golden rectangle (p. 460) A rectangle in which the ratio of the lengths of the longer side to the shorter side is the golden ratio.	**rectángulo áureo** Rectángulo en el cual la razón entre la longitud del lado más largo y la longitud del lado más corto es la razón áurea.	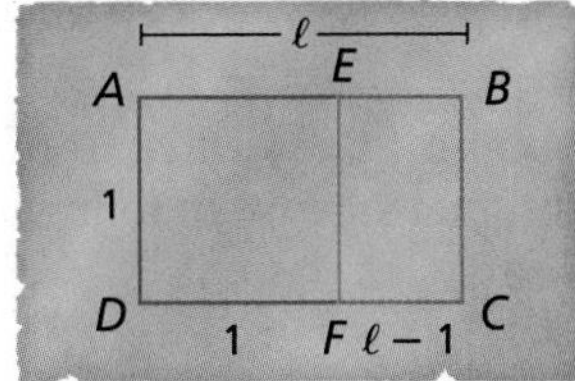
great circle (p. 714) A circle on a sphere that divides the sphere into two hemispheres.	**círculo máximo** En una esfera, círculo que divide la esfera en dos hemisferios.	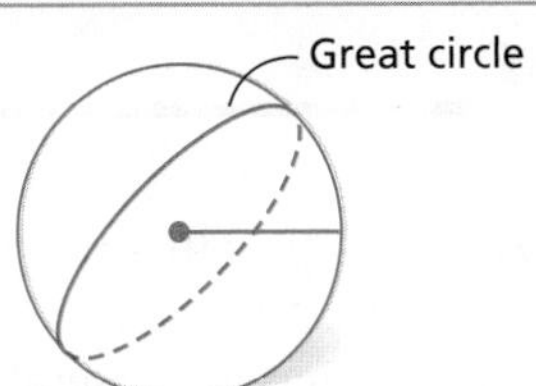

ENGLISH	SPANISH	EXAMPLES
head-to-tail method (p. 561) A method of adding two vectors by placing the tail of the second vector on the head of the first vector; the sum is the vector drawn from the tail of the first vector to the head of the second vector.	**método de cola a punta** Método para sumar dos vectores colocando la cola del segundo vector en la punta del primer vector. La suma es el vector trazado desde la cola del primer vector hasta la punta del segundo vector.	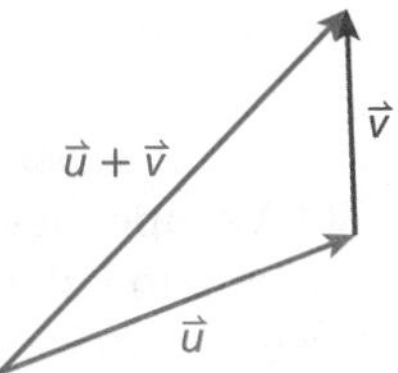
height of a figure (p. 36) The length of an altitude of the figure.	**altura de una figura** Longitud de la altura de la figura.	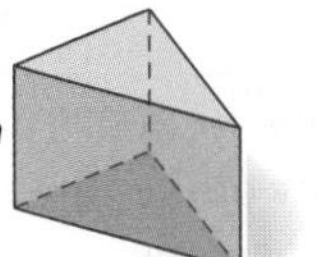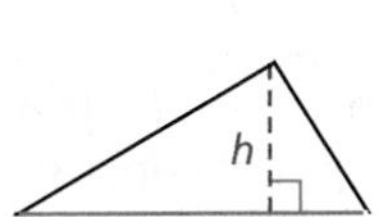
height of a triangle (p. 36) A segment from a vertex that forms a right angle with a line containing the base.	**altura de un triángulo** Segmento que se extiende desde el vértice y forma un ángulo recto con la línea de la base.	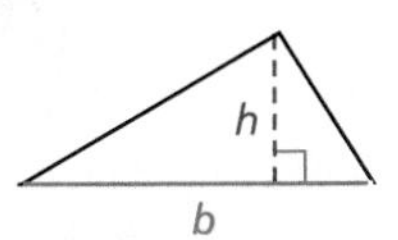
hemisphere (p. 714) Half of a sphere.	**hemisferio** Mitad de una esfera.	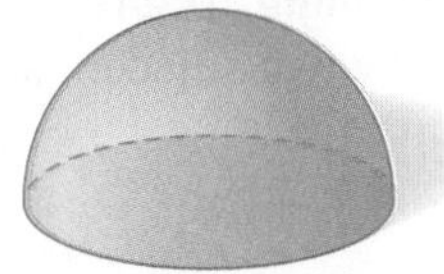

Glossary/Glosario G17

ENGLISH	SPANISH	EXAMPLES
heptagon (p. 382) A seven-sided polygon.	**heptágono** Polígono de siete lados.	
hexagon (p. 382) A six-sided polygon.	**hexágono** Polígono de seis lados.	
horizon (p. 662) The horizontal line in a perspective drawing that contains the vanishing point(s).	**horizonte** Línea horizontal en un dibujo en perspectiva que contiene el punto de fuga o los puntos de fuga.	Vanishing point Horizon
hypotenuse (p. 45) The side opposite the right angle in a right triangle.	**hipotenusa** Lado opuesto al ángulo recto de un triángulo rectángulo.	hypotenuse
hypothesis (p. 81) The part of a conditional statement following the word *if*.	**hipótesis** La parte de un enunciado condicional que sigue a la palabra *si*.	If $x + 1 = 5$, then $x = 4$. Hypothesis

I

ENGLISH	SPANISH	EXAMPLES
icosahedron (p. 669) A polyhedron with 20 faces. A regular icosahedron has equilateral triangles as faces, with 5 faces meeting at each vertex.	**icosaedro** Poliedro con 20 caras. Las caras de un icosaedro regular son triángulos equiláteros y cada vértice es compartido por 5 caras.	
identity (p. 531) An equation that is true for all values of the variables.	**identidad** Ecuación verdadera para todos los valores de las variables.	$3 = 3$ $2(x - 1) = 2x - 2$
image (p. 50) A shape that results from a transformation of a figure known as the preimage.	**imagen** Forma resultante de la transformación de una figura conocida como imagen original.	B, A, C B′, A′, C′
incenter of a triangle (p. 309) The point of concurrency of the three angle bisectors of a triangle.	**incentro de un triángulo** Punto donde se encuentran las tres bisectrices de los ángulos de un triángulo.	G, K, M, P, H, L, J *P* is the incenter.
included angle (p. 242) The angle formed by two adjacent sides of a polygon.	**ángulo incluido** Ángulo formado por dos lados adyacentes de un polígono.	A, B, C $\angle B$ is the included angle between $\overline{AB}$ and $\overline{BC}$.

G18 Glossary/Glosario

Glossary/Glosario

ENGLISH	SPANISH	EXAMPLES
included side (p. 252) The common side of two consecutive angles of a polygon.	**lado incluido** Lado común de dos ángulos consecutivos de un polígono.	$\overline{PQ}$ is the included side between $\angle P$ and $\angle Q$.
indirect measurement (p. 488) A method of measurement that uses formulas, similar figures, and/or proportions.	**medición indirecta** Método para medir objetos mediante fórmulas, figuras semejantes y/o proporciones.	
indirect proof (p. 332) A proof in which the statement to be proved is assumed to be false and a contradiction is shown.	**demostración indirecta** Prueba en la que se supone que el enunciado a demostrar es falso y se muestra una contradicción.	
indirect reasoning (p. 332) *See* indirect proof.	**razonamiento indirecto** *Ver* demostración indirecta.	
inductive reasoning (p. 74) The process of reasoning that a rule or statement is true because specific cases are true.	**razonamiento inductivo** Proceso de razonamiento por el que se determina que una regla o enunciado son verdaderos porque ciertos casos específicos son verdaderos.	
inequality (p. 92) A statement that compares two expressions by using one of the following signs: $<, >, \leq, \geq$, or $\neq$.	**desigualdad** Enunciado que compara dos expresiones utilizando uno de los siguientes signos: $<, >, \leq, \geq$ o $\neq$.	$x > 2$
initial point of a vector (p. 559) The starting point of a vector.	**punto inicial de un vector** Punto donde comienza un vector.	Initial point
initial side (p. 570) The ray that lies on the positive x-axis when an angle is drawn in standard position.	**lado inicial** Rayo que se encuentra sobre el eje x positivo cuando se traza un ángulo en posición estándar.	
inscribed angle (p. 772) An angle whose vertex is on a circle and whose sides contain chords of the circle.	**ángulo inscrito** Ángulo cuyo vértice se encuentra sobre un círculo y cuyos lados contienen cuerdas del círculo.	
inscribed circle (p. 309) A circle in which each side of the polygon is tangent to the circle.	**círculo inscrito** Círculo en el que cada lado del polígono es tangente al círculo.	
inscribed polygon (p. 599) A polygon in which every vertex of the polygon lies on the circle.	**polígono inscrito** Polígono cuyos vértices se encuentran sobre el círculo.	

Glossary/Glosario

Glossary/Glosario G19

ENGLISH	SPANISH	EXAMPLES
integer (p. 559) A member of the set of whole numbers and their opposites.	**entero** Miembro del conjunto de números cabales y sus opuestos.	$\{\ldots -3, -2, -1, 0, 1, 2, 3, \ldots\}$
intercepted arc (p. 772) An arc that consists of endpoints that lie on the sides of an inscribed angle and all the points of the circle between the endpoints.	**arco abarcado** Arco cuyos extremos se encuentran en los lados de un ángulo inscrito y consta de todos los puntos del círculo ubicados entre dichos extremos.	$\overset{\frown}{DF}$ is the intercepted arc.
interior angle (p. 225) An angle formed by two sides of a polygon with a common vertex.	**ángulo interno** Ángulo formado por dos lados de un polígono con un vértice común.	$\angle 1$ is an interior angle.
interior of a circle (p. 746) The set of all points inside a circle.	**interior de un círculo** Conjunto de todos los puntos que se encuentran dentro de un círculo.	Interior
interior of an angle (p. 20) The set of all points between the sides of an angle.	**interior de un ángulo** Conjunto de todos los puntos entre los lados de un ángulo.	Interior
interior of a polygon (p. 225) The set of all points inside a polygon.	**interior de un polígono** Conjunto de todos los puntos que se encuentran dentro de un polígono.	Interior
inverse (p. 83) The statement formed by negating the hypothesis and conclusion of a conditional statement.	**inverso** Enunciado formado al negar la hipótesis y la conclusión de un enunciado condicional.	Statement: If $n + 1 = 3$, then $n = 2$ Inverse: If $n + 1 \neq 3$, then $n \neq 2$
inverse cosine (p. 534) The measure of an angle whose cosine ratio is known.	**coseno inverso** Medida de un ángulo cuya razón coseno es conocida.	If $\cos A = x$, then $\cos^{-1} x = m\angle A$.
inverse function (p. 533) The function that results from exchanging the input and output values of a one-to-one function. The inverse of $f(x)$ is denoted $f^{-1}(x)$.	**función inversa** Función que resulta de intercambiar los valores de entrada y salida de una función uno a uno. La función inversa de $f(x)$ se indica $f^{-1}(x)$.	The function $y = \frac{1}{2}x - 2$ is the inverse of the function $y = 2x + 4$.

G20 Glossary/Glosario

ENGLISH	SPANISH	EXAMPLES
inverse sine (p. 534) The measure of an angle whose sine ratio is known.	**seno inverso** Medida de un ángulo cuya razón seno es conocida.	If $\sin A = x$, then $\sin^{-1} x = m\angle A$.
inverse tangent (p. 534) The measure of an angle whose tangent ratio is known.	**tangente inversa** Medida de un ángulo cuya razón tangente es conocida.	If $\tan A = x$, then $\tan^{-1} x = m\angle A$.
irrational number (p. 80) A real number that cannot be expressed as the ratio of two integers.	**número irracional** Número real que no se puede expresar como una razón de dos enteros.	$\sqrt{2}$, π, e
irregular polygon (p. 382) A polygon that is not regular.	**polígono irregular** Polígono que no es regular.	
isometric drawing (p. 662) A way of drawing three-dimensional figures using *isometric dot paper*, which has equally spaced dots in a repeating triangular pattern.	**dibujo isométrico** Forma de dibujar figuras tridimensionales utilizando *papel punteado isométrico*, que tiene puntos espaciados uniformemente en un patrón triangular que se repite.	
isometry (p. 824) A transformation that does not change the size or shape of a figure.	**isometría** Transformación que no cambia el tamaño ni la forma de una figura.	Reflections, translations, and rotations are all examples of isometries.
isosceles trapezoid (p. 429) A trapezoid in which the legs are congruent.	**trapecio isósceles** Trapecio cuyos lados no paralelos son congruentes.	B C A D
isosceles triangle (p. 217) A triangle with at least two congruent sides.	**triángulo isósceles** Triángulo que tiene al menos dos lados congruentes.	
iteration (p. 882) The repetitive application of the same rule.	**iteración** Aplicación repetitiva de la misma regla.	

K

ENGLISH	SPANISH	EXAMPLES
kite (p. 427) A quadrilateral with exactly two pairs of congruent consecutive sides.	**cometa o papalote** Cuadrilátero con exactamente dos pares de lados congruentes consecutivos.	B A C D Kite *ABCD*
Koch snowflake (p. 882) A fractal formed from a triangle by replacing the middle third of each segment with two segments that form a 60° angle.	**copo de nieve de Koch** Fractal formado a partir de un triángulo sustituyendo el tercio central de cada segmento por dos segmentos que forman un ángulo de 60°.	

Glossary/Glosario

Glossary/Glosario **G21**

ENGLISH	SPANISH	EXAMPLES

L

lateral area (p. 680) The sum of the areas of the lateral faces of a prism or pyramid, or the area of the lateral surface of a cylinder or cone.	**área lateral** Suma de las áreas de las caras laterales de un prisma o pirámide, o área de la superficie lateral de un cilindro o cono.	12 cm; 6 cm; 8 cm Lateral area = $(28)(12) = 336\text{ cm}^2$
lateral edge (p. 680) An edge of a prism or pyramid that is not an edge of a base.	**arista lateral** Arista de un prisma o pirámide que no es la arista de una base.	Bases; Lateral edge Right prism
lateral face (p. 680) A face of a prism or a pyramid that is not a base.	**cara lateral** Cara de un prisma o pirámide que no es la base.	Bases; Lateral face Right prism
lateral surface (p. 681) The curved surface of a cylinder or cone.	**superficie lateral** Superficie curva de un cilindro o cono.	Lateral surface Right cylinder
leg of a right triangle (p. 45) One of the two sides of the right triangle that form the right angle.	**cateto de un triángulo rectángulo** Uno de los dos lados de un triángulo rectángulo que forman el ángulo recto.	leg; leg
leg of a trapezoid (p. 429) One of the two nonparallel sides of the trapezoid.	**cateto de un trapecio** Uno de los dos lados no paralelos del trapecio.	B; C; Leg; Leg; A; D
leg of an isosceles triangle (p. 273) One of the two congruent sides of the isosceles triangle.	**cateto de un triángulo isósceles** Uno de los dos lados congruentes del triángulo isósceles.	leg; leg
length (p. 13) The distance between the two endpoints of a segment.	**longitud** Distancia entre los dos extremos de un segmento.	A; B; a; b $AB = \lvert a - b\rvert = \lvert b - a\rvert$
line (p. 6) An undefined term in geometry, a line is a straight path that has no thickness and extends forever.	**línea** Término indefinido en geometría; una línea es un trazo recto que no tiene grosor y se extiende infinitamente.	ℓ

Glossary/Glosario

G22 Glossary/Glosario

ENGLISH	SPANISH	 EXAMPLES
line of best fit (p. 198) The line that comes closest to all of the points in a data set.	**línea de mejor ajuste** Línea que más se acerca a todos los puntos de un conjunto de datos.	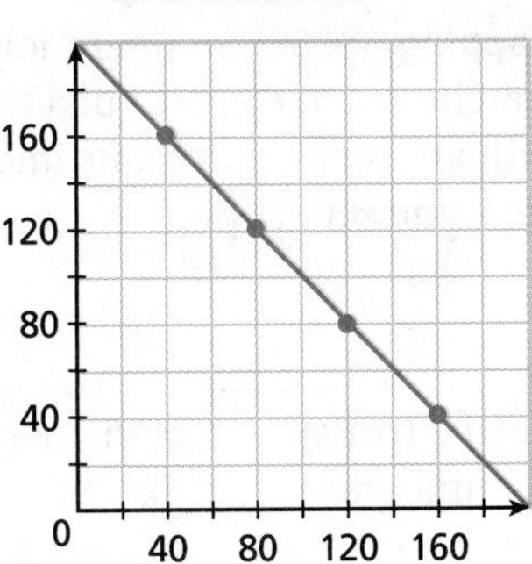
line of symmetry (p. 856) A line that divides a plane figure into two congruent reflected halves.	**eje de simetría** Línea que divide una figura plana en dos mitades reflejas congruentes.	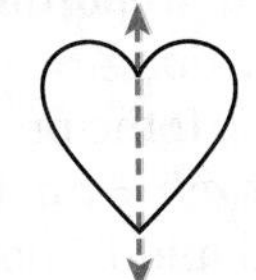
line symmetry (p. 856) A figure that can be reflected across a line so that the image coincides with the preimage.	**simetría axial** Figura que puede reflejarse sobre una línea de forma tal que la imagen coincida con la imagen original.	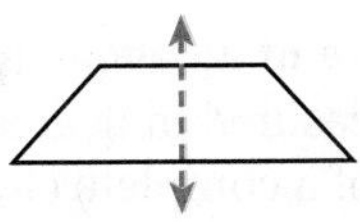
linear pair (p. 28) A pair of adjacent angles whose noncommon sides are opposite rays.	**par lineal** Par de ángulos adyacentes cuyos lados no comunes son rayos opuestos.	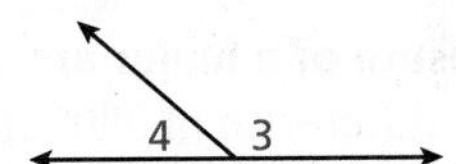 $\angle 3$ and $\angle 4$ form a linear pair.
literal equation (p. 588) An equation that contains two or more variables.	**ecuación literal** Ecuación que contiene dos o más variables.	$d = rt$ $\quad A = \frac{1}{2}h(b_1 + b_2)$
locus (p. 300) A set of points that satisfies a given condition.	**lugar geométrico** Conjunto de puntos que cumple con una condición determinada.	
logically equivalent statements (p. 83) Statements that have the same truth value.	**enunciados lógicamente equivalentes** Enunciados que tienen el mismo valor de verdad.	

M

ENGLISH	SPANISH	EXAMPLES
magnitude (p. 560) The length of a vector, written $\lvert\overrightarrow{AB}\rvert$ or $\lvert\vec{v}\rvert$.	**magnitud** Longitud de un vector, que se expresa $\lvert\overrightarrow{AB}\rvert$ o $\lvert\vec{v}\rvert$.	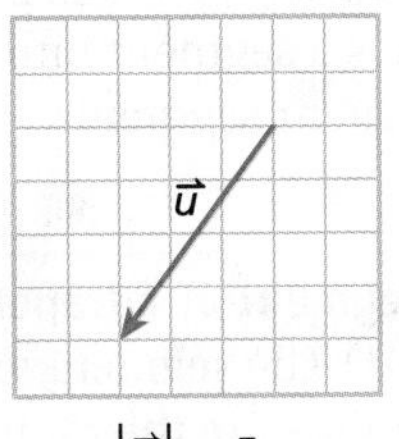 $\lvert\vec{u}\rvert = 5$
major arc (p. 756) An arc of a circle whose points are on or in the exterior of a central angle.	**arco mayor** Arco de un círculo cuyos puntos están sobre un ángulo central o en su exterior.	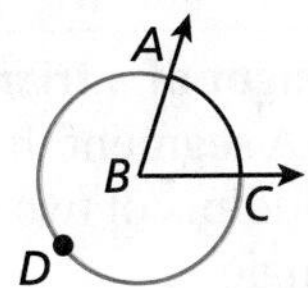 $\widehat{ADC}$ is a major arc of the circle.

Glossary/Glosario

Glossary/Glosario G23

ENGLISH	SPANISH	EXAMPLES
mapping (p. 50) An operation that matches each element of a set with another element, its image, in the same set.	**correspondencia** Operación que establece una correlación entre cada elemento de un conjunto con otro elemento, su imagen, en el mismo conjunto.	A, B, C → A′, B′, C′
matrix (p. 846) A rectangular array of numbers.	**matriz** Arreglo rectangular de números.	$\begin{bmatrix} 1 & 0 & 3 \\ -2 & 2 & -5 \\ 7 & -6 & 3 \end{bmatrix}$
means of a proportion (p. 455) In the proportion $\frac{a}{b} = \frac{c}{d}$, b and c are the means. If the proportion is written as $a{:}b = c{:}d$, the means are in the two middle positions.	**valores medios de una proporción** En la proporción $\frac{a}{b} = \frac{c}{d}$, b y c son los valores medios. Si la proporción se expresa como $a{:}b = c{:}d$, los valores medios están en las dos posiciones del medio.	
measure of an angle (p. 20) Angles are measured in degrees. A degree is $\frac{1}{360}$ of a complete circle.	**medida de un ángulo** Los ángulos se miden en grados. Un grado es $\frac{1}{360}$ de un círculo completo.	M, 26.8° $m\angle M = 26.8°$
measure of a major arc (p. 756) The difference of 360° and the measure of the associated minor arc.	**medida de un arco mayor** Diferencia entre 360° y la medida del arco menor asociado.	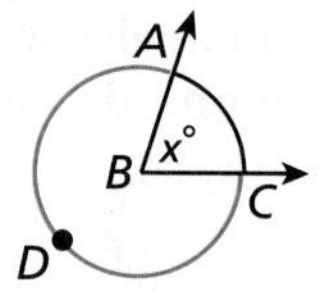 A, B, C, D, x° $m\widehat{ADC} = 360° - x°$
measure of a minor arc (p. 756) The measure of its central angle.	**medida de un arco menor** Medida de su ángulo central.	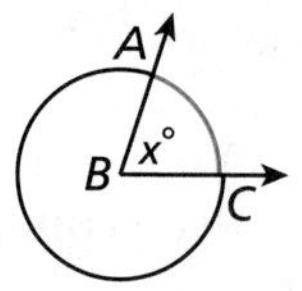 A, B, C, x° $m\widehat{AC} = x°$
median of a triangle (p. 314) A segment whose endpoints are a vertex of the triangle and the midpoint of the opposite side.	**mediana de un triángulo** Segmento cuyos extremos son un vértice del triángulo y el punto medio del lado opuesto.	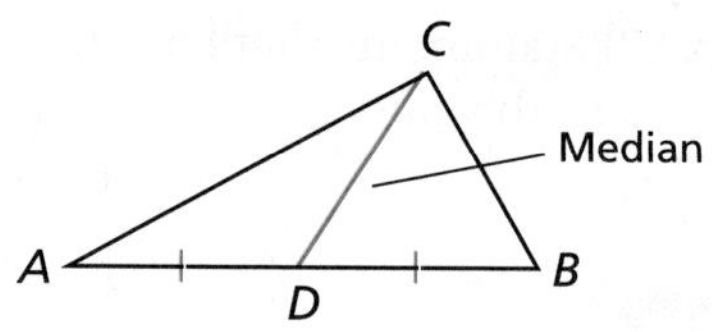 C, Median, A, D, B
midpoint (p. 15) The point that divides a segment into two congruent segments.	**punto medio** Punto que divide un segmento en dos segmentos congruentes.	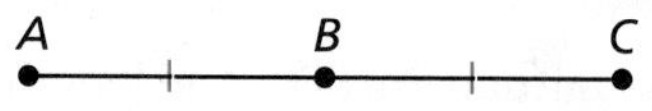 A, B, C B is the midpoint of $\overline{AC}$.
midsegment of a trapezoid (p. 431) The segment whose endpoints are the midpoints of the legs of the trapezoid.	**segmento medio de un trapecio** Segmento cuyos extremos son los puntos medios de los catetos del trapecio.	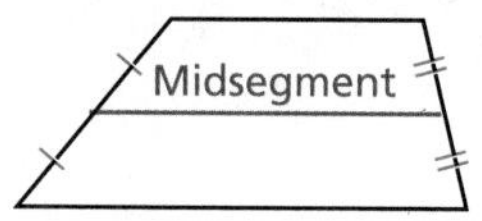 Midsegment
midsegment of a triangle (p. 322) A segment that joins the midpoints of two sides of the triangle.	**segmento medio de un triángulo** Segmento que une los puntos medios de dos lados del triángulo.	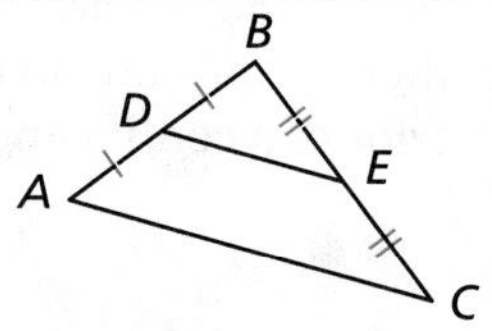 B, D, E, A, C

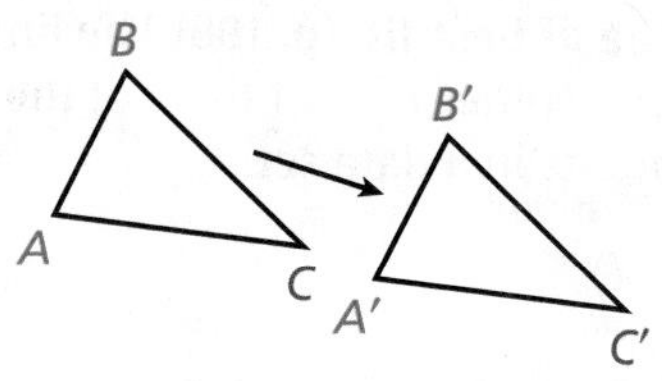

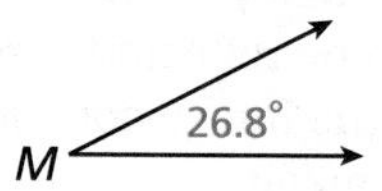

G24 Glossary/Glosario

ENGLISH	SPANISH	EXAMPLES
midsegment triangle (p. 322) The triangle formed by the three midsegments of a triangle.	**triángulo de segmentos medios** Triángulo formado por los tres segmentos medios de un triángulo.	Q, X, Y, P, Z, R Midsegment triangle: $\triangle XYZ$
minor arc (p. 756) An arc of a circle whose points are on or in the interior of a central angle.	**arco menor** Arco de un círculo cuyos puntos están sobre un ángulo central o en su interior.	A, B, C $\overset{\frown}{AC}$ is a minor arc of the circle.

N

ENGLISH	SPANISH	EXAMPLES
natural number (p. 80) A counting number.	**número natural** Número que sirve para contar.	1, 2, 3, 4, 5, 6, ...
negation (p. 82) The negation of statement p is "not p," written as $\sim p$.	**negación** La negación de un enunciado p es "no p", que se escribe p.	
negation of a vector (p. 566) The vector obtained by negating each component of a given vector.	**negación de un vector** Vector que se obtiene por la negación de cada componente de un vector dado.	The negation of $\langle 3, -2\rangle$ is $\langle -3, 2\rangle$.
net (p. 655) A diagram of the faces of a three-dimensional figure arranged in such a way that the diagram can be folded to form the three-dimensional figure.	**plantilla** Diagrama de las caras de una figura tridimensional que se puede plegar para formar la figura tridimensional.	10 m, 6 m 10 m, 6 m
network (p. 95) A diagram of vertices and edges.	**red** Diagrama de vértices y aristas.	(0, 0) (1, 0) $\left(0, \frac{3}{4}\right)$
***n*-gon** (p. 382) An n-sided polygon.	***n*-ágono** Polígono de n lados.	
nonagon (p. 382) A nine-sided polygon.	**nonágono** Polígono de nueve lados.	
noncollinear (p. 6) Points that do not lie on the same line.	**no colineal** Puntos que no se encuentran sobre la misma línea.	A, B, D Points A, B, and D are not collinear.
non-Euclidean geometry (p. 726) A system of geometry in which the Parallel Postulate, which states that there is exactly one line through a given point parallel to a given line, does not hold.	**geometría no euclidiana** Sistema de geometría en el cual no se cumple el postulado de las paralelas, que establece que por un punto dado se puede trazar una única línea paralela a una línea dada.	In spherical geometry, there are no parallel lines. The sum of the angles in a triangle is always greater than 180°.

Glossary/Glosario

Glossary/Glosario **G25**

ENGLISH	SPANISH	EXAMPLES
noncoplanar (p. 6) Points that do not lie on the same plane.	**no coplanar** Puntos que no se encuentran en el mismo plano.	S, T, U, V, ℛ *T*, *U*, *V*, and *S* are not coplanar.
numerator (p. 451) The top number of a fraction, which tells how many parts of a whole are being considered.	**numerador** El número superior de una fracción, que indica la cantidad de partes de un entero que se consideran.	The numerator of $\frac{3}{7}$ is 3.

O

ENGLISH	SPANISH	EXAMPLES
oblique cone (p. 690) A cone whose axis is not perpendicular to the base.	**cono oblicuo** Cono cuyo eje no es perpendicular a la base.	
oblique cylinder (p. 681) A cylinder whose axis is not perpendicular to the bases.	**cilindro oblicuo** Cilindro cuyo eje no es perpendicular a las bases.	
oblique prism (p. 680) A prism that has at least one nonrectangular lateral face.	**prisma oblicuo** Prisma que tiene por lo menos una cara lateral no rectangular.	
obtuse angle (p. 21) An angle that measures greater than 90° and less than 180°.	**ángulo obtuso** Ángulo que mide más de 90° y menos de 180°.	
obtuse triangle (p. 216) A triangle with one obtuse angle.	**triángulo obtusángulo** Triángulo con un ángulo obtuso.	
octagon (p. 382) An eight-sided polygon.	**octágono** Polígono de ocho lados.	
octahedron (p. 669) A polyhedron with eight faces.	**octaedro** Poliedro con ocho caras.	
one-point perspective (p. 662) A perspective drawing with one vanishing point.	**perspectiva de un punto** Dibujo en perspectiva con un punto de fuga.	Vanishing point
opposite rays (p. 7) Two rays that have a common endpoint and form a line.	**rayos opuestos** Dos rayos que tienen un extremo común y forman una línea.	F E G $\overrightarrow{EF}$ and $\overrightarrow{EG}$ are opposite rays.

G26 Glossary/Glosario

ENGLISH	SPANISH	EXAMPLES
opposite reciprocal (p. 184) The opposite of the reciprocal of a number. The opposite reciprocal of a is $-\frac{1}{a}$.	**recíproco opuesto** Opuesto del recíproco de un número. El recíproco opuesto de a es $-\frac{1}{a}$.	The opposite reciprocal of $\frac{2}{3}$ is $\frac{-3}{2}$
order of rotational symmetry (p. 857) The number of times a figure with rotational symmetry coincides with itself as it rotates 360°.	**orden de simetría de rotación** Cantidad de veces que una figura con simetría de rotación coincide consigo misma cuando rota 360°.	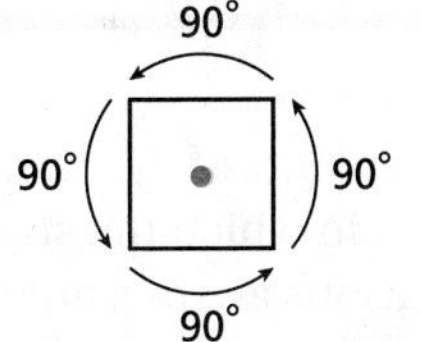 Order of rotational symmetry: 4
ordered pair (p. 42) A pair of numbers (x, y) that can be used to locate a point on a coordinate plane. The first number x indicates the distance to the left or right of the origin, and the second number y indicates the distance above or below the origin.	**par ordenado** Par de números (x, y) que se pueden utilizar para ubicar un punto en un plano cartesiano. El primer número indica la distancia a la izquierda o derecha del origen y el segundo número indica la distancia hacia arriba o hacia abajo del origen.	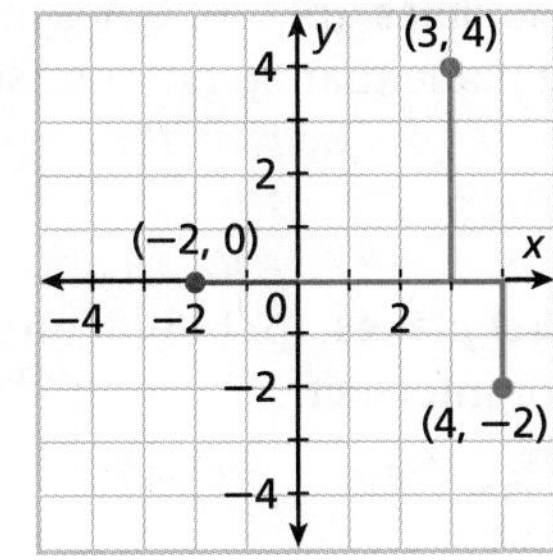
ordered triple (p. 671) A set of three numbers that can be used to locate a point (x, y, z) in a three-dimensional coordinate system.	**tripleta ordenada** Conjunto de tres números que se pueden utilizar para ubicar un punto (x, y, z) en un sistema de coordenadas tridimensional.	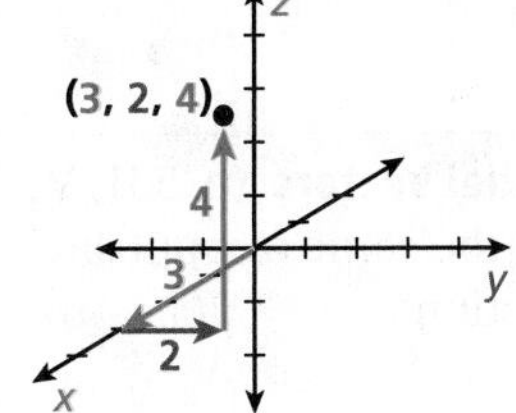
origin (p. 42) The intersection of the x- and y-axes in a coordinate plane. The coordinates of the origin are $(0, 0)$.	**origen** Intersección de los ejes x e y en un plano cartesiano. Las coordenadas de origen son $(0, 0)$.	
orthocenter of a triangle (p. 316) The point of concurrency of the three altitudes of a triangle.	**ortocentro de un triángulo** Punto de intersección de las tres alturas de un triángulo.	P is the orthocenter. 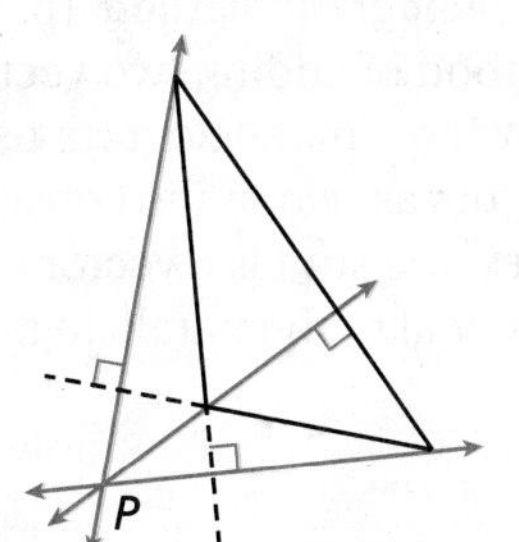
orthographic drawing (p. 661) A drawing that shows a three-dimensional object in which the line of sight for each view is perpendicular to the plane of the picture.	**dibujo ortográfico** Dibujo que muestra un objeto tridimensional en el que la línea visual para cada vista es perpendicular al plano de la imagen.	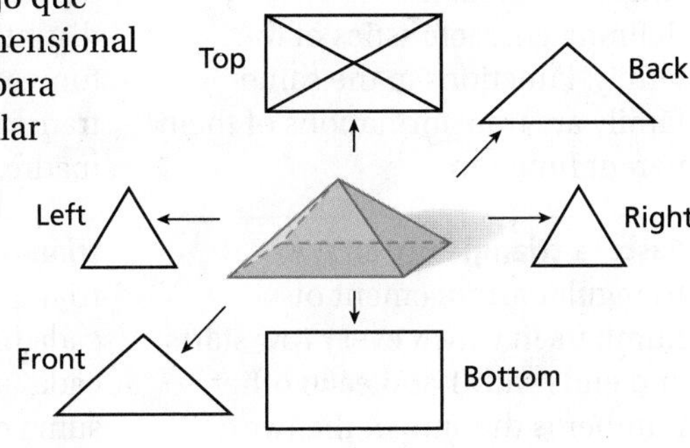

Glossary/Glosario G27

ENGLISH	SPANISH	EXAMPLES
outcome (p. 628) A possible result of a probability experiment.	**resultado** Resultado posible de un experimento de probabilidad.	In the experiment of rolling a number cube, the possible outcomes are 1, 2, 3, 4, 5, and 6.

ENGLISH	SPANISH	EXAMPLES
paragraph proof (p. 120) A style of proof in which the statements and reasons are presented in paragraph form.	**demostración con párrafos** Tipo de demostración en la cual los enunciados y las razones se presentan en forma de párrafo.	
parallel lines (p. 146) Lines in the same plane that do not intersect.	**líneas paralelas** Líneas rectas en el mismo plano que no se cruzan.	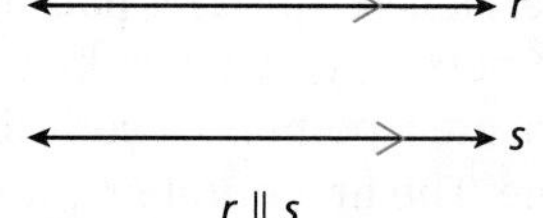 $r \parallel s$
parallel planes (p. 146) Planes that do not intersect.	**planos paralelos** Planos que no se cruzan.	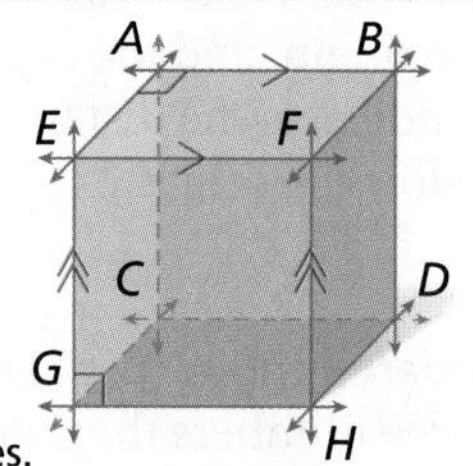 Plane *AEF* and plane *CGH* are parallel planes.
parallel vectors (p. 561) Vectors with the same or opposite direction.	**vectores paralelos** Vectores con dirección igual u opuesta.	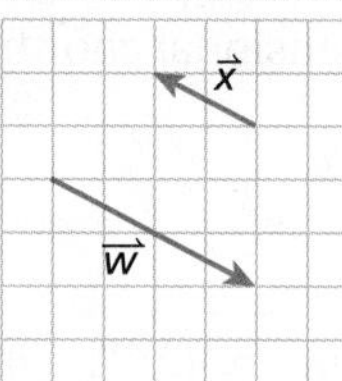 $\lvert\vec{w}\rvert = 2\sqrt{5}$ $\lvert\vec{x}\rvert = \sqrt{5}$
parallelogram (p. 391) A quadrilateral with two pairs of parallel sides.	**paralelogramo** Cuadrilátero con dos pares de lados paralelos.	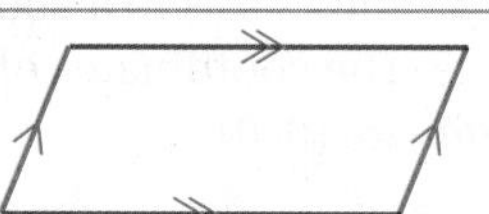
parallelogram method (p. 561) A method of adding two vectors by drawing a parallelogram using the vectors as two of the consecutive sides; the sum is a vector along the diagonal of the parallelogram.	**método del paralelogramo** Método mediante el cual se suman dos vectores dibujando un paralelogramo, utilizando los vectores como dos de los lados consecutivos; el resultado de la suma es un vector a lo largo de la diagonal del paralelogramo.	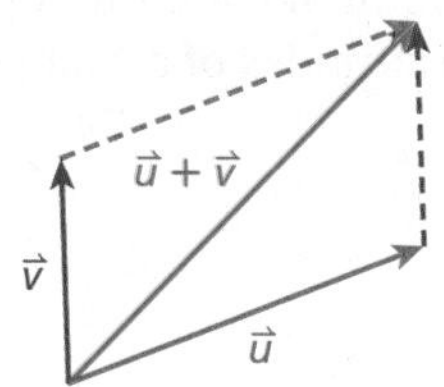
parent function (p. 221) The simplest function with the defining characteristics of the family. Functions in the same family are transformations of their parent function.	**función madre** La función más básica que tiene las características distintivas de una familia. Las funciones de la misma familia son transformaciones de su función madre.	$f(x) = x^2$ is the parent function for $g(x) = x^2 + 4$ and $h(x) = 5(x + 2)^2 - 3$.
Pascal's triangle (p. 883) A triangular arrangement of numbers in which every row starts and ends with 1 and each other number is the sum of the two numbers above it.	**triángulo de Pascal** Arreglo triangular de números en el cual cada fila comienza y termina con 1 y cada uno de los otros números es la suma de los dos números que están encima de él.	1 1 1 1 2 1 1 3 3 1 1 4 6 4 1

G28 Glossary/Glosario

ENGLISH	SPANISH	EXAMPLES
pentagon (p. 382) A five-sided polygon.	**pentágono** Polígono de cinco lados.	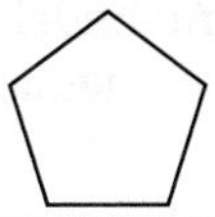
perimeter (p. 36) The sum of the side lengths of a closed plane figure.	**perímetro** Suma de las longitudes de los lados de una figura plana cerrada.	18 ft 6ft Perimeter = 18 + 6 + 18 + 6 = 48 ft
perpendicular (p. 146) Intersecting to form 90° angles, denoted by $\perp$.	**perpendicular** Que se cruza para formar ángulos de 90°, expresado por $\perp$.	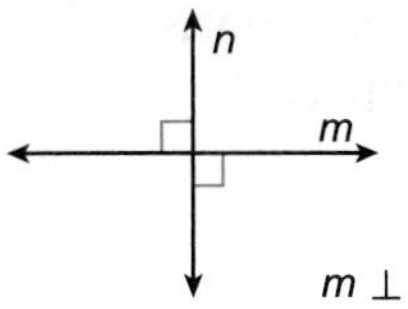 n m $m \perp n$
perpendicular bisector of a segment (p. 172) A line perpendicular to a segment at the segment's midpoint.	**mediatriz de un segmento** Línea perpendicular a un segmento en el punto medio del segmento.	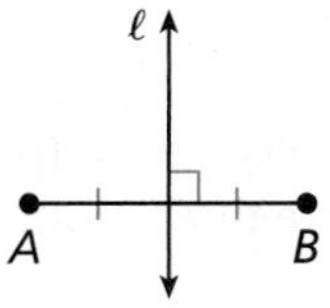 ℓ A B ℓ is the perpendicular bisector of $\overline{AB}$.
perpendicular lines (p. 146) Lines that intersect at 90° angles.	**líneas perpendiculares** Líneas que se cruzan en ángulos de 90°.	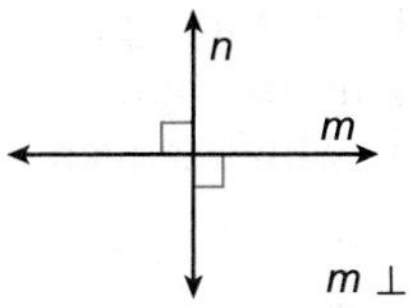 n m $m \perp n$
perspective drawing (p. 662) A drawing in which nonvertical parallel lines meet at a point called a *vanishing point.* Perspective drawings can have one or two vanishing points.	**dibujo en perspectiva** Dibujo en el cual las líneas paralelas no verticales se encuentran en un punto denominado *punto de fuga.* Los dibujos en perspectiva pueden tener uno o dos puntos de fuga.	Vanishing point 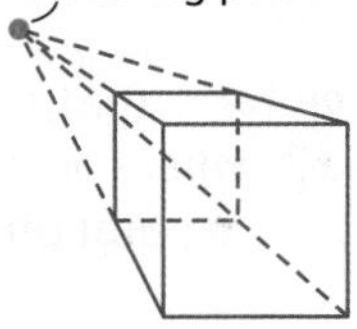
pi (p. 37) The ratio of the circumference of a circle to its diameter, denoted by the Greek letter π (pi). The value of π is irrational, often approximated by 3.14 or $\frac{22}{7}$.	**pi** Razón entre la circunferencia de un círculo y su diámetro, expresado por la letra griega π (pi). El valor de π es irracional y por lo general se aproxima a 3.14 ó $\frac{22}{7}$.	If a circle has a diameter of 5 inches and a circumference of C inches, then $\frac{C}{5} = \pi$, or $C = 5\pi$ inches, or about 15.7 inches.
plane (p. 6) An undefined term in geometry, it is a flat surface that has no thickness and extends forever.	**plano** Término indefinido en geometría; un plano es una superficie plana que no tiene grosor y se extiende infinitamente.	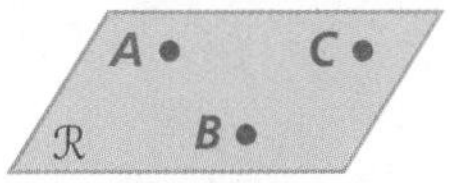 A C $\mathcal{R}$ B plane $\mathcal{R}$ or plane ABC
plane symmetry (p. 858) A three-dimensional figure that can be divided into two congruent reflected halves by a plane has plane symmetry.	**simetría de plano** Una figura tridimensional que se puede dividir en dos mitades congruentes reflejadas por un plano tiene simetría de plano.	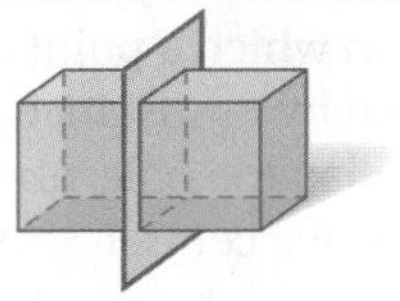 Plane symmetry
Platonic solid (p. 669) One of the five regular polyhedra: a tetrahedron, a cube, an octahedron, a dodecahedron, or an icosahedron.	**sólido platónico** Uno de los cinco poliedros regulares: tetraedro, cubo, octaedro, dodecaedro o icosaedro.	

Glossary/Glosario **G29**

ENGLISH	SPANISH	EXAMPLES

point (p. 6) An undefined term in geometry, it names a location and has no size.

punto Término indefinido de la geometría que denomina una ubicación y no tiene tamaño.

P •

point *P*

point matrix (p. 846) A matrix that represents the coordinates of the vertices of a polygon. The first row of the matrix consists of the *x*-coordinates of the points, and the second row consists of the *y*-coordinates.

matriz de puntos Matriz que representa las coordenadas de los vértices de un polígono. La primera fila de la matriz contiene las coordenadas *x* de los puntos y la segunda fila contiene las coordenadas *y*.

(1, 2)
(−2, 0)
(3, −4)

$$\begin{bmatrix} 1 & -2 & 3 \\ 2 & 0 & -4 \end{bmatrix}$$

point of concurrency (p. 307) A point where three or more lines coincide.

punto de concurrencia Punto donde se cruzan tres o más líneas.

B

point of tangency (p. 746) The point of intersection of a circle or sphere with a tangent line or plane.

punto de tangencia Punto de intersección de un círculo o esfera con una línea o plano tangente.

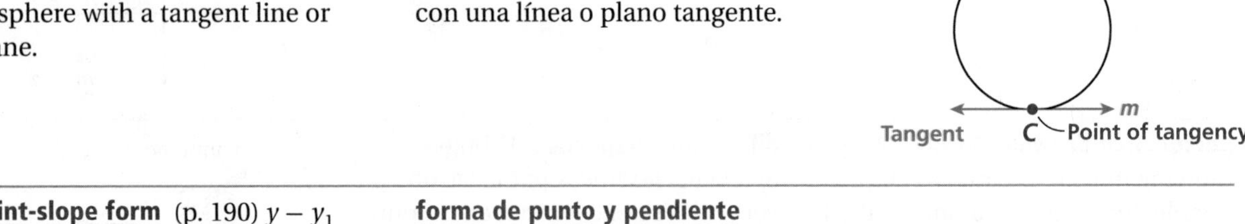

point-slope form (p. 190) $y - y_1 = m(x - x_1)$, where *m* is the slope and (x_1, y_1) is a point on the line.

forma de punto y pendiente $(y - y_1) = m(x - x_1)$, donde *m* es la pendiente y (x_1, y_1) es un punto en la línea.

polar axis (p. 808) In a polar coordinate system, the horizontal ray with the pole as its endpoint that lies along the positive *x*-axis.

eje polar En un sistema de coordenadas polares, el rayo horizontal, cuyo extremo es el polo, que se encuentra a lo largo del eje *x* positivo.

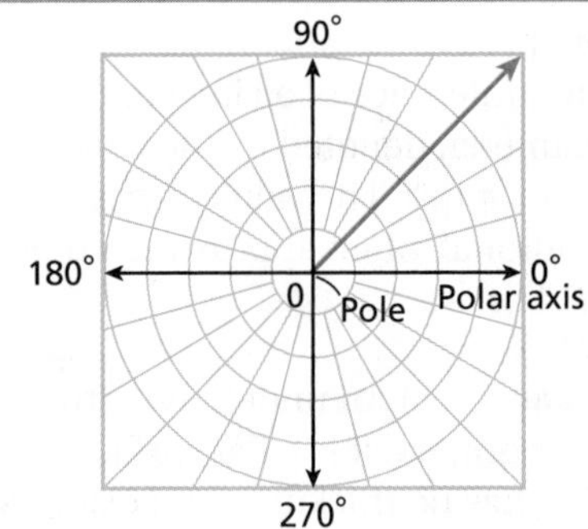

polar coordinate system (p. 808) A system in which a point in a plane is located by its distance *r* from a point called the pole, and by the measure of a central angle *θ*.

sistema de coordenadas polares Sistema en el cual un punto en un plano se ubica por su distancia *r* de un punto denominado polo y por la medida de un ángulo central *θ*.

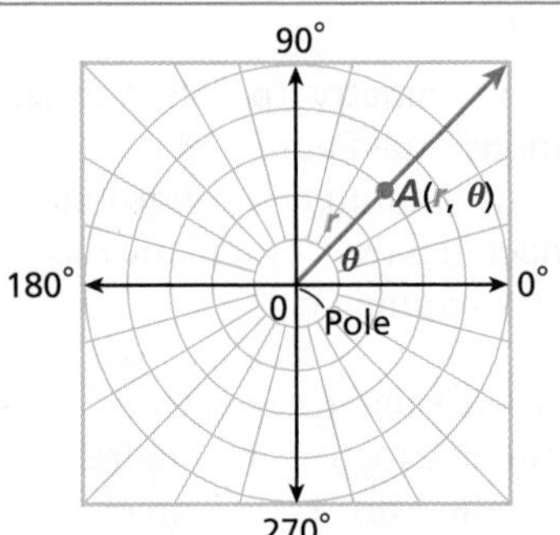

G30 Glossary/Glosario

ENGLISH	SPANISH	EXAMPLES
pole (p. 808) The point from which distances are measured in a polar coordinate system.	**polo** Punto desde el que se miden las distancias en un sistema de coordenadas polares.	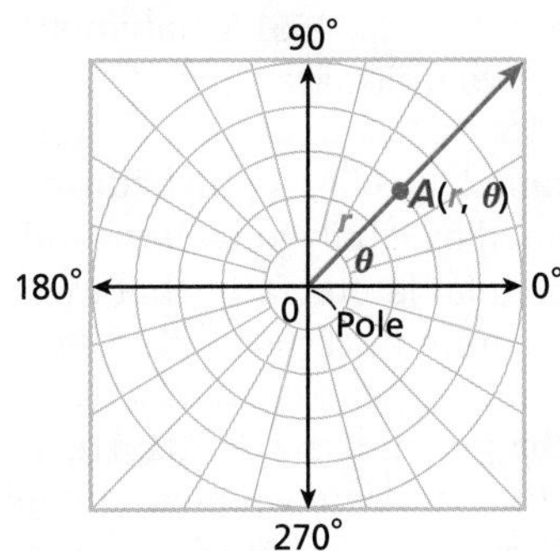
polygon (p. 98) A closed plane figure formed by three or more segments such that each segment intersects exactly two other segments only at their endpoints and no two segments with a common endpoint are collinear.	**polígono** Figura plana cerrada formada por tres o más segmentos tal que cada segmento se cruza únicamente con otros dos segmentos sólo en sus extremos y ningún segmento con un extremo común a otro es colineal con éste.	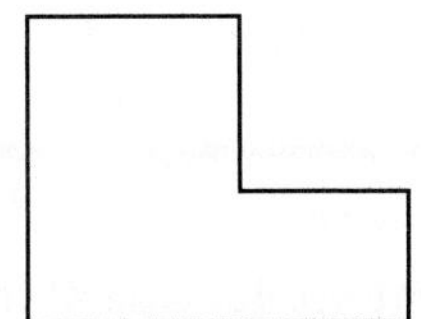
polyhedron (p. 670) A closed three-dimensional figure formed by four or more polygons that intersect only at their edges.	**poliedro** Figura tridimensional cerrada formada por cuatro o más polígonos que se cruzan sólo en sus aristas.	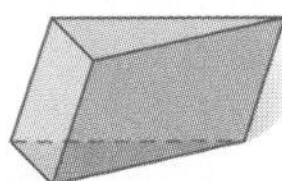
postulate (p. 7) A statement that is accepted as true without proof. Also called an *axiom*.	**postulado** Enunciado que se acepta como verdadero sin demostración. También denominado *axioma*.	
preimage (p. 50) The original figure in a transformation.	**imagen original** Figura original en una transformación.	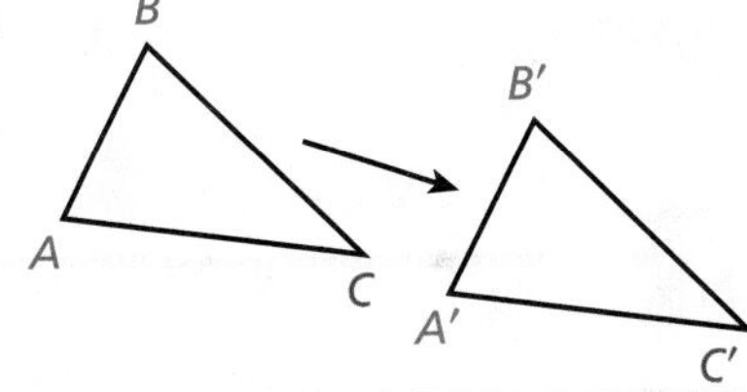
primes (p. 50) Symbols used to label the image in a transformation.	**apóstrofos** Símbolos utilizados para identificar la imagen en una transformación.	
prism (p. 654) A polyhedron formed by two parallel congruent polygonal bases connected by lateral faces that are parallelograms.	**prisma** Poliedro formado por dos bases poligonales congruentes y paralelas conectadas por caras laterales que son paralelogramos.	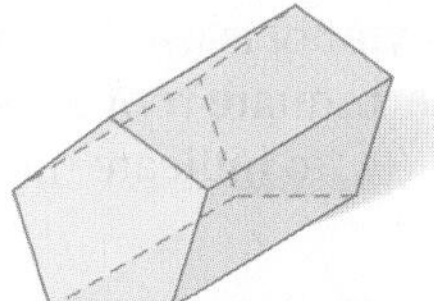
probability (p. 237) A number from 0 to 1 (or 0% to 100%) that is the measure of how likely an event is to occur.	**probabilidad** Número entre 0 y 1 (o entre 0% y 100%) que describe cuán probable es que ocurra un suceso.	A bag contains 3 red marbles and 4 blue marbles. The probability of randomly choosing a red marble is $\frac{3}{7}$.
proof (p. 104) An argument that uses logic to show that a conclusion is true.	**demostración** Argumento que se vale de la lógica para probar que una conclusión es verdadera.	
proof by contradiction (p. 322) *See* indirect proof.	**demostración por contradicción** *Ver* demostración indirecta.	

Glossary/Glosario G31

ENGLISH	SPANISH	EXAMPLES
proportion (p. 455) A statement that two ratios are equal; $\frac{a}{b} = \frac{c}{d}$.	**proporción** Ecuación que establece que dos razones son iguales; $\frac{a}{b} = \frac{c}{d}$.	$\frac{2}{3} = \frac{4}{6}$
pyramid (p. 654) A polyhedron formed by a polygonal base and triangular lateral faces that meet at a common vertex.	**pirámide** Poliedro formado por una base poligonal y caras laterales triangulares que se encuentran en un vértice común.	
Pythagorean triple (p. 349) A set of three nonzero whole numbers *a*, *b*, and *c* such that $a^2 + b^2 = c^2$.	**Tripleta de Pitágoras** Conjunto de tres números cabales distintos de cero *a*, *b* y *c* tal que $a^2 + b^2 = c^2$.	$\{3, 4, 5\}$ $3^2 + 4^2 = 5^2$

Q

ENGLISH	SPANISH	EXAMPLES
quadrant (p. 42) One of the four regions into which the *x*- and *y*-axes divide the coordinate plane.	**cuadrante** Una de las cuatro regiones en las que los ejes *x* e *y* dividen el plano cartesiano.	*y*-axis; Quadrant II; Quadrant I; *x*-axis; 0; Quadrant III; Quadrant IV
quadrilateral (p. 98) A four-sided polygon.	**cuadrilátero** Polígono de cuatro lados.	

R

ENGLISH	SPANISH	EXAMPLES
radial symmetry (p. 857) *See* rotational symmetry.	**simetría radial** *Ver* simetría de rotación.	
radical symbol (p. 346) The symbol $\sqrt{}$ used to denote a root. The symbol is used alone to indicate a square root or with an index, $\sqrt[n]{}$, to indicate the *n*th root.	**símbolo de radical** Símbolo $\sqrt{}$ que se utiliza para expresar una raíz. Puede utilizarse solo para indicar una raíz cuadrada, o con un índice, $\sqrt[n]{}$, para indicar la enésima raíz.	$\sqrt{36} = 6$ $\sqrt[3]{27} = 3$
radicand (p. 346) The expression under a radical sign.	**radicando** Número o expresión debajo del signo de radical.	Expression: $\sqrt{x + 3}$ Radicand: $x + 3$
radius of a circle (p. 37) A segment whose endpoints are the center of a circle and a point on the circle; the distance from the center of a circle to any point on the circle.	**radio de un círculo** Segmento cuyos extremos son el centro y un punto de la circunferencia; distancia desde el centro de un círculo hasta cualquier punto de la circunferencia.	Radius
radius of a cone (p. 690) The radius of the circular base.	**radio de un cono** El radio de la base circular.	r

G32 Glossary/Glosario

ENGLISH	SPANISH	EXAMPLES

radius of a cylinder (p. 681) The radius of the circular base.

radio de ´un cilindro El radio de la base circular.

---

radius of a sphere (p. 714) A segment whose endpoints are the center of a sphere and any point on the sphere; the distance from the center of a sphere to any point on the sphere.

radio de una esfera Segmento cuyos extremos son el centro de una esfera y cualquier punto sobre la esfera; distancia desde el centro de una esfera hasta cualquier punto sobre la esfera.

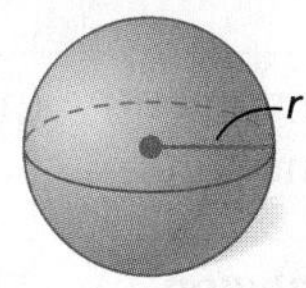

---

rate of change (p. 97) A ratio that compares the amount of change in a dependent variable to the amount of change in an independent variable.

tasa de cambio Razón que compara la cantidad de cambio de la variable dependiente con la cantidad de cambio de la variable independiente.

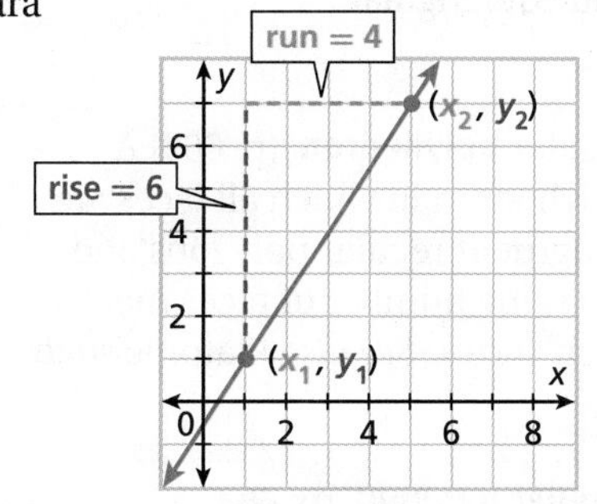

$$\text{Rate of change} = \frac{\text{change in } y}{\text{change in } x} = \frac{6}{4} = \frac{3}{2}$$

---

ratio (p. 454) A comparison of two quantities by division.

razón Comparación de dos cantidades mediante una división.

---

rational number (p. 80) A number that can be written in the form $\frac{a}{b}$, where a and b are integers and $b \neq 0$.

número racional Número que se puede expresar como $\frac{a}{b}$, donde a y b son números enteros y $b \neq 0$.

$3, 1.75, 0.\overline{3}, -\frac{2}{3}, 0$

---

ray (p. 7) A part of a line that starts at an endpoint and extends forever in one direction.

rayo Parte de una línea que comienza en un extremo y se extiende infinitamente en una dirección.

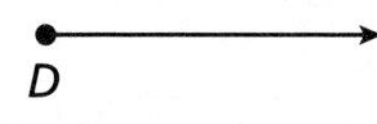

---

rectangle (p. 408) A quadrilateral with four right angles.

rectángulo Cuadrilátero con cuatro ángulos rectos.

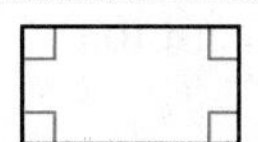

---

reduction (p. 873) A dilation with a scale factor greater than 0 but less than 1. In a reduction, the image is smaller than the preimage.

reducción Dilatación con un factor de escala mayor que 0 pero menor que 1. En una reducción, la imagen es más pequeña que la imagen original.

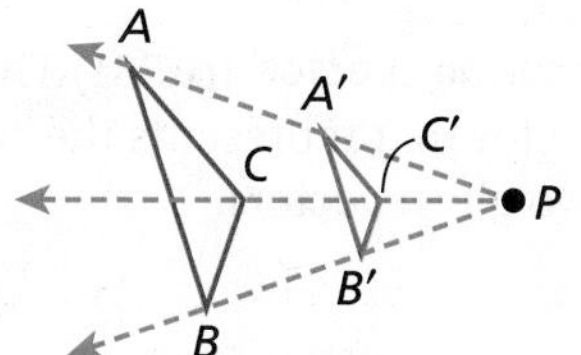

---

reference angle (p. 570) For an angle in standard position, the reference angle is the positive acute angle formed by the terminal side of the angle and the x-axis.

ángulo de referencia Dado un ángulo en posición estándar, el ángulo de referencia es el ángulo agudo positivo formado por el lado terminal del ángulo y el eje x.

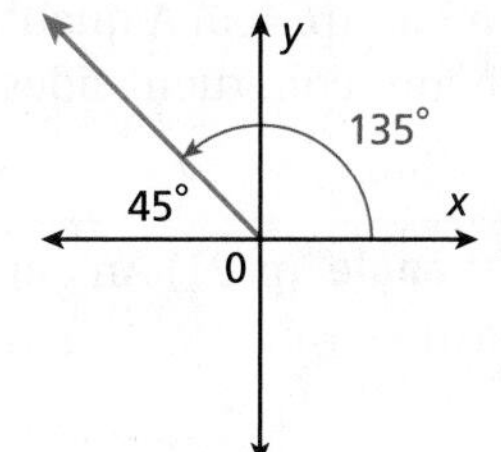

Glossary/Glosario **G33**

ENGLISH	SPANISH	EXAMPLES
reflection (p. 50) A transformation across a line, called the line of reflection, such that the line of reflection is the perpendicular bisector of each segment joining each point and its image.	**reflexión** Transformación sobre una línea, denominada la línea de reflexión. La línea de reflexión es la mediatriz de cada segmento que une un punto con su imagen.	A B C B′ C′ A′
reflection symmetry (p. 856) *See* line symmetry.	**simetría de reflexión** *Ver* simetría axial.	
regular polygon (p. 382) A polygon that is both equilateral and equiangular.	**polígono regular** Polígono equilátero de ángulos iguales.	
regular polyhedron (p. 669) A polyhedron in which all faces are congruent regular polygons and the same number of faces meet at each vertex. *See also* Platonic solid.	**poliedro regular** Poliedro cuyas caras son todas polígonos regulares congruentes y en el que el mismo número de caras se encuentran en cada vértice. *Ver también* sólido platónico.	s s s
regular pyramid (p. 689) A pyramid whose base is a regular polygon and whose lateral faces are congruent isosceles triangles.	**pirámide regular** Pirámide cuya base es un polígono regular y cuyas caras laterales son triángulos isósceles congruentes.	
regular tessellation (p. 866) A repeating pattern of congruent regular polygons that completely covers a plane with no gaps or overlaps.	**teselado regular** Patrón que se repite formado por polígonos regulares congruentes que cubren completamente un plano sin dejar espacios y sin superponerse.	
relation (p. 389) A set of ordered pairs.	**relación** Conjunto de pares ordenados.	$\{(0, 5), (0, 4), (2, 3), (4, 0)\}$
remote interior angle (p. 225) An interior angle of a polygon that is not adjacent to the exterior angle.	**ángulo interno remoto** Ángulo interno de un polígono que no es adyacente al ángulo externo.	2 1 3 4 The remote interior angles of $\angle 4$ are $\angle 1$ and $\angle 2$
resultant vector (p. 561) The vector that represents the sum of two given vectors.	**vector resultante** Vector que representa la suma de dos vectores dados.	$\vec{u} + \vec{v}$ $\vec{v}$ $\vec{u}$
rhombus (p. 409) A quadrilateral with four congruent sides.	**rombo** Cuadrilátero con cuatro lados congruentes.	
right angle (p. 21) An angle that measures 90°.	**ángulo recto** Ángulo que mide 90°.	

G34 Glossary/Glosario

ENGLISH	SPANISH	EXAMPLES
right cone (p. 690) A cone whose axis is perpendicular to the base.	**cono recto** Cono cuyo eje es perpendicular a la base.	Axis Right cone
right cylinder (p. 681) A cylinder whose axis is perpendicular to its bases.	**cilindro recto** Cilindro cuyo eje es perpendicular a sus bases.	Axis
right prism (p. 680) A prism whose lateral faces are all rectangles.	**prisma recto** Prisma cuyas caras laterales son todas rectángulos.	
right triangle (p. 216) A triangle with one right angle.	**triángulo rectángulo** Triángulo con un ángulo recto.	
rigid motion (p. 824) *See* isometry.	**movimiento rígido** *Ver* isometría.	
rise (p. 182) The difference in the *y*-values of two points on a line.	**distancia vertical** Diferencia entre los valores de *y* de dos puntos de una línea.	For the points $(3, -1)$ and $(6, 5)$, the rise is $5 - (-1) = 6$.
rotation (p. 50) A transformation about a point *P*, also known as the center of rotation, such that each point and its image are the same distance from *P*. All of the angles with vertex *P* formed by a point and its image are congruent.	**rotación** Transformación sobre un punto *P*, también conocido como el centro de rotación, tal que cada punto y su imagen estén a la misma distancia de *P*. Todos los ángulos con vértice *P* formados por un punto y su imagen son congruentes.	F' E' G' D' G F P D E
rotational symmetry (p. 857) A figure that can be rotated about a point by an angle less than 360° so that the image coincides with the preimage has rotational symmetry.	**simetría de rotación** Una figura que puede rotarse alrededor de un punto en un ángulo menor de 360° de forma tal que la imagen coincide con la imagen original tiene simetría de rotación.	90° 90° 90° 90° Order of rotational symmetry: 4
run (p. 182) The difference in the *x*-values of two points on a line.	**distancia horizontal** Diferencia entre los valores de *x* de dos puntos de una línea.	For the points $(3, -1)$ and $(6, 5)$, the run is $6 - 3 = 3$.

same-side interior angles (p. 147) For two lines intersected by a transversal, a pair of angles that lie on the same side of the transversal and between the two lines.	**ángulos internos del mismo lado** Dadas dos líneas cortadas por una transversal, el par de ángulos ubicados en el mismo lado de la transversal y entre las dos líneas.	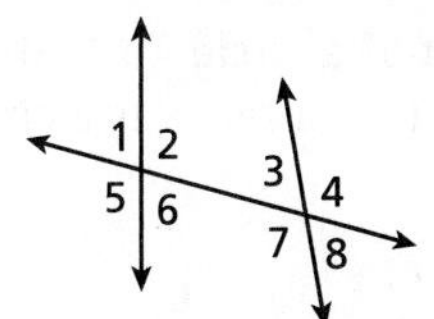 $\angle 2$ and $\angle 3$ are same-side interior angles.

Glossary/Glosario

Glossary/Glosario G35

ENGLISH	SPANISH	EXAMPLES
sample space (p. 628) The set of all possible outcomes of a probability experiment.	**espacio muestral** Conjunto de todos los resultados posibles de un experimento de probabilidad.	in the experiment of rolling a number cube, the sample space is {1, 2, 3, 4, 5, 6}.
scalar multiplication of a vector (p. 566) The process of multiplying a vector by a constant.	**multiplicación escalar de un vector** Proceso por el cual se multiplica un vector por una constante.	$3\langle -8, 1\rangle = \langle -24, 3\rangle$
scale (p. 489) The ratio between two corresponding measurements.	**escala** Razón entre dos medidas correspondientes.	1 cm : 5 mi
scale drawing (p. 489) A drawing that uses a scale to represent an object as smaller or larger than the actual object.	**dibujo a escala** Dibujo que utiliza una escala para representar un objeto como más pequeño o más grande que el objeto original.	 A blueprint is an example of a scale drawing.
scale factor (p. 495) The multiplier used on each dimension to change one figure into a similar figure.	**factor de escala** El multiplicador utilizado en cada dimensión para transformar una figura en una figura semejante.	 Scale factor: 2
scale model (p. 456) A three-dimensional model that uses a scale to represent an object as smaller or larger than the actual object.	**modelo a escala** Modelo tridimensional que utiliza una escala para representar un objeto como más pequeño o más grande que el objeto real.	
scalene triangle (p. 217) A triangle with no congruent sides.	**triángulo escaleno** Triángulo sin lados congruentes.	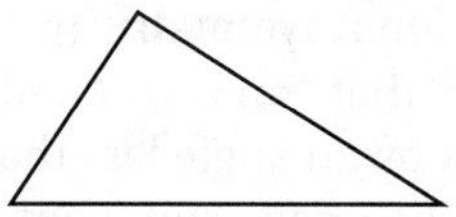
scatter plot (p. 198) A graph with points plotted to show a possible relationship between two sets of data.	**diagrama de dispersión** Gráfica con puntos que se usa para demostrar una relación posible entre dos conjuntos de datos.	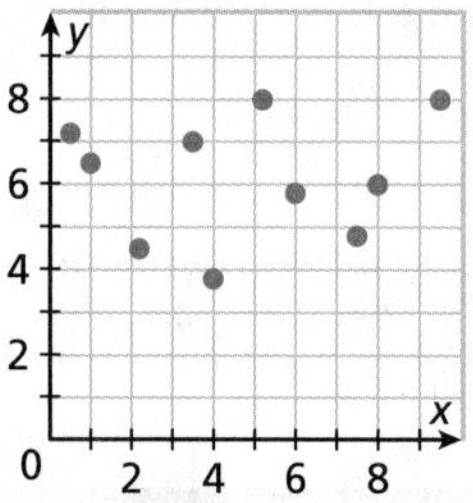
secant of a circle (p. 746) A line that intersects a circle at two points.	**secante de un círculo** Línea que corta un círculo en dos puntos.	

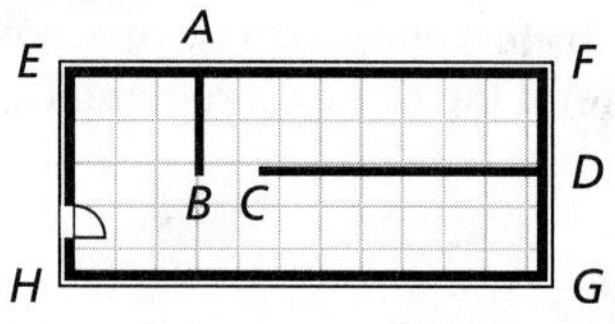

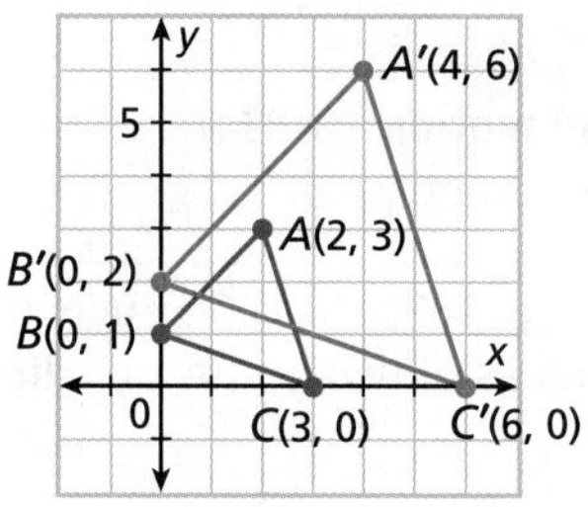

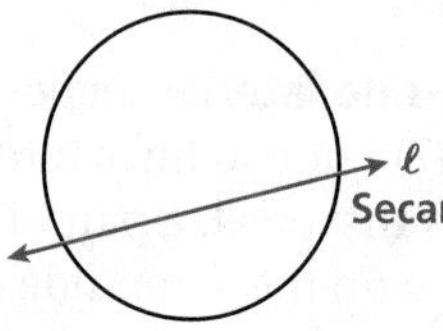

Glossary/Glosario

G36 *Glossary/Glosario*

ENGLISH	SPANISH	EXAMPLES
secant of an angle (p. 532) In a right triangle, the ratio of the length of the hypotenuse to the length of the side adjacent to angle *A*. It is the reciprocal of the cosine function.	**secante de un ángulo** En un triángulo rectángulo, la razón entre la longitud de la hipotenusa y la longitud del cateto adyacente al ángulo *A*. Es la inversa de la función coseno.	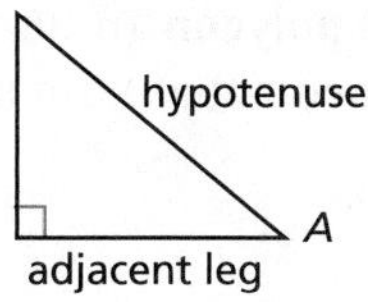 $\sec A = \frac{\text{hypotenuse}}{\text{adjacent}} = \frac{1}{\cos A}$
secant segment (p. 793) A segment of a secant with at least one endpoint on the circle.	**segmento secante** Segmento de una secante que tiene al menos un extremo sobre el círculo.	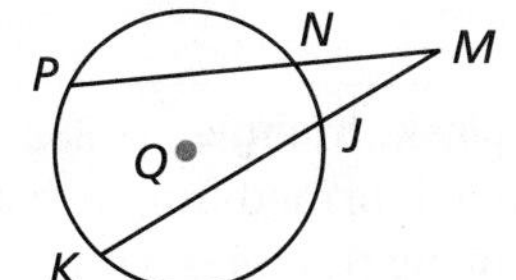 $\overline{NM}$ is an external secant segment. $\overline{JK}$ is an internal secant segment.
sector of a circle (p. 764) A region inside a circle bounded by two radii of the circle and their intercepted arc.	**sector de un círculo** Región dentro de un círculo delimitado por dos radios del círculo y por su arco abarcado.	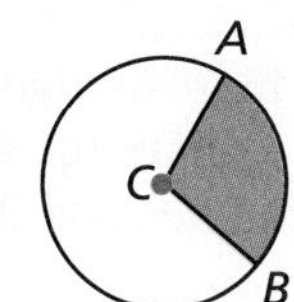
segment bisector (p. 16) A line, ray, or segment that divides a segment into two congruent segments.	**bisectriz de un segmento** Línea, rayo o segmento que divide un segmento en dos segmentos congruentes.	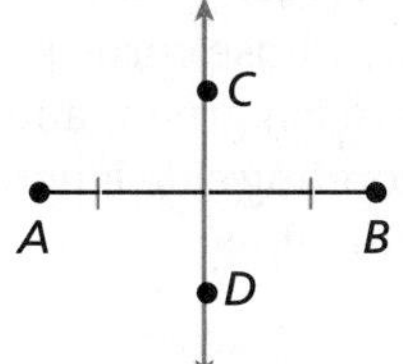
segment of a circle (p. 765) A region inside a circle bounded by a chord and an arc.	**segmento de un círculo** Región dentro de un círculo delimitada por una cuerda y un arco.	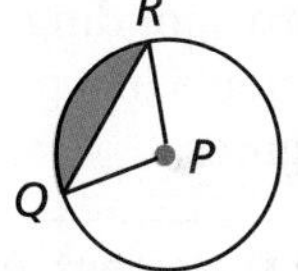
segment of a line (p. 7) A part of a line consisting of two endpoints and all points between them.	**segmento de una línea** Parte de una línea que consiste en dos extremos y todos los puntos entre éstos.	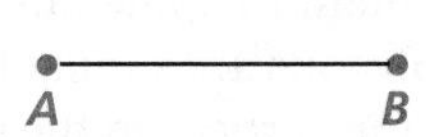
self-similar (p. 882) A figure that can be divided into parts, each of which is similar to the entire figure.	**autosemejante** Figura que se puede dividir en partes, cada una de las cuales es semejante a la figura entera.	
semicircle (p. 756) An arc of a circle whose endpoints lie on a diameter.	**semicírculo** Arco de un círculo cuyos extremos se encuentran sobre un diámetro.	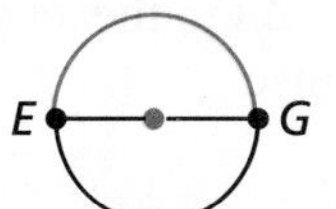
semiregular tessellation (p. 866) A repeating pattern formed by two or more regular polygons in which the same number of each polygon occur in the same order at every vertex and completely cover a plane with no gaps or overlaps.	**teselado semirregular** Patrón formado por dos o más polígonos regulares en el que el mismo número de cada polígono se presenta en el mismo orden en cada vértice y cubren un plano completamente sin dejar espacios vacíos ni superponerse.	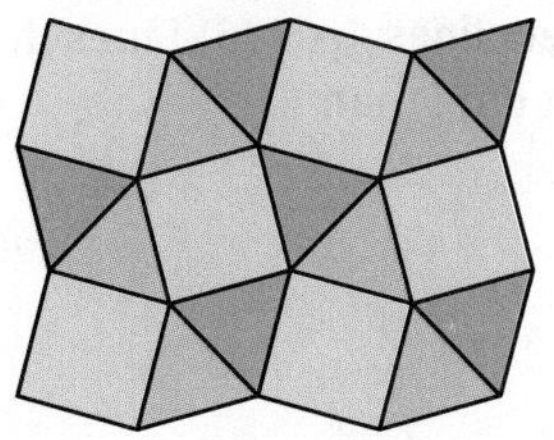

Glossary/Glosario G37

ENGLISH	SPANISH	EXAMPLES
side of a polygon (p. 382) One of the segments that form a polygon.	**lado de un polígono** Uno de los segmentos que forman un polígono.	Side
side of an angle (p. 20) One of the two rays that form an angle.	**lado de un ángulo** Uno de los dos rayos que forman un ángulo.	$\overrightarrow{AC}$ and $\overrightarrow{AB}$ are sides of $\angle CAB$.
Sierpinski triangle (p. 882) A fractal formed from a triangle by removing triangles with vertices at the midpoints of the sides of each remaining triangle.	**triángulo de Sierpinski** Fractal formado a partir de un triángulo al cual se le recortan triángulos cuyos vértices se encuentran en los puntos medios de los lados de cada triángulo restante.	
similar (p. 462) Two figures are similar if they have the same shape but not necessarily the same size.	**semejantes** Dos figuras con la misma forma pero no necesariamente del mismo tamaño.	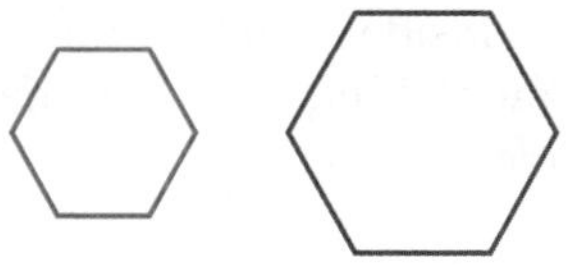
similar polygons (p. 462) Two polygons whose corresponding angles are congruent and whose corresponding side lengths are proportional.	**polígonos semejantes** Dos polígonos cuyos ángulos correspondientes son congruentes y cuyos lados correspondientes tienen longitudes proporcionales.	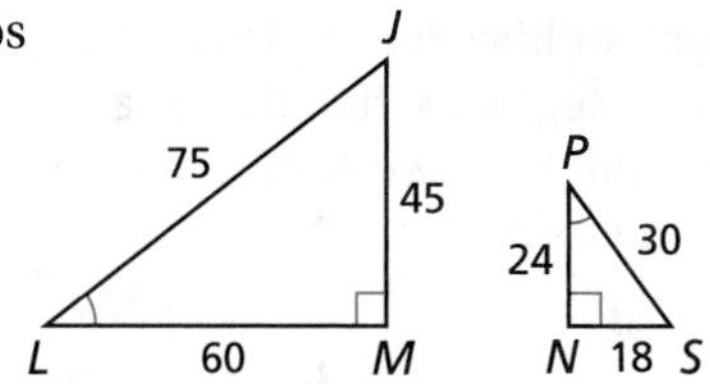
similarity ratio (p. 463) The ratio of two corresponding linear measurements in a pair of similar figures.	**razón de semejanza** Razón de dos medidas lineales correspondientes en un par de figuras semejantes.	Similarity ratio: $\frac{3.5}{2.1} = \frac{5}{3}$
similarity statement (p. 463) A statement that indicates that two polygons are similar by listing the vertices in the order of correspondence.	**enunciado de semejanza** Enunciado que indica que dos polígonos son semejantes enumerando los vértices en orden de correspondencia.	quadrilateral $ABCD \sim$ quadrilateral $EFGH$
sine (p. 525) In a right triangle, the ratio of the length of the leg opposite $\angle A$ to the length of the hypotenuse.	**seno** En un triángulo rectángulo, razón entre la longitud del cateto opuesto a $\angle A$ y la longitud de la hipotenusa.	$\sin A = \frac{\text{opposite}}{\text{hypotenuse}}$
skew lines (p. 146) Lines that are not coplanar.	**líneas oblicuas** Líneas que no son coplanares.	$\overleftrightarrow{AE}$ and $\overleftrightarrow{CD}$ are skew lines.

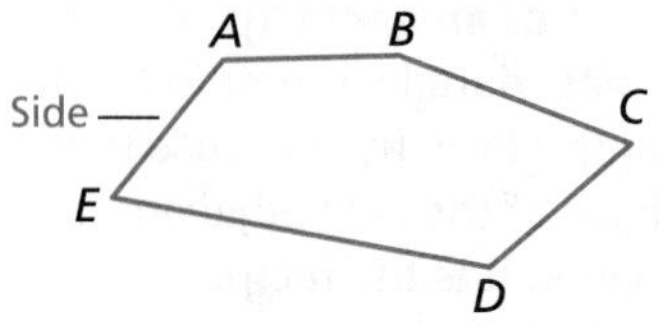

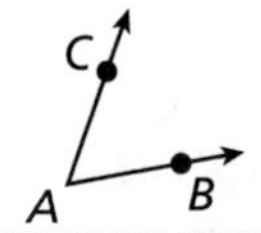

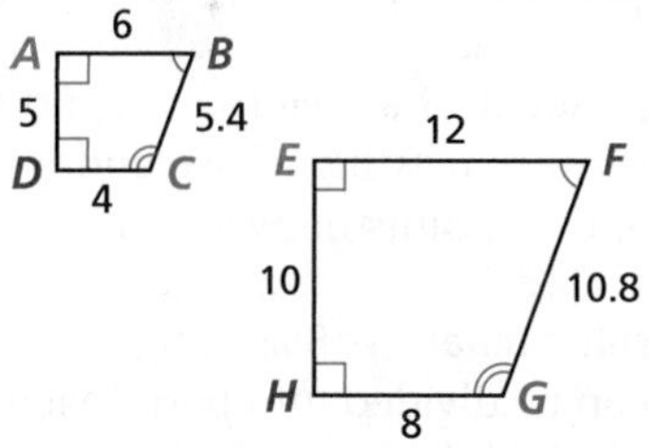

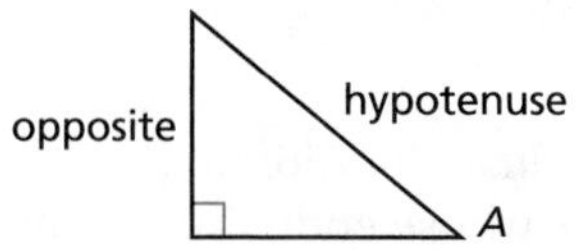

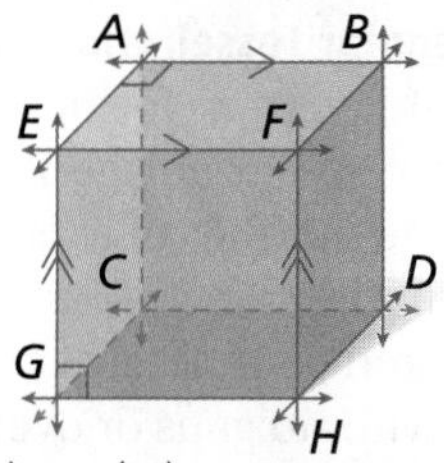

G38 Glossary/Glosario

ENGLISH	SPANISH	EXAMPLES
slant height of a regular pyramid (p. 689) The distance from the vertex of a regular pyramid to the midpoint of an edge of the base.	**altura inclinada de una pirámide regular** Distancia desde el vértice de una pirámide regular hasta el punto medio de una arista de la base.	Slant height
slant height of a right cone (p. 690) The distance from the vertex of a right cone to a point on the edge of the base.	**altura inclinada de un cono recto** Distancia desde el vértice de un cono recto hasta un punto en el borde de la base.	Slant height
slide (p. 50) *See* translation.	**deslizamiento** *Ver* traslación.	
slope (p. 182) A measure of the steepness of a line. If (x_1, y_1) and (x_2, y_2) are any two points on the line, the slope of the line, known as m, is represented by the equation $m = \frac{y_2 - y_1}{x_2 - x_1}$.	**pendiente** Medida de la inclinación de una línea. Dados dos puntos (x_1, y_1) y (x_2, y_2) en una línea, la pendiente de la línea, denominada m, se representa con la ecuación $m = \frac{y_2 - y_1}{x_2 - x_1}$.	
slope-intercept form (p. 190) The slope-intercept form of a linear equation is $y = mx + b$, where m is the slope and b is the y-intercept.	**forma de pendiente-intersección** La forma de pendiente-intersección de una ecuación lineal es $y = mx + b$, donde m es la pendiente y b es la intersección con el eje y.	$y = -2x + 4$ The slope is -2. The y-intercept is 4.
solid (p. 654) A three-dimensional figure.	**cuerpo geométrico** Figura tridimensional.	
solving a triangle (p. 535) Using given measures to find unknown angle measures or side lengths of a triangle.	**resolución de un triángulo** Utilizar medidas dadas para hallar las medidas desconocidas de los ángulos o las longitudes de los lados de un triángulo.	
space (p. 671) The set of all points in three dimensions.	**espacio** Conjunto de todos los puntos en tres dimensiones.	
special parallelogram (p. 410) A rectangle, rhombus, or square.	**paralelogramo especial** Un rectángulo, rombo o cuadrado.	
special quadrilateral (p. 391) A parallelogram, rectangle, rhombus, square, kite, or trapezoid.	**cuadrilátero especial** Un paralelogramo, rectángulo, rombo, cuadrado, cometa o trapecio.	
special right triangle (p. 356) A 45°-45°-90° triangle or a 30°-60°-90° triangle.	**triángulo rectángulo especial** Triángulo de 45°-45°-90° o triángulo de 30°-60°-90°.	A, B, C, 2s, 60°, s, 30°, $s\sqrt{3}$; B, A, C, $\ell\sqrt{2}$, 45°, ℓ, 45°, ℓ

Glossary/Glosario

Glossary/Glosario G39

ENGLISH	SPANISH	EXAMPLES
sphere (p. 714) The set of points in space that are a fixed distance from a given point called the center of the sphere.	**esfera** Conjunto de puntos en el espacio que se encuentran a una distancia fija de un punto determinado denominado centro de la esfera.	
spherical geometry (p. 726) A system of geometry defined on a sphere. A line is defined as a great circle of the sphere, and there are no parallel lines.	**geometría esférica** Sistema de geometría definido sobre una esfera. Una línea se define como un gran círculo de la esfera y no existen líneas paralelas.	
square (p. 410) A quadrilateral with four congruent sides and four right angles.	**cuadrado** Cuadrilátero con cuatro lados congruentes y cuatro ángulos rectos.	
standard position (p. 687) An angle in standard position has its vertex at the origin and its initial side on the positive x-axis.	**posición estándar** Ángulo cuyo vértice se encuentra en el origen y cuyo lado inicial se encuentra sobre el eje x positivo.	y; 236°; x; 0
straight angle (p. 21) A 180° angle.	**ángulo llano** Ángulo que mide 180°.	
subtend (p. 772) A segment or arc subtends an angle if the endpoints of the segment or arc lie on the sides of the angle.	**subtender** Un segmento o arco subtiende un ángulo si los extremos del segmento o arco se encuentran sobre los lados del ángulo.	D; E; F If D and F are the endpoints of an arc or chord, and E is a point not on $\overline{DF}$, then $\widehat{DF}$ or $\overline{DF}$ is said to subtend $\angle DEF$.
supplementary angles (p. 29) Two angles whose measures have a sum of 180°.	**ángulos suplementarios** Dos ángulos cuyas medidas suman 180°.	4; 3 $\angle 3$ and $\angle 4$ are supplementary angles.
surface area (p. 680) The total area of all faces and curved surfaces of a three-dimensional figure.	**área total** Área total de todas las caras y superficies curvas de una figura tridimensional.	12 cm; 6 cm; 8 cm Surface area $= 2(8)(12) + 2(8)(6) + 2(12)(6) = 432\text{ cm}^2$
symmetry (p. 856) In the transformation of a figure such that the image coincides with the preimage, the image and preimage have symmetry.	**simetría** En la transformación de una figura tal que la imagen coincide con la imagen original, la imagen y la imagen original tienen simetría.	

G40 Glossary/Glosario

ENGLISH	SPANISH	EXAMPLES
symmetry about an axis (p. 858) In the transformation of a figure such that there is a line about which a three-dimensional figure can be rotated by an angle greater than 0° and less than 360° so that the image coincides with the preimage, the image and preimage have symmetry about an axis.	**simetría axial** En la transformación de una figura tal que existe una línea sobre la cual se puede rotar una figura tridimensional a un ángulo mayor que 0° y menor que 360° de forma que la imagen coincida con la imagen original, la imagen y la imagen original tienen simetría axial.	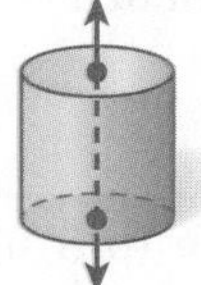
system of equations (p. 8) A set of two or more equations that have two or more variables.	**sistema de ecuaciones** Conjunto de dos o más ecuaciones que contienen dos o más variables.	$2x + 3y = -1$ $3x - 3y = 4$

tangent circles (p. 747) Two coplanar circles that intersect at exactly one point. If one circle is contained inside the other, they are *internally tangent*. If not, they are *externally tangent*.	**círculos tangentes** Dos círculos coplanares que se cruzan únicamente en un punto. Si un círculo contiene a otro, son *tangentes internamente*. De lo contrario, son *tangentes externamente*.	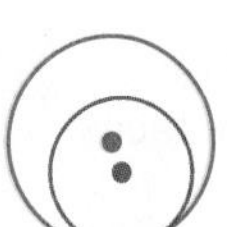 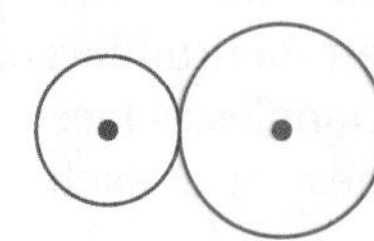
tangent of an angle (p. 525) In a right triangle, the ratio of the length of the leg opposite $\angle A$ to the length of the leg adjacent to $\angle A$.	**tangente de un ángulo** En un triángulo rectángulo, razón entre la longitud del cateto opuesto a $\angle A$ y la longitud del cateto adyacente a $\angle A$.	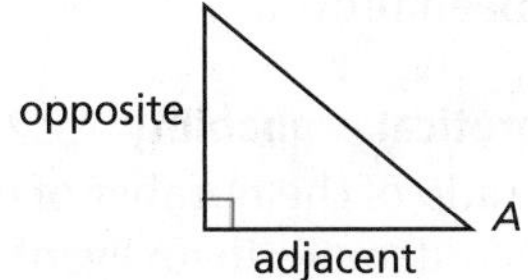 $\tan A = \frac{\text{opposite}}{\text{adjacent}}$
tangent segment (p. 794) A segment of a tangent with one endpoint on the circle.	**segmento tangente** Segmento de una tangente con un extremo en el círculo.	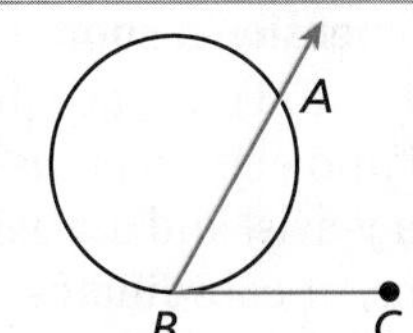 $\overline{BC}$ is a tangent segment.
tangent of a circle (p. 746) A line that is in the same plane as a circle and intersects the circle at exactly one point.	**tangente de un círculo** Línea que se encuentra en el mismo plano que un círculo y lo cruza únicamente en un punto.	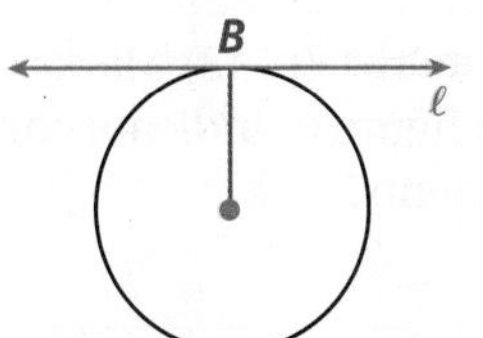
tangent of a sphere (p. 805) A line that intersects the sphere at exactly one point.	**tangente de una esfera** Línea que toca la esfera únicamente en un punto.	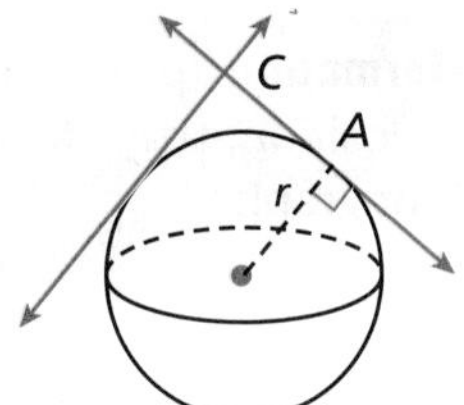

ENGLISH	SPANISH	EXAMPLES
terminal point of a vector (p. 559) The endpoint of a vector.	**punto terminal de un vector** Extremo de un vector.	
terminal side (p. 570) For an angle in standard position, the ray that is rotated relative to the positive x-axis.	**lado terminal** Para un ángulo en posición estándar, el rayo que se rota en relación con el eje x positivo.	
tessellation (p. 865) A repeating pattern of plane figures that completely covers a plane with no gaps or overlaps.	**teselado** Patrón que se repite formado por figuras planas que cubren completamente un plano sin dejar espacios libres y sin superponerse.	
tetrahedron (p. 669) A polyhedron with four faces. A regular tetrahedron has equilateral triangles as faces, with three faces meeting at each vertex.	**tetraedro** Poliedro con cuatro caras. Las caras de un tetraedro regular son triángulos equiláteros y cada vértice es compartido por tres caras.	
theorem (p. 110) A statement that has been proven.	**teorema** Enunciado que ha sido demostrado.	
theoretical probability (p. 214) The ratio of the number of equally likely outcomes in an event to the total number of possible outcomes.	**probabilidad teórica** Razón entre el número de resultados igualmente probables de un suceso y el número total de resultados posibles.	In the experiment of rolling a number cube, the theoretical probability of rolling an odd number is $\frac{3}{6} = \frac{1}{2}$.
three-dimensional coordinate system (p. 671) A space that is divided into eight regions by an x-axis, a y-axis, and a z-axis. The locations, or coordinates, of points are given by ordered triples.	**sistema de coordenadas tridimensional** Espacio dividido en ocho regiones por un eje x, un eje y un eje z. Las ubicaciones, o coordenadas, de los puntos son dadas por tripletas ordenadas.	
tick marks (p. 13) Marks used on a figure to indicate congruent segments.	**marcas "|"** Marcas utilizadas en una figura para indicar segmentos congruentes.	
tiling (p. 865) *See* tessellation.	**teselación** *Ver* teselado	
transformation (p. 50) A change ... position, size, or shape of a ...raph.	**transformación** Cambio en la posición, tamaño o forma de una figura o gráfica.	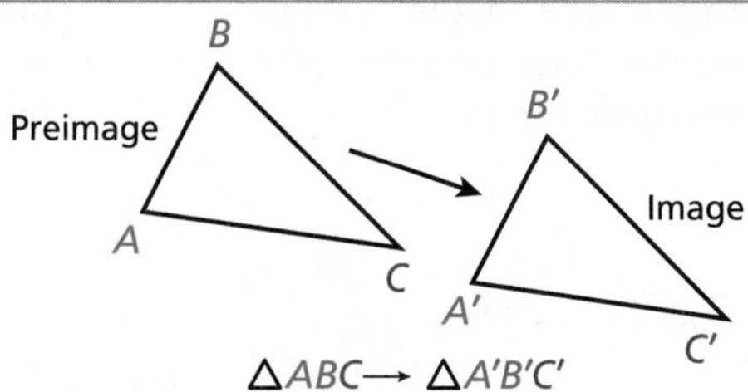

ENGLISH	SPANISH	EXAMPLES
translation (p. 50) A transformation that shifts or slides every point of a figure or graph the same distance in the same direction.	**traslación** Transformación en la que todos los puntos de una figura o gráfica se mueven la misma distancia en la misma dirección.	J′ M′ J M K′ L′ K L
translation symmetry (p. 865) A figure has translation symmetry if it can be translated along a vector so that the image coincides with the preimage.	**simetría de traslación** Una figura tiene simetría de traslación si se puede trasladar a lo largo de un vector de forma tal que la imagen coincida con la imagen original.	
transversal (p. 147) A line that intersects two coplanar lines at two different points.	**transversal** Línea que corta dos líneas coplanares en dos puntos diferentes.	1 2 5 6 3 4 7 8 Transversal
trapezoid (p. 429) A quadrilateral with exactly one pair of parallel sides.	**trapecio** Cuadrilátero con sólo un par de lados paralelos.	B C A D
triangle (p. 98) A three-sided polygon.	**triángulo** Polígono de tres lados.	
triangle rigidity (p. 242) A property of triangles that states that if the side lengths of a triangle are fixed, the triangle can have only one shape.	**rigidez del triángulo** Propiedad de los triángulos que establece que, si las longitudes de los lados de un triángulo son fijas, el triángulo puede tener sólo una forma.	
triangulation (p. 223) The method for finding the distance between two points by using them as vertices of a triangle in which one side has a known, or measurable, length.	**triangulación** Método para calcular la distancia entre dos puntos utilizándolos como vértices de un triángulo en el cual un lado tiene una longitud conocida o medible.	
trigonometric ratio (p. 525) A ratio of two sides of a right triangle.	**razón trigonométrica** Razón entre dos lados de un triángulo rectángulo.	B c a A b C $\sin A = \frac{a}{c}$; $\cos A = \frac{b}{c}$; $\tan A = \frac{a}{b}$
trigonometry (p. 514) The study of the measurement of triangles and of trigonometric functions and their applications.	**trigonometría** Estudio de la medición de los triángulos y de las funciones trigonométricas y sus aplicaciones.	
trisect (p. 25) To divide into three equal parts.	**trisecar** Dividir en tres partes iguales.	A B C D $\overline{AD}$ is trisected.
truth table (p. 128) A table that lists all possible combinations of truth values for a statement and its components.	**tabla de verdad** Tabla en la que se enumeran todas las combinaciones posibles de valores de verdad para un enunciado y sus componentes.	

Glossary/Glosario G43

ENGLISH	SPANISH	EXAMPLES
truth value (p. 82) A statement can have a truth value of true (T) or false (F).	**valor de verdad** Un enunciado puede tener un valor de verdad verdadero (V) o falso (F).	
turn (p. 50) *See* rotation.	**giro** *Ver* rotación.	
two-column proof (p. 111) A style of proof in which the statements are written in the left-hand column and the reasons are written in the right-hand column.	**demostración a dos columnas** Estilo de demostración en la que los enunciados se escriben en la columna de la izquierda y las razones en la columna de la derecha.	
two-point perspective (p. 662) A perspective drawing with two vanishing points.	**perspectiva de dos puntos** Dibujo en perspectiva con dos puntos de fuga.	

U

ENGLISH	SPANISH	EXAMPLES
undefined term (p. 6) A basic figure that is not defined in terms of other figures. The undefined terms in geometry are point, line, and plane.	**término indefinido** Figura básica que no está definida en función de otras figuras. Los términos indefinidos en geometría son el punto, la línea y el plano.	
unit circle (p. 570) A circle with a radius of 1, centered at the origin.	**círculo unitario** Círculo con un radio de 1, centrado en el origen.	Unit circle

V

ENGLISH	SPANISH	EXAMPLES
vanishing point (p. 662) In a perspective drawing, a point on the horizon where parallel lines appear to meet.	**punto de fuga** En un dibujo en perspectiva, punto en el horizonte donde todas las líneas paralelas parecen encontrarse.	
vector (p. 559) A quantity that has both magnitude and direction.	**vector** Cantidad que tiene magnitud y dirección.	
Venn diagram (p. 80) A diagram used to show relationships between sets.	**diagrama de Venn** Diagrama utilizado para mostrar la relación entre conjuntos.	

Glossary/Glosario

G44 Glossary/Glosario

ENGLISH	SPANISH	EXAMPLES
vertex angle of an isosceles triangle (p. 273) The angle formed by the legs of an isosceles triangle.	**ángulo del vértice de un triángulo isósceles** Ángulo formado por los catetos de un triángulo isósceles.	vertex angle; E; F
vertex of a cone (p. 654) The point opposite the base of the cone.	**vértice de un cono** Punto opuesto a la base del cono.	Vertex
vertex of a graph (p. 95) A point on a graph.	**vértice de una gráfica** Punto en una gráfica.	(0, 0); Vertex; (1, 0); $\left(0, \frac{3}{4}\right)$
vertex of a polygon (p. 382) The intersection of two sides of the polygon.	**vértice de un polígono** La intersección de dos lados del polígono.	A; B; C; Vertex; E; D. *A*, *B*, *C*, *D*, and *E* are vertices of the polygon.
vertex of a pyramid (p. 689) The point opposite the base of the pyramid.	**vértice de una pirámide** Punto opuesto a la base de la pirámide.	Vertex
vertex of a three-dimensional figure (p. 654) The point that is the intersection of three or more faces of the figure.	**vértice de una figura tridimensional** Punto que representa la intersección de tres o más caras de la figura.	Vertex
vertex of a triangle (p. 216) The intersection of two sides of the triangle.	**vértice de un triángulo** Intersección de dos lados del triángulo.	C; A; B. *A*, *B*, and *C* are vertices of $\triangle ABC$.
vertex of an angle (p. 20) The common endpoint of the sides of the angle.	**vértice de un ángulo** Extremo común de los lados del ángulo.	C; A; B. *A* is the vertex of $\angle CAB$.
vertical angles (p. 30) The nonadjacent angles formed by two intersecting lines.	**ángulos opuestos por el vértice** Ángulos no adyacentes formados por dos rectas que se cruzan.	2; 1; 3; 4. $\angle 1$ and $\angle 3$ are vertical angles. $\angle 2$ and $\angle 4$ are vertical angles.
volume (p. 697) The number of nonoverlapping unit cubes of a given size that will exactly fill the interior of a three-dimensional figure.	**volumen** Cantidad de cubos unitarios no superpuestos de un determinado tamaño que llenan exactamente el interior de una figura tridimensional.	4 ft; 3 ft; 12 ft. Volume $= (3)(4)(12) = 144 \text{ ft}^3$

Glossary/Glosario

Glossary/Glosario G45

ENGLISH	SPANISH	EXAMPLES

W

whole number (p. 80) The set of natural numbers and zero.	**número cabal** Conjunto de los números naturales y cero.	{0, 1, 2, 3, 4, 5, ...}

***x*-axis** (p. 42) The horizontal axis in a coordinate plane.	**eje *x*** Eje horizontal en un plano cartesiano.	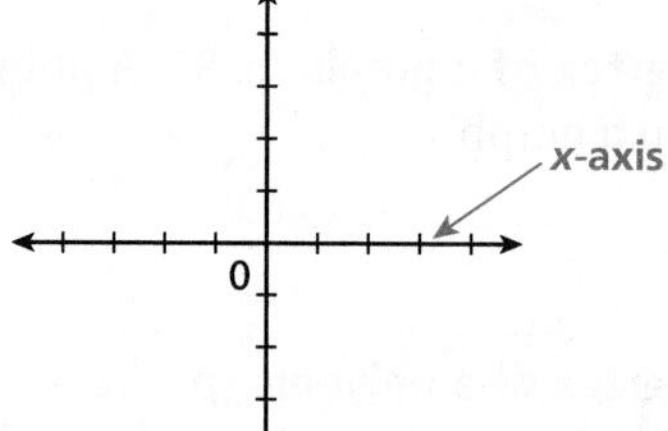

***y*-axis** (p. 42) The vertical axis in a coordinate plane.	**eje *y*** Eje vertical en un plano cartesiano.	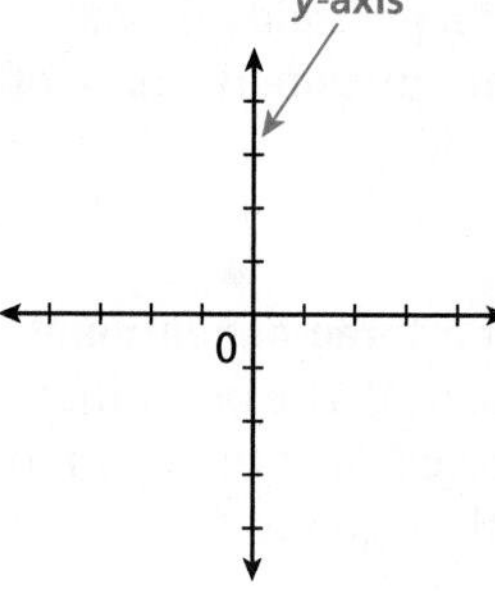

Z

***z*-axis** (p. 671) The third axis in a three-dimensional coordinate system.	**eje *z*** Tercer eje en un sistema de coordenadas tridimensional.	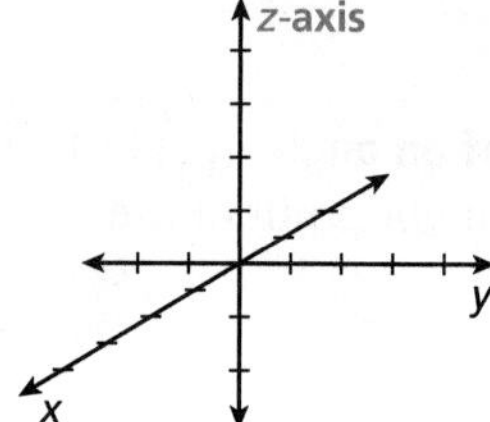

G46 *Glossary/Glosario*

Index

A

Index

Index

B

C

Index

Index

D

E

Index

Index

H

I

J

K

Index

Index

Index

S

T

Index

Index

U

V

W

Index

Notes

Credits

Abbreviations used: (t) top, (c) center, (b) bottom, (l) left, (r) right, (bkgd) background

Photo

All images HRW Photo unless otherwise noted.

Master Icons-teens, authors (all), Sam Dudgeon/HRW.

Front Matter: vi (l)Index Stock; vii (r) Kelly-Mooney Photography/CORBIS; viii (l) Victor Vasarely/Erich Lessing/Art Resource, NY; ix (r) Alamy Images; ix (teen) HRW Photo; x (l) Laurence Parent Photography; xi (r) Photo of Reptiles puzzle based on work by M.C. Escher 2006 The M.C. Escher Company–Holland. All rights reserved. *www.mcescher.com;* xii (l) Courtesy IMAX Corporation; xiv (l) Jim Wark; xv (r) Erik Pawassar/Getty Images Photo Assignments/HRW Photo; xvi (l) George B. Diebold/CORBIS; xvii (r) Michael Kevin Daly/CORBIS; xviii, (tc), Corbis images; (cr), ©Royalty Free/CORBIS; (bc), HRW Photo; xix (tc), Mark Sykes/Alamy Images; xix (cl), Photo by Walt Disney Studios/ZUMA Press ©Copyright 1998 by Courtesy of Walt Disney Studios; xix (c), ©Owaki-Kulla/CORBIS; xix (cr), The Image Bank/Getty Images; xx Victoria Smith/HRW Photo; xxi (cl) Sam Dudgeon/HRW

Front Cover: Scott Gilchrist/Masterfile

Chapter 1: 2-3 Index Stock; 6 (t)(b), Agence France Press/Newscom.com; 10 (tl), Photodisc Royalty Free; 10 (b)(inset), Reunion des Musee Nationaux/Art Resource, NY; 13 (tr), Tony Freeman/Photo Edit; 16 (tl) (tc) (tr), Andy Christiansen/HRW Photo; 18 (tl), Photodisc Royalty Free; 19 (c), Gabriel Bouys/AFP/Getty Images; 20 (tr), Gary Conner/Photo Edit; 21 (tl), HRW Photo; 26 (tl), Photodisc Royalty Free; 28 (t), Jon Feingersh/CORBIS; 32 (bl), Photodisc Royalty Free; 34 (tl), Photodisc Royalty Free; 34 (bc), Peter Casolino/Alamy; 38 (c-triangle), Victoria Smith/HRW Photo; 39 (bl), HRW Photo; 40 (l), Alamy Images; 41 (l), The Bridgeman Art Library/Getty Images; 43 (tl), HRW Photo; 43 (tr), Lee Foster/Bruce Coleman Photography; 46 (tl), Duomo/CORBIS; 48 (cl), Ilya Terntyev/Photodisc/Getty Images; 48 (bl), HRW Photo by Sam Dudgeon; 54 (tl), BrandX/Fotosearch.com; 54 (bl), HRW Photo; 58 (tl), HRW Photo by Sam Dudgeon; 58 (c), Marty Granger/HRW Photo

Chapter 2: 70-71 Kelly-Mooney Photography/CORBIS; 74 (tr), Francois Gohier/Photo Researchers, Inc.; 76 NASA Images; 78 (tl), Index Stock/Picturequest; 78 (bl), Victoria Smith/HRW Photo; 78 (br), The Granger Collection; 81 (tr), BARRY RUNK/STAN/Grant Heilman Photo; 83 (cl), Digital Vision/Getty; 83 (cr), Picturequest Images; 85 (bl), Victoria Smith/HRW Photo; 85 (br), Corbis; 86 Mark Sykes/Alamy Images; 87 (bl), Michael Newman/PhotoEdit; 88 (tr), Alamy Images; 88 (br), Taxi/Getty Images; 92 (cl), © Dennis MacDonald/Alamy; 92 (bl), Victoria Smith/HRW Photo; 95 (br), Sam Dudgeon/HRW Photo; 96 (tr), Steffan Hauser/botanikfoto/Alamy; 99 Getty/Stone; 100 (tl), Nibsc/Photo Researchers, Inc.; 100 (bl) Victoria Smith/HRW; 100 (br), The Granger Collection; 102 (tl), HRW/Victoria Smith; 102 (c-Alice and Chesire Cat), Corbis Images; 102 (br), Black and White Detail. The Pierpont Morgan Library/Art Resource, NY; 102 (tr), The Pierpont Morgan Library/Art Resource, NY; 104 Getty Images; 109 (tl), Photo-objects/Fotosearch; 109 (cr), Paul A. Souders/CORBIS; 110 (tr), REAL LIFE ADVENTURES c 2004 GarLanco. Reprinted with permission of UNIVERSAL PRESS SYNDICATE. All rights reserved.; 115 (cl), Corbis Images; 115 (cr), Digital Vision/Gettypix; 115 (bl), Photo-objects/Fotosearch; 118 (tr), HRW Photo; 120 Alamy Images; 121 (tl), Danilo Donadoni/Bruce Coleman Inc.; 124 (bl), Photo-objects/Fotosearch; 125 (cr) Victoria Smith/HRW; 125 Victoria Smith/HRW Photo; 126 (tl), Photo-objects/Fotosearch; 126 (tc), David Buffington/Photodisc/Getty; 140 (tl), Sam Dudgeon/HRW Photo; 140 (cr), Brightroom.com; 141 (cr), Rich Stevens Photography; 141 (bl) (bc), Brand X Royalty Free Photos

Chapter 3: 142-143 Victor Vasarely/Erich Lessing/Art Resource, NY; 146 (tr), © G. Baden/Corbis; 149 (bl), Mark McKenna Photography & Design; 150 (tl), Rick Davis/Darkhouse and Fun Enthusiast; 155 (tr), Alamy Photos; 157 (tl), Doug Menuez/Photodisc/Getty; 159 (cl), B.S.P.I./Corbis Images; 162 (tr), Ken Hawkins/Mira.com; 166 Alamy Images; 167 (cr), The Art Archive/Victoria and Albert Museum London/Sally Chappell; 168 (tl), Rick Davis/Darkhouse and Fun Enthusiast; 171 (tl)(tr)(cl)(tr)(bc), Andy Christiansen/HRW Photo; 172 (tr), Alamy Images; 175 Michael Melford/The Image Bank/Getty Images; 176 (tr), Klaus Lahnstein/Stone/Getty Images; 176 (bl), Rick Davis/Darkhouse and Fun Enthusiast; 177 (t), © David Jay Zimmerman/Corbis; 180 (tl) (br), Rick Davis/Darkhouse and Fun Enthusiast; 182 (tr), Craig Cameron Olsen/Stone/Getty; 186 (bl),Comstock/Fotosearch; 190 (tr), CLOSE TO HOME c 1996 John McPherson. Reprinted with permission of UNIVERSAL PRESS SYNDICATE. All rights reserved.; 193 (tr), Alamy Images; 195 Sipa Photos/ Newscom.com; 196 (tl), Comstock/Fotosearch; 200 (tl), Comstock/Fotosearch; 200 (tr), © Bobby Bogren/Alamy;

Chapter 4: 212-213 Alamy Images; 212 (inset-teen), HRW Photo; 216 (t), Philip Gould/CORBIS; 218 (t), Digital Image copyright 2007 PhotoDisc; 219 (cl), Sam Dudgeon/HRW; 220 (cl), Alamy Photo; 220 (bl), Andy Christiansen/HRW; 222 (c)(b)(t), Andy Christiansen/HRW; 223 (tr), ©Library of Congress/CORBIS; 227 (tr), Eckhard Slawik/Photo Researchers; 229 (bl), Andy Christiansen/HRW; 231 (br) (tr), NASA; 233 (tl), Getty Images/Rubberball; 233 (cr), John Foxx/ImageState; 234 (br), Gunter Marx Photographer/Corbis; 236 (tl), Andy Christiansen/HRW; 237 (bl), FotoSearch/COMSTOCK, Inc.; 238 (all), Andy Christiansen/HRW; 240 (t)(b), Sam Dudgeon/HRW; 241 (t)(b), Sam Dudgeon/HRW; 242 (tr), The image Bank/Getty Images; 247 (bl), Fotosearch; 248 (tl), Jack Fields/Photo Researchers, Inc.; 252 (tr), ©Steve Skjold/Alamy Photos; 252 (cr), Stockbyte Royalty-Free Images/HRW Library; 257 (tl), Mary Evans Picture Library; 258 (tl), Fotosearch/Photodisc; 259 (cr), Victoria Smith/HRW; 260 (tr) Chris Lisle/CORBIS; 262 (cr), Photonica; 264 (tl) Fotosearch/Photodisc; 267 (tr), Eric Vandeville, Rome; 271 (cl), Photodisc/Getty; 271 (bl), Fotosearch/Photodisc; 273 (tr), Jason T. Ware/ Photo Researchers, Inc.; 273 Jason T. Ware/Photo Researchers, Inc.; 278 (tl), Fotosearch/Photodisc; 278 (bl), Sam Dudgeon/HRW;280 (tl), Fotosearch/Photodisc; 280 (cr), ©Chuck Smith/Southern Stock/PictureQuest; 294 (tl), Sam Dudgeon/HRW Photo; 294-295 (b), Courtesy Queen's Cup Yacht Race; 295 (tr), Jon Hill Photography/Courtesty The Air Zoo

Chapter 5: 296-297 Laurence Parent Photography; 299 Sam Dudgeon/HRW Photo; 300 (tr), The Image Bank/Getty Images; 302 (br), ©Gunter Marx Photography/CORBIS; 305 (bl), Creatas/Punchstock.com; 305 (cr), Scott McDermott/IPN; 305 (cl), Lake Country Museum/CORBIS; 307 (tr), Firefly Productions/CORBIS; 307 (cl)(c)(cr), Sam Dudgeon/HRW Photo; 312 (bl), Creatas/Punchstock.com; 313 (cl), Corbis Images; 314 (tr), Calder, Alexander (1898-1976) ©ARS, NY Ordinary, 1969, 580 x 600 x 580 cm. (c) Copyright ARS, NY. Painted Steel. Private Collection Photo Credit: Art Resource, NYART127373; 318 (cl), Corbis Images; 319 (tl), Creatas/Punchstock.com; 320 (cl) (c) (cr), Sam Dudgeon/HRW Photo; 320 (bl), Corbis Images; 322 (tr), © Royalty Free/Dorian Weisel/CORBIS; 324 (cr), Imagebroker/Alamy Images; 326 (tl), Creatas/Punchstock.com; 328 (tl), Creatas/Punchstock.com; 328 (c), Photodisc Red/RF/Getty Images; 331 (tr)(br), Sam Dudgeon/HRW Photo; 332 (tr), Real Life Adventures by Gary Wise and Lance Aldrich; 337 (tl), AP PHOTO/CP/Winnipeg Free Press, Marc Gallan; 338 (tl), Photodisc Red/RF/Getty Images; 340 (tr), Stone/Getty; 343 (cl)(cr),Victoria Smith/HRW Photo; 344 (tl)(tr), Alamy Images; 344 (cr), Victoria Smith/HRW Photo; 344 (bl), Transtock Inc./Alamy; 347 (cr), Sam Dudgeon/HRW Photo; 348 (tr), Danny Lehman/CORBIS; 353 (tr), Peter Van Steen/ HRW Photo; 353 (cl), Erich Lessing/Art Resource; 354 (bl), Transtock Inc./Alamy Images; 356 (tr), Taxi/Getty Images; 357 (cr), HRW Photo; 359 (tl), Stockbyte/Getty Images; 359 (cr), Sam Dudgeon/HRW Photo; 360 (cr), Corbis Images/Punchstock.com; 360 (br), Sam Dudgeon/HRW Photo; 361 (cr), HRW Photo; 361 (bl), Transtock Inc./Alamy Images; 364 (tl), Transtock Inc./Alamy Images; 364 (b), Paul Doyle/Alamy

Chapter 6: 376–377 Photo of Reptiles puzzle based on work by M.C. Escher 2006 The M.C. Escher Company–Holland. All rights reserved. *www.mcescher.com;* 382 (tr), Staffan Widstrand/CORBIS; 385 (cr), Custom Medical Stock; 386 (tl), Ingram Image/Picturequest; 386 (tcl), Punchstock; 386 (tr), Comstock/Punchstock; 386 (tcr), Alamy Images; 386 (cr), Alamy Images; 387 (tr), Peter Van Steen/HRW Photo; 387 (bl), Sam Dudgeon/HRW Photo; 387 (br), HRW Photo by Peter Van Steen; 390 (t)(c)(b), HRW Photo; 391 (tr), George D. Lepp/CORBIS; 392 (br), Art Reference: BasketballHoopsUnlimited; 395 (tr), Robert Harding World Imagery/Getty Images; 395 (cr), Photo Edit Inc.; 396 (tr), Photo Courtesy Mohawk Lifts; 396 (bl), HRW Photo; 396 (br), HRW Photo by Peter Van Steen; 398 (tr), HRW Photo by Sam Dudgeon; 401 (cr), HRW Photo by Sam Dudgeon; 402 (cr-parallel rule) Victoria Smith/HRW Photo; 402 (cr-map), Alamy Images; 403 (tr)(inset), HRW Photo by Sam Dudgeon; 404 (cl), Historical Picture Archive/CORBIS; 404 (cr), Robervals's balance/Varnished wood, brass French, Late 18th century/700 mm x 360 mm; diam. 160 mm Inventory number 1983.26.36, Stewart Museum, Montreal, Canada; 404 (bl), Sam Dudgeon/HRW Photo; 404 (br), HRW Photo by Peter Van Steen; 405 (cr), © Andreas Karner/STOCK4B/Getty Images; 406 (tr), © Greg C. Grace/Alamy; 406 (cl), © Gabbro/Alamy; 406 (cr), © Harry Taylor/Dorling Kindersley/Getty Images; 407 (cr) Amazonite, HRW Photo; 406 (bl), Guinea REUTERS/Corbis Images; 407 (cr), HRW Photo; 408 (tr)(br), Courtesy of Wimberley Stain Glass/HRW Photo by Peter Van Steen; 411 (tl), Gareth Brown/CORBIS; 412 (tr), CORBIS; 412 (cr), Tony Freemman/Photo Edit Inc.; 413 (cl), Roger Ressmeyer/CORBIS; 413 (cr), Paul S. Calter; 414 (tl), BrandX/Fotosearch; 418 (tr), Digital Vision/Getty Images; 422 (cr), Peter Van Steen/HRW Photo; 424 (tl), BrandX/fotosearch; 425 (cr), HRW Photo; 427 (tr), CALVIN AND HOBBES c 1995 Watterson. Dist. By UNIVERSAL PRESS SYNDICATE. Reprinted with permission. All rights reserved.; 427 (tr), Spencer Grant/Photo Edit Inc.; 428 (tr), Victoria Smith/HRW Photo; 432 (r), HRW Photo by Sam Dudgeon; 434 (tl), BrandX/Fotosearch; 434 (cl), The Granger Collection; 434 (cr), Photo Edit Inc; 436 (tl), Punchstock; 436 (b), Punchstock; 437 (br), Royalty-Free/Corbis/Fotosearch; 442 (br), Royalty-Free/Fotosearch; 449 (tl), Sam Dudgeon/HRW Photo; 449 (cr), Alamy Images; 450 (tr) (b), AP Wide World

Chapter 7: 450-451 Courtesy IMAX Corporation; 453 (cr), Custom Medical Stock; 454 (tr), Photofest; 456 (cr), Photofest; 456 (br), Everett Collection OR Everett/CSU Archives; 457 (br), Joseph Sohm; ChromoSohm Inc./CORBIS; 458 (cl), ©John Elk III; 458 (cr), ©Zaw Min Yu/Lonely Planet Images; 458 (bl), ©Hemera Technologies/Alamy

Photo

All Teacher-to-Teacher photos courtesy of the teachers.

Chapter One TE wrap: Page 2 (tl), Photodisc; (cl), HRW Photo

Chapter Two TE wrap: Page 70 (tl), Victoria Smith/HRW, 70 (cl), Photo-objects/Fotosearch

Chapter Three TE wrap: Page 142 (tl), Rick Davis/Darkhouse and Fun Enthusiast, 142 (cl), Comstock/Fotosearch

Chapter Four TE wrap: Page 212 (tl), Andy Christiansen/HRW, 212 (cl), www.Fotosearch.com/Photodisc

Chapter Five TE wrap: Page 296 (tl), Transtock Inc./Alamy, 296 (cl), Creatas/Punchstock.com

Chapter Six TE wrap: Page 376 (tl), HRW Photo, 376 (cl), Comstock

Chapter Seven TE wrap: Page 450 (tl), ©Hemera Technologies/Alamy Photos, 450 (cl), Comstock/HRW Photo

Chapter Eight TE wrap: Page 513 (cl), (tl), Fotosearch

Chapter Nine TE wrap: Page 584 (cl), ©Royalty-Free/CORBIS, 584 (tr), ©Photodisc/gettyimages

Chapter Ten TE wrap: Page 650 (tl), HRW Photo, 650 (cl), David Young Wolf/Photoedit

Chapter Eleven TE wrap: Page 742 (tl), ©photolibrary.com/Index Stock Imagery, Inc., 742 (cl), Victoria Smith/HRW Photo

Chapter Twelve TE wrap: Page 820 (tl), ©Brian Hagiwara/Brand X Pictures/Getty Images, 820 (cl), M. C. Escher's Wooden Ball with Fish © 2005 The M.C. Escher Company-Holland. All rights reserved. www.mcescher.com

Photos; 461 (cr), George Post/Photo Researchers, Inc.; 461 (br), Wei Yan/Masterfile; 461 (cl), Age Fotostock/Morales; 461 (bl), Corbis Images; 462 (tr), Jens Meyer/AP/Wide World Photos; 463 (bl), ©Dennis Boissavy/Getty Images; 464 (t), ©Nathan Keay/HRW; 465 (cr), ©Cameron Cross; 466 (tr), ©Nathan Keay/HRW Photo; 466 (cl), Owaki-Kulla/CORBIS; 466 (bl), ©Hemera Technologies/Alamy Photos; 470 (tr), Royalty-Free/CORBIS; 472 (b), PhotoDisc/gettyimages; 476 (cl), ©Reuters/CORBIS; 476 (tl), ©Hemera Technologies/Alamy Photos; 478 (tl), ©Hemera Technologies/Alamy Photos; 478 (cr), ©David Young-Wolff/PHOTOEdit; 481 (tr), ©Christie's Images/CORBIS; 486 (tl), Royalty-Free/Comstock; 488 (tr), Cartoon Stock; 489 (br), ©Peter Gridley/Getty Images; 491 (br), Courtesy NASA/JPL/ASU; 492 (cl), ©Reuters/CORBIS; 492 (bl), Royalty-Free/Comstock; 493 (tl), ©Sygma/CORBIS; 493 (tr), ©Tom Bean/CORBIS; 494 (tr), © matt fowler photography/Alamy; 494 (bl), ©Mark Richards/PhotoEdit; 495 (tr), © moodboard/Corbis; 495 (cr), ©Photodisc/gettyimages; 495 (br), ©Photodisc/gettyimages; 499 (bl), Royalty-Free/Comstock; 502 (tr), Comstock/HRW Photo Research Library; 502 (cr), ©Jeff Cadge/Getty Images

Chapter 8: 518 (tr), Twisted Texas/Wesley Treat; 522 (bl), Fotosearch; 525 (tr), Alamy Images; 529 (br), Alamy Images; 530 (cr), Kevin Fleming/Corbis; 530 (bl), Fotosearch; 531 (tl), Alamy Images; 534 (tr), Photo Edit Inc.; 535 (bl), PhotoEdit; 536 (c), Getty Images; 538 (tr), Getty Images Sport/ Bobby Julich; 539 (tl), Fotosearch; 539 (cl), Photo Edit Inc.; 542 (tl), Fotosearch; 542 (b), Superstock; 544 (tr), Stone/Getty Images; 548 (tl), The Image Bank/Getty Images; 548 (bl), Fotosearch; 550 (tr), HRW Photo; 550 (cr), HRW Photo; 551 (tr), Alamy Images; 556 (tl), Brad Smith/News & Observer/AP/Wide World Photos; 557 (tl), Fotosearch; 559 (tr), Stone/Getty; 565 (tl), Fotosearch; 566 (t), FOXTROT c 1999 Bill Amend. Reprinted with permission of UNIVERSAL PRESS SYNDICATE. All rights reserved.; 566 (cl), Nick Koudis/Getty Images; 568 (tr), Fotosearch; 568 (b), Stone/Getty Images; 582 (tl), Sam Dudgeon/HRW Photo; 582 (b), Getty Images; 583 (tr), Ron Schramm Photography/Courtesy The Ernest Hemingway Foundation of Oak Park; 583 (bl), Time & Life Pictures/Getty Images

Chapter 9: 584 Air Photo/Jim Wark; 589 (tr), Victoria Smith/HRW Photo; 594 (c), HRW Photo by Sam Dudgeon; 594 (cr), HRW Photo by Sam Dudgeon; 595 (cl), The Granger Collection, New York; 595 (tl), Photodisc/Gettyimages; 596 (cr), HRW Photo; 598 (all) Sam Dudgeon/HRW Photo; 600 (tr), ©gkphotography/Alamy Photos; 604 (cl), ©Royalty-Free/CORBIS; 604 (bl), ©Photodisc/Gettyimages; 606 (tr), ©Rose/Zefa/Masterfile; 610 (bl), ©Photodisc/Gettyimages; 612 (bl), ©Royalty Free/CORBIS; 614 (tr), ©Photodisc/Gettyimages; 614 (c), ©Otto Rogge/CORBIS; 620 (bl), ©Royalty-Free/CORBIS; 626 (cl), ©Patrick Ray Dunn/Alamy Photos; 626 (bl), ©Royalty-Free/CORBIS; 628 (c), Peter Van Steen/HRW; 629 (t), Peter Van Steen/HRW; 630 (tr), ©Corbis/SuperStock; 628 (cr), Peter Van Steen/HRW; 632 (tl), Warren Morgan/CORBIS; 635 (tl), Romeo Gacad/AFP/Getty Images; 635 (bl), Royalty-Free/CORBIS; 637 (cr), HRW Photo by Sam Dudgeon; 638 (tl), Royalty-Free/CORBIS; 638 (b), Photofusion Picture Library/Alamy Photos; 638 (cr), Dennis MacDonald/PhotoEdit

Chapter 10: 650-651 Erik Pawassar/Getty Images Photo Assignments/HRW Photo/Sculpture by Dale Seymour; 654 (tr), AFP PHOTO/JIJI PRESS/Newscom; 655 (tl), Fotosearch; 655 (tr), David Young-Wolff/Photo Edit; 655 (cl), HRW Photo; 655 (cr), HRW Photo; 656 (cr), Newscom; 657 (tl) Bonillo/Photo Edit; 657 (tc), Photodisc/RF/Fotosearch; 657 (tr), HRW Photo; 658 (bl), David Young-Wolff/Photo Edit; 661 (cr)(br), HRW Photo; 662 (tr)(cr)(bc), HRW Photo; 662 (bl), Corbis Images; 664 (tr)(cr), Victoria Smith/HRW Photo; 665 (tl) Victoria Smith/HRW Photo; 665 (all cubes), Victoria Smith/HRW Photo; 666 (tl)(tc)(tr)(cr), Victoria Smith/HRW Photo; 666 (bl), David Young-Wolff/Photo Edit; 670 (tr), Jeff Hunter/The Image Bank/Getty Images; 675 (bl), David Young-Wolff/Photo Edit; 675 (tl), Stone/Getty Images; 678 (tl), David Young Wolf/Photoedit; 678 (b), Aurora Photo; 679 (cr), Victoria Smith/HRW Photo; 680 (tr), Robert Harding World Imagery/Getty Images; 686 (bl) HRW Photo; 687 (bl)(bc)(br), HRW Photo; 688 (all), HRW Photo; 692 (cl), Marc Golub/HRW Photo; 695 (tl), Victoria Smith/HRW; 695 (cl), Dennis MacDonald/Photo Edit; 697 (tr), Jeff Greenberg/Photoedit Inc.; 697 (tc), HRW Photo; 699 (tc)(tr), HRW Photo; 701 (cr), AFP/TIMOTHY A. CLARY/Getty Images; 703 (tl), Victoria Smith/HRW Photo; 703 (cl), AKG Images; 703 (cr), HRW Photo; 705 (tr), Goss Images/Alamy; 706 (cr), ©Lyndol Descant/LyndolDotCom; 711 (bl), HRW Photo; 718 (cl)(cr), Victoria Smith/HRW Photo; 719 (tr), ©Susan Van Etten/Photo Edit; 720 (Chart-Golf Ball), Martin Paul Ltd., Inc./Picturequest; 720 (Chart-Cricket ball), Photodisc/RF/Fotosearch; 720 (Chart-Tennis ball), Stockdisc/RF/Getty Images; 720 (Chart-Petanque ball), Dk Images/RF/Getty Images; 720 (cl), Ralph White/CORBIS; 720 (bl), HRW Photo; 721 (cr), Lyndol Descant/LyndolDotCom; 724 (tl), HRW Photo; 724 (b), Picturequest; 726 (bl), HRW Photo; 729 (tcl) (tcr), ©Dorling Kindersley/Getty Images; 729 (cr), Royalty-Free/Alamy Images; 729 (br), Stockbyte/RF Picturequest; 731 (tl)(tr)(c), Victoria Smith/HRW Photo; 734 (tc), HRW Photo; 740 (tl), Sam Dudgeon/HRW Photo; 740 (br), AP Photo/Keith Srakocic; 740 (bl), ©Doug Pensinger/Getty Images; 740 (tr) Terraserver; 741 (t), United States Mint; 741 (cr), ©Corbis Images; 741 (b), ©Gallery 19/Gregg Anderson

Chapter 11: 742 (tr), ©Getty Images; 746 (tr), PhotoDisc/Getty Images; 749 (tr), ©Alan Kearney/Getty Images; 749 (br), Gamma Press USA; 752 (cl), ©CORBIS; 752 (bc), Herbert Orth/Time Life Pictures/Getty Images; 753 (bl), Photolibrary.com.pty.ltd./Index Stock Imagery, Inc.; 756 (tr), ©Brand X Pictures/PunchStock; 762 (bl), ©photolibrary.com.pty.ltd./Index Stock Imagery, Inc.; 762 (c), Victoria Smith/HRW Photo; 764 (tr), AP/Wide World Photos; 764 (tr), Jim Wark/Airphoto; 767 (br), ©Christer Fredriksson/Lonely Planet Images; 768 (tl) ©Photolibrary.com.pty.ltd./Index Stock Imagery, Inc.; 768 (b), ©Tony Freeman/PhotoEdit; 768 (cl), Scala/Art Resource, NY; 768 (bl), ©Photolibrary.com.pty.ltd./Index Stock Imagery, Inc.; 768 (br), Photo by Eisenmann, N.Y./Library of Congress; 772 (tr), Victoria Smith/HRW Photo; 773 (br), Victoria Smith/HRW Photo; 776 (tc), Victoria Smith/HRW Photo; 777 (bl), Victoria Smith/HRW Photo; 777 (cr), H. Armstrong Roberts/RobertStock.com; 778 (tr), ©Archivo Iconografico, S.A./CORBIS; 787 (br) ©Jason Hawkes/CORBIS; 788 (bl) Victoria Smith/HRW Photo; 792 (tr), ©Joathan Blair/CORBIS; 795 (br), ©Chris Lisle/CORBIS; 796 (cr), ©Michael T. Sedam/CORBIS; 797 (tl), NASA Marshall Space Flight Center (NASA-MSFC); 797 (bl), Victoria Smith/HRW Photo; 799 (tr), Cartoon copyrighted by Mark Parisi, printed with permission.; 800 (bl), ©RuberBall/Alamy Photos; 802 (br) ©Alamy Photos; 803 (bl), Victoria Smith/HRW Photo; 804 (tl), The Granger Collection, New York; 805 (bl), Sam Dudgeon/HRW; 806 (tr), Victoria Smith/HRW Photo

Chapter 12: 820-821 ©Michael Kevin Daly/CORBIS; 823 (tl), Sam Dudgeon/HRW; 823 (tcl), Sam Dudgeon/HRW; 823 (bcl), Sam Dudgeon/HRW; 823 (bl), Sam Dudgeon/HRW; 824 (tr), ©Joe McDonald/CORBIS; 824 (cr), Sam Dudgeon/HRW; 824 (c), Sam Dudgeon/HRW; 824 (cl), Sam Dudgeon/HRW; 824 (br), Sam Dudgeon/HRW; 828 (cr), Musee d'Orsay, Paris, France/Erich Lessing/Art Resource, NY; 829 (tl), ©Brian Hagiwara/Brand X Pictures/Getty Images; 831 (tr), ©Steve Boyle/NewSport/CORBIS; 831 (cl), Sam Dudgeon/HRW; 831 (c), Sam Dudgeon/HRW; 831 (cr), Sam Dudgeon/HRW; 831 (br), Sam Dudgeon/HRW; 834 (cr), Bonhams, London, UK/The Bridgeman Art Library; 835 (tl), Photo by Walt Disney Studios/ZUMA Press c Copyright 1998 by Courtesy of Walt Disney Studios; 835 (bl), ©Brian Hagiwara/Brand X Pictures/Getty Images; 836 (tr), Victoria Smith/HRW; 839 (tr), Richard Wainscoat/Alamy; 839 (cl)(c)(cr)(br), Sam Dudgeon/HRW; 841 (cl), ©Robert Harding Picture Library Ltd/Alamy Photos; 843 (bl), ©Brian Hagiwara/Brand X Pictures/Getty Images; 844 (tr), PhotoDisc/Getty Images; 848 (tr), ©George B. Diebold/CORBIS; 853 (tl), ©Brian Hagiwara/Brand X Pictures/Getty Images; 854 (tl), ©Brian Hagiwara/Brand X Pictures/Getty Images; 854 (br), ©Brand X Pictures/Getty Images; 856 (tr), Jan Hinsch/Photo Researchers, Inc.; 856 (br), ©One Mile Up, Inc; 857 (c-purple diatoms) Alfred Pasieka/Photo Researchers, Inc.; 857 (bc), Eric Grave/Photo Researchers, Inc.; 857 (br), John Burbidge/Photo Researchers, Inc.; 859 (cr), Photo by spaceimaging.com/Getty Images; 859 (br), 859 (br), ©Brand X Pictures/Alamy Photos; 859 (tr), M. C. Escher's "Circle Limit III" c 2005 The M.C. Escher Company-Holland. All rights reserved. www.mcescher.com; 860 (tr), (c) ARS, NY/Art Resource, NY; 861 (tl), M. C. Escher's Wooden Ball with Fish c 2005 The M.C. Escher Company-Holland. All rights reserved. www.mcescher.com; 861 (cr), Comstock Images/PictureQuest; 861 (cr), ©bildagentur-online.com/de/Alamy Photos; 863 (tr), ©Russell Gordon/DanitaDelimont.com; 863 (tcl), ©Anna Zuckerman-Vdovenko/PhotoEdit; 863 (tcr), ©Danita Delimont/Alamy Photos; 863 (cl) ©Paul Souders/WorldFoto/Alamy Photos; 863 (cr), ©Jeff Greenberg/Alamy Photos; 863 (cbl)(cbr), ©Danita Delimont/Alamy Photos; 865 (tl), ©Comstock Images/Alamy Photos; 865 (cl), Darren Matthews/SDM Images/Photographer's Direct; 865 (c), ©G. Schuster/Photo-AG/CORBIS; 865 (cr), Brand X Pictures/PictureQuest; 866 (bc), ©M. Angelo/CORBIS; 867 (tl)(tc)(tr)(bl)(bc), Sam Dudgeon/HRW; 868 (cl)(br), Sam Dudgeon/HRW; 868 (bl), Lonely Planet Images/Alamy; 870 (tr)(cr)(br), Sam Dudgeon/HRW; 871 (tr)(cr)(cl)(br), Sam Dudgeon/HRW; 872 (tr), Mark Lennihan/AP/Wide World; 876 (bl), M. C. Escher's Wooden Ball with Fish c 2005 The M.C. Escher Company-Holland. All rights reserved. www.mcescher.com; 876 (br), M. C. Escher's "Drawing Hands" c 2005 The M.C. Escher Company-Holland. All rights reserved. www.mcescher.com; 876 (tl), AP Photo/The Truth, Jennifer Shephard; 877 (cl)(cr), Adam Hart-Davis/Photo Researchers, Inc.; 880 (tcl), M. C. Escher's "Symmetry Drawing E93" c 2005 The M.C. Escher Company-Holland. All rights reserved. www.mcescher.com; 880 (c), ©Alamy Photos; 881 (tl), M. C. Escher's Wooden Ball with Fish c 2005 The M.C. Escher Company-Holland. All rights reserved. www.mcescher.com; 880 (tcr), M. C. Escher's "Symmetry Drawing E91" c 2005 The M.C. Escher Company-Holland. All rights reserved. www.mcescher.com; 880 (bcl), M. C. Escher's "Path of Life III" c 2005 The M.C. Escher Company-Holland. All rights reserved. www.mcescher.com; 880 (bcr), M. C. Escher's "Symmetry Drawing E69" c 2005 The M.C. Escher Company-Holland. All rights reserved. www.mcescher.com; 880 (b), M. C. Escher's "Reptiles" c 2005 The M.C. Escher Company-Holland. All rights reserved. www.mcescher.com; 882 (tr), GEORGE POST/Photo Researchers, Inc.; 883 (cr), ©George W. Hart; 894 (cr), Index Stock Imagery/PictureQuest; 894 (bl) ©Dwight Hiscano; 894 ©Steven Anderson; 895 (cr), © Steven Richman; 895 (b), Susan Watts/NY Daily News Archive via Getty Images.

Back Matter: S2 Don Couch/HRW; S3 John Langford/HRW

CR2 Credits

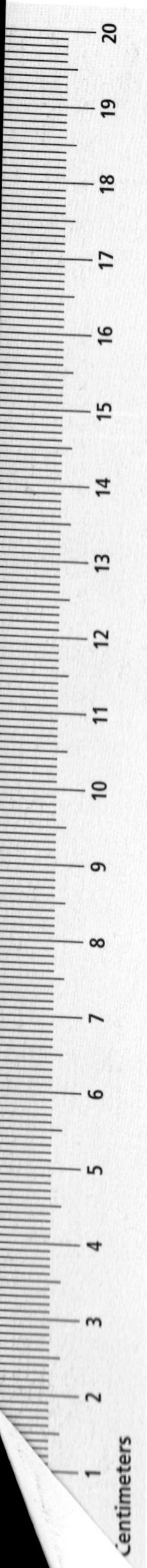

Symbols

$\overleftrightarrow{AB}$	line AB	$^\circ$	degree
$\overrightarrow{AB}$	ray AB	$\cong$	is congruent to
$\overline{AB}$	segment AB	$\sim$	is similar to
AB	the distance from A to B	$\parallel$	is parallel to
$\angle ABC$	angle ABC	$\perp$	is perpendicular to
$m\angle A$	the measure of $\angle A$	$\vec{v}$	vector v
$\overset{\frown}{AB}$	arc AB	$\overrightarrow{AB}$	vector AB
$\triangle ABC$	triangle ABC	π	pi
$\square ABCD$	parallelogram $ABCD$	A'	A prime
$\odot A$	circle A	$A \rightarrow A'$	A maps to A prime

Table of Measures

METRIC

Length

1 kilometer (km) = 1000 meters (m)
1 meter = 100 centimeters (cm)
1 centimeter = 10 millimeters (mm)

Capacity and Volume

1 liter (L) = 1000 milliliters (mL)

Mass

1 kilogram (kg) = 1000 grams (g)
1 gram = 1000 milligrams (mg)

CUSTOMARY

Length

1 mile (mi) = 1760 yards (yd)
1 mile = 5280 feet (ft)
1 yard = 3 feet
1 foot = 12 inches (in.)

Capacity and Volume

1 gallon (gal) = 4 quarts (qt)
1 quart = 2 pints (pt)
1 pint = 2 cups (c)
1 cup = 8 fluid ounces (fl oz)

Weight

1 ton = 2000 pounds (lb)
1 pound = 16 ounces (oz)

TIME

1 year (yr) = 365 days (d)
1 year = 12 months (mo)
1 year = 52 weeks (wk)
1 week = 7 days
1 day = 24 hours (h)
1 hour = 60 minutes (min)
1 minute = 60 seconds (s)